The COMPLETE CONCORDANCE TO THE BIBLE

New King James Version

The COMPLETE CONCORDANCE TO THE BIBLE

New King James Version

THOMAS NELSON PUBLISHERS

Nashville · Camden · New York

Published in Nashville, Tennessee, by Thomas Nelson, Inc., Publishers and distributed in Canada by Lawson Falle, Ltd., Cambridge, Ontario.

Library of Congress Cataloging in Publication Data
Main entry under title:
The Complete concordance to the Bible, New King James Version.

1. Bible—Concordances, English. I. Bible.
English. New King James. 1983.
BS425.C65 1983 220.5'2033 83-13271
ISBN 0-8407-4959-7

Printed in the United States of America

3 4 5 6 7 8 9 10 11 12 13 14 15 16 17 18 19 20—90 89

PREFACE

With the publication of the New King James Version (NKJV) of the Bible, the long-awaited fifth revision of the venerable King James Version, the first since 1769, was completed. It quickly became apparent that a useful concordance to the NKJV was needed, one that would be suitable for Bible students and readers alike; whereupon the publisher, Thomas Nelson Publishers, commissioned such a work. *The Complete Concordance to the Bible: New King James Version* is the result. Using this concordance as a key, the Bible student or reader can unlock the vocabulary of the NKJV text, find favorite verses, and discover how the revisers have enriched an already powerful English version.

As a complete concordance, this concordance lists all the references of every indexed word in the NKJV. Thus, for instance, every occurrence of the word *Lord*—from Genesis through Revelation—is listed under the entry LORD.

One of the lasting accomplishments of the NKJV has been to replace archaic English words with words that convey the original meaning of the King James Version. For instance, in the King James Version the word *let* occasionally means "to hinder," a meaning opposite to current English usage. The NKJV revisers replaced *let* with *hinder* in these passages, thus clarifying its meaning for the modern reader. Similar needed and helpful vocabulary changes in the NKJV have made a new concordance necessary. A studious use of *The Complete Concordance to the Bible: New King James Version* will result not only in an understanding of the methodology behind the NKJV, but also in a better understanding of the message of the text, which is the prime purpose of both the revision and the concordance.

LIST OF NON-INDEXED WORDS

The Complete Concordance to the Bible: New King James Version lists over 265,000 biblical references for the 13,331 words in the NKJV vocabulary. In order to allow space to index the more significant words, the references for 363 words have not been included; these words are listed immediately following this preface in the list of non-indexed words. In order that the reader will know how every word has been treated, the vocabulary of these non-indexed words is included within the concordance itself, along with the instruction to consult this list.

WORDS FOLLOWED BY ASTERISKS

Two types of entry words in the concordance are followed by asterisks. The first type is the indexed word that is spelled identically to a non-indexed word. Since the use of the indexed word is significant, it is included in the concordance, even though the more commonly used word with the same spelling is not indexed. The following ten words fit into this category:

—LEAVES (plural of *leaf*)
—LEFT (opposite of *right*)
—MIGHT (power)
—NO (proper noun)
—ON (proper noun)
—PUT (proper noun)
—SO (proper noun)
—SAW (a tool)
—WILL (a volition)
—WELL (a place where water is drawn)

The second type of entry word followed by an asterisk is the proper noun that is spelled identically to another word that also is indexed. When this occurs, separate entries are made for each word. For instance, references to the man *Lot* are separated from references to the *lot* used to make choices by chance and to one's *lot* in life. The nine proper nouns separated in this way are: CHERUB, EPHAH, EPHOD, HEN, IRON, LOT, MARK, RAM, and SIN. Also, the word *God* has been separated in order to distinguish the one true God of the Bible from other gods.

WORDS SET IN PARENTHESES

Another valuable feature of this book is its system of cross-references leading (1) to words within a larger "family" of words, (2) to variant spellings of proper names, (3) and to variant names for the same person or place. These cross-references are set within parentheses immediately following the entry word. By using the cross-referencing system, one finds, for instance, (1) that the entry MEAN also refers to entries for MEANING, MEANS, and MEANT, (2) that Baharumite and Barhumite are the same person, and (3) that Jerusalem is also called Ariel and that Augustus, Claudius, and Tiberius were personal names for the Roman rulers named Caesar.

The Complete Concordance to the Bible: New King James Version is designed to be a useful reference tool for the study of the Bible. To the degree that it assists the reader in knowing the Word of God, it will have accomplished its purpose.

LIST OF NON-INDEXED WORDS

a
about
above
according
accordingly
across
afar
after
afterward
again
against
ago
ah
aha
ahead
alas
alike
all
almost
alone
along
already
also
although
altogether
among
an
and
another
another's
answer
answered
answering
answers
any
anymore
anyone
anyone's
anything
anyway
anywhere
apart
are
around
as
aside
ask
asked
asking
asks
at
back
be
became
because
become
becomes
becoming
been
before
beforehand
began
begin
begins
begun
behind
being
below
beneath
beside
besides
better
between
beyond
both
bring
bringing
brings
brought
but
by
came
can
cannot
come

comes
coming
concerning
could
did
do
does
doing
done
down
during
each
either
else
elsewhere
enough
even
evenly
every
everyone
everyone's
everything
everywhere
except
excepted
far
far-off
farther
few
fewer
for
foremost
forth
fro
from
front
further
furthermore
go
goes
going
goings
gone
gotten
had
happen
happened
happening
happens
has
have
having
he
her
here
hereafter
hers
herself
him
himself
his

how
however
I
if
in
inasmuch
indeed
inside
instead
into
is
it
its
itself
large
largeness
larger
least
leave
leaves*
leaving
left*
less
lesser
lest
let
lets
letting
like
likewise
low
lower
lowest
many
matter
matters
may
me
meantime
meanwhile
mere
midst
might*
mine
more
moreover
most
much
my
myself
namely
near
nearby
nearer
nearest
nearly
neither
never
nevermore
nevertheless
next

no*
none
nor
not
nothing
now
nowhere
o
of
off
often
oh
on*
one's
ones
oneself
only
onto
or
other
other's
others
otherwise
ought
our
ours
ourselves
out
outside
over
overall
per
perhaps
place
placed
places
possibly
put*
puts
putting
rather
reach
reached
reaches
reaching
replied
replies
reply
said
same
saw*
sawn
say
saying
sayings
says
see
seeing
seem
seemed

seems
sees
self
set
sets
setting
settings
several
shall
she
should
since
so*
some
somebody
someday
somehow
someone
something
sometime
somewhat
somewhere
stay
stayed
staying
stays
stead
such
surely
talk
talked
talking
talks
tell
telling
tells
than
that
the
their
theirs
them
themselves
then
there
thereafter
thereby
therefore
therein
these
they
thing
things
this
thoroughly
those
though
through
throughout
thus

till
to
together
told
too
toward
under
underneath
unless
until
unto
up
upon
us
use
used
uses
using
very
was
we
well*
went
were
what
whatever
when
whence
whenever
where
whereas
whereby
wherein
whereof
whereupon
wherever
whether
which
whichever
while
who
whoever
whom
whomever
whose
why
will*
with
within
without
worse
worst
would
yes
yet
you
your
yours
yourself
yourselves

ABBREVIATIONS

Old Testament

Gen	Genesis	Eccl	Ecclesiastes
Ex	Exodus	Song	Song of Solomon
Lev	Leviticus	Is	Isaiah
Num	Numbers	Jer	Jeremiah
Deut	Deuteronomy	Lam	Lamentations
Josh	Joshua	Ezek	Ezekiel
Judg	Judges	Dan	Daniel
Ruth	Ruth	Hos	Hosea
1Sa	1 Samuel	Joel	Joel
2Sa	2 Samuel	Amos	Amos
1Ki	1 Kings	Obad	Obadiah
2Ki	2 Kings	Jon	Jonah
1Ch	1 Chronicles	Mic	Micah
2Ch	2 Chronicles	Nah	Nahum
Ezra	Ezra	Hab	Habakkuk
Neh	Nehemiah	Zeph	Zephaniah
Esth	Esther	Hag	Haggai
Job	Job	Zech	Zechariah
Ps	Psalms	Mal	Malachi
Prov	Proverbs		

New Testament

Matt	Matthew	1Ti	1 Timothy
Mark	Mark	2Ti	2 Timothy
Luke	Luke	Tit	Titus
John	John	Phm	Philemon
Acts	Acts	Heb	Hebrews
Rom	Romans	Jas	James
1Co	1 Corinthians	1Pe	1 Peter
2Co	2 Corinthians	2Pe	2 Peter
Gal	Galatians	1Jn	1 John
Eph	Ephesians	2Jn	2 John
Phil	Philippians	3Jn	3 John
Col	Colossians	Jude	Jude
1Th	1 Thessalonians	Rev	Revelation
2Th	2 Thessalonians		

Concordance

A

A (*see* PREFACE)

AARON (*see* AARONITES, AARON'S)

Ex 4:14 Is not **A** the Levite your
Ex 4:27 And the LORD said to **A**, "Go
Ex 4:28 So Moses told **A** all the words
Ex 4:29 **A** went and gathered together
Ex 4:30 **A** spoke all the words which
Ex 5: 1 **A** went in and told Pharaoh,
Ex 5: 4 Moses and **A**, why do you take
Ex 5:20 **A** who stood there to meet
Ex 6:13 the LORD spoke to Moses and **A**
Ex 6:20 and she bore him **A** and Moses
Ex 6:23 **A** took to himself Elisheba,
Ex 6:26 These are the same **A** and Moses
Ex 6:27 These are the same Moses and **A**
Ex 7: 1 **A** your brother shall be your
Ex 7: 2 **A** your brother shall speak to
Ex 7: 6 Then Moses and **A** did so
Ex 7: 7 **A** eighty-three years old when
Ex 7: 8 the LORD spoke to Moses and **A**
Ex 7: 9 then you shall say to **A**
Ex 7:10 **A** went in to Pharaoh, and they
Ex 7:10 **A** cast down his rod before
Ex 7:19 Say to **A**, 'Take your rod and
Ex 7:20 **A** did so, just as the LORD
Ex 8: 5 Say to **A**, 'Stretch out your
Ex 8: 6 So **A** stretched out his hand
Ex 8: 8 Pharaoh called for Moses and **A**
Ex 8:12 and **A** went out from Pharaoh
Ex 8:16 Say to **A**, 'Stretch out your
Ex 8:17 For **A** stretched out his hand
Ex 8:25 Pharaoh called for Moses and **A**
Ex 9: 8 the LORD said to Moses and **A**
Ex 9:27 sent and called for Moses and **A**
Ex 10: 3 **A** came in to Pharaoh and said
Ex 10: 8 and **A** were brought again to
Ex 10:16 Moses and **A** in haste, and said,
Ex 11:10 and **A** did all these wonders
Ex 12: 1 and **A** in the land of Egypt,
Ex 12:28 had commanded Moses and **A**
Ex 12:31 Moses and **A** by night, and said,
Ex 12:43 the LORD said to Moses and **A**
Ex 12:50 LORD commanded Moses and **A**
Ex 15:20 prophetess, the sister of **A**
Ex 16: 2 Moses and **A** in the wilderness
Ex 16: 6 **A** said to all the children of
Ex 16: 9 Then Moses spoke to **A**, "Say
Ex 16:10 pass, as **A** spoke to the whole
Ex 16:33 And Moses said to **A**, "Take a
Ex 16:34 so **A** laid it up before the
Ex 17:10 And Moses, **A**, and Hur went up
Ex 17:12 And **A** and Hur supported his
Ex 18:12 **A** came with all the elders of
Ex 19:24 come up, you and **A** with you
Ex 24: 1 Come up to the LORD, you and **A**
Ex 24: 9 Then Moses went up, also **A**
Ex 24:14 Indeed **A** and Hur are with you
Ex 27:21 is before the Testimony, **A**
Ex 28: 1 Now take **A** your brother, and
Ex 28: 1 minister to Me as priest, **A**
Ex 28: 2 garments for **A** your brother
Ex 28: 4 garments for **A** your brother
Ex 28:12 So **A** shall bear their names
Ex 28:29 So **A** shall bear the names of
Ex 28:30 So **A** shall bear the judgment
Ex 28:35 it shall be upon **A** when he
Ex 28:38 that **A** may bear the iniquity
Ex 28:41 put them on **A** your brother
Ex 28:43 They shall be on **A** and on his
Ex 29: 4 And **A** and his sons you shall
Ex 29: 5 garments, put the tunic on **A**
Ex 29: 9 gird them with sashes, **A** and
Ex 29: 9 So you shall consecrate **A**
Ex 29:10 tabernacle of meeting, and **A**
Ex 29:15 shall also take one ram, and **A**
Ex 29:19 also take the other ram, and **A**
Ex 29:20 the tip of the right ear of **A**
Ex 29:21 oil, and sprinkle it on **A** and
Ex 29:24 all these in the hands of **A**
Ex 29:27 of that which is for **A** and of
Ex 29:28 the children of Israel for **A**
Ex 29:29 the holy garments of **A** shall
Ex 29:32 Then **A** and his sons shall eat
Ex 29:35 Thus you shall do to **A** and his
Ex 29:44 I will also sanctify both **A**
Ex 30: 7 **A** shall burn on it sweet
Ex 30: 8 when **A** lights the lamps at
Ex 30:10 **A** shall make atonement upon
Ex 30:19 for **A** and his sons shall wash
Ex 30:30 And you shall anoint **A** and his
Ex 31:10 garments for **A** the priest
Ex 32: 1 people gathered together to **A**
Ex 32: 2 And **A** said to them,
Ex 32: 3 ears, and brought them to **A**
Ex 32: 5 So when **A** saw it, he built an
Ex 32: 5 **A** made a proclamation and said
Ex 32:21 And Moses said to **A**, "What
Ex 32:22 So **A** said, "Do not let the
Ex 32:25 were unrestrained (for **A** had
Ex 32:35 with the calf which **A** made
Ex 34:30 So when **A** and all the children
Ex 34:31 Moses called to them, and **A**
Ex 35:19 garments for **A** the priest
Ex 38:21 Ithamar, son of **A** the priest
Ex 39: 1 made the holy garments for **A**
Ex 39:27 woven of fine linen, for **A**
Ex 39:41 garments for **A** the priest
Ex 40:12 Then you shall bring **A** and his
Ex 40:13 put the holy garments on **A**
Ex 40:31 and Moses, **A**, and his sons
Lev 1: 7 The sons of **A** the priest
Lev 3:13 the sons of **A** shall sprinkle
Lev 6: 9 Command **A** and his sons
Lev 6:14 The sons of **A** shall offer it
Lev 6:16 And the remainder of it **A**
Lev 6:18 the children of **A** may eat it
Lev 6:20 This is the offering of **A**
Lev 6:25 Speak to **A** and to his sons,
Lev 7:10 belong to all the sons of **A**
Lev 7:33 He among the sons of **A**, who
Lev 7:34 given them to **A** the priest
Lev 7:35 the consecrated portion for **A**
Lev 8: 2 Take **A** and his sons with him,
Lev 8: 6 Then Moses brought **A** and his
Lev 8:14 Then **A** and his sons laid their
Lev 8:18 And **A** and his sons laid their
Lev 8:22 Then **A** and his sons laid their
Lev 8:30 altar, and sprinkled it on **A**
Lev 8:30 and he sanctified **A**, his
Lev 8:31 And Moses said to **A** and his
Lev 8:31 as I commanded, saying, '**A**
Lev 8:36 So **A** and his sons did all the
Lev 9: 1 day that Moses called **A** and
Lev 9: 2 And he said to **A**, "Take for
Lev 9: 7 And Moses said to **A**, "Go to
Lev 9: 8 **A** therefore went to the altar
Lev 9: 9 Then the sons of **A** brought
Lev 9:21 the right thigh **A** waved as a
Lev 9:22 Then **A** lifted his hand toward
Lev 9:23 **A** went into the tabernacle of
Lev 10: 1 Nadab and Abihu, the sons of **A**
Lev 10: 3 Then Moses said to **A**, "This
Lev 10: 3 So **A** held his peace
Lev 10: 4 sons of Uzziel the uncle of **A**
Lev 10: 6 And Moses said to **A**, and to
Lev 10: 8 Then the LORD spoke to **A**,
Lev 10:12 Then Moses spoke to **A**, and to
Lev 10:16 the sons of **A** who were left,
Lev 10:19 And **A** said to Moses,
Lev 11: 1 the LORD spoke to Moses and **A**
Lev 13: 1 the LORD spoke to Moses and **A**
Lev 13: 2 **A** the priest or to one of his
Lev 14:33 the LORD spoke to Moses and **A**
Lev 15: 1 the LORD spoke to Moses and **A**
Lev 16: 1 death of the two sons of **A**
Lev 16: 2 Tell **A** your brother not to
Lev 16: 3 Thus **A** shall come into the
Lev 16: 6 **A** shall offer the bull as a
Lev 16: 8 Then **A** shall cast lots for
Lev 16: 9 **A** shall bring the goat on
Lev 16:11 **A** shall bring the bull of the
Lev 16:21 **A** shall lay both his hands on
Lev 16:23 Then **A** shall come into the
Lev 17: 2 Speak to **A**, to his sons, and
Lev 21: 1 to the priests, the sons of **A**
Lev 21:17 Speak to **A**, saying
Lev 21:21 descendants of **A** the priest
Lev 21:24 And Moses told it to **A** and his
Lev 22: 2 Speak to **A** and his sons, that
Lev 22: 4 man of the descendants of **A**
Lev 22:18 Speak to **A** and his sons, and to
Lev 24: 3 **A** shall be in charge of it
Lev 24: 9 And it shall be for **A** and his
Num 1: 3 **A** shall number them by their
Num 1:17 **A** took these men who had been
Num 1:44 **A** numbered, with the leaders
Num 2: 1 the LORD spoke to Moses and **A**
Num 3: 1 these are the records of **A**
Num 3: 2 the names of the sons of **A**
Num 3: 3 the names of the sons of **A**
Num 3: 4 oversight of **A** their father
Num 3: 6 them before **A** the priest,
Num 3: 9 shall give the Levites to **A**
Num 3:10 So you shall appoint **A** and his
Num 3:32 And Eleazar the son of **A** the
Num 3:38 of meeting, were Moses, **A**
Num 3:39 **A** numbered at the
Num 3:48 of them is redeemed, to **A**
Num 3:51 their redemption money to **A**
Num 4: 1 the LORD spoke to Moses and **A**
Num 4: 5 camp prepares to journey, **A**
Num 4:15 And when **A** and his sons have
Num 4:16 **A** the priest is the oil for
Num 4:17 the LORD spoke to Moses and **A**
Num 4:19 **A** and his sons shall go in and
Num 4:27 **A** and his sons shall assign
Num 4:28 the son of **A** the priest
Num 4:33 the son of **A** the priest
Num 4:34 And Moses, **A**, and the leaders
Num 4:37 **A** numbered according to the
Num 4:41 **A** numbered according to the
Num 4:45 **A** numbered according to the
Num 4:46 of the Levites, whom Moses, **A**
Num 6:23 Speak to **A** and his sons,
Num 7: 8 the son of **A** the priest
Num 8: 2 Speak to **A**, and say to him
Num 8: 3 And **A** did so
Num 8:11 **A** shall offer the Levites
Num 8:13 stand the Levites before **A**
Num 8:19 the Levites as a gift to **A**
Num 8:20 Thus Moses and **A** and all the
Num 8:21 then **A** presented them, as
Num 8:21 **A** made atonement for them to
Num 8:22 of meeting before **A** and his
Num 9: 6 before Moses and **A** that day
Num 10: 8 The sons of **A**, the priests,
Num 12: 1 **A** spoke against Moses because
Num 12: 4 the LORD said to Moses, **A**
Num 12: 5 the tabernacle, and called **A**

Num 12:10 Then **A** turned toward Miriam,
Num 12:11 So **A** said to Moses, "Oh, my
Num 13:26 and came back to Moses and **A**
Num 14: 2 murmured against Moses and **A**
Num 14: 5 **A** fell on their faces before
Num 14:26 the LORD spoke to Moses and **A**
Num 15:33 brought him to Moses and **A**
Num 16: 3 together against Moses and **A**
Num 16:11 what is **A** that you murmur
Num 16:16 you and they, as well as **A**
Num 16:17 you also, and **A**, each of you
Num 16:18 of meeting with Moses and **A**
Num 16:20 the LORD spoke to Moses and **A**
Num 16:37 the son of **A** the priest, to
Num 16:40 who is not a descendant of **A**
Num 16:41 murmured against Moses and **A**
Num 16:42 gathered against Moses and **A**
Num 16:43 **A** came before the tabernacle
Num 16:46 So Moses said to **A**, "Take a
Num 16:47 Then **A** took it as Moses
Num 16:50 So **A** returned to Moses at the
Num 17: 6 the rod of **A** was among their
Num 17: 8 and behold, the rod of **A**, of
Num 18: 1 Then the LORD said to **A**
Num 18: 8 And the LORD spoke to **A**
Num 18:20 Then the LORD said to **A**
Num 18:28 from it to **A** the priest
Num 19: 1 the LORD spoke to Moses and **A**
Num 20: 2 together against Moses and **A**
Num 20: 6 **A** went from the presence of
Num 20: 8 your brother **A** gather the
Num 20:10 **A** gathered the congregation
Num 20:12 the LORD spoke to Moses and **A**
Num 20:23 **A** in Mount Hor by the border
Num 20:24 **A** shall be gathered to his
Num 20:25 Take **A** and Eleazar his son, and
Num 20:26 strip **A** of his garments and
Num 20:26 for **A** shall be gathered to
Num 20:28 Moses stripped **A** of his
Num 20:28 **A** died there on the top of
Num 20:29 saw that **A** was dead, all the
Num 20:29 mourned for **A** thirty days
Num 25: 7 the son of **A** the priest, saw
Num 25:11 the son of **A** the priest, has
Num 26: 1 the son of **A** the priest,
Num 26: 9 **A** in the company of Korah,
Num 26:59 and to Amram she bore **A** and
Num 26:60 To **A** were born Nadab and
Num 26:64 and **A** the priest when they
Num 27:13 people, as **A** your brother was
Num 33: 1 under the hand of Moses and **A**
Num 33:38 Then **A** the priest went up to
Num 33:39 **A** was one hundred and
Deut 9:20 LORD was very angry with **A**
Deut 9:20 so I prayed for **A** also at the
Deut 10: 6 the place where **A** died later
Deut 32:50 just as **A** your brother died
Josh 21: 4 the children of **A** the priest
Josh 21:10 were for the children of **A**
Josh 21:13 Thus to the children of **A** the
Josh 21:19 cities of the children of **A**
Josh 24: 5 Also I sent Moses and **A**, and I
Josh 24:33 And Eleazar the son of **A** died
Judg 20:28 son of Eleazar, the son of **A**
1Sa 12: 6 who raised up Moses and **A**
1Sa 12: 8 then the LORD sent Moses and **A**
1Ch 6: 3 The children of Amram were **A**
1Ch 6: 3 And the sons of **A** were Nadab
1Ch 6:49 But **A** and his sons offered
1Ch 6:50 Now these are the sons of **A**
1Ch 6:54 by lot to the sons of **A**, of
1Ch 6:57 to the sons of **A** they gave
1Ch 15: 4 assembled the children of **A**
1Ch 23:13 sons of Amram: **A** and Moses
1Ch 23:13 **A** was set apart, he and his
1Ch 23:28 was to help the sons of **A** in
1Ch 23:32 the needs of the sons of **A**
1Ch 24: 1 divisions of the sons of **A**
1Ch 24: 1 The sons of **A** were Nadab,
1Ch 24:19 by the hand of **A** their father
1Ch 24:31 brothers the sons of **A** did
2Ch 13: 9 of the LORD, the sons of **A**
2Ch 13:10 to the LORD are the sons of **A**
2Ch 26:18 the priests, the sons of **A**
2Ch 29:21 the priests, the sons of **A**
2Ch 31:19 for the sons of **A** the priests
2Ch 35:14 the priests, the sons of **A**
2Ch 35:14 the priests, the sons of **A**
Ezra 7: 5 the son of **A** the chief priest
Neh 10:38 priest, the descendant of **A**
Neh 12:47 them for the children of **A**
Ps 77:20 By the hand of Moses and **A**
Ps 99: 6 **A** were among His priests, And
Ps 105:26 And **A** whom He had chosen
Ps 106:16 And **A** the saint of the LORD,
Ps 115:10 O house of **A**, trust in the
Ps 115:12 He will bless the house of **A**
Ps 118: 3 Let the house of **A** now say
Ps 133: 2 on the beard, The beard of **A**
Ps 135:19 Bless the LORD, O house of **A**
Mic 6: 4 and I sent before you Moses, **A**
Luke 1: 5 was of the daughters of **A**
Acts 7:40 saying to **A**, 'Make us gods to
Heb 5: 4 called by God, just as **A** was
Heb 7:11 according to the order of **A**

AARONITES (*see* AARON)
1Ch 12:27 Jehoiada, the leader of the **A**
1Ch 27:17 over the **A**, Zadok

AARON'S (*see* AARON)
Ex 6:25 **A** son, took for himself one
Ex 7:12 But **A** rod swallowed up their
Ex 28: 1 Me as priest, Aaron and **A** sons
Ex 28: 3 that they may make **A** garments
Ex 28:30 they shall be over **A** heart
Ex 28:38 So it shall be on **A** forehead
Ex 28:40 For **A** sons you shall make
Ex 29:26 of the ram of **A** consecration
Lev 1: 5 **A** sons, shall bring the blood
Lev 1: 8 **A** sons, shall lay the parts,
Lev 1:11 **A** sons, shall sprinkle its
Lev 2: 2 He shall bring it to **A** sons
Lev 2: 3 the grain offering shall be **A**
Lev 2:10 the grain offering shall be **A**
Lev 3: 2 **A** sons, the priests, shall
Lev 3: 5 **A** sons shall burn it on the
Lev 3: 8 **A** sons shall sprinkle its
Lev 7:31 but the breast shall be **A**
Lev 8:12 the anointing oil on **A** head
Lev 8:13 Then Moses brought **A** sons
Lev 8:23 it on the tip of **A** right ear
Lev 8:24 Then he brought **A** sons
Lev 8:27 he put all these in **A** hands
Lev 9:12 **A** sons presented to him the
Lev 9:18 **A** sons presented to him the
Num 17: 3 you shall write **A** name on the
Num 17:10 Bring **A** rod back before the
Heb 9: 4 **A** rod that budded, and the

ABADDON
Rev 9:11 whose name in Hebrew is **A**

ABAGTHA
Esth 1:10 Biztha, Harbona, Bigtha, **A**

ABANAH
2Ki 5:12 Are not the **A** and the Pharpar,

ABANDON (*see* ABANDONED)
Prov 19: 7 with words, yet they **a** him

ABANDONED (*see* ABANDON)
Lam 2: 7 altar, He has **a** His sanctuary

ABARIM
Num 27:12 Go up into this Mount **A**, and
Num 33:47 camped in the mountains of **A**
Num 33:48 from the mountains of **A** and
Deut 32:49 Go up this mountain of the **A**
Jer 22:20 Cry from **A**, for all your

ABASE (*see* ABASED, ABASING)
Ezek 21:26 the lowly, and **a** the exalted
Dan 4:37 walk in pride He is able to **a**

ABASED (*see* ABASE)
Ezek 17:14 that the kingdom might be **a**
Matt 23:12 exalts himself will be **a**, and
Luke 14:11 exalts himself will be **a**, and
Luke 18:14 who exalts himself will be **a**
Phil 4:12 I know how to be **a**, and I know

ABASHED
Mic 3: 7 be ashamed, and the diviners **a**

ABASING (*see* ABASE)
2Co 11: 7 Did I commit sin in **a** myself

ABATED
Gen 8: 8 to see if the waters had **a**
Gen 8:11 waters had **a** from the earth
Deut 34: 7 dim nor his natural vigor **a**
Judg 8: 3 him **a** when he said that

ABBA
Mark 14:36 **A**, Father, all things are
Rom 8:15 **A**, Father
Gal 4: 6 **A**, Father

ABDA
1Ki 4: 6 and Adoniram the son of **A**,
Neh 11:17 **A** the son of Shammua, the son

ABDEEL
Jer 36:26 and Shelemiah the son of **A**

ABDI
1Ch 6:44 son of Kishi, the son of **A**
2Ch 29:12 of Merari, Kish the son of **A**
Ezra 10:26 Zechariah, Jehiel, **A**,

ABDIEL
1Ch 5:15 Ahi the son of **A**, the son of

ABDON
Josh 21:30 **A** with its common-land,
Judg 12:13 him, **A** the son of Hillel the
Judg 12:15 Then **A** the son of Hillel the
1Ch 6:74 **A** with its common-lands,
1Ch 8:23 **A**, Zichri, Hanan,
1Ch 8:30 And his firstborn son was **A**
1Ch 9:36 His firstborn son was **A**, then
2Ch 34:20 **A** the son of Micah, Shaphan

ABED-NEGO
Dan 1: 7 and to Azariah, **A**
Dan 2:49 **A** over the affairs of the
Dan 3:12 Shadrach, Meshach, and **A**
Dan 3:13 Shadrach, Meshach, and **A**
Dan 3:14 true, Shadrach, Meshach, and **A**
Dan 3:16 **A** answered and said to the
Dan 3:19 Shadrach, Meshach, and **A**
Dan 3:20 bind Shadrach, Meshach, and **A**
Dan 3:22 up Shadrach, Meshach, and **A**
Dan 3:23 men, Shadrach, Meshach, and **A**
Dan 3:26 Shadrach, Meshach, and **A**,
Dan 3:26 **A** came from the midst of the
Dan 3:28 of Shadrach, Meshach, and **A**
Dan 3:29 **A** shall be cut in pieces, and
Dan 3:30 **A** in the province of Babylon

ABEL
Gen 4: 2 this time his brother **A**
Gen 4: 2 Now **A** was a keeper of sheep,
Gen 4: 4 **A** also brought of the
Gen 4: 4 And the LORD respected **A** and
Gen 4: 8 talked with **A** his brother
Gen 4: 8 rose against **A** his brother
Gen 4: 9 Where is **A** your brother
Gen 4:25 seed for me instead of **A**,
1Sa 6:18 **A** on which they set the ark
2Sa 20:14 all the tribes of Israel to **A**
2Sa 20:15 him in **A** of Beth Maachah
2Sa 20:18 shall surely ask counsel at **A**
Matt 23:35 **A** to the blood of Zechariah
Luke 11:51 from the blood of **A** to the
Heb 11: 4 By faith **A** offered to God a
Heb 12:24 better things than that of **A**

ABEL ACACIA GROVE
Num 33:49 the **A** in the plains of Moab

ABEL BETH MAACHAH (*see* BETH MAACHAH)
1Ki 15:20 He attacked Ijon, Dan, **A**, and
2Ki 15:29 Assyria came and took Ijon, **A**

ABEL KERAMIM
Judg 11:33 and to **A**, with a very great

ABEL MAIM
2Ch 16: 4 They attacked Ijon, Dan, **A**

ABEL MEHOLAH (*see* MEHOLATHITE)
Judg 7:22 as far as the border of **A**
1Ki 4:12 Jezreel, from Beth Shean to **A**
1Ki 19:16 the son of Shaphat of **A** you

ABEL MIZRAIM (*see* MIZRAIM)
Gen 50:11 its name was called **A**, which

ABEZ
Josh 19:20 Rabbith, Kishion, **A**,

ABHOR (*see* ABHORRED, ABHORRENCE, ABHORRENT, ABHORS)
Lev 20:23 things, and therefore I **a** them
Lev 26:11 and My soul shall not **a** you
Lev 26:30 and My soul shall **a** you
Lev 26:44 them away, nor shall I **a** them
Deut 7:26 detest it and utterly **a** it
Deut 23: 7 You shall not **a** an Edomite

Deut 23: 7 You shall not **a** an Egyptian
1Sa 27:12 people Israel utterly **a** him
Job 9:31 and my own clothes will **a** me
Job 19:19 All my close friends **a** me
Job 30:10 They **a** me, they keep far from
Job 42: 6 Therefore I **a** myself, and
Ps 36: 4 He does not **a** evil
Ps 119:163 **a** lying, But I love Your law
Prov 24:24 nations will **a** him
Jer 14:21 Do not **a** us, for Your name's
Amos 5:10 they **a** the one who speaks
Amos 6: 8 I **a** the pride of Jacob, and
Mic 3: 9 who **a** justice and pervert all
Rom 2:22 You who **a** idols, do you rob
Rom 12: 9 **A** what is evil

ABHORRED (*see* ABHOR)
Lev 26:43 their soul **a** My statutes
1Sa 2:17 for men **a** the offering of the
2Sa 16:21 that you are **a** by your father
1Ki 11:25 he **a** Israel, and reigned over
Ps 22:24 nor **a** the affliction of the
Ps 78:59 furious, And greatly **a** Israel
Ps 89:38 But You have cast off and **a**
Ps 106:40 people, So that He **a** His own
Ps 107:18 Their soul **a** all manner of
Prov 22:14 he who is **a** of the LORD will
Ezek 16:25 and made your beauty to be **a**
Zech 11: 8 them, and their soul also **a** me

ABHORRENCE (*see* ABHOR)
Is 66:24 shall be an **a** to all flesh

ABHORRENT (*see* ABHOR)
Ex 5:21 us **a** in the sight of Pharaoh

ABHORS (*see* ABHOR)
Lev 26:15 if your soul **a** My judgments
Job 33:20 So that his life **a** bread, and
Ps 5: 6 The LORD **a** the bloodthirsty
Is 49: 7 to Him whom the nation **a**

ABI
2Ki 18: 2 His mother's name was **A** the

ABI-ALBON
2Sa 23:31 **A** the Arbathite, Azmaveth the

ABIASAPH (*see* EBIASAPH)
Ex 6:24 were Assir, Elkanah, and **A**

ABIATHAR (*see* ABIATHAR'S)
1Sa 22:20 the son of Ahitub, named **A**
1Sa 22:21 **A** told David that Saul had
1Sa 22:22 So David said to **A**, "I knew
1Sa 23: 6 when **A** the son of Ahimelech
1Sa 23: 9 him, he said to **A** the priest
1Sa 30: 7 David said to **A** the priest
1Sa 30: 7 **A** brought the ephod to David
2Sa 8:17 the son of **A** were the priests
2Sa 15:24 and **A** went up until all the
2Sa 15:27 son, and Jonathan the son of **A**
2Sa 15:29 **A** carried the ark of God back
2Sa 15:35 **A** the priests with you there
2Sa 15:35 to Zadok and **A** the priests
2Sa 17:15 to Zadok and **A** the priests,
2Sa 19:11 and **A** the priests, saying,
2Sa 20:25 Zadok and **A** were the priests
1Ki 1: 7 with **A** the priest, and they
1Ki 1:19 **A** the priest, and Joab the
1Ki 1:25 of the army, and **A** the priest
1Ki 1:42 the son of **A** the priest
1Ki 2:22 for **A** the priest, and for Joab
1Ki 2:26 to **A** the priest the king said
1Ki 2:27 So Solomon removed **A** from
1Ki 2:35 the priest in the place of **A**
1Ki 4: 4 Zadok and **A**, the priests
1Ch 15:11 **A** the priests, and for the
1Ch 18:16 the son of **A** were the priests
1Ch 24: 6 Ahimelech the son of **A**, and
1Ch 27:34 the son of Benaiah, then **A**
Mark 2:26 the days of **A** the high priest

ABIATHAR'S (*see* ABIATHAR)
2Sa 15:36 son, and Jonathan, **A** son

ABIB (*see* NISAN)
Ex 13: 4 are going out, in the month **A**
Ex 23:15 appointed in the month of **A**
Ex 34:18 time of the month of **A**
Ex 34:18 for in the month of **A** you
Deut 16: 1 Observe the month of **A**, and
Deut 16: 1 for in the month of **A** the

ABIDA (*see* ABIDAH)
1Ch 1:33 were Ephah, Epher, Hanoch, **A**

ABIDAH (*see* ABIDA)
Gen 25: 4 were Ephah, Epher, Hanoch, **A**

ABIDAN
Num 1:11 **A** the son of Gideoni
Num 2:22 shall be **A** the son of Gideoni
Num 7:60 On the ninth day **A** the son of
Num 7:65 of **A** the son of Gideoni
Num 10:24 was **A** the son of Gideoni

ABIDE (*see* ABIDES, ABIDING)
Lev 8:35 shall **a** at the door of the
Deut 12:11 chooses to make His name **a**
Deut 14:23 He chooses to make His name **a**
Deut 16: 6 chooses to make His name **a**
Deut 16:11 chooses to make His name **a**
Deut 26: 2 chooses to make His name **a**
Job 24:13 its ways nor **a** in its paths
Ps 15: 1 who may **a** in Your tabernacle
Ps 61: 4 I will **a** in Your tabernacle
Ps 61: 7 He shall **a** before God forever
Ps 91: 1 of the Most High Shall **a**
Prov 15:31 of life will **a** among the wise
Prov 19:23 has it will **a** in satisfaction
Jer 10:10 be able to **a** His indignation
Jer 42:10 you will still **a** in this land
Jer 49:18 No one shall **a** there, nor
Hos 3: 4 children of Israel shall **a**
Joel 3:20 But Judah shall **a** forever
Mic 5: 4 and they shall **a**, for now He
Luke 24:29 **A** with us, for it is toward
John 8:31 If you **a** in My word, you are
John 8:35 a slave does not **a** in the
John 12:46 Me should not **a** in darkness
John 14:16 that He may **a** with you
John 15: 4 **A** in Me, and I in you
John 15: 4 can you, unless you **a** in Me
John 15: 6 If anyone does not **a** in Me
John 15: 7 If you **a** in Me, and My words
John 15: 7 in Me, and My words **a** in you
John 15: 9 **a** in My love
John 15:10 you will **a** in My love, just
John 15:10 commandments and **a** in His
1Co 13:13 And now **a** faith, hope, love,
1Jn 2:24 Therefore let that **a** in you
1Jn 2:24 you also will **a** in the Son
1Jn 2:27 taught you, you will **a** in Him
1Jn 2:28 **a** in Him, that when He
1Jn 3:17 does the love of God **a** in him
1Jn 4:13 this we know that we **a** in Him
2Jn 9 does not **a** in the doctrine of

ABIDES (*see* ABIDE)
Ps 55:19 Even He who **a** from of old
Ps 119:90 the earth, and it **a**
Ps 125: 1 be moved, but **a** forever
Eccl 1: 4 but the earth **a** forever
John 3:36 but the wrath of God **a** on him
John 6:56 and drinks My blood **a** in Me
John 8:35 forever, but a son **a** forever
John 15: 4 unless it **a** in the vine,
John 15: 5 He who **a** in Me, and I in him,
1Pe 1:23 God which lives and **a** forever,
1Jn 2: 6 He who says he **a** in Him ought
1Jn 2:10 his brother **a** in the light
1Jn 2:14 and the word of God **a** in you
1Jn 2:17 the will of God **a** forever
1Jn 2:24 from the beginning **a** in you
1Jn 2:27 received from Him **a** in you
1Jn 3: 6 Whoever **a** in Him does not sin
1Jn 3:14 love his brother **a** in death
1Jn 3:24 His commandments **a** in Him
1Jn 3:24 this we know that He **a** in us
1Jn 4:12 God **a** in us, and His love has
1Jn 4:15 God **a** in him, and he in God
1Jn 4:16 who **a** in love **a** in God
2Jn 2 of the truth which **a** in us
2Jn 9 He who **a** in the doctrine of

ABIDING (*see* ABIDE)
1Sa 26:19 **a** in the inheritance of the
John 5:38 do not have His word **a** in you
1Jn 3:15 has eternal life **a** in him

ABIEL
1Sa 9: 1 name was Kish the son of **A**
1Sa 14:51 of Abner was the son of **A**
1Ch 11:32 of Gaash, **A** the Arbathite,

ABIEZER (*see* ABIEZRITE, EZER, JEEZER)
Josh 17: 2 for the children of **A**, the
Judg 8: 2 better than the vintage of **A**
2Sa 23:27 **A** the Anathothite, Mebunnai
1Ch 7:18 Hammoleketh bore Ishhod, **A**
1Ch 11:28 Tekoite, **A** the Anathothite,
1Ch 27:12 month was **A** the Anathothite

ABIEZRITE (*see* ABIEZER, ABIEZRITES)
Judg 6:11 which belonged to Joash the **A**

ABIEZRITES (*see* ABIEZRITE)
Judg 6:24 is still in Ophrah of the **A**
Judg 6:34 the **A** gathered behind him
Judg 8:32 father, in Ophrah of the **A**

ABIGAIL
1Sa 25: 3 and the name of his wife **A**
1Sa 25:14 one of the young men told **A**
1Sa 25:18 Then **A** made haste and took
1Sa 25:23 Now when **A** saw David, she
1Sa 25:32 Then David said to **A**
1Sa 25:36 Then **A** went to Nabal, and
1Sa 25:39 David sent and proposed to **A**
1Sa 25:40 David had come to **A** at Carmel
1Sa 25:42 So **A** rose in haste and rode on
1Sa 27: 3 **A** the Carmelitess, Nabal's
1Sa 30: 5 and **A** the widow of Nabal the
2Sa 2: 2 and **A** the widow of Nabal the
2Sa 3: 3 by **A** the widow of Nabal the
2Sa 17:25 who had gone in to **A** the
1Ch 2:16 sisters were Zeruiah and **A**
1Ch 2:17 **A** bore Amasa
1Ch 3: 1 Daniel, by **A** the Carmelitess

ABIHAIL
Num 3:35 was Zuriel the son of **A**
1Ch 2:29 of the wife of Abishur was **A**
1Ch 5:14 children of **A** the son of Huri
2Ch 11:18 of **A** the daughter of Eliah
Esth 2:15 of **A** the uncle of Mordecai
Esth 9:29 Esther, the daughter of **A**

ABIHU
Ex 6:23 and she bore him Nadab, **A**,
Ex 24: 1 you and Aaron, Nadab and **A**
Ex 24: 9 up, also Aaron, Nadab, and **A**
Ex 28: 1 Nadab, **A**, Eleazar, and Ithamar
Lev 10: 1 Then Nadab and **A**, the sons of
Num 3: 2 Nadab, the firstborn, and **A**
Num 3: 4 **A** had died before the LORD
Num 26:60 Aaron were born Nadab and **A**
Num 26:61 and **A** died when they offered
1Ch 6: 3 sons of Aaron were Nadab, **A**
1Ch 24: 1 sons of Aaron were Nadab, **A**
1Ch 24: 2 **A** died before their father,

ABIHUD
1Ch 8: 3 of Bela were Addar, Gera, **A**

ABIJAH (*see* ABIJAM)
1Sa 8: 2 and the name of his second, **A**
1Ki 14: 1 At that time **A** the son of
1Ch 2:24 Hezron's wife **A** bore him
1Ch 3:10 **A** was his son, Asa his son,
1Ch 6:28 firstborn, and **A** the second
1Ch 7: 8 Elioenai, Omri, Jerimoth, **A**
1Ch 24:10 to Hakkoz, the eighth to **A**
2Ch 11:20 and she bore him **A**, Attai,
2Ch 11:22 Rehoboam appointed **A** the son
2Ch 12:16 Then **A** his son reigned in his
2Ch 13: 1 **A** became king over Judah
2Ch 13: 2 And there was war between **A**
2Ch 13: 3 **A** set the battle in order
2Ch 13: 4 Then **A** stood on Mount
2Ch 13:15 and all Israel before **A** and
2Ch 13:17 Then **A** and his people struck
2Ch 13:19 **A** pursued Jeroboam and took
2Ch 13:20 again in the days of **A**
2Ch 13:21 But **A** grew mighty, married
2Ch 13:22 Now the rest of the acts of **A**
2Ch 14: 1 So **A** rested with his fathers,
2Ch 29: 1 His mother's name was **A** the
Neh 10: 7 Meshullam, **A**, Mijamin,
Neh 12: 4 Iddo, Ginnethoi, **A**,
Neh 12:17 of **A**, Zichri
Matt 1: 7 Rehoboam, Rehoboam begot **A**
Matt 1: 7 begot **A**, and **A** begot Asa
Luke 1: 5 of the division of **A**

ABIJAM (*see* ABIJAH)
1Ki 14:31 Then **A** his son reigned in his
1Ki 15: 1 **A** became king over Judah
1Ki 15: 7 Now the rest of the acts of **A**

1Ki 15: 7 And there was war between **A**
1Ki 15: 8 So **A** rested with his fathers,

ABILENE
Luke 3: 1 and Lysanias tetrarch of **A**

ABILITY (*see* ABLE)
Ex 35:34 in his heart the **a** to teach
Lev 27: 8 to the **a** of him who vowed
1Ch 26: 6 they were men of great **a**
Ezra 2:69 According to their **a**, they
Neh 5: 8 According to our **a** we have
Dan 1: 4 who had **a** to serve in the
Matt 25:15 each according to his own **a**
Acts 11:29 each according to his **a**,
2Co 8: 3 that according to their **a**
2Co 8: 3 yes, and beyond their **a**, they
1Pe 4:11 with the **a** which God supplies

ABIMAEL
Gen 10:28 Obal, **A**, Sheba,
1Ch 1:22 Ebal, **A**, Sheba,

ABIMELECH (*see* ABIMELECH'S, AHIMELECH)
Gen 20: 2 **A** king of Gerar sent and took
Gen 20: 3 But God came to **A** in a dream
Gen 20: 4 But **A** had not come near her
Gen 20: 8 So **A** rose early in the
Gen 20: 9 **A** called Abraham and said to
Gen 20:10 Then **A** said to Abraham
Gen 20:14 Then **A** took sheep, oxen, and
Gen 20:15 And **A** said, "See, my land is
Gen 20:17 and God healed **A**, his wife, and
Gen 20:18 house of **A** because of Sarah
Gen 21:22 to pass at that time that **A**
Gen 21:25 Then Abraham reproved **A**
Gen 21:26 And **A** said, "I do not know who
Gen 21:27 and oxen and gave them to **A**
Gen 21:29 Then **A** asked Abraham, "What
Gen 21:32 So **A** rose with Phichol, the
Gen 26: 1 Isaac went to **A** king of the
Gen 26: 8 long time, that **A** king of the
Gen 26: 9 Then **A** called Isaac and said,
Gen 26:10 And **A** said, "What is this you
Gen 26:11 So **A** charged all his people,
Gen 26:16 And **A** said to Isaac,
Gen 26:26 Then **A** came to him from Gerar
Judg 8:31 a son, whose name he called **A**
Judg 9: 1 **A** the son of Jerubbaal went
Judg 9: 3 was inclined to follow **A**, for
Judg 9: 4 with which **A** hired worthless
Judg 9: 6 and made **A** king beside the
Judg 9:16 and sincerity in making **A** king
Judg 9:18 sons on one stone, and made **A**
Judg 9:19 this day, then rejoice in **A**
Judg 9:20 if not, let fire come from **A**
Judg 9:20 from Beth Millo and devour **A**
Judg 9:21 for fear of **A** his brother
Judg 9:22 After **A** had reigned over
Judg 9:23 spirit of ill will between **A**
Judg 9:23 dealt treacherously with **A**
Judg 9:24 be laid on **A** their brother
Judg 9:25 and it was told **A**
Judg 9:27 and ate and drank, and cursed **A**
Judg 9:28 Who is **A**, and who is Shechem,
Judg 9:29 Then I would remove **A**
Judg 9:29 So he said to **A**, "Increase
Judg 9:31 sent messengers to **A** secretly
Judg 9:34 So **A** and all the people who
Judg 9:35 entrance to the city gate, **A**
Judg 9:38 which you said, 'Who is **A**
Judg 9:39 of Shechem, and fought with **A**
Judg 9:40 **A** chased him, and he fled from
Judg 9:41 Then **A** dwelt at Arumah, and
Judg 9:42 the field, and they told **A**
Judg 9:44 Then **A** and the company that
Judg 9:45 So **A** fought against the city
Judg 9:47 it was told **A** that all the
Judg 9:48 Then **A** went up to Mount
Judg 9:48 **A** took an ax in his hand and
Judg 9:49 his own bough and followed **A**
Judg 9:50 Then **A** went to Thebez, and he
Judg 9:52 So **A** came as far as the tower
Judg 9:55 of Israel saw that **A** was dead
Judg 9:56 repaid the wickedness of **A**
Judg 10: 1 After **A** there arose to save
2Sa 11:21 Who struck **A** the son of
1Ch 18:16 **A** the son of Abiathar were

ABIMELECH'S (*see* ABIMELECH)
Gen 21:25 which **A** servants had seized
Judg 9:53 an upper millstone on **A** head

ABINADAB
1Sa 7: 1 the house of **A** on the hill
1Sa 16: 8 So Jesse called **A**, and made
1Sa 17:13 the firstborn, next to him **A**
1Sa 31: 2 killed Jonathan, **A**, and
2Sa 6: 3 it out of the house of **A**,
2Sa 6: 3 Uzzah and Ahio, the sons of **A**
2Sa 6: 4 it out of the house of **A**,
1Ch 2:13 **A** the second, Shimea the
1Ch 8:33 begot Jonathan, Malchishua, **A**
1Ch 9:39 begot Jonathan, Malchishua, **A**
1Ch 10: 2 killed Jonathan, **A**, and
1Ch 13: 7 new cart from the house of **A**

ABINOAM
Judg 4: 6 of **A** from Kedesh in Naphtali
Judg 4:12 that Barak the son of **A** had
Judg 5: 1 the son of **A** sang on that day
Judg 5:12 captives away, O son of **A**

ABIRAM
Num 16: 1 **A** the sons of Eliab, and On
Num 16:12 **A** the sons of Eliab, but they
Num 16:24 tents of Korah, Dathan, and **A**
Num 16:25 rose and went to Dathan and **A**
Num 16:27 tents of Korah, Dathan, and **A**
Num 16:27 **A** came out and stood at the
Num 26: 9 were Nemuel, Dathan, and **A**
Num 26: 9 These are the Dathan and **A**
Deut 11: 6 **A** the sons of Eliab, the son
1Ki 16:34 with **A** his firstborn, and with
Ps 106:17 And covered the faction of **A**

ABISHAG
1Ki 1: 3 found **A** the Shunammite, and
1Ki 1:15 **A** the Shunammite was serving
1Ki 2:17 that he may give me **A** the
1Ki 2:21 Let **A** the Shunammite be given
1Ki 2:22 Now why do you ask **A** the

ABISHAI
1Sa 26: 6 and to **A** the son of Zeruiah,
1Sa 26: 6 And **A** said, "I will go down
1Sa 26: 7 **A** came to the people by night
1Sa 26: 8 Then **A** said to David, "God
1Sa 26: 9 And David said to **A**, "Do not
2Sa 2:18 Joab and **A** and Asahel
2Sa 2:24 Joab and **A** also pursued Abner
2Sa 3:30 **A** his brother killed Abner,
2Sa 10:10 the command of **A** his brother
2Sa 10:14 they also fled before **A**, and
2Sa 16: 9 Then **A** the son of Zeruiah
2Sa 16:11 And David said to **A** and all his
2Sa 18: 2 hand of **A** the son of Zeruiah
2Sa 18: 5 king had commanded Joab, **A**
2Sa 18:12 the king commanded you and **A**
2Sa 19:21 But **A** the son of Zeruiah
2Sa 20: 6 And David said to **A**, "Now
2Sa 20:10 **A** his brother pursued Sheba
2Sa 21:17 But **A** the son of Zeruiah came
2Sa 23:18 Now **A** the brother of Joab,
1Ch 2:16 And the sons of Zeruiah were **A**
1Ch 11:20 Now **A** the brother of Joab was
1Ch 18:12 Moreover **A** the son of Zeruiah
1Ch 19:11 the command of **A** his brother
1Ch 19:15 fled before **A** his brother

ABISHALOM (*see* ABSALOM)
1Ki 15: 2 the granddaughter of **A**
1Ki 15:10 the granddaughter of **A**

ABISHUA
1Ch 6: 4 Phinehas, and Phinehas begot **A**
1Ch 6: 5 **A** begot Bukki, and Bukki begot
1Ch 6:50 Phinehas his son, **A** his son,
1Ch 8: 4 **A**, Naaman, Ahoah,
Ezra 7: 5 the son of **A**, the son of

ABISHUR
1Ch 2:28 of Shammai were Nadab and **A**
1Ch 2:29 of the wife of **A** was Abihail

ABITAL
2Sa 3: 4 Shephatiah the son of **A**
1Ch 3: 3 the fifth, Shephatiah, by **A**

ABITUB
1Ch 8:11 And by Hushim he begot **A** and

ABIUD
Matt 1:13 Zerubbabel begot **A**
Matt 1:13 **A** begot Eliakim, and Eliakim

ABLE (*see* ABILITY)
Gen 13: 6 was not **a** to support them
Gen 15: 5 if you are **a** to number them
Gen 33:14 are **a** to endure, until I come
Ex 10: 5 will be **a** to see the earth
Ex 18:18 you are not **a** to perform it
Ex 18:21 from all the people **a** men
Ex 18:23 then you will be **a** to endure
Ex 18:25 Moses chose **a** men out of all
Ex 40:35 Moses was not **a** to enter the
Lev 5: 7 If he is not **a** to bring a
Lev 5:11 But if he is not **a** to bring
Lev 12: 8 if she is not **a** to bring a
Lev 14:22 such as he is **a** to afford
Lev 14:31 such as he is **a** to afford
Lev 25:26 becomes **a** to redeem it,
Lev 25:28 But if he is not **a** to have
Lev 25:49 or if he is **a** he may redeem
Num 1: 3 all who are **a** to go to war in
Num 1:20 all who were **a** to go to war
Num 1:22 all who were **a** to go to war
Num 1:24 all who were **a** to go to war
Num 1:26 all who were **a** to go to war
Num 1:28 all who were **a** to go to war
Num 1:30 all who were **a** to go to war
Num 1:32 all who were **a** to go to war
Num 1:34 all who were **a** to go to war
Num 1:36 all who were **a** to go to war
Num 1:38 all who were **a** to go to war
Num 1:40 all who were **a** to go to war
Num 1:42 all who were **a** to go to war
Num 1:45 all who were **a** to go to war
Num 6:21 else his hand is **a** to provide
Num 11:14 I am not **a** to bear all these
Num 13:30 we are well **a** to overcome it
Num 13:31 We are not **a** to go up against
Num 14:16 Because the LORD was not **a**
Num 22: 6 I shall be **a** to defeat them
Num 22:11 shall be **a** to overpower them
Num 22:37 Am I not **a** to honor you
Num 26: 2 all who are **a** to go to war in
Deut 1: 9 I alone am not **a** to bear you
Deut 7:24 no one shall be **a** to stand
Deut 9:28 Because the LORD was not **a** to
Deut 11:25 No man shall be **a** to stand
Deut 14:24 are not **a** to carry the tithe
Deut 16:17 man shall give as he is **a**
Josh 1: 5 No man shall be **a** to stand
Josh 14:12 I shall be **a** to drive them
Josh 23: 9 no one has been **a** to stand
Judg 8: 3 And what was I **a** to do in
1Sa 6:20 Who is **a** to stand before this
1Sa 17: 9 If he is **a** to fight with me
1Sa 17:33 You are not **a** to go against
1Ki 3: 9 For who is **a** to judge this
1Ki 9:21 been **a** to destroy completely
2Ki 3:21 all who were **a** to bear arms
2Ki 18:23 if you are **a** on your part to
2Ki 18:29 you, for he shall not be **a** to
1Ch 5:18 men **a** to bear shield and sword
1Ch 9:13 They were very **a** men for the
1Ch 12:36 **a** to keep battle formation,
1Ch 26: 7 Elihu and Semachiah were **a**
1Ch 26: 8 **a** men with strength for the
1Ch 26: 9 and brethren, eighteen **a** men
1Ch 26:30 thousand seven hundred **a** men
1Ch 26:32 thousand seven hundred **a** men
1Ch 29:14 that we should be **a** to offer
2Ch 2: 6 But who is **a** to build Him a
2Ch 7: 7 not **a** to receive the burnt
2Ch 20: 6 no one is **a** to withstand You
2Ch 20:37 were not **a** to go to Tarshish
2Ch 25: 5 **a** to go to war, who could
2Ch 25: 9 The LORD is **a** to give you
2Ch 32:13 of those lands in any way **a**
2Ch 32:14 that your God should be **a** to
2Ch 32:15 any nation or kingdom was **a**
Ezra 10:13 we are not **a** to stand outside
Neh 4:10 are not **a** to build the wall
Job 41:10 Who then is **a** to stand
Ps 18:38 that they were not **a** to rise
Ps 21:11 they are not **a** to perform
Ps 36:12 down and are not **a** to rise
Ps 40:12 so that I am not **a** to look up
Prov 27: 4 but who is **a** to stand before
Eccl 8:17 he will not be **a** to find it
Is 36: 8 if you are **a** on your part to
Is 36:14 will not be **a** to deliver you
Is 47:11 will not be **a** to put it off
Is 47:12 you will be **a** to profit,

2Ki 21: 2 according to the **a** of the
2Ki 21:11 of Judah has done these **a** (he
2Ki 23:24 all the **a** that were seen in
2Ch 28: 3 according to the **a** of the
2Ch 33: 2 according to the **a** of the
2Ch 34:33 **a** from all the country that
2Ch 36: 8 the **a** which he did, and what
2Ch 36:14 to all the **a** of the nations
Ezra 9: 1 to the **a** of the Canaanites
Ezra 9:11 with their **a** which have
Ezra 9:14 with the people of these **a**
Prov 26:25 are seven **a** in his heart
Is 66: 3 soul delights in their **a**,
Jer 4: 1 away your **a** out of My sight
Jer 7:10 delivered to do all these **a**'
Jer 7:30 They have set their **a** in the
Jer 13:27 your **a** on the hills in the
Jer 32:34 But they set their **a** in the
Jer 44:22 because of the **a** which you
Ezek 5: 9 again, because of all your **a**
Ezek 5:11 things and with all your **a**
Ezek 6: 9 they committed in all their **a**
Ezek 6:11 for all the evil **a** of the
Ezek 7: 3 will repay you for all your **a**
Ezek 7: 4 your **a** shall be in your midst
Ezek 7: 8 will repay you for all your **a**
Ezek 7: 9 your **a** will be in your midst
Ezek 7:20 from it the images of their **a**
Ezek 8: 6 the great **a** that the house of
Ezek 8: 6 again, you will see greater **a**
Ezek 8: 9 see the wicked **a** which they
Ezek 8:13 greater **a** that they are doing
Ezek 8:15 will see greater **a** than these
Ezek 8:17 the **a** which they commit here
Ezek 9: 4 cry over all the **a** that are
Ezek 11:18 and all its **a** from there
Ezek 11:21 detestable things and their **a**
Ezek 12:16 they may declare all their **a**
Ezek 14: 6 faces away from all your **a**
Ezek 16: 2 cause Jerusalem to know her **a**
Ezek 16:22 And in all your **a** and acts of
Ezek 16:43 in addition to all your **a**
Ezek 16:47 nor act according to their **a**
Ezek 16:51 your **a** more than they, and
Ezek 16:51 all the **a** which you have done
Ezek 16:58 for your lewdness and your **a**
Ezek 18:13 If he has done any of these **a**
Ezek 18:24 **a** that the wicked man does
Ezek 20: 4 them the **a** of their fathers
Ezek 20: 7 throw away the **a** which are
Ezek 20: 8 the **a** which were before their
Ezek 20:30 harlotry according to their **a**
Ezek 22: 2 Yes, show her all her **a**
Ezek 23:36 Then declare to them their **a**
Ezek 33:26 on your sword, you commit **a**
Ezek 33:29 because of all their **a** which
Ezek 36:31 for your iniquities and your **a**
Ezek 43: 8 by the **a** which they committed
Ezek 44: 6 us have no more of all your **a**
Ezek 44: 7 because of all your **a**
Ezek 44:13 and their **a** which they have
Dan 9:27 on the wing of **a** shall be one
Zech 9: 7 the **a** from between his teeth
Rev 17: 4 hand a golden cup full of **a**
Rev 17: 5 THE **A** OF THE EARTH

ABOUND (*see* ABOUNDED, ABOUNDING, ABOUNDS)
Gen 1:20 Let the waters **a** with an
Gen 8:17 that they may **a** on the earth
Deut 30: 9 you **a** in all the work of your
Prov 28:20 man will **a** with blessings
Matt 24:12 And because lawlessness will **a**
Rom 5:20 that the offense might **a**
Rom 6: 1 in sin that grace may **a**
Rom 15:13 that you may **a** in hope by the
2Co 1: 5 sufferings of Christ **a** in us
2Co 4:15 to **a** to the glory of God
2Co 8: 7 But as you **a** in everything
2Co 8: 7 see that you **a** in this grace
2Co 9: 8 make all grace **a** toward you
Eph 1: 8 which He made to **a** toward us
Phil 1: 9 your love may **a** still more
Phil 4:12 be abased, and I know how to **a**
Phil 4:12 and to be hungry, both to **a**
Phil 4:18 Indeed I have all and **a**
1Th 3:12 **a** in love to one another and
1Th 4: 1 Jesus that you should **a** more
2Pe 1: 8 these things are yours and **a**

ABOUNDED (*see* ABOUND)
Gen 1:21 with which the waters **a**,
Ps 105:30 Their land **a** with frogs, Even
Rom 5:15 Man, Jesus Christ, **a** to many
Rom 5:20 But where sin **a**, grace
Rom 5:20 **a**, grace **a** much more,
2Co 8: 2 their deep poverty **a** in the

ABOUNDING (*see* ABOUND)
Ex 34: 6 and **a** in goodness and truth,
Ps 103: 8 Slow to anger, and **a** in mercy
Prov 8:24 no fountains **a** with water
1Co 15:58 always **a** in the work of the
2Co 9:12 but also is **a** through many
Col 2: 7 **a** in it with thanksgiving

ABOUNDS (*see* ABOUND)
Prov 29:22 strife, and a furious man **a** in
2Co 1: 5 also **a** through Christ
Phil 4:17 fruit that **a** to your account
2Th 1: 3 you all **a** toward each other

ABOUT (*see* PREFACE)

ABOVE (*see* PREFACE)

ABRAHAM (*see* ABRAHAM'S, ABRAM)
Gen 17: 5 but your name shall be **A**
Gen 17: 9 And God said to **A**
Gen 17:15 Then God said to **A**, "As for
Gen 17:17 Then **A** fell on his face and
Gen 17:18 And **A** said to God,
Gen 17:22 him, and God went up from **A**
Gen 17:23 So **A** took Ishmael his son,
Gen 17:24 **A** was ninety-nine years old
Gen 17:26 same day **A** was circumcised
Gen 18: 6 So **A** hastened into the tent
Gen 18: 7 **A** ran to the herd, took a
Gen 18:11 Now **A** and Sarah were old,
Gen 18:13 And the LORD said to **A**, "Why
Gen 18:16 **A** went with them to send them
Gen 18:17 I hide from **A** what I am doing
Gen 18:18 since **A** shall surely become a
Gen 18:19 **A** what He has spoken to him
Gen 18:22 but **A** still stood before the
Gen 18:23 And **A** came near and said,
Gen 18:27 Then **A** answered and said
Gen 18:33 had finished speaking with **A**
Gen 18:33 and **A** returned to his place
Gen 19:27 **A** went early in the morning
Gen 19:29 plain, that God remembered **A**
Gen 20: 1 **A** journeyed from there to the
Gen 20: 2 Now **A** said of Sarah his wife,
Gen 20: 9 And Abimelech called **A** and
Gen 20:10 Then Abimelech said to **A**
Gen 20:11 And **A** said, "Because I thought
Gen 20:14 servants, and gave them to **A**
Gen 20:17 So **A** prayed to God
Gen 21: 2 bore **A** a son in his old age,
Gen 21: 3 **A** called the name of his son
Gen 21: 4 Then **A** circumcised his son
Gen 21: 5 Now **A** was one hundred years
Gen 21: 7 to **A** that Sarah would nurse
Gen 21: 8 **A** made a great feast on the
Gen 21: 9 whom she had borne to **A**,
Gen 21:10 Therefore she said to **A**
Gen 21:12 But God said to **A**, "Do not
Gen 21:14 So **A** rose early in the
Gen 21:22 of his army, spoke to **A**,
Gen 21:24 And **A** said, "I will swear."
Gen 21:25 Then **A** reproved Abimelech
Gen 21:27 So **A** took sheep and oxen and
Gen 21:28 **A** set seven ewe lambs of the
Gen 21:29 Then Abimelech asked **A**
Gen 21:33 Then **A** planted a tamarisk
Gen 21:34 **A** sojourned in the land of
Gen 22: 1 things that God tested **A**, and
Gen 22: 1 and said to him, "**A**!"
Gen 22: 3 So **A** rose early in the
Gen 22: 4 third day **A** lifted his eyes
Gen 22: 5 And **A** said to his young men,
Gen 22: 6 So **A** took the wood of the
Gen 22: 7 Isaac spoke to **A** his father
Gen 22: 8 **A** said, "My son, God will
Gen 22: 9 **A** built an altar there and
Gen 22:10 **A** stretched out his hand and
Gen 22:11 from heaven and said, "**A**, **A**!"
Gen 22:13 Then **A** lifted his eyes and
Gen 22:13 So **A** went and took the ram, and
Gen 22:14 And **A** called the name of the
Gen 22:15 **A** a second time out of heaven
Gen 22:19 So **A** returned to his young
Gen 22:19 and **A** dwelt at Beersheba
Gen 22:20 things that it was told **A**
Gen 23: 2 **A** came to mourn for Sarah and
Gen 23: 3 Then **A** stood up from before
Gen 23: 5 the sons of Heth answered **A**
Gen 23: 7 Then **A** stood up and bowed
Gen 23:10 **A** in the presence of the sons
Gen 23:12 Then **A** bowed himself down
Gen 23:14 And Ephron answered **A**, saying
Gen 23:16 And **A** listened to Ephron
Gen 23:16 **A** weighed out the silver for
Gen 23:18 to **A** as a possession in the
Gen 23:19 **A** buried Sarah his wife in
Gen 23:20 to **A** by the sons of Heth as
Gen 24: 1 Now **A** was old, well-advanced
Gen 24: 1 had blessed **A** in all things
Gen 24: 2 So **A** said to the oldest
Gen 24: 6 But **A** said to him, "Beware
Gen 24: 9 the thigh of **A** his master
Gen 24:12 O LORD God of my master **A**
Gen 24:12 show kindness to my master **A**
Gen 24:27 the LORD God of my master **A**
Gen 24:42 O LORD God of my master **A**
Gen 24:48 the LORD God of my master **A**
Gen 25: 1 **A** again took a wife, and her
Gen 25: 5 **A** gave all that he had to
Gen 25: 6 But **A** gave gifts to the sons
Gen 25: 6 of the concubines which **A** had
Gen 25: 8 Then **A** breathed his last and
Gen 25:10 the field which **A** purchased
Gen 25:10 There **A** was buried, and Sarah
Gen 25:11 to pass, after the death of **A**
Gen 25:12 maidservant, bore to **A**
Gen 25:19 **A** begot Isaac
Gen 26: 1 that was in the days of **A**
Gen 26: 3 I swore to **A** your father
Gen 26: 5 because **A** obeyed My voice and
Gen 26:15 in the days of **A** his father
Gen 26:18 in the days of **A** his father
Gen 26:18 them up after the death of **A**
Gen 26:24 I am the God of your father **A**
Gen 28: 4 and give you the blessing of **A**
Gen 28: 4 stranger, which God gave to **A**
Gen 28:13 the LORD God of **A** your father
Gen 31:42 of my father, the God of **A**
Gen 31:53 The God of **A**, the God of
Gen 32: 9 O God of my father **A** and God
Gen 35:12 The land which I gave **A** and
Gen 35:27 (that is, Hebron), where **A**
Gen 48:15 God, before whom my fathers **A**
Gen 48:16 and the name of my fathers **A**
Gen 49:30 which **A** bought with the field
Gen 49:31 There they buried **A** and Sarah
Gen 50:13 which **A** bought with the field
Gen 50:24 land of which He swore to **A**
Ex 2:24 His covenant with **A**, with
Ex 3: 6 the God of **A**, the God of
Ex 3:15 of your fathers, the God of **A**
Ex 3:16 of your fathers, the God of **A**
Ex 4: 5 their fathers, the God of **A**
Ex 6: 3 I appeared to **A**, to Isaac, and
Ex 6: 8 which I swore to give to **A**
Ex 32:13 Remember **A**, Isaac, and Israel,
Ex 33: 1 land of which I swore to **A**
Lev 26:42 with **A** I will remember
Num 32:11 land of which I swore to **A**
Deut 1: 8 to **A**, Isaac, and Jacob
Deut 6:10 swore to your fathers, to **A**
Deut 9: 5 swore to your fathers, to **A**
Deut 9:27 Remember Your servants, **A**
Deut 29:13 sworn to your fathers, to **A**
Deut 30:20 swore to your fathers, to **A**
Deut 34: 4 of which I swore to give **A**
Josh 24: 2 Terah, the father of **A** and the
Josh 24: 3 Then I took your father **A**
1Ki 18:36 LORD God of **A**, Isaac, and
2Ki 13:23 of His covenant with **A**, Isaac
1Ch 1:27 and Abram, that is **A**
1Ch 1:28 The sons of **A** were Isaac and
1Ch 1:34 And **A** begot Isaac
1Ch 16:16 covenant which He made with **A**
1Ch 29:18 O LORD God of **A**, Isaac, and
2Ch 20: 7 of **A** Your friend forever
2Ch 30: 6 return to the LORD God of **A**
Neh 9: 7 and gave him the name **A**
Ps 47: 9 The people of the God of **A**
Ps 105: 6 O seed of **A** His servant, You
Ps 105: 9 covenant which He made with **A**
Ps 105:42 promise, And **A** His servant
Is 29:22 says the LORD, who redeemed **A**
Is 41: 8 descendants of **A** My friend

Is 51: 2 Look to A your father, and to
Is 63:16 though A was ignorant of us,
Jer 33:26 over the descendants of A
Ezek 33:24 A was only one, and he
Mic 7:20 truth to Jacob and mercy to A
Matt 1: 1 Son of David, the Son of A
Matt 1: 2 A begot Isaac, Isaac begot
Matt 1:17 from A to David are fourteen
Matt 3: 9 We have A as our father
Matt 3: 9 to A from these stones
Matt 8:11 and west, and sit down with A
Matt 22:32 I am the God of A, the God
Mark 12:26 saying, I am the God of A
Luke 1:55 He spoke to our fathers, to A
Luke 1:73 He swore to our father A
Luke 3: 8 We have A as our father
Luke 3: 8 to A from these stones
Luke 3:34 son of Isaac, the son of A
Luke 13:16 woman, being a daughter of A
Luke 13:28 of teeth, when you see A and
Luke 16:23 saw A afar off, and Lazarus in
Luke 16:24 he cried and said, Father A
Luke 16:25 But A said, Son, remember
Luke 16:29 A said to him, They have
Luke 16:30 And he said, No, father A
Luke 19: 9 because he also is a son of A
Luke 20:37 called the Lord the God of A
John 8:39 to Him, "A is our father
John 8:39 you would do the works of A
John 8:40 A did not do this
John 8:52 A is dead, and the prophets
John 8:53 You greater than our father A
John 8:56 Your father A rejoiced to see
John 8:57 years old, and have You seen A
John 8:58 I say to you, before A was
Acts 3:13 The God of A, Isaac, and Jacob
Acts 3:25 with our fathers, saying to A
Acts 7: 2 appeared to our father A when
Acts 7: 5 But even when A had no child
Acts 7: 8 and so A begot Isaac and
Acts 7:16 and laid in the tomb that A
Acts 7:17 near which God had sworn to A
Acts 7:32 the God of A, the God of
Acts 13:26 sons of the family of A, and
Rom 4: 1 that A our father has found
Rom 4: 2 For if A was justified by
Rom 4: 3 A believed God, and it was
Rom 4: 9 to A for righteousness
Rom 4:12 our father A had while still
Rom 4:13 of the world was not to A or
Rom 4:16 who are of the faith of A
Rom 9: 7 they are the seed of A
Rom 11: 1 Israelite, of the seed of A
2Co 11:22 Are they the seed of A
Gal 3: 6 just as A believed God, and
Gal 3: 7 are of faith are sons of A
Gal 3: 8 the gospel to A beforehand
Gal 3: 9 are blessed with believing A
Gal 3:14 of A might come upon the
Gal 3:16 Now to A and his Seed were the
Gal 3:18 God gave it to A by promise
Gal 4:22 written that A had two sons
Heb 2:16 give aid to the seed of A
Heb 6:13 when God made a promise to A
Heb 7: 1 who met A returning from the
Heb 7: 2 to whom also A gave a tenth
Heb 7: 4 A gave a tenth of the spoils
Heb 7: 5 have come from the loins of A
Heb 7: 6 them received tithes from A
Heb 7: 9 tithes, paid tithes through A
Heb 11: 8 By faith A obeyed when he was
Heb 11:17 By faith A, when he was
Jas 2:21 Was not A our father
Jas 2:23 A believed God, and it was
1Pe 3: 6 as Sarah obeyed A, calling

ABRAHAM'S (*see* ABRAHAM)
Gen 17:23 male among the men of A house
Gen 20:18 because of Sarah, A wife
Gen 21:11 was very displeasing in A
Gen 22:23 bore to Nahor, A brother
Gen 24:15 A brother, came out with her
Gen 24:34 So he said, "I am A servant
Gen 24:52 when A servant heard their
Gen 24:59 and A servant and his men
Gen 25: 7 of A life which he lived
Gen 25:12 A son, whom Hagar the
Gen 25:19 the genealogy of Isaac, A son
Gen 26:24 for My servant A sake
Gen 28: 9 A son, the sister of Nebajoth
1Ch 1:32 A concubine, were Zimran,

Luke 16:22 by the angels to A bosom
John 8:33 We are A descendants, and have
John 8:37 that you are A descendants
John 8:39 If you were A children, you
Gal 3:29 Christ's, then you are A seed

ABRAM (*see* ABRAHAM, ABRAM'S)
Gen 11:26 seventy years, and begot A
Gen 11:27 Terah begot A, Nahor, and
Gen 11:29 Then A and Nahor took wives
Gen 11:31 And Terah took his son A and
Gen 12: 1 Now the LORD had said to A
Gen 12: 4 So A departed as the LORD had
Gen 12: 4 A was seventy-five years old
Gen 12: 5 Then A took Sarai his wife and
Gen 12: 6 A passed through the land to
Gen 12: 7 Then the LORD appeared to A
Gen 12: 9 So A journeyed, going on
Gen 12:10 and A went down to Egypt to
Gen 12:14 when A came into Egypt, that
Gen 12:16 He treated A well for her
Gen 12:18 And Pharaoh called A and said,
Gen 13: 1 Then A went up from Egypt, he
Gen 13: 2 A was very rich in livestock,
Gen 13: 4 there A called on the name of
Gen 13: 5 Lot also, who went with A
Gen 13: 8 So A said to Lot, Please
Gen 13:12 A dwelt in the land of Canaan
Gen 13:14 And the LORD said to A, after
Gen 13:18 Then A moved his tent, and
Gen 14:13 told A the Hebrew, for he
Gen 14:13 and they were allies with A
Gen 14:14 Now when A heard that his
Gen 14:19 Blessed be A of God Most High
Gen 14:21 the king of Sodom said to A
Gen 14:22 But A said to the king of
Gen 14:23 say, I have made A rich'
Gen 15: 1 LORD came to A in a vision
Gen 15: 1 Do not be afraid, A
Gen 15: 2 But A said, "Lord GOD, what
Gen 15: 3 Then A said, "Look, You have
Gen 15:11 carcasses, A drove them away
Gen 15:12 a deep sleep fell upon A
Gen 15:13 Then He said to A
Gen 15:18 LORD made a covenant with A
Gen 16: 2 So Sarai said to A, "See now
Gen 16: 2 A heeded the voice of Sarai
Gen 16: 3 her husband A to be his wife
Gen 16: 3 after A had dwelt ten years
Gen 16: 5 Then Sarai said to A, "My
Gen 16: 6 So A said to Sarai, "Indeed
Gen 16:15 So Hagar bore A a son
Gen 16:15 A named his son, whom Hagar
Gen 16:16 A was eighty-six years old
Gen 16:16 when Hagar bore Ishmael to A
Gen 17: 1 When A was ninety-nine years
Gen 17: 1 old, the LORD appeared to A
Gen 17: 3 Then A fell on his face, and
Gen 17: 5 shall your name be called A
1Ch 1:27 and A, that is Abraham
Neh 9: 7 are the LORD God, Who chose A

ABRAM'S (*see* ABRAM)
Gen 11:29 the name of A wife was Sarai,
Gen 11:31 Sarai, his son A wife, and
Gen 12:17 because of Sarai, A wife
Gen 13: 7 the herdsmen of A livestock
Gen 14:12 A brother's son who dwelt in
Gen 16: 1 A wife, had borne him no
Gen 16: 3 A wife, took Hagar her maid,

ABROAD
Gen 11: 4 lest we be scattered a over
Gen 11: 8 So the LORD scattered them a
Gen 11: 9 the LORD scattered them a
Gen 28:14 shall spread a to the west
Ex 5:12 the people were scattered a
Ps 112: 9 He has dispersed a, He has
Prov 5:16 your fountains be dispersed a
Is 24: 1 scatters a its inhabitants
Is 44:24 Who spreads a the earth by
Ezek 34:21 horns, and scattered them a
Zech 2: 6 for I have spread you a like
Matt 12:30 not gather with Me scatters a
John 11:52 of God who were scattered a
2Co 9: 9 He has dispersed a, He has
Jas 1: 1 tribes which are scattered a

ABRONAH
Num 33:34 from Jotbathah and camped at A
Num 33:35 They departed from A and

ABSALOM (*see* ABISHALOM, ABSALOM'S)
2Sa 3: 3 A the son of Maacah, the
2Sa 13: 1 that A the son of David had a
2Sa 13:20 A her brother said to her,
2Sa 13:22 A spoke to his brother Amnon
2Sa 13:22 For A hated Amnon, because he
2Sa 13:23 that A had sheepshearers in
2Sa 13:23 so A invited all the king's
2Sa 13:24 Then A came to the king and
2Sa 13:25 But the king said to A, "No,
2Sa 13:26 Then A said, "If not, please
2Sa 13:27 But A urged him
2Sa 13:28 Now A had commanded his
2Sa 13:29 So the servants of A did to
2Sa 13:29 to Amnon as A had commanded
2Sa 13:30 A has killed all the king's
2Sa 13:32 For by the command of A this
2Sa 13:34 Then A fled
2Sa 13:37 But A fled and went to Talmai
2Sa 13:38 So A fled and went to Geshur,
2Sa 13:39 King David longed to go to A
2Sa 14: 1 heart was concerned about A
2Sa 14:21 bring back the young man A
2Sa 14:23 and brought A to Jerusalem
2Sa 14:24 So A returned to his own
2Sa 14:25 much as A for his good looks
2Sa 14:27 To A were born three sons, and
2Sa 14:28 A dwelt two full years in
2Sa 14:29 Therefore A sent for Joab, to
2Sa 14:32 And A answered Joab,
2Sa 14:33 And when he had called for A
2Sa 14:33 Then the king kissed A
2Sa 15: 1 that A provided himself with
2Sa 15: 2 Now A would rise early and
2Sa 15: 2 that A would call to him and
2Sa 15: 3 Then A would say to him
2Sa 15: 4 Moreover A would say, "Oh,
2Sa 15: 6 In this manner A acted toward
2Sa 15: 6 So A stole the hearts of the
2Sa 15: 7 years that A said to the king
2Sa 15:10 Then A sent spies throughout
2Sa 15:10 say, A reigns in Hebron
2Sa 15:11 with A went two hundred men
2Sa 15:12 Then A sent for Ahithophel
2Sa 15:12 strong, for the people with A
2Sa 15:13 the men of Israel are with A
2Sa 15:14 we shall not escape from A
2Sa 15:31 among the conspirators with A
2Sa 15:34 to the city, and say to A, I
2Sa 15:37 And A came into Jerusalem
2Sa 16: 8 into the hand of A your son
2Sa 16:15 Meanwhile A and all the people
2Sa 16:16 David's friend, came to A
2Sa 16:16 that Hushai said to A
2Sa 16:17 So A said to Hushai, "Is
2Sa 16:18 And Hushai said to A, "No,
2Sa 16:20 Then A said to Ahithophel,
2Sa 16:21 And Ahithophel said to A, "Go
2Sa 16:22 for A on the top of the house
2Sa 16:22 A went in to his father's
2Sa 16:23 both with David and with A
2Sa 17: 1 Moreover Ahithophel said to A
2Sa 17: 4 And the saying pleased A and
2Sa 17: 5 Then A said, "Now call
2Sa 17: 6 And when Hushai came to A,
2Sa 17: 6 A spoke to him, saying,
2Sa 17: 7 So Hushai said to A
2Sa 17: 9 among the people who follow A
2Sa 17:14 So A and all the men of Israel
2Sa 17:14 might bring disaster on A
2Sa 17:15 and so Ahithophel counseled A
2Sa 17:18 a lad saw them, and told A
2Sa 17:24 A crossed over the Jordan, he
2Sa 17:25 A made Amasa captain of the
2Sa 17:26 A encamped in the land of
2Sa 18: 5 my sake with the young man A
2Sa 18: 5 captains orders concerning A
2Sa 18: 9 Then A met the servants of
2Sa 18: 9 A rode on a mule
2Sa 18:10 I just saw A hanging in a
2Sa 18:12 anyone touch the young man A
2Sa 18:15 Joab's armor surrounded A
2Sa 18:17 And they took A and cast him
2Sa 18:18 Now A in his lifetime had
2Sa 18:29 Is the young man A safe
2Sa 18:32 Is the young man A safe
2Sa 18:33 O my son A—my son
2Sa 18:33 my son, my son A
2Sa 18:33 O A my son, my son
2Sa 19: 1 is weeping and mourning for A

2Sa 19: 4 O my son A!
2Sa 19: 4 O A, my son, my son
2Sa 19: 6 perceive that if A had lived
2Sa 19: 9 from the land because of A
2Sa 19:10 But A, whom we anointed over
2Sa 20: 6 will do us more harm than A
1Ki 1: 6 mother had borne him after A
1Ki 2: 7 I fled from A your brother
1Ki 2:28 he had not defected to A
1Ch 3: 2 A the son of Maacah, the
2Ch 11:20 Maacah the granddaughter of A
2Ch 11:21 of A more than all his wives

ABSALOM'S (*see* ABSALOM)
2Sa 13: 4 Tamar, my brother A sister
2Sa 13:20 in her brother A house
2Sa 14:30 A servants set the field on
2Sa 14:31 Joab arose and came to A house
2Sa 17:20 when A servants came to the
2Sa 18:14 thrust them through A heart
2Sa 18:18 day it is called A Monument

ABSENCE (*see* ABSENT)
Luke 22: 6 in the a of the multitude
Phil 2:12 but now much more in my a

ABSENT (*see* ABSENCE)
Gen 31:49 me when we are a one from
1Co 5: 3 as a in body but present in
2Co 5: 6 body we are a from the Lord
2Co 5: 8 rather to be a from the body
2Co 5: 9 our aim, whether present or a
2Co 10: 1 but being a am bold toward
2Co 10:11 word by letters when we are a
2Co 13: 2 now being a I write to those
2Co 13:10 I write these things being a
Phil 1:27 I come and see you or am a
Col 2: 5 though I am a in the flesh

ABSTAIN (*see* ABSTINENCE)
Deut 23:22 But if you a from vowing, it
Acts 15:20 to a from things polluted by
Acts 15:29 that you a from things
1Th 4: 3 that you should a from sexual
1Th 5:22 A from every form of evil
1Ti 4: 3 commanding to a from foods
1Pe 2:11 a from fleshly lusts which

ABSTINENCE (*see* ABSTAIN)
Acts 27:21 But after long a from food

ABUNDANCE (*see* ABUNDANT)
Gen 1:20 with an a of living creatures
Deut 28:47 for the a of all things,
Deut 33:19 partake of the a of the seas
1Sa 1:16 woman, for out of the a of my
2Sa 12:30 spoil of the city in great a
1Ki 1:19 fattened cattle and sheep in a
1Ki 1:25 fattened cattle and sheep in a
1Ki 10:10 of gold, spices in great a
1Ki 10:10 a of spices as the queen of
1Ki 18:41 is the sound of a of rain
1Ch 20: 2 spoil of the city in great a
1Ch 22: 3 David prepared iron in a for
1Ch 22: 3 bronze in a beyond measure,
1Ch 22: 4 and cedar trees in a
1Ch 22:15 are workmen with you in a
1Ch 29: 2 stones, and marble slabs in a
1Ch 29:16 God, all this a that we have
1Ch 29:21 and sacrifices in a for all
2Ch 2: 9 to prepare timber for me in a
2Ch 4:18 a that the weight of the
2Ch 9: 1 that bore spices, gold in a
2Ch 9: 9 of gold, spices in great a
2Ch 11:23 he gave them provisions in a
2Ch 14:15 off sheep and camels in a, and
2Ch 17: 5 he had riches and honor in a
2Ch 18: 1 had riches and honor in a
2Ch 18: 2 sheep and oxen in a for him
2Ch 20:25 an a of valuables on the dead
2Ch 24:11 day, and gathered money in a
2Ch 29:35 the burnt offerings were in a
2Ch 31: 5 of Israel brought in a the
2Ch 31:10 what is left is this great a
2Ch 32: 5 made weapons and shields in a
2Ch 32:29 of flocks and herds in a
Neh 5:18 an a of all kinds of wine
Neh 9:25 groves, and fruit trees in a
Esth 1: 7 other, with royal wine in a
Job 22:11 and an a of water covers you
Job 36:31 He gives food in a
Job 38:34 that an a of water may cover
Ps 18:14 the foe, Lightnings in a, and
Ps 37:11 themselves in the a of peace
Ps 52: 7 in the a of his riches, And
Ps 65:11 And Your paths drip with a
Ps 72: 7 a of peace, Until the moon is
Ps 72:16 There will be an a of grain
Ps 73: 7 Their eyes bulge with a
Ps 78:15 drink in a like the depths
Eccl 5:10 nor he who loves a, with
Eccl 5:12 but the a of the rich will
Is 7:22 from the a of milk they give,
Is 15: 7 Therefore the a they have
Is 47: 9 for the great a of your
Is 55: 2 your soul delight itself in a
Is 60: 5 because the a of the sea
Is 66:11 with the a of her glory
Jer 31:14 soul of the priests with a
Jer 33: 6 reveal to them the a of peace
Jer 40:12 wine and summer fruit in a
Ezek 16:49 of food, and a of idleness
Ezek 26:10 of the a of his horses, their
Ezek 27:16 of the a of goods you made
Ezek 27:18 of the a of goods you made
Ezek 28:16 By the a of your trading you
Ezek 31: 5 because of the a of water
Zech 14:14 silver, and apparel in great a
Matt 12:34 For out of the a of the heart
Matt 13:12 be given, and he will have a
Matt 25:29 be given, and he will have a
Mark 12:44 all put in out of their a
Luke 6:45 For out of the a of the heart
Luke 12:15 does not consist in the a of
Luke 21: 4 a have put in offerings for
Rom 5:17 those who receive a of grace
2Co 8: 2 affliction the a of their joy
2Co 8:14 your a may supply their lack
2Co 8:14 that their a also may supply
2Co 9: 8 have an a for every good work
2Co 12: 7 by the a of the revelations
Rev 18: 3 through the a of her luxury

ABUNDANT (*see* ABUNDANCE, ABUNDANTLY)
Num 14:18 and a in mercy, forgiving
1Ki 10:27 he made cedars as a as the
1Ch 22: 5 So David made a
1Ch 22:14 measure, for it is so a
2Ch 1:15 he made cedars as a as the
2Ch 9:27 he made cedar trees as a as
Neh 9:17 a in kindness, and did not
Neh 9:27 according to Your a mercies
Job 37:23 in judgment and a justice
Ps 86: 5 a in mercy to all those who
Ps 86:15 and a in mercy and truth
Ps 130: 7 And with Him is a redemption
Is 56:12 be as today, and much more a
Jer 51:13 a in treasures, your end has
Ezek 17: 5 he placed it by a waters and
Ezek 31: 7 its roots reached to a waters
Dan 4:12 were lovely, its fruit a, and
Dan 4:21 were lovely and its fruit a
Jon 4: 2 a in lovingkindness, One who
2Co 11:23 in labors more a, in stripes
Phil 1:26 for me may be more a in Jesus
1Ti 1:14 of our Lord was exceedingly a
1Pe 1: 3 who according to His a mercy

ABUNDANTLY (*see* ABUNDANT)
Gen 9: 7 bring forth a in the earth and
Gen 41:47 the ground brought forth a
Ex 1: 7 were fruitful and increased a
Ex 8: 3 shall bring forth frogs a
Num 20:11 and water came out a, and the
1Ch 12:40 and oil and oxen and sheep a
2Ch 31: 5 they brought in a the tithe
Job 8: 7 latter end would increase a
Job 36:28 drop down and pour a on man
Ps 36: 8 They are a satisfied with the
Ps 65:10 You water its ridges a, You
Ps 132:15 I will a bless her provision
Is 35: 2 It shall blossom a and rejoice
Is 55: 7 our God, for He will a pardon
John 10:10 that they may have it more a
1Co 15:10 labored more a than they all
2Co 1:12 of God, and more a toward you
2Co 2: 4 which I have so a for you
2Co 12:15 though the more a I love you
Eph 3:20 a above all that we ask or
Tit 3: 6 us a through Jesus Christ our
Heb 6:17 determining to show more a to
2Pe 1:11 to you a into the everlasting

ABUSE (*see* ABUSED)
1Sa 31: 4 and thrust me through and a me
1Ch 10: 4 men come and a me
Jer 38:19 into their hand, and they a me
Acts 14: 5 Jews, with their rulers, to a
1Co 9:18 that I may not a my authority

ABUSED (*see* ABUSE)
Num 22:29 Because you have a me
Judg 19:25 a her all night until morning

ABYSS
Luke 8:31 them to go out into the a
Rom 10: 7 Who will descend into the a

ACACIA (*see* ACACIAS)
Ex 25: 5 red, badger skins, and a wood
Ex 25:10 shall make an ark of a wood
Ex 25:13 shall make poles of a wood
Ex 25:23 also make a table of a wood
Ex 25:28 make the poles of a wood, and
Ex 26:15 make the boards of a wood
Ex 26:26 you shall make bars of a wood
Ex 26:32 of a wood overlaid with gold
Ex 26:37 screen five pillars of a wood
Ex 27: 1 shall make an altar of a wood
Ex 27: 6 the altar, poles of a wood
Ex 30: 1 you shall make it of a wood
Ex 30: 5 make the poles of a wood, and
Ex 35: 7 red, badger skins, and a wood
Ex 35:24 with whom was found a wood
Ex 36:20 he made boards of a wood,
Ex 36:31 And he made bars of a wood
Ex 36:36 for it four pillars of a wood
Ex 37: 1 made the ark of a wood
Ex 37: 4 He made poles of a wood, and
Ex 37:10 He made the table of a wood
Ex 37:15 he made the poles of a wood
Ex 37:25 the incense altar of a wood
Ex 37:28 he made the poles of a wood
Ex 38: 1 of burnt offering of a wood
Ex 38: 6 he made the poles of a wood
Num 25: 1 Israel remained in A Grove
Deut 10: 3 So I made an ark of a wood
Josh 2: 1 from A Grove to spy secretly
Josh 3: 1 and they set out from A Grove
Is 41:19 the a tree, the myrtle and the
Mic 6: 5 from A Grove to Gilgal, that

ACACIAS (*see* ACACIA)
Joel 3:18 LORD and water the Valley of A

ACCAD
Gen 10:10 kingdom was Babel, Erech, A

ACCEPT (*see* ACCEPTABLE, ACCEPTANCE, ACCEPTED, ACCEPTING, ACCEPTS)
Gen 32:20 perhaps he will a me
Ex 8: 9 A the honor of saying when I
Ex 22:11 the owner of it shall a that
Lev 26:41 and they a their guilt
Lev 26:43 they will a their guilt,
Num 7: 5 A these from them, that they
Deut 20:11 if they a your offer of peace
Deut 33:11 and a the work of his hands
1Sa 26:19 me, let Him a an offering
2Sa 24:23 May the LORD your God a you
Esth 4: 4 him, but he would not a them
Job 2:10 we indeed a good from God
Job 2:10 and shall we not a adversity
Job 42: 8 For I will a him, lest I deal
Ps 20: 3 And a your burnt sacrifice
Ps 119:108 A, I pray, the freewill
Prov 6:35 He will a no recompense, nor
Jer 14:10 the LORD does not a them
Jer 14:12 offering, I will not a them
Ezek 20:40 there I will a them, and there
Ezek 20:41 I will a you as a sweet aroma
Ezek 43:27 and I will a you,' says the
Hos 8:13 but the LORD does not a them
Amos 5:22 offerings, I will not a them
Mal 1: 8 Would he a you favorably
Mal 1: 9 will He a you favorably
Mal 1:10 Nor will I a an offering from
Mal 1:13 Should I a this from your
Matt 19:11 All cannot a this saying, but
Matt 19:12 He who is able to a it, let
Matt 19:12 to a it, let him a it
Mark 4:20 the word, a it, and bear fruit
Acts 24: 3 we a it always and in all
Acts 24:15 which they themselves also a
1Co 6: 7 Why do you not rather a wrong

ACCUSE (*see* ACCUSATION, ACCUSED, ACCUSER, ACCUSES, ACCUSING)
Matt 12:10 that they might **a** Him
Mark 3: 2 so that they might **a** Him
Luke 3:14 anyone or **a** falsely, and be
Luke 11:54 say, that they might **a** Him
Luke 23: 2 And they began to **a** Him,
Luke 23:14 things of which you **a** Him
John 5:45 I shall **a** you to the Father
John 8: 6 something of which to **a** Him
Acts 24: 8 things of which we **a** him
Acts 24:13 things of which they now **a** me
Acts 25: 5 **a** this man, to see if there
Acts 25:11 of which these men **a** me, no
Acts 28:19 of which to **a** my nation

ACCUSED (*see* ACCUSE)
Dan 3: 8 came forward and **a** the Jews
Dan 6:24 those men who had **a** Daniel
Matt 27:12 while He was being **a** by the
Mark 15: 3 the chief priests **a** Him of
Luke 23:10 stood and vehemently **a** Him
Acts 22:30 why he was **a** by the Jews, he
Acts 23:28 to know the reason they **a** him
Acts 23:29 was **a** concerning questions of
Acts 25:16 to destruction before the **a**
Acts 26: 2 of which I am **a** by the Jews
Acts 26: 7 Agrippa, I am **a** by the Jews
Tit 1: 6 not **a** of dissipation or
Rev 12:10 who **a** them before our God day

ACCUSER (*see* ACCUSE, ACCUSERS)
Ps 109: 6 let an **a** stand at his right
Rev 12:10 for the **a** of our brethren,

ACCUSERS (*see* ACCUSER)
Ps 109: 4 for my love they are my **a**
Ps 109:20 be the LORD's reward to my **a**
Ps 109:29 Let my **a** be clothed with
John 8:10 where are those **a** of yours
Acts 23:30 also commanded his **a** to state
Acts 23:35 when your **a** also have come
Acts 24: 8 his **a** to come to you
Acts 25:16 meets the **a** face to face, and
Acts 25:18 When the **a** stood up, they

ACCUSES (*see* ACCUSE)
John 5:45 there is one who **a** you

ACCUSING (*see* ACCUSE)
Rom 2:15 **a** or else excusing them)

ACCUSTOMED
1Sa 30:31 and his men were **a** to rove
Jer 13:23 do good who are **a** to do evil
Matt 27:15 was **a** to releasing to the
Mark 10: 1 to Him again, and as He was **a**
Mark 15: 6 Now at the feast he was **a** to
Luke 22:39 Mount of Olives, as He was **a**

ACHAIA
Acts 18:12 Gallio was proconsul of **A**
Acts 18:27 when he desired to cross to **A**
Acts 19:21 through Macedonia and **A**
Rom 15:26 and **A** to make a certain
Rom 16: 5 firstfruits of **A** to Christ
1Co 16:15 it is the firstfruits of **A**
2Co 1: 1 the saints who are in all **A**
2Co 9: 2 that **A** was ready a year ago
2Co 11:10 boasting in the regions of **A**
1Th 1: 7 in Macedonia and **A** who believe
1Th 1: 8 not only in Macedonia and **A**

ACHAICUS
1Co 16:17 Stephanas, Fortunatus, and **A**

ACHAN (*see* ACHAR)
Josh 7: 1 for **A** the son of Carmi, the
Josh 7:18 **A** the son of Carmi, the son
Josh 7:19 So Joshua said to **A**, My son
Josh 7:20 **A** answered Joshua and said,
Josh 7:24 took **A** the son of Zerah, the
Josh 22:20 Did not **A** the son of Zerah

ACHAR (*see* ACHAN)
1Ch 2: 7 The son of Carmi was **A**, the

ACHBOR
Gen 36:38 son of **A** reigned in his place
Gen 36:39 Baal-Hanan the son of **A** died
2Ki 22:12 **A** the son of Michaiah,
2Ki 22:14 Hilkiah the priest, Ahikam, **A**
1Ch 1:49 son of **A** reigned in his place
Jer 26:22 Elnathan the son of **A**, and
Jer 36:12 Elnathan the son of **A**,

ACHIM
Matt 1:14 begot Zadok, Zadok begot **A**
Matt 1:14 and **A** begot Eliud.

ACHISH
1Sa 21:10 went to **A** the king of Gath
1Sa 21:11 the servants of **A** said to him
1Sa 21:12 afraid of **A** the king of Gath
1Sa 21:14 Then **A** said to his servants,
1Sa 27: 2 him to **A** the son of Maoch
1Sa 27: 3 So David dwelt with **A** at Gath
1Sa 27: 5 Then David said to **A**, "If I
1Sa 27: 6 So **A** gave him Ziklag that day
1Sa 27: 9 and returned and came to **A**
1Sa 27:10 Then **A** would say, "Where
1Sa 27:12 So **A** believed David, saying,
1Sa 28: 1 And **A** said to David,
1Sa 28: 2 And David said to **A**, "Surely
1Sa 28: 2 And **A** said to David,
1Sa 29: 2 in review at the rear with **A**
1Sa 29: 3 **A** said to the princes of the
1Sa 29: 6 Then **A** called David and said
1Sa 29: 8 Then David said to **A**, "But
1Sa 29: 9 But **A** answered and said to
1Ki 2:39 away to **A** the son of Maachah
1Ki 2:40 went to **A** at Gath to seek his

ACHMETHA
Ezra 6: 2 And at **A**, in the palace that

ACHOR
Josh 7:24 them to the Valley of **A**
Josh 7:26 the Valley of **A** to this day
Josh 15: 7 Debir from the Valley of **A**
Is 65:10 the Valley of **A** a place for
Hos 2:15 the Valley of **A** as a door of

ACHSAH
Josh 15:16 it, to him I will give **A** my
Josh 15:17 he gave him **A** his daughter as
Judg 1:12 give my daughter **A** as wife
Judg 1:13 him his daughter **A** as wife
1Ch 2:49 the daughter of Caleb was **A**

ACHSHAPH
Josh 11: 1 of Shimron, to the king of **A**
Josh 12:20 the king of **A**, one
Josh 19:25 Helkath, Hali, Beten, **A**,

ACHZIB (*see* CHEZIB)
Josh 15:44 Keilah, **A**, and Mareshah
Josh 19:29 at the sea by the region of **A**
Judg 1:31 of Sidon, or of Ahlab, **A**,
Mic 1:14 the houses of **A** shall be a

ACKNOWLEDGE (*see* ACKNOWLEDGED, ACKNOWLEDGES, ACKNOWLEDGMENT)
Deut 21:17 But he shall **a** the son of the
Deut 33: 9 nor did he **a** his brothers, Or
Ps 51: 3 For I **a** my transgressions, And
Prov 3: 6 in all your ways **a** Him, and He
Is 33:13 you who are near, **a** My might
Is 61: 9 All who see them shall **a** them
Is 63:16 us, and Israel does not **a** us
Jer 3:13 Only **a** your iniquity, that
Jer 14:20 We **a**, O LORD, our wickedness
Jer 24: 5 so will I **a** those who are
Dan 11:39 foreign god, which he shall **a**
Hos 5:15 till they **a** their offense
Hos 8: 4 princes, and I did not **a** it
1Co 14:37 let him **a** that the things
1Co 16:18 therefore **a** such men

ACKNOWLEDGED (*see* ACKNOWLEDGE)
Gen 38:26 So Judah **a** them and said
Ex 2:25 of Israel, and God **a** them
Ps 32: 5 I **a** my sin to You, And my
Acts 15: 8 **a** them, by giving them the

ACKNOWLEDGES (*see* ACKNOWLEDGE)
1Ki 2:44 You know, as your heart **a**
Ps 142: 4 For there is no one who **a** me
1Jn 2:23 he who **a** the Son has the

ACKNOWLEDGMENT (*see* ACKNOWLEDGE)
Tit 1: 1 the **a** of the truth which is
Phm 6 **a** of every good thing which

ACQUAINT (*see* ACQUAINTANCE, ACQUAINTED)
Job 22:21 Now **a** yourself with Him, and

ACQUAINTANCE (*see* ACQUAINT, ACQUAINTANCES)
Ps 55:13 equal, My companion and my **a**

ACQUAINTANCES (*see* ACQUAINTANCE)
2Ki 10:11 his great men and his close **a**
Job 19:13 my **a** are completely estranged
Job 42:11 who had been his **a** before
Ps 31:11 And am repulsive to my **a**
Ps 88: 8 put away my **a** far from me
Ps 88:18 me, And my **a** into darkness
Jer 20:10 All my **a** watched for my
Luke 2:44 among their relatives and **a**
Luke 23:49 But all His **a**, and the women

ACQUAINTED (*see* ACQUAINT)
Ps 139: 3 And are **a** with all my ways
Is 53: 3 of sorrows and **a** with grief

ACQUIRE (*see* ACQUIRED, ACQUIRES)
Gen 34:10 **a** possessions for yourselves

ACQUIRED (*see* ACQUIRE)
Gen 12: 5 whom they had **a** in Haran, and
Gen 31: 1 he has **a** all this wealth
Gen 31:18 his **a** livestock which he had
Gen 46: 6 which they had **a** in the land
Ruth 4:10 I have **a** as my wife, to raise
1Ki 9:28 and **a** four hundred and twenty
2Ch 1:17 They also **a** and imported from
2Ch 8:18 and **a** four hundred and fifty
Ps 78:54 which His right hand had **a**
Eccl 2: 7 I **a** male and female servants,
Eccl 2: 8 I **a** male and female singers,
Jer 13: 4 Take the sash that you **a**,
Jer 48:36 they have **a** have perished
Ezek 38:12 who have **a** livestock and goods

ACQUIRES (*see* ACQUIRE)
Prov 18:15 of the prudent **a** knowledge

ACQUIT (*see* ACQUITTED)
Job 10:14 will not **a** me of my iniquity
Joel 3:21 For I will **a** them of
Nah 1: 3 will not at all **a** the wicked

ACQUITTED (*see* ACQUIT)
Ex 21:19 he who struck him shall be **a**
Ex 21:28 owner of the ox shall be **a**
Is 43:26 your case, that you may be **a**
Joel 3:21 bloodguilt, whom I had not **a**

ACRE (*see* ACRES)
1Sa 14:14 about half an **a** of land

ACRES (*see* ACRE)
Is 5:10 For ten **a** of vineyard shall

ACROSS (*see* PREFACE)

ACT (*see* ACTED, ACTING, ACTS)
Deut 4: 5 that you should **a** according
Deut 4:16 lest you **a** corruptly and make
Deut 4:25 **a** corruptly and make a carved
Deut 11: 7 **a** of the LORD which He did
Deut 17:13 no longer **a** presumptuously
Judg 19:23 beg you, do not **a** so wickedly
2Sa 14: 2 but **a** like a woman who has
1Ki 8:32 then hear in heaven, and **a**
1Ki 8:39 place, and forgive, and **a**, and
2Ch 6:23 then hear from heaven, and **a**
2Ch 19: 9 Thus you shall **a** in the fear
Neh 6:13 **a** that way and sin, so that
Ps 119:126 It is time for You to **a**, O
Is 28:16 believes will not **a** hastily
Is 28:21 work, and bring to pass His **a**
Is 28:21 pass His **a**, His unusual **a**
Is 59: 6 the **a** of violence is in their
Ezek 8:18 I also will **a** in fury
Ezek 16:47 ways nor **a** according to their
Dan 9:19 O Lord, listen and **a**
Dan 11:23 him he shall **a** deceitfully
Dan 11:39 Thus he shall **a** against the
John 8: 4 in adultery, in the very **a**
Rom 5:18 **a** the free gift came to all

ACTED (*see* ACT)
Gen 42: 7 but he **a** as a stranger to
Deut 9:12 out of Egypt have **a** corruptly
Judg 9:16 if you have **a** in truth and
Judg 9:19 if then you have **a** in truth
2Sa 15: 6 In this manner Absalom **a**
2Ki 10:19 But Jehu **a** deceptively,
2Ki 21:11 **a** more wickedly than all the
2Ch 6:37 wrong, and have **a** wickedly'
2Ch 20:35 Israel, who **a** very wickedly

2Ch 27: 2 still the people **a** corruptly
Neh 1: 7 We have **a** very corruptly
Neh 9:10 they **a** proudly against them
Neh 9:16 they and our fathers **a** proudly
Neh 9:29 Yet they **a** proudly, and did
Job 36: 9 that they have **a** defiantly
Ps 78:57 **a** unfaithfully like their
Ezek 20: 9 But I **a** for My name's sake,
Ezek 20:14 But I **a** for My name's sake,
Ezek 20:22 **a** for My name's sake, that it

ACTING (*see* ACT)
Gen 19: 9 and he keeps **a** as a judge
Num 16:13 that you should keep **a** like a
Acts 17: 7 these are all **a** contrary to

ACTIONS
1Sa 2: 3 and by Him **a** are weighed

ACTIVE (*see* ACTIVITY)
Lev 13:51 the plague is an **a** leprosy
Lev 13:52 for it is an **a** leprosy
Lev 14:44 it is an **a** leprosy in the

ACTIVITIES (*see* ACTIVITY)
1Co 12: 6 And there are diversities of **a**

ACTIVITY (*see* ACTIVE, ACTIVITIES)
Eccl 5: 3 a dream comes through much **a**

ACTS (*see* ACT)
Ex 21:14 But if a man **a** with
Deut 11: 3 His **a** which He did in the
Deut 17:12 the man who **a** presumptuously
Judg 5:11 the righteous **a** of the LORD
Judg 5:11 LORD, the righteous **a** for His
1Sa 12: 7 all the righteous **a** of the
1Ki 11:41 the rest of the **a** of Solomon
1Ki 11:41 the book of the **a** of Solomon
1Ki 14:19 the rest of the **a** of Jeroboam
1Ki 14:29 the rest of the **a** of Rehoboam
1Ki 15: 7 the rest of the **a** of Abijam
1Ki 15:23 The rest of all the **a** of Asa
1Ki 15:31 the rest of the **a** of Nadab
1Ki 16: 5 the rest of the **a** of Baasha
1Ki 16:14 Now the rest of the **a** of Elah
1Ki 16:20 the rest of the **a** of Zimri
1Ki 16:27 Now the rest of the **a** of Omri
1Ki 22:39 Now the rest of the **a** of Ahab
1Ki 22:45 rest of the **a** of Jehoshaphat
2Ki 1:18 Now the rest of the **a** of
2Ki 8:23 the rest of the **a** of Joram
2Ki 10:34 Now the rest of the **a** of Jehu
2Ki 12:19 the rest of the **a** of Joash
2Ki 13: 8 the rest of the **a** of Jehoahaz
2Ki 13:12 the rest of the **a** of Joash
2Ki 14:15 Now the rest of the **a** of
2Ki 14:18 the rest of the **a** of Amaziah
2Ki 14:28 the rest of the **a** of Jeroboam
2Ki 15: 6 the rest of the **a** of Azariah
2Ki 15:11 rest of the **a** of Zechariah
2Ki 15:15 the rest of the **a** of Shallum
2Ki 15:21 the rest of the **a** of Menahem
2Ki 15:26 the rest of the **a** of Pekahiah
2Ki 15:31 the rest of the **a** of Pekah
2Ki 15:36 the rest of the **a** of Jotham
2Ki 16:19 Now the rest of the **a** of Ahaz
2Ki 20:20 the rest of the **a** of Hezekiah
2Ki 21:17 the rest of the **a** of Manasseh
2Ki 21:25 Now the rest of the **a** of Amon
2Ki 23:28 the rest of the **a** of Josiah
2Ki 24: 5 rest of the **a** of Jehoiakim
1Ch 29:29 Now the **a** of King David,
2Ch 9:29 the rest of the **a** of Solomon
2Ch 12:15 The **a** of Rehoboam, first and
2Ch 13:22 the rest of the **a** of Abijah
2Ch 16:11 Note that the **a** of Asa, first
2Ch 17: 4 according to the **a** of Israel
2Ch 20:34 rest of the **a** of Jehoshaphat
2Ch 25:26 the rest of the **a** of Amaziah
2Ch 26:22 the rest of the **a** of Uzziah
2Ch 27: 7 the rest of the **a** of Jotham
2Ch 28:26 Now the rest of his **a** and all
2Ch 32:32 the rest of the **a** of Hezekiah
2Ch 33:18 the rest of the **a** of Manasseh
2Ch 35:26 the rest of the **a** of Josiah
2Ch 36: 8 rest of the **a** of Jehoiakim
Esth 10: 2 Now all the **a** of his power and
Job 15:25 and **a** defiantly against the
Ps 103: 7 His **a** to the children of
Ps 106: 2 the mighty **a** of the LORD
Ps 145: 4 shall declare Your mighty **a**
Ps 145: 6 the might of Your awesome **a**
Ps 145:12 the sons of men His mighty **a**
Ps 150: 2 Praise Him for His mighty **a**
Prov 13:16 prudent man **a** with knowledge
Prov 14:17 is quick-tempered **a** foolishly
Prov 21:24 he **a** with arrogant pride
Is 64: 4 Who **a** for the one who waits
Ezek 16:20 Were your **a** of harlotry a
Ezek 16:22 **a** of harlotry you did not
Ezek 16:25 multiplied your **a** of harlotry
Ezek 16:26 increased your **a** of harlotry
Ezek 16:29 you multiplied your **a** of
Rev 19: 8 the righteous **a** of the saints

ACTUALLY
Gen 50:15 may **a** repay us for all the
2Ki 4:14 **A**, she has no son, and her
1Co 5: 1 It is **a** reported that there
Phil 1:12 me have **a** turned out for the
2Pe 2:18 the ones who have **a** escaped

ADADAH
Josh 15:22 Kinah, Dimonah, **A**,

ADAH
Gen 4:19 the name of one was **A**, and the
Gen 4:20 And **A** bore Jabal
Gen 4:23 **A** and Zillah, hear my voice
Gen 36: 2 **A** the daughter of Elon the
Gen 36: 4 Now **A** bore Eliphaz to Esau,
Gen 36:10 the son of **A** the wife of Esau
Gen 36:12 These were the sons of **A**,
Gen 36:16 They were the sons of **A**

ADAIAH
2Ki 22: 1 the daughter of **A** of Bozkath
1Ch 6:41 son of Zerah, the son of **A**
1Ch 8:21 **A**, Beraiah, and Shimrath were
1Ch 9:12 **A** the son of Jeroham, the son
2Ch 23: 1 Obed, Maaseiah the son of **A**
Ezra 10:29 Meshullam, Malluch, **A**, Jashub
Ezra 10:39 Shelemiah, Nathan, **A**,
Neh 11: 5 son of Hazaiah, the son of **A**
Neh 11:12 **A** the son of Jeroham, the son

ADALIA
Esth 9: 8 Poratha, **A**, Aridatha,

ADAM
Gen 2:19 brought them to **A** to see what
Gen 2:19 whatever **A** called each living
Gen 2:20 So **A** gave names to all cattle
Gen 2:20 But for **A** there was not found
Gen 2:21 a deep sleep to fall on **A**
Gen 2:23 And **A** said: "This is now
Gen 3: 8 in the cool of the day, and **A**
Gen 3: 9 Then the LORD God called to **A**
Gen 3:17 Then to **A** He said, "Because
Gen 3:20 **A** called his wife's name Eve,
Gen 3:21 Also for **A** and his wife the
Gen 4: 1 Now **A** knew Eve his wife, and
Gen 4:25 **A** knew his wife again, and she
Gen 5: 1 book of the genealogy of **A**
Gen 5: 3 **A** lived one hundred and thirty
Gen 5: 4 the days of **A** were eight
Gen 5: 5 So all the days that **A** lived
Deut 32: 8 He separated the sons of **A**
Josh 3:16 in a heap very far away at **A**
1Ch 1: 1 **A**, Seth, Enosh,
Job 31:33 my transgressions as **A**, by
Luke 3:38 the son of Seth, the son of **A**
Rom 5:14 death reigned from **A** to Moses
Rom 5:14 of the transgression of **A**
1Co 15:22 For as in **A** all die, even so
1Co 15:45 The first man **A** became a
1Co 15:45 The last **A** became a
1Ti 2:13 For **A** was formed first, then
1Ti 2:14 **A** was not deceived, but the
Jude 14 Now Enoch, the seventh from **A**

ADAMAH
Josh 19:36 **A**, Ramah, Hazor,

ADAMANT
Ezek 3: 9 Like a stone, harder than

ADAMI NEKEB
Josh 19:33 tree in Zaanannim, **A**, and

ADAR (*see* ADDAR)
Josh 15: 3 along to Hezron, went up to **A**
Ezra 6:15 third day of the month of **A**
Esth 3: 7 which is the month of **A**
Esth 3:13 which is the month of **A**, and
Esth 8:12 which is the month of **A**
Esth 9: 1 that is, the month of **A**, on
Esth 9:15 day of the month of **A** and
Esth 9:17 day of the month of **A**
Esth 9:19 day of the month of **A** as a
Esth 9:21 days of the month of **A**,

ADBEEL
Gen 25:13 then Kedar, **A**, Mibsam,
1Ch 1:29 then Kedar, **A**, Mibsam,

ADD (*see* ADDED, ADDING, ADDITION, ADDS)
Gen 30:24 The LORD shall **a** to me
Lev 5:16 shall **a** one-fifth to it and
Lev 6: 5 **a** one-fifth more to it, and
Lev 22:14 priest, and **a** one-fifth to it
Lev 27:13 then he must **a** one-fifth to
Lev 27:15 then he shall **a** one-fifth of
Lev 27:19 then he must **a** one-fifth of
Lev 27:27 and shall **a** one-fifth to it
Lev 27:31 he shall **a** one-fifth to it
Num 35: 6 you shall **a** forty-two cities
Deut 4: 2 You shall not **a** to the word
Deut 12:32 you shall not **a** to it nor
Deut 19: 9 then you shall **a** three more
2Sa 24: 3 Now may the LORD your God **a**
1Ki 12:11 on you, I will **a** to your yoke
1Ki 12:14 but I will **a** to your yoke
2Ki 20: 6 I will **a** to your days fifteen
1Ch 22:14 also, and you may **a** to them
2Ch 10:11 on you, I will **a** to your yoke
2Ch 10:14 heavy, but I will **a** to it
2Ch 28:13 You intend to **a** to our sins
Ps 69:27 **A** iniquity to their iniquity,
Prov 3: 2 and peace they will **a** to you
Prov 30: 6 Do not **a** to His words, lest
Is 5: 8 who **a** field to field, till
Is 29: 1 **A** year to year
Is 30: 1 that they may **a** sin to sin
Is 38: 5 I will **a** to your days fifteen
Jer 7:21 **A** your burnt offerings to
Matt 6:27 of you by worrying can **a** one
Luke 12:25 of you by worrying can **a** one
Phil 1:16 supposing to **a** affliction to
2Pe 1: 5 **a** to your faith virtue, to
Rev 22:18 God will **a** to him the plagues

ADDAN
Ezra 2:59 Melah, Tel Harsha, Cherub, **A**

ADDAR (*see* ADAR)
Josh 16: 5 the east side was Ataroth **A**
1Ch 8: 3 The sons of Bela were **A**, Gera

ADDED (*see* ADD)
Num 36: 3 and it will be **a** to the
Num 36: 4 **a** to the inheritance of the
Deut 5:22 and He **a** no more
1Sa 12:19 for we have **a** to all our sins
Neh 13:18 Yet you bring **a** wrath on
Prov 9:11 of life will be **a** to you
Eccl 3:14 Nothing can be **a** to it, and
Jer 36:32 there were **a** to them many
Jer 45: 3 For the LORD has **a** grief to
Dan 4:36 excellent majesty was **a** to me
Matt 6:33 things shall be **a** to you
Luke 3:20 also **a** this, above all, that
Luke 12:31 things shall be **a** to you
Acts 2:41 thousand souls were **a** to them
Acts 2:47 And the Lord **a** to the church
Acts 5:14 increasingly **a** to the Lord
Acts 11:24 people were **a** to the Lord
Gal 2: 6 be something **a** nothing to me
Gal 3:19 It was **a** because of

ADDI
Luke 3:28 son of Melchi, the son of **A**

ADDING (*see* ADD)
Ezra 10:10 **a** to the guilt of Israel
Eccl 7:27 **A** one thing to the other to

ADDITION (*see* ADD)
Gen 28: 9 to be his wife in **a** to the
Num 5: 8 in **a** to the ram of the
Ezek 16:43 not commit lewdness in **a** to

ADDON
Neh 7:61 Melah, Tel Harsha, Cherub, **A**

ADDS (*see* ADD)
Job 34:37 For he **a** rebellion to his sin
Prov 10:22 and He **a** no sorrow with it
Prov 16:23 and **a** learning to his lips
Gal 3:15 no one annuls or **a** to it
Heb 10:17 then He **a**, "Their sins and
Rev 22:18 If anyone **a** to these things,

ADHERE (*see* ADHERES)
Dan 2:43 will not **a** to one another

ADHERES (*see* ADHERE)
Job 31: 7 or if any spot **a** to my hands

ADIEL
1Ch 4:36 Jeshohaiah, Asaiah, **A**,
1Ch 9:12 Maasai the son of **A**, the son
1Ch 27:25 son of **A** was over the king's

ADIN
Ezra 2:15 the people of **A**, four hundred
Ezra 8: 6 of the sons of **A**, Ebed the
Neh 7:20 the children of **A**, six
Neh 10:16 Adonijah, Bigvai, **A**,

ADINA
1Ch 11:42 **A** the son of Shiza the

ADINO
2Sa 23: 8 He was called **A** the Eznite

ADITHAIM
Josh 15:36 Sharaim, **A**, Gederah, and

ADJACENT
Ezek 45: 6 **a** to the district of the holy
Ezek 48:18 It shall be **a** to the district
Ezek 48:21 **a** to the tribal portions

ADJOIN (*see* ADJOINED, ADJOINING)
Gen 49:13 and his border shall **a** Sidon

ADJOINED (*see* ADJOIN)
Josh 19:34 it **a** Zebulun on the south

ADJOINING (*see* ADJOIN)
Josh 17:10 was **a** Asher on the north and
Acts 2:10 the parts of Libya **a** Cyrene

ADJOURNED
Acts 24:22 he **a** the proceedings and said,

ADJURE
Matt 26:63 I **a** You by the living God
Acts 19:13 We **a** you by the Jesus whom

ADLAI
1Ch 27:29 Shaphat the son of **A** was over

ADMAH
Gen 10:19 go toward Sodom, Gomorrah, **A**
Gen 14: 2 of Gomorrah, Shinab king of **A**
Gen 14: 8 of Gomorrah, the king of **A**
Deut 29:23 of Sodom and Gomorrah, **A**,
Hos 11: 8 How can I make you like **A**

ADMATHA
Esth 1:14 being Carshena, Shethar, **A**

ADMINISTER (*see* ADMINISTERED, ADMINISTERS, ADMINISTRATION, ADMINISTRATOR)
1Ki 3:28 God was in him to **a** justice
Ps 9: 8 He shall **a** judgment for the

ADMINISTERED (*see* ADMINISTER)
Deut 33:21 He **a** the justice of the LORD,
2Sa 8:15 David **a** judgment and justice
1Ch 18:14 **a** judgment and justice to all
2Co 8:19 which is **a** by us to the glory
2Co 8:20 lavish gift which is **a** by us

ADMINISTERS (*see* ADMINISTER)
Deut 10:18 He **a** justice for the

ADMINISTRATION (*see* ADMINISTER, ADMINISTRATIONS)
2Co 9:12 For the **a** of this service not

ADMINISTRATIONS (*see* ADMINISTRATION)
1Co 12:28 gifts of healings, helps, **a**

ADMINISTRATOR (*see* ADMINISTER, ADMINISTRATORS)
Dan 2:48 chief **a** over all the wise men

ADMINISTRATORS (*see* ADMINISTRATOR)
Dan 3: 2 together the satraps, the **a**
Dan 3: 3 So the satraps, the **a**, the
Dan 3:27 And the satraps, **a**, governors,
Dan 6: 7 of the kingdom, the **a** and

ADMIRED
2Th 1:10 to be **a** among all those who

ADMONISH (*see* ADMONISHED, ADMONISHING, ADMONITION)
Ps 81: 8 O My people, and I will **a** you
Rom 15:14 able also to **a** one another
1Th 5:12 you in the Lord and **a** you,
2Th 3:15 enemy, but **a** him as a brother
Tit 2: 4 that they **a** the young women

ADMONISHED (*see* ADMONISH)
Eccl 4:13 king who will be **a** no more
Eccl 12:12 my son, be **a** by these
Jer 42:19 that I have **a** you this day
Zech 3: 6 Angel of the LORD **a** Joshua

ADMONISHING (*see* ADMONISH)
Col 3:16 **a** one another in psalms and

ADMONITION (*see* ADMONISH)
1Co 10:11 they were written for our **a**
Eph 6: 4 the training and **a** of the Lord
Tit 3:10 after the first and second **a**

ADNA (*see* ADNAH)
Ezra 10:30 **A**, Chelal, Benaiah, Maaseiah,
Neh 12:15 of Harim, **A**

ADNAH (*see* ADNA)
1Ch 12:20 who defected to him were **A**
2Ch 17:14 **A** the captain, and with him

ADONI-BEZEK (*see* BEZEK)
Judg 1: 5 And they found **A** in Bezek, and
Judg 1: 6 Then **A** fled, and they pursued
Judg 1: 7 And **A** said, "Seventy kings

ADONIJAH
2Sa 3: 4 fourth, **A** the son of Haggith
1Ki 1: 5 Now **A** the son of Haggith
1Ki 1: 7 and they followed and helped **A**
1Ki 1: 8 to David were not with **A**
1Ki 1: 9 **A** sacrificed sheep and oxen and
1Ki 1:11 that **A** the son of Haggith has
1Ki 1:13 Why then has **A** become king
1Ki 1:18 **A** has become king
1Ki 1:24 **A** shall reign after me, and
1Ki 1:25 they say, Long live King **A**
1Ki 1:41 So **A** and all the guests who
1Ki 1:42 And **A** said to him,
1Ki 1:43 answered and said to **A**, "No
1Ki 1:49 who were with **A** were afraid
1Ki 1:50 Now **A** was afraid of Solomon
1Ki 1:51 Indeed **A** is afraid of King
1Ki 2:13 Now **A** the son of Haggith came
1Ki 2:19 to speak to him for **A**
1Ki 2:21 to **A** your brother as wife
1Ki 2:22 Abishag the Shunammite for **A**
1Ki 2:23 if **A** has not spoken this word
1Ki 2:24 **A** shall be put to death today
1Ki 2:28 for Joab had defected to **A**
1Ch 3: 2 fourth, **A** the son of Haggith
2Ch 17: 8 Shemiramoth, Jehonathan, **A**
Neh 10:16 **A**, Bigvai, Adin,

ADONIKAM
Ezra 2:13 the people of **A**, six hundred
Ezra 8:13 of the last sons of **A**, whose
Neh 7:18 the children of **A**, six

ADONIRAM (*see* ADORAM)
1Ki 4: 6 **A** the son of Abda, over the
1Ki 5:14 **A** was in charge of the labor

ADONI-ZEDEK
Josh 10: 1 Now it came to pass when **A**
Josh 10: 3 Therefore **A** king of Jerusalem

ADOPTION
Rom 8:15 of **a** by whom we cry out
Rom 8:23 eagerly waiting for the **a**
Rom 9: 4 to whom pertain the **a**, the
Gal 4: 5 might receive the **a** as sons
Eph 1: 5 having predestined us to **a** as

ADORAIM
2Ch 11: 9 **A**, Lachish, Azekah,

ADORAM (*see* ADONIRAM)
2Sa 20:24 **A** was in charge of revenue
1Ki 12:18 Then King Rehoboam sent **A**

ADORN (*see* ADORNED, ADORNING, ADORNS)
Job 40:10 Then **a** yourself with majesty
Jer 4:30 though you **a** yourself with
Matt 23:29 and **a** the monuments of the
1Ti 2: 9 that the women **a** themselves
Tit 2:10 that they may **a** the doctrine

ADORNED (*see* ADORN)
2Ki 9:30 **a** her head, and looked through
Job 26:13 His Spirit He **a** the heavens
Jer 31: 4 You shall again be **a** with
Ezek 16:11 I **a** you with ornaments, put
Ezek 16:13 Thus you were **a** with gold
Ezek 16:16 **a** multicolored high places
Ezek 23:40 **a** yourself with ornaments
Luke 21: 5 how it was **a** with beautiful
1Pe 3: 5 in God also **a** themselves,
Rev 17: 4 and **a** with gold and precious
Rev 18:16 and **a** with gold and precious
Rev 21: 2 as a bride **a** for her husband
Rev 21:19 the wall of the city were **a**

ADORNING (*see* ADORN)
1Pe 3: 3 **a** of arranging the hair, of

ADORNS (*see* ADORN)
Ps 93: 5 Holiness **a** Your house, O LORD
Is 61:10 as a bride **a** herself with her

ADRAMMELECH
2Ki 17:31 their children in fire to **A**
2Ki 19:37 his god, that his sons **A** and
Is 37:38 of Nisroch his god, that **A**

ADRAMYTTIUM
Acts 27: 2 So, entering a ship of **A**, we

ADRIATIC
Acts 27:27 up and down in the **A** Sea,

ADRIEL
1Sa 18:19 that she was given to **A** the
2Sa 21: 8 whom she brought up for **A** the

ADRIFT
Ps 88: 5 **A** among the dead, Like the

ADULLAM (*see* ADULLAMITE)
Josh 12:15 the king of **A**, one
Josh 15:35 Jarmuth, **A**, Socoh, Azekah,
1Sa 22: 1 and escaped to the cave of **A**
2Sa 23:13 to David at the cave of **A**
1Ch 11:15 to David, into the cave of **A**
2Ch 11: 7 Beth Zur, Sochoh, **A**,
Neh 11:30 Zanoah, **A**, and their villages
Mic 1:15 of Israel shall come to **A**

ADULLAMITE (*see* ADULLAM)
Gen 38: 1 visited a certain **A** whose
Gen 38:12 he and his friend Hirah the **A**
Gen 38:20 the hand of his friend the **A**

ADULTERER (*see* ADULTERERS, ADULTERY)
Lev 20:10 his neighbor's wife, the **a**
Job 24:15 The eye of the **a** waits for
Is 57: 3 you offspring of the **a** and

ADULTERERS (*see* ADULTERER)
Ps 50:18 have been a partaker with **a**
Jer 9: 2 For they are all **a**, an
Jer 23:10 For the land is full of **a**
Hos 7: 4 They are all **a**
Mal 3: 5 against sorcerers, against **a**
Luke 18:11 extortioners, unjust, **a**, or
1Co 6: 9 nor idolaters, nor **a**, nor
Heb 13: 4 and **a** God will judge
Jas 4: 4 **A** and adulteresses

ADULTERESS (*see* ADULTERESSES, ADULTERY)
Lev 20:10 wife, the adulterer and the **a**
Prov 6:26 and an **a** will prey upon his
Rom 7: 3 man, she will be called an **a**
Rom 7: 3 that law, so that she is no **a**

ADULTERESSES (*see* ADULTERESS)
Ezek 23:45 them after the manner of **a**
Ezek 23:45 blood, because they are **a**
Jas 4: 4 Adulterers and **a**

ADULTERIES (*see* ADULTERY)
Jer 13:27 I have seen your **a** and your
Ezek 23:43 her who had grown old in **a**
Hos 2: 2 and her **a** from between her
Matt 15:19 evil thoughts, murders, **a**
Mark 7:21 men, proceed evil thoughts, **a**

ADULTEROUS (*see* ADULTERY)
Prov 30:20 This is the way of an **a** woman
Ezek 6: 9 I was crushed by their **a**
Ezek 16:32 You are an **a** wife, who takes
Matt 12:39 **a** generation seeks after a
Matt 16: 4 **a** generation seeks after a
Mark 8:38 of Me and My words in this **a**

ADULTERY (*see* ADULTERER, ADULTERESS, ADULTERIES, ADULTEROUS)
Ex 20:14 You shall not commit **a**
Lev 20:10 The man who commits **a** with
Lev 20:10 he who commits **a** with his

Deut 5:18 You shall not commit a
Prov 6:32 Whoever commits a with a
Jer 3: 8 Israel had committed a, I had
Jer 3: 9 committed a with stones and
Jer 5: 7 full, then they committed a
Jer 7: 9 you steal, murder, commit a
Jer 23:14 they commit a and walk in lies
Jer 29:23 have committed a with their
Ezek 23:37 For they have committed a
Ezek 23:37 committed a with their idols
Hos 3: 1 by a lover and is committing a
Hos 4: 2 and stealing and committing a
Hos 4:13 and your brides commit a
Hos 4:14 brides when they commit a
Matt 5:27 old, 'You shall not commit a
Matt 5:28 a with her in his heart
Matt 5:32 causes her to commit a
Matt 5:32 who is divorced commits a
Matt 19: 9 and marries another, commits a
Matt 19: 9 her who is divorced commits a
Matt 19:18 You shall not commit a
Mark 10:11 another commits a against her
Mark 10:12 another, she commits a
Mark 10:19 Do not commit a', 'Do not
Luke 16:18 and marries another commits a
Luke 16:18 from her husband commits a
Luke 18:20 Do not commit a', 'Do not
John 8: 3 to Him a woman caught in a
John 8: 4 this woman was caught in a
Rom 2:22 Do not commit a," do you
Rom 2:22 a," do you commit a
Rom 13: 9 You shall not commit a,"
Gal 5:19 a, fornication, uncleanness,
Jas 2:11 Do not commit a," also said,
Jas 2:11 Now if you do not commit a
2Pe 2:14 having eyes full of a and that
Rev 2:22 those who commit a with her

ADUMMIM
Josh 15: 7 is before the Ascent of A
Josh 18:17 is before the Ascent of A

ADVANCE (*see* ADVANCED, WELL-ADVANCED)
Num 10: 5 When you sound the a, the
Num 10: 6 sound the a the second time
Num 10: 7 blow, but not sound the a
Josh 6: 7 let him who is armed a before
2Sa 5:24 then you shall a quickly
Prov 30:27 king, yet they all a in ranks
Dan 11:39 acknowledge, and a its glory

ADVANCED (*see* ADVANCE)
Josh 6: 8 rams' horns before the LORD a
Josh 13: 1 Joshua was old, a in years
Josh 13: 1 a in years, and there remains
Josh 23: 1 that Joshua was old, a in age
Josh 23: 2 I am old, a in age
Judg 11:29 from Mizpah of Gilead he a
Judg 11:32 So Jephthah a toward the
1Sa 17:12 a in years, in the days of
1Ki 1: 1 David was old, a in years
Esth 3: 1 a him and set his seat above
Esth 5:11 how he had a him above the
Esth 10: 2 to which the king a him, are
Luke 1: 7 were both well a in years
Luke 1:18 and my wife is well a in years
Gal 1:14 I a in Judaism beyond many of

ADVANTAGE
Job 35: 3 What a will it be to You
Eccl 3:19 man has no a over beasts, for
Luke 9:25 For what a is it to a man if
John 16: 7 It is to your a that I go
Rom 3: 1 What a then has the Jew, or
1Co 15:32 Ephesus, what a is it to me
2Co 2:11 Satan should take a of us
2Co 8:10 It is to your a not only to
2Co 12:17 Did I take a of you by any of
2Co 12:18 Did Titus take a of you
1Th 4: 6 that no one should take a of
Jude 16 flattering people to gain a

ADVERSARIES (*see* ADVERSARY)
Ex 23:22 and an adversary to your a
Deut 32:27 enemy, lest their a should
Deut 32:43 and render vengeance to His a
Josh 5:13 Are You for us or for our a
1Sa 2:10 The a of the LORD shall be
2Sa 19:22 you should be a to me today
Ezra 4: 1 Now when the a of Judah and
Neh 4:11 And our a said,
Job 22:20 Surely our a are cut down,
Ps 27:12 me to the will of my a
Ps 38:20 evil for good, They are my a
Ps 69:19 My a are all before You
Ps 71:13 consumed Who are a of my life
Ps 81:14 turn My hand against their a
Ps 89:42 the right hand of his a
Is 1:24 Ah, I will rid Myself of My a
Is 9:11 up the a of Rezin against him
Is 11:13 the a of Judah shall be cut
Is 59:18 He will repay. fury to His a
Is 63:18 our a have trodden down Your
Is 64: 2 Your name known to Your a
Jer 30:16 and all your a, every one of
Jer 46:10 may avenge Himself on His a
Jer 50: 7 and their a said, 'We have not
Lam 1: 5 Her a have become the master,
Lam 1: 7 the a saw her and mocked at
Lam 1:17 those around him become his a
Lam 2:17 exalted the horn of your a
Mic 5: 9 be lifted against your a, and
Nah 1: 2 will take vengeance on His a
Luke 13:17 all His a were put to shame
Luke 21:15 your a will not be able to
1Co 16: 9 to me, and there are many a
Phil 1:28 any way terrified by your a
Heb 10:27 which will devour the a

ADVERSARY (*see* ADVERSARIES)
Ex 23:22 and an a to your adversaries
Num 22:22 the way as an a against him
1Sa 29: 4 in the battle he become our a
1Ki 5: 4 neither a nor evil occurrence
1Ki 11:14 up an a against Solomon,
1Ki 11:23 up another a against him,
1Ki 11:25 He was an a of Israel all the
Esth 7: 6 The a and enemy is this wicked
Job 16: 9 my a sharpens His gaze on me
Ps 74:10 how long will the a reproach
Is 50: 8 who is My a
Lam 1:10 The a has spread his hand
Lam 2: 4 His right hand, like an a
Lam 4:12 not have believed that the a
Amos 3:11 An a shall be all around the
Matt 5:25 Agree with your a quickly
Matt 5:25 lest your a deliver you to
Luke 12:58 with your a to the magistrate
Luke 18: 3 saying, "Avenge me of my a
1Ti 5:14 the a to speak reproachfully
1Pe 5: 8 because your a the devil

ADVERSITIES (*see* ADVERSITY)
1Sa 10:19 saved you out of all your a
Ps 31: 7 You have known my soul in a
Jer 36: 3 a which I purpose to bring

ADVERSITY (*see* ADVERSITIES)
Deut 29:21 the tribes of Israel for a
2Sa 4: 9 redeemed my life from all a
2Sa 12:11 I will raise up a against you
2Ch 15: 6 troubled them with every a
Job 2:10 God, and shall we not accept a
Job 2:11 this a that had come upon him
Job 42:11 a that the LORD had brought
Ps 10: 6 I shall never be in a
Ps 35:15 But in my a they rejoiced And
Ps 94:13 him rest from the days of a
Prov 17:17 and a brother is born for a
Prov 24:10 If you faint in the day of a
Eccl 7:14 but in the day of a consider
Is 30:20 Lord gives you the bread of a
Jer 15:11 with you in the time of a
Jer 21:10 face against this city for a
Jer 39:16 My words upon this city for a
Jer 44:27 I will watch over them for a
Jer 44:29 stand against you for a
Jer 45: 5 I will bring a on all flesh

ADVICE (*see* ADVISE)
Gen 41:37 So the a was good in the eyes
Judg 20: 7 give your a and counsel here
1Sa 25:33 And blessed is your a and
2Ch 10: 9 to them, "What a do you give
Job 26: 3 you declared sound a to many
Is 30: 2 Egypt, and have not asked My a
2Co 8:10 And in this I give my a

ADVISE (*see* ADVICE, ADVISED, ADVISORS, WELL-ADVISED)
Num 24:14 I will a you what this people
2Sa 19:43 to a bringing back our king
1Ki 12: 6 How do you a me to answer
2Ch 10: 6 How do you a me to answer

ADVISED (*see* ADVISE)
2Ki 5: 6 Now be a, when this letter
Esth 2:15 the custodian of the women, a
Acts 27: 9 was already over, Paul a them
Acts 27:12 the majority a to set sail

ADVISORS (*see* ADVISE)
Dan 6: 7 satraps, the counselors and a

ADVOCATE
1Jn 2: 1 we have an A with the Father,

AENEAS
Acts 9:33 found a certain man named A
Acts 9:34 A, Jesus the Christ heals you

AENON
John 3:23 was baptizing in A near Salim

AFAR (*see* PREFACE)

AFFAIRS
2Sa 14:20 a your servant Joab has done
1Ki 12:15 for the turn of a was from
1Ch 26:32 to God and the a of the king
2Ch 10:15 the turn of a was from God
Ps 112: 5 guide his a with discretion
Dan 2:49 Abed-Nego over the a of the
Dan 3:12 a of the province of Babylon
Eph 6:21 that you also may know my a
Eph 6:22 that you may know our a, and
Phil 1:27 absent, I may hear of your a
2Ti 2: 4 with the a of this life, that

AFFECTED (*see* AFFECTS)
Dan 3:27 nor were their garments a

AFFECTION (*see* AFFECTIONATE, AFFECTIONS)
1Ch 29: 3 because I have set my a on
1Co 7: 3 to his wife the a due her
Phil 1: 8 with the a of Jesus Christ
Phil 2: 1 of the Spirit, if any a and

AFFECTIONATE (*see* AFFECTION, AFFECTIONATELY)
Rom 12:10 Be kindly a to one another

AFFECTIONATELY (*see* AFFECTIONATE)
1Th 2: 8 a longing for you, we were

AFFECTIONS (*see* AFFECTION)
2Co 6:12 are restricted by your own a
2Co 7:15 his a are greater for you as

AFFECTS (*see* AFFECTED)
Job 35: 8 Your wickedness a a man such

AFFIRM (*see* AFFIRMED)
Rom 3: 8 and as some a that we say
1Co 15:31 I a, by the boasting in you
1Ti 1: 7 nor the things which they a
Tit 3: 8 I want you to a constantly

AFFIRMED (*see* AFFIRM)
Luke 22:59 passed, another confidently a
Acts 25:19 died, whom Paul a to be alive

AFFLICT (*see* AFFLICTED, AFFLICTION)
Gen 15:13 they will a them four hundred
Gen 31:50 If you a my daughters, or if
Ex 1:11 to a them with their burdens
Ex 22:22 You shall not a any widow or
Ex 22:23 If you a them in any way, and
Lev 16:29 you shall a your souls, and do
Lev 16:31 and you shall a your souls
Lev 23:27 you shall a your souls, and
Lev 23:32 and you shall a your souls
Num 24:24 and they shall a Asshur and
Num 24:24 a Eber, and so shall Amalek,
Num 29: 7 You shall a your souls
Num 30:13 binding oath to a her soul
Deut 7:15 will a you with none of the
Judg 16: 5 that we may bind him to a him
Judg 16: 6 you may be bound to a you
1Ki 8:35 their sin because You a them
1Ki 11:39 I will a the descendants of
2Ch 6:26 their sin because You a them
Ps 55:19 a them, Even He who abides
Ps 89:22 the son of wickedness a him
Ps 94: 5 O LORD, And a Your heritage
Ps 143:12 all those who a my soul
Is 51:23 the hand of those who a you
Is 58: 5 a day for a man to a his soul
Is 64:12 peace, and a us very severely
Jer 31:28 down, to destroy, and to a
Lam 3:33 For He does not a willingly
Amos 5:12 You a the just and take bribes
Amos 6:14 And they will a you from the

Nah 1:12 you, I will **a** you no more
Zeph 3:19 will deal with all who **a** you

AFFLICTED (*see* AFFLICT)
Ex 1:12 But the more they **a** them, the
Lev 23:29 **a** of soul on that same day
Num 11:11 Why have You **a** Your servant
Num 20:15 time, and the Egyptians **a** us
Deut 26: 6 **a** us, and laid hard bondage on
Ruth 1:21 me, and the Almighty has **a** me
1Ki 2:26 because you were **a** every time
1Ki 2:26 every time my father was **a**
2Ki 17:20 **a** them, and delivered them
Job 6:14 To him who is **a**, kindness
Job 30:11 and **a** me, they have cast off
Job 34:28 for He hears the cry of the **a**
Ps 22:24 the affliction of the **a**
Ps 25:16 on me, For I am desolate and **a**
Ps 44: 2 How You **a** the peoples, and
Ps 82: 3 Do justice to the **a** and needy
Ps 88: 7 You have **a** me with all Your
Ps 88:15 I have been **a** and ready to die
Ps 90:15 days in which You have **a** us
Ps 107:17 of their iniquities, were **a**
Ps 116:10 I am greatly **a**
Ps 119:67 Before I was **a** I went astray,
Ps 119:71 for me that I have been **a**
Ps 119:75 in faithfulness You have **a** me
Ps 119:107 I am **a** very much
Ps 129: 1 they have **a** me from my youth
Ps 129: 2 they have **a** me from my youth
Ps 140:12 maintain The cause of the **a**
Prov 15:15 the days of the **a** are evil
Prov 22:22 nor oppress the **a** at the gate
Prov 31: 5 the justice of all the **a**
Is 49:13 and will have mercy on His **a**
Is 51:21 please hear this, you **a**, and
Is 53: 4 smitten by God, and **a**
Is 53: 7 He was oppressed and He was **a**
Is 54:11 O you **a** one, tossed with
Is 58: 3 Why have we **a** our souls, and
Is 58:10 hungry and satisfy the **a** soul
Is 60:14 **a** you shall come bowing to
Is 63: 9 all their affliction He was **a**
Lam 1: 4 sigh, her virgins are **a**, and
Lam 1: 5 for the LORD has **a** her
Mic 4: 6 and those whom I have **a**
Nah 1:12 Though I have **a** you, I will
Matt 4:24 were **a** with various diseases
2Co 1: 6 Now if we are **a**, it is for
1Ti 5:10 if she has relieved the **a**
Heb 11:37 goatskins, being destitute, **a**

AFFLICTION (*see* AFFLICT, AFFLICTIONS)
Gen 16:11 the LORD has heard your **a**
Gen 29:32 has surely looked on my **a**
Gen 31:42 God has seen my **a** and the
Gen 41:52 fruitful in the land of my **a**
Ex 3:17 bring you up out of the **a** of
Ex 4:31 that He had looked on their **a**
Deut 16: 3 the bread of **a** (for you came
Deut 26: 7 our voice and looked on our **a**
1Sa 1:11 on the **a** of your maidservant
2Sa 16:12 the LORD will look on my **a**
1Ki 22:27 bread of **a** and water of **a**
2Ki 14:26 **a** of Israel was very bitter
2Ch 18:26 and feed him with bread of **a**
2Ch 18:26 water of **a** until I return in
2Ch 20: 9 and cry out to You in our **a**
2Ch 21:14 your people with a serious **a**
2Ch 33:12 Now when he was in **a**, he
Neh 9: 9 You saw the **a** of our fathers
Job 5: 6 For **a** does not come from the
Job 30:16 the days of **a** take hold of me
Job 30:27 days of **a** confront me
Job 36: 8 held in the cords of **a**,
Job 36:15 delivers the poor in their **a**
Job 36:21 chosen this rather than **a**
Ps 22:24 the **a** of the afflicted
Ps 25:18 Look on my **a** and my pain, And
Ps 44:24 Your face, And forget our **a**
Ps 66:11 You laid **a** on our backs
Ps 88: 9 eye wastes away because of **a**
Ps 106:44 He regarded their **a**, When He
Ps 107:10 shadow of death, Bound in **a**
Ps 107:39 low Through oppression, **a**
Ps 107:41 the poor on high, far from **a**
Ps 119:50 This is my comfort in my **a**
Ps 119:92 then have perished in my **a**
Ps 119:153 Consider my **a** and deliver me,
Eccl 6: 2 is vanity, and it is an evil **a**
Is 30:20 adversity and the water of **a**
Is 48:10 you in the furnace of **a**
Is 63: 9 In all their **a** He was
Jer 4:15 and proclaims **a** from Mount
Jer 15:11 adversity and in the time of **a**
Jer 16:19 my refuge in the day of **a**
Jer 30:12 Your **a** is incurable, your
Jer 30:15 Why do you cry about your **a**
Jer 48:16 hand, and his **a** comes quickly
Lam 1: 3 gone into captivity, under **a**
Lam 1: 7 In the days of her **a** and
Lam 1: 9 O LORD, behold my **a**, for the
Lam 3: 1 **a** by the rod of His wrath
Lam 3:19 Remember my **a** and roaming,
Hos 5:15 in their **a** they will
Amos 6: 6 grieved for the **a** of Joseph
Obad 13 their **a** in the day of their
Jon 2: 2 to the LORD because of my **a**
Nah 1: 9 **A** will not rise up a second
Hab 3: 7 saw the tents of Cushan in **a**
Zech 10:11 pass through the sea with **a**
Mark 5:29 that she was healed of the **a**
Mark 5:34 peace, and be healed of your **a**
2Co 2: 4 For out of much **a** and anguish
2Co 4:17 For our light **a**, which is but
2Co 8: 2 that in a great trial of **a**
Phil 1:16 to add **a** to my chains
1Th 1: 6 received the word in much **a**
1Th 3: 7 brethren, in all our **a** and
Heb 11:25 choosing rather to suffer **a**

AFFLICTIONS (*see* AFFLICTION)
Ps 34:19 Many are the **a** of the
Ps 132: 1 remember David And all his **a**
Mark 3:10 so that as many as had **a**
Luke 7:21 of their infirmities, **a**, and
Col 1:24 is lacking in the **a** of Christ
1Th 3: 3 should be shaken by these **a**
2Ti 3:11 persecutions, **a**, which
2Ti 4: 5 in all things, endure **a**, do

AFFORD
Lev 14:21 if he is poor and cannot **a** it
Lev 14:22 such as he is able to **a**
Lev 14:30 pigeons, such as he can **a**
Lev 14:31 such as he is able to **a**, the
Lev 14:32 sore, who cannot **a** the usual

AFRAID
Gen 3:10 I was **a** because I was naked
Gen 15: 1 Do not be **a**, Abram
Gen 18:15 not laugh," for she was **a**
Gen 19:30 for he was **a** to dwell in Zoar
Gen 20: 8 and the men were very **a**
Gen 26: 7 for he was **a** to say, "She is
Gen 28:17 And he was **a** and said, "How
Gen 31:31 Because I was **a**, for I said
Gen 32: 7 So Jacob was greatly **a** and
Gen 42:28 failed them and they were **a**
Gen 42:35 bundles of money, they were **a**
Gen 43:18 Now the men were **a** because
Gen 43:23 be with you, do not be **a**
Gen 50:19 Do not be **a**, for am I in the
Gen 50:21 Now therefore, do not be **a**
Ex 3: 6 for he was **a** to look upon God
Ex 14:10 So they were very **a**, and the
Ex 14:13 Do not be **a**
Ex 15:14 The people will hear and be **a**
Ex 34:30 they were **a** to come near him
Lev 26: 6 down, and none will make you **a**
Num 12: 8 Why then were you not **a** to
Num 22: 3 Moab was exceedingly **a** of the
Deut 1:17 you shall not be **a** in any
Deut 1:29 be terrified, or be **a** of them
Deut 2: 4 and they will be **a** of you
Deut 5: 5 for you were **a** because of the
Deut 7:18 you shall not be **a** of them
Deut 7:19 the peoples of whom you are **a**
Deut 9:19 For I was **a** of the anger and
Deut 18:22 you shall not be **a** of him
Deut 20: 1 than you, do not be **a** of them
Deut 20: 3 your heart faint, do not be **a**
Deut 28:10 and they shall be **a** of you
Deut 28:60 of Egypt, of which you were **a**
Deut 31: 6 do not fear nor be **a** of them
Josh 1: 9 do not be **a**, nor be dismayed,
Josh 8: 1 Do not be **a**, nor be dismayed
Josh 9:24 **a** for our lives because of
Josh 10:25 Do not be **a**, nor be dismayed
Josh 11: 6 Do not be **a** because of them,
Judg 7: 3 Whoever is fearful and **a**
Judg 7:10 But if you are **a** to go down
Judg 8:20 for he was **a**, because he was
1Sa 3:15 Samuel was **a** to tell Eli the
1Sa 4: 7 So the Philistines were **a**
1Sa 7: 7 of it, they were **a** of the
1Sa 17:11 were dismayed and greatly **a**
1Sa 17:24 from him and were dreadfully **a**
1Sa 18:12 Now Saul was **a** of David,
1Sa 18:15 very wisely, he was **a** of him
1Sa 18:29 was still more **a** of David
1Sa 21: 1 Ahimelech was **a** when he met
1Sa 21:12 was very much **a** of Achish the
1Sa 23: 3 Look, we are **a** here in Judah
1Sa 28: 5 of the Philistines, he was **a**
1Sa 28:13 Do not be **a**
1Sa 28:20 was dreadfully **a** because of
1Sa 31: 4 not, for he was greatly **a**
2Sa 1:14 How was it you were not **a** to
2Sa 6: 9 David was **a** of the LORD that
2Sa 10:19 So the Syrians were **a** to help
2Sa 12:18 **a** to tell him that the child
2Sa 13:28 Do not be **a**
2Sa 14:15 the people have made me **a**
2Sa 17: 2 and weak, and make him **a**
2Sa 22: 5 of ungodliness made me **a**
1Ki 1:49 who were with Adonijah were **a**
1Ki 1:50 Adonijah was **a** of Solomon
1Ki 1:51 Adonijah is **a** of King Solomon
2Ki 1:15 do not be **a** of him
2Ki 10: 4 But they were exceedingly **a**
2Ki 19: 6 Do not be **a** of the words
2Ki 25:24 Do not be **a** of the servants
2Ki 25:26 for they were **a** of the
1Ch 10: 4 not, for he was greatly **a**
1Ch 13:12 David was **a** of God that day,
1Ch 21:30 for he was **a** of the sword of
2Ch 20:15 Do not be **a** nor dismayed
2Ch 32: 7 do not be **a** nor dismayed
Neh 2: 2 Then I became dreadfully **a**
Neh 4:14 Do not be **a** of them
Neh 6: 9 all were trying to make us **a**
Neh 6:13 was hired, that I should be **a**
Neh 6:14 who would have made me **a**
Job 5:21 and you shall not be **a** of
Job 5:22 you shall not be **a** of the
Job 6:21 you see terror and are **a**
Job 9:28 I am **a** of all my sufferings
Job 11:19 and no one would make you **a**
Job 13:11 not His excellence make you **a**
Job 13:21 the dread of You make me **a**
Job 15:24 Trouble and anguish make him **a**
Job 19:29 be **a** of the sword for
Job 23:15 consider this, I am **a** of Him
Job 32: 6 therefore I was **a**, and dared
Job 41:25 himself up, the mighty are **a**
Ps 3: 6 I will not be **a** of ten
Ps 18: 4 of ungodliness made me **a**
Ps 27: 1 Of whom shall I be **a**
Ps 49:16 Do not be **a** when one becomes
Ps 56: 3 Whenever I am **a**, I will trust
Ps 56:11 I will not be **a**
Ps 65: 8 parts are **a** of Your signs
Ps 77:16 waters saw You, they were **a**
Ps 91: 5 You shall not be **a** of the
Ps 112: 7 He will not be **a** of evil
Ps 112: 8 He will not be **a**, Until he
Ps 119:120 And I am **a** of Your judgments
Prov 3:24 lie down, you will not be **a**
Prov 3:25 Do not be **a** of sudden terror,
Prov 31:21 She is not **a** of snow for her
Eccl 12: 5 when they are **a** of height
Is 8:12 nor be **a** of their threats,
Is 10:24 do not be **a** of the Assyrian
Is 10:29 Ramah is **a**, Gibeah of Saul
Is 12: 2 I will trust and not be **a**
Is 13: 8 and they will be **a**
Is 17: 2 and no one will make them **a**
Is 19:16 be like women, and will be **a**
Is 19:17 of it will be **a** in himself
Is 20: 5 Then they shall be **a** and
Is 31: 4 he will not be **a** of their
Is 31: 9 shall be **a** of the banner,"
Is 33:14 The sinners in Zion are **a**
Is 37: 6 Do not be **a** of the words
Is 40: 9 lift it up, be not **a**
Is 41: 5 the ends of the earth were **a**
Is 44: 8 Do not fear, nor be **a**
Is 51: 7 nor be **a** of their revilings
Is 51:12 be **a** of a man who will die
Is 57:11 And of whom have you been **a**
Jer 1: 8 Do not be **a** of their faces,

Jer 2:12 at this, and be horribly **a**
Jer 10: 5 Do not be **a** of them, for they
Jer 26:21 Urijah heard it, he was **a**
Jer 30:10 and no one shall make him **a**
Jer 36:24 Yet they were not **a**, nor did
Jer 38:19 I am **a** of the Jews who have
Jer 39:17 of the men of whom you are **a**
Jer 40: 9 Do not be **a** to serve the
Jer 41:18 for they were **a** of them,
Jer 42:11 Do not be **a** of the king of
Jer 42:11 of Babylon, of whom you are **a**
Jer 42:11 do not be **a** of him,' says the
Jer 42:16 **a** shall follow close after
Jer 46:27 No one shall make him **a**
Ezek 2: 6 do not be **a** of them nor be
Ezek 2: 6 them nor be **a** of their words
Ezek 2: 6 do not be **a** of their words or
Ezek 3: 9 do not be **a** of them, nor be
Ezek 27:35 their kings will be greatly **a**
Ezek 30: 9 the careless Ethiopians **a**
Ezek 32:10 kings shall be horribly **a** of
Ezek 34:28 and no one shall make them **a**
Ezek 39:26 land and no one made them **a**
Dan 4: 5 I saw a dream which made me **a**
Dan 8:17 and when he came I was **a** and
Joel 2:22 Do not be **a**, you beasts of
Amos 3: 6 will not the people be **a**
Jon 1: 5 Then the mariners were **a**
Jon 1:10 the men were exceedingly **a**
Mic 4: 4 and no one shall make them **a**
Mic 7:17 They shall be **a** of the LORD
Nah 2:11 cub, and no one made them **a**
Hab 2:17 of beasts which made them **a**
Hab 3: 2 heard your speech and was **a**
Zeph 3:13 and no one shall make them **a**
Matt 1:20 do not be **a** to take to you
Matt 2:22 Herod, he was **a** to go there
Matt 14:27 do not be **a**
Matt 14:30 wind was boisterous, he was **a**
Matt 17: 6 their faces and were greatly **a**
Matt 17: 7 Arise, and do not be **a**
Matt 25:25 And I was **a**, and went and hid
Matt 28: 5 Do not be **a**, for I know that
Matt 28:10 Do not be **a**
Mark 5:15 And they were **a**
Mark 5:36 Do not be **a**
Mark 6:50 do not be **a**
Mark 9: 6 say, for they were greatly **a**
Mark 9:32 saying, and were **a** to ask Him
Mark 10:32 as they followed they were **a**
Mark 16: 8 to anyone, for they were **a**
Luke 1:13 Do not be **a**, Zacharias, for
Luke 1:30 Do not be **a**, Mary, for you
Luke 2: 9 them, and they were greatly **a**
Luke 2:10 Do not be **a**, for behold, I
Luke 5:10 Do not be **a**
Luke 8:25 And they were **a**, and marveled
Luke 8:35 And they were **a**
Luke 8:50 Do not be **a**
Luke 9:45 they were **a** to ask Him about
Luke 12: 4 do not be **a** of those who kill
Luke 24: 5 Then, as they were **a** and bowed
John 6:19 and they were **a**
John 6:20 do not be **a**
John 14:27 troubled, neither let it be **a**
John 19: 8 saying, he was the more **a**
Acts 9:26 but they were all **a** of him
Acts 10: 4 he observed him, he was **a**
Acts 16:38 they were **a** when they heard
Acts 18: 9 Do not be **a**, but speak, and do
Acts 22: 9 saw the light and were **a**, but
Acts 22:29 and the commander was also **a**
Acts 24:25 judgment to come, Felix was **a**
Acts 27:24 saying, "Do not be **a**, Paul
Rom 13: 4 But if you do evil, be **a**
Gal 4:11 I am **a** for you, lest I have
Heb 11:23 they were not **a** of the king's
Heb 12:21 I am exceedingly **a** and
1Pe 3: 6 are not **a** with any terror
1Pe 3:14 do not be **a** of their threats,
2Pe 2:10 they are not **a** to speak evil
Rev 1:17 Do not be **a**
Rev 11:13 killed, and the rest were **a**

AFRESH
Job 7: 5 is cracked and breaks out **a**

AFTER (*see* PREFACE)

AFTERNOON
Judg 19: 8 So they delayed until **a**

AFTERWARD (*see* PREFACE)

AGABUS
Acts 11:28 Then one of them, named **A**
Acts 21:10 named **A** came down from Judea

AGAG (*see* AGAGITE)
Num 24: 7 king shall be higher than **A**
1Sa 15: 8 He also took **A** king of the
1Sa 15: 9 Saul and the people spared **A**
1Sa 15:20 brought back **A** king of Amalek
1Sa 15:32 said, "Bring **A** king of the
1Sa 15:32 So **A** came to him cautiously
1Sa 15:32 And **A** said, "Surely the
1Sa 15:33 Samuel hacked **A** in pieces

AGAGITE (*see* AGAG)
Esth 3: 1 the son of Hammedatha the **A**
Esth 3:10 the son of Hammedatha the **A**
Esth 8: 3 the evil plot of Haman the **A**
Esth 8: 5 the son of Hammedatha the **A**
Esth 9:24 the son of Hammedatha the **A**

AGAIN (*see* PREFACE)

AGAINST (*see* PREFACE)

AGATE
Ex 28:19 third row, a jacinth, an **a**
Ex 39:12 third row, a jacinth, an **a**

AGE (*see* AGED, AGES)
Gen 15:15 be buried at a good old **a**
Gen 18:11 were old, well-advanced in **a**
Gen 18:11 passed the **a** of childbearing
Gen 21: 2 Abraham a son in his old **a**
Gen 21: 7 borne him a son in his old **a**
Gen 24: 1 was old, well-advanced in **a**
Gen 25: 8 last and died in a good old **a**
Gen 37: 3 he was the son of his old **a**
Gen 44:20 man, and a child of his old **a**
Gen 48:10 of Israel were dim with **a**
Num 8:25 at the **a** of fifty years they
Josh 23: 1 Joshua was old, advanced in **a**
Josh 23: 2 I am old, advanced in **a**
Judg 8:32 of Joash died at a good old **a**
Ruth 4:15 and a nourisher of your old **a**
1Sa 2:33 die in the flower of their **a**
1Ki 14: 4 glazed by reason of his **a**
1Ki 15:23 But in the time of his old **a**
1Ch 23: 3 from the **a** of thirty years
1Ch 23:24 from the **a** of twenty years and
1Ch 29:28 So he died in a good old **a**
Job 5:26 come to the grave at a full **a**
Job 8: 8 please, of the former **a**, and
Job 32: 7 **A** should speak, and multitude
Ps 39: 5 my **a** is as nothing before You
Ps 71: 9 me off in the time of old **a**
Ps 92:14 still bear fruit in old **a**
Is 46: 4 even to your old **a**, I am He,
Dan 1:10 the young men who are your **a**
Zech 8: 4 his hand because of great **a**
Matt 12:32 either in this **a** or in the
Matt 12:32 this **a** or in the **a** to come
Matt 13:39 harvest is the end of the **a**
Matt 13:40 will be at the end of this **a**
Matt 13:49 will be at the end of the **a**
Matt 24: 3 and of the end of the **a**
Matt 28:20 even to the end of the **a**
Mark 5:42 for she was twelve years of **a**
Mark 10:30 in the **a** to come, eternal
Luke 1:36 conceived a son in her old **a**
Luke 2:36 She was of a great **a**, and had
Luke 3:23 at about thirty years of **a**
Luke 8:42 about twelve years of **a**, and
Luke 18:30 in the **a** to come everlasting
Luke 20:34 The sons of this **a** marry and
Luke 20:35 worthy to attain that **a**, and
John 9:21 He is of **a**
John 9:23 He is of **a**
1Co 1:20 is the disputer of this **a**
1Co 2: 6 yet not the wisdom of this **a**
1Co 2: 6 nor of the rulers of this **a**
1Co 2: 8 of the rulers of this **a** knew
1Co 3:18 seems to be wise in this **a**
2Co 4: 4 the god of this **a** has blinded
Gal 1: 4 us from this present evil **a**
Eph 1:21 not only in this **a** but also
Eph 6:12 of the darkness of this **a**
1Ti 6:17 present **a** not to be haughty
Tit 2:12 and godly in the present **a**
Heb 5:14 to those who are of full **a**
Heb 6: 5 the powers of the **a** to come
Heb 11:11 child when she was past the **a**
Heb 11:24 Moses, when he became of **a**

AGED (*see* AGE)
2Sa 19:32 Barzillai was a very **a** man
2Ch 36:17 virgin, on the **a** or the weak
Job 12:12 Wisdom is with **a** men, and with
Job 15:10 and the **a** are among us, much
Job 29: 8 hid, and the **a** arose and stood
Job 32: 9 wise, nor do the **a** always
Jer 6:11 the **a** with him who is full of
Lam 3: 4 He has **a** my flesh and my skin,
Phm 9 such a one as Paul, the **a**

AGEE
2Sa 23:11 the son of **A** the Hararite

AGENTS
1Ki 10:29 and thus, through their **a**,
2Ch 1:17 thus, through their **a**, they

AGES (*see* AGE)
1Co 2: 7 before the **a** for our glory
1Co 10:11 the ends of the **a** have come
Eph 2: 7 that in the **a** to come He
Eph 3: 5 which in other **a** was not made
Eph 3: 9 from the beginning of the **a**
Eph 3:21 Christ Jesus throughout all **a**
Col 1:26 which has been hidden from **a**
Heb 9:26 now, once at the end of the **a**

AGITATED
Ezek 16:43 but **a** Me with all these

AGO (*see* PREFACE)

AGONY
Is 23: 5 they also will be in **a** at the
Luke 22:44 And being in **a**, He prayed more

AGREE (*see* AGREEABLE, AGREED, AGREEMENT)
Matt 5:25 **A** with your adversary quickly
Matt 18:19 of you **a** on earth concerning
Matt 20:13 Did you not **a** with me for a
Mark 14:56 their testimonies did not **a**
Mark 14:59 then did their testimony **a**
Acts 15:15 the words of the prophets **a**
Acts 28:25 did not **a** among themselves
Rom 7:16 I **a** with the law that it is
1Jn 5: 8 and these three **a** as one

AGREEABLE (*see* AGREE)
Zech 11:12 If it is **a** to you, give me my

AGREED (*see* AGREE)
2Ki 12: 8 the priests **a** that they would
2Ch 30: 2 in Jerusalem had **a** to keep
2Ch 30:23 Then the whole assembly **a** to
Dan 2: 9 For you have **a** to speak lying
Amos 3: 3 together, unless they are **a**
Matt 20: 2 Now when he had **a** with the
Luke 22: 5 glad, and **a** to give him money
John 9:22 for the Jews had **a** already
Acts 5: 9 How is it that you have **a**
Acts 5:40 they **a** with him, and when they
Acts 23:20 The Jews have **a** to ask that

AGREEMENT (*see* AGREE, AGREEMENTS)
Num 30: 2 to bind himself by some **a**
Num 30: 3 binds herself by some **a** while
Num 30: 4 the **a** by which she has bound
Num 30: 4 every **a** with which she has
Num 30:10 herself by an **a** with an oath
Num 30:11 every **a** by which she bound
Num 30:12 concerning the **a** binding her
Is 28:15 and with Sheol we are in **a**
Is 28:18 your **a** with Sheol will not
Dan 11: 6 of the North to make an **a**
2Co 6:16 what **a** has the temple of God

AGREEMENTS (*see* AGREEMENT)
Num 30: 5 her **a** by which she has bound
Num 30: 7 and her **a** by which she bound
Num 30:14 or all the **a** that bind her

AGRIPPA
Acts 25:13 And after some days King **A**
Acts 25:22 Then **A** said to Festus, "I
Acts 25:23 So the next day, when **A** and
Acts 25:24 King **A** and all the men who are
Acts 25:26 especially before you, King **A**
Acts 26: 1 Then **A** said to Paul, "You
Acts 26: 2 I think myself happy, King **A**
Acts 26: 7 For this hope's sake, King **A**

Acts 26:19 Therefore, King **A**, I was not
Acts 26:27 King **A**, do you believe the
Acts 26:28 Then **A** said to Paul, "You
Acts 26:32 Then **A** said to Festus, "This

AGROUND
Acts 27:17 run **a** on the Syrtis Sands
Acts 27:26 we must run **a** on a certain
Acts 27:29 we should run **a** on the rocks
Acts 27:41 seas met, they ran the ship **a**

AGUR
Prov 30: 1 The words of **A** the son of

AH (*see* PREFACE)

AHA (*see* PREFACE)

AHAB (*see* AHAB'S)
1Ki 16:28 Then **A** his son reigned in his
1Ki 16:29 **A** the son of Omri became king
1Ki 16:29 **A** the son of Omri reigned
1Ki 16:30 Now **A** the son of Omri did
1Ki 16:33 And **A** made a wooden image
1Ki 16:33 **A** did more to provoke the
1Ki 17: 1 of Gilead, said to **A**, "As
1Ki 18: 1 Go, present yourself to **A**
1Ki 18: 2 went to present himself to **A**
1Ki 18: 3 **A** had called Obadiah, who was
1Ki 18: 5 And **A** had said to Obadiah,
1Ki 18: 6 **A** went one way by himself, and
1Ki 18: 9 servant into the hand of **A**
1Ki 18:12 so when I go and tell **A**, and he
1Ki 18:16 So Obadiah went to meet **A**
1Ki 18:16 and **A** went to meet Elijah
1Ki 18:17 when **A** saw Elijah, that **A**
1Ki 18:20 So **A** sent for all the
1Ki 18:41 Then Elijah said to **A**, "Go
1Ki 18:42 So **A** went up to eat and drink
1Ki 18:44 Go up, say to **A**, 'Prepare
1Ki 18:45 So **A** rode away and went to
1Ki 18:46 and ran ahead of **A** to the
1Ki 19: 1 And **A** told Jezebel all that
1Ki 20: 2 the city to **A** king of Israel
1Ki 20:13 approached **A** king of Israel
1Ki 20:14 So **A** said, "By whom
1Ki 20:34 Then **A** said, "I will send
1Ki 21: 1 palace of **A** king of Samaria
1Ki 21: 2 So **A** spoke to Naboth, saying,
1Ki 21: 3 And Naboth said to **A**, "The
1Ki 21: 4 So **A** went into his house
1Ki 21:15 dead, that Jezebel said to **A**
1Ki 21:16 when **A** heard that Naboth was
1Ki 21:16 that **A** got up and went down to
1Ki 21:18 down to meet **A** king of Israel
1Ki 21:20 Then **A** said to Elijah, "Have
1Ki 21:21 will cut off from **A** every
1Ki 21:24 eat whoever belongs to **A** and
1Ki 21:25 like **A** who sold himself to do
1Ki 21:27 when **A** heard those words,
1Ki 21:29 See how **A** has humbled himself
1Ki 22:20 Who will persuade **A** to go up
1Ki 22:39 Now the rest of the acts of **A**
1Ki 22:40 So **A** rested with his fathers
1Ki 22:41 year of **A** king of Israel
1Ki 22:49 son of **A** said to Jehoshaphat
1Ki 22:51 Ahaziah the son of **A** became
2Ki 1: 1 Israel after the death of **A**
2Ki 3: 1 Now Jehoram the son of **A**
2Ki 3: 5 But it happened, when **A** died
2Ki 8:16 year of Joram the son of **A**
2Ki 8:18 as the house of **A** had done
2Ki 8:18 daughter of **A** was his wife
2Ki 8:25 year of Joram the son of **A**
2Ki 8:27 in the way of the house of **A**
2Ki 8:27 as the house of **A** had done
2Ki 8:27 son-in-law of the house of **A**
2Ki 8:28 **A** to war against Hazael king
2Ki 8:29 Joram the son of **A** in Jezreel
2Ki 9: 7 the house of **A** your master
2Ki 9: 8 whole house of **A** shall perish
2Ki 9: 8 I will cut off from **A** all the
2Ki 9: 9 **A** like the house of Jeroboam
2Ki 9:25 together behind **A** his father
2Ki 9:29 year of Joram the son of **A**
2Ki 10: 1 Now **A** had seventy sons in
2Ki 10:10 concerning the house of **A**
2Ki 10:11 of the house of **A** in Jezreel
2Ki 10:17 who remained to **A** in Samaria
2Ki 10:18 **A** served Baal a little, but
2Ki 10:30 of **A** all that was in My heart
2Ki 21: 3 as **A** king of Israel had done
2Ki 21:13 the plummet of the house of **A**
2Ch 18: 1 he allied himself with **A**
2Ch 18: 2 down to visit **A** in Samaria
2Ch 18: 2 **A** killed sheep and oxen in
2Ch 18: 3 So **A** king of Israel said to
2Ch 18:19 Who will persuade **A** king of
2Ch 21: 6 as the house of **A** had done
2Ch 21: 6 the daughter of **A** as a wife
2Ch 21:13 harlotry of the house of **A**
2Ch 22: 3 in the ways of the house of **A**
2Ch 22: 4 the LORD, like the house of **A**
2Ch 22: 5 with Jehoram the son of **A**
2Ch 22: 6 the son of **A** in Jezreel,
2Ch 22: 7 to cut off the house of **A**
2Ch 22: 8 judgment on the house of **A**
Jer 29:21 concerning **A** the son of
Jer 29:22 make you like Zedekiah and **A**

AHAB'S (*see* AHAB)
1Ki 21: 8 she wrote letters in **A** name
2Ki 10: 1 and to those who reared **A** sons
Mic 6:16 the works of **A** house are done

AHARAH (*see* AHER, AHIRAM, EHI)
1Ch 8: 1 the second, **A** the third,

AHARHEL
1Ch 4: 8 the families of **A** the son of

AHASBAI
2Sa 23:34 Eliphelet the son of **A**, the

AHASUERUS
Ezra 4: 6 Now in the reign of **A**, in the
Esth 1: 1 **A** (this was the **A** who
Esth 1: 2 in those days when King **A** sat
Esth 1: 9 which belonged to King **A**
Esth 1:10 in the presence of King **A**
Esth 1:15 King **A** brought to her by the
Esth 1:16 all the provinces of King **A**
Esth 1:17 King **A** commanded Queen
Esth 1:19 come no more before King **A**
Esth 2: 1 the wrath of King **A** subsided
Esth 2:12 **A** after she had completed
Esth 2:16 So Esther was taken to King **A**
Esth 2:21 sought to lay hands on King **A**
Esth 3: 1 things King **A** promoted Haman
Esth 3: 6 the whole kingdom of **A**
Esth 3: 7 in the twelfth year of King **A**
Esth 3: 8 Then Haman said to King **A**
Esth 3:12 name of King **A** it was written
Esth 6: 2 sought to lay hands on King **A**
Esth 7: 5 King **A** answered and said
Esth 8: 1 On that day King **A** gave Queen
Esth 8: 7 Then King **A** said to Queen
Esth 8:10 wrote in the name of King **A**
Esth 8:12 all the provinces of King **A**
Esth 9: 2 **A** to lay hands on those who
Esth 9:20 all the provinces of King **A**
Esth 9:30 provinces of the kingdom of **A**
Esth 10: 1 King **A** imposed tribute on the
Esth 10: 3 the Jew was second to King **A**
Dan 9: 1 year of Darius the son of **A**

AHAVA (*see* IVAH)
Ezra 8:15 by the river that flows to **A**
Ezra 8:21 fast there at the river of **A**
Ezra 8:31 **A** on the twelfth day of the

AHAZ
2Ki 15:38 Then **A** his son reigned in his
2Ki 16: 1 **A** the son of Jotham, king of
2Ki 16: 2 **A** was twenty years old when
2Ki 16: 5 they besieged **A** but could not
2Ki 16: 7 So **A** sent messengers to
2Ki 16: 8 **A** took the silver and gold
2Ki 16:10 Now King **A** went to Damascus
2Ki 16:10 King **A** sent to Urijah the
2Ki 16:11 King **A** had sent from Damascus
2Ki 16:11 King **A** came from Damascus
2Ki 16:15 King **A** commanded Urijah
2Ki 16:16 to all that King **A** commanded
2Ki 16:17 King **A** cut off the panels of
2Ki 16:19 of the acts of **A** which he did
2Ki 16:20 So **A** rested with his fathers,
2Ki 17: 1 year of **A** king of Judah,
2Ki 18: 1 that Hezekiah the son of **A**
2Ki 20:11 gone down on the sundial of **A**
2Ki 23:12 roof, the upper chamber of **A**
1Ch 3:13 **A** his son, Hezekiah his son,
1Ch 8:35 Pithon, Melech, Tarea, and **A**
1Ch 8:36 And **A** begot Jehoaddah
1Ch 9:41 Pithon, Melech, Tahrea, and **A**
1Ch 9:42 And **A** begot Jarah
2Ch 27: 9 Then **A** his son reigned in his
2Ch 28: 1 **A** was twenty years old when
2Ch 28:16 King **A** sent to the kings of
2Ch 28:19 because of **A** king of Israel
2Ch 28:21 For **A** took part of the
2Ch 28:22 King **A** became increasingly
2Ch 28:22 This is that King **A**
2Ch 28:24 So **A** gathered the articles of
2Ch 28:27 So **A** rested with his fathers,
2Ch 29:19 **A** in his reign had cast aside
Is 1: 1 the days of Uzziah, Jotham, **A**
Is 7: 1 days of **A** the son of Jotham
Is 7: 3 Go out now to meet **A**, you and
Is 7:10 the LORD spoke again to **A**
Is 7:12 But **A** said, "I will not ask,
Is 14:28 in the year that King **A** died
Is 38: 8 the sun on the sundial of **A**
Hos 1: 1 the days of Uzziah, Jotham, **A**
Mic 1: 1 in the days of Jotham, **A**, and
Matt 1: 9 begot Jotham, Jotham begot **A**
Matt 1: 9 **A**, and **A** begot Hezekiah

AHAZIAH (*see* AHAZIAH'S, AZARIAH, JEHOAHAZ)
1Ki 22:40 Then **A** his son reigned in his
1Ki 22:49 Then **A** the son of Ahab said
1Ki 22:51 **A** the son of Ahab became king
2Ki 1: 2 Now **A** fell through the
2Ki 1:17 So **A** died according to the
2Ki 1:18 of the acts of **A** which he did
2Ki 8:24 Then **A** his son reigned in his
2Ki 8:25 **A** the son of Jehoram, king of
2Ki 8:26 **A** was twenty-two years old
2Ki 8:29 **A** the son of Jehoram, king of
2Ki 9:16 **A** king of Judah had come down
2Ki 9:21 **A** king of Judah went out,
2Ki 9:23 around and fled, and said to **A**
2Ki 9:23 Treachery, **A**!"
2Ki 9:27 But when **A** king of Judah saw
2Ki 9:29 **A** had become king over Judah
2Ki 10:13 brothers of **A** king of Judah
2Ki 10:13 We are the brothers of **A**
2Ki 11: 1 **A** saw that her son was dead
2Ki 11: 2 of King Joram, sister of **A**
2Ki 11: 2 took Joash the son of **A**, and
2Ki 12:18 Jehoshaphat and Jehoram and **A**
2Ki 13: 1 year of Joash the son of **A**
2Ki 14:13 son of Jehoash, the son of **A**
1Ch 3:11 **A** his son, Joash his son,
2Ch 20:35 himself with **A** king of Israel
2Ch 20:37 have allied yourself with **A**
2Ch 22: 1 of Jerusalem made **A** his
2Ch 22: 1 So **A** the son of Jehoram, king
2Ch 22: 2 **A** was forty-two years old
2Ch 22: 8 brothers who served **A**, that
2Ch 22: 9 Then he searched for **A**
2Ch 22: 9 So the house of **A** had no
2Ch 22:10 **A** saw that her son was dead
2Ch 22:11 king, took Joash the son of **A**
2Ch 22:11 (for she was the sister of **A**)

AHAZIAH'S (*see* AHAZIAH)
2Ch 22: 7 God's occasion for **A** downfall
2Ch 22: 8 the sons of **A** brothers who

AHBAN
1Ch 2:29 Abihail, and she bore him **A**

AHEAD (*see* PREFACE)

AHER (*see* AHARAH)
1Ch 7:12 and Hushim was the son of **A**

AHI
1Ch 5:15 **A** the son of Abdiel, the son
1Ch 7:34 The sons of Shemer were **A**

AHIAM
2Sa 23:33 **A** the son of Sharar the
1Ch 11:35 **A** the son of Sacar the

AHIAN
1Ch 7:19 And the sons of Shemida were **A**

AHIEZER
Num 1:12 Dan, **A** the son of Ammishaddai
Num 2:25 be **A** the son of Ammishaddai
Num 7:66 On the tenth day **A** the son of
Num 7:71 of **A** the son of Ammishaddai
Num 10:25 over their army was **A** the son
1Ch 12: 3 The chief was **A**, then Joash,

AHIHUD
Num 34:27 Asher, **A** the son of Shelomi
1Ch 8: 7 He begot Uzza and **A**

AHIJAH (*see* AHIMELECH)
1Sa 14: 3 **A** the son of Ahitub,
1Sa 14:18 And Saul said to **A**, "Bring
1Ki 4: 3 Elihoreph and **A**, the sons of
1Ki 11:29 that the prophet **A** the
1Ki 11:30 Then **A** took hold of the new
1Ki 12:15 the LORD had spoken by **A** the
1Ki 14: 2 **A** the prophet is there, who
1Ki 14: 4 and came to the house of **A**
1Ki 14: 4 But **A** could not see, for his
1Ki 14: 5 Now the LORD had said to **A**
1Ki 14: 6 when **A** heard the sound of her
1Ki 14:18 His servant **A** the prophet
1Ki 15:27 Then Baasha the son of **A**, of
1Ki 15:29 His servant **A** the Shilonite
1Ki 15:33 Baasha the son of **A** became
1Ki 21:22 house of Baasha the son of **A**
2Ki 9: 9 house of Baasha the son of **A**
1Ch 2:25 and Bunah, Oren, Ozem, and **A**
1Ch 8: 7 Naaman, **A**, and Gera who
1Ch 11:36 Mecherathite, **A** the Pelonite,
1Ch 26:20 **A** was over the treasuries of
2Ch 9:29 prophecy of **A** the Shilonite
2Ch 10:15 **A** the Shilonite to Jeroboam
Neh 10:26 **A**, Hanan, Anan,

AHIKAM
2Ki 22:12 **A** the son of Shaphan, Achbor
2Ki 22:14 So Hilkiah the priest, **A**,
2Ki 25:22 he made Gedaliah the son of **A**
2Ch 34:20 **A** the son of Shaphan, Abdon
Jer 26:24 Nevertheless the hand of **A**
Jer 39:14 him to Gedaliah the son of **A**
Jer 40: 5 back to Gedaliah the son of **A**
Jer 40: 6 went to Gedaliah the son of **A**
Jer 40: 7 son of **A** governor in the land
Jer 40: 9 And Gedaliah the son of **A**, the
Jer 40:11 them Gedaliah the son of **A**
Jer 40:14 son of **A** did not believe them
Jer 40:16 But Gedaliah the son of **A**
Jer 41: 1 men to Gedaliah the son of **A**
Jer 41: 2 struck Gedaliah the son of **A**
Jer 41: 6 Come to Gedaliah the son of **A**
Jer 41:10 to Gedaliah the son of **A**
Jer 41:16 Gedaliah the son of **A**
Jer 41:18 Gedaliah the son of **A**, whom
Jer 43: 6 with Gedaliah the son of **A**

AHILUD
2Sa 8:16 the son of **A** was recorder
2Sa 20:24 the son of **A** was recorder
1Ki 4: 3 Jehoshaphat the son of **A**, the
1Ki 4:12 Baana the son of **A**, in
1Ch 18:15 the son of **A** was recorder

AHIMAAZ
1Sa 14:50 was Ahinoam the daughter of **A**
2Sa 15:27 **A** your son, and Jonathan the
2Sa 15:36 with them their two sons, **A**
2Sa 17:17 **A** stayed at En Rogel, for
2Sa 17:20 Where are **A** and Jonathan
2Sa 18:19 Then **A** the son of Zadok said,
2Sa 18:22 **A** the son of Zadok said again
2Sa 18:23 Then **A** ran by way of the
2Sa 18:27 running of **A** the son of Zadok
2Sa 18:28 **A** called out and said to the
2Sa 18:29 And **A** answered, "When Joab
1Ki 4:15 **A**, in Naphtali
1Ch 6: 8 Zadok, and Zadok begot **A**
1Ch 6: 9 **A** begot Azariah, and Azariah
1Ch 6:53 Zadok his son, and **A** his son

AHIMAN
Num 13:22 **A**, Sheshai, and Talmai, the
Josh 15:14 Sheshai, **A**, and Talmai, the
Judg 1:10 And they killed Sheshai, **A**
1Ch 9:17 Shallum, Akkub, Talmon, **A**

AHIMELECH (*see* ABIMELECH, AHIJAH, AHIMELECH'S)
1Sa 21: 1 came to Nob, to **A** the priest
1Sa 21: 1 And **A** was afraid when he met
1Sa 21: 2 So David said to **A** the priest
1Sa 21: 8 And David said to **A**, "Is
1Sa 22: 9 Nob, to **A** the son of Ahitub
1Sa 22:11 sent to call **A** the priest
1Sa 22:14 So **A** answered the king and
1Sa 22:16 You shall surely die, **A**, you
1Sa 22:20 sons of **A** the son of Ahitub
1Sa 23: 6 of **A** fled to David at Keilah
1Sa 26: 6 said to **A** the Hittite and to
2Sa 8:17 **A** the son of Abiathar were
1Ch 24: 3 **A** of the sons of Ithamar,
1Ch 24: 6 **A** the son of Abiathar, and the
1Ch 24:31 of King David, Zadok, **A**, and

AHIMELECH'S (*see* AHIMELECH)
1Sa 30: 7 Abiathar the priest, **A** son,

AHIMOTH (*see* MAHATH)
1Ch 6:25 of Elkanah were Amasai and **A**

AHINADAB
1Ki 4:14 **A** the son of Iddo, in

AHINOAM
1Sa 14:50 was **A** the daughter of Ahimaaz
1Sa 25:43 David also took **A** of Jezreel
1Sa 27: 3 wives, **A** the Jezreelitess, and
1Sa 30: 5 wives, **A** the Jezreelitess, and
2Sa 2: 2 also, **A** the Jezreelitess, and
2Sa 3: 2 Amnon by **A** the Jezreelitess
1Ch 3: 1 Amnon, by **A** the Jezreelitess

AHIO
2Sa 6: 3 and Uzzah and **A**, the sons of
2Sa 6: 4 and **A** went before the ark
1Ch 8:14 **A**, Shashak, Jeremoth,
1Ch 8:31 Gedor, **A**, Zecher,
1Ch 9:37 Gedor, **A**, Zechariah, and
1Ch 13: 7 and Uzza and **A** drove the cart

AHIRA
Num 1:15 Naphtali, **A** the son of Enan
Num 2:29 shall be **A** the son of Enan
Num 7:78 twelfth day **A** the son of Enan
Num 7:83 offering of **A** the son of Enan
Num 10:27 was **A** the son of Enan

AHIRAM (*see* AHARAH, AHIRAMITES)
Num 26:38 of **A**, the family of the

AHIRAMITES (*see* AHIRAM)
Num 26:38 Ahiram, the family of the **A**

AHISAMACH
Ex 31: 6 with him Aholiab the son of **A**
Ex 35:34 him and Aholiab the son of **A**
Ex 38:23 him was Aholiab the son of **A**

AHISHAHAR
1Ch 7:10 Zethan, Tharshish, and **A**

AHISHAR
1Ki 4: 6 **A**, over the household

AHITHOPHEL
2Sa 15:12 sent for **A** the Gilonite,
2Sa 15:31 **A** is among the conspirators
2Sa 15:31 counsel of **A** into foolishness
2Sa 15:34 the counsel of **A** for me
2Sa 16:15 and **A** was with him
2Sa 16:20 Then Absalom said to **A**
2Sa 16:21 And **A** said to Absalom,
2Sa 16:23 And the counsel of **A**, which he
2Sa 16:23 counsel of **A** both with David
2Sa 17: 1 Moreover **A** said to Absalom,
2Sa 17: 6 **A** has spoken in this manner
2Sa 17: 7 The counsel that **A** has given
2Sa 17:14 better than the counsel of **A**
2Sa 17:14 defeat the good counsel of **A**
2Sa 17:15 so **A** counseled Absalom and the
2Sa 17:21 For thus has **A** counseled
2Sa 17:23 Now when **A** saw that his
2Sa 23:34 the son of **A** the Gilonite
1Ch 27:33 **A** was the king's counselor,
1Ch 27:34 After **A** was Jehoiada the son

AHITUB
1Sa 14: 3 Ahijah the son of **A**,
1Sa 22: 9 to Ahimelech the son of **A**
1Sa 22:11 the priest, the son of **A**, and
1Sa 22:12 Hear now, son of **A**
1Sa 22:20 of Ahimelech the son of **A**
2Sa 8:17 Zadok the son of **A** and
1Ch 6: 7 Amariah, and Amariah begot **A**
1Ch 6: 8 **A** begot Zadok, and Zadok
1Ch 6:11 Amariah, and Amariah begot **A**
1Ch 6:12 **A** begot Zadok, and Zadok
1Ch 6:52 Amariah his son, **A** his son,
1Ch 9:11 son of Meraioth, the son of **A**
1Ch 18:16 Zadok the son of **A** and
Ezra 7: 2 son of Zadok, the son of **A**
Neh 11:11 son of Meraioth, the son of **A**

AHLAB
Judg 1:31 inhabitants of Sidon, or of **A**

AHLAI
1Ch 2:31 and Sheshan's child was **A**
1Ch 11:41 Hittite, Zabad the son of **A**

AHOAH (*see* AHOHITE)
1Ch 8: 4 Abishua, Naaman, **A**,

AHOHITE (*see* AHOAH)
2Sa 23: 9 the son of Dodo, the **A**, one
2Sa 23:28 Zalmon the **A**, Maharai the
1Ch 11:12 the son of Dodo, the **A**, who
1Ch 11:29 the Hushathite, Ilai the **A**
1Ch 27: 4 second month was Dodai an **A**

AHOLIAB
Ex 31: 6 him **A** the son of Ahisamach
Ex 35:34 **A** the son of Ahisamach, of
Ex 36: 1 And Bezaleel and **A**, and every
Ex 36: 2 Moses called Bezaleel and **A**
Ex 38:23 with him was **A** the son of

AHOLIBAMAH
Gen 36: 2 **A** the daughter of Anah, the
Gen 36: 5 And **A** bore Jeush, Jaalam, and
Gen 36:14 These were the sons of **A**,
Gen 36:18 And these were the sons of **A**
Gen 36:18 chiefs who descended from **A**
Gen 36:25 and **A** the daughter of Anah
Gen 36:41 Chief **A**, Chief Elah, Chief
1Ch 1:52 Chief **A**, Chief Elah, Chief

AHUMAI
1Ch 4: 2 Jahath, and Jahath begot **A**

AHUZZAM
1Ch 4: 6 Naarah bore him **A**, Hepher,

AHUZZATH
Gen 26:26 came to him from Gerar with **A**

AHZAI
Neh 11:13 son of Azareel, the son of **A**

AI (*see* AIATH, AIJA)
Gen 12: 8 on the west and **A** on the east
Gen 13: 3 between Bethel and **A**,
Josh 7: 2 sent men from Jericho to **A**
Josh 7: 2 men went up and spied out **A**
Josh 7: 3 men go up and attack **A**
Josh 7: 3 for the people of **A** are few
Josh 7: 4 they fled before the men of **A**
Josh 7: 5 And the men of **A** struck down
Josh 8: 1 you, and arise, go up to **A**
Josh 8: 1 into your hand the king of **A**
Josh 8: 2 And you shall do to **A** and its
Josh 8: 3 of war, to go up against **A**
Josh 8: 9 stayed between Bethel and **A**
Josh 8: 9 and **A**, on the west side of **A**
Josh 8:10 before the people to **A**
Josh 8:11 camped on the north side of **A**
Josh 8:11 a valley between them and **A**
Josh 8:12 between Bethel and **A**
Josh 8:14 when the king of **A** saw it
Josh 8:16 in **A** were called together to
Josh 8:17 in **A** or Bethel who did not go
Josh 8:18 that is in your hand toward **A**
Josh 8:20 And when the men of **A** looked
Josh 8:21 and struck down the men of **A**
Josh 8:23 the king of **A** they took alive
Josh 8:24 inhabitants of **A** in the field
Josh 8:24 the Israelites returned to **A**
Josh 8:25 all the people of **A**
Josh 8:26 all the inhabitants of **A**
Josh 8:28 So Joshua burned **A** and made it
Josh 8:29 the king of **A** he hanged on a
Josh 9: 3 had done to Jericho and **A**,
Josh 10: 1 heard how Joshua had taken **A**
Josh 10: 1 its king, so he had done to **A**
Josh 10: 2 because it was greater than **A**
Josh 12: 9 the king of **A**, which is
Ezra 2:28 the men of Bethel and **A**, two
Neh 7:32 the men of Bethel and **A**, one
Jer 49: 3 O Heshbon, for **A** is plundered

AIAH (*see* AIJA, AJAH)
2Sa 3: 7 was Rizpah, the daughter of **A**
2Sa 21: 8 of Rizpah the daughter of **A**
2Sa 21:10 daughter of **A** took sackcloth
2Sa 21:11 what Rizpah the daughter of **A**

AIATH (*see* AI)
Is 10:28 He has come to **A**, he has

AID (*see* AIDED, AIDES)
2Sa 21:17 son of Zeruiah came to his a
2Ki 23:29 the a of the king of Assyria
Phil 4:16 Thessalonica you sent a once
Heb 2:16 He does not give a to angels
Heb 2:16 but He does give a to the
Heb 2:18 He is able to a those who are

AIDED (*see* AID)
Judg 9:24 who a him in the killing of
Dan 11:34 they shall be a with a little

AIDES (*see* AID)
2Ki 5:15 man of God, he and all his a

AIJA (*see* AI, AIAH)
Neh 11:31 Geba dwelt in Michmash, A

AIJALON
Josh 10:12 and Moon, in the Valley of A
Josh 19:42 Shaalabbin, A, Jethlah,
Josh 21:24 A with its common-land, and
Judg 1:35 to dwell in Mount Heres, in A
Judg 12:12 and was buried at A in the
1Sa 14:31 that day from Michmash to A
1Ch 6:69 A with its common-lands, and
1Ch 8:13 of the inhabitants of A, who
2Ch 11:10 Zorah, A, and Hebron, which
2Ch 28:18 and had taken Beth Shemesh, A

AILS
Gen 21:17 What a you, Hagar
Judg 18:23 What a you, that you have
Judg 18:24 you say to me, What a you
Ps 114: 5 What a you, O sea, that you
Is 22: 1 What a you now, that you have

AIM (*see* AIMLESS)
Rom 15:20 it my a to preach the gospel
2Co 5: 9 Therefore we make it our a

AIMLESS (*see* AIM)
1Pe 1:18 from your a conduct received

AIN
Num 34:11 Riblah on the east side of A
Josh 15:32 Lebaoth, Shilhim, A, and
Josh 19: 7 A, Rimmon, Ether, and Ashan
Josh 21:16 A with its common-land,
1Ch 4:32 their villages were Etam, A

AIR
Gen 1:26 sea, over the birds of the a
Gen 1:28 sea, over the birds of the a
Gen 1:30 earth, to every bird of the a
Gen 2:19 field and every bird of the a
Gen 2:20 cattle, to the birds of the a
Gen 6: 7 thing and birds of the a, for
Gen 7: 3 seven each of birds of the a
Gen 7:23 thing and bird of the a
Gen 9: 2 earth, on every bird of the a
Deut 4:17 bird that flies in the a,
Deut 28:26 for all the birds of the a
1Sa 17:44 flesh to the birds of the a
1Sa 17:46 to the birds of the a and the
2Sa 21:10 a to rest on them by day nor
1Ki 14:11 the birds of the a shall eat
1Ki 16: 4 the birds of the a shall eat
1Ki 21:24 the birds of the a shall eat
Job 12: 7 and the birds of the a, and
Job 28:21 from the birds of the a
Job 41:16 no a can come between them
Ps 8: 8 The birds of the a, And the
Prov 30:19 the way of an eagle in the a
Eccl 10:20 for a bird of the a may carry
Hos 2:18 with the birds of the a, and
Hos 4: 3 field and the birds of the a
Hos 7:12 them down like birds of the a
Matt 6:26 Look at the birds of the a
Matt 8:20 and birds of the a have nests
Matt 13:32 that the birds of the a come
Mark 4: 4 and the birds of the a came
Mark 4:32 a may nest under its shade
Luke 8: 5 birds of the a devoured it
Luke 9:58 and birds of the a have nests
Luke 13:19 the birds of the a nested in
Acts 10:12 things, and birds of the a
Acts 11: 6 things, and birds of the a
Acts 22:23 and threw dust into the a,
1Co 9:26 not as one who beats the a
1Co 14: 9 will be speaking into the a
Eph 2: 2 prince of the power of the a
1Th 4:17 to meet the Lord in the a
Rev 9: 2 the a were darkened because
Rev 16:17 out his bowl into the a, and a

AJAH (*see* AIAH)
Gen 36:24 both A and Anah
1Ch 1:40 The sons of Zibeon were A

AKAN (*see* JAAKAN, JACHAN)
Gen 36:27 Bilhan, Zaavan, and A

AKEL DAMA
Acts 1:19 in their own language, A,

AKKUB
1Ch 3:24 Eliashib, Pelaiah, A,
1Ch 9:17 gatekeepers were Shallum, A
Ezra 2:42 sons of Talmon, the sons of A
Ezra 2:45 of Hagabah, the sons of A
Neh 7:45 of Talmon, the children of A
Neh 8: 7 Bani, Sherebiah, Jamin, A
Neh 11:19 Moreover the gatekeepers, A
Neh 12:25 A were gatekeepers keeping

AKRABBIM
Num 34: 4 side of the Ascent of A,
Josh 15: 3 side of the Ascent of A,
Judg 1:36 was from the Ascent of A,

ALABASTER
Esth 1: 6 on a mosaic pavement of a
Matt 26: 7 an a flask of very costly
Mark 14: 3 a woman came having an a
Luke 7:37 house, brought an a flask of

ALAMMELECH
Josh 19:26 A, Amad, and Mishal

ALAMOTH
1Ch 15:20 with strings according to A

ALARM (*see* ALARMED)
Num 10: 9 sound an a with the trumpets
2Ch 13:12 to sound the a against you
Jer 4:19 of the trumpet, the a of war
Jer 49: 2 an a of war in Rabbah of the
Joel 2: 1 and sound an a in My holy
Zeph 1:16 and a against the fortified

ALARMED (*see* ALARM)
Mark 16: 5 and they were a
Mark 16: 6 Do not be a

ALAS (*see* PREFACE)

ALEMETH
1Ch 6:60 A with its common-lands, and
1Ch 7: 8 Abijah, Anathoth, and A
1Ch 8:36 Jehoaddah begot A, Azmaveth,
1Ch 9:42 Jarah begot A, Azmaveth, and

ALEXANDER
Mark 15:21 a Cyrenian, the father of A
Acts 4: 6 priest, Caiaphas, John, and A
Acts 19:33 And they drew A out of the
Acts 19:33 A motioned with his hand, and
1Ti 1:20 of whom are Hymenaeus and A
2Ti 4:14 A the coppersmith did me much

ALEXANDRIA (*see* ALEXANDRIAN)
Acts 18:24 Jew named Apollos, born at A

ALEXANDRIAN (*see* ALEXANDRIA, ALEXANDRIANS)
Acts 27: 6 an A ship sailing to Italy
Acts 28:11 months we sailed in an A ship

ALEXANDRIANS (*see* ALEXANDRIAN)
Acts 6: 9 of the Freedmen (Cyrenians, A

ALGUM (*see* ALMUG)
2Ch 2: 8 a logs from Lebanon, for I
2Ch 9:10 from Ophir, brought a wood
2Ch 9:11 a wood for the house of the

ALIAH (*see* ALVAH, ALVAN)
1Ch 1:51 were Chief Timnah, Chief A

ALIAN (*see* ALVAN)
1Ch 1:40 The sons of Shobal were A

ALIEN (*see* ALIENS)
Deut 14:21 you may give it to the a who
Deut 23: 7 you were an a in his land
Deut 28:43 The a who is among you shall
2Sa 1:13 I am the son of an a, an
Job 15:19 and no a passed among them
Job 19:15 I am an a in their sight
Ps 69: 8 an a to my mother's children
Jer 2:21 degenerate plant of an a vine
Jer 3:13 scattered your charms to a
Jer 19: 4 Me and made this an a place
Zech 7:10 fatherless, the a or the poor
Mal 3: 5 those who turn away an a

ALIENATE (*see* ALIENATED)
Ezek 48:14 they may not a this best part

ALIENATED (*see* ALIENATE)
Ezek 23:17 them, and a herself from them
Ezek 23:18 then I a Myself from her, as
Ezek 23:18 as I had a Myself from her
Ezek 23:22 from whom you have a yourself
Ezek 23:28 from whom you a yourself
Eph 4:18 being a from the life of God,
Col 1:21 And you, who once were a and

ALIENS (*see* ALIEN)
Deut 24:14 a who is in your land within
1Ch 22: 2 the a who were in the land of
1Ch 29:15 For we are a and pilgrims
2Ch 2:17 the a who were in the land of
Prov 5:10 lest a be filled with your
Is 25: 5 will reduce the noise of a
Jer 2:25 For I have loved a, and after
Jer 5:19 so you shall serve a in a
Lam 5: 2 has been turned over to a
Ezek 28:10 by the hand of a
Ezek 30:12 is in it, by the hand of a
Ezek 31:12 And a, the most terrible of
Hos 7: 9 A have devoured his strength,
Hos 8: 7 a would swallow it up
Joel 3:17 no a shall ever pass through
Eph 2:12 being a from the commonwealth
Heb 11:34 to flight the armies of the a

ALIGHT (*see* ALIGHTED, ALIGHTING)
Prov 26: 2 without cause shall not a

ALIGHTED (*see* ALIGHT)
Judg 4:15 Sisera a from his chariot and

ALIGHTING (*see* ALIGHT)
Matt 3:16 like a dove and a upon Him

ALIKE (*see* PREFACE)

ALIVE
Gen 6:19 ark, to keep them a with you
Gen 6:20 come to you to keep them a
Gen 7: 3 to keep the species a on the
Gen 7:23 him in the ark remained a
Gen 43: 7 Is your father still a
Gen 43:27 Is he still a
Gen 43:28 he is still a
Gen 45:26 Joseph is still a, and he is
Gen 45:28 Joseph my son is still a
Gen 46:30 face, because you are still a
Gen 50:20 day, to save many people a
Ex 1:17 but saved the male children a
Ex 1:18 and saved the male children a
Ex 1:22 daughter you shall save a
Ex 4:18 see whether they are still a
Ex 21:21 if he remains a a day or two
Ex 22: 4 certainly found a in his hand
Lev 16:10 presented a before the LORD
Lev 18:18 while the other is a
Num 14:38 son of Jephunneh remained a
Num 16:30 they go down a into the pit
Num 16:33 them went down a into the pit
Num 31:15 Have you kept all the women a
Num 31:18 But keep a for yourselves all
Deut 4: 4 the LORD your God are a today
Deut 5: 3 today, all of us who are a
Deut 6:24 that He might preserve us a
Deut 20:16 that breathes remain a,
Deut 31:27 while I am yet a with you
Deut 32:39 I kill and I make a
Josh 8:23 the king of Ai they took a
Josh 14:10 the LORD has kept me a, as
Judg 21:14 a of the women of Jabesh
1Sa 2: 6 The LORD kills and makes a
1Sa 15: 8 Agag king of the Amalekites a
1Sa 27: 9 left neither man nor woman a
1Sa 27:11 save neither man nor woman a
2Sa 8: 2 full line those to be kept a
2Sa 12:18 while the child was still a
2Sa 12:21 for the child while he was a
2Sa 12:22 While the child was still a
2Sa 18:14 while he was still a in the
1Ki 18: 5 to keep the horses and mules a
1Ki 20:18 out for peace, take them a
1Ki 20:18 come out for war, take them a
1Ki 20:32 Is he still a
1Ki 21:15 for Naboth is not a, but dead
2Ki 5: 7 Am I God, to kill and make a
2Ki 7: 4 If they keep us a, we shall
2Ki 7:12 city, we shall catch them a
2Ki 10:14 Take them a

2Ki 10:14 So they took them **a**, and
2Ch 25:12 another ten thousand **a**,
Ps 22:29 he who cannot keep himself **a**
Ps 30: 3 You have kept me **a**, that I
Ps 33:19 And to keep them **a** in famine
Ps 41: 2 preserve him and keep him **a**
Ps 55:15 Let them go down **a** into hell
Ps 124: 3 would have swallowed us **a**
Prov 1:12 us swallow them **a** like Sheol
Eccl 4: 2 the living who are still **a**
Is 7:21 a man will keep **a** a young cow
Jer 49:11 I will preserve them **a**
Ezek 7:13 though he may still be **a**
Ezek 13:18 people, and keep yourselves **a**
Ezek 13:19 keeping people **a** who should
Ezek 18:27 right, he preserves himself **a**
Dan 5:19 whomever he wished, he kept **a**
Matt 27:63 while He was still **a**, how
Mark 16:11 when they heard that He was **a**
Luke 15:24 my son was dead and is **a** again
Luke 15:32 your brother was dead and is **a**
Luke 24:23 of angels who said He was **a**
Acts 1: 3 He also presented Himself **a**
Acts 9:41 and widows, he presented her **a**
Acts 20:12 brought the young man in **a**
Acts 25:19 whom Paul affirmed to be **a**
Rom 6:11 but **a** to God in Christ Jesus
Rom 6:13 God as being **a** from the dead
Rom 7: 9 I was **a** once without the law,
1Co 15:22 in Christ all shall be made **a**
1Co 15:36 is not made **a** unless it dies
Eph 2: 1 And you He made **a**, who were
Eph 2: 5 made us **a** together with
Col 2:13 He has made **a** together with
1Th 4:15 the Lord, that we who are **a**
1Th 4:17 Then we who are **a** and remain
1Pe 3:18 but made **a** by the Spirit,
Rev 1:18 and behold, I am **a** forevermore
Rev 3: 1 have a name that you are **a**
Rev 19:20 These two were cast **a** into

ALL (*see* PREFACE)

ALLAYS
Prov 15:18 is slow to anger **a** contention

ALLELUIA
Rev 19: 1 **A**! Salvation and glory and
Rev 19: 3 **A**! And her smoke rises up
Rev 19: 4 Amen! **A**!"
Rev 19: 6 **A**! For the Lord God

ALLIED (*see* ALLIES)
2Ch 18: 1 by marriage he **a** himself with
2Ch 20:35 **a** himself with Ahaziah king
2Ch 20:36 he **a** himself with him to make
2Ch 20:37 Because you have **a** yourself
Neh 13: 4 of our God, was **a** with Tobiah
Ezek 30: 5 men of the lands who are **a**

ALLIES (*see* ALLIED)
Gen 14:13 and they were **a** with Abram
Job 9:13 anger, the **a** of the proud lie
Jer 2:37 has rejected your trusted **a**

ALLON (*see* ELON)
1Ch 4:37 son of Shiphi, the son of **A**

ALLON BACHUTH (*see* BACHUTH)
Gen 35: 8 the name of it was called **A**

ALLOTMENT (*see* ALLOTMENTS, ALLOTTED)
1Ch 16:18 as the **a** of your inheritance
Job 31: 2 For what is the **a** of God from
Ps 105:11 As the **a** of your inheritance
Ezek 16:27 you, diminished your **a**, and
Acts 13:19 their land to them by **a**

ALLOTMENTS (*see* ALLOTMENT)
2Ch 31:15 to distribute **a** to their

ALLOTTED (*see* ALLOTMENT)
Gen 47:22 rations **a** to them by Pharaoh
Judg 1: 3 up with me to my **a** territory
Judg 1: 3 with you to your **a** territory
Job 7: 3 so I have been **a** months of
Ps 78:55 **A** them an inheritance by
Ps 125: 3 the land **a** to the righteous

ALLOW (*see* ALLOWANCE, ALLOWED)
Gen 31: 7 God did not **a** him to hurt me
Gen 31:28 you did not **a** me to kiss my
Ex 12:23 not **a** the destroyer to come
Lev 2:13 you shall not **a** the salt of
Lev 22:16 or **a** them to bear the guilt
Num 21:23 But Sihon would not **a** Israel
Josh 10:19 do not **a** them to enter their
Judg 1:34 for they would not **a** them to
Judg 3:28 did not **a** anyone to cross
1Sa 24: 7 and did not **a** them to rise
2Sa 21:10 she did not **a** the birds of
Job 9:18 He will not **a** me to catch my
Ps 16:10 Nor will You **a** Your Holy One
Ps 66: 9 does not **a** our feet to be
Ps 89:33 Nor **a** My faithfulness to fail
Ps 121: 3 He will not **a** your foot to be
Prov 10: 3 The LORD will not **a** the
Matt 23:13 nor do you **a** those who are
Mark 1:34 He did not **a** the demons to
Mark 11:16 And He would not **a** anyone to
Luke 4:41 did not **a** them to speak, for
Acts 2:27 nor will You **a** Your Holy One
Acts 13:35 You will not **a** Your Holy One
Acts 19:30 the disciples would not **a** him
Acts 28: 4 justice does not **a** to live
1Co 10:13 who will not **a** you to be
Rev 2:20 you, because you **a** that woman
Rev 11: 9 not **a** their dead bodies to be

ALLOWANCE (*see* ALLOW)
Esth 2: 9 to her, besides her **a**

ALLOWED (*see* ALLOW)
Deut 8: 3 **a** you to hunger, and fed you
Job 31:30 (Indeed I have not **a** my mouth
Matt 3:15 Then he **a** Him
Matt 24:43 not **a** his house to be broken
Luke 12:39 not **a** his house to be broken
Acts 14:16 **a** all nations to walk in

ALLOY
Is 1:25 and take away all your **a**

ALLURE
Prov 6:25 nor let her **a** you with her
Hos 2:14 behold, I will **a** her, will
2Pe 2:18 they **a** through the lusts of

ALMIGHTY
Gen 17: 1 I am **A** God
Gen 28: 3 May God **A** bless you, and make
Gen 35:11 I am God **A**
Gen 43:14 may God **A** give you mercy
Gen 48: 3 God **A** appeared to me at Luz
Gen 49:25 by the **A** who will bless you
Ex 6: 3 Isaac, and to Jacob, as God **A**
Num 24: 4 who sees the vision of the **A**
Num 24:16 who sees the vision of the **A**
Ruth 1:20 for the **A** has dealt very
Ruth 1:21 me, and the **A** has afflicted me
Job 5:17 the chastening of the **A**
Job 6: 4 arrows of the **A** are within me
Job 6:14 he forsakes the fear of the **A**
Job 8: 3 Or does the **A** pervert justice
Job 8: 5 your supplication to the **A**
Job 11: 7 find out the limits of the **A**
Job 13: 3 But I would speak to the **A**
Job 15:25 acts defiantly against the **A**
Job 21:15 Who is the **A**, that we should
Job 21:20 drink of the wrath of the **A**
Job 22: 3 the **A** that you are righteous
Job 22:17 What can the **A** do to them
Job 22:23 If you return to the **A**, you
Job 22:25 the **A** will be your gold and
Job 22:26 have your delight in the **A**
Job 23:16 weak, and the **A** terrifies me
Job 24: 1 are not hidden from the **A**
Job 27: 2 away my justice, and the **A**
Job 27:10 he delight himself in the **A**
Job 27:11 what is with the **A** I will not
Job 27:13 received from the **A**
Job 29: 5 when the **A** was yet with me,
Job 31: 2 of the **A** from on high
Job 31:35 that the **A** would answer me,
Job 32: 8 the breath of the **A** gives him
Job 33: 4 breath of the **A** gives me life
Job 34:10 from the **A** to commit iniquity
Job 34:12 nor will the **A** pervert
Job 35:13 nor will the **A** regard it
Job 37:23 As for the **A**, we cannot find
Job 40: 2 with the **A** correct Him
Ps 68:14 When the **A** scattered kings in
Ps 91: 1 under the shadow of the **A**
Is 13: 6 as destruction from the **A**
Ezek 1:24 like the voice of the **A**, a
Ezek 10: 5 like the voice of **A** God when
Joel 1:15 as destruction from the **A**
2Co 6:18 and daughters, says the LORD **A**
Rev 1: 8 was and who is to come, the **A**
Rev 4: 8 Holy, holy, holy, Lord God **A**
Rev 11:17 give You thanks, O Lord God **A**
Rev 15: 3 are Your works, Lord God **A**
Rev 16: 7 Even so, Lord God **A**, true and
Rev 16:14 of that great day of God **A**
Rev 19:15 fierceness and wrath of **A** God
Rev 21:22 in it, for the Lord God **A**

ALMODAD
Gen 10:26 Joktan begot **A**, Sheleph,
1Ch 1:20 Joktan begot **A**, Sheleph,

ALMON
Josh 21:18 and **A** with its common-land

ALMOND (*see* ALMONDS)
Gen 30:37 of green poplar and of the **a**
Ex 25:33 like **a** blossoms on one branch
Ex 25:33 like **a** blossoms on the other
Ex 25:34 shall be made like **a** blossoms
Ex 37:19 like **a** blossoms on one branch
Ex 37:19 like **a** blossoms on the other
Ex 37:20 bowls made like **a** blossoms
Eccl 12: 5 when the **a** tree blossoms, the
Jer 1:11 I see a branch of an **a** tree

ALMON DIBLATHAIM
Num 33:46 Dibon Gad and camped at **A**
Num 33:47 They moved from **A** and camped

ALMONDS (*see* ALMOND)
Gen 43:11 and myrrh, pistachio nuts and **a**
Num 17: 8 blossoms and yielded ripe **a**

ALMOST (*see* PREFACE)

ALMS
Luke 11:41 But rather give **a** of such
Luke 12:33 Sell what you have and give **a**
Acts 3: 2 to ask **a** from those who
Acts 3: 3 into the temple, asked for **a**
Acts 3:10 **a** at the Beautiful Gate of
Acts 10: 2 who gave **a** generously to the
Acts 10: 4 your **a** have come up for a
Acts 10:31 your **a** are remembered in the
Acts 24:17 many years I came to bring **a**

ALMUG (*see* ALGUM)
1Ki 10:11 great quantities of **a** wood
1Ki 10:12 **a** wood for the house of the
1Ki 10:12 never again came such **a** wood

ALOES
Num 24: 6 like **a** planted by the LORD,
Ps 45: 8 are scented with myrrh and **a**
Prov 7:17 perfumed my bed with myrrh, **a**
Song 4:14 of frankincense, myrrh and **a**
John 19:39 a mixture of myrrh and **a**,

ALONE (*see* PREFACE)

ALONG (*see* PREFACE)

ALONGSIDE
1Ch 8:32 They also dwelt **a** their
1Ch 9:38 They also dwelt **a** their
Ezek 48:18 **a** the district of the holy

ALOOF
Ps 38:11 stand **a** from my plague, And my

ALOTH (*see* BEALOTH)
1Ki 4:16 son of Hushai, in Asher and **A**

ALOUD
Gen 45: 2 And he wept **a**, and the
1Ki 18:27 Cry **a**, for he is a god
1Ki 18:28 So they cried **a**, and cut
1Ch 16:42 to sound **a** with trumpets and
Ezra 3:12 yet many shouted **a** for joy
Job 19: 7 If I cry **a**, there is no
Ps 51:14 my tongue shall sing **a** of
Ps 55:17 at noon I will pray, and cry **a**
Ps 59:16 I will sing **a** of Your mercy
Ps 81: 1 Sing **a** to God our strength
Ps 132:16 saints shall shout **a** for joy
Ps 149: 5 Let them sing **a** on their beds
Prov 1:20 Wisdom calls **a** outside
Is 24:14 they shall cry **a** from the sea
Is 42:13 shall cry out, yes, shout **a**
Is 54: 1 forth into singing, and cry **a**
Is 58: 1 Cry **a**, spare not
Dan 3: 4 Then a herald cried **a**
Dan 4:14 He cried **a** and said thus
Dan 5: 7 The king cried **a** to bring in
Hos 5: 8 Cry **a** at Beth Aven, 'Look
Mic 4: 9 Now why do you cry **a**
Mark 15: 8 Then the multitude, crying **a**

ALPHA
Rev 1: 8 I am the **A** and the Omega, the
Rev 1:11 I am the **A** and the Omega, the
Rev 21: 6 I am the **A** and the Omega, the
Rev 22:13 I am the **A** and the Omega, the

ALPHAEUS (*see* CLEOPAS)
Matt 10: 3 James the son of **A**, and
Mark 2:14 by, He saw Levi the son of **A**
Mark 3:18 Thomas, James the son of **A**
Luke 6:15 James the son of **A**, and Simon
Acts 1:13 James the son of **A** and Simon

ALREADY (*see* PREFACE)

ALSO (*see* PREFACE)

ALTAR (*see* ALTARS)
Gen 8:20 Noah built an **a** to the LORD
Gen 8:20 burnt offerings on the **a**
Gen 12: 7 he built an **a** to the LORD
Gen 12: 8 he built an **a** to the LORD
Gen 13: 4 to the place of the **a** which
Gen 13:18 built an **a** there to the LORD
Gen 22: 9 And Abraham built an **a** there
Gen 22: 9 his son and laid him on the **a**
Gen 26:25 So he built an **a** there and
Gen 33:20 Then he erected an **a** there
Gen 35: 1 make an **a** there to God, who
Gen 35: 3 I will make an **a** there to God
Gen 35: 7 And he built an **a** there and
Ex 17:15 And Moses built an **a** and called
Ex 20:24 An **a** of earth you shall make
Ex 20:25 if you make Me an **a** of stone
Ex 20:26 you go up by steps to My **a**
Ex 21:14 you shall take him from My **a**
Ex 24: 4 built an **a** at the foot of the
Ex 24: 6 blood he sprinkled on the **a**
Ex 27: 1 make an **a** of acacia wood,
Ex 27: 1 the **a** shall be square
Ex 27: 5 the rim of the **a** beneath,
Ex 27: 5 may be midway up the **a**
Ex 27: 6 shall make poles for the **a**
Ex 27: 7 two sides of the **a** to bear it
Ex 28:43 the **a** to minister in the holy
Ex 29:12 of the **a** with your finger
Ex 29:12 beside the base of the **a**
Ex 29:13 them, and burn them on the **a**
Ex 29:16 it all around on the **a**
Ex 29:18 burn the whole ram on the **a**
Ex 29:20 the blood all around on the **a**
Ex 29:21 of the blood that is on the **a**
Ex 29:25 burn them on the **a** as a burnt
Ex 29:36 You shall cleanse the **a** when
Ex 29:37 make atonement for the **a** and
Ex 29:37 And the **a** shall be most holy
Ex 29:37 touches the **a** must be holy
Ex 29:38 what you shall offer on the **a**
Ex 29:44 of meeting and the **a**
Ex 30: 1 You shall make an **a** to burn
Ex 30:18 of meeting and the **a**
Ex 30:20 come near the **a** to minister
Ex 30:27 utensils, and the **a** of incense
Ex 30:28 the **a** of burnt offering with
Ex 31: 8 utensils, the **a** of incense,
Ex 31: 9 the **a** of burnt offering with
Ex 32: 5 it, he built an **a** before it
Ex 35:15 the incense **a**, its poles,
Ex 35:16 the **a** of burnt offering with
Ex 37:25 the incense **a** of acacia wood
Ex 38: 1 He made the **a** of burnt
Ex 38: 3 all the utensils for the **a**
Ex 38: 4 of bronze network for the **a**
Ex 38: 7 rings on the sides of the **a**
Ex 38: 7 He made the **a** hollow with
Ex 38:30 of meeting, the bronze **a**, the
Ex 38:30 and all the utensils for the **a**
Ex 39:38 the gold **a**, the anointing oil
Ex 39:39 the bronze **a**, its grate of
Ex 40: 5 You shall also set the **a** of
Ex 40: 6 the **a** of the burnt offering
Ex 40: 7 of meeting and the **a**, and put
Ex 40:10 You shall anoint the **a** of the
Ex 40:10 utensils, and sanctify the **a**
Ex 40:10 The **a** shall be most holy
Ex 40:26 He put the gold **a** in the
Ex 40:29 And he put the **a** of burnt
Ex 40:30 of meeting and the **a**, and put
Ex 40:32 and when they came near the **a**
Ex 40:33 the tabernacle and the **a**, and
Lev 1: 5 **a** that is by the door of the
Lev 1: 7 shall put fire on the **a**, and
Lev 1: 8 is on the fire upon the **a**
Lev 1: 9 on the **a** as a burnt sacrifice
Lev 1:11 side of the **a** before the LORD
Lev 1:11 its blood all around on the **a**
Lev 1:12 is on the fire upon the **a**
Lev 1:13 it all and burn it on the **a**
Lev 1:15 shall bring it to the **a**,
Lev 1:15 its head, and burn it on the **a**
Lev 1:15 out at the side of the **a**
Lev 1:16 beside the **a** on the east side
Lev 1:17 priest shall burn it on the **a**
Lev 2: 2 it as a memorial on the **a**
Lev 2: 8 he shall bring it to the **a**
Lev 2: 9 portion, and burn it on the **a**
Lev 2:12 on the **a** for a sweet aroma
Lev 3: 2 the blood all around on the **a**
Lev 3: 5 **a** upon the burnt sacrifice
Lev 3: 8 its blood all around on the **a**
Lev 3:11 burn them on the **a** as food
Lev 3:13 its blood all around on the **a**
Lev 3:16 burn them on the **a** as food
Lev 4: 7 blood on the horns of the **a**
Lev 4: 7 the **a** of the burnt offering
Lev 4:10 the **a** of the burnt offering
Lev 4:18 **a** which is before the LORD
Lev 4:18 of the **a** of burnt offering
Lev 4:19 from it and burn it on the **a**
Lev 4:25 of the **a** of burnt offering
Lev 4:25 of the **a** of burnt offering
Lev 4:26 burn all its fat on the **a**
Lev 4:30 of the **a** of burnt offering
Lev 4:30 blood at the base of the **a**
Lev 4:31 **a** for a sweet aroma to the
Lev 4:34 of the **a** of burnt offering
Lev 4:34 blood at the base of the **a**
Lev 4:35 priest shall burn it on the **a**
Lev 5: 9 offering on the side of the **a**
Lev 5: 9 out at the base of the **a**
Lev 5:12 burn it on the **a** according to
Lev 6: 9 the **a** all night until morning
Lev 6: 9 the fire of the **a** shall be
Lev 6:10 fire has consumed on the **a**
Lev 6:10 shall put them beside the **a**
Lev 6:12 the fire on the **a** shall be
Lev 6:13 fire shall burn on the **a**
Lev 6:14 it on the **a** before the LORD
Lev 6:15 it on the **a** for a sweet aroma
Lev 7: 2 sprinkle all around on the **a**
Lev 7: 5 shall burn them on the **a** as
Lev 7:31 shall burn the fat on the **a**
Lev 8:11 of it on the **a** seven times
Lev 8:11 seven times, anointed the **a**
Lev 8:15 some on the horns of the **a**
Lev 8:15 his finger, and purified the **a**
Lev 8:15 blood at the base of the **a**
Lev 8:16 and Moses burned them on the **a**
Lev 8:19 the blood all around on the **a**
Lev 8:21 burned the whole ram on the **a**
Lev 8:24 the blood all around on the **a**
Lev 8:28 hands and burned them on the **a**
Lev 8:30 the blood which was on the **a**
Lev 9: 7 Go to the **a**, offer your sin
Lev 9: 8 Aaron therefore went to the **a**
Lev 9: 9 put it on the horns of the **a**
Lev 9: 9 blood at the base of the **a**
Lev 9:10 offering he burned on the **a**
Lev 9:12 sprinkled all around on the **a**
Lev 9:13 and he burned them on the **a**
Lev 9:14 the burnt offering on the **a**
Lev 9:17 of it, and burned it on the **a**
Lev 9:18 sprinkled all around on the **a**
Lev 9:20 he burned the fat on the **a**
Lev 9:24 offering and the fat on the **a**
Lev 10:12 without leaven beside the **a**
Lev 14:20 the grain offering on the **a**
Lev 16:12 from the **a** before the LORD
Lev 16:18 he shall go out to the **a** that
Lev 16:18 the horns of the **a** all around
Lev 16:20 of meeting, and the **a**, he
Lev 16:25 he shall burn on the **a**
Lev 16:33 of meeting and for the **a**, and
Lev 17: 6 sprinkle the blood on the **a**
Lev 17:11 given it to you upon the **a** to
Lev 21:23 the veil or approach the **a**
Lev 22:22 of them on the **a** to the LORD
Num 3:26 the tabernacle and the **a**, and
Num 4:11 Over the golden **a** they shall
Num 4:13 away the ashes from the **a**
Num 4:14 and all the utensils of the **a**
Num 4:26 around the tabernacle and **a**
Num 5:25 LORD, and bring it to the **a**
Num 5:26 portion, burn it on the **a**
Num 7: 1 all its furnishings, and the **a**
Num 7:10 the **a** when it was anointed
Num 7:10 their offering before the **a**
Num 7:11 for the dedication of the **a**
Num 7:84 **a** from the leaders of Israel
Num 7:88 the **a** after it was anointed
Num 16:38 as a covering for the **a**
Num 16:39 out as a covering on the **a**
Num 16:46 and put fire in it from the **a**
Num 18: 3 of the sanctuary and the **a**
Num 18: 5 and the duties of the **a**, that
Num 18: 7 for everything at the **a** and
Num 18:17 sprinkle their blood on the **a**
Num 23: 2 a bull and a ram on each **a**
Num 23: 4 have offered on each **a** a bull
Num 23:14 a bull and a ram on each **a**
Num 23:30 a bull and a ram on every **a**
Deut 12:27 on the **a** of the LORD your God
Deut 12:27 on the **a** of the LORD your God
Deut 16:21 near the **a** which you build
Deut 26: 4 the **a** of the LORD your God
Deut 27: 5 an **a** to the LORD your God
Deut 27: 5 LORD your God, an **a** of stones
Deut 27: 6 the **a** of the LORD your God
Deut 33:10 burnt sacrifice on Your **a**
Josh 8:30 Now Joshua built an **a** to the
Josh 8:31 an **a** of whole stones over
Josh 9:27 for the **a** of the LORD, in the
Josh 22:10 an **a** there by the Jordan
Josh 22:10 a great, impressive **a**
Josh 22:11 of Manasseh have built an **a**
Josh 22:16 built for yourselves an **a**
Josh 22:19 an **a** besides the **a** of the
Josh 22:19 the **a** of the LORD our God
Josh 22:23 **a** to turn from following the
Josh 22:26 to build ourselves an **a**, not
Josh 22:28 the **a** of the LORD which our
Josh 22:29 day, to build an **a** for burnt
Josh 22:29 besides the **a** of the LORD our
Josh 22:34 children of Gad called the **a**
Judg 6:24 built an **a** there to the LORD
Judg 6:25 tear down the **a** of Baal that
Judg 6:26 build an **a** to the LORD your
Judg 6:28 there was the **a** of Baal,
Judg 6:28 on the **a** which had been built
Judg 6:30 has torn down the **a** of Baal
Judg 6:31 because his **a** has been torn
Judg 6:32 he has torn down his **a**
Judg 13:20 up toward heaven from the **a**
Judg 13:20 in the flame of the **a**
Judg 21: 4 early and built an **a** there
1Sa 2:28 My priest, to offer upon My **a**
1Sa 2:33 My **a** shall consume your eyes
1Sa 7:17 he built an **a** to the LORD
1Sa 14:35 Saul built an **a** to the LORD
1Sa 14:35 This was the first **a** that he
2Sa 24:18 erect an **a** to the LORD on the
2Sa 24:21 to build an **a** to the LORD
2Sa 24:25 built there an **a** to the LORD
1Ki 1:50 hold of the horns of the **a**
1Ki 1:51 hold of the horns of the **a**
1Ki 1:53 to bring him down from the **a**
1Ki 2:28 hold of the horns of the **a**
1Ki 2:29 there he is, by the **a**
1Ki 3: 4 burnt offerings on that **a**
1Ki 6:20 and overlaid the **a** of cedar
1Ki 6:22 with gold the entire **a** that
1Ki 7:48 the **a** of gold, and the table
1Ki 8:22 Solomon stood before the **a** of
1Ki 8:31 before Your **a** in this temple
1Ki 8:54 from before the **a** of the LORD
1Ki 8:64 because the bronze **a** that was
1Ki 9:25 and peace offerings on the **a**
1Ki 9:25 **a** that was before the LORD
1Ki 12:32 offered sacrifices on the **a**
1Ki 12:33 **a** which he had made at Bethel
1Ki 12:33 offered sacrifices on the **a**
1Ki 13: 1 by the **a** to burn incense
1Ki 13: 2 the **a** by the word of the LORD
1Ki 13: 2 O **a**, **a**
1Ki 13: 3 Surely the **a** shall split
1Ki 13: 4 out against the **a** in Bethel
1Ki 13: 4 out his hand from the **a**,
1Ki 13: 5 The **a** also was split apart,
1Ki 13: 5 ashes poured out from the **a**
1Ki 13:32 LORD against the **a** in Bethel
1Ki 16:32 Then he set up an **a** for Baal
1Ki 18:26 the **a** which they had made

1Ki 18:30 he repaired the a of the LORD
1Ki 18:32 an a in the name of the LORD
1Ki 18:32 a large enough to hold two
1Ki 18:35 water ran all around the a
2Ki 11:11 side of the temple, by the a
2Ki 12: 9 lid, and set it beside the a
2Ki 16:10 saw an a that was at Damascus
2Ki 16:10 priest the design of the a
2Ki 16:11 a according to all that King
2Ki 16:12 Damascus, the king saw the a
2Ki 16:12 and the king approached the a
2Ki 16:13 his peace offerings on the a
2Ki 16:14 a which was before the LORD
2Ki 16:14 from between the new a and the
2Ki 16:14 the north side of the new a
2Ki 16:15 On the great new a burn the
2Ki 16:15 the bronze a shall be for me
2Ki 18:22 before this a in Jerusalem'
2Ki 23: 9 did not come up to the a of
2Ki 23:15 Moreover the a that was at
2Ki 23:15 sin, had made, both that a
2Ki 23:16 tombs and burned them on the a
2Ki 23:17 done against the a of Bethel
1Ch 6:49 on the a of burnt offering
1Ch 6:49 on the a of incense, for all
1Ch 16:40 to the LORD on the a of burnt
1Ch 21:18 erect an a to the LORD on the
1Ch 21:22 build an a on it to the LORD
1Ch 21:26 built there an a to the LORD
1Ch 21:26 on the a of burnt offering
1Ch 21:29 the a of the burnt offering,
1Ch 22: 1 and this is the a of burnt
1Ch 28:18 weight for the a of incense
2Ch 1: 5 Now the bronze a that
2Ch 1: 6 the bronze a before the LORD
2Ch 4: 1 Moreover he made a bronze a
2Ch 4:19 the a of gold and the tables
2Ch 5:12 at the east end of the a,
2Ch 6:12 Solomon stood before the a of
2Ch 6:22 before Your a in this temple
2Ch 7: 7 because the bronze a which
2Ch 7: 9 of the a seven days, and the
2Ch 8:12 to the LORD on the a of the
2Ch 15: 8 he restored the a of the LORD
2Ch 23:10 of the temple, along by the a
2Ch 26:16 incense on the a of incense
2Ch 26:19 LORD, beside the incense a
2Ch 29:18 the a of burnt offerings with
2Ch 29:19 are, before the a of the LORD
2Ch 29:21 them on the a of the LORD
2Ch 29:22 and sprinkled it on the a
2Ch 29:22 sprinkled the blood on the a
2Ch 29:22 sprinkled the blood on the a
2Ch 29:24 their blood on the a as a sin
2Ch 29:27 the burnt offering on the a
2Ch 32:12 shall worship before one a
2Ch 33:16 repaired the a of the LORD
2Ch 35:16 on the a of the LORD,
Ezra 3: 2 built the a of the God of
Ezra 3: 3 they set the a on its bases
Ezra 7:17 offer them on the a of the
Neh 10:34 to burn on the a of the LORD
Ps 26: 6 So I will go about Your a
Ps 43: 4 I will go to the a of God
Ps 51:19 shall offer bulls on Your a
Ps 118:27 cords to the horns of the a
Is 6: 6 with the tongs from the a
Is 19:19 that day there will be an a
Is 27: 9 a like chalkstones that are
Is 36: 7 shall worship before this a'
Is 56: 7 will be accepted on My a
Is 60: 7 with acceptance on My a, and I
Lam 2: 7 The Lord has spurned His a
Ezek 8: 5 and there, north of the a gate
Ezek 8:16 between the porch and the a
Ezek 9: 2 and stood beside the bronze a
Ezek 40:46 who have charge of the a
Ezek 40:47 The a was in front of the
Ezek 41:22 The a was of wood, three
Ezek 43:13 a in cubits (the cubit is one
Ezek 43:13 This is the height of the a
Ezek 43:15 The a hearth is four cubits
Ezek 43:16 The a hearth is twelve cubits
Ezek 43:18 a on the day when it is made
Ezek 43:20 it on the four horns of the a
Ezek 43:22 and they shall cleanse the a
Ezek 43:26 make atonement for the a and
Ezek 43:27 your peace offerings on the a
Ezek 45:19 corners of the ledge of the a
Ezek 47: 1 of the temple, south of the a
Joel 1:13 you who minister before the a
Joel 2:17 between the porch and the a
Amos 2: 8 They lie down by every a on
Amos 3:14 of the a shall be cut off
Amos 9: 1 the Lord standing by the a
Zech 9:15 like the corners of the a
Zech 14:20 like the bowls before the a
Mal 1: 7 offer defiled food on My a
Mal 1:10 kindle fire on My a in vain
Mal 2:13 you cover the a of the LORD
Matt 5:23 you bring your gift to the a
Matt 5:24 your gift there before the a
Matt 23:18 And, 'Whoever swears by the a
Matt 23:19 the gift or the a that
Matt 23:20 he who swears by the a,
Matt 23:35 between the temple and the a
Luke 1:11 side of the a of incense
Luke 11:51 who perished between the a
Acts 17:23 I even found an a with this
1Co 9:13 and those who serve at the a
1Co 9:13 of the offerings of the a
1Co 10:18 sacrifices partakers of the a
Heb 7:13 man has officiated at the a
Heb 9: 4 had the golden a of incense
Heb 13:10 We have an a from which those
Jas 2:21 Isaac his son on the a
Rev 6: 9 I saw under the a the souls
Rev 8: 3 came and stood at the a
Rev 8: 3 the saints upon the golden a
Rev 8: 5 it with fire from the a, and
Rev 9:13 golden a which is before God
Rev 11: 1 the temple of God, the a, and
Rev 14:18 angel came out from the a
Rev 16: 7 another from the a saying

ALTARS (*see* ALTAR)
Ex 34:13 But you shall destroy their a
Lev 26:30 cut down your incense a, and
Num 3:31 table, the lampstand, the a
Num 23: 1 Build seven a for me here
Num 23: 4 I have prepared the seven a
Num 23:14 of Pisgah, and built seven a
Num 23:29 Build for me here seven a
Deut 7: 5 you shall destroy their a
Deut 12: 3 And you shall destroy their a
Judg 2: 2 you shall tear down their a
1Ki 19:10 covenant, torn down Your a
1Ki 19:14 covenant, torn down Your a
2Ki 11:18 broke in pieces its a and
2Ki 11:18 priest of Baal before the a
2Ki 18:22 whose a Hezekiah has taken
2Ki 21: 3 he raised up a for Baal, and
2Ki 21: 4 He also built a in the house
2Ki 21: 5 he built a for all the host
2Ki 23:12 The a that were on the roof,
2Ki 23:12 the a which Manasseh had made
2Ki 23:20 who were there on the a, and
2Ch 14: 3 for he removed the a of the
2Ch 14: 5 the incense a from all the
2Ch 23:17 They broke in pieces its a
2Ch 23:17 priest of Baal before the a
2Ch 28:24 made for himself a in every
2Ch 30:14 took away the a that were in
2Ch 30:14 took away all the incense a
2Ch 31: 1 down the high places and the a
2Ch 32:12 away His high places and His a
2Ch 33: 3 he raised up a for the Baals,
2Ch 33: 4 He also built a in the house
2Ch 33: 5 he built a for all the host
2Ch 33:15 all the a that he had built
2Ch 34: 4 the a of the Baals in his
2Ch 34: 4 and the incense a which were
2Ch 34: 5 of the priests on their a
2Ch 34: 7 When he had broken down the a
2Ch 34: 7 cut down all the incense a
Ps 84: 3 Even Your a, O LORD of hosts,
Is 17: 8 He will not look to the a
Is 17: 8 images nor the incense a
Is 27: 9 incense a do not stand up
Is 36: 7 whose a Hezekiah has taken
Is 65: 3 and burn incense on a of brick
Jer 11:13 up a to that shameful thing
Jer 11:13 a to burn incense to Baal
Jer 17: 1 and on the horns of your a
Jer 17: 2 children remember their a
Ezek 6: 4 Then your a shall be desolate
Ezek 6: 4 your incense a shall be
Ezek 6: 5 your bones all around your a
Ezek 6: 6 so that your a may be laid
Ezek 6: 6 your incense a may be cut
Ezek 6:13 idols all around their a, on
Hos 8:11 has made many a for sin, they
Hos 8:11 become for him a for sinning
Hos 10: 1 fruit he has increased the a
Hos 10: 2 He will break down their a
Hos 10: 8 thistle shall grow on their a
Hos 12:11 indeed their a shall be heaps
Amos 3:14 on the a of Bethel
Rom 11: 3 prophets and torn down Your a

ALTER (*see* ALTERED, ALTERS)
Ezra 6:12 who put their hand to a it
Ps 89:34 Nor a the word that has gone
Dan 6: 8 and Persians, which does not a
Dan 6:12 and Persians, which does not a

ALTERED (*see* ALTER)
Esth 1:19 so that it will not be a
Luke 9:29 appearance of His face was a

ALTERNATING
Neh 12:24 group a with group, according

ALTERS (*see* ALTER)
Ezra 6:11 that whoever a this edict

ALTHOUGH (*see* PREFACE)

ALTOGETHER (*see* PREFACE)

ALUSH
Num 33:13 from Dophkah and camped at A
Num 33:14 They moved from A and camped

ALVAH (*see* ALIAH)
Gen 36:40 Chief Timnah, Chief A, Chief

ALVAN (*see* ALIAH, ALIAN)
Gen 36:23 A, Manahath, Ebal, Shepho,

ALWAYS
Ex 25:30 on the table before Me a
Ex 28:38 it shall a be on his forehead
Num 9:16 So it was a
Deut 5:29 a keep all My commandments,
Deut 6:24 LORD our God, for our good a
Deut 11: 1 and His commandments a
Deut 11:12 the LORD your God are a on it
Deut 14:23 to fear the LORD your God a
Deut 19: 9 to walk a in His ways, then
1Sa 7:17 But he a returned to Ramah,
2Sa 9:10 shall eat bread at my table a
1Ki 5: 1 for Hiram had a loved David
1Ki 11:36 a have a lamp before Me in
1Ch 16:15 Remember His covenant a, the
2Ch 18: 7 concerning me, but a evil
Job 27:10 Will he a call on God
Job 32: 9 Great men are not a wise, nor
Job 32: 9 nor do the aged a understand
Ps 9:18 shall not a be forgotten
Ps 10: 5 His ways are a prospering
Ps 16: 8 have set the LORD a before me
Ps 73:12 ungodly, Who are a at ease
Ps 103: 9 He will not a strive with us,
Prov 5:19 a be enraptured with her love
Prov 8:30 rejoicing a before Him,
Prov 28:14 is the man who is a reverent
Eccl 9: 8 Let your garments a be white
Is 57:16 nor will I a be angry
Jer 20:17 her womb a enlarged with me
Matt 18:10 a see the face of My Father
Matt 26:11 you have the poor with you a
Matt 26:11 but Me you do not have a
Matt 28:20 and lo, I am with you a, even
Mark 5: 5 And a, night and day, he was in
Mark 14: 7 you have the poor with you a
Mark 14: 7 but Me you do not have a
Mark 15: 8 as he had a done for them
Luke 15:31 him, 'Son, you are a with me
Luke 18: 1 that men a ought to pray and
Luke 21:36 and pray a that you may be
John 6:34 Lord, give us this bread a
John 7: 6 but your time is a ready
John 8:29 for I a do those things that
John 11:42 And I know that You a hear Me
John 12: 8 the poor you have with you a
John 12: 8 but Me you do not have a
John 18:20 I a taught in synagogues and
John 18:20 temple, where the Jews a meet
Acts 2:25 the LORD a before my face
Acts 7:51 You a resist the Holy Spirit
Acts 10: 2 people, and prayed to God a
Acts 20:18 manner I a lived among you
Acts 24: 3 we accept it a and in all
Acts 24:16 I myself a strive to have a
Rom 1: 9 of you a in my prayers,

Rom 11:10 see, and bow down their back **a**
1Co 1: 4 I thank my God **a** concerning
1Co 15:58 **a** abounding in the work of
2Co 2:14 who **a** leads us in triumph in
2Co 4:10 **a** carrying about in the body
2Co 4:11 For we who live are **a**
2Co 5: 6 Therefore we are **a** confident
2Co 6:10 as sorrowful, yet **a** rejoicing
2Co 9: 8 **a** having all sufficiency in
Gal 4:18 be zealous in a good thing **a**
Eph 5:20 giving thanks **a** for all
Eph 6:18 praying **a** with all prayer and
Phil 1: 4 **a** in every prayer of mine
Phil 1:20 that with all boldness, as **a**
Phil 2:12 beloved, as you have **a** obeyed
Phil 4: 4 Rejoice in the Lord **a**
Col 1: 3 Christ, praying **a** for you
Col 4: 6 your speech **a** be with grace
Col 4:12 **a** laboring fervently for you
1Th 1: 2 thanks to God **a** for you all
1Th 2:16 saved, so as **a** to fill up the
1Th 3: 6 love, and that you **a** have good
1Th 4:17 thus we shall **a** be with the
1Th 5:15 but **a** pursue what is good
1Th 5:16 Rejoice **a**,
2Th 1: 3 bound to thank God **a** for you
2Th 1:11 Therefore we also pray **a** for
2Th 2:13 give thanks to God **a** for you
2Th 3:16 give you peace **a** in every way
2Ti 3: 7 **a** learning and never able to
Tit 1:12 Cretans are **a** liars, evil
Phm 4 of you **a** in my prayers,
Heb 3:10 They **a** go astray in their
Heb 9: 6 the priests **a** went into the
1Pe 3:15 **a** be ready to give a defense
2Pe 1:12 remind you **a** of these things
2Pe 1:15 **a** have a reminder of these

AM

Gen 4: 9 **A** I my brother's keeper
Gen 6: 7 for I **a** sorry that I have
Gen 6:17 I Myself **a** bringing the flood
Gen 15: 1 I **a** your shield, your
Gen 15: 7 I **a** the LORD, who brought you
Gen 16: 8 I **a** fleeing from the presence
Gen 17: 1 to him, "I **a** Almighty God
Gen 18:13 bear a child, since I **a** old
Gen 18:17 from Abraham what I **a** doing
Gen 18:27 I who **a** but dust and ashes
Gen 22: 1 And he said, "Here I **a**."
Gen 22: 7 Here I **a**, my son
Gen 22:11 And he said, "Here I **a**."
Gen 23: 4 I **a** a foreigner and a
Gen 24:24 I **a** the daughter of Bethuel,
Gen 24:34 said, "I **a** Abraham's servant
Gen 25:22 all is well, why **a** I this way
Gen 25:30 same red stew, for I **a** weary
Gen 25:32 Look, I **a** about to die
Gen 26:24 I **a** the God of your father
Gen 26:24 do not fear, for I **a** with you
Gen 27: 1 answered him, "Here I **a**."
Gen 27: 2 said, "Behold now, I **a** old
Gen 27:11 and I **a** a smooth-skinned man
Gen 27:18 and he said, "Here I **a**. Who
Gen 27:19 I **a** Esau your firstborn
Gen 27:24 And he said, "I **a**."
Gen 27:32 I **a** your son, your firstborn,
Gen 27:46 I **a** weary of my life because
Gen 28:13 I **a** the LORD God of Abraham
Gen 28:15 I **a** with you and will keep you
Gen 28:20 me in this way that I **a** going
Gen 29:33 has heard that I **a** unloved
Gen 30: 2 **A** I in the place of God, who
Gen 30:13 I **a** happy, for the daughters
Gen 31:11 And I said, "Here I **a**
Gen 31:13 I **a** the God of Bethel, where
Gen 32:10 I **a** not worthy of the least
Gen 34:30 since I **a** few in number, they
Gen 35:11 I **a** God Almighty
Gen 37:13 he said to him, "Here I **a**."
Gen 37:16 I **a** seeking my brothers
Gen 38:25 these belong, I **a** with child
Gen 41:44 I **a** Pharaoh, and without your
Gen 43:14 I **a** bereaved, I **a** bereaved
Gen 45: 3 to his brothers, "I **a** Joseph
Gen 45: 4 I **a** Joseph your brother, whom
Gen 46: 2 And he said, "Here I **a**."
Gen 46: 3 I **a** God, the God of your
Gen 48:21 I **a** dying, but God will be
Gen 49:29 I **a** to be gathered to my
Gen 50: 5 saying, "Behold, I **a** dying
Gen 50:19 for **a** I in the place of God
Gen 50:24 to his brethren, "I **a** dying
Ex 3: 4 And he said, "Here I **a**."
Ex 3: 6 I **a** the God of your father
Ex 3:11 Who **a** I that I should go to
Ex 3:14 said to Moses, "I **A** WHO I **A**
Ex 3:14 I **A** has sent me to you
Ex 3:19 But I **a** sure that the king of
Ex 4:10 I **a** not eloquent, neither
Ex 4:10 but I **a** slow of speech and
Ex 6: 2 I **a** the LORD
Ex 6: 6 I **a** the LORD
Ex 6: 7 I **a** the LORD your God who
Ex 6: 8 I **a** the LORD
Ex 6:12 for I **a** of uncircumcised lips
Ex 6:29 Moses, saying, "I **a** the LORD
Ex 6:30 I **a** of uncircumcised lips, and
Ex 7: 5 shall know that I **a** the LORD
Ex 7:17 shall know that I **a** the LORD
Ex 8:22 I **a** the LORD in the midst of
Ex 8:29 Indeed I **a** going out from you
Ex 10: 2 may know that I **a** the LORD
Ex 12:12 I **a** the LORD
Ex 14: 4 may know that I **a** the LORD
Ex 14:18 shall know that I **a** the LORD
Ex 15:26 For I **a** the LORD who heals
Ex 16:12 that I **a** the LORD your God
Ex 18: 6 **a** coming to you with your
Ex 20: 2 I **a** the LORD your God, who
Ex 20: 5 **a** a jealous God, visiting the
Ex 22:27 I will hear, for I **a** gracious
Ex 29:46 that I **a** the LORD their God
Ex 29:46 I **a** the LORD their God
Ex 31:13 that you may know that I **a**
Ex 34:11 I **a** driving out from before
Lev 11:44 For I **a** the LORD your God
Lev 11:44 for I **a** holy
Lev 11:45 For I **a** the LORD who brings
Lev 11:45 be holy, for I **a** holy
Lev 18: 2 I **a** the LORD your God
Lev 18: 3 where I **a** bringing you, you
Lev 18: 4 I **a** the LORD your God
Lev 18: 5 I **a** the LORD
Lev 18: 6 I **a** the LORD
Lev 18:21 I **a** the LORD
Lev 18:24 which I **a** casting out before
Lev 18:30 I **a** the LORD your God
Lev 19: 2 I the LORD your God **a** holy
Lev 19: 3 I **a** the LORD your God
Lev 19: 4 I **a** the LORD your God
Lev 19:10 I **a** the LORD your God
Lev 19:12 I **a** the LORD
Lev 19:14 I **a** the LORD
Lev 19:16 I **a** the LORD
Lev 19:18 I **a** the LORD
Lev 19:25 I **a** the LORD your God
Lev 19:28 I **a** the LORD
Lev 19:30 I **a** the LORD
Lev 19:31 I **a** the LORD your God
Lev 19:32 I **a** the LORD
Lev 19:34 I **a** the LORD your God
Lev 19:36 I **a** the LORD your God, who
Lev 19:37 I **a** the LORD
Lev 20: 7 for I **a** the LORD your God
Lev 20: 8 I **a** the LORD who sanctifies
Lev 20:22 them, that the land where I **a**
Lev 20:23 of the nation which I **a**
Lev 20:24 I **a** the LORD your God, who
Lev 20:26 to Me, for I the LORD **a** holy
Lev 21: 8 who sanctify you, **a** holy
Lev 21:12 I **a** the LORD
Lev 22: 2 I **a** the LORD
Lev 22: 3 I **a** the LORD
Lev 22: 8 I **a** the LORD
Lev 22:30 I **a** the LORD
Lev 22:31 I **a** the LORD
Lev 22:32 I **a** the LORD who sanctifies
Lev 22:33 I **a** the LORD
Lev 23:22 I **a** the LORD your God
Lev 23:43 I **a** the LORD your God
Lev 24:22 for I **a** the LORD your God
Lev 25:17 for I **a** the LORD your God
Lev 25:38 I **a** the LORD your God, who
Lev 25:55 I **a** the LORD your God
Lev 26: 1 for I **a** the LORD your God
Lev 26: 2 I **a** the LORD
Lev 26:13 I **a** the LORD your God, who
Lev 26:44 for I **a** the LORD their God
Lev 26:45 I **a** the LORD
Num 3:13 I **a** the LORD
Num 3:41 I **a** the LORD
Num 3:45 I **a** the LORD
Num 10:10 I **a** the LORD your God
Num 11:13 Where **a** I to get meat to give
Num 11:14 I **a** not able to bear all
Num 11:21 The people whom I **a** among are
Num 13: 2 which I **a** giving to the
Num 15: 2 which I **a** giving to you,
Num 15:41 I **a** the LORD your God, who
Num 15:41 I **a** the LORD your God
Num 18:20 I **a** your portion and your
Num 22:30 **A** I not your donkey on which
Num 22:37 **A** I not able to honor you
Num 24:14 I **a** going to my people
Deut 1: 9 I alone **a** not able to bear
Deut 1:36 his children I **a** giving the
Deut 1:42 fight, for I **a** not among you
Deut 5: 6 I **a** the LORD your God who
Deut 5: 9 **a** a jealous God, visiting the
Deut 5:31 I **a** giving them to possess
Deut 29: 6 that I **a** the LORD your God
Deut 31: 2 I **a** one hundred and twenty
Deut 31:27 while I **a** yet alive with you,
Deut 32:39 I, **a** He, and there is no God
Deut 32:52 into the land which I **a**
Josh 1: 2 land which I **a** giving to them
Josh 14:10 and now, here I **a** this day,
Josh 14:11 As yet I **a** as strong this day
Josh 23: 2 I **a** old, advanced in age
Josh 23:14 this day I **a** going the way of
Judg 4:19 to drink, for I **a** thirsty
Judg 6:10 you, "I **a** the LORD your God
Judg 6:15 I **a** the least in my father's
Judg 8: 5 and I **a** pursuing Zebah and
Judg 9: 2 that I **a** your own flesh and
Judg 13:11 And He said, "I **a**."
Judg 16:17 If I **a** shaven, then my
Judg 17: 9 I **a** a Levite from Bethlehem
Judg 17: 9 I **a** on my way to find a place
Judg 19:18 I **a** from there
Judg 19:18 now I **a** going to the house of
Ruth 1:12 for I **a** too old to have a
Ruth 2:10 of me, since I **a** a foreigner
Ruth 2:13 though I **a** not like one of
Ruth 3: 9 I **a** Ruth, your maidservant
Ruth 3:12 that I **a** your near kinsman
Ruth 4: 4 it, and I **a** next after you
1Sa 1: 8 **A** I not better to you than
1Sa 1:15 I **a** a woman of sorrowful
1Sa 1:26 I **a** the woman who stood by
1Sa 3: 4 And he answered, "Here I **a**!"
1Sa 3: 5 Here I **a**, for you called me
1Sa 3: 6 Here I **a**, for you called me
1Sa 3: 8 Here I **a**, for you did call me
1Sa 3:16 And he answered, "Here I **a**."
1Sa 4:16 I **a** he who came from the
1Sa 9:19 Saul and said, "I **a** the seer
1Sa 9:21 **A** I not a Benjamite, of the
1Sa 12: 2 I **a** old and grayheaded, and
1Sa 12: 3 Here I **a**
1Sa 14: 7 here I **a** with you, according
1Sa 16: 1 I **a** sending you to Jesse the
1Sa 17: 8 **A** I not a Philistine, and you
1Sa 17:43 **A** I a dog, that you come to
1Sa 17:58 I **a** the son of your servant
1Sa 18:18 Who **a** I, and what is my life
1Sa 18:23 son-in-law, seeing I **a** a poor
1Sa 22:12 Here I **a**, my lord
1Sa 23:22 For I **a** told that he is very
1Sa 25:19 see, I **a** coming after you
1Sa 28:15 I **a** deeply distressed
1Sa 30:13 I **a** a young man from Egypt,
2Sa 1: 7 And I answered, 'Here I **a**
2Sa 1: 8 him, "I **a** an Amalekite
2Sa 1:13 I **a** the son of an alien, an
2Sa 1:26 I **a** distressed for you, my
2Sa 2:20 And he answered, "I **a**."
2Sa 3: 8 **A** I a dog's head that belongs
2Sa 3:39 And I **a** weak today, though
2Sa 7:18 Who **a** I, O Lord GOD
2Sa 11: 5 and said, "I **a** with child
2Sa 14: 5 Indeed I **a** a widow, my
2Sa 15:26 no delight in you,' here I **a**
2Sa 19:20 Therefore here I **a**, the first
2Sa 19:22 today I **a** king over Israel
2Sa 19:35 I **a** today eighty years old
2Sa 20:17 He answered, "I **a**."
2Sa 20:17 he answered, "I **a** listening
2Sa 20:19 I **a** among the peaceable and
2Sa 24:14 Gad, "I **a** in great distress

1Ki 3: 7 David, but I **a** a little child
1Ki 13:14 And he said, "I **a**."
1Ki 13:18 I too **a** a prophet as you are,
1Ki 13:31 When I **a** dead, then bury me
1Ki 17:12 I **a** gathering a couple of
1Ki 18:12 as soon as I **a** gone from you,
1Ki 18:22 I alone **a** left a prophet of
1Ki 18:36 that I **a** Your servant, and
1Ki 19: 4 for I **a** no better than my
1Ki 19:10 I alone **a** left
1Ki 19:14 I alone **a** left
1Ki 20:13 shall know that I **a** the LORD
1Ki 20:28 shall know that I **a** the LORD
1Ki 22: 4 I **a** as you are, my people as
1Ki 22:34 the battle, for I **a** wounded
2Ki 1:10 If I **a** a man of God, then let
2Ki 1:12 If I **a** a man of God, let fire
2Ki 2: 9 before I **a** taken away from
2Ki 2:10 me when I **a** taken from you
2Ki 3: 7 I **a** as you are, my people as
2Ki 5: 7 **A** I God, to kill and make
2Ki 16: 7 I **a** your servant and your son
2Ki 21:12 I **a** bringing such calamity
1Ch 17:16 Who **a** I, O LORD God
1Ch 21:13 Gad, "I **a** in great distress
1Ch 21:17 I **a** the one who has sinned and
1Ch 29:14 But who **a** I, and who are my
2Ch 2: 4 I **a** building a temple for the
2Ch 2: 6 Who **a** I then, that I should
2Ch 2: 9 for the temple which I **a**
2Ch 18: 3 I **a** as you are, and my people
2Ch 18:33 the battle, for I **a** wounded
2Ch 35:23 for I **a** severely wounded
Ezra 9: 6 I **a** too ashamed and humiliated
Neh 5:10 **a** lending them money and grain
Neh 6: 3 I **a** doing a great work, so
Esth 5:12 tomorrow I **a** again invited by
Esth 7: 8 queen while I **a** in the house
Esth 8: 5 I **a** pleasing in his eyes, let
Job 3:26 I **a** not at ease, nor **a** I
Job 3:26 **a** not at ease, nor **a** I quiet
Job 7:12 **A** I a sea, or a sea serpent,
Job 7:20 so that I **a** a burden to
Job 9:21 I **a** blameless, yet I do not
Job 9:28 I **a** afraid of all my
Job 9:29 If I **a** condemned, why then do
Job 9:32 For He is not a man, as I **a**
Job 10: 7 You know that I **a** not wicked
Job 10:15 If I **a** wicked, woe to me
Job 10:15 even if I **a** righteous, I
Job 10:15 I **a** full of disgrace
Job 11: 4 And I **a** clean in your eyes
Job 12: 3 I **a** not inferior to you
Job 12: 4 I **a** one mocked by his friends
Job 13: 2 I **a** not inferior to you
Job 16: 6 remain silent, how **a** I eased
Job 19: 7 wrong, I **a** not heard
Job 19:10 on every side, and I **a** gone
Job 19:15 I **a** an alien in their sight
Job 19:17 I **a** repulsive to the children
Job 21: 6 when I remember I **a** terrified
Job 23:15 Therefore I **a** terrified at
Job 23:15 this, I **a** afraid of Him
Job 30: 9 And now I **a** their taunt-song
Job 30: 9 yes, I **a** their byword
Job 30:29 I **a** a brother of jackals, and
Job 32: 6 I **a** young in years, and you
Job 32:18 For I **a** full of words
Job 33: 6 Truly I **a** as your spokesman
Job 33: 9 I **a** pure, without
Job 33: 9 I **a** innocent, and there is no
Job 34: 5 I **a** righteous, but God has
Job 34: 6 incurable, though I **a** without
Job 40: 4 Behold, I **a** vile
Ps 6: 2 on me, O LORD, for I **a** weak
Ps 6: 6 I **a** weary with my groaning
Ps 13: 4 me rejoice when I **a** moved
Ps 22: 2 night season, and **a** not silent
Ps 22: 6 But I **a** a worm, and no man
Ps 22:14 I **a** poured out like water, And
Ps 25:16 For I **a** desolate and afflicted
Ps 28: 7 trusted in Him, and I **a** helped
Ps 31: 9 O LORD, for I **a** in trouble
Ps 31:11 I **a** a reproach among all my
Ps 31:11 And **a** repulsive to my
Ps 31:12 I **a** forgotten like a dead man
Ps 31:12 I **a** like a broken vessel
Ps 31:22 I **a** cut off from before Your
Ps 35: 3 my soul, "I **a** your salvation
Ps 37:25 have been young, and now **a** old

Ps 38: 6 I **a** troubled, I **a** bowed down
Ps 38: 8 I **a** feeble and severely broken
Ps 38:13 I **a** like a mute who does not
Ps 38:14 Thus I **a** like a man who does
Ps 38:17 For I **a** ready to fall, And my
Ps 39: 4 That I may know how frail I **a**
Ps 39:10 I **a** consumed by the blow of
Ps 39:12 For I **a** a stranger with You,
Ps 39:13 Before I go away and **a** no more
Ps 40:12 so that I **a** not able to look
Ps 40:17 But I **a** poor and needy
Ps 46:10 still, and know that I **a** God
Ps 50: 7 I **a** God, your God
Ps 52: 8 But I **a** like a green olive
Ps 55: 2 I **a** restless in my complaint,
Ps 56: 3 Whenever I **a** afraid, I will
Ps 69: 3 I **a** weary with my crying
Ps 69:12 I **a** the song of the drunkards
Ps 69:17 servant, For I **a** in trouble
Ps 69:20 And I **a** full of heaviness
Ps 69:29 But I **a** poor and sorrowful
Ps 70: 5 But I **a** poor and needy
Ps 71:18 Now also when I **a** old and
Ps 73:23 Nevertheless I **a** continually
Ps 77: 4 I **a** so troubled that I cannot
Ps 81:10 I **a** the LORD your God, Who
Ps 86: 1 For I **a** poor and needy
Ps 86: 2 my life, for I **a** holy
Ps 88: 4 I **a** counted with those who go
Ps 88: 4 I **a** like a man who has no
Ps 88: 8 I **a** shut up, and I cannot get
Ps 88:15 I **a** distraught
Ps 102: 6 I **a** like a pelican of the
Ps 102: 6 I **a** like an owl of the desert
Ps 102: 7 **a** like a sparrow alone on the
Ps 109:22 For I **a** poor and needy, And my
Ps 109:23 I **a** gone like a shadow when
Ps 109:23 I **a** shaken off like a locust
Ps 116:10 I **a** greatly afflicted
Ps 116:16 LORD, truly I **a** Your servant
Ps 116:16 I **a** Your servant, the son of
Ps 119:19 I **a** a stranger in the earth
Ps 119:63 I **a** a companion of all those
Ps 119:94 I **a** Yours, save me
Ps 119:107 I **a** afflicted very much
Ps 119:120 I **a** afraid of Your judgments
Ps 119:125 I **a** Your servant
Ps 119:141 I **a** small and despised, Yet I
Ps 119:158 **a** disgusted, Because they do
Ps 120: 7 I **a** for peace
Ps 139:14 You, for I **a** fearfully and
Ps 139:18 I awake, I **a** still with You
Ps 142: 6 cry, For I **a** brought very low
Ps 143:12 For I **a** Your servant
Prov 8:14 I **a** understanding, I have
Prov 20: 9 clean, I **a** pure from my sin"
Prov 30: 2 Surely I **a** more stupid than
Song 1: 5 I **a** dark, but lovely, O
Song 1: 6 upon me, because I **a** dark
Song 2: 1 I **a** the rose of Sharon, and
Song 2: 5 with apples, for I **a** lovesick
Song 2:16 beloved is mine, and I **a** his
Song 5: 8 you tell him I **a** lovesick
Song 6: 3 I **a** my beloved's, and my
Song 7:10 I **a** my beloved's, and his
Song 8:10 I **a** a wall, and my breasts
Is 1:14 I **a** weary of bearing them
Is 6: 5 Woe is me, for I **a** undone
Is 6: 5 Because I **a** a man of unclean
Is 6: 8 Here **a** I
Is 8:18 Here **a** I and the children whom
Is 10:13 by my wisdom, for I **a** prudent
Is 19:11 I **a** the son of the wise, the
Is 24:16 I said, "I **a** ruined, ruined
Is 29:12 he says, "I **a** not literate
Is 33:24 will not say, "I **a** sick"
Is 38:10 I **a** deprived of the remainder
Is 38:14 O LORD, I **a** oppressed
Is 41: 4 I, the LORD, **a** the first
Is 41: 4 and with the last I **a** He
Is 41:10 Fear not, for I **a** with you
Is 41:10 dismayed, for I **a** your God
Is 42: 8 I **a** the LORD, that is My name
Is 43: 3 For I **a** the LORD your God,
Is 43: 5 Fear not, for I **a** with you
Is 43:10 Me, and understand that I **a** He
Is 43:11 **a** the LORD, and besides Me
Is 43:12 that I **a** God
Is 43:13 before the day was, I **a** He
Is 43:15 I **a** the LORD, your Holy One,

Is 43:25 I, **a** He who blots out your
Is 44: 5 will say, 'I **a** the LORD's'
Is 44: 6 **a** the First and I **a** the Last
Is 44:16 I **a** warm, I have seen the
Is 44:24 I **a** the LORD, who makes all
Is 45: 3 name, **a** the God of Israel
Is 45: 5 I **a** the LORD, and there is no
Is 45: 6 I **a** the LORD, and there is no
Is 45:18 I **a** the LORD, and there is no
Is 45:22 For I **a** God, and there is no
Is 46: 4 I **a** He, and even to gray hairs
Is 46: 9 things of old, for I **a** God
Is 46: 9 I **a** God, and there is none
Is 47: 8 who say in your heart, 'I **a**
Is 47:10 have said in your heart, 'I **a**
Is 48:12 I **a** He, I **a** the First, I **a**
Is 48:17 I **a** the LORD your God, Who
Is 49:21 **a** desolate, a captive, and
Is 49:23 will know that I **a** the LORD
Is 49:26 LORD, **a** your Savior, and your
Is 51:12 even I, **a** He who comforts you
Is 51:15 But I **a** the LORD your God,
Is 52: 6 day that I **a** He who speaks
Is 56: 3 Here I **a**, a dry tree
Is 58: 9 and He will say, 'Here I **a**
Is 60:16 LORD, **a** your Savior and your
Is 65: 1 I said, 'Here I **a**, here I **a**,
Is 65: 1 I said, 'Here I **a**, here I **a**
Is 65: 5 me, for I **a** holier than you
Jer 1: 6 cannot speak, for I **a** a youth
Jer 1: 7 I **a** a youth,' for you shall
Jer 1: 8 for I **a** with you to deliver
Jer 1:12 for I **a** ready to perform My
Jer 1:15 I **a** calling all the families
Jer 1:19 For I **a** with you," says the
Jer 2:23 I **a** not polluted, I have not
Jer 2:35 say, 'Because I **a** innocent
Jer 3:12 For I **a** merciful,' says the
Jer 3:14 for I **a** married to you
Jer 4:19 I **a** pained in my very heart
Jer 6:11 Therefore I **a** full of the
Jer 6:11 I **a** weary of holding it in
Jer 8:21 of my people I **a** hurt
Jer 8:21 I **a** mourning
Jer 9:24 that I **a** the LORD, exercising
Jer 15: 6 I **a** weary of relenting
Jer 15:16 for I **a** called by Your name,
Jer 15:20 for I **a** with you to save you
Jer 18:11 I **a** fashioning a disaster and
Jer 20: 7 I **a** in derision daily
Jer 21:13 I **a** against you, O inhabitant
Jer 23: 9 I **a** like a drunken man, and
Jer 23:23 **A** I a God near at hand,"
Jer 23:30 I **a** against the prophets,"
Jer 23:31 I **a** against the prophets,"
Jer 23:32 Behold, I **a** against those who
Jer 24: 7 to know Me, that I **a** the LORD
Jer 26:14 As for me, here I **a**, in your
Jer 29:23 **a** a witness, says the LORD
Jer 30:11 For I **a** with you,' says the
Jer 31: 9 for I **a** a Father to Israel,
Jer 32:27 I **a** the LORD, the God of all
Jer 36: 5 I **a** confined, I cannot go
Jer 37:14 I **a** not defecting to the
Jer 38:19 I **a** afraid of the Jews who
Jer 42:11 for I **a** with you, to save
Jer 46:28 the LORD, "For I **a** with you
Jer 50:31 I **a** against you, O you most
Jer 51:25 I **a** against you, O destroying
Lam 1:11 and consider, for I **a** scorned
Lam 1:14 I **a** not able to withstand
Lam 1:20 O LORD, that I **a** in distress
Lam 3: 1 I **a** the man who has seen
Lam 3:54 I said, "I **a** cut off
Lam 3:59 You have seen how I **a** wronged
Lam 3:63 I **a** their taunting song
Ezek 2: 3 man, I **a** sending you to the
Ezek 2: 4 I **a** sending you to them, and
Ezek 4:15 See, I **a** giving you cow dung
Ezek 5: 8 **a** against you and will execute
Ezek 6: 7 shall know that I **a** the LORD
Ezek 6:10 shall know that I **a** the LORD
Ezek 6:13 shall know that I **a** the LORD
Ezek 6:14 shall know that I **a** the LORD
Ezek 7: 4 shall know that I **a** the LORD
Ezek 7: 9 that I **a** the LORD who strikes
Ezek 7:27 shall know that I **a** the LORD
Ezek 11:10 shall know that I **a** the LORD
Ezek 11:12 shall know that I **a** the LORD
Ezek 12:11 Say, 'I **a** a sign to you

Ezek 12:15 shall know that I a the LORD
Ezek 12:16 shall know that I a the LORD
Ezek 12:20 shall know that I a the LORD
Ezek 12:25 For I a the LORD
Ezek 13: 8 therefore I a indeed against
Ezek 13: 9 know that I a the Lord GOD
Ezek 13:14 shall know that I a the LORD
Ezek 13:20 I a against your magic charms
Ezek 13:21 shall know that I a the LORD
Ezek 13:23 shall know that I a the LORD
Ezek 14: 8 shall know that I a the LORD
Ezek 15: 7 shall know that I a the LORD
Ezek 16:62 shall know that I a the LORD
Ezek 20: 5 I a the LORD your God
Ezek 20: 7 I a the LORD your God
Ezek 20:12 I a the LORD who sanctifies
Ezek 20:19 I a the LORD your God
Ezek 20:20 that I a the LORD your God
Ezek 20:26 might know that I a the LORD
Ezek 20:38 will know that I a the LORD
Ezek 20:42 shall know that I a the LORD
Ezek 20:44 shall know that I a the LORD
Ezek 21: 3 I a against you, and I will
Ezek 22:16 shall know that I a the LORD
Ezek 22:26 so that I a profaned among
Ezek 23:49 know that I a the Lord GOD
Ezek 24:24 know that I a the Lord GOD
Ezek 24:27 will know that I a the LORD
Ezek 25: 5 shall know that I a the LORD
Ezek 25: 7 shall know that I a the LORD
Ezek 25:11 shall know that I a the LORD
Ezek 25:17 shall know that I a the LORD
Ezek 26: 3 I a against you, O Tyre, and
Ezek 26: 6 shall know that I a the LORD
Ezek 27: 3 said, 'I a perfect in beauty
Ezek 28: 2 I a a god, I sit in the seat
Ezek 28: 9 who slays you, 'I a a god'
Ezek 28:22 I a against you, O Sidon
Ezek 28:22 shall know that I a the LORD
Ezek 28:22 in her and a hallowed in her
Ezek 28:23 shall know that I a the LORD
Ezek 28:24 know that I a the Lord GOD
Ezek 28:25 a hallowed in them in the
Ezek 28:26 that I a the LORD their God
Ezek 29: 3 I a against you, O Pharaoh
Ezek 29: 6 shall know that I a the LORD
Ezek 29: 9 will know that I a the LORD
Ezek 29:10 I a against you and against
Ezek 29:16 know that I a the Lord GOD
Ezek 29:21 shall know that I a the LORD
Ezek 30: 8 will know that I a the LORD
Ezek 30:19 shall know that I a the LORD
Ezek 30:22 Surely I a against Pharaoh
Ezek 30:25 shall know that I a the LORD
Ezek 30:26 shall know that I a the LORD
Ezek 32:15 shall know that I a the LORD
Ezek 33:29 shall know that I a the LORD
Ezek 34:10 I a against the shepherds, and
Ezek 34:27 shall know that I a the LORD
Ezek 34:30 a with them, and that they,
Ezek 34:31 I a your God," says the Lord
Ezek 35: 3 O Mount Seir, I a against you
Ezek 35: 4 shall know that I a the LORD
Ezek 35: 9 shall know that I a the LORD
Ezek 35:12 shall know that I a the LORD
Ezek 35:15 shall know that I a the LORD
Ezek 36: 9 For indeed I a for you, and I
Ezek 36:11 shall know that I a the LORD
Ezek 36:23 shall know that I a the LORD
Ezek 36:23 when I a hallowed in you
Ezek 36:38 shall know that I a the LORD
Ezek 37: 6 shall know that I a the LORD
Ezek 37:13 shall know that I a the LORD
Ezek 38: 3 I a against you, O Gog, the
Ezek 38:16 when I a hallowed in you, O
Ezek 38:23 shall know that I a the LORD
Ezek 39: 1 I a against you, O Gog,
Ezek 39: 6 shall know that I a the LORD
Ezek 39: 7 shall know that I a the LORD
Ezek 39:13 on the day that I a glorified
Ezek 39:17 which I a sacrificing for you
Ezek 39:19 which I a sacrificing for you
Ezek 39:22 I a the LORD their God from
Ezek 39:27 I a hallowed in them in the
Ezek 39:28 that I a the LORD their God
Ezek 44:28 that I a their inheritance
Ezek 44:28 for I a their possession
Dan 8:19 I a making known to you what
Hos 2: 2 My wife, nor a I her Husband
Hos 11: 9 For I a God, and not man, the
Hos 12: 9 But I a the LORD your God,
Hos 13: 4 Yet I a the LORD your God
Hos 14: 8 I a like a green cypress tree
Joel 2:27 I a in the midst of Israel
Joel 2:27 that I a the LORD your God and
Joel 3:10 let the weak say, 'I a strong
Joel 3:17 that I a the LORD your God
Amos 2:13 I a weighed down by you, as a
Amos 7: 8 I a setting a plumb line in
Jon 1: 9 said to them, "I a a Hebrew
Mic 2: 3 family I a devising disaster
Mic 3: 8 But truly I a full of power
Mic 7: 1 For I a like those who gather
Nah 2:13 I a against you," says the
Nah 3: 5 I a against you," says the
Hab 1: 6 For indeed I a raising up the
Hab 2: 1 will answer when I a reproved
Zeph 2:15 I a it, and there is none
Hag 1:13 I a with you, says the LORD
Hag 2: 4 for I a with you,' says the
Zech 1:14 I a zealous for Jerusalem and
Zech 1:15 I a exceedingly angry with
Zech 1:16 I a returning to Jerusalem
Zech 2:10 I a coming and I will dwell in
Zech 3: 8 I a bringing forth My Servant
Zech 4: 2 I a looking, and there is a
Zech 8: 2 I a zealous for Zion with
Zech 8: 2 fervor I a zealous for her
Zech 8:15 I a determined to do good to
Zech 10: 6 for I a the LORD their God,
Zech 11: 5 be the LORD, for I a rich'
Zech 13: 5 I a no prophet, I a a farmer
Mal 1: 6 If then I a the Father, where
Mal 1: 6 if I a a Master, where is My
Mal 1:14 for I a a great King," says
Mal 3: 6 For I a the LORD, I do not
Matt 3:11 whose sandals I a not worthy
Matt 3:17 Son, in whom I a well pleased
Matt 8: 3 him, saying, "I a willing
Matt 8: 8 Lord, I a not worthy that You
Matt 8: 9 For I also a a man under
Matt 9:28 that I a able to do this
Matt 11:29 for I a gentle and lowly in
Matt 16:13 say that I, the Son of Man, a
Matt 16:15 But who do you say that I a
Matt 17: 5 Son, in whom I a well pleased
Matt 18:20 I a there in the midst of
Matt 20:13 I a doing you no wrong
Matt 20:15 eye evil because I a good
Matt 20:22 cup that I a about to drink
Matt 20:22 that I a baptized with
Matt 20:23 that I a baptized with
Matt 22:32 I a the God of Abraham, the
Matt 24: 5 I a the Christ,' and will
Matt 26:61 I a able to destroy the
Matt 27:24 I a innocent of the blood of
Matt 27:43 He said, "I a the Son of God
Matt 28:20 I a with you always, even to
Mark 1: 7 whose sandal strap I a not
Mark 1:11 Son, in whom I a well pleased
Mark 1:41 and said to him, "I a willing
Mark 8:27 Who do men say that I a
Mark 8:29 But who do you say that I a
Mark 10:38 that I a baptized with
Mark 10:39 with the baptism I a baptized
Mark 12:26 I a the God of Abraham, the
Mark 13: 6 in My name, saying, 'I a He
Mark 14:62 And Jesus said, "I a.
Luke 1:18 For I a an old man, and my
Luke 1:19 I a Gabriel, who stands in
Luke 3:16 strap I a not worthy to loose
Luke 3:22 in You I a well pleased
Luke 5: 8 for I a a sinful man, O Lord
Luke 5:13 him, saying, "I a willing
Luke 7: 6 for I a not worthy that You
Luke 7: 8 For I also a a man placed
Luke 9:18 do the crowds say that I a
Luke 9:20 But who do you say that I a
Luke 12:50 how distressed I a till it is
Luke 14:19 and I a going to test them
Luke 15:19 I a no longer worthy to be
Luke 15:21 and a no longer worthy to be
Luke 16: 3 I a ashamed to beg
Luke 16: 4 that when I a put out of the
Luke 16:24 for I a tormented in this
Luke 18:11 that I a not like other men
Luke 21: 8 in My name, saying, 'I a He
Luke 22:27 Yet I a among you as the One
Luke 22:33 I a ready to go with You,
Luke 22:58 Peter said, "Man, I a not
Luke 22:70 You rightly say that I a
John 1:20 I a not the Christ
John 1:21 He said, "I a not
John 1:23 I a 'The voice of one crying
John 1:27 strap I a not worthy to loose
John 3:28 I a not the Christ,' but, 'I
John 4:26 I who speak to you a He
John 5: 7 but while I a coming, another
John 6:35 them, "I a the bread of life
John 6:41 I a the bread which came down
John 6:48 I a the bread of life
John 6:51 I a the living bread which
John 7: 8 I a not yet going up to this
John 7:28 and you know where I a from
John 7:29 for I a from Him, and He sent
John 7:34 where I a you cannot come
John 7:36 where I a you cannot come'
John 8:12 I a the light of the world
John 8:14 came from and where I a going
John 8:14 come from and where I a going
John 8:16 for I a not alone, but I a
John 8:16 but I a with the Father who
John 8:18 I a One who bears witness of
John 8:21 I a going away, and you will
John 8:23 I a from above
John 8:23 I a not of this world
John 8:24 do not believe that I a He
John 8:28 you will know that I a He
John 8:58 you, before Abraham was, I A
John 9: 5 As long as I a in the world
John 9: 5 I a the light of the world
John 9: 9 He said, "I a he
John 10: 7 I a the door of the sheep
John 10: 9 I a the door
John 10:11 I a the good shepherd
John 10:14 I a the good shepherd
John 10:14 sheep, and a known by My own
John 10:36 I said, 'I a the Son of God'
John 11:15 I a glad for your sakes that
John 11:25 I a the resurrection and the
John 12:26 and where I a, there My
John 12:32 if I a lifted up from the
John 13: 7 What I a doing you do not
John 13:13 and you say well, for so I a
John 13:19 you may believe that I a He
John 13:33 to the Jews, 'Where I a going
John 13:36 Where I a going you cannot
John 14: 3 that where I a, there you may
John 14: 6 I a the way, the truth, and
John 14:10 that I a in the Father, and
John 14:11 Me that I a in the Father
John 14:20 know that I a in My Father
John 14:28 I a going away and coming
John 14:28 I a going to the Father,'
John 15: 1 I a the true vine, and My
John 15: 5 I a the vine, you are the
John 16:32 yet I a not alone, because
John 17:10 and I a glorified in them
John 17:11 Now I a no longer in the
John 17:14 just as I a not of the world
John 17:16 just as I a not of the world
John 17:24 Me may be with Me where I a
John 18: 5 Jesus said to them, "I a He
John 18: 6 He said to them, "I a He,"
John 18: 8 I have told you that I a He
John 18:17 He said, "I a not
John 18:25 denied it and said, "I a not
John 18:35 Pilate answered, "A I a Jew
John 18:37 say rightly that I a a king
John 19: 4 I a bringing Him out to you,
John 19:21 I a the King of the Jews
John 20:17 I a ascending to My Father
John 21: 3 to them, "I a going fishing
Acts 7:32 I a the God of your fathers
Acts 9: 5 I a Jesus, whom you are
Acts 9:10 Here I a, Lord
Acts 10:21 Yes, I a he whom you seek
Acts 10:26 I myself a also a man
Acts 13:25 said, "Who do you think I a
Acts 13:25 I a not He
Acts 13:25 feet I a not worthy to loose
Acts 18: 6 I a clean
Acts 18:10 for I a with you, and no one
Acts 20:26 to you this day that I a
Acts 21:13 For I a ready not only to be
Acts 21:39 I a a Jew from Tarsus, in
Acts 22: 3 I a indeed a Jew, born in
Acts 22: 8 I a Jesus of Nazareth, whom
Acts 23: 6 I a a Pharisee, the son of a
Acts 23: 6 of the dead I a being judged

Acts 24:21 **I a** being judged by you this
Acts 25:11 For if **I a** an offender, or
Acts 26: 2 which **I a** accused by the Jews
Acts 26: 6 **a** judged for the hope of the
Acts 26: 7 **I a** accused by the Jews
Acts 26:15 **I a** Jesus, whom you are
Acts 26:25 **I a** not mad, most noble
Acts 26:26 for **I a** convinced that none
Acts 26:29 and altogether such as **I a**
Acts 28:20 **I a** bound with this chain
Rom 1:14 **I a** a debtor both to Greeks
Rom 1:15 me, **I a** ready to preach the
Rom 1:16 For **I a** not ashamed of the
Rom 3: 7 why **a** I also still judged as
Rom 7:14 but **I a** carnal, sold under
Rom 7:15 For what **I a** doing, I do not
Rom 7:24 O wretched man that **I a**
Rom 8:38 For **I a** persuaded that
Rom 9: 1 **I a** not lying, my conscience
Rom 11: 1 For I also **a** an Israelite, of
Rom 11: 3 altars, and I alone **a** left
Rom 11:13 inasmuch as **I a** an apostle to
Rom 14:14 **a** convinced by the Lord Jesus
Rom 15:14 Now I myself **a** confident
Rom 15:25 But now **I a** going to
Rom 16:19 Therefore **I a** glad on your
1Co 1:12 you says, "**I a** of Paul," or
1Co 1:12 or "**I a** of Apollos," or
1Co 1:12 or "**I a** of Cephas," or
1Co 1:12 Cephas," or "**I a** of Christ
1Co 3: 4 **I a** of Paul," and another,
1Co 3: 4 **I a** of Apollos," are you not
1Co 4: 4 yet **I a** not justified by this
1Co 7: 8 if they remain even as **I a**
1Co 9: 1 **A** I not an apostle
1Co 9: 1 **A** I not free
1Co 9: 2 If **I a** not an apostle to
1Co 9: 2 yet doubtless **I a** to you
1Co 9:19 For though **I a** free from all
1Co 10:19 What **a** I saying then
1Co 10:30 why **a** I evil spoken of for
1Co 12:15 Because **I a** not a hand
1Co 12:15 **I a** not of the body," is it
1Co 12:16 Because **I a** not an eye, **I a**
1Co 12:16 **I a** not of the body," is it
1Co 13: 2 have not love, **I a** nothing
1Co 13:12 know just as I also **a** known
1Co 15: 9 For **I a** the least of the
1Co 15: 9 who **a** not worthy to be called
1Co 15:10 grace of God **I a** what **I a**
1Co 16: 5 through Macedonia (for **I a**
1Co 16:11 for **I a** waiting for him with
1Co 16:17 **I a** glad about the coming of
2Co 7: 4 **I a** filled with comfort
2Co 7: 4 **I a** exceedingly joyful in all
2Co 7:14 about you, **I a** not ashamed
2Co 8: 8 but **I a** testing the sincerity
2Co 10: 1 myself **a** pleading with you by
2Co 10: 1 in presence **a** lowly among you
2Co 10: 1 absent **a** bold toward you
2Co 10: 2 **I a** present I may not be bold
2Co 11: 2 For **I a** jealous for you with
2Co 11: 5 For I consider that **I a** not
2Co 11: 6 Even though **I a** untrained in
2Co 11: 6 yet **I a** not in knowledge
2Co 11:21 **I a** bold also
2Co 11:22 Hebrews? So **a** I.
2Co 11:22 Israelites? So **a** I.
2Co 11:22 seed of Abraham? So **a** I.
2Co 11:23 I speak as a fool—**I a** more:
2Co 11:29 Who is weak, and **I a** not weak
2Co 11:31 knows that **I a** not lying
2Co 12:10 **I a** weak, then **I a** strong
2Co 12:11 apostles, though **I a** nothing
2Co 12:14 time **I a** ready to come to you
2Co 12:15 love you, the less **I a** loved
2Co 13: 1 third time **I a** coming to you
Gal 4:11 **I a** afraid for you, lest I
Gal 4:12 I urge you to become as **I a**
Gal 4:12 for **I a** as you are
Gal 4:18 not only when **I a** present
Eph 3: 8 who **a** less than the least of
Eph 6:20 for which **I a** an ambassador
Eph 6:21 my affairs and how **I a** doing
Phil 1:17 knowing that **I a** appointed
Phil 1:23 For **I a** hard pressed between
Phil 1:27 I come and see you or **a** absent
Phil 2:17 if **I a** being poured out as a
Phil 2:17 **I a** glad and rejoice with you
Phil 3:12 or **a** already perfected
Phil 4:11 learned in whatever state **I a**
Phil 4:18 **I a** full, having received
Col 2: 5 For though **I a** absent in the
Col 2: 5 yet **I a** with you in spirit,
Col 4: 3 for which **I a** also in chains,
Col 4: 8 **I a** sending him to you for
1Ti 1:15 sinners, of whom **I a** chief
1Ti 2: 7 **I a** speaking the truth in
1Ti 3:15 but if **I a** delayed, I write
2Ti 1: 5 **I a** persuaded is in you also
2Ti 1:12 nevertheless **I a** not ashamed
2Ti 1:12 **a** persuaded that He is able
2Ti 4: 6 For **I a** already being poured
Phm 12 **I a** sending him back
Phm 19 **a** writing with my own hand
Heb 2:13 Here **a** I and the children whom
Heb 12:21 **I a** exceedingly afraid and
Jas 1:13 **I a** tempted by God"
1Pe 1:16 Be holy, for **I a** holy
1Pe 5: 1 I who **a** a fellow elder and a
2Pe 1:13 as long as **I a** in this tent
2Pe 1:17 Son, in whom **I a** well pleased
Rev 1: 8 **I a** the Alpha and the Omega,
Rev 1:11 **I a** the Alpha and the Omega,
Rev 1:17 **I a** the First and the Last
Rev 1:18 **I a** He who lives, and was dead
Rev 1:18 behold, **I a** alive forevermore
Rev 2:23 **I a** He who searches the minds
Rev 3:17 say, '**I a** rich, have become
Rev 16:15 Behold, **I a** coming as a thief
Rev 18: 7 **a** no widow, and will not see
Rev 19:10 **I a** your fellow servant, and
Rev 21: 6 **I a** the Alpha and the Omega,
Rev 22: 7 Behold, **I a** coming quickly
Rev 22: 9 For **I a** your fellow servant,
Rev 22:12 **I a** coming quickly, and My
Rev 22:13 **I a** the Alpha and the Omega,
Rev 22:16 **I a** the Root and the Offspring
Rev 22:20 Surely **I a** coming quickly

AMAD
Josh 19:26 Alammelech, **A**, and Mishal

AMAL
1Ch 7:35 Zophah, Imna, Shelesh, and **A**

AMALEK (*see* AMALEKITE)
Gen 36:12 son, and she bore **A** to Eliphaz
Gen 36:16 Chief Gatam, and Chief **A**
Ex 17: 8 Now **A** came and fought with
Ex 17: 9 men and go out, fight with **A**
Ex 17:10 said to him, and fought with **A**
Ex 17:11 down his hand, **A** prevailed
Ex 17:13 So Joshua defeated **A** and his
Ex 17:14 of **A** from under heaven
Ex 17:16 war with **A** from generation to
Num 24:20 Then he looked on **A**, and he
Num 24:20 **A** was first among the nations
Num 24:24 afflict Eber, and so shall **A**
Deut 25:17 Remember what **A** did to you on
Deut 25:19 of **A** from under heaven
Judg 3:13 the people of Ammon and **A**,
Judg 5:14 those whose roots were in **A**
1Sa 15: 2 punish what **A** did to Israel
1Sa 15: 3 Now go and attack **A**, and
1Sa 15: 5 And Saul came to a city of **A**
1Sa 15:20 brought back Agag king of **A**
1Sa 28:18 His fierce wrath upon **A**,
2Sa 8:12 from the Philistines, from **A**
1Ch 1:36 and by Timna, **A**
1Ch 18:11 the Philistines, and from **A**
Ps 83: 7 Gebal, Ammon, and **A**

AMALEKITE (*see* AMALEK, AMALEKITES)
1Sa 30:13 from Egypt, servant of an **A**
2Sa 1: 8 So I answered him, I am an **A**
2Sa 1:13 am the son of an alien, an **A**

AMALEKITES (*see* AMALEKITE)
Gen 14: 7 all the country of the **A**, and
Num 13:29 The **A** dwell in the land of
Num 14:25 Now the **A** and the Canaanites
Num 14:43 For the **A** and the Canaanites
Num 14:45 Then the **A** and the Canaanites
Judg 6: 3 also **A** and the people of the
Judg 6:33 Then all the Midianites and **A**
Judg 7:12 Now the Midianites and **A**, all
Judg 10:12 Also the Sidonians and **A** and
Judg 12:15 in the mountains of the **A**
1Sa 14:48 an army and attacked the **A**
1Sa 15: 6 get down from among the **A**
1Sa 15: 6 departed from among the **A**
1Sa 15: 7 And Saul attacked the **A**, from
1Sa 15: 8 took Agag king of the **A** alive
1Sa 15:15 have brought them from the **A**
1Sa 15:18 destroy the sinners, the **A**
1Sa 15:20 have utterly destroyed the **A**
1Sa 15:32 Agag king of the **A** here to me
1Sa 27: 8 the Girzites, and the **A**
1Sa 30: 1 that the **A** had invaded the
1Sa 30:18 that the **A** had carried away
2Sa 1: 1 from the slaughter of the **A**
1Ch 4:43 rest of the **A** who had escaped

AMAM
Josh 15:26 **A**, Shema, Moladah,

AMANA
Song 4: 8 Look from the top of **A**, from

AMARIAH
1Ch 6: 7 Meraioth begot **A**
1Ch 6: 7 and **A** begot Ahitub
1Ch 6:11 Azariah begot **A**
1Ch 6:11 and **A** begot Ahitub
1Ch 6:52 **A** his son, Ahitub his son,
1Ch 23:19 **A** the second, Jahaziel the
1Ch 24:23 **A** the second, Jahaziel the
2Ch 19:11 **A** the chief priest is over
2Ch 31:15 Miniamin, Jeshua, Shemaiah, **A**
Ezra 7: 3 the son of **A**, the son of
Ezra 10:42 Shallum, **A**, and Joseph
Neh 10: 3 Pashhur, **A**, Malchijah,
Neh 11: 4 of Zechariah, the son of **A**
Neh 12: 2 **A**, Malluch, Hattush,
Neh 12:13 of **A**, Jehohanan
Zeph 1: 1 son of Gedaliah, the son of **A**

AMASA
2Sa 17:25 Absalom made **A** captain of the
2Sa 17:25 This **A** was the son of a man
2Sa 19:13 And say to **A**, 'Are you not my
2Sa 20: 4 Then the king said to **A**
2Sa 20: 5 So **A** went to assemble the men
2Sa 20: 8 in Gibeon, **A** came before them
2Sa 20: 9 Then Joab said to **A**, "Are
2Sa 20: 9 Joab took **A** by the beard with
2Sa 20:10 But **A** did not notice the
2Sa 20:11 of Joab's men stood near **A**
2Sa 20:12 But **A** wallowed in his blood
2Sa 20:12 he moved **A** from the highway
1Ki 2: 5 **A** the son of Jether, whom he
1Ki 2:32 and **A** the son of Jether, the
1Ch 2:17 Abigail bore **A**
1Ch 2:17 the father of **A** was Jether
2Ch 28:12 **A** the son of Hadlai, stood up

AMASAI
1Ch 6:25 The sons of Elkanah were **A**
1Ch 6:35 son of Mahath, the son of **A**
1Ch 12:18 Then the Spirit came upon **A**
1Ch 15:24 Joshaphat, Nethaneel, **A**,
2Ch 29:12 Mahath the son of **A** and Joel

AMASHAI
Neh 11:13 **A** the son of Azareel, the son

AMASIAH
2Ch 17:16 next to him was **A** the son of

AMAZED (*see* AMAZEMENT)
Is 13: 8 they will be **a** at one another
Matt 12:23 And all the multitudes were **a**
Matt 19:25 it, they were exceedingly **a**
Mark 1:27 Then they were all **a**, so that
Mark 2:12 them all, so that all were **a**
Mark 6:51 And they were greatly **a** in
Mark 9:15 all the people were greatly **a**
Mark 10:32 and they were **a**
Mark 16: 8 for they trembled and were **a**
Luke 2:48 they saw Him, they were **a**
Luke 4:36 So they were all **a** and spoke
Luke 5:26 And they were all **a**, and they
Luke 9:43 And they were all **a** at the
Acts 2: 7 Then they were all **a** and
Acts 2:12 So they were all **a** and
Acts 3:11 called Solomon's, greatly **a**
Acts 8:13 with Philip, and was **a**, seeing
Acts 9:21 Then all who heard were **a**

AMAZEMENT (*see* AMAZED)
Mark 5:42 were overcome with great **a**
Acts 3:10 **a** at what had happened to him
Rev 17: 6 her, I marveled with great **a**

AMAZIAH
2Ki 12:21 Then **A** his son reigned in his
2Ki 13:12 against **A** king of Judah, are
2Ki 14: 1 **A** the son of Joash, king of
2Ki 14: 8 Then **A** sent messengers to
2Ki 14: 9 sent to **A** king of Judah,
2Ki 14:11 But **A** would not heed
2Ki 14:11 **A** king of Judah faced one
2Ki 14:13 captured **A** king of Judah, the
2Ki 14:15 fought with **A** king of Judah
2Ki 14:17 **A** the son of Joash, king of
2Ki 14:18 Now the rest of the acts of **A**
2Ki 14:21 king instead of his father **A**
2Ki 14:23 year of **A** the son of Joash
2Ki 15: 1 Israel, Azariah the son of **A**
2Ki 15: 3 that his father **A** had done
1Ch 3:12 **A** his son, Azariah his son,
1Ch 4:34 and Joshah the son of **A**
1Ch 6:45 of Hashabiah, the son of **A**
2Ch 24:27 Then **A** his son reigned in his
2Ch 25: 1 **A** was twenty-five years old
2Ch 25: 5 Moreover **A** gathered Judah
2Ch 25: 9 Then **A** said to the man of God
2Ch 25:10 So **A** discharged the troops
2Ch 25:11 Then **A** strengthened himself,
2Ch 25:13 army which **A** had discharged
2Ch 25:14 was so, after **A** came from the
2Ch 25:15 LORD was aroused against **A**
2Ch 25:17 Then **A** king of Judah took
2Ch 25:18 sent to **A** king of Judah,
2Ch 25:20 But **A** would not heed, for it
2Ch 25:21 **A** king of Judah faced one
2Ch 25:23 captured **A** king of Judah, the
2Ch 25:25 **A** the son of Joash, king of
2Ch 25:26 Now the rest of the acts of **A**
2Ch 25:27 After the time that **A** turned
2Ch 26: 1 king instead of his father **A**
2Ch 26: 4 that his father **A** had done
Amos 7:10 Then **A** the priest of Bethel
Amos 7:12 Then **A** said to Amos
Amos 7:14 Amos answered, and said to **A**

AMBASSADOR (*see* AMBASSADORS)
Prov 13:17 a faithful **a** brings health
Jer 49:14 an **a** has been sent to the
Eph 6:20 for which I am an **a** in chains

AMBASSADORS (*see* AMBASSADOR)
Josh 9: 4 and went and pretended to be **a**
2Ch 32:31 regarding the **a** of the
Is 18: 2 which sends **a** by sea, even in
Is 30: 4 Zoan, and his **a** came to Hanes
Is 33: 7 the **a** of peace shall weep
Ezek 17:15 him by sending his **a** to Egypt
2Co 5:20 Therefore we are **a** for Christ

AMBER
Ezek 1: 4 its midst like the color of **a**
Ezek 1:27 were, the color of **a** with the
Ezek 8: 2 like the color of **a**

AMBITION (*see* AMBITIONS)
Phil 1:16 preach Christ from selfish **a**
Phil 2: 3 through selfish **a** or conceit

AMBITIONS (*see* AMBITION)
2Co 12:20 outbursts of wrath, selfish **a**
Gal 5:20 outbursts of wrath, selfish **a**

AMBUSH (*see* AMBUSHES)
Josh 8: 2 Lay an **a** for the city behind
Josh 8: 4 lie in **a** against the city
Josh 8: 7 you shall rise from the **a**
Josh 8: 9 and they went to lie in **a**, and
Josh 8:12 set them in **a** between Bethel
Josh 8:14 not know that there was an **a**
Josh 8:19 So those in **a** arose quickly
Josh 8:21 that the **a** had taken the city
Judg 9:25 men of Shechem set men in **a**
Judg 20:29 men in **a** all around Gibeah
Judg 20:33 Then Israel's men in **a** burst
Judg 20:36 **a** whom they had set against
Judg 20:37 the men in **a** quickly rushed
Judg 20:37 the men in **a** spread out and
Judg 20:38 the men in **a** was that they
2Ch 13:13 But Jeroboam caused an **a** to
2Ch 13:13 and the **a** was behind them
Ezra 8:31 and from **a** along the road
Lam 3:10 in wait, like a lion in **a**
Acts 23:16 sister's son heard of their **a**
Acts 25: 3 while they lay in **a** along the

AMBUSHES (*see* AMBUSH)
2Ch 20:22 the LORD set **a** against the
Jer 51:12 the watchmen, prepare the **a**

AMEN
Num 5:22 **A**, so be it
Deut 27:15 shall answer and say, '**A**
Deut 27:16 all the people shall say, '**A**
Deut 27:17 all the people shall say, '**A**
Deut 27:18 all the people shall say, '**A**
Deut 27:19 all the people shall say, '**A**
Deut 27:20 all the people shall say, '**A**
Deut 27:21 all the people shall say, '**A**
Deut 27:22 all the people shall say, '**A**
Deut 27:23 all the people shall say, '**A**
Deut 27:24 all the people shall say, '**A**
Deut 27:25 all the people shall say, '**A**
Deut 27:26 all the people shall say, '**A**
1Ki 1:36 **A**! May the LORD God of my
1Ch 16:36 all the people said, "**A**!"
Neh 5:13 the congregation said, "**A**!"
Neh 8: 6 the people answered, "**A**, **A**!"
Ps 41:13 **A** and **A**
Ps 72:19 **A** and **A**
Ps 89:52 **A** and **A**
Ps 106:48 let all the people say, "**A**!"
Jer 28: 6 **A**! The LORD do so
Matt 6:13 and the glory forever. **A**.
Matt 28:20 to the end of the age." **A**.
Mark 16:20 the accompanying signs. **A**.
Luke 24:53 praising and blessing God. **A**.
John 21:25 that would be written. **A**.
Rom 1:25 who is blessed forever. **A**.
Rom 9: 5 the eternally blessed God. **A**.
Rom 11:36 to whom be glory forever. **A**.
Rom 15:33 peace be with you all. **A**.
Rom 16:20 Jesus Christ be with you. **A**.
Rom 16:24 Christ be with you all. **A**.
Rom 16:27 Jesus Christ forever. **A**.
1Co 14:16 **A**" at your giving of thanks,
1Co 16:24 you all in Christ Jesus. **A**.
2Co 1:20 in Him are Yes, and in Him **A**
2Co 13:14 Spirit be with you all. **A**.
Gal 1: 5 glory forever and ever. **A**.
Gal 6:18 Christ be with your spirit. **A**
Eph 3:21 world without end. **A**.
Eph 6:24 Jesus Christ in sincerity. **A**.
Phil 4:20 be glory forever and ever. **A**
Phil 4:23 Christ be with you all. **A**.
Col 4:18 Grace be with you. **A**.
1Th 5:28 Jesus Christ be with you. **A**
2Th 3:18 Christ be with you all. **A**
1Ti 1:17 glory forever and ever. **A**.
1Ti 6:16 and everlasting power. **A**.
1Ti 6:21 Grace be with you. **A**.
2Ti 4:18 glory forever and ever. **A**!
2Ti 4:22 Grace be with you. **A**.
Tit 3:15 Grace be with you all. **A**.
Phm 25 Christ be with your spirit. **A**
Heb 13:21 be glory forever and ever. **A**
Heb 13:25 Grace be with you all. **A**.
1Pe 4:11 dominion forever and ever. **A**
1Pe 5:11 dominion forever and ever. **A**.
1Pe 5:14 who are in Christ Jesus. **A**.
2Pe 3:18 both now and forever. **A**.
1Jn 5:21 keep yourselves from idols. **A**.
2Jn 13 elect sister greet you. **A**.
Jude 25 both now and forever. **A**.
Rev 1: 6 forever and ever. **A**.
Rev 1: 7 Even so, **A**.
Rev 1:18 I am alive forevermore. **A**.
Rev 3:14 These things says the **A**
Rev 5:14 living creatures said, "**A**!"
Rev 7:12 **A**! Blessing and glory
Rev 7:12 our God forever and ever. **A**."
Rev 19: 4 saying, "**A**! Alleluia!"
Rev 22:20 I am coming quickly." **A**.
Rev 22:21 Christ be with you all. **A**.

AMEND
Jer 7: 3 **A** your ways and your doings,
Jer 7: 5 if you thoroughly **a** your ways
Jer 26:13 **a** your ways and your doings,
Jer 35:15 **a** your doings, and do not go

AMETHYST
Ex 28:19 a jacinth, an agate, and an **a**
Ex 39:12 a jacinth, an agate, and an **a**
Rev 21:20 jacinth, and the twelfth **a**

AMI
Ezra 2:57 of Zebaim, and the sons of **A**

AMID
Ezek 19:11 height **a** the dense foliage
Amos 1:14 **a** shouting in the day of

AMISS
Job 5:24 habitation and find nothing **a**
Dan 3:29 which speaks anything **a**
Jas 4: 3 receive, because you ask **a**

AMITTAI
2Ki 14:25 servant Jonah the son of **A**
Jon 1: 1 came to Jonah the son of **A**

AMMAH
2Sa 2:24 they came to the hill of **A**

AMMIEL (*see* ELIAM)
Num 13:12 of Dan, **A** the son of Gemalli
2Sa 9: 4 house of Machir the son of **A**
2Sa 9: 5 house of Machir the son of **A**
2Sa 17:27 the son of **A** from Lo Debar
1Ch 3: 5 by Bathshua the daughter of **A**
1Ch 26: 5 **A** the sixth, Issachar the

AMMIHUD
Num 1:10 Elishama the son of **A**
Num 2:18 be Elishama the son of **A**
Num 7:48 day Elishama the son of **A**
Num 7:53 of Elishama the son of **A**
Num 10:22 was Elishama the son of **A**
Num 34:20 Simeon, Shemuel the son of **A**
Num 34:28 Pedahel the son of **A**
2Sa 13:37 went to Talmai the son of **A**
1Ch 7:26 **A** his son, Elishama his son,
1Ch 9: 4 Uthai the son of **A**, the son

AMMINADAB
Ex 6:23 Elisheba, daughter of **A**,
Num 1: 7 Judah, Nahshon the son of **A**
Num 2: 3 Nahshon the son of **A** shall be
Num 7:12 day was Nahshon the son of **A**
Num 7:17 of Nahshon the son of **A**
Num 10:14 army was Nahshon the son of **A**
Ruth 4:19 begot Ram, and Ram begot **A**
Ruth 4:20 **A** begot Nahshon, and Nahshon
1Ch 2:10 Ram begot **A**, and
1Ch 2:10 **A** begot Nahshon, leader of
1Ch 6:22 sons of Kohath were **A** his son
1Ch 15:10 **A** the chief, and one hundred
1Ch 15:11 Joel, Shemaiah, Eliel, and **A**
Matt 1: 4 Ram begot **A**, **A** begot Nahshon
Luke 3:33 the son of **A**, the son of Ram,

AMMISHADDAI
Num 1:12 Dan, Ahiezer the son of **A**
Num 2:25 shall be Ahiezer the son of **A**
Num 7:66 day Ahiezer the son of **A**,
Num 7:71 of Ahiezer the son of **A**
Num 10:25 army was Ahiezer the son of **A**

AMMIZABAD
1Ch 27: 6 in his division was **A** his son

AMMON (*see* AMMONITE, AMMONITESS)
Gen 19:38 the people of **A** to this day
Num 21:24 as far as the people of **A**
Num 21:24 the people of **A** was fortified
Deut 2:19 you come near the people of **A**
Deut 2:19 people of **A** as a possession
Deut 2:37 the land of the people of **A**
Deut 3:11 in Rabbah of the people of **A**
Deut 3:16 the border of the people of **A**
Josh 13:10 border of the children of **A**
Judg 3:13 to himself the people of **A**
Judg 10: 6 the gods of the people of **A**
Judg 10: 7 the hands of the people of **A**
Judg 10: 9 Moreover the people of **A**
Judg 10:11 and from the people of **A** and
Judg 10:17 people of **A** gathered together
Judg 10:18 fight against the people of **A**
Judg 11: 4 of **A** made war against Israel
Judg 11: 5 when the people of **A** made war
Judg 11: 6 fight against the people of **A**
Judg 11: 8 fight against the people of **A**
Judg 11: 9 fight against the people of **A**
Judg 11:12 the king of the people of **A**
Judg 11:13 the king of the people of **A**
Judg 11:14 the king of the people of **A**
Judg 11:15 the land of the people of **A**
Judg 11:27 of Israel and the people of **A**
Judg 11:28 of **A** did not heed the words
Judg 11:29 toward the people of **A**

Judg 11:30 the people of A into my hands
Judg 11:31 in peace from the people of A
Judg 11:32 toward the people of A to
Judg 11:33 Thus the people of A were
Judg 11:36 your enemies, the people of A
Judg 12: 1 fight against the people of A
Judg 12: 2 struggle with the people of A
Judg 12: 3 over against the people of A
1Sa 14:47 Moab, against the people of A
2Sa 8:12 Moab, from the people of A
2Sa 10: 1 king of the people of A died
2Sa 10: 2 the land of the people of A
2Sa 10: 3 of A said to Hanun their lord
2Sa 10: 6 So when the people of A saw
2Sa 10: 6 David, the people of A sent
2Sa 10: 8 Then the people of A came out
2Sa 10:10 array against the people of A
2Sa 10:11 But if the people of A are
2Sa 10:14 when the people of A saw that
2Sa 10:14 returned from the people of A
2Sa 10:19 help the people of A anymore
2Sa 11: 1 destroyed the people of A
2Sa 12: 9 the sword of the people of A
2Sa 12:26 Rabbah of the people of A
2Sa 12:31 the cities of the people of A
2Sa 17:27 Rabbah of the people of A
1Ki 11: 7 of the people of A
1Ki 11:33 the god of the people of A
2Ki 23:13 of the people of A
2Ki 24: 2 and bands of the people of A
1Ch 18:11 Moab, from the people of A
1Ch 19: 1 king of the people of A died
1Ch 19: 2 people of A to comfort him
1Ch 19: 3 the people of A said to Hanun
1Ch 19: 6 When the people of A saw that
1Ch 19: 6 and the people of A sent a
1Ch 19: 7 Also the people of A gathered
1Ch 19: 9 Then the people of A came out
1Ch 19:11 array against the people of A
1Ch 19:12 but if the people of A are
1Ch 19:15 When the people of A saw that
1Ch 19:19 help the people of A anymore
1Ch 20: 1 country of the people of A
1Ch 20: 3 the cities of the people of A
2Ch 20: 1 of Moab with the people of A
2Ch 20:10 now, here are the people of A
2Ch 20:22 against the people of A, Moab
2Ch 20:23 For the people of A and Moab
2Ch 27: 5 the people of A gave him in
2Ch 27: 5 The people of A paid him this
Neh 13:23 married women of Ashdod, A
Ps 83: 7 Gebal, A, and Amalek
Is 11:14 the people of A shall obey
Jer 9:26 Judah, Edom, the people of A
Jer 25:21 Moab, and the people of A
Jer 49: 6 captives of the people of A
Ezek 25: 5 A a resting place for flocks
Dan 11:41 and the prominent people of A
Amos 1:13 of the people of A, and for
Zeph 2: 8 revilings of the people of A
Zeph 2: 9 the people of A like Gomorrah

AMMONITE (*see* AMMON, AMMONITES)
Deut 23: 3 An A or Moabite shall not
1Sa 11: 1 Then Nahash the A came up
1Sa 11: 2 Nahash the A answered them,
2Sa 23:37 Zelek the A, Naharai the
1Ch 11:39 Zelek the A, Naharai the
Neh 2:10 Tobiah the A official heard
Neh 2:19 Tobiah the A official, and
Neh 4: 3 Tobiah the A was beside him
Neh 13: 1 was found written that no A

AMMONITES (*see* AMMONITE)
Deut 2:20 A call them Zamzummim
Josh 12: 2 which is the border of the A
Josh 13:25 land of the A as far as Aroer
1Sa 11:11 killed A until the heat of
1Sa 12:12 of the A came against you
1Ki 11: 1 women of the Moabites, A,
1Ki 11: 5 the abomination of the A
2Ch 20: 1 with them besides the A, came
2Ch 26: 8 Also the A brought tribute to
2Ch 27: 5 fought with the king of the A
Ezra 9: 1 the Jebusites, the A, the
Neh 4: 7 Tobiah, the Arabs, the A
Jer 27: 3 of Moab, the king of the A
Jer 40:11 who were in Moab, among the A
Jer 40:14 A has sent Ishmael the son of
Jer 41:10 departed to go over to the A
Jer 41:15 eight men and went to the A
Jer 49: 1 Against the A
Jer 49: 2 of war in Rabbah of the A
Ezek 21:20 to go to Rabbah of the A, and
Ezek 21:28 the Lord GOD concerning the A
Ezek 25: 2 set your face against the A
Ezek 25: 3 Say to the A, 'Hear the word
Ezek 25:10 together with the A, that
Ezek 25:10 that the A may not be

AMMONITESS (*see* AMMON)
1Ki 14:21 name was Naamah, an A
1Ki 14:31 name was Naamah, an A
2Ch 12:13 name was Naamah, an A
2Ch 24:26 the son of Shimeath the A

AMNON (*see* AMNON'S)
2Sa 3: 2 His firstborn was A by
2Sa 13: 1 A the son of David loved her
2Sa 13: 2 A was so distressed over his
2Sa 13: 2 it was improper for A to do
2Sa 13: 3 But A had a friend whose name
2Sa 13: 4 And A said to him,
2Sa 13: 6 Then A lay down and pretended
2Sa 13: 6 see him, A said to the king,
2Sa 13: 9 Then A said, "Have everyone
2Sa 13:10 Then A said to Tamar, "Bring
2Sa 13:10 brought them to A her brother
2Sa 13:15 Then A hated her exceedingly,
2Sa 13:15 And A said to her,
2Sa 13:20 Has A your brother been with
2Sa 13:22 A neither good nor bad
2Sa 13:22 For Absalom hated A, because
2Sa 13:26 let my brother A go with us
2Sa 13:27 so he let A and all the king's
2Sa 13:28 when I say to you, "Strike A
2Sa 13:29 to A as Absalom had
2Sa 13:32 sons, for only A is dead
2Sa 13:33 For only A is dead
2Sa 13:39 been comforted concerning A
1Ch 3: 1 The firstborn was A, by
1Ch 4:20 And the sons of Shimon were A

AMNON'S (*see* AMNON)
2Sa 13: 7 go to your brother A house
2Sa 13: 8 went to her brother A house
2Sa 13:28 when A heart is merry with

AMOK
Neh 12: 7 Sallu, A, Hilkiah, and Jedaiah
Neh 12:20 of A, Eber

AMON
1Ki 22:26 return him to A the governor
2Ki 21:18 Then his son A reigned in his
2Ki 21:19 A was twenty-two years old
2Ki 21:23 Then the servants of A
2Ki 21:24 had conspired against King A
2Ki 21:25 of the acts of A which he did
1Ch 3:14 A his son, and Josiah his son
2Ch 18:25 return him to A the governor
2Ch 33:20 Then his son A reigned in his
2Ch 33:21 A was twenty-two years old
2Ch 33:22 for A sacrificed to all the
2Ch 33:23 but A trespassed more and more
2Ch 33:25 had conspired against King A
Neh 7:59 Zebaim, and the children of A
Jer 1: 2 days of Josiah the son of A
Jer 25: 3 year of Josiah the son of A
Jer 46:25 bring punishment on A of No
Nah 3: 8 Are you better than No A that
Zeph 1: 1 days of Josiah the son of A
Matt 1:10 Manasseh begot A
Matt 1:10 and A begot Josiah

AMONG (*see* PREFACE)

AMORITE (*see* AMORITES)
Gen 10:16 the Jebusite, the A, and the
Gen 14:13 trees of Mamre the A, brother
Gen 48:22 hand of the A with my sword
Ex 33: 2 out the Canaanite and the A
Ex 34:11 out from before you the A
Deut 2:24 into your hand Sihon the A
Deut 20:17 the Hittite and the A and the
Josh 9: 1 the Hittite, the A, the
Josh 11: 3 east and in the west, the A
1Ch 1:14 the Jebusite, the A, and the
Ezek 16: 3 your father was an A and your
Ezek 16:45 a Hittite and your father an A
Amos 2: 9 destroyed the A before them
Amos 2:10 to possess the land of the A

AMORITES (*see* AMORITE)
Gen 14: 7 and also the A who dwelt in
Gen 15:16 of the A is not yet complete
Gen 15:21 the A, the Canaanites, the
Ex 3: 8 and the Hittites and the A and
Ex 3:17 and the Hittites and the A and
Ex 13: 5 and the Hittites and the A and
Ex 23:23 you and bring you in to the A
Num 13:29 the A dwell in the mountains
Num 21:13 from the border of the A
Num 21:13 Moab, between Moab and the A
Num 21:21 to Sihon king of the A,
Num 21:25 in all the cities of the A
Num 21:26 city of Sihon king of the A
Num 21:29 to Sihon king of the A
Num 21:31 dwelt in the land of the A
Num 21:32 and drove out the A who were
Num 21:34 did to Sihon king of the A
Num 22: 2 that Israel had done to the A
Num 32:33 of Sihon king of the A and the
Num 32:39 the A who were in it
Deut 1: 4 killed Sihon king of the A
Deut 1: 7 go to the mountains of the A
Deut 1:19 way to the mountains of the A
Deut 1:20 to the mountains of the A
Deut 1:27 us into the hand of the A
Deut 1:44 And the A who dwelt in that
Deut 3: 2 did to Sihon king of the A
Deut 3: 8 of the two kings of the A who
Deut 3: 9 and the A call it Senir),
Deut 4:46 land of Sihon king of the A
Deut 4:47 of Bashan, two kings of the A
Deut 7: 1 and the Girgashites and the A
Deut 31: 4 and Og, the kings of the A
Josh 2:10 A who were on the other side
Josh 3:10 and the Girgashites and the A
Josh 5: 1 A who were on the west side
Josh 7: 7 us into the hand of the A
Josh 9:10 A who were beyond the Jordan
Josh 10: 5 the five kings of the A, the
Josh 10: 6 for all the kings of the A
Josh 10:12 the A before the children of
Josh 12: 2 Sihon king of the A, who
Josh 12: 8 the Hittites, the A, the
Josh 13: 4 Aphek, to the border of the A
Josh 13:10 cities of Sihon king of the A
Josh 13:21 of Sihon king of the A, who
Josh 24: 8 you into the land of the A
Josh 24:11 also the A, the Perizzites,
Josh 24:12 also the two kings of the A
Josh 24:15 River, or the gods of the A
Josh 24:18 even the A who dwelt in the
Judg 1:34 the A forced the children of
Judg 1:35 and the A were determined to
Judg 1:36 the A was from the Ascent of
Judg 3: 5 the Hittites, the A, the
Judg 6:10 do not fear the gods of the A
Judg 10: 8 Jordan in the land of the A
Judg 10:11 the Egyptians and from the A
Judg 11:19 to Sihon king of the A, king
Judg 11:21 of all the land of the A, who
Judg 11:22 of all the territory of the A
Judg 11:23 the A from before His people
1Sa 7:14 peace between Israel and the A
2Sa 21: 2 but of the remnant of the A
1Ki 4:19 of Sihon king of the A and of
1Ki 9:20 people who were left of the A
1Ki 21:26 to all that the A had done
2Ki 21:11 all the A who were before him
2Ch 8: 7 were left of the Hittites, A
Ezra 9: 1 the Egyptians, and the A
Neh 9: 8 the Hittites, the A, the
Ps 135:11 Sihon king of the A, Og king
Ps 136:19 Sihon king of the A, For His

AMOS
Amos 1: 1 The words of A, who was among
Amos 7: 8 A, what do you see
Amos 7:10 A has conspired against you
Amos 7:11 For thus A has said
Amos 7:12 Then Amaziah said to A
Amos 7:14 Then A answered, and said to
Amos 8: 2 A, what do you see
Luke 3:25 of Mattathiah, the son of A

AMOUNT (*see* AMOUNTS)
Gen 30:30 is now increased to a great a
2Sa 8: 8 took a large a of bronze
1Ch 18: 8 brought a large a of bronze
2Ch 27: 5 paid him this a in the second

AMOUNTS (*see* AMOUNT)
Ex 30:34 shall be equal **a** of each

AMOZ
2Ki 19: 2 the prophet, the son of **A**
2Ki 19:20 the son of **A** sent to Hezekiah
2Ki 20: 1 the prophet, the son of **A**
2Ch 26:22 Isaiah the son of **A** wrote
2Ch 32:20 prophet Isaiah, the son of **A**
2Ch 32:32 the prophet, the son of **A**
Is 1: 1 vision of Isaiah the son of **A**
Is 2: 1 son of **A** saw concerning Judah
Is 13: 1 which Isaiah the son of **A** saw
Is 20: 2 spoke by Isaiah the son of **A**
Is 37: 2 the prophet, the son of **A**
Is 37:21 the son of **A** sent to Hezekiah
Is 38: 1 the prophet, the son of **A**

AMPHIPOLIS
Acts 17: 1 they had passed through **A**

AMPLIAS
Rom 16: 8 Greet **A**, my beloved in the

AMRAM (*see* AMRAM'S, AMRAMITES, HEMDAN)
Ex 6:18 And the sons of Kohath were **A**
Ex 6:20 Now **A** took for himself
Ex 6:20 life of **A** were one hundred
Num 3:19 **A**, Izehar, Hebron, and Uzziel
Num 26:58 And Kohath begot **A**
Num 26:59 to **A** she bore Aaron and Moses
1Ch 6: 2 The sons of Kohath were **A**
1Ch 6: 3 The children of **A** were Aaron
1Ch 6:18 The sons of Kohath were **A**
1Ch 23:12 **A**, Izhar, Hebron, and Uzziel
1Ch 23:13 The sons of **A**
1Ch 24:20 of the sons of **A**, Shubael
Ezra 10:34 Maadai, **A**, Uel,

AMRAMITES (*see* AMRAM)
Num 3:27 came the family of the **A**, the
1Ch 26:23 Of the **A**, the Izharites, the

AMRAM'S (*see* AMRAM)
Num 26:59 The name of **A** wife was

AMRAPHEL
Gen 14: 1 the days of **A** king of Shinar
Gen 14: 9 **A** king of Shinar, and Arioch

AMZI
1Ch 6:46 the son of **A**, the son of Bani
Neh 11:12 son of Pelaliah, the son of **A**

AN (*see* PREFACE)

ANAB
Josh 11:21 Hebron, from Debir, from **A**
Josh 15:50 **A**, Eshtemoh, Anim,

ANAH
Gen 36: 2 Aholibamah the daughter of **A**
Gen 36:14 wife, the daughter of **A**, the
Gen 36:18 wife, the daughter of **A**
Gen 36:20 Lotan, Shobal, Zibeon, **A**,
Gen 36:24 both Ajah and **A**
Gen 36:24 This was the **A** who found the
Gen 36:25 These were the children of **A**
Gen 36:25 Aholibamah the daughter of **A**
Gen 36:29 Shobal, Chief Zibeon, Chief **A**
1Ch 1:38 were Lotan, Shobal, Zibeon, **A**
1Ch 1:40 sons of Zibeon were Ajah and **A**
1Ch 1:41 The son of **A** was Dishon

ANAHARATH
Josh 19:19 Haphraim, Shion, **A**,

ANAIAH
Neh 8: 4 stood Mattithiah, Shema, **A**
Neh 10:22 Pelatiah, Hanan, **A**,

ANAK (*see* ANAKIM)
Num 13:22 Talmai, the descendants of **A**
Num 13:28 the descendants of **A** there
Num 13:33 of **A** came from the giants)
Deut 9: 2 before the descendants of **A**
Josh 15:13 (Arba was the father of **A**)
Josh 15:14 three sons of **A** from there
Josh 15:14 and Talmai, the children of **A**
Josh 21:11 (Arba being the father of **A**)
Judg 1:20 there the three sons of **A**

ANAKIM (*see* ANAK)
Deut 1:28 seen the sons of the **A** there
Deut 2:10 and numerous and tall as the **A**
Deut 2:11 as giants, like the **A**, but
Deut 2:21 and numerous and tall as the **A**
Deut 9: 2 the descendants of the **A**
Josh 11:21 and cut off the **A** from the
Josh 11:22 None of the **A** were left in
Josh 14:12 that day how the **A** were there
Josh 14:15 the greatest man among the **A**

ANAMIM
Gen 10:13 Mizraim begot Ludim, **A**,
1Ch 1:11 Mizraim begot Ludim, **A**,

ANAMMELECH
2Ki 17:31 in fire to Adrammelech and **A**

ANAN
Neh 10:26 Ahijah, Hanan, **A**,

ANANI
1Ch 3:24 Johanan, Delaiah, and **A**

ANANIAH (*see* ANANIAS)
Neh 3:23 son of Maaseiah, the son of **A**
Neh 11:32 in Anathoth, Nob, **A**

ANANIAS (*see* ANANIAH)
Acts 5: 1 But a certain man named **A**
Acts 5: 3 **A**, why has Satan filled your
Acts 5: 5 Then **A**, hearing these words,
Acts 9:10 disciple at Damascus named **A**
Acts 9:10 Lord said in a vision, "**A**."
Acts 9:12 seen a man named **A** coming in
Acts 9:13 Then **A** answered, "Lord, I
Acts 9:17 **A** went his way and entered the
Acts 22:12 Then one, **A**, a devout man
Acts 23: 2 the high priest **A** commanded
Acts 24: 1 Now after five days **A** the

ANATH
Judg 3:31 him was Shamgar the son of **A**
Judg 5: 6 the days of Shamgar, son of **A**

ANATHOTH (*see* ANATHOTHITE)
Josh 21:18 **A** with its common-land, and
1Ki 2:26 Go to **A**, to your own fields,
1Ch 6:60 and **A** with its common-lands
1Ch 7: 8 Omri, Jerimoth, Abijah, **A**
Ezra 2:23 the men of **A**, one hundred and
Neh 7:27 the men of **A**, one hundred and
Neh 10:19 Hariph, **A**, Nebai,
Neh 11:32 in **A**, Nob, Ananiah
Is 10:30 O poor **A**!
Jer 1: 1 in **A** in the land of Benjamin
Jer 11:21 men of **A** who seek your life
Jer 11:23 catastrophe on the men of **A**
Jer 29:27 not reproved Jeremiah of **A**
Jer 32: 7 Buy my field which is in **A**
Jer 32: 8 buy my field that is in **A**
Jer 32: 9 son of my uncle who was in **A**

ANATHOTHITE (*see* ANATHOTH)
2Sa 23:27 Abiezer the **A**, Mebunnai the
1Ch 11:28 the Tekoite, Abiezer the **A**
1Ch 12: 3 Berachah, and Jehu the **A**
1Ch 27:12 ninth month was Abiezer the **A**

ANCESTORS (*see* ANCESTRY)
Gen 49:26 the blessings of my **a**, up to
Lev 26:45 the covenant of their **a**, whom

ANCESTRY (*see* ANCESTORS)
Num 1:18 recited their **a** by families

ANCHOR (*see* ANCHORED, ANCHORS)
Heb 6:19 we have as an **a** of the soul

ANCHORED (*see* ANCHOR)
Mark 6:53 land of Gennesaret and **a** there

ANCHORS (*see* ANCHOR)
Acts 27:29 dropped four **a** from the stern
Acts 27:30 putting out **a** from the prow
Acts 27:40 And they let go the **a** and left

ANCIENT (*see* ANCIENTS)
Deut 33:15 things of the **a** mountains
Judg 5:21 that **a** torrent, the torrent
2Ki 19:25 From **a** times that I formed it
1Ch 4:22 Now the records are **a**
Ps 77: 5 of old, The years of **a** times
Prov 22:28 Do not remove the **a** landmark
Prov 23:10 Do not remove the **a** landmark
Eccl 1:10 been in **a** times before us
Is 19:11 the wise, the son of **a** kings
Is 23: 7 antiquity is from **a** days,
Is 37:26 from **a** times that I formed it
Is 44: 7 I appointed the **a** people
Is 45:21 has declared this from **a** time
Is 46:10 from **a** times things that are
Is 51: 9 Awake as in the **a** days, in
Jer 5:15 nation, it is an **a** nation
Jer 18:15 their ways, from the **a** paths
Ezek 35: 5 you have had an **a** hatred, and
Ezek 36: 2 The **a** heights have become our
Dan 7: 9 and the **A** of Days was seated
Dan 7:13 He came to the **A** of Days, and
Dan 7:22 until the **A** of Days came, and
2Pe 2: 5 and did not spare the **a** world

ANCIENTS (*see* ANCIENT)
1Sa 24:13 As the proverb of the **a** says
Ps 119:100 I understand more than the **a**

AND (*see* PREFACE)

ANDREW
Matt 4:18 **A** his brother, casting a net
Matt 10: 2 Peter, and **A** his brother
Mark 1:16 **A** his brother casting a net
Mark 1:29 the house of Simon and **A**, with
Mark 3:18 **A**, Philip, Bartholomew,
Mark 13: 3 and **A** asked Him privately,
Luke 6:14 named Peter, and **A** his brother
John 1:40 speak, and followed Him, was **A**
John 1:44 from Bethsaida, the city of **A**
John 6: 8 One of His disciples, **A**,
John 12:22 Philip came and told **A**
John 12:22 and in turn **A** and Philip told
Acts 1:13 Peter, James, John, and **A**

ANDRONICUS
Rom 16: 7 Greet **A** and Junia, my kinsmen

ANEM
1Ch 6:73 and **A** with its common-lands

ANER
Gen 14:13 of Eshcol and brother of **A**
Gen 14:24 **A**, Eshcol, and Mamre
1Ch 6:70 **A** with its common-lands and

ANGEL (*see* ANGEL'S, ANGELS)
Gen 16: 7 Now the **A** of the LORD found
Gen 16: 9 So the **A** of the LORD said to
Gen 16:10 Then the **A** of the LORD said
Gen 16:11 the **A** of the LORD said to her
Gen 21:17 Then the **a** of God called to
Gen 22:11 But the **A** of the LORD called
Gen 22:15 Then the **A** of the LORD called
Gen 24: 7 He will send His **a** before you
Gen 24:40 will send His **a** with you
Gen 31:11 Then the **A** of God spoke to me
Gen 48:16 the **A** who has redeemed me
Ex 3: 2 the **A** of the LORD appeared to
Ex 14:19 the **A** of God, who went before
Ex 23:20 I send an **A** before you to
Ex 23:23 For My **A** will go before you
Ex 32:34 My **A** shall go before you
Ex 33: 2 I will send My **A** before you
Num 20:16 heard our voice and sent the **A**
Num 22:22 the **A** of the LORD took His
Num 22:23 Now the donkey saw the **A** of
Num 22:24 Then the **A** of the LORD stood
Num 22:25 donkey saw the **A** of the LORD
Num 22:26 Then the **A** of the LORD went
Num 22:27 donkey saw the **A** of the LORD
Num 22:31 and he saw the **A** of the LORD
Num 22:32 the **A** of the LORD said to him
Num 22:34 said to the **A** of the LORD
Num 22:35 Then the **A** of the LORD said
Judg 2: 1 Then the **A** of the LORD came
Judg 2: 4 when the **A** of the LORD spoke
Judg 5:23 said the **a** of the LORD
Judg 6:11 Now the **A** of the LORD came and
Judg 6:12 the **A** of the LORD appeared to
Judg 6:20 The **A** of God said to him,
Judg 6:21 Then the **A** of the LORD put
Judg 6:21 the **A** of the LORD departed
Judg 6:22 that He was the **A** of the LORD
Judg 6:22 For I have seen the **A** of the
Judg 13: 3 the **A** of the LORD appeared to
Judg 13: 6 countenance of the **A** of God
Judg 13: 9 and the **A** of God came to the
Judg 13:13 So the **A** of the LORD said to
Judg 13:15 said to the **A** of the LORD
Judg 13:16 the **A** of the LORD said to
Judg 13:16 know He was the **A** of the LORD
Judg 13:17 said to the **A** of the LORD
Judg 13:18 the **A** of the LORD said to him
Judg 13:20 it happened that the **A** of the
Judg 13:21 When the **A** of the LORD
Judg 13:21 that He was the **A** of the LORD
1Sa 29: 9 in my sight as an **a** of God
2Sa 14:17 for as the **a** of God, so is my

2Sa 14:20 to the wisdom of the a of God
2Sa 19:27 the king is like the a of God
2Sa 24:16 when the a stretched out His
2Sa 24:16 and said to the a who was
2Sa 24:16 the a of the LORD was by the
2Sa 24:17 a who was striking the people
1Ki 13:18 an a spoke to me by the word
1Ki 19: 5 suddenly an a touched him
1Ki 19: 7 the a of the LORD came back
2Ki 1: 3 But the a of the LORD said to
2Ki 1:15 the a of the LORD said to
2Ki 19:35 the a of the LORD went out
1Ch 21:12 land, with the a of the LORD
1Ch 21:15 God sent an a to Jerusalem to
1Ch 21:15 and said to the a who was
1Ch 21:15 the a of the LORD stood by
1Ch 21:16 eyes and saw the a of the LORD
1Ch 21:18 Then the a of the LORD
1Ch 21:20 Ornan turned and saw the a
1Ch 21:27 the LORD commanded the a
1Ch 21:30 sword of the a of the LORD
2Ch 32:21 Then the LORD sent an a who
Ps 34: 7 The a of the LORD encamps all
Ps 35: 5 let the a of the LORD chase
Ps 35: 6 let the a of the LORD pursue
Is 37:36 Then the a of the LORD went
Is 63: 9 the A of His Presence saved
Dan 3:28 and Abed-Nego, who sent His A
Dan 6:22 My God sent His a and shut the
Hos 12: 4 Yes, he struggled with the A
Zech 1: 9 So the a who talked with me
Zech 1:11 answered the A of the LORD
Zech 1:12 Then the A of the LORD
Zech 1:13 the a who talked to me, with
Zech 1:14 So the a who spoke with me
Zech 1:19 I said to the a who talked
Zech 2: 3 there was the a who talked
Zech 2: 3 another a was coming out to
Zech 3: 1 before the A of the LORD, and
Zech 3: 3 and was standing before the A
Zech 3: 5 the A of the LORD stood by
Zech 3: 6 Then the A of the LORD
Zech 4: 1 Now the a who talked with me
Zech 4: 4 spoke to the a who talked
Zech 4: 5 Then the a who talked with me
Zech 5: 5 Then the a who talked with me
Zech 5:10 So I said to the a who talked
Zech 6: 4 said to the a who talked with
Zech 6: 5 the a answered and said to me,
Zech 12: 8 like the A of the LORD before
Matt 1:20 an a of the Lord appeared to
Matt 1:24 did as the a of the Lord
Matt 2:13 an a of the Lord appeared to
Matt 2:19 an a of the Lord appeared in
Matt 28: 2 for an a of the Lord
Matt 28: 5 But the a answered and said to
Luke 1:11 Then an a of the Lord
Luke 1:13 But the a said to him, Do
Luke 1:18 And Zacharias said to the a
Luke 1:19 the a answered and said to him
Luke 1:26 a Gabriel was sent by God to
Luke 1:28 come in, the a said to her,
Luke 1:30 Then the a said to her, "Do
Luke 1:34 Then Mary said to the a
Luke 1:35 the a answered and said to her
Luke 1:38 And the a departed from her
Luke 2: 9 an a of the Lord stood before
Luke 2:10 Then the a said to them, "Do
Luke 2:13 a a multitude of the heavenly
Luke 2:21 the name given by the a
Luke 22:43 Then an a appeared to Him
John 5: 4 For an a went down at a
John 12:29 An a has spoken to Him
Acts 5:19 But at night an a of the Lord
Acts 7:30 an A of the Lord appeared to
Acts 7:35 by the hand of the A who
Acts 7:38 A who spoke to him on Mount
Acts 8:26 Now an a of the Lord spoke to
Acts 10: 3 vision an a of God coming in
Acts 10: 7 when the a who spoke to him
Acts 10:22 instructed by a holy a to
Acts 11:13 an a standing in his house
Acts 12: 7 an a of the Lord stood by him
Acts 12: 8 Then the a said to him
Acts 12: 9 was done by the a was real
Acts 12:10 immediately the a departed
Acts 12:11 that the Lord has sent His a
Acts 12:15 It is his a
Acts 12:23 Then immediately an a of the
Acts 23: 8 and no a or spirit
Acts 23: 9 or an a has spoken to him
Acts 27:23 stood by me this night an a
2Co 11:14 himself into an a of light
Gal 1: 8 or an a from heaven, preach
Gal 4:14 received me as an a of God
Rev 1: 1 by His a to His servant John
Rev 2: 1 To the a of the church of
Rev 2: 8 to the a of the church in
Rev 2:12 to the a of the church in
Rev 2:18 to the a of the church in
Rev 3: 1 to the a of the church in
Rev 3: 7 to the a of the church in
Rev 3:14 to the a of the church of the
Rev 5: 2 Then I saw a strong a
Rev 7: 2 Then I saw another a
Rev 8: 3 Then another a, having a
Rev 8: 5 Then the a took the censer,
Rev 8: 7 The first a sounded
Rev 8: 8 Then the second a sounded
Rev 8:10 Then the third a sounded
Rev 8:12 Then the fourth a sounded
Rev 8:13 I heard an a flying through
Rev 9: 1 Then the fifth a sounded
Rev 9:11 the a of the bottomless pit
Rev 9:13 Then the sixth a sounded
Rev 9:14 sixth a who had the trumpet
Rev 10: 1 a coming down from heaven
Rev 10: 5 the a whom I saw standing on
Rev 10: 7 the sounding of the seventh a
Rev 10: 8 the a who stands on the sea
Rev 10: 9 And I went to the a and said to
Rev 11: 1 And the a stood, saying,
Rev 11:15 Then the seventh a sounded
Rev 14: 6 Then I saw another a flying
Rev 14: 8 another a followed, saying,
Rev 14: 9 Then a third a followed them,
Rev 14:15 another a came out of the
Rev 14:17 Then another a came out of
Rev 14:18 another a came out from the
Rev 14:19 So the a thrust his sickle
Rev 16: 3 Then the second a poured out
Rev 16: 4 Then the third a poured out
Rev 16: 5 I heard the a of the waters
Rev 16: 8 Then the fourth a poured out
Rev 16:10 Then the fifth a poured out
Rev 16:12 Then the sixth a poured out
Rev 16:17 Then the seventh a poured out
Rev 17: 7 But the a said to me, Why
Rev 18: 1 a coming down from heaven
Rev 18:21 Then a mighty a took up a
Rev 19:17 Then I saw an a standing in
Rev 20: 1 Then I saw an a coming down
Rev 21:17 of a man, that is, of an a
Rev 22: 6 a to show His servants the
Rev 22: 8 before the feet of the a who
Rev 22:16 have sent My a to testify to

ANGEL'S (*see* ANGEL)
Rev 8: 4 before God from the a hand
Rev 10:10 little book out of the a hand

ANGELS (*see* ANGEL, ANGELS')
Gen 19: 1 Now the two a came to Sodom
Gen 19:15 the a urged Lot to hurry,
Gen 28:12 and there the a of God were
Gen 32: 1 way, and the a of God met him
Job 4:18 He charges His a with error
Ps 8: 5 him a little lower than the a
Ps 78:49 By sending a of destruction
Ps 91:11 give His a charge over you
Ps 103:20 Bless the LORD, you His a
Ps 104: 4 Who makes His a spirits, His
Ps 148: 2 Praise Him, all His a
Matt 4: 6 He shall give His a charge
Matt 4:11 a came and ministered to Him
Matt 13:39 age, and the reapers are the a
Matt 13:41 of Man will send out His a
Matt 13:49 The a will come forth,
Matt 16:27 of His Father with His a, and
Matt 18:10 a always see the face of My
Matt 22:30 but are like a of God in
Matt 24:31 He will send His a with a
Matt 24:36 no, not even the a of heaven
Matt 25:31 and all the holy a with Him
Matt 25:41 for the devil and his a
Matt 26:53 more than twelve legions of a
Mark 1:13 and the a ministered to Him
Mark 8:38 of His Father with the holy a
Mark 12:25 but are like a in heaven
Mark 13:27 And then He will send His a
Mark 13:32 neither the a in heaven, nor
Luke 2:15 when the a had gone away from
Luke 4:10 give His a charge over You
Luke 9:26 Father's, and of the holy a
Luke 12: 8 confess before the a of God
Luke 12: 9 be denied before the a of God
Luke 15:10 a of God over one sinner who
Luke 16:22 by the a to Abraham's bosom
Luke 20:36 for they are equal to the a
Luke 24:23 of a who said He was alive
John 1:51 the a of God ascending and
John 20:12 And she saw two a in white
Acts 7:53 the law by the direction of a
Rom 8:38 nor a nor principalities nor
1Co 4: 9 to the world, both to a and to
1Co 6: 3 know that we shall judge a
1Co 11:10 on her head, because of the a
1Co 13: 1 the tongues of men and of a
Gal 3:19 it was appointed through a by
Col 2:18 humility and worship of a,
2Th 1: 7 from heaven with His mighty a
1Ti 3:16 in the Spirit, seen by a,
1Ti 5:21 the elect a that you observe
Heb 1: 4 so much better than the a
Heb 1: 5 of the a did He ever say
Heb 1: 6 Let all the a of God worship
Heb 1: 7 And of the a He says
Heb 1: 7 Who makes His a spirits and
Heb 1:13 of the a has He ever said
Heb 2: 2 through a proved steadfast
Heb 2: 5 we speak, in subjection to a
Heb 2: 7 him a little lower than the a
Heb 2: 9 a little lower than the a
Heb 2:16 He does not give aid to a
Heb 12:22 an innumerable company of a
Heb 13: 2 unwittingly entertained a
1Pe 1:12 things which a desire to look
1Pe 3:22 at the right hand of God, a
2Pe 2: 4 not spare the a who sinned
2Pe 2:11 whereas a, who are greater in
Jude 6 the a who did not keep their
Rev 1:20 the a of the seven churches
Rev 3: 5 My Father and before His a
Rev 5:11 of many a around the throne
Rev 7: 1 four a standing at the four
Rev 7: 2 a loud voice to the four a to
Rev 7:11 all the a stood around the
Rev 8: 2 I saw the seven a who stand
Rev 8: 6 So the seven a who had the
Rev 8:13 a who are about to sound
Rev 9:14 Release the four a who are
Rev 9:15 So the four a, who had been
Rev 12: 7 and his a fought against the
Rev 12: 7 the dragon and his a fought,
Rev 12: 9 his a were cast out with him
Rev 14:10 in the presence of the holy a
Rev 15: 1 seven a having the seven last
Rev 15: 6 a having the seven plagues
Rev 15: 7 a seven golden bowls full of
Rev 15: 8 of the seven a were completed
Rev 16: 1 temple saying to the seven a
Rev 17: 1 Then one of the seven a who
Rev 21: 9 Then one of the seven a who
Rev 21:12 twelve a at the gates, and

ANGELS' (*see* ANGELS)
Ps 78:25 Men ate a food

ANGER (*see* ANGERED, ANGRY)
Gen 27:45 a turns away from you, and he
Gen 30: 2 Jacob's a was aroused against
Gen 39:19 that his a was aroused
Gen 44:18 and do not let your a burn
Gen 49: 6 for in their a they slew a
Gen 49: 7 Cursed be their a, for it is
Ex 4:14 So the a of the LORD was
Ex 11: 8 out from Pharaoh in great a
Ex 32:19 So Moses' a became hot, and he
Ex 32:22 Do not let the a of my lord
Num 11: 1 it, and His a was aroused
Num 11:10 the a of the LORD was greatly
Num 12: 9 So the a of the LORD was
Num 22:22 Then God's a was aroused
Num 22:27 so Balaam's a was aroused
Num 24:10 Then Balak's a was aroused
Num 25: 3 the a of the LORD was aroused
Num 25: 4 that the fierce a of the LORD
Num 32:10 So the LORD's a was aroused
Num 32:13 So the LORD's a was aroused
Num 32:14 still more the fierce a of
Deut 4:25 your God to provoke Him to a
Deut 6:15 lest the a of the LORD your

Deut 7: 4 so the **a** of the LORD will be
Deut 9:18 the LORD, to provoke Him to **a**
Deut 9:19 For I was afraid of the **a**
Deut 11:17 lest the LORD's **a** be aroused
Deut 13:17 from the fierceness of His **a**
Deut 19: 6 of blood, while his **a** is hot
Deut 29:20 for then the **a** of the LORD
Deut 29:23 the LORD overthrew in His **a**
Deut 29:24 the heat of this great **a** mean
Deut 29:27 Then the **a** of the LORD was
Deut 29:28 them from their land in **a**
Deut 31:17 Then My **a** shall be aroused
Deut 31:29 to provoke Him to **a** through
Deut 32:16 they provoked Him to **a**
Deut 32:21 they have moved Me to **a** by
Deut 32:21 them to **a** by a foolish nation
Deut 32:22 For a fire is kindled in My **a**
Josh 7: 1 so the **a** of the LORD burned
Josh 7:26 from the fierceness of His **a**
Josh 23:16 then the **a** of the LORD will
Judg 2:12 they provoked the LORD to **a**
Judg 2:14 the **a** of the LORD was hot
Judg 2:20 Then the **a** of the LORD was
Judg 3: 8 Therefore the **a** of the LORD
Judg 8: 3 Then their **a** toward him
Judg 9:30 of Ebed, his **a** was aroused
Judg 10: 7 So the **a** of the LORD was hot
Judg 14:19 So his **a** was aroused, and he
1Sa 11: 6 his **a** was greatly aroused
1Sa 17:28 Eliab's **a** was aroused against
1Sa 20:30 Then Saul's **a** was aroused
1Sa 20:34 from the table in fierce **a**
2Sa 6: 7 Then the **a** of the LORD was
2Sa 12: 5 Then David's **a** was greatly
2Sa 24: 1 Again the **a** of the LORD was
1Ki 14: 9 images to provoke Me to **a**
1Ki 14:15 provoking the LORD to **a**
1Ki 15:30 the LORD God of Israel to **a**
1Ki 16: 2 Me to **a** with their sins,
1Ki 16: 7 LORD in provoking Him to **a**
1Ki 16:13 Israel to **a** with their idols
1Ki 16:26 Israel to **a** with their idols
1Ki 16:33 to **a** than all the kings of
1Ki 21:22 you have provoked Me to **a**
1Ki 22:53 the LORD God of Israel to **a**
2Ki 13: 3 Then the **a** of the LORD was
2Ki 17:11 to provoke the LORD to **a**,
2Ki 17:17 the LORD, to provoke Him to **a**
2Ki 21: 6 the LORD, to provoke Him to **a**
2Ki 21:15 have provoked Me to **a** since
2Ki 22:17 they might provoke Me to **a**
2Ki 23:19 made to provoke the LORD to **a**
2Ki 23:26 with which His **a** was aroused
2Ki 24:20 For because of the **a** of the
1Ch 13:10 Then the **a** of the LORD was
2Ch 25:10 Therefore their **a** was greatly
2Ch 25:10 they returned home in great **a**
2Ch 25:15 Therefore the **a** of the LORD
2Ch 28:25 provoked to **a** the LORD God of
2Ch 33: 6 the LORD, to provoke Him to **a**
2Ch 34:25 they might provoke Me to **a**
Neh 4: 5 You to **a** before the builders
Neh 9:17 and merciful, slow to **a**,
Esth 1:12 and his **a** burned within him
Job 4: 9 of His **a** they are consumed
Job 9: 5 He overturns them in His **a**
Job 9:13 God will not withdraw His **a**
Job 18: 4 You who tear yourself in **a**
Job 21:17 God distributes in His **a**
Job 35:15 He has not punished in His **a**
Ps 6: 1 do not rebuke me in Your **a**
Ps 7: 6 Arise, O LORD, in Your **a**
Ps 21: 9 oven in the time of Your **a**
Ps 27: 9 turn Your servant away in **a**
Ps 30: 5 For His **a** is but for a moment
Ps 37: 8 Cease from **a**, and forsake
Ps 38: 3 in my flesh Because of Your **a**
Ps 56: 7 In **a** cast down the peoples, O
Ps 69:24 wrathful **a** take hold of them
Ps 74: 1 Why does Your **a** smoke against
Ps 77: 9 Has He in **a** shut up His
Ps 78:21 **a** also came up against Israel
Ps 78:38 a time He turned His **a** away
Ps 78:49 them the fierceness of His **a**
Ps 78:50 He made a path for His **a**
Ps 78:58 to **a** with their high places
Ps 85: 3 from the fierceness of Your **a**
Ps 85: 4 cause Your **a** toward us to
Ps 85: 5 Your **a** to all generations
Ps 90: 7 have been consumed by Your **a**
Ps 90:11 Who knows the power of Your **a**
Ps 103: 8 and gracious, Slow to **a**, and
Ps 103: 9 will He keep His **a** forever
Ps 106:29 Him to **a** with their deeds
Ps 145: 8 full of compassion, Slow to **a**
Prov 15: 1 but a harsh word stirs up **a**
Prov 15:18 slow to **a** allays contention
Prov 16:32 He who is slow to **a** is better
Prov 19:11 of a man makes him slow to **a**
Prov 20: 2 whoever provokes him to **a**
Prov 21:14 A gift in secret pacifies **a**
Prov 22: 8 and the rod of his **a** will fail
Prov 27: 4 **a** a torrent, but who is able
Eccl 5:17 much sorrow and sickness and **a**
Eccl 7: 9 for **a** rests in the bosom of
Is 1: 4 they have provoked to **a** the
Is 5:25 Therefore the **a** of the LORD
Is 5:25 For all this His **a** is not
Is 7: 4 for the fierce **a** of Rezin
Is 9:12 For all this His **a** is not
Is 9:17 For all this His **a** is not
Is 9:21 For all this His **a** is not
Is 10: 4 this His **a** is not turned away
Is 10: 5 to Assyria, the rod of My **a**
Is 10:25 cease, as will My **a** in their
Is 12: 1 Your **a** is turned away, and You
Is 13: 3 My mighty ones for My **a**
Is 13: 9 with both wrath and fierce **a**
Is 13:13 and in the day of His fierce **a**
Is 14: 6 he who ruled the nations in **a**
Is 30:27 from afar, burning with His **a**
Is 30:30 with the indignation of His **a**
Is 42:25 on him the fury of His **a** and
Is 48: 9 name's sake I will defer My **a**
Is 63: 3 I have trodden them in My **a**
Is 63: 6 down the peoples in My **a**,
Is 65: 3 to **a** continually to My face
Is 66:15 to render His **a** with fury
Jer 2:35 surely His **a** shall turn from
Jer 3:12 not cause My **a** to fall on you
Jer 4: 8 For the fierce **a** of the LORD
Jer 4:26 of the LORD, by His fierce **a**
Jer 7:18 that they may provoke Me to **a**
Jer 7:19 Do they provoke Me to **a**
Jer 7:20 Behold, My **a** and My fury will
Jer 8:19 to **a** with their carved images
Jer 10:24 not in Your **a**, lest You bring
Jer 11:17 **a** in offering incense to Baal
Jer 12:13 of the fierce **a** of the LORD
Jer 15:14 for a fire is kindled in My **a**
Jer 17: 4 My **a** which shall burn forever
Jer 18:23 them in the time of Your **a**
Jer 21: 5 with a strong arm, even in **a**
Jer 23:20 The **a** of the LORD will not
Jer 25: 6 do not provoke Me to **a** with
Jer 25: 7 to **a** with the works of your
Jer 25:37 of the fierce **a** of the LORD
Jer 25:38 and because of His fierce **a**
Jer 30:24 The fierce **a** of the LORD will
Jer 32:29 gods, to provoke Me to **a**
Jer 32:30 to **a** with the work of their
Jer 32:31 to Me a provocation of My **a**
Jer 32:32 have done to provoke Me to **a**
Jer 32:37 I have driven them in My **a**
Jer 33: 5 men whom I will slay in My **a**
Jer 36: 7 For great is the **a** and the
Jer 42:18 As My **a** and My fury have been
Jer 44: 3 committed to provoke Me to **a**
Jer 44: 6 and My **a** were poured out and
Jer 49:37 upon them, my fierce **a**,' says
Jer 51:45 from the fierce **a** of the LORD
Jer 52: 3 For because of the **a** of the
Lam 1:12 me in the day of His fierce **a**
Lam 2: 1 of Zion with a cloud in His **a**
Lam 2: 1 footstool in the day of His **a**
Lam 2: 3 fierce **a** every horn of Israel
Lam 2:21 them in the day of Your **a**
Lam 2:22 **a** there was no refugee or
Lam 3:43 have covered Yourself with **a**
Lam 3:66 In Your **a**, pursue and destroy
Lam 4:11 has poured out His fierce **a**
Ezek 5:13 Thus shall My **a** be spent
Ezek 5:15 judgments among you in **a** and
Ezek 7: 3 I will send My **a** against you
Ezek 7: 8 fury, and spend My **a** upon you
Ezek 8:17 returned to provoke Me to **a**
Ezek 13:13 be a flooding rain in My **a**
Ezek 16:26 harlotry to provoke Me to **a**
Ezek 20: 8 fulfill My **a** against them in
Ezek 20:21 fulfill My **a** against them in
Ezek 22:20 so I will gather you in My **a**
Ezek 25:14 do in Edom according to My **a**
Ezek 35:11 I will do according to your **a**
Ezek 43: 8 I have consumed them in My **a**
Dan 9:16 I pray, let Your **a** and Your
Dan 11:20 but not in **a** or in battle
Hos 8: 5 My **a** is aroused against them
Hos 11: 9 the fierceness of My **a**
Hos 12:14 Him to **a** most bitterly
Hos 13:11 I gave you a king in My **a**
Hos 14: 4 for My **a** has turned away from
Joel 2:13 and merciful, slow to **a**, and of
Amos 1:11 his **a** tore perpetually, and he
Jon 3: 9 turn away from His fierce **a**
Jon 4: 2 and merciful God, slow to **a**
Mic 5:15 I will execute vengeance in **a**
Mic 7:18 does not retain His **a** forever
Nah 1: 3 the LORD is slow to **a** and
Nah 1: 6 the fierceness of His **a**
Hab 3: 8 was Your **a** against the rivers
Hab 3:12 you trampled the nations in **a**
Zeph 2: 2 fierce **a** comes upon you,
Zeph 2: 2 the LORD's **a** comes upon you
Zeph 2: 3 in the day of the LORD's **a**
Zeph 3: 8 indignation, All my fierce **a**
Zech 10: 3 My **a** is kindled against the
Mark 3: 5 looked around at them with **a**
Rom 10:19 I will **a** you by a foolish
Eph 4:31 Let all bitterness, wrath, **a**
Col 3: 8 **a**, wrath, malice, blasphemy,

ANGERED (*see* ANGER)
Ps 106:32 They **a** Him also at the waters

ANGRY (*see* ANGER)
Gen 4: 5 And Cain was very **a**, and his
Gen 4: 6 Why are you **a**
Gen 18:30 Let not the Lord be **a**, and I
Gen 18:32 Let not the Lord be **a**, and I
Gen 31:36 Then Jacob was **a** and rebuked
Gen 34: 7 men were grieved and very **a**
Gen 40: 2 Pharaoh was **a** with his two
Gen 41:10 When Pharaoh was **a** with his
Gen 45: 5 therefore be grieved nor **a**
Ex 16:20 And Moses was **a** with them
Lev 10:16 And he was **a** with Eleazar and
Num 16:15 Then Moses was very **a**, and
Num 16:22 sin, and You be **a** with all the
Num 31:14 But Moses was **a** with the
Deut 1:34 sound of your words, and was **a**
Deut 1:37 The LORD was also **a** with me
Deut 3:26 But the LORD was **a** with me on
Deut 4:21 was **a** with me for your sakes
Deut 9: 8 so that the LORD was **a** enough
Deut 9:19 which the LORD was **a** with you
Deut 9:20 LORD was very **a** with Aaron
Josh 22:18 that tomorrow He will be **a**
Judg 6:39 Do not be **a** with me, and let
Judg 18:25 lest **a** men fall upon you, and
1Sa 18: 8 Then Saul was very **a**, and the
1Sa 20: 7 But if he is very **a**, then be
1Sa 29: 4 Philistines were **a** with him
2Sa 3: 8 Then Abner became very **a** at
2Sa 6: 8 David became **a** because of the
2Sa 13:21 these things, he was very **a**
2Sa 19:42 are you **a** over this matter
2Sa 22: 8 and shook, because He was **a**
1Ki 8:46 and You become **a** with them
1Ki 11: 9 LORD became **a** with Solomon
2Ki 13:19 the man of God was **a** with him
2Ki 17:18 LORD was very **a** with Israel
1Ch 13:11 David became **a** because of the
2Ch 6:36 and You become **a** with them
2Ch 16:10 Then Asa was **a** with the seer,
2Ch 26:19 And while he was **a** with the
2Ch 28: 9 your fathers was **a** with Judah
Ezra 9:14 Would You not be **a** with us
Neh 4: 7 that they became very **a**,
Neh 5: 6 I became very **a** when I heard
Ps 2:12 Kiss the Son, lest He be **a**
Ps 4: 4 Be **a**, and do not sin
Ps 7:11 And God is **a** with the wicked
Ps 18: 7 were shaken, Because He was **a**
Ps 76: 7 presence When once You are **a**
Ps 79: 5 Will You be **a** forever
Ps 80: 4 hosts, How long will You be **a**
Ps 85: 5 Will You be **a** with us forever
Prov 21:19 with a contentious and **a** woman
Prov 22:24 no friendship with an **a** man
Prov 25:23 tongue an **a** countenance
Prov 29:22 An **a** man stirs up strife, and

Eccl 5: 6 God be **a** at your excuse and
Eccl 7: 9 hasten in your spirit to be **a**
Song 1: 6 mother's sons were **a** with me
Is 12: 1 though You were **a** with me
Is 28:21 He will be **a** as in the Valley
Is 47: 6 I was **a** with My people
Is 54: 9 I would not be **a** with you
Is 57:16 nor will I always be **a**
Is 57:17 of his covetousness I was **a**
Is 57:17 I hid and was **a**, and he went on
Is 64: 5 You are indeed **a**, for we have
Jer 3: 5 Will He remain **a** forever
Jer 3:12 I will not remain **a** forever
Jer 37:15 princes were **a** with Jeremiah
Lam 5:22 us, and are very **a** with us
Ezek 16:42 be quiet, and be **a** no more
Dan 2:12 this reason the king was **a**
Jon 4: 1 exceedingly, and he became **a**
Jon 4: 4 Is it right for you to be **a**
Jon 4: 9 you to be **a** about the plant
Jon 4: 9 It is right for me to be **a**
Zech 1: 2 been very **a** with your fathers
Zech 1:12 were **a** these seventy years
Zech 1:15 I am exceedingly **a** with the
Zech 1:15 for I was a little **a**, and they
Matt 2:16 wise men, was exceedingly **a**
Matt 5:22 **a** with his brother without a
Matt 18:34 And his master was **a**, and
Luke 14:21 master of the house, being **a**
Luke 15:28 But he was **a** and would not go
John 7:23 are you **a** with Me because I
Acts 12:20 **a** with the people of Tyre
Eph 4:26 Be **a**, and do not sin"
Heb 3:10 Therefore I was **a** with that
Heb 3:17 whom was He **a** forty years
Rev 11:18 The nations were **a**, and Your

ANGUISH
Gen 42:21 for we saw the **a** of his soul
Ex 6: 9 Moses, because of **a** of spirit
Deut 2:25 and be in **a** because of you
Deut 28:65 failing eyes, and **a** of soul
1Sa 1:10 to the LORD and wept in **a**
2Sa 1: 9 for **a** has come upon me, but
Job 6:10 though in **a**, I would exult
Job 7:11 speak in the **a** of my spirit
Job 15:24 Trouble and **a** make him afraid
Ps 38:18 I will be in **a** over my sin
Ps 77:10 This is my **a**
Ps 119:143 **a** have overtaken me, Yet Your
Prov 1:27 distress and **a** come upon you
Is 8:22 and darkness, gloom of **a**
Is 30: 6 a land of trouble and **a**, from
Jer 4:31 the **a** as of her who brings
Jer 6:24 **A** has taken hold of us, pain
Jer 15: 8 I will cause **a** and terror to
Jer 49:24 **A** and sorrows have taken her
Jer 50:43 **a** has taken hold of him,
Ezek 30: 4 great **a** shall be in Ethiopia,
Ezek 30: 9 great **a** shall come upon them,
John 16:21 she no longer remembers the **a**
Rom 2: 9 tribulation and **a**, on every
2Co 2: 4 **a** of heart I wrote to you,

ANIAM
1Ch 7:19 Ahian, Shechem, Likhi, and **A**

ANIM
Josh 15:50 Anab, Eshtemoh, **A**,

ANIMAL (*see* ANIMALS)
Gen 7: 2 seven each of every clean **a**
Gen 8:20 and took of every clean **a**
Gen 34:23 every **a** of theirs be ours
Gen 43:16 to my home, and slaughter an **a**
Ex 13: 2 of Israel, both of man and **a**
Ex 13:12 from an **a** which you have
Ex 13:15 of man and the firstborn of **a**
Ex 22: 5 grazed, and lets loose his **a**
Ex 22:13 it is torn to pieces by an **a**
Lev 11:47 between the **a** that may be
Lev 11:47 the **a** that may not be eaten
Lev 17:13 catches any **a** or bird that
Lev 24:18 Whoever kills an **a** shall
Lev 24:18 make it good, **a** for **a**
Lev 24:21 kills an **a** shall restore it
Deut 14: 6 And you may eat every **a** with
Deut 27:21 who lies with any kind of **a**
Neh 2:12 nor was there any **a** with me
Neh 2:14 **a** that was under me to pass
Prov 12:10 man regards the life of his **a**
Dan 4:16 be given the heart of an **a**
Luke 10:34 and he set him on his own **a**

ANIMALS (*see* ANIMAL)
Gen 6:20 of **a** after their kind, and of
Gen 7: 2 two each of **a** that are
Gen 8: 1 all the **a** that were with him
Gen 36: 6 his cattle and all his **a**, and
Lev 7:24 fat of what is torn by wild **a**
Lev 11: 2 These are the **a** which you
Lev 11:27 among all kinds of **a** that go
Lev 25: 7 the **a** that are in your land
Num 18:15 of unclean **a** you shall redeem
Num 20: 4 we and our **a** should die here
Num 20: 8 the congregation and their **a**
Num 20:11 congregation and their **a** drank
Num 35: 3 herds, and for all their **a**
Deut 14: 4 These are the **a** which you may
Deut 14: 6 chews the cud, among the **a**
1Ki 4:33 he spoke also of **a**, of birds,
2Ki 3: 9 nor for the **a** that followed
2Ki 3:17 cattle, and your **a** may drink
2Ch 35:11 the Levites skinned the **a**
Job 37: 8 The **a** enter dens, and remain
Ps 66:15 You burnt sacrifices of fat **a**
Ezek 44:31 or was torn by wild **a**
Acts 7:42 you offer Me slaughtered **a**
Acts 10:12 of four-footed **a** of the earth
Acts 11: 6 four-footed **a** of the earth

ANISE
Matt 23:23 you pay tithe of mint and **a**

ANKLE (*see* ANKLES, ANKLETS)
Acts 3: 7 **a** bones received strength

ANKLES (*see* ANKLE)
Ezek 47: 3 the water came up to my **a**

ANKLETS (*see* ANKLE)
Is 3:18 the jingling **a**, the scarves,

ANNA
Luke 2:36 Now there was one, **A**, a

ANNALS
2Ch 13:22 in the **a** of the prophet Iddo
2Ch 24:27 they are written in the **a** of

ANNAS
Luke 3: 2 **A** and Caiaphas being high
John 18:13 they led Him away to **A** first
John 18:24 Then **A** sent Him bound to
Acts 4: 6 as well as **A** the high priest,

ANNIHILATE (*see* ANNIHILATED)
Esth 3:13 to **a** all the Jews, both young
Esth 8: 5 which he wrote to **a** the Jews
Esth 8:11 and **a** all the forces of any
Esth 9:24 against the Jews to **a** them
Dan 11:44 fury to destroy and **a** many

ANNIHILATED (*see* ANNIHILATE)
Esth 7: 4 to be killed, and to be **a**

ANNOUNCE (*see* ANNOUNCED)
Deut 30:18 I **a** to you today that you
1Sa 9:27 that I may **a** to you the word
Neh 8:15 and that they should **a** and
Amos 4: 5 and **a** the freewill offerings
Acts 21:26 entered the temple to **a** the

ANNOUNCED (*see* ANNOUNCE)
Judg 21:13 of Rimmon, and **a** peace to them
Lam 1:21 on the day that You have **a**
Acts 12:14 **a** that Peter stood before the
Rom 15:21 To whom He was not **a**, they

ANNOYED
Acts 16:18 But Paul, greatly **a**, turned

ANNUL (*see* ANNULLED, ANNULLING, ANNULS)
Job 40: 8 you indeed **a** My judgment
Is 14:27 purposed, and who will **a** it
Gal 3:17 cannot **a** the covenant that

ANNULLED (*see* ANNUL)
Is 28:18 covenant with death will be **a**

ANNULLING (*see* ANNUL)
Heb 7:18 **a** of the former commandment

ANNULS (*see* ANNUL)
Gal 3:15 no one **a** or adds to it

ANOINT (*see* ANOINTED, ANOINTING)
Ex 28:41 You shall **a** them, consecrate
Ex 29: 7 pour it on his head, and **a** him
Ex 29:36 you shall **a** it to sanctify it
Ex 30:26 With it you shall **a** the
Ex 30:30 And you shall **a** Aaron and his
Ex 40: 9 **a** the tabernacle and all that
Ex 40:10 You shall **a** the altar of the
Ex 40:11 And you shall **a** the laver and
Ex 40:13 **a** him and sanctify him, that
Ex 40:15 You shall **a** them, as you
Deut 28:40 but you shall not **a** yourself
Judg 9: 8 forth to **a** a king over them
Judg 9:15 If in truth you **a** me as king
Ruth 3: 3 **a** yourself, put on your best
1Sa 9:16 you shall **a** him commander
1Sa 15: 1 The LORD sent me to **a** you
1Sa 15:17 did not the LORD **a** you king
1Sa 16: 3 you shall **a** for Me the one I
1Sa 16:12 the LORD said, Arise, **a** him
2Sa 14: 2 do not **a** yourself with oil,
1Ki 1:34 Nathan the prophet **a** him king
1Ki 19:15 **a** Hazael as king over Syria
1Ki 19:16 Also you shall **a** Jehu the son
1Ki 19:16 **a** as prophet in your place
Ps 23: 5 You **a** my head with oil
Is 21: 5 you princes, **a** the shield
Dan 9:24 and to **a** the Most Holy
Dan 10: 3 nor did I **a** myself at all,
Amos 6: 6 **a** yourselves with the best
Mic 6:15 but not **a** yourselves with oil
Matt 6:17 **a** your head and wash your face
Mark 14: 8 to **a** My body for burial
Mark 16: 1 that they might come and **a** Him
Luke 7:46 You did not **a** My head with
Rev 3:18 **a** your eyes with eye salve,

ANOINTED (*see* ANOINT)
Gen 31:13 where you **a** the pillar and
Ex 29: 2 unleavened wafers **a** with oil
Ex 29:29 him, to be **a** in them and to be
Ex 40:15 as you **a** their father, that
Lev 2: 4 unleavened wafers **a** with oil
Lev 4: 3 if the **a** priest sins,
Lev 4: 5 Then the **a** priest shall take
Lev 4:16 The **a** priest shall bring
Lev 6:20 on the day when he is **a**
Lev 6:22 who is **a** in his place, shall
Lev 7:12 unleavened wafers **a** with oil
Lev 7:36 on the day that He **a** them
Lev 8:10 **a** the tabernacle and all that
Lev 8:11 times, **a** the altar and all its
Lev 8:12 and **a** him, to sanctify him
Lev 8:26 a cake of bread **a** with oil
Lev 16:32 And the priest, who is **a** and
Num 3: 3 Aaron, the **a** priests, whom he
Num 6:15 unleavened wafers **a** with oil
Num 7: 1 the tabernacle, that he **a** it
Num 7: 1 so he **a** them and sanctified
Num 7:10 for the altar when it was **a**
Num 7:84 of Israel, when it was **a**
Num 7:88 for the altar after it was **a**
Num 35:25 who was **a** with the holy oil
1Sa 2:10 and exalt the horn of His **a**
1Sa 2:35 walk before My **a** forever
1Sa 10: 1 has **a** you commander over His
1Sa 12: 3 the LORD and before His **a**
1Sa 12: 5 His **a** is witness this day,
1Sa 16: 6 the LORD's **a** is before Him
1Sa 16:13 **a** him in the midst of his
1Sa 24: 6 to my master, the LORD's **a**
1Sa 24: 6 he is the **a** of the LORD
1Sa 24:10 lord, for he is the LORD's **a**
1Sa 26: 9 his hand against the LORD's **a**
1Sa 26:11 my hand against the LORD's **a**
1Sa 26:16 your master, the LORD's **a**
1Sa 26:23 my hand against the LORD's **a**
2Sa 1:14 hand to destroy the LORD's **a**
2Sa 1:16 I have killed the LORD's **a**
2Sa 1:21 of Saul, not **a** with oil
2Sa 2: 4 there they **a** David king over
2Sa 2: 7 Judah has **a** me king over them
2Sa 3:39 am weak today, though **a** king
2Sa 5: 3 they **a** David king over Israel
2Sa 5:17 heard that they had **a** David
2Sa 12: 7 I **a** you king over Israel, and
2Sa 12:20 **a** himself, and changed his
2Sa 19:10 Absalom, whom we **a** over us
2Sa 19:21 he cursed the LORD's **a**
2Sa 22:51 king, and shows mercy to His **a**
2Sa 23: 1 the **a** of the God of Jacob, and
1Ki 1:39 the tabernacle and **a** Solomon
1Ki 1:45 have **a** him king at Gihon
1Ki 5: 1 he heard that they had **a** him
2Ki 9: 3 I have **a** you king over Israel

2Ki 9: 6 I have **a** you king over the
2Ki 9:12 I have **a** you king over Israel
2Ki 11:12 **a** him, and they clapped their
2Ki 23:30 **a** him, and made him king in
1Ch 11: 3 Then they **a** David king over
1Ch 14: 8 been **a** king over all Israel
1Ch 16:22 Do not touch My **a** ones, and do
1Ch 29:22 **a** him before the LORD to be
2Ch 6:42 turn away the face of Your **a**
2Ch 22: 7 whom the LORD had **a** to cut
2Ch 23:11 Jehoiada and his sons **a** him
2Ch 28:15 them food and drink, and **a** them
Ps 2: 2 the LORD and against His **A**
Ps 18:50 king, And shows mercy to His **a**
Ps 20: 6 that the LORD saves His **a**
Ps 28: 8 is the saving refuge of His **a**
Ps 45: 7 has **a** You With the oil of
Ps 84: 9 look upon the face of Your **a**
Ps 89:20 With My holy oil I have **a** him
Ps 89:38 have been furious with Your **a**
Ps 89:51 the footsteps of Your **a**
Ps 92:10 I have been **a** with fresh oil
Ps 105:15 Do not touch My **a** ones, And do
Ps 132:10 turn away the face of Your **A**
Ps 132:17 will prepare a lamp for My **A**
Is 45: 1 Thus says the LORD to His **a**
Is 61: 1 because the LORD has **a** Me to
Lam 4:20 the **a** of the LORD, was caught
Ezek 16: 9 blood, and I **a** you with oil
Ezek 28:14 You were the **a** cherub who
Hab 3:13 for salvation with Your **A**
Zech 4:14 These are the two **a** ones, who
Mark 6:13 **a** with oil many who were sick
Luke 4:18 because He has **a** Me to preach
Luke 7:38 **a** them with the fragrant oil
Luke 7:46 but this woman has **a** My feet
John 9: 6 He **a** the eyes of the blind
John 9:11 **a** my eyes and said to me, 'Go
John 11: 2 It was that Mary who **a** the
John 12: 3 **a** the feet of Jesus, and wiped
Acts 4:27 Servant Jesus, whom You **a**
Acts 10:38 how God **a** Jesus of Nazareth
2Co 1:21 in Christ and has **a** us is God,
Heb 1: 9 has **a** You with the oil of

ANOINTING (*see* ANOINT)
Ex 25: 6 and spices for the **a** oil and
Ex 29: 7 And you shall take the **a** oil
Ex 29:21 altar, and some of the **a** oil
Ex 30:25 make from these a holy **a** oil
Ex 30:25 It shall be a holy **a** oil
Ex 30:31 This shall be a holy **a** oil
Ex 31:11 and the **a** oil and sweet incense
Ex 35: 8 and spices for the **a** oil and
Ex 35:15 altar, its poles, the **a** oil
Ex 35:28 for the light, for the **a** oil
Ex 37:29 He also made the holy **a** oil
Ex 39:38 the gold altar, the **a** oil
Ex 40: 9 And you shall take the **a** oil
Ex 40:15 for their **a** shall surely be
Lev 8: 2 and the garments, the **a** oil
Lev 8:10 Then Moses took the **a** oil
Lev 8:12 of the **a** oil on Aaron's head
Lev 8:30 Moses took some of the **a** oil
Lev 10: 7 for the **a** oil of the LORD is
Lev 21:10 head the **a** oil was poured
Lev 21:12 **a** oil of his God is upon him
Num 4:16 grain offering, the **a** oil
Is 10:27 because of the **a** oil
Jas 5:14 **a** him with oil in the name of
1Jn 2:20 But you have an **a** from the
1Jn 2:27 But the **a** which you have
1Jn 2:27 but as the same **a** teaches you

ANOTHER (*see* PREFACE)

ANOTHER'S (*see* PREFACE)

ANSWER (*see* PREFACE)

ANSWERED (*see* PREFACE)

ANSWERING (*see* PREFACE)

ANSWERS (*see* PREFACE)

ANT (*see* ANTS)
Prov 6: 6 Go to the **a**, you sluggard

ANTELOPE
Deut 14: 5 the mountain goat, the **a**
Is 51:20 streets, like an **a** in a net

ANTICHRIST (*see* ANTICHRISTS)
1Jn 2:18 heard that the **A** is coming
1Jn 2:22 He is **a** who denies the Father
1Jn 4: 3 this is the spirit of the **A**
2Jn 7 This is a deceiver and an **a**

ANTICHRISTS (*see* ANTICHRIST)
1Jn 2:18 even now many **a** have come

ANTICIPATED
Matt 17:25 into the house, Jesus **a** him

ANTIOCH
Acts 6: 5 Nicolas, a proselyte from **A**
Acts 11:19 as Phoenicia, Cyprus, and **A**
Acts 11:20 who, when they had come to **A**
Acts 11:22 Barnabas to go as far as **A**
Acts 11:26 him, he brought him to **A**
Acts 11:26 first called Christians in **A**
Acts 11:27 came from Jerusalem to **A**
Acts 13: 1 in the church that was at **A**
Acts 13:14 they came to **A** in Pisidia
Acts 14:19 Then Jews from **A** and Iconium
Acts 14:21 to Lystra, Iconium, and **A**,
Acts 14:26 From there they sailed to **A**
Acts 15:22 own company to **A** with Paul
Acts 15:23 who are of the Gentiles in **A**
Acts 15:30 were sent off, they came to **A**
Acts 15:35 Barnabas also remained in **A**
Acts 18:22 the church, he went down to **A**
Gal 2:11 But when Peter had come to **A**
2Ti 3:11 which happened to me at **A**

ANTIPAS
Rev 2:13 **A** was My faithful martyr, who

ANTIPATRIS
Acts 23:31 and brought him by night to **A**

ANTIQUITY
Is 23: 7 whose **a** is from ancient days,
Ezek 26:20 in places desolate from **a**

ANTITYPE
1Pe 3:21 There is also an **a** which now

ANTOTHIJAH
1Ch 8:24 Hananiah, Elam, **A**,

ANTS (*see* ANT)
Prov 30:25 the **a** are a people not strong

ANUB
1Ch 4: 8 and Koz begot **A**, Zobebah, and

ANVIL
Is 41: 7 him who strikes the **a**, saying

ANXIETIES (*see* ANXIETY)
Ps 94:19 multitude of my **a** within me
Ps 139:23 Try me, and know my **a**

ANXIETY (*see* ANXIETIES, ANXIOUS)
Prov 12:25 **A** in the heart of man causes
Ezek 4:16 eat bread by weight and with **a**
Ezek 12:18 water with trembling and **a**
Ezek 12:19 shall eat their bread with **a**

ANXIOUS (*see* ANXIETY, ANXIOUSLY)
1Sa 9:20 do not be **a** about them, for
Job 20: 2 Therefore my **a** thoughts make
Jer 17: 8 will not be **a** in the year of
Dan 2: 3 my spirit is **a** to know the
Luke 12:26 why are you **a** for the rest
Luke 12:29 drink, nor have an **a** mind
Phil 4: 6 Be **a** for nothing, but in

ANXIOUSLY (*see* ANXIOUS)
Luke 2:48 father and I have sought You **a**

ANY (*see* PREFACE)

ANYMORE (*see* PREFACE)

ANYONE (*see* PREFACE)

ANYONE'S (*see* PREFACE)

ANYTHING (*see* PREFACE)

ANYWAY (*see* PREFACE)

ANYWHERE (*see* PREFACE)

APART (*see* PREFACE)

APELLES
Rom 16:10 Greet **A**, approved in Christ

APES
1Ki 10:22 gold, silver, ivory, **a**, and
2Ch 9:21 gold, silver, ivory, **a**, and

APHARSATHCHITES
Ezra 4: 9 of the Dinaites, the **A**, the

APHEK (*see* APHIK)
Josh 12:18 the king of **A**, one
Josh 13: 4 to the Sidonians as far as **A**
Josh 19:30 Also Ummah, **A**, and Rehob
1Sa 4: 1 the Philistines encamped in **A**
1Sa 29: 1 all their armies at **A**, and the
1Ki 20:26 went up to **A** to fight against
1Ki 20:30 But the rest fled to **A**, into
2Ki 13:17 at **A** till you have destroyed

APHEKAH
Josh 15:53 Janum, Beth Tappuah, **A**,

APHIAH
1Sa 9: 1 of Bechorath, the son of **A**

APHIK (*see* APHEK)
Judg 1:31 of Ahlab, Achzib, Helbah, **A**

APIECE
Num 7:86 incense weighed ten shekels **a**
Num 17: 6 leaders gave him a rod **a**, for
Ezek 41:24 The doors had two panels **a**
Luke 9: 3 and do not have two tunics **a**
John 2: 6 twenty or thirty gallons **a**

APOLLONIA
Acts 17: 1 through Amphipolis and **A**, they

APOLLOS
Acts 18:24 Now a certain Jew named **A**
Acts 19: 1 while **A** was at Corinth, that
1Co 1:12 I am of **A**," or "I am of
1Co 3: 4 I am of **A**," are you not
1Co 3: 5 Who then is Paul, and who is **A**
1Co 3: 6 **A** watered, but God gave the
1Co 3:22 whether Paul or **A** or Cephas
1Co 4: 6 **A** for your sakes, that you
1Co 16:12 Now concerning our brother **A**
Tit 3:13 **A** on their journey with haste

APOLLYON
Rev 9:11 in Greek he has the name **A**

APOSTLE (*see* APOSTLES, APOSTLESHIP)
Rom 1: 1 Christ, called to be an **a**
Rom 11:13 as I am an **a** to the Gentiles
1Co 1: 1 called to be an **a** of Jesus
1Co 9: 1 Am I not an **a**
1Co 9: 2 If I am not an **a** to others
1Co 15: 9 not worthy to be called an **a**
2Co 1: 1 an **a** of Jesus Christ by the
2Co 12:12 Truly the signs of an **a** were
Gal 1: 1 Paul, an **a** (not from men nor
Eph 1: 1 an **a** of Jesus Christ by the
Col 1: 1 an **a** of Jesus Christ by the
1Ti 1: 1 an **a** of Jesus Christ, by the
1Ti 2: 7 appointed a preacher and an **a**
2Ti 1: 1 an **a** of Jesus Christ by the
2Ti 1:11 appointed a preacher, an **a**
Tit 1: 1 God and an **a** of Jesus Christ,
Heb 3: 1 calling, consider the **A** and
1Pe 1: 1 an **a** of Jesus Christ, To the
2Pe 1: 1 **a** of Jesus Christ, To those

APOSTLES (*see* APOSTLE, APOSTLES')
Matt 10: 2 of the twelve **a** are these
Mark 6:30 Then the **a** gathered to Jesus
Luke 6:13 twelve whom He also named **a**
Luke 9:10 And the **a**, when they had
Luke 11:49 will send them prophets and **a**
Luke 17: 5 And the **a** said to the Lord,
Luke 22:14 and the twelve **a** with Him
Luke 24:10 told these things to the **a**
Acts 1: 2 to the **a** whom He had chosen
Acts 1:26 numbered with the eleven **a**
Acts 2:37 to Peter and the rest of the **a**
Acts 2:43 signs were done through the **a**
Acts 4:33 the **a** gave witness to the
Acts 4:36 also named Barnabas by the **a**
Acts 5:12 the hands of the **a** many signs
Acts 5:18 and laid their hands on the **a**
Acts 5:29 Peter and the other **a** answered
Acts 5:34 commanded them to put the **a**
Acts 5:40 they had called for the **a**
Acts 6: 6 whom they set before the **a**
Acts 8: 1 and Samaria, except the **a**
Acts 8:14 Now when the **a** who were at
Acts 9:27 him and brought him to the **a**
Acts 11: 1 Now the **a** and brethren who
Acts 14: 4 the Jews, and part with the **a**
Acts 14:14 But when the **a** Barnabas and

Acts 15: 2 go up to Jerusalem, to the **a**
Acts 15: 4 by the church and the **a** and the
Acts 15: 6 So the **a** and elders came
Acts 15:22 Then it pleased the **a** and
Acts 15:23 The **a**, the elders, and the
Acts 15:33 from the brethren to the **a**
Acts 16: 4 were determined by the **a** and
Rom 16: 7 who are of note among the **a**
1Co 4: 9 God has displayed us, the **a**
1Co 9: 5 wife, as do also the other **a**
1Co 12:28 first **a**, second prophets,
1Co 12:29 Are all **a**?
1Co 15: 7 by James, then by all the **a**
1Co 15: 9 For I am the least of the **a**
2Co 11: 5 to the most eminent **a**
2Co 11:13 For such are false **a**,
2Co 11:13 themselves into **a** of Christ
2Co 12:11 I behind the most eminent **a**
Gal 1:17 to those who were **a** before me
Gal 1:19 of the other **a** except James
Eph 2:20 on the foundation of the **a**
Eph 3: 5 by the Spirit to His holy **a**
Eph 4:11 He Himself gave some to be **a**
1Th 2: 6 made demands as **a** of Christ
2Pe 3: 2 of us the **a** of the Lord and
Jude 17 **a** of our Lord Jesus Christ
Rev 2: 2 those who say they are **a** and
Rev 18:20 her, O heaven, and you holy **a**
Rev 21:14 of the twelve **a** of the Lamb

APOSTLES' (*see* APOSTLES)
Acts 2:42 steadfastly in the **a** doctrine
Acts 4:35 and laid them at the **a** feet
Acts 4:37 and laid it at the **a** feet
Acts 5: 2 part and laid it at the **a** feet
Acts 8:18 the laying on of the **a** hands

APOSTLESHIP (*see* APOSTLE)
Acts 1:25 and **a** from which Judas by
Rom 1: 5 **a** for obedience to the faith
1Co 9: 2 the seal of my **a** in the Lord
Gal 2: 8 in Peter for the **a** to the

APPAIM
1Ch 2:30 sons of Nadab were Seled and **A**
1Ch 2:31 The son of **A** was Ishi, the

APPALLED
Ps 40:15 Let them be **a** because of

APPAREL (*see* APPARELED)
Judg 14:19 of their men, took their **a**
1Sa 27: 9 donkeys, the camels, and the **a**
2Sa 1:24 ornaments of gold on your **a**
2Sa 13:18 virgin daughters wore such **a**
2Sa 14: 2 mourner, and put on mourning **a**
1Ki 10: 5 of his waiters and their **a**
2Ch 9: 4 of his waiters and their **a**
2Ch 9: 4 his cupbearers and their **a**
Ezra 3:10 in their **a** with trumpets, and
Esth 8:15 the king in royal **a** of blue
Is 3:22 the festal **a**, and the mantles
Is 4: 1 own food and wear our own **a**
Is 63: 1 One who is glorious in His **a**
Is 63: 2 Why is Your **a** red, and Your
Ezek 27:24 in chests of multicolored **a**
Zeph 1: 8 as are clothed with foreign **a**
Zech 14:14 and **a** in great abundance
Acts 1:10 men stood by them in white **a**
Acts 12:21 day Herod, arrayed in royal **a**
Acts 20:33 no one's silver or gold or **a**
1Ti 2: 9 adorn themselves in modest **a**
Jas 2: 2 with gold rings, in fine **a**
1Pe 3: 3 gold, or of putting on fine **a**

APPARELED (*see* APPAREL)
Luke 7:25 those who are gorgeously **a**

APPEAL (*see* APPEALED, APPEALING)
2Ki 8: 3 she went to make an **a** to the
Acts 25:11 I **a** to Caesar
Acts 28:19 was compelled to **a** to Caesar
Phm 9 love's sake I rather **a** to you
Phm 10 I **a** to you for my son
Heb 13:22 I **a** to you, brethren, bear

APPEALED (*see* APPEAL)
Acts 25:12 You have **a** to Caesar
Acts 25:21 But when Paul **a** to be
Acts 25:25 he himself had **a** to Augustus
Acts 26:32 he had not **a** to Caesar

APPEALING (*see* APPEAL)
2Ki 8: 5 **a** to the king for her house
Is 4: 2 **a** for those of Israel who

APPEAR (*see* APPEARANCE, APPEARED, APPEARING, APPEARS)
Gen 1: 9 and let the dry land **a**"
Ex 23:15 none shall **a** before Me empty)
Ex 23:17 shall **a** before the Lord GOD
Ex 34:20 And none shall **a** before Me
Ex 34:23 men shall **a** before the Lord
Ex 34:24 to **a** before the LORD your God
Lev 9: 4 today the LORD will **a** to you
Lev 9: 6 of the LORD will **a** to you
Lev 13: 4 does not **a** to be deeper than
Lev 13:31 indeed it does not **a** deeper
Lev 13:32 the scall does not **a** deeper
Lev 13:34 does not **a** deeper than the
Lev 14:37 which **a** to be deep in the
Lev 16: 2 for I will **a** in the cloud
Deut 16:16 **a** before the LORD your God in
Deut 16:16 they shall not **a** before the
Deut 31:11 when all Israel comes to **a**
1Sa 1:22 that he may **a** before the LORD
Ps 42: 2 shall I come and **a** before God
Ps 90:16 Let Your work **a** to Your
Ps 102:16 He shall **a** in His glory
Song 2:12 The flowers **a** on the earth
Is 1:12 When you come to **a** before Me
Jer 13:26 face, that your shame may **a**
Ezek 21:24 all your doings your sins **a**
Matt 6:16 may **a** to men to be fasting
Matt 6:18 so that you do not **a** to men
Matt 23:27 tombs which indeed **a**
Matt 23:28 outwardly **a** righteous to men
Matt 24:30 Son of Man will **a** in heaven
Luke 19:11 of God would **a** immediately
Acts 22:30 and all their council to **a**
Rom 7:13 But sin, that it might **a** sin
2Co 5:10 For we must all **a** before the
2Co 7:12 sight of God might **a** to you
2Co 13: 7 not that we should **a** approved
Col 3: 4 also will **a** with Him in glory
Heb 9:24 now to **a** in the presence of
Heb 9:28 Him He will **a** a second time
1Pe 4:18 the ungodly and the sinner **a**

APPEARANCE (*see* APPEAR)
Gen 29:17 was beautiful of form and **a**
Gen 39: 6 was handsome in form and **a**
Lev 13:43 as the **a** of leprosy on the
Num 9:15 tabernacle like the **a** of fire
Num 9:16 and the **a** of fire by night
1Sa 16: 7 Do not look at his **a** or at
1Sa 16: 7 man looks at the outward **a**
1Sa 25: 3 understanding and beautiful **a**
2Sa 14:27 was a woman of beautiful **a**
Job 4:16 but I could not discern its **a**
Lam 4: 7 like sapphire in their **a**
Lam 4: 8 Now their **a** is blacker than
Ezek 1: 5 And this was their **a**
Ezek 1:13 their **a** was like burning
Ezek 1:13 and like the **a** of torches
Ezek 1:14 forth, in **a** like a flash of
Ezek 1:16 The **a** of the wheels and their
Ezek 1:16 The **a** of their works was, as
Ezek 1:26 in **a** like a sapphire stone
Ezek 1:26 the **a** of a man high above it
Ezek 1:27 Also from the **a** of His waist
Ezek 1:27 **a** of fire all around within
Ezek 1:27 from the **a** of His waist and
Ezek 1:27 the **a** of fire with brightness
Ezek 1:28 Like the **a** of a rainbow in a
Ezek 1:28 day, so was the **a** of the
Ezek 1:28 This was the **a** of the
Ezek 8: 2 likeness, like the **a** of fire
Ezek 8: 2 from the **a** of His waist and
Ezek 8: 2 like the **a** of brightness,
Ezek 10: 1 having the **a** of the likeness
Ezek 10:10 As for their **a**, all four
Ezek 10:22 by the River Chebar, their **a**
Ezek 40: 3 there was a man whose **a** was
Ezek 40: 3 was like the **a** of bronze
Ezek 41:21 the **a** of the one was like the
Ezek 41:21 was like the **a** of the other
Ezek 42:11 their **a** was like the chambers
Ezek 43: 3 It was like the **a** of the
Dan 7:20 whose **a** was greater than his
Dan 8:15 me one having the **a** of a man
Dan 10: 6 face like the **a** of lightning
Joel 2: 4 Their **a** is like the
Joel 2: 4 is like the **a** of horses
Luke 9:29 the **a** of His face was altered
John 7:24 Do not judge according to **a**
2Co 5:12 answer those who glory in **a**
2Co 10: 7 according to the outward **a**
Phil 2: 8 And being found in **a** as a man
Col 2:23 **a** of wisdom in self-imposed
Jas 1:11 and its beautiful **a** perishes
Rev 4: 3 and a sardius stone in **a**
Rev 4: 3 throne, in **a** like an emerald

APPEARED (*see* APPEAR)
Gen 12: 7 Then the LORD **a** to Abram and
Gen 12: 7 to the LORD, who had **a** to him
Gen 17: 1 old, the LORD **a** to Abram and
Gen 18: 1 Then the LORD **a** to him by the
Gen 26: 2 Then the LORD **a** to him and
Gen 26:24 the LORD **a** to him the same
Gen 35: 1 who **a** to you when you fled
Gen 35: 7 because there God **a** to him
Gen 35: 9 Then God **a** to Jacob again,
Gen 48: 3 God Almighty **a** to me at Luz
Ex 3: 2 the Angel of the LORD **a** to
Ex 3:16 and of Jacob, **a** to me, saying,
Ex 4: 1 The LORD has not **a** to you
Ex 4: 5 God of Jacob, has **a** to you
Ex 6: 3 I **a** to Abraham, to Isaac, and
Ex 14:27 and when the morning **a**, the
Ex 16:10 of the LORD **a** in the cloud
Lev 9:23 the LORD **a** to all the people
Num 14:10 LORD **a** in the tabernacle of
Num 16:19 **a** to all the congregation
Num 16:42 and the glory of the LORD **a**
Num 20: 6 glory of the LORD **a** to them
Deut 31:15 Now the LORD **a** at the
Judg 6:12 Angel of the LORD **a** to him
Judg 13: 3 of the LORD **a** to the woman
Judg 13:10 the Man has just now **a** to me
Judg 13:21 the LORD **a** no more to Manoah
1Sa 3:21 Then the LORD **a** again in
1Ki 3: 5 At Gibeon the LORD **a** to
1Ki 9: 2 that the LORD **a** to Solomon
1Ki 9: 2 as He had **a** to him at Gibeon
1Ki 11: 9 who had **a** to him twice,
2Ki 2:11 of fire **a** with horses of fire
2Ch 1: 7 that night God **a** to Solomon
2Ch 3: 1 where the LORD had **a** to his
2Ch 7:12 Then the LORD **a** to Solomon by
Neh 4:21 daybreak until the stars **a**
Jer 31: 3 The LORD has **a** of old to me
Ezek 10: 1 there **a** something like a
Ezek 10: 8 The cherubim **a** to have the
Ezek 10: 9 the wheels **a** to have the
Dan 1:15 their countenance **a** better
Dan 5: 5 the fingers of a man's hand **a**
Dan 8: 1 Belshazzar a vision **a** to me
Dan 8: 1 after the one that **a** to me
Matt 1:20 the Lord **a** to him in a dream
Matt 2: 7 them what time the star **a**
Matt 2:13 Lord **a** to Joseph in a dream
Matt 2:19 an angel of the Lord **a** in a
Matt 13:26 a crop, then the tares also **a**
Matt 17: 3 Elijah **a** to them, talking
Matt 27:53 the holy city and **a** to many
Mark 9: 4 Elijah **a** to them with Moses,
Mark 16: 9 He **a** first to Mary Magdalene,
Mark 16:12 He **a** in another form to two
Mark 16:14 Afterward He **a** to the eleven
Luke 1:11 an angel of the Lord **a** to him
Luke 9: 8 and by some that Elijah had **a**
Luke 9:31 who **a** in glory and spoke of
Luke 22:43 Then an angel **a** to Him from
Luke 24:34 indeed, and has **a** to Simon
Acts 2: 3 Then there **a** to them divided
Acts 7: 2 The God of glory **a** to our
Acts 7:26 the next day he **a** to two of
Acts 7:30 an Angel of the Lord **a** to him
Acts 7:35 who **a** to him in the bush
Acts 9:17 who **a** to you on the road as
Acts 16: 9 a vision **a** to Paul in the
Acts 26:16 for I have **a** to you for this
Acts 27:20 sun nor stars **a** for many days
Tit 2:11 salvation has **a** to all men
Tit 3: 4 God our Savior toward man **a**
Heb 9:26 He has **a** to put away sin by
Rev 12: 1 Now a great sign **a** in heaven
Rev 12: 3 And another sign **a** in heaven

APPEARING (*see* APPEAR)
1Ti 6:14 our Lord Jesus Christ's **a**
2Ti 1:10 now been revealed by the **a** of
2Ti 4: 1 living and the dead at His **a**
2Ti 4: 8 to all who have loved His **a**
Tit 2:13 glorious **a** of our great God

APPEARS (*see* APPEAR)
Lev 13: 3 the sore **a** to be deeper than
Lev 13: 5 if the sore **a** to be as it was
Lev 13:14 But when raw flesh **a** on him
Lev 13:20 it indeed **a** deeper than the
Lev 13:25 it **a** deeper than the skin, it
Lev 13:30 indeed if it **a** deeper than
Lev 13:37 But if the scall **a** to be at a
Lev 13:57 But if it **a** again in the
Ps 84: 7 Every one of them **a** before
Jer 6: 1 for disaster **a** out of the
Mal 3: 2 And who can stand when He **a**
Col 3: 4 When Christ who is our life **a**
Jas 4:14 that **a** for a little time and
1Pe 5: 4 and when the Chief Shepherd **a**
1Jn 2:28 abide in Him, that when He **a**

APPEASE (*see* APPEASED)
Gen 32:20 I will **a** him with the present
Prov 16:14 but a wise man will **a** it
Matt 28:14 ears, we will **a** him and make

APPEASED (*see* APPEASE)
Prov 6:35 nor will he be **a** though you

APPETITE
Job 38:39 or satisfy the **a** of the young
Prov 23: 2 if you are a man given to **a**

APPHIA
Phm 2 to the beloved **A**, Archippus

APPII
Acts 28:15 to meet us as far as **A** Forum

APPLE (*see* APPLES)
Deut 32:10 kept him as the **a** of His eye
Ps 17: 8 Keep me as the **a** of Your eye
Prov 7: 2 my law as the **a** of your eye
Song 2: 3 Like an **a** tree among the
Song 8: 5 awakened you under the **a** tree
Joel 1:12 palm tree also, and the **a** tree
Zech 2: 8 you touches the **a** of His eye

APPLES (*see* APPLE)
Prov 25:11 like **a** of gold in settings of
Song 2: 5 of raisins, refresh me with **a**
Song 7: 8 of your breath like **a**,

APPLIED (*see* APPLY)
1Ki 6:35 overlaid them with gold **a**
Eccl 7:25 I **a** my heart to know, to
Eccl 8: 9 **a** my heart to every work that
Eccl 8:16 When I **a** my heart to know

APPLY (*see* APPLIED)
Prov 2: 2 **a** your heart to understanding
Prov 22:17 **a** your heart to my knowledge
Prov 23:12 **A** your heart to instruction,
Is 38:21 **a** it as a poultice on the

APPOINT (*see* APPOINTED, APPOINTMENT, APPOINTS)
Gen 41:34 let him **a** officers over the
Ex 21:13 then I will **a** for you a place
Ex 30:16 shall **a** it for the service of
Lev 26:16 I will even **a** terror over you
Num 1:50 but you shall **a** the Levites
Num 3:10 So you shall **a** Aaron and his
Num 4:19 **a** each of them to his service
Num 4:27 you shall **a** to them all their
Num 35: 6 shall **a** six cities of refuge
Num 35:11 then you shall **a** cities to
Num 35:14 You shall **a** three cities on
Num 35:14 shall **a** in the land of Canaan
Deut 16:18 You shall **a** judges and
Josh 20: 2 **A** for yourselves cities of
1Sa 8:11 **a** them for his own chariots
1Sa 8:12 He will **a** captains over his
2Sa 6:21 to **a** me ruler over the people
2Sa 7:10 Moreover I will **a** a place for
1Ch 15:16 to **a** their brethren to be the
1Ch 17: 9 Moreover I will **a** a place for
Neh 7: 3 and **a** guards from among the
Esth 2: 3 let the king **a** officers in
Job 9:19 who will **a** my day in court
Job 14:13 You would **a** me a set time
Is 26: 1 God will **a** salvation for
Jer 15: 3 I will **a** over them four forms
Jer 49:19 man that I may **a** over her
Jer 50:44 man that I may **a** over her
Jer 51:27 **A** a marshal against her
Ezek 21:19 **a** for yourself two ways for
Ezek 21:20 **A** a road for the sword to go
Ezek 45: 6 You shall **a** as the property
Hos 1:11 **a** for themselves one head
Zeph 3:19 I will **a** them for praise and
Matt 24:51 **a** him his portion with the
Luke 12:46 **a** him his portion with the
Acts 6: 3 whom we may **a** over this
1Co 6: 4 do you **a** those who are least
1Th 5: 9 For God did not **a** us to wrath
Tit 1: 5 **a** elders in every city as I

APPOINTED (*see* APPOINT)
Gen 4:25 For God has **a** another seed
Gen 18:14 At the **a** time I will return
Gen 24:14 have **a** for Your servant Isaac
Gen 24:44 has **a** for my master's son
Ex 9: 5 Then the LORD **a** a set time
Ex 23:15 at the time **a** in the month of
Ex 31: 6 have **a** with him Aholiab the
Ex 34:18 in the **a** time of the month of
Lev 23: 4 proclaim at their **a** times
Num 3:36 the **a** duty of the children of
Num 4:16 The **a** duty of Eleazar the son
Num 9: 2 the Passover at its **a** time
Num 9: 3 shall keep it at its **a** time
Num 9: 7 **a** time among the children of
Num 9:13 of the LORD at its **a** time
Num 10:10 gladness, in your **a** feasts
Num 15: 3 offering or in your **a** feasts
Num 28: 2 offer to Me at their **a** time
Num 29:39 **a** feasts (besides your vowed
Deut 18:14 God has not **a** such for you
Deut 31:10 at the **a** time in the year of
Josh 4: 4 the twelve men whom he had **a**
Josh 8:14 at an **a** place before the
Josh 20: 7 So they **a** Kedesh in Galilee,
Josh 20: 9 These were the cities **a** for
Judg 20:38 Now the **a** signal between the
1Sa 13:11 not come within the days **a**
1Sa 20:35 at the time **a** with David, and
1Sa 25:30 has **a** you ruler over Israel,
1Sa 29: 4 which you have **a** for him, and
2Sa 20: 5 time which David had **a** him
2Sa 23:23 David **a** him over his guard
2Sa 24:15 the morning till the **a** time
1Ki 1:35 For I have **a** him to be ruler
1Ki 20:42 whom I **a** to utter destruction
2Ki 4:17 son when the **a** time had come
2Ki 7:17 Now the king had **a** the
2Ki 8: 6 So the king **a** a certain
2Ki 10:24 Now Jehu had **a** for himself
2Ki 11:18 the priest **a** officers over
2Ki 17:32 from every class they **a** for
1Ch 6:31 are the men whom David **a** over
1Ch 6:48 were **a** to every kind of
1Ch 9:22 Samuel the seer had **a** them to
1Ch 9:29 Some of them were **a** over the
1Ch 11:25 David **a** him over his guard
1Ch 15:17 So the Levites **a** Heman the
1Ch 16: 4 he **a** some of the Levites to
1Ch 22: 2 and he **a** masons to cut hewn
2Ch 8:13 the three **a** yearly feasts
2Ch 8:14 he **a** the divisions of the
2Ch 10:12 third day, as the king had **a**
2Ch 11:15 Then he **a** for himself priests
2Ch 11:22 Rehoboam **a** Abijah the son of
2Ch 19: 8 Jehoshaphat **a** some of the
2Ch 20:21 he **a** those who should sing to
2Ch 23:18 Also Jehoiada **a** the oversight
2Ch 31: 2 Hezekiah **a** the divisions of
2Ch 31: 3 The king also **a** a portion of
2Ch 33: 8 I have **a** for your fathers
2Ch 34:22 king had **a** went to Huldah the
Ezra 3: 5 for all the **a** feasts of the
Ezra 3: 8 **a** the Levites from twenty
Ezra 8:20 the leaders had **a** for the
Ezra 10:14 pagan wives come at **a** times
Neh 5:14 from the time that I was **a** to
Neh 6: 7 you have also **a** prophets to
Neh 7: 1 and the Levites had been **a**
Neh 9:17 in their rebellion they **a** a
Neh 10:34 at the **a** times year by year,
Neh 12:31 and **a** two large thanksgiving
Neh 12:44 were **a** over the rooms of the
Neh 13:13 I **a** as treasurers over the
Neh 13:31 and the firstfruits at **a** times
Esth 4: 5 whom he had **a** to attend her
Esth 8: 2 Esther **a** Mordecai over the
Esth 9:31 days of Purim at their **a** time
Job 1: 4 houses, each on his **a** day
Job 7: 3 nights have been **a** to me
Job 14: 5 You have **a** his limits, so
Job 20:29 the heritage **a** to him by God
Job 23:14 He performs what is **a** for me
Job 30:23 to the house **a** for all living
Job 34:13 Or who **a** Him over the whole
Ps 78: 5 **a** a law in Israel, Which He
Ps 79:11 those who are **a** to die
Ps 102:20 To loose those **a** to death
Ps 104:19 He **a** the moon for seasons
Prov 7:20 will come home on the **a** day
Prov 31: 8 cause of all who are **a** to die
Eccl 7:14 Surely God has **a** the one as
Is 1:14 your **a** feasts my soul hates
Is 14:31 will be alone in his **a** times
Is 28:25 the barley in the **a** place
Is 33:20 the city of our **a** feasts
Is 44: 7 since I **a** the ancient people
Jer 5:24 us the **a** weeks of the harvest
Jer 8: 7 the heavens knows her **a** times
Jer 33:25 night, and if I have not **a** the
Jer 43:11 to death those **a** for death
Jer 43:11 those **a** for captivity, and to
Jer 43:11 sword those **a** for the sword
Jer 46:17 He has passed by the **a** time
Jer 47: 7 There He has **a** it
Lam 2: 6 LORD has caused the **a** feasts
Ezek 43:21 burn it in the **a** place of the
Ezek 44:24 statutes in all My **a** meetings
Ezek 45:17 at all the **a** seasons of the
Ezek 46: 9 the LORD on the **a** feast days
Ezek 46:11 the **a** feast days the grain
Dan 1: 5 the king **a** for them a daily
Dan 1:10 who has **a** your food and drink
Dan 2:24 whom the king had **a** to
Dan 8:19 for at the **a** time the end
Dan 10: 1 true, but the **a** time was long
Dan 11:27 will still be at the **a** time
Dan 11:29 At the **a** time he shall return
Dan 11:35 it is still for the **a** time
Hos 2:11 all her **a** feasts
Hos 6:11 Judah, a harvest is **a** for you
Hos 9: 5 What will you do in the **a** day
Hos 12: 9 as in the days of the **a** feast
Mic 6: 9 Who has **a** it
Nah 1:15 O Judah, keep your **a** feasts
Hab 1:12 You have **a** them for judgment
Hab 2: 3 vision is yet for an **a** time
Zeph 3:18 sorrow over the **a** assembly
Matt 28:16 which Jesus had **a** for them
Mark 3:14 Then He **a** twelve, that they
Luke 3:13 more than what is **a** for you
Luke 10: 1 Lord **a** seventy others also
John 15:16 **a** you that you should go and
Acts 7:44 in the wilderness, as He **a**
Acts 13:48 And as many as had been **a** to
Acts 14:23 So when they had **a** elders in
Acts 17:31 because He has **a** a day on
Acts 22:10 which are **a** for you to do
Acts 28:23 So when they had **a** him a day
Rom 13: 1 that exist are **a** by God
1Co 12:28 God has **a** these in the church
2Co 10:13 of the sphere which God **a** us
Gal 3:19 it was **a** through angels by
Gal 4: 2 the time **a** by the father
Phil 1:17 knowing that I am **a** for the
1Th 3: 3 know that we are **a** to this
1Ti 2: 7 for which I was **a** a preacher
2Ti 1:11 to which I was **a** a preacher
Heb 1: 2 whom He has **a** heir of all
Heb 3: 2 was faithful to Him who **a** Him
Heb 5: 1 men is **a** for men in things
Heb 8: 3 is **a** to offer both gifts and
Heb 9:27 as it is **a** for men to die
1Pe 2: 8 to which they also were **a**

APPOINTMENT (*see* APPOINT)
Job 2:11 made an **a** together to come

APPOINTS (*see* APPOINT)
Dan 5:21 **a** over it whomever He chooses
Heb 7:28 For the law **a** as high priests
Heb 7:28 law, **a** the Son who has been

APPORTION (*see* APPORTIONED)
Job 41: 6 Will they **a** him among the

APPORTIONED (*see* APPORTION)
1Ki 11:18 **a** food for him, and gave him
2Ki 12:11 the money, which had been **a**
Esth 2:12 days of their preparation **a**

APPREHEND (*see* APPREHENDED)
2Co 11:32 a garrison, desiring to **a** me

APPREHENDED (*see* APPREHEND)
Acts 12: 4 So when he had **a** him, he put
Phil 3:13 do not count myself to have **a**

APPROACH (*see* APPROACHED, APPROACHES, APPROACHING)
Lev 18: 6 None of you shall **a** anyone
Lev 18:14 You shall not **a** his wife
Lev 18:19 Also you shall not **a** a woman
Lev 21:17 may **a** to offer the bread of
Lev 21:18 who has a defect shall not **a**
Lev 21:23 near the veil or **a** the altar
Num 4:19 not die when they **a** the most
Deut 20: 2 that the priest shall **a** and
Deut 31:14 the days **a** when you must die
Josh 8: 5 are with me will **a** the city
2Sa 11:20 Why did you **a** so near to the
Job 31:37 like a prince I would **a** Him
Job 41:13 Who can **a** him with a double
Ps 65: 4 You choose, And cause to **a** You
Jer 30:21 draw near, and he shall **a** Me
Jer 30:21 who pledged his heart to **a** Me
Ezek 42:13 where the priests who **a** the
Ezek 42:14 then they may **a** that which is
Ezek 43:19 who **a** Me to minister to Me,'
Luke 8:19 could not **a** Him because of
Heb 10: 1 make those who **a** perfect

APPROACHED (*see* APPROACH)
Judg 20:24 So the children of Israel **a**
1Ki 20:13 Suddenly a prophet **a** Ahab
2Ki 16:12 the king **a** the altar and made
Ezek 18: 6 nor **a** a woman during her
Dan 6:15 Then these men **a** the king
Luke 10:40 much serving, and she **a** Him

APPROACHES (*see* APPROACH)
Lev 20:16 If a woman **a** any beast and
Luke 12:33 where no thief **a** nor moth

APPROACHING (*see* APPROACH)
Is 58: 2 they take delight in **a** God
Heb 10:25 the more as you see the Day **a**

APPROVE (*see* APPROVED, APPROVES)
Ps 49:13 posterity who **a** their sayings
Lam 3:36 the Lord does not **a**
Luke 11:48 **a** the deeds of your fathers
Rom 1:32 only do the same but also **a**
Rom 2:18 and **a** the things that are
1Co 16: 3 come, whomever you **a** by your
Phil 1:10 that you may **a** the things

APPROVED (*see* APPROVE)
Job 29:11 the eye saw, then it **a** me
Rom 14:18 acceptable to God and **a** by men
Rom 16:10 Greet Apelles, **a** in Christ
1Co 11:19 that those who are **a** may be
2Co 10:18 he who commends himself is **a**
2Co 13: 7 not that we should appear **a**
1Th 2: 4 But as we have been **a** by God
2Ti 2:15 to present yourself **a** to God

APPROVES (*see* APPROVE)
Rom 14:22 condemn himself in what he **a**

APRONS
Acts 19:12 **a** were brought from his body

AQUEDUCT
2Ki 18:17 stood by the **a** from the upper
Is 7: 3 at the end of the **a** from the
Is 36: 2 he stood by the **a** from the

AQUILA
Acts 18: 2 found a certain Jew named **A**
Acts 18:18 Priscilla and **A** were with him
Acts 18:26 When **A** and Priscilla heard him
Rom 16: 3 Greet Priscilla and **A**, my
1Co 16:19 **A** and Priscilla greet you
2Ti 4:19 Greet Prisca and **A**, and the

AR
Num 21:15 reaches to the dwelling of **A**
Num 21:28 it consumed **A** of Moab, the
Deut 2: 9 because I have given **A** to the
Deut 2:18 you are to cross over at **A**
Deut 2:29 who dwell in **A** did for me
Is 15: 1 Because in the night **A** of

ARA
1Ch 7:38 were Jephunneh, Pispah, and **A**

ARAB (*see* ARABIA, ARABS, ARBITE)
Josh 15:52 **A**, Dumah, Eshean,
Neh 2:19 Geshem the **A** heard of it,
Neh 6: 1 Tobiah, Geshem the **A**, and the

ARABAH
Deut 3:17 Sea of the **A** (the Salt Sea)
Deut 4:49 as far as the Sea of the **A**
Josh 3:16 down into the Sea of the **A**
Josh 12: 3 Sea of the **A** (the Salt Sea)
Josh 18:18 toward the north side of **A**
Josh 18:18 and went down to **A**
2Ki 14:25 of Hamath to the Sea of the **A**
Amos 6:14 Hamath to the Valley of the **A**

ARABIA (*see* ARAB, ARABIAN, ARABS)
1Ki 10:15 from all the kings of **A**, and
2Ch 9:14 And all the kings of **A** and
Is 21:13 The burden against **A**
Is 21:13 forest in **A** you will lodge
Jer 25:24 all the kings of **A** and all the
Ezek 27:21 **A** and all the princes of Kedar
Gal 1:17 but I went to **A**, and returned
Gal 4:25 Hagar is Mount Sinai in **A**

ARABIAN (*see* ARABIA, ARABIANS)
Is 13:20 nor will the **A** pitch tents
Jer 3: 2 like an **A** in the wilderness

ARABIANS (*see* ARABIAN)
2Ch 17:11 the **A** brought him flocks,
2Ch 21:16 and the **A** who were near the
2Ch 22: 1 **A** into the camp had killed
2Ch 26: 7 against the **A** who lived in

ARABS (*see* ARAB, ARABIA)
Neh 4: 7 when Sanballat, Tobiah, the **A**
Acts 2:11 Cretans and **A**

ARAD
Num 21: 1 When the king of **A**, the
Num 33:40 Now the king of **A**, the
Josh 12:14 the king of **A**, one
Judg 1:16 lies in the South near **A**
1Ch 8:15 Zebadiah, **A**, Eder,

ARAH
1Ch 7:39 The sons of Ulla were **A**,
Ezra 2: 5 the people of **A**, seven
Neh 6:18 of Shechaniah the son of **A**
Neh 7:10 the children of **A**, six

ARAM (*see* ARAMAIC, MESOPOTAMIA, SYRIA)
Gen 10:22 Asshur, Arphaxad, Lud, and **A**
Gen 10:23 The sons of **A** were Uz, Hul,
Gen 22:21 Kemuel the father of **A**,
Num 23: 7 of Moab has brought me from **A**
1Ch 1:17 Asshur, Arphaxad, Lud, **A**
1Ch 7:34 Ahi, Rohgah, Jehubbah, and **A**

ARAMAIC (*see* ARAM)
2Ki 18:26 servants in the **A** language
Ezra 4: 7 was written in **A** script, and
Ezra 4: 7 into the **A** language
Is 36:11 servants in the **A** language
Dan 2: 4 spoke to the king in **A**, "O

ARAN
Gen 36:28 sons of Dishan: Uz and **A**.
1Ch 1:42 sons of Dishan were Uz and **A**

ARARAT
Gen 8: 4 month, on the mountains of **A**
2Ki 19:37 escaped into the land of **A**
Is 37:38 escaped into the land of **A**
Jer 51:27 **A**, Minni, and Ashchenaz

ARAUNAH (*see* ORNAN)
2Sa 24:16 floor of **A** the Jebusite
2Sa 24:18 floor of **A** the Jebusite
2Sa 24:20 Now **A** looked, and saw the king
2Sa 24:20 So **A** went out and bowed before
2Sa 24:21 Then **A** said, "Why has my
2Sa 24:22 Now **A** said to David, "Let my
2Sa 24:23 king, **A** has given to the king
2Sa 24:23 And **A** said to the king,
2Sa 24:24 Then the king said to **A**, "No

ARBA
Josh 14:15 for **A** was the greatest man
Josh 15:13 which is Hebron (**A** was the
Josh 21:11 gave them Kirjath **A** (**A**

ARBATHITE
2Sa 23:31 Abi-Albon the **A**, Azmaveth the
1Ch 11:32 brooks of Gaash, Abiel the **A**

ARBITE (*see* ARAB)
2Sa 23:35 the Carmelite, Paarai the **A**

ARBITRATE (*see* ARBITRATOR)
Is 47: 3 and I will not **a** with a man

ARBITRATOR (*see* ARBITRATE)
Luke 12:14 Me a judge or an **a** over you

ARCHANGEL
1Th 4:16 shout, with the voice of an **a**
Jude 9 Yet Michael the **a**, in

ARCHELAUS
Matt 2:22 But when he heard that **A** was

ARCHER (*see* ARCHERS)
Gen 21:20 wilderness, and became an **a**
Jer 51: 3 her let the **a** bend his bow

ARCHERS (*see* ARCHER)
Gen 49:23 The **a** have bitterly grieved
Judg 5:11 Far from the noise of the **a**
1Sa 31: 3 and the **a** hit him, and he was
1Sa 31: 3 was severely wounded by the **a**
2Sa 11:24 The **a** shot from the wall at
1Ch 8:40 were mighty men of valor—**a**.
1Ch 10: 3 and the **a** hit him, and he was
1Ch 10: 3 and he was wounded by the **a**
2Ch 35:23 And the **a** shot King Josiah
Job 16:13 His **a** surround me
Is 21:17 remainder of the number of **a**
Is 22: 3 they are captured by the **a**
Jer 50:29 the **a** against Babylon

ARCHIPPUS
Col 4:17 And say to **A**, "Take heed to
Phm 2 **A** our fellow soldier, and to

ARCHITE (*see* ARCHITES)
2Sa 15:32 that there was Hushai the **A**
2Sa 16:16 so it was, when Hushai the **A**
2Sa 17: 5 Now call Hushai the **A** also
2Sa 17:14 The counsel of Hushai the **A**
1Ch 27:33 Hushai the **A** was the king's

ARCHITES (*see* ARCHITE)
Josh 16: 2 border of the **A** at Ataroth

ARCHIVES
Ezra 6: 1 and a search was made in the **a**

ARCHWAY (*see* ARCHWAYS)
Ezek 40:22 and its **a** was in front of it
Ezek 40:26 its **a** was in front of them

ARCHWAYS (*see* ARCHWAY)
Ezek 40:16 **a** on the inside of the
Ezek 40:21 side, its gateposts and its **a**
Ezek 40:22 Its windows and those of its **a**
Ezek 40:24 **a** according to these same
Ezek 40:25 and in its **a** all around like
Ezek 40:29 its **a** were according to these
Ezek 40:29 in it and in its **a** all around
Ezek 40:30 There were **a** all around,
Ezek 40:31 Its **a** faced the outer court,
Ezek 40:33 its **a** were according to these
Ezek 40:33 in it and in its **a** all around
Ezek 40:34 Its **a** faced the outer court,
Ezek 40:36 its gateposts, and its **a**

ARD (*see* ARDITES)
Gen 46:21 Rosh, Muppim, Huppim, and **A**
Num 26:40 And the sons of Bela were **A**
Num 26:40 of **A**, the family of the

ARDITES (*see* ARD)
Num 26:40 of Ard, the family of the **A**

ARDON
1Ch 2:18 Jesher, Shobab, and **A**

ARE (*see* PREFACE)

AREA (*see* AREAS)
1Sa 27:10 the southern **a** of Judah, or
1Sa 27:10 **a** of the Jerahmeelites, or
1Sa 27:10 the southern **a** of the Kenites
1Sa 30:14 southern **a** of the Cherethites
1Sa 30:14 and of the southern **a** of Caleb
1Ch 5:10 the entire **a** east of Gilead
1Ch 11: 8 Millo to the surrounding **a**
2Ch 3: 9 the upper **a** with gold
Ezek 43:12 The whole **a** surrounding the
Ezek 45: 5 An **a** twenty-five thousand

Ezek 45: 6 **a** five thousand cubits wide
Ezek 48:13 the Levites shall have an **a**
Ezek 48:22 the **a** between the border of

AREAS (*see* AREA)
Josh 13:32 These are the **a** which Moses
Josh 14: 1 These are the **a** which the
Ezek 42:20 the holy **a** from the common

ARELI (*see* ARELITES)
Gen 46:16 Ezbon, Eri, Arodi, and **A**
Num 26:17 of **A**, the family of the

ARELITES (*see* ARELI)
Num 26:17 of Areli, the family of the **A**

AREOPAGITE (*see* AREOPAGUS)
Acts 17:34 among them Dionysius the **A**

AREOPAGUS (*see* AREOPAGITE)
Acts 17:19 him and brought him to the **A**
Acts 17:22 stood in the midst of the **A**

ARETAS
2Co 11:32 under **A** the king, was

ARGOB
Deut 3: 4 cities, all the region of **A**
Deut 3:13 (All the region of **A**, with
Deut 3:14 took all the region of **A**, as
1Ki 4:13 the region of **A** in Bashan
2Ki 15:25 king's house, along with **A**

ARGUING (*see* ARGUMENTS)
Job 6:25 But what does your **a** prove

ARGUMENTS (*see* ARGUING)
Job 23: 4 Him, and fill my mouth with **a**
2Co 10: 5 casting down **a** and every high
1Ti 6: 4 **a** over words, from which come

ARIDAI
Esth 9: 9 Parmashta, Arisai, **A**, and

ARIDATHA
Esth 9: 8 Poratha, Adalia, **A**,

ARIEH
2Ki 15:25 house, along with Argob and **A**

ARIEL (*see* JERUSALEM)
Ezra 8:16 Then I sent for Eliezer, **A**
Is 29: 1 Woe to **A**, to **A**, the city
Is 29: 2 Yet I will distress **A**
Is 29: 2 and it shall be to Me as **A**
Is 29: 7 nations who fight against **A**

ARIGHT
Ps 50:23 **a** I will show the salvation
Ps 78: 8 that did not set its heart **a**
Prov 11: 5 will direct his way **a**, but
Jer 8: 6 but they do not speak **a**

ARIMATHEA
Matt 27:57 there came a rich man from **A**
Mark 15:43 Joseph of **A**, a prominent
Luke 23:51 He was from **A**, a city of the
John 19:38 After this, Joseph of **A**,

ARIOCH
Gen 14: 1 of Shinar, **A** king of Ellasar,
Gen 14: 9 Shinar, and **A** king of Ellasar
Dan 2:14 and wisdom Daniel answered **A**
Dan 2:15 said to **A** the king's captain,
Dan 2:15 Then **A** made the decision
Dan 2:24 Therefore Daniel went to **A**
Dan 2:25 Then **A** quickly brought Daniel

ARISAI
Esth 9: 9 Parmashta, **A**, Aridai, and

ARISE (*see* ARISEN, ARISES, AROSE)
Gen 13:17 **A**, walk in the land through
Gen 19:15 **A**, take your wife and your two
Gen 21:18 **A**, lift up the lad and hold
Gen 27:19 please **a**, sit and eat of my
Gen 27:31 Let my father **a** and eat of his
Gen 27:43 **a**, flee to my brother Laban
Gen 28: 2 **A**, go to Padan Aram, to the
Gen 31:13 Now **a**, get out of this land,
Gen 35: 1 **A**, go up to Bethel and dwell
Gen 35: 3 Then let us **a** and go up to
Gen 41:30 seven years of famine will **a**
Gen 43: 8 the lad with me, and we will **a**
Gen 43:13 Take your brother also, and **a**
Deut 9:12 Then the LORD said to me, **A**
Deut 10:11 Then the LORD said to me, **A**
Deut 17: 8 your gates, then you shall **a**
Josh 1: 2 Now therefore, **a**, go over
Josh 8: 1 people of war with you, and **a**
Judg 5:12 **A**, Barak, and lead your
Judg 7: 9 **A**, go down against the camp,
Judg 7:15 **A**, for the LORD has delivered
Judg 18: 9 **A**, let us go up against them
1Sa 9: 3 the servants with you, and **a**
1Sa 16:12 **A**, anoint him
1Sa 23: 4 **A**, go down to Keilah
2Sa 2:14 Let the young men now **a** and
2Sa 2:14 Let them **a**
2Sa 3:21 I will **a** and go, and gather all
2Sa 13:15 **A**, be gone
2Sa 15:14 **A**, and let us flee
2Sa 17: 1 thousand men, and I will **a**
2Sa 17:21 **A** and cross over the water
2Sa 19: 7 Now therefore, **a**, go out and
1Ki 3:12 any like you **a** after you
1Ki 14: 2 Please **a**, and disguise
1Ki 14:12 **A** therefore, go to your own
1Ki 17: 9 **A**, go to Zarephath, which
1Ki 19: 5 **A** and eat
1Ki 19: 7 **A** and eat, because the journey
1Ki 21: 7 **A** and eat food, and let your
1Ki 21:15 **A**, take possession of the
1Ki 21:18 **A**, go down to meet Ahab king
2Ki 1: 3 **A**, go up to meet the
2Ki 8: 1 **A** and go, you and your
2Ki 23:25 after him did any **a** like him
1Ch 22:16 **A** and begin working, and the
1Ch 22:19 Therefore **a** and build the
2Ch 6:41 Now therefore, **a**, O LORD God,
Ezra 10: 4 **A**, for this matter is your
Neh 2:20 we His servants will **a** and
Esth 4:14 deliverance will **a** for the
Job 7: 4 down, I say, 'When shall I **a**
Job 19:18 I **a**, and they speak against me
Ps 3: 7 **A**, O LORD
Ps 7: 6 **A**, O LORD, in Your anger
Ps 9:19 **A**, O LORD, Do not let man
Ps 10:12 **A**, O LORD
Ps 12: 5 of the needy, Now I will **a**
Ps 17:13 **A**, O LORD, Confront him, cast
Ps 44:23 Why do You sleep, O Lord? **A**!
Ps 44:26 **A** for our help, And redeem us
Ps 68: 1 Let God **a**, Let His enemies be
Ps 74:22 **A**, O God, plead Your own
Ps 78: 6 be born, That they may **a** and
Ps 82: 8 **A**, O God, judge the earth
Ps 88:10 Shall the dead **a** and praise
Ps 102:13 You will **a** and have mercy on
Ps 109:28 When they **a**, let them be
Ps 132: 8 **A**, O LORD, to Your resting
Prov 28:12 but when the wicked **a**, men
Prov 28:28 When the wicked **a**, men hide
Is 21: 5 **A**, you princes, anoint the
Is 23:12 **A**, cross over to Cyprus
Is 26:19 my dead body they shall **a**
Is 31: 2 but will **a** against the house
Is 49: 7 Kings shall see and **a**, princes
Is 52: 2 yourself from the dust, **a**
Is 60: 1 **A**, shine
Is 60: 2 but the LORD will **a** over you
Jer 1:17 prepare yourself and **a**, and
Jer 2:27 trouble they will say, '**A**
Jer 2:28 Let them **a**, if they can save
Jer 6: 4 **a**, and let us go up at noon
Jer 6: 5 **A**, and let us go by night, and
Jer 13: 4 is around your waist, and **a**
Jer 13: 6 **A**, go to the Euphrates, and
Jer 18: 2 **A** and go down to the potter's
Jer 31: 6 will cry on Mount Ephraim, '**A**
Jer 46:16 And they said, '**A**
Jer 49:28 **A**, go up to Kedar, and
Jer 49:31 **A**, go up to the wealthy
Lam 2:19 **A**, cry out in the night, at
Ezek 3:22 **A**, go out into the plain, and
Ezek 38:10 thoughts will **a** in your mind
Dan 2:39 But after you shall **a** another
Dan 7: 5 **A**, devour much flesh
Dan 7:17 which **a** out of the earth
Dan 7:24 who shall **a** from this kingdom
Dan 8:22 shall **a** out of that nation
Dan 8:23 fullness, a king shall **a**,
Dan 11: 2 more kings will **a** in Persia
Dan 11: 3 Then a mighty king shall **a**
Dan 11: 7 one shall **a** in his place, who
Dan 11:20 There shall **a** in his place
Dan 11:21 place shall **a** a vile person
Dan 12:13 will **a** to your inheritance at
Hos 10:14 shall **a** among your people
Obad 1 **A**, and let us rise up against
Jon 1: 2 **A**, go to Nineveh, that great
Jon 1: 6 **A**, call on your God
Jon 3: 2 **A**, go to Nineveh, that great
Mic 2:10 **A** and depart, for this is not
Mic 4:13 **A** and thresh, O daughter of
Mic 6: 1 **A**, plead your case before the
Mic 7: 8 when I fall, I will **a**
Hab 2:19 to silent stone, '**A**
Mal 4: 2 **a** with healing in His wings
Matt 2:13 **A**, take the young Child and
Matt 2:20 **A**, take the young Child and
Matt 9: 5 forgiven you,' or to say, '**A**
Matt 9: 6 **A**, take up your bed, and go to
Matt 17: 7 **A**, and do not be afraid
Matt 24:24 and false prophets will **a** and
Mark 2: 9 forgiven you,' or to say, '**A**
Mark 2:11 I say to you, **a**, take up your
Mark 5:41 Little girl, I say to you, **a**
Luke 5:24 I say to you, **a**, take up your
Luke 6: 8 **A** and stand here
Luke 7:14 Young man, I say to you, **a**
Luke 8:54 Little girl, **a**.
Luke 15:18 I will **a** and go to my father,
Luke 17:19 **A**, go your way
Luke 24:38 And why do doubts **a** in your
John 14:31 **A**, let us go from here
Acts 8:26 **A** and go toward the south
Acts 9: 6 **A** and go into the city, and you
Acts 9:11 **A** and go to the street called
Acts 9:34 **A** and make your bed
Acts 9:40 Tabitha, **a**.
Acts 10:20 **A** therefore, go down and go
Acts 12: 7 him up, saying, "**A** quickly
Acts 22:10 And the Lord said to me, '**A**
Acts 22:16 **A** and be baptized, and wash
Eph 5:14 **a** from the dead, and Christ

ARISEN (*see* ARISE)
Deut 34:10 **a** in Israel a prophet like
Dan 11: 4 And when he has **a**, his kingdom
John 7:52 prophet has **a** out of Galilee

ARISES (*see* ARISE)
Deut 13: 1 If there **a** among you a
Deut 17: 8 If a matter **a** which is too
Job 30:12 At my right hand the rabble **a**
Ps 104:22 When the sun **a**, they gather
Ps 112: 4 there **a** light in the darkness
Is 2:19 when He **a** to shake the earth
Is 2:21 when He **a** to shake the earth
Is 47:11 not know from where it **a**
Hab 1: 3 is strife, and contention **a**
Matt 13:21 **a** because of the word,
Mark 4:17 **a** for the word's sake,
Heb 7:15 there **a** another priest

ARISTARCHUS
Acts 19:29 having seized Gaius and **A**
Acts 20: 4 also **A** and Secundus of the
Acts 27: 2 **A**, a Macedonian of
Col 4:10 **A** my fellow prisoner greets
Phm 24 as do Mark, **A**, Demas, Luke,

ARISTOBULUS
Rom 16:10 who are of the household of **A**

ARK
Gen 6:14 yourself an **a** of gopherwood
Gen 6:14 make rooms in the **a**, and cover
Gen 6:15 The length of the **a** shall be
Gen 6:16 shall make a window for the **a**
Gen 6:16 the door of the **a** in its side
Gen 6:18 and you shall go into the **a**
Gen 6:19 two of every sort into the **a**
Gen 7: 1 Come into the **a**, you and all
Gen 7: 7 went into the **a** because of
Gen 7: 9 they went into the **a** to Noah
Gen 7:13 sons with them, entered the **a**
Gen 7:15 they went into the **a** to Noah
Gen 7:17 increased and lifted up the **a**
Gen 7:18 and the **a** moved about on the
Gen 7:23 him in the **a** remained alive
Gen 8: 1 that were with him in the **a**
Gen 8: 4 Then the **a** rested in the
Gen 8: 6 of the **a** which he had made
Gen 8: 9 returned into the **a** to him
Gen 8: 9 her into the **a** to himself
Gen 8:10 sent the dove out from the **a**
Gen 8:13 removed the covering of the **a**
Gen 8:16 Go out of the **a**, you and your
Gen 8:19 families, went out of the **a**
Gen 9:10 of all that go out of the **a**

Gen 9:18 went out of the **a** were Shem
Ex 2: 3 she took an **a** of bulrushes
Ex 2: 5 she saw the **a** among the reeds
Ex 25:10 make an **a** of acacia wood
Ex 25:14 rings on the sides of the **a**
Ex 25:14 that the **a** may be carried by
Ex 25:15 be in the rings of the **a**
Ex 25:16 you shall put into the **a** the
Ex 25:21 mercy seat on top of the **a**
Ex 25:21 in the **a** you shall put the
Ex 25:22 are on the **a** of the Testimony
Ex 26:33 Then you shall bring the **a** of
Ex 26:34 the **a** of the Testimony in the
Ex 30: 6 before the **a** of the Testimony
Ex 30:26 and the **a** of the Testimony
Ex 31: 7 the **a** of the Testimony and the
Ex 35:12 the **a** and its poles, with the
Ex 37: 1 made the **a** of acacia wood
Ex 37: 5 rings at the sides of the **a**
Ex 37: 5 of the **a**, to bear the **a**
Ex 39:35 the **a** of the Testimony with
Ex 40: 3 in it the **a** of the Testimony
Ex 40: 3 off the **a** with the veil
Ex 40: 5 before the **a** of the Testimony
Ex 40:20 and put it into the **a**,
Ex 40:20 through the rings of the **a**
Ex 40:20 mercy seat on top of the **a**
Ex 40:21 he brought the **a** into the
Ex 40:21 off the **a** of the Testimony
Lev 16: 2 mercy seat which is on the **a**
Num 3:31 Their duty included the **a**
Num 4: 5 cover the **a** of the Testimony
Num 7:89 was on the **a** of the Testimony
Num 10:33 the **a** of the covenant of the
Num 10:35 was, whenever the **a** set out
Num 14:44 neither the **a** of the covenant
Deut 10: 1 and make yourself an **a** of wood
Deut 10: 2 you shall put them in the **a**
Deut 10: 3 So I made an **a** of acacia wood
Deut 10: 5 in the **a** which I had made
Deut 10: 8 tribe of Levi to bear the **a**
Deut 31: 9 Levi, who bore the **a** of the
Deut 31:25 who bore the **a** of the
Deut 31:26 put it beside the **a** of the
Josh 3: 3 When you see the **a** of the
Josh 3: 6 Take up the **a** of the covenant
Josh 3: 6 took up the **a** of the covenant
Josh 3: 8 bear the **a** of the covenant
Josh 3:11 the **a** of the covenant of the
Josh 3:13 who bear the **a** of the LORD
Josh 3:14 the priests bearing the **a** of
Josh 3:15 bore the **a** came to the Jordan
Josh 3:15 **a** dipped in the edge of the
Josh 3:17 the priests who bore the **a** of
Josh 4: 5 Cross over before the **a** of
Josh 4: 7 were cut off before the **a** of
Josh 4: 9 the **a** of the covenant stood
Josh 4:10 **a** stood in the midst of the
Josh 4:11 that the **a** of the LORD and the
Josh 4:16 the priests who bear the **a** of
Josh 4:18 the priests who bore the **a** of
Josh 6: 4 of rams' horns before the **a**
Josh 6: 6 Take up the **a** of the covenant
Josh 6: 6 before the **a** of the LORD
Josh 6: 7 before the **a** of the LORD
Josh 6: 8 the **a** of the covenant of the
Josh 6: 9 rear guard came after the **a**
Josh 6:11 So he had the **a** of the LORD
Josh 6:12 took up the **a** of the LORD
Josh 6:13 the **a** of the LORD went on
Josh 6:13 came after the **a** of the LORD
Josh 7: 6 on his face before the **a** of
Josh 8:33 of the **a** before the priests
Josh 8:33 who bore the **a** of the
Judg 20:27 inquired of the LORD (the **a**
1Sa 3: 3 LORD where the **a** of God was
1Sa 4: 3 Let us bring the **a** of the
1Sa 4: 4 might bring from there the **a**
1Sa 4: 4 were there with the **a** of the
1Sa 4: 5 when the **a** of the covenant of
1Sa 4: 6 they understood that the **a** of
1Sa 4:11 Also the **a** of God was
1Sa 4:13 trembled for the **a** of God
1Sa 4:17 and the **a** of God has been
1Sa 4:18 made mention of the **a** of God
1Sa 4:19 the **a** of God was captured
1Sa 4:21 because the **a** of God had
1Sa 4:22 for the **a** of God has been
1Sa 5: 1 Philistines took the **a** of God
1Sa 5: 2 Philistines took the **a** of God
1Sa 5: 3 before the **a** of the LORD
1Sa 5: 4 before the **a** of the LORD
1Sa 5: 7 The **a** of the God of Israel
1Sa 5: 8 the **a** of the God of Israel
1Sa 5: 8 Let the **a** of the God of
1Sa 5: 8 So they carried the **a** of
1Sa 5:10 sent the **a** of God to Ekron
1Sa 5:10 as the **a** of God came to Ekron
1Sa 5:10 They have brought the **a** of
1Sa 5:11 Send away the **a** of the God of
1Sa 6: 1 Now the **a** of the LORD was in
1Sa 6: 2 we do with the **a** of the LORD
1Sa 6: 3 the **a** of the God of Israel
1Sa 6: 8 Then take the **a** of the LORD
1Sa 6:11 they set the **a** of the LORD on
1Sa 6:13 their eyes and saw the **a**, and
1Sa 6:15 took down the **a** of the LORD
1Sa 6:18 they set the **a** of the LORD
1Sa 6:19 looked into the **a** of the LORD
1Sa 6:21 back the **a** of the LORD
1Sa 7: 1 took the **a** of the LORD, and
1Sa 7: 1 son to keep the **a** of the LORD
1Sa 7: 2 So it was that the **a** remained
1Sa 14:18 Bring the **a** of God here"
1Sa 14:18 the **a** of God was with the
2Sa 6: 2 up from there the **a** of God
2Sa 6: 3 So they set the **a** of God on a
2Sa 6: 4 accompanying the **a** of God
2Sa 6: 4 and Ahio went before the **a**
2Sa 6: 6 out his hand to the **a** of God
2Sa 6: 7 he died there by the **a** of God
2Sa 6: 9 How can the **a** of the LORD
2Sa 6:10 **a** of the LORD with him into
2Sa 6:11 The **a** of the LORD remained in
2Sa 6:12 him, because of the **a** of God
2Sa 6:12 brought up the **a** of God from
2Sa 6:13 when those bearing the **a** of
2Sa 6:15 of Israel brought up the **a** of
2Sa 6:16 as the **a** of the LORD came
2Sa 6:17 brought the **a** of the LORD
2Sa 7: 2 but the **a** of God dwells
2Sa 11:11 The **a** and Israel and Judah are
2Sa 15:24 bearing the **a** of the covenant
2Sa 15:24 And they set down the **a** of God
2Sa 15:25 Carry the **a** of God back into
2Sa 15:29 Abiathar carried the **a** of God
1Ki 2:26 because you carried the **a** of
1Ki 3:15 stood before the **a** of the
1Ki 6:19 to set the **a** of the covenant
1Ki 8: 1 they might bring up the **a** of
1Ki 8: 3 and the priests took up the **a**
1Ki 8: 4 brought up the **a** of the LORD
1Ki 8: 5 were with him before the **a**
1Ki 8: 6 the priests brought in the **a**
1Ki 8: 7 wings over the place of the **a**
1Ki 8: 7 cherubim overshadowed the **a**
1Ki 8: 9 There was nothing in the **a**
1Ki 8:21 I have made a place for the **a**
1Ch 6:31 after the **a** came to rest
1Ch 13: 3 let us bring the **a** of our God
1Ch 13: 5 to bring the **a** of God from
1Ch 13: 6 there the **a** of God the LORD
1Ch 13: 7 So they carried the **a** of God
1Ch 13: 9 out his hand to hold the **a**
1Ch 13:10 he put his hand to the **a**
1Ch 13:12 I bring the **a** of God to me
1Ch 13:13 David would not move the **a**
1Ch 13:14 The **a** of God remained with
1Ch 15: 1 a place for the **a** of God, and
1Ch 15: 2 No one may carry the **a** of God
1Ch 15: 2 them to carry the **a** of God
1Ch 15: 3 to bring up the **a** of the LORD
1Ch 15:12 **a** of the LORD God of Israel
1Ch 15:14 **a** of the LORD God of Israel
1Ch 15:15 of the Levites bore the **a** of
1Ch 15:23 were doorkeepers for the **a**
1Ch 15:24 trumpets before the **a** of God
1Ch 15:24 Jehiah, doorkeepers for the **a**
1Ch 15:25 went to bring up the **a** of the
1Ch 15:26 the Levites who bore the **a** of
1Ch 15:27 the Levites who bore the **a**
1Ch 15:28 all Israel brought up the **a**
1Ch 15:29 as the **a** of the covenant of
1Ch 16: 1 So they brought the **a** of God
1Ch 16: 4 before the **a** of the LORD, to
1Ch 16: 6 the **a** of the covenant of God
1Ch 16:37 brothers there before the **a**
1Ch 16:37 before the **a** regularly, as
1Ch 17: 1 but the **a** of the covenant of
1Ch 22:19 God, to bring the **a** of the
1Ch 28: 2 a house of rest for the **a** of
1Ch 28:18 overshadowed the **a** of the
2Ch 1: 4 David had brought up the **a** of
2Ch 5: 2 that they might bring the **a**
2Ch 5: 4 and the Levites took up the **a**
2Ch 5: 5 Then they brought up the **a**
2Ch 5: 6 with him before the **a**, were
2Ch 5: 7 the priests brought in the **a**
2Ch 5: 8 wings over the place of the **a**
2Ch 5: 8 cherubim overshadowed the **a**
2Ch 5: 9 ends of the poles of the **a**
2Ch 5:10 the **a** except the two tablets
2Ch 6:11 And there I have put the **a**
2Ch 6:41 You and the **a** of Your strength
2Ch 8:11 the places to which the **a** of
2Ch 35: 3 Put the holy **a** in the house
Ps 132: 8 You and the **a** of Your strength
Jer 3:16 The **a** of the covenant of the
Matt 24:38 day that Noah entered the **a**
Luke 17:27 day that Noah entered the **a**
Heb 9: 4 and the **a** of the covenant
Heb 11: 7 prepared an **a** for the saving
1Pe 3:20 Noah, while the **a** was being
Rev 11:19 the **a** of His covenant was

ARKITE
Gen 10:17 the Hivite, the **A**, and the
1Ch 1:15 the Hivite, the **A**, and the

ARM (*see* ARMED, ARMLETS, ARMPITS, ARMRESTS, ARMS)
Ex 6: 6 you with an outstretched **a**
Ex 15:16 by the greatness of Your **a**
Num 11:23 the LORD's **a** been shortened
Num 31: 3 **A** some of yourselves for the
Num 32:20 if you **a** yourselves before
Deut 4:34 hand and an outstretched **a**
Deut 5:15 hand and by an outstretched **a**
Deut 7:19 hand and the outstretched **a**
Deut 9:29 and by Your outstretched **a**
Deut 11: 2 hand and His outstretched **a**
Deut 26: 8 and with an outstretched **a**
Deut 33:20 as a lion, and tears the **a**
1Sa 2:31 that I will cut off your **a**
1Sa 2:31 the **a** of your father's house,
2Sa 1:10 bracelet that was on his **a**
1Ki 8:42 hand and Your outstretched **a**)
2Ki 17:36 power and an outstretched **a**
2Ch 6:32 hand and Your outstretched **a**
2Ch 32: 8 With him is an **a** of flesh
Job 26: 2 the **a** that has no strength
Job 31:22 Then let my **a** fall from my
Job 31:22 let my **a** be torn from the
Job 35: 9 of the **a** of the mighty
Job 38:15 and the upraised **a** is broken
Job 40: 9 Have you an **a** like God
Ps 10:15 Break the **a** of the wicked and
Ps 44: 3 Nor did their own **a** save them
Ps 44: 3 was Your right hand, Your **a**
Ps 77:15 You have with Your **a** redeemed
Ps 89:10 enemies with Your mighty **a**
Ps 89:13 You have a mighty **a**
Ps 89:21 Also My **a** shall strengthen
Ps 98: 1 His holy **a** have gained Him
Ps 136:12 and with an outstretched **a**
Song 8: 6 heart, as a seal upon your **a**
Is 9:20 eat the flesh of his own **a**
Is 17: 5 and reaps the heads with his **a**
Is 30:30 and show the descent of His **a**
Is 33: 2 Be their **a** every morning, our
Is 40:10 and His **a** shall rule for Him
Is 40:11 gather the lambs with His **a**
Is 48:14 His **a** shall be against the
Is 51: 5 and on My **a** they will trust
Is 51: 9 on strength, O **a** of the LORD
Is 51: 9 Are you not the **a** that cut
Is 52:10 holy **a** in the eyes of all the
Is 53: 1 to whom has the **a** of the LORD
Is 59:16 therefore His own **a** brought
Is 62: 8 and by the **a** of His strength
Is 63: 5 therefore My own **a** brought
Is 63:12 of Moses, with His glorious **a**
Jer 21: 5 hand and with a strong **a**, even
Jer 27: 5 power and by My outstretched **a**
Jer 32:17 great power and outstretched **a**
Jer 32:21 hand and an outstretched **a**
Jer 48:25 his **a** is broken," says the
Ezek 4: 7 your **a** shall be uncovered, and
Ezek 20:33 hand, with an outstretched **a**
Ezek 20:34 hand, with an outstretched **a**
Ezek 30:21 man, I have broken the **a** of

Ezek 31:17 those who were its strong a
Zech 11:17 sword shall be against his a
Zech 11:17 his a shall completely wither
Luke 1:51 has shown strength with His a
John 12:38 to whom has the a of the LORD
Acts 13:17 with an uplifted a He brought
1Pe 4: 1 a yourselves also with the

ARMAGEDDON
Rev 16:16 the place called in Hebrew, A

ARMED (*see* ARM)
Gen 14:14 he a his three hundred and
Num 31: 5 twelve thousand a for war
Num 32:17 but we ourselves will be a
Num 32:21 all your a men cross over the
Num 32:27 over, every man a for war
Num 32:29 every man a for battle before
Num 32:30 do not cross over a with you
Num 32:32 We will cross over a before
Deut 3:18 over a before your brethren
Josh 1:14 pass before your brethren a
Josh 4:12 over a before the children of
Josh 6: 7 and let him who is a advance
Josh 6: 9 The a men went before the
Josh 6:13 the a men went before them
Judg 7:11 to the outpost of the a men
Judg 18:11 a with weapons of war
Judg 18:16 The six hundred men a with
Judg 18:17 were a with weapons of war
1Sa 17: 5 he was a with a coat of mail,
2Sa 22:40 For You have a me with
2Sa 23: 7 them must be a with iron and
1Ch 12: 2 a with bows, using both the
1Ch 12:24 eight hundred a for war
1Ch 12:37 twenty thousand a for battle
1Ch 20: 1 Joab led out the a forces
2Ch 17:17 thousand men a with bow and
2Ch 28:14 So the a men left the
Ps 18:39 For You have a me with
Ps 78: 9 children of Ephraim, being a
Prov 6:11 and your need like an a man
Prov 24:34 and your want like an a man
Is 15: 4 therefore the a soldiers of
Luke 11:21 When a strong man, fully a

ARMIES (*see* ARMY)
Ex 6:26 of Egypt according to their a
Ex 7: 4 hand on Egypt and bring My a
Ex 12:17 a out of the land of Egypt
Ex 12:41 a of the LORD went out from
Ex 12:51 of Egypt according to their a
Num 1: 3 shall number them by their a
Num 1:52 according to their a
Num 2: 3 camp according to their a
Num 2: 9 a of the forces with Judah
Num 2:10 Reuben according to their a
Num 2:16 a of the forces with Reuben
Num 2:18 Ephraim according to their a
Num 2:24 a of the forces with Ephraim
Num 2:25 side according to their a
Num 2:32 a of the forces were six
Num 10:14 first according to their a
Num 10:18 set out according to their a
Num 10:22 set out according to their a
Num 10:25 set out according to their a
Num 10:28 Israel, according to their a
Num 33: 1 a under the hand of Moses
Deut 20: 9 of the a to lead the people
Josh 10: 5 went up, they and all their a
Josh 11: 4 they and all their a with them
Judg 8:10 and their a with them, about
1Sa 17: 1 their a together to battle
1Sa 17: 8 cried out to the a of Israel
1Sa 17:10 I defy the a of Israel this
1Sa 17:23 from the a of the Philistines
1Sa 17:26 defy the a of the living God
1Sa 17:36 the a of the living God
1Sa 17:45 the God of the a of Israel
1Sa 23: 3 the a of the Philistines
1Sa 28: 1 their a together for war, to
1Sa 29: 1 together all their a at Aphek
1Ki 2: 5 commanders of the a of Israel
1Ki 15:20 his a against the cities of
2Ki 25:23 all the captains of the a
2Ki 25:26 and the captains of the a
2Ch 16: 4 his a against the cities of
Job 25: 3 Is there any number to His a
Ps 44: 9 You do not go out with our a
Ps 60:10 who did not go out with our a
Ps 68:12 Kings of a flee, they flee,
Ps 108:11 who did not go out with our a
Is 34: 2 His fury against all their a
Jer 40: 7 the a who were in the fields
Matt 22: 7 And he sent out his a,
Luke 21:20 see Jerusalem surrounded by a
Heb 11:34 to flight the a of the aliens
Rev 19:14 the a in heaven, clothed in
Rev 19:19 of the earth, and their a,

ARMLETS (*see* ARM)
Num 31:50 a and bracelets and signet

ARMONI
2Sa 21: 8 So the king took A and

ARMOR (*see* ARMORBEARER, ARMORY)
1Sa 14: 1 the young man who bore his a
1Sa 14: 6 the young man who bore his a
1Sa 17:38 Saul clothed David with his a
1Sa 17:39 fastened his sword to his a
1Sa 17:54 but he put his a in his tent
1Sa 18: 4 gave it to David, with his a
1Sa 31: 9 head and stripped off his a
1Sa 31:10 Then they put his a in the
2Sa 2:21 and take his a for yourself
2Sa 18:15 Joab's a surrounded Absalom
2Sa 20: 8 Joab was dressed in battle a
1Ki 10:25 silver and gold, garments, a
1Ki 20:11 his a boast like the one who
1Ki 22:34 between the joints of his a
1Ch 10: 9 him and took his head and his a
1Ch 10:10 Then they put his a in the
2Ch 9:24 silver and gold, garments, a
2Ch 18:33 between the joints of his a
2Ch 26:14 spears, helmets, body a,
Neh 4:16 shields, the bows, and wore a
Is 22: 8 looked in that day to the a
Is 45: 1 him and loose the a of kings
Jer 46: 4 the spears, put on the a
Jer 51: 3 up against her in his a
Luke 11:22 all his a in which he trusted
Rom 13:12 let us put on the a of light
2Co 6: 7 by the a of righteousness on
Eph 6:11 Put on the whole a of God
Eph 6:13 take up the whole a of God

ARMORBEARER (*see* ARMOR)
Judg 9:54 to the young man, his a, and
1Sa 14: 7 So his a said to him, "Do
1Sa 14:12 called to Jonathan and his a
1Sa 14:12 So Jonathan said to his a
1Sa 14:13 and knees with his a after him
1Sa 14:13 after him, his a killed them
1Sa 14:14 his a made was about twenty
1Sa 14:17 and his a were not there
1Sa 16:21 greatly, and he became his a
1Sa 31: 4 Then Saul said to his a
1Sa 31: 4 But his a would not, for he
1Sa 31: 5 when his a saw that Saul was
1Sa 31: 6 Saul, his three sons, his a
2Sa 23:37 Naharai the Beerothite (a of
1Ch 10: 4 Then Saul said to his a
1Ch 10: 4 But his a would not, for he
1Ch 10: 5 when his a saw that Saul was
1Ch 11:39 Naharai the Berothite (the a

ARMORY (*see* ARMOR)
2Ki 20:13 ointment, and all his a
Neh 3:19 to the A at the buttress
Song 4: 4 of David, built for an a, on
Is 39: 2 ointment, and all his a
Jer 50:25 The LORD has opened His a

ARMPITS (*see* ARM)
Jer 38:12 clothes and rags under your a

ARMRESTS (*see* ARM)
1Ki 10:19 there were a on either side
1Ki 10:19 two lions stood beside the a
2Ch 9:18 there were a on either side
2Ch 9:18 two lions stood beside the a

ARMS (*see* ARM)
Gen 49:24 the a of his hands were made
Deut 33:27 are the everlasting a
Judg 15:14 a became like flax that is
Judg 16:12 them off his a like a thread
2Sa 22:35 so that my a can bend a bow
1Ki 17:19 So he took him out of her a
2Ki 3:21 all who were able to bear a
2Ki 9:24 and shot Jehoram between his a
Ezra 4:23 by force of a made them cease
Job 39:21 gallops into the clash of a
Ps 18:32 It is God who a me with
Ps 18:34 So that my a can bend a bow
Ps 37:17 For the a of the wicked shall
Ps 129: 7 he who binds sheaves, his a
Prov 5:20 in the a of a seductress
Prov 31:17 and strengthens her a
Is 44:12 it with the strength of his a
Is 49:22 bring your sons in their a
Is 51: 5 My a will judge the peoples
Ezek 13:20 I will tear them from your a
Ezek 30:22 of Egypt, and will break his a
Ezek 30:24 the a of the king of Babylon
Ezek 30:24 but I will break Pharaoh's a
Ezek 30:25 the a of the king of Babylon
Ezek 30:25 but the a of Pharaoh shall
Dan 2:32 a of silver, its belly and
Dan 10: 6 like torches of fire, his a
Hos 7:15 and strengthened their a, yet
Hos 11: 3 walk, taking them by their a
Mark 9:36 He had taken him in His a
Mark 10:16 And He took them up in His a
Luke 2:28 he took Him up in his a and

ARMY (*see* ARMIES)
Gen 21:22 the commander of his a,
Gen 21:32 the commander of his a, and
Gen 26:26 the commander of his a
Ex 14: 4 Pharaoh and over all his a
Ex 14: 9 his horsemen and his a, and
Ex 14:17 Pharaoh and over all his a
Ex 14:24 a of the Egyptians through
Ex 14:24 and He troubled the a of the
Ex 14:28 all the a of Pharaoh that
Ex 15: 4 his a He has cast into the
Num 2: 4 And his a was numbered at
Num 2: 6 And his a was numbered at
Num 2: 8 And his a was numbered at
Num 2:11 And his a was numbered at
Num 2:13 And his a was numbered at
Num 2:15 And his a was numbered at
Num 2:19 his a was numbered at forty
Num 2:21 And his a was numbered at
Num 2:23 And his a was numbered at
Num 2:26 And his a was numbered at
Num 2:28 And his a was numbered at
Num 2:30 And his a was numbered at
Num 10:14 over their a was Nahshon the
Num 10:15 Over the a of the tribe of
Num 10:16 over the a of the tribe of
Num 10:18 over their a was Elizur the
Num 10:19 Over the a of the tribe of
Num 10:20 over the a of the tribe of
Num 10:22 over their a was Elishama the
Num 10:23 Over the a of the tribe of
Num 10:24 over the a of the tribe of
Num 10:25 over their a was Ahiezer the
Num 10:26 Over the a of the tribe of
Num 10:27 over the a of the tribe of
Num 31:14 with the officers of the a
Num 31:48 were over thousands of the a
Deut 11: 4 what He did to the a of Egypt
Deut 23: 9 When the a goes out against
Josh 5:14 but as Commander of the a of
Josh 5:15 the LORD's a said to Joshua
Josh 8:13 all the a that was on the
Judg 4: 2 commander of his a was Sisera
Judg 4: 7 the commander of Jabin's a
Judg 4:15 all his a with the edge of
Judg 4:16 the a as far as Harosheth
Judg 4:16 all the a of Sisera fell by
Judg 7:21 and the whole a ran and cried
Judg 7:22 the a fled to Beth Acacia,
Judg 8: 6 should give bread to your a
Judg 8:10 who were left of all the a of
Judg 8:11 he attacked the a while the
Judg 8:12 and routed the whole a
Judg 9:29 Increase your a and come out
1Sa 4: 2 men of the a in the field
1Sa 12: 9 commander of the a of Hazor
1Sa 14:48 And he gathered an a and
1Sa 14:50 of the commander of his a was
1Sa 17:20 a was going out to the fight
1Sa 17:21 battle array, a against a
1Sa 17:22 supply keeper, ran to the a
1Sa 17:48 ran toward the a to meet the
1Sa 17:55 Abner, the commander of the a
1Sa 26: 5 Ner, the commander of his a
1Sa 28: 5 When Saul saw the a of the
1Sa 28:19 a of Israel into the hand of
1Sa 29: 6 in the a is good in my sight
2Sa 2: 8 of Ner, commander of Saul's a
2Sa 8: 9 all the a of Hadadezer,
2Sa 8:16 son of Zeruiah was over the a

2Sa 10: 7 all the **a** of the mighty men
2Sa 10:16 **a** went before them
2Sa 10:18 the commander of their **a**, who
2Sa 17:25 of the **a** instead of Joab
2Sa 19:13 **a** before me continually in
2Sa 20:23 was over all the **a** of Israel
2Sa 24: 2 of the **a** who was with him
2Sa 24: 4 against the captains of the **a**
2Sa 24: 4 the captains of the **a** went
1Ki 1:19 Joab the commander of the **a**
1Ki 1:25 and the commanders of the **a**
1Ki 2:32 commander of the **a** of Israel
1Ki 2:32 commander of the **a** of Judah
1Ki 2:35 in his place over the **a**, and
1Ki 4: 4 son of Jehoiada, over the **a**
1Ki 11:15 the **a** had gone up to bury the
1Ki 11:21 commander of the **a** was dead
1Ki 16:16 Omri, the commander of the **a**
1Ki 20:19 the **a** which followed them
1Ki 20:25 you shall muster an **a** like
1Ki 20:25 like the **a** that you have lost
1Ki 22:36 a shout went throughout the **a**
2Ki 3: 9 there was no water for the **a**
2Ki 4:13 or to the commander of the **a**
2Ki 5: 1 commander of the **a** of the
2Ki 6:14 chariots and a great **a** there
2Ki 6:15 and went out, there was an **a**
2Ki 6:24 of Syria gathered all his **a**
2Ki 7: 4 to the **a** of the Syrians
2Ki 7: 6 **a** of the Syrians to hear the
2Ki 7: 6 the noise of a great **a**
2Ki 7:14 the direction of the Syrian **a**
2Ki 9: 5 the captains of the **a** sitting
2Ki 11:15 the officers of the **a**, and
2Ki 13: 7 For He left of the **a** of
2Ki 18:17 with a great **a** against
2Ki 25: 1 and all his **a** came against
2Ki 25: 5 But the **a** of the Chaldeans
2Ki 25: 5 All his **a** was scattered from
2Ki 25:10 all the **a** of the Chaldeans
2Ki 25:19 **a** who mustered the people of
1Ch 7: 4 troops of the **a** ready for war
1Ch 7:40 among the **a** fit for battle
1Ch 11:15 and the **a** of the Philistines
1Ch 12:14 of Gad, captains of the **a**
1Ch 12:21 they were captains in the **a**
1Ch 12:22 a great **a**, like the **a** of God
1Ch 14:16 they drove back the **a** of the
1Ch 18: 9 **a** of Hadadezer king of Zobah
1Ch 18:15 son of Zeruiah was over the **a**
1Ch 19: 8 all the **a** of the mighty men
1Ch 19:16 **a** went before them
1Ch 19:18 the commander of the **a**
1Ch 25: 1 and the captains of the **a**
1Ch 26:26 and the captains of the **a**
1Ch 27: 3 of the **a** for the first month
1Ch 27: 5 the **a** for the third month was
1Ch 27:34 of the king's **a** was Joab
2Ch 13: 3 with an **a** of valiant warriors
2Ch 14: 8 Asa had an **a** of three hundred
2Ch 14: 9 with an **a** of a million men
2Ch 14:13 before the LORD and His **a**
2Ch 16: 7 therefore the **a** of the king
2Ch 16: 8 the Lubim not a huge **a** with
2Ch 20:21 as they went out before the **a**
2Ch 23:14 who were set over the **a**, and
2Ch 24:23 **a** of Syria came up against
2Ch 24:24 For the **a** of the Syrians came
2Ch 24:24 very great **a** into their hand
2Ch 25: 7 do not let the **a** of Israel go
2Ch 25:13 of the **a** which Amaziah had
2Ch 26:11 Moreover Uzziah had an **a** of
2Ch 26:13 was an **a** of three hundred
2Ch 26:14 for them, for the entire **a**
2Ch 28: 9 the **a** that came to Samaria
2Ch 33:11 the **a** of the king of Assyria
Neh 2: 9 had sent captains of the **a**
Neh 4: 2 the **a** of Samaria, and said,
Job 29:25 so I dwelt as a king in the **a**
Ps 27: 3 Though an **a** should encamp
Ps 33:16 by the multitude of an **a**
Ps 136:15 his **a** in the Red Sea, For His
Song 6: 4 awesome as an **a** with banners
Song 6:10 Awesome as an **a** with banners
Is 13: 4 musters the **a** for battle
Is 36: 2 great **a** from Lachish to King
Is 43:17 the chariot and horse, the **a**
Jer 32: 2 **a** besieged Jerusalem, and
Jer 34: 1 king of Babylon and all his **a**
Jer 34: 7 **a** fought against Jerusalem
Jer 34:21 **a** which has gone back from
Jer 35:11 of the **a** of the Chaldeans
Jer 35:11 fear of the **a** of the Syrians
Jer 37: 5 Then Pharaoh's **a** came up from
Jer 37: 7 Pharaoh's **a** which has come up
Jer 37:10 **a** of the Chaldeans who fight
Jer 37:11 when the **a** of the Chaldeans
Jer 37:11 for fear of Pharaoh's **a**,
Jer 38: 3 of the king of Babylon's **a**
Jer 39: 1 and all his **a** came against
Jer 39: 5 the Chaldean **a** pursued them
Jer 46: 2 Concerning the **a** of Pharaoh
Jer 46:22 they shall march with an **a**
Jer 51: 3 utterly destroy all her **a**
Jer 52: 4 and all his **a** came against
Jer 52: 8 But the **a** of the Chaldeans
Jer 52: 8 All his **a** was scattered from
Jer 52:14 all the **a** of the Chaldeans
Jer 52:25 **a** who mustered the people of
Ezek 1:24 tumult like the noise of an **a**
Ezek 17:17 Pharaoh with his mighty **a**
Ezek 26: 7 and an **a** with many people
Ezek 27:10 were in your **a** as men of war
Ezek 27:11 your **a** were on your walls all
Ezek 29:18 his **a** to labor strenuously
Ezek 29:18 yet neither he nor his **a**
Ezek 29:19 will be the wages for his **a**
Ezek 32:31 Pharaoh and all his **a**, slain
Ezek 37:10 feet, an exceedingly great **a**
Ezek 38: 4 lead you out, with all your **a**
Ezek 38:13 gathered your **a** to take booty
Ezek 38:15 a great company and a mighty **a**
Dan 3:20 in his **a** to bind Shadrach
Dan 4:35 His will in the **a** of heaven
Dan 8:12 an **a** was given over to the
Dan 11: 7 who shall come with an **a**
Dan 11:13 of some years with a great **a**
Dan 11:25 of the South with a great **a**
Dan 11:25 with a very great and mighty **a**
Dan 11:26 his **a** shall be swept away, and
Joel 2:11 LORD gives voice before His **a**
Joel 2:20 far from you the northern **a**
Joel 2:25 my great **a** which I sent among
Zech 9: 8 My house because of the **a**
Rev 9:16 Now the number of the **a** of
Rev 19:19 on the horse and against His **a**

ARNAN
1Ch 3:21 of Rephaiah, the sons of **A**

ARNON
Num 21:13 on the other side of the **A**
Num 21:13 for the **A** is the border of
Num 21:14 Suphah, the brooks of the **A**
Num 21:24 land from the **A** to the Jabbok
Num 21:26 from his hand as far as the **A**
Num 21:28 lords of the heights of the **A**
Num 22:36 is on the border at the **A**
Deut 2:24 and cross over the River **A**
Deut 2:36 is on the bank of the River **A**
Deut 3: 8 from the River **A** to Mount
Deut 3:12 which is by the River **A**, and
Deut 3:16 Gilead as far as the River **A**
Deut 4:48 is on the bank of the River **A**
Josh 12: 1 from the River **A** to Mount
Josh 12: 2 is on the bank of the River **A**
Josh 13: 9 is on the bank of the River **A**
Josh 13:16 is on the bank of the River **A**
Judg 11:13 from the **A** as far as the
Judg 11:18 on the other side of the **A**
Judg 11:18 for the **A** was the border of
Judg 11:22 from the **A** to the Jabbok and
Judg 11:26 along the banks of the **A**, for
2Ki 10:33 which is by the River **A**,
Is 16: 2 of Moab at the fords of the **A**
Jer 48:20 Tell it in **A**, that Moab is

AROD (*see* ARODI)
Num 26:17 of **A**, the family of the

ARODI (*see* AROD, ARODITES)
Gen 46:16 Haggi, Shuni, Ezbon, Eri, **A**

ARODITES (*see* ARODI)
Num 26:17 of Arod, the family of the **A**

AROER (*see* AROERITE)
Num 32:34 built Dibon and Ataroth and **A**
Deut 2:36 From **A**, which is on the bank
Deut 3:12 at that time, from **A**, which
Deut 4:48 from **A**, which is on the bank
Josh 12: 2 ruled half of Gilead, from **A**
Josh 13: 9 from **A** which is on the bank
Josh 13:16 Their territory was from **A**
Josh 13:25 of the Ammonites as far as **A**
Judg 11:26 Heshbon and its villages, in **A**
Judg 11:33 them from **A** as far as Minnith
1Sa 30:28 those who were in **A**, those
2Sa 24: 5 the Jordan and camped in **A**
2Ki 10:33 from **A**, which is by the River
1Ch 5: 8 son of Joel, who dwelt in **A**
Is 17: 2 The cities of **A** are forsaken
Jer 48:19 O inhabitant of **A**, stand by

AROERITE (*see* AROER)
1Ch 11:44 the sons of Hotham the **A**,

AROMA (*see* AROMAS)
Gen 8:21 the LORD smelled a soothing **a**
Ex 29:18 it is a sweet **a**, an offering
Ex 29:25 as a sweet **a** before the LORD
Ex 29:41 in the morning, for a sweet **a**
Lev 1: 9 fire, a sweet **a** to the LORD
Lev 1:13 fire, a sweet **a** to the LORD
Lev 1:17 fire, a sweet **a** to the LORD
Lev 2: 2 fire, a sweet **a** to the LORD
Lev 2: 9 fire, a sweet **a** to the LORD
Lev 2:12 on the altar for a sweet **a**
Lev 3: 5 fire, a sweet **a** to the LORD
Lev 3:16 made by fire for a sweet **a**
Lev 4:31 for a sweet **a** to the LORD
Lev 6:15 it on the altar for a sweet **a**
Lev 6:21 for a sweet **a** to the LORD
Lev 8:21 burnt sacrifice for a sweet **a**
Lev 8:28 offerings for a sweet **a**
Lev 17: 6 fat for a sweet **a** to the LORD
Lev 23:13 to the LORD, for a sweet **a**
Lev 23:18 for a sweet **a** to the LORD
Num 15: 3 to make a sweet **a** to the LORD
Num 15: 7 wine as a sweet **a** to the LORD
Num 15:10 fire, a sweet **a** to the LORD
Num 15:13 fire, a sweet **a** to the LORD
Num 15:14 a sweet **a** to the LORD, just
Num 15:24 as a sweet **a** to the LORD,
Num 18:17 for a sweet **a** to the LORD
Num 28: 2 by fire as a sweet **a** to Me
Num 28: 6 at Mount Sinai for a sweet **a**
Num 28: 8 fire, a sweet **a** to the LORD
Num 28:13 a burnt offering of sweet **a**
Num 28:24 as a sweet **a** to the LORD
Num 28:27 as a sweet **a** to the LORD
Num 29: 2 as a sweet **a** to the LORD
Num 29: 6 their ordinance, as a sweet **a**
Num 29: 8 to the LORD as a sweet **a**
Num 29:13 fire as a sweet **a** to the LORD
Num 29:36 fire as a sweet **a** to the LORD
Ezra 6:10 sweet **a** to the God of heaven
Ps 66:15 With the sweet **a** of rams
Ezek 20:28 also sent up their sweet **a**
Ezek 20:41 **a** when I bring you out from
2Co 2:16 are the **a** of death to death
2Co 2:16 other the **a** of life to life
Eph 5: 2 to God for a sweet-smelling **a**
Phil 4:18 from you, a sweet-smelling **a**

AROMAS (*see* AROMA)
Lev 26:31 the fragrance of your sweet **a**

AROSE (*see* ARISE)
Gen 19:33 she lay down or when she **a**
Gen 19:35 And the younger **a** and lay with
Gen 19:35 she lay down or when she **a**
Gen 22: 3 for the burnt offering, and **a**
Gen 24:10 And he **a** and went to
Gen 24:54 Then they **a** in the morning,
Gen 24:61 Then Rebekah and her maids **a**
Gen 25:34 then he ate and drank, **a**, and
Gen 26:31 Then they **a** early in the
Gen 31:21 He **a** and crossed the river, and
Gen 31:55 early in the morning Laban **a**
Gen 32:22 he **a** that night and took his
Gen 37: 7 Then behold, my sheaf **a** and
Gen 37:35 daughters **a** to comfort him
Gen 38:19 So she **a** and went away, and
Gen 43:15 money in their hand, and **a**
Gen 46: 5 Then Jacob **a** from Beersheba
Ex 1: 8 Now there **a** a new king over
Ex 24:13 So Moses **a** with his assistant
Josh 8: 3 So Joshua **a**, and all the
Josh 8:19 So those in ambush **a** quickly
Josh 18: 8 Then the men **a** to go away
Josh 24: 9 **a** to make war against Israel,
Judg 2:10 another generation **a** after
Judg 3:20 So he **a** from his seat
Judg 4: 9 Then Deborah **a** and went with

Judg 5: 7 Israel, until I, Deborah, **a**
Judg 5: 7 **a** a mother in Israel
Judg 6:28 city **a** early in the morning
Judg 8:21 So Gideon **a** and killed Zebah
Judg 10: 1 After Abimelech there **a** to
Judg 10: 3 After him **a** Jair, a Gileadite
Judg 13:11 So Manoah **a** and followed his
Judg 16: 3 then he **a** at midnight, took
Judg 19: 3 Then her husband **a** and went
Judg 19: 5 they **a** early in the morning
Judg 19: 8 Then he **a** early in the
Judg 19:27 her master **a** in the morning
Judg 20: 8 all the people **a** as one man
Judg 20:18 And the children of Israel **a**
Ruth 1: 6 Then she **a** with her
Ruth 3:14 and she **a** before one could
1Sa 1: 9 So Hannah **a** after they had
1Sa 3: 6 So Samuel **a** and went to Eli,
1Sa 3: 8 Then he **a** and went to Eli, and
1Sa 5: 3 Ashdod **a** early in the morning
1Sa 5: 4 when they **a** early the next
1Sa 9:26 They **a** early
1Sa 9:26 And Saul **a**, and both of them
1Sa 13:15 Then Samuel **a** and went up
1Sa 16:13 So Samuel **a** and went to Ramah
1Sa 17:35 and when it **a** against me, I
1Sa 17:48 was so, when the Philistine **a**
1Sa 17:52 the men of Israel and Judah **a**
1Sa 18:27 therefore David **a** and went, he
1Sa 20:25 And Jonathan **a**, and Abner sat
1Sa 20:34 So Jonathan **a** from the table
1Sa 20:41 David **a** from a place toward
1Sa 20:42 So he **a** and departed, and
1Sa 21:10 Then David **a** and fled that day
1Sa 23:13 his men, about six hundred, **a**
1Sa 23:16 Then Jonathan, Saul's son, **a**
1Sa 23:24 So they **a** and went to Ziph
1Sa 24: 4 And David **a** and secretly cut
1Sa 24: 8 David also **a** afterward, went
1Sa 25: 1 And David **a** and went down to
1Sa 25:41 Then she **a**, bowed her face to
1Sa 26: 2 Then Saul **a** and went down to
1Sa 26: 5 So David **a** and came to the
1Sa 27: 2 Then David **a** and went over
1Sa 28:23 So he **a** from the ground and
1Sa 31:12 all the valiant men **a** and
2Sa 2:15 So they **a** and went over by
2Sa 6: 2 And David **a** and went with all
2Sa 11: 2 that David **a** from his bed
2Sa 12:17 So the elders of his house **a**
2Sa 12:20 So David **a** from the ground,
2Sa 12:21 when the child died, you **a**
2Sa 13:29 Then all the king's sons **a**
2Sa 13:31 So the king **a** and tore his
2Sa 14:23 So Joab **a** and went to Geshur,
2Sa 14:31 Then Joab **a** and came to
2Sa 15: 9 So he **a** and went to Hebron
2Sa 17:22 people who were with him **a**
2Sa 17:23 he saddled his donkey, and **a**
2Sa 19: 8 Then the king **a** and sat in the
2Sa 23:10 He **a** and attacked the
2Sa 24:11 when David **a** in the morning
1Ki 1:49 Adonijah were afraid, and **a**
1Ki 1:50 so he **a**, and went and took hold
1Ki 2:40 So Shimei **a**, saddled his
1Ki 3:20 So she **a** in the middle of the
1Ki 8:54 that he **a** from before the
1Ki 11:18 Then they **a** from Midian and
1Ki 11:40 But Jeroboam **a** and fled to
1Ki 14: 4 she **a** and went to Shiloh, and
1Ki 14:17 Then Jeroboam's wife **a** and
1Ki 17:10 So he **a** and went to Zarephath
1Ki 19: 3 And when he saw that, he **a**
1Ki 19: 8 So he **a**, and ate and drank
1Ki 19:21 Then he **a** and followed Elijah,
2Ki 1:15 So he **a** and went down with
2Ki 4:30 So he **a** and followed her
2Ki 6:15 of the man of God **a** early
2Ki 7: 7 Therefore they **a** and fled at
2Ki 7:12 Then the king **a** in the night
2Ki 8: 2 So the woman **a** and did
2Ki 9: 6 Then he **a** and went into the
2Ki 10:12 And he **a** and departed and went
2Ki 11: 1 that her son was dead, she **a**
2Ki 12:20 And his servants **a** and made a
2Ki 19:35 when people **a** early in the
2Ki 25:26 the captains of the armies, **a**
1Ch 10:12 all the valiant men **a** and took
2Ch 22:10 that her son was dead, she **a**
2Ch 29:12 Then these Levites **a**
2Ch 30:14 They **a** and took away the
2Ch 30:27 the priests, the Levites, **a**
2Ch 36:16 the LORD **a** against His people
Ezra 1: 5 **a** to go up and build the house
Ezra 3: 2 Shealtiel and his brethren, **a**
Ezra 3: 9 **a** as one to oversee those
Ezra 9: 5 sacrifice I **a** from my fasting
Ezra 10: 5 Then Ezra **a**, and made the
Neh 2:12 Then I **a** in the night, I and a
Neh 4:14 And I looked, and **a** and said to
Esth 7: 7 Then the king **a** in his wrath
Esth 8: 4 So Esther **a** and stood before
Job 1:20 Then Job **a** and tore his robe
Job 29: 8 saw me and hid, and the aged **a**
Ps 76: 9 When God **a** to judgment, To
Eccl 1: 5 to the place where it **a**
Song 5: 5 I **a** to open for my beloved,
Is 37:36 when people **a** early in the
Jer 41: 2 ten men who were with him, **a**
Ezek 3:23 So I **a** and went out into the
Dan 6:19 Then the king **a** very early in
Dan 8:27 afterward I **a** and went about
Jon 1: 3 But Jonah **a** to flee to
Jon 3: 3 So Jonah **a** and went to Nineveh
Jon 3: 6 he **a** from his throne and laid
Jon 4: 8 it happened, when the sun **a**
Matt 2:14 When he **a**, he took the young
Matt 2:21 Then he **a**, took the young
Matt 8:15 Then she **a** and served them
Matt 8:24 a great tempest **a** on the sea
Matt 8:26 Then He **a** and rebuked the
Matt 9: 7 And he **a** and departed to his
Matt 9: 9 And he **a** and followed Him
Matt 9:19 So Jesus **a** and followed him,
Matt 9:25 by the hand, and the girl **a**
Matt 25: 7 Then all those virgins **a** and
Matt 26:62 And the high priest **a** and said
Mark 2:12 And immediately he **a**, took up
Mark 2:14 And he **a** and followed Him
Mark 4:37 And a great windstorm **a**, and
Mark 4:39 Then He **a** and rebuked the wind
Mark 5:42 Immediately the girl **a** and
Mark 7:24 And from there He **a** and went
Mark 9:27 and lifted him up, and he **a**
Mark 10: 1 Then He **a** from there and came
Luke 1:39 Now Mary **a** in those days and
Luke 4:38 Now He **a** from the synagogue
Luke 4:39 And immediately she **a** and
Luke 6: 8 And he **a** and stood
Luke 6:48 And when the flood **a**, the
Luke 8:24 Then He **a** and rebuked the
Luke 8:55 and she **a** immediately
Luke 9:46 Then a dispute **a** among them
Luke 15:14 there **a** a severe famine in
Luke 15:20 And he **a** and came to his father
Luke 23: 1 the whole multitude of them **a**
Luke 24:12 But Peter **a** and ran to the
John 3:25 Then there **a** a dispute
John 6:18 Then the sea **a** because a
John 11:29 she **a** quickly and came to Him
Acts 5: 6 young men **a** and wrapped
Acts 6: 1 there **a** a murmuring against
Acts 6: 9 Then there **a** some from what
Acts 7:18 till another king **a** who did
Acts 8: 1 **a** against the church which
Acts 8:27 So he **a** and went
Acts 9: 8 Then Saul **a** from the ground,
Acts 9:18 and he **a** and was baptized
Acts 9:34 Then he **a** immediately
Acts 9:39 Then Peter **a** and went with
Acts 10:41 Him after He **a** from the dead
Acts 11:19 **a** over Stephen traveled as
Acts 19:23 about that time there **a** a
Acts 23: 7 a dissension **a** between the
Acts 23: 9 Then there **a** a loud outcry
Acts 23: 9 of the Pharisees' party **a**
Acts 23:10 And when there **a** a great
Acts 27:14 a tempestuous head wind **a**
Heb 7:14 that our Lord **a** from Judah
Rev 9: 2 smoke **a** out of the pit like

AROUND (*see* PREFACE)

AROUSE (*see* AROUSED, AROUSES)
Job 3: 8 who are ready to **a** Leviathan

AROUSED (*see* AROUSE)
Gen 30: 2 anger was **a** against Rachel
Gen 39:19 that his anger was **a**
Num 11: 1 heard it, and His anger was **a**
Num 11:10 of the LORD was greatly **a**
Num 11:33 LORD was **a** against the people
Num 12: 9 the LORD was **a** against them
Num 22:22 anger was **a** because he went
Num 22:27 so Balaam's anger was **a**, and
Num 24:10 anger was **a** against Balaam
Num 25: 3 the LORD was **a** against Israel
Num 32:10 anger was **a** on that day, and
Num 32:13 anger was **a** against Israel
Deut 6:15 your God be **a** against you
Deut 7: 4 LORD will be **a** against you
Deut 11:17 LORD's anger be **a** against you
Deut 29:27 LORD was **a** against this land
Deut 31:17 Then My anger shall be **a**
Judg 9:30 son of Ebed, his anger was **a**
Judg 14:19 So his anger was **a**, and he
1Sa 11: 6 and his anger was greatly **a**
1Sa 17:28 anger was **a** against David
1Sa 20:30 anger was **a** against Jonathan
2Sa 6: 7 the LORD was **a** against Uzzah
2Sa 12: 5 was greatly **a** against the man
2Sa 24: 1 the LORD was **a** against Israel
2Ki 13: 3 the LORD was **a** against Israel
2Ki 22:13 the LORD that is **a** against us
2Ki 22:17 shall be **a** against this place
2Ki 23:26 His anger was **a** against Judah
1Ch 13:10 the LORD was **a** against Uzza
2Ch 25:10 was greatly **a** against Judah
2Ch 25:15 LORD was **a** against Amaziah
Job 32: 2 of Ram, was **a** against Job
Job 32: 2 his wrath was **a** because he
Job 32: 3 three friends his wrath was **a**
Job 32: 5 three men, his wrath was **a**
Job 42: 7 My wrath is **a** against you
Is 5:25 LORD is **a** against His people
Hos 8: 5 My anger is **a** against them
Zech 2:13 for He is **a** from His holy
Matt 1:24 being **a** from sleep, did as
Rom 7: 5 **a** by the law were at work in

AROUSES (*see* AROUSE)
Prov 20: 1 intoxicating drink **a** brawling

ARPAD
2Ki 18:34 are the gods of Hamath and **A**
2Ki 19:13 king of Hamath, the king of **A**
Is 10: 9 Is not Hamath like **A**
Is 36:19 are the gods of Hamath and **A**
Is 37:13 king of Hamath, the king of **A**
Jer 49:23 **A** are shamed, for they have

ARPHAXAD
Gen 10:22 of Shem were Elam, Asshur, **A**
Gen 10:24 **A** begot Salah, and Salah begot
Gen 11:10 begot **A** two years after the
Gen 11:11 After he begot **A**, Shem lived
Gen 11:12 **A** lived thirty-five years, and
Gen 11:13 **A** lived four hundred and three
1Ch 1:17 of Shem were Elam, Asshur, **A**
1Ch 1:18 **A** begot Shelah, and Shelah
1Ch 1:24 Shem, **A**, Shelah,
Luke 3:36 son of Cainan, the son of **A**

ARRAIGN
Jer 49:19 Who will **a** Me
Jer 50:44 Who will **a** Me

ARRANGE (*see* ARRANGED, ARRANGEMENT, ARRANGING)
Ex 25:37 they shall **a** its lamps so
Ex 40: 4 **a** the things that are to be
Num 8: 2 to him, "When you **a** the lamps

ARRANGED (*see* ARRANGE)
Num 8: 3 he **a** the lamps to face toward
Matt 22: 2 who **a** a marriage for his son

ARRANGEMENT (*see* ARRANGE)
Judg 6:26 of this rock in the proper **a**
Ezek 43:11 design of the temple and its **a**

ARRANGING (*see* ARRANGE)
1Pe 3: 3 adorning of **a** the hair, of

ARRAY (*see* ARRAYED)
Judg 20:20 **a** to fight against them at
Judg 20:22 in **a** on the first day
Judg 20:30 **a** against Gibeah as at the
Judg 20:33 in battle **a** at Baal Tamar
1Sa 4: 2 in battle **a** against Israel
1Sa 17: 2 drew up in battle **a** against
1Sa 17:21 had drawn up in battle **a**,
2Sa 10: 8 put themselves in battle **a** at
2Sa 10: 9 put them in battle **a** against
2Sa 10:10 **a** against the people of Ammon
2Sa 10:17 in battle **a** against David
1Ch 19: 9 put themselves in battle **a**

1Ch 19:10 put them in battle **a** against
1Ch 19:11 set themselves in battle **a**
1Ch 19:17 up in battle **a** against them
1Ch 19:17 battle **a** against the Syrians
2Ch 14:10 set the troops in battle **a** in
Esth 6: 9 that he may **a** the man whom
Job 40:10 and **a** yourself with glory and
Is 22: 7 themselves in **a** at the gate
Jer 6:23 of war set in **a** against you
Jer 43:12 he shall **a** himself with the
Jer 50: 9 and they shall **a** themselves
Jer 50:14 Put yourselves in **a** against
Jer 50:42 ride on horses, set in **a**,
Ezek 23:24 they shall **a** against you
Joel 2: 5 strong people set in battle **a**

ARRAYED (*see* ARRAY)
Esth 6:11 **a** Mordecai and led him on
Job 6: 4 of God are **a** against me
Matt 6:29 was not **a** like one of these
Luke 12:27 was not **a** like one of these
Luke 23:11 **a** Him in a gorgeous robe, and
Acts 12:21 **a** in royal apparel, sat on
Rev 7:13 Who are these **a** in white
Rev 17: 4 The woman was **a** in purple
Rev 19: 8 granted to be **a** in fine linen

ARREST (*see* ARRESTED)
Judg 15:10 We have come up to **a** Samson
Judg 15:12 We have come down to **a** you
1Ki 13: 4 the altar, saying, "**A** him
Mark 13:11 But when they **a** you and

ARRESTED (*see* ARREST)
2Sa 4:10 I **a** him and had him executed
Luke 22:54 Then, having **a** Him, they led
John 18:12 officers of the Jews **a** Jesus
Acts 1:16 a guide to those who **a** Jesus

ARRIVAL (*see* ARRIVALS, ARRIVE)
Num 10:21 would be prepared for their **a**

ARRIVALS (*see* ARRIVAL)
Deut 32:17 new **a** that your fathers did

ARRIVE (*see* ARRIVAL, ARRIVED)
Gen 19:22 do anything until you **a** there
Gen 24:41 when you **a** among my kindred
Ex 10:26 the LORD until we **a** there
1Ki 19:15 and when you **a**, anoint Hazael
2Ki 9: 2 Now when you **a** at that place,
Jer 51:61 When you **a** in Babylon and see

ARRIVED (*see* ARRIVE)
Judg 3:27 And it happened, when he **a**
Judg 12: 5 before the Ephraimites **a**
2Ki 9: 5 And when he **a**, there were the
2Ch 22: 7 for when he **a**, he went out
Esth 4: 3 king's command and decree **a**
Mark 6:33 They **a** before them and came
Luke 10:32 when he **a** at the place, came
Luke 24:22 who **a** at the tomb early,
Acts 13: 5 when they **a** in Salamis, they
Acts 17:10 When they **a**, they went into
Acts 18:27 and when he **a**, he greatly
Acts 20:15 following day we **a** at Samos
Acts 27: 7 **a** with difficulty off Cnidus,
2Ti 1:17 but when he **a** in Rome, he

ARROGANCE (*see* ARROGANT)
1Sa 2: 3 let no **a** come from your mouth
Prov 8:13 pride and **a** and the evil way and
Is 9: 9 say in pride and **a** of heart
Is 13:11 will halt the **a** of the proud
Jer 48:29 proud), of his loftiness and **a**
Jas 4:16 But now you boast in your **a**

ARROGANT (*see* ARROGANCE)
Prov 21:24 he acts with **a** pride
Is 10:12 of the **a** heart of the king of
Ezek 24:21 your **a** boast, the desire of
Ezek 30:18 her **a** strength shall cease in
Ezek 33:28 her **a** strength shall cease,
Zeph 2: 8 made **a** threats against their
Zeph 2:10 made **a** threats against the

ARROW (*see* ARROWS)
Ex 19:13 be stoned or shot with an **a**
1Sa 20:36 ran, he shot an **a** beyond him
1Sa 20:37 **a** was which Jonathan had shot
1Sa 20:37 Is not the **a** beyond you
2Ki 9:24 the **a** came out at his heart,
2Ki 13:17 said, "The **a** of the LORD's
2Ki 13:17 the **a** of deliverance from
2Ki 19:32 city, nor shoot an **a** there
Job 41:28 The **a** cannot make him flee
Ps 11: 2 ready their **a** on the string
Ps 64: 7 shall shoot at them with an **a**
Ps 91: 5 Nor of the **a** that flies by
Prov 7:23 till an **a** struck his liver
Prov 25:18 a club, a sword, and a sharp **a**
Is 34:15 There the **a** snake shall make
Is 37:33 city, nor shoot an **a** there
Jer 9: 8 Their tongue is an **a** shot out
Lam 3:12 me up as a target for the **a**
Zech 9:14 and His **a** will go forth like
Heb 12:20 or thrust through with an **a**

ARROWS (*see* ARROW)
Num 24: 8 and pierce them with his **a**
Deut 32:23 I will spend My **a** upon them
Deut 32:42 I will make My **a** drunk with
1Sa 20:20 three **a** to the side of it
1Sa 20:21 lad, saying, "Go, find the **a**
1Sa 20:21 the **a** are on this side of you
1Sa 20:22 Look, the **a** are beyond you'
1Sa 20:36 run, find the **a** which I shoot
1Sa 20:38 lad gathered up the **a** and came
2Sa 22:15 He sent out **a** and scattered
2Ki 13:15 Take a bow and some **a**
2Ki 13:15 took himself a bow and some **a**
2Ki 13:18 Then he said, "Take the **a**"
1Ch 12: 2 and shooting **a** with the bow
2Ch 26:15 and the corners, to shoot **a**
Job 6: 4 For the **a** of the Almighty are
Ps 7:13 He makes His **a** into fiery
Ps 18:14 He sent out His **a** and
Ps 21:12 You will make ready Your **a** on
Ps 38: 2 For Your **a** pierce me deeply,
Ps 45: 5 Your **a** are sharp in the heart
Ps 57: 4 Whose teeth are spears and **a**
Ps 58: 7 Let his **a** be as if cut in
Ps 64: 3 their bows to shoot their **a**
Ps 76: 3 He broke the **a** of the bow
Ps 77:17 Your **a** also flashed about
Ps 120: 4 Sharp **a** of the warrior, With
Ps 127: 4 Like **a** in the hand of a
Ps 144: 6 Shoot out Your **a** and destroy
Prov 26:18 who throws firebrands, **a**, and
Is 5:28 Whose **a** are sharp, and all
Is 7:24 With **a** and bows men will come
Jer 50: 9 Their **a** shall be like those
Jer 50:14 shoot at her, spare no **a**, for
Jer 51:11 Make the **a** bright
Lam 3:13 He has caused the **a** of His
Ezek 5:16 **a** of famine which shall be
Ezek 21:21 he shakes the **a**, he consults
Ezek 39: 3 cause the **a** to fall out of
Ezek 39: 9 and bucklers, the bows and **a**
Hab 3: 9 oaths were sworn over Your **a**
Hab 3:11 the light of Your **a** they went
Hab 3:14 **a** the head of his villages

ART (*see* ARTISTIC)
Ex 30:25 to the **a** of the perfumer
Ex 30:35 to the **a** of the perfumer,
Acts 17:29 stone, something shaped by **a**

ARTAXERXES
Ezra 4: 7 In the days of **A** also,
Ezra 4: 7 wrote to **A** king of Persia
Ezra 4: 8 to King **A** in this fashion
Ezra 4:11 To King **A** from your servants
Ezra 4:23 **A**' letter was read before
Ezra 6:14 Darius, and **A** king of Persia
Ezra 7: 1 the reign of **A** king of Persia
Ezra 7: 7 in the seventh year of King **A**
Ezra 7:11 King **A** gave Ezra the priest
Ezra 7:12 **A**, king of kings, To Ezra the
Ezra 7:21 **A** the king, do issue a decree
Ezra 8: 1 in the reign of King **A**
Neh 2: 1 the twentieth year of King **A**
Neh 5:14 thirty-second year of King **A**
Neh 13: 6 of **A** king of Babylon I had

ARTEMAS
Tit 3:12 When I send **A** to you, or

ARTICLES
Ex 3:22 **a** of silver, **a** of gold
Ex 11: 2 **a** of silver and **a** of gold
Ex 12:35 the Egyptians **a** of silver
Ex 12:35 **a** of gold, and clothing
Ex 22: 7 neighbor money or **a** to keep
Num 18: 3 near the **a** of the sanctuary
Num 31: 6 the priest, with the holy **a**
1Sa 6: 8 put the **a** of gold which you
1Sa 6:15 in which were the **a** of gold
2Sa 8:10 brought with him **a** of silver
2Sa 8:10 **a** of gold, and **a** of bronze
1Ki 7:45 All these **a** which Hiram made
1Ki 7:47 did not weigh all the **a**,
1Ki 10:25 **a** of silver and gold, garments
2Ki 12:13 any **a** of gold, or **a** of
2Ki 12:13 or **a** of silver, from the
2Ki 14:14 all the **a** that were found in
2Ki 23: 4 the **a** that were made for Baal
2Ki 24:13 he cut in pieces all the **a** of
2Ki 25:16 these **a** was beyond measure
1Ch 18: 8 pillars, and the **a** of bronze
1Ch 18:10 him all kinds of **a** of gold
1Ch 22:19 the holy **a** of God into the
1Ch 23:26 or any of the **a** for its
1Ch 28:13 for all the **a** of service in
1Ch 28:14 for all **a** used in every kind
1Ch 28:14 for all **a** of silver by weight
1Ch 28:14 for all **a** used in every kind
2Ch 4:16 all their **a** Huram his master
2Ch 4:18 these **a** made in such great
2Ch 9:24 **a** of silver and gold, garments
2Ch 24:14 they made from it **a** for the
2Ch 24:14 **a** for serving and offering,
2Ch 25:24 all the **a** that were found in
2Ch 28:24 the **a** of the house of God
2Ch 28:24 cut in pieces the **a** of the
2Ch 29:18 offerings with all its **a**, and
2Ch 29:18 the showbread with all its **a**
2Ch 29:19 Moreover all the **a** which King
2Ch 36: 7 carried off some of the **a**
2Ch 36:10 with the costly **a** from the
2Ch 36:18 all the **a** from the house of
Ezra 1: 6 them with **a** of silver and gold
Ezra 1: 7 **a** of the house of the LORD
Ezra 1:10 kind, and one thousand other **a**
Ezra 1:11 All the **a** of gold and silver
Ezra 5:14 silver **a** of the house of God,
Ezra 5:15 he said to him, "Take these **a**
Ezra 6: 5 silver **a** of the house of God,
Ezra 7:19 Also the **a** that are given to
Ezra 8:25 silver, the gold, and the **a**
Ezra 8:26 silver **a** weighing one hundred
Ezra 8:28 the **a** are holy also
Ezra 8:30 the **a** by weight, to bring
Ezra 8:33 the **a** were weighed in the
Neh 10:39 the **a** of the sanctuary are
Neh 13: 5 the frankincense, the **a**, the
Neh 13: 9 the **a** of the house of God
Jer 52:20 these **a** was beyond measure
Dan 1: 2 with some of the **a** of the
Dan 1: 2 he brought the **a** into the
Dan 11: 8 and their precious **a** of silver

ARTISAN (*see* ARTISANS)
Ex 36: 1 every gifted **a** in whom the
Ex 36: 2 every gifted **a** in whose heart
Is 3: 3 counselor and the skillful **a**

ARTISANS (*see* ARTISAN)
Ex 28: 3 speak to all who are gifted **a**
Ex 31: 6 of all who are gifted **a**, that
Ex 35:25 the women who were gifted **a**
Ex 36: 8 Then all the gifted **a** among

ARTISTIC (*see* ART, ARTISTICALLY)
Ex 26: 1 with **a** designs of cherubim
Ex 26:31 with an **a** design of cherubim
Ex 31: 4 to design **a** works, to work in
Ex 35:32 to design **a** works, to work in
Ex 35:33 all manner of **a** workmanship
Ex 35:35 and those who design **a** works
Ex 36: 8 with **a** designs of cherubim
Ex 36:35 with an **a** design of cherubim
Ex 39: 3 linen thread, into **a** designs

ARTISTICALLY (*see* ARTISTIC)
Ex 28: 6 and fine linen thread, **a** woven
Ex 28:15 **A** woven according to the
Ex 39: 8 **a** woven like the workmanship
Ex 39:27 **a** woven of fine linen, for

ARUBBOTH
1Ki 4:10 Ben-Hesed, in **A**

ARUMAH (*see* RUMAH)
Judg 9:41 Then Abimelech dwelt at **A**

ARVAD (*see* ARVADITE)
Ezek 27: 8 Sidon and **A** were your oarsmen
Ezek 27:11 Men of **A** with your army were

ARVADITE (*see* ARVAD)
Gen 10:18 the **A**, the Zemarite, and the
1Ch 1:16 the **A**, the Zemarite, and the

ARZA
1Ki 16: 9 drunk in the house of **A**,

AS (*see* PREFACE)

ASA (*see* ASA'S)
1Ki 15: 8 Then **A** his son reigned in his
1Ki 15: 9 **A** became king over Judah
1Ki 15:11 **A** did what was right in the
1Ki 15:13 **A** cut down her obscene image
1Ki 15:16 Now there was war between **A**
1Ki 15:17 or come in to **A** king of Judah
1Ki 15:18 Then **A** took all the silver and
1Ki 15:18 King **A** sent them to Ben-Hadad
1Ki 15:20 So Ben-Hadad heeded King **A**
1Ki 15:22 Then King **A** made a
1Ki 15:22 with them King **A** built Geba
1Ki 15:23 The rest of all the acts of **A**
1Ki 15:24 So **A** rested with his fathers,
1Ki 15:25 year of **A** king of Judah, and
1Ki 15:28 third year of **A** king of Judah
1Ki 15:32 And there was war between **A**
1Ki 15:33 third year of **A** king of Judah
1Ki 16: 8 year of **A** king of Judah, Elah
1Ki 16:10 year of **A** king of Judah, and
1Ki 16:15 year of **A** king of Judah,
1Ki 16:23 year of **A** king of Judah, Omri
1Ki 16:29 year of **A** king of Judah, Ahab
1Ki 22:41 **A** had become king over Judah
1Ki 22:43 all the ways of his father **A**
1Ki 22:46 in the days of his father **A**
1Ch 3:10 **A** his son, Jehoshaphat his
1Ch 9:16 and Berechiah the son of **A**
2Ch 14: 1 Then **A** his son reigned in his
2Ch 14: 2 **A** did what was good and right
2Ch 14: 8 And **A** had an army of three
2Ch 14:10 So **A** went out against him, and
2Ch 14:11 **A** cried out to the LORD his
2Ch 14:12 the Ethiopians before **A** and
2Ch 14:13 And **A** and the people who were
2Ch 15: 2 And he went out to meet **A**, and
2Ch 15: 2 Hear me, **A**, and all Judah and
2Ch 15: 8 when **A** heard these words and
2Ch 15:10 year of the reign of **A**
2Ch 15:16 the mother of **A** the king
2Ch 15:16 **A** cut down her obscene image,
2Ch 15:17 of **A** was loyal all his days
2Ch 15:19 year of the reign of **A**
2Ch 16: 1 year of the reign of **A**,
2Ch 16: 1 or come in to **A** king of Judah
2Ch 16: 2 Then **A** brought silver and gold
2Ch 16: 4 So Ben-Hadad heeded King **A**
2Ch 16: 6 Then King **A** took all Judah,
2Ch 16: 7 seer came to **A** king of Judah
2Ch 16:10 Then **A** was angry with the
2Ch 16:10 And **A** oppressed some of the
2Ch 16:11 Note that the acts of **A**,
2Ch 16:12 **A** became diseased in his feet
2Ch 16:13 So **A** rested with his fathers
2Ch 17: 2 which **A** his father had taken
2Ch 20:32 in the way of his father **A**
2Ch 21:12 the ways of **A** king of Judah
Jer 41: 9 was the same one **A** the king
Matt 1: 7 Abijah, and Abijah begot **A**
Matt 1: 8 **A** begot Jehoshaphat,

ASAHEL
2Sa 2:18 Joab and Abishai and **A**
2Sa 2:18 **A** was as fleet of foot as a
2Sa 2:19 So **A** pursued Abner, and in
2Sa 2:20 him and said, "Are you **A**?"
2Sa 2:21 But **A** would not turn aside
2Sa 2:22 So Abner said again to **A**
2Sa 2:23 the place where **A** fell down
2Sa 2:30 servants nineteen men and **A**
2Sa 2:32 Then they took up **A** and buried
2Sa 3:27 the blood of **A** his brother
2Sa 3:30 **A** at Gibeon in the battle
2Sa 23:24 **A** the brother of Joab was one
1Ch 2:16 were Abishai, Joab, and **A**
1Ch 11:26 were **A** the brother of Joab
1Ch 27: 7 was **A** the brother of Joab
2Ch 17: 8 Nethaniah, Zebadiah, **A**,
2Ch 31:13 Jehiel, Azaziah, Nahath, **A**
Ezra 10:15 Only Jonathan the son of **A**

ASAIAH
2Ki 22:12 and **A** a servant of the king,
2Ki 22:14 and **A** went to Huldah the
1Ch 4:36 Jaakobah, Jeshohaiah, **A**,
1Ch 6:30 Haggiah his son, and **A** his son
1Ch 9: 5 **A** the firstborn and his sons
1Ch 15: 6 **A** the chief, and two hundred
1Ch 15:11 for Uriel, **A**, Joel, Shemaiah,
2Ch 34:20 and **A** a servant of the king,

ASAPH
2Ki 18:18 scribe, and Joah the son of **A**
2Ki 18:37 scribe, and Joah the son of **A**
1Ch 6:39 And his brother **A**, who stood
1Ch 6:39 was **A** the son of Berachiah,
1Ch 9:15 son of Zichri, the son of **A**
1Ch 15:17 **A** the son of Berechiah
1Ch 15:19 the singers, Heman, **A**, and
1Ch 16: 5 **A** the chief, and next to him
1Ch 16: 5 but **A** made music with cymbals
1Ch 16: 7 this psalm into the hand of **A**
1Ch 16:37 So he left **A** and his brothers
1Ch 25: 1 service some of the sons of **A**
1Ch 25: 2 Of the sons of **A**
1Ch 25: 2 the sons of **A** were under the
1Ch 25: 2 were under the direction of **A**
1Ch 25: 6 **A**, Jeduthun, and Heman were
1Ch 25: 9 lot for **A** came out for Joseph
1Ch 26: 1 son of Kore, of the sons of **A**
2Ch 5:12 the singers, all those of **A**
2Ch 20:14 a Levite of the sons of **A**
2Ch 29:13 of the sons of **A**, Zechariah
2Ch 29:30 of David and of **A** the seer
2Ch 35:15 And the singers, the sons of **A**
2Ch 35:15 to the command of David, **A**
Ezra 2:41 the sons of **A**, one hundred and
Ezra 3:10 and the Levites, the sons of **A**
Neh 2: 8 a letter to **A** the keeper of
Neh 7:44 the children of **A**, one
Neh 11:17 son of Zabdi, the son of **A**
Neh 11:22 of Micha, of the sons of **A**
Neh 12:35 son of Zaccur, the son of **A**
Neh 12:46 **A** of old there were chiefs of
Is 36: 3 scribe, and Joah the son of **A**
Is 36:22 scribe, and Joah the son of **A**

ASAREL
1Ch 4:16 Ziph, Ziphah, Tiria, and **A**

ASA'S (*see* ASA)
1Ki 15:14 Nevertheless **A** heart was

ASCEND (*see* ASCENDED, ASCENDING, ASCENDS, ASCENT)
Deut 30:12 Who will **a** into heaven for
Deut 32:50 on the mountain which you **a**
Ps 24: 3 Who may **a** into the hill of
Ps 135: 7 He causes the vapors to **a**
Ps 139: 8 If I **a** into heaven, You are
Is 5:24 blossom will **a** like dust
Is 14:13 I will **a** into heaven, I will
Is 14:14 I will **a** above the heights of
Is 34:10 its smoke shall **a** forever
Is 60: 7 they shall **a** with acceptance
Jer 10:13 He causes the vapors to **a**
Jer 48: 5 they **a** with continual weeping
Jer 51:16 He causes the vapors to **a**
Ezek 38: 9 You will **a**, coming like a
John 6:62 of Man **a** where He was before
Acts 2:34 did not **a** into the heavens
Rom 10: 6 Who will **a** into heaven
Rev 17: 8 will **a** out of the bottomless

ASCENDED (*see* ASCEND)
Ex 19:18 Its smoke **a** like the smoke of
Josh 8:20 smoke of the city **a** to heaven
Josh 8:21 that the smoke of the city **a**
Josh 10: 7 So Joshua **a** from Gilgal, he
Josh 15: 3 **a** on the south side of Kadesh
Judg 13:20 **a** in the flame of the altar
Ps 68:18 You have **a** on high, You have
Prov 30: 4 Who has **a** into heaven, or
Ezek 40:22 it was **a** by seven steps, and
Ezek 41: 7 of the temple **a** like steps
John 3:13 No one has **a** to heaven but He
John 20:17 I have not yet **a** to My Father
Eph 4: 8 When He **a** on high, He led
Eph 4: 9 He **a**"—what does it mean
Eph 4:10 is also the One who **a** far
Rev 8: 4 **a** before God from the angel's
Rev 11:12 they **a** to heaven in a cloud,

ASCENDING (*see* ASCEND)
Gen 28:12 the angels of God were **a** and
1Sa 28:13 I saw a spirit **a** out of the
1Ch 26:16 Gate on the **a** highway
John 1:51 open, and the angels of God **a**
John 20:17 I am **a** to My Father and your
Rev 7: 2 another angel **a** from the east

ASCENDS (*see* ASCEND)
Rev 11: 7 the beast that **a** out of the
Rev 14:11 of their torment **a** forever

ASCENT (*see* ASCEND)
Num 34: 4 side of the **A** of Akrabbim
Josh 11:17 the **a** to Seir, even as far as
Josh 12: 7 the **a** to Seir, which Joshua
Josh 15: 3 side of the **A** of Akrabbim
Josh 15: 7 is before the **A** of Adummim
Josh 18:17 is before the **A** of Adummim
Judg 1:36 was from the **A** of Akrabbim
Judg 8:13 battle, from the **A** of Heres
2Sa 15:30 the **a** of the Mount of Olives
2Ki 9:27 they did so at the **a** to Gur
2Ch 20:16 come up by the **a** of Ziz, and
Neh 3:19 of the **A** to the Armory at the
Is 15: 5 For by the **a** of Luhith they
Jer 48: 5 For in the **a** of Luhith they

ASCERTAIN
Acts 21:34 when he could not **a** the truth
Acts 24: 8 him yourself you may **a** all
Acts 24:11 because you may **a** that it is

ASCRIBE (*see* ASCRIBED)
Deut 32: 3 **a** greatness to our God
Job 36: 3 I will **a** righteousness to my
Ps 68:34 **A** strength to God

ASCRIBED (*see* ASCRIBE)
1Sa 18: 8 They have **a** to David ten
1Sa 18: 8 me they have **a** but thousands

ASENATH
Gen 41:45 And he gave him as a wife **A**
Gen 41:50 years of famine came, whom **A**
Gen 46:20 and Ephraim, whom **A**

ASH (*see* ASHES)
1Sa 2: 8 the beggar from the **a** heap
Ps 113: 7 the needy out of the **a** heap
Lam 4: 5 up in scarlet embrace **a** heaps
Dan 2: 5 shall be made an **a** heap
Dan 3:29 shall be made an **a** heap

ASHAMED
Gen 2:25 and his wife, and were not **a**
2Sa 10: 5 the men were greatly **a**
2Sa 19: 3 as people who are **a** steal
2Ki 2:17 they urged him till he was **a**
2Ki 8:11 in a stare until he was **a**
1Ch 19: 5 the men were greatly **a**
2Ch 30:15 priests and the Levites were **a**
Ezra 8:22 For I was **a** to request of the
Ezra 9: 6 I am too **a** and humiliated to
Job 19: 3 you are not **a** that you have
Ps 6:10 Let all my enemies be **a** and
Ps 6:10 turn back and be **a** suddenly
Ps 22: 5 trusted in You, and were not **a**
Ps 25: 2 Let me not be **a**
Ps 25: 3 no one who waits on You be **a**
Ps 25: 3 Let those be **a** who deal
Ps 25:20 Let me not be **a**, for I put my
Ps 31: 1 Let me never be **a**
Ps 31:17 Do not let me be **a**, O LORD,
Ps 31:17 Let the wicked be **a**
Ps 34: 5 And their faces were not **a**
Ps 35:26 Let them be **a** and brought to
Ps 37:19 not be **a** in the evil time
Ps 40:14 Let them be **a** and brought to
Ps 69: 6 of hosts, be **a** because of me
Ps 70: 2 Let them be **a** and confounded
Ps 74:21 let the oppressed return **a**
Ps 86:17 hate me may see it and be **a**
Ps 109:28 they arise, let them be **a**
Ps 119: 6 Then I would not be **a**, When I
Ps 119:46 kings, And will not be **a**
Ps 119:78 Let the proud be **a**, For they
Ps 119:80 statutes, That I may not be **a**
Ps 119:116 do not let me be **a** of my hope
Ps 127: 5 They shall not be **a**, But
Is 1:29 For they shall be **a** of the
Is 19: 9 weave fine fabric will be **a**
Is 20: 5 afraid and **a** of Ethiopia their
Is 23: 4 Be **a**, O Sidon

Is 24:23 be disgraced and the sun **a**
Is 26:11 be **a** for their envy of people
Is 29:22 Jacob shall not now be **a**, nor
Is 30: 5 They were all **a** of a people
Is 41:11 against you shall be **a** and
Is 42:17 back, they shall be greatly **a**
Is 44: 9 nor know, that they may be **a**
Is 44:11 all his companions would be **a**
Is 44:11 they shall be **a** together
Is 45:16 They shall be **a** and also
Is 45:17 you shall not be **a** or
Is 45:24 and all shall be **a** who are
Is 49:23 not be **a** who wait for Me
Is 50: 7 I know that I will not be **a**
Is 54: 4 fear, for you will not be **a**
Is 65:13 rejoice, but you shall be **a**
Is 66: 5 But they shall be **a**
Jer 2:26 As the thief is **a** when he is
Jer 2:26 so is the house of Israel **a**
Jer 2:36 Also you shall be **a** of Egypt
Jer 2:36 as you were **a** of Assyria
Jer 3: 3 you refuse to be **a**
Jer 6:15 Were they **a** when they had
Jer 6:15 They were not at all **a**
Jer 8: 9 The wise men are **a**, they are
Jer 8:12 Were they **a** when they had
Jer 8:12 They were not at all **a**, nor
Jer 9:19 We are greatly **a**, because we
Jer 12:13 But be **a** of your harvest
Jer 14: 3 they were **a** and confounded and
Jer 14: 4 the land, the plowmen were **a**
Jer 15: 9 she has been **a** and confounded
Jer 17:13 who forsake You shall be **a**
Jer 17:18 Let them be **a** who persecute
Jer 20:11 They will be greatly **a**, for
Jer 22:22 surely then you will be **a**
Jer 31:19 I was **a**, yes, even humiliated
Jer 46:24 daughter of Egypt shall be **a**
Jer 48:13 Moab shall be **a** of Chemosh
Jer 48:13 of Israel was **a** of Bethel
Jer 50:12 your mother shall be deeply **a**
Jer 50:12 she who bore you shall be **a**
Jer 51:47 her whole land shall be **a**
Jer 51:51 We are **a** because we have
Ezek 16:27 who were **a** of your lewd
Ezek 16:61 remember your ways and be **a**
Ezek 16:63 that you may remember and be **a**
Ezek 36:32 Be **a** and confounded for your
Ezek 43:10 that they may be **a** of their
Ezek 43:11 if they are **a** of all that
Hos 4:19 they shall be **a** because of
Hos 10: 6 Israel shall be **a** of his own
Joel 1:11 Be **a**, you farmers, wail, you
Mic 3: 7 So the seers shall be **a**, and
Mic 7:16 and be **a** of all their might
Zech 13: 4 be **a** of his vision when he
Mark 8:38 For whoever is **a** of Me and My
Mark 8:38 **a** when He comes in the glory
Luke 9:26 For whoever is **a** of Me and My
Luke 9:26 be **a** when He comes in His own
Luke 16: 3 I am **a** to beg
Rom 1:16 For I am not **a** of the gospel
Rom 6:21 things of which you are now **a**
2Co 7:14 to him about you, I am not **a**
2Co 9: 4 should be **a** of this
2Co 10: 8 destruction, I shall not be **a**
Phil 1:20 that in nothing I shall be **a**
2Th 3:14 with him, that he may be **a**
2Ti 1: 8 Therefore do not be **a** of the
2Ti 1:12 nevertheless I am not **a**, for
2Ti 1:16 me, and was not **a** of my chain
2Ti 2:15 who does not need to be **a**
Tit 2: 8 who is an opponent may be **a**
Heb 2:11 not **a** to call them brethren
Heb 11:16 Therefore God is not **a** to be
1Pe 3:16 conduct in Christ may be **a**
1Pe 4:16 a Christian, let him not be **a**
1Jn 2:28 not be **a** before Him at His

ASHAN
Josh 15:42 Libnah, Ether, **A**,
Josh 19: 7 Ain, Rimmon, Ether, and **A**
1Ch 4:32 Ain, Rimmon, Tochen, and **A**
1Ch 6:59 **A** with its common-lands, and

ASHARELAH
1Ch 25: 2 Joseph, Nethaniah, and **A**

ASHBEA
1Ch 4:21 workers of the house of **A**

ASHBEL (*see* ASHBELITES)
Gen 46:21 were Belah, Becher, **A**, Gera,
Num 26:38 of **A**, the family of the
1Ch 8: 1 **A** the second, Aharah the

ASHBELITES (*see* ASHBEL)
Num 26:38 Ashbel, the family of the **A**

ASHCHENAZ (*see* ASHKENAZ)
Jer 51:27 Ararat, Minni, and **A**

ASHDOD (*see* ASHDODITES)
Josh 11:22 in Gaza, in Gath, and in **A**
Josh 15:46 the sea, all that lay near **A**
Josh 15:47 **A** with its towns and villages,
1Sa 5: 1 brought it from Ebenezer to **A**
1Sa 5: 3 when the people of **A** arose
1Sa 5: 5 of Dagon in **A** to this day
1Sa 5: 6 was heavy on the people of **A**
1Sa 5: 6 them with tumors, both **A** and
1Sa 5: 7 the men of **A** saw how it was
1Sa 6:17 one for **A**, one for Gaza, one
2Ch 26: 6 of Jabneh, and the wall of **A**
2Ch 26: 6 and he built cities around **A**
Neh 13:23 who had married women of **A**
Neh 13:24 spoke the language of **A**, and
Is 20: 1 year that Tartan came to **A**
Is 20: 1 him, and he fought against **A**
Jer 25:20 Ekron, and the remnant of **A**)
Amos 1: 8 cut off the inhabitant from **A**
Amos 3: 9 Proclaim in the palaces at **A**
Zeph 2: 4 shall drive out **A** at noonday
Zech 9: 6 mixed race shall settle in **A**

ASHDODITES (*see* ASHDOD)
Josh 13: 3 the Gazites, the **A**, the
Neh 4: 7 the **A** heard that the walls of

ASHER (*see* ASHERITES)
Gen 30:13 So she called his name **A**
Gen 35:26 maidservant, were Gad and **A**
Gen 46:17 The sons of **A** were Jimnah
Gen 49:20 Bread from **A** shall be rich,
Ex 1: 4 Dan, Naphtali, Gad, and **A**
Num 1:13 from **A**, Pagiel the son of
Num 1:40 From the children of **A**, their
Num 1:41 of **A** were forty-one thousand
Num 2:27 him shall be the tribe of **A**
Num 2:27 leader of the children of **A**
Num 7:72 leader of the children of **A**
Num 10:26 tribe of the children of **A**
Num 13:13 from the tribe of **A**, Sethur
Num 26:44 The sons of **A** according to
Num 26:46 the daughter of **A** was Serah
Num 26:47 **A** according to those who were
Num 34:27 tribe of the children of **A**
Deut 27:13 Reuben, Gad, **A**, Zebulun,
Deut 33:24 And of **A** he said
Deut 33:24 **A** is most blessed of sons
Josh 17: 7 was from **A** to Michmethath
Josh 17:10 was adjoining **A** on the north
Josh 17:11 And in Issachar and in **A**,
Josh 19:24 tribe of the children of **A**
Josh 19:31 tribe of the children of **A**
Josh 19:34 **A** on the west side, and ended
Josh 21: 6 Issachar, from the tribe of **A**
Josh 21:30 and from the tribe of **A**,
Judg 1:31 Nor did **A** drive out the
Judg 5:17 **A** continued at the seashore,
Judg 6:35 He also sent messengers to **A**
Judg 7:23 together from Naphtali, **A**
1Ki 4:16 the son of Hushai, in **A** and
1Ch 2: 2 Naphtali, Gad, and **A**
1Ch 6:62 Issachar, from the tribe of **A**
1Ch 6:74 And from the tribe of **A**
1Ch 7:30 The sons of **A** were Imnah,
1Ch 7:40 these were the children of **A**
1Ch 12:36 of **A**, those who could go out
2Ch 30:11 Nevertheless some from **A**,
Ezek 48: 2 the west, one portion for **A**
Ezek 48: 3 by the border of **A**, from the
Ezek 48:34 gate for Gad, one gate for **A**
Luke 2:36 of Phanuel, of the tribe of **A**
Rev 7: 6 of the tribe of **A** twelve

ASHERAH (*see* ASHERAHS)
1Ki 15:13 made an obscene image of **A**
1Ki 18:19 four hundred prophets of **A**
2Ki 21: 7 image of **A** that he had made
2Ki 23: 4 were made for Baal, for **A**
2Ch 15:16 made an obscene image of **A**

ASHERAHS (*see* ASHERAH)
Judg 3: 7 God, and served the Baals and **A**

ASHERITES (*see* ASHER)
Judg 1:32 So the **A** dwelt among the

ASHES (*see* ASH)
Gen 18:27 **a** have taken it upon myself
Ex 9: 8 handfuls of **a** from a furnace
Ex 9:10 Then they took **a** from the
Ex 27: 3 its pans to receive its **a**
Lev 1:16 side, into the place for **a**
Lev 4:12 where the **a** are poured out,
Lev 4:12 where the **a** are poured out it
Lev 6:10 take up the **a** of the burnt
Lev 6:11 carry the **a** outside the camp
Num 4:13 away the **a** from the altar
Num 19: 9 gather up the **a** of the heifer
Num 19:10 the one who gathers the **a** of
Num 19:17 the **a** of the heifer burnt for
2Sa 13:19 Then Tamar put **a** on her head
1Ki 13: 3 the **a** on it shall be poured
1Ki 13: 5 the **a** poured out from the
2Ki 23: 4 and carried their **a** to Bethel
2Ki 23: 6 Kidron and ground it to **a**, and
2Ki 23: 6 threw its **a** on the graves of
Esth 4: 1 and put on sackcloth and **a**, and
Esth 4: 3 and many lay in sackcloth and **a**
Job 2: 8 he sat in the midst of the **a**
Job 13:12 platitudes are proverbs of **a**
Job 30:19 I have become like dust and **a**
Job 42: 6 and repent in dust and **a**
Ps 102: 9 For I have eaten **a** like bread
Ps 147:16 He scatters the frost like **a**
Is 44:20 He feeds on **a**
Is 58: 5 to spread out sackcloth and **a**
Is 61: 3 to give them beauty for **a**
Jer 6:26 sackcloth, and roll about in **a**
Jer 25:34 Roll about in the **a**, you
Jer 31:40 the dead bodies and of the **a**
Lam 3:16 gravel, and covered me with **a**
Ezek 27:30 they will roll about in **a**
Ezek 28:18 I turned you to **a** upon the
Dan 9: 3 with fasting, sackcloth, and **a**
Jon 3: 6 with sackcloth and sat in **a**
Mal 4: 3 for they shall be **a** under the
Matt 11:21 long ago in sackcloth and **a**
Luke 10:13 sitting in sackcloth and **a**
Heb 9:13 the **a** of a heifer, sprinkling
2Pe 2: 6 of Sodom and Gomorrah into **a**

ASHHUR
1Ch 2:24 him **A** the father of Tekoa
1Ch 4: 5 **A** the father of Tekoa had two

ASHIMA
2Ki 17:30 the men of Hamath made **A**

ASHKELON (*see* ASHKELONITES)
Judg 1:18 **A** with its territory, and
Judg 14:19 and he went down to **A** and
1Sa 6:17 one for Gaza, one for **A**, one
2Sa 1:20 it not in the streets of **A**
Jer 25:20 of the Philistines (namely, **A**
Jer 47: 5 **A** is cut off with the remnant
Jer 47: 7 given it a charge against **A**
Amos 1: 8 who holds the scepter from **A**
Zeph 2: 4 be forsaken, and **A** desolate
Zeph 2: 7 in the houses of **A** they shall
Zech 9: 5 **A** shall see it and fear
Zech 9: 5 and **A** shall not be inhabited

ASHKELONITES (*see* ASHKELON)
Josh 13: 3 the Ashdodites, the **A**, the

ASHKENAZ (*see* ASHCHENAZ)
Gen 10: 3 The sons of Gomer were **A**,
1Ch 1: 6 The sons of Gomer were **A**,

ASHNAH
Josh 15:33 Eshtaol, Zorah, **A**,
Josh 15:43 Jiphtah, **A**, Nezib,

ASHPENAZ
Dan 1: 3 Then the king instructed **A**

ASHTAROTH (*see* ASHTEROTH, ASHTORETH)
Deut 1: 4 who dwelt at **A** in Edrei
Josh 9:10 king of Bashan, who was at **A**
Josh 12: 4 of the giants, who dwelt at **A**
Josh 13:12 in Bashan, who reigned in **A**
Josh 13:31 half of Gilead, and **A** and Edrei
1Ch 6:71 and **A** with its common-lands

ASHTERATHITE
1Ch 11:44 Uzzia the A, Shama and Jeiel

ASHTEROTH (*see* ASHTAROTH, KARNAIM)
Gen 14: 5 the Rephaim in A Karnaim, the

ASHTORETH (*see* ASHTAROTH, ASHTORETHS)
1Ki 11: 5 after A the goddess of the
1Ki 11:33 worshiped A the goddess of
2Ki 23:13 for A the abomination of the

ASHTORETHS (*see* ASHTORETH)
Judg 2:13 LORD and served Baal and the A
Judg 10: 6 and served the Baals and the A
1Sa 7: 3 and the A from among you, and
1Sa 7: 4 put away the Baals and the A
1Sa 12:10 and served the Baals and A
1Sa 31:10 armor in the temple of the A

ASHURITES
2Sa 2: 9 king over Gilead, over the A
Ezek 27: 6 the company of A have inlaid

ASHVATH
1Ch 7:33 were Pasach, Bimhal, and A

ASIA
Acts 2: 9 and Cappadocia, Pontus and A
Acts 6: 9 A), disputing with Stephen
Acts 16: 6 to preach the word in A
Acts 19:10 so that all who dwelt in A
Acts 19:22 stayed in A for a time
Acts 19:26 but throughout almost all A
Acts 19:27 destroyed, whom all A and the
Acts 19:31 some of the officials of A
Acts 20: 4 of Berea accompanied him to A
Acts 20: 4 Tychicus and Trophimus of A
Acts 20:16 not have to spend time in A
Acts 20:18 first day that I came to A
Acts 21:27 almost ended, the Jews from A
Acts 24:18 of which some Jews from A
Acts 27: 2 to sail along the coasts of A
1Co 16:19 The churches of A greet you
2Co 1: 8 trouble which came to us in A
2Ti 1:15 that all those in A have
1Pe 1: 1 Galatia, Cappadocia, A, and
Rev 1: 4 seven churches which are in A
Rev 1:11 seven churches which are in A

ASIDE (*see* PREFACE)

ASIEL
1Ch 4:35 son of Seraiah, the son of A

ASK (*see* PREFACE)

ASKED (*see* PREFACE)

ASKING (*see* PREFACE)

ASKS (*see* PREFACE)

ASLEEP
Judg 4:21 for he was fast a and weary
1Sa 26:12 For they were all a, because
Job 3:13 quiet, I would have been a
Jon 1: 5 had lain down, and was fast a
Matt 8:24 But He was a
Matt 26:40 the disciples and found them a
Matt 26:43 He came and found them a again
Matt 27:52 who had fallen a were raised
Mark 4:38 in the stern, a on a pillow
Mark 14:40 He found them a again, for
Luke 8:23 But as they sailed He fell a
Acts 7:60 he had said this, he fell a
Acts 13:36 by the will of God, fell a
1Co 15: 6 but some have fallen a
1Co 15:18 a in Christ have perished
1Co 15:20 of those who have fallen a
1Th 4:13 those who have fallen a, lest
1Th 4:15 means precede those who are a
2Pe 3: 4 For since the fathers fell a

ASNAH
Ezra 2:50 the sons of A, the sons of

ASPATHA
Esth 9: 7 Also Parshandatha, Dalphon, A

ASPHALT
Gen 11: 3 and they had a for mortar
Gen 14:10 of Siddim was full of a pits
Ex 2: 3 for him, daubed it with a

ASPIRE
1Th 4:11 that you also a to lead a

ASPS
Ps 140: 3 The poison of a is under
Rom 3:13 The poison of a is under

ASRIEL (*see* ASRIELITES)
Num 26:31 of A, the family of the
Josh 17: 2 of Helek, the children of A
1Ch 7:14 of Gilead, the father of A

ASRIELITES (*see* ASRIEL)
Num 26:31 Asriel, the family of the A

ASSAIL
Luke 11:53 began to a Him vehemently

ASSASSINS
Acts 21:38 led the four thousand a out

ASSAULT
Deut 21: 5 and every a shall be settled
Esth 7: 8 Will he also a the queen
Esth 8:11 or province that would a them

ASSAYER
Jer 6:27 I have set you as an a and a

ASSEMBLE (*see* ASSEMBLED, ASSEMBLES, ASSEMBLING, ASSEMBLY)
2Sa 20: 4 A the men of Judah for me
2Sa 20: 5 went to a the men of Judah
Is 11:12 will a the outcasts of Israel
Is 45:20 A yourselves and come
Is 48:14 of you, a yourselves, and hear
Is 54:15 Indeed they shall surely a
Jer 4: 5 A yourselves, and let us go
Jer 8:14 A yourselves, and let us enter
Jer 12: 9 a all the beasts of the field
Jer 21: 4 I will a them in the midst of
Ezek 11:17 a you from the countries
Ezek 39:17 A yourselves and come
Dan 11:10 a a multitude of great forces
Hos 7:14 They a together for grain and
Joel 2:16 a the elders, gather the
Joel 3:11 A and come, all you nations,
Amos 3: 9 A on the mountains of
Mic 2:12 I will surely a all of you
Mic 4: 6 I will a the lame, I will

ASSEMBLED (*see* ASSEMBLE)
Ex 38: 8 who a at the door of the
Num 1:18 they a all the congregation
Josh 18: 1 Israel a together at Shiloh
Judg 10:17 children of Israel a together
1Sa 2:22 who a at the door of the
1Sa 14:20 people who were with him a
1Ki 8: 1 Now Solomon a the elders of
1Ki 8: 2 all the men of Israel a to
1Ki 8: 5 of Israel who were a to him
1Ki 12:21 he a all the house of Judah
1Ch 15: 4 Then David a the children of
1Ch 28: 1 Now David a at Jerusalem all
2Ch 5: 2 Now Solomon a the elders of
2Ch 5: 3 all the men of Israel a
2Ch 5: 6 of Israel who were a with him
2Ch 11: 1 he a from the house of Judah
2Ch 20:26 on the fourth day they a in
2Ch 30:13 a at Jerusalem to keep the
Ezra 9: 4 of the God of Israel a to me
Ezra 10: 1 children a to him from Israel
Neh 9: 1 of Israel were a with fasting
Esth 9:18 Jews who were at Shushan a
Ps 48: 4 For behold, the kings a, They
Is 43: 9 and let the people be a
Jer 5: 7 a themselves by troops in the
Dan 6:11 Then these men a and found
Matt 26: 3 the elders of the people a at
Matt 26:57 scribes and the elders were a
Matt 28:12 When they had a with the
Mark 14:53 with him were a all the chief
John 20:19 where the disciples were a
Acts 1: 4 being a together with them,
Acts 4:31 were a together was shaken
Acts 11:26 year they a with the church
Acts 15:25 being a with one accord, to

ASSEMBLES (*see* ASSEMBLE)
Is 54:15 Whoever a against you shall

ASSEMBLIES (*see* ASSEMBLY)
Is 1:13 Sabbaths, and the calling of a
Is 4: 5 of Mount Zion, and above her a
Amos 5:21 I do not savor your sacred a

ASSEMBLING (*see* ASSEMBLE)
Heb 10:25 not forsaking the a of

ASSEMBLY (*see* ASSEMBLE, ASSEMBLIES)
Gen 28: 3 you may be an a of peoples
Gen 49: 6 my honor be united to their a
Ex 12: 6 Then the whole a of the
Ex 16: 3 kill this whole a with hunger
Lev 4:13 hidden from the eyes of the a
Lev 4:14 then the a shall offer a
Lev 4:21 is a sin offering for the a
Lev 8: 4 the a was gathered together
Lev 23:36 It is a sacred a, and you
Num 8: 9 a of the children of Israel
Num 10: 2 use them for calling the a
Num 10: 3 all the a shall gather before
Num 14: 5 a of the congregation of the
Num 20: 6 of the a to the door of the
Num 20: 8 Aaron gather the a together
Num 29:35 day you shall have a sacred a
Deut 5:22 the LORD spoke to all your a
Deut 9:10 the fire in the day of the a
Deut 10: 4 the fire in the day of the a
Deut 16: 8 sacred a to the LORD your God
Deut 18:16 in Horeb in the day of the a
Judg 20: 2 in the a of the people of God
Judg 21: 5 up with the a to the LORD
Judg 21: 8 from Jabesh Gilead to the a
1Sa 17:47 Then all this a shall know
2Ki 10:20 Proclaim a solemn a for Baal
2Ch 7: 9 day they held a sacred a, for
2Ch 30:23 Then the whole a agreed to
Neh 5: 7 called a great a against them
Neh 8:18 day there was a sacred a,
Ps 22:16 The a of the wicked has
Ps 89: 7 feared in the a of the saints
Ps 107:32 Him in the a of the elders
Ps 111: 1 In the a of the upright and in
Prov 5:14 of the congregation and a
Jer 6:11 and on the a of young men
Jer 9: 2 an a of treacherous men
Jer 15:17 sit in the a of the mockers
Jer 26:17 to all the a of the people
Jer 50: 9 a of great nations from the
Lam 1:15 He has called an a against me
Lam 2: 6 has destroyed His place of a
Ezek 13: 9 not be in the a of My people
Ezek 16:40 bring up an a against you
Ezek 23:46 Bring up an a against them
Ezek 23:47 The a shall stone them with
Joel 1:14 a fast, call a sacred a
Joel 2:15 a fast, call a sacred a
Zeph 3: 8 nations to My a of kingdoms
Zeph 3:18 sorrow over the appointed a
Acts 19:32 for the a was confused, and
Acts 19:39 be determined in the lawful a
Acts 19:41 things, he dismissed the a
Acts 21:22 The a must certainly meet,
Acts 23: 7 and the a was divided
Acts 25:24 man about whom the whole a of
Heb 12:23 to the general a and church of
Jas 2: 2 your a a man with gold rings

ASSENTED
Acts 24: 9 And the Jews also a,

ASSESSED (*see* ASSESSMENT)
2Ki 18:14 And the king of Assyria a

ASSESSMENT (*see* ASSESSED)
2Ki 12: 4 money, each man's a money
2Ki 23:35 every one according to his a

ASSHUR (*see* ASSHURIM)
Gen 10:22 The sons of Shem were Elam, A
Num 24:22 How long until A carries you
Num 24:24 and they shall afflict A and
1Ch 1:17 The sons of Shem were Elam, A

ASSHURIM (*see* ASSHUR)
Gen 25: 3 And the sons of Dedan were A

ASSIGN (*see* ASSIGNED, ASSIGNMENT)
Num 4:27 and his sons shall a all the
Num 4:32 you shall a to each man by

ASSIGNED (*see* ASSIGN)
Josh 20: 8 eastward, they a Bezer in the
2Sa 11:16 that he a Uriah to a place
1Ch 6:54 for they were a by lot to the
1Ch 9:24 The gatekeepers were a to the
1Ch 23:11 therefore they were a as one
2Ch 23:18 whom David had a in the house
Ezra 6:18 They a the priests to their

Neh 13:30 I also **a** duties to the
Job 36:23 Who has **a** Him His way, or who
Prov 8:29 When He **a** to the sea its

ASSIGNMENT (*see* ASSIGN)
1Ch 9:23 house of the tabernacle, by **a**

ASSIR
Ex 6:24 And the sons of Korah were **A**
1Ch 3:17 the sons of Jeconiah were **A**
1Ch 6:22 Korah his son, **A** his son,
1Ch 6:23 Ebiasaph his son, **A** his son,
1Ch 6:37 son of Tahath, the son of **A**

ASSIST (*see* ASSISTANT)
2Ch 28:20 him, and did not **a** him
Rom 16: 2 **a** her in whatever business

ASSISTANT (*see* ASSIST, ASSISTANTS)
Ex 24:13 Moses arose with his **a** Joshua
Num 11:28 the son of Nun, Moses' **a**, one
Josh 1: 1 the son of Nun, Moses' **a**,
Acts 13: 5 They also had John as their **a**

ASSISTANTS (*see* ASSISTANT)
2Ch 31:15 his faithful **a** in the cities

ASSOCIATE (*see* ASSOCIATED, ASSOCIATES)
Prov 20:19 therefore do not **a** with one
Prov 24:21 do not **a** with those given to
Rom 12:16 things, but **a** with the humble

ASSOCIATED (*see* ASSOCIATE)
Num 18: 1 **a** with your priesthood

ASSOCIATES (*see* ASSOCIATE)
2Ki 9: 2 him rise up from among his **a**
2Ki 25:19 men of the king's close **a** who
Jer 52:25 men of the king's close **a** who

ASSOS
Acts 20:13 to the ship and sailed to **A**
Acts 20:14 And when he met us at **A**, we

ASSUME
2Ch 22: 9 to **a** power over the kingdom

ASSURANCE (*see* ASSURE)
Deut 28:66 night, and have no **a** of life
Is 32:17 quietness and **a** forever
Acts 17:31 He has given **a** of this to all
Col 2: 2 the full **a** of understanding
1Th 1: 5 the Holy Spirit and in much **a**
Heb 6:11 full **a** of hope until the end
Heb 10:22 true heart in full **a** of faith

ASSURE (*see* ASSURANCE, ASSURED, ASSUREDLY)
1Jn 3:19 shall **a** our hearts before Him

ASSURED (*see* ASSURE)
Jer 14:13 you **a** peace in this place
Dan 4:26 kingdom shall be **a** to you
2Ti 3:14 you have learned and been **a** of
Heb 11:13 them afar off were **a** of them

ASSUREDLY (*see* ASSURE)
1Sa 28: 1 You **a** know that you will go
1Ki 1:13 **A** your son Solomon shall
1Ki 1:17 **A** Solomon your son shall
1Ki 1:30 **A** Solomon your son shall be
Jer 32:41 I will **a** plant them in this
Jer 49:12 drink of the cup have **a** drunk
Matt 5:18 For **a**, I say to you, till
Matt 5:26 **A**, I say to you, you will by
Matt 6: 2 **A**, I say to you, they have
Matt 6: 5 **A**, I say to you, they have
Matt 6:16 **A**, I say to you, they have
Matt 8:10 **A**, I say to you, I have not
Matt 10:15 **A**, I say to you, it will be
Matt 10:23 For **a**, I say to you, you will
Matt 10:42 in the name of a disciple, **a**
Matt 11:11 **A**, I say to you, among those
Matt 13:17 for **a**, I say to you that many
Matt 16:28 **A**, I say to you, there are
Matt 17:20 for **a**, I say to you, if you
Matt 18: 3 **A**, I say to you, unless you
Matt 18:13 And if he should find it, **a**
Matt 18:18 **A**, I say to you, whatever you
Matt 19:23 **A**, I say to you that it is
Matt 19:28 **A** I say to you, that in the
Matt 21:21 **A**, I say to you, if you have
Matt 21:31 **A**, I say to you that tax
Matt 23:36 **A**, I say to you, all these
Matt 24: 2 **A**, I say to you, not one
Matt 24:34 **A**, I say to you, this
Matt 24:47 **A**, I say to you that he will
Matt 25:12 But he answered and said, '**A**
Matt 25:40 answer and say to them, '**A**
Matt 25:45 will answer them, saying, '**A**
Matt 26:13 **A**, I say to you, wherever
Matt 26:21 **A**, I say to you, one of you
Matt 26:34 **A**, I say to you that this
Mark 3:28 **A**, I say to you, all sins
Mark 6:11 **A**, I say to you, it will be
Mark 8:12 **A**, I say to you, no sign
Mark 9: 1 **A**, I say to you that there
Mark 9:41 you belong to Christ, **a**, I
Mark 10:15 **A**, I say to you, whoever does
Mark 10:29 **A**, I say to you, there is no
Mark 11:23 For **a**, I say to you, whoever
Mark 12:43 **A**, I say to you that this
Mark 13:30 **A**, I say to you, this
Mark 14: 9 **A**, I say to you, wherever
Mark 14:18 **A**, I say to you, one of you
Mark 14:25 **A**, I say to you, I will no
Mark 14:30 **A**, I say to you that today,
Luke 4:24 **A**, I say to you, no prophet
Luke 12:37 **A**, I say to you that he will
Luke 13:35 and **a**, I say to you, you shall
Luke 18:17 **A**, I say to you, whoever does
Luke 18:29 **A**, I say to you, there is no
Luke 21:32 **A**, I say to you, this
Luke 23:43 **A**, I say to you, today you
John 1:51 Most **a**, I say to you,
John 3: 3 Most **a**, I say to you, unless
John 3: 5 Most **a**, I say to you, unless
John 3:11 Most **a**, I say to you, We
John 5:19 Most **a**, I say to you, the Son
John 5:24 Most **a**, I say to you, he who
John 5:25 Most **a**, I say to you, the
John 6:26 Most **a**, I say to you, you
John 6:32 Most **a**, I say to you, Moses
John 6:47 Most **a**, I say to you, he who
John 6:53 Most **a**, I say to you, unless
John 8:34 Most **a**, I say to you, whoever
John 8:51 Most **a**, I say to you, if
John 8:58 Most **a**, I say to you, before
John 10: 1 Most **a**, I say to you, he who
John 10: 7 Most **a**, I say to you, I am
John 12:24 Most **a**, I say to you, unless
John 13:16 Most **a**, I say to you, a
John 13:20 Most **a**, I say to you, he who
John 13:21 Most **a**, I say to you, one of
John 13:38 Most **a**, I say to you, the
John 14:12 Most **a**, I say to you, he who
John 16:20 Most **a**, I say to you that you
John 16:23 Most **a**, I say to you,
John 21:18 Most **a**, I say to you, when
Acts 2:36 know **a** that God has made this

ASSYRIA (*see* ASSYRIAN)
Gen 2:14 goes toward the east of **A**
Gen 10:11 From that land he went to **A**
Gen 25:18 of Egypt as you go toward **A**
2Ki 15:19 Pul king of **A** came against
2Ki 15:20 to give to the king of **A**
2Ki 15:20 So the king of **A** turned back
2Ki 15:29 king of **A** came and took Ijon,
2Ki 15:29 he carried them captive to **A**
2Ki 16: 7 to Tiglath-Pileser king of **A**
2Ki 16: 8 as a present to the king of **A**
2Ki 16: 9 So the king of **A** heeded him
2Ki 16: 9 for the king of **A** went up
2Ki 16:10 Tiglath-Pileser king of **A**
2Ki 16:18 on account of the king of **A**
2Ki 17: 3 king of **A** came up against him
2Ki 17: 4 the king of **A** uncovered a
2Ki 17: 4 no tribute to the king of **A**
2Ki 17: 4 the king of **A** shut him up
2Ki 17: 5 Now the king of **A** went
2Ki 17: 6 the king of **A** took Samaria and
2Ki 17: 6 and carried Israel away to **A**
2Ki 17:23 away from their own land to **A**
2Ki 17:24 Then the king of **A** brought
2Ki 17:26 they spoke to the king of **A**
2Ki 17:27 Then the king of **A** commanded
2Ki 18: 7 against the king of **A** and did
2Ki 18: 9 of **A** came up against Samaria
2Ki 18:11 Then the king of **A** carried
2Ki 18:11 Israel away captive to **A**, and
2Ki 18:13 Sennacherib king of **A** came up
2Ki 18:14 to the king of **A** at Lachish
2Ki 18:14 And the king of **A** assessed
2Ki 18:16 and gave it to the king of **A**
2Ki 18:17 the king of **A** sent the Tartan
2Ki 18:19 the great king, the king of **A**
2Ki 18:23 to my master the king of **A**
2Ki 18:28 the great king, the king of **A**
2Ki 18:30 the hand of the king of **A**
2Ki 18:31 for thus says the king of **A**
2Ki 18:33 the hand of the king of **A**
2Ki 19: 4 of **A** has sent to reproach the
2Ki 19: 6 king of **A** have blasphemed Me
2Ki 19: 8 found the king of **A** warring
2Ki 19:10 the hand of the king of **A**
2Ki 19:11 heard what the kings of **A**
2Ki 19:17 the kings of **A** have laid
2Ki 19:20 king of **A** I have heard
2Ki 19:32 LORD concerning the king of **A**
2Ki 19:36 king of **A** departed and went
2Ki 20: 6 the hand of the king of **A**
2Ki 23:29 to the aid of the king of **A**
1Ch 5: 6 of **A** carried into captivity
1Ch 5:26 the spirit of Pul king of **A**
1Ch 5:26 is, Tiglath-Pileser king of **A**
2Ch 28:16 to the kings of **A** to help him
2Ch 28:20 king of **A** came to him and
2Ch 28:21 he gave it to the king of **A**
2Ch 30: 6 the hand of the kings of **A**
2Ch 32: 1 Sennacherib king of **A** came
2Ch 32: 4 should the kings of **A** come
2Ch 32: 7 dismayed before the king of **A**
2Ch 32: 9 of **A** sent his servants to
2Ch 32:10 says Sennacherib king of **A**
2Ch 32:11 the hand of the king of **A**"
2Ch 32:21 in the camp of the king of **A**
2Ch 32:22 of Sennacherib the king of **A**
2Ch 33:11 of the army of the king of **A**
Ezra 4: 2 days of Esarhaddon king of **A**
Ezra 6:22 of the king of **A** toward them
Neh 9:32 the kings of **A** until this day
Ps 83: 8 **A** also has joined with them
Is 7:17 bring the king of **A** upon you
Is 7:18 bee that is in the land of **A**
Is 7:20 the River, with the king of **A**
Is 8: 4 away before the king of **A**
Is 8: 7 the king of **A** and all his
Is 10: 5 Woe to **A**, the rod of My anger
Is 10:12 heart of the king of **A**, and
Is 11:11 people who are left, from **A**
Is 11:16 who will be left from **A**, as
Is 19:23 be a highway from Egypt to **A**
Is 19:23 Egypt and the Egyptian into **A**
Is 19:24 one of three with Egypt and **A**
Is 19:25 **A** the work of My hands, and
Is 20: 1 Sargon the king of **A** sent him
Is 20: 4 so shall the king of **A** lead
Is 20: 6 delivered from the king of **A**
Is 23:13 **A** founded it for wild beasts
Is 27:13 to perish in the land of **A**
Is 30:31 LORD **A** will be beaten down
Is 31: 8 Then **A** shall fall by a sword
Is 36: 1 of **A** came up against all the
Is 36: 2 Then the king of **A** sent the
Is 36: 4 the great king, the king of **A**
Is 36: 8 to my master the king of **A**
Is 36:13 the great king, the king of **A**
Is 36:15 the hand of the king of **A**
Is 36:16 for thus says the king of **A**
Is 36:18 the hand of the king of **A**
Is 37: 4 of **A** has sent to reproach the
Is 37: 6 king of **A** have blasphemed Me
Is 37: 8 found the king of **A** warring
Is 37:10 the hand of the king of **A**
Is 37:11 heard what the kings of **A**
Is 37:18 the kings of **A** have laid
Is 37:21 against Sennacherib king of **A**
Is 37:33 LORD concerning the king of **A**
Is 37:37 king of **A** departed and went
Is 38: 6 the hand of the king of **A**
Jer 2:18 Or why take the road to **A**
Jer 2:36 as you were ashamed of **A**
Jer 50:17 the king of **A** devoured him
Jer 50:18 I have punished the king of **A**
Ezek 23: 7 all of them choice men of **A**
Ezek 27:23 the merchants of Sheba, **A**
Ezek 31: 3 Indeed **A** was a cedar in
Ezek 32:22 **A** is there, and all her
Hos 5:13 wound, then Ephraim went to **A**
Hos 7:11 call to Egypt, they go to **A**
Hos 8: 9 For they have gone up to **A**
Hos 9: 3 shall eat unclean things in **A**
Hos 10: 6 also shall be carried to **A** as
Hos 11:11 a dove from the land of **A**
Hos 14: 3 **A** shall not save us, we will
Mic 5: 6 with the sword the land of **A**
Mic 7:12 they shall come to you from **A**

Nah 3:18 slumber, O king of **A**
Zeph 2:13 against the north, destroy **A**
Zech 10:10 Egypt, and gather them from **A**
Zech 10:11 Then the pride of **A** shall be

ASSYRIAN (*see* ASSYRIA, ASSYRIANS)
Is 10:24 do not be afraid of the **A**
Is 14:25 I will break the **A** in My land
Is 19:23 the **A** will come into Egypt and
Is 52: 4 then the **A** oppressed them
Hos 11: 5 but the **A** shall be his king,
Mic 5: 5 when the **A** comes into our
Mic 5: 6 shall deliver us from the **A**

ASSYRIANS (*see* ASSYRIAN)
2Ki 19:35 the camp of the **A** one hundred
Is 19:23 will serve with the **A**
Is 37:36 the camp of the **A** one hundred
Lam 5: 6 to the Egyptians and the **A**
Ezek 16:28 played the harlot with the **A**
Ezek 23: 5 her lovers, the neighboring **A**
Ezek 23: 9 into the hand of the **A**, for
Ezek 23:12 lusted for the neighboring **A**
Ezek 23:23 all the **A** with them, all of
Hos 12: 1 make a covenant with the **A**

ASTONISHED (*see* ASTONISHING, ASTONISHMENT)
Lev 26:32 dwell in it shall be **a** at it
1Ki 9: 8 who passes by it will be **a**
2Ch 7:21 who passes by it will be **a**
Ezra 9: 3 head and beard, and sat down **a**
Ezra 9: 4 I sat **a** until the evening
Job 17: 8 Upright men are **a** at this
Job 18:20 in the west are **a** at his day
Job 21: 5 Look at me and be **a**
Job 26:11 and are **a** at His reproof
Is 52:14 Just as many were **a** at you
Jer 2:12 Be **a**, O heavens, at this, and
Jer 4: 9 the priests shall be **a**, and
Jer 14: 9 should You be like a man **a**
Jer 18:16 who passes by it will be **a**
Jer 19: 8 who passes by it will be **a**
Jer 49:17 who goes by it will be **a** and
Ezek 3:15 remained there **a** among them
Ezek 26:16 every moment, and be **a** at you
Ezek 27:35 of the isles will be **a** at you
Ezek 28:19 the peoples are **a** at you
Ezek 32:10 make many peoples **a** at you
Dan 3:24 King Nebuchadnezzar was **a**
Dan 4:19 was **a** for a time, and his
Dan 5: 9 changed, and his lords were **a**
Dan 8:27 I was **a** by the vision, but no
Matt 7:28 people were **a** at His teaching
Matt 13:54 so that they were **a** and said,
Matt 22:33 they were **a** at His teaching
Mark 1:22 they were **a** at His teaching,
Mark 6: 2 And many hearing Him were **a**
Mark 7:37 they were **a** beyond measure,
Mark 10:24 disciples were **a** at His words
Mark 10:26 they were **a** beyond measure,
Mark 11:18 people were **a** at His teaching
Luke 2:47 were **a** at His understanding
Luke 4:32 they were **a** at His teaching,
Luke 5: 9 **a** at the catch of fish which
Luke 8:56 And her parents were **a**, but He
Luke 24:22 at the tomb early, **a** us
Acts 8: 9 and **a** the people of Samaria,
Acts 8:11 heeded him because he had **a**
Acts 9: 6 So he, trembling and **a**, said,
Acts 10:45 who believed were **a**, as many
Acts 12:16 door and saw him, they were **a**
Acts 13:12 being **a** at the teaching of

ASTONISHING (*see* ASTONISHED)
Jer 5:30 An **a** and horrible thing has

ASTONISHMENT (*see* ASTONISHED)
Gen 43:33 looked in **a** at one another
Deut 28:37 And you shall become an **a**, a
2Ch 29: 8 them up to trouble, to **a**, and
2Ch 30: 7 so that He gave them up to **a**
Jer 8:21 **a** has taken hold of me
Jer 25: 9 them, and make them an **a**, a
Jer 25:11 shall be a desolation and an **a**
Jer 25:18 make them a desolation, an **a**
Jer 29:18 to be a curse, an **a**, a
Jer 42:18 And you shall be an oath, an **a**
Jer 44:12 they shall be an oath and an **a**
Jer 44:22 land is a desolation, an **a**
Jer 49:17 Edom also shall be an **a**
Jer 51:37 place for jackals, an **a** and a
Ezek 5:15 an **a** to the nations that are

ASTOUNDED
Hab 1: 5 be utterly **a**

ASTRAY
Ex 23: 4 ox or his donkey going **a**, you
Num 5:12 If any man's wife goes **a**
Num 5:19 if you have not gone **a** to
Num 5:20 But if you have gone **a** while
Num 5:29 husband's authority, goes **a**
Deut 22: 1 ox or his sheep going **a**, and
2Ch 21:11 harlotry, and led Judah **a**
Ps 58: 3 They go **a** as soon as they are
Ps 95:10 who go **a** in their hearts, And
Ps 119:67 I was afflicted I went **a**, But
Ps 119:176 I have gone **a** like a lost
Prov 5:23 of his folly he shall go **a**
Prov 10:17 he who refuses reproof goes **a**
Prov 12:26 of the wicked leads them **a**
Prov 14:22 Do they not go **a** who devise
Prov 20: 1 whoever is led **a** by it is not
Prov 28:10 to go **a** in an evil way, he
Is 35: 8 a fool, shall not go **a**
Is 53: 6 All we like sheep have gone **a**
Jer 50: 6 shepherds have led them **a**
Ezek 44:10 from Me, when Israel went **a**
Ezek 44:15 of Israel went **a** from Me,
Ezek 48:11 who did not go **a** when the
Ezek 48:11 the children of Israel went **a**
Ezek 48:11 **a**, as the Levites went **a**
Amos 2: 4 their lies lead them **a**, lies
Matt 18:12 sheep, and one of them goes **a**
Matt 18:13 ninety-nine that did not go **a**
Heb 3:10 always go **a** in their heart
Heb 5: 2 who are ignorant and going **a**
1Pe 2:25 you were like sheep going **a**
2Pe 2:15 the right way and gone **a**,

ASTROLOGER (*see* ASTROLOGERS)
Dan 2:10 things of any magician, **a**

ASTROLOGERS (*see* ASTROLOGER)
Is 47:13 let now the **a**, the stargazers
Dan 1:20 **a** who were in all his realm
Dan 2: 2 to call the magicians, the **a**
Dan 2:27 demanded, the wise men, the **a**
Dan 4: 7 Then the magicians, the **a**
Dan 5: 7 cried aloud to bring in the **a**
Dan 5:11 him chief of the magicians, **a**
Dan 5:15 Now the wise men, the **a**, have

ASYNCRITUS
Rom 16:14 Greet **A**, Phlegon, Hermas,

AT (*see* PREFACE)

ATAD
Gen 50:10 to the threshing floor of **A**
Gen 50:11 at the threshing floor of **A**

ATARAH
1Ch 2:26 wife, whose name was **A**

ATAROTH (*see* ATROTH, JOAB)
Num 32: 3 **A**, Dibon, Jazer, Nimrah,
Num 32:34 of Gad built Dibon and **A** and
Josh 16: 2 border of the Archites at **A**
Josh 16: 5 on the east side was **A** Addar
Josh 16: 7 went down from Janohah to **A**

ATAROTH ADAR
Josh 18:13 and the border descended to **A**

ATE (*see* EAT)
Gen 3: 6 she took of its fruit and **a**
Gen 3: 6 her husband with her, and he **a**
Gen 3:12 gave me of the tree, and I **a**
Gen 3:13 serpent deceived me, and I **a**
Gen 18: 8 them under the tree as they **a**
Gen 19: 3 unleavened bread, and they **a**
Gen 24:54 the men who were with him **a**
Gen 25:28 Esau because he **a** of his game
Gen 25:34 then he **a** and drank, arose, and
Gen 26:30 made them a feast, and they **a**
Gen 27:25 it near to him, and he **a**
Gen 27:33 I **a** all of it before you came
Gen 31:46 and they **a** there on the heap
Gen 31:54 they **a** bread and stayed all
Gen 39: 6 for the bread which he **a**
Gen 40:17 the birds **a** them out of the
Gen 41: 4 gaunt cows **a** up the seven
Gen 41:20 and ugly cows **a** up the first
Gen 43:32 the Egyptians who **a** with him
Gen 47:22 they **a** their rations which
Ex 10:15 they **a** every herb of the land
Ex 16: 3 when we **a** bread to the full
Ex 16:35 of Israel **a** manna forty years
Ex 16:35 they **a** manna until they came
Ex 24:11 So they saw God, and they **a**
Ex 34:28 he neither **a** bread nor drank
Num 11: 5 which we **a** freely in Egypt
Num 25: 2 their gods, and the people **a**
Deut 9: 9 I neither **a** bread nor drank
Deut 9:18 I neither **a** bread nor drank
Deut 32:38 Who **a** the fat of their
Josh 5:11 they **a** of the produce of the
Josh 5:12 but they **a** the food of the
Judg 9:27 the house of their god, and **a**
Judg 14: 9 some to them, and they also **a**
Judg 19: 4 So they **a** and drank and lodged
Judg 19: 6 down, and the two of them **a**
Judg 19: 8 and both of them **a**
Judg 19:21 they washed their feet, and **a**
Ruth 2:14 and she **a** and was satisfied, and
1Sa 1:18 the woman went her way and **a**
1Sa 9:24 So Saul **a** with Samuel that
1Sa 14:32 the people **a** them with the
1Sa 20:34 **a** no food the second day of
1Sa 28:25 and his servants, and they **a**
1Sa 30:11 they gave him bread and he **a**
2Sa 9:13 for he **a** continually at the
2Sa 11:13 when David called him, he **a**
2Sa 12: 3 It **a** of his own food and drank
2Sa 12:20 set food before him, and he **a**
2Sa 12:21 died, you arose and **a** food
1Ki 13:19 and **a** bread in his house, and
1Ki 13:22 **a** bread, and drank water in
1Ki 17:15 her household **a** for many days
1Ki 19: 6 So he **a** and drank, and lay down
1Ki 19: 8 So he arose, and **a** and drank
1Ki 19:21 it to the people, and they **a**
2Ki 4:44 and they **a** and had some left
2Ki 6:23 and after they **a** and drank, he
2Ki 6:29 So we boiled my son, and **a** him
2Ki 7: 8 they went into one tent and **a**
2Ki 9:34 And when he had gone in, he **a**
2Ki 23: 9 but they **a** unleavened bread
2Ki 25:29 he **a** bread regularly before
1Ch 29:22 So they **a** and drank before the
2Ch 30:18 yet they **a** the Passover
2Ch 30:22 they **a** throughout the feast
Ezra 6:21 **a** together with all who had
Ezra 10: 6 he **a** no bread and drank no
Neh 5:14 **a** the governor's provisions
Neh 9:25 So they **a** and were filled and
Job 42:11 **a** food with him in his house
Ps 41: 9 Who **a** my bread, Has lifted up
Ps 78:25 Men **a** angels' food
Ps 78:29 So they **a** and were well filled
Ps 105:35 **a** up all the vegetation in
Ps 106:28 **a** sacrifices made to the dead
Jer 15:16 I **a** them, and Your word was to
Jer 41: 1 there they **a** bread together
Jer 52:33 he **a** bread regularly before
Lam 4: 5 Those who **a** delicacies are
Ezek 3: 3 So I **a** it, and it was in my
Ezek 16:13 You **a** pastry of fine flour,
Dan 1:15 **a** the portion of the king's
Dan 4:33 from men and **a** grass like oxen
Dan 10: 3 I **a** no pleasant food, no meat
Matt 12: 4 **a** the showbread which was not
Matt 14:20 So they all **a** and were filled,
Matt 15:37 So they all **a** and were filled,
Matt 15:38 Now those who **a** were four
Mark 1: 6 he **a** locusts and wild honey
Mark 2:26 **a** the showbread, which is not
Mark 6:42 So they all **a** and were filled
Mark 8: 8 So they **a** and were filled, and
Mark 14:18 Now as they sat and **a**, Jesus
Luke 4: 2 And in those days He **a** nothing
Luke 6: 1 **a** them, rubbing them in their
Luke 6: 4 **a** the showbread, and also gave
Luke 9:17 So they all **a** and were filled,
Luke 13:26 you will begin to say, 'We **a**
Luke 15:16 the pods that the swine **a**
Luke 17:27 They **a**, they drank, they
Luke 17:28 They **a**, they drank, they
Luke 24:43 it and **a** in their presence
John 6:23 **a** bread after the Lord had
John 6:26 because you **a** of the loaves
John 6:31 Our fathers **a** the manna in
John 6:49 Your fathers **a** the manna in
John 6:58 as your fathers **a** the manna
Acts 2:46 house, they **a** their food with
Acts 9: 9 sight, and neither **a** nor drank
Acts 10:41 by God, even to us who **a** and

Acts 11: 3 men and **a** with them
1Co 10: 3 all **a** the same spiritual food
Rev 10:10 **a** it, and it was as sweet as

ATER
Ezra 2:16 the people of **A** of Hezekiah
Ezra 2:42 of Shallum, the sons of **A**
Neh 7:21 the children of **A** of Hezekiah
Neh 7:45 of Shallum, the children of **A**
Neh 10:17 **A**, Hezekiah, Azzur,

ATHACH
1Sa 30:30 those who were in **A**,

ATHAIAH
Neh 11: 4 **A** the son of Uzziah, the son

ATHALIAH
2Ki 8:26 His mother's name was **A** the
2Ki 11: 1 When **A** the mother of Ahaziah
2Ki 11: 2 nurse in the bedroom, from **A**
2Ki 11: 3 while **A** reigned over the land
2Ki 11:13 Now when **A** heard the noise of
2Ki 11:14 **A** tore her clothes and cried
2Ki 11:20 for they had slain **A** with the
1Ch 8:26 Shamsherai, Shehariah, **A**,
2Ch 22: 2 His mother's name was **A** the
2Ch 22:10 Now when **A** the mother of
2Ch 22:11 hid him from **A** so that she
2Ch 22:12 while **A** reigned over the land
2Ch 23:12 Now when **A** heard the noise of
2Ch 23:13 So **A** tore her clothes and said
2Ch 23:21 had slain **A** with the sword
2Ch 24: 7 For the sons of **A**, that
Ezra 8: 7 Elam, Jeshaiah the son of **A**

ATHARIM
Num 21: 1 was coming on the road to **A**

ATHENIANS (*see* ATHENS)
Acts 17:21 For all the **A** and the

ATHENS (*see* ATHENIANS)
Acts 17:15 Paul brought him to **A**
Acts 17:16 Paul waited for them at **A**
Acts 17:22 Men of **A**, I perceive that in
Acts 18: 1 things Paul departed from **A**
1Th 3: 1 it good to be left in **A** alone

ATHLAI
Ezra 10:28 Hananiah, Zabbai, and **A**

ATHLETICS
2Ti 2: 5 also if anyone competes in **a**

ATONED (*see* ATONEMENT, ATONING)
1Sa 3:14 not be **a** for by sacrifice or

ATONEMENT (*see* ATONED)
Ex 29:33 with which the **a** was made
Ex 29:36 day as a sin offering for **a**
Ex 29:36 altar when you make **a** for it
Ex 29:37 shall make **a** for the altar
Ex 30:10 Aaron shall make **a** upon its
Ex 30:10 of the sin offering of **a**
Ex 30:10 **a** upon it throughout your
Ex 30:15 to make **a** for yourselves
Ex 30:16 you shall take the **a** money of
Ex 30:16 to make **a** for yourselves
Ex 32:30 I can make **a** for your sin
Lev 1: 4 his behalf to make **a** for him
Lev 4:20 priest shall make **a** for them
Lev 4:26 So the priest shall make **a**
Lev 4:31 priest shall make **a** for him
Lev 4:35 **a** for his sin that he has
Lev 5: 6 So the priest shall make **a**
Lev 5:10 So the priest shall make **a** on
Lev 5:13 priest shall make **a** for him
Lev 5:16 So the priest shall make **a**
Lev 5:18 make **a** for him regarding his
Lev 6: 7 **a** for him before the LORD
Lev 6:30 to make **a** in the holy place,
Lev 7: 7 the priest who makes **a** with
Lev 8:15 it, to make **a** for it
Lev 8:34 to do, to make **a** for you
Lev 9: 7 make **a** for yourself and for
Lev 9: 7 make **a** for them, as the LORD
Lev 10:17 to make **a** for them before the
Lev 12: 7 the LORD, and make **a** for her
Lev 12: 8 priest shall make **a** for her
Lev 14:18 **a** for him before the LORD
Lev 14:19 make **a** for him who is to be
Lev 14:20 priest shall make **a** for him
Lev 14:21 be waved, to make **a** for him
Lev 14:29 to make **a** for him before the
Lev 14:31 make **a** for him who is to be
Lev 14:53 make **a** for the house, and it
Lev 15:15 **a** for him before the LORD
Lev 15:30 the priest shall make **a** for
Lev 16: 6 make **a** for himself and for his
Lev 16:10 the LORD, to make **a** upon it
Lev 16:11 make **a** for himself and for his
Lev 16:16 So he shall make **a** for the
Lev 16:17 to make **a** in the Holy Place
Lev 16:17 he may make **a** for himself
Lev 16:18 make **a** for it, and shall take
Lev 16:24 make **a** for himself and for the
Lev 16:27 to make **a** in the Holy Place
Lev 16:30 priest shall make **a** for you
Lev 16:32 father's place, shall make **a**
Lev 16:33 then he shall make **a** for the
Lev 16:33 and he shall make **a** for the
Lev 16:33 and he shall make **a** for the
Lev 16:34 to make **a** for the children of
Lev 17:11 to make **a** for your souls
Lev 17:11 that makes **a** for the soul
Lev 19:22 The priest shall make **a** for
Lev 23:27 month shall be the Day of **A**
Lev 23:28 day, for it is the Day of **A**
Lev 23:28 to make **a** for you before the
Lev 25: 9 on the Day of **A** you shall
Num 5: 8 the **a** with which **a** is made
Num 6:11 make **a** for him, because he
Num 8:12 to make **a** for the Levites
Num 8:19 to make **a** for the children of
Num 8:21 and Aaron made **a** for them to
Num 15:25 So the priest shall make **a**
Num 15:28 **a** for the person who sins
Num 15:28 the LORD, to make **a** for him
Num 16:46 and make **a** for them
Num 16:47 and made **a** for the people
Num 25:13 made **a** for the children of
Num 28:22 offering, to make **a** for you
Num 28:30 the goats, to make **a** for you
Num 29: 5 offering, to make **a** for you
Num 29:11 the sin offering for **a**, the
Num 31:50 to make **a** for ourselves
Num 35:33 no **a** can be made for the land
Deut 21: 8 Provide **a**, O LORD, for Your
Deut 21: 8 **a** shall be provided on their
Deut 32:43 will provide **a** for His land
2Sa 21: 3 And with what shall I make **a**
1Ch 6:49 and to make **a** for Israel,
2Ch 29:24 to make an **a** for all Israel
2Ch 30:18 LORD provide **a** for everyone
Neh 10:33 to make **a** for Israel, and all
Ps 65: 3 You will provide **a** for them
Ps 79: 9 provide **a** for our sins, For
Prov 16: 6 and truth **a** is provided for
Is 22:14 there will be no **a** for you
Jer 18:23 Provide no **a** for their
Ezek 16:63 an **a** for all you have done
Ezek 43:20 cleanse it and make **a** for it
Ezek 43:26 shall make **a** for the altar
Ezek 45:15 to make **a** for them," says
Ezek 45:17 **a** for the house of Israel
Ezek 45:20 shall make **a** for the temple

ATONING (*see* ATONED)
Lev 16:20 end of **a** for the Holy Place

ATROTH (*see* ATAROTH)
Num 32:35 **A** and Shophan and Jazer and

ATROTH BETH JOAB
1Ch 2:54 the Netophathites, **A**, half

ATTACHED
Gen 29:34 husband will become **a** to me
Ex 29:13 the fatty lobe **a** to the liver
Ex 29:22 the fatty lobe **a** to the liver
Lev 3: 4 the fatty lobe **a** to the liver
Lev 3:10 the fatty lobe **a** to the liver
Lev 3:15 the fatty lobe **a** to the liver
Lev 4: 9 the fatty lobe **a** to the liver
Lev 7: 4 the fatty lobe **a** to the liver
Lev 8:16 the fatty lobe **a** to the liver
Lev 8:25 the fatty lobe **a** to the liver
Lev 9:19 the fatty lobe **a** to the liver
1Ki 6:10 they were **a** to the temple

ATTACK (*see* ATTACKED, ATTACKERS, ATTACKING, ATTACKS)
Gen 32:11 **a** me and the mother with the
Num 25:17 the Midianites, and **a** them
Josh 7: 3 thousand men go up and **a** Ai
Josh 9:18 of Israel did not **a** them,
Josh 10: 4 help me, that we may **a** Gibeon
Josh 10:19 and **a** their rear ranks
1Sa 15: 3 **a** Amalek, and utterly destroy
1Sa 23: 2 I go and **a** these Philistines
1Sa 23: 2 **a** the Philistines, and save
2Sa 11:25 Strengthen your **a** against the
1Ki 20:12 they got ready to **a** the city
2Ki 3:19 Also you shall **a** every
2Ki 7: 6 of the Egyptians to **a** us
2Ch 18:31 they surrounded him to **a**
Neh 4: 8 **a** Jerusalem and create
Ps 62: 3 How long will you **a** a man
Jer 18:18 let us **a** him with the tongue,
Dan 11:40 king of the South shall **a** him
Zech 11: 6 They shall **a** the land, and I
Acts 18:10 no one will **a** you to hurt you

ATTACKED (*see* ATTACK)
Gen 14: 5 **a** the Rephaim in Ashteroth
Gen 14: 7 and **a** all the country of the
Gen 14:15 and he and his servants **a** them
Gen 36:35 who **a** Midian in the field of
Num 14:45 **a** them, and drove them back as
Deut 3: 3 and we **a** him until he had no
Deut 25:18 **a** your rear ranks, all the
Josh 11: 7 of Merom, and they **a** them
Josh 11: 8 they **a** them until they left
Judg 1:17 they **a** the Canaanites who
Judg 8:11 he **a** the army while the camp
Judg 9:43 rose against them and **a** them
Judg 15: 8 So he **a** them hip and thigh
1Sa 13: 3 Jonathan **a** the garrison of
1Sa 13: 4 Saul had **a** a garrison of the
1Sa 14:48 army and **a** the Amalekites, and
1Sa 15: 7 Saul **a** the Amalekites, from
1Sa 27: 9 Whenever David **a** the land
1Sa 30: 1 **a** Ziklag and burned it with
1Sa 30:17 David **a** them from twilight
2Sa 8: 1 that David **a** the Philistines
2Sa 23:10 **a** the Philistines until his
1Ki 15:20 He **a** Ijon, Dan, Abel Beth
1Ki 20:21 **a** the horses and chariots, and
2Ki 3:24 **a** the Moabites, so that they
2Ki 3:25 slingers surrounded and **a** it
2Ki 8:21 and **a** the Edomites who had
2Ki 15:16 Tirzah, Menahem **a** Tiphsah
2Ki 15:16 it to him, therefore he **a** it
1Ch 1:46 who **a** Midian in the field of
1Ch 4:41 they **a** their tents and the
1Ch 18: 1 that David **a** the Philistines
2Ch 14:15 They also **a** the livestock
2Ch 16: 4 They **a** Ijon, Dan, Abel Maim,
2Ch 21: 9 and **a** the Edomites who had
2Ch 28:17 **a** Judah, and carried away
Jer 47: 1 before Pharaoh **a** Gaza
Dan 8: 7 **a** the ram, and broke his two
Acts 17: 5 and **a** the house of Jason, and

ATTACKERS (*see* ATTACK)
Ps 35:15 **A** gathered against me, And I

ATTACKING (*see* ATTACK)
Deut 25:11 the hand of the one **a** him
2Ch 11: 4 turned back from **a** Jeroboam

ATTACKS (*see* ATTACK)
Gen 32: 8 **a** it, then the other company
Deut 27:24 who **a** his neighbor secretly
Josh 15:16 He who **a** Kirjath Sepher and
Judg 1:12 He who **a** Kirjath Sepher and
1Ch 11: 6 Whoever **a** the Jebusites first

ATTAI
1Ch 2:35 as wife, and she bore him **A**
1Ch 2:36 **A** begot Nathan, and Nathan
1Ch 12:11 **A** the sixth, Eliel the
2Ch 11:20 and she bore him Abijah, **A**

ATTAIN (*see* ATTAINED, ATTAINING)
2Sa 23:19 he did not **a** to the first
2Sa 23:23 but he did not **a** to the first
1Ch 11:21 did not **a** to the first three
1Ch 11:25 but he did not **a** to the first
Ps 139: 6 It is high, I cannot **a** it
Prov 1: 5 will **a** wise counsel,
Hos 8: 5 be until they **a** to innocence
Luke 20:35 counted worthy to **a** that age
Acts 26: 7 God night and day, hope to **a**
Phil 3:11 I may **a** to the resurrection

ATTAINED (*see* ATTAIN)
Gen 47: 9 they have not **a** to the days
Eccl 1:16 I have **a** greatness, and have
Rom 9:30 have **a** to righteousness, even
Rom 9:31 has not **a** to the law of
Phil 3:12 Not that I have already **a**

Phil 3:16 degree that we have already **a**

ATTAINING (*see* ATTAIN)
Col 2: 2 **a** to all riches of the full

ATTALIA
Acts 14:25 in Perga, they went down to **A**

ATTEMPT (*see* ATTEMPTED, ATTEMPTING, ATTEMPTS)
Acts 14: 5 when a violent **a** was made by
Gal 5: 4 you who **a** to be justified by

ATTEMPTED (*see* ATTEMPT)
Acts 9:29 but they **a** to kill him

ATTEMPTING (*see* ATTEMPT)
Heb 11:29 **a** to do so, were drowned

ATTEMPTS (*see* ATTEMPT)
Job 4: 2 If one **a** a word with you,
Eccl 8:17 a wise man **a** to know it, he

ATTEND (*see* ATTENDANT, ATTENDED, ATTENDING)
Num 1:50 they shall **a** to it and camp
Num 3: 7 they shall **a** to his needs and
Num 3: 8 Also they shall **a** to all the
Num 3:10 and they shall **a** to their
Num 8:26 to **a** to needs, but they
Num 18: 3 They shall **a** to your needs and
Num 18: 4 you and **a** to the needs of the
Num 18: 5 you shall **a** to the duties of
Num 18: 7 **a** to your priesthood for
1Sa 24: 3 went in to **a** to his needs
1Ch 23:32 that they should **a** to the
2Ch 13:10 the Levites **a** to their duties
Esth 4: 5 he had appointed to **a** her
Ps 17: 1 cause, O LORD, **A** to my cry
Ps 55: 2 **A** to me, and hear me
Ps 61: 1 **A** to my prayer
Ps 86: 6 And **a** to the voice of my
Ps 142: 6 **A** to my cry, For I am brought
Prov 27:23 flocks, and **a** to your herds
Jer 23: 2 I will **a** to you for the evil

ATTENDANT (*see* ATTEND)
Luke 4:20 and gave it back to the **a**

ATTENDED (*see* ATTEND)
Judg 3:19 all who **a** him went out from
1Sa 25:42 **a** by five of her maidens
2Sa 13:17 called his servant who **a** him
2Ch 7: 6 And the priests **a** to their
Esth 2: 2 servants who **a** him said
Esth 6: 3 servants who **a** him said
Ps 66:19 He has **a** to the voice of my
Is 10:28 he has **a** to his equipment
Jer 23: 2 them away, and not **a** to them

ATTENDING (*see* ATTEND)
Judg 3:24 He is probably **a** to his needs
Rom 13: 6 **a** continually to this very

ATTENTION (*see* ATTENTIVE)
1Ki 18:29 one answered, no one paid **a**
2Ki 21: 9 But they paid no **a**, and
Job 32:12 I paid close **a** to you
Prov 4: 1 give **a** to know understanding
Prov 4:20 My son, give **a** to my words
Prov 5: 1 My son, pay **a** to my wisdom
Prov 7:24 pay **a** to the words of my
Prov 29:12 If a ruler pays **a** to lies
Acts 3: 5 So he gave them his **a**,
Acts 26:26 of these things escapes his **a**
1Ti 4:13 I come, give **a** to reading, to
Jas 2: 3 you pay **a** to the one wearing

ATTENTIVE (*see* ATTENTION, ATTENTIVELY)
2Ki 20:13 And Hezekiah was **a** to them
2Ch 6:40 let Your ears be **a** to the
2Ch 7:15 My ears **a** to prayer made in
Neh 1: 6 please let Your ear be **a** and
Neh 1:11 be **a** to the prayer of Your
Neh 8: 3 were **a** to the Book of the Law
Ps 130: 2 Let Your ears be **a** To the
Luke 19:48 were very **a** to hear Him

ATTENTIVELY (*see* ATTENTIVE)
Job 37: 2 Hear **a** the thunder of His

ATTESTATION (*see* ATTESTED)
Ruth 4: 7 and this was an **a** in Israel

ATTESTED (*see* ATTESTATION)
Acts 2:22 a Man **a** by God to you by

ATTIRE (*see* ATTIRED)
Judg 5:10 donkeys, who sit in judges' **a**
Prov 7:10 with the **a** of a harlot, and a
Jer 2:32 ornaments, or a bride her **a**

ATTIRED (*see* ATTIRE)
Lev 16: 4 linen turban he shall be **a**

ATTRACTED
Gen 34: 3 His soul was strongly **a** to

ATTRIBUTES
Rom 1:20 invisible **a** are clearly seen

AUDITORIUM
Acts 25:23 had entered the **a** with the

AUGUSTAN (*see* AUGUSTUS)
Acts 27: 1 a centurion of the **A** Regiment

AUGUSTUS (*see* AUGUSTAN, CAESAR)
Luke 2: 1 **A** that all the world should
Acts 25:21 for the decision of **A**, I
Acts 25:25 he himself had appealed to **A**

AUNT
Lev 18:14 she is your **a**

AUSTERE
Luke 19:21 you, because you are an **a** man
Luke 19:22 You knew that I was an **a** man

AUTHOR
1Co 14:33 For God is not the **a** of
Heb 2:10 glory, to make the **a** of their
Heb 5: 9 He became the **a** of eternal
Heb 12: 2 looking unto Jesus, the **a**

AUTHORITIES (*see* AUTHORITY)
Luke 12:11 and magistrates and **a**, do not
Acts 16:19 into the marketplace to the **a**
Rom 13: 1 be subject to the governing **a**
Rom 13: 1 God, and the **a** that exist are
Tit 3: 1 to be subject to rulers and **a**
1Pe 3:22 hand of God, angels and **a** and

AUTHORITY (*see* AUTHORITIES)
Gen 41:35 grain under the **a** of Pharaoh
Num 5:19 while under your husband's **a**
Num 5:20 while under your husband's **a**
Num 5:29 while under her husband's **a**
Num 27:20 give some of your **a** to him
1Ki 21: 7 now exercise **a** over Israel
2Ki 8:20 revolted against Judah's **a**
2Ki 8:22 against Judah's **a** to this day
1Ch 25: 6 were under the **a** of the king
2Ch 21: 8 revolted against Judah's **a**
2Ch 21:10 against Judah's **a** to this day
Neh 13: 4 having **a** over the storerooms
Esth 9:29 wrote with full **a** to confirm
Prov 29: 2 When the righteous are in **a**
Dan 11: 6 not retain the power of her **a**
Dan 11: 6 he nor his **a** shall stand
Matt 7:29 taught them as one having **a**
Matt 8: 9 For I also am a man under **a**
Matt 20:25 great exercise **a** over them
Matt 21:23 By what **a** are You doing these
Matt 21:23 And who gave You this **a**
Matt 21:24 by what **a** I do these things
Matt 21:27 by what **a** I do these things
Matt 28:18 All **a** has been given to Me in
Mark 1:22 taught them as one having **a**
Mark 1:27 For with **a** He commands even
Mark 10:42 ones exercise **a** over them
Mark 11:28 By what **a** are You doing these
Mark 11:28 who gave You this **a** to do
Mark 11:29 by what **a** I do these things
Mark 11:33 by what **a** I do these things
Mark 13:34 gave **a** to his servants, and to
Luke 4: 6 All this **a** I will give You,
Luke 4:32 for His word was with **a**
Luke 4:36 For with **a** and power He
Luke 7: 8 also am a man placed under **a**
Luke 9: 1 **a** over all demons, and to cure
Luke 10:19 I give you the **a** to trample
Luke 19:17 have **a** over ten cities
Luke 20: 2 by what **a** are You doing these
Luke 20: 2 who is he who gave You this **a**
Luke 20: 8 by what **a** I do these things
Luke 20:20 and the **a** of the governor
Luke 22:25 those who exercise **a** over
John 5:27 has given Him **a** to execute
John 7:17 whether I speak on My own **a**
John 11:51 he did not say on his own **a**
John 12:49 I have not spoken on My own **a**
John 14:10 I do not speak on My own **a**
John 16:13 will not speak on His own **a**
John 17: 2 given Him **a** over all flesh
Acts 1: 7 Father has put in His own **a**
Acts 8:27 a eunuch of great **a** under
Acts 9:14 here he has **a** from the chief
Acts 25: 5 let those who have **a** among
Acts 26:10 having received **a** from the
Acts 26:12 journeyed to Damascus with **a**
Rom 13: 1 there is no **a** except from God
Rom 13: 2 whoever resists the **a** resists
Rom 13: 3 want to be unafraid of the **a**
1Co 7: 4 not have **a** over her own body
1Co 7: 4 not have **a** over his own body
1Co 9:18 not abuse my **a** in the gospel
1Co 11:10 a symbol of **a** on her head
1Co 15:24 an end to all rule and all **a**
2Co 10: 8 somewhat more about our **a**
2Co 13:10 according to the **a** which the
2Th 3: 9 not because we do not have **a**
1Ti 2: 2 for kings and all who are in **a**
1Ti 2:12 teach or to have **a** over a man
Tit 2:15 exhort, and rebuke with all **a**
2Pe 2:10 of uncleanness and despise **a**
Jude 8 defile the flesh, reject **a**
Rev 9: 5 were not given **a** to kill them
Rev 13: 2 power, his throne, and great **a**
Rev 13: 4 who gave **a** to the beast
Rev 13: 5 he was given **a** to continue
Rev 13: 7 **a** was given him over every
Rev 13:12 he exercises all the **a** of the
Rev 17:12 but they receive **a** for one
Rev 17:13 their power and **a** to the beast
Rev 18: 1 from heaven, having great **a**

AUTUMN
Jude 12 late **a** trees without fruit,

AVA (*see* IVAH)
2Ki 17:24 from Babylon, Cuthah, **A**,

AVAIL (*see* AVAILS)
Job 41:26 reaches him, it cannot **a**

AVAILS (*see* AVAIL)
Esth 5:13 Yet all this **a** me nothing
Gal 5: 6 nor uncircumcision **a** anything
Gal 6:15 nor uncircumcision **a** anything
Jas 5:16 of a righteous man **a** much

AVEN
Ezek 30:17 The young men of **A** and Pi
Hos 10: 8 Also the high places of **A**
Amos 1: 5 from the Valley of **A**, and the

AVENGE (*see* AVENGED, AVENGER, AVENGES, AVENGING)
Deut 32:43 for He will **a** the blood of
1Sa 24:12 and let the LORD **a** me on you
2Ki 9: 7 that I may **a** the blood of My
Esth 8:13 be ready on that day to **a**
Jer 5: 9 shall I not **a** Myself on such
Jer 5:29 Shall I not **a** Myself on such
Jer 9: 9 Shall I not **a** Myself on such
Jer 46:10 that He may **a** Himself on His
Hos 1: 4 in a little while I will **a**
Luke 18: 3 saying, "**A** me of my adversary
Luke 18: 5 troubles me I will **a** her,
Luke 18: 7 shall God not **a** His own elect
Luke 18: 8 that He will **a** them speedily
Rom 12:19 do not **a** yourselves, but
Rev 6:10 and **a** our blood on those who

AVENGED (*see* AVENGE)
Gen 4:24 If Cain shall be **a** sevenfold
Judg 11:36 has **a** you of your enemies
1Sa 25:31 or that my lord has **a** himself
2Sa 4: 8 the LORD has **a** my lord the
2Sa 18:19 how the LORD has **a** him of his
2Sa 18:31 For the LORD has **a** you this
Ezek 5:13 upon them, and I will be **a**
Acts 7:24 **a** him who was oppressed, and
Rev 18:20 for God has **a** you on her
Rev 19: 2 He has **a** on her the blood of

AVENGER (*see* AVENGE)
Num 35:12 of refuge for you from the **a**
Num 35:19 The **a** of blood himself shall
Num 35:21 the **a** of blood shall put the
Num 35:24 the **a** of blood according to
Num 35:25 the hand of the **a** of blood
Num 35:27 and the **a** of blood finds him
Num 35:27 and the **a** of blood kills the
Deut 19: 6 lest the **a** of blood, while
Deut 19:12 to the hand of the **a** of blood

Josh 20: 3 refuge from the **a** of blood
Josh 20: 5 Then if the **a** of blood
Josh 20: 9 the **a** of blood until he stood
2Sa 14:11 do not permit the **a** of blood
Ps 8: 2 silence the enemy and the **a**
Ps 44:16 Because of the enemy and the **a**
Rom 13: 4 an **a** to execute wrath on him
1Th 4: 6 the Lord is the **a** of all such

AVENGES (*see* AVENGE)
2Sa 22:48 It is God who **a** me, who
Ps 9:12 When He **a** blood, He
Ps 18:47 It is God who **a** me, And
Nah 1: 2 God is jealous, and the LORD **a**
Nah 1: 2 the LORD **a** and is furious

AVENGING (*see* AVENGE)
1Sa 25:26 from **a** yourself with your own
1Sa 25:33 from **a** myself with my own
Ps 79:10 The **a** of the blood of Your
Ezek 25:12 offended by **a** itself on them

AVIM (*see* AVITES)
Deut 2:23 And the **A**, who dwelt in
Josh 18:23 **A**, Parah, Ophrah,

AVITES (*see* AVIM)
Josh 13: 3 also the **A**
2Ki 17:31 the **A** made Nibhaz and Tartak

AVITH
Gen 36:35 And the name of his city was **A**
1Ch 1:46 The name of his city was **A**

AVOID (*see* AVOIDING)
Job 36:18 would not help you **a** it
Prov 4:15 **A** it, do not travel on it
Prov 14:27 to **a** the snares of death
Rom 16:17 which you learned, and **a** them
2Ti 2:23 But **a** foolish and ignorant
Tit 3: 9 But **a** foolish disputes,

AVOIDING (*see* AVOID)
2Co 8:20 **a** this
1Ti 6:20 trust, **a** the profane and vain

AWAIT (*see* AWAITING)
Acts 20:23 chains and tribulations **a** me

AWAITING (*see* AWAIT)
Ps 65: 1 Praise is **a** You, O God, in

AWAKE (*see* AWAKEN, AWAKES, AWAKING, AWOKE)
Judg 5:12 **A**, **a**, Deborah
Judg 5:12 **A**, **a**, Deborah
Judg 5:12 **A**, **a**, sing a song
Judg 5:12 **A**, **a**, sing a song
Job 8: 6 surely now He would **a** for you
Job 14:12 they will not **a** nor be roused
Ps 7: 6 **a** for me to the judgment You
Ps 17:15 when I **a** in Your likeness
Ps 35:23 **a** to my vindication, To my
Ps 44:23 **A**! Why do You sleep, O Lord?
Ps 57: 8 **A**, my glory
Ps 57: 8 **A**, lute and harp
Ps 59: 4 **A** to help me, and behold
Ps 59: 5 **A** to punish all the nations
Ps 73:20 awakes, So, Lord, when You **a**
Ps 102: 7 I lie **a**, And am like a sparrow
Ps 108: 2 **A**, lute and harp
Ps 119:148 My eyes are **a** through the
Ps 127: 1 The watchman stays **a** in vain
Ps 139:18 When I **a**, I am still with You
Prov 6:22 and when you **a**, they will
Prov 23:35 When shall I **a**, that I may
Song 4:16 **A**, O north wind, and come, O
Song 5: 2 I sleep, but my heart is **a**
Is 26:19 **A** and sing, you who dwell in
Is 51: 9 **A**, **a**, put on strength, O
Is 51: 9 **A**, **a**, put on strength, O
Is 51: 9 **A** as in the ancient days, in
Is 51:17 **A**, **a**! Stand up, O
Is 52: 1 **A**, **a**! Put on your strength
Jer 51:39 a perpetual sleep and not **a**
Jer 51:57 a perpetual sleep and not **a**
Dan 12: 2 the dust of the earth shall **a**
Joel 1: 5 **A**, you drunkards, and weep
Hab 2:19 to him who says to wood, '**A**
Zech 13: 7 **A**, O sword, against My
Mal 2:12 man who does this, being **a**
Luke 9:32 and when they were fully **a**
Rom 13:11 high time to **a** out of sleep
1Co 15:34 **A** to righteousness, and do not
Eph 5:14 **A**, you who sleep, arise from

AWAKEN (*see* AWAKE, AWAKENED, AWAKENS)
Ps 57: 8 I will **a** the dawn
Ps 108: 2 I will **a** the dawn
Song 2: 7 do not stir up nor **a** love
Song 3: 5 do not stir up nor **a** love
Song 8: 4 do not stir up nor **a** love
Hab 2: 7 Will they not **a** who oppress

AWAKENED (*see* AWAKEN)
1Ki 18:27 he is sleeping and must be **a**
2Ki 4:31 The child has not **a**
Song 8: 5 I **a** you under the apple tree

AWAKENS (*see* AWAKEN)
Is 50: 4 He **a** Me morning by morning,
Is 50: 4 he **a** My ear to hear as the

AWAKES (*see* AWAKE)
Ps 73:20 As a dream when one **a**, So,
Is 29: 8 but he **a**, and his soul is
Is 29: 8 but he **a**, and indeed he is

AWAKING (*see* AWAKE)
Acts 16:27 **a** from sleep and seeing the

AWARE
Song 6:12 Before I was even **a**, my soul
Jer 50:24 O Babylon, and you were not **a**
Obad 7 No one is **a** of it
Mal 2:12 does this, being awake and **a**
Matt 24:50 an hour that he is not **a** of
Matt 26:10 But when Jesus was **a** of it
Mark 8:17 And Jesus, being **a** of it, said
Luke 11:44 over them are not **a** of them
Luke 12:46 at an hour when he is not **a**
Acts 5: 2 his wife also being **a** of it
Acts 14: 6 they became **a** of it and fled

AWAY (*see* PREFACE)

AWE (*see* AWESOME)
Ps 33: 8 the world stand in **a** of Him
Ps 119:161 stands in **a** of Your word

AWESOME (*see* AWE)
Gen 28:17 said, "How **a** is this place
Ex 34:10 For it is an **a** thing that I
Deut 7:21 great and **a** God, is among you
Deut 10:17 the great God, mighty and **a**
Deut 10:21 **a** things which your eyes have
Deut 28:58 **a** name, THE LORD YOUR
Judg 13: 6 of the Angel of God, very **a**
2Sa 7:23 and **a** deeds for Your land
1Ch 17:21 and **a** deeds, by driving out
Neh 1: 5 and **a** God, You who keep Your
Neh 4:14 the Lord, great and **a**
Neh 9:32 **a** God, Who keeps covenant and
Job 10:16 show Yourself **a** against me
Job 37:22 with God is **a** majesty
Ps 45: 4 hand shall teach You **a** things
Ps 47: 2 For the LORD Most High is **a**
Ps 65: 5 By **a** deeds in righteousness
Ps 66: 3 God, "How **a** are Your works
Ps 66: 5 He is **a** in His doing toward
Ps 68:35 You are more **a** than Your holy
Ps 76:12 He is **a** to the kings of the
Ps 99: 3 praise Your great and **a** name
Ps 106:22 Ham, **A** things by the Red Sea
Ps 111: 9 Holy and **a** is His name
Ps 145: 6 of the might of Your **a** acts
Song 6: 4 **a** as an army with banners
Song 6:10 **A** as an army with banners
Is 28:21 His **a** work, and bring to pass
Is 64: 3 When You did **a** things for
Jer 20:11 is with me as a mighty, **a** one
Lam 1: 9 therefore her collapse was **a**
Ezek 1:18 they were so high they were **a**
Ezek 1:22 the color of an **a** crystal
Dan 2:31 and its form was **a**
Dan 9: 4 **a** God, who keeps His covenant
Zeph 2:11 The LORD will be **a** to them

AWHILE
1Sa 9:27 But you stand here **a**, that I

AWL
Ex 21: 6 pierce his ear with an **a**
Deut 15:17 then you shall take an **a** and

AWOKE (*see* AWAKE)
Gen 9:24 So Noah **a** from his wine, and
Gen 28:16 Then Jacob **a** from his sleep
Gen 41: 4 So Pharaoh **a**
Gen 41: 7 So Pharaoh **a**, and indeed, it
Gen 41:21 So I **a**.
Judg 16:14 But he **a** from his sleep, and
Judg 16:20 So he **a** from his sleep, and
1Sa 26:12 no man saw it or knew it or **a**
1Ki 3:15 Then Solomon **a**
Ps 3: 5 I **a**, for the LORD sustained
Ps 78:65 Then the Lord **a** as one out of
Jer 31:26 After this I **a** and looked
Matt 8:25 came to Him and **a** Him, saying,
Mark 4:38 And they **a** Him and said to
Luke 8:24 came to Him and **a** Him, saying,

AWRY
Prov 15:22 Without counsel, plans go **a**

AX (*see* AXES)
Deut 19: 5 the **a** to cut down the tree
Deut 20:19 by wielding an **a** against them
Judg 9:48 took an **a** in his hand and cut
1Sa 13:20 plowshare, his mattock, his **a**
2Ki 6: 5 the iron **a** head fell into the
Eccl 10:10 If the **a** is dull, and one does
Is 10:15 Shall the **a** boast itself
Jer 10: 3 of the workman, with the **a**
Matt 3:10 even now the **a** is laid to the
Luke 3: 9 even now the **a** is laid to the

AXES (*see* AX)
1Sa 13:21 mattocks, the forks, and the **a**
2Sa 12:31 saws and iron picks and iron **a**
1Ch 20: 3 with iron picks, and with **a**
2Ch 34: 6 and all around, with **a**
Ps 74: 5 up **A** among the thick trees
Ps 74: 6 work, all at once, With **a**
Jer 46:22 and come against her with **a**
Ezek 26: 9 with his **a** he will break down

AXLE (*see* AXLES)
1Ki 7:33 their **a** pins, their rims,

AXLES (*see* AXLE)
1Ki 7:30 **a** of bronze, and its four feet
1Ki 7:32 and the **a** of the wheels were

AYYAH
1Ch 7:28 and its towns, as far as **A**

AZAL
Zech 14: 5 valley shall reach to **A**

AZALIAH
2Ki 22: 3 the scribe, the son of **A**, the
2Ch 34: 8 he sent Shaphan the son of **A**

AZANIAH
Neh 10: 9 Jeshua the son of **A**, Binnui

AZAREEL
1Ch 12: 6 Elkanah, Jisshiah, **A**, Joezer,
Ezra 10:41 **A**, Shelemiah, Shemariah,
Neh 11:13 and Amashai the son of **A**, the

AZAREL
1Ch 25:18 the eleventh for **A**, his sons
1Ch 27:22 Dan, **A** the son of Jeroham
Neh 12:36 and his brethren, Shemaiah, **A**

AZARIAH (*see* AHAZIAH, EZRA)
1Ki 4: 2 **A** the son of Zadok, the
1Ki 4: 5 **A** the son of Nathan, over the
2Ki 14:21 the people of Judah took **A**
2Ki 15: 1 **A** the son of Amaziah, king of
2Ki 15: 6 Now the rest of the acts of **A**
2Ki 15: 7 So **A** rested with his fathers,
2Ki 15: 8 year of **A** king of Judah,
2Ki 15:17 year of **A** king of Judah,
2Ki 15:23 year of **A** king of Judah,
2Ki 15:27 year of **A** king of Judah,
1Ch 2: 8 The son of Ethan was **A**
1Ch 2:38 begot Jehu, and Jehu begot **A**
1Ch 2:39 **A** begot Helez, and Helez begot
1Ch 3:12 **A** his son, Jotham his son,
1Ch 6: 9 Ahimaaz begot **A**
1Ch 6: 9 and **A** begot Johanan
1Ch 6:10 Johanan begot **A** (it was he
1Ch 6:11 **A** begot Amariah, and Amariah
1Ch 6:13 Hilkiah, and Hilkiah begot **A**
1Ch 6:14 **A** begot Seraiah, and Seraiah
1Ch 6:36 the son of Joel, the son of **A**
1Ch 9:11 **A** the son of Hilkiah, the son
2Ch 15: 1 came upon **A** the son of Oded
2Ch 21: 2 **A**, Jehiel, Zechariah,
2Ch 22: 6 **A** the son of Jehoram, king of
2Ch 23: 1 **A** the son of Jeroham, Ishmael
2Ch 23: 1 **A** the son of Obed, Maaseiah
2Ch 26:17 So **A** the priest went in after
2Ch 26:20 **A** the chief priest and all the

2Ch 28:12 **A** the son of Johanan,
2Ch 29:12 Amasai and Joel the son of **A**
2Ch 29:12 and **A** the son of Jehalelel
2Ch 31:10 **A** the chief priest, from the
2Ch 31:13 **A** the ruler of the house of
Ezra 7: 1 son of Seraiah, the son of **A**
Ezra 7: 3 son of Amariah, the son of **A**
Neh 3:23 After them **A** the son of
Neh 3:24 house of **A** to the buttress
Neh 7: 7 were Jeshua, Nehemiah, **A**,
Neh 8: 7 Hodijah, Maaseiah, Kelita, **A**
Neh 10: 2 Seraiah, **A**, Jeremiah,
Neh 12:33 and **A**, Ezra, Meshullam,
Jer 43: 2 that **A** the son of Hoshaiah,
Dan 1: 6 Hananiah, Mishael, and **A**
Dan 1: 7 and to **A**, Abed-Nego
Dan 1:11 Hananiah, Mishael, and **A**,
Dan 1:19 Hananiah, Mishael, and **A**
Dan 2:17 to Hananiah, Mishael, and **A**

AZARYAHU
2Ch 21: 2 Azariah, Jehiel, Zechariah, **A**

AZAZ
1Ch 5: 8 and Bela the son of **A**, the son

AZAZIAH
1Ch 15:21 Obed-Edom, Jeiel, and **A**, to
1Ch 27:20 Ephraim, Hoshea the son of **A**
2Ch 31:13 Jehiel, **A**, Nahath, Asahel,

AZBUK
Neh 3:16 him Nehemiah the son of **A**

AZEKAH
Josh 10:10 struck them down as far as **A**
Josh 10:11 heaven on them as far as **A**
Josh 15:35 Jarmuth, Adullam, Socoh, **A**
1Sa 17: 1 between Sochoh and **A**
2Ch 11: 9 Adoraim, Lachish, **A**,
Neh 11:30 in **A** and its villages
Jer 34: 7 left, against Lachish and **A**

AZEL
1Ch 8:37 Eleasah his son, and **A** his son
1Ch 8:38 **A** had six sons whose names
1Ch 8:38 All these were the sons of **A**
1Ch 9:43 Eleasah his son, and **A** his son
1Ch 9:44 **A** had six sons whose names
1Ch 9:44 these were the sons of **A**

AZGAD
Ezra 2:12 the people of **A**, one thousand
Ezra 8:12 of the sons of **A**, Johanan the
Neh 7:17 the children of **A**, two
Neh 10:15 Bunni, **A**, Bebai,

AZIEL
1Ch 15:20 Zechariah, **A**, Shemiramoth,

AZIZA
Ezra 10:27 Jeremoth, Zabad, and **A**

AZMAVETH
2Sa 23:31 Arbathite, **A** the Barhumite,
1Ch 8:36 Jehoaddah begot Alemeth, **A**
1Ch 9:42 Jarah begot Alemeth, **A**, and
1Ch 11:33 **A** the Baharumite, Eliahba the
1Ch 12: 3 Jeziel and Pelet the sons of **A**
1Ch 27:25 **A** the son of Adiel was over
Ezra 2:24 the people of **A**, forty-two
Neh 12:29 from the fields of Geba and **A**

AZMON (*see* HESHMON)
Num 34: 4 Hazar Addar, and continue to **A**
Num 34: 5 from **A** to the Brook of Egypt
Josh 15: 4 From there it passed toward **A**

AZNOTH TABOR (*see* TABOR)
Josh 19:34 border extended westward to **A**

AZOR
Matt 1:13 Eliakim, and Eliakim begot **A**
Matt 1:14 **A** begot Zadok, Zadok begot

AZOTUS
Acts 8:40 But Philip was found at **A**

AZRIEL
1Ch 5:24 Epher, Ishi, Eliel, **A**,
1Ch 27:19 Jerimoth the son of **A**
Jer 36:26 son, Seraiah the son of **A**

AZRIKAM
1Ch 3:23 were Elioenai, Hezekiah, and **A**
1Ch 8:38 **A**, Bocheru, Ishmael, Sheariah
1Ch 9:14 son of Hasshub, the son of **A**
1Ch 9:44 **A**, Bocheru, Ishmael, Sheariah
2Ch 28: 7 **A** the officer over the house,
Neh 11:15 son of Hasshub, the son of **A**

AZUBAH
1Ki 22:42 His mother's name was **A** the
1Ch 2:18 of Hezron begot children by **A**
1Ch 2:19 When **A** died, Caleb took
2Ch 20:31 His mother's name was **A** the

AZUR (*see* AZZUR)
Jer 28: 1 the son of **A** the prophet, who

AZZAN
Num 34:26 Paltiel the son of **A**

AZZUR (*see* AZUR)
Neh 10:17 Ater, Hezekiah, **A**,
Ezek 11: 1 I saw Jaazaniah the son of **A**

B

BAAL (*see* BAAL'S, BAALE, BAALE JUDAH, BAALS, BEL)
Num 22:41 up to the high places of **B**
Num 25: 3 was joined to **B** of Peor, and
Num 25: 5 who were joined to **B** of Peor
Deut 4: 3 what the LORD did at **B** Peor
Deut 4: 3 men who followed **B** of Peor
Judg 2:13 forsook the LORD and served **B**
Judg 6:25 of **B** that your father has
Judg 6:28 there was the altar of **B**
Judg 6:30 has torn down the altar of **B**
Judg 6:31 Would you plead for **B**
Judg 6:32 Let **B** plead against him,
1Ki 16:31 and he went and served **B** and
1Ki 16:32 for **B** in the temple of **B**
1Ki 16:32 for **B** in the temple of **B**
1Ki 18:19 and fifty prophets of **B**, and
1Ki 18:21 but if **B**, then follow him
1Ki 18:25 said to the prophets of **B**
1Ki 18:26 called on the name of **B** from
1Ki 18:26 O **B**, hear us
1Ki 18:40 Seize the prophets of **B**
1Ki 19:18 knees have not bowed to **B**
1Ki 22:53 for he served **B** and worshiped
2Ki 3: 2 of **B** that his father had made
2Ki 10:18 Ahab served **B** a little, but
2Ki 10:19 to me all the prophets of **B**
2Ki 10:19 great sacrifice to make to **B**
2Ki 10:19 the worshipers of **B**
2Ki 10:20 a solemn assembly for **B**
2Ki 10:21 all the worshipers of **B** came
2Ki 10:21 came into the temple of **B**
2Ki 10:21 the temple of **B** was full from
2Ki 10:22 for all the worshipers of **B**
2Ki 10:23 went into the temple of **B**
2Ki 10:23 said to the worshipers of **B**
2Ki 10:23 but only the worshipers of **B**
2Ki 10:25 inner room of the temple of **B**
2Ki 10:26 out of the temple of **B** and
2Ki 10:27 down the sacred pillar of **B**
2Ki 10:27 and tore down the temple of **B**
2Ki 10:28 Jehu destroyed **B** from Israel
2Ki 11:18 land went to the temple of **B**
2Ki 11:18 priest of **B** before the altars
2Ki 17:16 host of heaven, and served **B**
2Ki 21: 3 he raised up altars for **B**
2Ki 23: 4 articles that were made for **B**
2Ki 23: 5 those who burned incense to **B**
1Ch 4:33 these cities as far as **B**
1Ch 5: 5 Reaiah his son, **B** his son,
1Ch 8:30 was Abdon, then Zur, Kish, **B**
1Ch 9:36 was Abdon, then Zur, Kish, **B**
2Ch 23:17 went to the temple of **B**, and
2Ch 23:17 priest of **B** before the altars
Ps 106:28 themselves also to **B** of Peor
Jer 2: 8 the prophets prophesied by **B**
Jer 7: 9 falsely, burn incense to **B**
Jer 11:13 altars to burn incense to **B**
Jer 11:17 in offering incense to **B**
Jer 12:16 My people to swear by **B**, then
Jer 19: 5 built the high places of **B**
Jer 19: 5 fire for burnt offerings to **B**
Jer 23:13 they prophesied by **B** and
Jer 23:27 fathers forgot My name for **B**
Jer 32:29 have offered incense to **B**
Jer 32:35 built the high places of **B**
Hos 2: 8 which they prepared for **B**
Hos 9:10 But they went to **B** Peor, and
Hos 13: 1 but when he offended in **B**
Zeph 1: 4 trace of **B** from this place
Rom 11: 4 have not bowed the knee to **B**

BAALAH (*see* BILHAH, KIRJATH BAAL)
Josh 15: 9 **B** (which is Kirjath Jearim)
Josh 15:10 westward from **B** to Mount Seir
Josh 15:11 passed along to Mount **B**, and
Josh 15:29 **B**, Ijim, Ezem,
1Ch 13: 6 and all Israel went up to **B**

BAALATH (*see* BAALATH BEER)
Josh 19:44 Eltekeh, Gibbethon, **B**,
1Ki 9:18 **B**, and Tadmor in the
2Ch 8: 6 also **B** and all the storage

BAALATH BEER (*see* BAALATH)
Josh 19: 8 these cities as far as **B**,

BAAL-BERITH (*see* BERITH)
Judg 8:33 Baals, and made **B** their god
Judg 9: 4 silver from the temple of **B**

BAALE JUDAH (*see* BAAL)
2Sa 6: 2 who were with him from **B** to

BAAL GAD (*see* GAD)
Josh 11:17 Seir, even as far as **B** in the
Josh 12: 7 west, from **B** in the Valley of
Josh 13: 5 from **B** below Mount Hermon as

BAAL HAMON
Song 8:11 Solomon had a vineyard at **B**

BAAL-HANAN (*see* HANAN)
Gen 36:38 **B** the son of Achbor reigned
Gen 36:39 when **B** the son of Achbor died
1Ch 1:49 **B** the son of Achbor reigned
1Ch 1:50 when **B** died, Hadad reigned
1Ch 27:28 **B** the Gederite was over the

BAAL HAZOR (*see* HAZOR)
2Sa 13:23 had sheepshearers in **B**, which

BAAL HERMON (*see* HERMON)
Judg 3: 3 from Mount **B** to the entrance
1Ch 5:23 increased from Bashan to **B**

BAALIS
Jer 40:14 **B** the king of the Ammonites

BAAL MEON (*see* BETH BAAL MEON)
Num 32:38 **B** (their names being changed)
Josh 13:17 Dibon, Bamoth Baal, Beth **B**
1Ch 5: 8 in Aroer, as far as Nebo and **B**
Ezek 25: 9 country, Beth Jeshimoth, **B**

BAAL PERAZIM (*see* PERAZIM)
2Sa 5:20 So David went to **B**, and David
2Sa 5:20 the name of that place **B**
1Ch 14:11 So they went up to **B**, and
1Ch 14:11 the name of that place **B**

BAAL'S (*see* BAAL)
1Ki 18:22 but **B** prophets are four

BAALS (*see* BAAL)
Judg 2:11 of the LORD, and served the **B**
Judg 3: 7 their God, and served the **B**
Judg 8:33 played the harlot with the **B**
Judg 10: 6 of the LORD, and served the **B**
Judg 10:10 our God and served the **B**
1Sa 7: 4 of Israel put away the **B** and
1Sa 12:10 the LORD and served the **B** and
1Ki 18:18 and you have followed the **B**
2Ch 17: 3 he did not seek the **B**,
2Ch 24: 7 house of the LORD to the **B**
2Ch 28: 2 made molded images for the **B**
2Ch 33: 3 he raised up altars for the **B**
2Ch 34: 4 of the **B** in his presence, and
Jer 2:23 I have not gone after the **B**'
Jer 9:14 own heart and after the **B**,
Hos 2:13 her for the days of the **B** to
Hos 2:17 her mouth the names of the **B**
Hos 11: 2 They sacrificed to the **B**

BAAL SHALISHA
2Ki 4:42 Then a man came from **B**, and

BAAL TAMAR (*see* TAMAR)
Judg 20:33 in battle array at **B**

BAAL-ZEBUB (*see* BEELZEBUB)
2Ki 1: 2 Go, inquire of **B**, the god of
2Ki 1: 3 you are going to inquire of **B**
2Ki 1: 6 are sending to inquire of **B**
2Ki 1:16 messengers to inquire of **B**

BAAL ZEPHON (*see* ZEPHON)
Ex 14: 2 Migdol and the sea, opposite **B**
Ex 14: 9 beside Pi Hahiroth, before **B**
Num 33: 7 Hahiroth, which is east of **B**

BAANA (*see* BAANAH)
1Ki 4:12 **B** the son of Ahilud, in
Neh 3: 4 the son of **B** made repairs

BAANAH (*see* BAANA)
2Sa 4: 2 The name of one was **B** and the
2Sa 4: 5 the Beerothite, Rechab and **B**
2Sa 4: 6 and **B** his brother escaped
2Sa 4: 9 **B** his brother, the sons of
2Sa 23:29 Heleb the son of **B** (the
1Ki 4:16 **B** the son of Hushai, in Asher
1Ch 11:30 the son of **B** the Netophathite
Ezra 2: 2 Mispar, Bigvai, Rehum, and **B**
Neh 7: 7 Bigvai, Nehum, and **B**
Neh 10:27 Malluch, Harim, and **B**

BAARA
1Ch 8: 8 away Hushim and **B** his wives

BAASEIAH
1Ch 6:40 son of Michael, the son of **B**

BAASHA
1Ki 15:16 **B** king of Israel all their
1Ki 15:17 And **B** king of Israel came up
1Ki 15:19 treaty with **B** king of Israel
1Ki 15:21 when **B** heard it, that he
1Ki 15:22 which **B** had used for building
1Ki 15:27 Then **B** the son of Ahijah, of
1Ki 15:27 **B** killed him at Gibbethon,
1Ki 15:28 **B** killed him in the third
1Ki 15:32 **B** king of Israel all their
1Ki 15:33 **B** the son of Ahijah became
1Ki 16: 1 the son of Hanani, against **B**
1Ki 16: 3 take away the posterity of **B**
1Ki 16: 4 eat whoever belongs to **B** and
1Ki 16: 5 Now the rest of the acts of **B**
1Ki 16: 6 So **B** rested with his fathers
1Ki 16: 7 the son of Hanani against **B**
1Ki 16: 8 Elah the son of **B** became king
1Ki 16:11 killed all the household of **B**
1Ki 16:12 all the household of **B**,
1Ki 16:12 against **B** by Jehu the prophet
1Ki 16:13 for all the sins of **B** and the
1Ki 21:22 house of **B** the son of Ahijah
2Ki 9: 9 house of **B** the son of Ahijah
2Ch 16: 1 Asa, **B** king of Israel came up
2Ch 16: 3 treaty with **B** king of Israel
2Ch 16: 5 when **B** heard it, that he
2Ch 16: 6 which **B** had used for building
Jer 41: 9 for fear of **B** king of Israel

BABBLE (*see* BABBLER, BABBLINGS)
2Ki 9:11 You know the man and his **b**

BABBLER (*see* BABBLE, BABBLERS)
Eccl 10:11 the **b** is no different
Acts 17:18 What does this **b** want to say

BABBLERS (*see* BABBLER)
Is 44:25 frustrates the signs of the **b**

BABBLINGS (*see* BABBLE)
1Ti 6:20 the profane and vain **b** and
2Ti 2:16 But shun profane and vain **b**

BABE (*see* BABES, BABY)
Luke 1:41 that the **b** leaped in her womb
Luke 1:44 the **b** leaped in my womb for
Luke 2:12 You will find a **B** wrapped in
Luke 2:16 and the **B** lying in a manger
Heb 5:13 righteousness, for he is a **b**

BABEL (*see* BABYLON)
Gen 10:10 of his kingdom was **B**, Erech,
Gen 11: 9 its name is called **B**, because

BABES (*see* BABE)
Ps 8: 2 Out of the mouth of **b** and
Ps 17:14 their substance for their **b**
Is 3: 4 and **b** shall rule over them
Joel 2:16 the children and nursing **b**
Matt 11:25 and have revealed them to **b**
Matt 21:16 read, 'Out of the mouth of **b**
Luke 10:21 prudent and revealed them to **b**
Rom 2:20 the foolish, a teacher of **b**
1Co 3: 1 to carnal, as to **b** in Christ
1Co 14:20 however, in malice be **b**, but
1Pe 2: 2 as newborn **b**, desire the pure

BABIES (*see* BABY)
Matt 24:19 with nursing **b** in those days
Mark 13:17 with nursing **b** in those days
Luke 21:23 are nursing **b** in those days
Acts 7:19 making them expose their **b**

BABY (*see* BABE, BABIES)
Ex 2: 6 child, and behold, the **b** wept

BABYLON (*see* BABEL, BABYLONIAN, BABYLON'S, CHALDEA, SHESHACH)
2Ki 17:24 Assyria brought people from **B**
2Ki 17:30 The men of **B** made Succoth
2Ki 20:12 the son of Baladan, king of **B**
2Ki 20:14 from a far country, from **B**
2Ki 20:17 day, shall be carried to **B**
2Ki 20:18 the palace of the king of **B**
2Ki 24: 1 king of **B** came up, and
2Ki 24: 7 for the king of **B** had taken
2Ki 24:10 **B** came up against Jerusalem
2Ki 24:11 of **B** came against the city
2Ki 24:12 went out to the king of **B**
2Ki 24:12 and the king of **B**, in the
2Ki 24:15 Jehoiachin captive to **B**
2Ki 24:15 captivity from Jerusalem to **B**
2Ki 24:16 of **B** brought captive to **B**
2Ki 24:17 the king of **B** made Mattaniah
2Ki 24:20 against the king of **B**
2Ki 25: 1 that Nebuchadnezzar king of **B**
2Ki 25: 6 up to the king of **B** at Riblah
2Ki 25: 7 fetters, and took him to **B**
2Ki 25: 8 Nebuchadnezzar king of **B**)
2Ki 25: 8 a servant of the king of **B**
2Ki 25:11 had deserted to the king of **B**
2Ki 25:13 and carried their bronze to **B**
2Ki 25:20 to the king of **B** at Riblah
2Ki 25:21 the king of **B** struck them
2Ki 25:22 king of **B** had left
2Ki 25:23 heard that the king of **B** had
2Ki 25:24 land and serve the king of **B**
2Ki 25:27 that Evil-Merodach king of **B**
2Ki 25:28 kings who were with him in **B**
1Ch 9: 1 captive to **B** because of their
2Ch 32:31 of the princes of **B**, whom
2Ch 33:11 and carried him off to **B**
2Ch 36: 6 king of **B** came up against him
2Ch 36: 6 fetters to carry him off to **B**
2Ch 36: 7 the house of the LORD to **B**
2Ch 36: 7 put them in his temple at **B**
2Ch 36:10 him and took him to **B**
2Ch 36:18 all these he took to **B**
2Ch 36:20 sword he carried away to **B**
Ezra 1:11 brought from **B** to Jerusalem
Ezra 2: 1 Nebuchadnezzar the king of **B**
Ezra 2: 1 **B** had carried away to **B**
Ezra 4: 9 of Persia and Erech and **B** and
Ezra 5:12 of Nebuchadnezzar king of **B**
Ezra 5:12 carried the people away to **B**
Ezra 5:13 first year of Cyrus king of **B**
Ezra 5:14 carried into the temple of **B**
Ezra 5:14 took from the temple of **B**
Ezra 5:17 house, which is there in **B**
Ezra 6: 1 treasures were stored in **B**
Ezra 6: 5 in Jerusalem and brought to **B**
Ezra 7: 6 this Ezra came up from **B**
Ezra 7: 9 he began his journey from **B**
Ezra 7:16 find in all the province of **B**
Ezra 8: 1 who went up with me from **B**
Neh 7: 6 of **B** had carried away captive
Neh 13: 6 **B** I had returned to the king
Esth 2: 6 king of **B** had carried away
Ps 87: 4 and **B** to those who know Me
Ps 137: 1 By the rivers of **B**, There we
Ps 137: 8 O daughter of **B**, who are to
Is 13: 1 The burden against **B** which
Is 13:19 And **B**, the glory of kingdoms,
Is 14: 4 proverb against the king of **B**
Is 14:22 And cut off from **B** the name
Is 21: 9 **B** is fallen, is fallen
Is 39: 1 the son of Baladan, king of **B**
Is 39: 3 me from a far country, from **B**
Is 39: 6 day, shall be carried to **B**
Is 39: 7 the palace of the king of **B**
Is 43:14 your sake I will send to **B**
Is 47: 1 dust, O virgin daughter of **B**
Is 48:14 he shall do His pleasure on **B**
Is 48:20 Go forth from **B**
Jer 20: 4 the hand of the king of **B**
Jer 20: 4 shall carry them captive to **B**
Jer 20: 5 them, and carry them to **B**
Jer 20: 6 You shall go to **B**, and there
Jer 21: 2 of **B** makes war against us
Jer 21: 4 fight against the king of **B**
Jer 21: 7 of Nebuchadnezzar king of **B**
Jer 21:10 the hand of the king of **B**
Jer 22:25 of Nebuchadnezzar king of **B**
Jer 24: 1 Nebuchadnezzar king of **B** had
Jer 24: 1 and had brought them to **B**
Jer 25: 1 of Nebuchadnezzar king of **B**)
Jer 25: 9 Nebuchadnezzar the king of **B**
Jer 25:11 the king of **B** seventy years
Jer 25:12 I will punish the king of **B**
Jer 27: 6 Nebuchadnezzar the king of **B**
Jer 27: 8 Nebuchadnezzar the king of **B**
Jer 27: 8 the yoke of the king of **B**
Jer 27: 9 shall not serve the king of **B**
Jer 27:11 the yoke of the king of **B**
Jer 27:12 the yoke of the king of **B**
Jer 27:13 will not serve the king of **B**
Jer 27:14 shall not serve the king of **B**
Jer 27:16 be brought back from **B**"
Jer 27:17 serve the king of **B**, and live
Jer 27:18 at Jerusalem, do not go to **B**
Jer 27:20 king of **B** did not take, when
Jer 27:20 of Judah, from Jerusalem to **B**
Jer 27:22 They shall be carried to **B**
Jer 28: 2 the yoke of the king of **B**
Jer 28: 3 **B** took away from this place
Jer 28: 3 this place and carried to **B**
Jer 28: 4 of Judah who went to **B**,' says
Jer 28: 4 the yoke of the king of **B**
Jer 28: 6 captive, from **B** to this place
Jer 28:11 of **B** from the neck of all
Jer 28:14 Nebuchadnezzar king of **B**
Jer 29: 1 captive from Jerusalem to **B**
Jer 29: 3 king of Judah sent to **B**, to
Jer 29: 3 to Nebuchadnezzar king of **B**
Jer 29: 4 away from Jerusalem to **B**
Jer 29:10 years are completed at **B**, I
Jer 29:15 up prophets for us in **B**"
Jer 29:20 have sent from Jerusalem to **B**
Jer 29:21 of Nebuchadnezzar king of **B**
Jer 29:22 of Judah who are in **B**, saying
Jer 29:22 whom the king of **B** roasted in
Jer 29:28 For he has sent to us in **B**
Jer 32: 3 the hand of the king of **B**
Jer 32: 4 the hand of the king of **B**
Jer 32: 5 he shall lead Zedekiah to **B**
Jer 32:28 of Nebuchadnezzar king of **B**
Jer 32:36 of the king of **B** by the sword
Jer 34: 1 when Nebuchadnezzar king of **B**
Jer 34: 2 the hand of the king of **B**
Jer 34: 3 see the eyes of the king of **B**
Jer 34: 3 to face, and you shall go to **B**
Jer 35:11 of **B** came up into the land
Jer 36:29 king of **B** will certainly come
Jer 37: 1 of **B** made king in the land of
Jer 37:17 the hand of the king of **B**
Jer 37:19 The king of **B** will not come
Jer 38:23 by the hand of the king of **B**
Jer 39: 1 Nebuchadnezzar king of **B**
Jer 39: 3 of the king of **B** came in and
Jer 39: 3 the princes of the king of **B**
Jer 39: 5 to Nebuchadnezzar king of **B**
Jer 39: 6 Then the king of **B** killed the
Jer 39: 6 the king of **B** also killed all
Jer 39: 7 fetters to carry him off to **B**
Jer 39: 9 carried away captive to **B** the
Jer 39:11 of **B** gave charge concerning
Jer 40: 1 carried away captive to **B**
Jer 40: 4 to you to come with me to **B**
Jer 40: 4 for you to come with me to **B**
Jer 40: 5 whom the king of **B** has made
Jer 40: 7 heard that the king of **B** had
Jer 40: 7 carried away captive to **B**
Jer 40: 9 land and serve the king of **B**
Jer 40:11 heard that the king of **B** had
Jer 41: 2 **B** had made governor over the
Jer 41:18 whom the king of **B** had made
Jer 42:11 be afraid of the king of **B**
Jer 43: 3 or carry us away captive to **B**
Jer 43:10 Nebuchadnezzar the king of **B**
Jer 44:30 of Nebuchadnezzar king of **B**
Jer 46: 2 Nebuchadnezzar king of **B**
Jer 46:13 king of **B** would come and
Jer 46:26 of Nebuchadnezzar king of **B**
Jer 49:28 king of **B** shall strike
Jer 49:30 **B** has taken counsel against
Jer 50: 1 that the LORD spoke against **B**
Jer 50: 2 **B** is taken, Bel is shamed
Jer 50: 8 Move from the midst of **B**, go

Jer 50: 9 **B** An assembly of great
Jer 50:13 goes by **B** shall be horrified
Jer 50:14 in array against **B** all around
Jer 50:16 Cut off the sower from **B**, and
Jer 50:17 of **B** has broken his bones
Jer 50:18 I will punish the king of **B**
Jer 50:23 How **B** has become a desolation
Jer 50:24 have indeed been trapped, O **B**
Jer 50:28 of **B** declares in Zion the
Jer 50:29 the archers against **B**
Jer 50:34 disquiet the inhabitants of **B**
Jer 50:35 Against the inhabitants of **B**
Jer 50:42 against you, O daughter of **B**
Jer 50:43 The king of **B** has heard the
Jer 50:45 that He has taken against **B**
Jer 50:46 of **B** the earth trembles, and
Jer 51: 1 I will raise up against **B**
Jer 51: 2 And I will send winnowers to **B**
Jer 51: 6 Flee from the midst of **B**, and
Jer 51: 7 **B** was a golden cup in the
Jer 51: 8 **B** has suddenly fallen and been
Jer 51: 9 We would have healed **B**, but
Jer 51:11 is against **B** to destroy it
Jer 51:12 standard on the walls of **B**
Jer 51:12 against the inhabitants of **B**
Jer 51:24 And I will repay **B** and all the
Jer 51:29 shall be performed against **B**
Jer 51:29 to make the land of **B** a
Jer 51:30 The mighty men of **B** have
Jer 51:31 to show the king of **B** that
Jer 51:33 The daughter of **B** is like a
Jer 51:34 the king of **B** has devoured me
Jer 51:35 to me and my flesh be upon **B**
Jer 51:37 **B** shall become a heap, a
Jer 51:41 How **B** has become desolate
Jer 51:42 The sea has come up over **B**
Jer 51:44 I will punish Bel in **B**, and I
Jer 51:44 Yes, the wall of **B** shall fall
Jer 51:47 on the carved images of **B**
Jer 51:48 shall sing joyously over **B**
Jer 51:49 As **B** has caused the slain of
Jer 51:49 so at **B** the slain of all the
Jer 51:53 Though **B** were to mount up to
Jer 51:54 sound of a cry comes from **B**
Jer 51:55 the LORD is plundering **B** and
Jer 51:56 comes against her, against **B**
Jer 51:58 The broad walls of **B** shall be
Jer 51:59 the king of Judah to **B** in the
Jer 51:60 evil that would come upon **B**
Jer 51:60 that are written against **B**
Jer 51:61 When you arrive in **B** and see
Jer 51:64 Thus **B** shall sink and not
Jer 52: 3 against the king of **B**
Jer 52: 4 that Nebuchadnezzar king of **B**
Jer 52: 9 him up to the king of **B** at
Jer 52:10 Then the king of **B** killed the
Jer 52:11 the king of **B** bound him in
Jer 52:11 bronze fetters, took him to **B**
Jer 52:12 Nebuchadnezzar king of **B**)
Jer 52:12 who served the king of **B**
Jer 52:15 had deserted to the king of **B**
Jer 52:17 carried all their bronze to **B**
Jer 52:26 to the king of **B** at Riblah
Jer 52:27 the king of **B** struck them
Jer 52:31 that Evil-Merodach king of **B**
Jer 52:32 kings who were with him in **B**
Jer 52:34 given him by the king of **B**
Ezek 12:13 I will bring him to **B**, to the
Ezek 17:12 king of **B** went to Jerusalem
Ezek 17:12 and led them with him to **B**
Ezek 17:16 the midst of **B** he shall die
Ezek 17:20 I will bring him to **B** and try
Ezek 19: 9 brought him to the king of **B**
Ezek 21:19 sword of the king of **B** to go
Ezek 21:21 For the king of **B** stands at
Ezek 24: 2 the king of **B** started his
Ezek 26: 7 Nebuchadnezzar king of **B**,
Ezek 29:18 man, Nebuchadnezzar king of **B**
Ezek 29:19 to Nebuchadnezzar king of **B**
Ezek 30:10 of Nebuchadnezzar king of **B**
Ezek 30:24 the arms of the king of **B**
Ezek 30:25 the arms of the king of **B**
Ezek 30:25 the hand of the king of **B**
Ezek 32:11 king of **B** shall come upon you
Dan 1: 1 king of **B** came to Jerusalem
Dan 2:12 destroy all the wise men of **B**
Dan 2:14 out to kill the wise men of **B**
Dan 2:18 the rest of the wise men of **B**
Dan 2:24 to destroy the wise men of **B**
Dan 2:24 not destroy the wise men of **B**
Dan 2:48 over the whole province of **B**
Dan 2:48 over all the wise men of **B**
Dan 2:49 affairs of the province of **B**
Dan 3: 1 of Dura, in the province of **B**
Dan 3:12 affairs of the province of **B**
Dan 3:30 in the province of **B**
Dan 4: 6 the wise men of **B** before me
Dan 4:29 about the royal palace of **B**
Dan 4:30 Is not this great **B**, that I
Dan 5: 7 saying to the wise men of **B**
Dan 7: 1 year of Belshazzar king of **B**
Mic 4:10 and you shall go even to **B**
Zech 2: 7 dwell with the daughter of **B**
Zech 6:10 Jedaiah, who have come from **B**
Matt 1:11 they were carried away to **B**
Matt 1:12 after they were brought to **B**
Matt 1:17 until the captivity in **B** are
Matt 1:17 in **B** until the Christ are
Acts 7:43 will carry you away beyond **B**
1Pe 5:13 She who is in **B**, elect
Rev 14: 8 **B** is fallen, is fallen, that
Rev 16:19 great **B** was remembered before
Rev 17: 5 **B** THE GREAT, THE
Rev 18: 2 **B** the great is fallen, is
Rev 18:10 Alas, alas, that great city **B**
Rev 18:21 city **B** shall be thrown down

BABYLONIAN (*see* BABYLON, BABYLONIANS)
Josh 7:21 spoils a beautiful **B** garment

BABYLONIANS (*see* BABYLONIAN)
Ezek 23:15 manner of the **B** of Chaldea
Ezek 23:17 Then the **B** came to her, into
Ezek 23:23 the **B**, all the Chaldeans,

BABYLON'S (*see* BABYLON)
Jer 32: 2 For then the king of **B** army
Jer 34: 7 when the king of **B** army
Jer 34:21 the hand of the king of **B**
Jer 38: 3 hand of the king of **B** army
Jer 38:17 to the king of **B** princes,
Jer 38:18 to the king of **B** princes,
Jer 38:22 to the king of **B** princes, and
Jer 39:13 the king of **B** chief officers

BACA
Ps 84: 6 pass through the Valley of **B**

BACHRITES (*see* BECHER)
Num 26:35 Becher, the family of the **B**

BACK (*see* PREFACE)

BACKBITE (*see* BACKBITERS, BACKBITING)
Ps 15: 3 does not **b** with his tongue

BACKBITERS (*see* BACKBITE)
Rom 1:30 **b**, haters of God, violent,

BACKBITING (*see* BACKBITE, BACKBITINGS)
Prov 25:23 rain, and a **b** tongue an angry

BACKBITINGS (*see* BACKBITING)
2Co 12:20 wrath, selfish ambitions, **b**

BACKBONE
Lev 3: 9 shall remove close to the **b**

BACKS
Ex 23:27 enemies turn their **b** to you
Josh 7:12 but turned their **b** before
Judg 20:42 **b** before the men of Israel in
2Ch 29: 6 and turned their **b** on Him
Neh 9:26 cast Your law behind their **b**
Ps 66:11 You laid affliction on our **b**
Prov 19:29 beatings for the **b** of fools
Is 30: 6 on the **b** of young donkeys
Ezek 8:16 **b** toward the temple of the

BACKSLIDER (*see* BACKSLIDING)
Prov 14:14 The **b** in heart will be filled

BACKSLIDING (*see* BACKSLIDER, BACKSLIDINGS)
Is 57:17 he went on **b** in the way of
Jer 3: 6 seen what **b** Israel has done
Jer 3: 8 which **b** Israel had committed
Jer 3:11 **B** Israel has shown herself
Jer 3:12 **b** Israel,' says the LORD, 'and
Jer 3:14 O **b** children," says the LORD
Jer 3:22 you **b** children, and I will
Jer 8: 5 Jerusalem, in a perpetual **b**
Jer 31:22 gad about, O you **b** daughter
Jer 49: 4 flowing valley, O **b** daughter
Hos 11: 7 people are bent on **b** from Me
Hos 14: 4 I will heal their **b**, I will

BACKSLIDINGS (*see* BACKSLIDING)
Jer 2:19 and your **b** will reprove you
Jer 3:22 and I will heal your **b**
Jer 5: 6 their **b** have increased
Jer 14: 7 for our **b** are many, we have

BACKWARD
Gen 9:23 their shoulders, and went **b**
Gen 49:17 that its rider shall fall **b**
1Sa 4:18 **b** by the side of the gate
2Ki 20: 9 degrees or go **b** ten degrees
2Ki 20:10 the shadow go **b** ten degrees
2Ki 20:11 the shadow ten degrees **b**, by
Job 23: 8 but He is not there, and **b**
Ps 40:14 Let them be driven **b** and
Is 1: 4 they have turned away **b**
Is 28:13 that they might go and fall **b**
Is 38: 8 of Ahaz, ten degrees **b**
Is 44:25 Who turns wise men **b**, and
Jer 7:24 their evil heart, and went **b**
Jer 15: 6 You have gone **b**

BAD
Gen 24:50 speak to you either **b** or good
Gen 31:24 to Jacob neither good nor **b**
Gen 31:29 to Jacob neither good nor **b**
Gen 37: 2 Joseph brought a **b** report of
Lev 27:10 good for **b** or **b** for good
Lev 27:12 it, whether it is good or **b**
Lev 27:14 it, whether it is good or **b**
Lev 27:33 whether it is good or **b**, nor
Num 13:19 they dwell in is good or **b**
Num 13:32 a **b** report of the land which
Num 14:36 a **b** report of the land,
Num 24:13 good or **b** of my own will
Deut 22:14 brings a **b** name on her, and
Deut 22:19 because he has brought a **b**
2Sa 13:22 Amnon neither good nor **b**
2Sa 19:35 discern between the good and **b**
1Ki 14: 6 been sent to you with **b** news
2Ki 2:19 but the water is **b**, and the
Prov 25:19 of trouble is like a **b** tooth
Jer 24: 2 **b** figs which could not be
Jer 24: 2 not be eaten, they were so **b**
Jer 24: 3 and the **b**, very **b**, which
Jer 24: 3 be eaten, they are so **b**
Jer 24: 8 as the **b** figs which cannot be
Jer 24: 8 be eaten, they are so **b**'
Jer 29:17 be eaten, they are so **b**
Jer 49:23 for they have heard **b** news
Amos 8: 6 even sell the **b** wheat
Matt 6:23 But if your eye is **b**, your
Matt 7:17 but a **b** tree bears **b** fruit
Matt 7:18 good tree cannot bear **b** fruit
Matt 7:18 nor can a **b** tree bear good
Matt 12:33 the tree **b** and its fruit **b**
Matt 13:48 vessels, but threw the **b** away
Matt 22:10 all whom they found, both **b**
Luke 6:43 tree does not bear **b** fruit
Luke 6:43 nor does a **b** tree bear good
Luke 11:34 But when your eye is **b**, your
2Co 5:10 has done, whether good or **b**

BADGER (*see* BADGERS)
Ex 25: 5 red, **b** skins, and acacia wood
Ex 26:14 a covering of **b** skins above
Ex 35: 7 red, **b** skins, and acacia wood
Ex 35:23 and **b** skins, brought them
Ex 36:19 a covering of **b** skins above
Ex 39:34 red, the covering of **b** skins
Num 4: 6 on it a covering of **b** skins
Num 4: 8 with a covering of **b** skins
Num 4:10 in a covering of **b** skins, and
Num 4:11 it with a covering of **b** skins
Num 4:12 with a covering of **b** skins
Num 4:14 on it a covering of **b** skins
Num 4:25 the covering of **b** skins that
Ezek 16:10 and gave you sandals of **b** skin

BADGERS (*see* BADGER)
Ps 104:18 are a refuge for the rock **b**
Prov 30:26 the rock **b** are a feeble folk,

BAG (*see* BAGS)
Deut 25:13 in your **b** differing weights
1Sa 17:40 and put them in a shepherd's **b**
1Sa 17:49 David put his hand in his **b**
Job 14:17 is sealed up in a **b**, and You
Prov 7:20 He has taken a **b** of money
Prov 16:11 weights in the **b** are His work
Is 46: 6 They lavish gold out of the **b**
Mic 6:11 and with the **b** of deceitful
Hag 1: 6 to put into a **b** with holes

Matt 10:10 nor **b** for your journey, nor
Mark 6: 8 no **b**, no bread, no copper in
Luke 9: 3 neither staffs nor **b** nor
Luke 10: 4 Carry neither money **b**, sack,
Luke 22:35 I sent you without money **b**
Luke 22:36 But now, he who has a money **b**

BAGS (*see* BAG)
2Ki 5:23 talents of silver in two **b**
2Ki 12:10 priest came up and put it in **b**
Luke 12:33 money **b** which do not grow old

BAHARUMITE
1Ch 11:33 Azmaveth the **B**, Eliahba the

BAHURIM
2Sa 3:16 went along with her to **B**,
2Sa 16: 5 when King David came to **B**
2Sa 17:18 and came to a man's house in **B**
2Sa 19:16 a Benjamite, who was from **B**
1Ki 2: 8 of Gera, a Benjamite from **B**

BAKBAKKAR
1Ch 9:15 **B**, Heresh, Galal, and

BAKBUK
Ezra 2:51 the sons of **B**, the sons of
Neh 7:53 the children of **B**, the

BAKBUKIAH
Neh 11:17 and **B** the second among his
Neh 12: 9 Also **B** and Unni, their
Neh 12:25 Mattaniah, **B**, Obadiah,

BAKE (*see* BAKED, BAKER, BAKES)
Gen 11: 3 bricks and **b** them thoroughly
Ex 16:23 **B** what you will **b** today,
Lev 24: 5 and **b** twelve cakes with it
Lev 26:26 ten women shall **b** your bread
Ezek 4:12 and **b** it using fuel of human
Ezek 46:20 where they shall **b** the grain

BAKED (*see* BAKE)
Gen 19: 3 **b** unleavened bread, and they
Gen 40:17 kinds of **b** goods for Pharaoh
Ex 12:39 they **b** unleavened cakes of
Lev 2: 4 grain offering **b** in the oven
Lev 2: 5 a grain offering **b** in a pan
Lev 2: 7 offering **b** in a covered pan
Lev 6:17 It shall not be **b** with leaven
Lev 6:21 the **b** pieces of the grain
Lev 7: 9 that is **b** in the oven and all
Lev 23:17 they shall be **b** with leaven
1Sa 28:24 **b** unleavened bread from it
2Sa 13: 8 in his sight, and **b** the cakes
1Ki 19: 6 head was a cake **b** on coals
1Ch 9:31 that were **b** in the pans
1Ch 23:29 what is **b** in the pan, with
Is 44:19 I have also **b** bread on its

BAKER (*see* BAKE, BAKERS)
Gen 40: 1 the **b** of the king of Egypt
Gen 40: 2 chief butler and the chief **b**
Gen 40: 5 the **b** of the king of Egypt,
Gen 40:16 When the chief **b** saw that the
Gen 40:20 and of the chief **b** among his
Gen 40:22 But he hanged the chief **b**
Gen 41:10 guard, both me and the chief **b**
Hos 7: 4 like an oven heated by a **b**
Hos 7: 6 their **b** sleeps all night

BAKERS (*see* BAKER, BAKERS')
1Sa 8:13 to be perfumers, cooks, and **b**

BAKERS' (*see* BAKERS)
Jer 37:21 of bread from the **b** street

BAKES (*see* BAKE)
Is 44:15 yes, he kindles it and **b** bread

BALAAM (*see* BALAAM'S)
Num 22: 5 **B** the son of Beor at Pethor
Num 22: 7 their hand, and they came to **B**
Num 22: 8 princes of Moab stayed with **B**
Num 22: 9 Then God came to **B** and said
Num 22:10 And **B** said to God,
Num 22:12 And God said to **B**, "You shall
Num 22:13 So **B** rose in the morning and
Num 22:14 **B** refuses to come with us
Num 22:16 And they came to **B** and said to
Num 22:18 Then **B** answered and said to
Num 22:20 And God came to **B** at night
Num 22:21 So **B** rose in the morning,
Num 22:23 So **B** struck the donkey to
Num 22:27 LORD, she lay down under **B**
Num 22:28 the donkey, and she said to **B**
Num 22:29 And **B** said to the donkey,
Num 22:30 So the donkey said to **B**, "Am
Num 22:34 **B** said to the Angel of the
Num 22:35 Angel of the LORD said to **B**
Num 22:35 So **B** went with the princes
Num 22:36 Balak heard that **B** was coming
Num 22:37 Then Balak said to **B**, "Did I
Num 22:38 And **B** said to Balak,
Num 22:39 So **B** went with Balak, and they
Num 22:40 sheep, and he sent some to **B**
Num 22:41 next day, that Balak took **B**
Num 23: 1 Then **B** said to Balak, "Build
Num 23: 2 did just as **B** had spoken, and
Num 23: 2 **B** offered a bull and a ram on
Num 23: 3 Then **B** said to Balak, "Stand
Num 23: 4 And God met **B**, and he said to
Num 23:11 Then Balak said to **B**, "What
Num 23:16 Then the LORD met **B**, and put a
Num 23:25 Then Balak said to **B**
Num 23:26 So **B** answered and said to
Num 23:27 Then Balak said to **B**
Num 23:28 So Balak took **B** to the top of
Num 23:29 Then **B** said to Balak, "Build
Num 23:30 And Balak did as **B** had said
Num 24: 1 Now when **B** saw that it
Num 24: 2 **B** raised his eyes, and saw
Num 24: 3 of **B** the son of Beor, the
Num 24:10 anger was aroused against **B**
Num 24:10 and Balak said to **B**, "I
Num 24:12 So **B** said to Balak, "Did I
Num 24:15 of **B** the son of Beor, and the
Num 24:25 Then **B** rose and departed and
Num 31: 8 **B** the son of Beor they also
Num 31:16 through the counsel of **B**
Deut 23: 4 they hired against you **B** the
Deut 23: 5 God would not listen to **B**
Josh 13:22 the sword **B** the son of Beor
Josh 24: 9 called **B** the son of Beor to
Josh 24:10 But I would not listen to **B**
Neh 13: 2 but hired **B** against them to
Mic 6: 5 and what **B** the son of Beor
2Pe 2:15 the way of **B** the son of Beor
Jude 11 in the error of **B** for profit
Rev 2:14 who hold the doctrine of **B**

BALAAM'S (*see* BALAAM)
Num 22:25 crushed **B** foot against the
Num 22:27 so **B** anger was aroused, and he
Num 22:31 Then the LORD opened **B** eyes
Num 23: 5 LORD put a word in **B** mouth

BALADAN (*see* BERODACH-BALADAN, MERODACH-BALADAN)
2Ki 20:12 Berodach-Baladan the son of **B**
Is 39: 1 Merodach-Baladan the son of **B**

BALAH
Josh 19: 3 Hazar Shual, **B**, Ezem,

BALAK (*see* BALAK'S)
Num 22: 2 Now **B** the son of Zippor saw
Num 22: 4 **B** the son of Zippor was king
Num 22: 7 spoke to him the words of **B**
Num 22:10 **B** the son of Zippor, king of
Num 22:13 and said to the princes of **B**
Num 22:14 of Moab rose and went to **B**
Num 22:15 Then **B** again sent princes,
Num 22:16 Thus says **B** the son of Zippor
Num 22:18 and said to the servants of **B**
Num 22:18 Though **B** were to give me his
Num 22:35 went with the princes of **B**
Num 22:36 Now when **B** heard that Balaam
Num 22:37 Then **B** said to Balaam, "Did
Num 22:38 And Balaam said to **B**, "Look,
Num 22:39 So Balaam went with **B**, and
Num 22:40 Then **B** offered oxen and sheep,
Num 22:41 that **B** took Balaam and brought
Num 23: 1 Then Balaam said to **B**
Num 23: 2 And **B** did just as Balaam had
Num 23: 2 as Balaam had spoken, and **B**
Num 23: 3 Then Balaam said to **B**
Num 23: 5 Return to **B**, and thus you
Num 23: 7 **B** the king of Moab has
Num 23:11 Then **B** said to Balaam, "What
Num 23:13 Then **B** said to him, "Please
Num 23:15 And he said to **B**, "Stand here
Num 23:16 Go back to **B**, and thus you
Num 23:17 And **B** said to him,
Num 23:18 Rise up, **B**, and hear
Num 23:25 Then **B** said to Balaam
Num 23:26 Balaam answered and said to **B**
Num 23:27 Then **B** said to Balaam
Num 23:28 So **B** took Balaam to the top
Num 23:29 Then Balaam said to **B**
Num 23:30 **B** did as Balaam had said, and
Num 24:10 and **B** said to Balaam,
Num 24:12 So Balaam said to **B**, "Did I
Num 24:13 Though **B** were to give me his
Num 24:25 **B** also went his way
Josh 24: 9 Then **B** the son of Zippor,
Judg 11:25 than **B** the son of Zippor,
Mic 6: 5 remember now what **B** king of
Rev 2:14 Balaam, who taught **B** to put a

BALAK'S (*see* BALAK)
Num 24:10 Then **B** anger was aroused

BALANCE (*see* BALANCES)
Lev 25:27 restore the **b** to the man to
Job 31: 6 Let me be weighed in a just **b**
Job 37:16 Do you know the **b** of clouds
Prov 11: 1 A false **b** is an abomination
Prov 16:11 weight and **b** are the LORD's
Prov 20:23 and a false **b** is not good
Is 40:12 in scales and the hills in a **b**
Is 40:15 as the small dust on the **b**
Is 46: 6 bag, and weigh silver in the **b**

BALANCES (*see* BALANCE)
Lev 19:36 You shall have just **b**, just
Job 6: 2 laid with it in the **b**
Ps 62: 9 If they are weighed in the **b**
Jer 32:10 and weighed the money in the **b**
Ezek 5: 1 then take **b** to weigh and
Ezek 45:10 You shall have just **b**, a just
Dan 5:27 have been weighed in the **b**
Amos 8: 5 falsifying the **b** by deceit
Mic 6:11 pure those with the wicked **b**

BALD (*see* BALDHEAD, BALDNESS)
Lev 13:40 fallen from his head, he is **b**
Lev 13:41 he is **b** on the forehead, but
Lev 13:42 is on the **b** head or **b**
Lev 13:42 **b** head or his **b** forehead
Lev 13:43 on his **b** head or on his **b**
Lev 21: 5 any **b** place on their heads
Jer 16: 6 make themselves **b** for them
Jer 48:37 For every head shall be **b**
Ezek 27:31 completely **b** because of you
Ezek 29:18 every head was made **b**, and
Mic 1:16 Make yourself **b** and cut off

BALDHEAD (*see* BALD)
2Ki 2:23 Go up, you **b**

BALDNESS (*see* BALD)
Is 3:24 instead of well-set hair, **b**
Is 15: 2 on all their heads will be **b**
Is 22:12 and for mourning, for **b** and for
Jer 47: 5 **B** has come upon Gaza,
Ezek 7:18 face, **b** on all their heads
Amos 8:10 waist, and **b** on every head
Mic 1:16 enlarge your **b** like an eagle,

BALL
Is 22:18 and toss you like a **b** into a

BALM
Gen 37:25 camels, bearing spices, **b**
Gen 43:11 a little **b** and a little honey,
Jer 8:22 Is there no **b** in Gilead, is
Jer 46:11 Go up to Gilead and take **b**
Jer 51: 8 Take **b** for her pain
Ezek 27:17 millet, honey, oil, and **b**

BAMAH (*see* BAMOTH)
Ezek 20:29 name is called **B** to this day

BAMOTH (*see* BAMAH, BAMOTH BAAL)
Num 21:19 Nahaliel, from Nahaliel to **B**
Num 21:20 and from **B**, in the valley that

BAMOTH BAAL (*see* BAMOTH)
Josh 13:17 Dibon, **B**, Beth Baal Meon,

BAN
Lev 27:29 No person under the **b**, who

BAND (*see* BANDED, BANDS)
Gen 49:15 and became a **b** of slaves
Ex 28: 8 woven **b** of the ephod, which
Ex 28:27 woven **b** of the ephod
Ex 28:28 woven **b** of the ephod, and so
Ex 29: 5 woven **b** of the ephod
Ex 39: 5 the intricately woven **b** of
Ex 39:20 woven **b** of the ephod
Ex 39:21 woven **b** of the ephod, and that
Lev 8: 7 woven **b** of the ephod, and with
1Ki 11:24 captain over a **b** of raiders
2Ki 13:21 they spied a **b** of raiders

Job 38: 9 darkness its swaddling **b**
Dan 4:15 earth, bound with a **b** of iron
Dan 4:23 earth, bound with a **b** of iron
Hos 7: 1 A **b** of robbers takes spoil
Rev 1:13 the chest with a golden **b**

BANDAGE (*see* BANDAGED)
1Ki 20:38 with a **b** over his eyes
1Ki 20:41 take the **b** away from his eyes

BANDAGED (*see* BANDAGE)
Ezek 30:21 it has not been **b** for healing
Luke 10:34 **b** his wounds, pouring on oil

BANDED (*see* BAND)
Judg 11: 3 worthless men **b** together with
Acts 23:12 some of the Jews **b** together

BANDS (*see* BAND)
Ex 27:10 their **b** shall be of silver
Ex 27:11 pillars and their **b** of silver
Ex 27:17 court shall have **b** of silver
Ex 38:10 and their **b** were of silver
Ex 38:11 and their **b** were of silver
Ex 38:12 and their **b** were of silver
Ex 38:17 their **b** were of silver, and
Ex 38:17 of the court had **b** of silver
Ex 38:19 and their **b** was of silver
Ex 38:28 capitals, and made **b** for them
Lev 26:13 broken the **b** of your yoke
2Ki 6:23 So the **b** of Syrian raiders
2Ki 13:20 And the raiding **b** from Moab
2Ki 24: 2 him raiding **b** of Chaldeans
2Ki 24: 2 **b** of Syrians, **b** of Moabites
2Ki 24: 2 and **b** of the people of Ammon
1Ch 12:21 against the **b** of raiders, for
Job 1:17 The Chaldeans formed three **b**
Ezek 34:27 broken the **b** of their yoke
Hos 6: 9 As **b** of robbers lie in wait
Hos 11: 4 with **b** of love, and I was to
Rev 15: 6 chests girded with golden **b**

BANI
2Sa 23:36 of Zobah, **B** the Gadite,
1Ch 6:46 the son of Amzi, the son of **B**
1Ch 9: 4 the son of Imri, the son of **B**
Ezra 2:10 the people of **B**, six hundred
Ezra 10:29 of the sons of **B**
Ezra 10:34 of the sons of **B**
Ezra 10:38 **B**, Binnui, Shimei,
Neh 3:17 under Rehum the son of **B**
Neh 8: 7 Also Jeshua, **B**, Sherebiah,
Neh 9: 4 Then Jeshua, **B**, Kadmiel,
Neh 9: 4 Bunni, Sherebiah, **B**, and
Neh 9: 5 Levites, Jeshua, Kadmiel, **B**
Neh 10:13 Hodijah, **B**, and Beninu
Neh 10:14 Pahath-Moab, Elam, Zattu, **B**
Neh 11:22 was Uzzi the son of **B**, the

BANISHED (*see* BANISHMENT)
2Sa 14:13 bring his **b** one home again
2Sa 14:14 so that His **b** ones are not
1Ki 15:12 he **b** the perverted persons
1Ki 22:46 Asa, he **b** from the land
Prov 14:32 The wicked is **b** in his

BANISHMENT (*see* BANISHED)
Ezra 7:26 whether it be death, or **b**

BANK (*see* BANKERS, BANKS)
Gen 41: 3 cows on the **b** of the river
Gen 41:17 I stood on the **b** of the river
Ex 2: 3 in the reeds by the river's **b**
Ex 7:15 by the river's **b** to meet him
Deut 2:36 which is on the **b** of the
Deut 4:48 which is on the **b** of the
Josh 12: 2 which is on the **b** of the
Josh 13: 9 on the **b** of the River Arnon
Josh 13:16 which is on the **b** of the
Josh 13:23 was the **b** of the Jordan
2Ki 2:13 stood by the **b** of the Jordan
Ezek 47: 6 me to the **b** of the river
Ezek 47: 7 along the **b** of the river,
Ezek 47:12 Along the **b** of the river, on
Luke 19:23 you not put my money in the **b**

BANKERS (*see* BANK)
Matt 25:27 deposited my money with the **b**

BANKS (*see* BANK)
Num 13:29 along the **b** of the Jordan
Josh 3:15 **b** during the whole time of
Josh 4:18 over all its **b** as before
Judg 11:26 along the **b** of the Arnon, for
1Ch 12:15 it had overflowed all its **b**

Song 5:13 like **b** of scented herbs
Is 8: 7 channels and go over all his **b**
Dan 8:16 between the **b** of the Ulai

BANNER (*see* BANNERS)
Ps 60: 4 You have given a **b** to those
Song 2: 4 and his **b** over me was love
Is 5:26 He will lift up a **b** to the
Is 11:10 stand as a **b** to the people
Is 11:12 set up a **b** for the nations
Is 13: 2 Lift up a **b** on the high
Is 18: 3 lifts up a **b** on the mountains
Is 30:17 mountain and as a **b** on a hill
Is 31: 9 shall be afraid of the **b**,"
Is 62:10 lift up a **b** for the peoples
Jer 51:27 Set up a **b** in the land, blow
Zech 9:16 lifted like a **b** over His land

BANNERS (*see* BANNER)
Ps 20: 5 our God we will set up our **b**
Ps 74: 4 They set up their **b** for signs
Song 6: 4 awesome as an army with **b**
Song 6:10 Awesome as an army with **b**

BANQUET (*see* BANQUETING, BANQUETS)
Esth 5: 4 Haman come today to the **b**
Esth 5: 5 and Haman went to the **b** that
Esth 5: 6 At the **b** of wine the king
Esth 5: 8 Haman come to the **b** which I
Esth 5:12 to the **b** that she prepared
Esth 5:14 with the king to the **b**
Esth 6:14 to bring Haman to the **b** which
Esth 7: 2 at the **b** of wine, the king
Esth 7: 7 his wrath from the **b** of wine
Esth 7: 8 to the place of the **b** of wine
Job 41: 6 companions make a **b** of him
Dan 5:10 his lords, came to the **b** hall

BANQUETING (*see* BANQUET)
Song 2: 4 He brought me to the **b** house

BANQUETS (*see* BANQUET)
Amos 6: 7 recline at **b** shall be removed

BAPTISM (*see* BAPTISMS, BAPTIZE)
Matt 3: 7 and Sadducees coming to his **b**
Matt 20:22 be baptized with the **b** that I
Matt 20:23 be baptized with the **b** that I
Matt 21:25 The **b** of John, where was it
Mark 1: 4 preaching a **b** of repentance
Mark 10:38 be baptized with the **b** that I
Mark 10:39 with the **b** I am baptized with
Mark 11:30 The **b** of John
Luke 3: 3 preaching a **b** of repentance
Luke 7:29 baptized with the **b** of John
Luke 12:50 But I have a **b** to be baptized
Luke 20: 4 The **b** of John
Acts 1:22 beginning from the **b** of John
Acts 10:37 the **b** which John preached
Acts 13:24 the **b** of repentance to all
Acts 18:25 he knew only the **b** of John
Acts 19: 3 they said, "Into John's **b**."
Acts 19: 4 with a **b** of repentance,
Rom 6: 4 with Him through **b** into death
Eph 4: 5 one Lord, one faith, one **b**
Col 2:12 buried with Him in **b**, in
1Pe 3:21 which now saves us, namely **b**

BAPTISMS (*see* BAPTISM)
Heb 6: 2 of the doctrine of **b**, of

BAPTIST (*see* BAPTIST'S, BAPTIZE, JOHN)
Matt 3: 1 the **B** came preaching in the
Matt 11:11 one greater than John the **B**
Matt 11:12 **B** until now the kingdom of
Matt 14: 2 This is John the **B**
Matt 16:14 Some say John the **B**, some
Matt 17:13 spoke to them of John the **B**
Mark 6:14 John the **B** is risen from the
Mark 6:24 The head of John the **B**
Mark 6:25 of John the **B** on a platter
Mark 8:28 they answered, "John the **B**
Luke 7:20 John the **B** has sent us to You
Luke 7:28 prophet than John the **B**
Luke 7:33 For John the **B** came neither
Luke 9:19 John the **B**, but some say

BAPTIST'S (*see* BAPTIST)
Matt 14: 8 Give me John the **B** head here

BAPTIZE (*see* BAPTISM, BAPTIST, BAPTIZED, BAPTIZES, BAPTIZING)
Matt 3:11 I indeed **b** you with water
Matt 3:11 He will **b** you with the Holy
Mark 1: 8 but He will **b** you with the

Luke 3:16 I indeed **b** you with water
Luke 3:16 He will **b** you with the Holy
John 1:25 Why then do you **b** if you are
John 1:26 I **b** with water, but there
John 1:33 me to **b** with water said to me
John 4: 2 Jesus Himself did not **b**, but
1Co 1:17 Christ did not send me to **b**

BAPTIZED (*see* BAPTIZE)
Matt 3: 6 were **b** by him in the Jordan,
Matt 3:13 at the Jordan to be **b** by him
Matt 3:14 I have need to be **b** by You
Matt 3:16 Jesus, when He had been **b**
Matt 20:22 be **b** with the baptism that I
Matt 20:22 the baptism that I am **b** with
Matt 20:23 be **b** with the baptism that I
Matt 20:23 the baptism that I am **b** with
Mark 1: 5 and were all **b** by him in the
Mark 1: 8 I indeed **b** you with water,
Mark 1: 9 was **b** by John in the Jordan
Mark 10:38 be **b** with the baptism that I
Mark 10:38 the baptism that I am **b** with
Mark 10:39 with the baptism I am **b** with
Mark 10:39 **b** with you will be **b**
Mark 16:16 and is **b** will be saved
Luke 3: 7 that came out to be **b** by him
Luke 3:12 collectors also came to be **b**
Luke 3:21 when all the people were **b**
Luke 3:21 to pass that Jesus also was **b**
Luke 7:29 God, having been **b** with the
Luke 7:30 not having been **b** by him
Luke 12:50 I have a baptism to be **b** with
John 3:22 He remained with them and **b**
John 3:23 And they came and were **b**
John 4: 1 **b** more disciples than John
Acts 1: 5 for John truly **b** with water
Acts 1: 5 but you shall be **b** with the
Acts 2:38 let every one of you be **b** in
Acts 2:41 received his word were **b**
Acts 8:12 both men and women were **b**
Acts 8:13 when he was **b** he continued
Acts 8:16 They had only been **b** in the
Acts 8:36 What hinders me from being **b**
Acts 8:38 into the water, and he **b** him
Acts 9:18 and he arose and was **b**
Acts 10:47 that these should not be **b**
Acts 10:48 be **b** in the name of the Lord
Acts 11:16 John indeed **b** with water
Acts 11:16 but you shall be **b** with the
Acts 16:15 she and her household were **b**
Acts 16:33 he and all his family were **b**
Acts 18: 8 hearing, believed and were **b**
Acts 19: 3 Into what then were you **b**
Acts 19: 4 John indeed **b** with a baptism
Acts 19: 5 they were **b** in the name of
Acts 22:16 Arise and be **b**, and wash away
Rom 6: 3 were **b** into Christ Jesus were
Rom 6: 3 Jesus were **b** into His death
1Co 1:13 Or were you **b** in the name of
1Co 1:14 I thank God that I **b** none of
1Co 1:15 that I had **b** in my own name
1Co 1:16 I also **b** the household of
1Co 1:16 know whether I **b** any other
1Co 10: 2 all were **b** into Moses in the
1Co 12:13 we were all **b** into one body
1Co 15:29 do who are **b** for the dead
1Co 15:29 then are they **b** for the dead
Gal 3:27 **b** into Christ have put on

BAPTIZES (*see* BAPTIZE)
John 1:33 this is He who **b** with the

BAPTIZING (*see* BAPTIZE)
Matt 28:19 **b** them in the name of the
Mark 1: 4 John came **b** in the wilderness
John 1:28 the Jordan, where John was **b**
John 1:31 therefore I came **b** with water
John 3:23 Now John also was **b** in Aenon
John 3:26 behold, He is **b**, and all are
John 10:40 where John was **b** at first

BAR (*see* BARS)
Ex 26:28 The middle **b** shall pass
Ex 36:33 he made the middle **b** to pass
Judg 16: 3 gateposts, pulled them up, **b**
Neh 7: 3 them shut the doors and **b** them
Amos 1: 5 break the gate **b** of Damascus

BARABBAS
Matt 27:16 a notorious prisoner called **B**
Matt 27:17 **B**, or Jesus who is called
Matt 27:20 that they should ask for **B**
Matt 27:21 They said, "**B**!"

Matt 27:26 Then he released **B** to them
Mark 15: 7 And there was one named **B**
Mark 15:11 rather release **B** to them
Mark 15:15 the crowd, released **B** to them
Luke 23:18 Man, and release to us **B**"
John 18:40 Not this Man, but **B**
John 18:40 Now **B** was a robber

BARACHEL
Job 32: 2 the son of **B** the Buzite, of
Job 32: 6 the son of **B** the Buzite,

BARAK
Judg 4: 6 and called for **B** the son of
Judg 4: 8 And **B** said to her,
Judg 4: 9 and went with **B** to Kedesh
Judg 4:10 **B** called Zebulun and Naphtali
Judg 4:12 reported to Sisera that **B** the
Judg 4:14 Then Deborah said to **B**, "Up
Judg 4:14 So **B** went down from Mount
Judg 4:15 edge of the sword before **B**
Judg 4:16 But **B** pursued the chariots and
Judg 4:22 as **B** pursued Sisera, Jael
Judg 5: 1 **B** the son of Abinoam sang on
Judg 5:12 Arise, **B**, and lead your
Judg 5:15 so was **B** sent into the valley
Heb 11:32 me to tell of Gideon and **B**

BARBARIAN (*see* BARBARIANS)
Col 3:11 nor uncircumcised, **b**,

BARBARIANS (*see* BARBARIAN)
Rom 1:14 debtor both to Greeks and to **b**

BARBER'S
Ezek 5: 1 sword, take it as a **b** razor

BARE (*see* BAREFOOT)
Lev 13:45 shall be torn and his head **b**
Ps 29: 9 And strips the forests **b**
Is 32:11 yourselves, make yourselves **b**
Is 52:10 The LORD has made **b** His holy
Jer 13:22 uncovered, your heels made **b**
Jer 26:18 the **b** hills of the forest
Jer 49:10 But I have made Esau **b**
Ezek 16: 7 grew, but you were naked and **b**
Ezek 16:22 when you were naked and **b**
Ezek 16:39 and leave you naked and **b**
Ezek 23:29 for, and leave you naked and **b**
Joel 1: 7 he has stripped it **b** and
Mic 3:12 the **b** hills of the forest
Hab 3:13 by laying **b** from foundation
Zeph 2:14 He will lay **b** the cedar work

BAREFOOT (*see* BARE)
2Sa 15:30 his head covered and went **b**
Is 20: 2 he did so, walking naked and **b**
Is 20: 3 **b** three years for a sign and a
Is 20: 4 young and old, naked and **b**

BARHUMITE
2Sa 23:31 the Arbathite, Azmaveth the **B**

BARIAH
1Ch 3:22 were Hattush, Igal, **B**,

BAR-JESUS
Acts 13: 6 a Jew whose name was **B**,

BAR-JONAH (*see* SIMON)
Matt 16:17 Blessed are you, Simon **B**, for

BARK
Is 56:10 all dumb dogs, they cannot **b**

BARKOS
Ezra 2:53 the sons of **B**, the sons of
Neh 7:55 the children of **B**, the

BARLEY
Ex 9:31 the **b** were struck, for the
Ex 9:31 for the **b** was in the head and
Lev 27:16 A homer of **b** seed shall be
Num 5:15 of an ephah of **b** meal
Deut 8: 8 a land of wheat and **b**, of
Judg 7:13 a loaf of **b** bread tumbled
Ruth 1:22 at the beginning of **b** harvest
Ruth 2:17 and it was about an ephah of **b**
Ruth 2:23 until the end of **b** harvest
Ruth 3: 2 he is winnowing **b** tonight at
Ruth 3:15 he measured six ephahs of **b**
Ruth 3:17 six ephahs of **b** he gave me
2Sa 14:30 near mine, and he has **b** there
2Sa 17:28 earthen vessels and wheat, **b**
2Sa 21: 9 in the beginning of **b** harvest
1Ki 4:28 They also brought **b** and straw
2Ki 4:42 twenty loaves of **b** bread
2Ki 7: 1 two seahs of **b** for a shekel
2Ki 7:16 two seahs of **b** for a shekel
2Ki 7:18 Two seahs of **b** for a shekel
1Ch 11:13 a piece of ground full of **b**
2Ch 2:10 twenty thousand kors of **b**
2Ch 2:15 therefore, the wheat, the **b**
2Ch 27: 5 wheat, and ten thousand of **b**
Job 31:40 wheat, and weeds instead of **b**
Is 28:25 the **b** in the appointed place,
Jer 41: 8 we have treasures of wheat, **b**
Ezek 4: 9 take for yourself wheat, **b**
Ezek 4:12 you shall eat it as **b** cakes
Ezek 13:19 My people for handfuls of **b**
Ezek 45:13 of an ephah. from a homer of **b**
Hos 3: 2 one and one-half homers of **b**
Joel 1:11 for the wheat and the **b**
John 6: 9 here who has five **b** loaves
John 6:13 the fragments of the five **b**
Rev 6: 6 quarts of **b** for a denarius

BARN (*see* BARNS)
Hag 2:19 Is the seed still in the **b**
Matt 3:12 gather His wheat into the **b**
Matt 13:30 gather the wheat into my **b**
Luke 3:17 gather the wheat into His **b**
Luke 12:24 have neither storehouse nor **b**

BARNABAS (*see* JOSES)
Acts 4:36 who was also named **B** by the
Acts 9:27 But **B** took him and brought him
Acts 11:22 they sent out **B** to go as far
Acts 11:25 Then **B** departed for Tarsus to
Acts 11:30 the elders by the hands of **B**
Acts 12:25 And **B** and Saul returned from
Acts 13: 1 **B**, Simeon who was called
Acts 13: 2 Now separate to Me **B** and Saul
Acts 13: 7 This man called for **B** and Saul
Acts 13:43 proselytes followed Paul and **B**
Acts 13:46 Paul and **B** grew bold and said,
Acts 13:50 persecution against Paul and **B**
Acts 14:12 **B** they called Zeus, and Paul,
Acts 14:14 But when the apostles **B** and
Acts 14:20 he departed with **B** to Derbe
Acts 15: 2 **B** had no small dissension and
Acts 15: 2 determined that Paul and **B**
Acts 15:12 kept silent and listened to **B**
Acts 15:22 to Antioch with Paul and **B**
Acts 15:25 men to you with our beloved **B**
Acts 15:35 **B** also remained in Antioch,
Acts 15:36 some days Paul said to **B**
Acts 15:37 Now **B** was determined to take
Acts 15:39 so **B** took Mark and sailed to
1Co 9: 6 Or is it only **B** and I who have
Gal 2: 1 up again to Jerusalem with **B**
Gal 2: 9 me and **B** the right hand of
Gal 2:13 so that even **B** was carried
Col 4:10 with Mark the cousin of **B**

BARNS (*see* BARN)
Ps 144:13 That our **b** may be full,
Prov 3:10 so your **b** will be filled with
Joel 1:17 **b** are broken down, for the
Matt 6:26 nor reap nor gather into **b**
Luke 12:18 I will pull down my **b** and

BARRACKS
Acts 21:34 him to be taken into the **b**
Acts 21:37 about to be led into the **b**
Acts 22:24 him to be brought into the **b**
Acts 23:10 them, and bring him into the **b**
Acts 23:16 he went and entered the **b**
Acts 23:32 him, and returned to the **b**

BARREN (*see* BARRENNESS)
Gen 11:30 But Sarai was **b**
Gen 25:21 his wife, because she was **b**
Gen 29:31 but Rachel was **b**
Ex 23:26 or be **b** in your land
Deut 7:14 **b** among you or among your
Judg 13: 2 and his wife was **b** and had no
Judg 13: 3 Indeed now, you are **b** and have
1Sa 2: 5 Even the **b** has borne seven,
2Ki 2:19 water is bad, and the ground **b**
Job 3: 7 Oh, may that night be **b**
Job 15:34 of hypocrites will be **b**, and
Job 24:21 on the **b** who do not bear, and
Job 39: 6 And the **b** land his dwelling
Ps 113: 9 He grants the **b** woman a home
Prov 30:16 the **b** womb, the earth that is
Song 4: 2 and none is **b** among them
Song 6: 6 and none is **b** among them
Is 54: 1 Sing, O **b**, you who have not
Joel 2:20 will drive him away into a **b**
Luke 1: 7 because Elizabeth was **b**, and
Luke 1:36 for her who was called **b**
Luke 23:29 will say, 'Blessed are the **b**
Gal 4:27 Rejoice, O **b**, you who do not
2Pe 1: 8 you will be neither **b** nor

BARRENNESS (*see* BARREN)
2Ki 2:21 shall be no more death or **b**
Ps 107:34 A fruitful land into **b**, For

BARS (*see* BAR)
Ex 26:26 shall make **b** of acacia wood
Ex 26:27 five **b** for the boards on the
Ex 26:27 five **b** for the boards of the
Ex 26:29 of gold as holders for the **b**
Ex 26:29 and overlay the **b** with gold
Ex 35:11 its clasps, its boards, its **b**
Ex 36:31 And he made **b** of acacia wood
Ex 36:32 five **b** for the boards on the
Ex 36:32 five **b** for the boards of the
Ex 36:34 gold to be holders for the **b**
Ex 36:34 and overlaid the **b** with gold
Ex 39:33 its clasps, its boards, its **b**
Ex 40:18 up its boards, put in its **b**
Num 3:36 of the tabernacle, its **b**, its
Num 4:31 of the tabernacle, its **b**, its
Deut 3: 5 with high walls, gates, and **b**
1Sa 23: 7 a town that has gates and **b**
2Ch 8: 5 with walls, gates, and **b**,
2Ch 14: 7 them, and towers, gates, and **b**
Neh 3: 3 its doors with its bolts and **b**
Neh 3: 6 doors, with its bolts and **b**
Neh 3:13 its doors with its bolts and **b**
Neh 3:14 its doors with its bolts and **b**
Neh 3:15 its doors with its bolts and **b**
Job 38:10 My limit for it, and set **b**
Job 40:18 his ribs like **b** of iron
Ps 107:16 And cut the **b** of iron in two
Ps 147:13 the **b** of your gates
Prov 18:19 are like the **b** of a castle
Is 45: 2 bronze and cut the **b** of iron
Jer 49:31 Which has neither gates nor **b**
Jer 51:30 the **b** of her gate are broken
Lam 2: 9 has destroyed and broken her **b**
Ezek 38:11 having neither **b** nor gates'
Jon 2: 6 the earth with its **b** closed
Nah 3:13 devour the **b** of your gates

BARSABAS (*see* JOSEPH, JUDAS, JUSTUS)
Acts 1:23 Joseph called **B**, who was
Acts 15:22 Judas who was also named **B**

BARTERED
Ezek 27:13 They **b** human lives and vessels

BARTHOLOMEW (*see* NATHANAEL)
Matt 10: 3 Philip and **B**
Mark 3:18 Andrew, Philip, **B**, Matthew,
Luke 6:14 Philip and **B**
Acts 1:13 **B** and Matthew

BARTIMAEUS (*see* TIMAEUS)
Mark 10:46 and a great multitude, blind **B**

BARUCH
Neh 3:20 After him **B** the son of Zabbai
Neh 10: 6 Daniel, Ginnethon, **B**,
Neh 11: 5 and Maaseiah the son of **B**, the
Jer 32:12 deed to **B** the son of Neriah
Jer 32:13 Then I charged **B** before them
Jer 32:16 deed to **B** the son of Neriah
Jer 36: 4 called **B** the son of Neriah
Jer 36: 4 **B** wrote on a scroll of a book
Jer 36: 5 And Jeremiah commanded **B**,
Jer 36: 8 And **B** the son of Neriah did
Jer 36:10 Then **B** read from the book the
Jer 36:13 when **B** read the book in the
Jer 36:14 the son of Cushi, to **B**,
Jer 36:14 So **B** the son of Neriah took
Jer 36:15 So **B** read it in their
Jer 36:16 one to another, and said to **B**
Jer 36:17 And they asked **B**, saying
Jer 36:18 So **B** answered them, "He
Jer 36:19 Then the princes said to **B**
Jer 36:26 to seize **B** the scribe and
Jer 36:27 which **B** had written at the
Jer 36:32 and gave it to **B** the scribe
Jer 43: 3 But **B** the son of Neriah has
Jer 43: 6 and **B** the son of Neriah
Jer 45: 1 spoke to **B** the son of Neriah
Jer 45: 2 God of Israel, to you, O **B**

BARZILLAI
2Sa 17:27 **B** the Gileadite from Rogelim,
2Sa 19:31 **B** the Gileadite came down
2Sa 19:32 Now **B** was a very aged man,
2Sa 19:33 And the king said to **B**, "Come
2Sa 19:34 But **B** said to the king, "How
2Sa 19:39 over, the king kissed **B** and
2Sa 21: 8 the son of **B** the Meholathite
1Ki 2: 7 the sons of **B** the Gileadite
Ezra 2:61 sons of Koz, and the sons of **B**
Ezra 2:61 daughters of **B** the Gileadite
Neh 7:63 of Koz, the children of **B**
Neh 7:63 daughters of **B** the Gileadite

BASE (*see* BASES)
Ex 19:12 the mountain or touch its **b**
Ex 29:12 beside the **b** of the altar
Ex 30:18 with its **b** also of bronze,
Ex 30:28 and the laver and its **b**
Ex 31: 9 and the laver and its **b**
Ex 35:16 and the laver and its **b**
Ex 38: 8 its **b** of bronze, from the
Ex 39:39 the laver with its **b**
Ex 40:11 anoint the laver and its **b**
Lev 4: 7 blood of the bull at the **b** of
Lev 4:18 the **b** of the altar of burnt
Lev 4:25 the **b** of the altar of burnt
Lev 4:30 blood at the **b** of the altar
Lev 4:34 blood at the **b** of the altar
Lev 5: 9 out at the **b** of the altar
Lev 8:11 and the laver and its **b**, to
Lev 8:15 blood at the **b** of the altar
Lev 9: 9 blood at the **b** of the altar
2Sa 6:20 as one of the **b** fellows
Is 3: 5 the **b** toward the honorable
Ezek 43:13 the **b** one cubit high and one
Ezek 43:14 from the **b** on the ground to
Ezek 43:17 its **b**, one cubit all around
Zech 5:11 will be set there on its **b**
Mal 2: 9 and **b** before all the people,
1Co 1:28 the **b** things of the world and

BASEMATH
Gen 26:34 **B** the daughter of Elon the
Gen 36: 3 and **B**, Ishmael's daughter,
Gen 36: 4 to Esau, and **B** bore Reuel
Gen 36:10 the son of **B** the wife of Esau
Gen 36:13 These were the sons of **B**,
Gen 36:17 These were the sons of **B**,
1Ki 4:15 he also took **B** the daughter

BASES (*see* BASE)
Ex 38:27 and the **b** of the veil
Ex 38:31 the **b** for the court gate, all
Ezra 3: 3 they set the altar on its **b**
Song 5:15 marble set on **b** of fine gold

BASHAN
Num 21:33 and went up by the way to **B**
Num 21:33 So Og king of **B** went out
Num 32:33 the kingdom of Og king of **B**
Deut 1: 4 in Heshbon, and Og king of **B**
Deut 3: 1 and went up the road to **B**
Deut 3: 1 Og king of **B** came out against
Deut 3: 3 into our hands Og king of **B**
Deut 3: 4 Argob, the kingdom of Og in **B**
Deut 3:10 plain, all Gilead, and all **B**
Deut 3:10 of the kingdom of Og in **B**
Deut 3:11 For only Og king of **B**
Deut 3:13 The rest of Gilead, and all **B**
Deut 3:13 region of Argob, with all **B**
Deut 3:14 called **B** after his own name,
Deut 4:43 Golan in **B** for the Manassites
Deut 4:47 and the land of Og king of **B**
Deut 29: 7 Og king of **B** came out against
Deut 32:14 and rams of the breed of **B**
Deut 33:22 he shall leap from **B**
Josh 9:10 of Heshbon, and Og king of **B**
Josh 12: 4 Og king of **B** and his territory
Josh 12: 5 over Salcah, over all **B**, as
Josh 13:11 and all **B** as far as Salcah
Josh 13:12 all the kingdom of Og in **B**
Josh 13:30 was from Mahanaim, all **B**, all
Josh 13:30 the kingdom of Og king of **B**
Josh 13:30 towns of Jair which are in **B**
Josh 13:31 of the kingdom of Og in **B**
Josh 17: 1 he was given Gilead and **B**
Josh 17: 5 the land of Gilead and **B**,
Josh 20: 8 tribe of Gad, and Golan in **B**
Josh 21: 6 half-tribe of Manasseh in **B**
Josh 21:27 they gave Golan in **B** with its
Josh 22: 7 had given a possession in **B**
1Ki 4:13 the region of Argob in **B**
1Ki 4:19 Amorites and of Og king of **B**
2Ki 10:33 Arnon, including Gilead and **B**
1Ch 5:11 land of **B** as far as Salcah
1Ch 5:12 then Jaanai and Shaphat in **B**
1Ch 5:16 Gadites dwelt in Gilead, in **B**
1Ch 5:23 from **B** to Baal Hermon, that
1Ch 6:62 the tribe of Manasseh in **B**
1Ch 6:71 in **B** with its common-lands
Neh 9:22 and the land of Og king of **B**
Ps 22:12 Strong bulls of **B** have
Ps 68:15 of God is the mountain of **B**
Ps 68:15 peaks is the mountain of **B**
Ps 68:22 I will bring back from **B**, I
Ps 135:11 of the Amorites, Og king of **B**
Ps 136:20 And Og king of **B**, For His
Is 2:13 up, and upon all the oaks of **B**
Is 33: 9 is like a wilderness, and **B**
Jer 22:20 and lift up your voice in **B**
Jer 50:19 he shall feed on Carmel and **B**
Ezek 27: 6 Of oaks from **B** they made your
Ezek 39:18 all of them fatlings of **B**
Amos 4: 1 Hear this word, you cows of **B**
Mic 7:14 let them feed in **B** and Gilead,
Nah 1: 4 **B** and Carmel wither, and the
Zech 11: 2 Wail, O oaks of **B**, for the

BASIC
Col 2: 8 according to the **b** principles
Col 2:20 the **b** principles of the world

BASIN (*see* BASINS)
Ex 12:22 in the blood that is in the **b**
Ex 12:22 the blood that is in the **b**
John 13: 5 He poured water into a **b**

BASINS (*see* BASIN)
Ex 24: 6 half the blood and put it in **b**
Ex 27: 3 and its shovels and its **b** and
Ex 38: 3 the pans, the shovels, the **b**
Num 4:14 the forks, the shovels, the **b**
2Sa 17:28 brought beds and **b**, earthen
1Ki 7:50 the **b**, the trimmers, the
2Ki 12:13 house of the LORD **b** of silver
2Ki 25:15 The firepans and the **b**, the
1Ch 28:17 gold for the forks, the **b**
Ezra 1:10 thirty gold **b**, four hundred
Ezra 1:10 ten silver **b** of a similar
Ezra 8:27 twenty gold **b** worth a
Neh 7:70 gold drachmas, fifty **b**, and
Jer 52:19 The **b**, the firepans, the
Zech 9:15 be filled with blood like **b**

BASKET (*see* BASKETS)
Gen 40:17 In the uppermost **b** there were
Gen 40:17 them out of the **b** on my head
Ex 29: 3 You shall put them in one **b**
Ex 29: 3 **b** and bring them in the **b**
Ex 29:23 one wafer from the **b** of the
Ex 29:32 and the bread that is in the **b**
Lev 8: 2 and a **b** of unleavened bread
Lev 8:26 and from the **b** of unleavened
Lev 8:31 the bread that is in the **b** of
Num 6:15 a **b** of unleavened bread,
Num 6:17 with the **b** of unleavened
Num 6:19 unleavened cake from the **b**
Deut 26: 2 giving you, and put it in a **b**
Deut 26: 4 take the **b** out of your hand
Deut 28: 5 Blessed shall be your **b** and
Deut 28:17 Cursed shall be your **b** and
Judg 6:19 The meat he put in a **b**, and he
Jer 24: 2 One **b** had very good figs,
Jer 24: 2 the other **b** had very bad figs
Amos 8: 1 Behold, a **b** of summer fruit
Amos 8: 2 I said, 'A **b** of summer fruit
Zech 5: 6 It is a **b** that is going forth
Zech 5: 7 woman sitting inside the **b**"
Zech 5: 8 he thrust her down into the **b**
Zech 5: 9 lifted up the **b** between earth
Zech 5:10 Where are they carrying the **b**
Zech 5:11 the **b** will be set there on
Matt 5:15 a lamp and put it under a **b**
Mark 4:21 put under a **b** or under a bed
Luke 11:33 a secret place or under a **b**
Acts 9:25 through the wall in a large **b**
2Co 11:33 a **b** through a window in the

BASKETS (*see* BASKET)
Gen 40:16 had three white **b** on my head
Gen 40:18 The three **b** are three days
2Ki 10: 7 persons, put their heads in **b**
Ps 81: 6 hands were freed from the **b**
Jer 24: 1 there were two **b** of figs set
Matt 14:20 they took up twelve **b** full of
Matt 15:37 they took up seven large **b**
Matt 16: 9 and how many **b** you took up
Matt 16:10 how many large **b** you took up
Mark 6:43 up twelve **b** full of fragments
Mark 8: 8 large **b** of leftover fragments
Mark 8:19 how many **b** full of fragments
Mark 8:20 how many large **b** full of
Luke 9:17 and twelve **b** of the leftover
John 6:13 and filled twelve **b** with the

BAT (*see* BATS)
Lev 11:19 kind, the hoopoe, and the **b**
Deut 14:18 kind, and the hoopoe and the **b**

BATH (*see* BATHS)
Is 5:10 of vineyard shall yield one **b**
Ezek 45:10 a just ephah, and a just **b**
Ezek 45:11 the **b** shall be of the same
Ezek 45:11 so that the **b** contains
Ezek 45:14 the **b** of oil, is one-tenth of
Ezek 45:14 one-tenth of a **b** from a kor

BATHE (*see* BATHED, BATHING)
Lev 15: 5 **b** in water, and be unclean
Lev 15: 6 **b** in water, and be unclean
Lev 15: 7 **b** in water, and be unclean
Lev 15: 8 **b** in water, and be unclean
Lev 15:10 **b** in water, and be unclean
Lev 15:11 **b** in water, and be unclean
Lev 15:13 **b** his body in running water
Lev 15:18 they both shall **b** in water
Lev 15:21 **b** in water, and be unclean
Lev 15:22 **b** in water, and be unclean
Lev 15:27 **b** in water, and be unclean
Lev 16:26 and **b** his body in water, and
Lev 16:28 and **b** his body in water, and
Lev 17:15 **b** in water, and be unclean
Lev 17:16 does not wash or **b** his body
Num 19: 7 clothes, he shall **b** in water
Num 19: 8 **b** in water, and shall be
Num 19:19 his clothes, and **b** in water

BATHED (*see* BATHE)
1Ki 22:38 his blood while the harlots **b**
Job 29: 6 my steps were **b** with cream
Is 34: 5 My sword shall be **b** in heaven
John 13:10 He who is **b** needs only to

BATHING (*see* BATHE)
2Sa 11: 2 the roof he saw a woman **b**

BATH RABBIM
Song 7: 4 in Heshbon by the gate of **B**

BATHS (*see* BATH)
1Ki 7:26 It contained two thousand **b**
1Ki 7:38 each laver contained forty **b**
2Ch 2:10 twenty thousand **b** of wine
2Ch 2:10 and twenty thousand **b** of oil
2Ch 4: 5 It contained three thousand **b**
Ezra 7:22 wheat, one hundred **b** of wine
Ezra 7:22 of wine, one hundred **b** of oil
Ezek 45:14 A kor is a homer or ten **b**
Ezek 45:14 for ten **b** are a homer
Hag 2:16 out fifty **b** from the press

BATHSHEBA (*see* BATHSHUA)
2Sa 11: 3 Is this not **B**, the daughter
2Sa 12:24 David comforted **B** his wife
1Ki 1:11 So Nathan spoke to **B** the
1Ki 1:15 So **B** went into the chamber to
1Ki 1:16 **B** bowed and did homage to the
1Ki 1:28 and said, "Call **B** to me
1Ki 1:31 Then **B** bowed with her face to
1Ki 2:13 to **B** the mother of Solomon
1Ki 2:18 So **B** said, "Very well, I
1Ki 2:19 **B** therefore went to King

BATHSHUA (*see* BATHSHEBA)
1Ch 3: 5 four by **B** the daughter of

BATS (*see* BAT)
Is 2:20 to worship, to the moles and **b**

BATTEN
Judg 16:14 with the **b** of the loom, and
Judg 16:14 sleep, and pulled out the **b**

BATTER (*see* BATTERED, BATTERING)
Num 24:17 and **b** the brow of Moab, and

BATTERED (*see* BATTER)
2Sa 20:15 **b** the wall to throw it down

BATTERING (*see* BATTER)
Ezek 4: 2 place **b** rams against it all
Ezek 21:22 to set up **b** rams, to call for
Ezek 21:22 to set **b** rams against the
Ezek 26: 9 He will direct his **b** rams

BATTLE (*see* BATTLEFIELD, BATTLEMENT, BATTLES)
Gen 14: 8 joined together in **b** in the
Num 21:33 all his people, to **b** at Edrei
Num 31:14 who had come from the **b**
Num 31:21 of war who had gone to the **b**
Num 31:27 in the war, who went out to **b**
Num 31:28 men of war who went out to **b**
Num 32:27 for war, before the LORD to **b**
Num 32:29 armed for **b** before the LORD
Deut 2: 9 nor contend with them in **b**
Deut 2:24 it, and engage him in **b**
Deut 3: 1 all his people, to **b** at Edrei
Deut 20: 1 When you go out to **b** against
Deut 20: 2 you are on the verge of **b**
Deut 20: 3 verge of **b** with your enemies
Deut 20: 5 house, lest he die in the **b**
Deut 20: 6 house, lest he die in the **b**
Deut 20: 7 house, lest he die in the **b**
Deut 29: 7 came out against us to **b**, and
Josh 4:13 over before the LORD for **b**
Josh 8:14 went out against Israel to **b**
Josh 11:19 All the others they took in **b**
Josh 11:20 come against Israel in **b**,
Josh 22:33 of going against them in **b**
Judg 8:13 son of Joash returned from **b**
Judg 20:14 to go to **b** against the
Judg 20:18 to **b** against the children of
Judg 20:20 out to **b** against Benjamin
Judg 20:20 **b** array to fight against them
Judg 20:22 again formed the **b** line at
Judg 20:23 **b** against the children of my
Judg 20:28 **b** against the children of my
Judg 20:30 put themselves in **b** array
Judg 20:33 put themselves in **b** array at
Judg 20:34 Gibeah, and the **b** was fierce
Judg 20:39 men of Israel would turn in **b**
Judg 20:39 before us, as in the first **b**
Judg 20:42 but the **b** overtook them, and
1Sa 4: 1 now Israel went out to **b**
1Sa 4: 2 put themselves in **b** array
1Sa 4: 2 And when they joined **b**, Israel
1Sa 4:12 from the **b** line the same day
1Sa 4:16 I am he who came from the **b**
1Sa 4:16 I fled today from the **b** line
1Sa 7:10 drew near to **b** against Israel
1Sa 11: 7 out with Saul and Samuel to **b**
1Sa 13:22 came about, on the day of **b**
1Sa 14:20 and they went to the **b**
1Sa 14:22 hard after them in the **b**
1Sa 14:23 the **b** shifted to Beth Aven
1Sa 17: 1 their armies together to **b**
1Sa 17: 2 drew up in **b** array against
1Sa 17: 8 you come out to line up for **b**
1Sa 17:13 gone to follow Saul to the **b**
1Sa 17:13 **b** were Eliab the firstborn
1Sa 17:20 fight and shouting for the **b**
1Sa 17:21 had drawn up in **b** array, army
1Sa 17:28 have come down to see the **b**
1Sa 17:47 for the **b** is the LORD's, and
1Sa 26:10 die, or he shall go out to **b**
1Sa 28: 1 you will go out with me to **b**
1Sa 29: 4 let him go down with us to **b**
1Sa 29: 4 lest in the **b** he become our
1Sa 29: 9 not go up with us to the **b**
1Sa 30:24 is who goes down to the **b**
1Sa 31: 3 Now the **b** became intense
2Sa 1: 4 people have fled from the **b**
2Sa 1:25 fallen in the midst of the **b**
2Sa 2:17 was a very fierce **b** that day
2Sa 3:30 Asahel at Gibeon in the **b**
2Sa 10: 8 put themselves in **b** array at
2Sa 10: 9 When Joab saw that the **b** line
2Sa 10: 9 put them in **b** array against
2Sa 10:10 that he might put them in **b**
2Sa 10:13 for the **b** against the Syrians
2Sa 10:17 in **b** array against David and
2Sa 11: 1 time when kings go out to **b**
2Sa 11:15 forefront of the hottest **b**
2Sa 17:11 and that you go to **b** in person
2Sa 18: 6 the field of **b** against Israel
2Sa 18: 6 the **b** was in the woods of
2Sa 18: 8 For the **b** there was scattered
2Sa 19: 3 away when they flee in **b**
2Sa 19:10 over us, has died in **b**
2Sa 20: 8 Joab was dressed in **b** armor
2Sa 21:17 go out no more with us to **b**
2Sa 21:18 that there was again a **b** with
2Sa 21:19 Again there was a **b** in Gob
2Sa 21:20 again there was a **b** in Gath
2Sa 22:40 me with strength for the **b**
2Sa 23: 9 who were gathered there for **b**
1Ki 8:44 out to **b** against their enemy
1Ki 20:14 Who will set the **b** in order
1Ki 20:29 seventh day the **b** was joined
1Ki 20:39 out into the midst of the **b**
1Ki 22:30 disguise myself and go into **b**
1Ki 22:30 himself and went into **b**
1Ki 22:34 and take me out of the **b**, for
1Ki 22:35 The **b** increased that day
2Ki 3:26 the **b** was too intense for him
2Ki 14: 8 let us face one another in **b**
1Ch 5:20 cried out to God in the **b**
1Ch 7:11 fit to go out for war and **b**
1Ch 7:40 among the army fit for **b**
1Ch 10: 3 The **b** became intense against
1Ch 11:13 were gathered for **b**, and there
1Ch 12: 8 of valor, men trained for **b**
1Ch 12:19 Philistines to **b** against Saul
1Ch 12:33 thousand who went out to **b**
1Ch 12:35 who could keep **b** formation
1Ch 12:36 war, able to keep **b** formation
1Ch 12:37 **b** with every kind of weapon
1Ch 14:15 then you shall go out to **b**
1Ch 19: 7 their cities, and came to **b**
1Ch 19: 9 put themselves in **b** array
1Ch 19:10 When Joab saw that the **b** line
1Ch 19:10 put them in **b** array against
1Ch 19:11 and they set themselves in **b**
1Ch 19:14 for the **b** against the Syrians
1Ch 19:17 set up in **b** array against
1Ch 19:17 **b** array against the Syrians
1Ch 20: 1 at the time kings go out to **b**
2Ch 6:34 to **b** against their enemies
2Ch 13: 3 Abijah set the **b** in order
2Ch 13: 3 Jeroboam also drew up in **b**
2Ch 13:14 to their surprise the **b** line
2Ch 14:10 in **b** array in the Valley of
2Ch 18:29 disguise myself and go into **b**
2Ch 18:29 himself, and they went into **b**
2Ch 18:33 and take me out of the **b**, for
2Ch 18:34 The **b** increased that day, and
2Ch 20: 1 came to **b** against Jehoshaphat
2Ch 20:15 for the **b** is not yours, but
2Ch 20:17 not need to fight in this **b**
2Ch 25: 8 Be strong in **b**
2Ch 25:13 would not go with him to **b**
2Ch 25:17 let us face one another in **b**
Job 15:24 him, like a king ready for **b**
Job 38:23 of trouble, for the day of **b**
Job 39:25 He smells the **b** from afar
Job 41: 8 remember the **b**
Ps 18:39 me with strength for the **b**
Ps 24: 8 mighty, The LORD mighty in **b**
Ps 55:18 the **b** which was against me
Ps 78: 9 Turned back in the day of **b**
Ps 89:43 not sustained him in the **b**
Ps 140: 7 my head in the day of **b**
Ps 144: 1 for war, And my fingers for **b**
Prov 21:31 is prepared for the day of **b**
Eccl 9:11 nor the **b** to the strong, nor
Is 9: 5 sandal from the noisy **b**, and
Is 13: 4 hosts musters the army for **b**
Is 16: 9 for **b** cries have fallen over
Is 22: 2 with the sword, Nor dead in **b**
Is 27: 4 and thorns against Me in **b**
Is 28: 6 turn back the **b** at the gate
Is 42:25 anger and the strength of **b**
Jer 8: 6 the horse rushes into the **b**
Jer 18:21 be slain by the sword in **b**
Jer 46: 3 and shield, and draw near to **b**
Jer 49:14 against her, and rise up to **b**
Jer 50:22 A sound of **b** is in the land,
Jer 50:42 array, like a man for the **b**
Ezek 7:14 ready, but no one goes to **b**
Ezek 13: 5 in **b** on the day of the LORD
Dan 11:20 but not in anger or in **b**
Dan 11:25 up to **b** with a very great
Hos 1: 7 by bow, nor by sword or **b**
Hos 2:18 sword of **b** I will shatter
Hos 10: 9 The **b** in Gibeah against the
Hos 10:14 Beth Arbel in the day of **b**
Joel 2: 5 strong people set in **b** array
Amos 1:14 amid shouting in the day of **b**
Obad 1 rise up against her for **b**")
Zech 9:10 the **b** bow shall be cut off
Zech 10: 3 as His royal horse in the **b**
Zech 10: 4 tent peg, from him the **b** bow
Zech 10: 5 mire of the streets in the **b**
Zech 14: 2 to **b** against Jerusalem
Zech 14: 3 as He fights in the day of **b**
1Co 14: 8 will prepare himself for **b**
Heb 11:34 strong, became valiant in **b**
Rev 9: 7 like horses prepared for **b**
Rev 9: 9 many horses running into **b**
Rev 16:14 to gather them to the **b** of
Rev 20: 8 to gather them together to **b**

BATTLE-AX
Ps 76: 3 shield and the sword and the **b**
Jer 51:20 You are My **b** and weapons of
Ezek 9: 2 each with his **b** in his hand

BATTLEFIELD (*see* BATTLE)
Judg 5:18 also, on the heights of the **b**

BATTLEMENT (*see* BATTLE)
Song 8: 9 build upon her a **b** of silver

BATTLES (*see* BATTLE)
1Sa 8:20 out before us and fight our **b**
1Sa 18:17 for me, and fight the LORD's **b**
1Sa 25:28 lord fights the **b** of the LORD
1Ch 26:27 Some of the spoils won in **b**
2Ch 32: 8 to help us and to fight our **b**
Is 30:32 in **b** of brandishing He will

BAVAI
Neh 3:18 under **B** the son of Henadad,

BAY
Josh 15: 2 Sea, from the **b** that faces
Josh 15: 5 quarter began at the **b** of the
Josh 18:19 the north **b** at the Salt Sea
Acts 27:39 observed a **b** with a beach

BAZLITH (*see* BAZLUTH)
Neh 7:54 the children of **B**, the

BAZLUTH (*see* BAZLITH)
Ezra 2:52 the sons of **B**, the sons of

BDELLIUM
Gen 2:12 **B** and the onyx stone are there
Num 11: 7 its color like the color of **b**

BE (*see* PREFACE)

BEACH
Acts 27:39 they observed a bay with a **b**

BEALIAH
1Ch 12: 5 Eluzai, Jerimoth, **B**,

BEALOTH (*see* ALOTH)
Josh 15:24 Ziph, Telem, **B**,

BEAM (*see* BEAMS)
Num 4:10 and put it on a carrying **b**
Num 4:12 and put them on a carrying **b**
1Sa 17: 7 spear was like a weaver's **b**
2Sa 21:19 spear was like a weaver's **b**
2Ki 6: 2 every man take a **b** from there
1Ch 11:23 a spear like a weaver's **b**
1Ch 20: 5 spear was like a weaver's **b**
Hab 2:11 the **b** from the timbers will

BEAMS (*see* BEAM)
1Ki 6: 6 so that the support **b** would
1Ki 6: 9 he paneled the temple with **b**
1Ki 6:10 to the temple with cedar **b**
1Ki 6:36 stone and a row of cedar **b**
1Ki 7: 2 and cedar **b** on the pillars
1Ki 7: 3 with cedar above the **b** that
1Ki 7:12 stones and a row of cedar **b**
2Ch 3: 7 the **b** and doorposts, its walls
2Ch 34:11 hewn stone and timber for **b**
Neh 2: 8 make **b** for the gates of the
Neh 3: 3 they laid its **b** and hung its
Neh 3: 6 they laid its **b** and hung its
Job 40:18 bones are like **b** of bronze
Ps 104: 3 He lays the **b** of His upper
Song 1:17 The **b** of our houses are cedar

BEANS
2Sa 17:28 and flour, parched grain and **b**
Ezek 4: 9 for yourself wheat, barley, **b**

BEAR (*see* BEARERS, BEARING, BEARS, BORE, BORNE)
Gen 4:13 is greater than I can **b**
Gen 16:11 child, and you shall **b** a son
Gen 17:17 ninety years old, **b** a child
Gen 17:19 your wife shall **b** you a son

Gen 17:21 whom Sarah shall **b** to you at
Gen 18:13 Shall I surely **b** a child
Gen 30: 3 and she will **b** a child on my
Gen 43: 9 you, then let me **b** the blame
Gen 44:32 you, then I shall **b** the blame
Gen 49:15 his shoulder to **b** a burden
Ex 18:22 for they will **b** the burden
Ex 20:16 You shall not **b** false witness
Ex 25:27 for the poles to **b** the table
Ex 27: 7 sides of the altar to **b** it
Ex 28:12 So Aaron shall **b** their names
Ex 28:29 So Aaron shall **b** the names of
Ex 28:30 So Aaron shall **b** the judgment
Ex 28:38 that Aaron may **b** the iniquity
Ex 30: 4 the poles with which to **b** it
Ex 37: 5 of the ark, to **b** the ark
Ex 37:14 for the poles to **b** the table
Ex 37:15 of acacia wood to **b** the table
Ex 37:27 the poles with which to **b** it
Ex 38: 7 the altar, with which to **b** it
Lev 5:17 and shall **b** his iniquity
Lev 7:18 who eats of it shall **b** guilt
Lev 10:17 to you to **b** the guilt of the
Lev 16:22 The goat shall **b** on itself
Lev 17:16 then he shall **b** his guilt
Lev 19: 8 eats it shall **b** his iniquity
Lev 19:17 and not **b** sin because of him
Lev 19:18 nor **b** any grudge against the
Lev 20:17 He shall **b** his guilt
Lev 20:19 They shall **b** their guilt
Lev 20:20 They shall **b** their sin
Lev 22: 9 lest they **b** sin for it and die
Lev 22:16 or allow them to **b** the guilt
Lev 24:15 his God shall **b** his sin
Num 5:31 that woman shall **b** her guilt
Num 9:13 that man shall **b** his sin
Num 11:14 I am not able to **b** all these
Num 11:17 they shall **b** the burden of
Num 11:17 you, that you may not **b** it
Num 14:27 How long shall I **b** with this
Num 14:33 years, and **b** the brunt of your
Num 14:34 shall **b** your guilt one year
Num 18: 1 house with you shall **b** the
Num 18: 1 **b** the iniquity associated
Num 18:22 of meeting, lest they **b** sin
Num 18:23 they shall **b** their iniquity
Num 18:32 you shall **b** no sin because of
Num 30:15 then he shall **b** her guilt
Deut 1: 9 I alone am not able to **b** you
Deut 1:12 can I alone **b** your problems
Deut 5:20 You shall not **b** false
Deut 10: 8 the tribe of Levi to **b** the
Deut 29:23 it is not sown, nor does it **b**
Josh 3: 8 who **b** the ark of the covenant
Josh 3:13 who **b** the ark of the LORD
Josh 4:16 Command the priests who **b** the
Josh 6: 4 seven priests shall **b** seven
Josh 6: 6 let seven priests **b** seven
Judg 5:14 who **b** the recruiter's staff
Judg 13: 3 you shall conceive and **b** a son
Judg 13: 5 you shall conceive and **b** a son
Judg 13: 7 you shall conceive and **b** a son
Ruth 1:12 tonight and should also **b** sons
1Sa 17:34 and when a lion or a **b** came
1Sa 17:36 has killed both lion and **b**
1Sa 17:37 lion and from the paw of the **b**
2Sa 17: 8 like a **b** robbed of her cubs
1Ki 21:10 before him to **b** witness
2Ki 3:21 all who were able to **b** arms
2Ki 19:30 downward, and **b** fruit upward
1Ch 5:18 men, men able to **b** shield
2Ch 2: 2 thousand men to **b** burdens
Job 9: 9 He made the **B**, Orion, and the
Job 21: 3 **B** with me that I may speak,
Job 24:21 on the barren who do not **b**
Job 36: 2 **B** with me a little, and I will
Job 38:32 the Great **B** with its cubs
Job 39: 1 wild mountain goats **b** young
Job 39: 2 the time when they **b** young
Ps 28: 9 also, And **b** them up forever
Ps 55:12 Then I could **b** it
Ps 89:50 How I **b** in my bosom the
Ps 91:12 They shall **b** you up in their
Ps 92:14 still **b** fruit in old age
Prov 9:12 scoff, you alone will **b** it
Prov 17:12 Let a man meet a **b** robbed of
Prov 18:14 but who can **b** a broken spirit
Prov 28:15 and a charging **b** is a wicked
Prov 30:21 yes, for four it cannot **b** up
Is 7:14 **b** a Son, and shall call His
Is 11: 7 The cow and the **b** shall graze
Is 37:31 downward, and **b** fruit upward
Is 46: 4 I have made, and I will **b**
Is 46: 7 They **b** it on the shoulder,
Is 52:11 you who **b** the vessels of the
Is 53:11 many, for He shall **b** their
Jer 10:19 an infirmity, and I must **b** it
Jer 12: 2 they grow, yes, they **b** fruit
Jer 17:21 **b** no burden on the Sabbath
Jer 29: 6 so that they may **b** sons and
Jer 44:22 the LORD could no longer **b** it
Lam 3:10 to me like a **b** lying in wait
Lam 3:27 to **b** the yoke in his youth
Lam 5: 7 but we **b** their iniquities
Ezek 4: 4 you shall **b** their iniquity
Ezek 4: 5 so you shall **b** the iniquity
Ezek 4: 6 then you shall **b** the iniquity
Ezek 12: 6 **b** them on your shoulders and
Ezek 12:12 shall **b** his belongings on his
Ezek 14:10 they shall **b** their iniquity
Ezek 16:52 **b** your own shame also,
Ezek 16:52 **b** your own shame, because you
Ezek 16:54 that you may **b** your own shame
Ezek 17: 8 **b** fruit, and become a majestic
Ezek 17:23 **b** fruit, and be a majestic
Ezek 18:19 not **b** the guilt of the father
Ezek 18:20 The son shall not **b** the guilt
Ezek 18:20 nor the father **b** the guilt of
Ezek 23:35 shall **b** the penalty of your
Ezek 32:24 now they **b** their shame with
Ezek 32:25 yet they **b** their shame with
Ezek 32:30 **b** their shame with those who
Ezek 34:29 land, nor **b** the shame of the
Ezek 36: 7 you shall **b** their own shame
Ezek 36:11 shall increase and **b** young
Ezek 36:15 nor **b** the reproach of the
Ezek 36:30 **b** the reproach of famine
Ezek 44:10 they shall **b** their iniquity
Ezek 44:12 they shall **b** their iniquity
Ezek 44:13 but they shall **b** their shame
Ezek 47:12 They will **b** fruit every month
Ezek 47:22 and who **b** children among you
Dan 7: 5 beast, a second, like a **b**
Hos 9:16 they shall **b** no fruit
Hos 9:16 Yes, were they to **b** children
Hos 13: 8 like a **b** deprived of her cubs
Amos 5:19 from a lion, and a **b** met him
Amos 7:10 not able to **b** all his words
Mic 6:16 therefore you shall **b** the
Mic 7: 9 I will **b** the indignation of
Zech 6:13 He shall **b** the glory, and
Mal 3:11 **b** fruit for you in the field
Matt 1:23 **b** a Son, and they shall call
Matt 3: 8 Therefore **b** fruits worthy of
Matt 3:10 not **b** good fruit is cut down
Matt 4: 6 hands they shall **b** you up
Matt 7:18 good tree cannot **b** bad fruit
Matt 7:18 can a bad tree **b** good fruit
Matt 7:19 not **b** good fruit is cut down
Matt 17:17 How long shall I **b** with you
Matt 19:18 You shall not **b** false witness
Matt 23: 4 bind heavy burdens, hard to **b**
Matt 27:32 they compelled to **b** His cross
Mark 4:20 word, accept it, and **b** fruit
Mark 9:19 How long shall I **b** with you
Mark 10:19 Do not **b** false witness,'
Mark 15:21 and passing by, to **b** His cross
Luke 1:13 Elizabeth will **b** you a son
Luke 3: 8 Therefore **b** fruits worthy of
Luke 3: 9 not **b** good fruit is cut down
Luke 4:11 hands they shall **b** You up
Luke 6:43 tree does not **b** bad fruit
Luke 6:43 does a bad tree **b** good fruit
Luke 8:15 it and **b** fruit with patience
Luke 9:41 I be with you and **b** with you
Luke 11:46 men with burdens hard to **b**
Luke 11:48 fact, you **b** witness that you
Luke 14:27 whoever does not **b** his cross
Luke 18:20 Do not **b** false witness,'
Luke 23:26 he might **b** it after Jesus
John 1: 7 to **b** witness of the Light,
John 1: 8 but was sent to **b** witness of
John 3:28 You yourselves **b** me witness
John 5:31 If I **b** witness of Myself, My
John 5:36 **b** witness of Me, that the
John 8:13 You **b** witness of Yourself
John 8:14 Even if I **b** witness of Myself
John 10:25 name, they **b** witness of Me
John 15: 2 not **b** fruit He takes away
John 15: 2 that it may **b** more fruit
John 15: 4 cannot **b** fruit of itself,
John 15: 8 that you **b** much fruit
John 15:16 **b** fruit, and that your fruit
John 15:27 And you also will **b** witness
John 16:12 but you cannot **b** them now
John 18:23 evil, **b** witness of the evil
John 18:37 that I should **b** witness to
Acts 9:15 to **b** My name before Gentiles
Acts 15:10 fathers nor we were able to **b**
Acts 18:14 why I should **b** with you
Acts 23:11 must also **b** witness at Rome
Rom 7: 4 that we should **b** fruit to God
Rom 7: 5 members to **b** fruit to death
Rom 10: 2 For I **b** them witness that
Rom 13: 4 for he does not **b** the sword
Rom 13: 9 You shall not **b** false witness
Rom 15: 1 who are strong ought to **b**
1Co 10:13 that you may be able to **b** it
1Co 15:49 we shall also **b** the image of
1Co 16: 3 I will send to **b** your gift to
2Co 8: 3 For I **b** witness that
2Co 11: 1 that you would **b** with me in a
2Co 11: 1 and indeed you do **b** with me
Gal 4:15 For I **b** you witness that, if
Gal 4:27 O barren, you who do not **b**
Gal 5:10 you shall **b** his judgment,
Gal 6: 2 **B** one another's burdens, and
Gal 6: 5 each one shall **b** his own load
Gal 6:17 for I **b** in my body the marks
Col 4:13 For I **b** him witness that he
1Ti 5:14 **b** children, manage the house,
Heb 9:28 once to **b** the sins of many
Heb 13:22 brethren, **b** with the word of
Jas 3:12 **b** olives, or a grapevine **b**
Jas 3:12 olives, or a grapevine **b** figs
1Jn 1: 2 **b** witness, and declare to you
1Jn 5: 7 three who **b** witness in heaven
1Jn 5: 8 three that **b** witness on earth
3Jn 12 And we also **b** witness, and you
Rev 2: 2 that you cannot **b** those who
Rev 13: 2 were like the feet of a **b**

BEARD (*see* BEARDS)
Lev 13:29 a sore on the head or the **b**
Lev 13:30 a leprosy of the head or **b**
Lev 14: 9 hair off his head and his **b**
Lev 19:27 disfigure the edges of your **b**
1Sa 17:35 me, I caught it by its **b**, and
1Sa 21:13 his saliva fall down on his **b**
2Sa 20: 9 Joab took Amasa by the **b** with
Ezra 9: 3 of the hair of my head and **b**
Ps 133: 2 head, Running down on the **b**
Ps 133: 2 The **b** of Aaron, Running down
Is 7:20 and will also remove the **b**
Is 15: 2 baldness, and every **b** cut off
Is 50: 6 those who plucked out the **b**
Jer 48:37 be bald, and every **b** clipped
Ezek 5: 1 it over your head and your **b**

BEARDS (*see* BEARD)
Lev 21: 5 **b** nor make any cuttings in
2Sa 10: 4 shaved off half of their **b**
2Sa 10: 5 until your **b** have grown, and
1Ch 19: 5 until your **b** have grown, and
Jer 41: 5 men with their **b** shaved and

BEARERS (*see* BEAR)
2Ch 2:18 thousand of them **b** of burdens
2Ch 34:13 were over the burden **b** and

BEARING (*see* BEAR)
Gen 16: 2 restrained me from **b** children
Gen 29:35 Then she stopped **b**
Gen 30: 9 saw that she had stopped **b**
Gen 37:25 **b** spices, balm, and myrrh, on
Num 4:47 the work of **b** burdens in the
Deut 29:18 root **b** bitterness or wormwood
Josh 3: 3 **b** it, then you shall set out
Josh 3:14 with the priests **b** the ark of
Josh 6: 8 that the seven priests **b** the
Josh 6:13 Then seven priests **b** seven
2Sa 6:13 when those **b** the ark of the
2Sa 15:24 **b** the ark of the covenant of
2Sa 21:16 who was **b** a new sword,
1Ch 12:24 children of Judah **b** shield
Ps 126: 6 **B** seed for sowing, Shall
Is 1:14 to Me, I am weary of **b** them
Matt 21:43 a nation **b** the fruits of it
John 19:17 **b** His cross, went out to a
Acts 14: 3 who was **b** witness to the word
Rom 2:15 conscience also **b** witness
Rom 9: 1 my conscience also **b** me

Eph 4: 2 **b** with one another in love,
Col 3:13 **b** with one another, and
Heb 2: 4 God also **b** witness both with
Heb 13:13 the camp, **b** His reproach

BEARS (*see* BEAR)
Lev 5: 1 does not tell it, he **b** guilt
Lev 12: 5 But if she **b** a female child,
Deut 25: 6 **b** will succeed to the name of
Deut 28:57 and her children whom she **b**
2Ki 2:24 two female **b** came out of the
Job 16: 8 me and **b** witness to my face
Prov 25:18 A man who **b** false witness
Song 4: 2 every one of which **b** twins
Song 6: 6 every one **b** twins, and none is
Is 59:11 We all growl like **b**, and moan
Joel 2:22 up, and the tree **b** its fruit
Matt 7:17 every good tree **b** good fruit
Matt 7:17 but a bad tree **b** bad fruit
Matt 13:23 it, who indeed **b** fruit and
Luke 13: 9 And if it **b** fruit, well
Luke 18: 7 though He **b** long with them
John 5:32 another who **b** witness of Me
John 8:18 I am One who **b** witness of
John 8:18 who sent Me **b** witness of Me
John 15: 2 branch that **b** fruit He prunes
John 15: 5 Me, and I in him, **b** much fruit
Acts 22: 5 the high priest **b** me witness
Rom 8:16 The Spirit Himself **b** witness
1Co 13: 7 **b** all things, believes all
Heb 6: 7 **b** herbs useful for those by
Heb 6: 8 but if it **b** thorns and briars,
1Jn 5: 6 is the Spirit who **b** witness

BEAST (*see* BEASTS)
Gen 1:24 thing and **b** of the earth, each
Gen 1:25 God made the **b** of the earth
Gen 1:30 to every **b** of the earth, to
Gen 2:19 formed every **b** of the field
Gen 2:20 and to every **b** of the field
Gen 3: 1 was more cunning than any **b**
Gen 3:14 than every **b** of the field
Gen 6: 7 of the earth, both man and **b**
Gen 7:14 every **b** after its kind, all
Gen 8:19 Every **b**, every creeping thing
Gen 9: 2 be on every **b** of the earth
Gen 9: 5 of every **b** I will require it
Gen 9:10 every **b** of the earth with you
Gen 9:10 the ark, every **b** of the earth
Gen 37:20 Some wild **b** has devoured him
Gen 37:33 A wild **b** has devoured him
Ex 8:17 and it became lice on man and **b**
Ex 8:18 there were lice on man and **b**
Ex 9: 9 **b** throughout all the land of
Ex 9:10 out in sores on man and **b**
Ex 9:19 every **b** which is found in the
Ex 9:22 on man, on **b**, and on every
Ex 9:25 in the field, both man and **b**
Ex 11: 7 its tongue, against man or **b**
Ex 12:12 land of Egypt, both man and **b**
Ex 19:13 whether man or **b**, he shall
Ex 21:34 but the dead **b** shall be his
Ex 21:36 the dead **b** shall be his own
Ex 22:10 or any **b** to keep, and it dies,
Ex 22:19 Whoever lies with a **b** shall
Ex 23:29 the **b** of the field become too
Lev 5: 2 the carcass of an unclean **b**
Lev 7:21 uncleanness, any unclean **b**
Lev 7:24 And the fat of a **b** that dies
Lev 7:25 the **b** of which men offer an
Lev 7:26 whether of bird or **b**
Lev 11:26 The carcass of any **b** which
Lev 11:39 if any **b** which you may eat
Lev 18:23 Nor shall you mate with any **b**
Lev 18:23 before a **b** to mate with it
Lev 20:15 If a man mates with a **b**, he
Lev 20:15 and you shall kill the **b**
Lev 20:16 If a woman approaches any **b**
Lev 20:16 shall kill the woman and the **b**
Lev 20:25 abominable by **b** or by bird
Lev 27: 9 if it is a **b** such as men may
Lev 27:10 at all exchanges **b** for **b**
Lev 27:11 If it is an unclean **b** which
Lev 27:11 the **b** before the priest
Lev 27:27 And if it is an unclean **b**
Lev 27:28 that he has, both man and **b**
Num 3:13 in Israel, both man and **b**
Num 8:17 are Mine, both man and **b**
Num 18:15 to the LORD, whether man or **b**
Num 31:11 the booty, both of man and **b**
Num 31:26 was taken, both of man and **b**
Num 31:47 fifty, drawn from man and **b**
Deut 4:17 the likeness of any **b** that is
2Ki 14: 9 a wild **b** that was in Lebanon
2Ch 25:18 a wild **b** that was in Lebanon
Job 39:15 that a wild **b** may break them
Ps 36: 6 LORD, You preserve man and **b**
Ps 50:10 For every **b** of the forest is
Ps 73:22 I was like a **b** before You
Ps 74:19 Your turtledove to the wild **b**
Ps 80:13 And the wild **b** of the field
Ps 104:11 drink to every **b** of the field
Ps 135: 8 of Egypt, Both of man and **b**
Ps 147: 9 He gives to the **b** its food
Eccl 3:21 and the spirit of the **b**,
Is 35: 9 any ravenous **b** go up on it
Is 43:20 The **b** of the field will honor
Is 46: 1 a burden to the weary **b**
Is 63:14 As a **b** goes down into the
Jer 7:20 on man and on **b**, on the trees
Jer 21: 6 of this city, both man and **b**
Jer 27: 5 the **b** that are on the ground,
Jer 31:27 seed of man and the seed of **b**
Jer 32:43 is desolate, without man or **b**
Jer 33:10 without man and without **b**"
Jer 33:10 inhabitant and without **b**,
Jer 33:12 without man and without **b**
Jer 36:29 man and **b** to cease from here
Jer 50: 3 shall depart, both man and **b**
Jer 51:62 in it, neither man nor **b**, but
Ezek 14:13 and cut off man and **b** from it
Ezek 14:17 I cut off man and **b** from it,
Ezek 14:19 and cut off from it man and **b**
Ezek 14:21 to cut off man and **b** from it
Ezek 25:13 man and **b** from it, and make it
Ezek 29: 8 and cut off from you man and **b**
Ezek 29:11 nor foot of **b** pass through it
Ezek 34: 8 food for every **b** of the field
Ezek 36:11 multiply upon you man and **b**
Ezek 39:17 and to every **b** of the field
Ezek 44:31 not eat anything, bird or **b**
Dan 7: 5 And suddenly another **b**, a
Dan 7: 6 The **b** also had four heads, and
Dan 7: 7 and behold, a fourth **b**,
Dan 7:11 watched till the **b** was slain
Dan 7:19 the truth about the fourth **b**
Dan 7:23 The fourth **b** shall be a
Dan 8: 4 so that no **b** could withstand
Hos 13: 8 The wild **b** shall tear them
Jon 3: 7 Let neither man nor **b**, herd
Jon 3: 8 **b** be covered with sackcloth,
Zeph 1: 3 I will consume man and **b**
Zeph 2:14 midst, every **b** of the nation
Zech 8:10 for man nor any hire for **b**
Heb 12:20 if so much as a **b** touches the
Jas 3: 7 For every kind of **b** and bird,
Rev 11: 7 the **b** that ascends out of the
Rev 13: 1 I saw a **b** rising up out of
Rev 13: 2 Now the **b** which I saw was
Rev 13: 3 marveled and followed the **b**
Rev 13: 4 who gave authority to the **b**
Rev 13: 4 and they worshiped the **b**,
Rev 13: 4 Who is like the **b**
Rev 13:11 Then I saw another **b** coming
Rev 13:12 the first **b** in his presence
Rev 13:12 in it to worship the first **b**
Rev 13:14 to do in the sight of the **b**
Rev 13:14 the **b** who was wounded by the
Rev 13:15 breath to the image of the **b**
Rev 13:15 of the **b** should both speak
Rev 13:15 image of the **b** to be killed
Rev 13:17 the mark or the name of the **b**
Rev 13:18 calculate the number of the **b**
Rev 14: 9 If anyone worships the **b** and
Rev 14:11 or night, who worship the **b**
Rev 15: 2 have the victory over the **b**
Rev 16: 2 men who had the mark of the **b**
Rev 16:10 bowl on the throne of the **b**
Rev 16:13 out of the mouth of the **b**
Rev 17: 3 **b** which was full of names of
Rev 17: 7 of the **b** that carries her,
Rev 17: 8 The **b** that you saw was, and is
Rev 17: 8 when they see the **b** that was
Rev 17:11 the **b** that was, and is not, is
Rev 17:12 one hour as kings with the **b**
Rev 17:13 power and authority to the **b**
Rev 17:16 horns which you saw on the **b**
Rev 17:17 give their kingdom to the **b**
Rev 19:19 And I saw the **b**, the kings of
Rev 19:20 Then the **b** was captured, and
Rev 19:20 received the mark of the **b**
Rev 20: 4 worshiped the **b** or his image
Rev 20:10 fire and brimstone where the **b**

BEASTS (*see* BEAST)
Gen 7: 8 Of clean **b**, of **b** that
Gen 7: 8 of **b** that are unclean, of
Gen 7:21 birds and cattle and **b** and every
Gen 31:39 by **b** I did not bring to you
Gen 45:17 Load your **b** and depart
Ex 11: 5 and all the firstborn of the **b**
Ex 22:31 is torn by **b** in the field
Ex 23:11 the **b** of the field may eat
Lev 11: 2 the **b** that are on the earth
Lev 11: 3 Among the **b**, whatever
Lev 11:46 This is the law of the **b**
Lev 17:15 or what was torn by **b**,
Lev 20:25 distinguish between clean **b**
Lev 22: 8 is torn by **b** he shall not eat
Lev 26: 6 I will rid the land of evil **b**
Lev 26:22 also send wild **b** among you
Lev 27:26 But the firstling of the **b**
Deut 7:22 once, lest the **b** of the field
Deut 28:26 the **b** of the earth, and no one
Deut 32:24 against them the teeth of **b**
Judg 20:48 from every city, men and **b**
1Sa 17:44 the air and the **b** of the field
1Sa 17:46 the wild **b** of the earth, that
2Sa 21:10 the **b** of the field by night
Job 5:22 afraid of the **b** of the earth
Job 5:23 the **b** of the field shall be
Job 12: 7 But now ask the **b**, and they
Job 18: 3 Why are we counted as **b**, and
Job 35:11 more than the **b** of the earth
Job 40:20 all the **b** of the field play
Ps 8: 7 Even the **b** of the field,
Ps 49:12 He is like the **b** that perish
Ps 49:20 Is like the **b** that perish
Ps 50:11 the wild **b** of the field are
Ps 68:30 Rebuke the **b** of the reeds,
Ps 79: 2 saints to the **b** of the earth
Ps 104:20 In which all the **b** of the
Ps 148:10 **B** and all cattle
Prov 30:30 lion, which is mighty among **b**
Eccl 3:18 they themselves are like **b**
Eccl 3:19 sons of men also happens to **b**
Eccl 3:19 man has no advantage over **b**
Is 13:21 But wild **b** of the desert will
Is 18: 6 and for the **b** of the earth
Is 18: 6 all the **b** of the earth will
Is 23:13 it for wild **b** of the desert
Is 30: 6 against the **b** of the South
Is 34:14 The wild **b** of the desert
Is 40:16 nor its **b** sufficient for a
Is 46: 1 their idols were on the **b**
Is 56: 9 All you **b** of the field, come
Is 56: 9 all you **b** in the forest
Jer 7:33 and for the **b** of the earth
Jer 9:10 heavens and the **b** have fled
Jer 12: 4 the **b** and birds are consumed,
Jer 12: 9 all the **b** of the field, bring
Jer 15: 3 the **b** of the earth to devour
Jer 16: 4 and for the **b** of the earth
Jer 19: 7 and for the **b** of the earth
Jer 27: 6 the **b** of the field I have
Jer 28:14 him the **b** of the field also
Jer 34:20 heaven and the **b** of the earth
Jer 50:39 Therefore the wild desert **b**
Ezek 4:14 of itself or was torn by **b**
Ezek 5:17 against you famine and wild **b**
Ezek 8:10 creeping thing, abominable **b**
Ezek 14:15 If I cause wild **b** to pass
Ezek 14:15 pass through because of the **b**
Ezek 14:21 the sword and famine and wild **b**
Ezek 29: 5 as food to the **b** of the field
Ezek 31: 6 **b** of the field brought forth
Ezek 31:13 all the **b** of the field will
Ezek 32: 4 fill the **b** of the whole earth
Ezek 32:13 its **b** from beside its great
Ezek 32:13 the hooves of **b** muddy them
Ezek 33:27 give to the **b** to be devoured
Ezek 34: 5 became food for all the **b** of
Ezek 34:25 cause wild **b** to cease from
Ezek 34:28 nor shall **b** of the land
Ezek 38:20 the **b** of the field, all
Ezek 39: 4 to the **b** of the field to be
Dan 2:38 or the **b** of the field and the
Dan 4:12 The **b** of the field found
Dan 4:14 Let the **b** get out from under
Dan 4:15 let him graze with the **b** on
Dan 4:21 all, under which the **b** of the
Dan 4:23 graze with the **b** of the field

Dan 4:25 be with the **b** of the field
Dan 4:32 be with the **b** of the field
Dan 5:21 his heart was made like the **b**
Dan 7: 3 four great **b** came up from the
Dan 7: 7 all the **b** that were before it
Dan 7:12 As for the rest of the **b**,
Dan 7:17 Those great **b**, which are
Hos 2:12 the **b** of the field shall eat
Hos 2:18 them with the **b** of the field
Hos 4: 3 away with the **b** of the field
Joel 1:18 How the **b** groan
Joel 1:20 The **b** of the field also cry
Joel 2:22 be afraid, you **b** of the field
Mic 5: 8 among the **b** of the forest
Hab 2:17 the plunder of **b** which made
Zeph 2:15 a place for **b** to lie down
Mark 1:13 Satan, and was with the wild **b**
Acts 10:12 animals of the earth, wild **b**
Acts 11: 6 animals of the earth, wild **b**
Rom 1:23 and birds and four-footed **b**
1Co 15:32 have fought with **b** at Ephesus
1Co 15:39 of men, another flesh of **b**
Tit 1:12 are always liars, evil **b**,
Heb 13:11 For the bodies of those **b**
2Pe 2:12 brute **b** made to be caught
Jude 10 know naturally, like brute **b**
Rev 6: 8 and by the **b** of the earth

BEAT (*see* BEATEN, BEATING, BEATINGS, BEATS)
Ex 30:36 you shall **b** some of it very
Ex 39: 3 they **b** the gold into thin
Num 11: 8 or **b** it in the mortar, cooked
Deut 24:20 When you **b** your olive trees,
Deut 25: 3 **b** him with many blows above
Judg 19:22 the house and **b** on the door
Ruth 2:17 **b** out what she had gleaned,
2Sa 22:43 Then I **b** them as fine as the
Ps 18:42 Then I **b** them as fine as the
Ps 78:66 And He **b** back His enemies
Ps 89:23 I will **b** down his foes before
Prov 23:13 for if you **b** him with a rod,
Prov 23:14 You shall **b** him with a rod,
Is 2: 4 they shall **b** their swords
Is 41:15 **b** them small, and make the
Ezek 21:17 I also will **b** My fists
Ezek 22:13 I **b** My fists at the dishonest
Joel 3:10 **B** your plowshares into swords
Jon 4: 8 the sun **b** on Jonah's head, so
Mic 4: 3 they shall **b** their swords
Mic 4:13 you shall **b** in pieces many
Matt 7:25 winds blew and **b** on that house
Matt 7:27 winds blew and **b** on that house
Matt 21:35 **b** one, killed one, and stoned
Matt 24:49 and begins to **b** his fellow
Matt 26:67 spat in His face and **b** Him
Mark 4:37 the waves **b** into the boat, so
Mark 12: 3 him and **b** him and sent him
Mark 14:65 to **b** Him, and to say to Him,
Luke 6:48 the stream **b** vehemently
Luke 6:49 which the stream **b** vehemently
Luke 12:45 begins to **b** the menservants
Luke 18:13 but **b** his breast, saying
Luke 20:10 But the vinedressers **b** him
Luke 20:11 they **b** him also, treated him
Luke 22:63 Jesus mocked Him and **b** Him
Luke 23:48 **b** their breasts and returned
Acts 18:17 **b** him before the judgment
Acts 22:19 **b** those who believe on You
Acts 27:20 and no small tempest **b** on us

BEATEN (*see* BEAT)
Ex 5:14 had set over them, were **b**
Ex 5:16 And indeed your servants are **b**
Ex 37: 7 made two cherubim of **b** gold
Lev 2:14 fire, grain **b** from full heads
Lev 2:16 part of its **b** grain and part
Lev 16:12 full of sweet incense **b** fine
Deut 25: 2 wicked man deserves to be **b**
Deut 25: 2 down and be **b** in his presence,
Josh 8:15 as if they were **b** before them
2Sa 2:17 were **b** before the servants of
2Ch 34: 7 had **b** the carved images into
Prov 23:35 They have **b** me, but I did not
Is 27: 9 that are **b** to dust, when
Is 28:27 cummin is **b** out with a stick
Is 30:31 LORD Assyria will be **b** down
Jer 10: 9 Silver is **b** into plates
Jer 46: 5 Their mighty ones are **b** down
Mic 1: 7 images shall be **b** to pieces
Mark 13: 9 and you will be **b** in the
Luke 12:47 shall be **b** with many stripes
Luke 12:48 stripes, shall be **b** with few
Acts 5:40 **b** them, they commanded that
Acts 16:22 them to be **b** with rods
Acts 16:37 They have **b** us openly,
1Co 4:11 we are poorly clothed, and **b**
2Co 11:25 Three times I was **b** with rods
1Pe 2:20 if, when you are **b** for your

BEATING (*see* BEAT)
Ex 2:11 he saw an Egyptian **b** a Hebrew
Nah 2: 7 of doves, **b** their breasts
Mark 12: 5 **b** some and killing some
Acts 21:32 soldiers, they stopped **b** Paul

BEATINGS (*see* BEAT)
Prov 19:29 and **b** for the backs of fools

BEATS (*see* BEAT)
Ex 21:20 if a man **b** his servant or his
1Co 9:26 not as one who **b** the air

BEAUTIES (*see* BEAUTIFY)
Ps 110: 3 In the **b** of holiness, from

BEAUTIFUL (*see* BEAUTY)
Gen 6: 2 of men, that they were **b**
Gen 12:11 are a woman of **b** countenance
Gen 12:14 woman, that she was very **b**
Gen 24:16 woman was very **b** to behold
Gen 26: 7 because she is **b** to behold
Gen 29:17 but Rachel was **b** of form
Ex 2: 2 she saw that he was a **b** child
Lev 23:40 day the fruit of **b** trees,
Deut 6:10 **b** cities which you did not
Deut 8:12 full, and have built **b** houses
Deut 21:11 among the captives a **b** woman
Josh 7:21 spoils a **b** Babylonian garment
1Sa 25: 3 and **b** appearance
2Sa 11: 2 woman was very **b** to behold
2Sa 14:27 was a woman of **b** appearance
Esth 1:11 for she was **b** to behold
Esth 2: 2 Let **b** young virgins be sought
Esth 2: 3 they may gather all the **b**
Esth 2: 7 young woman was lovely and **b**
Job 42:15 so **b** as the daughters of Job
Ps 33: 1 praise from the upright is **b**
Ps 48: 2 **B** in elevation, The joy of
Ps 147: 1 is pleasant, and praise is **b**
Eccl 3:11 made everything **b** in its time
Song 6: 4 love, you are as **b** as Tirzah
Song 7: 1 How **b** are your feet in
Is 2:16 and upon all the **b** sloops
Is 4: 2 Branch of the LORD shall be **b**
Is 5: 9 **b** ones, without inhabitant
Is 52: 1 put on your **b** garments, O
Is 52: 7 How **b** upon the mountains are
Is 64:11 **b** temple, where our fathers
Jer 3:19 a **b** heritage of the hosts of
Jer 13:20 given to you, your **b** sheep
Jer 48:17 staff is broken, the **b** rod
Ezek 16: 7 matured, and became very **b**
Ezek 16:12 and a **b** crown on your head
Ezek 16:13 You were exceedingly **b**, and
Ezek 16:17 your **b** jewelry from My gold
Ezek 16:39 clothes, take your **b** jewelry
Ezek 23:26 and take away your **b** jewelry
Ezek 23:42 and **b** crowns on their heads
Ezek 31: 7 Thus it was **b** in greatness
Ezek 31: 9 I made it **b** with a multitude
Matt 13:45 a merchant seeking **b** pearls
Matt 23:27 indeed appear **b** outwardly
Luke 21: 5 it was adorned with **b** stones
Acts 3: 2 the temple which is called **B**
Acts 3:10 at the **B** Gate of the temple
Rom 10:15 How **b** are the feet of those
Heb 11:23 they saw he was a **b** child
Jas 1:11 its **b** appearance perishes

BEAUTIFY (*see* BEAUTIES, BEAUTIFYING, BEAUTY)
Ezra 7:27 to **b** the house of the LORD
Ps 149: 4 He will **b** the humble with
Is 60:13 to **b** the place of My
Jer 2:33 Why do you **b** your way to seek

BEAUTIFYING (*see* BEAUTIFY)
Esth 2:12 and preparations for **b** women

BEAUTY (*see* BEAUTIFUL, BEAUTIFY)
Ex 28: 2 brother, for glory and for **b**
Ex 28:40 hats for them, for glory and **b**
2Sa 1:19 The **b** of Israel is slain on
1Ch 16:29 the LORD in the **b** of holiness
2Ch 3: 6 with precious stones for **b**
2Ch 20:21 praise the **b** of holiness, as
Esth 1:11 to show her **b** to the people
Esth 2: 3 let **b** preparations be given
Esth 2: 9 so he readily gave **b**
Job 40:10 yourself with glory and **b**
Ps 27: 4 To behold the **b** of the LORD
Ps 29: 2 the LORD in the **b** of holiness
Ps 39:11 You make his **b** melt away like
Ps 45:11 will greatly desire your **b**
Ps 49:14 their **b** shall be consumed in
Ps 50: 2 of Zion, the perfection of **b**
Ps 90:17 let the **b** of the LORD our God
Ps 96: 6 and **b** are in His sanctuary
Ps 96: 9 the LORD in the **b** of holiness
Prov 6:25 after her **b** in your heart
Prov 31:30 **b** is vain, but a woman who
Is 3:24 and branding instead of **b**
Is 13:19 the **b** of the Chaldeans' pride
Is 28: 1 whose glorious **b** is a fading
Is 28: 4 the glorious **b** is a fading
Is 28: 5 a diadem of **b** to the remnant
Is 33:17 will see the King in His **b**
Is 44:13 according to the **b** of a man
Is 53: 2 there is no **b** that we should
Is 61: 3 to give them **b** for ashes
Lam 2: 1 to the earth the **b** of Israel
Lam 2:15 called "the perfection of **b**
Ezek 7:20 As for the **b** of his
Ezek 16:14 the nations because of your **b**
Ezek 16:15 But you trusted in your own **b**
Ezek 16:25 made your **b** to be abhorred
Ezek 27: 3 have said, 'I am perfect in **b**
Ezek 27: 4 have perfected your **b**
Ezek 27:11 they made your **b** perfect
Ezek 28: 7 against the **b** of your wisdom
Ezek 28:12 of wisdom and perfect in **b**
Ezek 28:17 lifted up because of your **b**
Ezek 31: 8 of God was like it in **b**
Ezek 32:19 Whom do you surpass in **b**
Hos 14: 6 his **b** shall be like an olive
Zech 9:17 goodness And how great their **b**
Zech 11: 7 the one I called **B**, and the
Zech 11:10 And I took my staff, **B**, and cut
1Pe 3: 3 Do not let your **b** be that

BEBAI
Ezra 2:11 the people of **B**, six hundred
Ezra 8:11 of the sons of **B**, Zechariah
Ezra 8:11 **B**, Zechariah the son of **B**
Ezra 10:28 of the sons of **B**
Neh 7:16 the children of **B**, six
Neh 10:15 Bunni, Azgad, **B**,

BECAME (*see* PREFACE)

BECAUSE (*see* PREFACE)

BECHER (*see* BACHRITES)
Gen 46:21 of Benjamin were Belah, **B**
Num 26:35 of **B**, the family of the
1Ch 7: 6 sons of Benjamin were Bela, **B**
1Ch 7: 8 The sons of **B** were Zemirah,
1Ch 7: 8 All these are the sons of **B**

BECHORATH
1Sa 9: 1 son of Zeror, the son of **B**

BECKONED
Luke 1:22 for he **b** to them and remained

BECOME (*see* PREFACE)

BECOMES (*see* PREFACE)

BECOMING (*see* PREFACE)

BED (*see* BEDCHAMBER, BEDRIDDEN, BEDROOM, BEDS, BEDSTEAD)
Gen 47:31 himself on the head of the **b**
Gen 48: 2 himself and sat up on the **b**
Gen 49: 4 went up to your father's **b**
Gen 49:33 drew his feet up into the **b**
Ex 8: 3 your bedchamber, on your **b**
Ex 21:18 die but is confined to his **b**
Lev 15: 4 Every **b** is unclean on which
Lev 15: 5 whoever touches his **b** shall
Lev 15:21 Whoever touches her **b** shall
Lev 15:23 If anything is on her **b** or
Lev 15:24 and every **b** on which he lies
Lev 15:26 Every **b** on which she lies
Lev 15:26 her as the **b** of her impurity
Deut 22:30 nor uncover his father's **b**
Deut 27:20 has uncovered his father's **b**
1Sa 19:13 an image and laid it in the **b**
1Sa 19:15 Bring him up to me in the **b**

1Sa 19:16 there was the image in the **b**
1Sa 28:23 the ground and sat on the **b**
2Sa 4: 5 was lying on his **b** at noon
2Sa 4: 7 lying on his **b** in his bedroom
2Sa 4:11 in his own house on his **b**
2Sa 11: 2 that David arose from his **b**
2Sa 11:13 **b** with the servants of his
2Sa 13: 5 Lie down on your **b** and pretend
1Ki 1:47 king bowed himself on the **b**
1Ki 17:19 and laid him on his own **b**
1Ki 21: 4 And he lay down on his **b**
2Ki 1: 4 not come down from the **b** to
2Ki 1: 6 not come down from the **b** to
2Ki 1:16 not come down from the **b** to
2Ki 4:10 let us put a **b** for him there,
2Ki 4:21 laid him on the **b** of the man
2Ki 4:32 child, lying dead on his **b**
1Ch 5: 1 he defiled his father's **b**
2Ch 16:14 they laid him in the **b** which
2Ch 24:25 and killed him on his **b**
Job 7:13 My **b** will comfort me, my
Job 17:13 house, if I make my **b** in the
Job 33:19 chastened with pain on his **b**
Job 39: 9 Will he **b** by your manger
Ps 4: 4 within your heart on your **b**
Ps 6: 6 All night I make my **b** swim
Ps 36: 4 devises wickedness on his **b**
Ps 41: 3 him on his **b** of illness
Ps 63: 6 When I remember You on my **b**
Ps 132: 3 go up to the comfort of my **b**
Ps 139: 8 If I make my **b** in hell,
Prov 7:16 spread my **b** with tapestry
Prov 7:17 have perfumed my **b** with myrrh
Prov 22:27 away your **b** from under you
Prov 26:14 the slothful turn on his **b**
Song 1:16 Also our **b** is green
Song 3: 1 By night on my **b** I sought the
Song 5:13 cheeks are like a **b** of spices
Is 28:20 For the **b** is too short for a
Is 57: 7 mountain you have set your **b**
Is 57: 8 you have enlarged your **b** and
Is 57: 8 you have loved their **b**, where
Ezek 23:17 to her, into the **b** of love
Ezek 32:25 They have set her **b** in the
Dan 2:28 of your head upon your **b**,
Dan 2:29 to your mind while on your **b**
Dan 4: 5 and the thoughts on my **b** and
Dan 4:10 of my head while on my **b**
Dan 4:13 of my head while on my **b**, and
Dan 7: 1 of his head while on his **b**
Amos 3:12 in the corner of a **b** and on
Matt 9: 2 Him a paralytic lying on a **b**
Matt 9: 6 Arise, take up your **b**, and go
Mark 2: 4 they let down the **b** on which
Mark 2: 9 say, Arise, take up your **b**
Mark 2:11 to you, arise, take up your **b**
Mark 2:12 he arose, took up the **b**, and
Mark 4:21 under a basket or under a **b**
Mark 7:30 her daughter lying on the **b**
Luke 5:18 men brought on a **b** a man who
Luke 5:19 and let him down with his **b**
Luke 5:24 to you, arise, take up your **b**
Luke 8:16 a vessel or puts it under a **b**
Luke 11: 7 my children are with me in **b**
Luke 17:34 will be two men in one **b**
John 5: 8 Rise, take up your **b** and walk
John 5: 9 was made well, took up his **b**
John 5:10 for you to carry your **b**
John 5:11 said to me, 'Take up your **b**
John 5:12 said to you, 'Take up your **b**
Acts 9:34 Arise and make your **b**
Heb 13: 4 among all, and the **b** undefiled

BEDAD
Gen 36:35 died, Hadad the son of **B**, who
1Ch 1:46 died, Hadad the son of **B**, who

BEDAN
1Sa 12:11 And the LORD sent Jerubbaal, **B**
1Ch 7:17 The son of Ulam was **B**

BEDCHAMBER (*see* BED)
Ex 8: 3 into your house, into your **b**

BEDEIAH
Ezra 10:35 Benaiah, **B**, Cheluh,

BEDRIDDEN (*see* BED)
Acts 9:33 who had been **b** eight years

BEDROOM (*see* BED)
2Sa 4: 7 was lying on his bed in his **b**
2Sa 13:10 Bring the food into the **b**
2Sa 13:10 to Amnon her brother in the **b**
2Ki 6:12 that you speak in your **b**
2Ki 11: 2 hid him and his nurse in the **b**
2Ch 22:11 put him and his nurse in a **b**
Eccl 10:20 the rich, even in your **b**

BEDS (*see* BED)
2Sa 17:28 brought **b** and basins, earthen
Job 33:15 while slumbering on their **b**
Ps 149: 5 them sing aloud on their **b**
Song 6: 2 to the **b** of spices, to feed
Is 57: 2 they shall rest in their **b**
Hos 7:14 when they wailed upon their **b**
Amos 6: 4 who lie on **b** of ivory,
Mic 2: 1 And work out evil on their **b**
Mark 6:55 on **b** those who were sick to
Acts 5:15 the streets and laid them on **b**

BEDSTEAD (*see* BED)
Deut 3:11 his **b** was an iron **b**

BEE (*see* BEES)
Is 7:18 for the **b** that is in the land

BEELIADA
1Ch 14: 7 Elishama, **B**, and Eliphelet

BEELZEBUB (*see* BAAL-ZEBUB)
Matt 10:25 the master of the house **B**
Matt 12:24 cast out demons except by **B**
Matt 12:27 And if I cast out demons by **B**
Mark 3:22 He has **B**," and, "By the
Luke 11:15 He casts out demons by **B**, the
Luke 11:18 say I cast out demons by **B**
Luke 11:19 And if I cast out demons by **B**

BEEN (*see* PREFACE)

BEER
Num 21:16 And from there they went to **B**
Judg 9:21 and he went to **B** and dwelt

BEERA
1Ch 7:37 Shilshah, Jithran, and **B**

BEERAH
1Ch 5: 6 and **B** his son, whom

BEER ELIM (*see* ELIM)
Is 15: 8 to Eglaim and its wailing to **B**

BEERI
Gen 26:34 the daughter of **B** the Hittite
Hos 1: 1 came to Hosea the son of **B**

BEER LAHAI ROI (*see* LAHAI ROI)
Gen 16:14 the well was called **B**
Gen 24:62 Isaac came from the way of **B**
Gen 25:11 And Isaac dwelt at **B**

BEEROTH (*see* BEEROTHITE)
Josh 9:17 were Gibeon, Chephirah, **B**
Josh 18:25 Gibeon, Ramah, **B**,
2Sa 4: 2 (For **B** also was part of
Ezra 2:25 Kirjath Arim, Chephirah, and **B**
Neh 7:29 Jearim, Chephirah, and **B**,

BEEROTHITE (*see* BEEROTH, BEEROTHITES, BEROTHITE)
2Sa 4: 2 the sons of Rimmon the **B**
2Sa 4: 5 Then the sons of Rimmon the **B**
2Sa 4: 9 the sons of Rimmon the **B**
2Sa 23:37 Naharai the **B** (armorbearer of

BEEROTHITES (*see* BEEROTHITE)
2Sa 4: 3 because the **B** fled to Gittaim

BEERSHEBA
Gen 21:14 in the Wilderness of **B**
Gen 21:31 he called that place **B**,
Gen 21:32 they made a covenant at **B**
Gen 21:33 planted a tamarisk tree in **B**
Gen 22:19 rose and went together to **B**
Gen 22:19 and Abraham dwelt at **B**
Gen 26:23 he went up from there to **B**
Gen 26:33 of the city is **B** to this day
Gen 28:10 Now Jacob went out from **B**
Gen 46: 1 all that he had, and came to **B**
Gen 46: 5 Then Jacob arose from **B**
Josh 15:28 Hazar Shual, **B**, Bizjothjah,
Josh 19: 2 their inheritance **B** (Sheba)
Judg 20: 1 came out, from Dan to **B**, as
1Sa 3:20 all Israel from Dan to **B** knew
1Sa 8: 2 they were judges in **B**
2Sa 3:10 and over Judah, from Dan to **B**
2Sa 17:11 to you, from Dan to **B**, like
2Sa 24: 2 of Israel, from Dan to **B**, and
2Sa 24: 7 to South Judah as far as **B**
2Sa 24:15 From Dan to **B** seventy
1Ki 4:25 tree, from Dan as far as **B**
1Ki 19: 3 for his life, and went to **B**
2Ki 12: 1 mother's name was Zibiah of **B**
2Ki 23: 8 incense, from Geba to **B**
1Ch 4:28 They dwelt at **B**, Moladah,
1Ch 21: 2 number Israel from **B** to Dan
2Ch 19: 4 **B** to the mountains of Ephraim
2Ch 24: 1 mother's name was Zibiah of **B**
2Ch 30: 5 from **B** to Dan, that they
Neh 11:27 Hazar Shual, and **B** and its
Neh 11:30 They dwelt from **B** to the
Amos 5: 5 Gilgal, nor pass over to **B**
Amos 8:14 and, 'As the way of **B** lives

BEES (*see* BEE)
Deut 1:44 you and chased you as **b** do
Judg 14: 8 And behold, a swarm of **b** and
Ps 118:12 They surrounded me like **b**

BE ESHTERAH
Josh 21:27 and **B** with its common-land

BEFALL (*see* BEFALLEN, BEFALLS)
Gen 42: 4 Lest some calamity **b** him
Gen 42:38 If any calamity should **b** him
Gen 49: 1 shall **b** you in the last days
Num 11:23 My word will **b** you or not
Deut 31:17 and troubles shall **b** them, so
Deut 31:29 evil will **b** you in the latter
Ps 91:10 No evil shall **b** you, Nor

BEFALLEN (*see* BEFALL)
Lev 10:19 and such things have **b** me
Num 20:14 the hardship that has **b** us
Josh 2:23 told him all that had **b** them
2Sa 19: 7 **b** you from your youth until
Neh 9:33 are just in all that has **b** us

BEFALLS (*see* BEFALL)
Gen 44:29 from me, and calamity **b** him
Eccl 3:19 one thing **b** them

BEFITTING
Acts 26:20 God, and do works **b** repentance

BEFORE (*see* PREFACE)

BEFOREHAND (*see* PREFACE)

BEG (*see* BEGGAR, BEGGED, BEGGING)
Gen 50:17 I **b** you, please forgive the
Josh 2:12 I **b** you, swear to me by the
Josh 7:19 I **b** you, give glory to the
Judg 19:23 I **b** you, do not act so
Job 9:15 I would **b** mercy of my Judge
Job 19:16 I **b** him with my mouth
Ps 109:10 be vagabonds, and **b**
Prov 20: 4 therefore he will **b** during
Luke 8:28 I **b** You, do not torment me
Luke 16: 3 I am ashamed to **b**
Luke 16:27 I **b** you therefore, father,
Acts 24: 4 I **b** you to hear, by your
Acts 26: 3 Therefore I **b** you to hear me
Rom 15:30 Now I **b** you, brethren,
2Co 10: 2 But I **b** you that when I am
1Pe 2:11 I **b** you as sojourners and

BEGAN (*see* PREFACE)

BEGET (*see* BEGETS, BEGETTING, BEGOT, BEGOTTEN)
Gen 17:20 He shall **b** twelve princes, and
Gen 48: 6 Your offspring whom you **b**
Lev 25:45 which they **b** in your land
Num 11:12 Did I **b** them, that You should
Deut 4:25 When you **b** children and
Deut 28:41 You shall **b** sons and daughters
2Ki 20:18 from you, whom you will **b**
Is 39: 7 from you, whom you will **b**
Jer 29: 6 wives and **b** sons and daughters

BEGETS (*see* BEGET)
Prov 17:21 He who **b** a scoffer does so to
Prov 23:24 he who **b** a wise child will
Eccl 5:14 when he **b** a son, there is
Eccl 6: 3 If a man **b** a hundred children
Ezek 18:10 If he **b** a son who is a robber
Ezek 18:14 he **b** a son who sees all the

BEGETTING (*see* BEGET)
Is 45:10 his father, 'What are you **b**

BEGGAR (*see* BEG)
1Sa 2: 8 lifts the **b** from the ash heap
Luke 16:20 was a certain **b** named Lazarus
Luke 16:22 So it was that the **b** died

BEGGARLY
Gal 4: 9 and **b** elements, to which you

BEGGED (*see* BEG)
Matt 8:31 So the demons **b** Him, saying,
Matt 8:34 they **b** Him to depart from
Matt 14:36 **b** Him that they might only
Matt 18:29 **b** him, saying, "Have patience
Matt 18:32 that debt because you **b** me
Mark 5:10 he **b** Him earnestly that He
Mark 5:12 And all the demons **b** Him,
Mark 5:18 had been demon-possessed **b**
Mark 5:23 and **b** Him earnestly, saying,
Mark 6:56 **b** Him that they might just
Mark 7:32 they **b** Him to put His hand on
Mark 8:22 to Him, and **b** Him to touch him
Luke 7: 4 they **b** Him earnestly, saying
Luke 8:31 they **b** Him that He would not
Luke 8:32 And they **b** Him that He would
Luke 8:38 the demons had departed **b** Him
Luke 8:41 **b** Him to come to his house,
John 9: 8 Is not this he who sat and **b**
Acts 13:42 the Gentiles **b** that these
Acts 16:15 were baptized, she **b** us,
Heb 12:19 so that those who heard it **b**

BEGGING (*see* BEG)
Ps 37:25 Nor his descendants **b** bread
Mark 10:46 of Timaeus, sat by the road **b**
Luke 18:35 blind man sat by the road **b**
Acts 3:10 **b** alms at the Beautiful Gate

BEGIN (*see* PREFACE)

BEGINNING (*see* BEGINNINGS)
Gen 1: 1 In the **b** God created the
Gen 10:10 And the **b** of his kingdom was
Gen 13: 3 his tent had been at the **b**
Gen 41:21 were just as ugly as at the **b**
Gen 49: 3 the **b** of my strength, the
Ex 12: 2 shall be your **b** of months
Lev 6:20 LORD, **b** on the day when he is
Num 10:10 at the **b** of your months, you
Deut 11:12 from the **b** of the year to the
Deut 21:17 has, for he is the **b** of his
Judg 7:19 at the **b** of the middle watch
Ruth 1:22 at the **b** of barley harvest
Ruth 3:10 at the end than at the **b**, in
1Sa 3:12 his house, from **b** to end
2Sa 21: 9 in the **b** of barley harvest
2Sa 21:10 from the **b** of harvest until
2Ki 17:25 at the **b** of their dwelling
Ezra 4: 6 in the **b** of his reign, they
Neh 4: 7 the gaps were **b** to be closed
Job 8: 7 Though your **b** was small, yet
Job 42:12 days of Job more than his **b**
Ps 111:10 the LORD is the **b** of wisdom
Prov 1: 7 LORD is the **b** of knowledge
Prov 8:22 me at the **b** of His way,
Prov 8:23 from everlasting, from the **b**
Prov 9:10 the LORD is the **b** of wisdom
Prov 17:14 The **b** of strife is like
Prov 20:21 gained hastily at the **b** will
Eccl 3:11 that God does from **b** to end
Eccl 7: 8 a thing is better than its **b**
Is 1:26 your counselors as at the **b**
Is 18: 2 terrible from their **b** onward
Is 18: 7 terrible from their **b** onward
Is 40:21 not been told you from the **b**
Is 41: 4 the generations from the **b**
Is 41:26 Who has declared from the **b**
Is 46:10 Declaring the end from the **b**
Is 48: 3 the former things from the **b**
Is 48: 5 even from the **b** I have
Is 48: 7 created now and not from the **b**
Is 48:16 spoken in secret from the **b**
Is 64: 4 For since the **b** of the world
Jer 17:12 the **b** is the place of our
Jer 26: 1 In the **b** of the reign of
Jer 27: 1 In the **b** of the reign of
Jer 28: 1 at the **b** of the reign of
Jer 49:34 in the **b** of the reign of
Lam 2:19 at the **b** of the watches
Ezek 40: 1 at the **b** of the year, on the
Dan 9:21 seen in the vision at the **b**
Dan 9:23 At the **b** of your
Amos 7: 1 at the **b** of the late crop
Mic 1:13 **b** of sin to the daughter of
Matt 14:30 and **b** to sink he cried out,
Matt 19: 4 them at the **b** 'made them male
Matt 19: 8 but from the **b** it was not so
Matt 20: 8 **b** with the last to the first
Matt 24: 8 these are the **b** of sorrows
Matt 24:21 the **b** of the world until this
Mark 1: 1 The **b** of the gospel of Jesus
Mark 10: 6 But from the **b** of the
Mark 13:19 the **b** of creation which God
Luke 1: 2 from the **b** were eyewitnesses
Luke 23: 5 **b** from Galilee to this place
Luke 24:27 And **b** at Moses and all the
Luke 24:47 all nations, **b** at Jerusalem
John 1: 1 In the **b** was the Word, and the
John 1: 2 He was in the **b** with God
John 2:10 Every man at the **b** sets out
John 2:11 This **b** of signs Jesus did in
John 6:64 **b** who they were who did not
John 8: 9 **b** with the oldest even to the
John 8:25 been saying to you from the **b**
John 8:44 He was a murderer from the **b**
John 15:27 have been with Me from the **b**
John 16: 4 I did not say to you at the **b**
Acts 1:22 **b** from the baptism of John to
Acts 8:35 **b** at this Scripture, preached
Acts 11: 4 to them in order from the **b**
Acts 11:15 them, as upon us at the **b**
Acts 26: 4 the **b** among my own nation at
Eph 3: 9 which from the **b** of the ages
Phil 4:15 that in the **b** of the gospel
Col 1:18 the church, who is the **b**
2Th 2:13 because God from the **b** chose
Heb 1:10 in the **b** laid the foundation
Heb 3:14 of Christ if we hold the **b** of
Heb 7: 3 having neither **b** of days nor
2Pe 2:20 is worse for them than the **b**
2Pe 3: 4 were from the **b** of creation
1Jn 1: 1 That which was from the **b**
1Jn 2: 7 which you have had from the **b**
1Jn 2: 7 which you heard from the **b**
1Jn 2:13 known Him who is from the **b**
1Jn 2:14 known Him who is from the **b**
1Jn 2:24 which you heard from the **b**
1Jn 2:24 from the **b** abides in you, you
1Jn 3: 8 devil has sinned from the **b**
1Jn 3:11 that you heard from the **b**
2Jn 5 which we have had from the **b**
2Jn 6 as you have heard from the **b**
Rev 1: 8 the Alpha and the Omega, the **B**
Rev 3:14 the **B** of the creation of God
Rev 21: 6 the Alpha and the Omega, the **B**
Rev 22:13 the Alpha and the Omega, the **B**

BEGINNINGS (*see* BEGINNING)
Num 28:11 At the **b** of your months you
Ezek 36:11 better for you than at your **b**
Mark 13: 8 These are the **b** of sorrows

BEGINS (*see* PREFACE)

BEGOT (*see* BEGET)
Gen 4:18 Irad **b** Mehujael, and Mehujael
Gen 4:18 Mehujael **b** Methushael, and
Gen 4:18 and Methushael **b** Lamech
Gen 5: 3 **b** a son in his own likeness,
Gen 5: 4 After he **b** Seth, the days of
Gen 5: 4 and he **b** sons and daughters
Gen 5: 6 and five years, and **b** Enosh
Gen 5: 7 After he **b** Enosh, Seth lived
Gen 5: 7 years, and **b** sons and daughters
Gen 5: 9 ninety years, and **b** Cainan
Gen 5:10 After he **b** Cainan, Enosh
Gen 5:10 years, and **b** sons and daughters
Gen 5:12 years, and **b** Mahalaleel
Gen 5:13 After he **b** Mahalaleel, Cainan
Gen 5:13 years, and **b** sons and daughters
Gen 5:15 sixty-five years, and **b** Jared
Gen 5:16 After he **b** Jared, Mahalaleel
Gen 5:16 years, and **b** sons and daughters
Gen 5:18 sixty-two years, and **b** Enoch
Gen 5:19 After he **b** Enoch, Jared lived
Gen 5:19 years, and **b** sons and daughters
Gen 5:21 years, and **b** Methuselah
Gen 5:22 After he **b** Methuselah, Enoch
Gen 5:22 years, and **b** sons and daughters
Gen 5:25 years, and **b** Lamech
Gen 5:26 After he **b** Lamech, Methuselah
Gen 5:26 years, and **b** sons and daughters
Gen 5:28 eighty-two years, and **b** a son
Gen 5:30 After he **b** Noah, Lamech lived
Gen 5:30 years, and **b** sons and daughters
Gen 5:32 years old, and Noah **b** Shem
Gen 6:10 And Noah **b** three sons
Gen 10: 8 Cush **b** Nimrod
Gen 10:13 Mizraim **b** Ludim, Anamim,
Gen 10:15 Canaan **b** Sidon his firstborn,
Gen 10:24 Arphaxad **b** Salah
Gen 10:24 and Salah **b** Eber
Gen 10:26 Joktan **b** Almodad, Sheleph,
Gen 11:10 **b** Arphaxad two years after
Gen 11:11 After he **b** Arphaxad, Shem
Gen 11:11 years, and **b** sons and daughters
Gen 11:12 thirty-five years, and **b** Salah
Gen 11:13 After he **b** Salah, Arphaxad
Gen 11:13 years, and **b** sons and daughters
Gen 11:14 lived thirty years, and **b** Eber
Gen 11:15 After he **b** Eber, Salah lived
Gen 11:15 years, and **b** sons and daughters
Gen 11:16 thirty-four years, and **b** Peleg
Gen 11:17 After he **b** Peleg, Eber lived
Gen 11:17 years, and **b** sons and daughters
Gen 11:18 lived thirty years, and **b** Reu
Gen 11:19 After he **b** Reu, Peleg lived
Gen 11:19 years, and **b** sons and daughters
Gen 11:20 thirty-two years, and **b** Serug
Gen 11:21 After he **b** Serug, Reu lived
Gen 11:21 years, and **b** sons and daughters
Gen 11:22 thirty years, and **b** Nahor
Gen 11:23 After he **b** Nahor, Serug lived
Gen 11:23 years, and **b** sons and daughters
Gen 11:24 twenty-nine years, and **b** Terah
Gen 11:25 After he **b** Terah, Nahor lived
Gen 11:25 years, and **b** sons and daughters
Gen 11:26 and **b** Abram, Nahor, and
Gen 11:27 Terah **b** Abram, Nahor, and
Gen 11:27 Haran **b** Lot
Gen 22:23 And Bethuel **b** Rebekah
Gen 25: 3 Jokshan **b** Sheba and Dedan
Gen 25:19 Abraham **b** Isaac
Num 26:29 and Machir **b** Gilead
Num 26:58 And Kohath **b** Amram
Deut 32:18 Of the Rock who **b** you, you
Judg 11: 1 and Gilead **b** Jephthah
Ruth 4:18 Perez **b** Hezron
Ruth 4:19 Hezron **b** Ram
Ruth 4:19 and Ram **b** Amminadab
Ruth 4:20 Amminadab **b** Nahshon, and
Ruth 4:20 and Nahshon **b** Salmon
Ruth 4:21 Salmon **b** Boaz
Ruth 4:21 and Boaz **b** Obed
Ruth 4:22 Obed **b** Jesse
Ruth 4:22 and Jesse **b** David
1Ch 1:10 Cush **b** Nimrod
1Ch 1:11 Mizraim **b** Ludim, Anamim,
1Ch 1:13 Canaan **b** Sidon, his firstborn
1Ch 1:18 Arphaxad **b** Shelah, and Shelah
1Ch 1:18 Shelah, and Shelah **b** Eber
1Ch 1:20 Joktan **b** Almodad, Sheleph,
1Ch 1:34 And Abraham **b** Isaac
1Ch 2:10 Ram **b** Amminadab, and
1Ch 2:10 and Amminadab **b** Nahshon,
1Ch 2:11 Nahshon **b** Salma
1Ch 2:11 and Salma **b** Boaz
1Ch 2:12 Boaz **b** Obed
1Ch 2:12 and Obed **b** Jesse
1Ch 2:13 Jesse **b** Eliab his firstborn,
1Ch 2:18 Hezron **b** children by Azubah
1Ch 2:20 And Hur **b** Uri
1Ch 2:20 and Uri **b** Bezaleel
1Ch 2:22 Segub **b** Jair, who had
1Ch 2:36 Attai **b** Nathan, and Nathan
1Ch 2:36 Nathan, and Nathan **b** Zabad
1Ch 2:37 Zabad **b** Ephlal, and Ephlal
1Ch 2:37 Ephlal, and Ephlal **b** Obed
1Ch 2:38 Obed **b** Jehu
1Ch 2:38 and Jehu **b** Azariah
1Ch 2:39 Azariah **b** Helez, and Helez
1Ch 2:39 Helez, and Helez **b** Eleasah
1Ch 2:40 Eleasah **b** Sismai, and Sismai
1Ch 2:40 Sismai, and Sismai **b** Shallum
1Ch 2:41 Shallum **b** Jekamiah, and
1Ch 2:41 and Jekamiah **b** Elishama
1Ch 2:44 Shema **b** Raham the father of
1Ch 2:44 and Rekem **b** Shammai
1Ch 2:46 and Haran **b** Gazez
1Ch 4: 2 the son of Shobal **b** Jahath
1Ch 4: 2 Jahath, and Jahath **b** Ahumai
1Ch 4: 8 Koz **b** Anub, Zobebah, and the
1Ch 4:11 the brother of Shuhah **b** Mehir
1Ch 4:12 Eshton **b** Beth-Rapha, Paseah,
1Ch 4:14 and Meonothai who **b** Ophrah
1Ch 4:14 Seraiah **b** Joab the father of

1Ch 6: 4 Eleazar **b** Phinehas, and
1Ch 6: 4 and Phinehas **b** Abishua
1Ch 6: 5 Abishua **b** Bukki
1Ch 6: 5 and Bukki **b** Uzzi
1Ch 6: 6 Uzzi **b** Zerahiah, and Zerahiah
1Ch 6: 6 and Zerahiah **b** Meraioth
1Ch 6: 7 Meraioth **b** Amariah, and
1Ch 6: 7 and Amariah **b** Ahitub
1Ch 6: 8 Ahitub **b** Zadok, and Zadok
1Ch 6: 8 Zadok, and Zadok **b** Ahimaaz
1Ch 6: 9 Ahimaaz **b** Azariah, and
1Ch 6: 9 Azariah, and Azariah **b** Johanan
1Ch 6:10 Johanan **b** Azariah (it was he
1Ch 6:11 Azariah **b** Amariah, and
1Ch 6:11 and Amariah **b** Ahitub
1Ch 6:12 Ahitub **b** Zadok, and Zadok
1Ch 6:12 Zadok, and Zadok **b** Shallum
1Ch 6:13 Shallum **b** Hilkiah, and Hilkiah
1Ch 6:13 Hilkiah, and Hilkiah **b** Azariah
1Ch 6:14 Azariah **b** Seraiah, and Seraiah
1Ch 6:14 and Seraiah **b** Jehozadak
1Ch 7:15 Zelophehad **b** only daughters
1Ch 7:32 And Heber **b** Japhlet, Shomer,
1Ch 8: 1 Now Benjamin **b** Bela his
1Ch 8: 7 He **b** Uzza and Ahihud
1Ch 8: 8 Shaharaim **b** children in the
1Ch 8: 9 By Hodesh his wife he **b** Jobab
1Ch 8:11 And by Hushim he **b** Abitub and
1Ch 8:32 and Mikloth, who **b** Shimeah
1Ch 8:33 Ner **b** Kish, Kish **b** Saul,
1Ch 8:33 Saul **b** Jonathan, Malchishua,
1Ch 8:34 and Merib-Baal **b** Micah
1Ch 8:36 And Ahaz **b** Jehoaddah
1Ch 8:36 Jehoaddah **b** Alemeth,
1Ch 8:36 and Zimri **b** Moza
1Ch 8:37 Moza **b** Binea, Raphah his son,
1Ch 9:38 And Mikloth **b** Shimeam
1Ch 9:39 Ner **b** Kish, Kish **b** Saul,
1Ch 9:39 Saul **b** Jonathan, Malchishua,
1Ch 9:40 and Merib-Baal **b** Micah
1Ch 9:42 And Ahaz **b** Jarah
1Ch 9:42 Jarah **b** Alemeth, Azmaveth,
1Ch 9:42 and Zimri **b** Moza
1Ch 9:43 Moza **b** Binea, Rephaiah his
1Ch 14: 3 and David **b** more sons and
2Ch 11:21 **b** twenty-eight sons and sixty
2Ch 13:21 **b** twenty-two sons and sixteen
Neh 12:10 Jeshua **b** Joiakim, Joiakim
Neh 12:10 Joiakim **b** Eliashib
Neh 12:10 Eliashib **b** Joiada
Neh 12:11 Joiada **b** Jonathan, and
Neh 12:11 and Jonathan **b** Jaddua
Prov 23:22 to your father who **b** you, and
Jer 16: 3 who **b** them in this land
Dan 11: 6 her, and with him who **b** her
Zech 13: 3 mother who **b** him will say to
Zech 13: 3 mother who **b** him shall thrust
Matt 1: 2 Abraham **b** Isaac
Matt 1: 2 Isaac **b** Jacob
Matt 1: 2 and Jacob **b** Judah
Matt 1: 3 Judah **b** Perez and Zerah by
Matt 1: 3 Perez **b** Hezron
Matt 1: 3 and Hezron **b** Ram
Matt 1: 4 Ram **b** Amminadab
Matt 1: 4 Amminadab **b** Nahshon
Matt 1: 4 Nahshon **b** Salmon
Matt 1: 5 Salmon **b** Boaz by Rahab
Matt 1: 5 Boaz **b** Obed by Ruth
Matt 1: 5 Obed by Ruth, Obed **b** Jesse,
Matt 1: 6 and Jesse **b** David the king
Matt 1: 6 David the king **b** Solomon by
Matt 1: 7 Solomon **b** Rehoboam
Matt 1: 7 Rehoboam **b** Abijah
Matt 1: 7 and Abijah **b** Asa
Matt 1: 8 Asa **b** Jehoshaphat,
Matt 1: 8 Jehoshaphat **b** Joram
Matt 1: 8 and Joram **b** Uzziah
Matt 1: 9 Uzziah **b** Jotham
Matt 1: 9 Jotham **b** Ahaz
Matt 1: 9 and Ahaz **b** Hezekiah
Matt 1:10 Hezekiah **b** Manasseh
Matt 1:10 Manasseh **b** Amon
Matt 1:10 and Amon **b** Josiah
Matt 1:11 Josiah **b** Jeconiah and his
Matt 1:12 Jeconiah **b** Shealtiel
Matt 1:12 and Shealtiel **b** Zerubbabel
Matt 1:13 Zerubbabel **b** Abiud
Matt 1:13 Abiud **b** Eliakim
Matt 1:13 and Eliakim **b** Azor
Matt 1:14 Azor **b** Zadok, Zadok **b** Achim,
Matt 1:14 and Achim **b** Eliud
Matt 1:15 Eliud **b** Eleazar, Eleazar
Matt 1:15 Eleazar **b** Matthan
Matt 1:15 and Matthan **b** Jacob
Matt 1:16 Jacob **b** Joseph the husband of
Acts 7: 8 and so Abraham **b** Isaac
Acts 7: 8 and Isaac **b** Jacob
Acts 7: 8 Jacob **b** the twelve patriarchs
1Jn 5: 1 who **b** also loves him who is

BEGOTTEN (*see* BEGET)
Lev 18:11 daughter, **b** by your father
Job 38:28 or who has **b** the drops of dew
Ps 2: 7 My Son, Today I have **b** You
Is 49:21 Who has **b** these for me,
Hos 5: 7 LORD, for they have **b** pagan
John 1:14 of the only **b** of the Father
John 1:18 The only **b** Son, who is in the
John 3:16 that He gave His only **b** Son
John 3:18 name of the only **b** Son of God
Acts 13:33 My Son, today I have **b** You
1Co 4:15 have **b** you through the gospel
Phm 10 whom I have **b** while in my
Heb 1: 5 My Son, today I have **b** You"
Heb 5: 5 My Son, today I have **b** You
Heb 11:17 offered up his only **b** son
1Pe 1: 3 **b** us again to a living hope
1Jn 4: 9 His only **b** Son into the world
1Jn 5: 1 loves him who is **b** of Him

BEGUILE (*see* BEGUILING)
Rev 2:20 and **b** My servants to commit

BEGUILING (*see* BEGUILE)
2Pe 2:14 from sin, **b** unstable souls

BEGUN (*see* PREFACE)

BEHALF
Ex 27:21 to their generations on **b** of
Lev 1: 4 **b** to make atonement for him
Lev 5:10 **b** for his sin which he has
Lev 22:20 not be acceptable on your **b**
Lev 22:25 not be accepted on your **b**
Lev 23:11 to be accepted on your **b**
Deut 21: 8 on their **b** for the blood
2Sa 3:12 messengers on his **b** to David
2Ki 4:13 your **b** to the king or to the
2Ch 16: 9 on **b** of those whose heart is
Esth 7: 9 spoke good on the king's **b**
Job 36: 2 yet words to speak on God's **b**
Is 8:19 the dead on **b** of the living
Ezek 22:30 before Me on **b** of the land
Rom 16:19 Therefore I am glad on your **b**
1Co 4: 6 on **b** of one against the other
2Co 1:11 by many persons on our **b** for
2Co 5:12 opportunity to glory on our **b**
2Co 5:20 we implore you on Christ's **b**
2Co 7: 4 is my boasting on your **b**
2Co 8:24 and of our boasting on your **b**
Phil 1:29 been granted on **b** of Christ
Col 1: 7 minister of Christ on your **b**
Phm 13 me, that on your **b** he might

BEHAVE (*see* BEHAVED, BEHAVES, BEHAVING, BEHAVIOR)
Deut 25:16 all who **b** unrighteously, are
2Ch 19:11 **B** courageously, and the LORD
Job 27:12 why then do you **b** with
Ps 101: 2 I will **b** wisely in a perfect
Ezek 24:19 signify to us, that you **b** so
1Co 13: 5 does not **b** rudely, does not

BEHAVED (*see* BEHAVE)
Ex 18:11 thing in which they **b** proudly
Num 5:27 **b** unfaithfully toward her
Judg 2:19 **b** more corruptly than their
1Sa 18: 5 Saul sent him, and **b** wisely
1Sa 18:14 David **b** wisely in all his
1Sa 18:15 saw that he **b** very wisely
1Sa 18:30 that David **b** more wisely than
1Ki 21:26 And he **b** very abominably in
1Th 2:10 blamelessly we **b** ourselves

BEHAVES (*see* BEHAVE)
Num 5:12 **b** unfaithfully toward him,

BEHAVING (*see* BEHAVE)
1Co 3: 3 not carnal and **b** like mere men
1Co 7:36 he is **b** improperly toward his

BEHAVIOR (*see* BEHAVE)
Deut 31:21 inclination of their **b** today
1Sa 8: 9 show them the **b** of the king
1Sa 8:11 This will be the **b** of the
1Sa 10:25 the people the **b** of royalty
1Sa 21:13 he changed his **b** before them
1Sa 27:11 so was his **b** all the time he
Esth 1:17 For the queen's **b** will become
Esth 1:18 heard of the **b** of the queen
Ezek 16:27 were ashamed of your lewd **b**
1Ti 3: 2 sober-minded, of good **b**,
Tit 2: 3 that they be reverent in **b**

BEHEADED
2Sa 4: 7 **b** him and took his head, and
Matt 14:10 sent and had John **b** in prison
Mark 6:16 This is John, whom I **b**
Mark 6:27 he went and **b** him in prison,
Luke 9: 9 John I have **b**, but who is
Rev 20: 4 **b** for their witness to Jesus

BEHELD (*see* BEHOLD)
Jer 4:23 I **b** the earth, and indeed it
Jer 4:24 I **b** the mountains, and indeed
Jer 4:25 I **b**, and indeed there was no
Jer 4:26 I **b**, and indeed the fruitful
John 1:14 we **b** His glory, the glory as

BEHEMOTH
Job 40:15 Look now at the **b**, which I

BEHIND (*see* PREFACE)

BEHOLD (*see* BEHELD, BEHOLDING, BEHOLDS)
Gen 3:22 **B**, the man has become like
Gen 6:13 and **b**, I will destroy them
Gen 6:17 And **b**, I Myself am bringing
Gen 8:11 to him in the evening, and **b**
Gen 9: 9 And as for Me, **b**, I establish
Gen 15: 4 And **b**, the word of the LORD
Gen 15:12 and **b**, horror and great
Gen 15:17 down and it was dark, that **b**
Gen 16:11 **B**, you are with child, and you
Gen 17: 4 As for Me, **b**, My covenant is
Gen 17:20 **B**, I have blessed him, and
Gen 18: 2 his eyes and looked, and **b**,
Gen 18:10 to the time of life, and **b**
Gen 19:28 and he saw, and **b**, the smoke of
Gen 20:16 **B**, I have given your brother
Gen 24:13 **B**, I stand here by the well
Gen 24:15 had finished speaking, that **b**
Gen 24:16 woman was very beautiful to **b**
Gen 24:43 **b**, I stand by the well of
Gen 26: 7 because she is beautiful to **b**
Gen 27: 2 And he said, "**B** now, I am old
Gen 27:39 **B**, your dwelling shall be of
Gen 28:12 Then he dreamed, and **b**, a
Gen 28:13 And **b**, the LORD stood above it
Gen 28:15 **B**, I am with you and will keep
Gen 29: 2 and **b**, there were three flocks
Gen 29:25 pass in the morning, that **b**
Gen 31:10 eyes and saw in a dream, and **b**
Gen 32:18 and **b**, he also is behind us
Gen 32:20 and also say, '**B**, your servant
Gen 37: 7 Then **b**, my sheaf arose and
Gen 38:27 time for giving birth, that **b**
Gen 40: 9 **B**, in my dream a vine was
Gen 41: 1 and **b**, he stood by the river
Gen 41: 3 Then **b**, seven other cows came
Gen 41: 6 Then **b**, seven thin heads,
Gen 41:17 **B**, in my dream I stood on the
Gen 41:19 Then **b**, seven other cows came
Gen 41:23 Then **b**, seven heads, withered
Gen 42:22 Therefore **b**, his blood is now
Gen 45:12 And **b**, your eyes and the eyes
Gen 48: 4 and said to me, '**B**, I will
Gen 48:21 **B**, I am dying, but God will
Gen 50: 5 **B**, I am dying
Gen 50:18 **B**, we are your servants
Ex 2: 6 it, she saw the child, and **b**
Ex 2:13 he went out the second day, **b**
Ex 3: 2 So he looked, and **b**, the bush
Ex 3: 9 Now therefore, **b**, the cry of
Ex 4: 6 and when he took it out, **b**
Ex 4: 7 it out of his bosom, and **b**
Ex 6:30 **B**, I am of uncircumcised lips
Ex 7:17 **B**, I will strike the waters
Ex 8: 2 you refuse to let them go, **b**
Ex 8:21 will not let My people go, **b**
Ex 9: 3 **b**, the hand of the LORD will
Ex 9:18 **B**, tomorrow about this time I
Ex 10: 4 refuse to let My people go, **b**
Ex 14:10 lifted their eyes, and **b**, the
Ex 16: 4 **B**, I will rain bread from
Ex 16:10 toward the wilderness, and **b**
Ex 17: 6 **B**, I will stand before you
Ex 19: 9 **B**, I come to you in the thick

Ex 23:20 **B**, I send an Angel before you
Ex 24: 8 **B**, the blood of the covenant
Ex 32:34 **B**, My Angel shall go before
Ex 34:10 **B**, I make a covenant
Ex 34:11 **B**, I am driving out from
Ex 34:30 of Israel saw Moses, **b**, the
Num 3:12 Now **b**, I Myself have taken
Num 17: 8 tabernacle of witness, and **b**
Num 18: 6 **B**, I Myself have taken your
Num 18:21 **B**, I have given the children
Num 22:32 **B**, I have come out to stand
Num 23: 9 and from the hills I **b** him
Num 23:20 **B**, I have received a command
Num 24:17 I **b** Him, but not near
Num 25:12 Therefore say, '**B**, I give to
Deut 3:27 **b** it with your eyes, for you
Deut 11:26 **B**, I set before you today a
Deut 26:10 and now, **b**, I have brought
Deut 31:14 **B**, the days approach when you
Deut 31:16 **B**, you will rest with your
Josh 2: 2 **B**, men have come here tonight
Josh 3:11 **B**, the ark of the covenant of
Josh 5:13 his eyes and looked, and **b**, a
Josh 8: 4 **B**, you shall lie in ambush
Josh 8:20 behind them, they saw, and **b**
Josh 14:10 And now, **b**, the LORD has kept
Josh 22:11 **B**, the children of Reuben,
Josh 23:14 **B**, this day I am going the
Josh 24:27 **B**, this stone shall be a
Judg 13: 5 For **b**, you shall conceive and
Judg 13: 7 And He said to me, '**B**, you
Judg 14: 8 And **b**, a swarm of bees and
Ruth 2: 4 Now **b**, Boaz came from
Ruth 4: 1 and **b**, the near kinsman of
1Sa 2:31 **B**, the days are coming that
1Sa 3:11 **B**, I will do something in
1Sa 15:22 **B**, to obey is better than
1Sa 24: 4 the LORD said to you, '**B**, I
2Sa 1: 2 on the third day, **b**, it
2Sa 11: 2 woman was very beautiful to **b**
2Sa 12:11 **B**, I will raise up adversity
2Sa 19: 1 **B**, the king is weeping and
1Ki 3:12 **b**, I have done according to
1Ki 5: 5 And **b**, I propose to build a
1Ki 8:27 **B**, heaven and the heaven of
1Ki 11:31 **B**, I will tear the kingdom
1Ki 13: 1 And **b**, a man of God went from
1Ki 13: 2 **B**, a child, Josiah by name,
1Ki 14:10 therefore **b**
1Ki 19: 9 and **b**, the word of the LORD
1Ki 19:11 And **b**, the LORD passed by,
1Ki 20:13 **B**, I will deliver it into
1Ki 21:21 **B**, I will bring calamity on
2Ki 6:17 And **b**, the mountain was full
2Ki 20:17 **B**, the days are coming when
2Ki 21:12 **B**, I am bringing such
2Ki 22:16 **B**, I will bring calamity on
1Ch 22: 9 **B**, a son shall be born to
2Ch 2: 4 **B**, I am building a temple for
2Ch 6:18 **B**, heaven and the heaven of
2Ch 21:14 **b**, the LORD will strike your
2Ch 23: 3 **B**, the king's son shall reign
2Ch 34:24 **B**, I will bring calamity on
Esth 1:11 for she was beautiful to **b**
Job 1:12 **B**, all that he has is in your
Job 2: 6 **B**, he is in your hand, but
Job 5:17 **B**, happy is the man whom God
Job 5:27 **B**, this we have searched out
Job 8:19 **B**, this is the joy of His way
Job 8:20 **B**, God will not cast away the
Job 13: 1 **B**, my eye has seen all this,
Job 19:27 myself, and my eyes shall **b**
Job 20: 9 will his place **b** him anymore
Job 23: 9 the left hand, I cannot **b** Him
Job 28:28 And to man He said, '**B**, the
Job 33:29 **B**, God works all these things
Job 35: 5 **b** the clouds which are higher
Job 36: 5 **B**, God is mighty, but
Job 36:22 **B**, God is exalted by His
Job 36:26 **B**, God is great, and we do not
Job 40: 4 **B**, I am vile
Ps 7:14 **B**, the wicked travails with
Ps 11: 4 His eyes **b**, His eyelids test
Ps 27: 4 To **b** the beauty of the LORD,
Ps 33:18 **B**, the eye of the LORD is on
Ps 37:36 Yet he passed away, and **b**, he
Ps 40: 7 Then I said, "**B**, I come
Ps 46: 8 **b** the works of the LORD, Who
Ps 48: 4 For **b**, the kings assembled,
Ps 51: 5 **B**, I was brought forth in
Ps 51: 6 **B**, You desire truth in the
Ps 54: 4 **B**, God is my helper
Ps 59: 4 Awake to help me, and **b**
Ps 73:12 **B**, these are the ungodly, Who
Ps 73:15 I will speak thus," **B**, I
Ps 78:20 **B**, He struck the rock, So
Ps 83: 2 For **b**, Your enemies make a
Ps 84: 9 **b** our shield, And look upon
Ps 87: 4 **B**, O Philistia and Tyre, with
Ps 92: 9 For **b**, Your enemies, O LORD,
Ps 92: 9 Your enemies, O LORD, For **b**
Ps 113: 6 Who humbles Himself to **b** The
Ps 119:40 **B**, I long for Your precepts
Ps 121: 4 **B**, He who keeps Israel Shall
Ps 123: 2 **B**, as the eyes of servants
Ps 127: 3 **B**, children are a heritage
Ps 128: 4 **B**, thus shall the man be
Ps 132: 6 **B**, we heard of it in
Ps 133: 1 **B**, how good and how pleasant
Ps 134: 1 **B**, bless the LORD, All you
Ps 139: 4 a word on my tongue, But **b**
Ps 139: 8 If I make my bed in hell, **b**
Eccl 11: 7 for the eyes to **b** the sun
Song 1:15 **B**, you are fair, my love
Song 1:15 **B**, you are fair
Song 1:16 **B**, you are handsome, my
Song 2: 8 **B**, he comes leaping upon the
Song 2: 9 **b**, he stands behind our wall
Song 3: 7 **B**, it is Solomon's couch,
Song 4: 1 **B**, you are fair, my love
Song 4: 1 **B**, you are fair
Is 3: 1 For **b**, the Lord, the LORD of
Is 5: 7 He looked for justice, but **b**
Is 5: 7 for righteousness, but **b**,
Is 5:30 if one looks to the land, **b**
Is 6: 7 **B**, this has touched your lips
Is 7:14 **B**, the virgin shall conceive
Is 8: 7 now therefore, **b**, the Lord
Is 10:33 **B**, the Lord, the LORD of
Is 12: 2 **B**, God is my salvation, I
Is 13: 9 **B**, the day of the LORD comes,
Is 13:17 **B**, I will stir up the Medes
Is 17: 1 **B**, Damascus will cease from
Is 17:14 Then **b**, at eventide, trouble
Is 19: 1 **B**, the LORD rides on a swift
Is 23:13 **B**, the land of the Chaldeans,
Is 24: 1 **B**, the LORD makes the earth
Is 25: 9 **B**, this is our God
Is 26:10 will not **b** the majesty of the
Is 26:21 For **b**, the LORD comes out of
Is 28: 2 **B**, the Lord has a mighty and
Is 28:16 **B**, I lay in Zion a stone for
Is 29:14 Therefore, **b**, I will again do
Is 30:27 **B**, the name of the LORD comes
Is 32: 1 **B**, a king will reign in
Is 35: 4 **B**, your God will come with
Is 38: 8 **B**, I will bring the shadow on
Is 39: 6 **B**, the days are coming when
Is 40: 9 cities of Judah, "**B** your God
Is 40:10 **B**, the Lord GOD shall come
Is 40:10 **b**, His reward is with Him, and
Is 40:15 **B**, the nations are as a drop
Is 41:11 **B**, all those who were
Is 41:15 **B**, I will make you into a new
Is 42: 1 **B**! My Servant whom I uphold
Is 42: 9 **B**, the former things have
Is 43:19 **B**, I will do a new thing, now
Is 47:14 **B**, they shall be as stubble,
Is 48:10 **B**, I have refined you, but
Is 49:22 **B**, I will lift My hand in an
Is 52: 6 **B**, it is I
Is 52:13 **B**, My Servant shall deal
Is 54:11 tempest, and not comforted, **b**
Is 54:16 **B**, I have created the
Is 59: 1 **B**, the LORD's hand is not
Is 60: 2 For **b**, the darkness shall
Is 62:11 **b**, His reward is with Him, and
Is 65: 6 **B**, it is written before Me
Is 65:13 **B**, My servants shall eat, but
Is 65:13 **b**, My servants shall drink,
Is 65:13 **b**, My servants shall rejoice,
Is 65:14 **b**, My servants shall sing for
Is 65:17 For **b**, I create new heavens
Is 65:18 for **b**, I create Jerusalem as
Is 66:12 **B**, I will extend peace to her
Is 66:15 For **b**, the LORD will come
Jer 1: 6 **B**, I cannot speak, for I am a
Jer 1: 9 **B**, I have put My words in
Jer 1:15 For **b**, I am calling all the
Jer 1:18 For **b**, I have made you this
Jer 2:35 **B**, I will plead My case
Jer 3: 5 **B**, you have spoken and done
Jer 4:13 **B**, he shall come up like
Jer 5:14 you speak this word, **b**, I
Jer 5:15 **B**, I will bring a nation
Jer 6:10 **B**, the word of the LORD is a
Jer 6:19 **B**, I will certainly bring
Jer 6:21 **B**, I will lay stumbling
Jer 6:22 **B**, a people comes from the
Jer 7: 8 **B**, you trust in lying words
Jer 7:11 **B**, I, even I, have seen it,"
Jer 7:20 **B**, My anger and My fury will
Jer 7:32 Therefore **b**, the days are
Jer 8: 9 **B**, they have rejected the
Jer 8:17 For **b**, I will send serpents
Jer 9: 7 **B**, I will refine them and try
Jer 9:15 **B**, I will feed them, this
Jer 9:25 **B**, the days are coming,"
Jer 10:18 **B**, I will throw out at this
Jer 10:22 **B**, the noise of the report
Jer 11:11 **B**, I will surely bring
Jer 11:22 **B**, I will punish them
Jer 12:14 **b**, I will pluck them out of
Jer 13:13 **B**, I will fill all the
Jer 14:13 **B**, the prophets say to them
Jer 14:18 I go out to the field, then **b**
Jer 14:18 if I enter the city, then **b**
Jer 16: 9 **B**, I will cause to cease from
Jer 16:12 than your fathers, for **b**,
Jer 16:14 Therefore **b**, the days are
Jer 16:16 **B**, I will send for many
Jer 16:21 Therefore **b**, I will this once
Jer 18:11 **B**, I am fashioning a disaster
Jer 19: 3 **B**, I will bring such a
Jer 19: 6 therefore **b**, the days are
Jer 19:15 **B**, I will bring on this city
Jer 20: 4 **B**, I will make you a terror
Jer 21: 4 **B**, I will turn back the
Jer 21: 8 **B**, I set before you the way
Jer 21:13 **B**, I am against you, O
Jer 23: 2 **B**, I will attend to you for
Jer 23: 5 **B**, the days are coming,"
Jer 23: 7 Therefore, **b**, the days are
Jer 23:15 **B**, I will feed them with
Jer 23:19 **B**, a whirlwind of the LORD
Jer 23:30 Therefore **b**, I am against the
Jer 23:31 **B**, I am against the prophets,
Jer 23:32 **B**, I am against those who
Jer 23:39 therefore **b**, I, even I, will
Jer 25: 9 **b**, I will send and take all
Jer 25:29 For **b**, I begin to bring
Jer 25:32 **B**, disaster shall go forth
Jer 27:16 **B**, the vessels of the LORD's
Jer 28:16 **B**, I will cast you from the
Jer 29:17 **B**, I will send on them the
Jer 29:21 **B**, I will deliver them into
Jer 29:32 **B**, I will punish Shemaiah the
Jer 30: 3 For **b**, the days are coming,'
Jer 30:10 for **b**, I will save you from
Jer 30:18 **B**, I will bring back the
Jer 30:23 **B**, the whirlwind of the LORD
Jer 31: 8 **B**, I will bring them from the
Jer 31:27 **B**, the days are coming,"
Jer 31:31 **B**, the days are coming,"
Jer 31:38 **B**, the days are coming,"
Jer 32: 3 **B**, I will give this city into
Jer 32: 7 **B**, Hanameel the son of
Jer 32:17 **B**, You have made the heavens
Jer 32:27 **B**, I am the LORD, the God of
Jer 32:28 **B**, I will give this city into
Jer 32:37 **B**, I will gather them out of
Jer 33: 6 **B**, I will bring it health and
Jer 33:14 **B**, the days are coming,'
Jer 34: 2 **B**, I will give this city
Jer 34:17 **B**, I proclaim liberty to you,
Jer 34:22 **B**, I will command,' says the
Jer 35:17 **B**, I will bring on Judah and
Jer 37: 7 **B**, Pharaoh's army which has
Jer 38:22 Now **b**, all the women who are
Jer 39:16 **B**, I will bring My words upon
Jer 43:10 **B**, I will send and bring
Jer 44: 2 and **b**, this day they are a
Jer 44:11 **B**, I will set My face
Jer 44:26 **B**, I have sworn by My great
Jer 44:27 **B**, I will watch over them
Jer 44:30 **B**, I will give Pharaoh
Jer 45: 4 **B**, what I have built I will
Jer 45: 5 for **b**, I will bring adversity
Jer 46:25 **B**, I will bring punishment on
Jer 46:27 For **b**, I will save you from

Jer 47: 2 **B**, waters rise out of the
Jer 48:12 Therefore **b**, the days are
Jer 48:40 **B**, one shall fly like an
Jer 49: 2 Therefore **b**, the days are
Jer 49: 5 **B**, I will bring fear upon you
Jer 49:12 **B**, those whose judgment was
Jer 49:19 **B**, he shall come up like a
Jer 49:22 **B**, He shall come up and fly
Jer 49:35 **B**, I will break the bow of
Jer 50: 9 For **b**, I will raise and cause
Jer 50:12 **B**, the least of the nations
Jer 50:18 **B**, I will punish the king of
Jer 50:31 **B**, I am against you, O you
Jer 50:41 **B**, a people shall come from
Jer 50:44 **B**, he shall come up like a
Jer 51: 1 **B**, I will raise up against
Jer 51:25 **B**, I am against you, O
Jer 51:36 **B**, I will plead your case and
Jer 51:47 therefore **b**, the days are
Jer 51:52 Therefore **b**, the days are
Lam 1: 9 **b** my affliction, for the
Lam 1:12 **B** and see if there is any
Lam 1:18 all peoples, and **b** my sorrow
Lam 5: 1 look, and **b** our reproach
Ezek 1: 4 Then I looked, and **b**, a
Ezek 1:15 at the living creatures, **b**
Ezek 2: 9 and **b**, a scroll of a book was
Ezek 3: 8 **B**, I have made your face
Ezek 3:23 went out into the plain, and **b**
Ezek 7: 5 **b**, it has come
Ezek 7: 6 **b**, it has come
Ezek 7:10 **B**, the day! **B**, it has come
Ezek 8: 4 And **b**, the glory of the God of
Ezek 13:20 **B**, I am against your magic
Ezek 14:22 Yet **b**, there shall be left in
Ezek 16:27 **B**, therefore, I stretched out
Ezek 17: 7 and **b**, this vine bent its
Ezek 17:10 **B**, it is planted, will it
Ezek 18: 4 **B**, all souls are Mine
Ezek 18:18 not good among his people, **b**
Ezek 20:47 **B**, I will kindle a fire in
Ezek 21: 3 **B**, I am against you, and I
Ezek 21: 7 **B**, it is coming and shall be
Ezek 22:13 **B**, therefore, I beat My fists
Ezek 22:19 all become dross, therefore **b**
Ezek 23:22 **B**, I will stir up your
Ezek 24:16 Son of man, **b**, I take away
Ezek 24:21 **B**, I will profane My
Ezek 25: 9 therefore, **b**, I will clear
Ezek 26: 3 **B**, I am against you, O Tyre,
Ezek 26: 7 **B**, I will bring against Tyre
Ezek 28: 3 (**B**, you are wiser than Daniel
Ezek 28: 7 **b**, therefore, I will bring
Ezek 28:22 **B**, I am against you, O Sidon
Ezek 29: 3 **B**, I am against you, O
Ezek 34:10 **B**, I am against the shepherds
Ezek 34:17 **B**, I shall judge between
Ezek 34:20 **B**, I Myself will judge
Ezek 35: 3 **B**, O Mount Seir, I am against
Ezek 36: 6 **B**, I have spoken in My
Ezek 37: 2 pass by them all around, and **b**
Ezek 37:12 **B**, O My people, I will open
Ezek 38: 3 **B**, I am against you, O Gog,
Ezek 39: 1 **B**, I am against you, O Gog,
Ezek 40: 3 He took me there, and **b**, there
Ezek 43: 2 And **b**, the glory of the God of
Ezek 43: 5 and **b**, the glory of the LORD
Ezek 43:12 **B**, this is the law of the
Ezek 44: 4 so I looked, and **b**, the glory
Dan 2:31 and **b**, a great image
Dan 4:10 I was looking, and **b**, A tree
Dan 7: 2 in my vision by night, and **b**
Dan 7: 7 in the night visions, and **b**
Dan 7:13 in the night visions, and **b**
Dan 10: 5 my eyes and looked, and **b**, a
Dan 10:13 and **b**, Michael, one of the
Dan 11: 2 **B**, three more kings will
Hos 2: 6 Therefore, **b**, I will hedge up
Hos 2:14 Therefore, **b**, I will allure
Joel 2:19 **B**, I will send you grain and
Joel 3: 1 For **b**, in those days and at
Joel 3: 7 **B**, I will raise them out of
Amos 2:13 **B**, I am weighed down by you,
Amos 4: 2 **B**, the days shall come upon
Amos 4:13 For **b**, He who forms mountains
Amos 6:11 For **b**, the LORD gives a
Amos 6:14 But, **b**, I will raise up a
Amos 7: 1 **B**, He formed locust swarms at
Amos 7: 4 **B**, the Lord GOD called for
Amos 7: 7 **B**, the Lord stood on a wall
Amos 7: 8 **B**, I am setting a plumb line
Amos 8: 1 **B**, a basket of summer fruit
Amos 8:11 **B**, the days are coming,"
Amos 9: 8 **B**, the eyes of the Lord GOD
Amos 9:13 **B**, the days are coming,"
Obad 2 **B**, I will make you small
Mic 1: 3 For **b**, the LORD is coming out
Mic 2: 3 **B**, against this family I am
Nah 1:15 **B**, on the mountains the feet
Nah 2:13 **B**, I am against you," says
Nah 3: 5 **B**, I am against you," says
Hab 1:13 of purer eyes than to **b** evil
Hab 2: 4 **B** the proud, his soul is not
Hab 2:13 **B**, is it not of the LORD of
Hab 2:19 **B**, it is overlaid with gold
Zeph 3:19 **B**, at that time I will deal
Zech 1: 8 I saw by night, and **b**, a man
Zech 1:11 throughout the earth, and **b**
Zech 2: 1 my eyes and looked, and **b**, a
Zech 2:10 For **b**, I am coming and I will
Zech 3: 8 for **b**, I am bringing forth My
Zech 3: 9 For **b**, the stone that I have
Zech 3: 9 **B**, I will engrave its
Zech 6: 1 my eyes and looked, and **b**, four
Zech 6:12 **B**, the Man whose name is the
Zech 8: 7 **B**, I will save My people
Zech 9: 4 **B**, the LORD will cast her out
Zech 9: 9 **B**, your King is coming to you
Zech 12: 2 **B**, I will make Jerusalem a
Zech 14: 1 **B**, the day of the LORD is
Mal 2: 3 **B**, I will rebuke your
Mal 3: 1 **B**, I send My messenger, and he
Mal 3: 1 **B**, He is coming," says the
Mal 4: 1 For **b**, the day is coming,
Mal 4: 5 **B**, I will send you Elijah the
Matt 1:20 thought about these things, **b**
Matt 1:23 **B**, a virgin shall be with
Matt 2: 1 the days of Herod the king, **b**
Matt 2: 9 and **b**, the star which they had
Matt 2:13 Now when they had departed, **b**
Matt 2:19 But when Herod was dead, **b**
Matt 3:16 and **b**, the heavens were opened
Matt 4:11 Then the devil left Him, and **b**
Matt 8: 2 And **b**, a leper came and
Matt 8:34 And **b**, the whole city came out
Matt 9: 2 And **b**, they brought to Him a
Matt 9:10 table in the house, that **b**
Matt 9:18 spoke these things to them, **b**
Matt 9:32 As they went out, **b**, they
Matt 10:16 **B**, I send you out as sheep in
Matt 11:10 **B**, I send My messenger
Matt 12:10 And **b**, there was a man who had
Matt 12:18 **B**, My Servant whom I have
Matt 12:46 talking to the multitudes, **b**
Matt 13: 3 **B**, a sower went out to sow
Matt 15:22 And **b**, a woman of Canaan
Matt 17: 3 And **b**, Moses and Elijah
Matt 17: 5 he was still speaking, **b**, a
Matt 19:16 Now **b**, one came and said to
Matt 20:18 **B**, we are going up to
Matt 20:30 And **b**, two blind men sitting
Matt 21: 5 Tell the daughter of Zion, **B**
Matt 25: 6 **B**, the bridegroom is coming
Matt 26:45 **B**, the hour is at hand, and
Matt 26:47 He was still speaking, **b**,
Matt 27:51 And **b**, the veil of the temple
Matt 28: 2 And **b**, there was a great
Matt 28: 7 **B**, I have told you
Matt 28: 9 went to tell His disciples, **b**
Matt 28:11 Now while they were going, **b**
Mark 1: 2 **B**, I send My messenger before
Mark 4: 3 **B**, a sower went out to sow
Mark 5:22 And **b**, one of the rulers of
Mark 10:33 **B**, we are going up to
Mark 14:41 **b**, the Son of Man is being
Luke 1:20 But **b**, you will be mute and
Luke 1:31 And **b**, you will conceive in
Luke 1:38 **B** the maidservant of the Lord
Luke 1:48 for **b**, henceforth all
Luke 2: 9 And **b**, an angel of the Lord
Luke 2:10 Do not be afraid, for **b**, I
Luke 2:25 And **b**, there was a man in
Luke 2:34 **B**, this Child is destined for
Luke 5:12 was in a certain city, that **b**
Luke 5:18 Then **b**, men brought on a bed
Luke 7:12 near the gate of the city, **b**
Luke 7:27 **B**, I send My messenger
Luke 7:37 And **b**, a woman in the city who
Luke 8:41 And **b**, there came a man named
Luke 9:30 Then **b**, two men talked with
Luke 9:39 And **b**, a spirit seizes him, and
Luke 10: 3 **b**, I send you out as lambs
Luke 10:19 **B**, I give you the authority
Luke 10:25 And **b**, a certain lawyer stood
Luke 13:11 And **b**, there was a woman who
Luke 13:32 Go, tell that fox, '**B**, I cast
Luke 14: 2 And **b**, there was a certain man
Luke 18:31 **B**, we are going up to
Luke 19: 2 Now **b**, there was a man named
Luke 22:10 **B**, when you have entered the
Luke 22:21 But **b**, the hand of My
Luke 22:47 He was still speaking, **b**, a
Luke 23:50 And **b**, there was a man named
Luke 24: 4 perplexed about this, that **b**
Luke 24:13 Now **b**, two of them were
Luke 24:39 **B** My hands and My feet, that
Luke 24:49 **B**, I send the Promise of My
John 1:29 **B**! The Lamb of God
John 1:36 he said, "**B** the Lamb of God
John 1:47 **B**, an Israelite indeed, in
John 3:26 **b**, He is baptizing, and all
John 4:35 **B**, I say to you, lift up your
John 11: 3 Lord, **b**, he whom You love is
John 12:15 **b**, your King is coming,
John 17:24 am, that they may **b** My glory
John 19: 4 **B**, I am bringing Him out to
John 19: 5 said to them, "**B** the Man
John 19:14 to the Jews, "**B** your King
John 19:26 mother, "Woman, **b** your son
John 19:27 the disciple, **B** your mother
Acts 1:10 heaven as He went up, **b**, two
Acts 8:27 And **b**, a man of Ethiopia, a
Acts 9:11 called Saul of Tarsus, for **b**
Acts 10:17 which he had seen meant, **b**
Acts 10:19 **B**, three men are seeking you
Acts 10:30 I prayed in my house, and **b**
Acts 12: 7 Now **b**, an angel of the Lord
Acts 13:25 But **b**, there comes One after
Acts 13:41 **B**, you despisers, marvel and
Acts 13:46 of everlasting life, **b**, we
Acts 16: 1 And **b**, a certain disciple was
Rom 9:33 **B**, I lay in Zion a stumbling
1Co 15:51 **B**, I tell you a mystery
2Co 5:17 **b**, all things have become new
2Co 6: 2 **B**, now is the accepted time
2Co 6: 2 **b**, now is the day of
2Co 6: 9 as dying, and **b** we live
Heb 8: 8 **B**, the days are coming,"
Heb 10: 7 Then I said, '**B**, I have come
Heb 10: 9 **B**, I have come to do Your
Jas 5: 9 **B**, the Judge is standing at
1Pe 2: 6 **B**, I lay in Zion a chief
1Jn 3: 1 **B** what manner of love the
Jude 14 **B**, the Lord comes with ten
Rev 1: 7 **B**, He is coming with clouds,
Rev 1:18 who lives, and was dead, and **b**
Rev 3:11 **B**, I come quickly
Rev 3:20 **B**, I stand at the door and
Rev 4: 1 these things I looked, and **b**
Rev 4: 2 and **b**, a throne set in heaven,
Rev 5: 5 **B**, the Lion of the tribe of
Rev 5: 6 And I looked, and **b**, in the
Rev 6: 2 And I looked, and **b**, a white
Rev 6: 5 And I looked, and **b**, a black
Rev 6: 8 And I looked, and **b**, a pale
Rev 6:12 opened the sixth seal, and **b**
Rev 7: 9 these things I looked, and **b**
Rev 9:12 **B**, still two more woes are
Rev 11:14 **B**, the third woe is coming
Rev 12: 3 **b**, a great, fiery red dragon
Rev 14: 1 Then I looked, and **b**, a Lamb
Rev 14:14 And I looked, and **b**, a white
Rev 15: 5 these things I looked, and **b**
Rev 16:15 **B**, I am coming as a thief
Rev 19:11 I saw heaven opened, and **b**
Rev 21: 3 **B**, the tabernacle of God is
Rev 21: 5 **B**, I make all things new
Rev 22: 7 **B**, I am coming quickly
Rev 22:12 And **b**, I am coming quickly, and

BEHOLDING (*see* BEHOLD)
2Co 3:18 **b** as in a mirror the glory of

BEHOLDS (*see* BEHOLD)
Job 41:34 He **b** every high thing
Ps 11: 7 His countenance **b** the upright

BEING (*see* PREFACE)

BEKAH
Ex 38:26 a **b** for each man (that is,

BEL (*see* BAAL)
Is 46: 1 **B** bows down, Nebo stoops
Jer 50: 2 Babylon is taken, **B** is shamed
Jer 51:44 I will punish **B** in Babylon

BELA (*see* BELAH, BELAITES)
Gen 14: 2 and the king of **B** (that is
Gen 14: 8 and the king of **B** (that is
Gen 36:32 **B** the son of Beor reigned in
Gen 36:33 And when **B** died, Jobab the son
Num 26:38 of **B**, the family of the
Num 26:40 And the sons of **B** were Ard
1Ch 1:43 **B** the son of Beor, and the
1Ch 1:44 And when **B** died, Jobab the son
1Ch 5: 8 **B** the son of Azaz, the son of
1Ch 7: 6 The sons of Benjamin were **B**
1Ch 7: 7 The sons of **B** were Ezbon,
1Ch 8: 1 begot **B** his firstborn, Ashbel
1Ch 8: 3 The sons of **B** were Addar,

BELAH (*see* BELA)
Gen 46:21 The sons of Benjamin were **B**

BELAITES (*see* BELA)
Num 26:38 of Bela, the family of the **B**

BELCH
Ps 59: 7 they **b** out with their mouth

BELIAL
2Co 6:15 what accord has Christ with **B**

BELIEF (*see* BELIEVE, UNBELIEF)
2Th 2:13 the Spirit and **b** in the truth,

BELIEVE (*see* BELIEF, BELIEVED, BELIEVER, BELIEVES, BELIEVING)
Gen 45:26 because he did not **b** them
Ex 4: 1 **b** me or listen to my voice
Ex 4: 5 that they may **b** that the LORD
Ex 4: 8 will be, if they do not **b** you
Ex 4: 8 that they may **b** the message
Ex 4: 9 if they do not **b** even these
Ex 19: 9 with you, and **b** you forever
Num 14:11 how long will they not **b** Me
Num 20:12 Because you did not **b** Me, to
Deut 1:32 you did not **b** the LORD your
Deut 9:23 you did not **b** Him nor obey
1Ki 10: 7 However I did not **b** the words
2Ki 17:14 who did not **b** in the LORD
2Ch 9: 6 However I did not **b** their
2Ch 20:20 **B** in the LORD your God, and
2Ch 20:20 **b** His prophets, and you shall
2Ch 32:15 like this, and do not **b** him
Job 9:16 I would not **b** that He was
Job 15:22 He does not **b** that he will
Job 29:24 at them, they did not **b** it
Ps 78:22 Because they did not **b** in God
Ps 78:32 did not **b** in His wondrous
Ps 106:24 They did not **b** His word,
Ps 119:66 For I **b** Your commandments
Prov 26:25 speaks kindly, do not **b** him
Is 7: 9 If you will not **b**, surely you
Is 43:10 **b** Me, and understand that I am
Jer 12: 6 Do not **b** them, even though
Jer 40:14 son of Ahikam did not **b** them
Hab 1: 5 days which you would not **b**
Matt 9:28 Do you **b** that I am able to do
Matt 18: 6 ones who **b** in Me to sin, it
Matt 21:25 Why then did you not **b** him
Matt 21:32 and you did not **b** him
Matt 21:32 not afterward relent and **b** him
Matt 24:23 do not **b** it
Matt 24:26 do not **b** it
Matt 27:42 the cross, and we will **b** Him
Mark 1:15 Repent, and **b** in the gospel
Mark 5:36 Do not be afraid; only **b**
Mark 9:23 If you can **b**, all things are
Mark 9:24 Lord, I **b**; help my unbelief
Mark 9:42 ones who **b** in Me to stumble
Mark 11:24 **b** that you receive them, and
Mark 11:31 Why then did you not **b** him
Mark 13:21 do not **b** it
Mark 15:32 cross, that we may see and **b**
Mark 16:11 seen by her, they did not **b**
Mark 16:13 they did not **b** them either
Mark 16:14 because they did not **b** those
Mark 16:16 does not **b** will be condemned
Mark 16:17 signs will follow those who **b**
Luke 1:20 because you did not **b** my
Luke 8:12 hearts, lest they should **b**
Luke 8:13 who **b** for a while and in time
Luke 8:50 only **b**, and she will be made
Luke 20: 5 Why then did you not **b** him
Luke 22:67 you, you will by no means **b**
Luke 24:11 tales, and they did not **b** them
Luke 24:25 slow of heart to **b** in all
Luke 24:41 they still did not **b** for joy
John 1: 7 that all through him might **b**
John 1:12 to those who **b** in His name
John 1:50 under the fig tree,' do you **b**
John 3:12 things and you do not **b**, how
John 3:12 how will you **b** if I tell you
John 3:36 he who does not **b** the Son
John 4:21 **b** Me, the hour is coming when
John 4:42 Now we **b**, not because of what
John 4:48 you will by no means **b**
John 5:38 He sent, Him you do not **b**
John 5:44 How can you **b**, who receive
John 5:46 Moses, you would **b** Me
John 5:47 if you do not **b** his writings
John 5:47 how will you **b** My words
John 6:29 that you **b** in Him whom He
John 6:30 that we may see it and **b** You
John 6:36 have seen Me and yet do not **b**
John 6:64 are some of you who do not **b**
John 6:64 who they were who did not **b**
John 6:69 Also we have come to **b** and
John 7: 5 His brothers did not **b** in Him
John 8:24 if you do not **b** that I am He
John 8:45 the truth, you do not **b** Me
John 8:46 truth, why do you not **b** Me
John 9:18 Jews did not **b** concerning him
John 9:35 Do you **b** in the Son of God
John 9:36 He, Lord, that I may **b** in Him
John 9:38 Then he said, "Lord, I **b**!"
John 10:25 I told you, and you do not **b**
John 10:26 But you do not **b**, because you
John 10:37 of My Father, do not **b** Me
John 10:38 I do, though you do not **b** Me
John 10:38 **b** the works, that you may
John 10:38 **b** that the Father is in Me,
John 11:15 was not there, that you may **b**
John 11:26 Do you **b** this
John 11:27 I **b** that You are the Christ,
John 11:40 to you that if you would **b**
John 11:42 that they may **b** that You sent
John 11:48 this, everyone will **b** in Him
John 12:36 **b** in the light, that you may
John 12:37 them, they did not **b** in Him
John 12:39 Therefore they could not **b**
John 12:47 hears My words and does not **b**
John 13:19 pass, you may **b** that I am He
John 14: 1 you **b** in God, **b** also in Me
John 14:10 Do you not **b** that I am in the
John 14:11 **B** Me that I am in the Father
John 14:11 or else **b** Me for the sake of
John 14:29 does come to pass, you may **b**
John 16: 9 because they do not **b** in Me
John 16:30 By this we **b** that You came
John 16:31 Do you now **b**
John 17:20 **b** in Me through their word
John 17:21 world may **b** that You sent Me
John 19:35 the truth, so that you may **b**
John 20:25 into His side, I will not **b**
John 20:31 **b** that Jesus is the Christ
Acts 8:37 If you **b** with all your heart,
Acts 8:37 I **b** that Jesus Christ is the
Acts 9:26 and did not **b** that he was a
Acts 13:41 which you will by no means **b**
Acts 15: 7 the word of the gospel and **b**
Acts 15:11 But we **b** that through the
Acts 16:31 **B** on the Lord Jesus Christ,
Acts 19: 4 **b** on Him who would come after
Acts 19: 9 were hardened and did not **b**
Acts 21:25 concerning the Gentiles who **b**
Acts 22:19 and beat those who **b** on You
Acts 26:27 do you **b** the prophets
Acts 26:27 I know that you do **b**
Acts 27:25 for I **b** God that it will be
Rom 3: 3 For what if some did not **b**
Rom 3:22 Christ to all and on all who **b**
Rom 4:11 the father of all those who **b**
Rom 4:24 **b** in Him who raised up Jesus
Rom 6: 8 we **b** that we shall also live
Rom 10: 9 **b** in your heart that God has
Rom 10:14 how shall they **b** in Him of
Rom 15:31 those in Judea who do not **b**
1Co 1:21 preached to save those who **b**
1Co 7:12 has a wife who does not **b**
1Co 7:13 has a husband who does not **b**
1Co 10:27 not **b** invites you to dinner
1Co 11:18 among you, and in part I **b** it
1Co 14:22 not to those who **b** but to
1Co 14:22 but for those who **b**
2Co 4: 4 age has blinded, who do not **b**
2Co 4:13 I spoke," we also **b** and
Gal 3:22 might be given to those who **b**
Eph 1:19 of His power toward us who **b**
Phil 1:29 Christ, not only to **b** in Him
1Th 1: 7 in Macedonia and Achaia who **b**
1Th 2:10 ourselves among you who **b**
1Th 2:13 works in you who **b**
1Th 4:14 For if we **b** that Jesus died
2Th 1:10 admired among all those who **b**
2Th 2:11 that they should **b** the lie
2Th 2:12 be condemned who did not **b**
1Ti 1:16 to those who are going to **b**
1Ti 4: 3 thanksgiving by those who **b**
1Ti 4:10 especially of those who **b**
Heb 10:39 but of those who **b** to the
Heb 11: 6 to God must **b** that He is, and
Heb 11:31 with those who did not **b**,
Jas 2:19 You **b** that there is one God
Jas 2:19 Even the demons **b**
1Pe 1:21 who through Him **b** in God, who
1Pe 2: 7 Therefore, to you who **b**, He
1Jn 3:23 that we should **b** on the name
1Jn 4: 1 do not **b** every spirit, but
1Jn 5:10 he who does not **b** God has
1Jn 5:13 **b** in the name of the Son of
1Jn 5:13 that you may continue to **b** in
Jude 5 destroyed those who did not **b**

BELIEVED (*see* BELIEVE)
Gen 15: 6 And he **b** in the LORD, and He
Ex 4:31 So the people **b**
Ex 14:31 **b** the LORD and His servant
1Sa 27:12 So Achish **b** David, saying
Ps 27:13 unless I had **b** That I would
Ps 106:12 Then they **b** His words
Ps 116:10 I **b**, therefore I spoke, 'I
Is 53: 1 Who has **b** our report
Lam 4:12 would not have **b** that the
Dan 6:23 him, because he **b** in his God
Jon 3: 5 the people of Nineveh **b** God
Matt 8:13 and as you have **b**, so let it
Matt 21:32 collectors and harlots **b** him
Luke 1: 1 are most surely **b** among us
Luke 1:45 Blessed is she who **b**, for
John 2:11 and His disciples **b** in Him
John 2:22 they **b** the Scripture and the
John 2:23 many **b** in His name when they
John 3:18 because he has not **b** in the
John 4:39 **b** in Him because of the word
John 4:41 many more **b** because of His
John 4:50 So the man **b** the word that
John 4:53 And he himself **b**, and his
John 5:46 For if you **b** Moses, you would
John 7:31 many of the people **b** in Him
John 7:48 or the Pharisees **b** in Him
John 8:30 these words, many **b** in Him
John 8:31 said to those Jews who **b** Him
John 10:42 And many **b** in Him there
John 11:45 things Jesus did, **b** in Him
John 12:11 Jews went away and **b** in Jesus
John 12:38 Lord, who has **b** our report
John 12:42 the rulers many **b** in Him, but
John 16:27 have **b** that I came forth from
John 17: 8 they have **b** that You sent Me
John 20: 8 and he saw and **b**
John 20:29 you have seen Me, you have **b**
John 20:29 have not seen and yet have **b**
Acts 2:44 Now all who **b** were together,
Acts 4: 4 of those who heard the word **b**
Acts 4:32 those who **b** were of one heart
Acts 8:12 But when they **b** Philip as he
Acts 8:13 Then Simon himself also **b**
Acts 9:42 Joppa, and many **b** on the Lord
Acts 10:45 who **b** were astonished, as
Acts 11:17 we **b** on the Lord Jesus Christ
Acts 11:21 them, and a great number **b**
Acts 13:12 Then the proconsul **b**, when he
Acts 13:48 appointed to eternal life **b**
Acts 14: 1 the Jews and of the Greeks **b**
Acts 14:23 the Lord in whom they had **b**
Acts 15: 5 the Pharisees who **b** rose up
Acts 16: 1 a certain Jewish woman who **b**
Acts 16:34 having **b** in God with all his
Acts 17:12 Therefore many of them **b**, and
Acts 17:34 some men joined him and **b**
Acts 18: 8 **b** on the Lord with all his

Acts 18: 8 the Corinthians, hearing, **b**
Acts 18:27 those who had **b** through grace
Acts 19: 2 the Holy Spirit when you **b**
Acts 19:18 And many who had **b** came
Acts 21:20 of Jews there are who have **b**
Rom 4: 3 Abraham **b** God, and it was
Rom 4:17 the presence of Him whom he **b**
Rom 4:18 contrary to hope, in hope **b**
Rom 10:14 Him in whom they have not **b**
Rom 10:16 Lord, who has **b** our report
Rom 13:11 nearer than when we first **b**
1Co 3: 5 ministers through whom you **b**
1Co 15: 2 unless you **b** in vain
1Co 15:11 so we preach and so you **b**
2Co 4:13 I **b** and therefore I spoke,"
Gal 2:16 even we have **b** in Christ
Gal 3: 6 **b** God, and it was accounted to
Eph 1:13 in whom also, having **b**, you
2Th 1:10 our testimony among you was **b**
1Ti 3:16 **b** on in the world, received
2Ti 1:12 for I know whom I have **b**
Tit 3: 8 that those who have **b** in God
Heb 4: 3 For we who have **b** do enter
Jas 2:23 Abraham **b** God, and it was
1Jn 4:16 **b** the love that God has for
1Jn 5:10 because he has not **b** the

BELIEVER (*see* BELIEVE, BELIEVERS, UNBELIEVER)
2Co 6:15 has a **b** with an unbeliever

BELIEVERS (*see* BELIEVER)
Acts 5:14 **b** were increasingly added to
1Ti 4:12 an example to the **b** in word
1Ti 6: 2 those who are benefited are **b**

BELIEVES (*see* BELIEVE)
Prov 14:15 The simple **b** every word, but
Is 28:16 whoever **b** will not act
Mark 9:23 are possible to him who **b**
Mark 11:23 but **b** that those things he
Mark 16:16 He who **b** and is baptized will
John 3:15 that whoever **b** in Him should
John 3:16 that whoever **b** in Him should
John 3:18 He who **b** in Him is not
John 3:36 He who **b** in the Son has
John 5:24 and **b** in Him who sent Me has
John 6:35 he who **b** in Me shall never
John 6:40 **b** in Him may have everlasting
John 6:47 to you, he who **b** in Me has
John 7:38 He who **b** in Me, as the
John 11:25 He who **b** in Me, though he may
John 11:26 and **b** in Me shall never die
John 12:44 He who **b** in Me
John 12:44 **b** not in Me but in Him who
John 12:46 that whoever **b** in Me should
John 14:12 I say to you, he who **b** in Me
Acts 10:43 whoever **b** in Him will receive
Acts 13:39 and by Him everyone who **b** is
Rom 1:16 salvation for everyone who **b**
Rom 4: 5 **b** on Him who justifies the
Rom 9:33 whoever **b** on Him will not be
Rom 10: 4 to everyone who **b**
Rom 10:10 heart one **b** to righteousness
Rom 10:11 Whoever **b** on Him will not be
Rom 14: 2 For one **b** he may eat all
1Co 13: 7 **b** all things, hopes all
1Pe 2: 6 he who **b** on Him will by no
1Jn 5: 1 Whoever **b** that Jesus is the
1Jn 5: 5 but he who **b** that Jesus is
1Jn 5:10 He who **b** in the Son of God

BELIEVING (*see* BELIEVE)
Matt 21:22 whatever you ask in prayer, **b**
John 7:39 whom those **b** in Him would
John 20:27 Do not be unbelieving, but **b**
John 20:31 that **b** you may have life in
Acts 24:14 **b** all things which are
Rom 15:13 with all joy and peace in **b**
1Co 9: 5 right to take along a **b** wife
Gal 3: 9 are blessed with **b** Abraham
1Ti 5:16 If any **b** man or woman has
1Ti 6: 2 And those who have **b** masters
1Pe 1: 8 now you do not see Him, yet **b**

BELL (*see* BELLS)
Ex 28:34 a golden **b** and a pomegranate,
Ex 28:34 and a pomegranate, a golden **b**
Ex 39:26 a **b** and a pomegranate
Ex 39:26 a **b** and a pomegranate

BELLOW (*see* BELLOWS)
Jer 50:11 grain, and you **b** like bulls,

BELLOWS (*see* BELLOW)
Jer 6:29 the **b** blow fiercely, the lead

BELLS (*see* BELL)
Ex 28:33 **b** of gold between them all
Ex 39:25 they made **b** of pure gold, and
Ex 39:25 and put the **b** between the
Zech 14:20 on the **b** of the horses

BELLY
Gen 3:14 on your **b** you shall go, and
Lev 11:42 Whatever crawls on its **b**
Num 5:21 thigh rot and your **b** swell
Num 5:22 stomach, and make your **b** swell
Num 5:27 her **b** will swell, her thigh
Judg 3:21 and thrust it into his **b**
Judg 3:22 draw the dagger out of his **b**
Job 20:15 God casts them out of his **b**
Job 32:19 Indeed my **b** is like wine that
Ps 17:14 whose **b** You fill with Your
Ezek 3: 3 Son of man, feed your **b**, and
Dan 2:32 and arms of silver, its **b** and
Jon 1:17 Jonah was in the **b** of the
Jon 2: 1 his God from the fish's **b**
Jon 2: 2 out of the **b** of Sheol I cried
Matt 12:40 in the **b** of the great fish
Rom 16:18 Jesus Christ, but their own **b**
Phil 3:19 whose god is their **b**, and

BELONG (*see* BELONGED, BELONGING, BELONGS)
Gen 32:17 saying, "To whom do you **b**
Gen 38:25 By the man to whom these **b**
Gen 40: 8 not interpretations **b** to God
Lev 7:10 shall **b** to all the sons of
Lev 7:14 It shall **b** to the priest who
Lev 25:30 **b** permanently to him who
Lev 27:19 to it, and it shall **b** to him
Num 1:50 over all things that **b** to it
Num 35: 5 This shall **b** to them as
Deut 10:14 the highest heavens **b** to the
Deut 29:29 The secret things **b** to the
Deut 29:29 which are revealed **b** to us
1Sa 25:22 who **b** to him by morning light
1Sa 30:13 To whom do you **b**, and where
Job 25: 2 Dominion and fear **b** to Him
Ps 47: 9 shields of the earth **b** to God
Ps 68:20 to GOD the Lord **b** escapes
Prov 14:22 truth **b** to those who devise
Prov 16: 1 of the heart **b** to man, but
Prov 24:23 things also **b** to the wise
Ezek 45: 5 wide shall **b** to the Levites
Ezek 45: 6 it shall **b** to the whole house
Ezek 46:16 sons, it shall **b** to his sons
Ezek 46:17 shall **b** to his sons
Ezek 48:10 shall this holy district **b**
Ezek 48:21 rest shall **b** to the prince
Ezek 48:21 it shall **b** to the prince
Ezek 48:22 shall **b** to the prince
Dan 9: 9 To the Lord our God **b** mercy
Mark 9:41 name, because you **b** to Christ
Acts 27:23 angel of the God to whom I **b**
1Co 7:32 the things that **b** to the Lord
1Pe 4:11 to whom **b** the glory and the

BELONGED (*see* BELONG)
Josh 17: 8 on the border of Manasseh **b**
Josh 24:33 that **b** to Phinehas his son
Judg 6:11 Ophrah, which **b** to Joash the
Judg 18:27 the priest who had **b** to him
Ruth 4: 3 the piece of land which **b** to
1Sa 21: 7 of the herdsmen who **b** to Saul
1Sa 27: 6 Therefore Ziklag has **b** to the
2Sa 8: 7 that had **b** to the servants of
2Sa 9: 9 son all that **b** to Saul and to
1Ki 1: 8 the mighty men who **b** to David
1Ki 4:10 to him **b** Sochoh and all the
1Ki 4:13 to him **b** the towns of Jair
1Ki 4:13 to him also **b** the region of
1Ki 15:27 which **b** to the Philistines,
1Ki 16:15 which **b** to the Philistines
2Ki 11:10 which had **b** to King David
2Ki 12:16 It **b** to the priests
2Ki 14:28 Hamath, what had **b** to Judah
2Ki 24: 7 **b** to the king of Egypt from
1Ch 2:23 All these **b** to the sons of
1Ch 13: 6 which **b** to Judah, to bring up
2Ch 26:23 burial which **b** to the kings
2Ch 34:33 **b** to the children of Israel
Esth 1: 9 which **b** to King Ahasuerus
Luke 23: 7 He **b** to Herod's jurisdiction

BELONGING (*see* BELONG, BELONGINGS)
Num 31:43 now the half **b** to the
Ruth 2: 3 part of the field **b** to Boaz
1Sa 6:18 **b** to the five lords, both
Ezek 45: 4 land, **b** to the priests, the
Luke 9:10 place **b** to the city called

BELONGINGS (*see* BELONGING)
Ezek 12: 3 prepare your **b** for captivity,
Ezek 12: 4 out your **b** in their sight
Ezek 12: 5 carry your **b** out through it
Ezek 12: 7 I brought out my **b** by day
Ezek 12:12 among them shall bear his **b**

BELONGS (*see* BELONG)
Ex 9: 4 shall die of all that **b** to
Lev 6: 5 and give it to whomever it **b**
Lev 7:20 offering that **b** to the LORD
Lev 7:21 offering that **b** to the LORD
Num 16:30 up with all that **b** to them
Josh 13: 4 and Mearah that **b** to the
Judg 18:28 valley that **b** to Beth Rehob
Judg 19:14 Gibeah, which **b** to Benjamin
Judg 20: 4 which **b** to Benjamin, to spend
1Sa 17: 1 at Sochoh, which **b** to Judah
1Sa 25:21 missed of all that **b** to him
1Sa 30:14 territory which **b** to Judah
2Sa 3: 8 a dog's head that **b** to Judah
2Sa 6:12 and all that **b** to him, because
2Sa 16: 4 all that **b** to Mephibosheth is
1Ki 14:11 eat whoever **b** to Jeroboam
1Ki 16: 4 shall eat whoever **b** to Baasha
1Ki 17: 9 which **b** to Sidon, and dwell
1Ki 19: 3 which **b** to Judah, and left his
1Ki 21:24 shall eat whoever **b** to Ahab
2Ki 14:11 Shemesh, which **b** to Judah
2Ch 25:21 Shemesh, which **b** to Judah
Ps 3: 8 Salvation **b** to the LORD
Ps 62:11 That power **b** to God
Ps 62:12 Also to You, O Lord, **b** mercy
Ps 89:18 For our shield **b** to the LORD
Ps 94: 1 God, to whom vengeance **b**
Ps 94: 1 O God, to whom vengeance **b**
Ezek 48:22 midst of what **b** to the prince
Dan 9: 7 Lord, righteousness **b** to You
Dan 9: 8 to us **b** shame of face, to our
Heb 5:14 But solid food **b** to those who
Heb 7:13 are spoken **b** to another tribe
Rev 7:10 Salvation **b** to our God who

BELOVED (*see* BELOVED'S, WELL-BELOVED)
Deut 33:12 The **b** of the LORD shall dwell
2Sa 1:23 Saul and Jonathan were **b** and
Neh 13:26 him, who was **b** of his God
Ps 60: 5 That Your **b** may be delivered,
Ps 108: 6 That Your **b** may be delivered,
Ps 127: 2 For so He gives His **b** sleep
Song 1:13 bundle of myrrh is my **b** to me
Song 1:14 My **b** is to me a cluster of
Song 1:16 you are handsome, my **b**
Song 2: 3 so is my **b** among the sons
Song 2: 8 The voice of my **b**
Song 2: 9 My **b** is like a gazelle or a
Song 2:10 My **b** spoke, and said to me
Song 2:16 My **b** is mine, and I am his
Song 2:17 shadows flee away, turn, my **b**
Song 4:16 Let my **b** come to his garden
Song 5: 1 yes, drink deeply, O **b** ones
Song 5: 2 it is the voice of my **b**
Song 5: 4 my **b** put his hand by the
Song 5: 5 I arose to open for my **b**, and
Song 5: 6 I opened for my **b**, but my
Song 5: 6 but my **b** had turned away and
Song 5: 8 Jerusalem, if you find my **b**
Song 5: 9 your **b** more than another **b**
Song 5: 9 What is your **b** more than
Song 5: 9 your **b** more than another **b**
Song 5:10 My **b** is white and ruddy, chief
Song 5:16 This is my **b**, and this is my
Song 6: 1 Where has your **b** gone, O
Song 6: 1 Where has your **b** turned aside
Song 6: 2 My **b** has gone to his garden,
Song 6: 3 my beloved's, and my **b** is mine
Song 7: 9 goes down smoothly for my **b**
Song 7:11 Come, my **b**, let us go forth
Song 7:13 I have laid up for you, my **b**
Song 8: 5 leaning upon her **b**
Song 8:14 Make haste, my **b**, and be like
Is 5: 1 my **B** regarding His vineyard
Jer 11:15 What has My **b** to do in My

Jer 12: 7 I have given the dearly **b** of
Dan 9:23 you, for you are greatly **b**
Dan 10:11 O Daniel, man greatly **b**,
Dan 10:19 O man greatly **b**, fear not
Hos 9:16 I would kill the **b** fruit of
Matt 3:17 This is My **b** Son, in whom I
Matt 12:18 my **B** in whom My soul is well
Matt 17: 5 This is My **b** Son, in whom I
Mark 1:11 You are My **b** Son, in whom I
Mark 9: 7 This is My **b** Son
Mark 12: 6 still having one son, his **b**
Luke 3:22 You are My **b** Son
Luke 9:35 This is My **b** Son
Luke 20:13 I will send my **b** son
Acts 15:25 to you with our **b** Barnabas
Rom 1: 7 **b** of God, called to be saints
Rom 9:25 were not My people, and her **b**
Rom 9:25 and her **b**, who was not **b**
Rom 11:28 the election they are **b** for
Rom 12:19 **B**, do not avenge yourselves,
Rom 16: 5 Greet my **b** Epaenetus, who is
Rom 16: 8 Amplias, my **b** in the Lord
Rom 16: 9 in Christ, and Stachys, my **b**
Rom 16:12 Greet the **b** Persis, who
1Co 4:14 but as my **b** children I warn
1Co 4:17 Timothy to you, who is my **b**
1Co 10:14 Therefore, my **b**, flee from
1Co 15:58 my **b** brethren, be steadfast,
2Co 7: 1 having these promises, **b**
2Co 12:19 But we do all things, **b**, for
Eph 1: 6 has made us accepted in the **B**
Eph 6:21 a **b** brother and faithful
Phil 2:12 Therefore, my **b**, as you have
Phil 4: 1 Therefore, my **b** and longed-for
Phil 4: 1 so stand fast in the Lord, **b**
Col 3:12 the elect of God, holy and **b**
Col 4: 7 Tychicus, who is a **b** brother
Col 4: 9 **b** brother, who is one of you
Col 4:14 Luke the **b** physician and Demas
1Th 1: 4 **b** brethren, your election by
2Th 2:13 you, brethren **b** by the Lord,
1Ti 6: 2 benefited are believers and **b**
2Ti 1: 2 To Timothy, my **b** son
Phm 1 To Philemon our **b** friend
Phm 2 to the **b** Apphia, Archippus
Phm 16 as a **b** brother, especially to
Heb 6: 9 But, **b**, we are confident of
Jas 1:16 be deceived, my **b** brethren
Jas 1:19 my **b** brethren, let every man
Jas 2: 5 Listen, my **b** brethren
1Pe 2:11 **B**, I beg you as sojourners and
1Pe 4:12 **B**, do not think it strange
2Pe 1:17 This is My **b** Son, in whom I
2Pe 3: 1 **B**, I now write to you this
2Pe 3: 8 But, **b**, do not forget this
2Pe 3:14 Therefore, **b**, looking forward
2Pe 3:15 as also our **b** brother Paul,
2Pe 3:17 You therefore, **b**, since you
1Jn 3: 2 **B**, now we are children of God
1Jn 3:21 **B**, if our heart does not
1Jn 4: 1 **B**, do not believe every
1Jn 4: 7 **B**, let us love one another,
1Jn 4:11 **B**, if God so loved us, we
3Jn 1 THE ELDER, To the **b** Gaius
3Jn 2 **B**, I pray that you may
3Jn 5 **B**, you do faithfully whatever
3Jn 11 **B**, do not imitate what is
Jude 3 **B**, while I was very diligent
Jude 17 But you, **b**, remember the
Jude 20 But you, **b**, building
Rev 20: 9 of the saints and the **b** city

BELOVED'S (*see* BELOVED)
Song 6: 3 I am my **b**, and my beloved is
Song 7:10 I am my **b**, and his desire is

BELOW (*see* PREFACE)

BELSHAZZAR
Dan 5: 1 **B** the king made a great feast
Dan 5: 2 **B** gave the command to bring
Dan 5: 9 Then King **B** was greatly
Dan 5:22 But you his son, **B**, have not
Dan 5:29 Then **B** gave the command, and
Dan 5:30 That very night **B**, king of
Dan 7: 1 year of **B** king of Babylon
Dan 8: 1 **B** a vision appeared to me

BELT (*see* BELTS)
Ex 12:11 with a **b** on your waist, your
1Sa 18: 4 his sword and his bow and his **b**
2Sa 18:11 ten shekels of silver and a **b**
2Sa 20: 8 on it was a **b** with a sword
1Ki 2: 5 **b** that was around his waist
2Ki 1: 8 wore a leather **b** around his
Job 12:18 And binds their waist with a **b**
Job 38:31 or loose the **b** of Orion
Ps 109:19 for a **b** with which he girds
Is 5:27 nor will the **b** on their loins
Is 11: 5 shall be the **b** of His loins
Is 11: 5 the **b** of His waist
Is 22:21 and strengthen him with your **b**
Matt 3: 4 with a leather **b** around his
Mark 1: 6 with a leather **b** around his
Acts 21:11 come to us, he took Paul's **b**
Acts 21:11 bind the man who owns this **b**

BELTESHAZZAR (*see* DANIEL)
Dan 1: 7 he gave Daniel the name **B**
Dan 2:26 to Daniel, whose name was **B**
Dan 4: 8 came before me (his name is **B**
Dan 4: 9 **B**, chief of the magicians,
Dan 4:18 Now you, **B**, declare its
Dan 4:19 Then Daniel, whose name was **B**
Dan 4:19 **B**, do not let the dream or
Dan 4:19 **B** answered and said,
Dan 5:12 Daniel, whom the king named **B**
Dan 10: 1 whose name was called **B**

BELTS (*see* BELT)
Ezek 23:15 girded with **b** around their
Mark 6: 8 no copper in their money **b**

BEMOAN (*see* BEMOANING)
Jer 15: 5 Or who will **b** you
Jer 16: 5 nor go to lament or **b** them
Jer 22:10 not for the dead, nor **b** him
Jer 48:17 **B** him, all you who are around
Nah 3: 7 Who will **b** her

BEMOANING (*see* BEMOAN)
Jer 31:18 heard Ephraim **b** himself

BEN
1Ch 15:18 Zechariah, **B**, Jaaziel,

BEN-ABINADAB
1Ki 4:11 **B**, in all the regions of Dor

BENAIAH
2Sa 8:18 **B** the son of Jehoiada was
2Sa 20:23 **B** the son of Jehoiada was
2Sa 23:20 **B** was the son of Jehoiada,
2Sa 23:22 These things **B** the son of
2Sa 23:30 **B** a Pirathonite, Hiddai from
1Ki 1: 8 **B** the son of Jehoiada, Nathan
1Ki 1:10 invite Nathan the prophet, **B**
1Ki 1:26 nor **B** the son of Jehoiada,
1Ki 1:32 and **B** the son of Jehoiada
1Ki 1:36 And **B** the son of Jehoiada
1Ki 1:38 **B** the son of Jehoiada, the
1Ki 1:44 **B** the son of Jehoiada, the
1Ki 2:25 hand of **B** the son of Jehoiada
1Ki 2:29 sent **B** the son of Jehoiada
1Ki 2:30 So **B** went to the tabernacle
1Ki 2:30 **B** brought back word to the
1Ki 2:34 So **B** the son of Jehoiada went
1Ki 2:35 The king put **B** the son of
1Ki 2:46 **B** the son of Jehoiada
1Ki 4: 4 **B** the son of Jehoiada, over
1Ch 4:36 Asaiah, Adiel, Jesimiel, and **B**
1Ch 11:22 **B** was the son of Jehoiada,
1Ch 11:24 These things **B** the son of
1Ch 11:31 Benjamin, **B** the Pirathonite,
1Ch 15:18 Jehiel, Unni, Eliab, **B**,
1Ch 15:20 Unni, Eliab, Maaseiah, and **B**
1Ch 15:24 Amasai, Zechariah, **B**, and
1Ch 16: 5 Jehiel, Mattithiah, Eliab, **B**
1Ch 16: 6 **B** and Jahaziel the priests
1Ch 18:17 **B** the son of Jehoiada was
1Ch 27: 5 for the third month was **B**
1Ch 27: 6 This was the **B** who was mighty
1Ch 27:14 month was **B** the Pirathonite
1Ch 27:34 was Jehoiada the son of **B**
2Ch 20:14 of Zechariah, the son of **B**
2Ch 31:13 **B** were overseers under the
Ezra 10:25 Eleazar, Malchijah, and **B**
Ezra 10:30 Adna, Chelal, **B**, Maaseiah,
Ezra 10:35 **B**, Bedeiah, Cheluh,
Ezra 10:43 Zebina, Jaddai, Joel, and **B**
Ezek 11: 1 and Pelatiah the son of **B**
Ezek 11:13 Pelatiah the son of **B** died

BEN-AMMI
Gen 19:38 a son and called his name **B**

BEND (*see* BENDS, BENT)
2Sa 22:35 my arms can **b** a bow of bronze
Ps 11: 2 The wicked **b** their bow, They
Ps 18:34 my arms can **b** a bow of bronze
Ps 64: 3 **b** their bows to shoot their
Jer 46: 9 who handle and **b** the bow
Jer 50:14 around, all you who **b** the bow
Jer 50:29 All you who **b** the bow, encamp
Jer 51: 3 her let the archer **b** his bow

BEN-DEKER
1Ki 4: 9 **B**, in Makaz, Shaalbim, Beth

BENDS (*see* BEND)
Ps 7:12 He **b** His bow and makes it
Ps 58: 7 When he **b** his bow, Let his

BENEATH (*see* PREFACE)

BENE BERAK
Josh 19:45 Jehud, **B**, Gath Rimmon,

BENEFACTORS
Luke 22:25 over them are called **b**

BENEFIT (*see* BENEFITED, BENEFITS)
Ps 106: 5 That I may see the **b** of Your
Is 30: 5 a people who could not **b** them
Is 30: 5 or be help or **b**
Is 30: 6 a people who shall not **b** them
Jer 18:10 which I said I would **b** it
2Co 1:15 you might have a second **b**

BENEFITED (*see* BENEFIT)
1Ti 6: 2 those who are **b** are believers

BENEFITS (*see* BENEFIT)
Ps 68:19 Who daily loads us with **b**
Ps 103: 2 soul, And forget not all His **b**
Ps 116:12 LORD For all His **b** toward me

BENE JAAKAN
Num 33:31 from Moseroth and camped at **B**
Num 33:32 They moved from **B** and camped
Deut 10: 6 the wells of **B** to Moserah

BEN-GEBER
1Ki 4:13 **B**, in Ramoth Gilead

BEN-HADAD (*see* HADAD)
1Ki 15:18 to **B** the son of Tabrimmon
1Ki 15:20 So **B** heeded King Asa, and sent
1Ki 20: 1 Now **B** the king of Syria
1Ki 20: 2 Thus says **B**
1Ki 20: 5 Thus speaks **B**, saying
1Ki 20: 9 said to the messengers of **B**
1Ki 20:10 Then **B** sent to him and said,
1Ki 20:12 it happened when **B** heard this
1Ki 20:16 Meanwhile **B** and the thirty-two
1Ki 20:17 **B** sent out a patrol, and they
1Ki 20:20 **B** the king of Syria escaped
1Ki 20:26 that **B** mustered the Syrians
1Ki 20:30 **B** fled and went into the city,
1Ki 20:32 Your servant **B** says, 'Please
1Ki 20:33 Your brother **B**
1Ki 20:33 Then **B** came out to him
1Ki 20:34 Then **B** said to him, "The
2Ki 6:24 **B** king of Syria gathered all
2Ki 8: 7 and **B** king of Syria was sick
2Ki 8: 9 Your son **B** king of Syria has
2Ki 13: 3 into the hand of **B** the son of
2Ki 13:24 Then **B** his son reigned in his
2Ki 13:25 recaptured from the hand of **B**
2Ch 16: 2 sent to **B** king of Syria, who
2Ch 16: 4 So **B** heeded King Asa, and sent
Jer 49:27 consume the palaces of **B**
Amos 1: 4 shall devour the palaces of **B**

BEN-HAIL
2Ch 17: 7 reign he sent his leaders, **B**

BEN-HANAN (*see* HANAN)
1Ch 4:20 were Amnon, Rinnah, **B**

BEN-HESED
1Ki 4:10 **B**, in Arubboth

BEN-HUR
1Ki 4: 8 **B**, in the mountains of

BENINU
Neh 10:13 Hodijah, Bani, and **B**

BEN-JAHAZIEL
Ezra 8: 5 of the sons of Shechaniah, **B**

BENJAMIN (*see* BENJAMIN'S, BENJAMITE)
Gen 35:18 but his father called him **B**
Gen 35:24 of Rachel were Joseph and **B**
Gen 42: 4 brother **B** with his brothers
Gen 42:36 and you want to take **B** away
Gen 43:14 your other brother and **B**
Gen 43:15 men took that present and **B**
Gen 43:16 When Joseph saw **B** with them
Gen 43:29 his eyes and saw his brother **B**
Gen 45:12 the eyes of my brother **B** see
Gen 45:14 wept, and **B** wept on his neck
Gen 45:22 but to **B** he gave three
Gen 46:19 wife, were Joseph and **B**
Gen 46:21 The sons of **B** were Belah,
Gen 49:27 **B** is a ravenous wolf
Ex 1: 3 Issachar, Zebulun, and **B**
Num 1:11 from **B**, Abidan the son of
Num 1:36 From the children of **B**, their
Num 1:37 numbered of the tribe of **B**
Num 2:22 shall come the tribe of **B**
Num 2:22 leader of the children of **B**
Num 7:60 leader of the children of **B**
Num 10:24 of **B** was Abidan the son of
Num 13: 9 from the tribe of **B**, Palti
Num 26:38 The sons of **B** according to
Num 26:41 These are the sons of **B**
Num 34:21 from the tribe of **B**, Elidad
Deut 27:12 Judah, Issachar, Joseph, and **B**
Deut 33:12 Of **B** he said
Josh 18:11 tribe of the children of **B**
Josh 18:20 of the children of **B**,
Josh 18:21 tribe of the children of **B**
Josh 18:28 of the children of **B**
Josh 21: 4 and from the tribe of **B**
Josh 21:17 and from the tribe of **B**,
Judg 1:21 But the children of **B** did not
Judg 1:21 of **B** in Jerusalem to this day
Judg 5:14 After you, **B**, with your
Judg 10: 9 against Judah also, against **B**
Judg 19:14 Gibeah, which belongs to **B**
Judg 20: 3 (Now the children of **B** heard
Judg 20: 4 Gibeah, which belongs to **B**
Judg 20:10 when they come to Gibeah in **B**
Judg 20:12 through all the tribe of **B**
Judg 20:13 But the children of **B** would
Judg 20:14 the children of **B** gathered
Judg 20:15 of **B** numbered twenty-six
Judg 20:17 Now besides **B**, the men of
Judg 20:18 against the children of **B**
Judg 20:20 went out to battle against **B**
Judg 20:21 of **B** came out of Gibeah, and
Judg 20:23 the children of my brother **B**
Judg 20:24 of **B** on the second day
Judg 20:25 **B** went out against them from
Judg 20:28 the children of my brother **B**
Judg 20:30 of **B** on the third day, and put
Judg 20:31 So the children of **B** went out
Judg 20:32 And the children of **B** said
Judg 20:35 LORD defeated **B** before Israel
Judg 20:36 So the children of **B** saw that
Judg 20:39 Now **B** had begun to strike and
Judg 20:41 back, the men of **B** panicked
Judg 20:44 thousand men of **B** fell
Judg 20:46 So all who fell of **B** that day
Judg 20:48 against the children of **B**
Judg 21: 1 his daughter to **B** as a wife
Judg 21: 6 grieved for **B** their brother
Judg 21:13 of **B** who were at the rock of
Judg 21:14 So **B** came back at that time,
Judg 21:15 And the people grieved for **B**
Judg 21:16 since the women of **B** have
Judg 21:17 for the survivors of **B**, that
Judg 21:18 the one who gives a wife to **B**
Judg 21:20 instructed the children of **B**
Judg 21:21 then go to the land of **B**
Judg 21:23 And the children of **B** did so
1Sa 4:12 Then a man of **B** ran from the
1Sa 9: 1 There was a man of **B** whose
1Sa 9:16 you a man from the land of **B**
1Sa 9:21 families of the tribe of **B**
1Sa 10: 2 the territory of **B** at Zelzah
1Sa 10:20 the tribe of **B** was chosen
1Sa 10:21 of **B** to come near by their
1Sa 13: 2 with Jonathan in Gibeah of **B**
1Sa 13:15 up from Gilgal to Gibeah of **B**
1Sa 13:16 them remained in Gibeah of **B**
1Sa 14:16 of Saul in Gibeah of **B** looked
2Sa 2: 9 Jezreel, over Ephraim, over **B**
2Sa 2:15 over by number, twelve from **B**
2Sa 2:25 Now the children of **B**
2Sa 2:31 David had struck down, of **B**
2Sa 3:19 spoke in the hearing of **B**
2Sa 3:19 and the whole house of **B**
2Sa 4: 2 of the children of **B**
2Sa 4: 2 Beeroth also was part of **B**
2Sa 19:17 a thousand men of **B** with him
2Sa 21:14 in the country of **B** in Zelah
2Sa 23:29 Gibeah of the children of **B**
1Ki 4:18 Shimei the son of Elah, in **B**
1Ki 12:21 of Judah with the tribe of **B**
1Ki 12:23 all the house of Judah and **B**
1Ki 15:22 them King Asa built Geba of **B**
1Ch 2: 2 Dan, Joseph, **B**, Naphtali, Gad
1Ch 6:60 And from the tribe of **B**
1Ch 6:65 of **B** these cities which are
1Ch 7: 6 The sons of **B** were Bela,
1Ch 7:10 sons of Bilhan were Jeush, **B**
1Ch 8: 1 Now **B** begot Bela his
1Ch 8:40 These were all sons of **B**
1Ch 9: 3 and some of the children of **B**
1Ch 9: 7 Of the sons of **B**
1Ch 11:31 Gibeah, of the children of **B**
1Ch 12: 2 They were of **B**, Saul's
1Ch 12:16 some of the children of **B**
1Ch 12:29 of the children of **B**, kinsmen
1Ch 21: 6 **B** among them, for the king's
1Ch 27:21 over **B**, Jaasiel the son of
2Ch 11: 1 and **B** one hundred and eighty
2Ch 11: 3 to all Israel in Judah and **B**
2Ch 11:10 which are in Judah and **B**,
2Ch 11:12 having Judah and **B** on his side
2Ch 11:23 the territories of Judah and **B**
2Ch 14: 8 from **B** two hundred and eighty
2Ch 15: 2 me, Asa, and all Judah and **B**
2Ch 15: 8 all the land of Judah and **B**
2Ch 15: 9 he gathered all Judah and **B**
2Ch 17:17 Of **B**: Eliada a mighty man
2Ch 25: 5 throughout all Judah and **B**
2Ch 31: 1 from all Judah, **B**, Ephraim,
2Ch 34: 9 Israel, from all Judah and **B**
2Ch 34:32 **B** take their stand for it
Ezra 1: 5 fathers' houses of Judah and **B**
Ezra 4: 1 **B** heard that the descendants
Ezra 10: 9 and **B** gathered at Jerusalem
Ezra 10:32 **B**, Malluch, and Shemariah
Neh 3:23 After him **B** and Hasshub made
Neh 11: 4 Judah and of the children of **B**
Neh 11: 7 And these are the sons of **B**
Neh 11:31 Also the children of **B** from
Neh 11:36 of Levites were in **B**
Neh 12:34 Judah, **B**, Shemaiah, Jeremiah,
Ps 68:27 There is little **B**, their
Ps 80: 2 Before Ephraim, **B**, and
Jer 1: 1 in Anathoth in the land of **B**
Jer 6: 1 O you children of **B**, gather
Jer 17:26 Jerusalem, from the land of **B**
Jer 20: 2 were in the high gate of **B**
Jer 32: 8 which is in the country of **B**
Jer 32:44 witnesses, in the land of **B**
Jer 33:13 the South, in the land of **B**
Jer 37:12 to go into the land of **B** to
Jer 37:13 when he was in the gate of **B**
Jer 38: 7 was sitting at the Gate of **B**
Ezek 48:22 the border of **B** shall belong
Ezek 48:23 **B** shall have one portion
Ezek 48:24 by the border of **B**, from the
Ezek 48:32 for Joseph, one gate for **B**
Hos 5: 8 Aven, 'Look behind you, O **B**
Obad 19 **B** shall possess Gilead
Acts 13:21 Kish, a man of the tribe of **B**
Rom 11: 1 of Abraham, of the tribe of **B**
Phil 3: 5 of Israel, of the tribe of **B**
Rev 7: 8 of the tribe of **B** twelve

BENJAMIN'S (*see* BENJAMIN)
Gen 43:34 but **B** serving was five times
Gen 44:12 the cup was found in **B** sack
Gen 45:14 he fell on his brother **B** neck
Zech 14:10 **B** Gate to the place of the

BENJAMITE (*see* BENJAMIN, BENJAMITES)
Judg 3:15 Ehud the son of Gera, the **B**
1Sa 9: 1 the son of Aphiah, a **B**, a
1Sa 9:21 Am I not a **B**, of the smallest
2Sa 16:11 How much more now may this **B**
2Sa 19:16 Shimei the son of Gera, a **B**
2Sa 20: 1 Sheba the son of Bichri, a **B**
1Ki 2: 8 a **B** from Bahurim, who cursed
Esth 2: 5 Shimei, the son of Kish, a **B**

BENJAMITES (*see* BENJAMITE)
Judg 19:16 the men of the place were **B**
Judg 20:34 But the **B** did not know that
Judg 20:35 thousand one hundred **B**
Judg 20:36 had given ground to the **B**
Judg 20:40 the **B** looked behind them, and
Judg 20:43 They surrounded the **B** and
1Sa 9: 4 through the land of the **B**
1Sa 22: 7 Hear now, you **B**
1Ch 27:12 the Anathothite, of the **B**

BEN-JOSIPHIAH
Ezra 8:10 of the sons of Shelomith, **B**

BENO
1Ch 24:26 the son of Jaaziah, **B**
1Ch 24:27 of Merari by Jaaziah were **B**

BEN-ONI
Gen 35:18 that she called his name **B**

BENT (*see* BEND)
Ps 37:14 have **b** their bow, To cast
Is 5:28 sharp, and all their bows **b**
Is 21:15 drawn sword, from the **b** bow
Jer 9: 3 have **b** their tongues for lies
Lam 2: 4 an enemy, He has **b** His bow
Lam 3:12 He has **b** His bow and set me up
Ezek 17: 7 this vine **b** its roots toward
Dan 11:27 hearts shall be **b** on evil
Hos 11: 7 My people are **b** on
Zech 9:13 For I have **b** Judah, My bow,
Luke 13:11 was **b** over and could in no way

BEN-ZOHETH (*see* ZOHETH)
1Ch 4:20 sons of Ishi were Zoheth and **B**

BEON
Num 32: 3 Elealeh, Shebam, Nebo, and **B**

BEOR
Gen 36:32 the son of **B** reigned in Edom
Num 22: 5 Balaam the son of **B** at Pethor
Num 24: 3 of Balaam the son of **B**, the
Num 24:15 of Balaam the son of **B**, and
Num 31: 8 Balaam the son of **B** they also
Deut 23: 4 you Balaam the son of **B** from
Josh 13:22 the sword Balaam the son of **B**
Josh 24: 9 the son of **B** to curse you
1Ch 1:43 Bela the son of **B**, and the
Mic 6: 5 the son of **B** answered him
2Pe 2:15 way of Balaam the son of **B**

BEQUEATHS
Deut 21:16 shall be, on the day he **b** his

BERA
Gen 14: 2 made war with **B** king of Sodom

BERACHAH
1Ch 12: 3 **B**, and Jehu the Anathothite
2Ch 20:26 assembled in the Valley of **B**
2Ch 20:26 Valley of **B** until this day

BERACHIAH
1Ch 6:39 hand, was Asaph the son of **B**

BERAIAH
1Ch 8:21 Adaiah, **B**, and Shimrath were

BEREA
Acts 17:10 and Silas away by night to **B**
Acts 17:13 God was preached by Paul at **B**
Acts 20: 4 Sopater of **B** accompanied him

BEREAVE (*see* BEREAVED, BEREAVES)
Jer 15: 7 I will **b** them of children
Ezek 5:17 beasts, and they will **b** you
Ezek 36:12 no more shall you **b** them of
Ezek 36:13 **b** your nation of children,'
Ezek 36:14 nor **b** your nation anymore,"
Hos 9:12 yet I will **b** them to the last

BEREAVED (*see* BEREAVE)
Gen 27:45 Why should I be **b** also of you
Gen 42:36 You have **b** me of my children
Gen 43:14 If I am **b**, I am **b**
Jer 18:21 widows and **b** of their children

BEREAVES (*see* BEREAVE)
Lam 1:20 Outside the sword **b**, at home

BERECHIAH
1Ch 3:20 and Hashubah, Ohel, **B**,
1Ch 9:16 **B** the son of Asa, the son of
1Ch 15:17 brethren, Asaph the son of **B**
1Ch 15:23 **B** and Elkanah were
2Ch 28:12 **B** the son of Meshillemoth,
Neh 3: 4 them Meshullam the son of **B**

Neh 3:30 of **B** made repairs in front of
Neh 6:18 of Meshullam the son of **B**
Zech 1: 1 to Zechariah the son of **B**
Zech 1: 7 to Zechariah the son of **B**
Matt 23:35 blood of Zechariah, son of **B**

BERED
Gen 16:14 it is between Kadesh and **B**
1Ch 7:20 **B** his son, Tahath his son,

BERI (*see* BERIAH, BERIITES)
1Ch 7:36 Suah, Harnepher, Shual, **B**

BERIAH (*see* BERI)
Gen 46:17 were Jimnah, Ishuah, Isui, **B**
Gen 46:17 And the sons of **B** were Heber
Num 26:44 of **B**, the family of the
Num 26:45 Of the sons of **B**
1Ch 7:23 and he called his name **B**,
1Ch 7:30 were Imnah, Ishvah, Ishvi, **B**
1Ch 7:31 The sons of **B** were Heber and
1Ch 8:13 and **B** and Shema, who were
1Ch 8:16 and Joha were the sons of **B**
1Ch 23:10 Jahath, Zina, Jeush, and **B**
1Ch 23:11 and **B** did not have many sons

BERIITES (*see* BERI)
Num 26:44 Beriah, the family of the **B**

BERITES
2Sa 20:14 and Beth Maachah and all the **B**

BERITH (*see* BAAL-BERITH)
Judg 9:46 of the temple of the god **B**

BERNICE
Acts 25:13 **B** came to Caesarea to greet
Acts 25:23 **B** had come with great pomp,
Acts 26:30 as well as the governor and **B**

BERODACH-BALADAN (*see* BALADAN, MERODACH-BALADAN)
2Ki 20:12 At that time **B** the son of

BEROTHAH (*see* BEROTHAI)
Ezek 47:16 Hamath, **B**, Sibraim (which is

BEROTHAI (*see* BEROTHAH)
2Sa 8: 8 Also from Betah and from **B**

BEROTHITE (*see* BEEROTHITE)
1Ch 11:39 Ammonite, Naharai the **B** (the

BERYL
Ex 28:20 and the fourth row, a **b**, an
Ex 39:13 the fourth row, a **b**, an onyx,
Song 5:14 are rods of gold set with **b**
Ezek 1:16 works was like the color of **b**
Ezek 10: 9 have the color of a **b** stone
Ezek 28:13 sardius, topaz, and diamond, **b**
Dan 10: 6 His body was like **b**, his face
Rev 21:20 chrysolite, the eighth **b**, the

BESAI
Ezra 2:49 sons of Paseah, the sons of **B**
Neh 7:52 the children of **B**, the

BESEECH
Ps 80:14 we **b** You, O God of hosts
Rom 12: 1 I **b** you therefore, brethren,
Eph 4: 1 **b** you to have a walk worthy

BESET
Heb 5: 2 himself is also **b** by weakness

BESIDE (*see* PREFACE)

BESIDES (*see* PREFACE)

BESIEGE (*see* BESIEGED, BESIEGES, BESIEGING)
Deut 20:12 you, then you shall **b** it
Deut 20:19 When you **b** a city for a long
Deut 28:52 They shall **b** you at all your
Deut 28:52 they shall **b** you at all your
1Sa 23: 8 go down to Keilah to **b** David
2Ch 6:28 when their enemies **b** them in
Is 21: 2 **B**, O Media
Jer 21: 4 and the Chaldeans who **b** you
Jer 21: 9 to the Chaldeans who **b** you

BESIEGED (*see* BESIEGE)
2Sa 11: 1 of Ammon and **b** Rabbah
2Sa 11:16 while Joab **b** the city, that
2Sa 20:15 **b** him in Abel of Beth Maachah
1Ki 16:17 Gibbethon, and they **b** Tirzah
1Ki 20: 1 up and **b** Samaria, and made war
2Ki 6:24 and went up and **b** Samaria
2Ki 6:25 and indeed they **b** it until a
2Ki 16: 5 they **b** Ahaz but could not
2Ki 17: 5 and **b** it for three years
2Ki 18: 9 up against Samaria and **b** it
2Ki 24:10 Jerusalem, and the city was **b**
2Ki 25: 2 So the city was **b** until the
1Ch 20: 1 and came and **b** Rabbah
Eccl 9:14 **b** it, and built great snares
Is 1: 8 of cucumbers, as a **b** city
Jer 32: 2 of Babylon's army **b** Jerusalem
Jer 39: 1 against Jerusalem, and **b** it
Jer 52: 5 So the city was **b** until the
Lam 3: 5 He has **b** me and surrounded me
Ezek 4: 3 against it, and it shall be **b**
Ezek 6:12 is **b** shall die by the famine
Dan 1: 1 came to Jerusalem and **b** it

BESIEGES (*see* BESIEGE)
1Ki 8:37 when their enemy **b** them in

BESIEGING (*see* BESIEGE)
2Ki 24:11 as his servants were **b** it
Jer 37: 5 **b** Jerusalem heard news of

BESODEIAH
Neh 3: 6 and Meshullam the son of **B**

BESOR
1Sa 30: 9 him, and came to the Brook **B**
1Sa 30:10 could not cross the Brook **B**
1Sa 30:21 made to stay at the Brook **B**

BEST
Gen 43:11 Take some of the **b** fruits of
Gen 45:18 I will give you the **b** of the
Gen 45:20 for the **b** of all the land of
Gen 47: 6 dwell in the **b** of the land
Gen 47:11 in the **b** of the land, in the
Ex 22: 5 from the **b** of his own field
Ex 22: 5 the **b** of his own vineyard
Num 18:12 All the **b** of the oil, all the
Num 18:12 all the **b** of the new wine and
Num 18:29 LORD, from all the **b** of them
Num 18:30 have lifted up the **b** of it
Num 18:32 have lifted up the **b** of it
Num 36: 6 them marry whom they think **b**
Deut 23:16 where it seems **b** to him
Deut 33:15 with the **b** things of the
Judg 10:15 to us whatever seems **b** to You
Judg 14:20 who had been his **b** man
Ruth 3: 3 put on your **b** garment and go
1Sa 1:23 Do what seems **b** to you
1Sa 2:29 the **b** of all the offerings of
1Sa 8:14 take the **b** of your fields
1Sa 15: 9 the **b** of the sheep, the oxen,
1Sa 15:15 spared the **b** of the sheep
1Sa 15:21 the **b** of the things which
2Sa 18: 4 Whatever seems **b** to you I
2Ki 10: 3 choose the **b** qualified of
Esth 2: 9 her maidservants to the **b**
Ps 39: 5 at his **b** state is but vapor
Prov 16:28 separates the **b** of friends
Prov 17: 9 separates the **b** of friends
Song 7: 9 of your mouth like the **b** wine
Ezek 31:16 **b** of Lebanon, all that drink
Ezek 44:30 The **b** of all firstfruits of
Ezek 48:14 this **b** part of the land, for
Amos 6: 6 with the **b** ointments, but are
Mic 7: 4 The **b** of them is like a brier
Matt 23: 6 They love the **b** places at
Matt 23: 6 the **b** seats in the synagogues
Mark 12:39 the **b** seats in the synagogues
Mark 12:39 and the **b** places at feasts,
Luke 11:43 For you love the **b** seats in
Luke 14: 7 how they chose the **b** places
Luke 14: 8 not sit down in the **b** place
Luke 15:22 Bring out the **b** robe and put
Luke 20:46 the **b** seats in the synagogues
Luke 20:46 and the **b** places at feasts,
1Co 12:31 earnestly desire the **b** gifts
Heb 12:10 us as seemed **b** to them, but

BESTOW (*see* BESTOWED)
Ex 32:29 LORD, that He may **b** on you a
Deut 21:16 that he must not **b** firstborn
Luke 22:29 I **b** upon you a kingdom, just
1Co 12:23 on these we **b** greater honor
1Co 13: 3 though I **b** all my goods to

BESTOWED (*see* BESTOW)
1Ch 29:25 **b** on him such royal majesty
Esth 6: 3 been **b** on Mordecai for this
Is 63: 7 all that the LORD has **b** on us
Is 63: 7 which He has **b** on them
Ezek 16:14 splendor which I had **b** on you
Luke 22:29 as My Father **b** one upon Me
2Co 8: 1 of God **b** on the churches of
1Jn 3: 1 love the Father has **b** on us

BETAH
2Sa 8: 8 Also from **B** and from Berothai,

BETEN
Josh 19:25 included Helkath, Hali, **B**

BETHABARA (*see* BETH BARAH)
John 1:28 done in **B** beyond the Jordan

BETH ACACIA
Judg 7:22 and the army fled to **B**, toward

BETH ANATH
Josh 19:38 Iron, Migdal El, Horem, **B**
Judg 1:33 or the inhabitants of **B**
Judg 1:33 **B** were put under tribute to

BETH ANOTH
Josh 15:59 Maarath, **B**, and Eltekon

BETHANY
Matt 21:17 and went out of the city to **B**
Matt 26: 6 when Jesus was in **B** at the
Mark 11: 1 Jerusalem, to Bethphage and **B**
Mark 11:11 He went out to **B** with the
Mark 11:12 when they had come out from **B**
Mark 14: 3 being in **B** at the house of
Luke 19:29 came near to Bethphage and **B**
Luke 24:50 He led them out as far as **B**
John 11: 1 man was sick, Lazarus of **B**
John 11:18 Now **B** was near Jerusalem,
John 12: 1 the Passover, Jesus came to **B**

BETH APHRAH
Mic 1:10 in Gath, weep not at all in **B**

BETH ARABAH
Josh 15: 6 Hoglah and passed north of **B**
Josh 15:61 **B**, Middin, Secacah,
Josh 18:22 **B**, Zemaraim, Bethel,

BETH ARBEL
Hos 10:14 **B** in the day of battle

BETH AVEN
Josh 7: 2 to Ai, which is beside **B**, on
Josh 18:12 ended at the Wilderness of **B**
1Sa 13: 5 in Michmash, to the east of **B**
1Sa 14:23 and the battle shifted to **B**
Hos 4:15 up to Gilgal, nor go up to **B**
Hos 5: 8 Cry aloud at **B**, Look behind
Hos 10: 5 fear because of the calf of **B**

BETH AZMAVETH
Neh 7:28 the men of **B**, forty-two

BETH BAAL MEON (*see* BAAL MEON, BETH MEON)
Josh 13:17 Dibon, Bamoth Baal, **B**,

BETH BARAH (*see* BETHABARA)
Judg 7:24 watering places as far as **B**
Judg 7:24 watering places as far as **B**

BETH BIRI
1Ch 4:31 Marcaboth, Hazar Susim, **B**

BETH CAR
1Sa 7:11 them back as far as below **B**

BETH DAGON (*see* DAGON)
Josh 15:41 Gederoth, **B**, Naamah, and
Josh 19:27 toward the sunrise to **B**

BETH DIBLATHAIM
Jer 48:22 on Dibon and Nebo and **B**,

BETH EDEN
Amos 1: 5 who holds the scepter from **B**

BETH EKED
2Ki 10:12 way, at **B** of the Shepherds,
2Ki 10:14 killed them at the well of **B**

BETHEL (*see* EL BETHEL)
Gen 12: 8 to the mountain east of **B**
Gen 12: 8 his tent with **B** on the west
Gen 13: 3 from the South as far as **B**
Gen 13: 3 at the beginning, between **B**
Gen 28:19 the name of that place **B**
Gen 31:13 I am the God of **B**, where you
Gen 35: 1 Arise, go up to **B** and dwell
Gen 35: 3 let us arise and go up to **B**
Gen 35: 6 **B**), which is in the land of
Gen 35: 8 she was buried below **B** under
Gen 35:15 where God spoke with him, **B**
Gen 35:16 Then they journeyed from **B**
Josh 7: 2 Aven, on the east side of **B**

Josh 8: 9 ambush, and stayed between **B**
Josh 8:12 set them in ambush between **B**
Josh 8:17 or **B** who did not go out after
Josh 12: 9 king of Ai, which is beside **B**
Josh 12:16 the king of **B**, one
Josh 16: 1 through the mountains to **B**
Josh 16: 2 then went out from **B** to Luz
Josh 18:13 of Luz (which is **B**) southward
Josh 18:22 Beth Arabah, Zemaraim, **B**,
Judg 1:22 Joseph also went up against **B**
Judg 1:23 Joseph sent men to spy out **B**
Judg 4: 5 **B** in the mountains of Ephraim
Judg 20:31 (one of which goes up to **B**
Judg 21:19 Shiloh, which is north of **B**
Judg 21:19 goes up from **B** to Shechem
1Sa 7:16 to year on a circuit to **B**
1Sa 10: 3 up to God at **B** will meet you
1Sa 13: 2 and in the mountains of **B**, and
1Sa 30:27 to those who were in **B**, those
1Ki 12:29 And he set up one in **B**, and the
1Ki 12:32 So he did at **B**, sacrificing
1Ki 12:32 at **B** he installed the priests
1Ki 12:33 altar which he had made at **B**
1Ki 13: 1 to **B** by the word of the LORD
1Ki 13: 4 out against the altar in **B**
1Ki 13:10 by the way he came to **B**
1Ki 13:11 Now an old prophet dwelt in **B**
1Ki 13:11 of God had done that day in **B**
1Ki 13:32 LORD against the altar in **B**
1Ki 16:34 days Hiel of **B** built Jericho
2Ki 2: 2 the LORD has sent me on to **B**
2Ki 2: 2 So they went down to **B**
2Ki 2: 3 were at **B** came out to Elisha
2Ki 2:23 And he went up from there to **B**
2Ki 10:29 golden calves that were at **B**
2Ki 17:28 Samaria came and dwelt in **B**
2Ki 23: 4 and carried their ashes to **B**
2Ki 23:15 the altar that was at **B**, and
2Ki 23:17 done against the altar of **B**
2Ki 23:19 the deeds he had done in **B**
1Ch 7:28 and habitations were **B** and its
2Ch 13:19 **B** with its villages, Jeshanah
Ezra 2:28 the men of **B** and Ai, two
Neh 7:32 the men of **B** and Ai, one
Neh 11:31 dwelt in Michmash, Aija, and **B**
Jer 48:13 of Israel was ashamed of **B**
Hos 10:15 it shall be done to you, O **B**
Hos 12: 4 He found Him in **B**, and there
Amos 3:14 on the altars of **B**
Amos 4: 4 Come to **B** and transgress, at
Amos 5: 5 But do not seek **B**, nor enter
Amos 5: 5 and **B** shall come to nothing
Amos 5: 6 with no one to quench it in **B**
Amos 7:10 of **B** sent to Jeroboam king of
Amos 7:13 But never again prophesy at **B**

BETH EMEK
Josh 19:27 El, then northward beyond **B**

BETHER
Song 2:17 stag upon the mountains of **B**

BETHESDA
John 5: 2 which is called in Hebrew, **B**

BETH EZEL (*see* EZEL)
Mic 1:11 **B** mourns

BETH GADER (*see* GEDER)
1Ch 2:51 and Hareph the father of **B**

BETH GAMUL (*see* GAMUL)
Jer 48:23 on Kirjathaim and **B** and

BETH HACCEREM
Neh 3:14 leader of the district of **B**

BETH HACCHEREM
Jer 6: 1 and set up a signal-fire in **B**

BETH HAGGAN
2Ki 9:27 he fled by the road to **B**

BETH HARAM
Josh 13:27 and in the valley **B**

BETH HARAN (*see* HARAN)
Num 32:36 Beth Nimrah and **B**, fortified

BETH HOGLAH (*see* HOGLAH)
Josh 15: 6 The border went up to **B** and
Josh 18:19 along to the north side of **B**
Josh 18:21 families, were Jericho, **B**

BETH HORON
Josh 10:10 along the road that goes to **B**
Josh 10:11 and were on the descent of **B**
Josh 16: 3 boundary of Lower **B** to Gezer
Josh 16: 5 Addar as far as Upper **B**
Josh 18:13 on the south side of Lower **B**
Josh 18:14 that lies before **B** southward
Josh 21:22 and **B** with its common-land
1Sa 13:18 turned to the road to **B**, and
1Ki 9:17 Solomon built Gezer, Lower **B**
1Ch 6:68 **B** with its common-lands,
1Ch 7:24 who built Lower and Upper **B**
2Ch 8: 5 He built Upper **B** and Lower
2Ch 25:13 of Judah from Samaria to **B**

BETH JESHIMOTH
Josh 12: 3 (the Salt Sea), the road to **B**
Josh 13:20 the slopes of Pisgah, and **B**
Ezek 25: 9 the glory of the country, **B**

BETH JESIMOTH
Num 33:49 from **B** as far as the Abel

BETH LEBAOTH (*see* LEBAOTH)
Josh 19: 6 **B**, and Sharuhen

BETHLEHEM (*see* BETHLEHEMITE)
Gen 35:19 way to Ephrath (that is, **B**)
Gen 48: 7 way to Ephrath (that is, **B**)
Josh 19:15 Shimron, Idalah, and **B**
Judg 12: 8 him, Ibzan of **B** judged Israel
Judg 12:10 Ibzan died and was buried at **B**
Judg 17: 7 a young man from **B** in Judah
Judg 17: 8 city of **B** in Judah to sojourn
Judg 17: 9 I am a Levite from **B** in Judah
Judg 19: 1 a concubine from **B** in Judah
Judg 19: 2 father's house at **B** in Judah
Judg 19:18 We are passing from **B** in
Judg 19:18 I went to **B** in Judah, and now
Ruth 1: 1 And a certain man of **B**, Judah,
Ruth 1: 2 Ephrathites of **B**, Judah
Ruth 1:19 went until they came to **B**
Ruth 1:19 when they had come to **B**,
Ruth 1:22 Now they came to **B** at the
Ruth 2: 4 Now behold, Boaz came from **B**
Ruth 4:11 Ephrathah and be famous in **B**
1Sa 16: 4 the LORD said, and went to **B**
1Sa 17:12 of that Ephrathite of **B** Judah
1Sa 17:15 feed his father's sheep at **B**
1Sa 20: 6 that he might run over to **B**
1Sa 20:28 permission of me to go to **B**
2Sa 2:32 father's tomb, which was in **B**
2Sa 23:14 the Philistines was then in **B**
2Sa 23:15 the water from the well of **B**
2Sa 23:16 of **B** that was by the gate
2Sa 23:24 Elhanan the son of Dodo of **B**
1Ch 2:51 Salma the father of **B**, and
1Ch 2:54 The sons of Salma were **B**, the
1Ch 4: 4 of Ephrathah the father of **B**
1Ch 11:16 the Philistines was then in **B**
1Ch 11:17 of water from the well of **B**
1Ch 11:18 of **B** that was by the gate
1Ch 11:26 Elhanan the son of Dodo of **B**
2Ch 11: 6 And he built **B**, Etam, Tekoa,
Ezra 2:21 the people of **B**, one hundred
Neh 7:26 the men of **B** and Netophah, one
Jer 41:17 of Chimham, which is near **B**
Mic 5: 2 **B** Ephrathah, though you are
Matt 2: 1 in **B** of Judea in the days of
Matt 2: 5 In **B** of Judea, for thus it is
Matt 2: 6 But you, **B**, in the land of
Matt 2: 8 And he sent them to **B** and said,
Matt 2:16 male children who were in **B**
Luke 2: 4 of David, which is called **B**
Luke 2:15 Let us now go to **B** and see
John 7:42 David and from the town of **B**

BETHLEHEMITE (*see* BETHLEHEM, LAHMI)
1Sa 16: 1 am sending you to Jesse the **B**
1Sa 16:18 seen a son of Jesse the **B**
1Sa 17:58 of your servant Jesse the **B**
2Sa 21:19 the **B** killed the brother of

BETH MAACHAH (*see* ABEL BETH MAACHAH, MAACHAH)
2Sa 20:14 tribes of Israel to Abel and **B**
2Sa 20:15 and besieged him in Abel of **B**
1Ki 15:20 He attacked Ijon, Dan, Abel **B**
2Ki 15:29 came and took Ijon, Abel **B**

BETH MARCABOTH
Josh 19: 5 Ziklag, **B**, Hazar Susah,
1Ch 4:31 **B**, Hazar Susim, Beth Biri, and

BETH MEON (*see* BETH BAAL MEON)
Jer 48:23 and Beth Gamul and **B**

BETH MILLO
Judg 9: 6 gathered together, all of **B**
Judg 9:20 the men of Shechem and **B**
Judg 9:20 the men of Shechem and from **B**

BETH NIMRAH (*see* NIMRAH)
Num 32:36 **B** and Beth Haran, fortified
Josh 13:27 in the valley Beth Haram, **B**

BETH PAZZEZ
Josh 19:21 En Gannim, En Haddah, and **B**

BETH PELET (*see* PELET)
Josh 15:27 Hazar Gaddah, Heshmon, **B**,
Neh 11:26 in Jeshua, Moladah, **B**,

BETH PEOR
Deut 3:29 in the valley opposite **B**
Deut 4:46 in the valley opposite **B**
Deut 34: 6 the land of Moab, opposite **B**
Josh 13:20 **B**, the slopes of Pisgah, and

BETHPHAGE
Matt 21: 1 to Jerusalem, and came to **B**
Mark 11: 1 came near Jerusalem, to **B**
Luke 19:29 pass, when He came near to **B**

BETH-RAPHA (*see* RAPHA)
1Ch 4:12 And Eshton begot **B**, Paseah,

BETH REHOB (*see* REHOB)
Judg 18:28 the valley that belongs to **B**
2Sa 10: 6 and hired the Syrians of **B**

BETHSAIDA
Matt 11:21 Woe to you, **B**
Mark 6:45 Him to the other side, to **B**
Mark 8:22 Then He came to **B**
Luke 9:10 to the city called **B**
Luke 10:13 Woe to you, **B**
John 1:44 Now Philip was from **B**, the
John 12:21 who was from **B** of Galilee

BETH SHAN
1Sa 31:10 his body to the wall of **B**
1Sa 31:12 his sons from the wall of **B**
2Sa 21:12 them from the street of **B**

BETH SHEAN
Josh 17:11 and in Asher, Manasseh had **B**
Josh 17:16 iron, both those who are of **B**
Judg 1:27 out the inhabitants of **B** and
1Ki 4:12 in Taanach, Megiddo, and all **B**
1Ki 4:12 from **B** to Abel Meholah, as
1Ch 7:29 children of Manasseh were **B**

BETH SHEMESH
Josh 15:10 is Chesalon), went down to **B**
Josh 19:22 to Tabor, Shahazimah, and **B**
Josh 19:38 El, Horem, Beth Anath, and **B**
Josh 21:16 and **B** with its common-land
Judg 1:33 out the inhabitants of **B** or
Judg 1:33 the inhabitants of **B** and Beth
1Sa 6: 9 to its own territory, to **B**
1Sa 6:12 straight for the road to **B**
1Sa 6:12 after them to the border of **B**
1Sa 6:13 Now the people of **B** were
1Sa 6:14 into the field of Joshua of **B**
1Sa 6:15 Then the men of **B** offered
1Sa 6:18 in the field of Joshua of **B**
1Sa 6:19 Then He struck the men of **B**
1Sa 6:20 And the men of **B** said, "Who
1Ki 4: 9 in Makaz, Shaalbim, **B**, and
2Ki 14:11 Judah faced one another at **B**
2Ki 14:13 the son of Ahaziah, at **B**
1Ch 6:59 and **B** with its common-lands
2Ch 25:21 Judah faced one another at **B**
2Ch 25:23 the son of Jehoahaz, at **B**
2Ch 28:18 of Judah, and had taken **B**,
Jer 43:13 of **B** that are in the land of

BETH TAPPUAH (*see* TAPPUAH)
Josh 15:53 Janum, **B**, Aphekah,

BETHUEL (*see* BETHUL)
Gen 22:22 Hazo, Pildash, Jidlaph, and **B**
Gen 22:23 And **B** begot Rebekah
Gen 24:15 Rebekah, who was born to **B**
Gen 24:24 I am the daughter of **B**,
Gen 24:47 she said, "The daughter of **B**
Gen 24:50 Laban and **B** answered and said,
Gen 25:20 the daughter of **B** the Syrian
Gen 28: 2 Aram, to the house of **B** your
Gen 28: 5 Laban the son of **B** the Syrian

1Ch 4:30 **B**, Hormah, Ziklag,

BETHUL (*see* BETHUEL)
Josh 19: 4 Eltolad, **B**, Hormah,

BETH ZUR (*see* ZUR)
Josh 15:58 Halhul, **B**, Gedor,
1Ch 2:45 and Maon was the father of **B**
2Ch 11: 7 **B**, Sochoh, Adullam,
Neh 3:16 of half the district of **B**

BETONIM
Josh 13:26 to Ramath Mizpah and **B**

BETRAY (*see* BETRAYED, BETRAYER, BETRAYING, BETRAYS)
1Ch 12:17 but if to **b** me to my enemies,
Is 16: 3 do not **b** him who escapes
Matt 24:10 will **b** one another, and will
Matt 26:16 sought opportunity to **b** Him
Matt 26:21 to you, one of you will **b** Me
Matt 26:23 with Me in the dish will **b** Me
Mark 13:12 will **b** brother to death, and a
Mark 14:10 priests to **b** Him to them
Mark 14:11 he might conveniently **b** Him
Mark 14:18 who eats with Me will **b** Me
Luke 22: 4 how he might **b** Him to them
Luke 22: 6 sought opportunity to **b** Him
John 6:64 believe, and who would **b** Him
John 6:71 for it was he who would **b** Him
John 12: 4 Simon's son, who would **b** Him
John 13: 2 Simon's son, to **b** Him,
John 13:11 For He knew who would **b** Him
John 13:21 to you, one of you will **b** Me

BETRAYED (*see* BETRAY)
Matt 10: 4 Iscariot, who also **b** Him
Matt 17:22 to be **b** into the hands of men
Matt 20:18 be **b** to the chief priests
Matt 26:24 by whom the Son of Man is **b**
Matt 26:45 the Son of Man is being **b**
Mark 3:19 Iscariot, who also **b** Him
Mark 14:21 by whom the Son of Man is **b**
Mark 14:41 the Son of Man is being **b**
Luke 21:16 You will be **b** even by parents
Luke 22:22 to that man by whom He is **b**
John 18: 2 And Judas, who **b** Him, also
John 18: 5 And Judas, who **b** Him, also
1Co 11:23 in which He was **b** took bread

BETRAYER (*see* BETRAY, BETRAYERS)
Matt 26:48 Now His **b** had given them a
Matt 27: 3 Then Judas, His **b**, seeing
Mark 14:42 See, My **b** is at hand
Mark 14:44 Now His **b** had given them a
Luke 22:21 the hand of My **b** is with Me

BETRAYERS (*see* BETRAYER)
Acts 7:52 you now have become the **b**

BETRAYING (*see* BETRAY)
Matt 26:25 Then Judas, who was **b** Him
Matt 27: 4 sinned by **b** innocent blood
Luke 22:48 are you **b** the Son of Man with

BETRAYS (*see* BETRAY)
Matt 26:46 See, he who **b** Me is at hand
Matt 26:73 because your speech **b** you
John 21:20 who is the one who **b** You

BETROTH (*see* BETROTHAL, BETROTHED)
Deut 28:30 You shall **b** a wife, but
Hos 2:19 I will **b** you to Me forever
Hos 2:19 yes, I will **b** you to Me in
Hos 2:20 I will **b** you to Me in

BETROTHAL (*see* BETROTH)
Jer 2: 2 youth, the love of your **b**

BETROTHED (*see* BETROTH)
Ex 21: 8 who has **b** her to himself,
Ex 21: 9 if he has **b** her to his son,
Ex 22:16 entices a virgin who is not **b**
Lev 19:20 with a woman who is **b** as a
Deut 20: 7 is there who is **b** to a woman
Deut 22:23 is a virgin is **b** to a husband
Deut 22:25 finds a **b** young woman in the
Deut 22:27 the **b** young woman cried out,
Deut 22:28 who is a virgin, who is not **b**
2Sa 3:14 whom I **b** to myself for a
Matt 1:18 mother Mary was **b** to Joseph
Luke 1:27 to a virgin **b** to a man whose
Luke 2: 5 his **b** wife, who was with
2Co 11: 2 For I have **b** you to one

BETTER (*see* PREFACE)

BETWEEN (*see* PREFACE)

BEULAH
Is 62: 4 Hephzibah, and your land **B**

BEVELED
1Ki 6: 4 house windows with **b** frames
1Ki 7: 4 with **b** frames in three rows
Ezek 40:16 There were **b** window frames in
Ezek 41:16 and the **b** window frames
Ezek 41:26 There were **b** window frames

BEVERAGE
Song 7: 2 which lacks no blended **b**

BEWAIL (*see* BEWAILED, BEWAILING)
Lev 10: 6 **b** the burning which the LORD
Judg 11:37 **b** my virginity, my friends and
Is 16: 9 Therefore I will **b** the vine

BEWAILED (*see* BEWAIL)
Judg 11:38 and **b** her virginity on the

BEWAILING (*see* BEWAIL)
Jer 4:31 daughter of Zion **b** herself

BEWARE
Gen 24: 6 **B** that you do not take my son
Ex 10:10 **B**, for evil is ahead of you
Ex 23:21 **B** of Him and obey His voice
Deut 6:12 then **b**, lest you forget the
Deut 8:11 **B** that you do not forget the
Deut 15: 9 **B** lest there be a wicked
2Sa 18:12 **B** lest anyone touch the
2Ki 6: 9 **B** that you do not pass this
Job 36:18 **b** lest He take you away with
Is 36:18 **B** lest Hezekiah persuade you
Matt 7:15 **B** of false prophets, who come
Matt 10:17 But **b** of men, for they will
Matt 16: 6 and **b** of the leaven of the
Matt 16:11 but you should **b** of the
Matt 16:12 to **b** of the leaven of bread
Mark 8:15 heed, **b** of the leaven of the
Mark 12:38 **B** of the scribes, who desire
Luke 12: 1 all, '**B** of the leaven of the
Luke 12:15 **b** of covetousness, for one's
Luke 20:46 **B** of the scribes, who desire
Acts 13:40 **B** therefore, lest what has
1Co 8: 9 But **b** lest somehow this
Gal 5:15 **b** lest you be consumed by one
Phil 3: 2 **B** of dogs, **b** of evil workers,
Phil 3: 2 **b** of the mutilation
Col 2: 8 **B** lest anyone cheat you
2Ti 4:15 You also must **b** of him, for
Heb 3:12 **B**, brethren, lest there be in
2Pe 3:17 **b** lest you also fall from

BEWILDERED
Ex 14: 3 They are **b** by the land

BEWITCHED
Gal 3: 1 Who has **b** you that you should

BEYOND (*see* PREFACE)

BEZAI
Ezra 2:17 the people of **B**, three
Neh 7:23 the children of **B**, three
Neh 10:18 Hodijah, Hashum, **B**,

BEZALEEL
Ex 31: 2 by name **B** the son of Uri, the
Ex 35:30 by name **B** the son of Uri, the
Ex 36: 1 And **B** and Aholiab, and every
Ex 36: 2 Then Moses called **B** and
Ex 37: 1 Then **B** made the ark of acacia
Ex 38:22 **B** the son of Uri, the son of
1Ch 2:20 Hur begot Uri, and Uri begot **B**
2Ch 1: 5 altar that **B** the son of Uri
Ezra 10:30 Maaseiah, Mattaniah, **B**,

BEZEK (*see* ADONI-BEZEK)
Judg 1: 4 killed ten thousand men at **B**
Judg 1: 5 they found Adoni-Bezek in **B**
1Sa 11: 8 When he numbered them in **B**

BEZER
Deut 4:43 **B** in the wilderness on the
Josh 20: 8 they assigned **B** in the
Josh 21:36 **B** with its common-land, Jahaz
1Ch 6:78 **B** in the wilderness with its
1Ch 7:37 **B**, Hod, Shamma, Shilshah,

BICHRI
2Sa 20: 1 name was Sheba the son of **B**
2Sa 20: 2 followed Sheba the son of **B**
2Sa 20: 6 Now Sheba the son of **B** will
2Sa 20: 7 to pursue Sheba the son of **B**
2Sa 20:10 pursued Sheba the son of **B**
2Sa 20:13 to pursue Sheba the son of **B**
2Sa 20:21 Sheba the son of **B** by name
2Sa 20:22 head of Sheba the son of **B**

BID (*see* BIDDING)
Luke 9:61 **b** them farewell who are at my

BIDDING (*see* BID)
1Sa 22:14 who goes at your **b**, and is

BIDKAR
2Ki 9:25 Jehu said to **B** his captain

BIG
Ex 29:20 on the **b** toe of their right
Lev 8:23 on the **b** toe of his right
Lev 8:24 on the **b** toes of their right
Lev 14:14 on the **b** toe of his right
Lev 14:17 on the **b** toe of his right
Lev 14:25 on the **b** toe of his right
Lev 14:28 on the **b** toe of his right
Judg 1: 6 cut off his thumbs and **b** toes
Judg 1: 7 **b** toes cut off used to gather

BIGTHA
Esth 1:10 Mehuman, Biztha, Harbona, **B**

BIGTHAN (*see* BIGTHANA)
Esth 2:21 two of the king's eunuchs, **B**

BIGTHANA (*see* BIGTHAN)
Esth 6: 2 that Mordecai had told of **B**

BIGVAI
Ezra 2: 2 Mordecai, Bilshan, Mispar, **B**
Ezra 2:14 the people of **B**, two thousand
Ezra 8:14 also of the sons of **B**, Uthai
Neh 7: 7 Bilshan, Mispereth, **B**, Nehum
Neh 7:19 the children of **B**, two
Neh 10:16 Adonijah, **B**, Adin,

BILDAD
Job 2:11 **B** the Shuhite, and Zophar the
Job 8: 1 Then **B** the Shuhite answered
Job 18: 1 Then **B** the Shuhite answered
Job 25: 1 Then **B** the Shuhite answered
Job 42: 9 **B** the Shuhite and Zophar the

BILE
Lam 2:11 my **b** is poured on the ground

BILEAM (*see* IBLEAM)
1Ch 6:70 **B** with its common-lands, for

BILGAH
1Ch 24:14 the fifteenth to **B**, the
Neh 12: 5 Mijamin, Maadiah, **B**,
Neh 12:18 of **B**, Shammua

BILGAI
Neh 10: 8 Maaziah, **B**, and Shemaiah

BILHAH (*see* BAALAH)
Gen 29:29 Laban gave his maid **B** to his
Gen 30: 3 Here is my maid **B**
Gen 30: 4 gave him **B** her maid as wife
Gen 30: 5 **B** conceived and bore Jacob a
Gen 30: 7 Rachel's maid **B** conceived
Gen 35:22 and lay with **B** his father's
Gen 35:25 the sons of **B**, Rachel's
Gen 37: 2 lad was with the sons of **B**
Gen 46:25 These were the sons of **B**,
1Ch 4:29 **B**, Ezem, Tolad,
1Ch 7:13 and Shallum, the sons of **B**

BILHAN
Gen 36:27 **B**, Zaavan, and Akan
1Ch 1:42 The sons of Ezer were **B**,
1Ch 7:10 The son of Jediael was **B**, and
1Ch 7:10 and the sons of **B** were Jeush

BILL
Luke 16: 6 he said to him, 'Take your **b**
Luke 16: 7 he said to him, 'Take your **b**

BILLOWS
Ps 42: 7 waves and **b** have gone over me
Jon 2: 3 all Your **b** and Your waves

BILSHAN
Ezra 2: 2 Reelaiah, Mordecai, **B**,
Neh 7: 7 Nahamani, Mordecai, **B**,

BIMHAL
1Ch 7:33 of Japhlet were Pasach, **B**

BIN
1Ki 17:12 a handful of flour in a **b**
1Ki 17:14 The **b** of flour shall not be
1Ki 17:16 The **b** of flour was not used

BIND (*see* BINDING, BINDS, BOUND)
Ex 28:28 They shall **b** the breastplate
Num 30: 2 LORD, or swears an oath to **b**
Num 30:14 all the agreements that **b** her
Deut 6: 8 You shall **b** them as a sign on
Deut 11:18 **b** them as a sign on your hand
Josh 2:18 you **b** this line of scarlet
Judg 16: 5 that we may **b** him to afflict
Judg 16: 7 If they **b** me with seven fresh
Judg 16:11 If they **b** me securely with
Job 31:36 and **b** it on me like a crown
Job 38:31 Can you **b** the cluster of the
Job 39:10 Can you **b** the wild ox in the
Job 40:13 **b** their faces in hidden
Ps 105:22 To **b** his princes at his
Ps 118:27 **B** the sacrifice with cords to
Ps 149: 8 To **b** their kings with chains,
Prov 3: 3 **b** them around your neck,
Prov 6:21 **B** them continually upon your
Prov 7: 3 **B** them on your fingers
Is 8:16 **B** up the testimony, Seal the
Is 49:18 **b** them on you as a bride does
Ezek 3:25 **b** you with them, so that you
Ezek 5: 3 **b** them in the edge of your
Ezek 24:17 **b** your turban on your head,
Ezek 30:21 nor a splint put on to **b** it
Ezek 34:16 **b** up the broken and strengthen
Dan 3:20 in his army to **b** Shadrach
Hos 6: 1 stricken, but He will **b** us up
Hos 10:10 when I **b** them for their two
Matt 13:30 **b** them in bundles to burn
Matt 16:19 whatever you **b** on earth will
Matt 18:18 whatever you **b** on earth will
Matt 22:13 **B** him hand and foot, take him
Matt 23: 4 For they **b** heavy burdens,
Mark 5: 3 and no one could **b** him, not
Acts 9:14 **b** all who call on Your name
Acts 21:11 **b** the man who owns this belt

BINDING (*see* BIND)
Gen 37: 7 were, **b** sheaves in the field
Gen 49:11 **B** his donkey to the vine, and
Ex 26:17 board for **b** one to another
Ex 28:32 it shall have a woven **b** all
Ex 36:22 tenons for **b** one to another
Ex 39:23 with a woven **b** all around the
Num 30:12 the agreement **b** her, it shall
Num 30:13 every **b** oath to afflict her
Ps 56:12 made to You are **b** upon me
Acts 22: 4 this Way to the death, **b** and

BINDS (*see* BIND)
Num 30: 3 **b** herself by some agreement
Job 5:18 For He bruises, but He **b** up
Job 12:18 **b** their waist with a belt
Job 26: 8 He **b** up the water in His
Job 30:18 it **b** me about as the collar
Job 36:13 cry for help when He **b** them
Ps 129: 7 hand, Nor he who **b** sheaves
Ps 147: 3 And **b** up their wounds
Prov 26: 8 Like one who **b** a stone in a
Is 30:26 in the day that the LORD **b** up
Matt 12:29 he first **b** the strong man
Mark 3:27 he first **b** the strong man

BINEA
1Ch 8:37 Moza begot **B**, Raphah his son,
1Ch 9:43 Moza begot **B**, Rephaiah his

BINNUI
Ezra 8:33 and Noadiah the son of **B**,
Ezra 10:30 Mattaniah, Bezaleel, **B**, and
Ezra 10:38 Bani, **B**, Shimei,
Neh 3:24 After him **B** the son of
Neh 7:15 the children of **B**, six
Neh 10: 9 **B** of the sons of Henadad, and
Neh 12: 8 the Levites were Jeshua, **B**

BIRD (*see* BIRD'S, BIRDS)
Gen 1:21 every winged **b** according to
Gen 1:30 to every **b** of the air, and to
Gen 2:19 and every **b** of the air, and
Gen 7:14 every **b** after its kind, every
Gen 7:14 kind, every **b** of every sort
Gen 7:23 thing and **b** of the air
Gen 8:19 every creeping thing, every **b**
Gen 8:20 animal and of every clean **b**
Gen 9: 2 on every **b** of the air, on all
Lev 7:26 whether of **b** or beast
Lev 14: 6 As for the living **b**, he shall
Lev 14: 6 the living **b** in the blood of
Lev 14: 6 **b** that was killed over the
Lev 14: 7 shall let the living **b** loose
Lev 14:51 the scarlet, and the living **b**
Lev 14:51 in the blood of the slain **b**
Lev 14:52 house with the blood of the **b**
Lev 14:52 running water and the living **b**
Lev 14:53 he shall let the living **b**
Lev 17:13 animal or **b** that may be eaten
Lev 20:25 abominable by beast or by **b**
Deut 4:17 **b** that flies in the air,
Job 28: 7 That path no **b** knows, nor has
Job 41: 5 you play with him as with a **b**
Ps 11: 1 Flee as a **b** to your mountain
Ps 124: 7 as a **b** from the snare of the
Prov 1:17 spread in the sight of any **b**
Prov 6: 5 like a **b** from the hand of the
Prov 7:23 As a **b** hastens to the snare,
Prov 27: 8 Like a **b** that wanders from
Eccl 10:20 for a **b** of the air may carry
Eccl 10:20 a **b** in flight may tell the
Eccl 12: 4 rises up at the sound of a **b**
Is 16: 2 **b** thrown out of the nest
Is 46:11 calling a **b** of prey from the
Lam 3:52 cause hunted me down like a **b**
Ezek 39:17 Speak to every sort of **b**
Ezek 44:31 **b** or beast, that died
Dan 7: 6 on its back four wings of a **b**
Hos 9:11 glory shall fly away like a **b**
Hos 11:11 trembling like a **b** from Egypt
Amos 3: 5 Will a **b** fall into a snare on
Jas 3: 7 For every kind of beast and **b**
Rev 18: 2 for every unclean and hated **b**

BIRD'S (*see* BIRD)
Deut 22: 6 If a **b** nest happens to be

BIRDS (*see* BIRD, BIRDS')
Gen 1:20 let **b** fly above the earth
Gen 1:22 let **b** multiply on the earth
Gen 1:26 over the **b** of the air, and
Gen 1:28 over the **b** of the air, and
Gen 2:20 to the **b** of the air, and to
Gen 6: 7 **b** of the air, for I am sorry
Gen 6:20 Of the **b** after their kind, of
Gen 7: 3 seven each of **b** of the air
Gen 7: 8 beasts that are unclean, of **b**
Gen 7:21 **b** and cattle and beasts and
Gen 8:17 **b** and cattle and every creeping
Gen 9:10 the **b**, the cattle, and every
Gen 15:10 he did not cut the **b** in two
Gen 40:17 the **b** ate them out of the
Gen 40:19 the **b** will eat your flesh
Lev 1:14 offering to the LORD is of **b**
Lev 11:13 as an abomination among the **b**
Lev 11:46 law of the beasts and the **b**
Lev 14: 4 two living and clean **b**, cedar
Lev 14: 5 the **b** be killed in an earthen
Lev 14:49 to cleanse the house, two **b**
Lev 14:50 he shall kill one of the **b** in
Lev 20:25 and unclean, between unclean **b**
Deut 14:11 All clean **b** you may eat
Deut 14:20 You may eat all clean **b**
Deut 28:26 food for all the **b** of the air
1Sa 17:44 flesh to the **b** of the air
1Sa 17:46 to the **b** of the air and the
2Sa 21:10 she did not allow the **b** of
1Ki 4:33 spoke also of animals, of **b**
1Ki 14:11 the **b** of the air shall eat
1Ki 16: 4 the **b** of the air shall eat
1Ki 21:24 the **b** of the air shall eat
Job 12: 7 the **b** of the air, and they
Job 28:21 from the **b** of the air
Job 35:11 us wiser than the **b** of heaven
Ps 8: 8 The **b** of the air, And the fish
Ps 50:11 I know all the **b** of the
Ps 79: 2 food for the **b** of the heavens
Ps 104:12 By them the **b** of the heavens
Ps 104:17 Where the **b** make their nests
Eccl 9:12 like **b** caught in a snare, so
Is 18: 6 for the mountain **b** of prey
Is 18: 6 the **b** of prey will summer on
Is 31: 5 Like **b** flying about, so will
Jer 4:25 all the **b** of the heavens had
Jer 5:27 As a cage is full of **b**, so
Jer 7:33 food for the **b** of the heaven
Jer 9:10 Both the **b** of the heavens and
Jer 12: 4 and **b** are consumed, For the
Jer 15: 3 the **b** of the heavens and the
Jer 16: 4 be meat for the **b** of heaven
Jer 19: 7 meat for the **b** of the heaven
Jer 34:20 meat for the **b** of the heaven
Ezek 13:20 you hunt souls there like **b**
Ezek 13:20 go, the souls you hunt like **b**
Ezek 17:23 it will dwell **b** of every sort
Ezek 29: 5 and to the **b** of the heavens
Ezek 31: 6 All the **b** of the heavens made
Ezek 31:13 all the **b** of the heavens, and
Ezek 32: 4 you all the **b** of the heavens
Ezek 38:20 the **b** of the heavens, the
Ezek 39: 4 I will give you to **b** of prey
Dan 2:38 the **b** of the heaven, He has
Dan 4:12 the **b** of the heavens dwelt in
Dan 4:14 and the **b** from its branches
Dan 4:21 on whose branches the **b** of
Hos 2:18 with the **b** of the air, and
Hos 4: 3 the field and the **b** of the air
Hos 7:12 them down like **b** of the air
Zeph 1: 3 consume the **b** of the heavens
Matt 6:26 Look at the **b** of the air, for
Matt 8:20 **b** of the air have nests, but
Matt 13: 4 the **b** came and devoured them
Matt 13:32 so that the **b** of the air come
Mark 4: 4 and the **b** of the air came and
Mark 4:32 so that the **b** of the air may
Luke 8: 5 the **b** of the air devoured it
Luke 9:58 **b** of the air have nests, but
Luke 12:24 more value are you than the **b**
Luke 13:19 the **b** of the air nested in
Acts 10:12 things, and **b** of the air
Acts 11: 6 things, and **b** of the air
Rom 1:23 and **b** and four-footed beasts
1Co 15:39 of fish, and another of **b**
Rev 19:17 saying to all the **b** that fly
Rev 19:21 all the **b** were filled with

BIRDS' (*see* BIRDS)
Dan 4:33 and his nails like **b** claws

BIRSHA
Gen 14: 2 **B** king of Gomorrah, Shinab

BIRTH (*see* BIRTHDAY, BIRTHRIGHT, BIRTHSTOOLS, BORN, CHILDBIRTH)
Gen 25:24 fulfilled for her to give **b**
Gen 38:27 at the time for giving **b**
Gen 38:28 it was, when she was giving **b**
Ex 1:19 give **b** before the midwives
Ex 21:22 that she gives **b** prematurely
Ex 28:10 stone, according to their **b**
Deut 23: 2 **b** shall not enter the
Ruth 2:11 mother and the land of your **b**
1Sa 4:19 she bowed herself and gave **b**
1Ki 3:17 I gave **b** while she was in the
1Ki 3:18 third day after I had given **b**
1Ki 3:18 that this woman also gave **b**
2Ki 19: 3 the children have come to **b**
Job 3: 1 and cursed the day of his **b**
Job 3:11 Why did I not die at **b**
Job 38:29 of heaven, who gives it **b**
Job 39: 1 mark when the deer gives **b**
Ps 22:10 I was cast upon You from **b**
Ps 29: 9 LORD makes the deer give **b**
Ps 71: 6 I have been upheld from my **b**
Eccl 7: 1 death than the day of one's **b**
Is 37: 3 the children have come to **b**
Is 46: 3 have been upheld by Me from **b**
Is 66: 7 she travailed, she gave **b**
Is 66: 8 be made to give **b** in one day
Is 66: 8 she gave **b** to her children
Is 66: 9 I bring to the time of **b**, and
Jer 2:27 to a stone, 'You gave **b** to me
Jer 14: 5 deer also gave **b** in the field
Jer 48:41 heart of a woman in **b** pangs
Jer 49:22 heart of a woman in **b** pangs
Ezek 16: 3 Your **b** and your nativity are
Hos 9:11 no **b**, no pregnancy, and no
Mic 4:10 Zion, like a woman in **b** pangs
Mic 5: 3 who is in labor has given **b**
Matt 1:18 Now the **b** of Jesus Christ was
Mark 7:26 Greek, a Syro-Phoenician by **b**
Luke 1:14 and many will rejoice at his **b**
John 9: 1 a man who was blind from **b**
John 16:21 she has given **b** to the child
Rom 8:22 labors with **b** pangs together
Gal 4:19 for whom I labor in **b** again
Gal 4:24 which gives **b** to bondage,
Jas 1:15 conceived, it gives **b** to sin
Rev 12: 2 in labor and in pain to give **b**

Rev 12: 4 woman who was ready to give **b**
Rev 12:13 who gave **b** to the male Child

BIRTHDAY (*see* BIRTH)
Gen 40:20 day, which was Pharaoh's **b**
Matt 14: 6 when Herod's **b** was celebrated
Mark 6:21 day came when Herod on his **b**

BIRTHRIGHT (*see* BIRTH)
Gen 25:31 Sell me your **b** as of this day
Gen 25:32 profit shall this **b** be to me
Gen 25:33 him, and sold his **b** to Jacob
Gen 25:34 Thus Esau despised his **b**
Gen 27:36 He took away my **b**, and now
Gen 43:33 firstborn according to his **b**
1Ch 5: 1 his **b** was given to the sons
1Ch 5: 1 not listed according to the **b**
1Ch 5: 2 although the **b** was Joseph's
Heb 12:16 one morsel of food sold his **b**

BIRTHSTOOLS (*see* BIRTH)
Ex 1:16 women, and see them on the **b**

BIRZAITH
1Ch 7:31 who was the father of **B**

BISHLAM
Ezra 4: 7 days of Artaxerxes also, **B**

BISHOP (*see* BISHOPS)
1Ti 3: 1 desires the position of a **b**
1Ti 3: 2 A **b** then must be blameless,
Tit 1: 7 For a **b** must be blameless, as

BISHOPS (*see* BISHOP)
Phil 1: 1 are in Philippi, with the **b**

BIT (*see* BITE, BITS)
Num 21: 6 people, and they **b** the people
Ps 32: 9 must be harnessed with **b** and
Amos 5:19 the wall, and a serpent **b** him

BITE (*see* BIT, BITES, BITTEN)
Eccl 10:11 A serpent may **b** when it is
Jer 8:17 charmed, and they shall **b** you
Amos 9: 3 serpent, and it shall **b** them
Gal 5:15 But if you **b** and devour one

BITES (*see* BITE)
Gen 49:17 that **b** the horse's heels so
Prov 23:32 the last it **b** like a serpent

BITHIAH
1Ch 4:18 these were the sons of **B** the

BITHRON
2Sa 2:29 Jordan, and went through all **B**

BITHYNIA
Acts 16: 7 they tried to go into **B**, but
1Pe 1: 1 Cappadocia, Asia, and **B**,

BITS (*see* BIT)
Amos 6:11 break the great house into **b**
Jas 3: 3 we put **b** in horses' mouths

BITTEN (*see* BITE)
Num 21: 8 be that everyone who is **b**
Num 21: 9 if a serpent had **b** anyone
Eccl 10: 8 a wall will be **b** by a serpent

BITTER (*see* BITTERLY, BITTERNESS)
Gen 27:34 **b** cry, and said to his father,
Ex 1:14 lives **b** with hard bondage
Ex 12: 8 with **b** herbs they shall eat
Ex 15:23 of Marah, for they were **b**
Num 5:18 **b** water that brings a curse
Num 5:19 be free from this **b** water
Num 5:23 them off into the **b** water
Num 5:24 make the woman drink the **b**
Num 5:24 shall enter her to become **b**
Num 5:27 will enter her and become **b**
Num 9:11 unleavened bread and **b** herbs
Deut 32:24 pestilence and **b** destruction
Deut 32:32 of gall, their clusters are **b**
2Sa 2:26 will be **b** in the latter end
2Ki 14:26 of Israel was very **b**
Esth 4: 1 out with a loud and **b** cry
Job 3:20 and life to the **b** of soul
Job 13:26 For You write **b** things
Job 23: 2 Even today my complaint is **b**
Job 27: 2 who has made my soul **b**,
Ps 64: 3 shoot their arrows—**b** words
Prov 5: 4 the end she is **b** as wormwood
Prov 27: 7 soul every **b** thing is sweet
Prov 31: 6 to those who are **b** of heart
Eccl 7:26 I find more **b** than death the
Is 5:20 who put **b** for sweet, and sweet
Is 5:20 for sweet, and sweet for **b**
Is 24: 9 strong drink is **b** to those
Jer 2:19 evil and **b** thing that you have
Jer 4:18 wickedness, Because it is **b**
Jer 6:26 only son, most **b** lamentation
Jer 31:15 **b** weeping, Rachel weeping for
Ezek 27:31 of heart and **b** wailing
Amos 8:10 son, and its end like a **b** day
Mic 2: 4 lament with a **b** lamentation
Hab 1: 6 raising up the Chaldeans, a **b**
Zeph 1:14 of the day of the LORD is **b**
Col 3:19 and do not be **b** toward them
Jas 3:11 and **b** from the same opening
Jas 3:14 But if you have **b** envy and
Rev 8:11 water, because it was made **b**
Rev 10: 9 it will make your stomach **b**
Rev 10:10 eaten it, my stomach became **b**

BITTERLY (*see* BITTER)
Gen 49:23 archers have **b** grieved him
Judg 5:23 curse its inhabitants **b**
Judg 21: 2 up their voices and wept **b**
Ruth 1:20 has dealt very **b** with me
2Sa 13:19 head and went away crying **b**
2Sa 13:36 all his servants wept very **b**
2Ki 20: 3 And Hezekiah wept **b**
Ezra 10: 1 for the people wept very **b**
Neh 13: 8 And it grieved me **b**
Is 15: 3 everyone will wail, weeping **b**
Is 22: 4 away from me, I will weep **b**
Is 33: 7 of peace shall weep **b**
Is 38: 3 And Hezekiah wept **b**
Jer 13:17 my eyes will weep **b** and run
Jer 22:10 but weep **b** for him who goes
Lam 1: 2 She weeps **b** in the night, her
Ezek 27:30 they will cry **b** and cast dust
Hos 12:14 provoked Him to anger most **b**
Matt 26:75 Then he went out and wept **b**
Luke 22:62 Then Peter went out and wept **b**

BITTERN
Zeph 2:14 and the **b** shall lodge on the

BITTERNESS (*see* BITTER)
Deut 29:18 a root bearing **b** or wormwood
1Sa 1:10 And she was in **b** of soul, and
1Sa 15:32 Surely the **b** of death is past
Job 7:11 complain in the **b** of my soul
Job 9:18 breath, but fills me with **b**
Job 10: 1 speak in the **b** of my soul
Job 21:25 man dies in the **b** of his soul
Prov 14:10 The heart knows its own **b**
Prov 17:25 and **b** to her who bore him
Is 38:15 my years in the **b** of my soul
Is 38:17 own peace that I had great **b**
Lam 1: 4 are afflicted, and she is in **b**
Lam 3: 5 me and surrounded me with **b**
Lam 3:15 He has filled me with **b**, He
Ezek 3:14 took me away, and I went in **b**
Ezek 21: 6 sigh with **b** before their eyes
Ezek 27:31 weep for you with **b** of heart
Acts 8:23 that you are poisoned by **b**
Rom 3:14 mouth is full of cursing and **b**
Eph 4:31 Let all **b**, wrath, anger,
Heb 12:15 lest any root of **b** springing

BIZJOTHJAH
Josh 15:28 Hazar Shual, Beersheba, **B**

BIZTHA
Esth 1:10 he commanded Mehuman, **B**

BLACK (*see* BLACKER, BLACKNESS)
Lev 13:31 and there is no **b** hair in it
Lev 13:37 there is **b** hair grown up in
1Ki 18:45 the sky became **b** with clouds
Esth 1: 6 and white and **b** marble
Job 30:30 My skin grows **b** and falls from
Prov 7: 9 in the evening, in the **b**
Song 5:11 are wavy, and **b** as a raven
Is 28:25 does he not sow the **b** cummin
Is 28:27 For the **b** cummin is not
Is 28:27 but the **b** cummin is beaten
Jer 4:28 and the heavens above be **b**
Zech 6: 2 the second chariot **b** horses
Zech 6: 6 The one with the **b** horses is
Matt 5:36 make one hair white or **b**
Rev 6: 5 a **b** horse, and he who sat on
Rev 6:12 the sun became **b** as sackcloth

BLACKER (*see* BLACK)
Lam 4: 8 appearance is **b** than soot

BLACKNESS (*see* BLACK)
Job 3: 5 may the **b** of the day terrify
Is 50: 3 I clothe the heavens with **b**
Is 59: 9 brightness, but we walk in **b**
Heb 12:18 burned with fire, and to **b**
Jude 13 the **b** of darkness forever

BLACKSMITH
1Sa 13:19 Now there was no **b** to be
Is 44:12 The **b** with the tongs works
Is 54:16 I have created the **b** who

BLADE
Judg 3:22 the hilt went in after the **b**
Judg 3:22 and the fat closed over the **b**
Ezek 21:16 Set your **b**!
Mark 4:28 first the **b**, then the head,

BLAME (*see* BLAMED, BLAMELESS)
Gen 43: 9 let me bear the **b** forever
Gen 44:32 you, then I shall bear the **b**
2Co 8:20 that anyone should **b** us in
Eph 1: 4 without **b** before Him in love,

BLAMED (*see* BLAME)
2Co 6: 3 our ministry may not be **b**
Gal 2:11 face, because he was to be **b**

BLAMELESS (*see* BLAME, BLAMELESSLY)
Gen 17: 1 walk before Me and be **b**
Gen 44:10 my slave, and you shall be **b**
Num 32:22 and be **b** before the LORD and
Deut 18:13 You shall be **b** before the
Josh 2:17 We will be **b** of this oath of
Judg 15: 3 This time I shall be **b**
2Sa 22:24 I was also **b** before Him, and I
2Sa 22:26 with a **b** man You will show
2Sa 22:26 man You will show Yourself **b**
Job 1: 1 and that man was **b** and upright,
Job 1: 8 like him on the earth, a **b**
Job 2: 3 like him on the earth, a **b**
Job 8:20 God will not cast away the **b**
Job 9:20 though I were **b**, it would
Job 9:21 I am **b**, yet I do not know
Job 9:22 I say, 'He destroys the **b**
Job 12: 4 **b** who is laughed to scorn
Job 22: 3 Him that you make your ways **b**
Ps 18:23 I was also **b** before Him, And I
Ps 18:25 With a **b** man You will show
Ps 18:25 man You will show Yourself **b**
Ps 19:13 Then I shall be **b**, And I shall
Ps 37:37 Mark the **b** man, and observe
Ps 51: 4 speak, And **b** when You judge
Ps 64: 4 may shoot in secret at the **b**
Ps 119:80 Let my heart be **b** regarding
Prov 2:21 and the **b** will remain in it
Prov 11: 5 The righteousness of the **b**
Prov 11:20 but such as are **b** in their
Prov 13: 6 keeps him whose way is **b**, but
Prov 28:10 But the **b** will inherit good
Prov 29:10 The bloodthirsty hate the **b**
Matt 12: 5 profane the Sabbath, and are **b**
Luke 1: 6 and ordinances of the Lord **b**
1Co 1: 8 that you may be **b** in the day
Phil 2:15 that you may become **b** and
Phil 3: 6 which is in the law, **b**
Col 1:22 to present you holy, and **b**
1Th 3:13 may establish your hearts **b**
1Th 5:23 body be preserved **b** at the
1Ti 3: 2 A bishop then must be **b**, the
1Ti 3:10 as deacons, being found **b**
1Ti 5: 7 command, that they may be **b**
1Ti 6:14 spot, **b** until our Lord Jesus
Tit 1: 6 if a man is **b**, the husband of
Tit 1: 7 For a bishop must be **b**, as a
2Pe 3:14 in peace, without spot and **b**

BLAMELESSLY (*see* BLAMELESS)
Prov 28:18 Whoever walks **b** will be saved
1Th 2:10 **b** we behaved ourselves among

BLANKET
Judg 4:18 she covered him with a **b**

BLASPHEME (*see* BLASPHEMED, BLASPHEMER, BLASPHEMES, BLASPHEMING, BLASPHEMOUS, BLASPHEMY)
2Sa 12:14 the enemies of the LORD to **b**
Ps 74:10 Will the enemy **b** Your name
Acts 26:11 and compelled them to **b**
1Ti 1:20 that they may learn not to **b**
Jas 2: 7 Do they not **b** that noble name
Rev 13: 6 to **b** His name, His tabernacle

BLASPHEMED (*see* BLASPHEME)
Lev 24:11 son **b** the name of the LORD
1Ki 21:10 him, saying, "You have **b** God
1Ki 21:13 Naboth has **b** God and the king
2Ki 19: 6 the king of Assyria have **b** Me
2Ki 19:22 have you reproached and **b**
Ps 74:18 people has **b** Your name
Is 37: 6 the king of Assyria have **b** Me
Is 37:23 have you reproached and **b**
Is 52: 5 And My name is **b** continually
Is 65: 7 and **b** Me on the hills
Ezek 20:27 too your fathers have **b** Me
Matt 27:39 And those who passed by **b** Him
Mark 15:29 And those who passed by **b** Him
Luke 23:39 who were hanged **b** Him, saying
Acts 18: 6 when they opposed him and **b**
Rom 2:24 The name of God is **b** among
1Ti 6: 1 and His doctrine may not be **b**
Tit 2: 5 the word of God may not be **b**
1Pe 4:14 On their part He is **b**, but on
2Pe 2: 2 the way of truth will be **b**
Rev 16: 9 they **b** the name of God who
Rev 16:11 And they **b** the God of heaven
Rev 16:21 And men **b** God because of the

BLASPHEMER (*see* BLASPHEME, BLASPHEMERS)
1Ti 1:13 although I was formerly a **b**

BLASPHEMERS (*see* BLASPHEMER)
Acts 19:37 temples nor **b** of your goddess
2Ti 3: 2 of money, boasters, proud, **b**

BLASPHEMES (*see* BLASPHEME)
Lev 24:16 whoever **b** the name of the
Lev 24:16 When he **b** the name of the
Matt 9: 3 This Man **b**!"
Mark 3:29 but he who **b** against the Holy
Luke 12:10 but to him who **b** against the

BLASPHEMIES (*see* BLASPHEMY)
Ezek 35:12 your **b** which you have spoken
Dan 11:36 shall speak **b** against the God
Matt 15:19 thefts, false witness, **b**
Mark 2: 7 this Man speak **b** like this
Mark 3:28 whatever **b** they may utter
Luke 5:21 Who is this who speaks **b**
Rev 13: 5 speaking great things and **b**

BLASPHEMING (*see* BLASPHEME)
John 10:36 into the world, 'You are **b**
Acts 13:45 and contradicting and **b**, they

BLASPHEMOUS (*see* BLASPHEME, BLASPHEMOUSLY)
Acts 6:11 speak **b** words against Moses
Acts 6:13 **b** words against this holy
Rev 13: 1 and on his heads a **b** name

BLASPHEMOUSLY (*see* BLASPHEMOUS)
Luke 22:65 they **b** spoke against Him

BLASPHEMY (*see* BLASPHEME, BLASPHEMIES)
2Ki 19: 3 of trouble, and rebuke, and **b**
Is 37: 3 day of trouble and rebuke and **b**
Matt 12:31 **b** will be forgiven men, but
Matt 12:31 but the **b** against the Spirit
Matt 26:65 He has spoken **b**
Matt 26:65 now you have heard His **b**
Mark 7:22 an evil eye, **b**, pride,
Mark 14:64 You have heard the **b**
John 10:33 do not stone You, but for **b**
Col 3: 8 anger, wrath, malice, **b**,
Rev 2: 9 I know the **b** of those who say
Rev 13: 6 his mouth in **b** against God
Rev 17: 3 which was full of names of **b**

BLAST (*see* BLASTED, BLASTS)
Ex 15: 8 with the **b** of Your nostrils
Ex 19:19 when the **b** of the trumpet
Josh 6: 5 a long **b** with the ram's horn
2Sa 22:16 at the **b** of the breath of His
Job 4: 9 By the **b** of God they perish,
Job 39:25 At the **b** of the trumpet he
Ps 18:15 At the **b** of the breath of
Is 25: 4 for the **b** of the terrible

BLASTED (*see* BLAST)
Amos 4: 9 I **b** you with blight and mildew

BLASTS (*see* BLAST)
Rev 8:13 because of the remaining **b** of

BLASTUS
Acts 12:20 and having made **B** the king's

BLAZE (*see* BLAZED, BLAZING)
Num 16:37 up the censers out of the **b**

BLAZED (*see* BLAZE)
Lam 2: 3 He has **b** against Jacob like a

BLAZING (*see* BLAZE)
Ezek 20:47 the **b** flame shall not be

BLEAT (*see* BLEATING)
Is 34:14 goat shall **b** to its companion

BLEATING (*see* BLEAT)
1Sa 15:14 What then is this **b** of the

BLEMISH (*see* BLEMISHED, BLEMISHES)
Ex 12: 5 Your lamb shall be without **b**
Ex 29: 1 bull and two rams without **b**
Lev 1: 3 him offer a male without **b**
Lev 1:10 shall bring a male without **b**
Lev 3: 1 it without **b** before the LORD
Lev 3: 6 he shall offer it without **b**
Lev 4: 3 without **b** as a sin offering
Lev 4:23 the goats, a male without **b**
Lev 4:28 the goats, a female without **b**
Lev 4:32 bring a female without **b**
Lev 5:15 ram without **b** from the flocks
Lev 5:18 ram without **b** from the flock
Lev 6: 6 a ram without **b** from the
Lev 9: 2 a burnt offering, without **b**
Lev 9: 3 of the first year, without **b**
Lev 14:10 take two male lambs without **b**
Lev 14:10 of the first year without **b**
Lev 22:19 without **b** from the cattle
Lev 23:12 of the first year, without **b**
Lev 23:18 of the first year, without **b**
Num 6:14 without **b** as a burnt offering
Num 6:14 without **b** as a sin offering
Num 6:14 one ram without **b** as a peace
Num 19: 2 you a red heifer without **b**
Num 28: 3 in their first year without **b**
Num 28: 9 their first year, without **b**
Num 28:11 their first year, without **b**
Num 28:19 Be sure they are without **b**
Num 28:31 Be sure they are without **b**
Num 29: 2 their first year, without **b**
Num 29: 8 Be sure they are without **b**
Num 29:13 They shall be without **b**
Num 29:17 in their first year without **b**
Num 29:20 in their first year without **b**
Num 29:23 their first year, without **b**
Num 29:26 in their first year without **b**
Num 29:29 in their first year without **b**
Num 29:32 in their first year without **b**
Num 29:36 in their first year without **b**
Deut 17: 1 which has any **b** or defect
Deut 32: 5 children, because of their **b**
2Sa 14:25 head there was no **b** in him
Prov 9: 7 a wicked man gets himself a **b**
Ezek 43:22 without **b** for a sin offering
Ezek 43:23 offer a young bull without **b**
Ezek 43:23 ram from the flock without **b**
Ezek 43:25 the flock, both without **b**
Ezek 45:18 take a young bull without **b**
Ezek 45:23 bulls and seven rams without **b**
Ezek 46: 4 shall be six lambs without **b**
Ezek 46: 4 and a ram without **b**
Ezek 46: 6 be a young bull without **b**
Ezek 46: 6 they shall be without **b**
Ezek 46:13 of the first year without **b**
Dan 1: 4 men in whom there was no **b**
Eph 5:27 should be holy and without **b**
1Pe 1:19 as of a lamb without **b** and

BLEMISHED (*see* BLEMISH)
Mal 1:14 to the Lord what is **b**

BLEMISHES (*see* BLEMISH)
2Pe 2:13 They are spots and **b**,

BLENDED
Lev 7:12 or cakes of finely **b** flour
Song 7: 2 which lacks no **b** beverage

BLESS (*see* BLESSED, BLESSEDNESS, BLESSES, BLESSING)
Gen 12: 2 I will **b** you and make your
Gen 12: 3 I will **b** those who **b** you,
Gen 17:16 And I will **b** her and also give
Gen 17:16 then I will **b** her, and she
Gen 22:17 in blessing I will **b** you, and
Gen 26: 3 I will be with you and **b** you
Gen 26:24 I will **b** you and multiply your
Gen 27: 4 soul may **b** you before I die
Gen 27: 7 **b** you in the presence of the
Gen 27:10 that he may **b** you before his
Gen 27:19 game, that your soul may **b** me
Gen 27:25 so that my soul may **b** you
Gen 27:29 and blessed be those who **b** you
Gen 27:31 game, that your soul may **b** me
Gen 27:34 **B** me, even me also, O my
Gen 27:38 **B** me, even me also, O my
Gen 28: 3 May God Almighty **b** you, and
Gen 32:26 let You go unless You **b** me
Gen 48: 9 them to me, and I will **b** them
Gen 48:16 me from all evil, **b** the lads
Gen 48:20 By you Israel will **b**, saying,
Gen 49:25 will **b** you with blessings of
Ex 12:32 and **b** me also
Ex 20:24 come to you, and I will **b** you
Ex 23:25 He will **b** your bread and your
Num 6:23 **b** the children of Israel
Num 6:24 The LORD **b** you and keep you
Num 6:27 of Israel, and I will **b** them
Num 22: 6 that he whom you **b** is blessed
Num 23:20 have received a command to **b**
Num 23:25 at all, nor **b** them at all
Num 24: 1 pleased the LORD to **b** Israel
Deut 1:11 **b** you as He has promised you
Deut 7:13 you and **b** you and multiply you
Deut 7:13 He will also **b** the fruit of
Deut 8:10 then you shall **b** the LORD
Deut 10: 8 to **b** in His name, to this day
Deut 14:29 that the LORD your God may **b**
Deut 15: 4 **b** you in the land which the
Deut 15: 6 For the LORD your God will **b**
Deut 15:10 will **b** you in all your works
Deut 15:18 will **b** you in all that you do
Deut 16:15 the LORD your God will **b** you
Deut 21: 5 to **b** in the name of the LORD
Deut 23:20 that the LORD your God may **b**
Deut 24:13 in his own garment and **b** you
Deut 24:19 that the LORD your God may **b**
Deut 26:15 **b** Your people Israel and the
Deut 27:12 Mount Gerizim to **b** the people
Deut 28: 8 He will **b** you in the land
Deut 28:12 to **b** all the work of your
Deut 30:16 the LORD your God will **b** you
Deut 33:11 **B** his substance, LORD, and
Josh 8:33 that they should **b** the people
Josh 24:10 he continued to **b** you
Judg 5: 2 offer themselves, **b** the LORD
Judg 5: 9 **B** the LORD!
Ruth 2: 4 The LORD **b** you
1Sa 2:20 And Eli would **b** Elkanah and
1Sa 9:13 he must **b** the sacrifice
2Sa 6:20 returned to **b** his household
2Sa 7:29 let it please You to **b** the
2Sa 8:10 **b** him, because he had fought
2Sa 21: 3 atonement, that you may **b** the
1Ki 1:47 gone to **b** our lord King David
1Ch 4:10 that You would **b** me indeed
1Ch 16:43 David returned to **b** his house
1Ch 17:27 You have been pleased to **b**
1Ch 18:10 **b** him, because he had fought
1Ch 29:20 Now **b** the LORD your God
Neh 9: 5 **b** the LORD your God forever
Ps 5:12 O LORD, will **b** the righteous
Ps 16: 7 I will **b** the LORD who has
Ps 26:12 I will **b** the LORD
Ps 28: 9 people, And **b** Your inheritance
Ps 29:11 The LORD will **b** His people
Ps 34: 1 I will **b** the LORD at all
Ps 62: 4 They **b** with their mouth, But
Ps 63: 4 Thus I will **b** You while I
Ps 65:10 showers, You **b** its growth
Ps 66: 8 Oh, **b** our God, you peoples
Ps 67: 1 **b** us, And cause His face to
Ps 67: 6 God, our own God, shall **b** us
Ps 67: 7 God shall **b** us, And all the
Ps 68:26 **B** God in the congregations,
Ps 96: 2 Sing to the LORD, **b** His name
Ps 100: 4 to Him, and **b** His name
Ps 103: 1 **B** the LORD, O my soul
Ps 103: 1 is within me, **b** His holy name
Ps 103: 2 **B** the LORD, O my soul, And
Ps 103:20 **B** the LORD, you His angels,
Ps 103:21 **B** the LORD, all you His hosts
Ps 103:22 **B** the LORD, all His works, In
Ps 103:22 **B** the LORD, O my soul
Ps 104: 1 **B** the LORD, O my soul
Ps 104:35 **B** the LORD, O my soul

Ps 109:28 Let them curse, but You **b**
Ps 115:12 He will **b** us
Ps 115:12 He will **b** the house of Israel
Ps 115:12 He will **b** the house of Aaron
Ps 115:13 He will **b** those who fear the
Ps 115:18 But we will **b** the LORD From
Ps 128: 5 The LORD **b** you out of Zion,
Ps 129: 8 We **b** you in the name of the
Ps 132:15 abundantly **b** her provision
Ps 134: 1 **b** the LORD, All you servants
Ps 134: 2 the sanctuary, And **b** the LORD
Ps 134: 3 and earth **B** you from Zion
Ps 135:19 **B** the LORD, O house of Israel
Ps 135:19 **B** the LORD, O house of Aaron
Ps 135:20 **B** the LORD, O house of Levi
Ps 135:20 who fear the LORD, **b** the LORD
Ps 145: 1 I will **b** Your name forever and
Ps 145: 2 Every day I will **b** You, And I
Ps 145:10 And Your saints shall **b** You
Ps 145:21 all flesh shall **b** His holy
Prov 30:11 and does not **b** its mother
Is 19:25 the LORD of hosts shall **b**
Is 65:16 himself in the earth shall **b**
Jer 4: 2 shall **b** themselves in Him
Jer 31:23 The LORD **b** you, O habitation
Hag 2:19 this day forward I will **b** you
Matt 5:44 **b** those who curse you, do
Luke 6:28 **b** those who curse you, and
Acts 3:26 Jesus, sent Him to **b** you, in
Rom 12:14 **B** those who persecute you
Rom 12:14 **b** and do not curse
1Co 4:12 Being reviled, we **b**
1Co 10:16 cup of blessing which we **b**
1Co 14:16 if you **b** with the spirit, how
Heb 6:14 Surely blessing I will **b** you
Jas 3: 9 With it we **b** our God and

BLESSED (*see* BLESS)
Gen 1:22 And God **b** them, saying,
Gen 1:28 Then God **b** them, and God said
Gen 2: 3 Then God **b** the seventh day and
Gen 5: 2 **b** them and called them
Gen 9: 1 So God **b** Noah and his sons, and
Gen 9:26 **B** be the LORD, the God of
Gen 12: 3 of the earth shall be **b**
Gen 14:19 And he **b** him and said
Gen 14:19 **B** be Abram of God Most High,
Gen 14:20 **b** be God Most High, Who has
Gen 17:20 Behold, I have **b** him, and will
Gen 18:18 the earth shall be **b** in him
Gen 22:18 of the earth shall be **b**,
Gen 24: 1 the LORD had **b** Abraham in all
Gen 24:27 **B** be the LORD God of my
Gen 24:31 Come in, O **b** of the LORD
Gen 24:35 The LORD has **b** my master
Gen 24:48 **b** the LORD God of my master
Gen 24:60 they **b** Rebekah and said to her
Gen 25:11 that God **b** his son Isaac
Gen 26: 4 of the earth shall be **b**
Gen 26:12 and the LORD **b** him
Gen 26:29 You are now the **b** of the LORD
Gen 27:23 so he **b** him
Gen 27:27 clothing, and **b** him and said
Gen 27:27 a field which the LORD has **b**
Gen 27:29 and **b** be those who bless you
Gen 27:33 you came, and I have **b** him
Gen 27:33 and indeed he shall be **b**
Gen 27:41 with which his father **b** him
Gen 28: 1 **b** him, and charged him, and
Gen 28: 6 saw that Isaac had **b** Jacob
Gen 28: 6 that as he **b** him he gave him
Gen 28:14 of the earth shall be **b**
Gen 30:13 the daughters will call me **b**
Gen 30:27 LORD has **b** me for your sake
Gen 30:30 the LORD has **b** you since my
Gen 31:55 sons and daughters and **b** them
Gen 32:29 And He **b** him there
Gen 35: 9 from Padan Aram, and **b** him
Gen 39: 5 he had, that the LORD **b** the
Gen 47: 7 and Jacob **b** Pharaoh
Gen 47:10 So Jacob **b** Pharaoh, and went
Gen 48: 3 the land of Canaan and **b** me,
Gen 48:15 And he **b** Joseph, and said
Gen 48:20 So he **b** them that day, saying
Gen 49:28 And he **b** them
Gen 49:28 he **b** each one according to
Ex 18:10 **B** be the LORD, who has
Ex 20:11 the LORD **b** the Sabbath day
Ex 39:43 And Moses **b** them
Lev 9:22 **b** them, and came down from
Lev 9:23 and came out and **b** the people

Num 22: 6 that he whom you bless is **b**
Num 22:12 the people, for they are **b**
Num 23:11 you have **b** them bountifully
Num 23:20 He has **b**, and I cannot reverse
Num 24: 9 **B** is he who blesses you, and
Num 24:10 you have bountifully **b** them
Deut 2: 7 For the LORD your God has **b**
Deut 7:14 You shall be **b** above all
Deut 12: 7 the LORD your God has **b** you
Deut 14:24 the LORD your God has **b** you
Deut 15:14 what the LORD has **b** you with
Deut 28: 3 **B** shall you be in the city,
Deut 28: 3 **b** shall you be in the country
Deut 28: 4 **B** shall be the fruit of your
Deut 28: 5 **B** shall be your basket and
Deut 28: 6 **B** shall you be when you come
Deut 28: 6 **b** shall you be when you go
Deut 33: 1 God **b** the children of Israel
Deut 33:13 **B** of the LORD is his land,
Deut 33:20 **B** is he who enlarges Gad
Deut 33:24 Asher is most **b** of sons
Josh 14:13 And Joshua **b** him, and gave
Josh 17:14 the LORD has **b** us until now
Josh 22: 6 So Joshua **b** them and sent them
Josh 22: 7 to their tents, he **b** them,
Josh 22:33 the children of Israel **b** God
Judg 5:24 Most **b** among women is Jael,
Judg 5:24 **b** is she among women in tents
Judg 13:24 child grew, and the LORD **b** him
Judg 17: 2 May you be **b** by the LORD, my
Ruth 2:19 **B** be the one who took notice
Ruth 2:20 **B** be he of the LORD, who has
Ruth 3:10 **B** are you of the LORD, my
Ruth 4:14 **B** be the LORD, who has not
1Sa 15:13 him, "**B** are you of the LORD
1Sa 23:21 **B** are you of the LORD, for
1Sa 25:32 **B** be the LORD God of Israel,
1Sa 25:33 **b** is your advice and **b**
1Sa 25:33 **b** are you, because you have
1Sa 25:39 **B** be the LORD, who has
1Sa 26:25 May you be **b**, my son David
2Sa 2: 5 You are **b** of the LORD, for
2Sa 6:11 the LORD **b** Obed-Edom and all
2Sa 6:12 The LORD has **b** the house of
2Sa 6:18 he **b** the people in the name
2Sa 7:29 of Your servant be **b** forever
2Sa 13:25 and he **b** him
2Sa 18:28 **B** be the LORD your God, who
2Sa 19:39 **b** him, and he returned to his
2Sa 22:47 **B** be my Rock
1Ki 1:48 **B** be the LORD God of Israel,
1Ki 2:45 But King Solomon shall be **b**
1Ki 5: 7 **B** be the LORD this day, for
1Ki 8:14 **b** the whole congregation of
1Ki 8:15 **B** be the LORD God of Israel,
1Ki 8:55 **b** all the congregation of
1Ki 8:56 **B** be the LORD, who has given
1Ki 8:66 they **b** the king, and went to
1Ki 10: 9 **B** be the LORD your God, who
1Ch 13:14 And the LORD **b** the house of
1Ch 16: 2 he **b** the people in the name
1Ch 16:36 **B** be the LORD God of Israel
1Ch 17:27 for You have **b** it, O LORD, and
1Ch 17:27 and it shall be **b** forever
1Ch 26: 5 for God **b** him
1Ch 29:10 Therefore David **b** the LORD
1Ch 29:10 **B** are You, LORD God of Israel
1Ch 29:20 **b** the LORD God of their
2Ch 2:12 **B** be the LORD God of Israel,
2Ch 6: 3 **b** the whole congregation of
2Ch 6: 4 **B** be the LORD God of Israel,
2Ch 9: 8 **B** be the LORD your God, who
2Ch 20:26 for there they **b** the LORD
2Ch 30:27 **b** the people, and their voice
2Ch 31: 8 they **b** the LORD and His people
2Ch 31:10 for the LORD has **b** His people
Ezra 7:27 **B** be the LORD God of our
Neh 8: 6 Ezra **b** the LORD, the great
Neh 9: 5 **B** be Your glorious name,
Neh 11: 2 the people **b** all the men who
Job 1:10 You have **b** the work of his
Job 1:21 **b** be the name of the LORD
Job 29:11 the ear heard, then it **b** me
Job 31:20 if his heart has not **b** me
Job 42:12 Now the LORD **b** the latter
Ps 1: 1 **B** is the man Who walks not in
Ps 2:12 **B** are all those who put their
Ps 18:46 **B** be my Rock
Ps 21: 6 have made him most **b** forever
Ps 28: 6 **B** be the LORD, Because He has

Ps 31:21 **B** be the LORD, For He has
Ps 32: 1 **B** is he whose transgression
Ps 32: 2 **B** is the man to whom the LORD
Ps 33:12 **B** is the nation whose God is
Ps 34: 8 **B** is the man who trusts in
Ps 37:22 For those who are **b** by Him
Ps 37:26 And his descendants are **b**
Ps 40: 4 **B** is that man who makes the
Ps 41: 1 **B** is he who considers the
Ps 41: 2 he will be **b** on the earth
Ps 41:13 **B** be the LORD God of Israel
Ps 45: 2 God has **b** You forever
Ps 65: 4 **B** is the man whom You choose,
Ps 66:20 **B** be God, Who has not turned
Ps 68:19 **B** be the Lord, Who daily
Ps 68:35 **B** be God!
Ps 72:17 And men shall be **b** in Him
Ps 72:17 All nations shall call Him **b**
Ps 72:18 **B** be the LORD God, the God of
Ps 72:19 And **b** be His glorious name
Ps 84: 4 **B** are those who dwell in Your
Ps 84: 5 **B** is the man whose strength
Ps 84:12 **B** is the man who trusts in
Ps 89:15 **B** are the people who know the
Ps 89:52 **B** be the LORD forevermore
Ps 94:12 **B** is the man whom You
Ps 106: 3 **B** are those who keep justice,
Ps 106:48 **B** be the LORD God of Israel
Ps 112: 1 **B** is the man who fears the
Ps 112: 2 of the upright will be **b**
Ps 113: 2 **B** be the name of the LORD
Ps 115:15 May you be **b** by the LORD, Who
Ps 118:26 **B** is he who comes in the name
Ps 118:26 We have **b** you from the house
Ps 119: 1 **B** are the undefiled in the
Ps 119: 2 **B** are those who keep His
Ps 119:12 **B** are You, O LORD
Ps 124: 6 **B** be the LORD, Who has not
Ps 128: 1 **B** is every one who fears the
Ps 128: 4 man be **b** Who fears the LORD
Ps 135:21 **B** be the LORD out of Zion,
Ps 144: 1 **B** be the LORD my Rock, Who
Ps 147:13 He has **b** your children within
Prov 5:18 Let your fountain be **b**, and
Prov 8:32 for **b** are those who keep my
Prov 8:34 **B** is the man who listens to
Prov 10: 7 memory of the righteous is **b**
Prov 20: 7 his children are **b** after him
Prov 20:21 will not be **b** at the end
Prov 22: 9 has a bountiful eye will be **b**
Prov 31:28 rise up and call her **b**
Eccl 10:17 **B** are you, O land, when your
Song 6: 9 saw her and called her **b**, the
Is 19:25 **B** is Egypt My people, and
Is 30:18 **b** are all those who wait for
Is 32:20 **B** are you who sow beside all
Is 51: 2 and **b** him and increased him
Is 56: 2 **B** is the man who does this,
Is 61: 9 posterity whom the LORD has **b**
Is 65:23 of the **b** of the LORD, and
Jer 17: 7 **B** is the man who trusts in
Jer 20:14 Let the day not be **b** in which
Ezek 3:12 **B** is the glory of the LORD
Dan 2:19 So Daniel **b** the God of heaven
Dan 2:20 **B** be the name of God forever
Dan 3:28 **B** be the God of Shadrach,
Dan 4:34 I **b** the Most High and praised
Dan 12:12 **B** is he who waits, and comes
Zech 11: 5 **B** be the LORD, for I am rich
Mal 3:12 all nations will call you **b**
Mal 3:15 So now we call the proud **b**
Matt 5: 3 **B** are the poor in spirit, for
Matt 5: 4 **B** are those who mourn, for
Matt 5: 5 **B** are the meek, for they
Matt 5: 6 **B** are those who hunger and
Matt 5: 7 **B** are the merciful, for they
Matt 5: 8 **B** are the pure in heart, for
Matt 5: 9 **B** are the peacemakers, for
Matt 5:10 **B** are those who are
Matt 5:11 **B** are you when they revile and
Matt 11: 6 **b** is he who is not offended
Matt 13:16 But **b** are your eyes for they
Matt 14:19 and looking up to heaven, He **b**
Matt 16:17 **B** are you, Simon Bar-Jonah,
Matt 21: 9 **B** is He who comes in the
Matt 23:39 **B** is He who comes in the
Matt 24:46 **B** is that servant whom his
Matt 25:34 you **b** of My Father, inherit
Matt 26:26 **b** it and broke it, and gave it
Mark 6:41 He looked up to heaven, **b**

Mark 8: 7 and having **b** them, He said to
Mark 10:16 His hands on them, and **b** them
Mark 11: 9 **B** is He who comes in the
Mark 11:10 **B** is the kingdom of our
Mark 14:22 **b** it and broke it, and gave it
Mark 14:61 the Christ, the Son of the **B**
Luke 1:28 **b** are you among women
Luke 1:42 **B** are you among women, and
Luke 1:42 **b** is the fruit of your womb
Luke 1:45 **B** is she who believed, for
Luke 1:48 generations will call me **b**
Luke 1:68 **B** is the Lord God of Israel,
Luke 2:28 in his arms and **b** God and said
Luke 2:34 Then Simeon **b** them, and said
Luke 6:20 **B** are you poor, for yours is
Luke 6:21 **B** are you who hunger now, for
Luke 6:21 **B** are you who weep now, for
Luke 6:22 **B** are you when men hate you,
Luke 7:23 **b** is he who is not offended
Luke 9:16 and looking up to heaven, He **b**
Luke 10:23 **B** are the eyes which see the
Luke 11:27 **B** is the womb that bore You,
Luke 11:28 **b** are those who hear the word
Luke 12:37 **B** are those servants whom the
Luke 12:38 them so, **b** are those servants
Luke 12:43 **B** is that servant whom his
Luke 13:35 **B** is He who Comes in the
Luke 14:14 And you will be **b**, because
Luke 14:15 **B** is he who shall eat bread
Luke 19:38 **B** is the King who comes in
Luke 23:29 **B** are the barren, the wombs
Luke 24:30 them, that He took bread, **b**
Luke 24:50 lifted up His hands and **b** them
Luke 24:51 came to pass, while He **b** them
John 12:13 **B** is He who comes in the
John 20:29 **B** are those who have not seen
Acts 3:25 of the earth shall be **b**
Acts 20:35 It is more **b** to give than to
Rom 1:25 the Creator, who is **b** forever
Rom 4: 7 **B** are those whose lawless
Rom 4: 8 **b** is the man to whom the LORD
Rom 9: 5 over all, the eternally **b** God
2Co 1: 3 **B** be the God and Father of our
2Co 11:31 who is **b** forever, knows that
Gal 3: 8 all the nations shall be **b**
Gal 3: 9 are **b** with believing Abraham
Eph 1: 3 **B** be the God and Father of our
Eph 1: 3 who has **b** us with every
1Ti 1:11 **b** God which was committed to
1Ti 6:15 His own time, He who is the **b**
Tit 2:13 looking for the **b** hope and
Heb 7: 1 of the kings and **b** him,
Heb 7: 6 **b** him who had the promises
Heb 7: 7 the lesser is **b** by the better
Heb 11:20 By faith Isaac **b** Jacob and
Heb 11:21 **b** each of the sons of Joseph,
Jas 1:12 **B** is the man who endures
Jas 1:25 one will be **b** in what he does
Jas 5:11 we count them **b** who endure
1Pe 1: 3 **B** be the God and Father of our
1Pe 3:14 sake, you are **b**
1Pe 4:14 **b** are you, for the Spirit of
Rev 1: 3 **B** is he who reads and those
Rev 14:13 **B** are the dead who die in
Rev 16:15 **B** is he who watches, and keeps
Rev 19: 9 **B** are those who are called
Rev 20: 6 **B** and holy is he who has part
Rev 22: 7 **B** is he who keeps the words
Rev 22:14 **B** are those who do His

BLESSEDNESS (*see* BLESS)
Rom 4: 6 the **b** of the man to whom God
Rom 4: 9 Does this **b** then come upon

BLESSES (*see* BLESS)
Num 24: 9 Blessed is he who **b** you, and
Deut 16:10 as the LORD your God **b** you
Deut 29:19 that he **b** himself in his
Ps 10: 3 He **b** the greedy and renounces
Ps 49:18 he **b** himself (For men will
Ps 107:38 He also **b** them, and they
Prov 3:33 but He **b** the habitation of
Prov 27:14 He who **b** his friend with a
Is 65:16 So that he who **b** himself in
Is 66: 3 incense, as if he **b** an idol

BLESSING (*see* BLESS, BLESSINGS)
Gen 12: 2 and you shall be a **b**
Gen 22:17 in **b** I will bless you, and in
Gen 27:12 a curse on myself and not a **b**
Gen 27:30 as Isaac had finished **b** Jacob
Gen 27:35 and has taken away your **b**
Gen 27:36 look, he has taken away my **b**
Gen 27:36 you not reserved a **b** for me
Gen 27:38 Have you only one **b**, my
Gen 27:41 the **b** with which his father
Gen 28: 4 and give you the **b** of Abraham
Gen 33:11 take my **b** that is brought to
Gen 39: 5 the **b** of the LORD was on all
Gen 49:28 one according to his own **b**
Ex 32:29 bestow on you a **b** this day
Lev 25:21 Then I will command My **b** on
Deut 11:26 I set before you today a **b**
Deut 11:27 the **b**, if you obey the
Deut 11:29 put the **b** on Mount Gerizim
Deut 12:15 according to the **b** of the
Deut 16:17 according to the **b** of the
Deut 23: 5 the curse into a **b** for you
Deut 28: 8 The LORD will command the **b**
Deut 30: 1 things come upon you, the **b**
Deut 30:19 before you life and death, **b**
Deut 33: 1 Now this is the **b** with which
Deut 33:16 Let the **b** come on the head
Deut 33:23 and full of the **b** of the LORD
Josh 15:19 Give me a **b**
Judg 1:15 Give me a **b**
2Sa 7:29 with Your **b** let the house of
1Ch 23:13 to give the **b** in His name
Neh 9: 5 which is exalted above all **b**
Neh 13: 2 God turned the curse into a **b**
Job 29:13 The **b** of a perishing man came
Ps 3: 8 Your **b** is upon Your people
Ps 24: 5 shall receive **b** from the LORD
Ps 109:17 As he did not delight in **b**
Ps 129: 8 The **b** of the LORD be upon you
Ps 133: 3 the LORD commanded the **b**
Prov 10:22 The **b** of the LORD makes one
Prov 11:11 By the **b** of the upright the
Prov 11:26 but **b** will be on the head of
Prov 24:25 a good **b** will come upon them
Is 19:24 even a **b** in the midst of the
Is 44: 3 and My **b** on your offspring
Is 65: 8 for a **b** is in it,' so will I
Ezek 34:26 places all around My hill a **b**
Ezek 34:26 there shall be showers of **b**
Ezek 44:30 to cause a **b** to rest on your
Joel 2:14 and leave a **b** behind Him
Zech 8:13 save you, and you shall be a **b**
Mal 3:10 pour out for you such **b** That
Luke 24:53 the temple praising and **b** God
Rom 15:29 the **b** of the gospel of Christ
1Co 10:16 The cup of **b** which we bless,
Gal 3:14 that the **b** of Abraham might
Gal 4:15 then was the **b** you enjoyed
Eph 1: 3 us with every spiritual **b** in
Heb 6: 7 receives **b** from God
Heb 6:14 Surely **b** I will bless you, and
Heb 12:17 he wanted to inherit the **b**
Jas 3:10 of the same mouth proceed **b**
1Pe 3: 9 but on the contrary **b**,
1Pe 3: 9 that you may inherit a **b**
Rev 5:12 and honor and glory and **b**
Rev 5:13 **B** and honor and glory and
Rev 7:12 **B** and glory and wisdom,

BLESSINGS (*see* BLESSING)
Gen 49:25 you with **b** of heaven above
Gen 49:25 **b** of the deep that lies
Gen 49:25 **b** of the breasts and of the
Gen 49:26 The **b** of your father have
Gen 49:26 the **b** of my ancestors, up to
Deut 28: 2 all these **b** shall come upon
Josh 8:34 the words of the law, the **b**
Ps 21: 3 him with the **b** of goodness
Prov 10: 6 **B** are on the head of the
Prov 28:20 man will abound with **b**, but
Mal 2: 2 you, and I will curse your **b**

BLEW (*see* BLOW)
Ex 10:19 and **b** them into the Red Sea
Ex 15:10 You **b** with Your wind, the sea
Josh 6: 8 **b** the trumpets, and the ark of
Josh 6: 9 priests who **b** the trumpets
Josh 6:13 and **b** with the trumpets
Josh 6:16 the priests **b** the trumpets
Josh 6:20 the priests **b** the trumpets
Judg 3:27 that he **b** the trumpet in the
Judg 6:34 then he **b** the trumpet, and the
Judg 7:19 they **b** the trumpets and broke
Judg 7:20 companies **b** the trumpets and
Judg 7:22 three hundred **b** the trumpets
1Sa 13: 3 Then Saul **b** the trumpet
2Sa 2:28 So Joab **b** a trumpet
2Sa 18:16 Then Joab **b** the trumpet, and
2Sa 20: 1 And he **b** a trumpet, and said
2Sa 20:22 Then he **b** a trumpet, and they
1Ki 1:39 they **b** the horn, and all the
2Ki 9:13 and they **b** trumpets, saying,
1Ch 16: 6 the priests regularly **b** the
Hag 1: 9 brought it home, I **b** it away
Matt 7:25 floods came, and the winds **b**
Matt 7:27 floods came, and the winds **b**
Acts 27:13 When the south wind **b** softly
Acts 28:13 one day the south wind **b**

BLIGHT (*see* BLIGHTED)
1Ki 8:37 **b** or mildew, locusts or
2Ch 6:28 pestilence or **b** or mildew
Amos 4: 9 I blasted you with **b** and
Hag 2:17 I struck you with **b** and

BLIGHTED (*see* BLIGHT)
Gen 41: 6 **b** by the east wind, sprang up
Gen 41:23 **b** by the east wind, sprang up
Gen 41:27 the seven empty heads **b** by
2Ki 19:26 grain **b** before it is grown
Is 37:27 as grain **b** before it is grown

BLIND (*see* BLINDED, BLINDFOLD, BLINDNESS, BLINDS)
Ex 4:11 deaf, the seeing, or the **b**
Lev 19:14 a stumblingblock before the **b**
Lev 21:18 a man **b** or lame, who has a
Lev 22:22 Those that are **b** or broken
Deut 15:21 if it is lame or **b** or has any
Deut 27:18 the **b** to wander off the road
Deut 28:29 as a **b** man gropes in darkness
1Sa 12: 3 bribe with which to **b** my eyes
2Sa 5: 6 but the **b** and the lame will
2Sa 5: 8 Jebusites (the lame and the **b**
2Sa 5: 8 The **b** and the lame shall not
Job 29:15 I was eyes to the **b**, and I was
Ps 146: 8 LORD opens the eyes of the **b**
Is 29: 9 **B** yourselves and be **b**
Is 29: 9 **B** yourselves and be **b**
Is 29:18 the eyes of the **b** shall see
Is 35: 5 eyes of the **b** shall be opened
Is 42: 7 To open **b** eyes, to bring out
Is 42:16 I will bring the **b** by a way
Is 42:18 and look, you **b**, that you may
Is 42:19 Who is **b** but My servant, or
Is 42:19 Who is **b** as he who is perfect
Is 42:19 and **b** as the LORD's servant
Is 43: 8 Bring out the **b** people who
Is 56:10 His watchmen are **b**, they are
Is 59:10 grope for the wall like the **b**
Jer 31: 8 the earth, among them the **b**
Lam 4:14 They wandered **b** in the
Zeph 1:17 and they shall walk like **b** men
Mal 1: 8 offer the **b** as a sacrifice
Matt 9:27 two **b** men followed Him,
Matt 9:28 house, the **b** men came to Him
Matt 11: 5 The **b** receive their sight and
Matt 12:22 who was demon-possessed, **b**
Matt 12:22 He healed him, so that the **b**
Matt 15:14 are **b** leaders of the **b**
Matt 15:14 And if the **b** leads the **b**
Matt 15:30 them those who were lame, **b**
Matt 15:31 lame walking, and the **b** seeing
Matt 20:30 two **b** men sitting by the road
Matt 21:14 Then the **b** and the lame came
Matt 23:16 **b** guides, who say, "Whoever
Matt 23:17 Fools and **b**!
Matt 23:19 Fools and **b**!
Matt 23:24 **B** guides, who strain out a
Matt 23:26 **B** Pharisee, first cleanse the
Mark 8:22 they brought a **b** man to Him
Mark 8:23 So He took the **b** man by the
Mark 10:46 **b** Bartimaeus, the son of
Mark 10:49 Then they called the **b** man
Mark 10:51 The **b** man said to Him,
Luke 4:18 and recovery of sight to the **b**
Luke 6:39 Can the **b** lead the **b**
Luke 6:39 Can the **b** lead the **b**
Luke 7:21 many who were **b** He gave sight
Luke 7:22 that the **b** see, the lame walk
Luke 14:13 the maimed, the lame, the **b**
Luke 14:21 maimed and the lame and the **b**
Luke 18:35 that a certain **b** man sat by
John 5: 3 multitude of sick people, **b**
John 9: 1 a man who was **b** from birth
John 9: 2 parents, that he was born **b**
John 9: 6 of the **b** man with the clay
John 9: 8 had seen that he was **b** said
John 9:13 was **b** to the Pharisees

John 9:17 They said to the **b** man again
John 9:18 him, that he had been **b** and
John 9:19 son, who you say was born **b**
John 9:20 son, and that he was born **b**
John 9:24 called the man who was **b**, and
John 9:25 that though I was **b**, now I
John 9:32 eyes of one who was born **b**
John 9:39 those who see may be made **b**
John 9:40 Are we **b** also
John 9:41 If you were **b**, you would have
John 10:21 demon open the eyes of the **b**
John 11:37 who opened the eyes of the **b**
Acts 13:11 upon you, and you shall be **b**
Rom 2:19 yourself are a guide to the **b**
Rev 3:17 wretched, miserable, poor, **b**

BLINDED (*see* BLIND)
Zech 11:17 right eye shall be totally **b**
John 12:40 He has **b** their eyes and
2Co 4: 4 the god of this age has **b**
1Jn 2:11 the darkness has **b** his eyes

BLINDFOLD (*see* BLIND, BLINDFOLDED)
Mark 14:65 to **b** Him, and to beat Him, and

BLINDFOLDED (*see* BLINDFOLD)
Luke 22:64 And having **b** Him, they struck

BLINDNESS (*see* BLIND)
Gen 19:11 doorway of the house with **b**
Deut 28:28 strike you with madness and **b**
2Ki 6:18 this people, I pray, with **b**
2Ki 6:18 And He struck them with **b**
Zech 12: 4 horse of the peoples with **b**
2Pe 1: 9 is shortsighted, even to **b**

BLINDS (*see* BLIND)
Ex 23: 8 for a bribe **b** the discerning
Deut 16:19 for a bribe **b** the eyes of the

BLOCK (*see* BLOCKED, BLOCKS)
Is 44:19 fall down before a **b** of wood
Is 57:14 take the stumbling **b** out of
Ezek 3:20 lay a stumbling **b** before him
Ezek 7:19 their stumbling **b** of iniquity
Rom 11: 9 and a trap, a stumbling **b** and a
Rom 14:13 not to put a stumbling **b** or a
1Co 1:23 to the Jews a stumbling **b**
1Co 8: 9 **b** to those who are weak
Rev 2:14 **b** before the children of

BLOCKED (*see* BLOCK)
Jer 51:32 The passages are **b**, the reeds
Lam 3: 9 He has **b** my ways with hewn

BLOCKS (*see* BLOCK)
Jer 6:21 **b** before this people, And the
Zeph 1: 3 the stumbling **b** along with

BLOOD (*see* BLOODGUILT, BLOODLINE, BLOODSHED, BLOODTHIRSTY, BLOODY, LIFEBLOOD)
Gen 4:10 **b** cries out to Me from the
Gen 4:11 brother's **b** from your hand
Gen 9: 4 with its life, that is, its **b**
Gen 9: 6 Whoever sheds man's **b**, by man
Gen 9: 6 by man his **b** shall be shed
Gen 37:22 Shed no **b**, but cast him into
Gen 37:26 our brother and conceal his **b**
Gen 37:31 and dipped the tunic in the **b**
Gen 42:22 his **b** is now required of us
Gen 49:11 clothes in the **b** of grapes
Ex 4: 9 will become **b** on the dry land
Ex 4:25 you are a husband of **b** to me
Ex 4:26 You are a husband of **b**
Ex 7:17 and they shall be turned to **b**
Ex 7:19 water, that they may become **b**
Ex 7:19 there shall be **b** throughout
Ex 7:20 in the river were turned to **b**
Ex 7:21 So there was **b** throughout all
Ex 12: 7 they shall take some of the **b**
Ex 12:13 Now the **b** shall be a sign
Ex 12:13 And when I see the **b**, I will
Ex 12:22 dip it in the **b** that is in
Ex 12:22 the **b** that is in the basin
Ex 12:23 He sees the **b** on the lintel
Ex 23:18 the **b** of My sacrifice with
Ex 24: 6 And Moses took half the **b** and
Ex 24: 6 half the **b** he sprinkled on
Ex 24: 8 And Moses took the **b**,
Ex 24: 8 the **b** of the covenant which
Ex 29:12 some of the **b** of the bull
Ex 29:12 pour all the **b** beside the
Ex 29:16 ram, and you shall take its **b**
Ex 29:20 ram, and take some of its **b**
Ex 29:20 sprinkle the **b** all around on
Ex 29:21 of the **b** that is on the altar
Ex 30:10 the **b** of the sin offering of
Ex 34:25 You shall not offer the **b** of
Lev 1: 5 sons, shall bring the **b** and
Lev 1: 5 sprinkle the **b** all around on
Lev 1:11 shall sprinkle its **b** all
Lev 1:15 its **b** shall be drained out at
Lev 3: 2 shall sprinkle the **b** all
Lev 3: 8 its **b** all around on the altar
Lev 3:13 its **b** all around on the altar
Lev 3:17 shall eat neither fat nor **b**
Lev 4: 5 take some of the bull's **b**
Lev 4: 6 shall dip his finger in the **b**
Lev 4: 6 sprinkle some of the **b** seven
Lev 4: 7 shall put some of the **b** on
Lev 4: 7 **b** of the bull at the base of
Lev 4:16 bull's **b** to the tabernacle of
Lev 4:17 shall dip his finger in the **b**
Lev 4:18 he shall put some of the **b** on
Lev 4:18 **b** at the base of the altar of
Lev 4:25 shall take some of the **b** of
Lev 4:25 pour its **b** at the base of the
Lev 4:30 some of its **b** with his finger
Lev 4:30 pour its remaining **b** at the
Lev 4:34 shall take some of the **b** of
Lev 4:34 pour its remaining **b** at the
Lev 5: 9 **b** of the sin offering on the
Lev 5: 9 the rest of the **b** shall be
Lev 6:27 when its **b** is sprinkled on
Lev 6:30 of the **b** is brought into the
Lev 7: 2 its **b** he shall sprinkle all
Lev 7:14 the **b** of the peace offering
Lev 7:26 you shall not eat any **b** in
Lev 7:27 Whoever eats any **b**, that
Lev 7:33 who offers the **b** of the peace
Lev 8:15 Then he took the **b**, and put
Lev 8:15 he poured the **b** at the base
Lev 8:19 Then he sprinkled the **b** all
Lev 8:23 And he took some of its **b** and
Lev 8:24 Moses put some of the **b** on
Lev 8:24 Moses sprinkled the **b** all
Lev 8:30 some of the **b** which was on
Lev 9: 9 of Aaron brought the **b** to him
Lev 9: 9 he dipped his finger in the **b**
Lev 9: 9 poured the **b** at the base of
Lev 9:12 sons presented to him the **b**
Lev 9:18 sons presented to him the **b**
Lev 10:18 Its **b** was not brought inside
Lev 12: 4 in the **b** of her purification
Lev 12: 5 in the **b** of her purification
Lev 12: 7 clean from the flow of her **b**
Lev 14: 6 the living bird in the **b** of
Lev 14:14 shall take some of the **b** of
Lev 14:17 on the **b** of the trespass
Lev 14:25 shall take some of the **b** of
Lev 14:28 on the place of the **b** of the
Lev 14:51 and dip them in the **b** of the
Lev 14:52 house with the **b** of the bird
Lev 15:19 discharge from her body is **b**
Lev 15:25 discharge of **b** for many days
Lev 16: 3 with the **b** of a young bull as
Lev 16:14 some of the **b** of the bull
Lev 16:14 shall sprinkle some of the **b**
Lev 16:15 bring its **b** inside the veil,
Lev 16:15 do with that **b** as he did with
Lev 16:15 he did with the **b** of the bull
Lev 16:18 some of the **b** of the bull
Lev 16:18 and some of the **b** of the goat
Lev 16:19 shall sprinkle some of the **b**
Lev 16:27 whose **b** was brought in to
Lev 17: 4 He has shed **b**
Lev 17: 6 priest shall sprinkle the **b**
Lev 17:10 among you, who eats any **b**
Lev 17:10 that person who eats **b**, and
Lev 17:11 life of the flesh is in the **b**
Lev 17:11 for it is the **b** that makes
Lev 17:12 No one among you shall eat **b**
Lev 17:12 who sojourns among you eat **b**
Lev 17:13 he shall pour out its **b** and
Lev 17:14 Its **b** sustains its life
Lev 17:14 not eat the **b** of any flesh
Lev 17:14 life of all flesh is its **b**
Lev 19:26 not eat anything with the **b**
Lev 20: 9 His **b** shall be upon him
Lev 20:11 Their **b** shall be upon them
Lev 20:12 Their **b** shall be upon them
Lev 20:13 Their **b** shall be upon them
Lev 20:16 Their **b** is upon them
Lev 20:18 uncovered the flow of her **b**
Lev 20:27 Their **b** shall be upon them
Num 18:17 sprinkle their **b** on the altar
Num 19: 4 some of its **b** with his finger
Num 19: 4 sprinkle some of its **b** seven
Num 19: 5 its hide, its flesh, its **b**
Num 23:24 drinks the **b** of the slain
Num 35:19 The avenger of **b** himself
Num 35:21 the avenger of **b** shall put
Num 35:24 the avenger of **b** according to
Num 35:25 the hand of the avenger of **b**
Num 35:27 the avenger of **b** finds him
Num 35:27 the avenger of **b** kills the
Num 35:27 he shall not be guilty of **b**
Num 35:33 for **b** defiles the land, and no
Num 35:33 for the **b** that is shed on it,
Num 35:33 except by the **b** of him who
Deut 12:16 Only you shall not eat the **b**
Deut 12:23 that you do not eat the **b**
Deut 12:23 for the **b** is the life
Deut 12:27 offerings, the meat and the **b**
Deut 12:27 and the **b** of your sacrifices
Deut 15:23 Only you shall not eat its **b**
Deut 19: 6 lest the avenger of **b**, while
Deut 19:10 lest innocent **b** be shed in
Deut 19:12 the hand of the avenger of **b**
Deut 19:13 of innocent **b** from Israel
Deut 21: 7 hands have not shed this **b**
Deut 21: 8 do not lay innocent **b** to the
Deut 21: 8 on their behalf for the **b**
Deut 21: 9 **b** from among you when you do
Deut 32:14 wine, the **b** of the grapes
Deut 32:42 make My arrows drunk with **b**
Deut 32:42 with the **b** of the slain and
Deut 32:43 avenge the **b** of His servants
Josh 2:19 his **b** shall be on his own
Josh 2:19 his **b** shall be on our head if
Josh 20: 3 refuge from the avenger of **b**
Josh 20: 5 the avenger of **b** pursues him
Josh 20: 9 **b** until he stood before the
Judg 9:24 their **b** be laid on Abimelech
1Sa 14:32 people ate them with the **b**
1Sa 14:33 the LORD by eating with the **b**
1Sa 14:34 the LORD by eating with the **b**
1Sa 19: 5 you sin against innocent **b**
1Sa 25:31 you have shed **b** without cause
1Sa 26:20 do not let my **b** fall to the
2Sa 1:16 Your **b** is on your own head,
2Sa 1:22 From the **b** of the slain, from
2Sa 3:27 the **b** of Asahel his brother
2Sa 3:28 the **b** of Abner the son of Ner
2Sa 4:11 require his **b** at your hand
2Sa 14:11 of **b** to destroy anymore, lest
2Sa 16: 8 the **b** of the house of Saul
2Sa 20:12 in his **b** in the middle of the
2Sa 23:17 Is this not the **b** of the men
1Ki 2: 5 And he shed the **b** of war in
1Ki 2: 5 put the **b** of war on his belt
1Ki 2: 9 hair down to the grave with **b**
1Ki 2:31 innocent **b** which Joab shed
1Ki 2:32 will return his **b** on his head
1Ki 2:33 Their **b** shall therefore
1Ki 2:37 your **b** shall be on your own
1Ki 18:28 until the **b** gushed out on
1Ki 21:19 dogs licked the **b** of Naboth
1Ki 21:19 dogs shall lick your **b**, even
1Ki 22:35 The **b** ran out from the wound
1Ki 22:38 and the dogs licked up his **b**
2Ki 3:22 on the other side as red as **b**
2Ki 3:23 And they said, "This is **b**
2Ki 9: 7 that I may avenge the **b** of My
2Ki 9: 7 the **b** of all the servants of
2Ki 9:26 saw yesterday the **b** of Naboth
2Ki 9:26 the **b** of his sons,' says the
2Ki 9:33 some of her **b** spattered on
2Ki 16:13 sprinkled the **b** of his peace
2Ki 16:15 the **b** of the burnt offering
2Ki 16:15 all the **b** of the sacrifice
2Ki 21:16 shed very much innocent **b**
2Ki 24: 4 innocent **b** that he had shed
2Ki 24: 4 Jerusalem with innocent **b**
1Ch 11:19 Shall I drink the **b** of these
1Ch 22: 8 saying, "You have shed much **b**
1Ch 22: 8 **b** on the earth in My sight
1Ch 28: 3 a man of war and have shed **b**
2Ch 24:25 against him because of the **b**
2Ch 29:22 and the priests received the **b**
2Ch 29:22 sprinkled the **b** on the altar
2Ch 29:22 sprinkled the **b** on the altar
2Ch 29:24 they presented their **b** on the
2Ch 30:16 **b** which they received from

2Ch 35:11 the **b** with their hands, while
Job 16:18 O earth, do not cover my **b**
Job 39:30 Its young ones suck up **b**
Ps 9:12 When He avenges **b**, He
Ps 16: 4 of **b** I will not offer, Nor
Ps 30: 9 What profit is there in my **b**
Ps 50:13 Or drink the **b** of goats
Ps 58:10 feet in the **b** of the wicked
Ps 68:23 your foot may crush them in **b**
Ps 72:14 shall be their **b** in His sight
Ps 78:44 Turned their rivers into **b**
Ps 79: 3 Their **b** they have shed like
Ps 79:10 sight The avenging of the **b**
Ps 94:21 And condemn innocent **b**
Ps 105:29 He turned their waters into **b**
Ps 106:38 And shed innocent **b**, Even the
Ps 106:38 Even the **b** of their sons and
Ps 106:38 the land was polluted with **b**
Prov 1:11 let us lie in wait to shed **b**
Prov 1:16 and they make haste to shed **b**
Prov 1:18 lie in wait for their own **b**
Prov 6:17 hands that shed innocent **b**
Prov 12: 6 Lie in wait for **b**," but the
Prov 30:33 wringing the nose produces **b**
Is 1:11 not delight in the **b** of bulls
Is 1:15 Your hands are full of **b**
Is 4: 4 purged the **b** of Jerusalem
Is 9: 5 and garments rolled in **b**,
Is 15: 9 of Dimon will be full of **b**
Is 26:21 will also disclose her **b**, and
Is 34: 3 shall be melted with their **b**
Is 34: 6 of the LORD is filled with **b**
Is 34: 6 and with the **b** of lambs and
Is 34: 7 land shall be soaked with **b**
Is 49:26 own **b** as with sweet wine
Is 59: 3 your hands are defiled with **b**
Is 59: 7 make haste to shed innocent **b**
Is 63: 3 their **b** is sprinkled upon My
Is 66: 3 as if he offers swine's **b**
Jer 2:34 **b** of the lives of the poor
Jer 7: 6 shed innocent **b** in this place
Jer 18:21 pour out their **b** by the force
Jer 19: 4 with the **b** of the innocents
Jer 22: 3 shed innocent **b** in this place
Jer 22:17 for shedding innocent **b**, and
Jer 26:15 innocent **b** on yourselves, on
Jer 46:10 and made drunk with their **b**
Jer 48:10 keeps back his sword from **b**
Jer 51:35 my **b** be upon the inhabitants
Lam 4:13 her midst the **b** of the just
Lam 4:14 defiled themselves with **b**
Ezek 3:18 but his **b** I will require at
Ezek 3:20 but his **b** I will require at
Ezek 5:17 **b** shall pass through you, and
Ezek 7:23 is filled with crimes of **b**
Ezek 14:19 pour out My fury on it in **b**
Ezek 16: 6 you struggling in your own **b**
Ezek 16: 6 I said to you in your **b**
Ezek 16: 6 Yes, I said to you in your **b**
Ezek 16: 9 thoroughly washed off your **b**
Ezek 16:22 and bare, struggling in your **b**
Ezek 16:36 and because of the **b** of your
Ezek 16:38 wedlock or shed **b** are judged
Ezek 16:38 I will bring **b** upon you in
Ezek 18:10 is a robber or a shedder of **b**
Ezek 18:13 His **b** shall be upon him
Ezek 21:32 your **b** shall be in the midst
Ezek 22: 3 The city sheds **b** in her own
Ezek 22: 4 by the **b** which you have shed
Ezek 22: 6 his power to shed **b** in you
Ezek 22:12 they take bribes to shed **b**
Ezek 22:27 tearing the prey, to shed **b**
Ezek 23:37 and **b** is on their hands
Ezek 23:45 manner of women who shed **b**
Ezek 23:45 and **b** is on their hands
Ezek 24: 7 For her **b** is in her midst
Ezek 24: 8 I have set her **b** on top of a
Ezek 28:23 upon her, and **b** in her streets
Ezek 32: 6 land with the flow of your **b**
Ezek 33: 4 his **b** shall be on his own
Ezek 33: 5 his **b** shall be upon himself
Ezek 33: 6 but his **b** I will require at
Ezek 33: 8 but his **b** I will require at
Ezek 33:25 You eat meat with **b**, you lift
Ezek 33:25 toward your idols, and shed **b**
Ezek 35: 5 and have shed the **b** of the
Ezek 35: 6 I will prepare you for **b**
Ezek 35: 6 and **b** shall pursue you
Ezek 35: 6 since you have not hated **b**
Ezek 35: 6 therefore **b** shall pursue you
Ezek 36:18 **b** they had shed on the land
Ezek 39:17 you may eat flesh and drink **b**
Ezek 39:18 drink the **b** of the princes of
Ezek 39:19 drink **b** till you are drunk,
Ezek 43:18 it, and for sprinkling **b** on it
Ezek 43:20 You shall take some of its **b**
Ezek 44: 7 My food, the fat and the **b**
Ezek 44:15 offer to Me the fat and the **b**
Ezek 45:19 of the **b** of the sin offering
Hos 6: 8 and is defiled with **b**
Joel 2:30 **b** and fire and pillars of smoke
Joel 2:31 darkness, and the moon into **b**
Joel 3:19 shed innocent **b** in their land
Jon 1:14 not charge us with innocent **b**
Mic 7: 2 They all lie in wait for **b**
Hab 2: 8 you, because of men's **b** and
Hab 2:17 afraid, because of men's **b**
Zeph 1:17 their **b** shall be poured out
Zech 9: 7 away the **b** from his mouth
Zech 9:11 because of the **b** of your
Zech 9:15 be filled with **b** like basins
Matt 9:20 a woman who had a flow of **b**
Matt 16:17 **b** has not revealed this to
Matt 23:30 them in the **b** of the prophets
Matt 23:35 righteous **b** shed on the earth
Matt 23:35 from the **b** of righteous Abel
Matt 23:35 Abel to the **b** of Zechariah
Matt 26:28 For this is My **b** of the new
Matt 27: 4 by betraying innocent **b**
Matt 27: 6 they are the price of **b**
Matt 27: 8 the Field of **B** to this day
Matt 27:24 of the **b** of this just Person
Matt 27:25 His **b** be on us and on our
Mark 5:25 a flow of **b** for twelve years
Mark 5:29 of her **b** was dried up, and she
Mark 14:24 This is My **b** of the new
Luke 8:43 a flow of **b** for twelve years
Luke 8:44 her flow of **b** stopped
Luke 11:50 that the **b** of all the
Luke 11:51 the **b** of Abel to the **b** of
Luke 13: 1 **b** Pilate had mingled with
Luke 22:20 is the new covenant in My **b**
Luke 22:44 **b** falling down to the ground
John 1:13 who were born, not of **b**, nor
John 6:53 the Son of Man and drink His **b**
John 6:54 drinks My **b** has eternal life,
John 6:55 and My **b** is drink indeed
John 6:56 drinks My **b** abides in Me, and
John 19:34 a spear, and immediately **b**
Acts 1:19 Dama, that is, Field of **B**
Acts 2:19 **b** and fire and vapor of smoke
Acts 2:20 darkness, and the moon into **b**
Acts 5:28 to bring this Man's **b** on us
Acts 15:20 things strangled, and from **b**
Acts 15:29 offered to idols, from **b**,
Acts 17:26 He has made from one **b** every
Acts 18: 6 Your **b** be upon your own heads
Acts 20:26 innocent of the **b** of all men
Acts 20:28 He purchased with His own **b**
Acts 21:25 offered to idols, from **b**,
Acts 22:20 when the **b** of Your martyr
Rom 3:15 feet are swift to shed **b**
Rom 3:25 to be a propitiation by His **b**
Rom 5: 9 now been justified by His **b**
1Co 10:16 communion of the **b** of Christ
1Co 11:25 is the new covenant in My **b**
1Co 11:27 of the body and **b** of the Lord
1Co 15:50 **b** cannot inherit the kingdom
Gal 1:16 confer with flesh and **b**,
Eph 1: 7 have redemption through His **b**
Eph 2:13 made near by the **b** of Christ
Eph 6:12 wrestle against flesh and **b**
Col 1:14 have redemption through His **b**
Col 1:20 through the **b** of His cross
Heb 2:14 have partaken of flesh and **b**
Heb 9: 7 once a year, not without **b**
Heb 9:12 Not with the **b** of goats and
Heb 9:12 but with His own **b** He entered
Heb 9:13 For if the **b** of bulls and
Heb 9:14 more shall the **b** of Christ
Heb 9:18 was dedicated without **b**
Heb 9:19 law, he took the **b** of calves
Heb 9:20 This is the **b** of the covenant
Heb 9:21 with **b** both the tabernacle
Heb 9:22 all things are purged with **b**
Heb 9:22 without shedding of **b** there
Heb 9:25 every year with **b** of another
Heb 10: 4 possible that the **b** of bulls
Heb 10:19 the Holiest by the **b** of Jesus
Heb 10:29 counted the **b** of the covenant
Heb 11:28 and the sprinkling of **b**, lest
Heb 12:24 to the **b** of sprinkling that
Heb 13:11 whose **b** is brought into the
Heb 13:12 the people with His own **b**
Heb 13:20 sheep, through the **b** of the
1Pe 1: 2 of the **b** of Jesus Christ
1Pe 1:19 with the precious **b** of Christ
1Jn 1: 7 the **b** of Jesus Christ His Son
1Jn 5: 6 is He who came by water and **b**
1Jn 5: 6 by water, but by water and **b**
1Jn 5: 8 Spirit, the water, and the **b**
Rev 1: 5 us from our sins in His own **b**
Rev 5: 9 by Your **b** out of every tribe
Rev 6:10 avenge our **b** on those who
Rev 6:12 and the moon became like **b**
Rev 7:14 white in the **b** of the Lamb
Rev 8: 7 fire followed, mingled with **b**
Rev 8: 8 a third of the sea became **b**
Rev 11: 6 over waters to turn them to **b**
Rev 12:11 him by the **b** of the Lamb and
Rev 14:20 **b** came out of the winepress,
Rev 16: 3 it became **b** as of a dead man
Rev 16: 4 of water, and they became **b**
Rev 16: 6 have shed the **b** of saints
Rev 16: 6 have given them **b** to drink
Rev 17: 6 with the **b** of the saints and
Rev 17: 6 with the **b** of the martyrs of
Rev 18:24 was found the **b** of prophets
Rev 19: 2 He has avenged on her the **b**
Rev 19:13 with a robe dipped in **b**, and

BLOODGUILT (*see* BLOOD, BLOODGUILTINESS)
Lev 17: 4 **b** shall be imputed to that
Hos 12:14 Lord will leave on him his **b**
Joel 3:21 For I will acquit them of **b**

BLOODGUILTINESS (*see* BLOODGUILT)
Deut 17: 8 judge, between degrees of **b**
Deut 19:10 and thus **b** be upon you
Deut 22: 8 that you may not bring **b** on
Ps 51:14 Deliver me from **b**, O God, The

BLOODLINE (*see* BLOOD)
Ezek 19:10 was like a vine in your **b**

BLOODSHED (*see* BLOOD)
Ex 22: 2 shall be no guilt for his **b**
Ex 22: 3 shall be guilt for his **b**
1Sa 25:26 you back from coming to **b**
1Sa 25:33 me this day from coming to **b**
2Ch 19:10 whether of **b** or offenses
Prov 28:17 A man burdened with **b** will
Is 33:15 his ears from hearing of **b**
Ezek 9: 9 and the land is full of **b**
Ezek 22: 9 men who slander to cause **b**
Ezek 22:13 at the **b** which has been in
Ezek 38:22 judgment with pestilence and **b**
Hos 1: 4 while I will avenge the **b** of
Hos 4: 2 with **b** after **b**
Mic 3:10 Who build up Zion with **b** and
Hab 2:12 him who builds a town with **b**
Heb 12: 4 have not yet resisted to **b**

BLOODTHIRSTY (*see* BLOOD)
2Sa 16: 7 You **b** man, you rogue
2Sa 16: 8 evil, because you are a **b** man
2Sa 21: 1 and his **b** house, because he
Ps 5: 6 The LORD abhors the **b** and
Ps 26: 9 Nor my life with **b** men,
Ps 55:23 **B** and deceitful men shall not
Ps 59: 2 And save me from **b** men
Ps 139:19 from me, therefore, you **b** men
Prov 29:10 The **b** hate the blameless, but

BLOODY (*see* BLOOD)
Ezek 22: 2 will you judge the **b** city
Ezek 24: 6 Woe to the **b** city, to the pot
Ezek 24: 9 Woe to the **b** city
Nah 3: 1 Woe to the **b** city

BLOOM (*see* BLOOMED, BLOOMS)
Song 7:12 and the pomegranates are in **b**

BLOOMED (*see* BLOOM)
Song 6:11 and the pomegranates had **b**

BLOOMS (*see* BLOOM)
Song 1:14 **b** in the vineyards of En Gedi

BLOSSOM (*see* BLOSSOMED, BLOSSOMS)
Num 17: 5 the man whom I choose will **b**
1Ki 7:26 brim of a cup, like a lily **b**
2Ch 4: 5 brim of a cup, like a lily **b**
Job 15:33 cast off his **b** like an olive

Is 5:24 their **b** will ascend like dust
Is 27: 6 Israel shall **b** and bud, and
Is 35: 1 rejoice and **b** as the rose
Is 35: 2 It shall **b** abundantly and
Hab 3:17 Though the fig tree may not **b**

BLOSSOMED (*see* BLOSSOM)
Ezek 7:10 the rod has **b**, pride has

BLOSSOMS (*see* BLOSSOM, BLOSSOMS)
Gen 40:10 its **b** shot forth, and its
Ex 25:33 like almond **b** on one branch
Ex 25:33 almond **b** on the other branch
Ex 25:34 shall be made like almond **b**
Ex 37:19 like almond **b** on one branch
Ex 37:19 almond **b** on the other branch
Ex 37:20 four bowls made like almond **b**
Num 17: 8 forth buds, had produced **b**
Eccl 12: 5 when the almond tree **b**, the
Song 7:12 whether the grape **b** are open

BLOT (*see* BLOTS, BLOTTED)
Ex 17:14 that I will utterly **b** out the
Ex 32:32 **b** me out of Your book which
Ex 32:33 I will **b** him out of My book
Deut 9:14 **b** out their name from under
Deut 25:19 that you will **b** out the
Deut 29:20 the LORD would **b** out his name
2Ki 14:27 did not say that He would **b**
Ps 51: 1 **B** out my transgressions
Ps 51: 9 And **b** out all my iniquities
Jer 18:23 nor **b** out their sin from Your
Rev 3: 5 I will not **b** out his name

BLOTS (*see* BLOT)
Is 43:25 even I, am He who **b** out your

BLOTTED (*see* BLOT)
Deut 25: 6 may not be **b** out of Israel
Neh 4: 5 sin be **b** out from before You
Ps 9: 5 You have **b** out their name
Ps 69:28 Let them be **b** out of the book
Ps 109:13 let their name be **b** out
Ps 109:14 sin of his mother be **b** out
Is 44:22 I have **b** out, like a thick
Acts 3:19 that your sins may be **b** out

BLOW (*see* BLEW, BLOWING, BLOWN, BLOWS)
Num 10: 3 When they **b** both of them, all
Num 10: 4 But if they **b** only one, then
Num 10: 7 together, you shall **b**, but
Num 10: 8 priests, shall **b** the trumpets
Num 10:10 you shall **b** the trumpets over
Josh 6: 4 priests shall **b** the trumpets
Judg 7:18 When I **b** the trumpet, I and
Judg 7:18 then you also **b** the trumpets
Judg 16:28 that I may with one **b** take
1Sa 19: 8 struck them with a mighty **b**
1Sa 23: 5 struck them with a mighty **b**
1Ki 1:34 **b** the horn, and say, 'Long
1Ch 15:24 were to **b** the trumpets before
Job 36:18 He take you away with one **b**
Ps 39:10 by the **b** of Your hand
Ps 78:26 east wind to **b** in the heavens
Ps 81: 3 **B** the trumpet at the time of
Ps 147:18 He causes His wind to **b**, and
Song 4:16 **B** upon my garden, that its
Is 40:24 when He will also **b** on them
Jer 4: 5 **B** the trumpet in the land
Jer 6: 1 **B** the trumpet in Tekoa, and
Jer 6:29 the bellows **b** fiercely, the
Jer 14:17 stroke, with a very severe **b**
Jer 51:27 land, **b** the trumpet among the
Ezek 21:31 I will **b** against you with the
Ezek 22:20 to **b** fire on it, to melt it
Ezek 22:21 **b** on you with the fire of My
Ezek 33: 6 does not **b** the trumpet, and
Hos 5: 8 **B** the ram's horn in Gibeah,
Joel 2: 1 **B** the trumpet in Zion, and
Joel 2:15 **B** the trumpet in Zion,
Zech 9:14 Lord GOD will **b** the trumpet
Luke 12:55 when you see the south wind **b**
Rev 7: 1 should not **b** on the earth

BLOWING (*see* BLOW)
Lev 23:24 a memorial of **b** of trumpets
Num 29: 1 it is a day of **b** the trumpets
Josh 6: 9 continued **b** the trumpets
Josh 6:13 continued **b** the trumpets
Judg 7:20 in their right hands for **b**
2Ki 11:14 were rejoicing and **b** trumpets
2Ch 23:13 **b** trumpets, also the singers
John 6:18 because a great wind was **b**

BLOWN (*see* BLOW)
Is 27:13 the great trumpet will be **b**
Ezek 7:14 They have **b** the trumpet and
Hos 13: 3 away, like chaff **b** off from a
Amos 3: 6 If a trumpet is **b** in a city

BLOWS (*see* BLOW)
Deut 25: 2 with a certain number of **b**
Deut 25: 3 Forty **b** he may give him and no
Deut 25: 3 him with many **b** above these
2Sa 7:14 with the **b** of the sons of men
Prov 17:10 than a hundred **b** on a fool
Prov 18: 6 and his mouth calls for **b**
Prov 20:30 **B** that hurt cleanse away evil
Is 18: 3 when he **b** a trumpet, you hear
Is 40: 7 breath of the LORD **b** upon it
Is 54:16 who **b** the coals in the fire
Jer 4:11 of the desolate heights **b** in
Ezek 33: 3 if he **b** the trumpet and warns
John 3: 8 The wind **b** where it wishes,

BLUE
Ex 25: 4 **b** and purple and scarlet yarn,
Ex 26: 1 of fine linen thread, and **b**
Ex 26: 4 of **b** yarn on the edge of the
Ex 26:31 shall make a veil woven of **b**
Ex 26:36 of the tabernacle, woven of **b**
Ex 27:16 cubits long, woven of **b** and
Ex 28: 5 They shall take the gold and **b**
Ex 28: 6 make the ephod of gold and **b**
Ex 28: 8 woven of gold and **b** and purple
Ex 28:15 of gold and **b** and purple and
Ex 28:28 of the ephod, using a **b** cord
Ex 28:31 robe of the ephod all of **b**
Ex 28:33 shall make pomegranates of **b**
Ex 28:37 you shall put it on a **b** cord
Ex 35: 6 **b** and purple and scarlet yarn,
Ex 35:23 man, with whom was found **b**
Ex 35:25 what they had spun, of **b** and
Ex 35:35 and the tapestry maker, in **b**
Ex 36: 8 of fine linen thread, and **b**
Ex 36:11 He made loops of **b** yarn on
Ex 36:35 And he made a veil woven of **b**
Ex 36:37 tabernacle door, woven of **b**
Ex 38:18 of the court was woven of **b**
Ex 38:23 and designer, a weaver in **b**
Ex 39: 1 Of the **b** and purple and scarlet
Ex 39: 2 made the ephod of gold and **b**
Ex 39: 3 to work it in with the **b**
Ex 39: 5 woven of gold and **b** and purple
Ex 39: 8 of the ephod, of gold and **b**
Ex 39:21 of the ephod with a **b** cord
Ex 39:22 ephod of woven work, all of **b**
Ex 39:24 of the robe pomegranates of **b**
Ex 39:29 and a sash of fine linen and **b**
Ex 39:31 And they tied to it a **b** cord
Num 4: 6 that a cloth entirely of **b**
Num 4: 7 they shall spread a **b** cloth
Num 4: 9 And they shall take a **b** cloth
Num 4:11 they shall spread a **b** cloth
Num 4:12 put them in a **b** cloth, cover
Num 15:38 and to put a **b** thread in the
2Ch 2: 7 in purple and crimson and **b**
2Ch 2:14 stone and wood, purple and **b**
2Ch 3:14 And he made the veil of **b** and
Esth 1: 6 **b** linen curtains fastened
Esth 8:15 king in royal apparel of **b**
Jer 10: 9 **b** and purple are their
Ezek 27: 7 **b** and purple from the coasts
Rev 9:17 of fiery red, hyacinth **b**, and

BLUNT
2Sa 2:23 with the **b** end of the spear

BLUSH
Jer 6:15 nor did they know how to **b**
Jer 8:12 nor did they know how to **b**

BOANERGES
Mark 3:17 to whom He gave the name **B**

BOAR
Ps 80:13 The **b** out of the woods

BOARD (*see* BOARDED, BOARDS)
Ex 26:16 shall be the length of a **b**
Ex 26:16 shall be the width of each **b**
Ex 26:17 **b** for binding one to another
Ex 26:19 one **b** for its two tenons, and
Ex 26:19 another **b** for its two tenons
Ex 26:21 two sockets under one **b**, and
Ex 26:21 two sockets under another **b**
Ex 26:25 two sockets under one **b**, and
Ex 26:25 two sockets under another **b**
Ex 36:21 of each **b** was ten cubits, and
Ex 36:21 the width of each **b** a cubit
Ex 36:22 Each **b** had two tenons for
Ex 36:24 one **b** for its two tenons, and
Ex 36:24 another **b** for its two tenons
Ex 36:26 two sockets under one **b** and
Ex 36:26 two sockets under another **b**
Ex 36:30 two sockets under every **b**
Acts 20:13 intending to take Paul on **b**
Acts 20:14 us at Assos, we took him on **b**
Acts 27: 6 to Italy, and he put us on **b**
Acts 27:17 When they had taken it on **b**

BOARDED (*see* BOARD)
Acts 21: 6 we **b** the ship, and they

BOARDS (*see* BOARD)
Ex 26:15 make the **b** of acacia wood
Ex 26:17 all the **b** of the tabernacle
Ex 26:18 make the **b** for the tabernacle
Ex 26:18 twenty **b** for the south side
Ex 26:19 of silver under the twenty **b**
Ex 26:20 side, there shall be twenty **b**
Ex 26:22 you shall make six **b**
Ex 26:23 you shall also make two **b** for
Ex 26:25 eight **b** with their sockets of
Ex 26:26 five for the **b** on one side of
Ex 26:27 five bars for the **b** on the
Ex 26:27 five bars for the **b** of the
Ex 26:28 of the **b** from end to end
Ex 26:29 shall overlay the **b** with gold
Ex 27: 8 shall make it hollow with **b**
Ex 35:11 covering, its clasps, its **b**
Ex 36:20 he made **b** of acacia wood,
Ex 36:22 all the **b** of the tabernacle
Ex 36:23 he made **b** for the tabernacle,
Ex 36:23 twenty **b** for the south side
Ex 36:24 made to go under the twenty **b**
Ex 36:25 north side, he made twenty **b**
Ex 36:27 the tabernacle he made six **b**
Ex 36:28 He also made two **b** for the
Ex 36:30 So there were eight **b** and
Ex 36:31 five for the **b** on one side of
Ex 36:32 five bars for the **b** on the
Ex 36:32 five bars for the **b** of the
Ex 36:33 bar to pass through the **b**
Ex 36:34 He overlaid the **b** with gold
Ex 38: 7 made the altar hollow with **b**
Ex 39:33 its clasps, its **b**, its bars,
Ex 40:18 its sockets, set up its **b**
Num 3:36 the **b** of the tabernacle, its
Num 4:31 the **b** of the tabernacle, its
1Ki 6: 9 with beams and **b** of cedar
1Ki 6:15 of the temple with cedar **b**
1Ki 6:16 to ceiling, with cedar **b**
Song 8: 9 enclose her with **b** of cedar
Acts 27:44 and the rest, some on **b** and

BOAST (*see* BOASTED, BOASTERS, BOASTFUL, BOASTING, BOASTS)
1Ki 20:11 **b** like the one who takes it
2Ch 25:19 your heart is lifted up to **b**
Ps 34: 2 shall make its **b** in the LORD
Ps 44: 8 In God we **b** all day long, And
Ps 49: 6 **b** in the multitude of their
Ps 52: 1 Why do you **b** in evil, O
Ps 90:10 Yet their **b** is only labor and
Ps 94: 4 of iniquity **b** in themselves
Ps 97: 7 carved images, Who **b** of idols
Prov 27: 1 Do not **b** about tomorrow, for
Is 10:15 Shall the ax **b** itself against
Is 61: 6 and in their glory you shall **b**
Ezek 24:21 My sanctuary, your arrogant **b**
Rom 2:17 law, and make your **b** in God
Rom 2:23 who make your **b** in the law
Rom 4: 2 has something of which to **b**
Rom 11:18 do not **b** against the branches
Rom 11:18 But if you **b**, remember that
1Co 9:16 I have nothing to **b** of, for
2Co 1:14 that we are your **b** as you
2Co 9: 2 about which I **b** of you to the
2Co 10: 8 For even if I should **b**
2Co 10:13 will not **b** beyond measure,
2Co 10:16 not to **b** in another man's
2Co 11:12 in the things of which they **b**
2Co 11:16 that I also may **b** a little
2Co 11:18 Seeing that many **b** according
2Co 11:18 to the flesh, I also will **b**
2Co 11:30 If I must **b**, I will **b** in
2Co 12: 1 not profitable for me to **b**
2Co 12: 5 Of such a one I will **b**
2Co 12: 5 yet of myself I will not **b**

2Co 12: 6 though I might desire to **b**
2Co 12: 9 rather **b** in my infirmities
Eph 2: 9 works, lest anyone should **b**
2Th 1: 4 so that we ourselves **b** of you
Jas 3:14 in your hearts, do not **b** and
Jas 4:16 But now you **b** in your

BOASTED (*see* BOAST)
Ezek 35:13 mouth you have **b** against Me
2Co 7:14 I have **b** to him about you

BOASTERS (*see* BOAST)
Rom 1:30 of God, violent, proud, **b**
2Ti 3: 2 lovers of money, **b**, proud,

BOASTFUL (*see* BOAST, BOASTFULLY)
Ps 5: 5 The **b** shall not stand in Your
Ps 73: 3 For I was envious of the **b**
Ps 75: 4 I said to the **b**, 'Do not deal

BOASTFULLY (*see* BOASTFUL)
Ps 75: 4 the boastful, 'Do not deal **b**

BOASTING (*see* BOAST)
Rom 3:27 Where is **b** then
1Co 9:15 anyone should make my **b** void
1Co 15:31 by the **b** in you which I have
2Co 1:12 For our **b** is this
2Co 7: 4 great is my **b** on your behalf
2Co 7:14 even so our **b** to Titus was
2Co 8:24 and of our **b** on your behalf
2Co 9: 3 lest our **b** of you should be
2Co 9: 4 ashamed of this confident **b**
2Co 10:15 not **b** of things beyond
2Co 11:10 **b** in the regions of Achaia
2Co 11:17 in this confidence of **b**
2Co 12:11 I have become a fool in **b**
Jas 4:16 All such **b** is evil

BOASTS (*see* BOAST)
Ps 10: 3 For the wicked **b** of his
Prov 20:14 has gone his way, then he **b**
Prov 25:14 Whoever falsely **b** of giving
Jas 3: 5 member and **b** great things

BOAT (*see* BOATS)
Matt 4:21 in the **b** with Zebedee their
Matt 4:22 immediately they left the **b**
Matt 8:23 Now when He got into a **b**, His
Matt 8:24 so that the **b** was covered
Matt 9: 1 So He got into a **b**, crossed
Matt 13: 2 Him, so that He got into a **b**
Matt 14:13 by **b** to a deserted place by
Matt 14:22 His disciples get into the **b**
Matt 14:24 But the **b** was now in the
Matt 14:29 had come down out of the **b**
Matt 14:32 And when they got into the **b**
Matt 14:33 those who were in the **b** came
Matt 15:39 the multitude, got into the **b**
Mark 1:19 in the **b** mending their nets
Mark 1:20 the **b** with the hired servants
Mark 3: 9 **b** should be kept ready for
Mark 4: 1 Him, so that He got into a **b**
Mark 4:36 Him along in the **b** as He was
Mark 4:37 and the waves beat into the **b**
Mark 5: 2 when He had come out of the **b**
Mark 5:18 And when He got into the **b**
Mark 5:21 again by **b** to the other side
Mark 6:32 place in the **b** by themselves
Mark 6:45 His disciples get into the **b**
Mark 6:47 the **b** was in the middle of
Mark 6:51 He went up into the **b** to them
Mark 6:54 when they came out of the **b**
Mark 8:10 into the **b** with His disciples
Mark 8:13 and getting into the **b** again
Mark 8:14 one loaf with them in the **b**
Luke 5: 3 the multitudes from the **b**
Luke 5: 7 in the other **b** to come and
Luke 8:22 into a **b** with His disciples
Luke 8:37 And He got into the **b** and
John 6:17 got into the **b**, and went over
John 6:19 the sea and drawing near the **b**
John 6:21 received Him into the **b**, and
John 6:21 immediately the **b** was at the
John 6:22 there was no other **b** there
John 6:22 the **b** with His disciples, but
John 21: 3 and immediately got into the **b**
John 21: 6 on the right side of the **b**
John 21: 8 came in the little **b** (for

BOATS (*see* BOAT)
Mark 4:36 other little **b** were also with
Luke 5: 2 saw two **b** standing by the
Luke 5: 3 Then He got into one of the **b**
Luke 5: 7 came and filled both the **b**
Luke 5:11 had brought their **b** to land
John 6:23 other **b** came from Tiberias,
John 6:24 they also got into **b** and came

BOAZ
Ruth 2: 1 his name was **B**
Ruth 2: 3 of the field belonging to **B**
Ruth 2: 4 **B** came from Bethlehem, and
Ruth 2: 5 Then **B** said to his servant
Ruth 2: 8 Then **B** said to Ruth, "You
Ruth 2:11 **B** answered and said to her,
Ruth 2:14 Now **B** said to her at mealtime
Ruth 2:15 **B** commanded his young men,
Ruth 2:19 with whom I worked today is **B**
Ruth 2:23 close by the young women of **B**
Ruth 3: 2 Now **B**, whose young women
Ruth 3: 7 after **B** had eaten and drunk,
Ruth 4: 1 Now **B** went up to the gate and
Ruth 4: 1 of whom **B** had spoken came by
Ruth 4: 1 So **B** said, "Come aside
Ruth 4: 5 Then **B** said, "On the day you
Ruth 4: 8 the near kinsman said to **B**
Ruth 4: 9 **B** said to the elders and to
Ruth 4:13 So **B** took Ruth and she became
Ruth 4:21 Salmon begot **B**
Ruth 4:21 and **B** begot Obed
1Ki 7:21 the left and called its name **B**
1Ch 2:11 begot Salma, and Salma begot **B**
1Ch 2:12 **B** begot Obed, and Obed begot
2Ch 3:17 name of the one on the left **B**
Matt 1: 5 Salmon begot **B** by Rahab, **B**
Matt 1: 5 **B** begot Obed by Ruth, Obed
Luke 3:32 the son of Obed, the son of **B**

BOCHERU
1Ch 8:38 Azrikam, **B**, Ishmael, Sheariah
1Ch 9:44 Azrikam, **B**, Ishmael, Sheariah

BOCHIM
Judg 2: 1 LORD came up from Gilgal to **B**
Judg 2: 5 the name of that place **B**

BODIES (*see* BODY)
Gen 47:18 sight of my lord but our **b**
1Sa 31:12 the **b** of his sons from the
1Ch 10:12 of Saul and the **b** of his sons
2Ch 20:24 and there were their dead **b**
2Ch 20:25 of valuables on the dead **b**
Neh 9:37 they have dominion over our **b**
Ps 79: 2 The dead **b** of Your servants
Ps 110: 6 fill the places with dead **b**
Jer 31:40 whole valley of the dead **b**
Jer 33: 5 **b** of men whom I will slay in
Jer 34:20 Their dead **b** shall be for
Jer 41: 9 had cast all the dead **b** of
Ezek 1:11 and two covered their **b**
Ezek 39:14 bury those **b** remaining on the
Ezek 44:18 and linen trousers on their **b**
Dan 3:27 whose **b** the fire had no power
Dan 3:28 word, and yielded their **b**,
Amos 6:10 with one who will burn the **b**
Amos 6:10 picks up the **b** to take them
Amos 8: 3 Many dead **b** everywhere, They
Nah 3: 3 of slain, a great number of **b**
Matt 27:52 many **b** of the saints who had
John 19:31 that the **b** should not remain
Rom 1:24 their **b** among themselves,
Rom 8:11 **b** through His Spirit who
Rom 12: 1 your **b** a living sacrifice
1Co 6:15 your **b** are members of Christ
1Co 10: 5 for their **b** were scattered in
1Co 15:40 celestial **b** and terrestrial **b**
Eph 5:28 own wives as their own **b**
Heb 10:22 our **b** washed with pure water
Heb 13:11 For the **b** of those beasts,
Rev 11: 8 their dead **b** will lie in the
Rev 11: 9 will see their dead **b** three
Rev 11: 9 not allow their dead **b** to be
Rev 18:13 horses and chariots, and **b**

BODILY (*see* BODY)
Luke 3:22 Holy Spirit descended in **b**
2Co 10:10 but his **b** presence is weak,
Col 2: 9 the fullness of the Godhead **b**
1Ti 4: 8 For **b** exercise profits a

BODY (*see* BODIES, BODILY, BODYGUARDS)
Gen 15: 4 your own **b** shall be your heir
Gen 25:23 be separated from your **b**
Gen 35:11 kings shall come from your **b**
Gen 46:26 to Egypt, who came from his **b**
Lev 6:10 he shall put on his **b**, and
Lev 13: 2 the skin of his **b** a swelling
Lev 13: 2 of his **b** like a leprous sore
Lev 13: 3 the sore on the skin of the **b**
Lev 13: 3 deeper than the skin of his **b**
Lev 13: 4 is white on the skin of his **b**
Lev 13:11 leprosy on the skin of his **b**
Lev 13:13 leprosy has covered all his **b**
Lev 13:18 If the **b** develops a boil in
Lev 13:24 Or if the **b** receives a burn
Lev 13:38 spots on the skin of the **b**
Lev 13:39 skin of the **b** are dull white
Lev 13:43 leprosy on the skin of the **b**
Lev 14: 9 and wash his **b** in water, and he
Lev 15: 2 has a discharge from his **b**
Lev 15: 3 whether his **b** runs with his
Lev 15: 3 or his **b** is stopped up by his
Lev 15: 7 the **b** of him who has the
Lev 15:13 bathe his **b** in running water
Lev 15:16 shall wash all his **b** in water
Lev 15:19 discharge from her **b** is blood
Lev 16: 4 the linen trousers on his **b**
Lev 16: 4 he shall wash his **b** in water
Lev 16:24 And he shall wash his **b** with
Lev 16:26 and bathe his **b** in water, and
Lev 16:28 and bathe his **b** in water, and
Lev 17:16 does not wash or bathe his **b**
Lev 21:11 shall he go near any dead **b**
Lev 22: 6 he washes his **b** with water
Num 5: 2 becomes defiled by a dead **b**
Num 6: 6 he shall not go near a dead **b**
Num 6:11 by reason of the dead **b**
Num 8: 7 and let them shave all their **b**
Num 9: 6 by the dead **b** of a man, so
Num 9: 7 by the dead **b** of a man
Num 9:10 unclean because of a dead **b**
Num 19:11 He who touches the dead **b** of
Num 19:13 Whoever touches the **b** of
Num 25: 8 and the woman through her **b**
Deut 21:23 his **b** shall not remain
Deut 28: 4 shall be the fruit of your **b**
Deut 28:11 goods, in the fruit of your **b**
Deut 28:18 shall be the fruit of your **b**
Deut 28:53 eat the fruit of your own **b**
Deut 30: 9 hand, in the fruit of your **b**
1Sa 31:10 they fastened his **b** to the
1Sa 31:12 night, and took the **b** of Saul
2Sa 7:12 who will come from your **b**
2Sa 16:11 from my own **b** seeks my life
1Ki 21:27 and put sackcloth on his **b**
2Ki 6:30 he had sackcloth on his **b**
2Ki 23:30 **b** in a chariot from Megiddo
1Ch 10:12 arose and took the **b** of Saul
2Ch 26:14 **b** armor, bows, and slings to
Job 4:15 the hair on my **b** stood up
Job 7:15 and death rather than my **b**
Job 19:17 to the children of my own **b**
Job 20:25 drawn, and comes out of the **b**
Ps 31: 9 grief, Yes, my soul and my **b**
Ps 44:25 Our **b** clings to the ground
Ps 109:18 let it enter his **b** like water
Ps 132:11 throne the fruit of your **b**
Prov 5:11 flesh and your **b** are consumed,
Prov 14:30 sound heart is life to the **b**
Prov 18: 8 go down into the inmost **b**
Prov 26:22 go down into the inmost **b**
Song 5:14 His **b** is carved ivory inlaid
Is 10:18 field, both soul and **b**
Is 20: 2 the sackcloth from your **b**
Is 26:19 my dead **b** they shall arise
Is 48:19 the offspring of your **b** like
Is 51:23 laid your **b** like the ground
Jer 26:23 and cast his dead **b** into the
Jer 36:30 his dead **b** shall be cast out
Lam 4: 7 more ruddy in **b** than rubies
Ezek 1:23 the other side of the **b**
Ezek 10:12 And their whole **b**, with their
Dan 4:33 his **b** was wet with the dew of
Dan 5:21 his **b** was wet with the dew of
Dan 7:11 its **b** destroyed and given to
Dan 7:15 in my spirit within my **b**, and
Dan 10: 6 His **b** was like beryl, his
Mic 6: 7 the fruit of my **b** for the sin
Hab 3:16 When I heard, my **b** trembled
Hag 2:13 a dead **b** touches any of these
Matt 5:29 than for your whole **b** to be
Matt 5:30 than for your whole **b** to be
Matt 6:22 The lamp of the **b** is the eye
Matt 6:22 your whole **b** will be full of
Matt 6:23 your whole **b** will be full of
Matt 6:25 nor about your **b**, what you

Matt 6:25 and the **b** more than clothing
Matt 10:28 **b** but cannot kill the soul
Matt 10:28 both soul and **b** in hell
Matt 14:12 came and took away the **b** and
Matt 26:12 this fragrant oil on My **b**
Matt 26:26 this is My **b**
Matt 27:58 and asked for the **b** of Jesus
Matt 27:58 the **b** to be given to him
Matt 27:59 when Joseph had taken the **b**
Mark 5:29 she felt in her **b** that she
Mark 14: 8 to anoint My **b** for burial
Mark 14:22 this is My **b**
Mark 14:51 thrown around his naked **b**
Mark 15:43 and asked for the **b** of Jesus
Mark 15:45 he granted the **b** to Joseph
Luke 11:34 The lamp of the **b** is the eye
Luke 11:34 your whole **b** also is full of
Luke 11:34 bad, your **b** also is full of
Luke 11:36 your whole **b** is full of light
Luke 11:36 the whole **b** will be full of
Luke 12: 4 of those who kill the **b**, and
Luke 12:22 nor about the **b**, what you
Luke 12:23 the **b** is more than clothing
Luke 17:37 Wherever the **b** is, there the
Luke 22:19 This is My **b** which is given
Luke 23:52 and asked for the **b** of Jesus
Luke 23:55 tomb and how His **b** was laid
Luke 24: 3 did not find the **b** of the
Luke 24:23 When they did not find His **b**
John 2:21 of the temple of His **b**
John 19:38 take away the **b** of Jesus
John 19:38 came and took the **b** of Jesus
John 19:40 Then they took the **b** of Jesus
John 20:12 where the **b** of Jesus had lain
Acts 2:30 that of the fruit of his **b**
Acts 9:40 And turning to the **b** he said
Acts 19:12 from his **b** to the sick, and
Rom 4:19 he did not consider his own **b**
Rom 6: 6 that the **b** of sin might be
Rom 6:12 sin reign in your mortal **b**
Rom 7: 4 law through the **b** of Christ
Rom 7:24 me from this **b** of death
Rom 8:10 the **b** is dead because of sin,
Rom 8:13 to death the deeds of the **b**
Rom 8:23 the redemption of our **b**
Rom 12: 4 we have many members in one **b**
Rom 12: 5 many, are one **b** in Christ, and
1Co 5: 3 as absent in **b** but present in
1Co 6:13 Now the **b** is not for sexual
1Co 6:13 Lord, and the Lord for the **b**
1Co 6:16 to a harlot is one **b** with her
1Co 6:18 a man does is outside the **b**
1Co 6:18 sins against his own **b**
1Co 6:19 **b** is the temple of the Holy
1Co 6:20 glorify God in your **b** and in
1Co 7: 4 have authority over her own **b**
1Co 7: 4 have authority over his own **b**
1Co 7:34 she may be holy both in **b**
1Co 9:27 But I discipline my **b** and
1Co 10:16 communion of the **b** of Christ
1Co 10:17 many, are one bread and one **b**
1Co 11:24 this is My **b** which is broken
1Co 11:27 will be guilty of the **b** and
1Co 11:29 not discerning the Lord's **b**
1Co 12:12 For as the **b** is one and has
1Co 12:12 all the members of that one **b**
1Co 12:12 being many, are one **b**
1Co 12:13 were all baptized into one **b**
1Co 12:14 For in fact the **b** is not one
1Co 12:15 not a hand, I am not of the **b**
1Co 12:15 is it therefore not of the **b**
1Co 12:16 not an eye, I am not of the **b**
1Co 12:16 is it therefore not of the **b**
1Co 12:17 If the whole **b** were an eye
1Co 12:18 in the **b** just as He pleased
1Co 12:19 member, where would the **b** be
1Co 12:20 are many members, yet one **b**
1Co 12:22 those members of the **b** which
1Co 12:23 those members of the **b** which
1Co 12:24 But God composed the **b**,
1Co 12:25 should be no schism in the **b**
1Co 12:27 Now you are the **b** of Christ
1Co 13: 3 I give my **b** to be burned, but
1Co 15:35 And with what **b** do they come
1Co 15:37 not sow that **b** that shall be
1Co 15:38 gives it a **b** as He pleases
1Co 15:38 and to each seed its own **b**
1Co 15:42 The **b** is sown in corruption,
1Co 15:44 It is sown a natural **b**, it is
1Co 15:44 it is raised a spiritual **b**
1Co 15:44 There is a natural **b**, and
1Co 15:44 and there is a spiritual **b**
2Co 4:10 carrying about in the **b** the
2Co 4:10 may be manifested in our **b**
2Co 5: 6 **b** we are absent from the Lord
2Co 5: 8 to be absent from the **b** and to
2Co 5:10 the things done in the **b**,
2Co 12: 2 in the **b** I do not know, or
2Co 12: 2 out of the **b** I do not know
2Co 12: 3 whether in the **b** or out of
2Co 12: 3 or out of the **b** I do not know
Gal 6:17 for I bear in my **b** the marks
Eph 1:23 which is His **b**, the fullness
Eph 2:16 in one **b** through the cross
Eph 3: 6 fellow heirs, of the same **b**
Eph 4: 4 There is one **b** and one Spirit,
Eph 4:12 edifying of the **b** of Christ
Eph 4:16 from whom the whole **b**, joined
Eph 4:16 causes growth of the **b** for
Eph 5:23 and He is the Savior of the **b**
Eph 5:30 For we are members of His **b**
Phil 1:20 will be magnified in my **b**
Phil 3:21 will transform our lowly **b**
Phil 3:21 conformed to His glorious **b**
Col 1:18 And He is the head of the **b**
Col 1:22 in the **b** of His flesh through
Col 1:24 Christ, for the sake of His **b**
Col 2:11 by putting off the **b** of the
Col 2:19 the Head, from whom all the **b**
Col 2:23 humility, and neglect of the **b**
Col 3:15 also you were called in one **b**
1Th 5:23 **b** be preserved blameless at
Heb 10: 5 but a **b** You have prepared for
Heb 10:10 **b** of Jesus Christ once for
Heb 13: 3 yourselves are in the **b** also
Jas 2:16 which are needed for the **b**
Jas 2:26 For as the **b** without the
Jas 3: 2 also to bridle the whole **b**
Jas 3: 3 us, and we turn their whole **b**
Jas 3: 6 that it defiles the whole **b**
1Pe 2:24 sins in His own **b** on the tree
Jude 9 disputed about the **b** of Moses

BODYGUARDS (*see* BODY)
2Ki 11: 4 of hundreds, of the **b** and the
2Ki 11:19 captains of hundreds, the **b**

BOHAN
Josh 15: 6 stone of **B** the son of Reuben
Josh 18:17 stone of **B** the son of Reuben

BOIL (*see* BOILED, BOILING, BOILS)
Ex 16:23 and **b** what you will **b**
Ex 23:19 You shall not **b** a young goat
Ex 29:31 **b** its flesh in the holy place
Ex 34:26 You shall not **b** a young goat
Lev 8:31 **B** the flesh at the door of
Lev 13:18 body develops a **b** in the skin
Lev 13:19 of the **b** there comes a white
Lev 13:20 which has broken out of the **b**
Lev 13:23 it is the scar of the **b**
Deut 14:21 You shall not **b** a young goat
2Ki 4:38 **b** stew for the sons of the
2Ki 20: 7 they took and laid it on the **b**
Job 41:31 makes the deep **b** like a pot
Is 38:21 it as a poultice on the **b**
Is 64: 2 as fire causes water to **b**
Ezek 24: 5 under it, make it **b** well, and
Ezek 46:20 shall **b** the trespass offering
Ezek 46:24 of the temple shall **b** the

BOILED (*see* BOIL)
Ex 12: 9 nor **b** at all with water, but
Lev 6:28 which it is **b** shall be broken
Lev 6:28 if it is **b** in a bronze pot,
Num 6:19 the **b** shoulder of the ram
1Sa 2:15 will not take **b** meat from you
1Ki 19:21 and **b** their flesh, using the
2Ki 6:29 So we **b** my son, and ate him
2Ch 35:13 holy offerings they **b** in pots

BOILING (*see* BOIL)
1Sa 2:13 his hand while the meat was **b**
Job 41:20 his nostrils, as from a **b** pot
Jer 1:13 I see a **b** pot, and it is

BOILS (*see* BOIL)
Ex 9: 9 it will cause **b** that break
Ex 9:10 they caused **b** that break out
Ex 9:11 before Moses because of the **b**
Ex 9:11 for the **b** were on the
Deut 28:27 you with the **b** of Egypt, with
Deut 28:35 **b** which cannot be healed, and
Job 2: 7 struck Job with painful **b**

BOISTEROUS
Matt 14:30 he saw that the wind was **b**

BOLD (*see* BOLDLY, BOLDNESS)
Ps 138: 3 made me **b** with strength in my
Prov 28: 1 the righteous are **b** as a lion
Acts 13:46 Then Paul and Barnabas grew **b**
Rom 10:20 But Isaiah is very **b** and says
2Co 10: 1 being absent am **b** toward you
2Co 10: 2 be **b** with that confidence by
2Co 10: 2 I intend to be **b** against some
2Co 11:21 But in whatever anyone is **b**
2Co 11:21 I am **b** also
Phil 1:14 are much more **b** to speak the
1Th 2: 2 we were **b** in our God to speak
Phm 8 though I might be very **b** in

BOLDLY (*see* BOLD)
Gen 34:25 and came **b** upon the city and
John 7:26 He speaks **b**, and they say
Acts 9:27 and how he had preached **b** at
Acts 9:29 he spoke **b** in the name of the
Acts 14: 3 speaking **b** in the Lord, who
Acts 18:26 to speak **b** in the synagogue
Acts 19: 8 spoke **b** for three months,
Rom 15:15 I have written more **b** to you
Eph 6:19 that I may open my mouth **b** to
Eph 6:20 that in it I may speak **b**, as
Heb 4:16 Let us therefore come **b** to
Heb 13: 6 So we may **b** say

BOLDNESS (*see* BOLD)
Ex 14: 8 of Israel went out with **b**
Num 33: 3 **b** in the sight of all the
Acts 4:13 when they saw the **b** of Peter
Acts 4:29 **b** they may speak Your word
Acts 4:31 spoke the word of God with **b**
2Co 3:12 we use great **b** of speech
2Co 7: 4 Great is my **b** of speech
Eph 3:12 in whom we have **b** and access
Phil 1:20 ashamed, but that with all **b**
1Ti 3:13 great **b** in the faith which is
Heb 10:19 having **b** to enter the Holiest
1Jn 4:17 that we may have **b** in the day

BOLT (*see* BOLTED, BOLTS)
2Sa 13:17 me, and **b** the door behind her

BOLTED (*see* BOLT)
2Sa 13:18 out and **b** the door behind her

BOLTS (*see* BOLT)
2Sa 22:15 lightning **b**, and He vanquished
Neh 3: 3 and hung its doors with its **b**
Neh 3: 6 and hung its doors, with its **b**
Neh 3:13 it, hung its doors with its **b**
Neh 3:14 and hung its doors with its **b**
Neh 3:15 it, hung its doors with its **b**

BOND (*see* BONDAGE, BONDS, BONDWOMAN)
Deut 32:36 no one remaining, **b** or free
1Ki 14:10 every male in Israel, **b** and
1Ki 21:21 every male in Israel, both **b**
2Ki 9: 8 the males in Israel, both **b**
2Ki 14:26 and whether **b** or free, there
Ezek 20:37 into the **b** of the covenant
Luke 13:16 from this **b** on the Sabbath
Eph 4: 3 the Spirit in the **b** of peace
Col 3:14 which is the **b** of perfection

BONDAGE (*see* BOND)
Ex 1:14 lives bitter with hard **b**
Ex 2:23 groaned because of the **b**, and
Ex 2:23 up to God because of the **b**
Ex 6: 5 whom the Egyptians keep in **b**
Ex 6: 6 will rescue you from their **b**
Ex 6: 9 anguish of spirit and cruel **b**
Ex 13: 3 Egypt, out of the house of **b**
Ex 13:14 Egypt, out of the house of **b**
Ex 20: 2 Egypt, out of the house of **b**
Deut 5: 6 Egypt, out of the house of **b**
Deut 6:12 of Egypt, from the house of **b**
Deut 7: 8 you from the house of **b**, from
Deut 8:14 of Egypt, from the house of **b**
Deut 13: 5 you from the house of **b**, to
Deut 13:10 of Egypt, from the house of **b**
Deut 26: 6 us, and laid hard **b** on us
Josh 24:17 of Egypt, from the house of **b**
Judg 6: 8 you out of the house of **b**
Ezra 9: 8 a measure of revival in our **b**
Ezra 9: 9 did not forsake us in our **b**
Neh 5:18 because the **b** was heavy on
Neh 9:17 a leader to return to their **b**

Is 14: 3 the hard **b** in which you were
Jer 34: 9 keep a Jewish brother in **b**
Jer 34:10 should keep them in **b** anymore
Jer 34:13 Egypt, out of the house of **b**
Mic 6: 4 you from the house of **b**
John 8:33 never been in **b** to anyone
Acts 7: 6 they would bring them into **b**
Acts 7: 7 will be in **b** I will judge
Rom 8:15 the spirit of **b** again to fear
Rom 8:21 the **b** of corruption into the
1Co 7:15 is not under **b** in such cases
2Co 11:20 it if one brings you into **b**
Gal 2: 4 they might bring us into **b**)
Gal 4: 3 were in **b** under the elements
Gal 4: 9 you desire again to be in **b**
Gal 4:24 Sinai which gives birth to **b**
Gal 4:25 is in **b** with her children
Gal 5: 1 again with a yoke of **b**
Heb 2:15 their lifetime subject to **b**
2Pe 2:19 him also he is brought into **b**

BONDS (*see* BOND)
Judg 15:14 his **b** broke loose from his
Job 12:18 He loosens the **b** of kings
Job 39: 5 loosed the **b** of the onager
Ps 2: 3 us break Their **b** in pieces
Ps 116:16 You have loosed my **b**
Is 28:22 lest your **b** be made strong
Is 52: 2 from the **b** of your neck, O
Is 58: 6 to loose the **b** of wickedness,
Jer 2:20 your yoke and burst your **b**
Jer 5: 5 the yoke and burst the **b**
Jer 27: 2 Make for yourselves **b** and
Jer 30: 8 neck, and will burst your **b**
Nah 1:13 you, and burst your **b** apart
Zech 11: 7 and the other I called **B**
Zech 11:14 cut in two my other staff, **B**
Luke 8:29 and he broke the **b** and was
Acts 22:30 he released him from his **b**

BONDWOMAN (*see* BOND)
Gen 21:10 Cast out this **b** and her son
Gen 21:10 for the son of this **b** shall
Gen 21:12 the lad or because of your **b**
Gen 21:13 a nation of the son of the **b**
Gal 4:22 the one by a **b**, the other by
Gal 4:23 But he who was of the **b** was
Gal 4:30 Cast out the **b** and her son,
Gal 4:30 for the son of the **b** shall
Gal 4:31 of the **b** but of the free

BONE (*see* BONES)
Gen 2:23 This is now **b** of my bones
Gen 29:14 Surely you are my **b** and my
Num 19:16 or a **b** of a man, or a grave,
Num 19:18 or on the one who touched a **b**
Judg 9: 2 that I am your own flesh and **b**
2Sa 5: 1 Indeed we are your **b** and your
2Sa 19:12 are my brethren, you are my **b**
2Sa 19:13 to Amasa, "Are you not my **b**
1Ch 11: 1 Indeed we are your **b** and your
Job 2: 5 Your hand now, and touch his **b**
Job 19:20 My **b** clings to my skin and to
Prov 25:15 and a gentle tongue breaks a **b**
Ezek 37: 7 came together, **b** to **b**
Ezek 39:15 anyone sees a man's **b**, he
Zeph 3: 3 leave not a **b** till morning

BONES (*see* BONE)
Gen 2:23 This is now bone of my **b** and
Gen 50:25 shall carry up my **b** from here
Ex 12:46 shall you break one of its **b**
Ex 13:19 Moses took the **b** of Joseph
Ex 13:19 up my **b** from here with you
Num 9:12 nor break one of its **b**
Num 24: 8 he shall break their **b** and
Josh 24:32 The **b** of Joseph, which the
1Sa 31:13 Then they took their **b** and
2Sa 21:12 went and took the **b** of Saul
2Sa 21:12 the **b** of Jonathan his son,
2Sa 21:13 he brought up the **b** of Saul
2Sa 21:13 the **b** of Jonathan his son
2Sa 21:13 they gathered the **b** of those
2Sa 21:14 They buried the **b** of Saul
1Ki 13: 2 men's **b** shall be burned on
1Ki 13:31 lay my **b** beside his **b**
2Ki 13:21 and touched the **b** of Elisha
2Ki 23:14 places with the **b** of men
2Ki 23:16 took the **b** out of the tombs
2Ki 23:18 let no one move his **b**
2Ki 23:18 So they let his **b** alone
2Ki 23:18 with the **b** of the prophet who
2Ki 23:20 and burned men's **b** on them
1Ch 10:12 and buried their **b** under the
2Ch 34: 5 He also burned the **b** of the
Job 4:14 which made all my **b** shake
Job 10:11 and knit me together with **b**
Job 20:11 His **b** are full of his
Job 21:24 the marrow of his **b** is moist
Job 30:17 My **b** are pierced in me at
Job 30:30 my **b** burn with fever
Job 33:19 strong pain in many of his **b**
Job 33:21 his **b** stick out which once
Job 40:18 His **b** are like beams of
Ps 6: 2 me, for my **b** are troubled
Ps 22:14 all My **b** are out of joint
Ps 22:17 I can count all My **b**
Ps 31:10 iniquity, And my **b** waste away
Ps 32: 3 my **b** grew old Through my
Ps 34:20 He guards all his **b**
Ps 35:10 All my **b** shall say, "LORD,
Ps 38: 3 in my **b** Because of my sin
Ps 42:10 As with a breaking of my **b**
Ps 51: 8 That the **b** which You have
Ps 53: 5 For God has scattered the **b**
Ps 102: 3 my **b** are burned like a hearth
Ps 102: 5 My **b** cling to my skin
Ps 109:18 water, And like oil into his **b**
Ps 141: 7 Our **b** are scattered at the
Prov 3: 8 flesh, and strength to your **b**
Prov 12: 4 is like rottenness in his **b**
Prov 14:30 envy is rottenness to the **b**
Prov 15:30 report makes the **b** healthy
Prov 16:24 the soul and health to the **b**
Prov 17:22 a broken spirit dries the **b**
Eccl 11: 5 or how the **b** grow in the womb
Is 38:13 a lion, so He breaks all my **b**
Is 58:11 drought, and strengthen your **b**
Is 66:14 your **b** shall flourish like
Jer 8: 1 the **b** of the kings of Judah
Jer 8: 1 the **b** of its princes, and the
Jer 8: 1 the **b** of the priests, and the
Jer 8: 1 the **b** of the prophets, and the
Jer 8: 1 the **b** of the inhabitants of
Jer 20: 9 burning fire shut up in my **b**
Jer 23: 9 all my **b** shake
Jer 50:17 of Babylon has broken his **b**
Lam 1:13 He has sent fire into my **b**
Lam 3: 4 and my skin, and broken my **b**
Lam 4: 8 their skin clings to their **b**
Ezek 6: 5 I will scatter your **b** all
Ezek 24: 5 also pile fuel **b** under it
Ezek 32:27 iniquities will be on their **b**
Ezek 37: 1 and it was full of **b**
Ezek 37: 3 Son of man, can these **b** live
Ezek 37: 4 Prophesy to these **b**, and say
Ezek 37: 4 and say to them, 'O dry **b**
Ezek 37: 5 says the Lord GOD to these **b**
Ezek 37: 7 the **b** came together, bone to
Ezek 37:11 these **b** are the whole house
Ezek 37:11 Our **b** are dry, our hope is
Dan 6:24 broke all their **b** in pieces
Amos 2: 1 because he burned the **b** of
Mic 3: 2 and the flesh from their **b**
Mic 3: 3 skin from them, break their **b**
Hab 3:16 rottenness entered my **b**
Matt 23:27 are full of dead men's **b** and
Luke 24:39 flesh and **b** as you see I have
John 19:36 Not one of His **b** shall be
Acts 3: 7 ankle **b** received strength
Eph 5:30 of His flesh and of His **b**
Heb 11:22 instructions concerning his **b**

BOOK (*see* BOOKS)
Gen 5: 1 This is the **b** of the
Ex 17:14 this for a memorial in the **b**
Ex 24: 7 he took the **B** of the Covenant
Ex 32:32 blot me out of Your **b** which
Ex 32:33 I will blot him out of My **b**
Num 5:23 write these curses in a **b**
Num 21:14 the **B** of the Wars of the LORD
Deut 17:18 a copy of this law in a **b**
Deut 28:58 that are written in this **b**
Deut 28:61 written in the **b** of this law
Deut 29:20 in this **b** would settle on him
Deut 29:21 written in this **B** of the Law
Deut 29:27 that is written in this **b**
Deut 30:10 written in this **B** of the Law
Deut 31:24 the words of this law in a **b**
Deut 31:26 Take this **B** of the Law, and
Josh 1: 8 This **B** of the Law shall not
Josh 8:31 in the **B** of the Law of Moses
Josh 8:34 written in the **B** of the Law
Josh 10:13 written in the **B** of Jasher
Josh 18: 9 wrote the survey in a **b** in
Josh 23: 6 in the **B** of the Law of Moses
Josh 24:26 in the **B** of the Law of God
1Sa 10:25 royalty, and wrote it in a **b**
2Sa 1:18 is written in the **B** of Jasher
1Ki 11:41 the **b** of the acts of Solomon
1Ki 14:19 they are written in the **b** of
1Ki 14:29 **b** of the chronicles of the
1Ki 15: 7 **b** of the chronicles of the
1Ki 15:23 **b** of the chronicles of the
1Ki 15:31 **b** of the chronicles of the
1Ki 16: 5 **b** of the chronicles of the
1Ki 16:14 **b** of the chronicles of the
1Ki 16:20 **b** of the chronicles of the
1Ki 16:27 **b** of the chronicles of the
1Ki 22:39 **b** of the chronicles of the
1Ki 22:45 **b** of the chronicles of the
2Ki 1:18 **b** of the chronicles of the
2Ki 8:23 **b** of the chronicles of the
2Ki 10:34 **b** of the chronicles of the
2Ki 12:19 **b** of the chronicles of the
2Ki 13: 8 **b** of the chronicles of the
2Ki 13:12 **b** of the chronicles of the
2Ki 14: 6 in the **B** of the Law of Moses
2Ki 14:15 **b** of the chronicles of the
2Ki 14:18 **b** of the chronicles of the
2Ki 14:28 **b** of the chronicles of the
2Ki 15: 6 **b** of the chronicles of the
2Ki 15:11 they are written in the **b** of
2Ki 15:15 they are written in the **b** of
2Ki 15:21 **b** of the chronicles of the
2Ki 15:26 they are written in the **b** of
2Ki 15:31 they are written in the **b** of
2Ki 15:36 **b** of the chronicles of the
2Ki 16:19 **b** of the chronicles of the
2Ki 20:20 **b** of the chronicles of the
2Ki 21:17 **b** of the chronicles of the
2Ki 21:25 **b** of the chronicles of the
2Ki 22: 8 I have found the **B** of the Law
2Ki 22: 8 Hilkiah gave the **b** to Shaphan
2Ki 22:10 the priest has given me a **b**
2Ki 22:11 the words of the **B** of the Law
2Ki 22:13 the words of this **b** that has
2Ki 22:13 obeyed the words of this **b**
2Ki 22:16 all the words of the **b** which
2Ki 23: 2 all the words of the **B** of the
2Ki 23: 3 that were written in this **b**
2Ki 23:21 in this **B** of the Covenant
2Ki 23:24 the **b** that Hilkiah the priest
2Ki 23:28 **b** of the chronicles of the
2Ki 24: 5 **b** of the chronicles of the
1Ch 9: 1 the **b** of the kings of Israel
1Ch 29:29 in the **b** of Samuel the seer
1Ch 29:29 seer, in the **b** of Nathan the
1Ch 29:29 in the **b** of Gad the seer,
2Ch 9:29 the **b** of Nathan the prophet
2Ch 12:15 the **b** of Shemaiah the prophet
2Ch 16:11 the **b** of the kings of Judah
2Ch 17: 9 had the **B** of the Law of the
2Ch 20:34 they are written in the **b** of
2Ch 20:34 the **b** of the kings of Israel
2Ch 24:27 annals of the **b** of the kings
2Ch 25: 4 in the Law in the **B** of Moses
2Ch 25:26 the **b** of the kings of Judah
2Ch 27: 7 the **b** of the kings of Israel
2Ch 28:26 the **b** of the kings of Judah
2Ch 32:32 and in the **b** of the kings of
2Ch 33:18 the **b** of the kings of Israel
2Ch 34:14 the priest found the **B** of the
2Ch 34:15 I have found the **B** of the Law
2Ch 34:15 Hilkiah gave the **b** to Shaphan
2Ch 34:16 carried the **b** to the king
2Ch 34:18 the priest has given me a **b**
2Ch 34:21 words of the **b** that is found
2Ch 34:21 all that is written in this **b**
2Ch 34:24 that are written in the **b**
2Ch 34:30 all the words of the **b** of the
2Ch 34:31 that were written in this **b**
2Ch 35:12 is written in the **B** of Moses
2Ch 35:27 the **b** of the kings of Israel
2Ch 36: 8 the **b** of the kings of Israel
Ezra 4:15 the **b** of the records of your
Ezra 4:15 find in the **b** of the records
Ezra 6:18 is written in the **B** of Moses
Neh 8: 1 the **B** of the Law of Moses
Neh 8: 3 attentive to the **B** of the Law
Neh 8: 5 And Ezra opened the **b** in the
Neh 8: 8 read distinctly from the **b**
Neh 8:18 he read from the **B** of the Law

Neh 9: 3 read from the **B** of the Law of
Neh 12:23 in the **b** of the chronicles
Neh 13: 1 **B** of Moses in the hearing of
Esth 2:23 it was written in the **b** of
Esth 6: 1 the **b** of the records of the
Esth 10: 2 **b** of the chronicles of the
Job 19:23 they were inscribed in a **b**
Job 31:35 my Prosecutor had written a **b**
Ps 40: 7 of the **B** it is written of me
Ps 56: 8 Are they not in Your **b**
Ps 69:28 out of the **b** of the living
Ps 139:16 And in Your **b** they all were
Is 29:11 words of a **b** that is sealed
Is 29:12 Then the **b** is delivered to
Is 29:18 shall hear the words of the **b**
Is 34:16 Search from the **b** of the LORD
Jer 25:13 all that is written in this **b**
Jer 30: 2 Write in a **b** for yourself
Jer 36: 2 Take a scroll of a **b** and write
Jer 36: 4 wrote on a scroll of a **b**, at
Jer 36: 8 reading from the **b** the words
Jer 36:10 **b** the words of Jeremiah in
Jer 36:11 words of the LORD from the **b**
Jer 36:13 the **b** in the hearing of the
Jer 36:18 wrote them with ink in the **b**
Jer 36:32 all the words of the **b** which
Jer 45: 1 in a **b** at the instruction of
Jer 51:60 So Jeremiah wrote in a **b** all
Jer 51:63 have finished reading this **b**
Ezek 2: 9 a scroll of a **b** was in it
Dan 12: 1 who is found written in the **b**
Dan 12: 4 seal the **b** until the time of
Nah 1: 1 The **b** of the vision of Nahum
Mal 3:16 so a **b** of remembrance was
Matt 1: 1 The **b** of the genealogy of
Mark 12:26 not read in the **b** of Moses
Luke 3: 4 as it is written in the **b** of
Luke 4:17 He was handed the **b** of the
Luke 4:17 And when He had opened the **b**
Luke 4:20 Then He closed the **b**, and gave
Luke 20:42 said in the **B** of Psalms, 'The
John 20:30 are not written in this **b**
Acts 1:20 is written in the **b** of Psalms
Acts 7:42 in the **b** of the Prophets
Gal 3:10 written in the **b** of the law
Phil 4: 3 names are in the **B** of Life
Heb 9:19 sprinkled both the **b** itself
Heb 10: 7 of the **b** it is written of Me
Rev 1:11 What you see, write in a **b**
Rev 3: 5 his name from the **B** of Life
Rev 10: 2 he had a little **b** open in his
Rev 10: 8 take the little **b** which is
Rev 10: 9 Give me the little **b**
Rev 10:10 I took the little **b** out of
Rev 13: 8 not been written in the **B** of
Rev 17: 8 are not written in the **B** of
Rev 20:12 another **b** was opened, which
Rev 20:12 which is the **B** of Life
Rev 20:15 not found written in the **B** of
Rev 21:27 in the Lamb's **B** of Life
Rev 22: 7 of the prophecy of this **b**
Rev 22: 9 who keep the words of this **b**
Rev 22:10 of the prophecy of this **b**
Rev 22:18 of the prophecy of this **b**
Rev 22:18 that are written in this **b**
Rev 22:19 of the **b** of this prophecy
Rev 22:19 his part from the **B** of Life
Rev 22:19 which are written in this **b**

BOOKS (*see* BOOK)
Eccl 12:12 Of making many **b** there is no
Dan 7:10 seated, and the **b** were opened
Dan 9: 2 understood by the **b** the
John 21:25 the **b** that would be written
Acts 19:19 brought their **b** together and
2Ti 4:13 and the **b**, especially the
Rev 20:12 before God, and **b** were opened
Rev 20:12 which were written in the **b**

BOOTH (*see* BOOTHS)
Job 27:18 like a **b** which a watchman
Is 1: 8 is left as a **b** in a vineyard

BOOTHS (*see* BOOTH)
Gen 33:17 and made **b** for his livestock
Lev 23:42 dwell in **b** for seven days
Lev 23:42 Israelites shall dwell in **b**
Lev 23:43 **b** when I brought them out of
2Ki 23: 7 he tore down the ritual **b** of
Neh 8:14 in **b** during the feast of the
Neh 8:15 of leafy trees, to make **b**
Neh 8:16 them and made themselves **b**
Neh 8:17 from the captivity made **b**
Neh 8:17 and sat under the **b**

BOOTY
Num 31:11 all the spoil and all the **b**
Num 31:12 brought the captives, the **b**
Num 31:32 And the **b** remaining from the
Deut 3: 7 we took as **b** for ourselves
Josh 8: 2 take as **b** for yourselves
Josh 8:27 took as **b** for themselves,
Josh 11:14 took as **b** for themselves
Jer 49:32 Their camels shall be for **b**
Ezek 38:12 to take plunder and to take **b**
Ezek 38:13 gathered your army to take **b**
Hab 2: 7 And you will become their **b**
Zeph 1:13 their goods shall become **b**

BORDER (*see* BORDERING, BORDERS)
Gen 10:19 the **b** of the Canaanites was
Gen 49:13 and his **b** shall adjoin Sidon
Ex 16:35 the **b** of the land of Canaan
Num 20:16 a city on the edge of your **b**
Num 20:23 by the **b** of the land of Edom
Num 21:13 from the **b** of the Amorites
Num 21:13 the Arnon is the **b** of Moab
Num 21:15 Ar, and lies on the **b** of Moab
Num 21:24 for the **b** of the people of
Num 22:36 is on the **b** at the Arnon, the
Num 33:44 Ije Abarim, at the **b** of Moab
Num 34: 3 Your southern **b** shall be
Num 34: 3 of Zin along the **b** of Edom
Num 34: 3 then your southern **b** shall
Num 34: 4 your **b** shall turn from the
Num 34: 5 the **b** shall turn from Azmon
Num 34: 6 As for the western **b**, you
Num 34: 6 have the Great Sea for a **b**
Num 34: 6 this shall be your western **b**
Num 34: 7 this shall be your northern **b**
Num 34: 7 out your **b** line to Mount Hor
Num 34: 8 **b** to the entrance of Hamath
Num 34: 8 the **b** shall be toward Zedad
Num 34: 9 the **b** shall proceed to
Num 34: 9 This shall be your northern **b**
Num 34:10 **b** from Hazar Enan to Shepham
Num 34:11 the **b** shall go down from
Num 34:11 the **b** shall go down and reach
Num 34:12 the **b** shall go down along
Deut 3:14 Argob, as far as the **b** of the
Deut 3:16 middle of the river as the **b**
Deut 3:16 the **b** of the people of Ammon
Deut 3:17 with the Jordan as the **b**
Deut 12:20 your **b** as He has promised you
Josh 4:19 on the east **b** of Jericho
Josh 12: 2 Jabbok, which is the **b** of the
Josh 12: 5 as far as the **b** of the
Josh 12: 5 of Gilead as far as the **b** of
Josh 13: 3 as far as the **b** of Ekron
Josh 13: 4 to the **b** of the Amorites
Josh 13:10 as far as the **b** of the
Josh 13:11 the **b** of the Geshurites and
Josh 13:23 And the **b** of the children of
Josh 13:26 Mahanaim to the **b** of Debir
Josh 13:27 with the Jordan as its **b**
Josh 15: 1 The **b** of Edom at the
Josh 15: 2 their southern **b** began at the
Josh 15: 4 and the **b** ended at the sea
Josh 15: 4 This shall be your southern **b**
Josh 15: 5 The east **b** was the Salt Sea
Josh 15: 5 the **b** on the northern quarter
Josh 15: 6 The **b** went up to Beth Hoglah
Josh 15: 6 the **b** went up to the stone of
Josh 15: 7 Then the **b** went up toward
Josh 15: 7 The **b** continued toward the
Josh 15: 8 the **b** went up by the Valley
Josh 15: 8 The **b** went up to the top of
Josh 15: 9 Then the **b** went around from
Josh 15: 9 the **b** went around to Baalah
Josh 15:10 Then the **b** turned westward
Josh 15:11 the **b** went out to the side of
Josh 15:11 Then the **b** went around to
Josh 15:11 and the **b** ended at the sea
Josh 15:12 The west **b** was the coastline
Josh 15:21 toward the **b** of Edom in the
Josh 16: 2 passed along to the **b** of the
Josh 16: 5 The **b** of the children of
Josh 16: 5 The **b** of their inheritance on
Josh 16: 6 the **b** went out toward the sea
Josh 16: 6 then the **b** went around
Josh 16: 8 The **b** went out from Tappuah
Josh 17: 7 the **b** went along south to the
Josh 17: 8 but Tappuah on the **b** of
Josh 17: 9 the **b** descended to the Brook
Josh 17: 9 The **b** of Manasseh was on the
Josh 17:10 and the sea was its **b**
Josh 18:12 Their **b** on the north side
Josh 18:12 the **b** went up to the side of
Josh 18:13 The **b** went over from there
Josh 18:13 the **b** descended to Ataroth
Josh 18:14 Then the **b** extended from
Josh 18:15 the **b** extended on the west and
Josh 18:16 Then the **b** came down to the
Josh 18:19 the **b** passed along to the
Josh 18:19 then the **b** ended at the north
Josh 18:20 was its **b** on the east side
Josh 19:10 the **b** of their inheritance
Josh 19:11 Their **b** went toward the west
Josh 19:12 along the **b** of Chisloth Tabor
Josh 19:14 Then the **b** went around it on
Josh 19:22 And the **b** reached to Tabor,
Josh 19:22 their **b** ended at the Jordan
Josh 19:29 the **b** turned to Ramah and to
Josh 19:29 then the **b** turned to Hosah,
Josh 19:33 And their **b** began at Heleph,
Josh 19:34 From Heleph the **b** extended
Josh 19:47 the **b** of the children of Dan
Josh 22:25 the Jordan a **b** between you
Josh 24:30 the **b** of his inheritance at
Judg 2: 9 the **b** of his inheritance at
Judg 7:22 as far as the **b** of Abel
Judg 11:18 did not enter the **b** of Moab
Judg 11:18 the Arnon was the **b** of Moab
1Sa 6:12 them to the **b** of Beth Shemesh
1Sa 13:18 **b** that overlooks the Valley
1Ki 4:21 as far as the **b** of Egypt
2Ki 3:21 and they stood at the **b**
2Ch 9:26 as far as the **b** of Egypt
Ps 78:54 He brought them to His holy **b**
Is 19:19 a pillar to the LORD at its **b**
Jer 31:17 come back to their own **b**
Jer 50:26 her from the farthest **b**
Ezek 11:10 judge you at the **b** of Israel
Ezek 11:11 judge you at the **b** of Israel
Ezek 29:10 as far as the **b** of Ethiopia
Ezek 45: 7 the west **b** to the east **b**
Ezek 47:15 This shall be the **b** of the
Ezek 47:16 is between the **b** of Damascus
Ezek 47:16 the **b** of Hamath), to Hazar
Ezek 47:16 (which is on the **b** of Hauran)
Ezek 47:17 Hazar Enan, the **b** of Damascus
Ezek 47:17 it is the **b** of Hamath
Ezek 47:18 out the **b** from between Hauran
Ezek 48: 1 From the northern **b** along the
Ezek 48: 1 the **b** of Damascus northward,
Ezek 48: 2 by the **b** of Dan, from the
Ezek 48: 3 by the **b** of Asher, from the
Ezek 48: 4 by the **b** of Naphtali, from
Ezek 48: 5 by the **b** of Manasseh, from
Ezek 48: 6 by the **b** of Ephraim, from the
Ezek 48: 7 by the **b** of Reuben, from the
Ezek 48: 8 by the **b** of Judah, from the
Ezek 48:12 holy by the **b** of the Levites
Ezek 48:13 Opposite the **b** of the priests
Ezek 48:21 as far as the eastern **b**, and
Ezek 48:21 as far as the western **b**,
Ezek 48:22 area between the **b** of Judah
Ezek 48:22 and the **b** of Benjamin shall
Ezek 48:24 by the **b** of Benjamin, from
Ezek 48:25 by the **b** of Simeon, from the
Ezek 48:26 by the **b** of Issachar, from
Ezek 48:27 by the **b** of Zebulun, from the
Ezek 48:28 by the **b** of Gad, on the south
Ezek 48:28 the **b** shall be from Tamar to
Obad 7 shall force you to the **b**
Mal 1: 5 beyond the **b** of Israel
Mark 6:56 touch the **b** of His garment
Luke 8:44 touched the **b** of His garment

BORDERING (*see* BORDER)
Ezek 45: 7 **b** on the holy district and the

BORDERS (*see* BORDER)
Gen 23:17 within all the surrounding **b**
Gen 47:21 from one end of the **b** of
Ex 34:24 before you and enlarge your **b**
Num 32:33 with its cities within the **b**
Josh 19:13 to Rimmon, which **b** on Neah
Josh 19:49 according to their **b**, the
2Ki 19:23 enter the extremity of its **b**
1Ch 5:16 of Sharon within their **b**
1Ch 7:29 by the **b** of the children of
Ps 74:17 set all the **b** of the earth
Ps 147:14 He makes peace in your **b**, And

Is 15: 8 gone all around the **b** of Moab
Is 26:15 all the **b** of the land
Is 60:18 nor destruction within your **b**
Jer 17: 3 of sin within all your **b**
Ezek 27: 4 Your **b** are in the midst of
Ezek 47:13 These are the **b** by which you
Joel 3: 6 remove them far from their **b**
Mic 5: 6 when he treads within our **b**
Zeph 2: 8 threats against their **b**
Zech 9: 2 against Hamath, which **b** on it
Matt 23: 5 and enlarge the **b** of their

BORE (*see* BEAR)
Gen 4: 1 conceived and **b** Cain, and said,
Gen 4: 2 Then she **b** again, this time
Gen 4:17 and she conceived and **b** Enoch
Gen 4:20 And Adah **b** Jabal
Gen 4:22 she also **b** Tubal-Cain, an
Gen 4:25 she **b** a son and named him Seth
Gen 6: 4 and they **b** children to them
Gen 16:15 So Hagar **b** Abram a son
Gen 16:15 named his son, whom Hagar **b**
Gen 16:16 Hagar **b** Ishmael to Abram
Gen 19:37 The firstborn **b** a son and
Gen 19:38 the younger, she also **b** a son
Gen 20:17 Then they **b** children
Gen 21: 2 **b** Abraham a son in his old
Gen 21: 3 whom Sarah **b** to him
Gen 22:23 These eight Milcah **b** to Nahor
Gen 22:24 also **b** Tebah, Gaham, Thahash,
Gen 24:24 son, whom she **b** to Nahor
Gen 24:36 Sarah my master's wife **b** a
Gen 24:47 son, whom Milcah **b** to him
Gen 25: 2 she **b** him Zimran, Jokshan,
Gen 25:12 maidservant, **b** to Abraham
Gen 25:26 years old when she **b** them
Gen 29:32 **b** a son, and she called his
Gen 29:33 again and **b** a son, and said,
Gen 29:34 again and **b** a son, and said,
Gen 29:35 again and **b** a son, and said,
Gen 30: 1 that she **b** Jacob no children
Gen 30: 5 conceived and **b** Jacob a son
Gen 30: 7 again and **b** Jacob a second son
Gen 30:10 maid Zilpah **b** Jacob a son
Gen 30:12 Zilpah **b** Jacob a second son
Gen 30:17 and **b** Jacob a fifth son
Gen 30:19 again and **b** Jacob a sixth son
Gen 30:21 Afterward she **b** a daughter
Gen 30:23 and **b** a son, and said,
Gen 31: 8 all the flocks **b** speckled
Gen 31: 8 all the flocks **b** streaked
Gen 31:39 I **b** the loss of it
Gen 36: 4 Now Adah **b** Eliphaz to Esau,
Gen 36: 4 to Esau, and Basemath **b** Reuel
Gen 36: 5 And Aholibamah **b** Jeush,
Gen 36:12 and she **b** Amalek to Eliphaz
Gen 36:14 And she **b** to Esau
Gen 38: 3 **b** a son, and he called his
Gen 38: 4 **b** a son, and she called his
Gen 38: 5 **b** a son, and called his name
Gen 38: 5 was at Chezib when she **b** him
Gen 41:50 priest of On, **b** to him
Gen 44:27 that my wife **b** me two sons
Gen 46:15 whom she **b** to Jacob in Padan
Gen 46:18 and these she **b** to Jacob
Gen 46:20 priest of On, **b** to him
Gen 46:25 and she **b** these to Jacob
Ex 2: 2 woman conceived and **b** a son
Ex 2:22 she **b** him a son, and he called
Ex 6:20 and she **b** him Aaron and Moses
Ex 6:23 and she **b** him Nadab, Abihu,
Ex 6:25 and she **b** him Phinehas
Ex 19: 4 how I **b** you on eagles' wings
Num 26:59 and to Amram she **b** Aaron and
Deut 31: 9 who **b** the ark of the covenant
Deut 31:25 who **b** the ark of the covenant
Josh 3:15 as those who **b** the ark came
Josh 3:15 **b** the ark dipped in the edge
Josh 3:17 Then the priests who **b** the
Josh 4: 9 who **b** the ark of the covenant
Josh 4:10 So the priests who **b** the ark
Josh 4:18 when the priests who **b** the
Josh 8:33 who **b** the ark of the covenant
Judg 8:31 in Shechem also **b** him a son
Judg 11: 2 Gilead's wife **b** sons
Judg 13:24 So the woman **b** a son and
Ruth 4:12 Perez, whom Tamar **b** to Judah
Ruth 4:13 conception, and she **b** a son
1Sa 1:20 **b** a son, and called his name
1Sa 2:21 **b** three sons and two daughters
1Sa 14: 1 the young man who **b** his armor
1Sa 14: 6 the young man who **b** his armor
1Sa 17:41 the man who **b** the shield went
2Sa 11:27 his wife and **b** him a son
2Sa 12:15 that Uriah's wife **b** to David
2Sa 12:24 So she **b** a son, and he called
2Sa 18:15 ten young men who **b** Joab's
2Sa 21: 8 of Aiah, whom she **b** to Saul
1Ki 10: 2 with camels that **b** spices
1Ki 11:20 **b** him Genubath his son, whom
2Ki 4:17 **b** a son when the appointed
1Ch 2: 4 **b** him Perez and Zerah
1Ch 2:17 Abigail **b** Amasa
1Ch 2:19 as his wife, who **b** him Hur
1Ch 2:21 and she **b** him Segub
1Ch 2:24 Hezron's wife Abijah **b** him
1Ch 2:29 and she **b** him Ahban and Molid
1Ch 2:35 as wife, and she **b** him Attai
1Ch 2:46 **b** Haran, Moza, and Gazez
1Ch 2:48 **b** Sheber and Tirhanah
1Ch 2:49 She also **b** Shaaph the father
1Ch 4: 6 Naarah **b** him Ahuzzam,
1Ch 4: 9 Because I **b** him in pain
1Ch 4:17 And Mered's wife **b** Miriam,
1Ch 4:18 (His wife Jehudijah **b** Jered
1Ch 7:14 his Syrian concubine **b** him
1Ch 7:16 the wife of Machir **b** a son
1Ch 7:18 sister Hammoleketh **b** Ishhod
1Ch 7:23 she conceived and **b** a son
1Ch 15:15 **b** the ark of God on their
1Ch 15:26 **b** the ark of the covenant of
1Ch 15:27 all the Levites who **b** the ark
2Ch 9: 1 retinue, camels that **b** spices
2Ch 11:19 And she **b** him children
2Ch 11:20 she **b** him Abijah, Attai, Ziza
Neh 5:15 even their servants **b** rule
Prov 17:25 bitterness to her who **b** him
Prov 23:25 and let her who **b** you rejoice
Song 6: 9 favorite of the one who **b** her
Song 8: 5 there she who **b** you brought
Is 8: 3 and she conceived and **b** a son
Is 22: 6 Elam **b** the quiver with
Is 51: 2 father, and to Sarah who **b** you
Is 53:12 He **b** the sin of many, and made
Is 63: 9 He **b** them and carried them all
Jer 16: 3 their mothers who **b** them and
Jer 20:14 in which my mother **b** me
Jer 22:26 out, and your mother who **b** you
Jer 31:19 because I **b** the reproach of
Jer 50:12 she who **b** you shall be
Ezek 12: 7 I **b** them on my shoulder in
Ezek 16:20 daughters, whom you **b** to Me
Ezek 23: 4 were Mine, and they **b** sons
Ezek 23:37 their sons whom they **b** to Me
Hos 1: 3 she conceived and **b** him a son
Hos 1: 6 again and **b** a daughter
Hos 1: 8 she conceived and **b** a son
Matt 8:17 and **b** our sicknesses
Mark 14:56 For many **b** false witness
Mark 14:57 **b** false witness against Him,
Luke 4:22 So all **b** witness to Him, and
Luke 11:27 is the womb that **b** You, and
Luke 23:29 the wombs that never **b**, and
John 1:15 John **b** witness of Him and
John 1:32 And John **b** witness, saying,
John 5:33 he has **b** witness to the truth
John 12:17 him from the dead, **b** witness
Heb 11:11 she **b** a child when she was
1Pe 2:24 who Himself **b** our sins in His
Rev 1: 2 who **b** witness to the word of
Rev 12: 5 she **b** a male Child who was to
Rev 22: 2 which **b** twelve fruits, each

BORED
2Ki 12: 9 **b** a hole in its lid, and set

BORN (*see* BIRTH, BORNE)
Gen 4:18 To Enoch was **b** Irad
Gen 4:26 Seth, to him also a son was **b**
Gen 6: 1 and daughters were **b** to them
Gen 10: 1 sons were **b** to them after the
Gen 10:21 children were **b** also to Shem
Gen 10:25 To Eber were **b** two sons
Gen 14:14 who were **b** in his own house
Gen 15: 3 indeed one **b** in my house is
Gen 17:12 he who is **b** in your house or
Gen 17:13 He who is **b** in your house and
Gen 17:17 Shall a child be **b** to a man
Gen 17:23 all who were **b** in his house
Gen 17:27 **b** in the house or bought with
Gen 21: 3 of his son who was **b** to him
Gen 21: 5 his son Isaac was **b** to him
Gen 24:15 who was **b** to Bethuel, son of
Gen 35:26 were **b** to him in Padan Aram
Gen 36: 5 were **b** to him in the land of
Gen 41:50 to Joseph were **b** two sons
Gen 46:20 land of Egypt were **b** Manasseh
Gen 46:22 Rachel, who were **b** to Jacob
Gen 46:27 **b** to him in Egypt were two
Gen 48: 5 who were **b** to you in the land
Ex 1:22 Every son who is **b** you shall
Lev 18: 9 mother, whether **b** at home or
Lev 19:34 be to you as one **b** among you
Lev 22:11 one who is **b** in his house may
Lev 22:27 or a sheep or a goat is **b**
Lev 24:16 as him who is **b** in the land
Num 26:59 who was **b** to Levi in Egypt
Num 26:60 To Aaron were **b** Nadab and
Deut 23: 8 **b** to them may enter the
Josh 5: 5 **b** in the wilderness on the
Josh 8:33 as he who was **b** among them
Judg 13: 8 for the child who will be **b**
Judg 18:29 father, who was **b** to Israel
Ruth 4:17 There is a son **b** to Naomi
2Sa 3: 2 Sons were **b** to David in
2Sa 3: 5 These were **b** to David in
2Sa 5:13 and daughters were **b** to David
2Sa 5:14 were **b** to him in Jerusalem
2Sa 12:14 the child also who is **b** to
2Sa 14:27 To Absalom were **b** three sons
2Sa 21:20 he also was **b** to the giant
2Sa 21:22 These four were **b** to the
1Ki 13: 2 shall be **b** to the house of
1Ch 1:19 To Eber were **b** two sons
1Ch 1:32 Now the sons **b** to Keturah
1Ch 2: 3 These three were **b** to him by
1Ch 2: 9 were **b** to him were Jerahmeel
1Ch 3: 1 who were **b** to him in Hebron
1Ch 3: 4 These six were **b** to him in
1Ch 3: 5 And these were **b** to him in
1Ch 7:21 **b** in that land killed them
1Ch 20: 6 he also was **b** to the giant
1Ch 20: 8 These were **b** to the giant in
1Ch 22: 9 a son shall be **b** to you, who
1Ch 26: 6 Shemaiah his son were sons **b**
Ezra 10: 3 those who have been **b** to them
Job 1: 2 three daughters were **b** to him
Job 3: 3 day perish on which I was **b**
Job 5: 7 yet man is **b** to trouble, as
Job 11:12 wild donkey's colt is **b** a man
Job 14: 1 Man who is **b** of woman is of
Job 15: 7 you the first man who was **b**
Job 15:14 he who is **b** of a woman, that
Job 25: 4 be pure who is **b** of a woman
Job 38:21 it, because you were **b** then
Ps 22:31 to a people who will be **b**
Ps 58: 3 astray as soon as they are **b**
Ps 78: 6 The children who would be **b**
Ps 87: 4 This one was **b** there
Ps 87: 5 one and that one were **b** in her
Ps 87: 6 This one was **b** there
Prov 17:17 a brother is **b** for adversity
Eccl 2: 7 and had servants **b** in my house
Eccl 3: 2 A time to be **b**, and a time to
Eccl 4:14 although he was **b** poor in his
Is 9: 6 For unto us a Child is **b**,
Is 66: 8 shall a nation be **b** at once
Jer 1: 5 before you were **b** I
Jer 16: 3 who are **b** in this place, and
Jer 20:14 be the day in which I was **b**
Jer 20:15 male child has been **b** to you
Jer 22:26 country where you were not **b**
Ezek 16: 4 on the day you were **b** your
Ezek 16: 5 loathed on the day you were **b**
Hos 2: 3 her, as in the day she was **b**
Hos 13:13 long where children are **b**
Matt 1:16 of whom was **b** Jesus who is
Matt 2: 1 Now after Jesus was **b** in
Matt 2: 2 has been **b** King of the Jews
Matt 2: 4 where the Christ was to be **b**
Matt 11:11 among those **b** of women there
Matt 19:12 **b** thus from their mother's
Matt 26:24 that man if he had not been **b**
Mark 14:21 man if he had never been **b**
Luke 1:35 **b** will be called the Son of
Luke 2:11 For there is **b** to you this
Luke 7:28 among those **b** of women there
John 1:13 who were **b**, not of blood, nor
John 3: 3 to you, unless one is **b** again
John 3: 4 can a man be **b** when he is old
John 3: 4 his mother's womb and be **b**
John 3: 5 you, unless one is **b** of water

John 3: 6 That which is **b** of the flesh
John 3: 6 that which is **b** of the Spirit
John 3: 7 to you, 'You must be **b** again
John 3: 8 who is **b** of the Spirit
John 8:41 We were not **b** of fornication
John 9: 2 parents, that he was **b** blind
John 9:19 son, who you say was **b** blind
John 9:20 son, and that he was **b** blind
John 9:32 eyes of one who was **b** blind
John 9:34 You were completely **b** in sins
John 16:21 has been **b** into the world
John 18:37 For this cause I was **b**, and
Acts 2: 8 language in which we were **b**
Acts 7:20 At this time Moses was **b**, and
Acts 18: 2 **b** in Pontus, who had recently
Acts 18:24 **b** at Alexandria, an eloquent
Acts 22: 3 **b** in Tarsus of Cilicia, but
Acts 22:28 But I was **b** a citizen
Rom 1: 3 who was **b** of the seed of
Rom 9:11 the children not yet being **b**
1Co 15: 8 as by one **b** out of due time
Gal 4: 4 **b** of a woman, **b** under the law
Gal 4:23 was **b** according to the flesh
Gal 4:29 as he who was **b** according to
Gal 4:29 was **b** according to the Spirit
Heb 11:12 were **b** as many as the stars
Heb 11:23 By faith Moses, when he was **b**
1Pe 1:23 having been **b** again, not of
1Jn 2:29 righteousness is **b** of Him
1Jn 3: 9 Whoever has been **b** of God
1Jn 3: 9 because he has been **b** of God
1Jn 4: 7 who loves is **b** of God and
1Jn 5: 1 is the Christ is **b** of God
1Jn 5: 4 For whatever is **b** of God
1Jn 5:18 is **b** of God does not sin
1Jn 5:18 but he who has been **b** of God
Rev 12: 4 her Child as soon as it was **b**

BORNE (*see* BEAR, BORN)
Gen 16: 1 wife, had **b** him no children
Gen 21: 7 For I have **b** him a son in his
Gen 21: 9 whom she had **b** to Abraham
Gen 22:20 Indeed Milcah also has **b**
Gen 29:34 I have **b** him three sons
Gen 30:20 because I have **b** him six sons
Gen 30:25 when Rachel had **b** Joseph
Gen 31:43 children whom they have **b**
Gen 34: 1 Leah, whom she had **b** to Jacob
Ex 21: 4 and she has **b** him sons or
Lev 12: 2 and **b** a male child, then she
Lev 12: 7 who has **b** a male or a female
Deut 21:15 they have **b** him children,
Judg 13: 3 have **b** no children, but you
Ruth 4:15 than seven sons, has **b** him
1Sa 2: 5 Even the barren has **b** seven
1Sa 4:20 fear, for you have **b** a son
1Ki 1: 6 His mother had **b** him after
1Ki 3:21 was not my son whom I had **b**
Job 34:31 to God, 'I have **b** chastening
Ps 69: 7 Your sake I have **b** reproach
Is 53: 4 Surely He has **b** our griefs
Is 54: 1 O barren, you who have not **b**
Jer 15: 9 languishes who has **b** seven
Jer 15:10 my mother, that you have **b** me
Lam 2:22 Those whom I have **b** and
Ezek 36: 6 because you have **b** the shame
Ezek 39:26 after they have **b** their shame
Matt 20:12 to us who have **b** the burden
1Co 15:49 as we have **b** the image of the
3Jn 6 who have **b** witness of your

BORROW (*see* BORROWED, BORROWER, BORROWS)
Deut 15: 6 nations, but you shall not **b**
Deut 28:12 nations, but you shall not **b**
2Ki 4: 3 **b** vessels from everywhere,
Matt 5:42 from him who wants to **b** from

BORROWED (*see* BORROW)
2Ki 6: 5 For it was **b**
Neh 5: 4 We have **b** money for the

BORROWER (*see* BORROW)
Prov 22: 7 and the **b** is servant to the
Is 24: 2 the lender, so with the **b**

BORROWS (*see* BORROW)
Ex 22:14 if a man **b** anything from his
Ps 37:21 The wicked **b** and does not

BOSOM
Ex 4: 6 Now put your hand in your **b**
Ex 4: 6 And he put his hand in his **b**
Ex 4: 7 Put your hand in your **b** again
Ex 4: 7 put his hand in his **b** again
Ex 4: 7 and drew it out of his **b**, and
Num 11:12 to me, 'Carry them in your **b**
Deut 13: 6 daughter, the wife of your **b**
Deut 28:54 toward the wife of his **b**
Deut 28:56 to the husband of her **b**, and
Ruth 4:16 child and laid him on her **b**
2Sa 12: 3 his own cup and lay in his **b**
1Ki 1: 2 and let her lie in your **b**,
1Ki 3:20 slept, and laid him in her **b**
1Ki 3:20 laid her dead child in my **b**
Job 31:33 by hiding my iniquity in my **b**
Ps 74:11 Take it out of Your **b** and
Ps 79:12 sevenfold into their **b** Their
Ps 89:50 How I bear in my **b** the
Prov 6:27 can a man take fire to his **b**
Eccl 7: 9 anger rests in the **b** of fools
Is 40:11 arm, and carry them in His **b**
Is 65: 6 even repay into their **b**
Is 65: 7 former work into their **b**
Is 66:11 with the consolation of her **b**
Jer 32:18 the **b** of their children after
Lam 2:12 out in their mothers' **b**
Ezek 23: 3 their virgin **b** was there
Ezek 23: 8 her, pressed her virgin **b**
Ezek 23:21 **b** because of your youthful
Mic 7: 5 from her who lies in your **b**
Luke 6:38 over will be put into your **b**
Luke 16:22 by the angels to Abraham's **b**
Luke 16:23 afar off, and Lazarus in his **b**
John 1:18 who is in the **b** of the Father
John 13:23 Jesus' **b** one of His disciples

BOTH (*see* PREFACE)

BOTTLE (*see* BOTTLES)
Ps 56: 8 Put my tears into Your **b**
Jer 13:12 Every **b** shall be filled with
Jer 13:12 **b** will be filled with wine
Hab 2:15 pressing him to your **b**, even

BOTTLES (*see* BOTTLE)
Job 38:37 can pour out the **b** of heaven
Jer 48:12 his vessels and break the **b**

BOTTOM (*see* BOTTOMLESS)
Ex 15: 5 sank to the **b** like a stone
Ex 26:24 be coupled together at the **b**
Ex 36:29 And they were coupled at the **b**
Ex 38: 4 its rim, midway from the **b**
Dan 6:24 ever came to the **b** of the den
Amos 9: 3 My sight at the **b** of the sea
Matt 27:51 was torn in two from top to **b**
Mark 15:38 was torn in two from top to **b**

BOTTOMLESS (*see* BOTTOM)
Rev 9: 1 given the key to the **b** pit
Rev 9: 2 And he opened the **b** pit, and
Rev 9:11 them the angel of the **b** pit
Rev 11: 7 that ascends out of the **b** pit
Rev 17: 8 will ascend out of the **b** pit
Rev 20: 1 having the key to the **b** pit
Rev 20: 3 and he cast him into the **b** pit

BOUGH (*see* BOUGHS)
Gen 49:22 Joseph is a fruitful **b**
Gen 49:22 a fruitful **b** by a well
Judg 9:48 cut down a **b** from the trees,
Judg 9:49 likewise cut down his own **b**
Is 10:33 lop off the **b** with terror
Is 17: 6 at the top of the uppermost **b**
Is 17: 9 will be as a forsaken **b** and an

BOUGHS (*see* BOUGH)
Lev 23:40 the **b** of leafy trees, and
Deut 24:20 shall not go over the **b** again
2Sa 18: 9 **b** of a great terebinth tree
Ps 80:10 the mighty cedars with its **b**
Ps 80:11 She sent out her **b** to the Sea
Is 27:11 When its **b** are withered, they
Ezek 17:23 and it will bring forth **b**, and
Ezek 31: 3 its top was among the thick **b**
Ezek 31: 5 its **b** were multiplied, and its
Ezek 31: 6 made their nests in its **b**
Ezek 31: 8 fir trees were not like its **b**
Ezek 31:10 set its top among the thick **b**
Ezek 31:12 its **b** lie broken by all the
Ezek 31:14 their tops among the thick **b**

BOUGHT (*see* BUY)
Gen 17:12 or **b** with money from any
Gen 17:13 he who is **b** with your money
Gen 17:23 all who were **b** with his money
Gen 17:27 born in the house or **b** with
Gen 33:19 And he **b** the parcel of land,
Gen 39: 1 **b** him from the Ishmaelites
Gen 47:14 for the grain which they **b**
Gen 47:20 Then Joseph **b** all the land of
Gen 47:23 Indeed I have **b** you and your
Gen 49:30 which Abraham **b** with the
Gen 50:13 which Abraham **b** with the
Ex 12:44 servant who is **b** for money
Lev 25:28 who **b** it until the Year of
Lev 25:30 permanently to him who **b** it
Lev 25:50 reckon with him who **b** him
Lev 25:51 the money with which he was **b**
Lev 27:22 LORD a field which he has **b**
Lev 27:24 to him from whom it was **b**
Deut 32: 6 He not your Father, who **b** you
Josh 24:32 of ground which Jacob had **b**
Ruth 4: 9 this day that I have **b** all
2Sa 12: 3 ewe lamb which he had **b** and
2Sa 24:24 So David **b** the threshing
1Ki 10:28 **b** them in Keveh at the
1Ki 16:24 he **b** the hill of Samaria from
2Ch 1:16 **b** them in Keveh at the
Is 43:24 You have **b** Me no sweet cane
Jer 32: 9 So I **b** the field from
Jer 32:43 fields will be **b** in this land
Hos 3: 2 So I **b** her for myself for
Matt 13:46 sold all that he had and **b** it
Matt 21:12 and drove out all those who **b**
Matt 27: 7 and **b** with them the potter's
Mark 11:15 to drive out those who **b** and
Mark 15:46 Then he **b** fine linen, took
Mark 16: 1 of James, and Salome **b** spices
Luke 14:18 I have **b** a piece of ground,
Luke 14:19 I have **b** five yoke of oxen,
Luke 17:28 They ate, they drank, they **b**
Luke 19:45 to drive out those who **b** and
Acts 7:16 in the tomb that Abraham **b**
1Co 6:20 For you were **b** at a price
1Co 7:23 You were **b** at a price
2Pe 2: 1 denying the Lord who **b** them

BOUND (*see* BIND)
Gen 22: 9 he **b** Isaac his son and laid
Gen 38:28 **b** it on his hand, saying,
Gen 42:24 and **b** him before their eyes
Gen 44:30 since his life is **b** up in the
Gen 49:26 up to the utmost **b** of the
Ex 12:34 **b** up in their clothes on
Ex 39:21 they **b** the breastplate by
Num 30: 4 by which she has **b** herself
Num 30: 4 with which she has **b** herself
Num 30: 5 she has **b** herself shall stand
Num 30: 6 while **b** by her vows or by a
Num 30: 6 lips by which she **b** herself
Num 30: 7 she **b** herself shall stand
Num 30: 8 lips, by which she **b** herself
Num 30: 9 by which she has **b** herself
Num 30:10 or **b** herself by an agreement
Num 30:11 she **b** herself shall stand
Josh 2:21 she **b** the scarlet cord in the
Judg 15:13 they **b** him with two new ropes
Judg 16: 6 you may be **b** to afflict you
Judg 16: 8 dried, and she **b** him with them
Judg 16:10 me what you may be **b** with
Judg 16:12 **b** him with them, and said to
Judg 16:13 me what you may be **b** with
Judg 16:21 They **b** him with bronze
1Sa 25:29 life of my lord shall be **b** in
2Sa 3:34 Your hands were not **b** nor
2Ki 5:23 **b** two talents of silver in
2Ki 17: 4 him up, and **b** him in prison
2Ki 25: 7 **b** him with bronze fetters, and
2Ch 33:11 **b** him with bronze fetters, and
2Ch 36: 6 **b** him in bronze fetters to
Job 36: 8 And if they are **b** in fetters
Ps 68: 6 who are **b** into prosperity
Ps 107:10 **B** in affliction and irons
Ps 119:61 cords of the wicked have **b** me
Prov 22:15 Foolishness is **b** up in the
Prov 30: 4 Who has **b** the waters in a
Is 1: 6 have not been closed or **b** up
Is 22: 3 found in you are **b** together
Is 61: 1 the prison to those who are **b**
Jer 5:22 the sand as the **b** of the sea
Jer 30:13 cause, that you may be **b** up
Jer 39: 7 **b** him with bronze fetters to

Jer 40: 1 when he had taken him **b** in
Jer 52:11 the king of Babylon **b** him in
Lam 1:14 of my transgressions was **b**
Ezek 34: 4 nor **b** up the broken, nor
Dan 3:21 men were **b** in their coats
Dan 3:23 fell down **b** into the midst of
Dan 3:24 Did we not cast three men **b**
Dan 4:15 **b** with a band of iron and
Dan 4:23 **b** with a band of iron and
Hos 13:12 iniquity of Ephraim is **b** up
Nah 3:10 great men were **b** in chains
Matt 14: 3 **b** him, and put him in prison
Matt 16:19 on earth will be **b** in heaven
Matt 18:18 on earth will be **b** in heaven
Matt 27: 2 And when they had **b** Him, they
Mark 5: 4 often been **b** with shackles
Mark 6:17 **b** him in prison for the sake
Mark 15: 1 they **b** Jesus, led Him away,
Luke 8:29 **b** with chains and shackles
Luke 13:16 of Abraham, whom Satan has **b**
John 11:44 who had died came out **b** hand
John 18:12 Jews arrested Jesus and **b** Him
John 18:24 Then Annas sent Him **b** to
John 19:40 **b** it in strips of linen with
Acts 8:23 bitterness and **b** by iniquity
Acts 9: 2 bring them **b** to Jerusalem
Acts 9:21 them **b** to the chief priests
Acts 10:11 sheet **b** at the four corners
Acts 12: 6 **b** with two chains between two
Acts 20:22 now I go **b** in the spirit to
Acts 21:11 **b** his own hands and feet, and
Acts 21:13 I am ready not only to be **b**
Acts 21:33 him to be **b** with two chains
Acts 22:25 as they **b** him with thongs,
Acts 22:29 and because he had **b** him
Acts 23:12 **b** themselves under an oath,
Acts 23:14 We have **b** ourselves under a
Acts 23:21 men who have **b** themselves by
Acts 24:27 the Jews a favor, left Paul **b**
Acts 28:20 Israel I am **b** with this chain
Rom 7: 2 **b** by the law to her husband
1Co 7:27 Are you **b** to a wife
1Co 7:39 A wife is **b** by law as long as
2Th 1: 3 We are **b** to thank God always
2Th 2:13 But we are **b** to give thanks
Rev 9:14 who are **b** at the great river
Rev 20: 2 **b** him for a thousand years

BOUNDARIES (*see* BOUNDARY)
Num 34: 2 the land of Canaan to its **b**
Num 34:12 land with its surrounding **b**
Deut 32: 8 He set the **b** of the peoples
Josh 18:20 according to its **b** all around
Is 10:13 removed the **b** of the people
Mic 2: 5 have no one to determine **b** by
Acts 17:26 the **b** of their habitation,

BOUNDARY (*see* BOUNDARIES)
Num 22:36 Arnon, the **b** of the territory
Num 33:37 on the **b** of the land of Edom
Deut 2:18 over at Ar, the **b** of Moab
Josh 15: 1 was the extreme southern **b**
Josh 15:12 This is the **b** of the children
Josh 16: 3 to the **b** of the Japhletites
Josh 16: 3 as far as the **b** of Lower Beth
Josh 18:19 This was the southern **b**
Judg 1:36 Now the **b** of the Amorites was
Job 26:10 at the **b** of light and darkness
Ps 104: 9 You have set a **b** that they
Prov 15:25 establish the **b** of the widow
Ezek 13:10 and one builds a **b** wall, and
Ezek 47:17 Thus the **b** shall be from the
Ezek 47:20 from the southern **b** until one

BOUNDLESS (*see* BOUNDS)
Nah 3: 9 her strength, and it was **b**

BOUNDS (*see* BOUNDLESS)
Ex 19:12 You shall set **b** for the
Ex 19:23 Set **b** around the mountain and
Ex 23:31 I will set your **b** from the

BOUNTIFUL (*see* BOUNTIFULLY, BOUNTY)
Prov 22: 9 He who has a **b** eye will be
Is 32: 5 nor the miser said to be **b**
Jer 2: 7 brought you into a **b** country
2Co 9: 5 time, and prepare your **b** gift

BOUNTIFULLY (*see* BOUNTIFUL)
Num 23:11 look, you have blessed them **b**
Num 24:10 you have **b** blessed them these
Ps 13: 6 He has dealt **b** with me
Ps 116: 7 the LORD has dealt **b** with you
Ps 119:17 Deal **b** with Your servant,
Ps 142: 7 For You shall deal **b** with me
2Co 9: 6 who sows **b** will also reap **b**

BOUNTY (*see* BOUNTIFUL)
1Ki 10:13 her according to the royal **b**
Hos 10: 1 According to the **b** of his

BOW (*see* BOWED, BOWING, BOWMEN, BOWS, BOWSHOT, BOWSTRING)
Gen 27: 3 your quiver and your **b**, and go
Gen 27:29 you, and nations **b** down to you
Gen 27:29 mother's sons **b** down to you
Gen 37:10 brothers indeed come to **b**
Gen 41:43 out before him, "**B** the knee
Gen 48:22 with my sword and my **b**
Gen 49: 8 shall **b** down before you
Gen 49:24 But his **b** remained in
Ex 11: 8 **b** down to me, saying, 'Get
Ex 20: 5 you shall not **b** down to them
Ex 23:24 You shall not **b** down to their
Lev 26: 1 in your land, to **b** down to it
Deut 5: 9 you shall not **b** down to them
Josh 23: 7 serve them nor **b** down to them
Josh 24:12 your sword or with your **b**
Judg 2:19 serve them and **b** down to them
1Sa 2:36 **b** down to him for a piece of
1Sa 18: 4 even to his sword and his **b**
2Sa 1:18 of Judah the Song of the **B**
2Sa 1:22 the **b** of Jonathan did not
2Sa 15: 5 near him to **b** down to him
2Sa 16: 4 I humbly **b** before you, that I
2Sa 22:35 arms can bend a **b** of bronze
1Ki 22:34 man drew a **b** at random, and
2Ki 5:18 I **b** down in the temple of
2Ki 5:18 when I **b** down in the temple
2Ki 6:22 with your sword and your **b**
2Ki 9:24 Now Jehu drew his **b** with full
2Ki 13:15 Take a **b** and some arrows
2Ki 13:15 So he took himself a **b** and
2Ki 13:16 Put your hand on the **b**
2Ki 17:35 nor **b** down to them nor serve
1Ch 5:18 and sword, to shoot with the **b**
1Ch 12: 2 and shooting arrows with the **b**
2Ch 17:17 thousand men armed with **b**
2Ch 18:33 man drew a **b** at random, and
Esth 3: 2 would not **b** or pay homage
Esth 3: 5 did not **b** or pay him homage
Job 20:24 a bronze **b** will pierce him
Job 29:20 my **b** is renewed in my hand
Job 31:10 let others **b** down over her
Job 39: 3 They **b** down, they bring forth
Ps 7:12 He bends His **b** and makes it
Ps 11: 2 The wicked bend their **b**, They
Ps 18:34 arms can bend a **b** of bronze
Ps 22:29 the dust Shall **b** before Him
Ps 31: 2 **B** down Your ear to me,
Ps 37:14 sword And have bent their **b**
Ps 44: 6 For I will not trust in my **b**
Ps 46: 9 He breaks the **b** and cuts the
Ps 58: 7 When he bends his **b**, Let his
Ps 72: 9 wilderness will **b** before Him
Ps 76: 3 He broke the arrows of the **b**
Ps 78:57 aside like a deceitful **b**
Ps 86: 1 **B** down Your ear, O LORD, hear
Ps 95: 6 let us worship and **b** down
Ps 144: 5 **B** down Your heavens, O LORD,
Prov 14:19 The evil will **b** before the
Eccl 12: 3 and the strong men **b** down
Is 2: 9 People **b** down, and each man
Is 10: 4 Without Me they shall **b** down
Is 21:15 drawn sword, from the bent **b**
Is 41: 2 as driven stubble to his **b**
Is 45:14 and they shall **b** down to you
Is 45:23 that to Me every knee shall **b**
Is 46: 2 stoop, they **b** down together
Is 49:23 they shall **b** down to you with
Is 58: 5 Is it to **b** down his head like
Is 65:12 you shall all **b** down to the
Is 66:19 Pul and Lud, who draw the **b**
Jer 6:23 They will lay hold on **b** and
Jer 9: 3 like their **b** they have bent
Jer 46: 9 who handle and bend the **b**
Jer 49:35 I will break the **b** of Elam
Jer 50:14 all you who bend the **b**
Jer 50:29 All you who bend the **b**,
Jer 50:42 They shall hold the **b** and the
Jer 51: 3 her let the archer bend his **b**
Lam 2: 4 an enemy, He has bent His **b**
Lam 2:10 The virgins of Jerusalem **b**
Lam 3:12 He has bent His **b** and set me
Ezek 39: 3 the **b** out of your left hand
Hos 1: 5 day that I will break the **b**
Hos 1: 7 and will not save them by **b**
Hos 2:18 **B** and sword of battle I will
Hos 7:16 they are like a deceitful **b**
Amos 2:15 not stand who handles the **b**
Mic 6: 6 **b** myself before the High God
Hab 3: 9 Your **b** was made quite ready
Zech 9:10 the battle **b** shall be cut off
Zech 9:13 For I have bent Judah, My **b**
Zech 9:13 fitted the **b** with Ephraim, and
Zech 10: 4 peg, from him the battle **b**
Rom 11:10 and **b** down their back always
Rom 14:11 every knee shall **b** to Me
Eph 3:14 For this reason I **b** my knees
Phil 2:10 of Jesus every knee should **b**
Rev 6: 2 And he who sat on it had a **b**

BOWED (*see* BOW)
Gen 18: 2 and **b** himself to the ground,
Gen 19: 1 he **b** himself with his face
Gen 23: 7 **b** himself to the people of
Gen 23:12 Then Abraham **b** himself down
Gen 24:26 Then the man **b** down his head
Gen 24:48 I **b** my head and worshiped the
Gen 33: 3 **b** himself to the ground seven
Gen 33: 6 and their children, and **b** down
Gen 33: 7 her children, and they **b** down
Gen 33: 7 came near, and they **b** down
Gen 37: 7 around and **b** down to my sheaf
Gen 37: 9 the eleven stars **b** down to me
Gen 42: 6 **b** down before him with their
Gen 43:26 and **b** down before him to the
Gen 43:28 they **b** their heads down and
Gen 47:31 So Israel **b** himself on the
Gen 48:12 he **b** down with his face to
Gen 49:15 he **b** his shoulder to bear a
Ex 4:31 then they **b** their heads and
Ex 12:27 So the people **b** their heads
Ex 18: 7 **b** down, and kissed him
Ex 34: 8 **b** his head toward the earth,
Num 22:31 he **b** his head and fell flat on
Num 25: 2 ate and **b** down to their gods
Josh 23:16 and **b** down to them, then the
Judg 2:12 them, and they **b** down to them
Judg 2:17 other gods, and **b** down to them
Ruth 2:10 **b** down to the ground, and said
1Sa 4:19 she **b** herself and gave birth,
1Sa 20:41 ground, and **b** down three times
1Sa 24: 8 face to the earth, and **b** down
1Sa 25:23 and **b** down to the ground
1Sa 25:41 **b** her face to the earth, and
1Sa 28:14 face to the ground and **b** down
2Sa 9: 8 Then he **b** himself, and said
2Sa 14:22 **b** himself, and thanked the
2Sa 14:33 **b** himself on his face to the
2Sa 18:21 the Cushite **b** himself to Joab
2Sa 18:28 Then he **b** down with his
2Sa 22:10 He **b** the heavens also, and
2Sa 24:20 **b** before the king with his
1Ki 1:16 And Bathsheba **b** and did
1Ki 1:23 he **b** down before the king
1Ki 1:31 Then Bathsheba **b** with her
1Ki 1:47 Then the king **b** himself on
1Ki 2:19 **b** down to her, and sat down on
1Ki 18:42 then he **b** down on the ground,
1Ki 19:18 knees have not **b** to Baal, and
2Ki 2:15 **b** to the ground before him
2Ki 4:37 his feet, and **b** to the ground
1Ch 21:21 **b** down to David with his face
1Ch 29:20 **b** their heads and prostrated
2Ch 7: 3 they **b** their faces to the
2Ch 20:18 Jehoshaphat **b** his head with
2Ch 20:18 Jerusalem **b** before the LORD
2Ch 24:17 came and **b** down to the king
2Ch 25:14 **b** down before them and burned
2Ch 29:29 who were present with him **b**
2Ch 29:30 and they **b** their heads and
Neh 8: 6 And they **b** their heads and
Esth 3: 2 were within the king's gate **b**
Ps 18: 9 He **b** the heavens also, and
Ps 20: 8 They have **b** down and fallen
Ps 35:14 I **b** down heavily, as one who
Ps 38: 6 troubled, I am **b** down greatly
Ps 44:25 For our soul is **b** down to the
Ps 57: 6 My soul is **b** down
Ps 145:14 up all those who are **b** down
Ps 146: 8 raises those who are **b** down
Is 2:11 of men shall be **b** down, and
Is 2:17 of man shall be **b** down, and
Hab 3: 6 the perpetual hills **b**

Matt 27:29 they **b** the knee before Him and
Luke 24: 5 **b** their faces to the earth,
Rom 11: 4 have not **b** the knee to Baal

BOWING (*see* BOW)
Gen 24:52 LORD, **b** himself to the earth
Ezra 10: 1 **b** down before the house of
Is 60:14 you shall come **b** to you, and
Mark 15:19 **b** the knee, they worshiped
John 19:30 **b** His head, He gave up His

BOWL (*see* BOWL-SHAPED, BOWLS)
Num 7:13 and one silver **b** of seventy
Num 7:19 and one silver **b** of seventy
Num 7:25 and one silver **b** of seventy
Num 7:31 and one silver **b** of seventy
Num 7:37 and one silver **b** of seventy
Num 7:43 and one silver **b** of seventy
Num 7:49 and one silver **b** of seventy
Num 7:55 and one silver **b** of seventy
Num 7:61 and one silver **b** of seventy
Num 7:67 and one silver **b** of seventy
Num 7:73 and one silver **b** of seventy
Num 7:79 and one silver **b** of seventy
Num 7:85 and each **b** seventy shekels
Deut 28: 5 basket and your kneading **b**
Deut 28:17 basket and your kneading **b**
Judg 5:25 out cream in a lordly **b**
Judg 6:38 the fleece, a **b** full of water
2Ki 2:20 Bring me a new **b**, and put salt
1Ch 28:17 gold by weight for every **b**
1Ch 28:17 silver by weight for every **b**
Prov 19:24 man buries his hand in the **b**
Prov 26:15 man buries his hand in the **b**
Eccl 12: 6 or the golden **b** is broken
Zech 4: 2 gold with a **b** on top of it
Zech 4: 3 it, one at the right of the **b**
Rev 16: 2 out his **b** upon the earth, and
Rev 16: 3 poured out his **b** on the sea
Rev 16: 4 out his **b** on the rivers and
Rev 16: 8 poured out his **b** on the sun
Rev 16:10 **b** on the throne of the beast
Rev 16:12 out his **b** on the great river
Rev 16:17 poured out his **b** into the air

BOWLS (*see* BOWL)
Ex 8: 3 and into your kneading **b**
Ex 12:34 having their kneading **b** bound
Ex 25:29 and its **b** for pouring
Ex 25:31 shaft, its branches, its **b**
Ex 25:33 Three **b** shall be made like
Ex 25:33 and three **b** made like almond
Ex 25:34 **b** shall be made like almond
Ex 37:16 its dishes, its cups, its **b**
Ex 37:17 shaft, its branches, its **b**
Ex 37:19 There were three **b** made like
Ex 37:19 and three **b** made like almond
Ex 37:20 **b** made like almond blossoms
Num 4: 7 the dishes, the pans, the **b**
Num 7:84 platters, twelve silver **b**
1Ki 7:40 and the shovels and the **b**
1Ki 7:45 pots, the shovels, and the **b**
1Ki 7:50 basins, the trimmers, the **b**
1Ch 28:17 of pure gold, and the golden **b**
1Ch 28:17 and for the silver **b**, silver
2Ch 4: 8 he made one hundred **b** of gold
2Ch 4:11 pots and the shovels and the **b**
2Ch 4:22 the trimmers, the **b**, the
Jer 35: 5 the Rechabites **b** full of wine
Jer 52:18 shovels, the trimmers, the **b**
Jer 52:19 basins, the firepans, the **b**
Amos 6: 6 who drink wine from **b**, and
Zech 14:20 like the **b** before the altar
Rev 5: 8 golden **b** full of incense,
Rev 15: 7 **b** full of the wrath of God
Rev 16: 1 pour out the **b** of the wrath
Rev 17: 1 who had the seven **b** came and
Rev 21: 9 angels who had the seven **b**

BOWL-SHAPED (*see* BOWL)
1Ki 7:41 the two **b** capitals that were
1Ki 7:41 networks covering the two **b**
1Ki 7:42 to cover the two **b** capitals
2Ch 4:12 the **b** capitals that were on
2Ch 4:12 networks covering the two **b**
2Ch 4:13 to cover the two **b** capitals

BOWMEN (*see* BOW)
Jer 4:29 noise of the horsemen and **b**

BOWS (*see* BOW)
Gen 49: 9 He **b** down, he lies down as a
Num 24: 9 He **b** down, he lies down as a
1Sa 2: 4 The **b** of the mighty men are
1Ch 12: 2 armed with **b**, using both the
2Ch 14: 8 who carried shields and drew **b**
2Ch 26:14 helmets, body armor, **b**, and
Neh 4:13 their spears, and their **b**
Neh 4:16 spears, the shields, the **b**
Ps 37:15 And their **b** shall be broken
Ps 64: 3 bend their **b** to shoot their
Ps 78: 9 being armed and carrying **b**
Is 5:28 sharp, and all their **b** bent
Is 7:24 and **b** men will come there,
Is 13:18 Also their **b** will dash the
Is 46: 1 Bel **b** down, Nebo stoops
Jer 51:56 one of their **b** is broken
Ezek 39: 9 shields and bucklers, the **b**

BOWSHOT (*see* BOW)
Gen 21:16 at a distance of about a **b**

BOWSTRING (*see* BOW, BOWSTRINGS)
Job 30:11 Because He has loosed my **b**

BOWSTRINGS (*see* BOWSTRING)
Judg 16: 7 bind me with seven fresh **b**
Judg 16: 8 up to her seven fresh **b**, not
Judg 16: 9 But he broke the **b** as a

BOX (*see* BOXES)
Is 41:19 pine and the **b** tree together,
Is 60:13 and the **b** tree together, to
John 12: 6 a thief, and had the money **b**
John 13:29 because Judas had the money **b**

BOXES (*see* BOX)
Is 3:20 the perfume **b**, the charms,

BOY (*see* BOY'S, BOYS)
Gen 21:14 the **b** to Hagar, and sent her
Gen 21:15 she placed the **b** under one of
Gen 21:16 me not see the death of the **b**
Gen 42:22 Do not sin against the **b**'
1Sa 3: 1 Then the **b** Samuel ministered
1Sa 3: 8 the LORD had called the **b**
Joel 3: 3 have given a **b** in exchange
Luke 2:43 the **B** Jesus lingered behind

BOY'S (*see* BOY)
Judg 13:12 will be the **b** rule of life

BOYS (*see* BOY)
Gen 25:27 So the **b** grew
Lam 5:13 **b** staggered under loads of
Zech 8: 5 the city shall be full of **b**

BOZEZ
1Sa 14: 4 And the name of one was **B**, and

BOZKATH
Josh 15:39 Lachish, **B**, Eglon,
2Ki 22: 1 the daughter of Adaiah of **B**

BOZRAH
Gen 36:33 of **B** reigned in his place
1Ch 1:44 of **B** reigned in his place
Is 34: 6 the LORD has a sacrifice in **B**
Is 63: 1 with dyed garments from **B**
Jer 48:24 on Kerioth and **B**, on all the
Jer 49:13 LORD, "that **B** shall become a
Jer 49:22 and spread His wings over **B**
Amos 1:12 shall devour the palaces of **B**

BRACED
Judg 16:29 he **b** himself against them,

BRACELET (*see* BRACELETS)
2Sa 1:10 the **b** that was on his arm, and

BRACELETS (*see* BRACELET)
Gen 24:22 two **b** for her wrists weighing
Gen 24:30 the **b** on his sister's wrists,
Gen 24:47 nose and the **b** on her wrists
Num 31:50 armlets and **b** and signet rings
Is 3:19 the pendants, the **b**, and the
Ezek 16:11 put **b** on your wrists, and a
Ezek 23:42 who put **b** on their wrists and

BRAIDED
Ex 28:14 of pure gold like **b** cords
Ex 28:14 fasten the **b** chains to the
Ex 28:22 like **b** cords of pure gold
Ex 28:24 **b** chains of gold in the two
Ex 28:25 other two ends of the two **b**
Ex 39:15 like **b** cords of pure gold
Ex 39:17 they put the two **b** chains of
Ex 39:18 The two ends of the two **b**
1Ti 2: 9 not with **b** hair or gold or

BRAMBLE (*see* BRAMBLES)
Judg 9:14 all the trees said to the **b**
Judg 9:15 the **b** said to the trees, 'If
Judg 9:15 let fire come out of the **b**
Luke 6:44 gather grapes from a **b** bush

BRAMBLES (*see* BRAMBLE)
Is 34:13 and **b** in its fortresses

BRANCH (*see* BRANCHES)
Ex 25:33 like almond blossoms on one **b**
Ex 25:33 blossoms on the other **b**, with
Ex 37:19 like almond blossoms on one **b**
Ex 37:19 blossoms on the other **b**, with
Num 13:23 there cut down a **b** with one
Job 15:32 and his **b** will not be green
Job 18:16 below, and his **b** withers above
Job 29:19 dew lies all night on my **b**
Ps 80:15 the **b** that You made strong
Is 4: 2 In that day the **B** of the LORD
Is 9:14 and tail from Israel, palm **b**
Is 11: 1 a **B** shall grow out of his
Is 14:19 grave like an abominable **b**
Is 17: 9 bough and an uppermost **b**,
Is 19:15 palm **b** or bulrush, may do
Is 60:21 the **b** of My planting, the
Jer 1:11 I see a **b** of an almond tree
Jer 23: 5 to David a **B** of righteousness
Jer 33:15 to David a **B** of righteousness
Ezek 8:17 they put the **b** to their nose
Ezek 15: 2 the vine **b** which is among the
Ezek 17: 3 from the cedar the highest **b**
Ezek 19:14 so that she has no strong **b**
Dan 11: 7 But from a **b** of her roots one
Zech 3: 8 forth My Servant the **B**
Zech 6:12 the Man whose name is the **B**
Zech 6:12 From His place He shall **b** out
Mal 4: 1 leave them neither root nor **b**
Matt 24:32 When its **b** has already become
Mark 13:28 When its **b** has already become
John 15: 2 Every **b** in Me that does not
John 15: 2 every **b** that bears fruit He
John 15: 4 As the **b** cannot bear fruit of
John 15: 6 in Me, he is cast out as a **b**

BRANCHES (*see* BRANCH)
Gen 40:10 and in the vine were three **b**
Gen 40:12 The three **b** are three days
Gen 49:22 his **b** run over the wall
Ex 25:31 Its shaft, its **b**, its bowls,
Ex 25:32 six **b** shall come out of its
Ex 25:32 three **b** of the lampstand out
Ex 25:32 three **b** of the lampstand out
Ex 25:33 so for the six **b** that come
Ex 25:35 the first two **b** of the same
Ex 25:35 the second two **b** of the same
Ex 25:35 the third two **b** of the same
Ex 25:35 six **b** that extend from the
Ex 25:36 their **b** shall be of one piece
Ex 37:17 Its shaft, its **b**, its bowls,
Ex 37:18 six **b** came out of its sides
Ex 37:18 three **b** of the lampstand out
Ex 37:18 three **b** of the lampstand out
Ex 37:19 so for the six **b** coming out
Ex 37:21 the first two **b** of the same
Ex 37:21 the second two **b** of the same
Ex 37:21 the third two **b** of the same
Ex 37:21 the six **b** extending from it
Ex 37:22 their **b** were of one piece
Lev 23:40 **b** of palm trees, the boughs
Neh 8:15 mountain, and bring olive **b**
Neh 8:15 **b** of oil trees
Neh 8:15 myrtle **b**, palm **b**, and
Neh 8:15 **b** of leafy trees, to make
Job 8:16 and his **b** spread out in his
Job 14: 9 bring forth **b** like a plant
Job 15:30 the flame will dry out his **b**
Ps 80:11 Sea, And her **b** to the River
Ps 104:12 They sing among the **b**
Song 7: 8 I will take hold of its **b**
Is 16: 8 Her **b** are stretched out, they
Is 17: 6 five in its most fruitful **b**
Is 18: 5 take away and cut down the **b**
Is 27:10 lie down and consume its **b**
Jer 5:10 Take away her **b**, for they are
Jer 6: 9 put your hand back into the **b**
Jer 11:16 on it, and its **b** are broken
Ezek 17: 6 its **b** turned toward him, but
Ezek 17: 6 a vine, Brought forth **b**, and
Ezek 17: 7 and stretched its **b** toward him

Ezek 17: 8 many waters, to bring forth **b**
Ezek 17:22 highest **b** of the high cedar
Ezek 17:23 of its **b** they will dwell
Ezek 19:10 full of **b** because of many
Ezek 19:11 She had strong **b** for scepters
Ezek 19:11 in stature above the thick **b**
Ezek 19:12 Her strong **b** were broken and
Ezek 19:14 come out from a rod of her **b**
Ezek 31: 3 with fine **b** that shaded the
Ezek 31: 5 its **b** became long because of
Ezek 31: 6 under its **b** all the beasts of
Ezek 31: 7 and in the length of its **b**
Ezek 31: 8 trees were not like its **b**
Ezek 31: 9 with a multitude of **b**, so
Ezek 31:12 its **b** have fallen on the
Ezek 31:13 the field will come to its **b**
Ezek 36: 8 you shall shoot forth your **b**
Dan 4:12 of the heavens dwelt in its **b**
Dan 4:14 the tree and cut off its **b**
Dan 4:14 it, and the birds from its **b**
Dan 4:21 on whose **b** the birds of the
Hos 14: 6 His **b** shall spread
Joel 1: 7 its **b** are made white
Nah 2: 2 out and ruined their vine **b**
Zech 4:12 olive **b** that drip into the
Matt 13:32 the air come and nest in its **b**
Matt 21: 8 cut down **b** from the trees
Mark 4:32 herbs, and shoots out large **b**
Mark 11: 8 down leafy **b** from the trees
Luke 13:19 of the air nested in its **b**
John 12:13 took **b** of palm trees and went
John 15: 5 I am the vine, you are the **b**
Rom 11:16 root is holy, so are the **b**
Rom 11:17 if some of the **b** were broken
Rom 11:18 do not boast against the **b**
Rom 11:19 **B** were broken off that I
Rom 11:21 did not spare the natural **b**
Rom 11:24 these, who are the natural **b**
Rev 7: 9 with palm **b** in their hands,

BRAND (*see* BRANDING)
Zech 3: 2 Is this not a **b** plucked from

BRANDING (*see* BRAND)
Is 3:24 and **b** instead of beauty

BRANDISH (*see* BRANDISHED, BRANDISHING)
Ezek 32:10 when I **b** My sword before them

BRANDISHED (*see* BRANDISH)
Nah 2: 3 and the spears are **b**

BRANDISHING (*see* BRANDISH)
Is 30:32 in battles of **b** He will fight

BRASS
1Co 13: 1 **b** or a clanging cymbal
Rev 1:15 His feet were like fine **b**
Rev 2:18 fire, and His feet like fine **b**
Rev 9:20 and idols of gold, silver, **b**

BRAVE
1Co 16:13 stand fast in the faith, be **b**

BRAWLING
Prov 20: 1 intoxicating drink arouses **b**

BRAY (*see* BRAYED)
Job 6: 5 donkey **b** when it has grass

BRAYED (*see* BRAY)
Job 30: 7 Among the bushes they **b**,

BRAZEN
Ezek 16:30 the deeds of a **b** harlot

BREACH (*see* BREACHED, BREACHES)
Gen 38:29 This **b** be upon you
Ps 106:23 one stood before Him in the **b**
Is 30:13 to you like a **b** ready to fall
Is 58:12 called the Repairer of the **B**

BREACHED (*see* BREACH)
Ezek 26:10 enter a city that has been **b**

BREACHES (*see* BREACH)
Ps 60: 2 Heal its **b**, for it is shaking

BREAD
Gen 3:19 eat **b** till you return to the
Gen 14:18 king of Salem brought out **b**
Gen 18: 5 And I will bring a morsel of **b**
Gen 19: 3 feast, and baked unleavened **b**
Gen 21:14 in the morning, and took **b**
Gen 25:34 And Jacob gave Esau **b** and stew
Gen 27:17 gave the savory food and the **b**
Gen 28:20 am going, and give me **b** to eat
Gen 31:54 called his brethren to eat **b**
Gen 31:54 And they ate **b** and stayed all
Gen 39: 6 except for the **b** which he ate
Gen 41:54 the land of Egypt there was **b**
Gen 41:55 people cried to Pharaoh for **b**
Gen 43:25 that they would eat **b** there
Gen 43:31 Serve the **b**."
Gen 45:23 donkeys loaded with grain, **b**
Gen 47:12 his father's household with **b**
Gen 47:13 was no **b** in all the land
Gen 47:15 Give us **b**, for why should we
Gen 47:16 I will give you **b** for your
Gen 47:17 and Joseph gave them **b** in
Gen 47:17 Thus he fed them with **b** in
Gen 47:19 Buy us and our land for **b**, and
Gen 49:20 **B** from Asher shall be rich,
Ex 2:20 Call him, that he may eat **b**
Ex 12: 8 in fire, with unleavened **b**
Ex 12:15 you shall eat unleavened **b**
Ex 12:15 **b** from the first day until
Ex 12:17 the Feast of Unleavened **B**
Ex 12:18 you shall eat unleavened **b**
Ex 12:20 you shall eat unleavened **b**
Ex 13: 3 No leavened **b** shall be eaten
Ex 13: 6 you shall eat unleavened **b**
Ex 13: 7 Unleavened **b** shall be eaten
Ex 13: 7 no leavened **b** shall be seen
Ex 16: 3 and when we ate **b** to the full
Ex 16: 4 I will rain **b** from heaven for
Ex 16: 8 in the morning **b** to the full
Ex 16:12 you shall be filled with **b**
Ex 16:15 This is the **b** which the LORD
Ex 16:22 they gathered twice as much **b**
Ex 16:29 the sixth day **b** for two days
Ex 16:32 that they may see the **b** with
Ex 18:12 **b** with Moses' father-in-law
Ex 23:15 the Feast of Unleavened **B**
Ex 23:15 eat unleavened **b** seven days
Ex 23:18 My sacrifice with leavened **b**
Ex 23:25 God, and He will bless your **b**
Ex 29: 2 and unleavened **b**, unleavened
Ex 29:23 one loaf of **b**, one cake made
Ex 29:23 **b** that is before the LORD
Ex 29:32 the **b** that is in the basket,
Ex 29:34 offerings, or of the **b**,
Ex 34:18 Unleavened **B** you shall keep
Ex 34:18 you shall eat unleavened **b**
Ex 34:28 he neither ate **b** nor drank
Ex 40:23 he set the **b** in order upon it
Lev 6:16 with unleavened **b** it shall be
Lev 7:13 **b** with the sacrifice of
Lev 8: 2 and a basket of unleavened **b**
Lev 8:26 the basket of unleavened **b**
Lev 8:26 a cake of **b** anointed with oil
Lev 8:31 eat it there with the **b** that
Lev 8:32 of the **b** you shall burn with
Lev 21: 6 fire, and the **b** of their God
Lev 21: 8 he offers the **b** of your God
Lev 21:17 to offer the **b** of his God
Lev 21:21 to offer the **b** of his God
Lev 21:22 He may eat the **b** of his God
Lev 22:25 of these as the **b** of your God
Lev 23: 6 of Unleavened **B** to the LORD
Lev 23: 6 you must eat unleavened **b**
Lev 23:14 You shall eat neither **b** nor
Lev 23:18 **b** seven lambs of the first
Lev 23:20 the **b** of the firstfruits as a
Lev 24: 7 be on the **b** for a memorial
Lev 26: 5 shall eat your **b** to the full
Lev 26:26 have cut off your supply of **b**
Lev 26:26 shall bake your **b** in one oven
Lev 26:26 back to you your **b** by weight
Num 6:15 a basket of unleavened **b**
Num 6:17 the basket of unleavened **b**
Num 9:11 eat it with unleavened **b** and
Num 14: 9 the land, for they are our **b**
Num 15:19 you eat of the **b** of the land
Num 21: 5 soul loathes this worthless **b**
Num 28:17 unleavened **b** shall be eaten
Deut 8: 3 man shall not live by **b** alone
Deut 8: 9 will eat **b** without scarcity
Deut 9: 9 I neither ate **b** nor drank
Deut 9:18 I neither ate **b** nor drank
Deut 16: 3 eat no leavened **b** with it
Deut 16: 3 eat unleavened **b** with it,
Deut 16: 3 the **b** of affliction (for you
Deut 16: 8 you shall eat unleavened **b**
Deut 16:16 at the Feast of Unleavened **B**
Deut 23: 4 they did not meet you with **b**
Deut 29: 6 you have not eaten **b**, nor
Josh 5:11 the Passover, unleavened **b**
Josh 9: 5 all the **b** of their provision
Josh 9:12 This **b** of ours we took hot
Judg 6:19 unleavened **b** from an ephah of
Judg 6:20 the meat and the unleavened **b**
Judg 6:21 the meat and the unleavened **b**
Judg 6:21 the meat and the unleavened **b**
Judg 7:13 a loaf of barley **b** tumbled
Judg 8: 5 Please give loaves of **b** to
Judg 8: 6 we should give **b** to your army
Judg 8:15 give **b** to your weary men
Judg 19: 5 your heart with a morsel of **b**
Judg 19:19 fodder for our donkeys, and **b**
Ruth 1: 6 His people in giving them **b**
Ruth 2:14 Come here, and eat of the **b**
Ruth 2:14 piece of **b** in the vinegar
1Sa 2: 5 hired themselves out for **b**
1Sa 2:36 of silver and a morsel of **b**
1Sa 2:36 that I may eat a piece of **b**
1Sa 9: 7 For the **b** in our vessels is
1Sa 10: 3 carrying three loaves of **b**
1Sa 10: 4 and give you two loaves of **b**
1Sa 16:20 took a donkey loaded with **b**
1Sa 21: 3 five loaves of **b** in my hand
1Sa 21: 4 There is no common **b** on hand
1Sa 21: 4 but there is holy **b**, if the
1Sa 21: 5 the **b** is in effect common,
1Sa 21: 6 So the priest gave him holy **b**
1Sa 21: 6 for there was no **b** there but
1Sa 21: 6 in order to put hot **b** in its
1Sa 22:13 in that you have given him **b**
1Sa 25:11 Shall I then take my **b** and my
1Sa 25:18 took two hundred loaves of **b**
1Sa 28:22 set a piece of **b** before you
1Sa 28:24 and baked unleavened **b** from it
1Sa 30:11 and they gave him **b** and he ate,
1Sa 30:12 for he had eaten no **b** nor
2Sa 3:29 by the sword, or who lacks **b**
2Sa 3:35 if I taste **b** or anything else
2Sa 6:19 men, to everyone a loaf of **b**
2Sa 9: 7 you shall eat **b** at my table
2Sa 9:10 eat **b** at my table always
2Sa 16: 1 them two hundred loaves of **b**
2Sa 16: 2 household to ride on, the **b**
1Ki 13: 8 nor would I eat **b** nor drink
1Ki 13: 9 saying, "You shall not eat **b**
1Ki 13:15 Come home with me and eat **b**
1Ki 13:16 neither can I eat **b** nor drink
1Ki 13:17 You shall not eat **b** nor
1Ki 13:18 your house, that he may eat **b**
1Ki 13:19 ate **b** in his house, and drank
1Ki 13:22 but you came back, ate **b**
1Ki 13:22 Eat no **b** and drink no water,"
1Ki 13:23 it was, after he had eaten **b**
1Ki 17: 6 The ravens brought him **b** and
1Ki 17: 6 and meat in the morning, and **b**
1Ki 17:11 me a morsel of **b** in your hand
1Ki 17:12 God lives, I do not have **b**
1Ki 18: 4 cave, and had fed them with **b**
1Ki 18:13 to a cave, and fed them with **b**
1Ki 22:27 feed him with **b** of affliction
2Ki 4:42 of God **b** of the firstfruits
2Ki 4:42 twenty loaves of barley **b**
2Ki 18:32 and new wine, a land of **b** and
2Ki 23: 9 **b** among their brethren
2Ki 25:29 he ate **b** regularly before the
1Ch 16: 3 to everyone a loaf of **b**, a
2Ch 8:13 the Feast of Unleavened **B**
2Ch 18:26 feed him with **b** of affliction
2Ch 30:13 **B** in the second month
2Ch 30:21 **B** seven days with great
2Ch 35:17 Unleavened **B** for seven days
Ezra 6:22 **B** seven days with joy
Ezra 10: 6 he came there, he ate no **b**
Neh 5:15 people, and took from them **b**
Neh 9:15 You gave them **b** from heaven
Neh 13: 2 the children of Israel with **b**
Job 15:23 He wanders about for **b**,
Job 22: 7 withheld **b** from the hungry
Job 27:14 shall not be satisfied with **b**
Job 28: 5 the earth, from it comes **b**
Job 33:20 So that his life abhors **b**
Ps 14: 4 up my people as they eat **b**
Ps 37:25 Nor his descendants begging **b**
Ps 41: 9 whom I trusted, Who ate my **b**
Ps 53: 4 up my people as they eat **b**
Ps 78:20 Can He give **b** also
Ps 78:24 given them of the **b** of heaven
Ps 80: 5 fed them with the **b** of tears
Ps 102: 4 So that I forget to eat my **b**
Ps 102: 9 For I have eaten ashes like **b**

Ps 104:15 **b** which strengthens man's
Ps 105:16 all the provision of **b**
Ps 105:40 them with the **b** of heaven
Ps 109:10 Let them seek their **b** also
Ps 127: 2 late, To eat the **b** of sorrows
Ps 132:15 will satisfy her poor with **b**
Prov 4:17 they eat the **b** of wickedness
Prov 6:26 is reduced to a crust of **b**
Prov 9: 5 Come, eat of my **b** and drink of
Prov 9:17 **b** eaten in secret is pleasant
Prov 12: 9 honors himself but lacks **b**
Prov 12:11 land will be satisfied with **b**
Prov 20:13 you will be satisfied with **b**
Prov 20:17 **B** gained by deceit is sweet
Prov 22: 9 he gives of his **b** to the poor
Prov 23: 6 Do not eat the **b** of a miser
Prov 25:21 is hungry, give him **b** to eat
Prov 28:19 land will have plenty of **b**
Prov 28:21 of **b** a man will transgress
Prov 31:27 not eat the **b** of idleness
Eccl 9: 7 Go, eat your **b** with joy, and
Eccl 9:11 nor **b** to the wise, nor riches
Eccl 11: 1 Cast your **b** upon the waters,
Is 3: 1 store, the whole supply of **b**
Is 21:14 with their **b** they met him who
Is 28:28 **B** flour must be ground
Is 30:20 gives you the **b** of adversity
Is 30:23 and **b** of the increase of the
Is 33:16 **b** will be given him, his
Is 36:17 and new wine, a land of **b** and
Is 44:15 yes, he kindles it and bakes **b**
Is 44:19 also baked **b** on its coals
Is 51:14 that his **b** should not fail
Is 55: 2 spend money for what is not **b**
Is 55:10 the sower and **b** to the eater,
Is 58: 7 share your **b** with the hungry
Jer 5:17 eat up your harvest and your **b**
Jer 16: 7 Nor shall men break **b** in
Jer 37:21 of **b** from the bakers' street
Jer 37:21 until all the **b** in the city
Jer 38: 9 is no more **b** in the city
Jer 41: 1 there they ate **b** together in
Jer 42:14 trumpet, nor be hungry for **b**
Jer 52:33 he ate **b** regularly before the
Lam 1:11 her people sigh, they seek **b**
Lam 4: 4 the young children ask for **b**
Lam 5: 6 to be satisfied with **b**
Lam 5: 9 We get our **b** at the risk of
Ezek 4: 9 make **b** of them for yourself
Ezek 4:13 defiled **b** among the Gentiles
Ezek 4:15 shall prepare your **b** over it
Ezek 4:16 the supply of **b** in Jerusalem
Ezek 4:16 they shall eat **b** by weight
Ezek 4:17 that they may lack **b** and water
Ezek 5:16 and cut off your supply of **b**
Ezek 12:18 eat your **b** with quaking, and
Ezek 12:19 eat their **b** with anxiety, and
Ezek 13:19 of barley and for pieces of **b**
Ezek 14:13 will cut off its supply of **b**
Ezek 18: 7 has given his **b** to the hungry
Ezek 18:16 has given his **b** to the hungry
Ezek 24:17 do not eat man's **b** of sorrow
Ezek 24:22 nor eat man's **b** of sorrow
Ezek 44: 3 it to eat **b** before the LORD
Ezek 45:21 unleavened **b** shall be eaten
Hos 2: 5 my lovers, who give me my **b**
Hos 9: 4 It shall be like **b** of
Hos 9: 4 For their **b** shall be for
Amos 4: 6 lack of **b** in all your places
Amos 7:12 There eat **b**, and there
Amos 8:11 the land, not a famine of **b**
Obad 7 Those who eat your **b** shall
Hag 2:12 the edge he touches **b** or stew
Matt 4: 3 that these stones become **b**
Matt 4: 4 Man shall not live by **b** alone
Matt 6:11 Give us this day our daily **b**
Matt 7: 9 who, if his son asks for **b**
Matt 15: 2 their hands when they eat **b**
Matt 15:26 good to take the children's **b**
Matt 15:33 **b** in the wilderness to fill
Matt 16: 5 they had forgotten to take **b**
Matt 16: 7 is because we have taken no **b**
Matt 16: 8 because you have brought no **b**
Matt 16:11 not speak to you concerning **b**
Matt 16:12 to beware of the leaven of **b**
Matt 26:17 **B** the disciples came to Jesus
Matt 26:26 were eating, Jesus took **b**
Mark 3:20 could not so much as eat **b**
Mark 6: 8 no bag, no **b**, no copper in
Mark 6:36 villages and buy themselves **b**
Mark 6:37 hundred denarii worth of **b**
Mark 7: 2 disciples eat **b** with defiled
Mark 7: 5 but eat **b** with unwashed hands
Mark 7:27 good to take the children's **b**
Mark 8: 4 with **b** here in the wilderness
Mark 8:14 had forgotten to take **b**, and
Mark 8:16 It is because we have no **b**
Mark 8:17 reason because you have no **b**
Mark 14: 1 and the Feast of Unleavened **B**
Mark 14:12 the first day of Unleavened **B**
Mark 14:22 were eating, Jesus took **b**
Luke 4: 3 this stone to become **b**
Luke 4: 4 Man shall not live by **b** alone
Luke 7:33 eating **b** nor drinking wine
Luke 9: 3 nor bag nor **b** nor money
Luke 11: 3 us day by day our daily **b**
Luke 11:11 If a son asks for **b** from any
Luke 14: 1 to eat **b** on the Sabbath, that
Luke 14:15 eat **b** in the kingdom of God
Luke 15:17 hired servants have **b** enough
Luke 22: 1 of Unleavened **B** drew near
Luke 22: 7 came the Day of Unleavened **B**
Luke 22:19 And He took **b**, gave thanks and
Luke 24:30 with them, that He took **b**
Luke 24:35 to them in the breaking of **b**
John 6: 5 Where shall we buy **b**, that
John 6: 7 hundred denarii worth of **b** is
John 6:23 **b** after the Lord had given
John 6:31 He gave them **b** from heaven
John 6:32 give you the **b** from heaven
John 6:32 you the true **b** from heaven
John 6:33 For the **b** of God is He who
John 6:34 Lord, give us this **b** always
John 6:35 I am the **b** of life
John 6:41 I am the **b** which came down
John 6:48 I am the **b** of life
John 6:50 This is the **b** which comes
John 6:51 I am the living **b** which came
John 6:51 If anyone eats of this **b**, he
John 6:51 the **b** that I shall give is My
John 6:58 This is the **b** which came down
John 6:58 He who eats this **b** will live
John 13:18 He who eats **b** with Me has
John 13:26 of **b** when I have dipped it
John 13:26 And having dipped the **b**, He
John 13:27 Now after the piece of **b**,
John 13:30 received the piece of **b**, he
John 21: 9 and fish laid on it, and **b**
John 21:13 Jesus then came and took the **b**
Acts 2:42 in the breaking of **b**, and in
Acts 2:46 and breaking **b** from house to
Acts 12: 3 the Days of Unleavened **B**
Acts 20: 6 the Days of Unleavened **B**, and
Acts 20: 7 came together to break **b**,
Acts 20:11 he had come up, had broken **b**
Acts 27:35 said these things, he took **b**
1Co 5: 8 the unleavened **b** of sincerity
1Co 10:16 The **b** which we break, is it
1Co 10:17 For we, being many, are one **b**
1Co 10:17 we all partake of that one **b**
1Co 11:23 which He was betrayed took **b**
1Co 11:26 as often as you eat this **b**
1Co 11:27 **b** or drinks this cup of the
1Co 11:28 and so let him eat of that **b**
2Co 9:10 and **b** for food, supply and
2Th 3: 8 eat anyone's **b** free of charge
2Th 3:12 quietness and eat their own **b**

BREADTH

Judg 20:16 sling a stone at a hair's **b**
1Ki 6: 3 across the **b** of the house
Job 38:18 the **b** of the earth
Is 8: 8 will fill the **b** of Your land
Hab 1: 6 through the **b** of the earth
Rev 20: 9 went up on the **b** of the earth
Rev 21:16 length is as great as its **b**
Rev 21:16 Its length, **b**, and height are

BREAK (*see* BREAKER, BREAKING, BREAKS, BROKE, BROKEN)

Gen 19: 9 came near to **b** down the door
Gen 27:40 that you shall **b** his yoke
Gen 38:29 How did you **b** through
Ex 9: 9 that **b** out in sores on man
Ex 9:10 that **b** out in sores on man
Ex 12:46 nor shall you **b** one of its
Ex 13:13 it, then you shall **b** its neck
Ex 19:21 lest they **b** through to gaze
Ex 19:22 lest the LORD **b** out against
Ex 19:24 the people **b** through to come
Ex 19:24 lest He **b** out against them
Ex 23:24 and completely **b** down their
Ex 32: 2 **B** off the golden earrings
Ex 32:24 any gold, let them **b** it off
Ex 34:13 **b** their sacred pillars, and
Ex 34:20 then you shall **b** his neck
Lev 2: 6 You shall **b** it in pieces and
Lev 11:33 any of them falls you shall **b**
Lev 14:45 he shall **b** down the house,
Lev 26:15 but **b** My covenant,
Lev 26:19 I will **b** the pride of your
Lev 26:44 and **b** My covenant with them
Num 2: 9 these shall **b** camp first
Num 2:16 shall be the second to **b** camp
Num 2:24 shall be the third to **b** camp
Num 2:31 they shall **b** camp last, with
Num 9:12 nor **b** one of its bones
Num 24: 8 he shall **b** their bones and
Num 30: 2 he shall not **b** his word
Deut 7: 5 **b** down their sacred pillars,
Deut 12: 3 **b** their sacred pillars, and
Deut 21: 4 they shall **b** the heifer's
Deut 31:16 **b** My covenant which I have
Deut 31:20 provoke Me and **b** My covenant
Judg 2: 1 I will never **b** My covenant
Judg 19:25 and when the day began to **b**
1Sa 25:10 who **b** away each one from his
1Ki 15:19 **b** your treaty with Baasha
2Ki 3:26 to **b** through to the king of
2Ch 16: 3 **b** your treaty with Baasha
Ezra 9:14 should we again **b** Your
Neh 4: 3 he will **b** down their stone
Job 19: 2 **b** me in pieces with words
Job 24:16 In the dark they **b** into
Job 30:13 They **b** up my path, they
Job 39:15 that a wild beast may **b** them
Ps 2: 3 Let us **b** Their bonds in
Ps 2: 9 You shall **b** them with a rod
Ps 10:15 **B** the arm of the wicked and
Ps 46: 5 her, just at the **b** of dawn
Ps 48: 7 As when You **b** the ships of
Ps 58: 6 **B** their teeth in their mouth,
Ps 58: 6 **B** out the fangs of the young
Ps 72: 4 And will **b** in pieces the
Ps 74: 6 now they **b** down its carved
Ps 89:31 If they **b** My statutes And do
Ps 89:34 My covenant I will not **b**, Nor
Ps 94: 5 They **b** in pieces Your people,
Ps 98: 4 **B** forth in song, rejoice, and
Eccl 3: 3 a time to **b** down, and a time
Is 5: 5 **b** down its wall, and it shall
Is 14: 7 they **b** forth into singing
Is 14:25 that I will **b** the Assyrian in
Is 28:28 **b** it with his cartwheel, or
Is 30:14 And He shall **b** it like the
Is 42: 3 A bruised reed He will not **b**
Is 44:23 **b** forth into singing, you
Is 45: 2 I will **b** in pieces the gates
Is 49:13 **b** out in singing, O mountains
Is 52: 9 **B** forth into joy, sing
Is 54: 1 **B** forth into singing, and cry
Is 55:12 the hills shall **b** forth into
Is 58: 6 and that you **b** every yoke
Is 58: 8 Then your light shall **b** forth
Jer 1:14 shall **b** forth on all the
Jer 4: 3 **B** up your fallow ground, and
Jer 14:21 do not **b** Your covenant with
Jer 15:12 Can anyone **b** iron, the
Jer 16: 7 Nor shall men **b** bread in
Jer 19:10 Then you shall **b** the flask in
Jer 19:11 Even so I will **b** this people
Jer 28: 4 for I will **b** the yoke of the
Jer 28:11 Even so I will **b** the yoke of
Jer 30: 8 That I will **b** his yoke from
Jer 31:28 to **b** down, to throw down, to
Jer 33:20 If you can **b** My covenant
Jer 43:13 He shall also **b** the sacred
Jer 45: 4 I have built I will **b** down
Jer 48:12 his vessels and **b** the bottles
Jer 49:35 I will **b** the bow of Elam, the
Jer 51:20 for with you I will **b** the
Jer 51:21 with you I will **b** in pieces
Jer 51:21 with you I will **b** in pieces
Jer 51:22 also I will **b** in pieces man
Jer 51:22 you I will **b** in pieces old
Jer 51:22 with you I will **b** in pieces
Jer 51:23 with you also I will **b** in
Jer 51:23 with you I will **b** in pieces
Jer 51:23 with you I will **b** in pieces
Ezek 13:13 wind to **b** forth in My fury
Ezek 13:14 So I will **b** down the wall you

Ezek 16:38 **b** wedlock or shed blood are
Ezek 16:39 and **b** down your high places
Ezek 17:15 Can he **b** a covenant and still
Ezek 23:34 you shall **b** its shards, and
Ezek 26: 4 of Tyre and **b** down her towers
Ezek 26: 9 he will **b** down your towers
Ezek 26:12 they will **b** down your walls
Ezek 30:18 when I **b** the yokes of Egypt
Ezek 30:22 will **b** his arms, both the
Ezek 30:24 but I will **b** Pharaoh's arms,
Dan 2:40 that kingdom will **b** in pieces
Dan 2:44 it shall **b** in pieces and
Dan 4:27 **b** off your sins by being
Dan 7:23 trample it and **b** it in pieces
Hos 1: 5 in that day that I will **b** the
Hos 4: 2 they **b** all restraint, with
Hos 10: 2 He will **b** down their altars
Hos 10:11 Jacob shall **b** his clods
Hos 10:12 **b** up your fallow ground, for
Joel 2: 7 and they do not **b** ranks
Amos 1: 5 I will also **b** the gate bar of
Amos 5: 6 lest He **b** out like fire in
Amos 6:11 He will **b** the great house
Amos 9: 1 **b** them on the heads of them
Mic 2:13 they will **b** out, pass through
Mic 3: 3 **b** their bones, and chop them
Nah 1:13 for now I will **b** off his yoke
Zech 11:10 that I might **b** the covenant
Zech 11:14 Bonds, that I might **b** the
Matt 6:19 destroy and where thieves **b** in
Matt 6:20 and where thieves do not **b** in
Matt 9:17 or else the wineskins **b**, the
Matt 12:20 A bruised reed He will not **b**
John 19:33 dead, they did not **b** His legs
Acts 20: 7 came together to **b** bread,
1Co 10:16 The bread which we **b**, is it
Gal 4:27 **B** forth and shout, you who do

BREAKER (*see* BREAK, BREAKERS)
Rom 2:25 but if you are a **b** of the law

BREAKERS (*see* BREAKER)
Job 30:14 They come as broad **b**

BREAKFAST
John 21:12 Come and eat **b**
John 21:15 So when they had eaten **b**,

BREAKING (*see* BREAK)
Gen 32:24 with him until the **b** of day
Ex 22: 2 If the thief is found **b** in
Lev 13:42 it is leprosy **b** out on his
Ps 42:10 As with a **b** of my bones, My
Ps 144:14 there be no **b** in or going out
Is 22: 5 **b** down the walls and of crying
Is 28:24 his soil and **b** the clods
Is 30:13 whose **b** comes suddenly, in an
Is 30:14 the **b** of the potter's vessel
Jer 2:23 dromedary **b** loose in her ways
Ezek 16:59 the oath by **b** the covenant
Ezek 17:18 the oath by **b** the covenant
Ezek 21: 6 son of man, with a **b** heart
Dan 7: 7 **b** in pieces, and trampling the
Luke 5: 6 of fish, and their net was **b**
Luke 24:35 to them in the **b** of bread
Acts 2:42 in the **b** of bread, and in
Acts 2:46 **b** bread from house to house,
Acts 21:13 mean by weeping and **b** my heart
Rom 2:23 God through **b** the law

BREAKS (*see* BREAK)
Gen 32:26 Let Me go, for the day **b**
Ex 22: 6 If fire **b** out and catches in
Lev 13:12 if leprosy **b** out all over the
Lev 14:43 **b** out in the house, after he
Judg 16: 9 as a strand of yarn **b** when it
Neh 6: 1 that there were no **b** left in
Job 7: 5 is cracked and **b** out afresh
Job 12:14 If He **b** a thing down, it
Job 16:14 He **b** me with wound upon
Job 19:10 He **b** me down on every side,
Job 26:12 He **b** up the storm
Job 28: 4 He **b** open a shaft away from
Job 34:24 He **b** in pieces mighty men
Ps 29: 5 of the LORD **b** the cedars, Yes
Ps 46: 9 He **b** the bow and cuts the
Ps 119:20 My soul **b** with longing For
Ps 141: 7 one plows and **b** up the earth
Prov 15: 4 in it **b** the spirit
Prov 25:15 and a gentle tongue **b** a bone
Eccl 10: 8 whoever **b** through a wall will
Song 2:17 Until the day **b** and the
Song 4: 6 Until the day **b** and the

Is 38:13 a lion, so He **b** all my bones
Is 59: 5 is crushed a viper **b** out
Is 66: 3 lamb, as if he **b** a dog's neck
Jer 19:11 as one **b** a potter's vessel,
Jer 23:29 that **b** the rock in pieces
Lam 4: 4 but no one **b** it for them
Dan 2:40 inasmuch as iron **b** in pieces
Mic 2:13 The one who **b** open will come
Matt 5:19 Whoever therefore **b** one of

BREAKTHROUGH
2Sa 5:20 before me, like a **b** of water
1Ch 14:11 by my hand like a **b** of water

BREAST (*see* BREASTPLATE, BREASTS)
Ex 29:26 the **b** of the ram of Aaron's
Ex 29:27 you shall sanctify the **b** of
Lev 7:30 fat with the **b** he shall bring
Lev 7:30 that the **b** may be waved as a
Lev 7:31 but the **b** shall be Aaron's and
Lev 7:34 For the **b** of the wave
Lev 8:29 And Moses took the **b** and
Lev 10:14 The **b** of the wave offering and
Lev 10:15 the **b** of the wave offering
Num 6:20 together with the **b** of the
Num 18:18 be yours, just as the wave **b**
Job 24: 9 the fatherless from the **b**
Is 60:16 and shall milk the **b** of kings
Luke 18:13 to heaven, but beat his **b**
John 13:25 leaning back on Jesus' **b**
John 21:20 leaned on His **b** at the supper

BREASTPLATE (*see* BREAST, BREASTPLATES)
Ex 25: 7 set in the ephod and in the **b**
Ex 28: 4 a **b**, an ephod, a robe, a
Ex 28:15 shall make the **b** of judgment
Ex 28:22 chains for the **b** at the end
Ex 28:23 two rings of gold for the **b**
Ex 28:23 on the two ends of the **b**
Ex 28:24 are on the ends of the **b**
Ex 28:26 them on the two ends of the **b**
Ex 28:28 They shall bind the **b** by
Ex 28:28 so that the **b** does not come
Ex 28:29 the sons of Israel on the **b**
Ex 28:30 in the **b** of judgment the Urim
Ex 29: 5 ephod, the ephod, and the **b**
Ex 35: 9 set in the ephod and in the **b**
Ex 35:27 set in the ephod and in the **b**
Ex 39: 8 And he made the **b**,
Ex 39: 9 They made the **b** square by
Ex 39:15 chains for the **b** at the ends
Ex 39:16 on the two ends of the **b**
Ex 39:17 rings on the ends of the **b**
Ex 39:19 them on the two ends of the **b**
Ex 39:21 they bound the **b** by means of
Ex 39:21 that the **b** would not come
Lev 8: 8 Then he put the **b** on him, and
Lev 8: 8 Urim and the Thummim in the **b**
Is 59:17 put on righteousness as a **b**
Eph 6:14 put on the **b** of righteousness
1Th 5: 8 putting on the **b** of faith

BREASTPLATES (*see* BREASTPLATE)
Rev 9: 9 they had **b** like **b** of iron
Rev 9:17 on them had **b** of fiery red

BREASTS (*see* BREAST)
Gen 49:25 beneath, blessings of the **b**
Lev 9:20 and they put the fat on the **b**
Lev 9:21 but the **b** and the right thigh
Job 3:12 Or why the **b**, that I should
Ps 22: 9 when I was on My mother's **b**
Prov 5:19 let her **b** satisfy you at all
Song 1:13 lies all night between my **b**
Song 4: 5 Your two **b** are like two fawns
Song 7: 3 Your two **b** are like two fawns
Song 7: 7 and your **b** like its clusters
Song 7: 8 Let now your **b** be like
Song 8: 1 who nursed at my mother's **b**
Song 8: 8 sister, and she has no **b**
Song 8:10 a wall, and my **b** like towers
Is 28: 9 Those just drawn from the **b**
Is 32:12 shall mourn upon their **b** for
Lam 4: 3 their **b** to nurse their young
Ezek 16: 7 Your **b** were formed, your hair
Ezek 23: 3 their **b** were there embraced,
Ezek 23:21 because of your youthful **b**
Ezek 23:34 shards, and tear at your own **b**
Hos 2: 2 adulteries from between her **b**
Hos 9:14 a miscarrying womb and dry **b**
Nah 2: 7 of doves, beating their **b**
Luke 11:27 and the **b** which nursed You
Luke 23:29 and the **b** which never nursed

Luke 23:48 had been done, beat their **b**

BREATH (*see* BREATHE)
Gen 2: 7 his nostrils the **b** of life
Gen 6:17 in which is the **b** of life
Gen 7:15 in which is the **b** of life
Gen 7:22 the **b** of the spirit of life
2Sa 22:16 of the **b** of His nostrils
1Ki 17:17 there was no **b** left in him
Job 4: 9 by the **b** of His anger they
Job 7: 7 remember that my life is a **b**
Job 7:16 for my days are but a **b**
Job 9:18 not allow me to catch my **b**
Job 12:10 and the **b** of all mankind
Job 15:30 by the **b** of His mouth he will
Job 19:17 My **b** is offensive to my wife,
Job 27: 3 as long as my **b** is in me, and
Job 27: 3 the **b** of God in my nostrils,
Job 32: 8 the **b** of the Almighty gives
Job 33: 4 the **b** of the Almighty gives
Job 34:14 Himself His Spirit and His **b**
Job 37:10 By the **b** of God ice is given,
Job 41:21 His **b** kindles coals, and a
Ps 18:15 of the **b** of Your nostrils
Ps 33: 6 of them by the **b** of His mouth
Ps 78:39 A **b** that passes away and does
Ps 104:29 You take away their **b**, they
Ps 135:17 there any **b** in their mouths
Ps 144: 4 Man is like a **b**
Ps 150: 6 that has **b** praise the LORD
Eccl 3:19 Surely, they all have one **b**
Song 7: 8 of your **b** like apples,
Is 2:22 whose **b** is in his nostrils
Is 11: 4 with the **b** of His lips He
Is 30:28 His **b** is like an overflowing
Is 30:33 the **b** of the LORD, like a
Is 33:11 your **b**, as fire, shall devour
Is 40: 7 because the **b** of the LORD
Is 42: 5 Who gives **b** to the people on
Is 57:13 all away, a **b** will take them
Jer 10:14 and there is no **b** in them
Jer 51:17 And there is no **b** in them
Lam 4:20 The **b** of our nostrils, the
Ezek 37: 5 cause **b** to enter into you
Ezek 37: 6 you with skin and put **b** in you
Ezek 37: 8 but there was no **b** in them
Ezek 37: 9 Prophesy to the **b**, prophesy,
Ezek 37: 9 son of man, and say to the **b**
Ezek 37: 9 Come from the four winds, O **b**
Ezek 37:10 **b** came into them, and they
Dan 5:23 who holds your **b** in His hand
Dan 10:17 now, nor is any **b** left in me
Hab 2:19 and in it there is no **b** at all
Acts 17:25 since He gives to all life, **b**
2Th 2: 8 with the **b** of His mouth and
Rev 11:11 a half days the **b** of life
Rev 13:15 **b** to the image of the beast

BREATHE (*see* BREATH, BREATHED, BREATHES, BREATHING)
Ps 27:12 me, And such as **b** out violence
Ezek 37: 9 **b** on these slain, that they

BREATHED (*see* BREATHE)
Gen 2: 7 and **b** into his nostrils the
Gen 25: 8 Then Abraham **b** his last and
Gen 25:17 he **b** his last and died, and was
Gen 35:29 So Isaac **b** his last and died,
Gen 49:33 **b** his last, and was gathered
Josh 10:40 utterly destroyed all that **b**
1Ki 15:29 to Jeroboam anyone that **b**
Jer 15: 9 she has **b** her last
Lam 1:19 my elders **b** their last in the
Mark 15:37 a loud voice, and **b** His last
Mark 15:39 this and **b** His last, he said,
Luke 23:46 said this, He **b** His last
John 20:22 He **b** on them, and said to them
Acts 5: 5 fell down and **b** his last
Acts 5:10 at his feet and **b** her last

BREATHES (*see* BREATHE)
Deut 20:16 nothing that **b** remain alive
Job 14:10 indeed he **b** his last And where

BREATHING (*see* BREATHE)
Josh 11:11 There was none left **b**
Josh 11:14 them, and they left none **b**
Acts 9: 1 still **b** threats and murder

BRED (*see* BREED)
Ex 16:20 and it **b** worms and stank
Esth 8:10 horses **b** from swift steeds

Rom 1:13 not want you to be unaware, **b**
Rom 7: 1 **b** (for I speak to those who
Rom 7: 4 Therefore, my **b**, you also
Rom 8:12 Therefore, **b**, we are debtors
Rom 8:29 be the firstborn among many **b**
Rom 9: 3 accursed from Christ for my **b**
Rom 10: 1 **B**, my heart's desire and
Rom 11:25 For I do not desire, **b**, that
Rom 12: 1 I beseech you therefore, **b**
Rom 15:14 concerning you, my **b**, that
Rom 15:15 Nevertheless, **b**, I have
Rom 15:30 Now I beg you, **b**, through the
Rom 16:14 and the **b** who are with them
Rom 16:17 Now I urge you, **b**, note those
1Co 1:10 Now I plead with you, **b**, by
1Co 1:11 to me concerning you, my **b**
1Co 1:26 For you see your calling, **b**
1Co 2: 1 And I, **b**, when I came to you,
1Co 3: 1 And I, **b**, could not speak to
1Co 4: 6 Now these things, **b**, I have
1Co 6: 5 able to judge between his **b**
1Co 6: 8 you do these things to your **b**
1Co 7:24 **B**, let each one remain with
1Co 7:29 But this I say, **b**, the time
1Co 8:12 you thus sin against the **b**
1Co 10: 1 Moreover, **b**, I do not want
1Co 11: 2 Now I praise you, **b**, that you
1Co 11:33 Therefore, my **b**, when you
1Co 12: 1 concerning spiritual gifts, **b**
1Co 14: 6 But now, **b**, if I come to you
1Co 14:20 **B**, do not be children in
1Co 14:26 How is it then, **b**
1Co 14:39 Therefore, **b**, desire
1Co 15: 1 Moreover, **b**, I declare to you
1Co 15: 6 over five hundred **b** at once
1Co 15:50 Now this I say, **b**, that flesh
1Co 15:58 Therefore, my beloved **b**, be
1Co 16:11 am waiting for him with the **b**
1Co 16:12 him to come to you with the **b**
1Co 16:15 I urge you, **b**
1Co 16:20 All the **b** greet you
2Co 1: 8 want you to be ignorant, **b**
2Co 8: 1 Moreover, **b**, we make known to
2Co 8:23 Or if our **b** are inquired
2Co 9: 3 Yet I have sent the **b**, lest
2Co 9: 5 **b** to go to you ahead of time
2Co 11: 9 the **b** who came from Macedonia
2Co 11:26 sea, in perils among false **b**
2Co 13:11 Finally, **b**, farewell
Gal 1: 2 all the **b** who are with me, To
Gal 1:11 But I make known to you, **b**
Gal 2: 4 **b** secretly brought in (who
Gal 3:15 **B**, I speak in the manner of
Gal 4:12 **B**, I urge you to become as I
Gal 4:28 Now we, **b**, as Isaac was, are
Gal 4:31 So then, **b**, we are not
Gal 5:11 And I, **b**, if I still preach
Gal 5:13 For you, **b**, have been called
Gal 6: 1 **B**, if a man is overtaken in
Gal 6:18 **B**, the grace of our Lord
Eph 6:10 Finally, my **b**, be strong in
Eph 6:23 Peace to the **b**, and love with
Phil 1:12 But I want you to know, **b**
Phil 1:14 and most of the **b** in the Lord
Phil 3: 1 Finally, my **b**, rejoice in the
Phil 3:13 **B**, I do not count myself to
Phil 3:17 **B**, join in following my
Phil 4: 1 my beloved and longed-for **b**
Phil 4: 8 Finally, **b**, whatever things
Phil 4:21 The **b** who are with me greet
Col 1: 2 faithful **b** in Christ who are
Col 4:15 Greet the **b** who are in
1Th 1: 4 knowing, beloved **b**, your
1Th 2: 1 For you yourselves know, **b**
1Th 2: 9 For you remember, **b**, our
1Th 2:14 For you, **b**, became imitators
1Th 2:17 But we, **b**, having been taken
1Th 3: 7 therefore, **b**, in all our
1Th 4: 1 Finally then, **b**, we urge and
1Th 4:10 **b** who are in all Macedonia
1Th 4:10 But we urge you, **b**, that you
1Th 4:13 want you to be ignorant, **b**
1Th 5: 1 the times and the seasons, **b**
1Th 5: 4 But you, **b**, are not in
1Th 5:12 And we urge you, **b**, to
1Th 5:14 Now we exhort you, **b**, warn
1Th 5:25 **B**, pray for us
1Th 5:26 Greet all the **b** with a holy
1Th 5:27 be read to all the holy **b**
2Th 1: 3 thank God always for you, **b**
2Th 2: 1 Now, **b**, concerning the coming
2Th 2:13 you, **b** beloved by the Lord,
2Th 2:15 Therefore, **b**, stand fast and
2Th 3: 1 Finally, **b**, pray for us, that
2Th 3: 6 But we command you, **b**, in the
2Th 3:13 But as for you, **b**, do not
1Ti 4: 6 the **b** in these things, you
1Ti 6: 2 them because they are **b**, but
2Ti 4:21 Linus, Claudia, and all the **b**
Heb 2:11 is not ashamed to call them **b**
Heb 2:12 declare Your name to My **b**
Heb 2:17 He had to be made like His **b**
Heb 3: 1 Therefore, holy **b**, partakers
Heb 3:12 Beware, **b**, lest there be in
Heb 7: 5 law, that is, from their **b**
Heb 10:19 Therefore, **b**, having boldness
Heb 13:22 And I appeal to you, **b**, bear
Jas 1: 2 My **b**, count it all joy when
Jas 1:16 not be deceived, my beloved **b**
Jas 1:19 Therefore, my beloved **b**, let
Jas 2: 1 My **b**, do not hold the faith
Jas 2: 5 Listen, my beloved **b**
Jas 2:14 What does it profit, my **b**
Jas 3: 1 My **b**, let not many of you
Jas 3:10 My **b**, these things ought not
Jas 3:12 Can a fig tree, my **b**, bear
Jas 4:11 speak evil of one another, **b**
Jas 5: 7 Therefore be patient, **b**,
Jas 5: 9 against one another, **b**, lest
Jas 5:10 My **b**, take the prophets, who
Jas 5:12 But above all, my **b**, do not
Jas 5:19 **B**, if anyone among you
1Pe 1:22 in sincere love of the **b**,
2Pe 1:10 Therefore, **b**, be even more
1Jn 2: 7 **B**, I write no new commandment
1Jn 3:13 Do not marvel, my **b**, if the
1Jn 3:14 life, because we love the **b**
1Jn 3:16 lay down our lives for the **b**
3Jn 3 rejoiced greatly when **b** came
3Jn 5 whatever you do for the **b**
3Jn 10 does not receive the **b**, and
Rev 6:11 fellow servants and their **b**
Rev 12:10 for the accuser of our **b**
Rev 19:10 and of your **b** who have the
Rev 22: 9 of your **b** the prophets, and of

BRIARS
Heb 6: 8 but if it bears thorns and **b**

BRIBE (*see* BRIBERY, BRIBES)
Ex 23: 8 And you shall take no **b**, for a
Ex 23: 8 for a **b** blinds the discerning
Deut 10:17 no partiality nor takes a **b**
Deut 16:19 show partiality, nor take a **b**
Deut 16:19 for a **b** blinds the eyes of
Deut 27:25 is the one who takes a **b** to
1Sa 12: 3 hand have I received any **b**
Job 6:22 Offer a **b** for me from your
Ps 15: 5 Nor does he take a **b** against
Prov 17:23 A wicked man accepts a **b**
Prov 21:14 a **b** behind the back, strong
Eccl 7: 7 and a **b** debases the heart
Is 5:23 justify the wicked for a **b**
Mic 3:11 her heads judge for a **b**, her
Mic 7: 3 gifts, the judge seeks a **b**

BRIBERY (*see* BRIBE)
Job 15:34 will consume the tents of **b**

BRIBES (*see* BRIBE)
1Sa 8: 3 after dishonest gain, took **b**
2Ch 19: 7 partiality, nor taking of **b**
Ps 26:10 whose right hand is full of **b**
Prov 15:27 but he who hates **b** will live
Prov 29: 4 who receives **b** overthrows it
Is 1:23 Everyone loves **b**, and follows
Is 33:15 with his hands, refusing **b**
Ezek 22:12 you they take **b** to shed blood
Amos 5:12 afflict the just and take **b**

BRICK (*see* BRICKS)
Gen 11: 3 They had **b** for stone, and
Ex 1:14 in mortar, in **b**, and in all
Ex 5: 7 straw to make **b** as before
Ex 5:14 in making **b** both yesterday
Ex 5:16 and they say to us, 'Make **b**
2Sa 12:31 cross over to the **b** works
Is 65: 3 burn incense on altars of **b**
Jer 43: 9 Judah, in the clay in the **b**
Nah 3:14 Make strong the **b** kiln

BRICKS (*see* BRICK)
Gen 11: 3 Come, let us make **b** and bake
Ex 5: 8 of **b** which they made before
Ex 5:18 shall deliver the quota of **b**
Ex 5:19 any **b** from your daily quota
Is 9:10 The **b** have fallen down, but

BRIDE (*see* BRIDEGROOM, BRIDE-PRICE, BRIDES)
Is 49:18 bind them on you as a **b** does
Is 61:10 as a **b** adorns herself with
Is 62: 5 rejoices over the **b**, so shall
Jer 2:32 ornaments, or a **b** her attire
Jer 7:34 and the voice of the **b**
Jer 16: 9 and the voice of the **b**
Jer 25:10 and the voice of the **b**, the
Jer 33:11 and the voice of the **b**, the
Joel 2:16 the **b** from her dressing room
John 3:29 He who has the **b** is the
Rev 18:23 **b** shall not be heard in you
Rev 21: 2 prepared as a **b** adorned for
Rev 21: 9 Come, I will show you the **b**
Rev 22:17 And the Spirit and the **b** say

BRIDEGROOM (*see* BRIDE, BRIDEGROOM'S)
Ps 19: 5 Which is like a **b** coming out
Is 61:10 as a **b** decks himself with
Is 62: 5 as the **b** rejoices over the
Jer 7:34 gladness, the voice of the **b**
Jer 16: 9 gladness, the voice of the **b**
Jer 25:10 gladness, the voice of the **b**
Jer 33:11 gladness, the voice of the **b**
Joel 2:16 let the **b** go out from his
Matt 9:15 Can the friends of the **b** mourn
Matt 9:15 as long as the **b** is with them
Matt 9:15 the **b** will be taken away from
Matt 25: 1 and went out to meet the **b**
Matt 25: 5 But while the **b** was delayed
Matt 25: 6 Behold, the **b** is coming
Matt 25:10 the **b** came, and those who were
Mark 2:19 Can the friends of the **b** fast
Mark 2:19 fast while the **b** is with them
Mark 2:19 As long as they have the **b**
Mark 2:20 the **b** will be taken away from
Luke 5:34 **b** fast while the **b** is with
Luke 5:35 the **b** will be taken away from
John 2: 9 of the feast called the **b**
John 3:29 He who has the bride is the **b**
John 3:29 but the friend of the **b**, who
Rev 18:23 And the voice of **b** and bride

BRIDEGROOM'S (*see* BRIDEGROOM)
John 3:29 because of the **b** voice

BRIDE-PRICE (*see* BRIDE)
Ex 22:16 the **b** for her to be his wife
Ex 22:17 according to the **b** of virgins

BRIDES (*see* BRIDE)
Hos 4:13 and your **b** commit adultery
Hos 4:14 nor your **b** when they commit

BRIDLE (*see* BRIDLES)
2Ki 19:28 My **b** in your lips, and I will
Job 41:13 approach him with a double **b**
Ps 32: 9 be harnessed with bit and **b**
Prov 26: 3 a **b** for the donkey, and a rod
Is 30:28 there shall be a **b** in the
Is 37:29 My **b** in your lips, and I will
Jas 1:26 does not **b** his tongue but
Jas 3: 2 able also to **b** the whole body

BRIDLES (*see* BRIDLE)
Rev 14:20 up to the horses' **b**, for one

BRIEFLY
1Pe 5:12 him, I have written to you **b**

BRIER (*see* BRIERS)
Is 55:13 instead of the **b** shall come
Ezek 28:24 no longer be a pricking **b** or
Mic 7: 4 The best of them is like a **b**

BRIERS (*see* BRIER)
Judg 8: 7 of the wilderness and with **b**
Judg 8:16 thorns of the wilderness and **b**
Is 5: 6 but there shall come up **b**
Is 7:23 of silver, it will be for **b**
Is 7:24 all the land will become **b**
Is 7:25 not go there for fear of **b**
Is 9:18 it shall devour the **b** and
Is 10:17 thorns and his **b** in one day
Is 27: 4 who would set **b** and thorns
Is 32:13 will come up thorns and **b**, yes
Ezek 2: 6 of their words, though **b** and

BRIGHT (*see* BRIGHTENED, BRIGHTER, BRIGHTNESS)
Lev 13: 2 swelling, a scab, or a **b** spot
Lev 13: 4 But if the **b** spot is white on
Lev 13:19 a white swelling or a **b** spot
Lev 13:23 But if the **b** spot stays in
Lev 13:24 of the burn becomes a **b** spot
Lev 13:25 the **b** spot has turned white
Lev 13:26 no white hairs in the **b** spot
Lev 13:28 But if the **b** spot stays in
Lev 13:38 If a man or a woman has **b**
Lev 13:38 specifically white **b** spots
Lev 13:39 indeed if the **b** spots on the
Lev 14:56 and a scab and a **b** spot,
1Sa 16:12 Now he was ruddy, with **b** eyes
Job 37:11 He scatters His **b** clouds
Job 37:21 when it is **b** in the skies
Jer 51:11 Make the arrows **b**
Ezek 1:13 the fire was **b**, and out of the
Ezek 21:15 It is made **b**
Ezek 32: 8 All the **b** lights of the
Nah 3: 3 Horsemen charge with **b** sword
Matt 17: 5 a **b** cloud overshadowed them
Luke 11:36 as when the **b** shining of a
Acts 10:30 stood before me in **b** clothing
Rev 15: 6 clothed in pure **b** linen, and
Rev 19: 8 in fine linen, clean and **b**
Rev 22:16 the Offspring of David, the **B**

BRIGHTENED (*see* BRIGHT)
1Sa 14:27 and his countenance **b**
1Sa 14:29 now, how my countenance has **b**

BRIGHTER (*see* BRIGHT)
Job 11:17 life would be **b** than noonday
Prov 4:18 that shines ever **b** unto the
Lam 4: 7 Nazirites were **b** than snow
Acts 26:13 **b** than the sun, shining

BRIGHTNESS (*see* BRIGHT)
2Sa 22:13 From the **b** before Him coals
Job 31:26 or the moon moving in **b**,
Ps 18:12 From the **b** before Him, His
Is 59: 9 For **b**, but we walk in
Is 60: 3 kings to the **b** of your rising
Is 60:19 nor for **b** shall the moon give
Is 62: 1 righteousness goes forth as **b**
Ezek 1: 4 and **b** was all around it and
Ezek 1:27 of fire with **b** all around
Ezek 1:28 of the **b** all around it
Ezek 8: 2 like the appearance of **b**
Ezek 10: 4 of the **b** of the LORD's glory
Dan 12: 3 like the **b** of the firmament
Joel 2:10 and the stars diminish their **b**
Joel 3:15 stars will diminish their **b**
Amos 5:20 very dark, with no **b** in it
Hab 3: 4 His **b** was like the light
2Th 2: 8 with the **b** of His coming
Heb 1: 3 who being the **b** of His glory

BRIM
1Ki 7:23 from one **b** to the other
1Ki 7:24 below its **b** were ornamental
1Ki 7:26 its **b** was shaped like the
1Ki 7:26 shaped like the **b** of a cup
2Ch 4: 2 from one **b** to the other
2Ch 4: 5 its **b** was shaped like the
2Ch 4: 5 shaped like the **b** of a cup
John 2: 7 they filled them up to the **b**

BRIMSTONE
Gen 19:24 Then the LORD rained **b** and
Deut 29:23 The whole land is **b**, salt,
Job 18:15 **B** is scattered on his
Ps 11: 6 He will rain coals, Fire and **b**
Is 30:33 the LORD, like a stream of **b**
Is 34: 9 pitch, and its dust into **b**
Ezek 38:22 great hailstones, fire, and **b**
Luke 17:29 **b** from heaven and destroyed
Rev 9:17 mouths came fire, smoke, and **b**
Rev 9:18 the **b** which came out of their
Rev 14:10 **b** in the presence of the holy
Rev 19:20 lake of fire burning with **b**
Rev 20:10 and **b** where the beast and the
Rev 21: 8 which burns with fire and **b**

BRING (*see* PREFACE)

BRINGING (*see* PREFACE)

BRINGS (*see* PREFACE)

BRISTLING
Jer 51:27 to come up like the **b** locusts

BROAD (*see* BROADER)
Ex 27: 1 cubits long and five cubits **b**
2Sa 22:20 brought me out into a **b** place
1Ch 4:40 pasture, and the land was **b**
2Ch 6:13 cubits long, five cubits **b**
Neh 3: 8 as far as the **B** Wall
Neh 12:38 Ovens as far as the **B** Wall
Job 30:14 They come as **b** breakers
Job 36:16 into a **b** place where there is
Job 37:10 and the **b** waters are frozen
Ps 18:19 brought me out into a **b** place
Ps 118: 5 me and set me in a **b** place
Ps 119:96 commandment is exceedingly **b**
Is 33:21 be for us a place of **b** rivers
Jer 51:58 The **b** walls of Babylon shall
Amos 8: 9 the earth in **b** daylight
Nah 2: 4 one another in the **b** roads
Matt 7:13 **b** is the way that leads to
Matt 23: 5 make their phylacteries **b**

BROADER (*see* BROAD)
Job 11: 9 the earth and **b** than the sea

BROILED
Luke 24:42 gave Him a piece of a **b** fish

BROKE (*see* BREAK)
Ex 9:25 **b** every tree of the field
Ex 32: 3 So all the people **b** off the
Ex 32:19 **b** them at the foot of the
Ex 34: 1 the first tablets which you **b**
Num 2:34 standards and so they **b** camp
Deut 9:17 and **b** them before your eyes
Deut 10: 2 first tablets, which you **b**
Judg 7:19 **b** the pitchers that were in
Judg 7:20 trumpets and **b** the pitchers
Judg 15:14 his bonds **b** loose from his
Judg 16: 9 But he **b** the bowstrings as
Judg 16:12 But he **b** them off his arms
1Sa 5: 9 and tumors **b** out on them
2Sa 23:16 men **b** through the camp of the
1Ki 19:11 **b** the rocks in pieces before
2Ki 10:27 Then they **b** down the sacred
2Ki 11:18 They thoroughly **b** in pieces
2Ki 14:13 **b** down the wall of Jerusalem
2Ki 18: 4 **b** the sacred pillars, cut
2Ki 18: 4 and **b** in pieces the bronze
2Ki 23: 8 also he **b** down the high
2Ki 23:12 of the LORD, the king **b** down
2Ki 23:14 he **b** in pieces the sacred
2Ki 23:15 and the high place he **b** down
2Ki 25:10 the captain of the guard **b**
2Ki 25:13 the Chaldeans **b** in pieces
1Ch 11:18 So the three **b** through the
1Ch 15:13 LORD our God **b** out against us
1Ch 20: 4 war **b** out at Gezer with the
2Ch 14: 3 **b** down the sacred pillars and
2Ch 23:17 They **b** in pieces its altars
2Ch 25:23 **b** down the wall of Jerusalem
2Ch 26: 6 **b** down the wall of Gath, the
2Ch 26:19 leprosy **b** out on his forehead
2Ch 31: 1 and **b** the sacred pillars in
2Ch 34: 4 They **b** down the altars of the
2Ch 34: 4 molded images he **b** in pieces
2Ch 36:19 **b** down the wall of Jerusalem,
Job 29:17 I **b** the fangs of the wicked,
Ps 74:13 You **b** the heads of the sea
Ps 74:14 You **b** the heads of Leviathan
Ps 74:15 You **b** open the fountain and
Ps 76: 3 There He **b** the arrows of the
Ps 106:29 the plague **b** out among them
Ps 107:14 And **b** their chains in pieces
Is 22:10 and the houses you **b** down to
Jer 28:10 Jeremiah's neck and **b** it
Jer 31:32 My covenant which they **b**
Jer 39: 8 **b** down the walls of Jerusalem
Jer 52:14 guard **b** down all the walls of
Jer 52:17 the Chaldeans **b** in pieces
Ezek 17:16 and whose covenant he **b**
Ezek 17:19 and My covenant which he **b**
Ezek 27:26 but the east wind **b** you in
Ezek 29: 7 of you with the hand, you **b**
Ezek 29: 7 they leaned on you, you **b**
Ezek 44: 7 then they **b** My covenant
Dan 2:34 and clay, and **b** them in pieces
Dan 2:45 that it **b** in pieces the iron,
Dan 6:24 **b** all their bones in pieces
Dan 7:19 **b** in pieces, and trampled the
Dan 8: 7 the ram, and **b** his two horns
Matt 14:19 up to heaven, He blessed and **b**
Matt 15:36 **b** them and gave them to His
Matt 26:26 it and **b** it, and gave it to the
Mark 6:41 **b** the loaves, and gave them to
Mark 8: 6 **b** them and gave them to His
Mark 8:19 When I **b** the five loaves for
Mark 8:20 when I **b** the seven for the
Mark 14: 3 she **b** the flask and poured it
Mark 14:22 **b** it, and gave it to them and
Luke 8:29 he **b** the bonds and was driven
Luke 9:16 **b** them, and gave them to the
Luke 22:19 **b** it, and gave it to them,
Luke 24:30 and **b** it, and gave it to them
John 5:18 He not only **b** the Sabbath
John 19:32 **b** the legs of the first and of
1Co 11:24 He had given thanks, He **b** it
Rev 12: 7 And war **b** out in heaven

BROKEN (*see* BREAK, BROKEN-HEARTED, BROKENHEARTED)
Gen 7:11 of the great deep were **b** up
Gen 17:14 he has **b** My covenant
Lev 6:28 which it is boiled shall be **b**
Lev 11:35 stove, it shall be **b** down
Lev 13:20 which has **b** out of the boil
Lev 13:25 it is leprosy **b** out in the
Lev 15:12 discharge touches shall be **b**
Lev 21:19 has a **b** foot or **b** hand
Lev 22:22 that are blind or **b** or maimed
Lev 26:13 I have **b** the bands of your
Num 15:31 has **b** His commandment, that
Deut 21: 6 neck was **b** in the valley
1Sa 2: 4 bows of the mighty men are **b**
1Sa 2:10 the LORD shall be **b** in pieces
1Sa 4:18 and his neck was **b** and he died,
1Sa 5: 4 were **b** off on the threshold
2Sa 5:20 The LORD has **b** through my
1Ki 5: 9 will have them **b** apart there
1Ki 18:30 of the LORD that was **b** down
2Ki 11: 6 the house, lest it be **b** down
2Ki 18:21 in the staff of this **b** reed
2Ki 25: 4 the city wall was **b** through
1Ch 14:11 God has **b** through my enemies
2Ch 14:13 for they were **b** before the
2Ch 24: 7 had **b** into the house of God,
2Ch 32: 5 up all the wall that was **b**
2Ch 33: 3 his father had **b** down
2Ch 34: 7 When he had **b** down the altars
Neh 1: 3 of Jerusalem is also **b** down
Neh 2:13 Jerusalem which were **b** down
Job 4:10 of the young lions are **b**
Job 4:20 They are **b** in pieces from
Job 17: 1 My spirit is **b**, my days are
Job 17:11 past, my purposes are **b** off
Job 24:20 should be **b** like a tree
Job 26: 8 the clouds are not **b** under it
Job 38:15 and the upraised arm is **b**
Ps 3: 7 You have **b** the teeth of the
Ps 31:12 I am like a **b** vessel
Ps 34:18 to those who have a **b** heart
Ps 34:20 Not one of them is **b**
Ps 37:15 And their bows shall be **b**
Ps 37:17 arms of the wicked shall be **b**
Ps 38: 8 I am feeble and severely **b**
Ps 44:19 But You have severely **b** us in
Ps 51: 8 which You have **b** may rejoice
Ps 51:17 a **b** spirit, A **b** and a
Ps 55:20 He has **b** his covenant
Ps 60: 1 You have **b** us down
Ps 60: 2 You have **b** it
Ps 69:20 Reproach has **b** my heart, And I
Ps 80:12 Why have You **b** down her
Ps 89:10 You have **b** Rahab in pieces,
Ps 89:40 You have **b** down all his
Ps 107:16 For He has **b** the gates of
Ps 109:16 even slay the **b** in heart
Ps 124: 7 The snare is **b**, and we have
Prov 3:20 the depths were **b** up, and
Prov 6:15 he shall be **b** without remedy
Prov 15:13 of the heart the spirit is **b**
Prov 17:22 but a **b** spirit dries the
Prov 18:14 but who can bear a **b** spirit
Prov 24:31 its stone wall was **b** down
Prov 25:28 spirit is like a city **b** down
Eccl 4:12 cord is not quickly **b**
Eccl 12: 6 or the golden bowl is **b**, or
Eccl 12: 6 or the wheel **b** at the well
Is 5:27 strap of their sandals be **b**
Is 7: 8 years Ephraim will be **b**, so
Is 8: 9 peoples, and be **b** in pieces
Is 8: 9 but be **b** in pieces

Is 8: 9 but be **b** in pieces
Is 8:15 they shall fall and be **b**, be
Is 9: 4 For You have **b** the yoke of
Is 14: 5 The LORD has **b** the staff of
Is 14:29 the rod that struck you is **b**
Is 16: 8 have **b** down its choice plants
Is 19:10 And its foundations will be **b**
Is 21: 9 gods he has **b** to the ground
Is 24: 5 **B** the everlasting covenant
Is 24:10 city of confusion is **b** down
Is 24:19 The earth is violently **b**, the
Is 27:11 withered, they will be **b** off
Is 28:13 go and fall backward, and be **b**
Is 30:14 vessel, which is **b** in pieces
Is 33: 8 He has **b** the covenant, He has
Is 33:20 will any of its cords be **b**
Is 36: 6 in the staff of this **b** reed
Jer 2:13 **b** cisterns that can hold no
Jer 2:16 Tahpanhes have **b** the crown of
Jer 2:20 For of old I have **b** your yoke
Jer 4:26 all its cities were **b** down at
Jer 5: 5 have altogether **b** the yoke
Jer 10:20 and all my cords are **b**
Jer 11:10 the house of Judah have **b** My
Jer 11:16 on it, and its branches are **b**
Jer 14:17 been **b** with a mighty stroke
Jer 22:28 man Coniah a despised, **b** idol
Jer 23: 9 My heart within me is **b**
Jer 28: 2 I have **b** the yoke of the
Jer 28:12 Hananiah the prophet had **b**
Jer 28:13 You have **b** the yokes of wood,
Jer 33:21 be **b** with David My servant
Jer 48:17 How the strong staff is **b**
Jer 48:20 is shamed, for he is **b** down
Jer 48:25 is cut off, and his arm is **b**
Jer 48:38 for I have **b** Moab like a
Jer 48:39 How she is **b** down
Jer 50: 2 Merodach is **b** in pieces
Jer 50: 2 her images are **b** in pieces
Jer 50:17 of Babylon has **b** his bones
Jer 50:23 earth has been cut apart and **b**
Jer 51:30 the bars of her gate are **b**
Jer 51:56 Every one of their bows is **b**
Jer 51:58 of Babylon shall be utterly **b**
Jer 52: 7 the city wall was **b** through
Lam 2: 9 has destroyed and **b** her bars
Lam 3: 4 and my skin, and **b** my bones
Lam 3:16 He has also **b** my teeth with
Ezek 6: 4 incense altars shall be **b**
Ezek 6: 6 desolate, your idols may be **b**
Ezek 19:12 Her strong branches were **b**
Ezek 26: 2 She is **b** who was the gateway
Ezek 27:34 But when you are **b** by the
Ezek 30: 4 and her foundations are **b** down
Ezek 30:21 I have **b** the arm of Pharaoh
Ezek 30:22 one and the one that was **b**
Ezek 31:12 its boughs lie **b** by all the
Ezek 32:28 you shall be **b** in the midst
Ezek 34: 4 were sick, nor bound up the **b**
Ezek 34:16 driven away, bind up the **b**
Ezek 34:27 when I have **b** the bands of
Dan 8: 8 strong, the large horn was **b**
Dan 8:22 As for the **b** horn and the four
Dan 8:25 but he shall be **b** without
Dan 11: 4 his kingdom shall be **b** up
Dan 11:22 away from before him and be **b**
Hos 5:11 **b** in judgment, because he
Hos 8: 6 Samaria shall be **b** to pieces
Joel 1:17 barns are **b** down, for the
Amos 4: 3 will go out through **b** walls
Jon 1: 4 the ship was about to be **b** up
Zech 11:11 So it was **b** on that day
Zech 11:16 nor heal those that are **b**
Matt 21:44 falls on this stone will be **b**
Matt 24:43 his house to be **b** into
Mark 2: 4 And when they had **b** through
Mark 5: 4 and the shackles **b** in pieces
Luke 12:39 his house to be **b** into
Luke 20:18 falls on that stone will be **b**
John 7:23 law of Moses should not be **b**
John 10:35 and the Scripture cannot be **b**)
John 19:31 that their legs might be **b**
John 19:36 one of His bones shall be **b**
John 21:11 so many, the net was not **b**
Acts 13:43 the congregation had **b** up
Acts 20:11 up, had **b** bread and eaten, and
Acts 27:35 when he had **b** it he began to
Acts 27:41 but the stern was being **b** up
Acts 27:44 some on **b** pieces of the ship
Rom 11:17 of the branches were **b** off
Rom 11:19 Branches were **b** off that I
Rom 11:20 of unbelief they were **b** off
1Co 11:24 is My body which is **b** for you
Eph 2:14 has **b** down the middle wall of
Rev 2:27 vessels shall be **b** to pieces'

BROKEN-HEARTED (*see* BROKEN, HEART)
Ps 147: 3 He heals the **b** And binds up

BROKENHEARTED (*see* BROKEN, HEART)
Is 61: 1 He has sent Me to heal the **b**
Luke 4:18 He has sent Me to heal the **b**

BRONZE
Gen 4:22 of every craftsman in **b** and
Ex 25: 3 gold, silver, and **b**
Ex 26:11 you shall make fifty **b** clasps
Ex 26:37 five sockets of **b** for them
Ex 27: 2 you shall overlay it with **b**
Ex 27: 3 make all its utensils of **b**
Ex 27: 4 grate for it, a network of **b**
Ex 27: 4 **b** rings at its four corners
Ex 27: 6 wood, and overlay them with **b**
Ex 27:10 twenty sockets shall be of **b**
Ex 27:11 and their twenty sockets of **b**
Ex 27:17 silver and their sockets of **b**
Ex 27:18 thread, and its sockets of **b**
Ex 27:19 of the court, shall be of **b**
Ex 30:18 shall also make a laver of **b**
Ex 30:18 with its base also of **b**, for
Ex 31: 4 work in gold, in silver, in **b**
Ex 35: 5 gold, silver, and **b**
Ex 35:16 offering with its **b** grating
Ex 35:24 an offering of silver or **b**
Ex 35:32 work in gold and silver and **b**
Ex 36:18 He also made fifty **b** clasps
Ex 36:38 their five sockets were of **b**
Ex 38: 2 And he overlaid it with **b**
Ex 38: 3 all its utensils he made of **b**
Ex 38: 4 he made a grate of **b** network
Ex 38: 5 four corners of the **b** grating
Ex 38: 6 wood, and overlaid them with **b**
Ex 38: 8 laver of **b** and its base of **b**
Ex 38: 8 from the **b** mirrors of the
Ex 38:10 them, with twenty **b** sockets
Ex 38:11 and their twenty **b** sockets
Ex 38:17 for the pillars were of **b**
Ex 38:19 with their four sockets of **b**
Ex 38:20 court all around, were of **b**
Ex 38:29 The offering of **b** was seventy
Ex 38:30 the **b** altar, the **b** grating
Ex 39:39 **b** altar, its grate of **b**
Lev 6:28 And if it is boiled in a **b** pot
Lev 26:19 iron and your earth like **b**
Num 16:39 the priest took the **b** censers
Num 21: 9 So Moses made a **b** serpent
Num 21: 9 he looked at the **b** serpent
Num 31:22 the gold, the silver, the **b**
Deut 28:23 are over your head shall be **b**
Deut 33:25 sandals shall be iron and **b**
Josh 6:19 and gold, and vessels of **b** and
Josh 6:24 and gold, and the vessels of **b**
Josh 22: 8 silver, with gold, with **b**
Judg 16:21 They bound him with **b** fetters
1Sa 17: 5 He had a **b** helmet on his head
1Sa 17: 5 five thousand shekels of **b**
1Sa 17: 6 he had **b** greaves on his legs
1Sa 17: 6 and a **b** javelin between his
1Sa 17:38 he put a **b** helmet on his head
2Sa 8: 8 took a large amount of **b**
2Sa 8:10 of gold, and articles of **b**
2Sa 21:16 the weight of whose **b** spear
2Sa 22:35 my arms can bend a bow of **b**
1Ki 4:13 with walls and **b** gate-bars
1Ki 7:14 was a man of Tyre, a **b** worker
1Ki 7:14 with all kinds of **b** work
1Ki 7:15 And he cast two pillars of **b**
1Ki 7:16 made two capitals of cast **b**
1Ki 7:23 he made the Sea of cast **b**
1Ki 7:27 He also made ten carts of **b**
1Ki 7:30 four **b** wheels and axles of **b**
1Ki 7:30 of cast **b** beside each wreath
1Ki 7:33 their hubs were all of cast **b**
1Ki 7:38 Then he made ten lavers of **b**
1Ki 7:45 the LORD were of burnished **b**
1Ki 7:47 the weight of the **b** was not
1Ki 8:64 because the **b** altar that was
1Ki 14:27 made **b** shields in their place
2Ki 16:14 He also brought the **b** altar
2Ki 16:15 the **b** altar shall be for me
2Ki 16:17 the **b** oxen that were under it
2Ki 18: 4 broke in pieces the **b** serpent
2Ki 25: 7 bound him with **b** fetters
2Ki 25:13 The **b** pillars that were in
2Ki 25:13 the **b** Sea that were in the
2Ki 25:13 and carried their **b** to Babylon
2Ki 25:14 all the **b** utensils with which
2Ki 25:16 the **b** of all these articles
2Ki 25:17 and the capital on it was of **b**
2Ki 25:17 the capital were all of **b**
1Ch 15:19 to sound the cymbals of **b**
1Ch 18: 8 brought a large amount of **b**
1Ch 18: 8 which Solomon made the **b** Sea
1Ch 18: 8 pillars, and the articles of **b**
1Ch 18:10 of gold, silver, and **b**
1Ch 22: 3 **b** in abundance beyond measure
1Ch 22:14 talents of silver, and **b** and
1Ch 22:16 Of gold and silver and **b** and
1Ch 29: 2 **b** for things of **b**, iron
1Ch 29: 7 thousand talents of **b**, and one
2Ch 1: 5 Now the **b** altar that Bezaleel
2Ch 1: 6 went up there to the **b** altar
2Ch 2: 7 work in gold and silver, in **b**
2Ch 2:14 to work in gold and silver, **b**
2Ch 4: 1 Moreover he made a **b** altar
2Ch 4: 2 he made the Sea of cast **b**
2Ch 4: 9 overlaid these doors with **b**
2Ch 4:16 **b** for King Solomon for the
2Ch 4:18 of the **b** was not determined
2Ch 6:13 (for Solomon had made a **b**
2Ch 7: 7 because the **b** altar which
2Ch 12:10 King Rehoboam made **b** shields
2Ch 24:12 **b** to restore the house of the
2Ch 33:11 bound him with **b** fetters
2Ch 36: 6 bound him in **b** fetters to
Ezra 8:27 vessels of fine polished **b**
Job 6:12 Or is my flesh **b**
Job 20:24 a **b** bow will pierce him
Job 40:18 His bones are like beams of **b**
Job 41:27 as straw, and **b** as rotten wood
Ps 18:34 my arms can bend a bow of **b**
Ps 107:16 He has broken the gates of **b**
Is 45: 2 in pieces the gates of **b** and
Is 48: 4 an iron sinew, and your brow **b**
Is 60:17 Instead of **b** I will bring
Is 60:17 silver, instead of wood, **b**
Jer 1:18 **b** walls against the whole
Jer 6:28 They are **b** and iron, they are
Jer 15:12 the northern iron and the **b**
Jer 15:20 people a fortified **b** wall
Jer 39: 7 bound him with **b** fetters to
Jer 52:11 bound him in **b** fetters, took
Jer 52:17 The **b** pillars that were in
Jer 52:17 the **b** Sea that were in the
Jer 52:17 all their **b** to Babylon
Jer 52:18 all the **b** utensils with which
Jer 52:20 the twelve **b** bulls which were
Jer 52:20 the **b** of all these articles
Jer 52:22 A capital of **b** was on it
Jer 52:22 around the capital, all of **b**
Ezek 1: 7 like the color of burnished **b**
Ezek 9: 2 and stood beside the **b** altar
Ezek 22:18 they are all **b**, tin, iron, and
Ezek 22:20 As men gather silver, **b**,
Ezek 24:11 and its **b** may burn, that its
Ezek 27:13 and vessels of **b** for your
Ezek 40: 3 was like the appearance of **b**
Dan 2:32 its belly and thighs of **b**
Dan 2:35 the iron, the clay, the **b**
Dan 2:39 another, a third kingdom of **b**
Dan 2:45 in pieces the iron, the **b**
Dan 4:15 with a band of iron and **b**, in
Dan 4:23 **b** in the tender grass of the
Dan 5: 4 the gods of gold and silver, **b**
Dan 5:23 the gods of silver and gold, **b**
Dan 7:19 of iron and its nails of **b**
Dan 10: 6 like burnished **b** in color
Mic 4:13 and I will make your hooves **b**
Zech 6: 1 mountains were mountains of **b**
Rev 18:12 of most precious wood, **b**,

BROOD (*see* BROODS)
Num 32:14 place, a **b** of sinful men, to
Is 1: 4 a **b** of evildoers, children
Is 14:20 The **b** of evildoers shall
Matt 3: 7 said to them, "**B** of vipers
Matt 12:34 **B** of vipers!
Matt 23:33 Serpents, **b** of vipers
Luke 3: 7 by him, "**B** of vipers
Luke 13:34 gathers her **b** under her wings

BROODS (*see* BROOD)
Jer 17:11 that **b** but does not hatch

BROOK (*see* BROOKS)
Gen 32:23 them, sent them over the **b**
Lev 23:40 trees, and willows of the **b**
Num 34: 5 from Azmon to the **B** of Egypt
Deut 9:21 the **b** that descended from the
Josh 11: 8 to the **B** Misrephoth, and to
Josh 13: 6 as far as the **B** Misrephoth
Josh 15: 4 and went out to the **B** of Egypt
Josh 15:47 as far as the **B** of Egypt and
Josh 16: 8 westward to the **B** Kanah, and
Josh 17: 9 descended to the **B** Kanah,
Josh 17: 9 Kanah, southward to the **b**
Josh 17: 9 on the north side of the **b**
Josh 19:11 extended along the **b** that is
Josh 19:26 along the **B** Shihor Libnath
1Sa 17:40 five smooth stones from the **b**
1Sa 30: 9 him, and came to the **B** Besor
1Sa 30:10 could not cross the **B** Besor
1Sa 30:21 made to stay at the **B** Besor
2Sa 15:23 crossed over the **B** Kidron
2Sa 17:20 have gone over the water **b**
1Ki 2:37 go out and cross the **B** Kidron
1Ki 8:65 of Hamath to the **B** of Egypt
1Ki 15:13 and burned it by the **B** Kidron
1Ki 17: 3 and hide by the **B** Cherith
1Ki 17: 4 you shall drink from the **b**
1Ki 17: 5 and stayed by the **B** Cherith
1Ki 17: 6 and he drank from the **b**
1Ki 17: 7 a while that the **b** dried up
1Ki 18:40 them down to the **B** Kishon
2Ki 23: 6 LORD, to the **B** Kidron outside
2Ki 23: 6 burned it at the **B** Kidron
2Ki 23:12 their dust into the **B** Kidron
2Ki 24: 7 the **B** of Egypt to the River
2Ch 7: 8 of Hamath to the **B** of Egypt
2Ch 15:16 and burned it by the **B** Kidron
2Ch 20:16 **b** before the Wilderness of
2Ch 29:16 and carried it to the **B** Kidron
2Ch 30:14 cast them into the **B** Kidron
2Ch 32: 4 the **b** that ran through the
Job 6:15 dealt deceitfully like a **b**
Job 40:22 willows by the **b** surround him
Ps 83: 9 As with Jabin at the **B** Kishon
Ps 110: 7 drink of the **b** by the wayside
Prov 18: 4 of wisdom is a flowing **b**
Is 15: 7 away to the **B** of the Willows
Is 27:12 the River to the **B** of Egypt
Jer 31:40 fields as far as the **B** Kidron
Ezek 47:19 along the **b** to the Great Sea
Ezek 48:28 along the **b** to the Great Sea
John 18: 1 disciples over the **B** Kidron

BROOKS (*see* BROOK)
Num 21:14 Suphah, the **b** of the Arnon,
Num 21:15 and the slope of the **b** that
Deut 8: 7 land, a land of **b** of water
2Sa 23:30 Hiddai from the **b** of Gaash
1Ki 18: 5 of water and to all the **b**
2Ki 19:24 dried up all the **b** of defense
1Ch 11:32 Hurai of the **b** of Gaash,
Job 6:15 of the **b** that pass away,
Job 22:24 among the stones of the **b**
Ps 42: 1 deer pants for the water **b**
Is 19: 6 and the **b** of defense will be
Is 37:25 dried up all the **b** of defense
Joel 1:20 for the water **b** are dried up
Joel 3:18 all the **b** of Judah shall be

BROOM
1Ki 19: 4 and sat down under a **b** tree
1Ki 19: 5 lay and slept under a **b** tree
Job 30: 4 **b** tree roots for their food
Ps 120: 4 With coals of the **b** tree
Is 14:23 it with the **b** of destruction

BROTH
Judg 6:19 and he put the **b** in a pot
Judg 6:20 this rock, and pour out the **b**
Is 65: 4 the **b** of abominable things is

BROTHER (*see* BRETHREN, BROTHERHOOD, BROTHERLY, BROTHER'S, BROTHERS)
Gen 4: 2 again, this time his **b** Abel
Gen 4: 8 Cain talked with Abel his **b**
Gen 4: 8 Cain rose against Abel his **b**
Gen 4: 9 Where is Abel your **b**
Gen 9: 5 the hand of every man's **b** I
Gen 10:21 the **b** of Japheth the elder
Gen 14:13 **b** of Eshcol and **b** of Aner
Gen 14:14 that his **b** was taken captive
Gen 14:16 also brought back his **b** Lot
Gen 20: 5 she herself said, "He is my **b**
Gen 20:13 He is my **b**
Gen 20:16 Behold, I have given your **b** a
Gen 22:20 children to your **b** Nahor
Gen 22:21 Huz his firstborn, Buz his **b**
Gen 22:23 bore to Nahor, Abraham's **b**
Gen 24:15 wife of Nahor, Abraham's **b**
Gen 24:29 Now Rebekah had a **b** whose
Gen 24:48 of my master's **b** for his son
Gen 24:53 gave precious things to her **b**
Gen 24:55 But her **b** and her mother said,
Gen 25:26 Afterward his **b** came out, and
Gen 27: 6 father speak to Esau your **b**
Gen 27:11 Esau my **b** is a hairy man, and
Gen 27:23 hairy like his **b** Esau's hands
Gen 27:30 that Esau his **b** came in from
Gen 27:35 Your **b** came with deceit and
Gen 27:40 and you shall serve your **b**
Gen 27:41 then I will kill my **b** Jacob
Gen 27:42 Surely your **b** Esau comforts
Gen 27:43 flee to my **b** Laban in Haran
Gen 28: 2 of Laban your mother's **b**
Gen 28: 5 the **b** of Rebekah, the mother
Gen 29:10 of Laban his mother's **b**, and
Gen 29:10 sheep of Laban his mother's **b**
Gen 29:10 flock of Laban his mother's **b**
Gen 32: 3 his **b** in the land of Seir
Gen 32: 6 We came to your **b** Esau, and he
Gen 32:11 I pray, from the hand of my **b**
Gen 32:13 as a present for Esau his **b**
Gen 32:17 When Esau my **b** meets you and
Gen 33: 3 until he came near to his **b**
Gen 33: 9 I have enough, my **b**
Gen 35: 1 from the face of Esau your **b**
Gen 35: 7 fled from the face of his **b**
Gen 36: 6 the presence of his **b** Jacob
Gen 37:26 is there if we kill our **b**
Gen 37:27 be upon him, for he is our **b**
Gen 38: 8 and raise up an heir to your **b**
Gen 38: 9 should give an heir to his **b**
Gen 38:29 his hand, that his **b** came out
Gen 38:30 Afterward his **b** came out who
Gen 42: 4 **b** Benjamin with his brothers
Gen 42:15 your youngest **b** comes here
Gen 42:16 you, and let him bring your **b**
Gen 42:20 bring your youngest **b** to me
Gen 42:21 truly guilty concerning our **b**
Gen 42:34 bring your youngest **b** to me
Gen 42:34 I will deliver your **b** to you
Gen 42:38 with you, for his **b** is dead
Gen 43: 3 unless your **b** is with you
Gen 43: 4 If you send our **b** with us
Gen 43: 5 unless your **b** is with you
Gen 43: 6 you had still another **b**
Gen 43: 7 Have you another **b**
Gen 43: 7 say, 'Bring your **b** down'
Gen 43:13 Take your **b** also, and arise,
Gen 43:14 he may release your other **b**
Gen 43:29 and saw his **b** Benjamin, his
Gen 43:29 Is this your younger **b** of
Gen 43:30 his heart yearned for his **b**
Gen 44:19 Have you a father or a **b**
Gen 44:20 his **b** is dead, and he alone is
Gen 44:23 **b** comes down with you, you
Gen 44:26 if our youngest **b** is with us
Gen 44:26 our youngest **b** is with us
Gen 45: 4 I am Joseph your **b**, whom you
Gen 45:12 the eyes of my **b** Benjamin see
Gen 45:14 fell on his **b** Benjamin's neck
Gen 48:19 but truly his younger **b** shall
Ex 4:14 not Aaron the Levite your **b**
Ex 7: 1 Aaron your **b** shall be your
Ex 7: 2 Aaron your **b** shall speak to
Ex 28: 1 Now take Aaron your **b**, and his
Ex 28: 2 garments for Aaron your **b**
Ex 28: 4 garments for Aaron your **b**
Ex 28:41 put them on Aaron your **b** and
Ex 32:27 and let every man kill his **b**
Ex 32:29 has opposed his son and his **b**
Lev 16: 2 Tell Aaron your **b** not to come
Lev 18:14 nakedness of your father's **b**
Lev 19:17 not hate your **b** in your heart
Lev 21: 2 son, his daughter, and his **b**
Lev 25:25 he may redeem what his **b** sold
Lev 25:36 that your **b** may live with you
Num 6: 7 for his **b** or his sister, when
Num 20: 8 and your **b** Aaron gather the
Num 20:14 Thus says your **b** Israel
Num 27:13 as Aaron your **b** was gathered
Num 36: 2 **b** Zelophehad to his daughters
Deut 1:16 his **b** or the stranger who is
Deut 13: 6 If your **b**, the son of your
Deut 15: 2 it of his neighbor or his **b**
Deut 15: 3 what is owed by your **b**,
Deut 15: 7 your hand from your poor **b**
Deut 15: 9 be evil against your poor **b**
Deut 15:11 open your hand wide to your **b**
Deut 15:12 If your **b**, a Hebrew man, or a
Deut 17:15 over you, who is not your **b**
Deut 19:18 falsely against his **b**,
Deut 19:19 thought to have done to his **b**
Deut 22: 1 bring them back to your **b**
Deut 22: 2 if your **b** is not near you, or
Deut 22: 2 you until your **b** seeks it
Deut 23: 7 an Edomite, for he is your **b**
Deut 23:19 not charge interest to your **b**
Deut 23:20 but to your **b** you shall not
Deut 24:10 When you lend your **b** anything
Deut 25: 3 your **b** be humiliated in your
Deut 25: 5 her husband's **b** shall go in
Deut 25: 5 duty of a husband's **b** to her
Deut 25: 6 to the name of his dead **b**
Deut 25: 7 My husband's **b** refuses to
Deut 25: 7 up a name to his **b** in Israel
Deut 25: 7 the duty of my husband's **b**
Deut 28:54 will be hostile toward his **b**
Deut 32:50 your **b** died on Mount Hor and
Josh 15:17 the **b** of Caleb, took it
Judg 1: 3 So Judah said to Simeon his **b**
Judg 1:13 of Kenaz, Caleb's younger **b**
Judg 1:17 Judah went with his **b** Simeon
Judg 3: 9 of Kenaz, Caleb's younger **b**
Judg 9: 3 He is our **b**
Judg 9:18 Shechem, because he is your **b**
Judg 9:21 for fear of Abimelech his **b**
Judg 9:24 be laid on Abimelech their **b**
Judg 20:23 the children of my **b** Benjamin
Judg 20:28 the children of my **b** Benjamin
Judg 21: 6 grieved for Benjamin their **b**
Ruth 4: 3 belonged to our **b** Elimelech
1Sa 14: 3 son of Ahitub, Ichabod's **b**
1Sa 17:28 Now Eliab his oldest **b** heard
1Sa 20:29 my **b** has commanded me to be
1Sa 26: 6 Zeruiah, **b** of Joab, saying,
2Sa 1:26 for you, my **b** Jonathan
2Sa 2:22 then could I face your **b** Joab
2Sa 3:27 for the blood of Asahel his **b**
2Sa 3:30 Abishai his **b** killed Abner,
2Sa 3:30 **b** Asahel at Gibeon in the
2Sa 4: 6 and Baanah his **b** escaped
2Sa 4: 9 Rechab and Baanah his **b**, the
2Sa 10:10 the command of Abishai his **b**
2Sa 13: 3 the son of Shimeah, David's **b**
2Sa 13: 4 Tamar, my **b** Absalom's sister
2Sa 13: 7 go to your **b** Amnon's house
2Sa 13: 8 went to her **b** Amnon's house
2Sa 13:10 to Amnon her **b** in the bedroom
2Sa 13:12 No, my **b**, do not force me,
2Sa 13:20 And Absalom her **b** said to her
2Sa 13:20 Amnon your **b** been with you
2Sa 13:20 He is your **b**
2Sa 13:20 in her **b** Absalom's house
2Sa 13:22 Absalom spoke to his **b** Amnon
2Sa 13:26 please let my **b** Amnon go with
2Sa 13:32 the son of Shimeah, David's **b**
2Sa 14: 7 Deliver him who struck his **b**
2Sa 14: 7 life of his **b** whom he killed
2Sa 18: 2 the son of Zeruiah, Joab's **b**
2Sa 20: 9 Are you in health, my **b**
2Sa 20:10 Abishai his **b** pursued Sheba
2Sa 21:19 the **b** of Goliath the Gittite
2Sa 21:21 the **b** of David, killed him
2Sa 23:18 Now Abishai the **b** of Joab
2Sa 23:24 Asahel the **b** of Joab was one
1Ki 1:10 mighty men, or Solomon his **b**
1Ki 2: 7 I fled from Absalom your **b**
1Ki 2:21 to Adonijah your **b** as wife
1Ki 2:22 for he is my older **b**
1Ki 9:13 which you have given me, my **b**
1Ki 13:30 Alas, my **b**!"
1Ki 20:32 He is my **b**
1Ki 20:33 and said, "Your **b** Ben-Hadad
1Ch 2:32 the **b** of Shammai, were Jether
1Ch 2:42 the **b** of Jerahmeel were Mesha
1Ch 4:11 Chelub the **b** of Shuhah begot
1Ch 6:39 his **b** Asaph, who stood at his
1Ch 7:16 The name of his **b** was Sheresh
1Ch 7:35 the sons of his **b** Helem were
1Ch 8:39 the sons of Eshek his **b** were

1Ch 11:20 Now Abishai the **b** of Joab was
1Ch 11:26 were Asahel the **b** of Joab
1Ch 11:38 Joel the **b** of Nathan, Mibhar
1Ch 11:45 son of Shimri, and Joha his **b**
1Ch 19:11 the command of Abishai his **b**
1Ch 19:15 fled before Abishai his **b**
1Ch 20: 5 the **b** of Goliath the Gittite
1Ch 20: 7 the son of Shimea, David's **b**
1Ch 24:25 The **b** of Michah, Isshiah
1Ch 26:22 Jehieli, Zetham and Joel his **b**
1Ch 27: 7 was Asahel the **b** of Joab, and
2Ch 31:12 Shimei his **b** was the next
2Ch 31:13 of Cononiah and Shimei his **b**
2Ch 36: 4 his **b** Eliakim king over Judah
2Ch 36: 4 And Necho took Jehoahaz his **b**
2Ch 36:10 made Zedekiah, Jehoiakim's **b**
Neh 5: 7 is exacting usury from his **b**
Neh 7: 2 of Jerusalem to my **b** Hanani
Job 22: 6 from your **b** for no reason
Job 30:29 I am a **b** of jackals, and a
Ps 35:14 though he were my friend or **b**
Ps 49: 7 can by any means redeem his **b**
Ps 50:20 sit and speak against your **b**
Prov 17:17 a **b** is born for adversity
Prov 18: 9 is a **b** to him who is a great
Prov 18:19 A **b** offended is harder to win
Prov 18:24 who sticks closer than a **b**
Prov 27:10 nearby than a **b** far away
Eccl 4: 8 he has neither son nor **b**
Song 8: 1 Oh, that you were like my **b**
Is 3: 6 a man takes hold of his **b** In
Is 9:19 no man shall spare his **b**
Is 19: 2 will fight against his **b**, and
Is 41: 6 neighbor, and said to his **b**
Jer 9: 4 and do not trust any **b**
Jer 9: 4 for every **b** will utterly
Jer 22:18 for him, saying, 'Alas, my **b**
Jer 23:35 and every one to his **b**, 'What
Jer 31:34 neighbor, and every man his **b**
Jer 34: 9 keep a Jewish **b** in bondage
Jer 34:14 man set free his Hebrew **b**
Jer 34:17 liberty, every one to his **b**
Ezek 18:18 robbed his **b** by violence, and
Ezek 33:30 everyone saying to his **b**
Ezek 38:21 sword will be against his **b**
Ezek 44:25 for **b** or unmarried sister may
Hos 12: 3 He took his **b** by the heel in
Amos 1:11 pursued his **b** with the sword
Obad 10 violence against your **b** Jacob
Obad 12 gazed on the day of your **b** in
Mic 7: 2 man hunts his **b** with a net
Hag 2:22 one by the sword of his **b**
Zech 7: 9 compassion everyone to his **b**
Zech 7:10 in his heart against his **b**
Mal 1: 2 Was not Esau Jacob's **b**
Matt 4:18 called Peter, and Andrew his **b**
Matt 4:21 son of Zebedee, and John his **b**
Matt 5:22 whoever is angry with his **b**
Matt 5:22 And whoever says to his **b**
Matt 5:23 there remember that your **b**
Matt 5:24 First be reconciled to your **b**
Matt 7: 4 Or how can you say to your **b**
Matt 10: 2 called Peter, and Andrew his **b**
Matt 10: 2 son of Zebedee, and John his **b**
Matt 10:21 Now **b** will deliver up **b**
Matt 12:50 My Father in heaven is My **b**
Matt 14: 3 Herodias, his **b** Philip's wife
Matt 17: 1 Peter, James, and John his **b**
Matt 18:15 if your **b** sins against you
Matt 18:15 you, you have gained your **b**
Matt 18:21 shall my **b** sin against me
Matt 18:35 forgive his **b** his trespasses
Matt 22:24 his **b** shall marry his wife and
Matt 22:24 raise up offspring for his **b**
Matt 22:25 left his wife to his **b**
Mark 1:16 Andrew his **b** casting a net
Mark 1:19 son of Zebedee, and John his **b**
Mark 3:17 and John the **b** of James, to
Mark 3:35 does the will of God is My **b**
Mark 5:37 James, and John the **b** of James
Mark 6: 3 **b** of James, Joses, Judas, and
Mark 6:17 Herodias, his **b** Philip's wife
Mark 12:19 to us that if a man's **b** dies
Mark 12:19 his **b** should take his wife and
Mark 12:19 raise up offspring for his **b**
Mark 13:12 **b** will betray **b** to death
Luke 3: 1 his **b** Philip tetrarch of
Luke 3:19 his **b** Philip's wife, and for
Luke 6:14 named Peter, and Andrew his **b**
Luke 6:42 Or how can you say to your **b**
Luke 6:42 you say to your **b**, 'B
Luke 12:13 tell my **b** to divide the
Luke 15:27 Your **b** has come, and because
Luke 15:32 be glad, for your **b** was dead
Luke 17: 3 If your **b** sins against you,
Luke 20:28 to us that if a man's **b** dies
Luke 20:28 his **b** should take his wife and
Luke 20:28 raise up offspring for his **b**
John 1:40 was Andrew, Simon Peter's **b**
John 1:41 first found his own **b** Simon
John 6: 8 Andrew, Simon Peter's **b**,
John 11: 2 whose **b** Lazarus was sick
John 11:19 them concerning their **b**
John 11:21 my **b** would not have died
John 11:23 her, "Your **b** will rise again
John 11:32 my **b** would not have died
Acts 9:17 **B** Saul, the Lord Jesus, who
Acts 12: 2 the **b** of John with the sword
Acts 21:20 You see, **b**, how many myriads
Acts 22:13 **B** Saul, receive your sight
Rom 14:10 But why do you judge your **b**
Rom 14:10 you show contempt for your **b**
Rom 14:15 Yet if your **b** is grieved
Rom 14:21 do anything by which your **b**
Rom 16:23 greets you, and Quartus, a **b**
1Co 1: 1 of God, and Sosthenes our **b**
1Co 5:11 company with anyone named a **b**
1Co 6: 6 **b** goes to law against **b**
1Co 7:12 If any **b** has a wife who does
1Co 7:15 a **b** or a sister is not under
1Co 8:11 shall the weak **b** perish, for
1Co 8:13 if food makes my **b** stumble
1Co 8:13 lest I make my **b** stumble
1Co 16:12 Now concerning our **b** Apollos
2Co 1: 1 will of God, and Timothy our **b**
2Co 2:13 I did not find Titus my **b**
2Co 8:18 the **b** whose praise is in the
2Co 8:22 **b** whom we have often proved
2Co 12:18 Titus, and sent our **b** with him
Gal 1:19 except James, the Lord's **b**
Eph 6:21 doing, Tychicus, a beloved **b**
Phil 2:25 to you Epaphroditus, my **b**
Col 1: 1 will of God, and Timothy our **b**
Col 4: 7 Tychicus, who is a beloved **b**
Col 4: 9 a faithful and beloved **b**, who
1Th 3: 2 and sent Timothy, our **b** and
1Th 4: 6 defraud his **b** in this matter,
2Th 3: 6 every **b** who walks disorderly
2Th 3:15 but admonish him as a **b**
Phm 1 Jesus, and Timothy our **b**, To
Phm 7 have been refreshed by you, **b**
Phm 16 than a slave, as a beloved **b**
Phm 20 Yes, **b**, let me have joy from
Heb 8:11 his neighbor, and none his **b**
Heb 13:23 Know that our **b** Timothy has
Jas 1: 9 Let the lowly **b** glory in his
Jas 2:15 If a **b** or sister is naked and
Jas 4:11 He who speaks evil of a **b**
Jas 4:11 and judges his **b**, speaks evil
1Pe 5:12 our faithful **b** as I consider
2Pe 3:15 as also our beloved **b** Paul
1Jn 2: 9 in the light, and hates his **b**
1Jn 2:10 He who loves his **b** abides in
1Jn 2:11 hates his **b** is in darkness
1Jn 3:10 is he who does not love his **b**
1Jn 3:12 wicked one and murdered his **b**
1Jn 3:14 love his **b** abides in death
1Jn 3:15 hates his **b** is a murderer
1Jn 3:17 goods, and sees his **b** in need
1Jn 4:20 I love God," and hates his **b**
1Jn 4:20 love his **b** whom he has seen
1Jn 4:21 God must love his **b** also
1Jn 5:16 If anyone sees his **b** sinning
Jude 1 **b** of James, To those who are
Rev 1: 9 I, John, both your **b** and

BROTHERHOOD (*see* BROTHER)
Amos 1: 9 remember the covenant of **b**
Zech 11:14 break the **b** between Judah
1Pe 2:17 Love the **b**
1Pe 5: 9 by your **b** in the world

BROTHERLY (*see* BROTHER)
Rom 12:10 to one another with **b** love
1Th 4: 9 But concerning **b** love you
Heb 13: 1 Let **b** love continue
2Pe 1: 7 to godliness **b** kindness, and
2Pe 1: 7 and to **b** kindness love

BROTHER'S (*see* BROTHER)
Gen 4: 9 Am I my **b** keeper
Gen 4:10 The voice of your **b** blood
Gen 4:11 your **b** blood from your hand
Gen 4:21 His **b** name was Jubal
Gen 10:25 and his **b** name was Joktan
Gen 12: 5 his wife and Lot his **b** son
Gen 14:12 Abram's **b** son who dwelt in
Gen 27:44 until your **b** fury turns away,
Gen 27:45 until your **b** anger turns away
Gen 38: 8 Go in to your **b** wife and marry
Gen 38: 9 when he went in to his **b** wife
Lev 18:16 the nakedness of your **b** wife
Lev 18:16 it is your **b** nakedness
Lev 20:21 If a man takes his **b** wife
Lev 20:21 has uncovered his **b** nakedness
Deut 22: 1 your **b** ox or his sheep going
Deut 22: 3 with any lost thing of your **b**
Deut 22: 4 You shall not see your **b**
Deut 25: 7 not want to take his **b** wife
Deut 25: 7 then let his **b** wife go up to
Deut 25: 9 then his **b** wife shall come to
Deut 25: 9 will not build up his **b** house
1Ki 2:15 over, and has become my **b**
1Ch 1:19 and his **b** name was Joktan
Job 1:13 wine in their oldest **b** house
Job 1:18 wine in their oldest **b** house
Prov 27:10 nor go to your **b** house in the
Matt 7: 3 at the speck in your **b** eye
Matt 7: 5 the speck out of your **b** eye
Mark 6:18 for you to have your **b** wife
Luke 6:41 at the speck in your **b** eye
Luke 6:42 speck that is in your **b** eye
Rom 14:13 a cause to fall in our **b** way
1Jn 3:12 were evil and his **b** righteous

BROTHERS (*see* BROTHER)
Gen 9:22 and told his two **b** outside
Gen 34:11 said to her father and her **b**
Gen 34:25 Simeon and Levi, Dinah's **b**
Gen 37: 2 feeding the flock with his **b**
Gen 37: 4 But when his **b** saw that their
Gen 37: 4 loved him more than all his **b**
Gen 37: 5 dream, and he told it to his **b**
Gen 37: 8 And his **b** said to him,
Gen 37: 9 dream and told it to his **b**
Gen 37:10 it to his father and his **b**
Gen 37:10 your **b** indeed come to bow
Gen 37:11 his **b** envied him, but his
Gen 37:12 Then his **b** went to feed their
Gen 37:13 Are not your **b** feeding the
Gen 37:14 see if it is well with your **b**
Gen 37:16 I am seeking my **b**
Gen 37:17 So Joseph went after his **b**
Gen 37:23 when Joseph had come to his **b**
Gen 37:26 So Judah said to his **b**
Gen 37:27 And his **b** listened
Gen 37:28 so the **b** pulled Joseph up and
Gen 37:30 And he returned to his **b** and
Gen 38: 1 Judah departed from his **b**
Gen 38:11 Lest he also die as his **b** did
Gen 42: 3 So Joseph's ten **b** went down
Gen 42: 4 brother Benjamin with his **b**
Gen 42: 6 And Joseph's **b** came and bowed
Gen 42: 7 Joseph saw his **b** and
Gen 42: 8 So Joseph recognized his **b**
Gen 42:13 Your servants are twelve **b**
Gen 42:19 let one of your **b** be confined
Gen 42:28 So he said to his **b**, "My
Gen 42:32 We are twelve **b**, sons of our
Gen 42:33 one of your **b** here with me
Gen 44:14 his **b** came to Joseph's house,
Gen 44:33 let the lad go up with his **b**
Gen 45: 1 made himself known to his **b**
Gen 45: 3 Then Joseph said to his **b**
Gen 45: 3 But his **b** could not answer
Gen 45: 4 And Joseph said to his **b**
Gen 45:15 Moreover he kissed all his **b**
Gen 45:15 after that his **b** talked with
Gen 45:16 Joseph's **b** have come
Gen 45:17 Say to your **b**, 'Do this
Gen 45:24 So he sent his **b** away, and
Gen 46:31 Then Joseph said to his **b**
Gen 46:31 Pharaoh, and say to him, 'My **b**
Gen 47: 1 My father and my **b**, their
Gen 47: 2 five men from among his **b**
Gen 47: 3 Then Pharaoh said to his **b**
Gen 47: 5 and your **b** have come to you
Gen 47: 6 **b** dwell in the best of the
Gen 47:11 situated his father and his **b**
Gen 47:12 provided his father, his **b**

Gen 48: 6 their **b** in their inheritance
Gen 48:22 you one portion above your **b**
Gen 49: 5 Simeon and Levi are **b**
Gen 49: 8 he whom your **b** shall praise
Gen 49:26 who was separate from his **b**
Gen 50: 8 the house of Joseph, his **b**
Gen 50:14 to Egypt, he and his **b** and all
Gen 50:15 When Joseph's **b** saw that
Gen 50:17 the trespass of your **b** and
Gen 50:18 Then his **b** also went and fell
Ex 1: 6 And Joseph died, all his **b**
Lev 25:48 One of his **b** may redeem him
Num 27: 4 among the **b** of our father
Num 27: 7 among their father's **b**, and
Num 27: 9 give his inheritance to his **b**
Num 27:10 If he has no **b**, then you
Num 27:10 inheritance to his father's **b**
Num 27:11 And if his father has no **b**
Num 36:11 the sons of their father's **b**
Deut 25: 5 If **b** dwell together, and one
Deut 33: 9 nor did he acknowledge his **b**
Deut 33:16 who was separate from his **b**
Deut 33:24 let him be favored by his **b**
Josh 2:13 my father, my mother, my **b**
Josh 2:18 father, your mother, your **b**
Josh 6:23 her father, her mother, her **b**
Josh 17: 4 us an inheritance among our **b**
Josh 17: 4 among their father's **b**
Judg 8:19 They were my **b**, the sons of
Judg 9: 1 to Shechem, to his mother's **b**
Judg 9: 3 And his mother's **b** spoke all
Judg 9: 5 at Ophrah and killed his **b**
Judg 9:24 him in the killing of his **b**
Judg 9:26 son of Ebed came with his **b**
Judg 9:31 his **b** have come to Shechem
Judg 9:41 Zebul drove out Gaal and his **b**
Judg 9:56 by killing his seventy **b**
Judg 11: 3 Then Jephthah fled from his **b**
Judg 16:31 And his **b** and all his father's
Judg 21:22 **b** come to us to complain,
1Sa 16:13 him in the midst of his **b**
1Sa 17:17 Take now for your **b** an ephah
1Sa 17:17 and run to your **b** at the camp
1Sa 17:18 and see how your **b** fare, and
1Sa 17:22 and came and greeted his **b**
1Sa 20:29 let me get away and see my **b**
1Sa 22: 1 And when his **b** and all his
2Sa 3: 8 of Saul your father, to his **b**
1Ki 1: 9 he also invited all his **b**
2Ki 10:13 Jehu met with the **b** of
2Ki 10:13 We are the **b** of Ahaziah
1Ch 4: 9 was more honorable than his **b**
1Ch 4:27 but his **b** did not have many
1Ch 5: 2 Judah prevailed over his **b**
1Ch 16:37 his **b** there before the ark of
1Ch 24:31 their **b** the sons of Aaron did
1Ch 26: 7 and Elzabad, whose **b** Elihu
1Ch 27:18 Elihu, one of David's **b**
2Ch 11:22 to be leader among his **b**
2Ch 21: 2 He had **b**, the sons of
2Ch 21: 4 all his **b** with the sword, and
2Ch 21:13 and also have killed your **b**
2Ch 22: 8 **b** who served Ahaziah, that he
2Ch 35: 9 his **b** Shemaiah and Nethaneel,
Ezra 3: 9 Jeshua with his sons and **b**
Ezra 8:18 Sherebiah, with his sons and **b**
Ezra 8:19 of the sons of Merari, his **b**
Ezra 10:18 the son of Jozadak, and his **b**
Neh 5:14 neither I nor my **b** ate the
Neh 12:24 with their **b** across from them
Job 6:15 My **b** have dealt deceitfully
Job 19:13 has removed my **b** far from me
Job 42:11 Then all his **b**, all his
Job 42:15 an inheritance among their **b**
Ps 69: 8 become a stranger to my **b**
Prov 17: 2 an inheritance among the **b**
Prov 19: 7 All the **b** of the poor hate
Jer 12: 6 For even your **b**, the house of
Jer 35: 3 the son of Habazziniah, his **b**
Matt 1: 2 and Jacob begot Judah and his **b**
Matt 1:11 his **b** about the time they
Matt 4:18 the Sea of Galilee, saw two **b**
Matt 4:21 there, He saw two other **b**
Matt 12:46 **b** stood outside, seeking to
Matt 12:47 Your **b** are standing outside,
Matt 12:48 is My mother and who are My **b**
Matt 12:49 Here are My mother and My **b**
Matt 13:55 His **b** James, Joses, Simon, and
Matt 19:29 who has left houses or **b** or
Matt 20:24 indignation against the two **b**
Matt 22:25 there were with us seven **b**
Mark 3:31 His **b** and His mother came
Mark 3:32 Your **b** are outside seeking
Mark 3:33 Who is My mother, or My **b**
Mark 3:34 Here are My mother and My **b**
Mark 10:29 or **b** or sisters or father or
Mark 10:30 houses and **b** and sisters and
Mark 12:20 Now there were seven **b**
Luke 8:19 **b** came to Him, and could not
Luke 8:20 Your **b** are standing outside,
Luke 8:21 My **b** are these who hear the
Luke 14:12 not ask your friends, your **b**
Luke 14:26 mother, wife and children, **b**
Luke 16:28 for I have five **b**, that he
Luke 18:29 or **b** or wife or children, for
Luke 20:29 Now there were seven **b**
Luke 21:16 betrayed even by parents and **b**
John 2:12 He, His mother, His **b**, and
John 7: 3 His **b** therefore said to Him,
John 7: 5 For even His **b** did not
John 7:10 But when His **b** had gone up
Acts 1:14 of Jesus, and with His **b**
Acts 7:13 was made known to his **b**, and
Acts 28:11 figurehead was the Twin **B**
1Co 9: 5 the **b** of the Lord, and Cephas
1Ti 5: 1 father, the younger men as **b**
1Pe 3: 8 love as **b**, be tenderhearted,

BROUGHT (*see* PREFACE)

BROW
Num 24:17 and batter the **b** of Moab, and
Is 48: 4 iron sinew, and your **b** bronze,
Jer 48:45 and shall devour the **b** of Moab
Luke 4:29 they led Him to the **b** of the

BROWN
Gen 30:32 and all the **b** ones among the
Gen 30:33 **b** among the lambs, will be
Gen 30:35 and all the **b** ones among the
Gen 30:40 all the **b** in the flock of

BRUISE (*see* BRUISED, BRUISES, BRUISING)
Gen 3:15 He shall **b** your head, and you
Gen 3:15 head, and you shall **b** His heel
Is 30:26 binds up the **b** of His people
Is 53:10 it pleased the LORD to **b** Him

BRUISED (*see* BRUISE)
Lev 22:24 the LORD what is **b** or crushed
Is 42: 3 A **b** reed He will not break,
Is 53: 5 He was **b** for our iniquities
Matt 12:20 A **b** reed He will not break,

BRUISES (*see* BRUISE)
Job 5:18 For He **b**, but He binds up
Is 1: 6 in it, but wounds and **b** and

BRUISING (*see* BRUISE)
Luke 9:39 **b** him, it departs from him

BRUNT
Num 14:33 bear the **b** of your infidelity

BRUSHWOOD
Is 64: 2 as fire burns **b**, as fire

BRUTAL (*see* BRUTALLY, BRUTE)
Ezek 21:31 you into the hands of **b** men
2Ti 3: 3 without self-control, **b**,

BRUTALLY (*see* BRUTAL)
Deut 21:14 you shall not treat her **b**

BRUTE (*see* BRUTAL)
2Pe 2:12 like natural **b** beasts made to
Jude 10 like **b** beasts, in these

BUCKET (*see* BUCKETS)
Is 40:15 nations are as a drop in a **b**

BUCKETS (*see* BUCKET)
Num 24: 7 shall pour water from his **b**

BUCKLER (*see* BUCKLERS)
Ps 35: 2 Take hold of shield and **b**, And
Ps 91: 4 shall be your shield and **b**
Jer 46: 3 Order the **b** and shield, and
Ezek 23:24 shall array against you **b**

BUCKLERS (*see* BUCKLER)
Song 4: 4 on which hang a thousand **b**
Ezek 38: 4 a great company with **b** and
Ezek 39: 9 both the shields and **b**, the

BUD (*see* BUDDED, BUDDING, BUDS)
Ex 9:31 the head and the flax was in **b**
Job 14: 9 the scent of water it will **b**
Is 18: 5 when the **b** is perfect and the
Is 27: 6 Israel shall blossom and **b**
Is 55:10 and make it bring forth and **b**
Is 61:11 the earth brings forth its **b**
Hos 8: 7 The stalk has no **b**

BUDDED (*see* BUD)
Gen 40:10 it was as though it **b**, its
Song 6:11 to see whether the vine had **b**
Song 7:12 let us see if the vine has **b**
Ezek 7:10 has blossomed, pride has **b**
Heb 9: 4 the manna, Aaron's rod that **b**

BUDDING (*see* BUD)
Luke 21:30 When they are already **b**, you

BUDS (*see* BUD)
Num 17: 8 had sprouted and put forth **b**
1Ki 6:18 carved with ornamental **b**
1Ki 7:24 **b** encircling it all around
1Ki 7:24 The ornamental **b** were cast in

BUFFET
2Co 12: 7 a messenger of Satan to **b** me

BUILD (*see* BUILDER, BUILDING, BUILDS, BUILT)
Gen 11: 4 let us **b** ourselves a city, and
Ex 20:25 you shall not **b** it of hewn
Num 23: 1 **B** seven altars for me here,
Num 23:29 **B** for me here seven altars,
Num 32:16 We will **b** sheepfolds here for
Num 32:24 **B** cities for your little ones
Deut 6:10 cities which you did not **b**
Deut 16:21 **b** for yourself to the LORD
Deut 20:20 to **b** siegeworks against the
Deut 22: 8 When you **b** a new house, then
Deut 25: 9 not **b** up his brother's house
Deut 27: 5 there you shall **b** an altar to
Deut 27: 6 You shall **b** with whole stones
Deut 28:30 you shall **b** a house, but you
Josh 22:26 to **b** ourselves an altar, not
Josh 22:29 day, to **b** an altar for burnt
Josh 24:13 and cities which you did not **b**
Judg 6:26 **b** an altar to the LORD your
1Sa 2:35 I will **b** him a sure house, and
2Sa 7: 5 Would you **b** a house for Me to
2Sa 7:13 He shall **b** a house for My
2Sa 7:27 saying, 'I will **b** you a house
2Sa 24:21 to **b** an altar to the LORD,
1Ki 2:36 him, "**B** yourself a house in
1Ki 5: 3 my father David could not **b** a
1Ki 5: 5 I propose to **b** a house for
1Ki 5: 5 he shall **b** the house for My
1Ki 5:18 and stones to **b** the temple
1Ki 6: 1 that he began to **b** the house
1Ki 7: 1 years to **b** his own house
1Ki 8:16 Israel in which to **b** a house
1Ki 8:17 **b** a house for the name of the
1Ki 8:18 to **b** a house for My name, you
1Ki 8:19 you shall not **b** the house
1Ki 8:19 he shall **b** the house for My
1Ki 9:15 to **b** the house of the LORD,
1Ki 9:19 desired to **b** in Jerusalem
1Ki 11:38 **b** for you an enduring house,
2Ki 19:32 nor **b** a siege mound against
1Ch 14: 1 carpenters, to **b** him a house
1Ch 17: 4 You shall not **b** Me a house to
1Ch 17:10 the LORD will **b** you a house
1Ch 17:12 He shall **b** Me a house, and I
1Ch 17:25 that You will **b** him a house
1Ch 21:22 that I may **b** an altar on it
1Ch 22: 2 stones to **b** the house of God
1Ch 22: 6 charged him to **b** a house for
1Ch 22: 7 me, it was in my mind to **b** a
1Ch 22: 8 you shall not **b** a house for
1Ch 22:10 He shall **b** a house for My
1Ch 22:11 **b** the house of the LORD your
1Ch 22:19 **b** the sanctuary of the LORD
1Ch 28: 2 I had it in my heart to **b** a
1Ch 28: 2 had made preparations to **b** it
1Ch 28: 3 You shall not **b** a house for
1Ch 28: 6 Solomon who shall **b** My house
1Ch 28:10 **b** a house for the sanctuary
1Ch 29:16 that we have prepared to **b**
1Ch 29:19 to **b** the temple for which I
2Ch 2: 1 to **b** a temple for the name of
2Ch 2: 3 sent him cedars to **b** himself
2Ch 2: 5 which I **b** will be great, for
2Ch 2: 6 who is able to **b** Him a temple
2Ch 2: 6 that I should **b** Him a temple
2Ch 2: 9 am about to **b** shall be great
2Ch 2:12 who will **b** a temple for the
2Ch 3: 1 Now Solomon began to **b** the

2Ch 3: 2 he began to **b** on the second
2Ch 6: 5 Israel in which to **b** a house
2Ch 6: 7 to **b** a temple for the name of
2Ch 6: 8 to **b** a temple for My name
2Ch 6: 9 you shall not **b** the house
2Ch 6: 9 he shall **b** the temple for My
2Ch 8: 6 desired to **b** in Jerusalem
2Ch 14: 7 Let us **b** these cities and make
2Ch 36:23 He has commanded me to **b**
Ezra 1: 2 He has commanded me to **b**
Ezra 1: 3 **b** the house of the LORD God
Ezra 1: 5 **b** the house of the LORD which
Ezra 4: 2 Let us **b** with you, for we
Ezra 4: 3 us to **b** a house for our God
Ezra 4: 3 but we alone will **b** to the
Ezra 5: 2 began to **b** the house of God
Ezra 5: 3 you to **b** this temple and
Ezra 5: 9 you to **b** this temple and to
Ezra 5:13 decree to **b** this house of God
Ezra 5:17 to **b** this house of God at
Ezra 6: 7 the elders of the Jews **b** this
Neh 2:17 Come and let us **b** the wall of
Neh 2:18 Let us rise up and **b**
Neh 2:20 His servants will arise and **b**
Neh 4: 3 Whatever they **b**, if even a
Neh 4:10 we are not able to **b** the wall
Job 19:12 **b** up their road against me
Job 20:19 a house which he did not **b**
Ps 28: 5 destroy them And not **b** them up
Ps 51:18 **B** the walls of Jerusalem
Ps 69:35 **b** the cities of Judah, That
Ps 89: 4 And **b** up your throne to all
Ps 102:16 For the LORD shall **b** up Zion
Ps 127: 1 They labor in vain who **b** it
Prov 24:27 and afterward **b** your house
Eccl 3: 3 break down, and a time to **b** up
Song 8: 9 a wall, we will **b** upon her a
Is 37:33 nor **b** a siege mound against
Is 45:13 he shall **b** My city and let My
Is 58:12 shall **b** the old waste places
Is 60:10 shall **b** up your walls, and
Is 62:10 **b** up, **b** up the highway
Is 65:21 They shall **b** houses and
Is 65:22 They shall not **b** and another
Is 66: 1 the house that you will **b** Me
Jer 1:10 and to throw down, to **b** and to
Jer 6: 6 **b** a mound against Jerusalem
Jer 18: 9 and concerning a kingdom, to **b**
Jer 22:14 I will **b** myself a wide house
Jer 24: 6 I will **b** them and not pull
Jer 29: 5 **B** houses and dwell in them
Jer 29:28 **b** houses and dwell in them, and
Jer 31: 4 Again I will **b** you, and you
Jer 31:28 I will watch over them to **b**
Jer 35: 7 You shall not **b** a house, sow
Jer 35: 9 nor to **b** ourselves houses to
Jer 42:10 this land, then I will **b** you
Ezek 4: 2 **b** a siege wall against it, and
Ezek 11: 3 time is not near to **b** houses
Ezek 13: 5 to **b** a wall for the house of
Ezek 17:17 and **b** a wall to cut off many
Ezek 21:22 a siege mound, and to **b** a wall
Ezek 26: 8 you, **b** a wall against you, and
Ezek 28:26 **b** houses, and plant vineyards
Dan 9:25 **b** Jerusalem until Messiah the
Dan 11:15 **b** a siege mound, and take a
Amos 9:14 they shall **b** the waste cities
Mic 3:10 Who **b** up Zion with bloodshed
Zeph 1:13 They shall **b** houses, but not
Hag 1: 8 **b** the temple, that I may take
Zech 5:11 To **b** a house for it in the
Zech 6:12 He shall **b** the temple of the
Zech 6:13 He shall **b** the temple of the
Zech 6:15 and **b** the temple of the LORD
Mal 1: 4 **b** the desolate places," Thus
Mal 1: 4 They may **b**, but I will throw
Matt 16:18 this rock I will **b** My church
Matt 23:29 Because you **b** the tombs of
Matt 26:61 God and to **b** it in three days
Matt 27:40 and **b** it in three days, save
Mark 14:58 within three days I will **b**
Mark 15:29 temple and **b** it in three days,
Luke 11:47 For you **b** the tombs of the
Luke 11:48 them, and you **b** their tombs
Luke 12:18 **b** greater, and there I will
Luke 14:28 you, intending to **b** a tower
Luke 14:30 saying, 'This man began to **b**
Luke 19:43 **b** an embankment around you
John 2:20 years to **b** this temple, and
Acts 7:49 What house will you **b** for Me
Acts 20:32 which is able to **b** you up
Rom 15:20 lest I should **b** on another
Gal 2:18 For if I **b** again those things

BUILDER (*see* BUILD, BUILDERS)
1Co 3:10 as a wise master **b** I have
Heb 11:10 has foundations, whose **b** and

BUILDERS (*see* BUILDER)
1Ki 5:18 Solomon's **b**, Hiram's **b**
2Ki 12:11 **b** who worked on the house of
2Ki 22: 6 to carpenters and **b** and masons
2Ch 34:11 **b** to buy hewn stone and timber
Ezra 3:10 When the **b** laid the
Neh 4: 5 You to anger before the **b**
Neh 4:18 Every one of the **b** had his
Ps 118:22 The stone which the **b**
Ezek 27: 4 Your **b** have perfected your
Matt 21:42 The stone which the **b**
Mark 12:10 The stone which the **b**
Luke 20:17 The stone which the **b**
Acts 4:11 which was rejected by you **b**
1Pe 2: 7 The stone which the **b**

BUILDING (*see* BUILD, BUILDINGS)
Gen 11: 8 and they ceased **b** the city
Josh 22:19 us, by **b** yourselves an altar
1Ki 3: 1 had finished **b** his own house
1Ki 6:12 this temple which you are **b**
1Ki 6:38 So he was seven years in **b** it
1Ki 9: 1 **b** the house of the LORD and
1Ki 15:21 it, that he stopped **b** Ramah
1Ki 15:22 which Baasha had used for **b**
2Ch 2: 4 I am **b** a temple for the name
2Ch 3: 3 laid for **b** the house of God
2Ch 16: 5 it, that he stopped **b** Ramah
2Ch 16: 6 which Baasha had used for **b**
Ezra 4: 1 of the captivity were **b** the
Ezra 4: 4 They troubled them in **b**,
Ezra 4:12 are **b** the rebellious and evil
Ezra 5: 4 who were constructing this **b**
Ezra 6: 8 for the **b** of this house of
Eccl 10:18 of laziness the **b** decays, and
Ezek 41:12 The **b** that fronted the
Ezek 41:12 the wall of the **b** was five
Ezek 41:13 courtyard with the **b** and its
Ezek 41:15 the length of the **b** behind it
Ezek 42: 1 the **b** toward the north
Ezek 42: 5 and middle stories of the **b**
Ezek 42:10 courtyard and opposite the **b**
Ezek 46:23 There was a row of **b** stones
Luke 6:48 He is like a man **b** a house
1Co 3: 9 God's field, you are God's **b**
2Co 5: 1 we have a **b** from God, a
Eph 2:21 in whom the whole **b**, being
Jude 20 **b** yourselves up on your most

BUILDINGS (*see* BUILDING)
Matt 24: 1 show Him the **b** of the temple
Mark 13: 1 of stones and what **b** are here
Mark 13: 2 Do you see these great **b**

BUILDS (*see* BUILD)
Josh 6:26 up and **b** this city Jericho
Job 27:18 He **b** his house like a moth,
Ps 127: 1 Unless the LORD **b** the house
Ps 147: 2 The LORD **b** up Jerusalem
Prov 14: 1 Every wise woman **b** her house
Jer 22:13 Woe to him who **b** his house by
Ezek 13:10 one **b** a boundary wall, and
Amos 9: 6 He who **b** His layers in the
Hab 2:12 Woe to him who **b** a town with
1Co 3:10 and another **b** on it
1Co 3:10 one take heed how he **b** on it
1Co 3:12 Now if anyone **b** on this

BUILT (*see* BUILD)
Gen 4:17 he **b** a city, and called the
Gen 8:20 Then Noah **b** an altar to the
Gen 10:11 **b** Nineveh, Rehoboth Ir, Calah
Gen 11: 5 which the sons of men had **b**
Gen 12: 7 there he **b** an altar to the
Gen 12: 8 there he **b** an altar to the
Gen 13:18 **b** an altar there to the LORD
Gen 22: 9 Abraham **b** an altar there and
Gen 26:25 So he **b** an altar there and
Gen 33:17 **b** himself a house, and made
Gen 35: 7 he **b** an altar there and called
Ex 1:11 they **b** for Pharaoh supply
Ex 17:15 Moses **b** an altar and called
Ex 24: 4 **b** an altar at the foot of the
Ex 32: 5 it, he **b** an altar before it
Num 13:22 (Now Hebron was **b** seven years
Num 21:27 Come to Heshbon, let it be **b**
Num 23:14 **b** seven altars, and offered a
Num 32:34 the children of Gad **b** Dibon
Num 32:37 children of Reuben **b** Heshbon
Num 32:38 to the cities which they **b**
Deut 8:12 have **b** beautiful houses and
Deut 13:16 It shall not be **b** again
Deut 20: 5 there who has **b** a new house
Josh 8:30 Now Joshua **b** an altar to the
Josh 19:50 he **b** the city and dwelt in it
Josh 22:10 **b** an altar there by the
Josh 22:11 the tribe of Manasseh have **b**
Josh 22:16 LORD, in that you have **b** for
Josh 22:23 If we have **b** ourselves an
Judg 1:26 **b** a city, and called its name
Judg 6:24 So Gideon **b** an altar there to
Judg 6:28 on the altar which had been **b**
Judg 21: 4 **b** an altar there, and offered
Ruth 4:11 the two who **b** the house of
1Sa 7:17 there he **b** an altar to the
1Sa 14:35 Then Saul **b** an altar to the
1Sa 14:35 altar that he **b** to the LORD
2Sa 5: 9 Then David **b** all around from
2Sa 5:11 And they **b** David a house
2Sa 7: 7 Why have you not **b** Me a
2Sa 24:25 David **b** there an altar to the
1Ki 3: 2 **b** for the name of the LORD
1Ki 6: 2 King Solomon **b** for the LORD
1Ki 6: 5 he **b** chambers all around,
1Ki 6: 7 temple, when it was being **b**
1Ki 6: 7 was **b** with stone finished at
1Ki 6: 7 temple while it was being **b**
1Ki 6: 9 So he **b** the temple and
1Ki 6:10 he **b** side chambers against
1Ki 6:14 So Solomon **b** the temple and
1Ki 6:15 he **b** the inside walls of the
1Ki 6:16 Then he **b** the twenty-cubit
1Ki 6:16 he **b** it inside as the inner
1Ki 6:36 he **b** the inner court with
1Ki 7: 2 He also **b** the House of the
1Ki 8:13 I have surely **b** You an
1Ki 8:20 I have **b** a house for the name
1Ki 8:27 this temple which I have **b**
1Ki 8:43 have **b** is called by Your name
1Ki 8:44 which I have **b** for Your name
1Ki 8:48 which I have **b** for Your name
1Ki 9: 3 have **b** to put My name there
1Ki 9:10 Solomon had **b** the two houses
1Ki 9:17 And Solomon **b** Gezer, Lower
1Ki 9:24 which Solomon had **b** for her
1Ki 9:24 Then he **b** the Millo
1Ki 9:25 which he had **b** for the LORD
1Ki 9:26 King Solomon also **b** a fleet
1Ki 10: 4 the house that he had **b**,
1Ki 11: 7 Then Solomon **b** a high place
1Ki 11:27 Solomon had **b** the Millo and
1Ki 11:38 as I **b** for David, and will
1Ki 12:25 Then Jeroboam **b** Shechem in
1Ki 12:25 out from there and **b** Penuel
1Ki 14:23 For they also **b** for
1Ki 15:17 **b** Ramah, that he might let
1Ki 15:22 King Asa **b** Geba of Benjamin
1Ki 15:23 did, and the cities which he **b**
1Ki 16:24 then he **b** on the hill, and
1Ki 16:24 name of the city which he **b**
1Ki 16:32 which he had **b** in Samaria
1Ki 16:34 days Hiel of Bethel **b** Jericho
1Ki 18:32 Then with the stones he **b** an
1Ki 22:39 the ivory house which he **b**
1Ki 22:39 and all the cities that he **b**
2Ki 14:22 He **b** Elath and restored it to
2Ki 15:35 He **b** the Upper Gate of the
2Ki 16:11 Then Urijah the priest **b** an
2Ki 16:18 they had **b** in the temple, and
2Ki 17: 9 they **b** for themselves high
2Ki 21: 4 He also **b** altars in the house
2Ki 21: 5 he **b** altars for all the host
2Ki 23:13 had **b** for Ashtoreth the
2Ki 25: 1 they **b** a siege wall against
1Ch 6:10 that Solomon **b** in Jerusalem)
1Ch 6:32 until Solomon had **b** the house
1Ch 7:24 who **b** Lower and Upper Beth
1Ch 8:12 and Shemed, who **b** Ono
1Ch 11: 8 he **b** the city around it, from
1Ch 15: 1 David **b** houses for himself in
1Ch 17: 6 Why have you not **b** Me a
1Ch 21:26 David **b** there an altar to the
1Ch 22: 5 to be **b** for the LORD must be
1Ch 22:19 the house that is to be **b** for
2Ch 6: 2 But I have **b** You an exalted

2Ch 6:10 I have **b** the temple for the
2Ch 6:18 this temple which I have **b**
2Ch 6:33 have **b** is called by Your name
2Ch 6:34 which I have **b** for Your name
2Ch 6:38 which I have **b** for Your name
2Ch 8: 1 in which Solomon had **b** the
2Ch 8: 2 to Solomon, Solomon **b** them
2Ch 8: 4 He also **b** Tadmor in the
2Ch 8: 4 cities which he **b** in Hamath
2Ch 8: 5 He **b** Upper Beth Horon and
2Ch 8:11 to the house he had **b** for her
2Ch 8:12 he had **b** before the vestibule
2Ch 9: 3 the house that he had **b**,
2Ch 11: 5 **b** cities for defense in Judah
2Ch 11: 6 he **b** Bethlehem, Etam, Tekoa,
2Ch 14: 6 And he **b** fortified cities in
2Ch 14: 7 So they **b** and prospered
2Ch 16: 1 **b** Ramah, that he might let
2Ch 16: 6 and with them he **b** Geba and
2Ch 17:12 he **b** fortresses and storage
2Ch 20: 8 have **b** You a sanctuary in it
2Ch 26: 2 He **b** Elath and restored it to
2Ch 26: 6 he **b** cities around Ashdod and
2Ch 26: 9 Uzziah **b** towers in Jerusalem
2Ch 26:10 Also he **b** towers in the
2Ch 27: 3 he **b** extensively on the wall
2Ch 27: 4 Moreover he **b** cities in the
2Ch 27: 4 the forests he **b** fortresses
2Ch 32: 5 **b** up all the wall that was
2Ch 32: 5 and **b** another wall outside
2Ch 33: 4 He also **b** altars in the house
2Ch 33: 5 he **b** altars for all the host
2Ch 33:14 After this he **b** a wall
2Ch 33:15 **b** in the mount of the house
2Ch 33:19 sites where he **b** high places
2Ch 35: 3 of David, king of Israel, **b**
Ezra 3: 2 **b** the altar of the God of
Ezra 4:13 king that, if this city is **b**
Ezra 4:21 that this city may not be **b**
Ezra 5: 8 which is being **b** with heavy
Ezra 5:11 that was **b** many years ago
Ezra 5:11 a great king of Israel **b** and
Ezra 6:14 So the elders of the Jews **b**
Ezra 6:14 And they **b** and finished it,
Neh 3: 1 priests and **b** the Sheep Gate
Neh 3: 1 They **b** as far as the Tower of
Neh 3: 2 Eliashib the men of Jericho **b**
Neh 3: 2 them Zaccur the son of Imri **b**
Neh 3: 3 of Hassenaah **b** the Fish Gate
Neh 3:13 They **b** it, hung its doors
Neh 3:14 he **b** it and hung its doors
Neh 3:15 he **b** it, covered it, hung its
Neh 4: 6 So we **b** the wall, and the
Neh 4:17 Those who **b** on the wall, and
Neh 4:18 girded at his side as he **b**
Neh 7: 1 it was, when the wall was **b**
Neh 12:29 for the singers had **b**
Job 3:14 who **b** ruins for themselves,
Job 22:23 Almighty, you will be **b** up
Ps 78:69 He **b** His sanctuary like the
Ps 89: 2 Mercy shall be **b** up forever
Ps 122: 3 Jerusalem is **b** As a city that
Prov 9: 1 Wisdom has **b** her house, she
Prov 24: 3 Through wisdom a house is **b**
Eccl 2: 4 I **b** myself houses, and planted
Eccl 9:14 and **b** great snares around it
Song 4: 4 **b** for an armory, on which
Is 5: 2 He **b** a tower in its midst, and
Is 44:26 of Judah, 'You shall be **b**
Is 44:28 You shall be **b**," and to the
Jer 7:31 they have **b** the high places
Jer 19: 5 (they have also **b** the high
Jer 30:18 the city shall be **b** upon its
Jer 31:38 that the city shall be **b** for
Jer 32:31 from the day that they **b** it
Jer 32:35 they **b** the high places of
Jer 45: 4 what I have **b** I will break
Jer 52: 4 they **b** a siege wall against
Ezek 16:24 that you also **b** for yourself
Ezek 16:25 You **b** your high places at the
Ezek 16:31 **b** your high place in every
Dan 4:30 that I have **b** for a royal
Dan 9:25 the street shall be **b** again
Hos 8:14 his Maker, and has **b** temples
Amos 5:11 though you have **b** houses of
Mic 7:11 when your walls are to be **b**
Hag 1: 2 the LORD's house should be **b**
Zech 1:16 my house shall be **b** in it
Zech 8: 9 that the temple might be **b**
Zech 9: 3 for Tyre **b** herself a tower,
Matt 7:24 who **b** his house on the rock
Matt 7:26 who **b** his house on the sand
Matt 21:33 winepress in it and **b** a tower
Mark 12: 1 for the wine vat and **b** a tower
Luke 4:29 on which their city was **b**
Luke 6:49 who **b** a house on the earth
Luke 7: 5 and has **b** us a synagogue
Luke 17:28 sold, they planted, they **b**
Acts 7:47 But Solomon **b** Him a house
1Co 3:14 which he has **b** on it endures
Eph 2:20 having been **b** on the
Eph 2:22 **b** together for a habitation
Col 2: 7 **b** up in Him and established in
Heb 3: 3 inasmuch as He who **b** the
Heb 3: 4 every house is **b** by someone
Heb 3: 4 but He who **b** all things is
1Pe 2: 5 are being **b** up a spiritual

BUKKI
Num 34:22 of Dan, **B** the son of Jogli
1Ch 6: 5 Abishua begot **B**
1Ch 6: 5 and **B** begot Uzzi
1Ch 6:51 **B** his son, Uzzi his son,
Ezra 7: 4 the son of Uzzi, the son of **B**

BUKKIAH
1Ch 25: 4 **B**, Mattaniah, Uzziel, Shebuel
1Ch 25:13 the sixth for **B**, his sons and

BUL
1Ki 6:38 year, in the month of **B**,

BULGE
Ps 73: 7 Their eyes **b** with abundance
Is 30:13 a **b** in a high wall, whose

BULL (*see* BULL'S, BULLS)
Ex 29: 1 Take one young **b** and two rams
Ex 29: 3 in the basket, with the **b**
Ex 29:10 have the **b** brought before the
Ex 29:10 hands on the head of the **b**
Ex 29:11 kill the **b** before the LORD
Ex 29:12 some of the blood of the **b**
Ex 29:14 But the flesh of the **b**, with
Ex 29:36 you shall offer a **b** every day
Lev 1: 5 kill the **b** before the LORD
Lev 4: 3 **b** without blemish as a sin
Lev 4: 4 the **b** to the door of the
Lev 4: 4 kill the **b** before the LORD
Lev 4: 7 the remaining blood of the **b**
Lev 4: 8 of the **b** as the sin offering
Lev 4:10 the **b** of the sacrifice of the
Lev 4:12 the whole **b** he shall carry
Lev 4:14 offer a young **b** for the sin
Lev 4:15 head of the **b** before the LORD
Lev 4:15 Then the **b** shall be killed
Lev 4:20 he shall do with the **b** as he
Lev 4:20 with the **b** as a sin offering
Lev 4:21 carry the **b** outside the camp
Lev 4:21 it as he burned the first **b**
Lev 8: 2 a **b** as the sin offering, two
Lev 8:14 he brought the **b** for the sin
Lev 8:14 of the **b** for the sin offering
Lev 8:17 But the **b**, its hide, its
Lev 9: 2 a young **b** as a sin offering
Lev 9: 4 also a **b** and a ram as peace
Lev 9:18 He also killed the **b** and the
Lev 9:19 and the fat from the **b** and the
Lev 16: 3 a young **b** as a sin offering
Lev 16: 6 offer the **b** as a sin offering
Lev 16:11 the **b** of the sin offering
Lev 16:11 shall kill the **b** as the sin
Lev 16:14 some of the blood of the **b**
Lev 16:15 did with the blood of the **b**
Lev 16:18 some of the blood of the **b**
Lev 16:27 The **b** for the sin offering and
Lev 22:23 Either a **b** or a lamb that
Lev 22:27 When a **b** or a sheep or a goat
Lev 23:18 without blemish, one young **b**
Num 7:15 one young **b**, one ram, and one
Num 7:21 one young **b**, one ram, and one
Num 7:27 one young **b**, one ram, and one
Num 7:33 one young **b**, one ram, and one
Num 7:39 one young **b**, one ram, and one
Num 7:45 one young **b**, one ram, and one
Num 7:51 one young **b**, one ram, and one
Num 7:57 one young **b**, one ram, and one
Num 7:63 one young **b**, one ram, and one
Num 7:69 one young **b**, one ram, and one
Num 7:75 one young **b**, one ram, and one
Num 7:81 one young **b**, one ram, and one
Num 8: 8 **b** with its grain offering of
Num 8: 8 young **b** as a sin offering
Num 15: 8 a young **b** as a burnt offering
Num 15: 9 young **b** a grain offering of
Num 15:11 be done for each young **b**, for
Num 15:24 young **b** as a burnt offering
Num 23: 2 Balak and Balaam offered a **b**
Num 23: 4 offered on each altar a **b**
Num 23:14 seven altars, and offered a **b**
Num 23:30 had said, and offered a **b** and a
Num 28:12 mixed with oil, for each **b**
Num 28:14 be half a hin of wine for a **b**
Num 28:20 ephah you shall offer for a **b**
Num 28:28 of an ephah for each **b**,
Num 29: 2 one young **b**, one ram, and
Num 29: 3 of an ephah for the **b**,
Num 29: 8 one young **b**, one ram, and
Num 29: 9 of an ephah for the **b**,
Num 29:36 one **b**, one ram, seven lambs
Num 29:37 drink offerings for the **b**
Deut 17: 1 a **b** or sheep which has any
Deut 18: 3 whether it is **b** or sheep
Deut 33:17 glory is like a firstborn **b**
Judg 6:25 Take your father's young **b**
Judg 6:25 the second **b** of seven years
Judg 6:26 and take the second **b** and
Judg 6:28 and the second **b** was being
1Sa 1:25 Then they slaughtered a **b**
1Ki 18:23 choose one **b** for themselves
1Ki 18:23 and I will prepare the other **b**
1Ki 18:25 Choose one **b** for yourselves
1Ki 18:26 So they took the **b** which was
1Ki 18:33 cut the **b** in pieces, and laid
2Ch 13: 9 himself with a young **b** and
Job 21:10 Their **b** breeds without
Ps 50: 9 not take a **b** from your house
Ps 69:31 LORD better than an ox or **b**
Is 66: 3 He who kills a **b** is as if he
Jer 31:18 like an untrained **b**
Ezek 43:19 You shall give a young **b** for
Ezek 43:21 the **b** of the sin offering
Ezek 43:22 they cleansed it with the **b**
Ezek 43:23 a young **b** without blemish
Ezek 43:25 shall also prepare a young **b**
Ezek 45:18 a young **b** without blemish
Ezek 45:22 land a **b** for a sin offering
Ezek 45:24 of one ephah for each **b** and
Ezek 46: 6 be a young **b** without blemish
Ezek 46: 7 offering of an ephah for a **b**
Ezek 46:11 shall be an ephah for a **b**

BULL'S (*see* BULL)
Lev 4: 4 lay his hand on the **b** head
Lev 4: 5 take some of the **b** blood and
Lev 4:11 But the **b** hide and all its
Lev 4:16 shall bring some of the **b**

BULLS (*see* BULL)
Gen 32:15 colts, forty cows and ten **b**
Num 7:87 offering were twelve young **b**
Num 7:88 offerings were twenty-four **b**
Num 8:12 on the heads of the young **b**
Num 23: 1 prepare for me here seven **b**
Num 23:29 prepare for me here seven **b**
Num 28:11 two young **b**, one ram, and
Num 28:19 two young **b**, one ram, and
Num 28:27 two young **b**, one ram, and
Num 29:13 thirteen young **b**, two rams,
Num 29:14 for each of the thirteen **b**
Num 29:17 day present twelve young **b**
Num 29:18 drink offerings for the **b**
Num 29:20 third day present eleven **b**
Num 29:21 drink offerings for the **b**
Num 29:23 the fourth day present ten **b**
Num 29:24 drink offerings for the **b**
Num 29:26 the fifth day present nine **b**
Num 29:27 drink offerings for the **b**
Num 29:29 the sixth day present eight **b**
Num 29:30 drink offerings for the **b**
Num 29:32 seventh day present seven **b**
Num 29:33 drink offerings for the **b**
1Sa 1:24 him up with her, with three **b**
1Ki 8:63 LORD, twenty-two thousand **b**
1Ki 18:23 let them give us two **b**
1Ch 15:26 that they offered seven **b**
1Ch 29:21 a thousand **b**, a thousand rams
2Ch 7: 5 of twenty-two thousand **b** and
2Ch 15:11 at that time seven hundred **b**
2Ch 29:21 And they brought seven **b**,
2Ch 29:22 So they killed the **b**, and the
2Ch 29:32 brought was seventy **b**, one
2Ch 29:33 things were six hundred **b**
2Ch 30:24 the congregation a thousand **b**

2Ch 30:24 the congregation a thousand **b**
Ezra 6: 9 young **b**, rams, and lambs for
Ezra 6:17 house of God, one hundred **b**
Ezra 7:17 to buy with this money **b**,
Ezra 8:35 twelve **b** for all Israel,
Job 42: 8 take for yourselves seven **b**
Ps 22:12 Many **b** have surrounded Me
Ps 22:12 Strong **b** of Bashan have
Ps 50:13 Will I eat the flesh of **b**
Ps 51:19 shall offer **b** on Your altar
Ps 66:15 I will offer **b** with goats
Ps 68:30 The herd of **b** with the calves
Is 1:11 not delight in the blood of **b**
Is 34: 7 young **b** with the mighty **b**
Jer 46:21 are in her midst like fat **b**
Jer 50:11 grain, and you bellow like **b**
Jer 50:27 Slay all her **b**, let them go
Jer 52:20 the twelve bronze **b** which
Ezek 39:18 rams and lambs, of goats and **b**
Ezek 45:23 offering to the LORD, seven **b**
Hos 12:11 they sacrifice **b** in Gilgal
Heb 9:13 For if the blood of **b** and
Heb 10: 4 possible that the blood of **b**

BULRUSH (*see* BULRUSHES)
Is 9:14 palm branch and **b** in one day
Is 19:15 or tail, palm branch or **b**
Is 58: 5 to bow down his head like a **b**

BULRUSHES (*see* BULRUSH)
Ex 2: 3 she took an ark of **b** for him

BULWARKS
Ps 48:13 Mark well her **b**
Is 26: 1 salvation for walls and **b**

BUNAH
1Ch 2:25 were Ram, the firstborn, and **B**

BUNCH
Ex 12:22 you shall take a **b** of hyssop

BUNDLE (*see* BUNDLES)
Gen 42:35 surprisingly each man's **b** of
1Sa 25:29 lord shall be bound in the **b**
Song 1:13 A **b** of myrrh is my beloved to
Acts 28: 3 had gathered a **b** of sticks

BUNDLES (*see* BUNDLE)
Gen 42:35 father saw the **b** of money
Ruth 2:16 the **b** fall purposely for her
Matt 13:30 bind them in **b** to burn them

BUNNI
Neh 9: 4 Bani, Kadmiel, Shebaniah, **B**
Neh 10:15 **B**, Azgad, Bebai,
Neh 11:15 of Hashabiah, the son of **B**

BURDEN (*see* BURDENED, BURDENS, BURDENSOME)
Gen 49:15 his shoulder to bear a **b**, and
Ex 18:22 they will bear the **b** with you
Ex 23: 5 hates you lying under its **b**
Num 11:11 that You have laid the **b** of
Num 11:14 because the **b** is too heavy
Num 11:17 they shall bear the **b** of the
2Sa 13:25 go now, lest we be a **b** to you
2Sa 15:33 you will become a **b** to me
2Sa 19:35 further **b** to my lord the king
2Ki 9:25 the LORD laid this **b** upon him
2Ch 6:29 when each one knows his own **b**
2Ch 34:13 were over the **b** bearers and
2Ch 35: 3 be a **b** on your shoulders
Job 7:20 so that I am a **b** to myself
Ps 38: 4 Like a heavy **b** they are too
Ps 55:22 Cast your **b** on the LORD, And
Ps 81: 6 his shoulder from the **b**
Eccl 12: 5 the grasshopper is a **b**, and
Is 9: 4 have broken the yoke of his **b**
Is 10:27 his **b** will be taken away from
Is 13: 1 The **b** against Babylon which
Is 14:25 and his **b** removed from their
Is 14:28 This is the **b** which came in
Is 15: 1 The **b** against Moab
Is 17: 1 The **b** against Damascus
Is 19: 1 The **b** against Egypt
Is 21: 1 The **b** against the Wilderness
Is 21:11 The **b** against Dumah
Is 21:13 The **b** against Arabia
Is 22: 1 The **b** against the Valley of
Is 22:25 the **b** that was on it will be
Is 23: 1 The **b** against Tyre
Is 30: 6 The **b** against the beasts of
Is 30:27 His anger, and His **b** is heavy
Is 46: 1 a **b** to the weary beast
Is 46: 2 they could not deliver the **b**
Jer 17:21 bear no **b** on the Sabbath day,
Jer 17:22 nor carry a **b** out of your
Jer 17:24 to bring no **b** through the
Jer 17:27 such as not carrying a **b** when
Ezek 12:10 This **b** concerns the prince in
Hos 8:10 because of the **b** of the king
Nah 1: 1 The **b** against Nineveh
Hab 1: 1 The **b** which the prophet
Zeph 3:18 to whom its reproach is a **b**
Zech 9: 1 The **b** of the word of the LORD
Zech 12: 1 The **b** of the word of the LORD
Mal 1: 1 The **b** of the word of the LORD
Matt 11:30 yoke is easy and My **b** is light
Matt 20:12 to us who have borne the **b**
Acts 15:28 to lay upon you no greater **b**
2Co 11: 9 I was a **b** to no one, for what
2Co 12:16 as it may, I did not **b** you
1Th 2: 9 not be a **b** to any of you, we
2Th 3: 8 not be a **b** to any of you,
Rev 2:24 I will put on you no other **b**

BURDENED (*see* BURDEN)
Prov 28:17 A man **b** with bloodshed will
Is 43:24 but you have **b** Me with your
2Co 1: 8 that we were **b** beyond measure
2Co 5: 4 in this tent groan, being **b**
2Co 8:13 should be eased and you **b**
1Ti 5:16 and do not let the church be **b**

BURDENS (*see* BURDEN)
Gen 49:14 lying down between two **b**
Ex 1:11 to afflict them with their **b**
Ex 2:11 brethren and looked at their **b**
Ex 6: 6 under the **b** of the Egyptians
Ex 6: 7 under the **b** of the Egyptians
Num 4:47 the work of bearing **b** in the
Deut 1:12 bear your problems and your **b**
1Ki 5:15 thousand who carried **b**, and
2Ch 2: 2 thousand men to bear **b**,
2Ch 2:18 thousand of them bearers of **b**
Neh 4:17 wall, and those who carried **b**
Neh 5:15 me laid **b** on the people, and
Neh 13:15 figs, and all kinds of **b**,
Neh 13:19 so that no **b** would be brought
Is 58: 6 to undo the heavy **b**, to let
Matt 23: 4 For they bind heavy **b**, hard
Luke 11:46 load men with **b** hard to bear
Luke 11:46 **b** with one of your fingers
Gal 6: 2 Bear one another's **b**, and so

BURDENSOME (*see* BURDEN)
1Ki 12: 4 lighten the **b** service of your
2Ch 10: 4 lighten the **b** service of your
Is 15: 4 his life will be **b** to him
2Co 11: 9 myself from being **b** to you
2Co 12:13 I myself was not **b** to you
2Co 12:14 And I will not be **b** to you
1Jn 5: 3 His commandments are not **b**

BURIAL (*see* BURY)
Gen 23: 4 for a **b** place among you, that
Gen 23: 6 the choicest of our **b** places
Gen 23: 6 withhold from you his **b** place
Gen 23: 9 for a **b** place among you
Gen 23:20 as property for a **b** place
Gen 47:30 and bury me in their **b** place
Gen 49:30 as a possession for a **b** place
Gen 50:13 as property for a **b** place
2Ch 26:23 **b** which belonged to the kings
Eccl 6: 3 or indeed he has no **b**, I say
Is 14:20 not be joined with them in **b**
Jer 22:19 buried with the **b** of a donkey
Ezek 39:11 Gog a **b** place there in Israel
Matt 26:12 My body, she did it for My **b**
Mark 14: 8 to anoint My body for **b**
John 12: 7 kept this for the day of My **b**
Acts 8: 2 men carried Stephen to his **b**

BURIED (*see* BURY)
Gen 15:15 you shall be **b** at a good old
Gen 23:19 Abraham **b** Sarah his wife in
Gen 25: 9 Ishmael **b** him in the cave of
Gen 25:10 Abraham was **b**, and Sarah
Gen 35: 8 she was **b** below Bethel under
Gen 35:19 was **b** on the way to Ephrath
Gen 35:29 his sons Esau and Jacob **b** him
Gen 48: 7 I **b** her there on the way to
Gen 49:31 they **b** Abraham and Sarah
Gen 49:31 his wife, there they **b** Isaac
Gen 49:31 his wife, and there I **b** Leah
Gen 50:13 and **b** him in the cave of the
Gen 50:14 And after he had **b** his father
Num 11:34 because there they **b** the
Num 20: 1 died there and was **b** there
Deut 10: 6 died later, and where he was **b**
Deut 34: 6 He **b** him in a valley in the
Josh 24:30 they **b** him within the border
Josh 24:32 they **b** at Shechem, in the
Josh 24:33 they **b** him in a hill that
Judg 2: 9 they **b** him within the border
Judg 8:32 was **b** in the tomb of Joash
Judg 10: 2 and he died and was **b** in Shamir
Judg 10: 5 Jair died and was **b** in Camon
Judg 12: 7 was **b** in one of the cities of
Judg 12:10 died and was **b** at Bethlehem
Judg 12:12 and was **b** at Aijalon in the
Judg 12:15 was **b** in Pirathon in the land
Judg 16:31 up and **b** him between Zorah
Ruth 1:17 die, and there will I be **b**
1Sa 25: 1 **b** him at his home in Ramah
1Sa 28: 3 **b** him in Ramah, in his own
1Sa 31:13 **b** them under the tamarisk
2Sa 2: 4 were the ones who **b** Saul
2Sa 2: 5 lord, to Saul, and have **b** him
2Sa 2:32 **b** him in his father's tomb,
2Sa 3:32 So they **b** Abner in Hebron
2Sa 4:12 **b** it in the tomb of Abner in
2Sa 17:23 he was **b** in his father's tomb
2Sa 19:37 and be **b** by the grave of my
2Sa 21:14 They **b** the bones of Saul and
1Ki 2:10 was **b** in the City of David
1Ki 2:34 he was **b** in his own house in
1Ki 11:43 was **b** in the City of David
1Ki 13:31 So it was, after he had **b** him
1Ki 13:31 where the man of God is **b**
1Ki 14:18 And they **b** him
1Ki 14:31 was **b** with his fathers in the
1Ki 15: 8 they **b** him in the City of
1Ki 15:24 was **b** with his fathers in the
1Ki 16: 6 fathers and was **b** in Tirzah
1Ki 16:28 fathers and was **b** in Samaria
1Ki 22:37 they **b** the king in Samaria
1Ki 22:50 was **b** with his fathers in the
2Ki 8:24 was **b** with his fathers in the
2Ki 9:28 **b** him in his tomb with his
2Ki 10:35 and they **b** him in Samaria
2Ki 12:21 they **b** him with his fathers
2Ki 13: 9 and they **b** him in Samaria
2Ki 13:13 Joash was **b** in Samaria with
2Ki 13:20 Elisha died, and they **b** him
2Ki 14:16 was **b** in Samaria with the
2Ki 14:20 he was **b** at Jerusalem with
2Ki 15: 7 they **b** him with his fathers
2Ki 15:38 was **b** with his fathers in the
2Ki 16:20 was **b** with his fathers in the
2Ki 21:18 was **b** in the garden of his
2Ki 21:26 he was **b** in his tomb in the
2Ki 23:30 and **b** him in his own tomb
1Ch 10:12 and **b** their bones under the
2Ch 9:31 was **b** in the City of David
2Ch 12:16 was **b** in the City of David
2Ch 14: 1 they **b** him in the City of
2Ch 16:14 They **b** him in his own tomb,
2Ch 21: 1 was **b** with his fathers in the
2Ch 21:20 However they **b** him in the
2Ch 22: 9 had killed him, they **b** him
2Ch 24:16 they **b** him in the City of
2Ch 24:25 they **b** him in the City of
2Ch 25:28 **b** him with his fathers in the
2Ch 26:23 they **b** him with his fathers
2Ch 27: 9 they **b** him in the City of
2Ch 28:27 they **b** him in the city, in
2Ch 32:33 they **b** him in the upper tombs
2Ch 33:20 they **b** him in his own house
2Ch 35:24 was **b** in one of the tombs of
Job 27:15 him shall be **b** in death, and
Eccl 8:10 Then I saw the wicked **b**, who
Jer 8: 2 shall not be gathered nor **b**
Jer 16: 4 lamented nor shall they be **b**
Jer 16: 6 They shall not be **b**
Jer 20: 6 be **b** there, you and all your
Jer 22:19 He shall be **b** with the burial
Jer 25:33 lamented, or gathered, or **b**
Ezek 39:15 till the buriers have **b** it in
Matt 14:12 **b** it, and went and told Jesus
Luke 16:22 rich man also died and was **b**
Acts 2:29 that he is both dead and **b**
Acts 5: 6 up, carried him out, and **b** him
Acts 5: 9 **b** your husband are at the
Acts 5:10 her out, **b** her by her husband
Acts 13:36 was **b** with his fathers, and
Rom 6: 4 Therefore we were **b** with Him

1Co 15: 4 and that He was **b**, and that He
Col 2:12 **b** with Him in baptism, in

BURIERS (*see* BURY)
Ezek 39:15 till the **b** have buried it in

BURIES (*see* BURY)
Prov 19:24 A slothful man **b** his hand in
Prov 26:15 The slothful man **b** his hand

BURN (*see* BURNED, BURNING, BURNS, BURNT)
Gen 44:18 anger **b** against your servant
Ex 3: 3 why the bush does not **b**
Ex 12:10 morning you shall **b** with fire
Ex 21:25 **b** for **b**, wound for wound,
Ex 21:25 **b** for **b**, wound for wound,
Ex 27:20 the lamp to **b** continually
Ex 29:13 them, and **b** them on the altar
Ex 29:14 you shall **b** with fire outside
Ex 29:18 you shall **b** the whole ram on
Ex 29:25 and **b** them on the altar as a
Ex 29:34 morning, then you shall **b** the
Ex 30: 1 make an altar to **b** incense on
Ex 30: 7 Aaron shall **b** on it sweet
Ex 30: 7 he shall **b** incense on it
Ex 30: 8 he shall **b** incense on it, a
Ex 30:20 to **b** an offering made by fire
Ex 32:10 wrath may **b** hot against them
Ex 32:11 why does Your wrath **b** hot
Lev 1: 9 the priest shall **b** all on the
Lev 1:13 it all and **b** it on the altar
Lev 1:15 head, and **b** it on the altar
Lev 1:17 shall **b** it on the altar, on
Lev 2: 2 the priest shall **b** it as a
Lev 2: 9 portion, and **b** it on the altar
Lev 2:11 for you shall **b** no leaven nor
Lev 2:16 shall **b** the memorial portion
Lev 3: 5 Aaron's sons shall **b** it on
Lev 3:11 the priest shall **b** them on
Lev 3:16 the priest shall **b** them on
Lev 4:10 the priest shall **b** them on
Lev 4:12 and **b** it on wood with fire
Lev 4:19 from it and **b** it on the altar
Lev 4:21 **b** it as he burned the first
Lev 4:26 he shall **b** all its fat on the
Lev 4:31 the priest shall **b** it on the
Lev 4:35 shall **b** it on the altar,
Lev 5:12 **b** it on the altar according
Lev 6:12 the priest shall **b** wood on it
Lev 6:12 he shall **b** on it the fat of
Lev 6:13 fire shall **b** on the altar
Lev 6:15 shall **b** it on the altar for a
Lev 7: 5 the priest shall **b** them on
Lev 7:31 the priest shall **b** the fat on
Lev 8:32 bread you shall **b** with fire
Lev 13:24 a **b** on its skin by fire, and
Lev 13:24 and the raw flesh of the **b**
Lev 13:25 leprosy broken out in the **b**
Lev 13:28 it is a swelling from the **b**
Lev 13:28 for it is the scar from the **b**
Lev 13:52 He shall therefore **b** that
Lev 13:55 you shall **b** it in the fire
Lev 13:57 you shall **b** with fire that in
Lev 16:25 he shall **b** on the altar
Lev 16:27 And they shall **b** in the fire
Lev 17: 6 **b** the fat for a sweet aroma
Lev 24: 2 make the lamps **b** continually
Num 5:26 **b** it on the altar, and
Num 18:17 **b** their fat as an offering
Deut 7: 5 **b** their carved images with
Deut 7:25 You shall **b** the carved images
Deut 12: 3 **b** their wooden images with
Deut 12:31 for they **b** even their sons and
Deut 13:16 completely **b** with fire the
Deut 29:20 would **b** against that man, and
Deut 32:22 shall **b** to the lowest hell
Josh 11: 6 **b** their chariots with fire
Josh 23:16 the LORD will **b** against you
Judg 9:52 the tower to **b** it with fire
Judg 12: 1 We will **b** your house down on
Judg 14:15 to us, or else we will **b** you
1Sa 2:16 should really **b** the fat first
1Sa 2:28 to **b** incense, and to wear an
1Ki 13: 1 by the altar to **b** incense
1Ki 13: 2 places who **b** incense on you
2Ki 16:15 On the great new altar **b** the
2Ki 23: 5 of Judah had ordained to **b**
1Ch 23:13 to **b** incense before the LORD,
2Ch 2: 4 to **b** before Him sweet incense
2Ch 2: 6 except to **b** sacrifice before
2Ch 4:20 to **b** in the prescribed manner
2Ch 13:11 And they **b** to the LORD every
2Ch 13:11 its lamps to **b** every evening
2Ch 26:16 to **b** incense on the altar of
2Ch 26:18 to **b** incense to the LORD, but
2Ch 26:18 are consecrated to **b** incense
2Ch 26:19 in his hand to **b** incense
2Ch 28:25 to **b** incense to other gods
2Ch 29:11 minister to Him and **b** incense
2Ch 32:12 altar and **b** incense on it"
Neh 10:34 to **b** on the altar of the LORD
Job 30:30 my bones **b** with fever
Ps 79: 5 Your jealousy **b** like fire
Ps 89:46 Will Your wrath **b** like fire
Is 1:31 both will **b** together, and no
Is 10:17 it will **b** and devour his
Is 27: 4 them, I would **b** them together
Is 40:16 is not sufficient to **b**, nor
Is 44:15 it shall be for a man to **b**
Is 47:14 the fire shall **b** them
Is 65: 3 **b** incense on altars of brick
Jer 4: 4 **b** so that no one can quench
Jer 7: 9 **b** incense to Baal, and walk
Jer 7:20 And it will **b** and not be
Jer 7:31 to **b** their sons and their
Jer 9:12 **b** up like a wilderness, so
Jer 11:13 altars to **b** incense to Baal
Jer 15:14 anger, which shall **b** upon you
Jer 17: 4 anger which shall **b** forever
Jer 19: 5 to **b** their sons with fire for
Jer 21:10 and he shall **b** it with fire
Jer 21:12 **b** so that no one can quench
Jer 32:29 and **b** it, with the houses on
Jer 34: 2 and he shall **b** it with fire
Jer 34: 5 so they shall **b** incense for
Jer 34:22 and take it and **b** it with fire
Jer 36:25 the king not to **b** the scroll
Jer 37: 8 and take it and **b** it with fire
Jer 37:10 tent, and **b** the city with fire
Jer 38:18 they shall **b** it with fire, and
Jer 43:12 of Egypt, and he shall **b** them
Jer 43:13 he shall **b** with fire
Jer 44: 3 that they went to **b** incense
Jer 44: 5 to **b** no incense to other gods
Jer 44:17 to **b** incense to the queen of
Jer 44:25 to **b** incense to the queen of
Ezek 5: 2 You shall **b** with fire
Ezek 5: 4 fire, and **b** them in the fire
Ezek 16:41 They shall **b** your houses with
Ezek 23:47 and **b** their houses with fire
Ezek 24:11 hot and its bronze may **b**, that
Ezek 39: 9 and **b** the weapons, both the
Ezek 43:21 **b** it in the appointed place
Hos 4:13 **b** incense on the hills, under
Amos 6:10 one who will **b** the bodies
Nah 2:13 I will **b** your chariots in
Hab 1:16 **b** incense to their dragnet
Mal 4: 1 is coming shall **b** them up
Matt 3:12 but He will **b** up the chaff
Matt 13:30 them in bundles to **b** them
Luke 1: 9 his lot fell to **b** incense
Luke 3:17 but the chaff He will **b** with
Luke 24:32 Did not our heart **b** within us
1Co 7: 9 marry than to **b** with passion
2Co 11:29 I do not **b** with indignation
Rev 17:16 her flesh and **b** her with fire

BURNED (*see* BURN)
Gen 38:24 Bring her out and let her be **b**
Ex 3: 2 the bush **b** with fire, but the
Ex 32:20 **b** it in the fire, and ground
Ex 40:27 he **b** sweet incense on it, as
Lev 2:12 but they shall not be **b** on
Lev 4:12 are poured out it shall be **b**
Lev 4:21 burn it as he **b** the first
Lev 6:22 It shall be wholly **b**
Lev 6:23 the priest shall be wholly **b**
Lev 6:30 It shall be **b** in the fire
Lev 7:17 third day must be **b** with fire
Lev 7:19 It shall be **b** with fire
Lev 8:16 Moses **b** them on the altar
Lev 8:17 he **b** with fire outside the
Lev 8:20 Moses **b** the head, the pieces,
Lev 8:21 Moses **b** the whole ram on the
Lev 8:28 **b** them on the altar, on the
Lev 9:10 offering he **b** on the altar
Lev 9:11 and the hide he **b** with fire
Lev 9:13 and he **b** them on the altar
Lev 9:14 and **b** them with the burnt
Lev 9:17 **b** it on the altar, besides
Lev 9:20 Then he **b** the fat on the
Lev 10:16 and there it was, **b** up
Lev 13:52 it shall be **b** in the fire
Lev 19: 6 it shall be **b** in the fire
Lev 20:14 They shall be **b** with fire
Lev 21: 9 She shall be **b** with fire
Num 11: 1 fire of the LORD **b** among them
Num 11: 3 of the LORD had **b** among them
Num 16:39 who were **b** up had presented
Num 19: 5 shall be **b** in his sight
Num 19: 5 and its offal shall be **b**
Num 24:22 nevertheless Kain shall be **b**
Num 31:10 They also **b** with fire all the
Deut 4:11 the mountain **b** with fire to
Deut 9:15 and the mountain **b** with fire
Deut 9:21 **b** it with fire and crushed it
Josh 6:24 But they **b** the city and all
Josh 7: 1 **b** against the children of
Josh 7:15 thing shall be **b** with fire
Josh 7:25 they **b** them with fire after
Josh 8:28 So Joshua **b** Ai and made it a
Josh 11: 9 **b** their chariots with fire
Josh 11:11 Then he **b** Hazor with fire
Josh 11:13 Israel **b** none of them, except
Josh 11:13 Hazor only, which Joshua **b**
Judg 15: 5 **b** up both the shocks and the
Judg 15: 6 **b** her and her father with fire
Judg 15:14 like flax that is **b** with fire
Judg 18:27 sword and **b** the city with fire
1Sa 2:15 Also, before they **b** the fat
1Sa 30: 1 Ziklag and **b** it with fire,
1Sa 30: 3 and there it was, **b** with fire
1Sa 30:14 and we **b** Ziklag with fire
1Sa 31:12 to Jabesh and **b** them there
2Sa 23: 7 they shall be utterly **b** with
1Ki 3: 3 **b** incense at the high places
1Ki 9:16 **b** it with fire, had killed
1Ki 9:25 he **b** incense with them on the
1Ki 11: 8 who **b** incense and sacrificed
1Ki 12:33 on the altar and **b** incense
1Ki 13: 2 men's bones shall be **b** on you
1Ki 15:13 and **b** it by the Brook Kidron
1Ki 16:18 **b** the king's house down upon
1Ki 22:43 **b** incense on the high places
2Ki 1:14 **b** up the first two captains
2Ki 10:26 the temple of Baal and **b** them
2Ki 12: 3 **b** incense on the high places
2Ki 14: 4 **b** incense on the high places
2Ki 15: 4 **b** incense on the high places
2Ki 15:35 **b** incense on the high places
2Ki 16: 4 **b** incense on the high places,
2Ki 16:13 So he **b** his burnt offering and
2Ki 17:11 there they **b** incense on all
2Ki 17:31 and the Sepharvites **b** their
2Ki 18: 4 of Israel **b** incense to it
2Ki 22:17 **b** incense to other gods, that
2Ki 23: 4 he **b** them outside Jerusalem
2Ki 23: 5 those who **b** incense to Baal,
2Ki 23: 6 **b** it at the Brook Kidron and
2Ki 23: 8 the priests had **b** incense
2Ki 23:11 he **b** the chariots of the sun
2Ki 23:15 and he **b** the high place and
2Ki 23:15 and **b** the wooden image
2Ki 23:16 and **b** them on the altar, and
2Ki 23:20 and **b** men's bones on them
2Ki 25: 9 He **b** the house of the LORD and
2Ki 25: 9 the great men, he **b** with fire
1Ch 14:12 and they were **b** with fire
2Ch 15:16 and **b** it by the Brook Kidron
2Ch 25:14 them and **b** incense to them
2Ch 28: 3 He **b** incense in the Valley of
2Ch 28: 3 **b** his children in the fire,
2Ch 28: 4 **b** incense on the high places,
2Ch 29: 7 have not **b** incense or offered
2Ch 34: 5 He also **b** the bones of the
2Ch 34:25 **b** incense to other gods, that
2Ch 36:19 Then they **b** the house of God,
2Ch 36:19 **b** all its palaces with fire,
Neh 1: 3 and its gates are **b** with fire
Neh 2: 3 and its gates are **b** with fire
Neh 2:13 gates which were **b** with fire
Neh 2:17 and its gates are **b** with fire
Neh 4: 2 stones that are **b**
Esth 1:12 and his anger **b** within him
Job 1:16 and **b** up the sheep and the
Ps 39: 3 I was musing, the fire **b**
Ps 74: 8 They have **b** up all the
Ps 80:16 It is **b** with fire, it is cut
Ps 102: 3 my bones are **b** like a hearth
Ps 106:18 The flame **b** up the wicked
Prov 6:27 and his clothes not be **b**
Is 1: 7 your cities are **b** with fire
Is 5: 5 its hedge, and it shall be **b**

Is 9:19 of hosts the land is **b** up
Is 24: 6 of the earth are **b**, and few
Is 33:12 they shall be **b** in the fire
Is 42:25 it **b** him, yet he did not take
Is 43: 2 the fire, you shall not be **b**
Is 44:19 I have **b** half of it in the
Is 64:11 You, is **b** up with fire
Is 65: 7 Who have **b** incense on the
Jer 1:16 **b** incense to other gods, and
Jer 2:15 his cities are **b**, without
Jer 9:10 because they are **b** up, so
Jer 18:15 Me, they have **b** incense to
Jer 19: 4 because they have **b** incense
Jer 19:13 on whose roofs they have **b**
Jer 36:27 Now after the king had **b** the
Jer 36:28 the king of Judah has **b**
Jer 36:29 You have **b** this scroll,
Jer 36:32 of Judah had **b** in the fire
Jer 38:17 city shall not be **b** with fire
Jer 38:23 this city to be **b** with fire
Jer 39: 8 the Chaldeans **b** the king's
Jer 44:15 had **b** incense to other gods
Jer 44:19 And when we **b** incense to the
Jer 44:21 The incense that you **b** in the
Jer 44:23 Because you have **b** incense
Jer 49: 2 villages shall be **b** with fire
Jer 51:30 they have **b** her dwelling
Jer 51:32 reeds they have **b** with fire
Jer 51:58 gates shall be **b** with fire
Jer 52:13 He **b** the house of the LORD and
Jer 52:13 the great men, he **b** with fire
Ezek 15: 4 of it, and its middle is **b**
Ezek 15: 5 has devoured it, and it is **b**
Ezek 24:10 and let the cuts be **b** up
Hos 2:13 Baals to which she **b** incense
Hos 11: 2 **b** incense to carved images
Joel 1:19 a flame has **b** all the trees
Amos 2: 1 because he **b** the bones of the
Mic 1: 7 shall be **b** with the fire
Matt 13:40 **b** in the fire, so it will be
Matt 22: 7 murderers, and **b** up their city
John 15: 6 into the fire, and they are **b**
Acts 19:19 **b** them in the sight of all
Rom 1:27 **b** in their lust for one
1Co 3:15 If anyone's work is **b**, he
1Co 13: 3 though I give my body to be **b**
Heb 6: 8 cursed, whose end is to be **b**
Heb 12:18 and that **b** with fire, and to
Heb 13:11 sin, are **b** outside the camp
2Pe 3:10 that are in it will be **b** up
Rev 8: 7 third of the trees were **b** up
Rev 8: 7 and all green grass was **b** up
Rev 18: 8 will be utterly **b** with fire

BURNING (*see* BURN, BURNINGS)
Gen 15:17 a **b** torch that passed between
Lev 6: 9 altar shall be kept **b** on it
Lev 6:12 altar shall be kept **b** on it
Lev 10: 6 bewail the **b** which the LORD
Lev 16:12 of **b** coals of fire from the
Num 19: 6 of the fire **b** the heifer
Deut 5:23 the mountain was **b** with fire
Deut 28:22 with severe **b** fever, with
Deut 29:23 land is brimstone, salt, and **b**
2Ch 16:14 made a very great **b** for him
2Ch 21:19 his people made no **b** for him
2Ch 21:19 like the **b** for his fathers
Job 41:19 Out of his mouth go **b** lights
Job 41:20 a boiling pot and **b** rushes
Ps 11: 6 Fire and brimstone and a **b** wind
Ps 58: 9 pots can feel the **b** thorns
Ps 58: 9 As in His living and **b** wrath
Ps 140:10 Let **b** coals fall upon them
Prov 16:27 is on his lips like a **b** fire
Prov 26:21 As charcoal is to **b** coals
Is 4: 4 and by the spirit of **b**,
Is 9: 5 in blood, will be used for **b**
Is 10:16 **b** like the **b** of a fire
Is 30:27 **b** with His anger, and His
Is 34: 9 its land shall become **b** pitch
Jer 20: 9 a **b** fire shut up in my bones
Jer 36:22 with a fire **b** on the hearth
Jer 44: 8 **b** incense to other gods in
Jer 44:18 But since we stopped **b**
Lam 2: 6 In His **b** indignation He has
Ezek 1:13 was like **b** coals of fire, and
Ezek 36: 5 **b** jealousy against the rest
Dan 3: 6 midst of a **b** fiery furnace
Dan 3:11 midst of a **b** fiery furnace
Dan 3:15 midst of a **b** fiery furnace
Dan 3:17 us from the **b** fiery furnace
Dan 3:20 them into the **b** fiery furnace
Dan 3:21 midst of the **b** fiery furnace
Dan 3:23 midst of the **b** fiery furnace
Dan 3:26 mouth of the **b** fiery furnace
Dan 7: 9 flame, its wheels a **b** fire
Dan 7:11 and given to the **b** flame
Amos 4:11 firebrand plucked from the **b**
Mal 4: 1 **b** like an oven, and all the
Mark 12:26 in the **b** bush passage, how
Luke 12:35 be girded and your lamps **b**
Luke 20:37 even Moses showed in the **b**
John 5:35 He was the **b** and shining lamp,
Jas 1:11 a **b** heat than it withers the
Rev 4: 5 of fire **b** before the throne
Rev 8: 8 like a great mountain **b** with
Rev 8:10 **b** like a torch, and it fell on
Rev 18: 9 they see the smoke of her **b**
Rev 18:18 they saw the smoke of her **b**
Rev 19:20 lake of fire **b** with brimstone

BURNINGS (*see* BURNING)
Is 33:12 shall be like the **b** of lime
Is 33:14 dwell with everlasting **b**

BURNISHED
1Ki 7:45 of the LORD were of **b** bronze
2Ch 4:16 master craftsman made of **b**
Ezek 1: 7 like the color of **b** bronze
Dan 10: 6 feet like **b** bronze in color,

BURNS (*see* BURN)
Lev 16:28 Then he who **b** them shall wash
Num 19: 8 the one who **b** it shall wash
Ps 46: 9 He **b** the chariot in the fire
Ps 83:14 As the fire **b** the woods, And
Ps 97: 3 **b** up His enemies round about
Is 9:18 For wickedness **b** as the fire
Is 44:16 He **b** half of it in the fire
Is 62: 1 salvation as a lamp that **b**
Is 64: 2 as fire **b** brushwood, as fire
Is 65: 5 a fire that **b** all the day
Is 66: 3 he who **b** incense, as if he
Jer 48:35 and **b** incense to his gods
Hos 7: 6 in the morning it **b** like a
Joel 2: 3 and behind them a flame **b**
Rev 21: 8 in the lake which **b** with fire

BURNT (*see* BURN)
Gen 8:20 offered **b** offerings on the
Gen 22: 2 and offer him there as a **b**
Gen 22: 3 the wood for the **b** offering
Gen 22: 6 the wood of the **b** offering
Gen 22: 7 is the lamb for a **b** offering
Gen 22: 8 the lamb for a **b** offering
Gen 22:13 ram, and offered it up for a **b**
Ex 10:25 and **b** offerings, that we may
Ex 18:12 took a **b** offering and
Ex 20:24 on it your **b** offerings and
Ex 24: 5 who offered **b** offerings and
Ex 29:18 It is a **b** offering to the
Ex 29:25 on the altar as a **b** offering
Ex 29:42 **b** offering throughout your
Ex 30: 9 or a **b** offering, or a meal
Ex 30:28 the altar of **b** offering with
Ex 31: 9 the altar of **b** offering with
Ex 32: 6 day, offered **b** offerings, and
Ex 35:16 the altar of **b** offering with
Ex 38: 1 He made the altar of **b**
Ex 40: 6 shall set the altar of the **b**
Ex 40:10 the altar of the **b** offering
Ex 40:29 And he put the altar of **b**
Ex 40:29 upon it the **b** offering and the
Lev 1: 3 is a **b** sacrifice of the herd
Lev 1: 4 on the head of the **b** offering
Lev 1: 6 he shall skin the **b** offering
Lev 1: 9 on the altar as a **b** sacrifice
Lev 1:10 as a **b** sacrifice, he shall
Lev 1:13 it is a **b** sacrifice, an
Lev 1:14 if the **b** sacrifice of his
Lev 1:17 It is a **b** sacrifice, an
Lev 3: 5 altar upon the **b** sacrifice
Lev 4: 7 the altar of the **b** offering
Lev 4:10 the altar of the **b** offering
Lev 4:18 of the altar of **b** offering
Lev 4:24 **b** offering before the LORD
Lev 4:25 of the altar of **b** offering
Lev 4:25 of the altar of **b** offering
Lev 4:29 the place of the **b** offering
Lev 4:30 of the altar of **b** offering
Lev 4:33 they kill the **b** offering
Lev 4:34 of the altar of **b** offering
Lev 5: 7 and the other as a **b** offering
Lev 5:10 a **b** offering according to the
Lev 6: 9 is the law of the **b** offering
Lev 6: 9 The **b** offering shall be on
Lev 6:10 take up the ashes of the **b**
Lev 6:12 lay the **b** offering in order
Lev 6:25 the **b** offering is killed, the
Lev 7: 2 **b** offering they shall kill
Lev 7: 8 offers anyone's **b** offering
Lev 7: 8 the **b** offering which he has
Lev 7:37 is the law of the **b** offering
Lev 8:18 the ram as the **b** offering
Lev 8:21 It was a **b** sacrifice for a
Lev 8:28 the altar, on the **b** offering
Lev 9: 2 and a ram as a **b** offering,
Lev 9: 3 blemish, as a **b** offering,
Lev 9: 7 and your **b** offering, and make
Lev 9:12 And he killed the **b** offering
Lev 9:13 the **b** offering to him, with
Lev 9:14 and burned them with the **b**
Lev 9:16 And he brought the **b** offering
Lev 9:17 besides the **b** sacrifice of
Lev 9:22 the **b** offering, and peace
Lev 9:24 and consumed the **b** offering
Lev 10:19 their **b** offering before the
Lev 12: 6 first year as a **b** offering
Lev 12: 8 one as a **b** offering and the
Lev 14:13 the **b** offering, in a holy
Lev 14:19 he shall kill the **b** offering
Lev 14:20 shall offer the **b** offering
Lev 14:22 and the other a **b** offering
Lev 14:31 and the other as a **b** offering
Lev 15:15 and the other as a **b** offering
Lev 15:30 and the other as a **b** offering
Lev 16: 3 and of a ram as a **b** offering
Lev 16: 5 and one ram as a **b** offering
Lev 16:24 out and offer his **b** offering
Lev 16:24 the **b** offering of the people,
Lev 17: 8 who offers a **b** offering or
Lev 22:18 to the LORD as a **b** offering
Lev 23:12 as a **b** offering to the LORD
Lev 23:18 They shall be as a **b** offering
Lev 23:37 LORD, a **b** offering and a grain
Num 6:11 and the other as a **b** offering
Num 6:14 blemish as a **b** offering, one
Num 6:16 offering and his **b** offering
Num 7:15 first year, as a **b** offering
Num 7:21 first year, as a **b** offering
Num 7:27 first year, as a **b** offering
Num 7:33 first year, as a **b** offering
Num 7:39 first year, as a **b** offering
Num 7:45 first year, as a **b** offering
Num 7:51 first year, as a **b** offering
Num 7:57 first year, as a **b** offering
Num 7:63 first year, as a **b** offering
Num 7:69 first year, as a **b** offering
Num 7:75 first year, as a **b** offering
Num 7:81 first year, as a **b** offering
Num 7:87 All the oxen for the **b**
Num 8:12 the other as a **b** offering to
Num 10:10 over your **b** offerings and over
Num 15: 3 a **b** offering or a sacrifice,
Num 15: 5 **b** offering or the sacrifice
Num 15: 8 a young bull as a **b** offering
Num 15:24 young bull as a **b** offering
Num 19:17 **b** for purification from sin
Num 23: 3 Stand by your **b** offering, and
Num 23: 6 standing by his **b** offering
Num 23:15 Stand here by your **b** offering
Num 23:17 standing by his **b** offering
Num 28: 3 day, as a regular **b** offering
Num 28: 6 It is a regular **b** offering
Num 28:10 this is the **b** offering for
Num 28:10 besides the regular **b**
Num 28:11 a **b** offering to the LORD
Num 28:13 as a **b** offering of sweet
Num 28:14 this is the **b** offering for
Num 28:15 the regular **b** offering and its
Num 28:19 as a **b** offering to the LORD
Num 28:23 the **b** offering of the morning
Num 28:23 is for a regular **b** offering
Num 28:24 the regular **b** offering and its
Num 28:27 You shall present a **b**
Num 28:31 besides the regular **b**
Num 29: 2 You shall offer a **b** offering
Num 29: 6 besides the **b** offering with
Num 29: 6 the regular **b** offering with
Num 29: 8 You shall present a **b**
Num 29:11 the regular **b** offering with
Num 29:13 shall present a **b** offering
Num 29:16 the regular **b** offering, its

Num 29:19 besides the regular **b**
Num 29:22 the regular **b** offering, its
Num 29:25 the regular **b** offering, its
Num 29:28 the regular **b** offering, its
Num 29:31 the regular **b** offering, its
Num 29:34 the regular **b** offering, its
Num 29:36 shall present a **b** offering
Num 29:38 the regular **b** offering, its
Num 29:39 as your **b** offerings and your
Deut 12: 6 shall take your **b** offerings
Deut 12:11 your **b** offerings, your
Deut 12:13 **b** offerings in every place
Deut 12:14 shall offer your **b** offerings
Deut 12:27 shall offer your **b** offerings
Deut 27: 6 offer **b** offerings on it to
Deut 33:10 a whole **b** sacrifice on Your
Josh 8:31 And they offered on it **b**
Josh 22:23 on it **b** offerings or grain
Josh 22:26 not for **b** offering nor for
Josh 22:27 Him with our **b** offerings,
Josh 22:28 though not for **b** offerings
Josh 22:29 an altar for **b** offerings, for
Judg 6:26 offer a **b** sacrifice with the
Judg 11:31 offer it up as a **b** offering
Judg 13:16 But if you offer a **b** offering
Judg 13:23 have accepted a **b** offering
Judg 20:26 and they offered **b** offerings
Judg 21: 4 offered **b** offerings and peace
1Sa 6:14 as a **b** offering to the LORD
1Sa 6:15 Shemesh offered **b** offerings
1Sa 7: 9 whole **b** offering to the LORD
1Sa 7:10 offering up the **b** offering
1Sa 10: 8 to you to offer **b** offerings
1Sa 13: 9 Bring a **b** offering and peace
1Sa 13: 9 And he offered the **b** offering
1Sa 13:10 offering the **b** offering, that
1Sa 13:12 and offered a **b** offering
1Sa 15:22 great delight in **b** offerings
2Sa 6:17 David offered **b** offerings
2Sa 6:18 finished offering **b** offerings
2Sa 24:22 here are oxen for **b** sacrifice
2Sa 24:24 nor will I offer **b** offerings
2Sa 24:25 offered **b** offerings and peace
1Ki 3: 4 **b** offerings on that altar
1Ki 3:15 LORD, offered up **b** offerings
1Ki 8:64 there he offered **b** offerings
1Ki 8:64 to receive the **b** offerings
1Ki 9:25 Solomon offered **b** offerings
1Ki 18:33 and pour it on the **b** sacrifice
1Ki 18:38 and consumed the **b** sacrifice
2Ki 3:27 offered him as a **b** offering
2Ki 5:17 **b** offering or sacrifice to
2Ki 10:24 sacrifices and **b** offerings
2Ki 10:25 of offering the **b** offering
2Ki 16:13 So he burned his **b** offering
2Ki 16:15 burn the morning **b** offering
2Ki 16:15 the king's **b** sacrifice, and
2Ki 16:15 with the **b** offering of all
2Ki 16:15 the blood of the **b** offering
1Ch 6:49 on the altar of **b** offering
1Ch 16: 1 Then they offered **b** offerings
1Ch 16: 2 offering the **b** offerings and
1Ch 16:40 to offer **b** offerings to the
1Ch 16:40 **b** offering regularly morning
1Ch 21:23 you the oxen for **b** offerings
1Ch 21:24 nor offer **b** offerings with
1Ch 21:26 offered **b** offerings and peace
1Ch 21:26 on the altar of **b** offering
1Ch 21:29 the altar of the **b** offering
1Ch 22: 1 of **b** offering for Israel
1Ch 23:31 at every presentation of a **b**
1Ch 29:21 offered **b** offerings to the
2Ch 1: 6 a thousand **b** offerings on it
2Ch 2: 4 for the **b** offerings morning
2Ch 4: 6 as they offered for the **b**
2Ch 7: 1 and consumed the **b** offering
2Ch 7: 7 there he offered **b** offerings
2Ch 7: 7 to receive the **b** offerings
2Ch 8:12 Then Solomon offered **b**
2Ch 13:11 and every evening **b** sacrifices
2Ch 23:18 to offer the **b** offerings of
2Ch 24:14 they offered **b** offerings in
2Ch 29: 7 burned incense or offered **b**
2Ch 29:18 the altar of **b** offerings with
2Ch 29:24 commanded that the **b** offering
2Ch 29:27 the **b** offering on the altar
2Ch 29:27 when the **b** offering began,
2Ch 29:28 the **b** offering was finished
2Ch 29:31 heart brought **b** offerings
2Ch 29:32 the number of the **b** offerings
2Ch 29:32 for a **b** offering to the LORD
2Ch 29:34 not skin all the **b** offerings
2Ch 29:35 Also the **b** offerings were in
2Ch 29:35 for every **b** offering
2Ch 30:15 brought the **b** offerings to
2Ch 31: 2 and Levites for **b** offerings
2Ch 31: 3 for the **b** offerings
2Ch 31: 3 and evening **b** offerings, the
2Ch 31: 3 the **b** offerings for the
2Ch 35:12 Then they removed the **b**
2Ch 35:14 busy in offering **b** offerings
2Ch 35:16 to offer **b** offerings on the
Ezra 3: 2 to offer **b** offerings on it,
Ezra 3: 3 they offered **b** offerings on
Ezra 3: 3 and evening **b** offerings
Ezra 3: 4 offered the daily **b** offerings
Ezra 3: 5 the regular **b** offering, and
Ezra 3: 6 offer **b** offerings to the LORD
Ezra 6: 9 lambs for the **b** offerings of
Ezra 8:35 offered **b** offerings to the
Ezra 8:35 All this was a **b** offering to
Neh 10:33 for the regular **b** offering of
Job 1: 5 offer **b** offerings according
Job 42: 8 for yourselves a **b** offering
Ps 20: 3 And accept your **b** sacrifice
Ps 40: 6 **B** offering and sin offering
Ps 50: 8 Or your **b** offerings, Which
Ps 51:16 do not delight in **b** offering
Ps 51:19 With **b** offering and whole
Ps 51:19 offering and whole **b** offering
Ps 66:13 Your house with **b** offerings
Ps 66:15 I will offer You **b** sacrifices
Is 1:11 enough of **b** offerings of rams
Is 40:16 sufficient for a **b** offering
Is 43:23 sheep for your **b** offerings
Is 56: 7 Their **b** offerings and their
Is 61: 8 I hate robbery for **b** offering
Jer 6:20 Your **b** offerings are not
Jer 7:21 Add your **b** offerings to your
Jer 7:22 concerning **b** offerings or
Jer 14:12 and when they offer **b** offering
Jer 17:26 bringing **b** offerings and
Jer 19: 5 fire for **b** offerings to Baal
Jer 33:18 offer **b** offerings before Me
Jer 51:25 and make you a **b** mountain
Ezek 40:38 they washed the **b** offering
Ezek 40:39 which to slay the **b** offering
Ezek 40:42 hewn stone for the **b** offering
Ezek 40:42 slaughtered the **b** offering
Ezek 43:18 sacrificing **b** offerings on it
Ezek 43:24 as a **b** offering to the LORD
Ezek 43:27 shall offer your **b** offerings
Ezek 44:11 shall slay the **b** offering
Ezek 45:15 **b** offerings, and peace
Ezek 45:17 part to give **b** offerings,
Ezek 45:17 the **b** offering, and the peace
Ezek 45:23 a **b** offering to the LORD,
Ezek 45:25 the **b** offering, the grain
Ezek 46: 2 shall prepare his **b** offering
Ezek 46: 4 The **b** offering that the
Ezek 46:12 prince makes a voluntary **b**
Ezek 46:12 shall prepare his **b** offering
Ezek 46:13 You shall daily make a **b**
Ezek 46:15 as a regular **b** offering every
Hos 6: 6 of God more than **b** offerings
Amos 5:22 you offer Me **b** offerings and
Mic 6: 6 before Him with **b** offerings
Mark 12:33 all the whole **b** offerings
Heb 10: 6 In **b** offerings and sacrifices
Heb 10: 8 **b** offerings, and offerings for

BURST (*see* BURSTING, BURSTS)
Judg 20:33 **b** forth from their position
Job 32:19 it is ready to **b** like new
Job 38: 8 with doors, when it **b** forth
Is 35: 6 For waters shall **b** forth in
Jer 2:20 your yoke and **b** your bonds
Jer 5: 5 the yoke and **b** the bonds
Jer 30: 8 neck, and will **b** your bonds
Nah 1:13 you, and **b** your bonds apart
Luke 5:37 new wine will **b** the wineskins
Acts 1:18 he **b** open in the middle and

BURSTING (*see* BURST)
Ezek 32: 2 seas, **b** forth in your rivers,

BURSTS (*see* BURST)
Mark 2:22 the new wine **b** the wineskins

BURY (*see* BURIAL, BURIED, BURIERS, BURIES, BURYING)
Gen 23: 4 that I may **b** my dead out of
Gen 23: 6 **b** your dead in the choicest
Gen 23: 6 that you may **b** your dead
Gen 23: 8 I **b** my dead out of my sight
Gen 23:11 **B** your dead!"
Gen 23:13 me and I will **b** my dead there
Gen 23:15 So **b** your dead
Gen 47:29 Please do not **b** me in Egypt
Gen 47:30 **b** me in their burial place
Gen 49:29 **b** me with my fathers in the
Gen 50: 5 Canaan, there you shall **b** me
Gen 50: 5 **b** my father, and I will come
Gen 50: 6 **b** your father, as he made you
Gen 50: 7 went up to **b** his father
Gen 50:14 up with him to **b** his father
Deut 21:23 shall surely **b** him that day
1Ki 2:31 **b** him, that you may take away
1Ki 11:15 had gone up to **b** the slain
1Ki 13:29 city to mourn, and to **b** him
1Ki 13:31 then **b** me in the tomb where
1Ki 14:13 **b** him, for he is the only one
2Ki 9:10 there shall be none to **b** her
2Ki 9:34 **b** her, for she was a king's
2Ki 9:35 So they went to **b** her, but
2Ch 24:25 but they did not **b** him in the
Ps 79: 3 And there was no one to **b** them
Jer 7:32 for they will **b** in Tophet
Jer 14:16 will have no one to **b** them
Jer 19:11 they shall **b** them in Tophet
Jer 19:11 till there is no place to **b**
Ezek 39:11 because there they will **b** Gog
Ezek 39:14 **b** those bodies remaining on
Hos 9: 6 Memphis shall **b** them
Matt 8:21 me first go and **b** my father
Matt 8:22 let the dead **b** their own dead
Matt 27: 7 field, to **b** strangers in
Luke 9:59 me first go and **b** my father
Luke 9:60 Let the dead **b** their own dead
John 19:40 custom of the Jews is to **b**

BURYING (*see* BURY)
Num 33: 4 were **b** all their firstborn
2Ki 13:21 it was, as they were **b** a man
Ezek 39:12 of Israel will be **b** them, in
Ezek 39:13 of the land will be **b** them

BUSH (*see* BUSHES)
Ex 3: 2 of fire from the midst of a **b**
Ex 3: 2 the **b** burned with fire, but
Ex 3: 2 but the **b** was not consumed
Ex 3: 3 why the **b** does not burn
Ex 3: 4 him from the midst of the **b**
Deut 33:16 of Him who dwelt in the **b**
Mark 12:26 in the burning **b** passage
Luke 6:44 grapes from a bramble **b**
Luke 20:37 **b** passage that the dead are
Acts 7:30 him in a flame of fire in a **b**
Acts 7:35 who appeared to him in the **b**

BUSHES (*see* BUSH)
Job 30: 4 who pluck mallow by the **b**
Job 30: 7 Among the **b** they brayed,

BUSINESS
Deut 24: 5 war or be charged with any **b**
Josh 2:14 of you tell this **b** of ours
Josh 2:20 And if you tell this **b** of ours
1Sa 21: 2 king has ordered me on some **b**
1Sa 21: 2 the **b** on which I send you
1Sa 21: 8 the king's **b** required haste
1Sa 25: 2 in Maon whose **b** was in Carmel
1Ch 26:30 for all the **b** of the LORD
Neh 11:16 had the oversight of the **b**
Job 20:18 **b** he will get no enjoyment
Ps 107:23 Who do **b** on great waters,
Eccl 8:16 to see the **b** that is done on
Dan 8:27 and went about the king's **b**
Matt 22: 5 own farm, another to his **b**
Luke 2:49 I must be about My Father's **b**
Luke 19:13 to them, 'Do **b** till I come
John 2:14 and the moneychangers doing **b**
Acts 6: 3 we may appoint over this **b**
Rom 16: 2 **b** she has need of you
1Th 4:11 life, to mind your own **b**, and

BUSTLING
Is 32:14 the **b** city will be deserted

BUSY
1Ki 18:27 he is meditating, or he is **b**
1Ki 20:40 while your servant was **b** here
2Ch 35:14 were **b** in offering burnt
Ps 39: 6 Surely they **b** themselves in
Eccl 5:20 because God keeps him **b** with

BUSYBODIES (*see* BUSYBODY)
2Th 3:11 not working at all, but are **b**
1Ti 5:13 idle but also gossips and **b**

BUSYBODY (*see* BUSYBODIES)
1Pe 4:15 or as a **b** in other people's

BUT (*see* PREFACE)

BUTLER (*see* BUTLERSHIP)
Gen 40: 1 after these things that the **b**
Gen 40: 2 his two officers, the chief **b**
Gen 40: 5 Then the **b** and the baker of
Gen 40: 9 Then the chief **b** told his
Gen 40:13 manner, when you were his **b**
Gen 40:20 up the head of the chief **b**
Gen 40:21 **b** to his butlership again
Gen 40:23 Yet the chief **b** did not
Gen 41: 9 Then the chief **b** spoke to

BUTLERSHIP (*see* BUTLER)
Gen 40:21 chief butler to his **b** again

BUTTED
Ezek 34:21 **b** all the weak ones with your

BUTTER
Gen 18: 8 So he took **b** and milk and the
Ps 55:21 mouth were smoother than **b**
Prov 30:33 churning of milk produces **b**

BUTTOCKS
2Sa 10: 4 in the middle, at their **b**
1Ch 19: 4 in the middle, at their **b**
Is 20: 4 with their **b** uncovered, to

BUTTRESS
2Ch 26: 9 at the corner **b** of the wall
Neh 3:19 Ascent to the Armory at the **b**
Neh 3:20 from the **b** to the door of the
Neh 3:24 the house of Azariah to the **b**
Neh 3:25 made repairs opposite the **b**

BUY (*see* BOUGHT, BUYER, BUYING, BUYS)
Gen 41:57 to Joseph in Egypt to **b** grain
Gen 42: 2 **b** for us there, that we may
Gen 42: 3 went down to **b** grain in Egypt
Gen 42: 5 to **b** grain among those who
Gen 42: 7 the land of Canaan to **b** food
Gen 42:10 servants have come to **b** food
Gen 43: 2 Go back, **b** us a little food
Gen 43: 4 we will go down and **b** you food
Gen 43:20 down the first time to **b** food
Gen 43:22 money in our hands to **b** food
Gen 44:25 Go back and **b** us a little food
Gen 47:19 **B** us and our land for bread,
Gen 47:22 of the priests he did not **b**
Ex 21: 2 If you **b** a Hebrew servant, he
Lev 25:14 to your neighbor or **b** from
Lev 25:15 shall **b** from your neighbor
Lev 25:44 you, from them you may **b** male
Lev 25:45 Moreover you may **b** the
Deut 2: 6 You shall **b** food from them
Deut 2: 6 you shall also **b** water from
Deut 28:68 slaves, but no one will **b** you
Ruth 4: 4 **B** it back in the presence of
Ruth 4: 5 On the day you **b** the field
Ruth 4: 5 you must also **b** it from Ruth
Ruth 4: 8 to Boaz, "**B** it for yourself
2Sa 24:21 To **b** the threshing floor from
2Sa 24:24 but I will surely **b** it from
2Ki 22: 6 to **b** timber and hewn stone to
1Ch 21:24 but I will surely **b** it for
2Ch 34:11 and builders to **b** hewn stone
Ezra 7:17 be careful to **b** with this
Neh 5: 3 that we might **b** grain because
Neh 5:16 and we did not **b** any land
Neh 10:31 we would not **b** it from them
Prov 23:23 **B** the truth, and do not sell
Is 55: 1 who have no money, come, **b**
Is 55: 1 **b** wine and milk without money
Jer 32: 7 **B** my field which is in
Jer 32: 7 redemption is yours to **b** it
Jer 32: 8 Please **b** my field that is in
Jer 32: 8 **b** it for yourself
Jer 32:25 **B** the field for money, and
Jer 32:44 Men will **b** fields for money,
Amos 8: 6 that we may **b** the poor for
Matt 14:15 villages and **b** themselves food
Matt 25: 9 who sell, and **b** for yourselves
Matt 25:10 And while they went to **b**, the
Mark 6:36 and **b** themselves bread
Mark 6:37 **b** two hundred denarii worth
Luke 9:13 **b** food for all these people
Luke 22:36 him sell his garment and **b** one
John 4: 8 away into the city to **b** food
John 6: 5 Where shall we **b** bread, that
John 13:29 **B** those things we need for
1Co 7:30 those who **b** as though they
Jas 4:13 a city, spend a year there, **b**
Rev 3:18 I counsel you to **b** from Me
Rev 13:17 that no one may **b** or sell

BUYER (*see* BUY)
Prov 20:14 for nothing," cries the **b**
Is 24: 2 as with the **b**, so with the
Ezek 7:12 Let not the **b** rejoice, nor

BUYING (*see* BUY)
2Ki 12:12 for **b** timber and hewn stone,

BUYS (*see* BUY)
Lev 22:11 But if the priest **b** a person
Prov 31:16 She considers a field and **b** it
Matt 13:44 that he has and **b** that field
Rev 18:11 over her, for no one **b** their

BUZ
Gen 22:21 **B** his brother, Kemuel the
1Ch 5:14 son of Jahdo, the son of **B**
Jer 25:23 Dedan, Tema, **B**, and all who

BUZI (*see* BUZITE)
Ezek 1: 3 the priest, the son of **B**, in

BUZITE (*see* BUZI)
Job 32: 2 the son of Barachel the **B**
Job 32: 6 the son of Barachel the **B**

BUZZARD
Lev 11:13 the eagle, the vulture, the **b**
Deut 14:12 the eagle, the vulture, the **b**

BUZZING
Is 18: 1 land shadowed with **b** wings

BY (*see* PREFACE)

BYGONE
Acts 14:16 who in **b** generations allowed

BYPASSED (*see* BYPASSING)
Judg 11:18 **b** the land of Edom and the

BYPASSING (*see* BYPASSED)
Josh 19:12 out toward Daberath, **b** Japhia
Josh 19:27 **b** Cabul which was on the left

BYWAYS
Judg 5: 6 travelers walked along the **b**

BYWORD
Deut 28:37 a **b** among all nations where
1Ki 9: 7 and a **b** among all peoples
2Ch 7:20 and a **b** among all nations
Job 17: 6 has made me a **b** of the people
Job 30: 9 yes, I am their **b**
Ps 44:14 You make us a **b** among the
Ps 69:11 I became a **b** to them
Jer 24: 9 harm, to be a reproach and a **b**
Ezek 16:56 a **b** in your mouth in the days
Ezek 23:10 She became a **b** among women

C

CABBON
Josh 15:40 **C**, Lahmas, Kithlish,

CABLES
Acts 27:17 they used **c** to undergird the

CABUL
Josh 19:27 bypassing **C** which was on the
1Ki 9:13 he called them the land of **C**

CAESAR (*see* AUGUSTUS, CAESAR'S, CLAUDIUS, TIBERIUS)
Matt 22:17 it lawful to pay taxes to **C**
Matt 22:21 to **C** the things that are
Mark 12:14 it lawful to pay taxes to **C**
Mark 12:17 Render to **C** the things that
Luke 2: 1 **C** Augustus that all the world
Luke 3: 1 of the reign of Tiberius **C**
Luke 20:22 us to pay taxes to **C** or not
Luke 20:25 to **C** the things that are
Luke 23: 2 forbidding to pay taxes to **C**
John 19:12 a king speaks against **C**
John 19:15 We have no king but **C**
Acts 11:28 in the days of Claudius **C**
Acts 17: 7 contrary to the decrees of **C**
Acts 25: 8 nor against **C** have I offended
Acts 25:11 I appeal to **C**
Acts 25:12 You have appealed to **C**
Acts 25:12 To **C** you shall go
Acts 25:21 till I could send him to **C**
Acts 26:32 he had not appealed to **C**
Acts 27:24 you must be brought before **C**
Acts 28:19 was compelled to appeal to **C**

CAESAREA
Acts 8:40 the cities till he came to **C**
Acts 9:30 they brought him down to **C**
Acts 10: 1 man in **C** called Cornelius
Acts 10:24 following day they entered **C**
Acts 11:11 having been sent to me from **C**
Acts 12:19 he went down from Judea to **C**
Acts 18:22 And when he had landed at **C**
Acts 21: 8 departed and came to **C**, and
Acts 21:16 disciples from **C** went with us
Acts 23:23 to **C** at the third hour of the
Acts 23:33 When they came to **C** and had
Acts 25: 1 went up from **C** to Jerusalem
Acts 25: 4 that Paul should be kept at **C**
Acts 25: 6 ten days, he went down to **C**
Acts 25:13 came to **C** to greet Festus

CAESAREA PHILIPPI
Matt 16:13 came into the region of **C**
Mark 8:27 went out to the towns of **C**

CAESAR'S (*see* CAESAR)
Matt 22:21 They said to Him, "**C**."
Matt 22:21 Caesar the things that are **C**
Mark 12:16 they said to Him, "**C**."
Mark 12:17 Caesar the things that are **C**
Luke 20:24 They answered and said, "**C**."
Luke 20:25 Caesar the things that are **C**
John 19:12 Man go, you are not **C** friend
Acts 25:10 I stand at **C** judgment seat,
Phil 4:22 those who are of **C** household

CAGE
Jer 5:27 As a **c** is full of birds, so
Ezek 19: 9 put him in a **c** with chains
Hos 13: 8 I will tear open their rib **c**
Rev 18: 2 and a **c** for every unclean and

CAIAPHAS
Matt 26: 3 high priest, who was called **C**
Matt 26:57 Him away to **C** the high priest
Luke 3: 2 **C** being high priests, the
John 11:49 And one of them, **C**, being high
John 18:13 of **C** who was high priest that
John 18:14 Now it was **C** who gave counsel
John 18:24 bound to **C** the high priest
John 18:28 from **C** to the Praetorium, and
Acts 4: 6 as Annas the high priest, **C**

CAIN
Gen 4: 1 and she conceived and bore **C**
Gen 4: 2 but **C** was a tiller of the
Gen 4: 3 time it came to pass that **C**
Gen 4: 5 but He did not respect **C** and
Gen 4: 5 And **C** was very angry, and his
Gen 4: 6 So the LORD said to **C**, "Why
Gen 4: 8 Now **C** talked with Abel his
Gen 4: 8 that **C** rose against Abel his
Gen 4: 9 Then the LORD said to **C**
Gen 4:13 And **C** said to the LORD,
Gen 4:15 Therefore, whoever kills **C**
Gen 4:15 And the LORD set a mark on **C**
Gen 4:16 Then **C** went out from the
Gen 4:17 And **C** knew his wife, and she
Gen 4:24 If **C** shall be avenged
Gen 4:25 of Abel, whom **C** killed
Heb 11: 4 excellent sacrifice than **C**
1Jn 3:12 not as **C** who was of the
Jude 11 have gone in the way of **C**

CAINAN
Gen 5: 9 ninety years, and begot **C**
Gen 5:10 After he begot **C**, Enosh lived
Gen 5:12 **C** lived seventy years, and
Gen 5:13 **C** lived eight hundred and
Gen 5:14 days of **C** were nine hundred
1Ch 1: 2 **C**, Mahalaleel, Jared,
Luke 3:36 the son of **C**, the son of

Luke 3:37 of Mahalalel, the son of **C**

CAKE (*see* CAKED, CAKES)
Ex 29:23 one **c** made with oil, and one
Lev 7:14 one **c** from each offering as a
Lev 8:26 LORD he took one unleavened **c**
Lev 8:26 a **c** of bread anointed with
Lev 24: 5 an ephah shall be in each **c**
Num 6:19 one unleavened **c** from the
Num 15:20 You shall offer up a **c** of
1Sa 30:12 him a piece of a **c** of figs
2Sa 6:19 of meat, and a **c** of raisins
1Ki 17:13 me a small **c** from it first
1Ki 19: 6 head was a **c** baked on coals
1Ch 16: 3 of meat, and a **c** of raisins
Hos 7: 8 Ephraim is a **c** unturned

CAKED (*see* CAKE)
Job 7: 5 My flesh is **c** with worms and

CAKES (*see* CAKE)
Gen 18: 6 knead it and make **c**
Ex 12:39 they baked unleavened **c** of
Ex 29: 2 unleavened **c** mixed with oil,
Lev 2: 4 it shall be unleavened **c** of
Lev 7:12 unleavened **c** mixed with oil,
Lev 7:12 or **c** of finely blended flour
Lev 7:13 Besides the **c**, as his
Lev 24: 5 and bake twelve **c** with it
Num 6:15 **c** of fine flour mixed with
Num 11: 8 it in pans, and made **c** of it
1Sa 25:18 and two hundred **c** of figs
2Sa 13: 6 make a couple of **c** for me in
2Sa 13: 8 made **c** in his sight, and baked
2Sa 13: 8 in his sight, and baked the **c**
2Sa 13:10 Tamar took the **c** which she
1Ki 14: 3 with you ten loaves, some **c**
1Ch 12:40 **c** of figs and **c** of raisins
1Ch 23:29 with the unleavened **c** and
Song 2: 5 Sustain me with **c** of raisins
Jer 7:18 to make **c** for the queen of
Jer 44:19 to her, did we make **c** for her
Ezek 4:12 you shall eat it as barley **c**
Hos 3: 1 the raisin **c** of the pagans

CALAH
Gen 10:11 built Nineveh, Rehoboth Ir, **C**
Gen 10:12 **C** (that is the principal city

CALAMITIES (*see* CALAMITY)
Ps 57: 1 Until these **c** have passed by

CALAMITY (*see* CALAMITIES)
Gen 42: 4 Lest some **c** befall him
Gen 42:38 If any **c** should befall him
Gen 44:29 and **c** befalls him, you shall
Deut 32:35 the day of their **c** is at hand
Judg 2:15 LORD was against them for **c**
2Sa 22:19 me in the day of my **c**, but
1Ki 9: 9 brought all this **c** on them
1Ki 21:21 Behold, I will bring **c** on you
1Ki 21:29 not bring the **c** in his days
1Ki 21:29 will bring the **c** on his house
2Ki 6:33 Surely this **c** is from the
2Ki 21:12 such **c** upon Jerusalem and
2Ki 22:16 I will bring **c** on this place
2Ki 22:20 **c** which I will bring on this
2Ch 7:22 brought all this **c** on them
2Ch 34:24 I will bring **c** on this place
2Ch 34:28 **c** which I will bring on this
Job 6: 2 and my **c** laid with it in the
Job 30:13 up my path, they promote my **c**
Ps 18:18 me in the day of my **c**, But
Prov 1:26 I also will laugh at your **c**
Prov 6:15 Therefore his **c** shall come
Prov 17: 5 he who is glad at **c** will not
Prov 24:16 the wicked shall fall by **c**
Prov 24:22 for their **c** will rise
Prov 27:10 house in the day of your **c**
Prov 28:14 his heart will fall into **c**
Is 45: 7 I make peace and create **c**
Jer 1:14 Out of the north **c** shall
Jer 6:19 bring **c** on this people, even
Jer 11:11 I will surely bring **c** on them
Jer 18:17 face in the day of their **c**
Jer 25:29 I begin to bring **c** on the
Jer 26: 3 **c** which I purpose to bring on
Jer 32:23 all this **c** to come upon them
Jer 32:42 this great **c** on this people
Jer 44: 2 the **c** that I have brought on
Jer 44:23 therefore this **c** has happened
Jer 46:21 of their **c** had come upon them
Jer 48:16 The **c** of Moab is near at hand
Jer 49: 8 bring the **c** of Esau upon him
Jer 49:32 their **c** from all its sides
Ezek 6:10 would bring this **c** upon them
Ezek 35: 5 sword at the time of their **c**
Amos 3: 6 If there is **c** in a city, will
Amos 9:10 The **c** shall not overtake us
Obad 13 people in the day of their **c**
Obad 13 in the day of their **c**, nor
Obad 13 in the day of their **c**

CALAMUS
Song 4:14 spikenard and saffron, **c** and

CALCOL (*see* CHALCOL)
1Ch 2: 6 were Zimri, Ethan, Heman, **C**

CALCULATE (*see* CALCULATED)
Rev 13:18 **c** the number of the beast

CALCULATED (*see* CALCULATE)
Is 40:12 **c** the dust of the earth in a

CALDRON (*see* CALDRONS)
1Sa 2:14 into the pan, or kettle, or **c**
Ezek 11: 3 this city is the **c**, and we are
Ezek 11: 7 meat, and this city is the **c**
Ezek 11:11 This city shall not be your **c**
Mic 3: 3 the pot, Like flesh in the **c**

CALDRONS (*see* CALDRON)
2Ch 35:13 they boiled in pots, in **c**

CALEB (*see* CALEB'S, CHELUB, CHELUBAI)
Num 13: 6 Judah, **C** the son of Jephunneh
Num 13:30 Then **C** quieted the people
Num 14: 6 **C** the son of Jephunneh, who
Num 14:24 But My servant **C**, because he
Num 14:30 Except for **C** the son of
Num 14:38 Nun and **C** the son of Jephunneh
Num 26:65 except **C** the son of Jephunneh
Num 32:12 except **C** the son of
Num 34:19 Judah, **C** the son of Jephunneh
Deut 1:36 except **C** the son of
Josh 14: 6 **C** the son of Jephunneh the
Josh 14:13 gave Hebron to **C** the son of
Josh 14:14 of **C** the son of Jephunneh the
Josh 15:13 Now to **C** the son of Jephunneh
Josh 15:14 **C** drove out the three sons of
Josh 15:16 **C** said, "He who attacks
Josh 15:17 of Kenaz, the brother of **C**
Josh 15:18 her donkey, and **C** said to her,
Josh 21:12 its villages they gave to **C**
Judg 1:12 Then **C** said, "He who attacks
Judg 1:14 her donkey, and **C** said to her,
Judg 1:15 Then **C** gave her the upper
Judg 1:20 And they gave Hebron to **C**, as
1Sa 25: 3 And he was of the house of **C**
1Sa 30:14 and of the southern area of **C**
1Ch 2:18 **C** the son of Hezron begot
1Ch 2:19 **C** took Ephrath as his wife,
1Ch 2:42 The descendants of **C** the
1Ch 2:49 the daughter of **C** was Achsah
1Ch 2:50 were the descendants of **C**
1Ch 4:15 The sons of **C** the son of
1Ch 6:56 to **C** the son of Jephunneh

CALEB EPHRATHAH
1Ch 2:24 After Hezron died in **C**,

CALEB'S (*see* CALEB)
Judg 1:13 **C** younger brother, took it
Judg 3: 9 of Kenaz, **C** younger brother
1Ch 2:46 **C** concubine, bore Haran, Moza
1Ch 2:48 **C** concubine, bore Sheber and

CALF (*see* CALVES)
Gen 18: 7 herd, took a tender and good **c**
Gen 18: 8 the **c** which he had prepared,
Ex 32: 4 tool, and made a molded **c**
Ex 32: 8 made themselves a molded **c**
Ex 32:19 the camp, that he saw the **c**
Ex 32:20 Then he took the **c** which they
Ex 32:24 the fire, and this **c** came out
Ex 32:35 with the **c** which Aaron made
Lev 9: 3 as a sin offering, and a **c**
Lev 9: 8 and killed the **c** of the sin
Deut 9:16 for yourselves a molded **c**
Deut 9:21 the **c** which you had made, and
1Sa 28:24 had a fatted **c** in the house
2Ch 11:15 the **c** idols which he had made
Neh 9:18 a molded **c** for themselves
Ps 29: 6 makes them also skip like a **c**
Ps 106:19 They made a **c** in Horeb, And
Prov 15:17 than a fatted **c** with hatred
Is 11: 6 with the young goat, the **c**
Is 27:10 there the **c** will feed, and
Jer 34:18 when they cut the **c** in two
Jer 34:19 between the parts of the **c**
Hos 4:16 is stubborn like a stubborn **c**
Hos 8: 5 Your **c** is rejected, O Samaria
Hos 8: 6 But the **c** of Samaria shall be
Hos 10: 5 because of the **c** of Beth Aven
Luke 15:23 And bring the fatted **c** here
Luke 15:27 has killed the fatted **c**
Luke 15:30 killed the fatted **c** for him
Acts 7:41 they made a **c** in those days,
Rev 4: 7 living creature like a **c**, the

CALL (*see* CALLED, CALLING, CALLS)
Gen 2:19 to see what he would **c** them
Gen 4:26 Then men began to **c** on the
Gen 16:11 You shall **c** his name Ishmael,
Gen 17:15 you shall not **c** her name
Gen 17:19 you shall **c** his name Isaac
Gen 24:57 We will **c** the young woman and
Gen 30:13 daughters will **c** me blessed
Ex 2: 7 **c** a nurse for you from the
Ex 2:20 **C** him, that he may eat bread
Num 10: 6 they shall sound the **c** for
Num 16:12 And Moses sent to **c** Dathan
Num 22: 5 his people, to **c** him, saying
Num 22:20 If the men come to **c** you,
Deut 2:11 but the Moabites **c** them Emim
Deut 2:20 **c** them Zamzummim
Deut 3: 9 the Sidonians **c** Hermon Sirion
Deut 3: 9 and the Amorites **c** it Senir)
Deut 4: 7 reason we may **c** upon Him
Deut 4:26 I **c** heaven and earth to
Deut 25: 8 of his city shall **c** him and
Deut 30: 1 you **c** them to mind among all
Deut 30:19 I **c** heaven and earth as
Deut 31:14 **c** Joshua, and present
Deut 31:28 **c** heaven and earth to witness
Deut 33:19 They shall **c** the peoples to
Judg 12: 1 did not **c** us to go with you
Judg 16:25 **C** for Samson, that he may
Judg 18:12 (Therefore they **c** that place
Ruth 1:20 to them, "Do not **c** me Naomi
Ruth 1:20 **c** me Mara, for the Almighty
Ruth 1:21 Why do you **c** me Naomi, since
1Sa 3: 5 I did not **c**
1Sa 3: 6 I did not **c**, my son
1Sa 3: 8 Here I am, for you did **c** me
1Sa 12:17 I will **c** to the LORD, and He
1Sa 14:17 Now **c** the roll and see who has
1Sa 22:11 to **c** Ahimelech the priest
2Sa 15: 2 that Absalom would **c** to him
2Sa 17: 5 Now **c** Hushai the Archite also
2Sa 22: 4 I will **c** upon the LORD, who
1Ki 1:28 and said, "**C** Bathsheba to me
1Ki 1:32 **C** to me Zadok the priest,
1Ki 8:52 them whenever they **c** to You
1Ki 18:24 Then you **c** on the name of
1Ki 18:24 I will **c** on the name of the
1Ki 18:25 **c** on the name of your god,
1Ki 22:13 to **c** Micaiah spoke to him
2Ki 4:12 **C** this Shunammite woman
2Ki 4:15 And he said, "**C** her
2Ki 4:36 **C** this Shunammite woman
2Ki 5:11 **c** on the name of the LORD his
2Ki 10:19 **c** to me all the prophets of
1Ch 16: 8 **C** upon His name
2Ch 18:12 to **c** Micaiah spoke to him
Job 5: 1 **C** out now
Job 13:22 Then **c**, and I will answer
Job 14:15 You shall **c**, and I will answer
Job 19:16 I **c** my servant, but he gives
Job 27:10 Will he always **c** on God
Ps 4: 1 Hear me when I **c**, O God of my
Ps 4: 3 will hear when I **c** to Him
Ps 14: 4 And do not **c** on the LORD
Ps 18: 3 I will **c** upon the LORD, who
Ps 20: 9 the King answer us when we **c**
Ps 49:11 They **c** their lands after
Ps 50: 4 He shall **c** to the heavens
Ps 50:15 **C** upon Me in the day of
Ps 53: 4 bread, And do not **c** upon God
Ps 55:16 I will **c** upon God, And the
Ps 72:17 nations shall **c** Him blessed
Ps 77: 6 I **c** to remembrance my song in
Ps 79: 6 that do not **c** on Your name
Ps 80:18 and we will **c** upon Your name
Ps 86: 5 to all those who **c** upon You
Ps 86: 7 my trouble I will **c** upon You
Ps 91:15 He shall **c** upon Me, and I will
Ps 102: 2 In the day that I **c**, answer

Ps 105: 1 **C** upon His name
Ps 116: 2 Therefore I will **c** upon Him
Ps 116:13 **c** upon the name of the LORD
Ps 116:17 will **c** upon the name of the
Ps 145:18 is near to all who **c** upon Him
Ps 145:18 Him, To all who **c** upon Him in
Prov 1:28 Then they will **c** on me, but I
Prov 7: 4 **c** understanding your nearest
Prov 8: 4 To you, O men, I **c**, and my
Prov 9:15 to **c** to those who pass by,
Prov 31:28 rise up and **c** her blessed
Is 5:20 Woe to those who **c** evil good
Is 7:14 shall **c** His name Immanuel
Is 8: 3 LORD said to me, "**C** his name
Is 8:12 this people **c** a conspiracy
Is 12: 4 the LORD, **c** upon His name
Is 22:20 day, that I will **c** My servant
Is 31: 2 will not **c** back His words,
Is 34:12 They shall **c** its nobles to
Is 41:25 the sun he shall **c** on My name
Is 44: 5 another will **c** himself by the
Is 45: 3 Who **c** you by your name, am
Is 48: 2 for they **c** themselves after
Is 48:13 when I **c** to them, they stand
Is 55: 5 Surely you shall **c** a nation
Is 55: 6 **c** upon Him while He is near
Is 58: 5 Would you **c** this a fast, and
Is 58: 9 Then you shall **c**, and the LORD
Is 58:13 **c** the Sabbath a delight, the
Is 60:14 they shall **c** you The City of
Is 60:18 but you shall **c** your walls
Is 61: 6 men shall **c** you the Servants
Is 62:12 they shall **c** them The Holy
Is 65:15 **c** His servants by another
Is 65:24 to pass that before they **c**
Jer 3:19 You shall **c** Me, 'My Father,
Jer 6:30 People will **c** them rejected
Jer 7:27 You shall also **c** to them, but
Jer 9:17 **c** for the mourning women,
Jer 10:25 who do not **c** on Your name
Jer 25:29 for I will **c** for a sword on
Jer 29:12 Then you will **c** upon Me and go
Jer 33: 3 **C** to Me, and I will answer
Jer 50:29 **C** together the archers
Jer 51:27 her, **c** the kingdoms together
Ezek 21:22 to **c** for a slaughter, to lift
Ezek 36:29 I will **c** for the grain and
Ezek 38:21 I will **c** for a sword against
Ezek 39:11 Therefore they will **c** it the
Dan 2: 2 command to **c** the magicians
Hos 1: 4 **C** his name Jezreel, for in a
Hos 1: 6 **C** her name Lo-Ruhamah, for I
Hos 1: 9 **C** his name Lo-Ammi, for you
Hos 2:16 That you will **c** Me 'My
Hos 2:16 no longer **c** Me 'My Master,'
Hos 7:11 they **c** to Egypt, they go to
Hos 11: 7 Though they **c** to the Most
Joel 1:14 a fast, **c** a sacred assembly
Joel 2:15 a fast, **c** a sacred assembly
Amos 5:16 They shall **c** the farmer to
Jon 1: 6 Arise, **c** on your God
Zeph 3: 9 that they all may **c** on the
Zech 13: 9 They will **c** on My name, and I
Mal 3:12 nations will **c** you blessed
Mal 3:15 So now we **c** the proud blessed
Matt 1:21 you shall **c** His name JESUS,
Matt 1:23 Son, and they shall **c** His name
Matt 9:13 not come to **c** the righteous
Matt 10:25 they **c** those of his household
Matt 19:17 Why do you **c** Me good
Matt 20: 8 **C** the laborers and give them
Matt 22: 3 sent out his servants to **c**
Matt 22:43 in the Spirit **c** Him Lord
Matt 23: 9 Do not **c** anyone on earth your
Mark 2:17 not come to **c** the righteous
Mark 10:18 Why do you **c** Me good
Mark 15:12 you **c** the King of the Jews
Luke 1:13 you shall **c** his name John
Luke 1:31 and shall **c** His name JESUS
Luke 1:48 generations will **c** me blessed
Luke 5:32 not come to **c** the righteous
Luke 6:46 But why do you **c** Me 'Lord
Luke 18:19 Why do you **c** Me good
John 4:16 **c** your husband; and come here
John 13:13 You **c** me Teacher and Lord,
John 15:15 No longer do I **c** you servants
Acts 2:39 as the Lord our God will **c**
Acts 9:14 bind all who **c** on Your name
Acts 10:15 you must not **c** common
Acts 10:28 **c** any man common or unclean
Acts 10:32 **c** Simon here, whose surname
Acts 11: 9 you must not **c** common
Acts 11:13 **c** for Simon whose surname is
Acts 19:13 **c** the name of the Lord Jesus
Acts 24:14 the Way which they **c** a sect
Acts 24:25 time I will **c** for you
Rom 9:25 I will **c** them My people, who
Rom 10:12 is rich to all who **c** upon Him
Rom 10:14 How then shall they **c** on Him
1Co 1: 2 **c** on the name of Jesus Christ
2Co 1:23 Moreover I **c** God as witness
Phil 3:14 **c** of God in Christ Jesus
1Th 4: 7 For God did not **c** us to
2Ti 1: 5 when I **c** to remembrance the
2Ti 2:22 peace with those who **c** on the
Heb 2:11 ashamed to **c** them brethren
Jas 5:14 Let him **c** for the elders of
1Pe 1:17 if you **c** on the Father, who
3Jn 10 I will **c** to mind his deeds
Rev 2:24 of Satan, as they **c** them, I

CALLED (*see* CALL)
Gen 1: 5 God **c** the light Day, and the
Gen 1: 5 and the darkness He **c** Night
Gen 1: 8 God **c** the firmament Heaven
Gen 1:10 God **c** the dry land Earth, and
Gen 1:10 of the waters He **c** Seas
Gen 2:19 whatever Adam **c** each living
Gen 2:23 she shall be **c** Woman, because
Gen 3: 9 Then the LORD God **c** to Adam
Gen 3:20 Adam **c** his wife's name Eve,
Gen 4:17 **c** the name of the city after
Gen 5: 2 **c** them Mankind in the day
Gen 5:29 he **c** his name Noah, saying,
Gen 11: 9 Therefore its name is **c** Babel
Gen 12: 8 **c** on the name of the LORD
Gen 12:18 And Pharaoh **c** Abram and said
Gen 13: 4 there Abram **c** on the name of
Gen 16:13 Then she **c** the name of the
Gen 16:14 the well was **c** Beer Lahai Roi
Gen 17: 5 shall your name be **c** Abram
Gen 19: 5 they **c** to Lot and said to him,
Gen 19:22 name of the city was **c** Zoar
Gen 19:37 bore a son and **c** his name Moab
Gen 19:38 a son and **c** his name Ben-Ammi
Gen 20: 8 **c** all his servants, and told
Gen 20: 9 And Abimelech **c** Abraham and
Gen 21: 3 Abraham **c** the name of his son
Gen 21:12 in Isaac your seed shall be **c**
Gen 21:17 Then the angel of God **c** to
Gen 21:31 Therefore he **c** that place
Gen 21:33 there **c** on the name of the
Gen 22:11 the LORD **c** to him from heaven
Gen 22:14 Abraham **c** the name of the
Gen 22:15 **c** to Abraham a second time
Gen 24:58 Then they **c** Rebekah and said
Gen 25:25 so they **c** his name Esau
Gen 25:26 so his name was **c** Jacob
Gen 25:30 Therefore his name was **c** Edom
Gen 26: 9 Then Abimelech **c** Isaac and
Gen 26:18 He **c** them by the names which
Gen 26:18 which his father had **c** them
Gen 26:20 So he **c** the name of the
Gen 26:21 So he **c** its name Sitnah
Gen 26:22 So he **c** its name Rehoboth,
Gen 26:25 **c** on the name of the LORD, and
Gen 26:33 So he **c** it Shebah
Gen 27: 1 that he **c** Esau his older son
Gen 27:42 **c** Jacob her younger son, and
Gen 28: 1 Then Isaac **c** Jacob and blessed
Gen 28:19 he **c** the name of that place
Gen 29:32 son, and she **c** his name Reuben
Gen 29:33 And she **c** his name Simeon
Gen 29:34 Therefore his name was **c** Levi
Gen 29:35 she **c** his name Judah
Gen 30: 6 Therefore she **c** his name Dan
Gen 30: 8 So she **c** his name Naphtali
Gen 30:11 So she **c** his name Gad
Gen 30:13 So she **c** his name Asher
Gen 30:18 So she **c** his name Issachar
Gen 30:20 So she **c** his name Zebulun
Gen 30:21 daughter, and **c** her name Dinah
Gen 30:24 So she **c** his name Joseph, and
Gen 31: 4 **c** Rachel and Leah to the field
Gen 31:47 Laban **c** it Jegar Sahadutha,
Gen 31:47 but Jacob **c** it Galeed
Gen 31:48 its name was **c** Galeed,
Gen 31:54 **c** his brethren to eat bread
Gen 32: 2 he **c** the name of that place
Gen 32:28 shall no longer be **c** Jacob
Gen 32:30 Jacob **c** the name of the place
Gen 33:17 of the place is **c** Succoth
Gen 33:20 there and **c** it El Elohe Israel
Gen 35: 7 and **c** the place El Bethel,
Gen 35: 8 of it was **c** Allon Bachuth
Gen 35:10 shall not be **c** Jacob anymore
Gen 35:10 So He **c** his name Israel
Gen 35:15 Jacob **c** the name of the place
Gen 35:18 that she **c** his name Ben-Oni
Gen 35:18 but his father **c** him Benjamin
Gen 38: 3 a son, and he **c** his name Er
Gen 38: 4 a son, and she **c** his name Onan
Gen 38: 5 a son, and **c** his name Shelah
Gen 38:29 his name was **c** Perez
Gen 38:30 And his name was **c** Zerah
Gen 39:14 that she **c** to the men of her
Gen 41: 8 **c** for all the magicians of
Gen 41:14 **c** Joseph, and they brought him
Gen 41:45 And Pharaoh **c** Joseph's name
Gen 41:51 Joseph **c** the name of the
Gen 41:52 of the second he **c** Ephraim
Gen 47:29 he **c** his son Joseph and said
Gen 48: 6 and will be **c** by the name of
Gen 49: 1 Jacob **c** his sons and said,
Gen 50:11 its name was **c** Abel Mizraim
Ex 1:18 of Egypt **c** for the midwives
Ex 2: 8 went and **c** the child's mother
Ex 2:10 So she **c** his name Moses,
Ex 2:22 son, and he **c** his name Gershom
Ex 3: 4 God **c** to him from the midst
Ex 7:11 Pharaoh also **c** the wise men
Ex 8: 8 Then Pharaoh **c** for Moses and
Ex 8:25 Then Pharaoh **c** for Moses and
Ex 9:27 **c** for Moses and Aaron, and said
Ex 10:16 Then Pharaoh **c** for Moses and
Ex 10:24 Then Pharaoh **c** to Moses and
Ex 12:21 Then Moses **c** for all the
Ex 12:31 Then he **c** for Moses and Aaron
Ex 15:23 the name of it was **c** Marah
Ex 16:31 of Israel **c** its name Manna
Ex 17: 7 So he **c** the name of the place
Ex 17:15 built an altar and **c** its name,
Ex 19: 3 the LORD **c** to him from the
Ex 19: 7 and **c** for the elders of the
Ex 19:20 the LORD **c** Moses to the top
Ex 24:16 on the seventh day He **c** to
Ex 31: 2 I have **c** by name Bezaleel the
Ex 33: 7 and **c** it the tabernacle of
Ex 34:31 Then Moses **c** to them, and
Ex 35:30 See, the LORD has **c** by name
Ex 36: 2 Then Moses **c** Bezaleel and
Lev 1: 1 Now the LORD **c** to Moses, and
Lev 9: 1 eighth day that Moses **c** Aaron
Lev 10: 4 Moses **c** Mishael and Elzaphan,
Num 11: 3 So he **c** the name of the place
Num 11:34 So he **c** the name of that
Num 12: 5 and **c** Aaron and Miriam
Num 13:16 Moses **c** Hoshea the son of Nun
Num 13:24 The place was **c** the Valley of
Num 21: 3 of that place was **c** Hormah
Num 24:10 I **c** you to curse my enemies,
Num 32:41 towns, and **c** them Havoth Jair
Num 32:42 he **c** it Nobah, after his own
Deut 3:13 was **c** the land of the giants
Deut 3:14 **c** Bashan after his own name,
Deut 5: 1 Moses **c** all Israel, and said
Deut 15: 2 because it is **c** the LORD's
Deut 25:10 his name shall be **c** in Israel
Deut 28:10 shall see that you are **c** by
Deut 29: 2 Now Moses **c** all Israel and
Deut 31: 7 Then Moses **c** Joshua and said
Josh 4: 4 Then Joshua **c** the twelve men
Josh 5: 9 place is **c** Gilgal to this day
Josh 6: 6 the son of Nun **c** the priests
Josh 7:26 **c** the Valley of Achor to this
Josh 8:16 **c** together to pursue them
Josh 9:22 Then Joshua **c** for them, and he
Josh 10:24 that Joshua **c** for all the men
Josh 19:47 They **c** Leshem, Dan, after the
Josh 22: 1 Then Joshua **c** the Reubenites,
Josh 22:34 children of Gad **c** the altar
Josh 23: 2 Joshua **c** for all Israel, for
Josh 24: 1 **c** for the elders of Israel,
Josh 24: 9 **c** Balaam the son of Beor to
Judg 1:17 name of the city was **c** Hormah
Judg 1:26 **c** its name Luz, which is its
Judg 2: 5 Then they **c** the name of that
Judg 4: 6 and **c** for Barak the son of
Judg 4:10 Barak **c** Zebulun and Naphtali
Judg 6:24 **c** it the-LORD-Shalom
Judg 6:32 that day he **c** him Jerubbaal

Judg 8:31 whose name he **c** Abimelech
Judg 9:54 Then he **c** quickly to the
Judg 10: 4 had thirty towns, which are **c**
Judg 12: 2 and when I **c** you, you did not
Judg 13:24 a son and **c** his name Samson
Judg 15:17 and **c** that place Ramath Lehi
Judg 15:19 Therefore he **c** its name
Judg 16:18 and **c** for the lords of the
Judg 16:19 **c** for a man and had him shave
Judg 16:25 So they **c** for Samson from
Judg 16:28 Then Samson **c** to the LORD
Judg 18:23 they **c** out to the children of
Judg 18:29 they **c** the name of the city
Ruth 4:17 And they **c** his name Obed
1Sa 1:20 **c** his name Samuel, saying,
1Sa 3: 4 that the LORD **c** Samuel
1Sa 3: 5 Here I am, for you **c** me
1Sa 3: 6 And the LORD **c** yet again,
1Sa 3: 6 Here I am, for you **c** me
1Sa 3: 8 the LORD **c** Samuel again the
1Sa 3: 8 that the LORD had **c** the boy
1Sa 3:10 stood and **c** as at other times,
1Sa 3:16 Then Eli **c** Samuel and said
1Sa 6: 2 Philistines **c** for the priests
1Sa 7:12 **c** its name Ebenezer, saying,
1Sa 9: 9 for he who is now **c** a prophet
1Sa 9: 9 prophet was formerly **c** a seer
1Sa 9:26 of the day that Samuel **c** to
1Sa 10:17 Then Samuel **c** the people
1Sa 12:18 So Samuel **c** to the LORD, and
1Sa 13: 4 the people were **c** together to
1Sa 14:12 of the garrison **c** to Jonathan
1Sa 14:17 And when they had **c** the roll
1Sa 16: 8 So Jesse **c** Abinadab, and made
1Sa 19: 7 Then Jonathan **c** David, and
1Sa 23: 8 Then Saul **c** all the people
1Sa 23:28 so they **c** that place the Rock
1Sa 24: 8 and **c** out to Saul, saying,
1Sa 26:14 David **c** out to the people and
1Sa 28:15 Therefore I have **c** you, that
1Sa 29: 6 Then Achish **c** David and said
2Sa 1: 7 him, he saw me and **c** to me
2Sa 1:15 Then David **c** one of the young
2Sa 2:16 Therefore that place was **c**
2Sa 2:26 Then Abner **c** to Joab and said,
2Sa 5: 9 and **c** it the City of David
2Sa 5:20 Therefore he **c** the name of
2Sa 6: 2 whose name is **c** by the Name
2Sa 6: 8 he **c** the name of the place
2Sa 9: 2 when they had **c** him to David
2Sa 9: 9 And the king **c** to Ziba, Saul's
2Sa 11:13 Now when David **c** him, he ate
2Sa 12:24 son, and he **c** his name Solomon
2Sa 12:25 so he **c** his name Jedidiah,
2Sa 12:28 city and it be **c** after my name
2Sa 13:17 Then he **c** his servant who
2Sa 14:33 And when he had **c** for Absalom
2Sa 18:18 He **c** the pillar after his
2Sa 18:18 to this day it is **c** Absalom's
2Sa 18:26 and the watchman **c** to the
2Sa 18:28 And Ahimaaz **c** out and said to
2Sa 21: 2 So the king **c** the Gibeonites
2Sa 22: 7 my distress I **c** upon the LORD
2Sa 23: 8 He was **c** Adino the Eznite,
1Ki 2:36 **c** for Shimei, and said to him,
1Ki 2:42 **c** for Shimei, and said to him,
1Ki 7:21 **c** its name Jachin, and he set
1Ki 7:21 the left and **c** its name Boaz
1Ki 8:43 have built is **c** by Your name
1Ki 9:13 he **c** them the land of Cabul,
1Ki 12: 3 that they sent and **c** him
1Ki 12:20 **c** him to the congregation, and
1Ki 16:24 **c** the name of the city which
1Ki 17:10 And he **c** to her and said,
1Ki 17:11 get it, he **c** to her and said,
1Ki 18: 3 And Ahab had **c** Obadiah, who
1Ki 18:26 **c** on the name of Baal from
1Ki 20: 7 Then the king of Israel **c** all
1Ki 22: 9 king of Israel **c** an officer
2Ki 3:10 For the LORD has **c** these
2Ki 3:13 No, for the LORD has **c** these
2Ki 4:12 When he had **c** her, she
2Ki 4:15 When he had **c** her, she
2Ki 4:22 Then she **c** to her husband, and
2Ki 4:36 And he **c** Gehazi and said,
2Ki 4:36 So he **c** her
2Ki 6:11 he **c** his servants and said to
2Ki 7:10 **c** to the gatekeepers of the
2Ki 7:11 And the gatekeepers **c** out, and
2Ki 8: 1 the LORD has **c** for a famine
2Ki 9: 1 Elisha the prophet **c** one of
2Ki 12: 7 So King Jehoash **c** Jehoiada
2Ki 14: 7 **c** its name Joktheel to this
2Ki 18: 4 to it, and **c** it Nehushtan
2Ki 18:18 when they had **c** to the king
2Ki 18:28 **c** out with a loud voice in
1Ch 4: 9 his mother **c** his name Jabez,
1Ch 4:10 Jabez **c** on the God of Israel
1Ch 6:65 which are **c** by their names
1Ch 7:16 son, and she **c** his name Peresh
1Ch 7:23 he **c** his name Beriah, because
1Ch 11: 7 therefore they **c** it the City
1Ch 13:11 is **c** Perez Uzza to this day
1Ch 14:11 Therefore they **c** the name
1Ch 15:11 David **c** for Zadok and Abiathar
1Ch 21:26 offerings, and **c** on the LORD
1Ch 22: 6 Then he **c** for his son Solomon
2Ch 3:17 he **c** the name of the one on
2Ch 6:33 have built is **c** by Your name
2Ch 7:14 if My people who are **c** by My
2Ch 10: 3 they sent for him and **c** him
2Ch 18: 8 Israel **c** one of his officers
2Ch 20:26 was **c** The Valley of Berachah
2Ch 24: 6 So the king **c** Jehoiada the
2Ch 32:18 Then they **c** out with a loud
Ezra 2:61 and was **c** by their name
Neh 5: 7 So I **c** a great assembly
Neh 5:12 Then I **c** the priests, and
Neh 7:63 and was **c** by their name
Esth 2:14 in her and **c** for her by name
Esth 3:12 the king's scribes were **c** on
Esth 4: 5 Then Esther **c** Hathach, one of
Esth 4:11 the king, who has not been **c**
Esth 4:11 **c** to go in to the king these
Esth 5:10 **c** for his friends and his wife
Esth 8: 9 scribes were **c** at that time
Esth 9:26 So they **c** these days Purim,
Job 9:16 If I **c** and He answered me, I
Job 12: 4 who **c** on God, and He answered
Job 42:14 he **c** the name of the first
Ps 17: 6 I have **c** upon You, for You
Ps 18: 6 my distress I **c** upon the LORD
Ps 31:17 O LORD, for I have **c** upon You
Ps 50: 1 **c** the earth From the rising
Ps 81: 7 You **c** in trouble, and I
Ps 88: 9 LORD, I have **c** daily upon You
Ps 99: 6 those who **c** upon His name
Ps 99: 6 They **c** upon the LORD, and He
Ps 105:16 Moreover He **c** for a famine in
Ps 116: 4 Then I **c** upon the name of the
Ps 118: 5 I **c** on the LORD in distress
Prov 1:24 Because I have **c** and you
Prov 16:21 in heart will be **c** prudent
Prov 24: 8 do evil will be **c** a schemer
Song 5: 6 I **c** him, but he gave me no
Song 6: 9 **c** her blessed, the queens and
Is 1:26 Afterward you shall be **c** the
Is 4: 1 only let us be **c** by your name
Is 4: 3 in Jerusalem will be **c** holy
Is 9: 6 His name will be **c** Wonderful
Is 13: 3 I have also **c** My mighty ones
Is 19:18 one will be **c** the City of
Is 22:12 GOD of hosts **c** for weeping
Is 30: 7 Therefore I have **c** her
Is 32: 5 will no longer be **c** generous
Is 35: 8 it shall be **c** the Highway of
Is 36:13 **c** out with a loud voice in
Is 41: 2 **c** him to His feet
Is 41: 9 **c** from its farthest regions,
Is 42: 6 have **c** You in righteousness,
Is 43: 1 I have **c** you by your name
Is 43: 7 everyone who is **c** by My name
Is 43:22 But you have not **c** upon Me
Is 45: 4 I have even **c** you by your
Is 47: 1 you shall no more be **c** tender
Is 47: 5 be **c** the Lady of Kingdoms
Is 48: 1 who are **c** by the name of
Is 48: 8 were **c** a transgressor from
Is 48:12 Me, O Jacob, and Israel, My **c**
Is 48:15 yes, I have **c** him, I have
Is 49: 1 The LORD has **c** Me from the
Is 50: 2 Why, when I **c**, was there none
Is 51: 2 for I **c** him alone, and blessed
Is 54: 5 He is **c** the God of the whole
Is 54: 6 For the LORD has **c** you like a
Is 56: 7 for My house shall be **c** a
Is 58:12 you shall be **c** the Repairer
Is 61: 3 that they may be **c** trees of
Is 62: 2 You shall be **c** by a new name,
Is 62: 4 But you shall be **c** Hephzibah
Is 62:12 and you shall be **c** Sought Out
Is 63:19 who were never **c** by Your name
Is 65: 1 that was not **c** by My name
Is 65:12 because, when I **c**, you did
Is 66: 4 Because, when I **c**, no one
Jer 3:17 be **c** The Throne of the LORD
Jer 7:10 house which is **c** by My name
Jer 7:11 which is **c** by My name, become
Jer 7:13 and I **c** you, but you did not
Jer 7:14 house which is **c** by My name
Jer 7:30 house which is **c** by My name
Jer 7:32 it will no more be **c** Tophet
Jer 11:16 The LORD **c** your name, green
Jer 12: 6 they have **c** a multitude after
Jer 14: 9 and we are **c** by Your name
Jer 15:16 for I am **c** by Your name, O
Jer 19: 6 **c** Tophet or the Valley of the
Jer 20: 3 The LORD has not **c** your name
Jer 23: 6 name by which He will be **c**
Jer 25:29 city which is **c** by My name
Jer 30:17 LORD, "Because they **c** you an
Jer 32:34 house which is **c** by My name
Jer 33:16 name by which she will be **c**
Jer 34:15 house which is **c** by My name
Jer 35:17 I have **c** to them but they
Jer 36: 4 Then Jeremiah **c** Baruch the
Jer 42: 8 Then he **c** Johanan the son of
Lam 1:15 He has **c** an assembly against
Lam 1:19 I **c** for my lovers, but they
Lam 2:15 Is this the city that is **c**
Lam 3:55 I **c** on Your name, O LORD,
Lam 3:57 near on the day I **c** on You
Ezek 9: 1 Then He **c** out in my hearing
Ezek 9: 3 He **c** to the man clothed with
Ezek 10:13 they were **c** in my hearing,
Ezek 20:29 So its name is **c** Bamah to
Ezek 23:21 Thus you **c** to remembrance the
Dan 5:12 now let Daniel be **c**, and he
Dan 8:16 the banks of the Ulai, who **c**
Dan 9:18 city which is **c** by Your name
Dan 9:19 people are **c** by Your name
Dan 10: 1 whose name was **c** Belteshazzar
Hos 11: 1 and out of Egypt I **c** My son
Hos 11: 2 As they **c** them
Amos 7: 4 the Lord GOD **c** for conflict
Amos 9:12 Gentiles who are **c** by My name
Hag 1:11 For I **c** for a drought on the
Zech 6: 8 He **c** to me, and spoke to me,
Zech 7:13 would not hear, so they **c** out
Zech 8: 3 shall be **c** the City of Truth
Zech 11: 7 the one I **c** Beauty, and the
Zech 11: 7 and the other I **c** Bonds
Mal 1: 4 they shall be **c** the Territory
Matt 1:16 born Jesus who is **c** Christ
Matt 1:25 And he **c** His name JESUS
Matt 2: 7 had secretly **c** the wise men
Matt 2:15 Out of Egypt I **c** My Son
Matt 2:23 and dwelt in a city **c** Nazareth
Matt 2:23 He shall be **c** a Nazarene
Matt 4:18 two brothers, Simon **c** Peter
Matt 4:21 And He **c** them,
Matt 5: 9 they shall be **c** sons of God
Matt 5:19 so, shall be **c** least in the
Matt 5:19 he shall be **c** great in the
Matt 10: 1 And when He had **c** His twelve
Matt 10: 2 first, Simon, who is **c** Peter
Matt 10:25 If they have **c** the master of
Matt 13:55 Is not His mother **c** Mary
Matt 15:10 Then He **c** the multitude and
Matt 15:32 Then Jesus **c** His disciples to
Matt 18: 2 Jesus **c** a little child to Him
Matt 18:32 master, after he had **c** him
Matt 20:16 For many are **c**, but few
Matt 20:25 But Jesus **c** them to Himself
Matt 20:32 still and **c** them, and said,
Matt 21:13 shall be **c** a house of prayer
Matt 22:14 For many are **c**, but few are
Matt 23: 7 to be **c** by men, 'Rabbi, Rabbi
Matt 23: 8 But you, do not be **c** 'Rabbi'
Matt 23:10 And do not be **c** teachers
Matt 25:14 who **c** his own servants and
Matt 26: 3 priest, who was **c** Caiaphas,
Matt 26:14 **c** Judas Iscariot, went to the
Matt 26:36 them to a place **c** Gethsemane
Matt 27: 8 that field has been **c** the
Matt 27:16 notorious prisoner **c** Barabbas
Matt 27:17 or Jesus who is **c** Christ
Matt 27:22 do with Jesus who is **c** Christ
Matt 27:33 come to a place **c** Golgotha
Mark 1:20 And immediately He **c** them,

Mark 3:13 c to Him those He Himself
Mark 3:23 So He c them to Him and said
Mark 6: 7 He c the twelve to Him, and
Mark 7:14 And when He had c all the
Mark 8: 1 Jesus c His disciples to Him
Mark 8:34 when He had c the people to
Mark 9:35 c the twelve, and said to them
Mark 10:42 But Jesus c them to Himself
Mark 10:49 and commanded him to be c
Mark 10:49 Then they c the blind man,
Mark 11:17 My house shall be c a house
Mark 12:43 So He c His disciples to Him
Mark 14:72 Peter c to mind the word that
Mark 15:16 into the hall c Praetorium
Mark 15:16 they c together the whole
Luke 1:32 and will be c the Son of the
Luke 1:35 born will be c the Son of God
Luke 1:36 for her who was c barren
Luke 1:59 they would have c him by the
Luke 1:60 he shall be c John
Luke 1:61 who is c by this name
Luke 1:62 what he would have him c
Luke 1:76 will be c the prophet of the
Luke 2: 4 which is c Bethlehem, because
Luke 2:21 Child, His name was c JESUS
Luke 2:23 be c holy to the LORD"),
Luke 6:13 He c His disciples to Him
Luke 6:15 and Simon c the Zealot
Luke 7:11 He went into a city c Nain
Luke 8: 2 Mary c Magdalene, out of whom
Luke 8:54 took her by the hand and c
Luke 9: 1 Then He c His twelve
Luke 9:10 to the city c Bethsaida
Luke 10:39 And she had a sister c Mary
Luke 13:12 He c her to Him and said to
Luke 15:19 worthy to be c your son
Luke 15:21 worthy to be c your son
Luke 15:26 So he c one of the servants
Luke 16: 2 So he c him and said to him
Luke 16: 5 So he c every one of his
Luke 18:16 But Jesus c them to Him and
Luke 19:13 So he c ten of his servants,
Luke 19:15 to be c to him, that he might
Luke 19:29 at the mountain c Olivet
Luke 19:39 c to Him from the crowd
Luke 20:37 when he c the Lord the God
Luke 21:37 on the mountain c Olivet
Luke 22: 1 near, which is c Passover
Luke 22:25 over them are c benefactors
Luke 22:47 and he who was c Judas, one of
Luke 23:13 when he had c together the
Luke 23:20 Jesus, again c out to them
Luke 23:33 come to the place c Calvary
Luke 24:13 day to a village c Emmaus
John 1:42 You shall be c Cephas"
John 1:48 Before Philip c you, when you
John 2: 9 of the feast c the bridegroom
John 4: 5 of Samaria which is c Sychar
John 4:25 is coming" (who is c Christ)
John 5: 2 a pool, which is c in Hebrew,
John 9:11 A Man c Jesus made clay and
John 9:18 until they c the parents of
John 9:24 So they again c the man who
John 10:35 If He c them gods, to whom
John 11:16 who is c Didymus, said to his
John 11:28 secretly c Mary her sister,
John 11:54 to a city c Ephraim, and
John 12:17 He c Lazarus out of his tomb
John 15:15 but I have c you friends, for
John 18:33 c Jesus, and said to Him,
John 19:13 place that is c The Pavement
John 19:17 went out to a place c the
John 19:17 Skull, which is c in Hebrew,
John 20:24 c Didymus, one of the twelve,
John 21: 2 Thomas c Didymus, Nathanael
Acts 1:12 from the Mount c Olivet,
Acts 1:19 so that field is c in their
Acts 1:23 Joseph c Barsabas, who was
Acts 3: 2 temple which is c Beautiful
Acts 3:11 porch which is c Solomon's
Acts 4:18 And they c them and
Acts 5:21 c the council together, with
Acts 5:40 and when they had c for the
Acts 6: 9 is c the Synagogue of the
Acts 7:14 c his father Jacob and all his
Acts 8: 9 was a certain man c Simon
Acts 9:11 go to the street c Straight
Acts 9:11 for one c Saul of Tarsus, for
Acts 9:21 c on this name in Jerusalem
Acts 9:41 and when he had c the saints
Acts 10: 1 man in Caesarea c Cornelius
Acts 10: 1 was c the Italian Regiment
Acts 10: 7 Cornelius c two of his
Acts 10:18 And they c and asked whether
Acts 10:24 had c together his relatives
Acts 11:26 first c Christians in Antioch
Acts 13: 1 Simeon who was c Niger,
Acts 13: 2 work to which I have c them
Acts 13: 7 This man c for Barnabas and
Acts 13: 9 Then Saul, who also is c Paul
Acts 14:12 And Barnabas they c Zeus, and
Acts 15:17 Gentiles who are c by My name
Acts 15:37 to take with them John c Mark
Acts 16:10 that the Lord had c us to
Acts 16:28 But Paul c with a loud voice,
Acts 16:29 Then he c for a light, ran in
Acts 19:25 He c them together with the
Acts 19:40 c in question for today's
Acts 20: 1 Paul c the disciples to him,
Acts 20:17 and c for the elders of the
Acts 23:17 Then Paul c one of the
Acts 23:18 Paul the prisoner c me to him
Acts 23:23 And he c for two centurions,
Acts 24: 2 And when he was c upon,
Acts 27: 8 came to a place c Fair Havens
Acts 27:14 head wind arose, c Euroclydon
Acts 27:16 shelter of an island c Clauda
Acts 28: 1 that the island was c Malta
Acts 28:17 c the leaders of the Jews
Acts 28:20 therefore I have c for you
Rom 1: 1 c to be an apostle, separated
Rom 1: 6 are the c of Jesus Christ
Rom 1: 7 of God, c to be saints
Rom 2:17 Indeed you are c a Jew, and
Rom 7: 3 she will be c an adulteress
Rom 8:28 God, to those who are the c
Rom 8:30 predestined, these He also c
Rom 8:30 whom He c, these He also
Rom 9: 7 In Isaac your seed shall be c
Rom 9:24 even us whom He c, not of the
Rom 9:26 there they will be c sons of
1Co 1: 1 c to be an apostle of Jesus
1Co 1: 2 c to be saints, with all who
1Co 1: 9 by whom you were c into the
1Co 1:24 but to those who are c, both
1Co 1:26 mighty, not many noble, are c
1Co 7:15 But God has c us to peace
1Co 7:17 as the Lord has c each one
1Co 7:18 Was anyone c while
1Co 7:18 Was anyone c while
1Co 7:20 calling in which he was c
1Co 7:21 Were you c while a slave
1Co 7:22 For he who is c in the Lord
1Co 7:22 Likewise he who is c while
1Co 7:24 calling in which he was c
1Co 15: 9 not worthy to be c an apostle
Gal 1: 6 away so soon from Him who c
Gal 1:15 and c me through His grace,
Gal 5:13 have been c to liberty
Eph 2:11 who are c Uncircumcision by
Eph 2:11 is c the Circumcision made in
Eph 4: 1 calling with which you were c
Eph 4: 4 just as you were c in one
Col 3:15 also you were c in one body
Col 4:11 and Jesus who is c Justus
2Th 2: 4 is c God or that is worshiped
2Th 2:14 to which He c you by our
1Ti 6:12 to which you were also c
1Ti 6:20 what is falsely c knowledge
2Ti 1: 9 c us with a holy calling, not
Heb 3:13 another daily, while it is c
Heb 5: 4 but he who is c by God, just
Heb 5:10 c by God as High Priest
Heb 7:11 not be c according to the
Heb 9: 2 which is c the sanctuary
Heb 9: 3 which is c the Holiest of All
Heb 9:15 that those who are c may
Heb 11: 8 was c to go out to the place
Heb 11:15 truly if they had c to mind
Heb 11:16 not ashamed to be c their God
Heb 11:18 In Isaac your seed shall be c
Heb 11:24 refused to be c the son of
Jas 2: 7 noble name by which you are c
Jas 2:23 he was c the friend of God
1Pe 1:15 but as He who c you is holy
1Pe 2: 9 the praises of Him who c you
1Pe 2:21 For to this you were c,
1Pe 3: 9 that you were c to this, that
1Pe 5:10 who c us to His eternal glory
2Pe 1: 3 of Him who c us by glory and
1Jn 3: 1 should be c children of God
Jude 1 of James, To those who are c
Rev 1: 9 was on the island that is c
Rev 11: 8 which spiritually is c Sodom
Rev 12: 9 c the Devil and Satan, who
Rev 16:16 to the place c in Hebrew,
Rev 17:14 those who are with Him are c
Rev 19: 9 c to the marriage supper of
Rev 19:11 who sat on him was c Faithful
Rev 19:13 His name is c The Word of God

CALLING (*see* CALL)
Num 10: 2 use them for c the assembly
Num 22:37 send to you, c for you
Judg 8: 1 c us when you went to fight
1Sa 26:14 are you, c out to the king
Is 1:13 and the c of assemblies
Is 41: 4 c the generations from the
Is 46:11 c a bird of prey from the
Jer 1:15 I am c all the families of
Ezek 23:19 c to remembrance the days of
Matt 11:16 and c to their companions,
Matt 27:47 This Man is c for Elijah
Mark 3:31 they sent to Him, c Him
Mark 10:49 Rise, He is c you
Mark 15:35 Look, He is c for Elijah
Luke 7:19 c two of his disciples to him
Luke 7:32 and c to one another, saying
John 11:28 has come and is c for you
Acts 7:59 Stephen as he was c on God
Acts 22:16 c on the name of the Lord
Rom 11:29 the c of God are irrevocable
1Co 1:26 For you see your c, brethren,
1Co 7:20 same c in which he was called
1Co 7:24 that c in which he was called
Eph 1:18 what is the hope of His c
Eph 4: 1 have a walk worthy of the c
Eph 4: 4 called in one hope of your c
2Th 1:11 count you worthy of this c
2Ti 1: 9 us and called us with a holy c
Heb 3: 1 partakers of the heavenly c
1Pe 3: 6 c him lord, whose daughters
2Pe 1:10 more diligent to make your c

CALLS (*see* CALL)
Gen 46:33 shall be, when Pharaoh c you
Deut 18:11 or one who c up the dead
1Sa 3: 9 and it shall be, if He c you
1Ki 8:43 which the foreigner c to You
2Ch 6:33 which the foreigner c to You
Ps 42: 7 Deep c unto deep at the noise
Ps 147: 4 He c them all by name
Prov 1:20 Wisdom c aloud outside
Prov 18: 6 and his mouth c for blows
Is 21:11 He c to me out of Seir,
Is 40:26 He c them all by name, by the
Is 59: 4 No one c for justice, nor
Is 64: 7 is no one who c on Your name
Hos 7: 7 none among them who c upon
Joel 2:32 c on the name of the LORD
Joel 2:32 the remnant whom the LORD c
Amos 5: 8 He c for the waters of the
Amos 9: 6 who c for the waters of the
Matt 22:45 If David then c Him 'Lord
Mark 12:37 David himself c Him 'Lord'
Luke 15: 6 he c together his friends and
Luke 15: 9 it, she c her friends and
Luke 20:44 David therefore c Him 'Lord'
John 10: 3 he c his own sheep by name and
Acts 2:21 c on the name of the LORD
Rom 4:17 c those things which do not
Rom 9:11 of works but of Him who c)
Rom 10:13 whoever c upon the name of
1Co 12: 3 of God c Jesus accursed, and
Gal 5: 8 not come from Him who c you
1Th 2:12 c you into His own kingdom
1Th 5:24 He who c you is faithful, who
Rev 2:20 who c herself a prophetess,

CALM (*see* CALMED, CALMS)
Prov 17:27 is of a c spirit
Jon 1:11 that the sea may be c for us
Jon 1:12 the sea will become c for you
Matt 8:26 And there was a great c
Mark 4:39 ceased and there was a great c
Luke 8:24 they ceased, and there was a c

CALMED (*see* CALM)
Ps 131: 2 Surely I have c and quieted my

1Ch 14:15 the **c** of the Philistines
2Ch 22: 1 **c** had killed all the older
2Ch 31: 2 gates of the **c** of the LORD
2Ch 32:21 captain in the **c** of the king
Ps 78:28 fall in the midst of their **c**
Ps 106:16 they envied Moses in the **c**
Song 6:13 the dance of the double **c**
Is 37:36 and killed in the **c** of the
Joel 2:11 army, for His **c** is very great
Nah 3:17 which **c** in the hedges on a
Zech 9: 8 I will **c** around My house
Heb 13:11 sin, are burned outside the **c**
Heb 13:13 forth to Him, outside the **c**
Rev 20: 9 the **c** of the saints and the

CAMPED (*see* CAMP)
Ex 13:20 **c** in Etham at the edge of the
Ex 15:27 so they **c** there by the waters
Ex 17: 1 of the LORD, and **c** in Rephidim
Ex 19: 2 Sinai, and **c** in the wilderness
Ex 19: 2 So Israel **c** there before the
Num 2:34 so they **c** by their standards
Num 11:35 to Hazeroth, and **c** at Hazeroth
Num 12:16 **c** in the Wilderness of Paran
Num 21:10 Israel moved on and **c** in Oboth
Num 21:11 and **c** at Ije Abarim, in the
Num 21:12 and **c** in the Valley of Zered
Num 21:13 **c** on the other side of the
Num 22: 1 **c** in the plains of Moab on
Num 33: 5 from Rameses and **c** at Succoth
Num 33: 6 **c** at Etham, which is on the
Num 33: 7 and they **c** near Migdol
Num 33: 8 of Etham, and **c** at Marah
Num 33: 9 so they **c** there
Num 33:10 from Elim and **c** by the Red Sea
Num 33:11 **c** in the Wilderness of Sin
Num 33:12 of Sin and **c** at Dophkah
Num 33:13 from Dophkah and **c** at Alush
Num 33:14 **c** at Rephidim, where there
Num 33:15 **c** in the Wilderness of Sinai
Num 33:16 and **c** at Kibroth Hattaavah
Num 33:17 Hattaavah and **c** at Hazeroth
Num 33:18 from Hazeroth and **c** at Rithmah
Num 33:19 Rithmah and **c** at Rimmon Perez
Num 33:20 Rimmon Perez and **c** at Libnah
Num 33:21 from Libnah and **c** at Rissah
Num 33:22 Rissah and **c** at Kehelathah
Num 33:23 and **c** at Mount Shepher
Num 33:24 Mount Shepher and **c** at
Num 33:25 Haradah and **c** at Makheloth
Num 33:26 from Makheloth and **c** at Tahath
Num 33:27 from Tahath and **c** at Terah
Num 33:28 from Terah and **c** at Mithkah
Num 33:29 Mithkah and **c** at Hashmonah
Num 33:30 Hashmonah and **c** at Moseroth
Num 33:31 Moseroth and **c** at Bene Jaakan
Num 33:32 Jaakan and **c** at Hor Hagidgad
Num 33:33 Hagidgad and **c** at Jotbathah
Num 33:34 Jotbathah and **c** at Abronah
Num 33:35 Abronah and **c** at Ezion Geber
Num 33:36 **c** in the Wilderness of Zin,
Num 33:37 and **c** at Mount Hor, on the
Num 33:41 Mount Hor and **c** at Zalmonah
Num 33:42 from Zalmonah and **c** at Punon
Num 33:43 from Punon and **c** at Oboth
Num 33:44 and **c** at Ije Abarim, at the
Num 33:45 from Ijim and **c** at Dibon Gad
Num 33:46 Gad and **c** at Almon Diblathaim
Num 33:47 **c** in the mountains of Abarim,
Num 33:48 **c** in the plains of Moab by
Num 33:49 They **c** by the Jordan, from
Josh 4:19 they **c** in Gilgal on the east
Josh 5:10 of Israel **c** in Gilgal, and
Josh 8:11 **c** on the north side of Ai
Josh 10: 5 **c** before Gibeon and made war
Josh 11: 5 **c** together at the waters of
2Sa 24: 5 **c** in Aroer, on the right side
Ezra 8:15 and we **c** there three days

CAMPING (*see* CAMP)
Ex 14: 9 overtook them **c** by the sea

CAMPS (*see* CAMP)
Num 2:17 in the middle of the **c**
Num 5: 3 **c** in the midst of which I
Num 10: 2 the movement of the **c**
Num 10: 5 the **c** that lie on the east
Num 10: 6 then the **c** that lie on the
Num 10:25 the rear guard of all the **c**
Num 13:19 are like **c** or strongholds
1Ch 9:18 been gatekeepers for the **c** of
Ezek 4: 2 set **c** against it also, and
Amos 4:10 I made the stench of your **c**
Zech 14:15 that will be in those **c**

CAN (*see* PREFACE)

CANA
John 2: 1 was a wedding in **C** of Galilee
John 2:11 Jesus did in **C** of Galilee
John 4:46 So Jesus came again to **C** of
John 21: 2 Nathanael of **C** in Galilee

CANAAN (*see* CANAANITE, CANAANITESS)
Gen 9:18 And Ham was the father of **C**
Gen 9:22 And Ham, the father of **C**, saw
Gen 9:25 Cursed be **C**
Gen 9:26 Shem, and may **C** be his servant
Gen 9:27 and may **C** be his servant
Gen 10: 6 were Cush, Mizraim, Put, and **C**
Gen 10:15 **C** begot Sidon his firstborn,
Gen 11:31 to go to the land of **C**
Gen 12: 5 to go to the land of **C**
Gen 12: 5 So they came to the land of **C**
Gen 13:12 Abram dwelt in the land of **C**
Gen 16: 3 ten years in the land of **C**
Gen 17: 8 a stranger, all the land of **C**
Gen 23: 2 is, Hebron) in the land of **C**
Gen 23:19 is, Hebron) in the land of **C**
Gen 28: 1 wife from the daughters of **C**
Gen 28: 6 wife from the daughters of **C**
Gen 28: 8 **C** did not please his father
Gen 31:18 father Isaac in the land of **C**
Gen 33:18 which is in the land of **C**
Gen 35: 6 which is in the land of **C**
Gen 36: 2 wives from the daughters of **C**
Gen 36: 5 born to him in the land of **C**
Gen 36: 6 had gained in the land of **C**
Gen 37: 1 a stranger, in the land of **C**
Gen 42: 5 famine was in the land of **C**
Gen 42: 7 the land of **C** to buy food
Gen 42:13 of one man in the land of **C**
Gen 42:29 their father in the land of **C**
Gen 42:32 this day in the land of **C**
Gen 44: 8 to you from the land of **C** the
Gen 45:17 go to the land of **C**
Gen 45:25 and came to the land of **C** to
Gen 46: 6 had acquired in the land of **C**
Gen 46:12 Onan died in the land of **C**)
Gen 46:31 who were in the land of **C**
Gen 47: 1 have come from the land of **C**
Gen 47: 4 is severe in the land of **C**
Gen 47:13 all the land of **C** languished
Gen 47:14 of Egypt and in the land of **C**
Gen 47:15 of Egypt and in the land of **C**
Gen 48: 3 to me at Luz in the land of **C**
Gen 48: 7 in the land of **C** on the way
Gen 49:30 before Mamre in the land of **C**
Gen 50: 5 for myself in the land of **C**
Gen 50:13 carried him to the land of **C**
Ex 6: 4 to give them the land of **C**
Ex 15:15 of **C** will melt away
Ex 16:35 the border of the land of **C**
Lev 14:34 have come into the land of **C**
Lev 18: 3 the doings of the land of **C**
Lev 25:38 to give you the land of **C**
Num 13: 2 men to spy out the land of **C**
Num 13:17 them to spy out the land of **C**
Num 26:19 and Onan died in the land of **C**
Num 32:30 among you in the land of **C**
Num 32:32 the LORD into the land of **C**
Num 33:40 in the South in the land of **C**
Num 33:51 the Jordan into the land of **C**
Num 34: 2 you come into the land of **C**
Num 34: 2 the land of **C** to its
Num 34:29 of Israel in the land of **C**
Num 35:10 the Jordan into the land of **C**
Num 35:14 appoint in the land of **C**,
Deut 32:49 view the land of **C**, which I
Josh 5:12 of the land of **C** that year
Josh 14: 1 inherited in the land of **C**
Josh 21: 2 at Shiloh in the land of **C**
Josh 22: 9 which is in the land of **C**
Josh 22:10 which is in the land of **C**
Josh 22:11 the frontier of the land of **C**
Josh 22:32 of Gilead to the land of **C**
Josh 24: 3 throughout all the land of **C**
Judg 3: 1 known any of the wars in **C**
Judg 4: 2 the hand of Jabin king of **C**
Judg 4:23 of **C** in the presence of the
Judg 4:24 against Jabin king of **C**,
Judg 4:24 had destroyed Jabin king of **C**
Judg 5:19 kings of **C** fought in Taanach
Judg 21:12 which is in the land of **C**
1Ch 1: 8 were Cush, Mizraim, Put, and **C**
1Ch 1:13 **C** begot Sidon, his firstborn,
1Ch 16:18 of **C** as the allotment of your
Ps 105:11 of **C** As the allotment of your
Ps 106:38 sacrificed to the idols of **C**
Ps 135:11 And all the kingdoms of **C**
Is 19:18 will speak the language of **C**
Is 23:11 **C** to destroy its strongholds
Ezek 16: 3 are from the land of **C**
Zeph 2: 5 the LORD is against you, O **C**
Matt 15:22 a woman of **C** came from that
Acts 7:11 all the land of Egypt and **C**
Acts 13:19 nations in the land of **C**, He

CANAANITE (*see* CANAAN, CANAANITES)
Gen 38: 2 certain **C** whose name was Shua
Gen 46:10 Shaul, the son of a **C** woman
Ex 6:15 and Shaul the son of a **C** woman
Ex 23:28 drive out the Hivite, the **C**
Ex 33: 2 and I will drive out the **C**
Ex 34:11 you the Amorite and the **C** and
Num 21: 1 When the king of Arad, the **C**
Num 33:40 Now the king of Arad, the **C**
Deut 20:17 and the Amorite and the **C** and
Josh 9: 1 Hittite, the Amorite, the **C**
Josh 13: 3 (which is counted as **C**)
Hos 12: 7 A cunning **C**!
Zech 14:21 there shall no longer be a **C**
Matt 10: 4 Simon the **C**, and Judas
Mark 3:18 Thaddaeus, Simon the **C**

CANAANITES (*see* CANAANITE)
Gen 10:18 of the **C** were dispersed
Gen 10:19 the border of the **C** was from
Gen 12: 6 the **C** were then in the land
Gen 13: 7 The **C** and the Perizzites then
Gen 15:21 the Amorites, the **C**, the
Gen 24: 3 from the daughters of the **C**
Gen 24:37 from the daughters of the **C**
Gen 34:30 of the land, among the **C** and
Gen 50:11 of the land, the **C**, saw the
Ex 3: 8 honey, to the place of the **C**
Ex 3:17 of Egypt to the land of the **C**
Ex 13: 5 you into the land of the **C**
Ex 13:11 you into the land of the **C**
Ex 23:23 and the Perizzites and the **C**
Num 13:29 the **C** dwell by the sea and
Num 14:25 the **C** dwell in the valley
Num 14:43 the **C** are there before you,
Num 14:45 and the **C** who dwelt in that
Num 21: 3 Israel and delivered up the **C**
Deut 1: 7 to the land of the **C** and to
Deut 7: 1 and the Amorites and the **C** and
Deut 11:30 sun, in the land of the **C** who
Josh 3:10 out from before you the **C**
Josh 5: 1 of the **C** who were by the sea
Josh 7: 9 For the **C** and all the
Josh 11: 3 to the **C** in the east and in
Josh 12: 8 Hittites, the Amorites, the **C**
Josh 13: 4 south, all the land of the **C**
Josh 16:10 out the **C** who dwelt in Gezer
Josh 16:10 but the **C** dwell among the
Josh 17:12 but the **C** were determined to
Josh 17:13 put the **C** to forced labor
Josh 17:16 all the **C** who dwell in the
Josh 17:18 for you shall drive out the **C**
Josh 24:11 the Perizzites, the **C**, the
Judg 1: 1 the **C** to fight against them
Judg 1: 3 we may fight against the **C**
Judg 1: 4 and the LORD delivered the **C**
Judg 1: 5 and they defeated the **C** and the
Judg 1: 9 down to fight against the **C**
Judg 1:10 the **C** who dwelt in Hebron
Judg 1:17 and they attacked the **C** who
Judg 1:27 for the **C** were determined to
Judg 1:28 they put the **C** under tribute
Judg 1:29 out the **C** who dwelt in Gezer
Judg 1:29 so the **C** dwelt in Gezer among
Judg 1:30 so the **C** dwelt among them, and
Judg 1:32 Asherites dwelt among the **C**
Judg 1:33 but they dwelt among the **C**
Judg 3: 3 of the Philistines, all the **C**
Judg 3: 5 of Israel dwelt among the **C**
2Sa 24: 7 of the Hivites and the **C**
1Ki 9:16 had killed the **C** who dwelt in
Ezra 9: 1 to the abominations of the **C**
Neh 9: 8 him to give the land of the **C**
Neh 9:24 of the land, the **C**, and gave
Obad 20 of the **C** as far as Zarephath

CANAANITESS (*see* CANAAN)
1Ch 2: 3 the daughter of Shua, the **C**

CANCER
2Ti 2:17 message will spread like **c**

CANDACE
Acts 8:27 of great authority under **C**

CANE
Ex 30:23 shekels of sweet-smelling **c**
Is 43:24 Me no sweet **c** with money, nor
Jer 6:20 sweet **c** from a far country
Ezek 27:19 **c** were among your merchandise

CANNEH (*see* CALNEH)
Ezek 27:23 Haran, **C**, Eden, the merchants

CANNOT (*see* PREFACE)

CANOPIES (*see* CANOPY)
2Sa 22:12 made darkness **c** around Him
Ezek 41:26 of the temple and on the **c**

CANOPY (*see* CANOPIES)
1Ki 7: 6 and a **c** was in front of them
Job 36:29 the thunder from His **c**
Ps 18:11 His **c** around Him was dark
Ezek 41:25 A wooden **c** was on the front

CAPABLE
1Ch 26:31 them **c** men at Jazer of Gilead

CAPER
Is 13:21 And wild goats will **c** there

CAPERNAUM
Matt 4:13 He came and dwelt in **C**, which
Matt 8: 5 Now when Jesus had entered **C**
Matt 11:23 And you, **C**, who are exalted to
Matt 17:24 And when they had come to **C**
Mark 1:21 Then they went into **C**, and
Mark 2: 1 He entered **C** after some days
Mark 9:33 Then He came to **C**
Luke 4:23 we have heard done in **C**, do
Luke 4:31 Then He went down to **C**, a
Luke 7: 1 of the people, He entered **C**
Luke 10:15 And you, **C**, who are exalted to
John 2:12 After this He went down to **C**
John 4:46 whose son was sick at **C**
John 6:17 and went over the sea toward **C**
John 6:24 got into boats and came to **C**
John 6:59 synagogue as He taught in **C**

CAPHTOR (*see* CAPHTORIM)
Deut 2:23 Caphtorim, who came from **C**
Jer 47: 4 remnant of the country of **C**
Amos 9: 7 Egypt, the Philistines from **C**

CAPHTORIM (*see* CAPHTOR)
Gen 10:14 came the Philistines and **C**)
Deut 2:23 the **C**, who came from Caphtor,
1Ch 1:12 the Philistines and the **C**)

CAPITAL (*see* CAPITALS)
1Ki 7:16 of one **c** was five cubits, and
1Ki 7:16 the other **c** was five cubits
1Ki 7:17 seven chains for one **c** and
1Ki 7:17 and seven for the other **c**
1Ki 7:18 thus he did for the other **c**
2Ki 25:17 the **c** on it was of bronze
2Ki 25:17 of the **c** was three cubits
2Ki 25:17 the **c** were all of bronze
2Ch 3:15 the **c** that was on the top of
Jer 52:22 A **c** of bronze was on it
Jer 52:22 of one **c** was five cubits,
Jer 52:22 pomegranates all around the **c**

CAPITALS (*see* CAPITAL)
Ex 36:38 And he overlaid their **c** and
Ex 38:17 of their **c** was of silver
Ex 38:19 and the overlay of their **c**
Ex 38:28 the pillars, overlaid their **c**
1Ki 7:16 he made two **c** of cast bronze
1Ki 7:17 for the **c** which were on top
1Ki 7:18 cover the **c** that were on top
1Ki 7:19 the **c** which were on top of
1Ki 7:20 The **c** on the two pillars also
1Ki 7:20 on each of the **c** all around
1Ki 7:41 the two bowl-shaped **c** that
1Ki 7:41 the two bowl-shaped **c** which
1Ki 7:42 **c** that were on top of the
2Ch 4:12 the bowl-shaped **c** that were
2Ch 4:12 the two bowl-shaped **c** which
2Ch 4:13 **c** that were on the pillars)
Zeph 2:14 lodge on the **c** of her pillars

CAPPADOCIA
Acts 2: 9 in Mesopotamia, Judea and **C**
1Pe 1: 1 in Pontus, Galatia, **C**, Asia,

CAPSTONE
Zech 4: 7 forth the **c** with shouts of

CAPTAIN (*see* CAPTAINS)
Gen 37:36 of Pharaoh and **c** of the guard
Gen 39: 1 **c** of the guard, an Egyptian,
Gen 40: 3 house of the **c** of the guard
Gen 40: 4 the **c** of the guard charged
Gen 41:10 house of the **c** of the guard
Gen 41:12 servant of the **c** of the guard
1Sa 17:18 to the **c** of their thousand
1Sa 18:13 and made him his **c** over a
1Sa 22: 2 So he became **c** over them
2Sa 5: 8 soul), he shall be chief and **c**
2Sa 17:25 Absalom made Amasa **c** of the
2Sa 23:19 Therefore he became their **c**
1Ki 11:24 and became **c** over a band of
2Ki 1: 9 **c** of fifty with his fifty men
2Ki 1:10 and said to the **c** of fifty
2Ki 1:11 **c** of fifty with his fifty men
2Ki 1:13 he sent a third **c** of fifty
2Ki 1:13 the third **c** of fifty went up,
2Ki 9:25 Jehu said to Bidkar his **c**
2Ki 18:24 **c** of the least of my master's
2Ki 25: 8 the **c** of the guard, a servant
2Ki 25:10 **c** of the guard broke down the
2Ki 25:11 Then Nebuzaradan the **c** of the
2Ki 25:12 But the **c** of the guard left
2Ki 25:15 the **c** of the guard took away
2Ki 25:18 And the **c** of the guard took
2Ki 25:20 **c** of the guard, took these and
1Ch 11: 6 first shall be chief and **c**
1Ch 11:21 Therefore he became their **c**
1Ch 27: 5 The third **c** of the army for
1Ch 27: 7 The fourth **c** for the fourth
1Ch 27: 8 The fifth **c** for the fifth
1Ch 27: 9 The sixth **c** for the sixth
1Ch 27:10 The seventh **c** for the seventh
1Ch 27:11 The eighth **c** for the eighth
1Ch 27:12 The ninth **c** for the ninth
1Ch 27:13 The tenth **c** for the tenth
1Ch 27:14 The eleventh **c** for the
1Ch 27:15 The twelfth **c** for the twelfth
2Ch 17:14 Adnah the **c**, and with him
2Ch 17:15 to him was Jehohanan the **c**
2Ch 32:21 **c** in the camp of the king of
Prov 6: 7 which, having no **c**, overseer
Is 3: 3 the **c** of fifty and the
Is 36: 9 **c** of the least of my master's
Jer 37:13 a **c** of the guard was there
Jer 39: 9 Then Nebuzaradan the **c** of the
Jer 39:10 But Nebuzaradan the **c** of the
Jer 39:11 the **c** of the guard, saying,
Jer 39:13 the **c** of the guard sent
Jer 40: 1 LORD after Nebuzaradan the **c**
Jer 40: 2 And the **c** of the guard took
Jer 40: 5 So the **c** of the guard gave
Jer 41:10 whom Nebuzaradan the **c** of the
Jer 43: 6 **c** of the guard had left with
Jer 52:12 the **c** of the guard, who
Jer 52:14 **c** of the guard broke down all
Jer 52:15 Then Nebuzaradan the **c** of the
Jer 52:16 But Nebuzaradan the **c** of the
Jer 52:19 the **c** of the guard took away
Jer 52:24 The **c** of the guard took
Jer 52:26 And Nebuzaradan the **c** of the
Jer 52:30 Nebuzaradan the **c** of the
Dan 2:14 the **c** of the king's guard,
Dan 2:15 said to Arioch the king's **c**
Jon 1: 6 So the **c** came to him, and said
John 18:12 detachment of troops and the **c**
Acts 4: 1 the **c** of the temple, and the
Acts 5:24 the **c** of the temple, and the
Acts 5:26 Then the **c** went with the
Acts 28:16 to the **c** of the guard

CAPTAINS (*see* CAPTAIN)
Ex 14: 7 with **c** over every one of them
Ex 15: 4 His chosen **c** also are drowned
Num 31:14 with the **c** over thousands and
Num 31:14 **c** over hundreds, who had come
Num 31:48 army, the **c** of thousands and
Num 31:48 **c** of hundreds, came near to
Num 31:52 from the **c** of thousands and
Num 31:52 **c** of hundreds, was sixteen
Num 31:54 gold from the **c** of thousands
Deut 20: 9 that they shall make **c** of the
Josh 10:24 said to the **c** of the men of
1Sa 8:12 He will appoint **c** over his
1Sa 8:12 **c** over his fifties, will set
1Sa 22: 7 make you all **c** of thousands
1Sa 22: 7 of thousands and **c** of hundreds
2Sa 4: 2 two men who were **c** of troops
2Sa 18: 1 him, and set **c** of thousands and
2Sa 18: 1 and **c** of hundreds over them
2Sa 18: 5 **c** orders concerning Absalom
2Sa 23: 8 Tachmonite, chief among the **c**
2Sa 24: 4 and against the **c** of the army
2Sa 24: 4 the **c** of the army went out
1Ki 9:22 his officers, his **c**,
1Ki 14:27 hands of the **c** of the guards
1Ki 15:20 and sent the **c** of his armies
1Ki 20:24 and put **c** in their places
1Ki 22:31 thirty-two **c** of his chariots
1Ki 22:32 when the **c** of the chariots
1Ki 22:33 when the **c** of the chariots
2Ki 1:14 two **c** of fifties with their
2Ki 8:21 the **c** of the chariots, but
2Ki 9: 5 there were the **c** of the army
2Ki 10:25 said to the guard and to the **c**
2Ki 11: 4 and brought the **c** of hundreds
2Ki 11: 9 So the **c** of the hundreds did
2Ki 11:10 And the priest gave the **c** of
2Ki 11:15 the **c** of the hundreds, the
2Ki 11:19 he took the **c** of hundreds
2Ki 24:14 all the **c** and all the mighty
2Ki 25:23 when all the **c** of the armies
2Ki 25:26 the **c** of the armies, arose and
1Ch 4:42 having as their **c** Pelatiah
1Ch 11:11 a Hachmonite, chief of the **c**
1Ch 12:14 sons of Gad, **c** of the army
1Ch 12:18 upon Amasai, chief of the **c**
1Ch 12:18 and made them **c** of the troop
1Ch 12:20 **c** of the thousands who were
1Ch 12:21 and they were **c** in the army
1Ch 12:28 father's house twenty-two **c**
1Ch 12:34 of Naphtali one thousand **c**
1Ch 13: 1 with the **c** of thousands and
1Ch 15:25 the **c** over thousands went to
1Ch 25: 1 the **c** of the army separated
1Ch 26:26 the **c** over thousands and
1Ch 26:26 and the **c** of the army, had
1Ch 27: 1 houses, the **c** of thousands and
1Ch 27: 3 the chief of all the **c** of the
1Ch 28: 1 the **c** of the divisions who
1Ch 28: 1 king, the **c** over thousands and
1Ch 28: 1 and **c** over hundreds, and the
1Ch 29: 6 the **c** of thousands and of
2Ch 1: 2 to the **c** of thousands and of
2Ch 8: 9 **c** of his officers
2Ch 8: 9 **c** of his chariots
2Ch 11:11 put **c** in them, and stores of
2Ch 12:10 hands of the **c** of the guard
2Ch 16: 4 and sent the **c** of his armies
2Ch 17:14 Of Judah, the **c** of thousands
2Ch 18:30 **c** of the chariots who were
2Ch 18:31 when the **c** of the chariots
2Ch 18:32 when the **c** of the chariots
2Ch 21: 9 him and the **c** of the chariots
2Ch 23: 1 with the **c** of hundreds
2Ch 23: 9 the **c** of hundreds the spears
2Ch 23:14 **c** of hundreds who were set
2Ch 23:20 he took the **c** of hundreds
2Ch 25: 5 set over them **c** of thousands
2Ch 25: 5 **c** of hundreds, according to
2Ch 26:11 Hananiah, one of the king's **c**
2Ch 32: 6 military **c** over the people
2Ch 33:11 **c** of the army of the king of
2Ch 33:14 Then he put military **c** in all
Neh 2: 9 king had sent **c** of the army
Job 39:25 from afar, the thunder of **c**
Jer 40: 7 Now when all the **c** of the
Jer 40:13 all the **c** of the forces that
Jer 41:11 all the **c** of the forces that
Jer 41:13 all the **c** of the forces who
Jer 41:16 all the **c** of the forces that
Jer 42: 1 Then all the **c** of the forces,
Jer 42: 8 all the **c** of the forces which
Jer 43: 4 all the **c** of the forces, and
Jer 43: 5 all the **c** of the forces took
Ezek 23: 6 who were clothed in purple, **c**
Ezek 23:12 the neighboring Assyrians, **C**
Ezek 23:15 all of them looking like **c**
Ezek 23:23 men, governors and rulers, **c**
Nah 3:17 locusts, and your **c** like great
Luke 22: 4 with the chief priests and **c**
Luke 22:52 **c** of the temple, and the
Rev 19:18 of kings, the flesh of **c**, the

CAPTIVE (*see* CAPTIVES, CAPTIVITY, CAPTURED)
Gen 14:14 that his brother was taken **c**
Gen 34:29 and their wives they took **c**
Ex 12:29 the **c** who was in the dungeon
Num 24:22 Asshur carries you away **c**
Num 31: 9 all the women of Midian **c**
Deut 21:10 your hand, and you take them **c**
1Sa 30: 2 and had taken **c** the women and
1Sa 30: 3 daughters had been taken **c**
1Sa 30: 5 Carmelite, had been taken **c**
1Ki 8:46 they take them **c** to the land
1Ki 8:47 where they were carried **c**
1Ki 8:47 land of those who took them **c**
1Ki 8:48 enemies who led them away **c**
1Ki 8:50 before those who took them **c**
2Ki 5: 2 had brought back **c** a young
2Ki 6:22 have taken **c** with your sword
2Ki 15:29 he carried them **c** to Assyria
2Ki 16: 9 carried its people **c** to Kir
2Ki 18:11 Israel away **c** to Assyria, and
2Ki 24:15 Jehoiachin **c** to Babylon
2Ki 24:16 Babylon brought **c** to Babylon
2Ki 25:11 of the guard carried away **c**
2Ki 25:21 away **c** from its own land
1Ch 9: 1 But Judah was carried away **c**
2Ch 6:36 they take them **c** to a land
2Ch 6:37 where they were carried **c**
2Ch 6:38 they have been carried **c**, and
2Ch 25:12 **c** another ten thousand alive
2Ch 28: 8 away **c** of their brethren two
2Ch 28:11 taken **c** from your brethren
2Ch 30: 9 by those who lead them **c**, so
Ezra 4:10 and noble Osnapper took **c** and
Ezra 8:35 who had been carried away **c**
Ezra 9: 4 who had been carried away **c**
Neh 7: 6 of Babylon had carried away **c**
Ps 68:18 You have led captivity **c**
Ps 106:46 those who carried them away **c**
Ps 137: 3 away **c** required of us a song
Song 7: 5 king is held **c** by its tresses
Is 14: 2 they will take them **c** whose
Is 49:21 children and am desolate, a **c**
Is 51:14 The **c** exile hastens, that he
Is 52: 2 neck, O **c** daughter of Zion
Jer 1: 3 **c** in the fifth month
Jer 13:17 LORD's flock has been taken **c**
Jer 13:19 Judah shall be carried away **c**
Jer 13:19 be wholly carried away **c**
Jer 20: 4 shall carry them **c** to Babylon
Jer 22:12 where they have led him **c**
Jer 24: 1 away **c** Jeconiah the son of
Jer 24: 5 are carried away **c** from Judah
Jer 27:20 away **c** Jeconiah the son of
Jer 28: 6 all who were carried away **c**
Jer 29: 1 who were carried away **c**
Jer 29: 1 had carried away **c** from
Jer 29: 4 all who were carried away **c**
Jer 29: 7 you to be carried away **c**, and
Jer 29:14 you to be carried away **c**
Jer 39: 9 **c** to Babylon the remnant of
Jer 40: 1 carried away **c** from Jerusalem
Jer 40: 1 carried away **c** to Babylon
Jer 40: 7 carried away **c** to Babylon
Jer 41:10 Then Ishmael carried away **c**
Jer 41:10 Nethaniah carried them away **c**
Jer 41:14 Ishmael had carried away **c**
Jer 43: 3 or carry us away **c** to Babylon
Jer 43:12 them and carry them away **c**
Jer 48:46 your sons have been taken **c**
Jer 48:46 **c**, and your daughters **c**
Jer 50:33 all who took them **c** have held
Jer 52:15 **c** some of the poor people
Jer 52:27 away **c** from its own land
Jer 52:28 Nebuchadnezzar carried away **c**
Jer 52:29 he carried away **c** from
Jer 52:30 **c** of the Jews seven hundred
Ezek 6: 9 where they are carried **c**,
Ezek 39:28 none of them **c** any longer
Dan 11: 8 carry their gods **c** to Egypt
Amos 1: 5 of Syria shall go **c** to Kir
Amos 1: 6 because they took **c** the whole
Amos 4:10 along with your **c** horses
Amos 6: 7 now go **c** as the first of the
Amos 7:11 away **c** from their own land
Amos 7:17 led away **c** from his own land
Obad 11 carried **c** his forces, when
Nah 2: 7 she shall be led away **c**, she
Luke 21:24 and be led away **c** into all
Eph 4: 8 on high, He led captivity **c**
2Ti 2:26 having been taken **c** by him to

CAPTIVES (*see* CAPTIVE)
Gen 31:26 like **c** taken with the sword
Num 31:12 Then they brought the **c**, the
Num 31:19 your **c** on the third day and on
Deut 21:11 among the **c** a beautiful woman
Deut 32:42 blood of the slain and the **c**
Judg 5:12 Barak, and lead your **c** away
2Ki 24:14 men of valor, ten thousand **c**
2Ch 28: 5 great multitude of them as **c**
2Ch 28:11 therefore, and return the **c**
2Ch 28:13 shall not bring the **c** here
2Ch 28:14 So the armed men left the **c**
2Ch 28:15 by name rose up and took the **c**
2Ch 28:17 Judah, and carried away **c**
Ezra 1:11 the **c** who were brought from
Esth 2: 6 from Jerusalem with the **c** who
Is 14: 2 captive whose **c** they were
Is 20: 4 and the Ethiopians as **c**, young
Is 49:24 or the **c** of the righteous be
Is 49:25 "Even the **c** of the mighty
Is 61: 1 to proclaim liberty to the **c**
Jer 28: 4 with all the **c** of Judah who
Jer 32:44 will cause their **c** to return
Jer 33: 7 I will cause the **c** of Judah
Jer 33: 7 the **c** of Israel to return, and
Jer 33:11 For I will cause the **c** of the
Jer 33:26 will cause their **c** to return
Jer 48:47 Yet I will bring back the **c**
Jer 49: 6 I will bring back the **c** of
Jer 49:39 will bring back the **c** of Elam
Lam 2:14 to bring back your **c**, but
Ezek 1: 1 as I was among the **c** by the
Ezek 3:11 And go, get to the **c**, to the
Ezek 3:15 I came to the **c** at Tel Abib
Ezek 16:53 When I bring back their **c**
Ezek 16:53 the **c** of Sodom and her
Ezek 16:53 and the **c** of Samaria and her
Ezek 16:53 the **c** of your captivity among
Ezek 29:14 bring back the **c** of Egypt
Ezek 39:25 bring back the **c** of Jacob
Dan 2:25 found a man of the **c** of Judah
Dan 5:13 is one of the **c** from Judah
Dan 6:13 is one of the **c** from Judah
Hos 6:11 I return the **c** of My people
Joel 3: 1 I bring back the **c** of Judah
Amos 6: 7 captive as the first of the **c**
Amos 9:14 the **c** of My people Israel
Obad 20 the **c** of this host of the
Obad 20 The **c** of Jerusalem who are in
Hab 1: 9 They gather **c** like sand
Zeph 2: 7 for them, and return their **c**
Zeph 3:20 your **c** before your eyes,"
Zech 6:10 Receive the gift from the **c**
Luke 4:18 preach deliverance to the **c**
2Ti 3: 6 and make **c** of gullible women

CAPTIVITY (*see* CAPTIVE)
Num 21:29 and his daughters into **c**, to
Deut 21:13 put off the clothes of her **c**
Deut 28:41 for they shall go into **c**
Deut 30: 3 will bring you back from **c**
Judg 18:30 the day of the **c** of the land
2Ki 24:14 carried into **c** all Jerusalem
2Ki 24:15 **c** from Jerusalem to Babylon
2Ki 25:27 thirty-seventh year of the **c**
1Ch 5: 6 of Assyria carried into **c**
1Ch 5:22 in their place until the **c**
1Ch 5:26 half-tribe of Manasseh into **c**
1Ch 6:15 Jehozadak went into **c** when
1Ch 6:15 into **c** by the hand of
2Ch 6:37 to You in the land of their **c**
2Ch 6:38 soul in the land of their **c**
2Ch 29: 9 and our wives are in **c**
Ezra 2: 1 who came back from the **c**, of
Ezra 3: 8 out of the **c** to Jerusalem
Ezra 4: 1 **c** were building the temple of
Ezra 6:16 of the descendants of the **c**
Ezra 6:19 the descendants of the **c** kept
Ezra 6:20 all the descendants of the **c**
Ezra 6:21 **c** ate together with all who
Ezra 8:35 who had come from the **c**,
Ezra 9: 7 the lands, to the sword, to **c**
Ezra 10: 6 the guilt of those from the **c**
Ezra 10: 7 all the descendants of the **c**
Ezra 10: 8 of those from the **c**
Ezra 10:16 descendants of the **c** did so
Neh 1: 2 who had survived the **c**, and
Neh 1: 3 who are left from the **c** in
Neh 4: 4 as plunder to a land of **c**
Neh 7: 6 who came back from the **c**, of
Neh 8:17 from the **c** made booths and sat
Ps 14: 7 back the **c** of His people, Let
Ps 53: 6 back the **c** of His people, Let
Ps 68:18 high, You have led **c** captive
Ps 78:61 delivered His strength into **c**
Ps 85: 1 brought back the **c** of Jacob
Ps 126: 1 brought back the **c** of Zion
Ps 126: 4 Bring back our **c**, O LORD, As
Is 5:13 my people have gone into **c**
Is 46: 2 have themselves gone into **c**
Jer 15: 2 for the **c**, to the **c**
Jer 20: 6 your house, shall go into **c**
Jer 22:22 your lovers shall go into **c**
Jer 29:14 bring you back from your **c**
Jer 29:16 not gone out with you into **c**
Jer 29:20 of the LORD, all you of the **c**
Jer 29:22 be taken up by all the **c** of
Jer 29:28 saying, 'This **c** is long
Jer 29:31 Send to all those in **c**,
Jer 30: 3 back from **c** My people Israel
Jer 30:10 seed from the land of their **c**
Jer 30:16 one of them, shall go into **c**
Jer 30:18 back the **c** of Jacob's tents
Jer 31:23 when I bring back their **c**
Jer 43:11 and to **c** those appointed for
Jer 43:11 those appointed for **c**, and to
Jer 46:19 prepare yourself to go into **c**
Jer 46:27 from the land of their **c**
Jer 48: 7 Chemosh shall go forth into **c**
Jer 48:11 nor has he gone into **c**
Jer 49: 3 go into **c** with his priests
Jer 52:31 thirty-seventh year of the **c**
Lam 1: 3 Judah has gone into **c**, under
Lam 1: 5 gone into **c** before the enemy
Lam 1:18 my young men have gone into **c**
Lam 4:22 no longer send you into **c**
Ezek 1: 2 year of King Jehoiachin's **c**
Ezek 11:24 into Chaldea, to those in **c**
Ezek 11:25 So I spoke to those in **c** of
Ezek 12: 3 prepare your belongings for **c**
Ezek 12: 3 go into **c** by day in their
Ezek 12: 3 go from your place into **c** to
Ezek 12: 4 sight, as though going into **c**
Ezek 12: 4 like those who go into **c**
Ezek 12: 7 day, as though going into **c**
Ezek 12:11 shall be carried away into **c**
Ezek 16:53 captives of your **c** among them
Ezek 25: 3 Judah when they went into **c**
Ezek 30:17 these cities shall go into **c**
Ezek 30:18 her daughters shall go into **c**
Ezek 33:21 in the twelfth year of our **c**
Ezek 39:23 into **c** for their iniquity
Ezek 39:28 them into **c** among the nations
Ezek 40: 1 twenty-fifth year of our **c**
Dan 11:33 fall by sword and flame, by **c**
Amos 1: 6 **c** to deliver them up to Edom
Amos 1: 9 up the whole **c** to Edom, and
Amos 1:15 Their king shall go into **c**
Amos 5: 5 Gilgal shall surely go into **c**
Amos 5:27 you into **c** beyond Damascus
Amos 9: 4 Though they go into **c** before
Obad 12 brother in the day of his **c**
Mic 1:16 they shall go from you into **c**
Nah 3:10 carried away, she went into **c**
Zech 14: 2 of the city shall go into **c**
Matt 1:17 from David until the **c** in
Matt 1:17 from the **c** in Babylon until
Rom 7:23 bringing me into **c** to the law
2Co 10: 5 **c** to the obedience of Christ
Eph 4: 8 He led **c** captive, and gave
Rev 13:10 leads into **c** shall go into **c**

CAPTURED (*see* CAPTIVE)
Josh 11:17 He **c** all their kings, and
Judg 7:25 they **c** two princes of the
1Sa 4:11 Also the ark of God was **c**
1Sa 4:17 and the ark of God has been **c**
1Sa 4:19 that the ark of God was **c**
1Sa 4:21 the ark of God had been **c**
1Sa 4:22 for the ark of God has been **c**
2Ki 14:13 **c** Amaziah king of Judah, the
2Ki 16: 6 of Syria **c** Elath for Syria
2Ch 25:23 **c** Amaziah king of Judah, the
Esth 2: 6 the captives who had been **c**
Is 13:15 everyone who is **c** will fall
Is 22: 3 they are **c** by the archers
Jer 39: 5 And when they had **c** him, they
Jer 50: 9 from there she shall be **c**
Ezek 33:21 The city has been **c**
Ezek 40: 1 year after the city was **c**
Rev 19:20 Then the beast was **c**, and with

CARAVANS
Job 6:19 The **c** of Tema look, the

CARCAS
Esth 1:10 Bigtha, Abagtha, Zethar, and **C**

CARCASS (*see* CARCASSES)
Lev 5: 2 whether it is the **c** of an
Lev 5: 2 or the **c** of unclean livestock
Lev 5: 2 or the **c** of unclean creeping
Lev 11:24 whoever touches the **c** of any
Lev 11:25 **c** of any of them shall wash
Lev 11:26 'The **c** of any beast which
Lev 11:27 such **c** shall be unclean until
Lev 11:28 such **c** shall wash his clothes
Lev 11:35 such **c** falls shall be unclean
Lev 11:36 any such **c** becomes unclean
Lev 11:37 if a part of any such **c** falls
Lev 11:38 of any such **c** falls on it
Lev 11:39 he who touches its **c** shall be
Lev 11:40 'He who eats of its **c** shall
Lev 11:40 its **c** shall wash his clothes
Judg 14: 8 to see the **c** of the lion
Judg 14: 8 were in the **c** of the lion
Judg 14: 9 out of the **c** of the lion
Ezek 32: 5 fill the valleys with your **c**
Matt 24:28 For wherever the **c** is, there

CARCASSES (*see* CARCASS)
Gen 15:11 vultures came down on the **c**
Lev 11: 8 their **c** you shall not touch
Lev 11:11 their **c** as an abomination
Lev 26:30 cast your **c** on the lifeless
Num 14:29 'The **c** of you who have
Num 14:32 your **c** shall fall in this
Num 14:33 until your **c** are consumed in
Deut 14: 8 flesh or touch their dead **c**
Deut 28:26 Your **c** shall be food for all
1Sa 17:46 give the **c** of the camp of the
Is 5:25 Their **c** were as refuse in the
Jer 9:22 'Even the **c** of men shall fall
Jer 16:18 the **c** of their detestable
Ezek 43: 7 the **c** of their kings on their
Ezek 43: 9 the **c** of their kings far away

CARCHEMISH
2Ch 35:20 against **C** by the Euphrates
Is 10: 9 Is not Calno like **C**
Jer 46: 2 by the River Euphrates in **C**

CARE (*see* CARED, CAREFREE, CAREFUL, CARELESS, CARES, CARING)
Deut 15: 5 to observe with **c** all these
2Sa 18: 3 they will not **c** about us
2Sa 18: 3 us die, will they **c** about us
1Ki 1: 2 king, and let her **c** for him
2Ki 4:13 for us with all this **c**
1Ch 22:13 if you take **c** to fulfill the
2Ch 19: 7 take **c** and do it, for there is
Esth 2: 8 into the **c** of Hegai the
Job 10:12 and Your **c** has preserved my
Job 21:21 For what does he **c** about his
Ps 27:10 the LORD will take **c** of me
Is 21: 7 diligently with great **c**
Zech 11:16 in the land who will not **c**
Matt 22:16 nor do You **c** about anyone,
Mark 4:38 do You not **c** that we are
Mark 12:14 are true, and **c** about no one
Luke 10:34 to an inn, and took **c** of him
Luke 10:35 said to him, 'Take **c** of him
Luke 10:40 do You not **c** that my sister
John 10:13 does not **c** about the sheep
Acts 22:26 Take **c** what you do, for this
Acts 27: 3 to his friends and receive **c**
1Co 7:32 I want you to be without **c**
1Co 12:25 the same **c** for one another
2Co 7:12 but that our **c** for you in the
2Co 8:16 **c** for you into the heart of
Phil 2:20 sincerely **c** for your state
Phil 4:10 that now at last your **c** for
Phil 4:10 though you surely did **c**, but
1Ti 3: 5 how will he take **c** of the
Heb 2: 6 of man that You take **c** of him
1Pe 5: 7 casting all your **c** upon Him

CAREAH (*see* KAREAH)
2Ki 25:23 Johanan the son of **C**,

CARED (*see* CARE)
2Sa 19:24 he had not **c** for his feet,
1Ki 1: 4 she **c** for the king, and served
John 12: 6 not that he **c** for the poor,

CAREFREE (*see* CARE)
Ezek 23:42 The sound of a **c** multitude

CAREFUL (*see* CARE, CAREFULLY)
Gen 31:24 Be **c** that you speak to Jacob
Gen 31:29 'Be **c** that you speak to Jacob
Num 28: 2 you shall be **c** to offer to Me
Deut 4: 6 Therefore be **c** to observe
Deut 4:15 Take **c** heed to yourselves,
Deut 5: 1 them and be **c** to observe them
Deut 5:32 Therefore you shall be **c** to
Deut 6: 3 be **c** to observe it, that it
Deut 6:25 if we are **c** to observe all
Deut 8: 1 you must be **c** to observe,
Deut 11:32 you shall be **c** to observe all
Deut 12: 1 which you shall be **c** to
Deut 12:32 you, be **c** to observe it
Deut 16:12 you shall be **c** to observe
Deut 17:10 And you shall be **c** to do
Deut 17:19 be **c** to observe all the words
Deut 24: 8 them, so you shall be **c** to do
Deut 26:16 therefore you shall be **c** to
Deut 28:13 and are **c** to observe them
Deut 32:46 children to be **c** to observe
Judg 13: 4 please be **c** not to drink wine
Judg 13:13 to the woman let her be **c**
2Ki 17:37 you shall be **c** to observe
2Ki 21: 8 only if they are **c** to do
1Ch 28: 8 God, be **c** to seek out all the
2Ch 33: 8 only if they are **c** to do all
Ezra 7:17 be **c** to buy with this money
Ezek 20:21 and were not **c** to observe My
Tit 3: 8 be **c** to maintain good works
2Pe 1:15 Moreover I will be **c** to

CAREFULLY (*see* CAREFUL)
Deut 2: 4 Therefore watch yourselves **c**
Deut 11:22 For if you **c** keep all these
Deut 15: 5 only if you **c** obey the voice
Deut 28: 1 God, to observe **c** all His
Deut 28:15 God, to observe **c** all His
Deut 28:58 If you do not **c** observe all
Deut 31:12 **c** observe all the words of
Job 21: 2 Listen **c** to my speech, and let
Prov 12:26 should choose his friends **c**
Prov 23: 1 Consider **c** what is before you
Prov 27: 5 better than love **c** concealed
Is 38:15 I shall walk **c** all my years
Hag 2:15 now, **c** consider from this day
1Ti 4: 6 which you have **c** followed
2Ti 3:10 But you have **c** followed my

CARELESS (*see* CARE)
Prov 19:16 but he who is **c** of his ways
Ezek 30: 9 make the **c** Ethiopians afraid

CARES (*see* CARE)
Deut 11:12 for which the LORD your God **c**
Ps 142: 4 No one **c** for my soul
Matt 13:22 the **c** of this world and the
Mark 4:19 "and the **c** of this world, the
Luke 8:14 go out and are choked with **c**
Luke 21:34 **c** of this life, and that Day
1Co 7:32 He who is unmarried **c** for the
1Co 7:33 But he who is married **c** about
1Co 7:34 The unmarried woman **c** about
1Co 7:34 But she who is married **c**
1Pe 5: 7 upon Him, for He **c** for you

CARGO
Jon 1: 5 threw the **c** that was in the
Acts 21: 3 the ship was to unload her **c**
Acts 27:10 much loss, not only of the **c**

CARING (*see* CARE)
1Sa 9: 5 cease **c** about the donkeys
1Sa 10: 2 ceased **c** about the donkeys

CARMEL (*see* CARMELITE, CARMELITESS)
Josh 12:22 the king of Jokneam in **C**, one
Josh 15:55 Maon, **C**, Ziph, Juttah,
Josh 19:26 reached to Mount **C** westward
1Sa 15:12 Saul went to **C**, and indeed, he
1Sa 25: 2 Maon whose business was in **C**
1Sa 25: 2 was shearing his sheep in **C**
1Sa 25: 5 Go up to **C**, go to Nabal, and
1Sa 25: 7 all the while they were in **C**
1Sa 25:40 had come to Abigail at **C**,
1Ki 18:19 all Israel to me on Mount **C**
1Ki 18:20 prophets together on Mount **C**
1Ki 18:42 went up to the top of **C**
2Ki 2:25 he went from there to Mount **C**
2Ki 4:25 to the man of God at Mount **C**
2Ch 26:10 in the mountains and in **C**, for
Song 7: 5 head crowns you like Mount **C**
Is 33: 9 and **C** shake off their fruits
Is 35: 2 to it, the excellence of **C**
Jer 46:18 as **C** by the sea, so he shall
Jer 50:19 and he shall feed on **C** and
Amos 1: 2 and the top of **C** withers
Amos 9: 3 hide themselves on top of **C**
Mic 7:14 a woodland, in the midst of **C**
Nah 1: 4 **C** wither, and the flower of

CARMELITE (*see* CARMEL)
1Sa 30: 5 the widow of Nabal the **C**, had
2Sa 2: 2 the widow of Nabal the **C**
2Sa 3: 3 the widow of Nabal the **C**
2Sa 23:35 Hezrai the **C**, Paarai the
1Ch 11:37 Hezro the **C**, Naarai the son

CARMELITESS (*see* CARMEL)
1Sa 27: 3 and Abigail the **C**, Nabal's
1Ch 3: 1 Daniel, by Abigail the **C**

CARMI (*see* CARMITES)
Gen 46: 9 Hanoch, Pallu, Hezron, and **C**
Ex 6:14 Hanoch, Pallu, Hezron, and **C**
Num 26: 6 of **C**, the family of the
Josh 7: 1 for Achan the son of **C**, the
Josh 7:18 by man, and Achan the son of **C**
1Ch 2: 7 The son of **C** was Achar, the
1Ch 4: 1 Judah were Perez, Hezron, **C**
1Ch 5: 3 Hanoch, Pallu, Hezron, and **C**

CARMITES (*see* CARMI)
Num 26: 6 of Carmi, the family of the **C**

CARNAL (*see* CARNALLY)
Rom 7:14 law is spiritual, but I am **c**
Rom 8: 7 Because the **c** mind is enmity
1Co 3: 1 spiritual people but as to **c**
1Co 3: 3 for you are still **c**
1Co 3: 3 among you, are you not **c** and
1Co 3: 4 of Apollos," are you not **c**
2Co 10: 4 not **c** but mighty in God for

CARNALLY (*see* CARNAL)
Gen 19: 5 to us that we may know them **c**
Lev 18:20 **c** with your neighbor's wife
Lev 19:20 'Whoever lies **c** with a woman
Num 5:13 'and a man lies with her **c**
Judg 19:22 house, that we may know him **c**
Rom 8: 6 For to be **c** minded is death,

CAROUSE (*see* CAROUSING)
2Pe 2:13 pleasure to **c** in the daytime

CAROUSING (*see* CAROUSE)
Luke 21:34 hearts be weighed down with **c**
2Pe 2:13 **c** in their own deceptions

CARPENTER (*see* CARPENTER'S, CARPENTERS)
Mark 6: 3 Is this not the **c**, the Son of

CARPENTER'S (*see* CARPENTER)
Matt 13:55 Is this not the **c** son

CARPENTERS (*see* CARPENTER)
2Sa 5:11 David, and cedar trees, and **c**
2Ki 12:11 and they paid it out to the **c**
2Ki 22: 6 to **c** and builders and masons
1Ch 14: 1 cedar trees, with masons and **c**
2Ch 24:12 **c** to repair the house of the
Ezra 3: 7 money to the masons and the **c**

CARPUS
2Ti 4:13 with **C** at Troas when you come

CARRIAGES
Is 46: 1 Your **c** were heavily loaded, a

CARRIED (*see* CARRY)
Gen 31:18 he **c** away all his livestock
Gen 31:26 and **c** away my daughters like
Gen 46: 5 Israel **c** their father Jacob
Gen 50:13 For his sons **c** him to the
Ex 25:14 that the ark may be **c** by them
Ex 25:28 the table may be **c** with them
Lev 10: 5 **c** them by their tunics out of
Lev 16:27 shall be **c** outside the camp
Num 7: 9 things, which they **c** on their
Num 13:23 they **c** it between two of them
Deut 1:31 how the LORD your God **c** you
Josh 4: 8 **c** them over with them to the
Judg 3:18 people who had **c** the tribute
Judg 11:39 he **c** out his vow with her
Judg 16: 3 **c** them to the top of the hill
1Sa 5: 8 of Israel be **c** away to Gath
1Sa 5: 8 So they **c** the ark of the
1Sa 5: 9 was, after they had **c** it away
1Sa 30: 2 but **c** them away and went their
1Sa 30:18 the Amalekites had **c** away

2Sa 5:21 David and his men **c** them away
2Sa 15:29 Abiathar **c** the ark of God
1Ki 2:26 because you **c** the ark of the
1Ki 5:15 thousand who **c** burdens, and
1Ki 8:47 where they were **c** captive
1Ki 14:28 LORD, that the guards **c** them
1Ki 17:19 **c** him to the upper room where
2Ki 5:23 they **c** them on ahead of him
2Ki 7: 8 **c** from it silver and gold and
2Ki 7: 8 **c** some from there also, and
2Ki 9:28 his servants **c** him in the
2Ki 15:29 he **c** them captive to Assyria
2Ki 16: 9 **c** its people captive to Kir,
2Ki 17: 6 **c** Israel away to Assyria, and
2Ki 17:11 LORD had **c** away before them
2Ki 17:23 So Israel was **c** away from
2Ki 17:28 had **c** away from Samaria came
2Ki 17:33 among whom they were **c** away
2Ki 18:11 **c** Israel away captive to
2Ki 20:17 day, shall be **c** to Babylon
2Ki 23: 4 and **c** their ashes to Bethel
2Ki 24:13 he **c** out from there all the
2Ki 24:14 Also he **c** into captivity all
2Ki 24:15 he **c** Jehoiachin captive to
2Ki 24:15 land he **c** into captivity from
2Ki 25:11 **c** away captive the rest of
2Ki 25:13 **c** their bronze to Babylon
2Ki 25:21 Thus Judah was **c** away captive
1Ch 5: 6 of Assyria **c** into captivity
1Ch 5:26 He **c** the Reubenites, the
1Ch 6:15 when the LORD **c** Judah and
1Ch 9: 1 But Judah was **c** away captive
1Ch 13: 7 So they **c** the ark of God on a
2Ch 6:37 where they were **c** captive
2Ch 6:38 they have been **c** captive, and
2Ch 12: 9 He also **c** away the gold
2Ch 14: 8 men from Judah who **c** shields
2Ch 14: 8 thousand men who **c** shields
2Ch 14:13 they **c** away very much spoil
2Ch 14:15 and **c** off sheep and camels in
2Ch 16: 6 they **c** away the stones and
2Ch 21:17 **c** away all the possessions
2Ch 28: 5 **c** away a great multitude of
2Ch 28: 8 **c** away captive of their
2Ch 28:17 Judah, and **c** away captives
2Ch 29:16 and **c** it to the Brook Kidron
2Ch 33:11 and **c** him off to Babylon
2Ch 34:16 So Shaphan **c** the book to the
2Ch 36: 4 brother and **c** him off to Egypt
2Ch 36: 7 Nebuchadnezzar also **c** off
2Ch 36:20 sword he **c** away to Babylon
Ezra 2: 1 of those who had been **c** away
Ezra 2: 1 Babylon had **c** away to Babylon
Ezra 5:12 **c** the people away to Babylon
Ezra 5:14 **c** into the temple of Babylon
Ezra 8:35 who had been **c** away captive
Ezra 9: 4 who had been **c** away captive
Neh 4:17 wall, and those who **c** burdens
Neh 7: 6 of those who had been **c** away
Neh 7: 6 of Babylon had **c** away captive
Esth 2: 6 Kish had been **c** away from
Esth 2: 6 king of Babylon had **c** away
Job 10:19 I would have been **c** from the
Ps 46: 2 though the mountains be **c**
Ps 106:46 those who **c** them away captive
Ps 137: 3 For there those who **c** us away
Is 23: 7 whose feet **c** her far off to
Is 39: 6 day, shall be **c** to Babylon
Is 46: 3 who have been **c** from the womb
Is 49:22 shall be **c** on their shoulders
Is 53: 4 our griefs and **c** our sorrows
Is 63: 9 **c** them all the days of old
Is 66:12 on her sides shall you be **c**
Jer 10: 5 they must be **c**, because they
Jer 13:19 Judah shall be **c** away captive
Jer 13:19 be wholly **c** away captive
Jer 24: 1 king of Babylon had **c** away
Jer 24: 5 are **c** away captive from Judah
Jer 27:20 take, when he **c** away captive
Jer 27:22 'They shall be **c** to Babylon
Jer 28: 3 this place and **c** to Babylon
Jer 28: 6 all who were **c** away captive
Jer 29: 1 who were **c** away captive
Jer 29: 1 whom Nebuchadnezzar had **c**
Jer 29: 4 all who were **c** away captive
Jer 29: 4 be **c** away from Jerusalem to
Jer 29: 7 you to be **c** away captive, and
Jer 29:14 you to be **c** away captive
Jer 39: 9 the captain of the guard **c**
Jer 40: 1 chains among all who were **c**
Jer 40: 1 who were **c** away captive to
Jer 40: 7 **c** away captive to Babylon
Jer 41:10 Then Ishmael **c** away captive
Jer 41:10 Nethaniah **c** them away captive
Jer 41:14 **c** away captive from Mizpah
Jer 52:15 **c** away captive some of the
Jer 52:17 **c** all their bronze to Babylon
Jer 52:27 Thus Judah was **c** away captive
Jer 52:28 Nebuchadnezzar **c** away captive
Jer 52:29 year of Nebuchadnezzar he **c**
Jer 52:30 **c** away captive of the Jews
Ezek 6: 9 where they are **c** captive,
Ezek 12:11 they shall be **c** away into
Ezek 17: 4 and **c** it to a land of trade
Dan 1: 2 which he **c** into the land of
Dan 2:35 the wind **c** them away so that
Hos 10: 6 The idol also shall be **c** to
Hos 12: 1 and oil is **c** to Egypt
Joel 3: 5 have **c** into your temples My
Amos 5:26 You also **c** Sikkuth your king
Obad 11 **c** captive his forces, when
Nah 3:10 Yet she was **c** away, she went
Matt 1:11 they were **c** away to Babylon
Mark 2: 3 who was **c** by four men
Luke 7:12 a dead man was being **c** out
Luke 7:14 those who **c** him stood still
Luke 16:22 and was **c** by the angels to
Luke 24:51 from them and **c** up into heaven
John 20:15 Sir, if You have **c** Him away
Acts 3: 2 from his mother's womb was **c**
Acts 5: 6 up, **c** him out, and buried him
Acts 7:16 they were **c** back to Shechem
Acts 8: 2 devout men **c** Stephen to his
Acts 21:35 stairs, he had to be **c** by the
1Co 12: 2 **c** away to these dumb idols,
Gal 2:13 **c** away with their hypocrisy
Eph 4:14 **c** about with every wind of
Heb 13: 9 Do not be **c** about with
2Pe 2:17 clouds **c** by a tempest, to
Jude 12 water, **c** about by the winds
Rev 12:15 her to be **c** away by the flood
Rev 17: 3 So he **c** me away in the Spirit
Rev 21:10 he **c** me away in the Spirit to

CARRIERS (*see* CARRY)
Josh 9:21 and water **c** for all the
Josh 9:23 water **c** for the house of my
Josh 9:27 water **c** for the congregation
Ezek 27:25 were **c** of your merchandise

CARRIES (*see* CARRY)
Lev 11:25 'whoever **c** part of the
Lev 11:28 'Whoever **c** any such carcass
Lev 11:40 He also who **c** its carcass
Lev 15:10 He who **c** any of those things
Num 11:12 as a guardian **c** a nursing
Num 24:22 Asshur **c** you away captive
Deut 1:31 you, as a man **c** his son, in
Job 21:18 chaff that a storm **c** away
Job 27:21 The east wind **c** him away, and
Hag 2:12 If one **c** holy meat in the
Rev 17: 7 and of the beast that **c** her

CARRION
Lev 11:18 the jackdaw, and the **c** vulture
Deut 14:17 the **c** vulture, the fisher owl

CARRY (*see* CARRIED, CARRIERS, CARRIES, CARRYING)
Gen 37:25 on their way to **c** them down
Gen 42:19 **c** grain for the famine of
Gen 43:11 **c** down a present for the man
Gen 44: 1 food, as much as they can **c**
Gen 45:27 Joseph had sent to **c** him, the
Gen 46: 5 Pharaoh had sent to **c** him
Gen 47:30 you shall **c** me out of Egypt
Gen 50:25 you shall **c** up my bones from
Ex 12:46 you shall not **c** any of the
Ex 13:19 you shall **c** up my bones from
Lev 4:12 'the whole bull he shall **c**
Lev 4:21 'Then he shall **c** the bull
Lev 6:11 **c** the ashes outside the camp
Lev 10: 4 **c** your brethren from before
Lev 14:45 he shall **c** them outside the
Num 1:50 they shall **c** the tabernacle
Num 4:15 Kohath shall come to **c** them
Num 4:15 the sons of Kohath are to **c**
Num 4:25 They shall **c** the curtains of
Num 4:31 this is what they must **c** as
Num 4:32 by name the items he must **c**
Num 11:12 '**C** them in your bosom, as a
Deut 14:24 are not able to **c** the tithe
Deut 28:38 You shall **c** much seed out to
Josh 4: 3 You shall **c** them over with
1Sa 17:18 **c** these ten cheeses to the
1Sa 20:40 him, "Go, **c** them to the city
2Sa 15:25 **C** the ark of God back into
2Sa 19:18 **c** over the king's household
1Ki 18:12 **c** you to a place I do not
2Ki 4:19 "**C** him to his mother
1Ch 15: 2 No one may **c** the ark of God
1Ch 15: 2 them to **c** the ark of God and
1Ch 23:26 no longer **c** the tabernacle
2Ch 2:16 you will **c** it up to Jerusalem
2Ch 20:25 more than they could **c** away
2Ch 29: 5 **c** out the rubbish from the
2Ch 36: 6 to **c** him off to Babylon
Ezra 5:15 **c** them to the temple site
Ezra 7:15 you are to **c** the silver and
Job 5:12 cannot **c** out their plans
Job 15:12 does your heart **c** you away
Job 31:36 Surely I would **c** it on my
Ps 49:17 dies he shall **c** nothing away
Ps 90: 5 You **c** them away like a flood
Eccl 5:15 he may **c** away in his hand
Eccl 10:20 of the air may **c** your voice
Is 5:29 they will **c** it away safely,
Is 15: 7 they will **c** away to the Brook
Is 30: 6 they will **c** their riches on
Is 40:11 and **c** them in His bosom, and
Is 41:16 the wind shall **c** them away
Is 45:20 who **c** the wood of their
Is 46: 4 to gray hairs I will **c** you
Is 46: 4 even I will **c**, and will
Is 46: 7 it on the shoulder, they **c** it
Is 57:13 the wind will **c** them all away
Jer 17:22 nor **c** a burden out of your
Jer 20: 4 he shall **c** them captive to
Jer 20: 5 them, and **c** them to Babylon
Jer 39: 7 to **c** him off to Babylon
Jer 43: 3 **c** us away captive to Babylon
Jer 43:12 them and **c** them away captive
Ezek 12: 5 **c** your belongings out through
Ezek 12: 6 and **c** them out at twilight
Ezek 12:12 wall to **c** them out through it
Ezek 29:19 **c** off her spoil, and remove
Ezek 38:13 to **c** away silver and gold, to
Dan 11: 8 he shall also **c** their gods
Dan 11:32 and **c** out great exploits
Mic 6:14 You may **c** some away, but
Matt 3:11 sandals I am not worthy to **c**
Mark 6:55 and began to **c** about on beds
Mark 11:16 to **c** wares through the temple
Luke 10: 4 **C** neither money bag, sack,
John 5:10 lawful for you to **c** your bed
John 21:18 **c** you where you do not wish
Acts 5: 9 door, and they will **c** you out
Acts 7:43 and I will **c** you away beyond
1Ti 6: 7 certain we can **c** nothing out

CARRYING (*see* CARRY)
Num 4:10 skins, and put it on a **c** beam
Num 4:12 and put them on a **c** beam
Num 4:24 Gershonites, in serving and **c**
Num 10:17 set out, **c** the tabernacle
Num 10:21 set out, **c** the holy things
Deut 32:11 them up, **c** them on its wings,
1Sa 10: 3 you, one **c** three young goats,
1Sa 10: 3 another **c** three loaves of
1Sa 10: 3 and another **c** a skin of wine
Ps 78: 9 **c** bows, Turned back in the
Jer 1: 3 until the **c** away of Jerusalem
Jer 17:27 such as not **c** a burden when
Zech 5:10 Where are they **c** the basket
Mark 14:13 meet you **c** a pitcher of water
Luke 22:10 meet you **c** a pitcher of water
Acts 5:10 **c** her out, buried her by her
2Co 4:10 always **c** about in the body

CARSHENA
Esth 1:14 those closest to him being **C**

CART (*see* CARTS, CARTWHEEL)
Num 7: 3 a **c** for every two of the
1Sa 6: 7 Now therefore, make a new **c**
1Sa 6: 7 and hitch the cows to the **c**
1Sa 6: 8 the LORD and set it on the **c**
1Sa 6:10 cows and hitched them to the **c**
1Sa 6:11 the ark of the LORD on the **c**
1Sa 6:14 Then the **c** came into the
1Sa 6:14 they split the wood of the **c**
2Sa 6: 3 set the ark of God on a new **c**
2Sa 6: 3 of Abinadab, drove the new **c**

1Ki 7:27 was the length of each **c**,
1Ki 7:30 Every **c** had four bronze
1Ki 7:32 wheels were joined to the **c**
1Ki 7:34 at the four corners of each **c**
1Ki 7:34 were part of the **c** itself
1Ki 7:35 On the top of the **c**, at the
1Ki 7:35 And on the top of the **c**, its
1Ch 13: 7 the ark of God on a new **c**
1Ch 13: 7 and Uzza and Ahio drove the **c**
Is 5:18 and sin as if with a **c** rope
Amos 2:13 as a **c** is weighed down that

CARTS (*see* CART)
Gen 45:19 Take **c** out of the land of
Gen 45:21 and Joseph gave them **c**,
Gen 45:27 and when he saw the **c** which
Gen 46: 5 in the **c** which Pharaoh had
Num 7: 3 the LORD, six covered **c** and
Num 7: 6 So Moses took the **c** and the
Num 7: 7 Two **c** and four oxen he gave to
Num 7: 8 and four **c** and eight oxen he
1Ki 7:27 He also made ten **c** of bronze
1Ki 7:28 this was the design of the **c**
1Ki 7:37 this manner he made the ten **c**
1Ki 7:38 each of the ten **c** was a laver
1Ki 7:39 he put five **c** on the right
1Ki 7:43 the ten **c**, and ten lavers on
1Ki 7:43 **c**, and ten lavers on the **c**
2Ki 16:17 cut off the panels of the **c**
2Ki 25:13 house of the LORD, and the **c**
2Ki 25:16 pillars, one Sea, and the **c**
2Ch 4:14 made **c** and the lavers on the **c**
Jer 27:19 the Sea, concerning the **c**
Jer 52:17 house of the LORD, and the **c**
Jer 52:20 which were under it, and the **c**

CARTWHEEL (*see* CART)
Is 28:27 nor is a **c** rolled over the
Is 28:28 forever, break it with his **c**

CARVE (*see* CARVED, CARVES, CARVING)
Hab 2:18 that its maker should **c** it

CARVED (*see* CARVE)
Ex 20: 4 make for yourself any **c** image
Lev 26: 1 neither a **c** image nor a
Deut 4:16 make for yourselves a **c** image
Deut 4:23 a **c** image in the form of
Deut 4:25 make a **c** image in the form of
Deut 5: 8 make for yourself any **c** image
Deut 7: 5 burn their **c** images with fire
Deut 7:25 You shall burn the **c** images
Deut 12: 3 the **c** images of their gods
Deut 27:15 makes any **c** or molded image
Judg 17: 3 for my son, to make a **c** image
Judg 17: 4 and he made it into a **c** image
Judg 18:14 a **c** image, and a molded image
Judg 18:17 there, they took the **c** image
Judg 18:20 and the **c** image, and took his
Judg 18:30 up for themselves the **c** image
Judg 18:31 Micah's **c** image which he made
1Ki 6:18 **c** with ornamental buds and
1Ki 6:29 Then he **c** all the walls of
1Ki 6:29 with **c** figures of cherubim,
1Ki 6:32 and he **c** on them figures of
1Ki 6:35 Then he **c** cherubim, palm
1Ki 6:35 applied evenly on the **c** work
2Ki 17:41 yet served their **c** images
2Ki 21: 7 He even set a **c** image of
2Ch 3: 5 he **c** palm trees and chainwork
2Ch 3: 7 he **c** cherubim on the walls
2Ch 33: 7 He even set a **c** image, the
2Ch 33:19 and **c** images, before he was
2Ch 33:22 the **c** images which his father
2Ch 34: 3 the **c** images, and the molded
2Ch 34: 4 the **c** images, and the molded
2Ch 34: 7 had beaten the **c** images into
Ps 74: 6 they break down its **c** work
Ps 78:58 jealousy with their **c** images
Ps 97: 7 to shame who serve **c** images
Song 5:14 His body is **c** ivory inlaid
Is 10:10 whose **c** images excelled those
Is 21: 9 all the **c** images of her gods
Is 40:20 workman to prepare a **c** image
Is 42:17 who trust in **c** images, who
Is 44:15 he makes it a **c** image, and
Is 44:17 makes into a god, his **c** image
Is 45:20 the wood of their **c** image
Is 48: 5 my **c** image and my molded image
Jer 8:19 to anger with their **c** images
Jer 50:38 it is the land of **c** images
Jer 51:17 put to shame by the **c** image
Jer 51:47 on the **c** images of Babylon
Jer 51:52 judgment on her **c** images, and
Ezek 41:20 cherubim and palm trees were **c**
Ezek 41:25 and palm trees were **c** on the
Ezek 41:25 as they were **c** on the walls
Hos 11: 2 and burned incense to **c** images
Mic 1: 7 All her **c** images shall be
Mic 5:13 Your **c** images I will also cut
Nah 1:14 I will cut off the **c** image

CARVES (*see* CARVE)
Is 22:16 who **c** a tomb for himself in a

CARVING (*see* CARVE)
Ex 31: 5 in **c** wood, and to work in all
Ex 35:33 in **c** wood, and to work in all
2Ch 3:10 two cherubim, fashioned by **c**

CASE (*see* CASES)
Gen 30: 6 God has judged my **c**
Ex 18:26 every small **c** themselves
Num 27: 5 their **c** before the LORD
Deut 1:17 The **c** that is too hard for
Deut 19: 4 "And this is the **c** of the
Deut 24:13 You shall in any **c** return the
Josh 20: 4 declares his **c** in the hearing
1Sa 24:15 and me, and see and plead my **c**
2Sa 15: 3 Look, your **c** is good and right
2Ch 19:10 Whatever **c** comes to you from
Job 13:18 See now, I have prepared my **c**
Job 23: 4 would present my **c** before Him
Job 29:16 I searched out the **c** that I
Prov 25: 9 Debate your **c** with your
Is 41:21 Present your **c**," says the
Is 43:26 state your **c**, that you may be
Is 45:21 Tell and bring forth your **c**
Jer 2:35 I will plead My **c** against you
Jer 25:31 plead His **c** with all flesh
Jer 50:34 will thoroughly plead their **c**
Jer 51:36 Behold, I will plead your **c**
Lam 3:58 pleaded the **c** for my soul
Lam 3:59 judge my **c**
Ezek 20:35 My **c** with you face to face
Ezek 20:36 Just as I pleaded My **c** with
Ezek 20:36 so I will plead My **c** with you
Dan 3:17 If that is the **c**, our God
Mic 6: 1 plead your **c** before the
Mic 7: 9 Him, until He pleads my **c**
Matt 19:10 If such is the **c** of the man
Acts 19:38 have a **c** against anyone, the
Acts 24:22 make a decision on your **c**
Acts 25:14 laid Paul's **c** before the king

CASES (*see* CASE)
Ex 18:26 the hard **c** they brought to
Deut 1:16 'Hear the **c** between your
1Co 7:15 not under bondage in such **c**

CASIPHIA
Ezra 8:17 the chief man at the place **C**
Ezra 8:17 the Nethinim at the place **C**

CASLUHIM
Gen 10:14 and **C** (from whom came the
1Ch 1:12 **C** (from whom came the

CASSIA
Ex 30:24 five hundred shekels of **c**
Ps 45: 8 with myrrh and aloes and **c**, Out
Ezek 27:19 Wrought iron, **c**, and cane were

CAST (*see* CASTING, CASTS)
Gen 21:10 **C** out this bondwoman and her
Gen 37:20 him and **c** him into some pit
Gen 37:22 but **c** him into this pit which
Gen 37:24 took him and **c** him into a pit
Gen 39: 7 wife **c** longing eyes on Joseph
Ex 1:22 you shall **c** into the river
Ex 4: 3 He said, "**C** it on the ground
Ex 4: 3 So he **c** it on the ground,
Ex 4:25 **c** it at Moses' feet, and said,
Ex 7: 9 **c** it before Pharaoh, and let
Ex 7:10 Aaron **c** down his rod before
Ex 15: 4 army He has **c** into the sea
Ex 15:25 when he **c** it into the waters,
Ex 25:12 You shall **c** four rings of
Ex 26:37 you shall **c** five sockets of
Ex 32:19 he **c** the tablets out of his
Ex 32:24 I **c** it into the fire, and this
Ex 34:24 For I will **c** out the nations
Ex 36:36 he **c** four sockets of silver
Ex 37: 3 he **c** for it four rings of
Ex 37:13 he **c** for it four rings of
Ex 38: 5 He **c** four rings for the four
Ex 38:27 were **c** the sockets of the
Lev 1:16 **c** it beside the altar on the
Lev 14:40 they shall **c** them into an
Lev 16: 8 Then Aaron shall **c** lots for
Lev 26:30 and **c** your carcasses on the
Lev 26:44 I will not **c** them away, nor
Num 19: 6 **c** them into the midst of the
Deut 6:19 to **c** out all your enemies
Deut 7: 1 has **c** out many nations before
Deut 9: 4 God has **c** them out before you
Deut 29:28 **c** them into another land, as
Josh 8:29 **c** it at the entrance of the
Josh 10:11 that the LORD **c** down large
Josh 10:27 **c** them into the cave where
Josh 13:12 had defeated and **c** out these
Josh 18: 6 that I may **c** lots for you
Josh 18: 8 that I may **c** lots for you
Josh 18:10 Then Joshua **c** lots for them
1Sa 14:42 said, "**C** lots between my son
1Sa 18:11 Saul **c** the spear, for he said
1Sa 20:33 Then Saul **c** a spear at him to
2Sa 1:21 of the mighty is **c** away there
2Sa 11:21 Was it not a woman who **c** a
2Sa 18:17 **c** him into a large pit in the
2Sa 20:15 and they **c** up a siege mound
1Ki 7:15 he **c** two pillars of bronze,
1Ki 7:16 made two capitals of **c** bronze
1Ki 7:23 he made the Sea of **c** bronze
1Ki 7:24 **c** in two rows when it was
1Ki 7:24 in two rows when it was **c**
1Ki 7:30 **c** bronze beside each wreath
1Ki 7:33 hubs were all of **c** bronze
1Ki 7:46 king had them **c** in clay molds
1Ki 9: 7 name I will **c** out of My sight
1Ki 14: 9 have **c** Me behind your back
1Ki 14:24 **c** out before the children of
1Ki 21:26 done, whom the LORD had **c** out
2Ki 2:16 **c** him upon some mountain or
2Ki 2:21 **c** in the salt there, and said,
2Ki 13:23 or **c** them from His presence
2Ki 16: 3 had **c** out from before the
2Ki 17: 8 had **c** out from before the
2Ki 17:20 until He had **c** them from His
2Ki 19:18 have **c** their gods into the
2Ki 21: 2 nations whom the LORD had **c**
2Ki 23:27 and will **c** off this city
2Ki 24:20 that He finally **c** them out
1Ch 24:31 These also **c** lots just as
1Ch 25: 8 they **c** lots for their duty,
1Ch 26:13 they **c** lots for each gate,
1Ch 26:14 Then they **c** lots for his son
1Ch 28: 9 He will **c** you off forever
2Ch 4: 2 he made the Sea of **c** bronze
2Ch 4: 3 The oxen were **c** in two rows
2Ch 4: 3 in two rows, when it was **c**
2Ch 4:17 king had them **c** in clay molds
2Ch 7:20 name I will **c** out of My sight
2Ch 13: 9 "Have you not **c** out the
2Ch 25:12 **c** them down from the top of
2Ch 26:14 bows, and slings to **c** stones
2Ch 28: 3 nations whom the LORD had **c**
2Ch 29:19 **c** aside in his transgression
2Ch 30:14 **c** them into the Brook Kidron
2Ch 33: 2 nations whom the LORD had **c**
2Ch 33:15 he **c** them out of the city
Neh 1: 9 though some of you were **c** out
Neh 9:26 **c** Your law behind their backs
Neh 10:34 We **c** lots among the priests,
Neh 11: 1 the rest of the people **c** lots
Esth 3: 7 they **c** Pur (that is, the lot)
Esth 9:24 had **c** Pur (that is, the lot),
Job 8: 4 He has **c** them away for their
Job 8:20 God will not **c** away the
Job 15: 4 you **c** off fear, and restrain
Job 15:33 **c** off his blossom like an
Job 18: 8 For he is **c** into a net by his
Job 20:23 God will **c** on him the fury of
Job 22:29 When they **c** you down, and you
Job 29:24 they did not **c** down
Job 30:11 they have **c** off restraint
Job 30:19 He has **c** me into the mire, and
Job 37:18 strong as a **c** metal mirror
Ps 2: 3 **c** away Their cords from us
Ps 5:10 **C** them out in the multitude
Ps 17:13 Confront him, **c** him down
Ps 18:42 I **c** them out like dirt in the
Ps 22:10 I was **c** upon You from birth
Ps 22:18 for My clothing they **c** lots
Ps 36:12 They have been **c** down and are
Ps 37:14 To **c** down the poor and needy,
Ps 37:24 shall not be utterly **c** down

Ps 42: 5 Why are you **c** down, O my soul
Ps 42: 6 my soul is **c** down within me
Ps 42:11 Why are you **c** down, O my soul
Ps 43: 2 Why do You **c** me off
Ps 43: 5 Why are you **c** down, O my soul
Ps 44: 2 the peoples, and **c** them out
Ps 44: 9 But You have **c** us off and put
Ps 44:23 Do not **c** us off forever
Ps 50:17 And **c** My words behind you
Ps 51:11 Do not **c** me away from Your
Ps 55:22 **C** your burden on the LORD,
Ps 56: 7 In anger **c** down the peoples,
Ps 60: 1 O God, You have **c** us off
Ps 60: 8 Over Edom I will **c** My shoe
Ps 60:10 not You, O God, who **c** us off
Ps 62: 4 They only consult to **c** him
Ps 71: 9 Do not **c** me off in the time
Ps 73:18 You **c** them down to
Ps 74: 1 why have You **c** us off forever
Ps 76: 6 and horse were **c** into a dead
Ps 77: 7 Will the Lord **c** off forever
Ps 78:49 He **c** on them the fierceness
Ps 80: 8 You have **c** out the nations,
Ps 88:14 why do You **c** off my soul
Ps 89:38 But You have **c** off and
Ps 89:44 And **c** his throne down to the
Ps 94:14 will not **c** off His people
Ps 102:10 lifted me up and **c** me away
Ps 108: 9 Over Edom I will **c** My shoe
Ps 108:11 not You, O God, who **c** us off
Ps 140:10 Let them be **c** into the fire,
Prov 1:14 **c** in your lot among us, let
Prov 7:26 for she has **c** down many
Prov 16:33 The lot is **c** into the lap,
Prov 22:10 **C** out the scoffer, and
Prov 29:18 the people **c** off restraint
Eccl 3: 5 a time to **c** away stones, and a
Eccl 11: 1 **C** your bread upon the waters,
Is 2:20 In that day a man will **c** away
Is 14:19 but you are **c** out of your
Is 19: 8 who **c** hooks into the River
Is 25: 7 covering **c** over all people
Is 26:19 earth shall **c** out the dead
Is 34:17 He has **c** the lot for them, and
Is 37:19 have **c** their gods into the
Is 38:17 for You have **c** all my sins
Is 41: 9 you and have not **c** you away
Is 44:10 Who would form a god or **c** a
Is 57:20 rest, whose waters **c** up mire
Is 58: 7 house the poor who are **c** out
Is 66: 5 who **c** you out for My name's
Jer 6:15 them, they shall be **c** down
Jer 7:15 I will **c** you out of My sight,
Jer 7:15 as I have **c** out all your
Jer 7:29 and **c** it away, and take up a
Jer 8:12 they shall be **c** down," says
Jer 9:19 been **c** out of our dwellings
Jer 14:16 be **c** out in the streets of
Jer 15: 1 **C** them out of My sight, and
Jer 16:13 Therefore I will **c** you out
Jer 22: 7 and **c** them into the fire
Jer 22:19 **c** out beyond the gates of
Jer 22:26 So I will **c** you out, and your
Jer 22:28 Why are they **c** out, he and his
Jer 22:28 **c** into a land which they do
Jer 23:39 will **c** you out of My presence
Jer 26:23 and **c** his dead body into the
Jer 28:16 I will **c** you from the face of
Jer 31:37 I will also **c** off all the
Jer 33:24 He has also **c** them off'
Jer 33:26 then I will **c** away the
Jer 36:23 **c** it into the fire that was
Jer 36:30 his dead body shall be **c** out
Jer 38: 6 **c** him into the dungeon of
Jer 38: 9 whom they have **c** into the
Jer 41: 7 **c** them into the midst of a
Jer 41: 9 **c** all the dead bodies of the
Jer 50:26 **c** her up as heaps of ruins,
Jer 52: 3 till He finally **c** them out
Lam 2: 1 He **c** down from heaven to the
Lam 3:31 Lord will not **c** off forever
Ezek 6: 4 I will **c** down your slain men
Ezek 11:16 Although I have **c** them far
Ezek 18:31 **C** away from you all the
Ezek 19:12 she was **c** down to the ground,
Ezek 20: 8 They did not all **c** away the
Ezek 23:35 Me and **c** Me behind your back,
Ezek 27:30 and **c** dust on their heads
Ezek 28:16 therefore I **c** you as a
Ezek 28:17 I **c** you to the ground, I laid
Ezek 31:16 when I **c** it down to hell
Ezek 32: 4 I will **c** you out on the open
Ezek 32:18 **c** them down to the depths of
Dan 3: 6 down and worship shall be **c**
Dan 3:11 worship shall be **c** into the
Dan 3:15 you shall be **c** immediately
Dan 3:20 **c** them into the burning fiery
Dan 3:21 were **c** into the midst of the
Dan 3:24 Did we not **c** three men bound
Dan 6: 7 shall be **c** into the den of
Dan 6:12 shall be **c** into the den of
Dan 6:16 **c** him into the den of lions
Dan 6:24 they **c** them into the den of
Dan 8: 7 him, but he **c** him down to the
Dan 8:10 it **c** down some of the host and
Dan 8:11 of His sanctuary was **c** down
Dan 8:12 he **c** truth down to the ground
Dan 11:12 and he will **c** down tens of
Hos 8: 3 Israel has **c** off the good
Hos 9:17 My God will **c** them away,
Joel 3: 3 They have **c** lots for My
Amos 1:11 the sword, and **c** off all pity
Amos 4: 3 and you will be **c** into Harmon
Obad 11 gates and **c** lots for Jerusalem
Jon 1: 7 Come, let us **c** lots, that we
Jon 1: 7 So they **c** lots, and the lot
Jon 2: 3 For You **c** me into the deep,
Jon 2: 4 I have been **c** out of Your
Mic 2: 9 you **c** out from their pleasant
Mic 7:19 You will **c** all our sins into
Nah 3: 6 I will **c** abominable filth
Nah 3:10 they **c** lots for her honorable
Zeph 3:15 he has **c** out your enemy
Zech 1:21 to **c** out the horns of the
Zech 9: 4 the LORD will **c** her out
Zech 10: 6 though I had not **c** them aside
Matt 5:29 pluck it out and **c** it from you
Matt 5:29 whole body to be **c** into hell
Matt 5:30 cut it off and **c** it from you
Matt 5:30 whole body to be **c** into hell
Matt 7: 6 nor **c** your pearls before
Matt 7:22 **c** out demons in Your name, and
Matt 8:12 be **c** out into outer darkness
Matt 8:16 He **c** out the spirits with a
Matt 8:31 If You **c** us out, permit us to
Matt 9:33 And when the demon was **c** out
Matt 10: 1 to **c** them out, and to heal all
Matt 10: 8 raise the dead, **c** out demons
Matt 12:24 not **c** out demons except by
Matt 12:27 And if I **c** out demons by
Matt 12:27 whom do your sons **c** them out
Matt 12:28 But if I **c** out demons by the
Matt 13:42 will **c** them into the furnace
Matt 13:47 that was **c** into the sea and
Matt 13:50 **c** them into the furnace of
Matt 17:19 Why could we not **c** him out
Matt 17:27 **c** in a hook, and take the fish
Matt 18: 8 cut it off and **c** it from you
Matt 18: 8 to be **c** into the everlasting
Matt 18: 9 pluck it out and **c** it from you
Matt 18: 9 eyes, to be **c** into hell fire
Matt 21:21 be **c** into the sea,' it will
Matt 21:39 **c** him out of the vineyard, and
Matt 22:13 **c** him into outer darkness
Matt 25:30 **c** the unprofitable servant
Matt 27:35 for My clothing they **c** lots
Mark 1:34 and **c** out many demons
Mark 3:15 sicknesses and to **c** out demons
Mark 3:23 How can Satan **c** out Satan
Mark 6:13 they **c** out many demons, and
Mark 7:26 Him to **c** the demon out of her
Mark 9:18 that they should **c** him out
Mark 9:28 Why could we not **c** him out
Mark 9:45 to be **c** into hell, into the
Mark 9:47 eyes, to be **c** into hell fire
Mark 11:23 be **c** into the sea,' and does
Mark 12: 8 **c** him out of the vineyard
Mark 16: 9 of whom He had **c** seven demons
Mark 16:17 name they will **c** out demons
Luke 6:22 **c** out your name as evil, for
Luke 9:40 Your disciples to **c** it out
Luke 11:18 Because you say I **c** out
Luke 11:19 And if I **c** out demons by
Luke 11:19 whom do your sons **c** them out
Luke 11:20 But if I **c** out demons with
Luke 12: 5 has power to **c** into hell
Luke 13:32 I **c** out demons and perform
Luke 20:12 wounded him also and **c** him out
Luke 20:15 So they **c** him out of the
Luke 23:34 His garments and **c** lots
John 6:37 Me I will by no means **c** out
John 9:34 And they **c** him out
John 9:35 heard that they had **c** him out
John 12:31 of this world will be **c** out
John 15: 6 he is **c** out as a branch and is
John 19:24 but **c** lots for it, whose it
John 19:24 for My clothing they **c** lots
John 21: 6 **C** the net on the right side
John 21: 6 So they **c**, and now they were
Acts 1:26 they **c** their lots, and the lot
Acts 7:58 they **c** him out of the city and
Acts 26:10 I **c** my vote against them
Rom 11: 1 has God **c** away His people
Rom 11: 2 God has not **c** away His people
Rom 11:15 For if their being **c** away is
Rom 13:12 Therefore let us **c** off the
Gal 4:30 **C** out the bondwoman and her
1Ti 5:12 because they have **c** off their
Heb 10:35 Therefore do not **c** away your
2Pe 2: 4 but **c** them down to hell and
Rev 2:22 Indeed I will **c** her into a
Rev 4:10 **c** their crowns before the
Rev 12: 9 So the great dragon was **c** out
Rev 12: 9 he was **c** to the earth, and his
Rev 12: 9 angels were **c** out with him
Rev 12:10 day and night, has been **c** down
Rev 12:13 he had been **c** to the earth
Rev 19:20 These two were **c** alive into
Rev 20: 3 he **c** him into the bottomless
Rev 20:10 was **c** into the lake of fire
Rev 20:14 Hades were **c** into the lake of
Rev 20:15 was **c** into the lake of fire

CASTING (*see* CAST)
Lev 18:24 which I am **c** out before you
Lev 20:23 which I am **c** out before you
1Ki 7:35 its panels were of the same **c**
Ps 89:39 crown by **c** it to the ground
Prov 18:18 **C** lots causes contentions to
Matt 4:18 brother, **c** a net into the sea
Matt 27:35 **c** lots, that it might be
Mark 1:16 brother **c** a net into the sea
Mark 1:39 all Galilee, and **c** out demons
Mark 9:38 who does not follow us **c** out
Mark 15:24 **c** lots for them to determine
Luke 9:49 we saw someone **c** out demons
Luke 11:14 He was **c** out a demon, and it
2Co 10: 5 **c** down arguments and every
1Pe 5: 7 **c** all your care upon Him, for

CASTLE
Prov 18:19 are like the bars of a **c**

CASTS (*see* CAST)
Job 18: 7 and his own counsel **c** him down
Job 20:15 God **c** them out of his belly
Ps 147: 6 He **c** the wicked down to the
Ps 147:17 He **c** out His hail like
Prov 10: 3 but He **c** away the desire of
Prov 19:15 Slothfulness **c** one into a
Is 40:19 silversmith **c** silver chains
Matt 9:34 He **c** out demons by the ruler
Matt 12:26 if Satan **c** out Satan, he is
Mark 3:22 of the demons He **c** out demons
Luke 11:15 He **c** out demons by Beelzebub,
1Jn 4:18 but perfect love **c** out fear

CASUAL
Jer 3: 9 pass, through her **c** harlotry

CATASTROPHE
Jer 11:23 for I will bring **c** on the men
Jer 19: 3 bring such a **c** on this place
Jer 44:11 set My face against you for **c**
Jer 51:64 not rise from the **c** that I

CATCH (*see* CATCHES, CAUGHT)
Judg 21:21 and every man **c** a wife for
2Ki 7:12 we shall **c** them alive, and get
Job 9:18 not allow me to **c** my breath
Ps 10: 9 He lies in wait to **c** the poor
Ps 35: 8 that he has hidden **c** himself
Prov 12:12 covet the **c** of evil men, but
Song 2:15 **C** us the foxes, the little
Jer 5:26 they set a trap; they **c** men.
Ezek 19: 3 he learned to **c** prey, and he
Ezek 19: 6 he learned to **c** prey
Hab 1:15 they **c** them in their net, and
Mark 12:13 to **c** Him in His words
Luke 5: 4 and let down your nets for a **c**
Luke 5: 9 the **c** of fish which they had
Luke 5:10 From now on you will **c** men
Luke 11:54 seeking to **c** Him in something

Luke 20:26 But they could not **c** Him in

CATCHES (*see* CATCH)
Ex 22: 6 **c** in thorns, so that stacked
Lev 17:13 **c** any animal or bird that may
Job 5:13 He **c** the wise in their own
Ps 10: 9 He **c** the poor when he draws
John 10:12 and the wolf **c** the sheep and
1Co 3:19 He **c** the wise in their own

CATERPILLAR
Ps 78:46 gave their crops to the **c**
Is 33: 4 like the gathering of the **c**

CATTLE
Gen 1:24 **c** and creeping thing and beast
Gen 1:25 **c** according to its kind, and
Gen 1:26 of the air, and over the **c**
Gen 2:20 So Adam gave names to all **c**
Gen 3:14 are cursed more than all **c**
Gen 7:14 all **c** after their kind, every
Gen 7:21 birds and **c** and beasts and every
Gen 7:23 both man and **c**, creeping thing
Gen 8:17 birds and **c** and every creeping
Gen 9:10 the birds, the **c**, and every
Gen 29: 7 it is not time for the **c** to
Gen 36: 6 of his household, his **c** and
Gen 47:17 the **c** of the herds, and for
Ex 9: 3 be on your **c** in the field
Ex 20:10 your maidservant, nor your **c**
Lev 22:19 without blemish from the **c**
Lev 22:21 from the **c** or the sheep, it
Num 31: 9 and took as spoil all their **c**
Num 31:28 hundred of the persons, the **c**
Num 31:30 drawn from the persons, the **c**
Num 31:33 seventy-two thousand **c**,
Num 31:38 The **c** were thirty-six
Num 31:44 thirty-six thousand **c**,
Num 35: 3 shall be for their **c**, for
Deut 5:14 donkey, nor any of your **c**
Deut 7:13 oil, the increase of your **c**
Deut 28: 4 herds, the increase of your **c**
Deut 28:18 land, the increase of your **c**
Deut 28:51 or the increase of your **c** or
Deut 32:14 curds from the **c**, and milk of
Josh 8: 2 its **c** you shall take as booty
1Ki 1: 9 fattened **c** by the stone of
1Ki 1:19 sacrificed oxen and fattened **c**
1Ki 1:25 sacrificed oxen and fattened **c**
2Ki 3:17 water, so that you, your **c**
1Ch 5: 9 because their **c** had
1Ch 7:21 down to take away their **c**
2Ch 35: 7 as well as three thousand **c**
2Ch 35: 8 the flock, and three hundred **c**
2Ch 35: 9 the flock and five hundred **c**
2Ch 35:12 And so they did with the **c**
Neh 9:37 and our **c** at their pleasure
Neh 10:36 of our sons and our **c**, as it
Job 36:33 the **c** also, concerning the
Ps 50:10 the **c** on a thousand hills
Ps 78:48 gave up their **c** to the hail
Ps 104:14 the grass to grow for the **c**
Ps 107:38 does not let their **c** decrease
Ps 148:10 Beasts and all **c**
Is 1:11 of rams and the fat of fed **c**
Is 30:23 In that day your **c** will feed
Is 46: 1 on the beasts and on the **c**
Jer 9:10 men hear the voice of the **c**
Jer 49:32 of their **c** for plunder
Joel 1:18 The herds of **c** are restless
Zech 13: 5 me to keep **c** from my youth
Zech 14:15 on all the **c** that will be in
Matt 22: 4 fatted **c** are killed, and all
Rev 18:13 oil, fine flour and wheat, **c**

CAUGHT (*see* CATCH)
Gen 22:13 **c** in a thicket by its horns
Gen 39:12 that she **c** him by his garment
Ex 4: 4 **c** it, and it became a rod in
Num 5:13 against her, nor was she **c**
Josh 8:22 so they were **c** in the midst
Judg 1: 6 **c** him and cut off his thumbs
Judg 8:14 he **c** a young man of the men
Judg 15: 4 went and **c** three hundred foxes
Judg 21:23 those who danced, whom they **c**
1Sa 17:35 me, I **c** it by its beard, and
2Sa 16: 8 So now you are **c** in your own
2Sa 18: 9 his head **c** in the terebinth
2Ki 4:27 she **c** him by the feet, but
2Ch 22: 9 they **c** him (he was hiding in
Ps 9:15 they hid, their own foot is **c**
Ps 10: 2 Let them be **c** in the plots
Prov 3:26 keep your foot from being **c**
Prov 5:22 he is **c** in the cords of his
Prov 7:13 So she **c** him and kissed him
Eccl 9:12 net, like birds **c** in a snare
Is 24:18 pit shall be **c** in the snare
Is 28:13 and be broken and snared and **c**
Jer 48:44 pit shall be **c** in the snare
Jer 50:24 you have been found and also **c**
Lam 4:20 was **c** in their pits, of whom
Ezek 12:13 and he shall be **c** in My snare
Amos 3: 4 his den, if he has **c** nothing
Amos 3: 5 if it has **c** nothing at all
Matt 14:31 and **c** him, and said to him,
Matt 21:39 And they **c** him, and cast him
Luke 5: 5 toiled all night and **c** nothing
Luke 5: 6 they **c** a great number of fish
John 8: 3 to Him a woman **c** in adultery
John 8: 4 this woman was **c** in adultery
John 21: 3 and that night they **c** nothing
John 21:10 fish which you have just **c**
Acts 8:39 of the Lord **c** Philip away
Acts 27:15 So when the ship was **c**, and
2Co 12: 2 such a one was **c** up to the
2Co 12: 4 how he was **c** up into Paradise
2Co 12:16 crafty, I **c** you with guile
1Th 4:17 remain shall be **c** up together
2Pe 2:12 brute beasts made to be **c**
Rev 12: 5 And her Child was **c** up to God

CAULK (*see* CAULKERS)
Ezek 27: 9 were in you to **c** your seams

CAULKERS (*see* CAULK)
Ezek 27:27 mariners and pilots, your **c**

CAUSE (*see* CAUSED, CAUSES, CAUSING)
Gen 7: 4 seven more days I will **c** it
Ex 8: 5 **c** frogs to come up on the
Ex 9: 9 it will **c** boils that break
Ex 9:18 about this time I will **c** very
Ex 22: 9 the **c** of both parties shall
Ex 23:27 I will **c** confusion among all
Ex 27:20 light, to **c** the lamp to burn
Lev 14:41 he shall **c** the house to be
Lev 19:29 to **c** her to be a harlot, lest
Lev 25: 9 Then you shall **c** the trumpet
Lev 26:16 the eyes and **c** sorrow of heart
Lev 26:36 leaf shall **c** them to flee
Num 16: 5 will **c** him to come near to
Num 16: 5 He will **c** to come near to Him
Num 27: 7 **c** the inheritance of their
Num 27: 8 no son, then you shall **c** his
Deut 1:38 him, for he shall **c** Israel to
Deut 3:28 he shall **c** them to inherit
Deut 17:16 nor **c** the people to return to
Deut 25: 2 judge will **c** him to lie down
Deut 28: 7 The LORD will **c** your enemies
Deut 28:25 The LORD will **c** you to be
Deut 31: 7 you shall **c** them to inherit
Josh 23: 7 nor **c** anyone to swear by them
Judg 8: 7 For this **c**, when the LORD has
1Sa 17:29 Is there not a **c**
1Sa 19: 5 to kill David without a **c**
1Sa 25:31 you have shed blood without **c**
1Sa 25:39 who has pleaded the **c** of my
1Sa 28: 9 for my life, to **c** me to die
2Sa 15: 4 suit or **c** would come to me
1Ki 8:45 and maintain their **c**
1Ki 8:49 and maintain their **c**,
1Ki 8:59 maintain the **c** of His servant
1Ki 8:59 the **c** of His people Israel,
2Ki 19: 7 I will **c** him to fall by the
1Ch 4:10 evil, that I may not **c** pain
1Ch 21: 3 he be a **c** of guilt in Israel
2Ch 6:35 and maintain their **c**
2Ch 6:39 and maintain their **c**, and
2Ch 32:20 Now for this **c** King Hezekiah
Ezra 4:15 for which **c** this city was
Neh 4:11 them and **c** the work to cease
Job 2: 3 him, to destroy him without **c**
Job 5: 8 and to God I would commit my **c**
Job 6:24 **c** me to understand wherein I
Job 9:17 my wounds without **c**
Job 24:10 They **c** the poor to go naked,
Job 30:22 wind and **c** me to ride on it
Job 31:13 the **c** of my manservant or my
Job 38:26 to **c** it to rain on a land
Job 38:27 **c** to spring forth the growth
Ps 7: 4 plundered my enemy without **c**
Ps 9: 4 maintained my right and my **c**
Ps 10:17 You will **c** Your ear to hear,
Ps 17: 1 Hear a just **c**, O LORD, Attend
Ps 25: 3 deal treacherously without **c**
Ps 32: 6 For this **c** everyone who is
Ps 35: 1 Plead my **c**, O LORD, with
Ps 35: 7 For without **c** they have
Ps 35: 7 dug without **c** for my life
Ps 35:19 eye who hate me without a **c**
Ps 35:23 to my vindication, To my **c**
Ps 35:27 Who favor my righteous **c**
Ps 43: 1 plead my **c** against an ungodly
Ps 65: 4 **c** to approach You, That he
Ps 67: 1 **c** His face to shine upon us
Ps 69: 4 **c** Are more than the hairs of
Ps 71: 2 and **c** me to escape
Ps 74:22 O God, plead Your own **c**
Ps 80: 3 **C** Your face to shine, And we
Ps 80: 7 **C** Your face to shine, And we
Ps 80:19 **C** Your face to shine, And we
Ps 85: 4 **c** Your anger toward us to
Ps 109: 3 fought against me without a **c**
Ps 119:154 Plead my **c** and redeem me
Ps 119:161 persecute me without a **c**, But
Ps 140:12 The **c** of the afflicted, And
Ps 143: 8 **C** me to hear Your
Ps 143: 8 **C** me to know the way in which
Prov 1:11 for the innocent without **c**
Prov 3:30 strive with a man without **c**
Prov 8:21 that I may **c** those who love
Prov 18:17 to plead his **c** seems right
Prov 22:23 the LORD will plead their **c**
Prov 23:11 plead their **c** against you
Prov 23:29 Who has wounds without **c**
Prov 24:28 your neighbor without **c**, for
Prov 26: 2 without **c** shall not alight
Prov 29: 7 considers the **c** of the poor
Prov 31: 8 in the **c** of all who are
Prov 31: 9 plead the **c** of the poor and
Eccl 5: 6 mouth **c** your flesh to sin
Eccl 10: 1 **c** it to give off a foul odor
Song 8: 2 I would **c** you to drink of
Is 1:23 nor does the **c** of the widow
Is 3:12 who lead you **c** you to err
Is 9:16 of this people **c** them to err
Is 10:30 **C** it to be heard as far as
Is 13:10 the moon will not **c** its light
Is 27: 6 shall **c** to take root in Jacob
Is 28:12 you may **c** the weary to rest
Is 30:11 **c** the Holy One of Israel to
Is 30:30 The LORD will **c** His glorious
Is 32: 6 he will **c** the drink of the
Is 34: 8 recompense for the **c** of Zion
Is 37: 7 I will **c** him to fall by the
Is 42: 2 nor **c** His voice to be heard
Is 49: 8 to **c** them to inherit the
Is 51:22 pleads the **c** of His people
Is 52: 4 oppressed them without **c**
Is 58:14 I will **c** you to ride on the
Is 61:11 Lord GOD will **c** righteousness
Is 66: 9 of birth, and not **c** delivery
Is 66: 9 Shall I who **c** delivery shut
Jer 3:12 I will not **c** My anger to fall
Jer 5:28 they do not plead the **c**, the
Jer 5:28 the **c** of the fatherless
Jer 7: 3 I will **c** you to dwell in this
Jer 7: 7 then I will **c** you to dwell in
Jer 7:34 Then I will **c** to cease from
Jer 11:20 to You I have revealed my **c**
Jer 14:22 the nations that can **c** rain
Jer 15: 8 I will **c** anguish and terror to
Jer 15:11 surely I will **c** the enemy to
Jer 16: 9 I will **c** to cease from this
Jer 16:21 will this once **c** them to know
Jer 16:21 I will **c** them to know My hand
Jer 17: 4 I will **c** you to serve your
Jer 18: 2 there I will **c** you to hear My
Jer 19: 7 I will **c** them to fall by the
Jer 19: 9 And I will **c** them to eat the
Jer 20:12 have pleaded my **c** before You
Jer 22:16 He judged the **c** of the poor
Jer 23:32 **c** My people to err by their
Jer 25:15 **c** all the nations, to whom I
Jer 29: 8 which you **c** to be dreamed
Jer 29:10 **c** you to return to this place
Jer 29:14 I **c** you to be carried away
Jer 30: 3 I will **c** them to return to
Jer 30:13 is no one to plead your **c**
Jer 30:21 then I will **c** him to draw
Jer 31: 9 I will **c** them to walk by the
Jer 32:35 to **c** their sons and their
Jer 32:35 to **c** Judah to sin
Jer 32:37 I will **c** them to dwell safely

Jer 32:44 for I will **c** their captives
Jer 33: 7 And I will **c** the captives of
Jer 33:11 For I will **c** the captives of
Jer 33:15 at that time I will **c** to grow
Jer 33:26 For I will **c** their captives
Jer 34:22 **c** them to return to this city
Jer 36:29 **c** man and beast to cease from
Jer 38:23 you shall **c** this city to be
Jer 42:12 **c** you to return to your own
Jer 48:35 I will **c** to cease in Moab the
Jer 49: 2 That I will **c** to be heard an
Jer 49:37 For I will **c** Elam to be
Jer 50: 9 **c** to come up against Babylon
Jer 51:27 **c** the horses to come up like
Lam 3:36 or subvert a man in his **c**
Lam 3:52 My enemies without **c** hunted
Ezek 5:13 I will **c** My fury to rest upon
Ezek 7:24 I will **c** the pomp of the
Ezek 13:13 I will **c** a stormy wind to
Ezek 14:15 If I **c** wild beasts to pass
Ezek 14:23 **c** that I have done in it,"
Ezek 16: 2 man, **c** Jerusalem to know her
Ezek 21:17 and I will **c** My fury to rest
Ezek 22: 9 who slander to **c** bloodshed
Ezek 23:48 Thus I will **c** lewdness to
Ezek 25: 7 I will **c** you to perish from
Ezek 26: 3 will **c** many nations to come
Ezek 29: 4 **c** the fish of your rivers to
Ezek 29:14 **c** them to return to the land
Ezek 29:21 In that day I will **c** the
Ezek 30:13 **c** the images to cease from
Ezek 32: 4 **c** to settle on you all the
Ezek 32:12 I will **c** your multitude to
Ezek 34:10 I will **c** them to cease
Ezek 34:25 **c** wild beasts to cease from
Ezek 34:26 I will **c** showers to come down
Ezek 36:12 I will **c** men to walk on you,
Ezek 36:15 nor shall you **c** your nation
Ezek 36:27 **c** you to walk in My statutes,
Ezek 37: 5 Surely I will **c** breath to
Ezek 37:12 **c** you to come up from your
Ezek 39: 3 **c** the arrows to fall out of
Ezek 44:23 **c** them to discern between the
Ezek 44:30 to **c** a blessing to rest on
Dan 8:25 his cunning he shall **c** deceit
Dan 9:17 for the Lord's sake **c** Your
Dan 11:39 he shall **c** them to rule over
Hos 2:11 I will also **c** all her mirth
Joel 2:23 He will **c** the rain to come
Joel 3:11 **C** Your mighty ones to go down
Amos 6: 3 who **c** the seat of violence to
Jon 1: 7 **c** this trouble has come upon
Jon 1: 8 For whose **c** is this trouble
Hab 1: 3 and **c** me to see trouble
Zech 8:12 I will **c** the remnant of this
Zech 13: 2 I will also **c** the prophets and
Matt 5:22 a **c** shall be in danger of the
Matt 10:21 **c** them to be put to death
Mark 13:12 **c** them to be put to death
John 15:25 They hated Me without a **c**
John 18:37 For this **c** I was born, and for
John 18:37 for this **c** I have come into
Acts 13:28 found no **c** for death in Him
Acts 28:18 because there was no **c** for
Rom 14:13 a **c** to fall in our brother's
Rom 16:17 note those who **c** divisions
2Co 4:15 may **c** thanksgiving to abound
1Ti 1: 4 which **c** disputes rather than
Heb 12:15 springing up **c** trouble, and by
1Jn 2:10 there is no **c** for stumbling
Jude 19 who **c** divisions, not having
Rev 12:15 that he might **c** her to be
Rev 13:15 and **c** as many as would not

CAUSED (*see* CAUSE)
Gen 2: 5 not **c** it to rain on the earth
Gen 2:21 the LORD God **c** a deep sleep
Gen 20:13 when God **c** me to wander from
Gen 41:52 For God has **c** me to be
Ex 9:10 they **c** boils that break out
Ex 14:21 the LORD **c** the sea to go back
Ex 36: 6 they **c** it to be proclaimed
Lev 24:20 as he has **c** disfigurement of
Num 31:16 these women **c** the children of
Deut 34: 4 I have **c** you to see it with
1Sa 10:20 when Samuel had **c** all the
1Sa 10:21 When he had **c** the tribe of
1Sa 20:17 Jonathan again **c** David to vow
1Sa 22:22 I have **c** the death of all the
2Sa 7:11 have **c** you to rest from all
1Ki 11:25 the trouble that Hadad **c**)
1Ki 11:27 this is what **c** him to rebel
2Ki 7: 6 For the LORD had **c** the army
2Ki 17:17 And they **c** their sons and
2Ch 13:13 But Jeroboam **c** an ambush to
2Ch 21:11 and **c** the inhabitants of
2Ch 33: 6 Also he **c** his sons to pass
Neh 13:26 pagan women **c** even him to sin
Job 29:13 I **c** the widow's heart to sing
Job 31:16 or **c** the eyes of the widow to
Job 31:39 or **c** its owners to lose their
Job 34:28 so that they **c** the cry of the
Job 38:12 **c** the dawn to know its place,
Ps 66:12 You have **c** men to ride over
Ps 76: 8 You **c** judgment to be heard
Ps 78:13 sea and **c** them to pass through
Ps 78:16 **c** waters to run down like
Ps 78:26 He **c** an east wind to blow in
Ps 80: 9 **c** it to take deep root, And it
Ps 119:49 which You have **c** me to hope
Prov 7:21 speech she **c** him to yield
Is 19:14 they have **c** Egypt to err in
Is 43:23 I have not **c** you to serve
Is 48: 3 mouth, and I **c** them to hear it
Is 48:21 He **c** the waters to flow from
Jer 12:14 inheritance which I have **c** My
Jer 13:11 so I have **c** the whole house
Jer 18:15 they have **c** themselves to
Jer 23:13 **c** My people Israel to err
Jer 23:22 had **c** My people to hear My
Jer 29: 4 whom I have **c** to be carried
Jer 29: 7 have **c** you to be carried away
Jer 29:31 he has **c** you to trust in a
Jer 32:23 therefore You have **c** all this
Jer 48: 4 ones have **c** a cry to be heard
Jer 48:33 I have **c** wine to fail from
Jer 51:49 As Babylon has **c** the slain of
Lam 2: 6 the LORD has **c** the appointed
Lam 2: 8 He has **c** the rampart and wall
Lam 2:17 and He has **c** your enemy to
Lam 3:13 He has **c** the arrows of His
Ezek 3: 2 He **c** me to eat that scroll
Ezek 20:26 in that they **c** all their
Ezek 22: 4 You have **c** your days to draw
Ezek 24:13 till I have **c** My fury to rest
Ezek 26:17 who **c** their terror to be on
Ezek 29:18 king of Babylon **c** his army to
Ezek 31:15 down to hell, I **c** mourning
Ezek 31:15 I **c** Lebanon to mourn for it,
Ezek 32:23 who **c** terror in the land of
Ezek 32:24 who **c** their terror in the
Ezek 32:25 though their terror was **c** in
Ezek 32:26 though they **c** their terror in
Ezek 32:30 which they **c** by their might
Ezek 32:32 For I have **c** My terror in the
Ezek 37: 2 Then He **c** me to pass by them
Ezek 44:12 **c** the house of Israel to fall
Ezek 46:21 and **c** me to pass by the four
Dan 9:21 being **c** to fly swiftly,
Hos 4:12 harlotry has **c** them to stray
Jon 3: 7 he **c** it to be proclaimed and
Mal 2: 8 you have **c** many to stumble at
Acts 15: 3 they **c** great joy to all the
2Co 2: 5 But if anyone has **c** grief

CAUSES (*see* CAUSE)
Ex 22: 5 If a man **c** a field or
Lev 24:19 If a man **c** disfigurement of
Num 5:22 may this water that **c** the
Ezra 6:12 may the God who **c** His name to
Job 20: 3 understanding **c** me to answer
Job 37:13 He **c** it to come, whether for
Job 37:15 **c** the light of His cloud to
Ps 37: 8 it only **c** harm
Ps 104:14 He **c** the grass to grow for
Ps 107:40 And **c** them to wander in the
Ps 119:165 nothing **c** them to stumble
Ps 135: 7 He **c** the vapors to ascend
Ps 147:18 He **c** His wind to blow, and the
Prov 10: 5 harvest is a son who **c** shame
Prov 10:10 winks with the eye **c** trouble
Prov 12: 4 but she who **c** shame is like
Prov 12:25 the heart of man **c** depression
Prov 14:35 is against him who **c** shame
Prov 17: 2 rule over a son who **c** shame
Prov 18:18 Casting lots **c** contentions to
Prov 19:26 mother is a son who **c** shame
Prov 28:10 Whoever **c** the upright to go
Is 61:11 as the garden **c** the things
Is 63:14 of the LORD **c** him to rest
Is 64: 2 as fire **c** water to boil
Jer 3: 8 the **c** for which backsliding
Jer 10:13 He **c** the vapors to ascend
Jer 13:16 your God before He **c** darkness
Jer 51:16 He **c** the vapors to ascend
Lam 3:32 Though He **c** grief, yet He
Ezek 14: 3 which **c** them to stumble into
Ezek 14: 4 what **c** him to stumble into
Ezek 14: 7 what **c** him to stumble into
Ezek 26: 3 as the sea **c** its waves to
Ezek 44:18 with anything that **c** sweat
Matt 5:29 your right eye **c** you to sin
Matt 5:30 your right hand **c** you to sin
Matt 5:32 **c** her to commit adultery
Matt 18: 6 But whoever **c** one of these
Matt 18: 8 hand or foot **c** you to sin
Matt 18: 9 And if your eye **c** you to sin
Mark 9:42 whoever **c** one of these little
2Co 9:11 which **c** thanksgiving through
Eph 4:16 **c** growth of the body for the
Rev 13:12 and **c** the earth and those who
Rev 13:16 he **c** all, both small and great
Rev 21:27 or **c** an abomination or a lie,

CAUSING (*see* CAUSE)
Is 30:28 of the people, **c** them to err
Jer 33:12 **c** their flocks to lie down
Ezek 16:21 by **c** them to pass through the

CAUTIOUSLY
1Sa 15:32 So Agag came to him **c**

CAVALRY
1Ki 9:19 chariots and cities for his **c**
1Ki 9:22 of his chariots, and his **c**
1Ki 20:20 escaped on a horse with the **c**
2Ch 8: 6 cities and the cities of the **c**
2Ch 8: 9 of his chariots, and his **c**
Hab 1: 8 their **c** comes from afar

CAVE (*see* CAVE'S, CAVES)
Gen 19:30 two daughters dwelt in a **c**
Gen 23: 9 that he may give me the **c** of
Gen 23:11 field and the **c** that is in it
Gen 23:17 the **c** which was in it, and all
Gen 23:19 Sarah his wife in the **c** of
Gen 23:20 and the **c** that is in it were
Gen 25: 9 him in the **c** of Machpelah
Gen 49:29 the **c** that is in the field of
Gen 49:30 in the **c** that is in the field
Gen 49:32 and the **c** that is there were
Gen 50:13 buried him in the **c** of the
Josh 10:16 themselves in a **c** at Makkedah
Josh 10:17 hidden in the **c** at Makkedah
Josh 10:18 against the mouth of the **c**
Josh 10:22 Open the mouth of the **c**, and
Josh 10:22 five kings to me from the **c**
Josh 10:23 five kings to him from the **c**
Josh 10:27 cast them into the **c** where
1Sa 22: 1 escaped to the **c** of Adullam
1Sa 24: 3 the road, where there was a **c**
1Sa 24: 3 in the recesses of the **c**
1Sa 24: 7 And Saul got up from the **c**
1Sa 24: 8 afterward, went out of the **c**
1Sa 24:10 today into my hand in the **c**
2Sa 23:13 to David at the **c** of Adullam
1Ki 18: 4 and hidden them, fifty to a **c**
1Ki 18:13 LORD's prophets, fifty to a **c**
1Ki 19: 9 And there he went into a **c**
1Ki 19:13 in the entrance of the **c**
1Ch 11:15 David, into the **c** of Adullam
John 11:38 It was a **c**, and a stone lay

CAVE'S (*see* CAVE)
Josh 10:27 stones against the **c** mouth
Jer 48:28 in the sides of the **c** mouth

CAVES (*see* CAVE)
Judg 6: 2 themselves the dens, the **c**
1Sa 13: 6 then the people hid in **c**
Job 30: 6 In **c** of the earth and the
Is 2:19 into the **c** of the earth, from
Ezek 33:27 **c** shall die of the pestilence
Nah 2:12 filled his **c** with prey, and
Heb 11:38 in dens and **c** of the earth
Rev 6:15 man, hid themselves in the **c**

CEASE (*see* CEASED, CEASES, CEASING)
Gen 8:22 and day and night shall not **c**
Ex 9:29 the thunder will **c**, and there
Num 8:25 must **c** performing this work
Deut 15:11 will never **c** from the land
Deut 32:26 of them to **c** from among men
Josh 22:25 **c** fearing the LORD
Judg 2:19 They did not **c** from their own
Judg 9: 9 Should I **c** giving my oil,

Judg 9:11 Should I **c** my sweetness and
Judg 9:13 Should I **c** my new wine,
Judg 15: 7 you, and after that I will **c**
Judg 20:28 Benjamin, or shall I **c**
1Sa 7: 8 Do not **c** to cry out to the
1Sa 9: 5 lest my father **c** caring about
2Ch 25:16 **C**! Why should you be killed
Ezra 4:21 command to make these men **c**
Ezra 4:23 by force of arms made them **c**
Ezra 5: 5 they could not make them **c**
Neh 4:11 them and cause the work to **c**
Neh 6: 3 the work **c** while I leave it
Job 3:17 the wicked **c** from troubling
Job 6:17 it is warm, they **c** to flow
Job 10:20 **C**! Leave me alone
Job 14: 7 its tender shoots will not **c**
Ps 35:15 They tore at me and did not **c**
Ps 37: 8 **C** from anger, and forsake
Ps 46: 9 He makes wars **c** to the end of
Ps 49: 8 costly, And it shall **c** forever
Ps 85: 4 Your anger toward us to **c**
Ps 89:44 You have made his glory **c**
Prov 18:18 lots causes contentions to **c**
Prov 19:27 **C** listening to instruction,
Prov 22:10 strife and reproach will **c**
Prov 23: 4 of your own understanding, **c**
Eccl 12: 3 when the grinders **c** because
Is 1:16 **C** to do evil,
Is 10:25 and the indignation will **c**
Is 16:10 I have made their shouting **c**
Is 17: 1 Damascus will **c** from being a
Is 17: 3 also will **c** from Ephraim, the
Is 21: 2 its sighing I have made to **c**
Is 30:11 of Israel to **c** from before us
Is 33: 1 When you **c** plundering, you
Jer 7:34 Then I will cause to **c** from
Jer 14:17 and day, and let them not **c**
Jer 16: 9 cause to **c** from this place
Jer 17: 8 nor will **c** from yielding
Jer 31:36 seed of Israel shall also **c**
Jer 36:29 man and beast to **c** from here
Jer 48:35 I will cause to **c** in Moab the
Lam 3:49 My eyes flow and do not **c**,
Ezek 6: 6 may be broken and made to **c**
Ezek 7:24 the pomp of the strong to **c**
Ezek 16:41 I will make you **c** playing the
Ezek 23:27 will make you **c** your lewdness
Ezek 23:48 lewdness to **c** from the land
Ezek 30:10 of Egypt to **c** by the hand of
Ezek 30:13 the images to **c** from Noph
Ezek 30:18 strength shall **c** in her
Ezek 33:28 her arrogant strength shall **c**
Ezek 34:10 them to **c** feeding the sheep
Ezek 34:25 beasts to **c** from the land
Hos 2:11 also cause all her mirth to **c**
Amos 7: 5 O Lord GOD, **c**, I pray
Acts 5:42 they did not **c** teaching and
Acts 6:13 This man does not **c** to speak
Acts 13:10 will you not **c** perverting the
Acts 20:31 not **c** to warn everyone night
1Co 13: 8 are tongues, they will **c**
Eph 1:16 do not **c** to give thanks for
Col 1: 9 do not **c** to pray for you, and
2Pe 2:14 and that cannot **c** from sin

CEASED (*see* CEASE)
Gen 11: 8 and they **c** building the city
Ex 9:33 the thunder and the hail **c**
Ex 9:34 hail, and the thunder had **c**
Josh 5:12 Now the manna **c** on the day
Judg 5: 7 life **c**, it **c** in Israel
1Sa 2: 5 were hungry have **c** to hunger
1Sa 10: 2 now your father has **c** caring
2Ki 4: 6 So the oil **c**
2Ch 16: 5 building Ramah and **c** his work
2Ch 25:16 Then the prophet **c**, and said
Ezra 4:24 God which is at Jerusalem **c**
Job 32: 1 three men **c** answering Job
Ps 36: 3 He has **c** to be wise and to do
Ps 77: 8 Has His mercy **c** forever
Is 14: 4 How the oppressor has **c**, the
Is 14: 4 has **c**, the golden city **c**
Jer 51:30 of Babylon have **c** fighting
Lam 5:14 The elders have **c** gathering
Lam 5:15 The joy of our heart has **c**
Hos 4:10 they have **c** obeying the LORD
Jon 1:15 the sea **c** from its raging
Matt 14:32 got into the boat, the wind **c**
Mark 4:39 And the wind **c** and there was
Mark 6:51 boat to them, and the wind **c**
Luke 7:45 but this woman has not **c** to
Luke 8:24 And they **c**, and there was a
Luke 9:36 And when the voice had **c**,
Luke 11: 1 in a certain place, when He **c**
Acts 20: 1 After the uproar had **c**, Paul
Acts 21:14 would not be persuaded, we **c**
Gal 5:11 offense of the cross has **c**
Heb 4:10 **c** from his works as God did
Heb 10: 2 they not have **c** to be offered
1Pe 4: 1 in the flesh has **c** from sin

CEASES (*see* CEASE)
Num 9:13 **c** to keep the Passover, that
Ps 12: 1 LORD, for the godly man **c**
Prov 26:20 is no talebearer, strife **c**
Is 16: 4 is at an end, devastation **c**
Is 24: 8 The mirth of the tambourine **c**
Is 24: 8 ends, the joy of the harp **c**
Is 33: 8 waste, the wayfaring man **c**
Hos 7: 4 he **c** stirring the fire after

CEASING (*see* CEASE)
1Sa 12:23 the LORD in **c** to pray for you
Ps 77: 2 out in the night without **c**
Rom 1: 9 that without **c** I make mention
1Th 1: 3 without **c** your work of faith
1Th 2:13 we also thank God without **c**
1Th 5:17 pray without **c**,
2Ti 1: 3 as without **c** I remember you

CEDAR (*see* CEDARS)
Lev 14: 4 **c** wood, scarlet, and hyssop
Lev 14: 6 the **c** wood and the scarlet and
Lev 14:49 **c** wood, scarlet, and hyssop
Lev 14:51 and he shall take the **c** wood
Lev 14:52 living bird, with the **c** wood
Num 19: 6 the priest shall take **c** wood
2Sa 5:11 **c** trees, and carpenters and
2Sa 7: 2 now, I dwell in a house of **c**
2Sa 7: 7 you not built Me a house of **c**
1Ki 4:33 from the **c** tree of Lebanon
1Ki 5: 8 you desire concerning the **c**
1Ki 5:10 So Hiram gave Solomon **c** and
1Ki 6: 9 with beams and boards of **c**
1Ki 6:10 to the temple with **c** beams
1Ki 6:15 of the temple with **c** boards
1Ki 6:16 to ceiling, with **c** boards
1Ki 6:18 inside of the temple was **c**
1Ki 6:18 All was **c**
1Ki 6:20 and overlaid the altar of **c**
1Ki 6:36 stone and a row of **c** beams
1Ki 7: 2 with four rows of **c** pillars
1Ki 7: 2 and **c** beams on the pillars
1Ki 7: 3 it was paneled with **c** above
1Ki 7: 7 it was paneled with **c** from
1Ki 7:11 hewn to size, and **c** wood
1Ki 7:12 stones and a row of **c** beams
1Ki 9:11 had supplied Solomon with **c**
2Ki 14: 9 to the **c** that was in Lebanon
1Ch 14: 1 and **c** trees, with masons and
1Ch 17: 1 now, I dwell in a house of **c**
1Ch 17: 6 you not built Me a house of **c**
1Ch 22: 4 and **c** trees in abundance
1Ch 22: 4 brought much **c** wood to David
2Ch 2: 8 Also send me **c** and cypress and
2Ch 9:27 he made **c** trees as abundant
2Ch 25:18 to the **c** that was in Lebanon
Ezra 3: 7 Tyre to bring **c** logs from
Job 40:17 He moves his tail like a **c**
Ps 92:12 grow like a **c** in Lebanon
Song 1:17 The beams of our houses are **c**
Song 8: 9 enclose her with boards of **c**
Is 41:19 plant in the wilderness the **c**
Jer 22:14 for it, paneling it with **c**
Jer 22:15 you enclose yourself in **c**
Ezek 17: 3 took from the **c** the highest
Ezek 17:22 branches of the high **c** and set
Ezek 17:23 fruit, and be a majestic **c**
Ezek 27: 5 they took a **c** from Lebanon to
Ezek 31: 3 Assyria was a **c** in Lebanon
Zeph 2:14 He will lay bare the **c** work
Zech 11: 2 for the **c** has fallen, because

CEDARS (*see* CEDAR)
Num 24: 6 like **c** beside the waters
Judg 9:15 and devour the **c** of Lebanon
1Ki 5: 6 down **c** for me from Lebanon
1Ki 10:27 he made **c** as abundant as the
2Ki 19:23 I will cut down its tall **c**
2Ch 1:15 he made **c** as abundant as the
2Ch 2: 3 sent him **c** to build himself a
Ps 29: 5 of the LORD breaks the **c**, Yes
Ps 29: 5 splinters the **c** of Lebanon
Ps 80:10 the mighty **c** with its boughs
Ps 104:16 The **c** of Lebanon which He
Ps 148: 9 Fruitful trees and all **c**
Song 5:15 Lebanon, excellent as the **c**
Is 2:13 upon all the **c** of Lebanon
Is 9:10 we will replace them with **c**
Is 14: 8 the **c** of Lebanon, saying
Is 37:24 I will cut down its tall **c**
Is 44:14 He hews down **c** for himself
Jer 22: 7 shall cut down your choice **c**
Jer 22:23 making your nest in the **c**
Ezek 31: 8 The **c** in the garden of God
Amos 2: 9 was like the height of the **c**
Zech 11: 1 that fire may devour your **c**

CEILING
1Ki 6:15 the **c** he paneled them on the
1Ki 6:16 the temple, from floor to **c**
1Ki 7: 7 with cedar from floor to **c**

CELEBRATE (*see* CELEBRATED)
Lev 23:32 you shall **c** your sabbath
Lev 23:41 You shall **c** it in the seventh
Neh 12:27 to **c** the dedication with
Esth 9:21 **c** yearly the fourteenth and
Esth 9:27 without fail they should **c**

CELEBRATED (*see* CELEBRATE)
Ezra 6:16 **c** the dedication of this
Esth 9:19 **c** the fourteenth day of the
Matt 14: 6 when Herod's birthday was **c**

CELESTIAL
1Co 15:40 There are also **c** bodies and
1Co 15:40 but the glory of the **c** is one

CELLS
Jer 37:16 entered the dungeon and the **c**

CENCHREA
Acts 18:18 He had his hair cut off at **C**
Rom 16: 1 a servant of the church in **C**

CENSER (*see* CENSERS)
Lev 10: 1 of Aaron, each took his **c**
Lev 16:12 Then he shall take a **c** full
Num 16:17 Each of you take his **c** and put
Num 16:17 bring his **c** before the LORD
Num 16:17 Aaron, each of you with his **c**
Num 16:18 So every man took his **c**, put
Num 16:46 Take a **c** and put fire in it
2Ch 26:19 he had a **c** in his hand to
Ezek 8:11 Each man had a **c** in his hand
Rev 8: 3 angel, having a golden **c**,
Rev 8: 5 Then the angel took the **c**

CENSERS (*see* CENSER)
Num 16: 6 Take **c**, Korah and all your
Num 16:17 LORD, two hundred and fifty **c**
Num 16:37 to pick up the **c** out of the
Num 16:38 The **c** of these men who sinned
Num 16:39 the priest took the bronze **c**
1Ki 7:50 ladles, and the **c** of pure gold
2Ch 4:22 ladles, and the **c** of pure gold

CENSUS
Ex 30:12 When you take the **c** of the
Num 1: 2 Take a **c** of all the
Num 1:49 nor take a **c** of them among
Num 4: 2 Take a **c** of the sons of
Num 4:22 Also take a **c** of the sons of
Num 26: 2 Take a **c** of all the
Num 26: 4 Take a **c** of the people from
2Ki 12: 4 each man's **c** money, each
1Ch 27:24 the son of Zeruiah began a **c**
1Ch 27:24 upon Israel because of this **c**
2Ch 2:17 after the **c** in which David
Luke 2: 2 This **c** first took place while
Acts 5:37 rose up in the days of the **c**

CENTER
Judg 9:37 down from the **c** of the land
Ezek 48: 8 with the sanctuary in the **c**
Ezek 48:10 of the LORD shall be in the **c**
Ezek 48:15 and the city shall be in the **c**
Ezek 48:21 the temple shall be in the **c**
John 19:18 side, and Jesus in the **c**

CENTURION (*see* CENTURION'S, CENTURIONS)
Matt 8: 5 a **c** came to Him, pleading
Matt 8: 8 The **c** answered and said
Matt 8:13 Then Jesus said to the **c**
Matt 27:54 Now when the **c** and those with
Mark 15:39 Now when the **c**, who stood
Mark 15:44 and summoning the **c**, he asked

Mark 15:45 when he found out from the **c**
Luke 7: 6 the **c** sent friends to Him,
Luke 23:47 Now when the **c** saw what had
Acts 10: 1 a **c** of what was called the
Acts 10:22 Cornelius the **c**, a just man,
Acts 22:25 said to the **c** who stood by
Acts 22:26 When the **c** heard that, he
Acts 24:23 commanded the **c** to keep Paul
Acts 27: 1 a **c** of the Augustan Regiment
Acts 27: 6 There the **c** found an
Acts 27:11 Nevertheless the **c** was more
Acts 27:31 Paul said to the **c** and the
Acts 27:43 But the **c**, wanting to save
Acts 28:16 the **c** delivered the prisoners

CENTURION'S (*see* CENTURION)
Luke 7: 2 And a certain **c** servant, who

CENTURIONS (*see* CENTURION)
Acts 21:32 took soldiers and **c**, and ran
Acts 23:17 called one of the **c** to him
Acts 23:23 And he called for two **c**,

CEPHAS (*see* PETER, SIMON)
John 1:42 You shall be called **C**"
1Co 1:12 I am of **C**," or "I am of
1Co 3:22 whether Paul or Apollos or **C**
1Co 9: 5 brothers of the Lord, and **C**
1Co 15: 5 and that He was seen by **C**,
Gal 2: 9 and when James, **C**, and John,

CERAMIC
Dan 2:41 the iron mixed with **c** clay
Dan 2:43 saw iron mixed with **c** clay

CEREMONIALLY (*see* CEREMONY)
Num 8: 6 of Israel and cleanse them **c**

CEREMONIES (*see* CEREMONY)
Num 9: 3 rites and **c** you shall keep it
Jer 34: 5 as in the **c** of your fathers,

CEREMONY (*see* CEREMONIALLY, CEREMONIES)
Num 9:14 and according to its **c**

CERTAIN (*see* CERTAINLY, CERTAINTY, UNCERTAIN)
Gen 28:11 So he came to a **c** place and
Gen 37:15 Now a **c** man found him, and
Gen 38: 1 visited a **c** Adullamite whose
Gen 38: 2 a **c** Canaanite whose name was
Ex 16: 4 gather a **c** quota every day,
Lev 27: 2 a vow **c** persons to the LORD
Num 9: 6 Now there were **c** men who were
Deut 13:13 **C** corrupt men have gone out
Deut 13:14 **c** that such an abomination
Deut 17: 4 **c** that such an abomination
Deut 25: 2 with a **c** number of blows
Josh 23:13 know for **c** that the LORD your
Judg 9:53 But a **c** woman dropped an
Judg 13: 2 there was a **c** man from Zorah
Judg 19: 1 that there was a **c** Levite
Judg 19:22 suddenly **c** men of the city,
Ruth 1: 1 a **c** man of Bethlehem, Judah,
1Sa 1: 1 Now there was a **c** man of
1Sa 21: 7 Now a **c** man of the servants
2Sa 18:10 Now a **c** man saw it and told
1Ki 2:37 know for **c** you shall surely
1Ki 2:42 Know for **c** that on the day
1Ki 11:17 **c** Edomites of his father's
1Ki 20:35 Now a **c** man of the sons of
1Ki 22:34 Now a **c** man drew a bow at
2Ki 4: 1 A **c** woman of the wives of the
2Ki 8: 6 appointed a **c** officer for her
2Ki 19:35 it came to pass on a **c** night
2Ch 18:33 Now a **c** man drew a bow at
Ezra 10:16 with **c** heads of the fathers'
Neh 11: 4 Also in Jerusalem dwelt **c** of
Neh 11:23 concerning them that a **c**
Neh 12:35 **c** of the priests' sons with
Neh 13: 6 Then after **c** days I obtained
Esth 2: 5 the citadel there was a **c** Jew
Esth 3: 8 There is a **c** people scattered
Jer 26:15 But know for **c** that if you
Jer 26:17 Then **c** of the elders of the
Jer 41: 5 that **c** men came from Shechem,
Ezek 20: 1 that **c** of the elders of
Dan 2: 8 I know for **c** that you would
Dan 2:45 The dream is **c**, and its
Dan 3: 8 time **c** Chaldeans came forward
Dan 3:12 There are **c** Jews whom you
Dan 3:20 he commanded **c** mighty men of
Dan 8:13 that **c** one who was speaking
Dan 10: 5 a **c** man clothed in linen,
Dan 11:14 also **c** violent men of your
Matt 8:19 Then a **c** scribe came and said
Matt 18:23 a **c** king who wanted to settle
Matt 21:33 There was a **c** landowner who
Matt 22: 2 like a **c** king who arranged a
Matt 26:18 Go into the city to a **c** man
Mark 5:25 Now a **c** woman had a flow of
Mark 14:51 Now a **c** young man followed
Mark 15:21 Now they compelled a **c** man
Luke 1: 5 a **c** priest named Zacharias,
Luke 5:12 when He was in a **c** city, that
Luke 5:17 Now it happened on a **c** day
Luke 7: 2 a **c** centurion's servant, who
Luke 7:41 There was a **c** creditor who
Luke 8: 2 **c** women who had been healed
Luke 8:22 Now it happened, on a **c** day
Luke 8:27 there met Him a **c** man from
Luke 10:25 a **c** lawyer stood up and tested
Luke 10:30 A **c** man went down from
Luke 10:31 Now by chance a **c** priest came
Luke 10:33 But a **c** Samaritan, as he
Luke 10:38 that He entered a **c** village
Luke 10:38 and a **c** woman named Martha
Luke 11: 1 He was praying in a **c** place
Luke 11:27 that a **c** woman from the crowd
Luke 11:37 a **c** Pharisee asked Him to
Luke 12:16 The ground of a **c** rich man
Luke 13: 6 A **c** man had a fig tree
Luke 14: 2 there was a **c** man before Him
Luke 14:16 A **c** man gave a great supper
Luke 15:11 A **c** man had two sons
Luke 16: 1 There was a **c** rich man who
Luke 16:19 There was a **c** rich man who
Luke 16:20 But there was a **c** beggar
Luke 17:12 as He entered a **c** village
Luke 18: 2 There was in a **c** city a judge
Luke 18:18 Now a **c** ruler asked Him,
Luke 18:35 that a **c** blind man sat by the
Luke 19:12 A **c** nobleman went into a far
Luke 20: 9 A **c** man planted a vineyard,
Luke 21: 2 He saw also a **c** poor widow
Luke 22:56 a **c** servant girl, seeing him
Luke 23:19 a **c** insurrection made in the
Luke 23:26 they laid hold of a **c** man
Luke 24: 1 **c** other women with them, came
Luke 24:22 **c** women of our company, who
Luke 24:24 **c** of those who were with us
John 4:46 there was a **c** nobleman whose
John 5: 4 at a **c** time into the pool
John 5: 5 Now a **c** man was there who had
John 11: 1 Now a **c** man was sick, Lazarus
John 12:20 Now there were **c** Greeks among
Acts 3: 2 And a **c** man lame from his
Acts 5: 1 But a **c** man named Ananias,
Acts 5: 2 of it, and brought a **c** part
Acts 8: 9 But there was a **c** man called
Acts 9:10 Now there was a **c** disciple at
Acts 9:33 he found a **c** man named Aeneas
Acts 9:36 At Joppa there was a **c**
Acts 10: 1 There was a **c** man in Caesarea
Acts 12:11 Now I know for **c** that the
Acts 13: 1 Antioch there were **c** prophets
Acts 13: 6 they found a **c** sorcerer, a
Acts 14: 8 in Lystra a **c** man without
Acts 15: 1 **c** men came down from Judea
Acts 15: 2 **c** others of them should go up
Acts 16: 1 a **c** disciple was there, named
Acts 16: 1 the son of a **c** Jewish woman
Acts 16:14 Now a **c** woman named Lydia
Acts 16:16 that a **c** slave girl possessed
Acts 17:18 Then **c** Epicurean and Stoic
Acts 18: 2 he found a **c** Jew named Aquila
Acts 18: 7 house of a **c** man named Justus
Acts 18:24 Now a **c** Jew named Apollos,
Acts 19:24 For a **c** man named Demetrius,
Acts 20: 9 in a window sat a **c** young man
Acts 21:10 a **c** prophet named Agabus came
Acts 22:30 he wanted to know for **c** why
Acts 24: 1 a **c** orator named Tertullus
Acts 25:14 There is a **c** man left a
Acts 25:26 I have nothing **c** to write to
Acts 27:26 run aground on a **c** island
Rom 15:26 and Achaia to make a **c**
Gal 2:12 for before **c** men came from
1Ti 6: 7 it is **c** we can carry nothing
Heb 2: 6 one testified in a **c** place
Heb 4: 4 For He has spoken in a **c**
Heb 4: 7 again He designates a **c** day
Heb 10:27 but a **c** fearful expectation
Jude 4 For **c** men have crept in

CERTAINLY (*see* CERTAIN)
Gen 15:13 Know **c** that your descendants
Gen 18:10 I will **c** return to you
Gen 26:28 We have **c** seen that the LORD
Gen 44:15 I can **c** practice divination
Ex 3:12 said, "I will **c** be with you
Ex 22: 4 If the theft is **c** found alive
Lev 5:19 he has **c** trespassed against
Lev 24:16 shall **c** stone him, the
Num 14:23 they **c** shall not see the land
Num 22:17 for I will **c** honor you
Deut 21:14 but you **c** shall not sell her
Deut 22: 1 you shall **c** bring them back
Josh 9:24 Because it was **c** told your
1Sa 14:45 **C** not!
1Sa 20: 3 Your father **c** knows that I
1Sa 20: 9 For if I knew **c** that evil was
1Sa 23:10 Your servant has **c** heard that
1Sa 25:28 For the LORD will **c** make for
1Ki 1:30 so I **c** will do this day
2Ki 8:10 to him, "You shall **c** recover
Ps 39: 5 **C** every man at his best state
Ps 66:19 But **c** God has heard me
Prov 23: 5 For riches **c** make themselves
Jer 6:19 I will **c** bring calamity on
Jer 8: 8 the scribe **c** works falsehood
Jer 13:12 Do we not **c** know that every
Jer 25:28 You shall **c** drink
Jer 36:29 king of Babylon will **c** come
Jer 40:14 Do you **c** know that Baalis the
Jer 42:19 Know **c** that I have
Jer 42:22 know **c** that you shall die by
Jer 44:17 But we will **c** do whatever has
Dan 11:10 and one shall **c** come and
Dan 11:13 shall **c** come at the end of
Luke 20:16 heard it they said, "**C** not
Luke 23:47 **C** this was a righteous Man
Acts 7:34 I have **c** seen the oppression
Acts 21:22 The assembly must **c** meet, for
Rom 3: 4 **C** not! Indeed, let God be
Rom 3: 6 **C** not! For then how will God
Rom 3:31 law through faith? **C** not!
Rom 6: 2 **C** not! How shall we who
Rom 6: 5 **c** we also shall be in the
Rom 6:15 law but under grace? **C** not!
Rom 7: 7 Is the law sin? **C** not!
Rom 7:13 become death to me? **C** not!
Rom 9:14 with God? **C** not!
Rom 11: 1 cast away His people? **C** not!
Rom 11:11 that they should fall? **C** not!
1Co 5:10 Yet I **c** did not mean with the
1Co 6:15 members of a harlot? **C** not!
Gal 2:17 a minister of sin? **C** not!
Gal 3:21 the promises of God? **C** not!

CERTAINTY (*see* CERTAIN)
1Sa 23:23 and come back to me with **c**
Prov 22:21 the **c** of the words of truth
Luke 1: 4 that you may know the **c** of

CERTIFICATE (*see* CERTIFIED)
Deut 24: 1 he writes her a **c** of divorce
Deut 24: 3 and writes her a **c** of divorce
Is 50: 1 Where is the **c** of your
Jer 3: 8 and given her a **c** of divorce
Matt 5:31 him give her a **c** of divorce
Matt 19: 7 to give a **c** of divorce, and to
Mark 10: 4 a man to write a **c** of divorce

CERTIFIED (*see* CERTIFICATE)
John 3:33 has **c** that God is true

CHAFF
Job 21:18 like **c** that a storm carries
Ps 1: 4 But are like the **c** which the
Ps 35: 5 be like **c** before the wind
Ps 83:13 Like the **c** before the wind
Is 5:24 and the flame consumes the **c**
Is 17:13 be chased like the **c** of the
Is 29: 5 be as **c** that passes away
Is 33:11 You shall conceive **c**, you
Is 41:15 and make the hills like **c**
Jer 23:28 What is the **c** to the wheat
Dan 2:35 became like **c** from the summer
Hos 13: 3 away, like **c** blown off from a
Zeph 2: 2 before the day passes like **c**
Matt 3:12 the **c** with unquenchable fire
Luke 3:17 but the **c** He will burn with

CHAIN (*see* CHAINED, CHAINS, CHAINWORK)
Gen 41:42 put a gold **c** around his neck
Lam 3: 7 he has made my **c** heavy
Ezek 7:23 Make a **c**, for the land is
Ezek 16:11 wrists, and a **c** on your neck
Dan 5: 7 have a **c** of gold around his
Dan 5:16 have a **c** of gold around your
Dan 5:29 put a **c** of gold around his
Acts 28:20 Israel I am bound with this **c**
2Ti 1:16 and was not ashamed of my **c**
Rev 20: 1 pit and a great **c** in his hand

CHAINED (*see* CHAIN)
Mark 15: 7 who was **c** with his fellow
2Ti 2: 9 but the word of God is not **c**
Heb 13: 3 prisoners as if **c** with them

CHAINS (*see* CHAIN)
Ex 28:14 you shall make two **c** of pure
Ex 28:14 the braided **c** to the settings
Ex 28:22 You shall make **c** for the
Ex 28:24 **c** of gold in the two rings
Ex 28:25 **c** you shall fasten to the two
Ex 39:15 And they made **c** for the
Ex 39:17 they put the two braided **c** of
Ex 39:18 **c** they fastened in the two
Judg 8:26 and besides the **c** that were
1Ki 6:21 He stretched gold **c** across
1Ki 7:17 seven **c** for one capital and
Ps 107:14 And broke their **c** in pieces
Ps 149: 8 To bind their kings with **c**
Prov 1: 9 head, and **c** about your neck
Song 1:10 your neck with **c** of gold
Is 40:19 silversmith casts silver **c**
Is 45:14 they shall come over in **c**
Jer 40: 1 he had taken him bound in **c**
Jer 40: 4 the **c** that were on your hand
Ezek 19: 4 with **c** to the land of Egypt
Ezek 19: 9 They put him in a cage with **c**
Nah 3:10 her great men were bound in **c**
Mark 5: 3 bind him, not even with **c**
Mark 5: 4 been bound with shackles and **c**
Mark 5: 4 the **c** had been pulled apart
Luke 8:29 under guard, bound with **c**
Acts 12: 6 bound with two **c** between two
Acts 12: 7 And his **c** fell off his hands
Acts 16:26 and everyone's **c** were loosed
Acts 20:23 in every city, saying that **c**
Acts 21:33 him to be bound with two **c**
Acts 22: 5 to Damascus to bring in **c**
Acts 23:29 him worthy of death or **c**
Acts 26:29 as I am, except for these **c**
Acts 26:31 nothing worthy of death or **c**
Eph 6:20 which I am an ambassador in **c**
Phil 1: 7 inasmuch as both in my **c**
Phil 1:13 rest, that my **c** are in Christ
Phil 1:14 become confident by my **c**, are
Phil 1:16 to add affliction to my **c**
Col 4: 3 for which I am also in **c**
Col 4:18 Remember my **c**
2Ti 2: 9 even to the point of **c**
Phm 10 I have begotten while in my **c**
Phm 13 to me in my **c** for the gospel
Heb 10:34 had compassion on me in my **c**
Heb 11:36 and scourgings, yes, and of **c**
2Pe 2: 4 them into **c** of darkness, to
Jude 6 **c** under darkness for the

CHAINWORK (*see* CHAIN)
1Ki 7:17 network, with wreaths of **c**
2Ch 3: 5 carved palm trees and **c** on it
2Ch 3:16 He made wreaths of **c**, as in
2Ch 3:16 put them on the wreaths of **c**

CHAIR
2Ki 4:10 him there, and a table and a **c**

CHALCEDONY
Rev 21:19 second sapphire, the third **c**

CHALCOL (*see* CALCOL)
1Ki 4:31 the Ezrahite, and Heman, **C**

CHALDEA (*see* BABYLON, CHALDEAN, CHALDEANS)
Jer 50:10 And **C** shall become plunder
Jer 51:24 all the inhabitants of **C** for
Jer 51:35 be upon the inhabitants of **C**
Ezek 11:24 by the Spirit of God into **C**
Ezek 16:29 as the land of the trader, **C**
Ezek 23:15 of the Babylonians of **C**, the
Ezek 23:16 sent messengers to them in **C**

CHALDEAN (*see* CHALDEA, CHALDEANS)
Ezra 5:12 king of Babylon, the **C**, who
Jer 39: 5 But the **C** army pursued them
Dan 2:10 magician, astrologer, or **C**

CHALDEANS (*see* CHALDEA, CHALDEAN, CHALDEANS', CHALDEES)
Gen 11:28 native land, in Ur of the **C**
Gen 11:31 with them from Ur of the **C** to
Gen 15: 7 you out of Ur of the **C**, to
2Ki 24: 2 him raiding bands of **C**, bands
2Ki 25: 4 even though the **C** were still
2Ki 25: 5 of the **C** pursued the king
2Ki 25:10 all the army of the **C** who
2Ki 25:13 the **C** broke in pieces, and
2Ki 25:24 of the servants of the **C**
2Ki 25:25 the **C** who were with him at
2Ki 25:26 for they were afraid of the **C**
2Ch 36:17 them the king of the **C**, who
Job 1:17 The **C** formed three bands,
Is 23:13 Behold, the land of the **C**
Is 43:14 the **C**, who rejoice in their
Is 47: 1 a throne, O daughter of the **C**
Is 47: 5 darkness, O daughter of the **C**
Is 48:14 arm shall be against the **C**
Jer 21: 4 the **C** who besiege you outside
Jer 21: 9 defects to the **C** who besiege
Jer 22:25 Babylon and the hand of the **C**
Jer 24: 5 good, into the land of the **C**
Jer 25:12 nation, the land of the **C**
Jer 32: 4 escape from the hand of the **C**
Jer 32: 5 though you fight with the **C**
Jer 32:24 of the **C** who fight against it
Jer 32:25 given into the hand of the **C**
Jer 32:28 city into the hand of the **C**
Jer 32:29 the **C** who fight against this
Jer 32:43 given into the hand of the **C**
Jer 33: 5 They come to fight with the **C**
Jer 35:11 for fear of the army of the **C**
Jer 37: 5 when the **C** who were besieging
Jer 37: 8 And the **C** shall come back and
Jer 37: 9 The **C** will surely depart from
Jer 37:10 the **C** who fight against you
Jer 37:11 when the army of the **C** left
Jer 37:13 You are defecting to the **C**
Jer 37:14 I am not defecting to the **C**
Jer 38: 2 goes over to the **C** shall live
Jer 38:18 given into the hand of the **C**
Jer 38:19 who have defected to the **C**
Jer 38:23 wives and children to the **C**
Jer 39: 8 the **C** burned the king's house
Jer 40: 9 not be afraid to serve the **C**
Jer 40:10 serve the **C** who come to us
Jer 41: 3 the **C** who were found there,
Jer 41:18 because of the **C**
Jer 43: 3 us into the hand of the **C**
Jer 50: 1 the **C** by Jeremiah the prophet
Jer 50: 8 go out of the land of the **C**
Jer 50:25 of hosts in the land of the **C**
Jer 50:35 A sword is against the **C**,"
Jer 50:45 against the land of the **C**
Jer 51: 4 fall in the land of the **C**
Jer 51:54 from the land of the **C**,
Jer 52: 7 even though the **C** were near
Jer 52: 8 of the **C** pursued the king
Jer 52:14 all the army of the **C** who
Jer 52:17 the **C** broke in pieces, and
Ezek 1: 3 in the land of the **C** by the
Ezek 12:13 Babylon, to the land of the **C**
Ezek 23:14 images of **C** portrayed in
Ezek 23:23 the Babylonians, all the **C**
Dan 1: 4 and literature of the **C**
Dan 2: 2 the **C** to tell the king his
Dan 2: 4 Then the **C** spoke to the king
Dan 2: 5 answered and said to the **C**
Dan 2:10 The **C** answered the king, and
Dan 3: 8 time certain **C** came forward
Dan 4: 7 the astrologers, the **C**, and
Dan 5: 7 in the astrologers, the **C**
Dan 5:11 the magicians, astrologers, **C**
Dan 5:30 Belshazzar, king of the **C**
Dan 9: 1 king over the realm of the **C**
Hab 1: 6 indeed I am raising up the **C**
Acts 7: 4 came out of the land of the **C**

CHALDEANS' (*see* CHALDEANS)
Is 13:19 the beauty of the **C** pride

CHALDEES (*see* CHALDEANS)
Neh 9: 7 him out of Ur of the **C**, and
Is 48:20 Flee from the **C**

CHALK (*see* CHALKSTONES)
Is 44:13 rule, he marks one out with **c**

CHALKSTONES (*see* CHALK)
Is 27: 9 **c** that are beaten to dust

CHAMBER (*see* CHAMBERS)
Gen 43:30 And he went into his **c** and wept
Judg 3:20 in his cool private **c**)
Judg 3:24 to his needs in the cool **c**
2Sa 18:33 up to the **c** over the gate
1Ki 1:15 went into the **c** to the king
1Ki 6: 6 The lowest **c** was five cubits
1Ki 14:28 them back into the guard **c**
1Ki 20:30 the city, into an inner **c**
1Ki 22:25 go into an inner **c** to hide
2Ki 23:11 by the **c** of Nathan-Melech,
2Ki 23:12 the roof, the upper **c** of Ahaz
2Ch 18:24 go into an inner **c** to hide
Ezra 10: 6 went into the **c** of Jehohanan
Job 37: 9 From the **c** of the south comes
Ps 19: 5 coming out of his **c**, And
Ps 132: 3 not go into the **c** of my house
Song 3: 4 and into the **c** of her who
Jer 35: 4 into the **c** of the sons of
Jer 35: 4 was by the **c** of the princes
Jer 35: 4 above the **c** of Maaseiah the
Jer 36:10 in the **c** of Gemariah the son
Jer 36:12 house, into the scribe's **c**
Jer 36:20 the **c** of Elishama the scribe
Jer 36:21 from Elishama the scribe's **c**
Ezek 40: 7 Each gate **c** was one rod long
Ezek 40:13 **c** to the roof of the other
Ezek 40:38 There was a **c** and its entrance
Ezek 40:45 This **c** which faces south is
Ezek 40:46 The **c** which faces north is
Ezek 41: 5 The width of each side **c** all
Ezek 42: 1 the **c** which was opposite the
Ezek 42:14 holy **c** into the outer court
Joel 2:16 bridegroom go out from his **c**

CHAMBERLAIN
Acts 12:20 the king's **c** their friend

CHAMBERS (*see* CHAMBER)
1Ki 6: 5 temple he built **c** all around
1Ki 6: 5 he made side **c** all around it
1Ki 6:10 he built side **c** against the
1Ch 9:26 And they had charge over the **c**
1Ch 9:33 Levites, who lodged in the **c**
1Ch 23:28 in the courts and in the **c**
1Ch 28:11 its upper **c**, its inner **c**
1Ch 28:12 LORD, of all the **c** all around
Ezra 8:29 in the **c** of the house of the
Job 9: 9 and the **c** of the south
Ps 104: 3 of His upper **c** in the waters
Ps 104:13 the hills from His upper **c**
Ps 105:30 Even in the **c** of their kings
Prov 7:27 descending to the **c** of death
Song 1: 4 has brought me into his **c**
Is 26:20 Come, my people, enter your **c**
Jer 22:13 his **c** by injustice, who uses
Jer 22:14 a wide house with spacious **c**
Jer 35: 2 the LORD, into one of the **c**
Ezek 21:14 that enters their private **c**
Ezek 40: 7 between the gate **c** was a
Ezek 40:10 were three gate **c** on one side
Ezek 40:12 space in front of the gate **c**
Ezek 40:12 the gate **c** were six cubits on
Ezek 40:16 window frames in the gate **c**
Ezek 40:17 and there were **c** and a pavement
Ezek 40:17 thirty **c** faced the pavement
Ezek 40:21 Its gate **c**, three on this
Ezek 40:29 Also its gate **c**, its
Ezek 40:33 Also its gate **c**, its
Ezek 40:36 also its gate **c**, its
Ezek 40:44 the **c** for the singers in the
Ezek 41: 6 The side **c** were in three
Ezek 41: 6 other, thirty **c** in each story
Ezek 41: 6 for the side **c** all around
Ezek 41: 7 the side **c** became wider all
Ezek 41: 8 the foundation of the side **c**
Ezek 41: 9 of the side **c** was five cubits
Ezek 41: 9 of the side **c** of the temple
Ezek 41:10 the wall **c** was a width of
Ezek 41:11 side **c** opened on the terrace
Ezek 41:26 on the side **c** of the temple
Ezek 42: 4 In front of the **c**, toward the
Ezek 42: 5 Now the upper **c** were shorter
Ezek 42: 7 outside ran parallel to the **c**
Ezek 42: 7 at the front of the **c**,
Ezek 42: 8 The length of the **c** toward

Ezek 42: 9 At the lower **c** was the
Ezek 42:10 There were also **c** in the
Ezek 42:11 appearance was like the **c**
Ezek 42:12 to the doors of the **c** that
Ezek 42:13 north **c** and the south **c**
Ezek 42:13 are the holy **c** where the
Ezek 44:19 leave them in the holy **c**
Ezek 45: 5 have twenty **c** as a possession
Ezek 46:19 gate, into the holy **c** of the

CHAMELEON
Lev 11:30 the sand lizard, and the **c**

CHAMPION
1Sa 17: 4 a **c** went out from the camp of
1Sa 17:23 with them, there was the **c**
1Sa 17:51 saw that their **c** was dead

CHANCE
1Sa 6: 9 it was by **c** that it happened
2Sa 1: 6 As I happened by **c** to be on
Eccl 9:11 time and **c** happen to them all
Luke 10:31 Now by **c** a certain priest

CHANGE (*see* CHANGED, CHANGERS', CHANGES, UNCHANGEABLE)
Gen 35: 2 and **c** your garments
Ex 13:17 Lest perhaps the people **c**
Num 36: 7 of Israel shall not **c** hands
Num 36: 9 **c** hands from one tribe to
Deut 28:24 The LORD will **c** the rain of
2Sa 14:20 To bring about this **c** of
Job 14:14 I will wait, till my **c** comes
Job 14:20 You **c** his countenance and send
Job 17:12 They **c** the night into day
Job 23:13 and who can make Him **c**
Ps 15: 4 to his own hurt and does not **c**
Ps 55:19 Selah Because they do not **c**
Ps 102:26 Like a cloak You will **c** them
Prov 24:21 with those given to **c**
Jer 2:36 about so much to **c** your way
Jer 13:23 Can the Ethiopian **c** his skin
Dan 5:10 nor let your countenance **c**
Dan 7:25 and shall intend to **c** times
Hos 4: 7 I will **c** their glory into
Mal 3: 6 For I am the LORD, I do not **c**
Acts 6:14 **c** the customs which Moses
Gal 4:20 with you now and to **c** my tone
Heb 7:12 there is also a **c** of the law

CHANGED (*see* CHANGE)
Gen 31: 7 **c** my wages ten times, but God
Gen 31:41 you have **c** my wages ten times
Gen 41:14 **c** his clothing, and came to
Lev 13:55 plague has not **c** its color
Num 32:38 Meon (their names being **c**)
1Sa 21:13 So he **c** his behavior before
2Sa 12:20 himself, and **c** his clothes
2Ki 23:34 and **c** his name to Jehoiakim
2Ki 24:17 and **c** his name to Zedekiah
2Ki 25:29 So Jehoiachin **c** from his
2Ch 36: 4 and **c** his name to Jehoiakim
Ps 102:26 them, And they will be **c**
Ps 106:20 Thus they **c** their glory Into
Eccl 8: 1 sternness of his face is **c**
Is 24: 5 **c** the ordinance, Broken the
Jer 2:11 Has a nation **c** its gods,
Jer 2:11 But My people have **c** their
Jer 34:11 afterward they **c** their minds
Jer 48:11 him, and his scent has not **c**
Jer 52:33 So Jehoiachin **c** from his
Lam 4: 1 How **c** the fine gold
Dan 2: 9 before me till the time has **c**
Dan 3:19 on his face **c** toward Shadrach
Dan 4:16 Let his heart be **c** from that
Dan 5: 6 Then the king's countenance **c**
Dan 5: 9 his countenance was **c**, and
Dan 6: 8 so that it cannot be **c**,
Dan 6:15 the king establishes may be **c**
Dan 6:17 Daniel might not be **c**
Dan 7:28 me, and my countenance **c**
Mic 2: 4 He has **c** the heritage of my
Acts 28: 6 they **c** their minds and said
Rom 1:23 and **c** the glory of the
1Co 15:51 sleep, but we shall all be **c**
1Co 15:52 and we shall be **c**
Heb 1:12 them up, and they will be **c**
Heb 7:12 For the priesthood being **c**

CHANGERS' (*see* CHANGE)
John 2:15 and poured out the **c** money

CHANGES (*see* CHANGE)
Gen 45:22 to each man, **c** of garments
Gen 45:22 silver and five **c** of garments
Lev 13:16 Or if the raw flesh **c** and
Judg 14:12 and thirty **c** of clothing
Judg 14:13 and thirty **c** of clothing
Judg 14:19 gave the **c** of clothing to
2Ki 5: 5 of gold, and ten **c** of clothing
2Ki 5:22 silver and two **c** of garments
2Ki 5:23 with two **c** of garments, and
Job 10:17 **c** and war are ever with me
Dan 2:21 He **c** the times and the seasons
Hab 1:11 Then his mind **c**, and he

CHANNEL (*see* CHANNELS)
Job 38:25 Who has divided a **c** for the
Is 27:12 from the **c** of the River to

CHANNELS (*see* CHANNEL)
2Sa 22:16 Then the **c** of the sea were
Job 28:10 He cuts out **c** in the rocks,
Ps 18:15 Then the **c** of waters were
Is 8: 7 he will go up over all his **c**

CHANT
Amos 6: 5 who **c** to the sound of
Mic 3: 5 who **c** "Peace" while they

CHARACTER
Rom 5: 4 and perseverance, **c**
Rom 5: 4 and **c**, hope
Phil 2:22 But you know his proven **c**

CHARCOAL
Prov 26:21 As **c** is to burning coals, and

CHARGE (*see* CHARGED, CHARGERS, CHARGES, CHARGING)
Gen 26: 5 obeyed My voice and kept My **c**
Gen 28: 6 blessed him he gave him a **c**
Ex 22:25 you shall not **c** him interest
Lev 8:35 keep the **c** of the LORD, so
Lev 24: 3 Aaron shall be in **c** of it
Lev 24: 4 He shall be in **c** of the lamps
Num 1:53 the Levites shall keep **c** of
Num 3:28 keeping **c** of the sanctuary
Num 3:32 who kept **c** of the sanctuary
Num 3:38 keeping **c** of the sanctuary,
Num 9:19 Israel kept the **c** of the LORD
Num 9:23 they kept the **c** of the LORD
Num 18: 8 you **c** of My heave offerings
Num 31:30 to the Levites who keep **c** of
Num 31:47 who kept **c** of the tabernacle
Deut 11: 1 LORD your God, and keep His **c**
Deut 21: 8 the **c** of Your people Israel
Deut 23:19 You shall not **c** interest to
Deut 23:20 foreigner you may **c** interest
Deut 23:20 you shall not **c** interest,
Josh 22: 3 but have kept the **c** of the
Ruth 2: 5 who was in **c** of the reapers
Ruth 2: 6 in **c** of the reapers answered
1Sa 13:21 the **c** for a sharpening was a
1Sa 14:27 **c** the people with the oath
2Sa 3: 8 you **c** me today with a fault
2Sa 20:24 Adoram was in **c** of revenue
1Ki 2: 3 keep the **c** of the LORD your
1Ki 4:28 each man according to his **c**
1Ki 5:14 Adoniram was in **c** of the
1Ki 12:18 who was in **c** of the revenue
1Ki 18: 3 who was in **c** of his house
2Ki 7:17 leaned to have **c** of the gate
2Ki 10: 5 he who was in **c** of the house
2Ki 10: 5 he who was in **c** of the city
2Ki 10:22 the one in **c** of the wardrobe
2Ki 25:19 who had **c** of the men of war
1Ch 9:19 were in **c** of the work of the
1Ch 9:23 their children were in **c** of
1Ch 9:26 they had **c** over the chambers
1Ch 9:27 they were in **c** of opening it
1Ch 9:28 in **c** of the serving vessels
1Ch 9:32 of the Kohathites were in **c**
1Ch 15:22 instructor in **c** of the music
1Ch 22:12 give you **c** concerning Israel,
2Ch 10:18 who was in **c** of revenue
2Ch 30:17 had **c** of the slaughter of the
Neh 7: 2 that I gave the **c** of
Neh 11:22 the singers in **c** of the
Neh 12:45 kept the **c** of their God and
Neh 12:45 the **c** of the purification,
Job 1:22 not sin nor **c** God with wrong
Job 24:12 does not **c** them with wrong
Job 34:13 Who gave Him **c** over the earth
Ps 91:11 give His angels **c** over you
Song 2: 7 I **c** you, O daughters of
Song 3: 5 I **c** you, O daughters of
Song 5: 8 I **c** you, O daughters of
Song 5: 9 beloved, that you so **c** us
Song 8: 4 I **c** you, O daughters of
Is 10: 6 of My wrath I will give him **c**
Jer 39:11 king of Babylon gave **c**
Jer 47: 7 given it a **c** against Ashkelon
Jer 52:25 who had **c** of the men of war
Ezek 9: 1 Let those who have **c** over the
Ezek 40:45 who have **c** of the temple
Ezek 40:46 who have **c** of the altar
Ezek 44: 8 not kept **c** of My holy things
Ezek 44: 8 **c** of My sanctuary for you
Ezek 44:14 them keep **c** of the temple
Ezek 44:15 who kept **c** of My sanctuary
Ezek 44:16 Me, and they shall keep My **c**
Ezek 48:11 who have kept My **c**, who did
Dan 6: 4 **c** against Daniel concerning
Dan 6: 4 they could find no **c** or fault
Dan 6: 5 We shall not find any **c**
Hos 4: 1 for the LORD brings a **c**
Hos 12: 2 also brings a **c** against Judah
Jon 1:14 do not **c** us with innocent
Nah 3: 3 Horsemen **c** with bright sword
Hab 1: 8 Their chargers **c** ahead
Zech 3: 7 likewise have **c** of My courts
Matt 4: 6 His angels **c** concerning you
Luke 4:10 give His angels **c** over You
Acts 7:60 do not **c** them with this sin
Acts 8:27 who had **c** of all her treasury
Acts 16:24 Having received such a **c**, he
Acts 25:16 concerning the **c** against him
Rom 8:33 Who shall bring a **c** against
1Co 9:18 gospel of Christ without **c**
2Co 11: 7 of God to you free of **c**
1Th 5:27 I **c** you by the Lord that this
2Th 3: 8 eat anyone's bread free of **c**
1Ti 1: 3 may **c** some that they teach no
1Ti 1:18 This **c** I commit to you, son
1Ti 5:21 I **c** you before God and the
2Ti 4: 1 I **c** you therefore before God

CHARGED (*see* CHARGE)
Gen 26:11 So Abimelech **c** all his people
Gen 28: 1 him, and **c** him, and said to him
Gen 40: 4 the guard **c** Joseph with them
Gen 49:29 Then he **c** them and said to
Deut 22:17 now he has **c** her with
Deut 24: 5 war or be **c** with any business
Josh 6:26 Then Joshua **c** them at that
Josh 18: 8 Joshua **c** those who went to
1Sa 14:28 Your father strictly **c** the
2Sa 11:19 and **c** the messenger, saying,
1Ki 2: 1 he **c** Solomon his son, saying
2Ki 17:15 whom the LORD had **c** them that
2Ki 17:35 a covenant and **c** them, saying
1Ch 22: 6 **c** him to build a house for
1Ch 22:13 with which the LORD **c** Moses
Neh 5:11 the oil, that you have **c** them
Neh 13:19 and **c** that they must not be
Esth 2:10 for Mordecai had **c** her not to
Esth 2:20 just as Mordecai had **c** her
Jer 32:13 Then I **c** Baruch before them,
Jer 35: 8 father, in all that he **c** us
Mark 8:15 Then He **c** them, saying
Mark 8:30 Then He **c** them that they
Luke 5:14 And He **c** him to tell no one,
Luke 8:56 but He **c** them to tell no one
Acts 23:29 but had nothing **c** against him
Rom 3: 9 have previously **c** both Jews
1Th 2:11 and **c** every one of you, as a
2Ti 4:16 May it not be **c** against them

CHARGERS (*see* CHARGE)
Hab 1: 8 Their **c** charge ahead

CHARGES (*see* CHARGE)
Deut 22:14 **c** her with shameful conduct,
Job 4:18 if He **c** His angels with error
Jer 2: 9 will yet bring **c** against you
Jer 2: 9 children I will bring **c**
Hos 2: 2 Bring **c** against your mother,
Hos 2: 2 against your mother, bring **c**
Acts 19:38 Let them bring **c** against one
Acts 23:30 before you the **c** against him
Acts 25:27 to specify the **c** against him

CHARGING (*see* CHARGE)
Prov 28:15 a **c** bear is a wicked ruler
2Ti 2:14 **c** them before the Lord not to

CHARIOT (*see* CHARIOTEERS, CHARIOTS)
Gen 41:43 in the second **c** which he had
Gen 46:29 So Joseph made ready his **c**
Ex 14: 6 So he made ready his **c** and
Ex 14:25 And He took off their **c** wheels
Judg 4:15 and Sisera alighted from his **c**
Judg 5:28 Why is his **c** so long in
2Sa 8: 4 hamstrung all the **c** horses
1Ki 7:33 the workmanship of a **c** wheel
1Ki 10:26 he stationed in the **c** cities
1Ki 10:29 Now a **c** that was imported
1Ki 12:18 his **c** in haste to flee to
1Ki 18:44 say to Ahab, "Prepare your **c**
1Ki 20:25 for horse and **c** for **c**
1Ki 20:33 he had him come up into the **c**
1Ki 22:34 said to the driver of his **c**
1Ki 22:35 king was propped up in his **c**
1Ki 22:35 wound onto the floor of the **c**
1Ki 22:38 the **c** at a pool in Samaria
2Ki 2:11 that suddenly a **c** of fire
2Ki 2:12 the **c** of Israel and its
2Ki 5: 9 went with his horses and **c**
2Ki 5:21 down from the **c** to meet him
2Ki 5:26 back from his **c** to meet you
2Ki 9:16 So Jehu rode in a **c** and went
2Ki 9:21 And his **c** was made ready
2Ki 9:21 Judah went out, each in his **c**
2Ki 9:24 and he sank down in his **c**
2Ki 9:27 Shoot him also in the **c**
2Ki 9:28 him in the **c** to Jerusalem
2Ki 10:15 took him up to him into the **c**
2Ki 10:16 So they had him ride in his **c**
2Ki 23:30 his body in a **c** from Megiddo
1Ch 18: 4 hamstrung all the **c** horses
1Ch 28:18 for the construction of the **c**
2Ch 1:14 he stationed in the **c** cities
2Ch 1:17 imported from Egypt a **c** for
2Ch 8: 6 had, and all the **c** cities and
2Ch 9:25 he stationed in the **c** cities
2Ch 10:18 his **c** in haste to flee to
2Ch 18:33 said to the driver of his **c**
2Ch 18:34 **c** facing the Syrians until
2Ch 35:24 took him out of that **c** and put
2Ch 35:24 in the second **c** that he had
Ps 46: 9 He burns the **c** in the fire
Ps 76: 6 O God of Jacob, Both the **c**
Ps 104: 3 Who makes the clouds His **c**
Is 21: 7 he saw a **c** with a pair of
Is 21: 7 a **c** of donkeys
Is 21: 7 a **c** of camels, and he listened
Is 21: 9 here comes a **c** of men with a
Is 43:17 who brings forth the **c** and
Jer 51:21 I will break in pieces the **c**
Mic 1:13 harness the **c** to the swift
Zech 6: 2 With the first **c** were red
Zech 6: 2 the second **c** black horses
Zech 6: 3 with the third **c** white horses
Zech 6: 3 the fourth **c** dappled horses
Zech 9:10 cut off the **c** from Ephraim
Acts 8:28 And sitting in his **c**, he was
Acts 8:29 Go near and overtake this **c**
Acts 8:38 the **c** to stand still

CHARIOTEERS (*see* CHARIOT)
2Sa 10:18 David killed seven hundred **c**
1Ch 19:18 David killed seven thousand **c**

CHARIOTS (*see* CHARIOT)
Gen 50: 9 there went up with him both **c**
Ex 14: 7 he took six hundred choice **c**
Ex 14: 7 and all the **c** of Egypt with
Ex 14: 9 **c** of Pharaoh, his horsemen and
Ex 14:17 and over all his army, his **c**
Ex 14:18 Myself over Pharaoh, his **c**
Ex 14:23 all Pharaoh's horses, his **c**
Ex 14:26 the Egyptians, on their **c**
Ex 14:28 returned and covered the **c**
Ex 15: 4 Pharaoh's **c** and his army He
Ex 15:19 of Pharaoh went with his **c**
Deut 11: 4 to their horses and their **c**
Deut 20: 1 enemies, and see horses and **c**
Josh 11: 4 with very many horses and **c**
Josh 11: 6 and burn their **c** with fire
Josh 11: 9 and burned their **c** with fire
Josh 17:16 of the valley have **c** of iron
Josh 17:18 though they have iron **c** and
Josh 24: 6 pursued your fathers with **c**
Judg 1:19 because they had **c** of iron
Judg 4: 3 had nine hundred **c** of iron
Judg 4: 7 of Jabin's army, with his **c**
Judg 4:13 gathered together all his **c**
Judg 4:13 nine hundred **c** of iron, and
Judg 4:15 routed Sisera and all his **c**
Judg 4:16 But Barak pursued the **c** and
Judg 5:28 tarries the clatter of his **c**
1Sa 8:11 and appoint them for his own **c**
1Sa 8:11 and some will run before his **c**
1Sa 8:12 of war and equipment for his **c**
1Sa 13: 5 Israel, thirty thousand **c**
2Sa 1: 6 and indeed the **c** and horsemen
2Sa 8: 4 took from him one thousand **c**
2Sa 8: 4 of them for one hundred **c**
2Sa 15: 1 provided himself with **c** and
1Ki 1: 5 and he prepared for himself **c**
1Ki 4:26 stalls of horses for his **c**
1Ki 9:19 Solomon had, cities for his **c**
1Ki 9:22 captains, commanders of his **c**
1Ki 10:26 And Solomon gathered **c** and
1Ki 10:26 one thousand four hundred **c**
1Ki 16: 9 commander of half his **c**,
1Ki 20: 1 with him, with horses and **c**
1Ki 20:21 and attacked the horses and **c**
1Ki 22:31 thirty-two captains of his **c**
1Ki 22:32 of the **c** saw Jehoshaphat,
1Ki 22:33 the **c** saw that it was not the
2Ki 6:14 Therefore he sent horses and **c**
2Ki 6:15 the city with horses and **c**
2Ki 6:17 **c** of fire all around Elisha
2Ki 7: 6 to hear the noise of **c** and the
2Ki 7:14 they took two **c** with horses
2Ki 8:21 Zair, and all his **c** with him
2Ki 8:21 him and the captains of the **c**
2Ki 10: 2 are with you, and you have **c**
2Ki 13: 7 only fifty horsemen, ten **c**
2Ki 13:14 the **c** of Israel and their
2Ki 18:24 put your trust in Egypt for **c**
2Ki 19:23 of my **c** I have come up to the
2Ki 23:11 he burned the **c** of the sun
1Ch 18: 4 took from him one thousand **c**
1Ch 18: 4 of them for one hundred **c**
1Ch 19: 6 to hire for themselves **c** and
1Ch 19: 7 thirty-two thousand **c**, with
2Ch 1:14 And Solomon gathered **c** and
2Ch 1:14 one thousand four hundred **c**
2Ch 8: 9 officers, captains of his **c**
2Ch 9:25 stalls for horses and **c**, and
2Ch 12: 3 with twelve hundred **c**, sixty
2Ch 14: 9 men and three hundred **c**, and
2Ch 16: 8 a huge army with very many **c**
2Ch 18:30 of the **c** who were with him
2Ch 18:31 of the **c** saw Jehoshaphat,
2Ch 18:32 the **c** saw that it was not the
2Ch 21: 9 and all his **c** with him
2Ch 21: 9 him and the captains of the **c**
Ps 20: 7 Some trust in **c**, and some in
Ps 68:17 The **c** of God are twenty
Song 1: 9 to my filly among Pharaoh's **c**
Song 6:12 as the **c** of my noble people
Is 2: 7 and there is no end to their **c**
Is 22: 6 bore the quiver with **c** of men
Is 22: 7 valleys shall be full of **c**
Is 22:18 there your glorious **c** shall
Is 31: 1 who trust in **c** because they
Is 36: 9 put your trust in Egypt for **c**
Is 37:24 of my **c** I have come up to the
Is 66:15 come with fire and with His **c**
Is 66:20 nations, on horses and in **c**
Jer 4:13 and his **c** like a whirlwind
Jer 17:25 throne of David, riding in **c**
Jer 22: 4 riding on horses and in **c**
Jer 46: 9 up, O horses, and rage, O **c**
Jer 47: 3 at the rushing of his **c**, at
Jer 50:37 their horses, against their **c**
Ezek 23:24 shall come against you with **c**
Ezek 26: 7 of kings, with horses, with **c**
Ezek 26:10 the wagons, and the **c**, when
Dan 11:40 him like a whirlwind, with **c**
Joel 2: 5 With a noise like **c** over
Mic 5:10 your midst and destroy your **c**
Nah 2: 3 The **c** come with flaming
Nah 2: 4 The **c** rage in the streets,
Nah 2:13 I will burn your **c** in smoke
Nah 3: 2 horses, of clattering **c**
Hab 3: 8 horses, your **c** of salvation
Hag 2:22 I will overthrow the **c** and
Zech 6: 1 four **c** were coming from
Rev 9: 9 of **c** with many horses running
Rev 18:13 cattle and sheep, horses and **c**

CHARITABLE
Matt 6: 1 do your **c** deeds before men
Matt 6: 2 when you do a **c** deed, do not
Matt 6: 3 But when you do a **c** deed, do
Matt 6: 4 that your **c** deed may be in
Acts 9:36 and **c** deeds which she did

CHARM (*see* CHARMED, CHARMERS, CHARMING, CHARMS)
Prov 31:30 **C** is deceitful and beauty is

CHARMED (*see* CHARM)
Eccl 10:11 may bite when it is not **c**
Jer 8:17 you, vipers which cannot be **c**

CHARMERS (*see* CHARM)
Ps 58: 5 will not heed the voice of **c**
Is 19: 3 consult the idols and the **c**

CHARMING (*see* CHARM)
Ps 58: 5 **C** ever so skillfully

CHARMS (*see* CHARM)
Is 3:20 the perfume boxes, the **c**,
Jer 3:13 and have scattered your **c** to
Ezek 13:18 sew magic **c** on their sleeves
Ezek 13:20 **c** by which you hunt souls

CHASE (*see* CHASED, CHASES, CHASING)
Lev 26: 7 You will **c** your enemies, and
Lev 26: 8 Five of you shall **c** a hundred
Deut 32:30 How could one **c** a thousand
Josh 23:10 man of you shall **c** a thousand
Ps 35: 5 the angel of the LORD **c** them
Hos 2: 7 She will **c** her lovers, but

CHASED (*see* CHASE)
Deut 1:44 **c** you as bees do, and drove
Josh 7: 5 for they **c** them from before
Josh 10:10 **c** them along the road that
Josh 11: 8 **c** them to Greater Sidon, to
Judg 9:40 And Abimelech **c** him, and he
Judg 20:43 **c** them, and easily trampled
Job 18:18 and **c** out of the world
Job 20: 8 Yes, he will be **c** away like a
Is 17:13 be **c** like the chaff of the

CHASES (*see* CHASE)
Prov 19:26 **c** away his mother is a son

CHASING (*see* CHASE)
1Sa 17:53 from **c** the Philistines, and

CHASTE
2Co 11: 2 you as a **c** virgin to Christ
Tit 2: 5 to be discreet, **c**, homemakers
1Pe 3: 2 when they observe your **c**

CHASTEN (*see* CHASTENED, CHASTENING, CHASTENS)
2Sa 7:14 I will **c** him with the rod of
Ps 6: 1 anger, Nor **c** me in Your hot
Ps 38: 1 wrath, Nor **c** me in Your hot
Prov 19:18 **C** your son while there is
Hos 10:10 is My desire, I will **c** them
Heb 12: 7 whom a father does not **c**
Rev 3:19 many as I love, I rebuke and **c**

CHASTENED (*see* CHASTEN)
Deut 21:18 and who, when they have **c** him
Job 33:19 Man is also **c** with pain on
Ps 69:10 **c** my soul with fasting, That
Ps 73:14 plagued, And **c** every morning
Ps 118:18 The LORD has **c** me severely
Jer 2:30 vain I have **c** your children
1Co 11:32 we are **c** by the Lord, that we
2Co 6: 9 as **c**, and yet not killed
Heb 12:10 **c** us as seemed best to them

CHASTENING (*see* CHASTEN)
Deut 11: 2 the **c** of the LORD your God
Job 5:17 despise the **c** of the Almighty
Job 34:31 said to God, "I have borne **c**
Prov 3:11 not despise the **c** of the LORD
Is 26:16 when Your **c** was upon them
Heb 12: 5 not despise the **c** of the LORD
Heb 12: 7 If you endure **c**, God deals
Heb 12: 8 But if you are without **c**, of
Heb 12:11 Now no **c** seems to be joyful

CHASTENS (*see* CHASTEN)
Deut 8: 5 heart that as a man **c** his son
Deut 8: 5 so the LORD your God **c** you
Heb 12: 6 For whom the LORD loves He **c**

CHASTISE (*see* CHASTISED, CHASTISEMENT)
Lev 26:28 will **c** you seven times for
1Ki 12:11 whips, but I will **c** you with
1Ki 12:14 whips, but I will **c** you with
2Ch 10:11 whips, but I will **c** you with
2Ch 10:14 whips, but I will **c** you with
Hos 7:12 I will **c** them according to
Luke 23:16 I will therefore **c** Him and
Luke 23:22 I will therefore **c** Him and let

CHASTISED (*see* CHASTISE)
1Ki 12:11 my father **c** you with whips,
1Ki 12:14 my father **c** you with whips,
2Ch 10:11 my father **c** you with whips,
2Ch 10:14 my father **c** you with whips,
Jer 31:18 You have **c** me, and I was **c**

CHASTISEMENT (*see* CHASTISE)
Is 53: 5 the **c** for our peace was upon
Jer 30:14 with the **c** of a cruel one,

CHATTER (*see* CHATTERED)
Prov 14:23 but idle **c** leads only to

CHATTERED (*see* CHATTER)
Is 38:14 a crane or a swallow, so I **c**

CHEAT
Col 2: 8 Beware lest anyone **c** you

CHEBAR
Ezek 1: 1 the captives by the River **C**
Ezek 1: 3 the Chaldeans by the River **C**
Ezek 3:15 who dwelt by the River **C**
Ezek 3:23 which I saw by the River **C**
Ezek 10:15 creature I saw by the River **C**
Ezek 10:20 God of Israel by the River **C**
Ezek 10:22 I had seen by the River **C**
Ezek 43: 3 which I saw by the River **C**

CHEDORLAOMER
Gen 14: 1 **C** king of Elam, and Tidal king
Gen 14: 4 Twelve years they served **C**
Gen 14: 5 In the fourteenth year **C** and
Gen 14: 9 against **C** king of Elam, Tidal
Gen 14:17 return from the defeat of **C**

CHEEK (*see* CHEEKBONE, CHEEKS)
1Ki 22:24 and struck Micaiah on the **c**
2Ch 18:23 and struck Micaiah on the **c**
Job 16:10 me reproachfully on the **c**
Lam 3:30 Let him give his **c** to the one
Mic 5: 1 of Israel with a rod on the **c**
Matt 5:39 slaps you on your right **c**
Luke 6:29 who strikes you on the one **c**

CHEEKBONE (*see* CHEEK)
Ps 3: 7 all my enemies on the **c**

CHEEKS (*see* CHEEK)
Deut 18: 3 priest the shoulder, the **c**
Song 1:10 Your **c** are lovely with
Song 5:13 His **c** are like a bed of
Is 50: 6 My **c** to those who plucked out
Lam 1: 2 night, her tears are on her **c**

CHEER (*see* CHEERFUL, CHEERS)
Eccl 11: 9 let your heart **c** you in the
Matt 9: 2 Son, be of good **c**
Matt 9:22 Be of good **c**, daughter
Matt 14:27 Be of good **c**! It is I
Mark 6:50 Be of good **c**! It is I
Mark 10:49 saying to him, "Be of good **c**
Luke 8:48 Daughter, be of good **c**
John 16:33 but be of good **c**, I have
Acts 23:11 Be of good **c**, Paul

CHEERFUL (*see* CHEER, CHEERFULLY, CHEERFULNESS)
Ruth 3: 7 and drunk, and his heart was **c**
1Ki 21: 7 food, and let your heart be **c**
Prov 15:13 heart makes a **c** countenance
Zech 8:19 **c** feasts for the house of
2Co 9: 7 for God loves a **c** giver
Jas 5:13 Is anyone **c**? Let him sing

CHEERFULLY (*see* CHEERFUL)
Acts 24:10 I do the more **c** answer for

CHEERFULNESS (*see* CHEERFUL)
Rom 12: 8 he who shows mercy, with **c**

CHEERS (*see* CHEER)
Judg 9:13 which **c** both God and men, and

CHEESE (*see* CHEESES)
2Sa 17:29 **c** of the herd, for David and
Job 10:10 milk, and curdle me like **c**

CHEESES (*see* CHEESE)
1Sa 17:18 And carry these ten **c** to the

CHELAL
Ezra 10:30 Adna, **C**, Benaiah, Maaseiah,

CHELUB (*see* CALEB)
1Ch 4:11 **C** the brother of Shuhah begot
1Ch 27:26 Ezri the son of **C** was over

CHELUBAI (*see* CALEB)
1Ch 2: 9 were Jerahmeel, Ram, and **C**

CHELUH
Ezra 10:35 Benaiah, Bedeiah, **C**,

CHEMOSH
Num 21:29 have perished, O people of **C**
Judg 11:24 **C** your god gives you to
1Ki 11: 7 built a high place for **C** the
1Ki 11:33 **C** the god of the Moabites, and
2Ki 23:13 for **C** the abomination of the
Jer 48: 7 And **C** shall go forth into
Jer 48:13 Moab shall be ashamed of **C**
Jer 48:46 The people of **C** perish

CHENAANAH
1Ki 22:11 Now Zedekiah the son of **C** had
1Ki 22:24 the son of **C** went near and
1Ch 7:10 were Jeush, Benjamin, Ehud, **C**
2Ch 18:10 Now Zedekiah the son of **C** had
2Ch 18:23 the son of **C** went near and

CHENANI
Neh 9: 4 **C** stood on the stairs of the

CHENANIAH (*see* CONONIAH)
1Ch 15:22 **C**, leader of the Levites, was
1Ch 15:27 **C** the music master with the
1Ch 26:29 Of the Izharites, **C** and his

CHEPHAR HAAMMONI
Josh 18:24 **C**, Ophni, and Gaba

CHEPHIRAH
Josh 9:17 their cities were Gibeon, **C**
Josh 18:26 Mizpah, **C**, Mozah,
Ezra 2:25 the people of Kirjath Arim, **C**
Neh 7:29 the men of Kirjath Jearim, **C**

CHERAN
Gen 36:26 Hemdan, Eshban, Ithran, and **C**
1Ch 1:41 Hamran, Eshban, Ithran, and **C**

CHERETHITES
1Sa 30:14 of the southern area of the **C**
2Sa 8:18 Jehoiada was over both the **C**
2Sa 15:18 and all the **C**, all the
2Sa 20: 7 So Joab's men, with the **C**
2Sa 20:23 of Jehoiada was over the **C**
1Ki 1:38 the son of Jehoiada, the **C**
1Ki 1:44 the son of Jehoiada, the **C**
1Ch 18:17 of Jehoiada was over the **C**
Ezek 25:16 and I will cut off the **C** and
Zeph 2: 5 seacoast, the nation of the **C**

CHERISHES
Eph 5:29 **c** it, just as the Lord does
1Th 2: 7 mother **c** her own children

CHERITH
1Ki 17: 3 and hide by the Brook **C**,
1Ki 17: 5 went and stayed by the Brook **C**

CHERUB (*see* CHERUBIM)
Ex 25:19 Make one **c** at one end, and the
Ex 25:19 the other **c** at the other end
Ex 37: 8 one **c** at one end on this side
Ex 37: 8 the other **c** at the other end
2Sa 22:11 He rode upon a **c**, and flew
1Ki 6:24 wing of the **c** was five cubits
1Ki 6:24 wing of the **c** five cubits
1Ki 6:25 the other **c** was ten cubits
1Ki 6:26 of one **c** was ten cubits, and
1Ki 6:26 cubits, and so was the other **c**
1Ki 6:27 and the wing of the other **c**
2Ch 3:11 of the one **c** was five cubits
2Ch 3:11 the wing of the other **c**
2Ch 3:12 the other **c** was five cubits
2Ch 3:12 the wing of the other **c**
Ps 18:10 And He rode upon a **c**, and flew
Ezek 9: 3 Israel had gone up from the **c**
Ezek 10: 2 among the wheels, under the **c**
Ezek 10: 4 the LORD went up from the **c**
Ezek 10: 7 the **c** stretched out his hand
Ezek 10: 9 cherubim, one wheel by one **c**
Ezek 10: 9 another wheel by each other **c**
Ezek 10:14 face was the face of a **c**, the
Ezek 28:14 the anointed **c** who covers
Ezek 28:16 I destroyed you, O covering **c**
Ezek 41:18 a palm tree between **c** and **c**
Ezek 41:18 Each **c** had two faces,

CHERUB*
Ezra 2:59 from Tel Melah, Tel Harsha, **C**
Neh 7:61 from Tel Melah, Tel Harsha, **C**

CHERUBIM (*see* CHERUB)
Gen 3:24 He placed **c** at the east of
Ex 25:18 you shall make two **c** of gold
Ex 25:19 you shall make the **c** at the
Ex 25:20 the **c** shall stretch out their
Ex 25:20 the faces of the **c** shall be
Ex 25:22 from between the two **c** which
Ex 26: 1 of **c** you shall weave them
Ex 26:31 with an artistic design of **c**
Ex 36: 8 designs of **c** they made them
Ex 36:35 with an artistic design of **c**
Ex 37: 7 He made two **c** of beaten gold
Ex 37: 8 He made the **c** at the two ends
Ex 37: 9 The **c** spread out their wings
Ex 37: 9 the faces of the **c** were
Num 7:89 from between the two **c**
1Sa 4: 4 who dwells between the **c**
2Sa 6: 2 who dwells between the **c**
1Ki 6:23 he made two **c** of olive wood
1Ki 6:25 both **c** were of the same size
1Ki 6:27 Then he set the **c** inside the
1Ki 6:27 out the wings of the **c** so
1Ki 6:28 he overlaid the **c** with gold
1Ki 6:29 with carved figures of **c**
1Ki 6:32 carved on them figures of **c**
1Ki 6:32 and he spread gold on the **c**
1Ki 6:35 Then he carved **c**, palm trees,
1Ki 7:29 frames were lions, oxen, and **c**
1Ki 7:36 on its panels he engraved **c**
1Ki 8: 6 under the wings of the **c**
1Ki 8: 7 For the **c** spread their two
1Ki 8: 7 the **c** overshadowed the ark and
2Ki 19:15 One who dwells between the **c**
1Ch 13: 6 who dwells between the **c**
1Ch 28:18 the gold **c** that spread their
2Ch 3: 7 and he carved **c** on the walls
2Ch 3:10 Most Holy Place he made two **c**
2Ch 3:11 The wings of the **c** were
2Ch 3:13 The wings of these **c** spanned
2Ch 3:14 fine linen, and wove **c** into it
2Ch 5: 7 under the wings of the **c**
2Ch 5: 8 For the **c** spread their wings
2Ch 5: 8 the **c** overshadowed the ark and
Ps 80: 1 You who dwell between the **c**
Ps 99: 1 He dwells between the **c**
Is 37:16 One who dwells between the **c**
Ezek 10: 1 was above the head of the **c**
Ezek 10: 2 of fire from among the **c**, and
Ezek 10: 3 Now the **c** were standing on
Ezek 10: 5 sound of the wings of the **c**
Ezek 10: 6 the wheels, from among the **c**
Ezek 10: 7 **c** to the fire that was among
Ezek 10: 7 the fire that was among the **c**
Ezek 10: 8 The **c** appeared to have the
Ezek 10: 9 were four wheels by the **c**
Ezek 10:15 And the **c** were lifted up
Ezek 10:16 When the **c** went, the wheels
Ezek 10:16 when the **c** lifted their wings
Ezek 10:17 When the **c** stood still, the
Ezek 10:18 temple and stood over the **c**
Ezek 10:19 the **c** lifted their wings and
Ezek 10:20 Chebar, and I knew they were **c**
Ezek 11:22 Then the **c** lifted up their
Ezek 41:18 And it was made with **c** and palm
Ezek 41:20 the wall of the sanctuary, **c**
Ezek 41:25 **C** and palm trees were carved
Heb 9: 5 above it were the **c** of glory

CHESALON
Josh 15:10 on the north (which is **C**)

CHESED
Gen 22:22 **C**, Hazo, Pildash, Jidlaph, and

CHESIL
Josh 15:30 Eltolad, **C**, Hormah,

CHEST (*see* CHESTS)
1Sa 6: 8 offering in a c by its side
1Sa 6:11 the c with the gold rats and
1Sa 6:15 the c that was with it, in
2Ki 12: 9 Jehoiada the priest took a c
2Ki 12:10 there was much money in the c
2Ch 24: 8 commandment they made a c
2Ch 24:10 put them into the c until all
2Ch 24:11 when the c was brought to the
2Ch 24:11 officer came and emptied the c
Dan 2:32 head was of fine gold, its c
Rev 1:13 girded about the c with a

CHESTNUT
Gen 30:37 c trees, peeled white strips
Ezek 31: 8 the c trees were not like its

CHESTS (*see* CHEST)
Ezek 27:24 in c of multicolored apparel,
Rev 15: 6 having their c girded with

CHESULLOTH (*see* CHISLOTH TABOR)
Josh 19:18 to Jezreel, and included C

CHEW (*see* CHEWED, CHEWING, CHEWS)
Lev 11: 4 not eat among those that c
Lev 11: 7 yet does not c the cud, is
Lev 11:26 or does not c the cud, is
Deut 14: 7 of those that c the cud or
Deut 14: 7 for they c the cud but do not
Deut 14: 8 yet does not c the cud
Mic 3: 5 while they c with their teeth

CHEWED (*see* CHEW)
Num 11:33 their teeth, before it was c

CHEWING (*see* CHEW)
Lev 11: 3 cloven hooves and c the cud
Joel 1: 4 What the c locust left, the
Joel 2:25 the c locust, my great army

CHEWS (*see* CHEW)
Lev 11: 4 because it c the cud but does
Lev 11: 5 because it c the cud but does
Lev 11: 6 because it c the cud but does
Deut 14: 6 that c the cud, among the

CHEZIB (*see* ACHZIB, CHOZEBA)
Gen 38: 5 He was at C when she bore him

CHICKS
Matt 23:37 gathers her c under her wings

CHIDON'S (*see* NACHON'S)
1Ch 13: 9 came to C threshing floor

CHIEF (*see* CHIEFLY, CHIEFS, CHIEFTAINS)
Gen 36:15 were C Teman, C Omar,
Gen 36:15 C Omar, C Zepho, C
Gen 36:15 Omar, C Zepho, C Kenaz,
Gen 36:16 C Korah, C Gatam, and
Gen 36:16 C Amalek
Gen 36:17 C Nahath, C Zerah
Gen 36:17 C Shammah, and C Mizzah
Gen 36:18 C Jeush, C Jaalam, and
Gen 36:18 C Jaalam, and C Korah
Gen 36:29 C Lotan, C Shobal
Gen 36:29 C Zibeon, C Anah
Gen 36:30 C Dishon, C Ezer
Gen 36:30 C Ezer, and C Dishan
Gen 36:40 C Timnah, C Alvah
Gen 36:40 C Alvah, C Jetheth,
Gen 36:41 C Aholibamah, C Elah,
Gen 36:41 C Elah, C Pinon,
Gen 36:42 C Kenaz, C Teman
Gen 36:42 C Teman, C Mibzar
Gen 36:43 C Magdiel, and C Iram
Gen 40: 2 c butler and the c baker
Gen 40: 9 Then the c butler told his
Gen 40:16 When the c baker saw that the
Gen 40:20 up the head of the c butler
Gen 40:20 and of the c baker among his
Gen 40:21 Then he restored the c butler
Gen 40:22 But he hanged the c baker
Gen 40:23 Yet the c butler did not
Gen 41: 9 Then the c butler spoke to
Gen 41:10 both me and the c baker,
Gen 47: 6 then make them c herdsmen
Lev 21: 4 being a c man among his
Num 3:32 be c over the leaders of the
Num 31:26 and the c fathers of the
Num 32:28 and to the c fathers of the
Num 36: 1 Now the c fathers of the
Num 36: 1 the c fathers of the children
Josh 22:14 the c house of every tribe of
1Sa 21: 7 the c of the herdsmen who
1Sa 28: 2 one of my c guardians forever
2Sa 5: 8 David's soul), he shall be c
2Sa 8:18 David's sons were c ministers
2Sa 20:26 was a c minister under David
2Sa 23: 8 c among the captains
2Sa 23:13 c men went down at harvest
2Sa 23:18 was c of another three
1Ki 8: 1 the c fathers of the children
2Ki 25:18 took Seraiah the c priest
1Ch 1:51 chiefs of Edom were C Timnah
1Ch 1:51 C Aliah, C Jetheth,
1Ch 1:52 C Aholibamah, C Elah,
1Ch 1:52 C Elah, C Pinon,
1Ch 1:53 C Kenaz, C Teman
1Ch 1:53 C Teman, C Mibzar
1Ch 1:54 C Magdiel, and C Iram
1Ch 5: 7 the c, Jeiel, and Zechariah,
1Ch 5:12 Joel was the c, Shapham the
1Ch 5:15 was c of their father's house
1Ch 7: 3 All five of them were c men
1Ch 7:40 men of valor, c leaders
1Ch 8:28 by their generations, c men
1Ch 9:17 Shallum was the c
1Ch 9:26 were four c gatekeepers
1Ch 11: 6 Jebusites first shall be c
1Ch 11: 6 went up first, and became c
1Ch 11:11 Hachmonite, c of the captains
1Ch 11:15 Now three of the thirty c men
1Ch 11:20 Joab was c of another three
1Ch 11:42 (a c of the Reubenites) and
1Ch 12: 3 The c was Ahiezer, then Joash
1Ch 12:18 c of the captains, and he said
1Ch 15: 5 sons of Kohath, Uriel the c
1Ch 15: 6 sons of Merari, Asaiah the c
1Ch 15: 7 sons of Gershom, Joel the c
1Ch 15: 8 of Elizaphan, Shemaiah the c
1Ch 15: 9 sons of Hebron, Eliel the c
1Ch 15:10 of Uzziel, Amminadab the c
1Ch 16: 5 Asaph the c, and next to him
1Ch 18:17 David's sons were c ministers
1Ch 24:31 The c fathers did just as
1Ch 26:12 gatekeepers, among the c men
1Ch 27: 3 the c of all the captains of
1Ch 27: 5 the priest, who was c
2Ch 5: 2 the c fathers the son of the children
2Ch 11:22 Abijah the son of Maacah as c
2Ch 19: 8 and some of the c fathers of
2Ch 19:11 Amariah the c priest is over
2Ch 23: 2 the c fathers of Israel, and
2Ch 24: 6 called Jehoiada the c priest
2Ch 26:12 The total number of c
2Ch 26:20 And Azariah the c priest and
2Ch 31:10 And Azariah the c priest, from
2Ch 35: 9 c of the Levites, gave to the
Ezra 5:10 the men who were c among them
Ezra 7: 5 the son of Aaron the c priest
Ezra 7:28 I gathered c men of Israel to
Ezra 8:17 c man at the place Casiphia
Job 29:25 the way for them, and sat as c
Ps 118:22 Has become the c cornerstone
Ps 137: 6 Jerusalem Above my c joy
Prov 1:21 cries out in the c concourses
Song 4:14 aloes, with all the c spices
Song 5:10 ruddy, c among ten thousand
Is 14: 9 all the c ones of the earth
Jer 20: 1 the priest who was also c
Jer 31: 7 among the c of the nations
Jer 39:13 king of Babylon's c officers
Jer 52:24 took Seraiah the c priest
Dan 1: 7 To them the c of the eunuchs
Dan 1: 8 he requested of the c of the
Dan 1: 9 will of the c of the eunuchs
Dan 1:10 the c of the eunuchs said to
Dan 1:11 to the steward whom the c of
Dan 1:18 the c of the eunuchs brought
Dan 2:48 c administrator over all the
Dan 4: 9 c of the magicians, because I
Dan 5:11 made him c of the magicians,
Dan 10:13 Michael, one of the c princes
Amos 6: 1 persons in the c nation, to
Hab 3:19 To the C Musician
Matt 2: 4 gathered all the c priests
Matt 16:21 c priests and scribes, and be
Matt 20:18 be betrayed to the c priests
Matt 21:15 But when the c priests and
Matt 21:23 the c priests and the elders
Matt 21:42 has become the c cornerstone
Matt 21:45 Now when the c priests and
Matt 26: 3 Then the c priests, the
Matt 26:14 went to the c priests
Matt 26:47 came from the c priests and
Matt 26:59 Now the c priests, the elders
Matt 27: 1 came, all the c priests and
Matt 27: 3 of silver to the c priests
Matt 27: 6 But the c priests took the
Matt 27:12 accused by the c priests and
Matt 27:20 But the c priests and elders
Matt 27:41 Likewise the c priests, also
Matt 27:62 the c priests and Pharisees
Matt 28:11 reported to the c priests all
Mark 6:21 and the c men of Galilee
Mark 8:31 c priests and scribes, and be
Mark 10:33 be delivered to the c priests
Mark 11:18 c priests heard it and sought
Mark 11:27 the c priests, the scribes,
Mark 12:10 has become the c cornerstone
Mark 14: 1 the c priests and the scribes
Mark 14:10 went to the c priests to
Mark 14:43 came from the c priests and
Mark 14:53 assembled all the c priests
Mark 14:55 And the c priests and all the
Mark 15: 1 morning, the c priests held a
Mark 15: 3 the c priests accused Him of
Mark 15:10 For he knew that the c
Mark 15:11 But the c priests stirred up
Mark 15:31 Likewise the c priests also
Luke 9:22 c priests and scribes, and be
Luke 19: 2 who was a c tax collector
Luke 19:47 But the c priests, the
Luke 20: 1 gospel, that the c priests
Luke 20:17 has become the c cornerstone'
Luke 20:19 the c priests and the scribes
Luke 22: 2 the c priests and the scribes
Luke 22: 4 conferred with the c priests
Luke 22:52 Jesus said to the c priests
Luke 22:66 both c priests and scribes,
Luke 23: 4 Pilate said to the c priests
Luke 23:10 And the c priests and scribes
Luke 23:13 called together the c priests
Luke 23:23 of the c priests prevailed
Luke 24:20 and how the c priests and our
John 7:32 the c priests sent officers
John 7:45 came to the c priests and
John 11:47 Then the c priests and the
John 11:57 Now both the c priests and the
John 12:10 But the c priests took
John 18: 3 officers from the c priests
John 18:35 the c priests have delivered
John 19: 6 Therefore, when the c priests
John 19:15 The c priests answered,
John 19:21 Then the c priests of the
Acts 4:11 has become the c cornerstone
Acts 4:23 all that the c priests and
Acts 5:24 the c priests heard these
Acts 9:14 the c priests to bind all who
Acts 9:21 them bound to the c priests
Acts 13:50 the c men of the city, raised
Acts 14:12 because he was the c speaker
Acts 19:14 of Sceva, a Jewish c priest
Acts 22:30 and commanded the c priests
Acts 23:14 They came to the c priests
Acts 25: 2 and the c men of the Jews
Acts 25:15 about whom the c priests and
Acts 26:10 authority from the c priests
Acts 26:12 commission from the c priests
Eph 2:20 being the c cornerstone,
1Ti 1:15 save sinners, of whom I am c
1Pe 2: 6 I lay in Zion a c cornerstone
1Pe 2: 7 has become the c cornerstone
1Pe 5: 4 when the C Shepherd appears,

CHIEFLY (*see* CHIEF)
Rom 3: 2 C because to them were

CHIEFS (*see* CHIEF)
Gen 36:15 These were the c of the sons
Gen 36:16 These were the c of Eliphaz
Gen 36:17 These were the c of Reuel in
Gen 36:18 These were the c who
Gen 36:19 Edom, and these were their c
Gen 36:21 were the c of the Horites
Gen 36:29 were the c of the Horites
Gen 36:30 were the c of the Horites
Gen 36:30 according to their c in the
Gen 36:40 the names of the c of Esau
Gen 36:43 These were the c of Edom,
Ex 15:15 Then the c of Edom will be
1Sa 14:38 all you c of the people, and
1Ki 5:16 the c of Solomon's deputies
1Ki 9:23 Others were c of the

1Ch 1:51 And the **c** of Edom were Chief
1Ch 1:54 These were the **c** of Edom
1Ch 12:32 do, their **c** were two hundred
2Ch 8:10 And others were **c** of the
Neh 12:46 there were **c** of the singers
Job 12:24 the understanding of the **c** of

CHIEFTAINS (*see* CHIEF)
Jer 13:21 you have taught them to be **c**

CHILD (*see* CHILDHOOD, CHILDISH, CHILDLESS, CHILDREN, CHILD'S)
Gen 11:30 she had no **c**
Gen 16:11 Behold, you are with **c**, and
Gen 17:10 Every male **c** among you shall
Gen 17:12 every male **c** in your
Gen 17:14 And the uncircumcised male **c**
Gen 17:17 Shall a **c** be born to a man
Gen 17:17 is ninety years old, bear a **c**
Gen 18:13 Shall I surely bear a **c**
Gen 19:36 were with **c** by their father
Gen 21: 8 So the **c** grew and was weaned
Gen 30: 3 she will bear a **c** on my knees
Gen 38:24 she is with **c** by harlotry
Gen 38:25 these belong, I am with **c**
Gen 44:20 a **c** of his old age, who is
Ex 2: 2 saw that he was a beautiful **c**
Ex 2: 3 and pitch, put the **c** in it
Ex 2: 6 had opened it, she saw the **c**
Ex 2: 7 she may nurse the **c** for you
Ex 2: 9 Take this **c** away and nurse him
Ex 2: 9 So the woman took the **c**
Ex 2:10 the **c** grew, and she brought
Ex 21:22 fight, and hurt a woman with **c**
Ex 22:22 any widow or fatherless **c**
Lev 12: 2 conceived, and borne a male **c**
Lev 12: 5 But if she bears a female **c**
Lev 22:13 or divorced, and has no **c**, and
Num 11:12 guardian carries a nursing **c**
Deut 32:25 the nursing **c** with the man of
Judg 11:34 and she was his only **c**
Judg 13: 5 for the **c** shall be a Nazirite
Judg 13: 7 for the **c** shall be a Nazirite
Judg 13: 8 do for the **c** who will be born
Judg 13:24 and the **c** grew, and the LORD
Ruth 4:16 Then Naomi took the **c** and laid
1Sa 1:11 your maidservant a male **c**
1Sa 1:22 go up until the **c** is weaned
1Sa 1:24 And the **c** was young
1Sa 1:25 bull, and brought the **c** to Eli
1Sa 1:27 For this **c** I prayed, and the
1Sa 2:11 But the **c** ministered to the
1Sa 2:18 before the LORD, even as a **c**
1Sa 2:21 Meanwhile the **c** Samuel grew
1Sa 2:26 the **c** Samuel grew in stature,
1Sa 4:19 Phinehas' wife, was with **c**
1Sa 4:21 Then she named the **c** Ichabod
1Sa 15: 3 and woman, infant and nursing **c**
2Sa 11: 5 I am with **c**
2Sa 12:14 the **c** also who is born to you
2Sa 12:15 the LORD struck the **c** that
2Sa 12:16 pleaded with God for the **c**
2Sa 12:18 came to pass that the **c** died
2Sa 12:18 tell him that the **c** was dead
2Sa 12:18 while the **c** was still alive,
2Sa 12:18 tell him that the **c** is dead
2Sa 12:19 perceived that the **c** was dead
2Sa 12:19 Is the **c** dead?
2Sa 12:21 wept for the **c** while he was
2Sa 12:21 alive, but when the **c** died
2Sa 12:22 While the **c** was still alive,
2Sa 12:22 to me, that the **c** may live
1Ki 3: 7 David, but I am a little **c**
1Ki 3:20 laid her dead **c** in my bosom
1Ki 3:25 Divide the living **c** in two
1Ki 3:26 lord, give her the living **c**
1Ki 3:27 the first woman the living **c**
1Ki 11:17 Hadad was still a little **c**
1Ki 13: 2 Behold, a **c**, Josiah by name,
1Ki 14: 3 you what will become of the **c**
1Ki 14:12 the city, the **c** shall die
1Ki 14:17 of the house, the **c** died
1Ki 17:21 out on the **c** three times, and
1Ki 17:22 the soul of the **c** came back
1Ki 17:23 And Elijah took the **c** and
2Ki 4:18 So the **c** grew
2Ki 4:26 Is it well with the **c**
2Ki 4:29 my staff on the face of the **c**
2Ki 4:30 And the mother of the **c** said
2Ki 4:31 staff on the face of the **c**
2Ki 4:31 The **c** has not awakened
2Ki 4:32 the house, there was the **c**
2Ki 4:34 And he went up and lay on the **c**
2Ki 4:34 himself out on the **c**, and the
2Ki 4:34 flesh of the **c** became warm
2Ki 4:35 then the **c** sneezed seven
2Ki 4:35 and the **c** opened his eyes
2Ki 5:14 like the flesh of a little **c**
2Ki 8:12 rip open their women with **c**
2Ki 15:16 were with **c** he ripped open
1Ch 2:31 and Sheshan's **c** was Ahlai
Job 3: 3 said, "A male **c** is conceived
Job 3:16 not hidden like a stillborn **c**
Ps 58: 8 Like a stillborn **c** of a woman
Ps 131: 2 Like a weaned **c** with his
Ps 131: 2 Like a weaned **c** is my soul
Prov 20:11 Even a **c** is known by his
Prov 22: 6 Train up a **c** in the way he
Prov 22:15 bound up in the heart of a **c**
Prov 23:13 withhold correction from a **c**
Prov 23:24 a wise **c** will delight in him
Prov 29:15 but a **c** left to himself
Eccl 6: 3 stillborn **c** is better than he
Eccl 10:16 O land, when your king is a **c**
Eccl 11: 5 the womb of her who is with **c**
Is 3: 5 the **c** will be insolent toward
Is 7:16 For before the **C** shall know
Is 8: 4 for before the **c** shall have
Is 9: 6 For unto us a **C** is born, unto
Is 10:19 that a **c** may write them
Is 11: 6 a little **c** shall lead them
Is 11: 8 The nursing **c** shall play by
Is 11: 8 the weaned **c** shall put his
Is 26:17 As a woman with **c** is in pain
Is 26:18 We have been with **c**, we have
Is 49:15 a woman forget her nursing **c**
Is 54: 1 who have not travailed with **c**
Is 65:20 for the **c** shall die one
Is 66: 7 came, she delivered a male **c**
Jer 4:31 who brings forth her first **c**
Jer 20:15 A male **c** has been born to you
Jer 30: 6 a man is ever in labor with **c**
Jer 31: 8 and the lame, the woman with **c**
Jer 31: 8 and the one who labors with **c**
Jer 31:20 Is he a pleasant **c**
Jer 44: 7 off from you man and woman, **c**
Hos 11: 1 When Israel was a **c**, I loved
Hos 13:16 women with **c** ripped open
Amos 1:13 the women with **c** in Gilead
Matt 1:18 with **c** of the Holy Spirit
Matt 1:23 a virgin shall be with **c**
Matt 2: 8 diligently for the young **C**
Matt 2: 9 over where the young **C** was
Matt 2:11 they saw the young **C** with
Matt 2:13 Arise, take the young **C** and
Matt 2:13 the young **C** to destroy Him
Matt 2:14 he arose, he took the young **C**
Matt 2:20 Arise, take the young **C** and
Matt 2:21 he arose, took the young **C**
Matt 10:21 to death, and a father his **c**
Matt 17:18 the **c** was cured from that
Matt 18: 2 called a little **c** to Him, set
Matt 18: 4 **c** is the greatest in the
Matt 18: 5 little **c** like this in My name
Mark 5:39 The **c** is not dead, but
Mark 5:40 father and the mother of the **c**
Mark 5:40 entered where the **c** was lying
Mark 5:41 He took the **c** by the hand
Mark 9:24 the father of the **c** cried out
Mark 9:36 Then He took a little **c** and
Mark 10:15 **c** will by no means enter it
Mark 13:12 to death, and a father his **c**
Luke 1: 7 But they had no **c**, because
Luke 1:59 they came to circumcise the **c**
Luke 1:66 What kind of **c** will this be
Luke 1:76 and you, **c**, will be called the
Luke 1:80 So the **c** grew and became
Luke 2: 5 wife, who was with **c**
Luke 2:17 told them concerning this **C**
Luke 2:21 for the circumcision of the **C**
Luke 2:27 brought in the **C** Jesus, to do
Luke 2:34 this **C** is destined for the
Luke 2:40 the **C** grew and became strong
Luke 9:38 my son, for he is my only **c**
Luke 9:42 unclean spirit, healed the **c**
Luke 9:47 their heart, took a little **c**
Luke 9:48 receives this little **c** in My
Luke 18:17 **c** will by no means enter it
John 4:49 come down before my **c** dies
John 16:21 she has given birth to the **c**
Acts 7: 5 even when Abraham had no **c**
1Co 13:11 I was a **c**, I spoke as a **c**
1Co 13:11 I understood as a **c**
1Co 13:11 I thought as a **c**
Gal 4: 1 heir, as long as he is a **c**
Heb 11:11 she bore a **c** when she was
Heb 11:23 they saw he was a beautiful **c**
Rev 12: 2 Then being with **c**, she cried
Rev 12: 4 to devour her **C** as soon as it
Rev 12: 5 she bore a male **C** who was to
Rev 12: 5 her **C** was caught up to God and
Rev 12:13 who gave birth to the male **C**

CHILDBEARING
Gen 18:11 Sarah had passed the age of **c**
1Ti 2:15 she will be saved in **c** if

CHILDBIRTH (*see* BIRTH)
Gen 35:16 Rachel travailed in **c**, and
Is 13: 8 be in pain as a woman in **c**
Jer 50:43 him, pangs as of a woman in **c**
Hos 13:13 in **c** shall come upon him

CHILDHOOD (*see* CHILD)
1Sa 12: 2 you from my **c** to this day
Prov 29:21 pampers his servant from **c**
Eccl 11:10 evil from your flesh, for **c**
Mark 9:21 he said, "From **c**.
2Ti 3:15 that from **c** you have known

CHILDISH (*see* CHILD)
1Co 13:11 a man, I put away **c** things

CHILDLESS (*see* CHILD)
Gen 15: 2 You give me, seeing I go **c**
Lev 20:20 they shall die **c**
Lev 20:21 They shall be **c**
1Sa 15:33 your sword has made women **c**
1Sa 15:33 your mother be **c** among women
Jer 22:30 Write this man down as **c**
Luke 20:30 her as wife, and he died **c**

CHILDREN (*see* CHILD, CHILDREN'S, GRANDCHILDREN)
Gen 3:16 pain you shall bring forth **c**
Gen 6: 4 of men and they bore **c** to them
Gen 10:21 **c** were born also to Shem, the
Gen 10:21 father of all the **c** of Eber
Gen 16: 1 wife, had borne him no **c**
Gen 16: 2 restrained me from bearing **c**
Gen 16: 2 I shall obtain **c** by her
Gen 18:19 that he may command his **c**
Gen 20:17 Then they bore **c**
Gen 21: 7 that Sarah would nurse **c**
Gen 22:20 borne **c** to your brother Nahor
Gen 25: 4 these were the **c** of Keturah
Gen 25:22 But the **c** struggled together
Gen 30: 1 saw that she bore Jacob no **c**
Gen 30: 1 Give me **c**, or else I die
Gen 30: 3 that I also may have **c** by her
Gen 30:26 my **c** for whom I have served
Gen 31:43 and these **c** are my **c**
Gen 31:43 their **c** whom they have borne
Gen 32:11 me and the mother with the **c**
Gen 32:32 **c** of Israel do not eat the
Gen 33: 1 he divided the **c** among Leah
Gen 33: 2 their **c** in front, Leah and her
Gen 33: 2 her **c** behind, and Rachel and
Gen 33: 5 eyes and saw the women and **c**
Gen 33: 5 The **c** whom God has graciously
Gen 33: 6 came near, they and their **c**
Gen 33: 7 also came near with her **c**
Gen 33:13 knows that the **c** are weak
Gen 33:14 that go before me, and the **c**
Gen 33:19 his tent, from the **c** of Hamor
Gen 36:25 These were the **c** of Anah
Gen 36:31 reigned over the **c** of Israel
Gen 37: 3 Joseph more than all his **c**
Gen 42:36 You have bereaved me of my **c**
Gen 44:20 is left of his mother's **c**
Gen 45:10 your **c**, your children's **c**
Gen 46: 8 the names of the **c** of Israel
Gen 49: 8 your father's **c** shall bow
Gen 50:23 Joseph saw Ephraim's **c** to the
Gen 50:23 The **c** of Machir, the son of
Gen 50:25 an oath from the **c** of Israel
Ex 1: 1 these are the names of the **c**
Ex 1: 7 But the **c** of Israel were
Ex 1: 9 the people of the **c** of Israel
Ex 1:12 in dread of the **c** of Israel
Ex 1:13 So the Egyptians made the **c**
Ex 1:17 but saved the male **c** alive
Ex 1:18 and saved the male **c** alive
Ex 2: 6 This is one of the Hebrews' **c**

Ex 2:23 Then the **c** of Israel groaned
Ex 2:25 looked upon the **c** of Israel
Ex 3: 9 the cry of the **c** of Israel
Ex 3:10 the **c** of Israel, out of Egypt
Ex 3:11 the **c** of Israel out of Egypt
Ex 3:13 I come to the **c** of Israel
Ex 3:14 shall say to the **c** of Israel
Ex 3:15 shall say to the **c** of Israel
Ex 4:29 the elders of the **c** of Israel
Ex 4:31 had visited the **c** of Israel
Ex 5:14 officers of the **c** of Israel
Ex 5:15 of the **c** of Israel came and
Ex 5:19 And the officers of the **c** of
Ex 6: 5 of the **c** of Israel whom the
Ex 6: 6 say to the **c** of Israel
Ex 6: 9 spoke thus to the **c** of Israel
Ex 6:11 that he must let the **c** of
Ex 6:12 The **c** of Israel have not
Ex 6:13 a command for the **c** of Israel
Ex 6:13 to bring the **c** of Israel out
Ex 6:26 Bring out the **c** of Israel
Ex 6:27 to bring out the **c** of Israel
Ex 7: 2 that he must send the **c** of
Ex 7: 4 the **c** of Israel, out of the
Ex 7: 5 bring out the **c** of Israel
Ex 9: 4 belongs to the **c** of Israel
Ex 9: 6 livestock of the **c** of Israel
Ex 9:26 where the **c** of Israel were,
Ex 9:35 he let the **c** of Israel go
Ex 10:20 not let the **c** of Israel go
Ex 10:23 But all the **c** of Israel had
Ex 11: 7 But against none of the **c** of
Ex 11:10 and he did not let the **c** of
Ex 12:26 when your **c** say to you, "What
Ex 12:27 over the houses of the **c** of
Ex 12:28 Then the **c** of Israel went
Ex 12:31 both you and the **c** of Israel
Ex 12:35 Now the **c** of Israel had done
Ex 12:37 Then the **c** of Israel
Ex 12:37 men on foot, besides **c**
Ex 12:40 the **c** of Israel who lived in
Ex 12:42 observance for all the **c** of
Ex 12:50 Thus all the **c** of Israel did
Ex 12:51 **c** of Israel out of the land
Ex 13: 2 womb among the **c** of Israel
Ex 13:18 the **c** of Israel went up in
Ex 13:19 for he had placed the **c** of
Ex 14: 2 Speak to the **c** of Israel,
Ex 14: 3 will say of the **c** of Israel
Ex 14: 8 and he pursued the **c** of Israel
Ex 14: 8 the **c** of Israel went out with
Ex 14:10 the **c** of Israel lifted their
Ex 14:10 the **c** of Israel cried out to
Ex 14:15 Tell the **c** of Israel to go
Ex 14:16 the **c** of Israel shall go on
Ex 14:22 So the **c** of Israel went into
Ex 14:29 But the **c** of Israel had
Ex 15: 1 the **c** of Israel sang this
Ex 15:19 But the **c** of Israel went on
Ex 16: 1 the **c** of Israel came to the
Ex 16: 2 whole congregation of the **c**
Ex 16: 3 the **c** of Israel said to them,
Ex 16: 6 said to all the **c** of Israel
Ex 16: 9 of the **c** of Israel, "Come
Ex 16:10 of the **c** of Israel, that they
Ex 16:12 murmurings of the **c** of Israel
Ex 16:15 So when the **c** of Israel saw
Ex 16:17 the **c** of Israel did so and
Ex 16:35 the **c** of Israel ate manna
Ex 17: 1 **c** of Israel set out on their
Ex 17: 3 of Egypt, to kill us and our **c**
Ex 17: 7 contention of the **c** of Israel
Ex 19: 1 **c** of Israel had gone out of
Ex 19: 3 and tell the **c** of Israel
Ex 19: 6 speak to the **c** of Israel
Ex 20: 5 fathers on the **c** to the third
Ex 20:22 shall say to the **c** of Israel
Ex 21: 4 her **c** shall be her master's,
Ex 21: 5 my master, my wife, and my **c**
Ex 22:24 widows, and your **c** fatherless
Ex 24: 5 young men of the **c** of Israel
Ex 24:11 **c** of Israel He did not lay
Ex 24:17 the eyes of the **c** of Israel
Ex 25: 2 Speak to the **c** of Israel,
Ex 25:22 to the **c** of Israel
Ex 27:20 you shall command the **c** of
Ex 27:21 on behalf of the **c** of Israel
Ex 28: 1 from among the **c** of Israel
Ex 28:30 **c** of Israel over his heart
Ex 28:38 the **c** of Israel hallow in all
Ex 29:28 the **c** of Israel for Aaron
Ex 29:28 from the **c** of Israel from the
Ex 29:43 meet with the **c** of Israel
Ex 29:45 dwell among the **c** of Israel
Ex 30:12 **c** of Israel for their number
Ex 30:16 money of the **c** of Israel, and
Ex 30:16 **c** of Israel before the LORD
Ex 30:31 speak to the **c** of Israel,
Ex 31:13 Speak also to the **c** of Israel
Ex 31:16 Therefore the **c** of Israel
Ex 31:17 Me and the **c** of Israel forever
Ex 32:20 made the **c** of Israel drink it
Ex 33: 5 Say to the **c** of Israel, "You
Ex 33: 6 So the **c** of Israel stripped
Ex 34: 7 of the fathers upon the **c**
Ex 34: 7 the children's **c** to the third
Ex 34:30 all the **c** of Israel saw Moses
Ex 34:32 Afterward all the **c** of Israel
Ex 34:34 and speak to the **c** of Israel
Ex 34:35 whenever the **c** of Israel saw
Ex 35: 1 of the **c** of Israel together
Ex 35: 4 of the **c** of Israel, saying
Ex 35:20 **c** of Israel departed from the
Ex 35:29 The **c** of Israel brought a
Ex 35:30 Moses said to the **c** of Israel
Ex 36: 3 **c** of Israel had brought for
Ex 39:32 the **c** of Israel did according
Ex 39:42 so the **c** of Israel did all
Ex 40:36 the **c** of Israel went onward
Lev 1: 2 Speak to the **c** of Israel, and
Lev 4: 2 Speak to the **c** of Israel,
Lev 6:18 the **c** of Aaron may eat it
Lev 7:23 Speak to the **c** of Israel,
Lev 7:29 Speak to the **c** of Israel,
Lev 7:34 taken from the **c** of Israel
Lev 7:34 to his sons from the **c** of
Lev 7:36 to them by the **c** of Israel
Lev 7:38 **c** of Israel to offer their
Lev 9: 3 to the **c** of Israel you shall
Lev 10:11 that you may teach the **c** of
Lev 10:14 offerings of the **c** of Israel
Lev 11: 2 Speak to the **c** of Israel,
Lev 12: 2 Speak to the **c** of Israel,
Lev 15: 2 Speak to the **c** of Israel, and
Lev 15:31 the **c** of Israel from their
Lev 16: 5 the congregation of the **c** of
Lev 16:16 of the **c** of Israel, and
Lev 16:19 of the **c** of Israel
Lev 16:21 iniquities of the **c** of Israel
Lev 16:34 atonement for the **c** of Israel
Lev 17: 2 and to all the **c** of Israel
Lev 17: 5 to the end that the **c** of
Lev 17:12 I said to the **c** of Israel
Lev 17:13 man of the **c** of Israel, or of
Lev 17:14 I said to the **c** of Israel
Lev 18: 2 Speak to the **c** of Israel, and
Lev 19: 2 of the **c** of Israel, and say to
Lev 19:18 against the **c** of your people
Lev 20: 2 shall say to the **c** of Israel
Lev 20: 2 Whoever of the **c** of Israel
Lev 21:24 and to all the **c** of Israel
Lev 22: 2 things of the **c** of Israel
Lev 22: 3 **c** of Israel sanctify to the
Lev 22:15 offerings of the **c** of Israel
Lev 22:18 and to all the **c** of Israel
Lev 22:32 among the **c** of Israel
Lev 23: 2 Speak to the **c** of Israel, and
Lev 23:10 Speak to the **c** of Israel, and
Lev 23:24 Speak to the **c** of Israel,
Lev 23:34 Speak to the **c** of Israel,
Lev 23:43 may know that I made the **c** of
Lev 23:44 So Moses declared to the **c** of
Lev 24: 2 Command the **c** of Israel that
Lev 24: 8 being taken from the **c** of
Lev 24:10 out among the **c** of Israel
Lev 24:15 speak to the **c** of Israel,
Lev 24:23 spoke to the **c** of Israel
Lev 24:23 So the **c** of Israel did as the
Lev 25: 2 Speak to the **c** of Israel, and
Lev 25:33 among the **c** of Israel
Lev 25:41 and his **c** with him, and shall
Lev 25:45 the **c** of the strangers who
Lev 25:46 for your **c** after you, to
Lev 25:46 the **c** of Israel, you shall
Lev 25:54 both he and his **c** with him
Lev 25:55 For the **c** of Israel are
Lev 26:22 which shall rob you of your **c**
Lev 26:46 and the **c** of Israel on Mount
Lev 27: 2 Speak to the **c** of Israel, and
Lev 27:34 commanded Moses for the **c** of
Num 1: 2 of the **c** of Israel, by their
Num 1:20 Now the **c** of Reuben, Israel's
Num 1:22 From the **c** of Simeon, their
Num 1:24 From the **c** of Gad, their
Num 1:26 From the **c** of Judah, their
Num 1:28 From the **c** of Issachar, their
Num 1:30 From the **c** of Zebulun, their
Num 1:32 the **c** of Ephraim, their
Num 1:34 From the **c** of Manasseh, their
Num 1:36 From the **c** of Benjamin, their
Num 1:38 From the **c** of Dan, their
Num 1:40 From the **c** of Asher, their
Num 1:42 From the **c** of Naphtali, their
Num 1:45 numbered of the **c** of Israel
Num 1:49 of them among the **c** of Israel
Num 1:52 The **c** of Israel shall pitch
Num 1:53 of the **c** of Israel
Num 1:54 Thus the **c** of Israel did
Num 2: 2 Everyone of the **c** of Israel
Num 2: 3 the leader of the **c** of Judah
Num 2: 5 leader of the **c** of Issachar
Num 2: 7 leader of the **c** of Zebulun
Num 2:10 the leader of the **c** of Reuben
Num 2:12 the leader of the **c** of Simeon
Num 2:14 the leader of the **c** of Gad
Num 2:18 and the leader of the **c** of
Num 2:20 and the leader of the **c** of
Num 2:22 and the leader of the **c** of
Num 2:25 the leader of the **c** of Dan
Num 2:27 the leader of the **c** of Asher
Num 2:29 and the leader of the **c** of
Num 2:32 who were numbered of the **c** of
Num 2:33 among the **c** of Israel, just
Num 2:34 Thus the **c** of Israel did
Num 3: 4 and they had no **c**
Num 3: 8 the needs of the **c** of Israel
Num 3: 9 from among the **c** of Israel
Num 3:12 **c** of Israel instead of every
Num 3:12 womb among the **c** of Israel
Num 3:15 Number the **c** of Levi by their
Num 3:25 of the **c** of Gershon in the
Num 3:29 The families of the **c** of
Num 3:36 the **c** of Merari included the
Num 3:38 the needs of the **c** of Israel
Num 3:40 **c** of Israel from a month old
Num 3:41 among the **c** of Israel, and the
Num 3:41 livestock of the **c** of Israel
Num 3:42 among the **c** of Israel, as the
Num 3:45 among the **c** of Israel, and the
Num 3:46 firstborn of the **c** of Israel
Num 3:50 From the firstborn of the **c**
Num 4: 2 from among the **c** of Levi, by
Num 5: 2 Command the **c** of Israel that
Num 5: 4 the **c** of Israel did so, and
Num 5: 4 Moses, so the **c** of Israel did
Num 5: 6 Speak to the **c** of Israel
Num 5: 9 things of the **c** of Israel
Num 5:12 Speak to the **c** of Israel, and
Num 5:28 be free and may conceive **c**
Num 6: 2 Speak to the **c** of Israel, and
Num 6:23 shall bless the **c** of Israel
Num 6:27 My name on the **c** of Israel
Num 7:24 leader of the **c** of Zebulun
Num 7:30 leader of the **c** of Reuben
Num 7:36 leader of the **c** of Simeon
Num 7:42 Deuel, leader of the **c** of Gad
Num 7:48 leader of the **c** of Ephraim
Num 7:54 leader of the **c** of Manasseh
Num 7:60 leader of the **c** of Benjamin
Num 7:66 leader of the **c** of Dan,
Num 7:72 leader of the **c** of Asher
Num 7:78 leader of the **c** of Naphtali
Num 8: 6 from among the **c** of Israel
Num 8: 9 assembly of the **c** of Israel
Num 8:10 the **c** of Israel shall lay
Num 8:11 offering from the **c** of Israel
Num 8:14 from among the **c** of Israel
Num 8:16 Me from among the **c** of Israel
Num 8:16 of all the **c** of Israel
Num 8:17 the **c** of Israel are Mine,
Num 8:18 firstborn of the **c** of Israel
Num 8:19 from among the **c** of Israel
Num 8:19 to do the work for the **c** of
Num 8:19 atonement for the **c** of Israel
Num 8:19 be no plague among the **c** of
Num 8:19 the **c** of Israel come near the
Num 8:20 of the **c** of Israel did to the
Num 8:20 so the **c** of Israel did to
Num 9: 2 Let the **c** of Israel keep the
Num 9: 4 So Moses told the **c** of Israel

Num 9: 5 Moses, so the **c** of Israel did
Num 9: 7 time among the **c** of Israel
Num 9:10 Speak to the **c** of Israel,
Num 9:17 after that the **c** of Israel
Num 9:17 there the **c** of Israel would
Num 9:18 the **c** of Israel would journey
Num 9:19 the **c** of Israel kept the
Num 9:22 the **c** of Israel would remain
Num 10:12 the **c** of Israel set out from
Num 10:14 the **c** of Judah set out first
Num 10:15 army of the tribe of the **c** of
Num 10:16 **c** of Zebulun was Eliab the
Num 10:19 army of the tribe of the **c** of
Num 10:20 army of the tribe of the **c** of
Num 10:22 of the **c** of Ephraim set out
Num 10:23 **c** of Manasseh was Gamaliel
Num 10:24 army of the tribe of the **c** of
Num 10:25 of the camp of the **c** of Dan
Num 10:26 army of the tribe of the **c** of
Num 10:27 army of the tribe of the **c** of
Num 10:28 of march of the **c** of Israel
Num 11: 4 so the **c** of Israel also wept
Num 13: 2 am giving to the **c** of Israel
Num 13: 3 were heads of the **c** of Israel
Num 13:26 **c** of Israel in the Wilderness
Num 13:32 they gave the **c** of Israel a
Num 14: 2 all the **c** of Israel murmured
Num 14: 3 and **c** should become victims
Num 14: 5 of the **c** of Israel
Num 14: 7 of the **c** of Israel, saying
Num 14:10 before all the **c** of Israel
Num 14:18 fathers on the **c** to the third
Num 14:27 the murmurings which the **c** of
Num 14:39 words to all the **c** of Israel
Num 15: 2 Speak to the **c** of Israel, and
Num 15:18 Speak to the **c** of Israel, and
Num 15:25 of the **c** of Israel, and it
Num 15:26 of the **c** of Israel and the
Num 15:29 among the **c** of Israel and for
Num 15:32 Now while the **c** of Israel
Num 15:38 Speak to the **c** of Israel
Num 16: 2 with some of the **c** of Israel
Num 16:27 their sons, and their little **c**
Num 16:38 be a sign to the **c** of Israel
Num 16:40 to be a memorial to the **c** of
Num 16:41 **c** of Israel murmured against
Num 17: 2 Speak to the **c** of Israel, and
Num 17: 5 murmurings of the **c** of Israel
Num 17: 6 spoke to the **c** of Israel, and
Num 17: 9 LORD to all the **c** of Israel
Num 17:12 And the **c** of Israel spoke to
Num 18: 5 more wrath on the **c** of Israel
Num 18: 6 from among the **c** of Israel
Num 18: 8 holy gifts of the **c** of Israel
Num 18:11 offerings of the **c** of Israel
Num 18:19 which the **c** of Israel offer
Num 18:20 among the **c** of Israel
Num 18:21 I have given the **c** of Levi
Num 18:22 Hereafter the **c** of Israel
Num 18:23 that among the **c** of Israel
Num 18:24 the tithes of the **c** of Israel
Num 18:24 Among the **c** of Israel they
Num 18:26 When you take from the **c** of
Num 18:28 receive from the **c** of Israel
Num 18:32 holy gifts of the **c** of Israel
Num 19: 2 Speak to the **c** of Israel
Num 19: 9 **c** of Israel for the water of
Num 19:10 forever to the **c** of Israel
Num 20: 1 Then the **c** of Israel, the
Num 20:12 the eyes of the **c** of Israel
Num 20:13 because the **c** of Israel
Num 20:19 So the **c** of Israel said to
Num 20:22 Then the **c** of Israel, the
Num 20:24 have given to the **c** of Israel
Num 21:10 Now the **c** of Israel moved on
Num 22: 1 Then the **c** of Israel moved,
Num 22: 3 because of the **c** of Israel
Num 25: 6 one of the **c** of Israel came
Num 25: 6 of the **c** of Israel, who were
Num 25: 8 stopped among the **c** of Israel
Num 25:11 My wrath from the **c** of Israel
Num 25:11 the **c** of Israel in My zeal
Num 25:13 atonement for the **c** of Israel
Num 26: 2 **c** of Israel from twenty years
Num 26: 4 the **c** of Israel who came out
Num 26: 5 The **c** of Reuben were
Num 26:11 Nevertheless the **c** of Korah
Num 26:51 numbered of the **c** of Israel
Num 26:62 among the other **c** of Israel
Num 26:62 to them among the **c** of Israel
Num 26:63 who numbered the **c** of Israel
Num 26:64 when they numbered the **c** of
Num 27: 8 speak to the **c** of Israel,
Num 27:11 And it shall be to the **c** of
Num 27:12 have given to the **c** of Israel
Num 27:20 **c** of Israel may be obedient
Num 27:21 all the **c** of Israel with him,
Num 28: 2 Command the **c** of Israel, and
Num 29:40 So Moses told the **c** of Israel
Num 30: 1 concerning the **c** of Israel
Num 31: 2 Take vengeance for the **c** of
Num 31: 9 the **c** of Israel took all the
Num 31:12 of the **c** of Israel, to the
Num 31:16 women caused the **c** of Israel
Num 31:30 from the **c** of Israel's half
Num 31:42 from the **c** of Israel's half,
Num 31:47 from the **c** of Israel's half
Num 31:54 as a memorial for the **c** of
Num 32: 1 Now the **c** of Reuben and the
Num 32: 1 the **c** of Gad had a very great
Num 32: 2 **c** of Gad and the **c** of Reuben
Num 32: 6 And Moses said to the **c** of Gad
Num 32: 6 of Gad and to the **c** of Reuben
Num 32: 7 **c** of Israel from going over
Num 32: 9 the heart of the **c** of Israel
Num 32:17 ready to go before the **c** of
Num 32:18 until every one of the **c** of
Num 32:25 the **c** of Gad and the **c**
Num 32:25 and the **c** of Reuben spoke to
Num 32:28 the tribes of the **c** of Israel
Num 32:29 If the **c** of Gad and the
Num 32:29 the **c** of Reuben cross over
Num 32:31 Then the **c** of Gad and the
Num 32:31 the **c** of Reuben answered,
Num 32:33 So Moses gave to the **c** of Gad
Num 32:33 to the **c** of Reuben, and to
Num 32:34 the **c** of Gad built Dibon and
Num 32:37 the **c** of Reuben built Heshbon
Num 32:39 the **c** of Machir the son of
Num 33: 1 journeys of the **c** of Israel
Num 33: 3 the **c** of Israel went out with
Num 33: 5 Then the **c** of Israel moved
Num 33:38 **c** of Israel had come out of
Num 33:40 the coming of the **c** of Israel
Num 33:51 Speak to the **c** of Israel, and
Num 34: 2 Command the **c** of Israel, and
Num 34:13 commanded the **c** of Israel
Num 34:14 For the tribe of the **c** of
Num 34:14 the tribe of the **c** of Gad
Num 34:20 the tribe of the **c** of Simeon
Num 34:22 the tribe of the **c** of Dan
Num 34:23 tribe of the **c** of Manasseh
Num 34:24 the tribe of the **c** of Ephraim
Num 34:25 the tribe of the **c** of Zebulun
Num 34:26 tribe of the **c** of Issachar
Num 34:27 the tribe of the **c** of Asher
Num 34:28 tribe of the **c** of Naphtali
Num 34:29 **c** of Israel in the land of
Num 35: 2 Command the **c** of Israel that
Num 35: 8 possession of the **c** of Israel
Num 35:10 Speak to the **c** of Israel, and
Num 35:15 refuge for the **c** of Israel
Num 35:34 dwell among the **c** of Israel
Num 36: 1 of the families of the **c** of
Num 36: 1 fathers of the **c** of Israel
Num 36: 2 by lot to the **c** of Israel
Num 36: 3 tribes of the **c** of Israel
Num 36: 4 of the **c** of Israel comes,
Num 36: 5 Then Moses commanded the **c**
Num 36: 7 So the inheritance of the **c**
Num 36: 7 for every one of the **c** of
Num 36: 8 in any tribe of the **c** of
Num 36: 8 so that the **c** of Israel each
Num 36: 9 but every tribe of the **c** of
Num 36:12 the **c** of Manasseh the son of
Num 36:13 the LORD commanded the **c** of
Deut 1: 3 that Moses spoke to the **c** of
Deut 1:36 his **c** I am giving the land on
Deut 1:39 your little ones and your **c**
Deut 3: 6 women, and **c** of every city
Deut 3:18 brethren, the **c** of Israel
Deut 4: 9 And teach them to your **c** and
Deut 4:10 that they may teach their **c**
Deut 4:25 When you beget **c** and
Deut 4:40 you and with your **c** after you
Deut 4:44 set before the **c** of Israel
Deut 4:45 which Moses spoke to the **c** of
Deut 4:46 and the **c** of Israel defeated
Deut 5: 9 upon the **c** to the third and
Deut 5:29 them and with their **c** forever
Deut 6: 7 them diligently to your **c**
Deut 10: 6 (Now the **c** of Israel
Deut 11: 2 I do not speak with your **c**
Deut 11:19 shall teach them to your **c**
Deut 11:21 the days of your **c** may be
Deut 12:25 your **c** after you, when you do
Deut 12:28 your **c** after you forever,
Deut 14: 1 You are the **c** of the LORD
Deut 17:20 his **c** in the midst of Israel
Deut 21:15 and they have borne him **c**
Deut 23: 8 The **c** of the third generation
Deut 24: 7 brethren of the **c** of Israel
Deut 24:16 be put to death for their **c**
Deut 24:16 nor shall the **c** be put to
Deut 28:54 his **c** whom he leaves behind
Deut 28:55 of his **c** whom he will eat
Deut 28:57 feet, and her **c** whom she bears
Deut 29: 1 Moses to make with the **c** of
Deut 29:22 your **c** who rise up after you
Deut 29:29 to our **c** forever, that we may
Deut 30: 2 you today, you and your **c**,
Deut 31:13 and that their **c**, who have not
Deut 31:19 teach it to the **c** of Israel
Deut 31:19 Me against the **c** of Israel
Deut 31:22 taught it to the **c** of Israel
Deut 31:23 for you shall bring the **c** of
Deut 32: 5 they are not His **c**, because
Deut 32: 8 the number of the **c** of Israel
Deut 32:20 **c** in whom is no faith
Deut 32:46 you shall command your **c** to
Deut 32:49 which I give to the **c** of
Deut 32:51 against Me among the **c** of
Deut 32:51 the midst of the **c** of Israel
Deut 32:52 am giving to the **c** of Israel
Deut 33: 1 **c** of Israel before his death
Deut 33: 9 brothers, Or know his own **c**
Deut 34: 8 And the **c** of Israel wept for
Deut 34: 9 so the **c** of Israel heeded him
Josh 1: 2 the **c** of Israel
Josh 2: 2 come here tonight from the **c**
Josh 3: 1 he and all the **c** of Israel, and
Josh 3: 9 said to the **c** of Israel
Josh 4: 4 from the **c** of Israel, one man
Josh 4: 5 the tribes of the **c** of Israel
Josh 4: 6 your **c** ask in time to come
Josh 4: 7 to the **c** of Israel forever
Josh 4: 8 the **c** of Israel did so, just
Josh 4: 8 the tribes of the **c** of Israel
Josh 4:12 armed before the **c** of Israel
Josh 4:21 he spoke to the **c** of Israel
Josh 4:21 When your **c** ask their fathers
Josh 4:22 you shall let your **c** know
Josh 5: 1 the **c** of Israel until we had
Josh 5: 1 because of the **c** of Israel
Josh 5: 6 For the **c** of Israel walked
Josh 5:10 So the **c** of Israel camped in
Josh 5:12 the **c** of Israel no longer had
Josh 6: 1 up because of the **c** of Israel
Josh 7: 1 But the **c** of Israel committed
Josh 7: 1 against the **c** of Israel
Josh 7:12 Therefore the **c** of Israel
Josh 7:23 and to all the **c** of Israel
Josh 8:31 had commanded the **c** of Israel
Josh 8:32 presence of the **c** of Israel
Josh 9:17 Then the **c** of Israel
Josh 9:18 But the **c** of Israel did not
Josh 9:26 the hand of the **c** of Israel
Josh 10: 4 and with the **c** of Israel
Josh 10:11 than those whom the **c** of
Josh 10:12 before the **c** of Israel, and he
Josh 10:20 the **c** of Israel made an end
Josh 10:21 any of the **c** of Israel
Josh 11:14 the **c** of Israel took as booty
Josh 11:19 peace with the **c** of Israel
Josh 11:22 the land of the **c** of Israel
Josh 12: 1 whom the **c** of Israel defeated
Josh 12: 6 the **c** of Israel had conquered
Josh 12: 7 the **c** of Israel conquered on
Josh 13: 6 from before the **c** of Israel
Josh 13:10 the border of the **c** of Ammon
Josh 13:13 Nevertheless the **c** of Israel
Josh 13:15 **c** of Reuben an inheritance
Josh 13:22 The **c** of Israel also killed
Josh 13:23 the border of the **c** of Reuben
Josh 13:23 the **c** of Reuben according to
Josh 13:24 to the **c** of Gad according to
Josh 13:28 **c** of Gad according to their
Josh 13:29 **c** of Manasseh according to
Josh 13:31 were for the **c** of Machir the
Josh 13:31 for half of the **c** of Machir

Josh 14: 1 are the areas which the **c** of
Josh 14: 1 of the tribes of the **c** of
Josh 14: 4 For the **c** of Joseph were two
Josh 14: 5 Moses, so the **c** of Israel did
Josh 14: 6 Then the **c** of Judah came to
Josh 15: 1 **c** of Judah according to their
Josh 15:12 of the **c** of Judah all around
Josh 15:13 portion among the **c** of Judah
Josh 15:14 and Talmai, the **c** of Anak
Josh 15:20 of the tribe of the **c** of
Josh 15:21 the tribe of the **c** of Judah
Josh 15:63 the **c** of Judah could not
Josh 15:63 **c** of Judah at Jerusalem to
Josh 16: 1 The lot fell to the **c** of
Josh 16: 4 So the **c** of Joseph, Manasseh
Josh 16: 5 border of the **c** of Ephraim
Josh 16: 8 of the tribe of the **c** of
Josh 16: 9 **c** of Ephraim were among the
Josh 16: 9 of the **c** of Manasseh, all the
Josh 17: 2 **c** of Manasseh according to
Josh 17: 2 for the **c** of Abiezer
Josh 17: 2 the **c** of Helek
Josh 17: 2 the **c** of Asriel
Josh 17: 2 the **c** of Shechem
Josh 17: 2 the **c** of Hepher
Josh 17: 2 and the **c** of Shemida
Josh 17: 2 these were the male **c** of
Josh 17: 8 belonged to the **c** of Ephraim
Josh 17:12 Yet the **c** of Manasseh could
Josh 17:13 when the **c** of Israel grew
Josh 17:14 Then the **c** of Joseph spoke to
Josh 17:16 But the **c** of Joseph said,
Josh 18: 1 of the **c** of Israel assembled
Josh 18: 2 the **c** of Israel seven tribes
Josh 18: 3 said to the **c** of Israel
Josh 18:10 the **c** of Israel according to
Josh 18:11 of the **c** of Benjamin came up
Josh 18:11 out between the **c** of Judah
Josh 18:11 of Judah and the **c** of Joseph
Josh 18:14 a city of the **c** of Judah
Josh 18:20 of the **c** of Benjamin,
Josh 18:21 tribe of the **c** of Benjamin
Josh 18:28 **c** of Benjamin according to
Josh 19: 1 for the tribe of the **c** of
Josh 19: 1 inheritance of the **c** of Judah
Josh 19: 8 of the tribe of the **c** of
Josh 19: 9 The inheritance of the **c** of
Josh 19: 9 the portion of the **c** of Judah
Josh 19: 9 for the portion of the **c** of
Josh 19: 9 Therefore the **c** of Simeon had
Josh 19:10 the **c** of Zebulun according to
Josh 19:16 the **c** of Zebulun according to
Josh 19:17 for the **c** of Issachar
Josh 19:23 of the tribe of the **c** of
Josh 19:24 out for the tribe of the **c** of
Josh 19:31 of the tribe of the **c** of
Josh 19:32 came out to the **c** of Naphtali
Josh 19:32 for the **c** of Naphtali
Josh 19:39 of the tribe of the **c** of
Josh 19:40 out for the tribe of the **c** of
Josh 19:47 the border of the **c** of Dan
Josh 19:47 because the **c** of Dan went up
Josh 19:48 of the tribe of the **c** of Dan
Josh 19:49 the **c** of Israel gave an
Josh 19:51 of the tribes of the **c** of
Josh 20: 2 Speak to the **c** of Israel,
Josh 20: 9 for all the **c** of Israel and
Josh 21: 1 the tribes of the **c** of Israel
Josh 21: 3 So the **c** of Israel gave to
Josh 21: 4 the **c** of Aaron the priest,
Josh 21: 5 The rest of the **c** of Kohath
Josh 21: 6 the **c** of Gershon had thirteen
Josh 21: 7 The **c** of Merari according to
Josh 21: 8 the **c** of Israel gave these
Josh 21: 9 the tribe of the **c** of Judah
Josh 21: 9 from the tribe of the **c** of
Josh 21:10 which were for the **c** of Aaron
Josh 21:10 who were of the **c** of Levi
Josh 21:13 Thus to the **c** of Aaron the
Josh 21:19 the cities of the **c** of Aaron
Josh 21:20 families of the **c** of Kohath
Josh 21:20 the rest of the **c** of Kohath
Josh 21:26 families of the **c** of Kohath
Josh 21:27 to the **c** of Gershon, of the
Josh 21:34 families of the **c** of Merari
Josh 21:40 the **c** of Merari according to
Josh 21:41 the possession of the **c** of
Josh 22: 9 So the **c** of Reuben, the
Josh 22: 9 the **c** of Gad, and half the
Josh 22: 9 departed from the **c** of Israel
Josh 22:10 **c** of Reuben, the **c** of Gad
Josh 22:11 Now the **c** of Israel heard
Josh 22:11 the **c** of Reuben, the **c**
Josh 22:11 the **c** of Gad, and half the
Josh 22:11 occupied by the **c** of Israel
Josh 22:12 when the **c** of Israel heard of
Josh 22:12 whole congregation of the **c**
Josh 22:13 Then the **c** of Israel sent
Josh 22:13 the priest to the **c** of Reuben
Josh 22:13 of Reuben, to the **c** of Gad
Josh 22:15 they came to the **c** of Reuben
Josh 22:15 of Reuben, to the **c** of Gad
Josh 22:21 Then the **c** of Reuben, the
Josh 22:21 the **c** of Gad, and half the
Josh 22:25 **c** of Reuben and **c** of Gad
Josh 22:30 words that the **c** of Reuben
Josh 22:30 the **c** of Gad, and the **c**
Josh 22:30 the **c** of Manasseh spoke, it
Josh 22:31 said to the **c** of Reuben, the
Josh 22:31 the **c** of Gad, and the **c**
Josh 22:31 of Gad, and the **c** of Manasseh,
Josh 22:31 **c** of Israel out of the hand
Josh 22:32 returned from the **c** of Reuben
Josh 22:32 the **c** of Gad, from the land
Josh 22:32 to the **c** of Israel, and
Josh 22:33 thing pleased the **c** of Israel
Josh 22:33 the **c** of Israel blessed God
Josh 22:33 land where the **c** of Reuben
Josh 22:34 And the **c** of Reuben and the
Josh 22:34 the **c** of Gad called the altar
Josh 24: 4 and his **c** went down to Egypt
Josh 24:32 which the **c** of Israel had
Josh 24:32 of the **c** of Joseph
Judg 1: 1 **c** of Israel asked the LORD
Judg 1: 8 Now the **c** of Judah fought
Judg 1: 9 afterward the **c** of Judah went
Judg 1:16 Now the **c** of the Kenite,
Judg 1:16 with the **c** of Judah into the
Judg 1:21 But the **c** of Benjamin did not
Judg 1:21 Jebusites dwell with the **c** of
Judg 1:34 the Amorites forced the **c** of
Judg 2: 4 words to all the **c** of Israel
Judg 2: 6 the **c** of Israel went each to
Judg 2:11 Then the **c** of Israel did evil
Judg 3: 2 **c** of Israel might be taught
Judg 3: 5 So the **c** of Israel dwelt
Judg 3: 7 So the **c** of Israel did evil
Judg 3: 8 and the **c** of Israel served
Judg 3: 9 When the **c** of Israel cried
Judg 3: 9 deliverer for the **c** of Israel
Judg 3:12 the **c** of Israel again did
Judg 3:14 So the **c** of Israel served
Judg 3:15 when the **c** of Israel cried
Judg 3:15 By him the **c** of Israel sent
Judg 3:27 the **c** of Israel went down
Judg 4: 1 the **c** of Israel again did
Judg 4: 3 the **c** of Israel cried out to
Judg 4: 3 oppressed the **c** of Israel
Judg 4: 5 the **c** of Israel came up to
Judg 4:11 Kenite, of the **c** of Hobab the
Judg 4:23 presence of the **c** of Israel
Judg 4:24 the hand of the **c** of Israel
Judg 6: 1 the **c** of Israel did evil in
Judg 6: 2 the **c** of Israel made for
Judg 6: 6 the **c** of Israel cried out to
Judg 6: 7 when the **c** of Israel cried
Judg 6: 8 a prophet to the **c** of Israel
Judg 8:28 before the **c** of Israel, so
Judg 8:33 that the **c** of Israel again
Judg 8:34 Thus the **c** of Israel did not
Judg 10: 6 Then the **c** of Israel again
Judg 10: 8 oppressed the **c** of Israel for
Judg 10: 8 all the **c** of Israel who were
Judg 10:10 the **c** of Israel cried out to
Judg 10:11 LORD said to the **c** of Israel
Judg 10:15 Then the **c** of Israel said to
Judg 10:17 the **c** of Israel assembled
Judg 11:27 day between the **c** of Israel
Judg 11:33 before the **c** of Israel
Judg 13: 1 Again the **c** of Israel did
Judg 13: 2 wife was barren and had no **c**
Judg 13: 3 are barren and have borne no **c**
Judg 18: 2 So the **c** of Dan sent five men
Judg 18:16 war, who were of the **c** of Dan
Judg 18:22 and overtook the **c** of Dan
Judg 18:23 called out to the **c** of Dan
Judg 18:25 the **c** of Dan said to him,
Judg 18:26 Then the **c** of Dan went their
Judg 18:30 Then the **c** of Dan set up for
Judg 19:12 are not of the **c** of Israel
Judg 19:30 **c** of Israel came up from the
Judg 20: 1 Then all the **c** of Israel came
Judg 20: 3 (Now the **c** of Benjamin heard
Judg 20: 3 **c** of Israel had gone up to
Judg 20: 3 Then the **c** of Israel said,
Judg 20: 7 All of you are **c** of Israel
Judg 20:13 But the **c** of Benjamin would
Judg 20:13 brethren, the **c** of Israel
Judg 20:14 the **c** of Benjamin gathered
Judg 20:14 against the **c** of Israel
Judg 20:15 the **c** of Benjamin numbered
Judg 20:18 the **c** of Israel arose and went
Judg 20:18 against the **c** of Benjamin
Judg 20:19 So the **c** of Israel rose in
Judg 20:21 Then the **c** of Benjamin came
Judg 20:23 Then the **c** of Israel went up
Judg 20:23 the **c** of my brother Benjamin
Judg 20:24 So the **c** of Israel approached
Judg 20:24 of Israel approached the **c** of
Judg 20:25 more of the **c** of Israel
Judg 20:26 Then all the **c** of Israel,
Judg 20:27 So the **c** of Israel inquired
Judg 20:28 the **c** of my brother Benjamin
Judg 20:30 And the **c** of Israel went up
Judg 20:30 **c** of Benjamin on the third
Judg 20:31 So the **c** of Benjamin went out
Judg 20:32 And the **c** of Benjamin said,
Judg 20:32 But the **c** of Israel said,
Judg 20:35 the **c** of Israel destroyed
Judg 20:36 So the **c** of Benjamin saw that
Judg 20:48 against the **c** of Benjamin
Judg 21: 5 The **c** of Israel said, "Who
Judg 21: 6 the **c** of Israel grieved for
Judg 21:10 including the women and **c**
Judg 21:13 sent word to the **c** of
Judg 21:18 for the **c** of Israel have
Judg 21:20 instructed the **c** of Benjamin
Judg 21:23 And the **c** of Benjamin did so
Judg 21:24 So the **c** of Israel departed
1Sa 1: 2 Peninnah had **c**
1Sa 1: 2 but Hannah had no **c**
1Sa 2: 5 she who has many **c** has become
1Sa 2:28 the **c** of Israel made by fire
1Sa 7: 4 So the **c** of Israel put away
1Sa 7: 6 Samuel judged the **c** of Israel
1Sa 7: 7 the **c** of Israel had gathered
1Sa 7: 7 when the **c** of Israel heard of
1Sa 7: 8 So the **c** of Israel said to
1Sa 9: 2 than he among the **c** of Israel
1Sa 10:18 and said to the **c** of Israel
1Sa 11: 8 the **c** of Israel were three
1Sa 14:18 God was with the **c** of Israel)
1Sa 15: 6 showed kindness to all the **c**
1Sa 17:53 Then the **c** of Israel returned
1Sa 22:19 sword, both men and women, **c**
1Sa 26:19 But if it is the **c** of men
1Sa 30:22 for every man's wife and **c**
2Sa 1:18 **c** of Judah the Song of the
2Sa 2:25 Now the **c** of Benjamin
2Sa 4: 2 of the **c** of Benjamin
2Sa 6:23 no **c** to the day of her death
2Sa 7: 6 the **c** of Israel up from Egypt
2Sa 7: 7 with all the **c** of Israel,
2Sa 12: 3 with him and with his **c**
2Sa 21: 2 were not of the **c** of Israel
2Sa 21: 2 the **c** of Israel had sworn
2Sa 21: 2 his zeal for the **c** of Israel
2Sa 23:29 Gibeah of the **c** of Benjamin
1Ki 6: 1 eightieth year after the **c** of
1Ki 6:13 dwell among the **c** of Israel
1Ki 8: 1 fathers of the **c** of Israel
1Ki 8: 9 covenant with the **c** of Israel
1Ki 8:63 all the **c** of Israel dedicated
1Ki 9:20 were not of the **c** of Israel
1Ki 9:21 whom the **c** of Israel had not
1Ki 9:22 But of the **c** of Israel
1Ki 11: 2 had said to the **c** of Israel
1Ki 12:17 Rehoboam reigned over the **c**
1Ki 12:24 your brethren the **c** of Israel
1Ki 12:33 a feast for the **c** of Israel
1Ki 14:24 out before the **c** of Israel
1Ki 18:20 sent for all the **c** of Israel
1Ki 19:10 for the **c** of Israel have
1Ki 19:14 because the **c** of Israel have
1Ki 20: 3 loveliest wives and **c** are mine
1Ki 20: 5 gold, your wives and your **c**"
1Ki 20: 7 sent to me for my wives, my **c**
1Ki 20:15 people, all the **c** of Israel
1Ki 20:27 the **c** of Israel were mustered
1Ki 20:27 Now the **c** of Israel encamped

1Ki 20:29 the **c** of Israel killed one
1Ki 21:26 out before the **c** of Israel
2Ki 8:12 will do to the **c** of Israel
2Ki 8:12 and you will dash their **c**, and
2Ki 13: 5 and the **c** of Israel dwelt in
2Ki 14: 6 But the **c** of the murderers he
2Ki 14: 6 not be put to death for the **c**
2Ki 14: 6 nor shall the **c** be put to
2Ki 16: 3 from before the **c** of Israel
2Ki 17: 7 the **c** of Israel had sinned
2Ki 17: 8 from before the **c** of Israel
2Ki 17: 9 Also the **c** of Israel secretly
2Ki 17:22 For the **c** of Israel walked in
2Ki 17:24 instead of the **c** of Israel
2Ki 17:31 **c** in fire to Adrammelech and
2Ki 17:34 had commanded the **c** of Jacob
2Ki 17:41 also their **c** and their
2Ki 17:41 and their children's **c** have
2Ki 18: 4 for until those days the **c** of
2Ki 19: 3 for the **c** have come to birth,
2Ki 21: 2 out before the **c** of Israel
2Ki 21: 9 before the **c** of Israel
1Ch 1:33 these were the **c** of Keturah
1Ch 1:43 reigned over the **c** of Israel
1Ch 2:10 leader of the **c** of Judah
1Ch 2:18 of Hezron begot **c** by Azubah
1Ch 2:30 Seled died without **c**
1Ch 2:32 Jether died without **c**
1Ch 4:27 brothers did not have many **c**
1Ch 4:27 as much as the **c** of Judah
1Ch 5:11 the **c** of Gad dwelt next to
1Ch 5:14 These were the **c** of Abihail
1Ch 5:23 So the **c** of the half-tribe of
1Ch 6: 3 The **c** of Amram were Aaron,
1Ch 6:64 So the **c** of Israel gave these
1Ch 6:65 the tribe of the **c** of Judah
1Ch 6:65 the tribe of the **c** of Simeon
1Ch 6:65 from the tribe of the **c** of
1Ch 6:77 of Zebulun the rest of the **c**
1Ch 7:29 by the borders of the **c** of
1Ch 7:29 these dwelt the **c** of Joseph
1Ch 7:33 These were the **c** of Japhlet
1Ch 7:40 All these were the **c** of Asher
1Ch 8: 8 And Shaharaim begot **c** in the
1Ch 9: 3 the **c** of Judah dwelt, and some
1Ch 9: 3 and some of the **c** of Benjamin
1Ch 9: 3 and of the **c** of Ephraim and
1Ch 9:18 for the camps of the **c** of
1Ch 9:23 their **c** were in charge of the
1Ch 11:31 of the **c** of Benjamin, Benaiah
1Ch 12:16 some of the **c** of Benjamin
1Ch 12:24 of the **c** of Judah bearing
1Ch 12:25 of the **c** of Simeon, mighty
1Ch 12:26 of the **c** of Levi four
1Ch 12:29 of the **c** of Benjamin, kinsmen
1Ch 12:30 of the **c** of Ephraim twenty
1Ch 12:32 of the **c** of Issachar who had
1Ch 14: 4 **c** whom he had in Jerusalem
1Ch 15: 4 assembled the **c** of Aaron and
1Ch 15:15 the **c** of the Levites bore the
1Ch 16:13 you **c** of Jacob, His chosen
1Ch 24: 2 their father, and had no **c**
1Ch 26:10 of the **c** of Merari, had sons
1Ch 27: 1 the **c** of Israel, according to
1Ch 27: 3 he was of the **c** of Perez, and
1Ch 27:10 Pelonite, of the **c** of Ephraim
1Ch 27:14 of the **c** of Ephraim
1Ch 27:20 over the **c** of Ephraim, Hoshea
1Ch 28: 8 for your **c** after you forever
2Ch 5: 2 fathers of the **c** of Israel
2Ch 5:10 covenant with the **c** of Israel
2Ch 6:11 He made with the **c** of Israel
2Ch 7: 3 When all the **c** of Israel saw
2Ch 8: 2 he settled the **c** of Israel
2Ch 8: 8 whom the **c** of Israel did not
2Ch 8: 9 Solomon did not make the **c** of
2Ch 10:17 Rehoboam reigned over the **c**
2Ch 10:18 but the **c** of Israel stoned
2Ch 11:19 And she bore him **c**
2Ch 13:12 O **c** of Israel, do not fight
2Ch 13:16 the **c** of Israel fled before
2Ch 13:18 Thus the **c** of Israel were
2Ch 13:18 the **c** of Judah prevailed,
2Ch 20:13 ones, their wives, and their **c**
2Ch 20:19 of the **c** of the Kohathites
2Ch 20:19 of the **c** of the Korahites
2Ch 21:14 your **c**, your wives, and all
2Ch 25: 4 he did not execute their **c**
2Ch 25: 4 be put to death for their **c**
2Ch 25: 4 nor shall the **c** be put to
2Ch 25: 7 with any of the **c** of Ephraim
2Ch 25:12 the **c** of Judah took captive
2Ch 28: 3 burned his **c** in the fire,
2Ch 28: 3 out before the **c** of Israel
2Ch 28: 8 the **c** of Israel carried away
2Ch 28:10 to force the **c** of Judah and
2Ch 28:12 the heads of the **c** of Ephraim
2Ch 30: 6 **C** of Israel, return to the
2Ch 30: 9 your **c** will be treated with
2Ch 30:21 So the **c** of Israel who were
2Ch 31: 1 Then all the **c** of Israel
2Ch 31: 5 the **c** of Israel brought in
2Ch 31: 6 the **c** of Israel and Judah, who
2Ch 33: 2 out before the **c** of Israel
2Ch 33: 9 before the **c** of Israel
2Ch 34:33 belonged to the **c** of Israel
2Ch 35:17 And the **c** of Israel who were
Ezra 2:58 the **c** of Solomon's servants
Ezra 3: 1 the **c** of Israel were in the
Ezra 6:16 Then the **c** of Israel, the
Ezra 6:21 Then the **c** of Israel who had
Ezra 7: 7 Some of the **c** of Israel, the
Ezra 8:35 The **c** of those who had been
Ezra 9:12 inheritance to your **c** forever
Ezra 10: 1 and **c** assembled to him from
Ezra 10:44 had wives by whom they had **c**
Neh 1: 6 for the **c** of Israel Your
Neh 1: 6 the **c** of Israel which we have
Neh 2:10 well-being of the **c** of Israel
Neh 5: 5 our **c** as their **c**
Neh 5: 5 our **c** as their **c**
Neh 7: 8 the **c** of Parosh, two thousand
Neh 7: 9 the **c** of Shephatiah, three
Neh 7:10 the **c** of Arah, six hundred and
Neh 7:11 the **c** of Pahath-Moab, of the
Neh 7:11 of the **c** of Jeshua and Joab,
Neh 7:12 the **c** of Elam, one thousand
Neh 7:13 the **c** of Zattu, eight hundred
Neh 7:14 the **c** of Zaccai, seven
Neh 7:15 the **c** of Binnui, six hundred
Neh 7:16 the **c** of Bebai, six hundred
Neh 7:17 the **c** of Azgad, two thousand
Neh 7:18 the **c** of Adonikam, six
Neh 7:19 the **c** of Bigvai, two thousand
Neh 7:20 the **c** of Adin, six hundred and
Neh 7:21 the **c** of Ater of Hezekiah,
Neh 7:22 the **c** of Hashum, three
Neh 7:23 the **c** of Bezai, three hundred
Neh 7:24 the **c** of Hariph, one hundred
Neh 7:25 the **c** of Gibeon, ninety-five
Neh 7:34 the **c** of the other Elam, one
Neh 7:35 the **c** of Harim, three hundred
Neh 7:36 the **c** of Jericho, three
Neh 7:37 the **c** of Lod, Hadid, and Ono,
Neh 7:38 the **c** of Senaah, three
Neh 7:39 the **c** of Jedaiah, of the
Neh 7:40 the **c** of Immer, one thousand
Neh 7:41 the **c** of Pashhur, one
Neh 7:42 the **c** of Harim, one thousand
Neh 7:43 the **c** of Jeshua, of Kadmiel,
Neh 7:43 and of the **c** of Hodevah,
Neh 7:44 the **c** of Asaph, one hundred
Neh 7:45 the **c** of Shallum
Neh 7:45 the **c** of Ater
Neh 7:45 the **c** of Talmon
Neh 7:45 the **c** of Akkub
Neh 7:45 the **c** of Hatita
Neh 7:45 the **c** of Shobai, one hundred
Neh 7:46 the **c** of Ziha
Neh 7:46 the **c** of Hasupha
Neh 7:46 the **c** of Tabbaoth
Neh 7:47 the **c** of Keros
Neh 7:47 the **c** of Sia
Neh 7:47 the **c** of Padon
Neh 7:48 the **c** of Lebana
Neh 7:48 the **c** of Hagaba
Neh 7:48 the **c** of Salmai
Neh 7:49 the **c** of Hanan
Neh 7:49 the **c** of Giddel
Neh 7:49 the **c** of Gahar
Neh 7:50 the **c** of Reaiah
Neh 7:50 the **c** of Rezin
Neh 7:50 the **c** of Nekoda
Neh 7:51 the **c** of Gazzam
Neh 7:51 the **c** of Uzza
Neh 7:51 the **c** of Paseah
Neh 7:52 the **c** of Besai
Neh 7:52 the **c** of Meunim
Neh 7:52 the **c** of Nephishesim
Neh 7:53 the **c** of Bakbuk
Neh 7:53 the **c** of Hakupha
Neh 7:53 the **c** of Harhur
Neh 7:54 the **c** of Bazlith
Neh 7:54 the **c** of Mehida
Neh 7:54 the **c** of Harsha
Neh 7:55 the **c** of Barkos
Neh 7:55 the **c** of Sisera
Neh 7:55 the **c** of Tamah
Neh 7:56 the **c** of Neziah
Neh 7:56 and the **c** of Hatipha
Neh 7:57 The **c** of Solomon's servants
Neh 7:57 the **c** of Sotai
Neh 7:57 the **c** of Sophereth
Neh 7:57 the **c** of Perida
Neh 7:58 the **c** of Jaala
Neh 7:58 the **c** of Darkon
Neh 7:58 the **c** of Giddel
Neh 7:59 the **c** of Shephatiah
Neh 7:59 the **c** of Hattil
Neh 7:59 the **c** of Pochereth of Zebaim,
Neh 7:59 and the **c** of Amon
Neh 7:60 the **c** of Solomon's servants,
Neh 7:62 the **c** of Delaiah
Neh 7:62 the **c** of Tobiah
Neh 7:62 the **c** of Nekoda, six hundred
Neh 7:63 the **c** of Habaiah
Neh 7:63 the **c** of Koz
Neh 7:63 the **c** of Barzillai, who took
Neh 7:73 the **c** of Israel were in their
Neh 8:14 that the **c** of Israel should
Neh 8:17 **c** of Israel had not done so
Neh 9: 1 day of this month the **c** of
Neh 9:23 **c** as the stars of heaven, and
Neh 10:39 For the **c** of Israel and the
Neh 10:39 the **c** of Levi shall bring the
Neh 11: 4 certain of the **c** of Judah
Neh 11: 4 and of the **c** of Benjamin
Neh 11: 4 The **c** of Judah
Neh 11: 4 Mahalaleel, of the **c** of Perez
Neh 11:24 of the **c** of Zerah the son of
Neh 11:25 some of the **c** of Judah dwelt
Neh 11:31 Also the **c** of Benjamin from
Neh 12:43 the **c** also rejoiced, so that
Neh 12:47 them for the **c** of Aaron
Neh 13: 2 the **c** of Israel with bread
Neh 13:16 the Sabbath to the **c** of Judah
Neh 13:24 half of their **c** spoke the
Esth 3:13 both young and old, little **c**
Esth 5:11 the multitude of his **c**, all
Esth 8:11 assault them, both little **c**
Job 17: 5 the eyes of his **c** will fail
Job 19:17 to the **c** of my own body
Job 19:18 Even young **c** despise me
Job 20:10 His **c** will seek the favor of
Job 21:11 a flock, and their **c** dance
Job 21:19 up one's iniquity for his **c**'
Job 24: 5 food for them and for their **c**
Job 27:14 If his **c** are multiplied, it
Job 29: 5 me, when my **c** were around me
Job 41:34 king over all the **c** of pride
Job 42:16 and forty years, and saw his **c**
Ps 14: 2 from heaven upon the **c** of men
Ps 17:14 They are satisfied with **c**
Ps 34:11 Come, you **c**, listen to me
Ps 36: 7 Therefore the **c** of men put
Ps 53: 2 from heaven upon the **c** of men
Ps 69: 8 And an alien to my mother's **c**
Ps 72: 4 will save the **c** of the needy
Ps 73:15 to the generation of Your **c**
Ps 78: 4 not hide them from their **c**
Ps 78: 5 make them known to their **c**
Ps 78: 6 The **c** who would be born, That
Ps 78: 6 and declare them to their **c**
Ps 78: 9 The **c** of Ephraim, being armed
Ps 82: 6 all of you are **c** of the Most
Ps 83: 8 They have helped the **c** of Lot
Ps 89:47 You created all the **c** of men
Ps 90: 3 And say, "Return, O **c** of men
Ps 90:16 And Your glory to their **c**
Ps 102:28 The **c** of Your servants will
Ps 103: 7 His acts to the **c** of Israel
Ps 103:13 As a father pities his **c**, So
Ps 103:17 righteousness to children's **c**
Ps 105: 6 You **c** of Jacob, His chosen
Ps 107: 8 works to the **c** of men
Ps 107:15 works to the **c** of men
Ps 107:21 works to the **c** of men
Ps 107:31 works to the **c** of men
Ps 109: 9 Let his **c** be fatherless, And
Ps 109:10 Let his **c** continually be

Ps 109:12 any to favor his fatherless **c**
Ps 113: 9 Like a joyful mother of **c**
Ps 115:14 more and more, You and your **c**
Ps 115:16 He has given to the **c** of men
Ps 127: 3 **c** are a heritage from the
Ps 127: 4 So are the **c** of one's youth
Ps 128: 3 Your **c** like olive plants All
Ps 128: 6 may you see your children's **c**
Ps 147:13 has blessed your **c** within you
Ps 148:12 Old men and **c**
Ps 148:14 Of the **c** of Israel, A people
Ps 149: 2 Let the **c** of Zion be joyful
Prov 4: 1 Hear, my **c**, the instruction
Prov 5: 7 Therefore hear me now, my **c**
Prov 7:24 therefore, listen to me, my **c**
Prov 8:32 therefore, listen to me, my **c**
Prov 13:22 to his children's **c**, but the
Prov 14:26 His **c** will have a place of
Prov 17: 6 Children's **c** are the crown of
Prov 17: 6 and the glory of **c** is their
Prov 20: 7 his **c** are blessed after him
Prov 31:28 Her **c** rise up and call her
Eccl 6: 3 If a man begets a hundred **c**
Is 1: 2 nourished and brought up **c**
Is 1: 4 **c** who are corrupters
Is 2: 6 with the **c** of foreigners
Is 3: 4 I will give **c** to be their
Is 3:12 **c** are their oppressors, and
Is 8:18 the **c** whom the LORD has given
Is 13:16 Their **c** also will be dashed
Is 13:18 their eye will not spare **c**
Is 14:21 Prepare slaughter for his **c**
Is 17: 3 the glory of the **c** of Israel
Is 17: 9 because of the **c** of Israel
Is 23: 4 not labor, nor bring forth **c**
Is 27:12 one by one, O you **c** of Israel
Is 29:23 but when he sees his **c**, the
Is 30: 1 Woe to the rebellious **c**,"
Is 30: 9 a rebellious people, lying **c**
Is 30: 9 **c** who will not hear the law
Is 31: 6 the **c** of Israel have deeply
Is 37: 3 for the **c** have come to birth,
Is 38:19 known Your truth to the **c**
Is 47: 8 shall I know the loss of **c**'
Is 47: 9 the loss of **c**, and widowhood
Is 49:20 The **c** you will have, after
Is 49:21 me, since I have lost my **c**
Is 49:25 you, and I will save your **c**
Is 54: 1 For more are the **c** of the
Is 54: 1 the **c** of the married woman
Is 54:13 All your **c** shall be taught by
Is 54:13 shall be the peace of your **c**
Is 57: 4 Are you not **c** of
Is 57: 5 slaying the **c** in the valleys,
Is 63: 8 My people, **c** who will not lie
Is 65:23 nor bring forth **c** for trouble
Is 66: 8 she gave birth to her **c**
Is 66:20 as the **c** of Israel bring an
Jer 2: 9 **c** I will bring charges
Jer 2:30 vain I have chastened your **c**
Jer 3:14 Return, O backsliding **c**,"
Jer 3:19 How can I put you among the **c**
Jer 3:21 of the **c** of Israel
Jer 3:22 Return, you backsliding **c**
Jer 4:22 They are silly **c**, and they
Jer 5: 7 Your **c** have forsaken Me and
Jer 6: 1 O you **c** of Benjamin, gather
Jer 6:11 pour it out on the **c** outside
Jer 7:18 The **c** gather wood, the
Jer 7:30 For the **c** of Judah have done
Jer 9:21 palaces, to kill off the **c**
Jer 10:20 my **c** have gone from me, and
Jer 15: 7 I will bereave them of **c**
Jer 16:14 lives who brought up the **c** of
Jer 16:15 lives who brought up the **c** of
Jer 17: 2 while their **c** remember their
Jer 17:19 gate of the **c** of the people
Jer 18:21 up their **c** to the famine, and
Jer 18:21 widows and bereaved of their **c**
Jer 23: 7 lives who brought up the **c** of
Jer 30:20 Their **c** also shall be as
Jer 31:15 Rachel weeping for her **c**
Jer 31:15 to be comforted for her **c**
Jer 31:17 That your **c** shall come back
Jer 32:18 bosom of their **c** after them
Jer 32:30 because the **c** of Israel and
Jer 32:30 the **c** of Judah have done only
Jer 32:30 For the **c** of Israel have
Jer 32:32 the evil of the **c** of Israel
Jer 32:32 the **c** of Judah, which they
Jer 32:39 of them and their **c** after them
Jer 38:23 wives and **c** to the Chaldeans
Jer 40: 7 to him men, women, **c**, and the
Jer 41:16 of war and the women and the **c**
Jer 43: 6 men, women, **c**, the king's
Jer 47: 3 not look back for their **c**
Jer 49:11 Leave your fatherless **c**, I
Jer 50: 4 The **c** of Israel shall come,
Jer 50: 4 and the **c** of Judah together
Jer 50:33 The **c** of Israel were
Jer 50:33 along with the **c** of Judah
Lam 1: 5 Her **c** have gone into
Lam 1:16 My **c** are desolate because the
Lam 2:11 of my people, because the **c**
Lam 2:19 for the life of your young **c**
Lam 2:20 the **c** they have cuddled
Lam 3:33 nor grieve the **c** of men
Lam 4: 4 the young **c** ask for bread,
Lam 4:10 women have cooked their own **c**
Ezek 2: 3 you to the **c** of Israel, to a
Ezek 2: 4 are impudent and stubborn **c**
Ezek 3:11 to the **c** of your people, and
Ezek 4:13 So shall the **c** of Israel eat
Ezek 6: 5 the **c** of Israel before their
Ezek 9: 6 men, maidens and little **c** and
Ezek 16:21 that you have slain My **c** and
Ezek 16:36 of the blood of your **c** which
Ezek 16:45 loathing husband and **c**
Ezek 16:45 loathed their husbands and **c**
Ezek 20:18 to their **c** in the wilderness
Ezek 20:21 the **c** rebelled against Me
Ezek 23:39 slain their **c** for their idols
Ezek 31:14 among the **c** of men who go
Ezek 33: 2 speak to the **c** of your people
Ezek 33:12 say to the **c** of your people
Ezek 33:17 Yet the **c** of your people say,
Ezek 33:30 man, the **c** of your people are
Ezek 35: 5 **c** of Israel by the power of
Ezek 36:12 you bereave them of their **c**
Ezek 36:13 and bereave your nation of **c**
Ezek 37:16 and for the **c** of Israel, his
Ezek 37:18 when the **c** of your people
Ezek 37:21 Surely I will take the **c** of
Ezek 37:25 dwell there, they, their **c**
Ezek 37:25 and their children's **c**,
Ezek 43: 7 of the **c** of Israel forever
Ezek 44: 9 who is among the **c** of Israel
Ezek 44:15 of My sanctuary when the **c** of
Ezek 47:22 you and who bear **c** among you
Ezek 47:22 among the **c** of Israel
Ezek 48:11 the **c** of Israel went astray
Dan 1: 3 bring some of the **c** of Israel
Dan 2:38 wherever the **c** of men dwell
Dan 6:24 them, their **c**, and their wives
Hos 1: 2 **c** of harlotry, for the land
Hos 1:10 Yet the number of the **c** of
Hos 1:11 Then the **c** of Judah and the
Hos 1:11 and the **c** of Israel shall be
Hos 2: 4 will not have mercy on her **c**
Hos 2: 4 they are the **c** of harlotry
Hos 3: 1 the LORD for the **c** of Israel
Hos 3: 4 For the **c** of Israel shall
Hos 3: 5 Afterward the **c** of Israel
Hos 4: 1 you **c** of Israel, for the LORD
Hos 4: 6 I also will forget your **c**
Hos 5: 7 they have begotten pagan **c**
Hos 9:12 Though they bring up their **c**
Hos 9:13 out his **c** to the murderer
Hos 9:16 Yes, were they to bear **c**, I
Hos 10: 9 the **c** of iniquity did not
Hos 10:14 dashed in pieces upon her **c**
Hos 13:13 stay long where **c** are born
Joel 1: 3 Tell your **c** about it
Joel 1: 3 let your **c** tell their **c**
Joel 1: 3 their **c** another generation
Joel 2:16 the elders, gather the **c** and
Joel 2:23 you **c** of Zion, and rejoice in
Joel 3:16 strength of the **c** of Israel
Amos 2:11 it not so, O you **c** of Israel
Amos 3: 1 O **c** of Israel, against the
Amos 3:12 so shall the **c** of Israel be
Amos 4: 5 you love, you **c** of Israel
Amos 9: 7 Ethiopia to Me, O **c** of Israel
Obad 12 the **c** of Judah in the day of
Obad 20 of this host of the **c** of
Mic 1:16 because of your precious **c**
Mic 2: 9 from their **c** you have taken
Mic 5: 3 return to the **c** of Israel
Nah 3:10 her young **c** also were dashed
Zeph 1: 8 the princes and the king's **c**
Zech 10: 7 their **c** shall see it and be
Zech 10: 9 live, together with their **c**
Mal 4: 6 of the fathers to the **c**, and
Mal 4: 6 of the **c** to their fathers
Matt 2:16 male **c** who were in Bethlehem
Matt 2:18 Rachel weeping for her **c**
Matt 3: 9 up **c** to Abraham from these
Matt 7:11 to give good gifts to your **c**
Matt 10:21 and **c** will rise up against
Matt 11:16 It is like **c** sitting in the
Matt 11:19 wisdom is justified by her **c**
Matt 14:21 men, besides women and **c**
Matt 15:38 men, besides women and **c**
Matt 18: 3 and become as little **c**, you
Matt 18:25 be sold, with his wife and **c**
Matt 19:13 Then little **c** were brought to
Matt 19:14 Let the little **c** come to Me
Matt 19:29 mother or wife or **c** or lands
Matt 21:15 and the **c** crying out in the
Matt 22:24 if a man dies, having no **c**
Matt 23:37 to gather your **c** together
Matt 27: 9 of the **c** of Israel priced
Matt 27:25 blood be on us and on our **c**
Mark 7:27 Let the **c** be filled first,
Mark 9:37 one of these little **c** in My
Mark 10:13 they brought young **c** to Him
Mark 10:14 Let the little **c** come to Me
Mark 10:24 **C**, how hard it is for those
Mark 10:29 mother or wife or **c** or lands
Mark 10:30 and sisters and mothers and **c**
Mark 12:19 wife behind, and leaves no **c**
Mark 13:12 and **c** will rise up against
Luke 1:16 he will turn many of the **c** of
Luke 1:17 of the fathers to the **c**,' and
Luke 3: 8 up **c** to Abraham from these
Luke 7:32 They are like **c** sitting in
Luke 7:35 is justified by all her **c**
Luke 11: 7 and my **c** are with me in bed
Luke 11:13 to give good gifts to your **c**
Luke 13:34 to gather your **c** together
Luke 14:26 father and mother, wife and **c**
Luke 18:16 Let the little **c** come to Me
Luke 18:29 or brothers or wife or **c**, for
Luke 19:44 your **c** within you, to the
Luke 20:28 a wife, and he dies without **c**
Luke 20:29 a wife, and died without **c**
Luke 20:31 and they left no **c**, and died
Luke 23:28 for yourselves and for your **c**
John 1:12 the right to become **c** of God
John 8:39 If you were Abraham's **c**, you
John 11:52 **c** of God who were scattered
John 13:33 Little **c**, I shall be with you
John 21: 5 **C**, have you any food
Acts 2:39 is to you and to your **c**, and to
Acts 5:21 the elders of the **c** of Israel
Acts 7:23 his brethren, the **c** of Israel
Acts 7:37 who said to the **c** of Israel
Acts 9:15 kings, and the **c** of Israel
Acts 10:36 God sent to the **c** of Israel
Acts 13:33 fulfilled this for us their **c**
Acts 21: 5 us, with wives and **c**, till we
Acts 21:21 not to circumcise their **c** nor
Rom 8:16 spirit that we are **c** of God
Rom 8:17 and if **c**, then heirs
Rom 8:21 liberty of the **c** of God
Rom 9: 7 nor are they all **c** because
Rom 9: 8 who are the **c** of the flesh
Rom 9: 8 these are not the **c** of God
Rom 9: 8 but the **c** of the promise are
Rom 9:11 (for the **c** not yet being born
Rom 9:27 Though the number of the **c** of
1Co 4:14 as my beloved **c** I warn you
1Co 7:14 otherwise your **c** would be
1Co 14:20 do not be **c** in understanding
2Co 3: 7 so that the **c** of Israel could
2Co 3:13 **c** of Israel could not look
2Co 6:13 the same (I speak as to **c**)
2Co 12:14 For the **c** ought not to lay up
2Co 12:14 but the parents for the **c**
Gal 4: 3 Even so we, when we were **c**
Gal 4:19 My little **c**, for whom I labor
Gal 4:25 and is in bondage with her **c**
Gal 4:27 **c** than she who has a husband
Gal 4:28 Isaac was, are **c** of promise
Gal 4:31 we are not **c** of the bondwoman
Eph 2: 3 and were by nature **c** of wrath
Eph 4:14 that we should no longer be **c**
Eph 5: 1 be followers of God as dear **c**
Eph 5: 8 Walk as **c** of light
Eph 6: 1 **C**, obey your parents in the

Eph 6: 4 not provoke your **c** to wrath
Phil 2:15 **c** of God without fault in the
Col 3:20 **C**, obey your parents in all
Col 3:21 do not provoke your **c**, lest
1Th 2: 7 mother cherishes her own **c**
1Th 2:11 as a father does his own **c**
1Ti 3: 4 having his **c** in submission
1Ti 3:12 of one wife, ruling their **c**
1Ti 5: 4 widow has **c** or grandchildren
1Ti 5:10 if she has brought up **c**, if
1Ti 5:14 younger widows marry, bear **c**
Tit 1: 6 having faithful **c** not accused
Tit 2: 4 husbands, to love their **c**
Heb 2:13 the **c** whom God has given Me
Heb 2:14 Inasmuch then as the **c** have
Heb 11:22 departure of the **c** of Israel
1Pe 1:14 as obedient **c**, not conforming
2Pe 2:14 practices, and are accursed **c**
1Jn 2: 1 My little **c**, these things I
1Jn 2:12 I write to you, little **c**,
1Jn 2:13 I write to you, little **c**,
1Jn 2:18 Little **c**, it is the last hour
1Jn 2:28 And now, little **c**, abide in
1Jn 3: 1 we should be called **c** of God
1Jn 3: 2 Beloved, now we are **c** of God
1Jn 3: 7 Little **c**, let no one deceive
1Jn 3:10 In this the **c** of God and the
1Jn 3:10 God and the **c** of the devil are
1Jn 3:18 My little **c**, let us not love
1Jn 4: 4 You are of God, little **c**, and
1Jn 5: 2 that we love the **c** of God
1Jn 5:21 Little **c**, keep yourselves
2Jn 1 To the elect lady and her **c**
2Jn 4 of your **c** walking in truth
2Jn 13 The **c** of your elect sister
3Jn 4 hear that my **c** walk in truth
Rev 2:14 block before the **c** of Israel
Rev 2:23 I will kill her **c** with death
Rev 7: 4 the **c** of Israel were sealed
Rev 21:12 tribes of the **c** of Israel

CHILDREN'S (*see* CHILDREN)
Gen 31:16 are really ours and our **c**
Gen 45:10 your **c** children, your flocks
Ex 34: 7 the **c** children to the third
Josh 14: 9 your **c** forever, because you
2Ki 17:41 and their **c** children have
Ps 103:17 righteousness to **c** children
Ps 128: 6 may you see your **c** children
Prov 13:22 inheritance to his **c** children
Prov 17: 6 **C** children are the crown of
Jer 2: 9 against your **c** children I
Jer 31:29 the **c** teeth are set on edge
Ezek 18: 2 the **c** teeth are set on edge'
Ezek 37:25 their **c** children, forever
Matt 15:26 not good to take the **c** bread
Mark 7:27 not good to take the **c** bread
Mark 7:28 table eat from the **c** crumbs

CHILD'S (*see* CHILD)
Ex 2: 8 went and called the **c** mother
1Ki 17:21 let this **c** soul come back to
Job 33:25 flesh shall be young like a **c**
Matt 2:20 the young **C** life are dead

CHILEAB
2Sa 3: 3 his second, **C**, by Abigail the

CHILION (*see* CHILION'S)
Ruth 1: 2 his two sons were Mahlon and **C**
Ruth 1: 5 both Mahlon and **C** also died

CHILION'S (*see* CHILION)
Ruth 4: 9 and all that was **C** and

CHILMAD
Ezek 27:23 and **C** were your merchants

CHIMHAM
2Sa 19:37 But here is your servant **C**
2Sa 19:38 **C** shall cross over with me,
2Sa 19:40 Gilgal, and **C** went on with him
Jer 41:17 dwelt in the habitation of **C**

CHIMNEY
Hos 13: 3 floor and like smoke from a **c**

CHINNERETH (*see* CHINNEROTH, GENNESARET)
Num 34:11 eastern side of the Sea of **C**
Deut 3:17 from **C** as far as the east
Josh 13:27 as the edge of the Sea of **C**
Josh 19:35 Zer, Hammath, Rakkath, **C**

CHINNEROTH (*see* CHINNERETH)
Josh 11: 2 in the plain south of **C**, in
Josh 12: 3 plain from the Sea of **C** as
1Ki 15:20 Abel Beth Maachah, and all **C**

CHIOS
Acts 20:15 the next day came opposite **C**

CHISEL
1Ki 6: 7 so that no hammer or **c** or any

CHISLEV
Neh 1: 1 to pass in the month of **C**
Zech 7: 1 the ninth month, which is **C**

CHISLON
Num 34:21 Benjamin, Elidad the son of **C**

CHISLOTH TABOR (*see* CHESULLOTH, TABOR)
Josh 19:12 sunrise along the border of **C**

CHIUN (*see* REMPHAN)
Amos 5:26 Sikkuth your king and **C**, your

CHLOE'S
1Co 1:11 by those of **C** household,

CHOICE (*see* CHOICEST, CHOOSE)
Gen 27: 9 there two **c** kids of the goats
Gen 27:15 Then Rebekah took the **c**
Gen 49:11 donkey's colt to the **c** vine
Ex 14: 7 took six hundred **c** chariots
Num 11:28 assistant, one of his **c** men
Deut 12:11 all your **c** offerings which
1Sa 9: 2 son whose name was Saul, a **c**
2Sa 6: 1 all the **c** men of Israel,
2Sa 10: 9 some of the **c** men of Israel
2Ki 3:19 city and every **c** city, and
2Ki 19:23 cedars and its **c** cypress trees
1Ch 7:40 **c** men, mighty men of valor,
1Ch 19:10 some of the **c** men of Israel
2Ch 13: 3 four hundred thousand **c** men
2Ch 13: 3 eight hundred thousand **c** men
2Ch 13:17 **c** men of Israel fell slain
2Ch 25: 5 three hundred thousand **c** men
Neh 5:18 was one ox and six **c** sheep
Esth 2: 9 Then seven **c** maidservants
Ps 78:31 down the **c** men of Israel
Prov 8:10 knowledge rather than **c** gold
Prov 8:19 and my revenue than **c** silver
Prov 10:20 of the righteous is **c** silver
Is 16: 8 have broken down its **c** plants
Is 25: 6 people a feast of **c** pieces
Is 37:24 cedars and its **c** cypress trees
Jer 22: 7 shall cut down your **c** cedars
Ezek 23: 7 all of them **c** men of Assyria
Ezek 24: 4 fill it with **c** cuts
Ezek 24: 5 take the **c** of the flock
Ezek 27:24 your merchants in **c** items
Ezek 31:16 all the trees of Eden, the **c**
Dan 11:15 Even his **c** troops shall have

CHOICEST (*see* CHOICE)
Gen 23: 6 in the **c** of our burial places
Deut 32:14 and goats, with the **c** wheat
Is 5: 2 and planted it with the **c** vine
Is 22: 7 come to pass that your **c**
Ezek 27:22 for your wares the **c** spices

CHOIR (*see* CHOIRS)
Neh 12:38 **c** went the opposite way, and I

CHOIRS (*see* CHOIR)
Neh 12:31 two large thanksgiving **c**, one
Neh 12:40 So the two thanksgiving **c**

CHOKE (*see* CHOKED)
Matt 13:22 of riches **c** the word, and he
Mark 4:19 things entering in **c** the word

CHOKED (*see* CHOKE)
Matt 13: 7 thorns sprang up and **c** them
Mark 4: 7 **c** it, and it yielded no crop
Luke 8: 7 sprang up with it and **c** it
Luke 8:14 are **c** with cares, riches, and

CHOOSE (*see* CHOICE, CHOOSES, CHOOSING, CHOSE, CHOSEN)
Ex 17: 9 **C** us some men and go out,
Num 17: 5 the man whom I **c** will blossom
Deut 1:13 **C** wise, understanding, and
Deut 7: 7 **c** you because you were more
Deut 30:19 therefore **c** life, that both
Josh 9:27 in the place which He would **c**
Josh 24:15 **c** for yourselves this day
1Sa 2:28 Did I not **c** him out of all
1Sa 17: 8 **C** a man for yourselves, and
2Sa 16:18 and all the men of Israel **c**
2Sa 17: 1 Now let me **c** twelve thousand
2Sa 24:12 **c** one of them for yourself,
1Ki 18:23 and let them **c** one bull for
1Ki 18:25 **C** one bull for yourselves and
2Ki 10: 3 **c** the best qualified of your
1Ch 21:10 **c** one of them for yourself,
1Ch 21:11 **C** for yourself,
2Ch 6: 5 nor did I **c** any man to be a
Job 9:14 **c** my words to reason with Him
Job 15: 5 and you **c** the tongue of the
Job 34: 4 Let us **c** justice for
Job 34:33 You must **c**, and not I
Ps 47: 4 He will **c** our inheritance for
Ps 65: 4 Blessed is the man whom You **c**
Ps 75: 2 When I **c** the proper time, I
Ps 78:67 And did not **c** the tribe of
Prov 1:29 did not **c** the fear of the
Prov 3:31 and **c** none of his ways
Prov 12:26 The righteous should **c** his
Is 7:15 refuse the evil and **c** the good
Is 7:16 **c** the good, the land that you
Is 14: 1 Jacob, and will still **c** Israel
Is 56: 4 **c** what pleases Me, and hold
Is 66: 4 so will I **c** their delusions,
Zech 1:17 and will again **c** Jerusalem
Zech 2:12 and will again **c** Jerusalem
John 6:70 Did I not **c** you, the twelve,
John 15:16 You did not **c** Me, but I chose
Phil 1:22 what I shall **c** I cannot tell

CHOOSES (*see* CHOOSE)
Num 16: 5 that one whom He **c** He will
Num 16: 7 LORD **c** shall be the holy one
Deut 12: 5 where the LORD your God **c**
Deut 12:11 God **c** to make His name abide
Deut 12:14 in the place which the LORD **c**
Deut 12:18 which the LORD your God **c**
Deut 12:21 where the LORD your God **c** to
Deut 12:26 to the place which the LORD **c**
Deut 14:23 in the place where He **c** to
Deut 14:24 where the LORD your God **c** to
Deut 14:25 which the LORD your God **c**
Deut 15:20 in the place which the LORD **c**
Deut 16: 2 the LORD **c** to put His name
Deut 16: 6 God **c** to make His name abide
Deut 16: 7 which the LORD your God **c**
Deut 16:11 God **c** to make His name abide
Deut 16:15 in the place which the LORD **c**
Deut 16:16 God in the place which He **c**
Deut 17: 8 which the LORD your God **c**
Deut 17:10 that place which the LORD **c**
Deut 17:15 you whom the LORD your God **c**
Deut 18: 6 to the place which the LORD **c**
Deut 23:16 in the place which he **c**
Deut 26: 2 God **c** to make His name abide
Deut 31:11 God in the place which He **c**
Job 7:15 so that my soul **c** strangling
Ps 25:12 He teach in the way He **c**
Is 40:20 for such a contribution **c** a
Is 41:24 he who **c** you is an
Dan 4:25 and gives it to whomever He **c**
Dan 4:32 and gives it to whomever He **c**
Dan 5:21 over it whomever He **c**

CHOOSING (*see* CHOOSE)
Heb 11:25 **c** rather to suffer affliction

CHOP (*see* CHOPS)
Jer 46:22 axes, like those who **c** wood
Dan 4:14 **C** down the tree and cut off
Dan 4:23 **C** down the tree and destroy
Mic 3: 3 **c** them in pieces like meat

CHOPS (*see* CHOP)
Is 10:15 against him who **c** with it

CHORASHAN
1Sa 30:30 Hormah, those who were in **C**

CHORAZIN
Matt 11:21 Woe to you, **C**
Luke 10:13 Woe to you, **C**

CHOSE (*see* CHOOSE)
Gen 6: 2 themselves of all whom they **c**
Gen 13:11 Then Lot **c** for himself all
Ex 18:25 Moses **c** able men out of all
Deut 4:37 fathers, therefore He **c** their
Deut 10:10 the LORD **c** not to destroy you
Deut 10:15 He **c** their descendants after
Josh 8: 3 and Joshua **c** thirty thousand
Judg 5: 8 They **c** new gods

1Sa 13: 2 Saul c for himself three
1Sa 17:40 he c for himself five smooth
2Sa 6:21 who c me instead of your
2Sa 10: 9 he c some of the choice men
2Sa 21: 6 of Saul, whom the LORD c
1Ki 8:16 but I c David to be over My
1Ki 11:34 whom I c because he kept My
1Ch 19:10 he c some of the choice men
1Ch 28: 4 the LORD God of Israel c me
Neh 9: 7 Who c Abram, and brought him
Job 29:25 I c the way for them, and sat
Ps 78:68 But c the tribe of Judah,
Ps 78:70 He also c David His servant,
Is 65:12 and c that in which I do not
Is 66: 4 and c that in which I do not
Ezek 20: 5 On the day when I c Israel
Mark 13:20 the elect's sake, whom He c
Luke 6:13 from them He c twelve whom
Luke 14: 7 how they c the best places
John 15:16 not choose Me, but I c you
John 15:19 but I c you out of the world,
Acts 6: 5 they c Stephen, a man full of
Acts 13:17 people Israel c our fathers
Acts 15: 7 good while ago God c among us
Acts 15:40 but Paul c Silas and departed,
Eph 1: 4 just as He c us in Him before
2Th 2:13 God from the beginning c you

CHOSEN (*see* CHOOSE)
Ex 15: 4 His c captains also are
Num 1:16 These were c from the
Deut 7: 6 the LORD your God has c you
Deut 14: 2 the LORD has c you to be a
Deut 18: 5 For the LORD your God has c
Deut 21: 5 has c them to minister to Him
Josh 24:22 c the LORD for yourselves
Judg 10:14 to the gods which you have c
1Sa 8:18 you have c for yourselves
1Sa 10:20 the tribe of Benjamin was c
1Sa 10:21 the family of Matri was c
1Sa 10:21 And Saul the son of Kish was c
1Sa 10:24 see him whom the LORD has c
1Sa 12:13 is the king whom you have c
1Sa 16: 8 has the LORD c this one
1Sa 16: 9 has the LORD c this one
1Sa 16:10 The LORD has not c these
1Sa 20:30 c the son of Jesse to your
1Sa 24: 2 c men from all Israel, and
1Sa 26: 2 having three thousand c men
1Ki 3: 8 Your people whom You have c
1Ki 8:16 I have c no city from any
1Ki 8:44 the city which You have c
1Ki 8:48 the city which You have c
1Ki 11:13 of Jerusalem which I have c
1Ki 11:32 the city which I have c out
1Ki 11:36 which I have c for Myself
1Ki 12:21 eighty thousand c men who
1Ki 14:21 c out of all the tribes of
2Ki 21: 7 which I have c out of all the
2Ki 23:27 city Jerusalem which I have c
1Ch 9:22 All those c as gatekeepers
1Ch 15: 2 for the LORD has c them to
1Ch 16:13 children of Jacob, His c ones
1Ch 16:41 and the rest who were c, who
1Ch 28: 4 for He has c Judah to be the
1Ch 28: 5 c my son Solomon to sit on
1Ch 28: 6 for I have c him to be My son
1Ch 28:10 for the LORD has c you to
1Ch 29: 1 whom alone God has c
2Ch 6: 5 I have c no city from any
2Ch 6: 6 but I have c Jerusalem, that
2Ch 6: 6 I have c David to be over My
2Ch 6:34 this city which You have c
2Ch 6:38 the city which You have c
2Ch 7:12 have c this place for Myself
2Ch 7:16 For now I have c and
2Ch 11: 1 eighty thousand c men who
2Ch 12:13 c out of all the tribes of
2Ch 29:11 for the LORD has c you to
2Ch 33: 7 which I have c out of all the
Neh 1: 9 c as a dwelling for My name
Job 36:21 for you have c this rather
Ps 33:12 has c as His own inheritance
Ps 89: 3 made a covenant with My c
Ps 89:19 exalted one c from the people
Ps 105: 6 children of Jacob, His c ones
Ps 105:26 And Aaron whom He had c
Ps 105:43 joy, His c ones with gladness
Ps 106: 5 the benefit of Your c ones
Ps 106:23 Had not Moses His c one stood
Ps 119:30 I have c the way of truth
Ps 119:173 For I have c Your precepts
Ps 132:13 For the LORD has c Zion
Ps 135: 4 For the LORD has c Jacob for
Prov 16:16 is to be c rather than silver
Prov 22: 1 A good name is to be c rather
Is 1:29 the gardens which you have c
Is 41: 8 servant, Jacob, whom I have c
Is 41: 9 are My servant, I have c you
Is 43:10 And My servant whom I have c
Is 43:20 give drink to My people, My c
Is 44: 1 and Israel whom I have c
Is 44: 2 you, Jeshurun, whom I have c
Is 49: 7 and He has c You
Is 58: 5 Is it a fast that I have c
Is 58: 6 not the fast that I have c
Is 65:15 your name as a curse to My c
Is 66: 3 as they have c their own ways
Jer 8: 3 Then death shall be c rather
Jer 33:24 families which the LORD has c
Jer 48:15 Her c young men have gone
Jer 49:19 who is a c man that I may
Jer 50:44 who is a c man that I may
Hag 2:23 for I have c you,' says the
Zech 3: 2 The LORD who has c Jerusalem
Matt 12:18 My Servant whom I have c
Matt 20:16 many are called, but few c
Matt 22:14 are called, but few are c
Luke 10:42 Mary has c that good part,
Luke 23:35 is the Christ, the c of God
John 13:18 I know whom I have c
Acts 1: 2 to the apostles whom He had c
Acts 1:24 which of these two You have c
Acts 9:15 for he is a c vessel of Mine
Acts 10:41 to witnesses c before by God
Acts 15:22 to send c men of their own
Acts 15:25 to send c men to you with our
Acts 22:14 c you that you should know
Rom 16:13 c in the Lord, and his mother
1Co 1:27 But God has c the foolish
1Co 1:27 God has c the weak things of
1Co 1:28 which are despised God has c
2Co 8:19 but who was also c by the
Jas 2: 5 Has God not c the poor of
1Pe 2: 4 but c by God and precious,
1Pe 2: 9 But you are a c generation
Rev 17:14 are with Him are called, c

CHOZEBA (*see* CHEZIB)
1Ch 4:22 also Jokim, the men of C, and

CHRIST (*see* CHRIST'S, CHRISTS, JESUS)
Matt 1: 1 of the genealogy of Jesus C
Matt 1:16 born Jesus who is called C
Matt 1:17 in Babylon until the C are
Matt 1:18 of Jesus C was as follows
Matt 2: 4 where the C was to be born
Matt 11: 2 prison about the works of C
Matt 16:16 You are the C, the Son of the
Matt 16:20 one that He was Jesus the C
Matt 22:42 What do you think about the C
Matt 23: 8 One is your Teacher, the C
Matt 23:10 One is your Teacher, the C
Matt 24: 5 My name, saying, 'I am the C
Matt 24:23 to you, 'Look, here is the C
Matt 26:63 You tell us if You are the C
Matt 26:68 Prophesy to us, C
Matt 27:17 or Jesus who is called C
Matt 27:22 do with Jesus who is called C
Mark 1: 1 of the gospel of Jesus C, the
Mark 8:29 You are the C
Mark 9:41 name, because you belong to C
Mark 12:35 the C is the Son of David
Mark 13:21 to you, 'Look, here is the C
Mark 14:61 Are You the C, the Son of the
Mark 15:32 Let the C, the King of Israel
Luke 2:11 a Savior, who is C the Lord
Luke 2:26 he had seen the Lord's C
Luke 3:15 whether he was the C or not
Luke 4:41 You are the C, the Son of God
Luke 4:41 they knew that He was the C
Luke 9:20 and said, "The C of God
Luke 20:41 say that the C is David's Son
Luke 22:67 If You are the C, tell us
Luke 23: 2 saying that He Himself is C
Luke 23:35 save Himself if He is the C
Luke 23:39 If You are the C, save
Luke 24:26 Ought not the C to have
Luke 24:46 necessary for the C to suffer
John 1:17 and truth came through Jesus C
John 1:20 I am not the C
John 1:25 baptize if you are not the C
John 1:41 (which is translated, the C)
John 3:28 that I said, 'I am not the C
John 4:25 is coming" (who is called C)
John 4:29 Could this be the C
John 4:42 that this is indeed the C
John 6:69 and know that You are the C
John 7:26 that this is truly the C
John 7:27 but when the C comes, no one
John 7:31 When the C comes, will He do
John 7:41 This is the C," but some
John 7:41 Will the C come out of
John 7:42 the C comes from the seed of
John 9:22 confessed that He was C, he
John 10:24 If You are the C, tell us
John 11:27 I believe that You are the C
John 12:34 that the C remains forever
John 17: 3 Jesus C whom You have sent
John 20:31 believe that Jesus is the C
Acts 2:30 up the C to sit on his throne
Acts 2:31 the resurrection of the C
Acts 2:36 you crucified, both Lord and C
Acts 2:38 in the name of Jesus C for
Acts 3: 6 name of Jesus C of Nazareth
Acts 3:18 that the C would suffer, He
Acts 3:20 and that He may send Jesus C
Acts 4:10 name of Jesus C of Nazareth
Acts 4:26 the LORD and against His C
Acts 5:42 and preaching Jesus as the C
Acts 8: 5 Samaria and preached C to them
Acts 8:12 of God and the name of Jesus C
Acts 8:37 Jesus C is the Son of God
Acts 9:20 the C in the synagogues, that
Acts 9:22 that this Jesus is the C
Acts 9:34 Aeneas, Jesus the C heals you
Acts 10:36 peace through Jesus C
Acts 11:17 believed on the Lord Jesus C
Acts 15:11 C we shall be saved in the
Acts 15:26 the name of our Lord Jesus C
Acts 16:18 of Jesus C to come out of her
Acts 16:31 Believe on the Lord Jesus C
Acts 17: 3 that the C had to suffer and
Acts 17: 3 whom I preach to you is the C
Acts 18: 5 the Jews that Jesus is the C
Acts 18:28 that Jesus is the C
Acts 19: 4 him, that is, on C Jesus
Acts 20:21 faith toward our Lord Jesus C
Acts 24:24 him concerning the faith in C
Acts 26:23 that the C would suffer, that
Acts 28:31 Jesus C with all confidence
Rom 1: 1 Paul, a servant of Jesus C
Rom 1: 3 His Son Jesus C our Lord, who
Rom 1: 6 are the called of Jesus C
Rom 1: 7 Father and the Lord Jesus C
Rom 1: 8 through Jesus C for you all
Rom 1:16 ashamed of the gospel of C
Rom 2:16 the secrets of men by Jesus C
Rom 3:22 faith in Jesus C to all and on
Rom 3:24 redemption that is in C Jesus
Rom 5: 1 God through our Lord Jesus C
Rom 5: 6 in due time C died for the
Rom 5: 8 still sinners, C died for us
Rom 5:11 God through our Lord Jesus C
Rom 5:15 grace of the one Man, Jesus C
Rom 5:17 life through the One, Jesus C
Rom 5:21 life through Jesus C our Lord
Rom 6: 3 C Jesus were baptized into
Rom 6: 4 that just as C was raised
Rom 6: 8 Now if we died with C, we
Rom 6: 9 knowing that C, having been
Rom 6:11 to God in C Jesus our Lord
Rom 6:23 life in C Jesus our Lord
Rom 7: 4 the law through the body of C
Rom 7:25 through Jesus C our Lord
Rom 8: 1 to those who are in C Jesus
Rom 8: 2 of the Spirit of life in C
Rom 8: 9 does not have the Spirit of C
Rom 8:10 if C is in you, the body is
Rom 8:11 He who raised C from the dead
Rom 8:17 of God and joint heirs with C
Rom 8:34 It is C who died, and
Rom 8:35 us from the love of C
Rom 8:39 which is in C Jesus our Lord
Rom 9: 1 I tell the truth in C, I am
Rom 9: 3 from C for my brethren, my
Rom 9: 5 C came, who is over all, the
Rom 10: 4 For C is the end of the law
Rom 10: 6 to bring C down from above)
Rom 10: 7 to bring C up from the dead)
Rom 12: 5 being many, are one body in C
Rom 13:14 But put on the Lord Jesus C

Rom 14: 9 For to this end **C** died and
Rom 14:10 before the judgment seat of **C**
Rom 14:15 food the one for whom **C** died
Rom 14:18 For he who serves **C** in these
Rom 15: 3 For even **C** did not please
Rom 15: 5 another, according to **C** Jesus
Rom 15: 6 and Father of our Lord Jesus **C**
Rom 15: 7 just as **C** also received us,
Rom 15: 8 Now I say that Jesus **C** has
Rom 15:16 of Jesus **C** to the Gentiles
Rom 15:17 **C** Jesus in the things which
Rom 15:18 which **C** has not accomplished
Rom 15:19 preached the gospel of **C**
Rom 15:20 gospel, not where **C** was named
Rom 15:29 blessing of the gospel of **C**
Rom 15:30 through the Lord Jesus **C**
Rom 16: 3 my fellow workers in **C** Jesus
Rom 16: 5 firstfruits of Achaia to **C**
Rom 16: 7 who also were in **C** before me
Rom 16: 9 our fellow worker in **C**, and
Rom 16:10 Greet Apelles, approved in **C**
Rom 16:16 The churches of **C** greet you
Rom 16:18 do not serve our Lord Jesus **C**
Rom 16:20 our Lord Jesus **C** be with you
Rom 16:24 Lord Jesus **C** be with you all
Rom 16:25 and the preaching of Jesus **C**
Rom 16:27 glory through Jesus **C** forever
1Co 1: 1 **C** through the will of God
1Co 1: 2 who are sanctified in **C** Jesus
1Co 1: 2 the name of Jesus **C** our Lord
1Co 1: 3 Father and the Lord Jesus **C**
1Co 1: 4 was given to you by **C** Jesus
1Co 1: 6 of **C** was confirmed in you
1Co 1: 7 of our Lord Jesus **C**,
1Co 1: 8 the day of our Lord Jesus **C**
1Co 1: 9 of His Son, Jesus **C** our Lord
1Co 1:10 the name of our Lord Jesus **C**
1Co 1:12 "I am of **C**."
1Co 1:13 Is **C** divided?
1Co 1:17 For **C** did not send me to
1Co 1:17 lest the cross of **C** should be
1Co 1:23 but we preach **C** crucified
1Co 1:24 **C** the power of God and the
1Co 1:30 But of Him you are in **C** Jesus
1Co 2: 2 among you except Jesus **C** and
1Co 2:16 But we have the mind of **C**
1Co 3: 1 to carnal, as to babes in **C**
1Co 3:11 is laid, which is Jesus **C**
1Co 3:23 are Christ's, and **C** is God's
1Co 4: 1 consider us, as servants of **C**
1Co 4:10 sake, but you are wise in **C**
1Co 4:15 ten thousand instructors in **C**
1Co 4:15 for in **C** Jesus I have
1Co 4:17 remind you of my ways in **C**
1Co 5: 4 the name of our Lord Jesus **C**
1Co 5: 4 the power of our Lord Jesus **C**
1Co 5: 7 For indeed **C**, our Passover,
1Co 6:15 your bodies are members of **C**
1Co 6:15 I then take the members of **C**
1Co 8: 6 and one Lord Jesus **C**, through
1Co 8:11 perish, for whom **C** died
1Co 8:12 conscience, you sin against **C**
1Co 9: 1 I not seen Jesus **C** our Lord
1Co 9:12 we hinder the gospel of **C**
1Co 9:18 gospel of **C** without charge
1Co 9:21 God, but under law toward **C**)
1Co 10: 4 them, and that Rock was **C**
1Co 10: 9 nor let us tempt **C**, as some
1Co 10:16 communion of the blood of **C**
1Co 10:16 communion of the body of **C**
1Co 11: 1 me, just as I also imitate **C**
1Co 11: 3 the head of every man is **C**
1Co 11: 3 man, and the head of **C** is God
1Co 12:12 are one body, so also is **C**
1Co 12:27 Now you are the body of **C**
1Co 15: 3 that **C** died for our sins
1Co 15:12 Now if **C** is preached that He
1Co 15:13 the dead, then **C** is not risen
1Co 15:14 if **C** is not risen, then our
1Co 15:15 of God that He raised up **C**
1Co 15:16 not rise, then **C** is not risen
1Co 15:17 if **C** is not risen, your faith
1Co 15:18 asleep in **C** have perished
1Co 15:19 life only we have hope in **C**
1Co 15:20 But now **C** is risen from the
1Co 15:22 even so in **C** all shall be
1Co 15:23 **C** the firstfruits, afterward
1Co 15:31 I have in **C** Jesus our Lord
1Co 15:57 through our Lord Jesus **C**
1Co 16:22 not love the Lord Jesus **C**
1Co 16:23 our Lord Jesus **C** be with you
1Co 16:24 be with you all in **C** Jesus
2Co 1: 1 of Jesus **C** by the will of God
2Co 1: 2 Father and the Lord Jesus **C**
2Co 1: 3 and Father of our Lord Jesus **C**
2Co 1: 5 sufferings of **C** abound in us
2Co 1: 5 also abounds through **C**
2Co 1:19 For the Son of God, Jesus **C**
2Co 1:21 establishes us with you in **C**
2Co 2:10 sakes in the presence of **C**
2Co 2:14 leads us in triumph in **C**, and
2Co 2:15 **C** among those who are being
2Co 2:17 in the sight of God in **C**
2Co 3: 3 manifestly an epistle of **C**
2Co 3: 4 trust through **C** toward God
2Co 3:14 the veil is taken away in **C**
2Co 4: 4 the gospel of the glory of **C**
2Co 4: 5 but **C** Jesus the Lord, and
2Co 4: 6 of God in the face of Jesus **C**
2Co 5:10 before the judgment seat of **C**
2Co 5:14 the love of **C** constrains us
2Co 5:16 **C** according to the flesh, yet
2Co 5:17 Therefore, if anyone is in **C**
2Co 5:18 us to Himself through Jesus **C**
2Co 5:19 that God was in **C** reconciling
2Co 5:20 we are ambassadors for **C**, as
2Co 6:15 what accord has **C** with Belial
2Co 8: 9 the grace of our Lord Jesus **C**
2Co 8:23 the churches, the glory of **C**
2Co 9:13 confession to the gospel of **C**
2Co 10: 1 meekness and gentleness of **C**
2Co 10: 5 to the obedience of **C**,
2Co 10:14 we came with the gospel of **C**
2Co 11: 2 you as a chaste virgin to **C**
2Co 11: 3 the simplicity that is in **C**
2Co 11:10 As the truth of **C** is in me
2Co 11:13 themselves into apostles of **C**
2Co 11:23 Are they ministers of **C**
2Co 11:31 and Father of our Lord Jesus **C**
2Co 12: 2 I know a man in **C** who
2Co 12: 9 power of **C** may rest upon me
2Co 12:19 We speak before God in **C**
2Co 13: 3 a proof of **C** speaking in me
2Co 13: 5 that Jesus **C** is in you
2Co 13:14 The grace of the Lord Jesus **C**
Gal 1: 1 man, but through Jesus **C** and
Gal 1: 3 Father and our Lord Jesus **C**
Gal 1: 6 called you in the grace of **C**
Gal 1: 7 to pervert the gospel of **C**
Gal 1:10 I would not be a servant of **C**
Gal 1:12 the revelation of Jesus **C**
Gal 1:22 of Judea which were in **C**
Gal 2: 4 which we have in **C** Jesus,
Gal 2:16 law but by faith in Jesus **C**
Gal 2:16 we have believed in **C** Jesus
Gal 2:16 be justified by faith in **C**
Gal 2:17 we seek to be justified by **C**
Gal 2:17 is **C** therefore a minister of
Gal 2:20 I have been crucified with **C**
Gal 2:20 I who live, but **C** lives in me
Gal 2:21 the law, then **C** died in vain
Gal 3: 1 before whose eyes Jesus **C** was
Gal 3:13 **C** has redeemed us from the
Gal 3:14 upon the Gentiles in **C** Jesus
Gal 3:16 And to your Seed," who is **C**
Gal 3:17 confirmed before by God in **C**
Gal 3:22 promise by faith in Jesus **C**
Gal 3:24 our tutor to bring us to **C**
Gal 3:26 God through faith in **C** Jesus
Gal 3:27 into **C** have put on **C**
Gal 3:28 you are all one in **C** Jesus
Gal 4: 7 then an heir of God through **C**
Gal 4:14 angel of God, even as **C** Jesus
Gal 4:19 until **C** is formed in you,
Gal 5: 1 by which **C** has made us free
Gal 5: 2 **C** will profit you nothing
Gal 5: 4 have become estranged from **C**
Gal 5: 6 For in **C** Jesus neither
Gal 6: 2 and so fulfill the law of **C**
Gal 6:12 for the cross of **C**
Gal 6:14 the cross of our Lord Jesus **C**
Gal 6:15 For in **C** Jesus neither
Gal 6:18 Jesus **C** be with your spirit
Eph 1: 1 of Jesus **C** by the will of God
Eph 1: 1 and faithful in **C** Jesus
Eph 1: 2 Father and the Lord Jesus **C**
Eph 1: 3 and Father of our Lord Jesus **C**
Eph 1: 3 in the heavenly places in **C**
Eph 1: 5 as sons by Jesus **C** to Himself
Eph 1:10 in one all things in **C**, both
Eph 1:12 we who first trusted in **C**
Eph 1:17 the God of our Lord Jesus **C**
Eph 1:20 which He worked in **C** when He
Eph 2: 5 **C** (by grace you have been
Eph 2: 6 heavenly places in **C** Jesus
Eph 2: 7 kindness toward us in **C** Jesus
Eph 2:10 created in **C** Jesus for good
Eph 2:12 that time you were without **C**
Eph 2:13 But now in **C** Jesus you who
Eph 2:13 made near by the blood of **C**
Eph 2:20 Jesus **C** Himself being the
Eph 3: 1 of Jesus **C** for you Gentiles
Eph 3: 4 in the mystery of **C**),
Eph 3: 6 in **C** through the gospel,
Eph 3: 8 the unsearchable riches of **C**
Eph 3: 9 all things through Jesus **C**
Eph 3:11 in **C** Jesus our Lord,
Eph 3:14 Father of our Lord Jesus **C**
Eph 3:17 that **C** may dwell in your
Eph 3:19 to know the love of **C** which
Eph 3:21 **C** Jesus throughout all ages
Eph 4:12 the edifying of the body of **C**
Eph 4:13 stature of the fullness of **C**
Eph 4:15 into Him who is the head—**C**
Eph 4:20 But you have not so learned **C**
Eph 4:32 just as God in **C** also forgave
Eph 5: 2 as **C** also has loved us and
Eph 5: 5 in the kingdom of **C** and God
Eph 5:14 and **C** will give you light
Eph 5:20 the name of our Lord Jesus **C**
Eph 5:23 as also **C** is head of the
Eph 5:24 as the church is subject to **C**
Eph 5:25 just as **C** also loved the
Eph 5:32 but I speak concerning **C**
Eph 6: 5 sincerity of heart, as to **C**
Eph 6: 6 but as servants of **C**, doing
Eph 6:23 Father and the Lord Jesus **C**
Eph 6:24 our Lord Jesus **C** in sincerity
Phil 1: 1 Timothy, servants of Jesus **C**
Phil 1: 1 To all the saints in **C** Jesus
Phil 1: 2 Father and the Lord Jesus **C**
Phil 1: 6 it until the day of Jesus **C**
Phil 1: 8 with the affection of Jesus **C**
Phil 1:10 offense till the day of **C**
Phil 1:11 which are by Jesus **C**, to the
Phil 1:13 rest, that my chains are in **C**
Phil 1:15 preach **C** even from envy and
Phil 1:16 The former preach **C** from
Phil 1:18 or in truth, **C** is preached
Phil 1:19 of the Spirit of Jesus **C**,
Phil 1:20 always, so now also **C** will be
Phil 1:21 For to me, to live is **C**, and
Phil 1:23 desire to depart and be with **C**
Phil 1:26 **C** by my coming to you again
Phil 1:27 be worthy of the gospel of **C**
Phil 1:29 been granted on behalf of **C**
Phil 2: 1 there is any consolation in **C**
Phil 2: 5 you which was also in **C** Jesus
Phil 2:11 confess that Jesus **C** is Lord
Phil 2:16 **C** that I have not run in vain
Phil 2:21 things which are of **C** Jesus
Phil 2:30 of **C** he came close to death
Phil 3: 3 Spirit, rejoice in **C** Jesus
Phil 3: 7 I have counted loss for **C**
Phil 3: 8 knowledge of **C** Jesus my Lord
Phil 3: 8 as rubbish, that I may gain **C**
Phil 3: 9 which is through faith in **C**
Phil 3:12 lay hold of that for which **C**
Phil 3:14 upward call of God in **C** Jesus
Phil 3:18 the enemies of the cross of **C**
Phil 3:20 the Savior, the Lord Jesus **C**
Phil 4: 7 and minds through **C** Jesus
Phil 4:13 through **C** who strengthens me
Phil 4:19 riches in glory by **C** Jesus
Phil 4:21 Greet every saint in **C** Jesus
Phil 4:23 Lord Jesus **C** be with you all
Col 1: 1 of Jesus **C** by the will of God
Col 1: 2 in **C** who are in Colosse
Col 1: 2 Father and the Lord Jesus **C**
Col 1: 3 and Father of our Lord Jesus **C**
Col 1: 4 of your faith in **C** Jesus and
Col 1: 7 minister of **C** on your behalf
Col 1:24 in the afflictions of **C**, for
Col 1:27 which is **C** in you, the hope
Col 1:28 every man perfect in **C** Jesus
Col 2: 2 both of the Father and of **C**
Col 2: 5 of your faith in **C**
Col 2: 6 received **C** Jesus the Lord
Col 2: 8 world, and not according to **C**
Col 2:11 by the circumcision of **C**

Col 2:17 but the substance is of **C**
Col 2:20 if you died with **C** from the
Col 3: 1 then you were raised with **C**
Col 3: 1 which are above, where **C** is
Col 3: 3 life is hidden with **C** in God
Col 3: 4 When **C** who is our life
Col 3:11 free, but **C** is all and in all
Col 3:13 even as **C** forgave you, so you
Col 3:16 Let the word of **C** dwell in
Col 3:24 for you serve the Lord **C**
Col 4: 3 to speak the mystery of **C**
Col 4:12 is one of you, a servant of **C**
1Th 1: 1 Father and the Lord Jesus **C**
1Th 1: 1 Father and the Lord Jesus **C**
1Th 1: 3 **C** in the sight of our God
1Th 2: 6 made demands as apostles of **C**
1Th 2:14 which are in Judea in **C** Jesus
1Th 2:19 Lord Jesus **C** at His coming
1Th 3: 2 laborer in the gospel of **C**
1Th 3:11 Himself, and our Lord Jesus **C**
1Th 3:13 Jesus **C** with all His saints
1Th 4:16 the dead in **C** will rise first
1Th 5: 9 through our Lord Jesus **C**,
1Th 5:18 of God in **C** Jesus for you
1Th 5:23 coming of our Lord Jesus **C**
1Th 5:28 our Lord Jesus **C** be with you
2Th 1: 1 Father and the Lord Jesus **C**
2Th 1: 2 Father and the Lord Jesus **C**
2Th 1: 8 gospel of our Lord Jesus **C**
2Th 1:12 **C** may be glorified in you
2Th 1:12 our God and the Lord Jesus **C**
2Th 2: 1 coming of our Lord Jesus **C**
2Th 2: 2 though the day of **C** had come
2Th 2:14 the glory of our Lord Jesus **C**
2Th 2:16 may our Lord Jesus **C** Himself
2Th 3: 5 God and into the patience of **C**
2Th 3: 6 the name of our Lord Jesus **C**
2Th 3:12 through our Lord Jesus **C** that
2Th 3:18 Lord Jesus **C** be with you all
1Ti 1: 1 Paul, an apostle of Jesus **C**
1Ti 1: 1 Savior and the Lord Jesus **C**
1Ti 1: 2 Father and Jesus **C** our Lord
1Ti 1:12 I thank **C** Jesus our Lord who
1Ti 1:14 and love which are in **C** Jesus
1Ti 1:15 that **C** Jesus came into the
1Ti 1:16 first Jesus **C** might show all
1Ti 2: 5 God and men, the Man **C** Jesus
1Ti 2: 7 I am speaking the truth in **C**
1Ti 3:13 the faith which is in **C** Jesus
1Ti 4: 6 be a good minister of Jesus **C**
1Ti 5:11 to grow wanton against **C**,
1Ti 5:21 God and the Lord Jesus **C** and
1Ti 6: 3 the words of our Lord Jesus **C**
1Ti 6:13 before **C** Jesus who witnessed
2Ti 1: 1 of Jesus **C** by the will of God
2Ti 1: 1 of life which is in **C** Jesus
2Ti 1: 2 Father and **C** Jesus our Lord
2Ti 1: 9 in **C** Jesus before time began
2Ti 1:10 of our Savior Jesus **C**, who
2Ti 1:13 and love which are in **C** Jesus
2Ti 2: 1 the grace that is in **C** Jesus
2Ti 2: 3 as a good soldier of Jesus **C**
2Ti 2: 8 Remember that Jesus **C**, of the
2Ti 2:10 in **C** Jesus with eternal glory
2Ti 2:19 of **C** depart from iniquity
2Ti 3:12 godly in **C** Jesus will suffer
2Ti 3:15 faith which is in **C** Jesus
2Ti 4: 1 God and the Lord Jesus **C**, who
2Ti 4:22 The Lord Jesus **C** be with your
Tit 1: 1 God and an apostle of Jesus **C**
Tit 1: 4 the Lord Jesus **C** our Savior
Tit 2:13 great God and Savior Jesus **C**
Tit 3: 6 through Jesus **C** our Savior
Phm 1 Paul, a prisoner of **C** Jesus
Phm 3 Father and the Lord Jesus **C**
Phm 6 which is in you in **C** Jesus
Phm 8 in **C** to command you what is
Phm 9 also a prisoner of Jesus **C**
Phm 23 my fellow prisoner in **C** Jesus
Phm 25 Jesus **C** be with your spirit
Heb 3: 1 of our confession, **C** Jesus,
Heb 3: 6 but **C** as a Son over His own
Heb 3:14 **C** if we hold the beginning of
Heb 5: 5 So also **C** did not glorify
Heb 6: 1 elementary principles of **C**
Heb 9:11 But **C** came as High Priest of
Heb 9:14 more shall the blood of **C**
Heb 9:24 For **C** has not entered the
Heb 9:28 so **C** was offered once to bear
Heb 10:10 body of Jesus **C** once for all
Heb 11:26 of **C** greater riches than the
Heb 13: 8 Jesus **C** is the same yesterday
Heb 13:21 in His sight, through Jesus **C**
Jas 1: 1 of God and of the Lord Jesus **C**
Jas 2: 1 the faith of our Lord Jesus **C**
1Pe 1: 1 Peter, an apostle of Jesus **C**
1Pe 1: 2 of the blood of Jesus **C**
1Pe 1: 3 and Father of our Lord Jesus **C**
1Pe 1: 3 of Jesus **C** from the dead,
1Pe 1: 7 at the revelation of Jesus **C**
1Pe 1:11 the Spirit of **C** who was in
1Pe 1:11 the sufferings of **C** and the
1Pe 1:13 at the revelation of Jesus **C**
1Pe 1:19 with the precious blood of **C**
1Pe 2: 5 to God through Jesus **C**
1Pe 2:21 because **C** also suffered for
1Pe 3:16 conduct in **C** may be ashamed
1Pe 3:18 For **C** also suffered once for
1Pe 3:21 the resurrection of Jesus **C**
1Pe 4: 1 since **C** suffered for us in
1Pe 4:11 be glorified through Jesus **C**
1Pe 4:14 reproached for the name of **C**
1Pe 5: 1 of the sufferings of **C**, and
1Pe 5:10 His eternal glory by **C** Jesus
1Pe 5:14 to you all who are in **C** Jesus
2Pe 1: 1 servant and apostle of Jesus **C**
2Pe 1: 1 of our God and Savior Jesus **C**
2Pe 1: 8 knowledge of our Lord Jesus **C**
2Pe 1:11 of our Lord and Savior Jesus **C**
2Pe 1:14 as our Lord Jesus **C** showed me
2Pe 1:16 and coming of our Lord Jesus **C**
2Pe 2:20 of the Lord and Savior Jesus **C**
2Pe 3:18 of our Lord and Savior Jesus **C**
1Jn 1: 3 and with His Son Jesus **C**
1Jn 1: 7 the blood of Jesus **C** His Son
1Jn 2: 1 Father, Jesus **C** the righteous
1Jn 2:22 denies that Jesus is the **C**
1Jn 3:23 the name of His Son Jesus **C**
1Jn 4: 2 that confesses that Jesus **C**
1Jn 4: 3 **C** has come in the flesh is
1Jn 5: 1 Jesus is the **C** is born of God
1Jn 5: 6 by water and blood—Jesus **C**
1Jn 5:20 is true, in His Son Jesus **C**
2Jn 3 and from the Lord Jesus **C**, the
2Jn 7 **C** as coming in the flesh
2Jn 9 of **C** does not have God
2Jn 9 of **C** has both the Father and
Jude 1 Jude, a servant of Jesus **C**
Jude 1 and preserved in Jesus **C**
Jude 4 Lord God and our Lord Jesus **C**
Jude 17 apostles of our Lord Jesus **C**
Jude 21 Jesus **C** unto eternal life
Rev 1: 1 The Revelation of Jesus **C**
Rev 1: 2 to the testimony of Jesus **C**
Rev 1: 5 and from Jesus **C**, the faithful
Rev 1: 9 and patience of Jesus **C**, was
Rev 1: 9 for the testimony of Jesus **C**
Rev 11:15 of our Lord and of His **C**, and
Rev 12:10 the power of His **C** have come
Rev 12:17 have the testimony of Jesus **C**
Rev 20: 4 reigned with **C** for a thousand
Rev 20: 6 be priests of God and of **C**
Rev 22:21 Lord Jesus **C** be with you all

CHRISTIAN (*see* CHRISTIANS)
Acts 26:28 persuade me to become a **C**
1Pe 4:16 Yet if anyone suffers as a **C**

CHRISTIANS (*see* CHRISTIAN)
Acts 11:26 first called **C** in Antioch

CHRIST'S (*see* CHRIST)
1Co 3:23 And you are **C**, and Christ is
1Co 4:10 We are fools for **C** sake, but
1Co 7:22 called while free is **C** slave
1Co 15:23 those who are **C** at His coming
2Co 2:12 to Troas to preach **C** gospel
2Co 5:20 we implore you on **C** behalf
2Co 10: 7 in himself that he is **C**, let
2Co 10: 7 himself, that just as he is **C**
2Co 10: 7 even so we are **C**
2Co 12:10 in distresses, for **C** sake
Gal 3:29 And if you are **C**, then you are
Gal 5:24 And those who are **C** have
Eph 4: 7 to the measure of **C** gift
1Ti 6:14 our Lord Jesus **C** appearing
1Pe 4:13 you partake of **C** sufferings

CHRISTS (*see* CHRIST)
Matt 24:24 For false **c** and false prophets
Mark 13:22 For false **c** and false prophets

CHRONICLES
1Ki 14:19 the **c** of the kings of Israel
1Ki 14:29 the **c** of the kings of Judah
1Ki 15: 7 the **c** of the kings of Judah
1Ki 15:23 the **c** of the kings of Judah
1Ki 15:31 the **c** of the kings of Israel
1Ki 16: 5 the **c** of the kings of Israel
1Ki 16:14 the **c** of the kings of Israel
1Ki 16:20 the **c** of the kings of Israel
1Ki 16:27 the **c** of the kings of Israel
1Ki 22:39 the **c** of the kings of Israel
1Ki 22:45 the **c** of the kings of Judah
2Ki 1:18 the **c** of the kings of Israel
2Ki 8:23 the **c** of the kings of Judah
2Ki 10:34 the **c** of the kings of Israel
2Ki 12:19 the **c** of the kings of Judah
2Ki 13: 8 the **c** of the kings of Israel
2Ki 13:12 the **c** of the kings of Israel
2Ki 14:15 the **c** of the kings of Israel
2Ki 14:18 the **c** of the kings of Judah
2Ki 14:28 the **c** of the kings of Israel
2Ki 15: 6 the **c** of the kings of Judah
2Ki 15:11 the **c** of the kings of Israel
2Ki 15:15 the **c** of the kings of Israel
2Ki 15:21 the **c** of the kings of Israel
2Ki 15:26 the **c** of the kings of Israel
2Ki 15:31 the **c** of the kings of Israel
2Ki 15:36 the **c** of the kings of Judah
2Ki 16:19 the **c** of the kings of Judah
2Ki 20:20 the **c** of the kings of Judah
2Ki 21:17 the **c** of the kings of Judah
2Ki 21:25 the **c** of the kings of Judah
2Ki 23:28 the **c** of the kings of Judah
2Ki 24: 5 the **c** of the kings of Judah
1Ch 27:24 of the **c** of King David
Neh 12:23 written in the book of the **c**
Esth 2:23 written in the book of the **c**
Esth 6: 1 book of the records of the **c**
Esth 10: 2 the **c** of the kings of Media

CHRYSOLITE
Rev 21:20 sixth sardius, the seventh **c**

CHRYSOPRASE
Rev 21:20 the ninth topaz, the tenth **c**

CHUB
Ezek 30: 5 all the mingled people, **C**

CHUN
1Ch 18: 8 Also from Tibhath and from **C**

CHURCH (*see* CHURCHES)
Matt 16:18 this rock I will build My **c**
Matt 18:17 hear them, tell it to the **c**
Matt 18:17 he refuses even to hear the **c**
Acts 2:47 the Lord added to the **c** daily
Acts 5:11 fear came upon all the **c** and
Acts 8: 1 arose against the **c** which was
Acts 8: 3 Saul, he made havoc of the **c**
Acts 11:22 ears of the **c** in Jerusalem
Acts 11:26 they assembled with the **c**
Acts 12: 1 to harass some from the **c**
Acts 12: 5 to God for him by the **c**
Acts 13: 1 Now in the **c** that was at
Acts 14:23 appointed elders in every **c**
Acts 14:27 and gathered the **c** together
Acts 15: 3 sent on their way by the **c**
Acts 15: 4 they were received by the **c**
Acts 15:22 and elders, with the whole **c**
Acts 18:22 and gone up and greeted the **c**
Acts 20:17 for the elders of the **c**
Acts 20:28 to shepherd the **c** of God
Rom 16: 1 servant of the **c** in Cenchrea
Rom 16: 5 Likewise greet the **c** that is
Rom 16:23 and the host of the whole **c**
1Co 1: 2 To the **c** of God which is at
1Co 4:17 I teach everywhere in every **c**
1Co 6: 4 esteemed by the **c** to judge
1Co 10:32 the Greeks or to the **c** of God
1Co 11:18 when you come together as a **c**
1Co 11:22 do you despise the **c** of God
1Co 12:28 has appointed these in the **c**
1Co 14: 4 who prophesies edifies the **c**
1Co 14: 5 that the **c** may receive
1Co 14:12 the **c** that you seek to excel
1Co 14:19 yet in the **c** I would rather
1Co 14:23 Therefore if the whole **c**
1Co 14:28 let him keep silent in **c**
1Co 14:35 for women to speak in **c**
1Co 15: 9 I persecuted the **c** of God
1Co 16:19 with the **c** that is in their
2Co 1: 1 To the **c** of God which is at

Gal 1:13 how I persecuted the **c** of God
Eph 1:22 head over all things to the **c**
Eph 3:10 the **c** to the principalities
Eph 3:21 to Him be glory in the **c** by
Eph 5:23 also Christ is head of the **c**
Eph 5:24 just as the **c** is subject to
Eph 5:25 as Christ also loved the **c**
Eph 5:27 it to Himself a glorious **c**
Eph 5:29 just as the Lord does the **c**
Eph 5:32 concerning Christ and the **c**
Phil 3: 6 zeal, persecuting the **c**
Phil 4:15 no **c** shared with me
Col 1:18 the head of the body, the **c**
Col 1:24 of His body, which is the **c**
Col 4:15 the **c** that is in his house
Col 4:16 in the **c** of the Laodiceans
1Th 1: 1 To the **c** of the Thessalonians
2Th 1: 1 To the **c** of the Thessalonians
1Ti 3: 5 he take care of the **c** of God
1Ti 3:15 which is the **c** of the living
1Ti 5:16 do not let the **c** be burdened
Phm 2 and to the **c** in your house
Heb 12:23 **c** of the firstborn who are
Jas 5:14 call for the elders of the **c**
3Jn 6 of your love before the **c**
3Jn 9 I wrote to the **c**, but
3Jn 10 to, putting them out of the **c**
Rev 2: 1 of the **c** of Ephesus write
Rev 2: 8 of the **c** in Smyrna write
Rev 2:12 of the **c** in Pergamos write
Rev 2:18 of the **c** in Thyatira write
Rev 3: 1 of the **c** in Sardis write
Rev 3: 7 And to the angel of the **c** in
Rev 3:14 to the angel of the **c** of the

CHURCHES (*see* CHURCH)
Acts 9:31 Then the **c** throughout all
Acts 15:41 Cilicia, strengthening the **c**
Acts 16: 5 So the **c** were strengthened in
Rom 16: 4 all the **c** of the Gentiles
Rom 16:16 The **c** of Christ greet you
1Co 7:17 And so I ordain in all the **c**
1Co 11:16 custom, nor do the **c** of God
1Co 14:33 as in all the **c** of the saints
1Co 14:34 women keep silent in the **c**
1Co 16: 1 orders to the **c** of Galatia
1Co 16:19 The **c** of Asia greet you
2Co 8: 1 on the **c** of Macedonia
2Co 8:18 gospel throughout all the **c**
2Co 8:19 who was also chosen by the **c**
2Co 8:23 they are messengers of the **c**
2Co 8:24 show to them, and before the **c**
2Co 11: 8 I robbed other **c**, taking
2Co 11:28 my deep concern for all the **c**
2Co 12:13 you were inferior to other **c**
Gal 1: 2 with me, To the **c** of Galatia
Gal 1:22 the **c** of Judea which were in
1Th 2:14 became imitators of the **c** of
2Th 1: 4 boast of you among the **c** of
Rev 1: 4 to the seven **c** which are in
Rev 1:11 the seven **c** which are in Asia
Rev 1:20 are the angels of the seven **c**
Rev 1:20 which you saw are the seven **c**
Rev 2: 7 what the Spirit says to the **c**
Rev 2:11 what the Spirit says to the **c**
Rev 2:17 what the Spirit says to the **c**
Rev 2:23 all the **c** shall know that I
Rev 2:29 what the Spirit says to the **c**
Rev 3: 6 what the Spirit says to the **c**
Rev 3:13 what the Spirit says to the **c**
Rev 3:22 what the Spirit says to the **c**
Rev 22:16 to you these things in the **c**

CHURNING (*see* CHURNS)
Prov 30:33 For as the **c** of milk produces

CHURNS (*see* CHURNING)
Hos 11: 8 My heart **c** within Me

CHUZA
Luke 8: 3 and Joanna the wife of **C**,

CILICIA
Acts 6: 9 Alexandrians, and those from **C**
Acts 15:23 in Antioch, Syria, and **C**
Acts 15:41 he went through Syria and **C**
Acts 21:39 I am a Jew from Tarsus, in **C**
Acts 22: 3 a Jew, born in Tarsus of **C**
Acts 23:34 understood that he was from **C**
Acts 27: 5 over the sea which is off **C**
Gal 1:21 the regions of Syria and **C**

CINNAMON
Ex 30:23 sweet-smelling **c** (two hundred
Prov 7:17 bed with myrrh, aloes, and **c**
Song 4:14 and saffron, calamus and **c**,
Rev 18:13 and **c** and incense, fragrant oil

CIRCLE (*see* CIRCLED, CIRCULAR)
Josh 6:11 ark of the LORD **c** the city
2Sa 5:23 **c** around behind them, and
1Ch 14:14 **c** around them, and come upon
Job 22:14 walks above the **c** of heaven
Prov 8:27 when He drew a **c** on the face
Is 40:22 sits above the **c** of the earth
Mark 3:34 He looked around in a **c** at

CIRCLED (*see* CIRCLE)
Acts 28:13 From there we **c** round and

CIRCUIT
1Sa 7:16 year to year on a **c** to Bethel
Ps 19: 6 And its **c** to the other end
Eccl 1: 6 and comes again on its **c**
Mark 6: 6 about the villages in a **c**

CIRCULAR (*see* CIRCLE)
Job 26:10 He drew a **c** horizon on the

CIRCULATE (*see* CIRCULATED)
Ex 23: 1 You shall not **c** a false

CIRCULATED (*see* CIRCULATE)
2Ch 31: 5 soon as the commandment was **c**

CIRCUMCISE (*see* CIRCUMCISED, CIRCUMCISING, CIRCUMCISION, UNCIRCUMCISED)
Deut 10:16 Therefore **c** the foreskin of
Deut 30: 6 your God will **c** your heart
Josh 5: 2 **c** the sons of Israel again
Jer 4: 4 **C** yourselves to the LORD, and
Luke 1:59 that they came to **c** the child
John 7:22 you **c** a man on the Sabbath
Acts 15: 5 It is necessary to **c** them
Acts 21:21 that they ought not to **c**

CIRCUMCISED (*see* CIRCUMCISE)
Gen 17:10 child among you shall be **c**
Gen 17:11 you shall be **c** in the flesh
Gen 17:12 days old among you shall be **c**
Gen 17:13 with your money must be **c**
Gen 17:14 who is not **c** in the flesh of
Gen 17:23 and **c** the flesh of their
Gen 17:24 he was **c** in the flesh of his
Gen 17:25 he was **c** in the flesh of his
Gen 17:26 very same day Abraham was **c**
Gen 17:27 a stranger, were **c** with him
Gen 21: 4 Then Abraham **c** his son Isaac
Gen 34:15 if every male of you is **c**
Gen 34:17 you will not heed us and be **c**
Gen 34:22 is **c** as they are **c**
Gen 34:24 every male was **c**, all who
Ex 12:44 money, when you have **c** him
Ex 12:48 LORD, let all his males be **c**
Lev 12: 3 of his foreskin shall be **c**
Josh 5: 3 **c** the sons of Israel at the
Josh 5: 4 the reason why Joshua **c** them
Josh 5: 5 who came out had been **c**, but
Josh 5: 5 out of Egypt had not been **c**
Josh 5: 7 So Joshua **c** their sons whom
Josh 5: 7 had not been **c** on the way
Jer 9:25 are **c** with the uncircumcised
Acts 7: 8 and **c** him on the eighth day
Acts 15: 1 Unless you are **c** according to
Acts 15:24 souls, saying, "You must be **c**
Acts 16: 3 **c** him because of the Jews who
Rom 3:30 will justify the **c** by faith
Rom 4: 9 then come upon the **c** only
Rom 4:10 While he was **c**, or
Rom 4:10 Not while **c**, but while
1Co 7:18 Was anyone called while **c**
1Co 7:18 Let him not be **c**
Gal 2: 3 Greek, was compelled to be **c**
Gal 2: 7 gospel for the **c** was to Peter
Gal 2: 8 **c** also worked effectively in
Gal 2: 9 the Gentiles and they to the **c**
Gal 5: 2 to you that if you become **c**
Gal 5: 3 to every man who becomes **c**
Gal 6:12 try to compel you to be **c**
Gal 6:13 those who are **c** keep the law
Gal 6:13 **c** that they may glory in your
Phil 3: 5 **c** the eighth day, of the
Col 2:11 In Him you were also **c** with
Col 3:11 nor Jew, **c** nor uncircumcised,

CIRCUMCISING (*see* CIRCUMCISE)
Josh 5: 8 had finished **c** all the people

CIRCUMCISION (*see* CIRCUMCISE)
Ex 4:26 because of the **c**
Luke 2:21 for the **c** of the Child, His
John 7:22 Moses therefore gave you **c**
John 7:23 man receives **c** on the Sabbath
Acts 7: 8 He gave him the covenant of **c**
Acts 10:45 those of the **c** who believed
Acts 11: 2 those of the **c** contended with
Rom 2:25 For **c** is indeed profitable if
Rom 2:25 of the law, your **c** has become
Rom 2:26 be counted as **c**
Rom 2:27 with your written code and **c**
Rom 2:28 nor is that **c** which is
Rom 2:29 **c** is that of the heart, in
Rom 3: 1 or what is the profit of **c**
Rom 4:11 And he received the sign of **c**
Rom 4:12 the father of **c** to those who
Rom 4:12 who not only are of the **c**
Rom 15: 8 to the **c** for the truth of God
1Co 7:19 **C** is nothing and
Gal 2:12 those who were of the **c**
Gal 5: 6 **c** nor uncircumcision avails
Gal 5:11 brethren, if I still preach **c**
Gal 6:15 **c** nor uncircumcision avails
Eph 2:11 by what is called the **C** made
Phil 3: 3 For we are the **c**, who worship
Col 2:11 with the **c** made without hands
Col 2:11 flesh, by the **c** of Christ,
Col 4:11 of God who are of the **c**
Tit 1:10 especially those of the **c**

CIRCUMFERENCE
1Ki 7:15 cubits measured the **c** of each
1Ki 7:23 thirty cubits measured its **c**
2Ch 4: 2 thirty cubits measured its **c**
Jer 52:21 cubits could measure its **c**

CIRCUMSPECT (*see* CIRCUMSPECTLY)
Ex 23:13 that I have said to you, be **c**

CIRCUMSPECTLY (*see* CIRCUMSPECT)
Eph 5:15 See then that you walk **c**, not

CIRCUMSTANCES
Col 4: 8 that he may know your **c** and

CISTERN (*see* CISTERNS)
Lev 11:36 Nevertheless a spring or a **c**
2Ki 18:31 drink the waters of his own **c**
Prov 5:15 Drink water from your own **c**
Is 30:14 or to take water from the **c**
Is 36:16 drink the waters of his own **c**

CISTERNS (*see* CISTERN)
Neh 9:25 **c** already dug, vineyards,
Jer 2:13 waters, and hewn themselves **c**
Jer 2:13 broken **c** that can hold no
Jer 14: 3 they went to the **c** and found

CITADEL (*see* CITADELS)
1Ki 16:18 the **c** of the king's house
2Ki 5:24 When he came to the **c**, he
2Ki 15:25 in the **c** of the king's house,
Neh 1: 1 as I was in Shushan the **c**
Neh 2: 8 the **c** which pertains to the
Neh 7: 2 Hananiah the leader of the **c**
Esth 1: 2 which was in Shushan the **c**
Esth 1: 5 were present in Shushan the **c**
Esth 2: 3 virgins to Shushan the **c**,
Esth 2: 5 Now in Shushan the **c** there
Esth 2: 8 gathered at Shushan the **c**
Esth 3:15 proclaimed in Shushan the **c**
Esth 8:14 was issued in Shushan the **c**
Esth 9: 6 in Shushan the **c** the Jews
Esth 9:11 the **c** was brought to the king
Esth 9:12 hundred men in Shushan the **c**
Dan 8: 2 that I was in Shushan, the **c**

CITADELS (*see* CITADEL)
Is 13:22 hyenas will howl in their **c**

CITIES (*see* CITY)
Gen 13:12 dwelt in the **c** of the plain
Gen 19:25 So He overthrew those **c**, all
Gen 19:25 all the inhabitants of the **c**
Gen 19:29 destroyed the **c** of the plain
Gen 19:29 when He overthrew the **c** in
Gen 35: 5 **c** that were all around them
Gen 41:35 let them keep food in the **c**
Gen 41:48 and laid up the food in the **c**
Gen 47:21 he moved them into the **c**
Ex 1:11 built for Pharaoh supply **c**

Lev 25:32 the **c** of the Levites, and the
Lev 25:32 the houses in the **c** of their
Lev 25:33 for the houses in the **c** of
Lev 25:34 of their **c** may not be sold
Lev 26:25 together within your **c** I will
Lev 26:31 I will lay your **c** waste and
Lev 26:33 be desolate and your **c** waste
Num 13:19 whether the **c** they inhabit
Num 13:28 the **c** are fortified and very
Num 21: 2 will utterly destroy their **c**
Num 21: 3 destroyed them and their **c**
Num 21:25 So Israel took all these **c**
Num 21:25 in all the **c** of the Amorites
Num 31:10 all the **c** where they dwelt
Num 32:16 and **c** for our little ones,
Num 32:17 **c** because of the inhabitants
Num 32:24 Build **c** for your little ones
Num 32:26 be there in the **c** of Gilead
Num 32:33 the land with its **c** within
Num 32:33 the **c** of the surrounding
Num 32:36 and Beth Haran, fortified **c**
Num 32:38 to the **c** which they built
Num 35: 2 **c** to dwell in from the
Num 35: 2 common-land around the **c**
Num 35: 3 shall have the **c** to dwell in
Num 35: 4 The common-land of the **c**
Num 35: 5 them as common-land for the **c**
Num 35: 6 Now among the **c** which you
Num 35: 6 shall appoint six **c** of refuge
Num 35: 6 you shall add forty-two **c**
Num 35: 7 So all the **c** you will give to
Num 35: 8 the **c** which you will give
Num 35: 8 some of its **c** to the Levites
Num 35:11 then you shall appoint **c** to
Num 35:11 to be **c** of refuge for you
Num 35:12 They shall be **c** of refuge
Num 35:13 of the **c** which you give, you
Num 35:13 shall have six **c** of refuge
Num 35:14 You shall appoint three **c** on
Num 35:14 three **c** you shall appoint in
Num 35:14 which will be **c** of refuge
Num 35:15 These six **c** shall be for
Deut 1:22 of the **c** into which we shall
Deut 1:28 the **c** are great and fortified
Deut 2:34 took all his **c** at that time
Deut 2:35 spoil of the **c** which we took
Deut 2:37 or to the **c** of the mountains,
Deut 3: 4 took all his **c** at that time
Deut 3: 4 sixty **c**, all the region of
Deut 3: 5 All these **c** were fortified
Deut 3: 7 the spoil of the **c** we took as
Deut 3:10 all the **c** of the plain, all
Deut 3:10 **c** of the kingdom of Og in
Deut 3:12 mountains of Gilead and its **c**
Deut 3:19 shall stay in your **c** which I
Deut 4:41 **c** on this side of the Jordan
Deut 4:42 one of these **c** he might live
Deut 6:10 beautiful **c** which you did not
Deut 9: 1 **c** great and fortified up to
Deut 13:12 hear someone in one of your **c**
Deut 19: 1 them and dwell in their **c** and
Deut 19: 2 you shall separate three **c**
Deut 19: 5 shall flee to one of these **c**
Deut 19: 7 separate three **c** for yourself
Deut 19: 9 you shall add three more **c**
Deut 19:11 and he flees to one of these **c**
Deut 20:15 you shall do to all the **c**
Deut 20:15 not of the **c** of these nations
Deut 20:16 But of the **c** of these peoples
Deut 21: 2 man to the surrounding **c**
Josh 9:17 came to their **c** on the third
Josh 9:17 Now their **c** were Gibeon,
Josh 10: 2 city, like one of the royal **c**
Josh 10:19 allow them to enter their **c**
Josh 10:20 escaped entered fortified **c**
Josh 10:37 its king, all its **c**, and all
Josh 10:39 it and its king and all its **c**
Josh 11:12 So all the **c** of those kings,
Josh 11:13 But as for the **c** that stood
Josh 11:14 And all the spoil of these **c**
Josh 11:21 destroyed them with their **c**
Josh 13:10 all the **c** of Sihon king of
Josh 13:17 all its **c** that are in the
Josh 13:21 all the **c** of the plain and all
Josh 13:23 to their families, the **c** and
Josh 13:25 all the **c** of Gilead, and half
Josh 13:28 to their families, the **c** and
Josh 13:30 which are in Bashan, sixty **c**
Josh 13:31 **c** of the kingdom of Og in
Josh 14: 4 except **c** to dwell in, with
Josh 14:12 and that the **c** were great and
Josh 15: 9 to the **c** of Mount Ephron
Josh 15:21 The **c** at the limits of the
Josh 15:32 all the **c** are twenty-nine,
Josh 15:36 fourteen **c** with their
Josh 15:41 sixteen **c** with their villages
Josh 15:44 nine **c** with their villages
Josh 15:51 eleven **c** with their villages
Josh 15:54 nine **c** with their villages
Josh 15:57 ten **c** with their villages
Josh 15:59 six **c** with their villages
Josh 15:60 two **c** with their villages
Josh 15:62 six **c** with their villages
Josh 16: 9 The separate **c** for the
Josh 16: 9 all the **c** with their villages
Josh 17: 9 These **c** of Ephraim are among
Josh 17: 9 are among the **c** of Manasseh
Josh 17:12 the inhabitants of those **c**
Josh 18: 9 in a book in seven parts by **c**
Josh 18:21 Now the **c** of the tribe of the
Josh 18:24 twelve **c** with their villages
Josh 18:28 fourteen **c** with their
Josh 19: 6 thirteen **c** and their villages
Josh 19: 7 four **c** and their villages
Josh 19: 8 **c** as far as Baalath Beer,
Josh 19:15 twelve **c** with their villages
Josh 19:16 these **c** with their villages
Josh 19:22 sixteen **c** with their villages
Josh 19:23 to their families, the **c** and
Josh 19:30 twenty-two **c** with their
Josh 19:31 these **c** with their villages
Josh 19:35 And the fortified **c** are Ziddim
Josh 19:38 nineteen **c** with their
Josh 19:39 to their families, the **c** and
Josh 19:48 these **c** with their villages
Josh 20: 2 for yourselves **c** of refuge
Josh 20: 4 he flees to one of those **c**
Josh 20: 9 These were the **c** appointed
Josh 21: 2 to give us **c** to dwell in,
Josh 21: 3 of the LORD, these **c** and their
Josh 21: 4 had thirteen **c** by lot from
Josh 21: 5 children of Kohath had ten **c**
Josh 21: 6 of Gershon had thirteen **c** by
Josh 21: 7 **c** from the tribe of Reuben
Josh 21: 8 of Israel gave these **c** with
Josh 21: 9 children of Simeon these **c**
Josh 21:16 nine **c** from those two tribes
Josh 21:18 with its common-land: four **c**
Josh 21:19 All the **c** of the children of
Josh 21:19 were thirteen **c** with their
Josh 21:20 even they had the **c** of their
Josh 21:22 with its common-land: four **c**
Josh 21:24 with its common-land: four **c**
Josh 21:25 with its common-land: two **c**
Josh 21:26 All the ten **c** with their
Josh 21:27 with its common-land: two **c**
Josh 21:29 with its common-land: four **c**
Josh 21:31 with its common-land: four **c**
Josh 21:32 with its common-land: three **c**
Josh 21:33 All the **c** of the Gershonites
Josh 21:33 families were thirteen **c** with
Josh 21:35 with its common-land: four **c**
Josh 21:37 with its common-land: four **c**
Josh 21:39 four **c** in all
Josh 21:40 So all the **c** for the children
Josh 21:40 were by their lot twelve **c**
Josh 21:41 All the **c** of the Levites
Josh 21:41 **c** with their common-lands
Josh 21:42 Every one of these **c** had its
Josh 21:42 thus were all these **c**
Josh 24:13 **c** which you did not build, and
Judg 11:26 in all the **c** along the banks
Judg 11:33 as far as Minnith—twenty **c**
Judg 12: 7 in one of the **c** of Gilead
Judg 20:14 from their **c** to Gibeah, to go
Judg 20:15 from their **c** at that time the
Judg 20:42 the **c** they destroyed in their
Judg 20:48 to all the **c** they came to
Judg 21:23 and they rebuilt the **c** and
1Sa 6:18 all the **c** of the Philistines
1Sa 6:18 five lords, both fortified **c**
1Sa 7:14 Then the **c** which the
1Sa 18: 6 out of all the **c** of Israel
1Sa 30:29 in the **c** of the Jerahmeelites
1Sa 30:29 were in the **c** of the Kenites
1Sa 31: 7 were dead, they forsook the **c**
2Sa 2: 1 up to any of the **c** of Judah
2Sa 2: 3 they dwelt in the **c** of Hebron
2Sa 8: 8 **c** of Hadadezer, King David
2Sa 10:12 and for the **c** of our God
2Sa 12:31 the **c** of the people of Ammon
2Sa 20: 6 find for himself fortified **c**
2Sa 24: 7 to all the **c** of the Hivites
1Ki 4:13 sixty large **c** with walls and
1Ki 8:37 them in the land of their **c**
1Ki 9:11 **c** in the land of Galilee
1Ki 9:12 went from Tyre to see the **c**
1Ki 9:13 What kind of **c** are these
1Ki 9:19 all the storage **c** that
1Ki 9:19 **c** for his chariots
1Ki 9:19 and **c** for his cavalry, and
1Ki 10:26 he stationed in the chariot **c**
1Ki 12:17 who dwelt in the **c** of Judah
1Ki 13:32 which are in the **c** of Samaria
1Ki 15:20 against the **c** of Israel
1Ki 15:23 the **c** which he built, are
1Ki 20:34 The **c** which my father took
1Ki 22:39 all the **c** that he built, are
2Ki 3:25 Then they destroyed the **c**
2Ki 13:25 the **c** which he had taken out
2Ki 13:25 and recaptured the **c** of Israel
2Ki 17: 6 and in the **c** of the Medes
2Ki 17: 9 high places in all their **c**
2Ki 17:24 and placed them in the **c** of
2Ki 17:24 of Samaria and dwelt in its **c**
2Ki 17:26 placed in the **c** of Samaria do
2Ki 17:29 in the **c** where they dwelt
2Ki 18:11 and in the **c** of the Medes,
2Ki 18:13 all the fortified **c** of Judah
2Ki 19:25 **c** into heaps of ruins
2Ki 23: 5 high places in the **c** of Judah
2Ki 23: 8 priests from the **c** of Judah
2Ki 23:19 that were in the **c** of Samaria
1Ch 2:22 who had twenty-three **c** in the
1Ch 4:31 These were their **c** until the
1Ch 4:32 Tochen, and Ashan—five **c**
1Ch 4:33 around these **c** as far as Baal
1Ch 6:57 gave one of the **c** of refuge
1Ch 6:60 All their **c** among their
1Ch 6:61 they gave by lot ten **c** from
1Ch 6:62 they gave thirteen **c** from the
1Ch 6:63 they gave twelve **c** from the
1Ch 6:64 of Israel gave these **c** with
1Ch 6:65 **c** which are called by their
1Ch 6:66 sons of Kohath were given **c**
1Ch 6:67 them one of the **c** of refuge
1Ch 9: 2 in their **c** were Israelites
1Ch 10: 7 dead, they forsook their **c**
1Ch 13: 2 and Levites who are in their **c**
1Ch 18: 8 **c** of Hadadezer, David brought
1Ch 19: 7 together from their **c**, and
1Ch 19:13 and for the **c** of our God
1Ch 20: 3 the **c** of the people of Ammon
1Ch 27:25 in the field, in the **c**, in
2Ch 1:14 he stationed in the chariot **c**
2Ch 6:28 them in the land of their **c**
2Ch 8: 2 that the **c** which Hiram had
2Ch 8: 4 all the storage **c** which he
2Ch 8: 5 fortified **c** with walls, gates
2Ch 8: 6 and all the storage **c** that
2Ch 8: 6 had, and all the chariot **c**
2Ch 8: 6 the **c** of the cavalry, and all
2Ch 9:25 he stationed in the chariot **c**
2Ch 10:17 who dwelt in the **c** of Judah
2Ch 11: 5 built **c** for defense in Judah
2Ch 11:10 and Benjamin, fortified **c**
2Ch 12: 4 took the fortified **c** of Judah
2Ch 13:19 Jeroboam and took **c** from him
2Ch 14: 5 from all the **c** of Judah, and
2Ch 14: 6 he built fortified **c** in Judah
2Ch 14: 7 Let us build these **c** and make
2Ch 14:14 all the **c** around Gerar, for
2Ch 14:14 and they plundered all the **c**
2Ch 15: 8 from the **c** which he had taken
2Ch 16: 4 against the **c** of Israel
2Ch 16: 4 all the storage **c** of Naphtali
2Ch 17: 2 all the fortified **c** of Judah
2Ch 17: 2 in the **c** of Ephraim which Asa
2Ch 17: 7 to teach in the **c** of Judah
2Ch 17: 9 throughout all the **c** of Judah
2Ch 17:12 and storage **c** in Judah
2Ch 17:13 property in the **c** of Judah
2Ch 17:19 **c** throughout all Judah
2Ch 19: 5 all the fortified **c** of Judah
2Ch 19:10 brethren who dwell in their **c**
2Ch 20: 4 from all the **c** of Judah they
2Ch 21: 3 with fortified **c** in Judah
2Ch 23: 2 from all the **c** of Judah, and
2Ch 24: 5 Go out to the **c** of Judah, and
2Ch 25:13 they raided the **c** of Judah

2Ch 26: 6 he built **c** around Ashdod and
2Ch 27: 4 Moreover he built **c** in the
2Ch 28:18 invaded the **c** of the lowland
2Ch 31: 1 went out to the **c** of Judah
2Ch 31: 1 returned to their own **c**,
2Ch 31: 6 who dwelt in the **c** of Judah
2Ch 31:15 in the **c** of the priests, to
2Ch 31:19 the common-lands of their **c**
2Ch 32: 1 against the fortified **c**,
2Ch 32:29 he provided **c** for himself
2Ch 33:14 all the fortified **c** of Judah
2Ch 34: 6 he did in the **c** of Manasseh
Ezra 2:70 Nethinim, dwelt in their **c**
Ezra 2:70 and all Israel in their **c**
Ezra 3: 1 of Israel were in the **c**, the
Ezra 4:10 settled in the **c** of Samaria
Ezra 10:14 let all those in our **c** who
Ezra 10:14 elders and judges of their **c**
Neh 7:73 all Israel dwelt in their **c**
Neh 7:73 of Israel were in their **c**
Neh 8:15 and proclaim in all their **c**
Neh 9:25 And they took strong **c** and a
Neh 11: 1 were to dwell in other **c**
Neh 11: 3 (But in the **c** of Judah
Neh 11: 3 his own possession in their **c**
Neh 11:20 were in all the **c** of Judah
Neh 12:44 **c** the portions specified by
Esth 9: 2 in their **c** throughout all the
Job 15:28 He dwells in desolate **c**, in
Ps 9: 6 And you have destroyed **c**
Ps 69:35 Zion And build the **c** of Judah
Is 1: 7 your **c** are burned with fire
Is 6:11 Until the **c** are laid waste and
Is 14:17 wilderness and destroyed its **c**
Is 14:21 the face of the world with **c**
Is 17: 2 The **c** of Aroer are forsaken
Is 17: 9 In that day his strong **c** will
Is 19:18 In that day five **c** in the
Is 33: 8 He has despised the **c**, He
Is 36: 1 all the fortified **c** of Judah
Is 37:26 **c** into heaps of ruins
Is 40: 9 say to the **c** of Judah
Is 42:11 its **c** lift up their voice,
Is 44:26 to the **c** of Judah, 'You
Is 54: 3 make the desolate **c** inhabited
Is 61: 4 shall repair the ruined **c**
Is 64:10 Your holy **c** are a wilderness,
Jer 1:15 and against all the **c** of Judah
Jer 2:15 his **c** are burned, without
Jer 2:28 of your **c** are your gods, O
Jer 4: 5 us go into the fortified **c**
Jer 4: 7 Your **c** will be laid waste,
Jer 4:16 voice against the **c** of Judah
Jer 4:26 all its **c** were broken down at
Jer 5: 6 will watch over their **c**
Jer 5:17 destroy your fortified **c**, in
Jer 7:17 they do in the **c** of Judah
Jer 7:34 to cease from the **c** of Judah
Jer 8:14 let us enter the fortified **c**
Jer 9:11 I will make the **c** of Judah
Jer 10:22 to make the **c** of Judah
Jer 11: 6 these words in the **c** of Judah
Jer 11:12 Then the **c** of Judah and the
Jer 11:13 of your **c** were your gods, O
Jer 13:19 The **c** of the South shall be
Jer 17:26 come from the **c** of Judah and
Jer 20:16 **c** which the LORD overthrew
Jer 22: 6 **c** which are not inhabited
Jer 25:18 the **c** of Judah, its kings and
Jer 26: 2 speak to all the **c** of Judah
Jer 31:21 turn back to these your **c**
Jer 31:23 the land of Judah and in its **c**
Jer 31:24 and in all its **c** together
Jer 32:44 in the **c** of Judah, in the
Jer 32:44 in the **c** of the mountains, in
Jer 32:44 in the **c** of the lowland, and
Jer 32:44 and in the **c** of the South
Jer 33:10 in the **c** of Judah, in the
Jer 33:12 beast, and in all its **c**, there
Jer 33:13 In the **c** of the mountains,
Jer 33:13 in the **c** of the lowland, in
Jer 33:13 in the **c** of the South, in the
Jer 33:13 in the **c** of Judah, the flocks
Jer 34: 1 Jerusalem and all its **c**,
Jer 34: 7 all the **c** of Judah that were
Jer 34: 7 for only these fortified **c**
Jer 34: 7 remained of the **c** of Judah
Jer 34:22 I will make the **c** of Judah a
Jer 36: 6 Judah who come from their **c**
Jer 36: 9 the **c** of Judah to Jerusalem
Jer 40: 5 governor over the **c** of Judah
Jer 40:10 dwell in your **c** that you have
Jer 44: 2 and on all the **c** of Judah
Jer 44: 6 and kindled in the **c** of Judah
Jer 44:17 in the **c** of Judah and in the
Jer 44:21 you burned in the **c** of Judah
Jer 48: 9 for her **c** shall be desolate,
Jer 48:15 and gone up from her **c**
Jer 48:24 on all the **c** of the land of
Jer 48:28 dwell in Moab, leave the **c**
Jer 49: 1 and his people dwell in its **c**
Jer 49:13 all its **c** shall be perpetual
Jer 49:18 and their neighboring **c**,"
Jer 50:32 I will kindle a fire in his **c**
Jer 50:40 and their neighboring **c**,"
Jer 51:43 Her **c** are a desolation, a dry
Lam 5:11 the maidens in the **c** of Judah
Ezek 6: 6 the **c** shall be laid waste
Ezek 12:20 Then the **c** that are inhabited
Ezek 19: 7 places, and laid waste their **c**
Ezek 25: 9 the territory of Moab of **c**
Ezek 25: 9 of the **c** on its frontier, the
Ezek 26:19 like **c** that are not inhabited
Ezek 29:12 among the **c** that are laid
Ezek 29:12 her **c** shall be desolate forty
Ezek 30: 7 her **c** shall be in the midst
Ezek 30: 7 of the **c** that are laid waste
Ezek 30:17 and these **c** shall go into
Ezek 35: 4 I shall lay your **c** waste, and
Ezek 35: 9 your **c** shall be uninhabited
Ezek 36: 4 the **c** that have been forsaken
Ezek 36:10 the **c** shall be inhabited and
Ezek 36:33 enable you to dwell in the **c**
Ezek 36:35 ruined **c** are now fortified and
Ezek 36:38 so shall the ruined **c** be
Ezek 39: 9 the **c** of Israel will go out
Hos 8:14 has multiplied fortified **c**
Hos 8:14 I will send fire upon his **c**
Hos 11: 6 sword shall slash in his **c**
Hos 13:10 he may save you in all your **c**
Amos 4: 6 of teeth in all your **c**
Amos 4: 8 So two or three **c** wandered to
Amos 9:14 they shall build the waste **c**
Obad 20 possess the **c** of the South
Mic 5:11 cut off the **c** of your land
Mic 5:14 thus I will destroy your **c**
Mic 7:12 Assyria and the fortified **c**
Zeph 1:16 alarm against the fortified **c**
Zeph 3: 6 their **c** are destroyed
Zech 1:12 on the **c** of Judah, against
Zech 1:17 My **c** shall again spread out
Zech 7: 7 and the **c** around it were
Zech 8:20 come, inhabitants of many **c**
Matt 9:35 And Jesus went about all the **c**
Matt 10:23 not have gone through the **c**
Matt 11: 1 teach and to preach in their **c**
Matt 11:20 He began to upbraid the **c** in
Matt 14:13 Him on foot from the **c**
Mark 6:33 there on foot from all the **c**
Mark 6:56 He entered, into villages, **c**
Luke 4:43 of God to the other **c** also
Luke 13:22 And He went through the **c** and
Luke 19:17 have authority over ten **c**
Luke 19:19 him, 'You also be over five **c**
Acts 5:16 surrounding **c** to Jerusalem
Acts 8:40 he preached in all the **c** till
Acts 14: 6 **c** of Lycaonia, and to the
Acts 16: 4 And as they went through the **c**
Acts 26:11 them even to foreign **c**
2Pe 2: 6 and turning the **c** of Sodom
Jude 7 and the **c** around them in a
Rev 16:19 the **c** of the nations fell

CITIZEN (*see* CITIZENS)
Luke 15:15 to a **c** of that country, and he
Acts 21:39 Cilicia, a **c** of no mean city
Acts 22:28 But I was born a **c**
Acts 28: 7 the leading **c** of the island

CITIZENS (*see* CITIZEN)
Luke 19:14 But his **c** hated him, and sent
Eph 2:19 but fellow **c** with the saints

CITIZENSHIP
Acts 22:28 a large sum I obtained this **c**
Phil 3:20 For our **c** is in heaven, from

CITRON
Rev 18:12 scarlet, every kind of **c** wood

CITY (*see* CITIES, CITY'S)
Gen 4:17 And he built a **c**, and called
Gen 4:17 and called the name of the **c**
Gen 10:12 (that is the principal **c**)
Gen 11: 4 let us build ourselves a **c**
Gen 11: 5 LORD came down to see the **c**
Gen 11: 8 and they ceased building the **c**
Gen 18:24 fifty righteous within the **c**
Gen 18:26 fifty righteous within the **c**
Gen 18:28 all of the **c** for lack of five
Gen 19: 4 lay down, the men of the **c**
Gen 19:12 and whomever you have in the **c**
Gen 19:14 the LORD will destroy this **c**
Gen 19:15 in the punishment of the **c**
Gen 19:16 out and set him outside the **c**
Gen 19:20 this **c** is near enough to flee
Gen 19:21 **c** for which you have spoken
Gen 19:22 name of the **c** was called Zoar
Gen 23:10 entered at the gate of his **c**
Gen 23:18 went in at the gate of his **c**
Gen 24:10 to the **c** of Nahor
Gen 24:11 the **c** by a well of water at
Gen 24:13 the **c** are coming out to draw
Gen 26:33 **c** is Beersheba to this day
Gen 28:19 but the name of that **c** had
Gen 33:18 safely to the **c** of Shechem
Gen 33:18 pitched his tent before the **c**
Gen 34:20 came to the gate of their **c**
Gen 34:20 spoke with the men of their **c**
Gen 34:24 gate of his **c** heeded Hamor
Gen 34:24 went out of the gate of his **c**
Gen 34:25 and came boldly upon the **c**
Gen 34:27 the slain, and plundered the **c**
Gen 34:28 donkeys, what was in the **c**
Gen 36:32 name of his **c** was Dinhabah
Gen 36:35 the name of his **c** was Avith
Gen 36:39 and the name of his **c** was Pau
Gen 41:48 he laid up in every **c** the
Gen 44: 4 they had gone out of the **c**
Gen 44:13 donkey and returned to the **c**
Ex 9:29 as I have gone out of the **c**
Ex 9:33 out of the **c** from Pharaoh
Lev 14:40 unclean place outside the **c**
Lev 14:41 unclean place outside the **c**
Lev 14:45 the **c** to an unclean place
Lev 14:53 the **c** in the open field, and
Lev 25:29 sells a house in a walled **c**
Lev 25:30 the house in the walled **c**
Lev 25:33 **c** of his possession shall be
Num 20:16 a **c** on the edge of your
Num 21:26 For Heshbon was the **c** of
Num 21:27 let the **c** of Sihon be
Num 21:28 a flame from the **c** of Sihon
Num 22:36 to meet him at the **c** of Moab
Num 24:19 destroy the remains of the **c**
Num 35: 4 **c** outward a thousand cubits
Num 35: 5 the **c** on the east side two
Num 35: 5 The **c** shall be in the middle
Num 35:25 shall return him to the **c** of
Num 35:26 the **c** of refuge where he fled
Num 35:27 the limits of his **c** of refuge
Num 35:28 **c** of refuge until the death
Num 35:32 has fled to his **c** of refuge
Deut 2:34 and little ones of every **c**
Deut 2:36 from the **c** that is in the
Deut 2:36 not one **c** too strong for us
Deut 3: 4 there was not a **c** which we
Deut 3: 6 women, and children of every **c**
Deut 13:13 the inhabitants of their **c**
Deut 13:15 the inhabitants of that **c**
Deut 13:16 burn with fire the **c** and all
Deut 19:12 elders of his **c** shall send
Deut 20:10 When you go near a **c** to fight
Deut 20:12 Now if the **c** will not make
Deut 20:14 and all that is in the **c**, all
Deut 20:19 besiege a **c** for a long time
Deut 20:20 siegeworks against the **c** that
Deut 21: 3 **c** nearest to the slain man
Deut 21: 4 the elders of that **c** shall
Deut 21: 6 And all the elders of that **c**
Deut 21:19 out to the elders of his **c**
Deut 21:19 **c**, to the gate of his **c**
Deut 21:20 say to the elders of his **c**
Deut 21:21 Then all the men of his **c**
Deut 22:15 elders of the **c** at the gate
Deut 22:17 before the elders of the **c**
Deut 22:18 of that **c** shall take that man
Deut 22:21 the men of her **c** shall stone
Deut 22:23 and a man finds her in the **c**
Deut 22:24 out to the gate of that **c**

Deut 22:24 she did not cry out in the c
Deut 25: 8 of his c shall call him and
Deut 28: 3 Blessed shall you be in the c
Deut 28:16 Cursed shall you be in the c
Deut 34: 3 the c of palm trees, as far
Josh 2:15 her house was on the c wall
Josh 3:16 the c that is beside Zaretan
Josh 6: 3 You shall march around the c
Josh 6: 3 go all around the c once
Josh 6: 4 around the c seven times, and
Josh 6: 5 of the c will fall down flat
Josh 6: 7 and march around the c, and
Josh 6:11 ark of the LORD circle the c
Josh 6:14 marched around the c once
Josh 6:15 marched around the c seven
Josh 6:15 around the c seven times
Josh 6:16 the LORD has given you the c
Josh 6:17 Now the c shall be doomed by
Josh 6:20 the people went up into the c
Josh 6:20 him, and they took the c
Josh 6:21 all that was in the c, both
Josh 6:24 But they burned the c and all
Josh 6:26 up and builds this c Jericho
Josh 8: 1 king of Ai, his people, his c
Josh 8: 2 an ambush for the c behind it
Josh 8: 4 lie in ambush against the c
Josh 8: 4 the c, behind the c
Josh 8: 4 Do not go very far from the c
Josh 8: 5 with me will approach the c
Josh 8: 6 we have drawn them from the c
Josh 8: 7 the ambush and seize the c
Josh 8: 8 be, when you have taken the c
Josh 8: 8 you shall set the c on fire
Josh 8:11 and they came before the c
Josh 8:12 Ai, on the west side of the c
Josh 8:13 was on the north of the c
Josh 8:13 guard on the west of the c
Josh 8:14 the men of the c hastened
Josh 8:14 against him behind the c
Josh 8:16 and were drawn away from the c
Josh 8:17 So they left the c open and
Josh 8:18 had in his hand toward the c
Josh 8:19 hand, and they entered the c
Josh 8:19 hastened to set the c on fire
Josh 8:20 the smoke of the c ascended
Josh 8:21 the ambush had taken the c
Josh 8:21 the smoke of the c ascended
Josh 8:22 out of the c against them
Josh 8:27 the spoil of that c Israel
Josh 8:29 entrance of the gate of the c
Josh 10: 2 because Gibeon was a great c
Josh 11:19 There was not a c that made
Josh 13:16 the c that is in the midst of
Josh 15: 8 c (which is Jerusalem)
Josh 15:62 the C of Salt, and En Gedi
Josh 18:14 a c of the children of Judah
Josh 18:16 the Jebusite c on the south
Josh 19:29 and to the fortified c of Tyre
Josh 19:50 him the c which he asked for
Josh 19:50 and he built the c and dwelt in
Josh 20: 4 entrance of the gate of the c
Josh 20: 4 of the elders of that c, they
Josh 20: 4 him into the c as one of them
Josh 20: 6 And he shall dwell in that c
Josh 20: 6 return and come to his own c
Josh 20: 6 to the c from which he fled
Josh 21:12 But the fields of the c and
Josh 21:13 with its common-land (a c of
Josh 21:21 a c of refuge for the slayer)
Josh 21:27 with its common-land (a c of
Josh 21:32 with its common-land (a c of
Josh 21:38 with its common-land (a c of
Judg 1: 8 sword and set the c on fire
Judg 1:16 went up from the c of palms
Judg 1:17 of the c was called Hormah
Judg 1:23 of the c was formerly Luz
Judg 1:24 saw a man coming out of the c
Judg 1:24 show us the entrance to the c
Judg 1:25 them the entrance to the c
Judg 1:25 they struck the c with the
Judg 1:26 of the Hittites, built a c
Judg 3:13 possession of the c of palms
Judg 6:27 the men of the c too much to
Judg 6:28 when the men of the c arose
Judg 6:30 men of the c said to Joash
Judg 8:16 he took the elders of the c
Judg 8:17 and killed the men of the c
Judg 8:27 ephod and set it up in his c
Judg 9:30 Zebul, the ruler of the c
Judg 9:31 fortifying the c against you
Judg 9:33 rise early and rush upon the c
Judg 9:35 in the entrance to the c gate
Judg 9:43 people, coming out of the c
Judg 9:44 entrance of the gate of the c
Judg 9:45 against the c all that day
Judg 9:45 he took the c and killed the
Judg 9:45 and he demolished the c and
Judg 9:51 was a strong tower in the c
Judg 9:51 all the people of the c
Judg 14:18 So the men of the c said to
Judg 16: 2 night at the gate of the c
Judg 16: 3 doors of the gate of the c
Judg 17: 8 c of Bethlehem in Judah to
Judg 18:27 and burned the c with fire
Judg 18:28 So they rebuilt the c and
Judg 18:29 called the name of the c Dan
Judg 18:29 the name of the c formerly
Judg 19:11 into this c of the Jebusites
Judg 19:12 here into a c of foreigners
Judg 19:15 in the open square of the c
Judg 19:17 in the open square of the c
Judg 19:22 suddenly certain men of the c
Judg 20:11 were gathered against the c
Judg 20:31 and were drawn away from the c
Judg 20:32 from the c to the highways
Judg 20:37 struck the whole c with the
Judg 20:38 of smoke rise up from the c
Judg 20:40 the c in a column of smoke
Judg 20:40 there was the whole c going
Judg 20:48 from every c, men and beasts,
Ruth 1:19 that all the c was excited
Ruth 2:18 took it up and went into the c
Ruth 3:15 Then she went into the c
Ruth 4: 2 men of the elders of the c
1Sa 1: 3 from his c yearly to worship
1Sa 4:13 when the man came into the c
1Sa 4:13 told it, all the c cried out
1Sa 5: 9 the c with a very great
1Sa 5: 9 and He struck the men of the c
1Sa 5:11 throughout all the c
1Sa 5:12 the cry of the c went up to
1Sa 8:22 Every man go to his c
1Sa 9: 6 is in this c a man of God
1Sa 9:10 So they went to the c where
1Sa 9:11 went up the hill to the c
1Sa 9:12 for today he came to this c
1Sa 9:13 soon as you come into the c
1Sa 9:14 So they went up to the c
1Sa 9:14 they were coming into the c
1Sa 9:25 the high place into the c
1Sa 9:27 to the outskirts of the c
1Sa 10: 5 you have come there to the c
1Sa 15: 5 And Saul came to a c of Amalek
1Sa 20: 6 run over to Bethlehem, his c
1Sa 20:29 has a sacrifice in the c, and
1Sa 20:40 Go, carry them to the c
1Sa 20:42 and Jonathan went into the c
1Sa 22:19 Nob, the c of the priests, he
1Sa 23:10 to destroy the c for my sake
1Sa 27: 5 dwell in the royal c with you
1Sa 28: 3 him in Ramah, in his own c
1Sa 30: 3 and his men came to the c, and
2Sa 5: 7 (that is, the C of David)
2Sa 5: 9 and called it the C of David
2Sa 6:10 with him into the C of David
2Sa 6:12 the C of David with gladness
2Sa 6:16 LORD came into the C of David
2Sa 10: 3 to you to search the c, to
2Sa 10:14 Abishai, and entered the c
2Sa 11:16 while Joab besieged the c
2Sa 11:17 the men of the c came out
2Sa 11:20 near to the c when you fought
2Sa 11:25 your attack against the c
2Sa 12: 1 There were two men in one c
2Sa 12:26 of Ammon, and took the royal c
2Sa 12:28 and encamp against the c and
2Sa 12:28 and take it, lest I take the c
2Sa 12:30 of the c in great abundance
2Sa 15: 2 and say, "What c are you from
2Sa 15:12 David's counselor, from his c
2Sa 15:14 strike the c with the edge of
2Sa 15:24 crossing over from the c
2Sa 15:25 ark of God back into the c
2Sa 15:27 Return to the c in peace, and
2Sa 15:34 But if you return to the c
2Sa 15:37 friend, went into the c
2Sa 17:13 if he has withdrawn into a c
2Sa 17:13 shall bring ropes to that c
2Sa 17:17 not be seen coming into the c
2Sa 17:23 home to his house, to his c
2Sa 18: 3 now more help to us in the c
2Sa 19: 3 back into the c that day, as
2Sa 19:37 that I may die in my own c
2Sa 20:15 a siege mound against the c
2Sa 20:16 woman cried out from the c
2Sa 20:19 You seek to destroy a c and a
2Sa 20:21 and I will depart from the c
2Sa 20:22 and they withdrew from the c
1Ki 1:41 Why is the c in such a noisy
1Ki 1:45 so that the c is in an uproar
1Ki 2:10 was buried in the C of David
1Ki 3: 1 the C of David until he had
1Ki 8: 1 the LORD from the C of David
1Ki 8:16 I have chosen no c from any
1Ki 8:44 the c which You have chosen
1Ki 8:48 the c which You have chosen
1Ki 9:16 Canaanites who dwelt in the c
1Ki 9:24 daughter came up from the C
1Ki 11:27 to the C of David his father
1Ki 11:32 the c which I have chosen out
1Ki 11:36 the c which I have chosen for
1Ki 11:43 was buried in the C of David
1Ki 13:25 told it in the c where the
1Ki 13:29 came to the c to mourn, and to
1Ki 14:11 to Jeroboam and dies in the c
1Ki 14:12 When your feet enter the c
1Ki 14:21 the c which the LORD had
1Ki 14:31 his fathers in the C of David
1Ki 15: 8 buried him in the C of David
1Ki 15:24 in the C of David his father
1Ki 16: 4 to Baasha and dies in the c
1Ki 16:18 saw that the c was taken,
1Ki 16:24 name of the c which he built
1Ki 17:10 he came to the gate of the c
1Ki 20: 2 the c to Ahab king of Israel
1Ki 20:12 got ready to attack the c
1Ki 20:19 of the c with the army which
1Ki 20:30 fled to Aphek, into the c
1Ki 20:30 fled and went into the c, into
1Ki 21: 8 dwelling in the c with Naboth
1Ki 21:11 So the men of his c, the
1Ki 21:11 who were inhabitants of his c
1Ki 21:13 they took him outside the c
1Ki 21:24 to Ahab and dies in the c, and
1Ki 22:26 to Amon the governor of the c
1Ki 22:36 Every man to his c, and every
1Ki 22:50 in the C of David his father
2Ki 2:19 men of the c said to Elisha
2Ki 2:19 of this c is pleasant, as my
2Ki 2:23 some youths came from the c
2Ki 3:19 attack every fortified c and
2Ki 3:19 and every choice c, and
2Ki 6:14 by night and surrounded the c
2Ki 6:15 surrounding the c with horses
2Ki 6:19 the way, nor is this the c
2Ki 7: 4 we say, 'We will enter the c
2Ki 7: 4 c,' the famine is in the c
2Ki 7:10 to the gatekeepers of the c
2Ki 7:12 When they come out of the c
2Ki 7:12 them alive, and get into the c
2Ki 7:13 which are left in the c
2Ki 8:24 his fathers in the C of David
2Ki 9:15 or escape from the c to go
2Ki 9:28 his fathers in the C of David
2Ki 10: 2 and horses, a fortified c also
2Ki 10: 5 he who was in charge of the c
2Ki 10: 6 with the great men of the c
2Ki 11:20 the c was quiet, for they had
2Ki 12:21 his fathers in the C of David
2Ki 14:20 his fathers in the C of David
2Ki 15: 7 his fathers in the C of David
2Ki 15:38 in the C of David his father
2Ki 16:20 his fathers in the C of David
2Ki 17: 9 watchtower to fortified c
2Ki 18: 8 watchtower to fortified c
2Ki 18:30 this c shall not be given
2Ki 19:13 king of the c of Sepharvaim
2Ki 19:32 He shall not come into this c
2Ki 19:33 he shall not come into this c
2Ki 19:34 For I will defend this c
2Ki 20: 6 this c from the hand of the
2Ki 20: 6 defend this c for My own sake
2Ki 20:20 and brought water into the c
2Ki 23: 8 Joshua the governor of the c
2Ki 23: 8 to the left of the c gate
2Ki 23:17 And the men of the c told him
2Ki 23:27 and will cast off this c
2Ki 24:10 and the c was besieged
2Ki 24:11 of Babylon came against the c
2Ki 25: 2 So the c was besieged until

2Ki 25: 3 c that there was no food for
2Ki 25: 4 Then the c wall was broken
2Ki 25: 4 all around against the c
2Ki 25:11 people who remained in the c
2Ki 25:19 He also took out of the c an
2Ki 25:19 who were found in the c, the
2Ki 25:19 land who were found in the c
1Ch 1:43 name of his c was Dinhabah
1Ch 1:46 The name of his c was Avith
1Ch 1:50 and the name of his c was Pai
1Ch 6:56 But the fields of the c and
1Ch 11: 5 (that is, the C of David)
1Ch 11: 7 they called it the C of David
1Ch 11: 8 And he built the c around it
1Ch 11: 8 repaired the rest of the c
1Ch 13:13 with him into the C of David
1Ch 15: 1 for himself in the C of David
1Ch 15:29 LORD came to the C of David
1Ch 19: 9 before the gate of the c, and
1Ch 19:15 his brother, and entered the c
1Ch 20: 2 of the c in great abundance
2Ch 5: 2 LORD up from the C of David
2Ch 6: 5 I have chosen no c from any
2Ch 6:34 this c which You have chosen
2Ch 6:38 toward the c which You have
•2Ch 8:11 of Pharaoh up from the C of
2Ch 9:31 was buried in the C of David
2Ch 11:12 Also in every c he put
2Ch 11:23 to every fortified c
2Ch 12:13 the c which the LORD had
2Ch 12:16 was buried in the C of David
2Ch 14: 1 buried him in the C of David
2Ch 15: 6 c by c, for God troubled
2Ch 16:14 for himself in the C of David
2Ch 18:25 to Amon the governor of the c
2Ch 19: 5 cities of Judah, c by c,
2Ch 21: 1 his fathers in the C of David
2Ch 21:20 buried him in the C of David
2Ch 23:21 the c was quiet, for they had
2Ch 24:16 they buried him in the C of
2Ch 24:25 buried him in the C of David
2Ch 25:28 his fathers in the C of Judah
2Ch 27: 9 buried him in the C of David
2Ch 28:15 Jericho, the c of palm trees
2Ch 28:25 in every single c of Judah he
2Ch 28:27 and they buried him in the c
2Ch 29:20 gathered the rulers of the c
2Ch 30:10 So the runners passed from c
2Ch 30:10 to c through the country of
2Ch 31:19 cities, in every single c
2Ch 32: 3 which were outside the c
2Ch 32: 5 the Millo in the C of David
2Ch 32: 6 the open square of the c gate
2Ch 32:18 that they might take the c
2Ch 32:30 west side of the C of David
2Ch 33:14 C of David on the west side
2Ch 33:15 and he cast them out of the c
2Ch 34: 8 the governor of the c, and
Ezra 2: 1 Judah, everyone to his own c
Ezra 4:12 the rebellious and evil c, and
Ezra 4:13 if this c is built and the
Ezra 4:15 this c is a rebellious c
Ezra 4:15 within the c in former times
Ezra 4:15 cause this c was destroyed
Ezra 4:16 that if this c is rebuilt
Ezra 4:19 it was found that this c in
Ezra 4:21 that this c may not be built
Neh 2: 3 face not be sad, when the c
Neh 2: 5 to the c of my fathers' tombs
Neh 2: 8 to the temple, for the c wall
Neh 3:15 go down from the C of David
Neh 7: 4 Now the c was large and
Neh 7: 6 Judah, everyone to his own c
Neh 11: 1 in Jerusalem, the holy c, and
Neh 11: 9 Senuah was second over the c
Neh 11:18 the holy c were two hundred
Neh 12:37 the stairs of the C of David
Neh 13:18 disaster on us and on this c
Esth 3:15 but the c of Shushan was
Esth 4: 1 out into the midst of the c
Esth 4: 6 c square that was in front of
Esth 6: 9 through the c square, and
Esth 6:11 through the c square, and
Esth 8:11 in every c to gather together
Esth 8:15 the c of Shushan rejoiced and
Esth 8:17 And in every province and c
Esth 9:28 every province, and every c
Job 24:12 The dying groan in the c, and
Job 29: 7 went out to the gate by the c
Job 39: 7 he scorns the tumult of the c

Ps 31:21 kindness in a strong c
Ps 46: 4 shall make glad the c of God
Ps 48: 1 praised In the c of our God
Ps 48: 2 The c of the great King
Ps 48: 8 In the c of the LORD of hosts
Ps 48: 8 of hosts, In the c of our God
Ps 55: 9 violence and strife in the c
Ps 59: 6 a dog, And go all around the c
Ps 59:14 a dog, And go all around the c
Ps 60: 9 bring me into the strong c
Ps 72:16 those of the c shall flourish
Ps 87: 3 are spoken of you, O c of God
Ps 101: 8 from the c of the LORD
Ps 107: 4 They found no c to dwell in
Ps 107: 7 go to a c for habitation
Ps 107:36 establish a c for habitation
Ps 108:10 bring me into the strong c
Ps 122: 3 Jerusalem is built As a c
Ps 127: 1 Unless the LORD guards the c
Prov 1:21 of the gates in the c she
Prov 8: 3 gates, at the entry of the c
Prov 9: 3 the highest places of the c
Prov 9:14 the highest places of the c
Prov 10:15 man's wealth is his strong c
Prov 11:10 the righteous, the c rejoices
Prov 11:11 the upright the c is exalted
Prov 16:32 spirit than he who takes a c
Prov 18:11 man's wealth is his strong c
Prov 18:19 harder to win than a strong c
Prov 21:22 scales the c of the mighty
Prov 25:28 is like a c broken down,
Prov 29: 8 Scoffers ensnare a c, but
Eccl 7:19 more than ten rulers of the c
Eccl 8:10 the c where they had so done
Eccl 9:14 a little c with few men in it
Eccl 9:15 by his wisdom delivered the c
Eccl 10:15 even know how to go to the c
Song 3: 2 And go about the c
Song 3: 3 who go about the c found me
Song 5: 7 who went about the c found me
Is 1: 8 of cucumbers, as a besieged c
Is 1:21 How the faithful c has become
Is 1:26 called the c of righteousness
Is 1:26 righteousness, the faithful c
Is 14: 4 ceased, the golden c ceased
Is 14:31 Cry, O c!
Is 17: 1 will cease from being a c
Is 19: 2 his neighbor, c against c
Is 19:18 called the C of Destruction
Is 22: 2 a tumultuous c, a joyous c
Is 22: 9 the damage to the c of David
Is 23: 7 Is this your joyous c, whose
Is 23: 8 against Tyre, the crowning c
Is 23:16 Take a harp, go about the c
Is 24:10 The c of confusion is broken
Is 24:12 In the c desolation is left,
Is 25: 2 For You have made a c a ruin
Is 25: 2 a ruin, a fortified c a ruin
Is 25: 2 foreigners to be a c no more
Is 25: 3 the c of the terrible nations
Is 26: 1 We have a strong c
Is 26: 5 dwell on high, the lofty c
Is 27:10 fortified c will be desolate
Is 29: 1 the c where David dwelt
Is 32:13 happy homes in the joyous c
Is 32:14 the bustling c will be
Is 32:19 and the c is brought low in
Is 33:20 the c of our appointed feasts
Is 36:15 this c will not be given into
Is 37:13 king of the c of Sepharvaim
Is 37:33 He shall not come into this c
Is 37:34 he shall not come into this c
Is 37:35 For I will defend this c
Is 38: 6 this c from the hand of the
Is 38: 6 and I will defend this c
Is 45:13 he shall build My c and let My
Is 48: 2 themselves after the holy c
Is 52: 1 O Jerusalem, the holy c
Is 60:14 call you The C of the LORD
Is 62:12 Sought Out, a C Not Forsaken
Is 66: 6 The sound of noise from the c
Jer 1:18 you this day a fortified c
Jer 3:14 I will take you, one from a c
Jer 4:29 The whole c shall flee from
Jer 4:29 Every c shall be forsaken, and
Jer 6: 6 This is the c to be punished
Jer 8:16 and all that is in it, the c
Jer 14:18 And if I enter the c, then
Jer 17:24 of this c on the Sabbath day
Jer 17:25 the gates of this c kings

Jer 17:25 this c shall remain forever
Jer 19: 8 I will make this c desolate
Jer 19:11 break this people and this c
Jer 19:12 and make this c like Tophet
Jer 19:15 I will bring on this c and on
Jer 20: 5 all the wealth of this c, all
Jer 21: 4 them in the midst of this c
Jer 21: 6 the inhabitants of this c
Jer 21: 7 in this c from the pestilence
Jer 21: 9 this c shall die by the sword
Jer 21:10 against this c for adversity
Jer 22: 8 nations will pass by this c
Jer 22: 8 LORD done so to this great c
Jer 23:39 the c that I gave you and your
Jer 25:29 to bring calamity on the c
Jer 26: 6 will make this c a curse to
Jer 26: 9 this c shall be desolate,
Jer 26:11 has prophesied against this c
Jer 26:12 against this c with all the
Jer 26:15 on yourselves, on this c, and
Jer 26:20 who prophesied against this c
Jer 27:17 should this c be laid waste
Jer 27:19 vessels that remain in this c
Jer 29: 7 seek the peace of the c where
Jer 29:16 people who dwell in this c
Jer 30:18 the c shall be built upon its
Jer 31:38 that the c shall be built for
Jer 32: 3 I will give this c into the
Jer 32:24 have come to the c to take it
Jer 32:24 the c has been given into the
Jer 32:25 yet the c has been given into
Jer 32:28 I will give this c into the
Jer 32:29 against this c shall come
Jer 32:29 come and set fire to this c
Jer 32:31 For this c has been to Me a
Jer 32:36 concerning this c of which
Jer 33: 4 the houses of this c and the
Jer 33: 5 hidden My face from this c
Jer 34: 2 I will give this c into the
Jer 34:22 them to return to this c
Jer 37: 8 back and fight against this c
Jer 37:10 tent, and burn the c with fire
Jer 37:21 the bread in the c was gone
Jer 38: 2 this c shall die by the sword
Jer 38: 3 This c shall surely be given
Jer 38: 4 of war who remain in this c
Jer 38: 9 is no more bread in the c
Jer 38:17 this c shall not be burned
Jer 38:18 then this c shall be given
Jer 38:23 you shall cause this c to be
Jer 39: 2 month, the c was penetrated
Jer 39: 4 and went out of the c by night
Jer 39: 9 people who remained in the c
Jer 39:16 upon this c for adversity
Jer 41: 7 came into the midst of the c
Jer 46: 8 earth, I will destroy the c
Jer 47: 2 and all that is in it, the c
Jer 48: 8 shall come against every c
Jer 49:25 Why is the c of praise not
Jer 49:25 not deserted, the c of My joy
Jer 51:31 his c is taken on all sides
Jer 52: 5 So the c was besieged until
Jer 52: 6 c that there was no food for
Jer 52: 7 Then the c wall was broken
Jer 52: 7 went out of the c at night by
Jer 52: 7 were near the c all around
Jer 52:15 people who remained in the c
Jer 52:25 He also took out of the c an
Jer 52:25 who were found in the c, the
Jer 52:25 found in the midst of the c
Lam 1: 1 How lonely sits the c that
Lam 1:19 breathed their last in the c
Lam 2:11 faint in the streets of the c
Lam 2:12 in the streets of the c, as
Lam 2:15 Is this the c that is called
Lam 3:51 of all the daughters of my c
Ezek 4: 1 you, and portray on it a c
Ezek 4: 3 wall between you and the c
Ezek 5: 2 in the midst of the c, when
Ezek 7:15 and whoever is in the c,
Ezek 7:23 the c is full of violence
Ezek 9: 1 charge over the c draw near
Ezek 9: 4 Go through the midst of the c
Ezek 9: 5 Go after him through the c
Ezek 9: 7 went out and killed in the c
Ezek 9: 9 and the c full of perversity
Ezek 10: 2 and scatter them over the c
Ezek 11: 2 give wicked counsel in this c
Ezek 11: 3 this c is the caldron, and we
Ezek 11: 6 your slain in this c, and you

Ezek 11: 7 and this c is the caldron
Ezek 11:11 This c shall not be your
Ezek 11:23 up from the midst of the c
Ezek 11:23 is on the east side of the c
Ezek 17: 4 he set it in a c of merchants
Ezek 21:19 the head of the road to the c
Ezek 22: 2 will you judge the bloody c
Ezek 22: 3 The c sheds blood in her own
Ezek 24: 6 Woe to the bloody c, to the
Ezek 24: 9 Woe to the bloody c
Ezek 26:10 as men enter a c that has
Ezek 26:17 seafaring men, O renowned c
Ezek 26:19 When I make you a desolate c
Ezek 27:32 you, 'What c is like Tyre,
Ezek 33:21 The c has been captured
Ezek 39:16 The name of the c will also
Ezek 40: 1 year after the c was captured
Ezek 40: 2 like the structure of a c
Ezek 43: 3 when I came to destroy the c
Ezek 45: 6 the c an area five thousand
Ezek 48:15 be for general use by the c
Ezek 48:15 the c shall be in the center
Ezek 48:17 common-land of the c shall be
Ezek 48:18 food for the workers of the c
Ezek 48:19 The workers of the c, from
Ezek 48:20 with the property of the c
Ezek 48:22 the possession of the c which
Ezek 48:30 These are the exits of the c
Ezek 48:31 (the gates of the c shall be
Ezek 48:35 the name of the c from that
Dan 9:16 away from Your c Jerusalem
Dan 9:18 the c which is called by Your
Dan 9:19 own sake, my God, for Your c
Dan 9:24 people and for your holy c
Dan 9:26 to come shall destroy the c
Dan 11:15 mound, and take a fortified c
Hos 6: 8 Gilead is a c of evildoers,
Joel 2: 9 They run to and fro in the c
Amos 3: 6 If a trumpet is blown in a c
Amos 3: 6 If there is calamity in a c
Amos 4: 7 I made it rain on one c, I
Amos 4: 7 withheld rain from another c
Amos 4: 8 to another c to drink water
Amos 5: 3 The c that goes out by a
Amos 6: 8 I will deliver up the c and
Amos 7:17 shall be a harlot in the c
Jon 1: 2 go to Nineveh, that great c
Jon 3: 2 go to Nineveh, that great c
Jon 3: 3 was an exceedingly great c
Jon 3: 4 the c on the first day's walk
Jon 4: 5 So Jonah went out of the c
Jon 4: 5 sat on the east side of the c
Jon 4: 5 what would become of the c
Jon 4:11 pity Nineveh, that great c
Mic 4:10 you shall go forth from the c
Mic 6: 9 LORD's voice cries to the c
Nah 3: 1 Woe to the bloody c
Hab 2: 8 violence of the land and the c
Hab 2:12 establishes a c by iniquity
Hab 2:17 violence of the land and the c
Zeph 2:15 c that dwelt securely, that
Zeph 3: 1 polluted, to the oppressing c
Zech 8: 3 be called the C of Truth, the
Zech 8: 5 The streets of the c shall be
Zech 8:21 of one c shall go to another
Zech 14: 2 the c shall be taken, the
Zech 14: 2 Half of the c shall go into
Zech 14: 2 not be cut off from the c
Matt 2:23 dwelt in a c called Nazareth,
Matt 4: 5 took Him up into the holy c
Matt 5:14 A c that is set on a hill
Matt 5:35 for it is the c of the great
Matt 8:33 and they went away into the c
Matt 8:34 the whole c came out to meet
Matt 9: 1 over, and came to His own c
Matt 10: 5 and do not enter a c of the
Matt 10:11 Now whatever c or town you
Matt 10:14 depart from that house or c
Matt 10:15 of judgment than for that c
Matt 10:23 they persecute you in this c
Matt 12:25 and every c or house divided
Matt 21:10 all the c was moved, saying,
Matt 21:17 went out of the c to Bethany
Matt 21:18 as He returned to the c, He
Matt 22: 7 and burned up their c
Matt 23:34 and persecute from c to c
Matt 26:18 Go into the c to a certain
Matt 27:53 they went into the holy c
Matt 28:11 of the guard came into the c
Mark 1:33 And the whole c was gathered
Mark 1:45 no longer openly enter the c
Mark 5:14 and they told it in the c
Mark 6:11 of judgment than for that c
Mark 11:19 come, He went out of the c
Mark 14:13 Go into the c, and a man will
Mark 14:16 went out, and came into the c
Luke 1:26 was sent by God to a c of
Luke 1:39 with haste, to a c of Judah,
Luke 2: 3 everyone to his own c
Luke 2: 4 out of the c of Nazareth,
Luke 2: 4 to the c of David, which is
Luke 2:11 in the c of David a Savior
Luke 2:39 to Galilee, to their own c
Luke 4:29 up and thrust Him out of the c
Luke 4:29 on which their c was built
Luke 4:31 a c of Galilee, and was
Luke 5:12 when He was in a certain c
Luke 7:11 He went into a c called Nain
Luke 7:12 came near the gate of the c
Luke 7:12 crowd from the c was with her
Luke 7:37 a woman in the c who was a
Luke 8: 1 that He went through every c
Luke 8: 4 had come to Him from every c
Luke 8:27 c who had demons for a long
Luke 8:34 they fled and told it in the c
Luke 8:39 throughout the whole c what
Luke 9: 5 when you go out of that c
Luke 9:10 to the c called Bethsaida
Luke 10: 1 before His face into every c
Luke 10: 8 Whatever c you enter, and they
Luke 10:10 But whatever c you enter, and
Luke 10:11 The very dust of your c
Luke 10:12 Day for Sodom than for that c
Luke 14:21 the streets and lanes of the c
Luke 18: 2 There was in a certain c a
Luke 18: 3 there was a widow in that c
Luke 19:41 as He drew near, He saw the c
Luke 22:10 when you have entered the c
Luke 23:19 insurrection made in the c
Luke 23:51 a c of the Jews, who himself
Luke 24:49 but tarry in the c of
John 1:44 the c of Andrew and Peter
John 4: 5 So He came to a c of Samaria
John 4: 8 away into the c to buy food
John 4:28 went her way into the c, and
John 4:30 Then they went out of the c
John 4:39 of the Samaritans of that c
John 11:54 to a c called Ephraim, and
John 19:20 was crucified was near the c
Acts 7:58 and they cast him out of the c
Acts 8: 5 went down to the c of Samaria
Acts 8: 8 there was great joy in that c
Acts 8: 9 practiced sorcery in the c
Acts 9: 6 Arise and go into the c, and
Acts 10: 9 journey and drew near the c
Acts 11: 5 I was in the c of Joppa
Acts 12:10 iron gate that leads to the c
Acts 13:44 Sabbath almost the whole c
Acts 13:50 and the chief men of the c
Acts 14: 4 of the c was divided
Acts 14:13 was in front of their c,
Acts 14:19 and dragged him out of the c
Acts 14:20 he rose up and went into the c
Acts 14:21 preached the gospel to that c
Acts 15:21 who preach him in every c
Acts 15:36 c where we have preached the
Acts 16:12 which is the foremost c of
Acts 16:12 in that c for some days
Acts 16:13 out of the c to the riverside
Acts 16:14 purple from the c of Thyatira
Acts 16:20 exceedingly trouble our c
Acts 16:39 them to depart from the c
Acts 17: 5 set all the c in an uproar and
Acts 17: 6 to the rulers of the c,
Acts 17: 8 the rulers of the c when they
Acts 17:16 the c was given over to idols
Acts 18:10 I have many people in this c
Acts 19:29 So the whole c was filled
Acts 19:35 when the c clerk had quieted
Acts 19:35 c of the Ephesians is temple
Acts 20:23 Spirit testifies in every c
Acts 21: 5 till we were out of the c
Acts 21:29 Ephesian with him in the c
Acts 21:30 And all the c was disturbed
Acts 21:39 a citizen of no mean c
Acts 22: 3 but brought up in this c at
Acts 24:12 in the synagogues or in the c
Acts 25:23 and the prominent men of the c
Acts 27: 5 we came to Myra, a c of Lycia
Acts 27: 8 Havens, near the c of Lasea
Rom 16:23 the treasurer of the c,
2Co 11:26 Gentiles, in perils in the c
2Co 11:32 was guarding the c of the
Tit 1: 5 in every c as I commanded you
Heb 11:10 the c which has foundations
Heb 11:16 He has prepared a c for them
Heb 12:22 to the c of the living God,
Heb 13:14 here we have no continuing c
Jas 4:13 will go to such and such a c
Rev 3:12 the name of the c of My God
Rev 11: 2 c under foot for forty-two
Rev 11: 8 in the street of the great c
Rev 11:13 and a tenth of the c fell
Rev 14: 8 is fallen, that great c,
Rev 14:20 was trampled outside the c
Rev 16:19 Now the great c was divided
Rev 17:18 whom you saw is that great c
Rev 18:10 c Babylon, that mighty c
Rev 18:16 that great c that was clothed
Rev 18:18 What is like this great c
Rev 18:19 Alas, alas, that great c
Rev 18:21 c Babylon shall be thrown
Rev 20: 9 the saints and the beloved c
Rev 21: 2 Then I, John, saw the holy c
Rev 21:10 and showed me the great c
Rev 21:14 Now the wall of the c had
Rev 21:15 a gold reed to measure the c
Rev 21:16 the c is laid out as a square
Rev 21:16 measured the c with the reed
Rev 21:18 the c was pure gold, like
Rev 21:19 of the wall of the c were
Rev 21:21 street of the c was pure gold
Rev 21:23 the c had no need of the sun
Rev 22:14 through the gates into the c
Rev 22:19 Book of Life, from the holy c

CITY'S (*see* CITY)
2Sa 12:27 have taken the c water supply
Ezek 45: 7 district and the c property
Ezek 45: 7 the c property, extending
Ezek 48:21 of the c property, next to

CLAD
Is 59:17 was c with zeal as a cloak

CLAIM (*see* CLAIMING, CLAIMS)
Judg 7: 2 lest Israel c glory for
Job 3: 5 and the shadow of death c it
Is 40:27 my just c is passed over by
Jer 37:12 the land of Benjamin to c his

CLAIMING (*see* CLAIM)
Acts 5:36 rose up, c to be somebody
Acts 8: 9 c that he was someone great,

CLAIMS (*see* CLAIM)
Ex 22: 9 which another c to be his

CLAMOR (*see* CLAMOROUS)
Eph 4:31 bitterness, wrath, anger, c

CLAMOROUS (*see* CLAMOR)
Prov 9:13 A foolish woman is c

CLAN (*see* CLANS)
Josh 7:17 and he brought the c of Judah
Judg 6:15 Indeed my c is the weakest in

CLANGING
1Co 13: 1 sounding brass or a c cymbal

CLANS (*see* CLAN)
1Sa 10:19 by your tribes and by your c
1Sa 23:23 throughout all the c of Judah

CLAP (*see* CLAPPED, CLAPS)
Job 27:23 Men shall c their hands at
Ps 47: 1 c your hands, all you peoples
Ps 98: 8 Let the rivers c their hands
Is 55:12 the field shall c their hands
Lam 2:15 All who pass by c their hands
Nah 3:19 will c their hands over you

CLAPPED (*see* CLAP)
2Ki 11:12 they c their hands and said,
Ezek 25: 6 Because you c your hands,

CLAPS (*see* CLAP)
Job 34:37 he c his hands among us, and

CLARITY
Ex 24:10 the very heavens in its c

CLASH
Job 39:21 he gallops into the c of arms

CLASPED (*see* CLASPS)
Ex 26: 5 loops may be **c** to one another

CLASPS (*see* CLASPED)
Ex 26: 6 shall make fifty **c** of gold
Ex 26: 6 curtains together with the **c**
Ex 26:11 you shall make fifty bronze **c**
Ex 26:11 put the **c** into the loops, and
Ex 26:33 hang the veil from the **c**
Ex 35:11 its tent, its covering, its **c**
Ex 36:13 And he made fifty **c** of gold
Ex 36:13 to one another with the **c**
Ex 36:18 He also made fifty bronze **c**
Ex 39:33 its **c**, its boards, its bars,

CLASS
1Ki 12:31 from every **c** of people, who
1Ki 13:33 **c** of people for the high
2Ki 17:32 from every **c** they appointed
2Co 10:12 For we dare not **c** ourselves

CLATTER (*see* CLATTERING)
Judg 5:28 tarries the **c** of his chariots

CLATTERING (*see* CLATTER)
Nah 3: 2 horses, of **c** chariots

CLAUDA
Acts 27:16 shelter of an island called **C**

CLAUDIA
2Ti 4:21 as well as Pudens, Linus, **C**

CLAUDIUS (*see* CAESAR)
Acts 11:28 in the days of **C** Caesar
Acts 18: 2 **C** had commanded all the Jews
Acts 23:26 **C** Lysias, to the most

CLAWS
Dan 4:33 and his nails like birds' **c**

CLAY
1Ki 7:46 king had them cast in **c** molds
2Ch 4:17 king had them cast in **c** molds
Job 4:19 who dwell in houses of **c**,
Job 10: 9 that You have made me like **c**
Job 13:12 defenses are defenses of **c**
Job 27:16 and piles up clothing like **c**
Job 33: 6 have been formed out of **c**
Job 38:14 on form like **c** under a seal
Ps 40: 2 pit, Out of the miry **c**, And
Is 29:16 potter be esteemed as the **c**
Is 41:25 as the potter treads **c**
Is 45: 9 Shall the **c** say to him who
Is 64: 8 we are the **c**, and You our
Jer 18: 4 **c** was marred in the hand of
Jer 18: 6 as the **c** is in the potter's
Jer 43: 9 Judah, in the **c** in the brick
Lam 4: 2 they are regarded as **c** pots
Ezek 4: 1 son of man, take a **c** tablet
Dan 2:33 partly of iron and partly of **c**
Dan 2:34 on its feet of iron and **c**, and
Dan 2:35 Then the iron, the **c**, the
Dan 2:41 and toes, partly of potter's **c**
Dan 2:41 the iron mixed with ceramic **c**
Dan 2:42 partly of iron and partly of **c**
Dan 2:43 saw iron mixed with ceramic **c**
Dan 2:43 as iron does not mix with **c**
Dan 2:45 the iron, the bronze, the **c**
Nah 3:14 Go into the **c** and tread the
John 9: 6 and made **c** with the saliva
John 9: 6 of the blind man with the **c**
John 9:11 A Man called Jesus made **c**
John 9:14 Sabbath when Jesus made the **c**
John 9:15 He put **c** on my eyes, and I
Rom 9:21 potter have power over the **c**
2Ti 2:20 silver, but also of wood and **c**

CLEAN (*see* CLEANNESS, CLEANSE, UNCLEAN)
Gen 7: 2 seven each of every **c** animal
Gen 7: 8 Of **c** beasts, of beasts that
Gen 8:20 and took of every **c** animal
Gen 8:20 animal and of every **c** bird
Lev 4:12 outside the camp to a **c** place
Lev 6:11 outside the camp to a **c** place
Lev 7:19 And as for the **c** flesh, all
Lev 7:19 all who are **c** may eat of it
Lev 10:10 and between unclean and **c**,
Lev 10:14 you shall eat in a **c** place
Lev 11:32 then it shall be **c**
Lev 11:36 plenty of water, shall be **c**
Lev 11:37 is to be sown, it remains **c**
Lev 11:47 between the unclean and the **c**
Lev 12: 7 she shall be **c** from the flow
Lev 12: 8 for her, and she will be **c**
Lev 13: 6 priest shall pronounce him **c**
Lev 13: 6 wash his clothes and be **c**
Lev 13:13 him **c** who has the sore
Lev 13:13 He is **c**
Lev 13:17 him **c** who has the sore
Lev 13:17 He is **c**
Lev 13:23 priest shall pronounce him **c**
Lev 13:28 priest shall pronounce him **c**
Lev 13:34 priest shall pronounce him **c**
Lev 13:34 wash his clothes and be **c**
Lev 13:37 He is **c**, and the priest shall
Lev 13:37 priest shall pronounce him **c**
Lev 13:39 He is **c**
Lev 13:40 head, he is bald, but he is **c**
Lev 13:41 on the forehead, but he is **c**
Lev 13:58 a second time, and shall be **c**
Lev 13:59 to pronounce it **c** or to
Lev 14: 4 **c** birds, cedar wood, scarlet,
Lev 14: 7 and shall pronounce him **c**
Lev 14: 8 in water, that he may be **c**
Lev 14: 9 in water, and he shall be **c**
Lev 14:11 the priest who makes him **c**
Lev 14:11 the man who is to be made **c**
Lev 14:20 for him, and he shall be **c**
Lev 14:48 shall pronounce the house **c**
Lev 14:53 the house, and it shall be **c**
Lev 14:57 it is unclean and when it is **c**
Lev 15: 8 spits on him who is **c**, then
Lev 15:13 then he shall be **c**
Lev 15:28 and after that she shall be **c**
Lev 16:30 that you may be **c** from all
Lev 17:15 Then he shall be **c**
Lev 20:25 distinguish between **c** beasts
Lev 20:25 between unclean birds and **c**
Lev 22: 4 holy offerings until he is **c**
Lev 22: 7 sun goes down he shall be **c**
Num 5:28 not defiled herself, and is **c**
Num 8: 7 and so make themselves **c**
Num 9:13 But the man who is **c** and is
Num 18:11 Everyone who is **c** in your
Num 18:13 Everyone who is **c** in your
Num 19: 9 Then a man who is **c** shall
Num 19: 9 outside the camp in a **c** place
Num 19:12 then he will be **c**
Num 19:12 seventh day, he will not be **c**
Num 19:18 A **c** person shall take hyssop
Num 19:19 The **c** person shall sprinkle
Num 19:19 and at evening he shall be **c**
Num 31:23 the fire, and it shall be **c**
Num 31:24 on the seventh day and be **c**
Deut 12:15 the **c** may eat of it, of the
Deut 12:22 and the **c** alike may eat them
Deut 14:11 All **c** birds you may eat
Deut 14:20 You may eat all **c** birds
Deut 15:22 the **c** person alike may eat it
2Ki 5:10 to you, and you shall be **c**
2Ki 5:12 I not wash in them and be **c**
2Ki 5:13 says to you, 'Wash, and be **c**'
2Ki 5:14 a little child, and he was **c**
2Ch 30:17 for everyone who was not **c**
Ezra 6:20 all of them were ritually **c**
Job 11: 4 pure, And I am **c** in your eyes
Job 14: 4 Who can bring a **c** thing out
Job 17: 9 he who has **c** hands will be
Ps 19: 9 The fear of the LORD is **c**
Ps 24: 4 He who has **c** hands and a pure
Ps 51: 7 with hyssop, and I shall be **c**
Ps 51:10 Create in me a **c** heart, O God
Prov 14: 4 no oxen are, the trough is **c**
Prov 20: 9 I have made my heart **c**, I am
Eccl 9: 2 to the good, the **c**, and the
Is 1:16 yourselves, make yourselves **c**
Is 28: 8 so that no place is **c**
Is 52:11 from the midst of her, be **c**
Is 66:20 bring an offering in a **c**
Jer 13:27 Will you still not be made **c**
Ezek 22:26 between the unclean and the **c**
Ezek 36:25 will sprinkle **c** water on you
Ezek 36:25 on you, and you shall be **c**
Ezek 44:23 between the unclean and the **c**
Zech 3: 5 Let them put a **c** turban on
Zech 3: 5 So they put a **c** turban on
Matt 8: 2 willing, You can make me **c**
Matt 23:26 outside of them may be **c** also
Matt 27:59 wrapped it in a **c** linen cloth
Mark 1:40 willing, You can make me **c**
Luke 5:12 willing, You can make me **c**
Luke 11:39 outside of the cup and dish **c**
Luke 11:41 all things are **c** to you
John 13:10 his feet, but is completely **c**
John 13:10 and you are **c**, but not all of
John 13:11 You are not all **c**
John 15: 3 You are already **c** because of
Acts 18: 6 I am **c**
Rev 19: 8 be arrayed in fine linen, **c**
Rev 19:14 in fine linen, white and **c**

CLEANNESS (*see* CLEAN)
2Sa 22:21 according to the **c** of my
2Sa 22:25 according to my **c** in His eyes
Ps 18:20 According to the **c** of my
Ps 18:24 According to the **c** of my
Amos 4: 6 Also I gave you **c** of teeth in

CLEANSE (*see* CLEAN, CLEANSED, CLEANSES, CLEANSING)
Ex 29:36 You shall **c** the altar when
Lev 14:49 to **c** the house, two birds,
Lev 14:52 he shall **c** the house with the
Lev 16:19 **c** it, and sanctify it from the
Lev 16:30 to **c** you, that you may be
Num 8: 6 Israel and **c** them ceremonially
Num 8: 7 shall do to them to **c** them
Num 8:15 So you shall **c** them and offer
Num 8:21 atonement for them to **c** them
2Ch 29:15 to **c** the house of the LORD
2Ch 29:16 the house of the LORD to **c** it
Neh 13: 9 commanded them to **c** the rooms
Neh 13:22 that they should **c** themselves
Job 9:30 and **c** my hands with soap,
Ps 19:12 **C** me from secret faults
Ps 51: 2 iniquity, And **c** me from my sin
Ps 119: 9 How can a young man **c** his way
Prov 20:30 Blows that hurt **c** away evil
Jer 4:11 not to fan or to **c**
Jer 33: 8 I will **c** them from all their
Ezek 16: 4 you washed in water to **c** you
Ezek 36:25 I will **c** you from all your
Ezek 36:33 that I **c** you from all your
Ezek 37:23 have sinned, and will **c** them
Ezek 39:12 them, in order to **c** the land
Ezek 39:14 the ground, in order to **c** it
Ezek 39:16 Thus they shall **c** the land
Ezek 43:20 thus you shall **c** it and make
Ezek 43:22 and they shall **c** the altar
Ezek 45:18 blemish and **c** the sanctuary
Matt 10: 8 **c** the lepers, raise the dead,
Matt 23:25 For you **c** the outside of the
Matt 23:26 first **c** the inside of the cup
2Co 7: 1 let us **c** ourselves from all
Eph 5:26 and **c** it with the washing of
Jas 4: 8 **C** your hands, you sinners
1Jn 1: 9 our sins and to **c** us from all

CLEANSED (*see* CLEANSE)
Lev 14: 4 him who is to be **c** two living
Lev 14: 7 is to be **c** from the leprosy
Lev 14: 8 He who is to be **c** shall wash
Lev 14:14 ear of him who is to be **c**
Lev 14:17 ear of him who is to be **c**
Lev 14:18 head of him who is to be **c**
Lev 14:19 to be **c** from his uncleanness
Lev 14:25 ear of him who is to be **c**
Lev 14:28 ear of him who is to be **c**
Lev 14:29 head of him who is to be **c**
Lev 14:31 is to be **c** before the LORD
Lev 15:13 is **c** of his discharge, then
Lev 15:28 But if she is **c** of her
Josh 22:17 we are not **c** until this day
2Sa 11: 4 her, for she was **c** from her
2Ch 29:18 We have **c** all the house of
2Ch 30:18 had not **c** themselves, yet
2Ch 30:19 he is not **c** according to the
2Ch 34: 5 and **c** Judah and Jerusalem
Neh 13:30 Thus I **c** them of everything
Ps 73:13 Surely I have **c** my heart in
Ezek 22:24 **c** or rained on in the day of
Ezek 43:22 as they **c** it with the bull
Ezek 44:26 After he is **c**, they shall
Dan 8:14 then the sanctuary shall be **c**
Matt 8: 3 I am willing; be **c**."
Matt 8: 3 immediately his leprosy was **c**
Matt 11: 5 the lepers are **c** and the deaf
Mark 1:41 I am willing; be **c**."
Mark 1:42 leprosy left him, and he was **c**
Luke 4:27 none of them was **c** except
Luke 5:13 I am willing; be **c**."
Luke 7:22 lame walk, the lepers are **c**
Luke 17:14 as they went, they were **c**
Luke 17:17 Were there not ten **c**
Acts 10:15 What God has **c** you must not
Acts 11: 9 What God has **c** you must not

CLEANSES (*see* CLEANSE)
2Ti 2:21 Therefore if anyone **c** himself
1Jn 1: 7 His Son **c** us from all sin

CLEANSING (*see* CLEANSE)
Lev 13: 7 seen by the priest for his **c**
Lev 13:35 over the skin after his **c**
Lev 14: 2 leper for the day of his **c**
Lev 14:23 on the eighth day for his **c**
Lev 14:32 who cannot afford the usual **c**
Lev 15:13 himself seven days for his **c**
Num 6: 9 his head on the day of his **c**
Ezek 43:23 When you have finished **c** it
Mark 1:44 offer for your **c** those things
Luke 5:14 make an offering for your **c**

CLEAR (*see* CLEARED, CLEARING, CLEARLY, CLEARS)
Gen 24:41 You will be **c** from this oath
Gen 44:16 Or how shall we **c** ourselves
Lev 26:10 **c** out the old because of the
Josh 17:15 **c** a place for yourself there
2Sa 23: 4 by **c** shining after rain
1Ki 7:36 there was a **c** space on each
Song 6:10 **c** as the sun, Awesome as an
Is 18: 4 place like **c** heat in sunshine
Ezek 25: 9 I will **c** the territory of
Ezek 32:14 I will make their waters **c**
Ezek 34:18 to have drunk of the **c** waters
2Co 7:11 to be **c** in this matter
Rev 21:11 a jasper stone, **c** as crystal
Rev 21:18 was pure gold, like **c** glass
Rev 22: 1 **c** as crystal, proceeding from

CLEARED (*see* CLEAR)
Job 37:21 the wind has passed and **c** them
Is 5: 2 **c** out its stones, and planted

CLEARING (*see* CLEAR)
Ex 34: 7 sin, by no means **c** the guilty
2Co 7:11 what **c** of yourselves, what

CLEARLY (*see* CLEAR)
1Sa 2:27 Did I not **c** reveal Myself to
Ezra 4:18 us has been **c** read before me
Matt 7: 5 then you will see **c** to remove
Mark 8:25 restored and saw everyone **c**
Luke 6:42 then you will see **c** to remove
John 3:21 that his deeds may be **c** seen
Acts 10: 3 hour of the day he saw **c** in a
Rom 1:20 attributes are **c** seen, being
Gal 3: 1 was **c** portrayed among you as
1Ti 5:24 Some men's sins are **c** evident
1Ti 5:25 works of some are **c** evident

CLEARS (*see* CLEAR)
Num 14:18 He by no means **c** the guilty

CLEFT (*see* CLEFTS)
Ex 33:22 put you in the **c** of the rock
Judg 15: 8 dwelt in the **c** of the rock of
Judg 15:11 to the **c** of the rock of Etam

CLEFTS (*see* CLEFT)
Job 30: 6 live in the **c** of the valleys
Song 2:14 in the **c** of the rock, in the
Is 2:21 to go into the **c** of the rocks
Is 7:19 in the **c** of the rocks, and on
Is 57: 5 under the **c** of the rocks
Jer 49:16 dwell in the **c** of the rock
Obad 3 dwell in the **c** of the rock

CLEMENT
Phil 4: 3 me in the gospel, with **C** also

CLEOPAS (*see* ALPHAEUS)
Luke 24:18 one whose name was **C**

CLERK
Acts 19:35 when the city **c** had quieted

CLIFF (*see* CLIFFS)
Ps 141: 6 by the sides of the **c**, And
Song 2:14 in the secret places of the **c**
Luke 4:29 throw Him down over the **c**

CLIFFS (*see* CLIFF)
Ps 104:18 The **c** are a refuge for the

CLIMB (*see* CLIMBED, CLIMBS)
Jer 4:29 thickets and **c** up on the rocks
Joel 2: 7 they **c** the wall like men of
Joel 2: 9 they **c** into the houses, they
Amos 9: 2 though they **c** up to heaven,

CLIMBED (*see* CLIMB)
1Sa 14:13 Jonathan **c** up on his hands and
Luke 19: 4 **c** up into a sycamore tree to

CLIMBS (*see* CLIMB)
2Sa 5: 8 Whoever **c** up by way of the
John 10: 1 but **c** up some other way, the

CLING (*see* CLINGS, CLUNG)
Deut 28:21 plague **c** to you until He has
Deut 28:60 and they shall **c** to you
Deut 30:20 and that you may **c** to Him
Josh 23:12 **c** to the remnant of these
2Ki 5:27 of Naaman shall **c** to you and
Job 38:38 and the clods **c** together
Ps 101: 3 It shall not **c** to me
Ps 102: 5 My bones **c** to my skin
Ps 119:31 I **c** to Your testimonies
Ps 137: 6 Let my tongue **c** to the roof
Is 14: 1 they will **c** to the house of
Jer 13:11 house of Judah to **c** to Me
Ezek 3:26 I will make your tongue **c** to
John 20:17 Do not **c** to Me, for I have
Rom 12: 9 **C** to what is good

CLINGS (*see* CLING)
Job 19:20 My bone **c** to my skin and to my
Ps 22:15 And My tongue **c** to My jaws
Ps 41: 8 they say, "**c** to him
Ps 44:25 Our body **c** to the ground
Ps 119:25 My soul **c** to the dust
Jer 13:11 For as the sash **c** to the
Lam 4: 4 **c** to the roof of its mouth
Lam 4: 8 their skin **c** to their bones,
Luke 10:11 dust of your city which **c** to

CLIPPED
Jer 48:37 be bald, and every beard **c**

CLOAK
Ps 102:26 Like a **c** You will change them
Is 59:17 and was clad with zeal as a **c**
Matt 5:40 let him have your **c** also
Luke 6:29 him who takes away your **c**
1Th 2: 5 nor a **c** for covetousness
2Ti 4:13 Bring the **c** that I left with
Heb 1:12 Like a **c** You will fold them
1Pe 2:16 your liberty as a **c** for vice

CLODS
Job 21:33 The **c** of the valley shall be
Job 38:38 and the **c** cling together
Is 28:24 his soil and breaking the **c**
Hos 10:11 Jacob shall break his **c**
Joel 1:17 grain shrivels under the **c**

CLOPAS
John 19:25 sister, Mary the wife of **C**

CLOSE (*see* CLOSED, CLOSELY, CLOSER, CLOSEST)
Gen 12:11 when he was **c** to entering
Ex 25:27 rings shall be **c** to the frame
Ex 37:14 The rings were **c** to the frame
Lev 3: 9 remove **c** to the backbone
Lev 25:47 **c** to you becomes rich, and one
Lev 25:47 or sojourner **c** to you, or to
Ruth 2: 8 but stay **c** by my young women
Ruth 2:21 You shall stay **c** by my young
Ruth 2:23 So she stayed **c** by the young
2Sa 19:42 king is a **c** relative of ours
2Ki 10:11 his **c** acquaintances and his
2Ki 25:19 war, five men of the king's **c**
Neh 6:10 let us **c** the doors of the
Job 19:14 my **c** friends have forgotten
Job 19:19 All my **c** friends abhor me, and
Job 32:12 I paid **c** attention to you
Ps 63: 8 My soul follows **c** behind You
Jer 38:22 Your **c** friends have set upon
Jer 42:16 **c** after you there in Egypt
Jer 52:25 seven men of the king's **c**
Luke 19:43 and **c** you in on every side,
Acts 10:24 his relatives and **c** friends
Acts 27:13 sea, they sailed **c** by Crete
Phil 2:30 of Christ he came **c** to death

CLOSED (*see* CLOSE)
Gen 2:21 **c** up the flesh in its place
Gen 20:18 for the LORD had **c** up all the
Ex 14: 3 the wilderness has **c** them in
Num 16:33 the earth **c** over them, and
Judg 3:22 the fat **c** over the blade, for
1Sa 1: 5 the LORD had **c** her womb
1Sa 1: 6 the LORD had **c** her womb
Neh 4: 7 gaps were beginning to be **c**
Ps 17:10 They have **c** up their fat
Is 1: 6 have not been **c** or bound up
Is 29:10 has **c** your eyes, namely, the
Dan 12: 9 for the words are **c** up and
Jon 2: 5 the deep **c** around me
Jon 2: 6 its bars **c** behind me forever
Matt 13:15 and their eyes they have **c**
Luke 4:20 Then He **c** the book, and gave
Acts 28:27 and their eyes they have **c**

CLOSELY (*see* CLOSE)
Job 13:27 and watch **c** all my paths
Mark 3: 2 And they watched Him **c**,
Luke 6: 7 and Pharisees watched Him **c**
Luke 14: 1 that they watched Him **c**

CLOSER (*see* CLOSE)
Prov 18:24 who sticks **c** than a brother

CLOSEST (*see* CLOSE)
Esth 1:14 those **c** to him being Carshena

CLOTH (*see* CLOTHS)
Num 4: 6 that a **c** entirely of blue
Num 4: 7 they shall spread a blue **c**
Num 4: 8 spread over them a scarlet **c**
Num 4: 9 And they shall take a blue **c**
Num 4:11 they shall spread a blue **c**
Num 4:12 put them in a blue **c**, cover
Num 4:13 and spread a purple **c** over it
Deut 22:17 And they shall spread the **c**
1Sa 21: 9 wrapped in a **c** behind the
2Ki 8:15 day that he took a thick **c**
Ezek 16:10 clothed you in embroidered **c**
Ezek 16:13 linen, silk, and embroidered **c**
Matt 9:16 unshrunk **c** on an old garment
Matt 27:59 wrapped it in a clean linen **c**
Mark 2:21 unshrunk **c** on an old garment
Mark 14:51 Him, having a linen **c** thrown
Mark 14:52 and he left the linen **c** and
John 11:44 his face was wrapped with a **c**

CLOTHE (*see* CLOTHED, CLOTHES, UNCLOTHED)
Ex 40:14 sons and **c** them with tunics
Esth 4: 4 sent garments to **c** Mordecai
Job 10:11 **c** me with skin and flesh, and
Ps 132:16 I will also **c** her priests
Ps 132:18 enemies I will **c** with shame
Prov 23:21 will **c** a man with rags
Is 15: 3 **c** themselves with sackcloth
Is 22:21 I will **c** him with your robe
Is 49:18 You shall surely **c** yourselves
Is 50: 3 I **c** the heavens with
Jer 4: 8 **c** yourself with sackcloth,
Jer 4:30 Though you **c** yourself with
Jer 6:26 **c** yourself with sackcloth, and
Ezek 26:16 they will **c** themselves with
Ezek 34: 3 **c** yourselves with the wool
Ezek 44:18 they shall not **c** themselves
Hag 1: 6 you **c** yourselves, but no one
Zech 3: 4 I will **c** you with rich robes
Matt 6:30 will He not much more **c** you
Matt 25:38 You in, or naked and **c** You
Matt 25:43 in, naked and you did not **c** Me
Luke 12:28 how much more will He **c** you

CLOTHED (*see* CLOTHE)
Gen 3:21 tunics of skin, and **c** them
Gen 41:42 he **c** him in garments of fine
Lev 8: 7 **c** him with the robe, and put
1Sa 17:38 So Saul **c** David with his
1Sa 17:38 he also **c** him with a coat of
2Sa 1:24 who **c** you in scarlet, with
1Ki 11:29 he had **c** himself with a new
1Ch 15:27 David was **c** with a robe of
1Ch 21:16 **c** in sackcloth, fell on their
2Ch 5:12 **c** in white linen, having
2Ch 6:41 be **c** with salvation, and let
2Ch 18: 9 **c** in their robes, sat each on
2Ch 28:15 from the spoil they **c** all who
Esth 4: 2 king's gate **c** with sackcloth
Job 8:22 hate you will be **c** with shame
Job 29:14 on righteousness, and it **c** me
Job 39:19 Have you **c** his neck with
Ps 30:11 and **c** me with gladness,
Ps 35:26 Let them be **c** with shame and
Ps 65: 6 strength, Being **c** with power
Ps 65:13 pastures are **c** with flocks
Ps 93: 1 reigns, He is **c** with majesty
Ps 93: 1 The LORD is **c**, He has girded
Ps 104: 1 You are **c** with honor and
Ps 109:18 As he **c** himself with cursing

Ps 109:29 my accusers be **c** with shame
Ps 132: 9 be **c** with righteousness, And
Prov 31:21 household is **c** with scarlet
Is 61:10 for He has **c** me with the
Ezek 7:27 will be **c** with desolation
Ezek 9: 2 among them was **c** with linen
Ezek 9: 3 to the man **c** with linen, who
Ezek 9:11 the man **c** with linen, who had
Ezek 10: 2 spoke to the man **c** with linen
Ezek 10: 6 commanded the man **c** in linen
Ezek 10: 7 hands of the man **c** with linen
Ezek 16:10 I **c** you in embroidered cloth
Ezek 16:10 I **c** you with fine linen and
Ezek 23: 6 who were **c** in purple,
Ezek 23:12 **c** most gorgeously, horsemen
Ezek 38: 4 and horsemen, all splendidly **c**
Dan 5: 7 shall be **c** with purple and
Dan 5:16 you shall be **c** with purple
Dan 5:29 they **c** Daniel with purple and
Dan 10: 5 a certain man **c** in linen
Dan 12: 6 said to the man **c** in linen
Dan 12: 7 I heard the man **c** in linen
Zeph 1: 8 and all such as are **c** with
Zech 3: 3 Now Joshua was **c** with filthy
Matt 3: 4 himself was **c** in camel's hair
Matt 11: 8 A man **c** in soft garments
Matt 25:36 I was naked and you **c** Me
Mark 1: 6 Now John was **c** with camel's
Mark 5:15 had the legion, sitting and **c**
Mark 15:17 And they **c** Him with purple
Mark 16: 5 man **c** in a long white robe
Luke 7:25 A man **c** in soft garments
Luke 8:35 at the feet of Jesus, **c** and in
Luke 16:19 rich man who was **c** in purple
1Co 4:11 and thirst, and we are poorly **c**
2Co 5: 2 earnestly desiring to be **c**
2Co 5: 3 if indeed, having been **c**, we
2Co 5: 4 be unclothed, but further **c**
1Pe 5: 5 and be **c** with humility, for
Rev 1:13 **c** with a garment down to the
Rev 3: 5 shall be **c** in white garments
Rev 3:18 garments, that you may be **c**
Rev 4: 4 sitting, **c** in white robes
Rev 7: 9 **c** with white robes, with palm
Rev 10: 1 from heaven, **c** with a cloud
Rev 11: 3 and sixty days, **c** in sackcloth
Rev 12: 1 a woman **c** with the sun, with
Rev 15: 6 **c** in pure bright linen, and
Rev 18:16 city that was **c** in fine linen
Rev 19:13 He was **c** with a robe dipped
Rev 19:14 **c** in fine linen, white and

CLOTHES (*see* CLOTHE, CLOTHING)
Gen 27:15 **c** of her elder son Esau,
Gen 37:29 and he tore his **c**
Gen 37:34 Then Jacob tore his **c**, put
Gen 44:13 Then they tore their **c**, and
Gen 49:11 his **c** in the blood of grapes
Ex 12:34 in their **c** on their shoulders
Ex 19:10 and let them wash their **c**
Ex 19:14 and they washed their **c**
Lev 10: 6 your heads nor tear your **c**
Lev 11:25 any of them shall wash his **c**
Lev 11:28 such carcass shall wash his **c**
Lev 11:40 its carcass shall wash his **c**
Lev 11:40 its carcass shall wash his **c**
Lev 13: 6 scab, and he shall wash his **c**
Lev 13:34 He shall wash his **c** and be
Lev 13:45 his **c** shall be torn and his
Lev 14: 8 be cleansed shall wash his **c**
Lev 14: 9 He shall wash his **c** and wash
Lev 14:47 in the house shall wash his **c**
Lev 14:47 in the house shall wash his **c**
Lev 15: 5 his bed shall wash his **c** and
Lev 15: 6 sat shall wash his **c** and bathe
Lev 15: 7 discharge shall wash his **c**
Lev 15: 8 then he shall wash his **c**
Lev 15:10 those things shall wash his **c**
Lev 15:11 in water, he shall wash his **c**
Lev 15:13 for his cleansing, wash his **c**
Lev 15:21 her bed shall wash his **c** and
Lev 15:22 she sat on shall wash his **c**
Lev 15:27 he shall wash his **c** and bathe
Lev 16:26 scapegoat shall wash his **c**
Lev 16:28 burns them shall wash his **c**
Lev 16:32 and put on the linen **c**, the
Lev 17:15 he shall both wash his **c**
Lev 21:10 his head nor tear his **c**
Num 8: 7 and let them wash their **c**
Num 8:21 themselves and washed their **c**
Num 14: 6 out the land, tore their **c**
Num 19: 7 the priest shall wash his **c**
Num 19: 8 it shall wash his **c** in water
Num 19:10 the heifer shall wash his **c**
Num 19:19 purify himself, wash his **c**
Num 19:21 purification shall wash his **c**
Num 31:24 your **c** on the seventh day
Deut 21:13 off the **c** of her captivity
Deut 29: 5 Your **c** have not worn out on
Josh 7: 6 Then Joshua tore his **c**, and
Judg 3:16 his **c** on his right thigh
Judg 11:35 saw her, that he tore his **c**
Judg 17:10 silver per year, a suit of **c**
1Sa 4:12 to Shiloh with his **c** torn
1Sa 19:13 head, and covered it with **c**
1Sa 19:24 And he also stripped off his **c**
1Sa 28: 8 himself and put on other **c**
2Sa 1: 2 Saul's camp with his **c** torn
2Sa 1:11 David took hold of his own **c**
2Sa 3:31 Tear your **c**, gird yourselves
2Sa 12:20 himself, and changed his **c**
2Sa 13:31 stood by with their **c** torn
2Sa 19:24 mustache, nor washed his **c**
1Ki 21:27 words, that he tore his **c**
2Ki 2:12 And he took hold of his own **c**
2Ki 5: 7 letter, that he tore his **c**
2Ki 5: 8 king of Israel had torn his **c**
2Ki 5: 8 Why have you torn your **c**
2Ki 6:30 the woman, that he tore his **c**
2Ki 11:14 And Athaliah tore her **c** and
2Ki 18:37 to Hezekiah with their **c** torn
2Ki 19: 1 heard it, that he tore his **c**
2Ki 22:11 the Law, that he tore his **c**
2Ki 22:19 a curse, and you tore your **c**
2Ch 23:13 So Athaliah tore her **c** and
2Ch 34:19 the Law, that he tore his **c**
2Ch 34:27 before Me, and you tore your **c**
Neh 4:23 followed me took off our **c**
Neh 9:21 their **c** did not wear out and
Esth 4: 1 had happened, he tore his **c**
Job 9:31 and my own **c** will abhor me
Prov 6:27 bosom, and his **c** not be burned
Is 36:22 to Hezekiah with their **c** torn
Is 37: 1 heard it, that he tore his **c**
Jer 38:11 and took from there old **c**
Jer 38:12 Please put these old **c** and
Jer 41: 5 beards shaved and their **c** torn
Ezek 16:39 also strip you of your **c**,
Ezek 23:26 also strip you of your **c** and
Ezek 27:24 in purple **c**, in embroidered
Amos 2: 8 altar on **c** taken in pledge
Zech 3: 5 and they put the **c** on him
Matt 6:30 Now if God so **c** the grass of
Matt 17: 2 His **c** became as white as the
Matt 21: 7 colt, laid their **c** on them
Matt 24:18 not go back to get his **c**
Matt 26:65 the high priest tore his **c**
Matt 27:31 off Him, put His own **c** on Him
Mark 5:28 If only I may touch His **c**
Mark 5:30 Who touched My **c**
Mark 9: 3 His **c** became shining,
Mark 14:63 the high priest tore his **c**
Mark 15:20 off Him, put His own **c** on Him
Luke 8:27 And he wore no **c**, nor did he
Luke 12:28 If then God so **c** the grass
Luke 19:36 spread their **c** on the road
Acts 7:58 witnesses laid down their **c**
Acts 14:14 heard this, they tore their **c**
Acts 16:22 magistrates tore off their **c**
Acts 22:20 guarding the **c** of those who
Acts 22:23 cried out and tore off their **c**
Jas 2: 2 in a poor man in filthy **c**
Jas 2: 3 to the one wearing the fine **c**

CLOTHING (*see* CLOTHES)
Gen 24:53 silver, jewelry of gold, and **c**
Gen 27:27 he smelled the smell of his **c**
Gen 28:20 bread to eat and **c** to put on,
Gen 41:14 and he shaved, changed his **c**
Ex 3:22 articles of gold, and **c**
Ex 12:35 articles of gold, and **c**
Ex 21:10 not diminish her food, her **c**
Ex 22: 9 ox, a donkey, a sheep, or **c**
Lev 11:32 of wood or **c** or skin or sack
Deut 10:18 giving him food and **c**
Deut 22:12 of the **c** with which you cover
Josh 22: 8 iron, and with very much **c**
Judg 14:12 and thirty changes of **c**
Judg 14:13 and thirty changes of **c**
Judg 14:19 and gave the changes of **c** to
2Ki 5: 5 of gold, and ten changes of **c**
2Ki 5:26 receive money and to receive **c**
2Ki 7: 8 from it silver and gold and **c**
Job 22: 6 stripped the naked of their **c**
Job 24: 7 the night naked, without **c**
Job 24:10 poor to go naked, without **c**
Job 27:16 dust, and piles up **c** like clay
Job 31:19 anyone perish for lack of **c**
Ps 22:18 And for My **c** they cast lots
Ps 35:13 were sick, My **c** was sackcloth
Ps 45:13 Her **c** is woven with gold
Prov 27:26 the lambs will provide your **c**
Prov 31:22 her **c** is fine linen and purple
Prov 31:25 Strength and honor are her **c**
Is 3: 6 You have **c**; you be our ruler
Is 3: 7 house is neither food nor **c**
Is 23:18 sufficiently, and for fine **c**
Is 59:17 garments of vengeance for **c**
Jer 10: 9 blue and purple are their **c**
Ezek 16:13 your **c** was of fine linen,
Ezek 18: 7 and covered the naked with **c**
Ezek 18:16 and covered the naked with **c**
Matt 6:25 food and the body more than **c**
Matt 6:28 So why do you worry about **c**
Matt 7:15 who come to you in sheep's **c**
Matt 11: 8 those who wear soft **c** are in
Matt 27:35 and for My **c** they cast lots
Matt 28: 3 and his **c** as white as snow
Luke 10:30 who stripped him of his **c**
Luke 12:23 and the body is more than **c**
John 19:24 and for My **c** they cast lots
Acts 10:30 stood before me in bright **c**
1Ti 2: 9 or gold or pearls or costly **c**
1Ti 6: 8 And having food and **c**, with

CLOTHS (*see* CLOTH)
Ezek 16: 4 nor swathed in swaddling **c**
Luke 2: 7 and wrapped Him in swaddling **c**
Luke 2:12 a Babe wrapped in swaddling **c**
Luke 24:12 he saw the linen **c** lying by
John 20: 5 saw the linen **c** lying there
John 20: 6 saw the linen **c** lying there
John 20: 7 not lying with the linen **c**

CLOUD (*see* CLOUDS, CLOUDY)
Gen 9:13 I set My rainbow in the **c**
Gen 9:14 I bring a **c** over the earth
Gen 9:14 shall be seen in the **c**
Gen 9:16 The rainbow shall be in the **c**
Ex 13:21 a pillar of **c** to lead the way
Ex 13:22 of **c** by day or the pillar of
Ex 14:19 the pillar of **c** went from
Ex 14:20 Thus it was a **c** and darkness
Ex 14:24 the pillar of fire and **c**, and
Ex 16:10 of the LORD appeared in the **c**
Ex 19: 9 I come to you in the thick **c**
Ex 19:16 a thick **c** on the mountain
Ex 24:15 and a **c** covered the mountain
Ex 24:16 the **c** covered it six days
Ex 24:16 out of the midst of the **c**
Ex 24:18 went into the midst of the **c**
Ex 33: 9 the pillar of **c** descended
Ex 33:10 people saw the pillar of **c**
Ex 34: 5 the LORD descended in the **c**
Ex 40:34 Then the **c** covered the
Ex 40:35 because the **c** rested above it
Ex 40:36 When the **c** was taken up from
Ex 40:37 But if the **c** was not taken up
Ex 40:38 For the **c** of the LORD was
Lev 16: 2 in the **c** above the mercy seat
Lev 16:13 that the **c** of incense may
Num 9:15 the **c** covered the tabernacle,
Num 9:16 the **c** covered it by day, and
Num 9:17 Whenever the **c** was taken up
Num 9:17 the place where the **c** settled
Num 9:18 as long as the **c** stayed above
Num 9:19 Even when the **c** continued
Num 9:20 was, when the **c** was above the
Num 9:21 when the **c** remained only from
Num 9:21 when the **c** was taken up in
Num 9:21 whenever the **c** was taken up
Num 9:22 that the **c** remained above the
Num 10:11 that the **c** was taken up from
Num 10:12 then the **c** settled down in
Num 10:34 the **c** of the LORD was above
Num 11:25 the LORD came down in the **c**
Num 12: 5 came down in the pillar of **c**
Num 12:10 And when the **c** departed from
Num 14:14 that Your **c** stands above them
Num 14:14 them in a pillar of **c** by day
Num 16:42 and suddenly the **c** covered it
Deut 1:33 by night and in the **c** by day
Deut 4:11 of heaven, with darkness, **c**

Deut 5:22 the midst of the fire, the **c**
Deut 31:15 tabernacle in a pillar of **c**
Deut 31:15 the pillar of **c** stood above
Judg 20:38 they would make a great **c** of
Judg 20:40 But when the **c** began to rise
1Ki 8:10 that the **c** filled the house
1Ki 8:11 ministering because of the **c**
1Ki 8:12 He would dwell in the dark **c**
1Ki 18:44 There is a **c**, as small as a
2Ch 5:13 the LORD, was filled with a **c**
2Ch 5:14 ministering because of the **c**
2Ch 6: 1 He would dwell in the dark **c**
Neh 9:19 The pillar of the **c** did not
Job 3: 5 may a **c** settle on it
Job 7: 9 As the **c** disappears and
Job 26: 9 and spreads His **c** over it
Job 30:15 has passed like a **c**
Job 37:15 the light of His **c** to shine
Ps 78:14 also He led them with the **c**
Ps 105:39 He spread a **c** for a covering,
Prov 16:15 like a **c** of the latter rain
Is 4: 5 and above her assemblies, a **c**
Is 18: 4 like a **c** of dew in the heat
Is 19: 1 the LORD rides on a swift **c**
Is 25: 5 as heat in the shadow of a **c**
Is 44:22 blotted out, like a thick **c**
Is 44:22 transgressions, and like a **c**
Is 60: 8 are these who fly like a **c**
Lam 2: 1 of Zion with a **c** in His anger
Lam 3:44 covered Yourself with a **c**
Ezek 1: 4 a great **c** with raging fire
Ezek 1:28 rainbow in a **c** on a rainy day
Ezek 8:11 a thick **c** of incense went up
Ezek 10: 3 the **c** filled the inner court
Ezek 10: 4 house was filled with the **c**
Ezek 30:18 a **c** shall cover her, and her
Ezek 32: 7 I will cover the sun with a **c**
Ezek 38: 9 covering the land like a **c**
Ezek 38:16 My people Israel like a **c**
Hos 6: 4 is like a morning **c**, and like
Hos 13: 3 shall be like the morning **c**
Matt 17: 5 a bright **c** overshadowed them
Matt 17: 5 a voice came out of the **c**
Mark 9: 7 a **c** came and overshadowed
Mark 9: 7 and a voice came out of the **c**
Luke 9:34 a **c** came and overshadowed
Luke 9:34 fearful as they entered the **c**
Luke 9:35 a voice came out of the **c**
Luke 12:54 When you see a **c** rising out
Luke 21:27 Man coming in a **c** with power
Acts 1: 9 a **c** received Him out of their
1Co 10: 1 our fathers were under the **c**
1Co 10: 2 baptized into Moses in the **c**
Heb 12: 1 by so great a **c** of witnesses
Rev 10: 1 from heaven, clothed with a **c**
Rev 11:12 ascended to heaven in a **c**
Rev 14:14 looked, and behold, a white **c**
Rev 14:14 on the **c** sat One like the Son
Rev 14:15 voice to Him who sat on the **c**
Rev 14:16 So He who sat on the **c** thrust

CLOUDS (*see* CLOUD)
Deut 33:26 And in His excellency on the **c**
Judg 5: 4 the **c** also poured water
2Sa 22:12 and thick **c** of the skies
2Sa 23: 4 rises, a morning without **c**
1Ki 18:45 the sky became black with **c**
Job 20: 6 and his head reaches to the **c**
Job 22:14 Thick **c** cover Him, so that He
Job 26: 8 up the water in His thick **c**
Job 26: 8 yet the **c** are not broken
Job 35: 5 behold the **c** which are higher
Job 36:28 Which the **c** drop down and pour
Job 36:29 understand the spreading of **c**
Job 37:11 He saturates the thick **c**
Job 37:11 He scatters His bright **c**
Job 37:16 Do you know the balance of **c**
Job 38: 9 when I made the **c** its garment
Job 38:34 lift up your voice to the **c**
Job 38:37 can number the **c** by wisdom
Ps 18:11 And thick **c** of the skies
Ps 18:12 Him, His thick **c** passed with
Ps 36: 5 faithfulness reaches to the **c**
Ps 57:10 And Your truth unto the **c**
Ps 68: 4 Extol Him who rides on the **c**
Ps 68:34 And His strength is in the **c**
Ps 77:17 The **c** poured out water
Ps 78:23 He had commanded the **c** above
Ps 97: 2 **C** and darkness surround Him
Ps 104: 3 Who makes the **c** His chariot
Ps 108: 4 Your truth reaches to the **c**
Ps 147: 8 Who covers the heavens with **c**
Ps 148: 8 Fire and hail, snow and **c**
Prov 3:20 up, and **c** drop down the dew
Prov 8:28 He established the **c** above
Prov 25:14 boasts of giving is like **c**
Eccl 11: 3 If the **c** are full of rain,
Eccl 11: 4 regards the **c** will not reap
Eccl 12: 2 the **c** do not return after the
Is 5: 6 I will also command the **c**
Is 5:30 light is darkened by the **c**
Is 14:14 above the heights of the **c**
Jer 4:13 he shall come up like **c**, and
Ezek 30: 3 it will be a day of **c**, the
Dan 7:13 coming with the **c** of heaven
Joel 2: 2 and gloominess, a day of **c**
Joel 2: 2 like the morning **c** spread
Nah 1: 3 the **c** are the dust of His
Zeph 1:15 and gloominess, a day of **c**
Zech 10: 1 the LORD will make flashing **c**
Matt 24:30 on the **c** of heaven with power
Matt 26:64 and coming on the **c** of heaven
Mark 13:26 in the **c** with great power
Mark 14:62 coming with the **c** of heaven
1Th 4:17 together with them in the **c**
2Pe 2:17 **c** carried by a tempest, to
Jude 12 they are **c** without water,
Rev 1: 7 Behold, He is coming with **c**

CLOUDY (*see* CLOUD)
Neh 9:12 them by day with a **c** pillar
Ps 99: 7 spoke to them in the **c** pillar
Ezek 34:12 they were scattered on a **c**

CLOVEN (*see* CLOVEN-HOOFED)
Lev 11: 3 the hoof, having **c** hooves
Lev 11: 4 or those that have **c** hooves
Lev 11: 4 but does not have **c** hooves
Lev 11: 5 but does not have **c** hooves
Lev 11: 6 but does not have **c** hooves
Lev 11: 7 the hoof, having **c** hooves
Deut 14: 6 every animal with **c** hooves
Deut 14: 7 chew the cud or have **c** hooves
Deut 14: 7 cud but do not have **c** hooves
Deut 14: 8 you, because it has **c** hooves

CLOVEN-HOOFED (*see* CLOVEN)
Lev 11:26 but is not **c** or does not chew

CLUB (*see* CLUBS)
Prov 25:18 his neighbor is like a **c**, a

CLUBS (*see* CLUB)
Matt 26:47 multitude with swords and **c**
Matt 26:55 with swords and **c** to take Me
Mark 14:43 multitude with swords and **c**
Mark 14:48 with swords and **c** to take Me
Luke 22:52 a robber, with swords and **c**

CLUMPS
Job 38:38 when the dust hardens in **c**

CLUNG (*see* CLING)
Ruth 1:14 but Ruth **c** to her
1Ki 11: 2 Solomon **c** to these in love

CLUSTER (*see* CLUSTERS)
Num 13:23 a branch with one **c** of grapes
Num 13:24 because of the **c** which the
Job 38:31 bind the **c** of the Pleiades
Song 1:14 My beloved is to me a **c** of
Is 65: 8 new wine is found in the **c**
Mic 7: 1 there is no **c** to eat of the

CLUSTERS (*see* CLUSTER)
Gen 40:10 and its **c** brought forth ripe
Deut 32:32 of gall, their **c** are bitter
1Sa 25:18 one hundred **c** of raisins
1Sa 30:12 of figs and two **c** of raisins
2Sa 16: 1 one hundred **c** of raisins
Song 7: 7 and your breasts like its **c**
Song 7: 8 breasts be like **c** of the vine
Rev 14:18 gather the **c** of the vine of

CNIDUS
Acts 27: 7 arrived with difficulty off **C**

COAL (*see* COALS)
Is 6: 6 having in his hand a live **c**
Is 47:14 not be a **c** to be warmed by

COALS (*see* COAL)
Lev 16:12 **c** of fire from the altar
2Sa 22: 9 **c** were kindled by it
2Sa 22:13 Him **c** of fire were kindled
1Ki 19: 6 head was a cake baked on **c**
Job 41:21 His breath kindles **c**, and a
Ps 11: 6 the wicked He will rain **c**
Ps 18: 8 **C** were kindled by it
Ps 18:12 with hailstones and **c** of fire
Ps 18:13 Hailstones and **c** of fire
Ps 120: 4 With **c** of the broom tree
Ps 140:10 Let burning **c** fall upon them
Prov 6:28 Can one walk on hot **c**, and his
Prov 25:22 heap **c** of fire on his head
Prov 26:21 As charcoal is to burning **c**
Is 44:12 the tongs works one in the **c**
Is 44:19 also baked bread on its **c**
Is 54:16 who blows the **c** in the fire
Ezek 1:13 was like burning **c** of fire
Ezek 10: 2 fill your hands with **c** of
Ezek 24:11 set the pot empty on the **c**
John 18:18 made a fire of **c** stood there
John 21: 9 they saw a fire of **c** there
Rom 12:20 heap **c** of fire on his head

COARSE
Zech 13: 4 a robe of **c** hair to deceive
Eph 5: 4 nor **c** jesting, which are not

COAST (*see* COASTLAND, COASTLINE, COASTS)
Zeph 2: 7 The **c** shall be for the

COASTLAND (*see* COAST, COASTLANDS)
Gen 10: 5 From these the **c** peoples of
Is 23: 2 you inhabitants of the **c**
Is 23: 6 you inhabitants of the **c**

COASTLANDS (*see* COASTLAND)
Is 24:15 of Israel in the **c** of the sea
Is 41: 1 Keep silence before Me, O **c**
Is 41: 5 The **c** saw it and feared, the
Is 42: 4 the **c** shall wait for His law
Is 42:10 and all that is in it, you **c**
Is 42:12 declare His praise in the **c**
Is 42:15 I will make the rivers **c**, and
Is 49: 1 Listen, O **c**, to Me, and take
Is 51: 5 the **c** will wait upon Me, and
Is 59:18 the **c** He will fully repay
Is 60: 9 Surely the **c** shall wait for
Is 66:19 to the **c** afar off who have
Jer 25:22 the kings of the **c** which are
Ezek 26:15 Will the **c** not shake at the
Ezek 26:18 Now the **c** tremble on the day
Ezek 26:18 the **c** by the sea are troubled
Ezek 27: 3 of the peoples on many **c**,
Ezek 39: 6 who live in security in the **c**
Dan 11:18 shall turn his face to the **c**

COASTLINE (*see* COAST)
Josh 15:12 was the **c** of the Great Sea
Josh 15:47 and the Great Sea with its **c**

COASTS (*see* COAST)
Num 24:24 come from the **c** of Cyprus
Josh 9: 1 in all the **c** of the Great Sea
Jer 2:10 pass beyond the **c** of Cyprus
Ezek 27: 6 ivory from the **c** of Cyprus
Ezek 27: 7 purple from the **c** of Elishah
Joel 3: 4 and all the **c** of Philistia
Acts 27: 2 to sail along the **c** of Asia

COAT (*see* COATS)
Ex 28:32 the opening in a **c** of mail
Ex 39:23 the opening in a **c** of mail
1Sa 17: 5 he was armed with a **c** of mail
1Sa 17: 5 the weight of the **c** was five
1Sa 17:38 clothed him with a **c** of mail
Job 30:18 about as the collar of my **c**
Job 41:13 Who can remove his outer **c**

COATS (*see* COAT)
Dan 3:21 men were bound in their **c**

COBRA (*see* COBRA'S, COBRAS)
Job 20:14 it becomes **c** venom within him
Ps 58: 4 the deaf **c** that stops its ear
Ps 91:13 tread upon the lion and the **c**

COBRA'S (*see* COBRA)
Is 11: 8 shall play by the **c** hole, and

COBRAS (*see* COBRA)
Deut 32:33 and the cruel venom of **c**
Job 20:16 He will suck the poison of **c**

CODE
Rom 2:27 who, even with your written **c**

COFFIN
Gen 50:26 and he was put in a **c** in Egypt
2Sa 3:31 And King David followed the **c**
Luke 7:14 He came and touched the open **c**

COIN (*see* COINS)
Matt 10:29 sparrows sold for a copper **c**
Luke 15: 8 coins, if she loses one **c**

COINS (*see* COIN)
Luke 12: 6 sold for two copper **c**
Luke 15: 8 woman, having ten silver **c**

COLD
Gen 8:22 seedtime and harvest, and **c**
Job 24: 7 and have no covering in the **c**
Job 37: 9 **c** from the scattering winds
Ps 147:17 Who can stand before His **c**
Prov 25:13 Like the **c** of snow in time of
Prov 25:20 away a garment in **c** weather
Prov 25:25 As **c** water to a weary soul,
Jer 18:14 Will the **c** flowing waters be
Nah 3:17 camp in the hedges on a **c** day
Matt 10:42 of **c** water in the name of a
Matt 24:12 the love of many will grow **c**
John 18:18 stood there, for it was **c**
Acts 28: 2 falling and because of the **c**
2Co 11:27 in fastings often, in **c** and
Rev 3:15 you are neither **c** nor hot
Rev 3:15 could wish you were **c** or hot
Rev 3:16 and neither **c** nor hot, I will

COL-HOZEH
Neh 3:15 Shallun the son of **C**, leader
Neh 11: 5 son of Baruch, the son of **C**

COLLAPSE (*see* COLLAPSED)
Jer 13:18 down, for your rule shall **c**
Lam 1: 9 therefore her **c** was awesome

COLLAPSED (*see* COLLAPSE)
Judg 7:13 and overturned, and the tent **c**

COLLAR
Job 30:18 me about as the **c** of my coat

COLLECT (*see* COLLECTED, COLLECTING, COLLECTION, COLLECTOR)
Gen 41:34 to **c** one-fifth of the produce
Luke 3:13 **C** no more than what is
Luke 19:21 You **c** what you did not

COLLECTED (*see* COLLECT)
Luke 19:23 might have **c** it with interest

COLLECTING (*see* COLLECT)
Eccl 2:26 the work of gathering and **c**
Luke 19:22 **c** what I did not deposit and

COLLECTION (*see* COLLECT, COLLECTIONS)
2Ch 24: 6 Judah and from Jerusalem the **c**
2Ch 24: 9 to bring to the LORD the **c**
Is 57:13 let your **c** of idols deliver
1Co 16: 1 the **c** for the saints, as I

COLLECTIONS (*see* COLLECTION)
1Co 16: 2 there be no **c** when I come

COLLECTOR (*see* COLLECT, COLLECTORS)
Matt 10: 3 Thomas and Matthew the tax **c**
Matt 18:17 you like a heathen and a tax **c**
Luke 5:27 and saw a tax **c** named Levi,
Luke 18:10 Pharisee and the other a tax **c**
Luke 18:11 or even as this tax **c**
Luke 18:13 And the tax **c**, standing afar
Luke 19: 2 who was a chief tax **c**, and he

COLLECTORS (*see* COLLECTOR)
Matt 5:46 even the tax **c** do the same
Matt 5:47 Do not even the tax **c** do so
Matt 9:10 that behold, many tax **c** and
Matt 9:11 your Teacher eat with tax **c**
Matt 11:19 winebibber, a friend of tax **c**
Matt 21:31 I say to you that tax **c** and
Matt 21:32 but tax **c** and harlots believed
Mark 2:15 Levi's house, that many tax **c**
Mark 2:16 saw Him eating with the tax **c**
Mark 2:16 He eats and drinks with tax **c**
Luke 3:12 Then tax **c** also came to be
Luke 5:29 were a great number of tax **c**
Luke 5:30 You eat and drink with tax **c**
Luke 7:29 even the tax **c** justified God,
Luke 7:34 winebibber, a friend of tax **c**
Luke 15: 1 Then all the tax **c** and the

COLONY
Acts 16:12 that part of Macedonia, a **c**

COLOR (*see* COLORED, COLORFUL, COLORS)
Lev 13:55 plague has not changed its **c**
Num 11: 7 **c** like the **c** of bdellium
Ezek 1: 4 its midst like the **c** of amber
Ezek 1: 7 the **c** of burnished bronze
Ezek 1:16 works was like the **c** of beryl
Ezek 1:22 the **c** of an awesome crystal
Ezek 1:27 were, the **c** of amber with the
Ezek 8: 2 like the **c** of amber
Ezek 10: 9 have the **c** of a beryl stone
Dan 10: 6 like burnished bronze in **c**
Joel 2: 6 all faces are drained of **c**
Nah 2:10 their faces are drained of **c**

COLORED (*see* COLOR)
Prov 7:16 **C** coverings of Egyptian linen

COLORFUL (*see* COLOR)
Is 54:11 lay your stones with **c** gems

COLORS (*see* COLOR)
Gen 37: 3 he made him a tunic of many **c**
Gen 37:23 of many **c** that was on him
Gen 37:32 they sent the tunic of many **c**
2Sa 13:18 she had on a robe of many **c**
2Sa 13:19 of many **c** that was on her
1Ch 29: 2 stones of various **c**, all
Ps 45:14 the King in robes of many **c**
Ezek 17: 3 full of feathers of various **c**

COLOSSE
Col 1: 2 in Christ who are in **C**

COLT (*see* COLTS)
Gen 49:11 his donkey's **c** to the choice
Job 11:12 wild donkey's **c** is born a man
Zech 9: 9 and riding on a donkey, a **c**
Matt 21: 2 donkey tied, and a **c** with her
Matt 21: 5 and sitting on a donkey, a **c**
Matt 21: 7 brought the donkey and the **c**
Mark 11: 2 it you will find a **c** tied
Mark 11: 4 found the **c** tied by the door
Mark 11: 5 are you doing, loosing the **c**
Mark 11: 7 they brought the **c** to Jesus
Luke 19:30 enter you will find a **c** tied
Luke 19:33 as they were loosing the **c**
Luke 19:33 Why are you loosing the **c**
Luke 19:35 their own garments on the **c**
John 12:15 sitting on a donkey's **c**

COLTS (*see* COLT)
Gen 32:15 milk camels with their **c**,

COLUMN (*see* COLUMNS)
Judg 20:40 from the city in a **c** of smoke
Joel 2: 8 one marches in his own **c**

COLUMNS (*see* COLUMN)
Jer 36:23 had read three or four **c**,

COME (*see* PREFACE)

COMELINESS
Is 53: 2 He has no form or **c**

COMES (*see* PREFACE)

COMFORT (*see* COMFORTED, COMFORTER, COMFORTING, COMFORTS)
Gen 5:29 This one will **c** us concerning
Gen 37:35 his daughters arose to **c** him
2Sa 10: 2 **c** him concerning his father
2Sa 19: 7 and speak **c** to your servants
1Ch 7:22 and his brethren came to **c** him
1Ch 19: 2 **c** him concerning his father
1Ch 19: 2 the people of Ammon to **c** him
Job 2:11 mourn with him, and to **c** him
Job 6:10 Then I would still have **c**
Job 7:13 When I say, "My bed will **c** me
Job 10:20 that I may take a little **c**
Job 16: 5 and the **c** of my lips would
Job 21:34 How then can you **c** me with
Ps 23: 4 rod and Your staff, they **c** me
Ps 71:21 And **c** me on every side
Ps 119:50 This is my **c** in my affliction
Ps 119:76 merciful kindness be for my **c**
Ps 119:82 When will You **c** me
Ps 132: 3 Or go up to the **c** of my bed
Is 12: 1 is turned away, and You **c** me
Is 22: 4 do not labor to **c** me because
Is 40: 1 **C**, yes, **c** My people
Is 40: 2 Speak **c** to Jerusalem, and cry
Is 51: 3 For the LORD will **c** Zion, He
Is 51: 3 Zion, He will **c** all her waste
Is 51:19 by whom will I **c** you
Is 57: 6 Should I receive **c** in these
Is 61: 2 to **c** all who mourn,
Is 66:13 comforts, so I will **c** you
Jer 8:18 I would **c** myself in sorrow
Jer 16: 7 them, to **c** them for the dead
Jer 31:13 mourning to joy, will **c** them
Lam 1: 2 lovers she has none to **c** her
Lam 1:17 but there is no one to **c** her
Lam 1:21 I sigh, with no one to **c** me
Lam 2:13 with you, that I may **c** you
Ezek 14:23 And they will **c** you, when you
Hos 2:14 wilderness, and speak **c** to her
Zech 1:17 the LORD will again **c** Zion
Zech 10: 2 they **c** in vain
John 11:19 to **c** them concerning their
Acts 9:31 in the **c** of the Holy Spirit,
Rom 15: 4 **c** of the Scriptures might
Rom 15: 5 **c** grant you to be like-minded
1Co 14: 3 and exhortation and **c** to men
2Co 1: 3 of mercies and God of all **c**
2Co 1: 4 to **c** those who are in any
2Co 1: 4 with the **c** with which we
2Co 2: 7 **c** him, lest perhaps such a
2Co 7: 4 I am filled with **c**
2Co 7:13 have been comforted in your **c**
2Co 13:11 Be of good **c**, be of one mind,
Eph 6:22 and that he may **c** your hearts
Phil 2: 1 if any **c** of love, if any
Col 4: 8 and **c** your hearts,
Col 4:11 have proved to be a **c** to me
1Th 4:18 Therefore **c** one another with
1Th 5:11 Therefore **c** each other and
1Th 5:14 **c** the fainthearted, uphold
2Th 2:17 **c** your hearts and establish

COMFORTED (*see* COMFORT)
Gen 24:67 So Isaac was **c** after his
Gen 37:35 but he refused to be **c**, and he
Gen 38:12 and Judah was **c**, and went up to
Gen 50:21 he **c** them and spoke kindly to
Ruth 2:13 for you have **c** me, and have
2Sa 12:24 Then David **c** Bathsheba his
2Sa 13:39 For he had been **c** concerning
Job 42:11 **c** him for all the adversity
Ps 77: 2 My soul refused to be **c**
Ps 86:17 LORD, have helped me and **c** me
Ps 119:52 old, O LORD, And have **c** myself
Is 49:13 For the LORD has **c** His people
Is 52: 9 For the LORD has **c** His people
Is 54:11 tossed with tempest, and not **c**
Is 66:13 you shall be **c** in Jerusalem
Jer 31:15 refusing to be **c** for her
Ezek 14:22 Then you will be **c** concerning
Ezek 16:54 that you did when you **c** them
Ezek 31:16 were **c** in the depths of the
Ezek 32:31 be **c** over all his multitude,
Matt 2:18 children, refusing to be **c**
Matt 5: 4 mourn, for they shall be **c**
Luke 16:25 but now he is **c** and you are
Acts 20:12 and they were not a little **c**
2Co 1: 4 we ourselves are **c** by God
2Co 1: 6 Or if we are **c**, it is for
2Co 7: 6 **c** us by the coming of Titus,
2Co 7: 7 with which he was **c** in you
2Co 7:13 have been **c** in your comfort
1Th 2:11 know how we exhorted, and **c**
1Th 3: 7 distress we were **c** concerning

COMFORTER (*see* COMFORT, COMFORTERS)
Eccl 4: 1 oppressed, but they have no **c**
Eccl 4: 1 was power, but they have no **c**
Lam 1: 9 she had no **c**
Lam 1:16 because the **c**, who should

COMFORTERS (*see* COMFORTER)
2Sa 10: 3 because he has sent **c** to you
1Ch 19: 3 because he has sent **c** to you
Job 16: 2 miserable **c** are you all
Ps 69:20 And for **c**, but I found none
Nah 3: 7 Where shall I seek **c** for you

COMFORTING (*see* COMFORT)
2Sa 14:17 lord the king will now be **c**
Zech 1:13 to me, with good and **c** words
John 11:31 **c** her, when they saw that

COMFORTS (*see* COMFORT)
Gen 27:42 Surely your brother Esau **c**
Job 29:25 army, as one who **c** mourners
Ps 94:19 me, Your **c** delight my soul
Is 51:12 I, even I, am He who **c** you
Is 57:18 lead him, and restore **c** to him
Is 66:13 As one whom his mother **c**, so
2Co 1: 4 who **c** us in all our
2Co 7: 6 who **c** the downcast, comforted

COMING (*see* PREFACE)

COMMAND (*see* COMMANDED, COMMANDER, COMMANDING, COMMANDMENT, COMMANDS)

Gen 18:19 that he may **c** his children
Gen 27: 8 according to what I **c** you
Gen 42:25 Then Joseph gave a **c** to fill
Gen 45:21 according to the **c** of Pharaoh
Ex 6:13 and gave them a **c** for the
Ex 7: 2 shall speak all that I **c** you
Ex 8:27 LORD our God as He will **c** us
Ex 27:20 you shall **c** the children of
Ex 34:11 Observe what I **c** you this day
Lev 6: 9 **C** Aaron and his sons, saying
Lev 13:54 then the priest shall **c** that
Lev 14: 4 then the priest shall **c** to
Lev 14: 5 the priest shall **c** that one
Lev 14:36 then the priest shall **c** that
Lev 14:40 then the priest shall **c** that
Lev 24: 2 **C** the children of Israel that
Lev 25:21 Then I will **c** My blessing on
Num 5: 2 **C** the children of Israel that
Num 9: 8 LORD will **c** concerning you
Num 9:18 At the **c** of the LORD the
Num 9:18 at the **c** of the LORD they
Num 9:20 according to the **c** of the
Num 9:20 according to the **c** of the
Num 9:23 At the **c** of the LORD they
Num 9:23 at the **c** of the LORD they
Num 9:23 at the **c** of the LORD by the
Num 10:13 **c** of the LORD by the hand of
Num 13: 3 to the **c** of the LORD, all of
Num 14:41 transgress the **c** of the LORD
Num 23:20 I have received a **c** to bless
Num 27:14 you rebelled against My **c** to
Num 28: 2 **C** the children of Israel, and
Num 31:49 of war who are under our **c**
Num 32:28 So Moses gave **c** concerning
Num 33: 2 journeys at the **c** of the LORD
Num 33:38 Hor at the **c** of the LORD, and
Num 34: 2 **C** the children of Israel, and
Num 35: 2 **C** the children of Israel that
Deut 1:26 the **c** of the LORD your God
Deut 1:43 against the **c** of the LORD
Deut 2: 4 And **c** the people, saying,
Deut 3:28 But **c** Joshua, and encourage
Deut 4: 2 add to the word which I **c** you
Deut 4: 2 LORD your God which I **c** you
Deut 4:40 which I **c** you today, that it
Deut 6: 2 commandments which I **c** you
Deut 6: 6 these words which I **c** you
Deut 7:11 judgments which I **c** you today
Deut 8: 1 I **c** you today you must be
Deut 8:11 statutes which I **c** you today
Deut 10:13 His statutes which I **c** you
Deut 11: 8 which I **c** you today, that you
Deut 11:13 which I **c** you today, to love
Deut 11:22 which I **c** you to do
Deut 11:27 your God which I **c** you today
Deut 11:28 the way which I **c** you today
Deut 12:11 shall bring all that I **c** you
Deut 12:14 you shall do all that I **c** you
Deut 12:28 all these words which I **c** you
Deut 12:32 Whatever I **c** you, be careful
Deut 13:18 which I **c** you today, to do
Deut 15: 5 which I **c** you today
Deut 15:11 therefore I **c** you, saying
Deut 15:15 therefore I **c** you this thing
Deut 18:18 to them all that I **c** Him
Deut 19: 7 Therefore I **c** you, saying
Deut 19: 9 which I **c** you today, to love
Deut 24:18 therefore I **c** you to do this
Deut 24:22 therefore I **c** you to do this
Deut 27: 1 which I **c** you today
Deut 27: 4 which I **c** you today, and you
Deut 27:10 statutes which I **c** you today
Deut 28: 1 which I **c** you today, that the
Deut 28: 8 The LORD will **c** the blessing
Deut 28:13 which I **c** you today, and are
Deut 28:14 words which I **c** you this day
Deut 28:15 statutes which I **c** you today
Deut 30: 2 to all that I **c** you today
Deut 30: 8 which I **c** you today
Deut 30:11 which I **c** you today, it is
Deut 30:16 in that I **c** you today to love
Deut 32:46 today, which you shall **c** your
Josh 1:11 and **c** the people, saying
Josh 1:16 All that you **c** us we will do,
Josh 1:18 Whoever rebels against your **c**
Josh 1:18 words, in all that you **c** him
Josh 3: 8 You shall **c** the priests who
Josh 4: 3 **c** them, saying, "Take for
Josh 4:16 **C** the priests who bear the
Judg 4:10 ten thousand men under his **c**
Judg 5:15 into the valley under his **c**
1Sa 16:16 master now **c** your servants
2Sa 10:10 the **c** of Abishai his brother
2Sa 13:32 For by the **c** of Absalom this
1Ki 5: 6 **c** that they cut down cedars
1Ki 11:38 if you heed all that I **c** you
1Ki 20:12 were drinking at the **c** post
1Ki 20:16 getting drunk at the **c** post
1Ch 12:32 brethren were at their **c**
1Ch 19:11 the **c** of Abishai his brother
1Ch 28:21 will be completely at your **c**
2Ch 7:13 or **c** the locusts to devour
2Ch 8:15 did not depart from the **c** of
2Ch 13:11 for we keep the **c** of the LORD
2Ch 35:10 according to the king's **c**
2Ch 35:15 according to the **c** of David
2Ch 35:16 to the **c** of King Josiah
Ezra 4:19 And I gave the **c**, and a search
Ezra 4:21 Now give the **c** to make these
Ezra 4:21 until the **c** is given by me
Ezra 6:14 according to the **c** of Cyrus
Ezra 8:17 I gave them a **c** for Iddo the
Neh 11:23 For it was the king's **c**
Neh 12:24 according to the **c** of David
Neh 12:45 according to the **c** of David
Esth 1:12 to come at the king's **c**
Esth 1:15 she did not obey the **c** of
Esth 2: 8 So it was, when the king's **c**
Esth 2:20 for Esther obeyed the **c** of
Esth 3: 3 you transgress the king's **c**
Esth 3:15 out, hastened by the king's **c**
Esth 4: 3 province where the king's **c**
Esth 4: 5 she gave him a **c** concerning
Esth 4: 8 that he might **c** her to go in
Esth 4:10 gave him a **c** for Mordecai
Esth 8:14 and pressed on by the king's **c**
Esth 8:17 city, wherever the king's **c**
Esth 9: 1 time came for the king's **c**
Job 39:27 the eagle mount up at your **c**
Ps 42: 8 The LORD will **c** His
Ps 44: 4 **C** victories for Jacob
Ps 147:15 sends out His **c** to the earth
Prov 6:20 My son, keep your father's **c**
Prov 8:29 would not transgress His **c**
Eccl 8: 5 He who keeps his **c** will
Is 5: 6 I will also **c** the clouds that
Is 45:11 work of My hands, you **c** Me
Jer 1: 7 send you, and whatever I **c** you
Jer 1:17 to them all that I **c** you
Jer 7:22 or **c** them in the day that I
Jer 7:31 the fire, which I did not **c**
Jer 11: 4 according to all that I **c** you
Jer 19: 5 which I did not **c** or speak
Jer 23:32 I did not send them or **c** them
Jer 26: 2 that I **c** you to speak to them
Jer 27: 4 And **c** them to say to their
Jer 32:35 which I did not **c** them, nor
Jer 34:22 Behold, I will **c**,' says the
Dan 2: 2 the **c** to call the magicians
Dan 2:12 gave a **c** to destroy all the
Dan 3:13 gave the **c** to bring Shadrach,
Dan 3:22 the king's **c** was urgent, and
Dan 4:26 gave the **c** to leave the stump
Dan 5: 2 gave the **c** to bring the gold
Dan 5:29 Then Belshazzar gave the **c**
Dan 6:16 So the king gave the **c**, and
Dan 6:24 And the king gave the **c**, and
Dan 9:23 supplications the **c** went out
Dan 9:25 forth of the **c** to restore
Amos 6:11 behold, the LORD gives a **c**
Amos 9: 3 there I will **c** the serpent
Amos 9: 4 from there I will **c** the sword
Amos 9: 9 For surely I will **c**, and will
Nah 1:14 has given a **c** concerning you
Zech 3: 7 and if you will keep My **c**
Matt 4: 3 **c** that these stones become
Matt 8:18 He gave a **c** to depart to the
Matt 14:28 **c** me to come to You on the
Matt 19: 7 Why then did Moses **c** to give
Matt 27:64 Therefore **c** that the tomb be
Mark 9:25 I **c** you, come out of him, and
Mark 10: 3 What did Moses **c** you
Luke 4: 3 **c** this stone to become bread
Luke 8:31 Him that He would not **c** them
Luke 9:54 do You want us to **c** fire to
John 10:18 This **c** I have received from
John 11:57 the Pharisees had given a **c**
John 12:49 who sent Me gave Me a **c**, what
John 12:50 And I know that His **c** is
John 15:14 if you do whatever I **c** you
John 15:17 These things I **c** you, that
Acts 5:28 Did we not strictly **c** you not
Acts 15: 5 to **c** them to keep the law of
Acts 16:18 I **c** you in the name of Jesus
Acts 17:15 and receiving a **c** for Silas
Acts 23: 3 and do you **c** me to be struck
Acts 25:23 at Festus' **c** Paul was brought
1Co 7:10 Now to the married I **c**, yet
2Th 3: 4 will do the things we **c** you
2Th 3: 6 But we **c** you, brethren, in
2Th 3:12 Now those who are such we **c**
1Ti 4:11 These things **c** and teach
1Ti 5: 7 And these things **c**, that they
1Ti 6:17 **C** those who are rich in this
Phm 8 to **c** you what is fitting,
Heb 11:23 not afraid of the king's **c**
Rev 3:10 have kept My **c** to persevere

COMMANDED (*see* COMMAND)

Gen 2:16 And the LORD God **c** the man
Gen 3:11 from the tree of which I **c**
Gen 3:17 the tree of which I **c** you
Gen 6:22 to all that God **c** him, so he
Gen 7: 5 to all that the LORD **c** him
Gen 7: 9 and female, as God had **c** Noah
Gen 7:16 went in as God had **c** him
Gen 12:20 So Pharaoh **c** his men
Gen 21: 4 days old, as God had **c** him
Gen 32: 4 And he **c** them, saying,
Gen 32:17 he **c** the first one, saying,
Gen 32:19 So he **c** the second, the third
Gen 44: 1 he **c** the steward of his house
Gen 45:19 Now you are **c**
Gen 47:11 of Rameses, as Pharaoh had **c**
Gen 50: 2 Joseph **c** his servants the
Gen 50:12 for him just as he had **c** them
Gen 50:16 Before your father died he **c**
Ex 1:17 as the king of Egypt **c** them
Ex 1:22 So Pharaoh **c** all his people,
Ex 4:28 the signs which He had **c** him
Ex 5: 6 **c** the taskmasters of the
Ex 7: 6 just as the LORD **c** them, so
Ex 7:10 did so, just as the LORD **c**
Ex 7:20 did so, just as the LORD **c**
Ex 12:28 just as the LORD had **c** Moses
Ex 12:50 as the LORD **c** Moses and Aaron,
Ex 16:16 thing which the LORD has **c**
Ex 16:24 up till morning, as Moses **c**
Ex 16:32 thing which the LORD has **c**
Ex 16:34 As the LORD **c** Moses, so Aaron
Ex 19: 7 words which the LORD **c** him
Ex 23:15 bread seven days, as I **c** you
Ex 29:35 to all that I have **c** you
Ex 31: 6 make all that I have **c** you
Ex 31:11 I have **c** you they shall do
Ex 32: 8 out of the way which I **c** them
Ex 34: 4 Sinai, as the LORD had **c** him
Ex 34:18 unleavened bread, as I **c** you
Ex 34:34 Israel whatever he had been **c**
Ex 35: 1 the LORD has **c** you to do
Ex 35: 4 is the thing which the LORD **c**
Ex 35:10 make all that the LORD has **c**
Ex 35:29 of Moses, had **c** to be done
Ex 36: 1 to all that the LORD has **c**
Ex 36: 5 which the LORD **c** us to do
Ex 38:22 all that the LORD had **c** Moses
Ex 39: 1 as the LORD had **c** Moses
Ex 39: 5 as the LORD had **c** Moses
Ex 39: 7 as the LORD had **c** Moses
Ex 39:21 as the LORD had **c** Moses
Ex 39:26 in, as the LORD had **c** Moses
Ex 39:29 woven as the LORD had **c** Moses
Ex 39:31 as the LORD had **c** Moses
Ex 39:32 all that the LORD had **c** Moses
Ex 39:42 all that the LORD had **c** Moses
Ex 39:43 as the LORD had **c**, just so
Ex 40:16 all that the LORD had **c** him
Ex 40:19 it, as the LORD had **c** Moses
Ex 40:21 as the LORD had **c** Moses
Ex 40:23 LORD, as the LORD had **c** Moses
Ex 40:25 LORD, as the LORD had **c** Moses
Ex 40:27 it, as the LORD had **c** Moses
Ex 40:29 as the LORD had **c** Moses
Ex 40:32 as the LORD had **c** Moses
Lev 7:36 The LORD **c** this to be given
Lev 7:38 which the LORD **c** Moses on
Lev 7:38 on the day when He **c** the
Lev 8: 4 Moses did as the LORD **c** him

Lev 8: 5 is what the LORD c to be done
Lev 8: 9 as the LORD had c Moses
Lev 8:13 them, as the LORD had c Moses
Lev 8:17 camp, as the LORD had c Moses
Lev 8:21 LORD, as the LORD had c Moses
Lev 8:29 as the LORD had c Moses
Lev 8:31 offerings, as I c, saying
Lev 8:34 day, so the LORD has c to do
Lev 8:35 for so I have been c
Lev 8:36 had c by the hand of Moses
Lev 9: 5 c before the tabernacle of
Lev 9: 6 which the LORD c you to do
Lev 9: 7 for them, as the LORD c
Lev 9:10 as the LORD had c Moses
Lev 9:21 the LORD, as Moses had c
Lev 10: 1 LORD, which He had not c them
Lev 10:13 for so I have been c
Lev 10:15 forever, as the LORD has c
Lev 10:18 it in a holy place, as I c
Lev 16:34 And he did as the LORD c Moses
Lev 17: 2 thing which the LORD has c
Lev 24:23 did as the LORD c Moses
Lev 27:34 c Moses for the children of
Num 1:19 As the LORD c Moses, so he
Num 1:54 to all that the LORD c Moses
Num 2:33 just as the LORD c Moses
Num 2:34 to all that the LORD c Moses
Num 3:16 word of the LORD, as he was c
Num 3:42 of Israel, as the LORD c him
Num 3:51 the LORD, as the LORD c Moses
Num 4:49 by him, as the LORD c Moses
Num 8: 3 as the LORD c Moses
Num 8:20 LORD c Moses concerning the
Num 8:22 as the LORD c Moses
Num 9: 5 to all that the LORD c Moses
Num 15:23 all that the LORD has c you
Num 15:36 So, as the LORD c Moses, all
Num 16:47 Then Aaron took it as Moses c
Num 17:11 just as the LORD had c him
Num 19: 2 the law which the LORD has c
Num 20: 9 before the LORD as He c him
Num 20:27 Moses did just as the LORD c
Num 26: 4 just as the LORD c Moses
Num 27:11 just as the LORD c Moses
Num 27:22 Moses did as the LORD c him
Num 27:23 just as the LORD c by the
Num 29:40 just as the LORD c Moses
Num 30: 1 thing which the LORD has c
Num 30:16 which the LORD c Moses,
Num 31: 7 just as the LORD c Moses
Num 31:21 law which the LORD c Moses
Num 31:31 did as the LORD c Moses
Num 31:41 priest, as the LORD c Moses
Num 31:47 the LORD, as the LORD c Moses
Num 34:13 Then Moses c the children of
Num 34:13 which the LORD has c to give
Num 34:29 c to divide the inheritance
Num 36: 2 The LORD c my lord Moses to
Num 36: 2 my lord was c by the LORD to
Num 36: 5 Then Moses c the children of
Num 36:10 Just as the LORD c Moses, so
Num 36:13 judgments which the LORD c
Deut 1:16 Then I c your judges at that
Deut 1:18 I c you at that time all the
Deut 1:19 as the LORD our God had c us
Deut 1:41 just as the LORD our God c us
Deut 3:18 I c you at that time, saying
Deut 3:21 And I c Joshua at that time,
Deut 4: 5 just as the LORD my God c me
Deut 4:13 which He c you to perform
Deut 4:14 the LORD c me at that time to
Deut 5:12 as the LORD your God c you
Deut 5:15 c you to keep the Sabbath day
Deut 5:16 the LORD your God has c you
Deut 5:32 the LORD your God has c you
Deut 5:33 the LORD your God has c you
Deut 6: 1 your God has c to teach you
Deut 6:17 statutes which He has c you
Deut 6:20 the LORD our God has c you
Deut 6:24 the LORD c us to observe all
Deut 6:25 LORD our God, as He has c us
Deut 9:12 from the way which I c them
Deut 9:16 way which the LORD had c you
Deut 10: 5 are, just as the LORD c me
Deut 12:21 you, just as I have c you
Deut 13: 5 LORD your God c you to walk
Deut 17: 3 of heaven, which I have not c
Deut 18:20 I have not c him to speak
Deut 20:17 the LORD your God has c you
Deut 24: 8 just as I c them, so you
Deut 26:13 which You have c me
Deut 26:14 to all that You have c me
Deut 27: 1 Israel, c the people, saying
Deut 27:11 Moses c the people on the
Deut 28:45 His statutes which He c you
Deut 29: 1 LORD c Moses to make with the
Deut 31: 5 which I have c you
Deut 31:10 And Moses c them, saying
Deut 31:25 that Moses c the Levites, who
Deut 31:29 the way which I have c you
Deut 33: 4 Moses c a law for us, a
Deut 34: 9 did as the LORD had c Moses
Josh 1: 7 which Moses My servant c you
Josh 1: 9 Have I not c you
Josh 1:10 Then Joshua c the officers of
Josh 1:13 the servant of the LORD c you
Josh 3: 3 they c the people, saying,
Josh 4: 8 did so, just as Joshua c, and
Josh 4:10 had c Joshua to speak to the
Josh 4:10 all that Moses had c Joshua
Josh 4:17 therefore c the priests,
Josh 6:10 Now Joshua had c the people
Josh 7:11 My covenant which I c them
Josh 8: 4 And he c them, saying
Josh 8: 8 See, I have c you
Josh 8:27 LORD which He had c Joshua
Josh 8:29 Joshua c that they should
Josh 8:31 had c the children of Israel
Josh 8:33 of the LORD had c before,
Josh 8:35 c which Joshua did not read
Josh 9:24 that the LORD your God c His
Josh 10:27 down of the sun that Joshua c
Josh 10:40 the LORD God of Israel had c
Josh 11:12 the servant of the LORD had c
Josh 11:15 As the LORD had c Moses his
Josh 11:15 servant, so Moses c Joshua
Josh 11:15 all that the LORD had c Moses
Josh 11:20 them, as the LORD had c Moses
Josh 13: 6 inheritance, as I have c you
Josh 14: 2 as the LORD had c by the hand
Josh 14: 5 As the LORD had c Moses, so
Josh 17: 4 The LORD c Moses to give us
Josh 21: 2 The LORD c through Moses to
Josh 21: 8 as the LORD had c by the hand
Josh 22: 2 the servant of the LORD c you
Josh 22: 2 my voice in all that I c you
Josh 22: 5 the servant of the LORD c you
Josh 23:16 LORD your God, which He c you
Judg 2:20 which I c their fathers, and
Judg 3: 4 which He had c their fathers
Judg 4: 6 not the LORD God of Israel c
Judg 13:14 All that I c her let her
Judg 21:10 men, and c them, saying,
Ruth 2: 9 Have I not c the young men
Ruth 2:15 Boaz c his young men, saying,
1Sa 2:29 I have c in My habitation
1Sa 13:13 LORD your God, which He c you
1Sa 13:14 and the LORD has c him to be
1Sa 13:14 not kept what the LORD c you
1Sa 17:20 and went as Jesse had c him
1Sa 18:22 And Saul c his servants,
1Sa 20:29 brother has c me to be there
1Sa 21: 2 you, or what I have c you
2Sa 4:12 So David c his young men, and
2Sa 5:25 did so, as the LORD c him
2Sa 7: 7 whom I c to shepherd My
2Sa 7:11 since the time that I c
2Sa 9:11 the king has c his servant
2Sa 13:28 Absalom had c his servants
2Sa 13:28 Have I not c you
2Sa 13:29 did to Amnon as Absalom had c
2Sa 14:19 For your servant Joab c me
2Sa 18: 5 Now the king had c Joab,
2Sa 18:12 in our hearing the king c you
2Sa 21:14 performed all that the king c
2Sa 24:19 of Gad, went up as the LORD c
1Ki 2:46 So the king c Benaiah the son
1Ki 5:17 the king c them to quarry
1Ki 8:58 which He c our fathers
1Ki 9: 4 to all that I have c you, and
1Ki 11:10 had c him concerning this
1Ki 11:10 not keep what the LORD had c
1Ki 11:11 statutes, which I have c you
1Ki 13: 9 For so it was c me by the
1Ki 13:21 which the LORD your God c you
1Ki 15: 5 He c him all the days of his
1Ki 17: 4 I have c the ravens to feed
1Ki 17: 9 I have c a widow there to
1Ki 22:31 Now the king of Syria had c
2Ki 11: 5 Then he c them, saying
2Ki 11: 9 that Jehoiada the priest c
2Ki 11:15 priest c the captains of the
2Ki 14: 6 of Moses, in which the LORD c
2Ki 16:15 Then King Ahaz c Urijah the
2Ki 16:16 to all that King Ahaz c
2Ki 17:13 law which I c your fathers
2Ki 17:27 Then the king of Assyria c
2Ki 17:34 which the LORD had c the
2Ki 18: 6 which the LORD had c Moses
2Ki 18:12 the servant of the LORD had c
2Ki 21: 8 to all that I have c them
2Ki 21: 8 that My servant Moses c them
2Ki 22:12 Then the king c Hilkiah the
2Ki 23: 4 the king c Hilkiah the high
2Ki 23:21 Then the king c all the
1Ch 6:49 the servant of God had c
1Ch 14:16 So David did as God c him
1Ch 15:15 as Moses had c according to
1Ch 16:15 always, the word which He c
1Ch 16:40 of the LORD which He c Israel
1Ch 17: 6 whom I c to shepherd My
1Ch 17:10 since the time that I c
1Ch 21:17 Was it not I who c the people
1Ch 21:18 c Gad to say to David that
1Ch 21:27 Then the LORD c the angel
1Ch 22: 2 So David c to gather the
1Ch 22:17 David also c all the leaders
1Ch 24:19 LORD God of Israel had c him
2Ch 7:17 to all that I have c you, and
2Ch 8:14 so David the man of God had c
2Ch 14: 4 He c Judah to seek the LORD
2Ch 18:30 had c the captains of the
2Ch 19: 9 And he c them, saying,
2Ch 23: 8 that Jehoiada the priest c
2Ch 25: 4 of Moses, where the LORD c
2Ch 29:21 Then he c the priests, the
2Ch 29:24 for the king c that the burnt
2Ch 29:27 Then Hezekiah c them to offer
2Ch 29:30 the leaders c the Levites to
2Ch 31: 4 Moreover he c the people who
2Ch 31:11 Now Hezekiah c them to
2Ch 32:12 c Judah and Jerusalem, saying,
2Ch 33: 8 to do all that I have c them
2Ch 33:16 c Judah to serve the LORD God
2Ch 34:20 Then the king c Hilkiah,
2Ch 35:21 for God c me to make haste
2Ch 36:23 He has c me to build Him a
Ezra 1: 2 He has c me to build Him a
Ezra 4: 3 the king of Persia has c us
Ezra 5: 3 Who has c you to build this
Ezra 5: 9 Who c you to build this
Ezra 7:23 Whatever is c by the God of
Ezra 9:11 which You have c by Your
Neh 1: 7 You c Your servant Moses
Neh 1: 8 the word that You c Your
Neh 8: 1 which the LORD had c Israel
Neh 8:14 which the LORD had c by Moses
Neh 9:14 c them precepts, statutes and
Neh 13: 5 which were c to be given to
Neh 13: 9 Then I c them to cleanse the
Neh 13:19 that I c the gates to be shut
Neh 13:22 I c the Levites that they
Esth 1:10 he c Mehuman, Biztha,
Esth 1:17 King Ahasuerus c Queen
Esth 3: 2 the king had c concerning him
Esth 3:12 according to all that Haman c
Esth 4:17 to all that Esther c him
Esth 6: 1 So one was c to bring the
Esth 8: 9 to all that Mordecai c, to
Esth 9:14 So the king c this to be done
Esth 9:25 he c by letter that this
Job 38:12 Have you c the morning since
Job 42: 9 and did as the LORD c them
Ps 7: 6 me to the judgment You have c
Ps 33: 9 He c, and it stood fast
Ps 68:28 Your God has c your strength
Ps 78: 5 Which He c our fathers, That
Ps 78:23 Yet He had c the clouds above
Ps 105: 8 forever, The word which He c
Ps 106:34 whom the LORD had c them,
Ps 111: 9 He has c His covenant forever
Ps 119: 4 You have c us To keep Your
Ps 119:138 testimonies, which You have c
Ps 133: 3 there the LORD c the blessing
Ps 148: 5 name of the LORD, For He c
Is 13: 3 I have c My sanctified ones
Is 34:16 For My mouth has c it, and His
Is 45:12 and all their host I have c
Is 48: 5 my molded image have c them
Jer 7:23 But this is what I c them

Jer 7:23 the ways that I have **c** you
Jer 11: 4 which I **c** your fathers in the
Jer 11: 8 which I **c** them to do, but
Jer 13: 5 Euphrates, as the LORD **c** me
Jer 13: 6 which I **c** you to hide there
Jer 14:14 **c** them, nor spoken to them
Jer 17:22 day, as I **c** your fathers
Jer 26: 8 all that the LORD had **c** him
Jer 29:23 name, which I have not **c** them
Jer 32:23 of all that You **c** them to do
Jer 35: 6 **c** us, saying, 'You shall
Jer 35:10 that Jonadab our father **c** us
Jer 35:14 Rechab, which he **c** his sons
Jer 35:16 their father, which he **c** them
Jer 35:18 to all that he **c** you,
Jer 36: 5 And Jeremiah **c** Baruch, saying,
Jer 36: 8 Jeremiah the prophet **c** him
Jer 36:26 And the king **c** Jerahmeel the
Jer 37:21 Then Zedekiah the king **c** that
Jer 38:10 Then the king **c** Ebed-Melech
Jer 38:27 words that the king had **c**
Jer 50:21 to all that I have **c** you
Jer 51:59 **c** Seraiah the son of Neriah
Lam 1:10 those whom You **c** not to enter
Lam 1:17 the LORD has **c** concerning
Lam 2:17 which He **c** in days of old
Lam 3:37 when the Lord has not **c** it
Ezek 9:11 I have done as You **c** me
Ezek 10: 6 when He **c** the man clothed in
Ezek 12: 7 So I did as I was **c**
Ezek 24:18 next morning I did as I was **c**
Ezek 37: 7 So I prophesied as I was **c**
Ezek 37:10 So I prophesied as He **c** me
Dan 2:46 **c** that they should present an
Dan 3: 4 To you it is **c**, O peoples,
Dan 3:19 **c** that they heat the furnace
Dan 3:20 he **c** certain mighty men of
Dan 6:23 and **c** that they should take
Amos 2:12 **c** the prophets saying, 'Do
Zech 1: 6 which I **c** My servants the
Mal 4: 4 which I **c** him in Horeb for
Matt 1:24 the angel of the Lord **c** him
Matt 8: 4 offer the gift that Moses **c**
Matt 10: 5 sent out and **c** them, saying
Matt 14: 9 he **c** it to be given to her
Matt 14:19 Then He **c** the multitudes to
Matt 15: 4 For God **c**, saying, 'Honor
Matt 15:35 He **c** the multitude to sit
Matt 16:20 Then He **c** His disciples that
Matt 17: 9 the mountain, Jesus **c** them
Matt 18:25 his master **c** that he be sold,
Matt 21: 6 went and did as Jesus **c** them
Matt 27:58 Then Pilate **c** the body to be
Matt 28:20 all things that I have **c** you
Mark 1:44 those things which Moses **c**
Mark 5:43 But He **c** them strictly that
Mark 6: 8 He **c** them to take nothing for
Mark 6:27 and **c** his head to be brought
Mark 6:39 Then He **c** them to make them
Mark 7:36 Then He **c** them that they
Mark 7:36 but the more He **c** them, the
Mark 8: 6 He **c** the multitude to sit
Mark 9: 9 He **c** them that they should
Mark 10:49 still and **c** him to be called
Mark 11: 6 to them just as Jesus had **c**
Mark 13:34 **c** the doorkeeper to watch
Luke 5:14 to them, just as Moses **c**
Luke 8:29 For He had **c** the unclean
Luke 8:55 And He **c** that she be given
Luke 9:21 **c** them to tell this to no one
Luke 14:22 Master, it is done as you **c**
Luke 17: 9 the things that were **c** him
Luke 17:10 those things which you are **c**
Luke 18:40 **c** him to be brought to Him
Luke 19:15 he then **c** these servants, to
John 8: 5 law, **c** us that such should be
Acts 1: 4 He **c** them not to depart from
Acts 4:15 But when they had **c** them to
Acts 4:18 **c** them not to speak at all
Acts 5:34 **c** them to put the apostles
Acts 5:40 they **c** that they should not
Acts 8:38 So he **c** the chariot to stand
Acts 10:33 all the things **c** you by God
Acts 10:42 And He **c** us to preach to the
Acts 10:48 he **c** them to be baptized in
Acts 12:19 **c** that they should be put to
Acts 13:47 For so the Lord has **c** us
Acts 16:22 **c** them to be beaten with rods
Acts 18: 2 (because Claudius had **c** all
Acts 21:33 **c** him to be bound with two
Acts 21:34 he **c** him to be taken into the
Acts 22:30 **c** the chief priests and all
Acts 23: 2 the high priest Ananias **c**
Acts 23:10 **c** the soldiers to go down and
Acts 23:22 young man depart, and **c** him,
Acts 23:30 also **c** his accusers to state
Acts 23:31 the soldiers, as they were **c**
Acts 23:35 And he **c** him to be kept in
Acts 24:23 So he **c** the centurion to keep
Acts 25: 6 seat, he **c** Paul to be brought
Acts 25:17 **c** the man to be brought in
Acts 25:21 I **c** him to be kept till I
Acts 27:43 **c** that those who could swim
1Co 9:14 Even so the Lord has **c** that
2Co 4: 6 who **c** light to shine out of
1Th 4:11 your own hands, as we **c** you
2Th 3:10 were with you, we **c** you this
Tit 1: 5 in every city as I **c** you
Heb 9:20 covenant which God has **c** you
Heb 12:20 could not endure what was **c**
Rev 9: 4 They were **c** not to harm the

COMMANDER (*see* COMMAND, COMMANDERS)
Gen 21:22 the **c** of his army, spoke to
Gen 21:32 the **c** of his army, and they
Gen 26:26 and Phichol the **c** of his army
Josh 5:14 but as **C** of the army of the
Josh 5:15 Then the **C** of the LORD's army
Judg 4: 2 The **c** of his army was Sisera,
Judg 4: 7 the **c** of Jabin's army, with
Judg 11: 6 Come and be our **c**, that we may
Judg 11:11 made him head and **c** over them
1Sa 9:16 you shall anoint him **c** over
1Sa 10: 1 you **c** over His inheritance
1Sa 12: 9 **c** of the army of Hazor, into
1Sa 13:14 him to be **c** over His people
1Sa 14:50 the name of the **c** of his army
1Sa 17:55 to Abner, the **c** of the army,
1Sa 26: 5 son of Ner, the **c** of his army
2Sa 2: 8 Ner, **c** of Saul's army, took
2Sa 10:16 Shobach the **c** of Hadadezer's
2Sa 10:18 Shobach the **c** of their army
2Sa 19:13 if you are not **c** of the army
2Sa 24: 2 **c** of the army who was with
1Ki 1:19 and Joab the **c** of the army
1Ki 2:32 the **c** of the army of Israel,
1Ki 2:32 the **c** of the army of Judah
1Ki 11:15 Joab the **c** of the army had
1Ki 11:21 that Joab the **c** of the army
1Ki 16: 9 **c** of half his chariots,
1Ki 16:16 the **c** of the army, king over
2Ki 4:13 king or to the **c** of the army
2Ki 5: 1 **c** of the army of the king of
2Ki 9: 5 I have a message for you, O **c**
2Ki 9: 5 And he said, "For you, **c**."
1Ch 19:16 Shophach the **c** of Hadadezer's
1Ch 19:18 Shophach the **c** of the army
Ezra 4: 8 Rehum the **c** and Shimshai the
Ezra 4: 9 From Rehum the **c**, Shimshai
Ezra 4:17 To Rehum the **c**, to Shimshai
Is 55: 4 a leader and **c** for the people
Acts 21:31 news came to the **c** of the
Acts 21:32 And when they saw the **c** and the
Acts 21:33 Then the **c** came near and took
Acts 21:37 barracks, he said to the **c**
Acts 22:24 the **c** ordered him to be
Acts 22:26 that, he went and told the **c**
Acts 22:27 Then the **c** came and said to
Acts 22:28 And the **c** answered,
Acts 22:29 the **c** was also afraid after
Acts 23:10 a great dissension, the **c**
Acts 23:15 suggest to the **c** that he be
Acts 23:17 Take this young man to the **c**
Acts 23:18 him and brought him to the **c**
Acts 23:19 Then the **c** took him by the
Acts 23:22 So the **c** let the young man
Acts 24: 7 But the **c** Lysias came by and
Acts 24:22 When Lysias the **c** comes down

COMMANDERS (*see* COMMANDER)
1Ki 1:25 and the **c** of the army, and
1Ki 2: 5 what he did to the two **c** of
1Ki 9:22 **c** of his chariots, and his
2Ch 32: 3 **c** to stop the water from the
Nah 3:17 Your **c** are like swarming
Acts 25:23 the auditorium with the **c**
Rev 6:15 men, the rich men, the **c**, the

COMMANDING (*see* COMMAND)
Gen 49:33 Jacob had finished **c** his sons
Matt 11: 1 when Jesus finished **c** His
Acts 16:23 **c** the jailer to keep them
Acts 24: 8 **c** his accusers to come to you
1Ti 4: 3 **c** to abstain from foods which

COMMANDMENT (*see* COMMAND, COMMANDMENTS)
Ex 17: 1 to the **c** of the LORD, and
Ex 25:22 which I will give you in **c** to
Ex 36: 6 So Moses gave a **c**, and they
Ex 38:21 according to the **c** of Moses
Num 3:39 numbered at the **c** of the LORD
Num 4:37 numbered according to the **c**
Num 4:41 to the **c** of the LORD
Num 4:49 According to the **c** of the
Num 15:23 from the day the LORD gave **c**
Num 15:31 the LORD, and has broken His **c**
Deut 6: 1 Now this is the **c**, and these
Deut 7:11 you shall keep the **c**, the
Deut 8: 1 Every **c** which I command you
Deut 9:23 the **c** of the LORD your God
Deut 11: 8 you shall keep every **c** which
Deut 17:20 **c** to the right hand or to the
Deut 30:11 For this **c** which I command
Deut 31: 5 **c** which I have commanded you
Josh 8: 8 According to the **c** of the
Josh 15:13 according to the **c** of the
Josh 17: 4 to the **c** of the LORD, he gave
Josh 21: 3 at the **c** of the LORD, these
Josh 22: 3 of the **c** of the LORD your God
Josh 22: 5 diligent heed to do the **c**
1Sa 12:14 against the **c** of the LORD
1Sa 12:15 against the **c** of the LORD
1Sa 13:13 the **c** of the LORD your God
1Sa 15:13 performed the **c** of the LORD
1Sa 15:24 the **c** of the LORD and your
2Sa 12: 9 despised the **c** of the LORD
1Ki 2:43 LORD and the **c** that I gave you
1Ki 13:21 have not kept the **c** which the
2Ki 17:34 law and **c** which the LORD had
2Ki 17:37 the **c** which He wrote for you,
2Ki 18:36 for the king's **c** was, "Do
2Ki 23:35 according to the **c** of Pharaoh
2Ki 24: 3 Surely at the **c** of the LORD
1Ch 14:12 gods there, David gave a **c**
2Ch 8:13 according to the **c** of Moses
2Ch 14: 4 to observe the law and the **c**
2Ch 19:10 or offenses against law or **c**
2Ch 24: 6 according to the **c** of Moses
2Ch 24: 8 king's **c** they made a chest
2Ch 24:21 at the **c** of the king they
2Ch 29:15 to the **c** of the king, at the
2Ch 29:25 according to the **c** of David
2Ch 29:25 for thus was the **c** of the
2Ch 30: 6 to the **c** of the king
2Ch 30:12 heart to do the **c** of the king
2Ch 31: 5 soon as the **c** was circulated
2Ch 31:13 at the **c** of Hezekiah the king
2Ch 31:21 God, in the law and in the **c**
Ezra 6:14 according to the **c** of the God
Ezra 10: 3 tremble at the **c** of our God
Job 23:12 from the **c** of His lips
Ps 19: 8 The **c** of the LORD is pure,
Ps 71: 3 have given the **c** to save me
Ps 119:96 But Your **c** is exceedingly
Prov 6:23 For the **c** is a lamp, and the
Prov 13:13 fears the **c** will be rewarded
Prov 19:16 keeps the **c** keeps his soul
Eccl 8: 2 Keep the king's **c** for the
Is 23:11 the LORD has given a **c**
Is 29:13 Me is taught by the **c** of men
Is 36:21 for the king's **c** was, "Do
Jer 35:14 and obey their father's **c**
Jer 35:16 the **c** of their father, which
Jer 35:18 the **c** of Jonadab your father
Lam 1:18 for I rebelled against His **c**
Mal 2: 1 O priests, this **c** is for you
Mal 2: 4 I have sent this **c** to you
Matt 15: 3 the **c** of God because of your
Matt 15: 6 Thus you have made the **c** of
Matt 22:36 is the great **c** in the law
Matt 22:38 This is the first and great **c**
Mark 7: 8 For laying aside the **c** of God
Mark 7: 9 well you reject the **c** of God
Mark 12:28 Which is the first **c** of all
Mark 12:30 This is the first **c**
Mark 12:31 no other **c** greater than these
Luke 15:29 your **c** at any time
Luke 23:56 Sabbath according to the **c**

John 13:34 A new **c** I give to you, that
John 14:31 and as the Father gave Me **c**
John 15:12 This is My **c**, that you love
Acts 15:24 to whom we gave no such **c**
Rom 7: 8 taking opportunity by the **c**
Rom 7: 9 the law, but when the **c** came
Rom 7:10 And the **c**, which was to bring
Rom 7:11 sin, taking occasion by the **c**
Rom 7:12 the **c** holy and just and good
Rom 7:13 so that sin through the **c**
Rom 13: 9 and if there is any other **c**
Rom 16:26 according to the **c** of the
1Co 7: 6 as a concession, not as a **c**
1Co 7:25 I have no **c** from the Lord
2Co 8: 8 I speak not by **c**, but I am
Eph 6: 2 is the first **c** with promise
1Ti 1: 1 by the **c** of God our Savior and
1Ti 1: 5 Now the purpose of the **c** is
1Ti 6:14 you keep this **c** without spot
Tit 1: 3 to the **c** of God our Savior
Heb 7: 5 have a **c** to receive tithes
Heb 7:16 to the law of a fleshly **c**
Heb 7:18 **c** because of its weakness
2Pe 2:21 the holy **c** delivered to them
2Pe 3: 2 of the **c** of us the apostles
1Jn 2: 7 I write no new **c** to you, but
1Jn 2: 7 but an old **c** which you have
1Jn 2: 7 The old **c** is the word which
1Jn 2: 8 a new **c** I write to you, which
1Jn 3:23 And this is His **c**
1Jn 3:23 one another, as He gave us **c**
1Jn 4:21 And this **c** we have from Him
2Jn 4 as we received **c** from the
2Jn 5 though I wrote a new **c** to you
2Jn 6 This is the **c**, that as you

COMMANDMENTS (*see* COMMANDMENT)
Gen 26: 5 voice and kept My charge, My **c**
Ex 15:26 His sight, give ear to His **c**
Ex 16:28 do you refuse to keep My **c**
Ex 20: 6 who love Me and keep My **c**
Ex 24:12 **c** which I have written, that
Ex 34:28 of the covenant, the Ten **C**
Ex 34:32 he gave them as **c** all that
Lev 4: 2 against any of the **c** of the
Lev 4:13 against any of the **c** of the
Lev 4:22 against any of the **c** of the
Lev 4:27 against any of the **c** of the
Lev 5:17 be done by the **c** of the LORD
Lev 22:31 Therefore you shall keep My **c**
Lev 26: 3 in My statutes and keep My **c**
Lev 26:14 and do not observe all these **c**
Lev 26:15 you do not perform all My **c**
Lev 27:34 These are the **c** which the
Num 15:22 do not observe all these **c**
Num 15:39 all the **c** of the LORD and do
Num 15:40 may remember and do all My **c**
Num 36:13 These are the **c** and the
Deut 1: 3 had given him as **c** to them
Deut 4: 2 that you may keep the **c** of
Deut 4:13 perform, that is, the Ten **C**
Deut 4:40 His **c** which I command you
Deut 5:10 who love Me and keep My **c**
Deut 5:29 Me and always keep all My **c**
Deut 5:31 I will speak to you all the **c**
Deut 6: 2 His **c** which I command you,
Deut 6:17 the **c** of the LORD your God
Deut 6:25 to observe all these **c** before
Deut 7: 9 who love Him and keep His **c**
Deut 8: 2 you would keep His **c** or not
Deut 8: 6 you shall keep the **c** of the
Deut 8:11 your God by not keeping His **c**
Deut 10: 4 the first writing, the Ten **C**
Deut 10:13 and to keep the **c** of the LORD
Deut 11: 1 judgments, and His **c** always
Deut 11:13 **c** which I command you today
Deut 11:22 carefully keep all these **c**
Deut 11:27 if you obey the **c** of the LORD
Deut 11:28 the **c** of the LORD your God
Deut 13: 4 and fear Him, and keep His **c**
Deut 13:18 to keep all His **c** which I
Deut 15: 5 **c** which I command you today
Deut 19: 9 and if you keep all these **c**
Deut 26:13 according to all Your **c** which
Deut 26:13 have not transgressed Your **c**
Deut 26:17 and keep His statutes, His **c**
Deut 26:18 you should keep all His **c**
Deut 27: 1 Keep all the **c** which I
Deut 27:10 your God, and observe His **c**
Deut 28: 1 **c** which I command you today
Deut 28: 9 if you keep the **c** of the LORD
Deut 28:13 if you heed the **c** of the LORD
Deut 28:15 observe carefully all His **c**
Deut 28:45 LORD your God, to keep His **c**
Deut 30: 8 do all His **c** which I command
Deut 30:10 LORD your God, to keep His **c**
Deut 30:16 in His ways, and to keep His **c**
Josh 22: 5 all His ways, to keep His **c**
Judg 2:17 in obeying the **c** of the LORD
Judg 3: 4 would obey the **c** of the LORD
1Sa 15:11 Me, and has not performed My **c**
1Ki 2: 3 to keep His statutes, His **c**
1Ki 3:14 to keep My statutes and My **c**
1Ki 6:12 My judgments, keep all My **c**
1Ki 8:58 His ways, and to keep His **c**
1Ki 8:61 in His statutes and keep His **c**
1Ki 9: 6 and do not keep My **c** and My
1Ki 11:34 I chose because he kept My **c**
1Ki 11:38 to keep My statutes and My **c**
1Ki 14: 8 servant David, who kept My **c**
1Ki 18:18 forsaken the **c** of the LORD
2Ki 17:13 your evil ways, and keep My **c**
2Ki 17:16 So they left all the **c** of the
2Ki 17:19 the **c** of the LORD their God
2Ki 18: 6 following Him, but kept His **c**
2Ki 23: 3 the LORD and to keep His **c**
1Ch 28: 7 is steadfast to observe My **c**
1Ch 28: 8 the **c** of the LORD your God
1Ch 29:19 a loyal heart to keep Your **c**
2Ch 7:19 My **c** which I have set before
2Ch 17: 4 father, and walked in His **c**
2Ch 24:20 transgress the **c** of the LORD
2Ch 34:31 the LORD, and to keep His **c**
Ezra 7:11 words of the **c** of the LORD
Ezra 9:10 For we have forsaken Your **c**
Ezra 9:14 should we again break Your **c**
Neh 1: 5 love You and observe Your **c**
Neh 1: 7 You, and have not kept the **c**
Neh 1: 9 return to Me, and keep My **c**
Neh 9:13 true laws, good statutes and **c**
Neh 9:16 necks, and did not heed Your **c**
Neh 9:29 and did not heed Your **c**, but
Neh 9:34 Your law, nor heeded Your **c**
Neh 10:29 do all the **c** of the LORD our
Ps 78: 7 works of God, But keep His **c**
Ps 89:31 statutes And do not keep My **c**
Ps 103:18 who remember His **c** to do them
Ps 111:10 have all those who do His **c**
Ps 112: 1 Who delights greatly in His **c**
Ps 119: 6 When I look into all Your **c**
Ps 119:10 let me not wander from Your **c**
Ps 119:19 Do not hide Your **c** from me
Ps 119:21 cursed, Who stray from Your **c**
Ps 119:32 will run in the way of Your **c**
Ps 119:35 me walk in the path of Your **c**
Ps 119:47 will delight myself in Your **c**
Ps 119:48 also I will lift up to Your **c**
Ps 119:60 did not delay To keep Your **c**
Ps 119:66 For I believe Your **c**
Ps 119:73 that I may learn Your **c**
Ps 119:86 All Your **c** are faithful
Ps 119:98 You, through Your **c**, make me
Ps 119:115 I will keep the **c** of my God
Ps 119:127 I love Your **c** More than gold
Ps 119:131 For I longed for Your **c**
Ps 119:143 Yet Your **c** are my delights
Ps 119:151 LORD, And all Your **c** are truth
Ps 119:166 salvation, And I do Your **c**
Ps 119:172 Your word, For all Your **c** are
Ps 119:176 For I do not forget Your **c**
Eccl 12:13 Fear God and keep His **c**, for
Is 48:18 Oh, that you had heeded My **c**
Dan 9: 4 and with those who keep His **c**
Amos 2: 4 LORD, and have not kept His **c**
Matt 5:19 one of the least of these **c**
Matt 15: 9 as doctrines the **c** of men
Matt 19:17 enter into life, keep the **c**
Matt 22:40 On these two **c** hang all the
Mark 7: 7 as doctrines the **c** of men
Mark 10:19 You know the **c**
Mark 12:29 The first of all the **c** is
Luke 1: 6 God, walking in all the **c**
Luke 18:20 You know the **c**
John 14:15 If you love Me, keep My **c**
John 14:21 He who has My **c** and keeps
John 15:10 If you keep My **c**, you will
John 15:10 as I have kept My Father's **c**
Acts 1: 2 the Holy Spirit had given **c**
Rom 13: 9 For the **c**, "You shall not
1Co 7:19 but keeping the **c** of God is
1Co 14:37 to you are the **c** of the Lord
Eph 2:15 the law of **c** contained in
Col 2:22 according to the **c** and
1Th 4: 2 for you know what **c** we gave
Tit 1:14 **c** of men who turn from the
1Jn 2: 3 we know Him, if we keep His **c**
1Jn 2: 4 Him," and does not keep His **c**
1Jn 3:22 Him, because we keep His **c**
1Jn 3:24 who keeps His **c** abides in Him
1Jn 5: 2 we love God and keep His **c**
1Jn 5: 3 of God, that we keep His **c**
1Jn 5: 3 And His **c** are not burdensome
2Jn 6 we walk according to His **c**
Rev 12:17 who keep the **c** of God and
Rev 14:12 those who keep the **c** of God
Rev 22:14 are those who do His **c**, that

COMMANDS (*see* COMMAND)
Ex 18:23 this thing, and God so **c** you
Num 32:25 servants will do as my lord **c**
Num 36: 6 This is what the LORD **c**
Deut 26:16 God **c** you to observe these
2Sa 15:15 whatever my lord the king **c**
Job 9: 7 He **c** the sun, and it does not
Job 36:10 and **c** that they turn from
Job 36:32 lightning, and **c** it to strike
Job 37:12 He **c** them on the face of the
Ps 107:25 For He **c** and raises the stormy
Prov 2: 1 and treasure my **c** within you
Prov 3: 1 but let your heart keep my **c**
Prov 4: 4 keep my **c**, and live
Prov 7: 1 and treasure my **c** within you
Prov 7: 2 Keep my **c** and live, and my law
Prov 10: 8 wise in heart will receive **c**
Mark 1:27 For with authority He **c** even
Luke 4:36 and power He **c** the unclean
Luke 8:25 For He **c** even the winds and
Acts 17:30 but now **c** all men everywhere

COMMEMORATE
1Ch 16: 4 the ark of the LORD, to **c**

COMMEND (*see* COMMENDABLE, COMMENDATION, COMMENDED, COMMENDING, COMMENDS)
Luke 23:46 into Your hands I **c** My spirit
Acts 20:32 I **c** you to God and to the word
Rom 16: 1 I **c** to you Phoebe our sister,
1Co 8: 8 But food does not **c** us to God
2Co 3: 1 we begin again to **c** ourselves
2Co 5:12 For we do not **c** ourselves
2Co 6: 4 But in all things we **c**
2Co 10:12 with those who **c** themselves

COMMENDABLE (*see* COMMEND)
1Pe 2:19 For this is **c**, if because of
1Pe 2:20 this is **c** before God

COMMENDATION (*see* COMMEND)
2Co 3: 1 epistles of **c** to you or
2Co 3: 1 you or letters of **c** from you

COMMENDED (*see* COMMEND)
Gen 12:15 saw her and **c** her to Pharaoh
Prov 12: 8 A man will be **c** according to
Eccl 8:15 So I **c** enjoyment, because a
Luke 16: 8 So the master **c** the unjust
Acts 14:23 they **c** them to the Lord in
Acts 14:26 where they had been **c** to the
Acts 15:40 being **c** by the brethren to
2Co 12:11 I ought to have been **c** by you

COMMENDING (*see* COMMEND)
2Co 4: 2 **c** ourselves to every man's

COMMENDS (*see* COMMEND)
2Co 10:18 For not he who **c** himself is
2Co 10:18 approved, but whom the Lord **c**

COMMISSION
Acts 26:12 **c** from the chief priests,

COMMIT (*see* COMMITS, COMMITTED, COMMITTING)
Ex 20:14 You shall not **c** adultery
Lev 18:26 and shall not **c** any of these
Lev 18:29 the persons who **c** them shall
Lev 18:30 so that you do not **c** any of
Lev 20: 5 him to **c** harlotry with Molech
Lev 20:23 for they **c** all these things,
Num 5: 6 commits any sin that men **c** in
Num 25: 1 and the people began to **c**
Deut 5:18 You shall not **c** adultery
Deut 19:20 again **c** such evil among you
Josh 22:20 **c** a trespass in the accursed
Judg 19:23 house, do not **c** this outrage

2Ki 17:21 and made them **c** a great sin
2Ch 21:11 of Jerusalem to **c** harlotry
Job 5: 8 and to God I would **c** my cause
Job 34:10 the Almighty to **c** iniquity
Ps 31: 5 Into Your hand I **c** my spirit
Ps 37: 5 **C** your way to the LORD, Trust
Prov 16: 3 **C** your works to the LORD, and
Prov 16:12 for kings to **c** wickedness
Is 22:21 I will **c** your responsibility
Is 23:17 **c** fornication with all the
Jer 7: 9 **c** adultery, swear falsely,
Jer 9: 5 themselves to **c** iniquity
Jer 23:14 they **c** adultery and walk in
Jer 37:21 **c** Jeremiah to the court of
Jer 44: 7 Why do you **c** this great evil
Ezek 8:17 to the house of Judah to **c**
Ezek 8:17 which they **c** here
Ezek 16:43 you shall not **c** lewdness in
Ezek 16:51 Samaria did not **c** half of
Ezek 22: 9 in your midst they **c** lewdness
Ezek 23:43 Will they **c** harlotry with
Ezek 33:26 you **c** abominations, and you
Hos 4:10 they shall **c** harlotry, but
Hos 4:13 your daughters **c** harlotry
Hos 4:13 and your brides **c** adultery
Hos 4:14 when they **c** harlotry, nor
Hos 4:14 brides when they **c** adultery
Hos 4:18 they **c** harlotry continually
Hos 5: 3 O Ephraim, you **c** harlotry
Hos 6: 9 surely they **c** lewdness
Matt 5:27 You shall not **c** adultery
Matt 5:32 causes her to **c** adultery
Matt 19:18 You shall not **c** adultery
Mark 10:19 Do not **c** adultery,' Do not
Luke 16:11 who will **c** to your trust the
Luke 18:20 Do not **c** adultery,' Do not
John 2:24 did not **c** Himself to them
Rom 2:22 Do not **c** adultery," do you
Rom 2:22 adultery," do you **c** adultery
Rom 13: 9 You shall not **c** adultery,"
1Co 10: 8 Nor let us **c** sexual
2Co 11: 7 Did I **c** sin in abasing myself
1Ti 1:18 This charge I **c** to you, son
2Ti 2: 2 **c** these to faithful men who
Jas 2: 9 show partiality, you **c** sin
Jas 2:11 Do not **c** adultery," also
Jas 2:11 Now if you do not **c** adultery
1Pe 4:19 to the will of God **c** their
1Jn 5:16 **c** sin not leading to death
Rev 2:14 and to **c** sexual immorality
Rev 2:20 to **c** sexual immorality and to
Rev 2:22 those who **c** adultery with her

COMMITS (*see* COMMIT)
Lev 5:15 If a person **c** a trespass, and
Lev 5:17 **c** any of these things which
Lev 6: 2 **c** a trespass against the LORD
Lev 18:29 For whoever **c** any of these
Lev 20:10 The man who **c** adultery with
Lev 20:10 he who **c** adultery with his
Num 5: 6 When a man or woman **c** any
Deut 19:15 iniquity or any sin that he **c**
2Sa 7:14 If he **c** iniquity, I will
Ps 10:14 The helpless **c** himself to You
Prov 6:32 Whoever **c** adultery with a
Ezek 3:20 and **c** iniquity, and I lay a
Ezek 8: 6 the house of Israel **c** here
Ezek 18:24 **c** iniquity, and does according
Ezek 18:26 **c** iniquity, and dies in it, it
Ezek 22:11 One **c** abomination with his
Ezek 33:13 and **c** iniquity, none of his
Ezek 33:18 and **c** iniquity, he shall die
Hab 1:11 he **c** offense, imputing this
Matt 5:32 who is divorced **c** adultery
Matt 19: 9 marries another, **c** adultery
Matt 19: 9 who is divorced **c** adultery
Mark 10:11 marries another **c** adultery
Mark 10:12 another, she **c** adultery
Luke 16:18 and marries another **c** adultery
Luke 16:18 from her husband **c** adultery
John 8:34 whoever **c** sin is a slave of
1Co 6:18 the body, but he who **c** sexual
1Jn 3: 4 Whoever **c** sin also **c**
1Jn 3: 4 sin also **c** lawlessness, and

COMMITTED (*see* COMMIT)
Gen 39: 8 he has **c** all that he has to
Gen 39:22 **c** to Joseph's hand all the
Lev 4:35 for his sin that he has **c**
Lev 5: 7 his trespass which he has **c**
Lev 18:30 which were **c** before you, and
Lev 20:12 They have **c** perversion
Lev 20:13 of them have **c** an abomination
Num 15:24 if it is unintentionally **c**
Deut 9:18 **c** in doing wickedly in the
Deut 13:14 abomination was **c** among you
Deut 17: 4 has been **c** in Israel,
Deut 17: 5 who has **c** that wicked thing
Deut 21:22 If a man has **c** a sin worthy
Josh 7: 1 **c** a trespass regarding the
Josh 22:16 is this that you have **c**
Josh 22:31 because you have not **c** this
Judg 20: 6 because they **c** lewdness and
1Ki 8:47 wrong, we have **c** wickedness'
1Ki 14:22 with their sins which they **c**
1Ki 14:27 **c** them to the hands of the
1Ki 16:19 he had **c** to make Israel sin
1Ki 16:20 of Zimri, and the treason he **c**
2Ki 21:17 he did, and the sin that he **c**
1Ch 10:13 he had **c** against the LORD
2Ch 12:10 **c** them to the hands of the
2Ch 34:16 All that was **c** to your
Ps 106: 6 We have **c** iniquity, We have
Jer 2:13 My people have **c** two evils
Jer 3: 8 Israel had **c** adultery, I had
Jer 3: 9 **c** adultery with stones and
Jer 5: 7 full, then they **c** adultery
Jer 5:30 thing has been **c** in the land
Jer 6:15 when they had **c** abomination
Jer 8:12 when they had **c** abomination
Jer 16:10 is our sin that we have **c**
Jer 29:23 have **c** adultery with their
Jer 37:18 offense have I **c** against you
Jer 39:14 **c** him to Gedaliah the son of
Jer 40: 7 and had **c** to him men, women,
Jer 41:10 had **c** to Gedaliah the son of
Jer 44: 3 have **c** to provoke Me to anger
Jer 44: 9 which they **c** in the land of
Jer 44:22 the abominations which you **c**
Ezek 6: 9 for the evils which they **c** in
Ezek 16:26 You also **c** harlotry with the
Ezek 16:50 and **c** abomination before Me
Ezek 16:52 **c** were more abominable than
Ezek 17:20 treason which he **c** against Me
Ezek 18:12 the idols, or **c** abomination
Ezek 18:21 all his sins which he has **c**
Ezek 18:22 **c** shall be remembered against
Ezek 18:24 and the sin which he has **c**
Ezek 18:27 the wickedness which he **c**
Ezek 18:28 the transgressions which he **c**
Ezek 18:31 which you have **c**, and get
Ezek 20:43 all the evils that you have **c**
Ezek 22:29 **c** robbery, and mistreated the
Ezek 23: 3 They **c** harlotry in Egypt,
Ezek 23: 3 they **c** harlotry in their
Ezek 23: 7 Thus she **c** her harlotry with
Ezek 23:37 For they have **c** adultery, and
Ezek 23:37 They have **c** adultery with
Ezek 33:13 of the iniquity that he has **c**
Ezek 33:16 of his sins which he has **c**
Ezek 33:29 which they have **c**
Ezek 43: 8 the abominations which they **c**
Ezek 44:13 which they have **c**
Dan 9: 5 and **c** iniquity, we have done
Dan 9: 7 which they have **c** against You
Hos 1: 2 for the land has **c** great
Hos 7: 1 For they have **c** fraud
Mal 2:11 has been **c** in Israel and in
Matt 5:28 **c** adultery with her in his
Mark 15: 7 they had **c** murder in the
Luke 12:48 know, yet **c** things worthy of
Luke 12:48 and to whom much has been **c**
John 5:22 but has **c** all judgment to the
Acts 25:11 or have **c** anything worthy of
Acts 25:25 had **c** nothing worthy of death
Rom 3: 2 were **c** the oracles of God
Rom 3:25 sins that were previously **c**
Rom 11:32 For God has **c** them all to
2Co 5:19 and has **c** to us the word of
Gal 2: 7 had been **c** to me, as the
1Ti 1:11 God which was **c** to my trust
1Ti 6:20 what was **c** to your trust,
2Ti 1:12 have **c** to Him until that Day
2Ti 1:14 good thing which was **c** to you
Tit 1: 3 which was **c** to me according
Heb 9: 7 people's sins **c** in ignorance
Jas 5:15 And if he has **c** sins, he will
1Pe 2:22 Who **c** no sin, nor was guile
1Pe 2:23 but **c** Himself to Him who
Jude 15 they have **c** in an ungodly way
Rev 17: 2 of the earth **c** fornication
Rev 18: 3 have **c** fornication with her
Rev 18: 9 the earth who **c** fornication
Rev 20: 4 and judgment was **c** to them

COMMITTING (*see* COMMIT)
Ezek 20:30 **c** harlotry according to their
Ezek 33:15 of life without **c** iniquity
Hos 3: 1 is **c** adultery, just like the
Hos 4: 2 **c** adultery, they break all
Acts 8: 3 and women, **c** them to prison
Rom 1:27 men with men **c** what is

COMMON (*see* COMMON-LAND, COMMONLY)
Lev 4:27 If anyone of the **c** people
Num 16:29 by the **c** fate of all men,
1Sa 21: 4 There is no **c** bread on hand
1Sa 21: 5 and the bread is in effect **c**
1Ki 10:27 as **c** in Jerusalem as stones
2Ki 23: 6 on the graves of the **c** people
2Ch 1:15 gold as **c** in Jerusalem as
2Ch 9:27 as **c** in Jerusalem as stones
Prov 22: 2 and the poor have this in **c**
Prov 29:13 the oppressor have this in **c**
Eccl 6: 1 the sun, and it is **c** among men
Jer 26:23 the graves of the **c** people
Ezek 7:27 the hands of the **c** people
Ezek 23:42 with men of the **c** sort, who
Ezek 42:20 the holy areas from the **c**
Mark 12:37 the **c** people heard Him gladly
Acts 2:44 and had all things in **c**,
Acts 4:32 but they had all things in **c**
Acts 5:18 and put them in the **c** prison
Acts 10:14 eaten anything **c** or unclean
Acts 10:15 cleansed you must not call **c**
Acts 10:28 not call any man **c** or unclean
Acts 11: 8 For nothing **c** or unclean has
Acts 11: 9 cleansed you must not call **c**
1Co 10:13 except such as is **c** to man
Tit 1: 4 my true son in our **c** faith
Heb 10:29 he was sanctified a **c** thing
Jude 3 concerning our **c** salvation

COMMON-LAND (*see* COMMON, COMMON-LANDS)
Lev 25:34 But the field of the **c** of
Num 35: 2 Levites **c** around the cities
Num 35: 3 their **c** shall be for their
Num 35: 4 The **c** of the cities which you
Num 35: 5 to them as **c** for the cities
Num 35: 7 you shall give with their **c**
Josh 21:11 with the **c** surrounding it
Josh 21:13 **c** (a city of refuge for the
Josh 21:13 slayer), Libnah with its **c**
Josh 21:14 Jattir with its **c**
Josh 21:14 Eshtemoa with its **c**,
Josh 21:15 Holon with its **c**
Josh 21:15 Debir with its **c**
Josh 21:16 Ain with its **c**
Josh 21:16 Juttah with its **c**
Josh 21:16 and Beth Shemesh with its **c**
Josh 21:17 Benjamin, Gibeon with its **c**
Josh 21:17 Geba with its **c**
Josh 21:18 Anathoth with its **c**
Josh 21:18 and Almon with its **c**
Josh 21:21 gave them Shechem with its **c**
Josh 21:21 the slayer), Gezer with its **c**
Josh 21:22 Kibzaim with its **c**
Josh 21:22 and Beth Horon with its **c**
Josh 21:23 of Dan, Eltekeh with its **c**
Josh 21:23 Gibbethon with its **c**,
Josh 21:24 Aijalon with its **c**, and Gath
Josh 21:24 and Gath Rimmon with its **c**
Josh 21:25 Manasseh, Tanach with its **c**
Josh 21:25 and Gath Rimmon with its **c**
Josh 21:27 Golan in Bashan with its **c**
Josh 21:27 and Be Eshterah with its **c**
Josh 21:28 Issachar, Kishion with its **c**
Josh 21:28 Daberath with its **c**,
Josh 21:29 Jarmuth with its **c**
Josh 21:29 and En Gannim with its **c**
Josh 21:30 of Asher, Mishal with its **c**
Josh 21:30 **c**, Abdon with its **c**
Josh 21:31 Helkath with its **c**
Josh 21:31 and Rehob with its **c**
Josh 21:32 Kedesh in Galilee with its **c**
Josh 21:32 Hammoth Dor with its **c**
Josh 21:32 and Kartan with its **c**
Josh 21:34 Zebulun, Jokneam with its **c**
Josh 21:34 Kartah with its **c**,
Josh 21:35 Dimnah with its **c**
Josh 21:35 and Nahalal with its **c**
Josh 21:36 of Reuben, Bezer with its **c**

Josh 21:36 Jahaz with its **c**
Josh 21:37 Kedemoth with its **c**, and
Josh 21:37 and Mephaath with its **c**
Josh 21:38 Ramoth in Gilead with its **c**
Josh 21:38 slayer), Mahanaim with its **c**
Josh 21:39 Heshbon with its **c**
Josh 21:39 and Jazer with its **c**
Josh 21:42 had its **c** surrounding it
Ezek 27:28 The **c** will shake at the sound
Ezek 48:15 the city, for dwellings and **c**
Ezek 48:17 The **c** of the city shall be

COMMON-LANDS (*see* COMMON-LAND)
Josh 14: 4 in, with their **c** for their
Josh 21: 2 in, with their **c** for our
Josh 21: 3 LORD, these cities and their **c**
Josh 21: 8 their **c** by lot to the Levites
Josh 21:19 thirteen cities with their **c**
Josh 21:26 **c** were for the rest of the
Josh 21:33 thirteen cities with their **c**
Josh 21:41 cities with their **c**
1Ch 5:16 in all the **c** of Sharon within
1Ch 6:55 Judah, with its surrounding **c**
1Ch 6:57 also Libnah with its **c**,
1Ch 6:57 Jattir, Eshtemoa with its **c**
1Ch 6:58 Hilen with its **c**, Debir with
1Ch 6:58 Debir with its **c**,
1Ch 6:59 Ashan with its **c**, and Beth
1Ch 6:59 and Beth Shemesh with its **c**
1Ch 6:60 Geba with its **c**, Alemeth with
1Ch 6:60 Alemeth with its **c**, and
1Ch 6:60 and Anathoth with its **c**
1Ch 6:64 with their **c** to the Levites
1Ch 6:67 of refuge, Shechem with its **c**
1Ch 6:67 also Gezer with its **c**,
1Ch 6:68 Jokmeam with its **c**, Beth
1Ch 6:68 Beth Horon with its **c**,
1Ch 6:69 Aijalon with its **c**, and Gath
1Ch 6:69 and Gath Rimmon with its **c**
1Ch 6:70 Aner with its **c** and Bileam
1Ch 6:70 and Bileam with its **c**, for the
1Ch 6:71 Golan in Bashan with its **c**
1Ch 6:71 and Ashtaroth with its **c**
1Ch 6:72 Kedesh with its **c**, Daberath
1Ch 6:72 Daberath with its **c**,
1Ch 6:73 Ramoth with its **c**, and Anem
1Ch 6:73 and Anem with its **c**
1Ch 6:74 Mashal with its **c**, Abdon with
1Ch 6:74 Abdon with its **c**,
1Ch 6:75 Hukok with its **c**, and Rehob
1Ch 6:75 and Rehob with its **c**
1Ch 6:76 Kedesh in Galilee with its **c**
1Ch 6:76 Hammon with its **c**, and
1Ch 6:76 and Kirjathaim with its **c**
1Ch 6:77 were given Rimmon with its **c**
1Ch 6:77 and Tabor with its **c**
1Ch 6:78 in the wilderness with its **c**
1Ch 6:78 Jahzah with its **c**,
1Ch 6:79 Kedemoth with its **c**, and
1Ch 6:79 and Mephaath with its **c**
1Ch 6:80 Ramoth in Gilead with its **c**
1Ch 6:80 Mahanaim with its **c**,
1Ch 6:81 Heshbon with its **c**, and Jazer
1Ch 6:81 and Jazer with its **c**
1Ch 13: 2 in their cities and their **c**
2Ch 11:14 For the Levites left their **c**
2Ch 31:19 of the **c** of their cities, in

COMMONLY (*see* COMMON)
Matt 28:15 this saying is **c** reported

COMMONWEALTH
Eph 2:12 aliens from the **c** of Israel

COMMOTION (*see* COMMOTIONS)
Jer 10:22 a great **c** out of the north
Mark 5:39 Why make this **c** and weep
Acts 19:23 arose a great **c** about the Way

COMMOTIONS (*see* COMMOTION)
Luke 21: 9 when you hear of wars and **c**

COMMUNED (*see* COMMUNION)
Eccl 1:16 I **c** with my heart, saying,

COMMUNICATE (*see* COMMUNICATED, COMMUNICATION)
1Sa 18:22 **C** with David secretly, and say

COMMUNICATED (*see* COMMUNICATE)
2Sa 3:17 Now Abner had **c** with the
Gal 2: 2 **c** to them that gospel which I

COMMUNICATION (*see* COMMUNICATE)
Eph 4:29 Let no corrupt **c** proceed out

COMMUNION (*see* COMMUNED)
1Co 10:16 is it not the **c** of the blood
1Co 10:16 is it not the **c** of the body
2Co 6:14 And what **c** has light with
2Co 13:14 the **c** of the Holy Spirit be

COMMUNITIES
Neh 10:37 tithes in all our farming **c**

COMPACT
Ps 122: 3 As a city that is **c** together

COMPANIES (*see* COMPANY)
Gen 32: 7 herds and camels, into two **c**
Gen 32:10 and now I have become two **c**
Judg 7:16 hundred men into three **c**, and
Judg 7:20 Then the three **c** blew the
Judg 9:34 against Shechem in four **c**
Judg 9:43 divided them into three **c**
Judg 9:44 the other two **c** rushed upon
1Sa 11:11 put the people in three **c**
1Sa 13:17 of the Philistines in three **c**
2Ch 26:11 men who went out to war by **c**
Is 21:13 you traveling **c** of Dedanites
Ezek 38: 7 all your **c** that are gathered

COMPANION (*see* COMPANIONS)
Ex 2:13 Why are you striking your **c**
Ex 32:27 his brother, every man his **c**
Judg 7:13 man telling a dream to his **c**
Judg 7:14 Then his **c** answered and said,
Judg 7:22 man's sword against his **c**
Judg 14:20 wife was given to his **c**, who
Judg 15: 2 I gave her to your **c**
Judg 15: 6 wife and given her to his **c**
1Ch 27:33 the Archite was the king's **c**
Job 30:29 jackals, and a **c** of ostriches
Ps 55:13 was you, a man my equal, My **c**
Ps 119:63 I am a **c** of all those who
Prov 2:17 forsakes the **c** of her youth
Prov 13:20 but the **c** of fools will be
Prov 28: 7 but a **c** of gluttons shames
Prov 28:24 the same is **c** to a
Prov 29: 3 but a **c** of harlots wastes his
Eccl 4: 8 There is one alone, without **c**
Eccl 4:10 fall, one will lift up his **c**
Is 34:14 goat shall bleat to its **c**
Mic 7: 5 put your confidence in a **c**
Zech 13: 7 against the Man who is My **C**
Mal 2:14 yet she is your **c** and your
Phil 4: 3 And I urge you also, true **c**
Rev 1: 9 **c** in tribulation, and in the

COMPANIONS (*see* COMPANION)
Num 16:40 become like Korah and his **c**
Judg 14:11 thirty **c** to be with him
Ezra 4: 7 the rest of their **c** wrote to
Ezra 4: 9 and the rest of their **c**
Ezra 4:17 their **c** who dwell in Samaria
Ezra 4:23 the scribe, and their **c**, they
Ezra 5: 3 their **c** came to them and spoke
Ezra 5: 6 and Shethar-Baznai, and his **c**
Ezra 6: 6 your **c** the Persians who are
Ezra 6:13 and their **c** diligently did
Job 35: 4 you, and your **c** with you
Job 41: 6 Will your **c** make a banquet of
Ps 45: 7 of gladness more than Your **c**
Ps 45:14 her **c** who follow her, shall
Ps 122: 8 the sake of my brethren and **c**
Song 1: 7 by the flocks of your **c**
Song 8:13 the **c** listen for your voice
Is 1:23 rebellious, and **c** of thieves
Is 44:11 surely all his **c** would be
Ezek 37:16 the children of Israel, his **c**
Ezek 37:16 the house of Israel, his **c**
Ezek 37:19 the tribes of Israel, his **c**
Dan 2:13 they sought Daniel and his **c**
Dan 2:17 Mishael, and Azariah, his **c**
Dan 2:18 his **c** might not perish with
Zech 3: 8 your **c** who sit before you,
Matt 11:16 and calling to their **c**,
Acts 4:23 go, they went to their own **c**
Acts 19:29 Macedonians, Paul's travel **c**
Acts 21: 8 we who were Paul's **c** departed
Heb 1: 9 of gladness more than Your **c**
Heb 10:33 became **c** of those who were so

COMPANY (*see* COMPANIES)
Gen 32: 8 If Esau comes to the one **c**
Gen 32: 8 then the other **c** which is
Gen 33: 8 by all this **c** which I met
Gen 35:11 a **c** of nations shall proceed
Gen 37:25 there was a **c** of Ishmaelites,
Num 16: 5 spoke to Korah and all his **c**
Num 16: 6 censers, Korah and all your **c**
Num 16:11 and all your **c** are gathered
Num 16:16 all your **c** be present before
Num 22: 4 Now this **c** will lick up all
Num 26: 9 and Aaron in the **c** of Korah
Num 26:10 with Korah when that **c** died
Num 27: 3 the **c** of those who gathered
Num 27: 3 in **c** with Korah, but he died
Judg 9:37 another **c** is coming from the
Judg 9:44 and the **c** that was with him
Judg 18:23 you have gathered such a **c**
1Sa 13:17 One **c** turned to the road that
1Sa 13:18 another **c** turned to the road
1Sa 13:18 another **c** turned to the road
2Ki 9:17 he saw the **c** of Jehu as he
2Ki 9:17 I see a **c** of men
2Ch 24:24 came with a small **c** of men
2Ch 31:18 the whole **c** of them
Job 15:34 For the **c** of hypocrites will
Job 16: 7 have made desolate all my **c**
Job 34: 8 who goes in **c** with the
Ps 68:11 Great was the **c** of those who
Ps 68:27 princes of Judah and their **c**
Ps 106:18 A fire was kindled in their **c**
Ezek 17:17 great **c** do anything in the
Ezek 27: 6 the **c** of Ashurites have
Ezek 27:27 the entire **c** which is in your
Ezek 27:34 the entire **c** will fall in
Ezek 32: 3 you with a **c** of many people
Ezek 32:22 is there, and all her **c**, with
Ezek 32:23 her **c** is all around her grave
Ezek 38: 4 a great **c** with bucklers and
Ezek 38:15 riding on horses, a great **c**
Hos 6: 9 so the **c** of priests murder on
Luke 2:44 Him to have been in the **c**
Luke 24:22 and certain women of our **c**
Acts 10:28 keep **c** with or go to one of
Acts 15:22 own **c** to Antioch with Paul
Rom 15:24 may enjoy your **c** for a while
1Co 5: 9 keep **c** with sexually immoral
1Co 5:11 written to you not to keep **c**
1Co 15:33 Evil **c** corrupts good habits
2Th 3:14 and do not keep **c** with him
Heb 12:22 to an innumerable **c** of angels

COMPARABLE (*see* COMPARE)
Gen 2:18 make him a helper **c** to him
Gen 2:20 not found a helper **c** to him

COMPARE (*see* COMPARABLE, COMPARED, COMPARING, COMPARISON)
Prov 3:15 may desire cannot **c** with her
Is 40:18 likeness will you **c** to Him
Is 46: 5 **c** Me, that we should be alike
Lam 2:13 what shall I **c** with you, that
Luke 13:18 And to what shall I **c** it
2Co 10:12 or **c** ourselves with those who

COMPARED (*see* COMPARE)
Ps 89: 6 heavens can be **c** to the LORD
Prov 8:11 desire cannot be **c** with her
Song 1: 9 I have **c** you, my love, to my
Rom 8:18 time are not worthy to be **c**

COMPARING (*see* COMPARE)
1Co 2:13 **c** spiritual things with
2Co 10:12 **c** themselves among themselves

COMPARISON (*see* COMPARE)
Judg 8: 2 have I done now in **c** with you
Judg 8: 3 I able to do in **c** with you
Hag 2: 3 In **c** with it, is this not in

COMPASS
Is 44:13 he marks it out with the **c**

COMPASSION (*see* COMPASSIONATE, COMPASSIONS)
Ex 2: 6 So she had **c** on him, and said,
Ex 33:19 I will have **c** on whom I will
Ex 33:19 on whom I will have **c**
Deut 13:17 have **c** on you and multiply you
Deut 30: 3 have **c** on you, and gather you
Deut 32:36 have **c** on His servants, when
1Sa 23:21 LORD, for you have **c** on me
1Ki 3:26 yearned with **c** for her son
1Ki 8:50 grant them **c** before those who
1Ki 8:50 that they may have **c** on them
2Ki 13:23 had **c** on them, and regarded
2Ch 30: 9 will be treated with **c** by
2Ch 36:15 He had **c** on His people and on

Gen 29:34 She **c** again and bore a son, and
Gen 29:35 she **c** again and bore a son, and
Gen 30: 5 And Bilhah **c** and bore Jacob a
Gen 30: 7 Rachel's maid Bilhah **c** again
Gen 30:17 listened to Leah, and she **c**
Gen 30:19 Then Leah **c** again and bore
Gen 30:23 And she **c** and bore a son, and
Gen 30:39 So the flocks **c** before the
Gen 30:41 the stronger livestock **c**,
Gen 31:10 at the time when the flocks **c**
Gen 38: 3 So she **c** and bore a son, and he
Gen 38: 4 She **c** again and bore a son, and
Gen 38: 5 she **c** yet again and bore a son
Gen 38:18 in to her, and she **c** by him
Ex 2: 2 So the woman **c** and bore a son
Lev 12: 2 If a woman has **c**, and borne a
1Sa 1:20 process of time that Hannah **c**
1Sa 2:21 visited Hannah, so that she **c**
2Sa 11: 5 And the woman **c**
2Ki 4:17 the woman **c**, and bore a son
1Ch 7:23 he went in to his wife, she **c**
Job 3: 3 was said, 'A male child is **c**
Ps 51: 5 And in sin my mother **c** me
Song 3: 4 the chamber of her who **c** me
Is 8: 3 to the prophetess, and she **c**
Jer 49:30 and has **c** a plan against you
Hos 1: 3 daughter of Diblaim, and she **c**
Hos 1: 6 And she **c** again and bore a
Hos 1: 8 had weaned Lo-Ruhamah, she **c**
Hos 2: 5 she who **c** them has done
Matt 1:20 for that which is **c** in her is
Luke 1:24 days his wife Elizabeth **c**
Luke 1:36 also **c** a son in her old age
Luke 2:21 before He was **c** in the womb
Acts 5: 4 Why have you **c** this thing in
Rom 9:10 Rebecca also had **c** by one man
Jas 1:15 Then, when desire has **c**, it

CONCEIVES (*see* CONCEIVE)
Ps 7:14 **C** trouble and brings forth

CONCEIVING (*see* CONCEIVE)
Is 59:13 oppression and revolt, **c** and

CONCEPTION (*see* CONCEIVE)
Gen 3:16 your sorrow and your **c**
Ruth 4:13 to her, the LORD gave her **c**
Hos 9:11 birth, no pregnancy, and no **c**

CONCERN (*see* CONCERNED, CONCERNS)
Job 39:16 labor is in vain, without **c**
Ps 131: 1 Neither do I **c** myself with
Ezek 36:21 But I had **c** for My holy name,
Dan 4:19 may the dream **c** those who
Dan 4:19 interpretation **c** your enemies
John 2: 4 what does your **c** have to do
Acts 28:31 teaching the things which **c**
2Co 11:28 my deep **c** for all the
2Co 11:30 things which **c** my infirmity
Col 2:22 which all **c** things which

CONCERNED (*see* CONCERN)
Gen 45:20 Also do not be **c** about your
2Sa 14: 1 heart was **c** about Absalom
2Ki 4:13 you have been **c** for us with
1Co 7:21 Do not be **c** about it
1Co 9: 9 Is it oxen God is **c** about
Heb 9:10 **c** only with foods and drinks,

CONCERNING (*see* PREFACE)

CONCERNS (*see* CONCERN)
Ex 22: 9 trespass, whether it **c** an ox
Ps 138: 8 will perfect that which **c** me
Ezek 7:13 for the vision **c** the whole
Ezek 12:10 This burden **c** the prince in

CONCESSION
1Co 7: 6 But I say this as a **c**, not as

CONCILIATION
Eccl 10: 4 for **c** pacifies great offenses

CONCLUDE (*see* CONCLUDED, CONCLUDING, CONCLUSION)
Rom 3:28 Therefore we **c** that a man is

CONCLUDED (*see* CONCLUDE)
Ruth 3:18 he has **c** the matter this day
Luke 7: 1 Now when He **c** all His sayings

CONCLUDING (*see* CONCLUDE)
Acts 16:10 **c** that the Lord had called us

CONCLUSION (*see* CONCLUDE)
Eccl 12:13 Let us hear the **c** of the

CONCOURSES
Prov 1:21 She cries out in the chief **c**

CONCUBINE (*see* CONCUBINES)
Gen 22:24 His **c**, whose name was
Gen 35:22 with Bilhah his father's **c**
Gen 36:12 Timna was the **c** of Eliphaz
Lev 19:20 as a **c** to another man, and who
Judg 8:31 his **c** who was in Shechem also
Judg 19: 1 He took for himself a **c** from
Judg 19: 2 But his **c** played the harlot
Judg 19: 9 he and his **c** and his servant
Judg 19:10 his **c** was also with him
Judg 19:24 daughter and the man's **c**
Judg 19:25 So the man took his **c** and
Judg 19:27 go his way, there was his **c**
Judg 19:29 a knife, laid hold of his **c**
Judg 20: 4 My **c** and I went into Gibeah,
Judg 20: 5 my **c** so that she died
Judg 20: 6 So I took hold of my **c**, cut
2Sa 3: 7 And Saul had a **c**, whose name
2Sa 3: 7 you gone in to my father's **c**
2Sa 21:11 Aiah, the **c** of Saul, had done
1Ch 1:32 born to Keturah, Abraham's **c**
1Ch 2:46 Ephah, Caleb's **c**, bore Haran,
1Ch 2:48 Maachah, Caleb's **c**, bore
1Ch 7:14 his Syrian **c** bore him Machir

CONCUBINES (*see* CONCUBINE)
Gen 25: 6 of the **c** which Abraham had
2Sa 5:13 And David took more **c** and
2Sa 15:16 the king left ten women, **c**
2Sa 16:21 Go in to your father's **c**,
2Sa 16:22 went in to his father's **c** in
2Sa 19: 5 wives and the lives of your **c**
2Sa 20: 3 his **c** whom he had left to
1Ki 11: 3 and three hundred **c**
1Ch 3: 9 besides the sons of the **c**
2Ch 11:21 than all his wives and his **c**
2Ch 11:21 eighteen wives and sixty **c**
Esth 2:14 king's eunuch who kept the **c**
Song 6: 8 are sixty queens and eighty **c**
Song 6: 9 blessed, the queens and the **c**
Dan 5: 2 his **c** might drink from them
Dan 5: 3 and his **c** drank from them
Dan 5:23 lords, your wives and your **c**

CONDEMN (*see* CONDEMNATION, CONDEMNED, CONDEMNING, CONDEMNS, UNCONDEMNED)
Ex 22: 9 whomever the judges **c** shall
Deut 25: 1 righteous and **c** the wicked,
Job 9:20 my own mouth would **c** me
Job 10: 2 will say to God, 'Do not **c** me
Job 34:17 will you **c** Him who is most
Job 40: 8 Would you **c** Me that you may
Ps 37:33 Nor **c** him when he is judged
Ps 94:21 And **c** innocent blood
Ps 109:31 save him from those who **c** him
Prov 12: 2 of wicked devices He will **c**
Is 50: 9 who is he who will **c** Me
Is 54:17 you in judgment you shall **c**
Matt 12:41 **c** it, because they repented
Matt 12:42 **c** it, for she came from the
Matt 20:18 they will **c** Him to death,
Mark 10:33 they will **c** Him to death and
Luke 6:37 **C** not, and you shall not be
Luke 11:31 **c** them, for she came from the
Luke 11:32 **c** it, for they repented at
John 3:17 into the world to **c** the world
John 8:11 Neither do I **c** you
Rom 2: 1 judge another you **c** yourself
Rom 14:22 Happy is he who does not **c**
2Co 7: 3 I do not say this to **c**
1Jn 3:21 if our heart does not **c** us

CONDEMNATION (*see* CONDEMN)
Matt 23:14 you will receive greater **c**
Matt 23:33 can you escape the **c** of hell
Mark 3:29 but is subject to eternal **c**"
Mark 12:40 These will receive greater **c**
Luke 20:47 These will receive greater **c**
Luke 23:40 you are under the same **c**
John 3:19 And this is the **c**, that the
John 5:29 to the resurrection of **c**
Rom 3: 8 Their **c** is just
Rom 5:16 one offense resulted in **c**
Rom 5:18 to all men, resulting in **c**
Rom 8: 1 There is therefore now no **c**
2Co 3: 9 the ministry of **c** had glory
1Ti 3: 6 into the same **c** as the devil
1Ti 5:12 having **c** because they have
Jude 4 were marked out for this **c**

CONDEMNED (*see* CONDEMN)
2Sa 24:10 David's heart **c** him after he
Job 9:29 If I am **c**, why then do I
Job 32: 3 no answer, and yet had **c** Job
Ps 34:21 hate the righteous shall be **c**
Ps 34:22 who trust in Him shall be **c**
Amos 2: 8 drink the wine of the **c** in
Matt 12: 7 not have **c** the guiltless
Matt 12:37 by your words you will be **c**
Matt 27: 3 seeing that He had been **c**
Mark 14:64 they all **c** Him to be worthy
Mark 16:16 does not believe will be **c**
Luke 6:37 not, and you shall not be **c**
Luke 24:20 Him to be **c** to death, and
John 3:18 who believes in Him is not **c**
John 3:18 does not believe is **c** already
John 8:10 Has no one **c** you
Rom 8: 3 He **c** sin in the flesh,
Rom 14:23 he who doubts is **c** if he eats
1Co 4: 9 last, as men **c** to death
1Co 11:32 may not be **c** with the world
2Th 2:12 that they all may be **c** who
Tit 2: 8 sound speech that cannot be **c**
Heb 11: 7 by which he **c** the world and
Jas 5: 6 You have **c**, you have murdered
Jas 5: 9 brethren, lest you be **c**
2Pe 2: 6 **c** them to destruction, making

CONDEMNING (*see* CONDEMN)
1Ki 8:32 **c** the wicked, bringing his
Acts 13:27 have fulfilled them in **c** Him

CONDEMNS (*see* CONDEMN)
Job 15: 6 Your own mouth **c** you, and not
Job 21:31 Who **c** his way to his face
Prov 17:15 he who **c** the just, both of
Rom 8:34 Who is he who **c**
1Jn 3:20 For if our heart **c** us, God is

CONDITION (*see* CONDITIONS)
Gen 34:15 But on this **c** we will consent
Gen 34:22 Only on this **c** will the men
1Sa 11: 2 On this **c** I will make a
2Ch 24:13 of God to its original **c** and
John 5: 6 been in that **c** a long time

CONDITIONS (*see* CONDITION)
Luke 14:32 delegation and asks **c** of peace

CONDUCT (*see* CONDUCTED)
Deut 22:14 charges her with shameful **c**
Deut 22:17 charged her with shameful **c**
1Sa 4: 9 **c** yourselves like men, you
1Sa 4: 9 **C** yourselves like men, and
1Sa 28: 8 Please **c** a seance for me, and
Ps 37:14 those who are of upright **c**
Ps 50:23 And to him who orders his **c**
Gal 1:13 of my former **c** in Judaism
Eph 4:22 off, concerning your former **c**
Phil 1:27 Only let your **c** be worthy of
1Ti 3:15 to **c** yourself in the house of
1Ti 4:12 the believers in word, in **c**
Heb 13: 5 Let your **c** be without
Heb 13: 7 the outcome of their **c**
Jas 3:13 Let him show by good **c** that
1Pe 1:15 also be holy in all your **c**
1Pe 1:17 **c** yourselves throughout the
1Pe 1:18 from your aimless **c** received
1Pe 2:12 having your **c** honorable among
1Pe 3: 1 won by the **c** of their wives
1Pe 3: 2 chaste **c** accompanied by fear
1Pe 3:16 **c** in Christ may be ashamed
2Pe 2: 7 the filthy **c** of the wicked
2Pe 3:11 ought you to be in holy **c**

CONDUCTED (*see* CONDUCT)
Acts 17:15 So those who **c** Paul brought
2Co 1:12 **c** ourselves in the world in
Eph 2: 3 **c** ourselves in the lusts of

CONFEDERACY
Ps 83: 5 They form a **c** against You
Obad 7 All the men in your **c** shall

CONFER (*see* CONFERRED)
Gal 1:16 not immediately **c** with flesh

CONFERRED (*see* CONFER)
1Ki 1: 7 Then he c with Joab the son
Luke 22: 4 c with the chief priests and
Acts 4:15 they c among themselves,
Acts 25:12 when he had c with the

CONFESS (*see* CONFESSED, CONFESSES, CONFESSING, CONFESSION)
Lev 5: 5 that he shall c that he has
Lev 16:21 c over it all the iniquities
Lev 26:40 But if they c their iniquity
Num 5: 7 then he shall c the sin
1Ki 8:33 c Your name, and pray and
1Ki 8:35 c Your name, and turn from
2Ch 6:24 c Your name, and pray and
2Ch 6:26 c Your name, and turn from
Neh 1: 6 c the sins of the children of
Job 40:14 Then I will also c to you
Ps 32: 5 I will c my transgressions to
Matt 10:32 him I will also c before My
Luke 12: 8 c before the angels of God
John 12:42 Pharisees they did not c Him
Acts 23: 8 but the Pharisees c both
Acts 24:14 But this I c to you, that
Rom 10: 9 that if you c with your mouth
Rom 14:11 every tongue shall c to God
Rom 15: 9 For this reason I will c to
Phil 2:11 that every tongue should c
Jas 5:16 C your trespasses to one
1Jn 1: 9 If we c our sins, He is
1Jn 4: 3 c that Jesus Christ has come
2Jn 7 c Jesus Christ as coming in
Rev 3: 5 but I will c his name before

CONFESSED (*see* CONFESS)
Neh 9: 2 stood and c their sins and the
Neh 9: 3 and for another fourth they c
John 1:20 He c, and did not deny, but
John 1:20 and did not deny, but c, "I
John 9:22 anyone c that He was Christ
1Ti 6:12 have c the good confession in
Heb 11:13 c that they were strangers and

CONFESSES (*see* CONFESS)
Prov 28:13 not prosper, but whoever c
Matt 10:32 whoever c Me before men, him
Luke 12: 8 whoever c Me before men, him
1Jn 4: 2 Every spirit that c that
1Jn 4:15 Whoever c that Jesus is the

CONFESSING (*see* CONFESS)
Ezra 10: 1 praying, and while he was c
Dan 9:20 c my sin and the sin of my
Matt 3: 6 in the Jordan, c their sins
Mark 1: 5 Jordan River, c their sins
Acts 19:18 many who had believed came c

CONFESSION (*see* CONFESS)
Josh 7:19 make c to Him, and tell me now
2Ch 30:22 making c to the LORD God of
Ezra 10:11 make c to the LORD God of
Dan 9: 4 to the LORD my God, and made c
Rom 10:10 with the mouth c is made to
2Co 9:13 c to the gospel of Christ
1Ti 6:12 c in the presence of many
1Ti 6:13 good c before Pontius Pilate
Heb 3: 1 and High Priest of our c,
Heb 4:14 God, let us hold fast our c
Heb 10:23 the c of our hope without

CONFIDENCE (*see* CONFIDENT)
Judg 9:26 of Shechem put their c in him
2Ki 18:19 What c is this in which you
Job 4: 6 Is not your reverence your c
Job 8:14 whose c shall be cut off, and
Job 31:24 to fine gold, 'You are my c'
Ps 65: 5 You who are the c of all the
Ps 118: 8 the LORD Than to put c in man
Ps 118: 9 LORD Than to put c in princes
Prov 3:26 for the LORD will be your c
Prov 14:26 of the LORD there is strong c
Prov 25:19 C in an unfaithful man in
Is 30:15 and c shall be your strength
Is 36: 4 What c is this in which you
Jer 48:13 ashamed of Bethel, their c
Ezek 29:16 the c of the house of Israel
Mic 7: 5 not put your c in a companion
Acts 28:31 Lord Jesus Christ with all c
2Co 1:15 in this c I intended to come
2Co 2: 3 having c in you all that my
2Co 7:16 I have c in you in everything
2Co 8:22 great c which we have in you
2Co 10: 2 c by which I intend to be
2Co 11:17 in this c of boasting
Gal 5:10 I have c in you, in the Lord,
Eph 3:12 access with c through faith
Phil 3: 3 and have no c in the flesh,
Phil 3: 4 might have c in the flesh
Phil 3: 4 he may have c in the flesh
2Th 3: 4 And we have c in the Lord
Phm 21 Having c in your obedience, I
Heb 3: 6 we are if we hold fast the c
Heb 3:14 of our c steadfast to the end
Heb 10:35 do not cast away your c,
1Jn 2:28 He appears, we may have c
1Jn 3:21 us, we have c toward God
1Jn 5:14 Now this is the c that we

CONFIDENT (*see* CONFIDENCE, CONFIDENTLY)
Job 6:20 because they were c
Job 40:23 he is c, though the Jordan
Ps 27: 3 me, In this I will be c
Rom 2:19 are c that you yourself are a
Rom 15:14 I myself am c concerning you
2Co 5: 6 Therefore we are always c
2Co 5: 8 We are c, yes, well pleased
2Co 9: 4 be ashamed of this c boasting
Phil 1: 6 being c of this very thing,
Phil 1:14 having become c by my chains
Phil 1:25 being c of this, I know that
Heb 6: 9 we are c of better things
Heb 13:18 for we are c that we have a

CONFIDENTLY (*see* CONFIDENT)
Luke 22:59 another c affirmed, saying,

CONFINED
Gen 39:20 the king's prisoners were c
Gen 40: 3 the place where Joseph was c
Gen 40: 5 who were c in the prison,
Gen 42:19 be c to your prison house
Ex 21:18 not die but is c to his bed
Ex 21:29 and he has not kept it c, so
Ex 21:36 its owner has not kept it c
Josh 17:15 of Ephraim are too c for you
Jer 36: 5 I am c, I cannot go into the
Gal 3:22 Scripture has c all under sin

CONFIRM (*see* CONFIRMATION, CONFIRMED, CONFIRMING, CONFIRMS)
Lev 26: 9 you and c My covenant with you
Num 30:13 soul, her husband may c it
Deut 27:26 is the one who does not c all
Ruth 4: 7 and exchanging, to c anything
1Ki 1:14 in after you and c your words
Esth 9:29 with full authority to c this
Esth 9:31 to c these days of Purim at
Dan 9:27 Then he shall c a covenant
Dan 11: 1 I, even I, stood up to c
Rom 15: 8 to c the promises made to the
1Co 1: 8 who will also c you to the

CONFIRMATION (*see* CONFIRM)
Phil 1: 7 c of the gospel, you all are
Heb 6:16 an oath for c is for them an

CONFIRMED (*see* CONFIRM)
1Ch 16:17 c it to Jacob for a statute,
Esth 2:23 into the matter, it was c
Esth 9:32 c these matters of Purim, and
Ps 68: 9 rain, Whereby You c Your
Ps 105:10 c it to Jacob for a statute,
Ps 119:106 and c That I will keep Your
Ezek 13: 6 hope that the word may be c
Dan 9:12 He has c His words, which He
1Co 1: 6 of Christ was c in you,
Gal 3:15 covenant, yet if it is c, no
Gal 3:17 was c before by God in Christ
Heb 2: 3 and was c to us by those who
Heb 6:17 His counsel, c it by an oath,

CONFIRMING (*see* CONFIRM)
Mark 16:20 and c the word through the

CONFIRMS (*see* CONFIRM)
Num 30:14 then he c all her vows or all
Num 30:14 he c them, because he made no
Is 44:26 Who c the word of His servant

CONFISCATED (*see* CONFISCATION)
Ezra 10: 8 all his property would be c

CONFISCATION (*see confiscated*)
Ezra 7:26 banishment, or c of goods, or

CONFLICT (*see* CONFLICTS)
Amos 7: 4 Lord GOD called for c by fire
Phil 1:30 having the same c which you
Col 2: 1 what a great c I have for you
1Th 2: 2 the gospel of God in much c

CONFLICTS (*see* CONFLICT)
2Co 7: 5 Outside were c, inside were

CONFORMED (*see* CONFORMING)
Rom 8:29 be c to the image of His Son
Rom 12: 2 do not be c to this world,
Phil 3:10 being c to His death,
Phil 3:21 may be c to His glorious body

CONFORMING (*see* CONFORMED)
1Pe 1:14 not c yourselves to the

CONFOUNDED
2Ki 19:26 they were dismayed and c
Ps 69: 6 seek You be c because of me
Ps 70: 2 ashamed and c Who seek my life
Ps 71:13 Let them be c and consumed
Ps 71:24 For they are c, For they are
Ps 83:17 Let them be c and dismayed
Is 37:27 they were dismayed and c
Jer 14: 3 they were ashamed and c and
Jer 15: 9 she has been ashamed and c
Ezek 36:32 c for your own ways, O house
Acts 9:22 and c the Jews who dwelt in

CONFRONT (*see* CONFRONTED, CONFRONTING)
Job 30:27 days of affliction c me
Ps 17:13 O LORD, C him, cast him down
Amos 9:10 not overtake us nor c us

CONFRONTED (*see* CONFRONT)
2Sa 22: 6 me, the snares of death c me
2Sa 22:19 They c me in the day of my
2Ki 23:29 him at Megiddo when he c him
Ps 18: 5 The snares of death c me
Ps 18:18 They c me in the day of my
Matt 21:23 c Him as He was teaching, and
Luke 20: 1 with the elders, c Him

CONFRONTING (*see* CONFRONT)
Dan 8: 7 And I saw him c the ram

CONFUSE (*see* CONFUSED, CONFUSION)
Gen 11: 7 there c their language, that

CONFUSED (*see* CONFUSE)
Gen 11: 9 because there the LORD c the
1Sa 7:10 and so c them that they were
Job 6:20 they come there and are c
Ps 70: 2 back and c Who desire my hurt
Acts 2: 6 came together, and were c,
Acts 19:32 for the assembly was c, and

CONFUSION (*see* CONFUSE)
Ex 23:27 I will cause c among all the
Deut 28:20 will send on you cursing, c
Deut 28:28 and blindness and c of heart
1Sa 14:20 and there was very great c
Neh 4: 8 attack Jerusalem and create c
Ps 35: 4 brought to c Who plot my hurt
Ps 35:26 and brought to mutual c Who
Ps 40:14 brought to mutual c Who seek
Ps 60: 3 made us drink the wine of c
Is 24:10 The city of c is broken down
Is 34:11 out over it the line of c
Is 41:29 molded images are wind and c
Is 45:16 they shall go in c together
Is 61: 7 and instead of c they shall
Jer 20:11 Their everlasting c will
Zech 12: 4 strike every horse with c
Acts 19:29 whole city was filled with c
1Co 14:33 the author of c but of peace
Jas 3:16 envy and self-seeking exist, c

CONGEALED
Ex 15: 8 the depths c in the heart of

CONGREGATION (*see* CONGREGATIONS)
Ex 12: 3 Speak to all the c of Israel
Ex 12: 6 the whole assembly of the c
Ex 12:19 cut off from the c of Israel
Ex 12:47 All the c of Israel shall
Ex 16: 1 all the c of the children of
Ex 16: 2 Then the whole c of the
Ex 16: 9 Say to all the c of the
Ex 16:10 c of the children of Israel
Ex 16:22 all the rulers of the c came
Ex 17: 1 Then all the c of the
Ex 34:31 of the c returned to him

Ex 35: 1 **c** of the children of Israel
Ex 35: 4 Moses spoke to all the **c** of
Ex 35:20 all the **c** of the children of
Ex 38:25 the **c** was one hundred talents
Lev 4:15 the elders of the **c** shall lay
Lev 8: 3 gather all the **c** together at
Lev 8: 5 And Moses said to the **c**
Lev 9: 5 all the **c** drew near and stood
Lev 10:17 to bear the guilt of the **c**
Lev 16: 5 he shall take from the **c** of
Lev 16:17 and for all the **c** of Israel
Lev 16:33 for all the people of the **c**
Lev 19: 2 Speak to all the **c** of the
Lev 24:14 and let all the **c** stone him
Lev 24:16 all the **c** shall certainly
Num 1: 2 Take a census of all the **c** of
Num 1:16 These were chosen from the **c**
Num 1:18 and they assembled all the **c**
Num 1:53 may be no wrath on the **c** of
Num 3: 7 and the needs of the whole **c**
Num 4:34 the leaders of the **c** numbered
Num 8:20 all the **c** of the children of
Num 10: 7 when the **c** is to be gathered
Num 13:26 all the **c** of the children of
Num 13:26 word to them and to all the **c**
Num 14: 1 Then all the **c** lifted up
Num 14: 2 the whole **c** said to them,
Num 14: 5 all the assembly of the **c** of
Num 14: 7 they spoke to all the **c** of
Num 14:10 all the **c** said to stone them
Num 14:27 evil **c** who murmur against Me
Num 14:35 do so to all this evil **c** who
Num 14:36 made all the **c** murmur against
Num 15:15 shall be for you of the **c**
Num 15:24 the knowledge of the **c**, that
Num 15:24 that the whole **c** shall offer
Num 15:25 atonement for the whole **c** of
Num 15:26 **c** of the children of Israel
Num 15:33 and Aaron, and to all the **c**
Num 15:35 all the **c** shall stone him
Num 15:36 all the **c** brought him outside
Num 16: 2 and fifty leaders of the **c**
Num 16: 2 representatives of the **c**
Num 16: 3 for all the **c** is holy, every
Num 16: 3 above the **c** of the LORD
Num 16: 9 you from the **c** of Israel, to
Num 16: 9 before the **c** to serve them
Num 16:19 And Korah gathered all the **c**
Num 16:19 LORD appeared to all the **c**
Num 16:21 yourselves from among this **c**
Num 16:22 You be angry with all the **c**
Num 16:24 Speak to the **c**, saying, 'Get
Num 16:26 And he spoke to the **c**, saying,
Num 16:33 perished from among the **c**
Num 16:41 On the next day all the **c** of
Num 16:42 when the **c** had gathered
Num 16:45 Get away from among this **c**
Num 16:46 and take it quickly to the **c**
Num 16:47 ran into the midst of the **c**
Num 19: 9 **c** of the children of Israel
Num 19:20 be cut off from among the **c**
Num 20: 1 of Israel, the whole **c**, came
Num 20: 2 there was no water for the **c**
Num 20: 4 the **c** of the LORD into this
Num 20: 8 rock, and give drink to the **c**
Num 20:10 Aaron gathered the **c** together
Num 20:11 came out abundantly, and the **c**
Num 20:12 you shall not bring this **c**
Num 20:22 of Israel, the whole **c**,
Num 20:27 Hor in the sight of all the **c**
Num 20:29 Now when all the **c** saw that
Num 25: 6 in the sight of all the **c** of
Num 25: 7 it, he rose from among the **c**
Num 26: 2 Take a census of all the **c** of
Num 26: 9 representatives of the **c**
Num 27: 2 the leaders and all the **c**, by
Num 27:14 during the strife of the **c**
Num 27:16 flesh, set a man over the **c**
Num 27:17 that the **c** of the LORD may
Num 27:19 priest and before all the **c**
Num 27:20 to him, that all the **c** of the
Num 27:21 of Israel with him, all the **c**
Num 27:22 priest and before all the **c**
Num 31:12 to the **c** of the children of
Num 31:13 and all the leaders of the **c**
Num 31:16 among the **c** of the LORD
Num 31:26 and the chief fathers of the **c**
Num 31:27 out to battle, and all the **c**
Num 31:43 to the **c** was three hundred
Num 32: 2 and to the leaders of the **c**
Num 32: 4 before the **c** of Israel, is a
Num 35:12 before the **c** in judgment
Num 35:24 then the **c** shall judge
Num 35:25 So the **c** shall deliver the
Num 35:25 the **c** shall return him to the
Deut 23: 1 not enter the **c** of the LORD
Deut 23: 2 not enter the **c** of the LORD
Deut 23: 2 shall enter the **c** of the LORD
Deut 23: 3 not enter the **c** of the LORD
Deut 23: 3 the **c** of the LORD forever
Deut 23: 8 may enter the **c** of the LORD
Deut 31:30 in the hearing of all the **c**
Deut 33: 4 a heritage of the **c** of Jacob
Josh 8:35 before all the **c** of Israel
Josh 9:15 rulers of the **c** swore to them
Josh 9:18 **c** had sworn to them by the
Josh 9:18 all the **c** murmured against
Josh 9:19 the rulers said to all the **c**
Josh 9:21 water carriers for all the **c**
Josh 9:27 and water carriers for the **c**
Josh 18: 1 Then the whole **c** of the
Josh 20: 6 before the **c** for judgment
Josh 20: 9 until he stood before the **c**
Josh 22:12 the whole **c** of the children
Josh 22:16 says the whole **c** of the LORD
Josh 22:17 a plague in the **c** of the LORD
Josh 22:18 with the whole **c** of Israel
Josh 22:20 fell on all the **c** of Israel
Josh 22:30 priest and the rulers of the **c**
Judg 20: 1 the **c** gathered together as
Judg 21:10 So the **c** sent out there
Judg 21:13 Then the whole **c** sent word to
Judg 21:16 Then the elders of the **c** said
1Ki 8: 5 all the **c** of Israel who were
1Ki 8:14 blessed the whole **c** of Israel
1Ki 8:14 while all the **c** of Israel was
1Ki 8:22 of all the **c** of Israel, and
1Ki 8:55 blessed all the **c** of Israel
1Ki 8:65 a great **c** from the entrance
1Ki 12: 3 the whole **c** of Israel came and
1Ki 12:20 him and called him to the **c**
1Ch 13: 2 said to all the **c** of Israel
1Ch 13: 4 Then all the **c** said that they
1Ch 28: 8 the **c** of the LORD, and in the
1Ch 29: 1 King David said to all the **c**
1Ch 29:10 the LORD before all the **c**
1Ch 29:20 Then David said to all the **c**
1Ch 29:20 So all the **c** blessed the
2Ch 1: 3 all the **c** with him, went to
2Ch 1: 5 and the **c** sought Him there
2Ch 5: 6 all the **c** of Israel who were
2Ch 6: 3 blessed the whole **c** of Israel
2Ch 6: 3 while all the **c** of Israel
2Ch 6:12 of all the **c** of Israel, and
2Ch 6:13 before all the **c** of Israel
2Ch 7: 8 him, a very great **c** from the
2Ch 20: 5 stood in the **c** of Judah and
2Ch 20:14 Asaph, in the midst of the **c**
2Ch 23: 3 Then all the **c** made a
2Ch 24: 6 of the **c** of Israel, for the
2Ch 28:14 the leaders and all the **c**
2Ch 29:23 before the king and the **c**, and
2Ch 29:28 So all the **c** worshiped, the
2Ch 29:31 So the **c** brought in
2Ch 29:32 **c** brought was seventy bulls
2Ch 30: 2 all the **c** in Jerusalem had
2Ch 30: 4 pleased the king and all the **c**
2Ch 30:13 many people, a very great **c**
2Ch 30:17 the **c** who had not sanctified
2Ch 30:24 to the **c** a thousand bulls
2Ch 30:24 to the **c** a thousand bulls
2Ch 30:25 The whole **c** of Judah rejoiced
2Ch 30:25 all the **c** that came from
Ezra 2:64 The whole **c** together was
Ezra 10: 1 of God, a very large **c** of men
Ezra 10: 8 **c** of those from the captivity
Ezra 10:12 Then all the **c** answered and
Ezra 10:14 leaders of our entire **c** stand
Neh 5:13 And all the **c** said, "Amen
Neh 7:66 Altogether the whole **c** was
Neh 8: 2 brought the Law before the **c**
Neh 8:17 So the whole **c** of those who
Neh 13: 1 ever come into the **c** of God
Job 30:28 I stand up in the **c** and cry
Ps 1: 5 in the **c** of the righteous
Ps 7: 7 So the **c** of the peoples shall
Ps 22:22 of the **c** I will praise You
Ps 22:25 be of You in the great **c**
Ps 26: 5 have hated the **c** of evildoers
Ps 35:18 You thanks in the great **c**
Ps 40: 9 righteousness In the great **c**
Ps 40:10 Your truth From the great **c**
Ps 68:10 Your **c** dwelt in it
Ps 74: 2 Remember Your **c**, which You
Ps 82: 1 stands in the **c** of the mighty
Ps 89: 5 also in the **c** of the saints
Ps 107:32 also in the **c** of the people
Ps 111: 1 of the upright and in the **c**
Ps 149: 1 His praise in the **c** of saints
Prov 5:14 ruin, in the midst of the **c**
Prov 21:16 rest in the **c** of the dead
Prov 26:26 revealed before the whole **c**
Is 14:13 sit on the mount of the **c** on
Jer 6:18 you nations, and know, O **c**
Jer 30:20 their **c** shall be established
Lam 1:10 commanded not to enter Your **c**
Hos 7:12 to what their **c** has heard
Joel 2:16 the people, sanctify the **c**
Mic 2: 5 by lot in the **c** of the LORD
Acts 7:38 This is he who was in the **c**
Acts 13:43 Now when the **c** had broken up,
Heb 2:12 in the midst of the **c** I will

CONGREGATIONS (*see* CONGREGATION)
Ps 26:12 In the **c** I will bless the
Ps 68:26 Bless God in the **c**, The Lord,

CONIAH (*see* JECONIAH, JEHOIACHIN)
Jer 22:24 though **C** the son of Jehoiakim
Jer 22:28 Is this man **C** a despised,
Jer 37: 1 of **C** the son of Jehoiakim

CONJURES
Deut 18:11 or one who **c** spells, or a

CONONIAH (*see* CHENANIAH)
2Ch 31:12 **C** the Levite was ruler over
2Ch 31:13 overseers under the hand of **C**

CONQUER (*see* CONQUERED, CONQUERING, CONQUERORS)
Deut 7: 2 over to you, you shall **c** them
Rev 6: 2 went out conquering and to **c**

CONQUERED (*see* CONQUER)
Deut 29: 7 us to battle, and we **c** them
Josh 10:40 So Joshua **c** all the land
Josh 10:41 Joshua **c** them from Kadesh
Josh 12: 6 the children of Israel had **c**
Josh 12: 7 the children of Israel **c** on
2Ki 10:32 and Hazael **c** them in all the

CONQUERING (*see* CONQUER)
Rev 6: 2 to him, and he went out **c** and

CONQUERORS (*see* CONQUER)
Rom 8:37 things we are more than **c**

CONSCIENCE (*see* CONSCIENCE', CONSCIENCES)
John 8: 9 being convicted by their **c**
Acts 23: 1 I have lived in all good **c**
Acts 24:16 always strive to have a **c**
Rom 2:15 their **c** also bearing witness,
Rom 9: 1 my **c** also bearing me witness
1Co 8: 7 and their **c**, being weak, is
1Co 8:10 will not the **c** of him who is
1Co 8:12 and wound their weak **c**, you
1Co 10:29 **C**, I say, not your own, but
1Co 10:29 judged by another man's **c**
2Co 1:12 the testimony of our **c** that
2Co 4: 2 man's **c** in the sight of God
1Ti 1: 5 a pure heart, from a good **c**
1Ti 1:19 having faith and a good **c**,
1Ti 3: 9 of the faith with a pure **c**
1Ti 4: 2 having their own **c** seared
2Ti 1: 3 whom I serve with a pure **c**
Tit 1:15 their mind and **c** are defiled
Heb 9: 9 perfect in regard to the **c**
Heb 9:14 purge your **c** from dead works
Heb 10:22 sprinkled from an evil **c** and
Heb 13:18 that we have a good **c**, in all
1Pe 2:19 if because of **c** toward God
1Pe 3:16 having a good **c**, that when
1Pe 3:21 of a good **c** toward God),

CONSCIENCE' (*see* CONSCIENCE)
Rom 13: 5 of wrath but also for **c** sake
1Co 10:25 no questions for **c** sake
1Co 10:27 asking no question for **c** sake
1Co 10:28 who told you, and for **c** sake

CONSCIENCES (*see* CONSCIENCE)
2Co 5:11 are well-known in your **c**

CONSCIOUSNESS
1Co 8: 7 with **c** of the idol, until now
Heb 10: 2 have had no more **c** of sins

CONSECRATE (*see* CONSECRATED, CONSECRATES, CONSECRATION)
Ex 28:41 **c** them, and sanctify them,
Ex 29: 9 So you shall **c** Aaron and his
Ex 29:33 the atonement was made, to **c**
Ex 29:35 Seven days you shall **c** them
Ex 32:29 **C** yourselves today to the
Lev 8:33 For seven days he shall **c** you
Lev 25:10 you shall **c** the fiftieth year
Num 6:12 He shall **c** to the LORD the
1Ch 29: 5 Who then is willing to **c**
2Ch 13: 9 so that whoever comes to **c**
Ezek 43:26 and purify it, and so **c** it
Joel 1:14 **C** a fast, call a sacred
Joel 2:15 Zion, **c** a fast, call a sacred
Mic 4:13 I will **c** their gain to the

CONSECRATED (*see* CONSECRATE)
Ex 29:29 in them and to be **c** in them
Lev 7:35 This is the **c** portion for
Lev 16:32 **c** to minister as priest in
Lev 21:10 who is **c** to wear the garments
Num 3: 3 whom he **c** to minister as
Num 6: 9 him, and he defiles his **c** head
Num 6:18 his **c** head at the door of the
Num 6:18 take the hair from his **c** head
Num 6:19 he has shaved his **c** hair,
Josh 6:19 and iron, are **c** to the LORD
Judg 17: 5 he **c** one of his sons, who
Judg 17:12 So Micah **c** the Levite, and the
1Sa 7: 1 **c** Eleazar his son to keep the
1Ki 8:64 **c** the middle of the court
1Ki 13:33 he **c** him, and he became one of
2Ch 7: 7 Furthermore Solomon **c** the
2Ch 26:18 who are **c** to burn incense
2Ch 29:31 said, "Now that you have **c**
2Ch 29:33 The **c** things were six hundred
2Ch 31: 6 of holy things which were **c**
2Ch 36:14 which He had **c** in Jerusalem
Ezra 3: 5 of the LORD that were **c**, and
Neh 3: 1 they **c** it and hung its doors
Neh 3: 1 and **c** it, then as far as the
Neh 12:47 They also **c** holy things for
Neh 12:47 the Levites **c** them for the
Heb 10:20 living way which He **c** for us

CONSECRATES (*see* CONSECRATE)
Lev 27: 2 When a man **c** by a vow
Num 6: 2 **c** an offering to take the vow

CONSECRATION (*see* CONSECRATE, CONSECRATIONS)
Ex 29:22 thigh (for it is a ram of **c**)
Ex 29:26 of the ram of Aaron's **c** and
Ex 29:27 from the ram of the **c** you
Ex 29:31 shall take the ram of the **c**
Ex 29:34 the flesh of the **c** offerings
Lev 8:22 the second ram, the ram of **c**
Lev 8:28 They were **c** offerings for a
Lev 8:29 Moses' part of the ram of **c**
Lev 8:31 in the basket of **c** offerings
Lev 8:33 the days of your **c** are ended
Lev 21:12 for the **c** of the anointing

CONSECRATIONS (*see* CONSECRATION)
Lev 7:37 the trespass offering, the **c**

CONSENT (*see* CONSENTED, CONSENTING)
Gen 34:15 condition we will **c** to you
Gen 34:22 the men **c** to dwell with us
Gen 34:23 Only let us **c** to them, and
Gen 41:44 without your **c** no man may
Deut 13: 8 you shall not **c** to him or
Judg 11:17 of Moab, but he would not **c**
1Sa 11: 7 and they came out with one **c**
1Ki 20: 8 Do not listen or **c**
2Ki 6: 3 Please **c** to go with your
Ps 83: 5 consulted together with one **c**
Prov 1:10 sinners entice you, do not **c**
Acts 18:20 time with them, he did not **c**
1Co 7: 5 except with **c** for a time,
1Ti 6: 3 does not **c** to wholesome words
Phm 14 But without your **c** I wanted

CONSENTED (*see* CONSENT)
Ps 50:18 you **c** with him, And have been
Dan 1:14 So he **c** with them in this
Luke 23:51 He had not **c** to their counsel

CONSENTING (*see* CONSENT)
Acts 8: 1 Now Saul was **c** to his death
Acts 22:20 standing by **c** to his death

CONSIDER (*see* CONSIDERED, CONSIDERING, CONSIDERS)
Ex 33:13 **c** that this nation is Your
Lev 13:13 then the priest shall **c**
Deut 4:39 **c** it in your heart, that the
Deut 32: 7 of old, **c** the years of many
Deut 32:29 this, that they would **c** their
Judg 18:14 **c** what you should do
Judg 19:30 **C** it, take counsel, and speak
1Sa 1:16 Do not **c** your maidservant a
1Sa 12:24 for **c** what great things He
1Sa 25:17 **c** what you will do, for harm
2Sa 24:13 Now **c** and see what answer I
2Ki 5: 7 Therefore please **c**, and see
1Ch 21:12 Now **c** what answer I should
1Ch 28:10 **C** now, for the LORD has
Job 8: 8 **c** the things discovered by
Job 11:11 Will He not then **c** it
Job 23:15 when I **c** this, I am afraid of
Job 34:23 He need not further **c** a man
Job 34:27 would not **c** any of His ways,
Job 37:14 **c** the wondrous works of God
Ps 5: 1 O LORD, **C** my meditation
Ps 8: 3 When I **c** Your heavens, the
Ps 9:13 **C** my trouble from those who
Ps 13: 3 **C** and hear me, O LORD my God
Ps 25:19 **C** my enemies, for they are
Ps 45:10 Listen, O daughter, **C** and
Ps 48:13 **C** her palaces
Ps 50:22 Now **c** this, you who forget
Ps 64: 9 they shall wisely **c** His doing
Ps 119:95 But I will **c** Your testimonies
Ps 119:128 all things I **c** to be right
Ps 119:153 **C** my affliction and deliver me
Ps 119:159 **C** how I love Your precepts
Prov 6: 6 **C** her ways and be wise,
Prov 23: 1 **C** carefully what is before
Prov 24:12 He who weighs the hearts **c** it
Prov 28:22 does not **c** that poverty will
Eccl 2:12 I turned myself to **c** wisdom
Eccl 7:13 **C** the work of God
Eccl 7:14 but in the day of adversity **c**
Is 1: 3 not know, My people do not **c**
Is 5:12 nor **c** the operation of His
Is 14:16 gaze at you, and **c** you, saying
Is 41:20 they may see and know, and **c**
Is 41:22 they were, that we may **c** them
Is 43:18 nor **c** the things of old
Is 52:15 had not heard they shall **c**
Jer 2:10 **c** diligently, and see if there
Jer 9:17 **C** and call for the mourning
Jer 30:24 the latter days you will **c** it
Lam 1: 9 she did not **c** her destiny
Lam 1:11 See, O LORD, and **c**, for I am
Lam 2:20 See, O LORD, and **c**
Ezek 12: 3 It may be that they will **c**
Dan 9:23 therefore **c** the matter, and
Hos 7: 2 They do not **c** in their hearts
Jon 1: 6 perhaps your God will **c** us
Hag 1: 5 **C** your ways
Hag 1: 7 **C** your ways
Hag 2:15 carefully **c** from this day
Hag 2:18 **C** now from this day forward,
Hag 2:18 LORD's temple was laid—**c** it
Matt 6:28 **C** the lilies of the field,
Matt 7: 3 but do not **c** the plank in
Luke 12:24 **C** the ravens, for they
Luke 12:27 **C** the lilies, how they grow
Luke 14:31 **c** whether he is able with ten
John 11:50 nor do you **c** that it is
Acts 15: 6 together to **c** this matter
Rom 4:19 he did not **c** his own body,
Rom 8:18 For I **c** that the sufferings
Rom 11:22 Therefore **c** the goodness and
1Co 4: 1 Let a man so **c** us, as
2Co 10: 7 let him again **c** this in
2Co 10:11 Let such a person **c** this,
2Co 11: 5 For I **c** that I am not at all
Phil 2: 6 did not **c** it robbery to be
2Ti 2: 7 **C** what I say, and may the Lord
Heb 3: 1 **c** the Apostle and High Priest
Heb 7: 4 Now **c** how great this man was,
Heb 10:24 let us **c** one another in order
Heb 12: 3 For **c** Him who endured such
1Pe 5:12 faithful brother as I **c** him

CONSIDERED (*see* CONSIDER)
Gen 30:33 the lambs, will be **c** stolen
Gen 31:15 Are we not **c** strangers by him
1Ki 5: 8 I have **c** the message which
Neh 13:13 for they were **c** faithful, and
Job 1: 8 Have you **c** My servant Job,
Job 2: 3 Have you **c** My servant Job,
Ps 31: 7 For You have **c** my trouble
Ps 77: 5 I have **c** the days of old, The
Prov 17:28 his lips, he is **c** perceptive
Prov 24:32 When I saw it, I **c** it well
Eccl 4: 1 **c** all the oppression that is
Eccl 9: 1 For I **c** all this in my heart,
Is 38:13 I have **c** until morning
Jer 33:24 Have you not **c** what these
Hos 8:12 But they were **c** a strange
Mark 10:42 **c** rulers over the Gentiles
Luke 1:29 **c** what manner of greeting
Luke 22:24 them should be **c** the greatest
Acts 11: 6 I observed it intently and **c**
Acts 12:12 So, when he had **c** this, he
Phil 2:25 Yet I **c** it necessary to send

CONSIDERING (*see* CONSIDER)
Dan 7: 8 I was **c** the horns, and there
Dan 8: 5 And as I was **c**, suddenly a
Acts 17:23 **c** the objects of your worship
Gal 6: 1 **c** yourself lest you also be
Heb 13: 7 **c** the outcome of their

CONSIDERS (*see* CONSIDER)
Ps 33:15 He **c** all their works
Ps 41: 1 Blessed is he who **c** the poor
Prov 14:15 prudent man **c** well his steps
Prov 21:12 **c** the house of the wicked
Prov 29: 7 The righteous **c** the cause of
Prov 31:16 She **c** a field and buys it
Is 44:19 no one **c** in his heart, nor is
Is 57: 1 away, while no one **c** that the
Jer 29:26 **c** himself a prophet, that you
Ezek 18:14 **c** but does not do likewise
Ezek 18:28 Because he **c** and turns away
Rom 14:14 but to him who **c** anything to

CONSIST
Luke 12:15 not **c** in the abundance of the
Col 1:17 and in Him all things **c**

CONSOLATION (*see* CONSOLATIONS, CONSOLE)
Job 21: 2 speech, and let this be your **c**
Is 66:11 with the **c** of her bosom, that
Jer 16: 7 men give them the cup of **c** to
Luke 2:25 waiting for the **C** of Israel
Luke 6:24 For you have received your **c**
2Co 1: 5 so our **c** also abounds through
2Co 1: 6 afflicted, it is for your **c**
2Co 1: 6 comforted, it is for your **c**
2Co 1: 7 you will partake of the **c**
2Co 7: 7 but also by the **c** with which
Phil 2: 1 if there is any **c** in Christ
2Th 2:16 us and given us everlasting **c**
Phm 7 **c** in your love, because the
Heb 6:18 lie, we might have strong **c**

CONSOLATIONS (*see* CONSOLATION)
Job 15:11 Are the **c** of God too small

CONSOLE (*see* CONSOLATION, CONSOLED)
Is 61: 3 to **c** those who mourn in Zion,
Lam 2:13 How shall I **c** you

CONSOLED (*see* CONSOLE)
Job 42:11 and they **c** him and comforted

CONSPIRACY (*see* CONSPIRE)
2Sa 15:12 the **c** grew strong, for the
2Ki 12:20 servants arose and made a **c**
2Ki 14:19 they made a **c** against him in
2Ki 15:15 the **c** which he led, indeed
2Ki 15:30 the son of Elah led a **c**
2Ki 17: 4 uncovered a **c** by Hoshea
2Ch 25:27 they made a **c** against him in
Is 8:12 Do not say, 'A **c**,' concerning
Is 8:12 all that this people call a **c**
Jer 11: 9 A **c** has been found among the
Ezek 22:25 The **c** of her prophets in her
Acts 23:13 forty who had formed this **c**

CONSPIRATORS (*see* CONSPIRE)
2Sa 15:31 is among the **c** with Absalom

Rom 14:10 you show **c** for your brother

CONTEMPTIBLE (*see* CONTEMPT)
Mal 1: 7 The table of the LORD is **c**
Mal 1:12 and its fruit, its food, is **c**
Mal 2: 9 I also have made you **c** and
2Co 10:10 is weak, and his speech **c**

CONTEMPTUOUSLY (*see* CONTEMPT)
Ps 31:18 and **c** against the righteous

CONTEND (*see* CONTENDED, CONTENDING, CONTENDS)
Ex 17: 2 Why do you **c** with me
Ex 21:18 If men **c** with each other, and
Deut 2: 9 nor **c** with them in battle,
Job 9: 3 If one wished to **c** with Him
Job 10: 2 show me why You **c** with me
Job 13: 8 Will you **c** for God
Job 13:19 Who is he who will **c** with me
Job 23: 6 Would He **c** with me in His
Job 33:13 Why do you **c** with Him
Prov 28: 4 as keep the law **c** with them
Eccl 6:10 he cannot **c** with Him who is
Is 43:26 let us **c** together
Is 49:25 for I will **c** with him who
Is 50: 8 who will **c** with Me
Is 57:16 For I will not **c** forever, nor
Jer 12: 5 how can you **c** with horses
Jer 18:19 voice of those who **c** with me
Hos 4: 4 Now let no man **c**, or reprove
Hos 4: 4 those who **c** with the priest
Mic 6: 2 and He will **c** with Israel
Jude 3 to **c** earnestly for the faith

CONTENDED (*see* CONTEND)
Ex 17: 2 the people **c** with Moses, and
Num 20: 3 And the people **c** with Moses
Num 20:13 of Israel **c** with the LORD
Num 26: 9 who **c** against Moses and Aaron
Num 26: 9 when they **c** against the LORD
Deut 33: 8 with whom You **c** at the waters
Neh 13:11 So I **c** with the rulers, and
Neh 13:17 Then I **c** with the nobles of
Neh 13:25 So I **c** with them and cursed
Is 27: 8 it away, you **c** with it
Is 41:12 those who **c** with you
Jer 50:24 you have **c** against the Lord
Acts 11: 2 the circumcision **c** with him

CONTENDING (*see* CONTEND)
Jude 9 in **c** with the devil, when he

CONTENDS (*see* CONTEND)
Job 40: 2 Shall the one who **c** with the
Prov 29: 9 If a wise man **c** with a
Is 49:25 with him who **c** with you, and I

CONTENT (*see* CONTENTMENT)
Ex 2:21 Then Moses was **c** to live with
Lev 10:20 Moses heard that, he was **c**
Josh 7: 7 Oh, that we had been **c**, and
Judg 17:11 Then the Levite was **c** to
Judg 19: 6 Please be **c** to stay all night
Luke 3:14 and be **c** with your wages
Phil 4:11 whatever state I am, to be **c**
1Ti 6: 8 with these we shall be **c**
Heb 13: 5 be **c** with such things as you
3Jn 10 not **c** with that, he himself

CONTENTION (*see* CONTENTIONS, CONTENTIOUS)
Ex 17: 7 because of the **c** of the
Prov 13:10 By pride comes only **c**, but
Prov 15:18 who is slow to anger allays **c**
Prov 17:14 therefore stop **c** before a
Prov 18: 6 A fool's lips enter into **c**
Prov 22:10 the scoffer, and **c** will leave
Jer 15:10 a man of **c** to the whole earth
Hab 1: 3 there is strife, and **c** arises
Acts 15:39 Then the **c** became so sharp

CONTENTIONS (*see* CONTENTION)
Prov 18:18 lots causes **c** to cease, and
Prov 18:19 and **c** are like the bars of a
Prov 19:13 and the **c** of a wife are a
Prov 23:29 Who has sorrow? Who has **c**?
1Co 1:11 that there are **c** among you
2Co 12:20 lest there be **c**, jealousies,
Gal 5:20 idolatry, sorcery, hatred, **c**
Tit 3: 9 disputes, genealogies, **c**, and

CONTENTIOUS (*see* CONTENTION)
Prov 21: 9 a house shared with a **c** woman
Prov 21:19 the wilderness, than with a **c**
Prov 25:24 a house shared with a **c** woman
Prov 26:21 fire, so is a **c** man to kindle
Prov 27:15 day and a **c** woman are alike
1Co 11:16 But if anyone seems to be **c**

CONTENTMENT (*see* CONTENT)
1Ti 6: 6 with **c** is great gain

CONTINGENTS
2Ki 11: 7 The two **c** of you who go off

CONTINUAL (*see* CONTINUALLY, CONTINUE)
Ex 29:42 This shall be a **c** burnt
2Ch 2: 4 for the **c** showbread, for the
Prov 15:15 a merry heart has a **c** feast
Prov 19:13 of a wife are a **c** dripping
Prov 27:15 A **c** dripping on a very rainy
Is 14: 6 in wrath with a **c** stroke, he
Jer 48: 5 they ascend with **c** weeping
Jer 50: 4 with **c** weeping they shall
Luke 18: 5 her, lest by her **c** coming she
Rom 9: 2 sorrow and **c** grief in my heart

CONTINUALLY (*see* CONTINUAL)
Gen 6: 5 of his heart was only evil **c**
Gen 8: 3 receded **c** from the earth
Gen 8: 5 the waters decreased **c** until
Ex 27:20 to cause the lamp to burn **c**
Ex 28:29 a memorial before the LORD **c**
Ex 28:30 his heart before the LORD **c**
Ex 29:38 the first year, day by day **c**
Lev 24: 2 to make the lamps burn **c**
Lev 24: 3 morning before the LORD **c**
Lev 24: 4 lampstand before the LORD **c**
Lev 24: 8 it in order before the LORD **c**
Deut 28:29 only oppressed and plundered **c**
Deut 28:33 only oppressed and crushed **c**
Josh 6:13 the ark of the LORD went on **c**
1Sa 18:29 Saul became David's enemy **c**
2Sa 9: 7 shall eat bread at my table **c**
2Sa 9:13 for he ate **c** at the king's
2Sa 15:12 Absalom **c** increased in number
2Sa 19:13 before me **c** in place of Joab
1Ki 10: 8 who stand **c** before you and
2Ch 9: 7 who stand **c** before you and
2Ch 24:14 **c** all the days of Jehoiada
2Ch 28:19 had been **c** unfaithful to the
Ps 34: 1 praise shall **c** be in my mouth
Ps 35:27 And let them say **c**, "Let the
Ps 38:17 And my sorrow is **c** before me
Ps 40:11 and Your truth **c** preserve me
Ps 40:16 as love Your salvation say **c**
Ps 42: 3 night, While they **c** say to me
Ps 44:15 My dishonor is **c** before me
Ps 50: 8 Which are **c** before Me
Ps 52: 1 The goodness of God endures **c**
Ps 58: 7 away as waters which run **c**
Ps 69:23 And make their loins shake **c**
Ps 70: 4 who love Your salvation say **c**
Ps 71: 3 To which I may resort **c**
Ps 71: 6 My praise shall be **c** of You
Ps 71:14 But I will hope **c**, And will
Ps 72:15 also will be made for Him **c**
Ps 73:23 Nevertheless I am **c** with You
Ps 74:23 up against You increases **c**
Ps 109:10 his children **c** be vagabonds
Ps 109:15 Let them be **c** before the LORD
Ps 109:19 with which he girds himself **c**
Ps 119:44 So shall I keep Your law **c**
Ps 119:109 My life is **c** in my hand, Yet
Ps 119:117 shall observe Your statutes **c**
Ps 126: 6 He who **c** goes forth weeping,
Ps 140: 2 They **c** gather together for
Prov 6:14 his heart, he devises evil **c**
Prov 6:21 Bind them **c** upon your heart
Eccl 1: 6 the wind whirls about **c**, and
Is 21: 8 I stand **c** on the watchtower
Is 49:16 your walls are **c** before Me
Is 51:13 you have feared **c** every day
Is 52: 5 is blasphemed **c** every day
Is 58:11 The LORD will guide you **c**
Is 60:11 your gates shall be open **c**
Is 65: 3 Me to anger **c** to My face
Jer 6: 7 Before Me **c** are grief and
Jer 23:17 They **c** say to those who
Jer 33:18 offerings, and to sacrifice **c**
Dan 6:16 Your God, whom you serve **c**
Dan 6:20 your God, whom you serve **c**
Hos 4:18 they commit harlotry **c**
Hos 12: 6 and wait on your God **c**
Obad 16 shall all the nations drink **c**
Nah 3:19 not your wickedness passed **c**
Luke 24:53 were **c** in the temple praising
Acts 6: 4 give ourselves **c** to prayer
Acts 10: 7 those who waited on him **c**
Rom 13: 6 **c** to this very thing
Heb 7: 3 of God, remains a priest **c**
Heb 10: 1 they offer **c** year by year
Heb 13:15 us **c** offer the sacrifice of

CONTINUANCE (*see* CONTINUE)
Rom 2: 7 **c** in doing good seek for

CONTINUE (*see* CONTINUAL, CONTINUANCE, CONTINUED, CONTINUES, CONTINUING, CONTINUOUSLY)
Lev 12: 4 She shall then **c** in the
Lev 12: 5 she shall **c** in the blood of
Num 34: 4 **c** to Zin, and be on the south
Num 34: 4 to Hazar Addar, and **c** to
1Sa 12:14 who reigns over you will **c**
1Sa 13:14 now your kingdom shall not **c**
2Sa 7:29 that it may **c** forever before
1Ki 8:11 **c** ministering because of the
2Ki 17:34 To this day they **c** practicing
1Ch 17:27 that it may **c** before You
2Ch 5:14 **c** ministering because of the
Job 14: 2 like a shadow and does not **c**
Job 15:29 rich, nor will his wealth **c**
Ps 36:10 Oh, **c** Your lovingkindness to
Ps 49: 9 That he should **c** to live
Ps 49:11 their houses will **c** forever
Ps 72:17 His name shall **c** as long as
Ps 101: 7 shall not **c** in my presence
Ps 102:28 of Your servants will **c**, And
Ps 119:91 They **c** this day according to
Prov 23:17 of the LORD **c** all day long
Is 5:11 who **c** until night, till wine
Is 64: 5 in these ways we **c**
Dan 11: 8 he shall **c** more years than
Hab 1:17 **c** to slay nations without
Zech 8:21 Let us **c** to go and pray before
Mal 2: 4 My covenant with Levi may **c**
Acts 11:23 they should **c** with the Lord
Acts 13:43 persuaded them to **c** in the
Acts 14:22 them to **c** in the faith, and
Rom 6: 1 Shall we **c** in sin that grace
Rom 11:22 if you **c** in His goodness
Rom 11:23 if they do not **c** in unbelief
2Co 11:12 I do, I will also **c** to do
Gal 2: 5 the gospel might **c** with you
Gal 3:10 not **c** in all things which are
Phil 1:25 and **c** with you all for your
Col 1:23 if indeed you **c** in the faith
Col 4: 2 **C** earnestly in prayer, being
1Ti 2:15 if they **c** in faith, love, and
1Ti 4:16 **C** in them, for in doing this
2Ti 3:14 **c** in the things which you
Heb 8: 9 they did not **c** in My covenant
Heb 13: 1 Let brotherly love **c**
2Pe 3: 4 all things **c** as they were
1Jn 5:13 that you may **c** to believe in
Rev 13: 5 to **c** for forty-two months
Rev 17:10 comes, he must **c** a short time

CONTINUED (*see* CONTINUE)
Gen 26:13 **c** prospering until he became
Ex 36: 3 So they **c** bringing to him
Num 9:19 Even when the cloud **c** long
Josh 6: 9 while the priests **c** blowing
Josh 6:13 while the priests **c** blowing
Josh 15: 7 The border **c** toward the
Josh 24:10 therefore he **c** to bless you
Judg 5:17 Asher **c** at the seashore, and
Ruth 2: 7 has **c** from morning until now,
1Sa 1:12 as she **c** praying before the
1Sa 14:19 the Philistines **c** to increase
1Ki 3: 6 You have **c** this great
2Ki 2:11 it happened, as they **c** on
2Ki 17:29 However every nation **c** to
2Ki 17:41 children's children have **c**
1Ch 21:20 but Ornan **c** threshing wheat
2Ch 29:28 all this **c** until the burnt
Neh 5:16 I also **c** the work on this
Job 27: 1 Moreover Job **c** his discourse,
Job 29: 1 Job further **c** his discourse,
Dan 1:21 Thus Daniel **c** until the first
Jon 1:13 for the sea **c** to grow more
Matt 15:32 have now **c** with Me three days
Luke 6:12 **c** all night in prayer to God
Luke 22:28 have **c** with Me in My trials

John 8: 7 So when they c asking Him
Acts 1:14 These all c with one accord
Acts 2:42 they c steadfastly in the
Acts 8:13 was baptized he c with Philip
Acts 12:16 Now Peter c knocking
Acts 18:11 And he c there a year and six
Acts 19:10 this c for two years, so that
Acts 20: 7 c his message until midnight
Acts 20: 9 as Paul c speaking, he fell
Acts 27:33 and c without food, and eaten
1Jn 2:19 us, they would have c with us

CONTINUES (see CONTINUE)
Lev 13:55 it c eating away, whether the
1Ti 5: 5 c in supplications and prayers
Heb 7:24 But He, because He c forever
Jas 1:25 and c in it, and is not a

CONTINUING (see CONTINUE)
Jer 30:23 with fury, a c whirlwind
Acts 2:46 So c daily with one accord in
Rom 12:12 c steadfastly in prayer
Heb 7:23 prevented by death from c
Heb 13:14 For here we have no c city

CONTINUOUSLY (see CONTINUE)
2Sa 16: 5 out, cursing c as he came

CONTRADICT (see CONTRADICTING,
CONTRADICTION, CONTRADICTIONS,
CONTRARY)
Luke 21:15 not be able to c or resist
Tit 1: 9 exhort and convict those who c

CONTRADICTING (see CONTRADICT)
Acts 13:45 and c and blaspheming, they

CONTRADICTION (see CONTRADICT)
Heb 7: 7 Now beyond all c the lesser

CONTRADICTIONS (see CONTRADICT)
1Ti 6:20 c of what is falsely called

CONTRARY (see CONTRADICT)
Lev 26:21 Then, if you walk c to Me
Lev 26:23 by Me, but walk c to Me,
Lev 26:24 I also will walk c to you
Lev 26:27 not obey Me, but walk c to Me
Lev 26:28 will walk c to you in fury
Lev 26:40 they also have walked c to Me
Lev 26:41 I also have walked c to them
2Ch 30:18 c to what was written
Matt 14:24 the waves, for the wind was c
Luke 22:26 on the c, he who is greatest
John 7:12 No, on the c, He deceives the
Acts 17: 7 these are all acting c to the
Acts 18:13 to worship God c to the law
Acts 23: 3 me to be struck c to the law
Acts 26: 9 I must do many things c to
Acts 27: 4 because the winds were c
Rom 3:31 On the c, we establish the
Rom 4:18 c to hope, in hope believed,
Rom 7: 7 On the c, I would not have
Rom 10:21 to a disobedient and c people
Rom 11:24 were grafted c to nature into
Rom 16:17 c to the doctrine which you
2Co 2: 7 so that, on the c, you ought
Gal 2: 7 But on the c, when they saw
Gal 5:17 these are c to one another,
Col 2:14 against us, which was c to us
1Th 2:15 God and are c to all men,
1Ti 1:10 that is c to sound doctrine
1Pe 3: 9 but on the c blessing,

CONTRIBUTE (see CONTRIBUTION)
2Ch 31: 4 to c support for the priests

CONTRIBUTION (see CONTRIBUTE,
CONTRIBUTIONS)
Is 40:20 a c chooses a tree that will
Rom 15:26 c for the poor among the

CONTRIBUTIONS (see CONTRIBUTION)
2Ch 24:10 rejoiced, brought their c

CONTRITE
Ps 34:18 saves such as have a c spirit
Ps 51:17 spirit, A broken and a c heart
Is 57:15 place, with him who has a c
Is 57:15 the heart of the c ones
Is 66: 2 poor and of a c spirit, and who

CONTROL
Acts 5: 4 was it not in your own c

CONTROVERSIES (see CONTROVERSY)
2Ch 19: 8 judgment of the LORD and for c

CONTROVERSY (see CONTROVERSIES)
Deut 17: 8 matters of c within your
Deut 19:17 then both men in the c shall
Deut 21: 5 by their word every c and
Jer 25:31 LORD has a c with the nations
Ezek 44:24 In c they shall stand as
1Ti 3:16 And without c great is the

CONVENIENT (see CONVENIENTLY)
Jer 40: 4 c for you to go, go there
Jer 40: 5 it seems c for you to go
Acts 24:25 when I have a c time I will
1Co 16:12 come when he has a c time

CONVENIENTLY (see CONVENIENT)
Mark 14:11 how he might c betray Him

CONVERSATION (see CONVERSED)
Jer 38:27 for the c had not been heard
Luke 24:17 What kind of c is this that

CONVERSED (see CONVERSATION)
Luke 24:15 So it was, while they c and
Acts 24:26 him more often and c with him

CONVERSION (see CONVERTED)
Acts 15: 3 describing the c of the

CONVERTED (see CONVERSION,
CONVERTING)
Ps 51:13 And sinners shall be c to You
Matt 18: 3 say to you, unless you are c
Acts 3:19 Repent therefore and be c,

CONVERTING (see CONVERTED)
Ps 19: 7 LORD is perfect, c the soul

CONVEX
1Ki 7:20 by the c surface which was

CONVICT (see CONVICTED, CONVICTS)
John 16: 8 He will c the world of sin,
Tit 1: 9 and c those who contradict
Jude 15 all, to c all who are ungodly

CONVICTED (see CONVICT)
John 8: 9 being c by their conscience,
Jas 2: 9 sin, and are c by the law as

CONVICTS (see CONVICT)
John 8:46 Which of you c Me of sin

CONVINCE (see CONVINCED)
2Ti 4: 2 C, rebuke, exhort, with all

CONVINCED (see CONVINCE)
Job 32:12 surely not one of you c Job
Acts 26:26 for I am c that none of these
Rom 4:21 being fully c that what He
Rom 14: 5 be fully c in his own mind
Rom 14:14 am c by the Lord Jesus that
1Co 14:24 he is c by all, he is judged
2Co 10: 7 If anyone is c in himself

CONVOCATION (see CONVOCATIONS)
Ex 12:16 day there shall be a holy c
Ex 12:16 shall be a holy c for you
Lev 23: 3 of solemn rest, a holy c
Lev 23: 7 day you shall have a holy c
Lev 23: 8 seventh day shall be a holy c
Lev 23:21 that it is a holy c to you
Lev 23:24 blowing of trumpets, a holy c
Lev 23:27 It shall be a holy c for you
Lev 23:35 day there shall be a holy c
Lev 23:36 day you shall have a holy c
Num 28:18 day you shall have a holy c
Num 28:25 day you shall have a holy c
Num 28:26 you shall have a holy c
Num 29: 1 you shall have a holy c
Num 29: 7 month you shall have a holy c
Num 29:12 month you shall have a holy c

CONVOCATIONS (see CONVOCATION)
Lev 23: 2 shall proclaim to be holy c
Lev 23: 4 LORD, holy c which you shall
Lev 23:37 shall proclaim to be holy c

CONVULSED (see CONVULSES)
Mark 1:26 the unclean spirit had c him
Mark 9:20 immediately the spirit c him
Mark 9:26 c him greatly, and came out of
Luke 9:42 threw him down and c him

CONVULSES (see CONVULSED)
Luke 9:39 it c him so that he foams at

COOK (see COOKED, COOKING, COOKS)
1Sa 9:23 And Samuel said to the c
1Sa 9:24 So the c took up the thigh
Ezek 24:10 c the meat well, Mix in the
Zech 14:21 and take them and c in them

COOKED (see COOK)
Gen 25:29 Now Jacob c a stew
Num 11: 8 c it in pans, and made cakes
Lam 4:10 have c their own children

COOKING (see COOK)
Lev 11:35 is an oven or c stove, it
Ezek 46:23 c hearths were made under the

COOKS (see COOK)
1Sa 8:13 daughters to be perfumers, c

COOL
Gen 3: 8 garden in the c of the day
Judg 3:20 in his c private chamber)
Judg 3:24 to his needs in the c chamber
Luke 16:24 in water and c my tongue

COPIED (see COPY)
Prov 25: 1 of Hezekiah king of Judah c

COPIES (see COPY)
Heb 9:23 the c of the things in the
Heb 9:24 which are c of the true, but

COPPER (see COPPERSMITH)
Deut 8: 9 of whose hills you can dig c
Job 28: 2 and c is smelted from ore
Matt 10: 9 nor c in your moneybelts,
Matt 10:29 sparrows sold for a c coin
Mark 6: 8 no c in their money belts
Mark 7: 4 c vessels, and couches
Luke 12: 6 sparrows sold for two c coins

COPPERSMITH (see COPPER)
2Ti 4:14 Alexander the c did me much

COPY (see COPIED, COPIES)
Deut 17:18 a c of this law in a book
Josh 8:32 a c of the law of Moses,
Ezra 4:11 This is a c of the letter
Ezra 4:23 Now when the c of King
Ezra 5: 6 This is a c of the letter
Ezra 7:11 Now this is the c of the
Esth 3:14 A c of the document was to be
Esth 4: 8 He also gave him a c of the
Esth 8:13 A c of the document was to be
Heb 8: 5 who serve the c and shadow of

CORAL (see CORALS)
Job 28:18 shall be made of c or quartz

CORALS (see CORAL)
Ezek 27:16 embroidery, fine linen, c

CORBAN
Mark 7:11 from me is C (that is,

CORD (see CORDS)
Gen 38:18 Your signet and c, and your
Gen 38:25 the signet and c, and staff
Ex 28:28 of the ephod, using a blue c
Ex 28:37 you shall put it on a blue c
Ex 39:21 of the ephod with a blue c
Ex 39:31 And they tied to it a blue c
Josh 2:18 bind this line of scarlet c
Josh 2:21 the scarlet c in the window
Eccl 4:12 a threefold c is not quickly
Eccl 12: 6 before the silver c is loosed
Ezek 16: 4 born your navel c was not cut

CORDS (see CORD)
Ex 28:14 of pure gold like braided c
Ex 28:22 like braided c of pure gold
Ex 35:18 pegs of the court, and their c
Ex 39:15 like braided c of pure gold
Ex 39:40 for the court gate, its c
Num 3:26 and the altar, and their c,
Num 3:37 their pegs, and their c
Num 4:26 and altar, and their c, all the
Num 4:32 their sockets, pegs, and c
Esth 1: 6 fastened with c of fine linen
Job 36: 8 held in the c of affliction,
Ps 2: 3 And cast away Their c from us
Ps 118:27 Bind the sacrifice with c to
Ps 119:61 The c of the wicked have
Ps 129: 4 in pieces the c of the wicked
Ps 140: 5 hidden a snare for me, and c
Prov 5:22 is caught in the c of his sin

Is 5:18 iniquity with **c** of vanity
Is 33:20 will any of its **c** be broken
Is 54: 2 lengthen your **c**, and
Jer 10:20 and all my **c** are broken
Ezek 27:24 apparel, in strong twined **c**
Hos 11: 4 I drew them with gentle **c**
John 2:15 When He had made a whip of **c**

CORIANDER
Ex 16:31 And it was like white **c** seed
Num 11: 7 Now the manna was like **c** seed

CORINTH (*see* CORINTHIANS)
Acts 18: 1 from Athens and went to **C**
Acts 19: 1 while Apollos was at **C**, that
1Co 1: 2 church of God which is at **C**
2Co 1: 1 church of God which is at **C**
2Co 1:23 spare you I came no more to **C**
2Ti 4:20 Erastus stayed in **C**, but

CORINTHIANS (*see* CORINTH)
Acts 18: 8 And many of the **C**, hearing,
2Co 6:11 O **C**! We have

CORNELIUS
Acts 10: 1 man in Caesarea called **C**, a
Acts 10: 3 and saying to him, "**C**!"
Acts 10: 7 **C** called two of his household
Acts 10:17 from **C** had made inquiry for
Acts 10:21 had been sent to him from **C**
Acts 10:22 **C** the centurion, a just man,
Acts 10:24 Now **C** was waiting for them,
Acts 10:25 **C** met him and fell down at his
Acts 10:30 **C** said, "Four days ago I was
Acts 10:31 and said, "**C**, your prayer has

CORNER (*see* CORNERS, CORNERSTONE)
1Sa 24: 4 cut off a **c** of Saul's robe
1Sa 24:11 see the **c** of your robe in my
1Sa 24:11 I cut off the **c** of your robe
2Ki 14:13 Gate of Ephraim to the **C** Gate
2Ch 25:23 Gate of Ephraim to the **C** Gate
2Ch 26: 9 in Jerusalem at the **C** Gate
2Ch 26: 9 at the **c** buttress of the wall
2Ch 28:24 in every **c** of Jerusalem
Neh 3:24 even as far as the **c**
Neh 3:31 as the upper room at the **c**
Neh 3:32 the upper room at the **c**, as
Prov 7: 8 along the street near her **c**
Prov 7:12 square, lurking at every **c**
Prov 21: 9 to dwell in a **c** of a housetop
Prov 25:24 to dwell in a **c** of a housetop
Is 30:20 not be moved into a **c** anymore
Jer 31:38 of Hananeel to the **C** Gate
Jer 31:40 to the **c** of the Horse Gate
Jer 51:26 for a **c** nor a stone for a
Ezek 46:21 in every **c** of the court there
Amos 3:12 in the **c** of a bed and on the
Zech 14:10 the **C** Gate, and from the Tower
Acts 26:26 thing was not done in a **c**

CORNERS (*see* CORNER)
Ex 25:12 it, and put them in its four **c**
Ex 25:26 **c** that are at its four legs
Ex 26:23 two back **c** of the tabernacle
Ex 26:24 They shall be for the two **c**
Ex 27: 2 make its horns on its four **c**
Ex 27: 4 bronze rings at its four **c**
Ex 36:28 two back **c** of the tabernacle
Ex 36:29 both of them for the two **c**
Ex 37: 3 gold to be set in its four **c**
Ex 37:13 put the rings on the four **c**
Ex 37:27 by its two **c** on both sides,
Ex 38: 2 made its horns on its four **c**
Ex 38: 5 four **c** of the bronze grating
Lev 19: 9 reap the **c** of your field, nor
Lev 23:22 shall not wholly reap the **c**
Num 15:38 on the **c** of their garments
Num 15:38 in the tassels of the **c**
Deut 22:12 make tassels on the four **c** of
1Ki 7:34 at the four **c** of each cart
2Ch 26:15 to be on the towers and the **c**
Job 1:19 the four **c** of the house, and
Is 11:12 from the four **c** of the earth
Jer 9:26 all who are in the farthest **c**
Jer 25:23 all who are in the farthest **c**
Jer 49:32 winds those in the farthest **c**
Ezek 7: 2 upon the four **c** of the land
Ezek 41:22 Its **c**, its length, and its
Ezek 43:16 wide, square at its four **c**
Ezek 43:20 on the four **c** of the ledge,
Ezek 45:19 on the four **c** of the ledge of
Ezek 46:21 by the four **c** of the court
Ezek 46:22 In the four **c** of the court
Ezek 46:22 all four **c** were the same size
Zech 9:15 like the **c** of the altar
Matt 6: 5 on the **c** of the streets, that
Acts 10:11 sheet bound at the four **c**
Acts 11: 5 down from heaven by four **c**
Rev 7: 1 at the four **c** of the earth
Rev 20: 8 in the four **c** of the earth

CORNERSTONE (*see* CORNER)
Job 38: 6 Or who laid its **c**,
Ps 118:22 Has become the chief **c**
Is 28:16 a tried stone, a precious **c**
Zech 10: 4 From him comes the **c**, from
Matt 21:42 has become the chief **c**
Mark 12:10 has become the chief **c**
Luke 20:17 has become the chief **c**'
Acts 4:11 which has become the chief **c**
Eph 2:20 Himself being the chief **c**
1Pe 2: 6 I lay in Zion a chief **c**,
1Pe 2: 7 has become the chief **c**,"

CORPSE (*see* CORPSES)
Lev 22: 4 anything made unclean by a **c**
Josh 8:29 take his **c** down from the tree
1Ki 13:22 your **c** shall not come to
1Ki 13:24 his **c** was thrown on the road,
1Ki 13:24 the lion also stood by the **c**
1Ki 13:25 saw the **c** thrown on the road,
1Ki 13:25 and the lion standing by the **c**
1Ki 13:28 found his **c** thrown on the
1Ki 13:28 and the lion standing by the **c**
1Ki 13:28 the **c** nor torn the donkey
1Ki 13:29 up the **c** of the man of God
1Ki 13:30 he laid the **c** in his own tomb
2Ki 9:37 the **c** of Jezebel shall be as
Is 14:19 like a **c** trodden under foot
Mark 6:29 they came and took away his **c**

CORPSES (*see* CORPSE)
2Ki 19:35 the morning, there were the **c**
Is 34: 3 shall rise from their **c**, and
Is 37:36 the morning, there were the **c**
Is 66:24 look upon the **c** of the men
Jer 7:33 The **c** of this people will be
Jer 16: 4 their **c** shall be meat for the
Jer 19: 7 their **c** I will give as meat
Ezek 6: 5 And I will lay the **c** of the
Nah 3: 3 number of bodies, countless **c**
Nah 3: 3 they stumble over the **c**
Heb 3:17 sinned, whose **c** fell in the

CORRECT (*see* CORRECTED, CORRECTING, CORRECTION, CORRECTLY, CORRECTS)
Job 40: 2 with the Almighty **c** Him
Ps 39:11 You **c** man for iniquity, You
Ps 94:10 the nations, shall He not **c**
Prov 29:17 **C** your son, and he will give
Jer 2:19 own wickedness will **c** you
Jer 10:24 LORD, **c** me, but with justice
Jer 30:11 But I will **c** you in justice,
Jer 46:28 I will rightly **c** you, for I

CORRECTED (*see* CORRECT)
Prov 29:19 will not be **c** by mere words
Heb 12: 9 had human fathers who **c** us

CORRECTING (*see* CORRECT)
2Ti 2:25 in humility **c** those who are

CORRECTION (*see* CORRECT)
Job 37:13 it to come, whether for **c**
Prov 3:11 of the LORD, nor detest His **c**
Prov 7:22 a fool to the **c** of the stocks
Prov 13:18 come to him who disdains **c**
Prov 15:10 Harsh **c** is for him who
Prov 16:22 but the **c** of fools is folly
Prov 22:15 but the rod of **c** will drive
Prov 23:13 not withhold **c** from a child
Jer 2:30 they received no **c**
Jer 5: 3 have refused to receive **c**
Jer 7:28 LORD their God nor receive **c**
Hab 1:12 You have marked them for **c**
Zeph 3: 2 voice, she has not received **c**
2Ti 3:16 doctrine, for reproof, for **c**

CORRECTLY (*see* CORRECT)
Judg 14:12 If you can **c** solve and explain

CORRECTS (*see* CORRECT)
Job 5:17 happy is the man whom God **c**
Prov 3:12 for whom the LORD loves He **c**

CORRESPONDING (*see* CORRESPONDS)
Ex 38:18 **c** to the hangings of the
Ezek 40:18 **c** to the length of the
Ezek 42:12 And **c** to the doors of the

CORRESPONDS (*see* CORRESPONDING)
Gal 4:25 **c** to Jerusalem which now is,

CORRODED (*see* CORROSION)
Jas 5: 3 Your gold and silver are **c**

CORROSION (*see* CORRODED)
Jas 5: 3 their **c** will be a witness

CORRUPT (*see* CORRUPTED, CORRUPTERS, CORRUPTIBLE, CORRUPTION, CORRUPTLY, CORRUPTS)
Gen 6:11 earth also was **c** before God
Gen 6:12 the earth, and indeed it was **c**
Deut 13:13 Certain **c** men have gone out
Deut 31:29 you will become utterly **c**
1Sa 2:12 Now the sons of Eli were **c**
Ps 14: 1 They are **c**, They have done
Ps 14: 3 They have together become **c**
Ps 53: 1 They are **c**, and have done
Ps 53: 3 They have together become **c**
Ezek 16:47 you became more **c** than they
Ezek 20:44 according to your **c** doings
Ezek 23:11 she became more **c** in her
Ezek 23:11 in her harlotry more **c** than
Dan 2: 9 **c** words before me till the
Dan 11:32 he shall **c** with flattery
Eph 4:22 the old man which grows **c**
Eph 4:29 Let no **c** communication
1Ti 6: 5 wranglings of men of **c** minds
2Ti 3: 8 men of **c** minds, disapproved
Jude 10 things they **c** themselves

CORRUPTED (*see* CORRUPT)
Gen 6:12 for all flesh had **c** their way
Ex 8:24 The land was **c** because of the
Ex 32: 7 of Egypt have **c** themselves
Deut 32: 5 They have **c** themselves
Ezek 28:17 you **c** your wisdom for the
Hos 9: 9 They are deeply **c**, as in the
Zeph 3: 7 early and **c** all their deeds
Mal 2: 8 You have **c** the covenant of
2Co 7: 2 no one, we have **c** no one, we
2Co 11: 3 so your minds may be **c** from
Jas 5: 2 Your riches are **c**, and your
Rev 19: 2 who **c** the earth with her

CORRUPTERS (*see* CORRUPT)
Is 1: 4 evildoers, children who are **c**
Jer 6:28 and iron, they are all **c**

CORRUPTIBLE (*see* CORRUPT)
Rom 1:23 into an image made like **c** man
1Co 15:53 For this **c** must put on
1Co 15:54 So when this **c** has put on
1Pe 1:18 not redeemed with **c** things
1Pe 1:23 born again, not of **c** seed but

CORRUPTION (*see* CORRUPT)
Lev 22:25 because their **c** is in them
2Ki 23:13 the south of the Mount of **C**
Job 17:14 if I say to **c**, 'You are my
Ps 16:10 allow Your Holy One to see **c**
Is 38:17 my soul from the pit of **c**
Acts 2:27 allow Your Holy One to see **c**
Acts 2:31 nor did His flesh see **c**
Acts 13:34 dead, no more to return to **c**
Acts 13:35 allow Your Holy One to see **c**
Acts 13:36 with his fathers, and saw **c**
Acts 13:37 whom God raised up saw no **c**
Rom 8:21 from the bondage of **c** into
1Co 15:42 The body is sown in **c**, it is
1Co 15:50 nor does **c** inherit
Gal 6: 8 will of the flesh reap **c**, but
2Pe 1: 4 having escaped the **c** that is
2Pe 2:12 utterly perish in their own **c**
2Pe 2:19 themselves are slaves of **c**

CORRUPTLY (*see* CORRUPT)
Deut 4:16 lest you act **c** and make for
Deut 4:25 grown old in the land, act **c**
Deut 9:12 out of Egypt have acted **c**
Judg 2:19 behaved more **c** than their
2Ch 27: 2 But still the people acted **c**
Neh 1: 7 have acted very **c** against You

CORRUPTS (*see* CORRUPT)
1Co 15:33 Evil company **c** good habits

COS
Acts 21: 1 straight course we came to C

COSAM
Luke 3:28 the son of Addi, the son of C

COST (*see* COSTLY, COSTS)
1Ki 10:29 c six hundred shekels of
Ezra 6: 8 Let the c be paid at the
Luke 14:28 sit down first and count the c

COSTLY (*see* COST)
1Ki 5:17 c stones, and hewn stones, to
1Ki 7: 9 All these were of c stones
1Ki 7:10 foundation was of c stones
1Ki 7:11 And above were c stones, hewn
2Ch 36:10 with the c articles from the
Ps 49: 8 of their souls is c, And it
Matt 26: 7 flask of very c fragrant oil
Mark 14: 3 of very c oil of spikenard
John 12: 3 of very c oil of spikenard
1Ti 2: 9 gold or pearls or c clothing

COSTS (*see* COST)
2Sa 24:24 with that which c me nothing
1Ch 21:24 with that which c me nothing

COUCH (*see* COUCHES)
Gen 49: 4 he went up to my c
Esth 7: 8 across the c where Esther was
Job 7:13 my c will ease my complaint,'
Ps 6: 6 I drench my c with my tears
Song 3: 7 Behold, it is Solomon's c
Ezek 23:41 You sat on a stately c, with
Amos 3:12 a bed and on the edge of a c

COUCHES (*see* COUCH)
Esth 1: 6 the c were of gold and silver
Amos 6: 4 ivory, stretch out on your c
Mark 7: 4 copper vessels, and c
Acts 5:15 and laid them on beds and c

COULD (*see* PREFACE)

COUNCIL (*see* COUNCILS)
Gen 49: 6 Let not my soul enter their c
Matt 5:22 shall be in danger of the c
Matt 26:59 and all the c sought false
Mark 14:55 all the c sought testimony
Mark 15: 1 and scribes and the whole c
Mark 15:43 a prominent c member, who
Luke 22:66 and led Him into their c,
Luke 23:50 a c member, a good and just
John 11:47 and the Pharisees gathered a c
Acts 4:15 them to go aside out of the c
Acts 5:21 came and called the c together
Acts 5:27 they set them before the c
Acts 5:34 Then one in the c stood up
Acts 5:41 from the presence of the c
Acts 6:12 him, and brought him to the c
Acts 6:15 And all who sat in the c,
Acts 22: 5 all the c of the elders, from
Acts 22:30 and all their c to appear, and
Acts 23: 1 looking earnestly at the c
Acts 23: 6 he cried out in the c, "Men
Acts 23:15 together with the c, suggest
Acts 23:20 Paul down to the c tomorrow
Acts 23:28 I brought him before their c
Acts 24:20 me while I stood before the c
Acts 25:12 he had conferred with the c

COUNCILS (*see* COUNCIL)
Matt 10:17 they will deliver you up to c
Mark 13: 9 they will deliver you up to c

COUNSEL (*see* COUNSELED, COUNSELOR, COUNSELS)
Ex 18:19 I will give you c, and God
Num 31:16 through the c of Balaam, to
Deut 32:28 they are a nation void of c
Josh 9:14 did not ask c of the LORD
Judg 19:30 Consider it, take c, and speak
Judg 20: 7 your advice and c here and now
Judg 20:18 house of God to ask c of God
Judg 20:23 asked c of the LORD, saying,
1Sa 14:37 So Saul asked c of God
2Sa 15:31 turn the c of Ahithophel into
2Sa 15:34 the c of Ahithophel for me
2Sa 16:20 Give c as to what we should
2Sa 16:23 the c of Ahithophel, which he
2Sa 16:23 So was all the c of
2Sa 17: 7 The c that Ahithophel has
2Sa 17:11 Therefore I c that all Israel
2Sa 17:14 The c of Hushai the Archite
2Sa 17:14 than the c of Ahithophel
2Sa 17:14 the good c of Ahithophel, to
2Sa 17:23 that his c was not followed
2Sa 20:18 shall surely ask c at Abel
1Ki 1:12 please, let me now give you c
1Ki 12: 8 But he rejected the c which
1Ki 12: 9 to them, "What c do you give
1Ki 12:13 and rejected the c which the
1Ki 12:14 to the c of the young men
1Ki 12:28 Therefore the king took c
2Ki 6: 8 he took c with his servants,
2Ki 18:20 You speak of having c and
1Ch 12:19 sent him away by c, saying
2Ch 10: 8 But he rejected the c which
2Ch 10:13 rejected the c of the elders
2Ch 10:14 to the c of the young men
2Ch 22: 5 He also walked in their c
2Ch 25:16 Have we made you the king's c
2Ch 25:16 this and have not heeded my c
2Ch 25:17 Amaziah king of Judah took c
2Ch 32: 3 he took c with his leaders and
Ezra 10: 3 to the c of my master and of
Ezra 10: 8 to the c of the leaders and
Neh 4:15 brought their c to nothing
Neh 6: 7 and let us take c together
Job 5:13 the c of the cunning comes
Job 10: 3 shine on the c of the wicked
Job 12:13 wisdom and strength, He has c
Job 15: 8 Have you heard the c of God
Job 18: 7 and his own c casts him down
Job 21:16 the c of the wicked is far
Job 22:18 but the c of the wicked is
Job 29: 4 when the friendly c of God
Job 29:21 and kept silence for my c
Job 38: 2 Who is this who darkens c by
Job 42: 3 who hides c without knowledge
Ps 1: 1 not in the c of the ungodly
Ps 2: 2 And the rulers take c together
Ps 13: 2 shall I take c in my soul
Ps 14: 6 You shame the c of the poor
Ps 16: 7 the LORD who has given me c
Ps 31:13 While they take c together
Ps 33:10 The LORD brings the c of the
Ps 33:11 The c of the LORD stands
Ps 55:14 We took sweet c together, And
Ps 64: 2 the secret c of the wicked
Ps 71:10 for my life take c together
Ps 73:24 You will guide me with Your c
Ps 83: 3 crafty c against Your people
Ps 106:13 They did not wait for His c
Ps 106:43 against Him by their c, And
Ps 107:11 despised the c of the Most
Prov 1: 5 will attain wise c,
Prov 1:25 you disdained all my c, and
Prov 1:30 they would have none of my c
Prov 3:32 but His secret c is with the
Prov 8:14 C is mine, and sound wisdom
Prov 11:14 Where there is no c, the
Prov 12:15 but he who heeds c is wise
Prov 15:22 Without c, plans go awry, but
Prov 19:20 Listen to c and receive
Prov 19:21 Nevertheless the LORD's c
Prov 20: 5 C in the heart of man is like
Prov 20:18 purpose is established by c
Prov 20:18 by wise c wage war
Prov 21:30 or c against the LORD
Prov 24: 6 for by wise c you will wage
Prov 27: 9 friend does so by hearty c
Eccl 8: 2 I c you, "Keep the king's
Is 5:19 let the c of the Holy One of
Is 7: 5 have taken evil c against you
Is 8:10 Take c together, but it will
Is 11: 2 the Spirit of c and might,
Is 16: 3 Take c, execute judgment
Is 19: 3 I will destroy their c, and
Is 19:11 counselors give foolish c
Is 19:17 because of the c of the LORD
Is 23: 8 has taken this c against Tyre
Is 28:29 hosts, Who is wonderful in c
Is 29:15 their c far from the LORD
Is 30: 1 Who take c, but not of Me, and
Is 36: 5 I say you speak of having c
Is 40:14 With whom did He take c, and
Is 44:26 and performs the c of His
Is 45:21 yes, let them take c together
Is 46:10 My c shall stand, and I will
Is 46:11 the man who executes My c
Jer 18:18 nor c from the wise, nor the
Jer 18:23 You know all their c which is
Jer 19: 7 will make void the c of Judah
Jer 23:18 stood in the c of the LORD
Jer 23:22 But if they had stood in My c
Jer 32:19 You are great in c and mighty
Jer 38:15 And if I give you c, you will
Jer 49: 7 has c perished from the
Jer 49:20 Therefore hear the c of the
Jer 49:30 has taken c against you, and
Jer 50:45 Therefore hear the c of the
Ezek 7:26 priest, and c from the elders
Ezek 11: 2 give wicked c in this city,
Dan 2:14 Then with c and wisdom Daniel
Dan 4:27 let my c be acceptable to you
Hos 4:12 My people ask c from their
Hos 10: 6 shall be ashamed of his own c
Mic 4:12 nor do they understand His c
Hab 2:10 gave shameful c to your house
Zech 6:13 and the c of peace shall be
Matt 12:14 took c against Him, how they
Matt 27: 1 elders of the people took c
Matt 27: 7 And they took c and bought with
Matt 28:12 with the elders and taken c
Luke 7:30 lawyers rejected the c of God
Luke 23:51 had not consented to their c
John 12:10 c that they might also put
John 18:14 c to the Jews that it was
Acts 2:23 delivered by the determined c
Acts 5:33 and took c to kill them
Acts 20:27 to you the whole c of God
Eph 1:11 to the c of His will,
Heb 6:17 the immutability of His c
Rev 3:18 I c you to buy from Me gold

COUNSELED (*see* COUNSEL)
2Sa 17:15 and so Ahithophel c Absalom
2Sa 17:15 and thus and so I have c
2Sa 17:21 has Ahithophel c against you
2Ch 22: 3 for his mother c him to do
Job 26: 3 How have you c one who has no
Mic 6: 5 now what Balak king of Moab c

COUNSELOR (*see* COUNSEL, COUNSELORS)
2Sa 15:12 the Gilonite, David's c, from
1Ch 26:14 his son Zechariah, a wise c
1Ch 27:32 David's uncle, was a c, a
1Ch 27:33 Ahithophel was the king's c
Is 3: 3 and the honorable man, the c
Is 9: 6 will be called Wonderful, C
Is 40:13 or as His c has taught Him
Is 41:28 them, but there was no c, who
Mic 4: 9 Has your c perished
Nah 1:11 against the LORD, a wicked c
Rom 11:34 Or who has become His c

COUNSELORS (*see* COUNSELOR)
2Ch 22: 4 for they were his c after the
Ezra 4: 5 and hired c against them to
Ezra 7:14 and his seven c to inquire
Ezra 7:15 his c have freely offered to
Ezra 7:28 me before the king and his c
Ezra 8:25 God which the king and his c
Job 3:14 c of the earth, who built
Job 12:17 He leads c away plundered, and
Ps 119:24 also are my delight And my c
Prov 11:14 of c there is safety
Prov 12:20 evil, but c of peace have joy
Prov 15:22 of c they are established
Prov 24: 6 of c there is safety
Is 1:26 your c as at the beginning
Is 19:11 Pharaoh's wise c give foolish
Dan 3: 2 the governors, the c, the
Dan 3: 3 the governors, the c, the
Dan 3:24 and spoke, saying to his c
Dan 3:27 and the king's c gathered
Dan 4:36 My c and nobles resorted to me
Dan 6: 7 and satraps, the c and advisors

COUNSELS (*see* COUNSEL)
Ps 5:10 Let them fall by their own c
Ps 81:12 heart, To walk in their own c
Prov 12: 5 but the c of the wicked are
Prov 22:20 to you excellent things of c
Is 25: 1 Your c of old are
Is 47:13 in the multitude of your c
Jer 7:24 ear, but walked in the c and
Hos 11: 6 them, because of their own c
Mic 6:16 and you walk in their c, that
1Co 4: 5 reveal the c of the hearts

COUNT (*see* COUNTED, COUNTING, COUNTLESS, COUNTS)
Gen 15: 5 c the stars if you are able
Ex 12: 4 make your c for the lamb
Lev 15:13 then he shall c for himself
Lev 15:28 then she shall c for herself

Lev 19:23 you shall **c** their fruit as
Lev 23:15 you shall **c** for yourselves
Lev 23:16 **C** fifty days to the day
Lev 25: 8 you shall **c** seven sabbaths of
Lev 25:27 then let him **c** the years
Num 23:10 Who can **c** the dust of Jacob,
Num 31:26 **C** up the plunder that was
Num 31:49 a **c** of the men of war who are
Deut 16: 9 You shall **c** seven weeks for
Deut 16: 9 begin to **c** the seven weeks
1Sa 18:27 them in full **c** to the king
2Sa 24: 2 **c** the people, that I may know
2Sa 24: 4 to **c** the people of Israel
2Ki 22: 4 that he may **c** the money which
1Ch 9:28 them in and took them out by **c**
1Ch 21: 6 But he did not **c** Levi and
Job 19:15 **c** me as a stranger
Job 31: 4 my ways, and **c** all my steps
Ps 22:17 I can **c** all My bones
Ps 48:12 **C** her towers
Ps 139:18 If I should **c** them, they
Ps 139:22 I **c** them my enemies
Ezek 44:26 they shall **c** seven days for
Mic 6:11 Shall I **c** pure those with the
Matt 21:26 for all **c** John as a prophet
Luke 14:28 **c** the cost, whether he has
Acts 20:24 nor do I **c** my life dear to
Phil 3: 8 But indeed I also **c** all
Phil 3: 8 **c** them as rubbish, that I may
Phil 3:13 I do not **c** myself to have
2Th 1:11 **c** you worthy of this calling
2Th 3:15 Yet do not **c** him as an enemy,
1Ti 6: 1 as are under the yoke **c** their
Phm 17 If then you **c** me as a partner
Jas 1: 2 **c** it all joy when you fall
Jas 5:11 Indeed we **c** them blessed who
2Pe 2:13 as those who **c** it pleasure to
2Pe 3: 9 as some **c** slackness, but is

COUNTED (*see* COUNT)
Gen 16:10 shall not be **c** for multitude
Ex 38:21 which was **c** according to the
Lev 25:31 be **c** as the fields of the
Josh 13: 3 (which is **c** as Canaanite)
Judg 21: 9 For when the people were **c**
1Ki 1:21 will be **c** as offenders
1Ki 3: 8 numerous to be numbered or **c**
1Ki 8: 5 oxen that could not be **c** or
2Ki 12:10 **c** the money that was found in
1Ch 23:24 houses as they were **c**
2Ch 5: 6 oxen that could not be **c** or
Ezra 1: 8 **c** them out to Sheshbazzar the
Job 18: 3 Why are we **c** as beasts, and
Ps 88: 4 I am **c** with those who go down
Prov 17:28 Even a fool is **c** wise when he
Prov 27:14 it will be **c** a curse to him
Is 32:15 field is **c** as a forest
Is 40:15 are **c** as the small dust on
Is 40:17 they are **c** by Him less than
Matt 14: 5 because they **c** him as a
Matt 26:15 And they **c** out to him thirty
Mark 11:32 for all **c** John to have been a
Luke 20:35 But those who are **c** worthy to
Luke 21:36 **c** worthy to escape all these
Acts 5:41 rejoicing that they were **c**
Acts 19:19 they **c** up the value of them,
Rom 2:26 be **c** as circumcision
Rom 4: 4 the wages are not **c** as grace
Rom 9: 8 the promise are **c** as the seed
Phil 3: 7 me, these I have **c** loss for
2Th 1: 5 that you may be **c** worthy of
1Ti 1:12 because He **c** me faithful,
1Ti 5:17 be **c** worthy of double honor
Heb 3: 3 For this One has been **c**
Heb 10:29 **c** the blood of the covenant

COUNTENANCE (*see* COUNTENANCES)
Gen 4: 5 was very angry, and his **c** fell
Gen 4: 6 And why has your **c** fallen
Gen 12:11 are a woman of beautiful **c**
Gen 31: 2 And Jacob saw the **c** of Laban
Gen 31: 5 I see your father's **c**, that
Num 6:26 LORD lift up His **c** upon you
Deut 28:50 a nation of fierce **c**, which
Judg 13: 6 to me, and His **c** was like the
Judg 13: 6 the **c** of the Angel of God
1Sa 14:27 and his **c** brightened
1Sa 14:29 now, how my **c** has brightened
2Ki 8:11 Then he set his **c** in a stare
Job 14:20 You change his **c** and send him
Job 29:24 the light of my **c** they did
Ps 4: 6 the light of Your **c** upon us
Ps 10: 4 his proud **c** does not seek God
Ps 11: 7 His **c** beholds the upright
Ps 42: 5 Him For the help of His **c**
Ps 42:11 praise Him, The help of my **c**
Ps 43: 5 praise Him, The help of my **c**
Ps 44: 3 arm, and the light of Your **c**
Ps 80:16 at the rebuke of Your **c**
Ps 89:15 LORD, in the light of Your **c**
Ps 90: 8 sins in the light of Your **c**
Prov 15:13 heart makes a cheerful **c**, but
Prov 25:23 backbiting tongue an angry **c**
Prov 27:17 sharpens the **c** of his friend
Eccl 7: 3 for by a sad **c** the heart is
Song 2:14 the cliff, let me see your **c**
Song 2:14 is sweet, and your **c** is lovely
Song 5:15 His **c** is like Lebanon,
Is 3: 9 The look on their **c** witnesses
Ezek 27:35 and their **c** will be troubled
Dan 1:15 days their **c** appeared better
Dan 5: 6 Then the king's **c** changed
Dan 5: 9 his **c** was changed, and his
Dan 5:10 you, nor let your **c** change
Dan 7:28 troubled me, and my **c** changed
Matt 6:16 the hypocrites, with a sad **c**
Matt 28: 3 His **c** was like lightning, and
2Co 3: 7 because of the glory of his **c**
Rev 1:16 and His **c** was like the sun

COUNTENANCES (*see* COUNTENANCE)
Dan 1:13 Then let our **c** be examined
Dan 1:13 the **c** of the young men who

COUNTERACT
Esth 8: 3 **c** the evil plot of Haman the

COUNTING (*see* COUNT)
Gen 41:49 the sea, until he stopped **c**

COUNTLESS (*see* COUNT)
Job 21:33 as **c** have gone before him
Nah 3: 3 number of bodies, **c** corpses

COUNTRIES (*see* COUNTRY)
Gen 41:57 So all **c** came to Joseph in
2Ki 18:35 their **c** from my hand, that
1Ch 22: 5 and glorious throughout all **c**
2Ch 20:29 **c** when they heard that the
Ezra 3: 3 of the people of those **c**,
Ps 110: 6 execute the heads of many **c**
Is 8: 9 Give ear, all you from far **c**
Is 36:20 their **c** from my hand, that
Jer 23: 3 of My flock out of all **c**
Jer 23: 8 from all the **c** where I had
Jer 28: 8 old prophesied against many **c**
Jer 32:37 **c** where I have driven them in
Jer 40:11 and who were in all the **c**
Ezek 5: 5 and the **c** all around her
Ezek 5: 6 the **c** that are all around her
Ezek 6: 8 are scattered through the **c**
Ezek 11:16 scattered them among the **c**
Ezek 11:16 in the **c** where they have gone
Ezek 11:17 the **c** where you have been
Ezek 12:15 them throughout the **c**
Ezek 20:23 them throughout the **c**,
Ezek 20:32 like the families in other **c**
Ezek 20:34 gather you out of the **c** where
Ezek 20:41 of the **c** where you have been
Ezek 22: 4 and a mockery to all **c**
Ezek 22:15 disperse you throughout the **c**
Ezek 25: 7 you to perish from the **c**
Ezek 29:12 of the **c** that are desolate
Ezek 29:12 them throughout the **c**
Ezek 30: 7 the midst of the desolate **c**
Ezek 30:23 them throughout the **c**
Ezek 30:26 them throughout the **c**
Ezek 32: 9 into the **c** which you have not
Ezek 34:13 and gather them from the **c**
Ezek 35:10 these two **c** shall be mine, and
Ezek 36:19 dispersed throughout the **c**
Ezek 36:24 gather you out of all **c**, and
Dan 9: 7 **c** to which You have driven
Dan 11:40 and he shall enter the **c**,
Dan 11:41 many **c** shall be overthrown
Dan 11:42 out his hand against the **c**
Zech 10: 9 shall remember Me in far **c**

COUNTRY (*see* COUNTRIES, COUNTRYSIDE)
Gen 12: 1 Get out of your **c**, from your
Gen 14: 7 attacked all the **c** of the
Gen 24: 4 but you shall go to my **c** and
Gen 25: 6 his son, to the **c** of the east
Gen 29:26 must not be done so in our **c**
Gen 30:25 go to my own place and to my **c**
Gen 32: 3 land of Seir, the **c** of Edom
Gen 32: 9 said to me, "Return to your **c**
Gen 34: 2 the Hivite, prince of the **c**
Gen 36: 6 went to a **c** away from the
Gen 42:30 and took us for spies of the **c**
Gen 42:33 the man, the lord of the **c**
Gen 47:27 of Egypt, in the **c** of Goshen
Lev 16:29 a native of your own **c** or a
Lev 17:15 of your own **c** or a stranger
Lev 24:22 and for one from your own **c**
Lev 25:31 as the fields of the **c**
Num 20:17 let us pass through your **c**
Num 21:20 that is in the **c** of Moab, to
Num 32: 4 the **c** which the LORD defeated
Num 32:33 cities of the surrounding **c**
Deut 26: 3 **c** which the LORD swore to our
Deut 28: 3 blessed shall you be in the **c**
Deut 28:16 cursed shall you be in the **c**
Josh 2: 2 of Israel to search out the **c**
Josh 2: 3 come to search out all the **c**
Josh 2:24 all the inhabitants of the **c**
Josh 6:22 men who had spied out the **c**
Josh 6:27 spread throughout all the **c**
Josh 7: 2 Go up and spy out the **c**
Josh 9: 6 We have come from a far **c**
Josh 9: 9 From a very far **c** your
Josh 9:11 of our **c** spoke to us, saying,
Josh 10:40 the mountain **c** and the South
Josh 10:41 all the **c** of Goshen, even as
Josh 11:16 the mountain **c**, all the South
Josh 12: 7 kings of the **c** which Joshua
Josh 12: 8 in the mountain **c**, in the
Josh 13:21 of Sihon dwelling in the **c**
Josh 15:48 And in the mountain **c**
Josh 17:15 then go up to the forest **c**
Josh 17:16 The mountain **c** is not enough
Josh 17:18 the mountain **c** shall be yours
Josh 19:51 made an end of dividing the **c**
Josh 22: 9 to go to the **c** of Gilead
Judg 8:28 the **c** was quiet for forty
Judg 11:21 who inhabited that **c**
Judg 12:12 Aijalon in the **c** of Zebulun
Judg 18:14 out the **c** of Laish answered
Ruth 1: 1 to sojourn in the **c** of Moab
Ruth 1: 2 And they went to the **c** of Moab
Ruth 1: 6 return from the **c** of Moab
Ruth 1: 6 for she had heard in the **c** of
Ruth 1:22 returned from the **c** of Moab
Ruth 2: 6 with Naomi from the **c** of Moab
Ruth 4: 3 come back from the **c** of Moab
1Sa 6: 1 **c** of the Philistines seven
1Sa 6:18 **c** villages, even as far as
1Sa 14:21 camp from the surrounding **c**
1Sa 27: 5 a place in some town in the **c**
1Sa 27: 7 that David dwelt in the **c** of
1Sa 27:11 in the **c** of the Philistines
2Sa 15:23 all the **c** wept with a loud
2Sa 21:14 in the **c** of Benjamin in Zelah
1Ki 4:19 in the **c** of Sihon king of the
1Ki 8:41 a far **c** for Your name's sake
1Ki 10:13 turned and went to her own **c**
1Ki 10:15 from the governors of the **c**
1Ki 11:21 that I may go to my own **c**
1Ki 11:22 you seek to go to your own **c**
1Ki 22:36 and every man to his own **c**
2Ki 20:14 They came from a far **c**, from
1Ch 8: 8 children in the **c** of Moab
1Ch 20: 1 ravaged the **c** of the people
2Ch 6:32 but who comes from a far **c**
2Ch 9:12 turned and went to her own **c**
2Ch 9:14 of the **c** brought gold and
2Ch 30:10 city through the **c** of Ephraim
2Ch 34:33 the **c** that belonged to the
Prov 25:25 so is good news from a far **c**
Is 1: 7 Your **c** is desolate, your
Is 13: 5 They come from a far **c**, from
Is 22:18 like a ball into a large **c**
Is 39: 3 They came to me from a far **c**
Is 46:11 My counsel, from a far **c**
Jer 2: 7 you into a bountiful **c**, to
Jer 4:16 watchers come from a far **c**
Jer 6:20 and sweet cane from a far **c**
Jer 6:22 people comes from the north **c**
Jer 8:19 of my people from a far **c**
Jer 10:22 commotion out of the north **c**
Jer 22:10 no more, nor see his native **c**
Jer 22:26 into another **c** where you were
Jer 23: 8 of Israel from the north **c**
Jer 31: 8 bring them from the north **c**

Jer 32: 8 which is in the **c** of Benjamin
Jer 44: 1 in the **c** of Pathros, saying,
Jer 46:10 **c** by the River Euphrates
Jer 47: 4 remnant of the **c** of Caphtor
Jer 48:21 has come on the plain **c**
Jer 50: 9 nations from the north **c**, and
Jer 51: 9 us go everyone to his own **c**
Ezek 20:38 of the **c** where they sojourn
Ezek 20:42 into the **c** for which I lifted
Ezek 25: 9 frontier, the glory of the **c**
Ezek 32:15 the **c** is destitute of all
Ezek 34:13 the inhabited places of the **c**
Ezek 36: 5 order to plunder its open **c**
Hos 4:16 forage like a lamb in open **c**
Hos 12:12 Jacob fled to the **c** of Syria
Jon 1: 8 What is your **c**
Jon 4: 2 said when I was still in my **c**
Zech 6: 6 is going to the north **c**, the
Zech 6: 6 are going toward the south **c**
Zech 6: 8 north **c** have given rest to My
Zech 6: 8 to My Spirit in the north **c**
Matt 2:12 for their own **c** another way
Matt 8:28 to the **c** of the Gergesenes,
Matt 9:31 news about Him in all that **c**
Matt 13:54 when He had come to His own **c**
Matt 13:57 honor except in his own **c**
Matt 21:33 and went into a far **c**
Matt 25:14 a man traveling to a far **c**
Mark 5: 1 to the **c** of the Gadarenes
Mark 5:10 not send them out of the **c**
Mark 5:14 it in the city and in the **c**
Mark 6: 1 there and came to His own **c**
Mark 6: 4 honor except in his own **c**
Mark 6:36 may go into the surrounding **c**
Mark 6:56 villages, cities, or the **c**
Mark 12: 1 and went into a far **c**
Mark 13:34 like a man going to a far **c**
Mark 15:21 as he was coming out of the **c**
Mark 16:12 walked and went into the **c**
Luke 1:39 into the hill **c** with haste
Luke 1:65 all the hill **c** of Judea
Luke 2: 8 Now there were in the same **c**
Luke 4:23 do also here in Your **c**
Luke 4:24 is accepted in his own **c**
Luke 8:26 to the **c** of the Gadarenes
Luke 8:34 it in the city and in the **c**
Luke 9:12 the surrounding towns and **c**
Luke 15:13 journeyed to a far **c**, and
Luke 15:15 to a citizen of that **c**, and he
Luke 19:12 **c** to receive for himself a
Luke 20: 9 into a far **c** for a long time
Luke 21:21 who are in the **c** enter her
Luke 23:26 who was coming from the **c**
John 4:44 has no honor in his own **c**
John 11:54 the **c** near the wilderness
John 11:55 many went from the **c** up to
Acts 4:36 a Levite of the **c** of Cyprus
Acts 7: 3 to him, 'Get out of your **c**
Acts 9:32 through all parts of the **c**
Acts 12:20 because their **c** was supplied
Acts 12:20 with food by the king's **c**
Heb 11: 9 of promise as in a foreign **c**
Heb 11:15 had called to mind that **c**
Heb 11:16 better, that is, a heavenly **c**

COUNTRYMEN
2Co 11:26 in perils of my own **c**, in
1Th 2:14 same things from your own **c**

COUNTRYSIDE (*see* COUNTRY)
Deut 22:25 young woman in the **c**, and the
Deut 22:27 for he found her in the **c**
2Sa 18: 8 over the face of the whole **c**
1Ki 20:27 the Syrians filled the **c**
Neh 12:28 from the **c** around Jerusalem

COUNTS (*see* COUNT)
Job 19:11 He **c** me as one of His enemies
Job 33:10 me, He **c** me as His enemy
Ps 147: 4 He **c** the number of the stars
Is 33:18 Where is he who **c** the towers
Jer 33:13 the hands of him who **c** them

COUPLE (*see* COUPLED)
Ex 26: 6 **c** the curtains together with
Ex 26: 9 you shall **c** five curtains by
Ex 26:11 **c** the tent together, that it
Ex 36:18 clasps to **c** the tent together
Ex 39: 4 for it to **c** it together
Judg 19: 3 and a **c** of donkeys with him
2Sa 13: 6 make a **c** of cakes for me in
2Sa 16: 1 with a **c** of saddled donkeys
1Ki 17:12 I am gathering a **c** of sticks

COUPLED (*see* COUPLE)
Ex 26: 3 shall be **c** to one another
Ex 26: 3 shall be **c** to one another
Ex 26:24 They shall be **c** together at
Ex 26:24 they shall be **c** together at
Ex 36:10 he **c** five curtains to one
Ex 36:10 curtains he **c** to one another
Ex 36:13 **c** the curtains to one another
Ex 36:16 He **c** five curtains by
Ex 36:29 they were **c** at the bottom and
Ex 36:29 **c** together at the top by one
Ex 39: 4 it was **c** together at its two

COURAGE (*see* COURAGEOUS)
Num 13:20 Be of good **c**
Deut 31: 6 Be strong and of good **c**, do
Deut 31: 7 Be strong and of good **c**, for
Deut 31:23 Be strong and of good **c**
Josh 1: 6 Be strong and of good **c**, for
Josh 1: 9 Be strong and of good **c**
Josh 1:18 Only be strong and of good **c**
Josh 2:11 **c** in anyone because of you
Josh 10:25 be strong and of good **c**, for
2Sa 10:12 Be of good **c**, and let us be
1Ch 19:13 Be of good **c**, and let us be
1Ch 22:13 Be strong and of good **c**
1Ch 28:20 Be strong and of good **c**, and do
2Ch 15: 8 Oded the prophet, he took **c**
Ezra 10: 4 Be of good **c**, and do it
Ps 27:14 Be of good **c**, And He shall
Ps 31:24 Be of good **c**, And He shall
Is 41: 6 Be of good **c**!"
Jer 47: 3 for their children, lacking **c**
Dan 11:25 his **c** against the king of the
Mark 15:43 of God, coming and taking **c**
Acts 28:15 he thanked God and took **c**

COURAGEOUS (*see* COURAGE, COURAGEOUSLY)
Josh 1: 7 Only be strong and very **c**,
Josh 23: 6 Therefore be very **c** to keep
2Sa 13:28 Be **c** and valiant
2Ch 32: 7 Be strong and **c**
Amos 2:16 The most **c** men of might shall

COURAGEOUSLY (*see* COURAGEOUS)
2Ch 19:11 Behave **c**, and the LORD will be

COURIERS
Esth 3:13 sent by **c** into all the king's
Esth 3:15 The **c** went out, hastened by
Esth 8:10 letters by **c** on horseback
Esth 8:14 Then the **c** who rode on royal

COURSE (*see* COURSES)
2Ch 21:19 it happened in the **c** of time
Job 1: 5 of feasting had run their **c**
Job 10: 1 give free **c** to my complaint
Is 48: 7 should say, 'Of **c** I knew them
Jer 8: 6 Everyone turned to his own **c**
Jer 23:10 Their **c** of life is evil, and
Acts 13:25 as John was finishing his **c**
Acts 16:11 a straight **c** to Samothrace
Acts 21: 1 a straight **c** we came to Cos
Eph 2: 2 to the **c** of this world,
2Th 3: 1 of the Lord may have free **c**
Jas 3: 6 sets on fire the **c** of nature

COURSES (*see* COURSE)
Judg 5:20 the stars from their **c** fought

COURT (*see* COURTS, COURTYARD)
Ex 27: 9 make the **c** of the tabernacle
Ex 27: 9 shall be hangings for the **c**
Ex 27:12 along the width of the **c** on
Ex 27:13 The width of the **c** on the
Ex 27:16 For the gate of the **c** there
Ex 27:17 **c** shall have bands of silver
Ex 27:18 The length of the **c** shall be
Ex 27:19 and all the pegs of the **c**
Ex 35:17 the hangings of the **c**, its
Ex 35:17 screen for the gate of the **c**
Ex 35:18 tabernacle, the pegs of the **c**
Ex 38: 9 Then he made the **c** on the
Ex 38: 9 the hangings of the **c** were
Ex 38:15 the other side of the **c** gate
Ex 38:16 All the hangings of the **c** all
Ex 38:17 of the **c** had bands of silver
Ex 38:18 of the **c** was woven of blue
Ex 38:18 to the hangings of the **c**
Ex 38:20 of the **c** all around, were of
Ex 38:31 sockets for the **c** all around
Ex 38:31 the bases for the **c** gate
Ex 38:31 the pegs for the **c** all around
Ex 39:40 the hangings of the **c**, its
Ex 39:40 the screen for the **c** gate
Ex 40: 8 shall set up the **c** all around
Ex 40: 8 up the screen at the **c** gate
Ex 40:33 he raised up the **c** all around
Ex 40:33 up the screen of the **c** gate
Lev 6:16 in the **c** of the tabernacle of
Lev 6:26 in the **c** of the tabernacle of
Num 3:26 screen for the door of the **c**
Num 3:26 the hangings of the **c** which
Num 3:37 pillars of the **c** all around
Num 4:26 the door of the gate of the **c**
Num 4:26 the hangings of the **c** which
Num 4:32 the **c** with their sockets,
Deut 25: 1 men, and they come to **c**, that
2Sa 17:18 who had a well in his **c**
1Ki 6:36 he built the inner **c** with
1Ki 7: 8 had another **c** inside the hall
1Ki 7: 9 on the outside to the great **c**
1Ki 7:12 The great **c** was enclosed with
1Ki 7:12 So were the inner **c** of the
1Ki 8:64 the middle of the **c** that was
2Ki 20: 4 gone out into the middle **c**
2Ki 23:11 the officer who was in the **c**
2Ch 4: 9 he made the **c** of the priests
2Ch 4: 9 great **c** and doors for the **c**
2Ch 6:13 set it in the midst of the **c**
2Ch 7: 7 the middle of the **c** that was
2Ch 20: 5 of the LORD, before the new **c**
2Ch 24:21 him with stones in the **c** of
2Ch 29:16 **c** of the house of the LORD
Neh 3:25 was by the **c** of the prison
Esth 1: 5 in the **c** of the garden of the
Esth 2:11 paced in front of the **c** of
Esth 4:11 into the inner **c** to the king
Esth 5: 1 stood in the inner **c** of the
Esth 5: 2 Esther standing in the **c**,
Esth 6: 4 Who is in the **c**
Esth 6: 4 **c** of the king's palace to
Esth 6: 5 is there, standing in the **c**
Job 9:19 who will appoint my day in **c**
Job 9:32 we should go to **c** together
Job 11:19 yes, many would **c** your favor
Prov 25: 8 Do not go hastily to **c**
Jer 19:14 and he stood in the **c** of the
Jer 26: 2 Stand in the **c** of the LORD's
Jer 32: 2 up in the **c** of the prison
Jer 32: 8 son came to me in the **c** of
Jer 32:12 sat in the **c** of the prison
Jer 33: 1 up in the **c** of the prison
Jer 36:10 in the upper **c** at the entry
Jer 36:20 went to the king, into the **c**
Jer 37:21 to the **c** of the prison, and
Jer 37:21 in the **c** of the prison
Jer 38: 6 was in the **c** of the prison
Jer 38:13 in the **c** of the prison
Jer 38:28 Jeremiah remained in the **c** of
Jer 39:14 from the **c** of the prison, and
Jer 39:15 up in the **c** of the prison
Ezek 8: 3 the north gate of the inner **c**
Ezek 8: 7 me to the door of the **c**
Ezek 8:16 inner **c** of the LORD's house
Ezek 10: 3 the cloud filled the inner **c**
Ezek 10: 4 and the **c** was full of the
Ezek 10: 5 was heard even in the outer **c**
Ezek 40:14 the **c** all around the gateway
Ezek 40:17 brought me into the outer **c**
Ezek 40:17 made all around the **c**
Ezek 40:19 front of the inner **c** exterior
Ezek 40:20 On the outer **c** was also a
Ezek 40:23 A gate of the inner **c** was
Ezek 40:27 also a gateway on the inner **c**
Ezek 40:28 inner **c** through the southern
Ezek 40:31 archways faced the outer **c**
Ezek 40:32 into the inner **c** facing east
Ezek 40:34 archways faced the outer **c**
Ezek 40:37 gateposts faced the outer **c**
Ezek 40:44 the singers in the inner **c**
Ezek 40:47 And he measured the **c**, one
Ezek 41:15 and the porches of the **c**,
Ezek 42: 1 me out into the outer **c**, by
Ezek 42: 3 the inner **c** of twenty cubits
Ezek 42: 3 the pavement of the outer **c**
Ezek 42: 7 chambers, toward the outer **c**
Ezek 42: 8 the outer **c** was fifty cubits
Ezek 42: 9 into them from the outer **c**
Ezek 42:10 wall of the **c** toward the east
Ezek 42:14 holy chamber into the outer **c**

Ezek 43: 5 brought me into the inner **c**
Ezek 44:17 the gates of the inner **c**,
Ezek 44:17 inner **c** or within the house
Ezek 44:19 they go out to the outer **c**
Ezek 44:19 to the outer **c** to the people,
Ezek 44:21 when he enters the inner **c**
Ezek 44:27 sin offering in the inner **c**
Ezek 45:19 of the gate of the inner **c**
Ezek 46: 1 The gateway of the inner **c**
Ezek 46:20 **c** to sanctify the people
Ezek 46:21 me out into the outer **c** and
Ezek 46:21 by the four corners of the **c**
Ezek 46:21 in every corner of the **c**
Ezek 46:21 there was another **c**
Ezek 46:22 of the **c** were enclosed courts
Dan 7:10 The **c** was seated, and the
Dan 7:26 But the **c** shall be seated,
1Co 4: 3 judged by you or by a human **c**
Gal 4:17 They zealously **c** you, but for
Rev 11: 2 But leave out the **c** which is

COURTEOUS (*see* COURTEOUSLY, COURTESY)
1Pe 3: 8 be tenderhearted, be **c**

COURTEOUSLY (*see* COURTEOUS)
Acts 28: 7 us **c** for three days

COURTESY (*see* COURTEOUS)
Acts 24: 4 I beg you to hear, by your **c**

COURTS (*see* COURT)
2Ki 21: 5 **c** of the house of the LORD
2Ki 23:12 had made in the two **c** of the
1Ch 23:28 house of the LORD, in the **c**
1Ch 28: 6 shall build My house and My **c**
1Ch 28:12 of the **c** of the house of the
2Ch 23: 5 **c** of the house of the LORD
2Ch 33: 5 **c** of the house of the LORD
Neh 8:16 or the **c** of the house of God
Neh 13: 7 in the **c** of the house of God
Ps 65: 4 That he may dwell in Your **c**
Ps 84: 2 faints For the **c** of the LORD
Ps 84:10 For a day in Your **c** is better
Ps 92:13 flourish in the **c** of our God
Ps 96: 8 offering, and come into His **c**
Ps 100: 4 And into His **c** with praise
Ps 116:19 In the **c** of the LORD's house,
Ps 135: 2 In the **c** of the house of our
Is 1:12 your hand, to trample My **c**
Is 62: 9 shall drink it in My holy **c**
Ezek 9: 7 fill the **c** with the slain
Ezek 42: 6 like the pillars of the **c**
Ezek 46:22 of the court were enclosed **c**
Zech 3: 7 likewise have charge of My **c**
Luke 7:25 in luxury are in kings' **c**
Acts 19:38 the **c** are open and there are
Jas 2: 6 you and drag you into the **c**

COURTYARD (*see* COURT, COURTYARDS)
Is 34:13 of jackals, a **c** for ostriches
Jer 43: 9 in the clay in the brick **c**
Ezek 41:12 **c** at its western end was
Ezek 41:13 the separating **c** with the
Ezek 41:14 including the separating **c**
Ezek 41:15 it, facing the separating **c**
Ezek 42: 1 was opposite the separating **c**
Ezek 42:10 opposite the separating **c**
Ezek 42:13 are opposite the separating **c**
Matt 26:58 to the high priest's **c**
Matt 26:69 Peter sat outside in the **c**
Mark 14:54 right into the **c** of the high
Mark 14:66 as Peter was below in the **c**
Luke 22:55 a fire in the midst of the **c**
John 18:15 into the **c** of the high priest

COURTYARDS (*see* COURTYARD)
Ex 8:13 of the houses, out of the **c**
Neh 8:16 or in their **c** or the courts

COUSIN
Col 4:10 with Mark the **c** of Barnabas

COVENANT (*see* COVENANTED, COVENANTS)
Gen 6:18 will establish My **c** with you
Gen 9: 9 I establish My **c** with you
Gen 9:11 I establish My **c** with you
Gen 9:12 the **c** which I make between Me
Gen 9:13 the sign of the **c** between Me
Gen 9:15 I will remember My **c** which is
Gen 9:16 the everlasting **c** between God
Gen 9:17 This is the sign of the **c**
Gen 15:18 the LORD made a **c** with Abram
Gen 17: 2 I will make My **c** between Me
Gen 17: 4 My **c** is with you, and you
Gen 17: 7 establish My **c** between Me
Gen 17: 7 for an everlasting **c**, to be
Gen 17: 9 for you, you shall keep My **c**
Gen 17:10 This is My **c** which you shall
Gen 17:11 be a sign of the **c** between Me
Gen 17:13 My **c** shall be in your flesh
Gen 17:13 flesh for an everlasting **c**
Gen 17:14 he has broken My **c**
Gen 17:19 I will establish My **c** with
Gen 17:19 with him for an everlasting **c**
Gen 17:21 But My **c** I will establish
Gen 21:27 and the two of them made a **c**
Gen 21:32 they made a **c** at Beersheba
Gen 26:28 and let us make a **c** with you
Gen 31:44 come, let us make a **c**, you
Ex 2:24 His **c** with Abraham
Ex 6: 4 established My **c** with them
Ex 6: 5 and I have remembered My **c**
Ex 19: 5 obey My voice and keep My **c**
Ex 23:32 You shall make no **c** with them
Ex 24: 7 he took the Book of the **C**
Ex 24: 8 the blood of the **c** which the
Ex 31:16 generations as a perpetual **c**
Ex 34:10 Behold, I make a **c**
Ex 34:12 lest you make a **c** with the
Ex 34:15 lest you make a **c** with the
Ex 34:27 I have made a **c** with you and
Ex 34:28 tablets the words of the **c**
Lev 2:13 **c** of your God to be lacking
Lev 24: 8 of Israel by an everlasting **c**
Lev 26: 9 you and confirm My **c** with you
Lev 26:15 commandments, but break My **c**
Lev 26:25 execute the vengeance of My **c**
Lev 26:42 will remember My **c** with Jacob
Lev 26:42 and My **c** with Isaac and My
Lev 26:42 and My **c** with Abraham I will
Lev 26:44 them and break My **c** with them
Lev 26:45 the **c** of their ancestors,
Num 10:33 the ark of the **c** of the LORD
Num 14:44 the **c** of the LORD nor Moses
Num 18:19 it is a **c** of salt forever
Num 25:12 I give to him My **c** of peace
Num 25:13 him a **c** of an everlasting
Deut 4:13 **c** which He commanded you to
Deut 4:23 lest you forget the **c** of the
Deut 4:31 you, nor forget the **c** of your
Deut 5: 2 God made a **c** with us in Horeb
Deut 5: 3 make this **c** with our fathers
Deut 7: 2 You shall make no **c** with them
Deut 7: 9 the faithful God who keeps **c**
Deut 7:12 God will keep with you the **c**
Deut 8:18 His **c** which He swore to your
Deut 9: 9 the tablets of the **c** which
Deut 9:11 stone, the tablets of the **c**
Deut 9:15 of the **c** were in my two hands
Deut 10: 8 the ark of the **c** of the LORD
Deut 17: 2 God, in transgressing His **c**
Deut 29: 1 **c** which the LORD commanded
Deut 29: 1 besides the **c** which He made
Deut 29: 9 keep the words of this **c**, and
Deut 29:12 into **c** with the LORD your God
Deut 29:14 I make this **c** and this oath,
Deut 29:21 **c** that are written in this
Deut 29:25 they have forsaken the **c** of
Deut 31: 9 the ark of the **c** of the LORD
Deut 31:16 break My **c** which I have made
Deut 31:20 will provoke Me and break My **c**
Deut 31:25 the ark of the **c** of the LORD
Deut 31:26 of the **c** of the LORD your God
Deut 33: 9 Your word and kept Your **c**
Josh 3: 3 of the **c** of the LORD your God
Josh 3: 6 Take up the ark of the **c** and
Josh 3: 6 they took up the ark of the **c**
Josh 3: 8 who bear the ark of the **c**
Josh 3:11 the ark of the **c** of the Lord
Josh 3:14 of the **c** before the people
Josh 3:17 who bore the ark of the **c** of
Josh 4: 7 the ark of the **c** of the LORD
Josh 4: 9 bore the ark of the **c** stood
Josh 4:18 who bore the ark of the **c** of
Josh 6: 6 Take up the ark of the **c**, and
Josh 6: 8 the ark of the **c** of the LORD
Josh 7:11 My **c** which I commanded them
Josh 7:15 the **c** of the LORD, and because
Josh 8:33 the ark of the **c** of the LORD
Josh 9: 6 therefore, make a **c** with us
Josh 9: 7 how can we make a **c** with you
Josh 9:11 therefore, make a **c** with us
Josh 9:15 made a **c** with them to let
Josh 9:16 they had made a **c** with them
Josh 23:16 the **c** of the LORD your God
Josh 24:25 So Joshua made a **c** with the
Judg 2: 1 never break My **c** with you
Judg 2: 2 you shall make no **c** with the
Judg 2:20 My **c** which I commanded their
Judg 20:27 **c** of God was there in those
1Sa 4: 3 **c** of the LORD from Shiloh to
1Sa 4: 4 of the **c** of the LORD of hosts
1Sa 4: 4 with the ark of the **c** of God
1Sa 4: 5 when the ark of the **c** of the
1Sa 11: 1 Make a **c** with us, and we will
1Sa 11: 2 I will make a **c** with you,
1Sa 18: 3 Jonathan and David made a **c**
1Sa 20: 8 into a **c** of the LORD with you
1Sa 20:16 So Jonathan made a **c** with the
1Sa 22: 8 a **c** with the son of Jesse
1Sa 23:18 them made a **c** before the LORD
2Sa 3:12 Make your **c** with me, and
2Sa 3:13 I will make a **c** with you
2Sa 3:21 they may make a **c** with you
2Sa 5: 3 King David made a **c** with them
2Sa 15:24 the ark of the **c** of God
2Sa 23: 5 made with me an everlasting **c**
1Ki 3:15 the ark of the **c** of the LORD
1Ki 6:19 of the **c** of the LORD there
1Ki 8: 1 bring up the ark of the **c** of
1Ki 8: 6 **c** of the LORD to its place
1Ki 8: 9 when the LORD made a **c** with
1Ki 8:21 in which is the **c** of the LORD
1Ki 8:23 like You, who keep Your **c**
1Ki 11:11 this, and have not kept My **c**
1Ki 19:10 Israel have forsaken Your **c**
1Ki 19:14 Israel have forsaken Your **c**
2Ki 11: 4 And he made a **c** with them and
2Ki 11:17 made a **c** between the LORD
2Ki 13:23 because of His **c** with Abraham
2Ki 17:15 His **c** that He had made with
2Ki 17:35 whom the LORD had made a **c**
2Ki 17:38 the **c** that I have made with
2Ki 18:12 God, but transgressed His **c**
2Ki 23: 2 words of the Book of the **C**
2Ki 23: 3 made a **c** before the LORD, to
2Ki 23: 3 **c** that were written in this
2Ki 23: 3 took their stand for the **c**
2Ki 23:21 written in this Book of the **C**
1Ch 11: 3 David made a **c** with them at
1Ch 15:25 **c** of the LORD from the house
1Ch 15:26 the ark of the **c** of the LORD
1Ch 15:28 **c** of the LORD with shouting
1Ch 15:29 as the ark of the **c** of the
1Ch 16: 6 the ark of the **c** of God
1Ch 16:15 Remember His **c** always, the
1Ch 16:16 the **c** which He made with
1Ch 16:17 Israel for an everlasting **c**
1Ch 16:37 the **c** of the LORD to minister
1Ch 17: 1 but the ark of the **c** of the
1Ch 22:19 the ark of the **c** of the LORD
1Ch 28: 2 the ark of the **c** of the LORD
1Ch 28:18 the ark of the **c** of the LORD
2Ch 5: 2 the **c** of the LORD up from the
2Ch 5: 7 **c** of the LORD to its place
2Ch 5:10 when the LORD made a **c** with
2Ch 6:11 in which is the **c** of the LORD
2Ch 6:14 like You, who keep Your **c**
2Ch 13: 5 and his sons, by a **c** of salt
2Ch 15:12 a **c** to seek the LORD God of
2Ch 21: 7 because of the **c** that He had
2Ch 23: 1 made a **c** with the captains of
2Ch 23: 3 **c** with the king in the house
2Ch 23:16 made a **c** between himself, the
2Ch 29:10 **c** with the LORD God of Israel
2Ch 34:30 words of the book of the **c**
2Ch 34:31 made a **c** before the LORD, to
2Ch 34:31 **c** that were written in this
2Ch 34:32 did according to the **c** of God
Ezra 10: 3 let us make a **c** with our God
Neh 1: 5 God, You who keep Your **c** and
Neh 9: 8 made a **c** with him to give the
Neh 9:32 and awesome God, Who keeps **c**
Neh 9:38 of all this, we make a sure **c**
Neh 13:29 the **c** of the priesthood and
Job 5:23 For you shall have a **c** with
Job 31: 1 I have made a **c** with my eyes
Job 41: 4 Will he make a **c** with you
Ps 25:10 truth, To such as keep His **c**
Ps 25:14 And He will show them His **c**
Ps 44:17 we dealt falsely with Your **c**
Ps 50: 5 made a **c** with Me by sacrifice
Ps 50:16 Or take My **c** in your mouth,
Ps 55:20 He has broken his **c**

Ps 74:20 Have respect to the **c**
Ps 78:10 did not keep the **c** of God
Ps 78:37 were they faithful in His **c**
Ps 89: 3 I have made a **c** with My
Ps 89:28 My **c** shall stand firm with
Ps 89:34 My **c** I will not break, Nor
Ps 89:39 the **c** of Your servant
Ps 103:18 To such as keep His **c**, And to
Ps 105: 8 has remembered His **c** forever
Ps 105: 9 The **c** which He made with
Ps 105:10 Israel for an everlasting **c**
Ps 106:45 sake He remembered His **c**,
Ps 111: 5 will ever be mindful of His **c**
Ps 111: 9 has commanded His **c** forever
Ps 132:12 If your sons will keep My **c**
Prov 2:17 and forgets the **c** of her God
Is 24: 5 Broken the everlasting **c**
Is 28:15 We have made a **c** with death
Is 28:18 Your **c** with death will be
Is 33: 8 He has broken the **c**, He has
Is 42: 6 give You as a **c** to the people
Is 49: 8 give You as a **c** to the people
Is 54:10 nor shall My **c** of peace be
Is 55: 3 an everlasting **c** with you
Is 56: 4 pleases Me, and hold fast My **c**
Is 56: 6 Sabbath, and holds fast My **c**
Is 57: 8 bed and made a **c** with them
Is 59:21 this is My **c** with them
Is 61: 8 with them an everlasting **c**
Jer 3:16 The ark of the **c** of the LORD
Jer 11: 2 Hear the words of this **c**, and
Jer 11: 3 not obey the words of this **c**
Jer 11: 6 Hear the words of this **c**
Jer 11: 8 them all the words of this **c**
Jer 11:10 My **c** which I made with their
Jer 14:21 do not break Your **c** with us
Jer 22: 9 the **c** of the LORD their God
Jer 31:31 when I will make a new **c** with
Jer 31:32 not according to the **c** that I
Jer 31:32 My **c** which they broke, though
Jer 31:33 But this is the **c** that I will
Jer 32:40 an everlasting **c** with them
Jer 33:20 can break My **c** with the day
Jer 33:20 My **c** with the night, so that
Jer 33:21 then My **c** may also be broken
Jer 33:25 If My **c** is not with day and
Jer 34: 8 a **c** with all the people who
Jer 34:10 who had entered into the **c**
Jer 34:13 I made a **c** with your fathers
Jer 34:15 you made a **c** before Me in the
Jer 34:18 who have transgressed My **c**
Jer 34:18 **c** which they made before Me
Jer 50: 5 **c** That will not be forgotten
Ezek 16: 8 and entered into a **c** with you
Ezek 16:59 the oath by breaking the **c**
Ezek 16:60 I will remember My **c** with you
Ezek 16:60 an everlasting **c** with you
Ezek 16:61 not because of My **c** with you
Ezek 16:62 will establish My **c** with you
Ezek 17:13 made a **c** with him, and put him
Ezek 17:14 keeping his **c** it might stand
Ezek 17:15 Can he break a **c** and still be
Ezek 17:16 despised and whose **c** he broke
Ezek 17:18 the oath by breaking the **c**
Ezek 17:19 My **c** which he broke, I will
Ezek 20:37 you into the bond of the **c**
Ezek 34:25 I will make a **c** of peace with
Ezek 37:26 make a **c** of peace with them
Ezek 37:26 be an everlasting **c** with them
Ezek 44: 7 then they broke My **c** because
Dan 9: 4 awesome God, who keeps His **c**
Dan 9:27 a **c** with many for one week
Dan 11:22 and also the prince of the **c**
Dan 11:28 be moved against the holy **c**
Dan 11:30 in rage against the holy **c**
Dan 11:30 those who forsake the holy **c**
Dan 11:32 the **c** he shall corrupt with
Hos 2:18 In that day I will make a **c**
Hos 6: 7 men they transgressed the **c**
Hos 8: 1 they have transgressed My **c**
Hos 10: 4 falsely in making a **c**
Hos 12: 1 Also they make a **c** with the
Amos 1: 9 remember the **c** of brotherhood
Zech 9:11 of the blood of your **c**, I
Zech 11:10 two, that I might break the **c**
Mal 2: 4 you, that My **c** with Levi may
Mal 2: 5 My **c** was with him, one of
Mal 2: 8 have corrupted the **c** of Levi
Mal 2:10 the **c** of the fathers
Mal 2:14 companion and your wife by **c**
Mal 3: 1 even the Messenger of the **c**
Matt 26:28 this is My blood of the new **c**
Mark 14:24 This is My blood of the new **c**
Luke 1:72 and to remember His holy **c**
Luke 22:20 cup is the new **c** in My blood
Acts 3:25 of the **c** which God made with
Acts 7: 8 him the **c** of circumcision
Rom 11:27 For this is My **c** with them
1Co 11:25 cup is the new **c** in My blood
2Co 3: 6 as ministers of the new **c**
Gal 3:15 Though it is only a man's **c**
Gal 3:17 cannot annul the **c** that was
Heb 7:22 become a surety of a better **c**
Heb 8: 6 also Mediator of a better **c**
Heb 8: 7 For if that first **c** had been
Heb 8: 8 when I will make a new **c** with
Heb 8: 9 not according to the **c** that I
Heb 8: 9 they did not continue in My **c**
Heb 8:10 For this is the **c** that I will
Heb 8:13 A new **c**," He has made the
Heb 9: 1 indeed, even the first **c** had
Heb 9: 4 the ark of the **c** overlaid on
Heb 9: 4 and the tablets of the **c**
Heb 9:15 is the Mediator of the new **c**
Heb 9:15 under the first **c**, that those
Heb 9:18 not even the first **c** was
Heb 9:20 This is the blood of the **c**
Heb 10:16 This is the **c** that I will
Heb 10:29 counted the blood of the **c** by
Heb 12:24 the Mediator of the new **c**
Heb 13:20 blood of the everlasting **c**
Rev 11:19 the ark of His **c** was seen in

COVENANTED (*see* COVENANT)
2Ch 7:18 as I **c** with David your father
Hag 2: 5 to the word that I **c** with you

COVENANTS (*see* COVENANT)
Rom 9: 4 adoption, the glory, the **c**
Gal 4:24 For these are the two **c**
Eph 2:12 from the **c** of promise, having

COVER (*see* COVERED, COVERING, COVERINGS, COVERS, UNCOVER)
Gen 6:14 **c** it inside and outside with
Ex 10: 5 they shall **c** the face of the
Ex 21:33 digs a pit and does not **c** it
Ex 26:13 side and on that side, to **c** it
Ex 28:42 trousers to **c** their nakedness
Ex 33:22 will **c** you with My hand while
Lev 13:45 he shall **c** his mustache, and
Lev 16:13 the cloud of incense may **c**
Lev 17:13 its blood and **c** it with dust
Num 4: 5 **c** the ark of the Testimony
Num 4: 8 **c** the same with a covering of
Num 4: 9 **c** the lampstand of the light,
Num 4:11 and **c** it with a covering of
Num 4:12 **c** them with a covering of
Num 19:15 which has no **c** fastened on it
Num 22: 5 they **c** the face of the earth,
Num 22:11 they **c** the face of the earth
Deut 22:12 with which you **c** yourself
Deut 23:13 it and turn and **c** your refuse
1Sa 19:13 put a **c** of goats' hair for
1Sa 19:16 with a **c** of goats' hair for
1Sa 25:20 went down under **c** of the hill
1Ki 7:18 **c** the capitals that were on
1Ki 7:42 to **c** the two bowl-shaped
2Ch 4:13 to **c** the two bowl-shaped
Neh 4: 5 Do not **c** their iniquity, and
Job 14:17 a bag, and You **c** my iniquity
Job 16:18 do not **c** my blood, and let my
Job 21:26 in the dust, and worms **c** them
Job 22:14 Thick clouds **c** Him, so that
Job 38:34 abundance of water may **c** you
Job 40:22 The lotus trees **c** him with
Ps 91: 4 He shall **c** you with His
Ps 104: 2 Who **c** Yourself with light as
Ps 104: 9 may not return to **c** the earth
Ps 109:29 let them **c** themselves with
Ps 140: 9 the evil of their lips **c** them
Is 11: 9 LORD as the waters **c** the sea
Is 14:11 under you, and worms **c** you
Is 26:21 and will no more **c** her slain
Is 32: 2 and a **c** from the tempest, as
Is 54: 9 would no longer **c** the earth
Is 58: 7 see the naked, that you **c** him
Is 59: 6 nor will they **c** themselves
Is 60: 2 darkness shall **c** the earth
Is 60: 6 of camels shall **c** your land
Jer 46: 8 **c** the earth, I will destroy
Ezek 7:18 horror will **c** them
Ezek 12: 6 you shall **c** your face, so
Ezek 12:12 He shall **c** his face, so that
Ezek 24: 7 the ground, to **c** it with dust
Ezek 24:17 do not **c** your lips, and do not
Ezek 24:22 you shall not **c** your lips nor
Ezek 26:10 horses, their dust will **c** you
Ezek 26:19 you, and great waters **c** you
Ezek 30:18 for her, a cloud shall **c** her
Ezek 32: 7 I will **c** the heavens, and make
Ezek 32: 7 I will **c** the sun with a cloud
Ezek 37: 6 **c** you with skin and put breath
Ezek 38:16 like a cloud, to **c** the land
Hos 2: 9 given to **c** her nakedness
Hos 10: 8 say to the mountains, "**C** us
Obad 10 Jacob, shame shall **c** you, and
Mic 3: 7 they shall all **c** their lips
Mic 7:10 shame will **c** her who said to
Hab 2:14 LORD, as the waters **c** the sea
Hab 2:17 done to Lebanon will **c** you
Zech 5: 8 the lead **c** over its mouth
Mal 2:13 you **c** the altar of the LORD
Luke 23:30 and to the hills, '**C** us
1Co 11: 7 ought not to **c** his head,
Jas 5:20 and **c** a multitude of sins
1Pe 4: 8 love will **c** a multitude of

COVERED (*see* COVER)
Gen 7:19 under the whole heaven were **c**
Gen 7:20 and the mountains were **c**
Gen 9:23 and **c** the nakedness of their
Gen 24:65 she took a veil and **c** herself
Gen 38:14 **c** herself with a veil and
Gen 38:15 because she had **c** her face
Ex 8: 6 up and **c** the land of Egypt
Ex 10:15 For they **c** the face of the
Ex 14:28 **c** the chariots, the horsemen,
Ex 15: 5 The depths have **c** them
Ex 15:10 Your wind, the sea **c** them
Ex 16:13 **c** the camp, and in the morning
Ex 24:15 and a cloud **c** the mountain
Ex 24:16 and the cloud **c** it six days
Ex 37: 9 **c** the mercy seat with their
Ex 40:34 Then the cloud **c** the
Lev 2: 7 offering baked in a **c** pan
Lev 7: 9 that is prepared in the **c** pan
Lev 13:13 leprosy has **c** all his body
Num 4:20 the holy things are being **c**
Num 7: 3 six **c** carts and twelve oxen, a
Num 9:15 the cloud **c** the tabernacle,
Num 9:16 the cloud **c** it by day, and the
Num 16:42 and suddenly the cloud **c** it
Deut 32:15 thick, you are **c** with fat
Josh 24: 7 the sea upon them, and **c** them
Judg 4:18 she **c** him with a blanket
Judg 4:19 gave him a drink, and **c** him
1Sa 19:13 head, and **c** it with clothes
1Sa 28:14 up, and he is **c** with a mantle
2Sa 15:30 and he had his head **c** and went
2Sa 15:30 were with him **c** their heads
2Sa 19: 4 But the king **c** his face, and
1Ki 6:15 he **c** the floor of the temple
2Ki 19: 1 **c** himself with sackcloth, and
2Ki 19: 2 **c** with sackcloth, to Isaiah
Neh 3:15 **c** it, hung its doors with its
Esth 6:12 mourning and with his head **c**
Esth 7: 8 mouth, they **c** Haman's face
Job 15:27 Though he has **c** his face with
Job 31:33 if I have **c** my transgressions
Ps 32: 1 is forgiven, Whose sin is **c**
Ps 44:15 the shame of my face has **c** me
Ps 44:19 **c** us with the shadow of death
Ps 65:13 valleys also are **c** with grain
Ps 68:13 wings of a dove **c** with silver
Ps 69: 7 Shame has **c** my face
Ps 71:13 Let them be **c** with reproach
Ps 80:10 The hills were **c** with its
Ps 85: 2 You have **c** all their sin
Ps 89:45 You have **c** him with shame
Ps 104: 6 You **c** it with the deep as
Ps 106:11 The waters **c** their enemies
Ps 106:17 And **c** the faction of Abiram
Ps 139:13 You have **c** me in my mother's
Ps 140: 7 You have **c** my head in the day
Prov 24:31 surface was **c** with nettles
Prov 26:23 **c** with silver dross
Prov 26:26 his hatred is **c** by deceit
Eccl 6: 4 its name is **c** with darkness
Song 5: 2 for my head is **c** with dew
Is 6: 2 with two he **c** his face, with
Is 6: 2 face, with two he **c** his feet
Is 27: 9 iniquity of Jacob will be **c**

Is 29:10 He has c your heads, namely,
Is 37: 1 c himself with sackcloth, and
Is 37: 2 c with sackcloth, to Isaiah
Is 51:16 I have c you with the shadow
Is 61:10 He has c me with the robe of
Jer 14: 3 confounded and c their heads
Jer 14: 4 they c their heads
Jer 51:42 she is c with the multitude
Jer 51:51 Shame has c our faces, for
Lam 2: 1 How the Lord has c the
Lam 3:16 gravel, and c me with ashes
Lam 3:43 You have c Yourself with
Lam 3:44 You have c Yourself with a
Ezek 1:11 and two c their bodies
Ezek 1:23 one had two which c one side
Ezek 1:23 each one had two which c the
Ezek 16: 8 over you and c your nakedness
Ezek 16:10 fine linen and c you with silk
Ezek 16:18 c them, and you set My oil and
Ezek 18: 7 c the naked with clothing
Ezek 18:16 c the naked with clothing
Ezek 24: 8 a rock, that it may not be c
Ezek 27: 7 of Elishah was what c you
Ezek 31:15 I c the deep because of it
Ezek 37: 8 them, and the skin c them over
Ezek 41:16 the windows were c
Jon 3: 6 c himself with sackcloth and
Jon 3: 8 beast be c with sackcloth, and
Hab 3: 3 Selah His glory c the heavens
Matt 8:24 the boat was c with the waves
Matt 10:26 For there is nothing c that
Luke 12: 2 For there is nothing c that
Rom 4: 7 forgiven, and whose sins are c
1Co 11: 4 having his head c, dishonors
1Co 11: 6 For if a woman is not c, let
1Co 11: 6 shorn or shaved, let her be c

COVERING (*see* COVER, COVERINGS)
Gen 8:13 Noah removed the c of the ark
Ex 22:27 For that is his only c, it is
Ex 25:20 c the mercy seat with their
Ex 26:14 You shall also make a c of
Ex 26:14 a c of badger skins above
Ex 35:11 tabernacle, its tent, its c
Ex 35:12 seat, and the veil of the c
Ex 36:19 Then he made a c for the tent
Ex 36:19 a c of badger skins above
Ex 39:34 the c of rams' skins dyed red
Ex 39:34 the c of badger skins, and the
Ex 39:34 skins, and the veil of the c
Ex 40:19 put the c of the tent on top
Ex 40:21 hung up the veil of the c
Num 3:25 the tent with its c, the
Num 4: 5 shall take down the c veil
Num 4: 6 put on it a c of badger skins
Num 4: 8 same with a c of badger skins
Num 4:10 in a c of badger skins, and
Num 4:11 it with a c of badger skins
Num 4:12 them with a c of badger skins
Num 4:14 on it a c of badger skins
Num 4:15 have finished c the sanctuary
Num 4:25 of meeting with its c, the
Num 4:25 the c of badger skins that is
Num 16:38 plates as a c for the altar
Num 16:39 out as a c on the altar,
2Sa 17:19 spread a c over the well's
1Ki 7:41 the two networks c the two
2Ch 4:12 the two networks c the two
Job 24: 7 and have no c in the cold
Job 26: 6 Him, and Destruction has no c
Job 31:19 or any poor man without c
Ps 105:39 He spread a cloud for a c
Is 4: 5 the glory there will be a c
Is 25: 7 of the c cast over all people
Is 28:20 and the c so narrow that he
Is 30:22 c of your graven images of
Is 50: 3 and I make sackcloth their c
Ezek 28:13 precious stone was your c
Ezek 28:16 O c cherub, from the midst of
Ezek 38: 9 c the land like a cloud, you
1Co 11:15 hair is given to her for a c

COVERINGS (*see* COVER, COVERING)
Gen 3: 7 together and made themselves c
Prov 7:16 Colored c of Egyptian linen

COVERS (*see* COVER)
Ex 29:13 the fat that c the entrails
Ex 29:22 the fat that c the entrails
Lev 3: 3 The fat that c the entrails
Lev 3: 9 the fat that c the entrails
Lev 3:14 The fat that c the entrails
Lev 4: 8 The fat that c the entrails
Lev 7: 3 the fat that c the entrails
Lev 9:19 what c the entrails and the
Lev 13:12 the leprosy c all the skin of
1Ki 1: 1 and they put c on him, but he
Job 9:24 He c the faces of its judges
Job 22:11 an abundance of water c you
Job 26: 9 He c the face of His throne,
Job 36:30 and c the depths of the sea
Job 36:32 He c His hands with lightning
Ps 73: 6 Violence c them like a
Ps 84: 6 The rain also c it with pools
Ps 109:19 like the garment which c him
Ps 147: 8 Who c the heavens with clouds
Prov 10: 6 but violence c the mouth of
Prov 10:11 but violence c the mouth of
Prov 10:12 strife, but love c all sins
Prov 12:16 but a prudent man c shame
Prov 17: 9 He who c a transgression
Prov 28:13 He who c his sins will not
Jer 3:25 shame, and our reproach c us
Ezek 28:14 the anointed cherub who c
Mal 2:16 for it c one's garment with
Luke 8:16 c it with a vessel or puts it

COVERT
Job 40:21 in a c of reeds and marsh

COVET (*see* COVETED, COVETOUS, COVETS)
Ex 20:17 You shall not c your
Ex 20:17 you shall not c your
Ex 34:24 neither will any man c your
Deut 5:21 You shall not c your
Deut 7:25 you shall not c the silver or
Prov 12:12 The wicked c the catch of
Mic 2: 2 They c fields and take them by
Rom 7: 7 You shall not c
Rom 13: 9 You shall not c," and if
Jas 4: 2 You murder and c and cannot

COVETED (*see* COVET)
Josh 7:21 I c them and took them
Acts 20:33 I have c no one's silver or

COVETOUS (*see* COVET, COVETOUSNESS)
1Co 5:10 of this world, or with the c
1Co 5:11 who is a fornicator, or c
1Co 6:10 nor thieves, nor c, nor
Eph 5: 5 unclean person, nor c man
1Ti 3: 3 not quarrelsome, not c
2Pe 2:14 heart trained in c practices

COVETOUSNESS (*see* COVETOUS)
Ex 18:21 God, men of truth, hating c
Ps 119:36 Your testimonies, And not to c
Prov 28:16 but he who hates c will
Is 57:17 iniquity of his c I was angry
Jer 6:13 them, everyone is given to c
Jer 8:10 everyone is given to c
Jer 22:17 are for nothing but your c
Jer 51:13 come, the measure of your c
Mark 7:22 thefts, c, wickedness, deceit
Luke 12:15 Take heed and beware of c, for
Rom 1:29 immorality, wickedness, c
Rom 7: 7 c unless the law had said
Eph 5: 3 and all uncleanness or c, let
Col 3: 5 passion, evil desire, and c
1Th 2: 5 you know, nor a cloak for c
Heb 13: 5 Let your conduct be without c
2Pe 2: 3 By c they will exploit you

COVETS (*see* COVET)
Prov 21:26 He c greedily all day long,
Hab 2: 9 Woe to him who c evil gain

COW (*see* COWS)
Lev 22:28 Whether it is a c or ewe, do
Num 18:17 But the firstborn of a c, the
Job 21:10 their c calves without
Is 7:21 man will keep alive a young c
Is 11: 7 The c and the bear shall graze
Ezek 4:15 See, I am giving you c dung

COWARDLY
Rev 21: 8 But the c, unbelieving,

COWS (*see* COW)
Gen 32:15 with their colts, forty c
Gen 41: 2 up out of the river seven c
Gen 41: 3 seven other c came up after
Gen 41: 3 stood by the other c on the
Gen 41: 4 gaunt c ate up the seven fine
Gen 41: 4 seven fine looking and fat c
Gen 41:18 Suddenly seven c came up out
Gen 41:19 seven other c came up after
Gen 41:20 ugly c ate up the first seven
Gen 41:20 up the first seven, the fat c
Gen 41:26 The seven good c are seven
Gen 41:27 ugly c which came up after
1Sa 6: 7 take two milk c which have
1Sa 6: 7 and hitch the c to the cart
1Sa 6:10 they took two milk c and
1Sa 6:12 Then the c headed straight
1Sa 6:14 and offered the c as a burnt
Amos 4: 1 you c of Bashan, who are on

COZBI
Num 25:15 was C the daughter of Zur
Num 25:18 of Peor and in the matter of C

CRACKED
Job 7: 5 worms and dust, my skin is c

CRACKLING
Eccl 7: 6 For like the c of thorns

CRAFT (*see* CRAFTSMAN)
Rev 18:22 no craftsman of any c shall

CRAFTILY (*see* CRAFTY)
Josh 9: 4 they worked c, and went and
Ps 105:25 To deal c with His servants

CRAFTINESS (*see* CRAFTY)
Job 5:13 the wise in their own c, and
Luke 20:23 But He perceived their c, and
1Co 3:19 the wise in their own c"
2Co 4: 2 not walking in c nor handling
2Co 11: 3 serpent deceived Eve by his c
Eph 4:14 in the cunning c by which

CRAFTSMAN (*see* CRAFT, CRAFTSMEN)
Gen 4:22 of every c in bronze and iron
Deut 27:15 work of the hands of the c
1Ch 28:21 every willing c will be with
2Ch 2:13 Huram my master c
2Ch 4:16 c made of burnished bronze
Prov 8:30 was beside Him, as a master c
Is 41: 7 So the c encouraged the
Is 44:13 The c stretches out his rule,
Jer 10: 9 from Uphaz, the work of the c
Rev 18:22 no c of any craft shall be

CRAFTSMEN (*see* CRAFTSMAN)
Ex 36: 4 Then all the c who were doing
2Ki 24:14 captives, and all the c and
2Ki 24:16 men, seven thousand, and c
1Ch 4:14 Ge-Harashim, for they were c
1Ch 29: 5 to be done by the hands of c
2Ch 34:11 They gave it to the c and
Neh 11:35 Lod, Ono, and the Valley of C
Jer 24: 1 princes of Judah with the c
Jer 29: 2 of Judah and Jerusalem, the c
Jer 52:15 Babylon, and the rest of the c
Hos 13: 2 all of it is the work of c
Zech 1:20 the LORD showed me four c
Zech 1:21 but the c are coming to
Acts 19:24 no small profit to the c
Acts 19:38 and his fellow c have a case

CRAFTY (*see* CRAFTILY, CRAFTINESS)
1Sa 23:22 I am told that he is very c
2Sa 13: 3 Now Jonadab was a very c man
Job 5:12 the devices of the c, so that
Job 15: 5 choose the tongue of the c
Ps 83: 3 They have taken c counsel
Prov 7:10 of a harlot, and a c heart
2Co 12:16 Nevertheless, being c, I

CRAG (*see* CRAGS)
Job 39:28 resides on the c of the rock

CRAGS (*see* CRAG)
Prov 30:26 make their homes in the c
Is 2:21 and into the c of the rugged

CRANE
Is 38:14 Like a c or a swallow, so I

CRASHING (*see* CRASHINGS)
Zeph 1:10 and a loud c from the hills

CRASHINGS (*see* CRASHING)
Job 41:25 because of his c they are

CRAVES (*see* CRAVING)
Is 29: 8 is faint, and his soul still c

CRAVING (*see* CRAVES)
Num 11: 4 them yielded to intense c
Num 11:34 people who had yielded to c
Ps 78:30 were not deprived of their c

CRAWL (*see* CRAWLING, CRAWLS)
Mic 7:17 they shall c from their holes

CRAWLING (*see* CRAWL)
Joel 1: 4 left, the c locust has eaten
Joel 1: 4 what the c locust left, the
Joel 2:25 the c locust, the consuming

CRAWLS (*see* CRAWL)
Lev 11:42 Whatever c on its belly,

CREAM
Judg 5:25 she brought out c in a lordly
Job 20:17 flowing with honey and c
Job 29: 6 my steps were bathed with c

CREATE (*see* CREATED, CREATES, CREATION, CREATOR, CREATURE)
Neh 4: 8 Jerusalem and c confusion
Ps 51:10 C in me a clean heart, O God,
Is 4: 5 then the LORD will c above
Is 45: 7 c darkness, I make peace and
Is 45: 7 I make peace and c calamity
Is 45:18 it, Who did not c it in vain
Is 57:19 I c the fruit of the lips
Is 65:17 I c new heavens and a new
Is 65:18 rejoice forever in what I c
Is 65:18 I c Jerusalem as a rejoicing,
Eph 2:15 so as to c in Himself one new

CREATED (*see* CREATE)
Gen 1: 1 beginning God c the heavens
Gen 1:21 So God c great sea creatures
Gen 1:27 So God c man in His own image
Gen 1:27 in the image of God He c him
Gen 1:27 male and female He c them
Gen 2: 3 all His work which God had c
Gen 2: 4 and the earth when they were c
Gen 5: 1 In the day that God c man
Gen 5: 2 He c them male and female, and
Gen 5: 2 in the day they were c
Gen 6: 7 destroy man whom I have c
Deut 4:32 that God c man on the earth
Ps 89:12 and the south, You have c them
Ps 89:47 You c all the children of men
Ps 102:18 to be c may praise the LORD
Ps 104:30 forth Your Spirit, they are c
Ps 148: 5 He commanded and they were c
Is 40:26 see who has c these things,
Is 41:20 Holy One of Israel has c it
Is 42: 5 LORD, Who c the heavens and
Is 43: 1 thus says the LORD, who c you
Is 43: 7 whom I have c for My glory
Is 45: 8 I, the LORD, have c it
Is 45:12 the earth, and c man on it
Is 45:18 Who c the heavens, Who is God
Is 48: 7 They are c now and not from
Is 54:16 I have c the blacksmith who
Is 54:16 and I have c the spoiler to
Jer 31:22 For the LORD has c a new
Ezek 21:30 in the place where you were c
Ezek 28:13 for you on the day you were c
Ezek 28:15 ways from the day you were c
Mal 2:10 Has not one God c us
Mark 13:19 which God c until this time
Rom 8:39 depth, nor any other c thing
1Co 11: 9 Nor was man c for the woman,
Eph 2:10 c in Christ Jesus for good
Eph 3: 9 c all things through Jesus
Eph 4:24 which was c according to God
Col 1:16 were c that are in heaven
Col 1:16 All things were c through Him
Col 3:10 to the image of Him who c him
1Ti 4: 3 God c to be received with
Rev 4:11 for You c all things, and by
Rev 4:11 will they exist and were c
Rev 10: 6 who c heaven and the things

CREATES (*see* CREATE)
Num 16:30 But if the LORD c a new thing
Amos 4:13 c the wind, who declares to

CREATION (*see* CREATE)
Mark 10: 6 from the beginning of the c
Mark 13:19 of c which God created until
Rom 1:20 For since the c of the world
Rom 8:19 the c eagerly waits for the
Rom 8:20 For the c was subjected to
Rom 8:21 because the c itself also
Rom 8:22 know that the whole c groans
2Co 5:17 is in Christ, he is a new c
Gal 6:15 avails anything, but a new c
Col 1:15 God, the firstborn over all c
Heb 9:11 hands, that is, not of this c
2Pe 3: 4 were from the beginning of c
Rev 3:14 the Beginning of the c of God

CREATOR (*see* CREATE)
Eccl 12: 1 Remember now your C in the
Eccl 12: 6 Remember your C before the
Is 40:28 the C of the ends of the
Is 43:15 the C of Israel, your King
Acts 24: 5 a c of dissension among all
Rom 1:25 creature rather than the C
1Pe 4:19 good, as to a faithful C

CREATURE (*see* CREATE, CREATURES)
Gen 1:24 c according to its kind
Gen 2:19 Adam called each living c
Gen 9:10 living c that is with you
Gen 9:12 every living c that is with
Gen 9:15 every living c of all flesh
Gen 9:16 every living c of all flesh
Lev 11:46 every living c that moves in
Lev 11:46 of every c that creeps on the
Is 34:14 also the night c shall rest
Ezek 1:15 living c with its four faces
Ezek 10:15 This was the living c I saw
Ezek 10:17 of the living c was in them
Ezek 10:20 This is the living c I saw
Mark 16:15 preach the gospel to every c
Acts 28: 4 the c hanging from his hand
Acts 28: 5 shook off the c into the fire
Rom 1:25 served the c rather than the
Col 1:23 to every c under heaven, of
1Ti 4: 4 For every c of God is good,
Heb 4:13 there is no c hidden from His
Jas 3: 7 c of the sea, is tamed and has
Rev 4: 7 living c was like a lion, the
Rev 4: 7 second living c like a calf
Rev 4: 7 the third living c had a face
Rev 4: 7 the fourth living c was like
Rev 5:13 every c which is in heaven and
Rev 6: 3 the second living c saying
Rev 6: 5 heard the third living c say
Rev 6: 7 of the fourth living c saying
Rev 16: 3 every living c in the sea

CREATURES (*see* CREATURE)
Gen 1:20 with an abundance of living c
Gen 1:21 So God created great sea c
Ps 148: 7 the earth, You great sea c
Ezek 1: 5 the likeness of four living c
Ezek 1: 9 The c did not turn when they
Ezek 1:13 the likeness of the living c
Ezek 1:13 and forth among the living c
Ezek 1:14 And the living c ran back and
Ezek 1:15 as I looked at the living c
Ezek 1:19 When the living c went, the
Ezek 1:19 when the living c were lifted
Ezek 1:20 living c was in the wheels
Ezek 1:21 living c was in the wheels
Ezek 1:22 the heads of the living c was
Ezek 3:13 c that touched one another
Jas 1:18 kind of firstfruits of His c
Rev 4: 6 were four living c full of
Rev 4: 8 And the four living c, each
Rev 4: 9 the living c give glory and
Rev 5: 6 and of the four living c, and
Rev 5: 8 the scroll, the four living c
Rev 5:11 the throne, the living c, and
Rev 5:14 Then the four living c said
Rev 6: 1 one of the four living c
Rev 6: 6 of the four living c saying
Rev 7:11 elders and the four living c
Rev 8: 9 the living c in the sea died
Rev 14: 3 before the four living c
Rev 15: 7 c gave to the seven angels
Rev 19: 4 the four living c fell down

CREDIT (*see* CREDITOR)
Luke 6:32 you, what c is that to you
Luke 6:33 to you, what c is that to you
Luke 6:34 back, what c is that to you
1Pe 2:20 For what c is it if, when you

CREDITOR (*see* CREDIT, CREDITORS)
Deut 15: 2 Every c who has lent anything
2Ki 4: 1 the c is coming to take my
Ps 109:11 Let the c seize all that he
Is 24: 2 as with the c, so with the
Luke 7:41 certain c who had two debtors

CREDITORS (*see* CREDITOR)
Is 50: 1 Or which of My c is it to
Hab 2: 7 Will not your c rise up

CREEP (*see* CREEPING, CREEPS, CREPT)
Lev 11:20 c on all fours shall be an
Lev 11:29 things that c on the earth
Lev 11:31 to you among all that c
Lev 11:42 things that c on the earth
Ps 104:20 beasts of the forest c about
Ezek 38:20 things that c on the earth
2Ti 3: 6 those who c into households

CREEPING (*see* CREEP)
Gen 1:24 c thing and beast of the earth
Gen 1:26 and over every c thing that
Gen 6: 7 c thing and birds of the air,
Gen 6:20 of every c thing of the earth
Gen 7:14 every c thing that creeps on
Gen 7:21 every c thing that creeps on
Gen 7:23 c thing and bird of the air
Gen 8:17 every c thing that creeps on
Gen 8:19 Every beast, every c thing
Lev 5: 2 carcass of unclean c things
Lev 11:29 c things that creep on the
Lev 11:41 every c thing that creeps on
Lev 11:42 has many feet among all c
Lev 11:43 with any c thing that creeps
Lev 11:44 c thing that creeps on the
Lev 22: 5 or whoever touches any c
Deut 14:19 Also every c thing that flies
1Ki 4:33 of c things, and of fish
Ps 148:10 C things and flying fowl
Ezek 8:10 every sort of c thing,
Ezek 38:20 all c things that creep on
Hos 2:18 and with the c things of the
Hab 1:14 like c things that have no
Acts 10:12 c things, and birds of the air
Acts 11: 6 c things, and birds of the air
Rom 1:23 beasts and c things

CREEPS (*see* CREEP)
Gen 1:25 and everything that c on the
Gen 1:26 thing that c on the earth
Gen 1:30 that c on the earth, in which
Gen 7: 8 that c on the earth,
Gen 7:14 every creeping thing that c
Gen 7:21 thing that c on the earth
Gen 8:17 thing that c on the earth
Gen 8:19 and whatever c on the earth,
Lev 11:21 insect that c on all fours
Lev 11:41 c on the earth shall be an
Lev 11:43 any creeping thing that c
Lev 11:44 thing that c on the earth
Lev 11:46 creature that c on the earth
Lev 20:25 thing that c on the ground
Deut 4:18 that c on the ground or the

CREPT (*see* CREEP)
Jude 4 men have c in unnoticed, who

CRESCENS
2Ti 4:10 C for Galatia, Titus for

CRESCENT (*see* CRESCENTS)
Judg 8:21 took the c ornaments that
Judg 8:26 gold, besides the c ornaments

CRESCENTS (*see* CRESCENT)
Is 3:18 the scarves, and the c

CREST
Esth 6: 8 which has a royal c placed on

CRETANS (*see* CRETE)
Acts 2:11 C and Arabs
Tit 1:12 C are always liars, evil

CRETE (*see* CRETANS)
Acts 27: 7 the shelter of C off Salmone
Acts 27:12 a harbor of C opening toward
Acts 27:13 sea, they sailed close by C
Acts 27:21 me, and not have sailed from C
Tit 1: 5 this reason I left you in C

CRIB
Is 1: 3 And the donkey its master's c

CRICKET
Lev 11:22 the c after its kind, and the

CRIED (*see* CRY)
Gen 27:34 he c with an exceedingly
Gen 39:14 I c out with a loud voice
Gen 39:15 and c out, that he left his
Gen 39:18 and c out, that he left his
Gen 41:43 and they c out before him,
Gen 41:55 the people c to Pharaoh for
Gen 45: 1 stood by him, and he c out,
Ex 2:23 of the bondage, and they c out

Ex 5:15 c out to Pharaoh, saying,
Ex 8:12 And Moses c out to the LORD
Ex 14:10 of Israel c out to the LORD
Ex 15:25 So he c out to the LORD, and
Ex 17: 4 So Moses c out to the LORD,
Num 11: 2 the people c out to Moses
Num 12:13 So Moses c out to the LORD,
Num 14: 1 lifted up their voices and c
Num 20:16 When we c out to the LORD,
Deut 22:27 betrothed young woman c out
Deut 26: 7 Then we c out to the LORD
Josh 24: 7 So they c out to the LORD
Judg 3: 9 of Israel c out to the LORD
Judg 3:15 of Israel c out to the LORD
Judg 4: 3 of Israel c out to the LORD
Judg 5:28 c out through the lattice
Judg 6: 6 of Israel c out to the LORD
Judg 6: 7 c out to the LORD because of
Judg 7:20 and they c, "The sword of the
Judg 7:21 army ran and c out and fled
Judg 9: 7 and c out, and said to them
Judg 10:10 of Israel c out to the LORD
Judg 10:12 and you c out to Me, and I
Judg 15:18 so he c out to the LORD and
1Sa 4:13 told it, all the city c out
1Sa 5:10 that the Ekronites c out
1Sa 7: 9 Then Samuel c out to the LORD
1Sa 12: 8 your fathers c out to the
1Sa 12:10 Then they c out to the LORD,
1Sa 15:11 and he c out to the LORD all
1Sa 17: 8 c out to the armies of Israel
1Sa 20:37 Jonathan c out after the lad
1Sa 20:38 Jonathan c out after the lad,
1Sa 28:12 she c out with a loud voice
2Sa 18:25 Then the watchman c out and
2Sa 19: 4 the king c out with a loud
2Sa 20:16 woman c out from the city
2Sa 22: 7 upon the LORD, and c to my God
1Ki 13: 2 Then he c out against the
1Ki 13: 4 who c out against the altar
1Ki 13:21 he c out to the man of God
1Ki 13:32 For the saying which he c out
1Ki 17:20 Then he c out to the LORD and
1Ki 17:21 c out to the LORD and said,
1Ki 18:28 So they c aloud, and cut
1Ki 20:39 he c out to the king and said,
1Ki 22:32 him, and Jehoshaphat c out
2Ki 2:12 Elisha saw it, and he c out,
2Ki 4: 1 the prophets c out to Elisha
2Ki 4:40 the stew, that they c out
2Ki 6: 5 and he c out and said,
2Ki 6:26 a woman c out to him, saying,
2Ki 11:14 tore her clothes and c out,
2Ki 20:11 the prophet c out to the LORD
1Ch 5:20 for they c out to God in the
2Ch 13:14 they c out to the LORD, and
2Ch 14:11 Asa c out to the LORD his God
2Ch 18:31 but Jehoshaphat c out, and the
2Ch 32:20 prayed and c out to heaven
Neh 9: 4 c out with a loud voice to
Neh 9:27 trouble, when they c to You
Neh 9:28 c out to You, You heard from
Esth 4: 1 He c out with a loud and
Job 29:12 delivered the poor who c out
Ps 3: 4 I c to the LORD with my voice
Ps 18: 6 the LORD, And c out to my God
Ps 18:41 They c out, but there was
Ps 22: 5 They c to You, and were
Ps 22:24 But when He c to Him, He
Ps 30: 2 I c out to You, And You have
Ps 30: 8 I c out to You, O LORD
Ps 31:22 When I c out to You
Ps 34: 6 This poor man c out, and the
Ps 66:17 I c to Him with my mouth, And
Ps 77: 1 I c out to God with my voice
Ps 88: 1 I have c out day and night
Ps 88:13 But to You I have c out, O
Ps 107: 6 Then they c out to the LORD
Ps 107:13 Then they c out to the LORD
Ps 107:19 Then they c out to the LORD
Ps 120: 1 my distress I c to the LORD
Ps 130: 1 of the depths I have c to You
Ps 138: 3 In the day when I c out, You
Ps 142: 5 I c out to You, O LORD
Is 6: 3 And one c to another and said
Is 6: 4 by the voice of him who c out
Is 21: 8 Then he c, "A lion, my Lord
Jer 4:20 upon destruction is c, for
Jer 20: 8 For when I spoke, "I c out
Jer 46:17 They c there, Pharaoh, king
Lam 2:18 Their heart c out to the Lord
Lam 4:15 They c out to them, "Go away
Ezek 9: 8 on my face and c out, and said,
Ezek 11:13 c with a loud voice, and said,
Dan 3: 4 Then a herald c aloud
Dan 4:14 He c aloud and said thus
Dan 5: 7 The king c aloud to bring in
Dan 6:20 he c out with a lamenting
Jon 1: 5 every man c out to his god,
Jon 1:14 Therefore they c out to the
Jon 2: 2 I c out to the LORD because
Jon 2: 2 out of the belly of Sheol I c
Jon 3: 4 Then he c out and said, "Yet
Matt 8:29 And suddenly they c out,
Matt 14:26 And they c out for fear
Matt 14:30 and beginning to sink he c out
Matt 15:22 and c out to Him, saying,
Matt 20:30 passing by, c out, saying,
Matt 20:31 but they c out all the more,
Matt 21: 9 and those who followed c out
Matt 27:23 But they c out all the more
Matt 27:46 Jesus c out with a loud voice
Matt 27:50 when He had c out again with
Mark 1:23 And he c out,
Mark 1:26 c out with a loud voice, he
Mark 3:11 before Him and c out, saying,
Mark 5: 7 he c out with a loud voice and
Mark 6:49 it was a ghost, and c out
Mark 9:24 the father of the child c out
Mark 9:26 Then the spirit c out,
Mark 10:48 but he c out all the more,
Mark 11: 9 and those who followed c out
Mark 15:13 So they c out again
Mark 15:14 they c out more exceedingly,
Mark 15:34 Jesus c out with a loud voice
Mark 15:37 Jesus c out with a loud voice
Mark 15:39 saw that He c out like this
Luke 4:33 he c out with a loud voice,
Luke 8: 8 He had said these things He c
Luke 8:28 he c out, fell down before
Luke 9:38 man from the multitude c out
Luke 16:24 Then he c and said, 'Father
Luke 18:38 And he c out, saying,
Luke 18:39 but he c out all the more,
Luke 23:18 And they all c out at once,
Luke 23:46 when Jesus had c out with a
John 1:15 of Him and c out, saying,
John 7:28 Then Jesus c out, as He
John 7:37 Jesus stood and c out, saying,
John 11:43 He c with a loud voice,
John 12:13 out to meet Him, and c out
John 12:44 Then Jesus c out and said
John 18:40 Then they all c again, saying
John 19: 6 officers saw Him, they c out
John 19:12 Him, but the Jews c out,
John 19:15 But they c out, "Away with
Acts 7:57 Then they c out with a loud
Acts 7:60 and c out with a loud voice,
Acts 16:17 Paul and us, and c out, saying,
Acts 19:28 of wrath and c out, saying,
Acts 19:32 Some therefore c one thing
Acts 19:34 all with one voice c out for
Acts 21:34 the multitude c one thing
Acts 22:23 Then, as they c out and tore
Acts 23: 6 he c out in the council,
Acts 24:21 one statement which I c out
Rev 6:10 they c with a loud voice,
Rev 7: 2 he c with a loud voice to the
Rev 10: 3 c with a loud voice, as when
Rev 10: 3 And when he c out, seven
Rev 12: 2 she c out in labor and in pain
Rev 14:18 he c with a loud cry to him
Rev 18: 2 he c mightily with a loud
Rev 18:18 c out when they saw the smoke
Rev 18:19 c out, weeping and wailing, and
Rev 19:17 and he c with a loud voice,

CRIES (*see* CRY)
Gen 4:10 of your brother's blood c out
Ex 22:27 will be that when he c to Me
Job 31:38 If my land c out against me,
Ps 72:12 deliver the needy when he c
Prov 1:21 She c out in the chief
Prov 8: 3 She c out by the gates, at
Prov 9: 3 she c out from the highest
Prov 20:14 for nothing," c the buyer
Is 16: 9 for battle c have fallen over
Is 26:17 c out in her pangs, when she
Is 46: 7 Though one c out to it, yet
Jer 12: 8 it c out against Me
Mic 6: 9 LORD's voice c to the city
Matt 15:23 away, for she c out after us
Luke 9:39 him, and he suddenly c out
Rom 9:27 Isaiah also c out concerning
Heb 5: 7 with vehement c and tears to
Jas 5: 4 the c of the reapers have

CRIME (*see* CRIMES, CRIMINALS)
Judg 9:24 that the c done to the

CRIMES (*see* CRIME)
Ezek 7:23 is filled with c of blood
Acts 18:14 of wrongdoing or wicked c

CRIMINALS (*see* CRIME)
Luke 23:32 There were also two others, c
Luke 23:33 they crucified Him, and the c
Luke 23:39 Then one of the c who were

CRIMSON
2Ch 2: 7 and iron, in purple and c and
2Ch 2:14 and blue, fine linen and c, and
2Ch 3:14 veil of blue and purple and c
Is 1:18 though they are red like c
Jer 4:30 you clothe yourself with c

CRIPPLE
Acts 14: 8 a c from his mother's womb,

CRISPUS
Acts 18: 8 Then C, the ruler of the
1Co 1:14 baptized none of you except C

CRITICIZED
Mark 14: 5 And they c her sharply

CROOKED
Deut 32: 5 a perverse and c generation
Ps 125: 5 as turn aside to their c ways
Prov 2:15 whose ways are c, and who are
Prov 8: 8 nothing c or perverse is in
Eccl 1:15 What is c cannot be made
Eccl 7:13 straight what He has made c
Is 40: 4 the c places shall be made
Is 42:16 them, and c places straight
Is 45: 2 make the c places straight
Is 59: 8 have made themselves c paths
Lam 3: 9 He has made my paths c
Luke 3: 5 the c places shall be made
Phil 2:15 fault in the midst of a c

CROP (*see* CROPPED, CROPS)
Lev 1:16 its c with its feathers and
Ezek 17:22 I will c off from the topmost
Amos 7: 1 the beginning of the late c
Amos 7: 1 indeed it was the late c
Matt 13: 8 on good ground and yielded a c
Matt 13:26 had sprouted and produced a c
Mark 4: 7 choked it, and it yielded no c
Mark 4: 8 yielded a c that sprang up,
Luke 8: 8 yielded a c a hundredfold

CROPPED (*see* CROP)
Ezek 17: 4 He c off its topmost young

CROPS (*see* CROP)
Ex 9:32 struck, for they are late c
Lev 25:15 of c he shall sell to you
Lev 25:16 number of the years of the c
Ps 78:46 their c to the caterpillar
Mark 4:28 the earth yields c by itself
Luke 12:17 I have no room to store my c
Luke 12:18 there I will store all my c
2Ti 2: 6 be first to partake of the c

CROSS (*see* CROSSED, CROSSES, CROSSING, CROSSROADS)
Num 32:21 all your armed men c over the
Num 32:27 but your servants will c over
Num 32:29 the children of Reuben c over
Num 32:30 But if they do not c over
Num 32:32 We will c over armed before
Num 35:10 When you c the Jordan into
Deut 2:13 and c over the Valley of the
Deut 2:18 day you are to c over at Ar
Deut 2:24 and c over the River Arnon
Deut 2:29 until I c the Jordan to the
Deut 3:18 c over armed before your
Deut 3:25 I pray, let me c over and see
Deut 3:27 shall not c over this Jordan
Deut 4:14 which you c over to possess
Deut 4:21 I would not c over the Jordan
Deut 4:22 I must not c over the Jordan
Deut 4:22 but you shall c over and
Deut 4:26 from the land which you c
Deut 9: 1 You are to c over the Jordan
Deut 11: 8 which you c over to possess

Deut 11:11 but the land which you **c** over
Deut 11:31 For you will **c** over the
Deut 12:10 But when you **c** over the
Deut 27: 2 on the day when you **c** over
Deut 30:18 **c** over the Jordan to go in
Deut 31: 2 You shall not **c** over this
Deut 31:13 you **c** the Jordan to possess
Deut 32:47 **c** over the Jordan to possess
Deut 34: 4 you shall not **c** over there
Josh 1:11 you will **c** over this Jordan
Josh 3: 6 and **c** over before the people
Josh 3:14 camp to **c** over the Jordan
Josh 4: 5 **C** over before the ark of the
Josh 22:19 then **c** over to the land of
Judg 3:28 not allow anyone to **c** over
Judg 12: 1 Why did you **c** over to fight
Judg 12: 5 Let me **c** over," the men of
1Sa 14: 8 let us **c** over to these men,
1Sa 30:10 could not **c** the Brook Besor
2Sa 12:31 made them **c** over to the brick
2Sa 15:22 to Ittai, "Go, and **c** over
2Sa 17:16 but speedily **c** over, lest
2Sa 17:21 and **c** over the water quickly
2Sa 19:37 let him **c** over with my lord
2Sa 19:38 Chimham shall **c** over with me
1Ki 2:37 **c** the Brook Kidron, know for
Is 11:15 and make men **c** over dryshod
Is 23: 2 whom those who **c** the sea have
Is 23: 6 **C** over to Tarshish
Is 23:12 Arise, **c** over to Cyprus
Is 31: 9 He shall **c** over to his
Is 51:10 for the redeemed to **c** over
Jer 15:14 I will make you **c** over with
Ezek 47: 5 a river that I could not **c**
Matt 10:38 And he who does not take his **c**
Matt 16:24 himself, and take up his **c**
Matt 27:32 they compelled to bear His **c**
Matt 27:40 of God, come down from the **c**
Matt 27:42 Him now come down from the **c**
Mark 4:35 Let us **c** over to the other
Mark 8:34 himself, and take up his **c**
Mark 10:21 and come, take up the **c**, and
Mark 15:21 and passing by, to bear His **c**
Mark 15:30 and come down from the **c**
Mark 15:32 descend now from the **c**, that
Luke 9:23 and take up his **c** daily, and
Luke 14:27 whoever does not bear his **c**
Luke 23:26 on him they laid the **c** that
John 19:17 And He, bearing His **c**, went
John 19:19 a title and put it on the **c**
John 19:25 by the **c** of Jesus His mother
John 19:31 **c** on the Sabbath (for that
Acts 18:27 he desired to **c** to Achaia
1Co 1:17 lest the **c** of Christ should
1Co 1:18 For the message of the **c** is
Gal 5:11 offense of the **c** has ceased
Gal 6:12 for the **c** of Christ
Gal 6:14 **c** of our Lord Jesus Christ
Eph 2:16 God in one body through the **c**
Phil 2: 8 even the death of the **c**
Phil 3:18 enemies of the **c** of Christ
Col 1:20 through the blood of His **c**
Col 2:14 having nailed it to the **c**
Heb 12: 2 set before Him endured the **c**

CROSSED (*see* CROSS)
Gen 31:21 **c** the river, and headed toward
Gen 32:10 for I **c** over this Jordan with
Gen 32:22 **c** over the ford of Jabbok
Gen 32:31 Just as he **c** over Penuel the
Gen 33: 3 Then he **c** over before them and
Num 33:51 When you have **c** the Jordan
Deut 2:13 So we **c** over the Valley of
Deut 2:14 we **c** over the Valley of the
Deut 27: 3 law, when you have **c** over
Deut 27: 4 be, when you have **c** over the
Deut 27:12 when you have **c** over the
Josh 2:23 from the mountain, and **c** over
Josh 3: 1 there before they **c** over
Josh 3:16 the people **c** over opposite
Josh 3:17 and all Israel **c** over on dry
Josh 3:17 until all the people had **c**
Josh 4: 1 completely **c** over the Jordan
Josh 4: 7 when it **c** over the Jordan,
Josh 4:10 the people hastened and **c** over
Josh 4:11 people had completely **c** over
Josh 4:11 the priests **c** over in the
Josh 4:12 **c** over armed before the
Josh 4:13 **c** over before the LORD for
Josh 4:22 Israel **c** over this Jordan on
Josh 4:23 you until you had **c** over, as
Josh 4:23 before us until we had **c** over
Josh 5: 1 of Israel until we had **c** over
Judg 6:33 and they **c** over and encamped in
Judg 8: 4 men who were with him **c** over
Judg 10: 9 the people of Ammon **c** over
Judg 12: 1 **c** over toward Zaphon, and said
Judg 12: 3 **c** over against the people of
1Sa 13: 7 some of the Hebrews **c** over
2Sa 2:29 **c** over the Jordan, and went
2Sa 10:17 **c** over the Jordan, and came to
2Sa 15:22 ones who were with him **c** over
2Sa 15:23 and all the people **c** over
2Sa 15:23 also **c** over the Brook Kidron
2Sa 15:23 all the people **c** over toward
2Sa 17:22 arose and **c** over the Jordan
2Sa 17:24 Absalom **c** over the Jordan, he
2Sa 19:18 king when he had **c** the Jordan
2Sa 19:39 And when the king had **c** over
2Sa 24: 5 they **c** over the Jordan and
2Ki 2: 8 of them **c** over on dry ground
2Ki 2: 9 it was, when they had **c** over
2Ki 2:14 and Elisha **c** over
1Ch 12:15 These are the ones who **c** the
1Ch 19:17 **c** over the Jordan and came
Jer 2: 6 through a land that no one **c**
Ezek 47: 5 a river that could not be **c**
Matt 9: 1 **c** over, and came to His own
Matt 14:34 When they had **c** over, they
Mark 5:21 Now when Jesus had **c** over
Mark 6:53 When they had **c** over, they

CROSSES (*see* CROSS)
Deut 31: 3 God Himself **c** over before you
Deut 31: 3 Joshua himself **c** over before

CROSS-EXAMINE
Luke 11:53 to **c** Him about many things,

CROSSING (*see* CROSS)
Deut 6: 1 you are **c** over to possess
Josh 3:11 is **c** over before you into the
2Sa 15:24 finished **c** over from the city

CROSSROADS (*see* CROSS)
Obad 14 not have stood at the **c** to

CROUCH (*see* CROUCHES, CROUCHING)
Job 38:40 when they **c** in their dens, or

CROUCHES (*see* CROUCH)
Ps 10:10 So he **c**, he lies low, That

CROUCHING (*see* CROUCH)
Ps 17:11 eyes, **c** down to the earth,

CROW (*see* CROWED, CROWING, CROWS)
Luke 22:34 the rooster will not **c** this
John 13:38 the rooster shall not **c** till

CROWD (*see* CROWDS)
Ex 23: 2 not follow a **c** to do evil
Matt 9:23 and the noisy **c** wailing,
Matt 9:25 But when the **c** was put
Mark 2: 4 near Him because of the **c**
Mark 5:27 she came behind Him in the **c**
Mark 5:30 Him, turned around in the **c**
Mark 7:17 a house away from the **c**, His
Mark 15:11 priests stirred up the **c**, so
Mark 15:15 wanting to gratify the **c**
Luke 4:42 the **c** sought Him and came to
Luke 5:19 him in, because of the **c**,
Luke 6:17 with a **c** of His disciples
Luke 7: 9 said to the **c** that followed
Luke 7:11 went with Him, and a large **c**
Luke 7:12 a large **c** from the city was
Luke 8:19 approach Him because of the **c**
Luke 11:27 from the **c** raised her voice
Luke 12:13 one from the **c** said to Him
Luke 13:14 and he said to the **c**, "There
Luke 19: 3 could not because of the **c**
Luke 19:39 called to Him from the **c**
Luke 23: 4 to the chief priests and the **c**
Luke 23:48 the whole **c** who came together
John 7:32 the **c** murmuring these things
John 7:40 Therefore many from the **c**
John 7:49 But this **c** that does not know
Acts 17: 8 And they troubled the **c** and the
Acts 19:35 city clerk had quieted the **c**
Acts 21:27 stirred up the whole **c** and
Acts 24:12 anyone nor inciting the **c**

CROWDS (*see* CROWD)
Luke 9:18 Who do the **c** say that I am
Luke 11:29 And while the **c** were thickly
Acts 17:13 also and stirred up the **c**

CROWED (*see* CROW)
Matt 26:74 And immediately a rooster **c**
Mark 14:68 on the porch, and a rooster **c**
Mark 14:72 a second time the rooster **c**
Luke 22:60 still speaking, the rooster **c**
John 18:27 and immediately a rooster **c**

CROWING (*see* CROW)
Mark 13:35 at the **c** of the rooster, or

CROWN (*see* CROWNED, CROWNING, CROWNS)
Gen 49:26 on the **c** of the head of him
Ex 29: 6 put the holy **c** on the turban
Ex 39:30 of the holy **c** of pure gold
Lev 8: 9 the golden plate, the holy **c**
Deut 33:16 on the **c** of the head of him
Deut 33:20 the arm and the **c** of his head
2Sa 1:10 I took the **c** that was on his
2Sa 12:30 their king's **c** from his head
2Sa 14:25 **c** of his head there was no
1Ki 7:31 Its opening inside the **c** at
2Ki 11:12 king's son, put the **c** on him
1Ch 20: 2 their king's **c** from his head
2Ch 23:11 king's son, put the **c** on him
Esth 1:11 the king, wearing her royal **c**
Esth 2:17 set the royal **c** upon her head
Esth 8:15 white, with a great **c** of gold
Job 2: 7 his foot to the **c** of his head
Job 19: 9 and taken the **c** from my head
Job 31:36 and bind it on me like a **c**
Ps 7:16 shall come down on his own **c**
Ps 21: 3 You set a **c** of pure gold upon
Ps 65:11 You **c** the year with Your
Ps 89:39 You have profaned his **c** by
Ps 132:18 Himself His **c** shall flourish
Prov 4: 9 a **c** of glory she will deliver
Prov 12: 4 wife is the **c** of her husband
Prov 14:24 The **c** of the wise is their
Prov 16:31 head is a **c** of glory, if it
Prov 17: 6 children are the **c** of old men
Prov 27:24 nor does a **c** endure to all
Song 3:11 the **c** with which his mother
Is 3:17 scab the **c** of the head of the
Is 28: 1 Woe to the **c** of pride, to the
Is 28: 3 The **c** of pride, the drunkards
Is 28: 5 will be for a **c** of glory and a
Is 62: 3 You shall also be a **c** of
Jer 2:16 broken the **c** of your head
Jer 13:18 collapse, the **c** of your glory
Jer 48:45 The **c** of the head of the sons
Lam 5:16 The **c** has fallen from our
Ezek 16:12 a beautiful **c** on your head
Ezek 21:26 the turban, and take off the **c**
Zech 6:11 and gold, make an elaborate **c**
Zech 6:14 Now the elaborate **c** shall be
Zech 9:16 be like the jewels of a **c**
Matt 27:29 had twisted a **c** of thorns
Mark 15:17 and they twisted a **c** of thorns
John 19: 2 twisted a **c** of thorns and put
John 19: 5 out, wearing the **c** of thorns
1Co 9:25 it to obtain a perishable **c**
1Co 9:25 but we for an imperishable **c**
Phil 4: 1 brethren, my joy and **c**, so
1Th 2:19 or joy, or **c** of rejoicing
2Ti 4: 8 for me the **c** of righteousness
Jas 1:12 he will receive the **c** of life
1Pe 5: 4 you will receive the **c** of
Rev 2:10 I will give you the **c** of life
Rev 3:11 that no one may take your **c**
Rev 6: 2 a **c** was given to him, and he
Rev 14:14 having on His head a golden **c**

CROWNED (*see* CROWN)
Ps 8: 5 You have **c** him with glory and
Prov 14:18 prudent are **c** with knowledge
Song 3:11 **c** him on the day of his
2Ti 2: 5 he is not **c** unless he
Heb 2: 7 You **c** him with glory and honor
Heb 2: 9 of death **c** with glory and

CROWNING (*see* CROWN)
Is 23: 8 the **c** city, whose merchants

CROWNS (*see* CROWN)
Ps 103: 4 Who **c** you with lovingkindness
Song 7: 5 Your head **c** you like Mount
Ezek 23:42 beautiful **c** on their heads
Rev 4: 4 they had **c** of gold on their
Rev 4:10 and cast their **c** before the
Rev 9: 7 and on their heads were **c** of
Rev 13: 1 horns, and on his horns ten **c**
Rev 19:12 and on His head were many **c**

CROWS (*see* CROW)
Matt 26:34 night, before the rooster **c**
Matt 26:75 Before the rooster **c**, you
Mark 14:30 before the rooster **c** twice
Mark 14:72 Before the rooster **c** twice
Luke 22:61 Before the rooster **c**, you

CRUCIFIED (*see* CRUCIFY)
Matt 26: 2 will be delivered up to be **c**
Matt 27:22 Let Him be **c**
Matt 27:23 Let Him be **c**
Matt 27:26 he delivered Him to be **c**
Matt 27:31 Him, and led Him away to be **c**
Matt 27:35 Then they **c** Him, and divided
Matt 27:38 two robbers were **c** with Him
Matt 27:44 **c** with Him reviled Him with
Matt 28: 5 that you seek Jesus who was **c**
Mark 15:15 he had scourged Him, to be **c**
Mark 15:24 And when they **c** Him, they
Mark 15:25 the third hour, and they **c** Him
Mark 15:27 Him they also **c** two robbers
Mark 15:32 those who were **c** with Him
Mark 16: 6 Jesus of Nazareth, who was **c**
Luke 23:23 with loud voices that He be **c**
Luke 23:33 Calvary, there they **c** Him
Luke 24: 7 hands of sinful men, and be **c**
Luke 24:20 condemned to death, and **c** Him
John 19:16 delivered Him to them to be **c**
John 19:18 where they **c** Him, and two
John 19:20 Jesus was **c** was near the city
John 19:23 when they had **c** Jesus, took
John 19:32 the other who was **c** with Him
John 19:41 He was **c** there was a garden
Acts 2:23 by lawless hands, have **c**, and
Acts 2:36 made this Jesus, whom you **c**
Acts 4:10 of Nazareth, whom you **c**, whom
Rom 6: 6 our old man was **c** with Him
1Co 1:13 Was Paul **c** for you
1Co 1:23 but we preach Christ **c**, to
1Co 2: 2 except Jesus Christ and Him **c**
1Co 2: 8 not have **c** the Lord of glory
2Co 13: 4 though He was **c** in weakness
Gal 2:20 I have been **c** with Christ
Gal 3: 1 portrayed among you as **c**
Gal 5:24 **c** the flesh with its passions
Gal 6:14 the world has been **c** to me
Rev 11: 8 where also our Lord was **c**

CRUCIFY (*see* CRUCIFIED)
Matt 20:19 to mock and to scourge and to **c**
Matt 23:34 of them you will kill and **c**
Mark 15:13 they cried out again, "**C** Him
Mark 15:14 out more exceedingly, "**C** Him
Mark 15:20 Him, and led Him out to **c** Him
Luke 23:21 saying, "**C** Him, **c** Him
John 19: 6 saying, "**C** Him, **c** Him
John 19: 6 You take Him and **c** Him
John 19:10 that I have power to **c** You
John 19:15 away with Him! **C** Him!
John 19:15 them, "Shall I **c** your King
Heb 6: 6 since they **c** again for

CRUEL (*see* CRUELLY, CRUELTY)
Gen 49: 7 and their wrath, for it is **c**
Ex 6: 9 of spirit and **c** bondage
Deut 32:33 and the **c** venom of cobras
Job 30:21 but You have become **c** to me
Ps 25:19 And they hate me with **c** hatred
Ps 71: 4 of the unrighteous and **c** man
Prov 5: 9 and your years to the **c** one
Prov 11:17 but he who is **c** troubles his
Prov 12:10 mercies of the wicked are **c**
Prov 17:11 therefore a **c** messenger will
Prov 27: 4 Wrath is **c** and anger a torrent
Eccl 9:12 Like fish taken in a **c** net
Song 8: 6 jealousy as **c** as the grave
Is 13: 9 the day of the LORD comes, **c**
Is 19: 4 into the hand of a **c** master
Jer 6:23 they are **c** and have no mercy
Jer 30:14 the chastisement of a **c** one
Jer 50:42 they are **c** and shall not show
Lam 4: 3 of my people has become **c**

CRUELLY (*see* CRUEL,)
Ezek 18:18 because he **c** oppressed,

CRUELTY (*see* CRUEL)
Gen 49: 5 instruments of **c** are in their
Ps 74:20 full of the habitations of **c**
Ezek 34: 4 and **c** you have ruled them

CRUMBLES
Job 14:18 **c** away, and as a rock is moved

CRUMBS
Matt 15:27 the **c** which fall from their
Mark 7:28 eat from the children's **c**
Luke 16:21 **c** which fell from the rich

CRUSH (*see* CRUSHED, CRUSHES, CRUSHING)
Job 6: 9 it would please God to **c** me
Job 39:15 that a foot may **c** them, or
Ps 68:23 your foot may **c** them in blood
Is 28:28 or **c** it with his horsemen
Lam 1:15 against me to **c** my young men
Lam 3:34 To **c** under His feet all the
Dan 2:40 in pieces and **c** all the others
Amos 4: 1 who **c** the needy, who say to
Mark 3: 9 lest they should **c** Him
Rom 16:20 will **c** Satan under your feet

CRUSHED (*see* CRUSH)
Lev 22:24 the LORD what is bruised or **c**
Num 22:25 **c** Balaam's foot against the
Deut 9:21 **c** it and ground it very small,
Deut 28:33 oppressed and **c** continually
Judg 9:53 head and **c** his skull
2Ki 23:15 **c** it to powder, and burned the
2Ch 15:16 **c** it, and burned it by the
Job 4:19 dust, who are **c** before a moth
Job 5: 4 they are **c** in the gate, and
Job 22: 9 of the fatherless was **c**
Job 34:25 in the night, and they are **c**
Ps 143: 3 He has **c** my life to the
Prov 26:28 hates those who are **c** by it
Prov 27:22 a pestle along with **c** grain
Is 59: 5 which is **c** a viper breaks out
Jer 51:34 has devoured me, he has **c** me
Ezek 6: 9 because I was **c** by their
Dan 2:35 and the gold were **c** together
2Co 4: 8 on every side, yet not **c**

CRUSHES (*see* CRUSH)
Job 9:17 For He **c** me with a tempest,
Dan 2:40 and like iron that **c**, that

CRUSHING (*see* CRUSH)
Deut 23: 1 by **c** or mutilation shall not
2Ki 19:25 that you should be for **c**
Is 3:15 do you mean by **c** My people
Is 37:26 that you should be for **c**

CRUST
Prov 6:26 is reduced to a **c** of bread

CRY (*see* CRIED, CRIES, CRYING)
Gen 27:34 exceedingly great and bitter **c**
Ex 2:23 and their **c** came up to God
Ex 3: 7 their **c** because of their
Ex 3: 9 the **c** of the children of
Ex 5: 8 therefore they **c** out, saying,
Ex 11: 6 **c** throughout all the land of
Ex 12:30 there was a great **c** in Egypt
Ex 14:15 Why do you **c** to Me
Ex 22:23 they **c** at all to Me, I will
Ex 22:23 I will surely hear their **c**
Ex 32:18 of those who **c** out in defeat
Lev 13:45 cover his mustache, and **c**
Num 16:34 around them fled at their **c**
Deut 15: 9 he **c** out to the LORD against
Deut 22:24 she did not **c** out in the city
Deut 24:15 lest he **c** out against you to
Judg 10:14 **c** out to the gods which you
1Sa 5:12 the **c** of the city went up to
1Sa 7: 8 Do not cease to **c** out to the
1Sa 8:18 you will **c** out in that day
1Sa 9:16 because their **c** has come to
2Sa 19:28 to **c** out anymore to the king
2Sa 22: 7 and my **c** entered His ears
1Ki 8:28 my God, and listen to the **c**
1Ki 18:27 **C** aloud, for he is a god
2Ch 6:19 my God, and listen to the **c**
2Ch 20: 9 and **c** out to You in our
Neh 9: 9 heard their **c** by the Red Sea
Esth 4: 1 out with a loud and bitter **c**
Job 16:18 and let my **c** have no resting
Job 19: 7 If I **c** out concerning wrong,
Job 19: 7 If I **c** aloud, there is no
Job 24:12 souls of the wounded **c** out
Job 27: 9 Will God hear his **c** when
Job 30:20 I **c** out to You, but You do
Job 30:24 ruins, if they **c** out when He
Job 30:28 and **c** out for help
Job 34:28 so that they caused the **c** of
Job 34:28 hears the **c** of the afflicted
Job 35: 9 of oppressions they **c** out
Job 35: 9 they **c** out for help because
Job 35:12 There they **c** out, but He does
Job 36:13 they do not **c** for help when
Job 38:41 when its young ones **c** to God
Ps 5: 2 heed to the voice of my **c**
Ps 9:12 forget the **c** of the humble
Ps 17: 1 cause, O LORD, Attend to my **c**
Ps 18: 6 my **c** came before Him, even to
Ps 22: 2 I **c** in the daytime, but You
Ps 27: 7 LORD, when I **c** with my voice
Ps 28: 1 To You I will **c**, O LORD my
Ps 28: 2 supplications When I **c** to You
Ps 34:15 His ears are open to their **c**
Ps 34:17 The righteous **c** out, and the
Ps 39:12 O LORD, And give ear to my **c**
Ps 40: 1 inclined to me, And heard my **c**
Ps 55:17 **c** aloud, And He shall hear my
Ps 56: 9 When I **c** out to You, Then my
Ps 57: 2 I will **c** out to God Most High
Ps 61: 1 Hear my **c**, O God
Ps 61: 2 of the earth I will **c** to You
Ps 84: 2 my flesh **c** out for the living
Ps 86: 3 For I **c** to You all day long
Ps 88: 2 Incline Your ear to my **c**
Ps 89:26 He shall **c** to Me, "You are my
Ps 102: 1 LORD, And let my **c** come to You
Ps 106:44 When He heard their **c**
Ps 107:28 Then they **c** out to the LORD
Ps 119:145 I **c** out with my whole heart
Ps 119:146 I **c** out to You
Ps 119:147 of the morning, And **c** for help
Ps 119:169 Let my **c** come before You, O
Ps 141: 1 Lord, I **c** out to You
Ps 141: 1 my voice when I **c** out to You
Ps 142: 1 I **c** out to the LORD with my
Ps 142: 6 Attend to my **c**, For I am
Ps 145:19 He also will hear their **c**
Ps 147: 9 And to the young ravens that **c**
Prov 2: 3 if you **c** out for discernment,
Prov 8: 1 Does not wisdom **c** out, and
Prov 21:13 shuts his ears to the **c** of
Prov 21:13 the poor will also **c** himself
Is 8: 4 knowledge to **c** 'My father'
Is 12: 6 **C** out and shout, O inhabitant
Is 14:31 Wail, O gate! **C**, O city!
Is 15: 4 Heshbon and Elealeh will **c** out
Is 15: 4 soldiers of Moab will **c** out
Is 15: 5 My heart will **c** out for Moab
Is 15: 5 raise up a **c** of destruction
Is 15: 8 For the **c** has gone all around
Is 19:20 for they will **c** to the LORD
Is 24:14 shall **c** aloud from the sea
Is 30:19 to you at the sound of your **c**
Is 33: 7 valiant ones shall **c** outside
Is 40: 2 and **c** out to her, that her
Is 40: 6 The voice said, "**C** out
Is 40: 6 What shall I **c**
Is 42: 2 He will not **c** out, nor raise
Is 42:13 He shall **c** out, yes, shout
Is 42:14 Now I will **c** like a woman in
Is 54: 1 **c** aloud, you who have not
Is 57:13 When you **c** out, let your
Is 58: 1 **C** aloud, spare not
Is 58: 9 you shall **c**, and He will say
Is 65:14 but you shall **c** for sorrow of
Jer 2: 2 **c** in the hearing of Jerusalem
Jer 3: 4 not from this time **c** to Me
Jer 4: 5 **c**, 'Gather together,' and say,
Jer 7:16 nor lift up a **c** or prayer for
Jer 8:19 the **c** of the daughter of my
Jer 11:11 and though they **c** out to Me
Jer 11:12 **c** out to the gods to whom
Jer 11:14 or lift up a **c** or prayer for
Jer 11:14 **c** out to Me because of their
Jer 14: 2 the **c** of Jerusalem has gone
Jer 14:12 fast, I will not hear their **c**
Jer 18:22 Let a **c** be heard from their
Jer 20:16 him hear the **c** in the morning
Jer 22:20 **c** out, and lift up your voice
Jer 22:20 **C** from Abarim, for all your
Jer 25:34 Wail, shepherds, and **c**
Jer 25:36 A voice of the **c** of the
Jer 30:15 Why do you **c** about your
Jer 31: 6 will **c** on Mount Ephraim
Jer 46:12 your **c** has filled the land
Jer 47: 2 then the men shall **c**, and all
Jer 48: 4 have caused a **c** to be heard
Jer 48: 5 have heard a **c** of destruction
Jer 48:20 Wail and **c**!

Jer 48:31 I will c out for all Moab
Jer 48:34 From the c of Heshbon to
Jer 49: 3 C, you daughters of Rabbah,
Jer 49:21 at the c its noise is heard
Jer 49:29 they shall c out to them
Jer 50:46 and the c is heard among the
Jer 51:54 The sound of a c comes from
Lam 2:19 c out in the night, at the
Lam 3: 8 Even when I c and shout, He
Lam 3:56 sighing, from my c for help
Ezek 8:18 though they c in My ears with
Ezek 9: 4 c over all the abominations
Ezek 21:12 C and wail, son of man
Ezek 26:15 your fall, when the wounded c
Ezek 27:28 sound of the c of your pilots
Ezek 27:30 they will c bitterly and cast
Hos 5: 8 C aloud at Beth Aven, "Look
Hos 7:14 They did not c out to Me with
Hos 8: 2 Israel will c to Me, 'My God,
Joel 1:14 God, and c out to the LORD
Joel 1:19 O LORD, to You I c out
Joel 1:20 the field also c out to You
Amos 3: 4 a young lion c out of his den
Jon 1: 2 city, and c out against it
Jon 3: 8 and c mightily to God
Mic 3: 4 Then they will c to the LORD
Mic 4: 9 Now why do you c aloud
Nah 2: 8 Halt! Halt!" they c
Hab 1: 2 O LORD, how long shall I c
Hab 1: 2 even c out to You,
Hab 2:11 will c out from the wall, and
Zeph 1:10 mournful c from the Fish Gate
Zeph 1:14 the mighty men shall c out
Matt 12:19 He will not quarrel nor c out
Matt 25: 6 And at midnight a c was heard
Mark 10:47 Nazareth, he began to c out
Luke 18: 7 His own elect who c out day
Luke 19:40 would immediately c out
Rom 8:15 of adoption by whom we c out
Jas 5: 4 you kept back by fraud, c out
Rev 14:18 he cried with a loud c to him

CRYING (*see* CRY)
2Sa 13:19 head and went away c bitterly
Ps 69: 3 I am weary with my c
Prov 30:15 leech has two daughters, c
Is 22: 5 walls and of c to the mountain
Is 24:11 There is a c for wine in the
Is 40: 3 The voice of one c in the
Is 65:19 in her, nor the voice of c
Jer 48: 3 a voice of c shall be from
Mal 2:13 with tears, with weeping and c
Matt 3: 3 The voice of one c in the
Matt 9:27 Him, c out and saying,
Matt 21:15 the children c out in the
Mark 1: 3 The voice of one c in the
Mark 5: 5 c out and cutting himself with
Mark 15: 8 c aloud, began to ask him to
Luke 3: 4 The voice of one c in the
Luke 4:41 out of many, c out and saying,
John 1:23 of one c in the wilderness
Acts 8: 7 c with a loud voice, came out
Acts 14:14 in among the multitude, c out
Acts 17: 6 rulers of the city, c out,
Acts 21:28 c out, "Men of Israel, help
Acts 21:36 people followed after, c out,
Acts 25:24 c out that he was not fit to
Gal 4: 6 Son into your hearts, c out,
Rev 7:10 and c out with a loud voice,
Rev 14:15 c with a loud voice to Him
Rev 21: 4 more death, nor sorrow, nor c

CRYSTAL
Job 28:17 gold nor c can equal it, nor
Is 54:12 of rubies, your gates of c
Ezek 1:22 the color of an awesome c
Rev 4: 6 was a sea of glass, like c
Rev 21:11 a jasper stone, clear as c
Rev 22: 1 of water of life, clear as c

CUB (*see* CUBS)
Nah 2:11 the lioness and lion's c, and

CUBIT (*see* CUBITS)
Gen 6:16 finish it to a c from above
Ex 25:10 shall be its length, a c and a
Ex 25:10 and a half its width, and a c
Ex 25:17 shall be its length and a c
Ex 25:23 a c its width, and a c and
Ex 26:13 a c on one side
Ex 26:13 a c on the other side
Ex 26:16 the length of a board, and a c
Ex 30: 2 A c shall be its length and a
Ex 30: 2 its length and a c its width
Ex 36:21 the width of each board a c
Ex 37: 1 cubits was its length, a c
Ex 37: 1 and a half its width, and a c
Ex 37: 6 cubits was its length and a c
Ex 37:10 a c its width, and a c and
Ex 37:25 Its length was a c
Ex 37:25 and its width a c
Deut 3:11 according to the standard c
Judg 3:16 a c in length) and fastened it
1Ki 7:24 it all around, ten to a c
1Ki 7:31 the top was one c in diameter
1Ki 7:35 at the height of half a c
2Ch 4: 3 it all around, ten to a c
Ezek 40: 5 cubits long, each being a c
Ezek 40:12 one c on this side
Ezek 40:12 and one c on that side
Ezek 40:42 for the burnt offering, one c
Ezek 40:42 c and a half long, one c
Ezek 40:42 and a half wide, and one c high
Ezek 42: 4 wide, at a distance of one c
Ezek 43:13 in cubits (the c is one c
Ezek 43:13 the base one c high and one
Ezek 43:13 one c wide, with a rim all
Ezek 43:14 the width of the ledge, one c
Ezek 43:14 the width of the ledge, one c
Ezek 43:17 a rim of half a c around it
Ezek 43:17 its base, one c all around
Matt 6:27 can add one c to his stature
Luke 12:25 can add one c to his stature

CUBITS (*see* CUBIT)
Gen 6:15 ark shall be three hundred c
Gen 6:15 its width fifty c
Gen 6:15 and its height thirty c
Gen 7:20 prevailed fifteen c upward
Ex 25:10 a half c shall be its length,
Ex 25:17 a half c shall be its length
Ex 25:23 two c shall be its length, a
Ex 26: 2 shall be twenty-eight c, and
Ex 26: 2 width of each curtain four c
Ex 26: 8 curtain shall be thirty c
Ex 26: 8 width of each curtain four c
Ex 26:16 Ten c shall be the length of
Ex 27: 1 five c long and five c broad
Ex 27: 1 its height shall be three c
Ex 27: 9 one hundred c long for one
Ex 27:11 hangings one hundred c long
Ex 27:12 shall be hangings of fifty c
Ex 27:13 east side shall be fifty c
Ex 27:14 the gate shall be fifteen c
Ex 27:15 be hangings of fifteen c,
Ex 27:16 be a screen twenty c long
Ex 27:18 court shall be one hundred c
Ex 27:18 and the height five c, woven
Ex 30: 2 two c shall be its height
Ex 36: 9 curtain was twenty-eight c
Ex 36: 9 width of each curtain four c
Ex 36:15 of each curtain was thirty c
Ex 36:15 width of each curtain four c
Ex 36:21 of each board was ten c, and
Ex 37: 1 a half c was its length, a
Ex 37: 6 a half c was its length and a
Ex 37:10 two c was its length, a cubit
Ex 37:25 and two c was its height
Ex 38: 1 five c was its length and five
Ex 38: 1 length and five c its width
Ex 38: 1 and its height was three c
Ex 38: 9 linen, one hundred c long
Ex 38:11 were one hundred c long, with
Ex 38:12 were hangings of fifty c,
Ex 38:13 the hangings were fifty c
Ex 38:14 the gate were fifteen c long
Ex 38:15 were hangings of fifteen c
Ex 38:18 The length was twenty c, and
Ex 38:18 along its width was five c
Num 11:31 about two c above the surface
Num 35: 4 a thousand c all around
Num 35: 5 the east side two thousand c
Num 35: 5 the south side two thousand c
Num 35: 5 the west side two thousand c
Num 35: 5 the north side two thousand c
Deut 3:11 Nine c is its length
Deut 3:11 four c its width, according
Josh 3: 4 two thousand c by measure
1Sa 17: 4 Gath, whose height was six c
1Ki 6: 2 LORD, its length was sixty c
1Ki 6: 2 and its height thirty c
1Ki 6: 3 of the house was twenty c
1Ki 6: 3 its width extended ten c from
1Ki 6: 6 chamber was five c
1Ki 6: 6 the middle was six c wide
1Ki 6: 6 and the third was seven c wide
1Ki 6:10 temple, each five c high
1Ki 6:17 sanctuary was forty c long
1Ki 6:20 twenty c long, twenty c wide
1Ki 6:20 and twenty c high
1Ki 6:23 olive wood, each ten c high
1Ki 6:24 wing of the cherub was five c
1Ki 6:24 wing of the cherub five c
1Ki 6:24 ten c from the tip of one
1Ki 6:25 And the other cherub was ten c
1Ki 6:26 of one cherub was ten c, and
1Ki 7: 2 its length was one hundred c
1Ki 7: 2 its width fifty c
1Ki 7: 2 and its height thirty c, with
1Ki 7: 6 its length was fifty c, and
1Ki 7: 6 and its width thirty c
1Ki 7:10 some ten c and some eight c
1Ki 7:15 each one eighteen c high
1Ki 7:15 a line of twelve c measured
1Ki 7:16 of one capital was five c
1Ki 7:16 the other capital was five c
1Ki 7:19 the shape of lilies, four c
1Ki 7:23 ten c from one brim to the
1Ki 7:23 Its height was five c, and a
1Ki 7:23 a line of thirty c measured
1Ki 7:27 four c was the length of each
1Ki 7:27 four c its width, and three
1Ki 7:27 width, and three c its height
1Ki 7:31 a half c in outside diameter
1Ki 7:32 a wheel was one and a half c
1Ki 7:38 and each laver was four c
2Ki 14:13 Corner Gate—four hundred c
2Ki 25:17 of one pillar was eighteen c
2Ki 25:17 of the capital was three c
1Ch 11:23 of great height, five c tall
2Ch 3: 3 The length was sixty c (by
2Ch 3: 3 (by c according to the former
2Ch 3: 3 and the width twenty c
2Ch 3: 4 c long across the width of
2Ch 3: 8 width of the house, twenty c
2Ch 3: 8 and its width twenty c
2Ch 3:11 twenty c in overall length
2Ch 3:11 of the one cherub was five c
2Ch 3:11 and the other wing was five c
2Ch 3:12 the other cherub was five c
2Ch 3:12 other wing also was five c
2Ch 3:13 spanned twenty c overall
2Ch 3:15 pillars thirty-five c high
2Ch 3:15 of each of them was five c
2Ch 4: 1 twenty c was its length,
2Ch 4: 1 twenty c its width
2Ch 4: 1 and ten c its height
2Ch 4: 2 ten c from one brim to the
2Ch 4: 2 Its height was five c
2Ch 4: 2 a line of thirty c measured
2Ch 6:13 a bronze platform five c long
2Ch 6:13 five c broad
2Ch 6:13 and three c high
2Ch 25:23 Corner Gate—four hundred c
Ezra 6: 3 laid, its height sixty c
Ezra 6: 3 its width sixty c
Neh 3:13 repaired a thousand c of the
Esth 5:14 gallows be made, fifty c high
Esth 7: 9 The gallows, fifty c high
Jer 52:21 of one pillar was eighteen c
Jer 52:21 of twelve c could measure its
Jer 52:22 of one capital was five c
Ezek 40: 5 a measuring rod six c long
Ezek 40: 7 was a space of five c
Ezek 40: 9 of the gateway, eight c
Ezek 40: 9 and the gateposts, two c
Ezek 40:11 to the gateway, ten c
Ezek 40:11 of the gate, thirteen c
Ezek 40:12 were six c on this side
Ezek 40:12 and six c on that side
Ezek 40:13 the width was twenty-five c
Ezek 40:14 the gateposts, sixty c high
Ezek 40:15 of the inner gate was fifty c
Ezek 40:19 one hundred c toward the east
Ezek 40:21 its length was fifty c
Ezek 40:21 and its width twenty-five c
Ezek 40:23 to gateway, one hundred c
Ezek 40:25 its length was fifty c
Ezek 40:25 and its width twenty-five c
Ezek 40:27 the south, one hundred c
Ezek 40:29 it was fifty c long
Ezek 40:29 and twenty-five c wide
Ezek 40:30 around, twenty-five c long

Ezek 40:30 **c** long and five **c** wide
Ezek 40:33 it was fifty **c** long and
Ezek 40:33 twenty-five **c** wide
Ezek 40:36 its length was fifty **c**
Ezek 40:36 and its width twenty-five **c**
Ezek 40:47 the court, one hundred **c** long
Ezek 40:47 one hundred **c** wide
Ezek 40:48 five **c** on this side
Ezek 40:48 and five **c** on that side
Ezek 40:48 was three **c** on this side
Ezek 40:48 and three **c** on that side
Ezek 40:49 of the vestibule was twenty **c**
Ezek 40:49 and the width eleven **c**
Ezek 41: 1 six **c** wide on one side
Ezek 41: 1 six **c** wide on the other side
Ezek 41: 2 of the entryway was ten **c**
Ezek 41: 2 were five **c** on this side and
Ezek 41: 2 and five **c** on the other side
Ezek 41: 2 measured its length, forty **c**
Ezek 41: 2 and its width, twenty **c**
Ezek 41: 3 measured the doorposts, two **c**
Ezek 41: 3 and the entrance, six **c** high
Ezek 41: 3 of the entrance, seven **c**
Ezek 41: 4 measured the length, twenty **c**
Ezek 41: 4 and the width, twenty **c**,
Ezek 41: 5 the wall of the temple, six **c**
Ezek 41: 5 was four **c** on every side
Ezek 41: 8 full rod, that is, six **c** high
Ezek 41: 9 the side chambers was five **c**
Ezek 41:10 was a width of twenty **c** all
Ezek 41:11 terrace was five **c** all around
Ezek 41:12 end was seventy **c** wide
Ezek 41:12 was five **c** thick all around
Ezek 41:12 and its length ninety **c**
Ezek 41:13 temple, one hundred **c** long
Ezek 41:13 walls was one hundred **c** long
Ezek 41:14 courtyard, was one hundred **c**
Ezek 41:15 the other side, one hundred **c**
Ezek 41:22 was of wood, three **c** high
Ezek 41:22 and its length two **c**
Ezek 42: 2 which was one hundred **c**
Ezek 42: 2 (the width was fifty **c**), was
Ezek 42: 3 the inner court of twenty **c**
Ezek 42: 4 inside, was a walk ten **c** wide
Ezek 42: 7 its length was fifty **c**
Ezek 42: 8 the outer court was fifty **c**
Ezek 42: 8 the temple was one hundred **c**
Ezek 42:20 around, five hundred **c** long
Ezek 43:13 of the altar in **c** (the cubit
Ezek 43:14 to the lower ledge, two **c**
Ezek 43:14 to the larger ledge, four **c**
Ezek 43:15 altar hearth is four **c** high
Ezek 43:16 altar hearth is twelve **c** long
Ezek 43:17 the ledge, fourteen **c** long
Ezek 45: 1 be twenty-five thousand **c**
Ezek 45: 2 with fifty **c** around it for an
Ezek 45: 3 twenty-five thousand **c** long
Ezek 45: 5 twenty-five thousand **c** long
Ezek 45: 6 an area five thousand **c** wide
Ezek 46:22 enclosed courts, forty **c** long
Ezek 47: 3 he measured one thousand **c**
Ezek 48: 8 thousand **c** in width, and in
Ezek 48: 9 thousand **c** in length and ten
Ezek 48:10 thousand **c** in length, on the
Ezek 48:13 thousand **c** in length and ten
Ezek 48:15 The five thousand **c** in width
Ezek 48:16 four thousand five hundred **c**
Ezek 48:17 north two hundred and fifty **c**
Ezek 48:18 be ten thousand **c** to the east
Ezek 48:20 be twenty-five thousand **c**
Ezek 48:20 by twenty-five thousand **c**
Ezek 48:21 **c** of the holy district as far
Ezek 48:30 four thousand five hundred **c**
Ezek 48:32 four thousand five hundred **c**
Ezek 48:33 four thousand five hundred **c**
Ezek 48:34 **c** with their three gates
Ezek 48:35 shall be eighteen thousand **c**
Dan 3: 1 whose height was sixty **c**
Dan 3: 1 and its width six **c**
Zech 5: 2 Its length is twenty **c** and its
Zech 5: 2 **c** and its width ten **c**
John 21: 8 but about two hundred **c**)
Rev 21:17 one hundred and forty-four **c**

CUBS (*see* CUB)
2Sa 17: 8 robbed of her **c** in the field
Job 4:11 and the **c** of the lioness are
Job 38:32 the Great Bear with its **c**
Prov 17:12 meet a bear robbed of her **c**
Ezek 19: 2 lions she nourished her **c**
Ezek 19: 3 She brought up one of her **c**
Ezek 19: 5 she took another of her **c**
Hos 13: 8 like a bear deprived of her **c**
Nah 2:12 in pieces enough for his **c**

CUCUMBERS
Num 11: 5 we ate freely in Egypt, the **c**
Is 1: 8 as a hut in a garden of **c**

CUD
Lev 11: 3 hooves and chewing the **c**
Lev 11: 4 **c** or those that have cloven
Lev 11: 4 because it chews the **c** but
Lev 11: 5 because it chews the **c** but
Lev 11: 6 because it chews the **c** but
Lev 11: 7 yet does not chew the **c**, is
Lev 11:26 or does not chew the **c**, is
Deut 14: 6 parts, and that chews the **c**
Deut 14: 7 the **c** or have cloven hooves
Deut 14: 7 for they chew the **c** but do
Deut 14: 8 yet does not chew the **c**

CUDDLED
Lam 2:20 the children they have **c**

CULTIVATE (*see* CULTIVATED)
Ezek 48:19 tribes of Israel, shall **c** it

CULTIVATED (*see* CULTIVATE)
Heb 6: 7 for those by whom it is **c**

CUMI
Mark 5:41 Talitha, **c**," which is

CUMIN
Matt 23:23 tithe of mint and anise and **c**

CUMMIN
Is 28:25 does he not sow the black **c**
Is 28:25 and scatter the **c**
Is 28:27 For the black **c** is not
Is 28:27 a cartwheel rolled over the **c**
Is 28:27 but the black **c** is beaten out
Is 28:27 a stick, and the **c** with a rod

CUNNING (*see* CUNNINGLY)
Gen 3: 1 Now the serpent was more **c**
Job 5:13 the counsel of the **c** comes
Dan 8:25 Through his **c** he shall cause
Hos 12: 7 A **c** Canaanite!
Eph 4:14 in the **c** craftiness by which

CUNNINGLY (*see* CUNNING)
2Pe 1:16 For we did not follow **c**

CUP (*see* CUPBEARER, CUPS)
Gen 40:11 Pharaoh's **c** was in my hand
Gen 40:11 pressed them into Pharaoh's **c**
Gen 40:11 placed the **c** in Pharaoh's
Gen 40:13 you will put Pharaoh's **c** in
Gen 40:21 he placed the **c** in Pharaoh's
Gen 44: 2 Also put my **c**, the silver **c**
Gen 44:12 the **c** was found in Benjamin's
Gen 44:16 with whom the **c** was found
Gen 44:17 in whose hand the **c** was found
2Sa 12: 3 food and drank from his own **c**
1Ki 7:26 shaped like the brim of a **c**
1Ki 17:10 me a little water in a **c**,
2Ch 4: 5 shaped like the brim of a **c**
Ps 11: 6 be the portion of their **c**
Ps 16: 5 of my inheritance and my **c**
Ps 23: 5 My **c** runs over
Ps 73:10 And waters of a full **c** are
Ps 75: 8 hand of the LORD there is a **c**
Ps 116:13 take up the **c** of salvation
Prov 23:31 when it sparkles in the **c**
Is 51:17 of the LORD the **c** of His fury
Is 51:17 dregs of the **c** of trembling
Is 51:22 your hand the **c** of trembling
Is 51:22 the dregs of the **c** of My fury
Jer 16: 7 **c** of consolation to drink for
Jer 25:15 Take this wine **c** of fury from
Jer 25:17 Then I took the **c** from the
Jer 25:28 the **c** from your hand to drink
Jer 49:12 of the **c** have assuredly drunk
Jer 51: 7 a golden **c** in the LORD's hand
Lam 4:21 The **c** shall also pass over to
Ezek 23:31 I will put her **c** in your hand
Ezek 23:32 drink of your sister's **c**, the
Ezek 23:33 the **c** of horror and desolation
Ezek 23:33 The **c** of your sister Samaria
Hab 2:16 The **c** of the LORD's right
Zech 12: 2 I will make Jerusalem a **c** of
Matt 10:42 a **c** of cold water in the name
Matt 20:22 **c** that I am about to drink
Matt 20:23 You will indeed drink My **c**
Matt 23:25 cleanse the outside of the **c**
Matt 23:26 cleanse the inside of the **c**
Matt 26:27 Then He took the **c**, and gave
Matt 26:39 let this **c** pass from Me
Matt 26:42 if this **c** cannot pass away
Mark 9:41 a **c** of water to drink in My
Mark 10:38 you drink the **c** that I drink
Mark 10:39 drink the **c** that I drink, and
Mark 14:23 Then He took the **c**, and when
Mark 14:36 Take this **c** away from Me
Luke 11:39 make the outside of the **c**
Luke 22:17 Then He took the **c**, and gave
Luke 22:20 also took the **c** after supper
Luke 22:20 This **c** is the new covenant in
Luke 22:42 will, remove this **c** from Me
John 18:11 Shall I not drink the **c** which
1Co 10:16 The **c** of blessing which we
1Co 10:21 drink the **c** of the Lord and
1Co 10:21 the Lord and the **c** of demons
1Co 11:25 also took the **c** after supper
1Co 11:25 This **c** is the new covenant in
1Co 11:26 this bread and drink this **c**
1Co 11:27 this bread or drinks this **c**
1Co 11:28 that bread and drink of that **c**
Rev 14:10 into the **c** of His indignation
Rev 16:19 to give her the **c** of the wine
Rev 17: 4 golden **c** full of abominations
Rev 18: 6 in the **c** which she has mixed,

CUPBEARER (*see* CUP, CUPBEARERS)
Neh 1:11 For I was the king's **c**

CUPBEARERS (*see* CUPBEARER)
1Ki 10: 5 and their apparel, his **c**, and
2Ch 9: 4 and their apparel, his **c** and

CUPS (*see* CUP)
Ex 37:16 its dishes, its **c**, its bowls,
Is 22:24 from the **c** to all the
Jer 35: 5 bowls full of wine, and **c**
Jer 52:19 the spoons, and the **c**,
Mark 7: 4 hold, like the washing of **c**
Mark 7: 8 the washing of pitchers and **c**

CURDLE (*see* CURDS)
Job 10:10 milk, and **c** me like cheese,

CURDS (*see* CURDLE)
Deut 32:14 **c** from the cattle, and milk of
2Sa 17:29 honey and **c**, sheep and cheese
Is 7:15 **C** and honey He shall eat, that
Is 7:22 they give, that he will eat **c**
Is 7:22 for **c** and honey everyone will

CURE (*see* CURED, CURES)
Is 3: 7 I cannot **c** your ills, for in
Hos 5:13 yet he cannot **c** you, nor heal
Matt 17:16 but they could not **c** him
Luke 9: 1 all demons, and to **c** diseases

CURED (*see* CURE)
Is 30:24 the ground will eat **c** fodder
Jer 46:11 you shall not be **c**
Matt 17:18 the child was **c** from that
Luke 7:21 And that very hour He **c** many
John 5:10 said to him who was **c**, "It

CURES (*see* CURE)
Luke 13:32 out demons and perform **c** today

CURRENCY
Gen 23:16 of silver, **c** of the merchants
Num 3:47 in the **c** of the shekel of the

CURRENT
1Ki 10:28 them in Keveh at the **c** price
2Ch 1:16 them in Keveh at the **c** price

CURSE (*see* CURSED, CURSES, CURSING)
Gen 8:21 I will never again **c** the
Gen 12: 3 I will **c** him who curses you
Gen 27:12 I shall bring a **c** on myself
Gen 27:13 Let your **c** be on me, my son
Ex 22:28 nor **c** a ruler of your people
Lev 19:14 You shall not **c** the deaf
Num 5:18 bitter water that brings a **c**
Num 5:19 bitter water that brings a **c**
Num 5:21 woman under the oath of the **c**
Num 5:21 the LORD make you a **c** and an
Num 5:22 the **c** go into your stomach
Num 5:24 bitter water that brings a **c**
Num 5:24 **c** shall enter her to become
Num 5:27 brings a **c** will enter her
Num 5:27 become a **c** among her people
Num 22: 6 **c** this people for me, for
Num 22: 6 and he whom you **c** is cursed
Num 22:11 Come now, **c** them for me

Num 22:12 you shall not **c** the people
Num 22:17 come, **c** this people for me
Num 23: 7 **c** Jacob for me, and come,
Num 23: 8 How shall I **c** whom God has
Num 23:11 I took you to **c** my enemies
Num 23:13 **c** them for me from there
Num 23:25 Neither **c** them at all, nor
Num 23:27 may **c** them for me from there
Num 24:10 I called you to **c** my enemies
Deut 11:26 you today a blessing and a **c**
Deut 11:28 and the **c**, if you do not obey
Deut 11:29 and the **c** on Mount Ebal
Deut 23: 4 of Mesopotamia, to **c** you
Deut 23: 5 the **c** into a blessing for you
Deut 27:13 stand on Mount Ebal to **c**
Deut 29:19 he hears the words of this **c**
Deut 29:20 every **c** that is written in
Deut 29:27 to bring on it every **c** that
Deut 30: 1 the **c** which I have set before
Josh 6:18 make the camp of Israel a **c**
Josh 24: 9 the son of Beor to **c** you
Judg 5:23 **C** Meroz,' said the angel of
Judg 5:23 **c** its inhabitants bitterly,
Judg 9:57 on them came the **c** of Jotham
Judg 17: 2 you, and on which you put a **c**
2Sa 16: 9 dead dog **c** my lord the king
2Sa 16:10 So let him **c**, because the
2Sa 16:10 has said to him, '**C** David
2Sa 16:11 Let him alone, and let him **c**
1Ki 2: 8 **c** in the day when I went to
2Ki 2:24 pronounced a **c** on them in the
2Ki 22:19 become a desolation and a **c**
Neh 10:29 nobles, and entered into a **c**
Neh 13: 2 Balaam against them to **c** them
Neh 13: 2 turned the **c** into a blessing
Job 1:11 he will surely **c** You to Your
Job 2: 5 he will surely **c** You to Your
Job 2: 9 **C** God and die
Job 3: 8 May those **c** it who **c** the day
Job 31:30 asking for a **c** on his soul)
Ps 62: 4 mouth, But they **c** inwardly
Ps 109:28 Let them **c**, but You bless
Prov 3:33 The **c** of the LORD is on the
Prov 11:26 The people will **c** him who
Prov 24:24 him the people will **c**
Prov 26: 2 so a **c** without cause shall
Prov 27:14 it will be counted a **c** to him
Prov 30:10 to his master, lest he **c** you
Eccl 10:20 Do not **c** the king, even in
Eccl 10:20 do not **c** the rich, even in
Is 8:21 **c** their king and their God, and
Is 24: 6 Therefore the **c** has devoured
Is 34: 5 and on the people of My **c**
Is 43:28 I will give Jacob to the **c**
Is 65:15 your name as a **c** to My chosen
Jer 23:10 of a **c** the land mourns
Jer 24: 9 and a byword, a taunt and a **c**
Jer 25:18 a hissing, and a **c**, as it is
Jer 26: 6 will make this city a **c** to
Jer 29:18 to be a **c**, an astonishment, a
Jer 29:22 because of them a **c** shall be
Jer 42:18 an oath, an astonishment, a **c**
Jer 44: 8 cut yourselves off and be a **c**
Jer 44:12 and an astonishment and a **c**
Jer 44:22 an astonishment, a **c**, and
Jer 49:13 a reproach, a waste, and a **c**
Lam 3:65 Your **c** be upon them
Dan 9:11 therefore the **c** and the oath
Zech 5: 3 This is the **c** that goes out
Zech 5: 4 I will send out the **c**," says
Zech 8:13 were a **c** among the nations
Mal 2: 2 I will send a **c** upon you, and
Mal 2: 2 and I will **c** your blessings
Mal 3: 9 You are cursed with a **c**, for
Mal 4: 6 and strike the earth with a **c**
Matt 5:44 bless those who **c** you, do
Matt 26:74 Then he began to **c** and swear,
Mark 14:71 But he began to **c** and swear
Luke 6:28 bless those who **c** you, and
Rom 12:14 bless and do not **c**
Gal 3:10 of the law are under the **c**
Gal 3:13 us from the **c** of the law,
Gal 3:13 having become a **c** for us (for
Jas 3: 9 Father, and with it we **c** men
Rev 22: 3 And there shall be no more **c**

CURSED (*see* CURSE)
Gen 3:14 this, you are **c** more than all
Gen 3:17 **C** is the ground for your sake
Gen 4:11 now you are **c** from the earth
Gen 5:29 ground which the LORD has **c**
Gen 9:25 **C** be Canaan
Gen 27:29 **C** be everyone who curses you,
Gen 49: 7 **C** be their anger, for it is
Lev 20: 9 He has **c** his father or his
Lev 24:11 the name of the LORD and **c**
Lev 24:14 the camp him who has **c**
Lev 24:23 the camp him who had **c**, and
Num 22: 6 and he whom you curse is **c**
Num 23: 8 I curse whom God has not **c**
Num 24: 9 and **c** is he who curses you
Deut 27:15 **C** is the one who makes any
Deut 27:16 **C** is the one who treats his
Deut 27:17 **C** is the one who moves his
Deut 27:18 **C** is the one who makes the
Deut 27:19 **C** is the one who perverts
Deut 27:20 **C** is the one who lies with
Deut 27:21 **C** is the one who lies with
Deut 27:22 **C** is the one who lies with
Deut 27:23 **C** is the one who lies with
Deut 27:24 **C** is the one who attacks his
Deut 27:25 **C** is the one who takes a
Deut 27:26 **C** is the one who does not
Deut 28:16 **C** shall you be in the city,
Deut 28:16 **c** shall you be in the country
Deut 28:17 **C** shall be your basket and
Deut 28:18 **C** shall be the fruit of your
Deut 28:19 **C** shall you be when you come
Deut 28:19 **c** shall you be when you go
Josh 6:26 **C** be the man before the LORD
Josh 9:23 Now therefore, you are **c**, and
Judg 9:27 ate and drank, and **c** Abimelech
Judg 21:18 **C** be the one who gives a
1Sa 14:24 **C** is the man who eats any
1Sa 14:28 **C** is the man who eats food
1Sa 17:43 the Philistine **c** David by his
1Sa 26:19 may they be **c** before the LORD
2Sa 16: 7 Shimei said thus when he **c**
2Sa 16:13 **c** as he went, threw stones at
2Sa 19:21 this, because he **c** the LORD's
1Ki 2: 8 who **c** me with a malicious
Neh 13:25 **c** them, struck some of them
Job 1: 5 and **c** God in their hearts
Job 3: 1 and **c** the day of his birth
Job 5: 3 suddenly I **c** his habitation
Job 24:18 should be **c** in the earth, so
Ps 37:22 But those who are **c** by Him
Ps 119:21 the **c**, Who stray from Your
Eccl 7:22 that even you have **c** others
Jer 11: 3 **C** is the man who does not
Jer 17: 5 **C** is the man who trusts in
Jer 20:14 **C** be the day in which I was
Jer 20:15 Let the man be **c** who brought
Jer 48:10 **C** is he who does the work of
Jer 48:10 **c** is he who keeps back his
Mal 1:14 But **c** be the deceiver who has
Mal 2: 2 Yes, I have **c** them already,
Mal 3: 9 You are **c** with a curse, for
Matt 25:41 hand, 'Depart from Me, you **c**
Mark 11:21 which You **c** has withered away
Gal 3:10 **C** is everyone who does not
Gal 3:13 **C** is everyone who hangs on a
Heb 6: 8 rejected and near to being **c**

CURSES (*see* CURSE)
Gen 12: 3 and I will curse him who **c** you
Gen 27:29 Cursed be everyone who **c** you
Ex 21:17 he who **c** his father or his
Lev 20: 9 For everyone who **c** his
Lev 24:15 Whoever **c** his God shall bear
Num 5:23 shall write these **c** in a book
Num 24: 9 and cursed is he who **c** you
Deut 28:15 that all these **c** will come
Deut 28:45 Moreover all these **c** shall
Deut 29:21 according to all the **c** of the
Deut 30: 7 all these **c** on your enemies
2Ch 34:24 all the **c** that are written in
Prov 20:20 Whoever **c** his father or his
Prov 28:27 his eyes will have many **c**
Prov 30:11 generation that **c** its father
Jer 15:10 every one of them **c** me
Matt 15: 4 He who **c** father or mother,
Mark 7:10 He who **c** father or mother,

CURSING (*see* CURSE, CURSINGS)
Deut 28:20 The LORD will send on you **c**
Deut 30:19 life and death, blessing and **c**
2Sa 16: 5 **c** continuously as he came
2Sa 16:12 with good for his **c** this day
Ps 10: 7 His mouth is full of **c** and
Ps 59:12 in their pride, And for the **c**
Ps 109:17 As he loved **c**, so let it come
Ps 109:18 with **c** as with his garment
Eccl 7:21 you hear your servant **c** you
Rom 3:14 Whose mouth is full of **c** and
Jas 3:10 mouth proceed blessing and **c**

CURSINGS (*see* CURSING)
Josh 8:34 law, the blessings and the **c**
Hos 7:16 for the **c** of their tongue

CURTAIN (*see* CURTAINS)
Ex 26: 2 The length of each **c** shall be
Ex 26: 2 width of each **c** four cubits
Ex 26: 4 yarn on the edge of the **c** on
Ex 26: 4 the other **c** of the second set
Ex 26: 5 you shall make in the one **c**
Ex 26: 5 make on the edge of the **c**
Ex 26: 8 The length of each **c** shall be
Ex 26: 8 width of each **c** four cubits
Ex 26: 9 **c** at the forefront of the
Ex 26:10 **c** that is outermost in one
Ex 26:10 of the **c** of the second set
Ex 26:12 the half **c** that remains,
Ex 36: 9 The length of each **c** was
Ex 36: 9 width of each **c** four cubits
Ex 36:11 yarn on the edge of the **c** on
Ex 36:11 the other **c** of the second set
Ex 36:12 Fifty loops he made on one **c**
Ex 36:12 **c** on the end of the second
Ex 36:12 loops held one **c** to another
Ex 36:15 of each **c** was thirty cubits
Ex 36:15 width of each **c** four cubits
Ex 36:17 **c** that is outermost in one
Ex 36:17 of the **c** of the second set
Ps 104: 2 out the heavens like a **c**
Is 40:22 out the heavens like a **c**, and

CURTAINS (*see* CURTAIN)
Ex 26: 1 the tabernacle with ten **c**
Ex 26: 2 every one of the **c** shall have
Ex 26: 3 Five **c** shall be coupled to
Ex 26: 3 the other five **c** shall be
Ex 26: 6 couple the **c** together with
Ex 26: 7 also make **c** of goats' hair
Ex 26: 7 You shall make eleven **c**
Ex 26: 8 the eleven **c** shall all have
Ex 26: 9 couple five **c** by themselves
Ex 26: 9 six **c** by themselves, and you
Ex 26:12 remains of the **c** of the tent
Ex 26:13 length of the **c** of the tent
Ex 36: 8 **c** woven of fine linen thread
Ex 36: 9 the **c** were all the same size
Ex 36:10 coupled five **c** to one another
Ex 36:10 the other five **c** he coupled
Ex 36:13 coupled the **c** to one another
Ex 36:14 He made **c** of goats' hair for
Ex 36:14 he made eleven **c**
Ex 36:15 the eleven **c** were the same
Ex 36:16 coupled five **c** by themselves
Ex 36:16 and six **c** by themselves
Num 4:25 carry the **c** of the tabernacle
2Sa 7: 2 of God dwells inside tent **c**
1Ch 17: 1 of the LORD is under tent **c**
Esth 1: 6 blue linen **c** fastened with
Song 1: 5 Kedar, like the **c** of Solomon
Is 54: 2 out the **c** of your habitations
Jer 4:20 and my **c** in a moment
Jer 10:20 tent anymore, or set up my **c**
Jer 49:29 take for themselves their **c**
Hab 3: 7 the **c** of the land of Midian

CURVES
Song 7: 1 The **c** of your thighs are like

CUSH (*see* ETHIOPIA)
Gen 2:13 the whole land of **C**
Gen 10: 6 The sons of Ham were **C**,
Gen 10: 7 The sons of **C** were Seba,
Gen 10: 8 **C** begot Nimrod
1Ch 1: 8 The sons of Ham were **C**,
1Ch 1: 9 The sons of **C** were Seba,
1Ch 1:10 **C** begot Nimrod
Is 11:11 and Egypt, from Pathros and **C**
Is 45:14 of Egypt and merchandise of **C**

CUSHAN
Hab 3: 7 the tents of **C** in affliction

CUSHAN-RISHATHAIM
Judg 3: 8 hand of **C** king of Mesopotamia
Judg 3: 8 Israel served **C** eight years
Judg 3:10 the LORD delivered **C** king of
Judg 3:10 and his hand prevailed over **C**

CUSHI
Jer 36:14 of Shelemiah, the son of **C**
Zeph 1: 1 to Zephaniah the son of **C**

CUSHITE
2Sa 18:21 Then Joab said to the **C**, "Go
2Sa 18:21 So the **C** bowed himself to
2Sa 18:22 let me also run after the **C**
2Sa 18:23 of the plain, and outran the **C**
2Sa 18:31 Just then the **C** came
2Sa 18:31 and the **C** said, There is
2Sa 18:32 to the **C**, "Is the young
2Sa 18:32 And the **C** answered,

CUSTODIAN (*see* CUSTODY)
Esth 2: 3 king's eunuch, **c** of the women
Esth 2: 8 of Hegai the **c** of the women
Esth 2:15 the **c** of the women, advised

CUSTODY (*see* CUSTODIAN)
Gen 40: 3 So he put them in **c** in the
Gen 40: 4 so they were in **c** for a while
Gen 40: 7 in the **c** of his lord's house
Gen 41:10 put me in **c** in the house of
Lev 24:12 Then they put him in **c**, that
Esth 2: 3 under the **c** of Hegai the
Esth 2: 8 citadel, under the **c** of Hegai
Esth 2:14 to the **c** of Shaashgaz, the
Acts 4: 3 put them in **c** until the next

CUSTOM (*see* CUSTOMARY, CUSTOMS)
Gen 19:31 as is the **c** of all the earth
Ex 21: 9 to the **c** of daughters
Num 15:16 one **c** shall be for you and for
Judg 11:39 And it became a **c** in Israel
Ruth 4: 7 Now this was the **c** in former
1Sa 2:13 And the priests' **c** with the
1Ki 18:28 themselves, as was their **c**
2Ki 11:14 by a pillar according to **c**
2Ch 30:16 place according to their **c**
2Ch 35:25 They made it a **c** in Israel
Ezra 4:13 not pay tax, tribute, or **c**
Ezra 4:20 and **c** were paid to them
Ezra 7:24 or **c** on any of the priests,
Esth 9:23 the **c** which they had begun
Ps 119:132 As Your **c** is toward those who
Jer 32:11 according to the law and **c**
Dan 6:10 as was his **c** since early days
Luke 1: 9 according to the **c** of the
Luke 2:27 according to the **c** of the law
Luke 2:42 to the **c** of the feast
Luke 4:16 And as His **c** was, He went into
John 18:39 But you have a **c** that I
John 19:40 as the **c** of the Jews is to
Acts 15: 1 according to the **c** of Moses
Acts 17: 2 Then Paul, as his **c** was, went
Acts 25:16 It is not the **c** of the
1Co 11:16 we have no such **c**, nor do

CUSTOMARILY (*see* CUSTOMARY)
Acts 16:13 where prayer was **c** made

CUSTOMARY (*see* CUSTOM, CUSTOMARILY)
Lev 12: 2 her **c** impurity she shall be
Lev 12: 5 weeks, as in her **c** impurity
Lev 15:25 at the time of her **c** impurity
Lev 15:25 as the days of her **c** impurity
Lev 15:33 because of her **c** impurity
Lev 18:19 as she is in her **c** impurity
Lev 23: 7 you shall do no **c** work on it
Lev 23: 8 you shall do no **c** work on it
Lev 23:21 You shall do no **c** work on it
Lev 23:25 You shall do no **c** work on it
Lev 23:35 You shall do no **c** work on it
Lev 23:36 you shall do no **c** work on it
Num 28:18 You shall do no **c** work
Num 28:25 You shall do no **c** work
Num 28:26 You shall do no **c** work
Num 29: 1 You shall do no **c** work
Num 29:12 You shall do no **c** work, and
Num 29:35 You shall do no **c** work
Ezek 36:17 of a woman in her **c** impurity

CUSTOMS (*see* CUSTOM)
Lev 18:30 any of these abominable **c**
Jer 10: 3 For the **c** of the peoples are
Ezek 11:12 **c** of the Gentiles which are
Matt 17:25 of the earth take **c** or taxes
Acts 6:14 and change the **c** which Moses
Acts 16:21 they teach **c** which are not
Acts 21:21 to walk according to the **c**
Acts 26: 3 you are expert in all **c** and
Acts 28:17 or the **c** of our fathers, yet
Rom 13: 7 **c** to whom **c**, fear to

CUT (*see* CUTS, CUTTING, WOODCUTTERS)
Gen 9:11 be **c** off by the waters of the
Gen 15:10 and **c** them in two, down the
Gen 15:10 but he did not **c** the birds in
Gen 17:14 be **c** off from his people
Ex 4:25 **c** off the foreskin of her son
Ex 9:15 been **c** off from the earth
Ex 12:15 shall be **c** off from Israel
Ex 12:19 **c** off from the congregation
Ex 23:23 and I will **c** them off
Ex 29:17 Then you shall **c** the ram in
Ex 30:33 shall be **c** off from his
Ex 30:38 he shall be **c** off from his
Ex 31:14 that person shall be **c** off
Ex 34: 1 **C** two tablets of stone like
Ex 34: 4 So he **c** two tablets of stone
Ex 34:13 **c** down their wooden images
Ex 39: 3 **c** it into threads, to work it
Lev 1: 6 and **c** it into its pieces
Lev 1:12 he shall **c** it into its pieces
Lev 7:20 be **c** off from his people
Lev 7:21 be **c** off from his people
Lev 7:25 be **c** off from his people
Lev 7:27 be **c** off from his people
Lev 8:20 And he **c** the ram into pieces
Lev 17: 4 that man shall be **c** off from
Lev 17: 9 that man shall be **c** off from
Lev 17:10 will **c** him off from among his
Lev 17:14 eats it shall be **c** off
Lev 18:29 who commit them shall be **c**
Lev 19: 8 be **c** off from his people
Lev 20: 3 and will **c** him off from his
Lev 20: 5 I will **c** him off from his
Lev 20: 6 **c** him off from his people
Lev 20:17 they shall be **c** off in the
Lev 20:18 be **c** off from their people
Lev 22: 3 be **c** off from My presence
Lev 22:24 or crushed, or torn or **c**
Lev 23:29 he shall be **c** off from his
Lev 26:26 When I have **c** off your supply
Lev 26:30 **c** down your incense altars,
Num 4:18 Do not **c** off the tribe of the
Num 9:13 **c** off from among his people
Num 13:23 there **c** down a branch with
Num 13:24 men of Israel **c** down there
Num 15:30 he shall be **c** off from among
Num 15:31 shall be completely **c** off
Num 19:13 shall be **c** off from Israel
Num 19:20 shall be **c** off from among the
Deut 7: 5 **c** down their wooden images,
Deut 12: 3 you shall **c** down the carved
Deut 14: 1 you shall not **c** yourselves
Deut 19: 1 **c** off the nations whose land
Deut 19: 5 with his neighbor to **c** timber
Deut 19: 5 the ax to **c** down the tree
Deut 20:19 do not **c** them down to use in
Deut 20:20 **c** down, to build siegeworks
Deut 25:12 then you shall **c** off her hand
Josh 3:13 of the Jordan shall be **c** off
Josh 3:16 Sea, failed, and were **c** off
Josh 4: 7 **c** off before the ark of the
Josh 4: 7 of the Jordan were **c** off
Josh 7: 9 **c** off our name from the earth
Josh 11:21 **c** off the Anakim from the
Josh 17:18 wooded, you shall **c** it down
Josh 23: 4 the nations that I have **c** off
Judg 1: 6 **c** off his thumbs and big toes
Judg 1: 7 big toes **c** off used to gather
Judg 6:25 **c** down the wooden image that
Judg 6:26 image which you shall **c** down
Judg 6:28 that was beside it was **c** down
Judg 6:30 because he has **c** down the
Judg 9:48 **c** down a bough from the trees
Judg 9:49 likewise **c** down his own bough
Judg 20: 6 **c** her in pieces, and sent her
Judg 20:21 on that day **c** down to the
Judg 20:25 **c** down to the ground eighteen
Judg 20:45 they **c** down five thousand of
Judg 21: 6 One tribe is **c** off from
Ruth 4:10 **c** off from among his brethren
1Sa 2:31 that I will **c** off your arm
1Sa 2:33 not **c** off from My altar shall
1Sa 11: 7 **c** them in pieces, and sent
1Sa 17:51 and **c** off his head with it
1Sa 20:15 but you shall not **c** off your
1Sa 20:15 has **c** off every one of the
1Sa 24: 4 secretly **c** off a corner of
1Sa 24: 5 because he had **c** Saul's robe
1Sa 24:11 For in that I **c** off the
1Sa 24:21 the LORD that you will not **c**
1Sa 28: 9 how he has **c** off the mediums
1Sa 31: 9 And they **c** off his head and
2Sa 4:12 **c** off their hands and feet, and
2Sa 7: 9 have **c** off all your enemies
2Sa 10: 4 **c** off their garments in the
2Sa 14:26 when he **c** the hair of his
2Sa 14:26 **c** it because it was heavy on
2Sa 14:26 when he **c** it, he weighed the
2Sa 20:22 they **c** off the head of Sheba
1Ki 5: 6 command that they **c** down
1Ki 5: 6 **c** timber like the Sidonians
1Ki 9: 7 then I will **c** off Israel from
1Ki 11:16 until he had **c** down every
1Ki 14:10 and will **c** off from Jeroboam
1Ki 14:14 **c** off the house of Jeroboam
1Ki 15:13 Asa **c** down her obscene image
1Ki 18:23 **c** it in pieces, and lay it on
1Ki 18:28 **c** themselves, as was their
1Ki 18:33 **c** the bull in pieces, and laid
1Ki 21:21 will **c** off from Ahab every
2Ki 3:19 shall **c** down every good tree,
2Ki 3:25 **c** down all the good trees,
2Ki 6: 4 the Jordan, they **c** down trees
2Ki 6: 6 So he **c** off a stick, and threw
2Ki 9: 8 I will **c** off from Ahab all
2Ki 10:32 to **c** off parts of Israel
2Ki 16:17 King Ahaz **c** off the panels of
2Ki 18: 4 **c** down the wooden images and
2Ki 19:23 I will **c** down its tall cedars
2Ki 23:14 **c** down the wooden images, and
2Ki 24:13 and he **c** in pieces all the
1Ch 17: 8 have **c** off all your enemies
1Ch 19: 4 **c** off their garments in the
1Ch 22: 2 he appointed masons to **c** hewn
2Ch 2: 8 skill to **c** timber in Lebanon
2Ch 2:10 the hewers who **c** timber,
2Ch 2:16 we will **c** wood from Lebanon,
2Ch 14: 3 and **c** down the wooden images
2Ch 15:16 Asa **c** down her obscene image,
2Ch 22: 7 to **c** off the house of Ahab
2Ch 26:21 for he was **c** off from the
2Ch 28:24 **c** in pieces the articles of
2Ch 31: 1 **c** down the wooden images, and
2Ch 32:21 **c** down every mighty man of
2Ch 34: 4 were above them he **c** down
2Ch 34: 7 **c** down all the incense altars
Job 4: 7 were the upright ever **c** off
Job 6: 9 loose his hand and **c** me off
Job 8:12 not **c** down, it withers before
Job 8:14 confidence shall be **c** off
Job 14: 7 for a tree, if it is **c** down
Job 21:21 of his months is **c** in half
Job 22:16 who were **c** down before their
Job 22:20 our adversaries are **c** down
Job 23:17 because I was not **c** off from
Job 36:20 when people are **c** off in
Ps 12: 3 May the LORD **c** off all
Ps 31:22 I am **c** off from before Your
Ps 34:16 To **c** off the remembrance of
Ps 37: 2 soon be **c** down like the grass
Ps 37: 9 For evildoers shall be **c** off
Ps 37:22 cursed by Him shall be **c** off
Ps 37:28 of the wicked shall be **c** off
Ps 37:34 When the wicked are **c** off
Ps 37:38 of the wicked shall be **c** off
Ps 54: 5 **C** them off in Your truth
Ps 58: 7 arrows be as if **c** in pieces
Ps 75:10 the wicked I will also **c** off
Ps 76:12 He shall **c** off the spirit of
Ps 80:16 with fire, it is **c** down
Ps 83: 4 let us **c** them off from being
Ps 88: 5 who are **c** off from Your hand
Ps 88:16 Your terrors have **c** me off
Ps 90: 6 In the evening it is **c** down
Ps 90:10 For it is soon **c** off, and we
Ps 94:23 shall **c** them off in their own
Ps 94:23 LORD our God shall **c** them off
Ps 101: 8 That I may **c** off all the
Ps 107:16 **c** the bars of iron in two
Ps 109:13 Let his posterity be **c** off
Ps 109:15 That He may **c** off the memory
Ps 129: 4 He has **c** in pieces the cords
Ps 143:12 In Your mercy **c** off my
Prov 2:22 will be **c** off from the earth
Prov 10:31 perverse tongue will be **c** out
Prov 23:18 your hope will not be **c** off
Prov 24:14 your hope will not be **c** off
Is 6:13 remains when it is **c** down
Is 9:10 the sycamores are **c** down, but
Is 9:14 the LORD will **c** off head and

Is 10: 7 and **c** off not a few nations
Is 10:34 He will **c** down the thickets
Is 11:13 of Judah shall be **c** off
Is 14: 8 Since you were **c** down, no
Is 14:12 How you are **c** down to the
Is 14:22 **c** off from Babylon the name
Is 15: 2 and every beard **c** off
Is 18: 5 he will both **c** off the sprigs
Is 18: 5 away and **c** down the branches
Is 22:25 be **c** down and fall, and the
Is 22:25 that was on it will be **c** off
Is 29:20 watch for iniquity are **c** off
Is 33:12 like thorns **c** up they shall
Is 37:24 I will **c** down its tall cedars
Is 38:12 I have **c** off my life like a
Is 45: 2 bronze and **c** the bars of iron
Is 48: 9 so that I do not **c** you off
Is 48:19 been **c** off nor destroyed from
Is 51: 9 the arm that **c** Rahab apart
Is 53: 8 For He was **c** off from the
Is 55:13 sign that shall not be **c** off
Is 56: 5 name that shall not be **c** off
Jer 7:28 has been **c** off from their
Jer 7:29 **C** off your hair and cast it
Jer 11:19 let us **c** him off from the
Jer 16: 6 them, **c** themselves, nor make
Jer 22: 7 they shall **c** down your choice
Jer 22:14 and **c** out windows for it,
Jer 25:37 peaceful habitations are **c**
Jer 34:18 when they **c** the calf in two
Jer 36:23 that the king **c** it with the
Jer 41: 5 having **c** themselves, with
Jer 44: 7 to **c** off from you man and
Jer 44: 8 that you may **c** yourselves off
Jer 46:23 They shall **c** down her forest,
Jer 47: 4 to **c** off from Tyre and Sidon
Jer 47: 5 Ashkelon is **c** off with the
Jer 47: 5 How long will you **c** yourself
Jer 48: 2 let us **c** her off as a nation
Jer 48: 2 You also shall be **c** down
Jer 48:25 The horn of Moab is **c** off
Jer 49:26 shall be **c** off in that day
Jer 50:16 **C** off the sower from Babylon,
Jer 50:23 whole earth has been **c** apart
Jer 50:30 shall be **c** off in that day
Jer 51: 6 Do not be **c** off in her
Jer 51:62 this place to **c** it off, so
Lam 2: 3 He has **c** off in fierce anger
Lam 3:54 I am **c** off
Ezek 4:16 man, surely I will **c** off the
Ezek 5:16 **c** off your supply of bread
Ezek 6: 6 incense altars may be **c** down
Ezek 14: 8 I will **c** him off from the
Ezek 14:13 I will **c** off its supply of
Ezek 14:13 **c** off man and beast from it
Ezek 14:17 I **c** off man and beast from it,
Ezek 14:19 **c** off from it man and beast,
Ezek 14:21 to **c** off man and beast from it
Ezek 16: 4 your navel cord was not **c**
Ezek 17: 9 **c** off its fruit, and leave it
Ezek 17:17 build a wall to **c** off many
Ezek 21: 3 and **c** off both righteous and
Ezek 21: 4 Because I will **c** off both
Ezek 25: 7 I will **c** you off from the
Ezek 25:13 **c** off man and beast from it,
Ezek 25:16 I will **c** off the Cherethites
Ezek 29: 8 **c** off from you man and beast
Ezek 30:15 I will **c** off the multitude of
Ezek 31:12 have **c** it down and left it
Ezek 35: 7 **c** off from it the one who
Ezek 37:11 and we ourselves are **c** off
Ezek 39:10 wood from the field nor **c**
Dan 2: 5 you shall be **c** in pieces
Dan 2:34 stone was **c** out without hands
Dan 2:45 you saw that the stone was **c**
Dan 3:29 shall be **c** in pieces, and
Dan 4:14 **c** off its branches, strip off
Dan 9:26 weeks Messiah shall be **c** off
Hos 8: 4 that they might be **c** off
Hos 10: 7 her king is **c** off like a twig
Hos 10:15 Israel shall be **c** off utterly
Joel 1: 5 for it has been **c** off from
Joel 1: 9 drink offering have been **c**
Joel 1:16 Is not the food **c** off before
Joel 2: 8 weapons, they are not **c** down
Amos 1: 5 **c** off the inhabitant from the
Amos 1: 8 I will **c** off the inhabitant
Amos 2: 3 I will **c** off the judge from
Amos 3:14 of the altar shall be **c** off
Obad 5 Oh, how you will be **c** off
Obad 9 may be **c** off by slaughter
Obad 10 and you shall be **c** off forever
Obad 14 to **c** off those among them who
Mic 1:16 **c** off your hair, because of
Mic 5: 9 your enemies shall be **c** off
Mic 5:10 That I will **c** off your horses
Mic 5:11 I will **c** off the cities of
Mic 5:12 I will **c** off sorceries from
Mic 5:13 images I will also **c** off, and
Nah 1:12 **c** down when he passes through
Nah 1:14 I will **c** off the carved image
Nah 1:15 he is utterly **c** off
Nah 2:13 I will **c** off your prey from
Nah 3:15 you, the sword will **c** you off
Hab 3:17 flock be **c** off from the fold
Zeph 1: 3 I will **c** off man from the
Zeph 1: 4 I will **c** off every trace of
Zeph 1:11 merchant people are **c** down
Zeph 1:11 who handle money are **c** off
Zeph 3: 6 I have **c** off nations, their
Zeph 3: 7 dwelling would not be **c** off
Zech 9: 6 I will **c** off the pride of the
Zech 9:10 I will **c** off the chariot from
Zech 9:10 the battle bow shall be **c** off
Zech 11:10 **c** it in two, that I might
Zech 11:14 Then I **c** in two my other
Zech 11:16 care for those who are **c** off
Zech 12: 3 will surely be **c** in pieces
Zech 13: 2 that I will **c** off the names
Zech 13: 8 thirds in it shall be **c** off
Zech 14: 2 not be **c** off from the city
Mal 2:12 May the LORD **c** off from the
Matt 3:10 not bear good fruit is **c** down
Matt 5:30 **c** it off and cast it from you
Matt 7:19 not bear good fruit is **c** down
Matt 18: 8 **c** it off and cast it from you
Matt 21: 8 others **c** down branches from
Matt 24:51 will **c** him in two and appoint
Matt 26:51 high priest, and **c** off his ear
Mark 9:43 hand makes you sin, **c** it off
Mark 9:45 foot makes you sin, **c** it off
Mark 11: 8 others **c** down leafy branches
Mark 14:47 high priest, and **c** off his ear
Luke 3: 9 not bear good fruit is **c** down
Luke 12:46 will **c** him in two and appoint
Luke 13: 7 **C** it down
Luke 13: 9 after that you can **c** it down
Luke 22:50 priest and **c** off his right ear
John 18:10 and **c** off his right ear
John 18:26 of him whose ear Peter **c** off
Acts 2:37 they were **c** to the heart, and
Acts 7:54 they were **c** to the heart, and
Acts 18:18 his hair **c** off at Cenchrea
Acts 27:32 Then the soldiers **c** away the
Rom 9:28 **c** it short in righteousness,
Rom 11:22 you also will be **c** off
Rom 11:24 For if you were **c** out of the
2Co 11:12 to do, that I may **c** off the
Gal 5:12 would even **c** themselves off

CUTH (*see* CUTHAH)
2Ki 17:30 the men of **C** made Nergal, the

CUTHAH (*see* CUTH)
2Ki 17:24 people from Babylon, **C**, Ava,

CUTS (*see* CUT)
Deut 12:29 When the LORD your God **c** off
Deut 29:11 from the one who **c** your wood
Job 28:10 He **c** out channels in the
Ps 46: 9 the bow and **c** the spear in two
Prov 26: 6 of a fool **c** off his own feet
Is 38:12 He **c** me off from the loom
Jer 10: 3 for one **c** a tree from the
Jer 48:37 on all the hands shall be **c**
Ezek 24: 4 fill it with choice **c**
Ezek 24: 5 and let the **c** simmer in it
Ezek 24:10 and let the **c** be burned up

CUTTING (*see* CUT, CUTTINGS)
Ex 31: 5 in **c** jewels for setting, in
Ex 35:33 in **c** jewels for setting, in
2Ki 6: 5 But as one was **c** down a tree
Jer 44:11 and for **c** off all Judah
Hab 2:10 **c** off many peoples, and sinned
Mark 5: 5 out and **c** himself with stones

CUTTINGS (*see* CUTTING)
Lev 19:28 You shall not make any **c** in
Lev 21: 5 nor make any **c** in their flesh
Jer 9:22 like **c** after the harvester,

CYMBAL (*see* CYMBALS)
1Co 13: 1 brass or a clanging **c**

CYMBALS (*see* CYMBAL)
2Sa 6: 5 on sistrums, and on **c**
1Ch 13: 8 on tambourines, on **c**, and
1Ch 15:16 instruments, harps, and **c**, by
1Ch 15:19 were to sound the **c** of bronze
1Ch 15:28 horn, with trumpets and with **c**
1Ch 16: 5 but Asaph made music with **c**
1Ch 16:42 aloud with trumpets and **c** and
1Ch 25: 1 stringed instruments, and **c**
1Ch 25: 6 the house of the LORD, with **c**
2Ch 5:12 in white linen, having **c**,
2Ch 5:13 voice with the trumpets and **c**
2Ch 29:25 the house of the LORD with **c**
Ezra 3:10 the sons of Asaph, with **c**
Neh 12:27 and singing, with **c** and
Ps 150: 5 Praise Him with loud **c**
Ps 150: 5 Him with high sounding **c**

CYPRESS
1Ki 5: 8 the cedar and **c** logs
1Ki 5:10 **c** logs according to all his
1Ki 6:15 the temple with planks of **c**
1Ki 6:34 the two doors were of **c** wood
1Ki 9:11 Solomon with cedar and **c** and
2Ki 19:23 cedars and its choice **c** trees
2Ch 2: 8 Also send me cedar and **c** and
2Ch 3: 5 **c** which he overlaid with fine
Is 14: 8 Indeed the **c** trees rejoice
Is 37:24 cedars and its choice **c** trees
Is 41:19 set in the desert the **c** tree
Is 44:14 for himself, and takes the **c**
Is 55:13 shall come up the **c** tree, and
Is 60:13 shall come to you, the **c**, the
Hos 14: 8 I am like a green **c** tree
Zech 11: 2 Wail, O **c**, for the cedar has

CYPRUS
Num 24:24 come from the coasts of **C**
Is 23: 1 from the land of **C** it is
Is 23:12 Arise, cross over to **C**
Jer 2:10 pass beyond the coasts of **C**
Ezek 27: 6 ivory from the coasts of **C**
Dan 11:30 For ships from **C** shall come
Acts 4:36 a Levite of the country of **C**
Acts 11:19 as far as Phoenicia, **C**, and
Acts 11:20 some of them were men from **C**
Acts 13: 4 from there they sailed to **C**
Acts 15:39 took Mark and sailed to **C**
Acts 21: 3 When we had sighted **C**, we
Acts 21:16 with them one, Mnason of **C**
Acts 27: 4 sailed under the shelter of **C**

CYRENE (*see* CYRENIAN)
Matt 27:32 out, they found a man of **C**
Acts 2:10 parts of Libya adjoining **C**
Acts 11:20 were men from Cyprus and **C**
Acts 13: 1 was called Niger, Lucius of **C**

CYRENIAN (*see* CYRENE, CYRENIANS)
Mark 15:21 a certain man, Simon a **C**, the
Luke 23:26 of a certain man, Simon a **C**

CYRENIANS (*see* CYRENIAN)
Acts 6: 9 Synagogue of the Freedmen (**C**

CYRUS
2Ch 36:22 year of **C** king of Persia,
2Ch 36:22 spirit of **C** king of Persia
2Ch 36:23 Thus says **C** king of Persia
Ezra 1: 1 year of **C** king of Persia,
Ezra 1: 1 spirit of **C** king of Persia
Ezra 1: 2 Thus says **C** king of Persia
Ezra 1: 7 King **C** also brought out the
Ezra 1: 8 **C** king of Persia brought them
Ezra 3: 7 had from **C** king of Persia
Ezra 4: 3 as King **C** the king of Persia
Ezra 4: 5 the days of **C** king of Persia
Ezra 5:13 year of **C** king of Babylon
Ezra 5:13 King **C** issued a decree to
Ezra 5:14 those King **C** took from the
Ezra 5:17 **C** to build this house of God
Ezra 6: 3 In the first year of King **C**
Ezra 6: 3 King **C** issued a decree
Ezra 6:14 according to the command of **C**
Is 44:28 who says of **C**, 'He is My
Is 45: 1 LORD to His anointed, to **C**
Dan 1:21 the first year of King **C**
Dan 6:28 in the reign of **C** the Persian
Dan 10: 1 In the third year of **C** king

DABBASHETH
Josh 19:11 west and to Maralah, went to **D**

DABERATH
Josh 19:12 Tabor, and went out toward **D**
Josh 21:28 **D** with its common-land,
1Ch 6:72 **D** with its common-lands,

DAGGER
Judg 3:16 a **d** (it was double-edged and a
Judg 3:21 took the **d** from his right
Judg 3:22 draw the **d** out of his belly

DAGON (*see* BETH DAGON, DAGON'S)
Judg 16:23 sacrifice to **D** their god, and
1Sa 5: 2 it into the temple of **D**
1Sa 5: 2 and set it by **D**
1Sa 5: 3 in the morning, there was **D**
1Sa 5: 3 So they took **D** and set it in
1Sa 5: 4 the next morning, there was **D**
1Sa 5: 4 The head of **D** and both the
1Sa 5: 4 the torso of **D** was left of it
1Sa 5: 5 of **D** nor any who come into
1Sa 5: 5 of **D** in Ashdod to this day
1Sa 5: 7 harsh toward us and **D** our god
1Ch 10:10 his head in the temple of **D**

DAGON'S (*see* DAGON)
1Sa 5: 5 into **D** temple tread on the

DAILY
Ex 5:13 your **d** quota, as when there
Ex 5:19 any bricks from your **d** quota
Ex 16: 5 as much as they gather **d**
Lev 6:20 flour as a **d** grain offering
Num 4:16 the **d** grain offering, the
Num 28:24 made by fire **d** for seven days
Judg 16:16 pestered him **d** with her words
2Ch 8:13 according to the **d** rate,
2Ch 31:16 the house of the LORD his **d**
Ezra 3: 4 offered the **d** burnt offerings
Neh 5:18 prepared for me **d** was one ox
Esth 3: 4 when they spoke to him **d**
Ps 13: 2 Having sorrow in my heart **d**
Ps 61: 8 That I may **d** perform my vows
Ps 68:19 Who **d** loads us with benefits,
Ps 72:15 And **d** He shall be praised
Ps 74:22 foolish man reproaches You **d**
Ps 88: 9 I have called **d** upon You
Prov 8:30 and I was **d** His delight,
Prov 8:34 me, watching **d** at my gates,
Is 58: 2 Yet they seek Me **d**, and
Jer 7:25 **d** rising up early and sending
Jer 20: 7 I am in derision **d**
Jer 20: 8 me a reproach and a derision **d**
Jer 37:21 **d** a piece of bread from the
Ezek 30:16 Noph shall be in distress **d**
Ezek 45:23 **d** for seven days, and a kid of
Ezek 45:23 goats **d** for a sin offering
Ezek 46:13 You shall **d** make a burnt
Dan 1: 5 a **d** provision of the king's
Dan 8:11 by him the **d** sacrifices were
Dan 8:12 to oppose the **d** sacrifices
Dan 8:13 concerning the **d** sacrifices
Dan 11:31 take away the **d** sacrifices
Dan 12:11 And from the time that the **d**
Hos 12: 1 He **d** increases lies and
Matt 6:11 Give us this day our **d** bread
Matt 26:55 I sat **d** with you, teaching in
Mark 14:49 I was **d** with you in the
Luke 9:23 and take up his cross **d**, and
Luke 11: 3 us day by day our **d** bread
Luke 19:47 was teaching **d** in the temple
Luke 22:53 was with you **d** in the temple
Acts 2:46 So continuing **d** with one
Acts 2:47 Lord added to the church **d**
Acts 3: 2 whom they laid **d** at the gate
Acts 5:42 **d** in the temple, and in every
Acts 6: 1 in the **d** distribution
Acts 16: 5 and increased in number **d**
Acts 17:11 searched the Scriptures **d** to
Acts 17:17 in the marketplace **d** with
Acts 19: 9 reasoning **d** in the school of
1Co 15:31 Jesus our Lord, I die **d**
2Co 11:28 things, what comes upon me **d**
Heb 3:13 but exhort one another **d**,
Heb 7:27 who does not need **d**, as those
Heb 10:11 priest stands ministering **d**
Jas 2:15 naked and destitute of **d** food

DAINTIES
Gen 49:20 and he shall yield royal **d**

DALMANUTHA
Mark 8:10 and came to the region of **D**

DALMATIA
2Ti 4:10 for Galatia, Titus for **D**

DALPHON
Esth 9: 7 Also Parshandatha, **D**, Aspatha

DAMAGE (*see* DAMAGED, DAMAGES)
Lev 13:55 whether the **d** is outside or
2Ki 12:12 to repair the **d** of the house
Ezra 4:22 Why should **d** increase to the
Is 22: 9 You also saw the **d** to the
Ezek 21:14 let the sword do double **d**
Dan 11:28 so he shall do **d** and return to
Dan 11:30 the holy covenant, and do **d**

DAMAGED (*see* DAMAGE)
Ps 74: 3 The enemy has **d** everything in
Jon 4: 7 it so **d** the plant that it

DAMAGES (*see* DAMAGE)
1Ki 11:27 repaired the **d** to the City of
2Ki 12: 5 repair the **d** of the temple
2Ki 12: 6 repaired the **d** of the temple
2Ki 12: 7 repaired the **d** of the temple
2Ki 12: 7 repairing the **d** of the temple
2Ki 12: 8 repair the **d** of the temple
2Ki 22: 5 to repair the **d** of the house
Amos 9:11 fallen down, and repair its **d**

DAMARIS
Acts 17:34 Areopagite, a woman named **D**

DAMASCENES (*see* DAMASCUS)
2Co 11:32 city of the **D** with a garrison

DAMASCUS (*see* DAMASCENES)
Gen 14:15 as Hobah, which is north of **D**
Gen 15: 2 of my house is Eliezer of **D**
2Sa 8: 5 When the Syrians of **D** came to
2Sa 8: 6 put garrisons in Syria of **D**
1Ki 11:24 And they went to **D** and dwelt
1Ki 11:24 dwelt there, and reigned in **D**
1Ki 15:18 king of Syria, who dwelt in **D**
1Ki 19:15 way to the Wilderness of **D**
1Ki 20:34 for yourself in **D**, as my
2Ki 5:12 the Pharpar, the rivers of **D**
2Ki 8: 7 Then Elisha went to **D**, and
2Ki 8: 9 him, of every good thing of **D**
2Ki 14:28 recaptured for Israel, from **D**
2Ki 16: 9 of Assyria went up against **D**
2Ki 16:10 Now King Ahaz went to **D** to
2Ki 16:10 and saw an altar that was at **D**
2Ki 16:11 King Ahaz had sent from **D**
2Ki 16:11 before King Ahaz came from **D**
2Ki 16:12 And when the king came from **D**
1Ch 18: 5 When the Syrians of **D** came to
1Ch 18: 6 put garrisons in Syria of **D**
2Ch 16: 2 king of Syria, who dwelt in **D**
2Ch 24:23 their spoil to the king of **D**
2Ch 28: 5 and brought them to **D**
2Ch 28:23 of **D** which had defeated him
Song 7: 4 Lebanon which looks toward **D**
Is 7: 8 For the head of Syria is **D**
Is 7: 8 and the head of **D** is Rezin
Is 8: 4 My mother,' the riches of **D**
Is 10: 9 Is not Samaria like **D**
Is 17: 1 The burden against **D**
Is 17: 1 **D** will cease from being a
Is 17: 3 Ephraim, the kingdom from **D**
Jer 49:23 Against **D**
Jer 49:24 **D** has grown feeble And turns
Jer 49:27 a fire in the wall of **D**, and
Ezek 27:18 **D** was your merchant because
Ezek 47:16 is between the border of **D**
Ezek 47:17 Hazar Enan, the border of **D**
Ezek 47:18 from between Hauran and **D**,
Ezek 48: 1 the border of **D** northward
Amos 1: 3 For three transgressions of **D**
Amos 1: 5 also break the gate bar of **D**
Amos 5:27 you into captivity beyond **D**
Zech 9: 1 **D** its resting place (for the
Acts 9: 2 him to the synagogues of **D**
Acts 9: 3 he journeyed he came near **D**
Acts 9: 8 hand and brought him into **D**
Acts 9:10 disciple at **D** named Ananias
Acts 9:19 days with the disciples at **D**
Acts 9:22 the Jews who dwelt in **D**,
Acts 9:27 at **D** in the name of Jesus
Acts 22: 5 went to **D** to bring in chains
Acts 22: 6 came near **D** at about noon,
Acts 22:10 to me, 'Arise and go into **D**
Acts 22:11 were with me, I came into **D**
Acts 26:12 journeyed to **D** with authority
Acts 26:20 declared first to those in **D**
2Co 11:32 In **D** the governor, under
Gal 1:17 and returned again to **D**

DAMS
Job 28:11 He **d** up the streams from

DAN (*see* DANITES, LAISH)
Gen 14:14 went in pursuit as far as **D**
Gen 30: 6 she called his name **D**
Gen 35:25 Rachel's maidservant, were **D**
Gen 46:23 The son of **D** was Hushim
Gen 49:16 **D** shall judge his people as
Gen 49:17 **D** shall be a serpent by the
Ex 1: 4 **D**, Naphtali, Gad, and Asher
Ex 31: 6 Ahisamach, of the tribe of **D**
Ex 35:34 Ahisamach, of the tribe of **D**
Ex 38:23 Ahisamach, of the tribe of **D**
Lev 24:11 of Dibri, of the tribe of **D**
Num 1:12 from **D**, Ahiezer the son of
Num 1:38 From the children of **D**, their
Num 1:39 of **D** were sixty-two thousand
Num 2:25 **D** shall be on the north side
Num 2:25 leader of the children of **D**
Num 2:31 numbered of the forces with **D**
Num 7:66 leader of the children of **D**
Num 10:25 the camp of the children of **D**
Num 13:12 from the tribe of **D**, Ammiel
Num 26:42 These are the sons of **D**
Num 26:42 These are the families of **D**
Num 34:22 tribe of the children of **D**
Deut 27:13 Gad, Asher, Zebulun, **D**, and
Deut 33:22 And of **D** he said
Deut 33:22 **D** is a lion's whelp
Deut 34: 1 land of Gilead as far as **D**
Josh 19:40 tribe of the children of **D**
Josh 19:47 of **D** went beyond these,
Josh 19:47 because the children of **D**
Josh 19:47 They called Leshem, **D**, after
Josh 19:47 the name of **D** their father
Josh 19:48 tribe of the children of **D**
Josh 21: 5 Ephraim, from the tribe of **D**
Josh 21:23 and from the tribe of **D**,
Judg 1:34 of **D** into the mountains, for
Judg 5:17 why did **D** remain on ships
Judg 18: 2 So the children of **D** sent
Judg 18:16 who were of the children of **D**
Judg 18:22 and overtook the children of **D**
Judg 18:23 out to the children of **D**
Judg 18:25 the children of **D** said to him
Judg 18:26 children of **D** went their way
Judg 18:29 called the name of the city **D**
Judg 18:29 the name of **D** their father
Judg 18:30 Then the children of **D** set up
Judg 18:30 of **D** until the day of the
Judg 20: 1 from **D** to Beersheba, as well
1Sa 3:20 And all Israel from **D** to
2Sa 3:10 Judah, from **D** to Beersheba
2Sa 17:11 from **D** to Beersheba, like the
2Sa 24: 2 from **D** to Beersheba, and count
2Sa 24:15 From **D** to Beersheba seventy
1Ki 4:25 from **D** as far as Beersheba,
1Ki 12:29 and the other he put in **D**
1Ki 12:30 before the one as far as **D**
1Ki 15:20 He attacked Ijon, **D**, Abel
2Ki 10:29 that were at Bethel and **D**
1Ch 2: 2 **D**, Joseph, Benjamin, Naphtali
1Ch 21: 2 Israel from Beersheba to **D**
1Ch 27:22 over **D**, Azarel the son of
2Ch 2:14 a woman of the daughters of **D**
2Ch 16: 4 They attacked Ijon, **D**, Abel
2Ch 30: 5 Israel, from Beersheba to **D**
Jer 4:15 For a voice declares from **D**
Jer 8:16 His horses was heard from **D**
Ezek 27:19 **D** and Javan paid for your
Ezek 48: 1 shall be one portion for **D**
Ezek 48: 2 by the border of **D**, from the
Ezek 48:32 Benjamin, and one gate for **D**
Amos 8:14 say, As your god lives, O **D**

DANCE (*see* DANCED, DANCES, DANCING)
Job 21:11 a flock, and their children **d**
Ps 149: 3 praise His name with the **d**
Ps 150: 4 Him with the timbrel and **d**
Eccl 3: 4 time to mourn, and a time to **d**

Song 6:13 the **d** of the double camp
Jer 31:13 the virgin rejoice in the **d**
Lam 5:15 our **d** has turned into
Matt 11:17 for you, and you did not **d**
Luke 7:32 for you, And you did not **d**

DANCED (*see* DANCE)
Judg 21:23 their number from those who **d**
1Sa 18: 7 So the women sang as they **d**
2Sa 6:14 Then David **d** before the LORD
Matt 14: 6 of Herodias **d** before them
Mark 6:22 daughter herself came in and **d**

DANCES (*see* DANCE)
Ex 15:20 her with timbrels and with **d**
Judg 21:21 come out to perform their **d**
1Sa 21:11 of him to one another in **d**
1Sa 29: 5 they sang to one another in **d**
Job 41:22 neck, and sorrow **d** before him
Jer 31: 4 in the **d** of those who rejoice

DANCING (*see* DANCE)
Ex 32:19 that he saw the calf and the **d**
Judg 11:34 meet him with timbrels and **d**
1Sa 18: 6 of Israel, singing and **d**, to
1Sa 30:16 land, eating and drinking and **d**
Ps 30:11 for me my mourning into **d**
Luke 15:25 house, he heard music and **d**

DANDLED
Is 66:12 carried, and be **d** on her knees

DANGER (*see* DANGEROUS)
1Sa 13: 6 in **d** (for the people were
Matt 5:21 will be in **d** of the judgment
Matt 5:22 shall be in **d** of the judgment
Matt 5:22 shall be in **d** of the council
Matt 5:22 shall be in **d** of hell fire
Acts 19:27 is this trade of ours in **d** of
Acts 19:40 For we are in **d** of being

DANGEROUS (*see* DANGER)
Acts 27: 9 sailing was now **d** because the

DANIEL (*see* BELTESHAZZAR)
1Ch 3: 1 the second, **D**, by Abigail the
Ezra 8: 2 of the sons of Ithamar, **D**
Neh 10: 6 **D**, Ginnethon, Baruch,
Ezek 14:14 these three men, Noah, **D**, and
Ezek 14:20 even though Noah, **D**, and Job
Ezek 28: 3 (Behold, you are wiser than **D**
Dan 1: 6 of the sons of Judah were **D**
Dan 1: 7 he gave **D** the name
Dan 1: 8 But **D** purposed in his heart
Dan 1: 9 had brought **D** into the favor
Dan 1:10 of the eunuchs said to **D**, "I
Dan 1:11 So **D** said to the steward whom
Dan 1:11 of the eunuchs had set over **D**
Dan 1:17 **D** had understanding in all
Dan 1:19 all none was found like **D**
Dan 1:21 Thus **D** continued until the
Dan 2:13 and they sought **D** and his
Dan 2:14 wisdom **D** answered Arioch, the
Dan 2:15 made the decision known to **D**
Dan 2:16 So **D** went in and asked the
Dan 2:17 Then **D** went to his house, and
Dan 2:18 this secret, so that **D** and his
Dan 2:19 to **D** in a night vision
Dan 2:19 So **D** blessed the God of
Dan 2:20 **D** answered and said
Dan 2:24 Therefore **D** went to Arioch,
Dan 2:25 brought **D** before the king
Dan 2:26 king answered and said to **D**
Dan 2:27 **D** answered in the presence of
Dan 2:46 his face, prostrate before **D**
Dan 2:47 The king answered **D**, and said,
Dan 2:48 Then the king promoted **D** and
Dan 2:49 Also **D** petitioned the king,
Dan 2:49 but **D** sat in the gate of the
Dan 4: 8 But at last **D** came before me
Dan 4:19 Then **D**, whose name was
Dan 5:12 enigmas were found in this **D**
Dan 5:12 now let **D** be called, and he
Dan 5:13 Then **D** was brought in before
Dan 5:13 the king spoke, and said to **D**
Dan 5:13 Are you that **D** who is one of
Dan 5:17 Then **D** answered, and said
Dan 5:29 and they clothed **D** with purple
Dan 6: 2 governors, of whom **D** was one
Dan 6: 3 Then this **D** distinguished
Dan 6: 4 **D** concerning the kingdom
Dan 6: 5 any charge against this **D**
Dan 6:10 Now when **D** knew that the
Dan 6:11 found **D** praying and making
Dan 6:13 That **D**, who is one of the
Dan 6:14 his heart on **D** to deliver him
Dan 6:16 command, and they brought **D**
Dan 6:16 the king spoke, saying to **D**
Dan 6:17 **D** might not be changed
Dan 6:20 with a lamenting voice to **D**
Dan 6:20 The king spoke, saying to **D**
Dan 6:20 **D**, servant of the living God,
Dan 6:21 Then **D** said to the king, "O
Dan 6:23 take **D** up out of the den
Dan 6:23 So **D** was taken up out of the
Dan 6:24 those men who had accused **D**
Dan 6:26 and fear before the God of **D**
Dan 6:27 Who has delivered **D** from the
Dan 6:28 So this **D** prospered in the
Dan 7: 1 **D** had a dream and visions of
Dan 7: 2 **D** spoke, saying, "I saw in
Dan 7:15 I, **D**, was grieved in my
Dan 7:28 As for me, **D**, my thoughts
Dan 8: 1 appeared to me—to me, **D**
Dan 8:15 Now it happened, when I, **D**
Dan 8:27 And I, **D**, fainted and was sick
Dan 9: 2 first year of his reign I, **D**
Dan 9:22 O **D**, I have now come forth to
Dan 10: 1 a message was revealed to **D**
Dan 10: 2 In those days I, **D**, was
Dan 10: 7 And I, **D**, alone saw the vision
Dan 10:11 O **D**, man greatly beloved,
Dan 10:12 Do not fear, **D**, for from the
Dan 12: 4 But you, **D**, shut up the words
Dan 12: 5 Then I, **D**, looked
Dan 12: 9 Go your way, **D**, for the words
Matt 24:15 spoken of by **D** the prophet
Mark 13:14 spoken of by **D** the prophet

DANITES (*see* DAN)
Judg 13: 2 Zorah, of the family of the **D**
Judg 18: 1 **D** was seeking an inheritance
Judg 18:11 of the **D** went from there,
1Ch 12:35 of the **D** who could keep

DAN JAAN
2Sa 24: 6 they came to **D** and around to

DANNAH
Josh 15:49 **D**, Kirjath Sannah (which is

DAPPLED
Zech 6: 3 the fourth chariot **d** horses
Zech 6: 6 the **d** are going toward the

DARA (*see* DARDA)
1Ch 2: 6 Ethan, Heman, Calcol, and **D**

DARDA (*see* DARA)
1Ki 4:31 and Heman, Chalcol, and **D**, the

DARE (*see* DARED)
Esth 7: 5 who would **d** presume in his
Job 41:10 that he would **d** stir him up
Amos 6:10 For we **d** not mention the name
Matt 22:46 anyone **d** question Him
Rom 5: 7 someone would even **d** to die
Rom 15:18 For I will not **d** to speak of
1Co 6: 1 **D** any of you, having a matter
2Co 10:12 For we **d** not class ourselves

DARED (*see* DARE)
2Sa 17:17 for they **d** not be seen coming
Job 32: 6 **d** not declare my opinion to
Mark 12:34 that no one **d** question Him
Luke 20:40 But after that they **d** not
John 21:12 of the disciples **d** ask Him
Acts 5:13 none of the rest **d** join them
Acts 7:32 Moses trembled and **d** not look
Jude 9 **d** not bring against him a

DARICS
1Ch 29: 7 and ten thousand **d** of gold

DARIUS
Ezra 4: 5 the reign of **D** king of Persia
Ezra 4:24 the reign of **D** king of Persia
Ezra 5: 5 till a report could go to **D**
Ezra 5: 6 the River, to **D** the king
Ezra 5: 7 To **D** the king: All peace
Ezra 6: 1 Then King **D** issued a decree,
Ezra 6:12 I **D** issue the decree
Ezra 6:13 to what King **D** had sent
Ezra 6:14 to the command of Cyrus, **D**
Ezra 6:15 year of the reign of King **D**
Neh 12:22 the reign of **D** the Persian
Dan 5:31 And **D** the Mede received the
Dan 6: 1 It pleased **D** to set over the
Dan 6: 6 King **D**, live forever
Dan 6: 9 Therefore King **D** signed the
Dan 6:25 Then King **D** wrote
Dan 6:28 prospered in the reign of **D**
Dan 9: 1 of **D** the son of Ahasuerus
Dan 11: 1 the first year of **D** the Mede
Hag 1: 1 In the second year of King **D**
Hag 1:15 in the second year of King **D**
Hag 2:10 in the second year of **D**, the
Zech 1: 1 month of the second year of **D**
Zech 1: 7 in the second year of **D**, the
Zech 7: 1 **D** it came to pass that the

DARK (*see* DARKEN, DARKER, DARKNESS)
Gen 15:17 the sun went down and it was **d**
Num 12: 8 plainly, and not in **d** sayings
Josh 2: 5 was being shut, when it was **d**
2Sa 22:12 **d** waters and thick clouds of
1Ki 8:12 He would dwell in the **d** cloud
2Ch 6: 1 He would dwell in the **d** cloud
Neh 13:19 as it began to be **d** before
Job 3: 9 the stars of its morning be **d**
Job 6:16 which are **d** because of the
Job 10:22 a land as **d** as darkness
Job 11:17 Though you were **d**, you would
Job 12:25 grope in the **d** without light
Job 18: 6 The light is **d** in his tent
Job 24:16 In the **d** they break into
Ps 18:11 around Him was **d** waters And
Ps 35: 6 Let their way be **d** and
Ps 49: 4 my **d** saying on the harp
Ps 74:20 For the **d** places of the earth
Ps 78: 2 I will utter **d** sayings of old
Ps 88:12 wonders be known in the **d**
Ps 105:28 sent darkness, and made it **d**
Prov 7: 9 in the black and **d** night
Song 1: 5 I am **d**, but lovely, O
Song 1: 6 look upon me, because I am **d**
Is 29:15 and their works are in the **d**
Is 45:19 in a **d** place of the earth
Jer 13:16 stumble on the **d** mountains
Lam 3: 6 He has set me in **d** places
Ezek 8:12 house of Israel do in the **d**
Ezek 32: 7 heavens, and make its stars **d**
Ezek 32: 8 I will make **d** over you, and
Ezek 34:12 on a cloudy and **d** day
Joel 2:10 the sun and moon grow **d**, and
Joel 3:15 The sun and moon will grow **d**
Amos 5: 8 and makes the day **d** as night
Amos 5:20 Is it not very **d**, with no
Mic 3: 6 the day shall be **d** for them
Matt 10:27 Whatever I tell you in the **d**
Luke 11:36 of light, having no part **d**
Luke 12: 3 you have spoken in the **d** will
John 6:17 And it was now **d**, and Jesus had
John 20: 1 early, while it was still **d**
Acts 13:11 immediately a **d** mist fell on
2Pe 1:19 that shines in a **d** place,

DARKEN (*see* DARK, DARKENED, DARKENS)
Amos 8: 9 I will **d** the earth in broad

DARKENED (*see* DARKEN)
Ex 10:15 earth, so that the land was **d**
Lev 13: 6 and indeed if the sore has **d**
Ps 69:23 Let their eyes be **d**, so that
Eccl 12: 2 moon and the stars, are not **d**
Is 5:30 the light is **d** by the clouds
Is 13:10 the sun will be **d** in its
Is 24:11 in the streets, all joy is **d**
Ezek 30:18 the day shall also be **d**, when
Matt 24:29 those days the sun will be **d**
Mark 13:24 the sun will be **d**, and the
Luke 23:45 Then the sun was **d**, and the
Rom 1:21 their foolish hearts were **d**
Rom 11:10 let their eyes be **d**, that
Eph 4:18 having their understanding **d**
Rev 8:12 that a third of them were **d**
Rev 9: 2 the air were **d** because of the

DARKENS (*see* DARKEN)
Job 38: 2 Who is this who **d** counsel by

DARKER (*see* DARK)
Gen 49:12 His eyes are **d** than wine, and

DARKNESS (*see* DARK)
Gen 1: 2 **d** was on the face of the deep
Gen 1: 4 divided the light from the **d**
Gen 1: 5 Day, and the **d** He called Night
Gen 1:18 divide the light from the **d**
Gen 15:12 and great **d** fell upon him
Ex 10:21 that there may be **d** over the
Ex 10:21 **d** which may even be felt

Ex 10:22 there was thick **d** in all the
Ex 14:20 and **d** to the one, and it gave
Ex 20:21 the thick **d** where God was
Deut 4:11 with **d**, cloud, and thick **d**
Deut 5:22 the cloud, and the thick **d**
Deut 5:23 voice from the midst of the **d**
Deut 28:29 as a blind man gropes in **d**
Josh 24: 7 He put **d** between you and the
1Sa 2: 9 wicked shall be silent in **d**
2Sa 22:10 down with **d** under His feet
2Sa 22:12 He made **d** canopies around
2Sa 22:29 the LORD shall enlighten my **d**
Job 3: 4 May that day be **d**
Job 3: 5 May **d** and the shadow of death
Job 3: 6 that night, may **d** seize it
Job 5:14 meet with **d** in the daytime
Job 10:21 not return, to the land of **d**
Job 10:22 a land as dark as **d** itself
Job 10:22 even the light is like **d**
Job 12:22 uncovers deep things out of **d**
Job 15:22 that he will return from **d**
Job 15:23 day of **d** is ready at his hand
Job 15:30 He will not depart from **d**
Job 17:12 they say, in the face of **d**
Job 17:13 if I make my bed in the **d**
Job 18:18 is driven from light into **d**
Job 19: 8 and He has set **d** in my paths
Job 20:26 Total **d** is reserved for his
Job 22:11 or **d** so that you cannot see
Job 22:13 He judge through the deep **d**
Job 23:17 off from the presence of **d**
Job 23:17 not hide deep **d** from my face
Job 26:10 at the boundary of light and **d**
Job 28: 3 Man puts an end to **d**, and
Job 28: 3 every recess for ore in the **d**
Job 29: 3 His light I walked through **d**
Job 30:26 waited for light, then came **d**
Job 34:22 There is no **d** nor shadow of
Job 37:19 nothing because of the **d**
Job 38: 9 thick **d** its swaddling band
Job 38:19 And **d**, where is its place,
Job 40:13 bind their faces in hidden **d**
Ps 18: 9 down With **d** under His feet
Ps 18:11 He made **d** His secret place
Ps 18:28 my God will enlighten my **d**
Ps 82: 5 They walk about in **d**
Ps 88: 6 me in the lowest pit, In **d**
Ps 88:18 And my acquaintances into **d**
Ps 91: 6 pestilence that walks in **d**
Ps 97: 2 Clouds and **d** surround Him
Ps 104:20 You make **d**, and it is night,
Ps 105:28 He sent **d**, and made it dark
Ps 107:10 Those who sat in **d** and in the
Ps 107:14 He brought them out of **d** and
Ps 112: 4 there arises light in the **d**
Ps 139:11 Surely the **d** shall fall on me
Ps 139:12 the **d** shall not hide from You
Ps 139:12 The **d** and the light are both
Ps 143: 3 He has made me dwell in **d**
Prov 2:13 to walk in the ways of **d**
Prov 4:19 way of the wicked is like **d**
Prov 20:20 will be put out in deep **d**
Eccl 2:13 folly as light excels **d**
Eccl 2:14 head, but the fool walks in **d**
Eccl 5:17 his days he also eats in **d**
Eccl 6: 4 in vanity and departs in **d**
Eccl 6: 4 and its name is covered with **d**
Eccl 11: 8 him remember the days of **d**
Is 5:20 who put **d** for light, and light
Is 5:20 for light, and light for **d**
Is 5:30 looks to the land, behold, **d**
Is 8:22 earth, and see trouble and **d**
Is 8:22 and they will be driven into **d**
Is 9: 2 in **d** have seen a great light
Is 29:18 out of obscurity and out of **d**
Is 42: 7 those who sit in **d** from the
Is 42:16 I will make **d** light before
Is 45: 3 give you the treasures of **d**
Is 45: 7 I form the light and create **d**
Is 47: 5 Sit in silence, and go into **d**
Is 49: 9 forth,' to those who are in **d**
Is 50:10 Who walks in **d** and has no
Is 58:10 light shall dawn in the **d**
Is 58:10 and your **d** shall be as the
Is 59: 9 for light, but there is **d**
Is 60: 2 the **d** shall cover the earth,
Is 60: 2 earth, and deep **d** the people
Jer 2:31 to Israel, Or a land of **d**
Jer 13:16 your God before He causes **d**
Jer 13:16 of death and makes it dense **d**
Jer 23:12 in the **d** they shall be driven
Lam 3: 2 led me and made me walk in **d**
Ezek 32: 8 bring **d** upon your land,' says
Dan 2:22 He knows what is in the **d**
Joel 2: 2 a day of **d** and gloominess, a
Joel 2: 2 a day of clouds and thick **d**
Joel 2:31 sun shall be turned into **d**
Amos 4:13 is, and makes the morning **d**
Amos 5:18 It will be **d**, and not light
Amos 5:20 Is not the day of the LORD **d**
Mic 3: 6 and you shall have **d** without
Mic 7: 8 when I sit in **d**, the LORD
Nah 1: 8 **d** will pursue His enemies
Zeph 1:15 and desolation, a day of **d**
Zeph 1:15 a day of clouds and thick **d**
Matt 4:16 sat in **d** saw a great light
Matt 6:23 whole body will be full of **d**
Matt 6:23 the light that is in you is **d**
Matt 6:23 how great is that **d**
Matt 8:12 will be cast out into outer **d**
Matt 22:13 and cast him into outer **d**
Matt 25:30 servant into the outer **d**
Matt 27:45 there was **d** over all the land
Mark 15:33 there was **d** over the whole
Luke 1:79 light to those who sit in **d**
Luke 11:34 your body also is full of **d**
Luke 11:35 which is in you is not **d**
Luke 22:53 your hour, and the power of **d**
Luke 23:44 and there was **d** over all the
John 1: 5 And the light shines in the **d**
John 1: 5 the **d** did not comprehend it
John 3:19 men loved **d** rather than light
John 8:12 Me shall not walk in **d**, but
John 12:35 light, lest **d** overtake you
John 12:35 he who walks in **d** does not
John 12:46 in Me should not abide in **d**
Acts 2:20 sun shall be turned into **d**
Acts 26:18 to turn them from **d** to light
Rom 2:19 a light to those who are in **d**
Rom 13:12 us cast off the works of **d**
1Co 4: 5 light the hidden things of **d**
2Co 4: 6 light to shine out of **d** who
2Co 6:14 communion has light with **d**
Eph 5: 8 For you were once **d**, but now
Eph 5:11 the unfruitful works of **d**
Eph 6:12 rulers of the **d** of this age
Col 1:13 us from the power of **d** and
1Th 5: 4 you, brethren, are not in **d**
1Th 5: 5 are not of the night nor of **d**
Heb 12:18 fire, and to blackness and **d**
1Pe 2: 9 of **d** into His marvelous light
2Pe 2: 4 them into chains of **d**, to be
2Pe 2:17 of **d** is reserved forever
1Jn 1: 5 and in Him is no **d** at all
1Jn 1: 6 with Him, and walk in **d**, we
1Jn 2: 8 because the **d** is passing away
1Jn 2: 9 brother, is in **d** until now
1Jn 2:11 who hates his brother is in **d**
1Jn 2:11 and walks in **d**
1Jn 2:11 because the **d** has blinded his
Jude 6 **d** for the judgment of the
Jude 13 the blackness of **d** forever
Rev 16:10 his kingdom became full of **d**

DARKON
Ezra 2:56 sons of Jaala, the sons of **D**
Neh 7:58 of Jaala, the children of **D**

DART (*see* DARTED, DARTS)
Job 41:26 nor does spear, **d**, or javelin

DARTED (*see* DART)
Ex 9:23 hail, and fire **d** to the ground

DARTS (*see* DART)
Job 41:29 **D** are regarded as straw
Eph 6:16 the fiery **d** of the wicked one

DASH (*see* DASHED, DASHES)
Deut 32:26 I will **d** them in pieces, I
2Ki 8:12 you will **d** their children, and
Ps 2: 9 You shall **d** them in pieces
Ps 91:12 Lest you **d** your foot against
Is 13:18 Also their bows will **d** the
Jer 13:14 I will **d** them one against
Matt 4: 6 lest you **d** your foot against
Luke 4:11 lest You **d** Your foot against

DASHED (*see* DASH)
Ex 15: 6 has **d** the enemy in pieces
2Ch 25:12 they all were **d** in pieces
Is 13:16 **d** to pieces before their eyes
Hos 10:14 a mother **d** in pieces upon her
Hos 13:16 infants shall be **d** in pieces
Nah 3:10 **d** to pieces at the head of

DASHES (*see* DASH)
Ps 137: 9 **d** Your little ones against

DATHAN
Num 16: 1 the son of Levi, with **D** and
Num 16:12 And Moses sent to call **D** and
Num 16:24 from the tents of Korah, **D**
Num 16:25 Then Moses rose and went to **D**
Num 16:27 around the tents of Korah, **D**
Num 16:27 and **D** and Abiram came out and
Num 26: 9 sons of Eliab were Nemuel, **D**
Num 26: 9 These are the **D** and Abiram,
Deut 11: 6 and what He did to **D**
Ps 106:17 opened up and swallowed **D**,

DAUBED
Ex 2: 3 **d** it with asphalt and pitch,

DAUGHTER (*see* DAUGHTER-IN-LAW, DAUGHTER'S, DAUGHTERS, GRANDDAUGHTER)
Gen 11:29 the **d** of Haran the father of
Gen 20:12 She is the **d** of my father,
Gen 20:12 but not the **d** of my mother
Gen 24:23 and said, Whose **d** are you
Gen 24:24 him, I am the **d** of Bethuel,
Gen 24:47 and said, Whose **d** are you
Gen 24:47 The **d** of Bethuel, Nahor's
Gen 24:48 way of truth to take the **d** of
Gen 25:20 the **d** of Bethuel the Syrian
Gen 26:34 the **d** of Beeri the Hittite
Gen 26:34 Basemath the **d** of Elon the
Gen 28: 9 Mahalath the **d** of Ishmael
Gen 29: 6 his **d** Rachel is coming with
Gen 29:10 the **d** of Laban his mother's
Gen 29:18 for Rachel your younger **d**
Gen 29:23 that he took Leah his **d** and
Gen 29:24 to his **d** Leah as a maid
Gen 29:28 So he gave him his **d** Rachel
Gen 29:29 to his **d** Rachel as a maid
Gen 30:21 Afterward she bore a **d**, and
Gen 34: 1 Now Dinah the **d** of Leah, whom
Gen 34: 3 to Dinah the **d** of Jacob, and
Gen 34: 5 he had defiled Dinah his **d**
Gen 34: 7 by lying with Jacob's **d**, a
Gen 34: 8 son Shechem longs for your **d**
Gen 34:17 then we will take our **d** and
Gen 34:19 he delighted in Jacob's **d**
Gen 36: 2 Adah the **d** of Elon the
Gen 36: 2 Aholibamah the **d** of Anah, the
Gen 36: 2 the **d** of Zibeon the Hivite
Gen 36: 3 and Basemath, Ishmael's **d**,
Gen 36:14 the **d** of Anah
Gen 36:14 the **d** of Zibeon
Gen 36:18 Esau's wife, the **d** of Anah
Gen 36:25 and Aholibamah the **d** of Anah
Gen 36:39 the **d** of Matred
Gen 36:39 the **d** of Mezahab
Gen 38: 2 And Judah saw there a **d** of a
Gen 38:12 process of time the **d** of Shua
Gen 41:45 the **d** of Poti-Pherah priest
Gen 41:50 the **d** of Poti-Pherah priest
Gen 46:15 Padan Aram, with his **d** Dinah
Gen 46:18 whom Laban gave to Leah his **d**
Gen 46:20 the **d** of Poti-Pherah priest
Gen 46:25 Laban gave to Rachel his **d**
Ex 1:16 but if it is a **d**, then she
Ex 1:22 every **d** you shall save alive
Ex 2: 1 and took as wife a **d** of Levi
Ex 2: 5 Then the **d** of Pharaoh came
Ex 2: 7 sister said to Pharaoh's **d**
Ex 2: 8 And Pharaoh's **d** said to her,
Ex 2: 9 Then Pharaoh's **d** said to her
Ex 2:10 brought him to Pharaoh's **d**
Ex 2:21 gave Zipporah his **d** to Moses
Ex 6:23 **d** of Amminadab, sister of
Ex 20:10 you, nor your son, nor your **d**
Ex 21: 7 if a man sells his **d** to be a
Ex 21:31 has gored a son or gored a **d**
Lev 12: 6 whether for a son or a **d**
Lev 18: 9 the **d** of your father, or the
Lev 18: 9 or the **d** of your mother,
Lev 18:10 son's **d** or your daughter's **d**
Lev 18:11 of your father's wife's **d**
Lev 18:17 nakedness of a woman and her **d**
Lev 18:17 shall you take her son's **d**
Lev 18:17 or her daughter's **d**
Lev 19:29 Do not prostitute your **d**
Lev 20:17 sister, his father's **d**

Lev 20:17 or his mother's **d**
Lev 21: 2 his father, his son, his **d**
Lev 21: 9 The **d** of any priest, if she
Lev 22:12 If the priest's **d** is married
Lev 22:13 But if the priest's **d** is a
Lev 24:11 was Shelomith the **d** of Dibri
Num 25:15 killed was Cozbi the **d** of Zur
Num 25:18 the **d** of a leader of Midian,
Num 26:46 the name of the **d** of Asher
Num 26:59 was Jochebed the **d** of Levi
Num 27: 8 inheritance to pass to his **d**
Num 27: 9 If he has no **d**, then you
Num 30:16 his **d** in her youth in her
Num 36: 8 And every **d** who possesses an
Deut 5:14 you, nor your son, nor your **d**
Deut 7: 3 not give your **d** to their son
Deut 7: 3 nor take their **d** for your son
Deut 12:18 you and your son and your **d**
Deut 13: 6 mother, your son or your **d**
Deut 16:11 you and your son and your **d**
Deut 16:14 you and your son and your **d**
Deut 18:10 his **d** pass through the fire
Deut 22:16 I gave my **d** to this man as
Deut 22:17 I found your **d** was not a
Deut 27:22 the **d** of his father
Deut 27:22 or the **d** of his mother
Deut 28:56 bosom, and to her son and her **d**
Josh 15:16 will give Achsah my **d** as wife
Josh 15:17 gave him Achsah his **d** as wife
Judg 1:12 will give my **d** Achsah as wife
Judg 1:13 gave him his **d** Achsah as wife
Judg 11:34 at Mizpah, there was his **d**
Judg 11:34 her he had neither son nor **d**
Judg 11:35 Alas, my **d**
Judg 11:40 each year to lament the **d** of
Judg 19:24 Look, here is my virgin **d**
Judg 21: 1 his **d** to Benjamin as a wife
Ruth 2: 2 Go, my **d**
Ruth 2: 8 You will listen, my **d**, will
Ruth 2:22 It is good, my **d**, that you go
Ruth 3: 1 My **d**, shall I not seek
Ruth 3:10 are you of the LORD, my **d**
Ruth 3:11 And now, my **d**, do not fear
Ruth 3:16 Is that you, my **d**
Ruth 3:18 Sit still, my **d**, until you
1Sa 14:50 was Ahinoam the **d** of Ahimaaz
1Sa 17:25 riches, will give him his **d**
1Sa 18:17 Here is my older **d** Merab
1Sa 18:19 the time when Merab, Saul's **d**
1Sa 18:20 Now Michal, Saul's **d**, loved
1Sa 18:27 him Michal his **d** as a wife
1Sa 18:28 and that Michal, Saul's **d**
1Sa 25:44 Saul had given Michal his **d**
2Sa 3: 3 the **d** of Talmai, king of
2Sa 3: 7 was Rizpah, the **d** of Aiah
2Sa 3:13 first bring Michal, Saul's **d**
2Sa 6:16 of David, Michal, Saul's **d**
2Sa 6:20 Michal the **d** of Saul came out
2Sa 6:23 Therefore Michal the **d** of
2Sa 11: 3 the **d** of Eliam, the wife of
2Sa 12: 3 and it was like a **d** to him
2Sa 14:27 one **d** whose name was Tamar
2Sa 17:25 in to Abigail the **d** of Nahash
2Sa 21: 8 sons of Rizpah the **d** of Aiah
2Sa 21: 8 sons of Michal the **d** of Saul
2Sa 21:10 Now Rizpah the **d** of Aiah took
2Sa 21:11 what Rizpah the **d** of Aiah
1Ki 3: 1 Egypt, and married Pharaoh's **d**
1Ki 4:11 the **d** of Solomon as wife
1Ki 4:15 the **d** of Solomon as wife
1Ki 7: 8 this hall for Pharaoh's **d**
1Ki 9:16 given it as a dowry to his **d**
1Ki 9:24 But Pharaoh's **d** came up from
1Ki 11: 1 as well as the **d** of Pharaoh
1Ki 16:31 wife Jezebel the **d** of Ethbaal
1Ki 22:42 was Azubah the **d** of Shilhi
2Ki 8:18 for the **d** of Ahab was his
2Ki 9:34 her, for she was a king's **d**
2Ki 11: 2 the **d** of King Joram, sister
2Ki 14: 9 Give your **d** to my son as
2Ki 15:33 was Jerusha the **d** of Zadok
2Ki 18: 2 was Abi the **d** of Zechariah
2Ki 19:21 the **d** of Zion, has despised
2Ki 19:21 the **d** of Jerusalem has shaken
2Ki 21:19 the **d** of Haruz of Jotbah
2Ki 22: 1 the **d** of Adaiah of Bozkath
2Ki 23:10 **d** pass through the fire to
2Ki 23:31 name was Hamutal the **d** of
2Ki 23:36 the **d** of Pedaiah of Rumah
2Ki 24: 8 name was Nehushta the **d** of
2Ki 24:18 name was Hamutal the **d** of
1Ch 1:50 was Mehetabel the **d** of Matred
1Ch 1:50 of Matred, the **d** of Mezahab
1Ch 2: 3 born to him by the **d** of Shua
1Ch 2:21 Hezron went in to the **d** of
1Ch 2:35 Sheshan gave his **d** to Jarha
1Ch 2:49 the **d** of Caleb was Achsah
1Ch 3: 2 the **d** of Talmai, king of
1Ch 3: 5 by Bathshua the **d** of Ammiel
1Ch 4:18 of Bithiah the **d** of Pharaoh
1Ch 7:24 Now his **d** was Sheerah, who
1Ch 15:29 that Michal the **d** of Saul
2Ch 8:11 Now Solomon brought the **d** of
2Ch 11:18 as wife Mahalath the **d** of
2Ch 11:18 of Abihail the **d** of Eliah the
2Ch 13: 2 the **d** of Uriel of Gibeah
2Ch 20:31 was Azubah the **d** of Shilhi
2Ch 21: 6 for he had the **d** of Ahab as a
2Ch 22:11 the **d** of the king, took Joash
2Ch 22:11 the **d** of King Jehoram, the
2Ch 25:18 Give your **d** to my son as
2Ch 27: 1 was Jerushah the **d** of Zadok
2Ch 29: 1 was Abijah the **d** of Zechariah
Neh 6:18 the **d** of Meshullam the son of
Esth 2: 7 is, Esther, his uncle's **d**
Esth 2: 7 took her as his own **d**
Esth 2:15 the **d** of Abihail the uncle of
Esth 2:15 who had taken her as his **d**
Esth 9:29 the **d** of Abihail, with
Ps 9:14 In the gates of the **d** of Zion
Ps 45:10 Listen, O **d**, Consider and
Ps 45:12 the **d** of Tyre will be there
Ps 45:13 The royal **d** is all glorious
Ps 137: 8 O **d** of Babylon, who are to be
Song 7: 1 feet in sandals, O prince's **d**
Is 1: 8 So the **d** of Zion is left as a
Is 10:30 up your voice, O **d** of Gallim
Is 10:32 at the mount of the **d** of Zion
Is 16: 1 to the mount of the **d** of Zion
Is 22: 4 of the **d** of my people
Is 23:10 the River, O **d** of Tarshish
Is 23:12 oppressed virgin **d** of Sidon
Is 37:22 the **d** of Zion, has despised
Is 37:22 the **d** of Jerusalem has shaken
Is 47: 1 dust, O virgin **d** of Babylon
Is 47: 1 throne, O **d** of the Chaldeans
Is 47: 5 O **d** of the Chaldeans
Is 52: 2 neck, O captive **d** of Zion
Is 62:11 Say to the **d** of Zion, 'Surely
Jer 4:11 toward the **d** of My people
Jer 4:31 the voice of the **d** of Zion
Jer 6: 2 I have likened the **d** of Zion
Jer 6:23 against you, O **d** of Zion
Jer 6:26 O **d** of my people, clothe
Jer 8:11 the **d** of My people slightly
Jer 8:19 the cry of the **d** of my people
Jer 8:21 For the hurt of the **d** of my
Jer 8:22 health of the **d** of my people
Jer 9: 1 slain of the **d** of my people
Jer 9: 7 deal with the **d** of My people
Jer 14:17 for the virgin **d** of my people
Jer 31:22 about, O you backsliding **d**
Jer 46:11 O virgin, the **d** of Egypt
Jer 46:19 O you **d** dwelling in Egypt,
Jer 46:24 The **d** of Egypt shall be
Jer 48:18 O **d** inhabiting Dibon, come
Jer 49: 4 valley, O backsliding **d**
Jer 50:42 against you, O **d** of Babylon
Jer 51:33 The **d** of Babylon is like a
Jer 52: 1 name was Hamutal the **d** of
Lam 1: 6 from the **d** of Zion all her
Lam 1:15 the virgin **d** of Judah
Lam 2: 1 the Lord has covered the **d** of
Lam 2: 2 strongholds of the **d** of Judah
Lam 2: 4 on the tent of the **d** of Zion
Lam 2: 5 lamentation in the **d** of Judah
Lam 2: 8 the wall of the **d** of Zion
Lam 2:10 The elders of the **d** of Zion
Lam 2:11 of the **d** of my people,
Lam 2:13 I liken you, O **d** of Jerusalem
Lam 2:13 you, O virgin **d** of Zion
Lam 2:15 heads at the **d** of Jerusalem
Lam 2:18 O wall of the **d** of Zion, let
Lam 3:48 of the **d** of my people
Lam 4: 3 but the **d** of my people has
Lam 4: 6 of the iniquity of the **d** of
Lam 4:10 of the **d** of my people
Lam 4:21 O **d** of Edom, you who dwell in
Lam 4:22 is accomplished, O **d** of Zion
Lam 4:22 your iniquity, O **d** of Edom
Ezek 14:20 deliver neither son nor **d**
Ezek 16:44 Like mother, like **d**
Ezek 16:45 You are your mother's **d**,
Ezek 16:49 her **d** had pride, fullness of
Ezek 22:11 his sister, his father's **d**
Ezek 26: 6 Also her **d** villages which
Ezek 26: 8 your **d** villages in the fields
Ezek 44:25 or mother, for son or **d**, for
Dan 11: 6 for the **d** of the king of the
Dan 11:17 he shall give him the **d** of
Hos 1: 3 took Gomer the **d** of Diblaim
Hos 1: 6 conceived again and bore a **d**
Mic 1:13 of sin to the **d** of Zion), for
Mic 4: 8 stronghold of the **d** of Zion
Mic 4: 8 kingdom of the **d** of Jerusalem
Mic 4:10 O **d** of Zion, like a woman in
Mic 4:13 Arise and thresh, O **d** of Zion
Mic 5: 1 in troops, O **d** of troops
Mic 7: 6 **d** rises against her mother,
Zeph 3:10 the **d** of My dispersed ones,
Zeph 3:14 Sing, O **d** of Zion
Zeph 3:14 your heart, O **d** of Jerusalem
Zech 2: 7 dwell with the **d** of Babylon
Zech 2:10 Sing and rejoice, O **d** of Zion
Zech 9: 9 Rejoice greatly, O **d** of Zion
Zech 9: 9 Shout, O **d** of Jerusalem
Mal 2:11 the **d** of a foreign god
Matt 9:18 My **d** has just died, but come
Matt 9:22 Be of good cheer, **d**
Matt 10:35 a **d** against her mother, and a
Matt 10:37 he who loves son or **d** more
Matt 14: 6 the **d** of Herodias danced
Matt 15:22 My **d** is severely
Matt 15:28 her **d** was healed from that
Matt 21: 5 Tell the **d** of Zion, 'Behold,
Mark 5:23 My little **d** lies at the point
Mark 5:34 **D**, your faith has made you
Mark 5:35 who said, "Your **d** is dead
Mark 6:22 when Herodias' **d** herself came
Mark 7:25 For a woman whose young **d** had
Mark 7:26 cast the demon out of her **d**
Mark 7:29 demon has gone out of your **d**
Mark 7:30 and her **d** lying on the bed
Luke 2:36 the **d** of Phanuel, of the
Luke 8:42 for he had an only **d** about
Luke 8:48 **D**, be of good cheer
Luke 8:49 to him, "Your **d** is dead
Luke 12:53 father, mother against **d** and
Luke 12:53 **d** and **d** against mother,
Luke 13:16 being a **d** of Abraham, whom
John 12:15 Fear not, **d** of Zion
Acts 7:21 Pharaoh's **d** took him away and
Heb 11:24 called the son of Pharaoh's **d**

DAUGHTER-IN-LAW (*see* DAUGHTER, DAUGHTERS-IN-LAW)
Gen 11:31 his **d** Sarai, his son Abram's
Gen 38:11 Judah said to Tamar his **d**
Gen 38:16 not know that she was his **d**
Gen 38:24 Tamar your **d** has played the
Lev 18:15 the nakedness of your **d**
Lev 20:12 If a man lies with his **d**
Ruth 1:22 the Moabitess her **d** with her
Ruth 2:20 Then Naomi said to her **d**
Ruth 2:22 And Naomi said to Ruth her **d**
Ruth 4:15 for your **d**, who loves you,
1Sa 4:19 Now his **d**, Phinehas' wife,
1Ch 2: 4 And Tamar, his **d**, bore him
Ezek 22:11 another lewdly defiles his **d**
Mic 7: 6 **d** against her mother-in-law
Matt 10:35 a **d** against her mother-in-law
Luke 12:53 mother-in-law against her **d**
Luke 12:53 **d** against her mother-in-law

DAUGHTER'S (*see* DAUGHTER)
Lev 18:10 daughter or your **d** daughter
Lev 18:17 daughter or her **d** daughter
Deut 22:17 evidences of my **d** virginity

DAUGHTERS (*see* DAUGHTER)
Gen 5: 4 and he begot sons and **d**
Gen 5: 7 years, and begot sons and **d**
Gen 5:10 years, and begot sons and **d**
Gen 5:13 years, and begot sons and **d**
Gen 5:16 years, and begot sons and **d**
Gen 5:19 years, and begot sons and **d**
Gen 5:22 years, and begot sons and **d**
Gen 5:26 years, and begot sons and **d**
Gen 5:30 years, and begot sons and **d**
Gen 6: 1 and **d** were born to them,
Gen 6: 2 sons of God saw the **d** of men
Gen 6: 4 God came in to the **d** of men

Gen 11:11 years, and begot sons and **d**
Gen 11:13 years, and begot sons and **d**
Gen 11:15 years, and begot sons and **d**
Gen 11:17 years, and begot sons and **d**
Gen 11:19 years, and begot sons and **d**
Gen 11:21 years, and begot sons and **d**
Gen 11:23 years, and begot sons and **d**
Gen 11:25 years, and begot sons and **d**
Gen 19: 8 I have two **d** who have not
Gen 19:12 Son-in-law, your sons, your **d**
Gen 19:14 who had married his **d**, and
Gen 19:15 your two **d** who are here, lest
Gen 19:16 and the hands of his two **d**
Gen 19:30 and his two **d** were with him
Gen 19:30 his two **d** dwelt in a cave
Gen 19:36 Thus both the **d** of Lot were
Gen 24: 3 from the **d** of the Canaanites
Gen 24:13 the **d** of the men of the city
Gen 24:37 from the **d** of the Canaanites
Gen 27:46 life because of the **d** of Heth
Gen 27:46 takes a wife of the **d** of Heth
Gen 27:46 who are the **d** of the land
Gen 28: 1 a wife from the **d** of Canaan
Gen 28: 2 the **d** of Laban your mother's
Gen 28: 6 a wife from the **d** of Canaan
Gen 28: 8 Also Esau saw that the **d** of
Gen 29:16 Now Laban had two **d**
Gen 30:13 happy, for the **d** will call me
Gen 31:26 me, and carried away my **d** like
Gen 31:28 me to kiss my sons and my **d**
Gen 31:31 take your **d** from me by force
Gen 31:41 fourteen years for your two **d**
Gen 31:43 These **d** are my **d**, and
Gen 31:43 **d** or to their children whom
Gen 31:50 If you afflict my **d**, or if
Gen 31:50 take other wives besides my **d**
Gen 31:55 and kissed his sons and **d** and
Gen 34: 1 out to see the **d** of the land
Gen 34: 9 give your **d** to us, and take
Gen 34: 9 and take our **d** to yourselves
Gen 34:16 we will give our **d** to you
Gen 34:16 and we will take your **d** to us
Gen 34:21 take their **d** to us as wives
Gen 34:21 and let us give them our **d**
Gen 36: 2 wives from the **d** of Canaan
Gen 36: 6 his wives, his sons, his **d**
Gen 37:35 all his **d** arose to comfort
Gen 46: 7 his **d** and his sons' **d**
Gen 46:15 persons, his sons and his **d**
Ex 2:16 priest of Midian had seven **d**
Ex 2:20 So he said to his **d**, "And
Ex 3:22 on your sons and on your **d**
Ex 6:25 of the **d** of Putiel as wife
Ex 10: 9 with our sons and our **d**, with
Ex 21: 4 she has borne him sons or **d**
Ex 21: 9 according to the custom of **d**
Ex 32: 2 wives, your sons, and your **d**
Ex 34:16 take of his **d** for your sons
Ex 34:16 his **d** play the harlot with
Lev 10:14 your sons, and your **d** with you
Lev 26:29 shall eat the flesh of your **d**
Num 18:11 **d** with you, as an ordinance
Num 18:19 **d** with you as an ordinance
Num 21:29 and his **d** into captivity, to
Num 26:33 of Hepher had no sons, but **d**
Num 26:33 and the names of the **d** of
Num 27: 1 Then came the **d** of Zelophehad
Num 27: 1 these were the names of his **d**
Num 27: 7 The **d** of Zelophehad speak
Num 36: 2 brother Zelophehad to his **d**
Num 36: 6 the **d** of Zelophehad, saying
Num 36:10 so did the **d** of Zelophehad
Num 36:11 the **d** of Zelophehad, were
Deut 12:12 you and your sons and your **d**
Deut 12:31 **d** in the fire to their gods
Deut 23:17 harlot of the **d** of Israel
Deut 28:32 and your **d** shall be given to
Deut 28:41 You shall beget sons and **d**
Deut 28:53 **d** whom the LORD your God
Deut 32:19 of His sons and His **d**
Josh 7:24 of gold, his sons, his **d**, his
Josh 17: 3 had no sons, but only **d**
Josh 17: 3 these are the names of his **d**
Josh 17: 6 because the **d** of Manasseh
Judg 3: 6 they took their **d** to be their
Judg 3: 6 gave their **d** to their sons
Judg 11:40 that the **d** of Israel went
Judg 12: 9 away thirty **d** in marriage
Judg 12: 9 and brought in thirty **d** from
Judg 14: 1 of the **d** of the Philistines
Judg 14: 2 of the **d** of the Philistines
Judg 14: 3 among the **d** of your brethren
Judg 21: 7 not give them our **d** as wives
Judg 21:18 give them wives from our **d**
Judg 21:21 just when the **d** of Shiloh
Judg 21:21 himself from the **d** of Shiloh
Ruth 1:11 Turn back, my **d**
Ruth 1:12 Turn back, my **d**, go your way
Ruth 1:13 No, my **d**; for it grieves me
1Sa 1: 4 wife and to all her sons and **d**
1Sa 2:21 and bore three sons and two **d**
1Sa 8:13 take your **d** to be perfumers
1Sa 14:49 names of his two **d** were these
1Sa 30: 3 and their **d** had been taken
1Sa 30: 6 man for his sons and his **d**
1Sa 30:19 small or great, sons or **d**
2Sa 1:20 lest the **d** of the Philistines
2Sa 1:20 rejoice, lest the **d** of the
2Sa 1:24 O **d** of Israel, weep over Saul
2Sa 5:13 sons and **d** were born to David
2Sa 13:18 virgin **d** wore such apparel
2Sa 19: 5 the lives of your sons and **d**
2Ki 17:17 **d** to pass through the fire,
1Ch 2:34 Sheshan had no sons, only **d**
1Ch 4:27 had sixteen sons and six **d**
1Ch 7:15 but Zelophehad begot only **d**
1Ch 14: 3 David begot more sons and **d**
1Ch 23:22 and had no sons, but only **d**
1Ch 25: 5 fourteen sons and three **d**
2Ch 2:14 of a woman of the **d** of Dan
2Ch 11:21 twenty-eight sons and sixty **d**
2Ch 13:21 twenty-two sons and sixteen **d**
2Ch 24: 3 wives, and he had sons and **d**
2Ch 28: 8 thousand women, sons, and **d**
2Ch 29: 9 and our sons, our **d**, and our
2Ch 31:18 their wives, their sons and **d**
Ezra 2:61 who took a wife of the **d** of
Ezra 9: 2 **d** as wives for themselves
Ezra 9:12 do not give your **d** as wives
Ezra 9:12 nor take their **d** to your sons
Neh 3:12 he and his **d** made repairs
Neh 4:14 brethren, your sons, your **d**
Neh 5: 2 our sons, and our **d** are many
Neh 5: 5 our **d** to be slaves, and some
Neh 5: 5 some of our **d** are brought
Neh 7:63 who took a wife of the **d** of
Neh 10:28 wives, their sons, and their **d**
Neh 10:30 **d** as wives to the peoples of
Neh 10:30 nor take their **d** for our sons
Neh 13:25 your **d** as wives to their sons
Neh 13:25 nor take their **d** for your
Job 1: 2 and three **d** were born to him
Job 1:13 **d** were eating and drinking
Job 1:18 **d** were eating and drinking
Job 42:13 had seven sons and three **d**
Job 42:15 so beautiful as the **d** of Job
Ps 45: 9 Kings' **d** are among Your
Ps 48:11 Let the **d** of Judah be glad,
Ps 97: 8 And the **d** of Judah rejoice
Ps 106:37 sons And their **d** to demons,
Ps 106:38 the blood of their sons and **d**
Ps 144:12 That our **d** may be as pillars,
Prov 30:15 The leech has two **d**, crying,
Prov 31:29 Many **d** have done well, but
Eccl 12: 4 and all the **d** of music are
Song 1: 5 O **d** of Jerusalem, like the
Song 2: 2 so is my love among the **d**
Song 2: 7 you, O **d** of Jerusalem, by the
Song 3: 5 you, O **d** of Jerusalem, by the
Song 3:10 love by the **d** of Jerusalem
Song 3:11 O **d** of Zion, and see King
Song 5: 8 O **d** of Jerusalem, if you find
Song 5:16 my friend, O **d** of Jerusalem
Song 6: 9 The **d** saw her and called her
Song 8: 4 O **d** of Jerusalem, do not stir
Is 3:16 Because the **d** of Zion are
Is 3:17 of the head of the **d** of Zion
Is 4: 4 the filth of the **d** of Zion
Is 16: 2 so shall be the **d** of Moab at
Is 32: 9 you complacent **d**, give ear to
Is 43: 6 My **d** from the ends of the
Is 49:22 your **d** shall be carried on
Is 56: 5 better than that of sons and **d**
Is 60: 4 your **d** shall be nursed at
Jer 3:24 herds, their sons and their **d**
Jer 5:17 your sons and **d** should eat
Jer 7:31 their **d** in the fire, which I
Jer 9:20 teach your **d** wailing, and
Jer 11:22 their **d** shall die by famine
Jer 14:16 wives, their sons nor their **d**
Jer 16: 2 have sons or **d** in this place
Jer 16: 3 **d** who are born in this place,
Jer 19: 9 sons and the flesh of their **d**
Jer 29: 6 Take wives and beget sons and **d**
Jer 29: 6 give your **d** to husbands, so
Jer 29: 6 that they may bear sons and **d**
Jer 32:35 their **d** to pass through the
Jer 35: 8 our wives, our sons, or our **d**
Jer 41:10 were in Mizpah, the king's **d**
Jer 43: 6 women, children, the king's **d**
Jer 48:46 captive, and your **d** captive
Jer 49: 3 Cry, you **d** of Rabbah, gird
Lam 3:51 of all the **d** of my city
Ezek 13:17 against the **d** of your people
Ezek 14:16 deliver neither sons nor **d**
Ezek 14:18 deliver neither sons nor **d**
Ezek 14:22 brought out, both sons and **d**
Ezek 16:20 you took your sons and your **d**
Ezek 16:27 the **d** of the Philistines, who
Ezek 16:46 her **d** to the north of you
Ezek 16:46 of you, is Sodom and her **d**
Ezek 16:48 nor her **d** have done as you
Ezek 16:48 as you and your **d** have done
Ezek 16:53 captives of Sodom and her **d**
Ezek 16:53 captives of Samaria and her **d**
Ezek 16:55 your sisters, Sodom and her **d**
Ezek 16:55 her **d** return to their former
Ezek 16:55 your **d** will return to your
Ezek 16:57 reproach of the **d** of Syria
Ezek 16:57 of the **d** of the Philistines,
Ezek 16:61 I will give them to you for **d**
Ezek 23: 2 women, the **d** of one mother
Ezek 23: 4 Mine, and they bore sons and **d**
Ezek 23:10 took away her sons and **d**, and
Ezek 23:25 take your sons and your **d**, and
Ezek 23:47 slay their sons and their **d**
Ezek 24:21 **d** whom you left behind shall
Ezek 24:25 minds, their sons and their **d**
Ezek 30:18 her **d** shall go into captivity
Ezek 32:16 the **d** of the nations shall
Ezek 32:18 the **d** of the famous nations,
Hos 4:13 Therefore your **d** commit
Hos 4:14 I will not punish your **d** when
Joel 2:28 your **d** shall prophesy, your
Joel 3: 8 your **d** into the hand of the
Amos 7:17 **d** shall fall by the sword
Luke 1: 5 wife was of the **d** of Aaron
Luke 23:28 **D** of Jerusalem, do not weep
Acts 2:17 your **d** shall prophesy, your
Acts 21: 9 four virgin **d** who prophesied
2Co 6:18 and you shall be My sons and **d**
1Pe 3: 6 whose **d** you are if you do

DAUGHTERS-IN-LAW (*see* DAUGHTER-IN-LAW)
Ruth 1: 6 Then she arose with her **d**
Ruth 1: 7 was, and her two **d** with her
Ruth 1: 8 And Naomi said to her two **d**

DAVID (*see* DAVID'S)
Ruth 4:17 of Jesse, the father of **D**
Ruth 4:22 begot Jesse, and Jesse begot **D**
1Sa 16:13 upon **D** from that day forward
1Sa 16:19 Send me your son **D**, who is
1Sa 16:20 them by his son **D** to Saul
1Sa 16:21 So **D** came to Saul and stood
1Sa 16:22 Please let **D** stand before me,
1Sa 16:23 that **D** would take a harp and
1Sa 17:12 Now **D** was the son of that
1Sa 17:14 **D** was the youngest
1Sa 17:15 But **D** occasionally went and
1Sa 17:17 Then Jesse said to his son **D**
1Sa 17:20 So **D** rose early in the
1Sa 17:22 **D** left his supplies in the
1Sa 17:23 So **D** heard them
1Sa 17:26 Then **D** spoke to the men who
1Sa 17:28 anger was aroused against **D**
1Sa 17:29 And **D** said, "What have I
1Sa 17:31 which **D** spoke were heard,
1Sa 17:32 Then **D** said to Saul, "Let no
1Sa 17:33 And Saul said to **D**, "You are
1Sa 17:34 But **D** said to Saul, "Your
1Sa 17:37 Moreover **D** said, "The LORD,
1Sa 17:37 And Saul said to **D**, "Go, and
1Sa 17:38 Saul clothed **D** with his armor
1Sa 17:39 **D** fastened his sword to his
1Sa 17:39 And **D** said to Saul,
1Sa 17:39 So **D** took them off
1Sa 17:41 and began drawing near to **D**
1Sa 17:42 looked about and saw **D**, he
1Sa 17:43 So the Philistine said to **D**

1Sa 17:43 cursed **D** by his gods
1Sa 17:44 And the Philistine said to **D**
1Sa 17:45 Then **D** said to the Philistine
1Sa 17:48 came and drew near to meet **D**
1Sa 17:48 that **D** hastened and ran toward
1Sa 17:49 Then **D** put his hand in his
1Sa 17:50 So **D** prevailed over the
1Sa 17:50 was no sword in the hand of **D**
1Sa 17:51 Therefore **D** ran and stood over
1Sa 17:54 And **D** took the head of the
1Sa 17:55 Now when Saul saw **D** going out
1Sa 17:57 Then, as **D** returned from the
1Sa 17:58 And **D** answered, "I am the son
1Sa 18: 1 was knit to the soul of **D**
1Sa 18: 3 **D** made a covenant, because he
1Sa 18: 4 was on him and gave it to **D**
1Sa 18: 5 So **D** went out wherever Saul
1Sa 18: 6 when **D** was returning from the
1Sa 18: 7 and **D** his ten thousands
1Sa 18: 8 ascribed to **D** ten thousands
1Sa 18: 9 So Saul eyed **D** from that day
1Sa 18:10 So **D** played music with his
1Sa 18:11 I will pin **D** to the wall with
1Sa 18:11 But **D** escaped his presence
1Sa 18:12 Now Saul was afraid of **D**,
1Sa 18:14 **D** behaved wisely in all his
1Sa 18:16 all Israel and Judah loved **D**
1Sa 18:17 Then Saul said to **D**, "Here
1Sa 18:18 So **D** said to Saul, "Who am I
1Sa 18:19 should have been given to **D**
1Sa 18:20 Saul's daughter, loved **D**
1Sa 18:21 Saul said to **D** a second time
1Sa 18:22 Communicate with **D** secretly
1Sa 18:23 words in the hearing of **D**
1Sa 18:23 And **D** said, "Does it seem
1Sa 18:24 In this manner **D** spoke
1Sa 18:25 Thus you shall say to **D**
1Sa 18:25 **D** fall by the hand of the
1Sa 18:26 servants told **D** these words
1Sa 18:26 it pleased **D** well to become
1Sa 18:27 therefore **D** arose and went, he
1Sa 18:27 **D** brought their foreskins, and
1Sa 18:28 knew that the LORD was with **D**
1Sa 18:29 was still more afraid of **D**
1Sa 18:30 that **D** behaved more wisely
1Sa 19: 1 that they should kill **D**
1Sa 19: 1 son, delighted much in **D**
1Sa 19: 2 So Jonathan told **D**, saying
1Sa 19: 4 well of **D** to Saul his father
1Sa 19: 4 his servant, against **D**,
1Sa 19: 5 to kill **D** without a cause
1Sa 19: 7 Then Jonathan called **D**, and
1Sa 19: 7 So Jonathan brought **D** to Saul
1Sa 19: 8 **D** went out and fought with the
1Sa 19: 9 **D** was playing music with his
1Sa 19:10 Then Saul sought to pin **D** to
1Sa 19:10 So **D** fled and escaped that
1Sa 19:12 So Michal let **D** down through
1Sa 19:14 sent messengers to take **D**
1Sa 19:15 the messengers back to see **D**
1Sa 19:18 So **D** fled and escaped, and went
1Sa 19:19 note, **D** is at Naioth in Ramah
1Sa 19:20 sent messengers to take **D**
1Sa 19:22 Where are Samuel and **D**
1Sa 20: 1 Then **D** fled from Naioth in
1Sa 20: 3 Then **D** took an oath again, and
1Sa 20: 4 So Jonathan said to **D**
1Sa 20: 5 And **D** said to Jonathan,
1Sa 20: 6 **D** earnestly asked permission
1Sa 20:10 Then **D** said to Jonathan
1Sa 20:11 And Jonathan said to **D**, "Come
1Sa 20:12 Then Jonathan said to **D**
1Sa 20:12 indeed there is good toward **D**
1Sa 20:15 **D** from the face of the earth
1Sa 20:16 covenant with the house of **D**
1Sa 20:17 again caused **D** to vow,
1Sa 20:18 Then Jonathan said to **D**
1Sa 20:24 So **D** hid in the field
1Sa 20:28 **D** earnestly asked permission
1Sa 20:33 by his father to kill **D**
1Sa 20:34 for he was grieved for **D**
1Sa 20:35 at the time appointed with **D**
1Sa 20:39 and **D** knew of the matter
1Sa 20:41 **D** arose from a place toward
1Sa 20:41 wept together, but **D** more so
1Sa 20:42 Then Jonathan said to **D**, "Go
1Sa 21: 1 Now **D** came to Nob, to
1Sa 21: 1 was afraid when he met **D**, and
1Sa 21: 2 So **D** said to Ahimelech the
1Sa 21: 4 And the priest answered **D** and
1Sa 21: 5 Then **D** answered the priest,
1Sa 21: 8 And **D** said to Ahimelech,
1Sa 21: 9 And **D** said, "There is none
1Sa 21:10 Then **D** arose and fled that day
1Sa 21:11 Is this not **D** the king of the
1Sa 21:11 and **D** his ten thousands'
1Sa 21:12 Now **D** took these words to
1Sa 22: 1 **D** therefore departed from
1Sa 22: 3 Then **D** went from there to
1Sa 22: 4 that **D** was in the stronghold
1Sa 22: 5 the prophet Gad said to **D**
1Sa 22: 5 So **D** departed and went into
1Sa 22: 6 When Saul heard that **D** and the
1Sa 22:14 servants is so faithful as **D**
1Sa 22:17 their hand also is with **D**
1Sa 22:20 escaped and fled after **D**
1Sa 22:21 Abiathar told **D** that Saul had
1Sa 22:22 So **D** said to Abiathar, "I
1Sa 23: 1 Then they told **D**, saying
1Sa 23: 2 Therefore **D** inquired of the
1Sa 23: 2 And the LORD said to **D**, "Go
1Sa 23: 4 Then **D** inquired of the LORD
1Sa 23: 5 And **D** and his men went to
1Sa 23: 5 So **D** saved the inhabitants of
1Sa 23: 6 Ahimelech fled to **D** at Keilah
1Sa 23: 7 that **D** had gone to Keilah
1Sa 23: 8 down to Keilah to besiege **D**
1Sa 23: 9 When **D** knew that Saul plotted
1Sa 23:10 Then **D** said, "O LORD God of
1Sa 23:12 Then **D** said, "Will the men
1Sa 23:13 So **D** and his men, about six
1Sa 23:13 **D** had escaped from Keilah
1Sa 23:14 **D** stayed in strongholds in
1Sa 23:15 So **D** saw that Saul had come
1Sa 23:15 **D** was in the Wilderness of
1Sa 23:16 went to **D** in the woods and
1Sa 23:18 **D** stayed in the woods, and
1Sa 23:19 Is **D** not hiding with us in
1Sa 23:24 But **D** and his men were in the
1Sa 23:25 went to seek him, they told **D**
1Sa 23:25 that, he pursued **D** in the
1Sa 23:26 side of the mountain, and **D**
1Sa 23:26 So **D** made haste to get away
1Sa 23:26 and his men were encircling **D**
1Sa 23:28 Saul returned from pursuing **D**
1Sa 23:29 Then **D** went up from there and
1Sa 24: 1 **D** is in the Wilderness of En
1Sa 24: 2 all Israel, and went to seek **D**
1Sa 24: 3 (**D** and his men were staying in
1Sa 24: 4 Then the men of **D** said to him
1Sa 24: 4 **D** arose and secretly cut off a
1Sa 24: 7 So **D** restrained his servants
1Sa 24: 8 **D** also arose afterward, went
1Sa 24: 8 **D** stooped with his face to
1Sa 24: 9 And **D** said to Saul
1Sa 24: 9 Indeed **D** seeks your harm'
1Sa 24:16 when **D** had finished speaking
1Sa 24:16 Is this your voice, my son **D**
1Sa 24:17 Then he said to **D**
1Sa 24:22 So **D** swore to Saul
1Sa 24:22 And Saul went home, but **D** and
1Sa 25: 1 **D** arose and went down to the
1Sa 25: 4 When **D** heard in the
1Sa 25: 5 **D** sent ten young men
1Sa 25: 5 and **D** said to the young men,
1Sa 25: 8 servants and to your son **D**
1Sa 25: 9 these words in the name of **D**
1Sa 25:10 Who is **D**, and who is the son
1Sa 25:13 Then **D** said to his men
1Sa 25:13 **D** also girded on his sword
1Sa 25:13 four hundred men went with **D**
1Sa 25:14 **D** sent messengers from the
1Sa 25:20 and there were **D** and his men,
1Sa 25:21 Now **D** had said, "Surely in
1Sa 25:22 also, to the enemies of **D**
1Sa 25:23 Now when Abigail saw **D**, she
1Sa 25:23 fell on her face before **D**
1Sa 25:32 Then **D** said to Abigail
1Sa 25:35 So **D** received from her hand
1Sa 25:39 So when **D** heard that Nabal
1Sa 25:39 **D** sent and proposed to Abigail
1Sa 25:40 when the servants of **D** had
1Sa 25:40 **D** sent us to you, to ask you
1Sa 25:42 followed the messengers of **D**
1Sa 25:43 **D** also took Ahinoam of
1Sa 26: 1 Is **D** not hiding in the hill
1Sa 26: 2 to seek **D** in the Wilderness
1Sa 26: 3 But **D** stayed in the
1Sa 26: 4 **D** therefore sent out spies,
1Sa 26: 5 So **D** arose and came to the
1Sa 26: 5 **D** saw the place where Saul
1Sa 26: 6 Then **D** answered, and said to
1Sa 26: 7 So **D** and Abishai came to the
1Sa 26: 8 Then Abishai said to **D**, "God
1Sa 26: 9 And **D** said to Abishai,
1Sa 26:10 **D** said furthermore, "As the
1Sa 26:12 So **D** took the spear and the
1Sa 26:13 Then **D** went over to the other
1Sa 26:14 **D** called out to the people and
1Sa 26:15 So **D** said to Abner, "Are you
1Sa 26:17 Is that your voice, my son **D**
1Sa 26:17 And **D** said, "It is my voice
1Sa 26:21 Return, my son **D**
1Sa 26:22 And **D** answered and said,
1Sa 26:25 Then Saul said to **D**, May
1Sa 26:25 May you be blessed, my son **D**
1Sa 26:25 So **D** went on his way, and
1Sa 27: 1 And **D** said in his heart,
1Sa 27: 2 Then **D** arose and went over
1Sa 27: 3 So **D** dwelt with Achish at
1Sa 27: 3 **D** with his two wives, Ahinoam
1Sa 27: 4 Saul that **D** had fled to Gath
1Sa 27: 5 Then **D** said to Achish, "If I
1Sa 27: 7 Now the time that **D** dwelt in
1Sa 27: 8 And **D** and his men went up and
1Sa 27: 9 Whenever **D** attacked the land,
1Sa 27:10 And **D** would say,
1Sa 27:11 **D** would save neither man nor
1Sa 27:11 on us, saying, "Thus **D** did
1Sa 27:12 So Achish believed **D**, saying,
1Sa 28: 1 And Achish said to **D**, "You
1Sa 28: 2 And **D** said to Achish,
1Sa 28: 2 And Achish said to **D**
1Sa 28:17 to your neighbor, namely, **D**
1Sa 29: 2 and by thousands, but **D** and his
1Sa 29: 3 Is this not **D**, the servant of
1Sa 29: 5 Is this not **D**, of whom they
1Sa 29: 5 and **D** his ten thousands'
1Sa 29: 6 Then Achish called **D** and said
1Sa 29: 8 Then **D** said to Achish, "But
1Sa 29: 9 Achish answered and said to **D**
1Sa 29:11 So **D** and his men rose early to
1Sa 30: 1 Now it happened, when **D** and
1Sa 30: 3 So **D** and his men came to the
1Sa 30: 4 **D** and the people who were
1Sa 30: 6 Then **D** was greatly distressed
1Sa 30: 6 But **D** strengthened himself in
1Sa 30: 7 Then **D** said to Abiathar the
1Sa 30: 7 brought the ephod to **D**
1Sa 30: 8 So **D** inquired of the LORD,
1Sa 30: 9 So **D** went, he and the six
1Sa 30:10 But **D** pursued, he and four
1Sa 30:11 field, and brought him to **D**
1Sa 30:13 Then **D** said to him, "To whom
1Sa 30:15 And **D** said to him,
1Sa 30:17 **D** attacked them from twilight
1Sa 30:18 So **D** recovered all that the
1Sa 30:18 and **D** rescued his two wives
1Sa 30:19 **D** recovered all
1Sa 30:20 Then **D** took all the flocks and
1Sa 30:21 Now **D** came to the two hundred
1Sa 30:21 that they could not follow **D**
1Sa 30:21 So they went out to meet **D**
1Sa 30:21 when **D** came near the people,
1Sa 30:22 who went with **D** answered and
1Sa 30:23 But **D** said, "My brethren,
1Sa 30:26 Now when **D** came to Ziklag, he
1Sa 30:31 the places where **D** himself
2Sa 1: 1 when **D** had returned from the
2Sa 1: 1 and **D** had stayed two days in
2Sa 1: 2 So it was, when he came to **D**
2Sa 1: 3 And **D** said to him,
2Sa 1: 4 Then **D** said to him, "How did
2Sa 1: 5 So **D** said to the young man
2Sa 1:11 Then **D** took hold of his own
2Sa 1:13 Then **D** said to the young man
2Sa 1:14 And **D** said to him,
2Sa 1:15 Then **D** called one of the
2Sa 1:16 So **D** said to him, "Your
2Sa 1:17 Then **D** lamented with this
2Sa 2: 1 that **D** inquired of the LORD
2Sa 2: 1 **D** said, "Where shall I go up
2Sa 2: 2 So **D** went up there, and his
2Sa 2: 3 **D** brought up the men who were
2Sa 2: 4 there they anointed **D** king
2Sa 2: 4 And they told **D**, saying, "The
2Sa 2: 5 So **D** sent messengers to the
2Sa 2:10 the house of Judah followed **D**
2Sa 2:11 the time that **D** was king in
2Sa 2:13 Zeruiah, and the servants of **D**

2Sa 2:15 twelve from the servants of **D**
2Sa 2:17 before the servants of **D**
2Sa 2:31 servants of **D** had struck down
2Sa 3: 1 of Saul and the house of **D**
2Sa 3: 1 But **D** grew stronger and
2Sa 3: 2 Sons were born to **D** in Hebron
2Sa 3: 5 were born to **D** in Hebron
2Sa 3: 6 of Saul and the house of **D**
2Sa 3: 8 you into the hand of **D**
2Sa 3: 9 if I do not do for **D** as the
2Sa 3:10 the throne of **D** over Israel
2Sa 3:12 messengers on his behalf to **D**
2Sa 3:13 And **D** said, "Good, I will
2Sa 3:14 So **D** sent messengers to
2Sa 3:17 for **D** to be king over you
2Sa 3:18 For the LORD has spoken of **D**
2Sa 3:18 By the hand of My servant **D**
2Sa 3:19 **D** in Hebron all that seemed
2Sa 3:20 with him came to **D** at Hebron
2Sa 3:20 **D** made a feast for Abner and
2Sa 3:21 Then Abner said to **D**, "I
2Sa 3:21 So **D** sent Abner away, and he
2Sa 3:22 that moment the servants of **D**
2Sa 3:22 was not with **D** in Hebron, for
2Sa 3:26 But **D** did not know it
2Sa 3:28 when **D** heard it, he said,
2Sa 3:31 Then **D** said to Joab and to all
2Sa 3:31 King **D** followed the coffin
2Sa 3:35 **D** to eat food while it was
2Sa 3:35 day, **D** took an oath, saying,
2Sa 4: 8 of Ishbosheth to **D** at Hebron
2Sa 4: 9 Then **D** answered Rechab and
2Sa 4:12 So **D** commanded his young
2Sa 5: 1 of Israel came to **D** at Hebron
2Sa 5: 3 King **D** made a covenant with
2Sa 5: 3 they anointed **D** king over
2Sa 5: 4 **D** was thirty years old when
2Sa 5: 6 of the land, who spoke to **D**
2Sa 5: 6 **D** cannot come in here
2Sa 5: 7 Nevertheless **D** took the
2Sa 5: 7 Zion (that is, the City of **D**)
2Sa 5: 8 Now **D** said on that day
2Sa 5: 9 So **D** dwelt in the stronghold,
2Sa 5: 9 and called it the City of **D**
2Sa 5: 9 Then **D** built all around from
2Sa 5:10 So **D** went on and became great,
2Sa 5:11 of Tyre sent messengers to **D**
2Sa 5:11 And they built **D** a house
2Sa 5:12 So **D** knew that the LORD had
2Sa 5:13 **D** took more concubines and
2Sa 5:13 and daughters were born to **D**
2Sa 5:17 anointed **D** king over Israel
2Sa 5:17 went up to search for **D**
2Sa 5:17 **D** heard of it and went down to
2Sa 5:19 And **D** inquired of the LORD,
2Sa 5:19 And the LORD said to **D**, "Go
2Sa 5:20 So **D** went to Baal Perazim, and
2Sa 5:20 and **D** defeated them there
2Sa 5:21 left their images there, and **D**
2Sa 5:23 when **D** inquired of the LORD,
2Sa 5:25 And **D** did so, as the LORD
2Sa 6: 1 Again **D** gathered all the
2Sa 6: 2 **D** arose and went with all the
2Sa 6: 5 Then **D** and all the house of
2Sa 6: 8 **D** became angry because of the
2Sa 6: 9 **D** was afraid of the LORD that
2Sa 6:10 So **D** would not move the ark
2Sa 6:10 with him into the City of **D**
2Sa 6:10 but **D** took it aside into the
2Sa 6:12 And it was told King **D**, saying
2Sa 6:12 So **D** went and brought up the
2Sa 6:12 the City of **D** with gladness
2Sa 6:14 Then **D** danced before the LORD
2Sa 6:14 **D** was wearing a linen ephod
2Sa 6:15 So **D** and all the house of
2Sa 6:16 LORD came into the City of **D**
2Sa 6:16 window and saw King **D** leaping
2Sa 6:17 that **D** had erected for it
2Sa 6:17 Then **D** offered burnt
2Sa 6:18 when **D** had finished offering
2Sa 6:20 Then **D** returned to bless his
2Sa 6:20 of Saul came out to meet **D**
2Sa 6:21 So **D** said to Michal, "It was
2Sa 7: 5 Go and tell My servant **D**
2Sa 7: 8 shall you say to My servant **D**
2Sa 7:17 vision, so Nathan spoke to **D**
2Sa 7:18 Then King **D** went in and sat
2Sa 7:20 what more can **D** say to You
2Sa 7:26 **D** be established before You
2Sa 8: 1 **D** attacked the Philistines
2Sa 8: 1 **D** took Metheg Ammah from
2Sa 8: 3 **D** also defeated Hadadezer the
2Sa 8: 4 **D** took from him one thousand
2Sa 8: 4 Also **D** hamstrung all the
2Sa 8: 5 **D** killed twenty-two thousand
2Sa 8: 6 Then **D** put garrisons in Syria
2Sa 8: 6 preserved **D** wherever he went
2Sa 8: 7 **D** took the shields of gold
2Sa 8: 8 King **D** took a large amount of
2Sa 8: 9 **D** had defeated all the army
2Sa 8:10 sent Joram his son to King **D**
2Sa 8:11 King **D** dedicated these to the
2Sa 8:13 **D** made himself a name when he
2Sa 8:14 preserved **D** wherever he went
2Sa 8:15 So **D** reigned over all Israel
2Sa 8:15 **D** administered judgment and
2Sa 9: 1 Now **D** said, "Is there still
2Sa 9: 2 when they had called him to **D**
2Sa 9: 5 Then King **D** sent and brought
2Sa 9: 6 son of Saul, had come to **D**
2Sa 9: 6 Then **D** said, "Mephibosheth
2Sa 9: 7 So **D** said to him, "Do not
2Sa 10: 2 Then **D** said, "I will show
2Sa 10: 2 So **D** sent by the hand of
2Sa 10: 3 Do you think that **D** really
2Sa 10: 3 Has **D** not rather sent his
2Sa 10: 5 When they told **D**, he sent to
2Sa 10: 6 themselves repulsive to **D**
2Sa 10: 7 Now when **D** heard of it, he
2Sa 10:17 When it was told **D**, he
2Sa 10:17 in battle array against **D**
2Sa 10:18 and **D** killed seven hundred
2Sa 11: 1 that **D** sent Joab and his
2Sa 11: 1 But **D** remained at Jerusalem
2Sa 11: 2 that **D** arose from his bed
2Sa 11: 3 So **D** sent and inquired about
2Sa 11: 4 Then **D** sent messengers, and
2Sa 11: 5 so she sent and told **D**, and
2Sa 11: 6 Then **D** sent to Joab, saying,
2Sa 11: 6 And Joab sent Uriah to **D**
2Sa 11: 7 **D** asked how Joab was doing,
2Sa 11: 8 And **D** said to Uriah,
2Sa 11:10 So when they told **D**, saying,
2Sa 11:10 his house," **D** said to Uriah,
2Sa 11:11 And Uriah said to **D**, "The ark
2Sa 11:12 Then **D** said to Uriah, "Wait
2Sa 11:13 Now when **D** called him, he ate
2Sa 11:14 that **D** wrote a letter to Joab
2Sa 11:17 of the servants of **D** fell
2Sa 11:18 sent and told **D** all the things
2Sa 11:22 told **D** all that Joab had sent
2Sa 11:23 And the messenger said to **D**
2Sa 11:25 Then **D** said to the messenger,
2Sa 11:27 **D** sent and brought her to his
2Sa 11:27 But the thing that **D** had done
2Sa 12: 1 the LORD sent Nathan to **D**
2Sa 12: 7 Then Nathan said to **D**, "You
2Sa 12:13 Then **D** said to Nathan, "I
2Sa 12:13 And Nathan said to **D**, "The
2Sa 12:15 that Uriah's wife bore to **D**
2Sa 12:16 **D** therefore pleaded with God
2Sa 12:16 **D** fasted and went in and lay
2Sa 12:18 the servants of **D** were afraid
2Sa 12:19 When **D** saw that his servants
2Sa 12:19 **D** perceived that the child
2Sa 12:19 Therefore **D** said to his
2Sa 12:20 So **D** arose from the ground,
2Sa 12:24 Then **D** comforted Bathsheba
2Sa 12:27 And Joab sent messengers to **D**
2Sa 12:29 So **D** gathered all the people
2Sa 12:31 Then **D** and all the people
2Sa 13: 1 son of **D** had a lovely sister
2Sa 13: 1 Amnon the son of **D** loved her
2Sa 13: 7 **D** sent home to Tamar, saying,
2Sa 13:21 But when King **D** heard of all
2Sa 13:30 the way, that news came to **D**
2Sa 13:37 **D** mourned for his son every
2Sa 13:39 And King **D** longed to go to
2Sa 15:13 And a messenger came to **D**,
2Sa 15:14 So **D** said to all his servants
2Sa 15:22 So **D** said to Ittai, "Go, and
2Sa 15:30 So **D** went up by the ascent of
2Sa 15:31 Then someone told **D**, saying,
2Sa 15:31 And **D** said, "O LORD, I pray
2Sa 15:32 Now it happened when **D** had
2Sa 15:33 **D** said to him, "If you go on
2Sa 16: 1 When **D** was a little past the
2Sa 16: 5 Now when King **D** came to
2Sa 16: 6 And he threw stones at **D** and at
2Sa 16: 6 at all the servants of King **D**
2Sa 16:10 has said to him, "Curse **D**
2Sa 16:11 **D** said to Abishai and all his
2Sa 16:13 And as **D** and his men went
2Sa 16:23 of Ahithophel both with **D**
2Sa 17: 1 arise and pursue **D** tonight
2Sa 17:16 send quickly and tell **D**,
2Sa 17:17 they would go and tell King **D**
2Sa 17:21 well and went and told King **D**
2Sa 17:21 and said to **D**, "Arise and
2Sa 17:22 So **D** and all the people who
2Sa 17:24 Then **D** went to Mahanaim
2Sa 17:27 when **D** had come to Mahanaim,
2Sa 17:29 and cheese of the herd, for **D**
2Sa 18: 1 **D** numbered the people who
2Sa 18: 2 Then **D** sent out one third of
2Sa 18: 7 before the servants of **D**, and
2Sa 18: 9 Absalom met the servants of **D**
2Sa 18:24 Now **D** was sitting between the
2Sa 19:11 Then King **D** sent to Zadok and
2Sa 19:16 men of Judah to meet King **D**
2Sa 19:22 And **D** said, "What have I
2Sa 19:43 have more right to **D** than you
2Sa 20: 1 We have no part in **D**, nor do
2Sa 20: 2 man of Israel deserted **D**, and
2Sa 20: 3 Now **D** came to his house at
2Sa 20: 5 which **D** had appointed him
2Sa 20: 6 And **D** said to Abishai,
2Sa 20:11 Joab and whoever is for **D**, let
2Sa 20:21 against the king, against **D**
2Sa 20:26 was a chief minister under **D**
2Sa 21: 1 the days of **D** for three years
2Sa 21: 1 and **D** inquired of the LORD
2Sa 21: 3 Therefore **D** said to the
2Sa 21: 7 was between them, between **D**
2Sa 21:11 **D** was told what Rizpah the
2Sa 21:12 Then **D** went and took the bones
2Sa 21:15 at war again with Israel, **D**
2Sa 21:15 and **D** grew faint
2Sa 21:16 thought he could kill **D**
2Sa 21:17 the men of **D** swore to him
2Sa 21:21 of Shimeah, the brother of **D**
2Sa 21:22 and fell by the hand of **D**
2Sa 22: 1 Then **D** spoke to the LORD the
2Sa 22:51 mercy to His anointed, to **D**
2Sa 23: 1 these are the last words of **D**
2Sa 23: 1 Thus says **D** the son of Jesse
2Sa 23: 8 of the mighty men whom **D** had
2Sa 23: 9 with **D** when they defied the
2Sa 23:13 and came to **D** at the cave of
2Sa 23:14 **D** was then in the stronghold,
2Sa 23:15 And **D** said with longing,
2Sa 23:16 and took it and brought it to **D**
2Sa 23:23 And **D** appointed him over his
2Sa 24: 1 He moved **D** against them to
2Sa 24:10 So **D** said to the LORD,
2Sa 24:11 Now when **D** arose in the
2Sa 24:12 Go and tell **D**, 'Thus says the
2Sa 24:13 So Gad came to **D** and told him
2Sa 24:14 And **D** said to Gad,
2Sa 24:17 Then **D** spoke to the LORD when
2Sa 24:18 And Gad came that day to **D**
2Sa 24:19 So **D**, according to the word
2Sa 24:21 And **D** said, "To buy the
2Sa 24:22 Now Araunah said to **D**, "Let
2Sa 24:24 So **D** bought the threshing
2Sa 24:25 **D** built there an altar to the
1Ki 1: 1 Now King **D** was old, advanced
1Ki 1: 8 to **D** were not with Adonijah
1Ki 1:11 **D** our lord does not know it
1Ki 1:13 Go immediately to King **D** and
1Ki 1:28 Then King **D** answered and said,
1Ki 1:31 my lord King **D** live forever
1Ki 1:32 And King **D** said, "Call to me
1Ki 1:37 the throne of my lord King **D**
1Ki 1:43 Our lord King **D** has made
1Ki 1:47 gone to bless our lord King **D**
1Ki 2: 1 Then the days of **D** drew near
1Ki 2:10 So **D** rested with his fathers,
1Ki 2:10 was buried in the City of **D**
1Ki 2:11 The period that **D** reigned
1Ki 2:12 on the throne of his father **D**
1Ki 2:24 on the throne of **D** my father
1Ki 2:26 Lord GOD before my father **D**
1Ki 2:32 my father **D** did not know it
1Ki 2:33 But upon **D** and his descendants
1Ki 2:44 that you did to my father **D**
1Ki 2:45 and the throne of **D** shall be
1Ki 3: 1 of **D** until he had finished
1Ki 3: 3 the statutes of his father **D**
1Ki 3: 6 to your servant **D** my father

1Ki 3: 7 king instead of my father **D**
1Ki 3:14 as your father **D** walked,
1Ki 5: 1 for Hiram had always loved **D**
1Ki 5: 3 You know how my father **D**
1Ki 5: 5 the LORD spoke to my father **D**
1Ki 5: 7 for He has given **D** a wise son
1Ki 6:12 I spoke to your father **D**
1Ki 7:51 his father **D** had dedicated
1Ki 8: 1 the LORD from the City of **D**
1Ki 8:15 with His mouth to my father **D**
1Ki 8:16 but I chose **D** to be over My
1Ki 8:17 **D** to build a house for the
1Ki 8:18 the LORD said to my father **D**
1Ki 8:20 the position of my father **D**
1Ki 8:24 Your servant **D** my father
1Ki 8:25 Your servant **D** my father,
1Ki 8:26 to Your servant **D** my father
1Ki 8:66 had done for His servant **D**
1Ki 9: 4 Me as your father **D** walked
1Ki 9: 5 as I promised **D** your father
1Ki 9:24 came up from the City of **D** to
1Ki 11: 4 was the heart of his father **D**
1Ki 11: 6 the LORD, as did his father **D**
1Ki 11:12 for the sake of your father **D**
1Ki 11:13 for the sake of my servant **D**
1Ki 11:15 when **D** was in Edom, and Joab
1Ki 11:21 **D** rested with his fathers
1Ki 11:24 when **D** killed those of Zobah
1Ki 11:27 to the City of **D** his father
1Ki 11:32 for the sake of My servant **D**
1Ki 11:33 as did his father **D**
1Ki 11:34 for the sake of My servant **D**
1Ki 11:36 that My servant **D** may always
1Ki 11:38 as My servant **D** did, then I
1Ki 11:38 house, as I built for **D**, and
1Ki 11:39 of **D** because of this, but not
1Ki 11:43 in the City of **D** his father
1Ki 12:16 What portion have we in **D**
1Ki 12:16 see to your own house, O **D**
1Ki 12:19 the house of **D** to this day
1Ki 12:20 who followed the house of **D**
1Ki 12:26 may return to the house of **D**
1Ki 13: 2 be born to the house of **D**
1Ki 14: 8 away from the house of **D**, and
1Ki 14: 8 have not been as My servant **D**
1Ki 14:31 his fathers in the City of **D**
1Ki 15: 3 was the heart of his father **D**
1Ki 15: 5 because **D** did what was right
1Ki 15: 8 buried him in the City of **D**
1Ki 15:11 the LORD, as did his father **D**
1Ki 15:24 in the City of **D** his father
1Ki 22:50 in the City of **D** his father
2Ki 8:19 for the sake of his servant **D**
2Ki 8:24 his fathers in the City of **D**
2Ki 9:28 his fathers in the City of **D**
2Ki 11:10 which had belonged to King **D**
2Ki 12:21 his fathers in the City of **D**
2Ki 14: 3 yet not like his father **D**
2Ki 14:20 his fathers in the City of **D**
2Ki 15: 7 his fathers in the City of **D**
2Ki 15:38 in the City of **D** his father
2Ki 16: 2 God, as his father **D** had done
2Ki 16:20 his fathers in the City of **D**
2Ki 17:21 Israel from the house of **D**
2Ki 18: 3 that his father **D** had done
2Ki 20: 5 the God of **D** your father
2Ki 20: 6 for the sake of My servant **D**
2Ki 21: 7 which the LORD had said to **D**
2Ki 22: 2 all the ways of his father **D**
1Ch 2:15 the sixth, and **D** the seventh
1Ch 3: 1 of **D** who were born to him in
1Ch 3: 9 These were all the sons of **D**
1Ch 4:31 cities until the reign of **D**
1Ch 6:31 **D** appointed over the service
1Ch 7: 2 **D** was twenty-two thousand six
1Ch 9:22 **D** and Samuel the seer had
1Ch 10:14 over to **D** the son of Jesse
1Ch 11: 1 came together to **D** at Hebron
1Ch 11: 3 **D** made a covenant with them
1Ch 11: 3 anointed **D** king over Israel
1Ch 11: 4 And **D** and all Israel went to
1Ch 11: 5 of Jebus said to **D**, "You
1Ch 11: 5 Nevertheless **D** took the
1Ch 11: 5 Zion (that is, the City of **D**)
1Ch 11: 6 Now **D** said, "Whoever attacks
1Ch 11: 7 Then **D** dwelt in the
1Ch 11: 7 they called it the City of **D**
1Ch 11: 9 Then **D** went on and became
1Ch 11:10 of the mighty men whom **D** had
1Ch 11:11 of the mighty men whom **D** had
1Ch 11:13 He was with **D** at Pasdammim
1Ch 11:15 went down to the rock to **D**
1Ch 11:16 **D** was then in the stronghold,
1Ch 11:17 And **D** said with longing,
1Ch 11:18 and took it and brought it to **D**
1Ch 11:18 Nevertheless **D** would not
1Ch 11:25 And **D** appointed him over his
1Ch 12: 1 to **D** at Ziklag while he was
1Ch 12: 8 Some Gadites joined **D** at the
1Ch 12:16 and Judah came to **D** at the
1Ch 12:17 **D** went out to meet them, and
1Ch 12:18 We are yours, O **D**
1Ch 12:18 So **D** received them, and made
1Ch 12:19 from Manasseh defected to **D**
1Ch 12:21 they helped **D** against the
1Ch 12:22 to **D** day by day to help him
1Ch 12:23 came to **D** at Hebron to turn
1Ch 12:31 name to come and make **D** king
1Ch 12:38 to make **D** king over all
1Ch 12:38 of one mind to make **D** king
1Ch 12:39 were there with **D** three days
1Ch 13: 1 Then **D** consulted with the
1Ch 13: 2 And **D** said to all the
1Ch 13: 5 So **D** gathered all Israel
1Ch 13: 6 And **D** and all Israel went up to
1Ch 13: 8 Then **D** and all Israel played
1Ch 13:11 **D** became angry because of the
1Ch 13:12 **D** was afraid of God that day,
1Ch 13:13 **D** would not move the ark with
1Ch 13:13 with him into the City of **D**
1Ch 14: 1 of Tyre sent messengers to **D**
1Ch 14: 2 **D** perceived that the LORD had
1Ch 14: 3 Then **D** took more wives in
1Ch 14: 3 and **D** begot more sons and
1Ch 14: 8 the Philistines heard that **D**
1Ch 14: 8 went up to search for **D**
1Ch 14: 8 **D** heard of it and went out
1Ch 14:10 **D** inquired of God, saying,
1Ch 14:11 and **D** defeated them there
1Ch 14:11 Then **D** said, "God has broken
1Ch 14:12 **D** gave a commandment, and
1Ch 14:14 Therefore **D** inquired again of
1Ch 14:16 So **D** did as God commanded
1Ch 14:17 Then the fame of **D** went out
1Ch 15: 1 **D** built houses for himself in
1Ch 15: 1 for himself in the City of **D**
1Ch 15: 2 Then **D** said, "No one may
1Ch 15: 3 And **D** gathered all Israel
1Ch 15: 4 Then **D** assembled the children
1Ch 15:11 And **D** called for Zadok and
1Ch 15:16 Then **D** spoke to the leaders
1Ch 15:25 So **D**, the elders of Israel,
1Ch 15:27 **D** was clothed with a robe of
1Ch 15:27 **D** also wore a linen ephod
1Ch 15:29 LORD came to the City of **D**
1Ch 15:29 a window, saw King **D** whirling
1Ch 16: 1 that **D** had erected for it
1Ch 16: 2 when **D** had finished offering
1Ch 16: 7 on that day **D** first delivered
1Ch 16:43 **D** returned to bless his house
1Ch 17: 1 when **D** was dwelling in his
1Ch 17: 1 that **D** said to Nathan the
1Ch 17: 2 Then Nathan said to **D**, "Do
1Ch 17: 4 Go and tell My servant **D**
1Ch 17: 7 shall you say to My servant **D**
1Ch 17:15 so did Nathan speak to **D**
1Ch 17:16 Then King **D** went in and sat
1Ch 17:18 What more can **D** say to You
1Ch 17:24 **D** be established before You
1Ch 18: 1 **D** attacked the Philistines
1Ch 18: 3 **D** defeated Hadadezer king of
1Ch 18: 4 **D** took from him one thousand
1Ch 18: 4 And **D** also hamstrung all the
1Ch 18: 5 **D** killed twenty-two thousand
1Ch 18: 6 Then **D** put garrisons in Syria
1Ch 18: 6 preserved **D** wherever he went
1Ch 18: 7 **D** took the shields of gold
1Ch 18: 8 **D** brought a large amount of
1Ch 18: 9 **D** had defeated all the army
1Ch 18:10 Hadoram his son to King **D**
1Ch 18:11 King **D** also dedicated these
1Ch 18:13 preserved **D** wherever he went
1Ch 18:14 So **D** reigned over all Israel,
1Ch 19: 2 Then **D** said, "I will show
1Ch 19: 2 So **D** sent messengers to
1Ch 19: 2 the servants of **D** came to
1Ch 19: 3 Do you think that **D** really
1Ch 19: 5 went and told **D** about the men
1Ch 19: 6 themselves repulsive to **D**
1Ch 19: 8 when **D** heard of it, he sent
1Ch 19:17 When it was told **D**, he
1Ch 19:17 So when **D** had set up in
1Ch 19:18 and **D** killed seven thousand
1Ch 19:19 they made peace with **D** and
1Ch 20: 1 But **D** stayed at Jerusalem
1Ch 20: 2 Then **D** took their king's
1Ch 20: 3 So **D** did to all the cities of
1Ch 20: 3 Then **D** and all the people
1Ch 20: 8 and they fell by the hand of **D**
1Ch 21: 1 and moved **D** to number Israel
1Ch 21: 2 So **D** said to Joab and to the
1Ch 21: 5 the number of the people to **D**
1Ch 21: 8 So **D** said to God, "I have
1Ch 21:10 Go and tell **D**, saying, "Thus
1Ch 21:11 So Gad came to **D** and said to
1Ch 21:13 And **D** said to Gad,
1Ch 21:16 Then **D** lifted his eyes and saw
1Ch 21:16 So **D** and the elders, clothed
1Ch 21:17 And **D** said to God,
1Ch 21:18 say to **D** that **D** should go
1Ch 21:19 So **D** went up at the word of
1Ch 21:21 Then **D** came to Ornan, and
1Ch 21:21 and Ornan looked and saw **D**
1Ch 21:21 bowed down to **D** with his face
1Ch 21:22 Then **D** said to Ornan, "Grant
1Ch 21:23 And Ornan said to **D**, "Take it
1Ch 21:24 Then King **D** said to Ornan,
1Ch 21:25 So **D** gave Ornan six hundred
1Ch 21:26 **D** built there an altar to the
1Ch 21:28 when **D** saw that the LORD had
1Ch 21:30 But **D** could not go before it
1Ch 22: 1 Then **D** said, "This is the
1Ch 22: 2 So **D** commanded to gather the
1Ch 22: 3 **D** prepared iron in abundance
1Ch 22: 4 brought much cedar wood to **D**
1Ch 22: 5 Now **D** said, "Solomon my son
1Ch 22: 5 So **D** made abundant
1Ch 22: 7 And **D** said to Solomon
1Ch 22:17 **D** also commanded all the
1Ch 23: 1 So when **D** was old and full of
1Ch 23: 5 which I made," said **D**, "for
1Ch 23: 6 **D** divided them into divisions
1Ch 23:25 For **D** said, "The LORD God of
1Ch 23:27 For by the last words of **D**
1Ch 24: 3 Then **D** with Zadok of the sons
1Ch 24:31 in the presence of King **D**
1Ch 25: 1 Moreover **D** and the captains of
1Ch 26:26 dedicated things which King **D**
1Ch 26:31 reign of **D** they were sought
1Ch 26:32 whom King **D** made officials
1Ch 27:23 But **D** did not take the number
1Ch 27:24 of the chronicles of King **D**
1Ch 28: 1 Now **D** assembled at Jerusalem
1Ch 28: 2 Then King **D** rose to his feet
1Ch 28:11 Then **D** gave his son Solomon
1Ch 28:19 All this," said **D**, "the
1Ch 28:20 **D** said to his son Solomon,
1Ch 29: 1 King **D** said to all the
1Ch 29: 9 King **D** also rejoiced greatly
1Ch 29:10 Therefore **D** blessed the LORD
1Ch 29:10 and **D** said: "Blessed are You
1Ch 29:20 Then **D** said to all the
1Ch 29:22 son of **D** king the second time
1Ch 29:23 king instead of **D** his father
1Ch 29:24 also all the sons of King **D**
1Ch 29:26 Thus **D** the son of Jesse
1Ch 29:29 Now the acts of King **D**, first
2Ch 1: 1 Now Solomon the son of **D** was
2Ch 1: 4 But **D** had brought up the ark
2Ch 1: 4 place **D** had prepared for it
2Ch 1: 8 great mercy to **D** my father
2Ch 1: 9 God, let Your promise to **D** my
2Ch 2: 3 have dealt with **D** my father
2Ch 2: 7 whom **D** my father provided
2Ch 2:12 has given King **D** a wise son
2Ch 2:14 men of my lord **D** your father
2Ch 2:17 **D** his father had numbered
2Ch 3: 1 had appeared to his father **D**
2Ch 3: 1 at the place that **D** had
2Ch 5: 1 his father **D** had dedicated
2Ch 5: 2 LORD up from the City of **D**
2Ch 6: 4 with His mouth to my father **D**
2Ch 6: 6 I have chosen **D** to be over My
2Ch 6: 7 **D** to build a temple for the
2Ch 6: 8 the LORD said to my father **D**
2Ch 6:10 the position of my father **D**
2Ch 6:15 Your servant **D** my father
2Ch 6:16 Your servant **D** my father,
2Ch 6:17 have spoken to Your servant **D**
2Ch 6:42 the mercies of Your servant **D**

2Ch 7: 6 which King **D** had made to
2Ch 7: 6 whenever **D** offered praise
2Ch 7:10 that the LORD had done for **D**
2Ch 7:17 Me as your father **D** walked
2Ch 7:18 covenanted with **D** your father
2Ch 8:11 **D** to the house he had built
2Ch 8:11 the house of **D** king of Israel
2Ch 8:14 to the order of **D** his father
2Ch 8:14 for so **D** the man of God had
2Ch 9:31 in the City of **D** his father
2Ch 10:16 What portion have we in **D**
2Ch 10:16 see to your own house, O **D**
2Ch 10:19 the house of **D** to this day
2Ch 11:17 they walked in the way of **D**
2Ch 11:18 of Jerimoth the son of **D**, and
2Ch 12:16 was buried in the City of **D**
2Ch 13: 5 over Israel to **D** forever, to
2Ch 13: 6 of Solomon the son of **D**, rose
2Ch 13: 8 in the hand of the sons of **D**
2Ch 14: 1 buried him in the City of **D**
2Ch 16:14 for himself in the City of **D**
2Ch 17: 3 former ways of his father **D**
2Ch 21: 1 his fathers in the City of **D**
2Ch 21: 7 not destroy the house of **D**
2Ch 21: 7 that He had made with **D**, and
2Ch 21:12 the LORD God of your father **D**
2Ch 21:20 buried him in the City of **D**
2Ch 23: 3 has said of the sons of **D**
2Ch 23:18 whom **D** had assigned in the
2Ch 23:18 as it was established by **D**
2Ch 24:16 the City of **D** among the kings
2Ch 24:25 buried him in the City of **D**
2Ch 27: 9 buried him in the City of **D**
2Ch 28: 1 as his father **D** had done
2Ch 29: 2 that his father **D** had done
2Ch 29:25 to the commandment of **D**, of
2Ch 29:26 with the instruments of **D**
2Ch 29:27 of **D** king of Israel
2Ch 29:30 the LORD with the words of **D**
2Ch 30:26 time of Solomon the son of **D**
2Ch 32: 5 the Millo in the City of **D**
2Ch 32:30 west side of the City of **D**
2Ch 32:33 upper tombs of the sons of **D**
2Ch 33: 7 of which God had said to **D**
2Ch 33:14 **D** on the west side of Gihon
2Ch 34: 2 in the ways of his father **D**
2Ch 34: 3 seek the God of his father **D**
2Ch 35: 3 which Solomon the son of **D**
2Ch 35: 4 of **D** king of Israel and the
2Ch 35:15 according to the command of **D**
Ezra 3:10 ordinance of **D** king of Israel
Ezra 8: 2 of the sons of **D**, Hattush
Ezra 8:20 also of the Nethinim, whom **D**
Neh 3:15 go down from the City of **D**
Neh 3:16 in front of the tombs of **D**
Neh 12:24 command of **D** the man of God
Neh 12:36 of **D** the man of God
Neh 12:37 the stairs of the City of **D**
Neh 12:37 wall, beyond the house of **D**
Neh 12:45 according to the command of **D**
Neh 12:46 For in the days of **D** and Asaph
Ps 18:50 mercy to His anointed, To **D**
Ps 72:20 The prayers of **D** the son of
Ps 78:70 He also chose **D** His servant
Ps 89: 3 I have sworn to My servant **D**
Ps 89:20 I have found My servant **D**
Ps 89:35 I will not lie to **D**
Ps 89:49 You swore to **D** in Your truth
Ps 122: 5 The thrones of the house of **D**
Ps 132: 1 Lord, remember **D** And all his
Ps 132:11 LORD has sworn in truth to **D**
Ps 132:17 will make the horn of **D** grow
Ps 144:10 Who delivers **D** His servant
Prov 1: 1 of Solomon the son of **D**, king
Eccl 1: 1 of the Preacher, the son of **D**
Song 4: 4 neck is like the tower of **D**
Is 7: 2 it was told to the house of **D**
Is 7:13 Hear now, O house of **D**
Is 9: 7 no end, upon the throne of **D**
Is 16: 5 truth, in the tabernacle of **D**
Is 22: 9 the damage to the city of **D**
Is 22:22 The key of the house of **D** I
Is 29: 1 Ariel, the city where **D** dwelt
Is 38: 5 the God of **D** your father
Is 55: 3 the sure mercies of **D**
Jer 17:25 sitting on the throne of **D**
Jer 21:12 O house of **D**!
Jer 22: 2 who sit on the throne of **D**
Jer 22: 4 who sit on the throne of **D**
Jer 22:30 sitting on the throne of **D**
Jer 23: 5 That I will raise to **D** a
Jer 29:16 who sits on the throne of **D**
Jer 30: 9 **D** their king, whom I will
Jer 33:15 **D** a Branch of righteousness
Jer 33:17 **D** shall never lack a man to
Jer 33:21 be broken with **D** My servant
Jer 33:22 descendants of **D** My servant
Jer 33:26 **D** My servant, so that I will
Jer 36:30 one to sit on the throne of **D**
Ezek 34:23 shall feed them—My servant **D**
Ezek 34:24 My servant **D** a prince among
Ezek 37:24 **D** My servant shall be king
Ezek 37:25 My servant **D** shall be their
Hos 3: 5 **D** their king, and fear the
Amos 6: 5 musical instruments like **D**
Amos 9:11 raise up The tabernacle of **D**
Zech 12: 7 the glory of the house of **D**
Zech 12: 8 in that day shall be like **D**
Zech 12: 8 the house of **D** shall be like
Zech 12:10 I will pour on the house of **D**
Zech 12:12 of the house of **D** by itself
Zech 13: 1 be opened for the house of **D**
Matt 1: 1 of Jesus Christ, the Son of **D**
Matt 1: 6 and Jesse begot **D** the king
Matt 1: 6 **D** the king begot Solomon by
Matt 1:17 to **D** are fourteen generations
Matt 1:17 from **D** until the captivity in
Matt 1:20 Joseph, son of **D**, do not be
Matt 9:27 Son of **D**, have mercy on us
Matt 12: 3 what **D** did when he was hungry
Matt 12:23 Could this be the Son of **D**
Matt 15:22 mercy on me, O Lord, Son of **D**
Matt 20:30 mercy on us, O Lord, Son of **D**
Matt 20:31 mercy on us, O Lord, Son of **D**
Matt 21: 9 Hosanna to the Son of **D**
Matt 21:15 Hosanna to the Son of **D**
Matt 22:42 said to Him, "The Son of **D**."
Matt 22:43 How then does **D** in the Spirit
Matt 22:45 If **D** then calls Him 'Lord,'
Mark 2:25 **D** did when he was in need
Mark 10:47 Jesus, Son of **D**, have mercy
Mark 10:48 Son of **D**, have mercy on me
Mark 11:10 **D** that comes in the name of
Mark 12:35 the Christ is the Son of **D**
Mark 12:36 For **D** himself said by the
Mark 12:37 Therefore **D** himself calls Him
Luke 1:27 was Joseph, of the house of **D**
Luke 1:32 the throne of His father **D**
Luke 1:69 in the house of His servant **D**
Luke 2: 4 into Judea, to the city of **D**
Luke 2: 4 of the house and lineage of **D**
Luke 2:11 day in the city of **D** a Savior
Luke 3:31 son of Nathan, the son of **D**
Luke 6: 3 what **D** did when he was hungry
Luke 18:38 Jesus, Son of **D**, have mercy
Luke 18:39 Son of **D**, have mercy on me
Luke 20:42 Now **D** himself said in the
Luke 20:44 **D** therefore calls Him 'Lord'
John 7:42 comes from the seed of **D** and
John 7:42 of Bethlehem, where **D** was
Acts 1:16 mouth of **D** concerning Judas
Acts 2:25 For **D** says concerning Him
Acts 2:29 to you of the patriarch **D**
Acts 2:34 For **D** did not ascend into the
Acts 4:25 of Your servant **D** have said
Acts 7:45 fathers until the days of **D**
Acts 13:22 raised up for them **D** as king
Acts 13:22 I have found **D** the son of
Acts 13:34 you the sure mercies of **D**
Acts 13:36 For **D**, after he had served
Acts 15:16 of **D** which has fallen down
Rom 1: 3 of **D** according to the flesh
Rom 4: 6 just as **D** also describes the
Rom 11: 9 And **D** says: "Let their table
2Ti 2: 8 Christ, of the seed of **D**, was
Heb 4: 7 a certain day, saying in **D**
Heb 11:32 Samson and Jephthah, also of **D**
Rev 3: 7 He who has the key of **D**, He
Rev 5: 5 tribe of Judah, the Root of **D**
Rev 22:16 Root and the Offspring of **D**

DAVID'S (*see* DAVID)
1Sa 18:29 So Saul became **D** enemy
1Sa 19:11 to **D** house to watch him and to
1Sa 19:11 **D** wife, told him, saying,
1Sa 20:16 it at the hand of **D** enemies
1Sa 20:25 side, but **D** place was empty
1Sa 20:27 month, that **D** place was empty
1Sa 23: 3 And **D** men said to him,
1Sa 24: 5 **D** heart troubled him because
1Sa 25: 9 So when **D** young men came,
1Sa 25:10 Nabal answered **D** servants
1Sa 25:12 So **D** young men turned on
1Sa 25:44 **D** wife, to Palti the son of
1Sa 26:17 Then Saul knew **D** voice, and
1Sa 30: 5 And **D** two wives, Ahinoam the
1Sa 30:20 This is **D** spoil
2Sa 2:30 of **D** servants nineteen men
2Sa 3: 5 Ithream, by **D** wife Eglah
2Sa 3:26 Joab had gone from **D** presence
2Sa 5: 8 who are hated by **D** soul)
2Sa 8: 2 Moabites became **D** servants
2Sa 8: 6 the Syrians became **D** servants
2Sa 8:14 Edomites became **D** servants
2Sa 8:18 **D** sons were chief ministers
2Sa 10: 2 **D** servants came into the land
2Sa 10: 4 Hanun took **D** servants, shaved
2Sa 12: 5 Then **D** anger was greatly
2Sa 12:30 And it was set on **D** head
2Sa 13: 3 the son of Shimeah, **D** brother
2Sa 13:32 **D** brother, answered and said,
2Sa 15:12 **D** counselor, from his city,
2Sa 15:37 **D** friend, went into the city
2Sa 16:16 **D** friend, came to Absalom,
2Sa 19:41 all **D** men with him across the
2Sa 24:10 **D** heart condemned him after
2Sa 24:11 prophet Gad, **D** seer, saying,
1Ki 1:38 Solomon ride on King **D** mule
1Ki 15: 4 Nevertheless for **D** sake the
2Ki 19:34 sake and for My servant **D** sake
1Ch 18: 2 Moabites became **D** servants
1Ch 18: 6 the Syrians became **D** servants
1Ch 18:13 Edomites became **D** servants
1Ch 18:17 **D** sons were chief ministers
1Ch 19: 4 Hanun took **D** servants, shaved
1Ch 20: 2 And it was set on **D** head
1Ch 20: 7 Shimea, **D** brother, killed him
1Ch 21: 9 spoke to Gad, **D** seer, saying,
1Ch 27:18 Elihu, one of **D** brothers
1Ch 27:31 over King **D** property
1Ch 27:32 **D** uncle, was a counselor, a
2Ch 23: 9 shields which had been King **D**
Ps 132:10 For Your servant **D** sake, Do
Is 37:35 sake and for My servant **D** sake
Jer 13:13 the kings who sit on **D** throne
Luke 20:41 say that the Christ is **D** Son

DAWN (*see* DAWNED, DAWNING, DAWNS)
Job 7: 4 had my fill of tossing till **d**
Job 38:12 and caused the **d** to know its
Ps 46: 5 her, just at the break of **d**
Ps 57: 8 I will awaken the **d**
Ps 108: 2 I will awaken the **d**
Is 58:10 light shall **d** in the darkness
Matt 28: 1 day of the week began to **d**
Acts 27:33 And as day was about to **d**,

DAWNED (*see* DAWN)
Gen 19:15 When the morning **d**, the
Gen 44: 3 As soon as the morning **d**, the
Deut 33: 2 Sinai, and **d** on them from Seir
Ezek 7: 6 it has **d** for you
Jon 4: 7 But as morning **d** the next day
Matt 4:16 shadow of death light has **d**

DAWNING (*see* DAWN)
Josh 6:15 about the **d** of the day, and
Judg 19:26 woman came as the day was **d**
1Sa 9:26 it was about the **d** of the day
Job 3: 9 and not see the **d** of the day
Ps 119:147 before the **d** of the morning
Is 24:15 the LORD in the **d** light, the

DAWNS (*see* DAWN)
2Pe 1:19 a dark place, until the day **d**

DAY (*see* DAYBREAK, DAYLIGHT, DAY'S, DAYS, DAYSPRING, DAYTIME)
Gen 1: 5 God called the light **D**, and
Gen 1: 5 the morning were the first **d**
Gen 1: 8 the morning were the second **d**
Gen 1:13 the morning were the third **d**
Gen 1:14 divide the **d** from the night
Gen 1:16 greater light to rule the **d**
Gen 1:18 and to rule over the **d** and over
Gen 1:19 the morning were the fourth **d**
Gen 1:23 the morning were the fifth **d**
Gen 1:31 the morning were the sixth **d**
Gen 2: 2 on the seventh **d** God ended
Gen 2: 2 He rested on the seventh **d**
Gen 2: 3 God blessed the seventh **d**
Gen 2: 4 in the **d** that the LORD God
Gen 2:17 for in the **d** that you eat of
Gen 3: 5 the **d** you eat of it your eyes

Gen 3: 8 garden in the cool of the **d**
Gen 4:14 **d** from the face of the ground
Gen 5: 1 In the **d** that God created man
Gen 5: 2 in the **d** they were created
Gen 7:11 seventeenth **d** of the month
Gen 7:11 on that **d** all the fountains
Gen 7:13 On the very same **d** Noah and
Gen 8: 4 seventeenth **d** of the month
Gen 8: 5 on the first **d** of the month
Gen 8:13 the first **d** of the month,
Gen 8:14 twenty-seventh **d** of the month
Gen 8:22 and winter and summer, and **d**
Gen 15:18 On the same **d** the LORD made a
Gen 17:23 foreskins that very same **d**
Gen 17:26 That very same **d** Abraham was
Gen 18: 1 door in the heat of the **d**
Gen 19:34 It happened on the next **d**
Gen 19:37 of the Moabites to this **d**
Gen 19:38 the people of Ammon to this **d**
Gen 21: 8 same **d** that Isaac was weaned
Gen 22: 4 Then on the third **d** Abraham
Gen 22:14 as it is said to this **d**, "In
Gen 24:12 please give me success this **d**
Gen 24:42 this **d** I came to the well and
Gen 25:31 your birthright as of this **d**
Gen 25:33 Swear to me as of this **d**
Gen 26:32 It came to pass the same **d**
Gen 26:33 city is Beersheba to this **d**
Gen 27: 2 do not know the **d** of my death
Gen 27:45 also of you both in one **d**
Gen 29: 7 Look, it is still high **d**
Gen 30:35 So he removed that **d** the male
Gen 31:22 third **d** that Jacob had fled
Gen 31:39 whether stolen by **d** or stolen
Gen 31:40 In the **d** the drought consumed
Gen 31:43 But what can I do this **d** to
Gen 31:48 between you and me this **d**
Gen 32:24 him until the breaking of **d**
Gen 32:26 Let Me go, for the **d** breaks
Gen 32:32 Therefore to this **d** the
Gen 33:13 should drive them hard one **d**
Gen 33:16 that **d** on his way to Seir
Gen 34:25 came to pass on the third **d**
Gen 35: 3 me in the **d** of my distress
Gen 35:20 of Rachel's grave to this **d**
Gen 39:10 she spoke to Joseph **d** by **d**
Gen 40:20 came to pass on the third **d**
Gen 41: 9 I remember my faults this **d**
Gen 42:18 said to them the third **d**
Gen 42:32 this **d** in the land of Canaan
Gen 47:23 your land this **d** for Pharaoh
Gen 47:26 the land of Egypt to this **d**
Gen 48:15 me all my life long to this **d**
Gen 48:20 So he blessed them that **d**
Gen 50:20 it about as it is this **d**, to
Ex 2:13 when he went out the second **d**
Ex 5: 6 So the same **d** Pharaoh
Ex 6:28 on the **d** when the LORD spoke
Ex 8:22 in that **d** I will set apart
Ex 9: 6 did this thing on the next **d**
Ex 10: 6 since the **d** that they were on
Ex 10: 6 were on the earth to this **d**
Ex 10:13 wind on the land all that **d**
Ex 10:28 For in the **d** you see my face
Ex 12: 3 On the tenth **d** of this month
Ex 12: 6 **d** of the same month
Ex 12:14 So this **d** shall be to you a
Ex 12:15 On the first **d** you shall
Ex 12:15 first **d** until the seventh **d**
Ex 12:16 On the first **d** there shall
Ex 12:16 on the seventh **d** there shall
Ex 12:17 for on this same **d** I will
Ex 12:17 you shall observe this **d**
Ex 12:18 on the fourteenth **d** of the
Ex 12:18 until the twenty-first **d** of
Ex 12:41 on that very same **d**
Ex 12:51 to pass, on that very same **d**
Ex 13: 3 Remember this **d** in which you
Ex 13: 4 On this **d** you are going out,
Ex 13: 6 on the seventh **d** there shall
Ex 13: 8 shall tell your son in that **d**
Ex 13:21 by **d** in a pillar of cloud to
Ex 13:21 them light, so as to go by **d**
Ex 13:22 by **d** or the pillar of fire by
Ex 14:30 that **d** out of the hand of the
Ex 16: 1 on the fifteenth **d** of the
Ex 16: 4 a certain quota every **d**, that
Ex 16: 5 **d** that they shall prepare
Ex 16:22 And so it was, on the sixth **d**
Ex 16:26 it, but on the seventh **d**,
Ex 16:27 on the seventh **d** to gather
Ex 16:29 sixth **d** bread for two days
Ex 16:29 of his place on the seventh **d**
Ex 16:30 rested on the seventh **d**
Ex 18:13 And so it was, on the next **d**
Ex 19: 1 land of Egypt, on the same **d**
Ex 19:11 them be ready for the third **d**
Ex 19:11 For on the third **d** the LORD
Ex 19:15 Be ready for the third **d**
Ex 19:16 came to pass on the third **d**
Ex 20: 8 Remember the Sabbath **d**, to
Ex 20:10 but the seventh **d** is the
Ex 20:11 them, and rested the seventh **d**
Ex 20:11 LORD blessed the Sabbath **d**
Ex 21:21 he remains alive a **d** or two
Ex 22:30 on the eighth **d** you shall
Ex 23:12 the seventh **d** you shall rest
Ex 24:16 on the seventh **d** He called to
Ex 29:36 every **d** as a sin offering for
Ex 29:38 year, **d** by **d** continually
Ex 31:15 any work on the Sabbath **d**
Ex 31:17 and on the seventh **d** He rested
Ex 32: 6 they rose early on the next **d**
Ex 32:28 men of the people fell that **d**
Ex 32:29 on you a blessing this **d**, for
Ex 32:30 next **d** that Moses said to the
Ex 32:34 in the **d** when I visit for
Ex 34:11 what I command you this **d**
Ex 34:21 the seventh **d** you shall rest
Ex 35: 2 seventh **d** shall be a holy **d**
Ex 35: 3 habitations on the Sabbath **d**
Ex 40: 2 On the first **d** of the first
Ex 40:17 on the first **d** of the month
Ex 40:37 the **d** that it was taken up
Ex 40:38 was above the tabernacle by **d**
Lev 6: 5 on the **d** of his trespass
Lev 6:20 beginning on the **d** when he is
Lev 7:15 the same **d** it is offered
Lev 7:16 the same **d** that he offers his
Lev 7:16 but on the next **d** the
Lev 7:17 **d** must be burned with fire
Lev 7:18 eaten at all on the third **d**
Lev 7:35 on the **d** when Moses presented
Lev 7:36 on the **d** that He anointed
Lev 7:38 on the **d** when He commanded
Lev 8:34 As he has done this **d**, so the
Lev 8:35 the tabernacle of meeting **d**
Lev 9: 1 **d** that Moses called Aaron
Lev 10:19 this **d** they have offered
Lev 12: 3 on the eighth **d** the flesh of
Lev 13: 5 look at him on the seventh **d**
Lev 13: 6 at him again on the seventh **d**
Lev 13:27 look at him on the seventh **d**
Lev 13:32 on the seventh **d** the priest
Lev 13:34 On the seventh **d** the priest
Lev 13:51 the plague on the seventh **d**
Lev 14: 2 for the **d** of his cleansing
Lev 14: 9 But on the seventh **d** he shall
Lev 14:10 on the eighth **d** he shall take
Lev 14:23 eighth **d** for his cleansing
Lev 14:39 come again on the seventh **d**
Lev 15:14 On the eighth **d** he shall
Lev 15:29 on the eighth **d** she shall
Lev 16:29 on the tenth **d** of the month
Lev 16:30 For on that **d** the priest
Lev 19: 6 eaten the same **d** you offer it
Lev 19: 6 offer it, and on the next **d**
Lev 19: 6 any remains until the third **d**
Lev 19: 7 eaten at all on the third **d**
Lev 22:27 and from the eighth **d** and
Lev 22:28 and her young on the same **d**
Lev 22:30 On the same **d** it shall be
Lev 23: 3 done, but the seventh **d** is a
Lev 23: 5 On the fourteenth **d** of the
Lev 23: 6 on the fifteenth **d** of the
Lev 23: 7 On the first **d** you shall
Lev 23: 8 The seventh **d** shall be a holy
Lev 23:11 on the **d** after the Sabbath
Lev 23:12 And you shall offer on that **d**
Lev 23:14 **d** that you have brought an
Lev 23:15 from the **d** after the Sabbath
Lev 23:15 from the **d** that you brought
Lev 23:16 Count fifty days to the **d**
Lev 23:21 the same **d** that it is a holy
Lev 23:24 on the first **d** of the month
Lev 23:27 Also the tenth **d** of this
Lev 23:27 shall be the **D** of Atonement
Lev 23:28 do no work on that same **d**
Lev 23:28 for it is the **D** of Atonement
Lev 23:29 of soul on that same **d**, he
Lev 23:30 does any work on that same **d**
Lev 23:32 on the ninth **d** of the month
Lev 23:34 The fifteenth **d** of this
Lev 23:35 On the first **d** there shall
Lev 23:36 On the eighth **d** you shall
Lev 23:37 everything on its **d**
Lev 23:39 **d** of the seventh month, when
Lev 23:39 on the first **d** there shall be
Lev 23:39 and on the eighth **d** a
Lev 23:40 **d** the fruit of beautiful
Lev 25: 9 tenth **d** of the seventh month
Lev 25: 9 on the **D** of Atonement you
Lev 27:23 **d** as a holy offering to the
Num 1: 1 on the first **d** of the second
Num 1:18 first **d** of the second month
Num 3:13 On the **d** that I struck all
Num 6: 9 on the **d** of his cleansing
Num 6: 9 on the seventh **d** he shall
Num 6:10 eighth **d** he shall bring two
Num 6:11 sanctify his head that same **d**
Num 7:11 offering, one leader each **d**
Num 7:12 **d** was Nahshon the son of
Num 7:18 On the second **d** Nethaneel the
Num 7:24 On the third **d** Eliab the son
Num 7:30 On the fourth **d** Elizur the
Num 7:36 On the fifth **d** Shelumiel the
Num 7:42 On the sixth **d** Eliasaph the
Num 7:48 On the seventh **d** Elishama the
Num 7:54 On the eighth **d** Gamaliel the
Num 7:60 On the ninth **d** Abidan the son
Num 7:66 On the tenth **d** Ahiezer the
Num 7:72 On the eleventh **d** Pagiel the
Num 7:78 On the twelfth **d** Ahira the
Num 8:17 on the **d** that I struck all
Num 9: 3 fourteenth **d** of this month
Num 9: 5 **d** of the first month, at
Num 9: 6 keep the Passover on that **d**
Num 9: 6 before Moses and Aaron that **d**
Num 9:11 On the fourteenth **d** of the
Num 9:15 on the **d** that the tabernacle
Num 9:16 the cloud covered it by **d**
Num 9:21 whether by **d** or by night,
Num 10:10 Also in the **d** of your
Num 10:11 **d** of the second month, in the
Num 10:34 the LORD was above them by **d**
Num 11:19 You shall eat, not one **d**
Num 11:32 people stayed up all that **d**
Num 11:32 that night, and all the next **d**
Num 14:14 in a pillar of cloud by **d**
Num 14:34 for each **d** you shall bear
Num 15:23 from the **d** the LORD gave
Num 15:32 sticks on the Sabbath **d**
Num 16:41 On the next **d** all the
Num 17: 8 **d** that Moses went into the
Num 19:12 with the water on the third **d**
Num 19:12 and on the seventh **d**
Num 19:12 purify himself on the third **d**
Num 19:12 and on the seventh **d**
Num 19:19 the unclean on the third **d**
Num 19:19 and on the seventh **d**
Num 19:19 on the seventh **d** he shall
Num 22:30 I became yours, to this **d**
Num 22:41 So it was the next **d**, that
Num 25:18 who was killed in the **d** of
Num 28: 3 **d** by **d**, as a regular burnt
Num 28: 9 on the Sabbath **d** two lambs in
Num 28:16 On the fourteenth **d** of the
Num 28:17 on the fifteenth **d** of this
Num 28:18 On the first **d** you shall
Num 28:25 on the seventh **d** you shall
Num 28:26 Also on the **d** of the
Num 29: 1 on the first **d** of the month
Num 29: 1 For you it is a **d** of blowing
Num 29: 7 On the tenth **d** of this
Num 29:12 On the fifteenth **d** of the
Num 29:17 On the second **d** present
Num 29:20 On the third **d** present
Num 29:23 On the fourth **d** present ten
Num 29:26 On the fifth **d** present nine
Num 29:29 On the sixth **d** present eight
Num 29:32 On the seventh **d** present
Num 29:35 On the eighth **d** you shall
Num 30: 5 her on the **d** that he hears
Num 30: 7 to her on the **d** that he hears
Num 30: 8 her on the **d** that he hears it
Num 30:12 void on the **d** he heard them
Num 30:14 whatever to her from **d** to **d**
Num 30:14 on the **d** that he heard them
Num 31:19 your captives on the third **d**
Num 31:19 and on the seventh **d**

Num 31:24 your clothes on the seventh **d**
Num 32:10 anger was aroused on that **d**
Num 33: 3 on the fifteenth **d** of the
Num 33: 3 on the **d** after the Passover
Num 33:38 on the first **d** of the fifth
Deut 1: 3 on the first **d** of the month
Deut 1:33 by night and in the cloud by **d**
Deut 2:18 This **d** you are to cross over
Deut 2:22 their place, even to this **d**
Deut 2:25 This **d** I will begin to put
Deut 2:30 your hand, as it is this **d**
Deut 3:14 name, Havoth Jair, to this **d**
Deut 4: 8 which I set before you this **d**
Deut 4:10 **d** you stood before the LORD
Deut 4:20 as you are this **d**
Deut 4:26 to witness against you this **d**
Deut 4:32 since the **d** that God created
Deut 4:38 inheritance, as it is this **d**
Deut 4:39 Therefore know this **d**, and
Deut 5:12 Observe the Sabbath **d**, to
Deut 5:14 but the seventh **d** is the
Deut 5:15 you to keep the Sabbath **d**
Deut 5:24 We have seen this **d** that God
Deut 6:24 us alive, as it is this **d**
Deut 8:18 your fathers, as it is this **d**
Deut 8:19 this **d** that you shall surely
Deut 9: 7 from the **d** that you departed
Deut 9:10 fire in the **d** of the assembly
Deut 9:24 from the **d** that I knew you
Deut 10: 4 fire in the **d** of the assembly
Deut 10: 8 bless in His name, to this **d**
Deut 10:15 all peoples, as it is this **d**
Deut 11: 4 has destroyed them to this **d**
Deut 16: 3 **d** in which you came out of
Deut 16: 4 first **d** at twilight remain
Deut 16: 8 on the seventh **d** there shall
Deut 18:16 in the **d** of the assembly,
Deut 21:16 on the **d** he bequeaths his
Deut 21:23 shall surely bury him that **d**
Deut 24:15 Each **d** you shall give him his
Deut 26:16 This **d** the LORD your God
Deut 27: 2 on the **d** when you cross over
Deut 27: 9 This **d** you have become the
Deut 27:11 the people on the same **d**,
Deut 28:14 which I command you this **d**
Deut 28:32 longing for them all **d** long
Deut 28:66 you shall fear **d** and night, and
Deut 29: 4 ears to hear, to this very **d**
Deut 29:28 another land, as it is this **d**
Deut 31:17 against them in that **d**, and I
Deut 31:17 that they will say in that **d**
Deut 31:18 **d** because of all the evil
Deut 31:22 wrote this song the same **d**
Deut 32:35 for the **d** of their calamity
Deut 32:48 to Moses that very same **d**
Deut 33:12 shelters him all the **d** long
Deut 34: 6 one knows his grave to this **d**
Josh 1: 8 you shall meditate in it **d**
Josh 3: 7 This **d** I will begin to
Josh 4: 9 and they are there to this **d**
Josh 4:14 On that **d** the LORD magnified
Josh 4:19 tenth **d** of the first month
Josh 5: 9 This **d** I have rolled away the
Josh 5: 9 is called Gilgal to this **d**
Josh 5:10 Passover on the fourteenth **d**
Josh 5:11 on the **d** after the Passover
Josh 5:11 grain on the very same **d**
Josh 5:12 **d** after they had eaten the
Josh 6: 4 But the seventh **d** you shall
Josh 6:10 until the **d** I say to you
Josh 6:14 the second **d** they marched
Josh 6:15 **d** that they rose early, about
Josh 6:15 about the dawning of the **d**
Josh 6:15 On that **d** only they marched
Josh 6:25 dwells in Israel to this **d**
Josh 7:25 LORD will trouble you this **d**
Josh 7:26 stones, still there to this **d**
Josh 7:26 the Valley of Achor to this **d**
Josh 8:25 was that all who fell that **d**
Josh 8:28 a desolation to this **d**
Josh 8:29 stones that remains to this **d**
Josh 9:12 from our houses on the **d** we
Josh 9:17 their cities on the third **d**
Josh 9:27 And that **d** Joshua made them
Josh 9:27 would choose, even to this **d**
Josh 10:12 spoke to the LORD in the **d**
Josh 10:13 go down for about a whole **d**
Josh 10:14 there has been no **d** like that
Josh 10:27 remain until this very **d**
Josh 10:28 On that **d** Joshua took
Josh 10:32 who took it on the second **d**
Josh 10:35 They took it on that **d** and
Josh 10:35 he utterly destroyed that **d**
Josh 13:13 the Israelites until this **d**
Josh 14: 9 So Moses swore on that **d**,
Josh 14:10 and now, here I am this **d**,
Josh 14:11 **d** as I was on the **d** that
Josh 14:11 on the **d** that Moses sent me
Josh 14:12 the LORD spoke in that **d**
Josh 14:12 for you heard in that **d** how
Josh 14:14 the Kenizzite to this **d**,
Josh 15:63 Judah at Jerusalem to this **d**
Josh 16:10 the Ephraimites to this **d**
Josh 22: 3 these many days, up to this **d**
Josh 22:16 to turn away this **d** from
Josh 22:16 rebel this **d** against the LORD
Josh 22:17 are not cleansed until this **d**
Josh 22:18 **d** from following the LORD
Josh 22:22 LORD, do not save us this **d**
Josh 22:29 following the LORD this **d**
Josh 22:31 This **d** we perceive that the
Josh 23: 8 as you have done to this **d**
Josh 23: 9 stand against you to this **d**
Josh 23:14 this **d** I am going the way of
Josh 24:15 this **d** whom you will serve
Josh 24:25 with the people that **d**, and
Judg 1:21 in Jerusalem to this **d**
Judg 1:26 which is its name to this **d**
Judg 3:30 **d** under the hand of Israel
Judg 4:14 For this is the **d** in which
Judg 4:23 So on that **d** God subdued
Judg 5: 1 son of Abinoam sang on that **d**
Judg 6:24 To this **d** it is still in
Judg 6:27 city too much to do it by **d**
Judg 6:32 Therefore on that **d** he called
Judg 9:18 my father's house this **d**, and
Judg 9:19 and with his house this **d**,
Judg 9:42 **d** that the people went out
Judg 9:45 against the city all that **d**
Judg 10: 4 Havoth Jair" to this **d**,
Judg 10:15 only deliver us this **d**, we
Judg 11:27 Judge, render judgment this **d**
Judg 12: 3 me this **d** to fight against me
Judg 13: 7 womb to the **d** of his death
Judg 13:10 who came to me the other **d**
Judg 14:15 **d** that they said to Samson's
Judg 14:17 seventh **d** that he told her
Judg 14:18 **d** before the sun went down
Judg 15:19 which is in Lehi to this **d**
Judg 18: 1 for until that **d** their whole
Judg 18:12 place Mahaneh Dan to this **d**
Judg 18:30 the **d** of the captivity of the
Judg 19: 5 **d** that they arose early in
Judg 19: 8 on the fifth **d** to depart, but
Judg 19: 9 the **d** is now drawing toward
Judg 19: 9 the **d** is coming to an end
Judg 19:11 Jebus, and the **d** was far spent
Judg 19:25 when the **d** began to break,
Judg 19:26 came as the **d** was dawning
Judg 19:30 been done or seen from the **d**
Judg 19:30 land of Egypt until this **d**
Judg 20:21 on that **d** cut down to the
Judg 20:22 in array on the first **d**
Judg 20:24 of Benjamin on the second **d**
Judg 20:25 from Gibeah on the second **d**
Judg 20:26 fasted that **d** until evening
Judg 20:30 of Benjamin on the third **d**
Judg 20:35 **d** twenty-five thousand one
Judg 20:46 **d** were twenty-five thousand
Ruth 3:18 concluded the matter this **d**
Ruth 4: 5 On the **d** you buy the field
Ruth 4: 9 You are witnesses this **d** that
Ruth 4:10 You are witnesses this **d**
Ruth 4:14 this **d** without a near kinsman
1Sa 2:34 in one **d** they shall die, both
1Sa 3:12 In that **d** I will perform
1Sa 4:12 the battle line the same **d**
1Sa 5: 5 of Dagon in Ashdod to this **d**
1Sa 6:15 the same **d** to the LORD
1Sa 6:16 returned to Ekron the same **d**
1Sa 6:18 **d** in the field of Joshua of
1Sa 7: 6 And they fasted that **d**, and
1Sa 7:10 upon the Philistines that **d**
1Sa 8: 8 they have done since the **d**
1Sa 8: 8 out of Egypt, even to this **d**
1Sa 8:18 you will cry out in that **d**
1Sa 8:18 will not hear you in that **d**
1Sa 9:15 ear the **d** before Saul came
1Sa 9:24 Saul ate with Samuel that **d**
1Sa 9:26 about the dawning of the **d**
1Sa 10: 9 signs came to pass that **d**
1Sa 11:11 So it was, on the next **d**,
1Sa 11:11 until the heat of the **d**
1Sa 11:13 shall be put to death this **d**
1Sa 12: 2 from my childhood to this **d**
1Sa 12: 5 anointed is witness this **d**
1Sa 12:18 sent thunder and rain that **d**
1Sa 13:22 on the **d** of battle, that
1Sa 14: 1 Now it happened one **d** that
1Sa 14:23 the LORD saved Israel that **d**
1Sa 14:24 Israel were distressed that **d**
1Sa 14:28 the man who eats food this **d**
1Sa 14:31 **d** from Michmash to Aijalon
1Sa 14:33 a large stone to me this **d**
1Sa 14:37 He did not answer him that **d**
1Sa 14:45 he has worked with God this **d**
1Sa 15:35 Saul until the **d** of his death
1Sa 16:13 David from that **d** forward
1Sa 17:10 the armies of Israel this **d**
1Sa 17:46 This **d** the LORD will deliver
1Sa 17:46 And this **d** I will give the
1Sa 18: 2 Saul took him that **d**, and
1Sa 18: 9 David from that **d** forward
1Sa 18:10 it happened on the next **d**
1Sa 19:24 and lay down naked all that **d**
1Sa 20: 5 until the third **d** at evening
1Sa 20:12 tomorrow, or the third **d**, and
1Sa 20:19 you hid on the **d** of the deed
1Sa 20:26 did not say anything that **d**
1Sa 20:27 And it happened the next **d**
1Sa 20:27 the second **d** of the month,
1Sa 20:34 the second **d** of the month
1Sa 21: 5 in the vessel this **d**
1Sa 21: 6 the **d** when it was taken away
1Sa 21: 7 of Saul was there that **d**,
1Sa 21:10 fled that **d** from before Saul,
1Sa 22: 8 lie in wait, as it is this **d**
1Sa 22:13 lie in wait, as it is this **d**
1Sa 22:18 killed on that **d** eighty-five
1Sa 22:22 I knew that **d**, when Doeg the
1Sa 23:14 Saul sought him every **d**, but
1Sa 24: 4 This is the **d** of which the
1Sa 24:10 this **d** your eyes have seen
1Sa 24:18 you have shown this **d** how you
1Sa 24:19 you have done to me this **d**
1Sa 25: 8 for we come on a feast **d**
1Sa 25:16 wall to us both by night and **d**
1Sa 25:32 sent you this **d** to meet me
1Sa 25:33 you have kept me this **d** from
1Sa 26: 8 enemy into your hand this **d**
1Sa 26:10 or his **d** shall come to die,
1Sa 26:19 this **d** from abiding in the
1Sa 26:21 precious in your eyes this **d**
1Sa 26:24 valued much this **d** in my eyes
1Sa 27: 6 Achish gave him Ziklag that **d**
1Sa 27: 6 the kings of Judah to this **d**
1Sa 28:18 done this thing to you this **d**
1Sa 28:20 no food all **d** or all night
1Sa 29: 3 to this **d** I have found no
1Sa 29: 6 For to this **d** I have not
1Sa 29: 6 the **d** of your coming to me
1Sa 29: 8 to this **d** what have you found
1Sa 30: 1 to Ziklag, on the third **d**
1Sa 30:17 the evening of the next **d**
1Sa 30:25 it was, from that **d** forward
1Sa 30:25 for Israel to this **d**
1Sa 31: 6 men died together that same **d**
1Sa 31: 8 So it came to pass the next **d**
2Sa 1: 2 on the third **d**, behold, it
2Sa 2:17 a very fierce battle that **d**
2Sa 3:35 eat food while it was still **d**
2Sa 3:37 **d** that it had not been the
2Sa 3:38 has fallen this **d** in Israel
2Sa 4: 3 sojourners there until this **d**
2Sa 4: 5 at about the heat of the **d** to
2Sa 4: 8 lord the king this **d** of Saul
2Sa 5: 8 Now David said on that **d**
2Sa 6: 8 place Perez Uzzah to this **d**
2Sa 6: 9 was afraid of the LORD that **d**
2Sa 6:23 to the **d** of her death
2Sa 7: 6 up from Egypt, even to this **d**
2Sa 11:12 remained in Jerusalem that **d**
2Sa 12:18 Then on the seventh **d** it came
2Sa 13: 4 becoming thinner **d** after **d**
2Sa 13:32 been determined from the **d**
2Sa 13:37 mourned for his son every **d**
2Sa 16:12 good for his cursing this **d**
2Sa 18: 7 men took place there that **d**
2Sa 18: 8 **d** than the sword devoured
2Sa 18:18 And to this **d** it is called

2Sa 18:20 not take the news this **d**, for
2Sa 18:20 shall take the news another **d**
2Sa 18:31 this **d** of all those who rose
2Sa 19: 2 So the victory that **d** was
2Sa 19: 2 people heard it said that **d**
2Sa 19: 3 back into the city that **d**
2Sa 19:19 your servant did on the **d**
2Sa 19:24 from the **d** the king departed
2Sa 19:24 the **d** he came back in peace
2Sa 20: 3 up to the **d** of their death
2Sa 21:10 the air to rest on them by **d**
2Sa 22: 1 on the **d** when the LORD had
2Sa 22:19 me in the **d** of my calamity
2Sa 23:10 about a great victory that **d**
2Sa 23:20 midst of a pit on a snowy **d**
2Sa 24:18 And Gad came that **d** to David
1Ki 1:30 so I certainly will do this **d**
1Ki 1:48 to sit on my throne this **d**
1Ki 2: 8 the **d** when I went to Mahanaim
1Ki 2:37 on the **d** you go out and cross
1Ki 2:42 that on the **d** you go out and
1Ki 3: 6 his throne, as it is this **d**
1Ki 3:18 the third **d** after I had given
1Ki 4:22 one **d** was thirty kors of fine
1Ki 5: 7 Blessed be the LORD this **d**
1Ki 8: 8 So they are there to this **d**
1Ki 8:16 Since the **d** that I brought
1Ki 8:24 Your hand, as it is this **d**
1Ki 8:29 toward this temple night and **d**
1Ki 8:59 be near the LORD our God **d**
1Ki 8:59 as each **d** may require,
1Ki 8:61 commandments, as at this **d**
1Ki 8:64 On the same **d** the king
1Ki 8:66 On the eighth **d** he sent the
1Ki 9:13 Cabul, as they are to this **d**
1Ki 9:21 labor, as it is to this **d**
1Ki 10:12 the like been seen to this **d**
1Ki 12:12 came to Rehoboam the third **d**
1Ki 12:12 Come back to me the third **d**
1Ki 12:19 the house of David to this **d**
1Ki 12:32 **d** of the eighth month, like
1Ki 12:33 **d** of the eighth month, in the
1Ki 13: 3 And he gave a sign the same **d**
1Ki 13:11 God had done that **d** in Bethel
1Ki 14:14 this is the **d**
1Ki 16:16 Israel that **d** in the camp
1Ki 17:14 until the **d** the LORD sends
1Ki 18:36 let it be known this **d** that
1Ki 20:29 **d** the battle was joined
1Ki 20:29 of the Syrians in one **d**
1Ki 22:25 you shall see on that **d** when
1Ki 22:35 The battle increased that **d**
2Ki 2:22 remains healed to this **d**,
2Ki 4: 8 Now it happened one **d** that
2Ki 4:11 it happened one **d** that he
2Ki 4:18 Now it happened one **d** that he
2Ki 6:29 I said to her on the next **d**
2Ki 7: 9 This **d** is a **d** of good news,
2Ki 8: 6 of the field from the **d** that
2Ki 8:15 **d** that he took a thick cloth
2Ki 8:22 Judah's authority to this **d**
2Ki 10:27 it a refuse dump to this **d**
2Ki 14: 7 its name Joktheel to this **d**
2Ki 15: 5 until the **d** of his death
2Ki 16: 6 and dwell there to this **d**
2Ki 17:23 Assyria, as it is to this **d**
2Ki 17:34 To this **d** they continue
2Ki 17:41 fathers did, even to this **d**
2Ki 19: 3 This **d** is a **d** of trouble,
2Ki 19: 3 This **d** is a **d** of trouble
2Ki 20: 5 On the third **d** you shall go
2Ki 20: 8 house of the LORD the third **d**
2Ki 20:17 have accumulated until this **d**
2Ki 21:15 Me to anger since the **d** their
2Ki 21:15 out of Egypt, even to this **d**
2Ki 25: 1 on the tenth **d** of the month
2Ki 25: 3 By the ninth **d** of the fourth
2Ki 25: 8 on the seventh **d** of the month
2Ki 25:27 twenty-seventh **d** of the month
2Ki 25:30 king, a portion for each **d**
1Ch 4:41 them, as it is to this **d**
1Ch 4:43 have dwelt there to this **d**
1Ch 5:26 the river of Gozan to this **d**
1Ch 9:33 were employed in that work **d**
1Ch 10: 8 So it happened the next **d**
1Ch 11:22 midst of a pit on a snowy **d**
1Ch 12:22 to David **d** by **d** to help him
1Ch 13:11 called Perez Uzza to this **d**
1Ch 13:12 was afraid of God that **d**,
1Ch 16: 7 And on that **d** David first
1Ch 16:23 His salvation from **d** to **d**
1Ch 17: 5 up Israel, even to this **d**
1Ch 26:17 on the north four each **d**
1Ch 26:17 **d**, on the south four each **d**
1Ch 28: 7 My judgments, as it is this **d**
1Ch 29: 5 himself this **d** to the LORD
1Ch 29:21 to the LORD on the next **d**
1Ch 29:22 with great gladness on that **d**
2Ch 3: 2 to build on the second **d** of
2Ch 5: 9 And they are there to this **d**
2Ch 6: 5 Since the **d** that I brought
2Ch 6:15 Your hand, as it is this **d**
2Ch 6:20 be open toward this temple **d**
2Ch 7: 9 on the eighth **d** they held a
2Ch 7:10 On the twenty-third **d** of the
2Ch 8: 8 labor, as it is to this **d**
2Ch 8:14 the duty of each **d** required
2Ch 8:16 **d** of the foundation of the
2Ch 10:12 to Rehoboam on the third **d**
2Ch 10:12 Come back to me the third **d**
2Ch 10:19 the house of David to this **d**
2Ch 18:24 you shall see on that **d** when
2Ch 18:34 The battle increased that **d**
2Ch 20:26 And on the fourth **d** they
2Ch 20:26 of Berachah until this **d**
2Ch 21:10 Judah's authority to this **d**
2Ch 21:15 of the sickness, **d** by **d**
2Ch 24:11 Thus they did **d** by **d**, and
2Ch 26:21 until the **d** of his death
2Ch 28: 6 thousand in Judah in one **d**
2Ch 29:17 first **d** of the first month
2Ch 29:17 on the eighth **d** of the month
2Ch 29:17 on the sixteenth **d** of the
2Ch 30:15 **d** of the second month
2Ch 30:21 praised the LORD **d** by **d**
2Ch 35: 1 **d** of the first month
2Ch 35:16 LORD was prepared the same **d**
2Ch 35:21 not come against you this **d**
2Ch 35:25 to this **d** all the singing men
Ezra 3: 4 by ordinance for each **d**
Ezra 3: 6 From the first **d** of the
Ezra 6: 9 them **d** by **d** without fail
Ezra 6:15 third **d** of the month of Adar
Ezra 6:19 **d** of the first month
Ezra 7: 9 On the first **d** of the first
Ezra 7: 9 on the first **d** of the fifth
Ezra 8:31 twelfth **d** of the first month
Ezra 8:33 on the fourth **d** the silver
Ezra 9: 7 **d** we have been very guilty
Ezra 9: 7 humiliation, as it is this **d**
Ezra 9:15 as a remnant, as it is this **d**
Ezra 10: 9 the twentieth **d** of the month
Ezra 10:16 first **d** of the tenth month to
Ezra 10:17 By the first **d** of the first
Neh 1: 6 I pray before You now, **d** and
Neh 1:11 Your servant prosper this **d**
Neh 4: 2 Will they complete it in a **d**
Neh 4: 9 we set a watch against them **d**
Neh 4:22 night and a working party by **d**
Neh 5:11 now to them, even this **d**,
Neh 6:15 on the twenty-fifth **d** of the
Neh 8: 2 on the first **d** of the seventh
Neh 8: 9 This **d** is holy to the LORD
Neh 8:10 for this **d** is holy to our
Neh 8:11 Be still, for the **d** is holy
Neh 8:13 Now on the second **d** the heads
Neh 8:17 the son of Nun until that **d**
Neh 8:18 Also **d** by **d**, from the first
Neh 8:18 first **d** until the last **d**
Neh 8:18 on the eighth **d** there was a
Neh 9: 1 Now on the twenty-fourth **d** of
Neh 9: 3 God for one-fourth of the **d**
Neh 9:10 for Yourself, as it is this **d**
Neh 9:12 by **d** with a cloudy pillar
Neh 9:19 did not depart from them by **d**
Neh 9:32 kings of Assyria until this **d**
Neh 10:31 to sell on the Sabbath **d**, we
Neh 10:31 the Sabbath, or on a holy **d**
Neh 11:23 the singers, a quota **d** by **d**
Neh 12:43 Also that **d** they offered
Neh 12:47 a portion for each **d**
Neh 13: 1 On that **d** they read from the
Neh 13:15 Jerusalem on the Sabbath **d**
Neh 13:15 I warned them about the **d** on
Neh 13:17 you profane the Sabbath **d**
Neh 13:19 brought in on the Sabbath **d**
Neh 13:22 to sanctify the Sabbath **d**
Esth 1:10 On the seventh **d**, when the
Esth 1:18 This very **d** the noble ladies
Esth 2:11 every **d** Mordecai paced in
Esth 3: 7 Haman to determine the **d** and
Esth 3:12 **d** of the first month, and a
Esth 3:13 children and women, in one **d**
Esth 3:13 on the thirteenth **d** of the
Esth 3:14 should be ready for that **d**
Esth 4:16 for three days, night or **d**
Esth 5: 1 **d** that Esther put on her
Esth 5: 9 Haman went out that **d** joyful
Esth 7: 2 And on the second **d**, at the
Esth 8: 1 On that **d** King Ahasuerus gave
Esth 8: 9 Sivan, on the twenty-third **d**
Esth 8:12 on one **d** in all the provinces
Esth 8:12 on the thirteenth **d** of the
Esth 8:13 **d** to avenge themselves on
Esth 9: 1 of Adar, on the thirteenth **d**
Esth 9: 1 On the **d** that the enemies of
Esth 9:11 On that **d** the number of those
Esth 9:15 **d** of the month of Adar and
Esth 9:17 **d** of the month of Adar
Esth 9:17 on the fourteenth **d** of the
Esth 9:17 made it a **d** of feasting and
Esth 9:18 together on the thirteenth **d**
Esth 9:18 well as on the fourteenth **d**
Esth 9:18 on the fifteenth **d** of the
Esth 9:18 made it a **d** of feasting and
Esth 9:19 **d** of the month of Adar as a
Esth 9:19 of Adar as a **d** of gladness
Job 1: 4 each on his appointed **d**, and
Job 1: 6 Now there was a **d** when the
Job 1:13 there was a **d** when his sons
Job 2: 1 Again there was a **d** when the
Job 3: 1 cursed the **d** of his birth
Job 3: 3 May the **d** perish on which I
Job 3: 4 May that **d** be darkness
Job 3: 5 blackness of the **d** terrify it
Job 3: 8 curse it who curse the **d**,
Job 3: 9 not see the dawning of the **d**
Job 9:19 will appoint my **d** in court
Job 14: 6 a hired man he finishes his **d**
Job 15:23 He knows that a **d** of
Job 17:12 They change the night into **d**
Job 18:20 west are astonished at his **d**
Job 20:28 away in the **d** of His wrath
Job 21:30 reserved for the **d** of doom
Job 21:30 brought out on the **d** of wrath
Job 38:23 for the **d** of battle and war
Ps 1: 2 And in His law he meditates **d**
Ps 7:11 angry with the wicked every **d**
Ps 18:18 me in the **d** of my calamity
Ps 19: 2 **D** unto **d** utters speech, And
Ps 20: 1 you in the **d** of trouble
Ps 25: 5 On You I wait all the **d**
Ps 32: 3 my groaning all the **d** long
Ps 32: 4 For **d** and night Your hand was
Ps 35:28 of Your praise all the **d** long
Ps 37:13 He sees that his **d** is coming
Ps 38: 6 I go mourning all the **d** long
Ps 38:12 plan deception all the **d** long
Ps 42: 3 My tears have been my food **d**
Ps 42:10 they say to me all **d** long
Ps 44: 8 In God we boast all **d** long
Ps 44:22 sake we are killed all **d** long
Ps 50:15 upon Me in the **d** of trouble
Ps 55:10 **D** and night they go around it
Ps 56: 1 Fighting all **d** he oppresses
Ps 56: 2 enemies would hound me all **d**
Ps 56: 5 All **d** they twist my words
Ps 59:16 refuge in the **d** of my trouble
Ps 71: 8 And with Your glory all the **d**
Ps 71:15 And Your salvation all the **d**
Ps 71:17 And to this **d** I declare Your
Ps 71:24 righteousness all the **d** long
Ps 73:14 For all **d** long I have been
Ps 74:16 The **d** is Yours, the night
Ps 77: 2 In the **d** of my trouble I
Ps 78: 9 back in the **d** of battle
Ps 78:42 The **d** when He redeemed them
Ps 81: 3 moon, on our solemn feast **d**
Ps 84:10 For a **d** in Your courts is
Ps 86: 3 For I cry to You all **d** long
Ps 86: 7 In the **d** of my trouble I will
Ps 88: 1 salvation, I have cried out **d**
Ps 88:17 me all **d** long like water
Ps 89:16 name they rejoice all **d** long
Ps 91: 5 of the arrow that flies by **d**
Ps 95: 8 as in the **d** of trial in the
Ps 96: 2 His salvation from **d** to **d**
Ps 102: 2 me in the **d** of my trouble
Ps 102: 2 In the **d** that I call, answer
Ps 102: 8 reproach me all **d** long, And

Ps 110: 3 In the **d** of Your power
Ps 110: 5 kings in the **d** of His wrath
Ps 118:24 This is the **d** which the LORD
Ps 119:91 this **d** according to Your
Ps 119:97 It is my meditation all the **d**
Ps 119:164 Seven times a **d** I praise You
Ps 121: 6 sun shall not strike you by **d**
Ps 136: 8 The sun to rule by **d**, For His
Ps 137: 7 of Edom The **d** of Jerusalem
Ps 138: 3 In the **d** when I cried out,
Ps 139:12 But the night shines as the **d**
Ps 140: 7 my head in the **d** of battle
Ps 145: 2 Every **d** I will bless You, And
Ps 146: 4 In that very **d** his plans
Prov 4:18 brighter unto the perfect **d**
Prov 6:34 spare in the **d** of vengeance
Prov 7:20 come home on the appointed **d**
Prov 11: 4 not profit in the **d** of wrath
Prov 16: 4 the wicked for the **d** of doom
Prov 21:26 He covets greedily all **d** long
Prov 21:31 prepared for the **d** of battle
Prov 23:17 the LORD continue all **d** long
Prov 24:10 faint in the **d** of adversity
Prov 27: 1 know what a **d** may bring forth
Prov 27:10 in the **d** of your calamity
Prov 27:15 dripping on a very rainy **d**
Eccl 7: 1 and the **d** of death
Eccl 7: 1 than the **d** of one's birth
Eccl 7:14 In the **d** of prosperity be
Eccl 7:14 but in the **d** of adversity
Eccl 8: 8 has power in the **d** of death
Eccl 8:16 one sees no sleep **d** or night
Eccl 12: 3 in the **d** when the keepers of
Song 2:17 Until the **d** breaks and the
Song 3:11 him on the **d** of his espousals
Song 3:11 the **d** of the gladness of his
Song 4: 6 Until the **d** breaks and the
Song 8: 8 the **d** when she is spoken for
Is 2:11 shall be exalted in that **d**
Is 2:12 For the **d** of the LORD of
Is 2:17 will be exalted in that **d**
Is 2:20 In that **d** a man will cast
Is 3: 7 in that **d** he will protest,
Is 3:18 In that **d** the Lord will take
Is 4: 1 in that **d** seven women shall
Is 4: 2 In that **d** the Branch of the
Is 4: 5 a cloud and smoke by **d** and the
Is 5:30 In that **d** they will roar
Is 7:17 have not come since the **d**
Is 7:18 **d** that the LORD will whistle
Is 7:20 In the same **d** the Lord will
Is 7:21 It shall be in that **d** that a
Is 7:23 It shall happen in that **d**
Is 9: 4 as in the **d** of Midian
Is 9:14 branch and bulrush in one **d**
Is 10: 3 you do in the **d** of punishment
Is 10:17 thorns and his briers in one **d**
Is 10:20 **d** that the remnant of Israel
Is 10:27 **d** that his burden will be
Is 10:32 he will remain at Nob that **d**
Is 11:10 in that **d** there shall be a
Is 11:11 shall come to pass in that **d**
Is 11:16 **d** that he came up from the
Is 12: 1 And in that **d** you will say
Is 12: 4 And in that **d** you will say
Is 13: 6 for the **d** of the LORD is at
Is 13: 9 the **d** of the LORD comes,
Is 13:13 in the **d** of His fierce anger
Is 14: 3 the **d** the LORD gives you rest
Is 16: 3 night in the middle of the **d**
Is 17: 4 In that **d** it shall come to
Is 17: 7 In that **d** a man will look to
Is 17: 9 In that **d** his strong cities
Is 17:11 in the **d** you will make your
Is 17:11 of ruins in the **d** of grief
Is 19:16 In that **d** Egypt will be like
Is 19:18 In that **d** five cities in the
Is 19:19 In that **d** there will be an
Is 19:21 will know the LORD in that **d**
Is 19:23 In that **d** there will be a
Is 19:24 In that **d** Israel will be one
Is 20: 6 territory will say in that **d**
Is 22: 5 For it is a **d** of trouble and
Is 22: 8 You looked in that **d** to the
Is 22:12 in that **d** the Lord GOD of
Is 22:20 Then it shall be in that **d**
Is 22:25 In that **d**,' says the LORD of
Is 23:15 shall come to pass in that **d**
Is 24:21 **d** that the LORD will punish
Is 25: 9 And it will be said in that **d**
Is 26: 1 In that **d** this song will be
Is 27: 1 In that **d** the LORD with His
Is 27: 2 In that **d** sing to her, A
Is 27: 3 hurt it, I keep it night and **d**
Is 27: 8 in the **d** of the east wind
Is 27:12 **d** that the LORD will thresh
Is 27:13 So it shall be in that **d**
Is 28: 5 In that **d** the LORD of hosts
Is 28:19 it will pass over, and by **d**
Is 28:24 keep plowing all **d** to sow
Is 29:18 In that **d** the deaf shall hear
Is 30:23 In that **d** your cattle will
Is 30:25 waters, in the **d** of the great
Is 30:26 in the **d** that the LORD binds
Is 31: 7 For in that **d** every man shall
Is 34: 8 For it is the **d** of the LORD's
Is 34:10 not be quenched night or **d**
Is 37: 3 This **d** is a **d** of trouble
Is 38:12 from **d** until night You make
Is 38:13 from **d** until night You make
Is 38:19 praise You, as I do this **d**
Is 39: 6 have accumulated until this **d**
Is 43:13 Indeed before the **d** was, I am
Is 47: 9 to you in a moment, in one **d**
Is 48: 7 before this **d** you have not
Is 49: 8 in the **d** of salvation I have
Is 51:13 feared continually every **d**
Is 52: 5 continually every **d**
Is 52: 6 **d** that I am He who speaks
Is 58: 3 in the **d** of your fast you
Is 58: 4 not fast as you do this **d**
Is 58: 5 a **d** for a man to afflict his
Is 58: 5 an acceptable **d** to the LORD
Is 58:13 your pleasure on My holy **d**
Is 58:13 the holy **d** of the LORD
Is 60:11 shall not be shut **d** or night
Is 60:19 no longer be your light by **d**
Is 61: 2 the **d** of vengeance of our God
Is 62: 6 hold their peace **d** or night
Is 63: 4 For the **d** of vengeance is in
Is 65: 2 stretched out My hands all **d**
Is 65: 5 a fire that burns all the **d**
Is 66: 8 made to give birth in one **d**
Jer 1:10 I have this **d** set you over
Jer 1:18 you this **d** a fortified city
Jer 3:25 from our youth even to this **d**
Jer 4: 9 shall come to pass in that **d**
Jer 6: 4 for the **d** goes away, for the
Jer 7:22 or command them in the **d** that
Jer 7:25 Since the **d** that your fathers
Jer 7:25 land of Egypt until this **d**
Jer 9: 1 of tears, that I might weep **d**
Jer 11: 4 your fathers in the **d** that I
Jer 11: 5 and honey, as it is this **d**
Jer 11: 7 your fathers in the **d** that I
Jer 11: 7 land of Egypt, until this **d**
Jer 12: 3 them for the **d** of slaughter
Jer 14:17 flow with tears night and **d**
Jer 15: 9 gone down while it was yet **d**
Jer 16:13 you shall serve other gods **d**
Jer 16:19 refuge in the **d** of affliction
Jer 17:16 have I desired the woeful **d**
Jer 17:17 are my hope in the **d** of doom
Jer 17:18 Bring on them the **d** of doom
Jer 17:21 no burden on the Sabbath **d**
Jer 17:22 your houses on the Sabbath **d**
Jer 17:22 but hallow the Sabbath **d**
Jer 17:24 of this city on the Sabbath **d**
Jer 17:24 but hallow the Sabbath **d**
Jer 17:27 Me to hallow the Sabbath **d**
Jer 17:27 of Jerusalem on the Sabbath **d**
Jer 18:17 in the **d** of their calamity
Jer 20: 3 next **d** that Pashhur brought
Jer 20:14 Cursed be the **d** in which I
Jer 20:14 Let the **d** not be blessed in
Jer 25: 3 king of Judah, even to this **d**
Jer 25:18 and a curse, as it is this **d**
Jer 25:33 at that **d** the slain of the
Jer 27:22 until the **d** that I visit them
Jer 30: 7 For that **d** is great, so that
Jer 30: 8 shall come to pass in that **d**
Jer 31: 6 For there shall be a **d** when
Jer 31:32 the **d** that I took them by the
Jer 31:35 the sun for a light by **d**, and
Jer 32:20 the land of Egypt, to this **d**
Jer 32:20 a name, as it is this **d**
Jer 32:31 My fury from the **d** that they
Jer 32:31 they built it, even to this **d**
Jer 33:20 break My covenant with the **d**
Jer 33:20 so that there will not be **d**
Jer 33:25 If My covenant is not with **d**
Jer 34:13 with your fathers in the **d**
Jer 35:14 for to this **d** they drink none
Jer 36: 2 from the **d** I spoke to you,
Jer 36: 2 days of Josiah even to this **d**
Jer 36: 6 house on the **d** of fasting
Jer 36:30 cast out to the heat of the **d**
Jer 38:28 of the prison until the **d**
Jer 39: 2 on the ninth **d** of the month
Jer 39:16 in that **d** before you
Jer 39:17 I will deliver you in that **d**
Jer 40: 4 I free you this **d** from the
Jer 41: 4 on the second **d** after he had
Jer 42:19 I have admonished you this **d**
Jer 42:21 I have this **d** declared it to
Jer 44: 2 this **d** they are a desolation,
Jer 44: 6 and desolate, as it is this **d**
Jer 44:10 not been humbled, to this **d**
Jer 44:22 inhabitant, as it is this **d**
Jer 44:23 happened to you, as at this **d**
Jer 46:10 For this is the **d** of the Lord
Jer 46:10 a **d** of vengeance, that He may
Jer 46:21 for the **d** of their calamity
Jer 47: 4 Because of the **d** that comes
Jer 48:41 hearts in Moab on that **d**
Jer 49:22 **d** shall be like the heart of
Jer 49:26 shall be cut off in that **d**
Jer 50:27 for their **d** has come, the
Jer 50:30 shall be cut off in that **d**
Jer 50:31 For your **d** has come, the time
Jer 51: 2 For in the **d** of doom they
Jer 52: 4 on the tenth **d** of the month
Jer 52: 6 on the ninth **d** of the month
Jer 52:11 till the **d** of his death
Jer 52:12 on the tenth **d** of the month
Jer 52:31 twenty-fifth **d** of the month
Jer 52:34 a portion for each **d**
Jer 52:34 until the **d** of his death
Lam 1:12 in the **d** of His fierce anger
Lam 1:13 desolate and faint all the **d**
Lam 1:21 Bring on the **d** that You have
Lam 2: 1 in the **d** of His anger
Lam 2: 7 as on the **d** of a set feast
Lam 2:16 is the **d** we have waited for
Lam 2:18 tears run down like a river **d**
Lam 2:21 them in the **d** of Your anger
Lam 2:22 **d** the terrors that surround
Lam 2:22 In the **d** of the LORD's anger
Lam 3: 3 time again throughout the **d**
Lam 3:14 their taunting song all the **d**
Lam 3:57 near on the **d** I called on You
Lam 3:62 against me all the **d**
Ezek 1: 1 on the fifth **d** of the month
Ezek 1: 2 On the fifth **d** of the month
Ezek 1:28 in a cloud on a rainy **d**, so
Ezek 2: 3 against Me to this very **d**
Ezek 4: 6 laid on you a **d** for each year
Ezek 4:10 by weight, twenty shekels a **d**
Ezek 7: 7 a **d** of trouble is near, and
Ezek 7:10 Behold, the **d**!
Ezek 7:12 has come, the **d** draws near
Ezek 7:19 **d** of the wrath of the LORD
Ezek 8: 1 on the fifth **d** of the month
Ezek 12: 3 captivity by **d** in their sight
Ezek 12: 4 By **d** you shall bring out your
Ezek 12: 7 out my belongings by **d**, as
Ezek 13: 5 battle on the **d** of the LORD
Ezek 16: 4 on the **d** you were born your
Ezek 16: 5 on the **d** you were born
Ezek 20: 1 on the tenth **d** of the month
Ezek 20: 5 On the **d** when I chose Israel
Ezek 20: 6 On that **d** I lifted My hand in
Ezek 20:29 is called Bamah to this **d**
Ezek 20:31 your idols, even to this **d**
Ezek 21:25 whose **d** has come, whose
Ezek 21:29 the slain whose **d** has come
Ezek 22:24 on in the **d** of indignation
Ezek 23:38 My sanctuary on the same **d**
Ezek 23:39 on the same **d** they came into
Ezek 24: 1 on the tenth **d** of the month
Ezek 24: 2 name of the **d**, this very **d**
Ezek 24: 2 against Jerusalem this very **d**
Ezek 24:25 will it not be in the **d** when
Ezek 24:26 on that **d** one who escapes
Ezek 24:27 on that **d** your mouth will be
Ezek 26: 1 on the first **d** of the month
Ezek 26:18 tremble on the **d** of your fall
Ezek 27:27 seas on the **d** of your ruin
Ezek 28:13 you on the **d** you were created
Ezek 28:15 from the **d** you were created

Ezek 29: 1 on the twelfth **d** of the month
Ezek 29:17 on the first **d** of the month
Ezek 29:21 In that **d** I will cause the
Ezek 30: 2 Wail, 'Woe to the **d**
Ezek 30: 3 For the **d** is near, even the
Ezek 30: 3 even the **d** of the LORD is
Ezek 30: 3 it will be a **d** of clouds, the
Ezek 30: 9 On that **d** messengers shall go
Ezek 30: 9 them, as on the **d** of Egypt
Ezek 30:18 At Tehaphnehes the **d** shall
Ezek 30:20 on the seventh **d** of the month
Ezek 31: 1 on the first **d** of the month
Ezek 31:15 In the **d** when it went down
Ezek 32: 1 on the first **d** of the month
Ezek 32:10 life, in the **d** of your fall
Ezek 32:17 the fifteenth **d** of the month
Ezek 33:12 in the **d** of his transgression
Ezek 33:12 the **d** that he turns from his
Ezek 33:12 in the **d** that he sins
Ezek 33:21 on the fifth **d** of the month
Ezek 34:12 **d** he is among his scattered
Ezek 34:12 on a cloudy and dark **d**
Ezek 36:33 On the **d** that I cleanse you
Ezek 38:10 On that **d** it shall come to
Ezek 38:14 On that **d** when My people
Ezek 38:19 Surely in that **d** there shall
Ezek 39: 8 This is the **d** of which I have
Ezek 39:11 that **d** that I will give Gog a
Ezek 39:13 on the **d** that I am glorified
Ezek 39:22 their God from that **d** forward
Ezek 40: 1 on the tenth **d** of the month
Ezek 40: 1 on the very same **d** the hand
Ezek 43:18 on the **d** when it is made, for
Ezek 43:22 On the second **d** you shall
Ezek 43:25 Every **d** for seven days you
Ezek 43:27 it shall be, on the eighth **d**
Ezek 44:27 on the **d** that he goes to the
Ezek 45:18 on the first **d** of the month
Ezek 45:20 **d** of the month for everyone
Ezek 45:21 the fourteenth **d** of the month
Ezek 45:22 on that **d** the prince shall
Ezek 45:25 the fifteenth **d** of the month
Ezek 46: 1 on the **d** of the New Moon it
Ezek 46: 4 **d** shall be six lambs without
Ezek 46: 6 On the **d** of the New Moon it
Ezek 46:12 as he did on the Sabbath **d**
Ezek 48:35 the city from that **d** shall be
Dan 6:10 his knees three times that **d**
Dan 6:13 his petition three times a **d**
Dan 9: 7 of face, as it is this **d**
Dan 9:15 a name, as it is this **d**
Dan 10: 4 **d** of the first month, as I
Dan 10:12 for from the first **d** that you
Hos 1: 5 **d** that I will break the bow
Hos 1:11 will be the **d** of Jezreel
Hos 2: 3 as in the **d** she was born, and
Hos 2:15 as in the **d** when she came up
Hos 2:16 And it shall be, in that **d**
Hos 2:18 In that **d** I will make a
Hos 2:21 in that **d** that I will answer
Hos 4: 5 you shall stumble in the **d**
Hos 5: 9 desolate in the **d** of rebuke
Hos 6: 2 on the third **d** He will raise
Hos 7: 5 In the **d** of our king princes
Hos 9: 5 you do in the appointed **d**
Hos 9: 5 in the **d** of the feast of the
Hos 10:14 Beth Arbel in the **d** of battle
Joel 1:15 Alas for the **d**
Joel 1:15 For the **d** of the LORD is at
Joel 2: 1 for the **d** of the LORD is
Joel 2: 2 a **d** of darkness and gloominess
Joel 2: 2 a **d** of clouds and thick
Joel 2:11 For the **d** of the LORD is
Joel 2:31 and terrible **d** of the LORD
Joel 3:14 For the **d** of the LORD is near
Joel 3:18 **d** that the mountains shall
Amos 1:14 shouting in the **d** of battle
Amos 1:14 in the **d** of the whirlwind
Amos 2:16 shall flee naked in that **d**
Amos 3:14 That in the **d** I punish Israel
Amos 5: 8 makes the **d** dark as night
Amos 5:18 who desire the **d** of the LORD
Amos 5:18 is the **d** of the LORD to you
Amos 5:20 Is not the **d** of the LORD
Amos 6: 3 who put far off the **d** of doom
Amos 8: 3 shall be wailing in that **d**
Amos 8: 9 shall come to pass in that **d**
Amos 8:10 and its end like a bitter **d**
Amos 8:13 In that **d** the fair virgins and
Amos 9:11 On that **d** I will raise up The
Obad 8 Will I not in that **d**," says
Obad 11 In the **d** that you stood on
Obad 11 in the **d** that strangers
Obad 12 not have gazed on the **d** of
Obad 12 in the **d** of his captivity
Obad 12 in the **d** of their destruction
Obad 12 proudly in the **d** of distress
Obad 13 in the **d** of their calamity
Obad 13 in the **d** of their calamity
Obad 13 in the **d** of their calamity
Obad 14 remained in the **d** of distress
Obad 15 For the **d** of the LORD upon
Jon 4: 7 next **d** God prepared a worm
Mic 2: 4 In that **d** one shall take up a
Mic 3: 6 the **d** shall be dark for them
Mic 4: 6 In that **d**," says the LORD
Mic 5:10 And it shall be in that **d**,"
Mic 7: 4 the **d** of your watchman and
Mic 7:11 In the **d** when your walls are
Mic 7:11 in that **d** the decree shall go
Mic 7:12 In that **d** they shall come to
Nah 1: 7 in the **d** of trouble
Nah 2: 3 in the **d** of his preparation
Nah 3:17 in the hedges on a cold **d**
Hab 3:16 rest in the **d** of trouble
Zeph 1: 7 for the **d** of the LORD is at
Zeph 1: 8 be, in the **d** of the LORD's
Zeph 1: 9 In the same **d** I will punish
Zeph 1:10 And there shall be on that **d**
Zeph 1:14 The great **d** of the LORD is
Zeph 1:14 The noise of the **d** of the
Zeph 1:15 That **d** is a **d** of wrath,
Zeph 1:15 a **d** of trouble and distress
Zeph 1:15 a **d** of devastation and
Zeph 1:15 a **d** of darkness and gloominess
Zeph 1:15 a **d** of clouds and thick
Zeph 1:16 a **d** of trumpet and alarm
Zeph 1:18 in the **d** of the LORD's wrath
Zeph 2: 2 before the **d** passes like
Zeph 2: 2 before the **d** of the LORD's
Zeph 2: 3 in the **d** of the LORD's anger
Zeph 3: 8 Until the **d** I rise up for
Zeph 3:11 In that **d** you shall not be
Zeph 3:16 In that **d** it shall be said to
Hag 1: 1 on the first **d** of the month
Hag 1:15 **d** of the sixth month, in the
Hag 2: 1 twenty-first **d** of the month
Hag 2:10 **d** of the ninth month, in the
Hag 2:15 consider from this **d** forward
Hag 2:18 now from this **d** forward, from
Hag 2:18 **d** of the ninth month, from
Hag 2:18 month, from the **d** that the
Hag 2:19 But from this **d** forward I
Hag 2:20 twenty-fourth **d** of the month
Hag 2:23 In that **d**,' says the LORD of
Zech 1: 7 On the twenty-fourth **d** of the
Zech 2:11 joined to the LORD in that **d**
Zech 3: 9 of that land in one **d**
Zech 3:10 In that **d**,' says the LORD of
Zech 4:10 the **d** of small things
Zech 6:10 and go the same **d** and enter the
Zech 7: 1 on the fourth **d** of the ninth
Zech 8: 9 who were in the **d** that the
Zech 9:16 God will save them in that **d**
Zech 11:11 So it was broken on that **d**
Zech 12: 3 it shall happen in that **d**
Zech 12: 4 In that **d**," says the LORD
Zech 12: 6 In that **d** I will make the
Zech 12: 8 In that **d** the LORD will
Zech 12: 8 in that **d** shall be like David
Zech 12: 9 It shall be in that **d** that I
Zech 12:11 In that **d** there shall be a
Zech 13: 1 In that **d** a fountain shall be
Zech 13: 2 It shall be in that **d**," says
Zech 13: 4 it shall be in that **d** that
Zech 14: 1 the **d** of the LORD is coming,
Zech 14: 3 He fights in the **d** of battle
Zech 14: 4 in that **d** His feet will stand
Zech 14: 6 shall come to pass in that **d**
Zech 14: 7 It shall be one **d** which is
Zech 14: 7 neither **d** nor night
Zech 14: 8 in that **d** it shall be that
Zech 14: 9 In that **d** it shall be
Zech 14:13 shall come to pass in that **d**
Zech 14:20 In that **d** "HOLINESS TO THE
Zech 14:21 In that **d** there shall no
Mal 3: 2 endure the **d** of His coming
Mal 3:17 On the **d** that I make them My
Mal 4: 1 the **d** is coming, burning like
Mal 4: 1 the **d** which is coming shall
Mal 4: 3 feet on the **d** that I do this
Mal 4: 5 and dreadful **d** of the LORD
Matt 6:11 Give us this **d** our daily
Matt 6:34 for the **d** is its own trouble
Matt 7:22 Many will say to Me in that **d**
Matt 10:15 Gomorrah in the **d** of judgment
Matt 11:22 Sidon in the **d** of judgment
Matt 11:23 have remained until this **d**
Matt 11:24 **d** of judgment than for you
Matt 12:36 of it in the **d** of judgment
Matt 13: 1 On the same **d** Jesus went out
Matt 16:21 be raised again the third **d**
Matt 17:23 the third **d** He will be raised
Matt 20: 2 laborers for a denarius a **d**
Matt 20: 6 been standing here idle all **d**
Matt 20:12 burden and the heat of the **d**
Matt 20:19 And the third **d** He will rise
Matt 22:23 The same **d** the Sadducees, who
Matt 22:46 nor from that **d** on did anyone
Matt 24:36 But of that **d** and hour no one
Matt 24:38 until the **d** that Noah entered
Matt 24:50 **d** when he is not looking for
Matt 25:13 for you know neither the **d**
Matt 26:17 Now on the first **d** of the
Matt 26:29 **d** when I drink it new with
Matt 27: 8 the Field of Blood to this **d**
Matt 27:62 On the next **d**, which followed
Matt 27:62 followed the **D** of Preparation
Matt 27:64 made secure until the third **d**
Matt 28: 1 as the first **d** of the week
Matt 28:15 among the Jews until this **d**
Mark 4:27 sleep by night and rise by **d**
Mark 4:35 On the same **d**, when evening
Mark 5: 5 And always, night and **d**, he was
Mark 6:11 Gomorrah in the **d** of judgment
Mark 6:21 Then an opportune **d** came
Mark 6:35 when the **d** was now far spent,
Mark 9:31 He will rise the third **d**
Mark 10:34 And the third **d** He will rise
Mark 11:12 Now the next **d**, when they had
Mark 13:32 But of that **d** and hour no one
Mark 14:12 Now on the first **d** of
Mark 14:25 of the vine until that **d** when
Mark 15:42 it was the Preparation **D**,
Mark 15:42 the **d** before the Sabbath,
Mark 16: 2 on the first **d** of the week
Mark 16: 9 on the first **d** of the week
Luke 1:20 the **d** these things take place
Luke 1:59 so it was, on the eighth **d**
Luke 1:80 the **d** of his manifestation to
Luke 2:11 this **d** in the city of David a
Luke 2:37 and prayers night and **d**
Luke 4:16 synagogue on the Sabbath **d**
Luke 4:42 Now when it was **d**, He
Luke 5:17 it happened on a certain **d**
Luke 6:13 And when it was **d**, He called
Luke 6:23 Rejoice in that **d** and leap for
Luke 7:11 the **d** after, that He went
Luke 8:22 it happened, on a certain **d**
Luke 9:12 When the **d** began to wear away
Luke 9:22 and be raised the third **d**
Luke 9:37 Now it happened on the next **d**
Luke 10:12 **D** for Sodom than for that
Luke 10:35 On the next **d**, when he
Luke 11: 3 Give us **d** by **d** our daily
Luke 12:46 **d** when he is not looking for
Luke 13:14 them, and not on the Sabbath **d**
Luke 13:31 On that very **d** some Pharisees
Luke 13:32 and the third **d** I shall be
Luke 13:33 tomorrow, and the **d** following
Luke 14: 5 pull him out on the Sabbath **d**
Luke 16:19 and fared sumptuously every **d**
Luke 17: 4 you seven times in a **d**, and
Luke 17: 4 times in a **d** returns to you
Luke 17:24 Son of Man will be in His **d**
Luke 17:27 until the **d** that Noah entered
Luke 17:29 but on the **d** that Lot went
Luke 17:30 the **d** when the Son of Man is
Luke 17:31 In that **d**, he who is on the
Luke 18: 7 His own elect who cry out **d**
Luke 18:33 And the third **d** He will rise
Luke 19:42 especially in this your **d**
Luke 21:34 life, and that **D** come on you
Luke 22: 7 Then came the **D** of Unleavened
Luke 22:34 **d** before you will deny three
Luke 22:66 As soon as it was **d**, the
Luke 23:12 That very **d** Pilate and Herod
Luke 23:54 That **d** was the Preparation,
Luke 24: 1 on the first **d** of the week
Luke 24: 7 and the third **d** rise again

Luke 24:13 were traveling that same **d** to
Luke 24:21 today is the third **d** since
Luke 24:29 and the **d** is far spent
Luke 24:46 from the dead the third **d**
John 1:29 The next **d** John saw Jesus
John 1:35 Again, the next **d**, John stood
John 1:39 remained with Him that **d** (now
John 1:43 The following **d** Jesus wanted
John 2: 1 On the third **d** there was a
John 5: 9 And that **d** was the Sabbath
John 6:22 On the following **d**, when the
John 6:39 raise it up at the last **d**
John 6:40 raise him up at the last **d**
John 6:44 raise him up at the last **d**
John 6:54 raise him up at the last **d**
John 7:37 On the last **d**, that great **d**
John 8:56 Abraham rejoiced to see My **d**
John 9: 4 Him who sent Me while it is **d**
John 11: 9 not twelve hours in the **d**
John 11: 9 If anyone walks in the **d**, he
John 11:24 resurrection at the last **d**
John 11:53 Then from that **d** on they
John 12: 7 this for the **d** of My burial
John 12:12 The next **d** a great multitude
John 12:48 will judge him in the last **d**
John 14:20 At that **d** you will know that
John 16:23 in that **d** you will ask Me
John 16:26 In that **d** you will ask in My
John 19:14 Preparation **D** of the Passover
John 19:31 it was the Preparation **D**,
John 19:31 that Sabbath was a high **d**)
John 19:42 of the Jews' Preparation **D**
John 20: 1 On the first **d** of the week
John 20:19 the same **d** at evening
John 20:19 being the first **d** of the week
Acts 1: 2 until the **d** in which He was
Acts 1:22 **d** when He was taken up from
Acts 2: 1 Now when the **D** of Pentecost
Acts 2:15 only the third hour of the **d**
Acts 2:20 and notable **d** of the LORD
Acts 2:29 his tomb is with us to this **d**
Acts 2:41 that **d** about three thousand
Acts 4: 3 in custody until the next **d**
Acts 4: 5 came to pass, on the next **d**
Acts 4: 9 If we this **d** are judged for a
Acts 7: 8 him on the eighth **d**
Acts 7:26 the next **d** he appeared to two
Acts 9:24 And they watched the gates **d**
Acts 10: 3 **d** he saw clearly in a vision
Acts 10: 9 The next **d**, as they went on
Acts 10:23 On the next **d** Peter went away
Acts 10:24 the following **d** they entered
Acts 10:40 God raised up on the third **d**
Acts 12:18 Then, as soon as it was **d**
Acts 12:21 So on a set **d** Herod, arrayed
Acts 13:14 synagogue on the Sabbath **d**
Acts 14:20 the next **d** he departed with
Acts 16:11 the next **d** came to Neapolis,
Acts 16:13 on the Sabbath **d** we went out
Acts 16:35 And when it was **d**, the
Acts 17:31 **d** on which He will judge the
Acts 20: 7 on the first **d** of the week
Acts 20: 7 ready to depart the next **d**
Acts 20:15 and the next **d** came opposite
Acts 20:15 the following **d** we arrived at
Acts 20:15 the next **d** we came to Miletus
Acts 20:16 on the **D** of Pentecost
Acts 20:18 from the first **d** that I came
Acts 20:26 I testify to you this **d** that
Acts 20:31 night and **d** with tears
Acts 21: 1 the following **d** to Rhodes
Acts 21: 7 and stayed with them one **d**
Acts 21: 8 On the next **d** we who were
Acts 21:18 On the following **d** Paul went
Acts 21:26 took the men, and the next **d**
Acts 22:30 The next **d**, because he wanted
Acts 23: 1 before God until this **d**
Acts 23:12 And when it was **d**, some of the
Acts 23:32 The next **d** they left the
Acts 24:21 am being judged by you this **d**
Acts 25: 6 And the next **d**, sitting on the
Acts 25:17 the next **d** I sat on the
Acts 25:23 So the next **d**, when Agrippa
Acts 26: 7 serving God night and **d**, hope
Acts 26:22 from God, to this **d** I stand
Acts 27: 3 the next **d** we landed at Sidon
Acts 27:18 the next **d** they lightened the
Acts 27:19 On the third **d** we threw the
Acts 27:29 and prayed for **d** to come
Acts 27:33 as **d** was about to dawn, Paul
Acts 27:33 fourteenth **d** you have waited
Acts 27:39 Now when it was **d**, they did
Acts 28:13 after one **d** the south wind
Acts 28:13 the next **d** we came to Puteoli
Acts 28:23 they had appointed him a **d**
Rom 2: 5 wrath in the **d** of wrath and
Rom 2:16 in the **d** when God will judge
Rom 8:36 sake we are killed all **d** long
Rom 10:21 All **d** long I have stretched
Rom 11: 8 not hear, to this very **d**
Rom 13:12 far spent, the **d** is at hand
Rom 13:13 us walk properly, as in the **d**
Rom 14: 5 esteems one **d** above another
Rom 14: 5 another esteems every **d** alike
Rom 14: 6 He who observes the **d**,
Rom 14: 6 he who does not observe the **d**
1Co 1: 8 **d** of our Lord Jesus Christ
1Co 3:13 for the **D** will declare it,
1Co 5: 5 in the **d** of the Lord Jesus
1Co 10: 8 did, and in one **d** twenty-three
1Co 15: 4 He rose again the third **d**
1Co 16: 2 On the first **d** of the week
2Co 1:14 in the **d** of the Lord Jesus
2Co 3:14 For until this **d** the same
2Co 3:15 But even to this **d**, when
2Co 4:16 man is being renewed **d** by **d**
2Co 6: 2 in the **d** of salvation I have
2Co 6: 2 now is the **d** of salvation
2Co 11:25 a **d** I have been in the deep
Eph 4:30 for the **d** of redemption
Eph 6:13 to withstand in the evil **d**
Phil 1: 5 from the first **d** until now
Phil 1: 6 until the **d** of Jesus Christ
Phil 1:10 offense till the **d** of Christ
Phil 2:16 **d** of Christ that I have not
Phil 3: 5 circumcised the eighth **d**, of
Col 1: 6 you since the **d** you heard
Col 1: 9 since the **d** we heard it, do
1Th 2: 9 for laboring night and **d**, that
1Th 3:10 **d** praying exceedingly that we
1Th 5: 2 know perfectly that the **d** of
1Th 5: 4 so that this **D** should
1Th 5: 5 of light and sons of the **d**
1Th 5: 8 us who are of the **d** be sober
2Th 1:10 when He comes, in that **D**, to
2Th 2: 2 as though the **d** of Christ had
2Th 2: 3 for that **D** will not come
2Th 3: 8 with labor and toil night and **d**
1Ti 5: 5 and prayers night and **d**
2Ti 1: 3 you in my prayers night and **d**
2Ti 1:12 committed to Him until that **D**
2Ti 1:18 mercy from the Lord in that **D**
2Ti 4: 8 will give to me on that **D**
Heb 3: 8 in the **d** of trial in the
Heb 4: 4 of the seventh **d** in this way
Heb 4: 4 **d** from all His works"
Heb 4: 7 He designates a certain **d**
Heb 4: 8 have spoken of another **d**
Heb 8: 9 the **d** when I took them by the
Heb 10:25 as you see the **D** approaching
Jas 5: 5 hearts as in a **d** of slaughter
1Pe 2:12 God in the **d** of visitation
2Pe 1:19 dark place, until the **d** dawns
2Pe 2: 8 soul from **d** to **d** by seeing
2Pe 2: 9 for the **d** of judgment,
2Pe 3: 7 fire until the **d** of judgment
2Pe 3: 8 one **d** is as a thousand years
2Pe 3: 8 and a thousand years as one **d**
2Pe 3:10 But the **d** of the Lord will
2Pe 3:12 the coming of the **d** of God
1Jn 4:17 boldness in the **d** of judgment
Jude 6 the judgment of the great **d**
Rev 1:10 in the Spirit on the Lord's **D**
Rev 4: 8 they do not rest **d** or night
Rev 6:17 For the great **d** of His wrath
Rev 7:15 throne of God, and serve Him **d**
Rev 8:12 third of the **d** did not shine
Rev 9:15 prepared for the hour and **d**
Rev 12:10 accused them before our God **d**
Rev 14:11 they have no rest **d** or night
Rev 16:14 that great **d** of God Almighty
Rev 18: 8 plagues will come in one **d**
Rev 20:10 And they will be tormented **d**
Rev 21:25 by **d** (there shall be no night

DAYBREAK (*see* DAY)
2Sa 2:32 and they came to Hebron at **d**
Neh 4:21 **d** until the stars appeared
Acts 20:11 a long while, even till **d**

DAYLIGHT (*see* DAY)
Judg 16: 2 In the morning, when it is **d**
Amos 8: 9 darken the earth in broad **d**
Mark 1:35 risen a long while before **d**

DAY'S (*see* DAY)
Num 11:31 about a **d** journey on this
Num 11:31 and about a **d** journey on the
1Ki 19: 4 But he himself went a **d**
1Ch 16:37 as every **d** work required
Jon 3: 4 the city on the first **d** walk
Luke 2:44 they went a **d** journey, and
Acts 1:12 a Sabbath **d** journey

DAYS (*see* DAY, DAYS')
Gen 1:14 signs and seasons, and for **d**
Gen 3:14 dust all the **d** of your life
Gen 3:17 of it all the **d** of your life
Gen 5: 4 the **d** of Adam were eight
Gen 5: 5 So all the **d** that Adam lived
Gen 5: 8 So all the **d** of Seth were
Gen 5:11 So all the **d** of Enosh were
Gen 5:14 So all the **d** of Cainan were
Gen 5:17 So all the **d** of Mahalaleel
Gen 5:20 So all the **d** of Jared were
Gen 5:23 So all the **d** of Enoch were
Gen 5:27 So all the **d** of Methuselah
Gen 5:31 So all the **d** of Lamech were
Gen 6: 3 yet his **d** shall be one
Gen 6: 4 on the earth in those **d**, and
Gen 7: 4 For after seven more **d** I will
Gen 7: 4 to rain on the earth forty **d**
Gen 7:10 **d** that the waters of the
Gen 7:12 rain was on the earth forty **d**
Gen 7:17 was on the earth forty **d**
Gen 7:24 earth one hundred and fifty **d**
Gen 8: 3 fifty **d** the waters decreased
Gen 8: 6 pass, at the end of forty **d**
Gen 8:10 he waited yet another seven **d**
Gen 8:12 he waited yet another seven **d**
Gen 9:29 So all the **d** of Noah were
Gen 10:25 for in his **d** the earth was
Gen 11:32 So the **d** of Terah were two
Gen 14: 1 it came to pass in the **d** of
Gen 17:12 He who is eight **d** old among
Gen 21: 4 Isaac when he was eight **d** old
Gen 21:34 of the Philistines many **d**
Gen 24:55 woman stay with us a few **d**
Gen 25:24 So when her **d** were fulfilled
Gen 26: 1 that was in the **d** of Abraham
Gen 26:15 the **d** of Abraham his father
Gen 26:18 the **d** of Abraham his father
Gen 27:41 The **d** of mourning for my
Gen 27:44 And stay with him a few **d**,
Gen 29:20 they seemed but a few **d** to
Gen 29:21 for my **d** are fulfilled, that
Gen 30:14 in the **d** of wheat harvest
Gen 35:28 Now the **d** of Isaac were one
Gen 35:29 being old and full of **d**
Gen 37:34 and mourned for his son many **d**
Gen 40:12 three branches are three **d**
Gen 40:13 Now within three **d** Pharaoh
Gen 40:18 The three baskets are three **d**
Gen 40:19 Within three **d** Pharaoh will
Gen 42:17 together in prison three **d**
Gen 47: 9 The **d** of the years of my
Gen 47: 9 evil have been the **d** of the
Gen 47: 9 have not attained to the **d** of
Gen 47: 9 in the **d** of their pilgrimage
Gen 49: 1 befall you in the last **d**
Gen 50: 3 Forty **d** were required for him
Gen 50: 3 for such are the **d** required
Gen 50: 3 mourned for him seventy **d**
Gen 50: 4 when the **d** of his mourning
Gen 50:10 He observed seven **d** of
Ex 2:11 it came to pass in those **d**
Ex 7:25 seven **d** passed after the LORD
Ex 10:22 all the land of Egypt three **d**
Ex 10:23 from his place for three **d**
Ex 12:15 Seven **d** you shall eat
Ex 12:19 For seven **d** no leaven shall
Ex 13: 6 Seven **d** you shall eat
Ex 13: 7 bread shall be eaten seven **d**
Ex 15:22 And they went three **d** in the
Ex 16:26 Six **d** you shall gather it,
Ex 16:29 the sixth day bread for two **d**
Ex 20: 9 Six **d** you shall labor and do
Ex 20:11 For in six **d** the LORD made
Ex 20:12 that your **d** may be long upon
Ex 22:30 be with its mother seven **d**
Ex 23:12 Six **d** you shall do your work,

Ex 23:15 eat unleavened bread seven **d**
Ex 23:26 fulfill the number of your **d**
Ex 24:16 and the cloud covered it six **d**
Ex 24:18 was on the mountain forty **d**
Ex 29:30 shall put them on for seven **d**
Ex 29:35 Seven **d** you shall consecrate
Ex 29:37 Seven **d** you shall make
Ex 31:15 Work shall be done for six **d**
Ex 31:17 for in six **d** the LORD made
Ex 34:18 Seven **d** you shall eat
Ex 34:21 Six **d** you shall work, but on
Ex 34:28 there with the LORD forty **d**
Ex 35: 2 Work shall be done for six **d**
Lev 8:33 of meeting for seven **d**
Lev 8:33 until the **d** of your
Lev 8:33 For seven **d** he shall
Lev 8:35 day and night for seven **d**, and
Lev 12: 2 she shall be unclean seven **d**
Lev 12: 2 as in the **d** of her customary
Lev 12: 4 purification thirty-three **d**
Lev 12: 4 the **d** of her purification are
Lev 12: 5 her purification sixty-six **d**
Lev 12: 6 When the **d** of her
Lev 13: 4 one who has the sore seven **d**
Lev 13: 5 isolate him another seven **d**
Lev 13:21 shall isolate him seven **d**
Lev 13:26 shall isolate him seven **d**
Lev 13:31 the sore of the scall seven **d**
Lev 13:33 has the scall another seven **d**
Lev 13:46 All the **d** he has the sore he
Lev 13:50 which has the plague seven **d**
Lev 13:54 isolate it another seven **d**
Lev 14: 8 stay outside his tent seven **d**
Lev 14:38 and shut up the house seven **d**
Lev 15:13 seven **d** for his cleansing
Lev 15:19 shall be set apart seven **d**
Lev 15:24 he shall be unclean seven **d**
Lev 15:25 discharge of blood for many **d**
Lev 15:25 all the **d** of her unclean
Lev 15:25 **d** of her customary impurity
Lev 15:26 **d** of her discharge shall be
Lev 15:28 count for herself seven **d**
Lev 22:27 be seven **d** with its mother
Lev 23: 3 Six **d** shall work be done,
Lev 23: 6 seven **d** you must eat
Lev 23: 8 fire to the LORD for seven **d**
Lev 23:16 Count fifty **d** to the day
Lev 23:34 for seven **d** to the LORD
Lev 23:36 For seven **d** you shall offer
Lev 23:39 feast of the LORD for seven **d**
Lev 23:40 the LORD your God for seven **d**
Lev 23:41 LORD for seven **d** in the year
Lev 23:42 dwell in booths for seven **d**
Num 6: 4 All the **d** of his separation
Num 6: 5 All the **d** of the vow of his
Num 6: 5 until the **d** are fulfilled for
Num 6: 6 All the **d** that he separates
Num 6: 8 All the **d** of his separation
Num 6:12 LORD the **d** of his separation
Num 6:12 the former **d** shall be lost
Num 6:13 When the **d** of his separation
Num 9:19 many **d** above the tabernacle,
Num 9:20 above the tabernacle a few **d**
Num 9:22 Whether it was two **d**, a month
Num 10:33 LORD on a journey of three **d**
Num 10:33 them for the three **d**' journey
Num 11:19 nor two **d**, nor five **d**
Num 11:19 nor ten **d**, nor twenty **d**
Num 12:14 she not be shamed seven **d**
Num 12:14 shut out of the camp seven **d**
Num 12:15 shut out of the camp seven **d**
Num 13:25 out the land after forty **d**
Num 14:34 to the number of the **d** in
Num 14:34 spied out the land, forty **d**
Num 19:11 shall be unclean seven **d**
Num 19:14 tent shall be unclean seven **d**
Num 19:16 shall be unclean seven **d**
Num 20:29 mourned for Aaron thirty **d**
Num 24:14 your people in the latter **d**
Num 28:17 shall be eaten for seven **d**
Num 28:24 by fire daily for seven **d**
Num 29:12 a feast to the LORD seven **d**
Num 31:19 outside the camp seven **d**
Deut 1:46 you remained in Kadesh many **d**
Deut 1:46 according to the **d** that you
Deut 2: 1 skirted Mount Seir for many **d**
Deut 4: 9 heart all the **d** of your life
Deut 4:10 the **d** they live on the earth
Deut 4:26 will not prolong your **d** in it
Deut 4:30 come upon you in the latter **d**
Deut 4:32 the **d** that are past, which
Deut 4:40 that you may prolong your **d**
Deut 5:13 Six **d** you shall labor and do
Deut 5:16 that your **d** may be long, and
Deut 5:33 that you may prolong your **d**
Deut 6: 2 all the **d** of your life, and
Deut 6: 2 that your **d** may be prolonged
Deut 9: 9 on the mountain forty **d** and
Deut 9:11 pass, at the end of forty **d**
Deut 9:18 as at the first, forty **d**
Deut 9:25 forty **d** and forty nights I
Deut 10:10 in the mountain forty **d** and
Deut 11: 9 that you may prolong your **d**
Deut 11:21 your **d** and the **d** of your
Deut 11:21 like the **d** of the heavens
Deut 12: 1 all the **d** that you live on
Deut 16: 3 seven **d** you shall eat
Deut 16: 3 Egypt all the **d** of your life
Deut 16: 4 your territory for seven **d**
Deut 16: 8 Six **d** you shall eat
Deut 16:13 Feast of Tabernacles seven **d**
Deut 16:15 Seven **d** you shall keep a
Deut 17: 9 to the judge there in those **d**
Deut 17:19 read it all the **d** of his life
Deut 17:20 prolong his **d** in his kingdom
Deut 19:17 judges who serve in those **d**
Deut 22: 7 that you may prolong your **d**
Deut 22:19 cannot divorce her all his **d**
Deut 22:29 to divorce her all his **d**
Deut 23: 6 prosperity all your **d** forever
Deut 25:15 that your **d** may be lengthened
Deut 26: 3 one who is priest in those **d**
Deut 30:18 you shall not prolong your **d**
Deut 30:20 life and the length of your **d**
Deut 31:14 the **d** approach when you must
Deut 31:29 befall you in the latter **d**
Deut 32: 7 Remember the **d** of old,
Deut 32:47 **d** in the land which you cross
Deut 33:25 as your **d**, so shall your
Deut 34: 8 the plains of Moab thirty **d**
Deut 34: 8 So the **d** of weeping and
Josh 1: 5 you all the **d** of your life
Josh 1:11 for within three **d** you will
Josh 2:16 Hide there three **d**, until the
Josh 2:22 stayed there three **d** until
Josh 3: 2 So it was, after three **d**,
Josh 4:14 Moses, all the **d** of his life
Josh 6: 3 This you shall do six **d**
Josh 6:14 So they did six **d**
Josh 9:16 at the end of three **d**, after
Josh 20: 6 who is high priest in those **d**
Josh 22: 3 your brethren these many **d**
Josh 24:31 the LORD all the **d** of Joshua
Josh 24:31 all the **d** of the elders who
Judg 2: 7 the LORD all the **d** of Joshua
Judg 2: 7 all the **d** of the elders who
Judg 2:18 all the **d** of the judge
Judg 5: 6 In the **d** of Shamgar, son of
Judg 5: 6 Anath, in the **d** of Jael, the
Judg 8:28 years in the **d** of Gideon
Judg 11:40 of Israel went four **d** each
Judg 14:12 the seven **d** of the feast,
Judg 14:14 Now for three **d** they could
Judg 14:17 **d** while their feast lasted
Judg 15:20 in the **d** of the Philistines
Judg 17: 6 In those **d** there was no king
Judg 18: 1 In those **d** there was no king
Judg 18: 1 in those **d** the tribe of the
Judg 19: 1 And it came to pass in those **d**
Judg 19: 4 and he stayed with him three **d**
Judg 20:27 of God was there in those **d**
Judg 20:28 stood before it in those **d**)
Judg 21:25 In those **d** there was no king
Ruth 1: 1 in the **d** when the judges
1Sa 1:11 LORD all the **d** of his life
1Sa 2:31 the **d** are coming that I will
1Sa 3: 1 the LORD was rare in those **d**
1Sa 7:13 all the **d** of Samuel
1Sa 7:15 Israel all the **d** of his life
1Sa 9:20 that were lost three **d** ago
1Sa 10: 8 Seven **d** you shall wait, till
1Sa 11: 3 Hold off for seven **d**, that we
1Sa 13: 8 Then he waited seven **d**,
1Sa 13:11 come within the **d** appointed
1Sa 14:52 Philistines all the **d** of Saul
1Sa 17:12 in years, in the **d** of Saul
1Sa 17:16 and presented himself forty **d**
1Sa 18:26 Now the **d** had not expired
1Sa 20:19 when you have stayed three **d**
1Sa 21: 5 three **d** since I came out
1Sa 25:28 in you throughout your **d**
1Sa 25:38 came about, after about ten **d**
1Sa 28: 1 those **d** that the Philistines
1Sa 29: 3 who has been with me these **d**
1Sa 30:12 drunk any water for three **d**
1Sa 30:13 because three **d** ago I fell
1Sa 31:13 at Jabesh, and fasted seven **d**
2Sa 1: 1 had stayed two **d** in Ziklag
2Sa 7:12 When your **d** are fulfilled and
2Sa 16:23 which he gave in those **d**
2Sa 20: 4 Judah for me within three **d**
2Sa 21: 1 **d** of David for three years
2Sa 21: 9 to death in the **d** of harvest
2Sa 21: 9 of harvest, in the first **d**
2Sa 24: 8 of nine months and twenty **d**
1Ki 2: 1 Then the **d** of David drew near
1Ki 2:38 dwelt in Jerusalem many **d**
1Ki 3: 2 of the LORD until those **d**
1Ki 3:13 among the kings all your **d**
1Ki 3:14 then I will lengthen your **d**
1Ki 4:21 Solomon all the **d** of his life
1Ki 4:25 all the **d** of Solomon
1Ki 8:40 they may fear You all the **d**
1Ki 8:65 the LORD our God, seven **d**
1Ki 8:65 seven more **d**—fourteen **d**
1Ki 10:21 nothing in the **d** of Solomon
1Ki 11:12 I will not do it in your **d**
1Ki 11:25 the **d** of Solomon (besides the
1Ki 11:34 **d** of his life for the sake of
1Ki 12: 5 Depart for three **d**, then come
1Ki 14:30 and Jeroboam all their **d**
1Ki 15: 5 him all the **d** of his life
1Ki 15: 6 all the **d** of his life
1Ki 15:14 loyal to the LORD all his **d**
1Ki 15:16 king of Israel all their **d**
1Ki 15:32 king of Israel all their **d**
1Ki 16:15 had reigned in Tirzah seven **d**
1Ki 16:34 In his **d** Hiel of Bethel built
1Ki 17:15 her household ate for many **d**
1Ki 18: 1 **d** that the word of the LORD
1Ki 19: 8 strength of that food forty **d**
1Ki 20:29 each other for seven **d**
1Ki 21:29 bring the calamity in his **d**
1Ki 21:29 but in the **d** of his son I
1Ki 22:46 in the **d** of his father Asa
2Ki 2:17 three **d** but did not find him
2Ki 3: 9 that roundabout route seven **d**
2Ki 8:20 In his **d** Edom revolted
2Ki 10:32 In those **d** the LORD began to
2Ki 12: 2 the **d** in which Jehoiada the
2Ki 13: 3 son of Hazael, all their **d**
2Ki 13:22 Israel all the **d** of Jehoahaz
2Ki 15:18 **d** from the sins of Jeroboam
2Ki 15:29 In the **d** of Pekah king of
2Ki 15:37 In those **d** the LORD began to
2Ki 18: 4 for until those **d** the
2Ki 20: 1 In those **d** Hezekiah was sick
2Ki 20: 6 add to your **d** fifteen years
2Ki 20:17 the **d** are coming when all
2Ki 20:19 and truth at least in my **d**
2Ki 23:22 **d** of the judges who judged
2Ki 23:22 nor in all the **d** of the kings
2Ki 23:29 In his **d** Pharaoh Necho king
2Ki 24: 1 In his **d** Nebuchadnezzar king
2Ki 25:29 king all the **d** of his life
2Ki 25:30 day, all the **d** of his life
1Ch 1:19 for in his **d** the earth was
1Ch 4:41 by name came in the **d** of
1Ch 5:10 Now in the **d** of Saul they
1Ch 5:17 by genealogies in the **d** of
1Ch 5:17 in the **d** of Jeroboam king of
1Ch 7: 2 their number in the **d** of
1Ch 7:22 their father mourned many **d**
1Ch 9:25 from time to time for seven **d**
1Ch 10:12 at Jabesh, and fasted seven **d**
1Ch 12:39 were there with David three **d**
1Ch 13: 3 at it since the **d** of Saul
1Ch 17:11 when your **d** are fulfilled,
1Ch 21:12 or else for three **d** the sword
1Ch 22: 9 quietness to Israel in his **d**
1Ch 23: 1 David was old and full of **d**
1Ch 29:15 our **d** on earth are as a
1Ch 29:28 in a good old age, full of **d**
2Ch 7: 8 kept the feast seven **d**, and
2Ch 7: 9 of the altar seven **d**
2Ch 7: 9 and the feast seven **d**
2Ch 9:20 nothing in the **d** of Solomon
2Ch 10: 5 Come back to me after three **d**
2Ch 12:15 and Jeroboam all their **d**
2Ch 13:20 again in the **d** of Abijah

2Ch 14: 1 In his **d** the land was quiet
2Ch 15:17 of Asa was loyal all his **d**
2Ch 20:25 they were three **d** gathering
2Ch 21: 8 In his **d** the Edomites
2Ch 24: 2 the **d** of Jehoiada the priest
2Ch 24:14 all the **d** of Jehoiada
2Ch 24:15 grew old and was full of **d**
2Ch 26: 5 God in the **d** of Zechariah
2Ch 29:17 house of the LORD in eight **d**
2Ch 30:21 seven **d** with great gladness
2Ch 30:22 throughout the feast seven **d**
2Ch 30:23 the feast another seven **d**
2Ch 30:23 another seven **d** with gladness
2Ch 32:24 In those **d** Hezekiah was sick
2Ch 32:26 them in the **d** of Hezekiah
2Ch 34:33 All his **d** they did not depart
2Ch 35:17 Unleavened Bread for seven **d**
2Ch 35:18 the **d** of Samuel the prophet
2Ch 36: 9 three months and ten **d**
Ezra 4: 2 the **d** of Esarhaddon king of
Ezra 4: 5 their purpose all the **d** of
Ezra 4: 7 In the **d** of Artaxerxes also,
Ezra 6:22 Bread seven **d** with joy
Ezra 8:15 and we camped there three **d**
Ezra 8:32 and stayed there three **d**
Ezra 9: 7 Since the **d** of our fathers to
Ezra 10: 8 would not come within three **d**
Ezra 10: 9 at Jerusalem within three **d**
Ezra 10:13 this the work of one or two **d**
Neh 1: 4 wept, and mourned for many **d**
Neh 2:11 and was there three **d**
Neh 5:18 once every ten **d** an abundance
Neh 6:15 month of Elul, in fifty-two **d**
Neh 6:17 Moreover in those **d** the
Neh 8:17 for since the **d** of Joshua the
Neh 8:18 they kept the feast seven **d**
Neh 9:32 from the **d** of the kings of
Neh 12: 7 brethren in the **d** of Jeshua
Neh 12:12 Now in the **d** of Joiakim, the
Neh 12:22 houses in the **d** of Eliashib
Neh 12:23 the **d** of Johanan the son of
Neh 12:26 These lived in the **d** of
Neh 12:26 and in the **d** of Nehemiah the
Neh 12:46 For in the **d** of David and
Neh 12:47 In the **d** of Zerubbabel and in
Neh 12:47 and in the **d** of Nehemiah all
Neh 13: 6 Then after certain **d** I
Neh 13:15 In those **d** I saw in Judah
Neh 13:23 In those **d** I also saw Jews
Esth 1: 1 **d** of Ahasuerus (this was the
Esth 1: 2 in those **d** when King
Esth 1: 4 excellent majesty for many **d**
Esth 1: 4 hundred and eighty **d** in all
Esth 1: 5 when these **d** were completed,
Esth 1: 5 made a feast lasting seven **d**
Esth 2:12 for thus were the **d** of their
Esth 2:21 In those **d**, while Mordecai
Esth 4:11 in to the king these thirty **d**
Esth 4:16 eat nor drink for three **d**
Esth 9:21 fifteenth **d** of the month of
Esth 9:22 as the **d** on which the Jews
Esth 9:22 make them **d** of feasting and
Esth 9:26 So they called these **d** Purim
Esth 9:27 these two **d** every year,
Esth 9:28 that these **d** should be
Esth 9:28 that these **d** of Purim should
Esth 9:31 to confirm these **d** of Purim
Job 1: 5 when the **d** of feasting had
Job 2:13 him on the ground seven **d**
Job 3: 6 among the **d** of the year, may
Job 7: 1 Are not his **d** also like the
Job 7: 1 like the **d** of a hired man
Job 7: 6 My **d** are swifter than a
Job 7:16 for my **d** are but a breath
Job 8: 9 because our **d** on earth are a
Job 9:25 Now my **d** are swifter than a
Job 10: 5 Are Your **d** like the **d** of a
Job 10: 5 like the **d** of a mighty man
Job 10:20 Are not my **d** few
Job 12:12 aged men, and with length of **d**
Job 14: 1 is born of woman is of few **d**
Job 14: 5 Since his **d** are determined,
Job 14:14 All the **d** of my hard service
Job 15:20 writhes with pain all his **d**
Job 17: 1 my **d** are extinguished, the
Job 17:11 My **d** are past, my purposes
Job 21:13 They spend their **d** in wealth
Job 24: 1 who know Him see not His **d**
Job 29: 2 as in the **d** when God watched
Job 29: 4 as I was in the **d** of my prime
Job 29:18 and multiply my **d** as the sand
Job 30:16 the **d** of affliction take hold
Job 30:27 **d** of affliction confront me
Job 33:25 return to the **d** of his youth
Job 36:11 spend their **d** in prosperity
Job 38:12 morning since your **d** began
Job 38:21 the number of your **d** is great
Job 42:12 latter **d** of Job more than his
Job 42:17 So Job died, old and full of **d**
Ps 21: 4 Length of **d** forever and ever
Ps 23: 6 me All the **d** of my life
Ps 27: 4 the LORD All the **d** of my life
Ps 34:12 desires life, And loves many **d**
Ps 37:18 knows the **d** of the upright
Ps 37:19 in the **d** of famine they shall
Ps 39: 4 what is the measure of my **d**
Ps 39: 5 made my **d** as handbreadths
Ps 44: 1 What deeds You did in their **d**
Ps 44: 1 In **d** of old
Ps 49: 5 I fear in the **d** of evil, When
Ps 55:23 not live out half their **d**
Ps 72: 7 In His **d** the righteous shall
Ps 77: 5 have considered the **d** of old
Ps 78:33 Therefore their **d** He consumed
Ps 89:29 his throne as the **d** of heaven
Ps 89:45 The **d** of his youth You have
Ps 90: 9 For all our **d** have passed
Ps 90:10 The **d** of our lives are
Ps 90:12 So teach us to number our **d**
Ps 90:14 rejoice and be glad all our **d**
Ps 90:15 us glad according to the **d** in
Ps 94:13 rest from the **d** of adversity
Ps 102: 3 For my **d** are consumed like
Ps 102:11 My **d** are like a shadow that
Ps 102:23 He shortened my **d**
Ps 102:24 me away in the midst of my **d**
Ps 103:15 for man, his **d** are like grass
Ps 109: 8 Let his **d** be few, And let
Ps 119:84 are the **d** of Your servant
Ps 128: 5 All the **d** of your life
Ps 139:16 The **d** fashioned for me, When
Ps 143: 5 I remember the **d** of old
Ps 144: 4 His **d** are like a passing
Prov 3: 2 for length of **d** and long life
Prov 3:16 Length of **d** is in her right
Prov 9:11 For by me your **d** will be
Prov 10:27 fear of the LORD prolongs **d**
Prov 15:15 All the **d** of the afflicted
Prov 19:20 may be wise in your latter **d**
Prov 28:16 will prolong his **d**
Prov 31:12 evil all the **d** of her life
Eccl 2: 3 all the **d** of their lives
Eccl 2:16 be forgotten in the **d** to come
Eccl 2:23 For all his **d** are sorrowful,
Eccl 5:17 All his **d** he also eats in
Eccl 5:18 **d** of his life which God gives
Eccl 5:20 unduly on the **d** of his life
Eccl 6: 3 so that the **d** of his years
Eccl 6:12 all the **d** of his vain life
Eccl 7:10 former **d** better than these
Eccl 7:15 all things in my **d** of vanity
Eccl 8:12 his **d** are prolonged, yet I
Eccl 8:13 nor will he prolong his **d**
Eccl 8:15 him in his labor for the **d** of
Eccl 9: 9 **d** of your vain life which He
Eccl 9: 9 the sun, all your **d** of vanity
Eccl 11: 1 you will find it after many **d**
Eccl 11: 8 remember the **d** of darkness
Eccl 11: 9 you in the **d** of your youth
Eccl 12: 1 in the **d** of your youth,
Eccl 12: 1 before the difficult **d** come
Is 1: 1 Jerusalem in the **d** of Uzziah
Is 2: 2 **d** that the mountain of the
Is 7: 1 **d** of Ahaz the son of Jotham
Is 7:17 **d** that have not come since
Is 13:22 her **d** will not be prolonged
Is 23: 7 antiquity is from ancient **d**
Is 23:15 to the **d** of one king
Is 24:22 after many **d** they will be
Is 30:26 as the light of seven **d**, in
Is 32:10 some **d** you will be troubled,
Is 38: 1 In those **d** Hezekiah was sick
Is 38: 5 add to your **d** fifteen years
Is 38:20 all the **d** of our life, in the
Is 39: 6 the **d** are coming when all
Is 39: 8 be peace and truth in my **d**
Is 51: 9 Awake as in the ancient **d**
Is 53:10 seed, He shall prolong His **d**
Is 60:20 the **d** of your mourning shall
Is 63: 9 carried them all the **d** of old
Is 63:11 he remembered the **d** of old
Is 65:20 from there live but a few **d**
Is 65:20 who has not fulfilled his **d**
Is 65:22 for as the **d** of a tree, so
Is 65:22 shall be the **d** of My people
Jer 1: 2 of the LORD came in the **d** of
Jer 1: 3 It came also in the **d** of
Jer 2:32 forgotten Me **d** without number
Jer 3: 6 in the **d** of Josiah the king
Jer 3:16 in the land in those **d**,"
Jer 3:18 In those **d** the house of Judah
Jer 5:18 Nevertheless in those **d**,"
Jer 6:11 with him who is full of **d**
Jer 7:32 the **d** are coming," says the
Jer 9:25 the **d** are coming," says the
Jer 13: 6 **d** that the LORD said to me
Jer 16: 9 before your eyes and in your **d**
Jer 16:14 the **d** are coming," says the
Jer 17:11 him in the midst of his **d**
Jer 19: 6 the **d** are coming," says the
Jer 20:18 that my **d** should be consumed
Jer 22:30 shall not prosper in his **d**
Jer 23: 5 the **d** are coming," says the
Jer 23: 6 In His **d** Judah will be saved,
Jer 23: 7 the **d** are coming," says the
Jer 23:20 In the latter **d** you will
Jer 25:34 For the **d** of your slaughter
Jer 26:18 **d** of Hezekiah king of Judah
Jer 30: 3 the **d** are coming,' says the
Jer 30:24 In the latter **d** you will
Jer 31:27 the **d** are coming," says the
Jer 31:29 In those **d** they shall say no
Jer 31:31 the **d** are coming," says the
Jer 31:33 After those **d**, says the LORD,
Jer 31:38 the **d** are coming," says the
Jer 32:14 that they may last many **d**
Jer 33:14 the **d** are coming,' says the
Jer 33:15 In those **d** and at that time I
Jer 33:16 In those **d** Judah will be
Jer 35: 1 from the LORD in the **d** of
Jer 35: 7 but all your **d** you shall
Jer 35: 7 that you may live many **d** in
Jer 35: 8 to drink no wine all our **d**
Jer 36: 2 from the **d** of Josiah even to
Jer 37:16 had remained there many **d**
Jer 42: 7 it happened after ten **d** that
Jer 46:26 inhabited as in the **d** of old
Jer 48:12 the **d** are coming," says the
Jer 48:47 of Moab in the latter **d**,"
Jer 49: 2 the **d** are coming," says the
Jer 49:39 come to pass in the latter **d**
Jer 50: 4 In those **d** and in that time,"
Jer 50:20 In those **d** and in that time,"
Jer 51:47 the **d** are coming that I will
Jer 51:52 the **d** are coming," says the
Jer 52:33 king all the **d** of his life
Jer 52:34 death, all the **d** of his life
Lam 1: 7 In the **d** of her affliction and
Lam 1: 7 that she had in the **d** of old
Lam 2:17 He commanded in **d** of old
Lam 4:18 our **d** were over, for our end
Lam 5:21 renew our **d** as of old,
Ezek 3:15 astonished among them seven **d**
Ezek 3:16 **d** that the word of the LORD
Ezek 4: 4 of the **d** that you lie on it
Ezek 4: 5 to the number of the **d**, three
Ezek 4: 5 three hundred and ninety **d**
Ezek 4: 6 of the house of Judah forty **d**
Ezek 4: 8 ended the **d** of your siege
Ezek 4: 9 During the number of **d** that
Ezek 4: 9 three hundred and ninety **d**
Ezek 5: 2 when the **d** of the siege are
Ezek 12:22 The **d** are prolonged, and
Ezek 12:23 The **d** are at hand, and the
Ezek 12:25 for in your **d**, O rebellious
Ezek 12:27 sees is for many **d** from now
Ezek 16:22 remember the **d** of your youth
Ezek 16:43 remember the **d** of your youth
Ezek 16:56 mouth in the **d** of your pride
Ezek 16:60 you in the **d** of your youth
Ezek 22: 4 caused your **d** to draw near
Ezek 22:14 in the **d** when I shall deal
Ezek 23:19 the **d** of her youth, when she
Ezek 36:38 at Jerusalem on its feast **d**
Ezek 38: 8 After many **d** you will be
Ezek 38:16 **d** that I will bring you
Ezek 38:17 I have spoken in former **d** by
Ezek 38:17 for years in those **d** that I
Ezek 43:25 Every day for seven **d** you
Ezek 43:26 Seven **d** they shall make

Ezek 43:27 When these **d** are over it
Ezek 44:26 shall count seven **d** for him
Ezek 45:21 Passover, a feast of seven **d**
Ezek 45:23 On the seven **d** of the feast
Ezek 45:23 blemish, daily for seven **d**
Ezek 45:25 shall do likewise for seven **d**
Ezek 46: 1 be shut the six working **d**
Ezek 46: 9 LORD on the appointed feast **d**
Ezek 46:11 the appointed feast **d** the
Dan 1:12 test your servants for ten **d**
Dan 1:14 matter, and tested them ten **d**
Dan 1:15 at the end of ten **d** their
Dan 1:18 Now at the end of the **d**, when
Dan 2:28 what will be in the latter **d**
Dan 2:44 in the **d** of these kings the
Dan 5:11 And in the **d** of your father,
Dan 6: 7 any god or man for thirty **d**
Dan 6:10 was his custom since early **d**
Dan 6:12 god or man within thirty **d**
Dan 7: 9 the Ancient of **D** was seated
Dan 7:13 He came to the Ancient of **D**
Dan 7:22 until the Ancient of **D** came
Dan 8:14 two thousand three hundred **d**
Dan 8:26 to many **d** in the future
Dan 8:27 fainted and was sick for **d**
Dan 10: 2 In those **d** I, Daniel, was
Dan 10:13 withstood me twenty-one **d**
Dan 10:14 your people in the latter **d**
Dan 10:14 refers to many **d** yet to come
Dan 11:20 but within a few **d** he shall
Dan 11:33 yet for many **d** they shall
Dan 12:11 two hundred and ninety **d**
Dan 12:12 hundred and thirty-five **d**
Dan 12:13 at the end of the **d**
Hos 1: 1 in the **d** of Uzziah, Jotham,
Hos 1: 1 in the **d** of Jeroboam the son
Hos 2:11 mirth to cease, her feast **d**
Hos 2:13 **d** of the Baals to which she
Hos 2:15 as in the **d** of her youth, as
Hos 3: 3 You shall stay with me many **d**
Hos 3: 4 many **d** without king or prince
Hos 3: 5 His goodness in the latter **d**
Hos 6: 2 After two **d** He will revive us
Hos 9: 7 The **d** of punishment have come
Hos 9: 7 the **d** of recompense have come
Hos 9: 9 as in the **d** of Gibeah
Hos 10: 9 sinned from the **d** of Gibeah
Hos 12: 9 as in the **d** of the appointed
Joel 1: 2 like this happened in your **d**
Joel 1: 2 or even in the **d** of your
Joel 2:29 pour out My Spirit in those **d**
Joel 3: 1 For behold, in those **d** and at
Amos 1: 1 the **d** of Uzziah king of Judah
Amos 1: 1 in the **d** of Jeroboam the son
Amos 4: 2 the **d** shall come upon you
Amos 4: 4 your tithes every three **d**
Amos 5:21 hate, I despise your feast **d**
Amos 8:11 the **d** are coming," says the
Amos 9:11 rebuild it as in the **d** of old
Amos 9:13 the **d** are coming," says the
Jon 1:17 the belly of the fish three **d**
Jon 3: 4 Yet forty **d**, and Nineveh shall
Mic 1: 1 Moresheth in the **d** of Jotham
Mic 4: 1 **d** That the mountain of the
Mic 7:14 and Gilead, as in **d** of old
Mic 7:15 As in the **d** when you came out
Mic 7:20 to our fathers from **d** of old
Hab 1: 5 I will work a work in your **d**
Zeph 1: 1 in the **d** of Josiah the son of
Hag 2:16 since those **d**, when one came
Zech 8: 6 of this people in these **d**
Zech 8: 9 have been hearing in these **d**
Zech 8:10 For before these **d** there were
Zech 8:11 people as in the former **d**
Zech 8:15 so again in these **d** I am
Zech 8:23 In those **d** ten men from
Zech 14: 5 the **d** of Uzziah king of Judah
Mal 3: 4 the LORD, as in the **d** of old
Mal 3: 7 Yet from the **d** of your
Matt 2: 1 in the **d** of Herod the king
Matt 3: 1 In those **d** John the Baptist
Matt 4: 2 And when He had fasted forty **d**
Matt 9:15 But the **d** will come when the
Matt 11:12 And from the **d** of John the
Matt 12:40 For as Jonah was three **d** and
Matt 12:40 the Son of Man be three **d**
Matt 15:32 now continued with Me three **d**
Matt 17: 1 Now after six **d** Jesus took
Matt 23:30 lived in the **d** of our fathers
Matt 24:19 nursing babies in those **d**
Matt 24:22 unless those **d** were shortened
Matt 24:22 those **d** will be shortened
Matt 24:29 **d** the sun will be darkened
Matt 24:37 But as the **d** of Noah were, so
Matt 24:38 For as in the **d** before the
Matt 26: 2 after two **d** is the Passover
Matt 26:61 God and to build it in three **d**
Matt 27:40 temple and build it in three **d**
Matt 27:63 After three **d** I will rise
Mark 1: 9 those **d** that Jesus came from
Mark 1:13 in the wilderness forty **d**
Mark 2: 1 Capernaum after some **d**, and it
Mark 2:20 But the **d** will come when the
Mark 2:20 they will fast in those **d**
Mark 2:26 the house of God in the **d** of
Mark 8: 1 In those **d**, the multitude
Mark 8: 2 have now been with Me three **d**
Mark 8:31 and after three **d** rise again
Mark 9: 2 Now after six **d** Jesus took
Mark 13:17 nursing babies in those **d**
Mark 13:19 For in those **d** there will be
Mark 13:20 Lord had shortened those **d**
Mark 13:20 He chose, He shortened the **d**
Mark 13:24 But in those **d**, after that
Mark 14: 1 After two **d** it was the
Mark 14:58 within three **d** I will build
Mark 15:29 temple and build it in three **d**
Luke 1: 5 There was in the **d** of Herod
Luke 1:23 was, as soon as the **d** of his
Luke 1:24 Now after those **d** his wife
Luke 1:25 in the **d** when He looked on me
Luke 1:39 Now Mary arose in those **d**
Luke 1:75 Him all the **d** of our life
Luke 2: 1 it came to pass in those **d**
Luke 2: 6 the **d** were completed for her
Luke 2:21 when eight **d** were completed
Luke 2:22 Now when the **d** of her
Luke 2:43 When they had finished the **d**
Luke 2:46 three **d** they found Him in the
Luke 4: 2 for forty **d** by the devil
Luke 4: 2 in those **d** He ate nothing, and
Luke 4:25 in Israel in the **d** of Elijah
Luke 5:35 But the **d** will come when the
Luke 5:35 they will fast in those **d**
Luke 6:12 **d** that He went out to the
Luke 9:28 about eight **d** after these
Luke 9:36 told no one in those **d** any of
Luke 13:14 There are six **d** on which men
Luke 15:13 And not many **d** after, the
Luke 17:22 The **d** will come when you will
Luke 17:22 of the **d** of the Son of Man
Luke 17:26 And as it was in the **d** of Noah
Luke 17:26 in the **d** of the Son of Man
Luke 17:28 it was also in the **d** of Lot
Luke 19:43 For the **d** will come upon you
Luke 20: 1 it happened on one of those **d**
Luke 21: 6 the **d** will come in which not
Luke 21:22 these are the **d** of vengeance
Luke 21:23 are nursing babies in those **d**
Luke 23:29 For indeed the **d** are coming
Luke 24:18 happened there in these **d**
John 2:12 did not stay there many **d**
John 2:19 in three **d** I will raise it up
John 2:20 You raise it up in three **d**
John 4:40 and He stayed there two **d**
John 4:43 Now after the two **d** He
John 11: 6 He stayed two more **d** in the
John 11:17 been in the tomb four **d**
John 11:39 for he has been dead four **d**
John 12: 1 six **d** before the Passover,
John 20:26 after eight **d** His disciples
Acts 1: 3 seen by them during forty **d**
Acts 1: 5 Spirit not many **d** from now
Acts 1:15 in those **d** Peter stood up in
Acts 2:17 come to pass in the last **d**
Acts 2:18 pour out My Spirit in those **d**
Acts 3:24 have also foretold these **d**
Acts 5:37 up in the **d** of the census
Acts 6: 1 Now in those **d**, when the
Acts 7:41 they made a calf in those **d**
Acts 7:45 fathers until the **d** of David
Acts 9: 9 he was three **d** without sight,
Acts 9:19 Then Saul spent some **d** with
Acts 9:23 Now after many **d** were past
Acts 9:37 those **d** that she became sick
Acts 9:43 many **d** in Joppa with Simon
Acts 10:30 Four **d** ago I was fasting
Acts 10:48 asked him to stay a few **d**
Acts 11:27 in these **d** prophets came from
Acts 11:28 in the **d** of Claudius Caesar
Acts 12: 3 the **D** of Unleavened Bread
Acts 13:31 He was seen for many **d** by
Acts 13:41 for I work a work in your **d**
Acts 15:36 Then after some **d** Paul said
Acts 16:12 in that city for some **d**
Acts 16:18 And this she did for many **d**
Acts 20: 6 the **D** of Unleavened Bread
Acts 20: 6 and in five **d** joined them at
Acts 20: 6 where we stayed seven **d**
Acts 21: 4 we stayed there seven **d**
Acts 21: 5 come to the end of those **d**
Acts 21:10 And as we stayed many **d**, a
Acts 21:15 And after those **d** we packed
Acts 21:26 of the **d** of purification, at
Acts 21:27 when the seven **d** were almost
Acts 24: 1 Now after five **d** Ananias the
Acts 24:11 twelve **d** since I went up to
Acts 24:24 And after some **d**, when Felix
Acts 25: 1 after three **d** he went up from
Acts 25: 6 among them more than ten **d**
Acts 25:13 after some **d** King Agrippa and
Acts 25:14 they had been there many **d**
Acts 27: 7 we had sailed slowly many **d**
Acts 27:20 nor stars appeared for many **d**
Acts 28: 7 us courteously for three **d**
Acts 28:12 Syracuse, we stayed three **d**
Acts 28:14 to stay with them seven **d**
Acts 28:17 three **d** that Paul called the
Gal 1:18 remained with him fifteen **d**
Gal 4:10 You observe **d** and months and
Eph 5:16 time, because the **d** are evil
2Ti 3: 1 that in the last **d** perilous
Heb 1: 2 has in these last **d** spoken to
Heb 5: 7 in the **d** of His flesh, when
Heb 7: 3 of **d** nor end of life, but
Heb 8: 8 the **d** are coming," says the
Heb 8:10 After those **d**," says the
Heb 10:16 make with them after those **d**
Heb 10:32 recall the former **d** in which
Heb 11:30 were encircled for seven **d**
Heb 12:10 For they indeed for a few **d**
Jas 5: 3 up treasure in the last **d**
1Pe 3:10 would love life and see good **d**
1Pe 3:20 God waited in the **d** of Noah
2Pe 3: 3 will come in the last **d**,
Rev 2:10 will have tribulation ten **d**
Rev 2:13 the **d** in which Antipas was My
Rev 9: 6 In those **d** men will seek
Rev 10: 7 but in the **d** of the sounding
Rev 11: 3 two hundred and sixty **d**,
Rev 11: 6 in the **d** of their prophecy
Rev 11: 9 dead bodies three and a half **d**
Rev 11:11 a half **d** the breath of life
Rev 12: 6 two hundred and sixty **d**

DAYS' (*see* DAYS)
Gen 30:36 Then he put three **d** journey
Gen 31:23 him for seven **d** journey, and
Ex 3:18 let us go three **d** journey
Ex 5: 3 let us go three **d** journey
Ex 8:27 We will go three **d** journey
Num 33: 8 went three **d** journey in the
Deut 1: 2 It is eleven **d** journey from
2Sa 24:13 three **d** plague in your land

DAYSPRING (*see* DAY)
Luke 1:78 with which the **D** from on high

DAYTIME (*see* DAY)
Job 5:14 meet with darkness in the **d**
Job 24:16 for themselves in the **d**
Ps 22: 2 O My God, I cry in the **d**, but
Ps 42: 8 His lovingkindness in the **d**
Ps 78:14 In the **d** also He led them
Is 4: 6 shade in the **d** from the heat
Is 21: 8 on the watchtower in the **d**
Luke 21:37 in the **d** He was teaching in
2Pe 2:13 pleasure to carouse in the **d**

DEACONS
Phil 1: 1 with the bishops and **d**
1Ti 3: 8 Likewise **d** must be reverent,
1Ti 3:10 then let them serve as **d**,
1Ti 3:12 Let **d** be the husbands of one
1Ti 3:13 as **d** obtain for themselves a

DEAD (*see* DEADLY, DEADNESS, DIE)
Gen 20: 3 him, "Indeed you are a **d** man
Gen 23: 3 stood up from before his **d**
Gen 23: 4 may bury my **d** out of my sight
Gen 23: 6 bury your **d** in the choicest
Gen 23: 6 that you may bury your **d**
Gen 23: 8 I bury my **d** out of my sight

Gen 23:11 Bury your **d**
Gen 23:13 me and I will bury my **d** there
Gen 23:15 So bury your **d**
Gen 42:38 you, for his brother is **d**
Gen 44:20 his brother is **d**, and he alone
Gen 50:15 saw that their father was **d**
Ex 4:19 for all the men are **d** who
Ex 9: 7 of the Israelites was **d**
Ex 12:30 where there was not one **d**
Ex 12:33 We shall all be **d**
Ex 14:30 Egyptians **d** on the seashore
Ex 21:34 but the **d** beast shall be his
Ex 21:35 and the **d** ox they shall also
Ex 21:36 the **d** beast shall be his own
Lev 11:31 are **d** shall be unclean until
Lev 11:32 when they are **d** shall be
Lev 19:28 in your flesh for the **d**, nor
Lev 21: 1 for the **d** among his people
Lev 21:11 shall he go near any **d** body
Num 5: 2 becomes defiled by a **d** body
Num 6: 6 he shall not go near a **d** body
Num 6:11 by reason of the **d** body
Num 9: 6 by the **d** body of a man, so
Num 9: 7 by the **d** body of a man
Num 9:10 unclean because of a **d** body
Num 12:12 do not let her be as one **d**
Num 16:48 And he stood between the **d**
Num 19:11 He who touches the **d** body of
Num 19:18 a bone, the slain, the **d**, or
Num 20:29 saw that Aaron was **d**, all the
Deut 14: 1 front of your head for the **d**
Deut 14: 8 or touch their **d** carcasses
Deut 18:11 or one who calls up the **d**
Deut 25: 5 the widow of the **d** man shall
Deut 25: 6 to the name of his **d** brother
Deut 26:14 nor given any of it for the **d**
Josh 1: 2 Moses My servant is **d**
Judg 2:19 to pass, when the judge was **d**
Judg 3:25 master, fallen **d** on the floor
Judg 4: 1 When Ehud was **d**, the children
Judg 4:22 **d** with the peg in his temple
Judg 5:27 he sank, there he fell **d**
Judg 8:33 so, as soon as Gideon was **d**
Judg 9:55 saw that Abimelech was **d**,
Judg 16:24 the one who multiplied our **d**
Judg 16:30 So the **d** that he killed at
Ruth 1: 8 as you have dealt with the **d**
Ruth 2:20 to the living and the **d**
Ruth 4: 5 Moabitess, the wife of the **d**
Ruth 4: 5 of the **d** on his inheritance
Ruth 4:10 of the **d** on his inheritance
Ruth 4:10 that the name of the **d** may
1Sa 4:17 Hophni and Phinehas, are **d**
1Sa 4:19 and her husband were **d**, she
1Sa 17:51 saw that their champion was **d**
1Sa 24:14 Whom do you pursue? A **d** dog?
1Sa 25:39 David heard that Nabal was **d**
1Sa 31: 5 saw that Saul was **d**, he also
1Sa 31: 7 that Saul and his sons were **d**
2Sa 1: 4 of the people are fallen and **d**
2Sa 1: 4 Jonathan his son are **d** also
2Sa 1: 5 and Jonathan his son are **d**
2Sa 2: 7 for your master Saul is **d**
2Sa 4:10 me, saying, 'Look, Saul is **d**
2Sa 9: 8 look upon such a **d** dog as I
2Sa 11:21 Uriah the Hittite is **d** also
2Sa 11:24 of the king's servants are **d**
2Sa 11:24 Uriah the Hittite is **d** also
2Sa 11:26 that Uriah her husband was **d**
2Sa 12:18 tell him that the child was **d**
2Sa 12:18 tell him that the child is **d**
2Sa 12:19 that the child was **d**
2Sa 12:19 Is the child **d**
2Sa 12:19 And they said, "He is **d**."
2Sa 12:23 But now he is **d**
2Sa 13:32 sons, for only Amnon is **d**
2Sa 13:33 all the king's sons are **d**
2Sa 13:33 For only Amnon is **d**
2Sa 13:39 Amnon, because he was **d**
2Sa 14: 2 a long time for the **d**
2Sa 14: 5 I am a widow, my husband is **d**
2Sa 16: 9 Why should this **d** dog curse
2Sa 18:20 because the king's son is **d**
2Sa 19:28 my father's house were but **d**
1Ki 3:20 laid her **d** child in my bosom
1Ki 3:21 nurse my son, there he was, **d**
1Ki 3:22 son, and the **d** one is your son
1Ki 3:22 But the **d** one is your son, and
1Ki 3:23 and your son is the **d** one'
1Ki 3:23 But your son is the **d** one
1Ki 11:21 commander of the army was **d**
1Ki 13:31 When I am **d**, then bury me in
1Ki 21:14 has been stoned and is **d**
1Ki 21:15 had been stoned and was **d**,
1Ki 21:15 Naboth is not alive, but **d**
1Ki 21:16 Ahab heard that Naboth was **d**
2Ki 4: 1 Your servant my husband is **d**
2Ki 4:32 the child, lying **d** on his bed
2Ki 8: 5 he had restored the **d** to life
2Ki 11: 1 saw that her son was **d**, she
2Ki 19:35 there were the corpses—all **d**
1Ch 5:22 for many fell **d**, because the
1Ch 10: 5 saw that Saul was **d**, he also
1Ch 10: 7 that Saul and his sons were **d**
2Ch 20:24 and there were their **d** bodies
2Ch 20:25 of valuables on the **d** bodies
2Ch 22:10 saw that her son was **d**, she
Job 1:19 the young men, and they are **d**
Job 26: 5 The **d** tremble, those under
Ps 31:12 I am forgotten like a **d** man
Ps 76: 6 were cast into a **d** sleep
Ps 79: 2 The **d** bodies of Your servants
Ps 88: 5 Adrift among the **d**, Like the
Ps 88:10 You work wonders for the **d**
Ps 88:10 Shall the **d** arise and praise
Ps 106:28 ate sacrifices made to the **d**
Ps 110: 6 fill the places with **d** bodies
Ps 115:17 The **d** do not praise the LORD,
Ps 143: 3 those who have long been **d**
Prov 2:18 death, and her paths to the **d**
Prov 9:18 not know that the **d** are there
Prov 21:16 in the congregation of the **d**
Eccl 4: 2 the **d** who were already **d**
Eccl 9: 3 after that they go to the **d**
Eccl 9: 4 dog is better than a **d** lion
Eccl 9: 5 but the **d** know nothing, and
Eccl 10: 1 **D** flies putrefy the
Is 8:19 Should they seek the **d** on
Is 14: 9 it stirs up the **d** for you
Is 22: 2 the sword, Nor **d** in battle
Is 26:14 They are **d**, they will not
Is 26:19 Your **d** shall live
Is 26:19 together with my **d** body they
Is 26:19 earth shall cast out the **d**
Is 37:36 there were the corpses—all **d**
Is 59:10 we are as **d** men in desolate
Jer 16: 7 to comfort them for the **d**
Jer 22:10 Weep not for the **d**, nor
Jer 26:23 and cast his **d** body into the
Jer 31:40 whole valley of the **d** bodies
Jer 33: 5 **d** bodies of men whom I will
Jer 34:20 Their **d** bodies shall be for
Jer 36:30 his **d** body shall be cast out
Jer 41: 9 Ishmael had cast all the **d**
Lam 3: 6 places like the **d** of long ago
Ezek 24:17 make no mourning for the **d**
Ezek 44:25 by coming near a **d** person
Amos 6:10 And when a kinsman of the **d**
Amos 8: 3 Many **d** bodies everywhere,
Hag 2:13 a **d** body touches any of these
Matt 2:19 But when Herod was **d**, behold,
Matt 2:20 the young Child's life are **d**
Matt 8:22 let the **d** bury their own **d**
Matt 9:24 room, for the girl is not **d**
Matt 10: 8 the lepers, raise the **d**, cast
Matt 11: 5 the **d** are raised up and the
Matt 14: 2 he is risen from the **d**, and
Matt 17: 9 of Man is risen from the **d**
Matt 22:31 the resurrection of the **d**
Matt 22:32 God is not the God of the **d**
Matt 23:27 are full of **d** men's bones
Matt 27:64 He has risen from the **d**
Matt 28: 4 of him, and became like **d** men
Matt 28: 7 that He is risen from the **d**
Mark 5:35 Your daughter is **d**
Mark 5:39 The child is not **d**, but
Mark 6:14 Baptist is risen from the **d**
Mark 6:16 he has been raised from the **d**
Mark 9: 9 of Man had risen from the **d**
Mark 9:10 the rising from the **d** meant
Mark 9:26 And he became as one **d**, so
Mark 9:26 that many said, "He is **d**."
Mark 12:25 For when they rise from the **d**
Mark 12:26 But concerning the **d**, that
Mark 12:27 He is not the God of the **d**
Mark 15:44 that He was already **d**
Mark 15:44 He had been **d** for some time
Luke 7:12 a **d** man was being carried out
Luke 7:15 And he who was **d** sat up and
Luke 7:22 the **d** are raised, the poor
Luke 8:49 Your daughter is **d**
Luke 8:52 she is not **d**, but sleeping
Luke 8:53 scorn, knowing that she was **d**
Luke 9: 7 John had risen from the **d**
Luke 9:60 Let the **d** bury their own **d**
Luke 10:30 departed, leaving him half **d**
Luke 15:24 for this my son was **d** and is
Luke 15:32 glad, for your brother was **d**
Luke 16:30 one goes to them from the **d**
Luke 16:31 though one rise from the **d**
Luke 20:35 the resurrection from the **d**
Luke 20:37 passage that the **d** are raised
Luke 20:38 of the **d** but of the living
Luke 24: 5 seek the living among the **d**
Luke 24:46 rise from the **d** the third day
John 2:22 when He had risen from the **d**
John 5:21 as the Father raises the **d**
John 5:25 is, when the **d** will hear the
John 6:49 in the wilderness, and are **d**
John 6:58 ate the manna, and are **d**
John 8:52 Abraham is **d**, and the prophets
John 8:53 our father Abraham, who is **d**
John 8:53 And the prophets are **d**
John 11:14 Lazarus is **d**
John 11:39 the sister of him who was **d**
John 11:39 for he has been **d** four days
John 11:41 where the **d** man was lying
John 12: 1 Lazarus was who had been **d**
John 12: 1 whom He had raised from the **d**
John 12: 9 whom He had raised from the **d**
John 12:17 tomb and raised him from the **d**
John 19:33 and saw that He was already **d**
John 20: 9 He must rise again from the **d**
John 21:14 He was raised from the **d**
Acts 2:29 David, that he is both **d** and
Acts 3:15 whom God raised from the **d**
Acts 4: 2 the resurrection from the **d**
Acts 4:10 whom God raised from the **d**
Acts 5:10 men came in and found her **d**
Acts 7: 4 there, when his father was **d**
Acts 10:41 Him after He arose from the **d**
Acts 10:42 Judge of the living and the **d**
Acts 13:30 But God raised Him from the **d**
Acts 13:34 that He raised Him from the **d**
Acts 14:19 city, supposing him to be **d**
Acts 17: 3 and rise again from the **d**, and
Acts 17:31 all by raising Him from the **d**
Acts 17:32 of the resurrection of the **d**
Acts 20: 9 third story and was taken up **d**
Acts 23: 6 of the **d** I am being judged
Acts 24:15 be a resurrection of the **d**
Acts 24:21 the resurrection of the **d** I
Acts 26: 8 by you that God raises the **d**
Acts 26:23 the first to rise from the **d**
Acts 28: 6 up or suddenly fall down **d**
Rom 1: 4 the resurrection from the **d**
Rom 4:17 God, who gives life to the **d**
Rom 4:19 already **d** (since he was about
Rom 4:24 up Jesus our Lord from the **d**
Rom 6: 4 **d** by the glory of the Father
Rom 6: 9 having been raised from the **d**
Rom 6:11 to be **d** indeed to sin, but
Rom 6:13 God as being alive from the **d**
Rom 7: 4 you also have become **d** to the
Rom 7: 4 Him who was raised from the **d**
Rom 7: 8 apart from the law sin was **d**
Rom 8:10 the body is **d** because of sin,
Rom 8:11 from the **d** dwells in you, He
Rom 8:11 who raised Christ from the **d**
Rom 10: 7 bring Christ up from the **d**)
Rom 10: 9 God has raised Him from the **d**
Rom 11:15 be but life from the **d**
Rom 14: 9 might be Lord of both the **d**
1Co 15:12 He has been raised from the **d**
1Co 15:12 is no resurrection of the **d**
1Co 15:13 is no resurrection of the **d**
1Co 15:15 if in fact the **d** do not rise
1Co 15:16 For if the **d** do not rise,
1Co 15:20 Christ is risen from the **d**
1Co 15:21 the resurrection of the **d**
1Co 15:29 do who are baptized for the **d**
1Co 15:29 if the **d** do not rise at all
1Co 15:29 are they baptized for the **d**
1Co 15:32 If the **d** do not rise,
1Co 15:35 How are the **d** raised up
1Co 15:42 is the resurrection of the **d**
1Co 15:52 and the **d** will be raised
2Co 1: 9 but in God who raises the **d**
Gal 1: 1 who raised Him from the **d**)
Eph 1:20 when He raised Him from the **d**

Eph 2: 1 who were **d** in trespasses and
Eph 2: 5 when we were **d** in trespasses
Eph 5:14 who sleep, arise from the **d**
Phil 3:11 the resurrection from the **d**
Col 1:18 the firstborn from the **d**
Col 2:12 who raised Him from the **d**
Col 2:13 being **d** in your trespasses and
1Th 1:10 whom He raised from the **d**
1Th 4:16 the **d** in Christ will rise
1Ti 5: 6 pleasure is **d** while she lives
2Ti 2: 8 David, was raised from the **d**
2Ti 4: 1 the **d** at His appearing and His
Heb 6: 1 of repentance from **d** works
Heb 6: 2 of resurrection of the **d**
Heb 9:14 **d** works to serve the living
Heb 9:17 is in force after men are **d**
Heb 11: 4 it the being **d** still speaks
Heb 11:12 one man, and him as good as **d**
Heb 11:19 raise him up, even from the **d**
Heb 11:35 their **d** raised to life again
Heb 13:20 up our Lord Jesus from the **d**
Jas 2:17 it does not have works, is **d**
Jas 2:20 that faith without works is **d**
Jas 2:26 body without the spirit is **d**
Jas 2:26 faith without works is **d** also
1Pe 1: 3 of Jesus Christ from the **d**
1Pe 1:21 who raised Him from the **d**
1Pe 4: 5 to judge the living and the **d**
1Pe 4: 6 also to those who are **d**, that
Jude 12 trees without fruit, twice **d**
Rev 1: 5 the firstborn from the **d**
Rev 1:17 Him, I fell at His feet as **d**
Rev 1:18 I am He who lives, and was **d**
Rev 2: 8 First and the Last, who was **d**
Rev 3: 1 you are alive, but you are **d**
Rev 11: 8 their **d** bodies will lie in
Rev 11: 9 will see their **d** bodies three
Rev 11: 9 not allow their **d** bodies to
Rev 11:18 come, and the time of the **d**
Rev 14:13 Blessed are the **d** who die in
Rev 16: 3 it became blood as of a **d** man
Rev 20: 5 But the rest of the **d** did not
Rev 20:12 And I saw the **d**, small and
Rev 20:12 the **d** were judged according
Rev 20:13 gave up the **d** who were in it
Rev 20:13 up the **d** who were in them

DEADLY (*see* DEAD)
1Sa 5:11 For there was a **d**
Ps 17: 9 me, From my **d** enemies who
Ps 144:10 His servant From the **d** sword
Ezek 9: 1 each with a **d** weapon in his
Mark 16:18 and if they drink anything **d**
Jas 3: 8 unruly evil, full of **d** poison
Rev 13: 3 and his **d** wound was healed
Rev 13:12 whose **d** wound was healed

DEADNESS (*see* DEAD)
Rom 4:19 and the **d** of Sarah's womb

DEAF
Ex 4:11 Or who makes the mute, the **d**
Lev 19:14 You shall not curse the **d**
Ps 38:13 But I, like a **d** man, do not
Ps 58: 4 They are like the **d** cobra
Is 29:18 In that day the **d** shall hear
Is 35: 5 the ears of the **d** shall be
Is 42:18 Hear, you **d**
Is 42:19 or **d** as My messenger whom I
Is 43: 8 eyes, and the **d** who have ears
Mic 7:16 their ears shall be **d**
Matt 11: 5 are cleansed and the **d** hear
Mark 7:32 brought to Him one who was **d**
Mark 7:37 He makes both the **d** to hear
Mark 9:25 You **d** and dumb spirit, I
Luke 7:22 the **d** hear, the dead are

DEAL (*see* DEALER, DEALING, DEALS, DEALT)
Gen 19: 9 now we will **d** worse with you
Gen 21:23 will not **d** falsely with me
Gen 24:49 Now if you will **d** kindly and
Gen 32: 9 and I will **d** well with you'
Gen 43: 6 Why did you **d** so wrongfully
Gen 47:29 **d** kindly and truly with me
Ex 1:10 let us **d** wisely with them,
Ex 8:29 But let Pharaoh not **d**
Ex 12:38 a great **d** of livestock
Ex 21: 9 he shall **d** with her according
Lev 19:11 nor **d** falsely, nor lie to one
Deut 7: 5 thus you shall **d** with them
Deut 32: 6 Do you thus **d** with the LORD,
Josh 2:14 land, that we will **d** kindly
Ruth 1: 8 The LORD **d** kindly with you,
1Sa 20: 8 Therefore you shall **d** kindly
2Sa 18: 5 **D** gently for my sake with the
2Ki 22: 7 because they **d** faithfully
2Ch 2: 3 to dwell in, so **d** with me
Job 42: 8 lest I **d** with you according
Ps 25: 3 Let those be ashamed who **d**
Ps 75: 4 Do not **d** boastfully,' And to
Ps 83: 9 **D** with them as with Midian,
Ps 105:25 To **d** craftily with His
Ps 109:21 **D** with me for Your name's
Ps 119:17 **D** bountifully with Your
Ps 119:124 **D** with Your servant according
Ps 142: 7 For You shall **d** bountifully
Prov 12:22 but those who **d** truthfully
Is 26:10 he will **d** unjustly, and will
Is 33: 1 and you who **d** treacherously,
Is 33: 1 they will **d** treacherously
Is 48: 8 would **d** very treacherously
Is 52:13 My Servant shall **d** prudently
Jer 9: 7 for how shall I **d** with the
Jer 12: 1 happy who **d** so treacherously
Jer 18:23 **D** thus with them in the time
Jer 21: 2 Perhaps the LORD will **d** with
Ezek 16:59 I will **d** with you as you have
Ezek 22:14 days when I shall **d** with you
Ezek 23:25 they shall **d** furiously with
Ezek 23:29 They will **d** hatefully with
Ezek 31:11 and he shall surely **d** with it
Dan 1:13 fit, so **d** with your servants
Dan 11: 7 and **d** with them and prevail
Hab 1:13 on those who **d** treacherously
Zeph 3:19 at that time I will **d** with
Mal 2:10 Why do we **d** treacherously
Mal 2:15 let none **d** treacherously with
Mal 2:16 you do not **d** treacherously

DEALER (*see* DEAL, DEALERS)
Is 21: 2 the treacherous **d** deals

DEALERS (*see* DEALER)
Is 24:16 The treacherous **d** have dealt
Is 24:16 treacherous **d** have dealt very

DEALING (*see* DEAL, DEALINGS)
Ex 5:15 Why are you **d** thus with your
Ps 7:16 his violent **d** shall come down
Is 33: 1 an end of **d** treacherously

DEALINGS (*see* DEALING)
1Sa 2:23 evil **d** from all the people
John 4: 9 have no **d** with Samaritans

DEALS (*see* DEAL)
Ps 112: 5 A good man **d** graciously and
Prov 10: 4 He who **d** with a slack hand
Is 21: 2 dealer **d** treacherously, and
Jer 6:13 priest, everyone **d** falsely
Jer 8:10 the priest Everyone **d** falsely
Heb 12: 7 God **d** with you as with sons

DEALT (*see* DEAL)
Gen 16: 6 when Sarai **d** harshly with her
Gen 33:11 because God has **d** graciously
Ex 1:20 Therefore God **d** well with the
Ex 14:11 Why have you so **d** with us
Ex 21: 8 since he has **d** deceitfully
Judg 9:16 and if you have **d** well with
Judg 9:23 Shechem **d** treacherously with
Ruth 1: 8 as you have **d** with the dead
Ruth 1:20 for the Almighty has **d** very
1Sa 14:33 You have **d** treacherously
1Sa 24:18 how you have **d** well with me
1Sa 25:31 LORD has **d** well with my lord
2Sa 18:13 Otherwise I would have **d**
2Ki 12:15 for they **d** faithfully
2Ch 2: 3 As you have **d** with David my
2Ch 11:23 He **d** wisely, and dispersed
Neh 9:33 for You have **d** faithfully
Job 6:15 My brothers have **d**
Ps 13: 6 Because He has **d** bountifully
Ps 44:17 Nor have we **d** falsely with
Ps 103:10 He has not **d** with us
Ps 116: 7 O my soul, For the LORD has **d**
Ps 119:65 You have **d** well with Your
Ps 147:20 He has not **d** thus with any
Is 24:16 dealers have **d** treacherously
Is 24:16 have **d** very treacherously
Is 33: 1 though they have not **d**
Jer 3:20 so have you **d** treacherously
Jer 5:11 the house of Judah have **d**
Jer 12: 6 your father, even they have **d**
Lam 1: 2 All her friends have **d**
Ezek 20:44 when I have **d** with you for My
Ezek 25:15 the Philistines **d** vengefully
Ezek 39:24 I have **d** with them, and hidden
Hos 5: 7 They have **d** treacherously
Hos 6: 7 There they **d** treacherously
Joel 2:26 who has **d** wondrously with you
Zech 1: 6 deeds, so He has **d** with us
Mal 2:11 Judah has **d** treacherously, and
Mal 2:14 whom you have **d** treacherously
Luke 1:25 Thus the Lord has **d** with me
Luke 16: 8 because he had **d** shrewdly
Acts 7:19 This man **d** treacherously with
Rom 12: 3 as God has **d** to each one a

DEAR (*see* DEARLY)
Jer 31:20 Is Ephraim My **d** son
Luke 7: 2 servant, who was **d** to him
Acts 20:24 I count my life **d** to myself
Eph 5: 1 of God as **d** children
Col 1: 7 our **d** fellow servant, who is
1Th 2: 8 you had become **d** to us

DEARLY (*see* DEAR)
Jer 12: 7 I have given the **d** beloved of
Hos 4:18 Her rulers **d** love dishonor

DEATH (*see* DEATHS, DIE)
Gen 21:16 me not see the **d** of the boy
Gen 24:67 after his mother's **d**
Gen 25:11 after the **d** of Abraham, that
Gen 26:11 wife shall surely be put to **d**
Gen 26:18 up after the **d** of Abraham
Gen 27: 2 I do not know the day of my **d**
Gen 27: 7 of the LORD before my **d**
Gen 27:10 he may bless you before his **d**
Ex 10:17 take away from me this **d** only
Ex 19:12 shall surely be put to **d**
Ex 21:12 dies shall surely be put to **d**
Ex 21:15 shall surely be put to **d**
Ex 21:16 shall surely be put to **d**
Ex 21:17 shall surely be put to **d**
Ex 21:28 gores a man or a woman to **d**
Ex 21:29 owner also shall be put to **d**
Ex 22:19 shall surely be put to **d**
Ex 31:14 it shall surely be put to **d**
Ex 31:15 he shall surely be put to **d**
Ex 35: 2 work on it shall be put to **d**
Lev 16: 1 **d** of the two sons of Aaron
Lev 19:20 they shall not be put to **d**
Lev 20: 2 he shall surely be put to **d**
Lev 20: 9 shall surely be put to **d**
Lev 20:10 shall surely be put to **d**
Lev 20:11 them shall surely be put to **d**
Lev 20:12 them shall surely be put to **d**
Lev 20:13 They shall surely be put to **d**
Lev 20:15 he shall surely be put to **d**
Lev 20:16 They shall surely be put to **d**
Lev 20:27 shall surely be put to **d**
Lev 24:16 LORD shall surely be put to **d**
Lev 24:16 LORD, he shall be put to **d**
Lev 24:17 man shall surely be put to **d**
Lev 24:21 kills a man shall be put to **d**
Lev 27:29 but shall surely be put to **d**
Num 1:51 comes near shall be put to **d**
Num 3:10 comes near shall be put to **d**
Num 3:38 came near was to be put to **d**
Num 15:35 man must surely be put to **d**
Num 18: 7 comes near shall be put to **d**
Num 23:10 Let me die the **d** of the
Num 35:16 shall surely be put to **d**
Num 35:17 shall surely be put to **d**
Num 35:18 shall surely be put to **d**
Num 35:19 shall put the murderer to **d**
Num 35:19 him, he shall put him to **d**
Num 35:21 him shall surely be put to **d**
Num 35:21 to **d** when he meets him
Num 35:25 remain there until the **d** of
Num 35:28 the **d** of the high priest
Num 35:28 But after the **d** of the high
Num 35:30 put to **d** on the testimony of
Num 35:30 a person for the **d** penalty
Num 35:31 a murderer who is guilty of **d**
Num 35:31 he shall surely be put to **d**
Num 35:32 before the **d** of the priest
Deut 13: 5 of dreams shall be put to **d**
Deut 13: 9 against him to put him to **d**
Deut 17: 5 shall stone to **d** that man or
Deut 17: 6 Whoever is worthy of **d** shall
Deut 17: 6 put to **d** on the testimony
Deut 17: 7 against him to put him to **d**
Deut 19: 6 though he was not worthy of **d**
Deut 21:21 stone him to **d** with stones

Deut 21:22 committed a sin worthy of **d**
Deut 21:22 and he is put to **d**
Deut 22:21 stone her to **d** with stones
Deut 22:24 stone them to **d** with stones
Deut 22:26 woman no sin worthy of **d**, for
Deut 24:16 put to **d** for their children
Deut 24:16 be put to **d** for their fathers
Deut 24:16 be put to **d** for his own sin
Deut 30:15 you today life and good, **d**
Deut 30:19 have set before you life and **d**
Deut 31:27 then how much more after my **d**
Deut 31:29 my **d** you will become utterly
Deut 33: 1 of Israel before his **d**
Josh 1: 1 After the **d** of Moses the
Josh 1:18 him, shall be put to **d**
Josh 2:13 and deliver our lives from **d**
Josh 20: 6 until the **d** of the one who is
Judg 1: 1 Now after the **d** of Joshua it
Judg 5:18 their lives to the point of **d**
Judg 6:31 him be put to **d** by morning
Judg 13: 7 the womb to the day of his **d**
Judg 16:16 that his soul was vexed to **d**
Judg 16:30 his **d** were more than he had
Judg 20:13 that we may put them to **d**
Judg 21: 5 He shall surely be put to **d**
Ruth 1:17 if anything but **d** parts you
Ruth 2:11 since the **d** of your husband
1Sa 4:20 about the time of her **d** the
1Sa 11:12 that we may put them to **d**
1Sa 11:13 shall be put to **d** this day
1Sa 15:32 the bitterness of **d** is past
1Sa 15:35 Saul until the day of his **d**
1Sa 20: 3 is but a step between me and **d**
1Sa 22:22 I have caused the **d** of all
2Sa 1: 1 to pass after the **d** of Saul
2Sa 1:23 and in their **d** they were not
2Sa 6:23 children to the day of her **d**
2Sa 8: 2 off those to be put to **d**, and
2Sa 15:21 be, whether in **d** or life,
2Sa 19:21 Shimei be put to **d** for this
2Sa 19:22 be put to **d** today in Israel
2Sa 20: 3 shut up to the day of their **d**
2Sa 21: 9 were put to **d** in the days of
2Sa 22: 5 the waves of **d** encompassed me
2Sa 22: 6 the snares of **d** confronted me
1Ki 1:51 servant to **d** with the sword
1Ki 2: 8 put you to **d** with the sword
1Ki 2:24 shall be put to **d** today
1Ki 2:26 for you are worthy of **d**
1Ki 2:26 not put you to **d** at this time
1Ki 11:40 Egypt until the **d** of Solomon
2Ki 1: 1 Israel after the **d** of Ahab
2Ki 2:21 be no more **d** or barrenness
2Ki 4:40 of God, there is **d** in the pot
2Ki 11: 8 range, let him be put to **d**
2Ki 14: 6 be put to **d** for the children
2Ki 14: 6 be put to **d** for the fathers
2Ki 14: 6 be put to **d** for his own sin
2Ki 14:17 the **d** of Jehoash the son of
2Ki 15: 5 leper until the day of his **d**
2Ki 20: 1 Hezekiah was sick and near **d**
2Ki 25:21 put them to **d** at Riblah in
1Ch 22: 5 preparations before his **d**
2Ch 15:13 of Israel was to be put to **d**
2Ch 22: 4 after the **d** of his father
2Ch 23: 7 house, let him be put to **d**
2Ch 24:17 Now after the **d** of Jehoiada
2Ch 25: 4 put to **d** for their children
2Ch 25: 4 be put to **d** for your fathers
2Ch 25:25 the **d** of Joash the son of
2Ch 26:21 leper until the day of his **d**
2Ch 32:24 Hezekiah was sick and near **d**
2Ch 32:33 honored him at his **d**
Ezra 7:26 on him, whether it be **d**, or
Esth 4:11 put all to **d**, except the one
Job 3: 5 and the shadow of **d** claim it
Job 3:21 who long for **d**, but it does
Job 5:20 He shall redeem you from **d**
Job 7:15 and **d** rather than my body
Job 10:21 darkness and the shadow of **d**
Job 10:22 itself, as the shadow of **d**
Job 12:22 the shadow of **d** to light
Job 16:16 my eyelids is the shadow of **d**
Job 18:13 the firstborn of **d** devours
Job 24:17 to them as the shadow of **d**
Job 24:17 terrors of the shadow of **d**
Job 27:15 him shall be buried in **d**, and
Job 28: 3 darkness and the shadow of **d**
Job 28:22 and **D** say, We have heard a
Job 30:23 that You will bring me to **d**
Job 34:22 of **d** where the workers of
Job 38:17 Have the gates of **d** been
Job 38:17 the doors of the shadow of **d**
Ps 6: 5 For in **d** there is no
Ps 7:13 for Himself instruments of **d**
Ps 9:13 me up from the gates of **d**
Ps 13: 3 Lest I sleep the sleep of **d**
Ps 18: 4 The pangs of **d** encompassed me
Ps 18: 5 The snares of **d** confronted me
Ps 22:15 brought Me to the dust of **d**
Ps 23: 4 the valley of the shadow of **d**
Ps 33:19 To deliver their soul from **d**
Ps 44:19 us with the shadow of **d**
Ps 48:14 will be our guide Even to **d**
Ps 49:14 **D** shall feed on them
Ps 55: 4 the terrors of **d** have fallen
Ps 55:15 Let **d** seize them
Ps 56:13 have delivered my soul from **d**
Ps 68:20 Lord belong escapes from **d**
Ps 73: 4 there are no pangs in their **d**
Ps 78:50 not spare their soul from **d**
Ps 89:48 man can live and not see **d**
Ps 102:20 To loose those appointed to **d**
Ps 107:10 and in the shadow of **d**, Bound
Ps 107:14 darkness and the shadow of **d**
Ps 107:18 drew near to the gates of **d**
Ps 116: 3 The pains of **d** encompassed me
Ps 116: 8 have delivered my soul from **d**
Ps 116:15 LORD Is the **d** of His saints
Ps 118:18 He has not given me over to **d**
Prov 2:18 for her house leads down to **d**
Prov 5: 5 Her feet go down to **d**, her
Prov 7:27 to the chambers of **d**
Prov 8:36 all those who hate me love **d**
Prov 10: 2 righteousness delivers from **d**
Prov 11: 4 righteousness delivers from **d**
Prov 11:19 evil pursues it to his own **d**
Prov 12:28 in its pathway there is no **d**
Prov 13:14 one away from the snares of **d**
Prov 14:12 but its end is the way of **d**
Prov 14:27 to avoid the snares of **d**
Prov 14:32 has a refuge in his **d**
Prov 16:14 As messengers of **d** is the
Prov 16:25 but its end is the way of **d**
Prov 18:21 **D** and life are in the power of
Prov 21: 6 fantasy of those who seek **d**
Prov 24:11 those who are drawn toward **d**
Prov 26:18 firebrands, arrows, and **d**,
Eccl 7: 1 the day of **d** than the day of
Eccl 7:26 I find more bitter than **d** the
Eccl 8: 8 one has power in the day of **d**
Song 8: 6 for love is as strong as **d**
Is 9: 2 the land of the shadow of **d**
Is 22:14 for you, even to your **d**,"
Is 25: 8 He will swallow up **d** forever
Is 28:15 have made a covenant with **d**
Is 28:18 with **d** will be annulled, and
Is 38: 1 Hezekiah was sick and near **d**
Is 38:18 You, **d** cannot praise You
Is 53: 9 but with the rich at His **d**
Is 53:12 He poured out His soul unto **d**
Jer 2: 6 of drought and the shadow of **d**
Jer 8: 3 Then **d** shall be chosen rather
Jer 9:21 For **d** has come through our
Jer 13:16 turns it into the shadow of **d**
Jer 15: 2 Such as are for **d**, to **d**
Jer 18:21 Let their men be put to **d**
Jer 21: 8 way of life and the way of **d**
Jer 26:15 that if you put me to **d**, you
Jer 26:19 all Judah ever put him to **d**
Jer 26:21 king sought to put him to **d**
Jer 26:24 of the people to put him to **d**
Jer 38: 4 let this man be put to **d**
Jer 38:15 you not surely put me to **d**
Jer 38:16 I will not put you to **d**, nor
Jer 38:25 and we will not put you to **d**
Jer 43: 3 that they may put us to **d** or
Jer 43:11 to **d** those appointed for **d**
Jer 52:11 prison till the day of his **d**
Jer 52:27 put them to **d** at Riblah in
Jer 52:34 day until the day of his **d**
Lam 1:20 at home it is like **d**
Ezek 18:32 in the **d** of one who dies,"
Ezek 28: 8 you shall die the **d** of the
Ezek 28:10 You shall die the **d** of the
Ezek 31:14 have all been delivered to **d**
Ezek 33:11 in the **d** of the wicked, but
Hos 13:14 I will redeem them from **d**
Hos 13:14 O **D**, I will be your plagues
Amos 5: 8 the shadow of **d** into morning
Jon 4: 8 Then he wished **d** for himself
Jon 4: 9 for me to be angry, even to **d**
Hab 2: 5 as hell, and he is like **d**, and
Matt 2:15 there until the **d** of Herod
Matt 2:16 and put to **d** all the male
Matt 4:16 shadow of **d** light has dawned
Matt 10:21 will deliver up brother to **d**
Matt 10:21 and cause them to be put to **d**
Matt 14: 5 he wanted to put him to **d**
Matt 15: 4 mother, let him be put to **d**
Matt 16:28 **d** till they see the Son of
Matt 20:18 and they will condemn Him to **d**
Matt 26:38 sorrowful, even to **d**
Matt 26:59 against Jesus to put Him to **d**
Matt 26:66 He is deserving of **d**
Matt 27: 1 against Jesus to put Him to **d**
Mark 5:23 lies at the point of **d**
Mark 7:10 mother, let him be put to **d**
Mark 9: 1 here who will not taste **d**
Mark 10:33 and they will condemn Him to **d**
Mark 13:12 will betray brother to **d**, and
Mark 13:12 and cause them to be put to **d**
Mark 14: 1 by trickery and put Him to **d**
Mark 14:34 sorrowful, even to **d**
Mark 14:55 against Jesus to put Him to **d**
Mark 14:64 Him to be worthy of **d**
Luke 1:79 darkness and the shadow of **d**
Luke 2:26 that he would not see **d**
Luke 9:27 here who shall not taste **d**
Luke 18:33 scourge Him and put Him to **d**
Luke 21:16 send some of you to your **d**
Luke 22:33 You, both to prison and to **d**
Luke 23:15 of **d** has been done by Him
Luke 23:22 found no reason for **d** in Him
Luke 23:32 led with Him to be put to **d**
Luke 24:20 Him to be condemned to **d**, and
John 4:47 for he was at the point of **d**
John 5:24 has passed from **d** into life
John 8:51 My word he shall never see **d**
John 8:52 word he shall never taste **d**
John 11: 4 This sickness is not unto **d**
John 11:13 However, Jesus spoke of his **d**
John 11:53 they plotted to put Him to **d**
John 12:10 might also put Lazarus to **d**
John 12:33 by what **d** He would die
John 18:31 for us to put anyone to **d**
John 18:32 by what **d** He would die
John 21:19 signifying by what **d** he would
Acts 2:23 have crucified, and put to **d**
Acts 2:24 having loosed the pains of **d**
Acts 8: 1 Saul was consenting to his **d**
Acts 12:19 that they should be put to **d**
Acts 13:28 found no cause for **d** in Him
Acts 13:28 that He should be put to **d**
Acts 22: 4 persecuted this Way to the **d**
Acts 22:20 by consenting to his **d**, and
Acts 23:29 him worthy of **d** or chains
Acts 25:11 anything worthy of **d**, I do
Acts 25:25 committed nothing worthy of **d**
Acts 26:10 and when they were put to **d**
Acts 26:31 nothing worthy of **d** or chains
Acts 28:18 no cause for putting me to **d**
Rom 1:32 such things are worthy of **d**
Rom 5:10 God through the **d** of His Son
Rom 5:12 and **d** through sin
Rom 5:12 thus **d** spread to all men,
Rom 5:14 Nevertheless **d** reigned from
Rom 5:17 **d** reigned through the one
Rom 5:21 so that as sin reigned in **d**
Rom 6: 3 were baptized into His **d**
Rom 6: 4 Him through baptism into **d**
Rom 6: 5 in the likeness of His **d**,
Rom 6: 9 **D** no longer has dominion over
Rom 6:10 For the **d** that He died, He
Rom 6:16 you obey, whether of sin to **d**
Rom 6:21 the end of those things is **d**
Rom 6:23 For the wages of sin is **d**
Rom 7: 5 members to bear fruit to **d**
Rom 7:10 life, I found to bring **d**
Rom 7:13 what is good become **d** to me
Rom 7:13 was producing **d** in me through
Rom 7:24 me from this body of **d**
Rom 8: 2 free from the law of sin and **d**
Rom 8: 6 to be carnally minded is **d**
Rom 8:13 to **d** the deeds of the body
Rom 8:38 that neither **d** nor life, nor
1Co 3:22 or the world or life or **d**
1Co 4: 9 last, as men condemned to **d**
1Co 11:26 the Lord's **d** till He comes
1Co 15:21 For since by man came **d**, by

1Co 15:26 that will be destroyed is **d**
1Co 15:54 **D** is swallowed up in victory
1Co 15:55 O **D**, where is your sting
1Co 15:56 The sting of **d** is sin, and the
2Co 1: 9 sentence of **d** in ourselves
2Co 1:10 us from so great a **d**, and does
2Co 2:16 are the aroma of **d** to **d**
2Co 3: 7 But if the ministry of **d**,
2Co 4:11 to **d** for Jesus' sake, that
2Co 4:12 So then **d** is working in us,
2Co 7:10 of the world produces **d**
Eph 2:16 putting to **d** the enmity
Phil 1:20 body, whether by life or by **d**
Phil 2: 8 obedient to the point of **d**
Phil 2: 8 even the **d** of the cross
Phil 2:27 he was sick almost unto **d**
Phil 2:30 of Christ he came close to **d**
Phil 3:10 being conformed to His **d**
Col 1:22 body of His flesh through **d**
Col 3: 5 Therefore put to **d** your
2Ti 1:10 Christ, who has abolished **d**
Heb 2: 9 of **d** crowned with glory and
Heb 2: 9 might taste **d** for everyone
Heb 2:14 same, that through **d** He might
Heb 2:14 him who had the power of **d**
Heb 2:15 of **d** were all their lifetime
Heb 5: 7 was able to save Him from **d**
Heb 7:23 by **d** from continuing
Heb 9:15 new covenant, by means of **d**
Heb 9:16 be the **d** of the testator
Heb 11: 5 so that he did not see **d**
Jas 1:15 is full-grown, brings forth **d**
Jas 5:20 way will save a soul from **d**
1Pe 3:18 being put to **d** in the flesh
1Jn 3:14 we have passed from **d** to life
1Jn 3:14 love his brother abides in **d**
1Jn 5:16 sin which does not lead to **d**
1Jn 5:16 commit sin not leading to **d**
1Jn 5:16 There is sin leading to **d**
1Jn 5:17 there is sin not leading to **d**
Rev 1:18 the keys of Hades and of **D**
Rev 2:10 Be faithful until **d**, and I
Rev 2:11 not be hurt by the second **d**
Rev 2:23 will kill her children with **d**
Rev 6: 8 of him who sat on it was **D**
Rev 6: 8 sword, with hunger, with **d**
Rev 9: 6 In those days men will seek **d**
Rev 9: 6 die, and **d** will flee from them
Rev 12:11 not love their lives to the **d**
Rev 18: 8 **d** and mourning and famine
Rev 20: 6 the second **d** has no power
Rev 20:13 the dead who were in it, and **D**
Rev 20:14 Then **D** and Hades were cast
Rev 20:14 This is the second **d**
Rev 21: 4 there shall be no more **d**, nor
Rev 21: 8 which is the second **d**

DEATHS (*see* DEATH)
Jer 16: 4 They shall die gruesome **d**
2Co 11:23 more frequently, in **d** often

DEBASED (*see* DEBASES)
Is 57: 9 and **d** yourself even to Sheol
Rom 1:28 gave them over to a **d** mind

DEBASES (*see* DEBASED)
Eccl 7: 7 and a bribe **d** the heart

DEBATE
Prov 25: 9 **D** your case with your
Is 58: 4 you fast for strife and **d**, and

DEBIR (*see* KIRJATH SANNAH, KIRJATH SEPHER)
Josh 10: 3 and **D** king of Eglon, saying,
Josh 10:38 and all Israel with him, to **D**
Josh 10:39 to Hebron, so he did to **D**
Josh 11:21 from Hebron, from **D**, from
Josh 12:13 the king of **D**, one
Josh 13:26 Mahanaim to the border of **D**
Josh 15: 7 **D** from the Valley of Achor
Josh 15:15 there to the inhabitants of **D**
Josh 15:15 name of **D** was Kirjath Sepher)
Josh 15:49 Kirjath Sannah (which is **D**)
Josh 21:15 **D** with its common-land,
Judg 1:11 against the inhabitants of **D**
Judg 1:11 (The name of **D** was formerly
1Ch 6:58 **D** with its common-lands,

DEBORAH
Gen 35: 8 Now **D**, Rebekah's nurse, died,
Judg 4: 4 Now **D**, a prophetess, the wife
Judg 4: 5 palm tree of **D** between Ramah
Judg 4: 9 Then **D** arose and went with
Judg 4:10 and **D** went up with him
Judg 4:14 Then **D** said to Barak, "Up
Judg 5: 1 Then **D** and Barak the son of
Judg 5: 7 ceased in Israel, until I, **D**
Judg 5:12 Awake, awake, **D**
Judg 5:15 of Issachar were with **D**

DEBRIS
2Ch 29:16 brought out all the **d** that

DEBT (*see* DEBTOR, DEBTS)
1Sa 22: 2 everyone who was in **d**, and
2Ki 4: 7 sell the oil and pay your **d**
Neh 10:31 and the exaction of every **d**
Matt 18:27 him, and forgave him the **d**
Matt 18:30 till he should pay the **d**
Matt 18:32 that **d** because you begged me
Rom 4: 4 not counted as grace but as **d**

DEBTOR (*see* DEBT, DEBTORS)
Is 24: 2 the creditor, so with the **d**
Ezek 18: 7 restored to the **d** his pledge
Rom 1:14 I am a **d** both to Greeks and to
Gal 5: 3 is a **d** to keep the whole law

DEBTORS (*see* DEBTOR)
Matt 6:12 debts, As we forgive our **d**
Luke 7:41 creditor who had two **d**
Luke 16: 5 one of his master's **d** to him
Rom 8:12 Therefore, brethren, we are **d**
Rom 15:27 indeed, and they are their **d**

DEBTS (*see* DEBT)
Deut 15: 1 shall grant a release of **d**
Prov 22:26 of those who is surety for **d**
Matt 6:12 And forgive us our **d**, As we

DECAPOLIS
Matt 4:25 from Galilee, and from **D**,
Mark 5:20 began to proclaim in **D** all
Mark 7:31 of **D** to the Sea of Galilee

DECAYS
Job 13:28 Man **d** like a rotten thing,
Eccl 10:18 of laziness the building **d**

DECEASE (*see* DECEASED)
Luke 9:31 spoke of His **d** which He was
2Pe 1:15 of these things after my **d**

DECEASED (*see* DECEASE)
Is 26:14 they are **d**, they will not

DECEIT (*see* DECEITFUL, DECEITS, DECEIVE)
Gen 27:35 Your brother came with **d** and
Job 15:35 their womb prepares **d**
Job 27: 4 nor my tongue utter **d**
Job 31: 5 if my foot has hastened to **d**
Ps 10: 7 mouth is full of cursing and **d**
Ps 36: 3 his mouth are wickedness and **d**
Ps 50:19 evil, And your tongue frames **d**
Ps 55:11 **D** and guile do not depart from
Ps 101: 7 He who works **d** shall not
Ps 119:118 For their **d** is falsehood
Prov 12:17 but a false witness, **d**
Prov 12:20 **D** is in the heart of those
Prov 14: 8 but the folly of fools is **d**
Prov 20:17 Bread gained by **d** is sweet to
Prov 26:24 and lays up **d** within himself
Prov 26:26 his hatred is covered by **d**
Is 53: 9 nor was any **d** in His mouth
Jer 5:27 so their houses are full of **d**
Jer 8: 5 They hold fast to **d**, they
Jer 9: 6 is in the midst of **d**
Jer 9: 6 through **d** they refuse to know
Jer 9: 8 it speaks **d**
Jer 14:14 and the **d** of their heart
Jer 23:26 of the **d** of their own heart
Dan 8:25 **d** to prosper under his hand
Hos 11:12 and the house of Israel with **d**
Amos 8: 5 falsifying the balances by **d**
Zeph 1: 9 houses with violence and **d**
Mark 7:22 covetousness, wickedness, **d**
Acts 13:10 O full of all **d** and all fraud,
Rom 1:29 of envy, murder, strife, **d**
Rom 3:13 they have practiced **d**"
Col 2: 8 through philosophy and empty **d**
1Th 2: 3 come from **d** or uncleanness

DECEITFUL (*see* DECEIT, DECEITFULLY, DECEITFULNESS)
Job 11:11 For He knows **d** men
Ps 5: 6 the bloodthirsty and **d** man
Ps 17: 1 that is not from **d** lips
Ps 35:20 But they devise **d** matters
Ps 43: 1 Oh, deliver me from the **d**
Ps 52: 4 devouring words, You **d** tongue
Ps 55:23 **d** men shall not live out half
Ps 78:57 turned aside like a **d** bow
Ps 109: 2 and the mouth of the **d** Have
Ps 120: 2 lying lips And from a **d** tongue
Prov 4:24 Put away from you a **d** mouth
Prov 12: 5 counsels of the wicked are **d**
Prov 14:25 but a **d** witness speaks lies
Prov 17:20 He who has a **d** heart finds no
Prov 27: 6 the kisses of an enemy are **d**
Prov 31:30 Charm is **d** and beauty is vain,
Jer 17: 9 The heart is **d** above all
Hos 7:16 they are like a **d** bow
Hos 12: 7 **d** scales are in his hand
Mic 6:11 and with the bag of **d** weights
Mic 6:12 tongue is **d** in their mouth
Zeph 3:13 nor shall a **d** tongue be found
2Co 11:13 **d** workers, transforming
Eph 4:22 according to the **d** lusts,

DECEITFULLY (*see* DECEITFUL)
Gen 34:13 Hamor his father, and spoke **d**
Ex 8:29 But let Pharaoh not deal **d**
Ex 21: 8 since he has dealt **d** with her
Lev 6: 4 thing which he has **d** obtained
Job 6:15 have dealt **d** like a brook
Job 13: 7 for God, and talk **d** for Him
Ps 24: 4 soul to an idol, Nor sworn **d**
Ps 52: 2 Like a sharp razor, working **d**
Jer 48:10 does the work of the LORD **d**
Dan 11:23 made with him he shall act **d**
2Co 4: 2 handling the word of God **d**

DECEITFULNESS (*see* DECEITFUL)
Matt 13:22 the **d** of riches choke the
Mark 4:19 the **d** of riches, and the
Heb 3:13 hardened through the **d** of sin

DECEITS (*see* DECEIT)
Is 30:10 us smooth things, prophesy **d**

DECEIVE (*see* DECEIT, DECEIVED, DECEIVER, DECEIVES, DECEIVING, DECEPTION, DECEPTIVE)
2Sa 3:25 the son of Ner came to **d** you
2Ki 4:28 Did I not say, 'Do not **d** me'
2Ki 18:29 Do not let Hezekiah **d** you
2Ki 19:10 God in whom you trust **d** you
2Ch 32:15 do not let Hezekiah **d** you or
Prov 24:28 for would you **d** with your
Is 36:14 Do not let Hezekiah **d** you
Is 37:10 God in whom you trust **d** you
Jer 9: 5 Everyone will **d** his neighbor
Jer 29: 8 who are in your midst **d** you
Jer 37: 9 Do not **d** yourselves, saying,
Obad 7 at peace with you shall **d** you
Zech 13: 4 a robe of coarse hair to **d**
Matt 24: 5 the Christ,' and will **d** many
Matt 24:11 will rise up and **d** many
Matt 24:24 signs and wonders, so as to **d**
Mark 13: 6 I am He,' and will **d** many
Mark 13:22 and show signs and wonders to **d**
Rom 16:18 and flattering speech **d** the
1Co 3:18 Let no one **d** himself
Eph 4:14 which they lie in wait to **d**
Eph 5: 6 Let no one **d** you with empty
Col 2: 4 I say lest anyone should **d**
2Th 2: 3 Let no one **d** you by any means
1Jn 1: 8 we **d** ourselves, and the truth
1Jn 2:26 those who try to **d** you
1Jn 3: 7 children, let no one **d** you
Rev 20: 3 him, so that he should **d** the
Rev 20: 8 will go out to **d** the nations

DECEIVED (*see* DECEIVE)
Gen 3:13 The serpent **d** me, and I ate
Gen 29:25 Why then have you **d** me
Gen 31: 7 Yet your father has **d** me and
Deut 11:16 lest your heart be **d**, and you
Josh 7:11 and have both stolen and **d**
Josh 9:22 Why have you **d** us, saying
1Sa 19:17 Why have you **d** me like this
1Sa 28:12 Why have you **d** me
2Sa 19:26 lord, O king, my servant **d** me
Job 12:16 the **d** and the deceiver are His
Is 19:13 the princes of Noph are **d**
Is 44:20 a **d** heart has turned him
Jer 4:10 have greatly **d** this people
Jer 49:16 Your fierceness has **d** you
Lam 1:19 for my lovers, but they **d** me
Obad 3 pride of your heart has **d** you
Matt 2:16 that he was **d** by the wise men
Luke 21: 8 Take heed that you not be **d**

John 7:47 Are you also **d**
Rom 7:11 **d** me, and by it killed me
1Co 6: 9 Do not be **d**
1Co 15:33 Do not be **d**
2Co 11: 3 as the serpent **d** Eve by his
Gal 6: 7 Do not be **d**, God is not
1Ti 2:14 And Adam was not **d**, but the
1Ti 2:14 but the woman being **d**, fell
2Ti 3:13 worse, deceiving and being **d**
Tit 3: 3 once foolish, disobedient, **d**
Jas 1:16 Do not be **d**, my beloved
Rev 18:23 all the nations were **d**
Rev 19:20 by which he **d** those who
Rev 20:10 who **d** them, was cast into the

DECEIVER (*see* DECEIVE, DECEIVERS)
Gen 27:12 I shall seem to be a **d** to him
Job 12:16 the deceived and the **d** are His
Mal 1:14 But cursed be the **d** who has
Matt 27:63 still alive, how that **d** said
2Jn 7 This is a **d** and an antichrist

DECEIVERS (*see* DECEIVER)
2Co 6: 8 as **d**, and yet true
Tit 1:10 both idle talkers and **d**,
2Jn 7 For many **d** have gone out into

DECEIVES (*see* DECEIVE)
Prov 26:19 is the man who **d** his neighbor
Matt 24: 4 Take heed that no one **d** you
Mark 13: 5 Take heed that no one **d** you
John 7:12 the contrary, He **d** the people
Gal 6: 3 he is nothing, he **d** himself
Jas 1:26 tongue but **d** his own heart
Rev 12: 9 Satan, who **d** the whole world
Rev 13:14 he **d** those who dwell on the

DECEIVING (*see* DECEIVE)
Job 15:31 **d** himself, for futility will
1Ti 4: 1 giving heed to **d** spirits
2Ti 3:13 will grow worse and worse, **d**
Jas 1:22 hearers only, **d** yourselves

DECENTLY
1Co 14:40 Let all things be done **d** and

DECEPTION (*see* DECEIVE, DECEPTIONS)
Ps 38:12 And plan **d** all the day long
Matt 27:64 So the last **d** will be worse
2Th 2:10 with all unrighteous **d** among

DECEPTIONS (*see* DECEPTION)
2Pe 2:13 carousing in their own **d**

DECEPTIVE (*see* DECEIVE, DECEPTIVELY)
Prov 11:18 The wicked man does **d** work
Prov 23: 3 for they are **d** food
Lam 2:14 for you false and **d** visions
2Pe 2: 3 will exploit you with **d** words

DECEPTIVELY (*see* DECEPTIVE)
2Ki 10:19 But Jehu acted **d**, with the

DECIDE (*see* DECIDED, DECISION)
Is 11: 3 nor **d** by the hearing of His
Is 11: 4 **d** with equity for the meek of

DECIDED (*see* DECIDE)
1Ki 20:40 you yourself have **d** it
Acts 20: 3 Syria, he **d** to return through
Acts 20:16 For Paul had **d** to sail past
Acts 21:25 **d** that they should observe no
Acts 25:25 to Augustus, I **d** to send him
Acts 27: 1 when it was **d** that we should
Tit 3:12 for I have **d** to spend the

DECISION (*see* DECIDE)
2Sa 15: 2 came to the king for a **d**,
Prov 16:33 but its every **d** is from the
Dan 2: 5 the Chaldeans, "My **d** is firm
Dan 2: 8 you see that my **d** is firm
Dan 2:15 made the **d** known to Daniel
Dan 2:17 made the **d** known to Hananiah,
Dan 4:17 This **d** is by the decree of
Joel 3:14 multitudes in the valley of **d**
Joel 3:14 is near in the valley of **d**
Acts 24:22 I will make a **d** on your case
Acts 25:21 for the **d** of Augustus, I

DECKED (*see* DECKS)
Hos 2:13 She **d** herself with her

DECKS (*see* DECKED)
Gen 6:16 lower, second, and third **d**
Is 61:10 as a bridegroom **d** himself

DECLARATION (*see* DECLARE)
Job 13:17 and to my **d** with your ears

DECLARE (*see* DECLARATION, DECLARED, DECLARES, DECLARING)
Deut 5: 5 to **d** to you the word of the
Deut 26: 3 I **d** today to the LORD your
1Ch 16:24 **D** His glory among the nations
Job 15:17 what I have seen I will **d**
Job 22:28 You will also **d** a thing, and
Job 31:37 I would **d** to Him the number
Job 32: 6 dared not **d** my opinion to you
Job 32:10 me, I also will **d** my opinion
Job 32:17 part, I too will **d** my opinion
Ps 2: 7 I will **d** the decree
Ps 9:11 **D** His deeds among the people
Ps 19: 1 The heavens **d** the glory of
Ps 22:22 I will **d** Your name to My
Ps 22:31 and **d** His righteousness to a
Ps 30: 9 Will it **d** Your truth
Ps 38:18 For I will **d** my iniquity
Ps 40: 5 If I would **d** and speak of them
Ps 50: 6 Let the heavens **d** His
Ps 50:16 have you to **d** My statutes
Ps 64: 9 And shall **d** the work of God
Ps 66:16 I will **d** what He has done for
Ps 71:17 to this day I **d** Your wondrous
Ps 71:18 Until I **d** Your strength to
Ps 73:28 That I may **d** all Your works
Ps 75: 1 **d** that Your name is near
Ps 75: 9 But I will **d** forever, I will
Ps 78: 6 **d** them to their children,
Ps 92: 2 To **d** Your lovingkindness in
Ps 92:15 To **d** that the LORD is upright
Ps 96: 3 **D** His glory among the nations
Ps 97: 6 The heavens **d** His
Ps 102:21 To **d** the name of the LORD in
Ps 106: 2 Or can **d** all His praise
Ps 107:22 **d** His works with rejoicing
Ps 118:17 And **d** the works of the LORD
Ps 142: 2 I **d** before Him my trouble
Ps 145: 4 And shall **d** Your mighty acts
Ps 145: 6 And I will **d** Your greatness
Eccl 9: 1 so that I could **d** it all
Is 3: 9 they **d** their sin as Sodom
Is 12: 4 **d** His deeds among the peoples
Is 21: 6 let him **d** what he sees
Is 41:22 or **d** to us things to come
Is 42: 9 to pass, and new things I **d**
Is 42:12 LORD, and **d** His praise in the
Is 43: 9 Who among them can **d** this
Is 43:21 they shall **d** My praise
Is 44: 7 Then let him **d** it and set it
Is 45:19 I **d** things that are right
Is 48: 6 and will you not **d** it
Is 48:20 With a voice of singing, **d**
Is 53: 8 who will **d** His generation
Is 57:12 I will **d** your righteousness
Is 66:19 they shall **d** My glory among
Jer 4: 5 **D** in Judah and proclaim in
Jer 5:20 **D** this in the house of Jacob
Jer 9:12 has spoken, that he may **d** it
Jer 31:10 **d** it in the isles afar off,
Jer 38:15 If I **d** it to you, will you
Jer 38:25 **D** to us now what you have
Jer 42: 4 you, I will **d** it to you
Jer 42:20 so **d** to us and we will do it
Jer 46:14 **D** in Egypt, and proclaim in
Jer 50: 2 **D** among the nations, Proclaim
Jer 51:10 let us **d** in Zion the work of
Ezek 12:16 that they may **d** all their
Ezek 23:36 Then **d** to them their
Ezek 40: 4 **D** to the house of Israel
Dan 2:27 cannot **d** to the king
Dan 4: 2 it good to **d** the signs and
Dan 4:18 **d** its interpretation, since
Mic 3: 8 and might, to **d** to Jacob his
Zech 9:12 Even today I **d** that I will
Matt 7:23 And then I will **d** to them, 'I
Matt 12:18 and He will **d** justice to the
John 16:14 what is Mine and **d** it to you
John 16:15 take of Mine and **d** it to you
John 17:26 them Your name, and will **d** it
Acts 8:33 who will **d** His generation
Acts 13:32 And we **d** to you glad tidings
Acts 13:41 one were to **d** it to you
Acts 20:27 For I have not shunned to **d**
1Co 3:13 for the Day will **d** it,
1Co 15: 1 I **d** to you the gospel which I
1Th 1: 9 For they themselves **d**
Heb 2:12 I will **d** Your name to My
Heb 11:14 **d** plainly that they seek a
1Jn 1: 2 **d** to you that eternal life
1Jn 1: 3 seen and heard we **d** to you
1Jn 1: 5 **d** to you, that God is light

DECLARED (*see* DECLARE)
Ex 9:16 may be **d** in all the earth
Lev 23:44 So Moses **d** to the children of
Deut 4:13 So He **d** to you His covenant
2Sa 19: 6 For you have **d** today that you
1Ki 22:23 and the LORD has **d** disaster
2Ch 18:22 and the LORD has **d** disaster
Neh 8:12 the words that were **d** to them
Job 26: 3 how have you **d** sound advice
Job 28:27 then He saw wisdom and **d** it
Ps 40:10 I have **d** Your faithfulness and
Ps 77:14 You have **d** Your strength
Ps 88:11 be **d** in the grave
Ps 111: 6 He has **d** to His people the
Ps 119:13 With my lips I have **d** All the
Ps 119:26 I have **d** my ways, and You
Prov 30: 1 This man **d** to Ithiel
Is 21: 2 distressing vision is **d** to me
Is 21:10 of Israel, I have **d** to you
Is 41:26 Who has **d** from the beginning,
Is 43:12 I have **d** and saved, I have
Is 44: 8 you from that time, and **d** it
Is 45:21 Who has **d** this from ancient
Is 48: 3 I have **d** the former things
Is 48: 5 beginning I have **d** it to you
Is 48:14 among them has **d** these things
Jer 36:13 Then Michaiah **d** to them all
Jer 42:21 I have this day **d** it to you
Luke 8:47 she **d** to Him in the presence
John 1:18 of the Father, He has **d** Him
John 17:26 I have **d** to them Your name,
Acts 9:27 he **d** to them how he had seen
Acts 12:17 he **d** to them how the Lord had
Acts 15:14 Simon has **d** how God at the
Acts 26:20 but **d** first to those in
Rom 1: 4 **d** to be the Son of God with
Rom 9:17 might be **d** in all the earth
1Co 1:11 For it has been **d** to me
Col 1: 8 who also **d** to us your love in
Rev 10: 7 as He **d** to His servants the

DECLARES (*see* DECLARE)
Josh 20: 4 **d** his case in the hearing of
Job 36:33 His thunder **d** it, the cattle
Ps 147:19 He **d** His word to Jacob, His
Prov 12:17 speaks truth **d** righteousness
Is 41:26 surely there is no one who **d**
Jer 4:15 For a voice **d** from Dan and
Jer 50:28 **d** in Zion the vengeance of
Amos 4:13 who **d** to man what his thought

DECLARING (*see* DECLARE)
Is 46:10 **D** the end from the beginning,
Acts 15:12 Paul **d** how many miracles and
1Co 2: 1 of speech or of wisdom **d** to

DECLINE
2Ch 28:19 encouraged moral **d** in Judah

DECORATE (*see* DECORATED)
Jer 10: 4 They **d** it with silver and gold

DECORATED (*see* DECORATE)
2Ch 3: 6 he **d** the house with precious

DECREASE (*see* DECREASED)
Ps 107:38 does not let their cattle **d**
John 3:30 must increase, but I must **d**

DECREASED (*see* DECREASE)
Gen 8: 3 and fifty days the waters **d**
Gen 8: 5 And the waters **d** continually

DECREE (*see* DECREED, DECREES)
Ezra 5:13 King Cyrus issued a **d** to
Ezra 5:17 whether it is so that a **d** was
Ezra 6: 1 Then King Darius issued a **d**
Ezra 6: 3 Cyrus, King Cyrus issued a **d**
Ezra 6: 8 Moreover I issue a **d** as to
Ezra 6:11 Also I issue a **d** that whoever
Ezra 6:12 I Darius issue the **d**
Ezra 7:13 I issue a **d** that all those of
Ezra 7:21 king, do issue a **d** to all the
Esth 1:19 let a royal **d** go out from him
Esth 1:20 When the king's **d** which he
Esth 2: 8 **d** were heard, and when many
Esth 3: 9 let a **d** be written that they
Esth 3:12 a **d** was written according to
Esth 3:15 and the **d** was proclaimed in
Esth 4: 3 **d** arrived, there was great

Esth 4: 8 **d** for their destruction,
Esth 8: 8 write a **d** for the Jews, as
Esth 8:13 as a **d** in every province and
Esth 8:14 the **d** was issued in Shushan
Esth 8:17 **d** came, the Jews had joy and
Esth 9: 1 and his **d** to be executed
Esth 9:13 according to today's **d**, and
Esth 9:14 the **d** was issued in Shushan,
Esth 9:32 So the **d** of Esther confirmed
Ps 2: 7 I will declare the **d**
Ps 148: 6 He has made a **d** which shall
Prov 8:15 reign, and rulers **d** justice
Is 10: 1 Woe to those who **d**
Jer 5:22 of the sea, by a perpetual **d**
Dan 2: 9 there is only one **d** for you
Dan 2:13 So the **d** went out, and they
Dan 2:15 Why is the **d** from the king so
Dan 3:10 have made a **d** that everyone
Dan 3:29 I make a **d** that any people
Dan 4: 6 Therefore I issued a **d** to
Dan 4:17 is by the **d** of the watchers
Dan 4:24 this is the **d** of the Most
Dan 6: 7 statute and to make a firm **d**
Dan 6: 8 Now, O king, establish the **d**
Dan 6: 9 Darius signed the written **d**
Dan 6:12 spoke concerning the king's **d**
Dan 6:12 signed a **d** that every man who
Dan 6:13 or for the **d** that you have
Dan 6:15 Persians that no **d** or statute
Dan 6:26 I make a **d** that in every
Jon 3: 7 Nineveh by the **d** of the king
Mic 7:11 that day the **d** shall go far
Zeph 2: 2 before the **d** is issued,
Luke 2: 1 that a **d** went out from Caesar

DECREED (*see* DECREE)
Esth 2: 1 what had been **d** against her
Esth 9:31 as they had **d** for themselves
Is 10:22 the destruction **d** shall
Nah 2: 7 It is **d**: she shall be led

DECREES (*see* DECREE)
Is 10: 1 who decree unrighteous **d**, who
Acts 16: 4 to them the **d** to keep, which
Acts 17: 7 contrary to the **d** of Caesar

DEDAN (*see* DEDANITES)
Gen 10: 7 of Raamah were Sheba and **D**
Gen 25: 3 Jokshan begot Sheba and **D**
Gen 25: 3 the sons of **D** were Asshurim,
1Ch 1: 9 of Raama were Sheba and **D**
1Ch 1:32 of Jokshan were Sheba and **D**
Jer 25:23 **D**, Tema, Buz, and all who are
Jer 49: 8 depths, O inhabitants of **D**
Ezek 25:13 **D** shall fall by the sword
Ezek 27:15 The men of **D** were your
Ezek 27:20 **D** was your merchant in
Ezek 38:13 Sheba, **D**, the merchants of

DEDANITES (*see* DEDAN)
Is 21:13 you traveling companies of **D**

DEDICATE (*see* DEDICATED, DEDICATION)
Deut 20: 5 battle and another man **d** it
2Ch 2: 4 God, to **d** it to Him, to burn

DEDICATED (*see* DEDICATE)
Deut 20: 5 a new house and has not **d** it
Judg 17: 3 I had wholly **d** the silver
2Sa 8:11 King David **d** these to the
2Sa 8:11 gold that he had **d** from all
1Ki 7:51 which his father David had **d**
1Ki 8:63 **d** the house of the LORD
1Ki 15:15 things which his father had **d**
1Ki 15:15 things which he himself had **d**
2Ki 12: 4 All the money of the **d** gifts
2Ki 12:18 kings of Judah, had **d**, and
2Ki 23:11 of Judah had **d** to the sun
1Ch 18:11 King David also **d** these to
1Ch 26:20 treasuries of the **d** things
1Ch 26:26 the **d** things which King David
1Ch 26:26 captains of the army, had **d**
1Ch 26:27 **d** to maintain the house of
1Ch 26:28 Joab the son of Zeruiah had **d**
1Ch 26:28 every **d** thing
1Ch 28:12 treasuries for the **d** things
2Ch 5: 1 which his father David had **d**
2Ch 7: 5 all the people **d** the house of
2Ch 15:18 things that his father had **d**
2Ch 15:18 and that he himself had **d**
2Ch 24: 7 **d** things of the house of the
2Ch 31:12 the tithes, and the **d** things
Ezek 44:29 every **d** thing in Israel shall
Matt 15: 5 me has been **d** to the temple"
Mark 7:11 (that is, **d** to the temple)"
Heb 9:18 covenant was **d** without blood

DEDICATION (*see* DEDICATE)
Num 7:10 **d** offering for the altar when
Num 7:11 day, for the **d** of the altar
Num 7:84 This was the **d** offering for
Num 7:88 This was the **d** offering for
2Ch 7: 9 for they observed the **d** of
Ezra 6:16 celebrated the **d** of this
Ezra 6:17 at the **d** of this house of God
Neh 12:27 Now at the **d** of the wall of
Neh 12:27 celebrate the **d** with gladness
Dan 3: 2 to come to the **d** of the image
Dan 3: 3 the **d** of the image that King
John 10:22 the Feast of **D** in Jerusalem

DEDUCTED
Lev 27:18 and it shall be **d** from your

DEED (*see* DEEDED, DEEDS)
Gen 44:15 What **d** is this you have done
Judg 19:30 No such **d** has been done or
Judg 20: 3 how did this wicked **d** happen
1Sa 20:19 you hid on the day of the **d**
2Sa 12:14 because by this **d** you have
Job 33:17 order to turn man from his **d**
Jer 32:10 And I signed the **d** and sealed
Jer 32:11 So I took the purchase **d**,
Jer 32:12 and I gave the purchase **d** to
Jer 32:12 who signed the purchase **d**
Jer 32:14 purchase **d** which is sealed
Jer 32:14 this **d** which is open, and put
Jer 32:16 had delivered the purchase **d**
Matt 6: 2 when you do a charitable **d**
Matt 6: 3 when you do a charitable **d**
Matt 6: 4 charitable **d** may be in secret
Luke 23:51 to their counsel and **d**
Luke 24:19 who was a Prophet mighty in **d**
Acts 4: 9 **d** done to the helpless man
Rom 15:18 through me, in word and **d**, to
1Co 5: 2 **d** might be taken away from
1Co 5: 3 him who has so done this **d**
2Co 10:11 be in **d** when we are present
Col 3:17 whatever you do in word or **d**
Tit 2:14 us from every lawless **d** and
Phm 14 that your good **d** might not be
1Jn 3:18 word or in tongue, but in **d**

DEEDED (*see* DEED)
Gen 23:17 surrounding borders, were **d**
Gen 23:20 **d** to Abraham by the sons of

DEEDS (*see* DEED)
Gen 20: 9 You have done **d** to me that
Deut 3:24 Your works and Your mighty **d**
2Sa 7:23 and awesome **d** for Your land
2Sa 23:20 Kabzeel, who had done many **d**
2Ki 23:19 the **d** he had done in Bethel
1Ch 11:22 Kabzeel, who had done many **d**
1Ch 16: 8 make known His **d** among the
1Ch 17:21 a name by great and awesome **d**
2Ch 32: 1 After these **d** of faithfulness
2Ch 35:27 his **d** from first to last,
Ezra 9:13 come upon us for our evil **d**
Neh 6:19 reported his good **d** before me
Neh 13:14 do not wipe out my good **d**
Ps 9:11 Declare His **d** among the
Ps 28: 4 to them according to their **d**
Ps 44: 1 What **d** You did in their days,
Ps 65: 5 By awesome **d** in righteousness
Ps 77:12 Your work, And talk of Your **d**
Ps 99: 8 You took vengeance on their **d**
Ps 105: 1 Make known His **d** among the
Ps 106:29 Him to anger with their **d**
Ps 106:39 the harlot by their own **d**
Ps 141: 5 against the **d** of the wicked
Prov 20:11 a child is known by his **d**
Prov 24:12 each man according to his **d**
Is 12: 4 declare His **d** among the
Is 59:18 According to their **d**,
Jer 5:28 surpass the **d** of the wicked
Jer 11:15 having done lewd **d** with many
Jer 25:14 them according to their **d**
Jer 32:14 Take these **d**, both this
Jer 32:44 buy fields for money, sign **d**
Ezek 9:10 their **d** on their own head
Ezek 11:21 their **d** on their own heads
Ezek 16:30 the **d** of a brazen harlot
Ezek 16:43 your **d** on your own head,"
Ezek 22:31 their **d** on their own heads
Ezek 24:14 according to your **d** they will
Ezek 36:17 it by their own ways and **d**
Ezek 36:19 to their ways and their **d**
Ezek 36:31 your **d** that were not good
Dan 9:18 because of our righteous **d**
Hos 4: 9 and reward them for their **d**
Hos 5: 4 They do not direct their **d**
Hos 7: 2 now their own **d** have
Hos 9:15 of the evil of their **d** I will
Hos 12: 2 according to his **d** He will
Mic 3: 4 have been evil in their **d**
Mic 7:13 and for the fruit of their **d**
Zeph 3: 7 and corrupted all their **d**
Zeph 3:11 **d** in which you transgress
Zech 1: 4 your evil ways and your evil **d**
Zech 1: 6 ways and according to our **d**
Matt 6: 1 your charitable **d** before men
Luke 11:48 approve the **d** of your fathers
Luke 23:41 the due reward of our **d**
John 3:19 because their **d** were evil
John 3:20 lest his **d** should be exposed
John 3:21 that his **d** may be clearly
John 8:41 You do the **d** of your father
Acts 7:22 and was mighty in words and **d**
Acts 9:36 charitable **d** which she did
Acts 19:18 confessing and telling their **d**
Rom 2: 6 each one according to his **d**"
Rom 3:20 Therefore by the **d** of the law
Rom 3:28 apart from the **d** of the law
Rom 4: 7 whose lawless **d** are forgiven
Rom 8:13 to death the **d** of the body
2Co 12:12 signs and wonders and mighty **d**
Col 3: 9 off the old man with his **d**
Heb 8:12 and their lawless **d** I will
Heb 10:17 and their lawless **d** I will
2Pe 2: 8 and hearing their lawless **d**)
2Jn 11 him shares in his evil **d**
3Jn 10 to mind his **d** which he does
Jude 15 **d** which they have committed
Rev 2: 6 that you hate the **d** of the
Rev 2:22 unless they repent of their **d**
Rev 16:11 and did not repent of their **d**

DEEP (*see* DEEPER, DEEPLY)
Gen 1: 2 was on the face of the **d**
Gen 2:21 a **d** sleep to fall on Adam
Gen 7:11 of the great **d** were broken up
Gen 8: 2 The fountains of the **d** and the
Gen 15:12 a **d** sleep fell upon Abram
Gen 49:25 blessings of the **d** that lies
Lev 14:37 appear to be **d** in the wall
Deut 33:13 dew, and the **d** lying beneath,
1Sa 26:12 because a **d** sleep from the
2Ki 4:27 for her soul is in **d** distress
Neh 9:11 You threw into the **d**, as a
Job 4:13 when **d** sleep falls on men,
Job 11: 7 out the **d** things of God
Job 12:22 He uncovers **d** things out of
Job 22:13 judge through the **d** darkness
Job 23:17 He did not hide **d** darkness
Job 28:14 The **d** says, 'It is not in me'
Job 33:15 when **d** sleep falls upon men,
Job 38:30 surface of the **d** is frozen
Job 41:31 He makes the **d** boil like a
Job 41:32 think the **d** had white hair
Ps 2: 5 them in His **d** displeasure
Ps 33: 7 lays up the **d** in storehouses
Ps 36: 6 Your judgments are a great **d**
Ps 42: 7 **D** calls unto **d** at the
Ps 64: 6 and the heart of man are **d**
Ps 69: 2 I sink in **d** mire, Where there
Ps 69: 2 I have come into **d** waters
Ps 69:14 me, And out of the **d** waters
Ps 69:15 Nor let the **d** swallow me up
Ps 80: 9 And caused it to take **d** root
Ps 92: 5 Your thoughts are very **d**
Ps 95: 4 are the **d** places of the earth
Ps 104: 6 with the **d** as with a garment
Ps 107:24 LORD, And His wonders in the **d**
Ps 135: 6 the seas and in all **d** places
Ps 140:10 into the fire, Into **d** pits
Prov 8:27 a circle on the face of the **d**
Prov 8:28 the fountains of the **d**,
Prov 18: 4 of a man's mouth are **d** waters
Prov 19:15 casts one into a **d** sleep, and
Prov 20: 5 heart of man is like **d** water
Prov 20:20 will be put out in **d** darkness
Prov 22:14 an immoral woman is a **d** pit
Prov 23:27 For a harlot is a **d** pit, and a
Eccl 7:24 is far off and exceedingly **d**
Is 29:10 on you the spirit of **d** sleep
Is 29:15 Woe to those who seek **d** to

Is 30:33 He has made it **d** and large
Is 44:27 Who says to the **d**, 'Be dry
Is 51:10 the waters of the great **d**
Is 60: 2 and **d** darkness the people
Is 63:13 Who led them through the **d**
Ezek 23:32 of your sister's cup, the **d**
Ezek 26:19 when I bring the **d** upon you
Ezek 31:15 I covered the **d** because of it
Ezek 47: 5 for the water was too **d**,
Dan 2:22 He reveals **d** and secret things
Dan 8:18 I was in a **d** sleep with my
Dan 10: 9 I was in a **d** sleep on my face
Amos 7: 4 and it consumed the great **d**
Jon 2: 3 For You cast me into the **d**
Jon 2: 5 the **d** closed around me
Hab 3:10 The **d** uttered its voice, and
Luke 5: 4 Launch out into the **d** and let
Luke 6:48 building a house, who dug **d**
John 4:11 draw with, and the well is **d**
Acts 20: 9 was sinking into a **d** sleep
1Co 2:10 yes, the **d** things of God
2Co 8: 2 their **d** poverty abounded in
2Co 11:25 and a day I have been in the **d**
2Co 11:28 my **d** concern for all the

DEEPER (*see* DEEP)
Lev 13: 3 the sore appears to be **d** than
Lev 13: 4 appear to be **d** than the skin
Lev 13:20 appears **d** than the skin, and
Lev 13:21 if it is not **d** than the skin,
Lev 13:25 it appears **d** than the skin,
Lev 13:26 it is not **d** than the skin,
Lev 13:30 if it appears **d** than the skin
Lev 13:31 not appear **d** than the skin
Lev 13:32 not appear **d** than the skin
Lev 13:34 not appear **d** than the skin
Job 11: 8 **D** than Sheol

DEEPLY (*see* DEEP)
1Sa 28:15 answered, "I am **d** distressed
2Sa 18:33 Then the king was **d** moved
Neh 2:10 they were **d** disturbed that a
Esth 4: 4 and the queen was **d** distressed
Ps 38: 2 For Your arrows pierce me **d**
Song 5: 1 Drink, yes, drink **d**, O
Is 31: 6 of Israel have **d** revolted
Is 66:11 bosom, that you may drink **d**
Jer 50:12 mother shall be **d** ashamed
Hos 5: 2 The revolters are **d** involved
Hos 9: 9 They are **d** corrupted, as in
Matt 26:37 be sorrowful and **d** distressed
Mark 8:12 But He sighed **d** in His spirit
Mark 14:33 be troubled and **d** distressed

DEER (*see* DEER'S)
Gen 49:21 Naphtali is a **d** let loose
Deut 12:15 of the gazelle and the **d** alike
Deut 12:22 the **d** are eaten, so you may
Deut 14: 5 the **d**, the gazelle, the roe **d**
Deut 15:22 if it were a gazelle or a **d**
2Sa 22:34 my feet like the feet of **d**
1Ki 4:23 one hundred sheep, besides **d**
Job 39: 1 mark when the **d** gives birth
Ps 18:33 my feet like the feet of **d**
Ps 29: 9 LORD makes the **d** give birth
Ps 42: 1 As the **d** pants for the water
Prov 5:19 As a loving **d** and a graceful
Is 35: 6 the lame shall leap like a **d**
Jer 14: 5 the **d** also gave birth in the
Lam 1: 6 like **d** that find no pasture

DEER'S (*see* DEER)
Hab 3:19 will make my feet like **d** feet

DEFAME (*see* DEFAMED)
1Pe 3:16 that when they **d** you as

DEFAMED (*see* DEFAME)
1Co 4:13 being **d**, we entreat

DEFEAT (*see* DEFEATED, DEFEATS)
Gen 14:17 from the **d** of Chedorlaomer
Ex 32:18 of those who cry out in **d**
Num 22: 6 I shall be able to **d** them
Deut 7:23 and will inflict **d** upon them
Judg 6:16 you shall **d** the Midianites as
2Sa 15:34 then you may **d** the counsel
2Sa 17:14 to **d** the good counsel of

DEFEATED (*see* DEFEAT)
Ex 17:13 So Joshua **d** Amalek and his
Lev 26:17 and you shall be **d** by your
Num 14:42 lest you be **d** by your enemies
Num 21:24 Then Israel **d** him with the
Num 21:35 So they **d** him, his sons, and
Num 32: 4 **d** before the congregation of
Deut 1:42 lest you be **d** before your
Deut 2:33 so we **d** him, his sons, and all
Deut 4:46 **d** after they came out of
Deut 28: 7 you to be **d** before your face
Deut 28:25 to be **d** before your enemies
Josh 11: 8 who **d** them and chased them to
Josh 12: 1 whom the children of Israel **d**
Josh 13:12 for Moses had **d** and cast out
Judg 1: 5 they **d** the Canaanites and the
Judg 3:13 **d** Israel, and took possession
Judg 11:21 of Israel, and they **d** them
Judg 11:33 he **d** them from Aroer as far
Judg 12: 4 the men of Gilead **d** Ephraim
Judg 20:35 The LORD **d** Benjamin before
Judg 20:36 Benjamin saw that they were **d**
Judg 20:39 Surely they are **d** before us
1Sa 4: 2 battle, Israel was **d** by the
1Sa 4: 3 Why has the LORD **d** us today
1Sa 4:10 fought, and Israel was **d**, and
2Sa 5:20 and David **d** them there
2Sa 8: 2 Then he **d** Moab
2Sa 8: 3 David also **d** Hadadezer the
2Sa 8: 9 **d** all the army of Hadadezer
2Sa 8:10 against Hadadezer and **d** him
2Sa 10:15 they had been **d** before Israel
2Sa 10:19 that they were **d** by Israel
1Ki 8:33 are **d** before an enemy because
2Ki 13:25 Three times Joash **d** him and
2Ki 14:10 You have indeed **d** Edom, and
2Ki 14:12 And Judah was **d** by Israel, and
1Ch 4:43 And they **d** the rest of the
1Ch 14:11 and David **d** them there
1Ch 18: 2 Then he **d** Moab, and the
1Ch 18: 3 David **d** Hadadezer king of
1Ch 18: 9 **d** all the army of Hadadezer
1Ch 18:10 **d** him (for Hadadezer had been
1Ch 19:16 they had been **d** by Israel
1Ch 19:19 that they were **d** by Israel
1Ch 20: 1 Joab **d** Rabbah and overthrew it
1Ch 21:12 or three months to be **d** by
2Ch 6:24 are **d** before an enemy because
2Ch 14:14 Then they **d** all the cities
2Ch 20:22 and they were **d**
2Ch 25:19 that you have **d** the Edomites
2Ch 25:22 And Judah was **d** by Israel, and
2Ch 27: 5 of the Ammonites and **d** them
2Ch 28: 5 They **d** him, and carried away a
2Ch 28: 5 who **d** him with a great
2Ch 28:23 of Damascus which had **d** him
Esth 9: 5 Thus the Jews **d** all their
Ps 135:10 He **d** many nations And slew
Is 10:20 depend on him who **d** them, but
Jer 37:10 For though you had **d** the
Jer 46: 2 king of Babylon **d** in the

DEFEATS (*see* DEFEAT)
2Sa 5: 8 **d** the Jebusites (the lame and

DEFECT (*see* DEFECTED, DEFECTING, DEFECTORS, DEFECTS)
Lev 21:17 generations, who has any **d**
Lev 21:18 has a **d** shall not approach
Lev 21:20 a man who has a **d** in his eye
Lev 21:21 Aaron the priest, who has a **d**
Lev 21:21 He has a **d**; he shall not come
Lev 21:23 the altar, because he has a **d**
Lev 22:20 But whatever has a **d**, you
Lev 22:21 there shall be no **d** in it
Num 19: 2 in which there is no **d** and on
Deut 15:21 But if there is any **d** in it
Deut 15:21 or blind or has any serious **d**
Deut 17: 1 which has any blemish or **d**
1Ch 12:19 He may **d** to his master Saul

DEFECTED (*see* DEFECT)
1Sa 29: 3 fault in him since he **d** to me
1Ki 2:28 for Joab had **d** to Adonijah
1Ki 2:28 he had not **d** to Absalom
1Ch 12:19 some from Manasseh **d** to David
1Ch 12:20 who **d** to him were Adnah,
Jer 38:19 who have **d** to the Chaldeans
Jer 39: 9 city and those who **d** to him

DEFECTING (*see* DEFECT)
Jer 37:13 You are **d** to the Chaldeans
Jer 37:14 I am not **d** to the Chaldeans

DEFECTORS (*see* DEFECT)
2Ki 25:11 the **d** who had deserted to the
Jer 52:15 the **d** who had deserted to the

DEFECTS (*see* DEFECT)
Lev 22:25 is in them, and **d** are in them
Jer 21: 9 out and **d** to the Chaldeans who

DEFEND (*see* DEFENDED, DEFENDER, DEFENDING, DEFENSE)
2Ki 19:34 For I will **d** this city, to
2Ki 20: 6 I will **d** this city for My own
Job 13:15 I will **d** my own ways before
Ps 5:11 for joy, because You **d** them
Ps 20: 1 of the God of Jacob **d** you
Ps 59: 1 **D** me from those who rise up
Ps 82: 3 **D** the poor and fatherless
Is 1:17 **d** the fatherless, plead for
Is 1:23 They do not **d** the fatherless,
Is 31: 5 the LORD of hosts **d** Jerusalem
Is 37:35 For I will **d** this city, to
Is 38: 6 and I will **d** this city
Jer 5:28 of the needy they do not **d**
Zech 9:15 The LORD of hosts will **d** them
Zech 12: 8 will **d** the inhabitants of

DEFENDED (*see* DEFEND)
2Sa 23:12 field, **d** it, and killed the
1Ch 11:14 field, **d** it, and killed the
Acts 7:24 of them suffer wrong, he **d**

DEFENDER (*see* DEFEND)
Ps 68: 5 a **d** of widows, Is God in His

DEFENDING (*see* DEFEND)
2Ki 9:14 had been **d** Ramoth Gilead, he
Is 31: 5 **D**, He will also deliver it

DEFENSE (*see* DEFEND, DEFENSES)
2Ki 19:24 dried up all the brooks of **d**
2Ch 11: 5 built cities for **d** in Judah
Ps 7:10 My **d** is of God, Who saves the
Ps 31: 2 A fortress of **d** to save me
Ps 59: 9 For God is my **d**
Ps 59:16 For You have been my **d** And
Ps 59:17 For God is my **d**, The God of
Ps 62: 2 He is my **d**; I shall not be
Ps 62: 6 He is my **d**; I shall not be
Ps 94:22 But the LORD has been my **d**
Eccl 7:12 For wisdom is a **d** as money is
Eccl 7:12 is a **d** as money is a **d**
Is 19: 6 and the brooks of **d** will be
Is 33:16 his place of **d** will be the
Is 37:25 dried up all the brooks of **d**
Ezek 26: 8 you, and raise a **d** against you
Nah 2: 5 walls, and the **d** is prepared
Acts 19:33 to make his **d** to the people
Acts 22: 1 hear my **d** before you now
Acts 26:24 Now as he thus made his **d**
1Co 9: 3 My **d** to those who examine me
Phil 1: 7 both in my chains and in the **d**
Phil 1:17 for the **d** of the gospel
2Ti 4:16 At my first **d** no one stood
1Pe 3:15 always be ready to give a **d**

DEFENSES (*see* DEFENSE)
Job 13:12 your **d** are **d** of clay

DEFER (*see* DEFERRED)
Is 48: 9 name's sake I will **d** My anger

DEFERRED (*see* DEFER)
Prov 13:12 Hope **d** makes the heart sick,

DEFIANT (*see* DEFIANTLY, DEFY)
Jer 5:23 But this people has a **d** and

DEFIANTLY (*see* DEFIANT)
Job 15:25 acts **d** against the Almighty,
Job 36: 9 that they have acted **d**

DEFIED (*see* DEFY)
1Sa 17:36 seeing he has **d** the armies of
1Sa 17:45 of Israel, whom you have **d**
2Sa 21:21 So when he **d** Israel, Jonathan
2Sa 23: 9 **d** the Philistines who were
1Ch 20: 7 So when he **d** Israel, Jonathan

DEFILE (*see* DEFILED, DEFILES, DEFILING, UNDEFILED)
Lev 11:44 Neither shall you **d**
Lev 15:31 **d** My tabernacle that is among
Lev 18:20 wife, to **d** yourself with her
Lev 18:23 beast, to **d** yourself with it
Lev 18:24 Do not **d** yourselves with any
Lev 18:28 you out also when you **d** it
Lev 18:30 that you do not **d** yourselves
Lev 20: 3 to **d** My sanctuary and profane
Lev 21: 1 None shall **d** himself for the
Lev 21: 3 for her he may **d** himself

Lev 21: 4 he shall not **d** himself, being
Lev 21:11 nor **d** himself for his father
Lev 22: 8 not eat, to **d** himself with it
Num 5: 3 that they may not **d** their
Num 35:34 Therefore do not **d** the land
Deut 21:23 so that you do not **d** the land
Song 5: 3 How can I **d** them
Is 30:22 You will also **d** the covering
Jer 32:34 is called by My name, to **d** it
Ezek 7:21 and they shall **d** it
Ezek 7:22 they will **d** My secret place
Ezek 7:22 shall enter it and **d** it
Ezek 9: 7 **D** the temple, and fill the
Ezek 20: 7 do not **d** yourselves with the
Ezek 20:18 nor **d** yourselves with their
Ezek 20:31 you **d** yourselves with all
Ezek 22: 3 within herself to **d** herself
Ezek 22:16 You shall **d** yourself in the
Ezek 28: 7 wisdom, and **d** your splendor
Ezek 33:26 you **d** one another's wives
Ezek 37:23 They shall not **d** themselves
Ezek 43: 7 of Israel **d** My holy name,
Ezek 44: 7 to be in My sanctuary to **d** it
Ezek 44:25 They shall not **d** themselves
Ezek 44:25 sister may they **d** themselves
Dan 1: 8 **d** himself with the portion of
Dan 1: 8 that he might not **d** himself
Dan 11:31 they shall **d** the sanctuary
Amos 2: 7 same girl, to **d** My holy name
Matt 15:18 the heart, and they **d** a man
Matt 15:20 are the things which **d** a man
Matt 15:20 hands does not **d** a man
Mark 7:15 from outside which can **d** him
Mark 7:15 are the things that **d** a man
Mark 7:18 man from outside cannot **d** him
Mark 7:23 come from within and **d** a man
Jude 8 these dreamers **d** the flesh

DEFILED (*see* DEFILE)
Gen 34: 5 he had **d** Dinah his daughter
Gen 34:13 because he had **d** Dinah their
Gen 34:27 their sister had been **d**
Gen 49: 4 then you **d** it
Lev 5: 3 is with which a man may be **d**
Lev 11:43 them, lest you be **d** by them
Lev 18:24 all these the nations are **d**
Lev 18:25 For the land is **d**
Lev 18:27 you, and thus the land is **d**)
Lev 19:31 after them, to be **d** by them
Lev 21: 7 who is a harlot or a **d** woman
Lev 21:14 or a **d** woman or a harlot
Num 5: 2 becomes **d** by a dead body
Num 5:13 that she has **d** herself, and
Num 5:14 his wife, who has **d** herself
Num 5:14 she has not **d** herself
Num 5:20 and if you have **d** yourself
Num 5:27 be, if she has **d** herself and
Num 5:28 the woman has not **d** herself
Num 6:12 because his separation was **d**
Num 9: 6 **d** by the dead body of a man
Num 9: 7 We became **d** by the dead body
Num 19:20 because he has **d** the
Deut 22: 9 fruit of your vineyard be **d**
Deut 24: 4 his wife after she has been **d**
2Ki 23: 8 **d** the high places where the
2Ki 23:10 he **d** Topheth, which is in the
2Ki 23:13 Then the king **d** the high
2Ki 23:16 **d** it according to the word of
1Ch 5: 1 but because he **d** his father's
2Ch 36:14 **d** the house of the LORD which
Ezra 2:62 from the priesthood as **d**
Neh 7:64 from the priesthood as **d**
Neh 13:29 they have **d** the priesthood
Ps 74: 7 They have **d** the dwelling
Ps 79: 1 Your holy temple they have **d**
Ps 106:39 Thus they were **d** by their own
Is 24: 5 The earth is also **d** under its
Is 59: 3 your hands are **d** with blood
Jer 2: 7 you **d** My land and made My
Jer 3: 9 harlotry, that she **d** the land
Jer 16:18 because they have **d** My land
Jer 19:13 be **d** like the place of Tophet
Lam 4:14 they have **d** themselves with
Ezek 4:13 of Israel eat their **d** bread
Ezek 4:14 Indeed I have never **d** myself
Ezek 5:11 surely, because you have **d** My
Ezek 7:24 their holy places shall be **d**
Ezek 18: 6 nor **d** his neighbor's wife,
Ezek 18:11 or **d** his neighbor's wife
Ezek 18:15 Nor **d** his neighbor's wife
Ezek 20:13 and they greatly **d** My Sabbaths
Ezek 20:43 doings with which you were **d**
Ezek 22: 4 and have **d** yourself with the
Ezek 23: 7 their idols, she **d** herself
Ezek 23:13 Then I saw that she was **d**
Ezek 23:17 and they **d** her with their
Ezek 23:17 so she was **d** by them, and
Ezek 23:30 have become **d** by their idols
Ezek 23:38 They have **d** My sanctuary on
Ezek 28:18 You **d** your sanctuaries by the
Ezek 36:17 they **d** it by their own ways
Ezek 36:18 with which they had **d** it
Ezek 43: 8 they **d** My holy name by the
Hos 5: 3 Israel is **d**
Hos 6: 8 evildoers, and is **d** with blood
Hos 6:10 Israel is **d**
Hos 9: 4 all who eat it shall be **d**
Amos 7:17 you shall die in a **d** land
Mic 2:10 because it is **d**, it shall
Mic 4:11 Let her be **d**, and let our eye
Mal 1: 7 You offer **d** food on My altar
Mal 1: 7 In what way have we **d** You
Mal 1:12 The table of the LORD is **d**
Mark 7: 2 disciples eat bread with **d**
John 18:28 lest they should be **d**, but
Acts 21:28 and has **d** this holy place
1Co 8: 7 conscience, being weak, is **d**
Tit 1:15 pure, but to those who are **d**
Tit 1:15 mind and conscience are **d**
Heb 12:15 and by this many become **d**
Jude 23 the garment **d** by the flesh
Rev 3: 4 who have not **d** their garments
Rev 14: 4 who were not **d** with women

DEFILES (*see* DEFILE)
Num 5:29 goes astray and **d** herself,
Num 6: 9 he **d** his consecrated head,
Num 19:13 **d** the tabernacle of the LORD
Num 35:33 for blood **d** the land, and no
Ezek 22:11 another lewdly **d** his
Matt 15:11 goes into the mouth **d** a man
Matt 15:11 of the mouth, this **d** a man
Mark 7:20 out of a man, that **d** a man
1Co 3:17 If anyone **d** the temple of God
Jas 3: 6 that it **d** the whole body, and
Rev 21:27 enter it anything that **d**, or

DEFILING (*see* DEFILE)
Is 56: 2 who keeps from **d** the Sabbath
Is 56: 6 who keeps from **d** the Sabbath
Ezek 20:30 Are you **d** yourselves in the

DEFRAUD (*see* DEFRAUDED)
Lev 19:13 You shall not **d** your neighbor
Mark 10:19 false witness,' 'Do not **d**
1Co 6: 8 you yourselves do wrong and **d**
Col 2:18 Let no one **d** you of your
1Th 4: 6 **d** his brother in this matter,

DEFRAUDED (*see* DEFRAUD)
1Sa 12: 3 I taken, or whom have I **d**
1Sa 12: 4 said, "You have not **d** us or
1Co 6: 7 rather let yourselves be **d**
2Co 7: 2 no one, we have **d** no one

DEFY (*see* DEFIANT, DEFIED)
1Sa 17:10 I **d** the armies of Israel this
1Sa 17:25 he has come up to **d** Israel
1Sa 17:26 that he should **d** the armies

DEGENERATE
Jer 2:21 the **d** plant of an alien vine
Ezek 16:30 How **d** is your heart

DEGREE (*see* DEGREES)
1Ch 17:17 the estate of a man of high **d**
Ps 62: 9 men of low **d** are a vapor, Men
Ps 62: 9 Men of high **d** are a lie
Phil 3:16 to the **d** that we have already

DEGREES (*see* DEGREE)
Deut 17: 8 between **d** of bloodguiltiness,
2Ki 20: 9 the shadow go forward ten **d**
2Ki 20: 9 or go backward ten **d**
2Ki 20:10 the shadow to go down ten **d**
2Ki 20:10 the shadow go backward ten **d**
2Ki 20:11 the shadow ten **d** backward
Is 38: 8 of Ahaz, ten **d** backward
Is 38: 8 So the sun returned ten **d**

DEHAVITES
Ezra 4: 9 and Babylon and Shushan, the **D**

DEITIES
Jer 3:13 your charms to alien **d** under

DELAIAH
1Ch 3:24 Pelaiah, Akkub, Johanan, **D**
1Ch 24:18 the twenty-third to **D**, the
Ezra 2:60 the sons of **D**, the sons of
Neh 6:10 of Shemaiah the son of **D**, the
Neh 7:62 the children of **D**, the
Jer 36:12 **D** the son of Shemaiah,
Jer 36:25 Nevertheless Elnathan, **D**, and

DELAY (*see* DELAYED, DELAYING)
Gen 34:19 man did not **d** to do the thing
Ex 22:29 You shall not **d** to offer the
Deut 23:21 you shall not **d** to pay it
1Sa 20:38 Make haste, hurry, do not **d**
2Ki 9: 3 the door and flee, and do not **d**
Ps 40:17 Do not **d**, O my God
Ps 70: 5 O LORD, do not **d**
Ps 119:60 and did not **d** To keep Your
Eccl 5: 4 to God, do not **d** to pay it
Jer 4: 6 Take refuge! Do not **d**!
Dan 9:19 Do not **d** for Your own sake,
Acts 9:38 not to **d** in coming to them
Acts 25:17 come together, without any **d**
Rev 10: 6 there should be **d** no longer

DELAYED (*see* DELAY)
Ex 32: 1 Moses **d** coming down from the
Judg 3:26 But Ehud escaped while they **d**
Judg 19: 8 So they **d** until afternoon
2Sa 20: 5 But he **d** longer than the set
Matt 25: 5 while the bridegroom was **d**
1Ti 3:15 but if I am **d**, I write so

DELAYING (*see* DELAY)
Matt 24:48 My master is **d** his coming
Luke 12:45 My master is **d** his coming

DELEGATE (*see* DELEGATION)
Ezek 23:24 I will **d** judgment to them,

DELEGATION (*see* DELEGATE)
Luke 14:32 a great way off, he sends a **d**
Luke 19:14 sent a **d** after him, saying

DELICACIES
Ps 141: 4 do not let me eat of their **d**
Prov 23: 3 Do not desire his **d**, for they
Prov 23: 6 of a miser, nor desire his **d**
Jer 51:34 filled his stomach with my **d**
Lam 4: 5 Those who ate **d** are desolate
Dan 1: 5 provision of the king's **d**
Dan 1: 8 the portion of the king's **d**
Dan 1:13 the portion of the king's **d**
Dan 1:15 the portion of the king's **d**
Dan 1:16 took away their portion of **d**
Dan 11:26 of his **d** shall destroy him

DELICATE (*see* DELICATENESS)
Gen 29:17 Leah's eyes were **d**, but
Deut 28:56 **d** woman among you, who
Is 47: 1 no more be called tender and **d**
Jer 6: 2 Zion to a lovely and **d** woman

DELICATENESS (*see* DELICATE)
Deut 28:56 the ground because of her **d**

DELIGHT (*see* DELIGHTED, DELIGHTFUL, DELIGHTS)
Deut 21:14 be, if you have no **d** in her
1Sa 15:22 as great **d** in burnt offerings
1Sa 18:22 Look, the king has **d** in you
2Sa 15:26 I have no **d** in you,' here I
2Ch 17: 6 his heart took **d** in the ways
Esth 6: 6 Whom would the king **d** to
Job 22:26 have your **d** in the Almighty
Job 27:10 Will he **d** himself in the
Job 33:26 to God, and He will **d** in him
Job 34: 9 that he should **d** in God
Ps 1: 2 But his **d** is in the law of
Ps 16: 3 ones, in whom is all my **d**
Ps 37: 4 **D** yourself also in the LORD,
Ps 37:11 shall **d** themselves in the
Ps 40: 8 I **d** to do Your will, O my God
Ps 51:16 You do not **d** in burnt
Ps 62: 4 They **d** in lies
Ps 68:30 the peoples who **d** in war
Ps 94:19 me, Your comforts **d** my soul
Ps 109:17 As he did not **d** in blessing
Ps 119:16 I will **d** myself in Your
Ps 119:24 testimonies also are my **d**
Ps 119:35 commandments, For I **d** in it
Ps 119:47 And I will **d** myself in Your

Ps 119:70 grease, But I **d** in Your law
Ps 119:77 For Your law is my **d**
Ps 119:92 Unless Your law had been my **d**
Ps 119:174 O LORD, And Your law is my **d**
Ps 147:10 He does not **d** in the strength
Prov 1:22 For scorners **d** in their
Prov 2:14 **d** in the perversity of the
Prov 7:18 let us **d** ourselves with love
Prov 8:30 and I was daily His **d**,
Prov 8:31 my **d** was with the sons of men
Prov 11: 1 but a just weight is His **d**
Prov 11:20 in their ways are His **d**
Prov 12:22 who deal truthfully are His **d**
Prov 15: 8 of the upright is His **d**
Prov 16:13 lips are the **d** of kings, and
Prov 18: 2 A fool has no **d** in
Prov 23:24 a wise child will **d** in him
Prov 24:25 rebuke the wicked will have **d**
Prov 27: 9 perfume **d** the heart, and the
Prov 29:17 he will give **d** to your soul
Song 2: 3 in his shade with great **d**
Is 1:11 I do not **d** in the blood of
Is 11: 3 His **d** is in the fear of the
Is 13:17 gold, they will not **d** in it
Is 55: 2 let your soul **d** itself in
Is 58: 2 and **d** to know My ways, as a
Is 58: 2 they take **d** in approaching
Is 58:13 day, and call the Sabbath a **d**
Is 58:14 Then you shall **d** yourself in
Is 65:12 that in which I do not **d**
Is 66: 4 that in which I do not **d**
Jer 6:10 they have no **d** in it
Jer 9:24 For in these I **d**," says the
Ezek 24:21 your eyes, the **d** of your soul
Mal 3: 1 the covenant, in whom you **d**
Rom 7:22 For I **d** in the law of God
Col 2:18 taking **d** in false humility and

DELIGHTED (*see* DELIGHT)
Gen 34:19 because he **d** in Jacob's
Deut 10:15 The LORD **d** only in your
1Sa 19: 1 Saul's son, **d** much in David
2Sa 22:20 me, because He **d** in me
1Ki 10: 9 who **d** in you, setting you on
2Ch 9: 8 who **d** in you, setting you on
Neh 9:25 **d** themselves in Your great
Esth 2:14 unless the king **d** in her and
Ps 18:19 me because He **d** in me
Is 66:11 be **d** with the abundance of

DELIGHTFUL (*see* DELIGHT)
Mal 3:12 for you will be a **d** land

DELIGHTS (*see* DELIGHT)
Num 14: 8 If the LORD **d** in us, then He
Esth 6: 6 man whom the king **d** to honor
Esth 6: 7 man whom the king **d** to honor
Esth 6: 9 man whom the king **d** to honor
Esth 6: 9 man whom the king **d** to honor
Esth 6:11 the man the king **d** to honor
Ps 22: 8 Him, since He **d** in Him
Ps 37:23 the LORD, And He **d** in his way
Ps 112: 1 LORD, Who **d** greatly in His
Ps 119:143 Your commandments are my **d**
Prov 3:12 a father the son in whom he **d**
Eccl 2: 8 the **d** of the sons of men, and
Song 7: 6 you are, O love, with your **d**
Is 42: 1 Elect One in whom My soul **d**
Is 62: 4 for the LORD **d** in you, and
Is 66: 3 and their soul **d** in their
Mic 7:18 because He **d** in mercy
Mal 2:17 LORD, and He **d** in them," or,

DELILAH
Judg 16: 4 of Sorek, whose name was **D**
Judg 16: 6 So **D** said to Samson, "Please
Judg 16:10 Then **D** said to Samson, "Look
Judg 16:12 Therefore **D** took new ropes and
Judg 16:13 Then **D** said to Samson
Judg 16:18 When **D** saw that he had told

DELIVER (*see* DELIVERANCE, DELIVERED, DELIVERER, DELIVERING, DELIVERS, DELIVERY)
Gen 32:11 **D** me, I pray, from the hand
Gen 37:22 that he might **d** him out of
Gen 42:34 I will **d** your brother to you,
Ex 3: 8 So I have come down to **d** them
Ex 5:18 yet you shall **d** the quota of
Ex 23:31 For I will **d** the inhabitants
Num 21: 2 If You will indeed **d** this
Num 35:25 So the congregation shall **d**
Deut 1:27 to **d** us into the hand of the
Deut 2:30 that He might **d** him into your
Deut 7:23 God will **d** them over to you
Deut 7:24 He will **d** their kings into
Deut 19:12 **d** him over to the hand of the
Deut 23:14 to **d** you and give your enemies
Deut 32:39 any who can **d** from My hand
Josh 2:13 and **d** our lives from death
Josh 7: 7 to **d** us into the hand of the
Josh 8: 7 God will **d** it into your hand
Josh 11: 6 about this time I will **d** all
Josh 20: 5 they shall not **d** the slayer
Judg 2:23 nor did He **d** them into the
Judg 4: 7 I will **d** him into your hand'
Judg 7: 7 **d** the Midianites into your
Judg 10:11 Did I not **d** you from the
Judg 10:13 I will **d** you no more
Judg 10:14 let them **d** you in your time
Judg 10:15 only **d** us this day, we pray
Judg 11:30 If You will indeed **d** the
Judg 12: 2 you did not **d** me out of their
Judg 12: 3 I saw that you would not **d** me
Judg 13: 5 he shall begin to **d** Israel
Judg 15:12 that we may **d** you into the
Judg 15:13 and **d** you into their hand
Judg 20:13 **d** up the men, the perverted
Judg 20:28 I will **d** them into your hand
1Sa 4: 8 Who will **d** us from the hand
1Sa 7: 3 He will **d** you from the hand
1Sa 12:10 but now **d** us from the hand of
1Sa 12:21 which cannot profit or **d**, for
1Sa 14:37 Will You **d** them into the hand
1Sa 17:37 He will **d** me from the hand of
1Sa 17:46 LORD will **d** you into my hand
1Sa 23: 4 For I will **d** the Philistines
1Sa 23:11 of Keilah **d** me into his hand
1Sa 23:12 Will the men of Keilah **d** me
1Sa 23:12 They will **d** you
1Sa 23:14 but God did not **d** him into
1Sa 23:20 our part shall be to **d** him
1Sa 24: 4 I will **d** your enemy into your
1Sa 24:15 and **d** me out of your hand
1Sa 26:24 and let Him **d** me out of all
1Sa 28:19 **d** Israel with you into the
1Sa 28:19 The LORD will also **d** the army
1Sa 30:15 nor **d** me into the hands of my
2Sa 5:19 Will You **d** them into my hand
2Sa 5:19 for I will doubtless **d** the
2Sa 14: 7 **D** him who struck his brother
2Sa 14:16 **d** his maidservant from the
2Sa 20:21 **D** him only, and I will depart
1Ki 8:46 **d** them to the enemy, and they
1Ki 20: 5 You shall **d** to me your silver
1Ki 20:13 I will **d** it into your hand
1Ki 20:28 therefore I will **d** all this
1Ki 22: 6 for the Lord will **d** it into
1Ki 22:12 for the LORD will **d** it into
1Ki 22:15 for the LORD will **d** it into
2Ki 3:10 three kings together to **d**
2Ki 3:13 three kings together to **d**
2Ki 3:18 He will also **d** the Moabites
2Ki 12: 7 but **d** it for repairing the
2Ki 17:39 He will **d** you from the hand
2Ki 18:29 able to **d** you from his hand
2Ki 18:30 The LORD will surely **d** us
2Ki 18:32 The LORD will **d** us
2Ki 18:35 hand, that the LORD should **d**
2Ki 20: 6 I will **d** you and this city
2Ki 21:14 **d** them into the hand of their
2Ki 22: 5 let them **d** it into the hand
1Ch 14:10 Will You **d** them into my hand
1Ch 14:10 for I will **d** them into your
1Ch 16:35 **d** us from the Gentiles, to
2Ch 6:36 **d** them to the enemy, and they
2Ch 18: 5 for God will **d** it into the
2Ch 18:11 for the LORD will **d** it into
2Ch 32:11 The LORD our God will **d** us
2Ch 32:13 lands in any way able to **d**
2Ch 32:14 destroyed that could **d** his
2Ch 32:14 be able to **d** you from my hand
2Ch 32:15 or kingdom was able to **d** his
2Ch 32:15 your God **d** you from my hand
2Ch 32:17 not **d** His people from my hand
Ezra 7:19 **d** in full before the God of
Job 5:19 He shall **d** you in six
Job 6:23 **D** me from the enemy's hand'
Job 10: 7 one who can **d** from Your hand
Job 22:30 He will even **d** one who is not
Job 33:24 **D** him from going down to the
Job 39: 3 young, they **d** their offspring
Ps 6: 4 Return, O LORD, **d** me
Ps 7: 1 And **d** me,
Ps 7: 2 while there is none to **d**
Ps 17:13 **D** my life from the wicked
Ps 22: 8 Let Him **d** Him, since He
Ps 22:20 **D** Me from the sword, My
Ps 25:20 Oh, keep my soul, and **d** me
Ps 27:12 Do not **d** me to the will of my
Ps 31: 1 **D** me in Your righteousness
Ps 31: 2 Your ear to me, **D** me speedily
Ps 31:15 **D** me from the hand of my
Ps 33:17 Neither shall it **d** any by its
Ps 33:19 To **d** their soul from death,
Ps 37:40 shall help them and **d** them
Ps 37:40 He shall **d** them from the
Ps 39: 8 **D** me from all my
Ps 40:13 Be pleased, O LORD, to **d** me
Ps 41: 1 The LORD will **d** him in time
Ps 41: 2 You will not **d** him to the
Ps 43: 1 **d** me from the deceitful and
Ps 50:15 I will **d** you, and you shall
Ps 50:22 pieces, And there be none to **d**
Ps 51:14 **D** me from bloodguiltiness, O
Ps 59: 1 **D** me from my enemies, O my
Ps 59: 2 **D** me from the workers of
Ps 69:14 **D** me out of the mire, And let
Ps 69:18 **D** me because of my enemies
Ps 70: 1 Make haste, O God, to **d** me
Ps 71: 2 **D** me in Your righteousness,
Ps 71: 4 **D** me, O my God, out of the
Ps 71:11 for there is none to **d** him
Ps 72:12 For He will **d** the needy when
Ps 74:19 do not **d** the life of Your
Ps 76: 9 To **d** all the oppressed of the
Ps 79: 9 **d** us, and provide atonement
Ps 82: 4 **D** the poor and needy
Ps 89:48 Can he **d** his life from the
Ps 91: 3 Surely He shall **d** you from
Ps 91:14 Me, therefore I will **d** him
Ps 91:15 I will **d** him and honor him
Ps 109:21 Your mercy is good, **d** me
Ps 116: 4 I implore You, **d** my soul
Ps 119:153 **d** me, For I do not forget
Ps 119:170 **D** me according to Your word
Ps 120: 2 **D** my soul, O LORD, from lying
Ps 140: 1 **D** me, O LORD, from evil men
Ps 142: 6 **D** me from my persecutors, For
Ps 143: 9 **D** me, O LORD, from my
Ps 144: 7 **d** me out of great waters,
Ps 144:11 me and **d** me from the hand of
Prov 2:12 to **d** you from the way of evil
Prov 2:16 to **d** you from the immoral
Prov 4: 9 of glory she will **d** to you
Prov 6: 3 this, my son, and **d** yourself
Prov 6: 5 **D** yourself like a gazelle
Prov 11: 6 of the upright will **d** them
Prov 12: 6 of the upright will **d** them
Prov 19:19 for if you **d** him, you will
Prov 23:14 rod, and **d** his soul from hell
Prov 24:11 **D** those who are drawn toward
Eccl 8: 8 wickedness will not **d** those
Is 5:29 away safely, and no one will **d**
Is 19:20 Mighty One, and He will **d** them
Is 29:11 which men **d** to one who is
Is 31: 5 Defending, He will also **d** it
Is 36:14 he will not be able to **d** you
Is 36:15 The LORD will surely **d** us
Is 36:18 The LORD will **d** us
Is 36:20 hand, that the LORD should **d**
Is 38: 6 I will **d** you and this city
Is 43:13 one who can **d** out of My hand
Is 44:17 **D** me, for you are my god
Is 44:20 and he cannot **d** his soul, nor
Is 46: 2 they could not **d** the burden
Is 46: 4 I will carry, and will **d** you
Is 47:14 they shall not **d** themselves
Is 50: 2 Or have I no power to **d**
Is 57:13 collection of idols **d** you
Jer 1: 8 for I am with you to **d** you
Jer 1:19 says the LORD, "to **d** you
Jer 15: 9 **d** to the sword before their
Jer 15:20 you and **d** you," says the LORD
Jer 15:21 I will **d** you from the hand of
Jer 18:21 Therefore **d** up their children
Jer 20: 5 Moreover I will **d** all the
Jer 21: 7 I will **d** Zedekiah king of
Jer 21:12 **d** him who is plundered out of
Jer 22: 3 **d** the plundered out of the
Jer 24: 9 I will **d** them to trouble
Jer 29:18 and I will **d** them to trouble
Jer 29:21 I will **d** them into the hand

Jer 34:17 I will **d** you to trouble among
Jer 38:19 lest they **d** me into their
Jer 38:20 They shall not **d** you
Jer 39:17 But I will **d** you in that day,
Jer 39:18 For I will surely **d** you, and
Jer 42:11 you and **d** you from his hand
Jer 43: 3 to **d** us into the hand of the
Jer 43:11 **d** to death those appointed
Jer 46:26 I will **d** them into the hand
Jer 51:45 let everyone **d** himself from
Lam 5: 8 there is none to **d** us from
Ezek 7:19 to **d** them in the day of the
Ezek 11: 9 and **d** you into the hands of
Ezek 13:21 **d** My people out of your hand,
Ezek 13:23 for I will **d** My people out of
Ezek 14:14 they would **d** only themselves
Ezek 14:16 they would **d** neither sons nor
Ezek 14:18 they would **d** neither sons nor
Ezek 14:20 they would **d** neither son nor
Ezek 14:20 they would **d** only themselves
Ezek 21:31 and **d** you into the hands of
Ezek 23:28 Surely I will **d** you into the
Ezek 25: 4 I will **d** you as a possession
Ezek 31:11 therefore I will **d** it into
Ezek 33:12 not **d** him in the day of his
Ezek 34:10 for I will **d** My flock from
Ezek 34:12 **d** them from all the places
Ezek 36:29 I will **d** you from all your
Ezek 37:23 but I will **d** them from all
Dan 3:15 who will **d** you from my hands
Dan 3:17 whom we serve is able to **d** us
Dan 3:17 He will **d** us from your hand,
Dan 3:29 other God who can **d** like this
Dan 6:14 his heart on Daniel to **d** him
Dan 6:14 down of the sun to **d** him
Dan 6:16 continually, He will **d** you
Dan 6:20 been able to **d** you from the
Dan 8: 4 that could **d** from his hand
Dan 8: 7 could **d** the ram from his hand
Hos 2:10 no one shall **d** her from My
Amos 1: 6 to **d** them up to Edom
Amos 2:14 shall the mighty **d** himself
Amos 2:15 of foot shall not **d** himself
Amos 2:15 who rides a horse **d** himself
Amos 6: 8 I will **d** up the city and all
Jon 4: 6 head to **d** him from his misery
Mic 5: 6 thus He shall **d** us from the
Mic 5: 8 in pieces, and none can **d**
Zeph 1:18 to **d** them in the day of the
Zech 11: 6 I will not **d** them from their
Matt 5:25 adversary **d** you to the judge
Matt 6:13 but **d** us from the evil one
Matt 10:17 for they will **d** you up to
Matt 10:19 But when they **d** you up, do
Matt 10:21 Now brother will **d** up brother
Matt 20:19 **d** Him to the Gentiles to mock
Matt 24: 9 Then they will **d** you up to
Matt 26:15 to give me if I **d** Him to you
Matt 27:43 let Him **d** Him now if He will
Mark 10:33 and **d** Him to the Gentiles
Mark 13: 9 for they will **d** you up to
Mark 13:11 you and **d** you up, do not worry
Luke 11: 4 but **d** us from the evil one
Luke 12:58 judge, the judge **d** you to the
Luke 20:20 in order to **d** Him to the
Acts 7:25 God would **d** them by his hand
Acts 7:34 and have come down to **d** them
Acts 21:11 **d** him into the hands of the
Acts 25:11 me, no one can **d** me to them
Acts 25:16 to **d** any man to destruction
Acts 26:17 I will **d** you from the Jewish
Rom 7:24 Who will **d** me from this body
1Co 5: 5 **d** such a one to Satan for the
2Co 1:10 great a death, and does **d** us
2Co 1:10 trust that He will still **d** us
Gal 1: 4 that He might **d** us from this
2Ti 4:18 the Lord will **d** me from every
2Pe 2: 9 how to **d** the godly out of

DELIVERANCE (*see* DELIVER)
Gen 45: 7 save your lives by a great **d**
Judg 15:18 You have given this great **d**
2Ki 13:17 The arrow of the LORD's **d**
2Ki 13:17 and the arrow of **d** from Syria
1Ch 11:14 LORD saved them by a great **d**
2Ch 12: 7 but I will grant them some **d**
Ezra 9:13 have given us such **d** as this
Esth 4:14 **d** will arise for the Jews
Ps 18:50 Great **d** He gives to His king,
Ps 32: 7 surround me with songs of **d**
Prov 21:31 battle, but **d** is of the LORD
Is 26:18 any **d** in the earth, nor have
Joel 2:32 in Jerusalem there shall be **d**
Obad 17 Mount Zion there shall be **d**
Luke 4:18 to preach **d** to the captives
Heb 11:35 tortured, not accepting **d**

DELIVERED (*see* DELIVER)
Gen 14:20 Who has **d** your enemies into
Gen 32:16 Then he **d** them to the hand of
Gen 37:21 he **d** him out of their hands,
Ex 2:19 An Egyptian **d** us from the
Ex 5:23 neither have You **d** Your
Ex 12:27 Egyptians and **d** our households
Ex 18: 4 and **d** me from the sword of
Ex 18: 8 and how the LORD had **d** them
Ex 18: 9 whom He had **d** out of the hand
Ex 18:10 who has **d** you out of the hand
Ex 18:10 who has **d** the people from
Ex 21:13 but God **d** him into his hand,
Lev 6: 2 was **d** to him for safekeeping
Lev 6: 4 or what was **d** to him for
Lev 26:25 you shall be **d** into the hand
Num 21: 3 **d** up the Canaanites, and they
Num 21:34 for I have **d** him into your
Deut 2:33 LORD our God **d** him over to us
Deut 2:36 the LORD our God **d** all to us
Deut 3: 2 fear him, for I have **d** him
Deut 3: 3 So the LORD our God also **d**
Deut 9:10 Then the LORD **d** to me two
Deut 31: 9 **d** it to the priests, the sons
Josh 2:24 Truly the LORD has **d** all the
Josh 9:26 **d** them out of the hand of the
Josh 10: 8 for I have **d** them into your
Josh 10:12 in the day when the LORD **d** up
Josh 10:19 God has **d** them into your hand
Josh 10:30 And the LORD also **d** it and its
Josh 10:32 the LORD **d** Lachish into the
Josh 11: 8 the LORD **d** them into the hand
Josh 21:44 the LORD **d** all their enemies
Josh 22:31 Now you have **d** the children
Josh 24:10 So I **d** you out of his hand
Josh 24:11 But I **d** them into your hand
Judg 1: 2 Indeed I have **d** the land into
Judg 1: 4 the LORD **d** the Canaanites and
Judg 2:14 So He **d** them into the hands
Judg 2:16 who **d** them out of the hand of
Judg 2:18 **d** them out of the hand of
Judg 3: 9 of Israel, who **d** them
Judg 3:10 the LORD **d** Cushan-Rishathaim
Judg 3:28 me, for the LORD has **d** your
Judg 3:31 and he also **d** Israel
Judg 4:14 has **d** Sisera into your hand
Judg 6: 1 So the LORD **d** them into the
Judg 6: 9 I **d** you out of the hand of
Judg 6:13 **d** us into the hands of the
Judg 7: 9 for I have **d** it into your
Judg 7:14 his hand God has **d** Midian
Judg 7:15 for the LORD has **d** the camp
Judg 8: 3 God has **d** into your hands the
Judg 8: 7 when the LORD has **d** Zebah
Judg 8:22 for you have **d** us from the
Judg 8:34 who had **d** them from the hands
Judg 9:17 and **d** you out of the hand of
Judg 10:12 and I **d** you from their hand
Judg 11:21 LORD God of Israel **d** Sihon
Judg 11:32 and the LORD **d** them into his
Judg 12: 3 the LORD **d** them into my hand
Judg 13: 1 the LORD **d** them into the hand
Judg 16:23 Our god has **d** into our hands
Judg 16:24 Our god has **d** into our hands
1Sa 4:19 was with child, due to be **d**
1Sa 10:18 **d** you from the hand of the
1Sa 12:11 **d** you out of the hand of your
1Sa 14:10 For the LORD has **d** them into
1Sa 14:12 for the LORD has **d** them into
1Sa 14:48 **d** Israel from the hands of
1Sa 17:35 **d** the lamb from its mouth
1Sa 17:37 who **d** me from the paw of the
1Sa 23: 7 God has **d** him into my hand,
1Sa 24:10 have seen that the LORD **d** you
1Sa 24:18 the LORD **d** me into your hand
1Sa 26: 8 God has **d** your enemy into
1Sa 26:23 for the LORD **d** you into my
1Sa 30:23 **d** into our hand the troop
2Sa 3: 8 have not **d** you into the hand
2Sa 12: 7 I **d** you from the hand of Saul
2Sa 16: 8 the LORD has **d** the kingdom
2Sa 18:28 God, who has **d** up the men who
2Sa 19: 9 he **d** us from the hand of the
2Sa 21: 6 of his descendants be **d** to us
2Sa 21: 9 he **d** them into the hands of
2Sa 22: 1 **d** him from the hand of all
2Sa 22:18 He **d** me from my strong enemy,
2Sa 22:20 He **d** me, because He delighted
2Sa 22:44 You have also **d** me from the
2Sa 22:49 you have **d** me from the
1Ki 13:26 LORD has **d** him to the lion
1Ki 15:18 **d** them into the hand of his
2Ki 12:15 **d** the money to be paid to
2Ki 13: 3 He **d** them into the hand of
2Ki 17:20 and **d** them into the hand of
2Ki 18:33 **d** its land from the hand of
2Ki 18:34 have they **d** Samaria from my
2Ki 18:35 **d** their countries from my
2Ki 19:11 and shall you be **d**
2Ki 19:12 the gods of the nations **d**
2Ki 22: 7 the money **d** into their hand
2Ki 22: 9 have **d** it into the hand of
1Ch 5:20 were **d** into their hand, and
1Ch 16: 7 on that day David first **d**
2Ch 13:16 God **d** them into their hand
2Ch 16: 8 He **d** them into your hand
2Ch 18:14 they shall be **d** into your
2Ch 24:24 but the LORD **d** a very great
2Ch 28: 5 **d** him into the hand of the
2Ch 28: 5 Then he was also **d** into the
2Ch 28: 9 He has **d** them into your hand
2Ch 32:17 of other lands have not **d**
2Ch 34: 9 they **d** the money that was
2Ch 34:17 have **d** it into the hand of
Ezra 8:31 He **d** us from the hand of the
Ezra 8:36 they **d** the king's orders to
Ezra 9: 7 our priests have been **d** into
Neh 9:27 Therefore You **d** them into the
Neh 9:28 and many times You **d** them
Esth 6: 9 horse be **d** to the hand of one
Job 16:11 God has **d** me to the ungodly,
Job 22:30 he will be **d** by the purity of
Job 23: 7 I would be **d** forever from my
Job 29:12 because I **d** the poor who
Ps 18:17 He **d** me from my strong enemy,
Ps 18:19 He **d** me because He delighted
Ps 18:43 You have **d** me from the
Ps 18:48 You have **d** me from the
Ps 22: 4 They trusted, and You **d** them
Ps 22: 5 They cried to You, and were **d**
Ps 33:16 is not **d** by great strength
Ps 34: 4 me, And **d** me from all my fears
Ps 54: 7 For He has **d** me out of all
Ps 56:13 For You have **d** my soul from
Ps 56:13 Have You not **d** my feet from
Ps 60: 5 That Your beloved may be **d**
Ps 69:14 Let me be **d** from those who
Ps 78:61 **d** His strength into captivity
Ps 81: 7 called in trouble, and I **d** you
Ps 86:13 You have **d** my soul from the
Ps 106:43 Many times He **d** them
Ps 107: 6 And He **d** them out of their
Ps 107:20 them, And **d** them from their
Ps 108: 6 That Your beloved may be **d**
Ps 116: 8 For You have **d** my soul from
Prov 11: 8 righteous is **d** from trouble
Prov 11: 9 the righteous will be **d**
Prov 11:21 of the righteous will be **d**
Prov 28:26 walks wisely will be **d**
Eccl 9:15 he by his wisdom **d** the city
Is 20: 6 we flee for help to be **d** from
Is 29:12 Then the book is **d** to one who
Is 36:18 **d** its land from the hand of
Is 36:19 have they **d** Samaria from my
Is 36:20 **d** their countries from my
Is 37:11 and will you be **d**
Is 37:12 the gods of the nations **d**
Is 38:17 but You have lovingly **d** my
Is 49:24 of the righteous be **d**
Is 49:25 the prey of the terrible be **d**
Is 66: 7 pain came, she **d** a male child
Jer 7:10 We are **d** to do all these
Jer 20:13 For He has **d** the life of the
Jer 32: 4 but shall surely be **d** into
Jer 32:16 Now when I had **d** the purchase
Jer 32:36 It shall be **d** into the hand
Jer 34: 3 be taken and **d** into his hand
Jer 37:17 You shall be **d** into the hand
Jer 46:24 she shall be **d** into the hand
Lam 1:14 the Lord **d** me into the hands
Ezek 3:19 but you have **d** your soul
Ezek 3:21 you will have **d** your soul
Ezek 14:16 only they would be **d**, and the
Ezek 14:18 they themselves would be **d**
Ezek 17:15 a covenant and still be **d**

Ezek 23: 9 Therefore I have **d** her into
Ezek 31:14 they have all been **d** to death
Ezek 32:20 She is **d** to the sword,
Ezek 33: 9 but you have **d** your soul
Ezek 34:27 **d** them from the hand of those
Dan 3:28 **d** His servants who trusted in
Dan 6:27 Who has **d** Daniel from the
Dan 12: 1 time your people shall be **d**
Amos 1: 9 because they **d** up the whole
Amos 9: 1 from them shall not be **d**
Obad 14 nor should you have **d** up
Mic 4:10 There you shall be **d**
Hab 2: 9 that he may be **d** from the
Matt 11:27 been **d** to Me by My Father
Matt 18:34 **d** him to the torturers until
Matt 25:14 and **d** his goods to them
Matt 25:20 you **d** to me five talents
Matt 25:22 Lord, you **d** to me two talents
Matt 26: 2 will be **d** up to be crucified
Matt 27: 2 **d** Him to Pontius Pilate the
Matt 27:18 of envy they had **d** Him
Matt 27:26 he **d** Him to be crucified
Mark 9:31 being **d** into the hands of men
Mark 10:33 be **d** to the chief priests
Mark 15: 1 Him away, and **d** Him to Pilate
Mark 15:15 and he **d** Jesus, after he had
Luke 1: 2 of the word **d** them to us,
Luke 1:57 time came for her to be **d**
Luke 1:74 Being **d** from the hand of our
Luke 2: 6 completed for her to be **d**
Luke 4: 6 for this has been **d** to me
Luke 9:44 to be **d** into the hands of men
Luke 10:22 been **d** to Me by My Father
Luke 18:32 For He will be **d** to the
Luke 19:13 **d** to them ten minas, and said
Luke 23:25 but he **d** Jesus to their will
Luke 24: 7 The Son of Man must be **d**
Luke 24:20 and our rulers **d** Him to be
John 18:30 not have **d** Him up to you
John 18:35 priests have **d** You to me
John 18:36 I should not be **d** to the Jews
John 19:11 Therefore the one who **d** Me to
John 19:16 So he **d** Him to them to be
Acts 2:23 being **d** by the determined
Acts 3:13 Servant Jesus, whom you **d** up
Acts 6:14 customs which Moses **d** to us
Acts 7:10 **d** him out of all his troubles
Acts 12: 4 and **d** him to four squads of
Acts 12:11 has **d** me from the hand of
Acts 15:30 together, they **d** the letter
Acts 16: 4 they **d** to them the decrees to
Acts 23:33 and had **d** the letter to the
Acts 27: 1 sail to Italy, they **d** Paul
Acts 28:16 the centurion **d** the prisoners
Acts 28:17 yet I was **d** as a prisoner
Rom 4:25 who was **d** up because of our
Rom 6:17 doctrine to which you were **d**
Rom 7: 6 we have been **d** from the law
Rom 8:21 will be **d** from the bondage of
Rom 8:32 but **d** Him up for us all, how
Rom 15:31 that I may be **d** from those in
1Co 11: 2 traditions as I **d** them to you
1Co 11:23 that which I also **d** to you
1Co 15: 3 For I **d** to you first of all
2Co 1:10 who **d** us from so great a
2Co 4:11 **d** to death for Jesus' sake
Col 1:13 He has **d** us from the power of
2Th 3: 2 and that we may be **d** from
1Ti 1:20 whom I **d** to Satan that they
2Ti 3:11 out of them all the Lord **d** me
2Ti 4:17 I was **d** out of the mouth of
2Pe 2: 4 hell and **d** them into chains of
2Pe 2: 7 and **d** righteous Lot, who was
2Pe 2:21 holy commandment **d** to them
Jude 3 once for all **d** to the saints
Rev 20:13 Hades **d** up the dead who were

DELIVERER (*see* DELIVER, DELIVERERS)
Judg 3: 9 the LORD raised up a **d** for
Judg 3:15 LORD raised up a **d** for them
Judg 18:28 There was no **d**, because it
2Sa 22: 2 my rock, my fortress and my **d**
2Ki 13: 5 Then the LORD gave Israel a **d**
Job 5: 4 in the gate, and there is no **d**
Ps 18: 2 rock and my fortress and my **d**
Ps 40:17 You are my help and my **d**
Ps 70: 5 You are my help and my **d**
Ps 144: 2 My high tower and my **d**, My
Acts 7:35 a **d** by the hand of the Angel
Rom 11:26 The **D** will come out of Zion,

DELIVERERS (*see* DELIVERER)
Neh 9:27 mercies You gave them **d** who

DELIVERING (*see* DELIVER)
1Ki 18: 9 that you are **d** your servant
Ps 35:10 **D** the poor from him who is
Luke 21:12 **d** you up to the synagogues and
Acts 22: 4 **d** into prisons both men and

DELIVERS (*see* DELIVER)
Ex 22: 7 If a man **d** to his neighbor
Ex 22:10 If a man **d** to his neighbor a
Deut 7: 2 your God **d** them over to you
Deut 7:16 LORD your God **d** over to you
Deut 20:13 your God **d** it into your hands
Deut 21:10 the LORD your God **d** them into
Judg 11: 9 the LORD **d** them to me, shall
2Sa 22:49 who **d** me from my enemies
Job 36:15 He **d** the poor in their
Ps 18:48 He **d** me from my enemies
Ps 34: 7 who fear Him, And **d** them
Ps 34:17 And **d** them out of all their
Ps 34:19 But the LORD **d** him out of
Ps 97:10 He **d** them out of the hand of
Ps 144:10 Who **d** David His servant From
Prov 10: 2 righteousness **d** from death
Prov 11: 4 righteousness **d** from death
Prov 14:25 A true witness **d** souls, but a
Is 42:22 are for prey, and no one **d**
Dan 6:27 He **d** and rescues, and He works
1Co 15:24 when He **d** the kingdom to God
1Th 1:10 even Jesus who **d** us from the

DELIVERY (*see* DELIVER)
Is 26:17 draws near the time of her **d**
Is 66: 9 time of birth, and not cause **d**
Is 66: 9 who cause **d** shut up the womb

DELUDED (*see* DELUSION)
Is 19:13 they have also **d** Egypt, those

DELUSION (*see* DELUDED, DELUSIONS)
Zech 10: 2 For the idols speak **d**
2Th 2:11 God will send them strong **d**

DELUSIONS (*see* DELUSION)
Is 66: 4 so will I choose their **d**, and
Lam 2:14 for you false prophecies and **d**

DEMAND (*see* DEMANDED, DEMANDING, DEMANDS)
Gen 9: 5 I will **d** a reckoning
Neh 5:18 **d** the governor's provisions
Dan 2:23 made known to us the king's **d**

DEMANDED (*see* DEMAND)
Dan 2:27 secret which the king has **d**

DEMANDING (*see* DEMAND)
Luke 23:23 **d** with loud voices that He be

DEMANDS (*see* DEMAND)
1Sa 10: 7 that you do as the occasion **d**
1Th 2: 6 made **d** as apostles of Christ

DEMAS
Col 4:14 physician and **D** greet you
2Ti 4:10 for **D** has forsaken me, having
Phm 24 as do Mark, Aristarchus, **D**

DEMENTED
Jer 29:26 LORD over every man who is **d**

DEMETRIUS
Acts 19:24 For a certain man named **D**
Acts 19:38 Therefore, if **D** and his fellow
3Jn 12 **D** has a good testimony from

DEMOLISH (*see* DEMOLISHED)
Num 33:52 and **d** all their high places

DEMOLISHED (*see* DEMOLISH)
Judg 9:45 he **d** the city and sowed it

DEMON (*see* DEMON-POSSESSED, DEMONIC, DEMONS)
Matt 9:33 when the **d** was cast out, the
Matt 11:18 and they say, 'He has a **d**
Matt 17:18 And Jesus rebuked the **d**, and he
Mark 7:26 the **d** out of her daughter
Mark 7:29 the **d** has gone out of your
Mark 7:30 she found the **d** gone out
Luke 4:33 had a spirit of an unclean **d**
Luke 4:35 when the **d** had thrown him in
Luke 7:33 wine, and you say, 'He has a **d**
Luke 8:29 was driven by the **d** into the
Luke 9:42 the **d** threw him down and
Luke 11:14 And He was casting out a **d**
Luke 11:14 when the **d** had gone out, that
John 7:20 You have a **d**
John 8:48 are a Samaritan and have a **d**
John 8:49 I do not have a **d**
John 8:52 Now we know that You have a **d**
John 10:20 He has a **d** and is mad
John 10:21 the words of one who has a **d**
John 10:21 Can a **d** open the eyes of the

DEMONIC (*see* DEMON)
Jas 3:15 but is earthly, sensual, **d**

DEMON-POSSESSED (*see* DEMON)
Matt 4:24 torments, and those who were **d**
Matt 8:16 to Him many who were **d**
Matt 8:28 there met Him two **d** men,
Matt 8:33 had happened to the **d** men
Matt 9:32 to Him a man, mute and **d**
Matt 12:22 was brought to Him who was **d**
Matt 15:22 My daughter is severely **d**
Mark 1:32 were sick and those who were **d**
Mark 5:15 and saw the one who had been **d**
Mark 5:16 to him who had been **d**, and
Mark 5:18 he who had been **d** begged Him
Luke 8:36 he who had been **d** was healed

DEMONS (*see* DEMON)
Lev 17: 7 offer their sacrifices to **d**
Deut 32:17 They sacrificed to **d**, not to
2Ch 11:15 the high places, for the **d**
Ps 106:37 sons And their daughters to **d**
Matt 7:22 cast out **d** in Your name, and
Matt 8:31 So the **d** begged Him, saying,
Matt 9:34 He casts out **d**
Matt 9:34 by the ruler of the **d**
Matt 10: 8 raise the dead, cast out **d**
Matt 12:24 out **d** except by Beelzebub
Matt 12:24 Beelzebub, the ruler of the **d**
Matt 12:27 if I cast out **d** by Beelzebub
Matt 12:28 But if I cast out **d** by the
Mark 1:34 diseases, and cast out many **d**
Mark 1:34 did not allow the **d** to speak
Mark 1:39 all Galilee, and casting out **d**
Mark 3:15 sicknesses and to cast out **d**
Mark 3:22 of the **d** He casts out **d**
Mark 5:12 all the **d** begged Him, saying,
Mark 6:13 And they cast out many **d**, and
Mark 9:38 us casting out **d** in Your name
Mark 16: 9 of whom He had cast seven **d**
Mark 16:17 My name they will cast out **d**
Luke 4:41 And **d** also came out of many,
Luke 8: 2 out of whom had come seven **d**
Luke 8:27 who had **d** for a long time
Luke 8:30 because many **d** had entered
Luke 8:33 Then the **d** went out of the
Luke 8:35 from whom the **d** had departed
Luke 8:38 the **d** had departed begged Him
Luke 9: 1 power and authority over all **d**
Luke 9:49 casting out **d** in Your name
Luke 10:17 even the **d** are subject to us
Luke 11:15 He casts out **d** by Beelzebub
Luke 11:15 Beelzebub, the ruler of the **d**
Luke 11:18 say I cast out **d** by Beelzebub
Luke 11:19 if I cast out **d** by Beelzebub
Luke 11:20 But if I cast out **d** with the
Luke 13:32 fox, 'Behold, I cast out **d**
1Co 10:20 sacrifice they sacrifice to **d**
1Co 10:20 you to have fellowship with **d**
1Co 10:21 of the Lord and the cup of **d**
1Co 10:21 table and of the table of **d**
1Ti 4: 1 spirits and doctrines of **d**
Jas 2:19 Even the **d** believe
Rev 9:20 they should not worship **d**
Rev 16:14 For they are spirits of **d**
Rev 18: 2 has become a habitation of **d**

DEMONSTRATE (*see* DEMONSTRATES, DEMONSTRATING, DEMONSTRATION)
Rom 3:25 to **d** His righteousness,
Rom 3:26 to **d** at the present time His

DEMONSTRATES (*see* DEMONSTRATE)
Rom 3: 5 **d** the righteousness of God
Rom 5: 8 But God **d** His own love toward

DEMONSTRATING (*see* DEMONSTRATE)
Acts 17: 3 and **d** that the Christ had to

DEMONSTRATION (*see* DEMONSTRATE)
1Co 2: 4 but in **d** of the Spirit and of

DEN (*see* DENS)
Ps 10: 9 secretly, as a lion in his **d**
Is 11: 8 put his hand in the viper's **d**
Jer 7:11 become a **d** of thieves in your
Jer 9:11 of ruins and a **d** of jackals
Jer 10:22 desolate, a **d** of jackals
Dan 6: 7 be cast into the **d** of lions
Dan 6:12 be cast into the **d** of lions
Dan 6:16 cast him into the **d** of lions
Dan 6:17 and laid on the mouth of the **d**
Dan 6:19 in haste to the **d** of lions
Dan 6:20 And when he came to the **d**, he
Dan 6:23 take Daniel up out of the **d**
Dan 6:23 was taken up out of the **d**
Dan 6:24 cast them into the **d** of lions
Dan 6:24 came to the bottom of the **d**
Amos 3: 4 a young lion cry out of his **d**
Matt 21:13 have made it a '**d** of thieves
Mark 11:17 have made it a '**d** of thieves
Luke 19:46 have made it a '**d** of thieves

DENARII (*see* DENARIUS)
Matt 18:28 who owed him a hundred **d**
Mark 6:37 two hundred **d** worth of bread
Mark 14: 5 for more than three hundred **d**
Luke 7:41 One owed five hundred **d**, and
Luke 10:35 departed, he took out two **d**
John 6: 7 Two hundred **d** worth of bread
John 12: 5 not sold for three hundred **d**

DENARIUS (*see* DENARII)
Matt 20: 2 the laborers for a **d** a day
Matt 20: 9 hour, they each received a **d**
Matt 20:10 likewise received each a **d**
Matt 20:13 you not agree with me for a **d**
Matt 22:19 So they brought Him a **d**
Mark 12:15 Bring Me a **d** that I may see
Luke 20:24 Show Me a **d**
Rev 6: 6 A quart of wheat for a **d**, and
Rev 6: 6 quarts of barley for a **d**

DENIED (*see* DENY)
Gen 18:15 But Sarah **d** it, saying, "I
Job 31:28 would have **d** God who is above
Matt 26:70 But he **d** it before them all,
Matt 26:72 But again he **d** with an oath
Mark 14:68 But he **d** it, saying, "I
Mark 14:70 But he **d** it again
Luke 8:45 When all **d** it, Peter and
Luke 12: 9 Me before men will be **d**
Luke 22:57 But he **d** Him, saying, "Woman
John 13:38 you have **d** Me three times
John 18:25 He **d** it and said, "I am not
John 18:27 Peter then **d** again
Acts 3:13 **d** in the presence of Pilate,
Acts 3:14 But you **d** the Holy One and the
Acts 19:36 these things cannot be **d**, you
1Ti 5: 8 he has **d** the faith and is
Rev 3: 8 word, and have not **d** My name

DENIES (*see* DENY)
Matt 10:33 But whoever **d** Me before men,
Luke 12: 9 But he who **d** Me before men
1Jn 2:22 **d** that Jesus is the Christ
1Jn 2:22 antichrist who **d** the Father
1Jn 2:23 Whoever **d** the Son does not

DENOUNCE (*see* DENOUNCED)
Num 23: 7 for me, and come, **d** Israel
Num 23: 8 how shall I **d** whom the LORD

DENOUNCED (*see* DENOUNCE)
Num 23: 8 whom the LORD has not **d**

DENS (*see* DEN)
Judg 6: 2 made for themselves the **d**
Job 37: 8 The animals enter **d**, and
Job 38:40 when they crouch in their **d**
Ps 104:22 And lie down in their **d**
Song 4: 8 and Hermon, from the lions' **d**
Nah 2:12 prey, and his **d** with flesh
Heb 11:38 in deserts and mountains, in **d**

DENSE
Jer 13:16 death and makes it **d** darkness
Ezek 19:11 her height amid the **d** foliage

DENY (*see* DENIED, DENIES, DENYING)
Josh 24:27 to you, lest you **d** your God
1Ki 2:16 do not **d** me
1Ki 20: 7 and I did not **d** him
Job 8:18 his place, then it will **d** him
Prov 30: 9 I be full and **d** You, and say,
Matt 10:33 him I will also **d** before My
Matt 16:24 after Me, let him **d** himself
Matt 26:34 you will **d** Me three times
Matt 26:35 with You, I will not **d** You
Matt 26:75 you will **d** Me three times
Mark 8:34 after Me, let him **d** himself
Mark 14:30 you will **d** Me three times
Mark 14:31 with You, I will not **d** You
Mark 14:72 you will **d** Me three times
Luke 9:23 after Me, let him **d** himself
Luke 20:27 who **d** that there is a
Luke 22:34 this day before you will **d**
Luke 22:61 you will **d** Me three times
John 1:20 He confessed, and did not **d**
Acts 4:16 Jerusalem, and we cannot **d** it
2Ti 2:12 If we **d** Him, He also will **d** us
2Ti 2:13 He cannot **d** Himself
Tit 1:16 God, but in works they **d** Him
Jude 4 **d** the only Lord God and our
Rev 2:13 did not **d** My faith even in

DENYING (*see* DENY)
2Ti 3: 5 of godliness but **d** its power
Tit 2:12 **d** ungodliness and worldly
2Pe 2: 1 even **d** the Lord who bought

DEPART (*see* DEPARTED, DEPARTING, DEPARTS, DEPARTURE)
Gen 45:17 Load your beasts and **d**
Gen 49:10 shall not **d** from Judah, nor a
Ex 8:11 And the frogs shall **d** from you
Ex 8:29 may **d** tomorrow from Pharaoh
Ex 18:27 Moses let his father-in-law **d**
Ex 33: 1 **D** and go up from here, you and
Ex 33:11 did not **d** from the tabernacle
Lev 25:41 And then he shall **d** from you
Num 10:30 but I will **d** to my own land
Num 16:26 **D** now from the tents of these
Deut 4: 9 lest they **d** from your heart
Josh 1: 8 shall not **d** from your mouth
Josh 24:28 So Joshua let the people **d**
Judg 6:18 Do not **d** from here, I pray,
Judg 7: 3 **d** at once from Mount Gilead
Judg 19: 5 the morning, and he stood to **d**
Judg 19: 7 And when the man stood to **d**
Judg 19: 8 morning on the fifth day to **d**
Judg 19: 9 And when the man stood to **d**
1Sa 6: 6 people go, that they might **d**
1Sa 15: 6 Go, **d**, get down from among
1Sa 16:23 spirit would **d** from him
1Sa 22: 5 **d**, and go to the land of Judah
1Sa 29:10 the morning and have light, **d**
1Sa 29:11 early to **d** in the morning
1Sa 30:22 they may lead them away and **d**
2Sa 7:15 My mercy shall not **d** from him
2Sa 11:12 and tomorrow I will let you **d**
2Sa 12:10 shall never **d** from your house
2Sa 15:14 Make haste to **d**, lest he
2Sa 20:21 and I will **d** from the city
2Sa 22:23 I did not **d** from them
1Ki 11:21 Let me **d**, that I may go to my
1Ki 12: 5 **D** for three days, then come
1Ki 20:36 as soon as you **d** from me
2Ki 3: 3 he did not **d** from them
2Ki 10:31 for he did not **d** from the
2Ki 13: 2 He did not **d** from them
2Ki 13: 6 Nevertheless they did not **d**
2Ki 13:11 he did not **d** from all the
2Ki 14:24 he did not **d** from all the
2Ki 15: 9 he did not **d** from the sins of
2Ki 15:18 he did not **d** all his days
2Ki 15:24 he did not **d** from the sins of
2Ki 15:28 he did not **d** from the sins of
2Ki 17:22 they did not **d** from them,
2Ki 18: 6 he did not **d** from following
2Ch 8:15 They did not **d** from the
2Ch 34:33 All his days they did not **d**
Neh 9:19 did not **d** from them by day
Job 15:30 He will not **d** from darkness
Job 20:28 increase of his house will **d**
Job 21:14 **D** from us, for we do not
Job 22:17 They said to God, '**D** from us
Job 28:28 wisdom, and to **d** from evil is
Job 39: 4 they **d** and do not return to
Ps 6: 8 **D** from me, all you workers of
Ps 34:14 **D** from evil, and do good
Ps 37:27 **D** from evil, and do good
Ps 55:11 and guile do not **d** from its
Ps 101: 4 heart shall **d** from me
Ps 119:115 **D** from me, you evildoers, For
Ps 139:19 **D** from me, therefore, you
Prov 3: 7 fear the LORD and **d** from evil
Prov 3:21 let them not **d** from your eyes
Prov 4:21 not let them **d** from your eyes
Prov 5: 7 do not **d** from the words of my
Prov 13:19 to fools to **d** from evil
Prov 16:17 the upright is to **d** from evil
Prov 17:13 evil will not **d** from his
Prov 22: 6 is old he will not **d** from it
Prov 27:22 will not **d** from him
Is 11:13 the envy of Ephraim shall **d**
Is 52:11 **D**! **D**! Go out from there
Is 54:10 For the mountains shall **d**
Is 54:10 kindness shall not **d** from you
Is 59:21 shall not **d** from your mouth,
Jer 6: 8 lest My soul **d** from you
Jer 17:13 Those who **d** from Me shall be
Jer 31:36 ordinances **d** from before Me
Jer 32:40 that they will not **d** from Me
Jer 37: 9 will surely **d** from us," for
Jer 37: 9 us," for they will not **d**
Jer 50: 3 They shall move, they shall **d**
Ezek 16:42 My jealousy shall **d** from you
Hos 9:12 to them when I **d** from them
Mic 2:10 Arise and **d**, for this is not
Zech 10:11 the scepter of Egypt shall **d**
Zech 13: 2 spirit to **d** from the land
Matt 7:23 **d** from Me, you who practice
Matt 8:18 to **d** to the other side
Matt 8:34 Him to **d** from their region
Matt 10:14 when you **d** from that house or
Matt 25:41 **D** from Me, you cursed, into
Mark 5:17 Him to **d** from their region
Mark 6:10 till you **d** from that place
Mark 6:11 when you **d** from there, shake
Luke 2:29 Your servant **d** in peace,
Luke 2:37 who did not **d** from the temple
Luke 5: 8 **D** from me, for I am a sinful
Luke 8:37 asked Him to **d** from them, for
Luke 9: 4 stay there, and from there **d**
Luke 12:59 you shall not **d** from there
Luke 13:27 **D** from Me, all you workers of
Luke 13:31 **d** from here, for Herod wants
Luke 21:21 who are in the midst of her **d**
John 7: 3 **D** from here and go into Judea,
John 13: 1 **d** from this world to the
John 16: 7 but if I **d**, I will send Him
Acts 1: 4 them not to **d** from Jerusalem
Acts 16:36 Now therefore **d**, and go in
Acts 16:39 asked them to **d** from the city
Acts 18: 2 all the Jews to **d** from Rome)
Acts 20: 7 ready to **d** the next day,
Acts 22:21 Then He said to me, '**D**, for I
Acts 23:22 commander let the young man **d**
1Co 7:10 is not to **d** from her husband
1Co 7:11 But even if she does **d**, let
1Co 7:15 unbeliever departs, let him **d**
2Co 12: 8 times that it might **d** from me
Phil 1:23 the two, having a desire to **d**
1Ti 4: 1 some will **d** from the faith
2Ti 2:19 of Christ **d** from iniquity
Jas 2:16 **D** in peace, be warmed and

DEPARTED (*see* DEPART)
Gen 12: 4 So Abram **d** as the LORD had
Gen 12: 4 old when he **d** from Haran
Gen 12: 5 they **d** to go to the land of
Gen 14:12 in Sodom, and his goods, and **d**
Gen 21:14 Then she **d** and wandered in the
Gen 24:10 of his master's camels and **d**
Gen 24:61 the servant took Rebekah and **d**
Gen 26:17 Then Isaac **d** from there and
Gen 26:31 and they **d** from him in peace
Gen 31:40 and my sleep **d** from my eyes
Gen 31:55 Then Laban **d** and returned to
Gen 37:17 They have **d** from here, for I
Gen 38: 1 Judah **d** from his brothers
Gen 42:26 the grain and **d** from there
Gen 45:24 his brothers away, and they **d**
Ex 16: 1 they **d** from the land of Egypt
Ex 19: 2 For they had **d** from Rephidim,
Ex 35:20 of the children of Israel **d**
Num 10:33 So they **d** from the mountain
Num 12: 9 aroused against them, and He **d**
Num 12:10 when the cloud **d** from above
Num 13:26 So they **d** and came back to
Num 14: 9 protection has **d** from them
Num 14:44 nor Moses **d** from the camp
Num 22: 7 the elders of Midian **d** with
Num 24:25 Then Balaam rose and **d** and
Num 33: 3 They **d** from Rameses in the
Num 33: 6 They **d** from Succoth and
Num 33: 8 They **d** from before Hahiroth
Num 33:13 They **d** from Dophkah and

Num 33:15 They **d** from Rephidim and
Num 33:17 They **d** from Kibroth Hattaavah
Num 33:18 They **d** from Hazeroth and
Num 33:19 They **d** from Rithmah and
Num 33:20 They **d** from Rimmon Perez and
Num 33:27 They **d** from Tahath and camped
Num 33:30 They **d** from Hashmonah and
Num 33:31 They **d** from Moseroth and
Num 33:35 They **d** from Abronah and
Num 33:41 So they **d** from Mount Hor and
Num 33:42 They **d** from Zalmonah and
Num 33:43 They **d** from Punon and camped
Num 33:44 They **d** from Oboth and camped
Num 33:45 They **d** from Ijim and camped at
Num 33:48 They **d** from the mountains of
Deut 1:19 So we **d** from Horeb, and went
Deut 1:24 And they **d** and went up into the
Deut 9: 7 from the day that you **d** from
Deut 24: 2 when she has **d** from his house
Josh 2:21 she sent them away, and they **d**
Josh 2:22 Then they **d** and went to the
Josh 9:12 the day we **d** to come to you
Josh 22: 9 **d** from the children of Israel
Judg 6:21 the LORD **d** out of his sight
Judg 9:55 Abimelech was dead, they **d**
Judg 16:20 that the LORD had **d** from him
Judg 17: 8 The man **d** from the city of
Judg 18: 7 So the five men **d** and went to
Judg 18:21 Then they turned and **d**, and put
Judg 19:10 so he rose and **d**, and came to a
Judg 21:24 **d** from there at that time
1Sa 4:21 The glory has **d** from Israel
1Sa 4:22 The glory has **d** from Israel
1Sa 10: 2 When you have **d** from me today
1Sa 15: 6 So the Kenites **d** from among
1Sa 16:14 of the LORD **d** from Saul, and a
1Sa 18:12 with him, but had **d** from Saul
1Sa 20:42 So he arose and **d**, and
1Sa 22: 1 David therefore **d** from there
1Sa 22: 5 So David **d** and went into the
1Sa 23:13 and **d** from Keilah and went
1Sa 28:15 me, and God has **d** from me and
1Sa 28:16 the LORD has **d** from you and
2Sa 6:19 So all the people **d**, everyone
2Sa 11: 8 So Uriah **d** from the king's
2Sa 12:15 Then Nathan **d** to his house
2Sa 17:21 to pass, after they had **d**
2Sa 19:24 from the day the king **d** until
2Sa 22:22 not wickedly **d** from my God
1Ki 12: 5 And the people **d**
1Ki 12:16 So Israel **d** to their tents
1Ki 14:17 Jeroboam's wife arose and **d**
1Ki 19:19 So he **d** from there, and found
1Ki 20: 9 And the messengers **d** and
1Ki 20:38 Then the prophet **d** and waited
2Ki 1: 4 So Elijah **d**
2Ki 3:27 So they **d** from him and
2Ki 4:25 So she **d**, and went to the man
2Ki 5: 5 So he **d** and took with him
2Ki 5:19 So he **d** from him a short
2Ki 5:24 he let the men go, and they **d**
2Ki 8:14 Then he **d** from Elisha, and
2Ki 10:12 And he arose and **d** and went to
2Ki 10:15 Now when he **d** from there, he
2Ki 19: 8 that he had **d** from Lachish
2Ki 19:36 Sennacherib king of Assyria **d**
1Ch 16:43 Then all the people **d**, every
1Ch 21: 4 Therefore Joab **d** and went
2Ch 10: 5 And the people **d**
2Ch 10:16 all Israel **d** to their tents
2Ch 21:20 and, to no one's sorrow, **d**
Ezra 8:31 Then we **d** from the river of
Job 23:12 I have not **d** from the
Ps 18:21 not wickedly **d** from my God
Ps 44:18 our steps **d** from Your way
Ps 105:38 Egypt was glad when they **d**
Ps 119:102 I have not **d** from Your
Is 7:17 day that Ephraim **d** from Judah
Is 37: 8 that he had **d** from Lachish
Is 37:37 Sennacherib king of Assyria **d**
Jer 5:23 they have revolted and **d**
Jer 29: 2 smiths had **d** from Jerusalem
Jer 37: 5 them, they **d** from Jerusalem
Jer 41:10 **d** to go over to the Ammonites
Jer 41:17 And they **d** and dwelt in the
Lam 1: 6 Zion all her splendor has **d**
Ezek 6: 9 heart which has **d** from Me
Ezek 10:18 **d** from the threshold of the
Dan 4:31 the kingdom has **d** from you
Dan 9:11 has **d** so as not to obey Your
Hos 10: 5 its glory has **d** from it
Mal 2: 8 But you have **d** from the way
Matt 2: 9 they heard the king, they **d**
Matt 2:12 they **d** for their own country
Matt 2:13 Now when they had **d**, behold,
Matt 2:14 by night and **d** for Egypt,
Matt 4:12 in prison, He **d** to Galilee
Matt 9: 7 And he arose and **d** to his house
Matt 9:27 When Jesus **d** from there, two
Matt 9:31 But when they had **d**, they
Matt 11: 1 that He **d** from there to teach
Matt 11: 7 As they **d**, Jesus began to say
Matt 12: 9 Now when He had **d** from there
Matt 13:53 that He **d** from there
Matt 14:13 He **d** from there by boat to a
Matt 15:21 **d** to the region of Tyre and
Matt 15:29 Jesus **d** from there, skirted
Matt 16: 4 And He left them and **d**
Matt 19: 1 that He **d** from Galilee and
Matt 19:15 hands on them and **d** from there
Matt 20:29 Now as they **d** from Jericho, a
Matt 24: 1 **d** from the temple, and His
Matt 27: 5 of silver in the temple and **d**
Matt 27:60 the door of the tomb, and **d**
Matt 28: 8 So they **d** quickly from the
Mark 1:35 out and **d** to a solitary place
Mark 5:20 And he **d** and began to proclaim
Mark 6:32 So they **d** to a deserted place
Mark 6:46 He **d** to the mountain to pray
Mark 8:13 again, **d** to the other side
Mark 9:30 Then they **d** from there and
Luke 1:23 that he **d** to his own house
Luke 1:38 And the angel **d** from her
Luke 4:13 he **d** from Him until an
Luke 4:42 Now when it was day, He **d**
Luke 5:25 on, and **d** to his own house,
Luke 7:24 the messengers of John had **d**
Luke 8:35 from whom the demons had **d**
Luke 8:38 from whom the demons had **d**
Luke 9: 6 So they **d** and went through the
Luke 10:30 clothing, wounded him, and **d**
Luke 10:35 On the next day, when he **d**
Luke 19:32 So those who were sent **d** and
Luke 24:12 and he **d**, marveling to himself
John 4: 3 Judea and **d** again to Galilee
John 4:43 the two days He **d** from there
John 5:15 The man **d** and told the Jews
John 6:15 He **d** again to a mountain by
John 12:36 things Jesus spoke, and **d**, and
Acts 5:41 So they **d** from the presence
Acts 10: 7 angel who spoke to him had **d**
Acts 11:25 Then Barnabas **d** for Tarsus to
Acts 12:10 the angel **d** from him
Acts 12:17 And he **d** and went to another
Acts 13:14 But when they **d** from Perga
Acts 14:20 And the next day he **d** with
Acts 15:38 had **d** from them in Pamphylia
Acts 15:40 but Paul chose Silas and **d**
Acts 16:40 they encouraged them and **d**
Acts 17:15 to him with all speed, they **d**
Acts 17:33 So Paul **d** from among them
Acts 18: 1 things Paul **d** from Athens
Acts 18: 7 he **d** from there and entered
Acts 18:23 spent some time there, he **d**
Acts 19: 9 he **d** from them and withdrew
Acts 20: 1 them, and **d** to go to Macedonia
Acts 20:11 even till daybreak, he **d**
Acts 21: 1 that when we had **d** from them
Acts 21: 5 the end of those days, we **d**
Acts 21: 8 who were Paul's companions **d**
Acts 28:10 and when we **d**, they provided
Acts 28:25 they **d** after Paul had said
Acts 28:29 said these words, the Jews **d**
2Co 2:13 of them, I **d** for Macedonia
Phil 4:15 when I **d** from Macedonia, no
2Ti 4:10 and has **d** for Thessalonica
Phm 15 For perhaps he **d** for a while

DEPARTING (*see* DEPART)
Gen 35:18 her soul was **d** (for she died)
Is 59:13 and **d** from our God, speaking
Dan 9: 5 even by **d** from Your precepts
Hos 1: 2 harlotry by **d** from the LORD
Mark 6:33 But the multitudes saw them **d**
Mark 7:31 **d** from the region of Tyre and
Acts 13:13 **d** from them, returned to
Heb 3:12 in **d** from the living God

DEPARTS (*see* DEPART)
Ps 146: 4 His spirit **d**, he returns to
Prov 14:16 **d** from evil, but a fool rages
Prov 16: 6 of the LORD one **d** from evil
Eccl 6: 4 **d** in darkness, and its name is
Is 59:15 and he who **d** from evil makes
Jer 3:20 **d** from her husband, so have
Jer 17: 5 whose heart **d** from the LORD
Nah 3: 1 Its victim never **d**
Luke 9:39 him, it **d** from him with great
1Co 7:15 But if the unbeliever **d**, let

DEPARTURE (*see* DEPART)
Ezek 26:18 sea are troubled at your **d**
Acts 20:29 that after my **d** savage wolves
2Ti 4: 6 the time of my **d** is at hand
Heb 11:22 made mention of the **d** of the

DEPEND (*see* DEPENDS)
Is 10:20 will never again **d** on him who
Is 10:20 but will **d** on the LORD, the

DEPENDS (*see* DEPEND)
Rom 12:18 possible, as much as **d** on you

DEPLETE
Gen 41:30 and the famine will **d** the land

DEPLOY (*see* DEPLOYED)
Judg 4: 6 Go and **d** troops at Mount Tabor
Judg 4: 7 against you I will **d** Sisera

DEPLOYED (*see* DEPLOY)
Judg 15: 9 **d** themselves against Lehi
2Sa 5:18 **d** themselves in the Valley of
2Sa 5:22 **d** themselves in the Valley of
Is 7: 2 forces are **d** in Ephraim

DEPOSED
2Ch 36: 3 of Egypt **d** him at Jerusalem
Dan 5:20 he was **d** from his kingly

DEPOSIT (*see* DEPOSITED)
Ezra 6: 5 **d** them in the house of God"
Luke 19:21 collect what you did not **d**
Luke 19:22 collecting what I did not **d**
2Co 1:22 Spirit in our hearts as a **d**

DEPOSITED (*see* DEPOSIT)
Matt 25:27 **d** my money with the bankers

DEPRESSION
Prov 12:25 in the heart of man causes **d**

DEPRIVE (*see* DEPRIVED, DEPRIVES)
Prov 30: 7 You (**D** me not before I die)
Eccl 4: 8 do I toil and **d** myself of good
1Co 7: 5 Do not **d** one another except

DEPRIVED (*see* DEPRIVE)
Job 39:17 because God **d** her of wisdom,
Ps 78:30 They were not **d** of their
Is 38:10 I am **d** of the remainder of my
Hos 13: 8 like a bear **d** of her cubs

DEPRIVES (*see* DEPRIVE)
Job 12:20 He **d** the trusted ones of

DEPTH (*see* DEPTHS)
Ex 14:27 sea returned to its full **d**
Prov 25: 3 for height and the earth for **d**
Is 7:11 ask it either in the **d** or in
Matt 13: 5 they had no **d** of earth
Matt 18: 6 drowned in the **d** of the sea
Mark 4: 5 because it had no **d** of earth
Rom 8:39 nor height nor **d**, nor any
Rom 11:33 the **d** of the riches both of
Eph 3:18 is the width and length and **d**

DEPTHS (*see* DEPTH)
Ex 15: 5 The **d** have covered them
Ex 15: 8 the **d** congealed in the heart
Job 36:30 and covers the **d** of the sea
Job 38:16 you walked in search of the **d**
Ps 68:22 back from the **d** of the sea
Ps 71:20 again from the **d** of the earth
Ps 77:16 The **d** also trembled
Ps 78:15 drink in abundance like the **d**
Ps 86:13 my soul from the **d** of Sheol
Ps 88: 6 pit, In darkness, in the **d**
Ps 106: 9 So He led them through the **d**
Ps 107:26 They go down again to the **d**
Ps 130: 1 Out of the **d** I have cried to
Ps 148: 7 sea creatures and all the **d**
Prov 3:20 the **d** were broken up, and
Prov 8:24 When there were no **d** I was
Prov 9:18 guests are in the **d** of hell
Prov 20:27 all the inner **d** of his heart

Prov 20:30 the inner **d** of the heart
Is 14:15 to the lowest **d** of the Pit
Is 51:10 that made the **d** of the sea a
Jer 49: 8 turn back, dwell in the **d**
Jer 49:30 Dwell in the **d**, O inhabitants
Ezek 27:34 seas in the **d** of the waters
Ezek 31:14 to the **d** of the earth, among
Ezek 31:16 in the **d** of the earth
Ezek 31:18 of Eden to the **d** of the earth
Ezek 32:18 down to the **d** of the earth
Mic 7:19 sins into the **d** of the sea
Zech 10:11 all the **d** of the River shall
Rev 2:24 have not known the **d** of Satan

DEPUTIES (*see* DEPUTY)
1Ki 5:16 the chiefs of Solomon's **d**
Jer 51:57 men, her governors, her **d**

DEPUTY (*see* DEPUTIES)
2Sa 15: 3 but there is no **d** of the king
1Ki 22:47 in Edom, only a **d** of the king
Neh 11:24 was the king's **d** in all

DERANGED
Jer 51: 7 therefore the nations are **d**

DERBE
Acts 14: 6 of it and fled to Lystra and **D**
Acts 14:20 departed with Barnabas to **D**
Acts 16: 1 Then he came to **D** and Lystra
Acts 20: 4 Thessalonians, and Gaius of **D**

DERIDE (*see* DERIDED, DERISION)
Ps 102: 8 those who **d** me swear an oath
Hab 1:10 They **d** every stronghold, for

DERIDED (*see* DERIDE)
Luke 16:14 these things, and they **d** Him

DERISION (*see* DERIDE)
Ps 2: 4 The LORD shall hold them in **d**
Ps 44:13 a **d** to those all around us
Ps 59: 8 have all the nations in **d**
Ps 79: 4 **d** to those who are around us
Ps 119:51 The proud have me in great **d**
Jer 20: 7 I am in **d** daily
Jer 20: 8 to me a reproach and a **d** daily
Jer 48:26 and he shall also be in **d**
Jer 48:27 For was not Israel a **d** to you
Jer 48:39 So Moab shall be a **d** and a
Ezek 23:32 laughed to scorn and held in **d**
Hos 7:16 This shall be their **d** in the

DERIVED
Heb 7: 6 **d** from them received tithes

DESCEND (*see* DESCENDANT, DESCENDED, DESCENDING, DESCENT)
2Ki 20:18 your sons who will **d** from you
Ps 49:17 glory shall not **d** after him
Is 5:14 is jubilant, shall **d** into it
Is 39: 7 your sons who will **d** from you
Ezek 26:20 with those who **d** into the Pit
Ezek 31:16 with those who **d** into the Pit
Mark 15:32 **d** now from the cross, that we
Rom 10: 7 Who will **d** into the abyss
1Th 4:16 **d** from heaven with a shout
Jas 3:15 wisdom does not **d** from above

DESCENDANT (*see* DESCEND, DESCENDANTS)
Gen 17:12 stranger who is not your **d**
Num 16:40 who is not a **d** of Aaron,
1Ki 11:14 he was a **d** of the king in
Neh 10:38 the **d** of Aaron, shall be with

DESCENDANTS (*see* DESCENDANT, DESCENDANTS')
Gen 9: 9 you and with your **d** after you
Gen 12: 7 To your **d** I will give this
Gen 13:15 give to you and your **d** forever
Gen 13:16 I will make your **d** as the
Gen 13:16 then your **d** also could be
Gen 15: 5 So shall your **d** be
Gen 15:13 Know certainly that your **d**
Gen 15:18 To your **d** I have given this
Gen 16:10 multiply your **d** exceedingly
Gen 17: 7 your **d** after you in their
Gen 17: 7 to you and your **d** after you
Gen 17: 8 your **d** after you the land in
Gen 17: 9 your **d** after you throughout
Gen 17:10 Me and you and your **d** after you
Gen 17:19 and with his **d** after him
Gen 22:17 I will multiply your **d** as the
Gen 22:17 your **d** shall possess the gate
Gen 24: 7 To your **d** I give this land,'
Gen 24:60 may your **d** possess the gates
Gen 26: 3 your **d** I give all these lands
Gen 26: 4 I will make your **d** multiply
Gen 26: 4 to your **d** all these lands
Gen 26:24 you and multiply your **d** for My
Gen 28: 4 your **d** with you, that you may
Gen 28:13 I will give to you and your **d**
Gen 28:14 Also your **d** shall be as the
Gen 32:12 make your **d** as the sand of
Gen 35:12 to your **d** after you I give
Gen 46: 6 Jacob and all his **d** with him
Gen 46: 7 all his **d** he brought with him
Gen 48: 4 and give this land to your **d**
Gen 48:19 he, and his **d** shall become a
Ex 1: 5 All those who were **d** of Jacob
Ex 28:43 to him and his **d** after him
Ex 30:21 him and his **d** throughout their
Ex 32:13 I will multiply your **d** as
Ex 32:13 spoken of I give to your **d**
Ex 33: 1 To your **d** I will give it
Lev 18:21 **d** pass through the fire to
Lev 20: 2 gives any of his **d** to Molech
Lev 20: 3 given some of his **d** to Molech
Lev 20: 4 gives some of his **d** to Molech
Lev 21:17 No man of your **d** in
Lev 21:21 No man of the **d** of Aaron the
Lev 22: 3 Whoever of all your **d**
Lev 22: 4 man of the **d** of Aaron, who is
Num 13:22 the **d** of Anak, were there
Num 13:28 we saw the **d** of Anak there
Num 13:33 (the **d** of Anak came from the
Num 14:24 and his **d** shall inherit it
Num 18:19 with you and your **d** with you
Num 25:13 his **d** after him a covenant of
Deut 1: 8 to them and their **d** after them
Deut 2: 4 the **d** of Esau, who live in
Deut 2: 8 the **d** of Esau who dwell in
Deut 2: 9 the **d** of Lot as a possession
Deut 2:12 in Seir, but the **d** of Esau
Deut 2:19 the **d** of Lot as a possession
Deut 2:22 He had done for the **d** of Esau
Deut 2:29 just as the **d** of Esau who
Deut 4:37 He chose their **d** after them
Deut 9: 2 the **d** of the Anakim, whom you
Deut 9: 2 stand before the **d** of Anak
Deut 10:15 He chose their **d** after them
Deut 11: 9 fathers, to them and their **d**
Deut 23: 2 none of his **d** shall enter the
Deut 23: 3 none of his **d** shall enter the
Deut 28:46 wonder, and on your **d** forever
Deut 28:59 your **d** extraordinary plagues
Deut 30: 6 heart and the heart of your **d**
Deut 30:19 both you and your **d** may live
Deut 31:21 in the mouths of their **d**, for
Deut 34: 4 I will give it to your **d**
Josh 22:24 come your **d** may speak to our
Josh 22:24 may speak to our **d**, saying
Josh 22:25 So your **d** would make our
Josh 22:25 our **d** cease fearing the LORD
Josh 22:27 that your **d** may not say to
Josh 22:27 say to our **d** in time to come
Josh 24: 3 Canaan, and multiplied his **d**
1Sa 2:20 The LORD give you **d** from this
1Sa 2:33 all the **d** of your house shall
1Sa 20:42 you and me, and between your **d**
1Sa 20:42 your **d** and my **d**,
1Sa 24:21 not cut off my **d** after me
2Sa 4: 8 this day of Saul and his **d**
2Sa 21: 6 of his **d** be delivered to us
2Sa 22:51 to David and his **d** forevermore
1Ki 2:33 the head of his **d** forever
1Ki 2:33 But upon David and his **d**, upon
1Ki 9:21 their **d** who were left in the
1Ki 11:39 I will afflict the **d** of David
2Ki 5:27 to you and your **d** forever
2Ki 17:20 rejected all the **d** of Israel
1Ch 2:42 The **d** of Caleb the brother of
1Ch 2:50 These were the **d** of Caleb
1Ch 2:52 of Kirjath Jearim had **d**
1Ch 7:14 The **d** of Manasseh
1Ch 7:17 These were the **d** of Gilead
1Ch 9: 4 of the **d** of Perez, the son of
1Ch 23:17 Of the **d** of Eliezer, Rehabiah
1Ch 26:21 the **d** of the Gershonites of
2Ch 8: 8 their **d** who were left in the
2Ch 20: 7 gave it to the **d** of Abraham
Ezra 4: 1 the **d** of the captivity were
Ezra 6:16 and the rest of the **d** of the
Ezra 6:19 the **d** of the captivity kept
Ezra 6:20 all the **d** of the captivity
Ezra 10: 7 to all the **d** of the captivity
Ezra 10:16 Then the **d** of the captivity
Neh 9: 8 to give it to his **d**
Neh 11: 3 and **d** of Solomon's servants
Esth 9:27 it upon themselves and their **d**
Esth 9:28 not perish among their **d**
Esth 9:31 their **d** concerning matters of
Job 5:25 that your **d** shall be many
Job 21: 8 Their **d** are established with
Ps 18:50 To David and his **d** forevermore
Ps 21:10 their **d** from among the sons
Ps 22:23 All you **d** of Jacob, glorify
Ps 25:13 his **d** shall inherit the earth
Ps 37:25 Nor his **d** begging bread
Ps 37:26 And his **d** are blessed
Ps 37:28 But the **d** of the wicked shall
Ps 69:36 the **d** of His servants shall
Ps 102:28 their **d** will be established
Ps 106:27 their **d** among the nations
Ps 112: 2 His **d** will be mighty on earth
Is 41: 8 the **d** of Abraham My friend
Is 43: 5 bring your **d** from the east
Is 44: 3 will pour My Spirit on your **d**
Is 45:25 all the **d** of Israel shall be
Is 48:19 Your **d** also would have been
Is 54: 3 and your **d** will inherit the
Is 59:21 nor from the mouth of your **d**
Is 59:21 mouth of your descendants' **d**
Is 61: 9 Their **d** shall be known among
Is 65: 9 will bring forth **d** from Jacob
Is 65:23 for they shall be the **d** of
Is 66:22 So shall your **d** and your name
Jer 22:28 they cast out, he and his **d**
Jer 22:30 none of his **d** shall prosper
Jer 23: 8 led the **d** of the house of
Jer 33:22 the **d** of David My servant
Jer 33:26 will cast away the **d** of Jacob
Jer 33:26 his **d** to be rulers over the
Jer 33:26 rulers over the **d** of Abraham
Jer 49:10 His **d** are plundered, his
Ezek 20: 5 the **d** of the house of Jacob
Ezek 44:22 the **d** of the house of Israel
Dan 1: 3 and some of the king's **d** and
Mal 2: 3 Behold, I will rebuke your **d**
John 8:33 We are Abraham's **d**, and have
John 8:37 know that you are Abraham's **d**
Acts 7: 5 and to his **d** after him
Acts 7: 6 that his **d** would sojourn in a
Rom 4:18 So shall your **d** be

DESCENDANTS' (*see* DESCENDANTS)
Is 59:21 mouth of your **d** descendants

DESCENDED (*see* DESCEND)
Gen 36:18 chiefs who **d** from Aholibamah
Ex 19:18 the LORD **d** upon it in fire
Ex 33: 9 that the pillar of cloud **d**
Ex 34: 5 Then the LORD **d** in the cloud
Deut 9:21 that **d** from the mountain
Josh 2:23 **d** from the mountain, and
Josh 17: 9 the border **d** to the Brook
Josh 18:13 the border **d** to Ataroth Adar,
Josh 18:16 **d** to the Valley of Hinnom, to
Josh 18:16 the south, and **d** to En Rogel
Josh 18:17 **d** to the stone of Bohan the
Prov 30: 4 ascended into heaven, or **d**
Matt 7:25 and the rain **d**, the floods
Matt 7:27 and the rain **d**, the floods
Matt 28: 2 of the Lord **d** from heaven
Luke 3:22 the Holy Spirit **d** in bodily
Eph 4: 9 **d** into the lower parts of the
Eph 4:10 He who **d** is also the One who

DESCENDING (*see* DESCEND)
Gen 28:12 God were ascending and **d** on it
Ps 133: 3 **D** upon the mountains of Zion
Prov 7:27 **d** to the chambers of death
Matt 3:16 Spirit of God **d** like a dove
Mark 1:10 the Spirit **d** upon Him like a
John 1:32 I saw the Spirit **d** from
John 1:33 whom you see the Spirit **d**
John 1:51 and **d** upon the Son of Man
Acts 10:11 **d** to him and let down to the
Acts 11: 5 an object **d** like a great
Rev 21:10 **d** out of heaven from God,

DESCENT (*see* DESCEND)
Josh 7: 5 and struck them down on the **d**
Josh 10:11 were on the **d** of Beth Horon,
Esth 6:13 begun to fall, is of Jewish **d**
Is 30:30 show the **d** of His arm, with
Jer 48: 5 for in the **d** of Horonaim the

Luke 19:37 the **d** of the Mount of Olives

DESCRIBE (*see* DESCRIBES, DESCRIBING)
Ezek 43:10 **d** the temple to the house of

DESCRIBES (*see* DESCRIBE)
Rom 4: 6 just as David also **d** the

DESCRIBING (*see* DESCRIBE)
Acts 15: 3 **d** the conversion of the

DESERT (*see* DESERTED, DESERTS)
Ex 3: 1 flock to the back of the **d**
Ex 5: 3 days' journey into the **d** and
Ex 19: 2 had come to the **D** of Sinai
Ex 23:31 and from the **d** to the River
Deut 32:10 He found him in a **d** land and
2Ch 26:10 Also he built towers in the **d**
Job 24: 5 like wild donkeys in the **d**
Ps 73:27 those who **d** You for harlotry
Ps 78:40 And grieved Him in the **d**
Ps 102: 6 I am like an owl of the **d**
Ps 106:14 And tested God in the **d**
Is 13:21 of the **d** will lie there, and
Is 21: 1 so it comes from the **d**, from
Is 23:13 it for wild beasts of the **d**
Is 34:14 The wild beasts of the **d**
Is 35: 1 and the **d** shall rejoice and
Is 35: 6 and streams in the **d**
Is 40: 3 make straight in the **d** a
Is 41:19 set in the **d** the cypress tree
Is 43:19 wilderness and rivers in the **d**
Is 43:20 wilderness and rivers in the **d**
Is 51: 3 her **d** like the garden of the
Jer 17: 6 be like a shrub in the **d**, and
Jer 25:24 multitude who dwell in the **d**
Jer 50:12 wilderness, a dry land and a **d**
Jer 50:39 Therefore the wild **d** beasts
Matt 24:26 to you, 'Look, He is in the **d**
John 6:31 ate the manna in the **d**
Acts 8:26 This is **d**

DESERTED (*see* DESERT)
Judg 5: 6 of Jael, the highways were **d**
2Sa 20: 2 every man of Israel **d** David
2Ki 25:11 the defectors who had **d** to
Is 32:14 the bustling city will be **d**
Jer 49:25 is the city of praise not **d**
Jer 52:15 the defectors who had **d** to
Matt 14:13 boat to a **d** place by Himself
Matt 14:15 This is a **d** place, and the
Mark 1:45 but was outside in **d** places
Mark 6:31 by yourselves to a **d** place
Mark 6:32 to a **d** place in the boat by
Mark 6:35 This is a **d** place, and already
Luke 4:42 and went into a **d** place
Luke 9:10 **d** place belonging to the city
Luke 9:12 for we are in a **d** place here

DESERTS (*see* DESERT)
Is 48:21 He led them through the **d**
Jer 2: 6 through a land of **d** and pits,
Jer 5: 6 a wolf of the **d** shall destroy
Ezek 13: 4 are like foxes in the **d**
Luke 1:80 was in the **d** till the day of
Heb 11:38 They wandered in **d** and

DESERVE (*see* DESERVES, DESERVING)
Ezra 9:13 us less than our iniquities **d**
Ps 28: 4 Render to them what they **d**
Jer 26:16 This man does not **d** to die
Ezek 7:27 what they **d** I will judge them

DESERVES (*see* DESERVE)
Deut 25: 2 the wicked man **d** to be beaten
Judg 9:16 and have done to him as he **d**
Job 11: 6 you less than your iniquity **d**
Jer 26:11 This man **d** to die

DESERVING (*see* DESERVE)
Matt 26:66 and said, 'He is **d** of death

DESIGN (*see* DESIGNER, DESIGNS)
Ex 26:31 an artistic **d** of cherubim
Ex 31: 4 to **d** artistic works, to work
Ex 35:32 to **d** artistic works, to work
Ex 35:35 those who **d** artistic works
Ex 36:35 an artistic **d** of cherubim
1Ki 7:28 this was the **d** of the carts
2Ki 16:10 the priest the **d** of the altar
2Ch 4: 7 of gold according to their **d**
Ezek 43:11 to them the **d** of the temple
Ezek 43:11 its entrances, its entire **d**
Ezek 43:11 they may keep its whole **d**

DESIGNATED (*see* DESIGNATES)
1Ch 12:31 who were **d** by name to come
1Ch 16:41 chosen, who were **d** by name
2Ch 28:15 who were **d** by name rose up
2Ch 31:19 were **d** by name to distribute
Ezra 8:20 All of them were **d** by name

DESIGNATES (*see* DESIGNATED)
Heb 4: 7 again He **d** a certain day,

DESIGNER (*see* DESIGN)
Ex 35:35 work of the engraver and the **d**
Ex 38:23 of Dan, an engraver and **d**, a

DESIGNS (*see* DESIGN)
Ex 26: 1 with artistic **d** of cherubim
Ex 36: 8 with artistic **d** of cherubim
Ex 39: 3 linen thread, into artistic **d**

DESIRABLE (*see* DESIRE)
Gen 3: 6 a tree **d** to make one wise,
2Ch 32:27 and for all kinds of **d** items
Prov 21:20 There is **d** treasure, and oil
Ezek 23: 6 all of them **d** young men,
Ezek 23:12 all of them **d** young men
Ezek 23:23 them, all of them **d** young men
Hos 13:15 the treasury of every **d** prize
Nah 2: 9 Or wealth of every **d** prize
Acts 6: 2 It is not **d** that we should

DESIRE (*see* DESIRABLE, DESIRED, DESIRES, DESIRING, UNDESIRABLE)
Gen 3:16 Your **d** shall be for your
Gen 4: 7 its **d** is for you, but you
Ex 15: 9 my **d** shall be satisfied on
Deut 5:21 and you shall not **d** your
Deut 18: 6 comes with all the **d** of his
Deut 21:11 **d** her and would take her for
1Sa 9:20 whom is all the **d** of Israel
1Sa 18:25 The king does not **d** any
1Sa 20: 4 Whatever you yourself **d**, I
1Sa 23:20 **d** of your soul to come down
2Sa 23: 5 all my salvation and all my **d**
2Sa 24: 3 my lord the king **d** this thing
1Ki 2:20 I **d** one small petition of you
1Ki 5: 8 me, and I will do all you **d**
1Ki 5: 9 you shall fulfill my **d** by
1Ki 5:10 logs according to all his **d**
1Ki 9: 1 and all Solomon's **d** which he
Neh 1:11 who **d** to fear Your name
Job 13: 3 and I **d** to reason with God
Job 14:15 You shall **d** the work of Your
Job 21:14 for we do not **d** the knowledge
Job 31:16 kept the poor from their **d**
Job 33:32 speak, for I **d** to justify you
Job 36:20 Do not **d** the night, when
Ps 10: 3 boasts of his heart's **d**
Ps 10:17 heard the **d** of the humble
Ps 20: 4 according to your heart's **d**
Ps 21: 2 have given him his heart's **d**
Ps 38: 9 Lord, all my **d** is before You
Ps 40: 6 and offering You did not **d**
Ps 45:11 will greatly **d** your beauty
Ps 51: 6 You **d** truth in the inward
Ps 51:16 For You do not **d** sacrifice
Ps 54: 7 seen its **d** upon my enemies
Ps 59:10 let me see my **d** on my enemies
Ps 70: 2 and confused Who **d** my hurt
Ps 73:25 earth that I **d** besides You
Ps 78:29 For He gave them their own **d**
Ps 92:11 has seen my **d** on my enemies
Ps 92:11 My ears hear my **d** on the
Ps 112: 8 sees his **d** upon his enemies
Ps 112:10 The **d** of the wicked shall
Ps 118: 7 see my **d** on those who hate me
Ps 145:16 satisfy the **d** of every living
Ps 145:19 He will fulfill the **d** of
Prov 3:15 and all the things you may **d**
Prov 8:11 and all the things one may **d**
Prov 10: 3 away the **d** of the wicked
Prov 10:24 the **d** of the righteous will
Prov 11:23 The **d** of the righteous is
Prov 13:12 sick, but when the **d** comes
Prov 13:19 A **d** accomplished is sweet to
Prov 18: 1 himself seeks his own **d**
Prov 21:25 The **d** of the slothful kills
Prov 23: 3 Do not **d** his delicacies, for
Prov 23: 6 a miser, nor **d** his delicacies
Prov 24: 1 men, nor **d** to be with them
Eccl 6: 9 eyes than the wandering of **d**
Eccl 12: 5 is a burden, and **d** fails
Song 7:10 and his **d** is toward me
Is 26: 8 the **d** of our soul is for Your
Is 53: 2 beauty that we should **d** Him
Jer 2:24 sniffs at the wind in her **d**
Jer 22:27 to which they **d** to return
Jer 42:22 where you **d** to go to sojourn
Jer 44:14 to which they **d** to return
Ezek 24:16 the **d** of your eyes with one
Ezek 24:21 the **d** of your eyes, the
Ezek 24:25 the **d** of their eyes, and that
Dan 11:37 fathers nor the **d** of women
Hos 6: 6 For I **d** mercy and not
Hos 10:10 When it is My **d**, I will
Amos 5:18 Woe to you who **d** the day of
Mic 7: 3 great man utters his evil **d**
Hab 2: 5 he enlarges his **d** as hell
Hag 2: 7 come to the **D** of All Nations
Matt 9:13 I **d** mercy and not sacrifice
Matt 12: 7 I **d** mercy and not sacrifice,'
Matt 15:28 Let it be to you as you **d**
Mark 12:38 who **d** to go around in long
Luke 17:22 will come when you will **d** to
Luke 20:46 who **d** to walk in long robes,
Luke 22:15 With fervent **d** I have desired
John 15: 7 you, you will ask what you **d**
John 17:24 I **d** that they also whom You
Acts 28:22 But we **d** to hear from you
Rom 7: 8 in me all manner of evil **d**
Rom 10: 1 Brethren, my heart's **d** and
Rom 11:25 For I do not **d**, brethren,
Rom 15:23 having a great **d** these many
1Co 10:27 you **d** to go, eat whatever is
1Co 12:31 But earnestly **d** the best
1Co 14: 1 and **d** spiritual gifts, but
1Co 14:39 **d** earnestly to prophesy, and
2Co 7: 7 he told us of your earnest **d**
2Co 7:11 what fear, what vehement **d**
2Co 8:11 there was a readiness to **d** it
2Co 11:12 who **d** an opportunity to be
2Co 12: 6 For though I might **d** to boast
Gal 4: 9 to which you **d** again to be in
Gal 4:21 you who **d** to be under the law
Gal 6:12 As many as **d** to make a good
Gal 6:13 law, but they **d** to have you
Phil 1:23 having a **d** to depart and be
Col 3: 5 uncleanness, passion, evil **d**
1Th 2:17 to see your face with great **d**
1Ti 2: 8 Therefore I **d** that the men
1Ti 5:11 Christ, they **d** to marry,
1Ti 5:14 Therefore I **d** that the
1Ti 6: 9 But those who **d** to be rich
2Ti 3:12 all who **d** to live godly in
Heb 6:11 we **d** that each one of you
Heb 10: 5 and offering You did not **d**
Heb 10: 8 for sin You did not **d**, nor
Heb 11:16 But now they **d** a better, that
Jas 1:15 when **d** has conceived, it
1Pe 1:12 which angels **d** to look into
1Pe 2: 2 **d** the pure milk of the word,
Rev 9: 6 they will **d** to die, and death
Rev 11: 6 plagues, as often as they **d**

DESIRED (*see* DESIRE)
Ex 10:11 LORD, for that is what you **d**
Deut 18:16 according to all you **d** of the
Judg 13:23 If the LORD had **d** to kill us
1Sa 2:25 the LORD **d** to kill them
1Sa 12:13 chosen and whom you have **d**
1Ki 9:11 and gold, as much as he **d**)
1Ki 9:19 whatever Solomon **d** to build
1Ki 10:13 the queen of Sheba all she **d**
2Ch 8: 6 all that Solomon **d** to build
2Ch 9:12 the queen of Sheba all she **d**
Esth 2:13 **d** to take with her from the
Ps 19:10 More to be **d** are they than
Ps 27: 4 thing I have **d** of the LORD
Ps 107:30 guides them to their **d** haven
Ps 132:13 He has **d** it for His
Ps 132:14 I will dwell, for I have **d** it
Prov 19:22 What is **d** in a man is
Eccl 2:10 Whatever my eyes **d** I did not
Is 1:29 trees which you have **d**
Is 26: 9 I have **d** You in the night
Jer 17:16 nor have I **d** the woeful day
Matt 13:17 righteous men **d** to see what
Luke 10:24 kings have **d** to see what you
Luke 22:15 **d** to eat this Passover with
Luke 23: 8 for he had **d** for a long time
John 16:19 knew that they **d** to ask Him
Acts 18:27 when he **d** to cross to Achaia,
Gal 2:10 They **d** only that we should

DESIRES (*see* DESIRE)
Deut 12:15 gates, whatever your heart **d**
Deut 12:20 as much meat as your heart **d**
Deut 12:21 gates as much as your heart **d**
Deut 14:26 for whatever your heart **d**
Deut 14:26 for whatever your heart **d**
1Sa 2:16 take as much as your heart **d**
2Sa 3:21 over all that your heart **d**
1Ki 11:37 reign over all your heart **d**
Job 7: 2 who earnestly **d** the shade
Job 20:20 will not save anything he **d**
Job 23:13 And whatever His soul **d**, that
Ps 34:12 Who is the man who **d** life
Ps 37: 4 give you the **d** of your heart
Ps 68:16 which God **d** to dwell in
Ps 140: 8 O LORD, the **d** of the wicked
Prov 13: 4 the soul of a sluggard **d**, and
Prov 21:10 The soul of the wicked **d** evil
Eccl 6: 2 for himself of all he **d**
Mic 7: 1 fruit which my soul **d**
Matt 16:24 If anyone **d** to come after Me,
Matt 16:25 For whoever **d** to save his
Matt 20:26 but whoever **d** to become great
Matt 20:27 whoever **d** to be first among
Mark 4:19 and the **d** for other things
Mark 8:34 Whoever **d** to come after Me,
Mark 8:35 For whoever **d** to save his
Mark 9:35 If anyone **d** to be first, he
Mark 10:43 but whoever **d** to become great
Mark 10:44 whoever of you **d** to be first
Luke 5:39 old wine, immediately **d** new
Luke 9:23 If anyone **d** to come after Me,
Luke 9:24 For whoever **d** to save his
John 8:44 the **d** of your father you want
Gal 5:24 flesh with its passions and **d**
Eph 2: 3 fulfilling the **d** of the flesh
1Ti 2: 4 who **d** all men to be saved and
1Ti 3: 1 If a man **d** the position of a
1Ti 3: 1 of a bishop, he **d** a good work
2Ti 4: 3 but according to their own **d**
Jas 1:14 he is drawn away by his own **d**
Jas 3: 4 rudder wherever the pilot **d**
Jas 4: 1 **d** for pleasure that war in
Rev 22:17 And whoever **d**, let him take

DESIRING (*see* DESIRE)
Luke 8:20 outside, **d** to see You
Luke 16:21 **d** to be fed with the crumbs
2Co 5: 2 earnestly **d** to be clothed
2Co 8:10 and were **d** to do a year ago
2Co 11:32 a garrison, **d** to apprehend me
1Th 3: 6 greatly **d** to see us, as we
1Ti 1: 7 **d** to be teachers of the law,
2Ti 1: 4 greatly **d** to see you, being
Heb 13:18 in all things **d** to live

DESISTED
Jer 41: 8 So he **d** and did not kill

DESOLATE (*see* DESOLATED, DESOLATION)
Gen 47:19 that the land may not be **d**
Ex 23:29 year, lest the land become **d**
Lev 26:22 and your highways shall be **d**
Lev 26:33 your land shall be **d** and your
Lev 26:34 sabbaths as long as it lies **d**
Lev 26:35 as it lies **d** it shall rest
Lev 26:43 while it lies **d** without them
Num 23: 3 So he went to a **d** height
2Sa 13:20 So Tamar remained **d** in her
2Ch 36:21 as she lay **d** she kept Sabbath
Job 15:28 He dwells in **d** cities, in
Job 16: 7 you have made **d** all my
Job 30: 3 late to the wilderness, **d**
Job 38:27 To satisfy the **d** waste, and
Ps 25:16 have mercy on me, For I am **d**
Ps 69:25 Let their habitation be **d**
Ps 107: 4 in the wilderness in a **d** way
Ps 109:10 also from their **d** places
Is 1: 7 Your country is **d**, your
Is 1: 7 and it is **d**, as overthrown by
Is 3:26 she being **d** shall sit on the
Is 5: 9 Truly, many houses shall be **d**
Is 6:11 a man, the land is utterly **d**
Is 7:19 will rest in the **d** valleys
Is 13: 9 anger, to lay the land **d**
Is 15: 6 waters of Nimrim will be **d**
Is 24: 6 those who dwell in it are **d**
Is 27:10 the fortified city will be **d**
Is 41:18 will open rivers in **d** heights
Is 49: 8 to inherit the **d** heritages
Is 49: 9 shall be on all **d** heights
Is 49:19 **d** places, and the land of your
Is 49:21 have lost my children and am **d**
Is 54: 1 are the children of the **d**
Is 54: 3 make the **d** cities inhabited
Is 59:10 are as dead men in **d** places
Is 62: 4 land any more be termed **D**
Jer 2:12 be very **d**," says the LORD
Jer 3: 2 up your eyes to the **d** heights
Jer 3:21 was heard on the **d** heights
Jer 4: 7 his place to make your land **d**
Jer 4:11 A dry wind of the **d** heights
Jer 4:27 The whole land shall be **d**
Jer 6: 8 lest I make you **d**, a land not
Jer 7:29 lamentation on the **d** heights
Jer 7:34 For the land shall be **d**
Jer 9:11 make the cities of Judah **d**
Jer 10:22 to make the cities of Judah **d**
Jer 10:25 him, and made his habitation **d**
Jer 12:10 portion a **d** wilderness
Jer 12:11 They have made it **d**
Jer 12:11 **d**, it mourns to Me
Jer 12:11 the whole land is made **d**,
Jer 12:12 have come on all the **d**
Jer 14: 6 stood in the **d** heights
Jer 18:16 to make their land **d** and a
Jer 19: 8 I will make this city **d** and a
Jer 25:38 for their land is **d** because
Jer 26: 9 and this city shall be **d**,
Jer 32:43 It is **d**, without man or beast
Jer 33:10 It is **d**, without man and
Jer 33:10 of Jerusalem that are **d**,
Jer 33:12 In this place which is **d**,
Jer 44: 6 and they are wasted and **d**, as
Jer 46:19 Noph shall be waste and be **d**
Jer 48: 9 for her cities shall be **d**
Jer 48:34 of Nimrim also shall be **d**
Jer 49: 2 It shall be a **d** mound, and her
Jer 49:20 their habitations **d** with them
Jer 50: 3 which shall make her land **d**
Jer 50:13 but she shall be wholly **d**
Jer 50:45 their habitation **d** with them
Jer 51:26 but you shall be **d** forever
Jer 51:41 become **d** among the nations
Jer 51:62 but it shall be **d** forever
Lam 1: 4 All her gates are **d**
Lam 1:13 He has made me **d** and faint all
Lam 1:16 My children are **d** because the
Lam 3:11 He has made me **d**
Lam 4: 5 are **d** in the streets
Lam 5:18 of Mount Zion which is **d**,
Ezek 6: 4 Then your altars shall be **d**
Ezek 6: 6 and the high places shall be **d**
Ezek 6: 6 may be laid waste and made **d**
Ezek 6:14 them and make the land **d**, yes,
Ezek 6:14 more **d** than the wilderness
Ezek 12:20 and the land shall become **d**
Ezek 14:15 make it so **d** that no man may
Ezek 14:16 and the land would be **d**
Ezek 15: 8 Thus I will make the land **d**
Ezek 19: 7 He knew their **d** places, and
Ezek 20:26 that I might make them **d**
Ezek 25: 3 land of Israel when it was **d**
Ezek 25:13 it, and make it **d** from Teman
Ezek 26:19 When I make you a **d** city
Ezek 26:20 in places **d** from antiquity,
Ezek 29: 9 land of Egypt shall become **d**
Ezek 29:10 of Egypt utterly waste and **d**
Ezek 29:12 Egypt **d** in the midst of the
Ezek 29:12 of the countries that are **d**
Ezek 29:12 cities shall be **d** forty years
Ezek 30: 7 They shall be **d** in the midst
Ezek 30: 7 the midst of the **d** countries
Ezek 30:14 I will make Pathros **d**, set
Ezek 32:15 I make the land of Egypt **d**
Ezek 33:28 I will make the land most **d**
Ezek 33:28 be so **d** that no one will pass
Ezek 33:29 most **d** because of all their
Ezek 35: 3 you, and make you most **d**
Ezek 35: 4 waste, and you shall be **d**
Ezek 35: 7 I will make Mount Seir most **d**
Ezek 35: 9 I will make you perpetually **d**
Ezek 35:12 Israel, saying, 'They are **d**
Ezek 35:14 rejoice when I make you **d**
Ezek 35:15 of the house of Israel was **d**
Ezek 35:15 you shall be **d**, O Mount Seir,
Ezek 36: 3 Because they made you **d** and
Ezek 36: 4 the **d** wastes, and the cities
Ezek 36:34 The **d** land shall be tilled
Ezek 36:34 **d** in the sight of all who
Ezek 36:35 This land that was **d** has
Ezek 36:35 and the wasted, **d**, and ruined
Ezek 36:36 places and planted what was **d**
Ezek 38: 8 Israel, which had long been **d**
Dan 9:17 on Your sanctuary, which is **d**
Dan 9:27 shall be one who makes **d**,
Dan 9:27 is poured out on the **d**
Hos 5: 9 Ephraim shall be **d** in the day
Joel 2: 3 and behind them a **d** wilderness
Joel 2:20 **d** land, with his face toward
Joel 3:19 Edom a **d** wilderness, because
Amos 7: 9 places of Isaac shall be **d**
Mic 1: 7 all her idols I will lay **d**
Mic 6:13 by making you **d** because of
Mic 7:13 Yet the land shall be **d**
Nah 2:10 She is empty, **d**, and waste
Zeph 2: 4 be forsaken, and Ashkelon **d**
Zeph 3: 6 I have made their streets **d**
Zech 7:14 the land became **d** after them
Zech 7:14 they made the pleasant land **d**
Mal 1: 4 return and build the **d** places
Matt 23:38 Your house is left to you **d**
Luke 13:35 Your house is left to you **d**
Acts 1:20 Let his habitation be **d**, and
Gal 4:27 for the **d** has many more
Rev 17:16 hate the harlot, make her **d**
Rev 18:19 For in one hour she is made **d**

DESOLATED (*see* DESOLATE)
Ezek 19: 7 land with its fullness was **d**

DESOLATION (*see* DESOLATE, DESOLATIONS)
Lev 26:31 bring your sanctuaries to **d**
Lev 26:32 I will bring the land to **d**
Josh 8:28 heap forever, a **d** to this day
2Ki 22:19 that they would become a **d**
Ps 73:19 Oh, how they are brought to **d**
Is 10: 3 in the **d** which will come from
Is 17: 9 and there will be **d**
Is 24:12 In the city **d** is left, and the
Is 47:11 And **d** shall come upon you
Is 51:19 **D** and destruction, famine and
Is 64:10 a wilderness, Jerusalem a **d**
Jer 22: 5 this house shall become a **d**
Jer 25:11 this whole land shall be a **d**
Jer 25:12 I will make it a perpetual **d**
Jer 25:18 its princes, to make them a **d**
Jer 34:22 Judah a **d** without inhabitant
Jer 44: 2 behold, this day they are a **d**
Jer 44:22 Therefore your land is a **d**
Jer 49:13 that Bozrah shall become a **d**
Jer 49:33 for jackals, a **d** forever
Jer 50:23 become a **d** among the nations
Jer 51:29 a **d** without inhabitant
Jer 51:43 Her cities are a **d**, a dry
Lam 3:47 a snare have come upon us, **d**
Ezek 7:27 prince will be clothed with **d**
Ezek 23:33 the cup of horror and **d**, The
Dan 8:13 and the transgression of **d**
Dan 11:31 there the abomination of **d**
Dan 12:11 abomination of **d** is set up
Hos 12: 1 He daily increases lies and **d**
Joel 3:19 Egypt shall be a **d**, and Edom a
Mic 6:16 that I may make you a **d**, and
Zeph 1:13 booty, and their houses a **d**
Zeph 1:15 a day of devastation and **d**
Zeph 2: 9 and saltpits, and a perpetual **d**
Zeph 2:13 Assyria, and make Nineveh a **d**
Zeph 2:14 **d** shall be at the threshold
Zeph 2:15 how has she become a **d**, a
Matt 12:25 itself is brought to **d**, and
Matt 24:15 you see the 'abomination of **d**
Mark 13:14 you see the 'abomination of **d**
Luke 11:17 itself is brought to **d**, and a
Luke 21:20 then know that its **d** is near

DESOLATIONS (*see* DESOLATION)
Ps 46: 8 Who has made **d** in the earth
Ps 74: 3 Your feet to the perpetual **d**
Is 61: 4 shall raise up the former **d**
Is 61: 4 the **d** of many generations
Jer 25: 9 a hissing, and perpetual **d**
Dan 9: 2 years in the **d** of Jerusalem
Dan 9:18 open Your eyes and see our **d**
Dan 9:26 of the war **d** are determined

DESPAIR (*see* DESPAIRED, DESPERATE)
1Sa 27: 1 and Saul will **d** of me, to seek
Jer 19: 9 lives shall drive them to **d**
2Co 4: 8 are perplexed, but not in **d**

DESPAIRED (*see* DESPAIR)
Eccl 2:20 **d** of all the labor in which I
2Co 1: 8 so that we **d** even of life

DESPERATE (*see* DESPAIR, DESPERATELY, DESPERATION)
Deut 28:53 **d** straits in which your enemy
Deut 28:55 **d** straits in which your enemy
Deut 28:57 **d** straits in which your enemy
Job 6:26 and the speeches of a **d** one
Is 17:11 the day of grief and **d** sorrow

DESPERATELY (*see* DESPERATE)
Job 27:22 he flees **d** from its power
Jer 17: 9 above all things, and **d** wicked

DESPERATION (*see* DESPERATE)
Jer 19: 9 in the **d** with which their

DESPISE (*see* DESPISED, DESPISERS, DESPISES, DESPISING)
Lev 26:15 if you **d** My statutes, or if
1Sa 2:30 and those who **d** Me shall be
2Sa 19:43 Why then do you **d** us
Esth 1:17 so that they will **d** their
Job 5:17 therefore do not **d** the
Job 9:21 I **d** my life
Job 10: 3 that You should **d** the work of
Job 19:18 Even young children **d** me
Ps 51:17 These, O God, You will not **d**
Ps 69:33 And does not **d** His prisoners
Ps 73:20 You shall **d** their image
Ps 102:17 And shall not **d** their prayer
Prov 1: 7 knowledge, but fools **d** wisdom
Prov 3:11 do not **d** the chastening of
Prov 6:30 People do not **d** a thief if he
Prov 23: 9 for he will **d** the wisdom of
Prov 23:22 do not **d** your mother when she
Is 30:12 Because you **d** this word, and
Jer 4:30 your lovers will **d** you
Jer 23:17 say to those who **d** Me, 'The
Lam 1: 8 All who honored her **d** her
Ezek 16:57 who **d** you everywhere
Ezek 28:24 are around them, who **d** them
Ezek 28:26 those around them who **d** them
Amos 5:21 I **d** your feast days, and I do
Mal 1: 6 to you priests who **d** My name
Matt 6:24 to the one and **d** the other
Matt 18:10 **d** one of these little ones
Luke 16:13 to the one and **d** the other
Rom 2: 4 Or do you **d** the riches of His
Rom 14: 3 eats **d** him who does not eat
1Co 11:22 Or do you **d** the church of God
1Co 16:11 Therefore let no one **d** him
Gal 4:14 flesh you did not **d** or reject
1Th 5:20 Do not **d** prophecies
1Ti 4:12 Let no one **d** your youth, but
1Ti 6: 2 let them not **d** them because
Tit 2:15 Let no one **d** you
Heb 12: 5 do not **d** the chastening of
2Pe 2:10 of uncleanness and **d** authority

DESPISED (*see* DESPISE)
Gen 16: 4 mistress became **d** in her eyes
Gen 16: 5 I became **d** in her eyes
Gen 25:34 Thus Esau **d** his birthright
Lev 26:43 because they **d** My judgments
Num 11:20 because you have **d** the LORD
Num 14:31 the land which you have **d**
Num 15:31 Because he has **d** the word of
Judg 9:38 these the people whom you **d**
1Sa 10:27 So they **d** him, and brought
1Sa 15: 9 But everything **d** and worthless
2Sa 6:16 and she **d** him in her heart
2Sa 12: 9 Why have you **d** the
2Sa 12:10 house, because you have **d** Me
2Ki 19:21 daughter of Zion, has **d** you
1Ch 15:29 and she **d** him in her heart
2Ch 36:16 **d** His words, and scoffed at
Neh 2:19 us to scorn and **d** us, and said,
Neh 4: 4 Hear, O our God, for we are **d**
Job 12: 5 A lamp is **d** in the thought of
Job 31:13 If I have **d** the cause of my
Ps 15: 4 whose eyes a vile person is **d**
Ps 22: 6 of men, and **d** of the people
Ps 22:24 For He has not **d** nor abhorred
Ps 53: 5 shame, Because God has **d** them
Ps 106:24 Then they **d** the pleasant land
Ps 107:11 **d** the counsel of the Most
Ps 119:141 I am small and **d**, Yet I do not
Prov 1:30 counsel and **d** all my reproof,
Prov 5:12 And my heart **d** reproof
Prov 12: 8 of a perverse heart will be **d**
Eccl 9:16 the poor man's wisdom is **d**
Song 8: 1 I would not be **d**
Song 8: 7 house, it would be utterly **d**
Is 5:24 **d** the word of the Holy One of
Is 16:14 will be **d** with all that great
Is 33: 8 He has **d** the cities, He
Is 37:22 daughter of Zion, has **d** you
Is 53: 3 He is **d** and rejected by men, a
Is 53: 3 He was **d**, and we did not
Is 60:14 all those who **d** you shall
Jer 22:28 Is this man Coniah a **d**,
Jer 33:24 Thus they have **d** My people
Jer 49:15 among nations, **d** among men
Ezek 16:59 who **d** the oath by breaking
Ezek 17:16 him king, whose oath he **d**
Ezek 17:18 Since he **d** the oath by
Ezek 17:19 surely My oath which he **d**
Ezek 20:13 they **d** My judgments, which,
Ezek 20:16 because they **d** My judgments
Ezek 20:24 but had **d** My statutes,
Ezek 22: 8 You have **d** My holy things and
Amos 2: 4 because they have **d** the law
Obad 2 you shall be greatly **d**
Zech 4:10 For who has **d** the day of
Mal 1: 6 what way have we **d** Your name
Luke 18: 9 were righteous, and **d** others
Acts 19:27 great goddess Diana may be **d**
1Co 1:28 which are **d** God has chosen

DESPISERS (*see* DESPISE)
Acts 13:41 Behold, you **d**, marvel and
2Ti 3: 3 brutal, **d** of good,

DESPISES (*see* DESPISE)
Job 36: 5 God is mighty, but **d** no one
Prov 11:12 of wisdom **d** his neighbor, but
Prov 13:13 He who **d** the word will be
Prov 14: 2 is perverse in his ways **d** Him
Prov 14:21 He who **d** his neighbor sins
Prov 15: 5 A fool **d** his father's
Prov 15:20 a foolish man **d** his mother
Prov 15:32 instruction **d** his own soul
Is 33:15 he who **d** the gain of
Is 49: 7 Holy One, to Him whom man **d**
Ezek 21:10 it **d** the scepter of My son,
Ezek 21:13 the sword **d** even the scepter

DESPISING (*see* DESPISE)
Heb 12: 2 **d** the shame, and has sat down

DESPITE
1Sa 2:32 **d** all the good which God does
Ezek 32:29 who **d** their might are laid
Zeph 3: 7 off, **d** everything for which I

DESPOILED
Judg 2:14 of plunderers who **d** them

DESTINED (*see* DESTINY)
Job 15:28 which are **d** to become ruins
Luke 2:34 this Child is **d** for the fall

DESTINY (*see* DESTINED)
Lam 1: 9 she did not consider her **d**

DESTITUTE
Ps 102:17 regard the prayer of the **d**
Ps 141: 8 Do not leave my soul **d**
Prov 15:21 him who is **d** of discernment
Ezek 32:15 the country is **d** of all that
1Ti 6: 5 **d** of the truth, who suppose
Heb 11:37 and goatskins, being **d**,
Jas 2:15 is naked and **d** of daily food,

DESTROY (*see* DESTROYED, DESTROYER, DESTROYING, DESTROYS, DESTRUCTION, DESTRUCTIVE)
Gen 6: 7 I will **d** man whom I have
Gen 6:13 I will **d** them with the earth
Gen 6:17 to **d** from under heaven all
Gen 7: 4 I will **d** from the face of the
Gen 8:21 nor will I again **d** every
Gen 9:11 be a flood to **d** the earth
Gen 9:15 become a flood to **d** all flesh
Gen 18:23 said, "Would You also **d** the
Gen 18:24 would You also **d** the place
Gen 18:28 would You **d** all of the city
Gen 18:28 forty-five, I will not **d** it
Gen 18:31 I will not **d** it for the sake
Gen 18:32 I will not **d** it for the sake
Gen 19:13 For we will **d** this place,
Gen 19:13 the LORD has sent us to **d** it
Gen 19:14 for the LORD will **d** this city
Ex 8: 9 to **d** the frogs from you and
Ex 12:13 shall not be on you to **d** you
Ex 15: 9 sword, my hand shall **d** them
Ex 34:13 But you shall **d** their altars
Lev 23:30 that person I will **d** from
Lev 26:22 **d** your livestock, and make you
Lev 26:30 I will **d** your high places,
Lev 26:44 abhor them, to utterly **d** them
Num 21: 2 I will utterly **d** their cities
Num 24:17 and **d** all the sons of tumult
Num 24:19 **d** the remains of the city
Num 32:15 you will **d** all these people
Num 33:52 **d** all their engraved stones,
Num 33:52 **d** all their molded images, and
Deut 1:27 hand of the Amorites, to **d** us
Deut 2:15 to **d** them from the midst of
Deut 4:31 not forsake you nor **d** you
Deut 6:15 **d** you from the face of the
Deut 7: 2 them and utterly **d** them
Deut 7: 4 against you and **d** you suddenly
Deut 7: 5 you shall **d** their altars, and
Deut 7:10 Him to their face, to **d** them
Deut 7:16 you shall **d** all the peoples
Deut 7:22 be unable to **d** them at once
Deut 7:24 you will **d** their name from
Deut 9: 3 He will **d** them and bring them
Deut 9: 3 **d** them quickly, as the LORD
Deut 9:14 Me alone, that I may **d** them
Deut 9:19 was angry with you, to **d** you
Deut 9:25 LORD had said He would **d** you
Deut 9:26 do not **d** Your people and Your
Deut 10:10 the LORD chose not to **d** you
Deut 12: 2 You shall utterly **d** all the
Deut 12: 3 you shall **d** their altars,
Deut 12: 3 **d** their names from that place
Deut 20:17 but you shall utterly **d** them
Deut 20:19 you shall not **d** its trees by
Deut 20:20 not trees for food you may **d**
Deut 28:63 rejoice over you to **d** you
Deut 31: 3 He will **d** these nations from
Deut 32:25 The sword shall **d** outside
Deut 33:27 before you, and will say, '**D**
Josh 7: 7 hand of the Amorites, to **d** us
Josh 7:12 unless you **d** the accursed
Josh 9:24 to **d** all the inhabitants of
Josh 11:20 that He might utterly **d** them
Josh 11:20 but that He might **d** them
Josh 22:33 to **d** the land where the
Judg 6: 4 **d** the produce of the earth as
Judg 6: 5 would enter the land to **d** it
Judg 21:11 shall utterly **d** every male
1Sa 15: 3 utterly **d** all that they have,
1Sa 15: 6 lest I **d** you with them
1Sa 15: 9 unwilling to utterly **d** them
1Sa 15:18 utterly **d** the sinners, the
1Sa 23:10 to **d** the city for my sake
1Sa 24:21 that you will not **d** my name
1Sa 26: 9 Do not **d** him
1Sa 26:15 in to **d** your lord the king
2Sa 1:14 hand to **d** the LORD's anointed
2Sa 14: 7 and we will **d** the heir also
2Sa 14:11 avenger of blood to **d** anymore
2Sa 14:11 anymore, lest they **d** my son
2Sa 14:16 of the man who would **d** me
2Sa 20:19 You seek to **d** a city and a
2Sa 20:20 that I should swallow up or **d**
2Sa 24:16 hand over Jerusalem to **d** it
1Ki 9:21 not been able to **d** completely
1Ki 13:34 **d** it from the face of the
2Ki 8:19 the LORD would not **d** Judah
2Ki 13:23 would not yet **d** them or cast
2Ki 18:25 against this place to **d** it
2Ki 18:25 up against this land, and **d** it
2Ki 24: 2 them against Judah to **d** it
1Ch 21:15 an angel to Jerusalem to **d** it
2Ch 8: 8 children of Israel did not **d**)
2Ch 12: 7 therefore I will not **d** them
2Ch 12:12 so as not to **d** him completely
2Ch 20:10 from them and did not **d** them
2Ch 20:23 to utterly kill and **d** them
2Ch 20:23 they helped to **d** one another
2Ch 21: 7 not **d** the house of David,
2Ch 25:16 God has determined to **d** you
2Ch 35:21 who is with me, lest He **d** you
Ezra 6:12 His name to dwell there **d** any
Ezra 6:12 or to **d** this house of God
Esth 3: 6 Haman sought to **d** all the
Esth 3:13 the king's provinces, to **d**
Esth 4: 7 treasuries to **d** the Jews
Esth 8:11 to **d**, kill, and annihilate all
Esth 9:24 to consume them and **d** them
Job 2: 3 him, to **d** him without cause

Job 10: 8 yet You would **d** me
Job 14:19 so You **d** the hope of man
Ps 5: 6 You shall **d** those who speak
Ps 21:10 You shall **d** from the earth
Ps 28: 5 of His hands, He shall **d** them
Ps 40:14 Who seek to **d** my life
Ps 52: 5 shall likewise **d** you forever
Ps 55: 9 **D**, O Lord, and divide their
Ps 63: 9 who seek my life, to **d** it
Ps 69: 4 are mighty who would **d** me
Ps 74: 8 Let us **d** them altogether
Ps 74:11 out of Your bosom and **d** them
Ps 78:38 iniquity, And did not **d** them
Ps 101: 5 his neighbor, Him I will **d**
Ps 101: 8 Early I will **d** all the wicked
Ps 106:23 He said that He would **d** them
Ps 106:23 His wrath, lest He **d** them
Ps 106:34 They did not **d** the peoples
Ps 118:10 of the LORD I will **d** them
Ps 118:11 of the LORD I will **d** them
Ps 118:12 of the LORD I will **d** them
Ps 119:95 wicked wait for me to **d** me
Ps 143:12 **d** all those who afflict my
Ps 144: 6 out Your arrows and **d** them
Ps 145:20 But all the wicked He will **d**
Prov 1:32 of fools will **d** them
Prov 11: 3 of the unfaithful will **d** them
Prov 15:25 The LORD will **d** the house of
Prov 21: 7 of the wicked will **d** them
Eccl 5: 6 and **d** the work of your hands
Eccl 7:16 why should you **d** yourself
Is 3:12 and **d** the way of your paths
Is 10: 7 but it is in his heart to **d**
Is 11: 9 nor **d** in all My holy mountain
Is 11:15 The LORD will utterly **d** the
Is 13: 5 to **d** the whole land
Is 13: 9 He will **d** its sinners from it
Is 19: 3 I will **d** their counsel, and
Is 23:11 Canaan to **d** its strongholds
Is 25: 7 He will **d** on this mountain
Is 32: 7 **d** the poor with lying words
Is 36:10 against this land to **d** it
Is 36:10 up against this land, and **d** it
Is 51:13 when he has prepared to **d**
Is 54:16 have created the spoiler to **d**
Is 65: 8 and one says, 'Do not **d** it
Is 65: 8 that I may not **d** them all
Is 65:25 nor **d** in all My holy mountain
Jer 1:10 out and to pull down, to **d**
Jer 5: 6 of the deserts shall **d** them
Jer 5:10 Go up on her walls and **d**, but
Jer 5:17 they shall **d** your fortified
Jer 6: 5 and let us **d** her palaces
Jer 11:19 Let us **d** the tree with its
Jer 12:17 **d** that nation," says the
Jer 13:14 have mercy, but will **d** them
Jer 15: 3 of the earth to devour and **d**
Jer 15: 6 My hand against you and **d** you
Jer 15: 7 I will **d** My people, since
Jer 17:18 doom, and **d** them with double
Jer 18: 7 up, to pull down, and to **d** it
Jer 23: 1 Woe to the shepherds who **d**
Jer 25: 9 and will utterly **d** them, and
Jer 31:28 down, to throw down, to **d**
Jer 36:29 **d** this land, and cause man and
Jer 46: 8 I will **d** the city and its
Jer 49: 9 would they not **d** until they
Jer 49:38 will **d** from there the king and
Jer 50:21 Waste and utterly **d** them,"
Jer 50:26 of ruins, and **d** her utterly
Jer 51: 3 utterly **d** all her army
Jer 51:11 is against Babylon to **d** it
Jer 51:20 with you I will **d** kingdoms
Lam 2: 8 The LORD has purposed to **d**
Lam 3:66 **d** them from under the heavens
Ezek 5:16 and which I will send to **d** you
Ezek 6: 3 I will **d** your high places
Ezek 9: 8 Will You **d** all the remnant of
Ezek 14: 9 **d** him from among My people
Ezek 21:31 men who are skillful to **d**
Ezek 22:27 blood, to **d** people, and to get
Ezek 22:30 land, that I should not **d** it
Ezek 25: 7 I will **d** you, and you shall
Ezek 25:15 to **d** because of the old
Ezek 25:16 **d** the remnant of the seacoast
Ezek 26: 4 they shall **d** the walls of
Ezek 26:12 and **d** your pleasant houses
Ezek 30:11 be brought to **d** the land
Ezek 30:13 I will also **d** the idols, and
Ezek 32:13 Also I will **d** all its beasts
Ezek 34:16 but I will **d** the fat and the
Ezek 43: 3 saw when I came to **d** the city
Dan 2:12 gave a command to **d** all the
Dan 2:24 to **d** the wise men of Babylon
Dan 2:24 Do not **d** the wise men of
Dan 4:23 **d** it, but leave its stump and
Dan 7:26 to consume and **d** it forever
Dan 8:24 he shall **d** fearfully, and
Dan 8:24 he shall **d** the mighty, and
Dan 8:25 He shall **d** many in their
Dan 9:26 is to come shall **d** the city
Dan 11:17 the daughter of women to **d** it
Dan 11:26 of his delicacies shall **d** him
Dan 11:44 go out with great fury to **d**
Hos 2:12 I will **d** her vines and her fig
Hos 4: 5 and I will **d** your mother
Hos 11: 9 I will not again **d** Ephraim
Amos 3:15 I will **d** the winter house
Amos 9: 8 I will **d** it from the face of
Amos 9: 8 utterly **d** the house of Jacob
Obad 8 Even **d** the wise men from Edom
Mic 2:10 it is defiled, it shall **d** you
Mic 5:10 your midst and **d** your chariots
Mic 5:14 thus I will **d** your cities
Zeph 2: 5 I will **d** you
Zeph 2:13 **d** Assyria, and make Nineveh a
Hag 2:22 I will **d** the strength of the
Zech 9: 4 He will **d** her power in the
Zech 12: 9 day that I will seek to **d** all
Mal 3:11 so that he will not **d** the
Matt 2:13 seek the young Child to **d** Him
Matt 5:17 to **d** the Law or the Prophets
Matt 5:17 not come to **d** but to fulfill
Matt 6:19 earth, where moth and rust **d**
Matt 10:28 who is able to **d** both soul
Matt 12:14 Him, how they might **d** Him
Matt 21:41 He will **d** those wicked men
Matt 26:61 I am able to **d** the temple of
Matt 27:20 ask for Barabbas and **d** Jesus
Matt 27:40 You who **d** the temple and build
Mark 1:24 Did You come to **d** us
Mark 3: 6 Him, how they might **d** Him
Mark 9:22 and into the water to **d** him
Mark 11:18 sought how they might **d** Him
Mark 12: 9 **d** the vinedressers, and give
Mark 14:58 I will **d** this temple that is
Mark 15:29 You who **d** the temple and build
Luke 4:34 Did You come to **d** us
Luke 6: 9 evil, to save life or to **d** it
Luke 9:56 to **d** men's lives but to save
Luke 19:47 of the people sought to **d** Him
Luke 20:16 **d** those vinedressers and give
John 2:19 **D** this temple, and in three
John 10:10 to steal, and to kill, and to **d**
Acts 6:14 of Nazareth will **d** this place
Rom 14:15 Do not **d** with your food the
Rom 14:20 Do not **d** the work of God for
1Co 1:19 I will **d** the wisdom of the
1Co 3:17 temple of God, God will **d** him
1Co 6:13 foods, but God will **d** both it
Gal 1:13 measure and tried to **d** it
Gal 1:23 which he once tried to **d**
2Th 2: 8 **d** with the brightness of His
Heb 2:14 **d** him who had the power of
Jas 4:12 who is able to save and to **d**
1Jn 3: 8 that He might **d** the works of
Rev 11:18 **d** those who **d** the earth

DESTROYED (*see* DESTROY)
Gen 7:23 So He **d** all living things
Gen 7:23 They were **d** from the earth
Gen 13:10 (before the LORD **d** Sodom and
Gen 19:17 the mountains, lest you be **d**
Gen 19:29 when God **d** the cities of the
Gen 34:30 I shall be **d**, my household and
Ex 10: 7 not yet know that Egypt is **d**
Ex 22:20 only, he shall be utterly **d**
Num 21: 3 and they utterly **d** them and
Deut 2:12 **d** them from before them, and
Deut 2:21 But the LORD **d** them before
Deut 2:22 when He **d** the Horites from
Deut 2:23 **d** them and dwelt in their
Deut 2:34 time, and we utterly **d** the men
Deut 3: 6 And we utterly **d** them, as we
Deut 4: 3 for the LORD your God has **d**
Deut 4:26 in it, but will be utterly **d**
Deut 7:20 themselves from you, are **d**
Deut 7:23 upon them until they are **d**
Deut 7:24 you until you have **d** them
Deut 9: 8 enough with you to have **d** you
Deut 9:20 Aaron and would have **d** him
Deut 11: 4 LORD has **d** them to this day
Deut 12:30 after they are **d** from before
Deut 28:20 hand to do, until you are **d**
Deut 28:24 down on you until you are **d**
Deut 28:45 overtake you, until you are **d**
Deut 28:48 your neck until He has **d** you
Deut 28:51 of your land, until you are **d**
Deut 28:51 flocks, until they have **d** you
Deut 28:61 upon you until you are **d**
Deut 31: 4 and their land, when He **d** them
Josh 2:10 and Og, whom you utterly **d**
Josh 6:21 they utterly **d** all that was
Josh 8:26 until he had utterly **d** all
Josh 10: 1 taken Ai and had utterly **d** it
Josh 10:28 He utterly **d** them
Josh 10:35 in it he utterly **d** that day
Josh 10:37 to Eglon, but utterly **d** it
Josh 10:39 utterly **d** all the people who
Josh 10:40 but utterly **d** all that
Josh 11:12 He utterly **d** them, as Moses
Josh 11:14 sword until they had **d** them
Josh 11:21 Joshua utterly **d** them with
Josh 23:15 until He has **d** you from this
Josh 24: 8 and I **d** them from before you
Judg 1:17 Zephath, and utterly **d** it
Judg 4:24 until they had **d** Jabin king
Judg 20:35 Israel **d** that day twenty-five
Judg 20:42 cities they **d** in their midst
Judg 21:16 of Benjamin have been **d**
Judg 21:17 may not be **d** from Israel
1Sa 15: 8 utterly **d** all the people with
1Sa 15: 9 that they utterly **d**
1Sa 15:15 and the rest we have utterly **d**
1Sa 15:20 have utterly **d** the Amalekites
1Sa 15:21 should have been utterly **d**
2Sa 11: 1 they **d** the people of Ammon
2Sa 21: 5 us, that we should be **d** from
2Sa 22:38 pursued my enemies and **d** them
2Sa 22:38 back again till they were **d**
2Sa 22:39 And I have **d** them and wounded
2Sa 22:41 so that I **d** those who hated
1Ki 15:29 breathed, until he had **d** him
1Ki 16:12 Thus Zimri **d** all the
1Ki 22:11 the Syrians until they are **d**
2Ki 3:25 Then they **d** the cities, and
2Ki 10:17 Samaria, till he had **d** them
2Ki 10:28 Thus Jehu **d** Baal from Israel
2Ki 11: 1 and **d** all the royal heirs
2Ki 13: 7 the king of Syria had **d** them
2Ki 13:17 at Aphek till you have **d** them
2Ki 13:19 Syria till you had **d** it
2Ki 19:12 those whom my fathers have **d**
2Ki 19:18 Therefore they have **d** them
2Ki 21: 3 Hezekiah his father had **d**
2Ki 21: 9 had **d** before the children of
1Ch 4:41 there, and utterly **d** them, as
1Ch 5:25 whom God had **d** before them
2Ch 15: 6 So nation was **d** by nation
2Ch 18:10 the Syrians until they are **d**
2Ch 20:37 the LORD has **d** your works
2Ch 22:10 **d** all the royal heirs of the
2Ch 24:23 and **d** all the leaders of the
2Ch 31: 1 they had utterly **d** them all
2Ch 32:14 **d** that could deliver his
2Ch 33: 9 had **d** before the children of
2Ch 34:11 the kings of Judah had **d**
2Ch 36:19 fire, and **d** all its precious
Ezra 4:15 which cause this city was **d**
Ezra 5:12 who **d** this temple and carried
Esth 3: 9 be written that they be **d**
Esth 7: 4 sold, my people and I, to be **d**
Esth 9: 6 killed and **d** five hundred men
Esth 9:12 **d** five hundred men in Shushan
Job 8:18 If he is **d** from his place,
Job 19:26 and after my skin is **d**, this I
Ps 9: 5 You have **d** the wicked
Ps 9: 6 And you have **d** cities
Ps 11: 3 If the foundations are **d**,
Ps 18:37 back again till they were **d**
Ps 18:40 So that I **d** those who hated
Ps 37:38 shall be **d** together
Ps 73:27 You have **d** all those who
Ps 78:45 them, And frogs, which **d** them
Ps 78:47 He **d** their vines with hail,
Ps 78:51 **d** all the firstborn in Egypt,
Ps 92: 7 is that they may be **d** forever
Ps 105:16 He **d** all the provision of
Ps 105:36 He also **d** all the firstborn
Ps 135: 8 He **d** the firstborn of Egypt,
Ps 137: 8 of Babylon, who are to be **d**

Prov 13:13 despises the word will be **d**
Prov 13:20 companion of fools will be **d**
Prov 29: 1 his neck, will suddenly be **d**
Is 9:16 who are led by them are **d**
Is 10:27 the yoke will be **d** because of
Is 14:17 **d** its cities, who did not
Is 14:20 because you have **d** your land
Is 15: 1 Ar of Moab is laid waste and **d**
Is 15: 1 of Moab is laid waste and **d**
Is 26:14 **d** them, and made all their
Is 34: 2 He has utterly **d** them, He has
Is 37:12 those whom my fathers have **d**
Is 37:19 Therefore they have **d** them
Is 48:19 cut off nor **d** from before Me
Jer 12:10 rulers have **d** My vineyard
Jer 22:20 for all your lovers are **d**
Jer 48: 4 Moab is **d**
Jer 48: 8 and the plain shall be **d**, as
Jer 48:18 he has **d** your strongholds
Jer 48:42 Moab shall be **d** as a people
Jer 51: 8 has suddenly fallen and been **d**
Lam 2: 5 He has **d** her strongholds, and
Lam 2: 6 He has **d** His place of
Lam 2: 9 He has **d** and broken her bars
Lam 2:22 brought up my enemies have **d**
Ezek 27:32 **d** in the midst of the sea
Ezek 28:16 I **d** you, O covering cherub,
Ezek 30: 8 and all her helpers are **d**
Ezek 32:12 all its multitude shall be **d**
Dan 2:44 which shall never be **d**
Dan 6:26 the one which shall not be **d**
Dan 7:11 was slain, and its body **d** and
Dan 7:14 the one which shall not be **d**
Dan 11:20 a few days he shall be **d**, but
Hos 4: 6 My people are **d** for lack of
Hos 10: 8 the sin of Israel, shall be **d**
Hos 13: 9 O Israel, you are **d**, but your
Amos 2: 9 Yet it was I who **d** the
Amos 2: 9 yet I **d** his fruit above and
Mic 2: 4 We are utterly **d**
Zeph 3: 6 their cities are **d**
Matt 22: 7 **d** those murderers, and burned
Luke 9:25 and is himself **d** or lost
Luke 17:27 the flood came and **d** them all
Luke 17:29 from heaven and **d** them all
Acts 3:23 **d** from among the people
Acts 9:21 Is this not he who **d** those
Acts 13:19 when He had **d** seven nations
Acts 19:27 and her magnificence **d**, whom
1Co 10: 9 and were **d** by serpents
1Co 10:10 and were **d** by the destroyer
1Co 15:26 enemy that will be **d** is death
2Co 4: 9 struck down, but not **d**
2Co 5: 1 house, this tent, is **d**, we
Gal 2:18 again those things which I **d**
Heb 11:28 lest he who **d** the firstborn
2Pe 2:12 beasts made to be caught and **d**
Jude 5 afterward **d** those who did not
Rev 8: 9 a third of the ships were **d**

DESTROYER (*see* DESTROY, DESTROYERS)
Ex 12:23 not allow the **d** to come into
Judg 16:24 the **d** of our land, and the one
Job 15:21 the **d** comes upon him
Ps 17: 4 from the paths of the **d**
Prov 18: 9 to him who is a great **d**
Prov 28:24 the same is companion to a **d**
Jer 4: 7 the **d** of nations is on his
1Co 10:10 and were destroyed by the **d**

DESTROYERS (*see* DESTROYER)
Is 49:17 your **d** and those who laid you
Jer 22: 7 I will prepare **d** against you
Jer 50:11 you **d** of My heritage, because

DESTROYING (*see* DESTROY)
Lev 11:22 the **d** locust after its kind,
Deut 3: 6 of Heshbon, utterly **d** the men
Deut 13:15 utterly **d** it, all that is in
Josh 11:11 of the sword, utterly **d** them
2Sa 24:16 angel who was **d** the people
2Ki 10:19 with the intent of **d** the
2Ki 19:11 all lands by utterly **d** them
1Ch 21:12 the LORD **d** throughout all the
1Ch 21:15 As he was **d**, the LORD looked
1Ch 21:15 said to the angel who was **d**
Is 28: 2 a **d** storm, like a flood of
Is 37:11 all lands by utterly **d** them
Jer 2:30 your prophets like a **d** lion
Jer 51: 1 dwell in Leb Kamai, a **d** wind
Jer 51:25 O **d** mountain, who destroys
Lam 2: 8 not withdrawn His hand from **d**

DESTROYS (*see* DESTROY)
Ex 21:26 **d** it, he shall let him go
Deut 8:20 which the LORD **d** before you
Job 9:22 He **d** the blameless and the
Job 12:23 nations great, and **d** them
Job 30:24 if they cry out when He **d** it
Prov 6:32 he who does so **d** his own soul
Prov 11: 9 with his mouth **d** his neighbor
Prov 31: 3 ways to that which **d** kings
Eccl 7: 7 Surely oppression **d** a wise
Eccl 9:18 but one sinner **d** much good
Jer 51:25 who **d** all the earth," says
Matt 6:20 where neither moth nor rust **d**
Luke 12:33 thief approaches nor moth **d**

DESTRUCTION (*see* DESTROY, DESTRUCTIONS)
Lev 27:29 become doomed to **d** among
Deut 7:26 you be doomed to **d** like it
Deut 32:24 by pestilence and bitter **d**
Josh 6:17 be doomed by the LORD to **d**
Josh 7:12 they have become doomed to **d**
1Sa 5: 9 the city with a very great **d**
1Sa 5:11 **d** throughout all the city
2Sa 24:16 the LORD relented from the **d**
1Ki 20:42 whom I appointed to utter **d**
2Ch 22: 4 death of his father, to his **d**
2Ch 26:16 heart was lifted up, to his **d**
Esth 4: 8 written decree for their **d**
Esth 8: 6 to see the **d** of my kindred
Esth 9: 5 sword, with slaughter and **d**
Job 5:21 be afraid of **d** when it comes
Job 5:22 You shall laugh at **d** and
Job 18:12 and **d** is ready at his side
Job 21:17 does their **d** come upon them
Job 21:20 Let his eyes see his **d**, and
Job 26: 6 Him, and **D** has no covering
Job 28:22 **D** and Death say, 'We have
Job 30:12 against me their ways of **d**
Job 31: 3 Is it not **d** for the wicked,
Job 31:12 be a fire that consumes to **d**
Job 31:23 For **d** from God is a terror to
Job 31:29 at the **d** of him who hated me
Ps 5: 9 Their inward part is **d**
Ps 35: 8 Let **d** come upon him
Ps 35: 8 Into that very **d** let him fall
Ps 38:12 who seek my hurt speak of **d**
Ps 52: 2 Your tongue devises **d**, Like a
Ps 55:11 **D** is in its midst
Ps 55:23 them down to the pit of **d**
Ps 73:18 You cast them down to **d**
Ps 78:49 angels of **d** among them
Ps 88:11 in the place of **d**
Ps 90: 3 You turn man to **d**, And say
Ps 91: 6 Nor of the **d** that lays waste
Ps 103: 4 Who redeems your life from **d**
Prov 1:27 your **d** comes like a whirlwind
Prov 10:14 of the foolish is near **d**
Prov 10:15 the **d** of the poor is their
Prov 10:29 but **d** will come to the
Prov 13: 3 wide his lips shall have **d**
Prov 15:11 Hell and **D** are before the LORD
Prov 16:18 Pride goes before **d**, and a
Prov 17:19 who exalts his gate seeks **d**
Prov 18: 7 A fool's mouth is his **d**, and
Prov 18:12 Before **d** the heart of a man
Prov 19:18 not set your heart on his **d**
Prov 21:15 but **d** will come to the
Prov 27:20 Hell and **D** are never full
Is 1:28 The **d** of transgressors and of
Is 10:22 the **d** decreed shall overflow
Is 10:25 as will My anger in their **d**
Is 13: 6 It will come as **d** from the
Is 14:23 sweep it with the broom of **d**
Is 15: 5 they will raise up a cry of **d**
Is 19:18 will be called the City of **D**
Is 24:12 the gate is stricken with **d**
Is 28:22 a **d** determined even upon the
Is 49:19 places, and the land of your **d**
Is 51:19 Desolation and **d**, famine and
Is 59: 7 and **d** are in their paths
Is 60:18 nor **d** within your borders
Jer 4: 6 from the north, and great **d**
Jer 4:20 **D** upon **d** is cried
Jer 6: 1 out of the north, and great **d**
Jer 15: 3 over them four forms of **d**
Jer 17:18 and destroy them with double **d**
Jer 46:20 But **d** comes, it comes from
Jer 48: 3 Plundering and great **d**
Jer 48: 5 enemies have heard a cry of **d**
Jer 50:22 is in the land, and of great **d**
Jer 51:54 great **d** from the land of the
Lam 2:11 the **d** of the daughter of my
Lam 3:47 come upon us, desolation and **d**
Lam 3:48 the **d** of the daughter of my
Lam 4:10 the **d** of the daughter of my
Ezek 5:16 which shall be for their **d**
Ezek 7:25 **D** comes
Ezek 20:17 My eye spared them from **d**
Ezek 32: 9 your **d** among the nations,
Dan 11:16 Land with **d** in his power
Hos 7:13 **D** to them, because they have
Hos 9: 6 they are gone because of **d**
Hos 13:14 O Grave, I will be your **d**
Joel 1:15 it shall come as **d** from the
Amos 3:14 I will also visit **d** on the
Obad 12 Judah in the day of their **d**
Mic 2:10 you, even with utter **d**
Zech 14:11 longer shall there be utter **d**
Matt 7:13 is the way that leads to **d**
Acts 25:16 to deliver any man to **d**
Rom 3:16 **d** and misery are in their ways
Rom 9:22 of wrath prepared for **d**,
1Co 5: 5 Satan for the **d** of the flesh
2Co 10: 8 edification and not for your **d**
2Co 13:10 for edification and not for **d**
Phil 3:19 whose end is **d**, whose god is
1Th 5: 3 then sudden **d** comes upon
2Th 1: 9 **d** from the presence of the
1Ti 6: 9 lusts which drown men in **d**
2Pe 2: 1 bring on themselves swift **d**
2Pe 2: 3 and their **d** does not slumber
2Pe 2: 6 ashes, condemned them to **d**
2Pe 3:16 unstable twist to their own **d**

DESTRUCTIONS (*see* DESTRUCTION)
Ps 9: 6 enemy, **d** are finished forever
Ps 35:17 Rescue me from their **d**, My
Ps 107:20 delivered them from their **d**

DESTRUCTIVE (*see* DESTROY)
2Pe 2: 1 secretly bring in **d** heresies
2Pe 2: 2 many will follow their **d** ways

DETACHMENT
John 18: 3 having received a **d** of troops
John 18:12 Then the **d** of troops and the

DETAIL (*see* DETAILS)
Acts 21:19 he told in **d** those things
Heb 9: 5 we cannot now speak in **d**

DETAILS (*see* DETAIL)
1Ki 6:38 was finished in all its **d**

DETAIN (*see* DETAINED)
Judg 13:15 Please let us **d** You, and we
Judg 13:16 Though you **d** Me, I will not

DETAINED (*see* DETAIN)
Judg 19: 4 young woman's father, **d** him
1Sa 21: 7 that day, **d** before the LORD

DETERMINATION (*see* DETERMINE)
Zeph 3: 8 My **d** is to gather the nations

DETERMINE (*see* DETERMINATION, DETERMINED, DETERMINING)
Gen 38:25 Please **d** whose these are
Ex 21:22 he shall pay as the judges **d**
Esth 3: 7 before Haman to **d** the day
Mic 2: 5 you will have no one to **d**
Mark 15:24 casting lots for them to **d**

DETERMINED (*see* DETERMINE)
Josh 17:12 were **d** to dwell in that land
Judg 1:27 were **d** to dwell in that land
Judg 1:35 the Amorites were **d** to dwell
Ruth 1:18 that she was **d** to go with her
1Sa 20: 7 be sure that evil is **d** by him
1Sa 20: 9 certainly that evil was **d** by
1Sa 20:33 Jonathan knew that it was **d**
1Sa 25:17 for harm is **d** against our
2Sa 13:32 of Absalom this has been **d**
1Ki 7:47 of the bronze was not **d**
2Ch 2: 1 Then Solomon **d** to build a
2Ch 4:18 of the bronze was not **d**
2Ch 25:16 that God has **d** to destroy you
Esth 7: 7 was **d** against him by the king
Job 14: 5 Since his days are **d**, the
Job 38: 5 Who **d** its measurements
Is 10:23 GOD of hosts will make a **d**
Is 19:17 which He has **d** against it
Is 28:22 a destruction **d** even upon the
Dan 9:24 weeks are **d** for your people
Dan 9:26 of the war desolations are **d**

Dan 9:27 the consummation, which is **d**
Dan 11:36 what has been **d** shall be done
Zech 1: 6 LORD of hosts **d** to do to us
Zech 8:14 Just as I **d** to punish you
Zech 8:15 am **d** to do good to Jerusalem
Matt 2: 7 **d** from them what time the
Matt 2:16 he had **d** from the wise men
Luke 22:22 of Man goes as it has been **d**
Acts 2:23 delivered by the **d** counsel
Acts 3:13 when he was **d** to let Him go
Acts 4:28 Your purpose **d** before to be
Acts 11:29 **d** to send relief to the
Acts 15: 2 they **d** that Paul and Barnabas
Acts 15:37 Now Barnabas was **d** to take
Acts 16: 4 which were **d** by the apostles
Acts 17:26 and has **d** their preappointed
Acts 19:39 it shall be **d** in the lawful
1Co 2: 2 For I **d** not to know anything
1Co 7:37 has so **d** in his heart that he
2Co 2: 1 But I **d** this within myself,

DETERMINING (*see* DETERMINE)
Heb 6:17 **d** to show more abundantly to

DETEST (*see* DETESTABLE, DETESTS)
Deut 7:26 but you shall utterly **d** it
Prov 3:11 LORD, nor **d** His correction

DETESTABLE (*see* DETEST)
Deut 14: 3 You shall not eat any **d** thing
Jer 16:18 with the carcasses of their **d**
Ezek 5:11 with all your **d** things and
Ezek 7:20 and their **d** things
Ezek 11:18 take away all its **d** things
Ezek 11:21 the heart of their **d** things
Ezek 37:23 nor with their **d** things, nor

DETESTS (*see* DETEST)
Deut 22:13 and goes in to her, and **d** her,
Deut 22:16 this man as wife, and he **d** her
Deut 24: 3 if the latter husband **d** her

DEUEL (*see* REUEL)
Num 1:14 Gad, Eliasaph the son of **D**
Num 7:42 day Eliasaph the son of **D**
Num 7:47 of Eliasaph the son of **D**
Num 10:20 Gad was Eliasaph the son of **D**

DEVASTATE (*see* DEVASTATED, DEVASTATION)
Jer 49:28 and **d** the men of the East

DEVASTATED (*see* DEVASTATE)
Zeph 3: 6 their fortresses are **d**

DEVASTATION (*see* DEVASTATE)
Is 16: 4 **d** ceases, the oppressors are
Zeph 1:15 and distress, a day of **d** and

DEVELOPS
Lev 13:18 If the body **d** a boil in the

DEVICE (*see* DEVICES)
Eccl 9:10 for there is no work or **d** or

DEVICES (*see* DEVICE)
2Ch 26:15 And he made **d** in Jerusalem,
Job 5:12 the **d** of the crafty, so that
Prov 12: 2 of wicked **d** He will condemn
2Co 2:11 we are not ignorant of his **d**

DEVIL
Matt 4: 1 to be tempted by the **d**
Matt 4: 5 Then the **d** took Him up into
Matt 4: 8 the **d** took Him up on an
Matt 4:11 Then the **d** left Him, and
Matt 13:39 enemy who sowed them is the **d**
Matt 25:41 fire prepared for the **d** and
Luke 4: 2 for forty days by the **d**
Luke 4: 3 And the **d** said to Him,
Luke 4: 5 Then the **d**, taking Him up on
Luke 4: 6 And the **d** said to Him,
Luke 4:13 Now when the **d** had ended
Luke 8:12 then the **d** comes and takes
John 6:70 twelve, and one of you is a **d**
John 8:44 You are of your father the **d**
John 13: 2 the **d** having already put it
Acts 10:38 who were oppressed by the **d**
Acts 13:10 all fraud, you son of the **d**
Eph 4:27 nor give place to the **d**
Eph 6:11 against the wiles of the **d**
1Ti 3: 6 same condemnation as the **d**
1Ti 3: 7 and the snare of the **d**
2Ti 2:26 and escape the snare of the **d**
Heb 2:14 of death, that is, the **d**,
Jas 4: 7 Resist the **d** and he will flee
1Pe 5: 8 **d** walks about like a roaring
1Jn 3: 8 He who sins is of the **d**, for
1Jn 3: 8 for the **d** has sinned from the
1Jn 3: 8 destroy the works of the **d**
1Jn 3:10 of the **d** are manifest
Jude 9 in contending with the **d**
Rev 2:10 the **d** is about to throw some
Rev 12: 9 serpent of old, called the **D**
Rev 12:12 For the **d** has come down to
Rev 20: 2 serpent of old, who is the **D**
Rev 20:10 And the **d**, who deceived them,

DEVIOUS (*see* DEVISE)
2Sa 22:27 and with the **d** You will show
Ps 18:26 And with the **d** You will show
Prov 2:15 and who are **d** in their paths

DEVISE (*see* DEVIOUS, DEVISED, DEVISES, DEVISING)
Ps 35:20 But they **d** deceitful matters
Ps 41: 7 Against me they **d** my hurt
Ps 64: 6 They **d** iniquities
Prov 3:29 Do not **d** evil against your
Prov 12:20 the heart of those who **d** evil
Prov 14:22 they not go astray who **d** evil
Prov 14:22 belong to those who **d** good
Prov 16:30 his eye to **d** perverse things
Is 30: 1 who **d** plans, but not of My
Jer 18:18 and let us **d** plans against
Ezek 11: 2 are the men who **d** iniquity
Dan 11:24 he shall **d** his plans against
Dan 11:25 stand, for they shall **d** plans
Hos 7:15 yet they **d** evil against Me
Mic 2: 1 Woe to those who **d** iniquity

DEVISED (*see* DEVISE)
1Ki 12:33 he had **d** in his own heart
Esth 8: 3 he had **d** against the Jews
Esth 8: 5 revoke the letters **d** by Haman
Esth 9:25 had **d** against the Jews should
Ps 10: 2 the plots which they have **d**
Ps 21:11 They **d** a plot which they are
Prov 30:32 or if you have **d** evil, put
Jer 11:19 they had **d** schemes against me
Jer 48: 2 they have **d** evil against her
Jer 51:12 For the LORD has both **d** and
2Pe 1:16 **d** fables when we made known

DEVISES (*see* DEVISE)
2Sa 14:14 but He **d** means, so that His
Ps 36: 4 He **d** wickedness on his bed
Ps 52: 2 Your tongue **d** destruction
Ps 94:20 which **d** evil by law, Have
Prov 6:14 he **d** evil continually, he
Prov 6:18 a heart that **d** wicked plans
Prov 24: 2 for their heart **d** violence
Is 32: 7 he **d** wicked plans to destroy
Is 32: 8 man **d** generous things, and by

DEVISING (*see* DEVISE)
Prov 24: 9 The **d** of foolishness is sin,
Jer 18:11 and **d** a plan against you
Mic 2: 3 this family I am **d** disaster
Acts 17:29 shaped by art and man's **d**

DEVOID
Prov 7: 7 the youths, a young man **d** of
Prov 10:13 him who is **d** of understanding
Prov 11:12 He who is **d** of wisdom
Prov 12:11 is **d** of understanding
Prov 17:18 A man **d** of understanding
Prov 24:30 of the man **d** of understanding

DEVOTE (*see* DEVOTED, DEVOUT)
Lev 27:28 offering that a man may **d** to
2Ch 31: 4 that they might **d** themselves
Prov 20:25 to **d** rashly something as holy

DEVOTED (*see* DEVOTE)
Lev 27:21 to the LORD, as a **d** field
Lev 27:28 Nevertheless no **d** offering
Lev 27:28 every **d** offering is most holy
Num 18:14 Every **d** thing in Israel shall
Num 18:16 And those redeemed of the **d**
Ps 119:38 Who is **d** to fearing You
1Co 16:15 that they have **d** themselves

DEVOUR (*see* DEVOURED, DEVOURER, DEVOURING, DEVOURS)
Gen 49:27 morning he shall **d** the prey
Deut 32:42 and My sword shall **d** flesh
Judg 9:15 and **d** the cedars of Lebanon
Judg 9:20 **d** the men of Shechem and Beth
Judg 9:20 Beth Millo and **d** Abimelech
2Sa 2:26 Shall the sword **d** forever
2Ch 7:13 the locusts to **d** the land
Ps 21: 9 And the fire shall **d** them
Ps 50: 3 A fire shall **d** before Him
Prov 30:14 to **d** the poor from off the
Is 1: 7 strangers **d** your land in your
Is 9:12 they shall **d** Israel with an
Is 9:18 it shall **d** the briers and
Is 9:20 He shall **d** on the left hand
Is 9:21 Manasseh shall **d** Ephraim, and
Is 10:17 **d** his thorns and his briers in
Is 26:11 of Your enemies shall **d** them
Is 31: 8 not of mankind shall **d** him
Is 33:11 breath, as fire, shall **d** you
Is 56: 9 of the field, come to **d**, all
Jer 2: 3 All that **d** him will offend
Jer 5:14 wood, and it shall **d** them
Jer 12: 9 of the field, bring them to **d**
Jer 12:12 **d** from one end of the land to
Jer 15: 3 the beasts of the earth to **d**
Jer 17:27 it shall **d** the palaces of
Jer 21:14 it shall **d** all things around
Jer 30:16 who **d** you shall be devoured
Jer 46:10 The sword shall **d**
Jer 48:45 shall **d** the brow of Moab, The
Jer 50:32 and it will **d** all around him
Ezek 7:15 and pestilence will **d** him
Ezek 15: 7 but another fire shall **d** them
Ezek 20:47 it shall **d** every green tree
Ezek 23:37 through the fire, to **d** them
Ezek 34:28 beasts of the land **d** them
Ezek 36:13 they say to you, 'You **d** men
Ezek 36:14 you shall **d** men no more, nor
Dan 7: 5 Arise, **d** much flesh
Dan 7:23 and shall **d** the whole earth,
Hos 5: 7 Now a New Moon shall **d** them
Hos 8:14 and it shall **d** his palaces
Hos 11: 6 **d** his districts, and consume
Hos 13: 8 there I will **d** them like a
Amos 1: 4 which shall **d** the palaces of
Amos 1: 7 which shall **d** its palaces
Amos 1:10 which shall **d** its palaces
Amos 1:12 which shall **d** the palaces of
Amos 1:14 it shall **d** its palaces, amid
Amos 2: 2 it shall **d** the palaces of
Amos 2: 5 it shall **d** the palaces of
Amos 5: 6 **d** it, with no one to quench
Obad 18 **d** them, and no survivor shall
Nah 2:13 the sword shall **d** your young
Nah 3:13 fire shall **d** the bars of your
Nah 3:15 There the fire will **d** you
Zech 9:15 They shall **d** and subdue with
Zech 11: 1 that fire may **d** your cedars
Zech 12: 6 they shall **d** all the
Matt 23:14 For you **d** widows' houses, and
Mark 12:40 who **d** widows' houses, and for
Luke 20:47 who **d** widows' houses, and for
Gal 5:15 **d** one another, beware lest
Heb 10:27 which will **d** the adversaries
1Pe 5: 8 lion, seeking whom he may **d**
Rev 12: 4 to **d** her Child as soon as it

DEVOURED (*see* DEVOUR)
Gen 37:20 Some wild beast has **d** him
Gen 37:33 A wild beast has **d** him
Gen 41: 7 thin heads **d** the seven plump
Gen 41:24 the thin heads **d** the seven
Lev 10: 2 **d** them, and they died before
Num 26:10 when the fire **d** two hundred
Deut 31:17 from them, and they shall be **d**
Deut 32:24 **d** by pestilence and bitter
2Sa 18: 8 the woods **d** more people that
2Sa 18: 8 that day than the sword **d**
Ps 78:45 among them, which **d** them,
Ps 79: 7 For they have **d** Jacob, And
Ps 105:35 **d** the fruit of their ground
Is 1:20 you shall be **d** by the sword"
Is 24: 6 the curse has **d** the earth
Jer 2:30 Your sword has **d** your
Jer 3:24 For shame has **d** the labor of
Jer 8:16 **d** the land and all that is in
Jer 10:25 **D** him and consumed him, and
Jer 30:16 who devour you shall be **d**
Jer 50: 7 who found them have **d** them
Jer 50:17 the king of Assyria **d** him
Jer 51:34 the king of Babylon has **d** me
Lam 4:11 and it has **d** its foundations
Ezek 15: 5 work when the fire has **d** it
Ezek 16:20 sacrificed to them to be **d**
Ezek 19: 3 to catch prey, and he **d** men
Ezek 19: 6 he **d** men
Ezek 19:14 **d** her fruit, so that she has

Ezek 22:25 they have **d** people
Ezek 23:25 remnant shall be **d** by fire
Ezek 28:18 it **d** you, and I turned you to
Ezek 33:27 give to the beasts to be **d**
Ezek 39: 4 beasts of the field to be **d**
Dan 7:19 its nails of bronze, which **d**
Hos 7: 7 oven, and have **d** their judges
Hos 7: 9 Aliens have **d** his strength,
Joel 1:19 for fire has **d** the open
Joel 1:20 fire has **d** the open pastures
Amos 4: 9 trees, The locust **d** them
Amos 7: 4 great deep and **d** the territory
Nah 1:10 They shall be **d** like stubble
Zeph 1:18 **d** by the fire of His jealousy
Zeph 3: 8 be **d** with the fire of My
Zech 9: 4 sea, and she will be **d** by fire
Matt 13: 4 and the birds came and **d** them
Mark 4: 4 birds of the air came and **d** it
Luke 8: 5 and the birds of the air **d** it
Luke 15:30 who has **d** your livelihood
Rev 20: 9 God out of heaven and **d** them

DEVOURER (*see* DEVOUR)
Mal 3:11 rebuke the **d** for your sakes

DEVOURING (*see* DEVOUR)
2Sa 22: 9 and **d** fire from His mouth
Ps 18: 8 And **d** fire from His mouth
Ps 52: 4 You love all **d** words, You
Is 29: 6 And the flame of **d** fire
Is 30:27 and His tongue like a **d** fire
Is 30:30 and the flame of a **d** fire,
Is 33:14 shall dwell with the **d** fire
Dan 7: 7 it was **d**, breaking in pieces,

DEVOURS (*see* DEVOUR)
Num 13:32 a land that **d** its inhabitants
Num 23:24 lie down until it **d** the prey
2Sa 11:25 for the sword **d** one as well
Job 18:13 It **d** patches of his skin
Job 18:13 of death **d** his limbs
Job 39:24 He **d** the distance with
Ps 80:13 wild beast of the field **d** it
Prov 19:28 of the wicked **d** iniquity
Is 5:24 as the fire **d** the stubble
Jer 46:14 for the sword **d** all around
Lam 2: 3 fire which **d** all around
Ezek 15: 4 the fire **d** both ends of it,
Joel 2: 3 A fire **d** before them, and
Joel 2: 5 fire that **d** the stubble, like
Hab 1:13 **d** one more rightous than he
2Co 11:20 into bondage, if one **d** you
Rev 11: 5 mouth and **d** their enemies

DEVOUT (*see* DEVOTE, DEVOUTLY)
Luke 2:25 and this man was just and **d**
Acts 2: 5 **d** men, from every nation
Acts 8: 2 **d** men carried Stephen to his
Acts 10: 2 a **d** man and one who feared
Acts 10: 7 a **d** soldier from among those
Acts 13:43 **d** proselytes followed Paul and
Acts 13:50 But the Jews stirred up the **d**
Acts 17: 4 multitude of the **d** Greeks
Acts 22:12 a **d** man according to the law,

DEVOUTLY (*see* DEVOUT)
1Th 2:10 witnesses, and God also, how **d**

DEW
Gen 27:28 give you of the **d** of heaven
Gen 27:39 of the **d** of heaven from above
Ex 16:13 in the morning the **d** lay all
Ex 16:14 And when the layer of **d** lifted
Num 11: 9 when the **d** fell on the camp
Deut 32: 2 my speech distill as the **d**
Deut 33:13 things of heaven, with the **d**
Deut 33:28 His Heavens shall also drop **d**
Judg 6:37 if there is **d** on the fleece
Judg 6:38 he wrung the **d** out of the
Judg 6:39 all the ground let there be **d**
Judg 6:40 but there was **d** on all the
2Sa 1:21 of Gilboa, let there be no **d**
2Sa 17:12 as the **d** falls on the ground
1Ki 17: 1 there shall not be **d** nor rain
Job 29:19 the **d** lies all night on my
Job 29:22 speech settled on them as **d**
Job 38:28 has begotten the drops of **d**
Ps 110: 3 You have the **d** of Your youth
Ps 133: 3 It is like the **d** of Hermon
Prov 3:20 up, and clouds drop down the **d**
Prov 19:12 favor is like **d** on the grass
Song 5: 2 for my head is covered with **d**
Is 18: 4 like a cloud of **d** in the heat
Is 26:19 **d** is like the **d** of herbs
Dan 4:15 be wet with the **d** of heaven
Dan 4:23 be wet with the **d** of heaven
Dan 4:25 wet you with the **d** of heaven
Dan 4:33 his body was wet with the **d**
Dan 5:21 was wet with the **d** of heaven
Hos 6: 4 like the early **d** it goes away
Hos 13: 3 like the early **d** that passes
Hos 14: 5 will be like the **d** to Israel
Mic 5: 7 like **d** from the LORD, like
Hag 1:10 above you withhold the **d**, and
Zech 8:12 heavens shall give their **d**

DIADEM (*see* DIADEMS)
Is 28: 5 a **d** of beauty to the remnant
Is 62: 3 a royal **d** in the hand of your

DIADEMS (*see* DIADEM)
Rev 12: 3 and seven **d** on his heads

DIAL
Is 38: 8 **d** by which it had gone down

DIAMETER
1Ki 7:31 at the top was one cubit in **d**
1Ki 7:31 and a half cubits in outside **d**

DIAMOND
Ex 28:18 turquoise, a sapphire, and a **d**
Ex 39:11 turquoise, a sapphire, and a **d**
Jer 17: 1 with the point of a **d** it is
Ezek 28:13 the sardius, topaz, and **d**,

DIANA
Acts 19:24 who made silver shrines of **D**
Acts 19:27 goddess **D** may be despised
Acts 19:28 Great is **D** of the Ephesians
Acts 19:34 Great is **D** of the Ephesians
Acts 19:35 of the great goddess **D**, and of

DIBLAH
Ezek 6:14 than the wilderness toward **D**

DIBLAIM
Hos 1: 3 took Gomer the daughter of **D**

DIBON (*see* DIMON)
Num 21:30 has perished as far as **D**
Num 32: 3 Ataroth, **D**, Jazer, Nimrah,
Num 32:34 the children of Gad built **D**
Josh 13: 9 plain of Medeba as far as **D**
Josh 13:17 **D**, Bamoth Baal, Beth Baal
Neh 11:25 Arba and its villages, **D** and
Is 15: 2 gone up to the temple and **D**
Jer 48:18 O daughter inhabiting **D**, come
Jer 48:22 on **D** and Nebo and Beth

DIBON GAD (*see* GAD)
Num 33:45 from Ijim and camped at **D**
Num 33:46 They moved from **D** and camped

DIBRI
Lev 24:11 Shelomith the daughter of **D**

DID (*see* PREFACE)

DIDYMUS (*see* THOMAS)
John 11:16 Then Thomas, who is called **D**
John 20:24 But Thomas, called **D**, one of
John 21: 2 Simon Peter, Thomas called **D**

DIE (*see* DEAD, DEATH, DIED, DIES)
Gen 2:17 eat of it you shall surely **d**
Gen 3: 3 you touch it, lest you **d**
Gen 3: 4 You will not surely **d**
Gen 6:17 that is on the earth shall **d**
Gen 19:19 some evil overtake me and I **d**
Gen 20: 7 know that you shall surely **d**
Gen 25:32 Look, I am about to **d**
Gen 26: 9 Lest I **d** on account of her
Gen 27: 4 soul may bless you before I **d**
Gen 30: 1 Give me children, or else I **d**
Gen 33:13 one day, all the flock will **d**
Gen 38:11 said, "Lest he also **d** as his
Gen 42: 2 that we may live and not **d**
Gen 42:20 verified, and you shall not **d**
Gen 43: 8 go, that we may live and not **d**
Gen 44: 9 it is found, let him **d**, and we
Gen 44:22 father, his father would **d**
Gen 44:31 not with us, that he will **d**
Gen 45:28 will go and see him before I **d**
Gen 46:30 Now let me **d**, since I have
Gen 47:15 should we **d** in your presence
Gen 47:19 Why should we **d** before your
Gen 47:19 that we may live and not **d**
Gen 47:29 drew near that Israel must **d**
Ex 7:18 that are in the river shall **d**
Ex 9: 4 So nothing shall **d** of all
Ex 9:19 and they shall **d**
Ex 10:28 you see my face you shall **d**
Ex 11: 5 in the land of Egypt shall **d**
Ex 14:11 away to **d** in the wilderness
Ex 14:12 we should **d** in the wilderness
Ex 20:19 God speak with us, lest we **d**
Ex 21:14 from My altar, that he may **d**
Ex 21:18 he does not **d** but is confined
Ex 28:35 comes out, that he may not **d**
Ex 28:43 do not incur iniquity and **d**
Ex 30:20 wash with water, lest they **d**
Ex 30:21 and their feet, lest they **d**
Lev 8:35 LORD, so that you may not **d**
Lev 10: 6 tear your clothes, lest you **d**
Lev 10: 7 of meeting, lest you **d**, for
Lev 10: 9 of meeting, lest you **d**
Lev 15:31 lest they **d** in their
Lev 16: 2 is on the ark, lest he **d**
Lev 16:13 on the Testimony, lest he **d**
Lev 20:20 they shall **d** childless
Lev 22: 9 **d** thereby, if they profane it
Num 4:15 any holy thing, lest they **d**
Num 4:19 not **d** when they approach the
Num 4:20 being covered, lest they **d**
Num 6: 7 or his sister, when they **d**
Num 14:35 and there they shall **d**
Num 16:29 If these men **d** naturally like
Num 17:10 away from Me, lest they **d**
Num 17:12 Surely we **d**, we perish, we
Num 17:13 tabernacle of the LORD must **d**
Num 17:13 Shall we all utterly **d**
Num 18: 3 and the altar, lest they **d**
Num 18:22 lest they bear sin and **d**
Num 18:32 of Israel, lest you **d**
Num 20: 4 and our animals should **d** here
Num 20:26 to his people and **d** there
Num 21: 5 Egypt to **d** in the wilderness
Num 23:10 Let me **d** the death of the
Num 26:11 children of Korah did not **d**
Num 26:65 surely **d** in the wilderness
Num 35:12 **d** until he stands before the
Num 35:17 one could **d**, and he does **d**
Num 35:18 one could **d**, and he does **d**
Num 35:23 stone, by which a man could **d**
Deut 4:22 But I must **d** in this land, I
Deut 5:25 therefore, why should we **d**
Deut 5:25 God anymore, then we shall **d**
Deut 17:12 the judge, that man shall **d**
Deut 18:16 great fire anymore, lest I **d**
Deut 18:20 gods, that prophet shall **d**
Deut 19:12 of blood, that he may **d**
Deut 20: 5 lest he **d** in the battle and
Deut 20: 6 lest he **d** in the battle and
Deut 20: 7 lest he **d** in the battle and
Deut 22:22 then both of them shall **d**
Deut 22:25 man who lay with her shall **d**
Deut 24: 7 then that kidnapper shall **d**
Deut 31:14 days approach when you must **d**
Deut 32:50 **d** on the mountain which you
Deut 33: 6 Let Reuben live, and not **d**
Josh 20: 9 and not **d** by the hand of the
Judg 6:23 do not fear, you shall not **d**
Judg 6:30 out your son, that he may **d**
Judg 13:22 We shall surely **d**, because we
Judg 15:18 and now shall I **d** of thirst
Judg 16:30 Let me **d** with the Philistines
Ruth 1:17 Where you **d**, I will **d**, and
1Sa 2:33 of your house shall **d** in the
1Sa 2:34 in one day they shall **d**, both
1Sa 5:12 the men who did not **d** were
1Sa 12:19 your God, that we may not **d**
1Sa 14:39 my son, he shall surely **d**
1Sa 14:43 So now I must **d**
1Sa 14:44 for you shall surely **d**,
1Sa 14:45 Shall Jonathan **d**, who has
1Sa 14:45 Jonathan, and he did not **d**
1Sa 20: 2 You shall not **d**
1Sa 20:14 still live, that I may not **d**
1Sa 20:31 to me, for he shall surely **d**
1Sa 22:16 You shall surely **d**, Ahimelech
1Sa 26:10 or his day shall come to **d**
1Sa 26:16 lives, you are worthy to **d**
1Sa 28: 9 for my life, to cause me to **d**
2Sa 3:33 Should Abner **d** as a fool dies
2Sa 11:15 he may be struck down and **d**
2Sa 12: 5 has done this shall surely **d**
2Sa 12:13 you shall not **d**
2Sa 12:14 is born to you shall surely **d**
2Sa 14:14 For we will surely **d** and

2Sa 18: 3 nor if half of us **d**, will
2Sa 19:23 You shall not **d**
2Sa 19:37 that I may **d** in my own city,
1Ki 1:52 is found in him, he shall **d**
1Ki 2: 1 drew near that he should **d**
1Ki 2:30 No, but I will **d** here
1Ki 2:37 certain you shall surely **d**
1Ki 2:42 anywhere, you shall surely **d**'
1Ki 14:12 the city, the child shall **d**
1Ki 17:12 son, that we may eat it, and **d**
1Ki 19: 4 And he prayed that he might **d**
1Ki 21:10 and stone him, that he may **d**
2Ki 1: 4 up, but you shall surely **d**
2Ki 1: 6 up, but you shall surely **d**
2Ki 1:16 up, but you shall surely **d**
2Ki 7: 3 we sitting here until we **d**
2Ki 7: 4 the city, and we shall **d** there
2Ki 7: 4 And if we sit here, we **d** also
2Ki 7: 4 they kill us, we shall but **d**
2Ki 8:10 me that he will really **d**
2Ki 13:14 illness of which he would **d**
2Ki 18:32 that you may live and not **d**
2Ki 20: 1 in order, for you shall **d**
2Ch 25: 4 shall **d** for his own sin
2Ch 32:11 over to **d** by famine and by
Job 2: 9 Curse God and **d**
Job 3:11 Why did I not **d** at birth
Job 4:21 They **d**, even without wisdom
Job 12: 2 and wisdom will **d** with you
Job 14: 8 its stump may **d** in the ground
Job 27: 5 till I **d** I will not put away
Job 29:18 I shall **d** in my nest, and
Job 34:20 In a moment they **d**, in the
Job 36:12 and they shall **d** without
Job 36:14 They **d** in youth, and their
Ps 41: 5 When will he **d**, and his name
Ps 49:10 For he sees that wise men **d**
Ps 79:11 those who are appointed to **d**
Ps 82: 7 But you shall **d** like men, And
Ps 88:15 ready to **d** from my youth up
Ps 104:29 away their breath, they **d**
Ps 118:17 I shall not **d**, but live, And
Prov 5:23 He shall **d** for lack of
Prov 10:21 many, but fools **d** for lack of
Prov 15:10 he who hates reproof will **d**
Prov 19:16 careless of his ways will **d**
Prov 23:13 him with a rod, he will not **d**
Prov 30: 7 (Deprive me not before I **d**)
Prov 31: 8 of all who are appointed to **d**
Eccl 2:16 and how does a wise man **d**
Eccl 3: 2 to be born, and a time to **d**
Eccl 7:17 why should you **d** before your
Eccl 9: 5 living know that they will **d**
Is 22:13 and drink, for tomorrow we **d**
Is 22:18 there you shall **d**, and there
Is 38: 1 in order, for you shall **d**
Is 50: 2 is no water, and **d** of thirst
Is 51: 6 in it will **d** in like manner
Is 51:12 be afraid of a man who will **d**
Is 51:14 he should not **d** in the pit
Is 65:20 for the child shall **d** one
Is 66:24 For their worm does not **d**
Jer 11:21 LORD, lest you **d** by our hand'
Jer 11:22 men shall **d** by the sword,
Jer 11:22 daughters shall **d** by famine
Jer 16: 4 They shall **d** gruesome deaths
Jer 16: 6 small shall **d** in this land
Jer 20: 6 Babylon, and there you shall **d**
Jer 21: 6 they shall **d** of a great
Jer 21: 9 city shall **d** by the sword
Jer 22:12 but he shall **d** in the place
Jer 22:26 and there you shall **d**
Jer 26: 8 You will surely **d**
Jer 26:11 This man deserves to **d**
Jer 26:16 man does not deserve to **d**
Jer 27:13 Why will you **d**, you and your
Jer 28:16 This year you shall **d**,
Jer 31:30 But every one shall **d** for his
Jer 34: 4 You shall not **d** by the sword
Jer 34: 5 But you shall **d** in peace
Jer 37:20 the scribe, lest I **d** there
Jer 38: 2 city shall **d** by the sword
Jer 38: 9 he is likely to **d** from hunger
Jer 38:24 words, and you shall not **d**
Jer 38:26 Jonathan's house to **d** there
Jer 42:16 and there you shall **d**
Jer 42:17 They shall **d** by the sword, by
Jer 42:22 that you shall **d** by the sword
Jer 44:12 They shall **d**, from the least
Lam 4: 9 than those who **d** of hunger
Ezek 3:18 wicked, 'You shall surely **d**
Ezek 3:18 man shall **d** in his iniquity
Ezek 3:19 he shall **d** in his iniquity
Ezek 3:20 block before him, he shall **d**
Ezek 3:20 he shall **d** in his sin, and his
Ezek 5:12 you shall **d** of the pestilence
Ezek 6:12 off shall **d** by the pestilence
Ezek 6:12 shall **d** by the famine
Ezek 7:15 the field will **d** by the sword
Ezek 12:13 it, though he shall **d** there
Ezek 13:19 people who should not **d**, and
Ezek 17:16 midst of Babylon he shall **d**
Ezek 18: 4 the soul who sins shall **d**
Ezek 18:13 he shall surely **d**
Ezek 18:17 he shall not **d** for the
Ezek 18:18 he shall **d** for his iniquity
Ezek 18:20 The soul who sins shall **d**
Ezek 18:21 he shall not **d**
Ezek 18:23 all that the wicked should **d**
Ezek 18:24 because of them he shall **d**
Ezek 18:28 he shall not **d**
Ezek 18:31 For why should you **d**, O house
Ezek 28: 8 you shall **d** the death of the
Ezek 28:10 You shall **d** the death of the
Ezek 33: 8 man, you shall surely **d**
Ezek 33: 8 man shall **d** in his iniquity
Ezek 33: 9 he shall **d** in his iniquity
Ezek 33:11 For why should you **d**, O house
Ezek 33:13 he has committed, he shall **d**
Ezek 33:14 wicked, 'You shall surely **d**
Ezek 33:15 he shall not **d**
Ezek 33:18 he shall **d** because of it
Ezek 33:27 and caves shall **d** of the
Amos 2: 2 Moab shall **d** with tumult,
Amos 6: 9 in one house, they shall **d**
Amos 7:11 Jeroboam shall **d** by the sword
Amos 7:17 you shall **d** in a defiled land
Amos 9:10 people shall **d** by the sword
Jon 4: 3 for me to **d** than to live
Jon 4: 8 for me to **d** than to live
Hab 1:12 We shall not **d**
Zech 11: 9 Let what is dying **d**, and what
Zech 13: 8 in it shall be cut off and **d**
Matt 26:35 Even if I have to **d** with You
Mark 9:44 where 'their worm does not **d**
Mark 9:46 where 'their worm does not **d**
Mark 9:48 where 'their worm does not **d**
Mark 14:31 If I have to **d** with You, I
Luke 7: 2 him, was sick and ready to **d**
Luke 20:36 nor can they **d** anymore, for
John 6:50 one may eat of it and not **d**
John 8:21 Me, and will **d** in your sin
John 8:24 that you will **d** in your sins
John 8:24 He, you will **d** in your sins
John 11:16 go, that we may **d** with Him
John 11:25 in Me, though he may **d**, he
John 11:26 believes in Me shall never **d**
John 11:50 man should **d** for the people
John 11:51 Jesus would **d** for the nation
John 12:33 by what death He would **d**
John 18:14 man should **d** for the people
John 18:32 by what death He would **d**
John 19: 7 to our law He ought to **d**,
John 21:23 this disciple would not **d**
John 21:23 to him that he would not **d**
Acts 21:13 but also to **d** at Jerusalem
Rom 5: 7 a righteous man will one **d**
Rom 5: 7 someone would even dare to **d**
Rom 8:13 to the flesh you will **d**
Rom 14: 8 if we **d**, we **d** to the Lord
Rom 14: 8 whether we live or **d**, we are
1Co 9:15 to **d** than that anyone should
1Co 15:22 For as in Adam all **d**, even so
1Co 15:31 Jesus our Lord, I **d** daily
1Co 15:32 and drink, for tomorrow we **d**
2Co 7: 3 to **d** together and to live
Phil 1:21 is Christ, and to **d** is gain
Heb 9:27 appointed for men to **d** once
Rev 3: 2 remain, that are ready to **d**
Rev 9: 6 they will desire to **d**, and
Rev 14:13 who **d** in the Lord from now on

DIED (*see* DIE)
Gen 5: 5 and he **d**
Gen 5: 8 and he **d**
Gen 5:11 and he **d**
Gen 5:14 and he **d**
Gen 5:17 and he **d**
Gen 5:20 and he **d**
Gen 5:27 and he **d**
Gen 5:31 and he **d**
Gen 7:21 all flesh **d** that moved on the
Gen 7:22 that was on the dry land, **d**
Gen 9:29 and he **d**
Gen 11:28 Haran **d** before his father
Gen 11:32 years, and Terah **d** in Haran
Gen 23: 2 So Sarah **d** in Kirjath Arba
Gen 25: 8 **d** in a good old age, an old
Gen 25:17 and he breathed his last and **d**
Gen 25:18 he **d** in the presence of all
Gen 35: 8 Deborah, Rebekah's nurse, **d**
Gen 35:18 was departing (for she **d**)
Gen 35:19 So Rachel **d** and was buried on
Gen 35:29 Isaac breathed his last and **d**
Gen 36:33 And when Bela **d**, Jobab the son
Gen 36:34 When Jobab **d**, Husham of the
Gen 36:35 And when Husham **d**, Hadad
Gen 36:36 When Hadad **d**, Samlah of
Gen 36:37 And when Samlah **d**, Saul of
Gen 36:38 When Saul **d**, Baal-Hanan the
Gen 36:39 the son of Achbor **d**, Hadar
Gen 38:12 of Shua, Judah's wife, **d**
Gen 46:12 Onan **d** in the land of Canaan)
Gen 48: 7 Rachel **d** beside me in the
Gen 50:16 your father **d** he commanded
Gen 50:26 So Joseph **d**, being one
Ex 1: 6 And Joseph **d**, all his brothers
Ex 2:23 time that the king of Egypt **d**
Ex 7:21 fish that were in the river **d**
Ex 8:13 the frogs **d** out of the houses
Ex 9: 6 all the livestock of Egypt **d**
Ex 9: 6 children of Israel, not one **d**
Ex 16: 3 that we had **d** by the hand of
Lev 10: 2 and they **d** before the LORD
Lev 16: 1 fire before the LORD, and **d**
Lev 17:15 **d** naturally or what was torn
Num 3: 4 Abihu had **d** before the LORD
Num 14: 2 If only we had **d** in the land
Num 14: 2 Or if only we had **d** in this
Num 14:37 **d** by the plague before the
Num 15:36 him with stones, and he **d**
Num 16:49 Now those who **d** in the plague
Num 16:49 besides those who **d** in the
Num 19:13 the body of anyone who has **d**
Num 19:16 slain by a sword or who has **d**
Num 20: 1 and Miriam **d** there and was
Num 20: 3 If only we had **d** when our
Num 20: 3 brethren **d** before the LORD
Num 20:28 Aaron **d** there on the top of
Num 21: 6 of the people of Israel **d**
Num 25: 9 those who **d** in the plague
Num 26:10 Korah when that company **d**
Num 26:19 Onan **d** in the land of Canaan
Num 26:61 Abihu **d** when they offered
Num 27: 3 Our father **d** in the
Num 27: 3 but he **d** in his own sin
Num 33:38 **d** there in the fortieth year
Num 33:39 old when he **d** on Mount Hor
Deut 10: 6 the place where Aaron **d** later
Deut 32:50 your brother **d** on Mount Hor
Deut 34: 5 the servant of the LORD **d**
Deut 34: 7 and twenty years old when he **d**
Josh 5: 4 had **d** in the wilderness on
Josh 10:11 as far as Azekah, and they **d**
Josh 10:11 There were more who **d** from
Josh 24:29 the servant of the LORD, **d**
Josh 24:33 And Eleazar the son of Aaron **d**
Judg 1: 7 to Jerusalem, and there he **d**
Judg 2: 8 **d** when he was one hundred and
Judg 2:21 which Joshua left when he **d**
Judg 3:11 Othniel the son of Kenaz **d**
Judg 4:21 asleep and weary. So he **d**.
Judg 8:32 of Joash **d** at a good old age
Judg 9:49 of the tower of Shechem **d**
Judg 9:54 thrust him through, and he **d**
Judg 10: 2 and he **d** and was buried in
Judg 10: 5 And Jair **d** and was buried in
Judg 12: 7 Then Jephthah the Gileadite **d**
Judg 12:10 Then Ibzan **d** and was buried at
Judg 12:12 And Elon the Zebulunite **d** and
Judg 12:15 of Hillel the Pirathonite **d**
Judg 20: 5 my concubine so that she **d**
Ruth 1: 3 Elimelech, Naomi's husband, **d**
Ruth 1: 5 both Mahlon and Chilion also **d**
1Sa 4:11 of Eli, Hophni and Phinehas, **d**
1Sa 4:18 his neck was broken and he **d**
1Sa 25: 1 Then Samuel **d**
1Sa 25:37 that his heart **d** within him
1Sa 25:38 LORD struck Nabal, and he **d**
1Sa 28: 3 Now Samuel had **d**, and all
1Sa 31: 5 on his sword, and **d** with him

1Sa 31: 6 all his men **d** together that
2Sa 1:15 And he struck him so that he **d**
2Sa 2:23 down there and **d** on the spot
2Sa 2:23 where Asahel fell down and **d**
2Sa 2:31 hundred and sixty men who **d**
2Sa 3:27 so that he **d** for the blood of
2Sa 4: 1 that Abner had **d** in Hebron
2Sa 6: 7 he **d** there by the ark of God
2Sa 10: 1 king of the people of Ammon **d**
2Sa 10:18 of their army, who **d** there
2Sa 11:17 and Uriah the Hittite **d** also
2Sa 11:21 wall, so that he **d** in Thebez
2Sa 12:18 came to pass that the child **d**
2Sa 12:21 alive, but when the child **d**
2Sa 17:23 and hanged himself, and **d**
2Sa 18:33 if only I had **d** in your place
2Sa 19: 6 and all of us had **d** today,
2Sa 19:10 over us, has **d** in battle
2Sa 20:10 Thus he **d**
2Sa 24:15 thousand men of the people **d**
1Ki 2:25 he struck him down, and he **d**
1Ki 2:46 and struck him down, and he **d**
1Ki 3:19 woman's son **d** in the night
1Ki 12:18 him with stones, and he **d**
1Ki 14:17 of the house, the child **d**
1Ki 16:18 upon himself with fire, and **d**
1Ki 16:22 So Tibni **d** and Omri reigned
1Ki 21:13 him with stones, so that he **d**
1Ki 22:35 the Syrians, and **d** at evening
1Ki 22:37 So the king **d**, and was brought
2Ki 1:17 So Ahaziah **d** according to the
2Ki 3: 5 But it happened, when Ahab **d**
2Ki 4:20 knees till noon, and then **d**
2Ki 7:17 him in the gate, and he **d**,
2Ki 7:20 him in the gate, and he **d**
2Ki 8:15 it over his face so that he **d**
2Ki 9:27 fled to Megiddo, and **d** there
2Ki 12:21 So he **d**, and they buried him
2Ki 13:20 Then Elisha **d**, and they buried
2Ki 13:24 Now Hazael king of Syria **d**
2Ki 23:34 went to Egypt, and he **d** there
1Ch 1:44 And when Bela **d**, Jobab the son
1Ch 1:45 When Jobab **d**, Husham of the
1Ch 1:46 And when Husham **d**, Hadad
1Ch 1:47 When Hadad **d**, Samlah of
1Ch 1:48 And when Samlah **d**, Saul of
1Ch 1:49 When Saul **d**, Baal-Hanan the
1Ch 1:50 And when Baal-Hanan **d**,
1Ch 1:51 Hadad **d** also
1Ch 2:19 When Azubah **d**, Caleb took
1Ch 2:24 After Hezron **d** in Caleb
1Ch 2:30 Seled **d** without children
1Ch 2:32 Jether **d** without children
1Ch 10: 5 also fell on his sword and **d**
1Ch 10: 6 So Saul and his three sons **d**
1Ch 10: 6 and all his house **d** together
1Ch 10:13 So Saul **d** for his
1Ch 13:10 and he **d** there before God
1Ch 19: 1 king of the people of Ammon **d**
1Ch 23:22 And Eleazar **d**, and had no sons,
1Ch 24: 2 Abihu **d** before their father,
1Ch 29:28 So he **d** in a good old age,
2Ch 10:18 him with stones, and he **d**
2Ch 13:20 the LORD struck him, and he **d**
2Ch 16:13 he **d** in the forty-first year
2Ch 18:34 about the time of sunset he **d**
2Ch 21:19 so he **d** in severe pain
2Ch 24:15 and was full of days, and he **d**
2Ch 24:15 and thirty years old when he **d**
2Ch 24:22 and as he **d**, he said, "The
2Ch 24:25 killed him on his bed. So he **d**
2Ch 35:24 So he **d**, and was buried in one
Esth 2: 7 When her father and mother **d**
Job 42:17 So Job **d**, old and full of days
Is 6: 1 the year that King Uzziah **d**
Is 14:28 in the year that King Ahaz **d**
Jer 28:17 **d** the same year in the
Ezek 4:14 I have never eaten what **d** of
Ezek 11:13 Pelatiah the son of Benaiah **d**
Ezek 24:18 and at evening my wife **d**
Ezek 44:31 that **d** naturally or was torn
Hos 13: 1 he offended in Baal, he **d**
Matt 9:18 My daughter has just **d**, but
Matt 22:25 The first **d** after he had
Matt 22:27 last of all the woman **d** also
Mark 12:21 the second took her, and he **d**
Mark 12:22 Last of all the woman **d** also
Luke 16:22 So it was that the beggar **d**
Luke 16:22 The rich man also **d** and was
Luke 20:29 a wife, and **d** without children
Luke 20:30 as wife, and he **d** childless
Luke 20:31 they left no children, and **d**
Luke 20:32 Last of all the woman **d** also
John 11:21 my brother would not have **d**
John 11:32 my brother would not have **d**
John 11:44 he who had **d** came out bound
Acts 7:15 and he **d**, he and our fathers
Acts 9:37 that she became sick and **d**
Acts 12:23 he was eaten by worms and **d**
Acts 25:19 about one, Jesus, who had **d**
Rom 5: 6 time Christ **d** for the ungodly
Rom 5: 8 sinners, Christ **d** for us
Rom 5:15 the one man's offense many **d**
Rom 6: 2 How shall we who **d** to sin
Rom 6: 7 For he who has **d** has been
Rom 6: 8 Now if we **d** with Christ, we
Rom 6:10 For the death that He **d**, He
Rom 6:10 He **d** to sin once for all
Rom 7: 6 having **d** to what we were held
Rom 7: 9 came, sin revived and I **d**
Rom 8:34 It is Christ who **d**, and
Rom 14: 9 For to this end Christ **d** and
Rom 14:15 the one for whom Christ **d**
1Co 8:11 perish, for whom Christ **d**
1Co 15: 3 that Christ **d** for our sins
2Co 5:14 One **d** for all, then all **d**
2Co 5:15 He **d** for all, that those who
2Co 5:15 but for Him who **d** for them
Gal 2:19 For I through the law **d** to
Gal 2:21 law, then Christ **d** in vain
Col 2:20 if you **d** with Christ from the
Col 3: 3 For you **d**, and your life is
1Th 4:14 if we believe that Jesus **d**
1Th 5:10 who **d** for us, that whether we
2Ti 2:11 For if we **d** with Him, we
Heb 11:13 These all **d** in faith, not
1Pe 2:24 having **d** to sins, might live
Rev 8: 9 living creatures in the sea **d**
Rev 8:11 many men **d** from the water,
Rev 16: 3 living creature in the sea **d**

DIES (*see* DIE)
Ex 21:12 he **d** shall surely be put to
Ex 21:20 so that he **d** under his hand,
Ex 21:35 hurts another's, so that it **d**
Ex 22: 2 and he is struck so that he **d**
Ex 22:10 or any beast to keep, and it **d**
Ex 22:14 and it becomes injured or **d**
Lev 7:24 of a beast that **d** naturally
Lev 11:39 any beast which you may eat **d**
Lev 22: 8 Whatever **d** naturally or is
Num 6: 9 if anyone **d** very suddenly
Num 19:14 law when a man **d** in a tent
Num 27: 8 If a man **d** and has no son,
Num 35:16 iron implement, so that he **d**
Num 35:20 something at him so that he **d**
Num 35:21 with his hand so that he **d**
Num 35:23 seeing him, so that he **d**,
Deut 13:10 him with stones until he **d**
Deut 14:21 eat anything that **d** of itself
Deut 19: 5 his neighbor so that he **d**
Deut 19:11 him mortally, so that he **d**
Deut 24: 3 or if the latter husband **d**
Deut 25: 5 together, and one of them **d**
2Sa 3:33 Should Abner die as a fool **d**
1Ki 14:11 **d** in the city, and the birds
1Ki 14:11 eat whoever **d** in the field
1Ki 16: 4 **d** in the city, and the birds
1Ki 16: 4 eat whoever **d** in the fields
1Ki 21:24 **d** in the city, and the birds
1Ki 21:24 eat whoever **d** in the field
Job 14:10 But man **d** and is laid away
Job 14:14 If a man **d**, shall he live
Job 21:23 One **d** in his full strength,
Job 21:25 Another man **d** in the
Ps 49:17 For when he **d** he shall carry
Prov 11: 7 When a wicked man **d**, his
Eccl 3:19 as one **d**, so **d** the other
Is 59: 5 he who eats of their eggs **d**
Jer 38:10 of the dungeon before he **d**
Ezek 18:26 **d** in it, it is because of the
Ezek 18:26 which he has done that he **d**
Ezek 18:32 in the death of one who **d**
Matt 22:24 Moses said that if a man **d**
Mark 12:19 us that if a man's brother **d**
Luke 20:28 us that if a man's brother **d**
Luke 20:28 he **d** without children, his
John 4:49 come down before my child **d**
John 12:24 falls into the ground and **d**
John 12:24 but if it **d**, it produces much
Rom 6: 9 from the dead, **d** no more
Rom 7: 2 But if the husband **d**, she is
Rom 7: 3 but if her husband **d**, she is
Rom 14: 7 and no one **d** to himself
1Co 7:39 but if her husband **d**, she is
1Co 15:36 is not made alive unless it **d**
Heb 10:28 law **d** without mercy on the

DIFFER (*see* DIFFERENCE, DIFFERENT, DIFFERING, DIFFERS)
1Co 4: 7 who makes you **d** from another
Gal 4: 1 does not **d** at all from a

DIFFERENCE (*see* DIFFER, DIFFERENCES)
Ex 8:23 I will make a **d** between My
Ex 9: 4 And the LORD will make a **d**
Ex 11: 7 a **d** between the Egyptians
Ezek 22:26 the **d** between the unclean
Ezek 44:23 people the **d** between the holy
Rom 3:22 For there is no **d**
1Co 7:34 There is a **d** between a wife
Gal 2: 6 were, it makes no **d** to me

DIFFERENCES (*see* DIFFERENCE)
1Co 12: 5 There are **d** of ministries,

DIFFERENT (*see* DIFFER)
Num 14:24 he has a **d** spirit in him and
Deut 22: 9 vineyard with **d** kinds of seed
Deut 22:11 not wear a garment of **d** sorts
Esth 1: 7 vessel being **d** from the other
Esth 3: 8 their laws are **d** from all
Eccl 10:11 the babbler is no **d**
Dan 7: 3 sea, each **d** from the other
Dan 7: 7 It was **d** from all the beasts
Dan 7:19 which was **d** from all the
Dan 7:23 which shall be **d** from all
Dan 7:24 he shall be **d** from the first
1Co 12:10 to another **d** kinds of tongues
2Co 11: 4 or if you receive a **d** spirit
2Co 11: 4 or a **d** gospel which you have
Gal 1: 6 of Christ, to a **d** gospel,
Heb 1: 1 in **d** ways spoke in time past

DIFFERING (*see* DIFFER)
Deut 25:13 have in your bag **d** weights
Deut 25:14 have in your house **d** measures
Rom 12: 6 Having then gifts **d** according

DIFFERS (*see* DIFFER)
1Co 15:41 for one star **d** from another

DIFFICULT (*see* DIFFICULTY)
1Ki 10: 3 there was nothing so **d** for
2Ch 9: 2 there was nothing so **d** for
Eccl 12: 1 youth, before the **d** days come
Dan 2:11 It is a **d** thing that the king
Matt 7:14 **d** is the way which leads to

DIFFICULTIES (*see* DIFFICULTY)
Ex 18:19 you may bring the **d** to God

DIFFICULTY (*see* DIFFICULT, DIFFICULTIES)
Ex 14:25 that they drove them with **d**
Ex 18:16 When they have a **d**, they come
Ex 24:14 If any man has a **d**, let him
Luke 9:39 departs from him with great **d**
Acts 27: 7 and arrived with **d** off Cnidus
Acts 27: 8 Passing it with **d**, we came to
Acts 27:16 we secured the skiff with **d**

DIFFUSED (*see* DIFFUSES)
Job 38:24 By what way is light **d**, or

DIFFUSES (*see* DIFFUSED)
2Co 2:14 through us **d** the fragrance of

DIG (*see* DIGS, DUG)
Deut 6:11 wells which you did not **d**
Deut 8: 9 whose hills you can **d** copper
Deut 23:13 outside, you shall **d** with it
Job 11:18 yes, you would **d** about you
Ezek 8: 8 Son of man, **d** into the wall"
Ezek 12: 5 **D** through the wall in their
Ezek 12:12 They shall **d** through the wall
Amos 9: 2 Though they **d** into hell, from
Nah 1:14 I will **d** your grave, for you
Luke 13: 8 also, until I **d** around it and
Luke 16: 3 I cannot **d**

DIGNITARIES (*see* DIGNITY)
2Pe 2:10 not afraid to speak evil of **d**
Jude 8 authority, and speak evil of **d**

DIGNITY (*see* DIGNITARIES)
Gen 49: 3 strength, the excellency of **d**
Esth 6: 3 What honor or **d** has been
Eccl 10: 6 folly is set in great **d**,

Hab 1: 7 and their **d** proceed from

DIGS (*see* DIG)
Ex 21:33 a pit, or if a man **d** a pit
Prov 16:27 An ungodly man **d** up evil, and
Prov 26:27 Whoever **d** a pit will fall
Eccl 10: 8 He who **d** a pit will fall into

DIKLAH
Gen 10:27 Hadoram, Uzal, **D**,
1Ch 1:21 Hadoram, Uzal, **D**,

DILAPIDATION
2Ki 12: 5 wherever any **d** is found

DILEAN
Josh 15:38 **D**, Mizpah, Joktheel,

DILIGENCE (*see* DILIGENT)
Prov 4:23 Keep your heart with all **d**
Prov 12:27 but **d** is man's precious
Rom 12: 8 he who leads, with **d**
Rom 12:11 not lagging in **d**, fervent in
2Co 7:11 What **d** it produced in you,
2Co 8: 7 in knowledge, in all **d**, and
2Co 8: 8 your love by the **d** of others
Heb 6:11 **d** to the full assurance of
2Pe 1: 5 very reason, giving all **d**

DILIGENT (*see* DILIGENCE, DILIGENTLY)
Deut 19:18 judges shall make **d** inquiry
Josh 22: 5 But take **d** heed to do the
Josh 23:11 Therefore take **d** heed to
2Ch 29:34 **d** in sanctifying themselves
Ps 77: 6 And my spirit makes **d** search
Prov 10: 4 hand of the **d** makes one rich
Prov 12:24 The hand of the **d** will rule
Prov 13: 4 of the **d** shall be made rich
Prov 21: 5 The plans of the **d** lead
Prov 27:23 Be **d** to know the state of
2Co 8:17 exhortation, but being more **d**
2Co 8:22 often proved **d** in many things
2Co 8:22 things, but now much more **d**
2Ti 2:15 Be **d** to present yourself
2Ti 4: 9 Be **d** to come to me quickly
Tit 3:12 be **d** to come to me at
Heb 4:11 be **d** to enter that rest, lest
2Pe 1:10 be even more **d** to make your
2Pe 3:14 be **d** to be found by Him in
Jude 3 while I was very **d** to write

DILIGENTLY (*see* DILIGENT)
Ex 15:26 If you **d** heed the voice of
Lev 10:16 Then Moses **d** made inquiry
Deut 4: 9 **d** keep yourself, lest you
Deut 6: 7 teach them **d** to your children
Deut 6:17 You shall **d** keep the
Deut 11:13 it shall be that if you **d**
Deut 13:14 inquire, search out, and ask **d**
Deut 17: 4 it, then you shall inquire **d**
Deut 24: 8 leprosy, that you **d** observe
Deut 28: 1 if you **d** obey the voice of
1Ki 20:33 Now the men were **d** watching
2Ch 34:33 **d** serve the LORD their God
Ezra 5: 8 and this work goes on **d** and
Ezra 6:12 let it be done **d**
Ezra 6:13 and their companions **d** did
Ezra 7:21 of you, let it be done **d**,
Ezra 7:23 let it **d** be done for the
Neh 3:20 Baruch the son of Zabbai **d**
Job 7:21 dust, and You will seek me **d**
Job 13:17 Listen **d** to my speech, and to
Job 24: 5 work, seeking **d** for food
Ps 37:10 you will look **d** for his place
Ps 78:34 returned and sought **d** for God
Ps 119: 4 us To keep Your precepts **d**
Prov 1:28 they will seek me **d**, but they
Prov 7:15 **d** to seek your face, and I
Prov 8:17 who seek me **d** will find me
Prov 11:27 He who **d** seeks good finds
Is 21: 7 he listened **d** with great care
Is 55: 2 Listen **d** to Me, and eat what
Jer 2:10 send to Kedar and consider **d**
Jer 12:16 if they will **d** learn the ways
Jer 17:24 if you **d** heed Me," says the
Hos 5:15 they will **d** seek Me
Zech 6:15 shall come to pass if you **d**
Matt 2: 8 search **d** for the young Child,
Luke 15: 8 seek **d** until she finds it
1Ti 5:10 if she has **d** followed every
2Ti 1:17 Rome, he sought me out very **d**
Heb 11: 6 of those who **d** seek Him
Heb 12:15 looking **d** lest anyone fall
Heb 12:17 he sought it **d** with tears

1Pe 1:10 have inquired and searched **d**

DIM (*see* DIMLY)
Gen 27: 1 his eyes were so **d** that he
Gen 48:10 of Israel were **d** with age
Deut 34: 7 His eyes were not **d** nor his
1Sa 3: 2 so **d** that he could not see
1Sa 4:15 his eyes were so **d** that he
Job 17: 7 grown **d** because of sorrow
Eccl 12: 3 through the windows grow **d**
Is 32: 3 those who see will not be **d**
Lam 4: 1 How the gold has become **d**
Lam 5:17 these things our eyes grow **d**

DIMINISH (*see* DIMINISHED)
Ex 5: 8 You shall not **d** it
Ex 5:19 You shall not **d** any bricks
Ex 21:10 wife, he shall not **d** her food
Lev 25:16 years you shall **d** its price
Jer 26: 2 Do not **d** a word
Jer 30:19 them, and they shall not **d**
Ezek 5:11 therefore I will also **d** you
Ezek 29:15 for I will **d** them so that
Joel 2:10 the stars **d** their brightness
Joel 3:15 and the stars will **d** their
Zech 14: 6 the lights will **d**

DIMINISHED (*see* DIMINISH)
Ex 5:11 none of your work will be **d**
Ezra 4:13 the king's treasury will be **d**
Ps 107:39 When they are **d** and brought
Prov 13:11 by dishonesty will be **d**, but
Is 21:17 people of Kedar, will be **d**
Is 25: 5 the terrible ones will be **d**
Jer 29: 6 be increased there, and not **d**
Ezek 16:27 **d** your allotment, and gave you

DIMLY (*see* DIM)
1Co 13:12 For now we see in a mirror, **d**

DIMNAH
Josh 21:35 **D** with its common-land, and

DIMON (*see* DIBON, DIMONAH)
Is 15: 9 For the waters of **D** will be
Is 15: 9 I will bring more upon **D**,

DIMONAH (*see* DIMON)
Josh 15:22 Kinah, **D**, Adadah,

DINAH (*see* DINAH'S)
Gen 30:21 and called her name **D**
Gen 34: 1 Now **D** the daughter of Leah,
Gen 34: 3 to **D** the daughter of Jacob
Gen 34: 5 he had defiled **D** his daughter
Gen 34:13 he had defiled **D** their sister
Gen 34:26 took **D** from Shechem's house,
Gen 46:15 Aram, with his daughter **D**

DINAH'S (*see* DINAH)
Gen 34:25 **D** brothers, each took his

DINAITES
Ezra 4: 9 representatives of the **D**, the

DINE (*see* DINING)
Gen 43:16 men will **d** with me at noon
Esth 7: 1 Haman went to **d** with Queen
Luke 11:37 asked Him to **d** with him
Rev 3:20 **d** with him, and he with Me

DINHABAH
Gen 36:32 and the name of his city was **D**
1Ch 1:43 and the name of his city was **D**

DINING (*see* DINE)
Mark 2:15 as He was **d** in Levi's house,

DINNER
Prov 15:17 Better is a **d** of herbs where
Matt 22: 4 See, I have prepared my **d**
Luke 11:38 had not first washed before **d**
Luke 14:12 When you give a **d** or a supper
1Co 10:27 not believe invites you to **d**

DIONYSIUS
Acts 17:34 among them **D** the Areopagite,

DIOTREPHES
3Jn 9 I wrote to the church, but **D**

DIP (*see* DIPPED, DIPS)
Ex 12:22 **d** it in the blood that is in
Lev 4: 6 The priest shall **d** his
Lev 4:17 Then the priest shall **d** his
Lev 14: 6 **d** them and the living bird in
Lev 14:16 Then the priest shall **d** his
Lev 14:51 **d** them in the blood of the
Num 19:18 **d** it in the water, sprinkle

Deut 33:24 let him **d** his foot in oil
Ruth 2:14 **d** your piece of bread in the
Luke 16:24 **d** the tip of his finger in

DIPHATH
1Ch 1: 6 of Gomer were Ashkenaz, **D**

DIPPED (*see* DIP)
Gen 37:31 and **d** the tunic in the blood
Lev 9: 9 he **d** his finger in the blood,
Josh 3:15 priests who bore the ark **d** in
1Sa 14:27 **d** it in a honeycomb, and put
2Ki 5:14 **d** seven times in the Jordan,
2Ki 8:15 **d** it in water, and spread it
Matt 26:23 He who **d** his hand with Me in
John 13:26 of bread when I have **d** it
John 13:26 having **d** the bread, He gave
Rev 19:13 with a robe **d** in blood, and

DIPS (*see* DIP)
Mark 14:20 who **d** with Me in the dish

DIRE
Job 36:16 brought you out of **d** distress
Lam 1: 3 overtake her in **d** straits

DIRECT (*see* DIRECTED, DIRECTING, DIRECTION, DIRECTLY, DIRECTOR, DIRECTS)
1Ch 15:21 to **d** with harps on the
Ps 5: 3 morning I will **d** it to You
Ps 119:133 **D** my steps by Your word, And
Prov 3: 6 Him, and He shall **d** your paths
Prov 11: 5 will **d** his way aright, but
Is 45:13 and I will **d** all his ways
Is 61: 8 I will **d** their work in truth,
Jer 10:23 who walks to **d** his own steps
Ezek 26: 9 He will **d** his battering rams
Hos 5: 4 They do not **d** their deeds
1Th 3:11 Christ, **d** our way to you
2Th 3: 5 Now may the Lord **d** your

DIRECTED (*see* DIRECT)
1Sa 21: 2 I have **d** my young men to such
1Ki 12:12 the third day, as the king **d**
2Ch 20:33 as yet the people had not **d**
Job 32:14 Now he has not **d** his words
Ps 119: 5 that my ways were **d** To keep
Is 40:13 Who has **d** the Spirit of the
Matt 26:19 did as Jesus had **d** them
Matt 27:10 field, as the LORD **d** me

DIRECTING (*see* DIRECT)
Num 10: 2 for **d** the movement of the

DIRECTION (*see* DIRECT, DIRECTIONS)
Num 34: 8 then the **d** of the border
Judg 20:42 in the **d** of the wilderness
2Ki 7:14 in the **d** of the Syrian army
1Ch 25: 2 were under the **d** of Asaph
1Ch 25: 3 under the **d** of their father
1Ch 25: 6 the **d** of their father for the
Ezek 9: 2 from the **d** of the upper gate
Ezek 10:11 in the **d** the head was facing
Ezek 48: 1 in the **d** of Hamath, there
Acts 7:53 the law by the **d** of angels

DIRECTIONS (*see* DIRECTION)
1Ch 9:24 were assigned to the four **d**
Ezek 1:17 went toward any one of four **d**
Ezek 10:11 toward any of their four **d**

DIRECTLY (*see* DIRECT)
Num 19: 4 of its blood seven times **d** in
Ezek 42:12 the way **d** in front of the

DIRECTOR (*see* DIRECT)
Neh 12:42 with Jezrahiah as their **d**

DIRECTS (*see* DIRECT)
Prov 16: 9 way, but the LORD **d** his steps

DIRT
1Sa 4:12 clothes torn and **d** on his head
2Sa 22:43 them like **d** in the streets
Ps 18:42 out like **d** in the streets
Is 57:20 waters cast up mire and **d**

DISAPPEAR (*see* DISAPPEARED, DISAPPEARS)
Ps 12: 1 For the faithful **d** from among

DISAPPEARED (*see* DISAPPEAR)
Lev 13:58 if the plague has **d** from it

DISAPPEARS (*see* DISAPPEAR)
Job 7: 9 As the cloud **d** and vanishes
Job 14:11 As water **d** from the sea, and a

Mark 10:13 but the **d** rebuked those who
Mark 10:23 around and said to His **d**
Mark 10:24 the **d** were astonished at His
Mark 10:46 out of Jericho with His **d**
Mark 11: 1 He sent out two of His **d**
Mark 11:14 And His **d** heard it
Mark 12:43 So He called His **d** to Him
Mark 13: 1 one of His **d** said to Him,
Mark 14:12 lamb, His **d** said to Him,
Mark 14:13 So He sent out two of His **d**
Mark 14:14 eat the Passover with My **d**
Mark 14:16 His **d** went out, and came into
Mark 14:32 and He said to His **d**, "Sit
Mark 16: 7 But go and tell His **d**
Luke 5:30 murmured against His **d**,
Luke 5:33 Why do the **d** of John fast
Luke 6: 1 His **d** plucked the heads of
Luke 6:13 day, He called His **d** to Him
Luke 6:17 place with a crowd of His **d**
Luke 6:20 up His eyes toward His **d**, and
Luke 7:11 many of His **d** went with Him,
Luke 7:18 Then the **d** of John reported
Luke 7:19 calling two of his **d** to him
Luke 8: 9 Then His **d** asked Him, saying,
Luke 8:22 He got into a boat with His **d**
Luke 9: 1 called His twelve **d** together
Luke 9:14 And He said to His **d**, "Make
Luke 9:16 gave them to the **d** to set
Luke 9:18 that His **d** joined Him, and He
Luke 9:40 Your **d** to cast it out, but
Luke 9:43 Jesus did, He said to His **d**
Luke 9:54 And when His **d** James and John
Luke 10:23 And He turned to His **d** and said
Luke 11: 1 that one of His **d** said to Him
Luke 11: 1 as John also taught his **d**
Luke 12: 1 to say to His **d** first of all
Luke 12:22 And He said to His **d**
Luke 16: 1 And He also said to His **d**
Luke 17: 1 Then He said to the **d**, "It
Luke 17:22 Then He said to the **d**, "The
Luke 18:15 but when His **d** saw it, they
Luke 19:29 that He sent two of His **d**
Luke 19:37 of the **d** began to rejoice
Luke 19:39 Teacher, rebuke Your **d**
Luke 20:45 the people, He said to His **d**
Luke 22:11 eat the Passover with My **d**
Luke 22:39 and His **d** also followed Him
Luke 22:45 prayer, and had come to His **d**
John 1:35 John stood with two of his **d**
John 1:37 The two **d** heard him speak, and
John 2: 2 His **d** were invited to the
John 2:11 and His **d** believed in Him
John 2:12 His brothers, and His **d**
John 2:17 Then His **d** remembered that it
John 2:22 His **d** remembered that He had
John 3:22 His **d** came into the land of
John 3:25 between some of John's **d** and
John 4: 1 and baptized more **d** than John
John 4: 2 did not baptize, but His **d**)
John 4: 8 For His **d** had gone away into
John 4:27 And at this point His **d** came
John 4:31 the meantime His **d** urged Him
John 4:33 Therefore the **d** said to one
John 6: 3 and there He sat with His **d**
John 6: 8 One of His **d**, Andrew, Simon
John 6:11 He distributed them to the **d**
John 6:11 the **d** to those sitting down
John 6:12 were filled, He said to His **d**
John 6:16 His **d** went down to the sea,
John 6:22 one which His **d** had entered
John 6:22 entered the boat with His **d**
John 6:22 but His **d** had gone away alone
John 6:24 was not there, nor His **d**,
John 6:60 Therefore many of His **d**, when
John 6:61 His **d** murmured about this
John 6:66 time many of His **d** went back
John 7: 3 that Your **d** also may see the
John 8:31 My word, you are My **d** indeed
John 9: 2 And His **d** asked Him, saying,
John 9:27 you also want to become His **d**
John 9:28 disciple, but we are Moses' **d**
John 11: 7 after this He said to the **d**
John 11: 8 The **d** said to Him, "Rabbi,
John 11:12 Then His **d** said, "Lord, if
John 11:16 Didymus, said to his fellow **d**
John 11:54 and there remained with His **d**
John 12: 4 Then one of His **d**, Judas
John 12:16 His **d** did not understand
John 13:22 Then the **d** looked at one
John 13:23 on Jesus' bosom one of His **d**
John 13:35 will know that you are My **d**
John 15: 8 so you will be My **d**
John 16:17 Then some of His **d** said among
John 16:29 His **d** said to Him, "See, now
John 18: 1 He went out with His **d** over
John 18: 1 which He and His **d** entered
John 18: 2 often met there with His **d**
John 18:17 not also one of this Man's **d**
John 18:19 then asked Jesus about His **d**
John 18:25 You are not also one of His **d**
John 20:10 Then the **d** went away again to
John 20:18 told the **d** that she had seen
John 20:19 where the **d** were assembled
John 20:20 Then the **d** were glad when
John 20:25 The other **d** therefore said to
John 20:26 days His **d** were again inside
John 20:30 in the presence of His **d**,
John 21: 1 the **d** at the Sea of Tiberias
John 21: 2 others of His **d** were together
John 21: 4 yet the **d** did not know that
John 21: 8 But the other **d** came in the
John 21:12 none of the **d** dared ask Him
John 21:14 **d** after He was raised from
Acts 1:15 up in the midst of the **d**
Acts 6: 1 of the **d** was multiplying,
Acts 6: 2 the multitude of the **d** and
Acts 6: 7 and the number of the **d**
Acts 9: 1 against the **d** of the Lord
Acts 9:19 days with the **d** at Damascus
Acts 9:25 Then the **d** took him by night
Acts 9:26 he tried to join the **d**
Acts 9:38 the **d** had heard that Peter
Acts 11:26 And the **d** were first called
Acts 11:29 Then the **d**, each according to
Acts 13:52 the **d** were filled with joy and
Acts 14:20 when the **d** gathered around
Acts 14:21 to that city and made many **d**
Acts 14:22 the souls of the **d**, exhorting
Acts 14:28 there a long time with the **d**
Acts 15:10 **d** which neither our fathers
Acts 18:23 strengthening all the **d**
Acts 18:27 exhorting the **d** to receive
Acts 19: 1 And finding some **d**
Acts 19: 9 from them and withdrew the **d**
Acts 19:30 the **d** would not allow him
Acts 20: 1 Paul called the **d** to him
Acts 20: 7 when the **d** came together to
Acts 20:30 away the **d** after themselves
Acts 21: 4 And finding **d**, we stayed there
Acts 21:16 Also some of the **d** from

DISCIPLES' (*see* DISCIPLES)
John 13: 5 and began to wash the **d** feet

DISCIPLINE (*see* DISCIPLE, DISCIPLINED, DISCIPLINES)
1Co 9:27 But I **d** my body and bring it

DISCIPLINED (*see* DISCIPLINE)
Hos 7:15 Though I **d** and strengthened

DISCIPLINES (*see* DISCIPLINE)
Prov 13:24 who loves him **d** him promptly

DISCLOSE
Ps 49: 4 I will **d** my dark saying on
Prov 25: 9 and do not **d** the secret to
Is 26:21 earth will also **d** her blood

DISCONTENTED
1Sa 22: 2 who was **d** gathered to him

DISCONTINUED
Ezra 4:24 it was **d** until the second

DISCORD
Prov 6:14 evil continually, he sows **d**
Prov 6:19 one who sows **d** among brethren

DISCOURAGE (*see* DISCOURAGED)
Num 32: 7 Now why will you **d** the heart
Ezra 4: 4 to **d** the people of Judah

DISCOURAGED (*see* DISCOURAGE)
Num 21: 4 became very **d** on the way
Num 32: 9 land, they **d** the heart of the
Deut 1:21 do not fear or be **d**
Deut 1:28 brethren have **d** our hearts
Is 42: 4 He will not fail nor be **d**
Col 3:21 children, lest they become **d**
Heb 12: 3 weary and **d** in your souls
Heb 12: 5 nor be **d** when you are rebuked

DISCOURSE
Job 27: 1 Moreover Job continued his **d**
Job 29: 1 Job further continued his **d**

DISCOVER (*see* DISCOVERED)
Eccl 8:17 though a man labors to **d** it

DISCOVERED (*see* DISCOVER)
Lev 20:18 he has **d** her flow, and she has
1Sa 22: 6 who were with him had been **d**
Neh 13: 7 **d** the evil that Eliashib had
Job 8: 8 the things **d** by their fathers
Job 36:26 the number of His years be **d**

DISCREET (*see* DISCRETION)
Tit 2: 5 to be **d**, chaste, homemakers,

DISCRETION (*see* DISCREET)
Ps 112: 5 will guide his affairs with **d**
Prov 1: 4 the young man knowledge and **d**
Prov 2:11 **d** will preserve you
Prov 3:21 keep sound wisdom and **d**
Prov 5: 2 that you may preserve **d**, and
Prov 8:12 and find out knowledge and **d**
Prov 11:22 is a lovely woman who lacks **d**
Prov 19:11 The **d** of a man makes him slow
Jer 10:12 out the heavens at His **d**

DISCUSSED (*see* DISCUSSING, DISCUSSION)
Luke 1:65 and all these sayings were **d**
Luke 6:11 **d** with one another what they

DISCUSSING (*see* DISCUSSED)
Mark 9:16 What are you **d** with them

DISCUSSION (*see* DISCUSSED)
Heb 6: 1 leaving the **d** of the

DISDAIN (*see* DISDAINED, DISDAINS)
Prov 8:33 and be wise, and do not **d** it
Ezek 25: 6 your **d** for the land of Israel

DISDAINED (*see* DISDAIN)
1Sa 17:42 about and saw David, he **d** him
Esth 3: 6 But he **d** to lay hands on
Job 30: 1 whose fathers I **d** to put with
Prov 1:25 because you **d** all my counsel,

DISDAINS (*see* DISDAIN)
Prov 13:18 come to him who **d** correction
Prov 15:32 He who **d** instruction despises

DISEASE (*see* DISEASED, DISEASES)
Lev 26:16 terror over you, wasting **d**
2Ki 8: 8 Shall I recover from this **d**
2Ki 8: 9 Shall I recover from this **d**
2Ch 16:12 yet in his **d** he did not seek
2Ch 21:15 with a **d** of your intestines
2Ch 21:18 with an incurable **d**
Ps 41: 8 An evil **d**," they say
Matt 4:23 and all kinds of **d** among the
Matt 9:35 and every **d** among the people
Matt 10: 1 of sickness and all kinds of **d**
John 5: 4 well of whatever **d** he had

DISEASED (*see* DISEASE)
1Ki 15:23 old age he was **d** in his feet
2Ch 16:12 Asa became **d** in his feet, and
John 6: 2 performed on those who were **d**

DISEASES (*see* DISEASE)
Ex 15:26 I will put none of the **d** on
Deut 7:15 **d** of Egypt which you have
Deut 28:60 on you all the **d** of Egypt
Ps 103: 3 Who heals all your **d**,
Matt 4:24 were afflicted with various **d**
Mark 1:34 who were sick with various **d**
Luke 4:40 various **d** brought them to Him
Luke 6:17 Him and be healed of their **d**
Luke 9: 1 over all demons, and to cure **d**
Acts 19:12 the **d** left them and the evil
Acts 28: 9 island who had **d** also came

DISFIGURE (*see* DISFIGURED, DISFIGUREMENT)
Lev 19:27 nor shall you **d** the edges of
Matt 6:16 For they **d** their faces that

DISFIGURED (*see* DISFIGURE)
Job 30:18 great force my garment is **d**

DISFIGUREMENT (*see* DISFIGURE)
Lev 24:19 man causes **d** of his neighbor
Lev 24:20 as he has caused **d** of a man

DISGRACE (*see* DISGRACED, DISGRACEFUL)
Job 10:15 I am full of **d**
Job 19: 5 me, and plead my **d** against me,
Ps 109:29 their own **d** as with a mantle

Jer 14:21 do not **d** the throne of Your

DISGRACED (*see* DISGRACE)
2Sa 19: 5 Today you have **d** all your
Is 24:23 Then the moon will be **d** and
Is 41:11 you shall be ashamed and **d**
Is 45:16 shall be ashamed and also **d**
Is 45:17 not be ashamed or **d** forever
Is 50: 7 therefore I will not be **d**
Is 54: 4 nor be **d**, for you will not be
Ezek 16:52 be **d** also, and bear your own
Ezek 16:54 be **d** by all that you did when

DISGRACEFUL (*see* DISGRACE)
Gen 34: 7 because he had done a **d** thing
Deut 22:21 has done a **d** thing in Israel
Josh 7:15 has done a **d** thing in Israel
2Sa 13:12 Do not do this **d** thing
Jer 29:23 have done **d** things in Israel

DISGUISE (*see* DISGUISED, DISGUISES)
1Ki 14: 2 **d** yourself, that they may not
1Ki 22:30 I will **d** myself and go into
2Ch 18:29 I will **d** myself and go into

DISGUISED (*see* DISGUISE)
1Sa 28: 8 So Saul **d** himself and put on
1Ki 20:38 **d** himself with a bandage over
1Ki 22:30 the king of Israel **d** himself
2Ch 18:29 the king of Israel **d** himself
2Ch 35:22 him, but **d** himself so that he

DISGUISES (*see* DISGUISE)
Job 24:15 and he **d** his face
Prov 26:24 **d** it with his lips, and lays

DISGUSTED
Ps 119:158 see the treacherous, and am **d**

DISH (*see* DISHES)
2Ki 21:13 Jerusalem as one wipes a **d**
Matt 23:25 the outside of the cup and **d**
Matt 23:26 the inside of the cup and **d**
Matt 26:23 Me in the **d** will betray Me
Mark 14:20 who dips with Me in the **d**
Luke 11:39 **d** clean, but your inward part

DISHAN (*see* DISHON)
Gen 36:21 Dishon, Ezer, and **D**
Gen 36:28 These were the sons of **D**
Gen 36:30 Chief Ezer, and Chief **D**
1Ch 1:38 Anah, Dishon, Ezer, and **D**
1Ch 1:42 The sons of **D** were Uz and Aran

DISHEARTENED
Neh 6:16 were very **d** in their own eyes

DISHES (*see* DISH)
Ex 25:29 You shall make its **d**, its
Ex 37:16 its **d**, its cups, its bowls,
Num 4: 7 cloth, and put on it the **d**

DISHON (*see* DISHAN)
Gen 36:21 **D**, Ezer, and Dishan
Gen 36:25 **D** and Aholibamah the daughter
Gen 36:26 These were the sons of **D**
Gen 36:30 Chief **D**, Chief Ezer, and Chief
1Ch 1:38 Shobal, Zibeon, Anah, **D**,
1Ch 1:41 The son of Anah was **D**
1Ch 1:41 The sons of **D** were Hamran

DISHONEST (*see* DISHONESTY)
1Sa 8: 3 turned aside after **d** gain
Ezek 22:13 I beat My fists at the **d**
Ezek 22:27 people, and to get **d** gain
Tit 1:11 not, for the sake of **d** gain
1Pe 5: 2 not for **d** gain but eagerly

DISHONESTY (*see* DISHONEST)
Prov 13:11 Wealth gained by **d** will be

DISHONOR (*see* DISHONORED, DISHONORS)
Ezra 4:14 for us to see the king's **d**
Ps 35: 4 brought to **d** Who seek after
Ps 35:26 and **d** Who magnify themselves
Ps 40:14 brought to **d** Who wish me evil
Ps 44:15 My **d** is continually before me
Ps 69:19 reproach, my shame, and my **d**
Ps 71:13 and **d** Who seek my hurt
Prov 6:33 and **d** he will get, and his
Prov 18: 3 and with **d** comes reproach
Is 23: 9 to bring to **d** the pride of
Hos 4:18 Her rulers dearly love **d**
John 8:49 honor My Father, and you **d** Me
Rom 1:24 to **d** their bodies among
Rom 2:23 do you **d** God through breaking
Rom 9:21 for honor and another for **d**
1Co 11:14 long hair, it is a **d** to him
1Co 15:43 It is sown in **d**, it is raised
2Co 6: 8 by honor and **d**, by evil report
2Ti 2:20 some for honor and some for **d**

DISHONORED (*see* DISHONOR)
1Co 4:10 distinguished, but we are **d**
Jas 2: 6 But you have **d** the poor man

DISHONORS (*see* DISHONOR)
Mic 7: 6 For son **d** father, daughter
1Co 11: 4 his head covered, **d** his head
1Co 11: 5 her head uncovered **d** her head

DISINHERIT
Num 14:12 **d** them, and I will make of you

DISLOCATED
Heb 12:13 what is lame may not be **d**

DISMAY (*see* DISMAYED)
Jer 1:17 lest I **d** you before them
Jer 48:39 a **d** to all those about her
Ezek 8:14 and to my **d**, women were

DISMAYED (*see* DISMAY)
Gen 45: 3 him, for they were **d** in his
Ex 15:15 the chiefs of Edom will be **d**
Deut 31: 8 do not fear nor be **d**
Josh 1: 9 do not be afraid, nor be **d**
Josh 8: 1 Do not be afraid, nor be **d**
Josh 10:25 Do not be afraid, nor be **d**
1Sa 17:11 the Philistine, they were **d**
2Ki 19:26 they were **d** and confounded
1Ch 22:13 do not fear nor be **d**
1Ch 28:20 do not fear nor be **d**, for the
2Ch 20:15 nor **d** because of this great
2Ch 20:17 Do not fear or be **d**
2Ch 32: 7 do not be afraid nor **d** before
Job 32:15 They are **d** and answer no more
Ps 83:17 be confounded and **d** forever
Is 21: 3 I was **d** when I saw it
Is 37:27 they were **d** and confounded
Is 41:10 be not **d**, for I am your God
Is 41:23 or do evil, that we may be **d**
Jer 1:17 Do not be **d** before their
Jer 8: 9 men are ashamed, they are **d**
Jer 10: 2 do not be **d** at the signs of
Jer 10: 2 the Gentiles are **d** at them
Jer 17:18 let them be **d**, but do not let
Jer 17:18 but do not let me be **d**
Jer 23: 4 shall fear no more, nor be **d**
Jer 30:10 says the LORD, 'nor be **d**
Jer 46: 5 Why have I seen them **d** and
Jer 46:27 servant Jacob, and do not be **d**
Jer 48: 1 stronghold is shamed and **d**
Jer 49:37 to be **d** before their enemies
Jer 50:36 mighty men, and they will be **d**
Ezek 2: 6 words or **d** by their looks
Ezek 3: 9 nor be **d** at their looks,
Ezek 4:17 be **d** with one another, and
Obad 9 men, O Teman, shall be **d**, to

DISMEMBERED
Judg 19:29 **d** her into twelve pieces,

DISMISS (*see* DISMISSED)
1Ki 20:24 **D** the kings, each from his
Mark 10: 4 of divorce, and to **d** her

DISMISSED (*see* DISMISS)
Judg 2: 6 when Joshua had **d** the people
2Ch 23: 8 had not **d** the divisions
Zech 11: 8 I **d** the three shepherds in
Acts 19:41 things, he **d** the assembly

DISMOUNT (*see* DISMOUNTED)
1Sa 25:23 hastened to **d** from the donkey

DISMOUNTED (*see* DISMOUNT)
Gen 24:64 Isaac she **d** from her camel
Josh 15:18 So she **d** from her donkey, and
Judg 1:14 she **d** from her donkey, and

DISOBEDIENCE (*see* DISOBEDIENT)
Ezek 5: 7 **d** more than the nations that
Rom 5:19 For as by one man's **d** many
Rom 11:30 mercy through their **d**,
Rom 11:32 has committed them all to **d**
2Co 10: 6 all **d** when your obedience is
Eph 2: 2 now works in the sons of **d**
Eph 5: 6 God comes upon the sons of **d**
Col 3: 6 is coming upon the sons of **d**
Heb 2: 2 **d** received a just reward,
Heb 4: 6 did not enter because of **d**
Heb 4:11 after the same example of **d**

DISOBEDIENT (*see* DISOBEDIENCE, DISOBEYED)
1Ki 13:26 was **d** to the word of the LORD
Neh 9:26 Nevertheless they were **d** and
Luke 1:17 the **d** to the wisdom of the
Acts 26:19 I was not **d** to the heavenly
Rom 1:30 of evil things, **d** to parents,
Rom 10:21 stretched out My hands to a **d**
Rom 11:30 For as you were once **d** to God
Rom 11:31 so these also have now been **d**
2Ti 3: 2 **d** to parents, unthankful,
Tit 1:16 deny Him, being abominable, **d**
Tit 3: 3 were also once foolish, **d**
1Pe 2: 7 but to those who are **d**, "The
1Pe 2: 8 being **d** to the word, to which
1Pe 3:20 who formerly were **d**, when

DISOBEYED (*see* DISOBEDIENT, DISOBEYING)
1Ki 13:21 Because you have **d** the word

DISOBEYING (*see* DISOBEYED)
Jer 42:13 **d** the voice of the LORD your

DISORDERLY
Acts 19:40 account for this **d** gathering
2Th 3: 6 every brother who walks **d**
2Th 3: 7 for we were not **d** among you
2Th 3:11 walk among you in a **d** manner

DISPATCHES
Job 37:15 Do you know when God **d** them

DISPENSATION
Eph 1:10 that in the **d** of the fullness
Eph 3: 2 you have heard of the **d** of

DISPERSE (*see* DISPERSED, DISPERSION)
1Sa 14:34 **D** yourselves among the people
Job 40:11 **D** the rage of your wrath
Prov 15: 7 lips of the wise **d** knowledge
Ezek 12:15 and **d** them throughout the
Ezek 20:23 and **d** them throughout the
Ezek 22:15 nations, **d** you throughout the
Ezek 29:12 and **d** them throughout the
Ezek 30:23 and **d** them throughout the
Ezek 30:26 and **d** them throughout the
Dan 11:24 he shall **d** among them the

DISPERSED (*see* DISPERSE)
Gen 10:18 of the Canaanites were **d**
2Ch 11:23 **d** some of his sons throughout
Esth 3: 8 **d** among the people in all the
Ps 112: 9 He has **d** abroad, He has given
Prov 5:16 your fountains be **d** abroad
Is 11:12 and gather together the **d** of
Ezek 36:19 they were **d** throughout the
Zeph 3:10 the daughter of My **d** ones
Acts 5:37 and all who obeyed him were **d**
2Co 9: 9 He has **d** abroad, He has given

DISPERSION (*see* DISPERSE, DISPERSIONS)
John 7:35 go to the **D** among the Greeks
1Pe 1: 1 pilgrims of the **D** in Pontus

DISPERSIONS (*see* DISPERSION)
Jer 25:34 and your **d** are fulfilled

DISPLACE
Deut 12:29 you **d** them and dwell in their

DISPLAYED
Ps 60: 4 That it may be **d** because of
1Co 4: 9 For I think that God has **d** us

DISPLEASE (*see* DISPLEASED, DISPLEASES, DISPLEASING, DISPLEASURE)
Gen 31:35 Let it not **d** my lord that I
1Sa 29: 7 may not **d** the lords of the
2Sa 11:25 Do not let this thing **d** you
Prov 24:18 it **d** Him, and He turn away His

DISPLEASED (*see* DISPLEASE)
Gen 38:10 thing which he did **d** the LORD
Gen 48:17 the head of Ephraim, it **d** him
Num 11: 1 complained, it **d** the LORD
Num 11:10 Moses also was **d**
1Sa 8: 6 But the thing **d** Samuel when
1Sa 18: 8 angry, and the saying **d** him
2Sa 11:27 David had done **d** the LORD
1Ki 20:43 went to his house sullen and **d**
1Ki 21: 4 **d** because of the word which
1Ch 21: 7 God was **d** with this thing
Ps 60: 1 You have been **d**
Is 59:15 it **d** Him that there was no
Dan 6:14 was greatly **d** with himself,
Jon 4: 1 But it **d** Jonah exceedingly,
Hab 3: 8 were You **d** with the rivers,

Mark 10:14 saw it, He was greatly **d** and
Mark 10:41 to be greatly **d** with James

DISPLEASES (*see* DISPLEASE)
Num 22:34 Now therefore, if it **d** You

DISPLEASING (*see* DISPLEASE)
Gen 21:11 And the matter was very **d** in
Gen 21:12 Do not let it be **d** in your
Jer 42: 6 Whether it is pleasing or **d**

DISPLEASURE (*see* DISPLEASE)
Deut 9:19 hot **d** with which the LORD was
Ps 2: 5 distress them in His deep **d**
Ps 6: 1 Nor chasten me in Your hot **d**
Ps 38: 1 Nor chasten me in Your hot **d**

DISPOSED (*see* DISPOSSESS)
Num 22:30 Was I ever **d** to do this to

DISPOSSESS (*see* DISPOSED, DISPOSSESSED, DISPOSSESSING)
Num 33:53 you shall **d** the inhabitants
Deut 7:17 how can I **d** them
Deut 9: 1 go in to **d** nations greater and
Deut 11:23 you, and you will **d** greater
Deut 12: 2 you shall **d** served their gods
Deut 12:29 the nations which you go to **d**
Deut 18:14 nations which you will **d**
Deut 19: 1 you **d** them and dwell in their
Deut 31: 3 you, and you shall **d** them

DISPOSSESSED (*see* DISPOSSESS)
Num 32:39 **d** the Amorites who were in it
Deut 2:12 descendants of Esau **d** them
Deut 2:21 before them, and they **d** them
Deut 2:22 They **d** them and dwelt in their
Judg 11:23 **d** the Amorites from before

DISPOSSESSING (*see* DISPOSSESS)
Ezek 45: 9 stop **d** My people," says the

DISPUTE (*see* DISPUTED, DISPUTER, DISPUTES, DISPUTING)
Ex 23: 2 a **d** so as to turn aside after
Ex 23: 3 to a poor man in his **d**
Ex 23: 6 of your poor in his **d**
Deut 25: 1 If there is a **d** between men
2Sa 19: 9 all the people were in a **d**
Mark 8:11 out and began to **d** with Him
Luke 9:46 Then a **d** arose among them as
John 3:25 Then there arose a **d** between
Acts 15: 2 **d** with them, they determined
Acts 15: 7 when there had been much **d**
Acts 28:29 and had a great **d** among
Heb 6:16 is for them an end of all **d**

DISPUTED (*see* DISPUTE)
Mark 9:33 What was it you **d** among
Mark 9:34 for on the road they had **d**
Acts 9:29 **d** against the Hellenists, but
Jude 9 when he **d** about the body of

DISPUTER (*see* DISPUTE)
1Co 1:20 Where is the **d** of this age

DISPUTES (*see* DISPUTE)
2Sa 20:18 Abel,' and so they would end **d**
Rom 14: 1 but not to **d** over doubtful
1Ti 1: 4 which cause **d** rather than
1Ti 6: 4 but is obsessed with **d** and
2Ti 2:23 avoid foolish and ignorant **d**
Tit 3: 9 But avoid foolish **d**,

DISPUTING (*see* DISPUTE)
Mark 9:14 them, and scribes **d** with them
Acts 6: 9 and Asia), **d** with Stephen
Acts 24:12 found me in the temple **d** with
Phil 2:14 things without murmuring and **d**

DISQUALIFIED
1Co 9:27 I myself should become **d**
2Co 13: 5 unless indeed you are **d**
2Co 13: 6 will know that we are not **d**
2Co 13: 7 though we may seem **d**
Tit 1:16 and **d** for every good work

DISQUIET (*see* DISQUIETED, DISQUIETING)
Jer 50:34 **d** the inhabitants of Babylon

DISQUIETED (*see* DISQUIET)
Ps 42: 5 And why are you **d** within me
Ps 42:11 And why are you **d** within me
Ps 43: 5 And why are you **d** within me

DISQUIETING (*see* DISQUIET)
Job 4:13 In **d** thoughts from the

DISREGARDED
Heb 8: 9 I **d** them," says the LORD

DISREPUTABLE (*see* DISREPUTE)
Prov 19:28 A **d** witness scorns justice,

DISREPUTE (*see* DISREPUTABLE)
Acts 19:27 in danger of falling into **d**

DISSENSION (*see* DISSENSIONS)
Acts 15: 2 and Barnabas had no small **d**
Acts 23: 7 this, a **d** arose between the
Acts 23:10 And when there arose a great **d**
Acts 24: 5 a creator of **d** among all the

DISSENSIONS (*see* DISSENSION)
Gal 5:20 wrath, selfish ambitions, **d**

DISSIPATION
Eph 5:18 with wine, in which is **d**
Tit 1: 6 of **d** or insubordination
1Pe 4: 4 them in the same flood of **d**

DISSOLVE (*see* DISSOLVED)
Zech 14:12 Their flesh shall **d** while
Zech 14:12 eyes shall **d** in their sockets
Zech 14:12 shall **d** in their mouths

DISSOLVED (*see* DISSOLVE)
Ps 75: 3 and all its inhabitants are **d**
Is 14:31 All you of Philistia are **d**
Is 34: 4 the host of heaven shall be **d**
Nah 2: 6 opened, and the palace is **d**
2Pe 3:11 all these things will be **d**
2Pe 3:12 will be **d** being on fire, and

DISTAFF
Prov 31:19 out her hands to the **d**, and

DISTANCE
Gen 21:16 him at a **d** of about a bowshot
Gen 32:16 put some **d** between successive
Gen 35:16 a little **d** to go to Ephrath
Gen 48: 7 a little **d** to go to Ephrath
Num 2: 2 they shall camp some **d** from
Num 16:37 scatter the fire some **d** away
Deut 21: 2 they shall measure the **d** from
1Sa 26:13 a great **d** being between them
2Ki 2: 7 and stood facing them at a **d**
2Ki 5:19 departed from him a short **d**
Job 39:24 He devours the **d** with
Ezek 42: 4 wide, at a **d** of one cubit
Matt 26:58 at a **d** to the high priest's
Mark 14:54 But Peter followed Him at a **d**
Luke 22:54 And Peter followed at a **d**
Luke 23:49 from Galilee, stood at a **d**
Rev 18:10 standing at a **d** for fear of
Rev 18:15 will stand at a **d** for fear of
Rev 18:17 on the sea, stood at a **d**

DISTILL
Deut 32: 2 my speech **d** as the dew, as
Job 36:27 which **d** as rain from the mist

DISTINCTION (*see* DISTINCTLY, DISTINGUISH)
Acts 15: 9 made no **d** between us and them,
Rom 10:12 For there is no **d** between Jew
1Co 14: 7 they make a **d** in the sounds
Jude 22 have compassion, making a **d**

DISTINCTLY (*see* DISTINCTION)
Neh 8: 8 So they read **d** from the book,

DISTINGUISH (*see* DISTINCTION, DISTINGUISHED)
Lev 10:10 that you may **d** between holy
Lev 11:47 To **d** between the unclean and
Lev 20:25 **d** between clean beasts and
2Ch 12: 8 that they may **d** My service

DISTINGUISHED (*see* DISTINGUISH)
Ezek 22:26 they have not **d** between the
Dan 6: 3 Then this Daniel **d** himself
1Co 4:10 You are **d**, but we are

DISTORTS
Is 24: 1 **d** its surface and scatters

DISTRACTED (*see* DISTRACTION)
Luke 10:40 But Martha was **d** with much

DISTRACTION (*see* DISTRACTED)
1Co 7:35 may serve the Lord without **d**

DISTRAUGHT
Ps 88:15 I am **d**

DISTRESS (*see* DISTRESSED, DISTRESSES, DISTRESSING)
Gen 35: 3 me in the day of my **d** and has
Gen 42:21 therefore this **d** has come
Deut 4:30 When you are in **d**, and all
Deut 28:53 which your enemy shall **d** you
Deut 28:55 shall **d** you at all your gates
Deut 28:57 shall **d** you at all your gates
Judg 10:14 deliver you in your time of **d**
Judg 11: 7 to me now when you are in **d**
1Sa 22: 2 And everyone who was in **d**,
2Sa 22: 7 In my **d** I called upon the
2Sa 24:14 I am in great **d**
1Ki 1:29 redeemed my life from every **d**
2Ki 4:27 for her soul is in deep **d**
1Ch 21:13 I am in great **d**
2Ch 28:22 of his **d** King Ahaz became
Neh 1: 3 province are there in great **d**
Neh 2:17 You see the **d** that we are in,
Neh 9:37 And we are in great **d**
Job 20:22 he will be in **d**
Job 36:16 brought you out of dire **d**
Job 36:19 forces, keep you from **d**
Ps 2: 5 wrath, And **d** them in His deep
Ps 4: 1 relieved me when I was in **d**
Ps 18: 6 In my **d** I called upon the
Ps 118: 5 I called on the LORD in **d**
Ps 120: 1 In my **d** I cried to the LORD,
Prov 1:27 like a whirlwind, when **d** and
Is 21:15 bow, and from the **d** of war
Is 25: 4 to the needy in his **d**, a
Is 29: 2 Yet I will **d** Ariel
Is 29: 7 **d** her, shall be as a dream of
Jer 10:18 of the land, and will **d** them
Lam 1:20 See, O LORD, that I am in **d**
Ezek 30:16 and Noph shall be in **d** daily
Obad 12 proudly in the day of **d**
Obad 14 who remained in the day of **d**
Zeph 1:15 wrath, a day of trouble and **d**
Zeph 1:17 I will bring **d** upon men, and
Luke 21:23 will be great **d** in the land
Luke 21:25 and on the earth **d** of nations
Rom 8:35 Shall tribulation, or **d**, or
1Co 7:26 good because of the present **d**
Phil 4:14 well that you shared in my **d**
1Th 3: 7 and **d** we were comforted

DISTRESSED (*see* DISTRESS)
Gen 32: 7 Jacob was greatly afraid and **d**
Judg 2:15 And they were greatly **d**
Judg 10: 9 so that Israel was severely **d**
1Sa 13: 6 (for the people were **d**), then
1Sa 14:24 men of Israel were **d** that day
1Sa 28:15 I am deeply **d**
1Sa 30: 6 Then David was greatly **d**, for
2Sa 1:26 I am **d** for you, my brother
2Sa 13: 2 Amnon was so **d** over his
2Ch 28:20 **d** him, and did not assist him
Esth 4: 4 and the queen was deeply **d**
Ps 143: 4 My heart within me is **d**
Is 9: 1 will not be upon her who is **d**
Is 21: 3 I was **d** when I heard it
Matt 26:37 to be sorrowful and deeply **d**
Mark 14:33 to be troubled and deeply **d**
Luke 12:50 and how **d** I am till it is
Phil 2:26 was **d** because you had heard

DISTRESSES (*see* DISTRESS)
Ps 25:17 Oh, bring me out of my **d**
Ps 107: 6 delivered them out of their **d**
Ps 107:13 He saved them out of their **d**
Ps 107:19 He saved them out of their **d**
Ps 107:28 He brings them out of their **d**
2Co 6: 4 tribulations, in needs, in **d**
2Co 12:10 needs, in persecutions, in **d**

DISTRESSING (*see* DISTRESS)
1Sa 16:14 and a **d** spirit from the LORD
1Sa 16:15 a **d** spirit from God is
1Sa 16:16 it with his hand when the **d**
1Sa 16:23 the **d** spirit would depart
1Sa 18:10 on the next day that the **d**
1Sa 19: 9 Now the **d** spirit from the
Is 21: 2 a **d** vision is declared to me

DISTRIBUTE (*see* DISTRIBUTED, DISTRIBUTES, DISTRIBUTING, DISTRIBUTION)
2Ch 31:14 to **d** the offerings of the
2Ch 31:15 to **d** allotments to their
2Ch 31:19 **d** portions to all the males

Neh 13:13 was to **d** to their brethren
Luke 18:22 **d** to the poor, and you will

DISTRIBUTED (*see* DISTRIBUTE)
Josh 13:32 **d** as an inheritance in the
Josh 14: 1 **d** as an inheritance to them
2Sa 6:19 Then he **d** among all the
1Ch 16: 3 Then he **d** to everyone of
2Ch 31:16 they **d** to everyone who
John 6:11 He **d** them to the disciples
Acts 4:35 they **d** to each as anyone had
Acts 13:19 He **d** their land to them by
1Co 7:17 But as God has **d** to each one

DISTRIBUTES (*see* DISTRIBUTE)
Job 21:17 sorrows God **d** in His anger

DISTRIBUTING (*see* DISTRIBUTE)
Rom 12:13 **d** to the needs of the saints,
1Co 12:11 **d** to each one individually as

DISTRIBUTION (*see* DISTRIBUTE)
Acts 6: 1 were neglected in the daily **d**

DISTRICT (*see* DISTRICTS)
Neh 3: 9 of half the **d** of Jerusalem
Neh 3:12 of half the **d** of Jerusalem
Neh 3:14 leader of the **d** of Beth
Neh 3:15 leader of the **d** of Mizpah
Neh 3:16 of half the **d** of Beth Zur
Neh 3:17 of half the **d** of Keilah, made
Neh 3:17 made repairs for his **d**
Neh 3:18 other half of the **d** of Keilah
Ezek 45: 1 set apart a **d** for the LORD
Ezek 45: 3 So this is the **d** you shall
Ezek 45: 6 adjacent to the **d** of the holy
Ezek 45: 7 and the other of the holy **d**
Ezek 45: 7 and bordering on the holy **d**
Ezek 48: 8 shall be the **d** which you
Ezek 48: 9 The **d** that you shall set
Ezek 48:10 shall this holy **d** belong
Ezek 48:12 this **d** of land that is set
Ezek 48:18 alongside the **d** of the holy
Ezek 48:18 to the **d** of the holy portion
Ezek 48:20 The entire **d** shall be
Ezek 48:20 **d** with the property of the
Ezek 48:21 and on the other of the holy **d**
Ezek 48:21 holy **d** as far as the eastern
Ezek 48:21 It shall be the holy **d**, and

DISTRICTS (*see* DISTRICT)
Neh 9:22 and divided them into **d**
Hos 11: 6 in his cities, devour his **d**
Matt 2:16 in Bethlehem and in all its **d**

DISTURBED (*see* DISTURBS)
1Sa 28:15 Why have you **d** me by bringing
Neh 2:10 they were deeply **d** that a man
Job 40:23 may rage, Yet he is not **d**
Is 31: 4 nor be **d** by their noise), so
Acts 4: 2 being greatly **d** that they
Acts 21:30 And all the city was **d**

DISTURBS (*see* DISTURBED)
Jer 31:35 Who **d** the sea, and its waves

DITCH (*see* DITCHES)
Ps 7:15 into the **d** which he made
Matt 15:14 both will fall into a **d**
Luke 6:39 they not both fall into the **d**

DITCHES (*see* DITCH)
2Ki 3:16 Make this valley full of **d**

DIVERSE (*see* DIVERSITIES)
Prov 20:10 **D** weights and **d** measures
Prov 20:23 **D** weights are an abomination

DIVERSITIES (*see* DIVERSE)
1Co 12: 4 Now there are **d** of gifts, but
1Co 12: 6 there are **d** of activities,

DIVERT
Amos 5:12 you **d** the poor from justice

DIVIDE (*see* DIVIDED, DIVIDER, DIVIDES, DIVIDING, DIVISION, DIVISIVE)
Gen 1: 6 let it **d** the waters from the
Gen 1:14 to **d** the day from the night
Gen 1:18 and to **d** the light from the
Gen 49: 7 I will **d** them in Jacob and
Gen 49:27 at night he shall **d** the spoil
Ex 14:16 hand over the sea and **d** it
Ex 15: 9 overtake, I will **d** the spoil
Ex 21:35 ox and **d** the money from it
Ex 21:35 the dead ox they shall also **d**
Lev 1:17 but shall not **d** it completely
Lev 5: 8 but shall not **d** it completely
Num 31:27 **d** the plunder into two parts,
Num 33:54 you shall **d** the land by lot
Num 34:17 **d** the land among you as an
Num 34:18 tribe to **d** the land for the
Num 34:29 **d** the inheritance among the
Deut 19: 3 and **d** into three parts the
Josh 1: 6 to this people you shall **d** as
Josh 13: 6 only **d** it by lot to Israel as
Josh 13: 7 **d** this land as an inheritance
Josh 18: 5 they shall **d** it into seven
Josh 22: 8 **D** the spoil of your enemies
2Sa 19:29 said, 'You and Ziba **d** the land
1Ki 3:25 **D** the living child in two, and
1Ki 3:26 mine nor yours, but **d** him
Job 27:17 innocent will **d** the silver
Ps 22:18 **d** My garments among them
Ps 55: 9 **d** their tongues, For I have
Ps 60: 6 I will **d** Shechem And measure
Ps 108: 7 I will **d** Shechem And measure
Prov 16:19 than to **d** the spoil with the
Is 9: 3 rejoice when they **d** the spoil
Is 18: 2 down, whose land the rivers **d**
Is 18: 7 down, whose land the rivers **d**
Is 53:12 Therefore I will **d** Him a
Is 53:12 He shall **d** the spoil with the
Ezek 5: 1 to weigh and **d** the hair
Ezek 45: 1 when you **d** the land by lot
Ezek 47:13 **d** the land as an inheritance
Ezek 47:21 Thus you shall **d** this land
Ezek 47:22 It shall be that you will **d**
Ezek 48:29 **d** by lot as an inheritance
Dan 11:39 many, and **d** the land for gain
Luke 12:13 tell my brother to **d** the
Luke 22:17 this and **d** it among yourselves

DIVIDED (*see* DIVIDE)
Gen 1: 4 and God **d** the light from the
Gen 1: 7 **d** the waters which were under
Gen 10:25 in his days the earth was **d**
Gen 10:32 were **d** on the earth after the
Gen 14:15 He **d** his forces against them
Gen 32: 7 he **d** the people that were
Gen 33: 1 So he **d** the children among
Ex 14:21 land, and the waters were **d**
Num 26:53 shall be **d** as an inheritance
Num 26:55 the land shall be **d** by lot
Num 26:56 shall be **d** between the larger
Deut 32: 8 when the Most High **d** their
Josh 14: 5 and they **d** the land
Josh 18:10 there Joshua **d** the land to
Josh 19:51 of the children of Israel **d**
Josh 23: 4 I have **d** to you by lot these
Judg 7:16 Then he **d** the three hundred
Judg 9:43 **d** them into three companies,
2Sa 1:23 their death they were not **d**
1Ki 16:21 Israel were **d** into two parts
1Ki 18: 6 So they **d** the land between
2Ki 2: 8 it was **d** this way and that, so
2Ki 2:14 it was **d** this way and that
1Ch 1:19 in his days the earth was **d**
1Ch 23: 6 David **d** them into divisions
1Ch 24: 3 **d** them according to the
1Ch 24: 4 Ithamar, and thus they were **d**
1Ch 24: 5 Thus they were **d** by lot, one
2Ch 35:13 **d** them quickly among all the
Neh 9:11 You **d** the sea before them, so
Neh 9:22 and **d** them into districts
Job 38:25 Who has **d** a channel for the
Ps 74:13 You **d** the sea by Your
Ps 78:13 He **d** the sea and caused them
Ps 136:13 To Him who **d** the Red Sea in
Is 33:23 prey of great plunder is **d**
Is 34:17 His hand has **d** it among them
Is 51:15 who **d** the sea whose waves
Ezek 37:22 nor shall they ever be **d** into
Dan 2:41 iron, the kingdom shall be **d**
Dan 5:28 Your kingdom has been **d**, and
Dan 11: 4 **d** toward the four winds of
Hos 10: 2 Their heart is **d**
Joel 3: 2 they have also **d** up My land
Amos 7:17 shall be **d** by survey line
Mic 2: 4 turncoat He has **d** our fields
Hab 3: 9 Selah You **d** the earth with
Zech 14: 1 spoil will be **d** in your midst
Matt 12:25 Every kingdom **d** against
Matt 12:25 every city or house **d** against
Matt 12:26 he is **d** against himself
Matt 27:35 **d** His garments, casting lots,
Matt 27:35 **d** My garments among them
Mark 3:24 a kingdom is **d** against itself
Mark 3:25 And if a house is **d** against
Mark 3:26 up against himself, and is **d**
Mark 6:41 two fish He **d** among them all
Mark 15:24 they **d** His garments, casting
Luke 11:17 Every kingdom **d** against
Luke 11:17 a house **d** against a house
Luke 11:18 also is **d** against himself
Luke 12:52 five in one house will be **d**
Luke 12:53 Father will be **d** against son
Luke 15:12 So he **d** to them his
Luke 23:34 they **d** His garments and cast
John 19:24 **d** My garments among them
Acts 2: 3 appeared to them **d** tongues
Acts 2:45 **d** them among all, as anyone
Acts 14: 4 multitude of the city was **d**
Acts 23: 7 and the assembly was **d**
1Co 1:13 Is Christ **d**?
Rev 16:19 city was **d** into three parts

DIVIDER (*see* DIVIDE)
Ex 26:33 The veil shall be a **d** for you

DIVIDES (*see* DIVIDE)
Lev 11: 3 beasts, whatever **d** the hoof
Lev 11: 7 swine, though it **d** the hoof
Lev 11:26 of any beast which **d** the foot
Ps 29: 7 the LORD **d** the flames of fire
Ps 68:12 remains at home **d** the spoil
Matt 25:32 as a shepherd **d** his sheep
Luke 11:22 he trusted, and **d** his spoils

DIVIDING (*see* DIVIDE)
Josh 19:49 they had made an end of **d** the
Josh 19:51 made an end of **d** the country
Judg 5:30 not finding and **d** the spoil
Is 63:12 **d** the water before them to
2Ti 2:15 rightly **d** the word of truth

DIVINATION (*see* DIVINE)
Gen 44: 5 which he indeed practices **d**
Gen 44:15 as I can certainly practice **d**
Lev 19:26 you practice **d** or soothsaying
Num 23:23 is there any **d** against Israel
Prov 16:10 Even though **d** is on the lips
Jer 14:14 to you a false vision, **d**, a
Ezek 12:24 **d** within the house of Israel
Ezek 13: 6 futility and false **d**, saying
Ezek 13: 7 have you not spoken false **d**
Ezek 13:23 futility nor practice **d**
Ezek 21:21 of the two roads, to use **d**
Ezek 21:22 hand is the **d** for Jerusalem
Ezek 21:23 be to them like a false **d** in
Mic 3: 6 shall have darkness without **d**
Acts 16:16 with a spirit of **d** met us

DIVINE (*see* DIVINATION, DIVINELY, DIVINER, DIVINING)
Ezek 13: 9 futility and who **d** lies
Ezek 21:29 while they **d** a lie to you, to
Mic 3:11 and her prophets **d** for money
Acts 17:29 the **D** Nature is like gold or
Rom 11: 4 But what does the **d** response
Heb 9: 1 had ordinances of **d** service
2Pe 1: 3 as His **d** power has given to
2Pe 1: 4 be partakers of the **d** nature

DIVINELY (*see* DIVINE)
Matt 2:12 being **d** warned in a dream
Acts 10:22 was **d** instructed by a holy
Heb 8: 5 as Moses was **d** instructed
Heb 11: 7 being **d** warned of things not

DIVINER (*see* DIVINE, DIVINER'S, DIVINERS)
Is 3: 2 and the prophet, and the **d** and

DIVINER'S (*see* DIVINER)
Num 22: 7 with the **d** fee in their hand

DIVINERS (*see* DIVINER, DIVINERS')
Deut 18:14 listened to soothsayers and **d**
1Sa 6: 2 for the priests and the **d**,
Is 44:25 the babblers, and drives **d** mad
Jer 27: 9 to your prophets, your **d**,
Jer 29: 8 your **d** who are in your midst
Mic 3: 7 be ashamed, and the **d** abashed
Zech 10: 2 the **d** envision lies, and tell

DIVINERS' (*see* DIVINERS)
Judg 9:37 from the **D** Terebinth Tree

DIVINING (*see* DIVINE)
Ezek 22:28 **d** lies for them, saying

DIVISION (*see* DIVIDE, DIVISIONS)
1Ch 27: 1 each **d** having twenty-four
1Ch 27: 2 Over the first **d** for the
1Ch 27: 2 in his **d** were twenty-four
1Ch 27: 4 Over the **d** of the second
1Ch 27: 4 of his **d** Mikloth also was the
1Ch 27: 4 in his **d** were twenty-four
1Ch 27: 5 in his **d** were twenty-four
1Ch 27: 6 in his **d** was Ammizabad his
1Ch 27: 7 in his **d** were twenty-four
1Ch 27: 8 in his **d** were twenty-four
1Ch 27: 9 in his **d** were twenty-four
1Ch 27:10 in his **d** were twenty-four
1Ch 27:11 in his **d** were twenty-four
1Ch 27:12 in his **d** were twenty-four
1Ch 27:13 in his **d** were twenty-four
1Ch 27:14 in his **d** were twenty-four
1Ch 27:15 in his **d** were twenty-four
1Ch 28:13 also for the **d** of the priests
2Ch 31:16 work of his service, by his **d**
2Ch 35: 5 according to the **d** of the
Luke 1: 5 Zacharias, of the **d** of Abijah
Luke 1: 8 God in the order of his **d**
Luke 12:51 you, not at all, but rather **d**
John 7:43 So there was a **d** among the
John 9:16 And there was a **d** among them
John 10:19 was a **d** again among the Jews
Eph 2:14 middle wall of **d** between us
Heb 4:12 even to the **d** of soul and

DIVISIONS (*see* DIVISION)
Num 1:16 heads of the **d** in Israel
Num 10: 4 the heads of the **d** of Israel
Num 31: 5 were recruited from the **d** of
Josh 11:23 to their **d** by their tribes
Josh 12: 7 according to their **d**,
Josh 18:10 Israel according to their **d**
Josh 22:14 father among the **d** of Israel
Josh 22:21 the heads of the **d** of Israel
Josh 22:30 the heads of the **d** of Israel
Judg 5:15 among the **d** of Reuben there
Judg 5:16 The **d** of Reuben have great
1Ch 12:23 were the numbers of the **d**
1Ch 23: 6 into **d** among the sons of Levi
1Ch 24: 1 Now these are the **d** of the
1Ch 26: 1 Concerning the **d** of the
1Ch 26:12 were the **d** of the gatekeepers
1Ch 26:19 These were the **d** of the
1Ch 27: 1 matter of the military **d**
1Ch 27: 1 These **d** came in and went out
1Ch 28: 1 of the **d** who served the king
1Ch 28:21 Here are the **d** of the priests
2Ch 5:11 without keeping to their **d**)
2Ch 8:14 he appointed the **d** of the
2Ch 8:14 by their **d** at each gate
2Ch 23: 8 had not dismissed the **d**
2Ch 31: 2 the **d** of the priests and the
2Ch 31: 2 Levites according to their **d**
2Ch 31:15 to their brethren by **d**, to
2Ch 31:17 to their work, by their **d**
2Ch 35: 4 houses, according to your **d**
2Ch 35: 5 **d** of the fathers' houses of
2Ch 35:10 and the Levites in their **d**
2Ch 35:12 **d** of the fathers' houses of
Ezra 6:18 the priests to their **d** and the
Ezra 6:18 and the Levites to their **d**
Neh 11:36 Some of the Judean **d** of
Rom 16:17 note those who cause **d** and
1Co 1:10 that there be no **d** among you
1Co 3: 3 and **d** among you, are you not
1Co 11:18 that there are **d** among you
Jude 19 sensual persons, who cause **d**

DIVISIVE (*see* DIVIDE)
Tit 3:10 Reject a **d** man after the

DIVORCE (*see* DIVORCED, DIVORCES)
Deut 22:19 he cannot **d** her all his days
Deut 22:29 to **d** her all his days
Deut 24: 1 writes her a certificate of **d**
Deut 24: 3 writes her a certificate of **d**
Is 50: 1 of your mother's **d**, whom I
Jer 3: 8 given her a certificate of **d**
Mal 2:16 Israel says that He hates **d**
Matt 5:31 give her a certificate of **d**
Matt 19: 3 to **d** his wife for just any
Matt 19: 7 to give a certificate of **d**
Matt 19: 8 permitted you to **d** your wives
Mark 10: 2 for a man to **d** his wife
Mark 10: 4 to write a certificate of **d**
1Co 7:11 husband is not to **d** his wife
1Co 7:12 with him, let him not **d** her
1Co 7:13 with her, let her not **d** him

DIVORCED (*see* DIVORCE)
Lev 21: 7 a woman **d** from her husband
Lev 21:14 A widow or a **d** woman or a
Lev 22:13 daughter is a widow or **d**, and
Num 30: 9 vow of a widow or a **d** woman
Deut 24: 4 **d** her must not take her back
Ezek 44:22 as wife a widow or a **d** woman
Matt 5:32 who is **d** commits adultery
Matt 19: 9 her who is **d** commits adultery
Luke 16:18 is **d** from her husband commits

DIVORCES (*see* DIVORCE)
Jer 3: 1 say, 'If a man **d** his wife
Matt 5:31 said, 'Whoever **d** his wife
Matt 5:32 **d** his wife for any reason
Matt 19: 9 whoever **d** his wife, except
Mark 10:11 Whoever **d** his wife and marries
Mark 10:12 if a woman **d** her husband and
Luke 16:18 Whoever **d** his wife and marries

DIZAHAB
Deut 1: 1 Laban, Hazeroth, and **D**

DO (*see* PREFACE)

DOCILE
Jer 11:19 But I was like a **d** lamb

DOCTRINE (*see* DOCTRINES)
Job 11: 4 My **d** is pure, And I am clean
Prov 4: 2 for I give you good **d**
Is 29:24 who murmured will learn **d**
Jer 10: 8 wooden idol is a worthless **d**
Matt 16:12 but of the **d** of the Pharisees
Mark 1:27 What new **d** is this
John 7:16 My **d** is not Mine, but His who
John 7:17 shall know concerning the **d**
John 18:19 about His disciples and His **d**
Acts 2:42 in the apostles' **d** and
Acts 5:28 filled Jerusalem with your **d**
Acts 17:19 new **d** is of which you speak
Rom 6:17 **d** to which you were delivered
Rom 16:17 contrary to the **d** which you
Eph 4:14 about with every wind of **d**
1Ti 1: 3 that they teach no other **d**
1Ti 1:10 that is contrary to sound **d**
1Ti 4: 6 of the good **d** which you have
1Ti 4:13 reading, to exhortation, to **d**
1Ti 4:16 heed to yourself and to the **d**
1Ti 5:17 who labor in the word and **d**
1Ti 6: 1 His **d** may not be blasphemed
1Ti 6: 3 to the **d** which is according
2Ti 3:10 have carefully followed my **d**
2Ti 3:16 God, and is profitable for **d**
2Ti 4: 3 they will not endure sound **d**
Tit 1: 9 he may be able, by sound **d**
Tit 2: 1 which are proper for sound **d**
Tit 2: 7 in **d** showing integrity,
Tit 2:10 that they may adorn the **d** of
Heb 6: 2 of the **d** of baptisms, of
2Jn 9 does not abide in the **d** of
2Jn 9 He who abides in the **d** of
2Jn 10 you and does not bring this **d**
Rev 2:14 who hold the **d** of Balaam, who
Rev 2:15 hold the **d** of the Nicolaitans
Rev 2:24 as many as do not have this **d**

DOCTRINES (*see* DOCTRINE)
Matt 15: 9 worship Me, teaching as **d** the
Mark 7: 7 worship Me, teaching as **d** the
Col 2:22 commandments and **d** of men
1Ti 4: 1 spirits and **d** of demons,
Heb 13: 9 with various and strange **d**

DOCUMENT
Neh 10: 1 their seal on the **d** were
Esth 3:14 A copy of the **d** was to be
Esth 8:13 A copy of the **d** was to be

DODAI (*see* DODO)
1Ch 27: 4 second month was **D** an Ahohite

DODANIM (*see* RODANIM)
Gen 10: 4 Tarshish, Kittim, and **D**

DODAVAH
2Ch 20:37 of **D** of Mareshah prophesied

DODO (*see* DODAI)
Judg 10: 1 the son of Puah, the son of **D**
2Sa 23: 9 him was Eleazar the son of **D**
2Sa 23:24 the son of **D** of Bethlehem
1Ch 11:12 him was Eleazar the son of **D**
1Ch 11:26 the son of **D** of Bethlehem

DOE
Prov 5:19 a loving deer and a graceful **d**

DOEG
1Sa 21: 7 name was **D**, an Edomite
1Sa 22: 9 Then answered **D** the Edomite
1Sa 22:18 And the king said to **D**, "You
1Sa 22:18 So **D** the Edomite turned and
1Sa 22:22 when **D** the Edomite was there,

DOER (*see* DOERS, DOINGS)
Jas 1:23 hearer of the word and not a **d**
Jas 1:25 hearer but a **d** of the work
Jas 4:11 you are not a **d** of the law

DOERS (*see* DOER)
Prov 24:19 Do not fret because of evil **d**
Rom 2:13 but the **d** of the law will be
Jas 1:22 But be **d** of the word, and not

DOES (*see* PREFACE)

DOG (*see* DOG'S, DOGS)
Ex 11: 7 shall a **d** move its tongue
Deut 23:18 a **d** to the house of the LORD
Judg 7: 5 with his tongue, as a **d** laps
1Sa 17:43 Am I a **d**, that you come to me
1Sa 24:14 do you pursue? A dead **d**?
2Sa 9: 8 look upon such a dead **d** as I
2Sa 16: 9 Why should this dead **d** curse
2Ki 8:13 a **d**, that he should do this
Ps 22:20 life from the power of the **d**
Ps 59: 6 return, They growl like a **d**
Ps 59:14 return, They growl like a **d**
Prov 26:11 As a **d** returns to his own
Prov 26:17 one who takes a **d** by the ears
Eccl 9: 4 for a living **d** is better than
2Pe 2:22 A **d** returns to his own vomit,

DOG'S (*see* DOG)
2Sa 3: 8 Am I a **d** head that belongs to
Is 66: 3 as if he breaks a **d** neck

DOGS (*see* DOG)
Ex 22:31 you shall throw it to the **d**
1Ki 14:11 The **d** shall eat whoever
1Ki 16: 4 The **d** shall eat whoever
1Ki 21:19 In the place where **d** licked
1Ki 21:19 **d** shall lick your blood, even
1Ki 21:23 The **d** shall eat Jezebel by
1Ki 21:24 The **d** shall eat whoever
1Ki 22:38 the **d** licked up his blood
2Ki 9:10 The **d** shall eat Jezebel in
2Ki 9:36 **d** shall eat the flesh of
Job 30: 1 to put with the **d** of my flock
Ps 22:16 For **d** have surrounded Me
Ps 68:23 the tongues of your **d** may
Is 56:10 they are all dumb **d**, they
Is 56:11 they are greedy **d** which never
Jer 15: 3 the **d** to drag, the birds of
Matt 7: 6 give what is holy to the **d**
Matt 15:26 and throw it to the little **d**
Matt 15:27 yet even the little **d** eat the
Mark 7:27 and throw it to the little **d**
Mark 7:28 yet even the little **d** under
Luke 16:21 Moreover the **d** came and licked
Phil 3: 2 Beware of **d**, beware of evil
Rev 22:15 But outside are **d** and

DOING (*see* PREFACE)

DOINGS (*see* DOER)
Lev 18: 3 According to the **d** of the
Lev 18: 3 according to the **d** of the
Deut 28:20 of the wickedness of your **d**
Judg 2:19 not cease from their own **d**
1Sa 25: 3 was harsh and evil in his **d**
Is 1:16 of your **d** from before My eyes
Is 3: 8 their **d** Are against the LORD,
Is 3:10 eat the fruit of their **d**
Jer 4: 4 because of the evil of your **d**
Jer 4:18 your **d** have procured these
Jer 7: 3 Amend your ways and your **d**
Jer 7: 5 amend your ways and your **d**
Jer 11:18 for You showed me their **d**
Jer 17:10 to the fruit of his **d**
Jer 18:11 make your ways and your **d** good
Jer 21:12 because of the evil of your **d**
Jer 21:14 to the fruit of your **d**,"
Jer 23: 2 to you for the evil of your **d**
Jer 23:22 and from the evil of their **d**
Jer 25: 5 of his evil way and his evil **d**
Jer 26: 3 of the evil of their **d**
Jer 26:13 amend your ways and your **d**
Jer 32:19 to the fruit of his **d**

Jer 35:15 his evil way, amend your **d**
Jer 44:22 because of the evil of your **d**
Ezek 14:22 see their ways and their **d**
Ezek 14:23 you see their ways and their **d**
Ezek 20:43 all your **d** with which you
Ezek 20:44 according to your corrupt **d**
Ezek 21:24 all your **d** your sins appear
Mic 2: 7 Are these His **d**

DOMAIN (*see* DOMINION)
Jude 6 did not keep their proper **d**

DOMINION (*see* DOMAIN, DOMINIONS)
Gen 1:26 let them have **d** over the fish
Gen 1:28 have **d** over the fish of the
Gen 37: 8 you indeed have **d** over us
Num 24:19 Out of Jacob One shall have **d**
Judg 14: 4 Philistines had **d** over Israel
1Ki 4:24 For he had **d** over all the
1Ki 9:19 and in all the land of his **d**
2Ki 20:13 **d** that Hezekiah did not show
2Ch 8: 6 all the land of his **d**
2Ch 13: 5 the **d** over Israel to David
Ezra 4:16 be that you will have no **d**
Neh 9:28 so that they had **d** over them
Neh 9:37 also they have **d** over our
Job 25: 2 **D** and fear belong to Him
Job 38:33 set their **d** over the earth
Ps 8: 6 have **d** over the works of Your
Ps 19:13 Let them not have **d** over me
Ps 49:14 The upright shall have **d** over
Ps 72: 8 He shall have **d** also from sea
Ps 103:22 works, In all places of His **d**
Ps 114: 2 sanctuary, And Israel His **d**
Ps 119:133 no iniquity have **d** over me
Ps 145:13 Your **d** endures throughout all
Is 26:13 You have had **d** over us
Is 39: 2 **d** that Hezekiah did not show
Jer 34: 1 of the earth under his **d**, and
Jer 51:28 rulers, All the land of his **d**
Dan 4: 3 His **d** is from generation to
Dan 4:22 and your **d** to the end of the
Dan 4:34 His **d** is an everlasting **d**
Dan 6:26 **d** of my kingdom men must
Dan 6:26 His **d** shall endure to the end
Dan 7: 6 heads, and **d** was given to it
Dan 7:12 they had their **d** taken away
Dan 7:14 Then to Him was given **d** and
Dan 7:14 His **d** is an everlasting
Dan 7:14 **d** is an everlasting **d**
Dan 7:26 and they shall take away his **d**
Dan 7:27 Then the kingdom and **d**, and
Dan 11: 3 who shall rule with great **d**
Dan 11: 4 to his **d** with which he ruled
Dan 11: 5 gain power over him and have **d**
Dan 11: 5 His **d** shall be a great **d**
Mic 4: 8 even the former **d** shall come
Zech 9:10 His **d** shall be 'from sea to
Rom 6: 9 no longer has **d** over Him
Rom 6:14 sin shall not have **d** over you
Rom 7: 1 that the law has **d** over a man
2Co 1:24 we have **d** over your faith
Eph 1:21 and power and might and **d**, and
1Pe 4:11 and the **d** forever and ever
1Pe 5:11 and the **d** forever and ever
Jude 25 wise, be glory and majesty, **d**
Rev 1: 6 be glory and **d** forever and ever

DOMINIONS (*see* DOMINION)
Dan 7:27 all **d** shall serve and obey Him
Col 1:16 whether thrones or **d** or

DONATIONS
Luke 21: 5 with beautiful stones and **d**

DONE (*see* PREFACE)

DONKEY (*see* DONKEY'S, DONKEYS)
Gen 22: 3 the morning and saddled his **d**
Gen 22: 5 Stay here with the **d**
Gen 42:27 his **d** feed at the encampment
Gen 44:13 and each man loaded his **d**
Gen 49:11 Binding his **d** to the vine
Gen 49:14 Issachar is a strong **d**, lying
Ex 4:20 his sons and set them on a **d**
Ex 13:13 a **d** you shall redeem with a
Ex 20:17 nor his ox, nor his **d**, nor
Ex 21:33 an ox or a **d** falls in it,
Ex 22: 4 it is an ox or **d** or sheep
Ex 22: 9 it concerns an ox, a **d**, a
Ex 22:10 delivers to his neighbor a **d**
Ex 23: 4 ox or his **d** going astray, you
Ex 23: 5 If you see the **d** of one who
Ex 23:12 your **d** may rest, and the son
Ex 34:20 But the firstling of a **d** you
Num 16:15 not taken one **d** from them
Num 22:21 in the morning, saddled his **d**
Num 22:22 And he was riding on his **d**
Num 22:23 Now the **d** saw the Angel of
Num 22:23 the **d** turned aside out of the
Num 22:23 So Balaam struck the **d** to
Num 22:25 when the **d** saw the Angel of
Num 22:27 when the **d** saw the Angel of
Num 22:27 and he struck the **d** with his
Num 22:28 opened the mouth of the **d**
Num 22:29 And Balaam said to the **d**
Num 22:30 So the **d** said to Balaam, "Am
Num 22:30 Am I not your **d** on which you
Num 22:32 your **d** these three times
Num 22:33 The **d** saw Me and turned aside
Deut 5:14 nor your ox, nor your **d**, nor
Deut 5:21 maidservant, his ox, his **d**
Deut 22: 3 shall do the same with his **d**
Deut 22: 4 not see your brother's **d** or
Deut 22:10 with an ox and a **d** together
Deut 28:31 your **d** shall be violently
Josh 6:21 and old, ox and sheep and **d**,
Josh 15:18 So she dismounted from her **d**
Judg 1:14 And she dismounted from her **d**
Judg 6: 4 neither sheep nor ox nor **d**
Judg 15:15 found a fresh jawbone of a **d**
Judg 15:16 With the jawbone of a **d**,
Judg 15:16 with the jawbone of a **d** I
Judg 19:28 the man lifted her onto the **d**
1Sa 12: 3 or whose **d** have I taken, or
1Sa 15: 3 ox and sheep, camel and **d**
1Sa 16:20 Jesse took a **d** loaded with
1Sa 25:20 it was, as she rode on the **d**
1Sa 25:23 to dismount from the **d**, fell
1Sa 25:42 rose in haste and rode on a **d**
2Sa 17:23 followed, he saddled his **d**
2Sa 19:26 I will saddle a **d** for myself
1Ki 2:40 Shimei arose, saddled his **d**
1Ki 13:13 Saddle the **d** for me
1Ki 13:13 So they saddled the **d** for him
1Ki 13:23 that he saddled the **d** for him
1Ki 13:24 road, and the **d** stood by it
1Ki 13:27 Saddle the **d** for me
1Ki 13:28 thrown on the road, and the **d**
1Ki 13:28 the corpse nor torn the **d**
1Ki 13:29 man of God, laid it on the **d**
2Ki 4:24 Then she saddled a **d**, and said
Job 6: 5 Does the wild **d** bray when it
Job 24: 3 away the **d** of the fatherless
Job 39: 5 Who set the wild **d** free
Prov 26: 3 the horse, a bridle for the **d**
Is 1: 3 And the **d** its master's crib
Is 32:20 the feet of the ox and the **d**
Jer 2:24 A wild **d** used to the
Jer 22:19 buried with the burial of a **d**
Hos 8: 9 like a wild **d** alone by itself
Zech 9: 9 lowly and riding on a **d**, a
Zech 9: 9 a colt, the foal of a **d**
Zech 14:15 mule, on the camel and the **d**
Matt 21: 2 you will find a **d** tied, and a
Matt 21: 5 you, lowly, and sitting on a **d**
Matt 21: 5 a colt, the foal of a **d**
Matt 21: 7 They brought the **d** and the
Luke 13:15 ox or his **d** from the stall
Luke 14: 5 having a **d** or an ox that has
John 12:14 when He had found a young **d**
2Pe 2:16 a dumb **d** speaking with a

DONKEY'S (*see* DONKEY)
Gen 49:11 his **d** colt to the choice vine
2Ki 6:25 a **d** head was sold for eighty
Job 11:12 when a wild **d** colt is born a
John 12:15 coming, sitting on a **d** colt

DONKEYS (*see* DONKEY)
Gen 12:16 He had sheep, oxen, male **d**
Gen 12:16 and female servants, female **d**
Gen 24:35 servants, and camels and **d**
Gen 30:43 male servants, and camels and **d**
Gen 32: 5 I have oxen, **d**, flocks, and
Gen 32:15 and ten bulls, twenty female **d**
Gen 34:28 sheep, their oxen, and their **d**
Gen 36:24 as he pastured the **d** of his
Gen 42:26 loaded their **d** with the grain
Gen 43:18 take us as slaves with our **d**
Gen 43:24 and he gave their **d** feed
Gen 44: 3 sent away, they and their **d**
Gen 45:23 ten **d** loaded with the good
Gen 45:23 and ten female **d** loaded with
Gen 47:17 of the herds, and for the **d**
Ex 9: 3 on the horses, on the **d**, on
Num 31:28 persons, the cattle, the **d**
Num 31:30 persons, the cattle, the **d**
Num 31:34 sixty-one thousand **d**,
Num 31:39 The **d** were thirty thousand
Num 31:45 thousand five hundred **d**,
Josh 7:24 daughters, his oxen, his **d**
Josh 9: 4 took old sacks on their **d**
Judg 5:10 you who ride on white **d**, who
Judg 10: 4 sons who rode on thirty **d**
Judg 12:14 who rode on seventy young **d**
Judg 19: 3 and a couple of **d** with him
Judg 19:10 him were the two saddled **d**
Judg 19:19 straw and fodder for our **d**
Judg 19:21 and gave fodder to the **d**
1Sa 8:16 finest young men and your **d**
1Sa 9: 3 Now the **d** of Kish, Saul's
1Sa 9: 3 arise, go and look for the **d**
1Sa 9: 5 cease caring about the **d** and
1Sa 9:20 But as for your **d** that were
1Sa 10: 2 The **d** which you went to look
1Sa 10: 2 has ceased caring about the **d**
1Sa 10:14 To look for the **d**
1Sa 10:16 that the **d** had been found
1Sa 22:19 and nursing infants, oxen and **d**
1Sa 25:18 of figs, and loaded them on **d**
1Sa 27: 9 the sheep, the oxen, the **d**
2Sa 16: 1 with a couple of saddled **d**
2Sa 16: 2 The **d** are for the king's
2Ki 4:22 the young men and one of the **d**
2Ki 7: 7 their horses, and their **d**
2Ki 7:10 **d** tied, and the tents intact
1Ch 5:21 and two thousand of their **d**
1Ch 12:40 were bringing food on **d** and
1Ch 27:30 Meronothite was over the **d**
2Ch 28:15 all the feeble ones ride on **d**
Ezra 2:67 their **d** six thousand seven
Neh 7:69 **d** six thousand seven hundred
Neh 13:15 loading **d** with wine, grapes,
Job 1:14 the **d** feeding beside them,
Job 24: 5 like wild **d** in the desert,
Job 42:12 and one thousand female **d**
Ps 104:11 The wild **d** quench their
Is 21: 7 of horsemen, a chariot of **d**
Is 30: 6 on the backs of young **d**, and
Is 30:24 the young **d** that work the
Is 32:14 forever, a joy of wild **d**, a
Jer 14: 6 And the wild **d** stood in the
Ezek 23:20 flesh is like the flesh of **d**
Dan 5:21 dwelling was with the wild **d**

DOOM (*see* DOOMED)
Job 21:30 are reserved for the day of **d**
Prov 16: 4 the wicked for the day of **d**
Jer 11:17 has pronounced **d** against you
Jer 17:17 are my hope in the day of **d**
Jer 17:18 Bring on them the day of **d**
Jer 19:15 the **d** that I have pronounced
Jer 26:13 the **d** that He has pronounced
Jer 26:19 the **d** which He had pronounced
Jer 35:17 of Jerusalem all the **d** that I
Jer 36:31 the **d** that I have pronounced
Jer 40: 2 this **d** on this place
Jer 51: 2 For in the day of **d** they
Ezek 7: 7 **D** has come to you, you who
Ezek 7:10 **D** has gone out
Amos 6: 3 who put far off the day of **d**

DOOMED (*see* DOOM)
Lev 27:29 the ban, who may become **d** to
Deut 7:26 lest you be **d** to destruction
Josh 6:17 Now the city shall be **d** by
Josh 7:12 have become **d** to destruction

DOOR (*see* DOORKEEPER, DOORPOST, DOORS, DOORWAY)
Gen 4: 7 do well, sin lies at the **d**
Gen 6:16 set the **d** of the ark in its
Gen 18: 1 tent **d** in the heat of the day
Gen 18: 2 from the tent **d** to meet them
Gen 18:10 tent **d** which was behind him
Gen 19: 6 shut the **d** behind him,
Gen 19: 9 came near to break down the **d**
Gen 19:10 with them, and shut the **d**
Gen 19:11 weary trying to find the **d**
Gen 43:19 him at the **d** of the house
Ex 12:22 **d** of his house until morning
Ex 12:23 the LORD will pass over the **d**
Ex 21: 6 shall also bring him to the **d**
Ex 26:36 for the **d** of the tabernacle
Ex 29: 4 to the **d** of the tabernacle of

Ex 29:11 by the **d** of the tabernacle of
Ex 29:32 by the **d** of the tabernacle of
Ex 29:42 at the **d** of the tabernacle of
Ex 33: 8 each man stood at his tent **d**
Ex 33: 9 and stood at the **d** of the
Ex 33:10 standing at the tabernacle **d**
Ex 33:10 each man in his tent **d**
Ex 35:15 the screen for the **d** at the
Ex 36:37 a screen for the tabernacle **d**
Ex 38: 8 at the **d** of the tabernacle of
Ex 38:30 the **d** of the tabernacle of
Ex 39:38 screen for the tabernacle **d**
Ex 40: 5 for the **d** of the tabernacle
Ex 40: 6 **d** of the tabernacle of the
Ex 40:12 and his sons to the **d** of the
Ex 40:28 at the **d** of the tabernacle
Ex 40:29 **d** of the tabernacle of the
Lev 1: 3 at the **d** of the tabernacle of
Lev 1: 5 by the **d** of the tabernacle of
Lev 3: 2 and kill it at the **d** of the
Lev 4: 4 to the **d** of the tabernacle of
Lev 4: 7 which is at the **d** of the
Lev 4:18 which is at the **d** of the
Lev 8: 3 together at the **d** of the
Lev 8: 4 at the **d** of the tabernacle of
Lev 8:31 at the **d** of the tabernacle of
Lev 8:33 the **d** of the tabernacle of
Lev 8:35 at the **d** of the tabernacle of
Lev 10: 7 the **d** of the tabernacle of
Lev 12: 6 to the **d** of the tabernacle of
Lev 14:11 at the **d** of the tabernacle of
Lev 14:23 to the **d** of the tabernacle of
Lev 14:38 to the **d** of the house, and
Lev 15:14 to the **d** of the tabernacle of
Lev 15:29 to the **d** of the tabernacle of
Lev 16: 7 at the **d** of the tabernacle of
Lev 17: 4 to the **d** of the tabernacle of
Lev 17: 5 at the **d** of the tabernacle of
Lev 17: 6 at the **d** of the tabernacle of
Lev 17: 9 to the **d** of the tabernacle of
Lev 19:21 to the **d** of the tabernacle of
Num 3:25 the screen for the **d** of the
Num 3:26 screen for the **d** of the court
Num 4:25 the screen for the **d** of the
Num 4:26 the screen for the **d** of the
Num 6:10 to the **d** of the tabernacle of
Num 6:13 to the **d** of the tabernacle of
Num 6:18 at the **d** of the tabernacle of
Num 10: 3 at the **d** of the tabernacle of
Num 11:10 everyone at the **d** of his tent
Num 12: 5 and stood in the **d** of the
Num 16:18 it, and stood at the **d** of the
Num 16:19 against them at the **d** of the
Num 16:27 stood at the **d** of their tents
Num 16:50 at the **d** of the tabernacle of
Num 20: 6 to the **d** of the tabernacle of
Num 25: 6 at the **d** of the tabernacle of
Deut 15:17 it through his ear to the **d**
Deut 22:21 the **d** of her father's house
Deut 31:15 above the **d** of the tabernacle
Josh 19:51 at the **d** of the tabernacle of
Judg 4:20 Stand at the **d** of the tent
Judg 9:52 he drew near the **d** of the
Judg 19:22 the house and beat on the **d**
Judg 19:26 fell down at the **d** of the
Judg 19:27 fallen at the **d** of the house
1Sa 2:22 at the **d** of the tabernacle of
2Sa 11: 9 But Uriah slept at the **d** of
2Sa 13:17 me, and bolt the **d** behind her
2Sa 13:18 and bolted the **d** behind her
1Ki 6:33 So for the **d** of the sanctuary
1Ki 6:34 comprised one folding **d**, and
1Ki 6:34 comprised the other folding **d**
1Ki 14: 6 as she came through the **d**
2Ki 4: 4 shall shut the **d** behind you
2Ki 4: 5 shut the **d** behind her and her
2Ki 4:21 of God, shut the **d** upon him
2Ki 4:33 shut the **d** behind the two of
2Ki 5: 9 and he stood at the **d** of the
2Ki 6:32 messenger comes, shut the **d**
2Ki 6:32 and hold him fast at the **d**
2Ki 9: 3 Then open the **d** and flee,
2Ki 9:10 And he opened the **d** and fled
2Ki 12: 9 the **d** put there all the money
1Ch 9:21 was keeper of the **d** of the
Neh 3:20 **d** of the house of Eliashib
Neh 3:21 from the **d** of the house of
Job 31: 9 lurked at my neighbor's **d**
Job 31:34 and did not go out of the **d**
Ps 141: 3 watch over the **d** of my lips
Prov 5: 8 go near the **d** of her house
Prov 9:14 sits at the **d** of her house
Prov 26:14 As a **d** turns on its hinges,
Song 5: 4 hand by the latch of the **d**
Song 8: 9 and if she is a **d**, we will
Is 6: 4 And the posts of the **d** were
Jer 35: 4 Shallum, the keeper of the **d**
Ezek 8: 3 to the **d** of the north gate of
Ezek 8: 7 me to the **d** of the court
Ezek 8: 8 into the wall, there was a **d**
Ezek 8:14 So He brought me to the **d** of
Ezek 8:16 at the **d** of the temple of the
Ezek 10:19 they stood at the **d** of the
Ezek 11: 1 there at the **d** of the gate
Ezek 40:13 cubits, as **d** faces **d**
Ezek 41:11 one **d** toward the north and
Ezek 41:17 from the space above the **d**
Ezek 41:20 to the space above the **d**, and
Ezek 41:24 two panels for one **d** and two
Ezek 41:24 and two panels for the other **d**
Ezek 42: 2 cubits), was the north **d**
Ezek 42:12 there was a **d** in front of the
Ezek 47: 1 back to the **d** of the temple
Hos 2:15 of Achor as a **d** of hope
Matt 6: 6 and when you have shut your **d**
Matt 25:10 and the **d** was shut
Matt 27:60 against the **d** of the tomb
Matt 28: 2 back the stone from the **d**
Mark 1:33 gathered together at the **d**
Mark 2: 2 them, not even near the **d**
Mark 11: 4 the **d** outside on the street
Mark 15:46 against the **d** of the tomb
Mark 16: 3 from the **d** of the tomb for us
Luke 11: 7 the **d** is now shut, and my
Luke 13:25 has risen up and shut the **d**
Luke 13:25 outside and knock at the **d**
John 10: 1 enter the sheepfold by the **d**
John 10: 2 the **d** is the shepherd of the
John 10: 7 you, I am the **d** of the sheep
John 10: 9 I am the **d**
John 18:16 Peter stood at the **d** outside
John 18:16 spoke to her who kept the **d**
John 18:17 who kept the **d** said to Peter
Acts 5: 9 your husband are at the **d**
Acts 12: 6 the guards before the **d** were
Acts 12:13 knocked at the **d** of the gate
Acts 12:16 and when they opened the **d**
Acts 14:27 that He had opened the **d** of
Acts 18: 7 was next **d** to the synagogue
1Co 16: 9 effective **d** has opened to me,
2Co 2:12 a **d** was opened to me by the
Col 4: 3 open to us a **d** for the word
Jas 5: 9 Judge is standing at the **d**
Rev 3: 8 have set before you an open **d**
Rev 3:20 Behold, I stand at the **d** and
Rev 3:20 hears My voice and opens the **d**
Rev 4: 1 a **d** standing open in heaven

DOORKEEPER (*see* DOOR, DOORKEEPERS)
Ps 84:10 I would rather be a **d** in the
Mark 13:34 and commanded the **d** to watch
John 10: 3 To him the **d** opens, and the

DOORKEEPERS (*see* DOORKEEPER)
2Ki 22: 4 which the **d** have gathered
2Ki 23: 4 of the second order, and the **d**
2Ki 25:18 second priest, and the three **d**
1Ch 15:23 and Elkanah were **d** for the ark
1Ch 15:24 and Jehiah, **d** for the ark
Esth 2:21 eunuchs, Bigthan and Teresh, **d**
Esth 6: 2 the **d** who had sought to lay
Jer 52:24 second priest, and the three **d**

DOORPOST (*see* DOOR, DOORPOSTS)
Ex 21: 6 him to the door, or to the **d**
1Sa 1: 9 **d** of the tabernacle of the
Ezek 43: 8 and their **d** by My **d**

DOORPOSTS (*see* DOORPOST)
Ex 12: 7 blood and put it on the two **d**
Ex 12:22 the two **d** with the blood that
Ex 12:23 on the lintel and on the two **d**
Deut 6: 9 them on the **d** of your house
Deut 11:20 them on the **d** of your house
1Ki 6:31 **d** were one-fifth of the wall
1Ki 6:33 he also made **d** of olive wood
1Ki 7: 5 and **d** had rectangular frames
2Ch 3: 7 the beams and **d**, its walls and
Ezek 40:48 and measured the **d** of the
Ezek 40:49 there were pillars by the **d**
Ezek 41: 1 sanctuary and measured the **d**
Ezek 41: 3 went inside and measured the **d**
Ezek 41:16 their **d** and the beveled window
Ezek 41:21 The **d** of the temple were
Ezek 45:19 put it on the **d** of the temple
Amos 9: 1 Strike the **d**, that the

DOORS (*see* DOOR)
Josh 2:19 the **d** of your house into the
Judg 3:23 shut the **d** of the upper room
Judg 3:24 the **d** of the upper room were
Judg 3:25 the **d** of the upper room
Judg 11:31 the **d** of my house to meet me
Judg 16: 3 took hold of the **d** of the
Judg 19:27 opened the **d** of the house and
1Sa 3:15 opened the **d** of the house of
1Sa 21:13 on the **d** of the gate, and let
1Ki 6:31 he made **d** of olive wood
1Ki 6:32 The two **d** were of olive wood
1Ki 6:34 the two **d** were of cypress
1Ki 7:50 both for the **d** of the inner
1Ki 7:50 for the **d** of the main hall of
2Ki 18:16 **d** of the temple of the LORD
1Ch 22: 3 nails of the **d** of the gates
2Ch 3: 7 and doorposts, its walls and **d**
2Ch 4: 9 court and **d** for the court
2Ch 4: 9 overlaid these **d** with bronze
2Ch 4:22 its inner **d** to the Most Holy
2Ch 4:22 the **d** of the main hall of the
2Ch 23: 4 be keeping watch over the **d**
2Ch 28:24 shut up the **d** of the house of
2Ch 29: 3 he opened the **d** of the house
2Ch 29: 7 up the **d** of the vestibule
2Ch 34: 9 the Levites who kept the **d**
Neh 3: 1 consecrated it and hung its **d**
Neh 3: 3 hung its **d** with its bolts and
Neh 3: 6 laid its beams and hung its **d**
Neh 3:13 hung its **d** with its bolts and
Neh 3:14 hung its **d** with its bolts and
Neh 3:15 hung its **d** with its bolts and
Neh 6: 1 not hung the **d** in the gates)
Neh 6:10 us close the **d** of the temple
Neh 7: 1 was built and I had hung the **d**
Neh 7: 3 guard, let them shut the **d**
Job 3:10 up the **d** of my mother's womb
Job 31:32 opened my **d** to the traveler)
Job 38: 8 Or who shut in the sea with **d**
Job 38:10 for it, and set bars and **d**
Job 38:17 Or have you seen the **d** of the
Job 41:14 can open the **d** of his face
Ps 24: 7 lifted up, you everlasting **d**
Ps 24: 9 them up, you everlasting **d**
Ps 78:23 And opened the **d** of heaven
Prov 8: 3 at the entrance of the **d**
Prov 8:34 waiting at the posts of my **d**
Eccl 12: 4 when the **d** are shut in the
Is 26:20 and shut your **d** behind you
Is 45: 1 open before him the double **d**
Is 57: 8 Also behind the **d** and their
Ezek 33:30 and in the **d** of the houses
Ezek 41:11 The **d** of the side chambers
Ezek 41:23 and the sanctuary had two **d**
Ezek 41:24 The **d** had two panels apiece,
Ezek 41:25 trees were carved on the **d** of
Ezek 42: 4 and their **d** faced north
Ezek 42:12 corresponding to the **d** of the
Mic 7: 5 Guard the **d** of your mouth
Zech 11: 1 Open your **d**, O Lebanon, that
Mal 1:10 you who would shut the **d**, So
Matt 24:33 it is near, at the very **d**
Mark 13:29 it is near, at the very **d**
John 20:19 when the **d** were shut where
John 20:26 the **d** being shut, and stood in
Acts 5:19 the Lord opened the prison **d**
Acts 5:23 standing outside before the **d**
Acts 16:26 all the **d** were opened and
Acts 16:27 and seeing the prison **d** open
Acts 21:30 immediately the **d** were shut

DOORWAY (*see* DOOR, DOORWAYS)
Gen 19: 6 out to them through the **d**
Gen 19:11 the men who were at the **d** of
Num 27: 2 by the **d** of the tabernacle of
1Ki 6: 8 The **d** for the middle story
1Ki 14:27 who guarded the **d** of the
2Ki 4:15 her, she stood in the **d**

DOORWAYS (*see* DOORWAY)
1Ki 7: 5 And all the **d** and doorposts had

DOPHKAH
Num 33:12 of Sin and camped at **D**
Num 33:13 They departed from **D** and

DOR (*see* EN DOR)
Josh 11: 2 the heights of **D** on the west
Josh 12:23 king of **D** in the heights of **D**
Josh 17:11 towns, the inhabitants of **D**
Judg 1:27 or the inhabitants of **D** and
1Ki 4:11 in all the regions of **D**
1Ch 7:29 Megiddo and its towns, **D** and

DORCAS (*see* TABITHA)
Acts 9:36 which is translated **D**
Acts 9:39 garments which **D** had made

DOTHAN
Gen 37:17 them say, 'Let us go to **D**
Gen 37:17 brothers and found them in **D**
2Ki 6:13 Surely he is in **D**

DOUBLE (*see* DOUBLED, DOUBLING)
Gen 43:12 Take **d** money in your hand, and
Gen 43:15 they took **d** money in their
Ex 22: 4 or sheep, he shall restore **d**
Ex 22: 7 is found, he shall pay **d**
Ex 22: 9 shall pay **d** to his neighbor
Ex 26: 9 you shall **d** over the sixth
Deut 15:18 for he has been worth a **d**
Deut 21:17 firstborn by giving him a **d**
1Sa 1: 5 he would give a **d** portion
2Ki 2: 9 Please let a **d** portion of
Job 11: 6 they would **d** your prudence
Job 41:13 approach him with a **d** bridle
Ps 12: 2 lips and a **d** heart they speak
Song 6:13 were, the dance of the **d** camp
Is 40: 2 hand **d** for all her sins
Is 45: 1 open before him the **d** doors
Is 61: 7 shame you shall have **d** honor
Is 61: 7 land they shall possess **d**
Jer 16:18 repay **d** for their iniquity
Jer 17:18 them with **d** destruction
Ezek 21:14 let the sword do **d** damage
Zech 9:12 that I will restore **d** to you
1Ti 5:17 be counted worthy of **d** honor
Rev 18: 6 repay her **d** according to her
Rev 18: 6 she has mixed, mix for her **d**

DOUBLED (*see* DOUBLE)
Ex 28:16 It shall be **d** into a square
Ex 39: 9 and a span its width when **d**

DOUBLE-EDGED
Judg 3:16 himself a dagger (it was **d**

DOUBLE-MINDED
Ps 119:113 I hate the **d**, But I love Your
Jas 1: 8 he is a **d** man, unstable in
Jas 4: 8 and purify your hearts, you **d**

DOUBLE-TONGUED
1Ti 3: 8 must be reverent, not **d**, not

DOUBLING (*see* DOUBLE)
Ex 39: 9 breastplate square by **d** it

DOUBT (*see* DOUBTED, DOUBTFUL, DOUBTING, DOUBTLESS, DOUBTS)
Gen 37:33 Without **d** Joseph is torn to
Deut 28:66 shall hang in **d** before you
Job 12: 2 No **d** you are the people, and
Matt 14:31 little faith, why did you **d**
Matt 21:21 if you have faith and do not **d**
Mark 11:23 does not **d** in his heart, but
John 10:24 How long do You keep us in **d**
Acts 28: 4 No **d** this man is a murderer,
1Co 9:10 For our sakes, no **d**, this is

DOUBTED (*see* DOUBT)
Matt 28:17 but some **d**

DOUBTFUL (*see* DOUBT)
Rom 14: 1 not to disputes over **d** things

DOUBTING (*see* DOUBT)
Acts 10:20 and go with them, **d** nothing
Acts 11:12 me to go with them, **d** nothing
1Ti 2: 8 hands, without wrath and **d**
Jas 1: 6 him ask in faith, with no **d**

DOUBTLESS (*see* DOUBT)
2Sa 5:19 up, for I will **d** deliver the
Ps 126: 6 Shall **d** come again with
Is 63:16 **D** You are our Father, though
1Co 9: 2 to others, yet **d** I am to you
2Co 12: 1 It is **d** not profitable for me

DOUBTS (*see* DOUBT)
Luke 24:38 why do **d** arise in your hearts
Rom 14:23 But he who **d** is condemned if
Gal 4:20 for I have **d** about you
Jas 1: 6 for he who **d** is like a wave

DOUGH
Ex 12:34 **d** before it was leavened,
Ex 12:39 unleavened cakes of the **d**
Neh 10:37 the firstfruits of our **d**, our
Jer 7:18 and the women knead their **d**
Hos 7: 4 the fire after kneading the **d**

DOVE (*see* DOVE'S, DOVES)
Gen 8: 8 sent out from himself a **d**
Gen 8: 9 But the **d** found no resting
Gen 8:10 sent the **d** out from the ark
Gen 8:11 Then the **d** came to him in the
Gen 8:12 seven days and sent out the **d**
2Ki 6:25 and one-fourth of a kab of **d**
Ps 55: 6 Oh, that I had wings like a **d**
Ps 68:13 of a **d** covered with silver
Song 2:14 O my **d**, in the clefts of the
Song 5: 2 me, my sister, my love, my **d**
Song 6: 9 My **d**, my perfect one, is the
Is 38:14 I mourned like a **d**
Jer 48:28 be like the **d** which makes her
Hos 7:11 also is like a silly **d**,
Hos 11:11 like a **d** from the land of
Matt 3:16 of God descending like a **d**
Mark 1:10 descending upon Him like a **d**
Luke 3:22 bodily form like a **d** upon Him
John 1:32 from heaven like a **d**, and He

DOVE'S (*see* DOVE)
Song 1:15 You have **d** eyes
Song 4: 1 You have **d** eyes behind your

DOVES (*see* DOVE)
Song 5:12 His eyes are like **d** by the
Is 59:11 bears, and moan sadly like **d**
Is 60: 8 and like **d** to their roosts
Ezek 7:16 like **d** of the valleys, all of
Nah 2: 7 her as with the voice of **d**
Matt 10:16 as serpents and harmless as **d**
Matt 21:12 the seats of those who sold **d**
Mark 11:15 the seats of those who sold **d**
John 2:14 who sold oxen and sheep and **d**
John 2:16 He said to those who sold **d**

DOWN (*see* PREFACE)

DOWNCAST
2Co 7: 6 God, who comforts the **d**,

DOWNFALL
2Ch 22: 7 occasion for Ahaziah's **d**
Prov 14:28 people is the **d** of a prince
Lam 1: 7 saw her and mocked at her **d**

DOWNWARD
2Ki 19:30 Judah shall again take root **d**
Is 37:31 Judah shall again take root **d**
Ezek 1:27 and **d** I saw, as it were, the
Ezek 8: 2 appearance of His waist and **d**

DOWRY
Gen 34:12 Ask me ever so much **d** and gift
1Sa 18:25 king does not desire any **d**
1Ki 9:16 it as a **d** to his daughter

DRACHMAS
Ezra 2:69 sixty-one thousand gold **d**
Ezra 8:27 basins worth a thousand **d**
Neh 7:70 treasury one thousand gold **d**
Neh 7:71 work twenty thousand gold **d**
Neh 7:72 was twenty thousand gold **d**

DRAG (*see* DRAGGED, DRAGGING)
Jer 15: 3 sword to slay, the dogs to **d**
Luke 12:58 lest he **d** you to the judge,
Jas 2: 6 you and **d** you into the courts

DRAGGED (*see* DRAG)
Jer 22:19 the burial of a donkey, **d**
John 21:11 **d** the net to land, full of
Acts 14:19 and **d** him out of the city,
Acts 16:19 **d** them into the marketplace
Acts 17: 6 they **d** Jason and some brethren
Acts 21:30 and **d** him out of the temple

DRAGGING (*see* DRAG)
John 21: 8 cubits), **d** the net with fish
Acts 8: 3 and **d** off men and women,

DRAGNET
Hab 1:15 and gather them in their **d**
Hab 1:16 and burn incense to their **d**
Matt 13:47 **d** that was cast into the sea

DRAGON
Rev 12: 3 fiery red **d** having seven
Rev 12: 4 the **d** stood before the woman
Rev 12: 7 angels fought against the **d**
Rev 12: 7 and the **d** and his angels fought
Rev 12: 9 So the great **d** was cast out
Rev 12:13 Now when the **d** saw that he
Rev 12:16 up the flood which the **d** had
Rev 12:17 the **d** was enraged with the
Rev 13: 2 the **d** gave him his power, his
Rev 13: 4 So they worshiped the **d** who
Rev 13:11 like a lamb and spoke like a **d**
Rev 16:13 out of the mouth of the **d**
Rev 20: 2 He laid hold of the **d**, that

DRAIN (*see* DRAINED, DRAINS)
Ps 75: 8 all the wicked of the earth **D**
Ezek 23:34 **d** it, you shall break its

DRAINED (*see* DRAIN)
Lev 1:15 its blood shall be **d** out at
Lev 5: 9 be **d** out at the base of the
Ps 73:10 of a full cup are **d** by them
Is 51:17 cup of trembling, and **d** it out
Joel 2: 6 all faces are **d** of color
Nah 2:10 their faces are **d** of color

DRAINS (*see* DRAIN)
Zech 4:12 from which the golden oil **d**

DRANK (*see* DRINK)
Gen 9:21 Then he **d** of the wine and was
Gen 24:46 So I **d**, and she gave the
Gen 24:54 who were with him ate and **d**
Gen 25:34 then he ate and **d**, arose, and
Gen 26:30 a feast, and they ate and **d**
Gen 27:25 he brought him wine, and he **d**
Gen 43:34 So they **d** and were merry with
Ex 24:11 saw God, and they ate and **d**
Ex 34:28 neither ate bread nor **d** water
Num 20:11 and their animals **d**
Deut 9: 9 neither ate bread nor **d** water
Deut 9:18 neither ate bread nor **d** water
Deut 32:14 you **d** wine, the blood of the
Deut 32:38 **d** the wine of their drink
Judg 9:27 of their god, and ate and **d**
Judg 15:19 and water came out, and he **d**
Judg 19: 4 So they ate and **d** and lodged
Judg 19: 6 two of them ate and **d** together
Judg 19:21 their feet, and ate and **d**
2Sa 11:13 him, he ate and **d** before him
2Sa 12: 3 **d** from his own cup and lay in
1Ki 13:19 in his house, and **d** water
1Ki 13:22 **d** water in the place of which
1Ki 17: 6 and he **d** from the brook
1Ki 19: 6 So he ate and **d**, and lay down
1Ki 19: 8 So he arose, and ate and **d**
2Ki 6:23 and after they ate and **d**, he
2Ki 7: 8 into one tent and ate and **d**
2Ki 9:34 he had gone in, he ate and **d**
1Ch 29:22 **d** before the LORD with great
Ezra 10: 6 **d** no water, for he mourned
Jer 51: 7 The nations **d** her wine
Dan 1: 5 and of the wine which he **d**
Dan 1: 8 nor with the wine which he **d**
Dan 5: 1 **d** wine in the presence of the
Dan 5: 3 and his concubines **d** from them
Dan 5: 4 They **d** wine, and praised the
Obad 16 For as you **d** on my holy
Mark 14:23 them, and they all **d** from it
Luke 13:26 **d** in Your presence, and You
Luke 17:27 They ate, they **d**, they
Luke 17:28 They ate, they **d**, they bought
John 4:12 **d** from it himself, as well as
Acts 9: 9 sight, and neither ate nor **d**
Acts 10:41 **d** with Him after He arose
1Co 10: 4 and all **d** the same spiritual
1Co 10: 4 For they **d** of that spiritual

DRAW (*see* DRAWING, DRAWN, DRAWS, DREW)
Gen 24:11 when women go out to **d** water
Gen 24:13 are coming out to **d** water
Gen 24:19 I will **d** water for your
Gen 24:20 back to the well to **d** water
Gen 24:43 virgin comes out to **d** water
Gen 24:44 I will **d** for your camels also
Ex 3: 5 Do not **d** near this place
Ex 15: 9 I will **d** my sword, my hand
Lev 26:33 and **d** out a sword after you
Deut 32:13 He made him to **d** honey from
Josh 8:26 did not **d** back his hand, with
Judg 3:22 for he did not **d** the dagger
Judg 8:20 youth would not **d** his sword

Judg 9:54 **D** your sword and kill me, lest
Judg 19:13 let us **d** near to one of these
Judg 20:23 Shall I again **d** near for
Judg 20:32 **d** them away from the city to
1Sa 9:11 women going out to **d** water
1Sa 14:36 Let us **d** near to God here
1Sa 31: 4 **D** your sword, and thrust me
1Ch 10: 4 **D** your sword, and thrust me
Job 41: 1 Can you **d** out Leviathan with
Ps 35: 3 Also **d** out the spear, And stop
Ps 69:18 **D** near to my soul, and redeem
Ps 73:28 good for me to **d** near to God
Ps 119:150 They **d** near who follow after
Prov 20: 5 understanding will **d** it out
Eccl 5: 1 **d** near to hear rather than to
Eccl 12: 1 the years **d** near when you say
Is 5:18 Woe to those who **d** iniquity
Is 5:19 the Holy One of Israel **d** near
Is 12: 3 **d** water from the wells of
Is 29:13 **d** near to Me with their
Is 45:20 **d** near together, you who have
Is 66:19 who **d** the bow, and Tubal and
Jer 30:21 I will cause him to **d** near
Jer 46: 3 shield, and **d** near to battle
Jer 49:20 of the flock shall **d** them out
Jer 50:45 of the flock shall **d** them out
Ezek 5: 2 I will **d** out a sword after
Ezek 5:12 I will **d** out a sword after
Ezek 9: 1 charge over the city **d** near
Ezek 12:14 I will **d** out the sword after
Ezek 21: 3 I will **d** My sword out of its
Ezek 22: 4 caused your days to **d** near
Ezek 28: 7 they shall **d** their swords
Ezek 30:11 they shall **d** their swords
Ezek 32: 3 they will **d** you up in My net
Joel 3: 9 let all the men of war **d** near
Nah 3:14 **D** your water for the siege
Hag 2:16 to **d** out fifty baths from the
Matt 15: 8 These people **d** near to Me
John 2: 8 **D** some out now, and take it to
John 4: 7 of Samaria came to **d** water
John 4:11 You have nothing to **d** with
John 4:15 thirst, nor come here to **d**
John 12:32 will **d** all peoples to Myself
John 21: 6 to **d** it in because of the
Acts 20:30 to **d** away the disciples after
Heb 7:19 which we **d** near to God
Heb 10:22 let us **d** near with a true
Heb 10:39 those who **d** back to perdition
Jas 4: 8 **D** near to God
Jas 4: 8 and He will **d** near to you

DRAWING (*see* DRAW)
Judg 19: 9 day is now **d** toward evening
1Sa 17:41 began **d** near to David, and the
Ezek 32:20 **d** her and all her multitudes
Luke 19:37 as He was now **d** near the
John 6:19 on the sea and **d** near the boat
Acts 27:27 they were **d** near some land

DRAWN (*see* DRAW)
Num 22:23 with His **d** sword in His hand
Num 22:31 with His **d** sword in His hand
Num 31:30 **d** from the persons, the
Num 31:47 **d** from man and beast, and gave
Deut 30:17 are **d** away, and worship other
Josh 5:13 with His sword **d** in His hand
Josh 8: 6 we have **d** them from the city
Josh 8:16 were **d** away from the city
Judg 20:31 were **d** away from the city
Ruth 2: 9 what the young men have **d**
1Sa 17:21 had **d** up in battle array,
1Ch 21:16 having in his hand a **d** sword
Job 20:25 It is **d**, and comes out of the
Ps 37:14 The wicked have **d** the sword
Ps 55:21 oil, Yet they were **d** swords
Prov 24:11 those who are **d** toward death
Is 21:15 the swords, from the **d** sword
Is 28: 9 Those just **d** from the breasts
Jer 6:29 for the wicked are not **d** off
Jer 31: 3 lovingkindness I have **d** you
Lam 2: 3 He has **d** back His right hand
Ezek 21: 5 have **d** My sword out of its
Ezek 21:28 A sword, a sword is **d**,
Zeph 3: 2 she has not **d** near to her God
Luke 21: 8 He,' and, 'The time has **d** near
John 2: 9 who had **d** the water knew)
Acts 11:10 and all were **d** up again into
Jas 1:14 is **d** away by his own desires

DRAWS (*see* DRAW)
Deut 25:11 the wife of one **d** near to
Deut 29:11 to the one who **d** your water
Job 24:22 But God **d** the mighty away
Job 33:22 his soul **d** near the Pit, and
Job 36:27 For He **d** up drops of water,
Ps 10: 9 when he **d** him into his net
Ps 88: 3 my life **d** near to the grave
Is 26:17 when she **d** near the time of
Ezek 7:12 time has come, the day **d** near
Luke 21:28 your redemption **d** near
John 6:44 the Father who sent Me **d** him
Heb 10:38 but if anyone **d** back, my soul

DREAD (*see* DREADED, DREADFUL)
Gen 9: 2 and the **d** of you shall be on
Ex 1:12 And they were in **d** of the
Ex 15:16 Fear and **d** will fall on them
Num 22: 3 Moab was sick with **d** because
Deut 2:25 day I will begin to put the **d**
Deut 11:25 God will put the **d** of you
Job 9:34 do not let **d** of Him terrify
Job 13:11 the **d** of Him fall upon you
Job 13:21 let not the **d** of You make me
Ps 119:39 away my reproach which I **d**
Is 7:16 the land that you **d** will be
Is 8:13 fear, and let Him be your **d**
Ezek 4:16 water by measure and with **d**
Ezek 12:19 and drink their water with **d**

DREADED (*see* DREAD)
Job 3:25 what I **d** has happened to me
Job 31:34 **d** the contempt of families,

DREADFUL (*see* DREAD, DREADFULLY)
Job 15:21 **D** sounds are in his ears
Ezek 21:10 to make a **d** slaughter,
Dan 7: 7 and behold, a fourth beast, **d**
Dan 7:19 all the others, exceedingly **d**
Hab 1: 7 They are terrible and **d**
Mal 4: 5 great and **d** day of the LORD

DREADFULLY (*see* DREADFUL)
1Sa 17:24 from him and were **d** afraid
1Sa 28:20 was **d** afraid because of the
Neh 2: 2 Then I became **d** afraid,
Matt 8: 6 home paralyzed, **d** tormented

DREAM (*see* DREAMED, DREAMER, DREAMS)
Gen 20: 3 to Abimelech in a **d** by night
Gen 20: 6 And God said to him in a **d**
Gen 31:10 lifted my eyes and saw in a **d**
Gen 31:11 of God spoke to me in a **d**
Gen 31:24 the Syrian in a **d** by night
Gen 37: 5 Now Joseph dreamed a **d**, and
Gen 37: 6 Please hear this **d** which I
Gen 37: 9 he dreamed still another **d**
Gen 37: 9 I have dreamed another **d**
Gen 37:10 What is this **d** that you have
Gen 40: 5 in the prison, dreamed a **d**
Gen 40: 5 each man's **d** in one night and
Gen 40: 5 each man's **d** with its own
Gen 40: 8 We each have dreamed a **d**, and
Gen 40: 9 butler told his **d** to Joseph
Gen 40: 9 in my **d** a vine was before me,
Gen 40:16 I also was in my **d**, and there
Gen 41: 1 years, that Pharaoh had a **d**
Gen 41: 7 awoke, and indeed, it was a **d**
Gen 41:11 each dreamed a **d** in one night
Gen 41:11 interpretation of his own **d**
Gen 41:12 according to his own **d**
Gen 41:15 I have dreamed a **d**, and there
Gen 41:15 that you can understand a **d**
Gen 41:17 in my **d** I stood on the bank
Gen 41:22 Also I saw in my **d**, and
Gen 41:32 the **d** was repeated to Pharaoh
Num 12: 6 and I speak to him in a **d**
Judg 7:13 telling a **d** to his companion
Judg 7:13 I have just had a **d**
Judg 7:15 heard the telling of the **d**
1Ki 3: 5 to Solomon in a **d** by night
1Ki 3:15 and indeed it had been a **d**
Job 20: 8 He will fly away like a **d**
Job 33:15 In a **d**, in a vision of the
Ps 73:20 As a **d** when one awakes, So,
Ps 126: 1 We were like those who **d**
Eccl 5: 3 For a **d** comes through much
Is 29: 7 shall be as a **d** of a night
Jer 23:28 has a **d**, let him tell a **d**
Dan 2: 3 I have had a **d**, and my spirit
Dan 2: 3 is anxious to know the **d**
Dan 2: 4 Tell your servants the **d**, and
Dan 2: 5 do not make known the **d** to me
Dan 2: 6 However, if you tell the **d**
Dan 2: 6 Therefore tell me the **d** and
Dan 2: 7 king tell his servants the **d**
Dan 2: 9 do not make known the **d** to me
Dan 2: 9 Therefore tell me the **d**, and I
Dan 2:26 to me the **d** which I have seen
Dan 2:28 Your **d**, and the visions of
Dan 2:36 This is the **d**
Dan 2:45 The **d** is certain, and its
Dan 4: 5 I saw a **d** which made me
Dan 4: 6 the interpretation of the **d**
Dan 4: 7 came in, and I told them the **d**
Dan 4: 8 and I told the **d** before him
Dan 4: 9 of my **d** that I have seen, and
Dan 4:18 This **d** I, King Nebuchadnezzar
Dan 4:19 do not let the **d** or its
Dan 4:19 may the **d** concern those who
Dan 7: 1 of Babylon, Daniel had a **d**
Dan 7: 1 Then he wrote down the **d**,
Joel 2:28 your old men shall **d** dreams
Matt 1:20 Lord appeared to him in a **d**
Matt 2:12 being divinely warned in a **d**
Matt 2:13 appeared to Joseph in a **d**
Matt 2:19 in a **d** to Joseph in Egypt
Matt 2:22 And being warned by God in a **d**
Matt 27:19 today in a **d** because of Him
Acts 2:17 your old men shall **d** dreams

DREAMED (*see* DREAM)
Gen 28:12 Then he **d**, and behold, a
Gen 37: 5 Now Joseph **d** a dream, and he
Gen 37: 6 this dream which I have **d**
Gen 37: 9 Then he **d** still another dream
Gen 37: 9 Look, I have **d** another dream
Gen 37:10 is this dream that you have **d**
Gen 40: 5 **d** a dream, both of them, each
Gen 40: 8 We each have **d** a dream, and
Gen 41: 5 He slept and **d** a second time
Gen 41:11 we each **d** a dream in one
Gen 41:11 Each of us **d** according to the
Gen 41:15 I have **d** a dream, and there is
Gen 42: 9 which he had **d** about them
Jer 23:25 I have **d**, I have **d**
Jer 29: 8 which you cause to be **d**

DREAMER (*see* DREAM, DREAMERS)
Gen 37:19 Look, this **d** is coming
Deut 13: 1 a prophet or a **d** of dreams
Deut 13: 3 prophet or that **d** of dreams
Deut 13: 5 But that prophet or that **d** of

DREAMERS (*see* DREAMER)
Jer 27: 9 your diviners, your **d**, your
Jude 8 also these **d** defile the flesh

DREAMS (*see* DREAM)
Gen 37: 8 hated him even more for his **d**
Gen 37:20 see what will become of his **d**
Gen 41: 8 And Pharaoh told them his **d**
Gen 41:12 he interpreted our **d** for us
Gen 41:25 The **d** of Pharaoh are one
Gen 41:26 the **d** are one
Gen 42: 9 **d** which he had dreamed about
Deut 13: 1 a prophet or a dreamer of **d**
Deut 13: 3 prophet or that dreamer of **d**
Deut 13: 5 of **d** shall be put to death
1Sa 28: 6 either by **d** or by Urim or by
1Sa 28:15 neither by prophets nor by **d**
Job 7:14 then You scare me with **d** and
Eccl 5: 7 For in the multitude of **d**
Is 29: 8 be as when a hungry man **d**
Is 29: 8 or as when a thirsty man **d**
Jer 23:27 forget My name by their **d**
Jer 23:32 those who prophesy false **d**
Jer 29: 8 nor listen to your **d** which
Dan 1:17 in all visions and **d**
Dan 2: 1 reign, Nebuchadnezzar had **d**
Dan 2: 2 to tell the king his **d**
Dan 5:12 understanding, interpreting **d**
Joel 2:28 your old men shall dream **d**
Zech 10: 2 lies, and tell false **d**
Acts 2:17 your old men shall dream **d**

DREGS
Ps 75: 8 Surely its **d** shall all the
Is 51:17 you have drunk the **d** of the
Is 51:22 the **d** of the cup of My fury
Jer 48:11 he has settled on his **d**, and

DRENCH
Ps 6: 6 I **d** my couch with my tears
Is 16: 9 I will **d** you with my tears

DRESSED (*see* DRESSING)
1Sa 25:18 of wine, five sheep already **d**
2Sa 20: 8 Now Joab was **d** in battle
2Ch 28:15 **d** them and gave them sandals,

DRESSING (*see* DRESSED)
Joel 2:16 and the bride from her **d** room

DREW (*see* DRAW)
Gen 8: 9 **d** her into the ark to himself
Gen 24:20 and **d** for all his camels
Gen 24:45 down to the well and **d** water
Gen 38:29 as he **d** back his hand, that
Gen 43:19 When they **d** near to the
Gen 47:29 When the time **d** near that
Gen 49:33 he **d** his feet up into the bed
Ex 2:10 Because I **d** him out of the
Ex 2:16 **d** water, and they filled the
Ex 2:19 he also **d** enough water for us
Ex 4: 7 **d** it out of his bosom, and
Ex 14:10 And when Pharaoh **d** near, the
Ex 20:21 but Moses **d** near the thick
Lev 9: 5 all the congregation **d** near
Josh 8:11 with him went up and **d** near
Josh 10:24 And they **d** near and put their
Judg 8:10 who **d** the sword had fallen
Judg 9:52 he **d** near the door of the
Judg 20: 2 foot soldiers who **d** the sword
Judg 20:15 thousand men who **d** the sword
Judg 20:17 thousand men who **d** the sword
Judg 20:25 all these **d** the sword
Judg 20:35 all these **d** the sword
Judg 20:46 thousand men who **d** the sword
1Sa 7: 6 **d** water, and poured it out
1Sa 7:10 the Philistines **d** near to
1Sa 9:18 Then Saul **d** near to Samuel in
1Sa 17: 2 **d** up in battle array against
1Sa 17:16 And the Philistine **d** near and
1Sa 17:40 he **d** near to the Philistine
1Sa 17:48 **d** near to meet David, that
1Sa 17:51 **d** it out of its sheath and
2Sa 10:13 people who were with him **d**
2Sa 18:25 And he came rapidly and **d** near
2Sa 22:17 He **d** me out of many waters
2Sa 23:16 **d** water from the well of
2Sa 24: 9 valiant men who **d** the sword
1Ki 2: 1 Then the days of David **d** near
1Ki 22:34 certain man **d** a bow at random
2Ki 3:26 hundred men who **d** swords, to
2Ki 9:24 Now Jehu **d** his bow with full
1Ch 11:18 **d** water from the well of
1Ch 19:14 people who were with him **d**
1Ch 21: 5 thousand men who **d** the sword
1Ch 21: 5 thousand men who **d** the sword
2Ch 13: 3 Jeroboam also **d** up in battle
2Ch 14: 8 who carried shields and **d** bows
2Ch 18:33 certain man **d** a bow at random
Job 26:10 He **d** a circular horizon on
Ps 18:16 He **d** me out of many waters
Ps 107:18 they **d** near to the gates of
Prov 8:27 when He **d** a circle on the
Is 41: 5 they **d** near and came
Lam 3:57 You **d** near on the day I
Hos 11: 4 I **d** them with gentle cords,
Matt 13:48 it was full, they **d** to shore
Matt 21: 1 Now when they **d** near to
Matt 21:34 Now when vintage-time **d** near
Matt 26:51 and **d** his sword, struck the
Mark 14:47 who stood by **d** his sword and
Luke 15: 1 the sinners **d** near to Him to
Luke 15:25 **d** near to the house, he heard
Luke 19:41 Now as He **d** near, He saw the
Luke 22: 1 of Unleavened Bread **d** near
Luke 22:47 **d** near to Jesus to kiss Him
Luke 23:54 and the Sabbath **d** near
Luke 24:15 that Jesus Himself **d** near
Luke 24:28 Then they **d** near to the
John 18: 6 they **d** back and fell to the
John 18:10 **d** it and struck the high
Acts 5:37 **d** away many people after him
Acts 7:17 the time of the promise **d**
Acts 7:31 as he **d** near to observe, the
Acts 10: 9 **d** near the city, Peter went
Acts 16:27 **d** his sword and was about to
Acts 19:33 they **d** Alexander out of the
Rev 12: 4 His tail **d** a third of the

DRIED (*see* DRY)
Gen 8: 7 had **d** up from the earth
Gen 8:13 were **d** up from the earth
Gen 8:14 of the month, the earth was **d**
Num 11: 6 now our whole being is **d** up
Josh 2:10 we have heard how the LORD **d**
Josh 4:23 for the LORD your God **d** up
Josh 4:23 which He **d** up before us until
Josh 5: 1 heard that the LORD had **d** up
Judg 16: 7 fresh bowstrings, not yet **d**
Judg 16: 8 fresh bowstrings, not yet **d**
1Sa 17:17 an ephah of this **d** grain and
1Ki 17: 7 a while that the brook **d** up
2Ki 19:24 I have **d** up all the brooks of
Job 18:16 His roots are **d** out below
Ps 22:15 My strength is **d** up like a
Ps 74:15 You **d** up mighty rivers
Ps 106: 9 the Red Sea also, and it **d** up
Is 5:13 multitude **d** up with thirst
Is 19: 5 river will be wasted and **d** up
Is 19: 6 will be emptied and **d** up
Is 37:25 I have **d** up all the brooks of
Is 51:10 not the One who **d** up the sea
Jer 23:10 of the wilderness are **d** up
Jer 50:38 waters, and they will be **d** up
Ezek 17:24 **d** up the green tree and made
Ezek 19:12 and the east wind **d** her fruit
Hos 9:16 stricken, their root is **d** up
Hos 13:15 and his fountain shall be **d** up
Joel 1:10 ruined, the new wine is **d** up
Joel 1:12 The vine has **d** up, and the fig
Joel 1:20 for the water brooks are **d** up
Nah 1:10 devoured like stubble fully **d**
Zech 9: 5 for He **d** up her expectation
Mark 5:29 of her blood was **d** up, and she
Mark 11:20 fig tree **d** up from the roots
Rev 16:12 and its water was **d** up, so

DRIES (*see* DRY)
Job 14:11 becomes parched and **d** up,
Prov 17:22 a broken spirit **d** the bones
Nah 1: 4 dry, and **d** up all the rivers

DRIFT
Heb 2: 1 we have heard, lest we **d** away

DRINK (*see* DRANK, DRINKERS, DRINKING, DRINKS, DRUNK)
Gen 19:32 let us make our father **d** wine
Gen 19:33 father **d** wine that night
Gen 19:34 let us make him **d** wine
Gen 19:35 father **d** wine that night also
Gen 21:19 water, and gave the lad a **d**
Gen 24:14 I may **d**,' and she says, '**D**
Gen 24:14 also give your camels a **d**'
Gen 24:17 Please let me **d** a little
Gen 24:18 So she said, "**D**, my lord."
Gen 24:18 to her hand, and gave him a **d**
Gen 24:19 had finished giving him a **d**
Gen 24:43 water from your pitcher to **d**
Gen 24:44 **D**, and I will draw for your
Gen 24:45 said to her, 'Please let me **d**
Gen 24:46 her shoulder, and said, '**D**
Gen 24:46 give your camels a **d** also
Gen 24:46 she gave the camels a **d** also
Gen 30:38 where the flocks came to **d**
Gen 30:38 conceive when they came to **d**
Gen 35:14 he poured a **d** offering on it,
Ex 7:18 to **d** the water of the river
Ex 7:21 not **d** the water of the river
Ex 7:24 the river for water to **d**,
Ex 7:24 not **d** the water of the river
Ex 15:23 they could not **d** the waters
Ex 15:24 What shall we **d**
Ex 17: 1 no water for the people to **d**
Ex 17: 2 Give us water, that we may **d**
Ex 17: 6 of it, that the people may **d**
Ex 29:40 a hin of wine as a **d** offering
Ex 29:41 the **d** offering, as in the
Ex 30: 9 you pour a **d** offering on it
Ex 32: 6 people sat down to eat and **d**
Ex 32:20 the children of Israel **d** it
Lev 10: 9 Do not **d** wine
Lev 10: 9 or intoxicating **d**
Lev 11:34 any **d** that may be drunk from
Lev 23:13 its **d** offering shall be of
Lev 23:18 and their **d** offerings, an
Lev 23:37 **d** offerings, everything on
Num 5:24 woman **d** the bitter water that
Num 5:26 make the woman **d** the water
Num 5:27 he has made her **d** the water
Num 6: 3 from wine and similar **d**
Num 6: 3 he shall **d** neither vinegar
Num 6: 3 vinegar made from similar **d**
Num 6: 3 shall he **d** any grape juice
Num 6:15 with their **d** offerings
Num 6:17 offering and its **d** offering
Num 6:20 that the Nazirite may **d** wine
Num 15: 5 of a hin of wine as a **d**
Num 15: 7 as a **d** offering you shall
Num 15:10 and you shall bring as the **d**
Num 15:24 its **d** offering, according to
Num 20: 5 nor is there any water to **d**
Num 20: 8 give **d** to the congregation and
Num 20:17 nor will we **d** water from
Num 20:19 livestock **d** any of your water
Num 21:22 we will not **d** water from
Num 28: 7 And its **d** offering shall be
Num 28: 7 you shall pour out the **d** to
Num 28: 8 its **d** offering, you shall
Num 28: 9 with oil, with its **d** offering
Num 28:10 offering with its **d** offering
Num 28:14 Their **d** offering shall be
Num 28:15 offering and its **d** offering
Num 28:24 offering and its **d** offering
Num 28:31 them with their **d** offerings
Num 29: 6 their **d** offerings, according
Num 29:11 and their **d** offerings
Num 29:16 offering, and its **d** offering
Num 29:18 their **d** offerings for the
Num 29:19 and their **d** offerings
Num 29:21 their **d** offerings for the
Num 29:22 offering, and its **d** offering
Num 29:24 their **d** offerings for the
Num 29:25 offering, and its **d** offering
Num 29:27 their **d** offerings for the
Num 29:28 offering, and its **d** offering
Num 29:30 their **d** offerings for the
Num 29:31 offering, and its **d** offering
Num 29:33 their **d** offerings for the
Num 29:34 offering, and its **d** offering
Num 29:37 their **d** offerings for the
Num 29:38 offering, and its **d** offering
Num 29:39 as your **d** offerings and your
Num 33:14 no water for the people to **d**
Deut 2: 6 with money, that you may **d**
Deut 2:28 water for money, that I may **d**
Deut 14:26 sheep, for wine or similar **d**
Deut 28:39 but you shall neither **d** of
Deut 29: 6 you drunk wine or similar **d**
Deut 32:38 the wine of their **d** offering
Judg 4:19 give me a little water to **d**
Judg 4:19 a jug of milk, gave him a **d**
Judg 7: 5 gets down on his knees to **d**
Judg 7: 6 on their knees to **d** water
Judg 13: 4 to **d** wine or similar **d**
Judg 13: 7 **d** no wine or similar **d**
Judg 13:14 nor may she **d** wine
Judg 13:14 or similar **d**
Ruth 2: 9 **d** from what the young men
1Sa 1:15 wine nor intoxicating **d**, but
1Sa 30:11 ate, and they let him **d** water
2Sa 11:11 go to my house to eat and **d**
2Sa 16: 2 faint in the wilderness to **d**
2Sa 19:35 taste what I eat or what I **d**
2Sa 23:15 someone would give me a **d** of
2Sa 23:16 he would not **d** it, but poured
2Sa 23:17 Therefore he would not **d** it
1Ki 13: 8 nor **d** water in this place
1Ki 13: 9 nor **d** water, nor return by
1Ki 13:16 nor **d** water with you in this
1Ki 13:17 eat bread nor **d** water there
1Ki 13:18 he may eat bread and **d** water
1Ki 13:22 **d** no water," your corpse
1Ki 17: 4 you shall **d** from the brook
1Ki 17:10 water in a cup, that I may **d**
1Ki 18:41 Go up, eat and **d**
1Ki 18:42 So Ahab went up to eat and **d**
2Ki 3:17 cattle, and your animals may **d**
2Ki 6:22 them, that they may eat and **d**
2Ki 16:13 and he poured his **d** offering
2Ki 16:15 and their **d** offerings
2Ki 18:27 **d** their own waste with you
2Ki 18:31 every one of you **d** the waters
1Ch 11:17 someone would give me a **d** of
1Ch 11:18 David would not **d** it, but
1Ch 11:19 Shall I **d** the blood of these
1Ch 11:19 Therefore he would not **d** it
1Ch 29:21 lambs, with their **d** offerings
2Ch 28:15 sandals, gave them food and **d**
2Ch 29:35 and with the **d** offerings for
Ezra 3: 7 and the carpenters, and food, **d**
Ezra 7:17 their **d** offerings, and offer
Neh 8:10 **d** the sweet, and send portions
Neh 8:12 went their way to eat and **d**
Esth 3:15 king and Haman sat down to **d**
Esth 4:16 eat nor **d** for three days,

Job 1: 4 sisters to eat and **d** with them
Job 21:20 let him **d** of the wrath of the
Job 22: 7 given the weary water to **d**
Ps 16: 4 Their **d** offerings of blood I
Ps 36: 8 And You give them **d** from the
Ps 50:13 Or **d** the blood of goats
Ps 60: 3 You have made us **d** the wine
Ps 69:21 they gave me vinegar to **d**
Ps 75: 8 of the earth Drain and **d** down
Ps 78:15 gave them **d** in abundance like
Ps 78:44 that they could not **d**
Ps 80: 5 tears to **d** in great measure
Ps 102: 9 mingled my **d** with weeping,
Ps 104:11 They give **d** to every beast of
Ps 110: 7 He shall **d** of the brook by
Prov 4:17 and **d** the wine of violence
Prov 5:15 **D** water from your own cistern
Prov 9: 5 **d** of the wine which I have
Prov 20: 1 intoxicating **d** arouses
Prov 23: 7 Eat and **d**
Prov 23:35 that I may seek another **d**
Prov 25:21 thirsty, give him water to **d**
Prov 31: 4 it is not for kings to **d** wine
Prov 31: 4 for princes intoxicating **d**
Prov 31: 5 lest they **d** and forget the law
Prov 31: 6 Give strong **d** to him who is
Prov 31: 7 Let him **d** and forget his
Eccl 2:24 than that he should eat and **d**
Eccl 3:13 every man should eat and **d**
Eccl 5:18 fitting for one to eat and **d**
Eccl 8:15 under the sun than to eat, **d**
Eccl 9: 7 and **d** your wine with a merry
Song 5: 1 **D**, yes, **d** deeply, O beloved
Song 8: 2 cause you to **d** of spiced wine
Is 5:11 may follow intoxicating **d**
Is 5:22 for mixing intoxicating **d**
Is 21: 5 in the tower, eat and **d**
Is 22:13 Let us eat and **d**, for tomorrow
Is 24: 9 They shall not **d** wine with a
Is 24: 9 strong **d** is bitter to those
Is 24: 9 is bitter to those who **d** it
Is 28: 7 **d** are out of the way
Is 28: 7 erred through intoxicating **d**
Is 28: 7 way through intoxicating **d**
Is 29: 9 but not with intoxicating **d**
Is 32: 6 he will cause the **d** of the
Is 36:12 **d** their own waste with you
Is 36:16 every one of you **d** the waters
Is 43:20 to give **d** to My people, My
Is 51:22 you shall no longer **d** it
Is 56:12 ourselves with intoxicating **d**
Is 57: 6 you have poured a **d** offering
Is 60:16 You shall **d** dry the milk of
Is 62: 8 shall not **d** your new wine
Is 62: 9 shall **d** it in My holy courts
Is 65:11 who furnish a **d** offering for
Is 65:13 behold, My servants shall **d**
Is 66:11 bosom, that you may **d** deeply
Jer 2:18 to **d** the waters of Sihor
Jer 2:18 to **d** the waters of the River
Jer 7:18 they pour out **d** offerings to
Jer 8:14 given us water of gall to **d**
Jer 9:15 give them water of gall to **d**
Jer 16: 7 **d** for their father or their
Jer 16: 8 to sit with them, to eat and **d**
Jer 19:13 poured out **d** offerings to
Jer 22:15 Did not your father eat and **d**
Jer 23:15 make them **d** the water of gall
Jer 25:15 to whom I send you, to **d** it
Jer 25:16 And they will **d** and stagger and
Jer 25:17 and made all the nations **d**
Jer 25:26 Sheshach shall **d** after them
Jer 25:27 **D**, be drunk, and vomit
Jer 25:28 the cup from your hand to **d**
Jer 25:28 You shall certainly **d**
Jer 32:29 poured out **d** offerings to
Jer 35: 2 and give them wine to **d**
Jer 35: 5 and I said to them, "**D** wine
Jer 35: 6 We will **d** no wine, for
Jer 35: 6 saying, 'You shall **d** no wine
Jer 35: 8 to **d** no wine all our days, we
Jer 35:14 his sons, not to **d** wine, are
Jer 35:14 for to this day they **d** none
Jer 44:17 pour out **d** offerings to her,
Jer 44:18 pouring out **d** offerings to
Jer 44:19 poured out **d** offerings to her
Jer 44:19 pour out **d** offerings to her
Jer 44:25 pour out **d** offerings to her
Jer 49:12 **d** of the cup have assuredly
Jer 49:12 but you shall surely **d** of it

Lam 3:15 He has made me **d** wormwood
Lam 5: 4 We pay for the water we **d**
Ezek 4:11 You shall also **d** water by
Ezek 4:11 from time to time you shall **d**
Ezek 4:16 shall **d** water by measure and
Ezek 12:18 **d** your water with trembling
Ezek 12:19 **d** their water with dread, so
Ezek 20:28 poured out their **d** offerings
Ezek 23:32 You shall **d** of your sister's
Ezek 23:34 You shall **d** and drain it, you
Ezek 25: 4 and they shall **d** your milk
Ezek 31:16 of Lebanon, all that **d** water
Ezek 34:19 they **d** what you have fouled
Ezek 39:17 you may eat flesh and **d** blood
Ezek 39:18 **d** the blood of the princes of
Ezek 39:19 **d** blood till you are drunk,
Ezek 44:21 No priest shall **d** wine when
Ezek 45:17 **d** offerings, at the feasts,
Dan 1:10 has appointed your food and **d**
Dan 1:12 to eat and water to **d**
Dan 1:16 the wine that they were to **d**
Dan 5: 2 concubines might **d** from them
Hos 2: 5 and my linen, my oil and my **d**
Hos 4:18 Their **d** is rebellion, they
Joel 1: 9 the **d** offering have been cut
Joel 1:13 the **d** offering are withheld
Joel 2:14 a **d** offering for the LORD
Joel 3: 3 for wine, that they may **d**
Amos 2: 8 **d** the wine of the condemned
Amos 2:12 gave the Nazirites wine to **d**
Amos 4: 1 Bring wine, let us **d**
Amos 4: 8 to another city to **d** water
Amos 5:11 shall not **d** wine from them
Amos 6: 6 who **d** wine from bowls, and
Amos 9:14 vineyards and **d** wine from them
Obad 16 all the nations **d** continually
Obad 16 yes, they shall **d**, and swallow
Jon 3: 7 not let them eat, or **d** water
Mic 2:11 prophesy to you of wine and **d**
Mic 6:15 sweet wine, but not **d** wine
Hab 2:15 who gives **d** to his neighbor
Hab 2:16 You also—**d**!
Zeph 1:13 but not **d** their wine
Hag 1: 6 you **d**, but you are not filled
Hag 1: 6 but you are not filled with **d**
Zech 7: 6 When you eat and when you **d**
Zech 7: 6 not eat and **d** for yourselves
Zech 9:15 They shall **d** and roar as if
Matt 6:25 will eat or what you will **d**
Matt 6:31 or 'What shall we **d**
Matt 20:22 Are you able to **d** the cup
Matt 20:22 the cup that I am about to **d**
Matt 20:23 You will indeed **d** My cup, and
Matt 24:49 eat and **d** with the drunkards,
Matt 25:35 was thirsty and you gave Me **d**
Matt 25:37 You, or thirsty and give You **d**
Matt 25:42 thirsty and you gave Me no **d**
Matt 26:27 **D** from it, all of you
Matt 26:29 I will not **d** of this fruit of
Matt 26:29 I **d** it new with you in My
Matt 26:42 away from Me unless I **d** it
Matt 27:34 wine mingled with gall to **d**
Matt 27:34 had tasted it, He would not **d**
Matt 27:48 reed, and gave it to Him to **d**
Mark 9:41 cup of water to **d** in My name
Mark 10:38 Can you **d** the cup that I **d**
Mark 10:39 indeed **d** the cup that I **d**
Mark 14:25 I will no longer **d** of the
Mark 14:25 I **d** it new in the kingdom of
Mark 15:23 wine mingled with myrrh to **d**
Mark 15:36 and offered it to Him to **d**
Mark 16:18 if they **d** anything deadly, it
Luke 1:15 and shall **d** neither wine nor
Luke 1:15 neither wine nor strong **d**
Luke 5:30 and **d** with tax collectors and
Luke 5:33 Pharisees, but Yours eat and **d**
Luke 12:19 eat, **d**, and be merry
Luke 12:29 eat or what you should **d**, nor
Luke 12:45 maidservants, and to eat and **d**
Luke 17: 8 afterward you will eat and **d**'
Luke 22:18 I will not **d** of the fruit of
Luke 22:30 **d** at My table in My kingdom,
John 4: 7 said to her, "Give Me a **d**."
John 4: 9 ask a **d** from me, a Samaritan
John 4:10 who says to you, 'Give Me a **d**
John 6:53 **d** His blood, you have no life
John 6:55 and My blood is **d** indeed
John 7:37 let him come to Me and **d**
John 18:11 Shall I not **d** the cup which
Acts 23:12 **d** till they had killed Paul

Acts 23:21 **d** till they have killed him
Rom 12:20 if he thirsts, give him a **d**
Rom 14:17 of God is not food and **d**, but
Rom 14:21 nor **d** wine nor do anything by
1Co 9: 4 we have no right to eat and **d**
1Co 9: 7 does not **d** of the milk of the
1Co 10: 4 drank the same spiritual **d**
1Co 10: 7 people sat down to eat and **d**
1Co 10:21 You cannot **d** the cup of the
1Co 10:31 whether you eat or **d**, or
1Co 11:22 have houses to eat and **d** in
1Co 11:25 This do, as often as you **d** it
1Co 11:26 **d** this cup, you proclaim the
1Co 11:28 that bread and **d** of that cup
1Co 12:13 made to **d** into one Spirit
1Co 15:32 Let us eat and **d**, for tomorrow
Phil 2:17 a **d** offering on the sacrifice
Col 2:16 one judge you in food or in **d**
1Ti 5:23 No longer **d** only water, but
2Ti 4: 6 poured out as a **d** offering
Rev 14: 8 she has made all nations **d** of
Rev 14:10 he himself shall also **d** of
Rev 16: 6 have given them blood to **d**

DRINKERS (*see* DRINK)
Joel 1: 5 and wail, all you **d** of wine

DRINKING (*see* DRINK)
Gen 24:19 until they have finished **d**
Gen 24:22 the camels had finished **d**
Ruth 3: 3 he has finished eating and **d**
1Sa 1: 9 eating and **d** in Shiloh
1Sa 30:16 all the land, eating and **d**
1Ki 1:25 are eating and **d** before him
1Ki 4:20 sea in multitude, eating and **d**
1Ki 10:21 All King Solomon's **d** vessels
1Ki 16: 9 him as he was in Tirzah **d**
1Ki 20:12 he and the kings were **d** at the
1Ch 12:39 David three days, eating and **d**
2Ch 9:20 All King Solomon's **d** vessels
Esth 1: 8 law, the **d** was not compulsory
Job 1:13 and **d** wine in their oldest
Job 1:18 and **d** wine in their oldest
Is 5:22 Woe to men mighty at **d** wine
Is 22:13 sheep, eating meat and **d** wine
Matt 11:18 came neither eating nor **d**
Matt 11:19 Son of Man came eating and **d**
Matt 24:38 flood, they were eating and **d**
Luke 7:33 eating bread nor **d** wine, and
Luke 7:34 of Man has come eating and **d**
Luke 10: 7 **d** such things as they give,
1Pe 4: 3 **d** parties, and abominable

DRINKS (*see* DRINK)
Gen 44: 5 the one from which my lord **d**
Num 23:24 and **d** the blood of the slain
Deut 11:11 which **d** water from the rain
Esth 1: 7 And they served **d** in golden
Job 6: 4 my spirit **d** in their poison
Job 15:16 Who **d** iniquity like water
Job 34: 7 Job, who **d** scorn like water,
Prov 26: 6 his own feet and **d** violence
Is 29: 8 man dreams, and look—he **d**
Is 44:12 he **d** no water and is faint
Ezek 31:14 that no tree which **d** water
Mark 2:16 and **d** with tax collectors and
John 4:13 Whoever **d** of this water will
John 4:14 but whoever **d** of the water
John 6:54 **d** My blood has eternal life,
John 6:56 **d** My blood abides in Me, and I
1Co 11:27 **d** this cup of the Lord in an
1Co 11:29 **d** in an unworthy manner eats
1Co 11:29 **d** judgment to himself, not
Heb 6: 7 For the earth which **d** in the
Heb 9:10 only with foods and **d**, various

DRIP (*see* DRIPPED, DRIPPING)
Ps 65:11 Your paths **d** with abundance
Prov 5: 3 of an immoral woman **d** honey
Song 4:11 my spouse, **d** as the honeycomb
Joel 3:18 shall **d** with new wine, the
Amos 9:13 shall **d** with sweet wine, and
Zech 4:12 two olive branches that **d**

DRIPPED (*see* DRIP)
Song 5: 5 my hands **d** with myrrh, My

DRIPPING (*see* DRIP)
1Sa 14:26 woods, there was the honey, **d**
Prov 19:13 of a wife are a continual **d**
Prov 27:15 A continual **d** on a very rainy
Song 5:13 are lilies, **d** liquid myrrh

DRIVE (*see* DRIVEN, DRIVER, DRIVES, DRIVING, DROVE, WELL-DRIVEN)

Gen 33:13 should **d** them hard one day
Ex 6: 1 will **d** them out of his land
Ex 11: 1 he will surely **d** you out of
Ex 23:28 which shall **d** out the Hivite,
Ex 23:29 I will not **d** them out from
Ex 23:30 Little by little I will **d**
Ex 23:31 you shall **d** them out before
Ex 33: 2 I will **d** out the Canaanite and
Num 22: 6 **d** them out of the land, for I
Num 22:11 overpower them and **d** them out
Num 33:52 then you shall **d** out all the
Num 33:55 But if you do not **d** out the
Deut 4:27 where the LORD will **d** you
Deut 7:22 the LORD your God will **d** out
Deut 9: 3 so you shall **d** them out and
Deut 11:23 then the LORD will **d** out all
Josh 3:10 **d** out from before you the
Josh 13: 6 them I will **d** out from before
Josh 13:13 **d** out the Geshurites or the
Josh 14:12 I shall be able to **d** them out
Josh 15:63 of Judah could not **d** them out
Josh 16:10 And they did not **d** out the
Josh 17:12 of Manasseh could not **d** out
Josh 17:13 did not utterly **d** them out
Josh 17:18 for you shall **d** out the
Josh 23: 5 and **d** them out of your sight
Josh 23:13 **d** out these nations from
Judg 1:19 but they could not **d** out the
Judg 1:21 of Benjamin did not **d** out the
Judg 1:27 Manasseh did not **d** out the
Judg 1:28 did not completely **d** them out
Judg 1:29 Nor did Ephraim **d** out the
Judg 1:30 Nor did Zebulun **d** out the
Judg 1:31 Nor did Asher **d** out the
Judg 1:32 for they did not **d** them out
Judg 1:33 Nor did Naphtali **d** out the
Judg 2: 3 I will not **d** them out before
Judg 2:21 I also will no longer **d** out
2Ki 4:24 **D**, and go forward
Job 18:11 side, and **d** him to his feet
Job 24: 3 they **d** away the donkey of the
Ps 36:11 hand of the wicked **d** me away
Ps 68: 2 driven away, So **d** them away
Prov 22:15 will **d** it far from him
Is 22:19 So I will **d** you out of your
Jer 19: 9 lives shall **d** them to despair
Jer 24: 9 places where I shall **d** them
Jer 27:10 I will **d** you out, and you will
Jer 27:15 My name, that I may **d** you out
Ezek 4:13 Gentiles, where I will **d** them
Dan 4:25 They shall **d** you from men,
Dan 4:32 they shall **d** you from men, and
Hos 9:15 I will **d** them from My house
Joel 2:20 will **d** him away into a barren
Zeph 2: 4 they shall **d** out Ashdod at
Mark 11:15 and began to **d** out those who
Luke 19:45 and began to **d** out those who
Acts 27:15 into the wind, we let her **d**

DRIVEN (*see* DRIVE)

Gen 4:14 Surely You have **d** me out this
Ex 10:11 And they were **d** out from
Ex 12:39 they were **d** out of Egypt and
Ex 22:10 or **d** away, no one seeing it,
Num 32:21 the LORD until He has **d** out
Deut 4:19 you feel **d** to worship them and
Deut 28:34 So you shall be **d** mad because
Deut 30: 4 If any of you are **d** out to
Josh 23: 9 For the LORD has **d** out from
1Sa 14:31 Now they had **d** back the
1Sa 26:19 for they have **d** me out this
1Sa 30:20 they had **d** before those other
Job 6:13 And is success **d** from me
Job 13:25 Will You frighten a leaf **d** to
Job 18:18 He is **d** from light into
Job 30: 5 They were **d** out from among
Ps 40:14 Let them be **d** backward and
Ps 68: 2 As smoke is **d** away, So drive
Is 8:22 they will be **d** into darkness
Is 19: 7 be **d** away, and be no more
Is 41: 2 as **d** stubble to his bow
Jer 8: 3 places where I have **d** them
Jer 16:15 the lands where He had **d** them
Jer 23: 2 **d** them away, and not attended
Jer 23: 3 countries where I have **d** them
Jer 23: 8 countries where I had **d** them
Jer 23:12 darkness they shall be **d** on
Jer 29:14 the places where I have **d** you
Jer 29:18 nations where I have **d** them
Jer 32:37 I have **d** them in My anger
Jer 40:12 places where they had been **d**
Jer 43: 5 nations where they had been **d**
Jer 46:28 nations to which I have **d** you
Jer 49: 5 you shall be **d** out, everyone
Jer 50:17 the lions have **d** him away
Ezek 31:11 I have **d** it out for its
Ezek 34: 4 brought back what was **d** away
Ezek 34:16 and bring back what was **d** away
Dan 4:33 he was **d** from men and ate
Dan 5:21 Then he was **d** from the sons
Dan 9: 7 to which You have **d** them,
Zeph 3:19 gather those who were **d** out
Luke 8:29 was **d** by the demon into the
Acts 27:17 they struck sail and so were **d**
Acts 27:27 had come, as we were **d** up
Jas 1: 6 is like a wave of the sea **d**
Jas 3: 4 are **d** by fierce winds, they

DRIVER (*see* DRIVE)

1Ki 22:34 said to the **d** of his chariot
2Ch 18:33 said to the **d** of his chariot
Job 39: 7 not heed the shouts of the **d**

DRIVES (*see* DRIVE)

Deut 9: 5 that the LORD your God **d** them
Deut 18:12 the LORD your God **d** them out
Deut 30: 1 where the LORD your God **d** you
2Ki 9:20 of Nimshi, for he **d** furiously
Ps 1: 4 chaff which the wind **d** away
Prov 16:26 for his hungry mouth **d** him on
Is 44:25 babblers, and **d** diviners mad

DRIVING (*see* DRIVE)

Ex 34:11 I am **d** out from before you
Deut 4:38 **d** out from before you nations
Deut 9: 4 is **d** them out from before you
Judg 2:23 nations, without **d** them out
2Ki 9:20 the **d** is like the **d** of
1Ch 17:21 by **d** out nations from before
Prov 28: 3 the poor is like a **d** rain
Acts 26:24 Much learning is **d** you mad

DROMEDARIES (*see* DROMEDARY)

Is 60: 6 the **d** of Midian and Ephah

DROMEDARY (*see* DROMEDARIES)

Jer 2:23 You are a swift **d** breaking

DROP (*see* DROPPED, DROPPINGS, DROPS)

Deut 28:40 for your olives shall **d** off
Deut 32: 2 Let my teaching **d** as the rain
Deut 33:28 His Heavens shall also **d** dew
Job 36:28 Which the clouds **d** down and
Ps 65:12 They **d** on the pastures of the
Prov 3:20 up, and clouds **d** down the dew
Is 40:15 are as a **d** in a bucket, and

DROPPED (*see* DROP)

Judg 9:53 But a certain woman **d** an
Ps 68: 8 The heavens also **d** rain at
Acts 27:29 they **d** four anchors from the

DROPPINGS (*see* DROP)

2Ki 6:25 **d** for five shekels of silver

DROPS (*see* DROP)

Job 36:27 For He draws up **d** of water
Job 38:28 who has begotten the **d** of dew
Song 5: 2 locks with the **d** of the night
Luke 22:44 **d** of blood falling down to
Rev 6:13 as a fig tree **d** its late figs

DROPSY

Luke 14: 2 man before Him who had **d**

DROSS

Ps 119:119 wicked of the earth like **d**
Prov 25: 4 Take away the **d** from silver
Prov 26:23 covered with silver **d**
Is 1:22 Your silver has become **d**,
Is 1:25 thoroughly purge away your **d**
Ezek 22:18 of Israel has become **d** to Me
Ezek 22:18 have become **d** from silver
Ezek 22:19 Because you have all become **d**

DROUGHT (*see* DROUGHTS)

Gen 31:40 In the day the **d** consumed me
Job 24:19 As **d** and heat consume the snow
Ps 32: 4 turned into the **d** of summer
Is 58:11 and satisfy your soul in **d**
Jer 2: 6 and pits, through a land of **d**
Jer 17: 8 be anxious in the year of **d**
Jer 50:38 A **d** is against her waters, and
Hos 13: 5 in the land of great **d**
Hag 1:11 I called for a **d** on the land

DROUGHTS (*see* DROUGHT)

Jer 14: 1 to Jeremiah concerning the **d**

DROVE (*see* DRIVE, DROVES)

Gen 3:24 So He **d** out the man
Gen 15:11 carcasses, Abram **d** them away
Gen 32:16 every **d** by itself, and said to
Ex 2:17 shepherds came and **d** them
Ex 14:25 so that they **d** them with
Num 14:45 **d** them back as far as Hormah
Num 21:32 **d** out the Amorites who were
Deut 1:44 and **d** you back from Seir to
Josh 15:14 Caleb **d** out the three sons of
Josh 24:12 **d** them out from before you
Josh 24:18 the LORD **d** out from before us
Judg 1:19 they **d** out the inhabitants of
Judg 4:21 **d** the peg into his temple, and
Judg 6: 9 **d** them out before you and gave
Judg 9:41 and Zebul **d** out Gaal and his
Judg 11: 2 they **d** Jephthah out, and said
1Sa 7:11 **d** them back as far as below
1Sa 19:10 he **d** the spear into the wall
2Sa 5:25 he **d** back the Philistines
2Sa 6: 3 of Abinadab, **d** the new cart
2Sa 11:23 then we **d** them back as far as
2Ki 16: 6 **d** the men of Judah from Elath
2Ki 17:21 Then Jeroboam **d** Israel from
1Ch 8:13 who **d** out the inhabitants of
1Ch 13: 7 and Uzza and Ahio **d** the cart
1Ch 14:16 they **d** back the army of the
2Ch 20: 7 who **d** out the inhabitants of
Neh 13:28 therefore I **d** him from me
Ps 44: 2 How You **d** out the nations
Ps 78:55 He also **d** out the nations
Jer 46:15 because the LORD **d** them away
Matt 21:12 **d** out all those who bought and
Mark 1:12 immediately the Spirit **d** Him
John 2:15 He **d** them all out of the
Acts 7:45 whom God **d** out before the
Acts 18:16 he **d** them from the judgment

DROVES (*see* DROVE)

Gen 32:16 distance between successive **d**
Gen 32:19 and all who followed the **d**

DROWN (*see* DROWNED)

Song 8: 7 love, nor can the floods **d** it
1Ti 6: 9 which **d** men in destruction

DROWNED (*see* DROWN)

Ex 15: 4 also are **d** in the Red Sea
Matt 18: 6 he were **d** in the depth of the
Mark 5:13 into the sea, and **d** in the sea
Luke 8:33 place into the lake and **d**
Heb 11:29 attempting to do so, were **d**

DROWSINESS

Prov 23:21 **d** will clothe a man with rags

DRUNK (*see* DRINK, DRUNKARD, DRUNKEN)

Gen 9:21 he drank of the wine and was **d**
Lev 11:34 any drink that may be **d** from
Deut 29: 6 bread, nor have you **d** wine or
Deut 32:42 make My arrows **d** with blood
Ruth 3: 7 And after Boaz had eaten and **d**
1Sa 1:13 Eli thought she was **d**
1Sa 1:14 How long will you be **d**
1Sa 1:15 I have **d** neither wine nor
1Sa 25:36 within him, for he was very **d**
1Sa 30:12 **d** any water for three days
2Sa 11:13 and he made him **d**
1Ki 13:23 eaten bread and after he had **d**
1Ki 16: 9 **d** in the house of Arza,
1Ki 20:16 getting **d** at the command post
2Ki 19:24 **d** strange water, and with the
Song 5: 1 I have **d** my wine with my milk
Is 29: 9 They are **d**, but not with wine
Is 37:25 **d** water, and with the soles of
Is 49:26 they shall be **d** with their
Is 51:17 you who have **d** at the hand of
Is 51:17 you have **d** the dregs of the
Is 51:21 and **d** but not with wine
Is 63: 6 made them **d** in My fury, and
Jer 25:27 Drink, be **d**, and vomit
Jer 46:10 and made **d** with their blood
Jer 48:26 Make him **d**, for he magnified
Jer 49:12 of the cup have assuredly **d**
Jer 51: 7 that made all the earth **d**
Jer 51:39 I will make them **d**, that they
Jer 51:57 And I will make **d** her princes
Lam 4:21 to you and you shall become **d**
Ezek 34:18 to have **d** of the clear waters
Ezek 39:19 and drink blood till you are **d**

Dan 5:23 have **d** wine from them
Nah 3:11 You also will be **d**
Hab 2:15 bottle, even to make him **d**
Luke 5:39 And no one, having **d** old wine,
Luke 12:45 and to eat and drink and be **d**
Luke 17: 8 me till I have eaten and **d**
John 2:10 when the guests have well **d**
Acts 2:15 For these are not **d**, as you
1Co 11:21 one is hungry and another is **d**
Eph 5:18 And do not be **d** with wine, in
1Th 5: 7 who get **d** are **d** at night
Rev 17: 2 made **d** with the wine of her
Rev 17: 6 **d** with the blood of the
Rev 18: 3 For all the nations have **d** of

DRUNKARD (*see* DRUNK, DRUNKARDS)
Deut 21:20 he is a glutton and a **d**
Deut 29:19 as though the **d** could be
Prov 23:21 for the **d** and the glutton will
Prov 26: 9 goes into the hand of a **d** is
Is 24:20 shall reel to and fro like a **d**
1Co 5:11 or a reviler, or a **d**, or an

DRUNKARDS (*see* DRUNKARD)
Ps 69:12 me, And I am the song of the **d**
Is 28: 1 to the **d** of Ephraim, whose
Is 28: 3 the **d** of Ephraim, will be
Joel 1: 5 Awake, you **d**, and weep
Nah 1:10 and while drunken like **d**,
Matt 24:49 and to eat and drink with the **d**
1Co 6:10 thieves, nor covetous, nor **d**

DRUNKEN (*see* DRUNK, DRUNKENNESS)
Job 12:25 them stagger like a **d** man
Ps 107:27 fro, and stagger like a **d** man
Is 19:14 as a **d** man staggers in his
Jer 23: 9 I am like a **d** man, and like a
Nah 1:10 while **d** like drunkards, They

DRUNKENNESS (*see* DRUNKEN)
Eccl 10:17 for strength and not for **d**
Jer 13:13 of Jerusalem—with **d**!
Ezek 23:33 You will be filled with **d**
Zech 12: 2 of **d** to all the surrounding
Luke 21:34 down with carousing, **d**, and
Rom 13:13 the day, not in revelry and **d**
Gal 5:21 envy, murders, **d**, revelries,
1Pe 4: 3 in licentiousness, lusts, **d**

DRUSILLA
Acts 24:24 Felix came with his wife **D**

DRY (*see* DRIED, DRIES, DRYSHOD)
Gen 1: 9 and let the **d** land appear"
Gen 1:10 God called the **d** land Earth
Gen 7:22 all that was on the **d** land
Gen 8:13 surface of the ground was **d**
Ex 4: 9 and pour it on the **d** land
Ex 4: 9 become blood on the **d** land
Ex 14:16 of Israel shall go on **d**
Ex 14:21 and made the sea into **d** land
Ex 14:22 of the sea on the **d** ground
Ex 14:29 of Israel had walked on **d**
Ex 15:19 on **d** land in the midst of the
Lev 7:10 offering mixed with oil, or **d**
Josh 3:17 of the LORD stood firm on **d**
Josh 3:17 crossed over on **d** ground,
Josh 4:18 feet touched the **d** land, that
Josh 4:22 over this Jordan on **d** land'
Josh 9: 5 of their provision was **d** and
Josh 9:12 But now look, it is **d** and
Judg 6:37 it is **d** on all the ground,
Judg 6:39 let it now be **d** only on the
Judg 6:40 It was **d** on the fleece only,
1Ki 17:14 shall the jar of oil run **d**
1Ki 17:16 nor did the jar of oil run **d**
2Ki 2: 8 them crossed over on **d** ground
Neh 9:11 of the sea on the **d** land
Job 12:15 the waters, they **d** up
Job 13:25 And will You pursue **d** stubble
Job 15:30 the flame will **d** out his
Job 24:24 they **d** out like the heads of
Ps 63: 1 My flesh longs for You In a **d**
Ps 66: 6 He turned the sea into **d** land
Ps 68: 6 rebellious dwell in a **d** land
Ps 69: 3 My throat is **d**
Ps 95: 5 His hands formed the **d** land
Ps 105:41 It ran in the **d** places like a
Ps 107:33 watersprings into **d** ground
Ps 107:35 And **d** land into watersprings
Prov 17: 1 Better is a **d** morsel with
Is 25: 5 aliens, as heat in a **d** place
Is 32: 2 rivers of water in a **d** place
Is 41:18 the **d** land springs of water
Is 42:15 **d** up all their vegetation
Is 42:15 and I will **d** up the pools
Is 44: 3 and floods on the **d** ground
Is 44:27 Who says to the deep, 'Be **d**
Is 44:27 and I will **d** up your rivers'
Is 50: 2 with My rebuke I **d** up the sea
Is 53: 2 and as a root out of **d** ground
Is 56: 3 say, "Here I am, a **d** tree
Is 60:16 You shall drink **d** the milk of
Jer 4:11 A **d** wind of the desolate
Jer 50:12 a **d** land and a desert
Jer 51:36 I will **d** up her sea and make
Jer 51:36 her sea and make her springs **d**
Jer 51:43 a **d** land and a wilderness, a
Lam 4: 8 it has become as **d** as wood
Ezek 17:24 and made the **d** tree flourish
Ezek 19:13 in the wilderness, in a **d**
Ezek 20:47 tree and every **d** tree in you
Ezek 30:12 I will make the rivers **d**, and
Ezek 37: 2 and indeed they were very **d**
Ezek 37: 4 O **d** bones, hear the word of
Ezek 37:11 indeed say, 'Our bones are **d**
Hos 2: 3 and set her like a **d** land
Hos 9:14 miscarrying womb and **d** breasts
Hos 13:15 his spring shall become **d**
Jon 1: 9 made the sea and the **d** land
Jon 2:10 it vomited Jonah onto **d** land
Nah 1: 4 rebukes the sea and makes it **d**
Zeph 2:13 as **d** as the wilderness
Hag 2: 6 and earth, the sea and **d** land
Zech 10:11 of the River shall **d** up
Matt 12:43 man, he goes through **d** places
Luke 11:24 man, he goes through **d** places
Luke 23:31 what will be done in the **d**
Heb 11:29 the Red Sea as by **d** land,

DRYSHOD (*see* DRY)
Is 11:15 and make men cross over **d**

DUE
Lev 10:13 is your **d** and your sons' **d**
Lev 10:14 are your **d** and your sons' **d**
Lev 27:18 reckon to him the money **d**
Num 18:29 heave offering **d** to the LORD
Deut 18: 3 priest's **d** from the people
Deut 24:17 justice **d** the stranger or the
Deut 27:19 the justice **d** the stranger
Deut 32:35 foot shall slip in **d** time
1Sa 4:19 with child, **d** to be delivered
1Ch 16:29 the LORD the glory **d** His name
Job 36:17 the judgment **d** the wicked
Ps 29: 2 LORD the glory **d** to His name
Ps 96: 8 the LORD the glory **d** His name
Ps 104:27 them their food in **d** season
Ps 145:15 them their food in **d** season
Prov 3:27 from those to whom it is **d**
Prov 15:23 and a word spoken in **d** season
Jer 10: 7 For this is Your rightful **d**
Lam 3:35 **d** a man before the face of
Dan 3:12 have not paid **d** regard to you
Dan 6:13 does not show **d** regard for
Matt 18:34 pay all that was **d** to him
Matt 24:45 to give them food in **d** season
Luke 12:42 portion of food in **d** season
Luke 23:41 for we receive the **d** reward
Rom 1:27 of their error which was **d**
Rom 5: 6 in **d** time Christ died for the
Rom 13: 7 therefore to all their **d**
Rom 13: 7 taxes to whom taxes are **d**
1Co 7: 3 his wife the affection **d** her
1Co 15: 8 as by one born out of **d** time
Gal 6: 9 for in **d** season we shall reap
1Ti 2: 6 to be testified in **d** time
Tit 1: 3 but has in **d** time manifested
1Pe 5: 6 He may exalt you in **d** time
Rev 16: 6 for it is their just **d**

DUG (*see* DIG)
Gen 21:30 that I have **d** this well
Gen 26:15 his father's servants had **d**
Gen 26:18 Isaac **d** again the wells of
Gen 26:18 of water which they had **d** in
Gen 26:19 servants **d** in the valley, and
Gen 26:21 Then they **d** another well, and
Gen 26:22 **d** another well, and they did
Gen 26:25 Isaac's servants **d** a well
Gen 26:32 the well which they had **d**
Gen 50: 5 in my grave which I **d** for
Ex 7:24 So all the Egyptians **d** all
Num 21:18 **d** by the nation's nobles, by
2Ki 19:24 I have **d** and drunk strange
2Ch 26:10 He **d** many wells, for he had
Neh 9:25 all goods, cisterns already **d**
Ps 7:15 **d** it out, And has fallen into
Ps 35: 7 Which they have **d** without
Ps 57: 6 They have **d** a pit before me
Ps 94:13 the pit is **d** for the wicked
Ps 119:85 The proud have **d** pits for me
Is 5: 2 He **d** it up and cleared out its
Is 5: 6 it shall not be pruned or **d**
Is 7:25 which could be **d** with the hoe
Is 37:25 I have **d** and drunk water, and
Is 51: 1 the pit from which you were **d**
Jer 13: 7 I went to the Euphrates and **d**
Jer 18:20 For they have **d** a pit for my
Jer 18:22 for they have **d** a pit to take
Ezek 8: 8 when I **d** into the wall, there
Ezek 12: 7 at evening I **d** through the
Matt 21:33 **d** a winepress in it and built
Matt 25:18 **d** in the ground, and hid his
Mark 12: 1 **d** a place for the wine vat and
Luke 6:48 house, who **d** deep and laid the

DULL (*see* DULL-HEARTED)
Lev 13:39 skin of the body are **d** white
Eccl 10:10 If the ax is **d**, and one does
Is 6:10 the heart of this people **d**
Matt 13:15 of this people has grown **d**
Acts 28:27 of this people has grown **d**
Heb 5:11 you have become **d** of hearing

DULL-HEARTED (*see* DULL)
Jer 10: 8 But they are altogether **d**
Jer 10:14 Everyone is **d**, without
Jer 10:21 the shepherds have become **d**
Jer 51:17 Everyone is **d**, without

DUMAH
Gen 25:14 Mishma, **D**, Massa,
Josh 15:52 Arab, **D**, Eshean,
1Ch 1:30 Mishma, **D**, Massa, Hadad,
Is 21:11 The burden against **D**

DUMB
Is 35: 6 and the tongue of the **d** sing
Is 56:10 they are all **d** dogs, they
Mark 9:25 **d** spirit, I command you, come
1Co 12: 2 carried away to these **d** idols
2Pe 2:16 a **d** donkey speaking with a

DUMP
2Ki 10:27 it a refuse **d** to this day

DUNG
Ezek 4:15 I am giving you cow **d** instead

DUNGEON
Gen 40:15 they should put me into the **d**
Gen 41:14 him hastily out of the **d**
Ex 12:29 the captive who was in the **d**
Jer 37:16 When Jeremiah entered the **d**
Jer 38: 6 and cast him into the **d** of
Jer 38: 6 in the **d** there was no water,
Jer 38: 7 had put Jeremiah in the **d**
Jer 38: 9 they have cast into the **d**
Jer 38:10 out of the **d** before he dies
Jer 38:11 ropes into the **d** to Jeremiah
Jer 38:13 and lifted him out of the **d**

DUNGHILL
Luke 14:35 for the land nor for the **d**

DURA
Dan 3: 1 set it up in the plain of **D**

DURING (*see* PREFACE)

DUST
Gen 2: 7 man of the **d** of the ground
Gen 3:14 you shall eat **d** all the days
Gen 3:19 for **d** you are, and to **d** you
Gen 3:19 and to **d** you shall return
Gen 13:16 as the **d** of the earth
Gen 13:16 number the **d** of the earth
Gen 18:27 Indeed now, I who am but **d**
Gen 28:14 be as the **d** of the earth
Ex 8:16 strike the **d** of the land, so
Ex 8:17 struck the **d** of the earth, and
Ex 8:17 All the **d** of the land became
Ex 9: 9 it will become fine **d** in all
Lev 14:41 the **d** that they scrape off
Lev 17:13 its blood and cover it with **d**
Num 5:17 take some of the **d** that is on
Num 23:10 Who can count the **d** of Jacob
Deut 9:21 until it was as fine as **d**
Deut 9:21 I threw its **d** into the brook
Deut 28:24 of your land to powder and **d**

Deut 32:24 poison of serpents of the **d**
Josh 7: 6 they put **d** on their heads
1Sa 2: 8 He raises the poor from the **d**
2Sa 1: 2 clothes torn and **d** on his head
2Sa 15:32 robe torn and **d** on his head
2Sa 16:13 stones at him and kicked up **d**
2Sa 22:43 as fine as the **d** of the earth
1Ki 16: 2 as I lifted you out of the **d**
1Ki 18:38 wood and the stones and the **d**
1Ki 20:10 also, if enough **d** is left of
2Ki 13: 7 them like the **d** at threshing
2Ki 23:12 threw their **d** into the Brook
2Ch 1: 9 **d** of the earth in multitude
2Ch 34: 4 made **d** of them and scattered
Neh 9: 1 and with **d** on their heads
Job 2:12 and sprinkled **d** on his head
Job 4:19 whose foundation is in the **d**
Job 5: 6 does not come from the **d**, nor
Job 7: 5 is caked with worms and **d**, my
Job 7:21 now I will lie down in the **d**
Job 10: 9 will You turn me into **d** again
Job 16:15 and laid my head in the **d**
Job 17:16 have rest together in the **d**
Job 20:11 lie down with him in the **d**
Job 21:26 They lie down alike in the **d**
Job 22:24 will lay your gold in the **d**
Job 27:16 he heaps up silver like **d**
Job 28: 6 and it contains gold **d**
Job 30:19 mire, and I have become like **d**
Job 34:15 and man would return to **d**
Job 38:38 when the **d** hardens in clumps,
Job 39:14 and warms them in the **d**
Job 40:13 Hide them in the **d** together
Job 42: 6 abhor myself, and repent in **d**
Ps 7: 5 And lay my honor in the **d**
Ps 18:42 fine as the **d** before the wind
Ps 22:15 brought Me to the **d** of death
Ps 22:29 to the **d** Shall bow before Him
Ps 30: 9 Will the **d** praise You
Ps 44:25 soul is bowed down to the **d**
Ps 72: 9 His enemies will lick the **d**
Ps 78:27 meat on them like the **d**,
Ps 83:13 make them like the whirling **d**
Ps 102:14 And show favor to her **d**
Ps 103:14 He remembers that we are **d**
Ps 104:29 they die and return to their **d**
Ps 113: 7 raises the poor out of the **d**
Ps 119:25 My soul clings to the **d**
Prov 8:26 the primeval **d** of the world
Eccl 3:20 all are from the **d**
Eccl 3:20 and all return to **d**
Eccl 12: 7 Then the **d** will return to the
Is 2:10 the rock, and hide in the **d**
Is 5:24 blossom will ascend like **d**
Is 25:12 to the ground, down to the **d**
Is 26: 5 He brings it down to the **d**
Is 26:19 and sing, you who dwell in **d**
Is 27: 9 that are beaten to **d**, when
Is 29: 4 shall be low, out of the **d**
Is 29: 4 shall whisper out of the **d**
Is 29: 5 foes shall be like fine **d**
Is 34: 7 and their **d** saturated with
Is 34: 9 and its **d** into brimstone
Is 40:12 calculated the **d** of the earth
Is 40:15 as the small **d** on the balance
Is 41: 2 them as the **d** to his sword
Is 47: 1 Come down and sit in the **d**
Is 49:23 lick up the **d** of your feet
Is 52: 2 Shake yourself from the **d**
Is 65:25 **d** shall be the serpent's food
Lam 2:10 they throw **d** on their heads
Lam 3:29 him put his mouth in the **d**
Ezek 24: 7 ground, to cover it with **d**
Ezek 26: 4 also scrape her **d** from her
Ezek 26:10 their **d** will cover you
Ezek 27:30 and cast **d** on their heads
Dan 12: 2 **d** of the earth shall awake
Amos 2: 7 They pant after the **d** of the
Mic 1:10 roll yourself in the **d**
Mic 7:17 lick the **d** like a serpent
Nah 1: 3 clouds are the **d** of His feet
Nah 3:18 your nobles rest in the **d**
Zeph 1:17 shall be poured out like **d**
Zech 9: 3 heaped up silver like the **d**
Matt 10:14 shake off the **d** from your
Mark 6:11 shake off the **d** under your
Luke 9: 5 shake off the very **d** from
Luke 10:11 The very **d** of your city
Acts 13:51 But they shook off the **d** from
Acts 22:23 and threw **d** into the air,
1Co 15:47 was of the earth, made of **d**
1Co 15:48 As was the man of **d**, so also
1Co 15:48 are those who are made of **d**
1Co 15:49 the image of the man of **d**
Rev 18:19 they threw **d** on their heads

DUTIES (*see* DUTY)
Ex 1:16 When you do the **d** of a
Num 3:25 The **d** of the children of
Num 4:28 their **d** shall be under the
Num 8:26 the Levites regarding their **d**
Num 18: 5 to the **d** of the sanctuary
Num 18: 5 and the **d** of the altar, that
1Ch 9:33 and were free from other **d**
1Ch 26:12 men, having **d** just like their
1Ch 26:29 sons performed **d** as officials
2Ch 8:14 for their **d** (to praise and
2Ch 13:10 the Levites attend to their **d**
2Ch 35: 2 he set the priests in their **d**
Neh 12: 9 across from them in their **d**
Neh 13:30 assigned **d** to the priests
Ezek 18:11 and does none of those **d**, but

DUTY (*see* DUTIES)
Num 3:31 Their **d** included the ark, the
Num 3:36 And the appointed **d** of the
Num 4:16 The appointed **d** of Eleazar
Num 4:27 all their tasks as their **d**
Deut 25: 5 perform the **d** of a husband's
Deut 25: 7 the **d** of my husband's brother
Ruth 3:13 **d** of a near kinsman for you
Ruth 3:13 want to perform the **d** for you
Ruth 3:13 I will perform the **d** for you
2Ki 11: 5 of you who come on **d** on the
2Ki 11: 7 of you who go off **d** on the
2Ki 11: 9 to be on **d** on the Sabbath
2Ki 11: 9 going off **d** on the Sabbath
1Ch 23:28 because their **d** was to help
1Ch 25: 8 And they cast lots for their **d**
2Ch 8:14 as the **d** of each day required
2Ch 23: 8 to be on **d** on the Sabbath
2Ch 23: 8 going off **d** on the Sabbath
Eccl 12:13 this is the whole **d** of man
Luke 17:10 done what was our **d** to do
Rom 15:27 their **d** is also to minister

DWARF
Lev 21:20 or is a hunchback or a **d**

DWELL (*see* DWELLERS, DWELLING, DWELLS, DWELT)
Gen 4:20 of those who **d** in tents and
Gen 9:27 may he **d** in the tents of Shem
Gen 13: 6 that they might **d** together
Gen 13: 6 they could not **d** together
Gen 16:12 he shall **d** in the presence of
Gen 19:30 he was afraid to **d** in Zoar
Gen 20:15 **d** where it pleases you
Gen 24: 3 Canaanites, among whom I **d**
Gen 24:37 Canaanites, in whose land I **d**
Gen 26: 2 **d** in the land of which I
Gen 30:20 now my husband will **d** with me
Gen 34:10 So you shall **d** with us, and
Gen 34:10 **D** and trade in it, and acquire
Gen 34:16 we will **d** with you, and we
Gen 34:21 let them **d** in the land and
Gen 34:22 the men consent to **d** with us
Gen 34:23 them, and they will **d** with us
Gen 35: 1 go up to Bethel and **d** there
Gen 36: 7 great for them to **d** together
Gen 45:10 You shall **d** in the land of
Gen 46:34 that you may **d** in the land
Gen 47: 4 **d** in the land of Goshen
Gen 47: 6 brothers **d** in the best of the
Gen 47: 6 let them **d** in the land of
Gen 49:13 Zebulun shall **d** by the haven
Ex 8:22 Goshen, in which My people **d**
Ex 23:33 They shall not **d** in your land
Ex 25: 8 that I may **d** among them
Ex 29:45 I will **d** among the children
Ex 29:46 that I may **d** among them
Lev 13:46 unclean, and he shall **d** alone
Lev 20:22 to **d** may not vomit you out
Lev 23:42 You shall **d** in booths for
Lev 23:42 Israelites shall **d** in booths
Lev 23:43 **d** in booths when I brought
Lev 25:18 you will **d** in the land in
Lev 25:19 fill, and **d** there in safety
Lev 26: 5 and **d** in your land safely
Lev 26:32 and your enemies who **d** in it
Num 5: 3 in the midst of which I **d**
Num 13:18 whether the people who **d** in
Num 13:19 land they **d** in is good or bad
Num 13:28 who **d** in the land are strong
Num 13:29 The Amalekites **d** in the land
Num 13:29 and the Amorites **d** in the
Num 13:29 the Canaanites **d** by the sea
Num 14:25 Canaanites **d** in the valley
Num 14:30 I swore I would make you **d** in
Num 32:17 our little ones will **d** in the
Num 33:53 **d** in it, for I have given you
Num 33:55 you in the land where you **d**
Num 35: 2 **d** in from the inheritance of
Num 35: 3 shall have the cities to **d** in
Num 35:32 that he may return to **d** in
Num 35:34 in the midst of which I **d**
Num 35:34 for I the LORD **d** among the
Deut 2: 8 of Esau who **d** in Seir, away
Deut 2:29 of Esau who **d** in Seir and the
Deut 2:29 who **d** in Ar did for me, until
Deut 8:12 beautiful houses and **d** in them
Deut 11:30 who **d** in the plain opposite
Deut 11:31 will possess it and **d** in it
Deut 12:10 **d** in the land which the LORD
Deut 12:10 so that you **d** in safety,
Deut 12:29 them and **d** in their land,
Deut 13:12 your God gives you to **d** in
Deut 17:14 **d** in it, and say, 'I will set
Deut 19: 1 **d** in their cities and in their
Deut 23:16 He may **d** with you in your
Deut 25: 5 If brothers **d** together, and
Deut 26: 1 and you possess it and **d** in it,
Deut 28:30 but you shall not **d** in it
Deut 30:20 that you may **d** in the land
Deut 33:12 LORD shall **d** in safety by Him
Deut 33:12 And he shall **d** between His
Deut 33:28 Then Israel shall **d** in safety
Josh 9: 7 Perhaps you **d** among us
Josh 9:22 from you,' when you **d** near us
Josh 10: 6 who **d** in the mountains have
Josh 13:13 the Maachathites **d** among the
Josh 14: 4 land, except cities to **d** in
Josh 15:63 but the Jebusites **d** with the
Josh 16:10 but the Canaanites **d** among
Josh 17:12 determined to **d** in that land
Josh 17:16 all the Canaanites who **d** in
Josh 20: 4 that he may **d** among them
Josh 20: 6 he shall **d** in that city until
Josh 21: 2 to give us cities to **d** in
Josh 24:13 not build, and you **d** in them
Josh 24:15 Amorites, in whose land you **d**
Judg 1:21 so the Jebusites **d** with the
Judg 1:27 determined to **d** in that land
Judg 1:35 to **d** in Mount Heres, in
Judg 6:10 Amorites, in whose land you **d**
Judg 8:11 who **d** in tents on the east of
Judg 9:41 they would not **d** in Shechem
Judg 17:10 **D** with me, and be a father and
Judg 17:11 was content to **d** with the man
Judg 18: 1 for itself to **d** in
1Sa 12: 8 made them **d** in this place
1Sa 27: 5 country, that I may **d** there
1Sa 27: 5 **d** in the royal city with you
2Sa 7: 2 I **d** in a house of cedar, but
2Sa 7: 5 build a house for Me to **d** in
2Sa 7:10 that they may **d** in a place of
1Ki 2:36 **d** there, and do not go out
1Ki 3:17 and I **d** in the same house
1Ki 6:13 I will **d** among the children
1Ki 8:12 He would **d** in the dark cloud
1Ki 8:13 place for You to **d** in forever
1Ki 8:27 God indeed **d** on the earth
1Ki 17: 9 belongs to Sidon, and **d** there
2Ki 4:13 I **d** among my own people
2Ki 6: 1 the place where we **d** with you
2Ki 6: 2 there a place where we may **d**
2Ki 16: 6 Elath, and **d** there to this day
2Ki 17:27 **d** there, and let him teach
2Ki 25:24 **D** in the land and serve the
1Ch 4:23 and those who **d** at Netaim and
1Ch 17: 1 I **d** in a house of cedar, but
1Ch 17: 4 not build Me a house to **d** in
1Ch 17: 9 that they may **d** in a place of
1Ch 23:25 that they may **d** in Jerusalem
2Ch 2: 3 build himself a house to **d** in
2Ch 6: 1 He would **d** in the dark cloud
2Ch 6: 2 place for You to **d** in forever
2Ch 6:18 But will God indeed **d** with
2Ch 8:11 My wife shall not **d** in the
2Ch 19:10 who **d** in their cities,
2Ch 20: 8 they **d** in it, and have built
Ezra 4:17 companions who **d** in Samaria

Ezra 6:12 **d** there destroy any king or
Neh 8:14 children of Israel should **d**
Neh 11: 1 out of ten to **d** in Jerusalem
Neh 11: 1 were to **d** in other cities
Neh 11: 2 themselves to **d** at Jerusalem
Job 4:19 those who **d** in houses of clay
Job 11:14 wickedness **d** in your tents
Job 17: 2 does not my eye **d** on their
Job 18:15 They **d** in his tent who are
Job 19:15 Those who **d** in my house, and
Ps 4: 8 O LORD, make me **d** in safety
Ps 5: 4 Nor shall evil **d** with You
Ps 15: 1 Who may **d** in Your holy hill
Ps 23: 6 I will **d** in the house of the
Ps 24: 1 world and those who **d** therein
Ps 25:13 himself shall **d** in prosperity
Ps 27: 4 That I may **d** in the house of
Ps 37: 3 **D** in the land, and feed on His
Ps 37:27 do good; And **d** forevermore.
Ps 37:29 the land, And **d** in it forever
Ps 65: 4 That he may **d** in Your courts
Ps 65: 8 They also who **d** in the
Ps 68: 6 rebellious **d** in a dry land
Ps 68:16 which God desires to **d** in
Ps 68:16 the LORD will **d** in it forever
Ps 68:18 the LORD God might **d** there
Ps 69:25 Let no one **d** in their tents
Ps 69:35 Judah, That they may **d** there
Ps 69:36 love His name shall **d** in it
Ps 72: 9 Those who **d** in the wilderness
Ps 78:55 of Israel **d** in their tents
Ps 80: 1 You who **d** between the
Ps 84: 4 are those who **d** in Your house
Ps 84:10 **d** in the tents of wickedness
Ps 85: 9 That glory may **d** in our land
Ps 98: 7 world and those who **d** in it
Ps 101: 6 land, That they may **d** with me
Ps 101: 7 shall not **d** within my house
Ps 107: 4 They found no city to **d** in
Ps 107:34 of those who **d** in it
Ps 107:36 There He makes the hungry **d**
Ps 120: 5 That I **d** among the tents of
Ps 123: 1 O You who **d** in the heavens
Ps 132:14 Here I will **d**, for I have
Ps 133: 1 to **d** together in unity
Ps 139: 9 **d** in the uttermost parts of
Ps 140:13 shall **d** in Your presence
Ps 143: 3 He has made me **d** in darkness
Prov 1:33 listens to me will **d** safely
Prov 2:21 upright will **d** in the land
Prov 8:12 **d** with prudence, and find out
Prov 21: 9 It is better to **d** in a corner
Prov 21:19 It is better to **d** in the
Prov 25:24 It is better to **d** in a corner
Eccl 5:20 For he will not **d** unduly on
Song 8:13 You who **d** in the gardens, the
Is 5: 8 **d** alone in the midst of the
Is 6: 5 I **d** in the midst of a people
Is 10:24 who **d** in Zion, do not be
Is 11: 6 also shall **d** with the lamb
Is 13:21 ostriches will **d** there, And
Is 16: 4 Let My outcasts **d** with you
Is 23:18 those who **d** before the LORD
Is 24: 6 and those who **d** in it are
Is 26: 5 down those who **d** on high, the
Is 26:19 and sing, you who **d** in dust
Is 30:19 shall **d** in Zion at Jerusalem
Is 32:16 will **d** in the wilderness, and
Is 32:18 My people will **d** in a
Is 33:14 Who among us shall **d** with the
Is 33:14 Who among us shall **d** with
Is 33:16 he will **d** on high
Is 33:24 the people who **d** in it will
Is 34:11 and the raven shall **d** in it
Is 34:17 generation they shall **d** in it
Is 40:22 them out like a tent to **d** in
Is 47: 8 who **d** securely, who say in
Is 49:20 give me a place where I may **d**
Is 51: 6 those who **d** in it will die in
Is 57:15 I **d** in the high and holy place
Is 58:12 Restorer of Streets to **D** In
Is 65: 9 and My servants shall **d** there
Jer 4:29 and not a man shall **d** in it
Jer 7: 3 cause you to **d** in this place
Jer 7: 7 cause you to **d** in this place
Jer 8:16 the city and those who **d** in it
Jer 9:26 who **d** in the wilderness
Jer 12: 4 of those who **d** there, because
Jer 20: 6 and all who **d** in your house,
Jer 23: 6 and Israel will **d** safely
Jer 23: 8 they shall **d** in their own
Jer 24: 8 those who **d** in the land of
Jer 25: 5 **d** in the land that the LORD
Jer 25:24 multitude who **d** in the desert
Jer 27:11 they shall till it and **d** in it
Jer 29: 5 Build houses and **d** in them
Jer 29:16 the people who **d** in this city
Jer 29:28 **d** in them, and plant gardens
Jer 29:32 anyone to **d** among this people
Jer 31:24 there shall **d** in Judah itself
Jer 32:37 I will cause them to **d** safely
Jer 33:16 and Jerusalem will **d** safely
Jer 35: 7 days you shall **d** in tents
Jer 35: 9 ourselves houses to **d** in
Jer 35:11 So we **d** at Jerusalem
Jer 35:15 then you will **d** in the land
Jer 40: 5 **d** with him among the people
Jer 40: 9 **D** in the land and serve the
Jer 40:10 me, I will indeed **d** at Mizpah
Jer 40:10 **d** in your cities that you
Jer 42:13 We will not **d** in this land
Jer 42:14 bread, and there we will **d**'
Jer 43: 5 to **d** in the land of Judah
Jer 44: 1 who **d** in the land of Egypt
Jer 44: 1 who **d** at Migdol, at Tahpanhes
Jer 44: 8 where you have gone to **d**,
Jer 44:13 who **d** in the land of Egypt
Jer 44:14 they desire to return and **d**
Jer 44:26 all Judah who **d** in the land
Jer 47: 2 city and those who **d** within
Jer 48: 9 without any to **d** in them
Jer 48:28 You who **d** in Moab, leave the
Jer 48:28 **d** in the rock, and be like the
Jer 49: 1 his people **d** in its cities
Jer 49: 8 turn back, **d** in the depths, O
Jer 49:16 O you who **d** in the clefts of
Jer 49:18 shall a son of man **d** in it
Jer 49:30 **D** in the depths, O
Jer 49:33 there, nor son of man **d** in it
Jer 50: 3 and no one shall **d** therein
Jer 50:39 **d** there with the jackals, and
Jer 50:39 the ostriches shall **d** in it
Jer 50:40 there, nor son of man **d** in it
Jer 51: 1 those who **d** in Leb Kamai, a
Jer 51:13 O you who **d** by many waters,
Lam 4:15 They shall no longer **d** here
Lam 4:21 you who **d** in the land of Uz
Ezek 2: 6 you and you **d** among scorpions
Ezek 7: 7 to you, you who **d** in the land
Ezek 12: 2 man, you **d** in the midst of a
Ezek 12:19 of all those who **d** in it
Ezek 17:23 Under it will **d** birds of
Ezek 17:23 of its branches they will **d**
Ezek 26:20 and I will make you **d** in the
Ezek 28:25 then they will **d** in their own
Ezek 28:26 they will **d** safely there,
Ezek 28:26 yes, they will **d** securely
Ezek 32:15 when I strike all who **d** in it
Ezek 34:25 they will **d** safely in the
Ezek 34:28 but they shall **d** safely, and
Ezek 36:28 Then you shall **d** in the land
Ezek 36:33 enable you to **d** in the cities
Ezek 37:25 Then they shall **d** in the land
Ezek 37:25 and they shall **d** there, they,
Ezek 38: 8 and now all of them **d** safely
Ezek 38:11 who **d** safely, all of them
Ezek 38:12 who **d** in the midst of the
Ezek 38:14 My people Israel **d** safely
Ezek 39: 9 Then those who **d** in the
Ezek 43: 7 where I will **d** in the midst
Ezek 43: 9 and I will **d** in their midst
Dan 2:38 the children of men **d**, or the
Dan 4: 1 languages that **d** in all the
Dan 6:25 languages that **d** in all the
Hos 9: 3 They shall not **d** in the
Hos 11:11 let them **d** in their houses
Hos 12: 9 again make you **d** in tents
Hos 14: 7 Those who **d** under his shadow
Amos 3:12 be taken out who **d** in Samaria
Amos 5:11 yet you shall not **d** in them
Amos 9: 5 and all who **d** there mourn
Obad 3 you who **d** in the clefts of
Mic 4:10 you shall **d** in the field, and
Mic 7:13 because of those who **d** in it
Mic 7:14 who **d** solitarily in a
Nah 1: 5 the world and all who **d** in it
Hab 2: 8 city, and of all who **d** in it
Hab 2:17 city, and of all who **d** in it
Zeph 1:18 all those who **d** in the land
Hag 1: 4 to **d** in your paneled houses
Zech 2: 7 you who **d** with the daughter
Zech 2:10 I will **d** in your midst,"
Zech 2:11 And I will **d** in your midst
Zech 8: 3 **d** in the midst of Jerusalem
Zech 8: 8 they shall **d** in the midst of
Zech 14:11 The people shall **d** in it
Matt 12:45 and they enter and **d** there
Luke 11:26 and they enter and **d** there
Luke 21:35 **d** on the face of the whole
Acts 2:14 all who **d** in Jerusalem, let
Acts 4:16 to all who **d** in Jerusalem
Acts 7: 4 this land in which you now **d**
Acts 7:48 the Most High does not **d** in
Acts 13:27 For those who **d** in Jerusalem
Acts 17:24 does not **d** in temples made
Acts 17:26 to **d** on all the face of the
Acts 28:16 but Paul was permitted to **d**
2Co 6:16 I will **d** in them and walk
Eph 3:17 that Christ may **d** in your
Col 1:19 Him all the fullness should **d**
Col 3:16 Let the word of Christ **d** in
1Pe 3: 7 husbands, **d** with them with
Rev 2:13 your works, and where you **d**
Rev 3:10 test those who **d** on the earth
Rev 6:10 on those who **d** on the earth
Rev 7:15 the throne will **d** among them
Rev 11:10 those who **d** on the earth will
Rev 11:10 those who **d** on the earth
Rev 12:12 heavens, and you who **d** in them
Rev 13: 6 and those who **d** in heaven
Rev 13: 8 all who **d** on the earth will
Rev 13:12 those who **d** in it to worship
Rev 13:14 he deceives those who **d** on
Rev 13:14 telling those who **d** on the
Rev 14: 6 to those who **d** on the earth
Rev 17: 8 those who **d** on the earth will
Rev 21: 3 He will **d** with them, and they

DWELLERS (*see* DWELL)
Is 18: 3 the world and **d** on the earth

DWELLING (*see* DWELL, DWELLINGS)
Gen 10:30 their **d** place was from Mesha
Gen 25:27 was a mild man, **d** in tents
Gen 27:39 your **d** shall be of the
Ex 15:17 You have made for Your own **d**
Num 21:15 that reaches to the **d** of Ar
Num 23: 9 A people **d** alone, not
Num 24:21 Firm is your **d** place, and your
Josh 13:21 of Sihon **d** in the country
2Sa 7: 1 the king was **d** in his house
2Sa 11:11 and Judah are **d** in tents, and
1Ki 8:30 hear in heaven Your **d** place
1Ki 8:39 hear in heaven Your **d** place
1Ki 8:43 hear in heaven Your **d** place
1Ki 8:49 Your **d** place their prayer
1Ki 12: 2 and had been **d** in Egypt),
1Ki 21: 8 the nobles who were **d** in the
2Ki 17:25 beginning of their **d** there
2Ki 19:27 But I know your **d** place,
1Ch 6:32 with music before the **d** place
1Ch 6:54 Now these are their **d** places
1Ch 17: 1 when David was **d** in his house
2Ch 6:21 hear from Your **d** place, in
2Ch 6:30 hear from heaven Your **d** place
2Ch 6:33 hear from heaven Your **d** place
2Ch 6:39 Your **d** place their prayer
2Ch 30:27 came up to His holy **d** place
2Ch 36:15 His people and on His **d** place
Ezra 7:15 whose **d** is in Jerusalem
Neh 1: 9 chosen as a **d** for My name
Neh 3:30 repairs in front of his **d**
Job 8:22 the **d** place of the wicked
Job 21:28 the **d** place of the wicked
Job 38:19 is the way to the **d** of light
Job 39: 6 And the barren land his **d**
Ps 49:11 And their **d** places to all
Ps 49:14 the grave, far from their **d**
Ps 52: 5 pluck you out of your **d** place
Ps 74: 7 They have defiled the **d** place
Ps 76: 2 And His **d** place in Zion
Ps 79: 7 And laid waste his **d** place
Ps 90: 1 You have been our **d** place in
Ps 91:10 any plague come near your **d**
Ps 132: 5 A **d** place for the Mighty God
Prov 21:20 oil in the **d** of the wise, but
Prov 24:15 man, against the **d** of the
Is 4: 5 every **d** place of Mount Zion
Is 18: 4 I will look from My **d** place
Is 37:28 But I know your **d** place, your
Jer 30:18 and have mercy on his **d** places

Jer 46:19 O you daughter **d** in Egypt
Jer 49:31 gates nor bars, **d** alone
Jer 49:33 shall be a **d** for jackals, a
Jer 51:30 they have burned her **d** places
Jer 51:37 a **d** place for jackals, an
Ezek 6: 6 In all your **d** places the
Ezek 37:23 **d** places in which they have
Ezek 38:11 all of them **d** without walls,
Dan 2:11 whose **d** is not with flesh
Dan 4:25 men, your **d** shall be with the
Dan 4:30 a royal **d** by my mighty power
Dan 4:32 and your **d** shall be with the
Dan 5:21 and his **d** was with the wild
Joel 3:17 **d** in Zion My holy mountain
Nah 2:11 Where is the **d** of the lions
Hab 1: 6 to possess **d** places that are
Zeph 3: 7 so that her **d** would not be
Mark 5: 3 who had his **d** among the tombs
Acts 1:19 to all those **d** in Jerusalem
Acts 2: 5 Now there were **d** in Jerusalem
Acts 2: 9 those **d** in Mesopotamia, Judea
Acts 7:46 asked to find a **d** for the God
Acts 11:29 to the brethren **d** in Judea
Acts 19:17 Jews and Greeks **d** in Ephesus
1Ti 6:16 **d** in unapproachable light,
Heb 11: 9 **d** in tents with Isaac and
2Pe 2: 8 **d** among them, tormented his

DWELLINGS (*see* DWELLING)
Ex 10:23 Israel had light in their **d**
Lev 3:17 generations in all your **d**
Lev 7:26 any blood in any of your **d**
Lev 23: 3 of the LORD in all your **d**
Lev 23:14 generations in all your **d**
Lev 23:21 **d** throughout your generations
Lev 23:31 generations in all your **d**
Num 24: 5 your **d**, O Israel
Num 35:29 generations in all your **d**
Job 18:19 nor any remaining in his **d**
Job 18:21 such are the **d** of the wicked
Ps 55:15 For wickedness is in their **d**
Ps 87: 2 More than all the **d** of Jacob
Is 32:18 habitation, in secure **d**, and
Jer 9:19 have been cast out of our **d**
Ezek 25: 4 you and make their **d** among you
Ezek 48:15 use by the city, for **d** and

DWELLS (*see* DWELL)
Ex 3:22 of her who **d** near her house,
Lev 19:34 But the stranger who **d** among
Lev 25:39 who **d** by you becomes poor
Lev 25:47 who **d** by him becomes poor
Deut 33:20 He **d** as a lion, and tears the
Josh 6:25 So she **d** in Israel to this
1Sa 4: 4 who **d** between the cherubim
2Sa 6: 2 who **d** between the cherubim
2Sa 7: 2 but the ark of God **d** inside
2Ki 19:15 the One who **d** between the
1Ch 13: 6 who **d** between the cherubim,
Job 15:28 He **d** in desolate cities, in
Job 39:28 It **d** on the rock, and resides
Job 41:22 Strength **d** in his neck, and
Ps 9:11 to the LORD, who **d** in Zion
Ps 26: 8 the place where Your glory **d**
Ps 91: 1 He who **d** in the secret place
Ps 99: 1 He **d** between the cherubim
Ps 113: 5 LORD our God, Who **d** on high,
Ps 135:21 of Zion, Who **d** in Jerusalem
Prov 3:29 for he **d** by you for safety's
Is 8:18 of hosts, Who **d** in Mount Zion
Is 33: 5 is exalted, for He **d** on high
Is 37:16 the One who **d** between the
Jer 44: 2 and no one **d** in them,
Jer 49:31 nation that **d** securely,"
Jer 51:43 a land where no one **d**,
Lam 1: 3 she **d** among the nations, she
Ezek 16:46 who **d** with her daughters to
Ezek 16:46 who **d** to the south of you, is
Ezek 17:16 the king **d** who made him king
Dan 2:22 darkness, and light **d** with Him
Hos 4: 3 everyone who **d** there will
Joel 3:21 for the LORD **d** in Zion
Amos 8: 8 and everyone mourn who **d** in it
Matt 23:21 by it and by Him who **d** in it
John 14:10 but the Father who **d** in Me
John 14:17 for He **d** with you and will be
Rom 7:17 do it, but sin that **d** in me
Rom 7:18 in my flesh) nothing good **d**
Rom 7:20 do it, but sin that **d** in me
Rom 8: 9 the Spirit of God **d** in you
Rom 8:11 Jesus from the dead **d** in you
Rom 8:11 His Spirit who **d** in you
1Co 3:16 the Spirit of God **d** in you
Col 2: 9 For in Him **d** all the fullness
2Ti 1:14 the Holy Spirit who **d** in us
Jas 4: 5 The Spirit who **d** in us yearns
2Pe 3:13 in which righteousness **d**
Rev 2:13 among you, where Satan **d**

DWELT (*see* DWELL)
Gen 4:16 **d** in the land of Nod on the
Gen 11: 2 of Shinar, and they **d** there
Gen 11:31 they came to Haran and **d** there
Gen 13: 7 Perizzites then **d** in the land
Gen 13:12 Abram **d** in the land of Canaan
Gen 13:12 Lot **d** in the cities of the
Gen 13:18 **d** by the terebinth trees of
Gen 14: 7 who **d** in Hazezon Tamar
Gen 14:12 brother's son who **d** in Sodom
Gen 14:13 for he **d** by the terebinth
Gen 16: 3 after Abram had **d** ten years
Gen 19:29 the cities in which Lot had **d**
Gen 19:30 **d** in the mountains, and his
Gen 19:30 his two daughters **d** in a cave
Gen 20: 1 **d** between Kadesh and Shur,
Gen 21:20 and **d** in the wilderness, and
Gen 21:21 He **d** in the Wilderness of
Gen 22:19 and Abraham **d** at Beersheba
Gen 23:10 Now Ephron **d** among the sons
Gen 24:62 Roi, for he **d** in the South
Gen 25:11 Isaac **d** at Beer Lahai Roi
Gen 25:18 (They **d** from Havilah as far
Gen 26: 6 So Isaac **d** in Gerar
Gen 26:17 Valley of Gerar, and **d** there
Gen 35:22 when Israel **d** in that land,
Gen 36: 8 So Esau **d** in Mount Seir
Gen 37: 1 Now Jacob **d** in the land where
Gen 38:11 and **d** in her father's house
Gen 47:27 So Israel **d** in the land of
Gen 50:22 So Joseph **d** in Egypt, he and
Ex 2:15 and **d** in the land of Midian
Lev 18: 3 land of Egypt, where you **d**
Lev 26:35 sabbaths when you **d** in it
Num 14:45 the Canaanites who **d** in that
Num 20:15 we **d** in Egypt a long time, and
Num 21: 1 who **d** in the South, heard
Num 21:25 Israel **d** in all the cities of
Num 21:31 Thus Israel **d** in the land of
Num 21:34 Amorites, who **d** at Heshbon
Num 31:10 all the cities where they **d**
Num 32:40 of Manasseh, and he **d** in it
Num 33:40 who **d** in the South in the
Deut 1: 4 who **d** in Heshbon, and Og king
Deut 1: 4 who **d** at Ashtaroth in Edrei
Deut 1: 6 You have **d** long enough at
Deut 1:44 the Amorites who **d** in that
Deut 2:10 (The Emim had **d** there in
Deut 2:12 Horites formerly **d** in Seir
Deut 2:12 **d** in their place, just as
Deut 2:20 giants formerly **d** there
Deut 2:21 them and **d** in their place,
Deut 2:22 Esau, who **d** in Seir, when He
Deut 2:22 **d** in their place, even to
Deut 2:23 who **d** in villages as far as
Deut 2:23 them and **d** in their place
Deut 3: 2 Amorites, who **d** at Heshbon
Deut 4:46 who **d** at Heshbon, whom Moses
Deut 29:16 we **d** in the land of Egypt
Deut 33:16 of Him who **d** in the bush
Josh 2:15 she **d** on the wall
Josh 7: 7 **d** on the other side of the
Josh 9:16 neighbors who **d** near them
Josh 12: 2 who **d** in Heshbon and ruled
Josh 12: 4 who **d** at Ashtaroth and at
Josh 16:10 the Canaanites who **d** in Gezer
Josh 19:47 possession of it, and **d** in it
Josh 19:50 he built the city and **d** in it
Josh 21:43 possession of it and **d** in it
Josh 22:33 children of Reuben and Gad **d**
Josh 24: 2 **d** on the other side of the
Josh 24: 7 Then you **d** in the wilderness
Josh 24: 8 who **d** on the other side of
Josh 24:18 Amorites who **d** in the land
Judg 1: 9 who **d** in the mountains, in
Judg 1:10 Canaanites who **d** in Hebron
Judg 1:16 went and **d** among the people
Judg 1:29 the Canaanites who **d** in Gezer
Judg 1:29 so the Canaanites **d** in Gezer
Judg 1:30 the Canaanites **d** among them
Judg 1:32 So the Asherites **d** among the
Judg 1:33 but they **d** among the
Judg 3: 3 the Hivites who **d** in Mount
Judg 3: 5 Israel **d** among the Canaanites
Judg 4: 2 who **d** in Harosheth Hagoyim
Judg 8:29 went and **d** in his own house
Judg 9:21 Beer and **d** there, for fear of
Judg 9:41 Then Abimelech **d** at Arumah
Judg 10: 1 and he **d** in Shamir in the
Judg 11: 3 and **d** in the land of Tob
Judg 11:26 While Israel **d** in Heshbon
Judg 15: 8 **d** in the cleft of the rock of
Judg 18: 7 were there, how they **d** safely
Judg 18:28 rebuilt the city and **d** there
Judg 21:23 the cities and **d** in them
Ruth 1: 4 they **d** there about ten years
Ruth 2:23 she **d** with her mother-in-law
1Sa 12:11 and you **d** in safety
1Sa 22: 4 they **d** with him all the time
1Sa 23:29 **d** in strongholds at En Gedi
1Sa 27: 3 So David **d** with Achish at
1Sa 27: 7 David **d** in the country of the
1Sa 27:11 he **d** in the country of the
1Sa 31: 7 Philistines came and **d** in them
2Sa 2: 3 So they **d** in the cities of
2Sa 5: 9 So David **d** in the stronghold,
2Sa 7: 6 For I have not **d** in a house
2Sa 9:12 all who **d** in the house of
2Sa 9:13 Mephibosheth **d** in Jerusalem
2Sa 14:28 Absalom **d** two full years in
2Sa 15: 8 while I **d** at Geshur in Syria
1Ki 2:38 So Shimei **d** in Jerusalem
1Ki 4:25 And Judah and Israel **d** safely
1Ki 7: 8 And the house where he **d** had
1Ki 9:16 Canaanites who **d** in the city
1Ki 11:24 and **d** there, and reigned in
1Ki 12:17 who **d** in the cities of Judah
1Ki 12:25 of Ephraim, and **d** there
1Ki 13:11 an old prophet **d** in Bethel
1Ki 13:25 city where the old prophet **d**
1Ki 15:18 who **d** in Damascus, saying,
2Ki 13: 5 the children of Israel **d** in
2Ki 15: 5 so he **d** in an isolated house
2Ki 17:24 of Samaria and **d** in its cities
2Ki 17:28 **d** in Bethel, and taught them
2Ki 17:29 in the cities where they **d**
2Ki 22:14 (She **d** in Jerusalem in the
1Ch 2:55 who **d** at Jabez were the
1Ch 4:23 there they **d** with the king
1Ch 4:28 They **d** at Beersheba, Moladah,
1Ch 4:41 So they **d** in their place,
1Ch 4:43 They have **d** there to this day
1Ch 5: 8 who **d** in Aroer, as far as
1Ch 5:10 and they **d** in their tents
1Ch 5:11 the children of Gad **d** next to
1Ch 5:16 And the Gadites **d** in Gilead
1Ch 5:22 they **d** in their place until
1Ch 5:23 of Manasseh **d** in the land
1Ch 7:29 In these **d** the children of
1Ch 8:28 These **d** in Jerusalem
1Ch 8:29 name was Maacah, **d** at Gibeon
1Ch 8:32 They also **d** alongside their
1Ch 9: 2 who **d** in their possessions in
1Ch 9: 3 the children of Judah **d**, and
1Ch 9:34 They **d** at Jerusalem
1Ch 9:35 name was Maacah, **d** at Gibeon
1Ch 9:38 They also **d** alongside their
1Ch 10: 7 Philistines came and **d** in them
1Ch 11: 7 Then David **d** in the
1Ch 17: 5 For I have not **d** in a house
2Ch 10:17 who **d** in the cities of Judah
2Ch 11: 5 So Rehoboam **d** in Jerusalem,
2Ch 16: 2 who **d** in Damascus, saying,
2Ch 19: 4 So Jehoshaphat **d** at Jerusalem
2Ch 26:21 He **d** in an isolated house,
2Ch 28:18 and they **d** there
2Ch 30:25 and those who **d** in Judah
2Ch 31: 4 **d** in Jerusalem to contribute
2Ch 31: 6 who **d** in the cities of Judah,
2Ch 34:22 (She **d** in Jerusalem in the
Ezra 2:70 **d** in their cities, and all
Neh 3:26 **d** in Ophel made repairs as
Neh 4:12 the Jews who **d** near them came
Neh 7:73 all Israel **d** in their cities
Neh 11: 1 of the people **d** at Jerusalem
Neh 11: 3 province who **d** in Jerusalem
Neh 11: 3 **d** in his own possession in
Neh 11: 4 Also in Jerusalem **d** certain
Neh 11: 6 who **d** at Jerusalem were four
Neh 11:21 But the Nethinim **d** in Ophel
Neh 11:25 of Judah **d** in Kirjath Arba
Neh 11:30 They **d** from Beersheba to the
Neh 11:31 from Geba **d** in Michmash, Aija

Neh 13:16 Men of Tyre **d** there also, who
Esth 9:19 who **d** in the unwalled towns
Job 22: 8 and the honorable man **d** in it
Job 29:25 so I **d** as a king in the army,
Ps 68:10 Your congregation **d** in it
Ps 74: 2 Mount Zion where You have **d**
Ps 120: 6 My soul has **d** too long With
Is 9: 2 those who **d** in the land of
Is 29: 1 Ariel, the city where David **d**
Jer 2: 6 one crossed and where no one **d**
Jer 35:10 But we have **d** in tents, and
Jer 39:14 So he **d** among the people
Jer 40: 6 **d** with him among the people
Jer 41:17 and **d** in the habitation of
Jer 44:15 all the people who **d** in the
Jer 50:39 nor shall it be **d** in from
Ezek 3:15 who **d** by the River Chebar
Ezek 31:17 who were its strong arm **d** in
Ezek 36:17 of Israel **d** in their own land
Ezek 37:25 servant, where your fathers **d**
Ezek 39:26 when they **d** safely in their
Dan 4:12 the heavens **d** in its branches
Dan 4:21 the beasts of the field **d**
Zeph 2:15 city that **d** securely, that
Matt 2:23 **d** in a city called Nazareth,
Matt 4:13 **d** in Capernaum, which is by
Luke 1:65 came on all who **d** around them
Luke 13: 4 other men who **d** in Jerusalem
John 1:14 **d** among us, and we beheld His
Acts 7: 2 before he **d** in Haran,
Acts 7: 4 the Chaldeans and **d** in Haran
Acts 9:22 the Jews who **d** in Damascus
Acts 9:32 to the saints who **d** in Lydda
Acts 9:35 So all who **d** at Lydda and
Acts 13:17 the people when they **d** as
Acts 19:10 so that all who **d** in Asia
Acts 22:12 with all the Jews who **d** there
Acts 28:30 Then Paul **d** two whole years
2Ti 1: 5 in you, which **d** first in your

DYED (*see* DYING)
Ex 25: 5 rams' skins **d** red, badger
Ex 26:14 skins **d** red for the tent, and
Ex 35: 7 rams' skins **d** red, badger
Ex 36:19 the tent of rams' skins **d** red
Ex 39:34 covering of rams' skins **d** red
Judg 5:30 Sisera, plunder of **d** garments
Judg 5:30 of garments embroidered and **d**
Judg 5:30 two pieces of **d** embroidery
Is 63: 1 with **d** garments from Bozrah,

DYING (*see* DYED)
Gen 48:21 Behold, I am **d**, but God will
Gen 50: 5 Behold, I am **d**
Gen 50:24 said to his brethren, "I am **d**
Job 24:12 The **d** groan in the city, and
Zech 11: 9 Let what is **d** die, and what is
Mark 12:20 and **d**, he left no offspring
Luke 8:42 years of age, and she was **d**
John 11:37 have kept this man from **d**
Acts 25:11 death, I do not object to **d**
2Co 4:10 body the **d** of the Lord Jesus
2Co 6: 9 as **d**, and behold we live
Heb 11:21 By faith Jacob, when he was **d**
Heb 11:22 faith Joseph, when he was **d**

DYSENTERY
Acts 28: 8 lay sick of a fever and **d**

E

EACH (*see* PREFACE)

EAGER (*see* EAGERLY)
Ps 17:12 that is **e** to tear his prey
Zech 6: 7 **e** to go, that they might walk
Gal 2:10 which I also was **e** to do

EAGERLY (*see* EAGER)
Job 7: 2 man who **e** looks for his wages
Prov 17: 4 a liar listens **e** to a
Rom 8:19 **e** waits for the revealing of
Rom 8:23 **e** waiting for the adoption,
Rom 8:25 then we **e** wait for it with
1Co 1: 7 **e** waiting for the revelation
Gal 5: 5 Spirit **e** wait for the hope of
Phil 2:28 I sent him the more **e**, that
Phil 3:20 from which we also **e** wait for
1Th 2:17 endeavored more **e** to see your
Heb 9:28 To those who **e** wait for Him
1Pe 5: 2 not for dishonest gain but **e**

EAGLE (*see* EAGLE'S, EAGLES)
Lev 11:13 the **e**, the vulture, the
Deut 14:12 the **e**, the vulture, the
Deut 28:49 as swift as the **e** flies, a
Deut 32:11 As an **e** stirs up its nest,
Job 9:26 like an **e** swooping on its
Job 39:27 Does the **e** mount up at your
Prov 23: 5 away like an **e** toward heaven
Prov 30:19 the way of an **e** in the air
Jer 48:40 one shall fly like an **e**, and
Jer 49:16 your nest as high as the **e**
Jer 49:22 come up and fly like the **e**
Ezek 1:10 the four had the face of an **e**
Ezek 10:14 the fourth the face of an **e**
Ezek 17: 3 A great **e** with large wings and
Ezek 17: 7 great **e** with large wings and
Hos 8: 1 He shall come like an **e**
Obad 4 yourself as high as the **e**
Mic 1:16 your baldness like an **e**, for
Hab 1: 8 they fly as the **e** that
Rev 4: 7 creature was like a flying **e**
Rev 12:14 given two wings of a great **e**

EAGLE'S (*see* EAGLE)
Ps 103: 5 youth is renewed like the **e**
Dan 7: 4 like a lion, and had **e** wings

EAGLES (*see* EAGLE, EAGLES')
2Sa 1:23 they were swifter than **e**,
Prov 30:17 and the young **e** will eat it
Is 40:31 mount up with wings like **e**
Jer 4:13 His horses are swifter than **e**
Lam 4:19 than the **e** of the heavens
Matt 24:28 there the **e** will be gathered
Luke 17:37 there the **e** will be gathered

EAGLES' (*see* EAGLES)
Ex 19: 4 and how I bore you on **e** wings
Dan 4:33 had grown like **e** feathers

EAR (*see* EARS)
Ex 15:26 give **e** to His commandments
Ex 21: 6 pierce his **e** with an awl
Ex 29:20 tip of the right **e** of Aaron
Ex 29:20 of the right **e** of his sons
Lev 8:23 on the tip of Aaron's right **e**
Lev 14:14 right **e** of him who is to be
Lev 14:17 right **e** of him who is to be
Lev 14:25 right **e** of him who is to be
Lev 14:28 right **e** of him who is to be
Deut 1:45 your voice nor give **e** to you
Deut 15:17 it through his **e** to the door
Deut 32: 1 Give **e**, O heavens, and I will
Judg 5: 3 Give **e**, O princes
1Sa 9:15 **e** the day before Saul came
2Ki 19:16 Incline Your **e**, O LORD, and
Neh 1: 6 let Your **e** be attentive and
Neh 1:11 I pray, please let Your **e** be
Job 4:12 my **e** received a whisper of it
Job 12:11 Does not the **e** test words
Job 13: 1 My **e** has heard and understood
Job 29:11 When the **e** heard, then it
Job 33:31 Give **e**, Job, listen to me
Job 34: 2 give **e** to me, you who have
Job 34: 3 For the **e** tests words as the
Job 36:10 opens their **e** to instruction
Job 42: 5 You by the hearing of the **e**
Ps 5: 1 Give **e** to my words, O LORD,
Ps 10:17 You will cause Your **e** to hear
Ps 17: 1 Give **e** to my prayer that is
Ps 17: 6 Incline Your **e** to me, and hear
Ps 31: 2 Bow down Your **e** to me,
Ps 39:12 O LORD, And give **e** to my cry
Ps 45:10 Consider and incline your **e**
Ps 49: 1 Give **e**, all you inhabitants
Ps 49: 4 incline my **e** to a proverb
Ps 54: 2 Give **e** to the words of my
Ps 55: 1 Give **e** to my prayer, O God,
Ps 58: 4 deaf cobra that stops its **e**
Ps 71: 2 Incline Your **e** to me, and save
Ps 77: 1 And He gave **e** to me
Ps 78: 1 Give **e**, O my people, to my
Ps 80: 1 Give **e**, O Shepherd of Israel,
Ps 84: 8 Give **e**, O God of Jacob
Ps 86: 1 Bow down Your **e**, O LORD,
Ps 86: 6 Give **e**, O LORD, to my prayer
Ps 88: 2 Incline Your **e** to my cry
Ps 94: 9 He who planted the **e**, shall
Ps 102: 2 Incline Your **e** to me
Ps 116: 2 He has inclined His **e** to me
Ps 141: 1 Give **e** to my voice when I cry
Ps 143: 1 Give **e** to my supplications
Prov 2: 2 you incline your **e** to wisdom
Prov 4:20 incline your **e** to my sayings
Prov 5: 1 lend your **e** to my
Prov 5:13 nor inclined my **e** to those
Prov 15:31 The **e** that hears the reproof
Prov 18:15 and the **e** of the wise seeks
Prov 20:12 The hearing **e** and the seeing
Prov 22:17 Incline your **e** and hear the
Prov 25:12 reprover to an obedient **e**
Prov 28: 9 his **e** from hearing the law
Eccl 1: 8 nor the **e** filled with hearing
Is 1: 2 Hear, O heavens, and give **e**
Is 1:10 give **e** to the law of our God,
Is 8: 9 Give **e**, all you from far
Is 28:23 Give **e** and hear my voice,
Is 32: 9 give **e** to my speech
Is 37:17 Incline Your **e**, O LORD, and
Is 42:23 among you will give **e** to this
Is 48: 8 ago your **e** was not opened
Is 50: 4 he awakens My **e** to hear as
Is 50: 5 The Lord GOD has opened My **e**
Is 51: 4 give **e** to Me, O My nation
Is 55: 3 Incline your **e**, and come to Me
Is 59: 1 nor His **e** heavy, that it
Is 64: 4 heard nor perceived by the **e**
Jer 6:10 Indeed their **e** is
Jer 7:24 not obey or incline their **e**
Jer 7:26 obey Me or incline their **e**
Jer 9:20 let your **e** receive the word
Jer 11: 8 not obey or incline their **e**
Jer 13:15 Hear and give **e**
Jer 17:23 not obey nor incline their **e**
Jer 25: 4 nor inclined your **e** to hear
Jer 34:14 obey Me nor incline their **e**
Jer 35:15 you have not inclined your **e**
Jer 44: 5 their **e** to turn from their
Lam 3:56 hide Your **e** from my sighing
Dan 9:18 O my God, incline Your **e** and
Hos 5: 1 Give **e**, O house of the king
Joel 1: 2 this, you elders, and give **e**
Amos 3:12 two legs or a piece of an **e**
Matt 10:27 and what you hear in the **e**
Matt 26:51 high priest, and cut off his **e**
Mark 14:47 high priest, and cut off his **e**
Luke 12: 3 the **e** in inner rooms will be
Luke 22:50 priest and cut off his right **e**
Luke 22:51 And He touched his **e** and
John 18:10 and cut off his right **e**
John 18:26 of him whose **e** Peter cut off
1Co 2: 9 nor **e** heard, nor have entered
1Co 12:16 And if the **e** should say,
Rev 2: 7 He who has an **e**, let him hear
Rev 2:11 He who has an **e**, let him hear
Rev 2:17 He who has an **e**, let him hear
Rev 2:29 He who has an **e**, let him hear
Rev 3: 6 He who has an **e**, let him hear
Rev 3:13 He who has an **e**, let him hear
Rev 3:22 He who has an **e**, let him hear
Rev 13: 9 If anyone has an **e**, let him

EARLY
Gen 19: 2 then you may rise **e** and go on
Gen 19:27 Abraham went **e** in the morning
Gen 20: 8 rose **e** in the morning, called
Gen 21:14 Abraham rose **e** in the morning
Gen 22: 3 Abraham rose **e** in the morning
Gen 26:31 they arose **e** in the morning
Gen 28:18 Jacob rose **e** in the morning
Gen 31:55 **e** in the morning Laban arose,
Ex 8:20 Rise **e** in the morning and
Ex 9:13 Rise **e** in the morning and
Ex 24: 4 he rose **e** in the morning, and
Ex 32: 6 Then they rose **e** on the next
Ex 34: 4 Moses rose **e** in the morning
Num 14:40 they rose **e** in the morning and
Deut 11:14 the **e** rain and the latter rain
Josh 3: 1 Joshua rose **e** in the morning
Josh 6:12 Joshua rose **e** in the morning,
Josh 6:15 seventh day that they rose **e**
Josh 7:16 Joshua rose **e** in the morning
Josh 8:10 rose up **e** in the morning and
Josh 8:14 the city hastened and rose **e**
Judg 6:28 city arose **e** in the morning
Judg 6:38 When he rose **e** the next
Judg 7: 1 who were with him rose **e** and
Judg 9:33 that you shall rise **e** and
Judg 19: 5 they arose **e** in the morning
Judg 19: 8 Then he arose **e** in the
Judg 19: 9 Tomorrow go your way **e**, so

Judg 21: 4 that the people rose **e** and
1Sa 1:19 they rose **e** in the morning
1Sa 5: 3 Ashdod arose **e** in the morning
1Sa 5: 4 when they arose **e** the next
1Sa 9:26 They arose **e**
1Sa 15:12 So when Samuel rose **e** in the
1Sa 17:20 So David rose **e** in the
1Sa 29:10 rise **e** in the morning with
1Sa 29:10 you are up **e** in the morning
1Sa 29:11 his men rose **e** to depart in
2Sa 15: 2 Now Absalom would rise **e** and
2Ki 3:22 they rose up **e** in the morning
2Ki 6:15 of the man of God arose **e**
2Ki 19:35 people arose **e** in the morning
2Ch 20:20 they rose **e** in the morning and
2Ch 29:20 Then King Hezekiah rose **e**
2Ch 36:15 His messengers, rising up **e**
Job 1: 5 and he would rise **e** in the
Ps 63: 1 **E** will I seek You
Ps 90:14 satisfy us **e** with Your mercy,
Ps 101: 8 **E** I will destroy all the
Ps 127: 2 is vain for you to rise up **e**
Prov 27:14 rising **e** in the morning, it
Song 7:12 Let us get up **e** to the
Is 5:11 who rise **e** in the morning
Is 26: 9 within me I will seek You **e**
Is 37:36 people arose **e** in the morning
Jer 7:13 I spoke to you, rising up **e**
Jer 7:25 prophets, daily rising up **e**
Jer 11: 7 until this day, rising **e**
Jer 25: 3 have spoken to you, rising **e**
Jer 25: 4 the prophets, rising **e** and
Jer 26: 5 sent to you, both rising up **e**
Jer 29:19 the prophets, rising up **e**
Jer 32:33 I taught them, rising up **e**
Jer 35:14 have spoken to you, rising **e**
Jer 35:15 the prophets, rising up **e**
Jer 44: 4 the prophets, rising **e** and
Dan 6:10 was his custom since **e** days
Dan 6:19 arose very **e** in the morning
Hos 6: 4 like the **e** dew it goes away
Hos 13: 3 like the **e** dew that passes
Zeph 3: 7 But they rose **e** and corrupted
Matt 20: 1 out **e** in the morning to hire
Mark 16: 2 Very **e** in the morning, on the
Mark 16: 9 Now when He rose **e** on the
Luke 21:38 Then **e** in the morning all the
Luke 24: 1 very **e** in the morning, they,
Luke 24:22 who arrived at the tomb **e**
John 8: 2 But **e** in the morning He came
John 18:28 and it was **e** morning
John 20: 1 Magdalene came to the tomb **e**
Acts 5:21 the temple **e** in the morning
Acts 21:16 an **e** disciple, with whom we
Jas 5: 7 it until it receives the **e**

EARNED (*see* EARNS)
Luke 19:16 your mina has **e** ten minas
Luke 19:18 your mina has **e** five minas

EARNERS (*see* EARNS)
Mal 3: 5 those who exploit wage **e** and

EARNEST (*see* EARNESTLY)
Rom 8:19 For the **e** expectation of the
2Co 7: 7 he told us of your **e** desire
2Co 8:16 **e** care for you into the heart
Phil 1:20 according to my **e** expectation
Heb 2: 1 we must give the more **e** heed

EARNESTLY (*see* EARNEST)
Num 22:37 Did I not **e** send to you,
1Sa 20: 6 David **e** asked permission of
1Sa 20:28 David **e** asked permission of
Job 7: 2 who **e** desires the shade, and
Job 8: 5 If you would **e** seek God and
Jer 11: 7 For I **e** exhorted your
Jer 31:20 him, I **e** remember him still
Mark 5:10 he begged Him **e** that He would
Mark 5:23 and begged Him **e**, saying, My
Luke 7: 4 to Jesus, they begged Him **e**
Luke 22:44 in agony, He prayed more **e**
Acts 23: 1 looking **e** at the council,
Acts 26: 7 **e** serving God night and day,
1Co 12:31 But **e** desire the best gifts
1Co 14:39 desire **e** to prophesy, and do
2Co 5: 2 **e** desiring to be clothed with
Col 4: 2 Continue **e** in prayer, being
Jas 5:17 he prayed **e** that it would not
Jude 3 **e** for the faith which was

EARNS (*see* EARNED, EARNERS)
Hag 1: 6 and he who **e** wages
Hag 1: 6 **e** wages to put into a bag

EARRING (*see* EARRINGS)
Prov 25:12 Like an **e** of gold and an

EARRINGS (*see* EARRING)
Gen 35: 4 all their **e** which were in
Ex 32: 2 Break off the golden **e** which
Ex 32: 3 **e** which were in their ears
Ex 35:22 a willing heart, and brought **e**
Num 31:50 and signet rings and **e** and
Judg 8:24 me the **e** from his plunder
Judg 8:24 For they had gold **e**,
Judg 8:25 it the **e** from his plunder
Judg 8:26 **e** that he requested was one
Ezek 16:12 nose, **e** in your ears, and a
Hos 2:13 She decked herself with her **e**

EARS (*see* EAR)
Gen 35: 4 which were in their **e**
Ex 32: 2 are in the **e** of your wives
Ex 32: 3 which were in their **e**, and
Lev 8:24 on the tips of their right **e**
Deut 29: 4 **e** to hear, to this very day
Judg 17: 2 curse, even saying it in my **e**
1Sa 3:11 in Israel at which both **e** of
1Sa 15:14 bleating of the sheep in my **e**
1Sa 25:24 maidservant speak in your **e**
2Sa 7:22 that we have heard with our **e**
2Sa 22: 7 and my cry entered His **e**
2Ki 19:28 tumult have come up to My **e**
2Ki 21:12 of it, both his **e** will tingle
1Ch 17:20 that we have heard with our **e**
2Ch 6:40 let Your **e** be attentive to
2Ch 7:15 My **e** attentive to prayer made
Neh 8: 3 the **e** of all the people were
Job 13:17 to my declaration with your **e**
Job 15:21 Dreadful sounds are in his **e**
Job 28:22 a report about it with our **e**
Job 33:16 Then He opens the **e** of men
Job 36:15 opens their **e** in oppression
Ps 18: 6 before Him, even to His **e**
Ps 34:15 His **e** are open to their cry
Ps 40: 6 My **e** You have opened
Ps 44: 1 We have heard with our **e**, O
Ps 78: 1 Incline your **e** to the words
Ps 92:11 My **e** hear my desire on the
Ps 115: 6 They have **e**, but they do not
Ps 130: 2 Let Your **e** be attentive To
Ps 135:17 They have **e**, but they do not
Prov 21:13 Whoever shuts his **e** to the
Prov 23:12 your **e** to words of knowledge
Prov 26:17 one who takes a dog by the **e**
Is 6:10 people dull, and their **e** heavy
Is 6:10 eyes, and hear with their **e**
Is 11: 3 by the hearing of His **e**
Is 30:21 Your **e** shall hear a word
Is 32: 3 the **e** of those who hear will
Is 33:15 who stops his **e** from hearing
Is 35: 5 the **e** of the deaf shall be
Is 37:29 tumult have come up to My **e**
Is 42:20 opening the **e**, but he does
Is 43: 8 eyes, and the deaf who have **e**
Is 49:20 will say again in your **e**
Jer 5:21 and see not, and who have **e**
Jer 19: 3 of it, his **e** will tingle
Jer 26:11 as you have heard with your **e**
Ezek 3:10 to you, and hear with your **e**
Ezek 8:18 cry in My **e** with a loud voice
Ezek 12: 2 **e** to hear but does not hear
Ezek 16:12 your nose, earrings in your **e**
Ezek 23:25 remove your nose and your **e**
Ezek 24:26 let you hear it with your **e**
Ezek 40: 4 your eyes and hear with your **e**
Ezek 44: 5 your eyes and hear with your **e**
Mic 7:16 their **e** shall be deaf
Zech 7:11 stopped their **e** so that they
Matt 11:15 He who has **e** to hear, let him
Matt 13: 9 He who has **e** to hear, let him
Matt 13:15 Their **e** are hard of hearing,
Matt 13:15 eyes and hear with their **e**
Matt 13:16 see, and your **e** for they hear
Matt 13:43 He who has **e** to hear, let him
Matt 28:14 comes to the governor's **e**
Mark 4: 9 He who has **e** to hear, let him
Mark 4:23 If anyone has **e** to hear, let
Mark 7:16 If anyone has **e** to hear, let
Mark 7:33 and put His fingers in his **e**
Mark 7:35 Immediately his **e** were opened
Mark 8:18 And having **e**, do you not hear
Luke 1:44 your greeting sounded in my **e**
Luke 8: 8 He who has **e** to hear, let him
Luke 9:44 words sink down into your **e**
Luke 14:35 He who has **e** to hear, let him
Acts 7:51 uncircumcised in heart and **e**
Acts 7:57 a loud voice, stopped their **e**
Acts 11:22 **e** of the church in Jerusalem
Acts 17:20 some strange things to our **e**
Acts 28:27 their **e** are hard of hearing,
Acts 28:27 eyes and hear with their **e**
Rom 11: 8 **e** that they should not hear,
2Ti 4: 3 because they have itching **e**
2Ti 4: 4 their **e** away from the truth
Jas 5: 4 the **e** of the Lord of Sabaoth
1Pe 3:12 and his **e** are open to their

EARTH (*see* EARTHEN, EARTHLY, EARTHQUAKE)
Gen 1: 1 created the heavens and the **e**
Gen 1: 2 The **e** was without form, and
Gen 1:10 And God called the dry land **E**
Gen 1:11 Let the **e** bring forth grass,
Gen 1:11 seed is in itself, on the **e**"
Gen 1:12 the **e** brought forth grass,
Gen 1:15 to give light on the **e**"
Gen 1:17 to give light on the **e**,
Gen 1:20 the **e** across the face of the
Gen 1:22 let birds multiply on the **e**
Gen 1:24 Let the **e** bring forth the
Gen 1:24 thing and beast of the **e**, each
Gen 1:25 the **e** according to its kind
Gen 1:25 that creeps on the **e**
Gen 1:26 the cattle, over all the **e**
Gen 1:26 thing that creeps on the **e**
Gen 1:28 fill the **e** and subdue it
Gen 1:28 thing that moves on the **e**
Gen 1:29 is on the face of all the **e**
Gen 1:30 Also, to every beast of the **e**
Gen 1:30 that creeps on the **e**, in
Gen 2: 1 Thus the heavens and the **e**
Gen 2: 4 the **e** when they were created,
Gen 2: 4 that the LORD God made the **e**
Gen 2: 5 of the field was in the **e**
Gen 2: 5 caused it to rain on the **e**
Gen 2: 6 but a mist went up from the **e**
Gen 4:11 now you are cursed from the **e**
Gen 4:12 you shall be on the **e**
Gen 4:14 and a vagabond on the **e**, and it
Gen 6: 1 multiply on the face of the **e**
Gen 6: 4 giants on the **e** in those days
Gen 6: 5 of man was great in the **e**
Gen 6: 6 that He had made man on the **e**
Gen 6: 7 from the face of the **e**, both
Gen 6:11 The **e** also was corrupt before
Gen 6:11 God, and the **e** was filled with
Gen 6:12 So God looked upon the **e**, and
Gen 6:12 corrupted their way on the **e**
Gen 6:13 Me, for the **e** is filled with
Gen 6:13 will destroy them with the **e**
Gen 6:17 the flood of waters on the **e**
Gen 6:17 that is on the **e** shall die
Gen 6:20 thing of the **e** after its kind
Gen 7: 3 on the face of all the **e**
Gen 7: 4 to rain on the **e** forty days
Gen 7: 4 from the face of the **e** all
Gen 7: 6 flood of waters was on the **e**
Gen 7: 8 that creeps on the **e**,
Gen 7:10 of the flood were on the **e**
Gen 7:12 rain was on the **e** forty days
Gen 7:14 on the **e** after its kind, and
Gen 7:17 flood was on the **e** forty days
Gen 7:17 and it rose high above the **e**
Gen 7:18 and greatly increased on the **e**
Gen 7:19 exceedingly on the **e**, and all
Gen 7:21 died that moved on the **e**
Gen 7:21 thing that creeps on the **e**
Gen 7:23 were destroyed from the **e**
Gen 7:24 on the **e** one hundred and fifty
Gen 8: 1 a wind to pass over the **e**
Gen 8: 3 continually from the **e**
Gen 8: 7 had dried up from the **e**
Gen 8: 9 on the face of the whole **e**
Gen 8:11 waters had abated from the **e**
Gen 8:13 were dried up from the **e**
Gen 8:14 of the month, the **e** was dried
Gen 8:17 thing that creeps on the **e**
Gen 8:17 that they may abound on the **e**
Gen 8:17 fruitful and multiply on the **e**
Gen 8:19 and whatever creeps on the **e**
Gen 8:22 While the **e** remains, seedtime
Gen 9: 1 and multiply, and fill the **e**

Gen 9: 2 be on every beast of the e
Gen 9: 2 on all that moves on the e
Gen 9: 7 forth abundantly in the e
Gen 9:10 every beast of the e with you
Gen 9:10 the ark, every beast of the e
Gen 9:11 be a flood to destroy the e
Gen 9:13 covenant between Me and the e
Gen 9:14 I bring a cloud over the e
Gen 9:16 of all flesh that is on the e
Gen 9:17 and all flesh that is on the e
Gen 9:19 the whole e was populated
Gen 10: 8 to be a mighty one on the e
Gen 10:25 in his days the e was divided
Gen 10:32 on the e after the flood
Gen 11: 1 Now the whole e had one
Gen 11: 4 over the face of the whole e
Gen 11: 8 over the face of all the e
Gen 11: 9 the language of all the e
Gen 11: 9 over the face of all the e
Gen 12: 3 of the e shall be blessed
Gen 13:16 as the dust of the e
Gen 13:16 number the dust of the e,
Gen 14:19 Possessor of heaven and e
Gen 14:22 the Possessor of heaven and e
Gen 18:18 and all the nations of the e
Gen 18:25 Judge of all the e do right
Gen 19:23 the e when Lot entered Zoar
Gen 19:31 there is no man on the e to
Gen 19:31 as is the custom of all the e
Gen 22:18 of the e shall be blessed
Gen 24: 3 of heaven and the God of the e
Gen 24:52 LORD, bowing himself to the e
Gen 26: 4 of the e shall be blessed
Gen 26:15 they had filled them with e
Gen 27:28 of the fatness of the e, and
Gen 27:39 be of the fatness of the e
Gen 28:12 a ladder was set up on the e
Gen 28:14 shall be as the dust of the e
Gen 28:14 of the e shall be blessed
Gen 37:10 bow down to the e before you
Gen 41:56 over all the face of the e
Gen 42: 6 him with their faces to the e
Gen 43:26 down before him to the e
Gen 45: 7 a posterity for you in the e
Gen 48:12 down with his face to the e
Gen 48:16 in the midst of the e
Ex 8:17 and struck the dust of the e
Ex 9:14 is none like Me in all the e
Ex 9:15 have been cut off from the e
Ex 9:16 may be declared in all the e
Ex 9:29 know that the e is the LORD's
Ex 9:33 rain was not poured on the e
Ex 10: 5 shall cover the face of the e
Ex 10: 5 one will be able to see the e
Ex 10: 6 were on the e to this day
Ex 10:15 the face of the whole e, so
Ex 15:12 the e swallowed them
Ex 19: 5 for all the e is Mine
Ex 20: 4 or that is in the e beneath
Ex 20: 4 is in the water under the e
Ex 20:11 made the heavens and the e
Ex 20:24 An altar of e you shall make
Ex 31:17 made the heavens and the e
Ex 32:12 them from the face of the e'
Ex 33:16 are upon the face of the e
Ex 34: 8 bowed his head toward the e
Ex 34:10 not been done in all the e
Lev 11: 2 the beasts that are on the e
Lev 11:21 with which to leap on the e
Lev 11:29 things that creep on the e
Lev 11:41 the e shall be an abomination
Lev 11:42 things that creep on the e
Lev 11:44 thing that creeps on the e
Lev 11:46 creature that creeps on the e
Lev 15:12 The vessel of e that he who
Lev 26:19 iron and your e like bronze
Num 12: 3 who were on the face of the e
Num 14:21 all the e shall be filled
Num 16:30 and the e opens its mouth and
Num 16:32 the e opened its mouth and
Num 16:33 the e closed over them, and
Num 16:34 Lest the e swallow us up also
Num 22: 5 they cover the face of the e
Num 22:11 they cover the face of the e
Num 26:10 the e opened its mouth and
Deut 3:24 on e who can do anything like
Deut 4:10 the days they live on the e
Deut 4:17 the e or the likeness of any
Deut 4:18 is in the water beneath the e
Deut 4:26 e to witness against you this
Deut 4:32 that God created man on the e
Deut 4:36 on e He showed you His great
Deut 4:39 above and on the e beneath
Deut 5: 8 or that is in the e beneath
Deut 5: 8 is in the water under the e
Deut 6:15 you from the face of the e
Deut 7: 6 peoples on the face of the e
Deut 10:14 also the e with all that is
Deut 11: 6 how the e opened its mouth and
Deut 11:21 of the heavens above the e
Deut 12: 1 days that you live on the e
Deut 12:16 pour it on the e like water
Deut 12:24 pour it on the e like water
Deut 13: 7 from one end of the e to the
Deut 13: 7 to the other end of the e
Deut 14: 2 who are on the face of the e
Deut 28: 1 above all nations of the e
Deut 28:10 the e shall see that you are
Deut 28:23 and the e which is under you
Deut 28:25 to all the kingdoms of the e
Deut 28:26 air and the beasts of the e
Deut 28:49 afar, from the end of the e
Deut 28:64 one end of the e to the other
Deut 30:19 e as witnesses today against
Deut 31:28 e to witness against them
Deut 32: 1 and hear, O e, the words of my
Deut 32:13 ride in the heights of the e
Deut 32:22 the e with her increase, and
Deut 33:16 the precious things of the e
Deut 33:17 peoples to the ends of the e
Josh 2:11 heaven above and on e beneath
Josh 3:11 of the Lord of all the e is
Josh 3:13 LORD, the Lord of all the e
Josh 4:24 e may know the hand of the
Josh 5:14 fell on his face to the e
Josh 7: 6 fell to the e on his face
Josh 7: 9 cut off our name from the e
Josh 7:21 hidden in the e in the midst
Josh 23:14 am going the way of all the e
Judg 5: 4 the e trembled and the heavens
Judg 6: 4 of the e as far as Gaza, and
Judg 18:10 of anything that is on the e
1Sa 2: 8 of the e are the LORD's, and
1Sa 2:10 will judge the ends of the e
1Sa 4: 5 so loudly that the e shook
1Sa 5: 3 fallen on its face to the e
1Sa 14:15 the e quaked, so that it was
1Sa 17:46 and the wild beasts of the e
1Sa 17:46 that all the e may know that
1Sa 17:49 he fell on his face to the e
1Sa 20:15 David from the face of the e
1Sa 20:31 son of Jesse lives on the e
1Sa 24: 8 with his face to the e, and
1Sa 25:41 bowed her face to the e, and
1Sa 26: 8 the spear, right to the e
1Sa 26:20 let my blood fall to the e
1Sa 28:13 spirit ascending out of the e
2Sa 4:11 hand and remove you from the e
2Sa 7: 9 great men who are on the e
2Sa 7:23 the one nation on the e whom
2Sa 14: 7 name nor remnant on the e
2Sa 14:20 all things that are in the e
2Sa 18: 9 hanging between heaven and e
2Sa 18:28 face to the e before the king
2Sa 22: 8 Then the e shook and trembled
2Sa 22:43 as fine as the dust of the e
2Sa 23: 4 grass springing out of the e
1Ki 1:31 bowed with her face to the e
1Ki 1:40 so that the e seemed to split
1Ki 1:52 of him shall fall to the e
1Ki 2: 2 I go the way of all the e
1Ki 4:34 from all the kings of the e
1Ki 8:23 above or on e below like You
1Ki 8:27 God indeed dwell on the e
1Ki 8:43 of the e may know Your name
1Ki 8:53 the e to be Your inheritance
1Ki 8:60 e may know that the LORD is
1Ki 10:23 the kings of the e in riches
1Ki 10:24 all the e sought the presence
1Ki 13:34 it from the face of the e
1Ki 17:14 the LORD sends rain on the e
1Ki 18: 1 and I will send rain on the e
2Ki 5:15 there is no God in all the e
2Ki 5:17 be given two mule-loads of e
2Ki 10:10 the e of the word of the LORD
2Ki 19:15 of all the kingdoms of the e
2Ki 19:15 You have made heaven and e
2Ki 19:19 all the kingdoms of the e may
1Ch 1:10 to be a mighty one on the e
1Ch 1:19 in his days the e was divided
1Ch 16:14 judgments are in all the e
1Ch 16:23 Sing to the LORD, all the e
1Ch 16:30 Tremble before Him, all the e
1Ch 16:31 rejoice, and let the e be glad
1Ch 16:33 He is coming to judge the e
1Ch 17: 8 great men who are on the e
1Ch 17:21 the one nation on the e whom
1Ch 21:16 the LORD standing between e
1Ch 22: 8 blood on the e in My sight
1Ch 29:11 is in heaven and in e is Yours
1Ch 29:15 our days on e are as a shadow
2Ch 1: 9 dust of the e in multitude
2Ch 2:12 Israel, who made heaven and e
2Ch 6:14 in heaven or on e like You
2Ch 6:18 dwell with men on the e
2Ch 6:33 of the e may know Your name
2Ch 9:22 the kings of the e in riches
2Ch 9:23 all the kings of the e sought
2Ch 16: 9 and fro throughout the whole e
2Ch 20:24 dead bodies, fallen on the e
2Ch 32:19 gods of the people of the e
2Ch 36:23 All the kingdoms of the e
Ezra 1: 2 All the kingdoms of the e the
Ezra 5:11 of the God of heaven and e
Neh 9: 6 with all their host, the e
Job 1: 7 From going to and fro on the e
Job 1: 8 is none like him on the e
Job 2: 2 From going to and fro on the e
Job 2: 3 is none like him on the e
Job 3:14 kings and counselors of the e
Job 5:10 He gives rain on the e, and
Job 5:22 afraid of the beasts of the e
Job 5:25 like the grass of the e
Job 7: 1 of hard service for man on e
Job 8: 9 our days on e are a shadow
Job 8:19 out of the e others will grow
Job 9: 6 He shakes the e out of its
Job 9:24 The e is given into the hand
Job 11: 9 measure is longer than the e
Job 12: 8 or speak to the e, and it will
Job 12:15 out, they overwhelm the e
Job 12:24 chiefs of the people of the e
Job 14: 8 root may grow old in the e
Job 14:19 wash away the soil of the e
Job 15:29 possessions overspread the e
Job 16:18 O e, do not cover my blood,
Job 18: 4 Shall the e be forsaken for
Job 18:17 of him perishes from the e
Job 19:25 shall stand at last on the e
Job 20: 4 since man was placed on e
Job 20:27 the e will rise up against
Job 24:18 should be cursed in the e
Job 26: 7 he hangs the e on nothing
Job 28: 2 Iron is taken from the e, and
Job 28: 5 As for the e, from it comes
Job 28:24 He looks to the ends of the e
Job 30: 6 valleys, In caves of the e
Job 34:13 gave Him charge over the e
Job 35:11 more than the beasts of the e
Job 37: 3 to the ends of the e
Job 37: 6 to the snow, Be on the e'
Job 37:12 on the face of the whole e
Job 37:17 the e by the south wind
Job 38: 4 laid the foundations of the e
Job 38:13 hold of the ends of the e
Job 38:18 the breadth of the e
Job 38:24 wind scattered over the e
Job 38:33 set their dominion over the e
Job 41:33 On e there is nothing like
Ps 2: 2 kings of the e set themselves
Ps 2: 8 the ends of the e for Your
Ps 2:10 you judges of the e
Ps 7: 5 him trample my life to the e
Ps 8: 1 is Your name in all the e
Ps 8: 9 is Your name in all the e
Ps 10:18 of the e may oppress no more
Ps 12: 6 tried in a furnace of e,
Ps 16: 3 the saints who are on the e
Ps 17:11 eyes, crouching down to the e
Ps 18: 7 Then the e shook and trembled
Ps 19: 4 gone out through all the e
Ps 21:10 You shall destroy from the e
Ps 22:29 prosperous of the e Shall eat
Ps 24: 1 The e is the LORD's, and all
Ps 25:13 shall inherit the e
Ps 33: 5 The e is full of the goodness
Ps 33: 8 Let all the e fear the LORD
Ps 33:14 all the inhabitants of the e
Ps 34:16 of them from the e
Ps 37: 9 They shall inherit the e

Ps 37:11 the meek shall inherit the e
Ps 37:22 by Him shall inherit the e
Ps 41: 2 he will be blessed on the e
Ps 45:16 make princes in all the e
Ps 46: 2 fear, Though the e be removed
Ps 46: 6 His voice, the e melted
Ps 46: 8 has made desolations in the e
Ps 46: 9 cease to the end of the e
Ps 46:10 I will be exalted in the e
Ps 47: 2 a great King over all the e
Ps 47: 7 God is the King of all the e
Ps 47: 9 of the e belong to God
Ps 48: 2 The joy of the whole e, Is
Ps 48:10 praise to the ends of the e
Ps 50: 1 called the e From the rising
Ps 50: 4 from above, And to the e, that
Ps 57: 5 Your glory be above all the e
Ps 57:11 Your glory be above all the e
Ps 58: 2 of your hands in the e
Ps 58:11 He is God who judges in the e
Ps 59:13 in Jacob To the ends of the e
Ps 60: 2 You have made the e tremble
Ps 61: 2 of the e I will cry to You
Ps 63: 9 into the lower parts of the e
Ps 65: 5 of all the ends of the e, And
Ps 65: 9 You visit the e and water it,
Ps 66: 1 shout to God, all the e
Ps 66: 4 All the e shall worship You
Ps 67: 2 Your way may be known on e
Ps 67: 4 And govern the nations on e
Ps 67: 6 Then the e shall yield her
Ps 67: 7 ends of the e shall fear Him
Ps 68: 8 The e shook
Ps 68:32 to God, you kingdoms of the e
Ps 69:34 e praise Him, The seas and
Ps 71:20 from the depths of the e
Ps 72: 6 Like showers that water the e
Ps 72: 8 River to the ends of the e
Ps 72:16 abundance of grain in the e
Ps 72:16 flourish like grass of the e
Ps 72:19 let the whole e be filled
Ps 73: 9 tongue walks through the e
Ps 73:25 there is none upon e that I
Ps 74:12 in the midst of the e
Ps 74:17 set all the borders of the e
Ps 74:20 For the dark places of the e
Ps 75: 3 The e and all its inhabitants
Ps 75: 8 all the wicked of the e Drain
Ps 76: 8 The e feared and was still,
Ps 76: 9 all the oppressed of the e
Ps 76:12 awesome to the kings of the e
Ps 77:18 The e trembled and shook
Ps 78:69 Like the e which He has
Ps 79: 2 saints to the beasts of the e
Ps 82: 5 of the e are unstable
Ps 82: 8 Arise, O God, judge the e
Ps 83:10 Who became as refuse on the e
Ps 83:18 the Most High over all the e
Ps 85:11 shall spring out of the e
Ps 89:11 Yours, the e also is Yours
Ps 89:27 highest of the kings of the e
Ps 90: 2 Or ever You had formed the e
Ps 94: 2 Rise up, O Judge of the e
Ps 95: 4 are the deep places of the e
Ps 96: 1 Sing to the LORD, all the e
Ps 96: 9 Tremble before Him, all the e
Ps 96:11 rejoice, and let the e be glad
Ps 96:13 He is coming to judge the e
Ps 97: 1 Let the e rejoice
Ps 97: 4 The e sees and trembles
Ps 97: 5 of the Lord of the whole e
Ps 97: 9 are most high above all the e
Ps 98: 3 All the ends of the e have
Ps 98: 4 to the LORD, all the e
Ps 98: 9 He is coming to judge the e
Ps 99: 1 Let the e be moved
Ps 102:15 the kings of the e Your glory
Ps 102:19 heaven the LORD viewed the e
Ps 102:25 laid the foundation of the e
Ps 103:11 heavens are high above the e
Ps 104: 5 laid the foundations of the e
Ps 104: 9 may not return to cover the e
Ps 104:13 The e is satisfied with the
Ps 104:14 bring forth food from the e
Ps 104:24 The e is full of Your
Ps 104:30 You renew the face of the e
Ps 104:32 He looks on the e, and it
Ps 104:35 be consumed from the e, And
Ps 105: 7 judgments are in all the e
Ps 106:17 The e opened up and swallowed
Ps 108: 5 And Your glory above all the e
Ps 109:15 the memory of them from the e
Ps 112: 2 will be mighty on e
Ps 113: 6 in the heavens and in the e
Ps 114: 7 Tremble, O e, at the presence
Ps 115:15 LORD, Who made heaven and e
Ps 115:16 But the e He has given to the
Ps 119:19 I am a stranger in the e
Ps 119:64 The e, O LORD, is full of
Ps 119:87 almost made an end of me on e
Ps 119:90 You established the e, and it
Ps 119:119 wicked of the e like dross
Ps 121: 2 LORD, Who made heaven and e
Ps 124: 8 LORD, Who made heaven and e
Ps 134: 3 and e Bless you from Zion
Ps 135: 6 He does, In heaven and in e
Ps 135: 7 ascend from the ends of the e
Ps 136: 6 out the e above the waters
Ps 138: 4 of the e shall praise You
Ps 139:15 in the lowest parts of the e
Ps 140:11 be established in the e
Ps 141: 7 one plows and breaks up the e
Ps 146: 4 departs, he returns to his e
Ps 146: 6 Who made heaven and e,
Ps 147: 8 Who prepares rain for the e
Ps 147:15 out His command to the e
Ps 148: 7 Praise the LORD from the e
Ps 148:11 Kings of the e and all peoples
Ps 148:11 and all judges of the e
Ps 148:13 His glory is above the e and
Prov 2:22 will be cut off from the e
Prov 3:19 LORD by wisdom founded the e
Prov 8:16 all the judges of the e
Prov 8:23 before there was ever an e
Prov 8:26 not made the e or the fields
Prov 8:29 out the foundations of the e
Prov 10:30 wicked will not inhabit the e
Prov 11:31 will be recompensed on the e
Prov 17:24 fool are on the ends of the e
Prov 25: 3 the e for depth, so the heart
Prov 30: 4 all the ends of the e
Prov 30:14 the poor from off the e, and
Prov 30:16 the e that is not satisfied
Prov 30:21 things the e is perturbed
Prov 30:24 which are little on the e
Eccl 1: 4 but the e abides forever
Eccl 3:21 which goes down to the e
Eccl 5: 2 God is in heaven, and you on e
Eccl 7:20 a just man on e who does good
Eccl 8:14 is a vanity which occurs on e
Eccl 8:16 business that is done on e
Eccl 11: 2 what evil will be on the e
Eccl 11: 3 empty themselves upon the e
Eccl 12: 7 return to the e as it was
Song 2:12 The flowers appear on the e
Is 1: 2 O heavens, and give ear, O e
Is 2:19 and into the caves of the e
Is 2:19 to shake the e mightily
Is 2:21 to shake the e mightily
Is 4: 2 the fruit of the e shall be
Is 5:26 to them from the end of the e
Is 6: 3 the whole e is full of His
Is 8:22 Then they will look to the e
Is 10:14 I have gathered all the e
Is 11: 4 equity for the meek of the e
Is 11: 4 He shall strike the e with
Is 11: 9 for the e shall be full of
Is 11:12 the four corners of the e
Is 12: 5 this is known in all the e
Is 13:13 the e will move out of her
Is 14: 7 The whole e is at rest and
Is 14: 9 all the chief ones of the e
Is 14:16 man who made the e tremble
Is 14:26 purposed against the whole e
Is 18: 3 world and dwellers on the e
Is 18: 6 and for the beasts of the e
Is 18: 6 of the e will winter on them
Is 23: 8 are the honorable of the e
Is 23: 9 all the honorable of the e
Is 23:17 world on the face of the e
Is 24: 1 the LORD makes the e empty
Is 24: 4 The e mourns and fades away,
Is 24: 4 people of the e languish
Is 24: 5 The e is also defiled under
Is 24: 6 the curse has devoured the e
Is 24: 6 of the e are burned, and few
Is 24:16 of the e we have heard songs
Is 24:17 you, O inhabitant of the e
Is 24:18 of the e are shaken
Is 24:19 The e is violently broken,
Is 24:19 the e is split open, the
Is 24:19 the e is shaken exceedingly
Is 24:20 The e shall reel to and fro
Is 24:21 on the e the kings of the e
Is 25: 8 will take away from all the e
Is 26: 9 Your judgments are in the e
Is 26:18 any deliverance in the e, nor
Is 26:19 the e shall cast out the dead
Is 26:21 of the e for their iniquity
Is 26:21 the e will also disclose her
Is 28: 2 down to the e with His hand
Is 28:22 even upon the whole e
Is 30:23 of the increase of the e
Is 33: 9 The e mourns and languishes,
Is 34: 1 Let the e hear, and all that
Is 37:16 of all the kingdoms of the e
Is 37:16 You have made heaven and e
Is 37:20 all the kingdoms of the e may
Is 40:12 dust of the e in a measure
Is 40:21 from the foundations of the e
Is 40:22 above the circle of the e
Is 40:23 the judges of the e useless
Is 40:24 stock take root in the e,
Is 40:28 Creator of the ends of the e
Is 41: 5 the ends of the e were afraid
Is 41: 9 taken from the ends of the e
Is 42: 4 established justice in the e
Is 42: 5 out, Who spread forth the e
Is 42:10 praise from the ends of the e
Is 43: 6 from the ends of the e
Is 44:23 you lower parts of the e
Is 44:24 abroad the e by Myself
Is 45: 8 let the e open, let them
Is 45: 9 with the potsherds of the e
Is 45:12 I have made the e, and created
Is 45:18 Who is God, Who formed the e
Is 45:19 in a dark place of the e
Is 45:22 saved, all you ends of the e
Is 48:13 laid the foundation of the e
Is 48:20 it even to the end of the e
Is 49: 6 to the ends of the e
Is 49: 8 the people, to restore the e
Is 49:13 Be joyful, O e
Is 49:23 you with their faces to the e
Is 51: 6 and look on the e beneath
Is 51: 6 the e will grow old like a
Is 51:13 laid the foundations of the e
Is 51:16 lay the foundations of the e
Is 52:10 all the ends of the e shall
Is 54: 5 called the God of the whole e
Is 54: 9 would no longer cover the e
Is 55: 9 heavens are higher than the e
Is 55:10 return there, but water the e
Is 58:14 on the high hills of the e
Is 60: 2 darkness shall cover the e
Is 61:11 For as the e brings forth its
Is 62: 7 Jerusalem a praise in the e
Is 63: 6 down their strength to the e
Is 65:16 e shall bless himself in the
Is 65:16 he who swears in the e shall
Is 65:17 create new heavens and a new e
Is 66: 1 throne, and e is My footstool
Is 66: 8 Shall the e be made to give
Is 66:22 the new e which I will make
Jer 4:23 I beheld the e, and indeed it
Jer 4:28 For this shall the e mourn
Jer 6:19 Hear, O e
Jer 6:22 the farthest parts of the e
Jer 7:33 and for the beasts of the e
Jer 8: 2 refuse on the face of the e
Jer 9: 3 for the truth on the e
Jer 9:24 and righteousness in the e
Jer 10:10 His wrath the e will tremble
Jer 10:11 e shall perish from the e
Jer 10:12 has made the e by His power
Jer 10:13 ascend from the ends of the e
Jer 15: 3 the beasts of the e to devour
Jer 15: 4 to all kingdoms of the e
Jer 15:10 of contention to the whole e
Jer 16: 4 refuse on the face of the e
Jer 16: 4 and for the beasts of the e
Jer 16:19 to You from the ends of the e
Jer 17:13 Me shall be written in the e
Jer 19: 7 and for the beasts of the e
Jer 22:29 O e, e, e, hear the word
Jer 23: 5 and righteousness in the e
Jer 23:24 do I not fill heaven and e
Jer 24: 9 all the kingdoms of the e
Jer 25:26 are on the face of the e
Jer 25:29 all the inhabitants of the e

Jer 25:30 all the inhabitants of the e
Jer 25:31 come to the ends of the e
Jer 25:32 the farthest parts of the e
Jer 25:33 be from one end of the e even
Jer 25:33 to the other end of the e
Jer 26: 6 to all the nations of the e
Jer 27: 5 I have made the e, the man
Jer 28:16 you from the face of the e
Jer 29:18 all the kingdoms of the e
Jer 31: 8 them from the ends of the e
Jer 31:22 created a new thing in the e
Jer 31:37 of the e searched out beneath
Jer 32:17 the e by Your great power and
Jer 33: 9 before all nations of the e
Jer 33:15 and righteousness in the e
Jer 33:25 the ordinances of heaven and e
Jer 34: 1 of the e under his dominion
Jer 34:17 all the kingdoms of the e
Jer 34:20 heaven and the beasts of the e
Jer 44: 8 all the nations of the e
Jer 46: 8 I will go up and cover the e
Jer 49:21 The e shakes at the noise of
Jer 50:23 whole e has been cut apart
Jer 50:41 up from the ends of the e
Jer 50:46 of Babylon the e trembles
Jer 51: 7 that made all the e drunk
Jer 51:15 has made the e by His power
Jer 51:16 ascend from the ends of the e
Jer 51:25 who destroys all the e,"
Jer 51:41 of the whole e is seized
Jer 51:48 Then the heavens and the e
Jer 51:49 slain of all the e shall fall
Lam 2: 1 to the e the beauty of Israel
Lam 2:15 the joy of the whole e'
Lam 3:34 all the prisoners of the e
Lam 4:12 The kings of the e, and all
Ezek 1:15 a wheel was on the e beside
Ezek 1:19 were lifted up from the e
Ezek 1:21 were lifted up from the e
Ezek 7:21 the wicked of the e as spoil
Ezek 8: 3 Spirit lifted me up between e
Ezek 10:16 wings to mount up from the e
Ezek 10:19 up from the e in my sight
Ezek 26:20 in the lowest part of the e
Ezek 27:33 enriched the kings of the e
Ezek 28:18 you to ashes upon the e in
Ezek 31:12 all the peoples of the e have
Ezek 31:14 death, to the depths of the e
Ezek 31:16 in the depths of the e
Ezek 31:18 Eden to the depths of the e
Ezek 32: 4 the beasts of the whole e
Ezek 32:18 down to the depths of the e
Ezek 32:24 to the lower parts of the e
Ezek 34: 6 over the whole face of the e
Ezek 34:27 and the e shall yield her
Ezek 35:14 The whole e will rejoice when
Ezek 38:20 things that creep on the e
Ezek 38:20 e shall shake at My presence
Ezek 39:18 blood of the princes of the e
Ezek 43: 2 the e shone with His glory
Dan 2:10 There is not a man on e who
Dan 2:35 and filled the whole e
Dan 2:39 shall rule over all the e
Dan 4: 1 that dwell in all the e
Dan 4:10 A tree in the midst of the e
Dan 4:11 seen to the ends of all the e
Dan 4:15 the stump and roots in the e
Dan 4:15 beasts on the grass of the e
Dan 4:20 could be seen by all the e
Dan 4:22 dominion to the end of the e
Dan 4:23 its stump and roots in the e
Dan 4:35 the e are reputed as nothing
Dan 4:35 the inhabitants of the e
Dan 6:25 that dwell in all the e
Dan 6:27 and wonders in heaven and on e
Dan 7: 4 it was lifted up from the e
Dan 7:17 which arise out of the e
Dan 7:23 be a fourth kingdom on e,
Dan 7:23 and shall devour the whole e
Dan 8: 5 the surface of the whole e
Dan 12: 2 the dust of the e shall awake
Hos 2:18 I will shatter from the e
Hos 2:21 and they shall answer the e
Hos 2:22 The e shall answer With grain
Hos 2:23 sow her for Myself in the e
Hos 6: 3 and former rain to the e
Joel 2:10 The e quakes before them, the
Joel 2:30 in the heavens and in the e
Joel 3:16 the heavens and e will shake
Amos 2: 7 pant after the dust of the e

Amos 3: 2 of all the families of the e
Amos 3: 5 fall into a snare on the e
Amos 3: 5 a snare spring up from the e
Amos 4:13 the high places of the e
Amos 5: 7 to rest in the e
Amos 5: 8 them out on the face of the e
Amos 8: 9 the e in broad daylight
Amos 9: 5 hosts, He who touches the e
Amos 9: 6 founded His strata in the e
Amos 9: 6 them out on the face of the e
Amos 9: 8 it from the face of the e
Jon 2: 6 the e with its bars closed
Mic 1: 2 listen, O e, and all that is
Mic 1: 3 on the high places of the e
Mic 4:13 to the Lord of the whole e
Mic 5: 4 be great to the ends of the e
Mic 6: 2 strong foundations of the e
Mic 7: 2 man has perished from the e
Mic 7:17 holes like snakes of the e
Nah 1: 5 the e heaves at His presence,
Nah 2:13 cut off your prey from the e
Hab 1: 6 through the breadth of the e
Hab 1:10 for they heap up mounds of e
Hab 2:14 For the e will be filled with
Hab 2:20 Let all the e keep silence
Hab 3: 3 the e was full of His praise
Hab 3: 6 He stood and measured the e
Hab 3: 9 You divided the e with rivers
Zeph 2: 3 LORD, all you meek of the e
Zeph 2:11 nothing all the gods of the e
Zeph 3: 8 all the e shall be devoured
Zeph 3:20 all the peoples of the e,
Hag 1:10 the e withholds its fruit
Hag 2: 6 I will shake heaven and e
Hag 2:21 I will shake heaven and e
Zech 1:10 to and fro throughout the e
Zech 1:11 to and fro throughout the e
Zech 1:11 all the e is resting quietly
Zech 4:10 and fro throughout the whole e
Zech 4:14 the Lord of the whole e
Zech 5: 3 over the face of the whole e
Zech 5: 6 resemblance throughout the e
Zech 5: 9 up the basket between e and
Zech 6: 5 before the Lord of all the e
Zech 6: 7 to and fro throughout the e
Zech 6: 7 to and fro throughout the e
Zech 6: 7 to and fro throughout the e
Zech 9:10 River to the ends of the e
Zech 12: 1 lays the foundation of the e
Zech 12: 3 the e are gathered against it
Zech 14: 9 shall be King over all the e
Zech 14:17 of the families of the e do
Mal 4: 6 strike the e with a curse
Matt 5: 5 for they shall inherit the e
Matt 5:13 You are the salt of the e
Matt 5:18 e pass away, one jot or one
Matt 5:35 nor by the e, for it is His
Matt 6:10 done on e as it is in heaven
Matt 6:19 for yourselves treasures on e
Matt 9: 6 power on e to forgive sins"
Matt 10:34 I came to bring peace on e
Matt 11:25 Father, Lord of heaven and e
Matt 12:40 nights in the heart of the e
Matt 12:42 the e to hear the wisdom of
Matt 13: 5 they did not have much e
Matt 13: 5 they had no depth of e
Matt 16:19 whatever you bind on e will
Matt 16:19 whatever you loose on e will
Matt 17:25 the e take customs or taxes
Matt 18:18 whatever you bind on e will
Matt 18:18 whatever you loose on e will
Matt 18:19 on e concerning anything that
Matt 23: 9 call anyone on e your father
Matt 23:35 righteous blood shed on the e
Matt 24:30 tribes of the e will mourn
Matt 24:35 and e will pass away, but My
Matt 27:51 the e quaked, and the rocks
Matt 28:18 given to Me in heaven and on e
Mark 2:10 power on e to forgive sins"
Mark 4: 5 where it did not have much e
Mark 4: 5 because it had no depth of e
Mark 4:28 For the e yields crops by
Mark 4:31 than all the seeds on e
Mark 9: 3 on e can whiten them
Mark 13:27 of e to the farthest part of
Mark 13:31 and e will pass away, but My
Luke 2:14 on e peace, good will toward
Luke 5:24 power on e to forgive sins"
Luke 6:49 on the e without a foundation
Luke 10:21 Father, Lord of heaven and e

Luke 11: 2 done On e as it is in heaven
Luke 11:31 the e to hear the wisdom of
Luke 12:49 I came to send fire on the e
Luke 12:51 I came to give peace on e
Luke 12:56 face of the sky and of the e
Luke 16:17 e to pass away than for one
Luke 18: 8 He really find faith on the e
Luke 21:25 on the e distress of nations,
Luke 21:26 which are coming on the e
Luke 21:33 and e will pass away, but My
Luke 21:35 on the face of the whole e
Luke 23:44 the e until the ninth hour
Luke 24: 5 and bowed their faces to the e
John 3:31 he who is of the e is earthly
John 3:31 is earthly and speaks of the e
John 12:32 if I am lifted up from the e
John 17: 4 I have glorified You on the e
Acts 1: 8 and to the end of the e
Acts 2:19 and signs in the e beneath
Acts 3:25 of the e shall be blessed
Acts 4:24 God, who made heaven and e
Acts 4:26 of the e took their stand
Acts 7:49 throne, and e is My footstool
Acts 8:33 His life is taken from the e
Acts 10:11 to him and let down to the e
Acts 10:12 four-footed animals of the e
Acts 11: 6 four-footed animals of the e
Acts 13:47 to the ends of the e
Acts 14:15 who made the heaven, the e
Acts 17:24 He is Lord of heaven and e
Acts 17:26 on all the face of the e, and
Acts 22:22 with such a fellow from the e
Rom 9:17 be declared in all the e
Rom 9:28 make a short work upon the e
Rom 10:18 has gone out to all the e
1Co 8: 5 on e (as there are many gods
1Co 10:26 The e is the LORD's, and all
1Co 10:28 The e is the LORD's, and all
1Co 15:47 The first man was of the e
Eph 1:10 in heaven and which are on e
Eph 3:15 in heaven and e is named,
Eph 4: 9 into the lower parts of the e
Eph 6: 3 and you may live long on the e
Phil 2:10 in heaven, and of those on e
Phil 2:10 and of those under the e,
Col 1:16 in heaven and that are on e
Col 1:20 whether things on e or things
Col 3: 2 above, not on things on the e
Col 3: 5 members which are on the e
Heb 1:10 laid the foundation of the e
Heb 6: 7 For the e which drinks in the
Heb 8: 4 For if He were on e, He would
Heb 11:13 and pilgrims on the e
Heb 11:38 in dens and caves of the e
Heb 12:25 refused Him who spoke on e
Heb 12:26 whose voice then shook the e
Heb 12:26 more I shake not only the e
Jas 5: 5 lived on the e in pleasure
Jas 5: 7 the precious fruit of the e
Jas 5:12 by e or with any other oath
Jas 5:18 and the e produced its fruit
2Pe 3: 5 the e standing out of water
2Pe 3: 7 the e which now exist are
2Pe 3:10 both the e and the works that
2Pe 3:13 heavens and a new e in which
1Jn 5: 8 three that bear witness on e
Rev 1: 5 ruler over the kings of the e
Rev 1: 7 all the tribes of the e will
Rev 3:10 test those who dwell on the e
Rev 5: 3 on the e or under the e
Rev 5: 6 God sent out into all the e
Rev 5:10 and we shall reign on the e
Rev 5:13 on the e and under the e
Rev 6: 4 it to take peace from the e
Rev 6: 8 them over a fourth of the e
Rev 6: 8 and by the beasts of the e
Rev 6:10 on those who dwell on the e
Rev 6:13 stars of heaven fell to the e
Rev 6:15 And the kings of the e, the
Rev 7: 1 at the four corners of the e
Rev 7: 1 the four winds of the e, that
Rev 7: 1 wind should not blow on the e
Rev 7: 2 it was granted to harm the e
Rev 7: 3 Do not harm the e, the sea,
Rev 8: 5 altar, and threw it to the e
Rev 8: 7 and they were thrown to the e
Rev 8:13 to the inhabitants of the e
Rev 9: 1 fallen from heaven to the e
Rev 9: 3 smoke locusts came upon the e
Rev 9: 3 scorpions of the e have power

Rev 9: 4 to harm the grass of the **e**
Rev 10: 6 things that are in it, the **e**
Rev 10: 8 stands on the sea and on the **e**
Rev 11: 4 before the God of the **e**
Rev 11: 6 and to strike the **e** with all
Rev 11:10 the **e** will rejoice over them
Rev 11:10 those who dwell on the **e**
Rev 11:18 those who destroy the **e**
Rev 12: 4 heaven and threw them to the **e**
Rev 12: 9 he was cast to the **e**, and his
Rev 12:12 to the inhabitants of the **e**
Rev 12:13 he had been cast to the **e**
Rev 12:16 But the **e** helped the woman,
Rev 12:16 the **e** opened its mouth and
Rev 13: 8 on the **e** will worship him
Rev 13:11 beast coming up out of the **e**
Rev 13:12 his presence, and causes the **e**
Rev 13:13 on the **e** in the sight of men
Rev 13:14 those who dwell on the **e** by
Rev 13:14 those who dwell on the **e** to
Rev 14: 3 who were redeemed from the **e**
Rev 14: 6 to those who dwell on the **e**
Rev 14: 7 Him who made heaven and **e**,
Rev 14:15 the harvest of the **e** is ripe
Rev 14:16 thrust in His sickle on the **e**
Rev 14:16 and the **e** was reaped
Rev 14:18 clusters of the vine of the **e**
Rev 14:19 thrust his sickle into the **e**
Rev 14:19 and gathered the vine of the **e**
Rev 16: 1 of the wrath of God on the **e**
Rev 16: 2 out his bowl upon the **e**, and a
Rev 16:14 go out to the kings of the **e**
Rev 16:18 since men were on the **e**
Rev 17: 2 the **e** committed fornication
Rev 17: 2 the inhabitants of the **e** were
Rev 17: 5 ABOMINATIONS OF THE **E**
Rev 17: 8 dwell on the **e** will marvel
Rev 17:18 over the kings of the **e**
Rev 18: 1 the **e** was illuminated with
Rev 18: 3 the kings of the **e** have
Rev 18: 3 the merchants of the **e** have
Rev 18: 9 And the kings of the **e** who
Rev 18:11 merchants of the **e** will weep
Rev 18:23 were the great men of the **e**
Rev 18:24 all who were slain on the **e**
Rev 19: 2 the **e** with her fornication
Rev 19:19 the beast, the kings of the **e**
Rev 20: 8 in the four corners of the **e**
Rev 20: 9 up on the breadth of the **e**
Rev 20:11 on it, from whose face the **e**
Rev 21: 1 I saw a new heaven and a new **e**
Rev 21: 1 the first **e** had passed away
Rev 21:24 and the kings of the **e** bring

EARTHEN (*see* EARTH, EARTHENWARE)
Lev 6:28 But the **e** vessel in which it
Lev 11:33 Any **e** vessel into which any
Lev 14: 5 **e** vessel over running water
Lev 14:50 **e** vessel over running water
Num 5:17 holy water in an **e** vessel
2Sa 17:28 **e** vessels and wheat, barley and
Jer 19: 1 Go and get a potter's **e** flask
Jer 32:14 and put them in an **e** vessel
2Co 4: 7 this treasure in **e** vessels

EARTHENWARE (*see* EARTHEN)
Prov 26:23 a wicked heart are like **e**

EARTHLY (*see* EARTH)
John 3:12 If I have told you **e** things
John 3:31 he who is of the earth is **e**
2Co 5: 1 we know that if our **e** house
Phil 3:19 set their mind on **e** things
Heb 9: 1 service and the **e** sanctuary
Jas 3:15 descend from above, but is **e**

EARTHQUAKE (*see* EARTH, EARTHQUAKES)
1Ki 19:11 and after the wind an **e**, but
1Ki 19:11 but the LORD was not in the **e**
1Ki 19:12 and after the **e** a fire, but
Is 29: 6 of hosts with thunder and **e**
Ezek 38:19 great **e** in the land of Israel
Amos 1: 1 two years before the **e**
Zech 14: 5 flee as you fled from the **e**
Matt 27:54 guarding Jesus, saw the **e**
Matt 28: 2 behold, there was a great **e**
Acts 16:26 Suddenly there was a great **e**
Rev 6:12 behold, there was a great **e**
Rev 8: 5 lightnings, and an **e**
Rev 11:13 same hour there was a great **e**
Rev 11:13 In the **e** seven thousand men
Rev 11:19 noises, thunderings, an **e**
Rev 16:18 and there was a great **e**, such
Rev 16:18 great **e** as had not occurred

EARTHQUAKES (*see* EARTHQUAKE)
Matt 24: 7 and **e** in various places
Mark 13: 8 there will be **e** in various
Luke 21:11 be great **e** in various places

EASE (*see* EASED)
Job 3:26 I am not at **e**, nor am I quiet
Job 7:13 my couch will **e** my complaint
Job 12: 5 thought of one who is at **e**
Job 16:12 I was at **e**, but He has
Job 21:23 strength, being wholly at **e**
Ps 73:12 ungodly, Who are always at **e**
Ps 123: 4 scorn of those who are at **e**
Is 32: 9 up, you women who are at **e**
Is 32:11 you women who are at **e**
Jer 46:27 return, have rest and be at **e**
Jer 48:11 has been at **e** from his youth
Amos 6: 1 to you who are at **e** in Zion
Zech 1:15 angry with the nations at **e**
Luke 12:19 take your **e**; eat, drink

EASED (*see* EASE)
Job 16: 6 I remain silent, how am I **e**
2Co 8:13 mean that others should be **e**

EASIER (*see* EASY)
Ex 18:22 So it will be **e** for you, for
Matt 9: 5 For which is **e**, to say, Your
Matt 19:24 it is **e** for a camel to go
Mark 2: 9 Which is **e**, to say to the
Mark 10:25 It is **e** for a camel to go
Luke 5:23 Which is **e**, to say, Your
Luke 16:17 it is **e** for heaven and earth
Luke 18:25 For it is **e** for a camel to go

EASILY (*see* EASY)
Judg 20:43 **e** trampled them down as far
Heb 12: 1 sin which so **e** ensnares us

EAST (*see* EASTERN, EASTWARD)
Gen 2:14 goes toward the **e** of Assyria
Gen 3:24 the **e** of the garden of Eden
Gen 4:16 land of Nod on the **e** of Eden
Gen 10:30 Sephar, the mountain of the **e**
Gen 11: 2 as they journeyed from the **e**
Gen 12: 8 to the mountain **e** of Bethel
Gen 12: 8 on the west and Ai on the **e**
Gen 13:11 of Jordan, and Lot journeyed **e**
Gen 25: 6 son, to the country of the **e**
Gen 25:18 which is **e** of Egypt as you go
Gen 28:14 abroad to the west and the **e**
Gen 29: 1 land of the people of the **e**
Gen 41: 6 heads, blighted by the **e** wind
Gen 41:23 and blighted by the **e** wind
Gen 41:27 the **e** wind are seven years of
Ex 10:13 the LORD brought an **e** wind on
Ex 10:13 the **e** wind brought the
Ex 14:21 strong **e** wind all that night
Ex 27:13 width of the court on the **e**
Ex 38:13 For the **e** side the hangings
Lev 1:16 the altar on the **e** side, into
Lev 16:14 the mercy seat on the **e** side
Num 2: 3 On the **e** side, toward the
Num 3:38 the tabernacle on the **e**,
Num 10: 5 the camps that lie on the **e**
Num 21:11 wilderness which is **e** of Moab
Num 23: 7 from the mountains of the **e**
Num 33: 7 which is **e** of Baal Zephon
Num 34:11 Riblah on the **e** side of Ain
Num 35: 5 outside the city on the **e**
Deut 3:17 the **e** side of the Sea of the
Deut 3:27 north, the south, and the **e**
Deut 4:49 all the plain on the **e** side
Josh 4:19 on the **e** border of Jericho
Josh 7: 2 on the **e** side of Bethel, and
Josh 11: 3 to the Canaanites in the **e**
Josh 13: 3 Sihor, which is **e** of Egypt
Josh 15: 5 The **e** border was the Salt Sea
Josh 16: 1 waters of Jericho on the **e**
Josh 16: 5 **e** side was Ataroth Addar as
Josh 16: 6 by it on the **e** of Janohah
Josh 17: 7 that lies **e** of Shechem
Josh 17:10 north and Issachar on the **e**
Josh 18: 7 beyond the Jordan on the **e**
Josh 18:20 was its border on the **e** side
Josh 19:11 brook that is **e** of Jokneam
Josh 19:13 along on the **e** of Gath Hepher
Judg 6: 3 the people of the **E** would
Judg 6:33 the people of the **E**,
Judg 7:12 all the people of the **E**,
Judg 8:10 army of the people of the **E**
Judg 8:11 in tents on the **e** of Nobah
Judg 11:18 came to the **e** side of the
Judg 20:43 front of Gibeah toward the **e**
Judg 21:19 on the **e** side of the highway
1Sa 13: 5 to the **e** of Beth Aven
1Sa 15: 7 to Shur, which is **e** of Egypt
1Ki 4:30 of all the men of the **E** and
1Ki 7:25 and three looking toward the **e**
1Ki 11: 7 hill that is **e** of Jerusalem
2Ki 13:17 Open the **e** window"
2Ki 23:13 that were **e** of Jerusalem,
1Ch 4:39 as far as the **e** side of the
1Ch 5:10 the entire area **e** of Gilead
1Ch 6:78 on the **e** side of the Jordan,
1Ch 7:28 to the **e** Naaran, to the west
1Ch 9:18 at the King's Gate on the **e**
1Ch 9:24 the **e**, west, north, and south
1Ch 12:15 in the valleys, to the **e** and
1Ch 26:14 The lot for the **E** Gate fell
1Ch 26:17 On the **e** were six Levites, on
2Ch 4: 4 and three looking toward the **e**
2Ch 5:12 stood at the **e** end of the
2Ch 29: 4 gathered them in the **E** Square
2Ch 31:14 the keeper of the **E** Gate
Neh 3:26 the Water Gate toward the **e**
Neh 3:29 the keeper of the **E** Gate
Job 15: 2 fill himself with the **e** wind
Job 18:20 those in the **e** are frightened
Job 27:21 The **e** wind carries him away,
Job 38:24 or the **e** wind scattered over
Ps 48: 7 of Tarshish With an **e** wind
Ps 75: 6 comes neither from the **e** Nor
Ps 78:26 He caused an **e** wind to blow
Ps 103:12 As far as the **e** is from the
Ps 107: 3 out of the lands, From the **e**
Is 11:14 plunder the people of the **e**
Is 27: 8 wind in the day of the **e** wind
Is 41: 2 Who raised up one from the **e**
Is 43: 5 your descendants from the **e**
Is 46:11 a bird of prey from the **e**
Jer 18:17 an **e** wind before the enemy
Jer 31:40 the Horse Gate toward the **e**
Jer 49:28 and devastate the men of the **E**
Ezek 8:16 and their faces toward the **e**
Ezek 8:16 the sun toward the **e**
Ezek 10:19 **e** gate of the LORD's house
Ezek 11: 1 brought me to the **e** gate of
Ezek 11:23 which is on the **e** side of the
Ezek 17:10 when the **e** wind touches it
Ezek 19:12 the **e** wind dried her fruit
Ezek 25: 4 to the men of the **E**, and they
Ezek 25:10 To the men of the **E** I will
Ezek 27:26 but the **e** wind broke you in
Ezek 39:11 who pass by **e** of the sea
Ezek 40: 6 to the gateway which faced **e**
Ezek 40:19 hundred cubits toward the **e**
Ezek 40:22 as the gateway facing **e**
Ezek 40:32 into the inner court facing **e**
Ezek 42: 9 the entrance on the **e** side
Ezek 42:10 of the court toward the **e**
Ezek 42:12 of the wall toward the **e**
Ezek 42:15 that faces toward the **e**, and
Ezek 42:16 He measured the **e** side with
Ezek 43: 1 gate that faces toward the **e**
Ezek 43: 2 came from the way of the **e**
Ezek 43: 4 gate which faces toward the **e**
Ezek 43:17 its steps face toward the **e**
Ezek 44: 1 which faces toward the **e**, but
Ezek 45: 7 and eastward on the **e** side
Ezek 45: 7 west border to the **e** border
Ezek 46: 1 the **e** shall be shut the six
Ezek 46:12 **e** shall then be opened for
Ezek 47: 1 of the temple toward the **e**
Ezek 47: 1 front of the temple faced **e**
Ezek 47: 2 outer gateway that faces **e**
Ezek 47: 3 the man went out to the **e**
Ezek 47:18 On the **e** side you shall mark
Ezek 47:18 This is the **e** side
Ezek 48: 1 from its **e** to its west side
Ezek 48: 2 from the **e** side to the west,
Ezek 48: 3 from the **e** side to the west,
Ezek 48: 4 from the **e** side to the west,
Ezek 48: 5 from the **e** side to the west,
Ezek 48: 6 from the **e** side to the west,
Ezek 48: 7 from the **e** side to the west,
Ezek 48: 8 from the **e** side to the west,
Ezek 48: 8 from the **e** side to the west,
Ezek 48:10 on the **e** ten thousand in
Ezek 48:16 the **e** side four thousand five

Ezek 48:17 to the **e** two hundred and fifty
Ezek 48:18 ten thousand cubits to the **e**
Ezek 48:23 from the **e** side to the west,
Ezek 48:24 from the **e** side to the west,
Ezek 48:25 from the **e** side to the west,
Ezek 48:26 from the **e** side to the west,
Ezek 48:27 from the **e** side to the west,
Ezek 48:32 on the **e** side, four thousand
Dan 8: 9 the south, toward the **e**, and
Dan 11:44 But news from the **e** and the
Hos 12: 1 wind, and pursues the **e** wind
Hos 13:15 an **e** wind shall come
Amos 8:12 to sea, and from north to **e**
Jon 4: 5 sat on the **e** side of the city
Jon 4: 8 prepared a vehement **e** wind
Hab 1: 9 faces are set like the **e** wind
Zech 8: 7 people from the land of the **e**
Zech 14: 4 faces Jerusalem on the **e**
Zech 14: 4 from **e** to west, making a very
Matt 2: 1 from the **E** came to Jerusalem
Matt 2: 2 have seen His star in the **E**
Matt 2: 9 in the **E** went before them
Matt 8:11 that many will come from **e**
Matt 24:27 lightning comes from the **e**
Luke 13:29 They will come from the **e**
Rev 7: 2 angel ascending from the **e**
Rev 16:12 from the **e** might be prepared
Rev 21:13 three gates on the **e**, three

EASTERN (*see* EAST)
Num 32:19 on this **e** side of the Jordan
Num 34:10 You shall mark out your **e**
Num 34:11 reach to the **e** side of the
Josh 12: 1 and all the **e** Jordan plain
Josh 12: 3 the **e** Jordan plain from the
Is 2: 6 they are filled with **e** ways
Ezek 40:10 In the **e** gateway were three
Ezek 40:23 just as the **e** gateway
Ezek 41:14 of the **e** face of the temple
Ezek 47: 8 flows toward the **e** region
Ezek 47:18 along the **e** side of the sea
Ezek 48:21 as far as the **e** border, and
Joel 2:20 his face toward the **e** sea
Zech 14: 8 half of them toward the **e** sea

EASTWARD (*see* EAST)
Gen 2: 8 planted a garden **e** in Eden
Gen 13:14 northward, southward, **e**, and
Gen 25: 6 still living he sent them **e**
Num 34: 3 border shall extend **e** to the
Num 34:15 Jordan, across from Jericho **e**
Josh 11: 8 and to the Valley of Mizpah **e**
Josh 13: 8 them, beyond the Jordan **e**
Josh 13:27 other side of the Jordan **e**
Josh 13:32 of the Jordan, by Jericho **e**
Josh 16: 6 around **e** to Taanath Shiloh
Josh 19:12 Then from Sarid it went **e**
Josh 20: 8 of the Jordan, by Jericho **e**
1Ki 17: 3 Get away from here and turn **e**
2Ki 10:33 from the Jordan **e**
1Ch 5: 9 **E** they settled as far as the
Neh 12:37 as far as the Water Gate **e**
Ezek 11: 1 LORD's house, which faces **e**
Ezek 45: 7 and **e** on the east side, the

EASY (*see* EASIER, EASILY)
2Ki 20:10 It is an **e** thing for the
Prov 14: 6 but knowledge is **e** to him who
Matt 11:30 For My yoke is **e** and My burden
1Co 14: 9 tongue words **e** to understand

EAT (*see* ATE, EATEN, EATER, EATING, EATS, EDIBLE)
Gen 2:16 the garden you may freely **e**
Gen 2:17 good and evil you shall not **e**
Gen 2:17 for in the day that you **e** of
Gen 3: 1 You shall not **e** of every
Gen 3: 2 We may **e** the fruit of the
Gen 3: 3 has said, You shall not **e** it
Gen 3: 5 you **e** of it your eyes will be
Gen 3:11 you that you should not **e**
Gen 3:14 you shall **e** dust all the days
Gen 3:17 You shall not **e** of it'
Gen 3:17 in toil you shall **e** of it all
Gen 3:18 you shall **e** the herb of the
Gen 3:19 of your face you shall **e**
Gen 3:22 of the tree of life, and **e**
Gen 9: 4 But you shall not **e** flesh
Gen 24:33 food was set before him to **e**
Gen 24:33 I will not **e** until I have
Gen 27: 4 bring it to me that I may **e**
Gen 27: 7 food for me, that I may **e** it
Gen 27:10 your father, that he may **e** it
Gen 27:19 **e** of my game, that your soul
Gen 27:25 I will **e** of my son's game, so
Gen 27:31 **e** of his son's game, that
Gen 28:20 going, and give me bread to **e**
Gen 31:54 his brethren to **e** bread
Gen 32:32 not **e** the muscle that shrank
Gen 37:25 And they sat down to **e** a meal
Gen 40:19 the birds will **e** your flesh
Gen 43:25 that they would **e** bread there
Gen 43:32 not **e** food with the Hebrews
Gen 45:18 you will **e** the fat of the
Ex 2:20 Call him, that he may **e** bread
Ex 10: 5 they shall **e** the residue of
Ex 10: 5 they shall **e** every tree which
Ex 10:12 and **e** every herb of the land
Ex 12: 7 of the houses where they **e** it
Ex 12: 8 Then they shall **e** the flesh
Ex 12: 8 bitter herbs they shall **e** it
Ex 12: 9 Do not **e** it raw, nor boiled
Ex 12:11 And thus you shall **e** it
Ex 12:11 So you shall **e** it in haste
Ex 12:15 you shall **e** unleavened bread
Ex 12:16 that which everyone must **e**
Ex 12:18 you shall **e** unleavened bread,
Ex 12:20 You shall **e** nothing leavened
Ex 12:20 you shall **e** unleavened bread
Ex 12:43 No outsider shall **e** it
Ex 12:44 him, then he may **e** it
Ex 12:45 hired servant shall not **e** it
Ex 12:48 person shall **e** it
Ex 13: 6 you shall **e** unleavened bread
Ex 16: 8 you meat to **e** in the evening
Ex 16:12 At twilight you shall **e** meat
Ex 16:15 the LORD has given you to **e**
Ex 16:25 **E** that today, for today is a
Ex 18:12 Israel to **e** bread with Moses'
Ex 22:31 you shall not **e** any meat
Ex 23:11 the poor of your people may **e**
Ex 23:11 the beasts of the field may **e**
Ex 23:15 **e** unleavened bread seven days
Ex 29:32 his sons shall **e** the flesh of
Ex 29:33 They shall **e** those things
Ex 29:33 a stranger shall not **e** them
Ex 32: 6 and the people sat down to **e**
Ex 34:15 and you **e** of his sacrifice,
Ex 34:18 you shall **e** unleavened bread
Lev 3:17 you shall **e** neither fat nor
Lev 6:16 it Aaron and his sons shall **e**
Lev 6:16 of meeting they shall **e** it
Lev 6:18 children of Aaron may **e** it
Lev 6:26 offers it for sin shall **e** it
Lev 6:29 among the priests may **e** it
Lev 7: 6 among the priests may **e** it
Lev 7:19 all who are clean may **e** of it
Lev 7:23 You shall not **e** any fat, of
Lev 7:24 you shall by no means **e** it
Lev 7:26 Moreover you shall not **e** any
Lev 8:31 **e** it there with the bread
Lev 8:31 Aaron and his sons shall **e** it
Lev 10:12 **e** it without leaven beside
Lev 10:13 And you shall **e** it in a holy
Lev 10:14 you shall **e** in a clean place
Lev 11: 2 **e** among all the beasts that
Lev 11: 3 that you may **e**
Lev 11: 4 these you shall not **e** among
Lev 11: 8 Their flesh you shall not **e**
Lev 11: 9 These you may **e** of all that
Lev 11: 9 that you may **e**
Lev 11:11 you shall not **e** their flesh
Lev 11:21 Yet these you may **e** of every
Lev 11:22 These you may **e**
Lev 11:39 beast which you may **e** dies
Lev 11:42 these you shall not **e**, for
Lev 17:12 one among you shall **e** blood
Lev 17:12 sojourns among you **e** blood
Lev 17:14 You shall not **e** the blood of
Lev 19:25 year you may **e** its fruit,
Lev 19:26 You shall not **e** anything
Lev 21:22 He may **e** the bread of his
Lev 22: 4 shall not **e** the holy
Lev 22: 6 and shall not **e** the holy
Lev 22: 7 afterward he may **e** the holy
Lev 22: 8 torn by beasts he shall not **e**
Lev 22:10 shall **e** the holy offering
Lev 22:10 shall not **e** the holy thing
Lev 22:11 with his money, he may **e** it
Lev 22:11 in his house may **e** his food
Lev 22:12 she may not **e** of the holy
Lev 22:13 she may **e** her father's food
Lev 22:13 but no outsider shall **e** it
Lev 22:16 they **e** their holy offerings
Lev 23: 6 you must **e** unleavened bread
Lev 23:14 You shall **e** neither bread
Lev 24: 9 they shall **e** it in a holy
Lev 25:12 you shall **e** its produce from
Lev 25:19 and you will **e** your fill, and
Lev 25:20 say, What shall we **e** in the
Lev 25:22 **e** old produce until the ninth
Lev 25:22 in, you shall **e** of the old
Lev 26: 5 you shall **e** your bread to the
Lev 26:10 You shall **e** the old harvest,
Lev 26:16 for your enemies shall **e** it
Lev 26:26 by weight, and you shall **e**
Lev 26:29 You shall **e** the flesh of your
Lev 26:29 you shall **e** the flesh of your
Lev 26:38 your enemies shall **e** you up
Num 6: 3 nor **e** fresh grapes or raisins
Num 6: 4 of his separation he shall **e**
Num 9:11 They shall **e** it with
Num 11: 4 Who will give us meat to **e**
Num 11:13 Give us meat, that we may **e**
Num 11:18 tomorrow, and you shall **e** meat
Num 11:18 Who will give us meat to **e**
Num 11:18 give you meat, and you shall **e**
Num 11:19 You shall **e**, not one day,
Num 11:21 that they may **e** for a whole
Num 15:19 when you **e** of the bread of
Num 18:10 holy place you shall **e** it
Num 18:10 every male shall **e** it
Num 18:11 clean in your house may **e** it
Num 18:13 clean in your house may **e** it
Num 18:31 You may **e** it in any place,
Deut 2: 6 with money, that you may **e**
Deut 2:28 food for money, that I may **e**
Deut 4:28 see nor hear nor **e** nor smell
Deut 8: 9 will **e** bread without scarcity
Deut 11:15 livestock, that you may **e**
Deut 12: 7 there you shall **e** before the
Deut 12:15 **e** meat within all your gates,
Deut 12:15 and the clean may **e** of it, of
Deut 12:16 you shall not **e** the blood
Deut 12:17 You may not **e** within your
Deut 12:18 But you must **e** them before
Deut 12:20 and you say, Let me **e** meat
Deut 12:20 because you long to **e** meat
Deut 12:20 you may **e** as much meat as
Deut 12:21 you may **e** within your gates
Deut 12:22 are eaten, so you may **e** them
Deut 12:22 and the clean alike may **e** them
Deut 12:23 that you do not **e** the blood
Deut 12:23 you may not **e** the life with
Deut 12:24 You shall not **e** it
Deut 12:25 You shall not **e** it, that it
Deut 12:27 God, and you shall **e** the meat
Deut 14: 3 You shall not **e** any
Deut 14: 4 the animals which you may **e**
Deut 14: 6 you may **e** every animal with
Deut 14: 7 hooves, you shall not **e**, such
Deut 14: 8 you shall not **e** their flesh
Deut 14: 9 These you may **e** of all that
Deut 14: 9 you may **e** all that have fins
Deut 14:10 and scales you shall not **e**
Deut 14:11 All clean birds you may **e**
Deut 14:12 But these you shall not **e**
Deut 14:20 You may **e** all clean birds
Deut 14:21 You shall not **e** anything that
Deut 14:21 your gates, that he may **e** it
Deut 14:23 you shall **e** before the LORD
Deut 14:26 you shall **e** there before the
Deut 14:29 your gates, may come and **e**
Deut 15:20 your household shall **e** it
Deut 15:22 You may **e** it within your
Deut 15:22 clean person alike may **e** it
Deut 15:23 you shall not **e** its blood
Deut 16: 3 You shall **e** no leavened bread
Deut 16: 3 seven days you shall **e**
Deut 16: 7 **e** it in the place which the
Deut 16: 8 you shall **e** unleavened bread
Deut 18: 1 they shall **e** the offerings of
Deut 18: 8 have equal portions to **e**,
Deut 20: 6 battle and another man **e** of it
Deut 20:14 and you shall **e** the enemies'
Deut 20:19 if you can **e** of them, do not
Deut 23:24 you may **e** your fill of grapes
Deut 26:12 so that they may **e** within
Deut 27: 7 offerings, and shall **e** there
Deut 28:31 but you shall not **e** of it
Deut 28:33 **e** the fruit of your land and
Deut 28:39 for the worms shall **e** them

Deut 28:51 they shall **e** the increase of
Deut 28:53 You shall **e** the fruit of your
Deut 28:55 his children whom he will **e**
Deut 28:57 for she will **e** them secretly
Deut 32:13 that he might **e** the produce
Josh 24:13 you **e** of the vineyards and
Judg 13: 4 not to **e** any unclean thing
Judg 13: 7 nor **e** anything unclean, for
Judg 13:14 She may not **e** anything that
Judg 13:14 drink, nor **e** anything unclean
Judg 13:16 Me, I will not **e** your food
Judg 14:14 the eater came something to **e**
Ruth 2:14 **e** of the bread, and dip your
1Sa 1: 7 she wept and did not **e**
1Sa 1: 8 Why do you not **e**
1Sa 2:36 that I may **e** a piece of bread
1Sa 9:13 up to the high place to **e**
1Sa 9:13 will not **e** until he comes
1Sa 9:13 those who are invited will **e**
1Sa 9:19 for you shall **e** with me today
1Sa 9:24 **E**; for until this time
1Sa 14:34 slaughter them here, and **e**
1Sa 20: 5 to sit with the king to **e**
1Sa 20:24 king sat down to **e** the feast
1Sa 20:27 son of Jesse not come to **e**
1Sa 28:22 and **e**, that you may have
1Sa 28:23 I will not **e**
2Sa 3:35 came to persuade David to **e**
2Sa 9: 7 you shall **e** bread at my table
2Sa 9:10 son may have food to **e**
2Sa 9:10 your master's son shall **e**
2Sa 9:11 he shall **e** at my table like
2Sa 11:11 I then go to my house to **e**
2Sa 12:17 nor did he **e** food with them
2Sa 13: 5 see it and **e** it from her hand
2Sa 13: 6 that I may **e** from her hand
2Sa 13: 9 him, but he refused to **e**
2Sa 13:10 that I may **e** from your hand
2Sa 13:11 had brought them to him to **e**
2Sa 16: 2 fruit for the young men to **e**
2Sa 17:29 people who were with him to **e**
2Sa 19:28 those who **e** at your own table
2Sa 19:35 what I **e** or what I drink
1Ki 2: 7 those who **e** at your table
1Ki 13: 8 nor would I **e** bread nor drink
1Ki 13: 9 You shall not **e** bread, nor
1Ki 13:15 Come home with me and **e** bread
1Ki 13:16 neither can I **e** bread nor
1Ki 13:17 You shall not **e** bread nor
1Ki 13:18 house, that he may **e** bread
1Ki 13:22 **E** no bread and drink no water,
1Ki 14:11 The dogs shall **e** whoever
1Ki 14:11 **e** whoever dies in the field
1Ki 16: 4 The dogs shall **e** whoever
1Ki 16: 4 **e** whoever dies in the fields
1Ki 17:12 and my son, that we may **e** it
1Ki 18:19 who **e** at Jezebel's table
1Ki 18:41 Go up, **e** and drink
1Ki 18:42 So Ahab went up to **e** and drink
1Ki 19: 5 said to him, Arise and **e**."
1Ki 19: 7 Arise and **e**, because the
1Ki 21: 4 his face, and would **e** no food
1Ki 21: 5 so sullen that you **e** no food
1Ki 21: 7 **e** food, and let your heart be
1Ki 21:23 The dogs shall **e** Jezebel by
1Ki 21:24 The dogs shall **e** whoever
1Ki 21:24 **e** whoever dies in the field
2Ki 4: 8 him to **e** some food
2Ki 4: 8 in there to **e** some food
2Ki 4:40 served it to the men to **e**
2Ki 4:40 And they could not **e** it
2Ki 4:41 the people, that they may **e**
2Ki 4:42 the people, that they may **e**
2Ki 4:43 the people, that they may **e**
2Ki 4:43 They shall **e** and have some
2Ki 6:22 before them, that they may **e**
2Ki 6:28 son, that we may **e** him today
2Ki 6:28 we will **e** my son tomorrow
2Ki 6:29 your son, that we may **e** him'
2Ki 7: 2 but you shall not **e** of it
2Ki 7:19 but you shall not **e** of it
2Ki 9:10 The dogs shall **e** Jezebel in
2Ki 9:36 shall **e** the flesh of Jezebel
2Ki 18:27 sit on the wall, who will **e**
2Ki 18:31 every one of you **e** from his
2Ki 19:29 You shall **e** this year such as
2Ki 19:29 and **e** the fruit of them
2Ch 31:10 LORD, we have had enough to **e**
Ezra 2:63 not **e** of the most holy things
Ezra 9:12 **e** the good of the land, and

Neh 5: 2 grain for them, that we may **e**
Neh 7:65 not **e** of the most holy things
Neh 8:10 **e** the fat, drink the sweet,
Neh 8:12 people went their way to **e**
Neh 9:36 to **e** its fruit and its good
Esth 4:16 neither **e** nor drink for three
Job 1: 4 their three sisters to **e** and
Job 3:24 my sighing comes before I **e**
Job 5: 5 the hungry **e** up his harvest
Job 20:21 Nothing is left for him to **e**
Job 31: 8 Then let me sow, and another **e**
Job 31:17 fatherless may not **e** of it
Ps 14: 4 Who **e** up my people as they
Ps 14: 4 up my people as they **e** bread
Ps 22:26 The poor shall **e** and be
Ps 22:29 of the earth Shall **e** and
Ps 27: 2 against me To **e** up my flesh
Ps 50:13 Will I **e** the flesh of bulls,
Ps 53: 4 Who **e** up my people as they
Ps 53: 4 up my people as they **e** bread
Ps 78:24 down manna on them to **e**, And
Ps 102: 4 that I forget to **e** my bread
Ps 127: 2 To **e** the bread of sorrows
Ps 128: 2 When you **e** the labor of your
Ps 141: 4 And do not let me **e** of their
Prov 1:31 therefore they shall **e** the
Prov 4:17 For they **e** the bread of
Prov 9: 5 **e** of my bread and drink of the
Prov 13: 2 A man shall **e** well by the
Prov 18:21 who love it will **e** its fruit
Prov 23: 1 sit down to **e** with a ruler
Prov 23: 6 Do not **e** the bread of a miser
Prov 23: 7 **E** and drink!" he says to you
Prov 24:13 **e** honey because it is good,
Prov 25:16 **E** only as much as you need,
Prov 25:21 hungry, give him bread to **e**
Prov 25:27 is not good to **e** much honey
Prov 27:18 the fig tree will **e** its fruit
Prov 30:17 and the young eagles will **e** it
Prov 31:27 and does not **e** the bread of
Eccl 2:24 a man than that he should **e**
Eccl 2:25 For who can **e**, or who can
Eccl 3:13 also that every man should **e**
Eccl 5:11 they increase who **e** them
Eccl 5:18 good and fitting for one to **e**
Eccl 5:19 and given him power to **e** of it
Eccl 6: 2 not give him power to **e** of it
Eccl 8:15 under the sun than to **e**,
Eccl 9: 7 **e** your bread with joy, and
Song 4:16 and **e** its pleasant fruits
Song 5: 1 (TO HIS FRIENDS) **E**, O friends
Is 1:19 you shall **e** the good of the
Is 3:10 for they shall **e** the fruit of
Is 4: 1 We will **e** our own food and
Is 5:17 fat ones strangers shall **e**
Is 7:15 Curds and honey He shall **e**
Is 7:22 give, that he will **e** curds
Is 7:22 honey everyone will **e** who is
Is 9:20 every man shall **e** the flesh
Is 11: 7 the lion shall **e** straw like
Is 21: 5 a watchman in the tower, **e**
Is 22:13 Let us **e** and drink, for
Is 23:18 to **e** sufficiently, and for
Is 30:24 ground will **e** cured fodder
Is 36:12 sit on the wall, who will **e**
Is 36:16 every one of you **e** from his
Is 37:30 You shall **e** this year such as
Is 37:30 and **e** the fruit of them
Is 50: 9 the moth will **e** them up
Is 51: 8 For the moth will **e** them up
Is 51: 8 the worm will **e** them like
Is 55: 1 have no money, come, buy and **e**
Is 55: 2 **e** what is good, and let your
Is 61: 6 you shall **e** the riches of the
Is 62: 9 have gathered it shall **e** it
Is 65: 4 who **e** swine's flesh, and the
Is 65:13 Behold, My servants shall **e**
Is 65:21 vineyards and **e** their fruit
Is 65:22 shall not plant and another **e**
Is 65:25 the lion shall **e** straw like
Jer 2: 7 to **e** its fruit and its
Jer 5:17 they shall **e** up your harvest
Jer 5:17 sons and daughters should **e**
Jer 5:17 They shall **e** up your flocks
Jer 5:17 they shall **e** up your vines and
Jer 7:21 to your sacrifices and **e** meat
Jer 16: 8 to sit with them, to **e** and
Jer 19: 9 I will cause them to **e** the
Jer 19: 9 everyone shall **e** the flesh of
Jer 22:15 Did not your father **e** and

Jer 22:22 The wind shall **e** up all your
Jer 29: 5 gardens and **e** their fruit
Jer 29:28 gardens and **e** their fruit
Jer 31: 5 and **e** them as ordinary food
Lam 2:20 the women **e** their offspring
Ezek 2: 8 mouth and **e** what I give you
Ezek 3: 1 Son of man, **e** what you find
Ezek 3: 1 **e** this scroll, and go, speak
Ezek 3: 2 He caused me to **e** that scroll
Ezek 4: 9 ninety days, you shall **e** it
Ezek 4:10 you **e** shall be by weight,
Ezek 4:10 time to time you shall **e** it
Ezek 4:12 And you shall **e** it as barley
Ezek 4:13 the children of Israel **e**
Ezek 4:16 they shall **e** bread by weight
Ezek 5:10 **e** their sons in your midst
Ezek 5:10 sons shall **e** their fathers
Ezek 12:18 **e** your bread with quaking, and
Ezek 12:19 They shall **e** their bread with
Ezek 22: 9 those who **e** on the mountains
Ezek 24:17 and do not **e** man's bread of
Ezek 24:22 nor **e** man's bread of sorrow
Ezek 25: 4 they shall **e** your fruit, and
Ezek 33:25 You **e** meat with blood, you
Ezek 34: 3 You **e** the fat and clothe
Ezek 34:19 they **e** what you have trampled
Ezek 39:17 Israel, that you may **e** flesh
Ezek 39:18 You shall **e** the flesh of the
Ezek 39:19 You shall **e** fat till you are
Ezek 42:13 **e** the most holy offerings
Ezek 44: 3 he may sit in it to **e** bread
Ezek 44:29 They shall **e** the grain
Ezek 44:31 priests shall not **e** anything
Dan 1:12 them give us vegetables to **e**
Dan 1:13 of the young men who **e** the
Dan 4:25 make you **e** grass like oxen
Dan 4:32 make you **e** grass like oxen
Dan 11:26 those who **e** of the portion of
Hos 2:12 of the field shall **e** them
Hos 4: 8 They **e** up the sin of My
Hos 4:10 For they shall **e**, but not
Hos 8:13 **e** it, but the LORD does not
Hos 9: 3 shall **e** unclean things in
Hos 9: 4 all who **e** it shall be defiled
Joel 2:26 You shall **e** in plenty and be
Amos 6: 4 **e** lambs from the flock and
Amos 7:12 There **e** bread, and there
Amos 9:14 gardens and **e** fruit from them
Obad 7 Those who **e** your bread shall
Jon 3: 7 do not let them **e**, or drink
Mic 3: 3 Who also **e** the flesh of My
Mic 6:14 You shall **e**, but not be
Mic 7: 1 there is no cluster to **e** of
Nah 3:15 it will **e** you up like a
Hab 1: 8 the eagle that hastens to **e**
Hag 1: 6 you **e**, but do not have enough
Zech 7: 6 When you **e** and when you drink
Zech 7: 6 when you drink, do you not **e**
Zech 11: 9 are left **e** each other's flesh
Zech 11:16 But he will **e** the flesh of
Matt 6:25 what you will **e** or what you
Matt 6:31 saying, What shall we **e**
Matt 9:11 Teacher **e** with tax collectors
Matt 12: 1 pluck heads of grain and to **e**
Matt 12: 4 was not lawful for him to **e**
Matt 14:16 You give them something to **e**
Matt 15: 2 their hands when they **e** bread
Matt 15:20 but to **e** with unwashed hands
Matt 15:27 yet even the little dogs **e**
Matt 15:32 days and have nothing to **e**
Matt 24:49 his fellow servants, and to **e**
Matt 26:17 for You to **e** the Passover
Matt 26:26 Take, **e**; this is My body."
Mark 2:26 which is not lawful to **e**
Mark 3:20 could not so much as **e** bread
Mark 5:43 should be given her to **e**
Mark 6:31 did not even have time to **e**
Mark 6:36 for they have nothing to **e**
Mark 6:37 You give them something to **e**
Mark 6:37 and give them something to **e**
Mark 7: 2 **e** bread with defiled, that is
Mark 7: 3 all the Jews do not **e** unless
Mark 7: 4 they do not **e** unless they
Mark 7: 5 but **e** bread with unwashed
Mark 7:28 **e** from the children's crumbs
Mark 8: 1 great and having nothing to **e**
Mark 8: 2 days and have nothing to **e**
Mark 11:14 Let no one **e** fruit from you
Mark 14:12 that You may **e** the Passover
Mark 14:14 I may **e** the Passover with My

Mark 14:22 Take, e; this is My body."
Luke 5:30 Why do You e and drink with
Luke 5:33 of the Pharisees, but Yours e
Luke 6: 4 for any but the priests to e
Luke 7:36 asked Him to e with him
Luke 7:36 house, and sat down to e
Luke 8:55 she be given something to e
Luke 9:13 You give them something to e
Luke 10: 8 you, e such things as are set
Luke 11:37 He went in and sat down to e
Luke 12:19 e, drink, and be merry
Luke 12:22 your life, what you will e
Luke 12:29 e or what you should drink
Luke 12:37 and have them sit down to e
Luke 12:45 and maidservants, and to e and
Luke 14: 1 to e bread on the Sabbath
Luke 14:15 Blessed is he who shall e
Luke 15:23 here and kill it, and let us e
Luke 17: 7 at once and sit down to e'
Luke 17: 8 and afterward you will e and
Luke 22: 8 for us, that we may e
Luke 22:11 I may e the Passover with My
Luke 22:15 to e this Passover with you
Luke 22:16 you, I will no longer e of it
Luke 22:30 that you may e and drink at My
John 4:31 saying, "Rabbi, e."
John 4:32 I have food to e of which you
John 4:33 brought Him anything to e
John 6: 5 buy bread, that these may e
John 6:31 them bread from heaven to e
John 6:50 heaven, that one may e of it
John 6:52 Man give us His flesh to e
John 6:53 unless you e the flesh of the
John 18:28 they might e the Passover
John 21:12 them, "Come and e breakfast
Acts 10:10 very hungry and wanted to e
Acts 10:13 Rise, Peter; kill and e."
Acts 11: 7 Rise, Peter; kill and e.'
Acts 23:12 e nor drink till they had
Acts 23:14 will e nothing until we have
Acts 23:21 e nor drink till they have
Acts 27:35 had broken it he began to e
Rom 14: 2 believes he may e all things
Rom 14: 3 despise him who does not e
Rom 14: 3 does not e judge him who eats
Rom 14: 6 and he who does not e, to the
Rom 14: 6 to the Lord he does not e
Rom 14:21 It is good neither to e meat
Rom 14:23 he does not e from faith
1Co 5:11 not even to e with such a
1Co 8: 7 until now e it as a thing
1Co 8: 8 if we e are we the better
1Co 8: 8 we do not e are we the worse
1Co 8:10 to e those things offered to
1Co 8:13 I will never again e meat
1Co 9: 4 Do we have no right to e and
1Co 9: 7 and does not e of its fruit
1Co 9:13 minister the holy things e of
1Co 10: 7 The people sat down to e and
1Co 10:18 Are not those who e of the
1Co 10:25 E whatever is sold in the
1Co 10:27 e whatever is set before you,
1Co 10:28 do not e it for the sake of
1Co 10:31 whether you e or drink, or
1Co 11:20 it is not to e the Lord's
1Co 11:22 Do you not have houses to e
1Co 11:24 Take, e; this is My body
1Co 11:26 as often as you e this bread
1Co 11:28 so let him e of that bread and
1Co 11:33 when you come together to e
1Co 11:34 is hungry, let him e at home
1Co 15:32 Let us e and drink, for
Gal 2:12 he would e with the Gentiles
2Th 3: 8 nor did we e anyone's bread
2Th 3:10 not work, neither shall he e
2Th 3:12 and e their own bread
Heb 13:10 tabernacle have no right to e
Jas 5: 3 will e your flesh like fire
Rev 2: 7 to e from the tree of life
Rev 2:14 to e things sacrificed to
Rev 2:17 some of the hidden manna to e
Rev 2:20 to e things sacrificed to
Rev 10: 9 he said to me, Take and e it
Rev 17:16 e her flesh and burn her with
Rev 19:18 that you may e the flesh of

EATEN (*see* EAT)
Gen 3:11 Have you e from the tree of
Gen 3:17 have e from the tree of which
Gen 6:21 of all food that is e, and you
Gen 14:24 what the young men have e
Gen 31:38 I have not e the rams of your
Gen 41:21 When they had e them up, no
Gen 41:21 known that they had e them
Gen 43: 2 when they had e up the grain
Ex 12:46 In one house it shall be e
Ex 13: 3 No leavened bread shall be e
Ex 13: 7 bread shall be e seven days
Ex 21:28 and its flesh shall not be e
Ex 29:34 It shall not be e, because it
Lev 6:16 it shall be e in a holy place
Lev 6:23 It shall not be e
Lev 6:26 In a holy place it shall be e
Lev 6:30 in the holy place, shall be e
Lev 7: 6 It shall be e in a holy place
Lev 7:15 for thanksgiving shall be e
Lev 7:16 it shall be e the same day
Lev 7:16 remainder of it also may be e
Lev 7:18 is e at all on the third day
Lev 7:19 unclean thing shall not be e
Lev 10:17 Why have you not e the sin
Lev 10:18 have e it in a holy place
Lev 10:19 If I had e the sin offering
Lev 11:13 they shall not be e, they are
Lev 11:41 It shall not be e
Lev 11:47 the animal that may be e and
Lev 11:47 the animal that may not be e
Lev 17:13 animal or bird that may be e
Lev 19: 6 It shall be e the same day
Lev 19: 7 And if it is e at all on the
Lev 19:23 It shall not be e
Lev 22:30 On the same day it shall be e
Num 28:17 shall be e for seven days
Deut 6:11 when you have e and are full
Deut 8:10 When you have e and are full,
Deut 8:12 when you have e and are full,
Deut 12:22 the gazelle and the deer are e
Deut 14:19 they shall not be e
Deut 20: 6 and has not yet e of it
Deut 26:14 I have not e any of it when
Deut 29: 6 you have not e bread, nor
Deut 31:20 their fathers, and they have e
Josh 5:12 had e the produce of the land
Ruth 3: 7 And after Boaz had e and drunk,
1Sa 14:30 better if the people had e
1Sa 28:20 for he had e no food all day
1Sa 30:12 So when he had e, his
1Sa 30:12 for he had e no bread nor
2Sa 19:42 Have we ever e at the king's
1Ki 13:23 it was, after he had e bread
1Ki 13:28 The lion had not e the corpse
Job 6: 6 food be e without salt
Job 21:25 never having e with pleasure
Job 31:17 or e my morsel by myself, so
Job 31:39 if I have e its fruit without
Ps 69: 9 for Your house has e me up
Ps 102: 9 For I have e ashes like bread
Prov 9:17 bread e in secret is pleasant
Prov 23: 8 The morsel you have e, you
Song 5: 1 I have e my honeycomb with my
Is 3:14 For you have e up the
Is 44:19 I have roasted meat and e it
Jer 10:25 for they have e up Jacob,
Jer 24: 2 bad figs which could not be e
Jer 24: 3 very bad, which cannot be e
Jer 24: 8 bad figs which cannot be e
Jer 29:17 rotten figs that cannot be e
Jer 31:29 fathers have e sour grapes
Ezek 4:14 I have never e what died of
Ezek 18: 2 fathers have e sour grapes
Ezek 18: 6 if he has not e on the
Ezek 18:11 but has e on the mountains or
Ezek 18:15 Who has not e on the
Ezek 34:18 to have e up the good pasture
Ezek 45:21 unleavened bread shall be e
Hos 10:13 You have e the fruit of lies,
Joel 1: 4 the swarming locust has e
Joel 1: 4 the crawling locust has e
Joel 1: 4 the consuming locust has e
Joel 2:25 the swarming locust has e
Matt 14:21 Now those who had e were
Mark 6:44 Now those who had e the
Mark 8: 9 Now those who had e were
Luke 17: 8 and serve me till I have e
John 2:17 for Your house has e Me up
John 6:13 left over by those who had e
John 21:15 So when they had e breakfast
Acts 10:14 For I have never e anything
Acts 12:23 he was e by worms and died
Acts 20:11 up, had broken bread and e
Acts 27:33 without food, and e nothing
Acts 27:38 So when they had e enough
Rev 10:10 But when I had e it, my

EATER (*see* EAT, EATERS)
Judg 14:14 Out of the e came something
Is 55:10 the sower and bread to the e
Nah 3:12 fall into the mouth of the e

EATERS (*see* EATER)
Prov 23:20 or with gluttonous e of meat

EATING (*see* EAT)
Lev 13:55 it continues e away, whether
Judg 14: 9 in his hands and went along, e
Ruth 3: 3 man until he has finished e
1Sa 1: 9 after they had finished e
1Sa 14:33 the LORD by e with the blood
1Sa 14:34 the LORD by e with the blood
1Sa 30:16 out over all the land, e and
1Ki 1:25 They are e and drinking before
1Ki 1:41 heard it as they finished e
1Ki 4:20 by the sea in multitude, e
2Ki 4:40 as they were e the stew,
1Ch 12:39 with David three days, e and
Job 1:13 his sons and daughters were e
Job 1:18 Your sons and daughters were e
Job 20:23 rain it on him while he is e
Is 22:13 e meat and drinking wine
Is 66:17 midst, e swine's flesh and the
Amos 7: 2 e the grass of the land, that
Matt 11:18 came neither e nor drinking
Matt 11:19 The Son of Man came e and
Matt 24:38 before the flood, they were e
Matt 26:21 Now as they were e, He said,
Matt 26:26 And as they were e, Jesus took
Mark 2:16 Pharisees saw Him e with the
Mark 14:22 And as they were e, Jesus took
Luke 7:33 e bread nor drinking wine
Luke 7:34 The Son of Man has come e
Luke 10: 7 remain in the same house, e
1Co 8: 4 Therefore concerning the e of
1Co 8:10 e in an idol's temple, will
1Co 11:21 For in e, each one takes his

EATS (*see* EAT)
Ex 12:15 For whoever e leavened bread
Ex 12:19 since whoever e what is
Lev 7:18 the person who e of it shall
Lev 7:20 But the person who e the
Lev 7:21 and who e the flesh of the
Lev 7:25 For whoever e the fat of the
Lev 7:25 the person who e it shall be
Lev 7:27 Whoever e any blood, that
Lev 11:40 He who e of its carcass
Lev 14:47 he who e in the house shall
Lev 17:10 who e any blood, I will set
Lev 17:10 that person who e blood, and
Lev 17:14 Whoever e it shall be cut off
Lev 17:15 every person who e what died
Lev 19: 8 Therefore everyone who e it
Lev 22:14 if a man e the holy offering
1Sa 14:24 Cursed is the man who e any
1Sa 14:28 the man who e food this day
Job 40:15 he e grass like an ox
Ps 106:20 image of an ox that e grass
Prov 13:25 The righteous e to the
Prov 30:20 she e and wipes her mouth, and
Eccl 5:12 whether he e little or much
Eccl 5:17 days he also e in darkness
Is 28: 4 he e it up while it is still
Is 29: 8 and look—he e
Is 44:16 with this half he e meat
Is 59: 5 he who e of their eggs dies,
Jer 31:30 every man who e the sour
Mark 2:16 How is it that He e and drinks
Mark 14:18 one of you who e with Me will
Luke 15: 2 sinners and e with them
John 6:51 If anyone e of this bread, he
John 6:54 Whoever e My flesh and drinks
John 6:56 He who e My flesh and drinks
John 6:58 He who e this bread will live
John 13:18 He who e bread with Me has
Rom 14: 2 who is weak e only vegetables
Rom 14: 3 Let not him who e despise him
Rom 14: 3 does not eat judge him who e
Rom 14: 6 He who e, e to the Lord,
Rom 14:20 the man who e with offense
Rom 14:23 doubts is condemned if he e
1Co 11:27 Therefore whoever e this
1Co 11:29 For he who e and drinks in an
1Co 11:29 in an unworthy manner e and

Jer 49:22 E in that day shall be like
Lam 4:21 and be glad, O daughter of E
Lam 4:22 iniquity, O daughter of E
Ezek 25:12 Because of what E did against
Ezek 25:13 stretch out My hand against E
Ezek 25:14 on E by the hand of My people
Ezek 25:14 Israel, that they may do in E
Ezek 32:29 There is E, her kings and all
Ezek 35:15 Seir, as well as all of E
Ezek 36: 5 the nations and against all E
Dan 11:41 E, Moab, and the prominent
Joel 3:19 and E a desolate wilderness,
Amos 1: 6 to deliver them up to E
Amos 1: 9 up the whole captivity to E
Amos 1:11 For three transgressions of E
Amos 2: 1 of the king of E to lime
Amos 9:12 may possess the remnant of E
Obad 1 E (We have heard a report
Obad 8 destroy the wise men from E
Mal 1: 4 Even though E has said, "We

EDOMITE (*see* EDOM, EDOMITES)
Deut 23: 7 You shall not abhor an E, for
1Sa 21: 7 And his name was Doeg, an E
1Sa 22: 9 Then answered Doeg the E, who
1Sa 22:18 So Doeg the E turned and
1Sa 22:22 when Doeg the E was there
1Ki 11:14 against Solomon, Hadad the E

EDOMITES (*see* EDOMITE)
Gen 36: 9 father of the E in Mount Seir
Gen 36:43 Esau was the father of the E
2Sa 8:14 and all the E became David's
1Ki 11: 1 of the Moabites, Ammonites, E
1Ki 11:17 certain E of his father's
2Ki 8:21 and attacked the E who had
2Ki 14: 7 E in the Valley of Salt, and
2Ki 16: 6 Then the E went to Elath, and
1Ch 18:12 E in the Valley of Salt
1Ch 18:13 and all the E became David's
2Ch 21: 8 In his days the E revolted
2Ch 21: 9 and attacked the E who had
2Ch 21:10 Thus the E have been in
2Ch 25:14 from the slaughter of the E
2Ch 25:19 that you have defeated the E
2Ch 28:17 For again the E had come,

EDREI
Num 21:33 his people, to battle at E
Deut 1: 4 who dwelt at Ashtaroth in E
Deut 3: 1 his people, to battle at E
Deut 3:10 Bashan, as far as Salcah and E
Josh 12: 4 dwelt at Ashtaroth and at E
Josh 13:12 who reigned in Ashtaroth and E
Josh 13:31 of Gilead, and Ashtaroth and E
Josh 19:37 Kedesh, E, En Hazor,

EFFECT (*see* EFFECTIVE)
1Sa 21: 5 and the bread is in e common
2Ch 34:22 they spoke to her to that e
Ps 33:10 plans of the peoples of no e
Is 32:17 and the e of righteousness,
Matt 15: 6 God of no e by your tradition
Mark 7:13 the word of God of no e
Rom 3: 3 faithfulness of God without e
Rom 4:14 and the promise made of no e
Rom 9: 6 word of God has taken no e
1Co 1:17 Christ should be made of no e
Gal 3:17 make the promise of no e

EFFECTIVE (*see* EFFECT, EFFECTIVELY)
Prov 17:10 Reproof is more e for a wise
1Co 16: 9 e door has opened to me, and
2Co 1: 6 which is e for enduring the
Eph 3: 7 by the e working of His power
Eph 4:16 according to the e working by
Phm 6 e by the acknowledgment of
Jas 5:16 The e, fervent prayer of a

EFFECTIVELY (*see* EFFECTIVE)
Gal 2: 8 who worked e in Peter for the
Gal 2: 8 e in me toward the Gentiles)
1Th 2:13 which also e works in you who

EFFORT
Luke 12:58 make every e along the way to

EGG (*see* EGGS)
Job 6: 6 taste in the white of an e
Luke 11:12 Or if he asks for an e, will

EGGS (*see* EGG)
Deut 22: 6 ground, with young ones or e
Deut 22: 6 on the young or on the e, you
Job 39:14 leaves her e on the ground
Is 10:14 one gathers e that are left
Is 34:15 shall make her nest and lay e
Is 59: 5 They hatch vipers' e and weave
Is 59: 5 he who eats of their e dies

EGLAH (*see* MICHAL)
2Sa 3: 5 Ithream, by David's wife E
1Ch 3: 3 sixth, Ithream, by his wife E

EGLAIM (*see* EN EGLAIM)
Is 15: 8 of Moab, its wailing to E

EGLON (*see* EGLON'S)
Josh 10: 3 Lachish, and Debir king of E
Josh 10: 5 of Lachish, and the king of E
Josh 10:23 of Lachish, and the king of E
Josh 10:34 Lachish Joshua passed to E
Josh 10:36 Then Joshua went up from E
Josh 10:37 to all that he had done to E
Josh 12:12 the king of E, one
Josh 15:39 Lachish, Bozkath, E,
Judg 3:12 So the LORD strengthened E
Judg 3:14 children of Israel served E
Judg 3:15 tribute to E king of Moab
Judg 3:17 the tribute to E king of Moab
Judg 3:17 (Now E was a very fat man

EGLON'S (*see* EGLON)
Judg 3:24 E servants came to look, and

EGYPT (*see* EGYPTIAN, GOSHEN, MIZRAIM)
Gen 12:10 down to E to sojourn there
Gen 12:11 he was close to entering E
Gen 12:14 was, when Abram came into E
Gen 13: 1 Then Abram went up from E
Gen 13:10 like the land of E as you go
Gen 15:18 from the river of E to the
Gen 21:21 for him from the land of E
Gen 25:18 which is east of E as you go
Gen 26: 2 Do not go down to E
Gen 37:25 way to carry them down to E
Gen 37:28 And they took Joseph to E
Gen 37:36 had sold him in E to Potiphar
Gen 39: 1 had been taken down to E
Gen 40: 1 king of E offended their lord
Gen 40: 1 their lord, the king of E
Gen 40: 5 and the baker of the king of E
Gen 41: 8 for all the magicians of E
Gen 41:19 seen in all the land of E
Gen 41:29 throughout all the land of E
Gen 41:30 be forgotten in the land of E
Gen 41:33 and set him over the land of E
Gen 41:34 of E in the seven plentiful
Gen 41:36 shall be in the land of E
Gen 41:41 you over all the land of E
Gen 41:43 him over all the land of E
Gen 41:44 or foot in all the land of E
Gen 41:45 out over all the land of E
Gen 41:46 before Pharaoh king of E
Gen 41:46 throughout all the land of E
Gen 41:48 which were in the land of E
Gen 41:53 were in the land of E ended
Gen 41:54 the land of E there was bread
Gen 41:55 the land of E was famished
Gen 41:56 severe in the land of E
Gen 41:57 to Joseph in E to buy grain
Gen 42: 1 saw that there was grain in E
Gen 42: 2 that there is grain in E
Gen 42: 3 went down to buy grain in E
Gen 43: 2 which they had brought from E
Gen 43:15 and arose and went down to E
Gen 45: 4 brother, whom you sold into E
Gen 45: 8 throughout all the land of E
Gen 45: 9 God has made me lord of all E
Gen 45:13 father of all my glory in E
Gen 45:18 you the best of the land of E
Gen 45:19 of E for your little ones
Gen 45:20 of all the land of E is yours
Gen 45:23 with the good things of E
Gen 45:25 Then they went up out of E
Gen 45:26 over all the land of E
Gen 46: 3 do not fear to go down to E
Gen 46: 4 I will go down with you to E
Gen 46: 6 land of Canaan, and went to E
Gen 46: 7 he brought with him to E
Gen 46: 8 and his sons, who went to E
Gen 46:20 land of E were born Manasseh
Gen 46:26 who went with Jacob to E, who
Gen 46:27 to him in E were two persons
Gen 46:27 who went to E were seventy
Gen 47: 6 The land of E is before you
Gen 47:11 a possession in the land of E
Gen 47:13 severe, so that the land of E
Gen 47:14 was found in the land of E
Gen 47:15 money failed in the land of E
Gen 47:20 all the land of E for Pharaoh
Gen 47:21 borders of E to the other end
Gen 47:26 the land of E to this day
Gen 47:27 Israel dwelt in the land of E
Gen 47:28 the land of E seventeen years
Gen 47:29 Please do not bury me in E
Gen 47:30 you shall carry me out of E
Gen 48: 5 of E before I came to you in
Gen 48: 5 before I came to you in E
Gen 50: 7 the elders of the land of E
Gen 50:14 father, Joseph returned to E
Gen 50:22 So Joseph dwelt in E, he and
Gen 50:26 he was put in a coffin in E
Ex 1: 1 of Israel who came to E
Ex 1: 5 (for Joseph was in E already)
Ex 1: 8 there arose a new king over E
Ex 1:15 Then the king of E spoke to
Ex 1:17 the king of E commanded them
Ex 1:18 So the king of E called for
Ex 2:23 time that the king of E died
Ex 3: 7 of My people who are in E
Ex 3:10 children of Israel, out of E
Ex 3:11 children of Israel out of E
Ex 3:12 brought the people out of E
Ex 3:16 seen what is done to you in E
Ex 3:17 of E to the land of the
Ex 3:18 of Israel, to the king of E
Ex 3:19 king of E will not let you go
Ex 3:20 strike E with all My wonders
Ex 4:18 to my brethren who are in E
Ex 4:19 Go, return to E
Ex 4:20 he returned to the land of E
Ex 4:21 When you go back to E, see
Ex 5: 4 the king of E said to them
Ex 5:12 E to gather stubble instead
Ex 6:11 speak to Pharaoh king of E
Ex 6:13 and for Pharaoh king of E, to
Ex 6:13 Israel out of the land of E
Ex 6:26 E according to their armies
Ex 6:27 spoke to Pharaoh king of E
Ex 6:27 the children of Israel from E
Ex 6:28 to Moses in the land of E
Ex 6:29 of E all that I say to you
Ex 7: 3 My wonders in the land of E
Ex 7: 4 that I may lay My hand on E
Ex 7: 4 land of E by great judgments
Ex 7: 5 I stretch out My hand on E
Ex 7:11 so the magicians of E, they
Ex 7:19 hand over the waters of E
Ex 7:19 throughout all the land of E
Ex 7:21 throughout all the land of E
Ex 7:22 of E did so with their
Ex 8: 5 to come up on the land of E
Ex 8: 6 his hand over the waters of E
Ex 8: 6 up and covered the land of E
Ex 8: 7 up frogs on the land of E
Ex 8:16 throughout all the land of E
Ex 8:17 throughout all the land of E
Ex 8:24 and into all the land of E
Ex 9: 4 Israel and the livestock of E
Ex 9: 6 all the livestock of E died
Ex 9: 9 dust in all the land of E
Ex 9: 9 throughout all the land of E
Ex 9:18 such as has not been in E
Ex 9:22 be hail in all the land of E
Ex 9:22 throughout the land of E
Ex 9:23 rained hail on the land of E
Ex 9:24 of E since it became a nation
Ex 9:25 the whole land of E, all that
Ex 10: 2 things I have done in E, and
Ex 10: 7 yet know that E is destroyed
Ex 10:12 the land of E for the locusts
Ex 10:12 may come upon the land of E
Ex 10:13 his rod over the land of E
Ex 10:14 up over all the land of E
Ex 10:14 on all the territory of E
Ex 10:15 throughout all the land of E
Ex 10:19 in all the territory of E
Ex 10:21 darkness over the land of E
Ex 10:22 all the land of E three days
Ex 11: 1 plague on Pharaoh and on E
Ex 11: 3 very great in the land of E
Ex 11: 4 go out into the midst of E
Ex 11: 5 in the land of E shall die
Ex 11: 6 throughout all the land of E
Ex 11: 9 multiplied in the land of E
Ex 12: 1 and Aaron in the land of E
Ex 12:12 the land of E on that night

Ex 12:12 firstborn in the land of **E**
Ex 12:12 of **E** I will execute judgment
Ex 12:13 when I strike the land of **E**
Ex 12:17 armies out of the land of **E**
Ex 12:27 in **E** when He struck the
Ex 12:29 firstborn in the land of **E**
Ex 12:30 and there was a great cry in **E**
Ex 12:39 they had brought out of **E**
Ex 12:39 they were driven out of **E**
Ex 12:40 lived in **E** was four hundred
Ex 12:41 went out from the land of **E**
Ex 12:42 them out of the land of **E**
Ex 12:51 **E** according to their armies
Ex 13: 3 in which you went out of **E**
Ex 13: 8 for me when I came up from **E**
Ex 13: 9 LORD has brought you out of **E**
Ex 13:14 the LORD brought us out of **E**
Ex 13:15 firstborn in the land of **E**
Ex 13:16 the LORD brought us out of **E**
Ex 13:17 they see war, and return to **E**
Ex 13:18 ranks out of the land of **E**
Ex 14: 5 of **E** that the people had fled
Ex 14: 7 all the chariots of **E** with
Ex 14: 8 heart of Pharaoh king of **E**
Ex 14:11 there were no graves in **E**
Ex 14:11 us, to bring us up out of **E**
Ex 14:12 word that we told you in **E**
Ex 14:31 which the LORD had done in **E**
Ex 16: 1 departed from the land of **E**
Ex 16: 3 of the LORD in the land of **E**
Ex 16: 6 you out of the land of **E**
Ex 16:32 you out of the land of **E**
Ex 17: 3 have brought us up out of **E**
Ex 18: 1 had brought Israel out of **E**
Ex 19: 1 had gone out of the land of **E**
Ex 20: 2 you out of the land of **E**, out
Ex 22:21 strangers in the land of **E**
Ex 23: 9 strangers in the land of **E**
Ex 23:15 for in it you came out of **E**
Ex 29:46 them up out of the land of **E**
Ex 32: 1 us up out of the land of **E**
Ex 32: 4 you out of the land of **E**
Ex 32: 7 **E** have corrupted themselves
Ex 32: 8 you out of the land of **E**
Ex 32:11 land of **E** with great power
Ex 32:23 us out of the land of **E**, we
Ex 33: 1 brought out of the land of **E**
Ex 34:18 of Abib you came out from **E**
Lev 11:45 you up out of the land of **E**
Lev 18: 3 the doings of the land of **E**
Lev 19:34 strangers in the land of **E**
Lev 19:36 you out of the land of **E**
Lev 22:33 you out of the land of **E**, to
Lev 23:43 them out of the land of **E**
Lev 25:38 you out of the land of **E**, to
Lev 25:42 brought out of the land of **E**
Lev 25:55 brought out of the land of **E**
Lev 26:13 you out of the land of **E**,
Lev 26:45 brought out of the land of **E**
Num 1: 1 had come out of the land of **E**
Num 3:13 firstborn in the land of **E**
Num 8:17 firstborn in the land of **E** I
Num 9: 1 had come out of the land of **E**
Num 11: 5 fish which we ate freely in **E**
Num 11:18 For it was well with us in **E**
Num 11:20 did we ever come up out of **E**
Num 13:22 seven years before Zoan in **E**
Num 14: 2 we had died in the land of **E**
Num 14: 3 better for us to return to **E**
Num 14: 4 a leader and return to **E**
Num 14:19 people, from **E** even until now
Num 14:22 and the signs which I did in **E**
Num 15:41 you out of the land of **E**, to
Num 20: 5 you made us come up out of **E**
Num 20:15 our fathers went down to **E**
Num 20:15 and we dwelt in **E** a long time
Num 20:16 and brought us up out of **E**
Num 21: 5 of **E** to die in the wilderness
Num 22: 5 a people has come from **E**
Num 22:11 a people has come out of **E**
Num 23:22 God brings them out of **E**
Num 24: 8 God brings him out of **E**
Num 26: 4 who came out of the land of **E**
Num 26:59 who was born to Levi in **E**
Num 32:11 of the men who came up from **E**
Num 33: 1 **E** by their armies under the
Num 33:38 had come out of the land of **E**
Num 34: 5 from Azmon to the Brook of **E**
Deut 1:27 us out of the land of **E** to
Deut 1:30 for you in **E** before your eyes
Deut 4:20 of the iron furnace, out of **E**
Deut 4:34 for you in **E** before your eyes
Deut 4:37 out of **E** with His Presence
Deut 4:45 after they came out of **E**,
Deut 4:46 after they came out of **E**
Deut 5: 6 you out of the land of **E**, out
Deut 5:15 were a slave in the land of **E**
Deut 6:12 you out of the land of **E**,
Deut 6:21 were slaves of Pharaoh in **E**
Deut 6:21 out of **E** with a mighty hand
Deut 6:22 great and severe, against **E**
Deut 7: 8 the hand of Pharaoh king of **E**
Deut 7:15 of **E** which you have known
Deut 7:18 did to Pharaoh and to all **E**
Deut 8:14 you out of the land of **E**,
Deut 9: 7 of **E** until you came to this
Deut 9:12 out of **E** have acted corruptly
Deut 9:26 out of **E** with a mighty hand
Deut 10:19 strangers in the land of **E**
Deut 10:22 to **E** with seventy persons
Deut 11: 3 He did in the midst of **E**
Deut 11: 3 to Pharaoh king of **E**
Deut 11: 4 what He did to the army of **E**
Deut 11:10 is not like the land of **E**
Deut 13: 5 you out of the land of **E** and
Deut 13:10 you out of the land of **E**,
Deut 15:15 were a slave in the land of **E**
Deut 16: 1 brought you out of **E** by night
Deut 16: 3 of the land of **E** in haste)
Deut 16: 3 **E** all the days of your life
Deut 16: 6 at the time you came out of **E**
Deut 16:12 that you were a slave in **E**
Deut 17:16 to **E** to multiply horses, for
Deut 20: 1 you up from the land of **E**
Deut 23: 4 road when you came out of **E**
Deut 24: 9 way when you came out of **E**
Deut 24:18 that you were a slave in **E**
Deut 24:22 were a slave in the land of **E**
Deut 25:17 as you were coming out of **E**
Deut 26: 5 perish, and he went down to **E**
Deut 26: 8 out of **E** with a mighty hand
Deut 28:27 you with the boils of **E**, with
Deut 28:60 on you all the diseases of **E**
Deut 28:68 take you back to **E** in ships
Deut 29: 2 your eyes in the land of **E**
Deut 29:16 we dwelt in the land of **E**
Deut 29:25 them out of the land of **E**
Deut 34:11 him to do in the land of **E**
Josh 2:10 you when you came out of **E**
Josh 5: 4 came out of **E** who were males
Josh 5: 4 after they had come out of **E**
Josh 5: 5 of **E** had not been circumcised
Josh 5: 6 men of war, who came out of **E**
Josh 5: 9 the reproach of **E** from you
Josh 9: 9 fame, and all that He did in **E**
Josh 13: 3 Sihor, which is east of **E**
Josh 15: 4 and went out to the Brook of **E**
Josh 15:47 as far as the Brook of **E** and
Josh 24: 4 his children went down to **E**
Josh 24: 5 and Aaron, and I plagued **E**,
Josh 24: 6 brought your fathers out of **E**
Josh 24: 7 your eyes saw what I did in **E**
Josh 24:14 side of the River and in **E**
Josh 24:17 up out of the land of **E**, from
Josh 24:32 had brought up out of **E**, they
Judg 2: 1 I led you up from **E** and
Judg 2:12 them out of the land of **E**
Judg 6: 8 I brought you up from **E** and
Judg 6:13 the LORD bring us up from **E**
Judg 11:13 when they came up out of **E**
Judg 11:16 when Israel came up from **E**
Judg 19:30 the land of **E** until this day
1Sa 2:27 were in **E** in Pharaoh's house
1Sa 8: 8 I brought them up out of **E**
1Sa 10:18 I brought up Israel out of **E**
1Sa 12: 6 fathers up from the land of **E**
1Sa 12: 8 When Jacob had gone into **E**
1Sa 12: 8 brought your fathers out of **E**
1Sa 15: 2 way when he came up from **E**
1Sa 15: 6 when they came up out of **E**
1Sa 15: 7 to Shur, which is east of **E**
1Sa 27: 8 even as far as the land of **E**
1Sa 30:13 I am a young man from **E**,
2Sa 7: 6 children of Israel up from **E**
2Sa 7:23 redeemed for Yourself from **E**
1Ki 3: 1 treaty with Pharaoh king of **E**
1Ki 4:21 as far as the border of **E**
1Ki 4:30 East and all the wisdom of **E**
1Ki 6: 1 had come out of the land of **E**
1Ki 8: 9 came out of the land of **E**
1Ki 8:16 My people Israel out of **E**
1Ki 8:21 them out of the land of **E**
1Ki 8:51 whom You brought out of **E**
1Ki 8:53 brought our fathers out of **E**
1Ki 8:65 of Hamath to the Brook of **E**
1Ki 9: 9 fathers out of the land of **E**
1Ki 9:16 Pharaoh king of **E** had gone up
1Ki 10:28 had horses imported from **E**
1Ki 10:29 that was imported from **E** cost
1Ki 11:17 that Hadad fled to go to **E**
1Ki 11:18 them from Paran and came to **E**
1Ki 11:18 to Pharaoh king of **E**
1Ki 11:21 Now when Hadad heard in **E**
1Ki 11:40 Jeroboam arose and fled to **E**
1Ki 11:40 to Shishak king of **E**
1Ki 11:40 was in **E** until the death of
1Ki 12: 2 heard it (he was still in **E**
1Ki 12: 2 and had been dwelling in **E**)
1Ki 12:28 you up from the land of **E**
1Ki 14:25 that Shishak king of **E** came
2Ki 17: 4 messengers to So, king of **E**
2Ki 17: 7 them up out of the land of **E**
2Ki 17: 7 the hand of Pharaoh king of **E**
2Ki 17:36 land of **E** with great power
2Ki 18:21 staff of this broken reed, **E**
2Ki 18:21 So is Pharaoh king of **E** to
2Ki 18:24 your trust in **E** for chariots
2Ki 21:15 their fathers came out of **E**
2Ki 23:29 days Pharaoh Necho king of **E**
2Ki 23:34 took Jehoahaz and went to **E**
2Ki 24: 7 the king of **E** did not come
2Ki 24: 7 belonged to the king of **E**
2Ki 24: 7 of **E** to the River Euphrates
2Ki 25:26 armies, arose and went to **E**
1Ch 13: 5 from Shihor in **E** to as far as
1Ch 17:21 whom You redeemed from **E**
2Ch 1:16 had horses imported from **E**
2Ch 1:17 imported from **E** a chariot for
2Ch 5:10 when they had come out of **E**
2Ch 6: 5 people out of the land of **E**
2Ch 7: 8 of Hamath to the Brook of **E**
2Ch 7:22 them out of the land of **E**
2Ch 9:26 as far as the border of **E**
2Ch 9:28 horses to Solomon from **E** and
2Ch 10: 2 Nebat heard it (he was in **E**
2Ch 10: 2 that Jeroboam returned from **E**
2Ch 12: 2 that Shishak king of **E** came
2Ch 12: 3 who came with him out of **E**
2Ch 12: 9 So Shishak king of **E** came up
2Ch 20:10 came out of the land of **E**
2Ch 26: 8 as far as the entrance of **E**
2Ch 35:20 Necho king of **E** came up to
2Ch 36: 3 Now the king of **E** deposed him
2Ch 36: 4 Then the king of **E** made his
2Ch 36: 4 and carried him off to **E**
Neh 9: 9 of our fathers in **E**, and heard
Neh 9:18 that brought you up out of **E**
Ps 68:31 Envoys will come out of **E**
Ps 78:12 fathers, In the land of **E**
Ps 78:43 When He worked His signs in **E**
Ps 78:51 all the firstborn in **E**, The
Ps 80: 8 have brought a vine out of **E**
Ps 81: 5 went throughout the land of **E**
Ps 81:10 you out of the land of **E**
Ps 105:23 Israel also came into **E**, And
Ps 105:38 **E** was glad when they departed
Ps 106: 7 Our fathers in **E** did not
Ps 106:21 had done great things in **E**
Ps 114: 1 When Israel went out of **E**
Ps 135: 8 destroyed the firstborn of **E**
Ps 135: 9 into the midst of you, O **E**
Ps 136:10 To Him who struck **E** in their
Is 7:18 part of the rivers of **E**, and
Is 10:24 you, in the manner of **E**
Is 10:26 lift it up in the manner of **E**
Is 11:11 are left, from Assyria and **E**
Is 11:15 the tongue of the Sea of **E**
Is 11:16 he came up from the land of **E**
Is 19: 1 The burden against **E**
Is 19: 1 cloud, and will come into **E**
Is 19: 1 the idols of **E** will totter at
Is 19: 1 the heart of **E** will melt in
Is 19: 3 The spirit of **E** will fail in
Is 19:12 hosts has purposed against **E**
Is 19:13 they have also deluded **E**,
Is 19:14 they have caused **E** to err in
Is 19:15 will there be any work for **E**
Is 19:16 In that day **E** will be like
Is 19:17 Judah will be a terror to **E**
Is 19:18 **E** will speak the language of

Is 19:19 in the midst of the land of **E**
Is 19:20 of hosts in the land of **E**
Is 19:21 the LORD will be known to **E**
Is 19:22 And the LORD will strike **E**
Is 19:23 a highway from **E** to Assyria
Is 19:23 the Assyrian will come into **E**
Is 19:24 will be one of three with **E**
Is 19:25 Blessed is **E** My people, and
Is 20: 3 a sign and a wonder against **E**
Is 20: 4 uncovered, to the shame of **E**
Is 20: 5 expectation and **E** their glory
Is 23: 5 When the report comes to **E**
Is 27:12 the River to the Brook of **E**
Is 27:13 are outcasts in the land of **E**
Is 30: 2 Who walk to go down to **E**, and
Is 30: 2 to trust in the shadow of **E**
Is 30: 3 and trust in the shadow of **E**
Is 31: 1 who go down to **E** for help
Is 36: 6 staff of this broken reed, **E**
Is 36: 6 So is Pharaoh king of **E** to
Is 36: 9 your trust in **E** for chariots
Is 43: 3 I gave **E** for your ransom,
Is 45:14 The labor of **E** and merchandise
Is 52: 4 first into **E** to sojourn there
Jer 2: 6 us up out of the land of **E**
Jer 2:18 And now why take the road to **E**
Jer 2:36 of **E** as you were ashamed of
Jer 7:22 them out of the land of **E**
Jer 7:25 the land of **E** until this day
Jer 9:26 **E**, Judah, Edom, the people of
Jer 11: 4 them out of the land of **E**
Jer 11: 7 them up out of the land of **E**
Jer 16:14 of Israel from the land of **E**
Jer 23: 7 of Israel from the land of **E**
Jer 24: 8 who dwell in the land of **E**
Jer 25:19 Pharaoh king of **E**, his
Jer 26:21 afraid and fled, and went to **E**
Jer 26:22 the king sent men to **E**
Jer 26:22 men who went with him to **E**
Jer 26:23 And they brought Urijah from **E**
Jer 31:32 them out of the land of **E**
Jer 32:20 and wonders in the land of **E**
Jer 32:21 of the land of **E** with signs
Jer 34:13 them out of the land of **E**
Jer 37: 5 Pharaoh's army came up from **E**
Jer 37: 7 to help you will return to **E**
Jer 41:17 they went on their way to **E**
Jer 42:14 **E** where we shall see no war
Jer 42:15 set your faces to enter **E**
Jer 42:16 you there in the land of **E**
Jer 42:16 close after you there in **E**
Jer 42:17 to go to **E** to sojourn there
Jer 42:18 out on you when you enter **E**
Jer 42:19 of Judah, "Do not go to **E**
Jer 43: 2 Do not go to **E** to sojourn
Jer 43: 7 So they went to the land of **E**
Jer 43:11 he shall strike the land of **E**
Jer 43:12 the houses of the gods of **E**
Jer 43:12 himself with the land of **E**
Jer 43:13 that are in the land of **E**
Jer 44: 1 who dwell in the land of **E**
Jer 44: 8 of **E** where you have gone to
Jer 44:12 land of **E** to sojourn there
Jer 44:12 and fall in the land of **E**
Jer 44:13 who dwell in the land of **E**
Jer 44:14 of **E** to sojourn there shall
Jer 44:15 who dwelt in the land of **E**
Jer 44:24 who are in the land of **E**
Jer 44:26 who dwell in the land of **E**
Jer 44:26 of Judah in all the land of **E**
Jer 44:27 who are in the land of **E**
Jer 44:28 of **E** to the land of Judah
Jer 44:28 land of **E** to sojourn there
Jer 44:30 of **E** into the hand of his
Jer 46: 2 Against **E**
Jer 46: 2 of Pharaoh Necho, king of **E**
Jer 46: 8 **E** rises up like a flood, and
Jer 46:11 O virgin, the daughter of **E**
Jer 46:13 come and strike the land of **E**
Jer 46:14 Declare in **E**, and proclaim in
Jer 46:17 there, Pharaoh, king of **E**
Jer 46:19 O you daughter dwelling in **E**
Jer 46:20 **E** is like a very pretty
Jer 46:24 The daughter of **E** shall be
Jer 46:25 of No, and Pharaoh and **E**
Ezek 17:15 sending his ambassadors to **E**
Ezek 19: 4 with chains to the land of **E**
Ezek 20: 5 to them in the land of **E**, I
Ezek 20: 6 of **E** into a land that I had
Ezek 20: 7 with the idols of **E**
Ezek 20: 8 they forsake the idols of **E**
Ezek 20: 8 in the midst of the land of **E**
Ezek 20: 9 them out of the land of **E**
Ezek 20:10 them go out of the land of **E**
Ezek 20:36 wilderness of the land of **E**
Ezek 23: 3 They committed harlotry in **E**
Ezek 23: 8 her harlotry brought from **E**
Ezek 23:19 the harlot in the land of **E**
Ezek 23:27 brought from the land of **E**
Ezek 23:27 them, nor remember **E** anymore
Ezek 27: 7 **E** was what you spread for
Ezek 29: 2 against Pharaoh king of **E**
Ezek 29: 2 against him, and against all **E**
Ezek 29: 3 you, O Pharaoh king of **E**, O
Ezek 29: 6 of **E** shall know that I am the
Ezek 29: 9 the land of **E** shall become
Ezek 29:10 the land of **E** utterly waste
Ezek 29:12 I will make the land of **E**
Ezek 29:14 bring back the captives of **E**
Ezek 29:19 I will give the land of **E** to
Ezek 29:20 the land of **E** for his labor
Ezek 30: 4 The sword shall come upon **E**
Ezek 30: 4 when the slain fall in **E**
Ezek 30: 6 Those who uphold **E** shall fall
Ezek 30: 8 when I have set a fire in **E**
Ezek 30: 9 upon them, as on the day of **E**
Ezek 30:10 of **E** to cease by the hand of
Ezek 30:11 draw their swords against **E**
Ezek 30:13 be princes from the land of **E**
Ezek 30:13 put fear in the land of **E**
Ezek 30:15 on Sin, the strength of **E**
Ezek 30:16 and set a fire in **E**
Ezek 30:18 I break the yokes of **E** there
Ezek 30:19 I will execute judgments on **E**
Ezek 30:21 the arm of Pharaoh king of **E**
Ezek 30:22 am against Pharaoh king of **E**
Ezek 30:25 it out against the land of **E**
Ezek 31: 2 man, say to Pharaoh king of **E**
Ezek 32: 2 for Pharaoh king of **E**, and say
Ezek 32:12 shall plunder the pomp of **E**
Ezek 32:15 I make the land of **E** desolate
Ezek 32:16 shall lament for her, for **E**
Ezek 32:18 wail over the multitude of **E**
Dan 9:15 land of **E** with a mighty hand
Dan 11: 8 carry their gods captive to **E**
Dan 11:42 and the land of **E** shall not
Dan 11:43 all the precious things of **E**
Hos 2:15 came up from the land of **E**
Hos 7:11 they call to **E**, they go to
Hos 7:16 derision in the land of **E**
Hos 8:13 They shall return to **E**
Hos 9: 3 but Ephraim shall return to **E**
Hos 9: 6 **E** shall gather them up
Hos 11: 1 and out of **E** I called My son
Hos 11: 5 not return to the land of **E**
Hos 11:11 trembling like a bird from **E**
Hos 12: 1 and oil is carried to **E**
Hos 12: 9 God, ever since the land of **E**
Hos 12:13 LORD brought Israel out of **E**
Hos 13: 4 God ever since the land of **E**
Joel 3:19 **E** shall be a desolation, and
Amos 2:10 you up from the land of **E**
Amos 3: 1 brought up from the land of **E**
Amos 3: 9 the palaces in the land of **E**
Amos 4:10 plague after the manner of **E**
Amos 8: 8 subside like the River of **E**
Amos 9: 5 subside like the River of **E**
Amos 9: 7 up Israel from the land of **E**
Mic 6: 4 you up from the land of **E**
Mic 7:15 you came out of the land of **E**
Nah 3: 9 **E** were her strength, and it
Hag 2: 5 you when you came out of **E**
Zech 10:10 them back from the land of **E**
Zech 10:11 the scepter of **E** shall depart
Zech 14:18 family of **E** will not come up
Zech 14:19 shall be the punishment of **E**
Matt 2:13 and His mother, flee to **E**, and
Matt 2:14 by night and departed for **E**
Matt 2:15 Out of **E** I called My Son
Matt 2:19 in a dream to Joseph in **E**
Acts 2:10 Phrygia and Pamphylia, **E** and
Acts 7: 9 envious, sold Joseph into **E**
Acts 7:10 of Pharaoh, king of **E**
Acts 7:10 he made him governor over **E**
Acts 7:11 came over all the land of **E**
Acts 7:12 that there was grain in **E**
Acts 7:15 So Jacob went down to **E**
Acts 7:17 grew and multiplied in **E**
Acts 7:34 of my people who are in **E**
Acts 7:34 come, I will send you to **E**
Acts 7:36 and signs in the land of **E**
Acts 7:39 hearts they turned back to **E**
Acts 7:40 us out of the land of **E**, we
Acts 13:17 as strangers in the land of **E**
Heb 3:16 it not all who came out of **E**
Heb 8: 9 them out of the land of **E**
Heb 11:26 than the treasures in **E**
Heb 11:27 By faith he forsook **E**, not
Jude 5 people out of the land of **E**
Rev 11: 8 is called Sodom and **E**, where

EGYPTIAN (*see* EGYPT, EGYPTIAN'S, EGYPTIANS)

Gen 16: 1 And she had an **E** maidservant
Gen 16: 3 took Hagar her maid, the **E**
Gen 21: 9 saw the son of Hagar the **E**
Gen 25:12 son, whom Hagar the **E**,
Gen 39: 1 captain of the guard, an **E**
Gen 39: 2 the house of his master the **E**
Ex 1:19 are not like the **E** women
Ex 2:11 he saw an **E** beating a Hebrew,
Ex 2:12 saw no one, he killed the **E**
Ex 2:14 kill me as you killed the **E**
Ex 2:19 An **E** delivered us from the
Lev 24:10 woman, whose father was an **E**
Deut 23: 7 You shall not abhor an **E**,
1Sa 30:11 they found an **E** in the field
2Sa 23:21 And he killed an **E**, a
2Sa 23:21 The **E** had a spear in his hand
1Ch 2:34 And Sheshan had an **E** servant
1Ch 11:23 And he killed an **E**, a man of
Prov 7:16 Colored coverings of **E** linen
Is 19:23 the **E** into Assyria, and the
Acts 7:24 and struck down the **E**
Acts 7:28 me as you did the **E** yesterday
Acts 21:38 Are you not the **E** who some

EGYPTIAN'S (*see* EGYPTIAN)

Gen 39: 5 the **E** house for Joseph's sake
2Sa 23:21 the spear out of the **E** hand
1Ch 11:23 In the **E** hand there had been
1Ch 11:23 the spear out of the **E** hand

EGYPTIANS (*see* EGYPTIAN)

Gen 12:12 happen, when the **E** see you
Gen 12:14 that the **E** saw the woman,
Gen 41:55 Pharaoh said to all the **E**
Gen 41:56 storehouses and sold to the **E**
Gen 43:32 the **E** who ate with him by
Gen 43:32 because the **E** could not eat
Gen 43:32 is an abomination to the **E**
Gen 45: 2 And he wept aloud, and the **E**
Gen 46:34 is an abomination to the **E**
Gen 47:15 all the **E** came to Joseph and
Gen 47:20 man of the **E** sold his field
Gen 50: 3 the **E** mourned for him seventy
Gen 50:11 a grievous mourning of the **E**
Ex 1:13 So the **E** made the children of
Ex 3: 8 them out of the hand of the **E**
Ex 3: 9 with which the **E** oppress them
Ex 3:21 favor in the sight of the **E**
Ex 3:22 So you shall plunder the **E**
Ex 6: 5 whom the **E** keep in bondage
Ex 6: 6 under the burdens of the **E**
Ex 6: 7 under the burdens of the **E**
Ex 7: 5 the **E** shall know that I am
Ex 7:18 the **E** will loathe to drink
Ex 7:21 the **E** could not drink the
Ex 7:24 So all the **E** dug all around
Ex 8:21 The houses of the **E** shall be
Ex 8:26 of the **E** to the LORD our God
Ex 8:26 of the **E** before their eyes
Ex 9:11 the magicians and on all the **E**
Ex 10: 6 and the houses of all the **E**
Ex 11: 3 favor in the sight of the **E**
Ex 11: 7 a difference between the **E**
Ex 12:23 pass through to strike the **E**
Ex 12:27 in Egypt when He struck the **E**
Ex 12:30 his servants, and all the **E**
Ex 12:33 the **E** urged the people, that
Ex 12:35 from the **E** articles of silver
Ex 12:36 favor in the sight of the **E**
Ex 12:36 Thus they plundered the **E**
Ex 14: 4 that the **E** may know that I am
Ex 14: 9 So the **E** pursued them, all
Ex 14:10 the **E** marched after them
Ex 14:12 alone that we may serve the **E**
Ex 14:12 **E** than that we should die in
Ex 14:13 For the **E** whom you see today,
Ex 14:17 harden the hearts of the **E**
Ex 14:18 Then the **E** shall know that I
Ex 14:20 between the camp of the **E**

EKRONITES (*see* EKRON)
Josh 13: 3 the Gittites, and the **E**
1Sa 5:10 that the **E** cried out, saying,

ELABORATE
Zech 6:11 and gold, make an **e** crown, and
Zech 6:14 Now the **e** crown shall be for

ELADAH
1Ch 7:20 **E** his son, Tahath his son,

ELAH
Gen 36:41 Chief Aholibamah, Chief **E**
1Sa 17: 2 encamped in the Valley of **E**
1Sa 17:19 were in the Valley of **E**,
1Sa 21: 9 you killed in the Valley of **E**
1Ki 4:18 Shimei the son of **E**, in
1Ki 16: 6 Then **E** his son reigned in his
1Ki 16: 8 **E** the son of Baasha became
1Ki 16:13 and the sins of **E** his son, by
1Ki 16:14 Now the rest of the acts of **E**
2Ki 15:30 Then Hoshea the son of **E** led
2Ki 17: 1 Hoshea the son of **E** became
2Ki 18: 1 year of Hoshea the son of **E**
2Ki 18: 9 year of Hoshea the son of **E**
1Ch 1:52 Chief Aholibamah, Chief **E**
1Ch 4:15 son of Jephunneh were Iru, **E**
1Ch 4:15 The son of **E** was Kenaz
1Ch 9: 8 **E** the son of Uzzi, the son of

ELAM (*see* ELAMITES, PERSIA)
Gen 10:22 The sons of Shem were **E**,
Gen 14: 1 Chedorlaomer king of **E**, and
Gen 14: 9 Chedorlaomer king of **E**, Tidal
1Ch 1:17 The sons of Shem were **E**,
1Ch 8:24 Hananiah, **E**, Antothijah,
1Ch 26: 3 **E** the fifth, Jehohanan the
Ezra 2: 7 the people of **E**, one thousand
Ezra 2:31 the people of the other **E**
Ezra 8: 7 of the sons of **E**, Jeshaiah
Ezra 10: 2 Jehiel, one of the sons of **E**
Ezra 10:26 of the sons of **E**
Neh 7:12 the children of **E**, one
Neh 7:34 the children of the other **E**
Neh 10:14 Parosh, Pahath-Moab, **E**, Zattu
Neh 12:42 Uzzi, Jehohanan, Malchijah, **E**
Is 11:11 from Pathros and Cush, from **E**
Is 21: 2 Go up, O **E**!
Is 22: 6 **E** bore the quiver with
Jer 25:25 of Zimri, all the kings of **E**
Jer 49:34 the prophet against **E**, in the
Jer 49:35 I will break the bow of **E**
Jer 49:36 Against **E** I will bring the
Jer 49:36 the outcasts of **E** will not go
Jer 49:37 For I will cause **E** to be
Jer 49:38 I will set My throne in **E**
Jer 49:39 bring back the captives of **E**
Ezek 32:24 There is **E** and all her
Dan 8: 2 which is in the province of **E**

ELAMITES (*see* ELAM, PERSIAN)
Ezra 4: 9 Shushan, the Dehavites, the **E**
Acts 2: 9 Parthians and Medes and **E**,

ELASAH (*see* ELEASAH)
Ezra 10:22 Nethaneel, Jozabad, and **E**
Jer 29: 3 hand of **E** the son of Shaphan

ELATH
Deut 2: 8 of the plain, away from **E**
1Ki 9:26 which is near **E** on the shore
2Ki 14:22 He built **E** and restored it to
2Ki 16: 6 of Syria captured **E** for Syria
2Ki 16: 6 drove the men of Judah from **E**
2Ki 16: 6 Then the Edomites went to **E**
2Ch 8:17 **E** on the seacoast, in the
2Ch 26: 2 He built **E** and restored it to

EL BETHEL (*see* BETHEL)
Gen 35: 7 there and called the place **E**

ELDAAH
Gen 25: 4 Epher, Hanoch, Abidah, and **E**
1Ch 1:33 Epher, Hanoch, Abida, and **E**

ELDAD
Num 11:26 the name of one was **E**, and the
Num 11:27 **E** and Medad are prophesying in

ELDER (*see* ELDERLY, ELDERS, ELDEST)
Gen 10:21 the brother of Japheth the **e**
Gen 27:15 clothes of her **e** son Esau
Gen 29:16 the name of the **e** was Leah
Is 3: 2 and the diviner and the **e**
Is 3: 5 will be insolent toward the **e**
Is 9:15 The **e** and honorable, he is the
Ezek 16:46 Your **e** sister is Samaria, who
Ezek 23: 4 Oholah the **e** and Oholibah her
1Ti 5:19 an **e** except from two or three
1Pe 5: 1 I exhort, I who am a fellow **e**
2Jn 1 THE **E**, To the elect lady and
3Jn 1 THE **E**, To the beloved Gaius,

ELDERLY (*see* ELDER)
Deut 28:50 which does not respect the **e**
Is 47: 6 on the **e** you laid your yoke

ELDERS (*see* ELDER)
Gen 50: 7 the **e** of his house, and all
Gen 50: 7 and all the **e** of the land of
Ex 3:16 Go and gather the **e** of Israel
Ex 3:18 the **e** of Israel, to the king
Ex 4:29 **e** of the children of Israel
Ex 12:21 for all the **e** of Israel and
Ex 17: 5 you some of the **e** of Israel
Ex 17: 6 the sight of the **e** of Israel
Ex 18:12 Aaron came with all the **e** of
Ex 19: 7 for the **e** of the people, and
Ex 24: 1 and seventy of the **e** of Israel
Ex 24: 9 and seventy of the **e** of Israel
Ex 24:14 And he said to the **e**, Wait
Lev 4:15 the **e** of the congregation
Lev 9: 1 his sons and the **e** of Israel
Num 11:16 men of the **e** of Israel, whom
Num 11:16 to be the **e** of the people
Num 11:24 men of the **e** of the people
Num 11:25 the same upon the seventy **e**
Num 11:30 both he and the **e** of Israel
Num 16:25 the **e** of Israel followed him
Num 22: 4 Moab said to the **e** of Midian
Num 22: 7 So the **e** of Moab and the
Num 22: 7 the **e** of Midian departed with
Deut 5:23 of your tribes and your **e**
Deut 19:12 then the **e** of his city shall
Deut 21: 2 then your **e** and your judges
Deut 21: 3 it shall be that the **e** of the
Deut 21: 4 and the **e** of that city shall
Deut 21: 6 And all the **e** of that city
Deut 21:19 him out to the **e** of his city
Deut 21:20 say to the **e** of his city
Deut 22:15 the **e** of the city at the gate
Deut 22:16 father shall say to the **e**
Deut 22:17 before the **e** of the city
Deut 22:18 Then the **e** of that city shall
Deut 25: 7 go up to the gate to the **e**
Deut 25: 8 Then the **e** of his city shall
Deut 25: 9 him in the presence of the **e**
Deut 27: 1 Moses, with the **e** of Israel,
Deut 29:10 and your tribes and your **e** and
Deut 31: 9 and to all the **e** of Israel
Deut 31:28 me all the **e** of your tribes
Deut 32: 7 your **e**, and they will tell you
Josh 7: 6 both he and the **e** of Israel
Josh 8:10 the **e** of Israel, before the
Josh 8:33 Then all Israel, with their **e**
Josh 9:11 Therefore our **e** and all the
Josh 20: 4 hearing of the **e** of that city
Josh 23: 2 for all Israel, for their **e**
Josh 24: 1 and called for the **e** of Israel
Josh 24:31 of the **e** who outlived Joshua
Judg 2: 7 of the **e** who outlived Joshua
Judg 8:14 leaders of Succoth and its **e**
Judg 8:16 And he took the **e** of the city
Judg 11: 5 that the **e** of Gilead went to
Judg 11: 7 said to the **e** of Gilead
Judg 11: 8 And the **e** of Gilead said to
Judg 11: 9 said to the **e** of Gilead, If
Judg 11:10 And the **e** of Gilead said to
Judg 11:11 went with the **e** of Gilead
Judg 21:16 Then the **e** of the
Ruth 4: 2 ten men of the **e** of the city
Ruth 4: 4 and the **e** of my people
Ruth 4: 9 And Boaz said to the **e** and to
Ruth 4:11 were at the gate, and the **e**
1Sa 4: 3 camp, the **e** of Israel said,
1Sa 8: 4 Then all the **e** of Israel
1Sa 11: 3 Then the **e** of Jabesh said to
1Sa 15:30 before the **e** of my people and
1Sa 16: 4 the **e** of the town trembled at
1Sa 30:26 the spoil to the **e** of Judah
2Sa 3:17 with the **e** of Israel, saying,
2Sa 5: 3 So all the **e** of Israel came
2Sa 12:17 So the **e** of his house arose
2Sa 17: 4 and all the **e** of Israel
2Sa 17:15 the **e** of Israel, and thus and
2Sa 19:11 Speak to the **e** of Judah,
1Ki 8: 1 assembled the **e** of Israel
1Ki 8: 3 Then all the **e** of Israel came
1Ki 12: 6 **e** who stood before his father
1Ki 12: 8 counsel which the **e** gave him
1Ki 12:13 which the **e** had given him
1Ki 20: 7 called all the **e** of the land
1Ki 20: 8 And all the **e** and all the
1Ki 21: 8 and sent the letters to the **e**
1Ki 21:11 So the men of his city, the **e**
2Ki 6:32 the **e** were sitting with him
2Ki 6:32 came to him, he said to the **e**
2Ki 10: 1 rulers of Jezreel, to the **e**
2Ki 10: 5 the **e** also, and those who
2Ki 19: 2 the **e** of the priests, covered
2Ki 23: 1 to gather all the **e** of Judah
1Ch 11: 3 Therefore all the **e** of Israel
1Ch 15:25 the **e** of Israel, and the
1Ch 21:16 So David and the **e**, clothed in
2Ch 5: 2 assembled the **e** of Israel
2Ch 5: 4 So all the **e** of Israel came,
2Ch 10: 6 **e** who stood before his father
2Ch 10: 8 which the **e** had given him
2Ch 10:13 rejected the counsel of the **e**
2Ch 34:29 gathered all the **e** of Judah
Ezra 5: 5 was upon the **e** of the Jews
Ezra 5: 9 Then we asked those **e**, and
Ezra 6: 7 the **e** of the Jews build this
Ezra 6: 8 do for the **e** of these Jews
Ezra 6:14 So the **e** of the Jews built,
Ezra 10: 8 counsel of the leaders and **e**
Ezra 10:14 times, together with the **e**
Job 12:20 away the discernment of the **e**
Ps 105:22 And teach his **e** wisdom
Ps 107:32 Him in the assembly of the **e**
Prov 31:23 sits among the **e** of the land
Is 3:14 with the **e** of His people and
Is 24:23 in Jerusalem and before His **e**
Is 37: 2 the **e** of the priests, covered
Jer 19: 1 some of the **e** of the people
Jer 19: 1 some of the **e** of the priests
Jer 26:17 of the **e** of the land rose up
Jer 29: 1 the **e** who were carried away
Lam 1:19 my **e** breathed their last in
Lam 2:10 The **e** of the daughter of Zion
Lam 4:16 nor show favor to the **e**
Lam 5:12 and **e** were not respected
Lam 5:14 The **e** have ceased gathering
Ezek 7:26 priest, and counsel from the **e**
Ezek 8: 1 **e** of Judah sitting before me
Ezek 8:11 the **e** of the house of Israel
Ezek 8:12 have you seen what the **e** of
Ezek 9: 6 So they began with the **e**
Ezek 14: 1 Now some of the **e** of Israel
Ezek 20: 1 that certain of the **e** of
Ezek 20: 3 man, speak to the **e** of Israel
Ezek 27: 9 **E** of Gebal and its wise men
Joel 1: 2 Hear this, you **e**, and give ear
Joel 1:14 gather the **e** and all the
Joel 2:16 congregation, assemble the **e**
Matt 15: 2 the tradition of the **e**
Matt 16:21 suffer many things from the **e**
Matt 21:23 and the **e** of the people
Matt 26: 3 the **e** of the people assembled
Matt 26:47 priests and **e** of the people
Matt 26:57 and the **e** were assembled
Matt 26:59 Now the chief priests, the **e**
Matt 27: 1 **e** of the people took counsel
Matt 27: 3 to the chief priests and **e**
Matt 27:12 by the chief priests and **e**
Matt 27:20 **e** persuaded the multitudes
Matt 27:41 mocking with the scribes and **e**
Matt 28:12 they had assembled with the **e**
Mark 7: 3 the tradition of the **e**
Mark 7: 5 to the tradition of the **e**
Mark 8:31 and be rejected by the **e** and
Mark 11:27 scribes, and the **e** came to Him
Mark 14:43 and the scribes and the **e**
Mark 14:53 all the chief priests, the **e**
Mark 15: 1 a consultation with the **e**
Luke 7: 3 he sent **e** of the Jews to Him,
Luke 9:22 and be rejected by the **e** and
Luke 20: 1 scribes, together with the **e**
Luke 22:52 the **e** who had come to Him,
Luke 22:66 the **e** of the people, both
Acts 4: 5 day, that their rulers, **e**
Acts 4: 8 of the people and **e** of Israel
Acts 4:23 priests and **e** had said to them
Acts 5:21 with all the **e** of the
Acts 6:12 stirred up the people, the **e**
Acts 11:30 sent it to the **e** by the hands
Acts 14:23 appointed **e** in every church

Acts 15: 2 to the apostles and e, about
Acts 15: 4 and the apostles and the e
Acts 15: 6 e came together to consider
Acts 15:22 it pleased the apostles and e
Acts 15:23 The apostles, the e, and the
Acts 16: 4 apostles and e at Jerusalem
Acts 20:17 for the e of the church
Acts 21:18 and all the e were present
Acts 22: 5 and all the council of the e
Acts 23:14 to the chief priests and e
Acts 24: 1 priest came down with the e
Acts 25:15 the e of the Jews informed me
1Ti 5:17 Let the e who rule well be
Tit 1: 5 appoint e in every city as I
Heb 11: 2 For by it the e obtained a
Jas 5:14 call for the e of the church
1Pe 5: 1 The e who are among you I
1Pe 5: 5 submit yourselves to your e
Rev 4: 4 I saw twenty-four e sitting
Rev 4:10 the twenty-four e fall down
Rev 5: 5 But one of the e said to me
Rev 5: 6 and in the midst of the e
Rev 5: 8 the twenty-four e fell down
Rev 5:11 living creatures, and the e
Rev 5:14 the twenty-four e fell down
Rev 7:11 around the throne and the e
Rev 7:13 Then one of the e answered
Rev 11:16 the twenty-four e who sat
Rev 14: 3 living creatures, and the e
Rev 19: 4 And the twenty-four e and the

ELDEST (*see* ELDER, OLD)
2Ki 3:27 Then he took his e son who

ELEAD
1Ch 7:21 his son, and Ezer and E

ELEALEH
Num 32: 3 Jazer, Nimrah, Heshbon, E
Num 32:37 of Reuben built Heshbon and E
Is 15: 4 E will cry out, their voice
Is 16: 9 with my tears, O Heshbon and E
Jer 48:34 From the cry of Heshbon to E

ELEASAH (*see* ELASAH)
1Ch 2:39 begot Helez, and Helez begot E
1Ch 2:40 E begot Sismai, and Sismai
1Ch 8:37 E his son, and Azel his son
1Ch 9:43 E his son, and Azel his son

ELEAZAR
Ex 6:23 she bore him Nadab, Abihu, E
Ex 6:25 E, Aaron's son, took for
Ex 28: 1 Nadab, Abihu, E, and Ithamar
Lev 10: 6 Moses said to Aaron, and to E
Lev 10:12 Moses spoke to Aaron, and to E
Lev 10:16 And he was angry with E and
Num 3: 2 the firstborn, and Abihu, E
Num 3: 4 So E and Ithamar ministered as
Num 3:32 E the son of Aaron the priest
Num 4:16 The appointed duty of E the
Num 16:37 Tell E, the son of Aaron the
Num 16:39 So E the priest took the
Num 19: 3 shall give it to E the priest
Num 19: 4 E the priest shall take some
Num 20:25 E his son, and bring them up
Num 20:26 and put them on E his son
Num 20:28 and put them on E his son
Num 20:28 E came down from the mountain
Num 25: 7 when Phinehas the son of E
Num 25:11 Phinehas the son of E, the
Num 26: 1 E the son of Aaron the priest
Num 26: 3 E the priest spoke with them
Num 26:60 were born Nadab and Abihu, E
Num 26:63 E the priest, who numbered
Num 27: 2 before E the priest, and
Num 27:19 set him before E the priest
Num 27:21 stand before E the priest
Num 27:22 set him before E the priest
Num 31: 6 the son of E the priest, with
Num 31:12 to E the priest, and to the
Num 31:13 E the priest, and all the
Num 31:21 Then E the priest said to the
Num 31:26 E the priest and the chief
Num 31:29 give it to E the priest as a
Num 31:31 E the priest did as the LORD
Num 31:41 offering to E the priest, as
Num 31:51 E the priest received the
Num 31:54 E the priest received the
Num 32: 2 to E the priest, and to the
Num 32:28 them to E the priest, to
Num 34:17 E the priest and Joshua the
Deut 10: 6 and E his son ministered as
Josh 14: 1 which E the priest, Joshua
Josh 17: 4 came near before E the priest
Josh 19:51 which E the priest, Joshua
Josh 21: 1 came near to E the priest
Josh 22:13 sent Phinehas the son of E
Josh 22:31 of E the priest said to the
Josh 22:32 the son of E the priest, and
Josh 24:33 And E the son of Aaron died
Judg 20:28 and Phinehas the son of E, the
1Sa 7: 1 consecrated E his son to keep
2Sa 23: 9 after him was E the son of
1Ch 6: 3 of Aaron were Nadab, Abihu, E
1Ch 6: 4 E begot Phinehas, and Phinehas
1Ch 6:50 E his son, Phinehas his son,
1Ch 9:20 Phinehas the son of E had
1Ch 11:12 After him was E the son of
1Ch 23:21 The sons of Mahli were E and
1Ch 23:22 E died, and had no sons, but
1Ch 24: 1 of Aaron were Nadab, Abihu, E
1Ch 24: 2 therefore E and Ithamar
1Ch 24: 3 with Zadok of the sons of E
1Ch 24: 4 found of the sons of E than
1Ch 24: 4 Among the sons of E there
1Ch 24: 5 of God, from the sons of E
1Ch 24: 6 father's house taken for E
1Ch 24:28 E, who had no sons
Ezra 7: 5 son of Phinehas, the son of E
Ezra 8:33 with him was E the son of
Ezra 10:25 Jeziah, Malchiah, Mijamin, E
Neh 12:42 also Maaseiah, Shemaiah, E
Matt 1:15 Eliud begot E
Matt 1:15 E begot Matthan

ELECT (*see* ELECTION, ELECT'S)
Is 42: 1 My E One in whom My soul
Is 45: 4 sake, and Israel My e, I have
Is 65: 9 My e shall inherit it, and My
Is 65:22 My e shall long enjoy the
Matt 24:24 if possible, even the e
Matt 24:31 His e from the four winds
Mark 13:22 if possible, even the e
Mark 13:27 His e from the four winds
Luke 18: 7 His own e who cry out day
Rom 8:33 a charge against God's e
Rom 11: 7 but the e have obtained it,
Col 3:12 Therefore, as the e of God
1Ti 5:21 the e angels that you observe
2Ti 2:10 things for the sake of the e
Tit 1: 1 to the faith of God's e and
1Pe 1: 2 e according to the
1Pe 2: 6 Zion a chief cornerstone, e
1Pe 5:13 e together with you, greets
2Jn 1 THE ELDER, To the e lady and
2Jn 13 of your e sister greet you

ELECTION (*see* ELECT)
Rom 9:11 according to e might stand
Rom 11: 5 according to the e of grace
Rom 11:28 but concerning the e they are
1Th 1: 4 brethren, your e by God
2Pe 1:10 e sure, for if you do these

ELECT'S (*see* ELECT)
Matt 24:22 but for the e sake those days
Mark 13:20 but for the e sake, whom He

EL ELOHE ISRAEL
Gen 33:20 an altar there and called it E

ELEMENTARY
Heb 6: 1 of the e principles of Christ

ELEMENTS
Gal 4: 3 under the e of the world
Gal 4: 9 to the weak and beggarly e
2Pe 3:10 the e will melt with fervent
2Pe 3:12 the e will melt with fervent

ELEPH
Josh 18:28 Zelah, E, Jebus (which is

ELEVATED (*see* ELEVATION)
Is 49:11 and My highways shall be e

ELEVATION (*see* ELEVATED)
Ps 48: 2 Beautiful in e, The joy of
Ezek 41: 8 I also saw an e all around

ELEVEN (*see* ELEVENTH)
Gen 32:22 his e sons, and crossed over
Gen 37: 9 the e stars bowed down to me
Ex 26: 7 You shall make e curtains
Ex 26: 8 the e curtains shall all have
Ex 36:14 he made e curtains
Ex 36:15 the e curtains were the same
Num 29:20 the third day present e bulls
Deut 1: 2 It is e days' journey from
Josh 15:51 e cities with their villages
Judg 16: 5 one of us will give you e
Judg 17: 2 The e hundred shekels of
Judg 17: 3 e hundred shekels of silver
2Ki 23:36 and he reigned e years in
2Ki 24:18 and he reigned e years in
2Ch 36: 5 and he reigned e years in
2Ch 36:11 and he reigned e years in
Jer 52: 1 and he reigned e years in
Ezek 40:49 cubits, and the width e cubits
Matt 28:16 Then the e disciples went
Mark 16:14 He appeared to the e as they
Luke 24: 9 all these things to the e
Luke 24:33 to Jerusalem, and found the e
Acts 1:26 numbered with the e apostles
Acts 2:14 Peter, standing up with the e

ELEVENTH (*see* ELEVEN)
Num 7:72 On the e day Pagiel the son
Deut 1: 3 fortieth year, in the e month
1Ki 6:38 And in the e year, in the
2Ki 9:29 In the e year of Joram the
2Ki 25: 2 the e year of King Zedekiah
1Ch 12:13 the tenth, and Machbanai the e
1Ch 24:12 the e to Eliashib, the
1Ch 25:18 the e for Azarel, his sons and
1Ch 27:14 The e captain for the
1Ch 27:14 the e month was Benaiah the
Jer 1: 3 until the end of the e year
Jer 39: 2 In the e year of Zedekiah, in
Jer 52: 5 the e year of King Zedekiah
Ezek 26: 1 it came to pass in the e year
Ezek 30:20 it came to pass in the e year
Ezek 31: 1 it came to pass in the e year
Zech 1: 7 day of the e month, which is
Matt 20: 6 about the e hour he went out
Matt 20: 9 were hired about the e hour
Rev 21:20 the e jacinth, and the twelfth

ELHANAN
2Sa 21:19 where E the son of
2Sa 23:24 E the son of Dodo of
1Ch 11:26 of Joab, E the son of Dodo of
1Ch 20: 5 and E the son of Jair killed

ELI (*see* ELI'S, ELOI)
1Sa 1: 3 Also the two sons of E,
1Sa 1: 9 Now E the priest was sitting
1Sa 1:12 that E watched her mouth
1Sa 1:13 Therefore E thought she was
1Sa 1:14 So E said to her, "How long
1Sa 1:17 Then E answered and said, "Go
1Sa 1:25 and brought the child to E
1Sa 2:11 the LORD before E the priest
1Sa 2:12 the sons of E were corrupt
1Sa 2:20 E would bless Elkanah and his
1Sa 2:22 Now E was very old
1Sa 2:27 Then a man of God came to E
1Sa 3: 1 to the LORD before E
1Sa 3: 2 while E was lying down in his
1Sa 3: 5 So he ran to E and said
1Sa 3: 6 So Samuel arose and went to E
1Sa 3: 8 Then he arose and went to E
1Sa 3: 8 Then E perceived that the
1Sa 3: 9 Therefore E said to Samuel,
1Sa 3:12 E all that I have spoken
1Sa 3:14 E that the iniquity of Eli's
1Sa 3:15 afraid to tell E the vision
1Sa 3:16 Then E called Samuel and said,
1Sa 4: 4 And the two sons of E, Hophni
1Sa 4:11 and the two sons of E, Hophni
1Sa 4:13 Now when he came, there was E
1Sa 4:14 When E heard the noise of the
1Sa 4:14 man came hastily and told E
1Sa 4:15 E was ninety-eight years old,
1Sa 4:16 Then the man said to E, "I
1Sa 4:18 God, that E fell off the seat
1Sa 14: 3 son of Phinehas, the son of E
1Ki 2:27 the house of E at Shiloh
Matt 27:46 E, E, lama sabachthani

ELIAB (*see* ELIAB'S, ELIEL)
Num 1: 9 Zebulun, E the son of Helon
Num 2: 7 E the son of Helon shall be
Num 7:24 third day E the son of Helon
Num 7:29 of E the son of Helon
Num 10:16 was E the son of Helon
Num 16: 1 and Abiram the sons of E, and
Num 16:12 and Abiram the sons of E, but
Num 26: 8 And the son of Pallu was E

Num 26: 9 The sons of E were Nemuel
Deut 11: 6 and Abiram the sons of E, the
1Sa 16: 6 came, that he looked at E
1Sa 17:13 battle were E the firstborn
1Sa 17:28 Now E his oldest brother
1Ch 2:13 Jesse begot E his firstborn,
1Ch 6:27 E his son, Jeroham his son,
1Ch 12: 9 the second, E the third,
1Ch 15:18 Shemiramoth, Jehiel, Unni, E
1Ch 15:20 Shemiramoth, Jehiel, Unni, E
1Ch 16: 5 Jehiel, Mattithiah, E,

ELIAB'S (*see* ELIAB)
1Sa 17:28 E anger was aroused against

ELIADA (*see* ELIADAH)
2Sa 5:16 Elishama, E, and Eliphelet
1Ch 3: 8 Elishama, E, and Eliphelet
2Ch 17:17 E a mighty man of valor, and

ELIADAH (*see* ELIADA)
1Ki 11:23 him, Rezon the son of E, who

ELIAH (*see* ELIEL, ELIJAH)
2Ch 11:18 of E the son of Jesse
Ezra 10:26 Jehiel, Abdi, Jeremoth, and E

ELIAHBA
2Sa 23:32 E the Shaalbonite (of the
1Ch 11:33 E the Shaalbonite,

ELIAKIM (*see* JEHOIAKIM)
2Ki 18:18 E the son of Hilkiah, who was
2Ki 18:26 Then E the son of Hilkiah,
2Ki 18:37 Then E the son of Hilkiah,
2Ki 19: 2 Then he sent E, who was over
2Ki 23:34 Then Pharaoh Necho made E
2Ch 36: 4 his brother E king over Judah
Neh 12:41 and the priests, E, Maaseiah,
Is 22:20 servant E the son of Hilkiah
Is 36: 3 E the son of Hilkiah, who was
Is 36:11 Then E, Shebna, and Joah said
Is 36:22 Then E the son of Hilkiah,
Is 37: 2 Then he sent E, who was over
Matt 1:13 Abiud begot E
Matt 1:13 and E begot Azor
Luke 3:30 son of Jonan, the son of E

ELIAM (*see* AMMIEL)
2Sa 11: 3 Bathsheba, the daughter of E
2Sa 23:34 E the son of Ahithophel the

ELIASAPH
Num 1:14 from Gad, E the son of Deuel
Num 2:14 shall be E the son of Reuel
Num 3:24 was E the son of Lael
Num 7:42 sixth day E the son of Deuel
Num 7:47 of E the son of Deuel
Num 10:20 of Gad was E the son of Deuel

ELIASHIB
1Ch 3:24 of Elioenai were Hodaviah, E
1Ch 24:12 the eleventh to E, the
Ezra 10: 6 of Jehohanan the son of E
Ezra 10:24 Also of the singers: E
Ezra 10:27 Elioenai, E, Mattaniah,
Ezra 10:36 Vaniah, Meremoth, E,
Neh 3: 1 Then E the high priest rose
Neh 3: 2 Next to E the men of Jericho
Neh 3:20 house of E the high priest
Neh 3:21 the door of the house of E to
Neh 3:21 to the end of the house of E
Neh 12:10 Joiakim begot E
Neh 12:10 E begot Joiada
Neh 12:22 houses in the days of E,
Neh 12:23 days of Johanan the son of E
Neh 13: 4 this, E the priest, having
Neh 13: 7 that E had done for Tobiah
Neh 13:28 the son of E the high priest,

ELIATHAH
1Ch 25: 4 Jerimoth, Hananiah, Hanani, E
1Ch 25:27 the twentieth for E, his sons

ELIDAD
Num 34:21 E the son of Chislon

ELIEL (*see* ELIAB, ELIAH)
1Ch 5:24 Epher, Ishi, E, Azriel,
1Ch 6:34 son of Jeroham, the son of E
1Ch 8:20 Elienai, Zillethai, E,
1Ch 8:22 Ishpan, Eber, E,
1Ch 11:46 E the Mahavite, Jeribai and
1Ch 11:47 E, Obed, and Jaasiel the
1Ch 12:11 the sixth, E the seventh,
1Ch 15: 9 E the chief, and eighty of his
1Ch 15:11 Asaiah, Joel, Shemaiah, E
2Ch 31:13 Asahel, Jerimoth, Jozabad, E

ELIENAI
1Ch 8:20 E, Zillethai, Eliel,

ELIEZER
Gen 15: 2 of my house is E of Damascus
Ex 18: 4 the other was E (for he said
1Ch 7: 8 Becher were Zemirah, Joash, E
1Ch 15:24 Zechariah, Benaiah, and E
1Ch 23:15 of Moses were Gershon and E
1Ch 23:17 Of the descendants of E,
1Ch 23:17 E had no other sons, but the
1Ch 26:25 And his brethren by E were
1Ch 27:16 was E the son of Zichri
2Ch 20:37 But E the son of Dodavah of
Ezra 8:16 Then I sent for E, Ariel,
Ezra 10:18 Maaseiah, E, Jarib, and
Ezra 10:23 Pethahiah, Judah, and E
Ezra 10:31 E, Ishijah, Malchijah,
Luke 3:29 the son of Jose, the son of E

ELIHOENAI (*see* ELIOENAI)
Ezra 8: 4 E the son of Zerahiah, and

ELIHOREPH
1Ki 4: 3 E and Ahijah, the sons of

ELIHU
1Sa 1: 1 son of Jeroham, the son of E
1Ch 12:20 Jediael, Michael, Jozabad, E
1Ch 26: 7 and Elzabad, whose brothers E
1Ch 27:18 over Judah, E, one of David's
Job 32: 2 Then the wrath of E, the son
Job 32: 4 E had waited to speak to Job
Job 32: 5 When E saw that there was no
Job 32: 6 So E, the son of Barachel the
Job 34: 1 E further answered and said
Job 35: 1 Moreover E answered and said
Job 36: 1 E also proceeded and said

ELIJAH (*see* ELIAH)
1Ki 17: 1 And E the Tishbite, of the
1Ki 17:13 And E said to her,
1Ki 17:15 according to the word of E
1Ki 17:16 the LORD which He spoke by E
1Ki 17:18 So she said to E, "What have
1Ki 17:22 the LORD heard the voice of E
1Ki 17:23 E took the child and brought
1Ki 17:23 E said, "See, your son lives
1Ki 17:24 Then the woman said to E
1Ki 18: 1 word of the LORD came to E
1Ki 18: 2 So E went to present himself
1Ki 18: 7 his way, suddenly E met him
1Ki 18: 7 Is that you, my lord E
1Ki 18: 8 tell your master, 'E is here
1Ki 18:11 your master, 'E is here"'
1Ki 18:14 tell your master, 'E is here
1Ki 18:15 Then E said, "As the LORD of
1Ki 18:16 and Ahab went to meet E
1Ki 18:17 it happened, when Ahab saw E
1Ki 18:21 E came to all the people, and
1Ki 18:22 Then E said to the people,
1Ki 18:25 Now E said to the prophets of
1Ki 18:27 that E mocked them and said,
1Ki 18:30 Then E said to all the people
1Ki 18:31 And E took twelve stones,
1Ki 18:36 that E the prophet came near
1Ki 18:40 And E said to them,
1Ki 18:40 E brought them down to the
1Ki 18:41 Then E said to Ahab, "Go up,
1Ki 18:42 And E went up to the top of
1Ki 18:46 hand of the LORD came upon E
1Ki 19: 1 Jezebel all that E had done
1Ki 19: 2 Jezebel sent a messenger to E
1Ki 19: 9 What are you doing here, E
1Ki 19:13 was, when E heard it, that he
1Ki 19:13 What are you doing here, E
1Ki 19:19 Then E passed by him and threw
1Ki 19:20 left the oxen and ran after E
1Ki 19:21 Then he arose and followed E
1Ki 21:17 LORD came to E the Tishbite
1Ki 21:20 Then Ahab said to E, "Have
1Ki 21:28 LORD came to E the Tishbite
2Ki 1: 3 LORD said to E the Tishbite
2Ki 1: 4 So E departed.
2Ki 1: 8 said, "It is E the Tishbite
2Ki 1:10 So E answered and said to the
2Ki 1:12 So E answered and said to them
2Ki 1:13 and fell on his knees before E
2Ki 1:15 angel of the LORD said to E
2Ki 1:17 the LORD which E had spoken
2Ki 2: 1 LORD was about to take up E
2Ki 2: 1 that E went with Elisha from
2Ki 2: 2 Then E said to Elisha, "Stay
2Ki 2: 4 Then E said to him, "Elisha,
2Ki 2: 6 Then E said to him, "Stay
2Ki 2: 8 Now E took his mantle, rolled
2Ki 2: 9 over, that E said to Elisha,
2Ki 2:11 E went up by a whirlwind into
2Ki 2:13 of E that had fallen from him
2Ki 2:14 of E that had fallen from him
2Ki 2:14 Where is the LORD God of E
2Ki 2:15 The spirit of E rests on
2Ki 3:11 water on the hands of E
2Ki 9:36 by His servant E the Tishbite
2Ki 10:10 He spoke by His servant E
2Ki 10:17 the LORD which He spoke to E
1Ch 8:27 Jaareshiah, E, and Zichri were
2Ch 21:12 to him from E the prophet
Ezra 10:21 Maaseiah, E, Shemaiah, Jehiel
Mal 4: 5 I will send you E the prophet
Matt 11:14 it, he is E who is to come
Matt 16:14 say John the Baptist, some E
Matt 17: 3 E appeared to them, talking
Matt 17: 4 one for Moses, and one for E
Matt 17:10 say that E must come first
Matt 17:11 E truly is coming first and
Matt 17:12 you that E has come already
Matt 27:47 This Man is calling for E
Matt 27:49 let us see if E will come to
Mark 6:15 Others said, "It is E."
Mark 8:28 but some say, E
Mark 9: 4 E appeared to them with Moses
Mark 9: 5 one for Moses, and one for E"
Mark 9:11 say that E must come first
Mark 9:12 them, "E does come first, and
Mark 9:13 to you that E has also come
Mark 15:35 Look, He is calling for E
Mark 15:36 let us see if E will come to
Luke 1:17 in the spirit and power of E
Luke 4:25 in Israel in the days of E
Luke 4:26 but to none of them was E
Luke 9: 8 by some that E had appeared
Luke 9:19 the Baptist, but some say E
Luke 9:30 Him, who were Moses and E
Luke 9:33 one for Moses, and one for E"
Luke 9:54 consume them, just as E did
John 1:21 What then? Are you E?"
John 1:25 you are not the Christ, nor E
Rom 11: 2 what the Scripture says of E
Jas 5:17 E was a man with a nature

ELIKA
2Sa 23:25 the Harodite, E the Harodite,

ELIM (*see* BEER ELIM)
Ex 15:27 Then they came to E, where
Ex 16: 1 And they journeyed from E, and
Ex 16: 1 of Sin, which is between E
Num 33: 9 from Marah and came to E
Num 33: 9 At E were twelve springs of
Num 33:10 They moved from E and camped

ELIMELECH (*see* ELIMELECH'S)
Ruth 1: 2 The name of the man was E
Ruth 1: 3 Then E, Naomi's husband, died
Ruth 2: 1 wealth, of the family of E
Ruth 2: 3 who was of the family of E
Ruth 4: 3 belonged to our brother E

ELIMELECH'S (*see* ELIMELECH)
Ruth 4: 9 I have bought all that was E

ELIMINATED
Matt 15:17 goes into the stomach and is e
Mark 7:19 but his stomach, and is e,

ELIOENAI (*see* ELIHOENAI)
1Ch 3:23 The sons of Neariah were E
1Ch 3:24 The sons of E were Hodaviah,
1Ch 4:36 E, Jaakobah, Jeshohaiah,
1Ch 7: 8 Zemirah, Joash, Eliezer, E
Ezra 10:22 E, Maaseiah, Ishmael,
Ezra 10:27 E, Eliashib, Mattaniah,
Neh 12:41 Minjamin, Michaiah, E,

ELIPHAL
1Ch 11:35 Hararite, E the son of Ur,

ELIPHAZ
Gen 36: 4 Now Adah bore E to Esau, and
Gen 36:10 E the son of Adah the wife of
Gen 36:11 And the sons of E were Teman
Gen 36:12 Timna was the concubine of E
Gen 36:12 son, and she bore Amalek to E

Gen 36:15 The sons of **E**, the firstborn
Gen 36:16 of **E** in the land of Edom
1Ch 1:35 The sons of Esau were **E**,
1Ch 1:36 And the sons of **E** were Teman
Job 2:11 **E** the Temanite, Bildad the
Job 4: 1 Then **E** the Temanite answered
Job 15: 1 Then **E** the Temanite answered
Job 22: 1 Then **E** the Temanite answered
Job 42: 7 LORD said to **E** the Temanite
Job 42: 9 So **E** the Temanite and Bildad

ELIPHELEH
1Ch 15:18 Maaseiah, Mattithiah, **E**,
1Ch 15:21 Mattithiah, **E**, Mikneiah,

ELIPHELET
2Sa 5:16 Elishama, Eliada, and **E**
2Sa 23:34 **E** the son of Ahasbai, the son
1Ch 3: 6 there were Ibhar, Elishama, **E**
1Ch 3: 8 Elishama, Eliada, and **E**
1Ch 8:39 the second, and **E** the third
1Ch 14: 7 Elishama, Beeliada, and **E**
Ezra 8:13 **E**, Jeiel, and Shemaiah
Ezra 10:33 Mattenai, Mattattah, Zabad, **E**

ELI'S (*see* ELI)
1Sa 3:14 **E** house shall not be atoned

ELISHA
1Ki 19:16 **E** the son of Shaphat of Abel
1Ki 19:17 sword of Jehu, **E** will kill
1Ki 19:19 found **E** the son of Shaphat,
1Ki 19:21 So **E** turned back from him, and
2Ki 2: 1 went with **E** from Gilgal
2Ki 2: 2 Then Elijah said to **E**, Stay
2Ki 2: 2 **E** said, As the LORD lives
2Ki 2: 3 were at Bethel came out to **E**
2Ki 2: 4 **E**, stay here, please, for the
2Ki 2: 5 who were at Jericho came to **E**
2Ki 2: 9 over, that Elijah said to **E**
2Ki 2: 9 **E** said, "Please let a double
2Ki 2:12 Now **E** saw it, and he cried out
2Ki 2:14 and **E** crossed over
2Ki 2:15 spirit of Elijah rests on **E**
2Ki 2:19 the men of the city said to **E**
2Ki 2:22 saying of **E** which he spoke
2Ki 3:11 **E** the son of Shaphat is here,
2Ki 3:13 Then **E** said to the king of
2Ki 3:14 **E** said, "As the LORD of
2Ki 4: 1 the prophets cried out to **E**
2Ki 4: 2 So **E** said to her, "What
2Ki 4: 8 one day that **E** went to Shunem
2Ki 4:17 come, of which **E** had told her
2Ki 4:32 when **E** came into the house,
2Ki 4:38 And **E** returned to Gilgal, and
2Ki 5: 8 when **E** the man of God heard
2Ki 5: 9 at the door of the house of **E**
2Ki 5:10 **E** sent a messenger to him,
2Ki 5:20 servant of **E** the man of God
2Ki 5:25 **E** said to him, "Where did you
2Ki 6: 1 of the prophets said to **E**
2Ki 6:12 but **E**, the prophet who is in
2Ki 6:17 And **E** prayed, and said,
2Ki 6:17 chariots of fire all around **E**
2Ki 6:18 **E** prayed to the LORD, and said
2Ki 6:18 according to the word of **E**
2Ki 6:19 Now **E** said to them, "This is
2Ki 6:20 come to Samaria, that **E** said
2Ki 6:21 Israel saw them, he said to **E**
2Ki 6:31 if the head of **E** the son of
2Ki 6:32 But **E** was sitting in his
2Ki 7: 1 Then **E** said, "Hear the word
2Ki 8: 1 Then **E** spoke to the woman
2Ki 8: 4 the great things **E** has done
2Ki 8: 5 son whom **E** restored to life
2Ki 8: 7 Then **E** went to Damascus, and
2Ki 8:10 **E** said to him, "Go, say to
2Ki 8:13 **E** answered, "The LORD has
2Ki 8:14 Then he departed from **E**, and
2Ki 8:14 him, "What did **E** say to you
2Ki 9: 1 **E** the prophet called one of
2Ki 13:14 **E** had become sick with the
2Ki 13:15 **E** said to him, "Take a bow
2Ki 13:16 **E** put his hands on the king's
2Ki 13:17 Then **E** said, "Shoot"
2Ki 13:20 Then **E** died, and they buried
2Ki 13:21 put the man in the tomb of **E**
2Ki 13:21 and touched the bones of **E**
Luke 4:27 in the time of **E** the prophet

ELISHAH
Gen 10: 4 The sons of Javan were **E**,
1Ch 1: 7 The sons of Javan were **E**,
Ezek 27: 7 of **E** was what covered you

ELISHAMA
Num 1:10 **E** the son of Ammihud
Num 2:18 shall be **E** the son of Ammihud
Num 7:48 day **E** the son of Ammihud,
Num 7:53 of **E** the son of Ammihud
Num 10:22 army was **E** the son of Ammihud
2Sa 5:16 **E**, Eliada, and Eliphelet
2Ki 25:25 of Nethaniah, the son of **E**
1Ch 2:41 and Jekamiah begot **E**
1Ch 3: 6 Also there were Ibhar, **E**,
1Ch 3: 8 **E**, Eliada, and Eliphelet
1Ch 7:26 Ammihud his son, **E** his son,
1Ch 14: 7 **E**, Beeliada, and Eliphelet
2Ch 17: 8 and with them **E** and Jehoram,
Jer 36:12 **E** the scribe, Delaiah the son
Jer 36:20 the chamber of **E** the scribe
Jer 36:21 and he took it from **E** the
Jer 41: 1 of Nethaniah, the son of **E**

ELISHAPHAT
2Ch 23: 1 and **E** the son of Zichri

ELISHEBA
Ex 6:23 Aaron took to himself **E**,

ELISHUA
2Sa 5:15 Ibhar, **E**, Nepheg, Japhia,
1Ch 14: 5 Ibhar, **E**, Elpelet,

ELIUD
Matt 1:14 Achim, and Achim begot **E**
Matt 1:15 **E** begot Eleazar, Eleazar

ELIZABETH (*see* ELIZABETH'S)
Luke 1: 5 of Aaron, and her name was **E**
Luke 1: 7 because **E** was barren, and they
Luke 1:13 your wife **E** will bear you a
Luke 1:24 days his wife **E** conceived
Luke 1:36 **E** your relative has also
Luke 1:40 of Zacharias and greeted **E**
Luke 1:41 when **E** heard the greeting of
Luke 1:41 **E** was filled with the Holy

ELIZABETH'S (*see* ELIZABETH)
Luke 1:57 Now **E** full time came for her

ELIZAPHAN (*see* ELZAPHAN)
Num 3:30 was **E** the son of Uzziel
Num 34:25 Zebulun, **E** the son of Parnach
1Ch 15: 8 of the sons of **E**, Shemaiah
2Ch 29:13 of the sons of **E**, Shimri and

ELIZUR
Num 1: 5 Reuben, **E** the son of Shedeur
Num 2:10 shall be **E** the son of Shedeur
Num 7:30 On the fourth day **E** the son
Num 7:35 of **E** the son of Shedeur
Num 10:18 army was **E** the son of Shedeur

ELJEHOENAI
1Ch 26: 3 the sixth, **E** the seventh

ELKANAH
Ex 6:24 sons of Korah were Assir, **E**
1Sa 1: 1 his name was **E** the son of
1Sa 1: 4 for **E** to make an offering
1Sa 1: 8 Then **E** her husband said to
1Sa 1:19 **E** knew Hannah his wife, and
1Sa 1:21 And the man **E** and all his house
1Sa 1:23 **E** her husband said to her,
1Sa 2:11 Then **E** went to his house at
1Sa 2:20 And Eli would bless **E** and his
1Ch 6:23 **E** his son, Ebiasaph his son,
1Ch 6:25 The sons of **E** were Amasai
1Ch 6:26 As for **E**, the sons of **E**
1Ch 6:27 Jeroham his son, and **E** his son
1Ch 6:34 the son of **E**, the son of
1Ch 6:35 the son of Zuph, the son of **E**
1Ch 6:36 the son of **E**, the son of Joel
1Ch 9:16 the son of Asa, the son of **E**
1Ch 12: 6 **E**, Jisshiah, Azareel, Joezer,
1Ch 15:23 **E** were doorkeepers for the
2Ch 28: 7 **E** who was second to the king

ELKOSHITE
Nah 1: 1 of the vision of Nahum the **E**

ELLASAR
Gen 14: 1 of Shinar, Arioch king of **E**
Gen 14: 9 Shinar, and Arioch king of **E**

ELMODAM
Luke 3:28 son of Cosam, the son of **E**

ELNAAM
1Ch 11:46 and Joshaviah the sons of **E**

ELNATHAN
2Ki 24: 8 daughter of **E** of Jerusalem
Ezra 8:16 Shemaiah, **E**, Jarib, **E**
Ezra 8:16 also for Joiarib and **E**, men of
Jer 26:22 **E** the son of Achbor, and other
Jer 36:12 **E** the son of Achbor, Gemariah
Jer 36:25 Nevertheless **E**, Delaiah, and

ELOI (*see* ELI)
Mark 15:34 **E**, **E**, lama sabachthani

ELON (*see* ALLON, ELONITES)
Gen 26:34 the daughter of **E** the Hittite
Gen 36: 2 the daughter of **E** the Hittite
Gen 46:14 sons of Zebulun were Sered, **E**
Num 26:26 of **E**, the family of the
Josh 19:43 **E**, Timnah, Ekron,
Judg 12:11 him, **E** the Zebulunite judged
Judg 12:12 **E** the Zebulunite died and was

ELON BETH HANAN (*see* HANAN)
1Ki 4: 9 Shaalbim, Beth Shemesh, and **E**

ELONITES (*see* ELON)
Num 26:26 of Elon, the family of the **E**

ELOQUENT
Ex 4:10 O my Lord, I am not **e**,
Acts 18:24 an **e** man and mighty in the

ELPAAL
1Ch 8:11 Hushim he begot Abitub and **E**
1Ch 8:12 The sons of **E** were Eber,
1Ch 8:18 and Jobab were the sons of **E**

EL PARAN (*see* PARAN)
Gen 14: 6 mountain of Seir, as far as **E**

ELPELET
1Ch 14: 5 Ibhar, Elishua, **E**,

ELSE (*see* PREFACE)

ELSEWHERE (*see* PREFACE)

ELTEKEH
Josh 19:44 **E**, Gibbethon, Baalath,
Josh 21:23 Dan, **E** with its common-land,

ELTEKON
Josh 15:59 Maarath, Beth Anoth, and **E**

ELTOLAD
Josh 15:30 **E**, Chesil, Hormah,
Josh 19: 4 **E**, Bethul, Hormah,

ELUL
Neh 6:15 day of the month of **E**, in

ELUZAI
1Ch 12: 5 **E**, Jerimoth, Bealiah,

ELYMAS
Acts 13: 8 But **E** the sorcerer (for so

ELZABAD
1Ch 12:12 the eighth, **E** the ninth,
1Ch 26: 7 Othni, Rephael, Obed, and **E**

ELZAPHAN (*see* ELIZAPHAN)
Ex 6:22 of Uzziel were Mishael, **E**
Lev 10: 4 And Moses called Mishael and **E**

EMASCULATED
Deut 23: 1 He who is **e** by crushing or

EMBALM (*see* EMBALMED)
Gen 50: 2 physicians to **e** his father

EMBALMED (*see* EMBALM)
Gen 50: 2 So the physicians **e** Israel
Gen 50: 3 required for those who are **e**
Gen 50:26 and they **e** him, and he was put

EMBANKMENT
Luke 19:43 will build an **e** around you

EMBARRASSED
Judg 3:25 they waited till they were **e**
Is 1:29 you shall be **e** because of the

EMBELLISHED
Hos 10: 1 have **e** his sacred pillars

EMBER
2Sa 14: 7 extinguish my **e** that is left

EMBLEMS
Num 2: 2 beside the e of his father's

EMBOLDENED
1Co 8:10 of him who is weak be e to

EMBOSSED
Job 15:26 Him with his strong, e shield

EMBRACE (*see* EMBRACED, EMBRACES, EMBRACING)
Gen 16: 5 I gave my maid into your e
2Ki 4:16 next year you shall e a son
Prov 4: 8 you honor, when you e her
Eccl 3: 5 a time to e, and a time to
Lam 4: 5 up in scarlet e ash heaps

EMBRACED (*see* EMBRACE)
Gen 29:13 and e him and kissed him, and
Gen 33: 4 e him, and fell on his neck and
Gen 48:10 and he kissed them and e them
1Ki 9: 9 and have e other gods, and
2Ch 7:22 e other gods, and worshiped
Prov 5:20 and be e in the arms of a
Ezek 23: 3 their breasts were there e
Acts 20: 1 e them, and departed to go to
Heb 11:13 e them, and confessed that

EMBRACES (*see* EMBRACE)
Song 2: 6 head, and his right hand e me
Song 8: 3 head, and his right hand e me

EMBRACING (*see* EMBRACE)
Eccl 3: 5 and a time to refrain from e
Acts 20:10 fell on him, and e him said,

EMBROIDERED (*see* EMBROIDERY)
Judg 5:30 plunder of garments e and
Ezek 16:10 I clothed you in e cloth and
Ezek 16:13 fine linen, silk, and e cloth
Ezek 16:18 You took your e garments and
Ezek 26:16 and take off their e garments
Ezek 27: 7 Fine e linen from Egypt was
Ezek 27:24 in e garments, in chests of

EMBROIDERY (*see* EMBROIDERED)
Judg 5:30 two pieces of dyed e for the
Ezek 27:16 wares emeralds, purple, e

EMEK KEZIZ
Josh 18:21 were Jericho, Beth Hoglah, E

EMERALD (*see* EMERALDS)
Ex 28:17 a sardius, a topaz, and an e
Ex 39:10 and an e was the first row
Ezek 28:13 turquoise, and e with gold
Rev 4: 3 in appearance like an e
Rev 21:19 chalcedony, the fourth e,

EMERALDS (*see* EMERALD)
Ezek 27:16 gave you for your wares e

EMIM
Gen 14: 5 the E in Shaveh Kiriathaim,
Deut 2:10 (The E had dwelt there in
Deut 2:11 but the Moabites call them E

EMINENT
2Co 11: 5 to the most e apostles
2Co 12:11 I behind the most e apostles

EMISSION (*see* EMITS)
Lev 15:16 If any man has an e of semen
Lev 15:18 and there is an e of semen
Lev 22: 4 man who has had an e of semen

EMITS (*see* EMISSION, EMITTED)
Lev 15:32 and for him who e semen and is

EMITTED (*see* EMITS)
Gen 38: 9 that he e on the ground, lest

EMMAUS
Luke 24:13 day to a village called E

EMPIRE
Esth 1:20 all his e (for it is great)

EMPLOYED
1Ch 9:33 for they were e in that work
Ezek 39:14 set apart men regularly e

EMPTIED (*see* EMPTY)
Gen 24:20 e her pitcher into the trough
Gen 42:35 as they e their sacks, that
2Ch 24:11 e the chest, and took it and
Neh 5:13 may he be shaken out and e
Is 19: 6 brooks of defense will be e
Is 24: 3 The land shall be entirely e
Jer 48:11 has not been e from vessel to
Ezek 12:19 may be e of all who are in it
Nah 2: 2 the emptiers have e them out

EMPTIERS (*see* EMPTY)
Nah 2: 2 for the e have emptied them

EMPTIES (*see* EMPTY)
Hos 10: 1 Israel e his vine

EMPTINESS (*see* EMPTY)
Is 34:11 confusion and the stones of e
2Pe 2:18 great swelling words of e

EMPTY (*see* EMPTIED, EMPTIERS, EMPTIES, EMPTINESS, EMPTY-HANDED, EMPTY-HEADED)
Gen 37:24 And the pit was e
Gen 41:27 the seven e heads blighted by
Ex 23:15 shall appear before Me e)
Lev 14:36 command that they e the house
Lev 26:43 also shall be left e by them
Judg 7:16 with e pitchers, and torches
Ruth 1:21 has brought me home again e
1Sa 6: 3 of Israel, do not send it e
1Sa 12:21 e things which cannot profit
1Sa 20:18 because your seat will be e
1Sa 20:25 side, but David's place was e
1Sa 20:27 that David's place was e
2Sa 1:22 of Saul did not return e
2Ki 4: 3 all your neighbors—e vessels
Job 11: 3 Should your e talk make men
Job 15: 2 man answer with e knowledge
Job 21:34 you comfort me with e words
Job 22: 9 You have sent widows away e
Job 26: 7 out the north over e space
Job 35:13 God will not listen to e talk
Eccl 11: 3 they e themselves upon the
Is 24: 1 the LORD makes the earth e
Is 29: 8 and his soul is still e
Is 59: 4 they trust in e words and
Jer 14: 3 returned with their vessels e
Jer 48:12 e his vessels and break the
Jer 51: 2 winnow her and e her land
Jer 51:34 he has made me an e vessel
Ezek 14:15 the land, and they e it, and
Ezek 24:11 set the pot e on the coals
Nah 2:10 She is e, desolate, and waste
Hab 1:17 they therefore e their net
Matt 12:44 when he comes, he finds it e
Luke 1:53 the rich He has sent away e
Eph 5: 6 one deceive you with e words
Col 2: 8 e deceit, according to the

EMPTY-HANDED (*see* EMPTY)
Gen 31:42 you would have sent me away e
Ex 3:21 go, that you shall not go e
Ex 34:20 none shall appear before Me e
Deut 15:13 shall not let him go away e
Deut 16:16 not appear before the LORD e
Ruth 3:17 to me, "Do not go e to your
Mark 12: 3 beat him and sent him away e
Luke 20:10 beat him and sent him away e
Luke 20:11 and sent him away e

EMPTY-HEADED (*see* EMPTY)
Job 11:12 For an e man will be wise,

ENABLE (*see* ENABLED)
Ezek 36:33 I will also e you to dwell in

ENABLED (*see* ENABLE)
1Ti 1:12 Jesus our Lord who has e me

ENAM
Josh 15:34 En Gannim, Tappuah, E

ENAN
Num 1:15 Naphtali, Ahira the son of E
Num 2:29 shall be Ahira the son of E
Num 7:78 day Ahira the son of E,
Num 7:83 of Ahira the son of E
Num 10:27 was Ahira the son of E

ENCAMP (*see* CAMP, ENCAMPED, ENCAMPMENT, ENCAMPS)
Judg 6: 4 they would e against them
2Sa 12:28 e against the city and take it
Job 19:12 they e all around my tent
Ps 27: 3 an army should e against me
Is 29: 3 I will e against you all
Jer 50:29 bow, e against it all around

ENCAMPED (*see* ENCAMP)
Ex 18: 5 where he was e at the
Num 9:18 tabernacle they remained e
Num 9:20 the LORD they would remain e
Num 9:22 of Israel would remain e and
Num 9:23 of the LORD they remained e
Num 24: 2 saw Israel e according to
Josh 10:31 they e against it and fought
Josh 10:34 they e against it and fought
Judg 6:33 e in the Valley of Jezreel
Judg 7: 1 e beside the well of Harod,
Judg 9:50 he e against Thebez and took
Judg 10:17 together and e in Gilead
Judg 10:17 together and e in Mizpah
Judg 11:18 e on the other side of the
Judg 11:20 e in Jahaz, and fought against
Judg 15: 9 up, e in Judah, and deployed
Judg 18:12 e in Kirjath Jearim in Judah
Judg 20:19 morning and e against Gibeah
1Sa 4: 1 and e beside Ebenezer
1Sa 4: 1 and the Philistines e in Aphek
1Sa 11: 1 up and e against Jabesh Gilead
1Sa 13: 5 e in Michmash, to the east of
1Sa 13:16 the Philistines e in Michmash
1Sa 17: 1 they e between Sochoh and
1Sa 17: 2 they e in the Valley of Elah,
1Sa 26: 3 And Saul e in the hill of
1Sa 26: 5 to the place where Saul had e
1Sa 26: 5 the people e all around him
1Sa 28: 4 and came and e at Shunem
1Sa 28: 4 together, and they e at Gilboa
1Sa 29: 1 and the Israelites e by a
2Sa 11:11 lord are e in the open fields
2Sa 17:26 and Absalom e in the land of
2Sa 23:13 e in the Valley of Rephaim
1Ki 16:15 the people were e against
1Ki 16:16 who were e heard it said
1Ki 20:27 Now the children of Israel e
1Ki 20:29 they e opposite each other
2Ki 25: 1 Jerusalem and e against it
2Ki 25: 4 the Chaldeans were still e
1Ch 11:15 e in the Valley of Rephaim
1Ch 19: 7 who came and e before Medeba
2Ch 32: 1 he e against the fortified
Jer 52: 4 Jerusalem and e against it

ENCAMPMENT (*see* ENCAMP, ENCAMPMENTS)
Gen 42:27 give his donkey feed at the e
Gen 43:21 when we came to the e, that
Ex 4:24 to pass on the way, at the e

ENCAMPMENTS (*see* ENCAMPMENT)
Ezek 25: 4 shall set their e among you

ENCAMPS (*see* ENCAMP)
Ps 34: 7 The angel of the LORD e all
Ps 53: 5 of him who e against you

ENCHANTER (*see* ENCHANTMENTS)
Is 3: 3 artisan, and the expert e

ENCHANTMENTS (*see* ENCHANTER)
Ex 7:11 in like manner with their e
Ex 7:22 of Egypt did so with their e
Ex 8: 7 magicians did so with their e
Ex 8:18 their e to bring forth lice
Is 47: 9 the great abundance of your e
Is 47:12 Stand now with your e and the

ENCIRCLE (*see* ENCIRCLED, ENCIRCLING)
Is 50:11 who e yourselves with sparks

ENCIRCLED (*see* ENCIRCLE)
Deut 32:10 He e him, He instructed him,
Ps 22:12 bulls of Bashan have e Me
Heb 11:30 they were e for seven days

ENCIRCLING (*see* ENCIRCLE)
1Sa 23:26 Saul and his men were e David
1Ki 7:24 buds e it all around, ten to
2Ch 4: 3 of oxen e it all around, ten

ENCLOSE (*see* ENCLOSED, ENCLOSING, ENCLOSURES)
Song 8: 9 we will e her with boards of
Jer 22:15 you e yourself in cedar

ENCLOSED (*see* ENCLOSE)
Ex 39: 6 stones, e in settings of gold
Ex 39:13 They were e in settings of
1Ki 7:12 The great court was e with
2Ch 33:14 it e Ophel, and he raised it
Ps 22:16 of the wicked has e Me
Song 4:12 A garden e is my sister, my
Ezek 46:22 of the court were e courts

ENCLOSING (*see* ENCLOSE)
Josh 19:33 e the territory from the

ENCLOSURES (*see* ENCLOSE)
2Ch 14:15 also attacked the livestock **e**

ENCOMPASS (*see* ENCOMPASSED, ENCOMPASSES)
Jer 31:22 a woman shall **e** a man

ENCOMPASSED (*see* ENCOMPASS)
2Sa 22: 5 When the waves of death **e** me
Ps 18: 4 The pangs of death **e** me, And
Ps 116: 3 The pains of death **e** me, And
Hos 11:12 Ephraim has **e** Me with lies,
Jon 2: 5 The waters **e** me, even to my

ENCOMPASSES (*see* ENCOMPASS)
Gen 2:11 it is the one which **e** the
Gen 2:13 it is the one which **e** the

ENCOUNTERED
Acts 17:18 and Stoic philosophers **e** him

ENCOURAGE (*see* ENCOURAGED, ENCOURAGEMENT)
Deut 1:38 **E** him, for he shall cause
Deut 3:28 and **e** him and strengthen him
2Sa 11:25 So **e** him.
1Ki 22:13 with one accord **e** the king
2Ch 18:12 with one accord **e** the king
Ps 64: 5 They **e** themselves in an evil
1Th 3: 2 **e** you concerning your faith,

ENCOURAGED (*see* ENCOURAGE)
Judg 20:22 **e** themselves and again formed
2Ch 28:19 for he had **e** moral decline in
2Ch 35: 2 **e** them for the service of the
Ezra 1: 6 them **e** them with articles of
Ezra 7:28 So I was **e**, as the hand of
Is 41: 7 the craftsman **e** the goldsmith
Acts 11:23 **e** them all that with purpose
Acts 16:40 the brethren, they **e** them
Acts 20: 2 **e** them with many words, he
Acts 27:36 Then they were all **e**, and also
Rom 1:12 that I may be **e** together with
1Co 14:31 all may learn and all may be **e**
Phil 2:19 that I also may be **e** when I
Col 2: 2 that their hearts may be **e**

ENCOURAGEMENT (*see* ENCOURAGE)
1Ki 22:13 of one of them, and speak **e**
2Ch 18:12 of one of them, and speak **e**
2Ch 30:22 Hezekiah gave **e** to all the
2Ch 32: 6 the city gate, and gave them **e**
Acts 4:36 which is translated Son of **E**)
Acts 15:31 it, they rejoiced over its **e**

END (*see* ENDED, ENDLESS, ENDS)
Gen 6:13 The **e** of all flesh has come
Gen 8: 3 At the **e** of the hundred and
Gen 8: 6 at the **e** of forty days, that
Gen 23: 9 is at the **e** of his field
Gen 41: 1 at the **e** of two full years,
Gen 47:21 from one **e** of the borders of
Gen 47:21 of Egypt to the other **e**
Ex 12:41 at the **e** of the four hundred
Ex 23:16 which is at the **e** of the year
Ex 25:19 Make one cherub at one **e**, and
Ex 25:19 other cherub at the other **e**
Ex 26: 5 is on the **e** of the second set
Ex 26:28 of the boards from **e** to **e**
Ex 28:22 for the breastplate at the **e**
Ex 31:18 And when He had made an **e** of
Ex 34:22 Ingathering at the year's **e**
Ex 36:12 on the **e** of the second set
Ex 36:33 from one **e** to the other
Ex 37: 8 cherub at one **e** on this side
Ex 37: 8 at the other **e** on that side
Lev 16:20 And when he has made an **e** of
Lev 17: 5 to the **e** that the children of
Num 23:10 and let my **e** be like his
Num 34: 3 to the **e** of the Salt Sea
Num 34: 5 and it shall **e** at the Sea
Num 34: 9 and it shall **e** at Hazar Enan
Num 34:12 it shall **e** at the Salt Sea
Deut 4:32 ask from one **e** of heaven to
Deut 8:16 you, to do you good in the **e**
Deut 9:11 at the **e** of forty days and
Deut 11:12 to the very **e** of the year
Deut 13: 7 from one **e** of the earth to
Deut 13: 7 to the other **e** of the earth
Deut 14:28 At the **e** of every third year
Deut 15: 1 At the **e** of every seven years
Deut 28:49 from the **e** of the earth, as
Deut 28:64 from one **e** of the earth to
Deut 31:10 At the **e** of every seven years
Deut 32:20 will see what their **e** will be
Deut 32:29 would consider their latter **e**
Josh 8:24 made an **e** of slaying all the
Josh 9:16 at the **e** of three days, after
Josh 10:20 children of Israel made an **e**
Josh 15: 8 which is at the **e** of the
Josh 18:15 at the **e** of Kirjath Jearim
Josh 18:16 **e** of the mountain that lies
Josh 18:19 at the south **e** of the Jordan
Josh 19:49 When they had made an **e** of
Josh 19:51 So they made an **e** of dividing
Judg 6:21 of the LORD put out the **e** of
Judg 11:39 it was so at the **e** of two
Judg 19: 9 the day is coming to an **e**
Ruth 2:23 until the **e** of barley harvest
Ruth 3: 7 at the **e** of the heap of grain
Ruth 3:10 the **e** than at the beginning
1Sa 3:12 house, from beginning to **e**
1Sa 14:27 he stretched out the **e** of the
1Sa 14:43 a little honey with the **e** of
2Sa 2:23 with the blunt **e** of the spear
2Sa 2:26 be bitter in the latter **e**
2Sa 14:26 at the **e** of every year he cut
2Sa 20:18 and so they would **e** disputes
2Sa 24: 8 at the **e** of nine months and
1Ki 2:39 at the **e** of three years, that
1Ki 9:10 at the **e** of twenty years,
2Ki 8: 3 at the **e** of seven years, that
2Ki 10:21 full from one **e** to the other
2Ki 10:25 an **e** of offering the burnt
2Ki 18:10 at the **e** of three years they
2Ki 21:16 from one **e** to another,
2Ch 5:12 at the east **e** of the altar
2Ch 8: 1 pass at the **e** of twenty years
2Ch 20:16 the **e** of the brook before the
2Ch 20:23 when they had made an **e** of
2Ch 21:19 after the **e** of two years,
Ezra 9:11 one **e** to another with their
Neh 3:21 **e** of the house of Eliashib
Job 6:11 And what is my **e**, that I
Job 8: 7 yet your latter **e** would
Job 16: 3 Shall words of wind have an **e**
Job 18: 2 till you put an **e** to words
Job 22: 5 And your iniquity without **e**
Job 28: 3 Man puts an **e** to darkness
Ps 7: 9 of the wicked come to an **e**
Ps 19: 4 words to the **e** of the world
Ps 19: 6 is from one **e** of heaven, And
Ps 19: 6 And its circuit to the other **e**
Ps 30:12 To the **e** that my glory may
Ps 39: 4 LORD, make me to know my **e**
Ps 46: 9 cease to the **e** of the earth
Ps 61: 2 From the **e** of the earth I
Ps 73:17 Then I understood their **e**
Ps 102:27 And Your years will have no **e**
Ps 107:27 man, And are at their wits' **e**
Ps 119:33 And I shall keep it to the **e**
Ps 119:87 made an **e** of me on earth, But
Ps 119:112 Forever, to the very **e**
Prov 5: 4 but in the **e** she is bitter as
Prov 14:12 but its **e** is the way of death
Prov 14:13 the **e** of mirth may be grief
Prov 16:25 but its **e** is the way of death
Prov 20:21 will not be blessed at the **e**
Prov 25: 8 for what will you do in the **e**
Prov 29:21 have him as a son in the **e**
Eccl 3:11 God does from beginning to **e**
Eccl 4: 8 Yet there is no **e** to all his
Eccl 4:16 There was no **e** of all the
Eccl 7: 2 for that is the **e** of all men
Eccl 7: 8 The **e** of a thing is better
Eccl 10:13 the **e** of his talk is raving
Eccl 12:12 many books there is no **e**, and
Is 2: 7 and there is no **e** to their
Is 2: 7 and there is no **e** to their
Is 5:26 them from the **e** of the earth
Is 7: 3 at the **e** of the aqueduct from
Is 9: 7 and peace there will be no **e**
Is 10:23 will make a determined **e** in
Is 13: 5 from the **e** of heaven, even
Is 16: 4 the extortioner is at an **e**
Is 23:15 At the **e** of seventy years it
Is 23:17 at the **e** of seventy years,
Is 33: 1 when you make an **e** of dealing
Is 38:12 night You make an **e** of me
Is 38:13 night You make an **e** of me
Is 41:22 and know the latter **e** of them
Is 46:10 Declaring the **e** from the
Is 47: 7 remember the latter **e** of them
Is 48:20 it even to the **e** of the earth
Is 62:11 to the **e** of the world
Jer 1: 3 until the **e** of the eleventh
Jer 3: 5 Will He keep it to the **e**
Jer 4:27 yet I will not make a full **e**
Jer 5:10 but do not make a complete **e**
Jer 5:18 not make a complete **e** of you
Jer 5:31 But what will you do in the **e**
Jer 12: 4 He will not see our final **e**
Jer 12:12 **e** of the land to the other
Jer 12:12 to the other **e** of the land
Jer 17:11 at his **e** he will be a fool
Jer 25:33 **e** of the earth even to the
Jer 25:33 to the other **e** of the earth
Jer 26: 8 an **e** of speaking all that the
Jer 30:11 though I make a full **e** of all
Jer 30:11 not make a complete **e** of you
Jer 34:14 At the **e** of seven years let
Jer 44:27 until there is an **e** to them
Jer 46:28 For I will make a complete **e**
Jer 46:28 not make a complete **e** of you
Jer 51:13 your **e** has come, the measure
Lam 4:18 Our **e** was near
Lam 4:18 were over, for our **e** had come
Ezek 3:16 Now it came to pass at the **e**
Ezek 7: 2 An **e**! The **e** has come
Ezek 7: 2 The **e** has come upon the four
Ezek 7: 3 Now the **e** has come upon you,
Ezek 7: 6 **e** has come, the **e** has come
Ezek 11:13 **e** of the remnant of Israel
Ezek 20:17 I did not make an **e** of them
Ezek 21:25 come, whose iniquity shall **e**
Ezek 21:29 come, whose iniquity shall **e**
Ezek 22: 4 come to the **e** of your years
Ezek 26:13 I will put an **e** to the sound
Ezek 29:13 At the **e** of forty years I
Ezek 35: 5 their iniquity came to an **e**
Ezek 39:14 At the **e** of seven months they
Ezek 41:12 **e** was seventy cubits wide
Ezek 46:19 at their extreme western **e**
Dan 1: 5 so that at the **e** of that time
Dan 1:15 at the **e** of ten days their
Dan 1:18 Now at the **e** of the days,
Dan 4:22 to the **e** of the earth
Dan 4:29 At the **e** of the twelve months
Dan 4:34 And at the **e** of the time I,
Dan 6:26 shall endure to the **e**
Dan 7:28 This is the **e** of the account
Dan 8:17 refers to the time of the **e**
Dan 8:19 appointed time the **e** shall be
Dan 9:24 to make an **e** of sins, to
Dan 9:26 the **e** of it shall be with a
Dan 9:26 And till the **e** of the war
Dan 9:27 shall bring an **e** to sacrifice
Dan 11: 6 at the **e** of some years they
Dan 11:13 **e** of some years with a great
Dan 11:18 reproach against them to an **e**
Dan 11:27 for the **e** will still be at
Dan 11:35 until the time of the **e**
Dan 11:40 At the time of the **e** the king
Dan 11:45 yet he shall come to his **e**
Dan 12: 4 book until the time of the **e**
Dan 12: 8 be the **e** of these things
Dan 12: 9 sealed till the time of the **e**
Dan 12:13 you, go your way till the **e**
Dan 12:13 at the **e** of the days
Hos 1: 4 bring an **e** to the kingdom of
Amos 3:15 great houses shall have an **e**
Amos 8: 2 The **e** has come upon my people
Amos 8:10 and its **e** like a bitter day
Obad 9 to the **e** that everyone from
Nah 1: 8 make an utter **e** of its place
Nah 1: 9 He will make an utter **e** of it
Nah 2: 9 There is no **e** of treasure
Hab 2: 3 but at the **e** it will speak,
Matt 10:22 to the **e** will be saved
Matt 13:39 harvest is the **e** of the age
Matt 13:40 will be at the **e** of this age
Matt 13:49 will be at the **e** of the age
Matt 24: 3 and of the **e** of the age
Matt 24: 6 to pass, but the **e** is not yet
Matt 24:13 to the **e** shall be saved
Matt 24:14 and then the **e** will come
Matt 24:31 from one **e** of heaven to the
Matt 26:58 the servants to see the **e**
Matt 28:20 even to the **e** of the age
Mark 3:26 he cannot stand, but has an **e**
Mark 13: 7 happen, but the **e** is not yet
Mark 13:13 to the **e** shall be saved
Luke 1:33 kingdom there will be no **e**
Luke 21: 9 but the **e** will not come

Luke 22:37 concerning Me have an e
John 13: 1 world, He loved them to the e
Acts 1: 8 and to the e of the earth
Acts 21: 5 come to the e of those days
Acts 27:10 voyage will e with disaster
Rom 6:21 For the e of those things is
Rom 6:22 fruit to holiness, and the e
Rom 10: 4 is the e of the law for
Rom 14: 9 For to this e Christ died
1Co 1: 8 also confirm you to the e
1Co 15:24 Then comes the e, when He
1Co 15:24 when He puts an e to all rule
2Co 1:13 understand, even to the e
2Co 2: 9 For to this e I also wrote,
2Co 3:13 e of what was passing away
2Co 11:15 whose e will be according to
Eph 3:21 all ages, world without e
Eph 6:18 this e with all perseverance
Phil 3:19 whose e is destruction, whose
Col 1:29 To this e I also labor,
1Ti 4:10 For to this e we both labor
Heb 3: 6 of the hope firm to the e
Heb 3:14 confidence steadfast to the e
Heb 6: 8 whose e is to be burned
Heb 6:11 assurance of hope until the e
Heb 6:16 for them an e of all dispute
Heb 7: 3 of days nor e of life, but
Heb 9:26 once at the e of the ages
Jas 5:11 seen the e intended by the
1Pe 1: 9 receiving the e of your faith
1Pe 4: 7 But the e of all things is at
1Pe 4:17 what will be the e of those
2Pe 2:20 the latter e is worse for
Rev 1: 8 Omega, the Beginning and the E
Rev 2:26 and keeps My works until the e
Rev 21: 6 Omega, the Beginning and the E
Rev 22:13 Omega, the Beginning and the E

ENDANGER (*see* ENDANGERED)
1Ch 12:19 master Saul and e our heads
Dan 1:10 Then you would e my head

ENDANGERED (*see* ENDANGER)
Eccl 10: 9 splits wood may be e by it

ENDEARMENT
Gen 26: 8 showing e to Rebekah his wife

ENDEAVORED (*see* ENDEAVORS)
1Th 2:17 e more eagerly to see your

ENDEAVORING (*see* ENDEAVORS)
Eph 4: 3 e to keep the unity of the

ENDEAVORS (*see* ENDEAVORED, ENDEAVORING)
Ps 28: 4 to the wickedness of their e

ENDED (*see* END)
Gen 2: 2 on the seventh day God e His
Gen 41:53 were in the land of Egypt e
Gen 47:18 When that year had e, they
Lev 8:33 of your consecration are e
Deut 31:30 this song until they were e
Deut 34: 8 and mourning for Moses e
Josh 15: 4 and the border e at the sea
Josh 15: 7 En Shemesh and e at En Rogel
Josh 15:11 and the border e at the sea
Josh 16: 3 and it e at the sea
Josh 16: 8 Kanah, and it e at the sea
Josh 17: 9 and it e at the sea
Josh 18:12 it e at the Wilderness of
Josh 18:14 it e at Kirjath Baal (which
Josh 18:19 then the border e at the
Josh 19:14 and it e in the Valley of
Josh 19:22 their border e at the Jordan
Josh 19:29 e at the sea by the region of
Josh 19:33 it e at the Jordan
Josh 19:34 and e at Judah by the Jordan
2Ch 29:34 them until the work was e
Job 7: 4 I arise, and the night be e
Job 31:40 The words of Job are e
Ps 72:20 David the son of Jesse are e
Is 40: 2 to her, that her warfare is e
Is 60:20 of your mourning shall be e
Jer 8:20 is past, the summer is e, and
Ezek 4: 8 have e the days of your siege
Matt 7:28 Jesus had e these sayings
Luke 4: 2 and afterward, when they had e
Luke 4:13 devil had e every temptation
John 13: 2 And supper being e, the devil
Acts 21:27 the seven days were almost e

ENDLESS (*see* END, ENDLESSLY)
1Ti 1: 4 e genealogies, which cause
Heb 7:16 to the power of an e life

ENDLESSLY (*see* ENDLESS)
Prov 21:28 who hears him will speak e

EN DOR (*see* DOR)
Josh 17:11 towns, the inhabitants of E
1Sa 28: 7 a woman who is a medium at E

ENDOR
Ps 83:10 Who perished at E, Who

ENDOW (*see* ENDOWED, ENDOWMENT)
Job 39:17 wisdom, and did not e her with

ENDOWED (*see* ENDOW)
Gen 30:20 God has e me with a good
2Ch 2:12 wise son, e with prudence and
2Ch 2:13 e with understanding, Huram

ENDOWMENT (*see* ENDOW)
Gen 30:20 has endowed me with a good e

ENDS (*see* END)
Ex 25:18 the two e of the mercy seat
Ex 25:19 the cherubim at the two e of
Ex 28:23 the two e of the breastplate
Ex 28:24 on the e of the breastplate
Ex 28:25 the other two e of the two
Ex 28:26 the two e of the breastplate
Ex 37: 7 the two e of the mercy seat
Ex 37: 8 the cherubim at the two e of
Ex 39:15 for the breastplate at the e
Ex 39:16 the two e of the breastplate
Ex 39:17 on the e of the breastplate
Ex 39:18 The two e of the two braided
Ex 39:19 the two e of the breastplate
Deut 33:17 peoples to the e of the earth
1Sa 2:10 will judge the e of the earth
1Ki 8: 8 e of the poles could be seen
2Ch 5: 9 the e of the poles of the ark
Job 28:24 looks to the e of the earth
Job 36:14 and their life e among the
Job 37: 3 to the e of the earth
Job 38:13 hold of the e of the earth
Ps 2: 8 the e of the earth for Your
Ps 22:27 All the e of the world Shall
Ps 48:10 praise to the e of the earth
Ps 59:13 Jacob To the e of the earth
Ps 65: 5 of all the e of the earth
Ps 67: 7 all the e of the earth shall
Ps 72: 8 River to the e of the earth
Ps 98: 3 All the e of the earth have
Ps 135: 7 from the e of the earth
Prov 17:24 are on the e of the earth
Prov 30: 4 all the e of the earth
Is 24: 8 the noise of the jubilant e
Is 24:16 From the e of the earth we
Is 40:28 Creator of the e of the earth
Is 41: 5 the e of the earth were
Is 41: 9 taken from the e of the earth
Is 42:10 from the e of the earth, you
Is 43: 6 from the e of the earth
Is 45:22 saved, all you e of the earth
Is 49: 6 to the e of the earth
Is 52:10 all the e of the earth shall
Jer 10:13 from the e of the earth
Jer 16:19 You from the e of the earth
Jer 25:31 come to the e of the earth
Jer 31: 8 them from the e of the earth
Jer 50:41 up from the e of the earth
Jer 51:16 from the e of the earth
Ezek 15: 4 the fire devours both e of it
Dan 4:11 to the e of all the earth
Mic 5: 4 great to the e of the earth
Zech 9:10 River to the e of the earth
Matt 12:42 for she came from the e of
Luke 11:31 for she came from the e of
Acts 13:47 to the e of the earth
Rom 10:18 words to the e of the world
1Co 10:11 on whom the e of the ages

ENDUED
Luke 24:49 are e with power from on high

ENDURANCE (*see* ENDURE)
Heb 10:36 For you have need of e, so
Heb 12: 1 let us run with e the race

ENDURE (*see* ENDURANCE, ENDURED, ENDURES, ENDURING)
Gen 33:14 the children, are able to e
Ex 18:23 then you will be able to e
Num 31:23 everything that can e fire
Num 31:23 But all that cannot e fire
Judg 10:16 longer e the misery of Israel
Esth 8: 6 For how can I e to see the
Esth 8: 6 Or how can I e to see the
Job 8:15 it fast, but it does not e
Job 31:23 magnificence I could not e
Ps 9: 7 But the LORD shall e forever
Ps 30: 5 Weeping may e for a night
Ps 72: 5 As long as the sun and moon e
Ps 72:17 His name shall e forever
Ps 81:15 their fate would e forever
Ps 89:29 also I will make to e forever
Ps 89:36 His seed shall e forever, And
Ps 101: 5 proud heart, Him I will not e
Ps 102:12 LORD, shall e forever, And the
Ps 102:26 will perish, but You will e
Ps 104:31 glory of the LORD e forever
Prov 27:24 nor does a crown e to all
Is 1:13 I cannot e iniquity and the
Ezek 22:14 Can your heart e, or can your
Dan 6:26 dominion shall e to the end
Joel 2:11 who can e it
Nah 1: 6 who can e the fierceness of
Mal 3: 2 But who can e the day of His
Mark 4:17 and so e only for a time
1Co 4:12 being persecuted, we e it
1Co 9:12 but e all things lest we
1Th 3: 1 when we could no longer e it
1Th 3: 5 when I could no longer e it
2Th 1: 4 and tribulations that you e
2Ti 2: 3 You therefore must e hardship
2Ti 2:10 Therefore I e all things for
2Ti 2:12 If we e, we shall also reign
2Ti 4: 3 will not e sound doctrine
2Ti 4: 5 e afflictions, do the work of
Heb 12: 7 If you e chastening, God
Heb 12:20 not e what was commanded
Jas 5:11 we count them blessed who e

ENDURED (*see* ENDURE)
Rom 9:22 e with much longsuffering the
2Ti 3:11 what persecutions I e
Heb 6:15 so, after he had patiently e
Heb 10:32 you e a great struggle with
Heb 11:27 for he e as seeing Him who is
Heb 12: 2 set before Him e the cross
Heb 12: 3 For consider Him who e such

ENDURES (*see* ENDURE)
1Ch 16:34 For His mercy e forever
1Ch 16:41 because His mercy e forever
2Ch 5:13 good, for His mercy e forever
2Ch 7: 3 good, for His mercy e forever
2Ch 7: 6 For His mercy e forever,"
2Ch 20:21 LORD, for His mercy e forever
Ezra 3:11 good, For His mercy e forever
Ps 52: 1 goodness of God e continually
Ps 100: 5 And His truth e to all
Ps 106: 1 For His mercy e forever
Ps 107: 1 For His mercy e forever
Ps 111: 3 His righteousness e forever
Ps 111:10 His praise e forever
Ps 112: 3 his righteousness e forever
Ps 112: 9 His righteousness e forever
Ps 117: 2 truth of the LORD e forever
Ps 118: 1 Because His mercy e forever
Ps 118: 2 His mercy e forever
Ps 118: 3 His mercy e forever
Ps 118: 4 His mercy e forever
Ps 118:29 For His mercy e forever
Ps 119:90 Your faithfulness e to all
Ps 119:160 righteous judgments e forever
Ps 135:13 e forever, Your fame, O LORD,
Ps 136: 1 For His mercy e forever
Ps 136: 2 For His mercy e forever
Ps 136: 3 For His mercy e forever
Ps 136: 4 For His mercy e forever
Ps 136: 5 For His mercy e forever
Ps 136: 6 For His mercy e forever
Ps 136: 7 For His mercy e forever
Ps 136: 8 For His mercy e forever
Ps 136: 9 For His mercy e forever
Ps 136:10 For His mercy e forever
Ps 136:11 For His mercy e forever
Ps 136:12 For His mercy e forever
Ps 136:13 For His mercy e forever
Ps 136:14 For His mercy e forever
Ps 136:15 For His mercy e forever
Ps 136:16 For His mercy e forever
Ps 136:17 For His mercy e forever

Ps 136:18 For His mercy e forever
Ps 136:19 For His mercy e forever
Ps 136:20 For His mercy e forever
Ps 136:21 For His mercy e forever
Ps 136:22 For His mercy e forever
Ps 136:23 For His mercy e forever
Ps 136:24 For His mercy e forever
Ps 136:25 For His mercy e forever
Ps 136:26 For His mercy e forever
Ps 138: 8 Your mercy, O LORD, e forever
Ps 145:13 Your dominion e throughout
Jer 33:11 for His mercy e forever"
Matt 10:22 But he who e to the end will
Matt 13:21 but e only for a while
Matt 24:13 But he who e to the end shall
Mark 13:13 But he who e to the end shall
John 6:27 which e to everlasting life
1Co 3:14 which he has built on it e
1Co 13: 7 all things, e all things
Jas 1:12 is the man who e temptation
1Pe 1:25 word of the LORD e forever
1Pe 2:19 toward God one e grief,

ENDURING (*see* ENDURE)
1Sa 25:28 make for my lord an e house
1Ki 11:38 and build for you an e house
Ps 19: 9 the LORD is clean, e forever
Prov 8:18 e riches and righteousness
2Co 1: 6 which is effective for e the
Heb 10:34 better and an e possession for

EN EGLAIM (*see* EGLAIM)
Ezek 47:10 stand by it from En Gedi to E

ENEMIES (*see* ENEMIES', ENEMY)
Gen 14:20 your e into your hand
Gen 22:17 possess the gate of their e
Gen 49: 8 be on the neck of your e
Ex 1:10 that they also join our e
Ex 23:22 I will be an enemy to your e
Ex 23:27 will make all your e turn
Ex 32:25 to their shame among their e)
Lev 26: 7 You will chase your e, and
Lev 26: 8 your e shall fall by the
Lev 26:16 vain, for your e shall eat it
Lev 26:17 shall be defeated by your e
Lev 26:32 your e who dwell in it shall
Lev 26:34 and you are in your e' land
Lev 26:36 in the lands of their e
Lev 26:37 power to stand before your e
Lev 26:38 of your e shall eat you up
Lev 26:39 iniquity in your e' lands
Lev 26:41 them into the land of their e
Lev 26:44 are in the land of their e
Num 10: 9 you will be saved from your e
Num 10:35 Let Your e be scattered, and
Num 14:42 you be defeated by your e
Num 23:11 I took you to curse my e, and
Num 24: 8 consume the nations, his e
Num 24:10 I called you to curse my e
Num 24:18 Seir also, his e, shall be a
Num 32:21 out His e from before Him
Deut 1:42 you be defeated before your e
Deut 6:19 all your e from before you
Deut 12:10 from all your e round about
Deut 20: 1 out to battle against your e
Deut 20: 3 verge of battle with your e
Deut 20: 4 fight for you against your e
Deut 20:14 you shall eat the e' plunder
Deut 21:10 go out to war against your e
Deut 23: 9 army goes out against your e
Deut 23:14 and give your e over to you
Deut 25:19 rest from your e all around
Deut 28: 7 The LORD will cause your e
Deut 28:25 to be defeated before your e
Deut 28:31 shall be given to your e, and
Deut 28:48 you shall serve your e, whom
Deut 28:68 for sale to your e as male
Deut 30: 7 all these curses on your e
Deut 32:31 even our e themselves being
Deut 32:41 will render vengeance to My e
Deut 33: 7 You be a help against his e
Deut 33:29 Your e shall submit to you,
Josh 7: 8 turns its back before its e
Josh 7:12 not stand before their e, but
Josh 7:12 their backs before their e
Josh 7:13 e until you take away the
Josh 10:13 had revenge upon their e
Josh 10:19 yourselves, but pursue your e
Josh 10:25 your e against whom you fight
Josh 21:44 their e stood against them
Josh 21:44 all their e into their hand
Josh 22: 8 of your e with your brethren
Josh 23: 1 from all their e round about
Judg 2:14 hands of their e all around
Judg 2:14 longer stand before their e
Judg 2:18 out of the hand of their e
Judg 3:28 e the Moabites into your hand
Judg 5:31 Thus let all Your e perish
Judg 8:34 of all their e on every side
Judg 11:36 has avenged you of your e
1Sa 2: 1 I smile at my e, because I
1Sa 4: 3 us from the hand of our e
1Sa 12:10 us from the hand of our e
1Sa 12:11 hand of your e on every side
1Sa 14:24 have taken vengeance on my e
1Sa 14:30 of their e which they found
1Sa 14:47 all his e on every side,
1Sa 18:25 vengeance on the king's e
1Sa 20:15 cut off every one of the e of
1Sa 20:16 it at the hand of David's e
1Sa 25:22 to the e of David, if I leave
1Sa 25:26 hand, now then, let your e
1Sa 25:29 the lives of your e He shall
1Sa 29: 8 fight against the e of my
1Sa 30:26 spoil of the e of the LORD"
2Sa 3:18 and the hand of all their e
2Sa 5:20 broken through my e before me
2Sa 7: 1 from all his e all around
2Sa 7: 9 all your e from before you
2Sa 7:11 you to rest from all your e
2Sa 12:14 e of the LORD to blaspheme
2Sa 18:19 LORD has avenged him of his e
2Sa 18:32 May the e of my lord the king
2Sa 19: 6 in that you love your e and
2Sa 19: 9 us from the hand of our e
2Sa 22: 1 from the hand of all his e
2Sa 22: 4 so shall I be saved from my e
2Sa 22:38 I have pursued my e and
2Sa 22:41 given me the necks of my e
2Sa 22:49 who delivers me from my e
2Sa 24:13 three months before your e
1Ki 3:11 have asked the life of your e
1Ki 8:48 e who led them away captive
2Ki 17:39 from the hand of all your e
2Ki 21:14 them into the hand of their e
2Ki 21:14 of plunder to all their e
1Ch 12:17 but if to betray me to my e
1Ch 14:11 my e by my hand like a
1Ch 17: 8 all your e from before you
1Ch 17:10 Also I will subdue all your e
1Ch 21:12 of your e overtaking you, or
1Ch 22: 9 from all his e all around
2Ch 1:11 honor or the life of your e
2Ch 6:28 when their e besiege them in
2Ch 6:34 out to battle against their e
2Ch 20:27 them rejoice over their e
2Ch 20:29 against the e of Israel
2Ch 25:20 them into the hand of their e
Neh 4:15 when our e heard that it was
Neh 5: 9 of the nations, our e
Neh 6: 1 the rest of our e heard that
Neh 6:16 when all our e heard of it
Neh 9:27 them into the hand of their e
Neh 9:27 them from the hand of their e
Neh 9:28 them in the hand of their e
Esth 8:13 avenge themselves on their e
Esth 9: 1 On the day that the e of the
Esth 9: 5 e with the stroke of the
Esth 9:16 lives, had rest from their e
Esth 9:16 thousand of their e
Esth 9:22 Jews had rest from their e
Job 19:11 He counts me as one of His e
Ps 3: 7 all my e on the cheekbone
Ps 5: 8 righteousness because of my e
Ps 6: 7 grows old because of all my e
Ps 6:10 Let all my e be ashamed and
Ps 7: 6 because of the rage of my e
Ps 8: 2 strength, Because of Your e
Ps 9: 3 When my e turn back, They
Ps 10: 5 As for all his e, he sneers
Ps 17: 9 From my deadly e who surround
Ps 18: 3 So shall I be saved from my e
Ps 18:37 I have pursued my e and
Ps 18:40 given me the necks of my e
Ps 18:48 He delivers me from my e
Ps 21: 8 hand will find all Your e
Ps 23: 5 me in the presence of my e
Ps 25: 2 Let not my e triumph over me
Ps 25:19 Consider my e, for they are
Ps 27: 2 me To eat up my flesh, My e
Ps 27: 6 up above my e all around me
Ps 27:11 smooth path, because of my e
Ps 31:11 am a reproach among all my e
Ps 31:15 me from the hand of my e, And
Ps 35:19 me who are wrongfully my e
Ps 37:20 the e of the LORD, Like the
Ps 38:19 But my e are vigorous, and
Ps 41: 2 him to the will of his e
Ps 41: 5 My e speak evil of me
Ps 42:10 My e reproach me, While they
Ps 44: 5 You we will push down our e
Ps 44: 7 You have saved us from our e
Ps 45: 5 in the heart of the King's e
Ps 54: 5 repay my e for their evil
Ps 54: 7 has seen its desire upon my e
Ps 56: 2 My e would hound me all day,
Ps 56: 9 You, Then my e will turn back
Ps 59: 1 Deliver me from my e, O my
Ps 59:10 let me see my desire on my e
Ps 60:12 He who shall tread down our e
Ps 66: 3 of Your power Your e shall
Ps 68: 1 arise, Let His e be scattered
Ps 68:21 will wound the head of His e
Ps 68:23 their portion from your e
Ps 69: 4 me, Being my e wrongfully
Ps 69:18 Deliver me because of my e
Ps 71:10 For my e speak against me
Ps 72: 9 And His e will lick the dust
Ps 74: 4 Your e roar in the midst of
Ps 74:23 forget the voice of Your e
Ps 78:53 the sea overwhelmed their e
Ps 78:66 And He beat back His e
Ps 80: 6 our e laugh among themselves
Ps 81:14 I would soon subdue their e
Ps 83: 2 behold, Your e make a tumult
Ps 89:10 Your e with Your mighty arm
Ps 89:42 have made all his e rejoice
Ps 89:51 which Your e have reproached
Ps 92: 9 For behold, Your e, O LORD,
Ps 92: 9 behold, Your e shall perish
Ps 92:11 has seen my desire on my e
Ps 97: 3 And burns up His e round about
Ps 102: 8 My e reproach me all day long
Ps 105:24 them stronger than their e
Ps 106:11 The waters covered their e
Ps 106:42 Their e also oppressed them,
Ps 108:13 He who shall tread down our e
Ps 110: 1 I make Your e Your footstool
Ps 110: 2 Rule in the midst of Your e
Ps 112: 8 he sees his desire upon his e
Ps 119:98 make me wiser than my e
Ps 119:139 Because my e have forgotten
Ps 119:157 are my persecutors and my e
Ps 127: 5 with their e in the gate
Ps 132:18 His e I will clothe with
Ps 136:24 And rescued us from our e, For
Ps 138: 7 Against the wrath of my e
Ps 139:20 Your e take Your name in vain
Ps 139:22 I count them my e
Ps 143: 9 Deliver me, O LORD, from my e
Ps 143:12 In Your mercy cut off my e
Prov 16: 7 he makes even his e to be at
Is 1:24 and take vengeance on My e
Is 9:11 against him, and spur his e on
Is 26:11 yes, the fire of Your e shall
Is 42:13 shall prevail against His e
Is 59:18 recompense to His e
Is 62: 8 grain to be food for your e
Is 66: 6 LORD, Who fully repays His e
Is 66:14 and His indignation to His e
Jer 12: 7 soul into the hand of her e
Jer 15: 9 to the sword before their e
Jer 15:14 e into a land which you do
Jer 17: 4 cause you to serve your e in
Jer 19: 7 by the sword before their e
Jer 19: 9 with which their e and those
Jer 20: 4 fall by the sword of their e
Jer 20: 5 give into the hand of their e
Jer 21: 7 into the hand of their e
Jer 34:20 them into the hand of their e
Jer 34:21 into the hand of their e,
Jer 44:30 Egypt into the hand of his e
Jer 48: 5 the e have heard a cry of
Jer 49:37 to be dismayed before their e
Lam 1: 2 they have become her e
Lam 1: 5 the master, her e prosper
Lam 1:21 All my e have heard of my
Lam 2:16 All your e have opened their
Lam 2:22 borne and brought up my e have
Lam 3:46 All our e have opened their
Lam 3:52 My e without cause hunted me

Lam 3:62 The lips of my **e** and their
Ezek 39:23 them into the hand of their **e**
Dan 4:19 interpretation concern your **e**
Amos 9: 4 into captivity before their **e**
Mic 4:10 you from the hand of your **e**
Mic 5: 9 all your **e** shall be cut off
Mic 7: 6 a man's **e** are the men of his
Nah 1: 2 He reserves wrath for His **e**
Nah 1: 8 and darkness will pursue His **e**
Nah 3:13 land are wide open for your **e**
Zech 10: 5 who tread down their **e** in the
Matt 5:44 But I say to you, love your **e**
Matt 22:44 hand, till I make Your **e** Your
Mark 12:36 I make Your **e** Your footstool
Luke 1:71 we should be saved from our **e**
Luke 1:74 from the hand of our **e**, might
Luke 6:27 Love your **e**, do good to those
Luke 6:35 But love your **e**, do good, and
Luke 19:27 bring here those **e** of mine
Luke 19:43 come upon you when your **e**
Luke 20:43 I make Your **e** Your footstool
Acts 2:35 I make Your **e** Your footstool
Rom 5:10 For if when we were **e** we were
Rom 11:28 they are **e** for your sake, but
1Co 15:25 has put all **e** under His feet
Phil 3:18 that they are the **e** of the
Col 1:21 and **e** in your mind by wicked
Heb 1:13 make Your **e** Your footstool"
Heb 10:13 His **e** are made His footstool
Rev 11: 5 mouth and devours their **e**
Rev 11:12 a cloud, and their **e** saw them

ENEMIES' (*see* ENEMIES)
Ezek 39:27 them out of their **e** lands

ENEMY (*see* ENEMIES, ENEMY'S)
Ex 15: 6 has dashed the **e** in pieces
Ex 15: 9 The **e** said, "I will pursue, I
Ex 23:22 will be an **e** to your enemies
Lev 26:25 into the hand of the **e**
Num 10: 9 the **e** who oppresses you, then
Num 35:23 not his **e** or seeking his harm
Deut 28:53 your **e** shall distress you
Deut 28:55 straits in which your **e** shall
Deut 28:57 straits in which your **e** shall
Deut 32:27 not feared the wrath of the **e**
Deut 32:42 heads of the leaders of the **e**
Deut 33:27 out the **e** from before you
Judg 16:23 into our hands Samson our **e**
Judg 16:24 into our hands our **e**, the
1Sa 2:32 And you will see an **e** in My
1Sa 18:29 became David's **e** continually
1Sa 19:17 like this, and sent my **e** away
1Sa 24: 4 deliver your **e** into your hand
1Sa 24:19 For if a man finds his **e**,
1Sa 26: 8 God has delivered your **e** into
1Sa 28:16 from you and has become your **e**
2Sa 4: 8 the son of Saul your **e**, who
2Sa 22:18 delivered me from my strong **e**
1Ki 8:33 are defeated before an **e**
1Ki 8:37 when their **e** besieges them in
1Ki 8:44 out to battle against their **e**
1Ki 8:46 them and deliver them to the **e**
1Ki 8:46 captive to the land of the **e**
1Ki 21:20 Have you found me, O my **e**
2Ch 6:24 are defeated before an **e**
2Ch 6:36 them and deliver them to the **e**
2Ch 25: 8 make you fall before the **e**
2Ch 26:13 help the king against the **e**
Ezra 8:22 us against the **e** on the road
Ezra 8:31 us from the hand of the **e**
Esth 3:10 Agagite, the **e** of the Jews
Esth 7: 4 although the **e** could never
Esth 7: 6 and **e** is this wicked Haman
Esth 8: 1 of Haman, the **e** of the Jews
Esth 9:10 Hammedatha, the **e** of the Jews
Esth 9:24 the **e** of all the Jews, had
Job 13:24 face, and regard me as Your **e**
Job 27: 7 May my **e** be like the wicked,
Job 33:10 me, He counts me as His **e**
Ps 7: 4 plundered my **e** without cause
Ps 7: 5 Let the **e** pursue me and
Ps 8: 2 That You may silence the **e**
Ps 9: 6 O **e**, destructions are
Ps 13: 2 How long will my **e** be exalted
Ps 13: 4 Lest my **e** say, "I have
Ps 18:17 delivered me from my strong **e**
Ps 31: 8 me up into the hand of the **e**
Ps 41:11 Because my **e** does not triumph
Ps 42: 9 of the oppression of the **e**
Ps 43: 2 of the oppression of the **e**
Ps 44:10 make us turn back from the **e**
Ps 44:16 and reviles, Because of the **e**
Ps 55: 3 Because of the voice of the **e**
Ps 55:12 For it is not an **e** who
Ps 61: 3 And a strong tower from the **e**
Ps 64: 1 my life from fear of the **e**
Ps 74: 3 The **e** has damaged everything
Ps 74:10 Will the **e** blaspheme Your
Ps 74:18 that the **e** has reproached, O
Ps 78:42 He redeemed them from the **e**
Ps 89:22 The **e** shall not outwit him,
Ps 106:10 them from the hand of the **e**
Ps 107: 2 from the hand of the **e**,
Ps 143: 3 For the **e** has persecuted my
Prov 24:17 not rejoice when your **e** falls
Prov 25:21 If your **e** is hungry, give him
Prov 27: 6 kisses of an **e** are deceitful
Is 59:19 when the **e** comes in like a
Is 63:10 Himself against them as an **e**
Jer 6:25 Because of the sword of the **e**
Jer 15:11 surely I will cause the **e** to
Jer 18:17 an east wind before the **e**
Jer 30:14 you with the wound of an **e**
Jer 31:16 back from the land of the **e**
Jer 44:30 his **e** who sought his life
Lam 1: 5 into captivity before the **e**
Lam 1: 7 fell into the hand of the **e**
Lam 1: 9 for the **e** has magnified
Lam 1:16 because the **e** prevailed
Lam 2: 3 right hand from before the **e**
Lam 2: 4 Standing like an **e**, He has
Lam 2: 5 The Lord was like an **e**
Lam 2: 7 into the hand of the **e**
Lam 2:17 and He has caused your **e** to
Lam 4:12 the **e** could enter the gates
Ezek 36: 2 Because the **e** has said of you
Dan 11:11 given into the hand of his **e**
Hos 8: 3 the **e** will pursue him
Mic 2: 8 people have risen up as an **e**
Mic 7: 8 Do not rejoice over me, my **e**
Mic 7:10 Then she who is my **e** will see
Nah 3:11 will seek refuge from the **e**
Zeph 3:15 he has cast out your **e**
Zech 8:10 the **e** for whoever went out or
Matt 5:43 your neighbor and hate your **e**
Matt 13:25 his **e** came and sowed tares
Matt 13:28 to them, 'An **e** has done this
Matt 13:39 The **e** who sowed them is the
Luke 10:19 over all the power of the **e**
Acts 13:10 you **e** of all righteousness,
Rom 12:20 Therefore if your **e** hungers
1Co 15:26 The last **e** that will be
Gal 4:16 your **e** because I tell you the
2Th 3:15 Yet do not count him as an **e**
Jas 4: 4 makes himself an **e** of God

ENEMY'S (*see* ENEMY)
Ex 23: 4 If you meet your **e** ox or his
Job 6:23 Deliver me from the **e** hand'
Ps 78:61 And His glory into the **e** hand

ENGAGE (*see* ENGAGED)
Deut 2:24 it, and **e** him in battle

ENGAGED (*see* ENGAGE)
2Ti 2: 4 No one **e** in warfare entangles

EN GANNIM
Josh 15:34 Zanoah, **E**, Tappuah, Enam,
Josh 19:21 Remeth, **E**, En Haddah, and
Josh 21:29 and **E** with its common-land

EN GEDI (*see* HAZAZON TAMAR, HAZEZON TAMAR)
Josh 15:62 the City of Salt, and **E**
1Sa 23:29 and dwelt in strongholds at **E**
1Sa 24: 1 is in the Wilderness of **E**
2Ch 20: 2 Hazazon Tamar" (which is **E**)
Song 1:14 blooms in the vineyards of **E**
Ezek 47:10 by it from **E** to En Eglaim

ENGRAVE (*see* ENGRAVED, ENGRAVER, ENGRAVING)
Ex 28: 9 **e** on them the names of the
Ex 28:11 you shall **e** the two stones
Ex 28:36 **e** on it, like the engraving
2Ch 2: 7 who has skill to **e** with the
Zech 3: 9 I will **e** its inscription,'

ENGRAVED (*see* ENGRAVE)
Ex 32:16 of God **e** on the tablets
Ex 39: 6 were **e**, as signets are **e**
Ex 39:14 **e** like a signet, each one
Lev 26: 1 up an **e** stone in your land
Num 33:52 destroy all their **e** stones
1Ki 7:36 on its panels he **e** cherubim
Job 19:24 that they were **e** on a rock
Jer 17: 1 is **e** on the tablet of their
Zech 14:20 TO THE LORD" shall be **e** on
2Co 3: 7 **e** on stones, was glorious, so

ENGRAVER (*see* ENGRAVE)
Ex 28:11 the work of an **e** in stone
Ex 35:35 all manner of work of the **e**
Ex 38:23 of the tribe of Dan, an **e**

ENGRAVING (*see* ENGRAVE, ENGRAVINGS)
Ex 28:36 on it, like the **e** of a signet
Ex 32: 4 fashioned it with an **e** tool
Ex 39:30 like the **e** of a signet
2Ch 2:14 and crimson, and to make any **e**

ENGRAVINGS (*see* ENGRAVING)
Ex 28:11 like the **e** of a signet, you
Ex 28:21 like the **e** of a signet, each
1Ki 7:31 and also on the opening were **e**

ENGULFED (*see* ENGULFING)
Ps 88:17 They **e** me altogether

ENGULFING (*see* ENGULFED)
Ezek 1: 4 with raging fire **e** itself

EN HADDAH
Josh 19:21 Remeth, En Gannim, **E**, and

EN HAKKORE
Judg 15:19 he called its name **E**, which

EN HAZOR
Josh 19:37 Kedesh, Edrei, **E**,

ENIGMA (*see* ENIGMAS)
Prov 1: 6 understand a proverb and an **e**

ENIGMAS (*see* ENIGMA)
Dan 5:12 explaining **e** were found in
Dan 5:16 interpretations and explain **e**

ENJOY (*see* ENJOYED, ENJOYING, ENJOYMENT)
Lev 26:34 Then the land shall **e** its
Lev 26:34 shall rest and **e** its sabbaths
Lev 26:43 will **e** its sabbaths while it
Josh 1:15 **e** it, which Moses the LORD's
Eccl 2: 1 therefore **e** pleasure"
Eccl 2:24 should **e** good in his labor
Eccl 3:13 **e** the good of all his labor
Eccl 5:18 and to **e** the good of all his
Is 65:22 My elect shall long **e** the
Acts 24: 2 through you we **e** great peace
Rom 15:24 if first I may **e** your company
1Ti 6:17 us richly all things to **e**
Heb 11:25 to **e** the passing pleasures of

ENJOYED (*see* ENJOY)
2Ch 36:21 the land had **e** her Sabbaths
Gal 4:15 then was the blessing you **e**

ENJOYING (*see* ENJOY)
Judg 19:22 Now as they were **e** themselves

ENJOYMENT (*see* ENJOY)
Job 20:18 his business he will get no **e**
Eccl 2:25 or who can have **e** more than I
Eccl 8:15 So I commended **e**, because a

ENLARGE (*see* ENLARGED, ENLARGES)
Gen 9:27 May God **e** Japheth, and may he
Ex 34:24 before you and **e** your borders
1Ch 4:10 **e** my territory, that Your
Ps 119:32 For You shall **e** my heart
Is 54: 2 **E** the place of your tent, and
Jer 4:30 though you **e** your eyes with
Amos 1:13 they might **e** their territory
Mic 1:16 **e** your baldness like an eagle
Matt 23: 5 and **e** the borders of their

ENLARGED (*see* ENLARGE)
2Sa 22:37 You **e** my path under me
Ps 18:36 You **e** my path under me
Ps 25:17 troubles of my heart have **e**
Is 5:14 Therefore Sheol has **e** itself
Is 57: 8 you have **e** your bed and made a
Jer 20:17 and her womb always **e** with me
2Co 10:15 we shall be greatly **e** by you

ENLARGES (*see* ENLARGE)
Deut 12:20 God **e** your border as He has
Deut 19: 8 your God **e** your territory
Deut 33:20 Blessed is he who **e** Gad
Job 12:23 He **e** nations, and guides them
Hab 2: 5 Because he **e** his desire as

ENLIGHTEN (*see* ENLIGHTENED, ENLIGHTENING)
2Sa 22:29 the LORD shall **e** my darkness
Ezra 9: 8 that our God may **e** our eyes
Ps 13: 3 **E** my eyes, Lest I sleep the
Ps 18:28 my God will **e** my darkness

ENLIGHTENED (*see* ENLIGHTEN)
Job 33:30 that he may be **e** with the
Eph 1:18 of your understanding being **e**
Heb 6: 4 for those who were once **e**

ENLIGHTENING (*see* ENLIGHTEN)
Ps 19: 8 the LORD is pure, **e** the eyes

ENLISTED
2Ti 2: 4 him who **e** him as a soldier

EN MISHPAT (*see* KADESH)
Gen 14: 7 came to **E** (that is, Kadesh),

ENMITY
Gen 3:15 I will put **e** between you and
Num 35:21 or in **e** he strikes him with
Num 35:22 pushes him suddenly without **e**
Hos 9: 7 of your iniquity and great **e**
Hos 9: 8 **e** in the house of his God
Luke 23:12 had been at **e** with each other
Rom 8: 7 carnal mind is **e** against God
Eph 2:15 abolished in His flesh the **e**
Eph 2:16 putting to death the **e**
Jas 4: 4 with the world is **e** with God

ENOCH
Gen 4:17 and she conceived and bore **E**
Gen 4:17 the name of his son—**E**.
Gen 4:18 To **E** was born Irad
Gen 5:18 sixty-two years, and begot **E**
Gen 5:19 After he begot **E**, Jared lived
Gen 5:21 **E** lived sixty-five years, and
Gen 5:22 **E** walked with God three
Gen 5:23 days of **E** were three hundred
Gen 5:24 And **E** walked with God
1Ch 1: 3 **E**, Methuselah, Lamech,
Luke 3:37 of Methuselah, the son of **E**
Heb 11: 5 By faith **E** was translated so
Jude 14 Now **E**, the seventh from Adam,

ENOS (*see* ENOSH)
Luke 3:38 the son of **E**, the son of Seth

ENOSH (*see* ENOS)
Gen 4:26 and he named him **E**
Gen 5: 6 and five years, and begot **E**
Gen 5: 7 After he begot **E**, Seth lived
Gen 5: 9 **E** lived ninety years, and
Gen 5:10 **E** lived eight hundred and
Gen 5:11 days of **E** were nine hundred
1Ch 1: 1 Adam, Seth, **E**,

ENOUGH (*see* PREFACE)

ENRAGED
2Sa 17: 8 they are **e** in their minds,
2Ch 16:10 for he was **e** at him because
Is 8:21 hungry, that they will be **e**
Acts 26:11 exceedingly **e** against them
Rev 12:17 dragon was **e** with the woman

ENRAPTURED
Prov 5:19 always be **e** with her love
Prov 5:20 be **e** by an immoral woman, and

ENRICH (*see* ENRICHED)
1Sa 17:25 king will **e** with great riches
Ps 65: 9 and water it, You greatly **e** it

ENRICHED (*see* ENRICH)
Ps 44:12 And are not **e** by their price
Ezek 27:33 you **e** the kings of the earth
1Co 1: 5 that you were **e** in everything
2Co 9:11 while you are **e** in everything

EN RIMMON
Neh 11:29 in **E**, Zorah, Jarmuth,

EN ROGEL
Josh 15: 7 of En Shemesh and ended at **E**
Josh 18:16 the south, and descended to **E**
2Sa 17:17 and Ahimaaz stayed at **E**, for
1Ki 1: 9 of Zoheleth, which is by **E**

EN SHEMESH
Josh 15: 7 toward the waters of **E** and
Josh 18:17 from the north, went out to **E**

ENSLAVE (*see* ENSLAVED)
Jer 30: 8 shall no more **e** them
Hos 4:11 wine, and new wine **e** the heart

ENSLAVED (*see* ENSLAVE)
Ezek 34:27 the hand of those who **e** them

ENSNARE (*see* ENSNARED, ENSNARES)
Prov 29: 8 Scoffers **e** a city, but wise

ENSNARED (*see* ENSNARE)
Deut 12:30 you are not **e** to follow them
Job 34:30 reign, lest the people be **e**
Prov 12:13 The wicked is **e** by the

ENSNARES (*see* ENSNARE)
Heb 12: 1 the sin which so easily **e** us

ENSURE
2Pe 1:15 I will be careful to **e** that

ENTANGLE (*see* ENTANGLED, ENTANGLES)
Matt 22:15 they might **e** Him in His talk

ENTANGLED (*see* ENTANGLE)
Gal 5: 1 do not be **e** again with a yoke
2Pe 2:20 they are again **e** in them

ENTANGLES (*see* ENTANGLE)
2Ti 2: 4 No one engaged in warfare **e**

EN TAPPUAH (*see* TAPPUAH)
Josh 17: 7 south to the inhabitants of **E**

ENTER (*see* ENTERED, ENTERING, ENTERS, ENTRY)
Gen 49: 6 not my soul **e** their council
Ex 40:35 Moses was not able to **e** the
Num 4: 3 all who **e** the service to do
Num 4:23 all who **e** to perform the
Num 5:24 shall **e** her to become bitter
Num 5:27 brings a curse will **e** her
Num 8:24 above one may **e** to perform
Num 14:30 you shall by no means **e** the
Num 20:24 for he shall not **e** the land
Deut 4:21 that I would not **e** the good
Deut 23: 1 not **e** the congregation of the
Deut 23: 2 birth shall not **e** the
Deut 23: 2 **e** the congregation of the
Deut 23: 3 or Moabite shall not **e** the
Deut 23: 3 **e** the congregation of the
Deut 23: 8 may **e** the congregation of the
Deut 27: 3 that you may **e** the land which
Deut 29:12 that you may **e** into covenant
Josh 10:19 allow them to **e** their cities
Judg 6: 5 and they would **e** the land to
Judg 11:18 But they did not **e** the border
Judg 18: 9 that you may **e** to possess the
1Ki 14:12 When your feet **e** the city
2Ki 7: 4 we say, 'We will **e** the city
2Ki 19:23 I will **e** the extremity of its
2Ch 7: 2 not **e** the house of the LORD
2Ch 23:19 in any way unclean should **e**
2Ch 27: 2 not **e** the temple of the LORD)
2Ch 30: 8 **e** His sanctuary, which He has
Esth 4: 2 for no one might **e** the king's
Job 37: 8 The animals **e** dens, and remain
Ps 37:15 sword shall **e** their own heart
Ps 45:15 They shall **e** the King's
Ps 95:11 They shall not **e** My rest
Ps 100: 4 **E** into His gates with
Ps 109:18 So let it **e** his body like
Ps 118:20 which the righteous shall **e**
Ps 143: 2 Do not **e** into judgment with
Prov 4:14 Do not **e** the path of the
Prov 18: 6 A fool's lips **e** into
Prov 23:10 nor **e** the fields of the
Is 2:10 **E** into the rock, and hide in
Is 3:14 The LORD will **e** into judgment
Is 13: 2 that they may **e** the gates of
Is 26: 2 keeps the truth may **e** in
Is 26:20 **e** your chambers, and shut your
Is 37:24 I will **e** its farthest height,
Is 57: 2 He shall **e** into peace
Is 59:14 street, and equity cannot **e**
Jer 7: 2 who **e** in at these gates to
Jer 8:14 let us **e** the fortified cities
Jer 14:18 if I **e** the city, then behold,
Jer 16: 5 Do not **e** the house of
Jer 17:20 who **e** by these gates
Jer 17:25 then shall **e** the gates of
Jer 21:13 Or who shall **e** our
Jer 22: 2 your people who **e** these gates
Jer 22: 4 then shall **e** the gates of
Jer 42:15 set your faces to **e** Egypt
Jer 42:18 out on you when you **e** Egypt
Lam 1:10 the nations **e** her sanctuary
Lam 1:10 not to **e** Your congregation
Lam 4:12 the enemy could **e** the gates
Ezek 7:22 for robbers shall **e** it and
Ezek 13: 9 nor shall they **e** into the
Ezek 20:38 not **e** the land of Israel
Ezek 26:10 as men **e** a city that has been
Ezek 37: 5 cause breath to **e** into you
Ezek 42:14 When the priests **e** them, they
Ezek 44: 2 and no man shall **e** by it,
Ezek 44: 3 he shall **e** by way of the
Ezek 44: 5 Mark well who may **e** the house
Ezek 44: 9 flesh, shall **e** My sanctuary,
Ezek 44:16 They shall **e** My sanctuary, and
Ezek 44:17 whenever they **e** the gates of
Ezek 46: 2 The prince shall **e** by way of
Dan 11: 7 **e** the fortress of the king of
Dan 11:17 to **e** with the strength of his
Dan 11:24 He shall **e** peaceably, even
Dan 11:40 he shall **e** the countries,
Dan 11:41 He shall also **e** the Glorious
Joel 2: 9 they **e** at the windows like a
Joel 3: 2 I will **e** into judgment with
Amos 5: 5 nor **e** Gilgal, nor pass over
Jon 3: 4 Jonah began to **e** the city on
Zech 5: 4 It shall **e** the house of the
Zech 6:10 **e** the house of Josiah the son
Zech 14:18 **e** in, they shall have no rain
Matt 5:20 you will by no means **e** the
Matt 7:13 **E** by the narrow gate
Matt 7:21 Lord,' shall **e** the kingdom of
Matt 10: 5 and do not **e** a city of the
Matt 10:11 whatever city or town you **e**
Matt 12:29 Or else how can one **e** a
Matt 12:45 than himself, and they **e** and
Matt 18: 3 you will by no means **e** the
Matt 18: 8 It is better for you to **e**
Matt 18: 9 to **e** into life with one eye
Matt 19:17 if you want to **e** into life
Matt 19:23 to **e** the kingdom of heaven
Matt 19:24 man to **e** the kingdom of God
Matt 21:31 harlots **e** the kingdom of God
Matt 25:21 **E** into the joy of your lord
Matt 25:23 **E** into the joy of your lord
Matt 26:41 lest you **e** into temptation
Mark 1:45 no longer openly **e** the city
Mark 3:27 No one can **e** a strong man's
Mark 5:12 the swine, that we may **e** them
Mark 6:10 whatever place you **e** a house
Mark 7:19 because it does not **e** his
Mark 9:25 out of him, and **e** him no more
Mark 9:43 for you to **e** into life maimed
Mark 9:45 better for you to **e** life lame
Mark 9:47 It is better for you to **e** the
Mark 10:15 child will by no means **e** it
Mark 10:23 to **e** the kingdom of God
Mark 10:24 to **e** the kingdom of God
Mark 10:25 man to **e** the kingdom of God
Mark 13:15 nor **e** to take anything out of
Mark 14:38 lest you **e** into temptation
Luke 7: 6 You should **e** under my roof
Luke 8:16 that those who **e** may see the
Luke 8:32 would permit them to **e** them
Luke 9: 4 Whatever house you **e**, stay
Luke 10: 5 But whatever house you **e**,
Luke 10: 8 Whatever city you **e**, and they
Luke 10:10 But whatever city you **e**, and
Luke 11:26 than himself, and they **e** and
Luke 11:52 You did not **e** in yourselves,
Luke 13:24 Strive to **e** through the
Luke 13:24 I say to you, will seek to **e**
Luke 18:17 child will by no means **e** it
Luke 18:24 to **e** the kingdom of God
Luke 18:25 man to **e** the kingdom of God
Luke 19:30 where as you **e** you will find
Luke 21:21 who are in the country **e** her
Luke 22:40 you may not **e** into temptation
Luke 22:46 lest you **e** into temptation
Luke 24:26 things and to **e** into His glory
John 3: 4 Can he **e** a second time into
John 3: 5 he cannot **e** the kingdom of
John 10: 1 to you, he who does not **e** the
Acts 14:22 **e** the kingdom of God
Heb 3:11 They shall not **e** My rest
Heb 3:18 they would not **e** His rest
Heb 3:19 not **e** in because of unbelief
Heb 4: 3 have believed do **e** that rest
Heb 4: 3 they shall not **e** My rest
Heb 4: 5 They shall not **e** My rest

Heb 4: 6 remains that some must e it
Heb 4: 6 not e because of disobedience
Heb 4:11 be diligent to e that rest
Heb 10:19 having boldness to e the
Rev 15: 8 and no one was able to e the
Rev 21:27 e it anything that defiles
Rev 22:14 may e through the gates into

ENTERED (*see* ENTER)
Gen 7:13 his sons with them, e the ark
Gen 7:16 So those that e, male and
Gen 19: 3 in to him and e his house
Gen 19:23 the earth when Lot e Zoar
Gen 23:10 all who e at the gate of his
Gen 31:33 tent and e Rachel's tent
Ex 33: 9 when Moses e the tabernacle,
Num 4:35 everyone who e the service
Num 4:39 everyone who e the service
Num 4:43 everyone who e the service
Josh 2: 3 who have e your house, for
Josh 8:19 they e the city and took it,
Josh 10:20 escaped e fortified cities
Judg 9:46 they e the stronghold of the
Judg 19:29 When he e his house he took a
2Sa 10:14 before Abishai, and e the city
2Sa 22: 7 temple, and my cry e His ears
2Ki 3:24 they e their land, killing
2Ki 7: 8 e another tent, and carried
2Ki 9:31 as Jehu e at the gate, she
1Ch 19:15 his brother, and e the city
2Ch 12:11 whenever the king e the house
2Ch 15:12 Then they e into a covenant
2Ch 31:16 e the house of the LORD his
2Ch 32: 1 of Assyria came and e Judah
Neh 2:15 e by the Valley Gate, and so
Neh 10:29 e into a curse and an oath to
Esth 6: 4 Now Haman had just e the
Job 38:16 Have you e the springs of the
Job 38:22 Have you e the treasury of
Jer 2: 7 But when you e, you defiled
Jer 9:21 has e our palaces, to kill
Jer 34:10 who had e into the covenant,
Jer 37:16 When Jeremiah e the dungeon
Ezek 2: 2 Then the Spirit e me when He
Ezek 3:24 Then the Spirit e me and set
Ezek 16: 8 e into a covenant with you,
Ezek 44: 2 God of Israel has e by it
Obad 11 when foreigners e his gates
Obad 13 You should not have e the
Hab 3:16 rottenness e my bones
Matt 8: 5 when Jesus had e Capernaum
Matt 12: 4 how he e the house of God and
Matt 24:38 the day that Noah e the ark
Mark 1:21 Sabbath He e the synagogue
Mark 1:29 they e the house of Simon and
Mark 2: 1 again He e Capernaum after
Mark 3: 1 He e the synagogue again, and
Mark 5:13 e the swine (there were about
Mark 5:40 e where the child was lying
Mark 6:56 Wherever He e, into villages,
Mark 7:17 when He had e a house away
Mark 7:24 He e a house and wanted no one
Mark 11: 2 as soon as you have e it you
Luke 1:40 e the house of Zacharias and
Luke 4:38 synagogue and e Simon's house
Luke 6: 6 that He e the synagogue and
Luke 7: 1 of the people, He e Capernaum
Luke 7:44 I e your house
Luke 8:30 because many demons had e him
Luke 8:33 e the swine, and the herd ran
Luke 9:34 fearful as they e the cloud
Luke 9:52 went, they e a village of the
Luke 10:38 that He e a certain village
Luke 17:12 Then as He e a certain
Luke 17:27 the day that Noah e the ark
Luke 19: 1 Then Jesus e and passed
Luke 22: 3 Then Satan e Judas, surnamed
Luke 22:10 when you have e the city
John 4:38 you have e into their labors
John 6:22 one which His disciples had e
John 6:22 that Jesus had not e the boat
John 13:27 piece of bread, Satan e him
John 18: 1 which He and His disciples e
John 18:33 Then Pilate e the Praetorium
Acts 1:13 And when they had e, they went
Acts 3: 2 from those who e the temple
Acts 3: 8 and e the temple with them
Acts 5:21 they e the temple early in
Acts 9:17 went his way and e the house
Acts 10:24 following day they e Caesarea
Acts 11: 8 has at any time e my mouth
Acts 11:12 me, and we e the man's house
Acts 16:40 and e the house of Lydia
Acts 18: 7 e the house of a certain man
Acts 18:19 he himself e the synagogue
Acts 21: 8 e the house of Philip the
Acts 21:26 e the temple to announce the
Acts 23:16 e the barracks and told Paul
Acts 25:23 had e the auditorium with the
Rom 5:12 one man sin e the world, and
Rom 5:20 Moreover the law e that the
1Co 2: 9 nor have e into the heart of
Heb 4:10 For he who has e His rest has
Heb 6:20 the forerunner has e for us
Heb 9:12 He e the Most Holy Place once
Heb 9:24 For Christ has not e the holy
Rev 11:11 of life from God e them, and

ENTERING (*see* ENTER)
Gen 12:11 when he was close to e Egypt
Deut 23:20 which you are e to possess
Judg 18:17 e there, they took the carved
1Sa 23: 7 in by e a town that has gates
2Ch 23: 4 of you e on the Sabbath, of
2Ch 26:16 e the temple of the LORD to
Ezra 9:11 The land which you are e to
Jer 17:27 e the gates of Jerusalem on
Matt 23:13 those who are e to go in
Mark 4:19 things e in choke the word
Mark 16: 5 e the tomb, they saw a young
Luke 11:52 and those who were e in you
Acts 8: 3 e every house, and dragging
Acts 27: 2 e a ship of Adramyttium, we
Heb 4: 1 promise remains of e His rest

ENTERS (*see* ENTER)
Ex 29:30 when he e the tabernacle of
Num 4:30 everyone who e the service to
Job 22: 4 and e into judgment with you
Prov 2:10 When wisdom e your heart, and
Ezek 21:14 that e their private chambers
Ezek 26:10 when he e your gates, as men
Ezek 42:12 facing south, as one e them
Ezek 44:21 when he e the inner court
Ezek 46: 8 When the prince e, he shall
Ezek 46: 9 whoever e by way of the north
Ezek 46: 9 whoever e by way of the south
Ezek 47: 8 into the valley, and e the sea
Matt 15:17 e the mouth goes into the
Mark 7:15 There is nothing that e a man
Mark 7:18 e a man from outside cannot
Luke 22:10 him into the house which he e
John 10: 2 But he who e by the door is
John 10: 9 If anyone e by Me, he will be
Heb 6:19 which e the Presence behind
Heb 9:25 as the high priest e the Most

ENTERTAIN (*see* ENTERTAINED)
Heb 13: 2 Do not forget to e strangers

ENTERTAINED (*see* ENTERTAIN)
Acts 28: 7 e us courteously for three
Heb 13: 2 have unwittingly e angels

ENTHRONED
Ps 29:10 The LORD sat e at the Flood

ENTICE (*see* ENTICED, ENTICES, ENTICING)
Deut 13: 5 to e you from the way in
Deut 13:10 because he sought to e you
Judg 14:15 E your husband, that he may
Judg 16: 5 E him, and find out where his
Prov 1:10 My son, if sinners e you, do

ENTICED (*see* ENTICE)
Deut 13:13 e the inhabitants of their
Job 31: 9 heart has been e by a woman
Job 31:27 my heart has been secretly e
Jas 1:14 away by his own desires and e

ENTICES (*see* ENTICE)
Ex 22:16 if a man e a virgin who is
Deut 13: 6 your own soul, secretly e you
Prov 16:29 A violent man e his neighbor

ENTICING (*see* ENTICE)
Prov 7:21 With her e speech she caused

ENTIRE (*see* ENTIRELY, ENTIRETY)
Num 14:29 according to your e number
1Ki 6:10 chambers against the e temple
1Ki 6:22 he overlaid with gold the e
1Ch 5:10 the e area east of Gilead
2Ch 26:14 for them, for the e army,
Ezra 10:14 of our e congregation stand
Neh 4: 6 and the e wall was joined
Ezek 27:27 the e company which is in
Ezek 27:34 the e company will fall in
Ezek 43:11 its e design and all its
Ezek 48:13 its e length shall be
Ezek 48:20 The e district shall be

ENTIRELY (*see* ENTIRE)
Num 3: 9 they are given e to him from
Num 4: 6 over that a cloth e of blue
Is 24: 3 The land shall be e emptied
1Ti 4:15 give yourself e to them, that

ENTIRETY (*see* ENTIRE)
Ps 119:160 The e of Your word is truth,
Ezek 11:15 the house of Israel in its e

ENTRAILS
Ex 12: 9 head with its legs and its e
Ex 29:13 all the fat that covers the e
Ex 29:17 the ram in pieces, wash its e
Ex 29:22 the fat that covers the e
Lev 1: 9 but he shall wash its e and
Lev 1:13 but he shall wash the e and
Lev 3: 3 The fat that covers the e
Lev 3: 3 all the fat that is on the e
Lev 3: 9 And the fat that covers the e
Lev 3: 9 all the fat that is on the e
Lev 3:14 The fat that covers the e
Lev 3:14 all the fat that is on the e
Lev 4: 8 The fat that covers the e
Lev 4: 8 all the fat which is on the e
Lev 4:11 with its head and legs, its e
Lev 7: 3 and the fat that covers the e
Lev 8:16 all the fat that was on the e
Lev 8:21 Then he washed the e and the
Lev 8:25 all the fat that was on the e
Lev 9:14 And he washed the e and the
Lev 9:19 fatty tail, what covers the e
Judg 3:22 and his e came out
2Sa 20:10 and his e poured out on the
Acts 1:18 and all his e gushed out

ENTRANCE (*see* ENTRANCES)
Ex 32:26 stood in the e of the camp
Ex 32:27 e to e throughout the camp
Ex 35:15 at the e of the tabernacle
Num 13:21 Rehob, near the e of Hamath
Num 34: 8 border to the e of Hamath
Josh 8:29 cast it at the e of the gate
Josh 13: 5 as far as the e to Hamath
Josh 20: 4 stands at the e of the gate
Judg 1:24 show us the e to the city
Judg 1:25 showed them the e to the city
Judg 3: 3 Hermon to the e of Hamath
Judg 9:35 stood in the e to the city
Judg 9:40 even to the e of the gate
Judg 9:44 stood at the e of the gate of
Judg 18:16 stood by the e of the gate
Judg 18:17 The priest stood at the e of
1Sa 17:52 as far as the e of the valley
2Sa 10: 8 array at the e of the gate
2Sa 11:23 as far as the e of the gate
1Ki 6:31 For the e of the inner
1Ki 8:65 e of Hamath to the Brook of
1Ki 18:46 of Ahab to the e of Jezreel
1Ki 19:13 and stood in the e of the cave
1Ki 22:10 the e of the gate of Samaria
2Ki 7: 3 men at the e of the gate
2Ki 10: 8 them in two heaps at the e of
2Ki 11:16 horses' e to the king's house
2Ki 14:25 of Israel from the e of
2Ki 16:18 e from the house of the LORD
2Ki 23: 8 e of the Gate of Joshua the
2Ki 23:11 at the e to the house of the
1Ch 4:39 they went to the e of Gedor
1Ch 5: 9 they settled as far as the e
1Ch 9:19 the e to the camp of the LORD
1Ch 13: 5 to as far as the e of Hamath
2Ch 7: 8 e of Hamath to the Brook of
2Ch 12:10 who guarded the e of the
2Ch 18: 9 the e of the gate of Samaria
2Ch 23:13 by his pillar at the e
2Ch 23:15 she went by way of the e of
2Ch 26: 8 as far as the e of Egypt, for
2Ch 33:14 as far as the e of the Fish
Esth 5: 1 facing the e of the house
Ps 119:130 The e of Your words gives
Prov 8: 3 city, at the e of the doors
Jer 1:15 e of the gates of Jerusalem
Jer 38:14 e of the house of the LORD
Jer 43: 9 the e to Pharaoh's house in
Ezek 8: 5 image of jealousy in the e

Ezek 27: 3 situated at the **e** of the sea
Ezek 40:11 width of the **e** to the gateway
Ezek 40:15 From the front of the **e** gate
Ezek 40:38 its **e** by the gateposts of the
Ezek 40:40 as one goes up to the **e** of
Ezek 41: 2 the side walls of the **e** were
Ezek 41: 3 and the **e**, six cubits high
Ezek 41: 3 and the width of the **e**, seven
Ezek 42: 9 was the **e** on the east side
Ezek 46: 3 land shall worship at the **e**
Ezek 46:19 he brought me through the **e**
Ezek 48: 1 to Hethlon at the **e** of Hamath
Amos 6:14 will afflict you from the **e**
2Pe 1:11 for so an **e** will be supplied

ENTRANCES (*see* ENTRANCE)
Ezek 42:11 and **e** were according to plan
Ezek 43:11 its exits and its **e**, its
Mic 5: 6 the land of Nimrod at its **e**

ENTRAP
Prov 5:22 iniquities **e** the wicked man

ENTREAT (*see* ENTREATED, ENTREATIES, ENTREATY)
Ex 8: 8 **E** the LORD that He may take
Ex 8:29 I will **e** the LORD, that the
Ex 9:28 **E** the LORD, that there may be
Ex 10:17 **e** the LORD your God, that He
Ruth 1:16 **E** me not to leave you, or to
1Ki 13: 6 Please **e** the favor of the
Prov 19: 6 Many **e** the favor of the
Mal 1: 9 But now **e** God's favor, that
1Co 4:13 being defamed, we **e**

ENTREATED (*see* ENTREAT)
Ex 8:30 from Pharaoh and **e** the LORD
Ex 10:18 from Pharaoh and **e** the LORD
1Ki 13: 6 So the man of God **e** the LORD
Ezra 8:23 **e** our God for this, and He
Ps 119:58 I **e** Your favor with my whole
Is 19:22 LORD, and He will be **e** by them

ENTREATIES (*see* ENTREAT)
Prov 18:23 The poor man uses **e**, but the

ENTREATY (*see* ENTREAT)
2Ch 33:13 and He received his **e**, heard
2Ch 33:19 and how God received his **e**

ENTRUSTED
1Co 9:17 my will, I have been **e** with a
1Th 2: 4 God to be **e** with the gospel
1Pe 5: 3 lords over those **e** to you

ENTRY (*see* ENTER, ENTRYWAY)
2Ch 4:22 As for the **e** of the sanctuary
Prov 8: 3 at the **e** of the city, at the
Jer 19: 2 which is by the **e** of the
Jer 26:10 sat down in the **e** of the new
Jer 36:10 the **e** of the New Gate of the
1Th 1: 9 manner of **e** we had to you

ENTRYWAY (*see* ENTRY)
1Ki 10: 5 his **e** by which he went up to
2Ch 9: 4 his **e** by which he went up to
Ezek 41: 2 width of the **e** was ten cubits

ENVIED (*see* ENVY)
Gen 26:14 So the Philistines **e** him
Gen 30: 1 Rachel **e** her sister, and said
Gen 37:11 And his brothers **e** him, but
Ps 106:16 When they **e** Moses in the camp
Eccl 4: 4 a man is **e** by his neighbor
Ezek 31: 9 all the trees of Eden **e** it

ENVIOUS (*see* ENVY)
Ps 37: 1 Nor be **e** of the workers of
Ps 73: 3 For I was **e** of the boastful,
Prov 24: 1 Do not be **e** of evil men, nor
Prov 24:19 doers, nor be **e** of the wicked
Acts 7: 9 And the patriarchs, becoming **e**
Acts 17: 5 not persuaded, becoming **e**

ENVISION (*see* ENVISIONED)
Ezek 13: 9 the prophets who **e** futility
Ezek 13:23 you shall no longer **e**
Zech 10: 2 the diviners **e** lies, and tell

ENVISIONED (*see* ENVISION)
Lam 2:14 but have **e** for you false
Ezek 13: 6 They have **e** futility and false
Ezek 13: 8 **e** lies, therefore I am indeed

ENVOYS
Ps 68:31 **E** will come out of Egypt

ENVY (*see* ENVIED, ENVIOUS, ENVYING)
Job 5: 2 man, and **e** slays a simple one
Ps 68:16 Why do you fume with **e**, you
Prov 3:31 Do not **e** the oppressor, and
Prov 14:30 but **e** is rottenness to the
Prov 23:17 not let your heart **e** sinners
Eccl 9: 6 their **e** have now perished
Is 11:13 Also the **e** of Ephraim shall
Is 11:13 Ephraim shall not **e** Judah
Is 26:11 ashamed for their **e** of people
Ezek 35:11 according to the **e** which you
Matt 27:18 of **e** they had delivered Him
Mark 15:10 handed Him over because of **e**
Acts 13:45 they were filled with **e**
Rom 1:29 full of **e**, murder, strife,
Rom 13:13 lewdness, not in strife and **e**
1Co 3: 3 For where there are **e**, strife
1Co 13: 4 love does not **e**
Gal 5:21 **e**, murders, drunkenness,
Phil 1:15 preach Christ even from **e**
1Ti 6: 4 over words, from which come **e**
Tit 3: 3 living in malice and **e**,
Jas 3:14 But if you have bitter **e** and
Jas 3:16 For where **e** and self-seeking
1Pe 2: 1 all guile, hypocrisy, **e**, and

ENVYING (*see* ENVY)
Gal 5:26 one another, **e** one another

EPAENETUS
Rom 16: 5 Greet my beloved **E**, who is

EPAPHRAS
Col 1: 7 as you also learned from **E**
Col 4:12 **E**, who is one of you, a
Phm 23 **E**, my fellow prisoner in

EPAPHRODITUS
Phil 2:25 it necessary to send to you **E**
Phil 4:18 having received from **E** the

EPHAH (*see* EPHAHS)
Ex 16:36 an omer is one-tenth of an **e**
Ex 29:40 of an **e** of flour mixed with
Lev 5:11 an **e** of fine flour as a sin
Lev 6:20 one-tenth of an **e** of fine
Lev 14:10 three-tenths of an **e** of fine
Lev 14:21 one-tenth of an **e** of fine
Lev 19:36 just weights, a just **e**, and a
Lev 23:13 an **e** of fine flour mixed with
Lev 23:17 loaves of two-tenths of an **e**
Lev 24: 5 Two-tenths of an **e** shall be
Num 5:15 of an **e** of barley meal
Num 15: 4 an **e** of fine flour mixed with
Num 15: 6 an **e** of fine flour mixed with
Num 15: 9 of three-tenths of an **e** of
Num 28: 5 one-tenth of an **e** of fine
Num 28: 9 two-tenths of an **e** of fine
Num 28:12 three-tenths of an **e** of fine
Num 28:12 two-tenths of an **e** of fine
Num 28:13 of an **e** of fine flour, mixed
Num 28:20 three-tenths of an **e** you
Num 28:21 **e** for each of the seven lambs
Num 28:28 of an **e** for each bull,
Num 29: 3 of an **e** for the bull,
Num 29: 9 of an **e** for the bull,
Num 29:14 three-tenths of an **e** for each
Judg 6:19 bread from an **e** of flour
Ruth 2:17 it was about an **e** of barley
1Sa 1:24 one **e** of flour, and a skin of
1Sa 17:17 an **e** of this dried grain and
Is 5:10 of seed shall yield one **e**
Ezek 45:10 have just balances, a just **e**
Ezek 45:11 The **e** and the bath shall be of
Ezek 45:11 the **e** one-tenth of a homer
Ezek 45:13 of an **e** from a homer of wheat
Ezek 45:13 and one-sixth of an **e** from a
Ezek 45:24 of one **e** for each bull and one
Ezek 45:24 one **e** for each ram, together
Ezek 45:24 with a hin of oil for each **e**
Ezek 46: 5 shall be one **e** for a ram, and
Ezek 46: 5 as a hin of oil with every **e**
Ezek 46: 7 offering of an **e** for a bull
Ezek 46: 7 an **e** for a ram, as much as he
Ezek 46: 7 and a hin of oil with every **e**
Ezek 46:11 shall be an **e** for a bull, an
Ezek 46:11 an **e** for a ram, as much as he
Ezek 46:11 and a hin of oil with every **e**
Ezek 46:14 morning, a sixth of an **e**, and
Amos 8: 5 Making the **e** small and the

EPHAH*
Gen 25: 4 And the sons of Midian were **E**
1Ch 1:33 The sons of Midian were **E**
1Ch 2:46 **E**, Caleb's concubine, bore
1Ch 2:47 Jotham, Geshan, Pelet, **E**
Is 60: 6 dromedaries of Midian and **E**

EPHAHS (*see* EPHAH)
Ruth 3:15 he measured six **e** of barley
Ruth 3:17 These six **e** of barley he gave
Hag 2:16 came to a heap of twenty **e**

EPHAI
Jer 40: 8 Tanhumeth, the sons of **E** the

EPHER
Gen 25: 4 sons of Midian were Ephah, **E**
1Ch 1:33 sons of Midian were Ephah, **E**
1Ch 4:17 Ezrah were Jether, Mered, **E**
1Ch 5:24 **E**, Ishi, Eliel, Azriel,

EPHES DAMMIM (*see* PASDAMMIM)
1Sa 17: 1 Sochoh and Azekah, in **E**

EPHESIAN (*see* EPHESIANS, EPHESUS)
Acts 21:29 seen Trophimus the **E** with him

EPHESIANS (*see* EPHESIAN)
Acts 19:28 Great is Diana of the **E**
Acts 19:34 Great is Diana of the **E**
Acts 19:35 **E** is temple guardian of the

EPHESUS (*see* EPHESIAN)
Acts 18:19 And he came to **E**, and left them
Acts 18:21 And he sailed from **E**
Acts 18:24 in the Scriptures, came to **E**
Acts 19: 1 the upper regions, came to **E**
Acts 19:17 Jews and Greeks dwelling in **E**
Acts 19:26 and hear that not only at **E**
Acts 19:35 Men of **E**, what man is there
Acts 20:16 had decided to sail past **E**
Acts 20:17 From Miletus he sent to **E**
1Co 15:32 have fought with beasts at **E**
1Co 16: 8 tarry in **E** until Pentecost
Eph 1: 1 To the saints who are in **E**
1Ti 1: 3 remain in **E** that you may
2Ti 1:18 ways he ministered to me at **E**
2Ti 4:12 And Tychicus I have sent to **E**
Rev 1:11 to **E**, to Smyrna, to Pergamos,
Rev 2: 1 of the church of **E** write

EPHLAL
1Ch 2:37 Zabad begot **E**
1Ch 2:37 and **E** begot Obed

EPHOD
Ex 25: 7 and stones to be set in the **e**
Ex 28: 4 a breastplate, an **e**, a robe,
Ex 28: 6 they shall make the **e** of gold
Ex 28: 8 woven band of the **e**, which is
Ex 28:12 on the shoulders of the **e** as
Ex 28:15 of the **e** you shall make it
Ex 28:25 straps of the **e** in the front
Ex 28:26 is on the inner side of the **e**
Ex 28:27 underneath the **e** toward its
Ex 28:27 woven band of the **e**
Ex 28:28 rings to the rings of the **e**
Ex 28:28 woven band of the **e**, and so
Ex 28:28 not come loose from the **e**
Ex 28:31 the robe of the **e** all of blue
Ex 29: 5 Aaron, and the robe of the **e**
Ex 29: 5 woven band of the **e**
Ex 35: 9 and stones to be set in the **e**
Ex 35:27 the stones to be set in the **e**
Ex 39: 2 He made the **e** of gold and blue
Ex 39: 5 woven band of his **e** that was
Ex 39: 7 on the shoulders of the **e**
Ex 39: 8 like the workmanship of the **e**
Ex 39:18 straps of the **e** in the front
Ex 39:19 on the inward side of the **e**
Ex 39:20 underneath the **e** toward its
Ex 39:20 woven band of the **e**
Ex 39:21 of the **e** with a blue cord
Ex 39:21 woven band of the **e**, and that
Ex 39:21 not come loose from the **e**
Ex 39:22 robe of the **e** of woven work
Lev 8: 7 the robe, and put the **e** on him
Lev 8: 7 woven band of the **e**, and with
Lev 8: 7 and with it tied the **e** on him
Judg 8:27 Then Gideon made it into an **e**
Judg 17: 5 had a shrine, and made an **e**
Judg 18:14 are in these houses an **e**,
Judg 18:17 took the carved image, the **e**
Judg 18:18 took the graven image, the **e**
Judg 18:20 and he took the **e**, the

1Sa 2:18 as a child, wearing a linen **e**
1Sa 2:28 and to wear an **e** before Me
1Sa 14: 3 in Shiloh, was wearing an **e**
1Sa 21: 9 in a cloth behind the **e**
1Sa 22:18 men who wore a linen **e**
1Sa 23: 6 down with an **e** in his hand
1Sa 23: 9 Bring the **e** here
1Sa 30: 7 Please bring the **e** here to me
1Sa 30: 7 brought the **e** to David
2Sa 6:14 David was wearing a linen **e**
1Ch 15:27 David also wore a linen **e**
Hos 3: 4 pillar, without **e** or teraphim

EPHOD*
Num 34:23 Hanniel the son of **E**,

EPHPHATHA
Mark 7:34 **E**," that is, "Be opened

EPHRAIM (*see* EPHRAIMITE, EPHRAIM'S, EPHRAIN, EPHRON)
Gen 41:52 of the second he called **E**
Gen 46:20 were born Manasseh and **E**
Gen 48: 1 his two sons, Manasseh and **E**
Gen 48: 5 And now your two sons, **E** and
Gen 48:13 **E** with his right hand toward
Gen 48:17 right hand on the head of **E**
Gen 48:20 May God make you as **E** and as
Gen 48:20 thus he set **E** before Manasseh
Num 1:10 from **E**, Elishama the son of
Num 1:32 of Joseph, the children of **E**
Num 1:33 of **E** were forty thousand five
Num 2:18 **E** according to their armies
Num 2:18 **E** shall be Elishama the son
Num 2:24 armies of the forces with **E**
Num 7:48 leader of the children of **E**
Num 10:22 **E** set out according to their
Num 13: 8 from the tribe of **E**, Hoshea
Num 26:28 families, by Manasseh and **E**
Num 26:35 These are the sons of **E**
Num 26:37 **E** according to those who were
Num 34:24 tribe of the children of **E**
Deut 33:17 are the ten thousands of **E**
Deut 34: 2 all Naphtali and the land of **E**
Josh 14: 4 two tribes: Manasseh and **E**
Josh 16: 4 of Joseph, Manasseh and **E**,
Josh 16: 5 border of the children of **E**
Josh 16: 8 tribe of the children of **E**
Josh 16: 9 **E** were among the inheritance
Josh 17: 8 belonged to the children of **E**
Josh 17: 9 These cities of **E** are among
Josh 17:15 since the mountains of **E** are
Josh 17:17 to **E** and Manasseh
Josh 19:50 Serah in the mountains of **E**
Josh 20: 7 Shechem in the mountains of **E**
Josh 21: 5 families of the tribe of **E**
Josh 21:20 their lot from the tribe of **E**
Josh 21:21 in the mountains of **E** (a city
Josh 24:30 is in the mountains of **E**, on
Josh 24:33 to him in the mountains of **E**
Judg 1:29 Nor did **E** drive out the
Judg 2: 9 Heres, in the mountains of **E**
Judg 3:27 trumpet in the mountains of **E**
Judg 4: 5 Bethel in the mountains of **E**
Judg 5:14 From **E** were those whose roots
Judg 7:24 all the mountains of **E**,
Judg 7:24 men of **E** gathered together
Judg 8: 1 Now the men of **E** said to him
Judg 8: 2 gleaning of the grapes of **E**
Judg 10: 1 Shamir in the mountains of **E**
Judg 10: 9 and against the house of **E**
Judg 12: 1 Then the men of **E** gathered
Judg 12: 4 of Gilead and fought against **E**
Judg 12: 4 the men of Gilead defeated **E**
Judg 12: 4 of **E** among the Ephraimites
Judg 12:15 in Pirathon in the land of **E**
Judg 17: 1 a man from the mountains of **E**
Judg 17: 8 he came to the mountains of **E**
Judg 18: 2 went to the mountains of **E**
Judg 18:13 there to the mountains of **E**
Judg 19: 1 in the remote mountains of **E**
Judg 19:16 was from the mountains of **E**
Judg 19:18 the remote mountains of **E**
1Sa 1: 1 Zophim, of the mountains of **E**
1Sa 9: 4 through the mountains of **E**
1Sa 14:22 hidden in the mountains of **E**
2Sa 2: 9 over Jezreel, over **E**, over
2Sa 13:23 Baal Hazor, which is near **E**
2Sa 18: 6 battle was in the woods of **E**
2Sa 20:21 a man from the mountains of **E**
1Ki 4: 8 in the mountains of **E**
1Ki 12:25 Shechem in the mountains of **E**
2Ki 5:22 to me from the mountains of **E**
2Ki 14:13 Gate of **E** to the Corner Gate
1Ch 6:66 territory from the tribe of **E**
1Ch 6:67 in the mountains of **E**, also
1Ch 7:20 The sons of **E** were Shuthelah,
1Ch 7:22 Then **E** their father mourned
1Ch 9: 3 and of the children of **E** and
1Ch 12:30 of the children of **E** twenty
1Ch 27:10 of the children of **E**
1Ch 27:14 of the children of **E**
1Ch 27:20 over the children of **E**,
2Ch 13: 4 is in the mountains of **E**, and
2Ch 15: 8 taken in the mountains of **E**
2Ch 15: 9 sojourned with them from **E**
2Ch 17: 2 in the cities of **E** which Asa
2Ch 19: 4 to the mountains of **E**, and
2Ch 25: 7 with any of the children of **E**
2Ch 25:10 that had come to him from **E**
2Ch 25:23 Gate of **E** to the Corner Gate
2Ch 28: 7 Zichri, a mighty man of **E**
2Ch 28:12 heads of the children of **E**
2Ch 30: 1 and also wrote letters to **E**
2Ch 30:10 city through the country of **E**
2Ch 30:18 of the people, many from **E**
2Ch 31: 1 from all Judah, Benjamin, **E**
2Ch 34: 6 in the cities of Manasseh, **E**
2Ch 34: 9 the hand of Manasseh and **E**
Neh 8:16 open square of the Gate of **E**
Neh 12:39 and above the Gate of **E**, above
Ps 60: 7 **E** also is the helmet for My
Ps 78: 9 The children of **E**, being
Ps 78:67 did not choose the tribe of **E**
Ps 80: 2 Before **E**, Benjamin, and
Ps 108: 8 **E** also is the helmet for My
Is 7: 2 forces are deployed in **E**
Is 7: 5 Because Syria, **E**, and the son
Is 7: 8 years **E** will be broken, so
Is 7: 9 The head of **E** is Samaria, and
Is 7:17 that **E** departed from Judah
Is 9: 9 **E** and the inhabitant of
Is 9:21 Manasseh shall devour **E**, and
Is 9:21 **E** Manasseh, and they together
Is 11:13 the envy of **E** shall depart
Is 11:13 **E** shall not envy Judah, and
Is 11:13 and Judah shall not harass **E**
Is 17: 3 also will cease from **E**, the
Is 28: 1 pride, to the drunkards of **E**
Is 28: 3 of pride, the drunkards of **E**
Jer 4:15 affliction from Mount **E**
Jer 7:15 the whole posterity of **E**
Jer 31: 6 watchmen will cry on Mount **E**
Jer 31: 9 Israel, and **E** is My firstborn
Jer 31:18 heard **E** bemoaning himself
Jer 31:20 Is **E** My dear son
Jer 50:19 shall be satisfied on Mount **E**
Ezek 37:16 For Joseph, the stick of **E**
Ezek 37:19 which is in the hand of **E**
Ezek 48: 5 the west, one portion for **E**
Ezek 48: 6 by the border of **E**, from the
Hos 4:17 **E** is joined to idols, let him
Hos 5: 3 I know **E**, and Israel is not
Hos 5: 3 for now, O **E**, you commit
Hos 5: 5 **E** stumble in their iniquity
Hos 5: 9 **E** shall be desolate in the
Hos 5:11 **E** is oppressed and broken in
Hos 5:12 I will be to **E** like a moth
Hos 5:13 When **E** saw his sickness, and
Hos 5:13 then **E** went to Assyria and
Hos 5:14 I will be like a lion to **E**
Hos 6: 4 O **E**, what shall I do to you
Hos 6:10 there is the harlotry of **E**
Hos 7: 1 iniquity of **E** was uncovered
Hos 7: 8 **E** has mixed himself among the
Hos 7: 8 **E** is a cake unturned
Hos 7:11 **E** also is like a silly dove,
Hos 8: 9 **E** has hired lovers
Hos 8:11 Because **E** has made many
Hos 9: 3 but **E** shall return to Egypt,
Hos 9: 8 watchman of **E** is with my God
Hos 9:11 As for **E**, their glory shall
Hos 9:13 Just as I saw **E** like Tyre
Hos 9:13 so **E** will bring out his
Hos 9:16 **E** is stricken, their root is
Hos 10: 6 **E** shall receive shame, and
Hos 10:11 **E** is a trained heifer that
Hos 10:11 I will make **E** pull a plow
Hos 11: 3 I taught **E** to walk, taking
Hos 11: 8 How can I give you up, **E**
Hos 11: 9 I will not again destroy **E**
Hos 11:12 **E** has encompassed Me with
Hos 12: 1 **E** feeds on the wind, and
Hos 12: 8 **E** said, "Surely I have
Hos 12:14 **E** provoked Him to anger most
Hos 13: 1 When **E** spoke, trembling, he
Hos 13:12 The iniquity of **E** is bound up
Hos 14: 8 **E** shall say, "What have I to
Obad 19 shall possess the fields of **E**
Zech 9:10 cut off the chariot from **E**
Zech 9:13 My bow, fitted the bow with **E**
Zech 10: 7 Those of **E** shall be like a
John 11:54 to a city called **E**, and there

EPHRAIMITE (*see* EPHRAIM, EPHRAIMITES)
Judg 12: 5 when any **E** who escaped said,
Judg 12: 5 Are you an **E**
1Sa 1: 1 Tohu, the son of Zuph, an **E**
1Ki 11:26 an **E** from Zereda, whose

EPHRAIMITES (*see* EPHRAIMITE)
Josh 16:10 dwell among the **E** to this day
Judg 12: 4 of Ephraim among the **E** and
Judg 12: 5 Jordan before the **E** arrived
Judg 12: 6 time forty-two thousand **E**

EPHRAIM'S (*see* EPHRAIM)
Gen 48:14 hand and laid it on **E** head
Gen 48:17 hand to remove it from **E** head
Gen 50:23 Joseph saw **E** children to the
Josh 17:10 Southward it was **E**, northward

EPHRAIN (*see* EPHRAIM, EPHRON)
2Ch 13:19 and **E** with its villages

EPHRATH (*see* EPHRATHITE)
Gen 35:16 a little distance to go to **E**
Gen 35:19 on the way to **E** (that is,
Gen 48: 7 a little distance to go to **E**
Gen 48: 7 on the way to **E** (that is,
1Ch 2:19 Caleb took **E** as his wife, who

EPHRATHAH
Ruth 4:11 and may you prosper in **E** and be
1Ch 2:50 of Hur, the firstborn of **E**
1Ch 4: 4 the firstborn of **E** the father
Ps 132: 6 Behold, we heard of it in **E**
Mic 5: 2 But you, Bethlehem **E**, though

EPHRATHITE (*see* EPHRATH, EPHRATHITES)
1Sa 17:12 of that **E** of Bethlehem Judah

EPHRATHITES (*see* EPHRATHITE)
Ruth 1: 2 **E** of Bethlehem, Judah

EPHRON (*see* EPHRAIM, EPHRAIN)
Gen 23: 8 meet with **E** the son of Zohar
Gen 23:10 Now **E** dwelt among the sons of
Gen 23:10 and **E** the Hittite answered
Gen 23:13 he spoke to **E** in the hearing
Gen 23:14 **E** answered Abraham, saying to
Gen 23:16 And Abraham listened to **E**
Gen 23:16 **E** which he had named in the
Gen 23:17 So the field of **E** which was
Gen 25: 9 in the field of **E** the son of
Gen 49:29 in the field of **E** the Hittite
Gen 49:30 bought with the field of **E**
Gen 50:13 bought with the field from **E**
Josh 15: 9 to the cities of Mount **E**

EPICUREAN
Acts 17:18 Then certain **E** and Stoic

EPILEPTIC (*see* EPILEPTICS)
Matt 17:15 on my son, for he is an **e**

EPILEPTICS (*see* EPILEPTIC)
Matt 4:24 who were demon-possessed, **e**

EPISTLE (*see* EPISTLES)
Rom 16:22 I, Tertius, who wrote this **e**
1Co 5: 9 I wrote to you in my **e** not to
2Co 3: 2 You are our **e** written in our
2Co 3: 3 are manifestly an **e** of Christ
2Co 7: 8 the same **e** made you sorry
Col 4:16 Now when this **e** is read among
Col 4:16 read the **e** from Laodicea
1Th 5:27 **e** be read to all the holy
2Th 2:15 whether by word or our **e**
2Th 3:14 not obey our word in this **e**
2Th 3:17 which is a sign in every **e**
2Pe 3: 1 write to you this second **e**

EPISTLES (*see* EPISTLE)
2Co 3: 1 **e** of commendation to you or
2Pe 3:16 as also in all his **e**,

EQUAL (*see* EQUALITY, EQUALLY, EQUITY, UNEQUALLY)
Ex 30:34 there shall be **e** amounts of
Deut 18: 8 shall have **e** portions to eat
Job 28:17 gold nor crystal can **e** it
Job 28:19 topaz of Ethiopia cannot **e** it
Ps 55:13 But it was you, a man my **e**
Is 40:25 Me, Or to whom shall I be **e**
Is 46: 5 you liken Me, and make Me **e**
Matt 20:12 you made them **e** to us who
Luke 20:36 for they are **e** to the angels
John 5:18 making Himself **e** with God
Phil 2: 6 it robbery to be **e** with God
Rev 21:16 breadth, and height are **e**

EQUALITY (*see* EQUAL)
2Co 8:14 but by an **e**, that now at this
2Co 8:14 that there may be **e**

EQUALLY (*see* EQUAL)
Ezek 47:14 inherit it **e** with one another

EQUIPMENT (*see* EQUIPPED)
Deut 23:13 an implement among your **e**
1Sa 8:12 of war and **e** for his chariots
1Sa 10:22 he is, hidden among the **e**
1Ki 19:21 flesh, using the oxen's **e**
Is 10:28 he has attended to his **e**
Dan 11:13 with a great army and much **e**

EQUIPPED (*see* EQUIPMENT, EQUIPPING)
1Ch 12:23 that were **e** for the war, and
2Ti 3:17 thoroughly **e** for every good

EQUIPPING (*see* EQUIPPED)
Eph 4:12 for the **e** of the saints for

EQUITY (*see* EQUAL)
Ps 98: 9 world, And the peoples with **e**
Ps 99: 4 You have established **e**
Prov 1: 3 Justice, judgment, and **e**
Prov 2: 9 righteousness and justice, **e**
Is 11: 4 decide with **e** for the meek of
Is 59:14 the street, and **e** cannot enter
Mic 3: 9 justice and pervert all **e**,
Mal 2: 6 walked with Me in peace and **e**

ER
Gen 38: 3 son, and he called his name **E**
Gen 38: 6 a wife for **E** his firstborn
Gen 38: 7 But **E**, Judah's firstborn, was
Gen 46:12 The sons of Judah were **E**,
Gen 46:12 Perez, and Zerah (but **E** and
Num 26:19 The sons of Judah were **E** and
Num 26:19 and **E** and Onan died in the land
1Ch 2: 3 The sons of Judah were **E**,
1Ch 2: 3 **E**, the firstborn of Judah,
1Ch 4:21 were **E** the father of Lecah
Luke 3:28 son of Elmodam, the son of **E**

ERAN (*see* ERANITES)
Num 26:36 of **E**, the family of the

ERANITES (*see* ERAN)
Num 26:36 of Eran, the family of the **E**

ERASTUS
Acts 19:22 to him, Timothy and **E**, but he
Rom 16:23 **E**, the treasurer of the city,
2Ti 4:20 **E** stayed in Corinth, but

ERECH
Gen 10:10 of his kingdom was Babel, **E**
Ezra 4: 9 the people of Persia and **E**

ERECT (*see* ERECTED)
2Sa 24:18 **e** an altar to the LORD on the
1Ch 21:18 **e** an altar to the LORD on the
Ezra 2:68 of God, to **e** it in its place

ERECTED (*see* ERECT)
Gen 33:20 Then he **e** an altar there and
2Sa 6:17 that David had **e** for it
1Ch 16: 1 that David had **e** for it
Ezra 6:11 be pulled from his house and **e**
Ezek 16:31 You **e** your shrine at the head
Heb 8: 2 tabernacle which the Lord **e**

ERI (*see* ERITES)
Gen 46:16 Haggi, Shuni, Ezbon, **E**,
Num 26:16 of **E**, the family of the

ERITES (*see* ERI)
Num 26:16 of Eri, the family of the **E**

ERR (*see* ERRED, ERROR)
Is 3:12 who lead you cause you to **e**
Is 9:16 this people cause them to **e**
Is 19:14 Egypt to **e** in all her work
Is 28: 7 they **e** in vision, they
Is 30:28 the people, causing them to **e**
Jer 23:13 caused My people Israel to **e**
Jer 23:32 My people to **e** by their lies

ERRAND
Gen 24:33 until I have told about my **e**

ERRED (*see* ERR)
Lev 5:18 his ignorance in which he **e**
1Sa 26:21 the fool and **e** exceedingly
Job 6:24 understand wherein I have **e**
Job 19: 4 And if indeed I have **e**, my
Is 28: 7 they also have **e** through wine
Is 28: 7 the prophet have **e** through
Is 29:24 These also who **e** in spirit

ERROR (*see* ERR, ERRORS)
2Sa 6: 7 struck him there for his **e**
Job 4:18 He charges His angels with **e**
Job 19: 4 erred, my **e** remains with me
Eccl 5: 6 of God that it was an **e**
Eccl 10: 5 as an **e** proceeding from the
Is 32: 6 to utter **e** against the LORD,
Dan 6: 4 nor was there any **e** or fault
Rom 1:27 of their **e** which was due
Jas 5:20 **e** of his way will save a soul
2Pe 2:18 from those who live in **e**
2Pe 3:17 away with the **e** of the wicked
1Jn 4: 6 of truth and the spirit of **e**
Jude 11 in the **e** of Balaam for profit

ERRORS (*see* ERROR)
Ps 19:12 Who can understand his **e**
Jer 10:15 They are futile, a work of **e**
Jer 51:18 They are futile, a work of **e**

ESARHADDON
2Ki 19:37 Then **E** his son reigned in his
Ezra 4: 2 the days of **E** king of Assyria
Is 37:38 Then **E** his son reigned in his

ESAU (*see* EDOM, ESAU'S)
Gen 25:25 so they called his name **E**
Gen 25:27 **E** was a skillful hunter, a
Gen 25:28 Isaac loved **E** because he ate
Gen 25:29 **E** came in from the field, and
Gen 25:30 And **E** said to Jacob,
Gen 25:32 **E** said, "Look, I am about
Gen 25:34 gave **E** bread and stew
Gen 25:34 Thus **E** despised his
Gen 26:34 When **E** was forty years old,
Gen 27: 1 he called **E** his older son
Gen 27: 5 when Isaac spoke to **E** his son
Gen 27: 5 **E** went to the field to hunt
Gen 27: 6 speak to **E** your brother,
Gen 27:11 **E** my brother is a hairy man,
Gen 27:15 clothes of her elder son **E**
Gen 27:19 I am **E** your firstborn
Gen 27:21 are really my son **E** or not
Gen 27:22 the hands are the hands of **E**
Gen 27:24 Are you really my son **E**
Gen 27:30 that **E** his brother came in
Gen 27:32 your son, your firstborn, **E**
Gen 27:34 When **E** heard the words of his
Gen 27:36 **E** said, "Is he not rightly
Gen 27:37 Isaac answered and said to **E**
Gen 27:38 And **E** said to his father,
Gen 27:38 **E** lifted up his voice and wept
Gen 27:41 So **E** hated Jacob because of
Gen 27:41 him, and **E** said in his heart,
Gen 27:42 the words of **E** her older son
Gen 27:42 him, "Surely your brother **E**
Gen 28: 5 the mother of Jacob and **E**
Gen 28: 6 **E** saw that Isaac had blessed
Gen 28: 8 Also **E** saw that the daughters
Gen 28: 9 So **E** went to Ishmael and took
Gen 32: 3 messengers before him to **E**
Gen 32: 4 Speak thus to my lord **E**
Gen 32: 6 We came to your brother **E**
Gen 32: 8 If **E** comes to the one company
Gen 32:11 brother, from the hand of **E**
Gen 32:13 a present for **E** his brother
Gen 32:17 When **E** my brother meets you
Gen 32:18 a present sent to my lord **E**
Gen 32:19 speak to **E** when you find him
Gen 33: 1 **E** was coming, and with him
Gen 33: 4 But **E** ran to meet him, and
Gen 33: 8 Then **E** said, "What do you
Gen 33: 9 But **E** said, "I have enough,
Gen 33:12 Then **E** said, "Let us take
Gen 33:15 **E** said, "Now let me leave
Gen 33:16 So **E** returned that day on his
Gen 35: 1 the face of **E** your brother
Gen 35:29 And his sons **E** and Jacob buried
Gen 36: 1 this is the genealogy of **E**
Gen 36: 2 **E** took his wives from the
Gen 36: 4 Now Adah bore Eliphaz to **E**
Gen 36: 5 These were the sons of **E** who
Gen 36: 6 Then **E** took his wives, his
Gen 36: 8 So **E** dwelt in Mount Seir
Gen 36: 8 **E** is Edom.
Gen 36: 9 this is the genealogy of **E**
Gen 36:10 the son of Adah the wife of **E**
Gen 36:10 son of Basemath the wife of **E**
Gen 36:14 And she bore to **E**
Gen 36:15 the chiefs of the sons of **E**
Gen 36:15 the firstborn son of **E**, were
Gen 36:19 These were the sons of **E**, who
Gen 36:40 the names of the chiefs of **E**
Gen 36:43 **E** was the father of the
Deut 2: 4 the descendants of **E**, who
Deut 2: 5 Seir to **E** as a possession
Deut 2: 8 of **E** who dwell in Seir, away
Deut 2:12 of **E** dispossessed them and
Deut 2:22 done for the descendants of **E**
Deut 2:29 of **E** who dwell in Seir and the
Josh 24: 4 To Isaac I gave Jacob and **E**
Josh 24: 4 To **E** I gave the mountains of
1Ch 1:34 The sons of Isaac were **E** and
1Ch 1:35 The sons of **E** were Eliphaz,
Jer 49: 8 the calamity of **E** upon him
Jer 49:10 But I have made **E** bare
Obad 6 how **E** shall be searched out
Obad 8 from the mountains of **E**
Obad 9 from the mountains of **E** may
Obad 18 house of **E** shall be stubble
Obad 18 remain of the house of **E**,"
Obad 19 possess the mountains of **E**
Obad 21 to judge the mountains of **E**
Mal 1: 2 Was not **E** Jacob's brother
Mal 1: 3 but **E** I have hated, and laid
Rom 9:13 loved, but **E** I have hated
Heb 11:20 **E** concerning things to come
Heb 12:16 or profane person like **E**, who

ESAU'S (*see* ESAU)
Gen 25:26 his hand took hold of **E** heel
Gen 27:23 like his brother **E** hands
Gen 36:10 were the names of **E** sons
Gen 36:12 **E** son, and she bore Amalek to
Gen 36:12 were the sons of Adah, **E** wife
Gen 36:13 the sons of Basemath, **E** wife
Gen 36:14 **E** wife, the daughter of Anah,
Gen 36:17 were the sons of Reuel, **E** son
Gen 36:17 the sons of Basemath, **E** wife
Gen 36:18 sons of Aholibamah, **E** wife
Gen 36:18 **E** wife, the daughter of Anah

ESCAPE (*see* ESCAPED, ESCAPES, ESCAPING)
Gen 19:17 he said, "**E** for your life
Gen 19:17 **E** to the mountains, lest you
Gen 19:19 but I cannot **e** to the
Gen 19:20 please let me **e** there (is it
Gen 19:22 Hurry, **e** there.
Gen 32: 8 company which is left will **e**
Josh 8:22 let none of them remain or **e**
1Sa 27: 1 speedily **e** to the land of the
1Sa 27: 1 So I shall **e** out of his hand
2Sa 15:14 we shall not **e** from Absalom
2Sa 20: 6 fortified cities, and **e** us
1Ki 18:40 Do not let one of them **e**
2Ki 9:15 or **e** from the city to go and
2Ki 10:24 escapes, whoever lets him **e**
2Ki 19:31 those who **e** from Mount Zion
Ezra 9: 8 to leave us a remnant to **e**
Esth 4:13 **e** in the king's palace any
Job 11:20 fail, and they shall not **e**
Job 32:15 words **e** them.
Ps 55: 8 I would hasten my **e** From the
Ps 56: 7 Shall they **e** by iniquity
Ps 71: 2 and cause me to **e**
Ps 141:10 own nets, While I **e** safely
Prov 19: 5 he who speaks lies will not **e**
Eccl 7:18 who fears God will **e** them all
Eccl 7:26 pleases God shall **e** from her
Is 20: 6 and how shall we **e**
Is 37:32 those who **e** from Mount Zion
Is 66:19 those among them who **e** I will
Jer 11:11 they will not be able to **e**

Jer 25:35 the leaders of the flock to **e**
Jer 32: 4 not **e** from the hand of the
Jer 34: 3 you shall not **e** from his hand
Jer 38:18 you shall not **e** from their
Jer 38:23 You shall not **e** from their
Jer 42:17 of them shall remain or **e**
Jer 44:14 there shall **e** or survive,
Jer 44:14 return except those who **e**
Jer 44:28 Yet a small number who **e** the
Jer 46: 6 away, nor the mighty man **e**
Jer 48: 8 No one shall **e**
Jer 50:28 **e** from the land of Babylon
Jer 50:29 let none of them **e**
Ezek 6: 8 that you may have some who **e**
Ezek 6: 9 Then those of you who **e** will
Ezek 7:16 Those who survive will **e**
Ezek 17:15 he who does such things **e**
Ezek 17:18 these things, he shall not **e**
Dan 11:41 these shall **e** from his hand
Dan 11:42 the land of Egypt shall not **e**
Joel 2: 3 surely nothing shall **e** them
Zech 2: 7 **E**, you who dwell with the
Matt 23:33 How can you **e** the
Luke 21:36 may be counted worthy to **e**
Acts 27:30 seeking to **e** from the ship
Acts 27:42 of them should swim away and **e**
Rom 2: 3 that you will **e** the judgment
1Co 10:13 will also make the way of **e**
1Th 5: 3 And they shall not **e**
2Ti 2:26 **e** the snare of the devil,
Heb 2: 3 how shall we **e** if we neglect
Heb 12:25 For if they did not **e** who
Heb 12:25 much more shall we not **e** if

ESCAPED (*see* ESCAPE)
Gen 14:13 Then one who had **e** came and
Deut 23:15 has **e** from his master to you
Josh 10:20 that those who **e** entered
Judg 3:26 But Ehud **e** while they delayed
Judg 3:26 stone images and **e** to Seirah
Judg 3:29 not a man **e**
Judg 12: 5 any Ephraimite who **e** said
1Sa 14:41 were taken, but the people **e**
1Sa 18:11 But David **e** his presence
1Sa 19:10 So David fled and **e** that night
1Sa 19:12 And he went and fled and **e**
1Sa 19:17 enemy away, so that he has **e**
1Sa 19:18 So David fled and **e**, and went
1Sa 22: 1 and **e** to the cave of Adullam
1Sa 22:20 of Ahitub, named Abiathar, **e**
1Sa 23:13 that David had **e** from Keilah
1Sa 30:17 Not a man of them **e**, except
2Sa 1: 3 I have **e** from the camp of
2Sa 4: 6 and Baanah his brother **e**
1Ki 20:20 **e** on a horse with the cavalry
2Ki 13: 5 so that they **e** from under the
2Ki 19:30 the remnant who have **e** of the
2Ki 19:37 and they **e** into the land of
1Ch 4:43 of the Amalekites who had **e**
2Ch 16: 7 of Syria has **e** from your hand
2Ch 20:24 No one had **e**
2Ch 30: 6 **e** from the hand of the kings
2Ch 36:20 those who **e** from the sword he
Neh 1: 2 concerning the Jews who had **e**
Job 1:15 and I alone have **e** to tell you
Job 1:16 and I alone have **e** to tell you
Job 1:17 and I alone have **e** to tell you
Job 1:19 and I alone have **e** to tell you
Job 19:20 I have **e** by the skin of my
Ps 124: 7 Our soul has **e** as a bird from
Ps 124: 7 snare is broken, and we have **e**
Is 4: 2 those of Israel who have **e**
Is 10:20 such as have **e** of the house
Is 37:31 the remnant who have **e** of the
Is 37:38 and they **e** into the land of
Is 45:20 you who have **e** from the
Jer 41:15 the son of Nethaniah **e** from
Jer 51:50 You who have **e** the sword, get
Ezek 24:27 be opened to him who has **e**
Ezek 33:21 that one who had **e** from
Ezek 33:22 before the man came who had **e**
Obad 14 off those among them who **e**
John 10:39 but He **e** out of their hand
Acts 27:44 they all **e** safely to land
Acts 28: 1 Now when they had **e**, they
Acts 28: 4 whom, though he has **e** the sea
2Co 11:33 the wall, and **e** from his hands
Heb 11:34 **e** the edge of the sword, out
2Pe 1: 4 having **e** the corruption that
2Pe 2:18 **e** from those who live in
2Pe 2:20 For if, after they have **e** the

ESCAPES (*see* ESCAPE)
1Ki 19:17 whoever **e** the sword of Hazael
1Ki 19:17 whoever **e** from the sword of
2Ki 10:24 brought into your hands **e**
Ps 68:20 the Lord belong **e** from death
Is 15: 9 upon him who **e** from Moab, and
Is 16: 3 do not betray him who **e**
Jer 48:19 him who flees and her who **e**
Ezek 24:26 on that day one who **e** will
Amos 9: 1 he who **e** from them shall not
Acts 26:26 these things **e** his attention

ESCAPING (*see* ESCAPE)
1Sa 23:28 that place the Rock of **E**
2Sa 4: 7 were all night **e** through the

ESCORT (*see* ESCORTED, ESCORTS)
2Sa 19:15 to **e** the king across the
2Sa 19:31 to **e** him across the Jordan
Ezra 8:22 of the king an **e** of soldiers

ESCORTED (*see* ESCORT)
2Sa 19:40 people of Judah **e** the king

ESCORTS (*see* ESCORT)
2Ki 11: 4 of the bodyguards and the **e**
2Ki 11: 6 at the gate behind the **e**
2Ki 11:11 Then the **e** stood, every man
2Ki 11:13 heard the noise of the **e** and
2Ki 11:19 the bodyguards, the **e**, and
2Ki 11:19 of the **e** to the king's house

ESEK
Gen 26:20 called the name of the well **E**

ESH-BAAL (*see* ISHBOSHETH)
1Ch 8:33 Malchishua, Abinadab, and **E**
1Ch 9:39 Malchishua, Abinadab, and **E**

ESHBAN
Gen 36:26 Hemdan, **E**, Ithran, and Cheran
1Ch 1:41 sons of Dishon were Hamran, **E**

ESHCOL
Gen 14:13 the Amorite, brother of **E**
Gen 14:24 Aner, **E**, and Mamre
Num 13:23 they came to the Valley of **E**
Num 13:24 was called the Valley of **E**
Num 32: 9 went up to the Valley of **E**
Deut 1:24 and came to the Valley of **E**

ESHEAN
Josh 15:52 Arab, Dumah, **E**,

ESHEK
1Ch 8:39 the sons of **E** his brother

ESHTAOL (*see* ESHTAOLITES)
Josh 15:33 **E**, Zorah, Ashnah,
Josh 19:41 inheritance was Zorah, **E**, Ir
Judg 13:25 Dan between Zorah and **E**
Judg 16:31 **E** in the tomb of his father
Judg 18: 2 men of valor from Zorah and **E**
Judg 18: 8 their brethren at Zorah and **E**
Judg 18:11 from there, from Zorah and **E**

ESHTAOLITES (*see* ESHTAOL)
1Ch 2:53 came the Zorathites and the **E**

ESHTEMOA (*see* ESHTEMOH)
Josh 21:14 **E** with its common-land,
1Sa 30:28 Siphmoth, those who were in **E**
1Ch 4:17 and Ishbah the father of **E**
1Ch 4:19 and of **E** the Maachathite
1Ch 6:57 **E** with its common-lands,

ESHTEMOH (*see* ESHTEMOA)
Josh 15:50 Anab, **E**, Anim,

ESHTON
1Ch 4:11 who was the father of **E**
1Ch 4:12 **E** begot Beth-Rapha, Paseah,

ESLI
Luke 3:25 son of Nahum, the son of **E**

ESPECIALLY
Deut 4:10 **e** concerning the day you
Josh 2: 1 Go, view the land, **e** Jericho
Ps 31:11 But **e** among my neighbors, And
Luke 19:42 you, **e** in this your day, the
Acts 25:26 **e** before you, King Agrippa,
Acts 26: 3 **e** because you are expert in
1Co 14: 1 but **e** that you may prophesy
2Co 10:13 a sphere which **e** includes you
Gal 6:10 **e** to those who are of the
Phil 4:22 you, but **e** those who are of
1Ti 4:10 men, **e** of those who believe
1Ti 5: 8 **e** for those of his household,
1Ti 5:17 **e** those who labor in the word
2Ti 4:13 the books, **e** the parchments
Tit 1:10 **e** those of the circumcision,
Phm 16 **e** to me but how much more to
Heb 13:19 But I **e** urge you to do this,
2Pe 2:10 **e** those who walk according to

ESPOUSALS
Song 3:11 him on the day of his **e**, the

ESTABLISH (*see* ESTABLISHED, ESTABLISHES, ESTABLISHING)
Gen 6:18 But I will **e** My covenant with
Gen 9: 9 I **e** My covenant with you and
Gen 9:11 Thus I **e** My covenant with you
Gen 17: 7 I will **e** My covenant between
Gen 17:19 I will **e** My covenant with him
Gen 17:21 covenant I will **e** with Isaac
Deut 8:18 that He may **e** His covenant
Deut 28: 9 The LORD will **e** you as a holy
Deut 29:13 that He may **e** you today as a
1Sa 1:23 Only let the LORD **e** His word
2Sa 7:12 body, and I will **e** his kingdom
2Sa 7:13 I will **e** the throne of his
2Sa 7:25 **e** it forever and do as You
1Ki 9: 5 then I will **e** the throne of
1Ch 17:11 and I will **e** his kingdom
1Ch 17:12 I will **e** his throne forever
1Ch 17:14 I will **e** him in My house and
1Ch 18: 3 as he went to **e** his power by
1Ch 22:10 I will **e** the throne of his
1Ch 28: 7 Moreover I will **e** his
2Ch 7:18 then I will **e** the throne of
2Ch 9: 8 to **e** them forever, therefore
Esth 9:21 to **e** among them that they
Job 28:25 to **e** a weight for the wind,
Ps 7: 9 to an end, But **e** the just
Ps 48: 8 God will **e** it forever
Ps 87: 5 Most High Himself shall **e** her
Ps 89: 2 shall **e** in the very heavens
Ps 89: 4 Your seed I will **e** forever
Ps 90:17 **e** the work of our hands for
Ps 90:17 Yes, **e** the work of our hands
Ps 107:36 That they may **e** a city for
Ps 119:38 **E** Your word to Your servant,
Prov 15:25 but He will **e** the boundary of
Is 9: 7 **e** it with judgment and justice
Is 26:12 You will **e** peace for us, for
Jer 11: 5 that I may **e** the oath which I
Jer 33: 2 **e** it (the LORD is His name)
Ezek 16:60 and I will **e** an everlasting
Ezek 16:62 I will **e** My covenant with you
Ezek 26:20 I shall **e** glory in the land
Ezek 34:23 I will **e** one shepherd over
Ezek 37:26 I will **e** them and multiply
Dan 6: 7 together to **e** a royal statute
Dan 6: 8 **e** the decree and sign the
Amos 5:15 **e** justice in the gate
Rom 3:31 On the contrary, we **e** the law
Rom 10: 3 and seeking to **e** their own
Rom 16:25 Now to Him who is able to **e**
1Th 3: 2 to **e** you and encourage you
1Th 3:13 so that He may **e** your hearts
2Th 2:17 **e** you in every good word and
2Th 3: 3 is faithful, who will **e** you
Heb 10: 9 that He may **e** the second
Jas 5: 8 **E** your hearts, for the coming
1Pe 5:10 suffered a while, perfect, **e**

ESTABLISHED (*see* ESTABLISH)
Gen 9:17 which I have **e** between Me
Gen 41:32 because the thing is **e** by God
Ex 6: 4 I have also **e** My covenant
Ex 15:17 LORD, which Your hands have **e**
Deut 19:15 the matter shall be **e**
Deut 32: 6 has He not made you and **e** you
1Sa 3:20 **e** as a prophet of the LORD
1Sa 13:13 **e** your kingdom over Israel
1Sa 14:47 So Saul **e** his sovereignty
1Sa 20:31 the earth, you shall not be **e**
1Sa 24:20 shall be **e** in your hand
2Sa 5:12 knew that the LORD had **e** him
2Sa 7:16 shall be **e** forever before you
2Sa 7:16 throne shall be **e** forever
2Sa 7:26 servant David be **e** before You
1Ki 2:12 and his kingdom was firmly **e**
1Ki 2:24 the LORD lives, who has **e** me
1Ki 2:45 be **e** before the LORD forever
1Ki 2:46 Thus the kingdom was **e** in the
2Ki 14: 5 the kingdom was **e** in his hand
1Ch 14: 2 had **e** him as king over Israel
1Ch 16:30 the world also is firmly **e**

1Ch 17:14 his throne shall be **e** forever
1Ch 17:23 house, let it be **e** forever
1Ch 17:24 So let it be **e**, that Your
1Ch 17:24 servant David be **e** before You
2Ch 1: 9 to David my father be **e**, for
2Ch 12: 1 Rehoboam had **e** the kingdom
2Ch 17: 5 Therefore the LORD **e** the
2Ch 20:20 your God, and you shall be **e**
2Ch 21: 4 Now when Jehoram was **e** over
2Ch 23:18 singing, as it was **e** by David
2Ch 25: 3 the kingdom was **e** for him
Esth 9:27 the Jews **e** and imposed it upon
Job 21: 8 Their descendants are **e** with
Job 22:28 and it will be **e** for you
Ps 24: 2 seas, And **e** it upon the waters
Ps 40: 2 upon a rock, And **e** my steps
Ps 65: 6 Who **e** the mountains by His
Ps 78: 5 For He **e** a testimony in Jacob
Ps 78:69 earth which He has **e** forever
Ps 81: 5 This He **e** in Joseph for a
Ps 89:21 With whom My hand shall be **e**
Ps 89:37 It shall be **e** forever like
Ps 93: 1 Surely the world is **e**, so
Ps 93: 2 Your throne is **e** from of old
Ps 96:10 The world also is firmly **e**
Ps 99: 4 You have **e** equity
Ps 102:28 will be **e** before You
Ps 103:19 The LORD has **e** His throne in
Ps 112: 8 His heart is **e**
Ps 119:90 You **e** the earth, and it abides
Ps 140:11 a slanderer be **e** in the earth
Ps 148: 6 He has also **e** them forever and
Prov 3:19 He **e** the heavens
Prov 4:26 and let all your ways be **e**
Prov 8:23 I have been **e** from
Prov 8:28 when He **e** the clouds above,
Prov 12: 3 A man is not **e** by wickedness,
Prov 12:19 lip shall be **e** forever, but a
Prov 15:22 of counselors they are **e**
Prov 16: 3 and your thoughts will be **e**
Prov 16:12 for a throne is **e** by
Prov 20:18 Every purpose is **e** by counsel
Prov 24: 3 and by understanding it is **e**
Prov 25: 5 will be **e** in righteousness
Prov 29:14 his throne will be **e** forever
Prov 30: 4 Who has **e** all the ends of the
Is 2: 2 the LORD's house shall be **e**
Is 7: 9 surely you shall not be **e**
Is 16: 5 In mercy the throne will be **e**
Is 30:33 For Tophet was **e** of old, yes,
Is 42: 4 till He has **e** justice in the
Is 45:18 and made it, Who has **e** it, Who
Is 54:14 righteousness you shall be **e**
Jer 10:12 He has **e** the world by His
Jer 12:16 then they shall be **e** in the
Jer 30:20 shall be **e** before Me
Jer 51:15 He has **e** the world by His
Ezek 28:14 I **e** you
Hos 6: 3 forth is **e** as the morning
Mic 4: 1 the LORD's house shall be **e**
Matt 18:16 witnesses every word may be **e**
Rom 1:11 gift, so that you may be **e**
2Co 13: 1 every word shall be **e**
Col 2: 7 **e** in the faith, as you have
Heb 8: 6 which was **e** on better
Heb 13: 9 that the heart be **e** by grace
2Pe 1:12 are **e** in the present truth

ESTABLISHES (*see* ESTABLISH)
Prov 21:29 for the upright, he **e** his way
Prov 29: 4 The king **e** the land by
Is 62: 7 and give Him no rest till He **e**
Dan 6:15 the king **e** may be changed
Hab 2:12 who **e** a city by iniquity
2Co 1:21 Now He who **e** us with you in

ESTABLISHING (*see* ESTABLISH)
1Ki 15: 4 after him and by **e** Jerusalem

ESTATE
1Ch 17:17 me according to the **e** of a
Eccl 3:18 Concerning the **e** of the sons
Acts 28: 7 **e** of the leading citizen of

ESTEEM (*see* ESTEEMED, ESTEEMING, ESTEEMS)
Prov 3: 4 high **e** in the sight of God and
Prov 18:11 like a high wall in his own **e**
Is 53: 3 despised, and we did not **e** Him
Phil 2: 3 **e** others better than himself
Phil 2:29 and hold such men in **e**
1Th 5:13 to **e** them very highly in love

ESTEEMED (*see* ESTEEM)
Deut 32:15 scornfully **e** the Rock of his
1Sa 2:30 despise Me shall be lightly **e**
1Sa 18:23 I am a poor and lightly **e** man
1Sa 18:30 that his name became highly **e**
Is 9: 1 lightly **e** the land of Zebulun
Is 29:16 the potter be **e** as the clay
Is 29:17 field be **e** as a forest
Is 53: 4 yet we **e** Him stricken,
Luke 16:15 For what is highly **e** among
Acts 5:13 but the people **e** them highly
1Co 6: 4 **e** by the church to judge

ESTEEMING (*see* ESTEEM)
Heb 11:26 **e** the reproach of Christ

ESTEEMS (*see* ESTEEM)
Rom 14: 5 One person **e** one day above
Rom 14: 5 another **e** every day alike

ESTHER (*see* ESTHER'S, HADASSAH)
Esth 2: 7 up Hadassah, that is, **E**, his
Esth 2: 8 that **E** also was taken to the
Esth 2:10 **E** had not revealed her people
Esth 2:15 Now when the turn came for **E**
Esth 2:15 **E** obtained favor in the sight
Esth 2:16 So **E** was taken to King
Esth 2:17 The king loved **E** more than
Esth 2:18 a great feast, the Feast of **E**
Esth 2:20 Now **E** had not yet revealed
Esth 2:20 for **E** obeyed the command of
Esth 2:22 to Mordecai, who told Queen **E**
Esth 2:22 and **E** informed the king in
Esth 4: 5 Then **E** called Hathach, one of
Esth 4: 8 that he might show it to **E**
Esth 4: 9 told **E** the words of Mordecai
Esth 4:10 Then **E** spoke to Hathach, and
Esth 4:13 told them to answer **E**
Esth 4:15 Then **E** told them to return
Esth 4:17 to all that **E** commanded him
Esth 5: 1 on the third day that **E** put
Esth 5: 2 Queen **E** standing in the court
Esth 5: 2 the king held out to **E** the
Esth 5: 2 Then **E** went near and touched
Esth 5: 3 What do you wish, Queen **E**
Esth 5: 4 So **E** answered, "If it
Esth 5: 5 that he may do as **E** has said
Esth 5: 5 banquet that **E** had prepared
Esth 5: 6 of wine the king said to **E**
Esth 5: 7 Then **E** answered and said, "My
Esth 5:12 Queen **E** invited no one but me
Esth 6:14 banquet which **E** had prepared
Esth 7: 1 went to dine with Queen **E**
Esth 7: 2 the king again said to **E**
Esth 7: 2 is your petition, Queen **E**
Esth 7: 3 Then Queen **E** answered and
Esth 7: 5 answered and said to Queen **E**
Esth 7: 6 **E** said, "The adversary
Esth 7: 7 Haman stood before Queen **E**
Esth 7: 8 across the couch where **E** was
Esth 8: 1 Queen **E** the house of Haman
Esth 8: 1 for **E** had told how he was
Esth 8: 2 **E** appointed Mordecai over the
Esth 8: 3 Now **E** spoke again to the king
Esth 8: 4 the golden scepter toward **E**
Esth 8: 4 So **E** arose and stood before
Esth 8: 7 Ahasuerus said to Queen **E**
Esth 8: 7 I have given **E** the house of
Esth 9:12 And the king said to Queen **E**
Esth 9:13 Then **E** said, "If it pleases
Esth 9:25 but when **E** came before the
Esth 9:29 Then Queen **E**, the daughter of
Esth 9:31 Queen **E** had prescribed for
Esth 9:32 So the decree of **E** confirmed

ESTHER'S (*see* ESTHER)
Esth 2:11 to learn of **E** welfare and
Esth 4: 4 So **E** maids and eunuchs came
Esth 4:12 So they told Mordecai **E** words

ESTRANGED
Job 19:13 are completely **e** from me
Ps 58: 3 wicked are **e** from the womb
Ezek 14: 5 because they are all **e** from
Gal 5: 4 You have become **e** from Christ

ETAM
Judg 15: 8 in the cleft of the rock of **E**
Judg 15:11 to the cleft of the rock of **E**
1Ch 4: 3 the sons of the father of **E**
1Ch 4:32 And their villages were **E**, Ain
2Ch 11: 6 And he built Bethlehem, **E**,

ETERNAL (*see* ETERNALLY, ETERNITY)
Deut 33:27 The **e** God is your refuge, and
Eccl 12: 5 For man goes to his **e** home
Is 60:15 will make you an **e** excellence
Matt 19:16 I do that I may have **e** life
Matt 25:46 but the righteous into **e** life
Mark 3:29 subject to **e** condemnation"
Mark 10:17 do that I may inherit **e** life
Mark 10:30 and in the age to come, **e** life
Luke 10:25 shall I do to inherit **e** life
Luke 18:18 shall I do to inherit **e** life
John 3:15 not perish but have **e** life
John 4:36 and gathers fruit for **e** life
John 5:39 you think you have **e** life
John 6:54 and drinks My blood has **e** life
John 6:68 You have the words of **e** life
John 10:28 And I give them **e** life, and
John 12:25 world will keep it for **e** life
John 17: 2 that He should give **e** life to
John 17: 3 And this is **e** life, that they
Acts 13:48 appointed to **e** life believed
Rom 1:20 are made, even His **e** power
Rom 2: 7 **e** life to those who by
Rom 5:21 through righteousness to **e**
Rom 6:23 but the gift of God is **e** life
2Co 4:17 and **e** weight of glory,
2Co 4:18 which are not seen are **e**
2Co 5: 1 with hands, **e** in the heavens
Eph 3:11 to the **e** purpose which He
1Ti 1:17 Now to the King **e**, immortal,
1Ti 6:12 of faith, lay hold on **e** life
1Ti 6:19 they may lay hold on **e** life
2Ti 2:10 in Christ Jesus with **e** glory
Tit 1: 2 in hope of **e** life which God,
Tit 3: 7 to the hope of **e** life
Heb 5: 9 He became the author of **e**
Heb 6: 2 of the dead, and of **e** judgment
Heb 9:12 having obtained **e** redemption
Heb 9:14 who through the **e** Spirit
Heb 9:15 promise of the **e** inheritance
1Pe 5:10 who called us to His **e** glory
1Jn 1: 2 declare to you that **e** life
1Jn 2:25 He has promised us—**e** life.
1Jn 3:15 has **e** life abiding in him
1Jn 5:11 that God has given us **e** life
1Jn 5:13 may know that you have **e** life
1Jn 5:20 is the true God and **e** life
Jude 7 the vengeance of **e** fire
Jude 21 Lord Jesus Christ unto **e** life

ETERNALLY (*see* ETERNAL)
Ps 49: 9 he should continue to live **e**
Rom 9: 5 over all, the **e** blessed God

ETERNITY (*see* ETERNAL)
Eccl 3:11 He has put **e** in their hearts
Is 57:15 and Lofty One Who inhabits **e**
Acts 15:18 God from **e** are all His works

ETHAM
Ex 13:20 camped in **E** at the edge of
Num 33: 6 from Succoth and camped at **E**
Num 33: 7 They moved from **E** and turned
Num 33: 8 in the Wilderness of **E**, and

ETHAN (*see* JOAH)
1Ki 4:31 than **E** the Ezrahite, and Heman
1Ch 2: 6 sons of Zerah were Zimri, **E**
1Ch 2: 8 The son of **E** was Azariah
1Ch 6:42 the son of **E**, the son of
1Ch 6:44 were **E** the son of Kishi, the
1Ch 15:17 Merari, **E** the son of Kushaiah
1Ch 15:19 singers, Heman, Asaph, and **E**

ETHANIM
1Ki 8: 2 the feast in the month of **E**

ETHBAAL
1Ki 16:31 Jezebel the daughter of **E**

ETHER
Josh 15:42 Libnah, **E**, Ashan,
Josh 19: 7 Ain, Rimmon, **E**, and Ashan

ETHIOPIA (*see* CUSH, ETHIOPIAN)
2Ki 19: 9 concerning Tirhakah king of **E**
Esth 1: 1 who reigned from India to **E**
Esth 8: 9 the provinces from India to **E**
Job 28:19 The topaz of **E** cannot equal
Ps 68:31 **E** will quickly stretch out
Ps 87: 4 O Philistia and Tyre, with **E**
Is 18: 1 is beyond the rivers of **E**
Is 20: 3 a wonder against Egypt and **E**
Is 20: 5 afraid and ashamed of **E** their

Is 37: 9 concerning Tirhakah king of E
Is 43: 3 gave Egypt for your ransom, E
Ezek 29:10 as far as the border of E
Ezek 30: 4 great anguish shall be in E
Ezek 30: 5 E, Libya, Lydia, all the
Ezek 38: 5 Persia, E, and Libya are with
Amos 9: 7 like the people of E to Me
Nah 3: 9 E and Egypt were her strength,
Zeph 3:10 the rivers of E my worshipers
Acts 8:27 And behold, a man of E, a

ETHIOPIAN (*see* ETHIOPIA, ETHIOPIANS)
Num 12: 1 Moses because of the E woman
Num 12: 1 for he had married an E woman
2Ch 14: 9 Then Zerah the E came out
Jer 13:23 Can the E change his skin or
Jer 38: 7 Now Ebed-Melech the E, one of
Jer 38:10 commanded Ebed-Melech the E
Jer 38:12 the E said to Jeremiah
Jer 39:16 and speak to Ebed-Melech the E

ETHIOPIANS (*see* ETHIOPIAN)
2Ch 12: 3 and the Sukkiim and the E
2Ch 14:12 LORD struck the E before Asa
2Ch 14:12 Asa and Judah, and the E fled
2Ch 14:13 So the E were overthrown, and
2Ch 16: 8 Were the E and the Lubim not a
2Ch 21:16 Arabians who were near the E
Is 20: 4 the E as captives, young and
Jer 46: 9 The E and the Libyans who
Ezek 30: 9 to make the careless E afraid
Dan 11:43 E shall follow at his heels
Zeph 2:12 You E also, you shall be
Acts 8:27 Candace the queen of the E

ETH KAZIN
Josh 19:13 east of Gath Hepher, toward E

ETHNAN
1Ch 4: 7 were Zereth, Zohar, and E

ETHNI (*see* JEATHERAI)
1Ch 6:41 the son of E, the son of

EUBULUS
2Ti 4:21 E greets you, as well as

EUNICE
2Ti 1: 5 Lois and your mother E, and I

EUNUCH (*see* EUNUCHS)
Lev 21:20 or eczema or scab, or is a e
Esth 2: 3 custody of Hegai the king's e
Esth 2:14 the king's e who kept the
Esth 2:15 but what Hegai the king's e
Is 56: 3 nor let the e say, "Here I
Acts 8:27 a e of great authority under
Acts 8:34 So the e answered Philip and
Acts 8:36 the e said, "See, here is
Acts 8:38 and the e went down into the
Acts 8:39 so that the e saw him no more

EUNUCHS (*see* EUNUCH)
2Ki 9:32 two or three e looked out at
2Ki 20:18 they shall be e in the palace
Esth 1:10 seven e who served in the
Esth 1:12 command brought by his e
Esth 1:15 brought to her by the e
Esth 2:21 gate, two of the king's e
Esth 4: 4 e came and told her, and the
Esth 4: 5 one of the king's e whom he
Esth 6: 2 Teresh, two of the king's e
Esth 6:14 with him, the king's e came
Esth 7: 9 Now Harbonah, one of the e
Is 39: 7 they shall be e in the palace
Is 56: 4 To the e who keep My Sabbaths
Jer 29: 2 king, the queen mother, the e
Jer 34:19 princes of Jerusalem, the e
Jer 38: 7 the Ethiopian, one of the e
Jer 41:16 and the children and the e,
Dan 1: 3 Ashpenaz, the master of his e
Dan 1: 7 the chief of the e gave names
Dan 1: 8 of the chief of the e that he
Dan 1: 9 will of the chief of the e
Dan 1:10 chief of the e said to Daniel
Dan 1:11 of the e had set over Daniel
Dan 1:18 the chief of the e brought
Matt 19:12 For there are e who were born
Matt 19:12 there are e who were made
Matt 19:12 who were made e by men, and
Matt 19:12 there are e who have made
Matt 19:12 who have made themselves e

EUODIA
Phil 4: 2 I implore E and I implore

EUPHRATES
Gen 2:14 The fourth river is the E
Gen 15:18 the great river, the River E
Deut 1: 7 the great river, the River E
Deut 11:24 from the river, the River E
Josh 1: 4 the great river, the River E
2Sa 8: 3 his territory at the River E
2Ki 23:29 of Assyria, to the River E
2Ki 24: 7 Brook of Egypt to the River E
1Ch 5: 9 this side of the River E,
1Ch 18: 3 his power by the River E
2Ch 35:20 against Carchemish by the E
Jer 13: 4 waist, and arise, go to the E
Jer 13: 5 So I went and hid it by the E
Jer 13: 6 Arise, go to the E, and take
Jer 13: 7 Then I went to the E and dug,
Jer 46: 2 by the River E in Carchemish
Jer 46: 6 the north, by the River E
Jer 46:10 north country by the River E
Jer 51:63 it and throw it out into the E
Rev 9:14 bound at the great river E
Rev 16:12 his bowl on the great river E

EUROCLYDON
Acts 27:14 head wind arose, called E

EUTYCHUS
Acts 20: 9 a certain young man named E

EVANGELIST (*see* EVANGELISTS)
Acts 21: 8 the house of Philip the e
2Ti 4: 5 do the work of an e, fulfill

EVANGELISTS (*see* EVANGELIST)
Eph 4:11 some prophets, some e, and

EVE
Gen 3:20 Adam called his wife's name E
Gen 4: 1 Now Adam knew E his wife, and
2Co 11: 3 deceived E by his craftiness
1Ti 2:13 Adam was formed first, then E

EVEN (*see* PREFACE)

EVENING (*see* EVENINGS, EVENTIDE)
Gen 1: 5 So the e and the morning were
Gen 1: 8 So the e and the morning were
Gen 1:13 So the e and the morning were
Gen 1:19 So the e and the morning were
Gen 1:23 So the e and the morning were
Gen 1:31 So the e and the morning were
Gen 8:11 the dove came to him in the e
Gen 19: 1 angels came to Sodom in the e
Gen 24:11 by a well of water at e time
Gen 24:63 in the field in the e
Gen 29:23 Now it came to pass in the e
Gen 30:16 out of the field in the e
Ex 12:18 day of the month at e, you
Ex 12:18 day of the month at e
Ex 16: 6 At e you shall know that the
Ex 16: 8 you meat to eat in the e, and
Ex 16:13 was that quails came up at e
Ex 18:13 Moses from morning until e
Ex 18:14 you from morning until e
Ex 27:21 e until morning before the
Lev 11:24 them shall be unclean until e
Lev 11:25 clothes and be unclean until e
Lev 11:27 shall be unclean until e
Lev 11:28 clothes and be unclean until e
Lev 11:31 dead shall be unclean until e
Lev 11:32 it shall be unclean until e
Lev 11:39 shall be unclean until e
Lev 11:40 clothes and be unclean until e
Lev 11:40 clothes and be unclean until e
Lev 14:46 up shall be unclean until e
Lev 15: 5 water, and be unclean until e
Lev 15: 6 water, and be unclean until e
Lev 15: 7 water, and be unclean until e
Lev 15: 8 water, and be unclean until e
Lev 15:10 him shall be unclean until e
Lev 15:10 water, and be unclean until e
Lev 15:11 water, and be unclean until e
Lev 15:16 water, and be unclean until e
Lev 15:17 water, and be unclean until e
Lev 15:18 water, and be unclean until e
Lev 15:19 her shall be unclean until e
Lev 15:21 water, and be unclean until e
Lev 15:22 water, and be unclean until e
Lev 15:23 he shall be unclean until e
Lev 15:27 water, and be unclean until e
Lev 17:15 water, and be unclean until e
Lev 22: 6 shall be unclean until e, and
Lev 23:32 ninth day of the month at e
Lev 23:32 from e to e, you shall
Lev 24: 3 be in charge of it from e
Num 9:15 from e until morning it was
Num 9:21 only from e until morning
Num 19: 7 shall be unclean until e
Num 19: 8 and shall be unclean until e
Num 19:10 and be unclean until e
Num 19:19 and at e he shall be clean
Num 19:21 shall be unclean until e
Num 19:22 it shall be unclean until e
Num 28: 4 lamb you shall offer in the e
Num 28: 8 lamb you shall offer in the e
Deut 23:11 when e comes, that he shall
Deut 28:67 say, "Oh, that it were e
Deut 28:67 at e you shall say, "Oh, that
Josh 7: 6 the ark of the LORD until e
Josh 8:29 he hanged on a tree until e
Josh 10:26 hanging on the trees until e
Judg 19: 9 day is now drawing toward e
Judg 19:16 his work in the field at e
Judg 20:23 wept before the LORD until e
Judg 20:26 and fasted that day until e
Judg 21: 2 there before God till e
Ruth 2:17 gleaned in the field until e
1Sa 14:24 man who eats any food until e
1Sa 17:16 forty days, morning and e
1Sa 20: 5 until the third day at e
1Sa 30:17 until the e of the next day
2Sa 1:12 and fasted until e for Saul
2Sa 11: 2 Then it happened one e that
2Sa 11:13 at e he went out to lie on
1Ki 17: 6 and bread and meat in the e
1Ki 18:29 offering of the e sacrifice
1Ki 18:36 offering of the e sacrifice
1Ki 22:35 the Syrians, and died at e
2Ki 16:15 the e grain offering, the
1Ch 16:40 regularly morning and e, and to
1Ch 23:30 the LORD, and likewise at e
2Ch 2: 4 burnt offerings morning and e
2Ch 13:11 every e burnt sacrifices and
2Ch 13:11 its lamps to burn every e
2Ch 18:34 facing the Syrians until e
2Ch 31: 3 e burnt offerings, the burnt
Ezra 3: 3 morning and e burnt offerings
Ezra 9: 4 until the e sacrifice
Ezra 9: 5 At the e sacrifice I arose
Esth 2:14 In the e she went, and in the
Job 4:20 in pieces from morning till e
Ps 55:17 E and morning and at noon I
Ps 59: 6 At e they return, They growl
Ps 59:14 at e they return, They growl
Ps 65: 8 of the morning and e rejoice
Ps 90: 6 In the e it is cut down and
Ps 104:23 And to his labor until the e
Ps 141: 2 my hands as the e sacrifice
Prov 7: 9 in the twilight, in the e
Eccl 11: 6 in the e do not withhold your
Jer 6: 4 of the e are lengthening
Ezek 12: 4 at e you shall go in their
Ezek 12: 7 at e I dug through the wall
Ezek 24:18 morning, and at e my wife died
Ezek 33:22 LORD had been upon me the e
Ezek 46: 2 shall not be shut until e
Dan 9:21 the time of the e offering
Hab 1: 8 and more fierce than e wolves
Zeph 2: 7 they shall lie down at e
Zeph 3: 3 her judges are e wolves that
Zech 14: 7 But at e time it shall happen
Matt 8:16 When e had come, they brought
Matt 14:15 When it was e, His disciples
Matt 14:23 when e had come, He was alone
Matt 16: 2 When it is e you say, It
Matt 20: 8 So when e had come, the owner
Matt 26:20 Now when e had come, He sat
Matt 27:57 Now when e had come, there
Mark 1:32 Now at e, when the sun had
Mark 4:35 when e had come, He said to
Mark 6:47 Now when e came, the boat was
Mark 11:19 when e had come, He went out
Mark 13:35 in the e, at midnight, at the
Mark 14:17 In the e He came with the
Mark 15:42 Now when e had come, because
Luke 24:29 with us, for it is toward e
John 6:16 And when e came, His disciples
John 20:19 Then, the same day at e,
Acts 4: 3 day, for it was already e
Acts 28:23 Prophets, from morning till e

EVENINGS (*see* EVENING)
Dan 8:26 And the vision of the e and

EVENLY (*see* PREFACE)

EVENT (*see* EVENTS)
Ex 1:10 and it happen, in the e of war
1Ki 13:33 After this e Jeroboam did not
Eccl 2:14 same e happens to them all
Eccl 9: 2 One e happens to the

EVENTIDE (*see* EVENING)
Is 17:14 Then behold, at e, trouble

EVENTS (*see* EVENT)
1Ch 29:30 the e that happened to him,
2Ch 29:36 since the e took place so

EVER
Gen 34:12 Ask me e so much dowry and
Ex 15:18 LORD shall reign forever and e
Ex 22:26 If you e take your neighbor's
Lev 27:19 field e wishes to redeem it
Num 11:20 Why did we e come up out of
Num 22:30 e since I became yours, to
Num 22:30 Was I e disposed to do this
Deut 4:33 Did any people e hear the
Deut 4:34 Or did God e try to go and
Josh 14:10 e since the LORD spoke this
Judg 11:25 Did he e strive against
Judg 11:25 Did he e fight against them
Judg 16:17 No razor has e come upon my
2Sa 7: 7 have I e spoken a word to
2Sa 19:42 Have we e eaten at the king's
1Ki 22:28 If you e return in peace, the
1Ch 17: 6 have I e spoken a word to any
1Ch 29:10 our Father, forever and e
2Ch 18:27 If you e return in peace, the
Neh 9: 5 LORD your God forever and e
Neh 13: 1 e come into the congregation
Job 4: 7 who e perished being innocent
Job 4: 7 were the upright e cut off
Job 6:22 Did I e say, Bring something
Job 10:17 changes and war are e with me
Ps 5:11 Let them e shout for joy,
Ps 9: 5 out their name forever and e
Ps 10:16 The LORD is King forever and e
Ps 21: 4 Length of days forever and e
Ps 25:15 My eyes are e toward the LORD
Ps 37:26 He is e merciful, and lends
Ps 45: 6 O God, is forever and e
Ps 45:17 shall praise You forever and e
Ps 48:14 is God, Our God forever and e
Ps 51: 3 And my sin is e before me
Ps 52: 8 the mercy of God forever and e
Ps 58: 5 Charming e so skillfully
Ps 90: 2 Or e You had formed the earth
Ps 111: 5 He will e be mindful of His
Ps 111: 8 They stand fast forever and e
Ps 119:44 law continually, Forever and e
Ps 119:98 For they are e with me
Ps 145: 1 bless Your name forever and e
Ps 145: 2 praise Your name forever and e
Ps 145:21 His holy name Forever and e
Ps 148: 6 established them forever and e
Prov 4:18 that shines e brighter unto
Prov 8:23 before there was e an earth
Is 30: 8 time to come, forever and e
Is 33:20 its stakes will e be removed
Is 34:10 pass through it forever and e
Is 45:17 or disgraced forever and e
Jer 7: 7 to your fathers forever and e
Jer 25: 5 and your fathers forever and e
Jer 26:19 all Judah e put him to death
Jer 30: 6 whether a man is e in labor
Ezek 4:14 flesh e come into my mouth
Ezek 31:14 e again exalt themselves for
Ezek 31:14 e be high enough to reach up
Ezek 37:22 nor shall they e be divided
Dan 2:10 or ruler has e asked such
Dan 2:20 the name of God forever and e
Dan 6:24 e came to the bottom of the
Dan 7:18 forever, even forever and e
Dan 12: 3 like the stars forever and e
Hos 12: 9 e since the land of Egypt
Hos 13: 4 God e since the land of Egypt
Joel 2: 2 nor will there e be any such
Joel 3:17 and no aliens shall e pass
Mic 4: 5 the LORD our God forever and e
Matt 21:19 no fruit grow on you e again
Matt 24:21 this time, no, nor e shall be
Mark 11:14 eat fruit from you e again
Mark 13:19 this time, nor e shall be
Luke 19:30 on which no one has e sat
Luke 23:53 no one had e lain before
John 4:29 me all things that I e did
John 4:39 He told me all that I e did
John 7:46 No man e spoke like this Man
John 10: 8 All who e came before Me are
1Co 9: 7 Who e goes to war at his own
Gal 1: 5 to whom be glory forever and e
Eph 5:29 For no one e hated his own
Phil 4:20 Father be glory forever and e
1Ti 1:17 honor and glory forever and e
2Ti 4:18 To Him be glory forever and e
Heb 1: 5 of the angels did He e say
Heb 1: 8 O God, is forever and e
Heb 1:13 of the angels has He e said
Heb 7:25 Him, since He e lives to make
Heb 13:21 to whom be glory forever and e
1Pe 4:11 and the dominion forever and e
1Pe 5:11 and the dominion forever and e
Rev 1: 6 and dominion forever and e
Rev 4: 9 who lives forever and e,
Rev 4:10 Him who lives forever and e
Rev 5:13 and to the Lamb, forever and e
Rev 5:14 Him who lives forever and e
Rev 7:12 be to our God forever and e
Rev 10: 6 by Him who lives forever and e
Rev 11:15 He shall reign forever and e
Rev 14:11 torment ascends forever and e
Rev 15: 7 of God who lives forever and e
Rev 19: 3 smoke rises up forever and e
Rev 20:10 day and night forever and e
Rev 22: 5 they shall reign forever and e

EVERLASTING (*see* EVERMORE)
Gen 9:16 the e covenant between God
Gen 17: 7 for an e covenant, to be God
Gen 17: 8 of Canaan, as an e possession
Gen 17:13 your flesh for an e covenant
Gen 17:19 with him for an e covenant
Gen 21:33 name of the LORD, the E God
Gen 48: 4 after you as an e possession
Gen 49:26 utmost bound of the e hills
Ex 12:14 as a feast by an e ordinance
Ex 12:17 generations as an e ordinance
Ex 40:15 shall surely be an e
Lev 16:34 shall be an e statute for you
Lev 24: 8 of Israel by an e covenant
Num 25:13 a covenant of an e priesthood
Deut 33:15 things of the e hills,
Deut 33:27 and underneath are the e arms
2Sa 23: 5 made with me an e covenant
1Ch 16:17 to Israel for an e covenant
1Ch 16:36 Israel from e to e
Ps 24: 7 And be lifted up, you e doors
Ps 24: 9 And lift them up, you e doors
Ps 41:13 Israel From e to e
Ps 90: 2 Even from e to e,
Ps 93: 2 You are from e
Ps 100: 5 His mercy is e, And His truth
Ps 103:17 mercy of the LORD is from e
Ps 103:17 to e On those who fear Him
Ps 105:10 To Israel for an e covenant
Ps 106:48 Israel From e to e
Ps 112: 6 will be in e remembrance
Ps 119:142 is an e righteousness, And
Ps 119:144 of Your testimonies is e
Ps 139:24 me, And lead me in the way e
Ps 145:13 Your kingdom is an e kingdom
Prov 8:23 have been established from e
Prov 10:25 righteous has an e foundation
Is 9: 6 E Father, Prince of Peace
Is 24: 5 Broken the e covenant
Is 26: 4 YAH, the LORD, is e strength
Is 33:14 shall dwell with e burnings
Is 35:10 with e joy on their heads
Is 40:28 The e God, the LORD, the
Is 45:17 the LORD with an e salvation
Is 51:11 with e joy on their heads
Is 54: 8 but with e kindness I will
Is 55: 3 I will make an e covenant
Is 55:13 for an e sign that shall not
Is 56: 5 I will give them an e name
Is 60:19 will be to you an e light
Is 60:20 the LORD will be your e light
Is 61: 7 e joy shall be theirs
Is 61: 8 make with them an e covenant
Is 63:12 to make for Himself an e name
Is 63:16 Redeemer from E is Your name
Jer 10:10 the living God and the e King
Jer 20:11 Their e confusion will never
Jer 23:40 I will bring an e reproach
Jer 31: 3 have loved you with an e love
Jer 32:40 I will make an e covenant
Ezek 16:60 an e covenant with you
Ezek 37:26 it shall be an e covenant
Dan 4: 3 His kingdom is an e kingdom
Dan 4:34 His dominion is an e dominion
Dan 7:14 His dominion is an e dominion
Dan 7:27 His kingdom is an e kingdom
Dan 9:24 to bring in e righteousness,
Dan 12: 2 shall awake, some to e life
Dan 12: 2 some to shame and e contempt
Mic 5: 2 have been from of old, from e
Hab 1:12 Are You not from e, O LORD my
Hab 3: 6 And the e mountains were
Hab 3: 6 His ways are e
Matt 18: 8 to be cast into the e fire
Matt 19:29 and inherit e life
Matt 25:41 into the e fire prepared for
Matt 25:46 go away into e punishment
Luke 16: 9 you into e habitations
Luke 18:30 and in the age to come e life
John 3:16 not perish but have e life
John 3:36 in the Son has e life
John 4:14 springing up into e life
John 5:24 in Him who sent Me has e life
John 6:27 food which endures to e life
John 6:40 in Him may have e life
John 6:47 who believes in Me has e life
John 12:50 that His command is e life
Acts 13:46 yourselves unworthy of e life
Rom 6:22 holiness, and the end, e life
Rom 16:26 the commandment of the e God
Gal 6: 8 of the Spirit reap e life
2Th 1: 9 with e destruction from the
2Th 2:16 given us e consolation and
1Ti 1:16 to believe on Him for e life
1Ti 6:16 to whom be honor and e power
Heb 13:20 the blood of the e covenant
2Pe 1:11 the e kingdom of our Lord
Jude 6 He has reserved in e chains
Rev 14: 6 having the e gospel to preach

EVERMORE (*see* EVERLASTING)
1Ch 16:11 seek His face e
Ps 105: 4 Seek His face e

EVERY (*see* PREFACE)

EVERYONE (*see* PREFACE)

EVERYONE'S (*see* PREFACE)

EVERYTHING (*see* PREFACE)

EVERYWHERE (*see* PREFACE)

EVI
Num 31: 8 E, Rekem, Zur, Hur, and Reba,
Josh 13:21 E, Rekem, Zur, Hur, and Reba,

EVICTING
Ezek 46:18 by e them from their property

EVIDENCE (*see* EVIDENCES, EVIDENT)
Ex 22:13 then he shall bring it as e
Deut 22:15 bring out the e of the young
Job 16:19 in heaven, and my e is on high
Acts 24: 1 These gave e to the governor
2Th 1: 5 which is manifest e of the
Heb 11: 1 for, the e of things not seen

EVIDENCES (*see* EVIDENCE)
Deut 22:17 yet these are the e of my
Deut 22:20 e of virginity are not found

EVIDENT (*see* EVIDENCE)
Acts 4:16 them is e to all who dwell in
1Co 15:27 it is e that He who put all
Gal 3:11 law in the sight of God is e
Gal 5:19 the works of the flesh are e
Phil 1:13 so that it has become e to
1Ti 4:15 your progress may be e to all
1Ti 5:24 Some men's sins are clearly e
1Ti 5:25 works of some are clearly e
Heb 7:14 For it is e that our Lord
Heb 7:15 And it is yet far more e if

EVIL (*see* EVILDOER, EVILS)
Gen 2: 9 of the knowledge of good and e
Gen 2:17 e you shall not eat, for in
Gen 3: 5 like God, knowing good and e
Gen 3:22 one of Us, to know good and e
Gen 6: 5 heart was only e continually
Gen 8:21 heart is e from his youth
Gen 19:19 lest some e overtake me and I
Gen 44: 4 have you repaid e for good

Gen 44: 5 You have done **e** in so doing
Gen 44:34 lest perhaps I see the **e** that
Gen 47: 9 **e** have been the days of the
Gen 48:16 has redeemed me from all **e**
Gen 50:15 all the **e** which we did to him
Gen 50:17 for they did **e** to you
Gen 50:20 you, you meant **e** against me
Ex 5:23 he has done **e** to this people
Ex 10:10 Beware, for **e** is ahead of you
Ex 23: 2 not follow a crowd to do **e**
Ex 32:22 that they are set on **e**
Lev 5: 4 lips to do **e** or to do good
Lev 26: 6 will rid the land of **e** beasts
Num 14:27 **e** congregation who murmur
Num 14:35 this **e** congregation who are
Num 14:37 the **e** report about the land
Num 20: 5 to bring us to this **e** place
Num 32:13 **e** in the sight of the LORD
Deut 1:35 one of these men of this **e**
Deut 1:39 no knowledge of good and **e**
Deut 4:25 do **e** in the sight of the LORD
Deut 13: 5 away the **e** from your midst
Deut 15: 9 your eye be **e** against your
Deut 17: 7 the **e** person from among you
Deut 17:12 away the **e** person from Israel
Deut 19:19 the **e** person from among you
Deut 19:20 again commit such **e** among you
Deut 21:21 the **e** person from among you
Deut 22:21 the **e** person from among you
Deut 22:22 away the **e** person from Israel
Deut 22:24 the **e** person from among you
Deut 24: 7 the **e** person from among you
Deut 30:15 life and good, death and **e**,
Deut 31:18 the **e** which they have done
Deut 31:29 and **e** will befall you in the
Deut 31:29 because you will do **e** in the
Josh 24:15 if it seems **e** to you to serve
Judg 2:11 **e** in the sight of the LORD
Judg 3: 7 **e** in the sight of the LORD
Judg 3:12 of Israel again did **e** in the
Judg 3:12 because they had done **e** in
Judg 4: 1 of Israel again did **e** in the
Judg 6: 1 **e** in the sight of the LORD
Judg 9:57 And all the **e** of the men of
Judg 10: 6 of Israel again did **e** in the
Judg 13: 1 **e** in the sight of the LORD
Judg 20:13 and remove the **e** from Israel
1Sa 2:23 For I hear of your **e** dealings
1Sa 6: 9 He has done us this great **e**
1Sa 12:19 the **e** of asking a king for
1Sa 15:19 do **e** in the sight of the LORD
1Sa 20: 7 angry, then be sure that **e** is
1Sa 20: 9 if I knew certainly that **e**
1Sa 20:13 pleases my father to do you **e**
1Sa 23: 9 Saul plotted **e** against him
1Sa 24:11 **e** nor rebellion in my hand
1Sa 24:17 I have rewarded you with **e**
1Sa 25: 3 was harsh and **e** in his doings
1Sa 25:21 he has repaid me **e** for good
1Sa 25:28 and **e** is not found in you
1Sa 25:39 has kept His servant from **e**
1Sa 26:18 done, or what **e** is in my hand
1Sa 29: 6 **e** in you since the day of
2Sa 12: 9 LORD, to do **e** in His sight
2Sa 13:16 This **e** of sending me away is
2Sa 14:17 king in discerning good and **e**
2Sa 16: 8 you are caught in your own **e**
2Sa 19: 7 **e** that has befallen you from
1Ki 3: 9 may discern between good and **e**
1Ki 5: 4 adversary nor **e** occurrence
1Ki 11: 6 Solomon did **e** in the sight of
1Ki 13:33 did not turn from his **e** way
1Ki 14: 9 but you have done more **e** than
1Ki 14:22 Now Judah did **e** in the sight
1Ki 15:26 he did **e** in the sight of the
1Ki 15:34 He did **e** in the sight of the
1Ki 16: 7 because of all the **e** that he
1Ki 16:19 he had sinned in doing **e** in
1Ki 16:25 Omri did **e** in the eyes of the
1Ki 16:30 **e** in the sight of the LORD
1Ki 21:20 do **e** in the sight of the LORD
1Ki 22: 8 good concerning me, but **e**
1Ki 22:18 good concerning me, but **e**
1Ki 22:52 He did **e** in the sight of the
2Ki 3: 2 he did **e** in the sight of the
2Ki 8:12 Because I know the **e** that you
2Ki 8:18 he did **e** in the sight of the
2Ki 8:27 did **e** in the sight of the
2Ki 13: 2 he did **e** in the sight of the
2Ki 13:11 he did **e** in the sight of the

2Ki 14:24 he did **e** in the sight of the
2Ki 15: 9 he did **e** in the sight of the
2Ki 15:18 he did **e** in the sight of the
2Ki 15:24 he did **e** in the sight of the
2Ki 15:28 he did **e** in the sight of the
2Ki 17: 2 he did **e** in the sight of the
2Ki 17:13 Turn from your **e** ways, and
2Ki 17:17 sold themselves to do **e** in
2Ki 21: 2 he did **e** in the sight of the
2Ki 21: 6 He did much **e** in the sight of
2Ki 21: 9 seduced them to do more **e**
2Ki 21:15 they have done **e** in My sight
2Ki 21:16 in doing **e** in the sight of
2Ki 21:20 he did **e** in the sight of the
2Ki 23:32 he did **e** in the sight of the
2Ki 23:37 he did **e** in the sight of the
2Ki 24: 9 he did **e** in the sight of the
2Ki 24:19 He also did **e** in the sight of
1Ch 4:10 that You would keep me from **e**
1Ch 21:17 has sinned and done **e** indeed
2Ch 12:14 And he did **e**, because he did
2Ch 18: 7 concerning me, but always **e**
2Ch 18:17 good concerning me, but **e**
2Ch 21: 6 he did **e** in the sight of the
2Ch 22: 4 Therefore he did **e** in the
2Ch 29: 6 done **e** in the eyes of the
2Ch 33: 2 But he did **e** in the sight of
2Ch 33: 6 He did much **e** in the sight of
2Ch 33: 9 of Jerusalem to do more **e**
2Ch 33:22 But he did **e** in the sight of
2Ch 36: 5 he did **e** in the sight of the
2Ch 36: 9 he did **e** in the sight of the
2Ch 36:12 He also did **e** in the sight of
Ezra 4:12 **e** city, and are finishing its
Ezra 9:13 come upon us for our **e** deeds
Neh 6:13 have occasion for an **e** report
Neh 9:28 they again did **e** before You
Neh 13: 7 and discovered the **e** that
Neh 13:17 What **e** thing is this that you
Neh 13:27 your doing all this great **e**
Esth 7: 7 life, for he saw that **e** was
Esth 8: 3 tears to counteract the **e**
Esth 8: 6 **e** that will come to my people
Job 1: 1 who feared God and shunned **e**
Job 1: 8 one who fears God and shuns **e**
Job 2: 3 one who fears God and shuns **e**
Job 5:19 in seven no **e** shall touch you
Job 20:12 Though **e** is sweet in his
Job 28:28 and to depart from **e** is
Job 30:26 looked for good, **e** came to me
Job 31:29 myself up when **e** found him
Job 35:12 because of the pride of **e** men
Ps 5: 4 Nor shall **e** dwell with You
Ps 7: 4 If I have repaid **e** to him who
Ps 10:15 of the wicked and the **e** man
Ps 15: 3 Nor does **e** to his neighbor,
Ps 21:11 they intended **e** against You
Ps 23: 4 of death, I will fear no **e**
Ps 28: 3 But **e** is in their hearts
Ps 34:13 Keep your tongue from **e**, And
Ps 34:14 Depart from **e**, and do good
Ps 34:16 is against those who do **e**
Ps 34:21 **E** shall slay the wicked, And
Ps 35:12 They reward me **e** for good
Ps 36: 4 He does not abhor **e**
Ps 37:19 not be ashamed in the **e** time
Ps 37:27 Depart from **e**, and do good
Ps 38:20 also who render **e** for good
Ps 40:14 to dishonor Who wish me **e**
Ps 41: 5 My enemies speak **e** of me
Ps 41: 8 An **e** disease," they say,
Ps 49: 5 I fear in the days of **e**, When
Ps 50:19 You give your mouth to **e**, And
Ps 51: 4 done this **e** in Your sight
Ps 52: 1 Why do you boast in **e**, O
Ps 52: 3 You love **e** more than good, And
Ps 54: 5 repay my enemies for their **e**
Ps 56: 5 thoughts are against me for **e**
Ps 64: 5 themselves in an **e** matter
Ps 90:15 years in which we have seen **e**
Ps 91:10 No **e** shall befall you, Nor
Ps 94:20 which devises **e** by law, Have
Ps 97:10 You who love the LORD, hate **e**
Ps 109: 5 have rewarded me **e** for good
Ps 109:20 who speak **e** against my person
Ps 112: 7 not be afraid of **e** tidings
Ps 119:101 my feet from every **e** way,
Ps 121: 7 shall preserve you from all **e**
Ps 140: 1 me, O LORD, from **e** men
Ps 140: 2 Who plan **e** things in their

Ps 140: 9 Let the **e** of their lips cover
Ps 140:11 Let **e** hunt the violent man to
Ps 141: 4 my heart to any **e** thing, To
Prov 1:16 for their feet run to **e**, and
Prov 1:33 be secure, without fear of **e**
Prov 2:12 deliver you from the way of **e**
Prov 2:14 who rejoice in doing **e**, and
Prov 3: 7 the LORD and depart from **e**
Prov 3:29 Do not devise **e** against your
Prov 4:14 do not walk in the way of **e**
Prov 4:16 sleep unless they have done **e**
Prov 4:27 remove your foot from **e**
Prov 6:14 he devises **e** continually, he
Prov 6:18 are swift in running to **e**
Prov 6:24 to keep you from the **e** woman
Prov 8:13 fear of the LORD is to hate **e**
Prov 8:13 and arrogance and the **e** way
Prov 10:23 To do **e** is like sport to a
Prov 11:19 so he who pursues **e** pursues
Prov 11:27 will come to him who seeks **e**
Prov 12:12 covet the catch of **e** men, but
Prov 12:20 heart of those who devise **e**
Prov 12:21 wicked shall be filled with **e**
Prov 13:19 to fools to depart from **e**
Prov 13:21 **E** pursues sinners, but to the
Prov 14:16 man fears and departs from **e**
Prov 14:19 The **e** will bow before the
Prov 14:22 not go astray who devise **e**
Prov 15: 3 place, keeping watch on the **e**
Prov 15:15 days of the afflicted are **e**
Prov 15:28 of the wicked pours forth **e**
Prov 16: 6 the LORD one departs from **e**
Prov 16:17 upright is to depart from **e**
Prov 16:27 An ungodly man digs up **e**, and
Prov 16:30 his lips and brings about **e**
Prov 17:11 An **e** man seeks only rebellion
Prov 17:13 Whoever rewards **e** for good
Prov 17:13 **e** will not depart from his
Prov 17:20 perverse tongue falls into **e**
Prov 19:23 he will not be visited with **e**
Prov 20: 8 scatters all **e** with his eyes
Prov 20:22 I will recompense **e**"
Prov 20:30 that hurt cleanse away **e**, as
Prov 21:10 soul of the wicked desires **e**
Prov 22: 3 A prudent man foresees **e** and
Prov 24: 1 Do not be envious of **e** men
Prov 24: 8 He who plots to do **e** will be
Prov 24:19 not fret because of **e** doers
Prov 24:20 be no prospect for the **e** man
Prov 27:12 A prudent man foresees **e** and
Prov 28: 5 **E** men do not understand
Prov 28:10 to go astray in an **e** way, he
Prov 28:22 A man with an **e** eye hastens
Prov 29: 6 an **e** man is snared, but the
Prov 30:32 or if you have devised **e**
Prov 31:12 not **e** all the days of her
Eccl 2:21 also is vanity and a great **e**
Eccl 4: 3 who has not seen the **e** work
Eccl 5: 1 do not know that they do **e**
Eccl 5:13 There is a severe **e** which I
Eccl 5:16 And this also is a severe **e**
Eccl 6: 1 There is an **e** which I have
Eccl 6: 2 and it is an **e** affliction
Eccl 8: 3 your stand for an **e** thing
Eccl 8:11 an **e** work is not executed
Eccl 8:11 is fully set in them to do **e**
Eccl 8:12 sinner does **e** a hundred times
Eccl 9: 3 This is an **e** in all that is
Eccl 9: 3 the sons of men are full of **e**
Eccl 9:12 men are snared in an **e** time
Eccl 10: 5 There is an **e** I have seen
Eccl 11: 2 what **e** will be on the earth
Eccl 11:10 put away **e** from your flesh,
Eccl 12:14 it is good or whether it is **e**
Is 1:16 put away the **e** of your doings
Is 1:16 Cease to do **e**,
Is 3: 9 brought **e** upon themselves
Is 5:20 who call **e** good, and good **e**
Is 7: 5 taken **e** counsel against you
Is 7:15 He may know to refuse the **e**
Is 7:16 shall know to refuse the **e**
Is 13:11 punish the world for its **e**
Is 32: 7 schemes of the schemer are **e**
Is 33:15 shuts his eyes from seeing **e**
Is 41:23 yes, do good or do **e**, that we
Is 47:11 Therefore **e** shall come upon
Is 56: 2 his hand from doing any **e**
Is 57: 1 is taken away from **e**
Is 59: 4 they conceive **e** and bring
Is 59: 7 Their feet run to **e**, and they

Is 59:15 he who departs from **e** makes
Is 65:12 but did **e** before My eyes, and
Is 66: 4 But they did **e** before My eyes
Jer 2:19 and see that it is an **e** and
Jer 3: 5 done **e** things, as you were
Jer 3:17 stubbornness of their **e** heart
Jer 4: 4 of the **e** of your doings
Jer 4:14 How long shall your **e**
Jer 4:22 They are wise to do **e**, but to
Jer 5:12 Neither will **e** come upon us
Jer 7:24 imagination of their **e** heart
Jer 7:30 Judah have done **e** in My sight
Jer 8: 3 who remain of this **e** family
Jer 9: 3 they proceed from **e** to **e**
Jer 10: 5 of them, for they cannot do **e**
Jer 11: 8 imagination of his **e** heart
Jer 11:15 When you do **e**, then you
Jer 11:17 the **e** of the house of Israel
Jer 12:14 Against all My **e** neighbors
Jer 13:10 This **e** people, who refuse to
Jer 13:23 who are accustomed to do **e**
Jer 16:12 of his own **e** heart, so that
Jer 18: 8 have spoken turns from its **e**
Jer 18:10 if it does **e** in My sight so
Jer 18:11 now every one from his **e** way
Jer 18:12 imagination of his **e** heart
Jer 18:20 Shall **e** be repaid for good
Jer 21:12 of the **e** of your doings
Jer 23: 2 you for the **e** of your doings
Jer 23:10 Their course of life is **e**
Jer 23:17 No **e** shall come upon you
Jer 23:22 turned them from their **e** way
Jer 23:22 from the **e** of their doings
Jer 25: 5 now everyone of his **e** way
Jer 25: 5 his **e** doings, and dwell in the
Jer 26: 3 listen and turn from his **e** way
Jer 26: 3 of the **e** of their doings
Jer 26:19 great **e** against ourselves
Jer 29:11 thoughts of peace and not of **e**
Jer 32:30 of Judah have done only **e**
Jer 32:32 because of all the **e** of the
Jer 35:15 now everyone from his **e** way
Jer 36: 3 may turn from his **e** way, that
Jer 36: 7 will turn from his **e** way
Jer 38: 9 these men have done **e** in all
Jer 41:11 the **e** that Ishmael the son of
Jer 44: 7 great **e** against yourselves
Jer 44:22 of the **e** of your doings and
Jer 48: 2 have devised **e** against her
Jer 51:24 of Chaldea for all the **e** they
Jer 51:60 the **e** that would come upon
Jer 52: 2 He also did **e** in the sight of
Ezek 6:11 for all the **e** abominations of
Ezek 33:11 Turn, turn from your **e** ways
Ezek 36:31 you will remember your **e** ways
Ezek 38:10 and you will make an **e** plan
Dan 11:27 hearts shall be bent on **e**
Hos 7:15 yet they devise **e** against Me
Hos 9:15 Because of the **e** of their
Amos 5:13 time, for it is an **e** time
Amos 5:14 Seek good and not **e**, that you
Amos 5:15 Hate **e**, love good
Jon 3: 8 every one turn from his **e** way
Jon 3:10 they turned from their **e** way
Mic 2: 1 And work out **e** on their beds
Mic 2: 3 for this is an **e** time
Mic 3: 2 You who hate good and love **e**
Mic 3: 4 have been **e** in their deeds
Mic 7: 3 do **e** with both hands
Mic 7: 3 great man utters his **e** desire
Nah 1:11 who plots **e** against the LORD
Hab 1:13 purer eyes than to behold **e**
Hab 2: 9 covets **e** gain for his house
Zeph 1:12 not do good, nor will He do **e**
Zech 1: 4 Turn now from your **e** ways
Zech 1: 4 and your **e** deeds
Zech 1:15 but with **e** intent
Zech 7:10 Let none of you plan **e** in his
Zech 8:17 let none of you think **e** in
Mal 1: 8 as a sacrifice, is it not **e**
Mal 1: 8 the lame and sick, is it not **e**
Mal 2:17 Everyone who does **e** is good
Matt 5:11 say all kinds of **e** against
Matt 5:37 than these is from the **e** one
Matt 5:39 you not to resist an **e** person
Matt 5:45 makes His sun rise on the **e**
Matt 6:13 but deliver us from the **e** one
Matt 7:11 If you then, being **e**, know
Matt 9: 4 do you think **e** in your hearts
Matt 12:34 How can you, being **e**, speak
Matt 12:35 and an **e** man out of the **e**
Matt 12:35 brings forth **e** things
Matt 12:39 An **e** and adulterous generation
Matt 15:19 the heart proceed **e** thoughts
Matt 20:15 Or is your eye **e** because I am
Matt 24:48 But if that **e** servant says in
Matt 27:23 Why, what **e** has He done
Mark 3: 4 Sabbath to do good or to do **e**
Mark 7:21 of men, proceed **e** thoughts,
Mark 7:22 an **e** eye, blasphemy, pride,
Mark 7:23 All these **e** things come from
Mark 9:39 soon afterward speak **e** of Me
Mark 15:14 Why, what **e** has He done
Luke 6: 9 Sabbath to do good or to do **e**
Luke 6:22 and cast out your name as **e**
Luke 6:35 kind to the unthankful and **e**
Luke 6:45 and an **e** man out of the **e**
Luke 6:45 **e** treasure of his heart brings
Luke 6:45 of his heart brings forth **e**
Luke 7:21 afflictions, and **e** spirits
Luke 8: 2 had been healed of **e** spirits
Luke 11: 4 but deliver us from the **e** one
Luke 11:13 If you then, being **e**, know
Luke 11:29 This is an **e** generation
Luke 16:25 and likewise Lazarus **e** things
Luke 23:22 Why, what **e** has He done
John 3:19 because their deeds were **e**
John 3:20 practicing **e** hates the light
John 5:29 and those who have done **e**
John 7: 7 of it that its works are **e**
John 17:15 keep them from the **e** one
John 18:23 If I have spoken **e**
John 18:23 bear witness of the **e**
Acts 17: 5 took some of the **e** men from
Acts 19: 9 but spoke **e** of the Way before
Acts 19:12 the **e** spirits went out of
Acts 19:13 over those who had **e** spirits
Acts 19:15 the **e** spirit answered and said
Acts 19:16 Then the man in whom the **e**
Acts 23: 5 You shall not speak **e** of the
Acts 23: 9 We find no **e** in this man
Acts 28:21 or spoken any **e** of you
Rom 1:30 inventors of **e** things,
Rom 2: 9 every soul of man who does **e**
Rom 3: 8 Let us do **e** that good may
Rom 7: 8 in me all manner of **e** desire
Rom 7:19 but the **e** I will not to do,
Rom 7:21 that **e** is present with me,
Rom 9:11 nor having done any good or **e**
Rom 12: 9 Abhor what is **e**
Rom 12:17 Repay no one **e** for **e**
Rom 12:21 Do not be overcome by **e**, but
Rom 12:21 but overcome **e** with good
Rom 13: 3 to good works, but to **e**
Rom 13: 4 But if you do **e**, be afraid
Rom 13: 4 wrath on him who practices **e**
Rom 14:16 your good be spoken of as **e**
Rom 14:20 but it is **e** for the man who
Rom 16:19 good, and simple concerning **e**
1Co 10: 6 we should not lust after **e**
1Co 10:30 why am I **e**spoken of for the
1Co 13: 5 is not provoked, thinks no **e**
1Co 15:33 **E** company corrupts good
2Co 6: 8 by **e** report and good report
2Co 13: 7 pray to God that you do no **e**
Gal 1: 4 us from this present **e** age
Eph 4:31 **e** speaking be put away from
Eph 5:16 time, because the days are **e**
Eph 6:13 to withstand in the **e** day
Phil 3: 2 of dogs, beware of **e** workers
Col 3: 5 **e** desire, and covetousness,
1Th 5:15 renders **e** for **e** to anyone
1Th 5:22 Abstain from every form of **e**
2Th 3: 3 and guard you from the **e** one
1Ti 6: 4 reviling, **e** suspicions,
1Ti 6:10 is a root of all kinds of **e**
2Ti 3:13 But **e** men and impostors will
2Ti 4:18 deliver me from every **e** work
Tit 1:12 **e** beasts, lazy gluttons
Tit 2: 8 nothing **e** to say of you
Tit 3: 2 to speak **e** of no one, to be
Heb 3:12 you an **e** heart of unbelief in
Heb 5:14 to discern both good and **e**
Heb 10:22 from an **e** conscience and our
Jas 1:13 God cannot be tempted by **e**
Jas 2: 4 become judges with **e** thoughts
Jas 3: 8 It is an unruly **e**, full of
Jas 3:16 every **e** thing will be there
Jas 4:11 Do not speak **e** of one another
Jas 4:11 He who speaks **e** of a brother
Jas 4:11 speaks **e** of the law and judges
Jas 4:16 All such boasting is **e**
1Pe 2: 1 envy, and all **e** speaking,
1Pe 3: 9 not returning **e** for **e** or
1Pe 3:10 him refrain his tongue from **e**
1Pe 3:11 let him turn away from **e** and
1Pe 3:12 is against those who do **e**
1Pe 3:17 doing good than for doing **e**
1Pe 4: 4 speaking **e** of you
2Pe 2:10 to speak **e** of dignitaries
2Pe 2:12 speak **e** of the things they do
1Jn 3:12 Because his works were **e** and
2Jn 11 him shares in his **e** deeds
3Jn 11 do not imitate what is **e**
3Jn 11 but he who does **e** has not
Jude 8 and speak **e** of dignitaries
Jude 10 But these speak **e** of whatever
Rev 2: 2 cannot bear those who are **e**

EVILDOER (*see* EVIL, EVILDOERS)
2Sa 3:39 The LORD shall repay the **e**
Prov 17: 4 An **e** gives heed to false lips
Is 9:17 is a hypocrite and an **e**, and
John 18:30 If He were not an **e**, we would
2Ti 2: 9 I suffer trouble as an **e**,
1Pe 4:15 as a murderer, a thief, an **e**

EVILDOERS (*see* EVILDOER)
Job 8:20 nor will He uphold the **e**
Ps 26: 5 hated the congregation of **e**
Ps 37: 1 Do not fret because of **e**, Nor
Ps 37: 9 For **e** shall be cut off
Ps 94:16 rise up for me against the **e**
Ps 101: 8 **e** from the city of the LORD
Ps 119:115 Depart from me, you **e**, For I
Is 1: 4 with iniquity, a brood of **e**
Is 14:20 The brood of **e** shall never be
Is 31: 2 arise against the house of **e**
Jer 20:13 the poor from the hand of **e**
Jer 23:14 strengthen the hands of **e**
Hos 6: 8 Gilead is a city of **e**, and is
1Pe 2:12 they speak against you as **e**
1Pe 2:14 him for the punishment of **e**
1Pe 3:16 when they defame you as **e**

EVIL-MERODACH (*see* MERODACH)
2Ki 25:27 that **E** king of Babylon, in
Jer 52:31 that **E** king of Babylon, in

EVIL-MINDEDNESS
Rom 1:29 murder, strife, deceit, **e**

EVILS (*see* EVIL)
Deut 31:17 And many **e** and troubles shall
Deut 31:17 Have not these **e** come upon
Deut 31:21 Then it shall be, when many **e**
Ps 40:12 For innumerable **e** have
Jer 2:13 people have committed two **e**
Ezek 6: 9 loathe themselves for the **e**
Ezek 20:43 the **e** that you have committed
Luke 3:19 for all the **e** which Herod had

EWE (*see* EWES)
Gen 21:28 Abraham set seven **e** lambs of
Gen 21:29 the meaning of these seven **e**
Gen 21:30 seven **e** lambs from my hand
Lev 14:10 one **e** lamb of the first year
Lev 22:28 Whether it is a cow or **e**, do
Num 6:14 one **e** lamb in its first year
2Sa 12: 3 except one little **e** lamb

EWES (*see* EWE)
Gen 31:38 your **e** and your female goats
Gen 32:14 male goats, two hundred **e**
Ps 78:71 From following the **e** that had

EXACT (*see* EXACTED, EXACTING, EXACTION, EXACTS)
Neh 10:32 to **e** from ourselves yearly

EXACTED (*see* EXACT)
2Ki 15:20 And Menahem **e** the money
2Ki 23:35 he **e** the silver and gold from
Ezek 18: 8 if he has not **e** usury nor
Ezek 18:13 if he has **e** usury or taken

EXACTING (*see* EXACT)
Neh 5: 7 Each of you is **e** usury from

EXACTION (*see* EXACT)
Neh 10:31 and the **e** of every debt

EXACTLY
Eccl 5:16 That just **e** as he came, so

EXACTS (*see* EXACT)
Job 11: 6 God **e** from you less than your

EXALT (*see* EXALTATION, EXALTED, EXALTING, EXALTS)
Ex 9:17 As yet you **e** yourself against
Ex 15: 2 father's God, and I will **e** Him
Num 16: 3 Why then do you **e** yourselves
1Sa 2:10 **e** the horn of His anointed
1Ch 25: 5 words of God, to **e** his horn
Job 17: 4 therefore You will not **e** them
Ps 34: 3 let us **e** His name together
Ps 37:34 He shall **e** you to inherit the
Ps 66: 7 the rebellious **e** themselves
Ps 99: 5 **E** the LORD our God, And
Ps 99: 9 **E** the LORD our God, And
Ps 107:32 Let them **e** Him also in the
Ps 118:28 You are my God, I will **e** You
Ps 137: 6 If I do not **e** Jerusalem Above
Prov 4: 8 **E** her, and she will promote
Prov 25: 6 Do not **e** yourself in the
Is 14:13 I will **e** my throne above the
Is 25: 1 I will **e** You, I will praise
Ezek 21:26 **E** the lowly, and abase the
Ezek 29:15 it shall never again **e** itself
Ezek 31:14 the waters may ever again **e**
Dan 11:14 men of your people shall **e**
Dan 11:36 he shall **e** and magnify himself
Hos 11: 7 Most High, none at all **e** Him
Obad 4 Though you **e** yourself as high
1Pe 5: 6 that He may **e** you in due time

EXALTATION (*see* EXALT)
Job 22:29 and you say, "**E** will come
Ps 75: 6 For **e** comes neither from the
Is 13: 3 those who rejoice in My **e**
Jas 1: 9 lowly brother glory in his **e**

EXALTED (*see* EXALT)
Num 24: 7 and his kingdom shall be **e**
1Sa 2: 1 my horn is **e** in the LORD
2Sa 5:12 that He had **e** His kingdom for
2Sa 22:47 Let God be **e**, the Rock of my
1Ki 1: 5 the son of Haggith **e** himself
1Ki 8:13 surely built You an **e** house
1Ki 9: 8 And this house will be **e**
1Ki 14: 7 Because I **e** you from among
1Ch 14: 2 **e** because of His people
1Ch 29:11 You are **e** as head over all
1Ch 29:25 So the LORD **e** Solomon
2Ch 1: 1 with him and **e** him exceedingly
2Ch 6: 2 I have built You an **e** house
2Ch 7:21 as for this house, which is **e**
2Ch 32:23 so that he was **e** in the sight
Neh 9: 5 which is **e** above all blessing
Job 10:16 If my head is **e**, you hunt me
Job 24:24 They are **e** for a little while
Job 36: 7 them forever, and they are **e**
Job 36:22 Behold, God is **e** by His power
Ps 12: 8 When vileness is **e** among the
Ps 13: 2 will my enemy be **e** over me
Ps 18:46 the God of my salvation be **e**
Ps 21:13 Be **e**, O LORD, in Your own
Ps 46:10 I will be **e** among the nations
Ps 46:10 I will be **e** in the earth
Ps 47: 9 He is greatly **e**
Ps 57: 5 Be **e**, O God, above the
Ps 57:11 Be **e**, O God, above the
Ps 75:10 of the righteous shall be **e**
Ps 89:16 Your righteousness they are **e**
Ps 89:17 in Your favor our horn is **e**
Ps 89:19 I have **e** one chosen from the
Ps 89:24 My name his horn shall be **e**
Ps 89:42 You have **e** the right hand of
Ps 92:10 You have **e** like a wild ox
Ps 97: 9 You are **e** far above all gods
Ps 108: 5 Be **e**, O God, above the
Ps 112: 9 His horn will be **e** with honor
Ps 118:16 right hand of the LORD is **e**
Ps 140: 8 wicked scheme, Lest they be **e**
Ps 148:13 LORD, For His name alone is **e**
Ps 148:14 And He has **e** the horn of His
Prov 11:11 of the upright the city is **e**
Is 2: 2 shall be **e** above the hills
Is 2:11 alone shall be **e** in that day
Is 2:17 alone will be **e** in that day
Is 5:16 hosts shall be **e** in judgment
Is 12: 4 mention that His name is **e**
Is 24:21 on high the host of **e** ones
Is 30:18 and therefore He will be **e**
Is 33: 5 The LORD is **e**, for He dwells
Is 33:10 Now I will be **e**, now I will
Is 40: 4 Every valley shall be **e**, and
Is 52:13 deal prudently, He shall be **e**
Lam 2:17 He has **e** the horn of your
Ezek 17:24 **e** the low tree, dried up the
Ezek 21:26 the lowly, and abase the **e**
Ezek 31: 5 Therefore its height was **e**
Dan 8:11 He even **e** himself as high as
Hos 13: 1 he **e** himself in Israel
Hos 13: 6 filled and their heart was **e**
Mic 4: 1 shall be **e** above the hills
Matt 11:23 who are **e** to heaven, will be
Matt 23:12 who humbles himself will be **e**
Luke 1:52 their thrones, and **e** the lowly
Luke 10:15 who are **e** to heaven, will be
Luke 14:11 who humbles himself will be **e**
Luke 18:14 who humbles himself will be **e**
Acts 2:33 Therefore being **e** to the
Acts 5:31 Him God has **e** to His right
Acts 13:17 **e** the people when they dwelt
2Co 11: 7 myself that you might be **e**
2Co 12: 7 And lest I should be **e** above
2Co 12: 7 lest I be **e** above measure
Phil 2: 9 God also has highly **e** Him

EXALTING (*see* EXALT)
Prov 30:32 been foolish in **e** yourself

EXALTS (*see* EXALT)
Ps 75: 7 puts down one, And **e** another
Prov 14:29 he who is impulsive **e** folly
Prov 14:34 Righteousness **e** a nation, but
Prov 17:19 and he who **e** his gate seeks
Matt 23:12 whoever **e** himself will be
Luke 14:11 For whoever **e** himself will be
Luke 18:14 for everyone who **e** himself
2Co 10: 5 that **e** itself against the
2Co 11:20 you, if one **e** himself, if one
2Th 2: 4 **e** himself above all that is

EXAMINATION (*see* EXAMINE)
Acts 25:26 so that after the **e** has taken

EXAMINE (*see* EXAMINATION, EXAMINES, EXAMINING)
Ezra 10:16 tenth month to **e** the matter
Ps 26: 2 **E** me, O LORD, and prove me
Lam 3:40 **e** our ways, and turn back to
Acts 22:29 to **e** him withdrew from him
1Co 9: 3 to those who **e** me is this
1Co 11:28 But let a man **e** himself, and
2Co 13: 5 **E** yourselves as to whether
Gal 6: 4 let each one **e** his own work

EXAMINED
1Ki 3:21 But when I had **e** him in the
Dan 1:13 countenances be **e** before you
Dan 1:20 about which the king **e** them
Luke 23:14 having **e** Him in your presence
Acts 12:19 he **e** the guards and commanded
Acts 22:24 should be **e** under scourging
Acts 28:18 who, when they had **e** me,

EXAMINES (*see* EXAMINE)
Prov 18:17 his neighbor comes and **e** him

EXAMINING (*see* EXAMINE)
Acts 24: 8 By **e** him yourself you may

EXAMPLE (*see* EXAMPLES)
Matt 1:19 to make her a public **e**, was
John 13:15 For I have given you an **e**
Phil 3:17 join in following my **e**, and
2Th 3: 9 but to make ourselves an **e** of
1Ti 4:12 but be an **e** to the believers
Heb 4:11 the same **e** of disobedience
Jas 5:10 Lord, as an **e** of suffering and
1Pe 2:21 for us, leaving us an **e**, that
2Pe 2: 6 making them an **e** to those who
Jude 7 flesh, are set forth as an **e**

EXAMPLES (*see* EXAMPLE)
1Co 10: 6 Now these things became our **e**
1Co 10:11 things happened to them as **e**
1Th 1: 7 so that you became **e** to all
1Pe 5: 3 you, but being **e** to the flock

EXCEED (*see* EXCEEDING, EXCEEDS)
Deut 25: 3 more, lest he should **e** this
1Ki 10: 7 and prosperity **e** the fame of
2Ch 9: 6 You **e** the fame of which I

EXCEEDING (*see* EXCEED, EXCEEDINGLY)
Ps 43: 4 altar of God, To God my **e** joy
2Co 4:17 working for us a far more **e**
2Co 9:14 of the **e** grace of God in you
Eph 1:19 what is the **e** greatness of
Eph 2: 7 to come He might show the **e**
1Pe 4:13 may also be glad with **e** joy
Jude 24 of His glory with **e** joy,

EXCEEDINGLY (*see* EXCEEDING)
Gen 7:19 prevailed **e** on the earth, and
Gen 13:13 men of Sodom were **e** wicked
Gen 15: 1 shield, your **e** great reward
Gen 16:10 multiply your descendants **e**
Gen 17: 2 you, and will multiply you **e**
Gen 17: 6 I will make you **e** fruitful
Gen 17:20 and will multiply him **e**
Gen 27:33 Then Isaac trembled **e**, and
Gen 27:34 he cried with an **e** great
Gen 30:43 the man became **e** prosperous
Gen 47:27 there and grew and multiplied **e**
Ex 1: 7 multiplied and grew **e** mighty
Num 14: 7 to spy out is an **e** good land
Num 22: 3 And Moab was **e** afraid of the
1Sa 26:21 played the fool and erred **e**
2Sa 12: 2 rich man had **e** many flocks
2Sa 13:15 Then Amnon hated her **e**, so
1Ki 4:29 **e** great understanding, and
2Ki 10: 4 But they were **e** afraid, and
1Ch 22: 5 LORD must be **e** magnificent
1Ch 29:25 **e** in the sight of all Israel
2Ch 1: 1 was with him and exalted him **e**
2Ch 14:14 for there was **e** much spoil in
2Ch 26: 8 for he strengthened himself **e**
Job 3:22 who rejoice **e**, and are glad
Ps 21: 6 You have made him **e** glad with
Ps 68: 3 Yes, let them rejoice **e**
Ps 106:14 But lusted **e** in the
Ps 119:96 Your commandment is **e** broad
Ps 119:167 testimonies, And I love them **e**
Ps 123: 3 For we are **e** filled with
Ps 123: 4 Our soul is **e** filled With the
Prov 30:24 earth, but they are **e** wise
Eccl 7:24 **e** deep, who can find it out
Is 24:19 open, the earth is shaken **e**
Jer 48:29 pride of Moab (he is **e** proud)
Ezek 9: 9 of Israel and Judah is **e** great
Ezek 16:13 You were **e** beautiful, and
Ezek 37:10 their feet, an **e** great army
Ezek 47:10 fish of the Great Sea, **e** many
Dan 3:22 urgent, and the furnace **e** hot
Dan 6:23 the king was **e** glad for him
Dan 7: 7 and terrible, **e** strong
Dan 7:19 **e** dreadful, with its teeth of
Dan 8: 9 grew **e** great toward the south
Jon 1:10 Then the men were **e** afraid
Jon 1:16 the men feared the LORD **e**
Jon 3: 3 Nineveh was an **e** great city
Jon 4: 1 But it displeased Jonah **e**
Zech 1:15 I am **e** angry with the nations
Matt 2:10 rejoiced with **e** great joy
Matt 2:16 by the wise men, was **e** angry
Matt 4: 8 Him up on an **e** high mountain
Matt 5:12 be **e** glad, for great is your
Matt 8:28 **e** fierce, so that no one
Matt 17:23 And they were **e** sorrowful
Matt 19:25 heard it, they were **e** amazed
Matt 26:22 And they were **e** sorrowful, and
Matt 26:38 My soul is **e** sorrowful, even
Mark 4:41 And they feared **e**, and said to
Mark 6:26 And the king was **e** sorry
Mark 9: 3 **e** white, like snow, such as
Mark 14:34 My soul is **e** sorrowful, even
Mark 15:14 And they cried out more **e**
Luke 23: 8 saw Jesus, he was **e** glad
Acts 16:20 Jews, **e** trouble our city
Acts 26:11 being **e** enraged against them,
Acts 27:18 we were **e** tempest-tossed, the
Rom 7:13 might become **e** sinful
2Co 7: 4 I am **e** joyful in all our
2Co 7:13 we rejoiced **e** more for the
Gal 1:14 being more **e** zealous for the
Eph 3:20 to Him who is able to do **e**
1Th 3:10 day praying **e** that we may see
2Th 1: 3 because your faith grows **e**
1Ti 1:14 of our Lord was **e** abundant
Heb 12:21 I am **e** afraid and trembling
2Pe 1: 4 have been given to us **e** great
Rev 16:21 since that plague was **e** great

EXCEEDS (*see* EXCEED)
Matt 5:20 e the righteousness of the
2Co 3: 9 e much more in glory

EXCEL (*see* EXCELLED, EXCELS)
Gen 49: 4 as water, you shall not e
Ps 103:20 Who e in strength, who do His
Prov 31:29 done well, but you e them all
1Co 14:12 the church that you seek to e

EXCELLED (*see* EXCEL)
Gen 49:26 have e the blessings of my
1Ki 4:30 Thus Solomon's wisdom e the
Eccl 2: 9 and e more than all who were
Is 10:10 images e those of Jerusalem

EXCELLENCE (*see* EXCELLENCY, EXCELLENT)
Ex 15: 7 in the greatness of Your e
Job 4:21 Does not their own e go away
Job 13:11 Will not His e make you
Ps 47: 4 The e of Jacob whom He loves
Ps 68:34 His e is over Israel, And His
Eccl 7:12 but the e of knowledge is
Is 35: 2 the e of Carmel and Sharon
Is 60:15 I will make you an eternal e
Nah 2: 2 the e of Jacob like the
Nah 2: 2 of Jacob like the e of Israel
1Co 2: 1 did not come with e of speech
2Co 4: 7 that the e of the power may
Phil 3: 8 all things loss for the e of

EXCELLENCY (*see* EXCELLENCE)
Gen 49: 3 the e of dignity and the
Gen 49: 3 of dignity and the e of power
Deut 33:26 And in His e on the clouds
Is 35: 2 of the LORD, the e of our God

EXCELLENT (*see* EXCELLENCE)
Esth 1: 4 the splendor of his e majesty
Job 37:23 He is e in power, in judgment
Ps 8: 1 How e is Your name in all the
Ps 8: 9 How e is Your name in all the
Ps 16: 3 They are the e ones, in whom
Ps 76: 4 e Than the mountains of prey
Ps 141: 5 It shall be as e oil
Ps 150: 2 according to His e greatness
Prov 8: 6 for I will speak of e things
Prov 12: 4 an e wife is the crown of her
Prov 17: 7 E speech is not becoming to a
Prov 22:20 to you e things of counsels
Song 5:15 like Lebanon, e as the cedars
Is 4: 2 fruit of the earth shall be e
Is 12: 5 For He has done e things
Is 28:29 in counsel and e in guidance
Dan 2:31 image, whose splendor was e
Dan 4:36 e majesty was added to me
Dan 5:12 Inasmuch as an e spirit,
Dan 5:14 e wisdom are found in you
Dan 6: 3 because an e spirit was in
Luke 1: 3 account, most e Theophilus,
Acts 23:26 to the most e governor Felix
Rom 2:18 approve the things that are e
1Co 12:31 yet I show you a more e way
Phil 1:10 approve the things that are e
Heb 1: 4 a more e name than they
Heb 8: 6 obtained a more e ministry
Heb 11: 4 a more e sacrifice than Cain
2Pe 1:17 came to Him from the E Glory

EXCELS (*see* EXCEL)
Prov 22:29 see a man who e in his work
Eccl 2:13 I saw that wisdom e folly
Eccl 2:13 as light e darkness
2Co 3:10 because of the glory that e

EXCEPT (*see* PREFACE)

EXCEPTED (*see* PREFACE)

EXCESS (*see* EXCESSIVE)
Num 3:48 with which the e number of

EXCESSIVE (*see* EXCESS)
Esth 1:18 Thus there will be e contempt

EXCHANGE (*see* EXCHANGED, EXCHANGES, EXCHANGING)
Gen 47:17 bread in e for the horses
Gen 47:17 in e for all their livestock
Lev 27:10 not substitute it or e it
Lev 27:33 or bad, nor shall he e it
Deut 14:25 then you shall e it for money
Ezek 48:14 shall not sell or e any of it
Joel 3: 3 given a boy in e for a harlot
Matt 16:26 a man give in e for his soul
Mark 8:37 a man give in e for his soul

EXCHANGED (*see* EXCHANGE)
Lev 27:10 the one e for it shall be
Lev 27:33 the one e for it shall be
Job 28:17 nor can it be e for jewelry
Rom 1:25 who e the truth of God for
Rom 1:26 For even their women e the

EXCHANGES (*see* EXCHANGE)
Lev 27:10 and if he at all e beast for
Lev 27:33 if he e it at all, then both

EXCHANGING (*see* EXCHANGE)
Ruth 4: 7 concerning redeeming and e

EXCITED (*see* EXCITEMENT)
Ruth 1:19 city was e because of them
Is 14: 9 from beneath is e about you

EXCITEMENT (*see* EXCITED)
Jer 51:39 In their e I will prepare

EXCLUDE (*see* EXCLUDED)
Luke 6:22 hate you, and when they e you
Gal 4:17 yes, they want to e you, that

EXCLUDED (*see* EXCLUDE)
Ezra 2:62 therefore they were e from
Neh 7:64 therefore they were e from
Rom 3:27 It is e. By what law?

EXCUSE (*see* EXCUSED, EXCUSES, EXCUSING)
Eccl 5: 6 should God be angry at your e
John 15:22 they have no e for their sin
Rom 1:20 so that they are without e
2Co 12:19 that we e ourselves to you

EXCUSED (*see* EXCUSE)
Luke 14:18 I ask you to have me e
Luke 14:19 I ask you to have me e

EXCUSES (*see* EXCUSE)
Luke 14:18 one accord began to make e

EXCUSING (*see* EXCUSE)
Rom 2:15 accusing or else e them)

EXECUTE (*see* EXECUTED, EXECUTES, EXECUTING, EXECUTIONER)
Ex 12:12 of Egypt I will e judgment
Lev 26:25 will e the vengeance of My
Num 5:30 the priest shall e all this
1Sa 28:18 nor e His fierce wrath upon
2Sa 1:15 and said, "Go near, and e him
2Sa 14: 7 that we may e him for the
2Sa 14:32 iniquity in me, let him e me
1Ki 6:12 e My judgments, keep all My
2Ki 14: 6 of the murderers he did not e
2Ch 25: 4 he did not e their children
Ps 110: 5 He shall e kings in the day
Ps 110: 6 He shall e the heads of many
Ps 119:84 When will You e judgment on
Ps 149: 7 To e vengeance on the nations
Ps 149: 9 To e on them the written
Is 16: 3 Take counsel, e judgment
Jer 7: 5 if you thoroughly e judgment
Jer 21:12 E judgment in the morning
Jer 22: 3 E judgment and righteousness,
Jer 23: 5 e judgment and righteousness
Jer 33:15 He shall e judgment and
Ezek 5: 8 and will e judgments in your
Ezek 5:10 I will e judgments among you,
Ezek 5:15 when I e judgments among you
Ezek 11: 9 and e judgments on you
Ezek 16:41 e judgments on you in the
Ezek 23:47 and e them with their swords
Ezek 25:11 I will e judgments upon Moab,
Ezek 25:17 I will e great vengeance on
Ezek 28:22 when I e judgments in her and
Ezek 28:26 when I e judgments on all
Ezek 30:14 to Zoan, and e judgments in No
Ezek 30:19 Thus I will e judgments on
Ezek 45: 9 e justice and righteousness,
Hos 11: 9 I will not e the fierceness
Mic 5:15 I will e vengeance in anger
Zech 7: 9 E true justice, show mercy
John 5:27 authority to e judgment also
Rom 13: 4 an avenger to e wrath on him
Jude 15 to e judgment on all, to

EXECUTED (*see* EXECUTE)
Num 33: 4 gods the LORD had e judgments
2Sa 4:10 him and had him e in Ziklag
2Sa 4:12 his young men, and they e them
1Ki 18:40 Brook Kishon and e them there
1Ki 19: 1 also how he had e all the
2Ki 14: 5 that he e his servants who
2Ki 21:24 But the people of the land e
2Ki 23:20 He e all the priests of the
2Ch 24:24 So they e judgment against
2Ch 25: 3 that he e his servants who
2Ch 33:25 But the people of the land e
Ezra 7:26 judgment be e speedily on him
Esth 9: 1 command and his decree to be e
Ps 99: 4 You have e justice and
Eccl 8:11 evil work is not e speedily
Jer 23:20 not turn back until He has e
Ezek 11:12 statutes nor e My judgments
Ezek 18: 8 e true judgment between man
Ezek 18:17 but has e My judgments and
Ezek 20:24 they had not e My judgments
Ezek 23:10 for they had e judgment on
Ezek 39:21 My judgment which I have e
Dan 5:19 Whomever he wished, he e

EXECUTES (*see* EXECUTE)
Ps 9:16 is known by the judgment He e
Ps 103: 6 The LORD e righteousness And
Ps 146: 7 Who e justice for the
Is 46:11 the man who e My counsel
Jer 5: 1 is anyone who e judgment, who
Joel 2:11 is the One who e His word
Mic 7: 9 my case and e justice for me

EXECUTING (*see* EXECUTE)
2Ch 22: 8 when Jehu was e judgment on

EXECUTIONER (*see* EXECUTE, EXECUTIONERS)
Mark 6:27 the king sent an e and

EXECUTIONERS (*see* EXECUTIONER)
Job 33:22 the Pit, and his life to the e

EXEMPTED (*see* EXEMPTION)
1Ki 15:22 none was e

EXEMPTION (*see* EXEMPTED)
1Sa 17:25 father's house e in Israel

EXERCISE (*see* EXERCISED, EXERCISES, EXERCISING)
1Ki 21: 7 You now e authority over
Matt 20:25 great e authority over them
Mark 10:42 their great ones e authority
Luke 22:25 Gentiles e lordship over them
Luke 22:25 those who e authority over
1Co 7: 9 if they cannot e self-control
1Ti 4: 7 and e yourself rather to
1Ti 4: 8 For bodily e profits a little

EXERCISED (*see* EXERCISE)
Eccl 1:13 man, by which they may be e
Heb 5:14 senses e to discern both good

EXERCISES (*see* EXERCISE)
Rev 13:12 he e all the authority of the

EXERCISING (*see* EXERCISE)
Jer 9:24 e lovingkindness, judgment,

EXHAUSTED (*see* EXHAUSTION)
Judg 8: 4 over, e but still in pursuit
Judg 8: 5 who follow me, for they are e

EXHAUSTION (*see* EXHAUSTED)
Jer 48:45 of Heshbon because of e

EXHORT (*see* EXHORTATION, EXHORTED, EXHORTING, EXHORTS)
2Co 9: 5 e the brethren to go to you
1Th 4: 1 e in the Lord Jesus that you
1Th 5:14 Now we e you, brethren, warn
2Th 3:12 and e through our Lord Jesus
1Ti 2: 1 Therefore I e first of all
1Ti 5: 1 but e him as a father, the
1Ti 6: 2 Teach and e these things
2Ti 4: 2 Convince, rebuke, e, with all
Tit 1: 9 by sound doctrine, both to e
Tit 2: 6 Likewise e the young men to
Tit 2: 9 E servants to be obedient to
Tit 2:15 Speak these things, e, and
Heb 3:13 but e one another daily,
1Pe 5: 1 elders who are among you I e

EXHORTATION (*see* EXHORT, EXHORTATIONS)
Acts 13:15 any word of e for the people
Rom 12: 8 he who exhorts, in e
1Co 14: 3 speaks edification and e and
2Co 8:17 he not only accepted the e
1Th 2: 3 For our e did not come from
1Ti 4:13 attention to reading, to e
Heb 12: 5 And you have forgotten the e

Heb 13:22 bear with the word of e, for

EXHORTATIONS (*see* EXHORTATION)
Luke 3:18 with many other e he preached

EXHORTED (*see* EXHORT)
Jer 11: 7 For I earnestly e your
Acts 2:40 testified and e them, saying,
Acts 15:32 e the brethren with many
1Th 2:11 as you know how we e, and

EXHORTING (*see* EXHORT)
Jer 11: 7 this day, rising early and e
Acts 14:22 e them to continue in the
Acts 18:27 e the disciples to receive
Heb 10:25 but e one another, and so much
1Pe 5:12 written to you briefly, e
Jude 3 e you to contend earnestly

EXHORTS (*see* EXHORT)
Rom 12: 8 he who e, in exhortation

EXILE (*see* EXILES)
2Sa 15:19 also an e from your own place
Is 51:14 The captive e hastens, that

EXILES (*see* EXILE)
Is 45:13 let My e go free, not for

EXIST (*see* EXISTED)
Is 66: 2 made, and all those things e
Rom 4:17 do not e as though they did
Rom 13: 1 that e are appointed by God
Jas 3:16 where envy and self-seeking e
2Pe 3: 7 the earth which now e are
Rev 4:11 and by Your will they e and

EXISTED (*see* EXIST)
Eccl 4: 3 both is he who has never e
2Pe 3: 6 world that then e perished

EXITS
Ezek 42:11 as the others, and all their e
Ezek 43:11 and its arrangement, its e
Ezek 48:30 These are the e of the city

EXORCISTS
Acts 19:13 of the itinerant Jewish e

EXPAND (*see* EXPANDED)
Is 54: 3 For you shall e to the right

EXPANDED (*see* EXPAND)
Is 26:15 you have e all the borders of

EXPECT (*see* EXPECTANTLY, EXPECTATION, EXPECTED, EXPECTING, UNEXPECTEDLY)
Matt 24:44 an hour when you do not e Him
Luke 12:40 at an hour you do not e

EXPECTANTLY (*see* EXPECT)
Ps 145:15 The eyes of all look e to You

EXPECTATION (*see* EXPECT, EXPECTATIONS)
Ps 9:18 The e of the poor shall not
Ps 62: 5 alone, For my e is from Him
Prov 10:28 but the e of the wicked will
Prov 11: 7 his e will perish, and the
Prov 11:23 but the e of the wicked is
Is 20: 5 ashamed of Ethiopia their e
Is 20: 6 day, Surely such is our e
Zech 9: 5 Ekron, for He dried up her e
Luke 3:15 Now as the people were in e
Luke 21:26 the e of those things which
Acts 12:11 from all the e of the Jewish
Rom 8:19 For the earnest e of the
Phil 1:20 according to my earnest e
Heb 10:27 certain fearful e of judgment

EXPECTATIONS (*see* EXPECTATION)
1Ki 2:15 Israel had set their e on me

EXPECTED (*see* EXPECT)
Is 5: 2 so He e it to bring forth
Is 5: 4 when I e it to bring forth

EXPECTING (*see* EXPECT)
Acts 3: 5 e to receive something from
Acts 28: 6 they were e that he would

EXPEDIENT
John 11:50 e for us that one man should
John 18:14 to the Jews that it was e

EXPEDITION
1Sa 23:13 so he halted the e

EXPEL (*see* EXPELLED)
Josh 23: 5 will e them from before you
Judg 11: 7 e me from my father's house

EXPELLED (*see* EXPEL)
Judg 1:20 Then he e from there the
2Sa 14:14 ones are not e from Him
Zech 5: 3 Every thief shall be e,'
Zech 5: 3 Every perjurer shall be e
Acts 13:50 and e them from their region

EXPENDED
Ezek 29:18 the labor which they e on it

EXPENSE (*see* EXPENSES)
2Sa 19:42 we ever eaten at the king's e
Ezra 6: 8 e from taxes on the region
1Co 9: 7 ever goes to war at his own e

EXPENSES (*see* EXPENSE)
Ezra 6: 4 Let the e be paid from the
Acts 21:24 pay their e so that they may

EXPERIENCE (*see* EXPERIENCED)
Gen 30:27 for I have learned by e that
Eccl 8: 5 will e nothing harmful

EXPERIENCED (*see* EXPERIENCE)
1Pe 5: 9 the same sufferings are e by

EXPERT
1Ch 12:33 e in war with all weapons of
Ezra 7:11 scribe, e in the words of the
Song 3: 8 hold swords, being e in war
Is 3: 3 artisan, and the e enchanter
Jer 50: 9 be like those of an e warrior
Acts 26: 3 you are e in all customs and

EXPIRATION (*see* EXPIRED)
Acts 21:26 the temple to announce the e

EXPIRED (*see* EXPIRATION)
1Sa 18:26 Now the days had not e
Rev 20: 7 the thousand years have e

EXPLAIN (*see* EXPLAINED, EXPLAINING)
Gen 41:24 no one who could e it to me
Deut 1: 5 Moses began to e this law
Judg 14:12 e it to me within the seven
Judg 14:13 But if you cannot e it to me
Judg 14:14 they could not e the riddle
Judg 14:15 that he may e the riddle to
Judg 14:16 so should I e it to you
1Ki 10: 3 that he could not e it to her
2Ch 9: 2 that he could not e it to her
Esth 4: 8 e it to her, and that he might
Job 12: 8 fish of the sea will e to you
Dan 4: 9 e to me the visions of my
Dan 5:16 interpretations and e enigmas
Matt 13:36 E to us the parable of the
Matt 15:15 Him, "E this parable to us
Heb 5:11 much to say, and hard to e

EXPLAINED (*see* EXPLAIN)
Num 15:34 because it had not been e
Judg 14:16 but you have not e it to me
Judg 14:16 I have not e it to my father
Judg 14:17 Then she e the riddle to the
Judg 14:19 to those who had e the riddle
1Sa 10:25 Then Samuel e to the people
Mark 4:34 alone, He e all things to His
Acts 10: 8 So when he had e all these
Acts 11: 4 But Peter e it to them in
Acts 18:26 e to him the way of God more
Acts 28:23 at his lodging, to whom he e

EXPLAINING (*see* EXPLAIN)
Dan 5:12 e enigmas were found in this
Acts 17: 3 e and demonstrating that the

EXPLOIT (*see* EXPLOITS)
Is 58: 3 and e all your laborers
Mal 3: 5 those who e wage earners and
2Pe 2: 3 e you with deceptive words

EXPLOITS (*see* EXPLOIT)
Dan 11:32 strong, and carry out great e

EXPLORE
1Ki 18: 6 the land between them to e it

EXPORTED
1Ki 10:29 they e them to all the kings
2Ch 1:17 they e them to all the kings

EXPOSE (*see* EXPOSED)
Prov 25:10 he who hears it e your shame
Hos 2: 3 e her, as in the day she was
Acts 7:19 making them e their babies,
Eph 5:11 darkness, but rather e them

EXPOSED (*see* EXPOSE)
Gen 30:37 e the white which was in the
Ex 20:26 nakedness may not be e on it
Hab 2:16 and be e as uncircumcised
John 3:20 lest his deeds should be e
Eph 5:13 But all things that are e are

EXPOUNDED
Luke 24:27 He e to them in all the

EXPRESS (*see* EXPRESSING, EXPRESSION, EXPRESSLY)
Eccl 1: 8 man cannot e it
Heb 1: 3 the e image of His person, and

EXPRESSING (*see* EXPRESS)
Prov 18: 2 but in e his own heart

EXPRESSION (*see* EXPRESS)
Dan 3:19 the e on his face changed

EXPRESSLY (*see* EXPRESS)
1Sa 20:21 If I e say to him, "Look,
Ezek 1: 3 came e to Ezekiel the priest
1Ti 4: 1 Now the Spirit e says that in

EXQUISITE
Ex 39:28 e hats of fine linen, short

EXTEND (*see* EXTENDED, EXTENDING, EXTENDS, EXTENT)
Ex 25:35 that e from the lampstand
Num 34: 3 e eastward to the end of the
Num 35: 4 give the Levites shall e from
Ps 109:12 be none to e mercy to him
Is 58:10 If you e your soul to the
Is 66:12 I will e peace to her like a
Jer 31:39 e straight forward over the

EXTENDED (*see* EXTEND)
Josh 15: 9 and e to the cities of Mount
Josh 15:11 Mount Baalah, and e to Jabneel
Josh 18:14 Then the border e from there
Josh 18:15 the border e on the west and
Josh 18:17 e toward Geliloth, which is
Josh 19:11 e along the brook that is
Josh 19:13 e to Rimmon, which borders on
Josh 19:34 From Heleph the border e
1Ki 6: 3 its width e ten cubits from
1Ki 8: 8 the poles e so that the ends
2Ch 5: 9 the poles e so that the ends
Ezra 7:28 has e mercy to me before the
Ezra 9: 9 but He e mercy to us in the
Ezek 40:14 the gateway e to the gatepost

EXTENDING (*see* EXTEND)
Ex 37:21 to the six branches e from it
Ezek 43:15 with four horns e upward from
Ezek 45: 7 e westward on the west side
2Co 10:14 For we are not e ourselves

EXTENDS (*see* EXTEND)
Num 21:13 that e from the border of the
Prov 31:20 She e her hand to the poor,

EXTENSIVE (*see* EXTENSIVELY, EXTENT)
Neh 4:19 The work is great and e, and we

EXTENSIVELY (*see* EXTENSIVE)
2Ch 27: 3 he built e on the wall of

EXTENT (*see* EXTEND, EXTENSIVE)
Num 22:41 observe the e of the people
Josh 17:18 its farthest e shall be yours
Jon 3: 3 a three-day journey in e
2Co 2: 5 me, but all of you to some e
1Pe 4:13 but rejoice to the e that you

EXTERIOR
Ezek 40:19 front of the inner court e

EXTERMINATE
1Ki 13:34 house of Jeroboam, so as to e

EXTINGUISH (*see* EXTINGUISHED)
2Sa 14: 7 So they would e my ember

EXTINGUISHED (*see* EXTINGUISH)
Job 17: 1 is broken, my days are e, the
Is 43:17 they are e, they are quenched

EXTOL (*see* EXTOLLED)
Ps 30: 1 I will e You, O LORD, for You
Ps 68: 4 E Him who rides on the clouds
Ps 145: 1 I will e You, my God, O King
Dan 4:37 Nebuchadnezzar, praise and e

EXTOLLED (*see* EXTOL)
Ps 66:17 And He was e with my tongue
Is 52:13 He shall be exalted and e

EXTORTED (*see* EXTORTION)
Lev 6: 2 or if he has e from his

EXTORTION (*see* EXTORTED, EXTORTIONER)
Prov 28: 8 e gathers it for him who will
Ezek 22:12 from your neighbors by e, and
Matt 23:25 but inside they are full of e

EXTORTIONER (*see* EXTORTION, EXTORTIONERS)
Is 16: 4 For the e is at an end,
1Co 5:11 or a drunkard, or an e

EXTORTIONERS (*see* EXTORTIONER)
Luke 18:11 e, unjust, adulterers, or
1Co 5:10 or with the covetous, or e
1Co 6:10 nor e will inherit the

EXTRAORDINARY
Deut 28:59 and your descendants e plagues

EXTREME (*see* EXTREMITY)
Josh 15: 1 was the e southern boundary
Ezek 46:19 at their e western end

EXTREMITY (*see* EXTREME)
2Ki 19:23 enter the e of its borders

EXULT
Job 6:10 though in anguish, I would e

EYE (*see* EYEBROWS, EYED, EYELIDS, EYES, EYESERVICE)
Ex 21:24 e for e, tooth for tooth,
Ex 21:26 strikes the e of his servant
Ex 21:26 or the e of his maidservant,
Ex 21:26 go free for the sake of his e
Lev 21:20 man who has a defect in his e
Lev 24:20 e for e, tooth for tooth
Deut 7:16 your e shall have no pity on
Deut 13: 8 nor shall your e pity him
Deut 15: 9 your e be evil against your
Deut 19:13 Your e shall not pity him,
Deut 19:21 Your e shall not pity
Deut 19:21 e for e, tooth for tooth,
Deut 25:12 your e shall not pity her
Deut 32:10 him as the apple of His e
1Sa 24:10 But my e spared you, and I
Ezra 5: 5 But the e of their God was
Job 7: 7 My e will never again see
Job 7: 8 The e of him who sees me will
Job 10:18 perished and no e had seen me
Job 13: 1 my e has seen all this, My
Job 17: 2 does not my e dwell on their
Job 17: 7 My e has also grown dim
Job 20: 9 The e that saw him will see
Job 24:15 The e of the adulterer waits
Job 24:15 saying, 'No e will see me'
Job 28: 7 has the falcon's e seen it
Job 28:10 his e sees every precious
Job 29:11 blessed me, and when the e saw
Job 42: 5 ear, but now my e sees You
Ps 6: 7 My e wastes away because of
Ps 17: 8 me as the apple of Your e
Ps 31: 9 My e wastes away with grief,
Ps 32: 8 I will guide you with My e
Ps 33:18 the e of the LORD is on those
Ps 35:19 Nor let them wink with the e
Ps 54: 7 my e has seen its desire upon
Ps 88: 9 My e wastes away because of
Ps 92:11 My e also has seen my desire
Ps 94: 9 He who formed the e, shall He
Prov 7: 2 my law as the apple of your e
Prov 10:10 with the e causes trouble
Prov 16:30 He winks his e to devise
Prov 20:12 hearing ear and the seeing e
Prov 22: 9 a bountiful e will be blessed
Prov 28:22 A man with an evil e hastens
Prov 30:17 The e that mocks his father,
Eccl 1: 8 The e is not satisfied with
Eccl 4: 8 nor is his e satisfied with
Is 13:18 their e will not spare
Is 52: 8 for they shall see e to e
Is 64: 4 nor has the e seen any God
Jer 32: 4 to face, and see him e to e
Lam 1:16 my e, my e overflows with
Lam 2: 4 who were pleasing to His e
Ezek 5:11 My e will not spare, nor will
Ezek 7: 4 My e will not spare you, nor
Ezek 7: 9 My e will not spare, nor
Ezek 8:18 My e will not spare nor will
Ezek 9: 5 do not let your e spare, nor
Ezek 9:10 My e will neither spare, nor
Ezek 16: 5 No e pitied you, to do any of
Ezek 20:17 Nevertheless My e spared them
Mic 4:11 and let our e look upon Zion
Zech 2: 8 touches the apple of His e
Zech 11:17 arm and against his right e
Zech 11:17 his right e shall be totally
Matt 5:29 if your right e causes you to
Matt 5:38 it was said, 'An e for an e
Matt 6:22 The lamp of the body is the e
Matt 6:22 If therefore your e is good
Matt 6:23 But if your e is bad, your
Matt 7: 3 the speck in your brother's e
Matt 7: 3 the plank in your own e
Matt 7: 4 the speck out of your e'
Matt 7: 4 a plank is in your own e
Matt 7: 5 the plank from your own e
Matt 7: 5 speck out of your brother's e
Matt 18: 9 if your e causes you to sin,
Matt 18: 9 to enter into life with one e
Matt 19:24 a camel to go through the e
Matt 20:15 Or is your e evil because I
Mark 7:22 licentiousness, an evil e
Mark 9:47 And if your e makes you sin,
Mark 9:47 the kingdom of God with one e
Mark 10:25 a camel to go through the e
Luke 6:41 the speck in your brother's e
Luke 6:41 the plank in your own e
Luke 6:42 the speck that is in your e
Luke 6:42 plank that is in your own e
Luke 6:42 the plank from your own e
Luke 6:42 that is in your brother's e
Luke 11:34 The lamp of the body is the e
Luke 11:34 when your e is good, your
Luke 11:34 But when your e is bad, your
Luke 18:25 e than for a rich man to
1Co 2: 9 E has not seen, nor ear heard
1Co 12:16 Because I am not an e, I am
1Co 12:17 If the whole body were an e
1Co 12:21 the e cannot say to the hand,
1Co 15:52 in the twinkling of an e
Rev 1: 7 every e will see Him, and they
Rev 3:18 anoint your eyes with e salve

EYEBROWS (*see* EYE)
Lev 14: 9 head and his beard and his e

EYED (*see* EYE)
1Sa 18: 9 So Saul e David from that day

EYELIDS (*see* EYE)
Job 16:16 and on my e is the shadow of
Job 41:18 are like the e of the morning
Ps 11: 4 His e test the sons of men
Ps 77: 4 You hold my e open
Ps 132: 4 to my eyes Or slumber to my e
Prov 4:25 your e look right before you
Prov 6: 4 eyes, nor slumber to your e
Prov 6:25 let her allure you with her e
Prov 30:13 And their e are lifted up
Jer 9:18 and our e gush with water

EYES (*see* EYE)
Gen 3: 5 of it your e will be opened
Gen 3: 6 that it was pleasant to the e
Gen 3: 7 Then the e of both of them
Gen 6: 8 grace in the e of the LORD
Gen 13:10 And Lot lifted his e and saw
Gen 13:14 Lift your e now and look from
Gen 16: 4 became despised in her e
Gen 16: 5 I became despised in her e
Gen 18: 2 So he lifted his e and looked,
Gen 21:19 And God opened her e, and she
Gen 22: 4 day Abraham lifted his e and
Gen 22:13 Then Abraham lifted his e
Gen 24:63 and he lifted his e and looked,
Gen 24:64 Then Rebekah lifted her e
Gen 27: 1 his e were so dim that he
Gen 29:17 Leah's e were delicate, but
Gen 30:27 I have found favor in your e
Gen 30:41 the e of the livestock in the
Gen 31:10 conceived, that I lifted my e
Gen 31:12 And He said, "Lift your e now
Gen 31:40 my sleep departed from my e
Gen 33: 1 Now Jacob lifted his e and
Gen 33: 5 And he lifted his e and saw the
Gen 34:11 Let me find favor in your e
Gen 37:25 Then they lifted their e and
Gen 39: 7 wife cast longing e on Joseph
Gen 41:37 was good in the e of Pharaoh
Gen 41:37 in the e of all his servants
Gen 42:24 and bound him before their e
Gen 43:29 Then he lifted his e and saw
Gen 44:21 that I may set my e on him
Gen 45:12 your e and the e of my brother
Gen 46: 4 will put his hand on your e
Gen 47:19 should we die before your e
Gen 48:10 Now the e of Israel were dim
Gen 49:12 His e are darker than wine,
Gen 50: 4 I have found favor in your e
Ex 8:26 the Egyptians before their e
Ex 13: 9 as a memorial between your e
Ex 13:16 as frontlets between your e
Ex 14:10 of Israel lifted their e, and
Ex 24:17 e of the children of Israel
Lev 4:13 from the e of the assembly
Lev 20: 4 way hide their e from the man
Lev 26:16 which shall consume the e
Num 5:13 from the e of her husband
Num 10:31 and you can be our e
Num 11: 6 this manna before our e
Num 15:39 and your own e are inclined,
Num 16:14 put out the e of these men
Num 20: 8 to the rock before their e
Num 20:12 to hallow Me in the e of the
Num 22:31 the LORD opened Balaam's e
Num 24: 2 And Balaam raised his e, and
Num 24: 3 of the man whose e are opened
Num 24: 4 down, with e opened wide
Num 24:15 of the man whose e are opened
Num 24:16 down, with e opened wide
Num 27:14 at the waters before their e
Num 33:55 shall be irritants in your e
Deut 1:30 you in Egypt before your e
Deut 3:21 Your e have seen all that
Deut 3:27 lift your e toward the west,
Deut 3:27 behold it with your e, for
Deut 4: 3 Your e have seen what the
Deut 4: 9 the things your e have seen
Deut 4:19 you lift your e to heaven
Deut 4:34 you in Egypt before your e
Deut 6: 8 as frontlets between your e
Deut 6:22 signs and wonders before our e
Deut 7:19 great trials which your e saw
Deut 9:17 and broke them before your e
Deut 10:21 things which your e have seen
Deut 11: 7 but your e have seen every
Deut 11:12 the e of the LORD your God
Deut 11:18 as frontlets between your e
Deut 12: 8 is right in his own e
Deut 13:18 in the e of the LORD your God
Deut 16:19 blinds the e of the wise and
Deut 21: 7 blood, nor have our e seen it
Deut 24: 1 e because he has found some
Deut 28:31 be slaughtered before your e
Deut 28:32 your e shall look and fail
Deut 28:34 of the sight which your e see
Deut 28:65 a trembling heart, failing e
Deut 28:67 of the sight which your e see
Deut 29: 2 your e in the land of Egypt
Deut 29: 3 trials which your e have seen
Deut 29: 4 e to see and ears to hear, to
Deut 34: 4 you to see it with your e
Deut 34: 7 His e were not dim nor his
Josh 5:13 Jericho, that he lifted his e
Josh 23:13 sides and thorns in your e
Josh 24: 7 And your e saw what I did in
Judg 16:21 took him and put out his e
Judg 16:28 the Philistines for my two e
Judg 17: 6 what was right in his own e
Judg 19:17 And when he raised his e, he
Judg 21:25 what was right in his own e
Ruth 2: 9 Let your e be on the field
Ruth 2:10 have I found favor in your e
1Sa 2:33 My altar shall consume your e
1Sa 3: 2 when his e had begun to grow
1Sa 4:15 his e were so dim that he
1Sa 6:13 and they lifted their e and saw
1Sa 11: 2 may put out all your right e
1Sa 12: 3 with which to blind my e
1Sa 12:16 LORD will do before your e
1Sa 15:17 you were little in your own e
1Sa 16:12 he was ruddy, with bright e
1Sa 20: 3 I have found favor in your e
1Sa 20:29 I have found favor in your e
1Sa 24:10 this day your e have seen
1Sa 25: 8 men find favor in your e, for
1Sa 26:21 precious in your e this day
1Sa 26:24 valued much this day in my e
1Sa 26:24 much in the e of the LORD
1Sa 27: 5 now found favor in your e

2Sa 6:20 in the **e** of the maids of his
2Sa 12:11 take your wives before your **e**
2Sa 13:34 keeping watch lifted his **e**
2Sa 15:25 favor in the **e** of the LORD
2Sa 18:24 to the wall, lifted his **e**
2Sa 19:27 do what is good in your **e**
2Sa 22:25 to my cleanness in His **e**
2Sa 22:28 but Your **e** are on the haughty
2Sa 24: 3 may the **e** of my lord the king
1Ki 1:20 the **e** of all Israel are on
1Ki 1:48 this day, while my **e** see it
1Ki 8:29 that Your **e** may be open
1Ki 8:52 that Your **e** may be open to
1Ki 9: 3 name there forever, and My **e**
1Ki 10: 7 came and saw it with my own **e**
1Ki 11:33 to do what is right in My **e**
1Ki 14: 4 see, for his **e** were glazed by
1Ki 14: 8 only what was right in My **e**
1Ki 15: 5 right in the **e** of the LORD
1Ki 15:11 right in the **e** of the LORD
1Ki 16:25 did evil in the **e** of the LORD
1Ki 20: 6 is pleasant in your **e**, they
1Ki 20:38 with a bandage over his **e**
1Ki 20:41 the bandage away from his **e**
1Ki 22:43 right in the **e** of the LORD
2Ki 4:34 his **e** on his **e**
2Ki 4:35 and the child opened his **e**
2Ki 5: 1 man in the **e** of his master
2Ki 6:17 open his **e** that he may see
2Ki 6:17 opened the **e** of the young man
2Ki 6:20 open the **e** of these men, that
2Ki 6:20 And the LORD opened their **e**
2Ki 7: 2 you shall see it with your **e**
2Ki 7:19 you shall see it with your **e**
2Ki 9:30 and she put paint on her **e**
2Ki 19:16 open Your **e**, O LORD, and see
2Ki 19:22 and lifted up your **e** on high
2Ki 22:20 your **e** shall not see all the
2Ki 25: 7 sons of Zedekiah before his **e**
2Ki 25: 7 put out the **e** of Zedekiah
1Ch 13: 4 in the **e** of all the people
1Ch 21:16 Then David lifted his **e** and
1Ch 21:23 king do what is good in his **e**
2Ch 6:20 that Your **e** may be open
2Ch 6:40 I pray, let Your **e** be open
2Ch 7:15 Now My **e** will be open and My
2Ch 7:16 and My **e** and My heart will be
2Ch 9: 6 I came and saw with my own **e**
2Ch 14: 2 right in the **e** of the LORD
2Ch 16: 9 For the **e** of the LORD run to
2Ch 20:12 to do, but our **e** are upon You
2Ch 29: 6 done evil in the **e** of the
2Ch 29: 8 as you see with your **e**
2Ch 34:28 your **e** shall not see all the
Ezra 3:12 was laid before their **e**
Ezra 9: 8 our God may enlighten our **e**
Neh 1: 6 be attentive and Your **e** open
Neh 6:16 disheartened in their own **e**
Esth 1:17 their husbands in their **e**
Esth 8: 5 and I am pleasing in his **e**
Job 2:12 they raised their **e** from afar
Job 3:10 nor hide sorrow from my **e**
Job 4:16 A form was before my **e**
Job 7: 8 while your **e** are upon me, I
Job 10: 4 Do You have **e** of flesh
Job 11: 4 pure, And I am clean in your **e**
Job 11:20 But the **e** of the wicked will
Job 14: 3 You open Your **e** on such a one
Job 15:12 and what do your **e** wink at
Job 16:20 my **e** pour out tears to God
Job 17: 5 even the **e** of his children
Job 19:27 my **e** shall behold, and not
Job 21: 8 offspring before their **e**
Job 21:20 Let his **e** see his destruction
Job 24:23 yet His **e** are on their ways
Job 27:19 he opens his **e**, and he is no
Job 28:21 from the **e** of all living, and
Job 29:15 I was **e** to the blind, and I
Job 31: 1 made a covenant with my **e**
Job 31: 7 or my heart walked after my **e**
Job 31:16 or caused the **e** of the widow
Job 32: 1 he was righteous in his own **e**
Job 34:21 For His **e** are on the ways of
Job 36: 7 His **e** from the righteous
Job 39:29 its **e** observe from afar
Job 40:24 Though he takes it in his **e**
Job 41:18 his **e** are like the eyelids of
Ps 10: 8 His **e** are secretly fixed on
Ps 11: 4 His **e** behold, His eyelids
Ps 13: 3 Enlighten my **e**, Lest I sleep
Ps 15: 4 In whose **e** a vile person is
Ps 17: 2 Let Your **e** look on the things
Ps 17:11 They have set their **e**,
Ps 19: 8 is pure, enlightening the **e**
Ps 25:15 My **e** are ever toward the LORD
Ps 26: 3 lovingkindness is before my **e**
Ps 31:22 cut off from before Your **e**"
Ps 34:15 The **e** of the LORD are on the
Ps 35:21 Our **e** have seen it
Ps 36: 1 no fear of God before his **e**
Ps 36: 2 flatters himself in his own **e**
Ps 38:10 As for the light of my **e**, it
Ps 50:21 them in order before your **e**
Ps 66: 7 His **e** observe the nations
Ps 69: 3 My **e** fail while I wait for my
Ps 69:23 Let their **e** be darkened, so
Ps 73: 7 Their **e** bulge with abundance
Ps 91: 8 with your **e** shall you look
Ps 101: 3 nothing wicked before my **e**
Ps 101: 6 My **e** shall be on the faithful
Ps 115: 5 **E** they have, but they do not
Ps 116: 8 My **e** from tears, And my feet
Ps 118:23 It is marvelous in our **e**
Ps 119:18 Open my **e**, that I may see
Ps 119:37 Turn away my **e** from looking
Ps 119:82 My **e** fail from seeking Your
Ps 119:123 My **e** fail from seeking Your
Ps 119:136 of water run down from my **e**
Ps 119:148 My **e** are awake through the
Ps 121: 1 lift up my **e** to the hills
Ps 123: 1 Unto You I lift up my **e**, O
Ps 123: 2 as the **e** of servants look to
Ps 123: 2 As the **e** of a maid to the
Ps 123: 2 So our **e** look to the LORD our
Ps 131: 1 not haughty, Nor my **e** lofty
Ps 132: 4 my **e** Or slumber to my eyelids
Ps 135:16 **E** they have, but they do not
Ps 139:16 Your **e** saw my substance,
Ps 141: 8 But my **e** are upon You, O GOD
Ps 145:15 The **e** of all look expectantly
Ps 146: 8 LORD opens the **e** of the blind
Prov 3: 7 Do not be wise in your own **e**
Prov 3:21 them not depart from your **e**
Prov 4:21 let them depart from your **e**
Prov 4:25 Let your **e** look straight
Prov 5:21 are before the **e** of the LORD
Prov 6: 4 Give no sleep to your **e**, nor
Prov 6:13 he winks with his **e**, he
Prov 10:26 the teeth and smoke to the **e**
Prov 12:15 a fool is right in his own **e**
Prov 15: 3 The **e** of the LORD are in
Prov 15:30 The light of the **e** rejoices
Prov 16: 2 a man are pure in his own **e**
Prov 17: 8 in the **e** of its possessor
Prov 17:24 but the **e** of a fool are on
Prov 20: 8 scatters all evil with his **e**
Prov 20:13 open your **e**, and you will be
Prov 21: 2 a man is right in his own **e**
Prov 21:10 finds no favor in his **e**
Prov 22:12 The **e** of the LORD preserve
Prov 23: 5 Will you set your **e** on that
Prov 23:26 let your **e** observe my ways
Prov 23:29 Who has redness of **e**
Prov 23:33 Your **e** will see strange
Prov 25: 7 prince, whom your **e** have seen
Prov 26: 5 lest he be wise in his own **e**
Prov 26:12 see a man wise in his own **e**
Prov 26:16 is wiser in his own **e** than
Prov 27:20 so the **e** of man are never
Prov 28:11 rich man is wise in his own **e**
Prov 28:27 but he who hides his **e** will
Prov 29:13 gives light to the **e** of both
Prov 30:12 that is pure in its own **e**
Prov 30:13 oh, how lofty are their **e**
Eccl 2:10 Whatever my **e** desired I did
Eccl 2:14 The wise man's **e** are in his
Eccl 5:11 to see them with their **e**
Eccl 6: 9 the **e** than the wandering of
Eccl 11: 7 for the **e** to behold the sun
Eccl 11: 9 and in the sight of your **e**
Song 1:15 You have dove's **e**
Song 4: 1 You have dove's **e** behind your
Song 4: 9 heart with one look of your **e**
Song 5:12 His **e** are like doves by the
Song 6: 5 Turn your **e** away from me, for
Song 7: 4 your **e** like the pools in
Song 8:10 then I became in his **e** as one
Is 1:15 I will hide My **e** from you
Is 1:16 your doings from before My **e**
Is 3: 8 to provoke the **e** of His glory
Is 3:16 necks and wanton **e**, walking
Is 5:15 the **e** of the lofty shall be
Is 5:21 who are wise in their own **e**
Is 6: 5 for my **e** have seen the King,
Is 6:10 ears heavy, and shut their **e**
Is 6:10 lest they see with their **e**
Is 11: 3 judge by the sight of His **e**
Is 13:16 to pieces before their **e**
Is 17: 7 his **e** will have respect for
Is 29:10 sleep, and has closed your **e**
Is 29:18 the **e** of the blind shall see
Is 30:20 but your **e** shall see your
Is 32: 3 The **e** of those who see will
Is 33:15 shuts his **e** from seeing evil
Is 33:17 Your **e** will see the King in
Is 33:20 your **e** will see Jerusalem, a
Is 35: 5 Then the **e** of the blind shall
Is 37:17 open Your **e**, O LORD, and see
Is 37:23 and lifted up your **e** on high
Is 38:14 my **e** fail from looking upward
Is 40:26 Lift up your **e** on high, and
Is 42: 7 To open blind **e**, to bring out
Is 43: 8 the blind people who have **e**
Is 44:18 for He has shut their **e**, so
Is 49: 5 glorious in the **e** of the LORD
Is 49:18 Lift up your **e**, look around
Is 51: 6 Lift up your **e** to the heavens
Is 52:10 in the **e** of all the nations
Is 59:10 and we grope as if we had no **e**
Is 60: 4 Lift up your **e** all around
Is 65:12 but did evil before My **e**
Is 65:16 they are hidden from My **e**
Is 66: 4 But they did evil before My **e**
Jer 3: 2 Lift up your **e** to the
Jer 4:30 you enlarge your **e** with paint
Jer 5: 3 are not Your **e** on the truth
Jer 5:21 understanding, who have **e**
Jer 7:11 a den of thieves in your **e**
Jer 9: 1 my **e** a fountain of tears,
Jer 9:18 that our **e** may run with tears
Jer 13:17 my **e** will weep bitterly and
Jer 13:20 Lift up your **e** and see those
Jer 14: 6 their **e** failed because there
Jer 14:17 Let my **e** flow with tears
Jer 16: 9 this place, before your **e**
Jer 16:17 For My **e** are on all their
Jer 16:17 iniquity hidden from My **e**
Jer 20: 4 and your **e** shall see it
Jer 22:17 Yet your **e** and your heart are
Jer 24: 6 set My **e** on them for good
Jer 29:21 shall slay them before your **e**
Jer 31:16 weeping, and your **e** from tears
Jer 32:19 for your **e** are open to all
Jer 34: 3 your **e** shall see the **e** of
Jer 34: 3 the **e** of the king of Babylon
Jer 39: 6 before his **e** in Riblah
Jer 39: 7 he put out Zedekiah's **e**, and
Jer 52:10 sons of Zedekiah before his **e**
Jer 52:11 put out the **e** of Zedekiah
Lam 2:11 My **e** fail with tears, my
Lam 2:18 give your **e** no rest
Lam 3:48 My **e** overflow with rivers of
Lam 3:49 My **e** flow and do not cease,
Lam 3:51 my **e** bring suffering to my
Lam 4:17 Still our **e** failed us,
Lam 5:17 these things our **e** grow dim
Ezek 1:18 and their rims were full of **e**
Ezek 6: 9 by their **e** which play the
Ezek 8: 5 lift your **e** now toward the
Ezek 8: 5 lifted my **e** toward the north
Ezek 10:12 were full of **e** all around
Ezek 12: 2 which has **e** to see but does
Ezek 12:12 see the ground with his **e**
Ezek 18: 6 nor lifted up his **e** to the
Ezek 18:12 lifted his **e** to the idols, or
Ezek 18:15 nor lifted his **e** to the idols
Ezek 20: 7 which are before his **e**, and do
Ezek 20: 8 which were before their **e**
Ezek 20:24 their **e** were fixed on their
Ezek 21: 6 bitterness before their **e**
Ezek 21:23 the **e** of those who have sworn
Ezek 22:26 their **e** from My Sabbaths, so
Ezek 23:16 As soon as her **e** saw them
Ezek 23:27 will not lift your **e** to them
Ezek 23:40 for them, painted your **e**, and
Ezek 24:16 of your **e** with one stroke
Ezek 24:21 boast, the desire of your **e**
Ezek 24:25 glory, the desire of their **e**
Ezek 33:25 you lift up your **e** toward
Ezek 36:23 in you before their **e**

Ezek 37:20 in your hand before their **e**
Ezek 38:16 in you, O Gog, before their **e**
Ezek 38:23 in the **e** of many nations
Ezek 40: 4 Son of man, look with your **e**
Ezek 44: 5 mark well, see with your **e**
Dan 4:34 lifted my **e** to heaven, and my
Dan 7: 8 were **e** like the **e** of a man
Dan 7: 8 were **e** like the **e** of a man
Dan 7:20 namely, that horn which had **e**
Dan 8: 3 Then I lifted my **e** and saw, and
Dan 8: 5 a notable horn between his **e**
Dan 8:21 its **e** is the first king
Dan 9:18 open Your **e** and see our
Dan 10: 5 I lifted my **e** and looked, and
Dan 10: 6 his **e** like torches of fire,
Hos 13:14 Pity is hidden from My **e**
Joel 1:16 the food cut off before our **e**
Amos 9: 4 I will set My **e** on them for
Amos 9: 8 the **e** of the Lord GOD are on
Mic 7:10 My **e** will see her
Hab 1:13 You are of purer **e** than to
Zeph 3:20 your captives before your **e**
Hag 2: 3 this not in your **e** as nothing
Zech 1:18 Then I raised my **e** and looked,
Zech 2: 1 Then I raised my **e** and looked,
Zech 3: 9 upon the stone are seven **e**
Zech 4:10 They are the **e** of the LORD
Zech 5: 1 Then I turned and raised my **e**
Zech 5: 5 Lift your **e** now, and see what
Zech 5: 9 Then I raised my **e** and looked,
Zech 6: 1 Then I turned and raised my **e**
Zech 8: 6 the **e** of the remnant of this
Zech 8: 6 it also be marvelous in My **e**
Zech 9: 1 place (for the **e** of men and
Zech 9: 8 for now I have seen with My **e**
Zech 12: 4 I will open My **e** on the house
Zech 14:12 their **e** shall dissolve in
Mal 1: 5 your **e** shall see, and you
Matt 9:29 Then He touched their **e**,
Matt 9:30 And their **e** were opened
Matt 13:15 their **e** they have closed,
Matt 13:15 they should see with their **e**
Matt 13:16 are your **e** for they see, and
Matt 17: 8 they had lifted up their **e**
Matt 18: 9 eye, rather than having two **e**
Matt 20:33 that our **e** may be opened
Matt 20:34 compassion and touched their **e**
Matt 20:34 their **e** received sight, and
Matt 21:42 and it is marvelous in our **e**'
Matt 26:43 again, for their **e** were heavy
Mark 8:18 Having **e**, do you not see
Mark 8:23 And when He had spit on his **e**
Mark 8:25 put His hands on his **e** again
Mark 9:47 one eye, than having two **e**
Mark 12:11 and it is marvelous in our **e**'
Mark 14:40 again, for their **e** were heavy
Luke 2:30 for my **e** have seen Your
Luke 4:20 the **e** of all who were in the
Luke 6:20 up His **e** toward His disciples
Luke 10:23 Blessed are the **e** which see
Luke 16:23 in Hades, he lifted up his **e**
Luke 18:13 much as raise his **e** to heaven
Luke 19:42 they are hidden from your **e**
Luke 24:16 But their **e** were restrained,
Luke 24:31 Then their **e** were opened and
John 4:35 I say to you, lift up your **e**
John 6: 5 Then Jesus lifted up His **e**
John 9: 6 and He anointed the **e** of the
John 9:10 How were your **e** opened
John 9:11 made clay and anointed my **e**
John 9:14 made the clay and opened his **e**
John 9:15 He put clay on my **e**, and I
John 9:17 Him because He opened your **e**
John 9:21 opened his **e** we do not know
John 9:26 How did He open your **e**
John 9:30 and yet He has opened my **e**
John 9:32 **e** of one who was born blind
John 10:21 demon open the **e** of the blind
John 11:37 who opened the **e** of the blind
John 11:41 And Jesus lifted up His **e** and
John 12:40 He has blinded their **e** and
John 12:40 they should see with their **e**
John 17: 1 lifted up His **e** to heaven
Acts 3: 4 And fixing his **e** on him, with
Acts 9: 8 when his **e** were opened he saw
Acts 9:18 there fell from his **e**
Acts 9:40 And she opened her **e**, and
Acts 26:18 to open their **e** and to turn
Acts 28:27 their **e** they have closed,
Acts 28:27 they should see with their **e**
Rom 3:18 no fear of God before their **e**
Rom 11: 8 **e** that they should not see and
Rom 11:10 let their **e** be darkened, that
Gal 3: 1 before whose **e** Jesus Christ
Gal 4:15 have plucked out your own **e**
Eph 1:18 the **e** of your understanding
Heb 4:13 open to the **e** of Him to whom
1Pe 3:12 For the **e** of the LORD are on
2Pe 2:14 having **e** full of adultery and
1Jn 1: 1 which we have seen with our **e**
1Jn 2:11 darkness has blinded his **e**
1Jn 2:16 the flesh, the lust of the **e**
Rev 1:14 His **e** like a flame of fire
Rev 2:18 who has **e** like a flame of
Rev 3:18 anoint your **e** with eye salve,
Rev 4: 6 creatures full of **e** in front
Rev 4: 8 wings, were full of **e** around
Rev 5: 6 having seven horns and seven **e**
Rev 7:17 away every tear from their **e**
Rev 19:12 His **e** were like a flame of
Rev 21: 4 away every tear from their **e**

EYESERVICE (*see* EYE)
Eph 6: 6 not with **e**, as men-pleasers,
Col 3:22 to the flesh, not with **e**, as

EYEWITNESSES (*see* WITNESS)
Luke 1: 2 who from the beginning were **e**
2Pe 1:16 but were **e** of His majesty

EZBAI
1Ch 11:37 Naarai the son of **E**,

EZBON
Gen 46:16 were Ziphion, Haggi, Shuni, **E**
1Ch 7: 7 The sons of Bela were **E**, Uzzi

EZEKIEL (*see* JEHEZEKEL)
Ezek 1: 3 expressly to **E** the priest
Ezek 24:24 Thus **E** is a sign to you

EZEL (*see* BETH EZEL)
1Sa 20:19 and remain by the stone **E**

EZEM
Josh 15:29 Baalah, Ijim, **E**,
Josh 19: 3 Hazar Shual, Balah, **E**,
1Ch 4:29 Bilhah, **E**, Tolad,

EZER (*see* ABIEZER, EBENEZER, ROMAMTI-EZER)
Gen 36:21 Dishon, **E**, and Dishan
Gen 36:27 These were the sons of **E**
Gen 36:30 Chief Dishon, Chief **E**, and
1Ch 1:38 Zibeon, Anah, Dishon, **E**, and
1Ch 1:42 The sons of **E** were Bilhan
1Ch 4: 4 **E** was the father of Hushah
1Ch 7:21 son, Shuthelah his son, and **E**
1Ch 12: 9 **E** the first, Obadiah the
Neh 3:19 And next to him **E** the son of
Neh 12:42 Malchijah, Elam, and **E**

EZION GEBER (*see* GEBER)
Num 33:35 from Abronah and camped at **E**
Num 33:36 They moved from **E** and camped
Deut 2: 8 plain, away from Elath and **E**
1Ki 9:26 built a fleet of ships at **E**
1Ki 22:48 the ships were wrecked at **E**
2Ch 8:17 Then Solomon went to **E** and
2Ch 20:36 and they made the ships in **E**

EZNITE
2Sa 23: 8 He was called Adino the **E**

EZRA (*see* AZARIAH)
Ezra 7: 1 **E** the son of Seraiah, the son
Ezra 7: 6 this **E** came up from Babylon
Ezra 7: 8 **E** came to Jerusalem in the
Ezra 7:10 For **E** had prepared his heart
Ezra 7:11 Artaxerxes gave **E** the priest
Ezra 7:12 To **E** the priest, a scribe of
Ezra 7:21 that whatever **E** the priest
Ezra 7:25 And you, **E**, according to your
Ezra 10: 1 Now while **E** was praying, and
Ezra 10: 2 Elam, spoke up and said to **E**
Ezra 10: 5 Then **E** arose, and made the
Ezra 10: 6 Then **E** rose up from before
Ezra 10:10 Then **E** the priest stood up and
Ezra 10:16 **E** the priest, with certain
Neh 8: 1 they told **E** the scribe to
Neh 8: 2 So **E** the priest brought the
Neh 8: 4 So **E** the scribe stood on a
Neh 8: 5 And **E** opened the book in the
Neh 8: 6 **E** blessed the LORD, the great
Neh 8: 9 **E** the priest and scribe, and
Neh 8:13 were gathered to **E** the scribe
Neh 12: 1 Seraiah, Jeremiah, **E**,
Neh 12:13 of **E**, Meshullam
Neh 12:26 of **E** the priest, the scribe
Neh 12:33 and Azariah, **E**, Meshullam,
Neh 12:36 **E** the scribe went before them

EZRAH (*see* EZRAHITE)
1Ch 4:17 The sons of **E** were Jether

EZRAHITE (*see* EZRAH, IZRAHITE, ZERAH)
1Ki 4:31 than Ethan the **E**, and Heman,

EZRI
1Ch 27:26 **E** the son of Chelub was over

F

FABLES
1Ti 1: 4 nor give heed to **f** and endless
1Ti 4: 7 profane and old wives' **f**, and
2Ti 4: 4 and be turned aside to **f**
Tit 1:14 not giving heed to Jewish **f**
2Pe 1:16 follow cunningly devised **f**

FABRIC
Is 19: 9 weave fine **f** will be ashamed

FACE (*see* FACED, FACES, FACING)
Gen 1: 2 was on the **f** of the deep
Gen 1: 2 over the **f** of the waters
Gen 1:20 the **f** of the firmament of the
Gen 1:29 is on the **f** of all the earth
Gen 2: 6 the whole **f** of the ground
Gen 3:19 In the sweat of your **f** you
Gen 4:14 day from the **f** of the ground
Gen 4:14 I shall be hidden from Your **f**
Gen 6: 1 on the **f** of the earth, and
Gen 6: 7 from the **f** of the earth, both
Gen 7: 3 on the **f** of all the earth
Gen 7: 4 the **f** of the earth all living
Gen 7:23 were on the **f** of the ground
Gen 8: 8 from the **f** of the ground
Gen 8: 9 on the **f** of the whole earth
Gen 11: 4 over the **f** of the whole earth
Gen 11: 8 over the **f** of all the earth
Gen 11: 9 over the **f** of all the earth
Gen 17: 3 Then Abram fell on his **f**, and
Gen 17:17 Then Abraham fell on his **f**
Gen 19: 1 with his **f** toward the ground
Gen 19:13 before the **f** of the LORD, and
Gen 30:40 made the flocks **f** toward the
Gen 32:20 and afterward I will see his **f**
Gen 32:30 For I have seen God **f** to **f**
Gen 33:10 as I have seen your **f** as
Gen 33:10 I had seen the **f** of God, and
Gen 35: 1 the **f** of Esau your brother
Gen 35: 7 from the **f** of his brother
Gen 38:15 because she had covered her **f**
Gen 41:56 over all the **f** of the earth
Gen 43: 3 You shall not see my **f**
Gen 43: 5 us, "You shall not see my **f**
Gen 43:31 Then he washed his **f** and came
Gen 44:23 you shall see my **f** no more
Gen 44:26 we may not see the man's **f**
Gen 46:30 die, since I have seen your **f**
Gen 48:11 had not thought to see your **f**
Gen 48:12 down with his **f** to the earth
Gen 50: 1 Joseph fell on his father's **f**
Gen 50:18 and fell down before his **f**
Ex 2:15 fled from the **f** of Pharaoh
Ex 3: 6 And Moses hid his **f**, for he
Ex 10: 5 cover the **f** of the earth, so
Ex 10:15 the **f** of the whole earth, so
Ex 10:28 yourself and see my **f** no more
Ex 10:28 you see my **f** you shall die
Ex 10:29 I will never see your **f** again
Ex 14:25 us flee from the **f** of Israel
Ex 25:20 and they shall **f** one another
Ex 32:12 them from the **f** of the earth'
Ex 33:11 LORD spoke to Moses **f** to **f**
Ex 33:16 are upon the **f** of the earth
Ex 33:20 You cannot see My **f**
Ex 33:23 but My **f** shall not be seen
Ex 34:29 know that the skin of his **f**
Ex 34:30 the skin of his **f** shone, and
Ex 34:33 them, he put a veil on his **f**
Ex 34:35 of Israel saw the **f** of Moses
Ex 34:35 the skin of Moses' **f** shone
Ex 34:35 put the veil on his **f** again

Lev 17:10 I will set My **f** against that
Lev 20: 3 I will set My **f** against that
Lev 20: 5 set My **f** against that man
Lev 20: 6 I will set My **f** against that
Lev 21:18 who has a marred **f** or any
Lev 26:17 I will set My **f** against you
Num 6:25 make His **f** shine upon you
Num 8: 3 to **f** toward the front of the
Num 12: 3 were on the **f** of the earth
Num 12: 8 I speak with him **f** to **f**
Num 12:14 father had but spit in her **f**
Num 14:14 You, LORD, are seen **f** to **f**
Num 16: 4 heard it, he fell on his **f**
Num 22: 5 they cover the **f** of the earth
Num 22:11 they cover the **f** of the earth
Num 22:31 head and fell flat on his **f**
Num 24: 1 but he set his **f** toward the
Deut 5: 4 talked with you **f** to **f** on
Deut 6:15 you from the **f** of the earth
Deut 7: 6 peoples on the **f** of the earth
Deut 7:10 those who hate Him to their **f**
Deut 7:10 He will repay him to his **f**
Deut 14: 2 who are on the **f** of the earth
Deut 25: 9 from his foot, spit in his **f**
Deut 28: 7 to be defeated before your **f**
Deut 31:17 and I will hide My **f** from them
Deut 31:18 I will surely hide My **f** in
Deut 32:20 I will hide My **f** from them
Deut 34:10 whom the LORD knew **f** to **f**
Josh 5:14 fell on his **f** to the earth
Josh 7: 6 fell to the earth on his **f**
Josh 7:10 Why do you lie thus on your **f**
Judg 6:22 Angel of the LORD **f** to **f**
Ruth 2:10 Then she fell on her **f**, bowed
1Sa 1:18 and her **f** was no longer sad
1Sa 5: 3 fallen on its **f** to the earth
1Sa 5: 4 fallen on its **f** to the ground
1Sa 17:49 he fell on his **f** to the earth
1Sa 20:15 David from the **f** of the earth
1Sa 20:41 fell on his **f** to the ground,
1Sa 24: 8 with his **f** to the earth, and
1Sa 25:23 fell on her **f** before David,
1Sa 25:41 bowed her **f** to the earth, and
1Sa 26:20 before the **f** of the LORD
1Sa 28:14 with his **f** to the ground and
2Sa 2:22 How then could I **f** your
2Sa 3:13 you shall not see my **f** unless
2Sa 3:13 when you come to see my **f**
2Sa 9: 6 to David, he fell on his **f**
2Sa 14: 4 fell on her **f** to the ground
2Sa 14:22 fell to the ground on his **f**
2Sa 14:24 but do not let him see my **f**
2Sa 14:24 but did not see the king's **f**
2Sa 14:28 but did not see the king's **f**
2Sa 14:32 let me see the king's **f**
2Sa 14:33 bowed himself on his **f** to the
2Sa 18: 8 was scattered over the **f** of
2Sa 18:28 his **f** to the earth before the
2Sa 19: 4 But the king covered his **f**
2Sa 24:20 king with his **f** to the ground
1Ki 1:23 king with his **f** to the ground
1Ki 1:31 bowed with her **f** to the earth
1Ki 13:34 it from the **f** of the earth
1Ki 18: 7 him, and fell on his **f**, and
1Ki 18:42 put his **f** between his knees,
1Ki 19:13 wrapped his **f** in his mantle
1Ki 21: 4 his bed, and turned away his **f**
2Ki 4:29 staff on the **f** of the child
2Ki 4:31 staff on the **f** of the child
2Ki 8:15 it over his **f** so that he died
2Ki 12:17 so Hazael set his **f** to go up
2Ki 13:14 to him, and wept over his **f**
2Ki 14: 8 Come, let us **f** one another in
2Ki 20: 2 turned his **f** toward the wall
1Ch 16:11 seek His **f** evermore
1Ch 21:21 with his **f** to the ground
2Ch 6:42 away the **f** of Your anointed
2Ch 7:14 and pray and seek My **f**, and
2Ch 20:18 head with his **f** to the ground
2Ch 25:17 Come, let us **f** one another in
2Ch 30: 9 will not turn His **f** from you
2Ch 35:22 would not turn his **f** from him
Ezra 9: 6 to lift up my **f** to You, my
Neh 2: 2 Why is your **f** sad, since you
Neh 2: 3 Why should my **f** not be sad
Esth 7: 8 mouth, they covered Haman's **f**
Job 1:11 surely curse You to Your **f**
Job 2: 5 surely curse You to Your **f**
Job 4:15 a spirit passed before my **f**
Job 6:28 I would never lie to your **f**

Job 9:27 I will put off my sad **f** and
Job 11:15 lift up your **f** without spot
Job 13:24 Why do You hide Your **f**, and
Job 15:27 his **f** with his fatness, and
Job 16: 8 me and bears witness to my **f**
Job 16:16 My **f** is flushed from weeping,
Job 17: 6 one in whose **f** men spit
Job 17:12 say, in the **f** of darkness
Job 21:31 Who condemns his way to his **f**
Job 22:26 and lift up your **f** to God
Job 23:17 hide deep darkness from my **f**
Job 24:15 and he disguises his **f**
Job 24:18 swift on the **f** of the waters
Job 26: 9 He covers the **f** of His throne
Job 26:10 on the **f** of the waters, at
Job 30:10 not hesitate to spit in my **f**
Job 33:26 He shall see His **f** with joy
Job 34:29 And when He hides His **f**, who
Job 37:12 on the **f** of the whole earth
Job 41:14 can open the doors of his **f**
Ps 5: 8 Your way straight before my **f**
Ps 10:11 He hides His **f**
Ps 13: 1 will You hide Your **f** from me
Ps 17:15 for me, I will see Your **f** in
Ps 22:24 has He hidden His **f** from Him
Ps 24: 6 who seek Him, Who seek Your **f**
Ps 27: 8 Seek My **f**," My heart said to
Ps 27: 8 Your **f**, LORD, I will seek
Ps 27: 9 Do not hide Your **f** from me
Ps 30: 7 You hid Your **f**, and I was
Ps 31:16 Make Your **f** shine upon Your
Ps 34:16 The **f** of the LORD is against
Ps 41:12 set me before Your **f** forever
Ps 44:15 shame of my **f** has covered me
Ps 44:24 Why do You hide Your **f**, And
Ps 51: 9 Hide Your **f** from my sins, And
Ps 67: 1 cause His **f** to shine upon us
Ps 69: 7 Shame has covered my **f**
Ps 69:17 do not hide Your **f** from Your
Ps 80: 3 Cause Your **f** to shine, And we
Ps 80: 7 Cause Your **f** to shine, And we
Ps 80:19 Cause Your **f** to shine, And we
Ps 84: 9 And look upon the **f** of Your
Ps 88:14 do You hide Your **f** from me
Ps 89:14 and truth go before Your **f**
Ps 89:23 down his foes before his **f**
Ps 102: 2 Do not hide Your **f** from me in
Ps 104:15 man, Oil to make his **f** shine
Ps 104:29 You hide Your **f**, they are
Ps 104:30 You renew the **f** of the earth
Ps 105: 4 Seek His **f** evermore
Ps 119:135 Make Your **f** shine upon Your
Ps 132:10 away the **f** of Your Anointed
Ps 143: 7 Do not hide Your **f** from me
Prov 7:13 an impudent **f** she said to him
Prov 7:15 diligently to seek your **f**
Prov 8:27 a circle on the **f** of the deep
Prov 16:15 light of the king's **f** is life
Prov 21:29 A wicked man hardens his **f**
Prov 27:19 As in water **f** reveals **f**,
Eccl 8: 1 wisdom makes his **f** shine, and
Eccl 8: 1 sternness of his **f** is changed
Is 6: 2 with two he covered his **f**
Is 8:17 Who hides His **f** from the
Is 14:21 fill the **f** of the world with
Is 16: 4 from the **f** of the spoiler
Is 23:17 world on the **f** of the earth
Is 27: 6 fill the **f** of the world with
Is 29:22 nor shall his **f** now grow pale
Is 38: 2 turned his **f** toward the wall
Is 50: 6 did not hide My **f** from shame
Is 50: 7 I have set My **f** like a flint
Is 54: 8 My **f** from you for a moment
Is 59: 2 have hidden His **f** from you
Is 64: 7 have hidden Your **f** from us
Is 65: 3 to anger continually to My **f**
Jer 2:27 back to Me, and not their **f**
Jer 8: 2 refuse on the **f** of the earth
Jer 13:26 your skirts over your **f**, that
Jer 16: 4 refuse on the **f** of the earth
Jer 16:17 they are not hidden from My **f**
Jer 18:17 not the **f** in the day of their
Jer 21:10 For I have set My **f** against
Jer 22:25 of those whose **f** you fear
Jer 25:26 are on the **f** of the earth
Jer 28:16 you from the **f** of the earth
Jer 32: 4 speak with him **f** to **f**, and
Jer 32:31 remove it from before My **f**
Jer 32:33 to Me the back, and not the **f**
Jer 33: 5 hidden My **f** from this city

Jer 34: 3 speak with you **f** to **f**, and
Jer 44:11 I will set My **f** against you
Lam 2:19 before the **f** of the Lord
Lam 3:35 before the **f** of the Most High
Lam 4:16 The **f** of the LORD scattered
Ezek 1:10 each had the **f** of a man,
Ezek 1:10 each of the four had the **f** of
Ezek 1:10 each of the four had the **f** of
Ezek 1:10 four had the **f** of an eagle
Ezek 1:28 when I saw it, I fell on my **f**
Ezek 3: 8 I have made your **f** strong
Ezek 3:23 and I fell on my **f**
Ezek 4: 3 Set your **f** against it, and it
Ezek 4: 7 you shall set your **f** toward
Ezek 6: 2 of man, set your **f** toward the
Ezek 7:18 shame will be on every **f**,
Ezek 7:22 I will turn My **f** from them
Ezek 9: 8 and I fell on my **f** and cried
Ezek 10:14 first **f** was the **f** of a cherub
Ezek 10:14 second **f** the **f** of a man
Ezek 10:14 the third the **f** of a lion
Ezek 10:14 the fourth the **f** of an eagle
Ezek 11:13 Then I fell on my **f** and cried
Ezek 12: 6 you shall cover your **f**, so
Ezek 12:12 He shall cover his **f**, so that
Ezek 13:17 man, set your **f** against the
Ezek 14: 8 I will set My **f** against that
Ezek 15: 7 I will set My **f** against them
Ezek 15: 7 when I set My **f** against them
Ezek 20:35 My case with you **f** to **f**
Ezek 20:46 set your **f** toward the south
Ezek 21: 2 set your **f** toward Jerusalem,
Ezek 25: 2 man, set your **f** against the
Ezek 28:21 set your **f** toward Sidon, and
Ezek 29: 2 set your **f** against Pharaoh
Ezek 34: 6 over the whole **f** of the earth
Ezek 35: 2 set your **f** against Mount Seir
Ezek 38: 2 set your **f** against Gog, of
Ezek 38:18 My fury will show in My **f**
Ezek 38:20 all men who are on the **f** of
Ezek 39:23 I hid My **f** from them
Ezek 39:24 and hidden My **f** from them
Ezek 39:29 hide My **f** from them anymore
Ezek 41:14 the eastern **f** of the temple
Ezek 41:19 so that the **f** of a man was
Ezek 41:19 the **f** of a young lion toward
Ezek 43: 3 and I fell on my **f**
Ezek 43:17 its steps **f** toward the east
Ezek 44: 4 and I fell on my **f**
Ezek 46:19 which **f** toward the north
Dan 2:46 Nebuchadnezzar fell on his **f**
Dan 3:19 and the expression on his **f**
Dan 8:17 I was afraid and fell on my **f**
Dan 8:18 sleep with my **f** to the ground
Dan 9: 3 Then I set my **f** toward the
Dan 9: 7 to You, but to us shame of **f**
Dan 9: 8 to us belongs shame of **f**
Dan 9:17 **f** to shine on Your sanctuary
Dan 10: 6 his **f** like the appearance of
Dan 10: 9 I was in a deep sleep on my **f**
Dan 10: 9 with my **f** to the ground
Dan 10:15 me, I turned my **f** toward the
Dan 11:17 He shall also set his **f** to
Dan 11:18 turn his **f** to the coastlands
Dan 11:19 Then he shall turn his **f**
Hos 5: 5 of Israel testifies to his **f**
Hos 5:15 Then they will seek My **f**
Hos 7: 2 they are before My **f**
Hos 7:10 of Israel testifies to his **f**
Joel 2:20 with his **f** toward the eastern
Amos 5: 8 out on the **f** of the earth
Amos 9: 6 out on the **f** of the earth
Amos 9: 8 it from the **f** of the earth
Mic 3: 4 He will even hide His **f** from
Nah 2: 1 has come up before your **f**
Nah 3: 5 lift your skirts over your **f**
Zeph 1: 2 things from the **f** of the land
Zeph 1: 3 man from the **f** of the land
Zech 5: 3 over the **f** of the whole earth
Matt 6:17 your head and wash your **f**,
Matt 11:10 My messenger before Your **f**
Matt 16: 3 to discern the **f** of the sky
Matt 17: 2 His **f** shone like the sun, and
Matt 18:10 the **f** of My Father who is in
Matt 26:39 farther and fell on His **f**, and
Matt 26:67 Then they spat in His **f** and
Mark 1: 2 My messenger before Your **f**
Luke 1:76 **f** of the Lord to prepare His
Luke 2:31 before the **f** of all peoples
Luke 5:12 and he fell on his **f** and

Luke 7:27 My messenger before Your **f**
Luke 9:29 of His **f** was altered, and His
Luke 9:51 set His **f** to go to Jerusalem
Luke 9:52 sent messengers before His **f**
Luke 9:53 because His **f** was set for the
Luke 10: 1 before His **f** into every city
Luke 12:56 can discern the **f** of the sky
Luke 17:16 down on his **f** at His feet
Luke 21:35 on the **f** of the whole earth
Luke 22:64 Him, they struck Him on the **f**
John 11:44 and his **f** was wrapped with a
Acts 2:25 the LORD always before my **f**
Acts 6:15 his **f** as the **f** of an angel
Acts 7:45 **f** of our fathers until the
Acts 17:26 on all the **f** of the earth
Acts 20:25 of God, will see my **f** no more
Acts 20:38 they would see his **f** no more
Acts 25:16 meets the accusers **f** to **f**
Acts 25:16 meets the accusers **f** to **f**
1Co 13:12 dimly, but then **f** to **f**
1Co 14:25 and so, falling down on his **f**
2Co 3: 7 the **f** of Moses because of the
2Co 3:13 his **f** so that the children of
2Co 3:18 But we all, with unveiled **f**
2Co 4: 6 God in the **f** of Jesus Christ
2Co 11:20 if one strikes you on the **f**
Gal 1:22 I was unknown by **f** to the
Gal 2:11 I withstood him to his **f**
Col 2: 1 not seen my **f** in the flesh
1Th 2:17 see your **f** with great desire
1Th 3:10 that we may see your **f** and
Jas 1:23 his natural **f** in a mirror
1Pe 3:12 but the **f** of the LORD is
2Jn 12 speak **f** to **f**, that our joy
3Jn 14 and we shall speak **f** to **f**
Rev 4: 7 creature had a **f** like a man
Rev 6:16 hide us from the **f** of Him who
Rev 10: 1 his **f** was like the sun, and
Rev 20:11 on it, from whose **f** the earth
Rev 22: 4 They shall see His **f**, and His

FACED (*see* FACE)
Ex 37: 9 They **f** one another
1Sa 14: 5 The front of one **f** northward
2Ki 14:11 Amaziah king of Judah **f** one
2Ch 3:13 their feet, and they **f** inward
2Ch 25:21 Amaziah king of Judah **f** one
Ezek 40: 6 to the gateway which **f** east
Ezek 40:17 chambers **f** the pavement
Ezek 40:31 Its archways **f** the outer
Ezek 40:34 Its archways **f** the outer
Ezek 40:37 Its gateposts **f** the outer
Ezek 42: 4 and their doors **f** north
Ezek 47: 1 front of the temple **f** east

FACES (*see* FACE)
Gen 9:23 Their **f** were turned away, and
Gen 42: 6 him with their **f** to the earth
Ex 25:20 the **f** of the cherubim shall
Ex 37: 9 the **f** of the cherubim were
Lev 9:24 shouted and fell on their **f**
Num 14: 5 Aaron fell on their **f** before
Num 16:22 Then they fell on their **f**
Num 16:45 And they fell on their **f**
Num 20: 6 and they fell on their **f**
Josh 15: 2 from the bay that **f** southward
Judg 13:20 fell on their **f** to the ground
Judg 16: 3 top of the hill that **f** Hebron
1Ki 18:39 saw it, they fell on their **f**
1Ch 12: 8 **f** were like the **f** of lions
1Ch 21:16 in sackcloth, fell on their **f**
2Ch 7: 3 they bowed their **f** to the
2Ch 29: 6 have turned their **f** away from
Neh 8: 6 with their **f** to the ground
Job 9:24 He covers the **f** of its judges
Job 40:13 bind their **f** in hidden
Ps 21:12 on Your string toward their **f**
Ps 34: 5 And their **f** were not ashamed
Ps 83:16 Fill their **f** with shame, That
Is 3:15 and grinding the **f** of the poor
Is 13: 8 their **f** will be like flames
Is 25: 8 wipe away tears from all **f**
Is 49:23 you with their **f** to the earth
Is 53: 3 as it were, our **f** from Him
Jer 1: 8 Do not be afraid of their **f**
Jer 1:17 be dismayed before their **f**
Jer 5: 3 made their **f** harder than rock
Jer 7:19 to the shame of their own **f**
Jer 30: 6 labor, and all **f** turned pale
Jer 42:15 set your **f** to enter Egypt
Jer 42:17 **f** to go to Egypt to sojourn
Jer 44:12 **f** to go into the land of
Jer 50: 5 Zion, with their **f** toward it
Jer 51:51 Shame has covered our **f**, for
Ezek 1: 6 Each one had four **f**, and each
Ezek 1: 8 and each of the four had **f**
Ezek 1:10 for the likeness of their **f**
Ezek 1:11 Thus were their **f**
Ezek 1:15 creature with its four **f**
Ezek 3: 8 face strong against their **f**
Ezek 8:16 their **f** toward the east, and
Ezek 9: 2 the upper gate, which **f** north
Ezek 10:14 Each one had four **f**
Ezek 10:21 Each one had four **f** and each
Ezek 10:22 the likeness of their **f** was
Ezek 10:22 the **f** which I had seen by the
Ezek 11: 1 house, which **f** eastward
Ezek 14: 6 turn your **f** away from all
Ezek 20:47 all **f** from the south to the
Ezek 40:13 cubits, as door **f** door
Ezek 40:45 This chamber which **f** south is
Ezek 40:46 The chamber which **f** north is
Ezek 41:18 Each cherub had two **f**,
Ezek 42:15 that **f** toward the east, and
Ezek 43: 1 the gate that **f** toward the
Ezek 43: 4 gate which **f** toward the east
Ezek 44: 1 which **f** toward the east, but
Ezek 46: 1 of the inner court that **f**
Ezek 46:12 the gate that **f** toward the
Ezek 47: 2 the outer gateway that **f** east
Dan 1:10 your **f** looking worse than the
Joel 2: 6 all **f** are drained of color
Nah 2:10 all their **f** are drained of
Hab 1: 9 Their **f** are set like the east
Zech 14: 4 which **f** Jerusalem on the east
Mal 2: 3 and spread refuse on your **f**
Matt 6:16 For they disfigure their **f**
Matt 17: 6 it, they fell on their **f** and
Luke 24: 5 bowed their **f** to the earth,
Rev 7:11 fell on their **f** before the
Rev 9: 7 **f** were like the **f** of men
Rev 11:16 their thrones fell on their **f**

FACING (*see* FACE)
1Ki 22:35 **f** the Syrians, and died at
2Ki 2: 7 stood **f** them at a distance,
2Ch 18:34 **f** the Syrians until evening
Esth 5: 1 **f** the entrance of the house
Jer 1:13 it is **f** away from the north
Ezek 10:11 the direction the head was **f**
Ezek 40:20 was also a gateway **f** north
Ezek 40:22 as the gateway **f** east
Ezek 40:24 there a gateway was **f** south
Ezek 40:27 on the inner court, **f** south
Ezek 40:32 into the inner court **f** east
Ezek 40:44 one **f** south at the side of
Ezek 40:44 the other **f** north at the side
Ezek 41:15 **f** the separating courtyard,
Ezek 42: 2 **F** the length, which was one
Ezek 42: 8 whereas that **f** the temple was
Ezek 42:12 chambers that were **f** south
Mark 4: 1 was on the land **f** the sea

FACT (*see* FACTS)
Gen 42:13 and in **f**, the youngest is with
Gen 48:11 but in **f**, God has also shown
Ex 22:12 But if, in **f**, it is stolen
Num 24:11 greatly honor you, but in **f**
Josh 22:24 But in **f** we have done it for
Judg 16:27 In **f**, there were about three
Judg 21: 8 And, in **f**, no one had come
Judg 21:19 In **f**, there is a yearly feast
Ruth 3: 2 In **f**, he is winnowing barley
1Sa 28: 7 In **f**, there is a woman who is
2Sa 15:20 In **f**, you came only yesterday
2Ki 7: 2 In **f**, you shall see it with
2Ki 7:19 In **f**, you shall see it with
Job 33:29 all these things, twice, in **f**
Is 58: 3 In **f**, in the day of your fast
Ezek 17:18 in **f** gave his hand and still
Ezek 46:21 and in **f**, in every corner of
Luke 11:48 In **f**, you bear witness that
1Co 4: 3 In **f**, I do not even judge
1Co 12:14 For in **f** the body is not one
1Co 15:15 if in **f** the dead do not rise
1Th 3: 4 For, in **f**, we told you before

FACTION (*see* FACTIONS)
Ps 106:17 And covered the **f** of Abiram

FACTIONS (*see* FACTION)
1Co 11:19 must also be **f** among you,

FACTS (*see* FACT)
Dan 7: 1 the dream, telling the main **f**

FADE (*see* FADED, FADES, FADING)
2Sa 22:46 The foreigners **f** away, and
Ps 18:45 The foreigners **f** away, And
Is 64: 6 we all **f** as a leaf, and our
Jer 8:13 fig tree, and the leaf shall **f**
Jas 1:11 will **f** away in his pursuits
1Pe 1: 4 and that does not **f** away,
1Pe 5: 4 of glory that does not **f** away

FADED (*see* FADE)
Lev 13:21 than the skin, but has **f**,
Lev 13:26 than the skin, but has **f**,
Lev 13:28 spread on the skin, but has **f**
Lev 13:56 plague has **f** after washing it

FADES (*see* FADE)
Job 14: 2 forth like a flower and **f** away
Is 1:30 as a terebinth whose leaf **f**
Is 24: 4 **f** away, the world languishes
Is 24: 4 world languishes and **f** away
Is 40: 7 grass withers, the flower **f**
Is 40: 8 grass withers, the flower **f**

FADING (*see* FADE)
Is 28: 1 whose glorious beauty is a **f**
Is 28: 4 the glorious beauty is a **f**

FAIL (*see* FAILED, FAILING, FAILS, FAILURE)
Deut 28:32 **f** with longing for them all
Josh 3:10 that He will without **f** drive
1Sa 17:32 man's heart **f** because of him
1Sa 20: 5 I should not **f** to sit with
1Sa 30: 8 them and without **f** recover all
2Sa 3:29 let there never **f** to be in
1Ki 8:25 You shall not **f** to have a
1Ki 9: 5 You shall not **f** to have a
2Ch 6:16 You shall not **f** to have a
2Ch 7:18 You shall never **f** to have a
Ezra 4:22 that you do not **f** to do this
Ezra 6: 9 them day by day without **f**
Esth 9:27 that without **f** they should
Esth 9:28 **f** to be observed among the
Job 11:20 the eyes of the wicked will **f**
Job 17: 5 eyes of his children will **f**
Job 31:16 the eyes of the widow to **f**
Ps 69: 3 My eyes **f** while I wait for my
Ps 73:26 My flesh and my heart **f**
Ps 89:33 allow My faithfulness to **f**
Ps 119:82 My eyes **f** from seeking Your
Ps 119:123 My eyes **f** from seeking Your
Prov 22: 8 the rod of his anger will **f**
Is 19: 3 of Egypt will **f** in its midst
Is 19: 5 waters will **f** from the sea
Is 21:16 all the glory of Kedar will **f**
Is 32: 6 the drink of the thirsty to **f**
Is 32:10 for the vintage will **f**, the
Is 34:16 not one of these shall **f**
Is 38:14 my eyes **f** from looking upward
Is 41:17 and their tongues **f** for thirst
Is 42: 4 He will not **f** nor be
Is 51:14 that his bread should not **f**
Is 57:16 the spirit would **f** before Me
Is 58:11 water, whose waters do not **f**
Jer 15:18 stream, as waters that **f**
Jer 48:33 to **f** from the winepresses
Lam 1:14 He made my strength **f**
Lam 2:11 My eyes **f** with tears, my
Lam 3:22 because His compassions **f** not
Ezek 47:12 and their fruit will not **f**
Hos 9: 2 the new wine shall **f** in her
Amos 8: 4 make the poor of the land **f**
Hab 3:17 the labor of the olive may **f**
Mal 3:11 nor shall the vine **f** to bear
Luke 12:33 the heavens that does not **f**
Luke 16: 9 mammon, that when you **f**, they
Luke 16:17 one tittle of the law to **f**
Luke 22:32 that your faith should not **f**
1Co 13: 8 are prophecies, they will **f**
Heb 1:12 and Your years will not **f**
Heb 11:32 For the time would **f** me to

FAILED (*see* FAIL)
Gen 42:28 Then their hearts **f** them
Gen 47:15 So when the money **f** in the
Gen 47:15 For the money has **f**
Josh 3:16 the Arabah, the Salt Sea, **f**
Josh 21:45 Not a word **f** of any good
Josh 23:14 has **f** of all the good things

Josh 23:14 and not one word of them has **f**
1Ki 8:56 There has not **f** one word of
Job 19:14 my relatives have **f**, and my
Ps 77: 8 Has His promise **f** forevermore
Ps 142: 4 Refuge has **f** me
Jer 14: 6 their eyes **f** because there
Jer 51:30 their might has **f**, they
Lam 4:17 Still our eyes **f** us, watching

FAILING (*see* FAIL)
Deut 28:65 **f** eyes, and anguish of soul
Neh 4:10 strength of the laborers is **f**
Luke 21:26 men's hearts **f** them from fear

FAILS (*see* FAIL)
Ps 31:10 My strength **f** because of my
Ps 38:10 heart pants, my strength **f** me
Ps 40:12 Therefore my heart **f** me
Ps 71: 9 forsake me when my strength **f**
Ps 143: 7 My spirit **f**
Eccl 12: 5 is a burden, and desire **f**
Is 15: 6 the grass **f**, there is nothing
Is 24: 7 The new wine **f**, the vine
Is 44:12 is hungry, and his strength **f**
Is 59:15 So truth **f**, and he who departs
Ezek 12:22 prolonged, and every vision **f**
Joel 1:10 wine is dried up, the oil **f**
Zeph 3: 5 He never **f**, But the unjust
1Co 13: 8 Love never **f**

FAILURE (*see* FAIL)
Job 21:10 Their bull breeds without **f**
Rom 11:12 and their **f** riches for the
1Co 6: 7 it is already an utter **f** for

FAINT (*see* FAINTED, FAINTHEARTED, FAINTNESS, FAINTS)
Deut 20: 3 do not let your heart **f**, do
Deut 20: 8 his brethren **f** like his heart
1Sa 14:28 And the people were **f**
1Sa 14:31 So the people were very **f**
2Sa 16: 2 **f** in the wilderness to drink
2Sa 21:15 and David grew **f**
Prov 24:10 If you **f** in the day of
Is 29: 8 he awakes, and indeed he is **f**
Is 40:30 Even the youths shall **f** and be
Is 40:31 they shall walk and not **f**
Is 44:12 he drinks no water and is **f**
Jer 8:18 my heart is **f** in me
Jer 51:46 And lest your heart **f**, and you
Lam 1:13 me desolate and **f** all the day
Lam 1:22 are many, and my heart is **f**
Lam 2:11 the infants **f** in the streets
Lam 2:19 who **f** from hunger at the head
Lam 5:17 of this our heart is **f**
Ezek 21: 7 feeble, every spirit will **f**
Amos 8:13 young men shall **f** from thirst
Jon 4: 8 head, so that he grew **f**
Matt 15:32 lest they **f** on the way
Mark 8: 3 they will **f** on the way

FAINTED (*see* FAINT)
Ps 107: 5 thirsty, Their soul **f** in them
Is 51:20 Your sons have **f**, they lie at
Jer 45: 3 I **f** in my sighing, and I find
Dan 8:27 And I, Daniel, **f** and was sick
Jon 2: 7 When my soul **f** within me, I

FAINTHEARTED (*see* FAINT)
Deut 20: 8 is there who is fearful and **f**
Josh 2: 9 the land are **f** because of you
Josh 2:24 country are **f** because of us
Is 7: 4 do not fear or be **f** for these
Jer 49:23 They are **f**
1Th 5:14 who are unruly, comfort the **f**

FAINTNESS (*see* FAINT)
Lev 26:36 I will send **f** into their

FAINTS (*see* FAINT)
Ps 84: 2 even **f** For the courts of the
Ps 119:81 My soul **f** for Your salvation,
Is 1: 5 is sick, and the whole heart **f**
Is 40:28 earth, neither **f** nor is weary

FAIR (*see* FAIRER, FAIREST, FAIR-MINDED)
Song 1:15 Behold, you are **f**, my love
Song 1:15 Behold, you are **f**
Song 2:10 love, my **f** one, and come away
Song 2:13 love, my **f** one, and come away
Song 4: 1 Behold, you are **f**, my love
Song 4: 1 Behold, you are **f**
Song 4: 7 You are all **f**, my love, and
Song 4:10 How **f** is your love, my sister
Song 6:10 **f** as the moon, clear as the
Song 7: 6 How **f** and how pleasant you are
Jer 4:30 vain you will make yourself **f**
Ezek 18:25 The way of the Lord is not **f**
Ezek 18:25 is it not My way which is **f**
Ezek 18:25 and your ways which are not **f**
Ezek 18:29 The way of the Lord is not **f**
Ezek 18:29 is it not My ways which are **f**
Ezek 18:29 and your ways which are not **f**
Ezek 33:17 The way of the LORD is not **f**
Ezek 33:17 is their way which is not **f**
Ezek 33:20 The way of the LORD is not **f**
Hos 10:11 but I harnessed her **f** neck
Amos 8:13 In that day the **f** virgins
Matt 16: 2 say, 'It will be **f** weather
Acts 27: 8 to a place called **F** Havens
Col 4: 1 servants what is just and **f**

FAIRER (*see* FAIR)
Ps 45: 2 You are **f** than the sons of

FAIREST (*see* FAIR)
Song 1: 8 O **f** among women, follow in
Song 5: 9 beloved, O **f** among women
Song 6: 1 gone, O **f** among women

FAIR-MINDED (*see* FAIR)
Acts 17:11 These were more **f** than those

FAITH (*see* FAITHFUL, FAITHLESS)
Deut 32:20 children in whom is no **f**
Hab 2: 4 the just shall live by his **f**
Matt 6:30 clothe you, O you of little **f**
Matt 8:10 I have not found such great **f**
Matt 8:26 fearful, O you of little **f**
Matt 9: 2 And Jesus, seeing their **f**,
Matt 9:22 your **f** has made you well
Matt 9:29 to your **f** let it be to you
Matt 14:31 O you of little **f**, why did
Matt 15:28 O woman, great is your **f**
Matt 16: 8 O you of little **f**, why do you
Matt 17:20 if you have **f** as a mustard
Matt 21:21 I say to you, if you have **f**
Matt 23:23 justice and mercy and **f**
Mark 2: 5 When Jesus saw their **f**, He
Mark 4:40 How is it that you have no **f**
Mark 5:34 your **f** has made you well
Mark 10:52 your **f** has made you well
Mark 11:22 said to them, "Have **f** in God
Luke 5:20 So when He saw their **f**, He
Luke 7: 9 I have not found such great **f**
Luke 7:50 woman, "Your **f** has saved you
Luke 8:25 Where is your **f**
Luke 8:48 your **f** has made you well
Luke 12:28 clothe you, O you of little **f**
Luke 17: 5 Increase our **f**
Luke 17: 6 If you have **f** as a mustard
Luke 17:19 Your **f** has made you well
Luke 18: 8 He really find **f** on the earth
Luke 18:42 your **f** has saved you
Luke 22:32 that your **f** should not fail
Acts 3:16 through **f** in His name, has
Acts 3:16 the **f** which comes through Him
Acts 6: 5 Stephen, a man full of **f** and
Acts 6: 7 were obedient to the **f**
Acts 6: 8 And Stephen, full of **f** and
Acts 11:24 of the Holy Spirit and of **f**
Acts 13: 8 the proconsul away from the **f**
Acts 14: 9 that he had **f** to be healed
Acts 14:22 them to continue in the **f**
Acts 14:27 the door of **f** to the Gentiles
Acts 15: 9 purifying their hearts by **f**
Acts 16: 5 were strengthened in the **f**
Acts 20:21 and **f** toward our Lord Jesus
Acts 24:24 concerning the **f** in Christ
Acts 26:18 who are sanctified by **f** in Me
Rom 1: 5 for obedience to the **f** among
Rom 1: 8 all, that your **f** is spoken of
Rom 1:12 by the mutual **f** both of you
Rom 1:17 is revealed from **f** to **f**
Rom 1:17 The just shall live by **f**
Rom 3:22 **f** in Jesus Christ to all and
Rom 3:25 by His blood, through **f**, to
Rom 3:26 of the one who has **f** in Jesus
Rom 3:27 No, but by the law of **f**
Rom 3:28 that a man is justified by **f**
Rom 3:30 justify the circumcised by **f**
Rom 3:30 the uncircumcised through **f**
Rom 3:31 make void the law through **f**
Rom 4: 5 his **f** is accounted for
Rom 4: 9 For we say that **f** was
Rom 4:11 **f** which he had while still
Rom 4:12 **f** which our father Abraham
Rom 4:13 the righteousness of **f**
Rom 4:14 **f** is made void and the promise
Rom 4:16 Therefore it is of **f** that it
Rom 4:16 who are of the **f** of Abraham
Rom 4:19 And not being weak in **f**, he
Rom 4:20 but was strengthened in **f**
Rom 5: 1 having been justified by **f**
Rom 5: 2 **f** into this grace in which we
Rom 9:30 even the righteousness of **f**
Rom 9:32 they did not seek it by **f**
Rom 10: 6 of **f** speaks in this way, "Do
Rom 10: 8 the word of **f** which we preach
Rom 10:17 So then **f** comes by hearing,
Rom 11:20 broken off, and you stand by **f**
Rom 12: 3 to each one a measure of **f**
Rom 12: 6 in proportion to our **f**
Rom 14: 1 one who is weak in the **f**, but
Rom 14:22 Do you have **f**
Rom 14:23 he does not eat from **f**
Rom 14:23 whatever is not from **f** is sin
Rom 16:26 God, for obedience to the **f**
1Co 2: 5 that your **f** should not be in
1Co 12: 9 to another **f** by the same
1Co 13: 2 and though I have all **f**, so
1Co 13:13 And now abide **f**, hope, love,
1Co 15:14 vain and your **f** is also vain
1Co 15:17 not risen, your **f** is futile
1Co 16:13 Watch, stand fast in the **f**
2Co 1:24 we have dominion over your **f**
2Co 1:24 for by **f** you stand
2Co 4:13 we have the same spirit of **f**
2Co 5: 7 For we walk by **f**, not by
2Co 8: 7 in **f**, in speech, in knowledge
2Co 10:15 that as your **f** is increased
2Co 13: 5 to whether you are in the **f**
Gal 1:23 us now preaches the **f** which
Gal 2:16 law but by **f** in Jesus Christ
Gal 2:16 be justified by **f** in Christ
Gal 2:20 I live by **f** in the Son of God
Gal 3: 2 law, or by the hearing of **f**
Gal 3: 5 law, or by the hearing of **f**
Gal 3: 7 are of **f** are sons of Abraham
Gal 3: 8 justify the nations by **f**,
Gal 3: 9 So then those who are of **f**
Gal 3:11 The just shall live by **f**
Gal 3:12 Yet the law is not of **f**, but
Gal 3:14 of the Spirit through **f**
Gal 3:22 sin, that the promise by **f** in
Gal 3:23 But before **f** came, we were
Gal 3:23 kept for the **f** which would
Gal 3:24 we might be justified by **f**
Gal 3:25 But after **f** has come, we are
Gal 3:26 God through **f** in Christ Jesus
Gal 5: 5 hope of righteousness by **f**
Gal 5: 6 but **f** working through love
Gal 6:10 who are of the household of **f**
Eph 1:15 of your **f** in the Lord Jesus
Eph 2: 8 you have been saved through **f**
Eph 3:12 confidence through **f** in Him
Eph 3:17 in your hearts through **f**
Eph 4: 5 one Lord, one **f**, one baptism
Eph 4:13 come to the unity of the **f**
Eph 6:16 taking the shield of **f** with
Eph 6:23 the brethren, and love with **f**
Phil 1:25 for your progress and joy of **f**
Phil 1:27 for the **f** of the gospel,
Phil 2:17 and service of your **f**, I am
Phil 3: 9 which is through **f** in Christ
Phil 3: 9 which is from God by **f**
Col 1: 4 of your **f** in Christ Jesus
Col 1:23 indeed you continue in the **f**
Col 2: 5 of your **f** in Christ
Col 2: 7 Him and established in the **f**
Col 2:12 **f** in the working of God, who
1Th 1: 3 ceasing your work of **f**, labor
1Th 1: 8 Your **f** toward God has gone
1Th 3: 2 you concerning your **f**,
1Th 3: 5 it, I sent to know your **f**
1Th 3: 6 us good news of your **f** and
1Th 3: 7 concerning you by your **f**
1Th 3:10 what is lacking in your **f**
1Th 5: 8 on the breastplate of **f** and
2Th 1: 3 fitting, because your **f** grows
2Th 1: 4 **f** in all your persecutions and
2Th 1:11 and the work of **f** with power
2Th 3: 2 for not all have **f**
1Ti 1: 2 Timothy, my true son in the **f**
1Ti 1: 4 edification which is in **f**
1Ti 1: 5 conscience, and from sincere **f**
1Ti 1:14 exceedingly abundant, with **f**

1Ti 1:19 having f and a good conscience
1Ti 1:19 concerning the f have
1Ti 2: 7 teacher of the Gentiles in f
1Ti 2:15 if they continue in f, love,
1Ti 3: 9 the f with a pure conscience
1Ti 3:13 great boldness in the f which
1Ti 4: 1 some will depart from the f
1Ti 4: 6 nourished in the words of f
1Ti 4:12 in love, in spirit, in f
1Ti 5: 8 he has denied the f and is
1Ti 5:12 have cast off their first f
1Ti 6:10 the f in their greediness
1Ti 6:11 righteousness, godliness, f
1Ti 6:12 Fight the good fight of f
1Ti 6:21 have strayed concerning the f
2Ti 1: 5 the genuine f that is in you
2Ti 1:13 you have heard from me, in f
2Ti 2:18 they overthrow the f of some
2Ti 2:22 but pursue righteousness, f
2Ti 3: 8 disapproved concerning the f
2Ti 3:10 manner of life, purpose, f
2Ti 3:15 f which is in Christ Jesus
2Ti 4: 7 the race, I have kept the f
Tit 1: 1 to the f of God's elect and
Tit 1: 4 my true son in our common f
Tit 1:13 they may be sound in the f
Tit 2: 2 temperate, sound in f, in
Tit 3:15 those who love us in the f
Phm 5 f which you have toward the
Phm 6 that the sharing of your f
Heb 4: 2 not being mixed with f in
Heb 6: 1 works and of f toward God,
Heb 6:12 imitate those who through f
Heb 10:22 heart in full assurance of f
Heb 10:38 Now the just shall live by f
Heb 11: 1 Now f is the substance of
Heb 11: 3 By f we understand that the
Heb 11: 4 By f Abel offered to God a
Heb 11: 5 By f Enoch was translated so
Heb 11: 6 But without f it is
Heb 11: 7 By f Noah, being divinely
Heb 11: 7 which is according to f
Heb 11: 8 By f Abraham obeyed when he
Heb 11: 9 By f he sojourned in the land
Heb 11:11 By f Sarah herself also
Heb 11:13 These all died in f, not
Heb 11:17 By f Abraham, when he was
Heb 11:20 By f Isaac blessed Jacob and
Heb 11:21 By f Jacob, when he was dying
Heb 11:22 By f Joseph, when he was
Heb 11:23 By f Moses, when he was born,
Heb 11:24 By f Moses, when he became of
Heb 11:27 By f he forsook Egypt, not
Heb 11:28 By f he kept the Passover and
Heb 11:29 By f they passed through the
Heb 11:30 By f the walls of Jericho
Heb 11:31 By f the harlot Rahab did not
Heb 11:33 who through f subdued
Heb 11:39 a good testimony through f
Heb 12: 2 author and finisher of our f
Heb 13: 7 whose f follow, considering
Jas 1: 3 of your f produces patience
Jas 1: 6 But let him ask in f, with no
Jas 2: 1 do not hold the f of our Lord
Jas 2: 5 of this world to be rich in f
Jas 2:14 if someone says he has f but
Jas 2:14 Can f save him
Jas 2:17 Thus also f by itself, if it
Jas 2:18 You have f, and I have works
Jas 2:18 Show me your f without your
Jas 2:18 show you my f by my works
Jas 2:20 that f without works is dead
Jas 2:22 Do you see that f was working
Jas 2:22 by works f was made perfect
Jas 2:24 by works, and not by f only
Jas 2:26 so f without works is dead
Jas 5:15 the prayer of f will save the
1Pe 1: 5 f for salvation ready to be
1Pe 1: 7 the genuineness of your f
1Pe 1: 9 receiving the end of your f
1Pe 1:21 Him glory, so that your f
1Pe 5: 9 him, steadfast in the f,
2Pe 1: 1 precious f with us by the
2Pe 1: 5 add to your f virtue, to
1Jn 5: 4 has overcome the world our f
Jude 3 the f which was once for all
Jude 20 up on your most holy f,
Rev 2:13 did not deny My f even in the
Rev 2:19 your works, love, service, f
Rev 13:10 and the f of the saints
Rev 14:12 of God and the f of Jesus

FAITHFUL (*see* FAITH, FAITHFULLY, FAITHFULNESS, UNFAITHFUL)
Num 12: 7 he is f in all My house
Deut 7: 9 the f God who keeps covenant
1Sa 2:35 a f priest who shall do
1Sa 22:14 servants is so f as David
2Sa 20:19 the peaceable and f in Israel
2Ch 31:15 his f assistants in the
Neh 7: 2 citadel, for he was a f man
Neh 9: 8 found his heart f before You
Neh 13:13 for they were considered f
Ps 12: 1 For the f disappear from
Ps 31:23 For the LORD preserves the f
Ps 78: 8 whose spirit was not f to God
Ps 78:37 Him, Nor were they f in His
Ps 89:37 Even like the f witness in
Ps 101: 6 shall be on the f of the land
Ps 119:86 All Your commandments are f
Ps 119:138 Are righteous and very f
Prov 11:13 but he who is of a f spirit
Prov 13:17 but a f ambassador brings
Prov 14: 5 A f witness does not lie, but
Prov 20: 6 but who can find a f man
Prov 25:13 in time of harvest is a f
Prov 27: 6 F are the wounds of a friend,
Prov 28:20 A f man will abound with
Is 1:21 How the f city has become a
Is 1:26 of righteousness, the f city
Is 8: 2 Myself f witnesses to record
Is 49: 7 because of the LORD who is f
Jer 42: 5 f witness between us, if we
Dan 6: 4 or fault, because he was f
Hos 11:12 with the Holy One who is f
Mic 7: 2 The f man has perished from
Matt 24:45 Who then is a f and wise
Matt 25:21 Well done, good and f servant
Matt 25:21 you were f over a few things,
Matt 25:23 Well done, good and f servant
Matt 25:23 you have been f over a few
Luke 12:42 Who then is that f and wise
Luke 16:10 He who is f in what is least
Luke 16:10 is least is f also in much
Luke 16:11 if you have not been f in the
Luke 16:12 if you have not been f in
Luke 19:17 you were f in a very little
Acts 16:15 judged me to be f to the Lord
1Co 1: 9 God is f, by whom you were
1Co 4: 2 stewards that one be found f
1Co 4:17 f son in the Lord, who will
1Co 10:13 but God is f, who will not
2Co 1:18 But as God is f, our word to
Eph 1: 1 Ephesus, and f in Christ Jesus
Eph 6:21 f minister in the Lord, will
Col 1: 2 f brethren in Christ who are
Col 1: 7 who is a f minister of Christ
Col 4: 7 a f minister, and a fellow
Col 4: 9 with Onesimus, a f and beloved
1Th 5:24 He who calls you is f, who
2Th 3: 3 But the Lord is f, who will
1Ti 1:12 me, because He counted me f
1Ti 1:15 This is a f saying and worthy
1Ti 3: 1 This is a f saying
1Ti 3:11 temperate, f in all things
1Ti 4: 9 This is a f saying and worthy
2Ti 2: 2 commit these to f men who
2Ti 2:11 This is a f saying
2Ti 2:13 are faithless, He remains f
Tit 1: 6 having f children not accused
Tit 1: 9 holding fast the f word as he
Tit 3: 8 This is a f saying, and these
Heb 2:17 and f High Priest in things
Heb 3: 2 who was f to Him who
Heb 3: 2 also was f in all His house
Heb 3: 5 Moses indeed was f in all His
Heb 10:23 for He who promised is f
Heb 11:11 judged Him f who had promised
1Pe 4:19 doing good, as to a f Creator
1Pe 5:12 our f brother as I consider
1Jn 1: 9 we confess our sins, He is f
Rev 1: 5 the f witness, the firstborn
Rev 2:10 Be f until death, and I will
Rev 2:13 which Antipas was My f martyr
Rev 3:14 things says the Amen, the F
Rev 17:14 Him are called, chosen, and f
Rev 19:11 who sat on him was called F
Rev 21: 5 for these words are true and f
Rev 22: 6 These words are f and true

FAITHFULLY (*see* FAITHFUL)
2Ki 12:15 to workmen, for they dealt f
2Ki 22: 7 hand, because they deal f
2Ch 19: 9 in the fear of the LORD, f
2Ch 31:12 Then they f brought in the
2Ch 34:12 And the men did the work f
Neh 9:33 for You have dealt f, but we
Jer 23:28 word, let him speak My word f
Ezek 18: 9 and kept My judgments f
Joel 2:23 given you the former rain f
3Jn 5 you do f whatever you do for

FAITHFULNESS (*see* FAITHFUL)
1Sa 26:23 his righteousness and his f
2Ch 31:18 for in their f they
2Ch 32: 1 After these deeds of f,
Ps 5: 9 there is no f in their mouth
Ps 36: 5 Your f reaches to the clouds
Ps 37: 3 in the land, and feed on His f
Ps 40:10 I have declared Your f and
Ps 71:22 And Your f, O my God
Ps 88:11 Or Your f in the place of
Ps 89: 1 Your f to all generations
Ps 89: 2 Your f You shall establish in
Ps 89: 5 Your f also in the
Ps 89: 8 Your f also surrounds You
Ps 89:24 But My f and My mercy shall be
Ps 89:33 him, Nor allow My f to fail
Ps 92: 2 And Your f every night,
Ps 98: 3 His f to the house of Israel
Ps 119:75 that in f You have afflicted
Ps 119:90 Your f endures to all
Ps 143: 1 In Your f answer me, And in
Is 11: 5 and f the belt of His waist
Is 25: 1 Your counsels of old are f
Lam 3:23 great is Your f
Hos 2:20 I will betroth you to Me in f
Hos 6: 4 For your f is like a morning
Rom 3: 3 the f of God without effect
Gal 5:22 kindness, goodness, f,

FAITHLESS (*see* FAITH)
Prov 22:12 overthrows the words of the f
Matt 17:17 O f and perverse generation,
Mark 9:19 O f generation, how long
Luke 9:41 O f and perverse generation,
2Ti 2:13 If we are f, He remains

FALCON (*see* FALCON'S)
Lev 11:14 kite, and the f after its kind
Deut 14:13 the red kite, the f, and the

FALCON'S (*see* FALCON)
Job 28: 7 nor has the f eye seen it

FALL (*see* FALLEN, FALLING, FALLS, FELL)
Gen 2:21 a deep sleep to f on Adam
Gen 43:18 and f upon us, to take us as
Gen 49:17 its rider shall f backward
Ex 5: 3 God, lest He f upon us with
Ex 15:16 Fear and dread will f on them
Lev 19:29 lest the land f into harlotry
Lev 26: 7 they shall f by the sword
Lev 26: 8 your enemies shall f by the
Lev 26:36 and they shall f when no one
Num 14: 3 this land to f by the sword
Num 14:29 Me shall f in this wilderness
Num 14:32 shall f in this wilderness
Num 14:43 and you shall f by the sword
Num 34: 2 f to you as an inheritance
Deut 22: 4 his ox f down along the road
Josh 6: 5 of the city will f down flat
Judg 15:18 and f into the hand of the
Judg 18:25 us, lest angry men f upon you
Ruth 2:16 bundles f purposely for her
1Sa 3:19 of his words f to the ground
1Sa 14:45 head shall f to the ground
1Sa 18:25 David f by the hand of the
1Sa 21:13 let his saliva f down on his
1Sa 26:20 do not let my blood f to the
2Sa 14:11 son shall f to the ground
2Sa 17:12 we will f on him as the dew
2Sa 24:14 Please let us f into the hand
2Sa 24:14 but do not let me f into the
1Ki 1:52 of him shall f to the earth
1Ki 22:20 up, that he may f at Ramoth
2Ki 6: 6 Where did it f
2Ki 10:10 f to the earth of the word of
2Ki 14:10 with trouble so that you f
2Ki 19: 7 I will cause him to f by the
1Ch 21:13 Please let me f into the hand
1Ch 21:13 but do not let me f into the
2Ch 18:19 up, that he may f at Ramoth

2Ch 25: 8 make you f before the enemy
2Ch 25:19 trouble, that you should f
Esth 6:13 whom you have begun to f, is
Esth 6:13 but will surely f before him
Job 13:11 the dread of Him f upon you
Job 31:22 Then let my arm f from my
Ps 5:10 Let them f by their own
Ps 9: 3 turn back, They shall f and
Ps 10:10 may f by his strength
Ps 35: 8 very destruction let him f
Ps 37:24 Though he f, he shall not be
Ps 38:17 For I am ready to f, And my
Ps 45: 5 The peoples f under You
Ps 63:10 They shall f by the sword
Ps 72:11 kings shall f down before Him
Ps 78:28 He let them f in the midst of
Ps 82: 7 f like one of the princes
Ps 91: 7 A thousand may f at your side
Ps 101: 3 the work of those who f away
Ps 118:13 me violently, that I might f
Ps 139:11 the darkness shall f on me
Ps 140:10 Let burning coals f upon them
Ps 141:10 Let the wicked f into their
Ps 145:14 The LORD upholds all who f
Prov 4:16 unless they make someone f
Prov 10: 8 but a prating fool will f
Prov 10:10 but a prating fool will f
Prov 11: 5 but the wicked will f by his
Prov 11:14 is no counsel, the people f
Prov 11:28 trusts in his riches will f
Prov 16:18 a haughty spirit before a f
Prov 22:14 of the LORD will f there
Prov 24:16 man may f seven times and rise
Prov 24:16 wicked shall f by calamity
Prov 26:27 digs a pit will f into it
Prov 28:10 he himself will f into his
Prov 28:14 heart will f into calamity
Prov 28:18 in his ways will f at once
Prov 29:16 righteous will see their f
Eccl 4:10 For if they f, one will lift
Eccl 10: 8 who digs a pit will f into it
Is 3:25 Your men shall f by the sword
Is 8:15 they shall f and be broken, be
Is 10: 4 they shall f among the slain
Is 10:34 Lebanon will f by the Mighty
Is 13:15 captured will f by the sword
Is 22:25 removed and be cut down and f
Is 24:18 the fear shall f into the pit
Is 24:20 heavy upon it, and it will f
Is 28:13 f backward, and be broken and
Is 30:13 you like a breach ready to f
Is 30:25 slaughter, when the towers f
Is 31: 3 both he who helps will f
Is 31: 3 he who is helped will f down
Is 31: 8 Then Assyria shall f by a
Is 34: 4 all their host shall f down
Is 37: 7 I will cause him to f by the
Is 40:30 the young men shall utterly f
Is 44:19 Shall I f down before a block
Is 47:11 And trouble shall f upon you
Is 54:15 you shall f for your sake
Is 60:14 who despised you shall f
Jer 3:12 cause My anger to f on you
Jer 6:15 shall f among those who f
Jer 6:21 sons together shall f on them
Jer 8: 4 Will they f and not rise
Jer 8:12 shall f among those who f
Jer 9:22 the carcasses of men shall f
Jer 15: 8 terror to f on them suddenly
Jer 19: 7 I will cause them to f by the
Jer 20: 4 they shall f by the sword of
Jer 23:12 be driven on and f in them
Jer 23:19 It will f violently on the
Jer 25:27 F and rise no more, because of
Jer 25:34 you shall f like a precious
Jer 30:23 it will f violently on the
Jer 39:18 you shall not f by the sword
Jer 44:12 and f in the land of Egypt
Jer 46: 6 f toward the north, by the
Jer 46:16 He made many f
Jer 48:44 the fear shall f into the pit
Jer 49:21 at the noise of their f
Jer 49:26 men shall f in her streets
Jer 50:30 men shall f in the streets
Jer 50:32 most proud shall stumble and f
Jer 51: 4 shall f in the land of the
Jer 51:44 the wall of Babylon shall f
Jer 51:47 slain shall f in her midst
Jer 51:49 the slain of Israel to f, so
Jer 51:49 of all the earth shall f
Ezek 5:12 and one-third shall f by the
Ezek 6: 7 slain shall f in your midst
Ezek 6:11 For they shall f by the sword
Ezek 6:12 is near shall f by the sword
Ezek 11:10 You shall f by the sword
Ezek 13:11 mortar, that it will f
Ezek 13:11 O great hailstones, shall f
Ezek 13:14 it will f, and you shall be
Ezek 17:21 troops shall f by the sword
Ezek 23:25 remnant shall f by the sword
Ezek 24:21 behind shall f by the sword
Ezek 25:13 Dedan shall f by the sword
Ezek 26:11 pillars will f to the ground
Ezek 26:15 shake at the sound of your f
Ezek 26:18 tremble on the day of your f
Ezek 27:27 will f into the midst of the
Ezek 27:34 company will f in your midst
Ezek 29: 5 you shall f on the open field
Ezek 30: 4 when the slain f in Egypt
Ezek 30: 5 shall f with them by the
Ezek 30: 6 who uphold Egypt shall f, and
Ezek 30: 6 her shall f by the sword,"
Ezek 30:17 Beseth shall f by the sword
Ezek 30:22 the sword f out of his hand
Ezek 30:25 arms of Pharaoh shall f down
Ezek 31:16 shake at the sound of its f
Ezek 32:10 life, in the day of your f
Ezek 32:12 cause your multitude to f
Ezek 32:20 They shall f in the midst of
Ezek 33:12 he shall not f because of it
Ezek 33:27 ruins shall f by the sword
Ezek 35: 8 slain by the sword shall f
Ezek 38:20 the steep places shall f
Ezek 38:20 wall shall f to the ground
Ezek 39: 3 cause the arrows to f out of
Ezek 39: 4 You shall f upon the
Ezek 39: 5 You shall f on the open field
Ezek 44:12 of Israel to f into iniquity
Ezek 47:14 this land shall f to you as
Dan 3: 5 of music, you shall f down
Dan 3: 6 and whoever does not f down
Dan 3:10 kinds of music, shall f down
Dan 3:11 and whoever does not f down
Dan 3:15 you f down and worship the
Dan 11:14 the vision, but they shall f
Dan 11:19 but he shall stumble and f
Dan 11:26 and many shall f down slain
Dan 11:33 days they shall f by sword
Dan 11:34 Now when they f, they shall
Dan 11:35 of understanding shall f, to
Hos 7:16 their princes shall f by the
Hos 10: 8 And to the hills, "F on us
Hos 13:16 They shall f by the sword,
Amos 3: 5 Will a bird f into a snare on
Amos 3:14 be cut off and f to the ground
Amos 7:17 shall f by the sword
Amos 8:14 They shall f and never rise
Amos 9: 9 grain shall f to the ground
Mic 7: 8 when I f, I will arise
Nah 3:12 they f into the mouth of the
Matt 4: 9 give You if You will f down
Matt 7:25 and it did not f, for it was
Matt 7:27 And great was its f
Matt 15:14 both will f into a ditch
Matt 15:27 f from their masters' table
Matt 24:29 the stars will f from heaven
Mark 13:25 the stars of heaven will f
Luke 2:34 Child is destined for the f
Luke 6:39 not both f into the ditch
Luke 8:13 in time of temptation f away
Luke 10:18 I saw Satan f like lightning
Luke 21:24 they will f by the edge of
Luke 23:30 to the mountains, "F on us
Acts 5:15 by might f on some of them
Acts 27:32 of the skiff and let it f off
Acts 27:34 since not a hair will f from
Acts 28: 6 up or suddenly f down dead
Rom 3:23 f short of the glory of God,
Rom 11:11 stumbled that they should f
Rom 11:11 But through their f, to
Rom 11:12 Now if their f is riches for
Rom 14:13 block or a cause to f in our
1Co 10:12 he stands take heed lest he f
1Ti 3: 6 puffed up with pride he f
1Ti 3: 7 lest he f into reproach and
1Ti 6: 9 to be rich f into temptation
Heb 4:11 lest anyone f after the same
Heb 6: 6 if they f away, to renew them
Heb 10:31 to f into the hands of the
Heb 12:15 diligently lest anyone f
Jas 1: 2 you f into various trials
Jas 5:12 lest you f into judgment
2Pe 3:17 beware lest you also f from
Rev 4:10 the twenty-four elders f down
Rev 6:16 F on us and hide us from the

FALLEN (*see* FALL)

Gen 4: 6 And why has your countenance f
Lev 13:40 hair has f from his head, he
Lev 13:41 hair has f from his forehead
Num 32:19 f to us on this eastern side
Josh 2: 9 the terror of you has f on us
Josh 8:24 when they all had f by the
Judg 3:25 master, f dead on the floor
Judg 8:10 men who drew the sword had f
Judg 18: 1 Israel had not yet f to them
Judg 19:27 f at the door of the house
1Sa 5: 3 f on its face to the earth
1Sa 5: 4 f on its face to the ground
1Sa 26:12 from the LORD had f on them
1Sa 31: 8 his three sons f on Mount
2Sa 1: 4 many of the people are f
2Sa 1:10 could not live after he had f
2Sa 1:12 they had f by the sword
2Sa 1:19 How the mighty have f
2Sa 1:25 How the mighty have f in the
2Sa 1:27 How the mighty have f, and the
2Sa 3:38 a great man has f this day in
2Sa 22:39 they have f under my feet
2Ki 2:13 of Elijah that had f from him
2Ki 2:14 of Elijah that had f from him
1Ch 10: 8 his sons f on Mount Gilboa
2Ch 20:24 dead bodies, f on the earth
2Ch 29: 9 fathers have f by the sword
Esth 7: 8 Haman had f across the couch
Ps 7:15 has f into the ditch which he
Ps 16: 6 The lines have f to me in
Ps 18:38 They have f under my feet
Ps 20: 8 They have bowed down and f
Ps 36:12 workers of iniquity have f
Ps 55: 4 of death have f upon me
Ps 57: 6 of it they themselves have f
Ps 69: 9 who reproach You have f on me
Ps 105:38 fear of them had f upon them
Is 3: 8 stumbled, and Judah is f,
Is 9: 8 Jacob, and it has f on Israel
Is 9:10 The bricks have f down, but
Is 14:12 How you are f from heaven
Is 16: 9 for battle cries have f over
Is 21: 9 Babylon is f, is f
Is 26:18 inhabitants of the world f
Is 59:14 for truth is f in the street,
Jer 46:12 they both have f together
Jer 48:32 The plunderer has f on your
Jer 50:15 hand, her foundations have f
Jer 51: 8 Babylon has suddenly f and
Lam 2:21 young men have f by the sword
Lam 5:16 The crown has f from our head
Ezek 13:12 Surely, when the wall has f
Ezek 24: 6 piece, on which no lot has f
Ezek 31:12 have f on the mountains and in
Ezek 32:22 of them slain, f by the sword
Ezek 32:23 f by the sword, who caused
Ezek 32:24 f by the sword, who have gone
Ezek 32:27 are f of the uncircumcised
Hos 7: 7 All their kings have f
Amos 5: 2 The virgin of Israel has f
Amos 9:11 of David, which has f down
Zech 11: 2 cypress, for the cedar has f
Matt 27:52 who had f asleep were raised
Luke 14: 5 an ox that has f into a pit
Acts 8:16 He had f upon none of them
Acts 15:16 of David which has f down
Acts 26:14 we all had f to the ground
1Co 15: 6 but some have f asleep
1Co 15:18 have f asleep in Christ have
1Co 15:20 of those who have f asleep
Gal 5: 4 you have f from grace
1Th 4:13 those who have f asleep, lest
Rev 2: 5 from where you have f
Rev 9: 1 I saw a star f from heaven to
Rev 14: 8 Babylon is f, is f, that
Rev 17:10 Five have f, one is, and the
Rev 18: 2 Babylon the great is f, is f

FALLING (*see* FALL)

Ps 56:13 not delivered my feet from f
Ps 116: 8 from tears, And my feet from f
Is 34: 4 as fruit f from a fig tree
Luke 8:47 and f down before Him, she
Luke 22:44 of blood f down to the ground

Acts 1:18 f headlong, he burst open in
Acts 19:27 in danger of f into disrepute
Acts 28: 2 of the rain that was f and
1Co 14:25 f down on his face, he will
2Th 2: 3 unless the f away comes first

FALLOW
Ex 23:11 shall let it rest and lie f
Prov 13:23 in the f ground of the poor
Jer 4: 3 Break up your f ground, and do
Hos 10:12 break up your f ground, for

FALLS (*see* FALL)
Ex 21:33 and an ox or a donkey f in it
Lev 11:32 on which any of them f, when
Lev 11:33 any of them f you shall break
Lev 11:34 which water f becomes unclean
Lev 11:35 carcass f shall be unclean
Lev 11:37 f on any planting seed which
Lev 11:38 of any such carcass f on it
Lev 25:35 f into poverty among you,
Num 24: 4 who f down, with eyes opened
Num 24:16 who f down, with eyes opened
Num 33:54 be whatever f to him by lot
Deut 22: 8 house if anyone f from it
2Sa 3:29 on a staff or f by the sword
2Sa 3:34 as a man f before wicked men,
2Sa 17:12 as the dew f on the ground
Job 4:13 when deep sleep f on men
Job 14:18 But as a mountain f and
Job 30:30 skin grows black and f from me
Job 33:15 when deep sleep f upon men
Prov 13:17 messenger f into trouble, but
Prov 17:20 a perverse tongue f into evil
Prov 24:17 not rejoice when your enemy f
Eccl 4:10 to him who is alone when he f
Eccl 9:12 when it f suddenly upon them
Eccl 11: 3 if a tree f to the south or
Eccl 11: 3 in the place where the tree f
Is 34: 4 as the leaf f from the vine
Is 44:15 carved image, and f down to it
Is 44:17 he f down before it and
Matt 10:29 And not one of them f to the
Matt 12:11 if it f into a pit on the
Matt 17:15 for he often f into the fire
Matt 21:44 whoever f on this stone will
Matt 21:44 but on whomever it f, it will
Luke 11:17 divided against a house f
Luke 15:12 portion of goods that f to me
Luke 20:18 Whoever f on that stone will
Luke 20:18 but on whomever it f, it will
John 12:24 of wheat f into the ground
Rom 14: 4 his own master he stands or f
Jas 1:11 its flower f, and its
1Pe 1:24 withers, and its flower f away
Rev 11: 6 so that no rain f in the days

FALSE (*see* FALSEHOOD, FALSELY, FALSIFYING)
Ex 5: 9 let them not regard f words
Ex 20:16 You shall not bear f witness
Ex 23: 1 not circulate a f report
Ex 23: 7 yourself far from a f matter
Deut 5:20 You shall not bear f witness
Deut 19:16 If a f witness rises against
Deut 19:18 if the witness is a f witness
Job 36: 4 For truly my words are not f
Ps 27:12 For f witnesses have risen
Ps 119:104 Therefore I hate every f way
Ps 119:128 I hate every f way
Ps 120: 3 be done to you, You f tongue
Prov 6:19 a f witness who speaks lies,
Prov 11: 1 A f balance is an abomination
Prov 12:17 but a f witness, deceit
Prov 14: 5 but a f witness will utter
Prov 17: 4 evildoer gives heed to f lips
Prov 19: 5 A f witness will not go
Prov 19: 9 A f witness will not go
Prov 20:23 and a f balance is not good
Prov 21:28 A f witness shall perish, but
Prov 25:18 A man who bears f witness
Jer 8: 8 Look, the f pen of the scribe
Jer 14:14 prophesy to you a f vision
Jer 23:32 those who prophesy f dreams
Jer 37:14 Jeremiah said, "It is f!
Lam 2:14 prophets have seen for you f
Lam 2:14 for you f prophecies and
Ezek 12:24 be any f vision or flattering
Ezek 13: 6 f divination, saying, "Thus
Ezek 13: 7 you not spoken f divination
Ezek 21:23 a f divination in the eyes of
Ezek 22:28 seeing f visions, and divining
Mic 2:11 man should walk in a f spirit
Zech 8:17 and do not love a f oath
Zech 10: 2 lies, and tell f dreams
Matt 7:15 Beware of f prophets, who
Matt 15:19 f witness, blasphemies
Matt 19:18 You shall not bear f witness
Matt 24:11 Then many f prophets will
Matt 24:24 For f christs and f
Matt 24:24 f prophets will arise and show
Matt 26:59 and all the council sought f
Matt 26:60 Even though many f witnesses
Matt 26:60 But at last two f witnesses
Mark 10:19 Do not bear f witness,'
Mark 13:22 For f christs and f
Mark 13:22 f prophets will rise and show
Mark 14:56 For many bore f witness
Mark 14:57 bore f witness against Him,
Luke 6:26 fathers to the f prophets
Luke 18:20 Do not bear f witness,'
Luke 19: 8 from anyone by f accusation
Acts 6:13 They also set up f witnesses
Acts 13: 6 a f prophet, a Jew whose name
Rom 13: 9 You shall not bear f witness
1Co 15:15 we are found f witnesses of
2Co 11:13 For such are f apostles,
2Co 11:26 in perils among f brethren
Gal 2: 4 this occurred because of f
Col 2:18 taking delight in f humility
Col 2:23 f humility, and neglect of the
2Pe 2: 1 But there were also f
2Pe 2: 1 will be f teachers among you
1Jn 4: 1 because many f prophets have
Rev 16:13 of the mouth of the f prophet
Rev 19:20 with him the f prophet who
Rev 20:10 beast and the f prophet are

FALSEHOOD (*see* FALSE)
Job 21:34 since f remains in your
Job 31: 5 If I have walked with f, or
Ps 4: 2 love worthlessness And seek f
Ps 5: 6 destroy those who speak f
Ps 7:14 trouble and brings forth f
Ps 119:78 treated me wrongfully with f
Ps 119:118 For their deceit is f
Ps 144: 8 hand is a right hand of f
Ps 144:11 hand is a right hand of f
Prov 30: 8 remove f and lies far from me
Is 28:15 and under f we have hidden
Is 57: 4 transgression, offspring of f
Is 59:13 from the heart words of f
Jer 8: 8 the scribe certainly works f
Jer 10:14 for his molded image is f
Jer 13:25 forgotten Me and trusted in f
Jer 51:17 for his molded image is f

FALSELY (*see* FALSE)
Gen 21:23 you will not deal f with me
Lev 6: 3 concerning it, and swears f
Lev 6: 5 about which he has sworn f
Lev 19:11 shall not steal, nor deal f
Lev 19:12 shall not swear by My name f
Deut 19:18 who has testified f against
2Sa 18:13 I would have dealt f against
Ps 44:17 Nor have we dealt f with Your
Prov 25:14 Whoever f boasts of giving is
Jer 5: 2 lives,' surely they swear f
Jer 5:31 the prophets prophesy f, and
Jer 6:13 the priest, everyone deals f
Jer 7: 9 commit adultery, swear f
Jer 8:10 the priest Everyone deals f
Jer 29: 9 prophesy f to you in My name
Jer 40:16 for you speak f concerning
Jer 43: 2 to Jeremiah, "You speak f!
Hos 10: 4 words, swearing f in making a
Zech 5: 4 one who swears f by My name
Matt 5:11 against you f for My sake
Matt 5:33 old, 'You shall not swear f
Luke 3:14 intimidate anyone or accuse f
1Ti 6:20 of what is f called knowledge

FALSIFYING (*see* FALSE)
Amos 8: 5 f the balances by deceit,

FALTER (*see* FALTERS)
1Ki 18:21 How long will you f between

FALTERS (*see* FALTER)
Prov 25:26 A righteous man who f before

FAME (*see* FAMOUS)
Num 14:15 heard of Your f will speak
Josh 6:27 his f spread throughout all
Josh 9: 9 for we have heard of His f
1Ki 4:31 and his f was in all the
1Ki 10: 1 f of Solomon concerning the
1Ki 10: 7 exceed the f of which I heard
1Ch 14:17 Then the f of David went out
2Ch 9: 1 heard of the f of Solomon
2Ch 9: 6 You exceed the f of which I
2Ch 26: 8 His f spread as far as the
2Ch 26:15 So his f spread far and wide,
Esth 9: 4 his f spread throughout all
Ps 135:13 LORD, endures forever, Your f
Is 66:19 heard My f nor seen My glory
Ezek 16:14 Your f went out among the
Ezek 16:15 the harlot because of your f
Zeph 3:19 f in every land where they
Zeph 3:20 for I will give you f and
Matt 4:24 Then His f went throughout
Mark 1:28 And immediately His f spread

FAMILIAR (*see* UNFAMILIAR)
Lev 19:31 to mediums and f spirits
Lev 20: 6 and f spirits, to prostitute
Lev 20:27 medium, or who has f spirits
Ps 41: 9 Even my own f friend in whom

FAMILIES (*see* FAMILY)
Gen 8:19 earth, according to their f
Gen 10: 5 according to their f, into
Gen 10:18 Afterward the f of the
Gen 10:20 of Ham, according to their f
Gen 10:31 of Shem, according to their f
Gen 10:32 These were the f of the sons
Gen 12: 3 in you all the f of the earth
Gen 28:14 in your seed all the f of the
Gen 36:40 of Esau, according to their f
Gen 47:12 to the number in their f
Ex 6:14 These are the f of Reuben
Ex 6:15 These are the f of Simeon
Ex 6:17 and Shimi according to their f
Ex 6:19 These are the f of Levi
Ex 6:24 These are the f of the
Ex 6:25 Levites according to their f
Ex 12:21 according to your f, and kill
Lev 25:45 their f who are with you,
Num 1: 2 of Israel, by their f, by
Num 1:18 recited their ancestry by f
Num 1:20 their genealogies by their f
Num 1:22 their genealogies by their f
Num 1:24 their genealogies by their f
Num 1:26 their genealogies by their f
Num 1:28 their genealogies by their f
Num 1:30 their genealogies by their f
Num 1:32 their genealogies by their f
Num 1:34 their genealogies by their f
Num 1:36 their genealogies by their f
Num 1:38 their genealogies by their f
Num 1:40 their genealogies by their f
Num 1:42 their genealogies by their f
Num 3:15 fathers' houses, by their f
Num 3:18 sons of Gershon by their f
Num 3:19 the sons of Kohath by their f
Num 3:20 the sons of Merari by their f
Num 3:20 These are the f of the
Num 3:21 these were the f of the
Num 3:23 The f of the Gershonites were
Num 3:27 these were the f of the
Num 3:29 The f of the children of
Num 3:30 the f of the Kohathites was
Num 3:33 these were the f of Merari
Num 3:35 f of Merari was Zuriel the
Num 3:39 of the LORD, by their f, all
Num 4: 2 children of Levi, by their f
Num 4:18 the f of the Kohathites from
Num 4:22 fathers' house, by their f
Num 4:24 of the f of the Gershonites
Num 4:28 f of the sons of Gershon in
Num 4:29 shall number them by their f
Num 4:33 the f of the sons of Merari
Num 4:34 of the Kohathites by their f
Num 4:36 f were two thousand seven
Num 4:37 of the f of the Kohathites
Num 4:38 sons of Gershon, by their f
Num 4:40 who were numbered by their f
Num 4:41 the f of the sons of Gershon
Num 4:42 Those of the f of the sons of
Num 4:42 who were numbered, by their f
Num 4:44 f were three thousand two
Num 4:45 the f of the sons of Merari
Num 4:46 Israel numbered, by their f
Num 11:10 weeping throughout their f
Num 26: 7 These are the f of the
Num 26:12 according to their f were
Num 26:14 These are the f of the

Num 26:15 Gad according to their **f** were
Num 26:18 These are the **f** of the sons
Num 26:20 according to their **f** were
Num 26:22 These are the **f** of Judah
Num 26:23 according to their **f** were
Num 26:25 These are the **f** of Issachar
Num 26:26 according to their **f** were
Num 26:27 These are the **f** of the
Num 26:28 Joseph according to their **f**
Num 26:34 These are the **f** of Manasseh
Num 26:35 Ephraim according to their **f**
Num 26:37 These are the **f** of the sons
Num 26:37 Joseph according to their **f**
Num 26:38 according to their **f** were
Num 26:41 Benjamin according to their **f**
Num 26:42 of Dan according to their **f**
Num 26:42 These are the **f** of Dan
Num 26:42 of Dan according to their **f**
Num 26:43 All the **f** of the Shuhamites,
Num 26:44 according to their **f** were
Num 26:47 These are the **f** of the sons
Num 26:48 according to their **f** were
Num 26:50 These are the **f** of Naphtali
Num 26:50 Naphtali according to their **f**
Num 26:57 Levites according to their **f**
Num 26:58 These are the **f** of the
Num 27: 1 from the **f** of Manasseh the
Num 33:54 an inheritance among your **f**
Num 36: 1 the chief fathers of the **f** of
Num 36: 1 of the **f** of the sons of
Num 36:12 They were married into the **f**
Josh 7:14 shall come according to **f**
Josh 13:15 according to their **f**
Josh 13:23 Reuben according to their **f**
Josh 13:24 of Gad according to their **f**
Josh 13:28 of Gad according to their **f**
Josh 13:29 Manasseh according to their **f**
Josh 13:31 Machir according to their **f**
Josh 15: 1 of Judah according to their **f**
Josh 15:12 around according to their **f**
Josh 15:20 of Judah according to their **f**
Josh 16: 5 Ephraim, according to their **f**
Josh 16: 8 Ephraim according to their **f**
Josh 17: 2 Manasseh according to their **f**
Josh 17: 2 Joseph according to their **f**
Josh 18:11 came up according to their **f**
Josh 18:20 around, according to their **f**
Josh 18:21 according to their **f**, were
Josh 18:28 Benjamin according to their **f**
Josh 19: 1 Simeon according to their **f**
Josh 19: 8 Simeon according to their **f**
Josh 19:10 Zebulun according to their **f**
Josh 19:16 Zebulun according to their **f**
Josh 19:17 Issachar according to their **f**
Josh 19:23 Issachar according to their **f**
Josh 19:24 of Asher according to their **f**
Josh 19:31 of Asher according to their **f**
Josh 19:32 Naphtali according to their **f**
Josh 19:39 Naphtali according to their **f**
Josh 19:40 of Dan according to their **f**
Josh 19:48 of Dan according to their **f**
Josh 21: 4 for the **f** of the Kohathites
Josh 21: 5 the **f** of the tribe of Ephraim
Josh 21: 6 cities by lot from the **f** of
Josh 21: 7 Merari according to their **f**
Josh 21:10 of Aaron, one of the **f** of the
Josh 21:20 And the **f** of the children of
Josh 21:26 were for the rest of the **f** of
Josh 21:27 of the **f** of the Levites, from
Josh 21:33 according to their **f** were
Josh 21:34 to the **f** of the children of
Josh 21:40 Merari according to their **f**
Josh 21:40 rest of the **f** of the Levites
1Sa 9:21 **f** of the tribe of Benjamin
1Sa 10:21 to come near by their **f**, the
1Ch 2:52 and half of the **f** of Manuhoth
1Ch 2:53 The **f** of Kirjath Jearim were
1Ch 2:55 And the **f** of the scribes who
1Ch 4: 2 These were the **f** of the
1Ch 4: 8 the **f** of Aharhel the son of
1Ch 4:21 the **f** of the house of the
1Ch 4:27 nor did any of their **f**
1Ch 4:38 name were leaders in their **f**
1Ch 5: 7 And his brethren by their **f**
1Ch 6:19 Now these are the **f** of the
1Ch 6:60 among their **f** were thirteen
1Ch 6:62 Gershon, throughout their **f**
1Ch 6:63 of Merari, throughout their **f**
1Ch 6:66 Now some of the **f** of the sons
1Ch 7: 5 brethren among all the **f** of
Neh 4:13 people according to their **f**
Job 31:34 and dreaded the contempt of **f**
Ps 22:27 And all the **f** of the nations
Ps 68: 6 God sets the solitary in **f**
Ps 107:41 makes their **f** like a flock
Jer 1:15 I am calling all the **f** of the
Jer 2: 4 all the **f** of the house of
Jer 10:25 on the **f** who do not call on
Jer 25: 9 take all the **f** of the north
Jer 31: 1 God of all the **f** of Israel
Jer 33:24 The two **f** which the LORD has
Ezek 20:32 like the **f** in other countries
Amos 3: 2 of all the **f** of the earth
Nah 3: 4 and **f** through her sorceries
Zech 12:14 all the **f** that remain, every
Zech 14:17 be that whichever of the **f** of
Acts 3:25 in your seed all the **f** of the

FAMILY (*see* FAMILIES)
Lev 20: 5 that man and against his **f**
Lev 25:10 of you shall return to his **f**
Lev 25:41 and shall return to his own **f**
Lev 25:47 a member of the stranger's **f**
Lev 25:49 him in his **f** may redeem him
Num 2:34 broke camp, each one by his **f**
Num 3:21 came the **f** of the Libnites
Num 3:21 and the **f** of the Shimites
Num 3:27 came the **f** of the Amramites
Num 3:27 the **f** of the Izharites, the
Num 3:27 the **f** of the Hebronites, and
Num 3:27 and the **f** of the Uzzielites
Num 3:33 came the **f** of the Mahlites
Num 3:33 and the **f** of the Mushites
Num 26: 5 the **f** of the Hanochites
Num 26: 5 Pallu, the **f** of the Palluites
Num 26: 6 the **f** of the Hezronites
Num 26: 6 Carmi, the **f** of the Carmites
Num 26:12 the **f** of the Nemuelites
Num 26:12 Jamin, the **f** of the Jaminites
Num 26:12 the **f** of the Jachinites
Num 26:13 Zerah, the **f** of the Zarhites
Num 26:13 Shaul, the **f** of the Shaulites
Num 26:15 the **f** of the Zephonites
Num 26:15 Haggi, the **f** of the Haggites
Num 26:15 Shuni, the **f** of the Shunites
Num 26:16 of Ozni, the **f** of the Oznites
Num 26:16 of Eri, the **f** of the Erites
Num 26:17 Arod, the **f** of the Arodites
Num 26:17 Areli, the **f** of the Arelites
Num 26:20 the **f** of the Shelanites
Num 26:20 Perez, the **f** of the Parzites
Num 26:20 Zerah, the **f** of the Zarhites
Num 26:21 the **f** of the Hezronites
Num 26:21 Hamul, the **f** of the Hamulites
Num 26:23 Tola, the **f** of the Tolaites
Num 26:23 of Puah, the **f** of the Punites
Num 26:24 the **f** of the Jashubites
Num 26:24 the **f** of the Shimronites
Num 26:26 Sered, the **f** of the Sardites
Num 26:26 Elon, the **f** of the Elonites
Num 26:26 the **f** of the Jahleelites
Num 26:29 the **f** of the Machirites
Num 26:29 the **f** of the Gileadites
Num 26:30 the **f** of the Jeezerites
Num 26:30 Helek, the **f** of the Helekites
Num 26:31 the **f** of the Asrielites
Num 26:31 the **f** of the Shechemites
Num 26:32 the **f** of the Shemidaites
Num 26:32 the **f** of the Hepherites
Num 26:35 the **f** of the Shuthalhites
Num 26:35 the **f** of the Bachrites
Num 26:35 Tahan, the **f** of the Tahanites
Num 26:36 Eran, the **f** of the Eranites
Num 26:38 Bela, the **f** of the Belaites
Num 26:38 the **f** of the Ashbelites
Num 26:38 the **f** of the Ahiramites
Num 26:39 the **f** of the Shuphamites
Num 26:39 the **f** of the Huphamites
Num 26:40 of Ard, the **f** of the Ardites
Num 26:40 Naaman, the **f** of the Naamites
Num 26:42 the **f** of the Shuhamites
Num 26:44 Jimna, the **f** of the Jimnites
Num 26:44 Jesui, the **f** of the Jesuites
Num 26:44 Beriah, the **f** of the Beriites
Num 26:45 Heber, the **f** of the Heberites
Num 26:45 the **f** of the Malchielites
Num 26:48 the **f** of the Jahzeelites
Num 26:48 of Guni, the **f** of the Gunites
Num 26:49 Jezer, the **f** of the Jezerites
Num 26:49 the **f** of the Shillemites
Num 26:57 the **f** of the Gershonites
Num 26:57 the **f** of the Kohathites
Num 26:57 the **f** of the Merarites
Num 26:58 the **f** of the Libnites, the
Num 26:58 the **f** of the Hebronites, the
Num 26:58 the **f** of the Mahlites, the
Num 26:58 the **f** of the Mushites, and the
Num 26:58 and the **f** of the Korathites
Num 27: 4 his **f** because he had no son
Num 27:11 kinsman nearest him in his **f**
Num 36: 6 the **f** of their father's tribe
Num 36: 8 the **f** of her father's tribe
Num 36:12 the tribe of their father's **f**
Deut 25: 5 to a stranger outside the **f**
Deut 29:18 man or woman or **f** or tribe
Josh 7:14 the **f** which the LORD takes
Josh 7:17 he took the **f** of the Zarhites
Josh 7:17 and he brought the **f** of the
Judg 1:25 let the man and all his **f** go
Judg 9: 1 with all the **f** of the house
Judg 13: 2 of the **f** of the Danites,
Judg 17: 7 in Judah, of the **f** of Judah
Judg 18: 2 their **f** from their territory
Judg 18:11 six hundred men of the **f** of
Judg 18:19 to a tribe and a **f** in Israel
Judg 21:24 every man to his tribe and **f**
Ruth 2: 1 wealth, of the **f** of Elimelech
Ruth 2: 3 who was of the **f** of Elimelech
1Sa 9:21 my **f** the least of all the
1Sa 10:21 the **f** of Matri was chosen
1Sa 18:18 or my father's **f** in Israel
1Sa 20: 6 sacrifice there for all the **f**
1Sa 20:29 for our **f** has a sacrifice in
2Sa 14: 7 now the whole **f** has risen up
2Sa 16: 5 the **f** of the house of Saul
2Ki 25:25 of Elishama, of the royal **f**
1Ch 6:54 of the **f** of the Kohathites
1Ch 6:61 To the rest of the **f** of the
1Ch 6:70 for the rest of the **f** of the
1Ch 6:71 From the **f** of the half-tribe
1Ch 13:14 of God remained with the **f** of
Esth 9:28 every generation, every **f**
Job 32: 2 the Buzite, of the **f** of Ram
Jer 3:14 from a city and two from a **f**
Jer 8: 3 who remain of this evil **f**
Jer 29:32 the Nehelamite and his **f**
Jer 36:31 I will punish him, his **f**, and
Jer 41: 1 of Elishama, of the royal **f**
Amos 3: 1 against the whole **f** which I
Mic 2: 3 against this **f** I am devising
Zech 12:12 mourn, every **f** by itself
Zech 12:12 the **f** of the house of David
Zech 12:12 the **f** of the house of Nathan
Zech 12:13 the **f** of the house of Levi by
Zech 12:13 the **f** of Shimei by itself, and
Zech 12:14 every **f** by itself, and their
Zech 14:18 If the **f** of Egypt will not
Acts 4: 6 of the **f** of the high priest
Acts 7:13 Joseph's **f** became known to
Acts 13:26 sons of the **f** of Abraham
Acts 16:33 he and all his **f** were baptized
Eph 3:15 whom the whole **f** in heaven

FAMINE (*see* FAMINES, FAMISH)
Gen 12:10 Now there was a **f** in the land
Gen 12:10 for the **f** was severe in the
Gen 26: 1 There was a **f** in the land
Gen 26: 1 besides the first **f** that was
Gen 41:27 wind are seven years of **f**
Gen 41:30 seven years of **f** will arise
Gen 41:30 the **f** will deplete the land
Gen 41:31 because of the **f** following
Gen 41:36 **f** which shall be in the land
Gen 41:36 may not perish during the **f**
Gen 41:50 before the years of **f** came
Gen 41:54 years of **f** began to come, as
Gen 41:54 The **f** was in all lands, but
Gen 41:56 The **f** was over all the face
Gen 41:56 the **f** became severe in the
Gen 41:57 because the **f** was severe in
Gen 42: 5 for the **f** was in the land of
Gen 42:19 for the **f** of your houses
Gen 42:33 take food for the **f** of your
Gen 43: 1 Now the **f** was severe in the
Gen 45: 6 the **f** has been in the land
Gen 45:11 are still five years of **f**
Gen 47: 4 for the **f** is severe in the
Gen 47:13 for the **f** was very severe, so
Gen 47:13 languished because of the **f**
Gen 47:20 because the **f** was severe upon
Ruth 1: 1 there was a **f** in the land
2Sa 21: 1 Now there was a **f** in the days

2Sa 24:13 Shall seven years of **f** come
1Ki 8:37 When there is **f** in the land
1Ki 18: 2 was a severe **f** in Samaria
2Ki 4:38 and there was a **f** in the land
2Ki 6:25 was a great **f** in Samaria
2Ki 7: 4 the **f** is in the city, and we
2Ki 8: 1 the LORD has called for a **f**
2Ki 25: 3 **f** had become so severe in the
1Ch 21:12 either three years of **f**, or
2Ch 6:28 When there is **f** in the land
2Ch 20: 9 judgment, pestilence, or **f**
2Ch 32:11 yourselves over to die by **f**
Neh 5: 3 buy grain because of the **f**
Job 5:20 In **f** He shall redeem you from
Job 5:22 laugh at destruction and **f**
Job 30: 3 They are gaunt from want and **f**
Ps 33:19 And to keep them alive in **f**
Ps 37:19 in the days of **f** they shall
Ps 105:16 He called for a **f** in the land
Is 14:30 I will kill your roots with **f**
Is 51:19 Desolation and destruction, **f**
Jer 5:12 nor shall we see sword or **f**
Jer 11:22 daughters shall die by **f**
Jer 14:12 them by the sword, by the **f**
Jer 14:13 sword, nor shall you have **f**
Jer 14:15 **f** shall not be in this land'
Jer 14:15 **f** those prophets shall be
Jer 14:16 of Jerusalem because of the **f**
Jer 14:18 behold, those sick from **f**
Jer 15: 2 are for the **f**, to the **f**
Jer 16: 4 consumed by the sword and by **f**
Jer 18:21 up their children to the **f**
Jer 21: 7 and the sword and the **f**, into
Jer 21: 9 shall die by the sword, by **f**
Jer 24:10 I will send the sword, the **f**
Jer 27: 8 LORD, with the sword, the **f**
Jer 27:13 by the sword, by the **f**, and
Jer 29:17 send on them the sword, the **f**
Jer 29:18 them with the sword, with **f**
Jer 32:24 it, because of the sword and **f**
Jer 32:36 by the sword, by the **f**, and by
Jer 34:17 sword, to pestilence, and to **f**
Jer 38: 2 shall die by the sword, by **f**
Jer 42:16 the **f** of which you were
Jer 42:17 shall die by the sword, by **f**
Jer 42:22 shall die by the sword, by **f**
Jer 44:12 consumed by the sword and by **f**
Jer 44:12 by the sword and by **f**
Jer 44:13 Jerusalem, by the sword, by **f**
Jer 44:18 consumed by the sword and by **f**
Jer 44:27 consumed by the sword and by **f**
Jer 52: 6 the **f** had become so severe in
Lam 5:10 because of the fever of **f**
Ezek 5:12 consumed with **f** in your midst
Ezek 5:16 of **f** which shall be for their
Ezek 5:16 will increase the **f** upon you
Ezek 5:17 So I will send against you **f**
Ezek 6:11 shall fall by the sword, by **f**
Ezek 6:12 besieged shall die by the **f**
Ezek 7:15 and the pestilence and **f** within
Ezek 7:15 and whoever is in the city, **f**
Ezek 12:16 men from the sword, from **f**
Ezek 14:13 send **f** on it, and cut off man
Ezek 14:21 the sword and **f** and wild beasts
Ezek 36:29 it, and bring no **f** upon you
Ezek 36:30 of **f** among the nations
Amos 8:11 I will send a **f** on the land
Amos 8:11 land, not a **f** of bread, nor a
Luke 4:25 and there was a great **f**
Luke 15:14 arose a severe **f** in that land
Acts 7:11 Now a **f** and great trouble came
Acts 11:28 was going to be a great **f**
Rom 8:35 or persecution, or **f**, or
Rev 18: 8 death and mourning and **f**

FAMINES (*see* FAMINE)
Matt 24: 7 And there will be **f**,
Mark 13: 8 places, and there will be **f**
Luke 21:11 in various places, and **f** and

FAMISH (*see* FAMINE, FAMISHED)
Prov 10: 3 allow the righteous soul to **f**

FAMISHED (*see* FAMISH)
Gen 41:55 all the land of Egypt was **f**
Is 5:13 their honorable men are **f**

FAMOUS (*see* FAME)
Ruth 4:11 and be **f** in Bethlehem
Ruth 4:14 may his name be **f** in Israel
1Ch 5:24 **f** men, and heads of their
1Ch 12:30 valor, **f** men throughout their
1Ch 22: 5 be exceedingly magnificent, **f**
Ps 136:18 slew **f** kings, For His mercy
Ezek 32:18 daughters of the **f** nations

FAN (*see* UNFANNED)
Is 30:24 winnowed with the shovel and **f**
Jer 4:11 not to **f** or to cleanse
Jer 15: 7 them with a winnowing **f** in
Matt 3:12 His winnowing **f** is in His
Luke 3:17 His winnowing **f** is in His

FANCIES (*see* FANCY)
Prov 1:31 to the full with their own **f**

FANCY (*see* FANCIES)
Ps 78:18 for the food of their **f**

FANGS
Job 29:17 I broke the **f** of the wicked,
Ps 58: 6 Break out the **f** of the young
Prov 30:14 whose **f** are like knives, to
Joel 1: 6 he has the **f** of a fierce lion

FANTASY
Prov 21: 6 tongue is the fleeting **f** of

FAR (*see* PREFACE)

FARE (*see* FARED)
1Sa 17:18 and see how your brothers **f**
Jon 1: 3 so he paid the **f**, and went

FARED (*see* FARE)
Luke 16:19 and **f** sumptuously every day

FAREWELL
Luke 9:61 and bid them **f** who are at my
Acts 15:29 you will do well. **F**.
Acts 23:30 the charges against him. **F**.
2Co 13:11 Finally, brethren, **f**

FARM (*see* FARMER, FARMING)
Matt 22: 5 their ways, one to his own **f**

FARMER (*see* FARM, FARMERS)
Gen 9:20 And Noah began to be a **f**, and
Jer 51:23 I will break in pieces the **f**
Amos 5:16 shall call the **f** to mourning
Zech 13: 5 I am no prophet, I am a **f**
2Ti 2: 6 The hard-working **f** must be
Jas 5: 7 See how the **f** waits for the

FARMERS (*see* FARMER)
2Ki 25:12 the land as vinedressers and **f**
2Ch 26:10 he also had **f** and vinedressers
Jer 31:24 in all its cities together, **f**
Jer 52:16 the land as vinedressers and **f**
Joel 1:11 Be ashamed, you **f**, wail, you

FARMING (*see* FARM)
Neh 10:37 in all our **f** communities

FAR-OFF (*see* PREFACE)

FARTHER (*see* PREFACE)

FARTHEST
Deut 30: 4 to the **f** parts under heaven
Josh 17:18 its **f** extent shall be yours
Neh 1: 9 to the **f** part of the heavens
Ps 65: 8 **f** parts are afraid of Your
Is 7:18 for the fly that is in the **f**
Is 14:13 on the **f** sides of the north
Is 37:24 I will enter its **f** height
Is 41: 9 and called from its **f** regions
Jer 6:22 from the **f** parts of the earth
Jer 9:26 all who are in the **f** corners
Jer 25:23 all who are in the **f** corners
Jer 25:32 from the **f** parts of the earth
Jer 49:32 winds those in the **f** corners
Jer 50:26 against her from the **f** border
Mark 13:27 from the **f** part of earth to
Mark 13:27 earth to the **f** part of heaven

FASHION (*see* FASHIONED, FASHIONING, FASHIONS)
Ezra 4: 8 to King Artaxerxes in this **f**
Job 31:15 the same One **f** us in the womb

FASHIONED (*see* FASHION)
Ex 32: 4 he **f** it with an engraving
Num 31:51 them, all the **f** ornaments
2Ch 3:10 **f** by carving, and overlaid
Job 10: 8 and **f** me, an intricate unity
Ps 119:73 hands have made me and **f** me
Ps 139:16 written, The days **f** for me
Is 22:11 for Him who **f** it long ago

FASHIONING (*see* FASHION)
Jer 18:11 I am **f** a disaster and devising

FASHIONS (*see* FASHION)
Ps 33:15 He **f** their hearts
Is 44:12 **f** it with hammers, and works
Is 44:13 he **f** it with a plane, he

FAST (*see* FASTED, FASTEN, FASTING)
Deut 4: 4 But you who held **f** to the
Deut 10:20 and to Him you shall hold **f**
Deut 11:22 His ways, and to hold **f** to Him
Deut 13: 4 serve Him and hold **f** to Him
Josh 22: 5 to hold **f** to Him, and to
Josh 23: 8 but you shall hold **f** to the
Judg 4:21 for he was **f** asleep and weary
2Sa 12:23 why should I **f**
1Ki 21: 9 Proclaim a **f**, and seat Naboth
1Ki 21:12 They proclaimed a **f**, and
2Ki 6:32 and hold him **f** at the door
2Ki 18: 6 For he held **f** to the LORD
2Ch 20: 3 proclaimed a **f** throughout all
Ezra 8:21 Then I proclaimed a **f** there
Esth 4:16 in Shushan, and **f** for me
Esth 4:16 My maids and I will **f** likewise
Job 2: 3 And still he holds **f** to his
Job 8:15 He holds it **f**, but it does
Job 23:11 foot has held **f** to His steps
Job 27: 6 My righteousness I hold **f**
Ps 33: 9 He commanded, and it stood **f**
Ps 111: 8 They stand **f** forever and ever,
Is 56: 4 Me, and hold **f** My covenant,
Is 56: 6 and holds **f** My covenant
Is 58: 3 of your **f** you find pleasure
Is 58: 4 Indeed you **f** for strife and
Is 58: 4 You will not **f** as you do this
Is 58: 5 Is it a **f** that I have chosen,
Is 58: 5 Would you call this a **f**, and
Is 58: 6 Is this not the **f** that I have
Jer 8: 5 They hold **f** to deceit, they
Jer 14:12 When they **f**, I will not hear
Jer 36: 9 that they proclaimed a **f**
Jer 46:14 say, 'Stand **f** and prepare
Jer 50:33 them captive have held them **f**
Joel 1:14 Consecrate a **f**, call a sacred
Joel 2:15 in Zion, consecrate a **f**, call
Jon 1: 5 lain down, and was **f** asleep
Jon 3: 5 believed God, proclaimed a **f**
Zech 7: 3 **f** as I have done for so many
Zech 7: 5 did you really **f** for Me
Zech 8:19 The **f** of the fourth month,
Zech 8:19 the **f** of the fifth
Zech 8:19 the **f** of the seventh
Zech 8:19 the **f** of the tenth
Matt 6:16 Moreover, when you **f**, do not
Matt 6:17 But you, when you **f**, anoint
Matt 9:14 we and the Pharisees **f** often
Matt 9:14 but Your disciples do not **f**
Matt 9:15 them, and then they will **f**
Mark 2:18 of John and of the Pharisees **f**
Mark 2:18 but Your disciples do not **f**
Mark 2:19 **f** while the bridegroom is
Mark 2:19 with them they cannot **f**
Mark 2:20 they will **f** in those days
Luke 5:33 the disciples of John **f** often
Luke 5:34 **f** while the bridegroom is
Luke 5:35 they will **f** in those days
Luke 18:12 I **f** twice a week
Acts 27: 9 the **F** was already over, Paul
Acts 27:41 and the prow stuck **f** and
1Co 15: 2 if you hold **f** that word which
1Co 16:13 stand **f** in the faith, be
Gal 5: 1 Stand **f** therefore in the
Phil 1:27 you stand **f** in one spirit
Phil 2:16 holding **f** the word of life,
Phil 4: 1 so stand **f** in the Lord,
Col 2:19 and not holding **f** to the Head
1Th 3: 8 if you stand **f** in the Lord
1Th 5:21 hold **f** what is good
2Th 2:15 Therefore, brethren, stand **f**
2Ti 1:13 Hold **f** the pattern of sound
Tit 1: 9 holding **f** the faithful word
Heb 3: 6 if we hold **f** the confidence
Heb 4:14 let us hold **f** our confession
Heb 10:23 Let us hold **f** the confession
Rev 2:13 you hold **f** to My name, and did
Rev 2:25 But hold **f** what you have till
Rev 3: 3 hold **f** and repent
Rev 3:11 Hold **f** what you have, that no

FASTED (*see* FAST)
Judg 20:26 and f that day until evening
1Sa 7: 6 And they f that day, and said
1Sa 31:13 at Jabesh, and f seven days
2Sa 1:12 f until evening for Saul and
2Sa 12:16 God for the child, and David f
2Sa 12:21 You f and wept for the child
2Sa 12:22 child was still alive, I f
1Ki 21:27 sackcloth on his body, and f
1Ch 10:12 at Jabesh, and f seven days
Ezra 8:23 So we f and entreated our God
Is 58: 3 Why have we f,' they say
Zech 7: 5 When you f and mourned in the
Matt 4: 2 And when He had f forty days
Acts 13: 2 ministered to the Lord and f
Acts 13: 3 Then, having f and prayed, and

FASTEN (*see* FAST, FASTENED)
Ex 28:14 f the braided chains to the
Ex 28:25 shall f to the two settings
Ex 39:31 to f it above on the turban,
Is 22:23 I will f him as a peg in a
Jer 10: 4 they f it with nails and

FASTENED (*see* FASTEN)
Ex 39:18 they f in the two settings
Ex 40:18 f its sockets, set up its
Num 19:15 which has no cover f on it
Judg 3:16 f it under his clothes on his
1Sa 17:39 And David f his sword to his
1Sa 31:10 they f his body to the wall
2Sa 20: 8 f in its sheath at his hips
1Ki 6: 6 be f into the walls of the
1Ch 10:10 f his head in the temple of
2Ch 9:18 which were f to the throne
Esth 1: 6 blue linen curtains f with
Job 38: 6 what were its foundations f
Is 22:25 the peg that is f in the
Is 41: 7 then he f it with pegs, that
Ezek 40:43 wide, f all around
Ezek 41: 6 but not f to the wall of the
Acts 16:24 f their feet in the stocks
Acts 28: 3 of the heat, and f on his hand

FASTING (*see* FAST, FASTINGS)
Ezra 9: 5 sacrifice I arose from my f
Neh 1: 4 I was f and praying before the
Neh 9: 1 Israel were assembled with f
Esth 4: 3 among the Jews, with f,
Esth 9:31 concerning matters of their f
Ps 35:13 I humbled myself with f
Ps 69:10 and chastened my soul with f
Ps 109:24 My knees are weak through f
Jer 36: 6 LORD's house on the day of f
Dan 6:18 palace and spent the night f
Dan 9: 3 and supplications, with f,
Joel 2:12 with all your heart, with f
Matt 6:16 may appear to men to be f
Matt 6:18 do not appear to men to be f
Matt 17:21 go out except by prayer and f
Mark 2:18 and of the Pharisees were f
Mark 9:29 by nothing but prayer and f
Acts 10:30 ago I was f until this hour
Acts 14:23 church, and prayed with f,
1Co 7: 5 you may give yourselves to f

FASTINGS (*see* FASTING)
Luke 2:37 temple, but served God with f
2Co 6: 5 in sleeplessness, in f
2Co 11:27 in f often, in cold and

FAT (*see* FATNESS, FATTED, FATTENED, FATTER, FATTY)
Gen 4: 4 of his flock and of their f
Gen 41: 2 seven cows, fine looking and f
Gen 41: 4 seven fine looking and f cows
Gen 41:18 the river, fine looking and f
Gen 41:20 the first seven, the f cows
Gen 45:18 will eat the f of the land
Ex 23:18 nor shall the f of My
Ex 29:13 you shall take all the f that
Ex 29:13 the f that is on them, and
Ex 29:22 shall take the f of the ram
Ex 29:22 ram, the f tail, the f that
Ex 29:22 f tail, the f that covers
Ex 29:22 and the f on them, the right
Lev 1: 8 the f in order on the wood
Lev 1:12 with its head and its f
Lev 3: 3 The f that covers the
Lev 3: 3 and all the f that is on the
Lev 3: 4 the f that is on them by the
Lev 3: 9 by fire to the LORD, its f
Lev 3: 9 the whole f tail which he
Lev 3: 9 And the f that covers the
Lev 3: 9 and all the f that is on the
Lev 3:10 the f that is on them by the
Lev 3:14 The f that covers the
Lev 3:14 and all the f that is on the
Lev 3:15 the f that is on them by the
Lev 3:16 all the f is the LORD's
Lev 3:17 shall eat neither f nor blood
Lev 4: 8 the f of the bull as the sin
Lev 4: 8 The f that covers the
Lev 4: 8 all the f which is on the
Lev 4: 9 the f that is on them by the
Lev 4:19 shall take all the f from it
Lev 4:26 burn all its f on the altar
Lev 4:26 like the f of the sacrifice
Lev 4:31 He shall remove all its f
Lev 4:31 as f is removed from the
Lev 4:35 He shall remove all its f
Lev 4:35 as the f of the lamb is
Lev 6:12 the f of the peace offerings
Lev 7: 3 shall offer from it all its f
Lev 7: 3 The f tail and the f that
Lev 7: 4 the f that is on them by the
Lev 7:23 You shall not eat any f, of
Lev 7:24 the f of a beast that dies
Lev 7:24 the f of what is torn by wild
Lev 7:25 For whoever eats the f of
Lev 7:30 The f with the breast he
Lev 7:31 shall burn the f on the altar
Lev 7:33 the peace offering, and the f
Lev 8:16 Then he took all the f that
Lev 8:16 the two kidneys with their f
Lev 8:20 head, the pieces, and the f
Lev 8:25 he took the f and the f tail
Lev 8:25 all the f that was on the
Lev 8:25 the two kidneys and their f
Lev 8:26 wafer, and put them on the f
Lev 9:10 But the f, the kidneys, and
Lev 9:19 the f from the bull and the
Lev 9:20 they put the f on the breasts
Lev 9:20 he burned the f on the altar
Lev 9:24 and the f on the altar
Lev 10:15 offerings of f made by fire
Lev 16:25 The f of the sin offering he
Lev 17: 6 burn the f for a sweet aroma
Num 18:17 burn their f as an offering
Deut 31:20 filled themselves and grown f
Deut 32:14 of the flock, with f of lambs
Deut 32:15 But Jeshurun grew f and kicked
Deut 32:15 you grew f, you grew thick,
Deut 32:15 thick, you are covered with f
Deut 32:38 Who ate the f of their
Judg 3:17 (Now Eglon was a very f man
Judg 3:22 the f closed over the blade,
1Sa 2:15 before they burned the f
1Sa 2:16 really burn the f first
1Sa 2:29 to make yourselves f with the
1Sa 15:22 and to heed than the f of rams
2Sa 1:22 from the f of the mighty, the
1Ki 8:64 the f of the peace offerings,
1Ki 8:64 the f of the peace offerings
2Ch 7: 7 the f of the peace offerings,
2Ch 7: 7 the grain offerings, and the f
2Ch 29:35 with the f of the peace
2Ch 35:14 offerings and f until night
Neh 8:10 Go your way, eat the f, drink
Neh 9:25 ate and were filled and grew f
Job 15:27 made his waist heavy with f
Ps 17:10 have closed up their f hearts
Ps 66:15 burnt sacrifices of f animals
Ps 119:70 Their heart is as f as grease
Is 1:11 rams and the f of fed cattle
Is 5:17 f ones strangers shall eat
Is 10:16 leanness among his f ones
Is 25: 6 of f things full of marrow,
Is 30:23 it will be f and plenteous
Is 34: 6 with the f of the kidneys of
Is 43:24 with the f of your sacrifices
Jer 5:28 They have grown f, they are
Jer 46:21 are in her midst like f bulls
Jer 50:11 because you have grown f like
Ezek 34: 3 You eat the f and clothe
Ezek 34:16 but I will destroy the f and
Ezek 34:20 will judge between the f and
Ezek 39:19 You shall eat f till you are
Ezek 44: 7 you offered My food, the f
Ezek 44:15 Me to offer to Me the f and
Zech 11:16 will eat the flesh of the f
Mal 4: 2 grow f like stall-fed calves

FATE
Num 16:29 by the common f of all men
Ps 81:15 Him, But their f would endure

FATHER (*see* FATHER-IN-LAW, FATHERED, FATHERLESS, FATHER'S, FATHERS, GRANDFATHER)
Gen 2:24 a man shall leave his f and
Gen 4:20 He was the f of those who
Gen 4:21 He was the f of all those who
Gen 9:18 And Ham was the f of Canaan
Gen 9:22 Ham, the f of Canaan, saw the
Gen 9:22 saw the nakedness of his f
Gen 9:23 the nakedness of their f
Gen 10:21 the f of all the children of
Gen 11:28 Haran died before his f Terah
Gen 11:29 of Haran the f of Milcah and
Gen 11:29 of Milcah and the f of Iscah
Gen 17: 4 and you shall be a f of many
Gen 17: 5 made you a f of many nations
Gen 19:31 Our f is old, and there is no
Gen 19:32 let us make our f drink wine
Gen 19:32 preserve the lineage of our f
Gen 19:33 So they made their f drink
Gen 19:33 went in and lay with her f
Gen 19:34 I lay with my f last night
Gen 19:34 preserve the lineage of our f
Gen 19:35 Then they made their f drink
Gen 19:36 were with child by their f
Gen 19:37 he is the f of the Moabites
Gen 19:38 he is the f of the people of
Gen 20:12 She is the daughter of my f
Gen 22: 7 Isaac spoke to Abraham his f
Gen 22: 7 his f and said, "My f!"
Gen 22:21 brother, Kemuel the f of Aram
Gen 26: 3 I swore to Abraham your f
Gen 26:15 in the days of Abraham his f
Gen 26:18 in the days of Abraham his f
Gen 26:18 which his f had called them
Gen 26:24 am the God of your f Abraham
Gen 27: 6 Indeed I heard your f speak
Gen 27: 9 food from them for your f
Gen 27:10 you shall take it to your f
Gen 27:12 Perhaps my f will feel me, and
Gen 27:14 food, such as his f loved
Gen 27:18 So he went to his f and said,
Gen 27:18 his f and said, "My f"
Gen 27:19 And Jacob said to his f, "I
Gen 27:22 went near to Isaac his f, and
Gen 27:26 Then his f Isaac said to him,
Gen 27:30 the presence of Isaac his f
Gen 27:31 food, and brought it to his f
Gen 27:31 and said to his f
Gen 27:31 Let my f arise and eat of his
Gen 27:32 And his f Isaac said to him,
Gen 27:34 Esau heard the words of his f
Gen 27:34 bitter cry, and said to his f
Gen 27:34 me, even me also, O my f
Gen 27:38 And Esau said to his f, "Have
Gen 27:38 you only one blessing, my f
Gen 27:38 me, even me also, O my f
Gen 27:39 Then Isaac his f answered
Gen 27:41 with which his f blessed him
Gen 27:41 mourning for my f are at hand
Gen 28: 2 of Bethuel your mother's f
Gen 28: 7 that Jacob had obeyed his f
Gen 28: 8 did not please his f Isaac
Gen 28:13 LORD God of Abraham your f
Gen 29:12 So she ran and told her f
Gen 31: 5 God of my f has been with me
Gen 31: 6 my might I have served your f
Gen 31: 7 Yet your f has deceived me and
Gen 31: 9 away the livestock of your f
Gen 31:16 from our f are really ours
Gen 31:18 to go to his f Isaac in the
Gen 31:29 but the God of your f spoke
Gen 31:35 And she said to her f, "Let
Gen 31:42 Unless the God of my f, the
Gen 31:53 by the Fear of his f Isaac
Gen 31:53 of their f judge between us
Gen 32: 9 O God of my f Abraham and
Gen 32: 9 Abraham and God of my f Isaac
Gen 33:19 of Hamor, Shechem's f, for
Gen 34: 4 Shechem spoke to his f Hamor
Gen 34: 6 Then Hamor the f of Shechem
Gen 34:11 Then Shechem said to her f
Gen 34:13 Shechem and Hamor his f, and
Gen 34:19 all the household of his f
Gen 35:18 but his f called him Benjamin
Gen 35:27 came to his f Isaac at Mamre
Gen 36: 9 f of the Edomites in Mount

Gen 36:24 the donkeys of his f Zibeon
Gen 36:43 Esau was the f of the
Gen 37: 1 where his f was a stranger
Gen 37: 2 a bad report of them to his f
Gen 37: 4 f loved him more than all his
Gen 37:10 So he told it to his f and his
Gen 37:10 his f rebuked him and said to
Gen 37:11 but his f kept the matter in
Gen 37:22 and bring him back to his f
Gen 37:32 and they brought it to their f
Gen 37:35 Thus his f wept for him
Gen 42:13 youngest is with our f today
Gen 42:29 their f in the land of Canaan
Gen 42:32 brothers, sons of our f
Gen 42:32 our f this day in the land of
Gen 42:35 their f saw the bundles of
Gen 42:36 Jacob their f said to them,
Gen 42:37 Then Reuben spoke to his f
Gen 43: 2 that their f said to them,
Gen 43: 7 Is your f still alive
Gen 43: 8 Judah said to Israel his f
Gen 43:11 their f Israel said to them,
Gen 43:23 the God of your f has given
Gen 43:27 Is your f well, the old man
Gen 43:28 Your servant our f is in good
Gen 44:17 you, go up in peace to your f
Gen 44:19 Have you a f or a brother
Gen 44:20 said to my lord, 'We have a f
Gen 44:20 children, and his f loves him
Gen 44:22 The lad cannot leave his f
Gen 44:22 for if he should leave his f
Gen 44:22 his f would die
Gen 44:24 went up to your servant my f
Gen 44:25 our f said, 'Go back and buy
Gen 44:27 your servant my f said to us
Gen 44:30 I come to your servant my f
Gen 44:31 f with sorrow to the grave
Gen 44:32 surety for the lad to my f
Gen 44:32 the blame before my f forever
Gen 44:34 f if the lad is not with me
Gen 44:34 that would come upon my f
Gen 45: 3 does my f still live
Gen 45: 8 He has made me a f to Pharaoh
Gen 45: 9 Hasten and go up to my f, and
Gen 45:13 So you shall tell my f of all
Gen 45:13 and bring my f down here
Gen 45:18 Bring your f and your
Gen 45:19 bring your f and come
Gen 45:23 he sent to his f these things
Gen 45:23 and food for his f for the
Gen 45:25 of Canaan to Jacob their f
Gen 45:27 of Jacob their f revived
Gen 46: 1 to the God of his f Isaac
Gen 46: 3 I am God, the God of your f
Gen 46: 5 Israel carried their f Jacob
Gen 46:29 Goshen to meet his f Israel
Gen 47: 1 My f and my brothers, their
Gen 47: 5 Your f and your brothers have
Gen 47: 6 Have your f and brothers dwell
Gen 47: 7 Joseph brought in his f Jacob
Gen 47:11 And Joseph situated his f and
Gen 47:12 Then Joseph provided his f
Gen 48: 1 Indeed your f is sick"
Gen 48: 9 And Joseph said to his f
Gen 48:17 when Joseph saw that his f
Gen 48:18 And Joseph said to his f
Gen 48:18 Not so, my f, for this one is
Gen 48:19 But his f refused and said
Gen 49: 2 and listen to Israel your f
Gen 49:25 of your f who will help you
Gen 49:26 The blessings of your f have
Gen 49:28 is what their f spoke to them
Gen 50: 2 physicians to embalm his f
Gen 50: 5 My f made me swear, saying,
Gen 50: 5 let me go up and bury my f
Gen 50: 6 Go up and bury your f, as he
Gen 50: 7 Joseph went up to bury his f
Gen 50:10 days of mourning for his f
Gen 50:14 And after he had buried his f
Gen 50:14 up with him to bury his f
Gen 50:15 saw that their f was dead
Gen 50:16 Before your f died he
Gen 50:17 servants of the God of your f
Ex 2:18 they came to Reuel their f
Ex 3: 6 I am the God of your f
Ex 12: 3 to the house of his f, a lamb
Ex 18: 4 The God of my f was my help
Ex 20:12 Honor your f and your mother,
Ex 21:15 he who strikes his f or his
Ex 21:17 he who curses his f or his
Ex 22:17 If her f utterly refuses to
Ex 40:15 them, as you anointed their f
Lev 18: 7 The nakedness of your f or
Lev 18: 9 the daughter of your f, or
Lev 18:11 daughter, begotten by your f
Lev 18:12 she is near of kin to your f
Lev 19: 3 revere his mother and his f
Lev 20: 9 f or his mother shall surely
Lev 20: 9 cursed his f or his mother
Lev 21: 2 his mother, his f, his son,
Lev 21: 9 harlot, she profanes her f
Lev 21:11 for his f or his mother
Lev 24:10 whose f was an Egyptian, went
Num 3: 4 oversight of Aaron their f
Num 6: 7 even for his f or his mother
Num 12:14 If her f had but spit in her
Num 18: 2 of Levi, the tribe of your f
Num 27: 3 Our f died in the wilderness
Num 27: 4 f be removed from among his
Num 27: 4 among the brothers of our f
Num 27: 7 of their f to pass to them
Num 27:11 if his f has no brothers,
Num 30: 4 her f hears her vow and the
Num 30: 4 her f holds his peace, then
Num 30: 5 But if her f overrules her on
Num 30: 5 because her f overruled her
Num 30:16 and his wife, and between a f
Deut 5:16 Honor your f and your mother,
Deut 21:13 in your house, and mourn her f
Deut 21:18 not obey the voice of his f
Deut 21:19 then his f and his mother
Deut 22:15 then the f and mother of the
Deut 22:16 the young woman's f shall say
Deut 22:19 give them to the f of the
Deut 22:29 f fifty shekels of silver
Deut 26: 5 My f was a Syrian, about to
Deut 27:16 is the one who treats his f
Deut 27:22 the daughter of his f or the
Deut 32: 6 Is He not your F, who bought
Deut 32: 7 Ask your f, and he will show
Deut 33: 9 who says of his f and mother
Josh 2:13 and spare my f, my mother, my
Josh 2:18 and unless you bring your f
Josh 6:23 and brought out Rahab, her f
Josh 15:13 (Arba was the f of Anak)
Josh 15:18 him to ask her f for a field
Josh 17: 1 the f of Gilead, because he
Josh 19:47 after the name of Dan their f
Josh 21:11 (Arba being the f of Anak)
Josh 22:14 his f among the divisions of
Josh 24: 2 the f of Abraham and the
Josh 24: 2 the f of Nahor, dwelt on the
Josh 24: 3 Then I took your f Abraham
Josh 24:32 f of Shechem for one hundred
Judg 1:14 him to ask her f for a field
Judg 6:25 altar of Baal that your f has
Judg 8:32 in the tomb of Joash his f
Judg 9: 1 the house of his mother's f
Judg 9:17 for my f fought for you,
Judg 9:28 men of Hamor the f of Shechem
Judg 9:56 his f by killing his seventy
Judg 11:36 My f, if you have given your
Judg 11:37 Then she said to her f, "Let
Judg 11:39 that she returned to her f
Judg 14: 2 So he went up and told his f
Judg 14: 3 Then his f and mother said to
Judg 14: 3 And Samson said to his f
Judg 14: 4 But his f and mother did not
Judg 14: 5 down to Timnah with his f
Judg 14: 6 But he did not tell his f or
Judg 14: 9 When he came to his f and
Judg 14:10 So his f went down to the
Judg 14:16 it to my f or my mother
Judg 15: 1 But her f would not permit
Judg 15: 2 Her f said, "I really
Judg 15: 6 burned her and her f with fire
Judg 16:31 in the tomb of his f Manoah
Judg 17:10 Dwell with me, and be a f and a
Judg 18:19 be a f and a priest to us
Judg 18:29 after the name of Dan their f
Judg 19: 3 when the f of the young woman
Judg 19: 4 the young woman's f,
Judg 19: 5 but the young woman's f said
Judg 19: 6 woman's f said to the man
Judg 19: 8 but the young woman's f said
Judg 19: 9 the young woman's f, said to
Ruth 2:11 and how you have left your f
Ruth 4:17 He is the f of Jesse, the
Ruth 4:17 of Jesse, the f of David
1Sa 2:25 not heed the voice of their f
1Sa 2:27 f when they were in Egypt in
1Sa 2:28 f all the offerings of the
1Sa 2:30 the house of your f would
1Sa 9: 3 the donkeys of Kish, Saul's f
1Sa 9: 5 lest my f cease caring about
1Sa 10: 2 now your f has ceased caring
1Sa 10:12 But who is their f
1Sa 14: 1 But he did not tell his f
1Sa 14:27 f charge the people with the
1Sa 14:28 Your f strictly charged the
1Sa 14:29 My f has troubled the land
1Sa 14:51 Kish was the f of Saul, and
1Sa 14:51 Ner the f of Abner was the
1Sa 19: 2 My f Saul seeks to kill you
1Sa 19: 3 and stand beside my f in the
1Sa 19: 3 speak with my f about you
1Sa 19: 4 well of David to Saul his f
1Sa 20: 1 what is my sin before your f
1Sa 20: 2 my f will do nothing either
1Sa 20: 2 why should my f hide this
1Sa 20: 3 Your f certainly knows that I
1Sa 20: 6 If your f misses me at all,
1Sa 20: 8 should you bring me to your f
1Sa 20: 9 by my f to come upon you,
1Sa 20:10 or what if your f answers you
1Sa 20:12 out my f sometime tomorrow
1Sa 20:13 pleases my f to do you evil
1Sa 20:13 you as He has been with my f
1Sa 20:32 Jonathan answered Saul his f
1Sa 20:33 by his f to kill David
1Sa 20:34 because his f had treated him
1Sa 22: 3 Please let my f and mother
1Sa 22:15 to any in the house of my f
1Sa 23:17 Saul my f shall not find you
1Sa 23:17 Even my f Saul knows that
1Sa 24:11 Moreover, my f, see
2Sa 3: 8 to the house of Saul your f
2Sa 6:21 chose me instead of your f
2Sa 7:14 I will be his F, and he shall
2Sa 10: 2 as his f showed kindness to
2Sa 10: 2 comfort him concerning his f
2Sa 10: 3 your f because he has sent
2Sa 13: 5 when your f comes to see you,
2Sa 16: 3 the kingdom of my f to me
2Sa 16:21 you are abhorred by your f
2Sa 17: 8 you know your f and his men,
2Sa 17: 8 your f is a man of war, and
2Sa 17:10 that your f is a mighty man
2Sa 19:37 buried by the grave of my f
2Sa 21:14 in the tomb of Kish his f
1Ki 1: 6 his f had not rebuked him at
1Ki 2:12 on the throne of his f David
1Ki 2:24 on the throne of David my f
1Ki 2:26 Lord GOD before my f David
1Ki 2:26 every time my f was afflicted
1Ki 2:31 from the house of my f the
1Ki 2:32 though my f David did not
1Ki 2:44 that you did to my f David
1Ki 3: 3 the statutes of his f David
1Ki 3: 6 to your servant David my f
1Ki 3: 7 king instead of my f David
1Ki 3:14 as your f David walked, then
1Ki 5: 1 him king in place of his f
1Ki 5: 3 You know how my f David could
1Ki 5: 5 the LORD spoke to my f David
1Ki 6:12 which I spoke to your f David
1Ki 7:14 his f was a man of Tyre, a
1Ki 7:51 his f David had dedicated
1Ki 8:15 with His mouth to my f David
1Ki 8:17 it was in the heart of my f
1Ki 8:18 the LORD said to my f David
1Ki 8:20 the position of my f David
1Ki 8:24 Your servant David my f
1Ki 8:25 Your servant David my f,
1Ki 8:26 to Your servant David my f
1Ki 9: 4 Me as your f David walked
1Ki 9: 5 as I promised David your f
1Ki 11: 4 was the heart of his f David
1Ki 11: 6 the LORD, as did his f David
1Ki 11:12 for the sake of your f David
1Ki 11:27 to the City of David his f
1Ki 11:33 judgments, as did his f David
1Ki 11:43 in the City of David his f
1Ki 12: 4 Your f made our yoke heavy
1Ki 12: 4 burdensome service of your f
1Ki 12: 6 his f Solomon while he still
1Ki 12: 9 yoke which your f put on us'
1Ki 12:10 Your f made our yoke heavy,
1Ki 12:11 whereas my f laid a heavy
1Ki 12:11 my f chastised you with whips

1Ki 12:14 My f made your yoke heavy,
1Ki 12:14 my f chastised you with whips
1Ki 13:11 they also told their f the
1Ki 13:12 And their f said to them,
1Ki 15: 3 in all the sins of his f,
1Ki 15: 3 was the heart of his f David
1Ki 15:11 the LORD, as did his f David
1Ki 15:15 which his f had dedicated
1Ki 15:19 between my f and your f
1Ki 15:24 in the City of David his f
1Ki 15:26 and walked in the way of his f
1Ki 19:20 Please let me kiss my f and my
1Ki 20:34 The cities which my f took
1Ki 20:34 from your f I will restore
1Ki 20:34 as my f did in Samaria
1Ki 22:43 in all the ways of his f Asa
1Ki 22:46 in the days of his f Asa, he
1Ki 22:50 in the City of David his f
1Ki 22:52 and walked in the way of his f
1Ki 22:53 to all that his f had done
2Ki 2:12 My f, my f, the chariot
2Ki 2:12 My f, my f, the chariot
2Ki 3: 2 the LORD, but not like his f
2Ki 3: 2 of Baal that his f had made
2Ki 3:13 Go to the prophets of your f
2Ki 4:18 day that he went out to his f
2Ki 4:19 And he said to his f, "My
2Ki 5:13 My f, if the prophet had told
2Ki 6:21 My f, shall I kill them
2Ki 9:25 together behind Ahab his f
2Ki 13:14 O my f, my f, the
2Ki 13:25 hand of Jehoahaz his f by war
2Ki 14: 3 yet not like his f David
2Ki 14: 3 as his f Joash had done
2Ki 14: 5 had murdered his f the king
2Ki 14:21 king instead of his f Amaziah
2Ki 15: 3 that his f Amaziah had done
2Ki 15:34 that his f Uzziah had done
2Ki 15:38 in the City of David his f
2Ki 16: 2 God, as his f David had done
2Ki 18: 3 all that his f David had done
2Ki 20: 5 LORD, the God of David your f
2Ki 21: 3 Hezekiah his f had destroyed
2Ki 21:20 as his f Manasseh had done
2Ki 21:21 ways that his f had walked
2Ki 21:21 idols that his f had served
2Ki 22: 2 all the ways of his f David
2Ki 23:34 king in place of his f Josiah
2Ki 24: 9 to all that his f had done
1Ch 2:17 the f of Amasa was Jether the
1Ch 2:21 of Machir the f of Gilead
1Ch 2:23 of Machir the f of Gilead
1Ch 2:24 him Ashhur the f of Tekoa
1Ch 2:42 who was the f of Ziph, and
1Ch 2:42 of Mareshah the f of Hebron
1Ch 2:44 begot Raham the f of Jorkoam
1Ch 2:45 and Maon was the f of Beth Zur
1Ch 2:49 Shaaph the f of Madmannah
1Ch 2:49 Sheva the f of Machbenah and
1Ch 2:49 Machbenah and the f of Gibea
1Ch 2:50 were Shobal the f of Kirjath
1Ch 2:51 Salma the f of Bethlehem, and
1Ch 2:51 Hareph the f of Beth Gader
1Ch 2:52 And Shobal the f of Kirjath
1Ch 2:55 the f of the house of Rechab
1Ch 4: 3 the sons of the f of Etam
1Ch 4: 4 and Penuel was the f of Gedor
1Ch 4: 4 and Ezer was the f of Hushah
1Ch 4: 4 Ephrathah the f of Bethlehem
1Ch 4: 5 Ashhur the f of Tekoa had two
1Ch 4:11 who was the f of Eshton
1Ch 4:12 Tehinnah the f of Ir-Nahash
1Ch 4:14 Joab the f of Ge-Harashim
1Ch 4:17 and Ishbah the f of Eshtemoa
1Ch 4:18 bore Jered the f of Gedor
1Ch 4:18 Gedor, Heber the f of Sochoh
1Ch 4:18 and Jekuthiel the f of Zanoah
1Ch 4:21 Judah were Er the f of Lecah
1Ch 4:21 Laadah the f of Mareshah, and
1Ch 7:14 him Machir the f of Gilead
1Ch 7:14 of Gilead, the f of Asriel
1Ch 7:22 their f mourned many days
1Ch 7:31 who was the f of Birzaith
1Ch 8:29 Now the f of Gibeon, whose
1Ch 9:35 Jeiel the f of Gibeon, whose
1Ch 17:13 I will be his F, and he shall
1Ch 19: 2 because his f showed kindness
1Ch 19: 2 comfort him concerning his f
1Ch 19: 3 your f because he has sent
1Ch 22:10 be My son, and I will be his F
1Ch 24: 2 and Abihu died before their f
1Ch 24:19 by the hand of Aaron their f
1Ch 25: 3 direction of their f Jeduthun
1Ch 25: 6 the direction of their f for
1Ch 26:10 his f made him the first),
1Ch 28: 4 my f to be king over Israel
1Ch 28: 4 of Judah, the house of my f
1Ch 28: 4 and among the sons of my f
1Ch 28: 6 be My son, and I will be his F
1Ch 28: 9 know the God of your f, and
1Ch 29:10 LORD God of Israel, our F
1Ch 29:23 king instead of David his f
2Ch 1: 8 great mercy to David my f
2Ch 1: 9 to David my f be established
2Ch 2: 3 have dealt with David my f
2Ch 2: 7 whom David my f provided
2Ch 2:14 his f was a man of Tyre),
2Ch 2:14 men of my lord David your f
2Ch 2:17 David his f had numbered them
2Ch 3: 1 had appeared to his f David
2Ch 5: 1 his f David had dedicated
2Ch 6: 4 with His mouth to my f David
2Ch 6: 7 it was in the heart of my f
2Ch 6: 8 the LORD said to my f David
2Ch 6:10 the position of my f David
2Ch 6:15 Your servant David my f
2Ch 6:16 Your servant David my f,
2Ch 7:17 Me as your f David walked
2Ch 7:18 covenanted with David your f
2Ch 8:14 to the order of David his f
2Ch 9:31 in the City of David his f
2Ch 10: 4 Your f made our yoke heavy
2Ch 10: 4 burdensome service of your f
2Ch 10: 6 his f Solomon while he still
2Ch 10: 9 yoke which your f put on us'
2Ch 10:10 Your f made our yoke heavy,
2Ch 10:11 whereas my f put a heavy yoke
2Ch 10:11 my f chastised you with whips
2Ch 10:14 My f made your yoke heavy,
2Ch 10:14 my f chastised you with whips
2Ch 15:18 that his f had dedicated and
2Ch 16: 3 between my f and your f
2Ch 17: 2 which Asa his f had taken
2Ch 17: 3 former ways of his f David
2Ch 17: 4 but sought the God of his f
2Ch 20:32 in the way of his f Asa, and
2Ch 21: 3 Their f gave them great gifts
2Ch 21: 4 over the kingdom of his f
2Ch 21:12 the LORD God of your f David
2Ch 21:12 ways of Jehoshaphat your f
2Ch 22: 4 after the death of his f, to
2Ch 24:22 his f had done to him, but
2Ch 25: 3 had murdered his f the king
2Ch 26: 1 king instead of his f Amaziah
2Ch 26: 4 that his f Amaziah had done
2Ch 27: 2 f Uzziah had done (although
2Ch 28: 1 LORD, as his f David had done
2Ch 29: 2 all that his f David had done
2Ch 33: 3 his f had broken down
2Ch 33:22 as his f Manasseh had done
2Ch 33:22 which his f Manasseh had made
2Ch 33:23 as his f Manasseh had humbled
2Ch 34: 2 in the ways of his f David
2Ch 34: 3 seek the God of his f David
Esth 2: 7 she had neither f nor mother
Esth 2: 7 When her f and mother died,
Job 15:10 us, much older than your f
Job 17:14 to corruption, 'You are my f
Job 29:16 I was a f to the poor, and I
Job 31:18 my youth I reared him as a f
Job 38:28 Has the rain a f
Job 42:15 and their f gave them an
Ps 27:10 When my f and my mother
Ps 68: 5 A f of the fatherless, a
Ps 89:26 cry to Me, 'You are my F, My
Ps 103:13 As a f pities his children,
Prov 1: 8 the instruction of your f
Prov 3:12 just as a f the son in whom
Prov 4: 1 the instruction of a f, and
Prov 10: 1 A wise son makes a glad f
Prov 15:20 A wise son makes a f glad
Prov 17: 6 glory of children is their f
Prov 17:21 the f of a fool has no joy
Prov 17:25 son is a grief to his f, and
Prov 19:13 son is the ruin of his f, and
Prov 19:26 He who mistreats his f and
Prov 20:20 curses his f or his mother
Prov 23:22 to your f who begot you, and
Prov 23:24 The f of the righteous will
Prov 23:25 Let your f and your mother be
Prov 28: 7 of gluttons shames his f
Prov 28:24 robs his f or his mother, and
Prov 29: 3 wisdom makes his f rejoice
Prov 30:11 generation that curses its f
Prov 30:17 The eye that mocks his f, and
Is 3: 6 brother In the house of his f
Is 8: 4 have knowledge to cry 'My f'
Is 9: 6 Mighty God, Everlasting F
Is 22:21 He shall be a f to the
Is 38: 5 LORD, the God of David your f
Is 38:19 the f shall make known Your
Is 43:27 Your first f sinned, and your
Is 45:10 Woe to him who says to his f
Is 51: 2 Look to Abraham your f, and to
Is 58:14 the heritage of Jacob your f
Is 63:16 Doubtless You are our F,
Is 63:16 You, O LORD, are our F
Is 64: 8 now, O LORD, You are our F
Jer 2:27 to a tree, 'You are my f,' and
Jer 3: 4 this time cry to Me, 'My f
Jer 3:19 My F," and not turn away from
Jer 12: 6 brothers, the house of your f
Jer 16: 7 for their f or their mother
Jer 20:15 who brought news to my f,
Jer 22:11 instead of Josiah his f, who
Jer 22:15 Did not your f eat and drink,
Jer 31: 9 for I am a F to Israel, and
Jer 35: 6 the son of Rechab, our f,
Jer 35: 8 the son of Rechab, our f, in
Jer 35:10 Jonadab our f commanded us
Jer 35:16 the commandment of their f
Jer 35:18 of Jonadab your f
Ezek 16: 3 your f was an Amorite and your
Ezek 16:45 Hittite and your f an Amorite
Ezek 18: 4 the soul of the f as well as
Ezek 18:14 the sins which his f has done
Ezek 18:17 die for the iniquity of his f
Ezek 18:18 As for his f, because he
Ezek 18:19 not bear the guilt of the f
Ezek 18:20 not bear the guilt of the f
Ezek 18:20 nor the f bear the guilt of
Ezek 22: 7 you they have made light of f
Ezek 44:25 Only for f or mother, for son
Dan 5: 2 f Nebuchadnezzar had taken
Dan 5:11 And in the days of your f,
Dan 5:11 King Nebuchadnezzar your f
Dan 5:11 your f the king
Dan 5:13 whom my f the king brought
Dan 5:18 your f a kingdom and majesty,
Amos 2: 7 his f go in to the same girl,
Mic 7: 6 For son dishonors f, daughter
Zech 13: 3 still prophesies, then his f
Zech 13: 3 And his f and mother who begot
Mal 1: 6 A son honors his f, and a
Mal 1: 6 If then I am the F, where is
Mal 2:10 Have we not all one F
Matt 2:22 Judea instead of his f Herod
Matt 3: 9 We have Abraham as our f
Matt 4:21 the boat with Zebedee their f
Matt 4:22 they left the boat and their f
Matt 5:16 and glorify your F in heaven
Matt 5:45 be sons of your F in heaven
Matt 5:48 just as your F in heaven is
Matt 6: 1 reward from your F in heaven
Matt 6: 4 your F who sees in secret
Matt 6: 6 pray to your F who is in the
Matt 6: 6 your F who sees in secret
Matt 6: 8 For your F knows the things
Matt 6: 9 Our F in heaven, hallowed be
Matt 6:14 your heavenly F will also
Matt 6:15 neither will your F forgive
Matt 6:18 but to your F who is in the
Matt 6:18 your F who sees in secret
Matt 6:26 your heavenly F feeds them
Matt 6:32 For your heavenly F knows
Matt 7:11 how much more will your F who
Matt 7:21 the will of My F in heaven
Matt 8:21 let me first go and bury my f
Matt 10:20 of your F who speaks in you
Matt 10:21 to death, and a f his child
Matt 10:32 before My F who is in heaven
Matt 10:33 before My F who is in heaven
Matt 10:35 to set a man against his f
Matt 10:37 He who loves f or mother more
Matt 11:25 I thank You, F, Lord of
Matt 11:26 Even so, F, for so it seemed
Matt 11:27 been delivered to Me by My F
Matt 11:27 knows the Son except the F
Matt 11:27 know the F except the Son
Matt 12:50 My F in heaven is My brother

Matt 13:43 sun in the kingdom of their F
Matt 15: 4 saying, 'Honor your f and
Matt 15: 4 He who curses f or mother
Matt 15: 5 says to his f or mother
Matt 15: 6 from honoring his f or mother
Matt 15:13 F has not planted will be
Matt 16:17 but My F who is in heaven
Matt 16:27 of His F with His angels, and
Matt 18:10 face of My F who is in heaven
Matt 18:14 F who is in heaven that one
Matt 18:19 for them by My F in heaven
Matt 18:35 So My heavenly F also will do
Matt 19: 5 a man shall leave his f and
Matt 19:19 Honor your f and your mother,
Matt 19:29 or f or mother or wife or
Matt 20:23 whom it is prepared by My F
Matt 21:31 the two did the will of his f
Matt 23: 9 call anyone on earth your f
Matt 23: 9 for One is your F, He who is
Matt 24:36 of heaven, but My F only
Matt 25:34 Come, you blessed of My F
Matt 26:39 O My F, if it is possible,
Matt 26:42 O My F, if this cup cannot
Matt 26:53 I cannot now pray to My F
Matt 28:19 them in the name of the F
Mark 1:20 they left their f Zebedee in
Mark 5:40 them all out, He took the f
Mark 7:10 For Moses said, 'Honor your f
Mark 7:10 He who curses f or mother
Mark 7:11 a man says to his f or mother
Mark 7:12 for his f or his mother,
Mark 8:38 of His F with the holy angels
Mark 9:21 So He asked his f, "How long
Mark 9:24 Immediately the f of the
Mark 10: 7 a man shall leave his f and
Mark 10:19 not defraud, 'Honor your f
Mark 10:29 or f or mother or wife or
Mark 11:10 is the kingdom of our f David
Mark 11:25 that your F in heaven may
Mark 11:26 neither will your F in heaven
Mark 13:12 to death, and a f his child
Mark 13:32 nor the Son, but only the F
Mark 14:36 Abba, F, all things are
Mark 15:21 the f of Alexander and Rufus,
Luke 1:32 Him the throne of His f David
Luke 1:59 him by the name of his f,
Luke 1:62 So they made signs to his f
Luke 1:67 Now his f Zacharias was
Luke 1:73 He swore to our f Abraham
Luke 2:48 Look, Your f and I have sought
Luke 3: 8 We have Abraham as our f
Luke 6:36 just as your F also is
Luke 8:51 James, and John, and the f
Luke 9:42 and gave him back to his f
Luke 9:59 let me first go and bury my f
Luke 10:21 I praise You, F, Lord of
Luke 10:21 Even so, F, for so it seemed
Luke 10:22 been delivered to Me by My F
Luke 10:22 who the Son is but the F, and
Luke 10:22 who the F is but the Son, and
Luke 11: 2 Our F in heaven, hallowed be
Luke 11:11 bread from any f among you
Luke 11:13 F give the Holy Spirit to
Luke 12:30 your F knows that you need
Luke 12:53 F will be divided against son
Luke 12:53 against son and son against f
Luke 14:26 to Me and does not hate his f
Luke 15:12 younger of them said to his f
Luke 15:12 F, give me the portion of goods
Luke 15:18 I will arise and go to my f
Luke 15:18 F, I have sinned against
Luke 15:20 And he arose and came to his f
Luke 15:20 way off, his f saw him and had
Luke 15:21 And the son said to him, 'F
Luke 15:22 But the f said to his
Luke 15:27 your f has killed the fatted
Luke 15:28 Therefore his f came out and
Luke 15:29 he answered and said to his f
Luke 16:24 F Abraham, have mercy on me,
Luke 16:27 said, 'I beg you therefore, f
Luke 16:30 And he said, 'No, f Abraham
Luke 18:20 false witness', 'Honor your f
Luke 22:29 just as My F bestowed one
Luke 22:42 F, if it is Your will, remove
Luke 23:34 F, forgive them, for they do
Luke 23:46 F, 'into Your hands I commend
Luke 24:49 the Promise of My F upon you
John 1:14 of the only begotten of the F
John 1:18 who is in the bosom of the F
John 3:35 The F loves the Son, and has
John 4:12 You greater than our f Jacob
John 4:21 in Jerusalem, worship the F
John 4:23 will worship the F in spirit
John 4:23 for the F is seeking such to
John 4:53 So the f knew that it was at
John 5:17 My F has been working until
John 5:18 also said that God was His F
John 5:19 but what He sees the F do
John 5:20 For the F loves the Son, and
John 5:21 For as the F raises the dead
John 5:22 For the F judges no one, but
John 5:23 Son just as they honor the F
John 5:23 not honor the F who sent Him
John 5:26 For as the F has life in
John 5:30 the will of the F who sent Me
John 5:36 the F has given Me to finish
John 5:36 of Me, that the F has sent Me
John 5:37 the F Himself, who sent Me,
John 5:45 I shall accuse you to the F
John 6:27 because God the F has set His
John 6:32 but My F gives you the true
John 6:37 All that the F gives Me will
John 6:39 the will of the F who sent Me
John 6:42 the son of Joseph, whose f
John 6:44 the F who sent Me draws him
John 6:45 from the F comes to Me
John 6:46 that anyone has seen the F
John 6:46 He has seen the F
John 6:57 As the living F sent Me, and I
John 6:57 and I live because of the F
John 6:65 been granted to him by My F
John 8:16 I am with the F who sent Me
John 8:18 and the F who sent Me bears
John 8:19 Where is Your F
John 8:19 You know neither Me nor My F
John 8:19 would have known My F also
John 8:27 He spoke to them of the F
John 8:28 but as My F taught Me, I
John 8:29 The F has not left Me alone,
John 8:38 what I have seen with My F
John 8:38 you have seen with your f
John 8:39 Abraham is our f
John 8:41 You do the deeds of your f
John 8:41 we have one F
John 8:42 If God were your F, you would
John 8:44 You are of your f the devil
John 8:44 of your f you want to do
John 8:44 he is a liar and the f of it
John 8:49 but I honor My F, and you
John 8:53 greater than our f Abraham
John 8:54 It is My F who honors Me, of
John 8:56 Your f Abraham rejoiced to
John 10:15 As the F knows Me, even so I
John 10:15 Me, even so I know the F
John 10:17 Therefore My F loves Me,
John 10:18 I have received from My F
John 10:29 My F, who has given them to
John 10:30 I and My F are one
John 10:32 I have shown you from My F
John 10:36 of Him whom the F sanctified
John 10:37 I do not do the works of My F
John 10:38 believe that the F is in Me
John 11:41 F, I thank You that You have
John 12:26 Me, him My F will honor
John 12:27 F, save Me from this hour'
John 12:28 F, glorify Your name
John 12:49 but the F who sent Me gave Me
John 12:50 just as the F has told Me
John 13: 1 from this world to the F,
John 13: 3 knowing that the F had given
John 14: 6 to the F except through Me
John 14: 7 would have known My F also
John 14: 8 Lord, show us the F, and it is
John 14: 9 has seen Me has seen the F
John 14: 9 can you say, 'Show us the F'
John 14:10 believe that I am in the F
John 14:10 and the F in Me
John 14:10 but the F who dwells in Me
John 14:11 Believe Me that I am in the F
John 14:11 the F in Me, or else believe
John 14:12 will do, because I go to My F
John 14:13 that the F may be glorified
John 14:16 And I will pray the F, and He
John 14:20 will know that I am in My F
John 14:21 Me will be loved by My F, and
John 14:23 My F will love him, and We
John 14:26 whom the F will send in My
John 14:28 I said, 'I am going to the F
John 14:28 for My F is greater than I
John 14:31 may know that I love the F
John 14:31 F gave Me commandment,
John 15: 1 and My F is the vinedresser
John 15: 8 By this My F is glorified,
John 15: 9 As the F loved Me, I also
John 15:15 My F I have made known to you
John 15:16 that whatever you ask the F
John 15:23 who hates Me hates My F also
John 15:24 also hated both Me and My F
John 15:26 shall send to you from the F
John 15:26 truth who proceeds from the F
John 16: 3 have not known the F nor Me
John 16:10 because I go to My F and you
John 16:15 that the F has are Mine
John 16:16 see Me, because I go to the F
John 16:17 and, 'because I go to the F'
John 16:23 whatever you ask the F in My
John 16:25 tell you plainly about the F
John 16:26 I shall pray the F for you
John 16:27 for the F Himself loves you,
John 16:28 I came forth from the F and
John 16:28 the world and go to the F
John 16:32 because the F is with Me
John 17: 1 F, the hour has come
John 17: 5 And now, O F, glorify Me
John 17:11 Holy F, keep through Your
John 17:21 all may be one, as You, F
John 17:24 F, I desire that they also
John 17:25 O righteous F
John 18:11 cup which My F has given Me
John 20:17 have not yet ascended to My F
John 20:17 ascending to My F and your F
John 20:21 As the F has sent Me, I also
Acts 1: 4 wait for the Promise of the F
Acts 1: 7 the F has put in His own
Acts 2:33 the F the promise of the Holy
Acts 7: 2 our f Abraham when he was in
Acts 7: 4 there, when his f was dead
Acts 7:14 sent and called his f Jacob
Acts 7:16 of Hamor, the f of Shechem
Acts 16: 1 believed, but his f was Greek
Acts 16: 3 all knew that his f was Greek
Acts 28: 8 it happened that the f of
Rom 1: 7 you and peace from God our F
Rom 4: 1 we say that Abraham our f has
Rom 4:11 that he might be the f of all
Rom 4:12 and the f of circumcision to
Rom 4:12 of the faith which our f
Rom 4:16 who is the f of us all
Rom 4:17 I have made you a f of many
Rom 4:18 became the f of many nations
Rom 6: 4 dead by the glory of the F
Rom 8:15 we cry out, "Abba, F."
Rom 9:10 one man, even by our f Isaac
Rom 15: 6 F of our Lord Jesus Christ
1Co 1: 3 you and peace from God our F
1Co 8: 6 there is only one God, the F
1Co 15:24 the kingdom to God the F,
2Co 1: 2 you and peace from God our F
2Co 1: 3 F of our Lord Jesus Christ,
2Co 1: 3 the F of mercies and God of
2Co 6:18 I will be a F to you, and you
2Co 11:31 F of our Lord Jesus Christ,
Gal 1: 1 God the F who raised Him from
Gal 1: 3 you and peace from God the F
Gal 1: 4 to the will of our God and F
Gal 4: 2 the time appointed by the f
Gal 4: 6 hearts, crying out, "Abba, F!"
Eph 1: 2 you and peace from God our F
Eph 1: 3 F of our Lord Jesus Christ,
Eph 1:17 the F of glory, may give to
Eph 2:18 access by one Spirit to the F
Eph 3:14 I bow my knees to the F of
Eph 4: 6 F of all, who is above all,
Eph 5:20 the F in the name of our Lord
Eph 5:31 a man shall leave his f and
Eph 6: 2 Honor your f and mother,"
Eph 6:23 with faith, from God the F
Phil 1: 2 you and peace from God our F
Phil 2:11 to the glory of God the F
Phil 2:22 that as a son with his f he
Phil 4:20 F be glory forever and ever
Col 1: 2 you and peace from God our F
Col 1: 3 F of our Lord Jesus Christ,
Col 1:12 giving thanks to the F who
Col 1:19 For it pleased the F that in
Col 2: 2 mystery of God, both of the F
Col 3:17 to God the F through Him
1Th 1: 1 Thessalonians in God the F
1Th 1: 1 you and peace from God our F

1Th 1: 3 in the sight of our God and F
1Th 2:11 as a f does his own children,
1Th 3:11 F Himself, and our Lord Jesus
1Th 3:13 F at the coming of our Lord
2Th 1: 1 Thessalonians in God our F
2Th 1: 2 you and peace from God our F
2Th 2:16 Himself, and our God and F,
1Ti 1: 2 and peace from God our F and
1Ti 5: 1 man, but exhort him as a f
2Ti 1: 2 and peace from God the F and
Tit 1: 4 and peace from God the F and
Phm 3 you and peace from God our F
Heb 1: 5 I will be to Him a F, and He
Heb 7: 3 without f, without mother,
Heb 7:10 f when Melchizedek met him
Heb 12: 7 whom a f does not chasten
Heb 12: 9 to the F of spirits and live
Jas 1:17 down from the F of lights
Jas 1:27 before God and the F is this
Jas 2:21 Was not Abraham our f
Jas 3: 9 With it we bless our God and F
1Pe 1: 2 foreknowledge of God the F
1Pe 1: 3 F of our Lord Jesus Christ,
1Pe 1:17 And if you call on the F, who
2Pe 1:17 received from God the F honor
1Jn 1: 2 life which was with the F
1Jn 1: 3 our fellowship is with the F
1Jn 2: 1 have an Advocate with the F
1Jn 2:13 because you have known the F
1Jn 2:15 love of the F is not in him
1Jn 2:16 is not of the F but is of the
1Jn 2:22 antichrist who denies the F
1Jn 2:23 does not have the F either
1Jn 2:23 the Son has the F also
1Jn 2:24 abide in the Son and in the F
1Jn 3: 1 love the F has bestowed on us
1Jn 4:14 testify that the F has sent
1Jn 5: 7 the F, the Word, and the Holy
2Jn 3 be with you from God the F
2Jn 3 Christ, the Son of the F, in
2Jn 4 commandment from the F
2Jn 9 of Christ has both the F and
Jude 1 sanctified by God the F, and
Rev 1: 6 and priests to His God and F
Rev 2:27 also have received from My F
Rev 3: 5 confess his name before My F
Rev 3:21 down with My F on His throne

FATHERED (*see* FATHER)
Deut 32:18 forgotten the God who f you

FATHER-IN-LAW (*see* FATHER)
Gen 38:13 your f is going up to Timnah
Gen 38:25 out, she sent to her f,
Ex 3: 1 the flock of Jethro his f
Ex 4:18 and returned to Jethro his f
Ex 18: 1 priest of Midian, Moses' f
Ex 18: 2 Then Jethro, Moses' f, took
Ex 18: 5 and Jethro, Moses' f, came
Ex 18: 6 your f Jethro, am coming to
Ex 18: 7 Moses went out to meet his f
Ex 18: 8 Moses told his f all that the
Ex 18:12 Then Jethro, Moses' f, took a
Ex 18:12 with Moses' f before God
Ex 18:14 So when Moses' f saw all that
Ex 18:15 And Moses said to his f
Ex 18:17 So Moses' f said to him
Ex 18:24 heeded the voice of his f
Ex 18:27 Then Moses let his f depart
Num 10:29 Reuel the Midianite, Moses' f
Judg 1:16 of the Kenite, Moses' f, went
Judg 4:11 of Hobab the f of Moses, had
Judg 19: 4 Now his f, the young woman's
Judg 19: 7 to depart, his f urged him
Judg 19: 9 his f, the young woman's
1Sa 4:19 was captured, and that her f
1Sa 4:21 captured and because of her f
John 18:13 for he was the f of Caiaphas

FATHERLESS (*see* FATHER)
Ex 22:22 afflict any widow or f child
Ex 22:24 be widows, and your children f
Deut 10:18 administers justice for the f
Deut 14:29 you, and the stranger and the f
Deut 16:11 gates, the stranger and the f
Deut 16:14 Levite, the stranger and the f
Deut 24:17 due the stranger or the f
Deut 24:19 be for the stranger, the f
Deut 24:20 be for the stranger, the f
Deut 24:21 be for the stranger, the f
Deut 26:12 Levite, the stranger, the f
Deut 26:13 Levite, the stranger, the f
Deut 27:19 due the stranger, the f, and
Job 6:27 Yes, you overwhelm the f, and
Job 22: 9 strength of the f was crushed
Job 24: 3 away the donkey of the f
Job 24: 9 snatch the f from the breast
Job 29:12 poor who cried out, and the f
Job 31:17 so that the f may not eat of
Job 31:21 raised my hand against the f
Ps 10:14 You are the helper of the f
Ps 10:18 To do justice to the f and the
Ps 68: 5 A father of the f, a defender
Ps 82: 3 Defend the poor and f
Ps 94: 6 the stranger, And murder the f
Ps 109: 9 Let his children be f, And his
Ps 109:12 any to favor his f children
Ps 146: 9 He relieves the f and widow
Prov 23:10 nor enter the fields of the f
Is 1:17 defend the f, plead for the
Is 1:23 They do not defend the f, nor
Is 9:17 nor have mercy on their f
Is 10: 2 and that they may rob the f
Jer 5:28 the cause, the cause of the f
Jer 7: 6 oppress the stranger, the f
Jer 22: 3 to the stranger, the f, or
Jer 49:11 Leave your f children, I will
Ezek 22: 7 they have mistreated the f
Hos 14: 3 For in You the f finds mercy
Zech 7:10 oppress the widow or the f
Mal 3: 5 earners and widows and the f

FATHER'S (*see* FATHER)
Gen 9:23 did not see their f nakedness
Gen 12: 1 kindred and from your f house
Gen 20:13 me to wander from my f house
Gen 24: 7 who took me from my f house
Gen 24:23 your f house for us to lodge
Gen 24:38 you shall go to my f house
Gen 24:40 my kindred and from my f house
Gen 26:15 his f servants had dug in the
Gen 28:21 back to my f house in peace
Gen 29: 9 Rachel came with her f sheep
Gen 29:12 that he was her f relative
Gen 31: 1 taken away all that was our f
Gen 31: 1 from what was our f he has
Gen 31: 5 I see your f countenance,
Gen 31:14 for us in our f house
Gen 31:19 idols that were her f
Gen 31:30 greatly long for your f house
Gen 35:22 with Bilhah his f concubine
Gen 37: 2 sons of Zilpah, his f wives
Gen 37:12 feed their f flock in Shechem
Gen 38:11 Remain a widow in your f
Gen 38:11 went and dwelt in her f house
Gen 41:51 all my toil and all my f house
Gen 46:31 and to his f household,
Gen 46:31 and those of my f house, who
Gen 47:12 and all his f household with
Gen 48:17 his f hand to remove it from
Gen 49: 4 you went up to your f bed
Gen 49: 8 your f children shall bow
Gen 50: 1 Joseph fell on his f face
Gen 50: 8 his brothers, and his f house
Gen 50:22 Egypt, he and his f household
Ex 2:16 to water their f flock
Ex 6:20 his f sister, as wife
Ex 15: 2 my f God, and I will exalt Him
Lev 16:32 as priest in his f place,
Lev 18: 8 The nakedness of your f wife
Lev 18: 8 it is your f nakedness
Lev 18:11 of your f wife's daughter
Lev 18:12 nakedness of your f sister
Lev 18:14 nakedness of your f brother
Lev 20:11 his f wife has uncovered his
Lev 20:11 has uncovered his f nakedness
Lev 20:17 sister, his f daughter or his
Lev 20:19 sister nor of your f sister
Lev 22:13 has returned to her f house
Lev 22:13 youth, she may eat her f food
Num 1: 4 one the head of his f house
Num 1:44 one representing his f house
Num 2: 2 the emblems of his f house
Num 17: 2 them a rod from each f house
Num 17: 3 for the head of each f house
Num 18: 1 your f house with you shall
Num 25:14 a leader of a f house among
Num 25:15 people of a f house in Midian
Num 27: 7 among their f brothers, and
Num 27:10 inheritance to his f brothers
Num 30: 3 in her f house in her youth
Num 30:16 in her youth in her f house
Num 32:14 have risen in your f place
Num 36: 6 the family of their f tribe
Num 36: 8 of the family of her f tribe
Num 36:11 the sons of their f brothers
Num 36:12 the tribe of their f family
Deut 22:21 to the door of her f house
Deut 22:21 the harlot in her f house
Deut 22:30 man shall not take his f wife
Deut 22:30 wife, nor uncover his f bed
Deut 27:20 one who lies with his f wife
Deut 27:20 he has uncovered his f bed
Josh 2:12 show kindness to my f house
Josh 2:18 all your f household to your
Josh 6:25 her f household, and all that
Josh 17: 4 among their f brothers
Judg 6:15 I am the least in my f house
Judg 6:25 Take your f young bull, the
Judg 6:27 he feared his f household
Judg 9: 5 went to his f house at Ophrah
Judg 9:18 against my f house this day
Judg 11: 2 no inheritance in our f house
Judg 11: 7 and expel me from my f house
Judg 14:15 you and your f house with fire
Judg 14:19 went back up to his f house
Judg 16:31 all his f household came down
Judg 19: 2 went away from him to her f
Judg 19: 3 brought him into her f house
1Sa 2:31 and the arm of your f house
1Sa 9:20 on you and on all your f house
1Sa 17:15 feed his f sheep at Bethlehem
1Sa 17:25 give his f house exemption in
1Sa 17:34 used to keep his f sheep, and
1Sa 18: 2 home to his f house anymore
1Sa 18:18 life or my f family in Israel
1Sa 22: 1 all his f house heard it,
1Sa 22:11 of Ahitub, and all his f house
1Sa 22:16 you and all your f house
1Sa 22:22 the persons of your f house
1Sa 24:21 my name from my f house
2Sa 2:32 and buried him in his f tomb
2Sa 3: 7 you gone in to my f concubine
2Sa 3:29 of Joab and on all his f house
2Sa 9: 7 for Jonathan your f sake, and
2Sa 14: 9 be on me and on my f house
2Sa 15:34 your f servant previously
2Sa 16:19 served in your f presence
2Sa 16:21 Go in to your f concubines
2Sa 16:22 and Absalom went in to his f
2Sa 17:23 he was buried in his f tomb
2Sa 19:28 For all of my f house were
2Sa 24:17 me and against my f house
1Ki 11:17 of his f servants with him
1Ki 12:10 be thicker than my f waist
1Ki 18:18 your f house have, in that
2Ki 10: 3 sons, set him on his f throne
2Ki 23:30 made him king in his f place
1Ch 4:38 and their f house increased
1Ch 5: 1 because he defiled his f bed
1Ch 5:13 brethren of their f house
1Ch 5:15 was chief of their f house
1Ch 7: 2 heads of their f house
1Ch 9: 9 a f house in their fathers'
1Ch 9:19 brethren, from his f house
1Ch 12:28 from his f house twenty-two
1Ch 12:30 men throughout their f house
1Ch 21:17 my f house, but not against
1Ch 23:11 were assigned as one f house
1Ch 24: 6 one f house taken for Eleazar
1Ch 26:13 according to their f house
2Ch 10:10 be thicker than my f waist
2Ch 21:13 those of your f household
2Ch 31:17 according to their f house
2Ch 35: 5 of the f house of the Levites
2Ch 36: 1 in his f place in Jerusalem
Ezra 2:59 f house or their genealogy
Neh 1: 6 Both my f house and I have
Neh 7:61 f house nor their lineage
Esth 4:14 and your f house will perish
Ps 45:10 people also, and your f house
Prov 4: 3 When I was my f son, tender
Prov 6:20 My son, keep your f command
Prov 13: 1 son heeds his f instruction
Prov 15: 5 despises his f instruction
Prov 27:10 own friend or your f friend
Is 7:17 your people and your f house
Is 22:23 throne to his f house
Is 22:24 all the glory of his f house
Jer 35:14 and obey their f commandment
Ezek 22:11 his sister, his f daughter
Matt 10:29 ground apart from your F will
Matt 26:29 new with you in My F kingdom

Luke 2:49 I must be about My F business
Luke 9:26 in His own glory, and in His F
Luke 12:32 flock, for it is your F good
Luke 15:17 said, 'How many of my f hired
Luke 16:27 would send him to my f house
John 2:16 Do not make My F house a
John 5:43 I have come in My F name, and
John 10:25 works that I do in My F name
John 10:29 snatch them out of My F hand
John 14: 2 In My F house are many
John 14:24 Mine but the F who sent Me
John 15:10 I have kept My F
Acts 7:20 his f house for three months
1Co 5: 1 that a man has his f wife
Rev 14: 1 having His F name written on

FATHERS (*see* FATHER, FATHERS', FOREFATHERS)
Gen 15:15 shall go to your f in peace
Gen 31: 3 Return to the land of your f
Gen 46:34 now, both we and also our f
Gen 47: 3 both we and also our f
Gen 47: 9 of my f in the days of their
Gen 47:30 but let me lie with my f
Gen 48:15 before whom my f Abraham
Gen 48:16 and the name of my f Abraham
Gen 48:21 back to the land of your f
Gen 49:29 bury me with my f in the cave
Ex 3:13 The God of your f has sent
Ex 3:15 The LORD God of your f, the
Ex 3:16 them, "The LORD God of your f
Ex 4: 5 that the LORD God of their f
Ex 6:25 These are the heads of the f
Ex 10: 6 which neither your f nor your
Ex 10: 6 nor your fathers' f have seen
Ex 13: 5 swore to your f to give you
Ex 13:11 as He swore to you and your f
Ex 20: 5 the iniquity of the f on the
Ex 34: 7 of the f upon the children
Lev 25:41 to the possession of his f
Lev 26:40 and the iniquity of their f
Num 13: 2 their f you shall send a man
Num 14:18 the iniquity of the f on the
Num 14:23 of which I swore to their f
Num 20:15 how our f went down to Egypt
Num 20:15 afflicted us and our f
Num 26:55 of the tribes of their f
Num 31:26 priest and the chief f of the
Num 32: 8 Thus your f did when I sent
Num 32:28 to the chief f of the tribes
Num 33:54 to the tribes of your f
Num 34:14 to the house of their f, and
Num 34:14 to the house of their f, have
Num 36: 1 Now the chief f of the
Num 36: 1 the chief f of the children
Num 36: 3 from the inheritance of our f
Num 36: 4 of the tribe of our f
Num 36: 7 of the tribe of his f
Num 36: 8 the inheritance of his f
Deut 1: 8 the LORD swore to your f
Deut 1:11 f make you a thousand times
Deut 1:21 of your f has spoken to you
Deut 1:35 I swore to give to your f
Deut 4: 1 God of your f is giving you
Deut 4:31 your f which He swore to them
Deut 4:37 And because He loved your f
Deut 5: 3 make this covenant with our f
Deut 5: 9 the iniquity of the f upon
Deut 6: 3 of your f has promised you
Deut 6:10 of which He swore to your f
Deut 6:18 the LORD swore to your f,
Deut 6:23 of which He swore to our f
Deut 7: 8 oath which He swore to your f
Deut 7:12 which He swore to your f
Deut 7:13 swore to your f to give you
Deut 8: 1 the LORD swore to your f
Deut 8: 3 not know nor did your f know
Deut 8:16 which your f did not know,
Deut 8:18 which He swore to your f, as
Deut 9: 5 the LORD swore to your f, to
Deut 10:11 swore to their f to give them
Deut 10:15 LORD delighted only in your f
Deut 10:22 Your f went down to Egypt
Deut 11: 9 the LORD swore to give your f
Deut 11:21 swore to your f to give them
Deut 12: 1 f is giving you to possess
Deut 13: 6 known, neither you nor your f
Deut 13:17 just as He swore to your f
Deut 19: 8 as He swore to your f, and
Deut 19: 8 He promised to give to your f
Deut 24:16 The f shall not be put to
Deut 24:16 be put to death for their f
Deut 26: 3 swore to our f to give us
Deut 26: 7 out to the LORD God of our f
Deut 26:15 just as You swore to our f
Deut 27: 3 of your f has promised you
Deut 28:11 swore to your f to give you
Deut 28:36 you nor your f have known
Deut 28:64 you nor your f have known
Deut 29:13 as He has sworn to your f
Deut 29:25 of the LORD God of their f
Deut 30: 5 land which your f possessed
Deut 30: 5 multiply you more than your f
Deut 30: 9 as He rejoiced over your f
Deut 30:20 the LORD swore to your f, to
Deut 31: 7 sworn to their f to give them
Deut 31:16 you will rest with your f
Deut 31:20 of which I swore to their f
Deut 32:17 that your f did not fear
Josh 1: 6 swore to their f to give them
Josh 4:21 ask their f in time to come
Josh 5: 6 their f that He would give us
Josh 14: 1 the heads of the f of the
Josh 18: 3 God of your f has given you
Josh 19:51 the heads of the f of the
Josh 21: 1 Now the heads of the f of the
Josh 21: 1 to the heads of the f of the
Josh 21:43 had sworn to give to their f
Josh 21:44 that He had sworn to their f
Josh 22:28 of the LORD which our f made
Josh 24: 2 Your f, including Terah, the
Josh 24: 6 I brought your f out of Egypt
Josh 24: 6 pursued your f with chariots
Josh 24:14 away the gods which your f
Josh 24:15 f served that were on the
Josh 24:17 our f up out of the land of
Judg 2: 1 of which I swore to your f
Judg 2:10 had been gathered to their f
Judg 2:12 the LORD God of their f, who
Judg 2:17 way in which their f walked
Judg 2:19 more corruptly than their f
Judg 2:20 which I commanded their f
Judg 2:22 in them as their f kept them
Judg 3: 4 their f by the hand of Moses
Judg 6:13 which our f told us about
Judg 21:22 be, when their f or their
1Sa 12: 6 who brought your f up from
1Sa 12: 7 which He did to you and your f
1Sa 12: 8 your f cried out to the LORD,
1Sa 12: 8 brought your f out of Egypt
1Sa 12:15 you, as it was against your f
2Sa 7:12 and you rest with your f, I
1Ki 1:21 the king rests with his f
1Ki 2:10 So David rested with his f
1Ki 8: 1 the chief f of the children
1Ki 8:21 LORD which He made with our f
1Ki 8:34 which You gave to their f
1Ki 8:40 land which You gave to our f
1Ki 8:48 which You gave to their f
1Ki 8:53 brought our f out of Egypt
1Ki 8:57 with us, as He was with our f
1Ki 8:58 which He commanded our f
1Ki 9: 9 who brought their f out of
1Ki 11:21 that David rested with his f
1Ki 11:43 Solomon rested with his f
1Ki 13:22 come to the tomb of your f
1Ki 14:15 land which He gave to their f
1Ki 14:20 So he rested with his f
1Ki 14:22 all that their f had done
1Ki 14:31 So Rehoboam rested with his f
1Ki 14:31 was buried with his f in the
1Ki 15: 8 So Abijam rested with his f
1Ki 15:12 the idols that his f had made
1Ki 15:24 So Asa rested with his f, and
1Ki 15:24 was buried with his f in the
1Ki 16: 6 So Baasha rested with his f
1Ki 16:28 So Omri rested with his f
1Ki 19: 4 for I am no better than my f
1Ki 21: 3 inheritance of my f to you
1Ki 21: 4 you the inheritance of my f
1Ki 22:40 So Ahab rested with his f
1Ki 22:50 Jehoshaphat rested with his f
1Ki 22:50 was buried with his f in the
2Ki 8:24 So Joram rested with his f
2Ki 8:24 was buried with his f in the
2Ki 9:28 his f in the City of David
2Ki 10:35 So Jehu rested with his f
2Ki 12:18 the sacred things that his f
2Ki 12:21 his f in the City of David
2Ki 13: 9 So Jehoahaz rested with his f
2Ki 13:13 So Joash rested with his f
2Ki 14: 6 The f shall not be put to
2Ki 14: 6 be put to death for the f
2Ki 14:16 So Jehoash rested with his f
2Ki 14:20 his f in the City of David
2Ki 14:22 the king rested with his f
2Ki 14:29 So Jeroboam rested with his f
2Ki 15: 7 So Azariah rested with his f
2Ki 15: 7 his f in the City of David
2Ki 15: 9 the LORD, as his f had done
2Ki 15:22 So Menahem rested with his f
2Ki 15:38 So Jotham rested with his f
2Ki 15:38 was buried with his f in the
2Ki 16:20 So Ahaz rested with his f
2Ki 16:20 was buried with his f in the
2Ki 17:13 law which I commanded your f
2Ki 17:14 like the necks of their f
2Ki 17:15 that He had made with their f
2Ki 17:41 doing as their f did, even to
2Ki 19:12 whom my f have destroyed,
2Ki 20:17 what your f have accumulated
2Ki 20:21 So Hezekiah rested with his f
2Ki 21: 8 the land which I gave their f
2Ki 21:15 day their f came out of Egypt
2Ki 21:18 So Manasseh rested with his f
2Ki 21:22 forsook the LORD God of his f
2Ki 22:13 because our f have not obeyed
2Ki 22:20 I will gather you to your f
2Ki 23:32 to all that his f had done
2Ki 23:37 to all that his f had done
2Ki 24: 6 Jehoiakim rested with his f
1Ch 4:19 were the f of Keilah the
1Ch 5:25 to the God of their f, and
1Ch 6:19 Levites according to their f
1Ch 9:19 Their f had been keepers of
1Ch 12:17 may the God of our f look
1Ch 17:11 you must go to be with your f
1Ch 24:31 The chief f did just as their
1Ch 26:31 to his genealogy of the f
1Ch 29:15 before You, as were all our f
1Ch 29:18 Isaac, and Israel, our f,
1Ch 29:20 the LORD God of their f, and
2Ch 5: 2 the chief f of the children
2Ch 6:25 You gave to them and their f
2Ch 6:31 land which You gave to our f
2Ch 6:38 which You gave to their f
2Ch 7:22 the LORD God of their f, who
2Ch 9:31 Solomon rested with his f
2Ch 11:16 to the LORD God of their f
2Ch 12:16 So Rehoboam rested with his f
2Ch 13:12 the LORD God of your f, for
2Ch 13:18 on the LORD God of their f
2Ch 14: 1 So Abijah rested with his f
2Ch 14: 4 seek the LORD God of their f
2Ch 15:12 their f with all their heart
2Ch 16:13 So Asa rested with his f
2Ch 19: 4 to the LORD God of their f
2Ch 19: 8 some of the chief f of Israel
2Ch 20: 6 O LORD God of our f, are You
2Ch 20:33 hearts to the God of their f
2Ch 21: 1 Jehoshaphat rested with his f
2Ch 21: 1 was buried with his f in the
2Ch 21:10 the LORD God of his f
2Ch 21:19 like the burning for his f
2Ch 23: 2 and the chief f of Israel
2Ch 24:18 of the LORD God of their f
2Ch 24:24 the LORD God of their f
2Ch 25: 4 The f shall not be put to
2Ch 25: 4 be put to death for their f
2Ch 25:28 buried him with his f in the
2Ch 26: 2 the king rested with his f
2Ch 26:23 So Uzziah rested with his f
2Ch 26:23 his f in the field of burial
2Ch 27: 9 So Jotham rested with his f
2Ch 28: 6 the LORD God of their f
2Ch 28: 9 your f was angry with Judah
2Ch 28:25 anger the LORD God of his f
2Ch 28:27 So Ahaz rested with his f
2Ch 29: 5 of the LORD God of your f
2Ch 29: 6 For our f have trespassed and
2Ch 29: 9 because of this our f have
2Ch 30: 7 And do not be like your f and
2Ch 30: 7 the LORD God of their f, so
2Ch 30: 8 stiffnecked, as your f were
2Ch 30:19 God, the LORD God of his f
2Ch 30:22 to the LORD God of their f
2Ch 32:13 my f have done to all the
2Ch 32:14 my f utterly destroyed that
2Ch 32:15 my hand or the hand of my f
2Ch 32:33 So Hezekiah rested with his f
2Ch 33: 8 I have appointed for your f

Neh 2: 3 city, the place of my **f** tombs
Neh 2: 5 to the city of my **f** tombs
Neh 7:70 the **f** houses gave to the work
Neh 7:71 Some of the heads of the **f**
Neh 8:13 **f** houses of all the people
Neh 10:34 according to our **f** houses
Neh 11:13 heads of the **f** houses, were
Neh 12:12 heads of the **f** houses were
Neh 12:22 their **f** houses in the days of
Neh 12:23 the heads of the **f** houses
Ezek 20:24 were fixed on their **f** idols
Ezek 22:10 men uncover their **f** nakedness
Matt 23:32 the measure of your **f** guilt
Acts 22: 3 the strictness of our **f** law

FATHOMS
Acts 27:28 and found it to be twenty **f**
Acts 27:28 and found it to be fifteen **f**

FATLING (*see* FATLINGS)
Is 11: 6 young lion and the **f** together

FATLINGS (*see* FATLING)
1Sa 15: 9 of the sheep, the oxen, the **f**
Ezek 34: 3 you slaughter the **f**, but you
Ezek 39:18 all of them **f** of Bashan

FATNESS (*see* FAT)
Gen 27:28 of the **f** of the earth, and
Gen 27:39 be of the **f** of the earth, and
Job 15:27 covered his face with his **f**
Ps 63: 5 satisfied as with marrow and **f**
Ps 109:24 is feeble from lack of **f**
Is 17: 4 the **f** of his flesh grow lean
Is 34: 6 it is made overflowing with **f**
Is 34: 7 their dust saturated with **f**
Rom 11:17 root and **f** of the olive tree,

FATTED (*see* FAT)
1Sa 28:24 had a **f** calf in the house
2Sa 6:13 he sacrificed oxen and **f** sheep
1Ki 4:23 ten **f** oxen, twenty oxen from
1Ki 4:23 gazelles, roebucks, and **f** fowl
Prov 15:17 than a **f** calf with hatred
Matt 22: 4 **f** cattle are killed, and all
Luke 15:23 And bring the **f** calf here
Luke 15:27 father has killed the **f** calf
Luke 15:30 you killed the **f** calf for him

FATTENED (*see* FAT)
1Ki 1: 9 and **f** cattle by the stone of
1Ki 1:19 oxen and **f** cattle and sheep in
1Ki 1:25 oxen and **f** cattle and sheep in
Amos 5:22 regard your **f** peace offerings
Jas 5: 5 you have **f** your hearts as in

FATTER (*see* FAT)
Dan 1:15 **f** in flesh than all the young

FATTY (*see* FAT)
Ex 29:13 the **f** lobe attached to the
Ex 29:22 the **f** lobe attached to the
Lev 3: 4 the **f** lobe attached to the
Lev 3:10 the **f** lobe attached to the
Lev 3:15 the **f** lobe attached to the
Lev 4: 9 the **f** lobe attached to the
Lev 7: 4 the **f** lobe attached to the
Lev 8:16 the **f** lobe attached to the
Lev 8:25 the **f** lobe attached to the
Lev 9:10 the **f** lobe from the liver of
Lev 9:19 the **f** tail, what covers the
Lev 9:19 the **f** lobe attached to the

FAULT (*see* FAULTLESS, FAULTS)
Ex 5:16 but the **f** is in your own
1Sa 29: 3 **f** in him since he defected to
2Sa 3: 8 a **f** concerning this woman
Ps 59: 4 through no **f** of mine
Dan 6: 4 could find no charge or **f**
Dan 6: 4 any error or **f** found in him
Matt 18:15 and tell him his **f** between you
Mark 7: 2 unwashed hands, they found **f**
Luke 23: 4 I find no **f** in this Man
Luke 23:14 I have found no **f** in this Man
John 18:38 I find no **f** in Him at all
John 19: 4 know that I find no **f** in Him
John 19: 6 Him, for I find no **f** in Him
Acts 25: 5 see if there is any **f** in him
Rom 9:19 Why does He still find **f**
Phil 2:15 children of God without **f** in
Heb 8: 8 Because finding **f** with them
Rev 14: 5 for they are without **f** before

FAULTLESS (*see* FAULT)
Heb 8: 7 first covenant had been **f**
Jude 24 to present you **f** before the

FAULTS (*see* FAULT)
Gen 41: 9 I remember my **f** this day
Ps 19:12 Cleanse me from secret **f**
1Pe 2:20 you are beaten for your **f**

FAVOR (*see* FAVORABLE, FAVORED, FAVORITE, FAVORS)
Gen 18: 3 now found **f** in Your sight
Gen 19:19 has found **f** in your sight
Gen 30:27 I have found **f** in your eyes
Gen 32: 5 I may find **f** in your sight
Gen 33: 8 These are to find **f** in the
Gen 33:10 now found **f** in your sight
Gen 33:15 Let me find **f** in the sight of
Gen 34:11 Let me find **f** in your eyes,
Gen 39: 4 Joseph found **f** in his sight
Gen 39:21 He gave him **f** in the sight of
Gen 47:25 let us find **f** in the sight of
Gen 47:29 I have found **f** in your sight
Gen 50: 4 I have found **f** in your eyes
Ex 3:21 people **f** in the sight of the
Ex 11: 3 people **f** in the sight of the
Ex 12:36 people **f** in the sight of the
Num 11:11 I not found **f** in Your sight
Num 11:15 I have found **f** in Your sight
Num 32: 5 we have found **f** in your sight
Deut 24: 1 happens that she finds no **f**
Deut 28:50 nor show **f** to the young
Deut 33:16 the **f** of Him who dwelt in the
Deut 33:23 O Naphtali, satisfied with **f**
Judg 6:17 I have found **f** in Your sight
Ruth 2: 2 in whose sight I may find **f**
Ruth 2:10 have I found **f** in your eyes
Ruth 2:13 Let me find **f** in your sight,
1Sa 1:18 find **f** in your sight
1Sa 2:26 in **f** both with the LORD and
1Sa 16:22 he has found **f** in my sight
1Sa 20: 3 I have found **f** in your eyes
1Sa 20:29 I have found **f** in your eyes
1Sa 25: 8 young men find **f** in your eyes
1Sa 27: 5 have now found **f** in your eyes
1Sa 29: 6 the lords do not **f** you
2Sa 14:22 I have found **f** in your sight
2Sa 15:25 If I find **f** in the eyes of
2Sa 16: 4 I may find **f** in your sight
1Ki 11:19 Hadad found great **f** in the
1Ki 13: 6 Please entreat the **f** of the
2Ch 32:25 according to the **f** shown him
Neh 2: 5 has found **f** in your sight
Esth 2: 9 him, and she obtained his **f**
Esth 2:15 And Esther obtained **f** in the
Esth 2:17 **f** in his sight more than all
Esth 5: 2 that she found **f** in his sight
Esth 5: 8 If I have found **f** in the
Esth 7: 3 I have found **f** in your sight
Esth 8: 5 I have found **f** in his sight
Job 10:12 You have granted me life and **f**
Job 11:19 yes, many would court your **f**
Job 20:10 will seek the **f** of the poor
Ps 5:12 With **f** You will surround him
Ps 30: 5 a moment, His **f** is for life
Ps 30: 7 by Your **f** You have made my
Ps 35:27 Who **f** my righteous cause
Ps 45:12 the people will seek your **f**
Ps 89:17 in Your **f** our horn is exalted
Ps 102:13 For the time to **f** her, Yes,
Ps 102:14 stones, And show **f** to her dust
Ps 106: 4 with the **f** You have toward
Ps 109:12 to **f** his fatherless children
Ps 119:58 I entreated Your **f** with my
Prov 3: 4 and so find **f** and high esteem
Prov 8:35 and obtains **f** from the LORD
Prov 11:27 diligently seeks good finds **f**
Prov 12: 2 man obtains **f** from the LORD
Prov 13:15 Good understanding gains **f**
Prov 14: 9 among the upright there is **f**
Prov 14:35 The king's **f** is toward a wise
Prov 16:15 his **f** is like a cloud of the
Prov 18:22 and obtains **f** from the LORD
Prov 19: 6 entreat the **f** of the nobility
Prov 19:12 but his **f** is like dew on the
Prov 21:10 finds no **f** in his eyes
Prov 22: 1 loving **f** rather than silver
Prov 28:23 a man will find more **f**
Prov 29:26 Many seek the ruler's **f**, but
Eccl 9:11 nor **f** to men of skill
Is 27:11 them will show them no **f**
Is 60:10 but in My **f** I have had mercy
Jer 16:13 where I will not show you **f**
Jer 26:19 the LORD and seek the LORD's **f**
Lam 4:16 nor show **f** to the elders
Dan 1: 9 had brought Daniel into the **f**
Dan 7:22 a judgment was made in **f** of
Hos 12: 4 he wept, and sought **f** from Him
Mal 1: 9 But now entreat God's **f**, that
Luke 1:30 for you have found **f** with God
Luke 2:52 and in **f** with God and men
Acts 2:47 having **f** with all the people
Acts 7:10 his troubles, and gave him **f**
Acts 7:46 who found **f** before God and
Acts 24:27 wanting to do the Jews a **f**
Acts 25: 3 asking a **f** against him, that
Acts 25: 9 wanting to do the Jews a **f**

FAVORABLE (*see* FAVOR, FAVORABLY)
Gen 31: 2 indeed it was not **f** toward
Gen 31: 5 that it is not **f** toward me as
Ps 77: 7 And will He be **f** no more
Ps 85: 1 You have been **f** to Your land
Jer 15: 1 not be **f** toward this people

FAVORABLY (*see* FAVORABLE)
Lev 26: 9 For I will look on you **f** and
Mal 1: 8 Would he accept you **f**
Mal 1: 9 hands, will He accept you **f**

FAVORED (*see* FAVOR)
Gen 19:21 I have **f** you concerning this
Deut 33:24 let him be **f** by his brothers,
Ps 44: 3 Because You **f** them
Luke 1:28 Rejoice, highly **f** one, the

FAVORITE (*see* FAVOR, FAVORITISM)
Song 6: 9 the **f** of the one who bore her

FAVORITISM (*see* FAVORITE)
Luke 20:21 and You do not show personal **f**
Gal 2: 6 shows personal **f** to no man

FAVORS (*see* FAVOR)
2Sa 20:11 Whoever **f** Joab and whoever is

FAWNS
Song 4: 5 two breasts are like two **f**
Song 7: 3 two breasts are like two **f**

FEAR (*see* FEARED, FEARFUL, FEARING, FEARS)
Gen 9: 2 the **f** of you and the dread of
Gen 20:11 surely the **f** of God is not in
Gen 21:17 **F** not, for God has heard the
Gen 22:12 for now I know that you **f** God
Gen 26:24 do not **f**, for I am with you
Gen 31:42 the **F** of Isaac, had been with
Gen 31:53 Jacob swore by the **F** of his
Gen 32:11 for I **f** him, lest he come and
Gen 35:17 Do not **f**
Gen 42:18 Do this and live, for I **f** God
Gen 46: 3 do not **f** to go down to Egypt,
Ex 9:30 will not yet **f** the LORD God
Ex 15:16 **F** and dread will fall on them
Ex 18:21 able men, such as **f** God, men
Ex 20:20 Do not **f**
Ex 20:20 that His **f** may be before you,
Ex 23:27 I will send My **f** before you
Lev 19:14 blind, but shall **f** your God
Lev 19:32 of an old man, and **f** your God
Lev 25:17 but you shall **f** your God
Lev 25:36 but **f** your God, that your
Lev 25:43 but you shall **f** your God
Num 14: 9 nor **f** the people of the land,
Num 14: 9 Do not **f** them
Num 21:34 Do not **f** him, for I have
Deut 1:21 do not **f** or be discouraged
Deut 2:25 **f** of you upon the nations
Deut 3: 2 said to me, 'Do not **f** him
Deut 3:22 You must not **f** them, for the
Deut 4:10 that they may learn to **f** Me
Deut 5:29 in them that they would **f** Me
Deut 6: 2 that you may **f** the LORD your
Deut 6:13 You shall **f** the LORD your God
Deut 6:24 to **f** the LORD our God, for
Deut 8: 6 walk in His ways and to **f** Him
Deut 10:12 but to **f** the LORD your God,
Deut 10:20 You shall **f** the LORD your God
Deut 11:25 the **f** of you upon all the
Deut 13: 4 God and **f** Him, and keep His
Deut 13:11 So all Israel shall hear and **f**
Deut 14:23 that you may learn to **f** the
Deut 17:13 the people shall hear and **f**
Deut 17:19 learn to **f** the LORD his God
Deut 19:20 who remain shall hear and **f**

Deut 21:21 and all Israel shall hear and f
Deut 25:18 and he did not f God
Deut 28:58 that you may f this glorious
Deut 28:66 you shall f day and night, and
Deut 28:67 because of the f which
Deut 31: 6 do not f nor be afraid of
Deut 31: 8 do not f nor be dismayed
Deut 31:12 learn to f the LORD your God
Deut 31:13 learn to f the LORD your God
Deut 32:17 that your fathers did not f
Josh 4:24 that you may f the LORD your
Josh 10: 8 Do not f them, for I have
Josh 22:24 in fact we have done it for f
Josh 24:14 f the LORD, serve Him in
Judg 4:18 turn aside to me; do not f.
Judg 6:10 do not f the gods of the
Judg 6:23 do not f, you shall not die
Judg 9:21 there, for f of Abimelech his
Ruth 3:11 And now, my daughter, do not f
1Sa 4:20 Do not f, for you have borne
1Sa 11: 7 the f of the LORD fell on the
1Sa 12:14 If you f the LORD and serve
1Sa 12:20 said to the people, "Do not f.
1Sa 12:24 Only f the LORD, and serve Him
1Sa 22:23 Stay with me; do not f.
1Sa 23:17 Do not f, for the hand of
2Sa 9: 7 Do not f, for I will surely
2Sa 23: 4 ruling in the f of God
1Ki 8:40 that they may f You all the
1Ki 8:43 and f You, as do Your people
1Ki 17:13 Elijah said to her, "Do not f
2Ki 6:16 Do not f, for those who are
2Ki 17:25 that they did not f the LORD
2Ki 17:28 how they should f the LORD
2Ki 17:34 they do not f the LORD, nor
2Ki 17:35 You shall not f other gods
2Ki 17:36 arm, Him you shall f, Him you
2Ki 17:37 you shall not f other gods
2Ki 17:38 nor shall you f other gods
2Ki 17:39 the LORD your God you shall f
1Ch 14:17 the LORD brought the f of him
1Ch 22:13 do not f nor be dismayed
1Ch 28:20 do not f nor be dismayed, for
2Ch 6:31 that they may f You, to walk
2Ch 6:33 and f You, as do Your people
2Ch 14:14 for the f of the LORD came
2Ch 17:10 the f of the LORD fell on all
2Ch 19: 7 let the f of the LORD be upon
2Ch 19: 9 act in the f of the LORD,
2Ch 20:17 Do not f or be dismayed
2Ch 20:29 the f of God was on all the
Ezra 3: 3 Though f had come upon them
Neh 1:11 who desire to f Your name
Neh 5: 9 f of our God because of the
Neh 5:15 so, because of the f of God
Esth 8:17 because f of the Jews fell
Esth 9: 2 because f of them fell upon
Esth 9: 3 because the f of Mordecai
Job 1: 9 Does Job f God for nothing
Job 4:14 f came upon me, and trembling,
Job 6:14 the f of the Almighty
Job 9:35 I would speak and not f Him
Job 11:15 could be steadfast, and not f
Job 15: 4 Yes, you cast off f, and
Job 21: 9 Their houses are safe from f
Job 22: 4 Is it because of your f of
Job 22:10 and sudden f troubles you,
Job 25: 2 Dominion and f belong to Him
Job 28:28 the f of the Lord, that is
Job 33: 7 Surely no f of me will
Job 37:24 Therefore men f Him
Job 39:22 He mocks at f, and is not
Job 41:33 him, which is made without f
Ps 2:11 Serve the LORD with f, And
Ps 5: 7 In f of You I will worship
Ps 9:20 Put them in f, O LORD, That
Ps 14: 5 There they are in great f
Ps 15: 4 honors those who f the LORD
Ps 19: 9 The f of the LORD is clean,
Ps 22:23 You who f the LORD, praise
Ps 22:23 f Him, all you offspring of
Ps 22:25 vows before those who f Him
Ps 23: 4 of death, I will f no evil
Ps 25:14 LORD is with those who f Him
Ps 27: 1 Whom shall I f
Ps 27: 3 me, My heart shall not f
Ps 31:13 F is on every side
Ps 31:19 laid up for those who f You
Ps 33: 8 Let all the earth f the LORD
Ps 33:18 LORD is on those who f Him
Ps 34: 7 all around those who f Him
Ps 34: 9 f the LORD, you His saints
Ps 34: 9 is no want to those who f Him
Ps 34:11 teach you the f of the LORD
Ps 36: 1 There is no f of God before
Ps 40: 3 Many will see it and f, And
Ps 46: 2 Therefore we will not f,
Ps 48: 6 F took hold of them there, And
Ps 49: 5 Why should I f in the days of
Ps 52: 6 righteous also shall see and f
Ps 53: 5 in great f Where no f was
Ps 55:19 Therefore they do not f God
Ps 56: 4 I will not f
Ps 60: 4 a banner to those who f You
Ps 61: 5 of those who f Your name
Ps 64: 1 my life from f of the enemy
Ps 64: 4 they shoot at him and do not f
Ps 64: 9 All men shall f, And shall
Ps 66:16 and hear, all you who f God
Ps 67: 7 ends of the earth shall f Him
Ps 72: 5 They shall f You As long as
Ps 78:33 futility, And their years in f
Ps 78:53 so that they did not f
Ps 85: 9 is near to those who f Him
Ps 86:11 Unite my heart to f Your name
Ps 90:11 For as the f of You, so is
Ps 102:15 shall f the name of the LORD
Ps 103:11 mercy toward those who f Him
Ps 103:13 LORD pities those who f Him
Ps 103:17 On those who f Him, And His
Ps 105:38 For the f of them had fallen
Ps 111: 5 given food to those who f Him
Ps 111:10 The f of the LORD is the
Ps 115:11 You who f the LORD, trust in
Ps 115:13 bless those who f the LORD
Ps 118: 4 Let those who f the LORD now
Ps 118: 6 I will not f
Ps 119:63 of all those who f You, And of
Ps 119:74 Those who f You will be glad
Ps 119:79 Let those who f You turn to
Ps 119:120 flesh trembles for f of You
Ps 135:20 You who f the LORD, bless the
Ps 145:19 the desire of those who f Him
Ps 147:11 pleasure in those who f Him
Prov 1: 7 The f of the LORD is the
Prov 1:29 not choose the f of the LORD
Prov 1:33 be secure, without f of evil
Prov 2: 5 understand the f of the LORD
Prov 3: 7 f the LORD and depart from
Prov 8:13 The f of the LORD is to hate
Prov 9:10 The f of the LORD is the
Prov 10:24 The f of the wicked will come
Prov 10:27 The f of the LORD prolongs
Prov 14:26 In the f of the LORD there is
Prov 14:27 The f of the LORD is a
Prov 15:16 little with the f of the LORD
Prov 15:33 The f of the LORD is the
Prov 16: 6 and by the f of the LORD one
Prov 19:23 The f of the LORD leads to
Prov 22: 4 the f of the LORD are riches
Prov 23:17 but in the f of the LORD
Prov 24:21 son, f the LORD and the king
Prov 29:25 The f of man brings a snare,
Eccl 3:14 that men should f before Him
Eccl 5: 7 But f God.
Eccl 8:12 who f God, who f before Him
Eccl 8:13 he does not f before God
Eccl 12:13 F God and keep His
Song 3: 8 because of f in the night
Is 7: 4 do not f or be fainthearted
Is 7:25 not go there for f of briers
Is 8:13 Let Him be your f, and let Him
Is 11: 2 and of the f of the LORD
Is 11: 3 is in the f of the LORD, and
Is 14: 3 your sorrow, and from your f
Is 19:16 f because of the waving of
Is 21: 4 He turned into f for me
Is 24:17 F and the pit and the snare are
Is 24:18 the f shall fall into the pit
Is 25: 3 terrible nations will f You
Is 29:13 their f toward Me is taught
Is 29:23 Jacob, and f the God of Israel
Is 31: 9 over to his stronghold for f
Is 33: 6 the f of the LORD is His
Is 35: 4 Be strong, do not f
Is 41:10 F not, for I am with you
Is 41:13 you, F not, I will help you
Is 41:14 F not, you worm Jacob, you
Is 43: 1 F not, for I have redeemed
Is 43: 5 F not, for I am with you
Is 44: 2 F not, O Jacob My servant
Is 44: 8 Do not f, nor be afraid
Is 44:11 yet they shall f, they shall
Is 51: 7 do not f the reproach of men,
Is 54: 4 Do not f, for you will not be
Is 54:14 for you shall not f
Is 57:11 of old that you do not f Me
Is 59:19 So shall they f the name of
Is 63:17 our heart from Your f
Jer 2:19 the f of Me is not in you,"
Jer 3: 8 sister Judah did not f, but
Jer 5:22 do you not f Me
Jer 5:24 Let us now f the LORD our God
Jer 6:25 the enemy, f is on every side
Jer 10: 7 who would not f You, O King
Jer 17: 8 will not f when heat comes
Jer 20:10 F on every side
Jer 22:25 of those whose face you f
Jer 23: 4 and they shall f no more, nor
Jer 26:19 Did he not f the LORD and seek
Jer 30: 5 a voice of trembling, of f
Jer 30:10 Therefore do not f, O My
Jer 32:39 that they may f Me forever
Jer 32:40 but I will put My f in their
Jer 33: 9 they shall f and tremble for
Jer 35:11 for f of the army of the
Jer 35:11 and for f of the army of the
Jer 36:16 in f from one to another, and
Jer 37:11 for f of Pharaoh's army,
Jer 41: 9 f of Baasha king of Israel
Jer 46: 5 For f was all around," says
Jer 46:27 But do not f, O My servant
Jer 46:28 Do not f, O Jacob My servant,
Jer 48:43 F and the pit and the snare
Jer 48:44 He who flees from the f shall
Jer 49: 5 I will bring f upon you,"
Jer 49:24 to flee, and f has seized her
Jer 49:29 to them, 'F is on every side
Jer 50:16 For f of the oppressing sword
Jer 51:46 you f for the rumor that will
Lam 3:47 F and a snare have come upon
Lam 3:57 Do not f!"
Ezek 30:13 I will put f in the land of
Dan 1:10 I f my lord the king, who has
Dan 6:26 f before the God of Daniel
Dan 10:12 Do not f, Daniel, for from
Dan 10:19 O man greatly beloved, f not
Hos 3: 5 f the LORD and His goodness in
Hos 10: 3 Because we did not f the LORD
Hos 10: 5 The inhabitants of Samaria f
Joel 2:21 F not, O land
Amos 3: 8 Who will not f
Jon 1: 9 and I f the LORD, the God of
Mic 7:17 and shall f because of You
Zeph 3: 7 I said, 'Surely you will f Me
Zeph 3:16 Do not f
Hag 2: 5 do not f
Zech 8:13 Do not f, let your hands be
Zech 8:15 Do not f
Zech 9: 5 Ashkelon shall see it and f
Mal 2: 5 to him that he might f Me
Mal 3: 5 because they do not f Me,"
Mal 3:16 Him for those who f the LORD
Mal 4: 2 But to you who f My name the
Matt 10:26 Therefore do not f them
Matt 10:28 do not f those who kill the
Matt 10:28 But rather f Him who is able
Matt 10:31 Do not f therefore
Matt 14:26 And they cried out for f
Matt 21:26 we f the multitude, for all
Matt 28: 4 the guards shook for f of him
Matt 28: 8 quickly from the tomb with f
Luke 1:12 troubled, and f fell upon him
Luke 1:50 who f Him from generation to
Luke 1:65 Then f came on all who dwelt
Luke 1:74 might serve Him without f
Luke 5:26 God and were filled with f
Luke 7:16 Then f came upon all, and they
Luke 8:37 they were seized with great f
Luke 12: 5 show you whom you should f
Luke 12: 5 F Him who, after He has
Luke 12: 5 yes, I say to you, f Him
Luke 12: 7 Do not f therefore
Luke 12:32 Do not f, little flock, for
Luke 18: 2 did not f God nor regard man
Luke 18: 4 Though I do not f God nor
Luke 21:26 hearts failing them from f
Luke 23:40 Do you not even f God, seeing
John 7:13 of Him for f of the Jews
John 12:15 F not, daughter of Zion

John 19:38 for f of the Jews, asked
John 20:19 for f of the Jews, Jesus came
Acts 2:43 Then f came upon every soul,
Acts 5: 5 So great f came upon all
Acts 5:11 So great f came upon all the
Acts 9:31 walking in the f of the Lord
Acts 13:16 of Israel, and you who f God
Acts 13:26 and those among you who f God
Acts 19:17 f fell on them all, and the
Rom 3:18 There is no f of God before
Rom 8:15 spirit of bondage again to f
Rom 11:20 Do not be haughty, but f
Rom 13: 7 f to whom f, honor to whom
Rom 13: 7 whom customs, f to whom f
1Co 2: 3 with you in weakness, in f
1Co 16:10 he may be with you without f
2Co 7: 1 holiness in the f of God
2Co 7:11 what indignation, what f
2Co 7:15 of you all, how with f and
2Co 11: 3 But I f, lest somehow, as the
2Co 12:20 For I f lest, when I come, I
Eph 5:21 one another in the f of God
Eph 6: 5 to the flesh, with f and
Phil 1:14 to speak the word without f
Phil 2:12 out your own salvation with f
1Ti 5:20 all, that the rest also may f
2Ti 1: 7 not given us a spirit of f
Heb 2:15 f of death were all their
Heb 4: 1 let us f lest any of you seem
Heb 5: 7 heard because of His godly f
Heb 11: 7 yet seen, moved with godly f
Heb 12:28 with reverence and godly f
Heb 13: 6 I will not f
1Pe 1:17 of your sojourning here in f
1Pe 2:17 F God. Honor the king.
1Pe 2:18 to your masters with all f
1Pe 3: 2 conduct accompanied by f
1Pe 3:15 is in you, with meekness and f
1Jn 4:18 There is no f in love
1Jn 4:18 but perfect love casts out f
1Jn 4:18 because f involves torment
Jude 12 they feast with you without f
Jude 23 but others save with f,
Rev 2:10 Do not f any of those things
Rev 11:11 great f fell on those who saw
Rev 11:18 and those who f Your name
Rev 14: 7 F God and give glory to Him,
Rev 15: 4 Who shall not f You, O Lord,
Rev 18:10 distance for f of her torment
Rev 18:15 distance for f of her torment
Rev 19: 5 servants and those who f Him

FEARED (*see* FEAR)
Ex 1:17 But the midwives f God, and
Ex 1:21 because the midwives f God
Ex 2:14 So Moses f and said
Ex 9:20 He who f the word of the LORD
Ex 14:31 so the people f the LORD, and
Deut 32:27 Had I not f the wrath of the
Josh 4:14 and they f him, as they had
Josh 4:14 him, as they had f Moses, all
Josh 10: 2 that they f greatly, because
Judg 6:27 But because he f his father's
1Sa 12:18 the people greatly f the LORD
1Sa 14:26 for the people f the oath
1Sa 15:24 because I f the people and
2Sa 3:11 word, because he f him
1Ki 3:28 they f the king, for they saw
1Ki 18: 3 (Now Obadiah f the LORD
1Ki 18:12 have f the LORD from my youth
2Ki 4: 1 that your servant f the LORD
2Ki 17: 7 and they had f other gods,
2Ki 17:32 So they f the LORD, and from
2Ki 17:33 They f the LORD, yet served
2Ki 17:41 So these nations f the LORD
1Ch 16:25 also to be f above all gods
2Ch 20: 3 And Jehoshaphat f, and set
Neh 7: 2 man and f God more than many
Job 1: 1 and upright, and one who f God
Job 3:25 I greatly f has come upon me
Job 31:34 because I f the great
Ps 76: 7 You, Yourself, are to be f
Ps 76: 8 The earth f and was still,
Ps 76:11 to Him who ought to be f
Ps 89: 7 God is greatly to be f in the
Ps 96: 4 He is to be f above all gods
Ps 130: 4 with You, That You may be f
Is 41: 5 The coastlands saw it and f
Is 51:13 you have f continually every
Is 57:11 have you been afraid, or f
Jer 42:16 f shall overtake you there in
Jer 44:10 to this day, nor have they f
Ezek 11: 8 You have f the sword
Dan 5:19 trembled and f before him
Jon 1:16 Then the men f the LORD
Hag 1:12 the people f the presence of
Mal 1:14 My name is to be f among the
Mal 2: 5 so he f Me and was reverent
Mal 3:16 Then those who f the LORD
Matt 14: 5 he f the multitude, because
Matt 21:46 Him, they f the multitudes,
Matt 27:54 they f greatly, saying,
Mark 4:41 they f exceedingly, and said
Mark 6:20 for Herod f John, knowing
Mark 11:18 for they f Him, because all
Mark 11:32 they f the people, for all
Mark 12:12 but f the multitude, for they
Luke 19:21 For I f you, because you are
Luke 20:19 on Him, but they f the people
Luke 22: 2 Him, for they f the people
John 9:22 because they f the Jews, for
Acts 5:26 for they f the people, lest
Acts 10: 2 one who f God with all his

FEARFUL (*see* FEAR, FEARFUL-HEARTED, FEARFULLY, FEARFULNESS)
Ex 15:11 f in praises, doing wonders
Deut 20: 8 What man is there who is f
Judg 7: 3 people, saying, 'Whoever is f
Matt 8:26 Why are you f, O you of
Mark 4:40 Why are you so f
Luke 9:34 they were f as they entered
Luke 21:11 and there will be f sights
Heb 10:27 but a certain f expectation
Heb 10:31 It is a f thing to fall into

FEARFUL-HEARTED (*see* FEARFUL)
Is 35: 4 Say to those who are f, Be

FEARFULLY (*see* FEARFUL)
Ps 139:14 I will praise You, for I am f
Dan 8:24 he shall destroy f, and shall

FEARFULNESS (*see* FEARFUL)
Ps 55: 5 F and trembling have come
Is 21: 4 wavered, f frightened me
Is 33:14 f has seized the hypocrites

FEARING (*see* FEAR)
Josh 22:25 descendants cease f the LORD
Ps 119:38 Who is devoted to f You
Mark 5:33 But the woman, f and trembling
Acts 23:10 f lest Paul might be pulled
Acts 27:17 and f lest they should run
Acts 27:29 f lest we should run aground
Gal 2:12 f those who were of the
Col 3:22 in sincerity of heart, f God
Heb 11:27 not f the wrath of the king

FEARS (*see* FEAR)
Job 1: 8 and upright man, one who f God
Job 2: 3 and upright man, one who f God
Ps 25:12 is the man that f the LORD
Ps 34: 4 And delivered me from all my f
Ps 112: 1 is the man who f the LORD
Ps 128: 1 is every one who f the LORD
Ps 128: 4 man be blessed Who f the LORD
Prov 13:13 but he who f the commandment
Prov 14: 2 in his uprightness f the LORD
Prov 14:16 A wise man f and departs from
Prov 31:30 but a woman who f the LORD
Eccl 7:18 for he who f God will escape
Eccl 9: 2 an oath as he who f an oath
Is 50:10 Who among you f the LORD
Is 66: 4 and bring their f on them
Acts 10:22 a just man, one who f God
Acts 10:35 in every nation whoever f Him
2Co 7: 5 were conflicts, inside were f
1Jn 4:18 But he who f has not been

FEAST (*see* FEASTING, FEASTS)
Gen 19: 3 Then he made them a f, and
Gen 21: 8 Abraham made a great f on the
Gen 26:30 So he made them a f, and they
Gen 29:22 men of the place and made a f
Gen 40:20 that he made a f for all his
Ex 5: 1 that they may hold a f to Me
Ex 10: 9 we must hold a f to the LORD
Ex 12:14 you shall keep it as a f to
Ex 12:14 You shall keep it as a f by
Ex 12:17 the F of Unleavened Bread
Ex 13: 6 shall be a f to the LORD
Ex 23:14 keep a f to Me in the year
Ex 23:15 You shall keep the F of
Ex 23:16 and the F of Harvest, the
Ex 23:16 the F of Ingathering, which
Ex 32: 5 Tomorrow is a f to the LORD
Ex 34:18 The F of Unleavened Bread you
Ex 34:22 shall observe the F of Weeks
Ex 34:22 the F of Ingathering at the
Ex 34:25 the F of the Passover be left
Lev 23: 6 of the same month is the F of
Lev 23:34 F of Tabernacles for seven
Lev 23:39 you shall keep the f of the
Lev 23:41 You shall keep it as a f to
Num 28:17 day of this month is the f
Num 28:26 the LORD at your F of Weeks
Num 29:12 you shall keep a f to the
Deut 16:10 Then you shall keep the F of
Deut 16:13 You shall observe the F of
Deut 16:14 you shall rejoice in your f
Deut 16:15 you shall keep a sacred f to
Deut 16:16 at the F of Unleavened Bread,
Deut 16:16 at the F of Weeks, and at the
Deut 16:16 and at the F of Tabernacles
Deut 31:10 at the F of Tabernacles,
Judg 14:10 And Samson gave a f there, for
Judg 14:12 the seven days of the f, then
Judg 14:17 days while their f lasted
Judg 21:19 there is a yearly f of the
1Sa 20:24 king sat down to eat the f
1Sa 25: 8 eyes, for we come on a f day
1Sa 25:36 holding a f in his house,
1Sa 25:36 house, like the f of a king
2Sa 3:20 And David made a f for Abner
1Ki 3:15 made a f for all his servants
1Ki 8: 2 to King Solomon at the f in
1Ki 8:65 At that time Solomon held a f
1Ki 12:32 Jeroboam ordained a f on the
1Ki 12:32 like the f that was in Judah,
1Ki 12:33 And he ordained a f for the
2Ki 6:23 prepared a great f for them
2Ch 5: 3 with the king at the f, which
2Ch 7: 8 Solomon kept the f seven days
2Ch 7: 9 days, and the f seven days
2Ch 8:13 the F of Unleavened Bread,
2Ch 8:13 the F of Weeks, and the F
2Ch 8:13 and the F of Tabernacles
2Ch 30:13 at Jerusalem to keep the F of
2Ch 30:21 at Jerusalem kept the F of
2Ch 30:22 throughout the f seven days
2Ch 30:23 keep the f another seven days
2Ch 35:17 the F of Unleavened Bread for
Ezra 3: 4 kept the F of Tabernacles
Ezra 6:22 they kept the F of Unleavened
Neh 8:14 the f of the seventh month
Neh 8:18 And they kept the f seven days
Esth 1: 3 a f for all his officials
Esth 1: 5 the king made a f lasting
Esth 1: 9 Queen Vashti also made a f
Esth 2:18 Then the king made a great f
Esth 2:18 the F of Esther, for all his
Esth 8:17 Jews had joy and gladness, a f
Job 1: 4 f in their houses, each on
Ps 42: 4 that kept a pilgrim f
Ps 81: 3 moon, on our solemn f day
Prov 15:15 merry heart has a continual f
Eccl 10:16 your princes f in the morning
Eccl 10:17 your princes f at the proper
Eccl 10:19 A f is made for laughter, and
Is 25: 6 people a f of choice pieces
Is 25: 6 a f of wines on the lees, of
Lam 2: 7 LORD as on the day of a set f
Lam 2:22 to a f day the terrors that
Ezek 36:38 at Jerusalem on its f days
Ezek 45:21 Passover, a f of seven days
Ezek 45:23 f he shall prepare a burnt
Ezek 45:25 day of the month, at the f
Ezek 46: 9 LORD on the appointed f days
Ezek 46:11 and the appointed f days the
Dan 5: 1 the king made a great f for a
Hos 2:11 her f days, her New Moons,
Hos 9: 5 the day of the f of the LORD
Hos 12: 9 the days of the appointed f
Amos 5:21 I hate, I despise your f days
Zech 14:16 to keep the F of Tabernacles
Zech 14:18 to keep the F of Tabernacles
Zech 14:19 to keep the F of Tabernacles
Matt 26: 5 Not during the f, lest there
Matt 26:17 F of the Unleavened Bread the
Matt 27:15 Now at the f the governor was
Mark 6:21 gave a f for his nobles, the
Mark 14: 1 the F of Unleavened Bread
Mark 14: 2 Not during the f, lest there
Mark 15: 6 Now at the f he was

Luke 2:41 year at the F of the Passover
Luke 2:42 to the custom of the f
Luke 5:29 a great f in his own house
Luke 14: 8 by anyone to a wedding f, do
Luke 14:13 But when you give a f, invite
Luke 22: 1 Now the F of Unleavened Bread
Luke 23:17 release one to them at the f)
John 2: 8 it to the master of the f
John 2: 9 When the master of the f had
John 2: 9 the master of the f called
John 2:23 at the Passover, during the f
John 4:45 He did in Jerusalem at the f
John 4:45 they also had gone to the f
John 5: 1 there was a f of the Jews
John 6: 4 a f of the Jews, was near
John 7: 2 Now the Jews' F of
John 7: 8 You go up to this f
John 7: 8 am not yet going up to this f
John 7:10 then He also went up to the f
John 7:11 the Jews sought Him at the f
John 7:14 the f Jesus went up into the
John 7:37 day, that great day of the f
John 10:22 Now it was the F of
John 11:56 He will not come to the f
John 12:12 that had come to the f, when
John 12:20 came up to worship at the f
John 13: 1 Now before the f of the
John 13:29 things we need for the f,"
Acts 18:21 this coming f in Jerusalem
1Co 5: 8 Therefore let us keep the f
2Pe 2:13 while they f with you,
Jude 12 while they f with you without

FEASTING (*see* FEAST)
Esth 9:17 rested and made it a day of f
Esth 9:18 rested, and made it a day of f
Esth 9:19 as a day of gladness and f
Esth 9:22 should make them days of f
Job 1: 5 when the days of f had run
Prov 17: 1 a house full of f with strife
Eccl 7: 2 than to go to the house of f
Jer 16: 8 house of f to sit with them
Hab 3:14 like f on the poor in secret

FEASTS (*see* FEAST)
Lev 23: 2 The f of the LORD, which you
Lev 23: 2 convocations, these are My f
Lev 23: 4 These are the f of the LORD
Lev 23:37 These are the f of the LORD
Lev 23:44 of Israel the f of the LORD
Num 10:10 gladness, in your appointed f
Num 15: 3 or in your appointed f, to
Num 29:39 the LORD at your appointed f
1Ch 23:31 the New Moons and on the set f
2Ch 2: 4 on the set f of the LORD our
2Ch 8:13 the three appointed yearly f
2Ch 31: 3 and the New Moons and the set f
Ezra 3: 5 f of the LORD that were
Neh 10:33 the New Moons, and the set f
Ps 35:16 at f They gnashed at me with
Is 1:14 appointed f my soul hates
Is 5:12 flute, and wine are in their f
Is 29: 1 let f come around
Is 33:20 the city of our appointed f
Jer 51:39 I will prepare their f
Lam 1: 4 no one comes to the set f
Lam 2: 6 has caused the appointed f
Ezek 45:17 and drink offerings, at the f
Hos 2:11 all her appointed f
Amos 8:10 turn your f into mourning
Nah 1:15 Judah, keep your appointed f
Zech 8:19 cheerful f for the house of
Mal 2: 3 the refuse of your solemn f
Matt 23: 6 love the best places at f
Mark 12:39 and the best places at f,
Luke 20:46 and the best places at f,
Jude 12 are spots in your love f,

FEATHERED (*see* FEATHERS)
Ps 78:27 F fowl like the sand of the

FEATHERS (*see* FEATHERED)
Lev 1:16 remove its crop with its f
Ps 68:13 And her f with yellow gold
Ps 91: 4 He shall cover you with His f
Ezek 17: 3 full of f of various colors,
Ezek 17: 7 with large wings and many f
Dan 4:33 hair had grown like eagles' f

FEATURES
Dan 8:23 shall arise, having fierce f

FED (*see* FEED)
Gen 30:36 Jacob f the rest of Laban's
Gen 41: 2 and they f in the meadow
Gen 41:18 and they f in the meadow
Gen 47:17 Thus he f them with bread in
Gen 48:15 the God who has f me all my
Ex 16:32 I f you in the wilderness
Deut 8: 3 f you with manna which you
Deut 8:16 who f you in the wilderness
1Ki 18: 4 and had f them with bread and
1Ki 18:13 f them with bread and water
1Ch 27:29 the herds that f in Sharon
Ps 80: 5 You have f them with the
Ps 81:16 He would have f them also
Is 1:11 rams and the fat of f cattle
Jer 5: 7 When I had f them to the full
Ezek 16:19 oil, and honey which I f you
Ezek 34: 8 the shepherds f themselves
Dan 4:12 and all flesh was f from it
Dan 5:21 They f him with grass like
Hos 11: 4 I stooped and f them
Zech 11: 7 So I f the flock for
Zech 11: 7 and I f the flock
Mark 5:14 Now those who f the swine
Luke 8:34 When those who f them saw
Luke 16:21 desiring to be f with the
1Co 3: 2 I f you with milk and not with

FEE
Num 22: 7 the diviner's f in their hand

FEEBLE (*see* FEEBLER)
Gen 30:42 But when the flocks were f
1Sa 2: 5 many children has become f
2Ch 28:15 they let all the f ones ride
Neh 4: 2 What are these f Jews doing
Job 4: 4 have strengthened the f knees
Ps 38: 8 I am f and severely broken
Ps 105:37 there was none f among His
Ps 109:24 my flesh is f from lack of
Prov 30:26 the rock badgers are a f folk
Is 16:14 will be very small and f
Is 35: 3 and make firm the f knees
Jer 6:24 our hands grow f
Jer 49:24 Damascus has grown f
Jer 50:43 them, and his hands grow f
Ezek 7:17 Every hand will be f, and
Ezek 21: 7 melt, all hands will be f
Zech 12: 8 the one who is f among them
Heb 12:12 hang down, and the f knees,

FEEBLER (*see* FEEBLE)
Gen 30:42 so the f were Laban's and the

FEED (*see* FED, FEEDING, FEEDS, WELL-FED)
Gen 24:25 f enough, and room to lodge
Gen 24:32 f for the camels, and water to
Gen 25:30 Please f me with that same
Gen 29: 7 the sheep, and go and f them
Gen 30:31 thing for me, I will again f
Gen 37:12 to f their father's flock in
Gen 42:27 donkey f at the encampment
Gen 43:24 and he gave their donkeys f
Gen 46:32 has been to f livestock
Ex 34: 3 herds f before that mountain
1Sa 17:15 to f his father's sheep at
1Ki 17: 4 the ravens to f you there
1Ki 22:27 and f him with bread of
2Ch 18:26 and f him with bread of
Job 24: 2 flocks violently and f on them
Job 24:20 worm should f sweetly on him
Ps 37: 3 and f on His faithfulness
Ps 49:14 Death shall f on them
Prov 10:21 lips of the righteous f many
Prov 30: 8 f me with the food You
Song 1: 7 where you f your flock, where
Song 1: 8 f your little goats beside
Song 4: 5 which f among the lilies
Song 6: 2 to f his flock in the gardens
Is 5:17 shall f in their pasture, and
Is 14:30 firstborn of the poor will f
Is 27:10 there the calf will f, and
Is 30:23 will f in large pastures
Is 40:11 He will f His flock like a
Is 49: 9 They shall f along the roads,
Is 49:26 I will f those who oppress
Is 58:14 f you with the heritage of
Is 61: 5 f your flocks, and the sons of
Is 65:25 and the lamb shall f together
Is 66:11 that you may f and be
Is 66:12 then you shall f
Jer 3:15 who will f you with knowledge
Jer 9:15 Behold, I will f them, this
Jer 23: 2 the shepherds who f My people
Jer 23: 4 over them who will f them
Jer 23:15 I will f them with wormwood,
Jer 50:19 and he shall f on Carmel and
Ezek 3: 3 f your belly, and fill your
Ezek 34: 2 of Israel who f themselves
Ezek 34: 2 the shepherds f the flocks
Ezek 34: 3 but you do not f the flock
Ezek 34: 8 and did not f My flock"
Ezek 34:10 shall f themselves no more
Ezek 34:13 I will f them on the
Ezek 34:14 I will f them in good pasture
Ezek 34:14 and f in rich pasture on the
Ezek 34:15 I will f My flock, and I will
Ezek 34:16 strong, and f them in judgment
Ezek 34:23 over them, and he shall f them
Ezek 34:23 He shall f them and be their
Hos 9: 2 winepress Shall not f them
Mic 5: 4 f His flock in the strength
Mic 7:14 let them f in Bashan and
Hab 2:13 peoples labor to f the fire
Zeph 2: 7 they shall f their flocks
Zeph 3:13 for they shall f their flocks
Zech 11: 4 F the flock for slaughter,
Zech 11: 9 I will not f you
Zech 11:16 nor f those that still stand
Matt 25:37 f You, or thirsty and give You
Luke 15:15 into his fields to f swine
John 21:15 He said to him, "F My lambs
John 21:17 said to him, "F My sheep
Rom 12:20 if your enemy hungers, f him
1Co 13: 3 all my goods to f the poor
Rev 12: 6 that they should f her there

FEEDING (*see* FEED)
Gen 37: 2 old, was f the flock with his
Gen 37:13 f the flock in Shechem
Gen 37:16 where they are f their flocks
Job 1:14 and the donkeys f beside them
Ezek 34:10 them to cease f the sheep
Nah 2:11 and the f place of the young
Matt 8:30 was a herd of many swine f
Mark 5:11 f there near the mountains
Luke 8:32 was f there on the mountain

FEEDS (*see* FEED)
Ex 22: 5 it f in another man's field,
Prov 13: 2 the unfaithful f on violence
Prov 15:14 of fools f on foolishness
Song 2:16 He f his flock among the
Song 6: 3 He f his flock among the
Is 44:20 He f on ashes
Hos 12: 1 Ephraim f on the wind, and
Matt 6:26 your heavenly Father f them
Luke 12:24 and God f them
John 6:57 so he who f on Me will live

FEEL (*see* FEELING, FEELINGS, FELT)
Gen 27:12 Perhaps my father will f me
Gen 27:21 come near, that I may f you
Deut 4:19 you f driven to worship them
Judg 16:26 Let me f the pillars which
Ps 58: 9 pots can f the burning thorns
Prov 23:35 beaten me, but I did not f it
Zech 11: 5 slaughter them and f no guilt

FEELING (*see* FEEL)
Eph 4:19 who, being past f, have given

FEELINGS (*see* FEEL)
Prov 29:11 A fool vents all his f, but a

FEET (*see* FOOT)
Gen 18: 4 be brought, and wash your f
Gen 19: 2 the night, and wash your f
Gen 24:32 and water to wash his f and
Gen 24:32 the f of the men who were
Gen 43:24 water, and they washed their f
Gen 49:10 a lawgiver from between his f
Gen 49:33 he drew his f up into the bed
Ex 3: 5 Take your sandals off your f
Ex 4:25 son and cast it at Moses' f
Ex 12:11 waist, your sandals on your f
Ex 24:10 there was under His f as it
Ex 30:19 and their f in water from it
Ex 30:21 wash their hands and their f
Ex 40:31 their f with water from it
Lev 8:24 the big toes of their right f
Lev 11:21 jointed legs above their f
Lev 11:23 insects which have four f
Lev 11:42 or whatever has many f among
Deut 28:57 comes out from between her f

Deut 29: 5 have not worn out on your **f**
Deut 33: 3 they sit down at Your **f**
Josh 3:13 **f** of the priests who bear the
Josh 3:15 the **f** of the priests who bore
Josh 4: 3 the priests' **f** stood firm
Josh 4: 9 in the place where the **f** of
Josh 4:18 **f** touched the dry land, that
Josh 9: 5 and patched sandals on their **f**
Josh 10:24 put your **f** on the necks of
Josh 10:24 put their **f** on their necks
Judg 5:27 At her **f** he sank, he fell, he
Judg 5:27 at her **f** he sank, he fell
Judg 19:21 And they washed their **f**, and
Ruth 3: 4 shall go in, uncover his **f**
Ruth 3: 7 came softly, uncovered his **f**
Ruth 3: 8 a woman was lying at his **f**
Ruth 3:14 lay at his **f** until morning
1Sa 2: 9 guard the **f** of His saints
1Sa 25:24 So she fell at his **f** and said
1Sa 25:41 a servant to wash the **f** of
2Sa 3:34 nor your **f** put into fetters
2Sa 4: 4 a son who was lame in his **f**
2Sa 4:12 cut off their hands and **f**
2Sa 9: 3 Jonathan who is lame in his **f**
2Sa 9:13 And he was lame in both his **f**
2Sa 11: 8 to your house and wash your **f**
2Sa 19:24 And he had not cared for his **f**
2Sa 22:10 with darkness under His **f**
2Sa 22:34 makes my **f** like the **f** of deer
2Sa 22:37 so my **f** did not slip
2Sa 22:39 they have fallen under my **f**
1Ki 2: 5 sandals that were on his **f**
1Ki 5: 3 foes under the soles of his **f**
1Ki 7:30 and its four **f** had supports
1Ki 14:12 When your **f** enter the city,
1Ki 15:23 age he was diseased in his **f**
2Ki 4:27 hill, she caught him by the **f**
2Ki 4:37 So she went in, fell at his **f**
2Ki 6:32 of his master's **f** behind him
2Ki 9:35 her than the skull and the **f**
2Ki 13:21 he revived and stood on his **f**
2Ki 19:24 with the soles of my **f** I have
2Ki 21: 8 and I will not make the **f** of
1Ch 28: 2 Then King David rose to his **f**
2Ch 3:13 They stood on their **f**, and
2Ch 16:12 Asa became diseased in his **f**
Neh 9:21 out and their **f** did not swell
Esth 8: 3 the king, fell down at his **f**
Job 12: 5 ready for those whose **f** slip
Job 13:27 You put my **f** in the stocks,
Job 13:27 a limit for the soles of my **f**
Job 18: 8 cast into a net by his own **f**
Job 18:11 side, and drive him to his **f**
Job 28: 4 in places forgotten by **f** they
Job 29:15 blind, and I was **f** to the lame
Job 30:12 they push away my **f**, and they
Job 33:11 He puts my **f** in the stocks,
Ps 8: 6 put all things under his **f**
Ps 18: 9 With darkness under His **f**
Ps 18:33 makes my **f** like the **f** of deer
Ps 18:36 So that my **f** did not slip
Ps 18:38 They have fallen under my **f**
Ps 22:16 They pierced My hands and My **f**
Ps 25:15 pluck my **f** out of the net
Ps 31: 8 have set my **f** in a wide place
Ps 40: 2 And set my **f** upon a rock, And
Ps 47: 3 And the nations under our **f**
Ps 56:13 delivered my **f** from falling
Ps 58:10 He shall wash his **f** in the
Ps 66: 9 not allow our **f** to be moved
Ps 73: 2 me, my **f** had almost stumbled
Ps 74: 3 Lift up Your **f** to the
Ps 105:18 They hurt his **f** with fetters
Ps 115: 7 **F** they have, but they do not
Ps 116: 8 tears, And my **f** from falling
Ps 119:59 ways, And turned my **f** to Your
Ps 119:101 my **f** from every evil way,
Ps 119:105 Your word is a lamp to my **f**
Ps 122: 2 Our **f** have been standing
Prov 1:16 for their **f** run to evil, and
Prov 4:26 Ponder the path of your **f**
Prov 5: 5 Her **f** go down to death, her
Prov 6:13 his eyes, he shuffles his **f**
Prov 6:18 **f** that are swift in running
Prov 6:28 coals, and his **f** not be seared
Prov 7:11 her **f** would not stay at home
Prov 19: 2 sins who hastens with his **f**
Prov 26: 6 of a fool cuts off his own **f**
Prov 29: 5 spreads a net for his **f**
Song 5: 3 I have washed my **f**
Song 7: 1 are your **f** in sandals, O
Is 3:16 a jingling with their **f**,
Is 6: 2 with two he covered his **f**
Is 20: 2 take your sandals off your **f**
Is 23: 7 whose **f** carried her far off
Is 26: 6 the **f** of the poor and the
Is 32:20 out freely the **f** of the ox
Is 37:25 with the soles of my **f** I have
Is 41: 2 called him to His **f**
Is 41: 3 he had not gone with his **f**
Is 49:23 and lick up the dust of your **f**
Is 52: 7 upon the mountains are the **f**
Is 59: 7 Their **f** run to evil, and they
Is 60:13 the place of My **f** glorious
Is 60:14 at the soles of your **f**
Jer 13:16 before your **f** stumble on the
Jer 14:10 have not restrained their **f**
Jer 18:22 me, and hidden snares for my **f**
Jer 38:22 your **f** have sunk in the mire,
Lam 1:13 He has spread a net for my **f**
Lam 3:34 To crush under His **f** all the
Ezek 1: 7 the soles of their **f** were
Ezek 1: 7 like the soles of calves' **f**
Ezek 2: 1 Son of man, stand on your **f**
Ezek 2: 2 to me, and set me on my **f**
Ezek 3:24 entered me and set me on my **f**
Ezek 6:11 your fists and stamp your **f**
Ezek 24:17 and put your sandals on your **f**
Ezek 24:23 and your sandals on your **f**
Ezek 25: 6 your hands, stamped your **f**
Ezek 32: 2 the waters with your **f**, and
Ezek 34:18 must tread down with your **f**
Ezek 34:18 foul the residue with your **f**
Ezek 34:19 you have trampled with your **f**
Ezek 34:19 you have fouled with your **f**
Ezek 37:10 lived, and stood upon their **f**
Ezek 43: 7 place of the soles of My **f**
Dan 2:33 iron, its **f** partly of iron and
Dan 2:34 the image on its **f** of iron
Dan 2:41 Whereas you saw the **f** and toes
Dan 2:42 as the toes of the **f** were
Dan 7: 4 to stand on two **f** like a man
Dan 7: 7 the residue with its **f**
Dan 7:19 the residue with its **f**
Dan 10: 6 **f** like burnished bronze in
Nah 1: 3 clouds are the dust of His **f**
Nah 1:15 on the mountains the **f** of him
Hab 3: 5 and fever followed at His **f**
Hab 3:19 make my **f** like deer's **f**
Zech 14: 4 in that day His **f** will stand
Zech 14:12 while they stand on their **f**
Mal 4: 3 under the soles of your **f** on
Matt 7: 6 trample them under their **f**
Matt 10:14 off the dust from your **f**
Matt 15:30 laid them down at Jesus' **f**
Matt 18: 8 having two hands or two **f**
Matt 18:29 servant fell down at his **f**
Matt 28: 9 came and held Him by the **f**
Mark 5:22 he saw Him, he fell at His **f**
Mark 6:11 off the dust under your **f** as
Mark 7:25 and she came and fell at His **f**
Mark 9:45 life lame, than having two **f**
Luke 1:79 to guide our **f** into the way
Luke 7:38 stood at His **f** behind Him
Luke 7:38 to wash His **f** with her tears
Luke 7:38 and she kissed His **f** and
Luke 7:44 you gave Me no water for My **f**
Luke 7:44 washed My **f** with her tears
Luke 7:45 My **f** since the time I came in
Luke 7:46 My **f** with fragrant oil
Luke 8:35 sitting at the **f** of Jesus
Luke 8:41 And he fell down at Jesus' **f**
Luke 9: 5 **f** as a testimony against them
Luke 10:39 who also sat at Jesus' **f**
Luke 15:22 his hand and sandals on his **f**
Luke 17:16 down on his face at His **f**
Luke 24:39 Behold My hands and My **f**, that
Luke 24:40 them His hands and His **f**
John 11: 2 wiped His **f** with her hair,
John 11:32 Him, she fell down at His **f**
John 12: 3 anointed the **f** of Jesus, and
John 12: 3 wiped His **f** with her hair
John 13: 5 to wash the disciples' **f**, and
John 13: 6 Lord, are You washing my **f**
John 13: 8 You shall never wash my **f**
John 13: 9 Lord, not my **f** only, but also
John 13:10 needs only to wash his **f**, but
John 13:12 So when He had washed their **f**
John 13:14 Teacher, have washed your **f**
John 13:14 ought to wash one another's **f**
John 20:12 head and the other at the **f**
Acts 3: 7 him up, and immediately his **f**
Acts 4:35 laid them at the apostles' **f**
Acts 4:37 and laid it at the apostles' **f**
Acts 5: 2 and laid it at the apostles' **f**
Acts 5: 9 Look, the **f** of those who have
Acts 5:10 she fell down at his **f** and
Acts 7:33 Take your sandals off your **f**
Acts 7:58 **f** of a young man named Saul
Acts 10:25 met him and fell down at his **f**
Acts 13:25 the sandals of whose **f** I am
Acts 13:51 from their **f** against them
Acts 14: 8 strength in his **f** was sitting
Acts 14:10 Stand up straight on your **f**
Acts 16:24 their **f** in the stocks
Acts 21:11 bound his own hands and **f**
Acts 22: 3 city at the **f** of Gamaliel
Acts 26:16 But rise and stand on your **f**
Rom 3:15 Their **f** are swift to shed
Rom 10:15 How beautiful are the **f** of
Rom 16:20 Satan under your **f** shortly
1Co 12:21 nor again the head to the **f**
1Co 15:25 put all enemies under His **f**
1Co 15:27 put all things under His **f**
Eph 1:22 He put all things under His **f**
Eph 6:15 having shod your **f** with the
1Ti 5:10 she has washed the saints' **f**
Heb 2: 8 in subjection under his **f**
Heb 12:13 straight paths for your **f**
Rev 1:13 with a garment down to the **f**
Rev 1:15 His **f** were like fine brass,
Rev 1:17 Him, I fell at His **f** as dead
Rev 2:18 and His **f** like fine brass
Rev 3: 9 come and worship before your **f**
Rev 10: 1 his **f** like pillars of fire
Rev 11:11 and they stood on their **f**
Rev 12: 1 with the moon under her **f**
Rev 13: 2 his **f** were like the **f** of a
Rev 13: 2 were like the **f** of a bear
Rev 19:10 I fell at his **f** to worship
Rev 22: 8 **f** of the angel who showed me

FEIGNED
1Sa 21:13 **f** madness in their hands,

FELIX
Acts 23:24 him safely to **F** the governor
Acts 23:26 the most excellent governor **F**
Acts 24: 3 in all places, most noble **F**
Acts 24:22 But when **F** heard these things
Acts 24:24 when **F** came with his wife
Acts 24:25 **F** was afraid and answered,
Acts 24:27 Porcius Festus succeeded **F**
Acts 24:27 and **F**, wanting to do the Jews
Acts 25:14 man left a prisoner by **F**,

FELL (*see* FALL)
Gen 4: 5 angry, and his countenance **f**
Gen 14:10 some **f** there, and the
Gen 15:12 a deep sleep **f** upon Abram
Gen 15:12 and great darkness **f** upon him
Gen 17: 3 Then Abram **f** on his face, and
Gen 17:17 Then Abraham **f** on his face
Gen 33: 4 **f** on his neck and kissed him,
Gen 44:14 and they **f** before him on the
Gen 45:14 Then he **f** on his brother
Gen 46:29 **f** on his neck and wept on his
Gen 50: 1 Then Joseph **f** on his father's
Gen 50:18 **f** down before his face, and
Ex 32:28 men of the people **f** that day
Lev 9:24 shouted and **f** on their faces
Lev 16: 9 on which the LORD's lot **f**
Lev 16:10 **f** to be the scapegoat shall
Num 11: 9 when the dew **f** on the camp in
Num 11: 9 the night, the manna **f** on it
Num 14: 5 Aaron **f** on their faces before
Num 16: 4 heard it, he **f** on his face
Num 16:22 Then they **f** on their faces,
Num 16:45 And they **f** on their faces
Num 20: 6 and they **f** on their faces
Num 22:31 head and **f** flat on his face
Deut 9:18 I **f** down before the LORD, as
Josh 5:14 Joshua **f** on his face to the
Josh 6:20 that the wall **f** down flat
Josh 7: 6 **f** to the earth on his face
Josh 8:25 was that all who **f** that day
Josh 16: 1 The lot **f** to the children of
Josh 17: 5 Ten portions **f** to Manasseh
Josh 22:20 thing, and wrath **f** on all the
Judg 4:16 all the army of Sisera **f** by
Judg 5:27 At her feet he sank, he **f**
Judg 5:27 he sank, there he **f** dead

Judg 7:13 and struck it so that it f
Judg 9:40 many f wounded, even to the
Judg 12: 6 There f at that time
Judg 13:20 they f on their faces to the
Judg 16:30 the temple f on the lords and
Judg 19:26 f down at the door of the
Judg 20:44 thousand men of Benjamin f
Judg 20:46 So all who f of Benjamin that
Ruth 2:10 Then she f on her face, bowed
1Sa 4:10 and there f of Israel thirty
1Sa 4:18 God, that Eli f off the seat
1Sa 11: 7 of the LORD f on the people
1Sa 14:13 and they f before Jonathan
1Sa 17:49 he f on his face to the earth
1Sa 17:52 f along the road to Shaaraim
1Sa 20:41 f on his face to the ground,
1Sa 25:23 f on her face before David,
1Sa 25:24 So she f at his feet and said
1Sa 28:20 Then immediately Saul f full
1Sa 30:13 three days ago I f sick
1Sa 31: 1 and f slain on Mount Gilboa
1Sa 31: 4 Saul took a sword and f on it
1Sa 31: 5 he also f on his sword, and
2Sa 1: 2 that he f to the ground and
2Sa 2:16 so they f down together
2Sa 2:23 he f down there and died on
2Sa 2:23 the place where Asahel f down
2Sa 3:34 before wicked men, so you f
2Sa 4: 4 made haste to flee, that he f
2Sa 9: 6 to David, he f on his face and
2Sa 11:17 of the servants of David f
2Sa 14: 4 she f on her face to the
2Sa 14:22 Then Joab f to the ground on
2Sa 19:18 f down before the king when
2Sa 20: 8 was going forward, it f out
2Sa 21: 9 So they f, all seven together
2Sa 21:22 f by the hand of David and by
1Ki 1:53 f down before King Solomon
1Ki 18: 7 and f on his face, and said,
1Ki 18:38 Then the fire of the LORD f
1Ki 18:39 saw it, they f on their faces
1Ki 20:30 then a wall f on twenty-seven
2Ki 1: 2 Now Ahaziah f through the
2Ki 1:13 f on his knees before Elijah,
2Ki 4:37 f at his feet, and bowed to
2Ki 6: 5 iron ax head f into the water
1Ch 5:10 Hagrites, who f by their hand
1Ch 5:22 for many f dead, because the
1Ch 10: 1 and f slain on Mount Gilboa
1Ch 10: 4 Saul took a sword and f on it
1Ch 10: 5 he also f on his sword and
1Ch 20: 8 they f by the hand of David
1Ch 21:14 thousand men of Israel f
1Ch 21:16 sackcloth, f on their faces
1Ch 24: 7 the first lot f to Jehoiarib
1Ch 26:14 the East Gate f to Shelemiah
2Ch 13:17 choice men of Israel f slain
2Ch 17:10 the fear of the LORD f on all
2Ch 29: 8 of the LORD f upon Judah and
Ezra 9: 5 I f on my knees and spread out
Esth 3: 7 until it f on the twelfth
Esth 8: 3 king, f down at his feet, and
Esth 8:17 fear of the Jews f upon them
Esth 9: 2 of them f upon all people
Esth 9: 3 fear of Mordecai f upon them
Job 1:16 The fire of God f from heaven
Job 1:19 it f on the young men, and
Job 1:20 and he f to the ground and
Ps 27: 2 and foes, They stumbled and f
Ps 78:64 Their priests f by the sword
Ps 107:12 They f down, and there was
Jer 46:16 yes, one f upon another
Lam 1: 7 When her people f into the
Ezek 1:28 I f on my face, and I heard a
Ezek 3:23 and I f on my face
Ezek 8: 1 the Lord GOD f upon me there
Ezek 9: 8 I f on my face and cried out,
Ezek 11: 5 Spirit of the LORD f upon me
Ezek 11:13 Then I f on my face and cried
Ezek 39:23 and they all f by the sword
Ezek 43: 3 and I f on my face
Ezek 44: 4 and I f on my face
Dan 2:46 Nebuchadnezzar f on his face
Dan 3: 7 nations, and languages f down
Dan 3:23 f down bound into the midst
Dan 4:31 mouth, a voice f from heaven
Dan 7:20 came up, before which three f
Dan 8:17 I was afraid and f on my face
Dan 10: 7 a great terror f upon them
Jon 1: 7 lots, and the lot f on Jonah
Matt 2:11 and f down and worshiped Him
Matt 7:27 beat on that house; and it f.
Matt 13: 4 some seed f by the wayside
Matt 13: 5 Some f on stony places, where
Matt 13: 7 some f among thorns, and the
Matt 13: 8 But others f on good ground
Matt 17: 6 they f on their faces and were
Matt 18:26 therefore f down before him
Matt 18:29 servant f down at his feet
Matt 26:39 f on His face, and prayed,
Mark 3:11 f down before Him and cried
Mark 4: 4 some seed f by the wayside
Mark 4: 5 Some f on stony ground, where
Mark 4: 7 And some seed f among thorns
Mark 4: 8 other seed f on good ground
Mark 5:22 he saw Him, he f at His feet
Mark 5:33 f down before Him and told Him
Mark 7:25 and she came and f at His feet
Mark 9:20 him, and he f on the ground and
Mark 14:35 f on the ground, and prayed
Luke 1: 9 his lot f to burn incense
Luke 1:12 troubled, and fear f upon him
Luke 5: 8 he f down at Jesus' knees,
Luke 5:12 he f on his face and implored
Luke 6:49 and immediately it f
Luke 8: 5 sowed, some f by the wayside
Luke 8: 6 Some f on rock
Luke 8: 7 some f among thorns, and the
Luke 8: 8 But others f on good ground,
Luke 8:14 the ones that f among thorns
Luke 8:15 But the ones that f on the
Luke 8:23 as they sailed He f asleep
Luke 8:28 f down before Him, and with a
Luke 8:41 he f down at Jesus' feet and
Luke 10:30 f among thieves, who stripped
Luke 10:36 him who f among the thieves
Luke 13: 4 on whom the tower in Siloam f
Luke 15:20 f on his neck and kissed him
Luke 16:21 f from the rich man's table
Luke 17:16 f down on his face at His
John 11:32 Him, she f down at His feet,
John 18: 6 drew back and f to the ground
Acts 1:25 Judas by transgression f,
Acts 1:26 and the lot f on Matthias
Acts 5: 5 f down and breathed his last
Acts 5:10 she f down at his feet and
Acts 7:60 he had said this, he f asleep
Acts 9: 4 Then he f to the ground, and
Acts 9:18 Immediately there f from his
Acts 10:10 ready, he f into a trance
Acts 10:25 him and f down at his feet and
Acts 10:44 the Holy Spirit f upon all
Acts 11:15 the Holy Spirit f upon them
Acts 12: 7 his chains f off his hands
Acts 13:11 a dark mist f on him, and he
Acts 13:36 f asleep, was buried with his
Acts 16:29 f down trembling before Paul
Acts 19:17 fear f on them all, and the
Acts 19:35 image which f down from Zeus
Acts 20: 9 he f down from the third
Acts 20:10 f on him, and embracing him
Acts 20:37 f on Paul's neck and kissed
Acts 22: 7 I f to the ground and heard a
Rom 11:22 on those who f, severity
Rom 15: 3 who reproached You f on Me
1Co 10: 8 day twenty-three thousand f
1Ti 2:14 f into transgression
Heb 3:17 whose corpses f in the
Heb 11:30 f down after they were
2Pe 3: 4 since the fathers f asleep
Rev 1:17 Him, I f at His feet as dead
Rev 5: 8 elders f down before the Lamb
Rev 5:14 the twenty-four elders f down
Rev 6:13 of heaven f to the earth, as
Rev 7:11 f on their faces before the
Rev 8:10 And a great star f from heaven
Rev 8:10 it f on a third of the rivers
Rev 11:11 great fear f on those who saw
Rev 11:13 and a tenth of the city f
Rev 11:16 thrones f on their faces and
Rev 16:19 the cities of the nations f
Rev 16:21 hail from heaven f upon men
Rev 19: 4 four living creatures f down
Rev 19:10 I f at his feet to worship
Rev 22: 8 I f down to worship before

FELLOW (*see* FELLOWS, FELLOWSHIP)
1Sa 21:15 f to play the madman in my
1Sa 21:15 Shall this f come into my
1Sa 25:21 this f has in the wilderness
1Sa 29: 4 Make this f return, that he
1Ki 22:27 Put this f in prison, and feed
2Ch 18:26 Put this f in prison, and feed
Matt 12:24 This f does not cast out
Matt 18:28 found one of his f servants
Matt 18:29 So his f servant fell down at
Matt 18:31 So when his f servants saw
Matt 18:33 compassion on your f servant
Matt 24:49 begins to beat his f servants
Matt 26:61 This f said, 'I am able to
Matt 26:71 This f also was with Jesus of
Mark 15: 7 with his f insurrectionists
Luke 22:59 Surely this f also was with
Luke 23: 2 We found this f perverting
John 9:29 as for this f, we do not know
John 11:16 said to his f disciples
Acts 18:13 This f persuades men to
Acts 19:38 his f craftsmen have a case
Acts 22:22 with such a f from the earth
Rom 16: 3 my f workers in Christ Jesus,
Rom 16: 7 my f prisoners, who are of
Rom 16: 9 our f worker in Christ, and
Rom 16:21 my f worker, and Lucius, Jason
1Co 3: 9 For we are God's f workers
2Co 1:24 but are f workers for your
2Co 8:23 and f worker concerning you
Eph 2:19 but f citizens with the
Eph 3: 6 Gentiles should be f heirs
Phil 2:25 f worker, and f soldier,
Phil 4: 3 and the rest of my f workers
Col 1: 7 Epaphras, our dear f servant
Col 4: 7 a f servant in the Lord, will
Col 4:10 Aristarchus my f prisoner
Col 4:11 These are my only f workers
1Th 3: 2 our f laborer in the gospel
Phm 1 beloved friend and f laborer,
Phm 2 Archippus our f soldier, and
Phm 23 my f prisoner in Christ Jesus
Phm 24 Demas, Luke, my f laborers
1Pe 5: 1 I exhort, I who am a f elder
3Jn 8 that we may become f workers
Rev 6:11 number of their f servants
Rev 19:10 I am your f servant, and of
Rev 22: 9 For I am your f servant, and

FELLOWS (*see* FELLOW)
2Sa 6:20 as one of the base f
Dan 7:20 was greater than his f

FELLOWSHIP (*see* FELLOW)
Ps 94:20 evil by law, Have f with You
Acts 2:42 the apostles' doctrine and f
1Co 1: 9 called into the f of His Son
1Co 10:20 you to have f with demons
2Co 6:14 For what f has righteousness
2Co 8: 4 the f of the ministering to
Gal 2: 9 Barnabas the right hand of f
Eph 3: 9 what is the f of the mystery
Eph 5:11 have no f with the unfruitful
Phil 1: 5 for your f in the gospel from
Phil 2: 1 if any f of the Spirit, if
Phil 3:10 and the f of His sufferings,
1Jn 1: 3 you also may have f with us
1Jn 1: 3 and truly our f is with the
1Jn 1: 6 say that we have f with Him
1Jn 1: 7 we have f with one another,

FELT (*see* FEEL)
Gen 27:22 father, and he f him and said,
Ex 10:21 darkness which may even be f
Judg 8:11 army while the camp f secure
1Sa 13:12 Therefore I f compelled, and
Mark 5:29 she f in her body that she

FEMALE
Gen 1:27 male and f He created them
Gen 5: 2 He created them male and f
Gen 6:19 they shall be male and f
Gen 7: 2 clean animal, a male and his f
Gen 7: 2 are unclean, a male and his f
Gen 7: 3 birds of the air, male and f
Gen 7: 9 the ark to Noah, male and f
Gen 7:16 f of all flesh, went in as
Gen 12:16 f servants, f donkeys,
Gen 12:16 f donkeys, and camels
Gen 15: 9 a three-year-old f goat, a
Gen 20:14 f servants, and gave them to
Gen 24:35 and f servants, and camels and
Gen 30:35 all the f goats that were
Gen 30:43 and had large flocks, f and
Gen 31:38 ewes and your f goats have not
Gen 32: 5 flocks, and male and f servants
Gen 32:14 two hundred f goats and twenty

Gen 32:15 twenty f donkeys and ten foals
Gen 45:23 ten f donkeys loaded with
Lev 3: 1 the herd, whether male or f
Lev 3: 6 the flock, whether male or f
Lev 4:28 a f without blemish, for his
Lev 4:32 bring a f without blemish
Lev 5: 6 a f from the flock, a lamb or
Lev 12: 5 But if she bears a f child
Lev 12: 7 who has borne a male or a f
Lev 25:44 f slaves whom you may have
Lev 25:44 you may buy male and f slaves
Lev 27: 4 If it is a f, then your
Lev 27: 5 and for a f ten shekels
Lev 27: 6 for a f your valuation shall
Lev 27: 7 and for a f ten shekels
Num 5: 3 shall put out both male and f
Num 15:27 then he shall bring a f goat
Deut 4:16 the likeness of male or f
Deut 7:14 shall not be a male or f
Deut 28:68 f slaves, but no one will buy
2Ki 2:24 two f bears came out of the
2Ki 5:26 and oxen, male and f servants
2Ch 28:10 to be your male and f slaves
Ezra 2:65 f servants, of whom there
Neh 7:67 f servants, of whom there
Esth 7: 4 f slaves, I would have held
Job 42:12 and one thousand f donkeys
Eccl 2: 7 f servants, and had servants
Eccl 2: 8 f singers, the delights of
Jer 34: 9 set free his male and f slave
Jer 34:10 f slaves, that no one should
Jer 34:11 f slaves return, whom they
Jer 34:11 as male and f slaves
Jer 34:16 f slaves, whom he had set at
Jer 34:16 to be your male and f slaves
Matt 19: 4 made them male and f,'
Mark 10: 6 God 'made them male and f
Gal 3:28 there is neither male nor f

FENCE (*see* FENCED)
Ps 62: 3 leaning wall and a tottering f

FENCED (*see* FENCE)
Job 19: 8 He has f up my way, so that I

FERRYBOAT
2Sa 19:18 Then a f went across to carry

FERTILE (*see* FERTILIZE)
Ezek 17: 5 and planted it in a f field

FERTILIZE (*see* FERTILE)
Luke 13: 8 until I dig around it and f it

FERVENT (*see* FERVENTLY, FERVOR)
Prov 26:23 F lips with a wicked heart
Luke 22:15 With f desire I have desired
Acts 18:25 being f in spirit, he spoke
Rom 12:11 f in spirit, serving the Lord
Jas 5:16 f prayer of a righteous man
1Pe 4: 8 have f love for one another
2Pe 3:10 will melt with f heat
2Pe 3:12 will melt with f heat

FERVENTLY (*see* FERVENT)
Col 4:12 always laboring f for you in
1Pe 1:22 love one another f with a

FERVOR (*see* FERVENT)
Zech 8: 2 with great f I am zealous for

FESTAL
Is 3:22 the f apparel, and the mantles

FESTERING
Ps 38: 5 f Because of my foolishness

FESTIVAL (*see* FESTIVALS)
Is 30:29 night when a holy f is kept
Col 2:16 or regarding a f or a new

FESTIVALS (*see* FESTIVAL)
Ezek 46:11 At the f and the appointed

FESTUS (*see* PORCIUS)
Acts 24:27 Porcius F succeeded Felix
Acts 25: 1 Now when F had come to the
Acts 25: 4 But F answered that Paul
Acts 25: 9 But F, wanting to do the Jews
Acts 25:12 Then F, when he had conferred
Acts 25:13 came to Caesarea to greet F
Acts 25:14 F laid Paul's case before the
Acts 25:22 Then Agrippa said to F, "I
Acts 25:23 city, at F' command Paul was
Acts 25:24 F said: "King Agrippa and all
Acts 26:24 F said with a loud voice,
Acts 26:25 I am not mad, most noble F
Acts 26:32 Then Agrippa said to F

FETCH
Job 36: 3 I will f my knowledge from

FETTERS
Judg 16:21 They bound him with bronze f
2Sa 3:34 nor your feet put into f
2Ki 25: 7 bound him with bronze f, and
2Ch 33:11 bound him with bronze f, and
2Ch 36: 6 and bound him in bronze f to
Job 36: 8 And if they are bound in f
Ps 105:18 They hurt his feet with f
Ps 149: 8 their nobles with f of iron
Eccl 7:26 and nets, whose hands are f
Jer 39: 7 bound him with bronze f to
Jer 52:11 Babylon bound him in bronze f

FEVER
Lev 26:16 f which shall consume the
Deut 28:22 you with consumption, with f
Deut 28:22 with severe burning f, with
Job 30:30 my bones burn with f
Lam 5:10 because of the f of famine
Hab 3: 5 and f followed at His feet
Matt 8:14 mother lying sick with a f
Matt 8:15 her hand, and the f left her
Mark 1:30 mother lay sick with a f, and
Mark 1:31 and immediately the f left her
Luke 4:38 mother was sick with a high f
Luke 4:39 over her and rebuked the f
John 4:52 seventh hour the f left him
Acts 28: 8 of Publius lay sick of a f

FEW (*see* PREFACE)

FEWER (*see* PREFACE)

FIDELITY
Tit 2:10 but showing all good f, that

FIELD (*see* FIELDS)
Gen 2: 5 of the f was in the earth
Gen 2: 5 any herb of the f had grown
Gen 2:19 formed every beast of the f
Gen 2:20 and to every beast of the f
Gen 3: 1 than any beast of the f which
Gen 3:14 than every beast of the f
Gen 3:18 shall eat the herb of the f
Gen 4: 8 pass, when they were in the f
Gen 23: 9 which is at the end of his f
Gen 23:11 I give you the f and the cave
Gen 23:13 will give you money for the f
Gen 23:17 So the f of Ephron which was
Gen 23:17 which was before Mamre, the f
Gen 23:17 the trees that were in the f
Gen 23:19 cave of the f of Machpelah
Gen 23:20 So the f and the cave that is
Gen 24:63 in the f in the evening
Gen 24:65 walking in the f to meet us
Gen 25: 9 in the f of Ephron the son of
Gen 25:10 the f which Abraham purchased
Gen 25:27 hunter, a man of the f
Gen 25:29 and Esau came in from the f
Gen 27: 3 your bow, and go out to the f
Gen 27: 5 went to the f to hunt game
Gen 27:27 f which the LORD has blessed
Gen 29: 2 and saw a well in the f
Gen 30:14 and found mandrakes in the f
Gen 30:16 out of the f in the evening
Gen 31: 4 Rachel and Leah to the f, to
Gen 34: 5 with his livestock in the f
Gen 34: 7 from the f when they heard it
Gen 34:28 the city and what was in the f
Gen 36:35 Midian in the f of Moab,
Gen 37: 7 binding sheaves in the f
Gen 37:15 he was, wandering in the f
Gen 39: 5 had in the house and in the f
Gen 47:20 of the Egyptians sold his f
Gen 47:24 your own, as seed for the f
Gen 49:29 the f of Ephron the Hittite
Gen 49:30 that is in the f of Machpelah
Gen 49:30 Abraham bought with the f of
Gen 49:32 The f and the cave that is
Gen 50:13 cave of the f of Machpelah
Gen 50:13 Abraham bought with the f
Ex 1:14 manner of service in the f
Ex 9: 3 be on your cattle in the f
Ex 9:19 and all that you have in the f
Ex 9:19 beast which is found in the f
Ex 9:21 and his livestock in the f
Ex 9:22 and on every herb of the f
Ex 9:25 Egypt, all that was in the f
Ex 9:25 struck every herb of the f
Ex 9:25 and broke every tree of the f
Ex 10: 5 grows up for you out of the f
Ex 10:15 or on the plants of the f
Ex 16:25 you will not find it in the f
Ex 22: 5 If a man causes a f or
Ex 22: 5 it feeds in another man's f
Ex 22: 5 from the best of his own f
Ex 22: 6 or the f is consumed, he who
Ex 22:31 is torn by beasts in the f
Ex 23:11 the beasts of the f may eat
Ex 23:16 which you have sown in the f
Ex 23:16 of your labors from the f
Ex 23:29 the beast of the f become too
Lev 14: 7 bird loose in the open f
Lev 14:53 the city in the open f, and
Lev 17: 5 they offer in the open f,
Lev 19: 9 reap the corners of your f
Lev 19:19 sow your f with mixed seed
Lev 23:22 of your f when you reap, nor
Lev 25: 3 years you shall sow your f
Lev 25: 4 f nor prune your vineyard
Lev 25:12 eat its produce from the f
Lev 25:34 But the f of the common-land
Lev 26: 4 and the trees of the f shall
Lev 27:16 part of a f of his possession
Lev 27:17 If he sanctifies his f from
Lev 27:18 his f after the Jubilee, then
Lev 27:19 f ever wishes to redeem it
Lev 27:20 does not want to redeem the f
Lev 27:20 has sold the f to another man
Lev 27:21 but the f, when it is
Lev 27:21 to the LORD, as a devoted f
Lev 27:22 LORD a f which he has bought
Lev 27:22 which is not the f of his
Lev 27:24 f shall return to him from
Lev 27:28 or the f of his possession,
Num 19:16 Whoever in the open f
Num 22: 4 licks up the grass of the f
Num 22:23 of the way and went into the f
Num 23:14 him to the f of Zophim, to
Deut 5:21 your neighbor's house, his f
Deut 7:22 lest the beasts of the f
Deut 14:22 the f produces year by year
Deut 20:19 tree of the f is man's food
Deut 21: 1 lying in the f in the land
Deut 24:19 reap your harvest in your f
Deut 24:19 and forget a sheaf in the f
Deut 28:38 carry much seed out to the f
Josh 8:24 inhabitants of Ai in the f
Josh 15:18 him to ask her father for a f
Judg 1:14 him to ask her father for a f
Judg 5: 4 marched from the f of Edom
Judg 9:32 you, and lie in wait in the f
Judg 9:42 people went out into the f
Judg 9:43 and laid in wait in the f
Judg 13: 9 as she was sitting in the f
Judg 19:16 his work in the f at evening
Judg 20:31 other to Gibeah) and in the f
Ruth 2: 2 Please let me go to the f
Ruth 2: 3 gleaned in the f after the
Ruth 2: 3 of the f belonging to Boaz
Ruth 2: 8 not go to glean in another f
Ruth 2: 9 be on the f which they reap
Ruth 2:17 in the f until evening, and
Ruth 2:22 not meet you in any other f
Ruth 4: 5 the f from the hand of Naomi
1Sa 4: 2 men of the army in the f
1Sa 6:14 f of Joshua of Beth Shemesh
1Sa 6:18 f of Joshua of Beth Shemesh
1Sa 11: 5 behind the herd from the f
1Sa 14:15 in the camp, in the f, and
1Sa 17:44 air and the beasts of the f
1Sa 19: 3 father in the f where you are
1Sa 20: 5 the f until the third day at
1Sa 20:11 and let us go out into the f
1Sa 20:11 of them went out into the f
1Sa 20:24 So David hid in the f
1Sa 20:35 f at the time appointed with
1Sa 30:11 found an Egyptian in the f
2Sa 2:16 called the F of Sharp Swords
2Sa 10: 8 were by themselves in the f
2Sa 11:23 us and came out to us in the f
2Sa 14: 6 with each other in the f, and
2Sa 14:30 Joab's f is near mine, and he
2Sa 14:30 servants set the f on fire
2Sa 14:31 servants set my f on fire
2Sa 17: 8 robbed of her cubs in the f
2Sa 18: 6 f of battle against Israel
2Sa 20:12 from the highway to the f
2Sa 21:10 the beasts of the f by night

2Sa 23:12 in the middle of the **f**,
1Ki 11:29 the two were alone in the **f**
1Ki 14:11 eat whoever dies in the **f**
1Ki 21:24 eat whoever dies in the **f**
2Ki 4:39 into the **f** to gather herbs
2Ki 7:12 to hide themselves in the **f**
2Ki 8: 6 all the proceeds of the **f**
2Ki 9:25 **f** of Naboth the Jezreelite
2Ki 9:37 on the surface of the **f**, in
2Ki 18:17 the highway to the Fuller's **F**
2Ki 19:26 were as the grass of the **f**
1Ch 1:46 Midian in the **f** of Moab,
1Ch 11:14 in the midst of that **f**,
1Ch 16:32 let the **f** rejoice, and all
1Ch 19: 9 were by themselves in the **f**
1Ch 27:25 over the storehouses in the **f**
1Ch 27:26 the **f** for tilling the ground
2Ch 26:23 **f** of burial which belonged to
2Ch 31: 5 of all the produce of the **f**
Neh 13:10 work had gone back to his **f**
Job 5:23 with the stones of the **f**, and
Job 5:23 the beasts of the **f** shall be
Job 24: 6 gather their fodder in the **f**
Job 40:20 beasts of the **f** play there
Ps 8: 7 Even the beasts of the **f**,
Ps 50:11 wild beasts of the **f** are Mine
Ps 78:12 of Egypt, in the **f** of Zoan
Ps 78:43 His wonders in the **f** of Zoan
Ps 80:13 beast of the **f** devours it
Ps 96:12 Let the **f** be joyful, and all
Ps 103:15 As a flower of the **f**, so he
Ps 104:11 drink to every beast of the **f**
Prov 24:27 it fit for yourself in the **f**
Prov 24:30 I went by the **f** of the
Prov 27:26 and the goats the price of a **f**
Prov 31:16 She considers a **f** and buys it
Eccl 5: 9 himself is served from the **f**
Song 2: 7 or by the does of the **f**, do
Song 3: 5 or by the does of the **f**, do
Song 7:11 let us go forth to the **f**
Is 5: 8 who add **f** to **f**, till
Is 7: 3 the highway to the Fuller's **F**
Is 10:18 forest and of his fruitful **f**
Is 16:10 and joy from the plentiful **f**
Is 29:17 be turned into a fruitful **f**
Is 29:17 the fruitful **f** be esteemed as
Is 32:15 becomes a fruitful **f**, and the
Is 32:15 the fruitful **f** is counted as
Is 32:16 remain in the fruitful **f**
Is 36: 2 the highway to the Fuller's **F**
Is 37:27 were as the grass of the **f**
Is 40: 6 is like the flower of the **f**
Is 43:20 beast of the **f** will honor Me
Is 55:12 all the trees of the **f** shall
Is 56: 9 All you beasts of the **f**, come
Jer 4:17 Like keepers of a **f** they are
Jer 6:25 Do not go out into the **f**, nor
Jer 7:20 beast, on the trees of the **f**
Jer 9:22 fall as refuse on the open **f**
Jer 12: 4 the herbs of every **f** wither
Jer 12: 9 all the beasts of the **f**,
Jer 14: 5 deer also gave birth in the **f**
Jer 14:18 If I go out to the **f**, then
Jer 17: 3 O My mountain in the **f**, I
Jer 18:14 comes from the rock of the **f**
Jer 26:18 Zion shall be plowed like a **f**
Jer 27: 6 the beasts of the **f** I have
Jer 28:14 him the beasts of the **f** also
Jer 32: 7 Buy my **f** which is in Anathoth
Jer 32: 8 Please buy my **f** that is in
Jer 32: 9 I bought the **f** from Hanameel
Jer 32:25 Buy the **f** for money, and take
Jer 35: 9 nor do we have vineyard, **f**
Jer 41: 8 oil, and honey in the **f**
Jer 48:33 taken from the plentiful **f**
Lam 4: 9 lack of the fruits of the **f**
Ezek 7:15 Whoever is in the **f** will die
Ezek 16: 5 thrown out into the open **f**
Ezek 16: 7 thrive like a plant in the **f**
Ezek 17: 5 and planted it in a fertile **f**
Ezek 17:24 of the **f** shall know that I
Ezek 29: 5 you shall fall on the open **f**
Ezek 29: 5 food to the beasts of the **f**
Ezek 31: 4 to all the trees of the **f**
Ezek 31: 5 above all the trees of the **f**
Ezek 31: 6 all the beasts of the **f**
Ezek 31:13 all the beasts of the **f** will
Ezek 31:15 of the **f** wilted because of it
Ezek 33:27 **f** I will give to the beasts
Ezek 34: 5 **f** when they were scattered
Ezek 34: 8 food for every beast of the **f**
Ezek 34:27 Then the trees of the **f** shall
Ezek 38:20 heavens, the beasts of the **f**
Ezek 39: 4 of the **f** to be devoured
Ezek 39: 5 You shall fall on the open **f**
Ezek 39:10 **f** nor cut down any from the
Ezek 39:17 and to every beast of the **f**
Dan 2:38 dwell, or the beasts of the **f**
Dan 4:12 The beasts of the **f** found
Dan 4:15 in the tender grass of the **f**
Dan 4:21 the beasts of the **f** dwelt
Dan 4:23 in the tender grass of the **f**
Dan 4:23 with the beasts of the **f**,
Dan 4:25 be with the beasts of the **f**
Dan 4:32 be with the beasts of the **f**
Hos 2:12 of the **f** shall eat them
Hos 2:18 them with the beasts of the **f**
Hos 4: 3 away with the beasts of the **f**
Hos 10: 4 in the furrows of the **f**
Hos 12:11 heaps in the furrows of the **f**
Joel 1:10 The **f** is wasted, the land
Joel 1:11 harvest of the **f** has perished
Joel 1:12 trees of the **f** are withered
Joel 1:19 burned all the trees of the **f**
Joel 1:20 The beasts of the **f** also cry
Joel 2:22 afraid, you beasts of the **f**
Mic 1: 6 a heap of ruins in the **f**,
Mic 3:12 Zion shall be plowed like a **f**
Mic 4:10 you shall dwell in the **f**
Zech 10: 1 grass in the **f** for everyone
Mal 3:11 bear fruit for you in the **f**
Matt 6:28 Consider the lilies of the **f**
Matt 6:30 so clothes the grass of the **f**
Matt 13:24 who sowed good seed in his **f**
Matt 13:27 not sow good seed in your **f**
Matt 13:31 a man took and sowed in his **f**
Matt 13:36 parable of the tares of the **f**
Matt 13:38 The **f** is the world, the good
Matt 13:44 like treasure hidden in a **f**
Matt 13:44 that he has and buys that **f**
Matt 24:18 let him who is in the **f** not
Matt 24:40 Then two men will be in the **f**
Matt 27: 7 with them the potter's **f**, to
Matt 27: 8 Therefore that **f** has been
Matt 27: 8 the **F** of Blood to this day
Matt 27:10 gave them for the potter's **f**
Mark 13:16 let him who is in the **f** not
Luke 12:28 which today is in the **f** and
Luke 15:25 his older son was in the **f**
Luke 17: 7 he has come in from the **f**
Luke 17:31 the one who is in the **f**, let
Luke 17:36 Two men will be in the **f**
Acts 1:18 (Now this man purchased a **f**
Acts 1:19 so that **f** is called in their
Acts 1:19 Dama, that is, **F** of Blood
1Co 3: 9 you are God's **f**, you are
Jas 1:10 of the **f** he will pass away

FIELDS (*see* FIELD)
Gen 41:48 the **f** which surrounded them
Ex 8:13 courtyards, and out of the **f**
Lev 25:31 as the **f** of the country
Num 16:14 nor given us inheritance of **f**
Num 20:17 pass through **f** or vineyards
Num 21:22 aside into **f** or vineyards
Deut 11:15 in your **f** for your livestock
Deut 32:13 eat the produce of the **f**
Deut 32:32 Sodom and of the **f** of Gomorrah
Josh 21:12 But the **f** of the city and its
Judg 9:27 So they went out into the **f**
Judg 9:44 upon all who were in the **f**
1Sa 8:14 will take the best of your **f**
1Sa 22: 7 Jesse give every one of you **f**
1Sa 25:15 them, when we were in the **f**
2Sa 1:21 upon you, nor **f** of offerings
2Sa 11:11 are encamped in the open **f**
1Ki 2:26 Go to Anathoth, to your own **f**
1Ki 16: 4 eat whoever dies in the **f**
2Ki 23: 4 Jerusalem in the **f** of Kidron
1Ch 6:56 But the **f** of the city and its
2Ch 31:19 who were in the **f** of the
Neh 11:25 for the villages with their **f**
Neh 11:30 in Lachish and its **f**
Neh 12:29 Gilgal, and from the **f** of Geba
Neh 12:44 gather into them from the **f**
Job 5:10 and sends waters on the **f**
Ps 107:37 And sow **f** and plant vineyards,
Ps 132: 6 it in the **f** of the woods
Ps 144:13 And ten thousands in our **f**
Prov 8:26 not made the earth or the **f**
Prov 23:10 nor enter the **f** of the
Is 16: 8 For the **f** of Heshbon languish
Is 32:12 breasts for the pleasant **f**
Jer 6:12 be turned over to others, **f**
Jer 8:10 their **f** to those who will
Jer 13:27 on the hills in the **f**
Jer 31:40 all the **f** as far as the Brook
Jer 32:15 Houses and **f** and vineyards
Jer 32:43 **f** will be bought in this land
Jer 32:44 Men will buy **f** for money
Jer 39:10 and **f** at the same time
Jer 40: 7 the armies who were in the **f**
Jer 40:13 **f** came to Gedaliah at Mizpah
Ezek 26: 6 villages which are in the **f**
Ezek 26: 8 daughter villages in the **f**
Ezek 32: 4 cast you out on the open **f**
Ezek 36:30 and the increase of your **f**
Obad 19 possess the **f** of Ephraim and
Obad 19 Ephraim and the **f** of Samaria
Mic 2: 2 They covet **f** and take them by
Mic 2: 4 turncoat He has divided our **f**
Hab 3:17 fail, and the **f** yield no food
Luke 2: 8 shepherds living out in the **f**
Luke 15:15 him into his **f** to feed swine
John 4:35 up your eyes and look at the **f**
Jas 5: 4 the laborers who mowed your **f**

FIERCE (*see* FIERCELY, FIERCENESS, FIERCER)
Gen 49: 7 be their anger, for it is **f**
Ex 32:12 Turn from Your **f** wrath, and
Num 25: 4 that the **f** anger of the LORD
Num 32:14 **f** anger of the LORD against
Deut 28:50 a nation of **f** countenance
Judg 20:34 Gibeah, and the battle was **f**
1Sa 14:52 Now there was **f** war with the
1Sa 20:34 from the table in **f** anger
1Sa 28:18 His **f** wrath upon Amalek,
2Sa 2:17 was a very **f** battle that day
2Ch 28:11 for the **f** wrath of the LORD
2Ch 28:13 and there is **f** wrath against
2Ch 29:10 that His **f** wrath may turn
Ezra 10:14 until the **f** wrath of our God
Job 4:10 lion, the voice of the **f** lion
Job 10:16 you hunt me like a **f** lion
Job 28: 8 nor has the **f** lion passed
Job 41:10 No one is so **f** that he would
Ps 35:11 **F** witnesses rise up
Ps 88:16 Your **f** wrath has gone over me
Prov 26:13 A **f** lion is in the streets
Is 7: 4 for the **f** anger of Rezin and
Is 13: 9 and **f** anger, to lay the land
Is 13:13 and in the day of His **f** anger
Is 19: 4 a **f** king will rule over them,
Is 33:19 You will not see a **f** people
Jer 4: 8 For the **f** anger of the LORD
Jer 4:26 of the LORD, by His **f** anger
Jer 12:13 of the **f** anger of the LORD
Jer 25:37 of the **f** anger of the LORD
Jer 25:38 and because of His **f** anger
Jer 30:24 The **f** anger of the LORD will
Jer 49:37 my **f** anger,' says the LORD
Jer 51:45 from the **f** anger of the LORD
Lam 1:12 me in the day of His **f** anger
Lam 2: 3 He has cut off in **f** anger
Lam 4:11 He has poured out His **f** anger
Dan 8:23 arise, having **f** features, Who
Joel 1: 6 he has the fangs of a **f** lion
Jon 3: 9 and turn away from His **f** anger
Hab 1: 8 more **f** than evening wolves
Zeph 2: 2 before the LORD's **f** anger
Zeph 3: 8 indignation, All my **f** anger
Matt 8:28 of the tombs, exceedingly **f**
Luke 23: 5 But they were the more **f**,
Jas 3: 4 and are driven by **f** winds,

FIERCELY (*see* FIERCE)
Jer 6:29 the bellows blow **f**, the lead

FIERCENESS (*see* FIERCE)
Deut 13:17 turn from the **f** of His anger
Josh 7:26 from the **f** of His anger
2Ki 23:26 from the **f** of His great wrath
2Ch 30: 8 that the **f** of His wrath may
Job 39:24 devours the distance with **f**
Ps 78:49 on them the **f** of His anger
Ps 85: 3 from the **f** of Your anger
Jer 25:38 of the **f** of the Oppressor
Jer 49:16 Your **f** has deceived you, the
Hos 11: 9 not execute the **f** of My anger
Nah 1: 6 can endure the **f** of His anger
Rev 16:19 wine of the **f** of His wrath
Rev 19:15 treads the winepress of the **f**

FIERCER (*see* FIERCE)
2Sa 19:43 of the men of Judah were **f**

FIERY (*see* FIRE)
Num 21: 6 So the LORD sent **f** serpents
Num 21: 8 Make a **f** serpent, and set it
Deut 8:15 in which were **f** serpents
Deut 33: 2 hand came a **f** law for them
Ps 7:13 His arrows into **f** shafts
Ps 21: 9 a **f** oven in the time of Your
Ps 78:48 their flocks to **f** lightning
Is 14:29 will be a **f** flying serpent
Is 30: 6 **f** flying serpent, they will
Ezek 28:14 in the midst of **f** stones
Ezek 28:16 the midst of the **f** stones
Dan 3: 6 midst of a burning **f** furnace
Dan 3:11 midst of a burning **f** furnace
Dan 3:15 midst of a burning **f** furnace
Dan 3:17 us from the burning **f** furnace
Dan 3:20 into the burning **f** furnace
Dan 3:21 of the burning **f** furnace
Dan 3:23 of the burning **f** furnace
Dan 3:26 of the burning **f** furnace and
Dan 7: 9 His throne was a **f** flame, its
Dan 7:10 A **f** stream issued and came
Zech 12: 6 like a **f** torch in the sheaves
Eph 6:16 the **f** darts of the wicked one
Heb 10:27 and **f** indignation which will
1Pe 4:12 **f** trial which is to try you
Rev 6: 4 horse, **f** red, went out
Rev 9:17 had breastplates of **f** red
Rev 12: 3 **f** red dragon having seven

FIFTEEN (*see* FIFTEENTH)
Gen 5:10 **f** years, and begot sons and
Gen 7:20 prevailed **f** cubits upward
Ex 27:14 of the gate shall be **f** cubits
Ex 27:15 shall be hangings of **f** cubits
Ex 38:14 the gate were **f** cubits long
Ex 38:15 were hangings of **f** cubits
Lev 27: 7 valuation shall be **f** shekels
Judg 8:10 about **f** thousand men, all who
2Sa 9:10 Now Ziba had **f** sons and
2Sa 19:17 and his **f** sons and his twenty
1Ki 7: 3 pillars, **f** to a row
2Ki 14:17 lived **f** years after the death
2Ki 20: 6 will add to your days **f** years
2Ch 25:25 lived **f** years after the death
Is 38: 5 will add to your days **f** years
Ezek 45:12 **f** shekels shall be your mina
Hos 3: 2 for **f** shekels of silver, and
Acts 27:28 and found it to be **f** fathoms
Gal 1:18 and remained with him **f** days

FIFTEENTH (*see* FIFTEEN)
Ex 16: 1 on the **f** day of the second
Lev 23: 6 And on the **f** day of the same
Lev 23:34 The **f** day of this seventh
Lev 23:39 Also on the **f** day of the
Num 28:17 on the **f** day of this month is
Num 29:12 On the **f** day of the seventh
Num 33: 3 on the **f** day of the first
1Ki 12:32 the **f** day of the eighth month
1Ki 12:33 the **f** day of the eighth month
2Ki 14:23 In the **f** year of Amaziah the
1Ch 24:14 the **f** to Bilgah, the
1Ch 25:22 the **f** for Jeremoth, his sons
2Ch 15:10 in the **f** year of the reign of
Esth 9:18 on the **f** day of the month
Esth 9:21 **f** days of the month of Adar,
Ezek 32:17 on the **f** day of the month,
Ezek 45:25 on the **f** day of the month, at
Luke 3: 1 Now in the **f** year of the

FIFTH (*see* FIVE)
Gen 1:23 and the morning were the **f** day
Gen 30:17 and bore Jacob a **f** son
Lev 19:25 in the **f** year you may eat its
Num 7:36 On the **f** day Shelumiel the
Num 29:26 On the **f** day present nine
Num 33:38 the first day of the **f** month
Josh 19:24 The **f** lot came out for the
Judg 19: 8 on the **f** day to depart, but
2Sa 3: 4 the **f**, Shephatiah the son of
1Ki 14:25 in the **f** year of King
2Ki 8:16 Now in the **f** year of Joram
2Ki 25: 8 Now in the **f** month, on the
1Ch 2:14 the fourth, Raddai the **f**,
1Ch 3: 3 the **f**, Shephatiah, by Abital
1Ch 8: 2 the fourth, and Rapha the **f**
1Ch 12:10 the fourth, Jeremiah the **f**
1Ch 24: 9 the **f** to Malchijah, the sixth
1Ch 25:12 the **f** for Nethaniah, his sons
1Ch 26: 3 Elam the **f**, Jehohanan the
1Ch 26: 4 the fourth, Nethanel the **f**
1Ch 27: 8 **f** captain for the **f** month
2Ch 12: 2 in the **f** year of King
Ezra 7: 8 to Jerusalem in the **f** month
Ezra 7: 9 on the first day of the **f**
Neh 6: 5 the **f** time, with an open
Jer 1: 3 captive in the **f** month
Jer 28: 1 fourth year and in the **f** month
Jer 36: 9 **f** year of Jehoiakim the son
Jer 52:12 Now in the **f** month, on the
Ezek 1: 1 on the **f** day of the month, as
Ezek 1: 2 On the **f** day of the month,
Ezek 1: 2 which was in the **f** year of
Ezek 8: 1 on the **f** day of the month, as
Ezek 20: 1 seventh year, in the **f** month
Ezek 33:21 on the **f** day of the month,
Zech 7: 3 Should I weep in the **f** month
Zech 7: 5 fasted and mourned in the **f**
Zech 8:19 month, the fast of the **f**, the
Rev 6: 9 When He opened the **f** seal
Rev 9: 1 Then the **f** angel sounded
Rev 16:10 Then the **f** angel poured out
Rev 21:20 the **f** sardonyx, the sixth

FIFTIES (*see* FIFTY)
Ex 18:21 of hundreds, rulers of **f**, and
Ex 18:25 of hundreds, rulers of **f**, and
Deut 1:15 of hundreds, leaders of **f**
1Sa 8:12 and captains over his **f**, will
2Ki 1:14 of **f** with their **f**
Mark 6:40 in ranks, in hundreds and in **f**

FIFTIETH (*see* FIFTY)
Lev 25:10 shall consecrate the **f** year
Lev 25:11 That **f** year shall be a
2Ki 15:23 In the **f** year of Azariah king

FIFTY (*see* FIFTIES, FIFTIETH)
Gen 6:15 cubits, its width **f** cubits
Gen 7:24 earth one hundred and **f** days
Gen 8: 3 **f** days the waters decreased
Gen 9:28 three hundred and **f** years
Gen 9:29 were nine hundred and **f** years
Gen 18:24 Suppose there were **f**
Gen 18:24 and not spare it for the **f**
Gen 18:26 said, "If I find in Sodom **f**
Gen 18:28 less than the **f** righteous
Ex 26: 5 **F** loops you shall make in the
Ex 26: 5 **f** loops you shall make on the
Ex 26: 6 shall make **f** clasps of gold
Ex 26:10 You shall make **f** loops on the
Ex 26:10 **f** loops on the edge of the
Ex 26:11 shall make **f** bronze clasps
Ex 27:12 shall be hangings of **f** cubits
Ex 27:13 east side shall be **f** cubits
Ex 27:18 the width **f** throughout, and
Ex 30:23 **f** shekels), two hundred and
Ex 30:23 **f** shekels of sweet-smelling
Ex 36:12 **F** loops he made on one
Ex 36:12 **f** loops he made on the edge
Ex 36:13 he made **f** clasps of gold, and
Ex 36:17 he made **f** loops on the edge
Ex 36:17 **f** loops he made on the edge
Ex 36:18 He also made **f** bronze clasps
Ex 38:12 were hangings of **f** cubits
Ex 38:13 the hangings were **f** cubits
Ex 38:26 five hundred and **f** men
Lev 23:16 Count **f** days to the day
Lev 27: 3 shall be **f** shekels of silver
Lev 27:16 valued at **f** shekels of silver
Num 1:25 thousand six hundred and **f**
Num 1:46 thousand five hundred and **f**
Num 2:15 thousand six hundred and **f**
Num 2:16 thousand four hundred and **f**
Num 2:32 thousand five hundred and **f**
Num 4: 3 even to **f** years old, all who
Num 4:23 even to **f** years old, you
Num 4:30 even to **f** years old, you
Num 4:35 even to **f** years old, everyone
Num 4:36 thousand seven hundred and **f**
Num 4:39 even to **f** years old, everyone
Num 4:43 even to **f** years old, everyone
Num 4:47 even to **f** years old, everyone
Num 8:25 at the age of **f** years they
Num 16: 2 **f** leaders of the congregation
Num 16:17 two hundred and **f** censers
Num 16:35 and **f** men who were offering
Num 26:10 devoured two hundred and **f**
Num 31:30 you shall take one of every **f**
Num 31:47 Moses took one of every **f**
Num 31:52 seven hundred and **f** shekels
Deut 22:29 father **f** shekels of silver
Josh 7:21 of gold weighing **f** shekels
1Sa 6:19 He struck **f** thousand and
2Sa 15: 1 and **f** men to run before him
2Sa 24:24 the oxen for **f** shekels of
1Ki 1: 5 and **f** men to run before him
1Ki 7: 2 cubits, its width **f** cubits
1Ki 7: 6 its length was **f** cubits, and
1Ki 9:23 five hundred and **f**, who ruled
1Ki 10:29 and a horse one hundred and **f**
1Ki 18: 4 **f** to a cave, and had fed them
1Ki 18:13 **f** to a cave, and fed them with
1Ki 18:19 **f** prophets of Baal, and the
1Ki 18:22 are four hundred and **f** men
2Ki 1: 9 of **f** with his **f** men
2Ki 1:10 and said to the captain of **f**
2Ki 1:10 and consume you and your **f**
2Ki 1:10 and consumed him and his **f**
2Ki 1:11 of **f** with his **f** men
2Ki 1:12 and consume you and your **f**
2Ki 1:12 and consumed him and his **f**
2Ki 1:13 of **f** with his **f** men
2Ki 1:13 third captain of **f** went up
2Ki 1:13 the life of these **f** servants
2Ki 2: 7 And **f** men of the sons of the
2Ki 2:16 there are **f** strong men with
2Ki 2:17 Therefore they sent **f** men
2Ki 13: 7 of Jehoahaz only **f** horsemen
2Ki 15:20 from each man **f** shekels of
2Ki 15:25 with him were **f** men of Gilead
1Ch 5:21 **f** thousand of their camels,
1Ch 5:21 **f** thousand of their sheep, and
1Ch 8:40 one hundred and **f** in all
1Ch 12:33 of Zebulun there were **f**
2Ch 1:17 a horse for one hundred and **f**
2Ch 3: 9 nails was **f** shekels of gold
2Ch 8:10 two hundred and **f**, who ruled
2Ch 8:18 **f** talents of gold from there,
Ezra 8: 3 were one hundred and **f** males
Ezra 8: 6 Jonathan, and with him **f** males
Ezra 8:26 **f** talents of silver, silver
Neh 5:17 **f** Jews and rulers, besides
Neh 7:70 **f** basins, and five hundred and
Esth 5:14 **f** cubits high, and in the
Esth 7: 9 **f** cubits high, which Haman
Is 3: 3 the captain of **f** and the
Ezek 40:15 the inner gate was **f** cubits
Ezek 40:21 its length was **f** cubits and
Ezek 40:25 its length was **f** cubits and
Ezek 40:29 it was **f** cubits long and
Ezek 40:33 it was **f** cubits long and
Ezek 40:36 its length was **f** cubits and
Ezek 42: 2 (the width was **f** cubits), was
Ezek 42: 7 its length was **f** cubits
Ezek 42: 8 the outer court was **f** cubits
Ezek 45: 2 with **f** cubits around it for
Ezek 48:17 **f** cubits, to the south two
Ezek 48:17 to the south two hundred and **f**
Ezek 48:17 to the east two hundred and **f**
Ezek 48:17 to the west two hundred and **f**
Hag 2:16 out **f** baths from the press
Luke 7:41 denarii, and the other **f**
Luke 9:14 them sit down in groups of **f**
Luke 16: 6 sit down quickly and write **f**
John 8:57 You are not yet **f** years old
Acts 13:20 **f** years, until Samuel the
Acts 19:19 it totaled **f** thousand pieces

FIFTY-FIVE
2Ki 21: 1 and he reigned **f** years in
2Ch 33: 1 and he reigned **f** years in
Neh 7:20 of Adin, six hundred and **f**

FIFTY-FOUR
Num 1:29 were **f** thousand four hundred
Num 2: 6 at **f** thousand four hundred
Ezra 2: 7 one thousand two hundred and **f**
Ezra 2:15 of Adin, four hundred and **f**
Ezra 2:31 one thousand two hundred and **f**
Neh 7:12 one thousand two hundred and **f**
Neh 7:34 one thousand two hundred and **f**

FIFTY-NINE
Num 1:23 were **f** thousand three hundred
Num 2:13 at **f** thousand three hundred

FIFTY-ONE
Num 2:16 **f** thousand four hundred and

FIFTY-SECOND
2Ki 15:27 In the **f** year of Azariah king

FIFTY-SEVEN
Num 1:31 were **f** thousand four hundred
Num 2: 8 at **f** thousand four hundred
Num 2:31 and **f** thousand six hundred

FIFTY-SIX
1Ch 9: 9 nine hundred and **f**
Ezra 2:14 of Bigvai, two thousand and **f**
Ezra 2:22 the men of Netophah, **f**
Ezra 2:30 of Magbish, one hundred and **f**

FIFTY-THREE
Num 1:43 were **f** thousand four hundred
Num 2:30 at **f** thousand four hundred
Num 26:47 **f** thousand four hundred
2Ch 2:17 and **f** thousand six hundred
John 21:11 large fish, one hundred and **f**

FIFTY-TWO
Num 26:34 were **f** thousand seven hundred
2Ki 15: 2 and he reigned **f** years in
2Ch 26: 3 and he reigned **f** years in
Ezra 2:29 the people of Nebo, **f**
Ezra 2:37 of Immer, one thousand and **f**
Ezra 2:60 of Nekoda, six hundred and **f**
Neh 6:15 the month of Elul, in **f** days
Neh 7:10 of Arah, six hundred and **f**
Neh 7:33 the men of the other Nebo, **f**
Neh 7:40 of Immer, one thousand and **f**

FIG (*see* FIGS)
Gen 3: 7 they sewed **f** leaves together
Deut 8: 8 **f** trees and pomegranates, a
Judg 9:10 the trees said to the **f** tree
Judg 9:11 But the **f** tree said to them
1Ki 4:25 his **f** tree, from Dan as far
2Ki 18:31 every one from his own **f** tree
Ps 105:33 vines also, and their **f** trees
Prov 27:18 Whoever keeps the **f** tree will
Song 2:13 The **f** tree puts forth her
Is 34: 4 fruit falling from a **f** tree
Is 36:16 every one from his own **f** tree
Jer 5:17 up your vines and your **f** trees
Jer 8:13 vine, nor figs on the **f** tree
Hos 2:12 her **f** trees, of which she has
Hos 9:10 **f** tree in its first season
Joel 1: 7 My vine, and ruined My **f** tree
Joel 1:12 and the **f** tree has withered
Joel 2:22 the **f** tree and the vine yield
Amos 4: 9 your **f** trees, and your olive
Mic 4: 4 his vine and under his **f** tree
Nah 3:12 are **f** trees with ripened figs
Hab 3:17 Though the **f** tree may not
Hag 2:19 the **f** tree, the pomegranate,
Zech 3:10 his vine and under his **f** tree
Matt 21:19 seeing a **f** tree by the road,
Matt 21:19 And immediately the **f** tree
Matt 21:20 How did the **f** tree wither
Matt 21:21 what was done to the **f** tree
Matt 24:32 this parable from the **f** tree
Mark 11:13 afar a **f** tree having leaves
Mark 11:20 they saw the **f** tree dried up
Mark 11:21 The **f** tree which You cursed
Mark 13:28 this parable from the **f** tree
Luke 13: 6 had a **f** tree planted in his
Luke 13: 7 seeking fruit on this **f** tree
Luke 21:29 Look at the **f** tree, and all
John 1:48 you were under the **f** tree
John 1:50 I saw you under the **f** tree
Jas 3:12 Can a **f** tree, my brethren,
Rev 6:13 as a **f** tree drops its late

FIGHT (*see* FIGHTING, FIGHTS, FOUGHT)
Ex 1:10 **f** against us, and so go up out
Ex 14:14 The LORD will **f** for you, and
Ex 17: 9 men and go out, **f** with Amalek
Ex 21:22 If men **f**, and hurt a woman
Deut 1:30 before you, He will **f** for you
Deut 1:41 we will go up and **f**, just as
Deut 1:42 Do not go up nor **f**, for I am
Deut 2:32 out against us to **f** at Jahaz
Deut 20: 4 to **f** for you against your
Deut 20:10 near a city to **f** against it
Deut 25:11 If two men **f** together, and the
Josh 9: 2 together to **f** with Joshua
Josh 10:25 enemies against whom you **f**
Josh 11: 5 of Merom to **f** against Israel
Josh 19:47 went up to **f** against Leshem
Judg 1: 1 Canaanites to **f** against them
Judg 1: 3 that we may **f** against the
Judg 1: 9 of Judah went down to **f**
Judg 8: 1 went to **f** with the Midianites
Judg 9:38 you will, and **f** with them now
Judg 10: 9 to **f** against Judah also,
Judg 10:18 the man who will begin the **f**
Judg 11: 6 that we may **f** against the
Judg 11: 8 **f** against the people of Ammon
Judg 11: 9 **f** against the people of Ammon
Judg 11:12 to **f** against me in my land
Judg 11:25 Did he ever **f** against them
Judg 11:32 of Ammon to **f** against them
Judg 12: 1 Why did you cross over to **f**
Judg 12: 3 me this day to **f** against me
Judg 20:20 in battle array to **f** against
1Sa 4: 9 yourselves like men, and **f**
1Sa 8:20 before us and **f** our battles
1Sa 13: 5 together to **f** with Israel
1Sa 15:18 **f** against them until they are
1Sa 17: 9 If he is able to **f** with me
1Sa 17:10 a man, that we may **f** together
1Sa 17:20 army was going out to the **f**
1Sa 17:32 go and **f** with this Philistine
1Sa 17:33 this Philistine to **f** with him
1Sa 18:17 me, and **f** the LORD's battles
1Sa 28: 1 for war, to **f** with Israel
1Sa 29: 8 **f** against the enemies of my
2Sa 2:28 nor did they **f** anymore
1Ki 12:21 to **f** against the house of
1Ki 12:24 You shall not go up nor **f**
1Ki 20:23 but if we **f** against them in
1Ki 20:25 Then we will **f** against them
1Ki 20:26 to Aphek to **f** against Israel
1Ki 22: 4 with me to **f** at Ramoth Gilead
1Ki 22: 6 go against Ramoth Gilead to **f**
1Ki 22:31 **F** with no one small or great,
1Ki 22:32 turned aside to **f** against him
2Ki 3: 7 go with me to **f** against Moab
2Ki 3:21 had come up to **f** against them
2Ki 10: 3 **f** for your master's house
2Ch 11: 1 to **f** against Israel, that he
2Ch 11: 4 up or **f** against your brethren
2Ch 13:12 do not **f** against the LORD God
2Ch 18:30 **F** with no one small or great,
2Ch 20:17 not need to **f** in this battle
2Ch 32: 8 help us and to **f** our battles
2Ch 35:20 king of Egypt came up to **f**
2Ch 35:22 so that he might **f** with him
2Ch 35:22 So he came to **f** in the Valley
Neh 4:14 **f** for your brethren, your
Neh 4:20 Our God will **f** for us
Ps 35: 1 **F** against those who **f**
Ps 56: 2 are many who **f** against me
Is 19: 2 everyone will **f** against his
Is 29: 7 nations who **f** against Ariel
Is 29: 7 even all who **f** against her
Is 29: 8 be, who **f** against Mount Zion
Is 30:32 brandishing He will **f** with it
Is 31: 4 come down to **f** for Mount Zion
Jer 1:19 They will **f** against you, but
Jer 15:20 they will **f** against you, but
Jer 21: 4 with which you **f** against the
Jer 21: 5 I Myself will **f** against you
Jer 32: 5 though you **f** with the
Jer 32:24 Chaldeans who **f** against it
Jer 32:29 the Chaldeans who **f** against
Jer 33: 5 They come to **f** with the
Jer 34:22 They will **f** against it and
Jer 37: 8 **f** against this city, and take
Jer 37:10 Chaldeans who **f** against you
Jer 41:12 went to **f** with Ishmael the
Dan 10:20 now I must return to **f** with
Dan 11:11 **f** with him, with the king of
Zech 10: 5 They shall **f** because the LORD
Zech 14: 3 **f** against those nations, as
Zech 14:14 also will **f** at Jerusalem
John 18:36 world, My servants would **f**
Acts 5:39 be found to **f** against God
Acts 23: 9 him, let us not **f** against God
1Co 9:26 Thus I **f**: not as one who
1Ti 6:12 **F** the good **f** of faith,
2Ti 4: 7 I have fought the good **f**, I
Jas 4: 2 You **f** and war.
Rev 2:16 will **f** against them with the

FIGHTING (*see* FIGHT)
Ex 2:13 behold, two Hebrew men were **f**
Judg 11:27 wronged me by **f** against me
1Sa 17:19 Elah, **f** with the Philistines
1Sa 23: 1 are **f** against Keilah, and they
2Ch 26:11 Uzziah had an army of **f** men
Ps 56: 1 **F** all day he oppresses me
Jer 51:30 men of Babylon have ceased **f**
Acts 7:26 to two of them as they were **f**

FIGHTS (*see* FIGHT)
Ex 14:25 for the LORD **f** for them
Deut 3:22 your God Himself **f** for you
Josh 23:10 your God is He who **f** for you
1Sa 25:28 because my lord **f** the battles
Zech 14: 3 as He **f** in the day of battle
Jas 4: 1 wars and **f** come from among

FIGS (*see* FIG)
Num 13:23 some of the pomegranates and **f**
Num 20: 5 or **f** or vines or pomegranates
1Sa 25:18 and two hundred cakes of **f**
1Sa 30:12 him a piece of a cake of **f**
2Ki 20: 7 Take a lump of **f**
1Ch 12:40 of flour and cakes of **f** and
Neh 13:15 donkeys with wine, grapes, **f**
Song 2:13 tree puts forth her green **f**
Is 38:21 Let them take a lump of **f**
Jer 8:13 nor **f** on the fig tree, and the
Jer 24: 1 of **f** set before the temple of
Jer 24: 2 One basket had very good **f**
Jer 24: 2 like the **f** that are first
Jer 24: 2 **f** which could not be eaten
Jer 24: 3 **F**, the good **f**, very good
Jer 24: 5 Like these good **f**, so will I
Jer 24: 8 as the bad **f** which cannot be
Jer 29:17 rotten **f** that cannot be eaten
Nah 3:12 are fig trees with ripened **f**
Matt 7:16 or **f** from thistles?
Mark 11:13 it was not the season for **f**
Luke 6:44 do not gather **f** from thorns
Jas 3:12 olives, or a grapevine bear **f**
Rev 6:13 late **f** when it is shaken by a

FIGURATIVE (*see* FIGURATIVELY, FIGURE)
John 16:25 spoken to you in **f** language
John 16:25 speak to you in **f** language
Heb 11:19 received him in a **f** sense

FIGURATIVELY (*see* FIGURATIVE)
1Co 4: 6 I have **f** transferred to

FIGURE (*see* FIGURATIVE, FIGUREHEAD, FIGURES)
Deut 4:16 image in the form of any **f**
Is 44:13 makes it like the **f** of a man
John 16:29 and using no **f** of speech

FIGUREHEAD (*see* FIGURE)
Acts 28:11 whose **f** was the Twin Brothers

FIGURES (*see* FIGURE)
1Ki 6:29 with carved **f** of cherubim
1Ki 6:32 carved on them **f** of cherubim

FILL (*see* FILLED, FILLING, FILLS, FULL)
Gen 1:22 **f** the waters in the seas, and
Gen 1:28 **f** the earth and subdue it
Gen 9: 1 and multiply, and **f** the earth
Gen 42:25 to **f** their sacks with grain
Gen 44: 1 **F** the men's sacks with food,
Ex 10: 6 They shall **f** your houses
Ex 16:32 **F** an omer with it, to be
Lev 25:19 fruit, and you will eat your **f**
Deut 6:11 things, which you did not **f**
Deut 23:24 you may eat your **f** of grapes
1Sa 16: 1 **F** your horn with oil, and go
1Ki 18:33 **F** four waterpots with water,
Job 7: 4 For I have had my **f** of
Job 8:21 He will yet **f** your mouth with
Job 15: 2 **f** himself with the east wind
Job 20:23 he is about to **f** his stomach
Job 23: 4 **f** my mouth with arguments
Job 41: 7 Can you **f** his skin with
Ps 17:14 whose belly You **f** with Your
Ps 81:10 mouth wide, and I will **f** it
Ps 83:16 **F** their faces with shame,
Ps 110: 6 He shall **f** the places with
Ps 129: 7 reaper does not **f** his hand
Prov 1:13 we shall **f** our houses with
Prov 7:18 let us take our **f** of love
Prov 8:21 that I may **f** their treasuries
Is 8: 8 out of his wings will **f** the
Is 14:21 **f** the face of the world with
Is 27: 6 **f** the face of the world with
Is 56:12 and we will **f** ourselves with
Jer 13:13 I will **f** all the inhabitants
Jer 23:24 do I not **f** heaven and earth
Jer 33: 5 but only to **f** their places
Jer 51:14 Surely I will **f** you with men
Ezek 3: 3 and **f** your stomach with this

Ezek 7:19 nor **f** their stomachs, because
Ezek 9: 7 **f** the courts with the slain
Ezek 10: 2 **f** your hands with coals of
Ezek 24: 4 **f** it with choice cuts
Ezek 30:11 **f** the land with the slain
Ezek 32: 4 with you I will **f** the beasts
Ezek 32: 5 and **f** the valleys with your
Ezek 35: 8 I will **f** its mountains with
Zeph 1: 9 who **f** their masters' houses
Hag 2: 7 I will **f** this temple with
Matt 15:33 to **f** such a great multitude
Matt 23:32 **F** up, then, the measure of
John 2: 7 **F** the waterpots with water
Rom 15:13 of hope **f** you with all joy
Eph 4:10 that He might **f** all things
Col 1:24 and **f** up in my flesh what is
1Th 2:16 so as always to **f** up the

FILLED (*see* FILL)
Gen 6:11 the earth was **f** with violence
Gen 6:13 Me, for the earth is **f** with
Gen 21:19 **f** the skin with water, and
Gen 24:16 **f** her pitcher, and came up
Gen 26:15 they had **f** them with earth
Ex 1: 7 and the land was **f** with them
Ex 2:16 they **f** the troughs to water
Ex 16:12 you shall be **f** with bread
Ex 28: 3 whom I have **f** with the spirit
Ex 31: 3 I have **f** him with the Spirit
Ex 35:31 He has **f** him with the Spirit
Ex 35:35 He has **f** them with skill to
Ex 40:34 of the LORD **f** the tabernacle
Ex 40:35 of the LORD **f** the tabernacle
Num 14:21 all the earth shall be **f** with
Deut 11:15 that you may eat and be **f**
Deut 26:12 eat within your gates and be **f**
Deut 31:20 **f** themselves and grown fat,
Josh 9:13 wineskins which we **f** were new
1Ki 7:14 he was **f** with wisdom and
1Ki 8:10 that the cloud **f** the house of
1Ki 8:11 LORD **f** the house of the LORD
1Ki 8:20 I have **f** the position of my
1Ki 18:35 he also **f** the trench with
1Ki 20:27 the Syrians **f** the countryside
2Ki 3:17 valley shall be **f** with water
2Ki 3:20 and the land was **f** with water
2Ki 3:25 good piece of land and **f** it
2Ki 21:16 till he had **f** Jerusalem from
2Ki 23:14 **f** their places with the bones
2Ki 24: 4 for he had **f** Jerusalem with
2Ch 5:13 the LORD, was **f** with a cloud,
2Ch 5:14 the LORD **f** the house of God
2Ch 6:10 I have **f** the position of my
2Ch 7: 1 of the LORD **f** the temple
2Ch 7: 2 LORD had **f** the LORD's house
2Ch 16:14 bed which was **f** with spices
Ezra 9:11 abominations which have **f** it
Neh 9:25 So they ate and were **f** and grew
Esth 3: 5 Haman was **f** with wrath
Esth 5: 9 he was **f** with indignation
Job 3:15 gold, who **f** their houses with
Job 22:18 Yet He **f** their houses with
Job 36:17 But you are **f** with the
Ps 71: 8 Let my mouth be **f** with Your
Ps 72:19 earth be **f** with His glory
Ps 78:29 So they ate and were well **f**
Ps 80: 9 deep root, And it **f** the land
Ps 104:28 hand, they are **f** with good
Ps 123: 3 exceedingly **f** with contempt
Ps 123: 4 Our soul is exceedingly **f**
Ps 126: 2 our mouth was **f** with laughter
Prov 1:31 be **f** to the full with their
Prov 3:10 barns will be **f** with plenty
Prov 5:10 lest aliens be **f** with your
Prov 12:21 wicked shall be **f** with evil
Prov 14:14 will be **f** with his own ways
Prov 18:20 of his lips he shall be **f**
Prov 20:17 mouth will be **f** with gravel
Prov 24: 4 rooms are **f** with all precious
Prov 25:16 need, lest you be **f** with it
Prov 30:22 a fool when he is **f** with food
Eccl 1: 8 nor the ear **f** with hearing
Is 2: 6 because they are **f** with
Is 6: 1 of His robe **f** the temple
Is 6: 4 and the house was **f** with smoke
Is 21: 3 my loins are **f** with pain
Is 23: 2 who cross the sea have **f**
Is 33: 5 He has **f** Zion with justice and
Is 34: 6 of the LORD is **f** with blood
Jer 13:12 bottle shall be **f** with wine
Jer 13:12 bottle will be **f** with wine
Jer 15:17 hand, for You have **f** me with
Jer 16:18 they have **f** My inheritance
Jer 19: 4 have **f** this place with the
Jer 41: 9 Nethaniah **f** it with the slain
Jer 46:12 and your cry has **f** the land
Jer 51: 5 though their land was **f** with
Jer 51:34 he has **f** his stomach with my
Lam 3:15 He has **f** me with bitterness,
Ezek 7:23 for the land is **f** with crimes
Ezek 8:17 For they have **f** the land with
Ezek 10: 3 the cloud **f** the inner court
Ezek 10: 4 and the house was **f** with the
Ezek 11: 6 you have **f** its streets with
Ezek 23:33 You will be **f** with
Ezek 26: 2 I shall be **f**
Ezek 27:25 You were **f** and very glorious
Ezek 28:16 became **f** with violence within
Ezek 32:15 of all that once **f** it, when I
Ezek 36:38 be **f** with flocks of men
Ezek 39:20 You shall be **f** at My table
Ezek 43: 5 of the LORD **f** the temple
Ezek 44: 4 LORD **f** the house of the LORD
Dan 2:35 mountain and **f** the whole earth
Hos 13: 6 they had pasture, they were **f**
Nah 2:12 **f** his caves with prey, and his
Hab 2:14 For the earth will be **f** with
Hab 2:16 You are **f** with shame instead
Hag 1: 6 but you are not **f** with drink
Zech 9:15 they shall be **f** with blood
Matt 5: 6 for they shall be **f**
Matt 14:20 So they all ate and were **f**
Matt 15:37 So they all ate and were **f**
Matt 22:10 hall was **f** with guests
Matt 27:48 **f** it with sour wine and put it
Mark 6:42 So they all ate and were **f**
Mark 7:27 Let the children be **f** first
Mark 8: 8 So they ate and were **f**, and
Mark 15:36 **f** a sponge full of sour wine,
Luke 1:15 He will also be **f** with the
Luke 1:41 Elizabeth was **f** with the Holy
Luke 1:53 He has **f** the hungry with good
Luke 1:67 was **f** with the Holy Spirit
Luke 2:40 in spirit, **f** with wisdom
Luke 3: 5 Every valley shall be **f** and
Luke 4: 1 being **f** with the Holy Spirit,
Luke 4:28 things, were **f** with wrath,
Luke 5: 7 **f** both the boats, so that
Luke 5:26 were **f** with fear, saying,
Luke 6:11 But they were **f** with rage
Luke 6:21 now, for you shall be **f**
Luke 9:17 So they all ate and were **f**
Luke 14:23 in, that my house may be **f**
Luke 15:16 he would gladly have **f** his
John 2: 7 they **f** them up to the brim
John 6:12 So when they were **f**, He said
John 6:13 **f** twelve baskets with the
John 6:26 ate of the loaves and were **f**
John 12: 3 And the house was **f** with the
John 16: 6 you, sorrow has **f** your heart
John 19:29 they **f** a sponge with sour
Acts 2: 2 it **f** the whole house where
Acts 2: 4 they were all **f** with the Holy
Acts 3:10 they were **f** with wonder and
Acts 4: 8 **f** with the Holy Spirit, said
Acts 4:31 they were all **f** with the Holy
Acts 5: 3 why has Satan **f** your heart to
Acts 5:17 they were **f** with indignation,
Acts 5:28 you have **f** Jerusalem with
Acts 9:17 be **f** with the Holy Spirit
Acts 13: 9 Paul, **f** with the Holy Spirit,
Acts 13:45 they were **f** with envy
Acts 13:52 the disciples were **f** with joy
Acts 19:29 city was **f** with confusion
Rom 1:29 being **f** with all
Rom 15:14 **f** with all knowledge, able
2Co 7: 4 I am **f** with comfort
Eph 3:19 that you may be **f** with all
Eph 5:18 but be **f** with the Spirit,
Phil 1:11 being **f** with the fruits of
Col 1: 9 to ask that you may be **f** with
2Ti 1: 4 that I may be **f** with joy
Jas 2:16 in peace, be warmed and **f**,"
Rev 8: 5 **f** it with fire from the altar
Rev 15: 8 The temple was **f** with smoke
Rev 19:21 birds were **f** with their flesh
Rev 21: 9 who had the seven bowls **f**

FILLING (*see* FILL)
Mark 4:37 so that it was already **f**
Luke 8:23 they were **f** with water, and
Acts 14:17 **f** our hearts with food and

FILLS (*see* FILL)
Job 9:18 but **f** me with bitterness
Ps 107: 9 And **f** the hungry soul with
Ps 147:14 **f** you with the finest wheat
Eph 1:23 of Him who **f** all in all

FILLY
Song 1: 9 love, to my **f** among Pharaoh's

FILTH (*see* FILTHY)
Ezra 6:21 themselves from the **f** of the
Is 4: 4 **f** of the daughters of Zion
Nah 3: 6 cast abominable **f** upon you
1Co 4:13 made as the **f** of the world
1Pe 3:21 removal of the **f** of the flesh

FILTHINESS (*see* FILTHY)
Prov 30:12 yet is not washed from its **f**
Is 28: 8 tables are full of vomit and **f**
Ezek 16:36 Because your **f** was poured out
Ezek 22:15 remove your **f** completely from
Ezek 24:11 that its **f** may be melted in
Ezek 24:13 In your **f** is lewdness
Ezek 24:13 be purged of your **f** anymore
Ezek 36:25 cleanse you from all your **f**
2Co 7: 1 from all **f** of the flesh and
Eph 5: 4 neither **f**, nor foolish
Jas 1:21 Therefore lay aside all **f**
Rev 17: 4 and the **f** of her fornication

FILTHY (*see* FILTH, FILTHINESS)
Job 15:16 man, who is abominable and **f**
Is 64: 6 are like **f** rags
Zech 3: 3 was clothed with **f** garments
Zech 3: 4 Take away the **f** garments from
Col 3: 8 **f** language out of your mouth
Jas 2: 2 in a poor man in **f** clothes
2Pe 2: 7 the **f** conduct of the wicked
Rev 22:11 he who is **f**, let him be **f**

FINAL (*see* FINALLY)
Jer 12: 4 He will not see our **f** end

FINALLY (*see* FINAL)
Deut 2:16 had **f** perished from among the
2Ki 24:20 that He **f** cast them out from
Jer 52: 3 till He **f** cast them out from
Acts 27:20 would be saved was **f** given up
2Co 13:11 **F**, brethren, farewell
Eph 6:10 **F**, my brethren, be strong in
Phil 3: 1 **F**, my brethren, rejoice in
Phil 4: 8 **F**, brethren, whatever things
1Th 4: 1 **F** then, brethren, we urge and
2Th 3: 1 **F**, brethren, pray for us,
2Ti 4: 8 **F**, there is laid up for me
1Pe 3: 8 **F**, all of you be of one mind,

FIND (*see* FINDING, FINDS, FOUND)
Gen 18:26 said, "If I **f** in Sodom fifty
Gen 18:28 If I **f** there forty-five, I
Gen 18:30 not do it if I **f** thirty there
Gen 19:11 weary trying to **f** the door
Gen 31:32 With whomever you **f** your gods
Gen 31:33 tents, but he did not **f** them
Gen 31:34 the tent but did not **f** them
Gen 31:35 did not **f** the household idols
Gen 32: 5 that I may **f** favor in your
Gen 32:19 speak to Esau when you **f** him
Gen 33: 8 These are to **f** favor in the
Gen 33:15 Let me **f** favor in the sight
Gen 34:11 Let me **f** favor in your eyes,
Gen 38:20 hand, but he did not **f** her
Gen 38:22 I cannot **f** her
Gen 41:38 Can we **f** such a one as this,
Gen 47:25 let us **f** favor in the sight
Ex 5:11 straw where you can **f** it
Ex 16:25 will not **f** it in the field
Ex 33:13 that I may **f** grace in Your
Num 32:23 sure your sin will **f** you out
Deut 4:29 you will **f** Him if you seek
Deut 28:65 nations you shall **f** no rest
Josh 2:22 the way, but did not **f** them
Judg 9:33 to them as you **f** opportunity
Judg 16: 5 him, and **f** out where his great
Judg 17: 8 wherever he could **f** a place
Judg 17: 9 I am on my way to **f** a place
Ruth 1: 9 grant that you may **f** rest
Ruth 2: 2 in whose sight I may **f** favor
Ruth 2:13 Let me **f** favor in your sight,
1Sa 1:18 **f** favor in your sight
1Sa 9: 4 but they did not **f** them
1Sa 9: 4 but they did not **f** them
1Sa 9:13 you will surely **f** him before
1Sa 9:13 this time you will **f** him

1Sa 10: 2 today, you will f two men by
1Sa 20:21 saying, "Go, f the arrows
1Sa 20:36 f the arrows which I shoot
1Sa 23:17 my father shall not f you
1Sa 23:22 f out for sure, and see the
1Sa 25: 8 men f favor in your eyes, for
1Sa 28: 7 F me a woman who is a medium,
2Sa 15:25 If I f favor in the eyes of
2Sa 16: 4 that I may f favor in your
2Sa 17:20 searched and could not f them
2Sa 20: 6 him, lest he f for himself
1Ki 18: 5 perhaps we may f grass to
1Ki 18:10 that they could not f you
1Ki 18:12 tell Ahab, and he cannot f you
2Ki 2:17 three days but did not f him
2Ki 6:27 where can I f help for you
2Ch 20:16 you will f them at the end of
2Ch 32: 4 Assyria come and f much water
Ezra 4:15 you will f in the book of the
Ezra 7:16 gold that you may f in all
Job 3:22 when they can f the grave
Job 5:24 habitation and f nothing amiss
Job 11: 7 Can you f out the limits of
Job 17:10 for I shall not f one wise
Job 23: 3 I knew where I might f Him
Job 32:20 speak, that I may f relief
Job 34:11 and makes man to f a reward
Job 37:23 the Almighty, we cannot f Him
Ps 10:15 wickedness until You f none
Ps 21: 8 Your hand will f all Your
Ps 21: 8 will f those who hate You
Ps 132: 5 Until I f a place for the
Prov 1:13 we shall f all kinds of
Prov 1:28 but they will not f me
Prov 2: 5 and f the knowledge of God
Prov 3: 4 so f favor and high esteem in
Prov 4:22 are life to those who f them
Prov 8: 9 to those who f knowledge
Prov 8:12 f out knowledge and discretion
Prov 8:17 seek me diligently will f me
Prov 14: 6 seeks wisdom and does not f it
Prov 16:20 the word wisely will f good
Prov 19: 8 understanding will f good
Prov 20: 6 but who can f a faithful man
Prov 28:23 f more favor afterward than
Prov 31:10 Who can f a virtuous wife
Eccl 3:11 except that no one can f out
Eccl 7:14 so that man can f nothing
Eccl 7:24 deep, who can f it out
Eccl 7:26 I f more bitter than death
Eccl 7:27 the other to f out the reason
Eccl 7:28 still seeks but I cannot f
Eccl 8:17 that a man cannot f out the
Eccl 8:17 it, yet he will not f it
Eccl 8:17 he will not be able to f it
Eccl 11: 1 for you will f it after many
Eccl 12:10 sought to f acceptable words
Song 3: 1 him, but I did not f him
Song 3: 2 him, but I did not f him
Song 5: 6 him, but I could not f him
Song 5: 8 if you f my beloved, that you
Song 8: 1 If I should f you outside
Is 34:14 f for herself a place of rest
Is 41:12 shall seek them and not f them
Is 58: 3 of your fast you f pleasure
Jer 2:24 in her month they will f her
Jer 5: 1 places if you can f a man
Jer 6:16 then you will f rest for your
Jer 10:18 them, that they may f it so
Jer 29:13 f Me, when you search for Me
Jer 45: 3 in my sighing, and I f no rest
Lam 1: 6 like deer that f no pasture
Lam 2: 9 her prophets f no vision from
Ezek 3: 1 Son of man, eat what you f
Dan 6: 4 and satraps sought to f some
Dan 6: 4 but they could f no charge or
Dan 6: 5 We shall not f any charge
Dan 6: 5 this Daniel unless we f it
Hos 2: 6 that she cannot f her paths
Hos 2: 7 seek them, but not f them
Hos 5: 6 LORD, but they will not f Him
Hos 12: 8 f in me no iniquity that is
Amos 8:12 the LORD, but shall not f it
Matt 7: 7 seek, and you will f
Matt 7:14 and there are few who f it
Matt 10:39 life for My sake will f it
Matt 11:29 and you will f rest for your
Matt 16:25 life for My sake will f it
Matt 17:27 you will f a piece of money
Matt 18:13 And if he should f it,
Matt 21: 2 you will f a donkey tied, and
Matt 22: 9 highways, and as many as you f
Matt 24:46 he comes, will f so doing
Mark 11: 2 it you will f a colt tied
Mark 11:13 He would f something on it
Mark 13:36 suddenly, he f you sleeping
Luke 2:12 You will f a Babe wrapped in
Luke 2:45 So when they did not f Him
Luke 5:19 when they could not f how
Luke 6: 7 Sabbath, that they might f an
Luke 11: 9 seek, and you will f
Luke 12:37 he comes, will f watching
Luke 12:38 f them so, blessed are those
Luke 12:43 whom his master will f so
Luke 13: 7 on this fig tree and f none
Luke 18: 8 will He really f faith on the
Luke 19:30 enter you will f a colt tied
Luke 23: 4 I f no fault in this Man
Luke 24: 3 did not f the body of the
Luke 24:23 When they did not f His body
John 7:34 You will seek Me and not f Me
John 7:35 to go that we shall not f Him
John 7:36 You will seek Me and not f Me
John 10: 9 go in and out and f pasture
John 18:38 I f no fault in Him at all
John 19: 4 know that I f no fault in Him
John 19: 6 Him, for I f no fault in Him
John 21: 6 the boat, and you will f some
Acts 5:22 did not f them in the prison,
Acts 7:46 asked to f a dwelling for the
Acts 17: 6 But when they did not f them
Acts 17:11 the Scriptures daily to f out
Acts 17:27 f Him, though He is not far
Acts 23: 9 We f no evil in this man
Rom 1:10 now at last I may f a way in
Rom 7:18 what is good I do not f
Rom 7:21 I f then a law, that evil is
Rom 9:19 Why does He still f fault
2Co 2:13 I did not f Titus my brother
2Co 9: 4 f you unprepared, we (not to
2Co 12:20 I shall not f you such as I
2Ti 1:18 grant to him that he may f
Heb 4:16 f grace to help in time of
Rev 9: 6 seek death and will not f it
Rev 18:14 you shall f them no more at

FINDING (*see* FIND)
Gen 4:15 lest anyone f him should kill
Judg 5:30 Are they not f and dividing
Job 9:10 does great things past f out
Is 58:13 nor f your own pleasure, nor
Luke 11:24 and f none, he says, 'I will
Acts 4:21 f no way of punishing them,
Acts 19: 1 And f some disciples
Acts 21: 2 And f a ship sailing over to
Acts 21: 4 f disciples, we stayed there
Rom 11:33 and His ways past f out
Heb 8: 8 Because f fault with them, He

FINDS (*see* FIND)
Gen 4:14 anyone who f me will kill me
Num 35:27 the avenger of blood f him
Deut 22:23 a man f her in the city and
Deut 22:25 But if a man f a betrothed
Deut 22:28 If a man f a young woman who
Deut 24: 1 and it happens that she f no
1Sa 24:19 For if a man f his enemy,
Job 33:10 Yet He f occasions against me
Ps 36: 2 When he f out his iniquity and
Ps 119:162 As one who f great treasure
Prov 3:13 Happy is the man who f wisdom
Prov 8:35 For whoever f me f life
Prov 11:27 diligently seeks good f favor
Prov 17:20 a deceitful heart f no good
Prov 18:22 He who f a wife f a good
Prov 18:22 f a wife f a good thing
Prov 21:10 his neighbor f no favor in
Prov 21:21 righteousness and mercy f life
Eccl 9:10 Whatever your hand f to do
Lam 1: 3 the nations, she f no rest
Hos 14: 3 in You the fatherless f mercy
Matt 7: 8 receives, and he who seeks f
Matt 10:39 He who f his life will lose
Matt 12:43 seeking rest, and f none
Matt 12:44 he f it empty, swept, and put
Luke 11:10 receives, and he who seeks f
Luke 11:25 he f it swept and put in order
Luke 15: 4 which is lost until he f it
Luke 15: 8 diligently until she f it

FINE (*see* FINELY, FINERY, FINEST)
Gen 18: 6 three measures of f meal
Gen 41: 2 seven cows, f looking and fat
Gen 41: 4 ate up the seven f looking
Gen 41:18 the river, f looking and fat
Gen 41:42 him in garments of f linen
Ex 9: 9 it will become f dust in all
Ex 16:14 as f as frost on the ground
Ex 25: 4 f linen thread, and goats'
Ex 26: 1 woven of f linen thread, and
Ex 26:31 yarn, and f linen thread
Ex 26:36 f linen thread, made by a
Ex 27: 9 court woven of f linen thread
Ex 27:16 f linen thread, made by a
Ex 27:18 woven of f linen thread, and
Ex 28: 5 scarlet thread, and f linen,
Ex 28: 6 f linen thread, artistically
Ex 28: 8 thread, and f linen thread
Ex 28:15 of f linen thread, you shall
Ex 28:39 the tunic of f linen thread
Ex 28:39 make the turban of f linen
Ex 30:36 shall beat some of it very f
Ex 35: 6 f linen thread, and goats'
Ex 35:23 f linen, goats' hair, red
Ex 35:25 purple and scarlet, and f linen
Ex 35:35 f linen, and of the weaver
Ex 36: 8 woven of f linen thread, and
Ex 36:35 yarn, and f linen thread
Ex 36:37 f linen thread, made by a
Ex 38: 9 court were woven of f linen
Ex 38:16 around were woven of f linen
Ex 38:18 yarn, and f linen thread
Ex 38:23 yarn, and f linen thread
Ex 39: 2 thread, and of f linen thread
Ex 39: 3 f linen thread, into artistic
Ex 39: 5 f linen thread, as the LORD
Ex 39: 8 thread, and f linen thread
Ex 39:24 and scarlet and f linen thread
Ex 39:27 artistically woven of f linen
Ex 39:28 a turban of f linen,
Ex 39:28 exquisite hats of f linen
Ex 39:28 short trousers of f linen
Ex 39:29 and a sash of f linen and blue
Lev 2: 1 offering shall be of f flour
Lev 2: 2 it his handful of f flour
Lev 2: 4 of f flour mixed with oil
Lev 2: 5 a pan, it shall be of f flour
Lev 2: 7 be made of f flour with oil
Lev 5:11 of f flour as a sin offering
Lev 6:15 from it his handful of the f
Lev 6:20 of f flour as a daily grain
Lev 14:10 f flour mixed with oil as a
Lev 14:21 one-tenth of an ephah of f
Lev 16:12 of sweet incense beaten f
Lev 23:13 of f flour mixed with oil
Lev 23:17 They shall be of f flour
Lev 24: 5 And you shall take f flour
Num 6:15 cakes of f flour mixed with
Num 7:13 both of them full of f flour
Num 7:19 both of them full of f flour
Num 7:25 both of them full of f flour
Num 7:31 both of them full of f flour
Num 7:37 both of them full of f flour
Num 7:43 both of them full of f flour
Num 7:49 both of them full of f flour
Num 7:55 both of them full of f flour
Num 7:61 both of them full of f flour
Num 7:67 both of them full of f flour
Num 7:73 both of them full of f flour
Num 7:79 both of them full of f flour
Num 8: 8 of f flour mixed with oil
Num 15: 4 f flour mixed with one-fourth
Num 15: 6 two-tenths of an ephah of f
Num 15: 9 f flour mixed with half a hin
Num 28: 5 one-tenth of an ephah of f
Num 28: 9 f flour as a grain offering
Num 28:12 f flour as a grain offering
Num 28:12 f flour as a grain offering
Num 28:13 of an ephah of f flour, mixed
Num 28:20 be of f flour mixed with oil
Num 28:28 of f flour mixed with oil
Num 29: 3 be f flour mixed with oil
Num 29: 9 be of f flour mixed with oil
Num 29:14 be of f flour mixed with oil
Deut 9:21 until it was as f as dust
Deut 22:19 they shall f him one hundred
2Sa 22:43 Then I beat them as f as the
1Ki 4:22 was thirty kors of f flour
2Ki 7: 1 f flour shall be sold for a
2Ki 7:16 So a seah of f flour was sold

2Ki 7:18 and a seah of **f** flour for a
1Ch 9:29 and over the **f** flour and the
1Ch 15:27 with a robe of **f** linen, as
1Ch 23:29 the **f** flour for the grain
2Ch 2:14 **f** linen and crimson, and to
2Ch 3: 5 which he overlaid with **f** gold
2Ch 3: 8 six hundred talents of **f** gold
2Ch 3:14 **f** linen, and wove cherubim
Ezra 8:27 two vessels of **f** polished
Esth 1: 6 with cords of **f** linen and
Esth 8:15 gold and a garment of **f** linen
Job 28:17 for jewelry of **f** gold
Job 31:24 my hope, or said to **f** gold
Ps 18:42 Then I beat them as **f** as the
Ps 19:10 gold, Yea, than much **f** gold
Ps 119:127 than gold, yes, than **f** gold
Prov 3:14 and her gain than **f** gold
Prov 8:19 than gold, yes, than **f** gold
Prov 25:12 an ornament of **f** gold is a
Prov 31:22 her clothing is **f** linen and
Song 5:15 marble set on bases of **f** gold
Is 3:23 the **f** linen, the turbans, and
Is 13:12 mortal more rare than **f** gold
Is 19: 9 those who work in **f** flax and
Is 19: 9 those who weave **f** fabric will
Is 23:18 and for **f** clothing
Is 29: 5 foes shall be like **f** dust
Lam 4: 1 How changed the **f** gold
Lam 4: 2 of Zion, valuable as **f** gold
Ezek 16:10 I clothed you with **f** linen
Ezek 16:13 your clothing was of **f** linen
Ezek 16:13 You ate pastry of **f** flour
Ezek 16:19 the pastry of **f** flour, oil,
Ezek 27: 7 **F** embroidered linen from
Ezek 27:16 **f** linen, corals, and rubies
Ezek 31: 3 with **f** branches that shaded
Ezek 46:14 of oil to moisten the **f** flour
Dan 2:32 image's head was of **f** gold
Mark 15:46 Then he bought **f** linen, took
Luke 16:19 **f** linen and fared sumptuously
Jas 2: 2 in **f** apparel, and there should
Jas 2: 3 the one wearing the **f** clothes
1Pe 3: 3 or of putting on **f** apparel
Rev 1:15 His feet were like **f** brass
Rev 2:18 and His feet like **f** brass
Rev 18:12 **f** linen and purple, silk and
Rev 18:13 **f** flour and wheat, cattle and
Rev 18:16 that was clothed in **f** linen
Rev 19: 8 to be arrayed in **f** linen,
Rev 19: 8 for the **f** linen is the
Rev 19:14 in heaven, clothed in **f** linen

FINELY (*see* FINE)
Lev 7:12 or cakes of **f** blended flour

FINERY (*see* FINE)
Is 3:18 the Lord will take away the **f**

FINEST (*see* FINE)
1Sa 8:16 and your **f** young men and your
Ps 81:16 them also with the **f** of wheat
Ps 147:14 And fills you with the **f** wheat
Song 5:11 His head is like the **f** gold

FINGER (*see* FINGERS)
Ex 8:19 This is the **f** of God
Ex 29:12 of the altar with your **f**, and
Ex 31:18 written with the **f** of God
Lev 4: 6 shall dip his **f** in the blood
Lev 4:17 shall dip his **f** in the blood
Lev 4:25 the sin offering with his **f**
Lev 4:30 some of its blood with his **f**
Lev 4:34 the sin offering with his **f**
Lev 8:15 altar all around with his **f**
Lev 9: 9 he dipped his **f** in the blood
Lev 14:16 **f** in the oil that is in his
Lev 14:16 some of the oil with his **f**
Lev 14:27 sprinkle with his right **f**
Lev 16:14 sprinkle it with his **f** on the
Lev 16:14 blood with his **f** seven times
Lev 16:19 on it with his **f** seven times
Num 19: 4 some of its blood with his **f**
Deut 9:10 written with the **f** of God
1Ki 12:10 My little **f** shall be thicker
2Ch 10:10 My little **f** shall be thicker
Is 58: 9 midst, the pointing of the **f**
Luke 11:20 out demons with the **f** of God
Luke 16:24 dip the tip of his **f** in water
John 8: 6 on the ground with His **f**, as
John 20:25 put my **f** into the print of
John 20:27 Reach your **f** here, and look at

FINGERS (*see* FINGER)
2Sa 21:20 who had six **f** on each hand and
1Ch 20: 6 stature, with twenty-four **f**
Ps 8: 3 heavens, the work of Your **f**
Ps 144: 1 for war, And my **f** for battle
Prov 6:13 feet, he points with his **f**
Prov 7: 3 Bind them on your **f**
Song 5: 5 My **f** with liquid myrrh, on
Is 2: 8 which their own **f** have made
Is 17: 8 respect what his **f** have made
Is 59: 3 and your **f** with iniquity
Jer 52:21 and its thickness was four **f**
Dan 5: 5 In the same hour the **f** of a
Dan 5:24 Then the **f** of the hand were
Matt 23: 4 move them with one of their **f**
Mark 7:33 put His **f** in his ears, and He
Luke 11:46 burdens with one of your **f**

FINISH (*see* FINISHED, FINISHER, FINISHES, FINISHING)
Gen 6:16 you shall **f** it to a cubit
1Ch 27:24 a census, but he did not **f**
Ezra 5: 3 this temple and **f** this wall
Ezra 5: 9 temple and to **f** these walls
Ps 90: 9 We **f** our years like a sigh
Dan 9:24 to **f** the transgression, to
Zech 4: 9 his hands shall also **f** it
Luke 14:28 whether he has enough to **f** it
Luke 14:29 and is not able to **f** it, all
Luke 14:30 to build and was not able to **f**
John 4:34 who sent Me, and to **f** His work
John 5:36 the Father has given Me to **f**
Acts 20:24 so that I may **f** my race with
Rom 9:28 For He will **f** the work and cut
Rev 11: 7 Now when they **f** their

FINISHED (*see* FINISH)
Gen 2: 1 all the host of them, were **f**
Gen 17:22 Then He **f** talking with him,
Gen 18:33 had **f** speaking with Abraham
Gen 24:15 before he had **f** speaking
Gen 24:19 when she had **f** giving him a
Gen 24:19 until they have **f** drinking
Gen 24:22 the camels had **f** drinking
Gen 24:45 But before I had **f** speaking
Gen 27:30 as Isaac had **f** blessing Jacob
Gen 49:33 when Jacob had **f** commanding
Ex 34:33 when Moses had **f** speaking
Ex 39:32 of the tent of meeting was **f**
Ex 40:33 So Moses **f** the work
Num 4:15 his sons have **f** covering the
Num 7: 1 when Moses had **f** setting up
Num 16:31 as he **f** speaking all these
Deut 20: 9 have **f** speaking to the people
Deut 26:12 When you have **f** laying aside
Deut 31:24 in a book, when they were **f**
Deut 32:45 Moses **f** speaking all these
Josh 4:10 **f** that the LORD had commanded
Josh 5: 8 when they had **f** circumcising
Josh 10:20 slaughter, till they had **f**
Judg 3:18 when he had **f** presenting the
Judg 15:17 was, when he had **f** speaking
Ruth 2:21 they have **f** all my harvest
Ruth 3: 3 the man until he has **f** eating
1Sa 1: 9 arose after they had **f** eating
1Sa 10:13 And when he had **f** prophesying
1Sa 13:10 as soon as he had **f** offering
1Sa 18: 1 when he had **f** speaking to
1Sa 24:16 when David had **f** speaking
2Sa 6:18 when David had **f** offering
2Sa 11:19 When you have **f** telling the
2Sa 13:36 as soon as he had **f** speaking
2Sa 15:24 **f** crossing over from the city
1Ki 1:41 him heard it as they **f** eating
1Ki 3: 1 had **f** building his own house
1Ki 6: 7 with stone **f** at the quarry
1Ki 6: 9 and **f** it, and he paneled the
1Ki 6:14 built the temple and **f** it
1Ki 6:22 until he had **f** all the temple
1Ki 6:38 the house was **f** in all its
1Ki 7: 1 so he **f** all his house
1Ki 7:22 the work of the pillars was **f**
1Ki 7:40 So Hiram **f** doing all the work
1Ki 7:51 the house of the LORD was **f**
1Ki 8:54 when Solomon had **f** praying
1Ki 9: 1 when Solomon had **f** building
1Ki 9:25 So he **f** the temple
1Ch 16: 2 when David had **f** offering the
1Ch 28:20 until you have **f** all the work
2Ch 4:11 So Huram **f** doing the work
2Ch 5: 1 the house of the LORD was **f**
2Ch 7: 1 when Solomon had **f** praying
2Ch 7:11 Thus Solomon **f** the house of
2Ch 8:16 of the LORD until it was **f**
2Ch 24:14 When they had **f**, they brought
2Ch 29:17 day of the first month they **f**
2Ch 29:28 the burnt offering was **f**
2Ch 29:29 And when they had **f** offering
2Ch 31: 1 Now when all this was **f**, all
2Ch 31: 7 they **f** in the seventh month
Ezra 5:16 and it is not yet **f**
Ezra 6:14 and **f** it, according to the
Ezra 6:15 Now the temple was **f** on the
Ezra 10:17 **f** questioning all the men who
Neh 6:15 So the wall was **f** on the
Job 16:22 For when a few years are **f**
Ps 9: 6 destructions are **f** forever
Jer 51:63 when you have **f** reading this
Ezek 5: 2 the days of the siege are **f**
Ezek 42:15 Now when he had **f** measuring
Ezek 43:23 When you have **f** cleansing it
Dan 5:26 your kingdom, and **f** it
Dan 12: 7 all these things shall be **f**
Amos 7: 2 when they had **f** eating the
Matt 11: 1 when Jesus **f** commanding His
Matt 13:53 Jesus had **f** these parables
Matt 19: 1 Jesus had **f** these sayings
Matt 26: 1 when Jesus had **f** all these
Luke 2:43 When they had **f** the days, as
John 17: 4 I have **f** the work which You
John 19:30 It is **f**
Acts 21: 7 when we had **f** our voyage from
2Ti 4: 7 I have **f** the race, I have
Heb 4: 3 although the works were **f**
Rev 10: 7 the mystery of God would be **f**
Rev 20: 3 the thousand years were **f**
Rev 20: 5 the thousand years were **f**

FINISHER (*see* FINISH)
Heb 12: 2 **f** of our faith, who for the

FINISHES (*see* FINISH)
Job 14: 6 like a hired man he **f** his day

FINISHING (*see* FINISH)
Ezra 4:12 are **f** its walls and repairing
Acts 13:25 And as John was **f** his course

FINS
Lev 11: 9 whatever in the water has **f**
Lev 11:10 the rivers that do not have **f**
Lev 11:12 does not have **f** or scales
Deut 14: 9 you may eat all that have **f**
Deut 14:10 And whatever does not have **f**

FIR
2Sa 6: 5 of instruments made of **f** wood
Ps 104:17 has her home in the **f** trees
Song 1:17 cedar, and our rafters of **f**
Ezek 27: 5 planks of **f** trees from Senir
Ezek 31: 8 the **f** trees were not like its

FIRE (*see* FIERY, FIREBRAND, FIREPAN, FIRES)
Gen 19:24 **f** on Sodom and Gomorrah,
Gen 22: 6 and he took the **f** in his hand
Gen 22: 7 Look, the **f** and the wood, but
Ex 3: 2 to him in a flame of **f** from
Ex 3: 2 the bush burned with **f**, but
Ex 9:23 and **f** darted to the ground
Ex 9:24 **f** mingled with the hail, so
Ex 12: 8 roasted in **f**, with unleavened
Ex 12: 9 with water, but roasted in **f**
Ex 12:10 morning you shall burn with **f**
Ex 13:21 of **f** to give them light, so
Ex 13:22 by day or the pillar of **f** by
Ex 14:24 through the pillar of **f** and
Ex 19:18 LORD descended upon it in **f**
Ex 22: 6 If **f** breaks out and catches in
Ex 22: 6 the **f** shall surely make
Ex 24:17 LORD was like a consuming **f**
Ex 29:14 burn with **f** outside the camp
Ex 29:18 made by **f** to the LORD
Ex 29:25 made by **f** to the LORD
Ex 29:34 burn the remainder with **f**
Ex 29:41 made by **f** to the LORD
Ex 30:20 made by **f** to the LORD, they
Ex 32:20 had made, burned it in the **f**
Ex 32:24 me, and I cast it into the **f**
Ex 35: 3 You shall kindle no **f**
Ex 40:38 **f** was over it by night, in
Lev 1: 7 shall put **f** on the altar, and
Lev 1: 7 the wood in order on the **f**
Lev 1: 8 is on the **f** upon the altar
Lev 1: 9 an offering made by **f**, a

Lev 1:12 is on the **f** upon the altar
Lev 1:13 an offering made by **f**, a
Lev 1:17 on the wood that is on the **f**
Lev 1:17 an offering made by **f**, a
Lev 2: 2 altar, an offering made by **f**
Lev 2: 3 to the LORD made by **f**
Lev 2: 9 It is an offering made by **f**
Lev 2:10 to the LORD made by **f**
Lev 2:11 to the LORD made by **f**
Lev 2:14 of grain roasted on the **f**
Lev 2:16 made by **f** to the LORD
Lev 3: 3 made by **f** to the LORD
Lev 3: 5 on the wood that is on the **f**
Lev 3: 5 as an offering made by **f**
Lev 3: 9 made by **f** to the LORD, its
Lev 3:11 made by **f** to the LORD
Lev 3:14 made by **f** to the LORD
Lev 3:16 made by **f** for a sweet aroma
Lev 4:12 and burn it on wood with **f**
Lev 4:35 made by **f** to the LORD
Lev 5:12 made by **f** to the LORD
Lev 6: 9 the **f** of the altar shall be
Lev 6:10 burnt offering which the **f**
Lev 6:12 the **f** on the altar shall be
Lev 6:13 A perpetual **f** shall burn on
Lev 6:17 of My offerings made by **f**
Lev 6:18 made by **f** to the LORD
Lev 6:30 It shall be burned in the **f**
Lev 7: 5 made by **f** to the LORD
Lev 7:17 day must be burned with **f**
Lev 7:19 It shall be burned with **f**
Lev 7:25 made by **f** to the LORD, the
Lev 7:30 made by **f** to the LORD
Lev 7:35 made by **f** to the LORD, on the
Lev 8:17 he burned with **f** outside the
Lev 8:21 made by **f** to the LORD, as the
Lev 8:28 made by **f** to the LORD
Lev 8:32 bread you shall burn with **f**
Lev 9:11 with **f** outside the camp
Lev 9:24 **f** came out from before the
Lev 10: 1 put **f** in it, put incense on
Lev 10: 1 profane **f** before the LORD
Lev 10: 2 So **f** went out from the LORD
Lev 10:12 made by **f** to the LORD, and eat
Lev 10:13 made by **f** to the LORD
Lev 10:15 offerings of fat made by **f**
Lev 13:24 a burn on its skin by **f**, and
Lev 13:52 it shall be burned in the **f**
Lev 13:55 and you shall burn it in the **f**
Lev 13:57 you shall burn with **f** that in
Lev 16: 1 profane **f** before the LORD
Lev 16:12 full of burning coals of **f**
Lev 16:13 on the **f** before the LORD,
Lev 16:27 burn in the **f** their skins
Lev 18:21 pass through the **f** to Molech
Lev 19: 6 it shall be burned in the **f**
Lev 20:14 They shall be burned with **f**
Lev 21: 6 of the LORD made by **f**, and the
Lev 21: 9 She shall be burned with **f**
Lev 21:21 made by **f** to the LORD
Lev 22:22 nor make an offering by **f** of
Lev 22:27 made by **f** to the LORD
Lev 23: 8 offer an offering made by **f**
Lev 23:13 made by **f** to the LORD, for a
Lev 23:18 an offering made by **f** for a
Lev 23:25 made by **f** to the LORD
Lev 23:27 made by **f** to the LORD
Lev 23:36 made by **f** to the LORD
Lev 23:36 made by **f** to the LORD
Lev 23:37 made by **f** to the LORD, a
Lev 24: 7 made by **f** to the LORD
Lev 24: 9 of the LORD made by **f**, by a
Num 3: 4 **f** before the LORD in the
Num 6:18 and put it on the **f** which is
Num 9:15 like the appearance of **f**
Num 9:16 the appearance of **f** by night
Num 11: 1 So the **f** of the LORD burned
Num 11: 2 the LORD, the **f** was quenched
Num 11: 3 because the **f** of the LORD had
Num 14:14 and in a pillar of **f** by night
Num 15: 3 an offering by **f** to the LORD
Num 15:10 wine as an offering made by **f**
Num 15:13 an offering made by **f**, a
Num 15:14 present an offering made by **f**
Num 15:25 made by **f** to the LORD, and
Num 16: 7 put **f** in them and put incense
Num 16:18 put **f** in it, laid incense on
Num 16:35 a **f** came out from the LORD and
Num 16:37 scatter the **f** some distance
Num 16:46 put **f** in it from the altar,
Num 18: 9 things reserved from the **f**
Num 18:17 by **f** for a sweet aroma to the
Num 19: 6 of the **f** burning the heifer
Num 21:28 For **f** went out from Heshbon,
Num 26:10 died, when the **f** devoured two
Num 26:61 profane **f** before the LORD
Num 28: 2 by **f** as a sweet aroma to Me
Num 28: 3 is the offering made by **f**
Num 28: 6 made by **f** to the LORD
Num 28: 8 it as an offering made by **f**
Num 28:13 made by **f** to the LORD
Num 28:19 **f** as a burnt offering to the
Num 28:24 by **f** daily for seven days
Num 29: 6 made by **f** to the LORD
Num 29:13 an offering made by **f** as a
Num 29:36 an offering made by **f** as a
Num 31:10 They also burned with **f** all
Num 31:23 everything that can endure **f**
Num 31:23 you shall put through the **f**
Num 31:23 But all that cannot endure **f**
Deut 1:33 in the **f** by night and in the
Deut 4:11 with **f** to the midst of heaven
Deut 4:12 you out of the midst of the **f**
Deut 4:15 out of the midst of the **f**
Deut 4:24 your God is a consuming **f**
Deut 4:33 out of the midst of the **f**
Deut 4:36 He showed you His great **f**
Deut 4:36 out of the midst of the **f**
Deut 5: 4 from the midst of the **f**
Deut 5: 5 were afraid because of the **f**
Deut 5:22 from the midst of the **f**, the
Deut 5:23 mountain was burning with **f**
Deut 5:24 voice from the midst of the **f**
Deut 5:25 For this great **f** will consume
Deut 5:26 from the midst of the **f**, as
Deut 7: 5 their carved images with **f**
Deut 7:25 images of their gods with **f**
Deut 9: 3 before you as a consuming **f**
Deut 9:10 from the midst of the **f** in
Deut 9:15 and the mountain burned with **f**
Deut 9:21 had made, and burned it with **f**
Deut 10: 4 from the midst of the **f** in
Deut 12: 3 their wooden images with **f**
Deut 12:31 in the **f** to their gods
Deut 13:16 burn with **f** the city and all
Deut 18: 1 of the LORD made by **f**, and His
Deut 18:10 daughter pass through the **f**
Deut 18:16 me see this great **f** anymore
Deut 32:22 For a **f** is kindled in My
Deut 32:22 set on **f** the foundations of
Josh 6:24 and all that was in it with **f**
Josh 7:15 thing shall be burned with **f**
Josh 7:25 they burned them with **f** after
Josh 8: 8 you shall set the city on **f**
Josh 8:19 hastened to set the city on **f**
Josh 11: 6 and burn their chariots with **f**
Josh 11: 9 burned their chariots with **f**
Josh 11:11 Then he burned Hazor with **f**
Josh 13:14 by **f** are their inheritance
Judg 1: 8 sword and set the city on **f**
Judg 6:21 **f** rose out of the rock and
Judg 9:15 let **f** come out of the bramble
Judg 9:20 let **f** come from Abimelech and
Judg 9:20 let **f** come from the men of
Judg 9:49 stronghold on **f** above them
Judg 9:52 the tower to burn it with **f**
Judg 12: 1 your house down on you with **f**
Judg 14:15 and your father's house with **f**
Judg 15: 5 he had set the torches on **f**
Judg 15: 6 her and her father with **f**
Judg 15:14 flax that is burned with **f**
Judg 16: 9 yarn breaks when it touches **f**
Judg 18:27 and burned the city with **f**
Judg 20:48 They also set **f** to all the
1Sa 2:28 children of Israel made by **f**
1Sa 30: 1 Ziklag and burned it with **f**
1Sa 30: 3 there it was, burned with **f**
1Sa 30:14 and we burned Ziklag with **f**
2Sa 14:30 go and set it on **f**
2Sa 14:30 servants set the field on **f**
2Sa 14:31 servants set my field on **f**
2Sa 22: 9 devouring **f** from His mouth
2Sa 22:13 Him coals of **f** were kindled
2Sa 23: 7 burned with **f** in their place
1Ki 9:16 Gezer and burned it with **f**
1Ki 16:18 down upon himself with **f**, and
1Ki 18:23 wood, but put no **f** under it
1Ki 18:23 wood, but put no **f** under it
1Ki 18:24 and the God who answers by **f**
1Ki 18:25 god, but put no **f** under it
1Ki 18:38 Then the **f** of the LORD fell
1Ki 19:12 and after the earthquake a **f**
1Ki 19:12 but the LORD was not in the **f**
1Ki 19:12 after the **f** a still small
2Ki 1:10 then let **f** come down from
2Ki 1:10 **f** came down from heaven and
2Ki 1:12 let **f** come down from heaven
2Ki 1:12 the **f** of God came down from
2Ki 1:14 **f** has come down from heaven
2Ki 2:11 of **f** appeared with horses of
2Ki 2:11 appeared with horses of **f**
2Ki 6:17 and chariots of **f** all around
2Ki 8:12 strongholds you will set on **f**
2Ki 16: 3 his son pass through the **f**
2Ki 17:17 to pass through the **f**,
2Ki 17:31 children in **f** to Adrammelech
2Ki 19:18 cast their gods into the **f**
2Ki 21: 6 his son pass through the **f**
2Ki 23:10 pass through the **f** to Molech
2Ki 23:11 chariots of the sun with **f**
2Ki 25: 9 great men, he burned with **f**
1Ch 14:12 and they were burned with **f**
1Ch 21:26 by **f** on the altar of burnt
2Ch 7: 1 **f** came down from heaven and
2Ch 7: 3 saw how the **f** came down, and
2Ch 28: 3 burned his children in the **f**
2Ch 33: 6 sons to pass through the **f** in
2Ch 35:13 **f** according to the ordinance
2Ch 36:19 burned all its palaces with **f**
Neh 1: 3 its gates are burned with **f**
Neh 2: 3 its gates are burned with **f**
Neh 2:13 which were burned with **f**
Neh 2:17 its gates are burned with **f**
Neh 9:12 by night with a pillar of **f**
Neh 9:19 nor the pillar of **f** by night
Job 1:16 The **f** of God fell from heaven
Job 15:34 **f** will consume the tents of
Job 18: 5 flame of his **f** does not shine
Job 20:26 an unfanned **f** will consume
Job 22:20 the **f** consumes their remnant
Job 28: 5 it is turned up as by **f**
Job 31:12 would be a **f** that consumes to
Job 41:19 sparks of **f** shoot out
Ps 11: 6 wicked He will rain coals, **F**
Ps 18: 8 devouring **f** from His mouth
Ps 18:12 with hailstones and coals of **f**
Ps 18:13 Hailstones and coals of **f**
Ps 21: 9 And the **f** shall devour them
Ps 29: 7 LORD divides the flames of **f**
Ps 39: 3 I was musing, the **f** burned
Ps 46: 9 He burns the chariot in the **f**
Ps 50: 3 A **f** shall devour before Him,
Ps 57: 4 sons of men Who are set on **f**
Ps 66:12 We went through **f** and through
Ps 68: 2 As wax melts before the **f**
Ps 74: 7 They have set **f** to Your
Ps 78:14 the night with a light of **f**
Ps 78:21 So a **f** was kindled against
Ps 78:63 The **f** consumed their young
Ps 79: 5 Your jealousy burn like **f**
Ps 80:16 It is burned with **f**, it is
Ps 83:14 As the **f** burns the woods, And
Ps 83:14 flame sets the mountains on **f**
Ps 89:46 Will Your wrath burn like **f**
Ps 97: 3 A **f** goes before Him, And burns
Ps 104: 4 His ministers a flame of **f**
Ps 105:32 And flaming **f** in their land
Ps 105:39 **f** to give light in the night
Ps 106:18 A **f** was kindled in their
Ps 118:12 quenched like a **f** of thorns
Ps 140:10 Let them be cast into the **f**
Ps 148: 8 **F** and hail, snow and clouds
Prov 6:27 can a man take **f** to his bosom
Prov 16:27 on his lips like a burning **f**
Prov 25:22 heap coals of **f** on his head
Prov 26:20 is no wood, the **f** goes out
Prov 26:21 burning coals, and wood to **f**
Prov 30:16 and the **f** that never says,
Song 8: 6 its flames are flames of **f**
Is 1: 7 your cities are burned with **f**
Is 4: 5 of a flaming **f** by night
Is 5:24 as the **f** devours the stubble,
Is 9: 5 used for burning and fuel of **f**
Is 9:18 For wickedness burns as the **f**
Is 9:19 shall be as fuel for the **f**
Is 10:16 like the burning of a **f**
Is 10:17 of Israel will be for a **f**
Is 26:11 the **f** of Your enemies shall
Is 27:11 women come and set them on **f**
Is 29: 6 And the flame of devouring **f**

Is 30:14 to take f from the hearth
Is 30:27 His tongue like a devouring f
Is 30:30 and the flame of a devouring f
Is 30:33 its pyre is f with much wood
Is 31: 9 whose f is in Zion and whose
Is 33:11 your breath, as f, shall
Is 33:12 they shall be burned in the f
Is 33:14 dwell with the devouring f
Is 37:19 cast their gods into the f
Is 42:25 has set him on f all around
Is 43: 2 When you walk through the f
Is 44:16 He burns half of it in the f
Is 44:16 I am warm, I have seen the f
Is 44:19 burned half of it in the f
Is 47:14 the f shall burn them
Is 47:14 by, nor a f to sit before
Is 50:11 Look, all you who kindle a f
Is 50:11 walk in the light of your f
Is 54:16 who blows the coals in the f
Is 64: 2 as f burns brushwood, as f
Is 64: 2 as f causes water to boil
Is 64:11 You, is burned up with f
Is 65: 5 a f that burns all the day
Is 66:15 the LORD will come with f
Is 66:15 His rebuke with flames of f
Is 66:16 For by f and by His sword the
Is 66:24 and their f is not quenched
Jer 4: 4 My fury come forth like f
Jer 5:14 make My words in your mouth f
Jer 6:29 the lead is consumed by the f
Jer 7:18 the fathers kindle the f
Jer 7:31 and their daughters in the f
Jer 11:16 tumult He has kindled f on it
Jer 15:14 for a f is kindled in My
Jer 17: 4 for you have kindled a f in
Jer 17:27 will kindle a f in its gates
Jer 19: 5 to burn their sons with f for
Jer 20: 9 burning f shut up in my bones
Jer 21:10 and he shall burn it with f
Jer 21:12 lest My fury go out like f
Jer 21:14 will kindle a f in its forest
Jer 22: 7 and cast them into the f
Jer 23:29 Is not My word like a f
Jer 29:22 of Babylon roasted in the f'
Jer 32:29 set f to this city and burn it
Jer 32:35 pass through the f to Molech
Jer 34: 2 and he shall burn it with f
Jer 34:22 and take it and burn it with f
Jer 36:22 with a f burning on the
Jer 36:23 cast it into the f that was
Jer 36:23 the f that was on the hearth
Jer 36:32 of Judah had burned in the f
Jer 37: 8 and take it and burn it with f
Jer 37:10 tent, and burn the city with f
Jer 38:17 shall not be burned with f
Jer 38:18 they shall burn it with f
Jer 38:23 this city to be burned with f
Jer 39: 8 houses of the people with f
Jer 43:12 I will kindle a f in the
Jer 43:13 he shall burn with f
Jer 48:45 But a f shall come out of
Jer 49: 2 shall be burned with f
Jer 49:27 I will kindle a f in the wall
Jer 50:32 will kindle a f in his cities
Jer 51:32 reeds they have burned with f
Jer 51:58 gates shall be burned with f
Jer 51:58 the nations, because of the f
Jer 52:13 great men, he burned with f
Lam 1:13 He has sent f into my bones
Lam 2: 3 Jacob like a flaming f which
Lam 2: 4 poured out His fury like f
Lam 4:11 He kindled a f in Zion, and it
Ezek 1: 4 raging f engulfing itself
Ezek 1: 4 out of the midst of the f
Ezek 1:13 was like burning coals of f
Ezek 1:13 F was going back and forth
Ezek 1:13 the f was bright, and out of
Ezek 1:13 out of the f went lightning
Ezek 1:27 of f all around within it
Ezek 1:27 the appearance of f with
Ezek 5: 2 You shall burn with f
Ezek 5: 4 them into the midst of the f
Ezek 5: 4 and burn them in the f
Ezek 5: 4 for from there a f will go
Ezek 8: 2 like the appearance of f
Ezek 8: 2 of His waist and downward, f
Ezek 10: 2 of f from among the cherubim
Ezek 10: 6 Take f from among the wheels,
Ezek 10: 7 among the cherubim to the f
Ezek 15: 4 is thrown into the f for fuel
Ezek 15: 4 the f devours both ends of it
Ezek 15: 5 when the f has devoured it
Ezek 15: 6 have given to the f for fuel
Ezek 15: 7 They will go out from one f
Ezek 15: 7 but another f shall devour
Ezek 16:21 them to pass through the f
Ezek 16:41 shall burn your houses with f
Ezek 19:12 the f consumed them
Ezek 19:14 F has come out from a rod of
Ezek 20:26 to pass through the f, that I
Ezek 20:31 your sons pass through the f
Ezek 20:47 I will kindle a f in you
Ezek 21:31 you with the f of My wrath
Ezek 21:32 You shall be fuel for the f
Ezek 22:20 of a furnace, to blow f on it
Ezek 22:21 on you with the f of My wrath
Ezek 22:31 them with the f of My wrath
Ezek 23:25 shall be devoured by f
Ezek 23:37 passing them through the f
Ezek 23:47 and burn their houses with f
Ezek 24:10 on the wood, kindle the f
Ezek 24:12 Let her scum be in the f
Ezek 28:18 I brought f from your midst
Ezek 30: 8 when I have set a f in Egypt
Ezek 30:14 set f to Zoan, and execute
Ezek 30:16 and set a f in Egypt
Ezek 38:19 in the f of My wrath I have
Ezek 38:22 rain, great hailstones, f
Ezek 39: 6 And I will send f on Magog
Ezek 39: 9 will go out and set on f and
Dan 3:22 the flame of the f killed
Dan 3:24 bound into the midst of the f
Dan 3:25 walking in the midst of the f
Dan 3:26 came from the midst of the f
Dan 3:27 bodies the f had no power
Dan 3:27 the smell of f was not on
Dan 7: 9 flame, its wheels a burning f
Dan 10: 6 his eyes like torches of f
Hos 7: 4 he ceases stirring the f
Hos 7: 6 it burns like a flaming f
Hos 8:14 I will send f upon his cities
Joel 1:19 for f has devoured the open
Joel 1:20 and f has devoured the open
Joel 2: 3 A f devours before them, and
Joel 2: 5 f that devours the stubble
Joel 2:30 blood and f and pillars of
Amos 1: 4 But I will send a f into the
Amos 1: 7 But I will send a f upon the
Amos 1:10 But I will send a f upon the
Amos 1:12 I will send a f upon Teman
Amos 1:14 But I will kindle a f in the
Amos 2: 2 But I will send a f upon Moab
Amos 2: 5 I will send a f upon Judah
Amos 5: 6 like f in the house of Joseph
Amos 7: 4 GOD called for conflict by f
Obad 18 house of Jacob shall be a f
Mic 1: 4 split like wax before the f
Mic 1: 7 shall be burned with the f
Nah 1: 6 His fury is poured out like f
Nah 3:13 f shall devour the bars of
Nah 3:15 There the f will devour you,
Hab 2:13 peoples labor to feed the f
Zeph 1:18 by the f of His jealousy, for
Zeph 3: 8 with the f of My jealousy
Zech 2: 5 be a wall of f all around her
Zech 3: 2 a brand plucked from the f
Zech 9: 4 and she will be devoured by f
Zech 11: 1 that f may devour your cedars
Zech 13: 9 the one third through the f
Mal 1:10 kindle f on My altar in vain
Mal 3: 2 For He is like a refiner's f
Matt 3:10 cut down and thrown into the f
Matt 3:11 you with the Holy Spirit and f
Matt 3:12 the chaff with unquenchable f
Matt 5:22 shall be in danger of hell f
Matt 7:19 cut down and thrown into the f
Matt 13:40 gathered and burned in the f
Matt 13:42 them into the furnace of f
Matt 13:50 them into the furnace of f
Matt 17:15 for he often falls into the f
Matt 18: 8 cast into the everlasting f
Matt 18: 9 eyes, to be cast into hell f
Matt 25:41 into the everlasting f
Mark 9:22 thrown him both into the f
Mark 9:43 into the f that shall never
Mark 9:44 die and the f is not quenched
Mark 9:45 into the f that shall never
Mark 9:46 die and the f is not quenched
Mark 9:47 eyes, to be cast into hell f
Mark 9:48 die and the f is not quenched
Mark 9:49 will be seasoned with f, and
Mark 14:54 and warmed himself at the f
Luke 3: 9 cut down and thrown into the f
Luke 3:16 the Holy Spirit and with f
Luke 3:17 will burn with unquenchable f
Luke 9:54 f to come down from heaven
Luke 12:49 I came to send f on the earth
Luke 17:29 went out of Sodom it rained f
Luke 22:55 a f in the midst of the
Luke 22:56 seeing him as he sat by the f
John 15: 6 them and throw them into the f
John 18:18 made a f of coals stood there
John 21: 9 they saw a f of coals there,
Acts 2: 3 them divided tongues, as of f
Acts 2:19 blood and f and vapor of smoke
Acts 7:30 him in a flame of f in a bush
Acts 28: 2 for they kindled a f and made
Acts 28: 3 sticks and laid them on the f
Acts 28: 5 off the creature into the f
Rom 12:20 heap coals of f on his head
1Co 3:13 it will be revealed by f
1Co 3:13 the f will test each one's
1Co 3:15 be saved, yet so as through f
2Th 1: 8 in flaming f taking vengeance
Heb 1: 7 and His ministers a flame of f
Heb 11:34 quenched the violence of f
Heb 12:18 touched and that burned with f
Heb 12:29 For our God is a consuming f
Jas 3: 5 a forest a little f kindles
Jas 3: 6 And the tongue is a f, a world
Jas 3: 6 and sets on f the course of
Jas 3: 6 and it is set on f by hell
Jas 5: 3 and will eat your flesh like f
1Pe 1: 7 though it is tested by f
2Pe 3: 7 reserved for f until the day
2Pe 3:12 will be dissolved being on f
Jude 7 the vengeance of eternal f
Jude 23 pulling them out of the f
Rev 1:14 and His eyes like a flame of f
Rev 2:18 has eyes like a flame of f
Rev 3:18 from Me gold refined in the f
Rev 4: 5 f burning before the throne
Rev 8: 5 it with f from the altar, and
Rev 8: 7 and f followed, mingled with
Rev 8: 8 f was thrown into the sea
Rev 9:17 and out of their mouths came f
Rev 9:18 by the f and the smoke and the
Rev 10: 1 and his feet like pillars of f
Rev 11: 5 f proceeds from their mouth
Rev 13:13 so that he even makes f come
Rev 14:10 he shall be tormented with f
Rev 14:18 altar, who had power over f
Rev 15: 2 a sea of glass mingled with f
Rev 16: 8 to him to scorch men with f
Rev 17:16 her flesh and burn her with f
Rev 18: 8 will be utterly burned with f
Rev 19:12 eyes were like a flame of f
Rev 19:20 of f burning with brimstone
Rev 20: 9 f came down from God out of
Rev 20:10 was cast into the lake of f
Rev 20:14 were cast into the lake of f
Rev 20:15 was cast into the lake of f
Rev 21: 8 the lake which burns with f

FIREBRAND (*see* FIRE, FIREBRANDS)
Amos 4:11 you were like a f plucked

FIREBRANDS (*see* FIREBRAND)
Prov 26:18 Like a madman who throws f
Is 7: 4 these two stubs of smoking f

FIREPAN (*see* FIRE, FIREPANS)
Zech 12: 6 like a f in the woodpile, and

FIREPANS (*see* FIREPAN)
Ex 27: 3 basins and its forks and its f
Ex 38: 3 basins, the forks, and the f
Num 4:14 the f, the forks, the shovels
2Ki 25:15 The f and the basins, the
Jer 52:19 The basins, the f, the bowls,

FIRES (*see* FIRE)
Ezek 39: 9 they will make f with them
Ezek 39:10 will make f with the weapons

FIRM (*see* FIRMLY)
Num 24:21 F is your dwelling place, and
Deut 25: 8 and if he stands f and says, I
Josh 3:17 f on dry ground in the midst
Josh 4: 3 the priests' feet stood f
Job 39:24 nor does he stand f, because
Job 41:23 they are f on him and cannot
Ps 73: 4 But their strength is f
Ps 89:28 shall stand f with him

Prov 4:13 Take f hold of instruction,
Is 35: 3 and make f the feeble knees
Dan 2: 5 My decision is f
Dan 2: 8 you see that my decision is f
Dan 6: 7 statute and to make a f decree
Heb 3: 6 of the hope f to the end

FIRMAMENT
Gen 1: 6 Let there be a f in the midst
Gen 1: 7 Thus God made the f, and
Gen 1: 7 f from the waters which were
Gen 1: 7 waters which were above the f
Gen 1: 8 And God called the f Heaven
Gen 1:14 f of the heavens to divide
Gen 1:15 the f of the heavens to give
Gen 1:17 God set them in the f of the
Gen 1:20 face of the f of the heavens
Ps 19: 1 the f shows His handiwork
Ps 150: 1 Praise Him in His mighty f
Ezek 1:22 The likeness of the f above
Ezek 1:23 And under the f their wings
Ezek 1:25 f that was over their heads
Ezek 1:26 above the f over their heads
Ezek 10: 1 there in the f that was above
Dan 12: 3 like the brightness of the f

FIRMLY (*see* FIRM)
1Ki 2:12 his kingdom was f established
1Ch 16:30 world also is f established
Ezra 6: 3 foundations of it be f laid
Ps 75: 3 I set up its pillars f
Ps 96:10 world also is f established

FIRST (*see* FIRSTBORN, FIRSTFRUIT, FIRSTLING, FIRST-RIPE)
Gen 1: 5 and the morning were the f day
Gen 2:11 The name of the f is Pishon
Gen 8: 5 on the f day of the month,
Gen 8:13 and f year, in the f month
Gen 8:13 the f day of the month, that
Gen 13: 4 which he had made there at f
Gen 25:25 And the f came out red
Gen 26: 1 besides the f famine that was
Gen 32:17 And he commanded the f one
Gen 38:28 This one came out f
Gen 41:20 ugly cows ate up the f seven
Gen 43:18 in our sacks the f time, that
Gen 43:20 down the f time to buy food
Ex 4: 8 the message of the f sign
Ex 12: 2 it shall be the f month of
Ex 12: 5 blemish, a male of the f year
Ex 12:15 On the f day you shall remove
Ex 12:15 leavened bread from the f day
Ex 12:16 On the f day there shall be
Ex 12:18 In the f month, on the
Ex 22:29 the f of your ripe produce
Ex 23:19 The f of the firstfruits of
Ex 25:35 f two branches of the same
Ex 28:17 The f row shall be a sardius,
Ex 28:17 this shall be the f row
Ex 29:38 two lambs of the f year, day
Ex 34: 1 of stone like the f ones, and
Ex 34: 1 the f tablets which you broke
Ex 34: 4 of stone like the f ones
Ex 34:26 The f of the firstfruits of
Ex 37:21 f two branches of the same
Ex 39:10 and an emerald was the f row
Ex 40: 2 On the f day of the f month
Ex 40:17 And it came to pass in the f
Ex 40:17 on the f day of the month,
Lev 4:21 it as he burned the f bull
Lev 5: 8 is for the sin offering f
Lev 9: 3 and a lamb, both of the f year
Lev 9:15 it for sin, like the f one
Lev 12: 6 f year as a burnt offering
Lev 14:10 one ewe lamb of the f year
Lev 23: 5 f month at twilight is the
Lev 23: 7 On the f day you shall have
Lev 23:12 a male lamb of the f year
Lev 23:18 seven lambs of the f year
Lev 23:19 two male lambs of the f year
Lev 23:24 on the f day of the month,
Lev 23:35 On the f day there shall be
Lev 23:39 on the f day there shall be a
Lev 23:40 f day the fruit of beautiful
Num 1: 1 on the f day of the second
Num 1:18 together on the f day of the
Num 2: 9 these shall break camp f
Num 6:12 bring a male lamb in its f
Num 6:14 one male lamb in its f year
Num 6:14 one ewe lamb in its f year
Num 7:12 f day was Nahshon the son of
Num 7:15 one male lamb in its f year
Num 7:17 male lambs in their f year
Num 7:21 one male lamb in its f year
Num 7:23 male lambs in their f year
Num 7:27 one male lamb in its f year
Num 7:29 male lambs in their f year
Num 7:33 one male lamb in its f year
Num 7:35 male lambs in their f year
Num 7:39 one male lamb in its f year
Num 7:41 male lambs in their f year
Num 7:45 one male lamb in its f year
Num 7:47 male lambs in their f year
Num 7:51 one male lamb in its f year
Num 7:53 male lambs in their f year
Num 7:57 one male lamb in its f year
Num 7:59 male lambs in their f year
Num 7:63 one male lamb in its f year
Num 7:65 male lambs in their f year
Num 7:69 one male lamb in its f year
Num 7:71 male lambs in their f year
Num 7:75 one male lamb in its f year
Num 7:77 male lambs in their f year
Num 7:81 one male lamb in its f year
Num 7:83 male lambs in their f year
Num 7:87 lambs in their f year twelve
Num 7:88 lambs in their f year sixty
Num 9: 1 in the f month of the second
Num 9: 5 fourteenth day of the f month
Num 10:13 the f time according to the
Num 10:14 f according to their armies
Num 13:20 season of the f ripe grapes
Num 15:20 offer up a cake of the f of
Num 15:21 Of the f of your ground meal
Num 15:27 its f year as a sin offering
Num 18:13 Whatever f ripe fruit is in
Num 18:15 Everything that f opens the
Num 20: 1 of Zin in the f month, and the
Num 24:20 Amalek was f among the
Num 28: 3 their f year without blemish
Num 28: 9 day two lambs in their f year
Num 28:11 seven lambs in their f year
Num 28:16 f month is the Passover of
Num 28:18 On the f day you shall have
Num 28:19 seven lambs in their f year
Num 28:27 seven lambs in their f year
Num 29: 1 on the f day of the month,
Num 29: 2 seven lambs in their f year
Num 29: 8 seven lambs in their f year
Num 29:13 lambs in their f year
Num 29:17 their f year without blemish
Num 29:20 their f year without blemish
Num 29:23 lambs in their f year,
Num 29:26 their f year without blemish
Num 29:29 their f year without blemish
Num 29:32 their f year without blemish
Num 29:36 their f year without blemish
Num 33: 3 from Rameses in the f month
Num 33: 3 fifteenth day of the f month
Num 33:38 on the f day of the fifth
Deut 1: 3 on the f day of the month,
Deut 9:18 before the LORD, as at the f
Deut 10: 1 tablets of stone like the f
Deut 10: 2 that were on the f tablets
Deut 10: 3 tablets of stone like the f
Deut 10: 4 according to the f writing
Deut 10:10 As at the f time, I stayed in
Deut 13: 9 your hand shall be f against
Deut 16: 4 the f day at twilight remain
Deut 17: 7 f against him to put him to
Deut 18: 4 the f of the fleece of your
Deut 26: 2 f of all the produce of the
Deut 33:21 He provided the f part for
Josh 4:19 the tenth day of the f month
Josh 8: 5 out against us as at the f
Josh 8: 6 fleeing before us as at the f
Josh 21:10 for the lot was theirs f
Judg 1: 1 Who shall be f to go up for
Judg 20:18 go up f to battle against the
Judg 20:18 Judah shall go up f
Judg 20:22 in array on the f day
Judg 20:32 down before us, as at f
Judg 20:39 before us, as in the f battle
1Sa 2:16 should really burn the fat f
1Sa 14:14 That f slaughter which
1Sa 14:35 This was the f altar that he
1Sa 17:30 him as the f ones did
1Sa 20: 2 or small without f telling me
2Sa 3:13 unless you f bring Michal
2Sa 17: 9 them are overthrown at the f
2Sa 18:27 the f is like the running of
2Sa 19:20 the f to come today of all
2Sa 19:43 were we not the f to advise
2Sa 21: 9 of harvest, in the f days
2Sa 23:19 did not attain to the f three
2Sa 23:23 did not attain to the f three
1Ki 3:22 And the f woman said,
1Ki 3:27 Give the f woman the living
1Ki 17:13 me a small cake from it f
1Ki 18:25 yourselves and prepare it f
1Ki 20: 9 servant the f time I will do
1Ki 20:17 of the provinces went out f
2Ki 1:14 burned up the f two captains
1Ch 9: 2 the f inhabitants who dwelt
1Ch 11: 6 Jebusites f shall be chief
1Ch 11: 6 the son of Zeruiah went up f
1Ch 11:21 did not attain to the f three
1Ch 11:25 did not attain to the f three
1Ch 12: 9 Ezer the f, Obadiah the
1Ch 12:15 the Jordan in the f month
1Ch 15:13 you did not do it the f time
1Ch 16: 7 on that day David f delivered
1Ch 23: 8 the f Jehiel, then Zetham and
1Ch 23:11 Jahath was the f and Zizah the
1Ch 23:16 of Gershon, Shebuel was the f
1Ch 23:17 Eliezer, Rehabiah was the f
1Ch 23:18 of Izhar, Shelomith was the f
1Ch 23:19 of Hebron, Jeriah was the f
1Ch 23:20 of Uzziel, Michah was the f
1Ch 24: 7 Now the f lot fell to
1Ch 24:21 Rehabiah, the f was Isshiah
1Ch 24:23 of Hebron, Jeriah was the f
1Ch 25: 9 Now the f lot for Asaph came
1Ch 26:10 Shimri the f (for though he
1Ch 26:10 his father made him the f)
1Ch 27: 2 the f division for the f
1Ch 27: 3 of the army for the f month
1Ch 29:29 Now the acts of King David, f
2Ch 9:29 of the acts of Solomon, f
2Ch 12:15 The acts of Rehoboam, f and
2Ch 16:11 Note that the acts of Asa, f
2Ch 20:34 of the acts of Jehoshaphat, f
2Ch 25:26 from f to last, indeed are
2Ch 26:22 from f to last, the prophet
2Ch 28:26 from f to last, indeed they
2Ch 29: 3 In the f year of his reign,
2Ch 29: 3 of his reign, in the f month
2Ch 29:17 the f day of the f month
2Ch 29:17 of the f month they finished
2Ch 35: 1 fourteenth day of the f month
2Ch 35:27 and his deeds from f to last
2Ch 36:22 Now in the f year of Cyrus
Ezra 1: 1 Now in the f year of Cyrus
Ezra 3: 6 From the f day of the seventh
Ezra 3:12 who had seen the f temple
Ezra 5:13 in the f year of Cyrus king
Ezra 6: 3 In the f year of King Cyrus,
Ezra 6:19 fourteenth day of the f month
Ezra 7: 9 On the f day of the f
Ezra 7: 9 On the f day of the f
Ezra 7: 9 on the f day of the fifth
Ezra 8:31 twelfth day of the f month
Ezra 10:16 they sat down on the f day of
Ezra 10:17 By the f day of the f
Ezra 10:17 of the f month they finished
Neh 7: 5 had come up in the f return
Neh 8: 2 on the f day of the seventh
Neh 8:18 from the f day until the last
Esth 3: 7 In the f month, which is the
Esth 3:12 thirteenth day of the f month
Job 15: 7 Are you the f man who was
Job 40:19 He is the f of the ways of
Job 42:14 the name of the f Jemimah
Ps 78:51 The f of their strength in
Ps 105:36 The f of all their strength
Prov 18:17 The f one to plead his cause
Is 1:26 your judges as at the f, and
Is 9: 1 as when at f He lightly
Is 28: 4 like the f fruit before the
Is 41: 4 I, the LORD, am the f
Is 41:27 The f time I said to Zion
Is 43:27 Your f father sinned, and your
Is 44: 6 I am the F and I am the Last
Is 48:12 I am He, I am the F, I am
Is 52: 4 My people went down at f into
Is 60: 9 ships of Tarshish will come f
Jer 4:31 who brings forth her f child
Jer 7:12 where I set My name at the f
Jer 16:18 f I will repay double for
Jer 24: 2 like the figs that are f ripe
Jer 25: 1 of Judah (which was the f
Jer 33: 7 those places as at the f

Jer 33:11 land to return as at the f
Jer 36:28 words that were in the f
Jer 50:17 F the king of Assyria
Jer 52:31 in the f year of his reign,
Ezek 10:14 the f face was the face of a
Ezek 26: 1 on the f day of the month,
Ezek 29:17 year, in the f month, on the
Ezek 29:17 on the f day of the month,
Ezek 30:20 eleventh year, in the f month
Ezek 31: 1 on the f day of the month,
Ezek 32: 1 on the f day of the month,
Ezek 40:21 measurements as the f gate
Ezek 44:30 the f of your ground meal
Ezek 45:18 the f month, on the f day
Ezek 45:21 In the f month, on the
Ezek 46:13 of the f year without blemish
Dan 1:21 the f year of King Cyrus
Dan 7: 1 In the f year of Belshazzar
Dan 7: 4 The f was like a lion, and had
Dan 7: 8 before whom three of the f
Dan 7:24 be different from the f ones
Dan 8: 1 appeared to me the f time
Dan 8:21 its eyes is the f king
Dan 9: 1 In the f year of Darius the
Dan 9: 2 in the f year of his reign I,
Dan 10: 4 day of the f month, as I was
Dan 10:12 for from the f day that you
Dan 11: 1 Also in the f year of Darius
Hos 2: 7 go and return to my f husband
Hos 9:10 the fig tree in its f season
Joel 2:23 latter rain in the f month
Amos 6: 7 as the f of the captives, and
Jon 3: 4 the city on the f day's walk
Hag 1: 1 on the f day of the month,
Zech 6: 2 With the f chariot were red
Zech 12: 7 save the tents of Judah f
Zech 14:10 to the place of the F Gate
Matt 5:24 F be reconciled to your
Matt 6:33 But seek f the kingdom of God
Matt 7: 5 F remove the plank from your
Matt 8:21 Lord, let me f go and bury my
Matt 10: 2 f, Simon, who is called Peter
Matt 12:29 unless he f binds the strong
Matt 12:45 that man is worse than the f
Matt 13:30 F gather together the tares
Matt 17:10 say that Elijah must come f
Matt 17:11 Elijah truly is coming f and
Matt 17:27 take the fish that comes up f
Matt 19:30 many who are f will be last
Matt 19:30 will be last, and the last f
Matt 20: 8 with the last to the f
Matt 20:10 But when the f came, they
Matt 20:16 So the last will be f
Matt 20:16 and the f last
Matt 20:27 desires to be f among you
Matt 21:28 two sons, and he came to the f
Matt 21:31 They said to Him, "The f."
Matt 21:36 servants, more than the f
Matt 22:25 The f died after he had
Matt 22:38 This is the f and great
Matt 23:26 f cleanse the inside of the
Matt 26:17 Now on the f day of the Feast
Matt 27:64 will be worse than the f
Matt 28: 1 as the f day of the week
Mark 3:27 unless he f binds the strong
Mark 4:28 f the blade, then the head,
Mark 7:27 Let the children be filled f
Mark 9:11 say that Elijah must come f
Mark 9:12 Elijah does come f, and
Mark 9:35 If anyone desires to be f
Mark 10:31 many who are f will be last
Mark 10:31 will be last, and the last f
Mark 10:44 of you desires to be f shall
Mark 12:20 The f took a wife
Mark 12:28 Which is the f commandment of
Mark 12:29 The f of all the commandments
Mark 12:30 This is the f commandment
Mark 13:10 the gospel must f be preached
Mark 14:12 Now on the f day of
Mark 16: 2 on the f day of the week,
Mark 16: 9 on the f day of the week, He
Mark 16: 9 week, He appeared f to Mary
Luke 1: 3 of all things from the very f
Luke 2: 2 This census f took place
Luke 6: 1 f that He went through the
Luke 6:42 F remove the plank from your
Luke 9:59 Lord, let me f go and bury my
Luke 9:61 follow You, but let me f go
Luke 10: 5 f say, 'Peace to this house
Luke 11:26 that man is worse than the f
Luke 11:38 not f washed before dinner
Luke 12: 1 say to His disciples f of all
Luke 13:30 there are last who will be f
Luke 13:30 there are f who will be last
Luke 14:18 The f said to him, 'I have
Luke 14:28 a tower, does not sit down f
Luke 14:31 king, does not sit down f
Luke 16: 5 to him, and said to the f
Luke 17:25 But f He must suffer many
Luke 19:16 Then came the f, saying
Luke 20:29 the f took a wife, and died
Luke 21: 9 things must come to pass f
Luke 24: 1 Now on the f day of the week,
John 1:41 He f found his own brother
John 5: 4 then whoever stepped in f
John 8: 7 him throw a stone at her f
John 10:40 where John was baptizing at f
John 12:16 understand these things at f
John 18:13 they led Him away to Annas f
John 19:32 and broke the legs of the f
John 19:39 who at f came to Jesus by
John 20: 1 On the f day of the week Mary
John 20: 4 Peter and came to the tomb f
John 20: 8 who came to the tomb f, went
John 20:19 being the f day of the week,
Acts 3:26 To you f, God, having raised
Acts 7:12 he sent out our fathers f
Acts 11:26 the disciples were f called
Acts 12:10 When they were past the f
Acts 13:24 after John had f preached
Acts 13:46 God should be spoken to you f
Acts 15:14 the f visited the Gentiles to
Acts 20: 7 Now on the f day of the week,
Acts 20:18 from the f day that I came to
Acts 26: 5 They knew me from the f, if
Acts 26:20 but declared f to those in
Acts 26:23 that He would be the f to
Acts 27:43 swim should jump overboard f
Rom 1: 8 F, I thank my God through
Rom 1:16 who believes, for the Jew f
Rom 2: 9 who does evil, of the Jew f
Rom 2:10 what is good, to the Jew f
Rom 10:19 F Moses says
Rom 11:35 Or who has f given to Him and
Rom 13:11 than when we f believed
Rom 15:24 if f I may enjoy your company
1Co 11:18 For f of all, when you come
1Co 12:28 f apostles, second prophets,
1Co 14:30 by, let the f keep silent
1Co 15: 3 For I delivered to you f of
1Co 15:45 The f man Adam became a
1Co 15:46 the spiritual is not f, but
1Co 15:47 The f man was of the earth,
1Co 16: 2 On the f day of the week let
2Co 8: 5 but f gave themselves to the
2Co 8:12 if there is f a willing mind
Gal 4:13 the gospel to you at the f
Eph 1:12 that we who f trusted in
Eph 4: 9 f descended into the lower
Eph 6: 2 which is the f commandment
Phil 1: 5 from the f day until now,
1Th 4:16 dead in Christ will rise f
2Th 2: 3 the falling away comes f, and
1Ti 1:16 that in me f Jesus Christ
1Ti 2: 1 Therefore I exhort f of all
1Ti 2:13 For Adam was formed f, then
1Ti 3:10 let these also f be proved
1Ti 5: 4 let them f learn to show
1Ti 5:12 have cast off their f faith
2Ti 1: 5 in you, which dwelt f in your
2Ti 2: 6 be f to partake of the crops
2Ti 4:16 At my f defense no one stood
Tit 3:10 a divisive man after the f
Heb 2: 3 which at the f began to be
Heb 4: 6 it, and those to whom it was f
Heb 5:12 to teach you again the f
Heb 7: 2 of all, f being translated
Heb 7:27 f for His own sins and then
Heb 8: 7 For if that f covenant had
Heb 8:13 He has made the f obsolete
Heb 9: 1 even the f covenant had
Heb 9: 2 the f part, in which was the
Heb 9: 6 always went into the f part
Heb 9: 8 the f tabernacle was still
Heb 9:15 under the f covenant, that
Heb 9:18 the f covenant was dedicated
Heb 10: 9 He takes away the f that He
Jas 3:17 that is from above is f pure
1Pe 4:17 and if it begins with us f
2Pe 1:20 knowing this f, that no
2Pe 3: 3 knowing this f: that scoffers
1Jn 4:19 Him because He f loved us
Rev 1:11 the Alpha and the Omega, the F
Rev 1:17 I am the F and the Last
Rev 2: 4 you have left your f love
Rev 2: 5 repent and do the f works, or
Rev 2: 8 These things says the F
Rev 2:19 the last are more than the f
Rev 4: 1 the f voice which I heard was
Rev 4: 7 The f living creature was
Rev 8: 7 The f angel sounded
Rev 13:12 the f beast in his presence
Rev 13:12 in it to worship the f beast
Rev 16: 2 So the f went and poured out
Rev 20: 5 This is the f resurrection
Rev 20: 6 part in the f resurrection
Rev 21: 1 a new earth, for the f heaven
Rev 21: 1 the f earth had passed away
Rev 21:19 the f foundation was jasper,
Rev 22:13 Beginning and the End, the F

FIRSTBORN (*see* FIRST)
Gen 10:15 Canaan begot Sidon his f, and
Gen 19:31 Now the f said to the younger
Gen 19:33 the f went in and lay with her
Gen 19:34 the f said to the younger
Gen 19:37 The f bore a son and called
Gen 22:21 Huz his f, Buz his brother,
Gen 25:13 The f of Ishmael, Nebajoth
Gen 27:19 I am Esau your f
Gen 27:32 I am your son, your f, Esau
Gen 29:26 give the younger before the f
Gen 35:23 Leah were Reuben, Jacob's f
Gen 36:15 the f son of Esau, were Chief
Gen 38: 6 took a wife for Er his f, and
Gen 38: 7 But Er, Judah's f, was wicked
Gen 41:51 the name of the f Manasseh
Gen 43:33 him, the f according to his
Gen 46: 8 Reuben was Jacob's f
Gen 48:14 for Manasseh was the f
Gen 48:18 father, for this one is the f
Gen 49: 3 Reuben, you are my f, my
Ex 4:22 Israel is My son, My f
Ex 4:23 I will kill your son, your f
Ex 6:14 the f of Israel, were Hanoch,
Ex 11: 5 and all the f in the land of
Ex 11: 5 from the f of Pharaoh who
Ex 11: 5 throne, even to the f of the
Ex 11: 5 and all the f of the beasts
Ex 12:12 will strike all the f in the
Ex 12:29 the f in the land of Egypt
Ex 12:29 from the f of Pharaoh who sat
Ex 12:29 sat on his throne to the f of
Ex 12:29 and all the f of livestock
Ex 13: 2 Sanctify to Me all the f,
Ex 13:13 all the f of man among your
Ex 13:15 the f in the land of Egypt
Ex 13:15 of Egypt, both the f of man
Ex 13:15 of man and the f of animal
Ex 13:15 but all the f of my sons I
Ex 22:29 The f of your sons you shall
Ex 34:20 All the f of your sons you
Num 3: 2 Nadab, the f, and Abihu,
Num 3:12 f who opens the womb among
Num 3:13 because all the f are Mine
Num 3:13 the f in the land of Egypt
Num 3:13 to Myself all the f in Israel
Num 3:40 Number all the f males of the
Num 3:41 instead of all the f among
Num 3:41 f among the livestock of the
Num 3:42 the f among the children of
Num 3:43 And all the f males, according
Num 3:45 the f among the children of
Num 3:46 seventy-three of the f of the
Num 3:50 From the f of the children of
Num 8:16 the f of all the children of
Num 8:17 For all the f among the
Num 8:17 the f in the land of Egypt I
Num 8:18 f of the children of Israel
Num 18:15 nevertheless the f of man you
Num 18:15 the f of unclean animals you
Num 18:17 But the f of a cow, the
Num 18:17 cow, the f of a sheep, or the
Num 18:17 or the f of a goat you shall
Num 26: 5 Reuben was the f of Israel
Num 33: 4 were burying all their f,
Deut 15:19 All the f males that come
Deut 15:19 work with the f of your herd
Deut 15:19 nor shear the f of your flock
Deut 21:15 if the f son is of her who is
Deut 21:16 that he must not bestow f

Deut 21:16 unloved, who is truly the f
Deut 21:17 the f by giving him a double
Deut 21:17 the right of the f is his
Deut 25: 6 it shall be that the f son
Deut 33:17 His glory is like a f bull
Josh 6:26 lay its foundation with his f
Josh 17: 1 for he was the f of Joseph
Josh 17: 1 for Machir the f of Manasseh
Judg 8:20 And he said to Jether his f
1Sa 8: 2 The name of his f was Joel
1Sa 14:49 the name of the f Merab, and
1Sa 17:13 the battle were Eliab the f
2Sa 3: 2 His f was Amnon by Ahinoam
1Ki 16:34 foundation with Abiram his f
1Ch 1:13 Canaan begot Sidon, his f
1Ch 1:29 The f of Ishmael was Nabajoth
1Ch 2: 3 the f of Judah, was wicked in
1Ch 2:13 Jesse begot Eliab his f,
1Ch 2:25 the f of Hezron, were Ram,
1Ch 2:25 of Hezron, were Ram, the f
1Ch 2:27 the f of Jerahmeel, were Maaz
1Ch 2:42 Jerahmeel were Mesha, his f
1Ch 2:50 Hur, the f of Ephrathah, were
1Ch 3: 1 The f was Amnon, by Ahinoam
1Ch 3:15 of Josiah were Johanan the f
1Ch 4: 4 the f of Ephrathah the father
1Ch 5: 1 of Reuben the f of Israel
1Ch 5: 1 he was indeed the f, but
1Ch 5: 3 the f of Israel were Hanoch
1Ch 6:28 of Samuel were Joel the f
1Ch 8: 1 Now Benjamin begot Bela his f
1Ch 8:30 his f son was Abdon; then Zur
1Ch 8:39 his brother were Ulam his f
1Ch 9: 5 Asaiah the f and his sons
1Ch 9:31 the f of Shallum the Korahite
1Ch 9:36 His f son was Abdon, then Zur
1Ch 26: 2 were Zechariah the f, Jediael
1Ch 26: 4 were Shemaiah the f
1Ch 26:10 (for though he was not the f
2Ch 21: 3 Jehoram, because he was the f
Neh 10:36 to bring the f of our sons
Job 18:13 the f of death devours his
Ps 78:51 destroyed all the f in Egypt
Ps 89:27 Also I will make him My f
Ps 105:36 all the f in their land, The
Ps 135: 8 He destroyed the f of Egypt
Ps 136:10 who struck Egypt in their f
Is 14:30 The f of the poor will feed,
Jer 31: 9 to Israel, and Ephraim is My f
Ezek 20:26 f to pass through the fire
Mic 6: 7 Shall I give my f for my
Zech 12:10 Him as one grieves for a f
Matt 1:25 had brought forth her f Son
Luke 2: 7 she brought forth her f Son
Rom 8:29 be the f among many brethren
Col 1:15 God, the f over all creation
Col 1:18 the f from the dead, that in
Heb 1: 6 brings the f into the world
Heb 11:28 the f should touch them
Heb 12:23 and church of the f who are
Rev 1: 5 the f from the dead, and the

FIRSTFRUIT (*see* FIRST, FIRSTFRUITS)
Rom 11:16 For if the f is holy, the

FIRSTFRUITS (*see* FIRSTFRUIT)
Ex 23:16 the f of your labors which
Ex 23:19 The first of the f of your
Ex 34:22 of the f of wheat harvest, and
Ex 34:26 The first of the f of your
Lev 2:12 As for the offering of the f
Lev 2:14 of your f to the LORD, you
Lev 2:14 your f green heads of grain
Lev 23:10 the f of your harvest to the
Lev 23:17 They are the f to the LORD
Lev 23:20 f as a wave offering before
Num 18:12 their f which they offer to
Num 28:26 Also on the day of the f
Deut 18: 4 The f of your grain and your
Deut 26:10 I have brought the f of the
2Ki 4:42 the man of God bread of the f
2Ch 31: 5 in abundance the f of grain
Neh 10:35 to bring the f of our ground
Neh 10:35 the f of all fruit of all
Neh 10:37 to bring the f of our dough
Neh 12:44 for the offerings, the f, and
Neh 13:31 and the f at appointed times
Prov 3: 9 and with the f of all your
Jer 2: 3 LORD, the f of His increase
Ezek 20:40 the f of your sacrifices,
Ezek 44:30 The best of all f of any kind
Hos 9:10 the f on the fig tree in its
Rom 8:23 who have the f of the Spirit
Rom 16: 5 who is the f of Achaia to
1Co 15:20 has become the f of those who
1Co 15:23 Christ the f, afterward those
1Co 16:15 that it is the f of Achaia
Jas 1:18 a kind of f of His creatures
Rev 14: 4 being f to God and to the Lamb

FIRSTLING (*see* FIRST, FIRSTLINGS)
Ex 13:12 every f that comes from an
Ex 13:13 But every f of a donkey you
Ex 34:19 and every male f among your
Ex 34:20 But the f of a donkey you
Lev 27:26 But the f of the beasts,
Lev 27:26 which should be the LORD's f

FIRSTLINGS (*see* FIRSTLING)
Gen 4: 4 brought of the f of his flock
Deut 12: 6 the f of your herds and flocks
Deut 12:17 of the f of your herd or your
Deut 14:23 of the f of your herds and
Neh 10:36 the f of our herds and our

FIRST-RIPE (*see* FIRST)
Mic 7: 1 f fruit which my soul desires

FISH (*see* FISHER, FISHHOOKS, FISHING, FISH'S)
Gen 1:26 over the f of the sea, over
Gen 1:28 over the f of the sea, over
Gen 9: 2 and on all the f of the sea
Ex 7:18 the f that are in the river
Ex 7:21 The f that were in the river
Num 11: 5 We remember the f which we
Num 11:22 Or shall all the f of the sea
Deut 4:18 of any f that is in the water
1Ki 4:33 of creeping things, and of f
2Ch 33:14 as the entrance of the F Gate
Neh 3: 3 of Hassenaah built the F Gate
Neh 12:39 Old Gate, above the F Gate
Neh 13:16 there also, who brought in f
Job 12: 8 the f of the sea will explain
Ps 8: 8 the f of the sea That pass
Ps 105:29 into blood, And killed their f
Eccl 9:12 Like f taken in a cruel net,
Is 50: 2 their f stink because there
Jer 16:16 and they shall f them
Ezek 29: 4 cause the f of your rivers to
Ezek 29: 4 all the f in your rivers will
Ezek 29: 5 and all the f of your rivers
Ezek 38:20 so that the f of the sea
Ezek 47: 9 a very great multitude of f
Ezek 47:10 Their f will be of the same
Ezek 47:10 as the f of the Great Sea
Hos 4: 3 even the f of the sea will be
Jon 1:17 a great f to swallow Jonah
Jon 1:17 the belly of the f three days
Jon 2:10 So the LORD spoke to the f
Hab 1:14 make men like f of the sea
Zeph 1: 3 the f of the sea, and the
Zeph 1:10 mournful cry from the F Gate
Matt 7:10 Or if he asks for a f, will
Matt 12:40 in the belly of the great f
Matt 14:17 only five loaves and two f
Matt 14:19 the five loaves and the two f
Matt 15:34 Seven, and a few little f
Matt 15:36 the seven loaves and the f
Matt 17:27 and take the f that comes up
Mark 6:38 Five, and two f."
Mark 6:41 the five loaves and the two f
Mark 6:41 the two f He divided among
Mark 6:43 full of fragments and of the f
Mark 8: 7 And they had a few small f
Luke 5: 6 caught a great number of f
Luke 5: 9 of f which they had taken
Luke 9:13 than five loaves and two f
Luke 9:16 the five loaves and the two f
Luke 11:11 Or if he asks for a f, will
Luke 11:11 him a serpent instead of a f
Luke 24:42 Him a piece of a broiled f
John 6: 9 barley loaves and two small f
John 6:11 and likewise of the f, as much
John 21: 6 because of the multitude of f
John 21: 8 dragging the net with f
John 21: 9 and f laid on it, and bread
John 21:10 Bring some of the f which you
John 21:11 net to land, full of large f
John 21:13 it to them, and likewise the f
1Co 15:39 flesh of beasts, another of f

FISHER (*see* FISH, FISHERS)
Lev 11:17 the little owl, the f owl
Deut 14:17 carrion vulture, the f owl

FISHERMEN (*see* FISHERS)
Is 19: 8 The f also will mourn
Jer 16:16 I will send for many f,"
Ezek 47:10 It shall be that f will stand
Matt 4:18 for they were f
Mark 1:16 for they were f
Luke 5: 2 but the f had gone from them

FISHERS (*see* FISHER, FISHERMEN)
Matt 4:19 and I will make you f of men
Mark 1:17 will make you become f of men

FISHHOOKS (*see* FISH)
Amos 4: 2 He will take you away with f
Amos 4: 2 and your posterity with f

FISHING (*see* FISH)
Job 41: 7 or his head with f spears
John 21: 3 I am going f

FISH'S (*see* FISH)
Jon 2: 1 LORD his God from the f belly

FIST (*see* FISTS)
Ex 21:18 with a stone or with his f
Is 10:32 he will shake his f at the
Is 11:15 shake His f over the River
Is 58: 4 with the f of wickedness
Zeph 2:15 her shall hiss and shake his f

FISTS (*see* FIST)
Prov 30: 4 gathered the wind in His f
Ezek 6:11 Pound your f and stamp your
Ezek 21:17 also will beat My f together
Ezek 22:13 I beat My f at the dishonest

FIT (*see* FITLY, FITTED, FITTING)
2Ki 24:16 f for war, these the king of
1Ch 7:11 of valor f to go out for war
1Ch 7:40 among the army f for battle
1Ch 12:25 mighty men of valor f for war
Prov 24:27 make it f for yourself in the
Ezek 16:50 I took them away as I saw f
Dan 1:13 and as you see f, so deal with
Luke 9:62 is f for the kingdom of God
Luke 14:35 It is neither f for the land
Acts 22:22 for he is not f to live
Acts 25:24 was not f to live any longer

FITLY (*see* FIT)
Prov 25:11 A word f spoken is like
Song 5:12 washed with milk, and f set

FITTED (*see* FIT)
Zech 9:13 f the bow with Ephraim, and

FITTING (*see* FIT)
Esth 3: 8 Therefore it is not f for the
Job 34:18 Is it f to say to a king
Prov 19:10 Luxury is not f for a fool
Prov 26: 1 so honor is not f for a fool
Eccl 5:18 f for one to eat and drink, and
Matt 3:15 for thus it is f for us to
Rom 1:28 those things which are not f
1Co 16: 4 But if it is f that I go also
Eph 5: 3 among you, as is f for saints
Eph 5: 4 jesting, which are not f, but
Col 3:18 husbands, as is f in the Lord
2Th 1: 3 for you, brethren, as it is f
Phm 8 to command you what is f,
Heb 2:10 For it was f for Him, for
Heb 7:26 a High Priest was f for us

FIVE (*see* FIFTH)
Gen 5: 6 and f years, and begot Enosh
Gen 5:11 were nine hundred and f years
Gen 5:30 Noah, Lamech lived f hundred
Gen 5:32 Noah was f hundred years old,
Gen 11:11 Shem lived f hundred years,
Gen 11:32 f years, and Terah died in
Gen 14: 9 four kings against f
Gen 18:28 Suppose there were f less
Gen 18:28 all of the city for lack of f
Gen 43:34 was f times as much as any of
Gen 45: 6 there are still f years in
Gen 45:11 are still f years of famine
Gen 45:22 and f changes of garments
Gen 47: 2 he took f men from among his
Ex 22: 1 restore f oxen for an ox and
Ex 26: 3 F curtains shall be coupled
Ex 26: 3 the other f curtains shall be
Ex 26: 9 you shall couple f curtains

Ex 26:26 f for the boards on one side
Ex 26:27 f bars for the boards on the
Ex 26:27 f bars for the boards of the
Ex 26:37 f pillars of acacia wood, and
Ex 26:37 you shall cast f sockets of
Ex 27: 1 f cubits long and f cubits
Ex 27:18 and the height f cubits,
Ex 30:23 f hundred shekels of liquid
Ex 30:24 f hundred shekels of cassia,
Ex 36:10 he coupled f curtains to one
Ex 36:10 and the other f curtains he
Ex 36:16 He coupled f curtains by
Ex 36:31 f for the boards on one side
Ex 36:32 f bars for the boards on the
Ex 36:32 f bars for the boards of the
Ex 36:38 and its f pillars with their
Ex 36:38 but their f sockets were of
Ex 38: 1 f cubits was its length and
Ex 38: 1 length and f cubits its width
Ex 38:18 along its width was f cubits
Ex 38:26 f hundred and fifty men
Lev 26: 8 F of you shall chase a
Lev 27: 5 if from f years old up to
Lev 27: 6 a month old up to f years old
Lev 27: 6 shall be f shekels of silver
Num 1:21 forty-six thousand f hundred
Num 1:33 were forty thousand f hundred
Num 1:41 forty-one thousand f hundred
Num 1:46 and three thousand f hundred
Num 2:11 forty-six thousand f hundred
Num 2:19 at forty thousand f hundred
Num 2:28 forty-one thousand f hundred
Num 2:32 and three thousand f hundred
Num 3:22 were seven thousand f hundred
Num 3:47 you shall take f shekels for
Num 4:48 were eight thousand f hundred
Num 7:17 f rams, f male goats, and
Num 7:17 f male lambs in their first
Num 7:23 f rams, f male goats, and
Num 7:23 f male lambs in their first
Num 7:29 f rams, f male goats, and
Num 7:29 f male lambs in their first
Num 7:35 f rams, f male goats, and
Num 7:35 f male lambs in their first
Num 7:41 f rams, f male goats, and
Num 7:41 f male lambs in their first
Num 7:47 f rams, f male goats, and
Num 7:47 f male lambs in their first
Num 7:53 f rams, f male goats, and
Num 7:53 f male lambs in their first
Num 7:59 f rams, f male goats, and
Num 7:59 f male lambs in their first
Num 7:65 f rams, f male goats, and
Num 7:65 f male lambs in their first
Num 7:71 f rams, f male goats, and
Num 7:71 f male lambs in their first
Num 7:77 f rams, f male goats, and
Num 7:77 f male lambs in their first
Num 7:83 f rams, f male goats, and
Num 7:83 f male lambs in their first
Num 11:19 nor f days, nor ten days, nor
Num 18:16 for f shekels of silver,
Num 26:18 forty thousand f hundred
Num 26:22 thousand f hundred
Num 26:27 sixty thousand f hundred
Num 26:37 thirty-two thousand f hundred
Num 31: 8 Reba, the f kings of Midian
Num 31:28 one of every f hundred of the
Num 31:36 thousand f hundred sheep
Num 31:39 thirty thousand f hundred
Num 31:43 thousand f hundred sheep,
Num 31:45 thousand f hundred donkeys
Josh 8:12 he took about f thousand men
Josh 10: 5 Therefore the f kings of the
Josh 10:16 But these f kings had fled and
Josh 10:17 The f kings have been found
Josh 10:22 bring out those f kings to me
Josh 10:23 brought out those f kings to
Josh 10:26 and hanged them on f trees
Josh 13: 3 f lords of the Philistines
Judg 3: 3 f lords of the Philistines,
Judg 18: 2 f men of their family from
Judg 18: 7 So the f men departed and went
Judg 18:14 Then the f men who had gone
Judg 18:17 Then the f men who had gone
Judg 20:45 they cut down f thousand of
1Sa 6: 4 F golden tumors
1Sa 6: 4 and f golden rats
1Sa 6:16 So when the f lords of the
1Sa 6:18 belonging to the f lords,
1Sa 17: 5 f thousand shekels of bronze
1Sa 17:40 he chose for himself f smooth
1Sa 21: 3 Give me f loaves of bread in
1Sa 25:18 f sheep already dressed
1Sa 25:18 f seahs of roasted grain, one
1Sa 25:42 attended by f of her maidens
2Sa 4: 4 He was f years old when the
2Sa 21: 8 and the f sons of Michal the
2Sa 24: 9 were f hundred thousand men
1Ki 4:32 songs were one thousand and f
1Ki 6: 6 chamber was f cubits wide
1Ki 6:10 temple, each f cubits high
1Ki 6:24 of the cherub was f cubits
1Ki 6:24 wing of the cherub f cubits
1Ki 7:16 of one capital was f cubits
1Ki 7:16 other capital was f cubits
1Ki 7:23 Its height was f cubits, and a
1Ki 7:39 he put f carts on the right
1Ki 7:39 f on the left side of the
1Ki 7:49 f on the right side
1Ki 7:49 f on the left in front of the
1Ki 9:23 f hundred and fifty, who ruled
2Ki 6:25 for f shekels of silver
2Ki 7:13 let several men take f of the
2Ki 13:19 have struck f or six times
2Ki 25:19 f men of the king's close
1Ch 2: 4 All the sons of Judah were f
1Ch 2: 6 f of them in all
1Ch 3:20 f in all
1Ch 4:32 f cities
1Ch 4:42 f hundred men of the sons of
1Ch 7: 3 All f of them were chief men
1Ch 7: 7 f in all
1Ch 11:23 great height, f cubits tall
1Ch 29: 7 of God f thousand talents
2Ch 3:11 the one cherub was f cubits
2Ch 3:11 the other wing was f cubits
2Ch 3:12 the other cherub was f cubits
2Ch 3:12 other wing also was f cubits
2Ch 3:15 of each of them was f cubits
2Ch 4: 2 Its height was f cubits, and a
2Ch 4: 6 put f on the right side and
2Ch 4: 6 f on the left, to wash in
2Ch 4: 7 f on the right side
2Ch 4: 7 and f on the left
2Ch 4: 8 f on the right side
2Ch 4: 8 and f on the left
2Ch 6:13 bronze platform f cubits long
2Ch 6:13 f cubits broad, and three
2Ch 13:17 so f hundred thousand choice
2Ch 26:13 and seven thousand f hundred
2Ch 35: 9 for Passover offerings f
2Ch 35: 9 the flock and f hundred cattle
Ezra 1:11 silver were f thousand four
Ezra 2:69 f thousand minas of silver,
Neh 7:70 f hundred and thirty priestly
Esth 9: 6 and destroyed f hundred men
Esth 9:12 destroyed f hundred men in
Job 1: 3 f hundred yoke of oxen
Job 1: 3 f hundred female donkeys, and
Is 17: 6 bough, four or f in its most
Is 19:18 In that day f cities in the
Is 30:17 threat of f you shall flee
Jer 52:22 of one capital was f cubits
Ezek 40: 7 was a space of f cubits
Ezek 40:30 cubits long and f cubits wide
Ezek 40:48 f cubits on this side
Ezek 40:48 and f cubits on that side
Ezek 41: 2 were f cubits on this side
Ezek 41: 2 f cubits on the other side
Ezek 41: 9 side chambers was f cubits
Ezek 41:11 was f cubits all around
Ezek 41:12 was f cubits thick all around
Ezek 42:16 rod, f hundred rods by the
Ezek 42:17 side, f hundred rods by the
Ezek 42:18 side, f hundred rods by the
Ezek 42:19 measured f hundred rods by
Ezek 42:20 f hundred cubits long
Ezek 42:20 f hundred wide, to separate
Ezek 45: 2 f hundred by f hundred rods
Ezek 45: 6 of the city an area f
Ezek 48:15 The f thousand cubits in
Ezek 48:16 thousand f hundred cubits
Ezek 48:16 side four thousand f hundred
Ezek 48:16 side four thousand f hundred
Ezek 48:16 side four thousand f hundred
Ezek 48:30 thousand f hundred cubits
Ezek 48:32 side, four thousand f hundred
Ezek 48:33 thousand f hundred cubits
Ezek 48:34 side, four thousand f hundred
Matt 14:17 We have here only f loaves
Matt 14:19 And He took the f loaves and
Matt 14:21 were about f thousand men
Matt 16: 9 f loaves of the f thousand
Matt 25: 2 Now f of them were wise, and
Matt 25: 2 were wise, and f were foolish
Matt 25:15 And to one he gave f talents
Matt 25:16 received the f talents went
Matt 25:16 and made another f talents
Matt 25:20 had received f talents came
Matt 25:20 and brought f other talents,
Matt 25:20 you delivered to me f talents
Matt 25:20 I have gained f more talents
Mark 6:38 F, and two fish."
Mark 6:41 He had taken the f loaves
Mark 6:44 were about f thousand men
Mark 8:19 When I broke the f loaves for
Mark 8:19 loaves for the f thousand
Luke 1:24 and she hid herself f months
Luke 7:41 One owed f hundred denarii,
Luke 9:13 We have no more than f loaves
Luke 9:14 were about f thousand men
Luke 9:16 Then He took the f loaves
Luke 12: 6 Are not f sparrows sold for
Luke 12:52 For from now on f in one
Luke 14:19 I have bought f yoke of oxen
Luke 16:28 for I have f brothers, that
Luke 19:18 your mina has earned f minas
Luke 19:19 You also be over f cities
John 4:18 for you have had f husbands
John 5: 2 Bethesda, having f porches
John 6: 9 here who has f barley loaves
John 6:10 in number about f thousand
John 6:13 f barley loaves which were
Acts 4: 4 came to be about f thousand
Acts 20: 6 and in f days joined them at
Acts 24: 1 Now after f days Ananias the
1Co 14:19 f words with my understanding
1Co 15: 6 f hundred brethren at once
2Co 11:24 From the Jews f times I
Rev 9: 5 to torment them for f months
Rev 9:10 was to hurt men f months
Rev 17:10 F have fallen, one is, and the

FIX (*see* FIXED, FIXING)
1Ch 29:18 and f their heart toward You
Ezek 40: 4 f your mind on everything I

FIXED (*see* FIX)
Job 38:10 when I f My limit for it, and
Ps 10: 8 secretly f on the helpless
Prov 22:18 them all be f upon your lips
Ezek 20:24 their eyes were f on their
Luke 4:20 the synagogue were f on Him
Luke 16:26 you there is a great gulf f

FIXING (*see* FIX)
Acts 3: 4 f his eyes on him, with John,

FLAME (*see* FLAMES, FLAMING)
Ex 3: 2 LORD appeared to him in a f
Num 21:28 a f from the city of Sihon
Judg 13:20 as the f went up toward
Judg 13:20 in the f of the altar
Job 15:30 the f will dry out his
Job 18: 5 the f of his fire does not
Job 41:21 a f goes out of his mouth
Ps 83:14 as the f sets the mountains
Ps 104: 4 His ministers a f of fire
Ps 106:18 The f burned up the wicked
Song 8: 6 of fire, a most vehement f
Is 5:24 the f consumes the chaff, so
Is 10:17 fire, and his Holy One for a f
Is 29: 6 And the f of devouring fire
Is 30:30 the f of a devouring fire,
Is 43: 2 nor shall the f scorch you
Is 47:14 from the power of the f
Jer 48:45 a f from the midst of Sihon,
Ezek 20:47 the blazing f shall not be
Dan 3:22 hot, the f of the fire killed
Dan 7: 9 His throne was a fiery f, its
Dan 7:11 and given to the burning f
Dan 11:33 they shall fall by sword and f
Joel 1:19 a f has burned all the trees
Joel 2: 3 and behind them a f burns
Obad 18 and the house of Joseph a f
Luke 16:24 for I am tormented in this f
Acts 7:30 him in a f of fire in a bush
Heb 1: 7 and His ministers a f of fire
Rev 1:14 and His eyes like a f of fire
Rev 2:18 who has eyes like a f of fire
Rev 19:12 eyes were like a f of fire

FLAMES (*see* FLAME)
Ps 29: 7 LORD divides the f of fire
Song 8: 6 its f are f of fire, a
Is 13: 8 their faces will be like f
Is 66:15 and His rebuke with f of fire

FLAMING (*see* FLAME)
Gen 3:24 a f sword which turned every
Ps 105:32 rain, And f fire in their land
Is 4: 5 shining of a f fire by night
Lam 2: 3 a f fire which devours all
Hos 7: 6 it burns like a f fire
Joel 2: 5 like the noise of a f fire
Nah 2: 3 The chariots come with f
2Th 1: 8 in f fire taking vengeance on

FLANGES
1Ki 7:35 on the top of the cart, its f
1Ki 7:36 On the plates of its f and on

FLANKS
Lev 3: 4 fat that is on them by the f
Lev 3:10 fat that is on them by the f
Lev 3:15 fat that is on them by the f
Lev 4: 9 fat that is on them by the f
Lev 7: 4 fat that is on them by the f
Nah 2: 1 Strengthen your f

FLASH (*see* FLASHED, FLASHES, FLASHING)
Job 41:18 His sneezings f forth light
Ps 144: 6 F forth lightning and scatter
Ezek 1:14 like a f of lightning
Ezek 21:10 polished to f like lightning

FLASHED (*see* FLASH)
Ps 77:17 Your arrows also f about

FLASHES (*see* FLASH)
Ex 20:18 thunderings, the lightning f
Matt 24:27 f to the west, so also will
Luke 17:24 that f out of one part under

FLASHING (*see* FLASH)
Ezek 21:28 for consuming, for f
Hab 3: 4 He had rays f from His hand,
Zech 10: 1 the LORD will make f clouds

FLASK
1Sa 10: 1 Then Samuel took a f of oil
2Ki 9: 1 take this f of oil in your
2Ki 9: 3 Then take the f of oil, and
Jer 19: 1 and get a potter's earthen f
Jer 19:10 Then you shall break the f in
Matt 26: 7 to Him having an alabaster f
Mark 14: 3 f of very costly oil of
Mark 14: 3 And she broke the f and poured
Luke 7:37 alabaster f of fragrant oil

FLAT
Num 22:31 head and fell f on his face
Josh 6: 5 of the city will fall down f
Josh 6:20 that the wall fell down f

FLATTER (*see* FLATTERED, FLATTERING, FLATTERS, FLATTERY)
Job 32:21 nor let me f any man
Job 32:22 For I do not know how to f
Ps 5: 9 They f with their tongue

FLATTERED (*see* FLATTER)
Ps 78:36 Nevertheless they f Him with

FLATTERING (*see* FLATTER)
Ps 12: 2 With f lips and a double heart
Ps 12: 3 the LORD cut off all f lips
Prov 6:24 woman, from the f tongue of a
Prov 7:21 with her f lips she seduced
Prov 26:28 it, and a f mouth works ruin
Ezek 12:24 be any false vision or f
Rom 16:18 f speech deceive the hearts
1Th 2: 5 any time did we use f words
Jude 16 f people to gain advantage

FLATTERS (*see* FLATTER)
Ps 36: 2 For he f himself in his own
Prov 2:16 who f with her words,
Prov 7: 5 who f with her words
Prov 20:19 with one who f with his lips
Prov 28:23 than he who f with the tongue
Prov 29: 5 A man who f his neighbor

FLATTERY (*see* FLATTER)
Job 17: 5 He who speaks f to his
Dan 11:32 he shall corrupt with f

FLAVOR (*see* FLAVORLESS)
Matt 5:13 but if the salt loses its f
Mark 9:50 but if the salt loses its f
Luke 14:34 if the salt has lost its f

FLAVORLESS (*see* FLAVOR)
Job 6: 6 Can f food be eaten without

FLAX
Ex 9:31 Now the f and the barley were
Ex 9:31 the head and the f was in bud
Josh 2: 6 them with the stalks of f
Judg 15:14 on his arms became like f
Prov 31:13 She seeks wool and f, and
Is 19: 9 those who work in fine f and
Is 42: 3 smoking f He will not quench
Ezek 40: 3 He had a line of f and a
Matt 12:20 smoking f He will not quench,

FLAY
Mic 3: 3 f their skin from them, break

FLEA
1Sa 24:14 A dead dog? A f
1Sa 26:20 has come out to seek a f, as

FLED (*see* FLEE)
Gen 14:10 kings of Sodom and Gomorrah f
Gen 14:10 and the remainder f to the
Gen 16: 6 her, she f from her presence
Gen 31:21 So he f with all that he had
Gen 31:22 third day that Jacob had f
Gen 35: 1 appeared to you when you f
Gen 35: 7 he f from the face of his
Gen 39:12 his garment in her hand, and f
Gen 39:13 in her hand and f outside,
Gen 39:15 his garment with me, and f
Gen 39:18 garment with me and f outside
Ex 2:15 But Moses f from the face of
Ex 4: 3 and Moses f from it
Ex 14: 5 Egypt that the people had f
Num 16:34 around them f at their cry
Num 35:25 city of refuge where he had f
Num 35:26 the city of refuge where he f
Num 35:32 has f to his city of refuge
Josh 7: 4 but they f before the men of
Josh 8:15 them, and f by the way of the
Josh 8:20 the people who had f to the
Josh 10:11 as they f before Israel and
Josh 10:16 But these five kings had f
Josh 20: 6 to the city from which he f
Judg 1: 6 Then Adoni-Bezek f, and they
Judg 4:15 his chariot and f away on foot
Judg 4:17 Sisera had f away on foot to
Judg 7:21 army ran and cried out and f
Judg 7:22 the army f to Beth Acacia,
Judg 8:12 When Zebah and Zalmunna f,
Judg 9:21 And Jotham ran away and f
Judg 9:40 chased him, and he f from him
Judg 9:51 f there and shut themselves in
Judg 11: 3 Then Jephthah f from his
Judg 20:45 f toward the wilderness to
Judg 20:47 f toward the wilderness to
1Sa 4:10 and every man f to his tent
1Sa 4:16 I f today from the battle
1Sa 4:17 Israel has f before the
1Sa 14:22 heard that the Philistines f
1Sa 17:24 f from him and were dreadfully
1Sa 17:51 champion was dead, they f
1Sa 19: 8 blow, and they f from him
1Sa 19:10 So David f and escaped that
1Sa 19:12 And he went and f and escaped
1Sa 19:18 So David f and escaped, and
1Sa 20: 1 Then David f from Naioth in
1Sa 21:10 f that day from before Saul,
1Sa 22:17 because they knew when he f
1Sa 22:20 escaped and f after David
1Sa 23: 6 f to David at Keilah, that he
1Sa 27: 4 Saul that David had f to Gath
1Sa 30:17 men who rode on camels and f
1Sa 31: 1 and the men of Israel f from
1Sa 31: 7 that the men of Israel had f
1Sa 31: 7 they forsook the cities and f
2Sa 1: 4 people have f from the battle
2Sa 4: 3 the Beerothites f to Gittaim
2Sa 4: 4 and his nurse took him up and f
2Sa 10:13 Syrians, and they f before him
2Sa 10:14 they also f before Abishai,
2Sa 10:18 the Syrians f before Israel
2Sa 13:29 each one got on his mule and f
2Sa 13:34 Then Absalom f
2Sa 13:37 But Absalom f and went to
2Sa 13:38 So Absalom f and went to
2Sa 18:17 Then all Israel f, everyone
2Sa 19: 8 of Israel had f to his tent
2Sa 19: 9 now he has f from the land
2Sa 23:11 Then the people f from the
1Ki 2: 7 I f from Absalom your brother
1Ki 2:28 So Joab f to the tabernacle
1Ki 2:29 Joab has f to the tabernacle
1Ki 11:17 that Hadad f to go to Egypt,
1Ki 11:23 who had f from his lord,
1Ki 11:40 f to Egypt, to Shishak king
1Ki 12: 2 Egypt, for he had f from the
1Ki 20:20 so the Syrians f, and Israel
1Ki 20:30 But the rest f to Aphek, into
1Ki 20:30 And Ben-Hadad f and went into
2Ki 3:24 so that they f before them
2Ki 7: 7 f at twilight, and left the
2Ki 7: 7 and they f for their lives
2Ki 8:21 his people f to their tents
2Ki 9:10 And he opened the door and f
2Ki 9:23 Then Joram turned around and f
2Ki 9:27 he f by the road to Beth
2Ki 9:27 Then he f to Megiddo, and died
2Ki 14:12 and every man f to his tent
2Ki 14:19 Jerusalem, and he f to Lachish
2Ki 25: 4 all the men of war f at night
1Ch 10: 1 and the men of Israel f from
1Ch 10: 7 valley saw that they had f
1Ch 10: 7 forsook their cities and f
1Ch 11:13 And the people f from the
1Ch 19:14 Syrians, and they f before him
1Ch 19:15 they also f before Abishai
1Ch 19:18 the Syrians f before Israel
2Ch 10: 2 where he had f from the
2Ch 13:16 of Israel f before Judah, and
2Ch 14:12 and Judah, and the Ethiopians f
2Ch 25:22 and every man f to his tent
2Ch 25:27 Jerusalem, and he f to Lachish
Ps 104: 7 At Your rebuke they f
Ps 114: 3 The sea saw it and f
Ps 114: 5 ails you, O sea, that you f
Is 10:29 afraid, Gibeah of Saul has f
Is 10:31 Madmenah has f, the
Is 21:14 bread they met him who f
Is 21:15 For they f from the swords,
Is 22: 3 your rulers have f together
Is 22: 3 who have f from afar
Jer 4:25 birds of the heavens had f
Jer 9:10 heavens and the beasts have f
Jer 26:21 heard it, he was afraid and f
Jer 39: 4 of war saw them, that they f
Jer 46: 5 They have speedily f, And did
Jer 46:21 they have f away together
Jer 48:45 Those who f stood under the
Jer 52: 7 and all the men of war f and
Lam 4:15 When they f and wandered,
Dan 10: 7 them, so that they f to hide
Hos 7:13 them, for they have f from Me
Hos 12:12 Jacob f to the country of
Amos 5:19 as though a man f from a lion
Jon 1:10 he f from the presence of the
Jon 4: 2 Therefore I f previously to
Zech 14: 5 you shall flee as you f from
Matt 8:33 Then those who kept them f
Matt 26:56 disciples forsook Him and f
Mark 5:14 Now those who fed the swine f
Mark 14:50 they all forsook Him and f
Mark 14:52 cloth and f from them naked
Mark 16: 8 f from the tomb, for they
Luke 8:34 saw what had happened, they f
Acts 7:29 Then, at this saying, Moses f
Acts 14: 6 f to Lystra and Derbe, cities
Acts 16:27 supposing the prisoners had f
Acts 19:16 so that they f out of that
Heb 6:18 who have f for refuge to lay
Rev 12: 6 Then the woman f into the
Rev 16:20 Then every island f away, and
Rev 20:11 earth and the heaven f away

FLEE (*see* FLED, FLEEING, FLEES)
Gen 19:20 city is near enough to f to
Gen 27:43 f to my brother Laban in
Gen 31:20 him that he intended to f
Gen 31:27 Why did you f away secretly,
Ex 9:20 his livestock f to the houses
Ex 14:25 Let us f from the face of
Ex 21:13 you a place where he may f
Lev 26:17 and you shall f when no one
Lev 26:36 leaf shall cause them to f
Lev 26:36 they shall f as though
Num 10:35 who hate You f before You
Num 24:11 therefore, f to your place

Num 35: 6 to which a manslayer may f
Num 35:11 accidentally may f there
Num 35:15 accidentally may f there
Deut 4:42 the manslayer might f there
Deut 19: 3 any manslayer may f there
Deut 19: 5 he shall f to one of these
Deut 28: 7 and f before you seven ways
Deut 28:25 and f seven ways before them
Josh 8: 5 that we shall f before them
Josh 8: 6 we will f before them
Josh 8:20 to f this way or that way
Josh 20: 3 unintentionally may f there
Josh 20: 9 accidentally might f there
Judg 20:32 Let us f and draw them away
2Sa 4: 4 as she made haste to f, that
2Sa 15:14 Arise, and let us f
2Sa 17: 2 who are with him will f, and I
2Sa 18: 3 For if we f away, they will
2Sa 19: 3 away when they f in battle
2Sa 24:13 Or shall you f three months
1Ki 12:18 in haste to f to Jerusalem
2Ki 9: 3 Then open the door and f
2Ch 10:18 in haste to f to Jerusalem
Neh 6:11 Should such a man as I f
Job 9:25 they f away, they see no good
Job 20:24 He will f from the iron
Job 41:28 The arrow cannot make him f
Ps 11: 1 F as a bird to your mountain
Ps 31:11 who see me outside f from me
Ps 64: 8 All who see them shall f away
Ps 68: 1 who hate Him f before Him
Ps 68:12 Kings of armies f, they f,
Ps 139: 7 Or where can I f from Your
Prov 28: 1 The wicked f when no one
Prov 28:17 bloodshed will f into a pit
Song 2:17 breaks and the shadows f away
Song 4: 6 breaks and the shadows f away
Is 10: 3 To whom will you f for help
Is 13:14 everyone will f to his own
Is 15: 5 his fugitives shall f to Zoar
Is 17:13 them and they will f far away
Is 20: 6 wherever we f for help to be
Is 30:16 No, for we will f on horses"
Is 30:16 therefore you shall f
Is 30:17 One thousand shall f at the
Is 30:17 threat of five you shall f
Is 31: 8 But he shall f from the sword
Is 33: 3 the tumult the people shall f
Is 35:10 and sighing shall f away
Is 48:20 F from the Chaldees
Is 51:11 and sighing shall f away
Jer 4:29 The whole city shall f from
Jer 6: 1 gather yourselves to f from
Jer 25:35 will have no way to f, nor
Jer 46: 6 Do not let the swift f away
Jer 48: 6 F, save your lives
Jer 48: 9 wings to Moab, that she may f
Jer 49: 8 F, turn back, dwell in the
Jer 49:24 grown feeble And turns to f
Jer 49:30 F, get far away
Jer 50:16 everyone shall f to his own
Jer 50:28 The voice of those who f and
Jer 51: 6 F from the midst of Babylon,
Lam 1: 6 that f without strength
Amos 2:16 shall f naked in that day
Amos 7:12 F to the land of Judah
Jon 1: 3 But Jonah arose to f to
Nah 2: 8 of water, now they f away
Nah 3: 7 look upon you Will f from you
Nah 3:17 the sun rises they f away
Zech 2: 6 F from the land of the north,
Zech 14: 5 Then you shall f through My
Zech 14: 5 you shall f as you fled from
Matt 2:13 f to Egypt, and stay there
Matt 3: 7 Who has warned you to f from
Matt 10:23 in this city, f to another
Matt 24:16 in Judea f to the mountains
Mark 13:14 in Judea f to the mountains
Luke 3: 7 Who warned you to f from the
Luke 21:21 in Judea f to the mountains
John 10: 5 stranger, but will f from him
1Co 6:18 F sexual immorality
1Co 10:14 my beloved, f from idolatry
1Ti 6:11 God, f these things and pursue
2Ti 2:22 F also youthful lusts
Jas 4: 7 devil and he will f from you
Rev 9: 6 and death will f from them

FLEECE
Deut 18: 4 first of the f of your sheep
Judg 6:37 I shall put a f of wool on
Judg 6:37 if there is dew on the f only
Judg 6:38 and squeezed the f together
Judg 6:38 he wrung the dew out of the f
Judg 6:39 just once more with the f
Judg 6:39 it now be dry only on the f
Judg 6:40 It was dry on the f only, but
Job 31:20 warmed with the f of my sheep

FLEEING (*see* FLEE)
Gen 16: 8 I am f from the presence of
Ex 14:27 the Egyptians were f into it
Lev 26:36 flee as though f from a sword
Deut 4:42 that by f to one of these
Josh 8: 6 They are f before us as at
2Sa 10:14 saw that the Syrians were f
1Ch 19:15 saw that the Syrians were f
Job 26:13 hand pierced the f serpent
Job 30: 3 f late to the wilderness,
Is 27: 1 Leviathan the f serpent,

FLEES (*see* FLEE)
Deut 19: 4 of the manslayer who f there
Deut 19:11 he f to one of these cities,
Josh 20: 4 when he f to one of those
Job 14: 2 He f like a shadow and does
Job 27:22 he f desperately from its
Is 24:18 it shall be that he who f
Jer 48:19 Ask him who f and her who
Jer 48:44 He who f from the fear shall
Amos 9: 1 He who f from them shall not
John 10:12 and leaves the sheep and f
John 10:13 The hireling f because he is

FLEET (*see* FLEETING)
2Sa 2:18 Asahel was as f of foot as a
1Ki 9:26 a f of ships at Ezion Geber
1Ki 9:27 sent his servants with the f
1Ki 10:22 at sea with the f of Hiram

FLEETING (*see* FLEET)
Prov 21: 6 by a lying tongue is the f

FLESH (*see* FLESHHOOK, FLESHLY)
Gen 2:21 closed up the f in its place
Gen 2:23 of my bones and f of my f
Gen 2:24 and they shall become one f
Gen 6: 3 forever, for he is indeed f
Gen 6:12 for all f had corrupted their
Gen 6:13 The end of all f has come
Gen 6:17 from under heaven all f in
Gen 6:19 all f you shall bring two of
Gen 7:15 two, of all f in which is the
Gen 7:16 male and female of all f,
Gen 7:21 all f died that moved on the
Gen 8:17 of all f that is with you
Gen 9: 4 shall not eat f with its life
Gen 9:11 Never again shall all f be
Gen 9:15 living creature of all f
Gen 9:15 a flood to destroy all f
Gen 9:16 of all f that is on the earth
Gen 9:17 all f that is on the earth
Gen 17:11 in the f of your foreskins
Gen 17:13 covenant shall be in your f
Gen 17:14 in the f of his foreskin,
Gen 17:23 circumcised the f of their
Gen 17:24 in the f of his foreskin
Gen 17:25 in the f of his foreskin
Gen 29:14 you are my bone and my f
Gen 37:27 he is our brother and our f
Gen 40:19 will eat your f from you
Ex 4: 7 was restored like his other f
Ex 12: 8 shall eat the f on that night
Ex 12:46 of the f outside the house
Ex 21:28 and its f shall not be eaten
Ex 29:14 But the f of the bull, with
Ex 29:31 boil its f in the holy place
Ex 29:32 shall eat the f of the ram
Ex 29:34 And if any of the f of the
Ex 30:32 not be poured on man's f
Lev 4:11 the bull's hide and all its f
Lev 6:27 touches its f must be holy
Lev 7:15 The f of the sacrifice of
Lev 7:17 the remainder of the f of
Lev 7:18 And if any of the f of the
Lev 7:19 The f that touches any
Lev 7:19 And as for the clean f, all
Lev 7:20 the f of the sacrifice of the
Lev 7:21 and who eats the f of the
Lev 8:17 But the bull, its hide, its f
Lev 8:31 Boil the f at the door of the
Lev 8:32 What remains of the f and of
Lev 9:11 The f and the hide he burned
Lev 11: 8 Their f you shall not eat,
Lev 11:11 you shall not eat their f
Lev 12: 3 on the eighth day the f of
Lev 13:10 spot of raw f in the swelling
Lev 13:14 But when raw f appears on him
Lev 13:15 shall look at the raw f and
Lev 13:15 for the raw f is unclean
Lev 13:16 Or if the raw f changes and
Lev 13:24 the raw f of the burn becomes
Lev 16:27 the fire their skins, their f
Lev 17:11 life of the f is in the blood
Lev 17:14 for it is the life of all f
Lev 17:14 not eat the blood of any f
Lev 17:14 life of all f is its blood
Lev 19:28 in your f for the dead, nor
Lev 21: 5 make any cuttings in their f
Lev 26:29 shall eat the f of your sons
Lev 26:29 eat the f of your daughters
Num 12:12 whose f is half consumed when
Num 16:22 God of the spirits of all f
Num 18:15 first opens the womb of all f
Num 18:18 their f shall be yours, just
Num 19: 5 its hide, its f, its blood,
Num 27:16 God of the spirits of all f
Deut 5:26 For who is there of all f
Deut 14: 8 their f or touch their dead
Deut 28:53 the f of your sons and your
Deut 28:55 the f of his children whom he
Deut 32:42 and My sword shall devour f
Judg 8: 7 then I will tear your f with
Judg 9: 2 Remember that I am your own f
1Sa 17:44 I will give your f to the
2Sa 5: 1 we are your bone and your f
2Sa 19:12 you are my bone and my f
2Sa 19:13 Are you not my bone and my f
1Ki 19:21 them and boiled their f, using
2Ki 4:34 the f of the child became
2Ki 5:10 your f shall be restored to
2Ki 5:14 his f was restored like the
2Ki 5:14 like the f of a little child
2Ki 9:36 shall eat the f of Jezebel
1Ch 11: 1 we are your bone and your f
2Ch 32: 8 With him is an arm of f
Neh 5: 5 Yet now our f is as the f
Job 2: 5 and touch his bone and his f
Job 6:12 Or is my f bronze
Job 7: 5 My f is caked with worms and
Job 10: 4 Do You have eyes of f
Job 10:11 clothe me with skin and f, and
Job 13:14 do I take my f in my teeth
Job 14:22 But his f will be in pain
Job 19:20 clings to my skin and to my f
Job 19:22 are not satisfied with my f
Job 19:26 that in my f I shall see God,
Job 21: 6 trembling takes hold of my f
Job 33:21 His f wastes away from sight,
Job 33:25 His f shall be young like a
Job 34:15 All f would perish together,
Job 41:23 The folds of his f are joined
Ps 16: 9 My f also will rest in hope
Ps 27: 2 against me To eat up my f
Ps 38: 3 in my f Because of Your anger
Ps 38: 7 there is no soundness in my f
Ps 50:13 Will I eat the f of bulls
Ps 56: 4 What can f do to me
Ps 63: 1 My f longs for You In a dry
Ps 65: 2 To You all f will come
Ps 73:26 My f and my heart fail
Ps 78:39 that they were but f, A
Ps 79: 2 The f of Your saints to the
Ps 84: 2 my f cry out for the living
Ps 109:24 my f is feeble from lack of
Ps 119:120 My f trembles for fear of You
Ps 136:25 Who gives food to all f, For
Ps 145:21 all f shall bless His holy
Prov 3: 8 It will be health to your f
Prov 4:22 and health to all their f
Prov 5:11 mourn at last, when your f
Prov 11:17 is cruel troubles his own f
Eccl 2: 3 how to gratify my f with wine
Eccl 4: 5 hands and consumes his own f
Eccl 5: 6 mouth cause your f to sin
Eccl 11:10 and put away evil from your f
Eccl 12:12 study is wearisome to the f
Is 9:20 eat the f of his own arm
Is 17: 4 fatness of his f grow lean
Is 31: 3 and their horses are f, and not
Is 40: 5 all f shall see it together

Is 40: 6 All f is grass, and all its
Is 49:26 oppress you with their own f
Is 49:26 All f shall know that I, the
Is 58: 7 hide yourself from your own f
Is 65: 4 who eat swine's f, and the
Is 66:16 the LORD will judge all f
Is 66:17 the midst, eating swine's f
Is 66:23 all f shall come to worship
Is 66:24 be an abhorrence to all f
Jer 11:15 the holy f has passed from
Jer 12:12 no f shall have peace
Jer 17: 5 makes f his strength, whose
Jer 19: 9 to eat the f of their sons
Jer 19: 9 the f of their daughters, and
Jer 19: 9 everyone shall eat the f of
Jer 25:31 plead His case with all f
Jer 32:27 am the LORD, the God of all f
Jer 45: 5 will bring adversity on all f
Jer 51:35 my f be upon Babylon," the
Lam 3: 4 He has aged my f and my skin,
Ezek 4:14 nor has abominable f ever
Ezek 11:19 stony heart out of their f
Ezek 11:19 and give them a heart of f
Ezek 20:48 All f shall see that I, the
Ezek 21: 4 all f from south to north
Ezek 21: 5 that all f may know that I,
Ezek 23:20 whose f is like the f of
Ezek 32: 5 I will lay your f on the
Ezek 36:26 heart of stone out of your f
Ezek 36:26 and give you a heart of f
Ezek 37: 6 bring f upon you, cover you
Ezek 37: 8 the f came upon them, and the
Ezek 39:17 of Israel, that you may eat f
Ezek 39:18 shall eat the f of the mighty
Ezek 40:43 the f of the sacrifices was
Ezek 44: 7 heart and uncircumcised in f
Ezek 44: 9 heart or uncircumcised in f
Dan 1:15 and fatter in f than all the
Dan 2:11 whose dwelling is not with f
Dan 4:12 and all f was fed from it
Dan 7: 5 Arise, devour much f
Hos 8:13 My offerings they sacrifice f
Joel 2:28 pour out My Spirit on all f
Mic 3: 2 and the f from their bones
Mic 3: 3 also eat the f of My people
Mic 3: 3 pot, Like f in the caldron
Nah 2:12 with prey, and his dens with f
Zeph 1:17 dust, and their f like refuse
Zech 2:13 Be silent, all f, before the
Zech 11: 9 are left eat each other's f
Zech 11:16 he will eat the f of the fat
Zech 14:12 Their f shall dissolve while
Matt 16:17 you, Simon Bar-Jonah, for f
Matt 19: 5 the two shall become one f'
Matt 19: 6 are no longer two but one f
Matt 24:22 no f would be saved
Matt 26:41 is willing, but the f is weak
Mark 10: 8 the two shall become one f'
Mark 10: 8 are no longer two, but one f
Mark 13:20 days, no f would be saved
Mark 14:38 is ready, but the f is weak
Luke 3: 6 all f shall see the salvation
Luke 24:39 for a spirit does not have f
John 1:13 nor of the will of the f
John 1:14 And the Word became f and
John 3: 6 is born of the f is f
John 6:51 that I shall give is My f
John 6:52 this Man give us His f to eat
John 6:53 eat the f of the Son of Man
John 6:54 Whoever eats My f and drinks
John 6:55 For My f is food indeed, and
John 6:56 He who eats My f and drinks My
John 6:63 the f profits nothing
John 8:15 You judge according to the f
John 17: 2 Him authority over all f,
Acts 2:17 out of My Spirit on all f
Acts 2:26 moreover my f will also rest
Acts 2:30 his body, according to the f
Acts 2:31 nor did His f see corruption
Rom 1: 3 of David according to the f
Rom 2:28 which is outward in the f
Rom 3:20 no f will be justified in His
Rom 4: 1 has found according to the f
Rom 6:19 of the weakness of your f
Rom 7: 5 For when we were in the f
Rom 7:18 in my f) nothing good dwells
Rom 7:25 but with the f the law of sin
Rom 8: 1 not walk according to the f
Rom 8: 3 it was weak through the f
Rom 8: 3 in the likeness of sinful f
Rom 8: 3 He condemned sin in the f
Rom 8: 4 not walk according to the f
Rom 8: 5 the f set their minds on the
Rom 8: 5 minds on the things of the f
Rom 8: 8 in the f cannot please God
Rom 8: 9 in the f but in the Spirit
Rom 8:12 not to the f, to live
Rom 8:12 to live according to the f
Rom 8:13 to the f you will die
Rom 9: 3 my kinsmen according to the f
Rom 9: 5 from whom, according to the f
Rom 9: 8 who are the children of the f
Rom 11:14 jealousy those who are my f
Rom 13:14 make no provision for the f
1Co 1:26 many wise according to the f
1Co 1:29 that no f should glory in His
1Co 5: 5 for the destruction of the f
1Co 6:16 shall become one f
1Co 7:28 will have trouble in the f
1Co 10:18 Observe Israel after the f
1Co 15:39 All f is not the same f,
1Co 15:39 there is one kind of f of men
1Co 15:39 another f of beasts, another
1Co 15:50 this I say, brethren, that f
2Co 1:17 do I plan according to the f
2Co 3: 3 of stone but on tablets of f
2Co 4:11 be manifested in our mortal f
2Co 5:16 no one according to the f
2Co 5:16 Christ according to the f
2Co 7: 1 from all filthiness of the f
2Co 7: 5 our f had no rest, but we
2Co 10: 2 we walked according to the f
2Co 10: 3 For though we walk in the f
2Co 10: 3 do not war according to the f
2Co 11:18 many boast according to the f
2Co 12: 7 a thorn in the f was given to
Gal 1:16 not immediately confer with f
Gal 2:16 law no f shall be justified
Gal 2:20 which I now live in the f I
Gal 3: 3 being made perfect by the f
Gal 4:14 my f you did not despise or
Gal 4:23 was born according to the f
Gal 4:29 was born according to the f
Gal 5:13 as an opportunity for the f
Gal 5:16 not fulfill the lust of the f
Gal 5:17 For the f lusts against the
Gal 5:17 and the Spirit against the f
Gal 5:19 works of the f are evident
Gal 5:24 the f with its passions and
Gal 6: 8 his f will of the f reap
Gal 6:12 make a good showing in the f
Gal 6:13 that they may glory in your f
Eph 2: 3 in the lusts of our f,
Eph 2: 3 the desires of the f and of
Eph 2:11 you, once Gentiles in the f
Eph 2:11 made in the f by hands
Eph 2:15 abolished in His f the enmity
Eph 5:29 no one ever hated his own f
Eph 5:30 members of His body, of His f
Eph 5:31 and the two shall become one f
Eph 6: 5 masters according to the f
Eph 6:12 we do not wrestle against f
Phil 1:22 But if I live on in the f
Phil 1:24 to remain in the f is more
Phil 3: 3 have no confidence in the f
Phil 3: 4 have confidence in the f
Phil 3: 4 may have confidence in the f
Col 1:22 body of His f through death
Col 1:24 and fill up in my f what is
Col 2: 1 not seen my face in the f
Col 2: 5 though I am absent in the f
Col 2:11 the body of the sins of the f
Col 2:13 the uncircumcision of your f
Col 2:23 the indulgence of the f
Col 3:22 masters according to the f
1Ti 3:16 God was manifested in the f
Phm 16 more to you, both in the f
Heb 2:14 children have partaken of f
Heb 5: 7 who, in the days of His f
Heb 9:13 for the purifying of the f
Heb 10:20 the veil, that is, His f,
Jas 5: 3 and will eat your f like fire
1Pe 1:24 All f is as grass, and all the
1Pe 3:18 the f but made alive by the
1Pe 3:21 removal of the filth of the f
1Pe 4: 1 suffered for us in the f, arm
1Pe 4: 1 in the f has ceased from sin
1Pe 4: 2 in the f for the lusts of men
1Pe 4: 6 according to men in the f
2Pe 2:10 who walk according to the f
2Pe 2:18 through the lusts of the f
1Jn 2:16 the lust of the f, the lust
1Jn 4: 2 has come in the f is of God
1Jn 4: 3 come in the f is not of God
2Jn 7 Christ as coming in the f
Jude 7 and gone after strange f, are
Jude 8 these dreamers defile the f
Jude 23 the garment defiled by the f
Rev 17:16 desolate and naked, eat her f
Rev 19:18 you may eat the f of kings
Rev 19:18 the f of captains
Rev 19:18 the f of mighty men
Rev 19:18 the f of horses and of those
Rev 19:18 the f of all people, free and
Rev 19:21 were filled with their f

FLESHHOOK (*see* FLESH)
1Sa 2:13 come with a three-pronged f
1Sa 2:14 all that the f brought up

FLESHLY (*see* FLESH)
Ezek 16:26 your very f neighbors, and
2Co 1:12 not with f wisdom but by the
Col 2:18 puffed up by his f mind,
Heb 7:16 to the law of a f commandment
Heb 9:10 f ordinances imposed until
1Pe 2:11 abstain from f lusts which

FLEW (*see* FLY)
2Sa 22:11 He rode upon a cherub, and f
Ps 18:10 He rode upon a cherub, and f
Ps 18:10 He f upon the wings of the
Is 6: 2 his feet, and with two he f
Is 6: 6 one of the seraphim f to me

FLIES (*see* FLY)
Ex 8:21 will send swarms of f on you
Ex 8:21 shall be full of swarms of f
Ex 8:22 no swarms of f shall be there
Ex 8:24 Thick swarms of f came into
Ex 8:24 because of the swarms of f
Ex 8:29 that the swarms of f may
Ex 8:31 the swarms of f from Pharaoh
Deut 4:17 winged bird that f in the air
Deut 14:19 that f is unclean for you
Deut 28:49 as swift as the eagle f, a
Ps 78:45 sent swarms of f among them
Ps 91: 5 of the arrow that f by day
Ps 105:31 and there came swarms of f
Eccl 10: 1 Dead f putrefy the perfumer's
Nah 3:16 The locust plunders and f away

FLIGHT (*see* FLY)
Lev 26: 8 shall put ten thousand to f
Deut 32:30 and two put ten thousand to f
1Ch 12:15 they put to f all those in
Eccl 10:20 and a bird in f may tell the
Is 52:12 out with haste, nor go by f
Amos 2:14 Therefore f shall perish from
Matt 24:20 pray that your f may not be
Mark 13:18 pray that your f may not be
Heb 11:34 turned to f the armies of the

FLINT (*see* FLINTY)
Deut 8:15 for you out of the rock of f
Josh 5: 2 Make f knives for yourself,
Josh 5: 3 So Joshua made f knives for
Job 28: 9 He puts his hand on the f
Ps 114: 8 The f into a fountain of
Is 5:28 hooves will seem like f, and
Is 50: 7 I have set My face like a f
Ezek 3: 9 adamant stone, harder than f
Zech 7:12 they made their hearts like f

FLINTY (*see* FLINT)
Deut 32:13 rock, and oil from the f rock

FLITTING
Prov 26: 2 Like a f sparrow, like a

FLOAT
1Ki 5: 9 I will f them in rafts by sea
2Ki 6: 6 and he made the iron f

FLOCK (*see* FLOCKS)
Gen 4: 4 of the firstlings of his f
Gen 21:28 lambs of the f by themselves
Gen 27: 9 Go now to the f and bring me
Gen 29:10 watered the f of Laban his
Gen 30:32 pass through all your f today
Gen 30:40 the brown in the f of Laban
Gen 30:40 not put them with Laban's f
Gen 31: 4 Leah to the field, to his f
Gen 31:38 not eaten the rams of your f
Gen 31:41 and six years for your f, and

Gen 31:43 and this **f** is my **f**
Gen 33:13 one day, all the **f** will die
Gen 37: 2 was feeding the **f** with his
Gen 37:12 their father's **f** in Shechem
Gen 37:13 feeding the **f** in Shechem
Gen 38:17 you a young goat from the **f**
Ex 2:16 to water their father's **f**
Ex 2:17 them, and watered their **f**
Ex 2:19 water for us and watered the **f**
Ex 3: 1 Now Moses kept the **f** of
Ex 3: 1 he led the **f** to the back of
Lev 1: 2 of the herd and of the **f**
Lev 3: 6 to the LORD is of the **f**,
Lev 5: 6 sinned, a female from the **f**
Lev 5:18 without blemish from the **f**
Lev 6: 6 without blemish from the **f**
Lev 27:32 tithe of the herd or the **f**
Num 15: 3 LORD, from the herd or the **f**
Deut 7:13 and the offspring of your **f**
Deut 12:17 of your herd or your **f**, of
Deut 12:21 from your **f** which the LORD
Deut 15:14 him liberally from your **f**
Deut 15:19 your **f** you shall sanctify to
Deut 15:19 shear the firstborn of your **f**
Deut 16: 2 the LORD your God, from the **f**
Deut 32:14 the cattle, and milk of the **f**
1Sa 17:34 and took a lamb out of the **f**
2Sa 12: 4 to take from his own **f** and
2Ch 35: 7 and young goats from the **f**
2Ch 35: 8 six hundred from the **f**, and
2Ch 35: 9 five thousand from the **f** and
Ezra 10:19 **f** as their trespass offering
Job 21:11 their little ones like a **f**
Job 30: 1 to put with the dogs of my **f**
Ps 77:20 like a **f** By the hand of Moses
Ps 78:52 in the wilderness like a **f**
Ps 80: 1 You who lead Joseph like a **f**
Ps 107:41 makes their families like a **f**
Song 1: 7 I love, where you feed your **f**
Song 1: 8 in the footsteps of the **f**
Song 2:16 He feeds his **f** among the
Song 4: 1 hair is like a **f** of goats
Song 4: 2 Your teeth are like a **f** of
Song 6: 2 to feed his **f** in the gardens,
Song 6: 3 He feeds his **f** among the
Song 6: 5 Your hair is like a **f** of
Song 6: 6 Your teeth are like a **f** of
Is 40:11 feed His **f** like a shepherd
Is 63:11 with the shepherd of His **f**
Jer 13:17 because the LORD's **f** has been
Jer 13:20 Where is the **f** that was given
Jer 23: 2 You have scattered My **f**,
Jer 23: 3 gather the remnant of My **f**
Jer 25:34 ashes, you leaders of the **f**
Jer 25:35 leaders of the **f** to escape
Jer 25:36 to the **f** will be heard
Jer 31:10 him as a shepherd does his **f**
Jer 31:12 oil, for the young of the **f**
Jer 49:20 of the **f** shall draw them out
Jer 50:45 of the **f** shall draw them out
Jer 51:23 pieces the shepherd and his **f**
Ezek 24: 5 take the choice of the **f**
Ezek 34: 3 but you do not feed the **f**
Ezek 34: 6 My **f** was scattered over the
Ezek 34: 8 because My **f** became a prey
Ezek 34: 8 My **f** became food for every
Ezek 34: 8 My shepherds search for My **f**
Ezek 34: 8 and did not feed My **f**"
Ezek 34:10 require My **f** at their hand
Ezek 34:10 My **f** from their mouths, that
Ezek 34:12 **f** on the day he is among his
Ezek 34:15 I will feed My **f**, and I will
Ezek 34:17 And as for you, O My **f**, thus
Ezek 34:19 And as for My **f**, they eat what
Ezek 34:22 therefore I will save My **f**
Ezek 34:31 My **f**, the **f** of My pasture
Ezek 36:37 increase their men like a **f**
Ezek 36:38 Like a **f** offered as holy
Ezek 36:38 like the **f** at Jerusalem on
Ezek 43:23 and a ram from the **f** without
Ezek 43:25 bull and a ram from the **f**,
Ezek 45:15 given from a **f** of two hundred
Amos 6: 4 couches, eat lambs from the **f**
Amos 7:15 took me as I followed the **f**
Jon 3: 7 man nor beast, herd nor **f**
Mic 2:12 like a **f** in the midst of
Mic 4: 8 And you, O tower of the **f**, the
Mic 5: 4 feed His **f** in the strength of
Mic 7:14 the **f** of Your heritage, who
Hab 3:17 though the **f** be cut off from
Zech 9:16 day, as the **f** of His people
Zech 10: 3 of hosts will visit His **f**
Zech 11: 4 Feed the **f** for slaughter,
Zech 11: 7 So I fed the **f** for slaughter,
Zech 11: 7 particular the poor of the **f**
Zech 11: 7 and I fed the **f**
Zech 11:11 Thus the poor of the **f**, who
Zech 11:17 shepherd, who leaves the **f**
Mal 1:14 who has in his **f** a male, and
Matt 26:31 the sheep of the **f** will be
Luke 2: 8 watch over their **f** by night
Luke 12:32 Do not fear, little **f**, for it
John 10:16 and there will be one **f** and one
Acts 20:28 to yourselves and to all the **f**
Acts 20:29 among you, not sparing the **f**
1Co 9: 7 Or who tends a **f** and does not
1Co 9: 7 drink of the milk of the **f**
1Pe 5: 2 Shepherd the **f** of God which
1Pe 5: 3 but being examples to the **f**

FLOCKS (*see* FLOCK)
Gen 13: 5 who went with Abram, had **f**
Gen 24:35 and He has given him **f** and
Gen 26:14 for he had possessions of **f**
Gen 29: 2 there were three **f** of sheep
Gen 29: 2 that well they watered the **f**
Gen 29: 3 Now all the **f** would be
Gen 29: 8 the **f** are gathered together
Gen 30:31 again feed and keep your **f**
Gen 30:36 fed the rest of Laban's **f**
Gen 30:38 before the **f** in the gutters
Gen 30:38 where the **f** came to drink
Gen 30:39 So the **f** conceived before the
Gen 30:39 the **f** brought forth streaked,
Gen 30:40 made the **f** face toward the
Gen 30:40 put his own **f** by themselves
Gen 30:42 But when the **f** were feeble
Gen 30:43 prosperous, and had large **f**
Gen 31: 8 then all the **f** bore speckled
Gen 31: 8 then all the **f** bore streaked
Gen 31:10 the time when the **f** conceived
Gen 31:10 upon the **f** were streaked,
Gen 31:12 leap on the **f** are streaked
Gen 32: 5 I have oxen, donkeys, **f**, and
Gen 32: 7 that were with him, and the **f**
Gen 33:13 children are weak, and the **f**
Gen 37:14 brothers and well with the **f**
Gen 37:16 they are feeding their **f**
Gen 45:10 children's children, your **f**
Gen 46:32 and they have brought their **f**
Gen 47: 1 and my brothers, their **f** and
Gen 47: 4 have no pasture for their **f**
Gen 47:17 for the horses, the **f**, the
Gen 50: 8 their little ones, their **f**
Ex 10: 9 and our daughters, with our **f**
Ex 10:24 only let your **f** and your herds
Ex 12:32 Also take your **f** and your
Ex 12:38 went up with them also, and **f**
Ex 34: 3 let neither **f** nor herds feed
Lev 1:10 if his offering is of the **f**
Lev 5:15 without blemish from the **f**
Num 11:22 Shall **f** and herds be
Num 31: 9 all their cattle, all their **f**
Num 32:26 little ones, our wives, our **f**
Deut 8:13 and your **f** multiply, and your
Deut 12: 6 firstlings of your herds and **f**
Deut 14:23 of your herds and your **f**, that
Deut 28: 4 and the offspring of your **f**
Deut 28:18 and the offspring of your **f**
Deut 28:51 or the offspring of your **f**
Judg 5:16 to hear the pipings for the **f**
1Sa 30:20 Then David took all the **f**
2Sa 12: 2 man had exceedingly many **f**
1Ki 20:27 like two little **f** of goats
1Ch 4:39 to seek pasture for their **f**
1Ch 4:41 was pasture for their **f** there
1Ch 27:31 the Hagerite was over the **f**
2Ch 17:11 and the Arabians brought him **f**
2Ch 32:28 of livestock, and folds for **f**
2Ch 32:29 himself, and possessions of **f**
Neh 10:36 of our herds and our **f**, to the
Job 24: 2 they seize **f** violently and
Ps 65:13 pastures are clothed with **f**
Ps 78:48 their **f** to fiery lightning
Prov 27:23 to know the state of your **f**
Eccl 2: 7 and **f** than all who were in
Song 1: 7 by the **f** of your companions
Is 17: 2 will be for **f** which lie down
Is 32:14 wild donkeys, a pasture of **f**
Is 60: 7 All the **f** of Kedar shall be
Is 61: 5 shall stand and feed your **f**
Is 65:10 Sharon shall be a fold of **f**
Jer 3:24 their **f** and their herds, their
Jer 5:17 They shall eat up your **f** and
Jer 6: 3 their **f** shall come to her
Jer 10:21 and all their **f** shall be
Jer 31:24 and those going out with **f**
Jer 33:12 causing their **f** to lie down
Jer 33:13 the **f** shall again pass under
Jer 49:29 their **f** they shall take away
Jer 50: 8 be like the rams before the **f**
Ezek 25: 5 Ammon a resting place for **f**
Ezek 34: 2 not the shepherds feed the **f**
Ezek 36:38 be filled with **f** of men
Hos 5: 6 With their **f** and herds they
Joel 1:18 even the **f** of sheep suffer
Mic 5: 8 a young lion among **f** of sheep
Zeph 2: 6 for shepherds and folds for **f**
Zeph 2: 7 they shall feed their **f** there
Zeph 3:13 for they shall feed their **f**

FLOOD (*see* FLOODED, FLOODING, FLOODS, FLOODWATER)
Gen 6:17 the **f** of waters on the earth
Gen 7: 6 **f** of waters was on the earth
Gen 7: 7 of the waters of the **f**
Gen 7:10 of the **f** were on the earth
Gen 7:17 Now the **f** was on the earth
Gen 9:11 off by the waters of the **f**
Gen 9:11 be a **f** to destroy the earth
Gen 9:15 a **f** to destroy all flesh
Gen 9:28 after the **f** three hundred
Gen 10: 1 were born to them after the **f**
Gen 10:32 on the earth after the **f**
Gen 11:10 two years after the **f**
Job 22:16 were swept away by a **f**
Job 27:20 Terrors overtake him like a **f**
Ps 29:10 LORD sat enthroned at the **F**
Ps 32: 6 Surely in a **f** of great waters
Ps 74:15 open the fountain and the **f**
Ps 90: 5 You carry them away like a **f**
Is 28: 2 like a **f** of mighty waters
Is 59:19 the enemy comes in like a **f**
Jer 46: 7 is this coming up like a **f**
Jer 46: 8 Egypt rises up like a **f**, and
Jer 47: 2 and shall be an overflowing **f**
Dan 9:26 end of it shall be with a **f**
Dan 11:22 With the force of a **f** they
Nah 1: 8 But with an overflowing **f** He
Matt 24:38 as in the days before the **f**
Matt 24:39 did not know until the **f** came
Luke 6:48 And when the **f** arose, the
Luke 17:27 the **f** came and destroyed them
1Pe 4: 4 in the same **f** of dissipation
2Pe 2: 5 bringing in the **f** on the
Rev 12:15 like a **f** after the woman,
Rev 12:15 to be carried away by the **f**
Rev 12:16 swallowed up the **f** which the

FLOODED (*see* FLOOD)
Joel 3:18 Judah shall be **f** with water
2Pe 3: 6 perished, being **f** with water

FLOODING (*see* FLOOD)
Jer 12: 5 you do in the **f** of the Jordan
Jer 49:19 up like a lion from the **f** of
Jer 50:44 up like a lion from the **f** of
Ezek 13:11 There will be **f** rain, and you,
Ezek 13:13 shall be a **f** rain in My anger
Ezek 38:22 **f** rain, great hailstones,

FLOODS (*see* FLOOD)
Ex 15: 8 the **f** stood upright like a
2Sa 22: 5 the **f** of ungodliness made me
Ps 18: 4 the **f** of ungodliness made me
Ps 69: 2 Where the **f** overflow me
Ps 93: 3 The **f** have lifted up, O LORD,
Ps 93: 3 The **f** have lifted up their
Ps 93: 3 The **f** lift up their waves
Song 8: 7 love, nor can the **f** drown it
Is 44: 3 and **f** on the dry ground
Jon 2: 3 seas, and the **f** surrounded me
Matt 7:25 the **f** came, and the winds blew
Matt 7:27 the **f** came, and the winds blew

FLOODWATER (*see* FLOOD)
Ps 69:15 Let not the **f** overflow me

FLOOR (*see* FLOORS)
Gen 50:10 to the threshing **f** of Atad
Gen 50:11 at the threshing **f** of Atad
Num 5:17 is on the **f** of the tabernacle
Num 15:20 offering of the threshing **f**
Num 18:27 the grain of the threshing **f**

Num 18:30 produce of the threshing **f**
Deut 15:14 flock, from your threshing **f**
Deut 16:13 from your threshing **f** and from
Judg 3:25 master, fallen dead on the **f**
Judg 6:37 of wool on the threshing **f**
Ruth 3: 2 tonight at the threshing **f**
Ruth 3: 3 and go down to the threshing **f**
Ruth 3: 6 went down to the threshing **f**
Ruth 3:14 woman came to the threshing **f**
2Sa 24:16 **f** of Araunah the Jebusite
2Sa 24:18 **f** of Araunah the Jebusite
2Sa 24:21 buy the threshing **f** from you
2Sa 24:24 David bought the threshing **f**
1Ki 6:15 from the **f** of the temple to
1Ki 6:15 and he covered the **f** of the
1Ki 6:16 from **f** to ceiling, with cedar
1Ki 6:30 And the **f** of the temple he
1Ki 7: 7 with cedar from **f** to ceiling
1Ki 22:10 at a threshing **f** at the
1Ki 22:35 onto the **f** of the chariot
2Ki 6:27 From the threshing **f** or from
1Ch 13: 9 came to Chidon's threshing **f**
1Ch 21:15 **f** of Ornan the Jebusite
1Ch 21:18 **f** of Ornan the Jebusite
1Ch 21:21 went out from the threshing **f**
1Ch 21:22 the place of this threshing **f**
1Ch 21:28 him on the threshing **f** of
2Ch 3: 1 **f** of Ornan the Jebusite
2Ch 18: 9 they sat at a threshing **f** at
2Ch 34:11 to **f** the houses which the
Job 39:12 gather it to your threshing **f**
Is 21:10 and the grain of my **f**
Jer 51:33 **f** when it is time to thresh
Ezek 41:20 From the **f** to the space above
Hos 9: 1 reward on every threshing **f**
Hos 9: 2 The threshing **f** and the
Hos 13: 3 blown off from a threshing **f**
Mic 4:12 sheaves to the threshing **f**
Matt 3:12 purge His threshing **f**, and
Luke 3:17 purge His threshing **f**, and

FLOORS (*see* FLOOR)
1Sa 23: 1 are robbing the threshing **f**
Dan 2:35 from the summer threshing **f**
Joel 2:24 The threshing **f** shall be full

FLOUR
Ex 29: 2 shall make them of wheat **f**)
Ex 29:40 **f** mixed with one-fourth of a
Lev 2: 1 offering shall be of fine **f**
Lev 2: 2 from it his handful of fine **f**
Lev 2: 4 of fine **f** mixed with oil, or
Lev 2: 5 a pan, it shall be of fine **f**
Lev 2: 7 be made of fine **f** with oil
Lev 5:11 of fine **f** as a sin offering
Lev 6:15 fine **f** of the grain offering
Lev 6:20 of an ephah of fine **f** as a
Lev 7:12 blended **f** mixed with oil
Lev 14:10 of an ephah of fine **f** mixed
Lev 14:21 of an ephah of fine **f** mixed
Lev 23:13 of fine **f** mixed with oil, an
Lev 23:17 They shall be of fine **f**
Lev 24: 5 And you shall take fine **f** and
Num 6:15 cakes of fine **f** mixed with
Num 7:13 **f** mixed with oil as a grain
Num 7:19 **f** mixed with oil as a grain
Num 7:25 **f** mixed with oil as a grain
Num 7:31 **f** mixed with oil as a grain
Num 7:37 **f** mixed with oil as a grain
Num 7:43 **f** mixed with oil as a grain
Num 7:49 **f** mixed with oil as a grain
Num 7:55 **f** mixed with oil as a grain
Num 7:61 **f** mixed with oil as a grain
Num 7:67 **f** mixed with oil as a grain
Num 7:73 **f** mixed with oil as a grain
Num 7:79 **f** mixed with oil as a grain
Num 8: 8 of fine **f** mixed with oil, and
Num 15: 4 of an ephah of fine **f** mixed
Num 15: 6 of an ephah of fine **f** mixed
Num 15: 9 of an ephah of fine **f** mixed
Num 28: 5 of an ephah of fine **f** as a
Num 28: 9 of fine **f** as a grain offering
Num 28:12 of fine **f** as a grain offering
Num 28:12 of fine **f** as a grain offering
Num 28:13 of an ephah of fine **f**, mixed
Num 28:20 be of fine **f** mixed with oil
Num 28:28 of fine **f** mixed with oil
Num 29: 3 be fine **f** mixed with oil
Num 29: 9 be of fine **f** mixed with oil
Num 29:14 be of fine **f** mixed with oil
Judg 6:19 bread from an ephah of **f**
1Sa 1:24 three bulls, one ephah of **f**
1Sa 28:24 And she took **f** and kneaded it,
2Sa 13: 8 Then she took **f** and kneaded it
2Sa 17:28 vessels and wheat, barley and **f**
1Ki 4:22 day was thirty kors of fine **f**
1Ki 17:12 only a handful of **f** in a bin
1Ki 17:14 The bin of **f** shall not be
1Ki 17:16 The bin of **f** was not used up,
2Ki 4:41 Then bring some **f**
2Ki 7: 1 this time a seah of fine **f**
2Ki 7:16 So a seah of fine **f** was sold
2Ki 7:18 a seah of fine **f** for a shekel
1Ch 9:29 sanctuary, and over the fine **f**
1Ch 12:40 provisions of **f** and cakes of
1Ch 23:29 and the fine **f** for the grain
Is 28:28 Bread **f** must be ground
Ezek 16:13 You ate pastry of fine **f**,
Ezek 16:19 the pastry of fine **f**, oil, and
Ezek 46:14 of oil to moisten the fine **f**
Rev 18:13 wine and oil, fine **f** and wheat

FLOURISH (*see* FLOURISHED, FLOURISHES, FLOURISHING)
Job 8:11 Can the reeds **f** without water
Ps 72: 7 days the righteous shall **f**
Ps 72:16 **f** like grass of the earth
Ps 92: 7 all the workers of iniquity **f**
Ps 92:12 shall **f** like a palm tree, He
Ps 92:13 **f** in the courts of our God
Ps 132:18 Himself His crown shall **f**
Prov 11:28 righteous will **f** like foliage
Prov 14:11 tent of the upright will **f**
Is 17:11 you will make your seed to **f**
Is 66:14 your bones shall **f** like grass
Ezek 17:24 tree and made the dry tree **f**

FLOURISHED (*see* FLOURISH)
Phil 4:10 your care for me has **f** again

FLOURISHES (*see* FLOURISH)
Ps 90: 6 In the morning it **f** and grows
Ps 103:15 flower of the field, so he **f**

FLOURISHING (*see* FLOURISH)
Ps 92:14 They shall be fresh and **f**,
Dan 4: 4 my house, and **f** in my palace

FLOW (*see* FLOWED, FLOWING, FLOWS)
Lev 12: 7 clean from the **f** of her blood
Lev 20:18 he has discovered her **f**, and
Lev 20:18 uncovered the **f** of her blood
Deut 8: 7 that **f** out of valleys and
Job 6:17 it is warm, they cease to **f**
Job 20:28 his goods will **f** away in the
Ps 58: 7 Let them **f** away as waters
Ps 104:10 Which **f** among the hills
Ps 147:18 wind to blow, and the waters **f**
Song 4:16 that its spices may **f** out
Is 2: 2 and all nations shall **f** to it
Is 8: 6 of Shiloah that **f** softly, and
Is 48:21 to **f** from the rock for them
Jer 14:17 Let my eyes **f** with tears
Lam 3:49 My eyes **f** and do not cease,
Ezek 32: 6 land with the **f** of your blood
Joel 3:18 the hills shall **f** with milk
Joel 3:18 a fountain shall **f** from the
Amos 9:13 all the hills shall **f** with it
Mic 4: 1 and peoples shall **f** to it
Zech 14: 8 waters shall **f** from Jerusalem
Matt 9:20 a woman who had a **f** of blood
Mark 5:25 a **f** of blood for twelve years
Luke 8:43 having a **f** of blood for
Luke 8:44 immediately her **f** of blood
John 7:38 said, out of his heart will **f**

FLOWED (*see* FLOW)
Josh 4:18 and **f** over all its banks as
Lam 3:54 The waters **f** over my head

FLOWER (*see* FLOWERS)
Ex 25:33 an ornamental knob and a **f**
Ex 25:33 an ornamental knob and a **f**
Ex 25:34 with its ornamental knob and **f**
Ex 37:19 an ornamental knob and a **f**
Ex 37:19 an ornamental knob and a **f**
Ex 37:20 with its ornamental knob and **f**
1Sa 2:33 die in the **f** of their age
Job 14: 2 He comes forth like a **f** and
Ps 103:15 As a **f** of the field, so he
Is 18: 5 grape is ripening in the **f**
Is 28: 1 **f** which is at the head of the
Is 28: 4 **f** which is at the head of the
Is 40: 6 is like the **f** of the field
Is 40: 7 the **f** fades, because the
Is 40: 8 the **f** fades, but the word of
Nah 1: 4 and the **f** of Lebanon wilts
1Co 7:36 is past the **f** of her youth
Jas 1:10 because as a **f** of the field
Jas 1:11 its **f** falls, and its beautiful
1Pe 1:24 of man as the **f** of the grass
1Pe 1:24 withers, and its **f** falls away,

FLOWERS (*see* FLOWER)
Ex 25:31 and **f** shall be of one piece
Ex 37:17 its **f** were of the same piece
Num 8: 4 to its **f** it was hammered work
1Ki 6:18 ornamental buds and open **f**
1Ki 6:29 palm trees, and open **f**
1Ki 6:32 palm trees, and open **f**, and
1Ki 6:35 open **f** on them, and overlaid
1Ki 7:49 inner sanctuary, with the **f**
2Ch 4:21 with the **f** and the lamps and
Song 2:12 The **f** appear on the earth

FLOWING (*see* FLOW)
Ex 3: 8 land, to a land **f** with milk
Ex 3:17 to a land **f** with milk and
Ex 13: 5 a land **f** with milk and honey,
Ex 33: 3 Go up to a land **f** with milk
Lev 20:24 a land **f** with milk and honey
Num 16:13 up out of a land **f** with milk
Num 16:14 us into a land **f** with milk
Deut 6: 3 a land **f** with milk and honey
Deut 11: 9 a land **f** with milk and honey
Deut 21: 4 down to a valley with **f** water
Deut 26: 9 a land **f** with milk and honey"
Deut 26:15 a land **f** with milk and honey
Deut 27: 3 a land **f** with milk and honey,
Deut 31:20 them to the land **f** with milk
Josh 5: 6 a land **f** with milk and honey
Job 20:17 the rivers **f** with honey and
Prov 18: 4 of wisdom is a **f** brook
Is 66:12 the Gentiles like a **f** stream
Jer 11: 5 give them a land **f** with milk
Jer 18:14 Will the cold **f** waters be
Jer 32:22 a land **f** with milk and honey
Jer 49: 4 your **f** valley, O backsliding
Ezek 20: 6 **f** with milk and honey, the
Ezek 20:15 **f** with milk and honey, the
Ezek 23:15 **f** turbans on their heads, all
Ezek 47: 1 **f** from under the threshold of
Ezek 47: 1 the water was **f** from under

FLOWS (*see* FLOW)
Num 13:27 It truly **f** with milk and honey
Num 14: 8 us, a land which **f** with milk
1Ki 17: 3 which **f** into the Jordan
1Ki 17: 5 which **f** into the Jordan
Ezra 8:15 by the river that **f** to Ahava
Ezek 47: 8 This water **f** toward the
Ezek 47:12 water **f** from the sanctuary

FLUSHED
Job 16:16 My face is **f** from weeping, and

FLUTE (*see* FLUTES, FLUTISTS)
Gen 4:21 those who play the harp and **f**
1Sa 10: 5 instrument, a tambourine, a **f**
Job 21:12 rejoice to the sound of the **f**
Job 30:31 my **f** to the voice of those
Is 5:12 strings, the tambourine and **f**
Is 30:29 as when one goes with a **f**
Dan 3: 5 hear the sound of the horn, **f**
Dan 3: 7 the sound of the horn, **f**,
Dan 3:10 the sound of the horn, **f**,
Dan 3:15 hear the sound of the horn, **f**
Matt 9:23 house, and saw the **f** players
Matt 11:17 We played the **f** for you, And
Luke 7:32 We played the **f** for you, and
1Co 14: 7 life, whether **f** or harp, when

FLUTES (*see* FLUTE)
1Ki 1:40 and the people played the **f**
Ps 150: 4 stringed instruments and **f**
Jer 48:36 shall wail like **f** for Moab
Jer 48:36 like **f** My heart shall wail

FLUTISTS (*see* FLUTE)
Rev 18:22 of harpists, musicians, **f**

FLUTTERING
Num 11:31 left them **f** near the camp,

FLY (*see* FLEW, FLIES, FLIGHT, FLYING)
Gen 1:20 let birds **f** above the earth
Job 5: 7 as the sparks **f** upward
Job 20: 8 He will **f** away like a dream,
Job 39:26 Does the hawk **f** by your
Ps 55: 6 For then I would **f** away and be

Ps 90:10 is soon cut off, and we **f** away
Prov 23: 5 they **f** away like an eagle
Is 7:18 the **f** that is in the farthest
Is 11:14 But they shall **f** down upon
Is 60: 8 are these who **f** like a cloud
Jer 48:40 one shall **f** like an eagle, and
Jer 49:22 **f** like the eagle, and spread
Dan 9:21 being caused to **f** swiftly
Hos 9:11 shall **f** away like a bird
Hab 1: 8 they **f** as the eagle that
Rev 12:14 that she might **f** into the
Rev 19:17 to all the birds that **f** in

FLYING (*see* FLY)
Lev 11:20 All **f** insects that creep on
Lev 11:21 **f** insect that creeps on all
Lev 11:23 But all other **f** insects
Ps 148:10 Creeping things and **f** fowl
Prov 26: 2 like a **f** swallow, so a curse
Is 14:29 will be a fiery **f** serpent
Is 30: 6 fiery **f** serpent, they will
Is 31: 5 Like birds **f** about, so will
Zech 5: 1 eyes, and saw there a **f** scroll
Zech 5: 2 I see a **f** scroll
Rev 4: 7 creature was like a **f** eagle
Rev 8:13 I heard an angel **f** through
Rev 14: 6 **f** in the midst of heaven,

FOAL (*see* FOALS)
Zech 9: 9 a colt, the **f** of a donkey
Matt 21: 5 a colt, the **f** of a donkey

FOALS (*see* FOAL)
Gen 32:15 female donkeys and ten **f**

FOAMING (*see* FOAMS)
Mark 9:20 and wallowed, **f** at the mouth
Jude 13 the sea, **f** up their own shame

FOAMS (*see* FOAMING)
Mark 9:18 he **f** at the mouth, gnashes
Luke 9:39 him so that he **f** at the mouth

FODDER
Judg 19:19 **f** for our donkeys, and bread
Judg 19:21 and gave **f** to the donkeys
Job 6: 5 or does the ox low over its **f**
Job 24: 6 gather their **f** in the field
Is 30:24 the ground will eat cured **f**

FOE (*see* FOES)
Ps 18:14 His arrows and scattered the **f**

FOES (*see* FOE)
1Ki 5: 3 until the LORD put his **f**
1Ch 21:12 your **f** with the sword of your
Ps 27: 2 up my flesh, My enemies and **f**
Ps 30: 1 not let my **f** rejoice over me
Ps 89:23 down his **f** before his face
Is 29: 5 the multitude of your **f** shall
Matt 10:36 a man's **f** will be those of

FOLD (*see* FOLDED, FOLDING, FOLDS)
Neh 5:13 shook out the **f** of my garment
Is 65:10 Sharon shall be a **f** of flocks
Jer 25:30 roar mightily against His **f**
Ezek 34:14 their **f** shall be on the high
Ezek 34:14 shall lie down in a good **f**
Mic 2:12 together like sheep of the **f**
Hab 3:17 flock be cut off from the **f**
Hag 2:12 meat in the **f** of his garment
John 10:16 have which are not of this **f**
Heb 1:12 a cloak You will **f** them up

FOLDED (*see* FOLD)
John 20: 7 but **f** together in a place by

FOLDING (*see* FOLD)
1Ki 6:34 panels comprised one **f** door
1Ki 6:34 comprised the other **f** door
Prov 6:10 a little **f** of the hands to
Prov 24:33 a little **f** of the hands to
Ezek 41:24 panels apiece, two **f** panels

FOLDS (*see* FOLD)
Num 32:24 **f** for your sheep, and do what
Num 32:36 cities, and **f** for sheep
2Ch 32:28 of livestock, and **f** for flocks
Job 41:23 The **f** of his flesh are joined
Ps 50: 9 Nor goats out of your **f**
Eccl 4: 5 The fool **f** his hands and
Jer 23: 3 and bring them back to their **f**
Zeph 2: 6 for shepherds and **f** for flocks

FOLIAGE
Prov 11:28 will flourish like **f**
Ezek 19:11 her height amid the dense **f**

FOLK
Prov 30:26 rock badgers are a feeble **f**

FOLLOW (*see* FOLLOWED, FOLLOWERS, FOLLOWING, FOLLOWS)
Gen 24: 5 willing to **f** me to this land
Gen 24: 8 woman is not willing to **f** you
Gen 24:39 the woman will not **f** me
Gen 44: 4 steward, "Get up, **f** the men
Ex 11: 8 and all the people who **f** you
Ex 14:17 and they shall **f** them
Ex 23: 2 You shall not **f** a crowd to do
Num 15:39 and that you may not **f** the
Deut 8:19 **f** other gods, and serve them
Deut 12:30 are not ensnared to **f** them
Deut 16:20 You shall **f** what is
Deut 18: 9 you shall not learn to **f** the
Judg 3:28 **F** me, for the LORD has
Judg 8: 5 bread to the people who **f** me
Judg 9: 3 was inclined to **f** Abimelech
1Sa 17:13 gone to **f** Saul to the battle
1Sa 25:27 the young men who **f** my lord
1Sa 30:21 that they could not **f** David
2Sa 17: 9 the people who **f** Absalom
2Sa 20:11 is for David, let him **f** Joab
1Ki 11: 6 and did not fully **f** the LORD
1Ki 18:21 If the LORD is God, **f** Him
1Ki 18:21 but if Baal, then **f** him
1Ki 19:20 mother, and then I will **f** you
1Ki 20:10 each of the people who **f** me
2Ki 6:19 **F** me, and I will bring you to
2Ki 9:18 Turn around and **f** me
2Ki 9:19 Turn around and **f** me
2Ki 17:34 nor do they **f** their statutes
2Ki 23: 3 to **f** the LORD and to keep His
2Ch 34:31 to **f** the LORD, and to keep His
Job 21:33 everyone shall **f** him, as
Ps 23: 6 mercy shall **f** me All the days
Ps 38:20 because I **f** what is good
Ps 45:14 her companions who **f** her
Ps 94:15 upright in heart will **f** it
Ps 119:150 near who **f** after wickedness
Song 1: 8 **f** in the footsteps of the
Is 5:11 that they may **f** intoxicating
Is 51: 1 you who **f** after righteousness
Jer 42:16 **f** close after you there in
Ezek 13: 3 who **f** their own spirit and
Ezek 29:16 when they turned to **f** them
Dan 11:43 shall **f** at his heels
Matt 4:19 **F** Me, and I will make you
Matt 8:19 I will **f** You wherever You go
Matt 8:22 **F** Me, and let the dead bury
Matt 9: 9 And He said to him, "**F** Me
Matt 10:38 **f** after Me is not worthy of
Matt 16:24 and take up his cross, and **f** Me
Matt 19:21 and come, **f** Me
Mark 2:14 and said to him, "**F** Me
Mark 5:37 no one to **f** Him except Peter
Mark 8:34 and take up his cross, and **f** Me
Mark 9:38 **f** us casting out demons in
Mark 9:38 him because he does not **f** us
Mark 10:21 take up the cross, and **f** Me
Mark 14:13 **f** him
Mark 16:17 these signs will **f** those who
Luke 5:27 And He said to him, "**F** Me
Luke 9:23 up his cross daily, and **f** Me
Luke 9:49 because he does not **f** with us
Luke 9:57 I will **f** You wherever You go
Luke 9:59 He said to another, "**F** Me
Luke 9:61 Lord, I will **f** You, but let
Luke 17:23 not go after them or **f** them
Luke 18:22 and come, **f** Me
Luke 22:10 **f** him into the house which he
John 1:43 Philip and said to him, "**F** Me
John 10: 4 and the sheep **f** him, for they
John 10: 5 will by no means **f** a stranger
John 10:27 and I know them, and they **f** Me
John 12:26 serves Me, let him **f** Me
John 13:36 am going you cannot **f** Me now
John 13:36 but you shall **f** Me afterward
John 13:37 Lord, why can I not **f** You now
John 21:19 this, He said to him, "**F** Me
John 21:22 You **f** Me
Acts 3:24 from Samuel and those who **f**
Acts 12: 8 Put on your garment and **f** me
2Th 3: 7 know how you ought to **f** us
2Th 3: 9 of how you should **f** us
1Ti 5:24 but those of some men **f** later
Heb 13: 7 of God to you, whose faith **f**
1Pe 1:11 and the glories that would **f**
1Pe 2:21 that you should **f** His steps
2Pe 1:16 For we did not **f** cunningly
2Pe 2: 2 many will **f** their destructive
Rev 14: 4 These are the ones who **f** the
Rev 14:13 labors, and their works **f** them

FOLLOWED (*see* FOLLOW)
Gen 24:61 on the camels and **f** the man
Gen 32:19 all who **f** the droves, saying,
Num 14:24 has **f** Me fully, I will bring
Num 16:25 and the elders of Israel **f** him
Num 32:11 they have not wholly **f** Me
Num 32:12 they have wholly **f** the LORD
Deut 1:36 because he wholly **f** the LORD
Deut 4: 3 the men who **f** Baal of Peor
Josh 6: 8 covenant of the LORD **f** them
Josh 14: 8 but I wholly **f** the LORD my
Josh 14: 9 have wholly **f** the LORD my God
Josh 14:14 because he wholly **f** the LORD
Judg 2:12 they **f** other gods from among
Judg 9: 4 and they **f** him
Judg 9:49 **f** Abimelech, put them against
Judg 13:11 So Manoah arose and **f** his wife
1Sa 13: 7 the people **f** him trembling
1Sa 14:22 they also **f** hard after them
1Sa 17:14 And the three oldest **f** Saul
1Sa 25:42 she **f** the messengers of David
1Sa 31: 2 Philistines **f** hard after Saul
2Sa 1: 6 horsemen **f** hard after him
2Sa 2:10 the house of Judah **f** David
2Sa 3:31 And King David **f** the coffin
2Sa 11: 8 of food from the king **f** him
2Sa 15:18 men who had **f** him from Gath
2Sa 17:23 that his counsel was not **f**
2Sa 20: 2 **f** Sheba the son of Bichri
1Ki 1: 7 the priest, and they **f** and
1Ki 12:20 none who **f** the house of David
1Ki 14: 8 who **f** Me with all his heart,
1Ki 16:21 half of the people **f** Tibni
1Ki 16:21 make him king, and half **f** Omri
1Ki 16:22 But the people who **f** Omri
1Ki 16:22 over the people who **f** Tibni
1Ki 18:18 LORD, and you have **f** the Baals
1Ki 19:21 and **f** Elijah, and served him
1Ki 20:19 with the army which **f** them
2Ki 3: 9 for the animals that **f** them
2Ki 4:30 So he arose and **f** her
2Ki 13: 2 **f** the sins of Jeroboam the
2Ki 17:15 they **f** idols, became
2Ki 17:40 obey, but they **f** their former
1Ch 10: 2 Philistines **f** hard after Saul
Neh 4:23 who **f** me took off our clothes
Ps 68:25 on instruments **f** after
Jer 2: 5 have **f** idols, and have become
Ezek 10:11 but **f** in the direction the
Amos 7:15 LORD took me as I **f** the flock
Hab 3: 5 and fever **f** at His feet
Matt 4:20 left their nets and **f** Him
Matt 4:22 and their father, and **f** Him
Matt 4:25 And great multitudes **f** Him
Matt 8: 1 great multitudes **f** Him
Matt 8:10 and said to those who **f**
Matt 8:23 a boat, His disciples **f** Him
Matt 9: 9 And he arose and **f** Him
Matt 9:19 arose and **f** him, and so did His
Matt 9:27 there, two blind men **f** Him
Matt 12:15 and great multitudes **f** Him
Matt 14:13 they **f** Him on foot from the
Matt 19: 2 And great multitudes **f** Him
Matt 19:27 we have left all and **f** You
Matt 19:28 you who have **f** Me will also
Matt 20:29 a great multitude **f** Him
Matt 20:34 received sight, and they **f** Him
Matt 21: 9 and those who **f** cried out,
Matt 26:58 But Peter **f** Him at a distance
Matt 27:55 many women who **f** Jesus from
Matt 27:62 next day, which **f** the Day of
Mark 1:18 they left their nets and **f** Him
Mark 2:14 And he arose and **f** Him
Mark 2:15 were many, and they **f** Him
Mark 3: 7 multitude from Galilee **f** Him
Mark 5:24 and a great multitude **f** Him
Mark 6: 1 and His disciples **f** Him
Mark 10:28 we have left all and **f** You
Mark 10:32 as they **f** they were afraid
Mark 10:52 sight and **f** Jesus on the road
Mark 11: 9 and those who **f** cried out,
Mark 14:51 Now a certain young man **f** Him

Mark 14:54 But Peter f Him at a distance
Mark 15:41 who also f Him and ministered
Luke 5:11 they forsook all and f Him
Luke 5:28 left all, rose up, and f Him
Luke 7: 9 said to the crowd that f Him
Luke 9:11 knew it, they f Him
Luke 18:28 we have left all and f You
Luke 18:43 and f Him, glorifying God
Luke 22:39 and His disciples also f Him
Luke 22:54 And Peter f at a distance
Luke 23:27 multitude of the people f Him
Luke 23:49 and the women who f Him from
Luke 23:55 with Him from Galilee f after
John 1:37 him speak, and they f Jesus
John 1:40 and f Him, was Andrew, Simon
John 6: 2 Then a great multitude f Him
John 11:31 and went out, f her, saying,
John 18:15 And Simon Peter f Jesus, and so
Acts 12: 9 f him, and did not know that
Acts 13:43 and devout proselytes f Paul
Acts 16:17 This girl f Paul and us, and
Acts 21:36 of the people f after, crying
1Co 10: 4 spiritual Rock that f them
1Ti 4: 6 which you have carefully f
1Ti 5:10 diligently f every good work
2Ti 3:10 have carefully f my doctrine
Rev 6: 8 Death, and Hades f with him
Rev 8: 7 And hail and fire f, mingled
Rev 13: 3 world marveled and f the beast
Rev 14: 8 And another angel f, saying
Rev 14: 9 Then a third angel f them
Rev 19:14 clean, f Him on white horses

FOLLOWERS (*see* FOLLOW)
2Sa 2:15 f of Ishbosheth the son of
Eph 5: 1 Therefore be f of God as dear
1Th 1: 6 And you became f of us and of
1Pe 3:13 you become f of what is good

FOLLOWING (*see* FOLLOW)
Gen 41:31 land because of the famine f
Num 32:15 if you turn away from f Him
Deut 7: 4 turn your sons away from f Me
Josh 22:16 away this day from f the LORD
Josh 22:18 away this day from f the LORD
Josh 22:23 altar to turn from f the LORD
Josh 22:29 turn from f the LORD this day
Judg 2:19 by f other gods, to serve
Judg 4:14 with ten thousand men f him
Ruth 1:16 to turn back from f after you
1Sa 12:14 continue f the LORD your God
1Sa 12:20 turn aside from f the LORD
1Sa 15:11 he has turned back from f Me
1Sa 24: 1 from f the Philistines, that
2Sa 2:19 or to the left from f Abner
2Sa 2:21 not turn aside from f him
2Sa 2:22 Turn aside from f me
2Sa 7: 8 from f the sheep, to be ruler
1Ki 9: 6 sons at all turn from f Me
1Ki 21:26 very abominably in f idols
2Ki 17:21 drove Israel from f the LORD
2Ki 18: 6 he did not depart from f Him
1Ch 17: 7 from f the sheep, that you
2Ch 25:27 turned away from f the LORD
2Ch 34:33 from f the LORD God of their
2Ch 35: 4 f the written instruction of
Ezra 10:18 f were found of the sons of
Ps 48:13 tell it to the generation f
Ps 78:71 From f the ewes that had
Ps 109:13 in the generation f let their
Zeph 1: 6 turned back from f the LORD
Luke 13:33 today, tomorrow, and the day f
John 1:38 turned, and seeing them f,
John 1:43 The f day Jesus wanted to go
John 6:22 On the f day, when the people
John 20: 6 f him, and went into the tomb
John 21:20 disciple whom Jesus loved f
Acts 10:24 And the f day they entered
Acts 20:15 the f day we arrived at Samos
Acts 21: 1 the f day to Rhodes, and from
Acts 21:18 On the f day Paul went in
Acts 23:11 But the f night the Lord
Acts 23:25 a letter in the f manner
Phil 3:17 join in f my example, and note
2Pe 2:15 f the way of Balaam the son

FOLLOWS (*see* FOLLOW)
Ex 21:22 yet no lasting harm f, he
Ex 21:23 But if any lasting harm f
2Ki 11:15 with the sword whoever f her
2Ch 23:14 with the sword whoever f her
Ps 63: 8 My soul f close behind You

Prov 12:11 but he who f frivolity is
Prov 15: 9 loves him who f righteousness
Prov 21:21 He who f righteousness and
Prov 28:19 but he who f frivolity will
Is 1:23 bribes, and f after rewards
Jer 17:16 being a shepherd who f You
Matt 1:18 of Jesus Christ was as f
John 8:12 He who f Me shall not walk in

FOLLY (*see* FOOL)
1Sa 25:25 is his name, and f is with him
Job 35:15 nor taken much notice of f
Job 42: 8 with you according to your f
Ps 85: 8 let them not turn back to f
Prov 5:23 of his f he shall go astray
Prov 13:16 but a fool lays open his f
Prov 14: 8 but the f of fools is deceit
Prov 14:18 The simple inherit f, but the
Prov 14:24 the foolishness of fools is f
Prov 14:29 he who is impulsive exalts f
Prov 15:21 F is joy to him who is
Prov 16:22 the correction of fools is f
Prov 17:12 rather than a fool in his f
Prov 18:13 before he hears it, it is f
Prov 26: 4 a fool according to his f
Prov 26: 5 a fool according to his f
Prov 26:11 so a fool repeats his f
Eccl 1:17 and to know madness and f
Eccl 2: 3 and how to lay hold on f,
Eccl 2:12 wisdom and madness and f
Eccl 2:13 f as light excels darkness
Eccl 7:25 to know the wickedness of f
Eccl 10: 1 so does a little f to one
Eccl 10: 6 f is set in great dignity,
Is 9:17 and every mouth speaks f
Jer 23:13 I have seen f in the prophets
2Co 11: 1 bear with me in a little f
2Ti 3: 9 for their f will be manifest

FOOD (*see* FOODS)
Gen 1:29 to you it shall be for f
Gen 1:30 every green herb for f'
Gen 2: 9 to the sight and good for f
Gen 3: 6 that the tree was good for f
Gen 6:21 of all f that is eaten, and
Gen 6:21 and it shall be f for you and
Gen 9: 3 that lives shall be f for you
Gen 24:33 f was set before him to eat,
Gen 27: 4 And make me savory f, such as
Gen 27: 7 game and make savory f for me
Gen 27: 9 I will make savory f from
Gen 27:14 and his mother made savory f
Gen 27:17 Then she gave the savory f
Gen 27:31 He also had made savory f
Gen 41:35 let them gather all the f of
Gen 41:35 let them keep f in the cities
Gen 41:36 Then that f shall be as a
Gen 41:48 f of the seven years which
Gen 41:48 laid up the f in the cities
Gen 41:48 the f of the fields which
Gen 42: 7 the land of Canaan to buy f
Gen 42:10 servants have come to buy f
Gen 42:33 take f for the famine of your
Gen 43: 2 Go back, buy us a little f
Gen 43: 4 we will go down and buy you f
Gen 43:20 down the first time to buy f
Gen 43:22 money in our hands to buy f
Gen 43:32 not eat f with the Hebrews
Gen 44: 1 Fill the men's sacks with f
Gen 44:25 Go back and buy us a little f
Gen 45:23 and f for his father for the
Gen 47:24 for the field and for your f
Gen 47:24 as f for your little ones
Ex 21:10 he shall not diminish her f
Lev 3:11 burn them on the altar as f
Lev 3:16 burn them on the altar as f
Lev 11:34 any edible f upon which water
Lev 19:23 all kinds of trees for f,
Lev 22: 7 because it is his f
Lev 22:11 in his house may eat his f
Lev 22:13 she may eat her father's f
Lev 25: 6 the land shall be f for you
Lev 25: 7 its produce shall be for f
Lev 25:37 lend him your f at a profit
Num 21: 5 For there is no f and no water
Num 28: 2 My f for My offerings made by
Num 28:24 the f of the offering made by
Deut 2: 6 You shall buy f from them
Deut 2:28 You shall sell me f for money
Deut 10:18 the stranger, giving him f
Deut 20:19 tree of the field is man's f

Deut 20:20 trees for f you may destroy
Deut 23:19 interest on money or f or
Deut 28:26 Your carcasses shall be f for
Josh 5:12 but they ate the f of the
Judg 1: 7 gather their f under my table
Judg 13:16 Me, I will not eat your f
1Sa 14:24 who eats any f until evening
1Sa 14:24 none of the people tasted f
1Sa 14:28 the man who eats f this day
1Sa 20:34 ate no f the second day of
1Sa 28:20 for he had eaten no f all day
2Sa 3:35 eat f while it was still day
2Sa 9:10 son may have f to eat
2Sa 11: 8 a gift of f from the king
2Sa 12: 3 It ate of his own f and drank
2Sa 12:17 nor did he eat f with them
2Sa 12:20 they set f before him, and he
2Sa 12:21 died, you arose and ate f
2Sa 13: 5 Tamar come and give me f, and
2Sa 13: 5 and prepare the f in my sight
2Sa 13: 7 house, and prepare f for him
2Sa 13:10 Bring the f into the bedroom,
1Ki 4: 7 who provided f for the king
1Ki 4:27 provided f for King Solomon
1Ki 5: 9 by giving f for my household
1Ki 5:11 wheat as f for his household
1Ki 10: 5 the f on his table, the
1Ki 11:18 house, apportioned f for him
1Ki 19: 8 strength of that f forty days
1Ki 21: 4 his face, and would eat no f
1Ki 21: 5 so sullen that you eat no f
1Ki 21: 7 Arise and eat f, and let your
2Ki 4: 8 constrained him to eat some f
2Ki 4: 8 turned in there to eat some f
2Ki 6:22 Set f and water before them,
2Ki 25: 3 f for the people of the land
1Ch 12:40 were bringing f on donkeys
2Ch 9: 4 the f on his table, the
2Ch 11:11 in them, and stores of f, oil,
2Ch 28:15 them sandals, gave them f
Ezra 3: 7 and the carpenters, and f,
Job 6: 6 Can flavorless f be eaten
Job 6: 7 they are as loathsome f to me
Job 12:11 and the mouth taste its f
Job 20:14 yet his f in his stomach
Job 23:12 more than my necessary f
Job 24: 5 seeking diligently for f
Job 24: 5 wilderness yields f for them
Job 30: 4 broom tree roots for their f
Job 33:20 and his soul succulent f
Job 34: 3 words as the palate tastes f
Job 36:31 He gives f in abundance
Job 38:41 Who provides f for the raven,
Job 38:41 and wander about for lack of f
Job 40:20 the mountains yield f for him
Job 42:11 ate f with him in his house
Ps 42: 3 My tears have been my f day
Ps 44:11 up like sheep intended for f
Ps 59:15 They wander up and down for f
Ps 69:21 also gave me gall for my f
Ps 74:14 gave him as f to the people
Ps 78:18 for the f of their fancy
Ps 78:25 Men ate angels' f
Ps 78:25 He sent them f to the full
Ps 78:30 But while their f was still
Ps 79: 2 as f for the birds of the
Ps 104:14 bring forth f from the earth
Ps 104:21 And seek their f from God
Ps 104:27 them their f in due season
Ps 107:18 soul abhorred all manner of f
Ps 111: 5 He has given f to those who
Ps 136:25 Who gives f to all flesh, For
Ps 145:15 them their f in due season
Ps 146: 7 Who gives f to the hungry
Ps 147: 9 He gives to the beast its f
Prov 6: 8 gathers her f in the harvest
Prov 13:23 Much f is in the fallow
Prov 23: 3 for they are deceptive f
Prov 27:27 enough goats' milk for your f
Prov 27:27 for the f of your household,
Prov 28: 3 rain which leaves no f
Prov 30: 8 feed me with the f You
Prov 30:22 fool when he is filled with f
Prov 30:25 prepare their f in the summer
Prov 31:14 she brings her f from afar
Prov 31:15 provides f for her household,
Is 3: 7 is neither f nor clothing
Is 4: 1 We will eat our own f and wear
Is 62: 8 to be f for your enemies
Is 65:25 dust shall be the serpent's f

Jer 7:33 of this people will be f for
Jer 31: 5 and eat them as ordinary f
Jer 44:17 For then we had plenty of f
Jer 52: 6 f for the people of the land
Lam 1:11 for f to restore life
Lam 1:19 city, while they sought f to
Lam 4:10 they became f for them in the
Ezek 4:10 your f which you eat shall be
Ezek 16:19 Also My f which I gave you
Ezek 16:49 had pride, fullness of f, and
Ezek 29: 5 I have given you as f to the
Ezek 34: 5 they became f for all the
Ezek 34: 8 My flock became f for every
Ezek 34:10 may no longer be f for them
Ezek 44: 7 and when you offered My f, the
Ezek 47:12 all kinds of trees used for f
Ezek 47:12 Their fruit will be for f
Ezek 48:18 its produce shall be f for
Dan 1:10 who has appointed your f
Dan 4:12 and in it was f for all
Dan 4:21 in which was f for all,
Dan 10: 3 I ate no pleasant f, no meat
Joel 1:16 Is not the f cut off before
Hab 1:16 and their f plenteous
Hab 3:17 and the fields yield no f
Hag 2:12 stew, wine or oil, or any f
Mal 1: 7 offer defiled f on My altar
Mal 1:12 and its fruit, its f, is
Mal 3:10 there may be f in My house
Matt 3: 4 his f was locusts and wild
Matt 6:25 Is not life more than f and
Matt 10:10 a worker is worthy of his f
Matt 14:15 villages and buy themselves f
Matt 24:45 to give them f in due season
Matt 25:35 I was hungry and you gave Me f
Matt 25:42 hungry and you gave Me no f
Luke 3:11 and he who has f, let him do
Luke 9:13 buy f for all these people
Luke 12:23 Life is more than f, and the
Luke 12:42 portion of f in due season
Luke 24:41 Have you any f here
John 4: 8 away into the city to buy f
John 4:32 I have f to eat of which you
John 4:34 My f is to do the will of Him
John 6:27 for the f which perishes, but
John 6:27 but for the f which endures
John 6:55 For My flesh is f indeed, and
John 21: 5 Children, have you any f
Acts 2:46 ate their f with gladness
Acts 9:19 And when he had received f
Acts 12:20 with f by the king's country
Acts 14:17 filling our hearts with f
Acts 16:34 house, he set f before them
Acts 27:21 after long abstinence from f
Acts 27:33 implored them all to take f
Acts 27:33 waited and continued without f
Acts 27:36 and also took f themselves
Rom 14:15 is grieved because of your f
Rom 14:15 f the one for whom Christ
Rom 14:17 the kingdom of God is not f
Rom 14:20 work of God for the sake of f
1Co 3: 2 with milk and not with solid f
1Co 8: 8 But f does not commend us to
1Co 8:13 if f makes my brother stumble
1Co 10: 3 all ate the same spiritual f
1Co 10:30 f over which I give thanks
2Co 9:10 to the sower, and bread for f
Col 2:16 judge you in f or in drink
1Ti 6: 8 And having f and clothing, with
Heb 5:12 to need milk and not solid f
Heb 5:14 But solid f belongs to those
Heb 12:16 of f sold his birthright
Jas 2:15 naked and destitute of daily f

FOODS (*see* FOOD)
Mark 7:19 thus purifying all f
1Co 6:13 F for the stomach and the
1Co 6:13 stomach and the stomach for f
1Ti 4: 3 f which God created to be
Heb 9:10 concerned only with f and
Heb 13: 9 not with f which have not

FOOL (*see* FOLLY, FOOLISH, FOOL'S, FOOLS)
1Sa 26:21 Indeed I have played the f
2Sa 3:33 Should Abner die as a f dies
Ps 14: 1 The f has said in his heart,
Ps 49:10 Likewise the f and the
Ps 53: 1 The f has said in his heart,
Ps 92: 6 Nor does a f understand this
Prov 7:22 or as a f to the correction
Prov 10: 8 but a prating f will fall
Prov 10:10 but a prating f will fall
Prov 10:18 spreads slander is a f
Prov 10:23 do evil is like sport to a f
Prov 11:29 the f will be servant to the
Prov 12:15 The way of a f is right in
Prov 13:16 but a f lays open his folly
Prov 14: 3 of a f is a rod of pride, but
Prov 14:16 from evil, but a f rages and
Prov 15: 5 A f despises his father's
Prov 15: 7 heart of the f does not do so
Prov 17: 7 speech is not becoming to a f
Prov 17:10 than a hundred blows on a f
Prov 17:12 rather than a f in his folly
Prov 17:16 of a f the purchase price of
Prov 17:21 the father of a f has no joy
Prov 17:24 but the eyes of a f are on
Prov 17:28 Even a f is counted wise when
Prov 18: 2 A f has no delight in
Prov 19: 1 in his lips, and is a f
Prov 19:10 Luxury is not fitting for a f
Prov 20: 3 since any f can start a
Prov 23: 9 speak in the hearing of a f
Prov 24: 7 Wisdom is too lofty for a f
Prov 26: 1 honor is not fitting for a f
Prov 26: 4 Do not answer a f according
Prov 26: 5 Answer a f according to his
Prov 26: 6 of a f cuts off his own feet
Prov 26: 8 is he who gives honor to a f
Prov 26:10 things gives the f his hire
Prov 26:11 so a f repeats his folly
Prov 26:12 hope for a f than for him
Prov 27:22 Though you grind a f in a
Prov 28:26 in his own heart is a f, but
Prov 29: 9 whether the f rages or laughs
Prov 29:11 A f vents all his feelings,
Prov 29:20 hope for a f than for him
Prov 30:22 a f when he is filled with
Eccl 2:14 but the f walks in darkness
Eccl 2:15 As it happens to the f, it
Eccl 2:16 wise than of the f forever
Eccl 2:16 does a wise man die? As the f!
Eccl 2:19 he will be a wise man or a f
Eccl 4: 5 The f folds his hands and
Eccl 6: 8 has the wise man than the f
Eccl 7: 6 so is the laughter of the f
Eccl 10: 3 Even when a f walks along the
Eccl 10: 3 shows everyone that he is a f
Eccl 10:12 but the lips of a f shall
Eccl 10:14 A f also multiplies words
Is 35: 8 walks the road, although a f
Jer 17:11 and at his end he will be a f
Hos 9: 7 The prophet is a f, the
Matt 5:22 But whoever says, You f
Luke 12:20 But God said to him, You f
1Co 3:18 let him become a f that he
2Co 11:16 let no one think me a f
2Co 11:16 at least receive me as a f
2Co 11:23 I speak as a f
2Co 12: 6 to boast, I will not be a f
2Co 12:11 I have become a f in boasting

FOOLISH (*see* FOOL, FOOLISHLY, FOOLISHNESS)
Deut 32: 6 thus deal with the LORD, O f
Deut 32:21 Me to anger by their f idols
Deut 32:21 them to anger by a f nation
Job 2:10 as one of the f women speaks
Job 5: 2 For wrath kills a f man, and
Job 5: 3 I have seen the f taking root
Ps 39: 8 make me the reproach of the f
Ps 49:13 is the way of those who are f
Ps 73:22 I was so f and ignorant
Ps 74:18 LORD, And that a f people has
Ps 74:22 Remember how the f man
Prov 9:13 A f woman is clamorous
Prov 10: 1 but a f son is the grief of
Prov 10:14 of the f is near destruction
Prov 14: 1 but the f pulls it down with
Prov 14: 7 from the presence of a f man
Prov 15:20 but a f man despises his
Prov 17:25 A f son is a grief to his
Prov 19:13 A f son is the ruin of his
Prov 21:20 but a f man squanders it
Prov 29: 9 man contends with a f man
Prov 30:32 If you have been f in
Eccl 4:13 f king who will be admonished
Eccl 7:17 be overly wicked, nor be f
Is 19:11 counselors give f counsel
Is 32: 5 The f person will no longer
Is 32: 6 for the f person will speak
Jer 4:22 For My people are f, they
Jer 5: 4 They are f
Jer 5:21 this now, O f people, without
Jer 10: 8 altogether dull-hearted and f
Ezek 13: 3 Woe to the f prophets, who
Zech 11:15 implements of a f shepherd
Matt 7:26 will be like a f man who
Matt 25: 2 were wise, and five were f
Matt 25: 3 Those who were f took their
Matt 25: 8 the f said to the wise, 'Give
Luke 11:40 F ones!
Luke 24:25 O f ones, and slow of heart to
Rom 1:21 their f hearts were darkened
Rom 2:20 an instructor of the f, a
Rom 10:19 will anger you by a f nation
1Co 1:20 Has not God made f the wisdom
1Co 1:27 But God has chosen the f
1Co 15:36 F one, what you sow is not
Gal 3: 1 O f Galatians!
Gal 3: 3 Are you so f?
Eph 5: 4 nor f talking, nor coarse
1Ti 6: 9 and a snare, and into many f
2Ti 2:23 But avoid f and ignorant
Tit 3: 3 we ourselves were also once f
Tit 3: 9 But avoid f disputes,
Jas 2:20 O f man, that faith without
1Pe 2:15 the ignorance of f men

FOOLISHLY (*see* FOOLISH)
Gen 31:28 you have done f in so doing
Num 12:11 us, in which we have done f
1Sa 13:13 You have done f
2Sa 24:10 for I have done very f
1Ch 21: 8 for I have done very f
2Ch 16: 9 In this you have done f
Prov 14:17 who is quick-tempered acts f
2Co 11:17 the Lord, but as it were, f
2Co 11:21 I speak f

FOOLISHNESS (*see* FOOLISH)
2Sa 15:31 counsel of Ahithophel into f
Ps 38: 5 and festering Because of my f
Ps 69: 5 O God, You know my f
Prov 9: 6 Forsake f and live, and go in
Prov 12:23 heart of fools proclaims f
Prov 14:24 but the f of fools is folly
Prov 15: 2 mouth of fools pours forth f
Prov 15:14 the mouth of fools feeds on f
Prov 19: 3 The f of a man twists his way
Prov 22:15 F is bound up in the heart of
Prov 24: 9 The devising of f is sin, and
Prov 27:22 yet his f will not depart
Eccl 7:25 of folly, even of f and
Eccl 10:13 of his mouth begin with f
Is 32: 6 foolish person will speak f
Is 44:25 and makes their knowledge f
Mark 7:22 evil eye, blasphemy, pride, f
1Co 1:18 f to those who are perishing
1Co 1:21 f of the message preached to
1Co 1:23 block and to the Greeks f,
1Co 1:25 Because the f of God is wiser
1Co 2:14 of God, for they are f to him
1Co 3:19 of this world is f with God

FOOL'S (*see* FOOL)
Prov 12:16 A f wrath is known at once,
Prov 18: 6 A f lips enter into
Prov 18: 7 A f mouth is his destruction,
Prov 26: 3 and a rod for the f back
Prov 27: 3 but a f wrath is heavier than
Eccl 5: 3 a f voice is known by his
Eccl 10: 2 but a f heart at his left

FOOLS (*see* FOOL)
2Sa 13:13 like one of the f in Israel
Job 12:17 and makes f of the judges
Job 30: 8 They were sons of f, yes,
Ps 94: 8 And you f, when will you be
Ps 107:17 F, because of their
Prov 1: 7 but f despise wisdom and
Prov 1:22 scorning, and f hate knowledge
Prov 1:32 of f will destroy them
Prov 3:35 shall be the legacy of f
Prov 8: 5 understand prudence, and you f
Prov 10:21 but f die for lack of wisdom
Prov 12:23 but the heart of f proclaims
Prov 13:19 to f to depart from evil
Prov 13:20 of f will be destroyed
Prov 14: 8 but the folly of f is deceit
Prov 14: 9 F mock at sin, but among the
Prov 14:24 the foolishness of f is folly
Prov 14:33 the heart of f is made known
Prov 15: 2 but the mouth of f pours

Prov 15:14 but the mouth of **f** feeds on
Prov 16:22 the correction of **f** is folly
Prov 19:29 beatings for the backs of **f**
Prov 26: 7 a proverb in the mouth of **f**
Prov 26: 9 a proverb in the mouth of **f**
Eccl 5: 1 to give the sacrifice of **f**
Eccl 5: 4 for He has no pleasure in **f**
Eccl 7: 4 but the heart of **f** is in the
Eccl 7: 5 a man to hear the song of **f**
Eccl 7: 9 anger rests in the bosom of **f**
Eccl 9:17 the shout of a ruler of **f**
Eccl 10:15 The labor of **f** wearies them
Is 19:11 the princes of Zoan are **f**
Is 19:13 princes of Zoan have become **f**
Jer 50:36 and they will be **f**
Matt 23:17 **F** and blind!
Matt 23:19 **F** and blind!
Rom 1:22 to be wise, they became **f**
1Co 4:10 We are **f** for Christ's sake,
2Co 11:19 For you put up with **f** gladly
Eph 5:15 not as **f** but as wise,

FOOT (*see* FEET, FOOTSTEP, FOOTSTOOL, FOUR-FOOTED)
Gen 8: 9 place for the sole of her **f**
Gen 41:44 or **f** in all the land of Egypt
Ex 12:37 six hundred thousand men on **f**
Ex 19:17 at the **f** of the mountain
Ex 21:24 hand for hand, **f** for **f**,
Ex 24: 4 at the **f** of the mountain, and
Ex 29:20 the big toe of their right **f**
Ex 32:19 them at the **f** of the mountain
Lev 8:23 on the big toe of his right **f**
Lev 11:26 any beast which divides the **f**
Lev 13:12 sore, from his head to his **f**
Lev 14:14 on the big toe of his right **f**
Lev 14:17 on the big toe of his right **f**
Lev 14:25 on the big toe of his right **f**
Lev 14:28 on the big toe of his right **f**
Lev 21:19 has a broken **f** or broken hand
Num 11:21 six hundred thousand men on **f**
Num 20:19 let me only pass through on **f**
Num 22:25 Balaam's **f** against the wall
Deut 2:28 only let me pass through on **f**
Deut 4:11 near and stood at the **f** of the
Deut 8: 4 nor did your **f** swell these
Deut 11:10 your seed and watered it by **f**
Deut 11:24 your **f** treads shall be yours
Deut 19:21 hand for hand, **f** for **f**
Deut 25: 9 remove his sandal from his **f**
Deut 28:35 from the sole of your **f** to
Deut 28:56 to set the sole of her **f** on
Deut 28:65 your **f** have a resting place
Deut 32:35 their **f** shall slip in due
Deut 33:24 and let him dip his **f** in oil
Josh 1: 3 your **f** will tread upon I have
Josh 5:15 Take your sandal off your **f**
Josh 14: 9 **f** has trodden shall be your
Judg 4:15 his chariot and fled away on **f**
Judg 4:17 away on **f** to the tent of Jael
Judg 20: 2 God, four hundred thousand **f**
1Sa 4:10 thirty thousand **f** soldiers
1Sa 15: 4 hundred thousand **f** soldiers
2Sa 2:18 fleet of **f** as a wild gazelle
2Sa 8: 4 and twenty thousand **f** soldiers
2Sa 10: 6 twenty thousand **f** soldiers
2Sa 14:25 From the sole of his **f** to the
2Sa 21:20 hand and six toes on each **f**
1Ki 20:29 **f** soldiers of the Syrians in
2Ki 9:33 and he trampled her under **f**
2Ki 13: 7 and ten thousand **f** soldiers
1Ch 18: 4 and twenty thousand **f** soldiers
1Ch 19:18 forty thousand **f** soldiers of
1Ch 20: 6 on each hand and six on each **f**
2Ch 33: 8 the **f** of Israel from the land
Job 2: 7 **f** to the crown of his head
Job 23:11 My **f** has held fast to His
Job 31: 5 or if my **f** has hastened to
Job 39:15 that a **f** may crush them, or
Ps 9:15 hid, their own **f** is caught
Ps 26:12 My **f** stands in an even place
Ps 36:11 Let not the **f** of pride come
Ps 38:16 me, Lest, when my **f** slips
Ps 66: 6 went through the river on **f**
Ps 68:23 That your **f** may crush them in
Ps 91:12 dash your **f** against a stone
Ps 91:13 you shall trample under **f**
Ps 94:18 My **f** slips," Your mercy, O
Ps 121: 3 not allow your **f** to be moved
Prov 1:15 keep your **f** from their path
Prov 3:23 and your **f** will not stumble
Prov 3:26 will keep your **f** from being
Prov 4:27 remove your **f** from evil
Prov 25:17 Seldom set **f** in your
Prov 25:19 bad tooth and a **f** out of joint
Is 1: 6 of the **f** even to the head
Is 14:19 like a corpse trodden under **f**
Is 14:25 mountains tread him under **f**
Is 26: 6 The **f** shall tread it down
Is 28: 3 will be trampled under **f**
Is 58:13 away your **f** from the Sabbath
Jer 2:25 Withhold your **f** from being
Jer 12:10 trodden My portion under **f**
Ezek 29:11 Neither **f** of man shall pass
Ezek 29:11 **f** of beast pass through it
Ezek 32:13 the **f** of man shall muddy them
Dan 8:13 host to be trampled under **f**
Amos 2:15 bow, the swift of **f** shall not
Matt 4: 6 dash your **f** against a stone
Matt 5:13 and trampled under **f** by men
Matt 14:13 Him on **f** from the cities
Matt 18: 8 if your hand or **f** causes you
Matt 22:13 servants, Bind him hand and **f**
Mark 6:33 ran there on **f** from all the
Mark 9:45 if your **f** makes you sin, cut
Luke 4:11 dash Your **f** against a stone
John 11:44 **f** with graveclothes, and his
Acts 7: 5 even enough to set his **f** on
Acts 20:13 intending himself to go on **f**
1Co 12:15 If the **f** should say
Rev 10: 2 he set his right **f** on the sea
Rev 10: 2 and his left **f** on the land,
Rev 11: 2 under **f** for forty-two months

FOOTMEN
Jer 12: 5 If you have run with the **f**

FOOTSTEP (*see* FOOT, FOOTSTEPS)
Deut 2: 5 no, not so much as one **f**

FOOTSTEPS (*see* FOOTSTEP)
1Ki 14: 6 heard the sound of her **f** as
Ps 17: 5 paths, That my **f** may not slip
Ps 77:19 And Your **f** were not known
Ps 85:13 shall make His **f** our pathway
Ps 89:51 the **f** of Your anointed
Song 1: 8 follow in the **f** of the flock

FOOTSTOOL (*see* FOOT)
1Ch 28: 2 for the **f** of our God, and had
2Ch 9:18 with a **f** of gold, which were
Ps 99: 5 our God, And worship at His **f**
Ps 110: 1 I make Your enemies Your **f**
Ps 132: 7 Let us worship at His **f**
Is 66: 1 My throne, and earth is My **f**
Lam 2: 1 did not remember His **f** in the
Matt 5:35 by the earth, for it is His **f**
Matt 22:44 I make Your enemies Your **f**"'
Mark 12:36 I make Your enemies Your **f**
Luke 20:43 I make Your enemies Your **f**
Acts 2:35 I make Your enemies Your **f**
Acts 7:49 My throne, and earth is My **f**
Heb 1:13 I make Your enemies Your **f**"
Heb 10:13 His enemies are made His **f**
Jas 2: 3 Sit here at my **f**,"

FOR (*see* PREFACE)

FORAGE
Hos 4:16 now the LORD will let them **f**

FORBADE (*see* FORBID)
Mark 9:38 we **f** him because he does not
Luke 9:49 we **f** him because he does not

FORBEAR (*see* FORBEARANCE)
2Co 12: 6 But I **f**, lest anyone should

FORBEARANCE (*see* FORBEAR)
Prov 25:15 By long **f** a ruler is
Rom 2: 4 the riches of His goodness, **f**
Rom 3:25 because in His **f** God had

FORBID (*see* FORBADE, FORBIDDEN, FORBIDDING, FORBIDS)
Num 11:28 said, "Moses my lord, **f** them
1Sa 24: 6 The LORD **f** that I should do
1Sa 26:11 The LORD **f** that I should
1Ki 21: 3 The LORD **f** that I should give
Matt 19:14 come to Me, and do not **f** them
Mark 9:39 Do not **f** him, for no one who
Mark 10:14 come to Me, and do not **f** them
Luke 9:50 Do not **f** him, for he who is
Luke 18:16 come to Me, and do not **f** them
Acts 10:47 Can anyone **f** water, that
Acts 24:23 told him not to **f** any of his
1Co 14:39 and do not **f** to speak with
Gal 6:14 But God **f** that I should glory

FORBIDDEN (*see* FORBID)
Lev 5:17 which are **f** to be done by the
Deut 2:37 the LORD our God had **f** us
Deut 4:23 the LORD your God has **f** you
Acts 16: 6 they were **f** by the Holy

FORBIDDING (*see* FORBID)
Luke 23: 2 **f** to pay taxes to Caesar,
Acts 28:31 all confidence, no one **f** him
1Th 2:16 **f** us to speak to the Gentiles
1Ti 4: 3 **f** to marry, and commanding to

FORBIDS (*see* FORBID)
3Jn 10 **f** those who wish to, putting

FORCE (*see* FORCED, FORCEFUL, FORCES, FORCING)
Gen 31:31 your daughters from me by **f**
1Sa 2:16 if not, I will take it by **f**
2Sa 13:12 No, my brother, do not **f** me
1Ki 4: 6 son of Abda, over the labor **f**
1Ki 5:13 a labor **f** out of all Israel
1Ki 5:13 and the labor **f** was thirty
1Ki 5:14 was in charge of the labor **f**
1Ki 9:15 **f** which King Solomon raised
1Ki 11:28 **f** of the house of Joseph
2Ch 28:10 And now you propose to **f** the
Ezra 4:23 by **f** of arms made them cease
Job 30:18 By great **f** my garment is
Jer 18:21 blood by the **f** of the sword
Ezek 34: 4 but with **f** and cruelty you
Dan 11:22 With the **f** of a flood they
Obad 7 shall **f** you to the border
Matt 11:12 and the violent take it by **f**
John 6:15 take Him by **f** to make Him
Acts 23:10 take him by **f** from among them
Heb 9:17 is in **f** after men are dead

FORCED (*see* FORCE)
Ex 5:13 taskmasters **f** them to hurry
Josh 16:10 day and have become **f** laborers
Josh 17:13 put the Canaanites to **f** labor
Judg 1:34 the Amorites **f** the children
2Sa 13:14 she, he **f** her and lay with her
2Sa 13:22 because he had **f** his sister
2Sa 13:32 that he **f** his sister Tamar
1Ki 8:31 and is **f** to take an oath, and
1Ki 9:21 these Solomon raised **f** labor
1Ki 9:22 Solomon made no **f** laborers
1Ch 8: 6 and who **f** them to move to
1Ch 8: 7 and Gera who **f** them to move
2Ch 6:22 and is **f** to take an oath, and
2Ch 8: 8 these Solomon raised **f** labor
Job 24: 4 of the land are **f** to hide
Prov 12:24 will be put to **f** labor
Is 31: 8 men shall become **f** labor

FORCEFUL (*see* FORCE)
Job 6:25 How **f** are right words

FORCES (*see* FORCE)
Gen 14:15 He divided his **f** against them
Num 2: 3 the **f** with Judah shall camp
Num 2: 9 armies of the **f** with Judah
Num 2:10 be the standard of the **f** with
Num 2:16 armies of the **f** with Reuben
Num 2:18 be the standard of the **f** with
Num 2:24 armies of the **f** with Ephraim
Num 2:25 The standard of the **f** with
Num 2:31 numbered of the **f** with Dan
Num 2:32 of the **f** were six hundred
Deut 22:25 countryside, and the man **f** her
1Ki 20: 1 gathered all his **f** together
1Ch 20: 1 that Joab led out the armed **f**
2Ch 32: 9 and all the **f** with him, laid
Esth 8:11 annihilate all the **f** of any
Job 36:19 riches, or all the mighty **f**
Prov 11:21 Though they join **f**, the
Prov 16: 5 though they join **f**, none will
Is 7: 2 Syria's **f** are deployed in
Jer 40:13 the **f** that were in the fields
Jer 41:11 all the captains of the **f**
Jer 41:13 of the **f** who were with him
Jer 41:16 of the **f** that were with him
Jer 42: 1 all the captains of the **f**
Jer 42: 8 of the **f** which were with him
Jer 43: 4 all the captains of the **f**
Jer 43: 5 the **f** took all the remnant of
Dan 11: 6 some years they shall join **f**
Dan 11:10 a multitude of great **f**
Dan 11:15 the **f** of the South shall not

Dan 11:31 **f** shall be mustered by him,
Obad 11 carried captive his **f**, when

FORCING (*see* FORCE)
2Sa 8: 2 **F** them down to the ground, he
Neh 5: 5 and indeed we are **f** our sons
Prov 30:33 so the **f** of wrath produces

FORD (*see* FORDS)
Gen 32:22 crossed over the **f** of Jabbok

FORDS (*see* FORD)
Josh 2: 7 road to the Jordan, to the **f**
Judg 3:28 seized the **f** of the Jordan
Judg 12: 5 **f** of the Jordan before the
Judg 12: 6 him at the **f** of the Jordan
Is 16: 2 of Moab at the **f** of the Arnon

FOREFATHERS (*see* FATHERS)
Jer 11:10 **f** who refused to hear My
Dan 11:24 have not done, nor his **f**
Acts 7:19 people, and oppressed our **f**
2Ti 1: 3 pure conscience, as my **f** did

FOREFRONT
Ex 26: 9 curtain at the **f** of the tent
2Sa 11:15 Set Uriah in the **f** of the

FOREGO
Neh 10:31 that we would **f** the seventh

FOREHEAD (*see* FOREHEADS)
Ex 28:38 So it shall be on Aaron's **f**
Ex 28:38 it shall always be on his **f**
Lev 13:41 hair has fallen from his **f**
Lev 13:41 he is bald on the **f**
Lev 13:42 bald **f** a reddish-white sore
Lev 13:42 his bald head or his bald **f**
Lev 13:43 bald head or on his bald **f**
1Sa 17:49 the Philistine in his **f**, so
1Sa 17:49 the stone sank into his **f**
2Ch 26:19 leprosy broke out on his **f**
2Ch 26:20 at him, and there, on his **f**
Jer 3: 3 You have had a harlot's **f**
Ezek 3: 8 your **f** strong against their
Ezek 3: 9 flint, I have made your **f**
Rev 14: 9 mark on his **f** or on his hand
Rev 17: 5 on her **f** a name was written

FOREHEADS (*see* FOREHEAD)
Ezek 3: 8 strong against their **f**
Ezek 9: 4 put a mark on the **f** of the
Rev 7: 3 of our God on their **f**
Rev 9: 4 the seal of God on their **f**
Rev 13:16 right hand or on their **f**,
Rev 14: 1 name written on their **f**
Rev 20: 4 on their **f** or on their hands
Rev 22: 4 His name shall be on their **f**

FOREIGN (*see* FOREIGNER)
Gen 35: 2 Put away the **f** gods that are
Gen 35: 4 **f** gods which were in their
Ex 2:22 been a stranger in a **f** land
Ex 18: 3 a stranger in a **f** land")
Ex 21: 8 to sell her to a **f** people
Deut 32:12 there was no **f** god with him
Deut 32:16 Him to jealousy with **f** gods
Josh 24:20 the LORD and serve **f** gods,
Josh 24:23 put away the **f** gods which are
Judg 10:16 the **f** gods from among them
1Sa 7: 3 then put away the **f** gods
1Ki 11: 1 Solomon loved many **f** women
1Ki 11: 8 likewise for all his **f** wives
2Ch 14: 3 the altars of the **f** gods and
2Ch 33:15 He took away the **f** gods and
Ps 44:20 out our hands to a **f** god,
Ps 81: 9 shall be no **f** god among you
Ps 81: 9 shall you worship any **f** god
Ps 137: 4 the LORD's song In a **f** land
Is 17:10 plants and set out **f** seedlings
Is 43:12 there was no **f** god among you
Jer 5:19 served **f** gods in your land,
Jer 8:19 images, and with **f** idols
Dan 11:39 fortresses with a **f** god,
Zeph 1: 8 as are clothed with **f** apparel
Mal 2:11 the daughter of a **f** god
Acts 7: 6 would sojourn in a **f** land
Acts 17:18 to be a proclaimer of **f** gods
Acts 26:11 them even to **f** cities
Heb 11: 9 of promise as in a **f** country

FOREIGNER (*see* FOREIGN, FOREIGNER'S, FOREIGNERS)
Gen 23: 4 I am a **f** and a sojourner among
Deut 14:21 it, or you may sell it to a **f**
Deut 15: 3 Of a **f** you may require it
Deut 17:15 you may not set a **f** over you
Deut 23:20 To a **f** you may charge
Deut 29:22 the **f** who comes from a far
Ruth 2:10 notice of me, since I am a **f**
2Sa 15:19 For you are a **f** and also an
1Ki 8:41 Moreover, concerning a **f**, who
1Ki 8:43 for which the **f** calls to You
2Ch 6:32 Moreover, concerning a **f**, who
2Ch 6:33 for which the **f** calls to You
Prov 5:10 labors go to the house of a **f**
Eccl 6: 2 of it, but a **f** consumes it
Is 56: 3 **f** who has joined himself to
Is 56: 6 Also the sons of the **f** who
Is 61: 5 the sons of the **f** shall be
Is 62: 8 the sons of the **f** shall not
Ezek 44: 9 No **f**, uncircumcised in heart
Ezek 44: 9 including any **f** who is among
Luke 17:18 glory to God except this **f**
1Co 14:11 I shall be a **f** to him who
1Co 14:11 who speaks will be a **f** to me

FOREIGNER'S (*see* FOREIGNER)
Lev 22:25 Nor from a **f** hand shall you

FOREIGNERS (*see* FOREIGNER)
Deut 31:16 the gods of the **f** of the land
Judg 19:12 aside here into a city of **f**
2Sa 22:45 The **f** submit to me
2Sa 22:46 The **f** fade away, and come
Neh 9: 2 themselves from all **f**
Ps 18:44 The **f** submit to me
Ps 18:45 The **f** fade away, And come
Ps 144: 7 waters, From the hand of **f**
Ps 144:11 deliver me from the hand of **f**
Is 2: 6 with the children of **f**
Is 25: 2 a palace of **f** to be a city no
Is 60:10 The sons of **f** shall build up
Jer 30: 8 **f** shall no more enslave them
Lam 5: 2 to aliens, and our houses to **f**
Ezek 44: 7 When you brought in **f**,
Obad 11 when **f** entered his gates and
Acts 17:21 the **f** who were there spent
Eph 2:19 are no longer strangers and **f**

FOREKNEW (*see* FOREKNOWLEDGE)
Rom 8:29 For whom He **f**, He also
Rom 11: 2 away His people whom He **f**

FOREKNOWLEDGE (*see* FOREKNEW)
Acts 2:23 **f** of God, you have taken by
1Pe 1: 2 to the **f** of God the Father

FOREMOST (*see* PREFACE)

FOREORDAINED
1Pe 1:20 He indeed was **f** before the

FORERUNNER
Heb 6:20 where the **f** has entered for

FORESAW (*see* FORESEES)
Acts 2:25 I **f** the LORD always before

FORESEEING (*see* FORESEES)
Acts 2:31 **f** this, spoke concerning the
Gal 3: 8 **f** that God would justify the

FORESEES (*see* FORESAW, FORESEEING, FORESIGHT)
Prov 22: 3 A prudent man **f** evil and hides
Prov 27:12 A prudent man **f** evil and hides

FORESIGHT (*see* FORESEES)
Acts 24: 2 to this nation by your **f**,

FORESKIN (*see* FORESKINS)
Gen 17:14 in the flesh of his **f**, that
Gen 17:24 in the flesh of his **f**
Gen 17:25 in the flesh of his **f**
Ex 4:25 and cut off the **f** of her son
Lev 12: 3 of his **f** shall be circumcised
Deut 10:16 the **f** of your heart, and be

FORESKINS (*see* FORESKIN)
Gen 17:11 in the flesh of your **f**, and it
Gen 17:23 of their **f** that very same day
Josh 5: 3 Israel at the hill of the **f**
1Sa 18:25 hundred **f** of the Philistines
1Sa 18:27 And David brought their **f**, and
2Sa 3:14 hundred **f** of the Philistines
Jer 4: 4 and take away the **f** of your

FOREST (*see* FORESTS)
Josh 17:15 then go up to the **f** country
1Sa 14:25 of the land came to a **f**
1Sa 22: 5 and went into the **f** of Hereth
1Sa 23:15 the Wilderness of Ziph in a **f**
1Ki 7: 2 the House of the **F** of Lebanon
1Ki 10:17 the House of the **F** of Lebanon
1Ki 10:21 the **F** of Lebanon were of pure
2Ki 19:23 borders, to its fruitful **f**
2Ch 9:16 the House of the **F** of Lebanon
2Ch 9:20 the **F** of Lebanon were of pure
Neh 2: 8 the keeper of the king's **f**
Ps 50:10 every beast of the **f** is Mine
Ps 104:20 beasts of the **f** creep about
Is 9:18 in the thickets of the **f**
Is 10:18 consume the glory of his **f**
Is 10:19 **f** will be so few in number
Is 10:34 thickets of the **f** with iron
Is 21:13 In the **f** in Arabia you will
Is 22: 8 armor of the House of the **F**
Is 29:17 field be esteemed as a **f**
Is 32:15 field is counted as a **f**
Is 32:19 hail comes down on the **f**, and
Is 37:24 height, to its fruitful **f**
Is 44:14 among the trees of the **f**
Is 44:23 singing, you mountains, O **f**
Is 56: 9 all you beasts in the **f**
Jer 5: 6 from the **f** shall slay them
Jer 10: 3 one cuts a tree from the **f**
Jer 12: 8 is to Me like a lion in the **f**
Jer 21:14 I will kindle a fire in its **f**
Jer 26:18 like the bare hills of the **f**
Jer 46:23 They shall cut down her **f**
Ezek 15: 2 is among the trees of the **f**
Ezek 15: 6 vine among the trees of the **f**
Ezek 20:46 prophesy against the **f** land
Ezek 20:47 say to the **f** of the South
Ezek 31: 3 branches that shaded the **f**
Hos 2:12 So I will make them a **f**, and
Amos 3: 4 Will a lion roar in the **f**
Mic 3:12 like the bare hills of the **f**
Mic 5: 8 among the beasts of the **f**
Zech 11: 2 for the thick **f** has come down
Jas 3: 5 See how great a **f** a little

FORESTS (*see* FOREST)
Num 13:20 there are **f** there or not
2Ch 27: 4 in the **f** he built fortresses
Ps 29: 9 birth, And strips the **f** bare
Ezek 39:10 nor cut down any from the **f**

FORETELL (*see* FORETOLD)
2Co 13: 2 **f** as if I were present the

FORETOLD (*see* FORETELL)
Acts 3:18 God **f** by the mouth of all His
Acts 3:24 have also **f** these days
Acts 7:52 they killed those who **f** the

FOREVER (*see* FOREVERMORE)
Gen 3:22 of life, and eat, and live **f**"
Gen 6: 3 shall not strive with man **f**
Gen 13:15 to you and your descendants **f**
Gen 43: 9 then let me bear the blame **f**
Gen 44:32 the blame before my father **f**
Ex 3:15 This is My name **f**, and this is
Ex 12:24 for you and your sons **f**
Ex 14:13 you shall see again no more **f**
Ex 15:18 The LORD shall reign **f** and
Ex 19: 9 with you, and believe you **f**
Ex 21: 6 and he shall serve him **f**
Ex 27:21 It shall be a statute **f** to
Ex 28:43 shall be a statute **f** to him
Ex 29:28 and his sons by a statute **f**
Ex 30:21 shall be a statute **f** to them
Ex 31:17 and the children of Israel **f**
Ex 32:13 and they shall inherit it **f**
Lev 6:18 statute **f** in your generations
Lev 6:22 It is a statute **f** to the LORD
Lev 7:34 of Israel by a statute **f**
Lev 7:36 by a statute **f** throughout
Lev 10: 9 It shall be a statute **f**
Lev 10:15 with you, by a statute **f**, as
Lev 16:29 shall be a statute **f** for you
Lev 16:31 It is a statute **f**
Lev 17: 7 This shall be a statute **f** for
Lev 23:14 it shall be a statute **f**
Lev 23:21 **f** in all your dwellings
Lev 23:31 it shall be a statute **f**
Lev 23:41 statute **f** in your generations
Lev 24: 3 statute **f** in your generations
Num 10: 8 be to you as an ordinance **f**
Num 15:15 an ordinance **f** throughout
Num 18: 8 your sons, as an ordinance **f**
Num 18:11 with you, as an ordinance **f**
Num 18:19 with you as an ordinance **f**

Lam 5:20 Why do You forget us **f**, and
Ezek 27:36 a horror, and be no more **f**
Ezek 28:19 horror, and shall be no more **f**
Ezek 37:25 their children's children, **f**
Ezek 37:25 David shall be their prince **f**
Ezek 43: 7 of the children of Israel **f**
Ezek 43: 9 I will dwell in their midst **f**
Dan 2: 4 O king, live **f**
Dan 2:20 Blessed be the name of God **f**
Dan 2:44 kingdoms, and it shall stand **f**
Dan 3: 9 O king, live **f**
Dan 4:34 and honored Him who lives **f**
Dan 5:10 O king, live **f**
Dan 6: 6 King Darius, live **f**
Dan 6:21 O king, live **f**
Dan 6:26 living God, and steadfast **f**
Dan 7:18 and possess the kingdom **f**
Dan 7:18 the kingdom **f**, even **f**
Dan 7:26 to consume and destroy it **f**
Dan 12: 3 like the stars **f** and ever
Dan 12: 7 and swore by Him who lives **f**
Hos 2:19 I will betroth you to Me **f**
Joel 3:20 But Judah shall abide **f**, and
Amos 1:11 and he kept his wrath **f**
Obad 10 and you shall be cut off **f**
Jon 2: 6 its bars closed behind me **f**
Mic 2: 9 have taken away My glory **f**
Mic 4: 5 name of the LORD our God **f**
Mic 4: 7 Zion From now on, even **f**
Mic 7:18 does not retain His anger **f**
Zech 1: 5 the prophets, do they live **f**
Mal 1: 4 LORD will have indignation **f**
Matt 6:13 and the power and the glory **f**
Luke 1:33 over the house of Jacob **f**
Luke 1:55 to Abraham and to his seed **f**
John 6:51 of this bread, he will live **f**
John 6:58 eats this bread will live **f**
John 8:35 does not abide in the house **f**
John 8:35 **f**, but a son abides **f**
John 12:34 law that the Christ remains **f**
John 14:16 that He may abide with you **f**
Rom 1:25 the Creator, who is blessed **f**
Rom 11:36 things, to whom be glory **f**
Rom 16:27 glory through Jesus Christ **f**
2Co 9: 9 His righteousness remains **f**
2Co 11:31 Christ, who is blessed **f**,
Gal 1: 5 to whom be glory **f** and ever
Phil 4:20 our God and Father be glory **f**
1Ti 1:17 is wise, be honor and glory **f**
2Ti 4:18 To Him be glory **f** and ever
Phm 15 that you might receive him **f**
Heb 1: 8 Your throne, O God, is **f** and
Heb 5: 6 You are a priest **f** according
Heb 6:20 **f** according to the order of
Heb 7:17 You are a priest **f** according
Heb 7:21 You are a priest **f** according
Heb 7:24 He, because He continues **f**
Heb 7:28 Son who has been perfected **f**
Heb 10:12 one sacrifice for sins **f**, sat
Heb 10:14 **f** those who are being
Heb 13: 8 same yesterday, today, and **f**
Heb 13:21 Christ, to whom be glory **f**
1Pe 1:23 God which lives and abides **f**
1Pe 1:25 word of the LORD endures **f**
1Pe 4:11 the glory and the dominion **f**
1Pe 5:11 the glory and the dominion **f**
2Pe 2:17 of darkness is reserved **f**
2Pe 3:18 be the glory both now and **f**
1Jn 2:17 does the will of God abides **f**
2Jn 2 in us and will be with us **f**
Jude 13 the blackness of darkness **f**
Jude 25 and power, both now and **f**
Rev 1: 6 to Him be glory and dominion **f**
Rev 4: 9 on the throne, who lives **f**
Rev 4:10 and worship Him who lives **f**
Rev 5:13 the throne, and to the Lamb, **f**
Rev 5:14 and worshiped Him who lives **f**
Rev 7:12 and might, be to our God **f**
Rev 10: 6 and swore by Him who lives **f**
Rev 11:15 Christ, and He shall reign **f**
Rev 14:11 of their torment ascends **f**
Rev 15: 7 the wrath of God who lives **f**
Rev 19: 3 And her smoke rises up **f** and
Rev 20:10 be tormented day and night **f**
Rev 22: 5 And they shall reign **f** and ever

FOREVERMORE (*see* FOREVER)
2Sa 22:51 to David and his descendants **f**
Ps 16:11 right hand are pleasures **f**
Ps 18:50 To David and his descendants **f**
Ps 37:27 do good; And dwell **f**
Ps 77: 8 Has His promise failed **f**
Ps 86:12 And I will glorify Your name **f**
Ps 89:52 Blessed be the LORD **f**
Ps 92: 8 But You, LORD, are on high **f**
Ps 106:31 To all generations **f**
Ps 113: 2 From this time forth and **f**
Ps 115:18 From this time forth and **f**
Ps 121: 8 this time forth, and even **f**
Ps 132:12 shall sit upon your throne **f**
Ps 133: 3 Life **f**.
Is 59:21 from this time and **f**
Ezek 37:26 My sanctuary in their midst **f**
Ezek 37:28 sanctuary is in their midst **f**
Rev 1:18 dead, and behold, I am alive **f**

FOREWARN (*see* FOREWARNED)
1Sa 8: 9 you shall solemnly **f** them

FOREWARNED (*see* FOREWARN)
1Th 4: 6 of all such, as we also **f** you

FORGAVE (*see* FORGIVE)
Ps 32: 5 You **f** the iniquity of my sin
Ps 78:38 **f** their iniquity, And did not
Matt 18:27 him, and **f** him the debt
Matt 18:32 I **f** you all that debt because
Luke 7:42 repay, he freely **f** them both
Luke 7:43 the one whom he **f** more
Eph 4:32 as God in Christ also **f** you
Col 3:13 even as Christ **f** you, so you

FORGED (*see* FORGERS)
Ps 119:69 The proud have **f** a lie

FORGERS (*see* FORGED)
Job 13: 4 But you **f** of lies, you are

FORGET (*see* FORGETFUL, FORGETS, FORGETTING, FORGOT, FORGOTTEN)
Gen 41:51 God has made me **f** all my toil
Deut 4: 9 lest you **f** the things your
Deut 4:23 lest you **f** the covenant of
Deut 4:31 nor **f** the covenant of your
Deut 6:12 lest you **f** the LORD who
Deut 8:11 Beware that you do not **f** the
Deut 8:14 you **f** the LORD your God who
Deut 8:19 any means **f** the LORD your God
Deut 9: 7 do not **f** how you provoked the
Deut 24:19 **f** a sheaf in the field, you
Deut 25:19 You shall not **f**
1Sa 1:11 not **f** your maidservant, but
2Ki 17:38 with you, you shall not **f**
Job 8:13 the paths of all who **f** God
Job 9:27 I will **f** my complaint, I
Job 11:16 you would **f** your misery, and
Job 24:20 The womb should **f** him, the
Ps 9:12 He does not **f** the cry of the
Ps 9:17 And all the nations that **f** God
Ps 10:12 Do not **f** the humble
Ps 13: 1 Will You **f** me forever
Ps 44:24 And **f** our affliction and our
Ps 45:10 **F** your own people also, and
Ps 50:22 consider this, you who **f** God
Ps 59:11 slay them, lest my people **f**
Ps 74:19 Do not **f** the life of Your
Ps 74:23 Do not **f** the voice of Your
Ps 78: 7 not **f** the works of God, But
Ps 102: 4 So that I **f** to eat my bread
Ps 103: 2 And **f** not all His benefits
Ps 119:16 I will not **f** Your word
Ps 119:83 Yet I do not **f** Your statutes
Ps 119:93 I will never **f** Your precepts,
Ps 119:109 hand, Yet I do not **f** Your law
Ps 119:141 Yet I do not **f** Your precepts
Ps 119:153 me, For I do not **f** Your law
Ps 119:176 servant, For I do not **f** Your
Ps 137: 5 If I **f** you, O Jerusalem, Let
Ps 137: 5 Let my right hand **f** her skill
Prov 3: 1 My son, do not **f** my law, but
Prov 4: 5 Do not **f**, nor turn away from
Prov 31: 5 **f** the law, and pervert the
Prov 31: 7 **f** his poverty, and remember
Is 49:15 Can a woman **f** her nursing
Is 49:15 Surely they may **f**
Is 49:15 yet I will not **f** you
Is 51:13 you **f** the LORD your Maker,
Is 54: 4 for you will **f** the shame of
Is 65:11 who **f** My holy mountain, who
Jer 2:32 Can a virgin **f** her ornaments,
Jer 23:27 **f** My name by their dreams
Jer 23:39 I, even I, will utterly **f** you
Lam 5:20 Why do You **f** us forever, and
Hos 4: 6 I also will **f** your children
Amos 8: 7 never **f** any of their works
Heb 6:10 is not unjust to **f** your work
Heb 13: 2 Do not **f** to entertain
Heb 13:16 But do not **f** to do good and to
2Pe 3: 5 For this they willfully **f**
2Pe 3: 8 do not **f** this one thing, that

FORGETFUL (*see* FORGET, FORGETFULNESS)
Jas 1:25 is not a **f** hearer but a doer

FORGETFULNESS (*see* FORGETFUL)
Ps 88:12 in the land of **f**

FORGETS (*see* FORGET)
Gen 27:45 he **f** what you have done to
Job 39:15 she **f** that a foot may crush
Prov 2:17 **f** the covenant of her God
Jas 1:24 immediately **f** what kind of

FORGETTING (*see* FORGET)
Phil 3:13 do, **f** those things which are

FORGIVE (*see* FORGAVE, FORGIVEN, FORGIVES, FORGIVING, UNFORGIVING)
Gen 50:17 please **f** the trespass of your
Gen 50:17 please, **f** the trespass of the
Ex 10:17 please **f** my sin only this
Ex 32:32 now, if You will **f** their sin
Num 30: 5 and the LORD will **f** her,
Num 30: 8 and the LORD will **f** her
Num 30:12 void, and the LORD will **f** her
Josh 24:19 He will not **f** your
1Sa 25:28 Please **f** the trespass of your
1Ki 8:30 and when You hear, **f**
1Ki 8:34 and **f** the sin of Your people
1Ki 8:36 **f** the sin of Your servants,
1Ki 8:39 Your dwelling place, and **f**
1Ki 8:50 **f** Your people who have sinned
2Ch 6:21 and when You hear, **f**
2Ch 6:25 and **f** the sin of Your people
2Ch 6:27 **f** the sin of Your servants,
2Ch 6:30 Your dwelling place, and **f**
2Ch 6:39 **f** Your people who have sinned
2Ch 7:14 and will **f** their sin and heal
Ps 25:18 and my pain, And **f** all my sins
Ps 86: 5 Lord, are good, and ready to **f**
Is 2: 9 therefore do not **f** them
Jer 31:34 For I will **f** their iniquity,
Jer 36: 3 that I may **f** their iniquity
Dan 9:19 O Lord, hear! O Lord, **f**!
Amos 7: 2 O Lord GOD, **f**, I pray
Matt 6:12 **f** us our debts
Matt 6:12 As we **f** our debtors
Matt 6:14 For if you **f** men their
Matt 6:14 Father will also **f** you
Matt 6:15 But if you do not **f** men their
Matt 6:15 your Father **f** your trespasses
Matt 9: 6 power on earth to **f** sins"
Matt 18:21 sin against me, and I **f** him
Matt 18:35 does not **f** his brother his
Mark 2: 7 Who can **f** sins but God alone
Mark 2:10 power on earth to **f** sins"
Mark 11:25 **f** him, that your Father in
Mark 11:25 also **f** you your trespasses
Mark 11:26 But if you do not **f**, neither
Mark 11:26 in heaven **f** your trespasses
Luke 5:21 Who can **f** sins but God alone
Luke 5:24 power on earth to **f** sins"
Luke 6:37 **F**, and you will be forgiven
Luke 11: 4 **f** us our sins, for we also
Luke 11: 4 for we also **f** everyone who is
Luke 17: 3 and if he repents, **f** him
Luke 17: 4 I repent,' you shall **f** him
Luke 23:34 **f** them, for they do not know
John 20:23 If you **f** the sins of any,
2Co 2: 7 you ought rather to **f** and
2Co 2:10 you **f** anything, I also **f**
2Co 12:13 **F** me this wrong
1Jn 1: 9 just to **f** us our sins and to

FORGIVEN (*see* FORGIVE, FORGIVENESS)
Lev 4:20 them, and it shall be **f** them
Lev 4:26 his sin, and it shall be **f** him
Lev 4:31 for him, and it shall be **f** him
Lev 4:35 and it shall be **f** him
Lev 5:10 sinned, and it shall be **f** him
Lev 5:13 and it shall be **f** him
Lev 5:16 and it shall be **f** him
Lev 5:18 know it, and it shall be **f** him
Lev 6: 7 he shall be **f** for any one of
Lev 19:22 he has done shall be **f** him
Num 14:19 as You have **f** this people
Num 15:25 Israel, and it shall be **f** them

Num 15:26 It shall be **f** the whole
Num 15:28 and it shall be **f** him
Ps 32: 1 he whose transgression is **f**
Ps 85: 2 You have **f** the iniquity of
Is 33:24 it will be **f** their iniquity
Matt 9: 2 your sins are **f** you
Matt 9: 5 to say, Your sins are **f** you
Matt 12:31 and blasphemy will be **f** men
Matt 12:31 the Spirit will not be **f** men
Matt 12:32 Son of Man, it will be **f** him
Matt 12:32 Spirit, it will not be **f** him
Mark 2: 5 Son, your sins are **f** you
Mark 2: 9 Your sins are **f** you,' or to
Mark 3:28 will be **f** the sons of men
Mark 4:12 turn, and their sins be **f** them
Luke 5:20 Man, your sins are **f** you
Luke 5:23 to say, Your sins are **f** you
Luke 6:37 Forgive, and you will be **f**
Luke 7:47 sins, which are many, are **f**
Luke 7:47 But to whom little is **f**, the
Luke 7:48 Your sins are **f**
Luke 12:10 Son of Man, it will be **f** him
Luke 12:10 Holy Spirit, it will not be **f**
John 20:23 sins of any, they are **f** them
Acts 8:22 of your heart may be **f** you
Rom 4: 7 whose lawless deeds are **f**
2Co 2:10 if indeed I have **f** anything
2Co 2:10 I have **f** that one for your
Col 2:13 having **f** you all trespasses,
Jas 5:15 committed sins, he will be **f**
1Jn 2:12 because your sins are **f** you

FORGIVENESS (*see* FORGIVEN)
Ps 130: 4 But there is **f** with You, That
Dan 9: 9 our God belong mercy and **f**
Mark 3:29 the Holy Spirit never has **f**
Acts 5:31 to Israel and **f** of sins
Acts 13:38 preached to you the **f** of sins
Acts 26:18 they may receive **f** of sins
Eph 1: 7 the **f** of sins, according to
Col 1:14 His blood, the **f** of sins

FORGIVES (*see* FORGIVE)
Ps 103: 3 Who **f** all your iniquities,
Luke 7:49 Who is this who even **f** sins

FORGIVING (*see* FORGIVE)
Ex 34: 7 **f** iniquity and transgression
Num 14:18 **f** iniquity and transgression
Eph 4:32 **f** one another, just as God in
Col 3:13 **f** one another, if anyone has

FORGOT (*see* FORGET)
Gen 40:23 remember Joseph, but **f** him
Judg 3: 7 They **f** the LORD their God, and
1Sa 12: 9 when they **f** the LORD their
Ps 78:11 **f** His works And His wonders
Ps 106:13 They soon **f** His works
Ps 106:21 They **f** God their Savior, Who
Jer 23:27 fathers **f** My name for Baal
Hos 2:13 Then she **f** Me," says the
Hos 13: 6 therefore they **f** Me

FORGOTTEN (*see* FORGET)
Gen 41:30 be **f** in the land of Egypt
Deut 26:13 nor have I **f** them
Deut 31:21 for it will not be **f** in the
Deut 32:18 have **f** the God who fathered
Job 19:14 and my close friends have **f** me
Job 28: 4 in places **f** by feet they hang
Ps 9:18 needy shall not always be **f**
Ps 10:11 God has **f**
Ps 31:12 I am **f** like a dead man, out
Ps 42: 9 Why have You **f** me
Ps 44:17 But we have not **f** You, Nor
Ps 44:20 If we had **f** the name of our
Ps 77: 9 Has God **f** to be gracious
Ps 119:61 me, But I have not **f** Your law
Ps 119:139 my enemies have **f** Your words
Eccl 2:16 will be **f** in the days to come
Eccl 8:10 they were **f** in the city where
Eccl 9: 5 for the memory of them is **f**
Is 17:10 Because you have **f** the God of
Is 23:15 Tyre will be **f** seventy years
Is 23:16 about the city, you **f** harlot
Is 44:21 you will not be **f** by Me
Is 49:14 me, and my Lord has **f** me
Is 65:16 the former troubles are **f**
Jer 2:32 Yet My people have **f** Me days
Jer 3:21 they have **f** the LORD their
Jer 13:25 Because you have **f** Me and
Jer 18:15 Because My people have **f** Me
Jer 20:11 confusion will never be **f**
Jer 23:40 shame, which shall not be **f**
Jer 30:14 All your lovers have **f** you
Jer 44: 9 Have you **f** the wickedness of
Jer 50: 5 covenant That will not be **f**
Jer 50: 6 they have **f** their resting
Lam 2: 6 and Sabbaths to be **f** in Zion
Lam 3:17 I have **f** prosperity
Ezek 22:12 by extortion, and have **f** Me
Ezek 23:35 Because you have **f** Me and
Hos 4: 6 Because you have **f** the law of
Hos 8:14 For Israel has **f** his Maker
Matt 16: 5 they had **f** to take bread
Mark 8:14 disciples had **f** to take bread
Luke 12: 6 one of them is **f** before God
Heb 12: 5 you have **f** the exhortation
2Pe 1: 9 has **f** that he was purged from

FORK (*see* FORKS)
Ezek 21:21 at the **f** of the two roads, to

FORKS (*see* FORK)
Ex 27: 3 and its basins and its **f** and its
Ex 38: 3 shovels, the basins, the **f**
Num 4:14 the firepans, the **f**, the
1Sa 13:21 the mattocks, the **f**, and the
1Ch 28:17 also pure gold for the **f**, the
2Ch 4:16 the pots, the shovels, the **f**

FORM (*see* FORMATION, FORMED, FORMS, UNFORMED)
Gen 1: 2 The earth was without **f**, and
Gen 29:17 but Rachel was beautiful of **f**
Gen 39: 6 And Joseph was handsome in **f**
Num 12: 8 and he sees the **f** of the LORD
Deut 4:12 of the words, but saw no **f**
Deut 4:15 for you saw no **f** when the
Deut 4:16 image in the **f** of any figure
Deut 4:23 a carved image in the **f** of
Deut 4:25 image in the **f** of anything
Deut 15: 2 this is the **f** of the release
1Sa 28:14 What is his **f**?"
Job 4:16 A **f** was before my eyes
Job 38:14 It takes on **f** like clay under
Ps 83: 5 They **f** a confederacy against
Is 44:10 Who would **f** a god or cast a
Is 45: 7 I **f** the light and create
Is 52:14 His **f** more than the sons of
Is 53: 2 He has no **f** or comeliness
Jer 4:23 and indeed it was without **f**
Ezek 8: 3 stretched out the **f** of a hand
Ezek 10: 8 appeared to have the **f** of a
Dan 2:31 and its **f** was awesome
Dan 3:25 the **f** of the fourth is like
Mark 16:12 **f** to two of them as they
Luke 3:22 bodily **f** like a dove upon Him
John 5:37 at any time, nor seen His **f**
Rom 2:20 having the **f** of knowledge and
Rom 6:17 **f** of doctrine to which you
1Co 7:31 For the **f** of this world is
Phil 2: 6 who, being in the **f** of God
Phil 2: 7 taking the **f** of a servant, and
1Th 5:22 Abstain from every **f** of evil
2Ti 3: 5 having a **f** of godliness but

FORMATION (*see* FORM)
1Ch 12:35 who could keep battle **f**,
1Ch 12:36 to war, able to keep battle **f**
2Ch 13: 3 **f** against him with eight
Joel 2: 7 every one marches in **f**, and

FORMED (*see* FORM)
Gen 2: 7 the LORD God **f** man of the
Gen 2: 8 He put the man whom He had **f**
Gen 2:19 **f** every beast of the field
Num 10:25 which **f** the rear guard of all
Judg 20:22 again **f** the battle line at
2Ki 19:25 ancient times that I **f** it
Job 1:17 The Chaldeans **f** three bands
Job 33: 6 also have been **f** out of clay
Ps 90: 2 Or ever You had **f** the earth
Ps 94: 9 He who **f** the eye, shall He
Ps 95: 5 And His hands **f** the dry land
Ps 139:13 For You have **f** my inward
Prov 26:10 The great God who **f** all
Is 27:11 He who **f** them will show them
Is 29:16 Or shall the thing **f** say of
Is 29:16 **f** say of him who **f** it
Is 37:26 ancient times that I **f** it
Is 43: 1 you, O Jacob, and He who **f** you
Is 43: 7 I have **f** him, yes, I have
Is 43:10 Before Me there was no God **f**
Is 43:21 people I have **f** for Myself
Is 44: 2 **f** you from the womb, who will
Is 44:21 I have **f** you, you are My
Is 44:24 He who **f** you from the womb
Is 45:18 Who **f** the earth and made it,
Is 45:18 Who **f** it to be inhabited
Is 49: 5 who **f** Me from the womb to be
Is 54:17 no weapon **f** against you shall
Jer 1: 5 Before I **f** you in the womb I
Jer 33: 2 made it, the LORD who **f** it to
Ezek 16: 7 Your breasts were **f**, your
Amos 7: 1 He **f** locust swarms at the
Acts 23:13 who had **f** this conspiracy
Rom 9:20 thing **f** say to him who **f** it
Gal 4:19 until Christ is **f** in you,
1Ti 2:13 For Adam was **f** first, then

FORMER (*see* FORMERLY)
Gen 40:13 according to the **f** manner
Num 6:12 but the **f** days shall be lost,
Num 21:26 against the **f** king of Moab
Deut 24: 4 then her **f** husband who
Ruth 4: 7 **f** times in Israel concerning
2Sa 20:18 They used to talk in **f** times
2Ki 17:34 practicing the **f** rituals
2Ki 17:40 they followed their **f** rituals
2Ch 3: 3 according to the **f** measure)
2Ch 17: 3 **f** ways of his father David
Ezra 4:15 within the city in **f** times
Ezra 4:19 **f** times has made insurrection
Ezra 5:15 God be rebuilt on its **f** site
Neh 5:15 But the **f** governors who had
Job 8: 8 inquire, please, of the **f** age
Ps 79: 8 do not remember **f** iniquities
Ps 89:49 Lord, where are Your **f**
Eccl 1:11 is no remembrance of **f** things
Eccl 7:10 Why were the **f** days better
Is 41:22 let them show the **f** things
Is 41:26 **f** times, that we may say, He
Is 42: 9 the **f** things have come to
Is 43: 9 this, and show us **f** things
Is 43:18 Do not remember the **f** things
Is 46: 9 Remember the **f** things of old,
Is 48: 3 I have declared the **f** things
Is 61: 4 raise up the **f** desolations
Is 65: 7 I will measure their **f** work
Is 65:16 because the **f** troubles are
Is 65:17 the **f** shall not be remembered
Jer 5:24 Who gives rain, both the **f**
Jer 34: 5 the **f** kings who were before
Jer 36:28 write on it all the **f** words
Ezek 16:55 return to their **f** state, and
Ezek 16:55 return to their **f** state, then
Ezek 16:55 will return to your **f** state
Ezek 36:11 you inhabited as in **f** times
Ezek 38:17 in **f** days by My servants the
Dan 11:13 multitude greater than the **f**
Dan 11:29 be like the **f** or the latter
Hos 6: 3 latter and **f** rain to the earth
Joel 2:23 you the **f** rain faithfully
Joel 2:23 the **f** rain, and the latter
Mic 4: 8 even the **f** dominion shall
Hag 2: 3 this temple in its **f** glory
Hag 2: 9 shall be greater than the **f**
Zech 1: 4 to whom the **f** prophets
Zech 7: 7 the **f** prophets when Jerusalem
Zech 7:12 Spirit through the **f** prophets
Zech 8:11 this people as in the **f** days
Mal 3: 4 days of old, as in **f** years
Acts 1: 1 The **f** account I made, O
Gal 1:13 of my **f** conduct in Judaism
Eph 4:22 concerning your **f** conduct
Phil 1:16 The **f** preach Christ from
Heb 7:18 is an annulling of the **f**
Heb 10:32 recall the **f** days in which
1Pe 1:14 yourselves to the **f** lusts
1Pe 3: 5 in **f** times, the holy women
Rev 21: 4 for the **f** things have passed

FORMERLY (*see* FORMER)
Deut 2:12 The Horites **f** dwelt in Seir,
Deut 2:20 giants **f** dwelt there
Josh 11:10 for Hazor was **f** the head of
Josh 14:15 of Hebron **f** was Kirjath Arba
Josh 15:15 (**f** the name of Debir was
Judg 1:10 of Hebron was **f** Kirjath Arba
Judg 1:11 of Debir was **f** Kirjath Sepher
Judg 1:23 name of the city was **f** Luz
Judg 3: 2 those who had not **f** known it)
Judg 18:29 name of the city **f** was Laish
1Sa 9: 9 (**F** in Israel, when a man went
1Sa 9: 9 a prophet was **f** called a seer
1Sa 10:11 knew him **f** saw that he indeed

1Ch 4:40 some Hamites **f** lived there
John 9:13 They brought him who **f** was
Gal 1:23 He who **f** persecuted us now
1Ti 1:13 although I was **f** a blasphemer
1Pe 3:20 who **f** were disobedient, when

FORMS (*see* FORM)
Lev 26:30 the lifeless **f** of your idols
Is 45: 9 the clay say to him who **f** it
Jer 15: 3 them four **f** of destruction
Ezek 43:11 all its ordinances, all its **f**
Amos 4:13 He who **f** mountains, and
Zech 12: 1 **f** the spirit of man within

FORNICATION (*see* FORNICATIONS, FORNICATOR)
Is 23:17 pay, and commit **f** with all the
John 8:41 We were not born of **f**
2Co 12:21 of the uncleanness, **f**, and
Gal 5:19 adultery, **f**, uncleanness,
Eph 5: 3 But **f** and all uncleanness or
Col 3: 5 **f**, uncleanness, passion, evil
Rev 14: 8 wine of the wrath of her **f**
Rev 17: 2 of the earth committed **f**, and
Rev 17: 2 drunk with the wine of her **f**
Rev 17: 4 and the filthiness of her **f**
Rev 18: 3 wine of the wrath of her **f**
Rev 18: 3 have committed **f** with her
Rev 18: 9 of the earth who committed **f**
Rev 19: 2 the earth with her **f**

FORNICATIONS (*see* FORNICATION)
Matt 15:19 murders, adulteries, **f**,
Mark 7:21 evil thoughts, adulteries, **f**

FORNICATOR (*see* FORNICATION, FORNICATORS)
1Co 5:11 named a brother, who is a **f**
Eph 5: 5 For this you know, that no **f**
Heb 12:16 lest there be any **f** or

FORNICATORS (*see* FORNICATOR)
1Co 6: 9 Neither **f**, nor idolaters, nor
1Ti 1:10 for **f**, for sodomites, for
Heb 13: 4 but **f** and adulterers God will

FORSAKE (*see* FORSAKEN, FORSAKES, FORSAKING, FORSOOK)
Deut 4:31 He will not **f** you nor destroy
Deut 12:19 **f** the Levite as long as you
Deut 14:27 You shall not **f** the Levite
Deut 31: 6 will not leave you nor **f** you
Deut 31: 8 will not leave you nor **f** you
Deut 31:16 among them, and they will **f** Me
Deut 31:17 in that day, and I will **f** them
Josh 1: 5 will not leave you nor **f** you
Josh 10: 6 Do not **f** your servants
Josh 24:16 **f** the LORD to serve other
Josh 24:20 If you **f** the LORD and serve
1Sa 12:22 LORD will not **f** His people
1Ki 6:13 will not **f** My people Israel
1Ki 8:57 May He not leave us nor **f** us
2Ki 21:14 So I will **f** the remnant of
1Ch 28: 9 but if you **f** Him, He will
1Ch 28:20 will not leave you nor **f** you
2Ch 7:19 away and **f** My statutes and My
2Ch 15: 2 if you **f** Him, He will **f** you
Ezra 8:22 against all those who **f** Him
Ezra 9: 9 did not **f** us in our bondage
Neh 9:17 kindness, and did not **f** them
Neh 9:19 mercies You did not **f** them in
Neh 9:31 consume them nor **f** them
Job 20:13 he spares it and does not **f** it
Ps 27: 9 Do not leave me nor **f** me, O
Ps 27:10 my father and my mother **f** me
Ps 37: 8 Cease from anger, and **f** wrath
Ps 37:28 And does not **f** His saints
Ps 38:21 Do not **f** me, O LORD
Ps 71: 9 Do not **f** me when my strength
Ps 71:18 O God, do not **f** me, Until I
Ps 89:30 If his sons **f** My law And do
Ps 94:14 Nor will He **f** His inheritance
Ps 119: 8 Oh, do not **f** me utterly
Ps 119:53 of the wicked, who **f** Your law
Ps 119:87 But I did not **f** Your precepts
Ps 138: 8 Do not **f** the works of Your
Prov 1: 8 and do not **f** the law of your
Prov 3: 3 let not mercy and truth **f** you
Prov 4: 2 do not **f** my law
Prov 4: 6 Do not **f** her, and she will
Prov 6:20 and do not **f** the law of your
Prov 9: 6 **F** foolishness and live, and go
Prov 27:10 Do not **f** your own friend or
Prov 28: 4 Those who **f** the law praise
Is 1:28 those who **f** the LORD shall be
Is 41:17 of Israel, will not **f** them
Is 42:16 do for them, and not **f** them
Is 55: 7 Let the wicked **f** his way, and
Is 58: 2 did not **f** the ordinance of
Is 65:11 you are those who **f** the LORD
Jer 17:13 all who **f** You shall be
Jer 23:33 I will even **f** you," says
Jer 23:39 **f** you, and the city that I
Jer 51: 9 **F** her, and let us go everyone
Lam 5:20 and **f** us for so long a time
Ezek 20: 8 nor did they **f** the idols of
Dan 11:30 those who **f** the holy covenant
Jon 2: 8 idols **f** their own Mercy
Luke 14:33 whoever of you does not **f** all
Acts 21:21 among the Gentiles to **f** Moses
Heb 13: 5 never leave you nor **f** you

FORSAKEN (*see* FORSAKE)
Gen 24:27 who has not **f** His mercy and
Deut 28:20 doings in which you have **f** Me
Deut 29:25 Because they have **f** the
Judg 6:13 But now the LORD has **f** us
Judg 10:10 we have both **f** our God and
Judg 10:13 Yet you have **f** Me and served
Ruth 2:20 who has not **f** His kindness to
1Sa 8: 8 with which they have **f** Me
1Sa 12:10 because we have **f** the LORD
1Ki 11:33 because they have **f** Me, and
1Ki 18:18 have, in that you have **f** the
1Ki 19:10 Israel have **f** Your covenant
1Ki 19:14 Israel have **f** Your covenant
2Ki 22:17 because they have **f** Me and
2Ch 12: 5 You have **f** Me, and therefore
2Ch 13:10 our God, and we have not **f** Him
2Ch 13:11 our God, but you have **f** Him
2Ch 21:10 because he had **f** the LORD God
2Ch 24:20 Because you have **f** the LORD
2Ch 24:20 the LORD, He also has **f** you
2Ch 24:24 because they had **f** the LORD
2Ch 28: 6 because they had **f** the LORD
2Ch 29: 6 they have **f** Him, have turned
2Ch 34:25 because they have **f** Me and
Ezra 9:10 For we have **f** Your
Neh 13:11 Why is the house of God **f**
Job 18: 4 Shall the earth be **f** for you
Job 20:19 **f** the poor, he has violently
Ps 9:10 have not **f** those who seek You
Ps 22: 1 My God, why have You **f** Me
Ps 37:25 have not seen the righteous **f**
Ps 71:11 God has **f** him
Is 1: 4 They have **f** the LORD, they
Is 2: 6 For You have **f** Your people
Is 6:12 the **f** places are many in the
Is 7:16 will be **f** by both her kings
Is 17: 2 The cities of Aroer are **f**
Is 17: 9 cities will be as a **f** bough
Is 27:10 be desolate, the habitation **f**
Is 32:14 Because the palaces will be **f**
Is 49:14 The LORD has **f** me, and my Lord
Is 54: 6 has called you like a woman **f**
Is 54: 7 a mere moment I have **f** you
Is 60:15 Whereas you have been **f** and
Is 62: 4 shall no longer be termed **F**
Is 62:12 Sought Out, a City Not **F**
Jer 1:16 because they have **f** Me,
Jer 2:13 they have **f** Me, the fountain
Jer 2:17 in that you have **f** the LORD
Jer 2:19 you have **f** the LORD your God
Jer 4:29 Every city shall be **f**, and not
Jer 5: 7 Your children have **f** Me and
Jer 5:19 them, 'Just as you have **f** Me
Jer 7:29 **f** the generation of His wrath
Jer 9:13 Because they have **f** My law
Jer 9:19 because we have **f** the land
Jer 12: 7 I have **f** My house, I have
Jer 15: 6 You have **f** Me," says the
Jer 16:11 your fathers have **f** Me,' says
Jer 16:11 worshiped them, and have **f** Me
Jer 17:13 because they have **f** the LORD
Jer 18:14 be **f** for strange waters
Jer 19: 4 Because they have **f** Me and
Jer 22: 9 Because they have **f** the
Jer 51: 5 For Israel is not **f**, nor
Ezek 8:12 us, the LORD has **f** the land
Ezek 9: 9 say, 'The LORD has **f** the land
Ezek 36: 4 the cities that have been **f**
Amos 5: 2 She lies **f** on her land
Zeph 2: 4 For Gaza shall be **f**, and
Matt 27:46 My God, why have You **f** Me
Mark 15:34 My God, why have You **f** Me
2Co 4: 9 persecuted, but not **f**
2Ti 4:10 for Demas has **f** me, having
2Pe 2:15 They have **f** the right way and

FORSAKES (*see* FORSAKE)
Job 6:14 even though he **f** the fear of
Prov 2:17 who **f** the companion of her
Prov 15:10 is for him who **f** the way, and
Prov 28:13 and **f** them will have mercy

FORSAKING (*see* FORSAKE)
Heb 10:25 not **f** the assembling of

FORSOOK (*see* FORSAKE)
Deut 32:15 then he **f** God who made him,
Judg 2:12 they **f** the LORD God of their
Judg 2:13 They **f** the LORD and served
Judg 10: 6 they **f** the LORD and did not
1Sa 31: 7 they **f** the cities and fled
1Ki 9: 9 Because they **f** the LORD
2Ki 21:22 He **f** the LORD God of his
1Ch 10: 7 they **f** their cities and fled
2Ch 7:22 Because they **f** the LORD God
2Ch 12: 1 that he **f** the law of the LORD
Ps 78:60 So that He **f** the tabernacle
Matt 26:56 Then all the disciples **f** Him
Mark 14:50 Then they all **f** Him and fled
Luke 5:11 boats to land, they **f** all
2Ti 4:16 stood with me, but all **f** me
Heb 11:27 By faith he **f** Egypt, not

FORT (*see* FORTIFY, FORTRESS, FORTS)
Is 25:12 The fortress of the high **f** of
Nah 2: 1 Man the **f**!

FORTH (*see* PREFACE)

FORTIETH (*see* FORTY)
Num 33:38 and died there in the **f** year
Deut 1: 3 it came to pass in the **f** year
1Ch 26:31 In the **f** year of the reign of

FORTIFIED (*see* FORTIFY)
Num 13:28 the cities are **f** and very
Num 21:24 of the people of Ammon was **f**
Num 32:17 the **f** cities because of the
Num 32:36 **f** cities, and folds for sheep
Deut 1:28 are great and **f** up to heaven
Deut 3: 5 cities were **f** with high walls
Deut 9: 1 great and **f** up to heaven,
Deut 28:52 **f** walls, in which you trust,
Josh 10:20 who escaped entered **f** cities
Josh 14:12 the cities were great and **f**
Josh 19:29 and to the **f** city of Tyre
Josh 19:35 the **f** cities are Ziddim, Zer,
1Sa 6:18 both **f** cities and country
2Sa 20: 6 he find for himself **f** cities
2Ki 3:19 you shall attack every **f** city
2Ki 10: 2 a **f** city also, and weapons,
2Ki 17: 9 from watchtower to **f** city
2Ki 18: 8 from watchtower to **f** city
2Ki 18:13 all the **f** cities of Judah
2Ki 19:25 **f** cities into heaps of ruins
2Ch 8: 5 **f** cities with walls, gates,
2Ch 11:10 Judah and Benjamin, **f** cities
2Ch 11:11 he **f** the strongholds, and put
2Ch 11:23 and Benjamin, to every **f** city
2Ch 12: 4 he took the **f** cities of Judah
2Ch 14: 6 he built **f** cities in Judah,
2Ch 17: 2 in all the **f** cities of Judah
2Ch 17:19 whom the king put in the **f**
2Ch 19: 5 all the **f** cities of Judah
2Ch 21: 3 with **f** cities in Judah
2Ch 26: 9 then he **f** them
2Ch 32: 1 encamped against the **f** cities
2Ch 33:14 in all the **f** cities of Judah
Neh 3: 8 they **f** Jerusalem as far as
Is 2:15 tower, and upon every **f** wall
Is 25: 2 a **f** city a ruin, a palace of
Is 27:10 Yet the **f** city will be
Is 36: 1 all the **f** cities of Judah
Is 37:26 **f** cities into heaps of ruins
Jer 1:18 made you this day a **f** city
Jer 4: 5 let us go into the **f** cities
Jer 5:17 shall destroy your **f** cities
Jer 8:14 and let us enter the **f** cities
Jer 15:20 this people a **f** bronze wall
Jer 34: 7 for only these **f** cities
Ezek 21:20 and to Judah, into **f** Jerusalem
Ezek 36:35 and ruined cities are now **f**
Dan 11:15 siege mound, and take a **f** city
Hos 8:14 also has multiplied **f** cities
Mic 7:12 and the **f** cities, from the

Zeph 1:16 and alarm against the f cities

FORTIFY (*see* FORT, FORTIFIED, FORTIFYING)
Neh 4: 2 Will they f themselves
Is 22:10 you broke down to f the wall
Jer 33: 4 to f against the siege mounds
Jer 51:53 and though she were to f the
Nah 2: 1 F your power mightily
Nah 3:14 F your strongholds

FORTIFYING (*see* FORTIFY)
Judg 9:31 are, f the city against you

FORTRESS (*see* FORT, FORTRESSES)
2Sa 22: 2 The LORD is my rock, my f
Ps 18: 2 The LORD is my rock and my f
Ps 31: 2 A f of defense to save me
Ps 31: 3 For You are my rock and my f
Ps 71: 3 For You are my rock and my f
Ps 91: 2 He is my refuge and my f
Ps 144: 2 My lovingkindness and my f
Is 17: 3 The f also will cease from
Is 25:12 The f of the high fort of
Is 29: 7 fight against her and her f
Is 33:16 will be the f of rocks
Jer 6:27 a f among My people, that you
Jer 10:17 land, O inhabitant of the f
Jer 16:19 O LORD, my strength and my f
Dan 11: 7 enter the f of the king of
Dan 11:10 then he shall return to his f
Dan 11:19 toward the f of his own land
Dan 11:31 shall defile the sanctuary f
Amos 5: 9 so that fury comes upon the f
Mic 7:12 from the f to the River, from

FORTRESSES (*see* FORTRESS)
1Ch 27:25 in the villages, and in the f
2Ch 17:12 powerful, and he built f and
2Ch 27: 4 and in the forests he built f
Is 34:13 nettles and brambles in its f
Dan 11:38 he shall honor a god of f
Dan 11:39 f with a foreign god, which
Hos 10:14 all your f shall be plundered
Zeph 3: 6 their f are devastated

FORTS (*see* FORT)
Num 31:10 they dwelt, and all their f
Is 32:14 The f and towers will become

FORTUNATUS
1Co 16:17 the coming of Stephanas, F

FORTUNE-TELLING
Acts 16:16 her masters much profit by f

FORTY (*see* FORTIETH)
Gen 5:13 f years, and begot sons and
Gen 7: 4 to rain on the earth f days
Gen 7: 4 f nights, and I will destroy
Gen 7:12 earth f days and f nights
Gen 7:17 flood was on the earth f days
Gen 8: 6 to pass, at the end of f days
Gen 18:29 there should be f found there
Gen 18:29 not do it for the sake of f
Gen 25:20 Isaac was f years old when he
Gen 26:34 When Esau was f years old
Gen 32:15 f cows and ten bulls, twenty
Gen 50: 3 F days were required for him,
Ex 16:35 of Israel ate manna f years
Ex 24:18 mountain f days and f nights
Ex 26:19 You shall make f sockets of
Ex 26:21 their f sockets of silver
Ex 34:28 LORD f days and f nights
Ex 36:24 F sockets of silver he made
Ex 36:26 their f sockets of silver
Num 1:33 were f thousand five hundred
Num 2:19 at f thousand five hundred
Num 13:25 out the land after f days
Num 14:33 in the wilderness f years
Num 14:34 f days, for each day you
Num 14:34 one year, namely f years, and
Num 26:18 f thousand five hundred
Num 32:13 in the wilderness f years
Deut 2: 7 These f years the LORD your
Deut 8: 2 f years in the wilderness
Deut 8: 4 your foot swell these f years
Deut 9: 9 mountain f days and f nights
Deut 9:11 to pass, at the end of f days
Deut 9:11 f nights, that the LORD gave
Deut 9:18 first, f days and f nights
Deut 9:18 first, f days and f nights
Deut 9:25 f days and f nights I kept
Deut 9:25 f nights I kept prostrating
Deut 10:10 mountain f days and f nights
Deut 25: 3 F blows he may give him and no
Deut 29: 5 I have led you f years in the
Josh 4:13 About f thousand prepared for
Josh 5: 6 f years in the wilderness
Josh 14: 7 I was f years old when Moses
Judg 3:11 the land had rest for f years
Judg 5: 8 among f thousand in Israel
Judg 5:31 the land had rest for f years
Judg 8:28 the country was quiet for f
Judg 12:14 He had f sons and thirty
Judg 13: 1 the Philistines for f years
1Sa 4:18 he had judged Israel f years
1Sa 17:16 and presented himself f days
2Sa 2:10 was f years old when he began
2Sa 5: 4 reign, and he reigned f years
2Sa 10:18 f thousand horsemen of the
2Sa 15: 7 it came to pass after f years
1Ki 2:11 over Israel was f years
1Ki 4:26 Solomon had f thousand stalls
1Ki 6:17 sanctuary was f cubits long
1Ki 7:38 each laver contained f baths
1Ki 11:42 over all Israel was f years
1Ki 19: 8 strength of that food f days
1Ki 19: 8 f nights as far as Horeb, the
2Ki 8: 9 of Damascus, f camel-loads
2Ki 12: 1 and he reigned f years in
1Ch 12:36 battle formation, f thousand
1Ch 19:18 f thousand foot soldiers of
1Ch 29:27 over Israel was f years
2Ch 9:30 over all Israel f years
2Ch 24: 1 and he reigned f years in
Neh 5:15 besides f shekels of silver
Neh 9:21 F years You sustained them in
Job 42:16 f years, and saw his children
Ps 95:10 For f years I was grieved
Ezek 4: 6 of the house of Judah f days
Ezek 29:11 shall be uninhabited f years
Ezek 29:12 shall be desolate f years
Ezek 29:13 At the end of f years I will
Ezek 41: 2 f cubits, and its width,
Ezek 46:22 f cubits long and thirty wide
Amos 2:10 led you f years through the
Amos 5:25 in the wilderness f years
Jon 3: 4 Yet f days, and Nineveh shall
Matt 4: 2 And when He had fasted f days
Matt 4: 2 f nights, afterward He was
Mark 1:13 in the wilderness f days,
Luke 4: 2 for f days by the devil
Acts 1: 3 seen by them during f days
Acts 4:22 For the man was over f years
Acts 7:23 But when he was f years old
Acts 7:30 when f years had passed, an
Acts 7:36 and in the wilderness f years
Acts 7:42 sacrifices during f years in
Acts 13:18 Now for a time of about f
Acts 13:21 of Benjamin, for f years
Acts 23:13 than f who had formed this
Acts 23:21 for more than f of them lie
2Co 11:24 received f stripes minus one
Heb 3: 9 Me, and saw My works f years
Heb 3:17 whom was He angry f years

FORTY-EIGHT
Num 35: 7 to the Levites shall be f
Josh 21:41 were f cities with their
Neh 7:15 of Binnui, six hundred and f
Neh 7:44 of Asaph, one hundred and f

FORTY-FIRST
2Ch 16:13 he died in the f year of his

FORTY-FIVE
Gen 18:28 If I find there f, I will not
Num 1:25 were f thousand six hundred
Num 2:15 at f thousand six hundred
Num 26:41 were f thousand six hundred
Num 26:50 were f thousand four hundred
Josh 14:10 as He said, these f years
1Ki 7: 3 beams that were on f pillars
Ezra 2: 8 of Zattu, nine hundred and f
Ezra 2:34 Jericho, three hundred and f
Ezra 2:66 their mules two hundred and f
Neh 7:13 of Zattu, eight hundred and f
Neh 7:36 Jericho, three hundred and f
Neh 7:67 and f men and women singers
Neh 7:68 their mules two hundred and f
Jer 52:30 seven hundred and f persons

FORTY-FOUR
1Ch 5:18 had f thousand seven hundred
Rev 7: 4 f thousand of all the tribes
Rev 14: 1 and f thousand, having His
Rev 14: 3 f thousand who were redeemed
Rev 21:17 f cubits, according to the

FORTY-NINE
Lev 25: 8 years shall be to you f years

FORTY-ONE
Num 1:41 were f thousand five hundred
Num 2:28 at f thousand five hundred
1Ki 14:21 Rehoboam was f years old when
1Ki 15:10 And he reigned f years in
2Ki 14:23 Samaria, and reigned f years
2Ch 12:13 Now Rehoboam was f years old

FORTY-SEVEN
Gen 47:28 was one hundred and f years
Ezra 2:38 one thousand two hundred and f
Neh 7:41 one thousand two hundred and f

FORTY-SIX
Num 1:21 were f thousand five hundred
Num 2:11 at f thousand five hundred
John 2:20 It has taken f years to build

FORTY-THREE
Num 26: 7 were f thousand seven hundred
Ezra 2:25 Beeroth, seven hundred and f
Neh 7:29 Beeroth, seven hundred and f

FORTY-TWO
Num 35: 6 these you shall add f cities
Judg 12: 6 time f thousand Ephraimites
2Ki 2:24 and mauled f of the youths
2Ki 10:14 the well of Beth Eked, f men
2Ch 22: 2 Ahaziah was f years old when
Ezra 2:10 of Bani, six hundred and f
Ezra 2:24 the people of Azmaveth, f
Ezra 2:64 was f thousand three hundred
Neh 7:28 the men of Beth Azmaveth, f
Neh 7:62 of Nekoda, six hundred and f
Neh 7:66 was f thousand three hundred
Neh 11:13 houses, were two hundred and f
Rev 11: 2 city under foot for f months
Rev 13: 5 to continue for f months

FORUM
Acts 28:15 to meet us as far as Appii F

FORWARD
Ex 14:15 children of Israel to go f
Num 1:51 the tabernacle is to go f
Num 12: 5 And they both went f
Judg 9:44 that was with him rushed f
1Sa 10: 3 you shall go on f from there
1Sa 16:13 upon David from that day f
1Sa 18: 9 eyed David from that day f
1Sa 30:25 And so it was, from that day f
2Sa 20: 8 and as he was going f, it fell
1Ki 22:21 Then a spirit came f and stood
2Ki 4:24 Drive, and go f
2Ki 20: 9 shall the shadow go f ten
2Ch 18:20 Then a spirit came f and stood
Job 23: 8 Look, I go f, but He is not
Is 9: 7 and justice from that time f
Jer 7:24 and went backward and not f
Jer 31:39 f over the hill Gareb
Ezek 1: 9 but each one went straight f
Ezek 1:12 And each one went straight f
Ezek 10:22 They each went straight f
Ezek 39:22 their God from that day f
Dan 3: 8 time certain Chaldeans came f
Hag 2:15 consider from this day f
Hag 2:18 Consider now from this day f
Hag 2:19 this day f I will bless you
Matt 26:60 many false witnesses came f
Matt 26:60 two false witnesses came f
Mark 3: 3 Step f
John 18: 4 would come upon Him, went f
Acts 19:33 the Jews putting him f
Phil 3:13 reaching f to those things
2Pe 3:14 looking f to these things, be
3Jn 6 If you send them f on their

FOSTER (*see* FOSTERED)
Is 49:23 Kings shall be your f fathers

FOSTERED (*see* FOSTER)
Ezra 4:19 and sedition have been f in it

FOUGHT (*see* FIGHT)
Ex 17: 8 f with Israel in Rephidim
Ex 17:10 said to him, and f with Amalek
Lev 24:10 a man of Israel f each other
Num 21: 1 then he f against Israel and
Num 21:23 to Jahaz and f against Israel
Num 21:26 who had f against the former

Ps 109: 7 judged, let him be f guilty
Ps 116: 3 I f trouble and sorrow
Ps 132: 6 We f it in the fields of the
Prov 6:31 Yet when he is f, he must
Prov 7:15 your face, and I have f you
Prov 10:13 Wisdom is f on the lips of
Prov 16:31 if it is f in the way of
Prov 24:14 if you have f it, there is a
Prov 25:16 Have you f honey
Prov 30: 6 you, and you be f a liar
Prov 30:10 curse you, and you be f guilty
Eccl 7:27 Here is what I have f," says
Eccl 7:28 man among a thousand I have f
Eccl 7:28 among all these I have not f
Eccl 7:29 Truly, this only I have f
Eccl 9:15 Now there was f in it a poor
Song 3: 3 who go about the city f me
Song 3: 4 them, when I f the one I love
Song 5: 7 who went about the city f me
Song 8:10 his eyes as one who f peace
Is 10:10 As my hand has f the kingdoms
Is 10:14 My hand has f like a nest the
Is 13:15 Everyone who is f will be
Is 22: 3 All who are f in you are
Is 30:14 So there shall not be f among
Is 35: 9 it shall not be f there
Is 37: 8 f the king of Assyria warring
Is 39: 2 all that was f among his
Is 51: 3 and gladness will be f in it
Is 55: 6 the LORD while He may be f
Is 57:10 You have f the life of your
Is 65: 1 I was f by those who did not
Is 65: 8 new wine is f in the cluster
Jer 2: 5 have your fathers f in Me
Jer 2:26 is ashamed when he is f out
Jer 2:34 Also on your skirts is f the
Jer 2:34 I have not f it by secret
Jer 5:26 My people are f wicked men
Jer 11: 9 A conspiracy has been f among
Jer 14: 3 to the cisterns and f no water
Jer 15:16 Your words were f, and I ate
Jer 23:11 I have f their wickedness
Jer 29:14 I will be f by you, says the
Jer 31: 2 who survived the sword f
Jer 41: 3 Chaldeans who were f there
Jer 41: 8 But ten men were f among them
Jer 41:12 they f him by the great pool
Jer 48:27 Was he f among thieves
Jer 50: 7 All who f them have devoured
Jer 50:20 but they shall not be f
Jer 50:24 you have been f and also
Jer 52:25 who were f in the city, the
Jer 52:25 f in the midst of the city
Lam 2:16 we have f it, we have seen it
Ezek 22:30 but I f no one
Ezek 26:21 you will never be f again
Ezek 28:15 till iniquity was f in you
Dan 1:19 all none was f like Daniel
Dan 1:20 he f them ten times better
Dan 2:25 him, "I have f a man of the
Dan 2:35 that no trace of them was f
Dan 4:12 of the field f shade under it
Dan 5:11 of the gods, were f in him
Dan 5:12 enigmas were f in this Daniel
Dan 5:14 excellent wisdom are f in you
Dan 5:27 in the balances, and f wanting
Dan 6: 4 any error or fault f in him
Dan 6:11 f Daniel praying and making
Dan 6:22 me, because I was f innocent
Dan 6:23 injury whatever was f on him
Dan 11:19 stumble and fall, and not be f
Dan 12: 1 every one who is f written in
Hos 9:10 I f Israel like grapes in the
Hos 12: 4 He f Him in Bethel, and there
Hos 12: 8 I have f wealth for myself
Hos 14: 8 Your fruit is f in Me
Jon 1: 3 f a ship going to Tarshish
Mic 1:13 of Israel were f in you
Zeph 3:13 tongue be f in their mouth
Zech 10:10 no more room is f for them
Mal 2: 6 was not f on his lips
Matt 1:18 she was f with child of the
Matt 2: 8 Child, and when you have f Him
Matt 8:10 I have not f such great faith
Matt 13:44 in a field, which a man f
Matt 13:46 when he had f one pearl of
Matt 18:28 f one of his fellow servants
Matt 20: 6 f others standing idle, and
Matt 21:19 f nothing on it but leaves,
Matt 22:10 together all whom they f,
Matt 26:40 f them asleep, and said to
Matt 26:43 and f them asleep again, for
Matt 26:60 but f none.
Matt 26:60 came forward, they f none
Matt 27:32 they f a man of Cyrene, Simon
Mark 1:37 When they f Him, they said to
Mark 6:38 when they f out they said,
Mark 7: 2 unwashed hands, they f fault
Mark 7:30 she f the demon gone out, and
Mark 11: 4 f the colt tied by the door
Mark 11:13 He f nothing but leaves, for
Mark 14:16 f it just as He had said to
Mark 14:37 f them sleeping, and said to
Mark 14:40 He f them asleep again, for
Mark 14:55 put Him to death, and f none
Mark 15:45 And when he f out from the
Luke 1:30 for you have f favor with God
Luke 2:16 f Mary and Joseph, and the
Luke 2:46 days they f Him in the temple
Luke 4:17 He f the place where it was
Luke 7: 9 I have not f such great faith
Luke 7:10 f the servant well who had
Luke 8:35 and f the man from whom the
Luke 9:36 had ceased, Jesus was f alone
Luke 13: 6 seeking fruit on it and f none
Luke 15: 5 And when he has f it, he lays
Luke 15: 6 for I have f my sheep which
Luke 15: 9 And when she has f it, she
Luke 15: 9 for I have f the piece which
Luke 15:24 he was lost and is f
Luke 15:32 is alive, and was lost and is f
Luke 17:18 Were there not any f who
Luke 19:32 f it just as He had said to
Luke 22:13 f it as He had said to them,
Luke 22:45 He f them sleeping from
Luke 23: 2 We f this fellow perverting
Luke 23:14 I have f no fault in this Man
Luke 23:22 I have f no reason for death
Luke 24: 2 But they f the stone rolled
Luke 24:24 f it just as the women had
Luke 24:33 f the eleven and those who
John 1:41 He first f his own brother
John 1:41 We have f the Messiah"
John 1:43 He f Philip and said to him,
John 1:45 Philip f Nathanael and said to
John 1:45 We have f Him of whom Moses
John 2:14 He f in the temple those who
John 5:14 Afterward Jesus f him in the
John 6:25 when they f Him on the other
John 9:35 and when He had f him, He said
John 11:17 He f that he had already been
John 12:14 when He had f a young donkey,
Acts 5:10 f her dead, and carrying her
Acts 5:23 Indeed we f the prison shut
Acts 5:23 them, we f no one inside
Acts 5:39 lest you even be f to fight
Acts 7:11 our fathers f no sustenance
Acts 7:46 who f favor before God and
Acts 8:40 But Philip was f at Azotus
Acts 9: 2 so that if he f any who were
Acts 9:30 When the brethren f out, they
Acts 9:33 There he f a certain man
Acts 10:27 f many who had come together
Acts 11:26 And when he had f him, he
Acts 12:19 searched for him and not f him
Acts 13: 6 they f a certain sorcerer, a
Acts 13:22 I have f David the son of
Acts 13:28 though they f no cause for
Acts 17:23 I even f an altar with this
Acts 18: 2 And he f a certain Jew named
Acts 19:34 But when they f out that he
Acts 22:29 he f out that he was a Roman
Acts 23:29 I f out that he was accused
Acts 24: 5 For we have f this man a
Acts 24:12 And they neither f me in the
Acts 24:18 f me purified in the temple
Acts 24:20 f any wrongdoing in me while
Acts 25:25 But when I f that he had
Acts 27: 6 There the centurion f an
Acts 27:28 f it to be twenty fathoms
Acts 27:28 f it to be fifteen fathoms
Acts 28: 1 they then f out that the
Acts 28:14 where we f brethren, and were
Rom 4: 1 has f according to the flesh
Rom 7:10 life, I f to bring death
Rom 10:20 I was f by those who did not
1Co 4: 2 that one be f faithful
1Co 15:15 we are f false witnesses of
2Co 5: 3 we shall not be f naked
2Co 7:14 boasting to Titus was f true
2Co 12:20 that I shall be f by you such
Gal 2:17 ourselves also are f sinners
Phil 2: 8 being f in appearance as a
Phil 3: 9 be f in Him, not having my
1Ti 3:10 as deacons, being f blameless
2Ti 1:17 out very diligently and f me
Heb 11: 5 was not f because God had
Heb 12:17 for he f no place for
1Pe 1: 7 may be f to praise, honor, and
1Pe 2:22 nor was guile f in His mouth
2Pe 3:14 to be f by Him in peace,
2Jn 4 greatly that I have f some of
Jude 3 I f it necessary to write to
Rev 2: 2 are not, and have f them liars
Rev 3: 2 for I have not f your works
Rev 5: 4 no one was f worthy to open
Rev 12: 8 nor was a place f for them in
Rev 14: 5 in their mouth was f no guile
Rev 16:20 and the mountains were not f
Rev 18:21 and shall not be f anymore
Rev 18:22 shall be f in you anymore
Rev 18:24 in her was f the blood of
Rev 20:11 there was f no place for them
Rev 20:15 anyone not f written in the

FOUNDATION (*see* FOUNDATIONS)
Josh 6:26 he shall lay its f with his
1Ki 5:17 to lay the f of the temple
1Ki 6:37 In the fourth year the f of
1Ki 7: 9 from the f to the eaves, and
1Ki 7:10 The f was of costly stones,
1Ki 16:34 He laid its f with Abiram his
2Ch 3: 3 This is the f which Solomon
2Ch 8:16 from the day of the f of the
2Ch 23: 5 at the Gate of the F
Ezra 3: 6 But the f of the temple of
Ezra 3:10 f of the temple of the LORD
Ezra 3:11 because the f of the house of
Ezra 3:12 the f of this temple was laid
Ezra 5:16 laid the f of the house of
Job 4:19 whose f is in the dust, who
Ps 87: 1 His f is in the holy
Ps 89:14 are the f of Your throne
Ps 97: 2 are the f of His throne
Ps 102:25 You laid the f of the earth
Ps 137: 7 it, raze it, To its very f
Prov 10:25 has an everlasting f
Is 28:16 I lay in Zion a stone for a f
Is 28:16 cornerstone, a sure f
Is 44:28 Your f shall be laid
Is 48:13 has laid the f of the earth
Jer 51:26 a corner nor a stone for a f
Ezek 13:14 ground, so that its f will be
Ezek 41: 8 it was the f of the side
Hab 3:13 by laying bare from f to neck
Hag 2:18 from the day that the f of
Zech 4: 9 laid the f of this temple
Zech 8: 9 were in the day that the f
Zech 12: 1 lays the f of the earth, and
Matt 13:35 from the f of the world
Matt 25:34 you from the f of the world
Luke 6:48 and laid the f on the rock
Luke 6:49 on the earth without a f,
Luke 11:50 the f of the world may be
Luke 14:29 lest, after he has laid the f
John 17:24 Me before the f of the world
Rom 15:20 build on another man's f,
1Co 3:10 builder I have laid the f
1Co 3:11 For no other f can anyone lay
1Co 3:12 builds on this f with gold
Eph 1: 4 Him before the f of the world
Eph 2:20 on the f of the apostles and
1Ti 6:19 a good f for the time to come
2Ti 2:19 the solid f of God stands
Heb 1:10 laid the f of the earth, and
Heb 4: 3 from the f of the world
Heb 6: 1 not laying again the f of
Heb 9:26 since the f of the world
1Pe 1:20 before the f of the world
Rev 13: 8 slain from the f of the world
Rev 17: 8 Life from the f of the world
Rev 21:19 the first f was jasper, the

FOUNDATIONS (*see* FOUNDATION)
Deut 32:22 and set on fire the f of the
2Sa 22: 8 the f of heaven moved and
2Sa 22:16 seen, the f of the world were
Ezra 4:12 its walls and repairing the f
Ezra 6: 3 let the f of it be firmly
Job 22:16 whose f were swept away by a
Job 38: 4 I laid the f of the earth

Job 38: 6 To what were its **f** fastened
Ps 11: 3 If the **f** are destroyed, What
Ps 18: 7 The **f** of the hills also
Ps 18:15 And the **f** of the world were
Ps 82: 5 All the **f** of the earth are
Ps 104: 5 who laid the **f** of the earth
Prov 8:29 marked out the **f** of the earth
Is 16: 7 For the **f** of Kir Hareseth you
Is 19:10 And its **f** will be broken
Is 24:18 the **f** of the earth are shaken
Is 40:21 from the **f** of the earth
Is 51:13 and laid the **f** of the earth
Is 51:16 lay the **f** of the earth, and
Is 54:11 lay your **f** with sapphires
Is 58:12 up the **f** of many generations
Jer 31:37 the **f** of the earth searched
Jer 50:15 her **f** have fallen, her walls
Lam 4:11 and it has devoured its **f**
Ezek 30: 4 and her **f** are broken down
Mic 1: 6 and I will uncover her **f**
Mic 6: 2 you strong **f** of the earth
Acts 16:26 so that the **f** of the prison
Heb 11:10 for the city which has **f**,
Rev 21:14 wall of the city had twelve **f**
Rev 21:19 the **f** of the wall of the city

FOUNDED (*see* FOUND)
Ps 24: 2 For He has **f** it upon the seas
Ps 89:11 its fullness, You have **f** them
Ps 104: 8 place which You **f** for them
Ps 119:152 that You have **f** them forever
Prov 3:19 LORD by wisdom **f** the earth
Is 14:32 That the LORD has **f** Zion, and
Is 23:13 Assyria **f** it for wild beasts
Amos 9: 6 has **f** His strata in the earth
Matt 7:25 for it was **f** on the rock
Luke 6:48 it, for it was **f** on the rock

FOUNDING (*see* FOUND)
Ex 9:18 Egypt since its **f** until now

FOUNTAIN (*see* FOUNTAINS)
Deut 33:28 the **f** of Jacob alone, in a
Josh 15: 9 **f** of the water of Nephtoah
1Sa 29: 1 by a **f** which is in Jezreel
Neh 2:14 Then I went on to the **F** Gate
Neh 3:15 Mizpah, repaired the **F** Gate
Neh 12:37 By the **F** Gate, in front of
Ps 36: 9 For with You is the **f** of life
Ps 68:26 Lord, from the **f** of Israel
Ps 74:15 You broke open the **f** and the
Ps 114: 8 The flint into a **f** of waters
Prov 5:18 Let your **f** be blessed, and
Prov 13:14 of the wise is a **f** of life
Prov 14:27 of the LORD is a **f** of life
Eccl 12: 6 pitcher shattered at the **f**
Song 4:12 a spring shut up, a **f** sealed
Song 4:15 a **f** of gardens, a well of
Jer 2:13 the **f** of living waters, and
Jer 6: 7 As a **f** wells up with water,
Jer 9: 1 and my eyes a **f** of tears,
Jer 17:13 LORD, the **f** of living waters
Hos 13:15 and his **f** shall be dried up
Joel 3:18 a **f** shall flow from the house
Zech 13: 1 In that day a **f** shall be
Mark 5:29 Immediately the **f** of her
John 4:14 him will become in him a **f** of
Rev 21: 6 I will give of the **f** of the

FOUNTAINS (*see* FOUNTAIN)
Gen 7:11 on that day all the **f** of the
Gen 8: 2 The **f** of the deep and the
Deut 8: 7 land of brooks of water, of **f**
Prov 5:16 Should your **f** be dispersed
Prov 8:24 forth, when there were no **f**
Prov 8:28 the **f** of the deep,
Is 41:18 **f** in the midst of the valleys
Rev 7:17 them to living **f** of waters

FOUR (*see* FOUR-FOOTED, FOURS, FOURSQUARE, FOURTH)
Gen 2:10 parted and became **f** riverheads
Gen 11:13 Arphaxad lived **f** hundred
Gen 11:15 Eber, Salah lived **f** hundred
Gen 11:17 Peleg, Eber lived **f** hundred
Gen 14: 9 **f** kings against five
Gen 15:13 afflict them **f** hundred years
Gen 23:15 the land is worth **f** hundred
Gen 23:16 **f** hundred shekels of silver,
Gen 32: 6 **f** hundred men are with him
Gen 33: 1 with him were **f** hundred men
Ex 12:40 lived in Egypt was **f** hundred
Ex 12:41 at the end of the **f** hundred
Ex 22: 1 an ox and **f** sheep for a sheep
Ex 25:12 You shall cast **f** rings of
Ex 25:12 and put them in its **f** corners
Ex 25:26 make for it **f** rings of gold
Ex 25:26 and put the rings on the **f**
Ex 25:26 that are at its **f** legs
Ex 25:34 On the lampstand itself **f**
Ex 26: 2 of each curtain **f** cubits
Ex 26: 8 of each curtain **f** cubits
Ex 26:32 the **f** pillars of acacia wood
Ex 26:32 upon **f** sockets of silver
Ex 27: 2 its horns on its **f** corners
Ex 27: 4 **f** bronze rings at its **f**
Ex 27:16 **f** pillars and **f** sockets
Ex 28:17 in it, **f** rows of stones
Ex 36: 9 of each curtain **f** cubits
Ex 36:15 of each curtain **f** cubits
Ex 36:36 He made for it **f** pillars of
Ex 36:36 he cast **f** sockets of silver
Ex 37: 3 he cast for it **f** rings of
Ex 37: 3 to be set in its **f** corners
Ex 37:13 cast for it **f** rings of gold
Ex 37:13 and put the rings on the **f**
Ex 37:13 that were at its **f** legs
Ex 37:20 were **f** bowls made like almond
Ex 38: 2 its horns on its **f** corners
Ex 38: 5 He cast **f** rings for the **f**
Ex 38:19 there were **f** pillars with
Ex 38:19 their **f** sockets of bronze
Ex 38:29 and two thousand **f** hundred
Ex 39:10 set in it **f** rows of stones
Lev 11:23 which have **f** feet shall be an
Num 1:29 fifty-four thousand **f** hundred
Num 1:31 thousand **f** hundred
Num 1:37 thousand **f** hundred
Num 1:43 thousand **f** hundred
Num 2: 6 fifty-four thousand **f** hundred
Num 2: 8 thousand **f** hundred
Num 2: 9 eighty-six thousand **f** hundred
Num 2:16 fifty-one thousand **f** hundred
Num 2:23 thousand **f** hundred
Num 2:30 thousand **f** hundred
Num 7: 7 **f** oxen he gave to the sons of
Num 7: 8 **f** carts and eight oxen he gave
Num 7:85 thousand **f** hundred shekels
Num 26:43 sixty-four thousand **f** hundred
Num 26:47 thousand **f** hundred
Num 26:50 forty-five thousand **f** hundred
Deut 3:11 **f** cubits its width, according
Deut 22:12 the **f** corners of the clothing
Josh 19: 7 **f** cities and their villages
Josh 21:18 its common-land: **f** cities
Josh 21:22 its common-land: **f** cities
Josh 21:24 its common-land: **f** cities
Josh 21:29 its common-land: **f** cities
Josh 21:31 its common-land: **f** cities
Josh 21:35 its common-land: **f** cities
Josh 21:37 its common-land: **f** cities
Josh 21:39 **f** cities in all
Judg 9:34 Shechem in **f** companies
Judg 11:40 **f** days each year to lament
Judg 19: 2 and was there **f** whole months
Judg 20: 2 God, **f** hundred thousand foot
Judg 20:17 **f** hundred thousand men who
Judg 20:47 rock of Rimmon for **f** months
Judg 21:12 of Jabesh Gilead **f** hundred
1Sa 4: 2 who killed about **f** thousand
1Sa 22: 2 there were about **f** hundred
1Sa 25:13 about **f** hundred men went with
1Sa 27: 7 was one full year and **f** months
1Sa 30:10 pursued, he and **f** hundred men
1Sa 30:17 except **f** hundred young men
2Sa 21:22 These **f** were born to the
1Ki 6: 1 came to pass in the **f** hundred
1Ki 7: 2 with **f** rows of cedar pillars,
1Ki 7:19 the shape of lilies, **f** cubits
1Ki 7:27 **f** cubits was the length of
1Ki 7:27 **f** cubits its width, and three
1Ki 7:30 cart had **f** bronze wheels and
1Ki 7:30 and its **f** feet had supports
1Ki 7:32 the panels were the **f** wheels
1Ki 7:34 there were **f** supports at the
1Ki 7:34 at the **f** corners of each cart
1Ki 7:38 and each laver was **f** cubits
1Ki 7:42 **f** hundred pomegranates for
1Ki 9:28 Ophir, and acquired **f** hundred
1Ki 10:26 thousand **f** hundred chariots
1Ki 18:19 the **f** hundred and fifty
1Ki 18:19 the **f** hundred prophets of
1Ki 18:22 Baal's prophets are **f** hundred
1Ki 18:33 Fill **f** waterpots with water,
1Ki 22: 6 about **f** hundred men, and said
2Ki 7: 3 Now there were **f** leprous men
2Ki 14:13 **f** hundred cubits
1Ch 3: 5 **f** by Bathshua the daughter of
1Ch 7: 1 **f** in all
1Ch 9:24 assigned to the **f** directions
1Ch 9:26 were **f** chief gatekeepers
1Ch 12:26 Levi **f** thousand six hundred
1Ch 21: 5 sword, and Judah had **f** hundred
1Ch 21:20 his **f** sons who were with him
1Ch 23: 5 **f** thousand were gatekeepers,
1Ch 23: 5 **f** thousand praised the LORD
1Ch 23:10 were the **f** sons of Shimei
1Ch 23:12 **f** in all
1Ch 26:17 on the north **f** each day, on
1Ch 26:17 day, on the south **f** each day
1Ch 26:18 there were **f** on the highway
2Ch 1:14 thousand **f** hundred chariots
2Ch 4:13 **f** hundred pomegranates for
2Ch 8:18 Ophir, and acquired **f** hundred
2Ch 9:25 Solomon had **f** thousand stalls
2Ch 13: 3 **f** hundred thousand choice men
2Ch 18: 5 **f** hundred men, and said to
2Ch 25:23 Corner Gate—**f** hundred cubits
Ezra 1:10 **f** hundred and ten silver
Ezra 1:11 were five thousand **f** hundred
Ezra 2:15 Adin, **f** hundred and fifty-four
Ezra 2:67 their camels **f** hundred and
Ezra 6:17 **f** hundred lambs, and as a sin
Neh 6: 4 sent me this message **f** times
Neh 7:69 their camels **f** hundred and
Neh 11: 6 at Jerusalem were **f** hundred
Job 1:19 struck the **f** corners of the
Job 42:16 for **f** generations
Prov 30:15 **f** things never say,
Prov 30:18 **f** which I do not understand
Prov 30:21 yes, for **f** it cannot bear up
Prov 30:24 There are **f** things which are
Prov 30:29 **f** which are stately in walk
Is 11:12 the **f** corners of the earth
Is 17: 6 bough, **f** or five in its most
Jer 15: 3 them **f** forms of destruction
Jer 36:23 had read three or **f** columns
Jer 49:36 the **f** winds from the **f**
Jer 49:36 from the **f** quarters of heaven
Jer 52:21 its thickness was **f** fingers
Jer 52:30 were **f** thousand six hundred
Ezek 1: 5 of **f** living creatures
Ezek 1: 6 Each one had **f** faces, and each
Ezek 1: 6 and each one had **f** wings
Ezek 1: 8 their wings on their **f** sides
Ezek 1: 8 and each of the **f** had faces
Ezek 1:10 each of the **f** had the face of
Ezek 1:10 each of the **f** had the face of
Ezek 1:10 each of the **f** had the face of
Ezek 1:15 creature with its **f** faces
Ezek 1:16 all **f** had the same likeness
Ezek 1:17 any one of **f** directions
Ezek 1:18 all around the **f** of them
Ezek 7: 2 the **f** corners of the land
Ezek 10: 9 there were **f** wheels by the
Ezek 10:10 all **f** looked alike
Ezek 10:11 any of their **f** directions
Ezek 10:12 and the wheels that the **f** had
Ezek 10:14 Each one had **f** faces
Ezek 10:21 Each one had **f** faces and each
Ezek 10:21 faces and each one **f** wings
Ezek 14:21 send My **f** severe judgments on
Ezek 37: 9 Come from the **f** winds, O
Ezek 40:41 **F** tables were on this side and
Ezek 40:41 **f** tables on that side, by the
Ezek 40:42 There were also **f** tables of
Ezek 41: 5 was **f** cubits on every side
Ezek 42:20 He measured it on the **f** sides
Ezek 43:14 to the larger ledge, **f** cubits
Ezek 43:15 altar hearth is **f** cubits high
Ezek 43:15 with **f** horns extending upward
Ezek 43:16 wide, square at its **f** corners
Ezek 43:17 fourteen wide on its **f** sides
Ezek 43:20 put it on the **f** horns of the
Ezek 43:20 on the **f** corners of the ledge
Ezek 45:19 on the **f** corners of the ledge
Ezek 46:21 by the **f** corners of the court
Ezek 46:22 In the **f** corners of the court
Ezek 46:22 all **f** corners were the same
Ezek 46:23 all around the **f** of them
Ezek 48:16 the north side **f** thousand
Ezek 48:16 the south side **f** thousand
Ezek 48:16 the east side **f** thousand five

Ezek 48:16 the west side f thousand five
Ezek 48:30 measuring f thousand five
Ezek 48:32 side, f thousand five hundred
Ezek 48:33 measuring f thousand five
Ezek 48:34 side, f thousand five hundred
Dan 1:17 As for these f young men, God
Dan 3:25 I see f men loose, walking in
Dan 7: 2 the f winds of heaven were
Dan 7: 3 f great beasts came up from
Dan 7: 6 on its back f wings of a bird
Dan 7: 6 The beast also had f heads
Dan 7:17 great beasts, which are f
Dan 7:17 are f kings which arise out
Dan 8: 8 in place of it f notable ones
Dan 8: 8 toward the f winds of heaven
Dan 8:22 the f that stood up in its
Dan 8:22 f kingdoms shall arise out of
Dan 11: 4 toward the f winds of heaven
Amos 1: 3 of Damascus, and for f, I will
Amos 1: 6 of Gaza, and for f, I will not
Amos 1: 9 of Tyre, and for f, I will not
Amos 1:11 of Edom, and for f, I will not
Amos 1:13 the people of Ammon, and for f
Amos 2: 1 of Moab, and for f, I will not
Amos 2: 4 of Judah, and for f, I will
Amos 2: 6 of Israel, and for f, I will
Zech 1:18 looked, and there were f horns
Zech 1:20 LORD showed me f craftsmen
Zech 2: 6 like the f winds of heaven
Zech 6: 1 f chariots were coming from
Zech 6: 5 These are f spirits of heaven
Matt 15:38 who ate were f thousand men
Matt 16:10 loaves of the f thousand and
Matt 24:31 His elect from the f winds
Mark 2: 3 who was carried by f men
Mark 8: 9 eaten were about f thousand
Mark 8:20 the seven for the f thousand
Mark 13:27 His elect from the f winds
John 4:35 There are still f months
John 6:19 rowed about three or f miles
John 11:17 been in the tomb f days
John 11:39 for he has been dead f days
John 19:23 made f parts, to each soldier
Acts 5:36 about f hundred, joined him
Acts 7: 6 oppress them f hundred years
Acts 10:11 sheet bound at the f corners
Acts 10:30 F days ago I was fasting
Acts 11: 5 down from heaven by f corners
Acts 12: 4 delivered him to f squads of
Acts 13:20 judges for about f hundred
Acts 21: 9 Now this man had f virgin
Acts 21:23 We have f men who have taken
Acts 21:38 led the f thousand assassins
Acts 27:29 they dropped f anchors from
Gal 3:17 the law, which was f hundred
Rev 4: 6 were f living creatures full
Rev 4: 8 the f living creatures, each
Rev 5: 6 of the f living creatures, and
Rev 5: 8 the f living creatures and the
Rev 5:14 Then the f living creatures
Rev 6: 1 I heard one of the f living
Rev 6: 6 the f living creatures saying
Rev 7: 1 After these things I saw f
Rev 7: 1 at the f corners of the earth
Rev 7: 1 holding the f winds of the
Rev 7: 2 the f angels to whom it was
Rev 7:11 the f living creatures, and
Rev 9:13 I heard a voice from the f
Rev 9:14 Release the f angels who are
Rev 9:15 So the f angels, who had been
Rev 14: 3 before the f living creatures
Rev 15: 7 Then one of the f living
Rev 19: 4 the f living creatures fell
Rev 20: 8 in the f corners of the earth

FOUR-FIFTHS
Gen 47:24 F shall be your own, as seed

FOURFOLD
2Sa 12: 6 shall restore f for the lamb
Luke 19: 8 false accusation, I restore f

FOUR-FOOTED (*see* FOOT, FOUR)
Acts 10:12 of f animals of the earth
Acts 11: 6 I saw f animals of the earth,
Rom 1:23 f beasts and creeping things

FOURS (*see* FOUR)
Lev 11:20 insects that creep on all f
Lev 11:21 insect that creeps on all f
Lev 11:27 of animals that go on all f
Lev 11:42 belly, whatever goes on all f

FOURSQUARE (*see* FOUR)
Ezek 40:47 and one hundred cubits wide, f
Ezek 48:20 thousand cubits, f

FOURTEEN (*see* FOURTEENTH)
Gen 31:41 I served you f years for your
Gen 46:22 f persons in all
Num 16:49 were f thousand seven hundred
Num 29:13 f lambs in their first year
Num 29:15 for each of the f lambs
Num 29:17 f lambs in their first year
Num 29:20 f lambs in their first year
Num 29:23 f lambs in their first year,
Num 29:26 f lambs in their first year
Num 29:29 f lambs in their first year
Num 29:32 f lambs in their first year
Josh 15:36 f cities with their villages
Josh 18:28 f cities with their villages
1Ki 8:65 seven more days—f days
1Ch 25: 5 For God gave Heman f sons
2Ch 13:21 grew mighty, married f wives
Job 42:12 for he had f thousand sheep,
Ezek 43:17 f cubits long and f wide
Matt 1:17 to David are f generations
Matt 1:17 in Babylon are f generations
Matt 1:17 the Christ are f generations
2Co 12: 2 man in Christ who f years ago
Gal 2: 1 Then after f years I went up

FOURTEENTH (*see* FOURTEEN)
Gen 14: 5 In the f year Chedorlaomer and
Ex 12: 6 the f day of the same month
Ex 12:18 on the f day of the month at
Lev 23: 5 On the f day of the first
Num 9: 3 On the f day of this month,
Num 9: 5 the f day of the first month
Num 9:11 On the f day of the second
Num 28:16 On the f day of the first
Josh 5:10 on the f day of the month at
2Ki 18:13 And in the f year of King
1Ch 24:13 Huppah, the f to Jeshebeab,
1Ch 25:21 the f for Mattithiah, his
2Ch 30:15 the f day of the second month
2Ch 35: 1 the f day of the first month
Ezra 6:19 the f day of the first month
Esth 9:15 together again on the f day
Esth 9:17 on the f day of the month
Esth 9:18 day, as well as on the f day
Esth 9:19 towns celebrated the f day of
Esth 9:21 should celebrate yearly the f
Is 36: 1 f year of King Hezekiah that
Ezek 40: 1 in the f year after the city
Ezek 45:21 on the f day of the month,
Acts 27:27 But when the f night had come
Acts 27:33 Today is the f day you have

FOURTH (*see* FOUR)
Gen 1:19 and the morning were the f day
Gen 2:14 The f river is the Euphrates
Gen 15:16 But in the f generation they
Ex 20: 5 f generations of those who
Ex 28:20 and the f row, a beryl, an
Ex 34: 7 the third and the f generation
Ex 39:13 the f row, a beryl, an onyx,
Lev 19:24 But in the f year all its
Num 7:30 On the f day Elizur the son
Num 14:18 to the third and f generation
Num 29:23 On the f day present ten
Deut 5: 9 f generations of those who
Josh 19:17 The f lot came out to
Judg 19: 5 f day that they arose early
1Sa 9: 8 one f of a shekel of silver
2Sa 3: 4 the f, Adonijah the son of
1Ki 6: 1 in the f year of Solomon's
1Ki 6:37 In the f year the foundation
1Ki 22:41 king over Judah in the f year
2Ki 10:30 of Israel to the f generation
2Ki 15:12 of Israel to the f generation
2Ki 18: 9 the f year of King Hezekiah
2Ki 25: 3 By the ninth day of the f
1Ch 2:14 Nethanel the f, Raddai the
1Ch 3: 2 the f, Adonijah the son of
1Ch 3:15 Zedekiah, and the f Shallum
1Ch 8: 2 Nohah the f, and Rapha the
1Ch 12:10 Mishmannah the f, Jeremiah
1Ch 23:19 the third, and Jekameam the f
1Ch 24: 8 to Harim, the f to Seorim,
1Ch 24:23 the third, and Jekameam the f
1Ch 25:11 the f for Jizri, his sons and
1Ch 26: 2 the third, Jathniel the f
1Ch 26: 4 Joah the third, Sacar the f
1Ch 26:11 the third, Zechariah the f
1Ch 27: 7 The f captain for the f
1Ch 27: 7 the f month was Asahel the
2Ch 3: 2 in the f year of his reign
2Ch 20:26 on the f day they assembled
Ezra 8:33 Now on the f day the silver
Neh 9: 3 for another f they confessed
Jer 25: 1 in the f year of Jehoiakim
Jer 28: 1 king of Judah, in the f year
Jer 36: 1 f year of Jehoiakim the son
Jer 39: 2 of Zedekiah, in the f month
Jer 45: 1 in the f year of Jehoiakim
Jer 46: 2 f year of Jehoiakim the son
Jer 51:59 in the f year of his reign
Jer 52: 6 By the f month, on the ninth
Ezek 1: 1 year, in the f month, on the
Ezek 10:14 the f the face of an eagle
Dan 2:40 the f kingdom shall be as
Dan 3:25 the form of the f is like the
Dan 7: 7 a f beast, dreadful and
Dan 7:19 the truth about the f beast
Dan 7:23 The f beast shall be a
Dan 7:23 shall be a f kingdom on earth
Dan 11: 2 the f shall be far richer
Zech 6: 3 with the f chariot dappled
Zech 7: 1 Now in the f year of King
Zech 7: 1 on the f day of the ninth
Zech 8:19 The fast of the f month, the
Matt 14:25 Now in the f watch of the
Mark 6:48 And about the f watch of the
Rev 4: 7 the f living creature was
Rev 6: 7 When He opened the f seal
Rev 6: 7 the f living creature saying
Rev 6: 8 to them over a f of the earth
Rev 8:12 Then the f angel sounded
Rev 16: 8 Then the f angel poured out
Rev 21:19 chalcedony, the f emerald,

FOWL (*see* FOWLER)
1Ki 4:23 roebucks, and fatted f
Neh 5:18 also f were prepared for me,
Ps 78:27 Feathered f like the sand of
Ps 148:10 Creeping things and flying f

FOWLER (*see* FOWL, FOWLER'S, FOWLERS)
Ps 91: 3 you from the snare of the f
Prov 6: 5 a bird from the hand of the f

FOWLER'S (*see* FOWLER)
Hos 9: 8 but the prophet is a f snare

FOWLERS (*see* FOWLER)
Ps 124: 7 bird from the snare of the f

FOX (*see* FOXES)
Neh 4: 3 if even a f goes up on it, he
Luke 13:32 Go, tell that f, Behold, I

FOXES (*see* FOX)
Judg 15: 4 and caught three hundred f
Judg 15: 4 turned the f tail to tail, and
Judg 15: 5 he let the f go into the
Song 2:15 Catch us the f, the little
Song 2:15 the little f that spoil the
Lam 5:18 with f walking about on it
Ezek 13: 4 are like f in the deserts
Matt 8:20 F have holes and birds of the
Luke 9:58 F have holes and birds of the

FRACTURE
Lev 24:20 f for f, eye for eye,

FRAGILE
Dan 2:42 be partly strong and partly f

FRAGMENTS
Is 30:14 not be found among its f a
Matt 14:20 full of the f that remained
Matt 15:37 full of the f that were left
Mark 6:43 up twelve baskets full of f
Mark 8: 8 large baskets of leftover f
Mark 8:19 full of f did you take up
Mark 8:20 full of f did you take up
Luke 9:17 f were taken up by them
John 6:12 Gather up the f that remain
John 6:13 twelve baskets with the f of

FRAGRANCE (*see* FRAGRANT)
Lev 26:31 the f of your sweet aromas
Song 1: 3 Because of the f of your good
Song 1:12 spikenard sends forth its f
Song 4:11 the f of your garments is
Song 4:11 is like the f of Lebanon
Song 7: 8 The f of your breath like
Song 7:13 The mandrakes give off a f
Hos 14: 6 tree, and his f like Lebanon

John 12: 3 filled with the f of the oil
2Co 2:14 through us diffuses the f of
2Co 2:15 For we are to God the f of

FRAGRANT (*see* FRAGRANCE)
Song 3: 6 all the merchant's f powders
Song 4:13 f henna with spikenard,
Matt 26: 7 flask of very costly f oil
Matt 26: 9 For this f oil might have
Matt 26:12 pouring this f oil on My body
Mark 14: 4 Why was this f oil wasted
Luke 7:37 an alabaster flask of f oil
Luke 7:38 anointed them with the f oil
Luke 7:46 anointed My feet with f oil
Luke 23:56 and prepared spices and f oils
John 11: 2 anointed the Lord with f oil
John 12: 5 Why was this f oil not sold
Rev 18:13 f oil and frankincense, wine

FRAIL (*see* FRAILTY)
Ps 39: 4 That I may know how f I am

FRAILTY (*see* FRAIL)
Dan 10: 8 vigor was turned to f in me

FRAME (*see* FRAMED, FRAMES)
Ex 25:25 You shall make for it a f of
Ex 25:25 molding for the f all around
Ex 25:27 rings shall be close to the f
Ex 37:12 Also he made a f of a
Ex 37:12 gold for the f all around it
Ex 37:14 The rings were close to the f
Ps 103:14 For He knows our f
Ps 139:15 My f was not hidden from You,

FRAMED (*see* FRAME)
Heb 11: 3 were f by the word of God

FRAMES (*see* FRAME)
1Ki 6: 4 house windows with beveled f
1Ki 7: 4 with beveled f in three rows
1Ki 7: 5 doorposts had rectangular f
1Ki 7:28 and the panels were between f
1Ki 7:29 were between the f were lions
1Ki 7:29 on the f was a pedestal on
Ps 50:19 evil, And your tongue f deceit
Ezek 40:16 window f in the gate chambers
Ezek 41:16 and the beveled window f
Ezek 41:26 There were beveled window f

FRANKINCENSE
Ex 30:34 and pure f with these sweet
Lev 2: 1 oil on it, and put f on it
Lev 2: 2 flour and oil with all the f
Lev 2:15 put oil on it, and lay f on it
Lev 2:16 of its oil, with all the f
Lev 5:11 nor shall he put any f on it
Lev 6:15 all the f which is on the
Lev 24: 7 shall put pure f on each row
Num 5:15 oil on it and put no f on it
Neh 13: 5 the grain offerings, the f
Neh 13: 9 the grain offering and the f
Song 3: 6 perfumed with myrrh and f
Song 4: 6 of myrrh and to the hill of f
Song 4:14 cinnamon, with all trees of f
Jer 6:20 to Me comes f from Sheba, and
Matt 2:11 gold, f, and myrrh
Rev 18:13 and incense, fragrant oil and f

FRAUD
Hos 7: 1 For they have committed f
Acts 13:10 O full of all deceit and all f
Jas 5: 4 which you kept back by f

FREE (*see* FREED, FREEDMAN, FREEDOM, FREELY, FREEWILL, FREEWOMAN)
Ex 21: 2 the seventh he shall go out f
Ex 21: 5 I will not go out f,'
Ex 21:11 her, then she shall go out f
Ex 21:26 he shall let him go f for the
Ex 21:27 he shall let him go f for the
Lev 1: 3 own f will at the door of the
Lev 19: 5 offer it of your own f will
Lev 19:20 death, because she was not f
Lev 22:19 f will a male without blemish
Lev 22:29 offer it of your own f will
Num 5:19 be f from this bitter water
Num 5:28 is clean, then she shall be f
Num 5:31 man shall be f from iniquity
Deut 15:12 shall let him go f from you
Deut 15:13 you send him away f from you
Deut 15:18 you send him away f from you
Deut 21:14 her, then you shall set her f
Deut 24: 5 he shall be f at home one
Deut 32:36 no one remaining, bond or f
Josh 2:20 then we will be f from your
Judg 16:20 times, and shake myself f
1Ki 14:10 male in Israel, bond and f
1Ki 21:21 in Israel, both bond and f
2Ki 9: 8 in Israel, both bond and f
2Ki 14:26 and whether bond or f, there
1Ch 9:33 and were f from other duties
Job 3:19 the servant is f from his
Job 10: 1 I will give f course to my
Job 39: 5 Who set the wild donkey f
Ps 82: 4 F them from the hand of the
Ps 105:20 of the people let him go f
Is 45:13 My city and let My exiles go f
Is 58: 6 to let the oppressed go f
Jer 34: 9 man should set f his male
Jer 34:10 should set f his male and
Jer 34:11 return, whom they had set f
Jer 34:14 man set f his Hebrew brother
Jer 34:14 shall let him go f from you
Jer 40: 4 I f you this day from the
Zech 9:11 f from the waterless pit
Mal 3:15 yes, those who tempt God go f
Matt 17:26 Then the sons are f
John 8:32 and the truth shall make you f
John 8:33 you say, 'You will be made f'
John 8:36 if the Son makes you f
John 8:36 you shall be f indeed
Acts 26:32 man might have been set f if
Rom 5:15 But the f gift is not like
Rom 5:16 but the f gift which came
Rom 5:18 the f gift came to all men
Rom 6:18 And having been set f from sin
Rom 6:20 sin, you were f in regard to
Rom 6:22 having been set f from sin
Rom 7: 3 she is f from that law, so
Rom 8: 2 made me f from the law of sin
1Co 7:21 but if you can be made f,
1Co 7:22 while f is Christ's slave
1Co 9: 1 Am I not f?
1Co 9:19 though I am f from all men
1Co 12:13 Greeks, whether slaves or f
2Co 11: 7 of God to you f of charge
Gal 3:28 there is neither slave nor f
Gal 4:26 but the Jerusalem above is f
Gal 4:31 of the bondwoman but of the f
Gal 5: 1 by which Christ has made us f
Eph 6: 8 whether he is a slave or f
Col 3:11 Scythian, slave nor f, but
2Th 3: 1 of the Lord may have f course
2Th 3: 8 anyone's bread f of charge
Heb 13:23 Timothy has been set f, with
1Pe 2:16 as f, yet not using your
Rev 6:15 every slave and every f man
Rev 13:16 and great, rich and poor, f
Rev 19:18 and the flesh of all people, f

FREED (*see* FREE)
Josh 9:23 shall be f from being slaves
Ps 81: 6 His hands were f from the
Rom 6: 7 has died has been f from sin

FREEDMAN (*see* FREE, FREEDMEN)
1Co 7:22 while a slave is the Lord's f

FREEDMEN (*see* FREEDMAN)
Acts 6: 9 Synagogue of the F (Cyrenians

FREEDOM (*see* FREE)
Lev 19:20 been redeemed nor given her f
Ps 146: 7 The LORD gives f to the

FREELY (*see* FREE)
Gen 2:16 of the garden you may f eat
Num 11: 5 fish which we ate f in Egypt
1Sa 14:30 if the people had eaten f
Ezra 2:68 offered f for the house of
Ezra 7:15 his counselors have f offered
Ezra 7:16 are to be f offered for the
Ps 54: 6 I will f sacrifice to You
Is 32:20 who send out f the feet of
Hos 14: 4 I will love them f, for My
Matt 10: 8 F you have received, f give
Mark 1:45 out and began to proclaim it f
Luke 7:42 repay, he f forgave them both
Acts 2:29 let me speak f to you of the
Acts 20:37 Then they all wept f, and fell
Acts 26:26 before whom I also speak f
Rom 3:24 being justified f by His
Rom 8:32 Him also f give us all things
1Co 2:12 been f given to us by God
2Co 8: 3 ability, they were f willing
Rev 21: 6 of life f to him who thirsts
Rev 22:17 him take the water of life f

FREEWILL (*see* FREE)
Ex 35:29 of Israel brought a f
Ex 36: 3 him f offerings every morning
Lev 22:18 or for any of his f offerings
Lev 22:21 vow, or a f offering from the
Lev 22:23 you may offer as a f offering
Lev 23:38 besides all your f offerings
Num 15: 3 or as a f offering or in your
Num 29:39 your f offerings) as your
Deut 12: 6 your f offerings, and the
Deut 12:17 of your f offerings, or of
Deut 16:10 a f offering from your hand
2Ch 31:14 was over the f offerings to
Ezra 1: 4 besides the f offerings for
Ezra 3: 5 a f offering to the LORD
Ezra 7:16 along with the f offering of
Ezra 8:28 the gold are a f offering to
Ps 119:108 the f offerings of my mouth,
Amos 4: 5 and announce the f offerings

FREEWOMAN (*see* FREE)
Gal 4:22 a bondwoman, the other by a f
Gal 4:23 he of the f through promise,
Gal 4:30 be heir with the son of the f

FREQUENT (*see* FREQUENTLY)
1Ti 5:23 sake and your f infirmities

FREQUENTLY (*see* FREQUENT)
2Co 11:23 measure, in prisons more f

FRESH (*see* FRESHLY)
Lev 23:14 f grain until the same day
Num 6: 3 nor eat f grapes or raisins
Judg 15:15 He found a f jawbone of a
Judg 16: 7 me with seven f bowstrings
Judg 16: 8 up to her seven f bowstrings
Job 29:20 My glory is f within me, and
Ps 92:10 have been anointed with f oil
Ps 92:14 They shall be f and
Jas 3:11 a spring send forth f water
Jas 3:12 yield both salt water and f

FRESHLY (*see* FRESH)
Gen 8:11 a f plucked olive leaf was in

FRET (*see* FRETS)
Ps 37: 1 Do not f because of evildoers
Ps 37: 7 Do not f because of him who
Ps 37: 8 Do not f—it only causes harm
Prov 24:19 Do not f because of evil

FRETS (*see* FRET)
Prov 19: 3 his heart f against the LORD

FRIEND (*see* FRIENDLY, FRIENDS, FRIENDSHIP)
Gen 38:12 his f Hirah the Adullamite
Gen 38:20 hand of his f the Adullamite
Ex 33:11 as a man speaks to his f
Deut 13: 6 or your f who is as your own
Ruth 4: 1 Come aside, f, sit down here
2Sa 13: 3 But Amnon had a f whose name
2Sa 15:37 So Hushai, David's f, went
2Sa 16:16 Hushai the Archite, David's f
2Sa 16:17 this your loyalty to your f
2Sa 16:17 did you not go with your f
1Ki 4: 5 a priest and the king's f
2Ch 20: 7 of Abraham Your f forever
Job 6:14 should be shown by his f,
Job 6:27 and you undermine your f
Ps 15: 3 up a reproach against his f
Ps 35:14 he were my f or brother
Ps 41: 9 familiar f in whom I trusted
Ps 88:18 f You have put far from me,
Prov 6: 1 you become surety for your f
Prov 6: 3 come into the hand of your f
Prov 6: 3 plead with your f
Prov 17:17 A f loves at all times, and a
Prov 17:18 and becomes surety for his f
Prov 18:24 but there is a f who sticks
Prov 19: 4 poor is separated from his f
Prov 19: 6 every man is a f to one who
Prov 22:11 lips, the king will be his f
Prov 27: 6 are the wounds of a f, but
Prov 27: 9 the sweetness of a man's f
Prov 27:10 own f or your father's f
Prov 27:14 his f with a loud voice,
Prov 27:17 the countenance of his f
Song 5:16 my beloved, and this is my f
Is 41: 8 descendants of Abraham My f
Jer 6:21 and his f shall perish
Jer 19: 9 flesh of his f in the siege
Mic 7: 5 Do not trust in a f
Matt 11:19 a f of tax collectors and

Matt 20:13 one of them and said, 'F, I am
Matt 22:12 So he said to him, F, how
Matt 26:50 F, why have you come
Luke 7:34 a f of tax collectors and
Luke 11: 5 Which of you shall have a f
Luke 11: 5 at midnight and say to him, 'F
Luke 11: 6 for a f of mine has come to
Luke 11: 8 to him because he is his f
Luke 14:10 comes he may say to you, 'F
John 3:29 but the f of the bridegroom,
John 11:11 Our f Lazarus sleeps, but I
John 19:12 go, you are not Caesar's f
Acts 12:20 king's chamberlain their f
Phm 1 To Philemon our beloved f
Jas 2:23 And he was called the f of God
Jas 4: 4 therefore wants to be a f of

FRIENDLY (*see* FRIEND)
Job 29: 4 when the f counsel of God was
Prov 18:24 has friends must himself be f

FRIENDS (*see* FRIEND)
Gen 26:26 with Ahuzzath, one of his f
Judg 11:37 and bewail my virginity, my f
Judg 11:38 and she went with her f, and
1Sa 30:26 the elders of Judah, to his f
2Sa 3: 8 to his brothers, and to his f
2Sa 19: 6 your enemies and hate your f
1Ki 16:11 of his kinsmen nor of his f
Esth 5:10 he sent and called for his f
Esth 5:14 and all his f said to him,
Esth 6:13 all his f everything that had
Job 2:11 Now when Job's three f heard
Job 12: 4 I am one mocked by his f, who
Job 16:20 My f scorn me
Job 17: 5 who speaks flattery to his f
Job 19:14 my close f have forgotten me
Job 19:19 All my close f abhor me, and
Job 19:21 have pity on me, O you my f
Job 32: 3 three f his wrath was aroused
Job 42: 7 against you and your two f
Job 42:10 when he prayed for his f
Ps 38:11 and my f stand aloof from my
Prov 12:26 should choose his f carefully
Prov 14:20 but the rich has many f
Prov 16:28 separates the best of f
Prov 17: 9 separates the best of f
Prov 18:24 A man who has f must himself
Prov 19: 4 Wealth makes many f, but the
Prov 19: 7 more do his f go far from him
Jer 20: 4 to yourself and to all your f
Jer 20: 6 there, you and all your f, to
Jer 38:22 Your close f have set upon
Lam 1: 2 All her f have dealt
Zech 13: 6 wounded in the house of my f
Matt 9:15 Can the f of the bridegroom
Mark 2:19 Can the f of the bridegroom
Mark 5:19 Go home to your f, and tell
Luke 5:34 Can you make the f of the
Luke 7: 6 the centurion sent f to Him
Luke 12: 4 And I say to you, My f, do not
Luke 14:12 a supper, do not ask your f
Luke 15: 6 home, he calls together his f
Luke 15: 9 has found it, she calls her f
Luke 15:29 I might make merry with my f
Luke 16: 9 you, make f for yourselves by
Luke 21:16 and brothers, relatives and f
Luke 23:12 and Herod became f with each
John 15:13 lay down one's life for his f
John 15:14 You are My f if you do
John 15:15 but I have called you f, for
Acts 10:24 his relatives and close f
Acts 19:31 of Asia, who were his f, sent
Acts 24:23 not to forbid any of his f to
Acts 27: 3 him liberty to go to his f
3Jn 14 Our f greet you
3Jn 14 Greet the f by name

FRIENDSHIP (*see* FRIEND)
Prov 22:24 Make no f with an angry man,
Jas 4: 4 Do you not know that f with

FRIGHTEN (*see* FRIGHTENED)
Deut 28:26 and no one shall f them away
2Ch 32:18 to f them and trouble them,
Neh 6:19 Tobiah sent letters to f me
Job 13:25 Will You f a leaf driven to
Job 18:11 Terrors f him on every side,
Job 39:20 Can you f him like a locust
Ps 83:15 And f them with Your storm
Jer 7:33 And no one will f them away

FRIGHTENED (*see* FRIGHTEN)
2Sa 22:46 come f from their hideouts
Job 18:20 as those in the east are f
Job 39:22 He mocks at fear, and is not f
Ps 18:45 come f from their hideouts
Is 21: 4 wavered, fearfulness f me
Luke 24:37 But they were terrified and f

FRIVOLITY
Prov 12:11 but he who follows f is
Prov 28:19 but he who follows f will

FRO (*see* PREFACE)

FROGS
Ex 8: 2 all your territory with f
Ex 8: 3 bring forth f abundantly,
Ex 8: 4 the f shall come up on you,
Ex 8: 5 cause f to come up on the
Ex 8: 6 the f came up and covered the
Ex 8: 7 brought up f on the land of
Ex 8: 8 may take away the f from me
Ex 8: 9 to destroy the f from you
Ex 8:11 the f shall depart from you,
Ex 8:12 the f which He had brought
Ex 8:13 the f died out of the houses,
Ps 78:45 which devoured them, And f
Ps 105:30 Their land abounded with f
Rev 16:13 f coming out of the mouth of

FROM (*see* PREFACE)

FRONT (*see* PREFACE)

FRONTED
Ezek 41:12 The building that f the

FRONTIER
Josh 22:11 the f of the land of Canaan
Ezek 25: 9 of the cities on its f, the

FRONTLETS
Ex 13:16 as f between your eyes, for
Deut 6: 8 they shall be as f between
Deut 11:18 they shall be as f between

FROST
Gen 31:40 the f by night, and my sleep
Ex 16:14 as fine as f on the ground
Job 38:29 the f of heaven, who gives it
Ps 78:47 their sycamore trees with f
Ps 147:16 He scatters the f like ashes
Jer 36:30 the day and the f of the night

FROZEN
Job 37:10 and the broad waters are f
Job 38:30 the surface of the deep is f

FRUIT (*see* FRUITFUL, FRUITS)
Gen 1:11 the f tree that yields f
Gen 1:12 and the tree that yields f
Gen 1:29 tree whose f yields seed
Gen 3: 2 We may eat the f of the trees
Gen 3: 3 but of the f of the tree
Gen 3: 6 one wise, she took of its f
Gen 4: 3 f of the ground to the LORD
Gen 30: 2 from you the f of the womb
Ex 10:15 all the f of the trees which
Ex 23:16 the f of your labors from the
Lev 19:23 their f as uncircumcised
Lev 19:24 year all its f shall be holy
Lev 19:25 fifth year you may eat its f
Lev 23:39 gathered in the f of the land
Lev 23:40 day the f of beautiful trees
Lev 25: 3 vineyard, and gather in its f
Lev 25:19 the land will yield its f
Lev 26: 4 the field shall yield their f
Lev 26:20 of the land yield their f
Lev 27:30 land or of the f of the tree
Num 13:20 some of the f of the land
Num 13:26 showed them the f of the land
Num 13:27 and honey, and this is its f
Num 18:13 first ripe f is in their land
Deut 1:25 f of the land in their hands
Deut 7:13 also bless the f of your womb
Deut 7:13 and the f of your land, your
Deut 22: 9 the f of your vineyard be
Deut 28: 4 shall be the f of your body
Deut 28:11 in the f of your body, in the
Deut 28:18 shall be the f of your body
Deut 28:33 shall eat the f of your land
Deut 28:53 eat the f of your own body
Deut 30: 9 in the f of your body, in the
Judg 9:11 my sweetness and my good f
2Sa 16: 2 summer f for the young men to
2Ki 19:29 and eat the f of them
2Ki 19:30 downward, and bear f upward
Neh 9:25 and f trees in abundance
Neh 9:36 to our fathers, to eat its f
Neh 10:35 of all f of all trees, year
Neh 10:37 the f from all kinds of trees
Job 31:39 eaten its f without money
Ps 1: 3 forth its f in its season
Ps 72:16 Its f shall wave like Lebanon
Ps 80:12 pass by the way pluck her f
Ps 92:14 shall still bear f in old age
Ps 104:13 with the f of Your works
Ps 105:35 And devoured the f of their
Ps 127: 3 The f of the womb is His
Ps 132:11 throne the f of your body
Prov 1:31 eat the f of their own way
Prov 8:19 My f is better than gold, yes
Prov 11:30 The f of the righteous is a
Prov 12:12 of the righteous yields f
Prov 12:14 good by the f of his mouth
Prov 13: 2 well by the f of his mouth
Prov 18:20 from the f of his mouth, and
Prov 18:21 who love it will eat its f
Prov 27:18 the fig tree will eat its f
Prov 31:31 her of the f of her hands
Eccl 2: 5 all kinds of f trees in them
Song 2: 3 his f was sweet to my taste
Song 8:11 was to bring for its f a
Song 8:12 who keep its f two hundred
Is 3:10 eat the f of their doings
Is 4: 2 the f of the earth shall be
Is 10:12 I will punish the f of the
Is 13:18 no pity on the f of the womb
Is 27: 6 the face of the world with f
Is 27: 9 this is all the f of taking
Is 28: 4 like the first f before the
Is 34: 4 as f falling from a fig tree
Is 37:30 and eat the f of them
Is 37:31 downward, and bear f upward
Is 57:19 I create the f of the lips
Is 65:21 vineyards and eat their f
Jer 2: 7 country, to eat its f and its
Jer 6:19 even the f of their thoughts,
Jer 7:20 and on the f of the ground
Jer 11:16 Tree, Lovely and of Good F
Jer 11:19 destroy the tree with its f
Jer 12: 2 they grow, yes, they bear f
Jer 17: 8 will cease from yielding f
Jer 17:10 to the f of his doings
Jer 21:14 to the f of your doings,"
Jer 29: 5 plant gardens and eat their f
Jer 29:28 plant gardens and eat their f
Jer 32:19 to the f of his doings
Jer 40:10 you, gather wine and summer f
Jer 40:12 wine and summer f in abundance
Jer 48:32 has fallen on your summer f
Ezek 17: 8 bring forth branches, bear f
Ezek 17: 9 up its roots, cut off its f
Ezek 17:23 bring forth boughs, and bear f
Ezek 19:12 and the east wind dried her f
Ezek 19:14 branches and devoured her f
Ezek 25: 4 they shall eat your f, and
Ezek 34:27 the field shall yield their f
Ezek 36: 8 yield your f to My people
Ezek 36:30 multiply the f of your trees
Ezek 47:12 and their f will not fail
Ezek 47:12 They will bear f every month
Ezek 47:12 Their f will be for food, and
Dan 4:12 its f abundant, and in it was
Dan 4:14 its leaves and scatter its f
Dan 4:21 its f abundant, in which was
Hos 9:16 they shall bear no f
Hos 9:16 the beloved f of their womb
Hos 10: 1 he brings forth f for himself
Hos 10: 1 to the multitude of his f he
Hos 10:13 You have eaten the f of lies
Hos 14: 8 Your f is found in Me
Joel 2:22 up, and the tree bears its f
Amos 2: 9 yet I destroyed his f above
Amos 6:12 the f of righteousness into
Amos 7:14 and a tender of sycamore f
Amos 8: 1 Behold, a basket of summer f
Amos 8: 2 A basket of summer f
Amos 9:14 gardens and eat f from them
Mic 6: 7 the f of my body for the sin
Mic 7: 1 f which my soul desires
Mic 7:13 and for the f of their deeds
Hab 3:17 nor f be on the vines
Hag 1:10 and the earth withholds its f
Hag 2:19 olive tree have not yielded f

Zech 8:12 the vine shall give its f
Mal 1:12 and its f, its food, is
Mal 3:11 destroy the f of your ground
Mal 3:11 bear f for you in the field
Matt 3:10 not bear good f is cut down
Matt 7:17 every good tree bears good f
Matt 7:17 but a bad tree bears bad f
Matt 7:18 A good tree cannot bear bad f
Matt 7:18 can a bad tree bear good f
Matt 7:19 not bear good f is cut down
Matt 12:33 its f good, or else make the
Matt 12:33 the tree bad and its f bad
Matt 12:33 for a tree is known by its f
Matt 13:23 it, who indeed bears f and
Matt 21:19 Let no f grow on you ever
Matt 21:34 that they might receive its f
Matt 26:29 f of the vine from now on
Mark 4:20 word, accept it, and bear f
Mark 11:14 Let no one eat f from you
Mark 12: 2 f of the vineyard from the
Mark 14:25 f of the vine until that day
Luke 1:42 blessed is the f of your womb
Luke 3: 9 not bear good f is cut down
Luke 6:43 good tree does not bear bad f
Luke 6:43 does a bad tree bear good f
Luke 6:44 tree is known by its own f
Luke 8:14 and bring no f to maturity
Luke 8:15 it and bear f with patience
Luke 13: 6 and he came seeking f on it
Luke 13: 7 seeking f on this fig tree
Luke 13: 9 And if it bears f, well
Luke 20:10 some of the f of the vineyard
Luke 22:18 the f of the vine until the
John 4:36 gathers f for eternal life,
John 15: 2 does not bear f He takes away
John 15: 2 branch that bears f He prunes
John 15: 2 that it may bear more f
John 15: 4 cannot bear f of itself,
John 15: 5 Me, and I in him, bears much f
John 15: 8 that you bear much f
John 15:16 that you should go and bear f
John 15:16 that your f should remain,
Acts 2:30 him that of the f of his body
Rom 1:13 have some f among you also
Rom 6:21 What f did you have then in
Rom 6:22 you have your f to holiness
Rom 7: 4 that we should bear f to God
Rom 7: 5 members to bear f to death
Rom 15:28 and have sealed to them this f
1Co 9: 7 and does not eat of its f
Gal 5:22 But the f of the Spirit is
Eph 5: 9 (for the f of the Spirit is
Phil 1:22 will mean f from my labor
Phil 4:17 but I seek the f that abounds
Col 1: 6 world, and is bringing forth f
Heb 12:11 it yields the peaceable f of
Heb 13:15 the f of our lips, giving
Jas 3:18 Now the f of righteousness is
Jas 5: 7 the precious f of the earth
Jas 5:18 and the earth produced its f
Jude 12 late autumn trees without f
Rev 18:14 the f that your soul longed
Rev 22: 2 yielding its f every month

FRUITFUL (*see* FRUIT, UNFRUITFUL)
Gen 1:22 Be f and multiply, and fill the
Gen 1:28 Be f and multiply
Gen 8:17 abound on the earth, and be f
Gen 9: 1 Be f and multiply, and fill the
Gen 9: 7 And as for you, be f and
Gen 17: 6 I will make you exceedingly f
Gen 17:20 him, and will make him f, and
Gen 26:22 and we shall be f in the land
Gen 28: 3 bless you, and make you f and
Gen 35:11 Be f and multiply
Gen 41:52 me to be f in the land of my
Gen 48: 4 Behold, I will make you f
Gen 49:22 Joseph is a f bough, a
Gen 49:22 bough, a f bough by a well
Ex 1: 7 the children of Israel were f
Lev 26: 9 you favorably and make you f
2Ki 19:23 its borders, to its f forest
Ps 107:34 A f land into barrenness, For
Ps 107:37 they may yield a f harvest
Ps 128: 3 a f vine In the very heart of
Ps 148: 9 F trees and all cedars
Is 5: 1 a vineyard On a very f hill
Is 10:18 his forest and of his f field
Is 17: 6 five in its most f branches
Is 29:17 be turned into a f field, and
Is 29:17 the f field be esteemed as a
Is 32:12 fields, for the f vine
Is 32:15 wilderness becomes a f field
Is 32:15 the f field is counted as a
Is 32:16 remain in the f field
Is 37:24 height, to its f forest
Jer 4:26 and indeed the f land was a
Jer 23: 3 and they shall be f and
Ezek 19:10 Planted by the waters, f
Hos 13:15 Though he is f among his
Acts 14:17 f seasons, filling our hearts
Col 1:10 being f in every good work and

FRUITS (*see* FRUIT)
Gen 43:11 Take some of the best f of
Deut 33:14 the precious f of the sun
2Sa 16: 1 raisins, one hundred summer f
Song 4:13 pomegranates with pleasant f
Song 4:16 garden and eat its pleasant f
Song 7:13 at our gates are pleasant f
Is 16: 9 fallen over your summer f
Is 33: 9 and Carmel shake off their f
Lam 4: 9 lack of the f of the field
Mic 7: 1 those who gather summer f
Matt 3: 8 Therefore bear f worthy of
Matt 7:16 You will know them by their f
Matt 7:20 by their f you will know them
Matt 21:41 to him the f in their seasons
Matt 21:43 a nation bearing the f of it
Luke 3: 8 Therefore bear f worthy of
2Co 9:10 and increase the f of your
Phil 1:11 being filled with the f of
Jas 3:17 full of mercy and good f,
Rev 22: 2 of life, which bore twelve f

FRUSTRATE (*see* FRUSTRATED, FRUSTRATES)
Ezra 4: 5 f their purpose all the days

FRUSTRATED (*see* FRUSTRATE)
Dan 3:28 they have f the king's word,

FRUSTRATES (*see* FRUSTRATE)
Job 5:12 He f the devices of the
Is 44:25 Who f the signs of the

FUEL
Is 9: 5 used for burning and f of fire
Is 9:19 shall be as f for the fire
Ezek 4:12 and bake it using f of human
Ezek 15: 4 is thrown into the fire for f
Ezek 15: 6 have given to the fire for f
Ezek 21:32 You shall be f for the fire
Ezek 24: 5 also pile f bones under it,

FUGITIVE (*see* FUGITIVES)
Gen 4:12 A f and a vagabond you shall
Gen 4:14 I shall be a f and a vagabond
1Ch 12: 1 a f from Saul the son of Kish

FUGITIVES (*see* FUGITIVE)
Num 21:29 He has given his sons as f
Judg 12: 4 You Gileadites are f of
Is 15: 5 his f shall flee to Zoar,
Is 43:14 and bring them all down as f
Ezek 17:21 All his f with all his troops

FULFILL (*see* FULFILLED, FULFILLING, FULFILLMENT, FULFILLS)
Gen 29:27 F her week, and we will give
Ex 5:13 F your work, your daily quota
Ex 23:26 I will f the number of your
Lev 22:21 to f his vow, or a freewill
Num 15: 3 to f a vow or as a freewill
Num 15: 8 or as a sacrifice to f a vow
Deut 9: 5 that He may f the word which
1Ki 2: 4 that the LORD may f His word
1Ki 2:27 that he might f the word of
1Ki 5: 9 And you shall f my desire by
1Ki 12:15 that He might f His word
1Ch 22:13 take care to f the statutes
2Ch 10:15 the LORD might f His word
2Ch 36:21 to f the word of the LORD by
2Ch 36:21 Sabbath, to f seventy years
Esth 5: 8 f my request, then let the
Job 39: 2 number the months that they f
Ps 20: 4 desire, And f all your purpose
Ps 20: 5 May the LORD f all your
Ps 145:19 He will f the desire of those
Jer 44:25 You will surely f your vows
Ezek 20: 8 f My anger against them in
Ezek 20:21 f My anger against them in
Matt 3:15 for us to f all righteousness
Matt 5:17 not come to destroy but to f
Rom 13:14 for the flesh, to f its lusts
Gal 5:16 you shall not f the lust of
Gal 6: 2 and so f the law of Christ
Phil 2: 2 f my joy by being like-minded
Col 1:25 you, to f the word of God,
Col 4:17 the Lord, that you may f it
2Th 1:11 f all the good pleasure of
2Ti 4: 5 evangelist, f your ministry
Jas 2: 8 If you really f the royal law
Rev 17:17 their hearts to f His purpose

FULFILLED (*see* FULFILL)
Gen 25:24 were f for her to give birth
Gen 29:21 me my wife, for my days are f
Gen 29:28 Jacob did so and f her week
Ex 5:14 Why have you not f your task
Lev 12: 4 of her purification are f
Lev 12: 6 of her purification are f
Num 6: 5 until the days are f for
Num 6:13 days of his separation are f
2Sa 7:12 When your days are f and you
2Sa 14:22 in that the king has f the
1Ki 8:15 and with His hand has f it
1Ki 8:20 So the LORD has f His word
1Ki 8:24 f it with Your hand, as it is
1Ch 17:11 be, when your days are f,
2Ch 6: 4 who has f with His hands what
2Ch 6:10 So the LORD has f His word
2Ch 6:15 f it with Your hand, as it is
2Ch 36:22 mouth of Jeremiah might be f
Ezra 1: 1 mouth of Jeremiah might be f
Is 65:20 man who has not f his days
Jer 25:34 and your dispersions are f
Jer 44:25 f with your hands, saying,
Lam 2:17 He has f His word which He
Lam 4:11 The LORD has f His fury, He
Dan 4:33 f concerning Nebuchadnezzar
Dan 10: 3 till three whole weeks were f
Matt 1:22 be f which was spoken by the
Matt 2:15 that it might be f which was
Matt 2:17 Then was f what was spoken by
Matt 2:23 that it might be f which was
Matt 4:14 that it might be f which was
Matt 5:18 from the law till all is f
Matt 8:17 that it might be f which was
Matt 12:17 that it might be f which was
Matt 13:14 the prophecy of Isaiah is f
Matt 13:35 that it might be f which was
Matt 21: 4 be f which was spoken by the
Matt 24:34 till all these things are f
Matt 26:54 could the Scriptures be f
Matt 26:56 of the prophets might be f
Matt 27: 9 Then was f what was spoken by
Matt 27:35 that it might be f which was
Mark 1:15 The time is f, and the kingdom
Mark 13: 4 all these things will be f
Mark 14:49 But the Scriptures must be f
Mark 15:28 Scripture was f which says
Luke 1:20 will be f in their own time
Luke 4:21 is f in your hearing
Luke 21:22 which are written may be f
Luke 21:24 times of the Gentiles are f
Luke 21:32 away till all things are f
Luke 22:16 it is f in the kingdom of God
Luke 24:44 that all things must be f
John 3:29 this joy of mine is f
John 12:38 Isaiah the prophet might be f
John 13:18 that the Scripture may be f
John 15:25 that the word might be f
John 17:12 that the Scripture might be f
John 17:13 have My joy f in themselves
John 18: 9 might be f which He spoke
John 18:32 might be f which He spoke
John 19:24 might be f which says
John 19:28 that the Scripture might be f
John 19:36 the Scripture should be f
Acts 1:16 this Scripture had to be f
Acts 3:18 would suffer, He has thus f
Acts 12:25 they had f their ministry
Acts 13:27 have f them in condemning Him
Acts 13:29 Now when they had f all that
Acts 13:33 God has f this for us their
Rom 8: 4 of the law might be f in us
Rom 13: 8 loves another has f the law
2Co 10: 6 when your obedience is f
Gal 5:14 all the law is f in one word
Jas 2:23 Scripture was f which says
Rev 17:17 until the words of God are f

FULFILLING (*see* FULFILL)
Ps 148: 8 Stormy wind, f His word
Eph 2: 3 f the desires of the flesh and

FULFILLMENT (*see* FULFILL)
Ps 66:12 You brought us out to rich f
Ezek 12:23 and the f of every vision
Dan 11:14 themselves in f of the vision
Dan 12: 6 How long shall the f of these
Luke 1:45 for there will be a f of
Rom 13:10 love is the f of the law

FULFILLS (*see* FULFILL)
Rom 2:27 if he f the law, judge you

FULL (*see* FILL, FULL-GROWN, FULLNESS, FULLY)
Gen 14:10 Siddim was f of asphalt pits
Gen 23: 9 give it to me at the f price
Gen 25: 8 f of years, and was gathered
Gen 35:29 being old and f of days
Gen 41: 1 at the end of two f years
Gen 41: 7 the seven plump and f heads
Gen 41:22 heads came up on one stalk, f
Gen 43:21 sack, our money in f weight
Ex 8:21 shall be f of swarms of flies
Ex 14:27 sea returned to its f depth
Ex 16: 3 and when we ate bread to the f
Ex 16: 8 in the morning bread to the f
Ex 22: 3 He should make f restitution
Lev 2:14 grain beaten from f heads
Lev 6: 5 He shall restore its f value
Lev 16:12 f of burning coals of fire
Lev 16:12 with his hands f of sweet
Lev 19:29 land become f of wickedness
Lev 25:29 within a f year he may redeem
Lev 25:30 within the space of a f year
Lev 26: 5 shall eat your bread to the f
Num 5: 7 for his trespass in f value
Num 7:13 both of them f of fine flour
Num 7:14 of ten shekels, f of incense
Num 7:19 both of them f of fine flour
Num 7:20 of ten shekels, f of incense
Num 7:25 both of them f of fine flour
Num 7:26 of ten shekels, f of incense
Num 7:31 both of them f of fine flour
Num 7:32 of ten shekels, f of incense
Num 7:37 both of them f of fine flour
Num 7:38 of ten shekels, f of incense
Num 7:43 both of them f of fine flour
Num 7:44 of ten shekels, f of incense
Num 7:49 both of them f of fine flour
Num 7:50 of ten shekels, f of incense
Num 7:55 both of them f of fine flour
Num 7:56 of ten shekels, f of incense
Num 7:61 both of them f of fine flour
Num 7:62 of ten shekels, f of incense
Num 7:67 both of them f of fine flour
Num 7:68 of ten shekels, f of incense
Num 7:73 both of them f of fine flour
Num 7:74 of ten shekels, f of incense
Num 7:79 both of them f of fine flour
Num 7:80 of ten shekels, f of incense
Num 7:86 The twelve gold pans f of
Num 22:18 give me his house f of silver
Num 24:13 give me his house f of silver
Deut 6:11 houses f of all good things,
Deut 6:11 when you have eaten and are f
Deut 8:10 When you have eaten and are f
Deut 8:12 when you have eaten and are f
Deut 21:13 and her mother a f month
Deut 33:23 f of the blessing of the LORD
Deut 34: 9 was f of the spirit of wisdom
Judg 5:31 it comes out in f strength
Judg 6:38 the fleece, a bowl f of water
Judg 16:27 Now the temple was f of men
Ruth 1:21 I went out f, and the LORD has
Ruth 2:12 a f reward be given you by
1Sa 2: 5 Those who were f have hired
1Sa 18:27 them in f count to the king
1Sa 27: 7 Philistines was one f year
1Sa 28:20 fell f length on the ground
2Sa 8: 2 with one f line those to be
2Sa 13:23 to pass, after two f years
2Sa 14:28 Absalom dwelt two f years in
2Sa 23:11 piece of ground f of lentils
2Ki 3:16 Make this valley f of ditches
2Ki 4: 4 and set aside the f ones
2Ki 4: 6 pass, when the vessels were f
2Ki 4:39 it a lap f of wild gourds
2Ki 6:17 the mountain was f of horses
2Ki 7:15 the road was f of garments
2Ki 9:24 drew his bow with f strength
2Ki 10:21 the temple of Baal was f from
2Ki 15:13 and he reigned a f month in
1Ch 11:13 a piece of ground f of barley
1Ch 21:22 grant it to me at the f price
1Ch 21:24 surely buy it for the f price
1Ch 23: 1 f of days, he made his son
1Ch 29:28 f of days and riches and honor
2Ch 24:15 was f of days, and he died
Ezra 7:19 deliver in f before the God
Neh 9:25 houses f of all goods,
Esth 9:29 wrote with f authority to
Job 5:26 come to the grave at a f age
Job 10:15 I am f of disgrace
Job 11: 2 should a man f of talk be
Job 14: 1 of few days and f of trouble
Job 20:11 His bones are f of his
Job 21:23 One dies in his f strength
Job 21:24 His pails are f of milk, and
Job 32:18 For I am f of words
Job 36:16 table would be f of richness
Job 42:17 So Job died, old and f of days
Ps 10: 7 His mouth is f of cursing
Ps 26:10 right hand is f of bribes
Ps 29: 4 of the LORD is f of majesty
Ps 33: 5 The earth is f of the
Ps 38: 7 loins are f of inflammation
Ps 48:10 hand is f of righteousness
Ps 65: 9 river of God is f of water
Ps 69:20 heart, And I am f of heaviness
Ps 73:10 waters of a f cup are drained
Ps 74:20 are f of the habitations of
Ps 78:25 He sent them food to the f
Ps 78:38 He, being f of compassion,
Ps 81: 3 the New Moon, At the f moon
Ps 86:15 are a God f of compassion, and
Ps 88: 3 For my soul is f of troubles
Ps 104:16 of the LORD are f of sap, The
Ps 104:24 The earth is f of Your
Ps 111: 4 gracious and f of compassion
Ps 112: 4 f of compassion, and righteous
Ps 119:64 O LORD, is f of Your mercy
Ps 127: 5 who has his quiver f of them
Ps 144:13 That our barns may be f,
Ps 145: 8 and f of compassion, Slow to
Prov 1:31 be filled to the f with their
Prov 17: 1 than a house f of feasting
Prov 27:20 and Destruction are never f
Prov 30: 9 Lest I be f and deny You, and
Eccl 1: 7 the sea, yet the sea is not f
Eccl 1: 8 All things are f of labor
Eccl 4: 6 quietness than both hands f
Eccl 9: 3 the sons of men are f of evil
Eccl 11: 3 If the clouds are f of rain
Is 1:15 Your hands are f of blood
Is 1:21 It was f of justice
Is 2: 7 land is also f of silver and
Is 2: 7 land is also f of horses, and
Is 2: 8 Their land is also f of idols
Is 6: 3 whole earth is f of His glory
Is 11: 9 for the earth shall be f of
Is 13:21 houses will be f of owls
Is 15: 9 of Dimon will be f of blood
Is 22: 2 you who are f of noise, a
Is 22: 7 shall be f of chariots, and
Is 25: 6 of fat things f of marrow
Is 28: 8 For all tables are f of vomit
Is 30:27 His lips are f of indignation
Is 51:20 they are f of the fury of the
Jer 4:27 yet I will not make a f end
Jer 5: 7 When I had fed them to the f
Jer 5:27 As a cage is f of birds, so
Jer 5:27 their houses are f of deceit
Jer 6: 6 She is f of oppression in her
Jer 6:11 Therefore I am f of the fury
Jer 6:11 with him who is f of days
Jer 23:10 the land is f of adulterers
Jer 28: 3 Within two f years I will
Jer 28:11 the space of two f years
Jer 30:11 though I make a f end of all
Jer 35: 5 Rechabites bowls f of wine
Lam 1: 1 the city that was f of people
Lam 3:30 him, and be f of reproach
Ezek 1:18 and their rims were f of eyes
Ezek 7:23 and the city is f of violence
Ezek 9: 9 the land is f of bloodshed,
Ezek 9: 9 and the city f of perversity
Ezek 10: 4 and the court was f of the
Ezek 10:12 were f of eyes all around
Ezek 17: 3 f of feathers of various
Ezek 19:10 f of branches because of many
Ezek 22: 5 as infamous and f of tumult
Ezek 28:12 f of wisdom and perfect in
Ezek 32: 6 riverbeds will be f of you
Ezek 37: 1 and it was f of bones
Ezek 39:19 shall eat fat till you are f
Ezek 41: 8 a f rod, that is, six cubits
Dan 3:19 Nebuchadnezzar was f of fury
Dan 10: 2 was mourning three f weeks
Joel 2:24 floors shall be f of wheat
Joel 3:13 for the winepress is f, the
Amos 2:13 down that is f of sheaves
Mic 3: 8 But truly I am f of power by
Mic 6:12 rich men are f of violence
Nah 3: 1 It is all f of lies and
Hab 3: 3 the earth was f of His praise
Zech 8: 5 the city shall be f of boys
Matt 6:22 whole body will be f of light
Matt 6:23 body will be f of darkness
Matt 13:48 which, when it was f, they
Matt 14:20 f of the fragments that
Matt 15:37 f of the fragments that were
Matt 23:25 they are f of extortion and
Matt 23:27 but inside are f of dead
Matt 23:28 inside you are f of hypocrisy
Mark 4:28 after that the f grain in the
Mark 6:43 twelve baskets f of fragments
Mark 8:19 how many baskets f of
Mark 8:20 how many large baskets f of
Mark 15:36 a sponge f of sour wine, put
Luke 1:57 Now Elizabeth's f time came
Luke 5:12 a man who was f of leprosy
Luke 6:25 Woe to you who are f, For you
Luke 11:34 whole body also is f of light
Luke 11:34 body also is f of darkness
Luke 11:36 your whole body is f of light
Luke 11:36 whole body will be f of light
Luke 11:39 inward part is f of greed
Luke 16:20 f of sores, who was laid at
John 1:14 Father, f of grace and truth
John 15:11 and that your joy may be f
John 16:24 that your joy may be f
John 19:29 Now a vessel f of sour wine
John 21:11 f of large fish, one hundred
Acts 2:13 They are f of new wine
Acts 2:28 you will make me f of joy in
Acts 6: 3 f of the Holy Spirit and
Acts 6: 5 a man f of faith and the Holy
Acts 6: 8 f of faith and power, did
Acts 7:55 being f of the Holy Spirit,
Acts 9:36 woman was f of good works
Acts 11:24 f of the Holy Spirit and of
Acts 13:10 O f of all deceit and all
Acts 19:28 this, they were f of wrath
Rom 1:29 f of envy, murder, strife,
Rom 3:14 Whose mouth is f of cursing
Rom 15:14 you also are f of goodness
1Co 4: 8 You are already f
Phil 4:12 I have learned both to be f
Phil 4:18 I am f, having received from
Col 2: 2 to all riches of the f
Heb 5:14 to those who are of f age
Heb 6:11 the same diligence to the f
Heb 10:22 heart in f assurance of faith
Jas 3: 8 evil, f of deadly poison
Jas 3:17 f of mercy and good fruits,
1Pe 1: 8 inexpressible and f of glory,
2Pe 2:14 having eyes f of adultery
1Jn 1: 4 to you that your joy may be f
2Jn 8 we may receive a f reward
2Jn 12 face, that our joy may be f
Rev 4: 6 creatures f of eyes in front
Rev 4: 8 were f of eyes around and
Rev 5: 8 and golden bowls f of incense
Rev 14:10 of God, which is poured out f
Rev 15: 7 f of the wrath of God who
Rev 16:10 kingdom became f of darkness
Rev 17: 3 was f of names of blasphemy
Rev 17: 4 golden cup f of abominations

FULLER'S
2Ki 18:17 on the highway to the F Field
Is 7: 3 on the highway to the F Field
Is 36: 2 on the highway to the F Field
Mal 3: 2 refiner's fire And like f soap

FULL-GROWN (*see* FULL, GROW)
Jas 1:15 and sin, when it is f, brings

FULLNESS (*see* FULL)
Num 18:27 as the f of the winepress
Deut 33:16 things of the earth and its f
1Ch 16:32 the sea roar, and all its f
Ps 16:11 In Your presence is f of joy
Ps 24: 1 is the LORD's, and all its f

Ps 36: 8 with the **f** of Your house, And
Ps 50:12 world is Mine, and all its **f**
Ps 89:11 The world and all its **f**, You
Ps 96:11 the sea roar, and all its **f**
Ps 98: 7 the sea roar, and all its **f**
Is 47: 9 come upon you in their **f**
Ezek 16:49 **f** of food, and abundance of
Ezek 19: 7 the land with its **f** was
Dan 8:23 have reached their **f**, a king
John 1:16 of His **f** we have all received
Rom 11:12 how much more their **f**
Rom 11:25 to Israel until the **f** of the
Rom 15:29 I shall come in the **f** of the
1Co 10:26 is the LORD's, and all its **f**
1Co 10:28 is the LORD's, and all its **f**
Gal 4: 4 But when the **f** of the time
Eph 1:10 the **f** of the times He might
Eph 1:23 the **f** of Him who fills all in
Eph 3:19 filled with all the **f** of God
Eph 4:13 stature of the **f** of Christ
Col 1:19 in Him all the **f** should dwell
Col 2: 9 the **f** of the Godhead bodily

FULLY (*see* FULL)
Num 14:24 in him and has followed Me **f**
Ruth 2:11 It has been **f** reported to me,
2Sa 17:11 Israel be **f** gathered to you
1Ki 11: 6 did not **f** follow the LORD, as
Job 6: 2 that my grief were **f** weighed
Ps 31:23 **f** repays the proud person
Ps 75: 8 It is **f** mixed, and He pours it
Eccl 8:11 is **f** set in them to do evil
Is 59:18 coastlands He will **f** repay
Is 66: 6 Who **f** repays His enemies
Nah 1:10 devoured like stubble **f** dried
Luke 9:32 and when they were **f** awake
Luke 11:21 man, **f** armed, guards his own
John 7: 8 My time has not yet **f** come
Acts 2: 1 Day of Pentecost had **f** come
Acts 23:20 to inquire more **f** about him
Rom 4:21 being **f** convinced that what
Rom 14: 5 Let each be **f** convinced in
Rom 15:19 have **f** preached the gospel of
Col 1:10 Lord, **f** pleasing Him, being
2Ti 4:17 be preached **f** through me, and
1Pe 1:13 rest your hope **f** upon the
Rev 14:18 for her grapes are **f** ripe

FUME
Ps 68:16 Why do you **f** with envy, you

FUNCTION
Rom 12: 4 do not have the same **f**,

FURIOUS (*see* FURIOUSLY, FURY)
2Ki 5:11 But Naaman became **f**, and went
2Ch 26:19 Then Uzziah became **f**
Neh 4: 1 the wall, that he was **f** and
Esth 1:12 therefore the king was **f**, and
Esth 2:21 Teresh, doorkeepers, became **f**
Ps 78:21 the LORD heard this and was **f**
Ps 78:59 When God heard this, He was **f**
Ps 78:62 was **f** with His inheritance
Ps 89:38 You have been **f** with Your
Prov 22:24 and with a **f** man do not go,
Prov 29:22 strife, and a **f** man abounds in
Is 64: 9 Do not be **f**, O LORD, nor
Ezek 5:15 and in fury and in **f** rebukes
Ezek 25:17 on them with **f** rebukes
Dan 2:12 the king was angry and very **f**
Dan 8: 6 and ran at him with **f** power
Nah 1: 2 the LORD avenges and is **f**
Matt 22: 7 king heard about it, he was **f**
Acts 5:33 they heard this, they were **f**

FURIOUSLY (*see* FURIOUS)
2Ki 9:20 of Nimshi, for he drives **f**
Ezek 23:25 and they shall deal **f** with you

FURLONGS
Rev 14:20 one thousand six hundred **f**
Rev 21:16 twelve thousand **f**

FURNACE
Gen 19:28 went up like the smoke of a **f**
Ex 9: 8 handfuls of ashes from a **f**
Ex 9:10 they took ashes from the **f**
Ex 19:18 like the smoke of a **f**, and the
Deut 4:20 brought you out of the iron **f**
1Ki 8:51 of Egypt, out of the iron **f**)
Ps 12: 6 silver tried in a **f** of earth
Prov 17: 3 the **f** for gold, but the LORD
Prov 27:21 the **f** for gold, and a man is
Is 31: 9 and whose **f** is in Jerusalem
Is 48:10 you in the **f** of affliction
Jer 11: 4 of Egypt, from the iron **f**
Ezek 22:18 and lead, in the midst of a **f**
Ezek 22:20 and tin into the midst of a **f**
Ezek 22:22 is melted in the midst of a **f**
Dan 3: 6 midst of a burning fiery **f**
Dan 3:11 midst of a burning fiery **f**
Dan 3:15 midst of a burning fiery **f**
Dan 3:17 us from the burning fiery **f**
Dan 3:19 that they heat the **f** seven
Dan 3:20 them into the burning fiery **f**
Dan 3:21 midst of the burning fiery **f**
Dan 3:22 the **f** exceedingly hot, the
Dan 3:23 midst of the burning fiery **f**
Dan 3:26 mouth of the burning fiery **f**
Matt 13:42 cast them into the **f** of fire
Matt 13:50 cast them into the **f** of fire
Rev 1:15 brass, as if refined in a **f**
Rev 9: 2 like the smoke of a great **f**

FURNISH (*see* FURNISHED, FURNISHINGS)
Is 65:11 who **f** a drink offering for

FURNISHED (*see* FURNISH)
Prov 9: 2 she has also **f** her table
Mark 14:15 you a large upper room, **f**
Luke 22:12 you a large, **f** upper room

FURNISHINGS (*see* FURNISH, FURNITURE)
Ex 25: 9 and the pattern of all its **f**
Ex 39:33 Moses, the tent and all its **f**
Num 1:50 the Testimony, over all its **f**
Num 1:50 the tabernacle and all its **f**
Num 3: 8 the **f** of the tabernacle of
Num 4:15 all the **f** of the sanctuary,
Num 4:16 with the sanctuary and its **f**
Num 4:26 all the **f** for their service
Num 4:32 and cords, with all their **f**
Num 7: 1 and sanctified it and all its **f**
1Ki 7:48 Solomon had all the **f** made
1Ki 7:51 silver and the gold and the **f**
1Ki 8: 4 all the holy **f** that were in
1Ch 9:29 were appointed over the **f**
2Ch 4:19 Thus Solomon had all the **f**
2Ch 5: 1 and the gold and all the **f**
2Ch 5: 5 all the holy **f** that were in

FURNITURE (*see* FURNISHINGS)
Ex 31: 7 all the **f** of the tabernacle

FURROW (*see* FURROWS)
Job 39:10 wild ox in the **f** with ropes

FURROWS (*see* FURROW)
Job 31:38 me, and its **f** weep together
Ps 65:10 abundantly, You settle its **f**
Ps 129: 3 They made their **f** long
Hos 10: 4 hemlock in the **f** of the field
Hos 12:11 heaps in the **f** of the field

FURTHER (*see* PREFACE)

FURTHERANCE
Phil 1:12 out for the **f** of the gospel

FURTHERMORE (*see* PREFACE)

FURY (*see* FURIOUS)
Gen 27:44 your brother's **f** turns away
Lev 26:28 walk contrary to you in **f**
Job 20:23 on him the **f** of His wrath
Prov 6:34 For jealousy is a husband's **f**
Is 27: 4 **F** is not in Me
Is 34: 2 and His **f** against all their
Is 42:25 on him the **f** of His anger
Is 51:13 of the **f** of the oppressor
Is 51:13 And where is the **f** of the
Is 51:17 of the LORD the cup of His **f**
Is 51:20 are full of the **f** of the LORD
Is 51:22 the dregs of the cup of My **f**
Is 59:18 repay, **f** to His adversaries,
Is 63: 3 and trampled them in My **f**
Is 63: 5 and My own **f**, it sustained Me
Is 63: 6 made them drunk in My **f**, and
Is 66:15 to render His anger with **f**
Jer 4: 4 lest My **f** come forth like
Jer 6:11 am full of the **f** of the LORD
Jer 7:20 My **f** will be poured out on
Jer 10:25 Pour out Your **f** on the
Jer 21: 5 arm, even in anger and **f** and
Jer 21:12 lest My **f** go out like fire and
Jer 23:19 the LORD has gone forth in **f**
Jer 25:15 wine cup of **f** from My hand
Jer 30:23 of the LORD goes forth with **f**
Jer 32:31 My **f** from the day that they
Jer 32:37 them in My anger, in My **f**
Jer 33: 5 will slay in My anger and My **f**
Jer 36: 7 and the **f** that the LORD has
Jer 42:18 My **f** have been poured out on
Jer 42:18 so will My **f** be poured out on
Jer 44: 6 So My **f** and My anger were
Lam 2: 4 poured out His **f** like fire
Lam 4:11 The LORD has fulfilled His **f**
Ezek 5:13 I will cause My **f** to rest
Ezek 5:13 I have spent My **f** upon them
Ezek 5:15 among you in anger and in **f**
Ezek 6:12 will I spend My **f** upon them
Ezek 7: 8 you I will soon pour out My **f**
Ezek 8:18 I also will act in **f**
Ezek 9: 8 out Your **f** on Jerusalem
Ezek 13:13 wind to break forth in My **f**
Ezek 13:13 hailstones in **f** to consume it
Ezek 14:19 pour out My **f** on it in blood,
Ezek 16:38 bring blood upon you in **f**
Ezek 16:42 lay to rest My **f** toward you
Ezek 19:12 But she was plucked up in **f**
Ezek 20: 8 I will pour out My **f** on them
Ezek 20:13 **f** on them in the wilderness
Ezek 20:21 I would pour out My **f** on them
Ezek 20:33 with **f** poured out, I will
Ezek 20:34 arm, and with **f** poured out
Ezek 21:17 and I will cause My **f** to rest
Ezek 22:20 you in My anger and in My **f**
Ezek 22:22 have poured out My **f** on you
Ezek 24: 8 That it may raise up **f** and
Ezek 24:13 caused My **f** to rest upon you
Ezek 25:14 My anger and according to My **f**
Ezek 30:15 I will pour My **f** on Sin, the
Ezek 36: 6 spoken in My jealousy and My **f**
Ezek 36:18 Therefore I poured out My **f**
Ezek 38:18 that My **f** will show in My
Dan 3:13 Nebuchadnezzar, in rage and **f**
Dan 3:19 Nebuchadnezzar was full of **f**
Dan 9:16 Your **f** be turned away from
Dan 11:44 out with great **f** to destroy
Amos 5: 9 so that **f** comes upon the
Mic 5:15 **f** on the nations that have
Nah 1: 6 His **f** is poured out like fire

FUTILE (*see* FUTILITY)
Deut 32:47 it is not a **f** thing for you
Job 15:31 Let him not trust in **f** things
Ps 94:11 of man, That they are **f**
Is 1:13 Bring no more **f** sacrifices
Jer 10: 3 customs of the peoples are **f**
Jer 10:15 They are **f**, a work of errors
Jer 51:18 They are **f**, a work of errors
Ezek 13: 7 Have you not seen a **f** vision
Rom 1:21 but became **f** in their
1Co 3:20 of the wise, that they are **f**
1Co 15:17 is not risen, your faith is **f**

FUTILITY (*see* FUTILE)
Job 7: 3 been allotted months of **f**
Job 15:31 for **f** will be his reward
Job 15:35 trouble and bring forth **f**
Ps 78:33 their days He consumed in **f**
Ps 89:47 For what **f** have You created
Is 30:28 nations with the sieve of **f**
Ezek 13: 6 They have envisioned **f** and
Ezek 13: 9 the prophets who envision **f**
Ezek 13:23 **f** nor practice divination
Rom 8:20 creation was subjected to **f**
Eph 4:17 walk, in the **f** of their mind,

FUTURE
Ps 37:37 For the **f** of that man is
Ps 37:38 The **f** of the wicked shall be
Jer 29:11 not of evil, to give you a **f**
Jer 31:17 There is hope in your **f**,"
Dan 8:26 refers to many days in the **f**

G

GAAL
Judg 9:26 Now **G** the son of Ebed came
Judg 9:28 Then **G** the son of Ebed said,
Judg 9:30 words of **G** the son of Ebed
Judg 9:31 **G** the son of Ebed and his
Judg 9:35 When **G** the son of Ebed went
Judg 9:36 when **G** saw the people, he
Judg 9:37 So **G** spoke again and said,
Judg 9:39 So **G** went out, leading the

Judg 9:41 Arumah, and Zebul drove out **G**

GAASH
Josh 24:30 on the north side of Mount **G**
Judg 2: 9 on the north side of Mount **G**
2Sa 23:30 Hiddai from the brooks of **G**
1Ch 11:32 Hurai of the brooks of **G**,

GABA (*see* GEBA)
Josh 18:24 Haammoni, Ophni, and **G**

GABBAI
Neh 11: 8 and after him **G** and Sallai,

GABBATHA
John 19:13 Pavement, but in Hebrew, **G**

GABRIEL
Dan 8:16 **G**, make this man understand
Dan 9:21 speaking in prayer, the man **G**
Luke 1:19 I am **G**, who stands in the
Luke 1:26 **G** was sent by God to a city

GAD (*see* BAAL GAD, DIBON GAD, GADITE, MIGDAL GAD)
Gen 30:11 So she called his name **G**
Gen 35:26 Leah's maidservant, were **G**
Gen 46:16 The sons of **G** were Ziphion,
Gen 49:19 **G**, a troop shall tramp upon
Ex 1: 4 Dan, Naphtali, **G**, and Asher
Num 1:14 from **G**, Eliasaph the son of
Num 1:24 From the children of **G**, their
Num 1:25 of **G** were forty-five thousand
Num 2:14 shall come the tribe of **G**
Num 2:14 **G** shall be Eliasaph the son
Num 7:42 leader of the children of **G**
Num 10:20 of **G** was Eliasaph the son of
Num 13:15 from the tribe of **G**, Geuel
Num 26:15 The sons of **G** according to
Num 26:18 **G** according to those who were
Num 32: 1 the children of **G** had a very
Num 32: 2 the children of **G** and the
Num 32: 6 said to the children of **G**
Num 32:25 And the children of **G** and the
Num 32:29 If the children of **G** and the
Num 32:31 Then the children of **G** and the
Num 32:33 gave to the children of **G**
Num 32:34 the children of **G** built Dibon
Num 34:14 tribe of the children of **G**
Deut 27:13 Reuben, **G**, Asher, Zebulun,
Deut 33:20 And of **G** he said
Deut 33:20 Blessed is he who enlarges **G**
Josh 4:12 men of Reuben, the men of **G**
Josh 13:24 inheritance to the tribe of **G**
Josh 13:24 to the children of **G**
Josh 13:28 of the children of **G**
Josh 18: 7 And **G**, Reuben, and half the
Josh 20: 8 Gilead, from the tribe of **G**
Josh 21: 7 Reuben, from the tribe of **G**
Josh 21:38 and from the tribe of **G**,
Josh 22: 9 of Reuben, the children of **G**
Josh 22:10 of Reuben, the children of **G**
Josh 22:11 of Reuben, the children of **G**
Josh 22:13 Reuben, to the children of **G**
Josh 22:15 Reuben, to the children of **G**
Josh 22:21 of Reuben, the children of **G**
Josh 22:25 of Reuben and children of **G**
Josh 22:30 of Reuben, the children of **G**
Josh 22:31 of Reuben, the children of **G**
Josh 22:32 Reuben and the children of **G**
Josh 22:33 children of Reuben and **G** dwelt
Josh 22:34 the children of **G** called the
1Sa 13: 7 the Jordan to the land of **G**
1Sa 22: 5 the prophet **G** said to David
2Sa 24: 5 the midst of the ravine of **G**
2Sa 24:11 LORD came to the prophet **G**
2Sa 24:13 So **G** came to David and told
2Sa 24:14 And David said to **G**, "I am in
2Sa 24:18 **G** came that day to David and
2Sa 24:19 according to the word of **G**
2Ki 10:33 **G**, Reuben, and Manasseh
1Ch 2: 2 Joseph, Benjamin, Naphtali, **G**
1Ch 5:11 the children of **G** dwelt next
1Ch 6:63 Reuben, from the tribe of **G**
1Ch 6:80 And from the tribe of **G**
1Ch 12:14 These were from the sons of **G**
1Ch 21: 9 And the LORD spoke to **G**,
1Ch 21:11 So **G** came to David and said to
1Ch 21:13 And David said to **G**, "I am in
1Ch 21:18 **G** to say to David that David
1Ch 21:19 went up at the word of **G**,
1Ch 29:29 and in the book of **G** the seer
2Ch 29:25 of **G** the king's seer, and of
Is 65:11 who prepare a table for **G**
Jer 2:36 Why do you **g** about so much to
Jer 31:22 How long will you **g** about
Jer 49: 1 then does Milcham inherit **G**
Ezek 48:27 **G** shall have one portion
Ezek 48:28 by the border of **G**, on the
Ezek 48:34 one gate for **G**, one gate for
Rev 7: 5 of the tribe of **G** twelve

GADARENES
Mark 5: 1 sea, to the country of the **G**
Luke 8:26 to the country of the **G**,
Luke 8:37 **G** asked Him to depart from

GADDI
Num 13:11 Manasseh, **G** the son of Susi

GADDIEL
Num 13:10 of Zebulun, **G** the son of Sodi

GADI
2Ki 15:14 son of **G** went up from Tirzah
2Ki 15:17 Menahem the son of **G** became

GADITE (*see* GAD, GADITES)
2Sa 23:36 Nathan of Zobah, Bani the **G**

GADITES (*see* GADITE)
Deut 3:12 to the Reubenites and the **G**
Deut 3:16 the **G** I gave from Gilead as
Deut 4:43 Ramoth in Gilead for the **G**
Deut 29: 8 to the Reubenites, to the **G**
Josh 1:12 And to the Reubenites, the **G**
Josh 12: 6 to the Reubenites, the **G**, and
Josh 13: 8 and the **G** received their
Josh 22: 1 called the Reubenites, the **G**
1Ch 5:16 the **G** dwelt in Gilead, in
1Ch 5:18 The sons of Reuben, the **G**
1Ch 5:26 carried the Reubenites, the **G**
1Ch 12: 8 Some **G** joined David at the
1Ch 12:37 of the Reubenites and the **G**
1Ch 26:32 over the Reubenites, the **G**

GAHAM
Gen 22:24 Reumah, also bore Tebah, **G**

GAHAR
Ezra 2:47 sons of Giddel, the sons of **G**
Neh 7:49 of Giddel, the children of **G**

GAIN (*see* GAINED, GAINS)
Ex 14: 4 I will **g** honor over Pharaoh
Ex 14:17 So I will **g** honor over
1Sa 8: 3 aside after dishonest **g**, took
Job 18: 2 **G** understanding, and afterward
Job 22: 3 Or is it **g** to Him that you
Job 27: 8 though he may **g** much, if God
Ps 44: 3 For they did not **g** possession
Ps 90:12 That we may **g** a heart of
Prov 1:19 everyone who is greedy for **g**
Prov 3:14 and her **g** than fine gold
Prov 15:27 He who is greedy for **g**
Prov 31:11 so he will have no lack of **g**
Eccl 3: 6 a time to **g**, and a time to
Is 23:18 Her **g** and her pay will be set
Is 23:18 for her **g** will be for those
Is 33:15 despises the **g** of oppressions
Is 56:11 way, every one for his own **g**
Ezek 22:27 people, and to get dishonest **g**
Ezek 33:31 hearts pursue their own **g**
Ezek 39:13 they will **g** renown for it on
Dan 2: 8 certain that you would **g** time
Dan 11: 5 he shall **g** power over him and
Dan 11:39 and divide the land for **g**
Mic 4:13 their **g** to the LORD, and their
Hab 2: 9 covets evil **g** for his house
Phil 1:21 is Christ, and to die is **g**
Phil 3: 7 But what things were **g** to me
Phil 3: 8 rubbish, that I may **g** Christ
1Ti 6: 5 godliness is a means of **g**
1Ti 6: 6 with contentment is great **g**
Tit 1:11 for the sake of dishonest **g**
1Pe 5: 2 for dishonest **g** but eagerly
Jude 16 people to **g** advantage

GAINED (*see* GAIN)
Gen 31:18 possessions which he had **g**
Gen 31:18 which he had **g** in Padan Aram
Gen 36: 6 had **g** in the land of Canaan
Ex 14:18 LORD, when I have **g** honor for
Deut 8:17 my hand have **g** me this wealth
Judg 11:21 Thus Israel **g** possession of
Job 31:25 and because my hand had **g**
Ps 98: 1 arm have **g** Him the victory
Prov 13:11 Wealth **g** by dishonesty will
Prov 20:17 Bread **g** by deceit is sweet to
Prov 20:21 An inheritance **g** hastily at
Eccl 1:16 have **g** more wisdom than all
Is 15: 7 the abundance they have **g**
Ezek 28: 4 have **g** riches for yourself
Matt 18:15 you, you have **g** your brother
Matt 25:17 received two **g** two more also
Matt 25:20 I have **g** five more talents
Matt 25:22 I have **g** two more talents
Luke 19:15 every man had **g** by trading

GAINS (*see* GAIN)
Prov 3:13 the man who **g** understanding
Prov 13:15 Good understanding **g** favor
Matt 16:26 if he **g** the whole world, and
Mark 8:36 a man if he **g** the whole world
Luke 9:25 a man if he **g** the whole world

GAIUS
Acts 19:29 one accord, having seized **G**
Acts 20: 4 **G** of Derbe, and Timothy, and
Rom 16:23 **G**, my host and the host of the
1Co 1:14 of you except Crispus and **G**
3Jn 1 ELDER, To the beloved **G**

GALAL
1Ch 9:15 Bakbakkar, Heresh, **G**, and
1Ch 9:16 son of Shemaiah, the son of **G**
Neh 11:17 son of Shammua, the son of **G**

GALATIA (*see* GALATIANS)
Acts 16: 6 Phrygia and the region of **G**
Acts 18:23 went over all the region of **G**
1Co 16: 1 orders to the churches of **G**
Gal 1: 2 with me, To the churches of **G**
2Ti 4:10 Crescens for **G**, Titus for
1Pe 1: 1 the Dispersion in Pontus, **G**

GALATIANS (*see* GALATIA)
Gal 3: 1 O foolish **G**

GALBANUM
Ex 30:34 spices, stacte and onycha and **g**

GALEED
Gen 31:47 but Jacob called it **G**
Gen 31:48 its name was called **G**,

GALILEAN (*see* GALILEANS, GALILEE)
Mark 14:70 for you are a **G**, and your
Luke 22:59 was with Him, for he is a **G**
Luke 23: 6 he asked if the Man were a **G**

GALILEANS (*see* GALILEAN)
Luke 13: 1 the **G** whose blood Pilate had
Luke 13: 2 Do you suppose that these **G**
Luke 13: 2 sinners than all other **G**,
John 4:45 the **G** received Him, having
Acts 2: 7 are not all these who speak **G**

GALILEE (*see* GALILEAN)
Josh 20: 7 So they appointed Kedesh in **G**
Josh 21:32 Kedesh in **G** with its
1Ki 9:11 cities in the land of **G**
2Ki 15:29 Kedesh, Hazor, Gilead, and **G**
1Ch 6:76 Kedesh in **G** with its
Is 9: 1 Jordan, in **G** of the Gentiles
Matt 2:22 aside into the region of **G**
Matt 3:13 Then Jesus came from **G** to
Matt 4:12 in prison, He departed to **G**
Matt 4:15 the Jordan, **G** of the Gentiles
Matt 4:18 walking by the Sea of **G**, saw
Matt 4:23 Now Jesus went about all **G**
Matt 4:25 from **G**, and from Decapolis,
Matt 15:29 there, skirted the Sea of **G**
Matt 17:22 while they were staying in **G**
Matt 19: 1 that He departed from **G** and
Matt 21:11 prophet from Nazareth of **G**
Matt 26:32 I will go before you to **G**
Matt 26:69 You also were with Jesus of **G**
Matt 27:55 who followed Jesus from **G**
Matt 28: 7 He is going before you into **G**
Matt 28:10 tell My brethren to go to **G**
Matt 28:16 disciples went away into **G**
Mark 1: 9 Jesus came from Nazareth of **G**
Mark 1:14 in prison, Jesus came to **G**
Mark 1:16 as He walked by the Sea of **G**
Mark 1:28 all the region around **G**
Mark 1:39 synagogues throughout all **G**
Mark 3: 7 multitude from **G** followed Him
Mark 6:21 and the chief men of **G**
Mark 7:31 of Decapolis to the Sea of **G**
Mark 9:30 there and passed through **G**
Mark 14:28 I will go before you to **G**
Mark 15:41 to Him when He was in **G**

Mark 16: 7 He is going before you into **G**
Luke 1:26 to a city of **G** named Nazareth
Luke 2: 4 And Joseph also went up from **G**
Luke 2:39 the Lord, they returned to **G**
Luke 3: 1 Herod being tetrarch of **G**
Luke 4:14 the power of the Spirit to **G**
Luke 4:31 to Capernaum, a city of **G**
Luke 4:44 in the synagogues of **G**
Luke 5:17 come out of every town of **G**
Luke 8:26 which is opposite **G**
Luke 17:11 the midst of Samaria and **G**
Luke 23: 5 from **G** to this place
Luke 23: 6 When Pilate heard of **G**, he
Luke 23:49 who followed Him from **G**
Luke 23:55 Him from **G** followed after
Luke 24: 6 to you when He was still in **G**
John 1:43 day Jesus wanted to go to **G**
John 2: 1 was a wedding in Cana of **G**
John 2:11 signs Jesus did in Cana of **G**
John 4: 3 Judea and departed again to **G**
John 4:43 from there and went to **G**
John 4:45 So when He came to **G**, the
John 4:46 **G** where He had made the water
John 4:47 had come out of Judea into **G**
John 4:54 had come out of Judea into **G**
John 6: 1 Jesus went over the Sea of **G**
John 7: 1 things Jesus walked in **G**
John 7: 9 to them, He remained in **G**
John 7:41 Will the Christ come out of **G**
John 7:52 Are you also from **G**
John 7:52 prophet has arisen out of **G**
John 12:21 who was from Bethsaida of **G**
John 21: 2 Nathanael of Cana in **G**, the
Acts 1:11 Men of **G**, why do you stand
Acts 5:37 Judas of **G** rose up in the
Acts 9:31 throughout all Judea, **G**, and
Acts 10:37 and began from **G** after the
Acts 13:31 with Him from **G** to Jerusalem

GALL
Deut 32:32 their grapes are grapes of **g**
Job 16:13 pours out my **g** on the ground
Job 20:25 point comes out of his **g**
Ps 69:21 also gave me **g** for my food
Jer 8:14 given us water of **g** to drink
Jer 9:15 give them water of **g** to drink
Jer 23:15 them drink the water of **g**
Lam 3:19 the wormwood and the **g**
Amos 6:12 have turned justice into **g**
Matt 27:34 wine mingled with **g** to drink

GALLERIES (*see* GALLERY)
Ezek 41:15 with its **g** on the one side and
Ezek 41:16 the **g** all around their three
Ezek 42: 5 because the **g** took away space

GALLERY (*see* GALLERIES)
Ezek 42: 3 was **g** against **g** in
Ezek 42: 3 against **g** in three stories

GALLEY
Is 33:21 in which no **g** with oars will

GALLIM
1Sa 25:44 son of Laish, who was from **G**
Is 10:30 your voice, O daughter of **G**

GALLIO
Acts 18:12 Now when **G** was proconsul of
Acts 18:14 mouth, **G** said to the Jews,
Acts 18:17 But **G** took no notice of these

GALLONS
John 2: 6 twenty or thirty **g** apiece

GALLOPING (*see* GALLOPS)
Judg 5:22 the **g**, **g** of his steeds
Nah 3: 2 of **g** horses, of clattering

GALLOPS (*see* GALLOPING)
Job 39:21 he **g** into the clash of arms

GALLOWS
Esth 2:23 and both were hanged on a **g**
Esth 5:14 Let a **g** be made, fifty cubits
Esth 5:14 so he had the **g** made
Esth 6: 4 **g** that he had prepared for
Esth 7: 9 The **g**, fifty cubits high,
Esth 7:10 **g** that he had prepared for
Esth 8: 7 **g** because he tried to lay his
Esth 9:13 ten sons be hanged on the **g**
Esth 9:25 should be hanged on the **g**

GAMALIEL
Num 1:10 **G** the son of Pedahzur
Num 2:20 be **G** the son of Pedahzur
Num 7:54 On the eighth day **G** the son
Num 7:59 of **G** the son of Pedahzur
Num 10:23 was **G** the son of Pedahzur
Acts 5:34 stood up, a Pharisee named **G**
Acts 22: 3 in this city at the feet of **G**

GAME
Gen 25:28 Esau because he ate of his **g**
Gen 27: 3 to the field and hunt **g** for me
Gen 27: 5 went to the field to hunt **g**
Gen 27: 7 Bring me **g** and make savory
Gen 27:19 arise, sit and eat of my **g**
Gen 27:25 and I will eat of my son's **g**
Gen 27:31 arise and eat of his son's **g**
Gen 27:33 Where is the one who hunted **g**

GAMMAD
Ezek 27:11 the men of **G** were in your

GAMUL (*see* BETH GAMUL)
1Ch 24:17 the twenty-second to **G**,

GAP (*see* GAPS)
Is 7: 6 let us make a **g** in its wall
Ezek 22:30 stand in the **g** before Me on

GAPE
Job 16:10 They **g** at me with their mouth
Ps 22:13 They **g** at Me with their

GAPS (*see* GAP)
Neh 4: 7 the **g** were beginning to be
Ezek 13: 5 the **g** to build a wall for the

GARDEN (*see* GARDENER, GARDENS)
Gen 2: 8 planted a **g** eastward in Eden
Gen 2: 9 also in the midst of the **g**
Gen 2:10 out of Eden to water the **g**
Gen 2:15 put him in the **g** of Eden to
Gen 2:16 of the **g** you may freely eat
Gen 3: 1 eat of every tree of the **g**'
Gen 3: 2 fruit of the trees of the **g**
Gen 3: 3 is in the midst of the **g**, God
Gen 3: 8 the **g** in the cool of the day
Gen 3: 8 God among the trees of the **g**
Gen 3:10 I heard Your voice in the **g**
Gen 3:23 God sent him out of the **g** of
Gen 3:24 at the east of the **g** of Eden
Gen 13:10 like the **g** of the LORD, like
Deut 11:10 it by foot, as a vegetable **g**
1Ki 21: 2 may have it for a vegetable **g**
2Ki 21:18 in the **g** of his own house
2Ki 21:18 own house, in the **g** of Uzza
2Ki 21:26 in his tomb in the **g** of Uzza
2Ki 25: 4 which was by the king's **g**
Neh 3:15 of Shelah by the King's **G**
Esth 1: 5 in the court of the **g** of the
Esth 7: 7 and went into the palace **g**
Esth 7: 8 returned from the palace **g** to
Job 8:16 branches spread out in his **g**
Song 4:12 A **g** enclosed is my sister, my
Song 4:16 Blow upon my **g**, that its
Song 4:16 Let my beloved come to his **g**
Song 5: 1 I have come to my **g**, my
Song 6: 2 My beloved has gone to his **g**
Song 6:11 I went down to the **g** of nuts
Is 1: 8 as a hut in a **g** of cucumbers
Is 1:30 and as a **g** that has no water
Is 51: 3 desert like the **g** of the LORD
Is 58:11 you shall be like a watered **g**
Is 61:11 as the **g** causes the things
Jer 31:12 be like a well-watered **g**, and
Jer 39: 4 night, by way of the king's **g**
Jer 52: 7 which was by the king's **g**
Lam 2: 6 tabernacle, As if it were a **g**
Ezek 17: 7 from the **g** terrace where it
Ezek 17:10 the **g** terrace where it grew
Ezek 28:13 were in Eden, the **g** of God
Ezek 31: 8 The cedars in the **g** of God
Ezek 31: 8 no tree in the **g** of God was
Ezek 31: 9 it, that were in the **g** of God
Ezek 34:29 up for them a **g** of renown
Ezek 36:35 has become like the **g** of Eden
Joel 2: 3 the **G** of Eden before them
Luke 13:19 a man took and put in his **g**
John 18: 1 Kidron, where there was a **g**
John 18:26 not see you in the **g** with Him
John 19:41 was crucified there was a **g**
John 19:41 in the **g** a new tomb in which

GARDENER (*see* GARDEN)
John 20:15 supposing Him to be the **g**

GARDENS (*see* GARDEN)
Num 24: 6 like **g** by the riverside, like
Eccl 2: 5 I made myself **g** and orchards,
Song 4:15 a fountain of **g**, a well of
Song 6: 2 to feed his flock in the **g**
Song 8:13 You who dwell in the **g**, the
Is 1:29 the **g** which you have chosen
Is 65: 3 who sacrifice in **g**, and burn
Is 66:17 to go to the **g** after an idol
Jer 29: 5 plant **g** and eat their fruit
Jer 29:28 and dwell in them, and plant **g**
Amos 4: 9 When your **g** increased, your
Amos 9:14 They shall also make **g** and eat

GAREB
2Sa 23:38 the Ithrite, **G** the Ithrite,
1Ch 11:40 the Ithrite, **G** the Ithrite,
Jer 31:39 forward over the hill **G**

GARLAND (*see* GARLANDS)
Rev 12: 1 on her head a **g** of twelve

GARLANDS (*see* GARLAND)
Acts 14:13 **g** to the gates, intending to

GARLIC
Num 11: 5 leeks, the onions, and the **g**

GARMENT (*see* GARMENTS)
Gen 9:23 But Shem and Japheth took a **g**
Gen 25:25 was like a hairy **g** all over
Gen 39:12 that she caught him by his **g**
Gen 39:12 But he left his **g** in her hand
Gen 39:13 he had left his **g** in her hand
Gen 39:15 that he left his **g** with me
Gen 39:16 So she kept his **g** with her
Gen 39:18 that he left his **g** with me
Ex 22:26 your neighbor's **g** as a pledge
Ex 22:27 it is his **g** for his skin
Lev 6:10 shall put on his linen **g**, and
Lev 6:27 blood is sprinkled on any **g**
Lev 13:47 if a **g** has a leprous plague
Lev 13:47 a woolen **g** or a linen **g**
Lev 13:47 a woolen **g** or a linen **g**
Lev 13:49 in the **g** or in the leather
Lev 13:51 plague has spread in the **g**
Lev 13:52 that **g** in which is the plague
Lev 13:53 has not spread in the **g**,
Lev 13:56 he shall tear it out of the **g**
Lev 13:57 if it appears again in the **g**
Lev 13:58 And if you wash the **g**, either
Lev 13:59 in a **g** of wool or linen,
Lev 14:55 for the leprosy of a **g** and of
Lev 15:17 And any **g** and any leather on
Lev 19:19 Nor shall a **g** of mixed linen
Num 31:20 Purify every **g**, everything
Deut 22: 3 and so shall you do with his **g**
Deut 22: 5 a man put on a woman's **g**, for
Deut 22:11 wear a **g** of different sorts
Deut 24:13 he may sleep in his own **g**
Deut 24:17 take a widow's **g** as a pledge
Josh 7:21 a beautiful Babylonian **g**, two
Josh 7:24 of Zerah, the silver, the **g**
Judg 8:25 And they spread out a **g**, and
Ruth 3: 3 yourself, put on your best **g**
2Sa 20:12 threw a **g** over him, when he
1Ki 11:29 clothed himself with a new **g**
1Ki 11:30 of the new **g** that was on him
2Ki 9:13 man hastened to take his **g**
Ezra 9: 3 heard this thing, I tore my **g**
Ezra 9: 5 and having torn my **g** and my
Neh 5:13 I shook out the fold of my **g**
Esth 8:15 a **g** of fine linen and purple
Job 13:28 like a **g** that is moth-eaten
Job 30:18 force my **g** is disfigured
Job 38: 9 when I made the clouds its **g**
Job 38:14 seal, and stands out like a **g**
Ps 69:11 I also made sackcloth my **g**
Ps 73: 6 Violence covers them like a **g**
Ps 102:26 them will grow old like a **g**
Ps 104: 2 with light as with a **g**, Who
Ps 104: 6 it with the deep as with a **g**
Ps 109:18 with cursing as with his **g**
Ps 109:19 like the **g** which covers him
Prov 20:16 Take the **g** of one who is
Prov 25:20 away a **g** in cold weather, and
Prov 27:13 Take the **g** of him who is
Prov 30: 4 has bound the waters in a **g**
Is 14:19 Like the **g** of those who are
Is 50: 9 will all grow old like a **g**

Is 51: 6 earth will grow old like a **g**
Is 51: 8 will eat them up like a **g**
Is 61: 3 the **g** of praise for the
Jer 43:12 as a shepherd puts on his **g**
Ezek 5: 3 them in the edge of your **g**
Dan 7: 9 His **g** was white as snow, and
Mic 2: 8 **g** from those who trust you
Hag 2:12 meat in the fold of his **g**
Mal 2:16 covers one's **g** with violence
Matt 9:16 of unshrunk cloth on an old **g**
Matt 9:16 patch pulls away from the **g**
Matt 9:20 and touched the hem of His **g**
Matt 9:21 If only I may touch His **g**
Matt 14:36 only touch the hem of His **g**
Matt 22:11 did not have on a wedding **g**
Matt 22:12 in here without a wedding **g**
Mark 2:21 of unshrunk cloth on an old **g**
Mark 5:27 in the crowd and touched His **g**
Mark 6:56 touch the border of His **g**
Mark 10:50 And throwing aside his **g**, he
Mark 13:16 not go back to get his **g**
Luke 5:36 from a new **g** on an old one
Luke 8:44 touched the border of His **g**
Luke 22:36 no sword, let him sell his **g**
John 21: 7 he put on his outer **g** (for he
Acts 12: 8 Put on your **g** and follow me
Heb 1:11 will all grow old like a **g**
Jude 23 hating even the **g** defiled by
Rev 1:13 clothed with a **g** down to the

GARMENTS (*see* GARMENT)
Gen 35: 2 yourselves, and change your **g**
Gen 38:14 So she took off her widow's **g**
Gen 38:19 put on the **g** of her widowhood
Gen 41:42 him in **g** of fine linen and put
Gen 45:22 to each man, changes of **g**
Gen 45:22 silver and five changes of **g**
Gen 49:11 vine, he washed his **g** in wine
Ex 28: 2 you shall make holy **g** for
Ex 28: 3 that they may make Aaron's **g**
Ex 28: 4 these are the **g** which they
Ex 28: 4 holy **g** for Aaron your brother
Ex 29: 5 Then you shall take the **g**
Ex 29:21 it on Aaron and on his **g**, on
Ex 29:21 on the **g** of his sons with him
Ex 29:21 his **g** shall be hallowed, and
Ex 29:21 sons and his sons' **g** with him
Ex 29:29 the holy **g** of Aaron shall be
Ex 31:10 the **g** of ministry, the holy
Ex 31:10 the holy **g** for Aaron the
Ex 31:10 and the **g** of his sons, to
Ex 35:19 the **g** of ministry, for
Ex 35:19 the holy **g** for Aaron the
Ex 35:19 and the **g** of his sons, to
Ex 35:21 service, and for the holy **g**
Ex 39: 1 they made **g** of ministry, for
Ex 39: 1 and made the holy **g** for Aaron
Ex 39:41 and the **g** of ministry, to
Ex 39:41 the holy **g** for Aaron the
Ex 39:41 the priest, and his sons' **g**
Ex 40:13 shall put the holy **g** on Aaron
Lev 6:11 Then he shall take off his **g**
Lev 6:11 put on other **g**
Lev 8: 2 his sons with him, and the **g**
Lev 8:30 it on Aaron, on his **g**, on his
Lev 8:30 on the **g** of his sons with him
Lev 8:30 and he sanctified Aaron, his **g**
Lev 8:30 the **g** of his sons with him
Lev 16: 4 These are holy **g**
Lev 16:23 **g** which he put on when he
Lev 16:24 in a holy place, put on his **g**
Lev 16:32 the linen clothes, the holy **g**
Lev 21:10 is consecrated to wear the **g**
Num 15:38 of their **g** throughout their
Num 20:26 and strip Aaron of his **g** and
Num 20:28 Moses stripped Aaron of his **g**
Deut 8: 4 Your **g** did not wear out on
Josh 9: 5 feet, and old **g** on themselves
Josh 9:13 and these our **g** and our sandals
Judg 5:30 for Sisera, plunder of dyed **g**
Judg 5:30 plunder of **g** embroidered and
Judg 14:12 will give you thirty linen **g**
Judg 14:13 shall give me thirty linen **g**
2Sa 10: 4 cut off their **g** in the middle
2Sa 13:31 the king arose and tore his **g**
1Ki 10:25 articles of silver and gold, **g**
2Ki 5:22 of silver and two changes of **g**
2Ki 5:23 bags, with two changes of **g**
2Ki 7:15 all the road was full of **g**
2Ki 25:29 changed from his prison **g**
1Ch 19: 4 cut off their **g** in the middle
2Ch 9:24 articles of silver and gold, **g**
Ezra 2:69 and one hundred priestly **g**
Neh 7:70 hundred and thirty priestly **g**
Neh 7:72 and sixty-seven priestly **g**
Esth 4: 4 Then she sent **g** to clothe
Job 37:17 Why are your **g** hot, when He
Ps 22:18 They divide My **g** among them
Ps 45: 8 All Your **g** are scented with
Ps 133: 2 down on the edge of his **g**
Prov 31:24 She makes linen **g** and sells
Eccl 9: 8 Let your **g** always be white,
Song 4:11 the fragrance of your **g** is
Is 3:22 the outer **g**, the purses,
Is 9: 5 **g** rolled in blood, will be
Is 52: 1 put on your beautiful **g**, O
Is 59: 6 Their webs will not become **g**
Is 59:17 He put on the **g** of vengeance
Is 61:10 me with the **g** of salvation
Is 63: 1 with dyed **g** from Bozrah, this
Is 63: 2 Your **g** like one who treads in
Is 63: 3 blood is sprinkled upon My **g**
Jer 36:24 nor did they tear their **g**
Jer 52:33 changed from his prison **g**
Lam 4:14 no one would touch their **g**
Ezek 16:16 You took some of your **g** and
Ezek 16:18 You took your embroidered **g**
Ezek 26:16 take off their embroidered **g**
Ezek 27:24 clothes, in embroidered **g**
Ezek 42:14 **g** in which they minister, for
Ezek 42:14 They shall put on other **g**
Ezek 44:17 they shall put on linen **g**
Ezek 44:19 their **g** in which they have
Ezek 44:19 chambers, and put on other **g**
Ezek 44:19 in their holy **g** they shall
Dan 3:21 turbans, and their other **g**
Dan 3:27 nor were their **g** affected
Joel 2:13 your heart, and not your **g**
Zech 3: 3 was clothed with filthy **g**
Zech 3: 4 away the filthy **g** from him
Matt 11: 8 A man clothed in soft **g**
Matt 21: 8 spread their **g** on the road
Matt 23: 5 the borders of their **g**
Matt 27:35 Him, and divided His **g**,
Matt 27:35 They divided My **g** among them
Mark 11: 7 Jesus and threw their **g** on it
Mark 11: 8 spread their **g** on the road
Mark 15:24 Him, they divided His **g**,
Luke 7:25 A man clothed in soft **g**
Luke 19:35 threw their own **g** on the colt
Luke 23:34 And they divided His **g** and
Luke 24: 4 stood by them in shining **g**
John 13: 4 supper and laid aside His **g**
John 13:12 their feet, taken His **g**, and
John 19:23 crucified Jesus, took His **g**
John 19:24 They divided My **g** among them
Acts 9:39 **g** which Dorcas had made while
Acts 18: 6 and blasphemed, he shook his **g**
Jas 5: 2 and your **g** are moth-eaten
Rev 3: 4 who have not defiled their **g**
Rev 3: 5 shall be clothed in white **g**
Rev 3:18 and white **g**, that you may be
Rev 16:15 who watches, and keeps his **g**

GARMITE
1Ch 4:19 the fathers of Keilah the **G**

GARRISON (*see* GARRISONS)
1Sa 10: 5 God where the Philistine **g** is
1Sa 13: 3 Jonathan attacked the **g** of
1Sa 13: 4 a **g** of the Philistines, and
1Sa 13:23 the **g** of the Philistines went
1Sa 14: 1 **g** that is on the other side
1Sa 14: 4 go over to the Philistines' **g**
1Sa 14: 6 let us go over to the **g** of
1Sa 14:11 to the **g** of the Philistines
1Sa 14:12 of the **g** called to Jonathan
1Sa 14:15 The **g** and the raiders also
2Sa 23:14 the **g** of the Philistines was
1Ch 11:16 the **g** of the Philistines was
Matt 27:27 the whole **g** around Him
Mark 15:16 called together the whole **g**
Acts 21:31 to the commander of the **g**
2Co 11:32 of the Damascenes with a **g**

GARRISONS (*see* GARRISON)
2Sa 8: 6 Then David put **g** in Syria of
2Sa 8:14 He also put **g** in Edom
2Sa 8:14 throughout all Edom he put **g**
1Ch 18: 6 Then David put **g** in Syria of
1Ch 18:13 He also put **g** in Edom, and all
2Ch 17: 2 set **g** in the land of Judah and

GASP
Is 42:14 I will pant and **g** at once

GATAM
Gen 36:11 were Teman, Omar, Zepho, **G**
Gen 36:16 Chief Korah, Chief **G**, and
1Ch 1:36 were Teman, Omar, Zephi, **G**

GATE (*see* GATE-BARS, GATEKEEPER, GATEPOST, GATES, GATEWAY)
Gen 19: 1 was sitting in the **g** of Sodom
Gen 22:17 the **g** of their enemies
Gen 23:10 entered at the **g** of his city
Gen 23:18 went in at the **g** of his city
Gen 28:17 and this is the **g** of heaven
Gen 34:20 came to the **g** of their city
Gen 34:24 all who went out of the **g** of
Gen 34:24 went out of the **g** of his city
Ex 27:14 the **g** shall be fifteen cubits
Ex 27:16 For the **g** of the court there
Ex 35:17 screen for the **g** of the court
Ex 38:14 **g** were fifteen cubits long
Ex 38:15 the other side of the court **g**
Ex 38:18 The screen for the **g** of the
Ex 38:31 the bases for the court **g**
Ex 39:40 the screen for the court **g**
Ex 40: 8 up the screen at the court **g**
Ex 40:33 up the screen of the court **g**
Num 4:26 door of the **g** of the court
Deut 21:19 city, to the **g** of his city
Deut 22:15 elders of the city at the **g**
Deut 22:24 out to the **g** of that city
Deut 25: 7 go up to the **g** to the elders
Josh 2: 5 as the **g** was being shut, when
Josh 2: 7 had gone out, they shut the **g**
Josh 7: 5 the **g** as far as Shebarim, and
Josh 8:29 entrance of the **g** of the city
Josh 20: 4 entrance of the **g** of the city
Judg 9:35 in the entrance to the city **g**
Judg 9:40 even to the entrance of the **g**
Judg 9:44 entrance of the **g** of the city
Judg 16: 2 night at the **g** of the city
Judg 16: 3 doors of the **g** of the city
Judg 18:16 by the entrance of the **g**
Judg 18:17 at the entrance of the **g** with
Ruth 4: 1 Now Boaz went up to the **g**
Ruth 4:10 and from the **g** of his place
Ruth 4:11 the people who were at the **g**
1Sa 4:18 backward by the side of the **g**
1Sa 9:18 drew near to Samuel in the **g**
1Sa 21:13 on the doors of the **g**, and let
2Sa 3:27 Joab took him aside in the **g**
2Sa 10: 8 at the entrance of the **g**
2Sa 11:23 far as the entrance of the **g**
2Sa 15: 2 stand beside the way to the **g**
2Sa 18: 4 the king stood beside the **g**
2Sa 18:24 up to the roof over the **g**
2Sa 18:33 up to the chamber over the **g**
2Sa 19: 8 king arose and sat in the **g**
2Sa 19: 8 is the king, sitting in the **g**
2Sa 23:15 Bethlehem, which is by the **g**
2Sa 23:16 Bethlehem that was by the **g**
1Ki 17:10 he came to the **g** of the city
1Ki 22:10 entrance of the **g** of Samaria
2Ki 7: 1 a shekel, at the **g** of Samaria
2Ki 7: 3 men at the entrance of the **g**
2Ki 7:17 to have charge of the **g**
2Ki 7:17 people trampled him in the **g**
2Ki 7:18 this time in the **g** of Samaria
2Ki 7:20 people trampled him in the **g**
2Ki 9:31 as Jehu entered at the **g**
2Ki 10: 8 of the **g** until morning
2Ki 11: 6 shall be at the **g** of Sur, and
2Ki 11: 6 one-third at the **g** behind the
2Ki 11:19 went by way of the **g** of the
2Ki 14:13 **G** of Ephraim to the Corner
2Ki 14:13 of Ephraim to the Corner **G**
2Ki 15:35 He built the Upper **G** of the
2Ki 23: 8 **G** of Joshua the governor of
2Ki 23: 8 to the left of the city **g**
2Ki 25: 4 of the **g** between two walls
1Ch 9:18 at the King's **G** on the east
1Ch 11:17 Bethlehem, which is by the **g**
1Ch 11:18 Bethlehem that was by the **g**
1Ch 19: 9 before the **g** of the city, and
1Ch 26:13 And they cast lots for each **g**
1Ch 26:14 the East **G** fell to Shelemiah
1Ch 26:14 lot came out for the North **G**
1Ch 26:15 to Obed-Edom the South **G**, and
1Ch 26:16 lot came out for the West **G**
1Ch 26:16 with the Shallecheth **G** on the

2Ch 8:14 by their divisions at each g
2Ch 18: 9 entrance of the g of Samaria
2Ch 23: 5 one-third at the G of the
2Ch 23:15 Horse G into the king's house
2Ch 23:20 Upper G to the king's house
2Ch 24: 8 set it outside at the g of
2Ch 25:23 G of Ephraim to the Corner
2Ch 25:23 of Ephraim to the Corner G
2Ch 26: 9 in Jerusalem at the Corner G
2Ch 26: 9 Corner G, at the Valley G
2Ch 27: 3 He built the Upper G of the
2Ch 31:14 the keeper of the East G
2Ch 32: 6 the open square of the city g
2Ch 33:14 as the entrance of the Fish G
2Ch 35:15 gatekeepers were at each g
Neh 2:13 Valley G to the Serpent Well
Neh 2:13 Serpent Well and the Refuse G
Neh 2:14 I went on to the Fountain G
Neh 2:15 and entered by the Valley G
Neh 3: 1 priests and built the Sheep G
Neh 3: 3 of Hassenaah built the Fish G
Neh 3: 6 Besodeiah repaired the Old G
Neh 3:13 Zanoah repaired the Valley G
Neh 3:13 wall as far as the Refuse G
Neh 3:14 repaired the Refuse G
Neh 3:15 repaired the Fountain G
Neh 3:26 the Water G toward the east
Neh 3:28 Beyond the Horse G the
Neh 3:29 the keeper of the East G
Neh 3:31 in front of the Miphkad G
Neh 3:32 corner, as far as the Sheep G
Neh 8: 1 was in front of the Water G
Neh 8: 3 G from morning until midday
Neh 8:16 open square of the Water G
Neh 8:16 square of the G of Ephraim
Neh 12:31 the wall toward the Refuse G
Neh 12:37 By the Fountain G, in front
Neh 12:37 far as the Water G eastward
Neh 12:39 above the G of Ephraim, above
Neh 12:39 the Old G, above the Fish G
Neh 12:39 as far as the Sheep G
Neh 12:39 by the G of the Prison
Esth 2:19 sat within the king's g
Esth 2:21 sat within the king's g, two
Esth 3: 2 within the king's g bowed
Esth 3: 3 the king's g said to Mordecai
Esth 4: 2 in front of the king's g, for
Esth 4: 2 g clothed with sackcloth
Esth 4: 6 was in front of the king's g
Esth 5: 9 saw Mordecai in the king's g
Esth 5:13 Jew sitting at the king's g
Esth 6:10 who sits within the king's g
Esth 6:12 went back to the king's g
Job 5: 4 they are crushed in the g
Job 29: 7 went out to the g by the city
Job 31:21 I saw I had help in the g
Ps 69:12 sit in the g speak against me
Ps 118:20 This is the g of the LORD
Ps 127: 5 with their enemies in the g
Prov 17:19 his g seeks destruction
Prov 22:22 the afflicted at the g
Prov 24: 7 not open his mouth in the g
Song 7: 4 by the g of Bath Rabbim
Is 14:31 Wail, O g
Is 22: 7 themselves in array at the g
Is 24:12 and the g is stricken with
Is 28: 6 turn back the battle at the g
Is 29:21 for him who reproves in the g
Jer 7: 2 Stand in the g of the LORD's
Jer 17:19 Go and stand in the g of the
Jer 19: 2 the entry of the Potsherd G
Jer 20: 2 in the high g of Benjamin
Jer 26:10 the new g of the LORD's house
Jer 31:38 of Hananeel to the Corner G
Jer 31:40 the Horse G toward the east
Jer 36:10 the New G of the LORD's house
Jer 37:13 he was in the g of Benjamin
Jer 38: 7 sitting at the G of Benjamin
Jer 39: 3 in and sat in the Middle G
Jer 39: 4 by the g between the two
Jer 51:30 the bars of her g are broken
Jer 52: 7 the g between the two walls
Lam 5:14 ceased gathering at the g
Ezek 8: 3 north g of the inner court
Ezek 8: 5 there, north of the altar g
Ezek 8:14 north g of the LORD's house
Ezek 9: 2 the direction of the upper g
Ezek 10:19 east g of the LORD's house
Ezek 11: 1 east g of the LORD's house
Ezek 11: 1 of the g were twenty-five men
Ezek 40: 7 Each g chamber was one rod
Ezek 40: 7 between the g chambers was a
Ezek 40: 7 of the inside g was one rod
Ezek 40: 8 the vestibule of the inside g
Ezek 40: 9 of the g was on the inside
Ezek 40:10 three g chambers on one side
Ezek 40:11 and the length of the g,
Ezek 40:12 in front of the g chambers
Ezek 40:12 the g chambers were six
Ezek 40:13 from the roof of one g
Ezek 40:15 g to the front of the
Ezek 40:15 the inner g was fifty cubits
Ezek 40:16 frames in the g chambers and
Ezek 40:21 Its g chambers, three on this
Ezek 40:21 measurements as the first g
Ezek 40:23 A g of the inner court was
Ezek 40:29 Also its g chambers, its
Ezek 40:33 Also its g chambers, its
Ezek 40:36 also its g chambers, its
Ezek 40:44 Outside the inner g were the
Ezek 43: 1 he brought me to the g, the
Ezek 43: 1 the g that faces toward the
Ezek 43: 4 the temple by way of the g
Ezek 44: 1 me back to the outer g of the
Ezek 44: 2 to me, "This g shall be shut
Ezek 44: 4 me by way of the north g to
Ezek 45:19 of the g of the inner court
Ezek 46: 2 at the threshold of the g
Ezek 46: 2 but the g shall not be shut
Ezek 46: 9 g to worship shall go out by
Ezek 46: 9 go out by way of the south g
Ezek 46: 9 g shall go out by way of the
Ezek 46: 9 go out by way of the north g
Ezek 46: 9 the g through which he came
Ezek 46: 9 go out through the opposite g
Ezek 46:12 the g that faces toward the
Ezek 46:12 goes out the g shall be shut
Ezek 46:19 was at the side of the g,
Ezek 47: 2 me out by way of the north g
Ezek 48:31 one g for Reuben
Ezek 48:31 one g for Judah
Ezek 48:31 and one g for Levi
Ezek 48:32 one g for Joseph
Ezek 48:32 one g for Benjamin
Ezek 48:32 and one g for Dan
Ezek 48:33 one g for Simeon
Ezek 48:33 one g for Issachar
Ezek 48:33 and one g for Zebulun
Ezek 48:34 one g for Gad
Ezek 48:34 one g for Asher
Ezek 48:34 and one g for Naphtali
Dan 2:49 sat in the g of the king
Amos 1: 5 break the g bar of Damascus
Amos 5:10 the one who rebukes in the g
Amos 5:12 poor from justice at the g
Amos 5:15 establish justice in the g
Obad 13 g of My people in the day of
Mic 1: 9 come to the g of My people
Mic 1:12 LORD to the g of Jerusalem
Mic 2:13 break out, pass through the g
Zeph 1:10 mournful cry from the Fish G
Zech 14:10 G to the place of the First
Zech 14:10 First G and the Corner G
Matt 7:13 Enter by the narrow g
Matt 7:13 for wide is the g and broad is
Matt 7:14 Because narrow is the g and
Luke 7:12 came near the g of the city
Luke 13:24 to enter through the narrow g
Luke 16:20 sores, who was laid at his g
John 5: 2 by the Sheep G a pool, which
Acts 3: 2 the g of the temple which is
Acts 3:10 the Beautiful G of the temple
Acts 10:17 house, and stood before the g
Acts 12:10 they came to the iron g that
Acts 12:13 knocked at the door of the g
Acts 12:14 she did not open the g, but
Acts 12:14 that Peter stood before the g
Heb 13:12 blood, suffered outside the g
Rev 21:21 each individual g was of one

GATE-BARS (*see* GATE)
1Ki 4:13 cities with walls and bronze g

GATEKEEPER (*see* GATE, GATEKEEPERS)
2Sa 18:26 the watchman called to the g

GATEKEEPERS (*see* GATEKEEPER)
2Ki 7:10 called to the g of the city
2Ki 7:11 the g called out, and they
1Ch 9:17 the g were Shallum, Akkub,
1Ch 9:18 been g for the camps of the
1Ch 9:19 service, g of the tabernacle
1Ch 9:22 chosen as g were two hundred
1Ch 9:24 The g were assigned to the
1Ch 9:26 office were four chief g
1Ch 15:18 Obed-Edom, and Jeiel, the g
1Ch 16:38 Jeduthun, and Hosah, to be g
1Ch 16:42 the sons of Jeduthun were g
1Ch 23: 5 four thousand were g, and four
1Ch 26: 1 the divisions of the g
1Ch 26:12 were the divisions of the g
1Ch 26:19 the g among the sons of Korah
2Ch 8:14 the g by their divisions at
2Ch 23:19 he set the g at the gates of
2Ch 34:13 were scribes, officers, and g
2Ch 35:15 Also the g were at each gate
Ezra 2:42 The sons of the g
Ezra 2:70 people, the singers, the g
Ezra 7: 7 Levites, the singers, the g
Ezra 7:24 priests, Levites, singers, g
Ezra 10:24 and of the g: Shallum, Telem
Neh 7: 1 hung the doors, when the g
Neh 7:45 The g: the children of
Neh 7:73 priests, the Levites, the g
Neh 10:28 priests, the Levites, the g
Neh 10:39 priests who minister and the g
Neh 11:19 Moreover the g, Akkub,
Neh 12:25 and Akkub were g keeping the
Neh 12:45 and the g kept the charge of
Neh 12:47 for the singers and the g, a
Neh 13: 5 the Levites and singers and g
Ezek 44:11 as g of the house and

GATEPOST (*see* GATE, GATEPOSTS)
Ezek 40:14 the gateway extended to the g
Ezek 40:16 on each g were palm trees
Ezek 46: 2 outside, and stand by the g

GATEPOSTS (*see* GATEPOST)
Judg 16: 3 gate of the city and the two g
Ezek 40: 9 and the g, two cubits
Ezek 40:10 also the g were of the same
Ezek 40:14 He measured the g, sixty
Ezek 40:21 and three on that side, its g
Ezek 40:24 and he measured its g and
Ezek 40:26 and it had palm trees on its g
Ezek 40:29 Also its gate chambers, its g
Ezek 40:31 palm trees were on its g
Ezek 40:33 Also its gate chambers, its g
Ezek 40:34 were on its g on this side
Ezek 40:36 also its gate chambers, its g
Ezek 40:37 Its g faced the outer court,
Ezek 40:37 were on its g on this side
Ezek 40:38 by the g of the gateway,
Ezek 45:19 on the g of the gate of the

GATES (*see* GATE)
Gen 24:60 the g of those who hate them
Ex 20:10 stranger who is within your g
Deut 3: 5 fortified with high walls, g
Deut 5:14 stranger who is within your g
Deut 6: 9 of your house and on your g
Deut 11:20 of your house and on your g
Deut 12:12 Levite who is within your g
Deut 12:15 and eat meat within all your g
Deut 12:17 g the tithe of your grain or
Deut 12:18 Levite who is within your g
Deut 12:21 your g as much as your heart
Deut 14:21 alien who is within your g
Deut 14:27 Levite who is within your g
Deut 14:28 and store it up within your g
Deut 14:29 widow who are within your g
Deut 15: 7 within any of the g in your
Deut 15:22 You may eat it within your g
Deut 16: 5 g which the LORD your God
Deut 16:11 Levite who is within your g
Deut 16:14 widow, who are within your g
Deut 16:18 and officers in all your g
Deut 17: 2 within any of your g which
Deut 17: 5 g that man or woman who has
Deut 17: 8 of controversy within your g
Deut 18: 6 comes from any of your g,
Deut 23:16 chooses within one of your g
Deut 24:14 is in your land within your g
Deut 26:12 they may eat within your g
Deut 28:52 at all your g until your high
Deut 28:52 besiege you at all your g
Deut 28:55 distress you at all your g
Deut 28:57 distress you at all your g
Deut 31:12 stranger who is within your g
Josh 6:26 he shall set up its g
Judg 5: 8 then there was war in the g
Judg 5:11 LORD shall go down to the g
1Sa 17:52 valley and to the g of Ekron

1Sa 23: 7 by entering a town that has **g**
2Sa 18:24 was sitting between the two **g**
1Ki 16:34 son Segub he set up its **g**
2Ki 23: 8 **g** which were at the entrance
1Ch 9:23 were in charge of the **g** of
1Ch 22: 3 nails of the doors of the **g**
2Ch 8: 5 cities with walls, **g**, and bars
2Ch 14: 7 around them, and towers, **g**
2Ch 23:19 **g** of the house of the LORD
2Ch 31: 2 to praise in the **g** of the
Neh 1: 3 its **g** are burned with fire
Neh 2: 3 its **g** are burned with fire
Neh 2: 8 the **g** of the citadel which
Neh 2:13 its **g** which were burned with
Neh 2:17 its **g** are burned with fire
Neh 6: 1 not hung the doors in the **g**)
Neh 7: 3 Do not let the **g** of Jerusalem
Neh 11:19 their brethren who kept the **g**
Neh 12:25 at the storerooms of the **g**
Neh 12:30 and purified the people, the **g**
Neh 13:19 at the **g** of Jerusalem, as it
Neh 13:19 I commanded the **g** to be shut
Neh 13:19 some of my servants at the **g**
Neh 13:22 they should go and guard the **g**
Job 17:16 go down to the **g** of Sheol
Job 38:17 Have the **g** of death been
Ps 9:13 me up from the **g** of death
Ps 9:14 the **g** of the daughter of Zion
Ps 24: 7 Lift up your heads, O you **g**
Ps 24: 9 Lift up your heads, O you **g**
Ps 87: 2 The LORD loves the **g** of Zion
Ps 100: 4 Enter into His **g** with
Ps 107:16 He has broken the **g** of bronze
Ps 107:18 drew near to the **g** of death
Ps 118:19 Open to me the **g** of
Ps 122: 2 been standing Within your **g**
Ps 147:13 the bars of your **g**
Prov 1:21 at the openings of the **g** in
Prov 8: 3 She cries out by the **g**, at
Prov 8:34 to me, watching daily at my **g**
Prov 14:19 at the **g** of the righteous
Prov 31:23 Her husband is known in the **g**
Prov 31:31 own works praise her in the **g**
Song 7:13 at our **g** are pleasant fruits,
Is 3:26 Her **g** shall lament and mourn,
Is 13: 2 may enter the **g** of the nobles
Is 26: 2 Open the **g**, that the
Is 38:10 I shall go to the **g** of Sheol
Is 45: 1 so that the **g** will not be
Is 45: 2 in pieces the **g** of bronze
Is 54:12 your **g** of crystal, and all
Is 60:11 Therefore your **g** shall be
Is 60:18 Salvation, and your **g** Praise
Is 62:10 Go through, go through the **g**
Jer 1:15 of the **g** of Jerusalem,
Jer 7: 2 these **g** to worship the LORD
Jer 14: 2 mourns, and her **g** languish
Jer 15: 7 fan in the **g** of the land
Jer 17:19 in all the **g** of Jerusalem
Jer 17:20 who enter by these **g**
Jer 17:21 it in by the **g** of Jerusalem
Jer 17:24 **g** of this city on the Sabbath
Jer 17:25 the **g** of this city kings and
Jer 17:27 a burden when entering the **g**
Jer 17:27 I will kindle a fire in its **g**
Jer 22: 2 your people who enter these **g**
Jer 22: 4 enter the **g** of this house
Jer 22:19 out beyond the **g** of Jerusalem
Jer 49:31 Which has neither **g** nor bars
Jer 51:58 her high **g** shall be burned
Lam 1: 4 All her **g** are desolate
Lam 2: 9 Her **g** have sunk into the
Lam 4:12 enter the **g** of Jerusalem
Ezek 21:15 the sword against all their **g**
Ezek 21:22 battering rams against the **g**
Ezek 26:10 when he enters your **g**, as
Ezek 38:11 and having neither bars nor **g**'
Ezek 44:17 the **g** of the inner court,
Ezek 44:17 the **g** of the inner court or
Ezek 48:31 (the **g** of the city shall be
Ezek 48:31 the three **g** northward
Ezek 48:32 five hundred cubits, three **g**
Ezek 48:33 five hundred cubits, three **g**
Ezek 48:34 cubits with their three **g**
Obad 11 when foreigners entered his **g**
Nah 2: 6 The **g** of the rivers are
Nah 3:13 The **g** of your land are wide
Nah 3:13 devour the bars of your **g**
Zech 8:16 judgment in your **g** for truth
Matt 16:18 and the **g** of Hades shall not
Acts 9:24 And they watched the **g** day
Acts 14:13 oxen and garlands to the **g**
Rev 21:12 and high wall with twelve **g**
Rev 21:12 and twelve angels at the **g**
Rev 21:13 three **g** on the east, three
Rev 21:13 three **g** on the north, three
Rev 21:13 three **g** on the south, and
Rev 21:13 south, and three **g** on the west
Rev 21:15 to measure the city, its **g**
Rev 21:21 And the twelve **g** were twelve
Rev 21:25 Its **g** shall not be shut at
Rev 22:14 through the **g** into the city

GATEWAY (*see* GATE, GATEWAYS)
Ezek 26: 2 who was the **g** of the peoples
Ezek 40: 3 hand, and he stood in the **g**
Ezek 40: 6 to the **g** which faced east
Ezek 40: 6 the threshold of the **g**, which
Ezek 40: 7 the threshold of the **g** by the
Ezek 40: 9 the vestibule of the **g**, eight
Ezek 40:10 In the eastern **g** were three
Ezek 40:11 of the entrance to the **g**, ten
Ezek 40:13 Then he measured the **g** from
Ezek 40:14 **g** extended to the gatepost
Ezek 40:16 inside of the **g** all around
Ezek 40:19 **g** to the front of the inner
Ezek 40:20 was also a **g** facing north
Ezek 40:22 as the **g** facing east
Ezek 40:23 was opposite the northern **g**
Ezek 40:23 just as the eastern **g**
Ezek 40:23 he measured from **g** to **g**
Ezek 40:24 there a **g** was facing south
Ezek 40:27 There was also a **g** on the
Ezek 40:27 he measured from **g** to **g**
Ezek 40:28 court through the southern **g**
Ezek 40:28 **g** according to these same
Ezek 40:32 he measured the **g** according
Ezek 40:35 he brought me to the north **g**
Ezek 40:38 by the gateposts of the **g**
Ezek 40:39 the **g** were two tables on this
Ezek 40:40 entrance of the northern **g**
Ezek 40:40 of the **g** were two tables
Ezek 40:41 side, by the side of the **g**
Ezek 40:44 at the side of the northern **g**
Ezek 40:44 at the side of the southern **g**
Ezek 40:48 the width of the **g** was three
Ezek 42:15 **g** that faces toward the east
Ezek 44: 3 way of the vestibule of the **g**
Ezek 46: 1 The **g** of the inner court that
Ezek 46: 2 of that **g** from the outside
Ezek 46: 3 this **g** before the LORD on the
Ezek 46: 8 of the vestibule of that **g**
Ezek 47: 2 the outer **g** that faces east
Matt 26:71 when he had gone out to the **g**

GATEWAYS (*see* GATEWAY)
Ezek 40:18 was by the side of the **g**,
Ezek 40:18 to the length of the **g**

GATH (*see* GITTITE, MORESHETH GATH)
Josh 11:22 remained only in Gaza, in **G**
1Sa 5: 8 Israel be carried away to **G**
1Sa 6:17 one for Ashkelon, one for **G**
1Sa 7:14 to Israel, from Ekron to **G**
1Sa 17: 4 named Goliath, from **G**, whose
1Sa 17:23 champion, the Philistine of **G**
1Sa 17:52 to Shaaraim, even as far as **G**
1Sa 21:10 went to Achish the king of **G**
1Sa 21:12 of Achish the king of **G**
1Sa 27: 2 the son of Maoch, king of **G**
1Sa 27: 3 David dwelt with Achish at **G**
1Sa 27: 4 Saul that David had fled to **G**
1Sa 27:11 alive, to bring news to **G**
2Sa 1:20 Tell it not in **G**, proclaim it
2Sa 15:18 who had followed him from **G**
2Sa 21:20 again there was a battle in **G**
2Sa 21:22 were born to the giant in **G**
1Ki 2:39 the son of Maachah, king of **G**
1Ki 2:39 Look, your slaves are in **G**
1Ki 2:40 went to Achish at **G** to seek
1Ki 2:40 and brought his slaves from **G**
1Ki 2:41 had gone from Jerusalem to **G**
2Ki 12:17 went up and fought against **G**
1Ch 7:21 The men of **G** who were born in
1Ch 8:13 out the inhabitants of **G**
1Ch 18: 1 subdued them, and took **G** and
1Ch 20: 6 Yet again there was war at **G**
1Ch 20: 8 were born to the giant in **G**
2Ch 11: 8 **G**, Mareshah, Ziph,
2Ch 26: 6 and broke down the wall of **G**
Amos 6: 2 Then go down to **G** of the
Mic 1:10 Tell it not in **G**, weep not at

GATHER (*see* GATHERED, GATHERING, GATHERS)
Gen 6:21 you shall **g** it to yourself
Gen 31:46 to his brethren, "**G** stones
Gen 34:30 they will **g** themselves
Gen 41:35 let them **g** all the food of
Gen 49: 1 **G** together, that I may tell
Gen 49: 2 **G** together and hear, you sons
Ex 3:16 Go and **g** the elders of Israel
Ex 5: 7 go and **g** straw for themselves
Ex 5:12 to **g** stubble instead of straw
Ex 9:19 **g** your livestock and all that
Ex 16: 4 **g** a certain quota every day,
Ex 16: 5 twice as much as they **g** daily
Ex 16:16 Let every man **g** it according
Ex 16:26 Six days you shall **g** it, but
Ex 16:27 out on the seventh day to **g**
Ex 23:10 land and **g** in its produce,
Lev 8: 3 and **g** all the congregation
Lev 19: 9 nor shall you **g** the gleanings
Lev 19:10 nor shall you **g** every grape
Lev 23:22 nor shall you **g** any gleaning
Lev 25: 3 vineyard, and **g** in its fruit
Lev 25: 5 nor **g** the grapes of your
Lev 25:11 nor **g** the grapes of your
Lev 25:20 not sow nor **g** in our produce
Num 8: 9 and you shall **g** together the
Num 10: 3 all the assembly shall **g**
Num 10: 4 of Israel, shall **g** to you
Num 11:16 **G** to Me seventy men of the
Num 19: 9 a man who is clean shall **g** up
Num 20: 8 and your brother Aaron **g** the
Num 21:16 **G** the people together, and I
Deut 4:10 **G** the people to Me, and I
Deut 11:14 that you may **g** in your grain,
Deut 13:16 you shall **g** all its plunder
Deut 24:21 When you **g** the grapes of your
Deut 28:30 but shall not **g** its grapes
Deut 28:38 and **g** but little in, for the
Deut 28:39 of the wine nor **g** the grapes
Deut 30: 3 and **g** you again from all the
Deut 30: 4 the LORD your God will **g** you
Deut 31:12 **G** the people together, men and
Deut 31:28 **G** to me all the elders of
Judg 1: 7 big toes cut off used to **g**
Ruth 2: 7 **g** after the reapers among the
1Sa 7: 5 **G** all Israel to Mizpah, and I
2Sa 3:21 **g** all Israel to my lord the
2Sa 12:28 **g** the rest of the people
1Ki 18:19 **g** all Israel to me on Mount
2Ki 4: 3 do not **g** just a few
2Ki 4:39 out into the field to **g** herbs
2Ki 22:20 I will **g** you to your fathers,
2Ki 23: 1 to **g** all the elders of Judah
1Ch 13: 2 that they may **g** together to
1Ch 16:35 **g** us together, and deliver us
1Ch 22: 2 So David commanded to **g** the
2Ch 24: 5 **g** from all Israel money to
2Ch 34:28 Surely I will **g** you to your
Ezra 10: 7 that they must **g** at Jerusalem
Neh 1: 9 yet I will **g** them from there,
Neh 7: 5 into my heart to **g** the nobles
Neh 12:44 to **g** into them from the
Esth 2: 3 that they may **g** all the
Esth 4:16 Go, **g** all the Jews who are
Esth 8:11 in every city to **g** together
Job 16:10 they **g** together against me
Job 24: 6 They **g** their fodder in the
Job 34:14 if He should **g** to Himself His
Job 39:12 **g** it to your threshing floor
Ps 26: 9 Do not **g** my soul together
Ps 39: 6 does not know who will **g** them
Ps 50: 5 **G** My saints together to Me,
Ps 56: 6 They **g** together, They hide,
Ps 59: 3 The mighty **g** against me, Not
Ps 94:21 They **g** together against the
Ps 104:22 they **g** together And lie down
Ps 104:28 What You give them they **g** in
Ps 106:47 **g** us from among the Gentiles,
Ps 140: 2 **g** together for war
Eccl 3: 5 stones, and a time to **g** stones
Song 6: 2 the gardens, and to **g** lilies
Is 11:12 **g** together the dispersed of
Is 34:15 and **g** them under her shadow
Is 40:11 He will **g** the lambs with His
Is 43: 5 east, and **g** you from the west
Is 49:18 all these **g** together and come
Is 54: 7 great mercies I will **g** you
Is 56: 8 Yet I will **g** to him others
Is 60: 4 they all **g** together, they

Is 66:18 be that I will **g** all nations
Jer 4: 5 cry, **G** together,' and say
Jer 6: 1 **g** yourselves to flee from the
Jer 7:18 The children **g** wood, the
Jer 9:22 and no one shall **g** them
Jer 10:17 **G** up your wares from the land
Jer 23: 3 But I will **g** the remnant of
Jer 29:14 I will **g** you from all the
Jer 31: 8 **g** them from the ends of the
Jer 31:10 scattered Israel will **g** him
Jer 32:37 I will **g** them out of all
Jer 40:10 **g** wine and summer fruit and oil
Jer 49: 5 and no one will **g** those who
Jer 49:14 **G** together, come against her,
Jer 51:11 **G** the shields
Ezek 11:17 I will **g** you from the peoples
Ezek 16:37 I will **g** all your lovers with
Ezek 16:37 I will **g** them from all around
Ezek 20:34 **g** you out of the countries
Ezek 20:41 **g** you out of the countries
Ezek 22:19 I will **g** you into the midst
Ezek 22:20 As men **g** silver, bronze,
Ezek 22:20 so I will **g** you in My anger
Ezek 22:21 Yes, I will **g** you and blow on
Ezek 24: 4 **G** pieces of meat in it, every
Ezek 29:13 will **g** the Egyptians from the
Ezek 34:13 **g** them from the countries, and
Ezek 36:24 **g** you out of all countries,
Ezek 37:21 will **g** them from every side
Ezek 39:17 **g** together from all sides to
Dan 3: 2 to **g** together the satraps
Hos 8:10 nations, now I will **g** them
Hos 9: 6 Egypt shall **g** them up
Joel 1:14 **g** the elders and all the
Joel 2:16 **g** the people, sanctify the
Joel 2:16 **g** the children and nursing
Joel 3: 2 I will also **g** all nations
Joel 3:11 and **g** together all around
Mic 2:12 I will surely **g** the remnant
Mic 4: 6 I will **g** the outcast and those
Mic 4:12 for He will **g** them like
Mic 5: 1 Now **g** yourself in troops, O
Mic 7: 1 those who **g** summer fruits
Hab 1: 9 They **g** captives like sand
Hab 1:15 and **g** them in their dragnet
Zeph 2: 1 **G** yourselves together, yes,
Zeph 2: 1 **g** together, O undesirable
Zeph 3: 8 My determination is to **g** the
Zeph 3:18 I will **g** those who sorrow
Zeph 3:19 **g** those who were driven out
Zeph 3:20 even at the time I **g** you
Zech 10: 8 **g** them, for I will redeem
Zech 10:10 Egypt, and **g** them from Assyria
Zech 14: 2 For I will **g** all the nations
Matt 3:12 **g** His wheat into the barn
Matt 6:26 sow nor reap nor **g** into barns
Matt 7:16 Do men **g** grapes from
Matt 12:30 he who does not **g** with Me
Matt 13:28 us then to go and **g** them up
Matt 13:29 lest while you **g** up the tares
Matt 13:30 First **g** together the tares and
Matt 13:30 but **g** the wheat into my barn
Matt 13:41 and they will **g** out of His
Matt 23:37 How often I wanted to **g** your
Matt 24:31 and they will **g** together His
Matt 25:26 **g** where I have not scattered
Mark 13:27 **g** together His elect from the
Luke 3:17 **g** the wheat into His barn
Luke 6:44 For men do not **g** figs from
Luke 6:44 nor do they **g** grapes from a
Luke 11:23 he who does not **g** with Me
Luke 13:34 How often I wanted to **g** your
John 6:12 **G** up the fragments that
John 11:52 would **g** together in one the
John 15: 6 and they **g** them and throw them
Eph 1:10 of the times He might **g**
Rev 14:18 **g** the clusters of the vine of
Rev 16:14 to **g** them to the battle of
Rev 19:17 **g** together for the supper of
Rev 20: 8 to **g** them together to battle,

GATHERED (*see* GATHER)

Gen 1: 9 be **g** together into one place
Gen 12: 5 possessions that they had **g**
Gen 25: 8 years, and was **g** to his people
Gen 25:17 died, and was **g** to his people
Gen 29: 3 the flocks would be **g** there
Gen 29: 7 the cattle to be **g** together
Gen 29: 8 all the flocks are **g** together
Gen 29:22 Laban **g** together all the men
Gen 35:29 was **g** to his people, being
Gen 41:48 So he **g** up all the food of
Gen 41:49 Joseph **g** very much grain, as
Gen 47:14 Joseph **g** up all the money
Gen 49:29 I am to be **g** to my people
Gen 49:33 last, and was **g** to his people
Ex 4:29 **g** together all the elders of
Ex 8:14 They **g** them together in heaps
Ex 15: 8 the waters were **g** together
Ex 16:17 of Israel did so and **g**, some
Ex 16:18 he who **g** much had nothing
Ex 16:18 he who **g** little had no lack
Ex 16:18 Every man had **g** according to
Ex 16:21 So they **g** it every morning,
Ex 16:22 that they **g** twice as much
Ex 23:16 when you have **g** in the fruit
Ex 32: 1 the people **g** together to
Ex 32:26 And all the sons of Levi **g**
Ex 35: 1 Then Moses **g** all the
Lev 8: 4 the assembly was **g** together
Lev 23:39 when you have **g** in the fruit
Lev 26:25 when you are **g** together
Num 10: 7 is to be **g** together, you
Num 11: 8 **g** it, ground it on millstones
Num 11:22 sea be **g** together for them
Num 11:24 he **g** the seventy men of the
Num 11:32 next day, and **g** the quail
Num 11:32 he who **g** least **g** ten homers
Num 14:35 who are **g** together against Me
Num 16: 3 They **g** together against Moses
Num 16:11 you and all your company are **g**
Num 16:19 Korah **g** all the congregation
Num 16:42 had **g** against Moses and Aaron,
Num 20: 2 so they **g** together against
Num 20:10 and Aaron **g** the congregation
Num 20:24 shall be **g** to his people, for
Num 20:26 shall be **g** to his people and
Num 21:23 So Sihon **g** all his people
Num 27: 3 **g** together against the LORD
Num 27:13 shall be **g** to your people
Num 27:13 as Aaron your brother was **g**
Num 31: 2 you shall be **g** to your people
Deut 16:13 when you have **g** from your
Deut 32:50 be **g** to your people, just as
Deut 32:50 Hor and was **g** to his people
Deut 33: 5 leaders of the people were **g**
Josh 9: 2 that they **g** together to fight
Josh 10: 5 **g** together and went up, they
Josh 10: 6 have **g** together against us
Josh 22:12 of the children of Israel **g**
Josh 24: 1 Then Joshua **g** all the tribes
Judg 2:10 had been **g** to their fathers
Judg 3:13 Then he **g** to himself the
Judg 4:13 So Sisera **g** together all his
Judg 6:33 of the East, **g** together
Judg 6:34 the Abiezrites **g** behind him
Judg 6:35 who also **g** behind him
Judg 7:23 the men of Israel **g** together
Judg 7:24 the men of Ephraim **g** together
Judg 9: 6 the men of Shechem **g** together
Judg 9:27 **g** grapes from their vineyards
Judg 9:47 of Shechem were **g** together
Judg 10:17 people of Ammon **g** together
Judg 11:20 So Sihon **g** all his people
Judg 12: 1 the men of Ephraim **g** together
Judg 12: 4 Now Jephthah **g** together all
Judg 16:23 lords of the Philistines **g**
Judg 18:22 near Micah's house **g** together
Judg 18:23 you, that you have **g** such a
Judg 20: 1 the congregation **g** together
Judg 20:11 were **g** against the city,
Judg 20:14 the children of Benjamin **g**
1Sa 5: 8 **g** to themselves all the lords
1Sa 5:11 **g** together all the lords of
1Sa 7: 6 So they **g** together at Mizpah,
1Sa 7: 7 had **g** together at Mizpah, the
1Sa 8: 4 elders of Israel **g** together
1Sa 13: 5 Then the Philistines **g**
1Sa 13:11 **g** together at Michmash,
1Sa 14:48 he **g** an army and attacked the
1Sa 15: 4 So Saul **g** the people together
1Sa 17: 1 Now the Philistines **g** their
1Sa 17: 1 were **g** together at Sochoh,
1Sa 17: 2 men of Israel were **g** together
1Sa 20:38 lad **g** up the arrows and came
1Sa 22: 2 who was discontented **g** to him
1Sa 25: 1 and the Israelites **g** together
1Sa 28: 1 **g** their armies together for
1Sa 28: 4 the Philistines **g** together
1Sa 28: 4 So Saul **g** all Israel together
1Sa 29: 1 Then the Philistines **g**
2Sa 2:25 **g** together behind Abner and
2Sa 2:30 when he had **g** all the people
2Sa 6: 1 Again David **g** all the choice
2Sa 10:15 Israel, they **g** together
2Sa 10:17 he **g** all Israel, crossed over
2Sa 12:29 So David **g** all the people
2Sa 14:14 which cannot be **g** up again
2Sa 17:11 all Israel be fully **g** to you
2Sa 20:14 So they were **g** together and
2Sa 21:13 they **g** the bones of those who
2Sa 23: 9 who were **g** there for battle
2Sa 23:11 The Philistines had **g**
1Ki 10:26 And Solomon **g** chariots and
1Ki 11:24 So he **g** men to him and became
1Ki 18:20 **g** the prophets together on
1Ki 20: 1 **g** all his forces together
1Ki 22: 6 **g** the prophets together,
2Ki 3:21 to bear arms and older were **g**
2Ki 4:39 **g** from it a lap full of wild
2Ki 6:24 king of Syria **g** all his army
2Ki 10:18 Then Jehu **g** all the people
2Ki 22: 4 have **g** from the people
2Ki 22: 9 Your servants have **g** the
2Ki 22:20 you shall be **g** to your grave
1Ch 11:13 Philistines were **g** for battle
1Ch 13: 5 So David **g** all Israel
1Ch 15: 3 David **g** all Israel together
1Ch 19: 7 Also the people of Ammon **g**
1Ch 19:17 he **g** all Israel, crossed over
1Ch 23: 2 he **g** together all the leaders
2Ch 1:14 And Solomon **g** chariots and
2Ch 12: 5 Judah, who were **g** together in
2Ch 13: 7 worthless rogues **g** to him
2Ch 15: 9 Then he **g** all Judah and
2Ch 15:10 So they **g** together at
2Ch 18: 5 **g** the prophets together, four
2Ch 20: 4 So Judah **g** together to ask
2Ch 23: 2 **g** the Levites from all the
2Ch 24: 5 Then he **g** the priests and the
2Ch 24:11 day, and **g** money in abundance
2Ch 25: 5 Amaziah **g** Judah together and
2Ch 28:24 So Ahaz **g** the articles of the
2Ch 29: 4 **g** them in the East Square,
2Ch 29:15 And they **g** their brethren,
2Ch 29:20 **g** the rulers of the city, and
2Ch 30: 3 nor had the people **g** together
2Ch 32: 4 Thus many people **g** together
2Ch 32: 6 **g** them together to him in the
2Ch 34: 9 who kept the doors had **g** from
2Ch 34:17 they have **g** the money that
2Ch 34:28 you shall be **g** to your grave
2Ch 34:29 **g** all the elders of Judah and
Ezra 3: 1 the people **g** together as one
Ezra 7:28 I **g** chief men of Israel to go
Ezra 8:15 Now I **g** them by the river
Ezra 10: 9 and Benjamin **g** at Jerusalem
Neh 5:16 were **g** there for the work
Neh 8: 1 Now all the people **g** together
Neh 8:13 were **g** to Ezra the scribe, in
Neh 12:28 singers **g** together from the
Neh 13:11 I **g** them together and set them
Esth 2: 8 were **g** at Shushan the citadel
Esth 2:19 When virgins were **g** together
Esth 9: 2 The Jews **g** together in their
Esth 9:15 **g** together again on the
Esth 9:16 king's provinces **g** together
Job 27:19 lie down, but not be **g** up
Ps 35:15 they rejoiced And **g** together
Ps 35:15 Attackers **g** against me, And I
Ps 47: 9 of the people have **g** together
Ps 102:22 the peoples are **g** together
Ps 107: 3 **g** out of the lands, From the
Prov 27:25 of the mountains are **g** in
Prov 30: 4 Who has **g** the wind in His
Eccl 2: 8 I also **g** for myself silver and
Song 5: 1 I have **g** my myrrh with my
Is 10:14 left, I have **g** all the earth
Is 13: 4 of nations **g** together
Is 22: 9 you **g** together the waters of
Is 24:22 They will be **g** together, as
Is 24:22 as prisoners are **g** in the pit
Is 27:12 and you will be **g** one by one
Is 33: 4 Your plunder shall be **g** like
Is 34:15 also shall the hawks be **g**
Is 34:16 it, and His Spirit has **g** them
Is 43: 9 all the nations be **g** together
Is 44:11 let them all be **g** together
Is 49: 5 so that Israel is **g** to Him
Is 56: 8 those who are **g** to him
Is 60: 7 shall be **g** together to you

Is 62: 9 who have **g** it shall eat it
Jer 3:17 the nations shall be **g** to it
Jer 8: 2 shall not be **g** nor buried
Jer 25:33 shall not be lamented, or **g**
Jer 26: 9 all the people were **g** against
Jer 40:12 **g** wine and summer fruit in
Jer 40:15 **g** to you would be scattered
Ezek 28: 4 **g** gold and silver into your
Ezek 28:25 When I have **g** the house of
Ezek 29: 5 shall not be picked up or **g**
Ezek 38: 7 that are **g** about you
Ezek 38: 8 **g** from many people on the
Ezek 38:12 a people **g** from the nations
Ezek 38:13 Have you **g** your army to take
Ezek 39:27 **g** them out of their enemies'
Dan 3: 3 officials of the provinces **g**
Dan 3:27 king's counselors **g** together
Hos 1:11 of Israel shall be **g** together
Hos 10:10 Peoples shall be **g** against
Mic 1: 7 for she **g** it from the pay of
Mic 4:11 nations have **g** against you
Zech 12: 3 of the earth are **g** against it
Zech 14:14 nations shall be **g** together
Matt 2: 4 when he had **g** all the chief
Matt 13: 2 were **g** together to Him, so
Matt 13:40 Therefore as the tares are **g**
Matt 13:47 sea and **g** some of every kind,
Matt 13:48 **g** the good into vessels, but
Matt 18:20 are **g** together in My name
Matt 22:10 and **g** together all whom they
Matt 22:34 Sadducees, they **g** together
Matt 22:41 the Pharisees were **g** together
Matt 24:28 the eagles will be **g** together
Matt 25:32 nations will be **g** before Him
Matt 27:17 when they had **g** together
Matt 27:27 **g** the whole garrison around
Matt 27:62 and Pharisees **g** together to
Mark 1:33 the whole city was **g** together
Mark 2: 2 Immediately many **g** together
Mark 4: 1 great multitude was **g** to Him
Mark 5:21 a great multitude **g** to Him
Mark 6:30 Then the apostles **g** to Jesus
Mark 10: 1 the people **g** to Him again, and
Luke 8: 4 when a great multitude had **g**
Luke 11:29 were thickly **g** together, He
Luke 12: 1 of people had **g** together, so
Luke 15:13 younger son **g** all together
Luke 17:37 the eagles will be **g** together
Luke 24:33 who were with them **g** together
John 6:13 Therefore they **g** them up, and
John 11:47 and the Pharisees **g** a council
Acts 4: 6 were **g** together at Jerusalem
Acts 4:26 the rulers were **g** together
Acts 4:27 of Israel, were **g** together
Acts 5:16 Also a multitude **g** from the
Acts 12:12 where many were **g** together
Acts 14:20 the disciples **g** around him
Acts 14:27 **g** the church together, they
Acts 15:30 when they had **g** the multitude
Acts 20: 8 where they were **g** together
Acts 28: 3 But when Paul had **g** a bundle
1Co 5: 4 when you are **g** together,
2Co 8:15 He who **g** much had nothing
2Co 8:15 he who **g** little had no lack
Rev 14:19 **g** the vine of the earth, and
Rev 16:16 they **g** them together to the
Rev 19:19 **g** together to make war

GATHERING (*see* GATHER)
Gen 1:10 the **g** together of the waters
Gen 50: 9 and it was a very great **g**
Num 15:32 they found a man **g** sticks on
Num 15:33 those who found him **g** sticks
1Ki 17:10 a widow was there **g** sticks
1Ki 17:12 I am **g** a couple of sticks
2Ch 20:25 they were three days **g** the
Eccl 2:26 sinner He gives the work of **g**
Is 32:10 fail, the **g** will not come
Is 33: 4 like the **g** of the caterpillar
Lam 5:14 have ceased **g** at the gate
Matt 25:24 sown, and **g** where you have not
Acts 17: 5 **g** a mob, set all the city in
Acts 19:40 account for this disorderly **g**
2Th 2: 1 our **g** together to Him, we ask

GATHERS (*see* GATHER)
Num 19:10 the one who **g** the ashes of
Job 11:10 **g** to judgment, then who can
Ps 33: 7 He **g** the waters of the sea
Ps 41: 6 His heart **g** iniquity to
Ps 147: 2 He **g** together the outcasts of
Prov 6: 8 **g** her food in the harvest
Prov 10: 5 He who **g** in summer is a wise
Prov 13:11 but he who **g** by labor will
Prov 28: 8 extortion **g** it for him who
Is 10:14 as one **g** eggs that are left,
Is 17: 5 the harvester **g** the grain
Is 17: 5 who **g** heads of grain in the
Is 56: 8 who **g** the outcasts of Israel,
Nah 3:18 mountains, and no one **g** them
Hab 2: 5 he **g** to himself all nations
Matt 23:37 as a hen **g** her chicks under
Luke 13:34 as a hen **g** her brood under
John 4:36 **g** fruit for eternal life,

GATH HEPHER
Josh 19:13 passed along on the east of **G**
2Ki 14:25 the prophet who was from **G**

GATH RIMMON
Josh 19:45 Jehud, Bene Berak, **G**,
Josh 21:24 and **G** with its common-land
Josh 21:25 and **G** with its common-land
1Ch 6:69 and **G** with its common-lands

GAUNT
Gen 41: 3 out of the river, ugly and **g**
Gen 41: 4 **g** cows ate up the seven fine
Gen 41:19 them, poor and very ugly and **g**
Gen 41:20 And the **g** and ugly cows ate up
Job 30: 3 They are **g** from want and

GAVE (*see* GIVE)
Gen 2:20 So Adam **g** names to all cattle
Gen 3: 6 She also **g** to her husband
Gen 3:12 whom You **g** to be with me, she
Gen 3:12 she **g** me of the tree, and I
Gen 14:20 And he **g** him a tithe of all
Gen 16: 3 **g** her to her husband Abram to
Gen 16: 5 I **g** my maid into your embrace
Gen 18: 7 **g** it to a young man, and he
Gen 20:14 and **g** them to Abraham
Gen 21:14 it on her shoulder, he **g** it
Gen 21:19 water, and **g** the lad a drink
Gen 21:27 **g** them to Abimelech, and the
Gen 24:18 to her hand, and **g** him a drink
Gen 24:46 she **g** the camels a drink also
Gen 24:53 and **g** them to Rebekah
Gen 24:53 He also **g** precious things to
Gen 25: 5 Abraham **g** all that he had to
Gen 25: 6 But Abraham **g** gifts to the
Gen 25:34 Jacob **g** Esau bread and stew of
Gen 27:17 Then she **g** the savory food and
Gen 28: 4 which God **g** to Abraham
Gen 28: 6 blessed him he **g** him a charge
Gen 29:24 Laban **g** his maid Zilpah to
Gen 29:28 So he **g** him his daughter
Gen 29:29 Laban **g** his maid Bilhah to
Gen 30: 4 Then she **g** him Bilhah her
Gen 30: 9 and **g** her to Jacob as wife
Gen 30:35 **g** them into the hand of his
Gen 35: 4 So they **g** Jacob all the
Gen 35:12 The land which I **g** Abraham
Gen 38:18 Then he **g** them to her, and
Gen 39:21 He **g** him favor in the sight
Gen 41:45 he **g** him as a wife Asenath,
Gen 42:25 Then Joseph **g** a command to
Gen 43:24 **g** them water, and they washed
Gen 43:24 and he **g** their donkeys feed
Gen 45:21 and Joseph **g** them carts,
Gen 45:21 he **g** them provisions for the
Gen 45:22 He **g** to all of them, to each
Gen 45:22 but to Benjamin he **g** three
Gen 46:18 whom Laban **g** to Leah his
Gen 46:25 whom Laban **g** to Rachel his
Gen 47:11 **g** them a possession in the
Gen 47:17 and Joseph **g** them bread in
Gen 47:22 rations which Pharaoh **g** them
Ex 2:21 he **g** Zipporah his daughter to
Ex 6:13 and **g** them a command for the
Ex 11: 3 the LORD **g** the people favor
Ex 14:20 it **g** light by night to the
Ex 31:18 He **g** Moses two tablets of the
Ex 32:24 So they **g** it to me, and I
Ex 34:32 he **g** them as commandments all
Ex 36: 6 So Moses **g** a commandment,
Num 3:51 And Moses **g** their redemption
Num 7: 6 and **g** them to the Levites
Num 7: 7 four oxen he **g** to the sons of
Num 7: 8 eight oxen he **g** to the sons
Num 7: 9 the sons of Kohath he **g** none
Num 13:32 they **g** the children of Israel
Num 15:23 day the LORD **g** commandment
Num 17: 6 leaders **g** him a rod apiece
Num 31:41 So Moses **g** the tribute which
Num 31:47 **g** them to the Levites, who
Num 32:28 So Moses **g** command
Num 32:33 So Moses **g** to the children of
Num 32:38 they **g** other names to the
Num 32:40 So Moses **g** Gilead to Machir
Deut 2:12 which the LORD **g** them
Deut 3:12 I **g** to the Reubenites and the
Deut 3:13 Og, I **g** to half the tribe of
Deut 3:15 And I **g** Gilead to Machir
Deut 3:16 the Gadites I **g** from Gilead
Deut 5:22 of stone and **g** them to me
Deut 9:11 that the LORD **g** me the two
Deut 10: 4 and the LORD **g** them to me
Deut 22:16 I **g** my daughter to this man
Deut 29: 8 **g** it as an inheritance to the
Josh 1:14 **g** you on this side of the
Josh 1:15 **g** you on this side of the
Josh 11:23 Joshua **g** it as an inheritance
Josh 12: 7 which Joshua **g** to the tribes
Josh 13:29 Moses also **g** an inheritance
Josh 14: 4 they **g** no part to the Levites
Josh 14:13 **g** Hebron to Caleb the son of
Josh 15:13 he **g** a portion among the
Josh 15:17 he **g** him Achsah his daughter
Josh 15:19 So he **g** her the upper
Josh 17: 4 he **g** them an inheritance
Josh 18: 7 servant of the LORD **g** them
Josh 19:49 the children of Israel **g** an
Josh 19:50 the word of the LORD they **g**
Josh 21: 3 **g** to the Levites from their
Josh 21: 8 And the children of Israel **g**
Josh 21: 9 So they **g** from the tribe of
Josh 21:11 they **g** them Kirjath Arba
Josh 21:12 its villages they **g** to Caleb
Josh 21:13 of Aaron the priest they **g**
Josh 21:21 For they **g** them Shechem with
Josh 21:27 they **g** Golan in Bashan with
Josh 21:43 So the LORD **g** to Israel all
Josh 21:44 The LORD **g** them rest all
Josh 22: 4 the servant of the LORD **g** you
Josh 22: 7 **g** a possession among their
Josh 24: 3 descendants and **g** him Isaac
Josh 24: 4 To Isaac I **g** Jacob and Esau
Josh 24: 4 To Esau I **g** the mountains of
Josh 24: 8 But I **g** them into your hand,
Judg 1:13 so he **g** him his daughter
Judg 1:15 Then Caleb **g** her the upper
Judg 1:20 they **g** Hebron to Caleb, as
Judg 3: 6 **g** their daughters to their
Judg 4:19 **g** him a drink, and covered him
Judg 5:25 asked for water, she **g** milk
Judg 6: 9 you and **g** you their land
Judg 9: 4 So they **g** him seventy shekels
Judg 12: 9 he **g** away thirty daughters in
Judg 14: 9 he **g** some to them, and they
Judg 14:10 Samson **g** a feast there, for
Judg 14:19 **g** the changes of clothing to
Judg 15: 2 therefore I **g** her to your
Judg 17: 4 **g** them to the silversmith, and
Judg 19:21 and **g** fodder to the donkeys
Judg 21:14 they **g** them the women whom
Ruth 2:18 **g** to her what she had kept
Ruth 3:17 six ephahs of barley he **g** me
Ruth 4: 7 **g** it to the other, and this
Ruth 4:13 the LORD **g** her conception, and
Ruth 4:17 neighbor women **g** him a name
1Sa 4:19 **g** birth, for her labor pains
1Sa 9:23 the portion which I **g** you
1Sa 10: 9 that God **g** him another heart
1Sa 18: 4 **g** it to David, with his armor
1Sa 18:27 they **g** them in full count to
1Sa 18:27 Then Saul **g** him Michal his
1Sa 20:40 Then Jonathan **g** his weapons
1Sa 21: 6 So the priest **g** him holy
1Sa 22:10 **g** him provisions
1Sa 22:10 **g** him the sword of Goliath
1Sa 27: 6 So Achish **g** him Ziklag that
1Sa 30:11 they **g** him bread and he ate,
1Sa 30:12 they **g** him a piece of a cake
2Sa 12: 8 I **g** you your master's house
2Sa 12: 8 **g** you the house of Israel and
2Sa 16:23 which he **g** in those days, was
2Sa 18: 5 **g** all the captains orders
2Sa 24: 9 Then Joab **g** the sum of the
1Ki 2:43 the commandment that I **g** you
1Ki 3:17 I **g** birth while she was in
1Ki 3:18 that this woman also **g** birth
1Ki 4:29 And God **g** Solomon wisdom

1Ki 5:10 So Hiram **g** Solomon cedar and
1Ki 5:11 And Solomon **g** Hiram twenty
1Ki 5:11 Thus Solomon **g** to Hiram year
1Ki 5:12 So the LORD **g** Solomon wisdom,
1Ki 8:34 which You **g** to their fathers
1Ki 8:40 which You **g** to our fathers
1Ki 8:48 which You **g** to their fathers
1Ki 9:11 that King Solomon then **g**
1Ki 10:10 Then she **g** the king one
1Ki 10:10 of Sheba **g** to King Solomon
1Ki 10:13 King Solomon **g** the queen of
1Ki 11:18 of Egypt, who **g** him a house,
1Ki 11:18 food for him, and **g** him land
1Ki 11:19 so that he **g** him as wife the
1Ki 12: 8 which the elders **g** him, and
1Ki 13: 3 he **g** a sign the same day,
1Ki 14: 8 of David, and **g** it to you
1Ki 14:15 which He **g** to their fathers
1Ki 15: 4 sake the LORD his God **g** him a
1Ki 17:23 house, and **g** him to his mother
1Ki 19:21 **g** it to the people, and they
2Ki 10:15 So he **g** him his hand, and he
2Ki 11:10 the priest **g** the captains of
2Ki 11:12 him, and **g** him the Testimony
2Ki 12:11 Then they **g** the money, which
2Ki 12:14 But they **g** that to the
2Ki 13: 5 Then the LORD **g** Israel a
2Ki 15:19 and Menahem **g** Pul a thousand
2Ki 18:15 So Hezekiah **g** him all the
2Ki 18:16 **g** it to the king of Assyria
2Ki 21: 8 land which I **g** their fathers
2Ki 22: 8 Hilkiah **g** the book to Shaphan
2Ki 23:35 So Jehoiakim **g** the silver
2Ki 25:28 **g** him a more prominent seat
1Ch 2:35 Sheshan **g** his daughter to
1Ch 6:55 They **g** them Hebron in the
1Ch 6:56 its villages they **g** to Caleb
1Ch 6:57 to the sons of Aaron they **g**
1Ch 6:61 of the Kohathites they **g** by
1Ch 6:62 they **g** thirteen cities from
1Ch 6:63 they **g** twelve cities from the
1Ch 6:64 **g** these cities with their
1Ch 6:65 they **g** by lot from the tribe
1Ch 6:67 they **g** them one of the cities
1Ch 14:12 David **g** a commandment, and
1Ch 21: 5 Then Joab **g** the sum of the
1Ch 21:25 So David **g** Ornan six hundred
1Ch 25: 5 For God **g** Heman fourteen sons
1Ch 28:11 Then David **g** his son Solomon
1Ch 28:14 He **g** gold by weight for
1Ch 28:16 by weight he **g** gold for the
1Ch 28:17 he **g** gold by weight for every
1Ch 29: 7 They **g** for the work of the
1Ch 29: 8 **g** them to the treasury of the
2Ch 6:25 the land which You **g** to them
2Ch 6:31 which You **g** to our fathers
2Ch 6:38 which You **g** to their fathers
2Ch 9: 9 Then she **g** the king one
2Ch 9: 9 of Sheba **g** to King Solomon
2Ch 9:12 Now King Solomon **g** to the
2Ch 11:23 and he **g** them provisions in
2Ch 13: 5 **g** the dominion over Israel to
2Ch 13:15 the men of Judah **g** a shout
2Ch 15:15 and the LORD **g** them rest all
2Ch 17: 5 and all Judah **g** presents to
2Ch 20: 7 **g** it to the descendants of
2Ch 20:30 for his God **g** him rest all
2Ch 21: 3 Their father **g** them great
2Ch 21: 3 but he **g** the kingdom to
2Ch 23: 9 Jehoiada the priest **g** to the
2Ch 23:11 **g** him the Testimony, and made
2Ch 24:12 Jehoiada **g** it to those who
2Ch 27: 5 the people of Ammon **g** him in
2Ch 28:15 **g** them sandals
2Ch 28:15 **g** them food and drink, and
2Ch 28:21 and he **g** it to the king of
2Ch 30: 7 so that He **g** them up to
2Ch 30:22 Hezekiah **g** encouragement to
2Ch 30:24 Judah **g** to the congregation a
2Ch 30:24 and the leaders **g** to the
2Ch 32: 6 **g** them encouragement, saying,
2Ch 32:24 spoke to him and **g** him a sign
2Ch 34:10 they **g** it to the workmen who
2Ch 34:11 They **g** it to the craftsmen and
2Ch 34:15 Hilkiah **g** the book to Shaphan
2Ch 35: 7 Then Josiah **g** the lay people
2Ch 35: 8 his leaders **g** willingly to
2Ch 35: 8 God, **g** to the priests for the
2Ch 35: 9 **g** to the Levites for Passover
2Ch 36:17 He **g** them all into his hand
Ezra 2:69 they **g** to the treasury for
Ezra 3: 7 They also **g** money to the
Ezra 4:19 I **g** the command, and a search
Ezra 5:12 He **g** them into the hand of
Ezra 7:11 Artaxerxes **g** Ezra the priest
Ezra 8:17 I **g** them a command for Iddo
Ezra 8:36 So they **g** support to the
Ezra 10:15 the Levite **g** them support
Ezra 10:19 they **g** their promise that
Neh 2: 1 the wine and **g** it to the king
Neh 2: 9 **g** them the king's letters
Neh 7: 2 that I **g** the charge of
Neh 7:70 fathers' houses **g** to the work
Neh 7:70 The governor **g** to the
Neh 7:71 of the fathers' houses **g** to
Neh 7:72 the rest of the people **g** was
Neh 8: 8 they **g** the sense, and helped
Neh 9: 7 and **g** him the name Abraham
Neh 9:13 **g** them just ordinances and
Neh 9:15 You **g** them bread from heaven
Neh 9:20 You also **g** Your good Spirit
Neh 9:20 **g** them water for their thirst
Neh 9:22 Moreover You **g** them kingdoms
Neh 9:24 **g** them into their hands, with
Neh 9:27 **g** them deliverers who saved
Neh 9:30 therefore You **g** them into the
Neh 9:35 good things that You **g** them
Neh 9:36 that You **g** to our fathers
Neh 12:47 Israel **g** the portions for the
Esth 2: 9 so he readily **g** beauty
Esth 2:18 and **g** gifts according to the
Esth 3:10 **g** it to Haman, the son of
Esth 4: 5 her, and she **g** him a command
Esth 4: 8 He also **g** him a copy of the
Esth 4:10 **g** him a command for Mordecai
Esth 8: 1 **g** Queen Esther the house of
Esth 8: 2 Haman, and **g** it to Mordecai
Job 1:21 The LORD **g**, and the LORD has
Job 34:13 Who **g** Him charge over the
Job 42:10 Indeed the LORD **g** Job twice
Job 42:11 Each one **g** him a piece of
Job 42:15 and their father **g** them an
Ps 21: 4 from You, and You **g** it to him
Ps 68:11 The Lord **g** the word
Ps 69:21 They also **g** me gall for my
Ps 69:21 And for my thirst they **g** me
Ps 74:14 **g** him as food to the people
Ps 77: 1 And He **g** ear to me
Ps 78:15 **g** them drink in abundance
Ps 78:29 For He **g** them their own
Ps 78:46 He also **g** their crops to the
Ps 78:48 He also **g** up their cattle to
Ps 78:50 But **g** their life over to the
Ps 78:62 He also **g** His people over to
Ps 81:12 So I **g** them over to their own
Ps 99: 7 the ordinance that He **g** them
Ps 105:32 He **g** them hail for rain, And
Ps 105:44 He **g** them the lands of the
Ps 106:15 He **g** them their request, But
Ps 106:41 He **g** them into the hand of
Ps 135:12 **g** their land as a heritage, A
Ps 136:21 **g** their land as a heritage,
Eccl 12: 7 will return to God who **g** it
Song 5: 6 him, but he **g** me no answer
Is 41: 2 Who **g** the nations before him,
Is 41: 2 Who **g** them as the dust to his
Is 42:24 Who **g** Jacob for plunder, and
Is 43: 3 I **g** Egypt for your ransom,
Is 50: 6 I **g** My back to those who
Is 66: 7 she travailed, she **g** birth
Is 66: 8 she **g** birth to her children
Jer 2:27 a stone, You **g** birth to me
Jer 7: 7 in the land that I **g** to your
Jer 7:14 this place which I **g** to you
Jer 11:18 Now the LORD **g** me knowledge
Jer 14: 5 the deer also **g** birth in the
Jer 16:15 which I **g** to their fathers
Jer 17: 4 your heritage which I **g** you
Jer 23:39 you, and the city that I **g** you
Jer 24:10 the land that I **g** to them
Jer 30: 3 that I **g** to their fathers
Jer 32:12 and I **g** the purchase deed to
Jer 36:32 **g** it to Baruch the scribe,
Jer 37: 2 **g** heed to the words of the
Jer 39:10 **g** them vineyards and fields at
Jer 39:11 king of Babylon **g** charge
Jer 40: 5 of the guard **g** him rations
Jer 44:30 as I **g** Zedekiah king of Judah
Jer 52:32 **g** him a more prominent seat
Ezek 16:10 **g** you sandals of badger skin
Ezek 16:19 Also My food which I **g** you
Ezek 16:27 **g** you up to the will of those
Ezek 16:34 In that you **g** payment but no
Ezek 16:36 children which you **g** to them
Ezek 17:18 in fact **g** his hand and still
Ezek 20:11 And I **g** them My statutes and
Ezek 20:12 Moreover I also **g** them My
Ezek 20:25 Therefore I also **g** them up to
Ezek 27:10 they **g** splendor to you
Ezek 27:12 They **g** you silver, iron, tin,
Ezek 27:16 They **g** you for your wares
Ezek 28:25 which I **g** to My servant Jacob
Ezek 31: 4 waters **g** it height, with
Ezek 36: 5 who **g** My land to themselves
Ezek 36:28 land that I **g** to your fathers
Ezek 39:23 I **g** them into the hand of
Dan 1: 2 the Lord **g** Jehoiakim king of
Dan 1: 7 chief of the eunuchs **g** names
Dan 1: 7 he **g** Daniel the name
Dan 1:16 drink, and **g** them vegetables
Dan 1:17 God **g** them knowledge and skill
Dan 2: 2 Then the king **g** the command
Dan 2:12 **g** a command to destroy all
Dan 2:48 and **g** him many great gifts
Dan 3:13 fury, **g** the command to bring
Dan 4:26 And inasmuch as they **g** the
Dan 5: 2 Belshazzar **g** the command to
Dan 5:18 O king, the Most High God **g**
Dan 5:19 of the majesty that He **g** him
Dan 5:29 Then Belshazzar **g** the command
Dan 6: 3 the king **g** thought to setting
Dan 6:10 **g** thanks before his God, as
Dan 6:16 So the king **g** the command
Dan 6:24 the king **g** the command, and
Hos 2: 8 not know that I **g** her grain
Hos 13:11 I **g** you a king in My anger,
Amos 2:12 But you **g** the Nazirites wine
Amos 4: 6 Also I **g** you cleanness of
Hab 2:10 You **g** shameful counsel to
Mal 2: 5 I **g** them to him that he might
Matt 8:18 He **g** a command to depart to
Matt 10: 1 He **g** them power over unclean
Matt 14:19 **g** the loaves to the disciples
Matt 14:19 and the disciples **g** to the
Matt 15:36 **g** thanks, broke them
Matt 15:36 and **g** them to His disciples
Matt 15:36 and the disciples **g** to the
Matt 21:23 And who **g** You this authority
Matt 25:15 to one he **g** five talents, to
Matt 25:35 I was hungry and you **g** Me food
Matt 25:35 was thirsty and you **g** Me drink
Matt 25:42 hungry and you **g** Me no food
Matt 25:42 thirsty and you **g** Me no drink
Matt 26:26 **g** it to the disciples and said
Matt 26:27 **g** thanks, and **g** it to them,
Matt 27:10 **g** them for the potter's field
Matt 27:34 they **g** Him sour wine mingled
Matt 27:48 reed, and **g** it to Him to drink
Matt 28:12 they **g** a large sum of money
Mark 2:26 also **g** some to those who were
Mark 3:16 to whom He **g** the name Peter
Mark 3:17 James, to whom He **g** the name
Mark 5:13 And at once Jesus **g** them
Mark 6: 7 **g** them power over unclean
Mark 6:21 **g** a feast for his nobles, the
Mark 6:28 platter, and **g** it to the girl
Mark 6:28 the girl **g** it to her mother
Mark 6:41 **g** them to His disciples to
Mark 8: 6 **g** thanks, broke them
Mark 8: 6 **g** them to His disciples to
Mark 11:28 who **g** You this authority to
Mark 13:34 **g** authority to his servants,
Mark 14:22 it, and **g** it to them and said,
Mark 14:23 given thanks He **g** it to them
Mark 15:23 Then they **g** Him wine mingled
Luke 2:38 she **g** thanks to the Lord, and
Luke 4:20 **g** it back to the attendant and
Luke 5:29 Then Levi **g** Him a great feast
Luke 6: 4 also **g** some to those who were
Luke 7:21 who were blind He **g** sight
Luke 7:44 you **g** Me no water for My feet
Luke 7:45 You **g** Me no kiss, but this
Luke 9: 1 **g** them power and authority
Luke 9:16 **g** them to the disciples to
Luke 9:42 and **g** him back to his father
Luke 10:35 **g** them to the innkeeper, and
Luke 14:16 A certain man **g** a great
Luke 15:16 ate, and no one **g** him anything
Luke 15:29 yet you never **g** me a young
Luke 18:43 they saw it, **g** praise to God

Luke 20: 2 Or who is he who **g** You this
Luke 22:17 cup, and **g** thanks, and said,
Luke 22:19 **g** thanks and broke it
Luke 22:19 and **g** it to them, saying
Luke 23:24 So Pilate **g** sentence that it
Luke 24:30 and broke it, and **g** it to them
Luke 24:42 So they **g** Him a piece of a
John 1:12 to them He **g** the right to
John 3:16 He **g** His only begotten Son
John 4: 5 Jacob **g** to his son Joseph
John 4:12 who **g** us the well, and drank
John 6:31 He **g** them bread from heaven
John 7:22 Moses therefore **g** you
John 12:49 who sent Me **g** Me a command
John 13:26 He **g** it to Judas Iscariot,
John 14:31 Father, and as the Father **g** Me
John 17: 6 You **g** them to Me, and they
John 17:12 whom You **g** Me I have kept
John 17:22 the glory which You **g** Me I
John 17:24 that they also whom You **g** Me
John 18: 9 Of those whom You **g** Me I have
John 18:14 Now it was Caiaphas who **g**
John 19: 9 But Jesus **g** him no answer
John 19:30 His head, He **g** up His spirit
John 19:38 and Pilate **g** him permission
John 21:13 **g** it to them, and likewise the
Acts 2: 4 tongues, as the Spirit **g** them
Acts 3: 5 So he **g** them his attention,
Acts 4:33 great power the apostles **g**
Acts 7: 5 God **g** him no inheritance in
Acts 7: 8 Then He **g** him the covenant of
Acts 7:10 **g** him favor and wisdom in the
Acts 7:42 **g** them up to worship the host
Acts 8:10 to whom they all **g** heed, from
Acts 9:41 Then he **g** her his hand and
Acts 10: 2 who **g** alms generously to the
Acts 11:17 If therefore God **g** them the
Acts 11:17 them the same gift as He **g** us
Acts 12:21 and **g** an oration to them
Acts 13:20 After that He **g** them judges
Acts 13:21 so God **g** them Saul the son of
Acts 13:22 to whom also He **g** testimony
Acts 14:17 **g** us rain from heaven and
Acts 15:24 to whom we **g** no such
Acts 24: 1 These **g** evidence to the
Acts 27: 3 **g** him liberty to go to his
Acts 27:35 and **g** thanks to God in the
Rom 1:24 Therefore God also **g** them up
Rom 1:26 For this reason God **g** them up
Rom 1:28 God **g** them over to a debased
1Co 3: 5 as the Lord **g** to each one
1Co 3: 6 but God **g** the increase
2Co 8: 5 but first **g** themselves to the
2Co 10: 8 which the Lord **g** us for
Gal 1: 4 who **g** Himself for our sins,
Gal 2: 9 been given to me, they **g** me
Gal 2:20 loved me and **g** Himself for me
Gal 3:18 but God **g** it to Abraham by
Eph 1:22 **g** Him to be head over all
Eph 4: 8 captive, and **g** gifts to men
Eph 4:11 And He Himself **g** some to be
Eph 5:25 church and **g** Himself for it,
1Th 4: 2 know what commandments we **g**
1Ti 2: 6 who **g** Himself a ransom for
Tit 2:14 who **g** Himself for us, that He
Heb 7: 2 Abraham **g** a tenth part of all
Heb 7: 4 **g** a tenth of the spoils
Heb 11:22 **g** instructions concerning his
Jas 5:18 again, and the heaven **g** rain
1Pe 1:21 **g** Him glory, so that your
1Jn 3:23 as He **g** us commandment
Rev 1: 1 which God **g** Him to show His
Rev 2:21 I **g** her time to repent of her
Rev 11:13 **g** glory to the God of heaven
Rev 12:13 who **g** birth to the male Child
Rev 13: 2 the dragon **g** him his power,
Rev 13: 4 who **g** authority to the beast
Rev 15: 7 **g** to the seven angels seven
Rev 20:13 The sea **g** up the dead who

GAZA (*see* GAZITES)
Gen 10:19 go toward Gerar, as far as **G**
Deut 2:23 dwelt in villages as far as **G**
Josh 10:41 Kadesh Barnea as far as **G**
Josh 11:22 they remained only in **G**, in
Josh 15:47 **G** with its towns and villages
Judg 1:18 Also Judah took **G** with its
Judg 6: 4 of the earth as far as **G**, and
Judg 16: 1 Then Samson went to **G** and saw
Judg 16:21 and brought him down to **G**
1Sa 6:17 one for Ashdod, one for **G**
1Ki 4:24 River from Tiphsah even to **G**
2Ki 18: 8 the Philistines, as far as **G**
Jer 25:20 (namely, Ashkelon, **G**, Ekron,
Jer 47: 1 before Pharaoh attacked **G**
Jer 47: 5 Baldness has come upon **G**,
Amos 1: 6 For three transgressions of **G**
Amos 1: 7 a fire upon the wall of **G**
Zeph 2: 4 For **G** shall be forsaken, and
Zech 9: 5 **G** also shall be very
Zech 9: 5 The king shall perish from **G**
Acts 8:26 goes down from Jerusalem to **G**

GAZE (*see* GAZED, GAZING)
Ex 19:21 through to **g** at the LORD, and
Job 16: 9 sharpens His **g** on me
Ps 39:13 Remove Your **g** from me, that I
Is 14:16 who see you will **g** at you
Ezek 28:17 that they might **g** at you

GAZED (*see* GAZE)
Obad 12 But you should not have **g** on
Obad 13 you should not have **g** on
Acts 7:55 **g** into heaven and saw the

GAZELLE (*see* GAZELLES)
Deut 12:15 clean may eat of it, of the **g**
Deut 12:22 Just as the **g** and the deer are
Deut 14: 5 the deer, the **g**, the roe deer
Deut 15:22 as if it were a **g** or a deer
2Sa 2:18 as fleet of foot as a wild **g**
Prov 6: 5 Deliver yourself like a **g**
Song 2: 9 is like a **g** or a young stag
Song 2:17 be like a **g** or a young stag
Song 4: 5 like two fawns, twins of a **g**
Song 7: 3 like two fawns, twins of a **g**
Song 8:14 be like a **g** or a young stag
Is 13:14 It shall be as the hunted **g**

GAZELLES (*see* GAZELLE)
1Ki 4:23 sheep, besides deer, **g**,
1Ch 12: 8 swift as **g** on the mountains
Song 2: 7 by the **g** or by the does of
Song 3: 5 by the **g** or by the does of

GAZEZ
1Ch 2:46 bore Haran, Moza, and **G**
1Ch 2:46 and Haran begot **G**

GAZING (*see* GAZE)
Song 2: 9 **g** through the lattice
Acts 1:11 do you stand **g** up into heaven

GAZITES (*see* GAZA)
Josh 13: 3 the **G**, the Ashdodites, the
Judg 16: 2 When the **G** were told

GAZZAM
Ezra 2:48 sons of Nekoda, the sons of **G**
Neh 7:51 the children of **G**, the

GEBA (*see* GABA, GIBEAH, GIBEON)
Josh 21:17 **G** with its common-land,
Judg 20:33 position in the plain of **G**
1Sa 13: 3 the Philistines that was in **G**
2Sa 5:25 from **G** as far as Gezer
1Ki 15:22 King Asa built **G** of Benjamin
2Ki 23: 8 incense, from **G** to Beersheba
1Ch 6:60 **G** with its common-lands,
1Ch 8: 6 of the inhabitants of **G**, and
2Ch 16: 6 and with them he built **G** and
Ezra 2:26 the people of Ramah and **G**, six
Neh 7:30 the men of Ramah and **G**, six
Neh 11:31 from **G** dwelt in Michmash,
Neh 12:29 and from the fields of **G** and
Is 10:29 have taken up lodging at **G**
Zech 14:10 from **G** to Rimmon south of

GEBAL (*see* GEBALITES)
Ps 83: 7 **G**, Ammon, and Amalek
Ezek 27: 9 Elders of **G** and its wise men

GEBALITES (*see* GEBAL)
Josh 13: 5 the land of the **G**, and all
1Ki 5:18 and the **G** quarried them

GEBER (*see* EZION GEBER)
1Ki 4:19 **G** the son of Uri, in the land

GEBIM
Is 10:31 inhabitants of **G** seek refuge

GECKO
Lev 11:30 the **g**, the monitor lizard,

GEDALIAH
2Ki 25:22 Then he made **G** the son of
2Ki 25:23 Babylon had made **G** governor
2Ki 25:23 they came to **G** at Mizpah
2Ki 25:24 **G** took an oath before them and
2Ki 25:25 ten men and struck and killed **G**
1Ch 25: 3 **G**, Zeri, Jeshaiah, Shimei,
1Ch 25: 9 the second for **G**, him with
Ezra 10:18 Eliezer, Jarib, and **G**
Jer 38: 1 **G** the son of Pashhur, Jucal
Jer 39:14 committed him to **G** the son of
Jer 40: 5 Go back to **G** the son of
Jer 40: 6 went to **G** the son of Ahikam
Jer 40: 7 king of Babylon had made **G**
Jer 40: 8 then they came to **G** at Mizpah
Jer 40: 9 **G** the son of Ahikam, the son
Jer 40:11 over them **G** the son of Ahikam
Jer 40:12 to **G** at Mizpah, and gathered
Jer 40:13 fields came to **G** at Mizpah
Jer 40:14 But **G** the son of Ahikam did
Jer 40:15 spoke secretly to **G** in Mizpah
Jer 40:16 But **G** the son of Ahikam said
Jer 41: 1 men to **G** the son of Ahikam
Jer 41: 2 struck **G** the son of Ahikam,
Jer 41: 3 is, with **G** at Mizpah, and the
Jer 41: 4 day after he had killed **G**
Jer 41: 6 Come to **G** the son of Ahikam
Jer 41: 9 he had slain, because of **G**
Jer 41:10 to **G** the son of Ahikam
Jer 41:16 murdered **G** the son of Ahikam
Jer 41:18 murdered **G** the son of Ahikam
Jer 43: 6 left with **G** the son of Ahikam
Zeph 1: 1 son of Cushi, the son of **G**

GEDER (*see* BETH GADER, BETH GEDER, GEDERITE, GEDOR)
Josh 12:13 the king of **G**, one

GEDERAH (*see* GEDERATHITE)
Josh 15:36 Sharaim, Adithaim, **G**, and
1Ch 4:23 who dwell at Netaim and **G**

GEDERATHITE (*see* GEDERAH)
1Ch 12: 4 Johanan, and Jozabad the **G**

GEDERITE (*see* GEDER)
1Ch 27:28 Baal-Hanan the **G** was over the

GEDEROTH
Josh 15:41 **G**, Beth Dagon, Naamah, and
2Ch 28:18 Beth Shemesh, Aijalon, **G**,

GEDEROTHAIM
Josh 15:36 Adithaim, Gederah, and **G**

GEDOR (*see* GEDER)
Josh 15:58 Halhul, Beth Zur, **G**,
1Ch 4: 4 and Penuel was the father of **G**
1Ch 4:18 bore Jered the father of **G**
1Ch 4:39 went to the entrance of **G**
1Ch 8:31 **G**, Ahio, Zecher,
1Ch 9:37 **G**, Ahio, Zechariah, and
1Ch 12: 7 the sons of Jeroham of **G**

GE-HARASHIM
1Ch 4:14 begot Joab the father of **G**

GEHAZI
2Ki 4:12 Then he said to **G** his servant
2Ki 4:14 And **G** answered, "Actually
2Ki 4:25 that he said to his servant **G**
2Ki 4:27 but **G** came near to push her
2Ki 4:29 Then he said to **G**, "Get
2Ki 4:31 Now **G** went on ahead of them,
2Ki 4:36 And he called **G** and said
2Ki 5:20 But **G**, the servant of Elisha
2Ki 5:21 So **G** pursued Naaman
2Ki 5:25 Where did you go, **G**
2Ki 8: 4 Then the king talked with **G**
2Ki 8: 5 **G** said, "My lord, O king

GELILOTH
Josh 18:17 and extended toward **G**

GEMALLI
Num 13:12 of Dan, Ammiel the son of **G**

GEMARIAH
Jer 29: 3 **G** the son of Hilkiah, whom
Jer 36:10 in the chamber of **G** the son
Jer 36:11 When Michaiah the son of **G**
Jer 36:12 Achbor, **G** the son of Shaphan,
Jer 36:25 **G** implored the king not to

GEMS
Is 54:11 your stones with colorful **g**

GENEALOGIES (*see* GENEALOGY)
Num 1:20 their **g** by their families, by
Num 1:22 their **g** by their families, by
Num 1:24 their **g** by their families, by

Num 1:26 their **g** by their families, by
Num 1:28 their **g** by their families, by
Num 1:30 their **g** by their families, by
Num 1:32 their **g** by their families, by
Num 1:34 their **g** by their families, by
Num 1:36 their **g** by their families, by
Num 1:38 their **g** by their families, by
Num 1:40 their **g** by their families, by
Num 1:42 their **g** by their families, by
1Ch 1:29 These are their **g**
1Ch 5:17 these were registered by **g** in
1Ch 7: 5 of valor, listed by their **g**
1Ch 7: 7 they were listed by their **g**
1Ch 7:40 they were recorded by **g** among
1Ch 9: 1 all Israel was recorded by **g**
2Ch 12:15 of Iddo the seer concerning **g**
2Ch 31:19 listed by **g** among the Levites
1Ti 1: 4 heed to fables and endless **g**
Tit 3: 9 But avoid foolish disputes, **g**

GENEALOGY (*see* GENEALOGIES)
Gen 5: 1 is the book of the **g** of Adam
Gen 6: 9 This is the **g** of Noah
Gen 10: 1 Now this is the **g** of the sons
Gen 11:10 This is the **g** of Shem
Gen 11:27 This is the **g** of Terah
Gen 25:12 Now this is the **g** of Ishmael
Gen 25:19 This is the **g** of Isaac,
Gen 36: 1 Now this is the **g** of Esau
Gen 36: 9 this is the **g** of Esau the
Gen 37: 2 This is the **g** of Jacob
Ruth 4:18 Now this is the **g** of Perez
1Ch 4:33 and they maintained their **g**
1Ch 5: 1 so that the **g** is not listed
1Ch 5: 7 families, when the **g** of their
1Ch 7: 9 by **g** according to their
1Ch 9:22 They were recorded by their **g**
1Ch 26:31 to his **g** of the fathers
2Ch 31:16 up who were written in the **g**
2Ch 31:17 who were written in the **g**
2Ch 31:18 all who were written in the **g**
Ezra 2:59 father's house or their **g**
Ezra 2:62 who were registered by **g**, but
Ezra 8: 1 this is the **g** of those who
Neh 7: 5 they might be registered by **g**
Neh 7: 5 I found a register of the **g**
Neh 7:64 who were registered by **g**, but
Matt 1: 1 book of the **g** of Jesus Christ
Heb 7: 3 without mother, without **g**
Heb 7: 6 but he whose **g** is not derived

GENERAL
1Ch 27:34 the **g** of the king's army was
Jer 48:38 A **g** lamentation on all the
Ezek 48:15 shall be for **g** use by the
Heb 12:23 to the **g** assembly and church

GENERATE
2Ti 2:23 knowing that they **g** strife

GENERATION (*see* GENERATIONS)
Gen 7: 1 righteous before Me in this **g**
Gen 15:16 But in the fourth **g** they
Gen 50:23 children to the third **g**
Ex 1: 6 his brothers, and all that **g**
Ex 17:16 Amalek from **g** to **g**
Ex 34: 7 to the third and the fourth **g**
Num 14:18 to the third and fourth **g**
Num 32:13 until all the **g** that had done
Deut 1:35 of these men of this evil **g**
Deut 2:14 until all the **g** of the men of
Deut 23: 2 even to the tenth **g** none of
Deut 23: 3 even to the tenth **g** none of
Deut 23: 8 The children of the third **g**
Deut 29:22 so that the coming **g** of your
Deut 32: 5 a perverse and crooked **g**
Deut 32:20 be, for they are a perverse **g**
Judg 2:10 When all that **g** had been
Judg 2:10 another **g** arose after them
2Ki 10:30 of Israel to the fourth **g**
2Ki 15:12 of Israel to the fourth **g**
Esth 9:28 and kept throughout every **g**
Ps 12: 7 them from this **g** forever
Ps 14: 5 with the **g** of the righteous
Ps 22:30 of the Lord to the next **g**
Ps 24: 6 the **g** of those who seek Him,
Ps 48:13 tell it to the **g** following
Ps 49:19 go to the **g** of his fathers
Ps 71:18 Your strength to this **g**, Your
Ps 73:15 to the **g** of Your children
Ps 78: 4 Telling to the **g** to come the
Ps 78: 6 That the **g** to come might know
Ps 78: 8 A stubborn and rebellious **g**
Ps 78: 8 A **g** that did not set its
Ps 95:10 I was grieved with that **g**
Ps 102:18 be written for the **g** to come
Ps 109:13 in the **g** following let their
Ps 112: 2 The **g** of the upright will be
Ps 145: 4 One **g** shall praise Your works
Prov 30:11 There is a **g** that curses its
Prov 30:12 There is a **g** that is pure in
Prov 30:13 There is a **g**—oh, how lofty
Prov 30:14 There is a **g** whose teeth are
Eccl 1: 4 One **g** passes away, and another
Eccl 1: 4 away, and another **g** comes
Is 13:20 will it be settled from **g** to **g**
Is 34:10 from **g** to **g** it shall lie
Is 34:17 from **g** to **g** they
Is 51: 8 from **g** to **g**."
Is 53: 8 and who will declare His **g**
Jer 2:31 O **g**, see the word of the LORD
Jer 7:29 forsaken the **g** of His wrath
Jer 50:39 dwelt in from **g** to **g**
Lam 5:19 Your throne from **g** to **g**
Dan 4: 3 His dominion is from **g** to **g**
Dan 4:34 His kingdom is from **g** to **g**
Joel 1: 3 and their children another **g**
Joel 3:20 Jerusalem from **g** to **g**
Matt 11:16 to what shall I liken this **g**
Matt 12:39 adulterous **g** seeks after a
Matt 12:41 in the judgment with this **g**
Matt 12:42 in the judgment with this **g**
Matt 12:45 it also be with this wicked **g**
Matt 16: 4 adulterous **g** seeks after a
Matt 17:17 O faithless and perverse **g**
Matt 23:36 things will come upon this **g**
Matt 24:34 this **g** will by no means pass
Mark 8:12 Why does this **g** seek a sign
Mark 8:12 sign shall be given to this **g**
Mark 8:38 this adulterous and sinful **g**
Mark 9:19 O faithless **g**, how long shall
Mark 13:30 this **g** will by no means pass
Luke 1:50 fear Him from **g** to **g**
Luke 7:31 I liken the men of this **g**
Luke 9:41 O faithless and perverse **g**
Luke 11:29 This is an evil **g**
Luke 11:30 Son of Man will be to this **g**
Luke 11:31 with the men of this **g** and
Luke 11:32 in the judgment with this **g**
Luke 11:50 may be required of this **g**
Luke 11:51 shall be required of this **g**
Luke 16: 8 **g** than the sons of light
Luke 17:25 and be rejected by this **g**
Luke 21:32 this **g** will by no means pass
Acts 2:40 Be saved from this perverse **g**
Acts 8:33 And who will declare His **g**
Acts 13:36 his own **g** by the will of God
Phil 2:15 of a crooked and perverse **g**
Heb 3:10 I was angry with that **g**, and
1Pe 2: 9 But you are a chosen **g**, a

GENERATIONS (*see* GENERATION)
Gen 6: 9 a just man, perfect in his **g**
Gen 9:12 is with you, for perpetual **g**
Gen 10:32 of Noah, according to their **g**
Gen 17: 7 after you in their **g**, for an
Gen 17: 9 after you throughout their **g**
Gen 17:12 every male child in your **g**
Gen 25:13 names, according to their **g**
Ex 3:15 this is My memorial to all **g**
Ex 6:16 of Levi according to their **g**
Ex 6:19 of Levi according to their **g**
Ex 12:14 to the LORD throughout your **g**
Ex 12:17 this day throughout your **g** as
Ex 12:42 of Israel throughout their **g**
Ex 16:32 it, to be kept for your **g**
Ex 16:33 LORD, to be kept for your **g**
Ex 20: 5 fourth **g** of those who hate Me
Ex 27:21 **g** on behalf of the children
Ex 29:42 your **g** at the door of the
Ex 30: 8 the LORD throughout your **g**
Ex 30:10 upon it throughout your **g**
Ex 30:21 throughout their **g**
Ex 30:31 oil to Me throughout your **g**
Ex 31:13 Me and you throughout your **g**
Ex 31:16 **g** as a perpetual covenant
Ex 40:15 priesthood throughout their **g**
Lev 3:17 your **g** in all your dwellings
Lev 6:18 **g** concerning the offerings
Lev 7:36 forever throughout their **g**
Lev 10: 9 forever throughout your **g**
Lev 17: 7 for them throughout their **g**
Lev 21:17 descendants in succeeding **g**
Lev 22: 3 descendants throughout your **g**
Lev 23:14 your **g** in all your dwellings
Lev 23:21 dwellings throughout your **g**
Lev 23:31 your **g** in all your dwellings
Lev 23:41 a statute forever in your **g**
Lev 23:43 that your **g** may know that I
Lev 24: 3 a statute forever in your **g**
Lev 25:30 bought it, throughout his **g**
Num 10: 8 forever throughout your **g**
Num 15:14 among you throughout your **g**
Num 15:15 forever throughout your **g**
Num 15:21 offering throughout your **g**
Num 15:23 and onward throughout your **g**
Num 15:38 garments throughout their **g**
Num 18:23 forever, throughout your **g**
Num 35:29 your **g** in all your dwellings
Deut 5: 9 fourth **g** of those who hate Me
Deut 7: 9 mercy for a thousand **g** with
Deut 32: 7 consider the years of many **g**
Josh 22:27 our **g** after us, that we may
Josh 22:28 or to our **g** in time to come
Judg 3: 2 **g** of the children of Israel
1Ch 5: 7 of their **g** was registered
1Ch 7: 2 men of valor in their **g**
1Ch 7: 4 And with them, by their **g**,
1Ch 7: 9 according to their **g**, heads
1Ch 8:28 fathers' houses by their **g**
1Ch 9: 9 according to their **g**
1Ch 9:34 were heads throughout their **g**
1Ch 16:15 commanded, for a thousand **g**
Job 42:16 and grandchildren for four **g**
Ps 33:11 plans of His heart to all **g**
Ps 45:17 to be remembered in all **g**
Ps 49:11 dwelling places to all **g**
Ps 61: 6 life, His years as many **g**
Ps 72: 5 moon endure, Throughout all **g**
Ps 79:13 forth Your praise to all **g**
Ps 85: 5 prolong Your anger to all **g**
Ps 89: 1 Your faithfulness to all **g**
Ps 89: 4 build up your throne to all **g**
Ps 90: 1 our dwelling place in all **g**
Ps 100: 5 And His truth endures to all **g**
Ps 102:12 of Your name to all **g**
Ps 102:24 years are throughout all **g**
Ps 105: 8 commanded, for a thousand **g**
Ps 106:31 To all **g** forevermore
Ps 119:90 faithfulness endures to all **g**
Ps 135:13 O LORD, throughout all **g**
Ps 145:13 endures throughout all **g**
Ps 146:10 Your God, O Zion, to all **g**
Prov 27:24 does a crown endure to all **g**
Is 41: 4 it, calling the **g** from the
Is 51: 9 ancient days, in the **g** of old
Is 58:12 up the foundations of many **g**
Is 60:15 excellence, a joy of many **g**
Is 61: 4 the desolations of many **g**
Joel 2: 2 even for many successive **g**
Matt 1:17 So all the **g** from Abraham to
Matt 1:17 to David are fourteen **g**, from
Matt 1:17 in Babylon are fourteen **g**
Matt 1:17 the Christ are fourteen **g**
Luke 1:48 henceforth all **g** will call me
Acts 14:16 who in bygone **g** allowed all
Acts 15:21 **g** those who preach him in
Col 1:26 hidden from ages and from **g**

GENEROSITY (*see* GENEROUS)
Esth 1: 7 to the **g** of the king
Esth 2:18 according to the **g** of a king
Is 32: 8 and by **g** he shall stand
2Co 9: 5 may be ready as a matter of **g**

GENEROUS (*see* GENEROSITY, GENEROUSLY)
Ps 51:12 uphold me with Your **g** Spirit
Prov 11:25 The **g** soul will be made rich,
Is 32: 5 will no longer be called **g**
Is 32: 8 But a **g** man devises **g** things

GENEROUSLY (*see* GENEROUS)
Acts 10: 2 who gave alms **g** to the people

GENITALS
Deut 25:11 hand and seizes him by the **g**

GENNESARET (*see* CHINNERETH)
Matt 14:34 they came to the land of **G**
Mark 6:53 they came to the land of **G**
Luke 5: 1 He stood by the Lake of **G**

GENTILE (*see* GENTILES)
Hag 2:22 strength of the **G** kingdoms
Acts 17:17 with the **G** worshipers, and in

GENTILES (*see* GENTILE)
Gen 10: 5 coastland peoples of the **G**
Deut 32:43 Rejoice, O **G**, with His people
2Sa 22:50 to You, O LORD, among the **G**
1Ch 16:35 and deliver us from the **G**
Ps 18:49 to You, O LORD, among the **G**
Ps 105:44 gave them the lands of the **G**
Ps 106:35 But they mingled with the **G**
Ps 106:41 them into the hand of the **G**
Ps 106:47 gather us from among the **G**
Ps 115: 2 Why should the **G** say,
Ps 117: 1 praise the LORD, all you **G**
Is 9: 1 Jordan, in Galilee of the **G**
Is 11:10 for the **G** shall seek Him, and
Is 42: 1 bring forth justice to the **G**
Is 42: 6 people, as a light to the **G**
Is 49: 6 give You as a light to the **G**
Is 60: 3 The **G** shall come to your
Is 60: 5 of the **G** shall come to you
Is 60:11 to you the wealth of the **G**
Is 60:16 drink dry the milk of the **G**
Is 61: 6 shall eat the riches of the **G**
Is 61: 9 shall be known among the **G**
Is 62: 2 The **G** shall see your
Is 66:12 the glory of the **G** like a
Is 66:19 declare My glory among the **G**
Jer 9:16 scatter them also among the **G**
Jer 10: 2 Do not learn the way of the **G**
Jer 10: 2 for the **G** are dismayed at
Jer 10:25 Pour out Your fury on the **G**
Jer 16:19 the **G** shall come to You from
Jer 18:13 Ask now among the **G**, who has
Ezek 4:13 defiled bread among the **G**
Ezek 7:24 will bring the worst of the **G**
Ezek 11:12 to the customs of the **G** which
Ezek 11:16 cast them far off among the **G**
Ezek 12:16 among the **G** wherever they go
Ezek 20: 9 the **G** among whom they were
Ezek 20:14 not be profaned before the **G**
Ezek 20:22 in the sight of the **G**, in
Ezek 20:23 scatter them among the **G** and
Ezek 20:32 say, We will be like the **G**
Ezek 20:41 hallowed in you before the **G**
Ezek 23:30 gone as a harlot after the **G**
Ezek 28:25 in them in the sight of the **G**
Ezek 30: 3 of clouds, the time of the **G**
Ezek 34:29 the shame of the **G** anymore
Ezek 39:23 The **G** shall know that the
Hos 8: 8 the **G** like a vessel in which
Amos 9:12 all the **G** who are called by
Mic 5: 8 of Jacob shall be among the **G**
Mal 1:11 shall be great among the **G**
Matt 4:15 the Jordan, Galilee of the **G**
Matt 6:32 all these things the **G** seek
Matt 10: 5 not go into the way of the **G**
Matt 10:18 testimony to them and to the **G**
Matt 12:18 will declare justice to the **G**
Matt 12:21 And in His name **G** will trust
Matt 20:19 deliver Him to the **G** to mock
Matt 20:25 of the **G** lord it over them
Mark 10:33 death and deliver Him to the **G**
Mark 10:42 over the **G** lord it over them
Luke 2:32 to bring revelation to the **G**
Luke 18:32 He will be delivered to the **G**
Luke 21:24 will be trampled by **G** until
Luke 21:24 times of the **G** are fulfilled
Luke 22:25 The kings of the **G** exercise
Acts 4:27 and Pontius Pilate, with the **G**
Acts 7:45 the land possessed by the **G**
Acts 9:15 Mine to bear My name before **G**
Acts 10:45 been poured out on the **G** also
Acts 11: 1 in Judea heard that the **G** had
Acts 11:18 to the **G** repentance to life
Acts 13:42 the **G** begged that these words
Acts 13:46 behold, we turn to the **G**
Acts 13:47 you to be a light to the **G**
Acts 13:48 Now when the **G** heard this
Acts 14: 2 Jews stirred up the **G** and
Acts 14: 5 was made by both the **G** and
Acts 14:27 the door of faith to the **G**
Acts 15: 3 the conversion of the **G**
Acts 15: 7 that by my mouth the **G** should
Acts 15:12 through them among the **G**
Acts 15:14 the **G** to take out of them a
Acts 15:17 even all the **G** who are called
Acts 15:19 those from among the **G** who
Acts 15:23 who are of the **G** in Antioch
Acts 18: 6 now on I will go to the **G**
Acts 21:11 him into the hands of the **G**
Acts 21:19 the **G** through his ministry
Acts 21:21 among the **G** to forsake Moses
Acts 21:25 concerning the **G** who believe
Acts 22:21 you far from here to the **G**
Acts 26:17 people, as well as from the **G**
Acts 26:20 of Judea, and then to the **G**
Acts 26:23 the Jewish people and to the **G**
Acts 28:28 of God has been sent to the **G**
Rom 1:13 just as among the other **G**
Rom 2:14 for when **G**, who do not have
Rom 2:24 among the **G** because of you
Rom 3:29 He not also the God of the **G**
Rom 3:29 Yes, of the **G** also,
Rom 9:24 Jews only, but also of the **G**
Rom 9:30 That **G**, who did not pursue
Rom 11:11 salvation has come to the **G**
Rom 11:12 failure riches for the **G**, how
Rom 11:13 For I speak to you **G**
Rom 11:13 as I am an apostle to the **G**
Rom 11:25 fullness of the **G** has come in
Rom 15: 9 that the **G** might glorify God
Rom 15: 9 confess to You among the **G**
Rom 15:10 Rejoice, O **G**, with His people
Rom 15:11 Praise the LORD, all you **G**
Rom 15:12 rise to reign over the **G**, in
Rom 15:12 in Him the **G** shall hope
Rom 15:16 of Jesus Christ to the **G**,
Rom 15:16 of the **G** might be acceptable
Rom 15:18 deed, to make the **G** obedient
Rom 15:27 For if the **G** have been
Rom 16: 4 all the churches of the **G**
1Co 5: 1 is not even named among the **G**
1Co 10:20 that the things which the **G**
1Co 12: 2 You know that you were **G**,
2Co 11:26 in perils of the **G**, in
Gal 1:16 might preach Him among the **G**
Gal 2: 2 which I preach among the **G**
Gal 2: 8 in me toward the **G**),
Gal 2: 9 that we should go to the **G**
Gal 2:12 he would eat with the **G**
Gal 2:14 Jew, live in the manner of **G**
Gal 2:14 you compel **G** to live as Jews
Gal 2:15 and not sinners of the **G**,
Gal 3:14 upon the **G** in Christ Jesus
Eph 2:11 that you, once **G** in the flesh
Eph 3: 1 of Jesus Christ for you **G**
Eph 3: 6 that the **G** should be fellow
Eph 3: 8 I should preach among the **G**
Eph 4:17 as the rest of the **G** walk
Col 1:27 of this mystery among the **G**
1Th 2:16 us to speak to the **G** that
1Th 4: 5 like the **G** who do not know
1Ti 2: 7 a teacher of the **G** in faith
1Ti 3:16 angels, preached among the **G**
2Ti 1:11 and a teacher of the **G**
2Ti 4:17 and that all the **G** might hear
1Pe 2:12 conduct honorable among the **G**
1Pe 4: 3 in doing the will of the **G**
3Jn 7 taking nothing from the **G**
Rev 11: 2 it has been given to the **G**

GENTLE (*see* GENTLENESS, GENTLY)
Job 37: 6 likewise to the **g** rain and the
Prov 25:15 and a **g** tongue breaks a bone
Hos 11: 4 I drew them with **g** cords,
Matt 11:29 and learn from Me, for I am **g**
1Th 2: 7 But we were **g** among you, just
1Ti 3: 3 not greedy for money, but **g**
2Ti 2:24 not quarrel but be **g** to all
Tit 3: 2 of no one, to be peaceable, **g**
Jas 3:17 first pure, then peaceable, **g**
1Pe 2:18 not only to the good and **g**
1Pe 3: 4 incorruptible ornament of a **g**

GENTLENESS (*see* GENTLE)
2Sa 22:36 and Your **g** has made me great
Ps 18:35 up, Your **g** has made me great
1Co 4:21 or in love and a spirit of **g**
2Co 10: 1 the meekness and **g** of Christ
Gal 5:23 **g**, self-control
Gal 6: 1 such a one in a spirit of **g**
Eph 4: 2 with all lowliness and **g**, with
Phil 4: 5 Let your **g** be known to all
1Ti 6:11 faith, love, patience, **g**

GENTLY (*see* GENTLE)
2Sa 18: 5 Deal **g** for my sake with the
Job 15:11 and the word spoken **g** with you
Song 7: 9 moving **g** the lips of sleepers
Is 40:11 **g** lead those who are with

GENUBATH
1Ki 11:20 Tahpenes bore him **G** his son
1Ki 11:20 **G** was in Pharaoh's household

GENUINE (*see* GENUINENESS)
2Ti 1: 5 the **g** faith that is in you

GENUINENESS (*see* GENUINE)
1Pe 1: 7 that the **g** of your faith,

GERA
Gen 46:21 were Belah, Becher, Ashbel, **G**
Judg 3:15 Ehud the son of **G**, the
2Sa 16: 5 name was Shimei the son of **G**
2Sa 19:16 And Shimei the son of **G**, a
2Sa 19:18 Now Shimei the son of **G** fell
1Ki 2: 8 with you Shimei the son of **G**
1Ch 8: 3 sons of Bela were Addar, **G**
1Ch 8: 5 **G**, Shephuphan, and Huram
1Ch 8: 7 **G** who forced them to move

GERAHS
Ex 30:13 (a shekel is twenty **g**)
Lev 27:25 twenty **g** to the shekel
Num 3:47 the shekel of twenty **g**
Num 18:16 sanctuary, which is twenty **g**
Ezek 45:12 The shekel shall be twenty **g**

GERAR
Gen 10:19 from Sidon as you go toward **G**
Gen 20: 1 and Shur, and sojourned in **G**
Gen 20: 2 And Abimelech king of **G** sent
Gen 26: 1 king of the Philistines, in **G**
Gen 26: 6 So Isaac dwelt in **G**
Gen 26:17 his tent in the Valley of **G**
Gen 26:20 But the herdsmen of **G**
Gen 26:26 to him from **G** with Ahuzzath
2Ch 14:13 with him pursued them to **G**
2Ch 14:14 all the cities around **G**, for

GERGESENES
Matt 8:28 side, to the country of the **G**

GERIZIM
Deut 11:29 put the blessing on Mount **G**
Deut 27:12 Mount **G** to bless the people
Josh 8:33 them were in front of Mount **G**
Judg 9: 7 and stood on top of Mount **G**

GERSHOM (*see* GERSHON)
Ex 2:22 son, and he called his name **G**
Ex 18: 3 of one was **G** (for he said
Judg 18:30 and Jonathan the son of **G**, the
1Ch 15: 7 of the sons of **G**, Joel the
1Ch 26:24 Shebuel the son of **G**, the son
Ezra 8: 2 of the sons of Phinehas, **G**

GERSHON (*see* GERSHOM, GERSHONITE)
Gen 46:11 The sons of Levi were **G**,
Ex 6:16 **G**, Kohath, and Merari
Ex 6:17 The sons of **G** were Libni and
Num 3:17 **G**, Kohath, and Merari
Num 3:18 sons of **G** by their families
Num 3:21 From **G** came the family of the
Num 3:25 of **G** in the tabernacle of
Num 4:22 a census of the sons of **G**
Num 4:28 of **G** in the tabernacle of
Num 4:38 numbered of the sons of **G**
Num 4:41 the families of the sons of **G**
Num 7: 7 oxen he gave to the sons of **G**
Num 10:17 and the sons of **G** and the sons
Num 26:57 of **G**, the family of the
Josh 21: 6 And the children of **G** had
Josh 21:27 And to the children of **G**, of
1Ch 6: 1 The sons of Levi were **G**,
1Ch 6:16 The sons of Levi were **G**,
1Ch 6:17 the names of the sons of **G**
1Ch 6:20 Of **G** were Libni his son,
1Ch 6:43 son of Jahath, the son of **G**
1Ch 6:62 And to the sons of **G**,
1Ch 6:71 of Manasseh the sons of **G**
1Ch 23: 6 **G**, Kohath, and Merari
1Ch 23:15 The sons of Moses were **G** and
1Ch 23:16 Of the sons of **G**, Shebuel was

GERSHONITE (*see* GERSHON, GERSHONITES)
1Ch 26:21 houses, of Laadan the **G**
1Ch 29: 8 into the hand of Jehiel the **G**

GERSHONITES (*see* GERSHONITE)
Num 3:21 were the families of the **G**
Num 3:23 The families of the **G** were to
Num 3:24 the **G** was Eliasaph the son of
Num 4:24 of the families of the **G**, in
Num 4:27 service of the sons of the **G**
Num 26:57 Gershon, the family of the **G**

Josh 21:33 All the cities of the **G**
1Ch 23: 7 the **G**: Laadan and Shimei
1Ch 26:21 of the **G** of Laadan, heads of
2Ch 29:12 of the **G**, Joah the son of

GESHAN
1Ch 2:47 Jahdai were Regem, Jotham, **G**

GESHEM
Neh 2:19 **G** the Arab heard of it, they
Neh 6: 1 **G** the Arab, and the rest of
Neh 6: 2 and **G** sent to me, saying,
Neh 6: 6 **G** says, that you and the Jews

GESHUR (*see* GESHURITES)
2Sa 3: 3 daughter of Talmai, king of **G**
2Sa 13:37 the son of Ammihud, king of **G**
2Sa 13:38 So Absalom fled and went to **G**
2Sa 14:23 So Joab arose and went to **G**
2Sa 14:32 Why have I come from **G**
2Sa 15: 8 while I dwelt at **G** in Syria
1Ch 2:23 (**G** and Syria took from them
1Ch 3: 2 daughter of Talmai, king of **G**

GESHURITES (*see* GESHUR)
Deut 3:14 as far as the border of the **G**
Josh 12: 5 as far as the border of the **G**
Josh 13: 2 and all that of the **G**,
Josh 13:11 and the border of the **G** and
Josh 13:13 out the **G** or the Maachathites
Josh 13:13 the Maachathites, but the **G**
1Sa 27: 8 men went up and raided the **G**

GESTURES
Is 33:15 who **g** with his hands,

GET (*see* GETS, GETTING, GOT)
Gen 12: 1 **G** out of your country, from
Gen 19:14 **G** up, **g** out of this place
Gen 27:13 voice, and go, **g** them for me
Gen 31:13 **g** out of this land, and return
Gen 34: 4 **G** me this young woman as a
Gen 40:14 and **g** me out of this house
Gen 44: 4 **G** up, follow the men
Ex 2: 5 she sent her maid to **g** it
Ex 5: 4 **G** back to your labor
Ex 5:11 **g** yourselves straw where you
Ex 10:28 said to him, "**G** away from me
Ex 11: 8 **G** out, and all the people who
Ex 19:24 **G** down and then come up, you
Ex 32: 7 said to Moses, "Go, **g** down
Num 11:13 Where am I to **g** meat to give
Num 16:24 **G** away from the tents of
Num 16:45 **G** away from among this
Num 17: 2 **g** from them a rod from each
Deut 8:18 gives you power to **g** wealth
Deut 24:10 his house to **g** his pledge
Deut 24:19 you shall not go back to **g** it
Josh 2:16 **G** to the mountain, lest the
Josh 7:10 **G** up! Why do you lie thus
Josh 7:13 **G** up, sanctify the people, and
Judg 9:32 **g** up by night, you and the
Judg 11: 5 elders of Gilead went to **g**
Judg 14: 2 **g** her for me as a wife
Judg 14: 3 must go and **g** a wife from the
Judg 14: 3 **G** her for me, for she pleases
Judg 14: 8 when he returned to **g** her
Judg 19: 9 early, so that you may **g** home
Judg 19:28 **G** up and let us be going
1Sa 9:26 **G** up, that I may send you on
1Sa 15: 6 depart, **g** down from among the
1Sa 20:21 **g** them and come'
1Sa 20:29 eyes, please let me **g** away
1Sa 23:26 haste to **g** away from Saul
1Sa 24:19 will he let him **g** away safely
1Sa 26:22 young men come over and **g** it
2Sa 4: 6 house, as though to **g** wheat
1Ki 1: 1 him, but he could not **g** warm
1Ki 17: 3 **G** away from here and turn
1Ki 17:11 And as she was going to **g** it
1Ki 20:12 to his servants, "**G** ready
2Ki 4:29 **G** yourself ready, and take my
2Ki 6:13 is, that I may send and **g** him
2Ki 7:12 alive, and **g** into the city
2Ki 9: 1 **G** yourself ready, take this
2Ki 9:17 **G** a horseman and send him to
2Ch 26:18 **G** out of the sanctuary, for
2Ch 26:20 he also hurried to **g** out,
Neh 5: 2 let us **g** grain for them, that
Job 20:18 he will **g** no enjoyment
Ps 88: 8 am shut up, and I cannot **g** out
Ps 119:104 precepts I **g** understanding
Prov 4: 5 **G** wisdom!
Prov 4: 5 **G** understanding!
Prov 4: 7 therefore **g** wisdom
Prov 4: 7 your getting, **g** understanding
Prov 6:33 Wounds and dishonor he will **g**
Prov 16:16 it is to **g** wisdom than gold
Prov 16:16 to **g** understanding is to be
Song 7:12 Let us **g** up early to the
Is 30:11 **G** out of the way, turn aside
Is 30:22 will say to them, "**G** away
Is 40: 9 **g** up into the high mountain
Jer 13: 1 **g** yourself a linen sash, and
Jer 19: 1 **g** a potter's earthen flask,
Jer 48: 9 that she may flee and **g** away
Jer 49:30 Flee, **g** far away
Jer 51:50 escaped the sword, **g** away
Lam 3: 7 me in so that I cannot **g** out
Lam 5: 9 We **g** our bread at the risk of
Ezek 3:11 **g** to the captives, to the
Ezek 11:15 **G** far away from the LORD
Ezek 18:31 **g** yourselves a new heart and a
Ezek 22:27 and to **g** dishonest gain
Dan 4:14 Let the beasts **g** out from
Amos 9: 1 from them shall not **g** away
Matt 5:26 you will by no means **g** out of
Matt 13:54 did this Man **g** this wisdom
Matt 13:56 this Man **g** all these things
Matt 14:22 His disciples **g** into the boat
Matt 15:33 Where could we **g** enough bread
Matt 16:23 Peter, "**G** behind Me, Satan
Matt 24:18 not go back to **g** his clothes
Mark 6: 2 did this Man **g** these things
Mark 6:45 His disciples **g** into the boat
Mark 8:33 saying, "**G** behind Me, Satan
Mark 13:16 not go back to **g** his garment
Luke 4: 8 to him, "**G** behind Me, Satan
Luke 9:12 and lodge and **g** provisions
Luke 13:31 **G** out and depart from here,
John 4:11 do You **g** that living water
John 11:12 if he sleeps he will **g** well
Acts 7: 3 **G** out of your country and
Acts 16:37 come themselves and **g** us out
Acts 22:18 **g** out of Jerusalem quickly,
Acts 27:43 overboard first and **g** to land,
1Th 5: 7 those who **g** drunk are drunk
2Ti 4:11 **G** Mark and bring him with you,

GETHER
Gen 10:23 sons of Aram were Uz, Hul, **G**
1Ch 1:17 Lud, Aram, Uz, Hul, **G**, and

GETHSEMANE
Matt 26:36 with them to a place called **G**
Mark 14:32 to a place which was named **G**

GETS (*see* GET)
Judg 7: 5 likewise everyone who **g** down
Prov 9: 7 a scoffer **g** shame for himself
Prov 9: 7 man **g** himself a blemish
Prov 15:32 heeds reproof **g** understanding
Prov 19: 8 He who **g** wisdom loves his own
Jer 17:11 hatch, so is he who **g** riches
Jer 48:44 he who **g** out of the pit shall

GETTING (*see* GET)
1Ki 20:16 kings helping him were **g**
Prov 4: 7 And in all your **g**, get
Prov 21: 6 **G** treasures by a lying tongue
Mark 8:13 and **g** into the boat again,

GEUEL
Num 13:15 of Gad, **G** the son of Machi

GEZER
Josh 10:33 Then Horam king of **G** came up
Josh 12:12 the king of **G**, one
Josh 16: 3 of Lower Beth Horon to **G**
Josh 16:10 the Canaanites who dwelt in **G**
Josh 21:21 **G** with its common-land,
Judg 1:29 the Canaanites who dwelt in **G**
Judg 1:29 dwelt in **G** among them
2Sa 5:25 from Geba as far as **G**
1Ki 9:15 Hazor, Megiddo, and **G**
1Ki 9:16 Egypt had gone up and taken **G**
1Ki 9:17 And Solomon built **G**, Lower
1Ch 6:67 also **G** with its common-lands,
1Ch 7:28 east Naaran, to the west **G**
1Ch 14:16 from Gibeon as far as **G**
1Ch 20: 4 out at **G** with the Philistines

GHOST
Matt 14:26 It is a **g**
Mark 6:49 sea, they supposed it was a **g**

GIAH
2Sa 2:24 which is before **G** by the road

GIANT (*see* GIANTS)
2Sa 21:16 was one of the sons of the **g**
2Sa 21:18 was one of the sons of the **g**
2Sa 21:20 and he also was born to the **g**
2Sa 21:22 were born to the **g** in Gath
1Ch 20: 4 was one of the sons of the **g**
1Ch 20: 6 and he also was born to the **g**
1Ch 20: 8 were born to the **g** in Gath

GIANTS (*see* GIANT)
Gen 6: 4 There were **g** on the earth in
Num 13:33 There we saw the **g** (the
Num 13:33 of Anak came from the **g**)
Deut 2:11 They were also regarded as **g**
Deut 2:20 also regarded as a land of **g**
Deut 2:20 **g** formerly dwelt there
Deut 3:11 of the remnant of the **g**
Deut 3:13 was called the land of the **g**
Josh 12: 4 was of the remnant of the **g**
Josh 13:12 of the remnant of the **g**
Josh 17:15 of the Perizzites and the **g**

GIBBAR (*see* GIBEON)
Ezra 2:20 the people of **G**, ninety-five

GIBBETHON
Josh 19:44 Eltekeh, **G**, Baalath,
Josh 21:23 **G** with its common-land,
1Ki 15:27 And Baasha killed him at **G**
1Ki 15:27 and all Israel laid siege to **G**
1Ki 16:15 were encamped against **G**,
1Ki 16:17 with him went up from **G**, and

GIBEA (*see* GIBEAH, GIBEON)
1Ch 2:49 Machbenah and the father of **G**

GIBEAH (*see* GEBA, GIBEA, GIBEATH, GIBEATHITE, GIBEON)
Josh 15:57 Kain, **G**, and Timnah
Judg 19:12 we will go on to **G**
Judg 19:13 the night in **G** or in Ramah
Judg 19:14 sun went down on them near **G**
Judg 19:15 there to go in to lodge in **G**
Judg 19:16 he was sojourning in **G**,
Judg 20: 4 My concubine and I went into **G**
Judg 20: 5 the men of **G** rose against me,
Judg 20: 9 thing which we will do to **G**
Judg 20:10 they come to **G** in Benjamin
Judg 20:13 perverted men who are in **G**
Judg 20:14 from their cities to **G**, to go
Judg 20:15 besides the inhabitants of **G**
Judg 20:19 and encamped against **G**
Judg 20:20 to fight against them at **G**
Judg 20:21 of Benjamin came out of **G**
Judg 20:25 them from **G** on the second day
Judg 20:29 men in ambush all around **G**
Judg 20:30 **G** as at the other times
Judg 20:31 to Bethel and the other to **G**)
Judg 20:34 all Israel came against **G**
Judg 20:36 whom they had set against **G**
Judg 20:37 ambush quickly rushed upon **G**
Judg 20:43 front of **G** toward the east
1Sa 10:26 And Saul also went home to **G**
1Sa 11: 4 messengers came to **G** of Saul
1Sa 13: 2 Jonathan in **G** of Benjamin
1Sa 13:15 from Gilgal to **G** of Benjamin
1Sa 13:16 remained in **G** of Benjamin
1Sa 14: 2 of **G** under a pomegranate tree
1Sa 14: 5 other southward opposite **G**
1Sa 14:16 Saul in **G** of Benjamin looked
1Sa 15:34 up to his house at **G** of Saul
1Sa 22: 6 now Saul was staying in **G**
1Sa 23:19 Ziphites came up to Saul at **G**
1Sa 26: 1 Ziphites came to Saul at **G**
2Sa 21: 6 before the LORD in **G** of Saul
2Sa 23:29 **G** of the children of Benjamin
1Ch 11:31 Ithai the son of Ribai of **G**
2Ch 13: 2 the daughter of Uriel of **G**
Is 10:29 is afraid, **G** of Saul has fled
Hos 5: 8 Blow the ram's horn in **G**, the
Hos 9: 9 as in the days of **G**
Hos 10: 9 sinned from the days of **G**
Hos 10: 9 The battle in **G** against the

GIBEATH (*see* GIBEAH)
Josh 18:28 Jebus (which is Jerusalem), **G**

GIBEATHITE (*see* GIBEAH)
1Ch 12: 3 the sons of Shemaah the **G**

GIBEON (*see* GEBA, GIBBAR, GIBEA, GIBEAH, GIBEONITE)
Josh 9: 3 **G** heard what Joshua had done
Josh 9:17 Now their cities were **G**,
Josh 10: 1 how the inhabitants of **G** had
Josh 10: 2 because **G** was a great city,
Josh 10: 4 help me, that we may attack **G**
Josh 10: 5 armies, and camped before **G**
Josh 10: 6 the men of **G** sent to Joshua
Josh 10:10 with a great slaughter at **G**
Josh 10:12 Sun, stand still over **G**
Josh 10:41 of Goshen, even as far as **G**
Josh 11:19 Hivites, the inhabitants of **G**
Josh 18:25 **G**, Ramah, Beeroth,
Josh 21:17 **G** with its common-land, Geba
2Sa 2:12 went out from Mahanaim to **G**
2Sa 2:13 and met them by the pool of **G**
2Sa 2:16 Sharp Swords, which is in **G**
2Sa 2:24 road to the Wilderness of **G**
2Sa 3:30 Asahel at **G** in the battle
2Sa 20: 8 the large stone which is in **G**
1Ki 3: 4 went to **G** to sacrifice there
1Ki 3: 5 At **G** the LORD appeared to
1Ki 9: 2 He had appeared to him at **G**
1Ch 8:29 Now the father of **G**, whose
1Ch 8:29 name was Maacah, dwelt at **G**
1Ch 9:35 Jeiel the father of **G**, whose
1Ch 9:35 name was Maacah, dwelt at **G**
1Ch 14:16 from **G** as far as Gezer
1Ch 16:39 the high place that was at **G**
1Ch 21:29 time at the high place in **G**
2Ch 1: 3 the high place that was at **G**
2Ch 1:13 the high place that was at **G**
Neh 3: 7 the Meronothite, the men of **G**
Neh 7:25 the children of **G**,
Is 28:21 angry as in the Valley of **G**
Jer 28: 1 the prophet, who was from **G**
Jer 41:12 the great pool that is in **G**
Jer 41:16 he had brought back from **G**

GIBEONITE (*see* GIBEON, GIBEONITES)
1Ch 12: 4 Ishmaiah the **G**, a mighty man
Neh 3: 7 next to them Melatiah the **G**

GIBEONITES (*see* GIBEONITE)
2Sa 21: 1 because he killed the **G**
2Sa 21: 2 So the king called the **G** and
2Sa 21: 2 Now the **G** were not of the
2Sa 21: 3 Therefore David said to the **G**
2Sa 21: 4 And the **G** said to him,
2Sa 21: 9 them into the hands of the **G**

GIDDALTI
1Ch 25: 4 Hananiah, Hanani, Eliathah, **G**
1Ch 25:29 the twenty-second for **G**, his

GIDDEL
Ezra 2:47 the sons of **G**, the sons of
Ezra 2:56 sons of Darkon, the sons of **G**
Neh 7:49 of Hanan, the children of **G**
Neh 7:58 of Darkon, the children of **G**

GIDEON (*see* JERUBBAAL)
Judg 6:11 while his son **G** threshed
Judg 6:13 **G** said to Him, "O my lord
Judg 6:19 Then **G** went in and prepared a
Judg 6:22 Now **G** perceived that He was
Judg 6:22 So **G** said, "Alas, O Lord GOD!
Judg 6:24 So **G** built an altar there to
Judg 6:27 So **G** took ten men from among
Judg 6:29 **G** the son of Joash has done
Judg 6:34 of the LORD came upon **G**
Judg 6:36 Then **G** said to God, "If You
Judg 6:39 Then **G** said to God, "Do not
Judg 7: 1 **G**) and all the people who were
Judg 7: 2 And the LORD said to **G**, "The
Judg 7: 4 And the LORD said to **G**, "The
Judg 7: 5 And the LORD said to **G**
Judg 7: 7 Then the LORD said to **G**, "By
Judg 7:13 when **G** had come, there was a
Judg 7:14 sword of **G** the son of Joash
Judg 7:15 when **G** heard the telling of
Judg 7:18 The sword of the LORD and of **G**
Judg 7:19 So **G** and the hundred men who
Judg 7:20 The sword of the LORD and of **G**
Judg 7:24 Then **G** sent messengers
Judg 7:25 Zeeb to **G** on the other side
Judg 8: 4 When **G** came to the Jordan, he
Judg 8: 7 So **G** said, "For this cause,
Judg 8:11 Then **G** went up by the road of
Judg 8:13 Then **G** the son of Joash
Judg 8:21 So **G** arose and killed Zebah
Judg 8:22 the men of Israel said to **G**
Judg 8:23 But **G** said to them, "I will
Judg 8:24 Then **G** said to them, "I
Judg 8:27 Then **G** made it into an ephod
Judg 8:27 It became a snare to **G** and to
Judg 8:28 forty years in the days of **G**
Judg 8:30 **G** had seventy sons who were
Judg 8:32 Now **G** the son of Joash died
Judg 8:33 was so, as soon as **G** was dead
Judg 8:35 **G**) in accordance with the
Heb 11:32 would fail me to tell of **G**

GIDEONI
Num 1:11 Benjamin, Abidan the son of **G**
Num 2:22 shall be Abidan the son of **G**
Num 7:60 ninth day Abidan the son of **G**
Num 7:65 of Abidan the son of **G**
Num 10:24 was Abidan the son of **G**

GIDOM
Judg 20:45 them relentlessly up to **G**

GIFT (*see* GIFTED, GIFTS, GIVE)
Gen 34:12 me ever so much dowry and **g**
Num 8:19 the Levites as a **g** to Aaron
Num 18: 6 they are a **g** to you, given by
Num 18: 7 to you as a **g** for service
Num 18:11 the heave offering of their **g**
2Sa 11: 8 a **g** of food from the king
2Sa 19:42 Or has he given us any **g**
2Ki 5:15 please take a **g** from your
Ps 45:12 Tyre will be there with a **g**
Prov 18:16 A man's **g** makes room for him,
Prov 21:14 A **g** in secret pacifies anger,
Eccl 3:13 it is the **g** of God
Eccl 5:19 this is the **g** of God
Jer 40: 5 guard gave him rations and a **g**
Ezek 46:16 If the prince gives a **g** of
Ezek 46:17 But if he gives a **g** of some
Zech 6:10 Receive the **g** from the
Matt 5:23 you bring your **g** to the altar
Matt 5:24 leave your **g** there before the
Matt 5:24 and then come and offer your **g**
Matt 8: 4 and offer the **g** that Moses
Matt 23:18 swears by the **g** that is on it
Matt 23:19 the **g** or the altar that
Matt 23:19 altar that sanctifies the **g**
John 4:10 If you knew the **g** of God, and
Acts 2:38 the **g** of the Holy Spirit
Acts 8:20 you thought that the **g** of God
Acts 10:45 because the **g** of the Holy
Acts 11:17 same **g** as He gave us when we
Rom 1:11 to you some spiritual **g**, so
Rom 5:15 But the free **g** is not like
Rom 5:15 the **g** by the grace of the one
Rom 5:16 the **g** is not like that which
Rom 5:16 but the free **g** which came
Rom 5:17 of the **g** of righteousness
Rom 5:18 the free **g** came to all men
Rom 6:23 but the **g** of God is eternal
1Co 1: 7 that you come short in no **g**
1Co 7: 7 one has his own **g** from God
1Co 13: 2 I have the **g** of prophecy, and
1Co 16: 3 to bear your **g** to Jerusalem
2Co 1:11 on our behalf for the **g**
2Co 8: 4 that we would receive the **g**
2Co 8:19 to travel with us with this **g**
2Co 8:20 blame us in this lavish **g**
2Co 9: 5 your bountiful **g** beforehand
2Co 9:15 God for His indescribable **g**
Eph 2: 8 it is the **g** of God,
Eph 3: 7 **g** of the grace of God given
Eph 4: 7 to the measure of Christ's **g**
Phil 4:17 Not that I seek the **g**, but I
1Ti 4:14 neglect the **g** that is in you
2Ti 1: 6 the **g** of God which is in you
Heb 6: 4 and have tasted the heavenly **g**
Jas 1:17 Every good **g** and every perfect
Jas 1:17 every perfect **g** is from above
1Pe 4:10 As each one has received a **g**

GIFTED (*see* GIFT)
Ex 28: 3 to all who are **g** artisans
Ex 31: 6 of all who are **g** artisans
Ex 35:25 All the women who were **g**
Ex 36: 1 every **g** artisan in whom the
Ex 36: 2 and every **g** artisan in whose
Ex 36: 8 Then all the **g** artisans among
Dan 1: 4 **g** in all wisdom, possessing

GIFTS (*see* GIFT)
Gen 25: 6 But Abraham gave **g** to the
Ex 28:38 hallow in all their holy **g**
Lev 23:38 of the LORD, besides your **g**
Num 18: 8 all the holy **g** of the
Num 18:29 Of all your **g** you shall
Num 18:32 **g** of the children of Israel
2Ki 12: 4 **g** that are brought into the
2Ch 21: 3 gave them great **g** of silver
2Ch 32:23 many brought **g** to the LORD at
Esth 2:18 and gave **g** according to the
Esth 9:22 one another and **g** to the poor
Ps 68:18 You have received **g** among men
Ps 72:10 of Sheba and Seba Will offer **g**
Prov 6:35 though you give many **g**
Prov 19: 6 a friend to one who gives **g**
Ezek 20:26 because of their ritual **g**
Ezek 20:31 For when you offer your **g**
Ezek 20:39 holy name no more with your **g**
Dan 2: 6 you shall receive from me **g**
Dan 2:48 and gave him many great **g**
Dan 5:17 Let your **g** be for yourself,
Mic 7: 3 the prince asks for **g**, the
Matt 2:11 they presented **g** to Him
Matt 7:11 give good **g** to your children
Luke 11:13 give good **g** to your children
Luke 21: 1 their **g** into the treasury
Rom 11:29 For the **g** and the calling of
Rom 12: 6 Having then **g** differing
1Co 12: 1 Now concerning spiritual **g**
1Co 12: 4 there are diversities of **g**
1Co 12: 9 to another **g** of healings by
1Co 12:28 then **g** of healings, helps,
1Co 12:30 Do all have **g** of healings
1Co 12:31 earnestly desire the best **g**
1Co 14: 1 love, and desire spiritual **g**
1Co 14:12 are zealous for spiritual **g**
Eph 4: 8 captive, and gave **g** to men
Heb 2: 4 and **g** of the Holy Spirit,
Heb 5: 1 God, that he may offer both **g**
Heb 8: 3 is appointed to offer both **g**
Heb 8: 4 the **g** according to the law
Heb 9: 9 present time in which both **g**
Heb 11: 4 God testifying of his **g**
Rev 11:10 and send **g** to one another,

GIHON
Gen 2:13 name of the second river is **G**
1Ki 1:33 mule, and take him down to **G**
1Ki 1:38 mule, and took him to **G**
1Ki 1:45 have anointed him king at **G**
2Ch 32:30 the water outlet of Upper **G**
2Ch 33:14 David on the west side of **G**

GILALAI
Neh 12:36 Shemaiah, Azarel, Milalai, **G**

GILBOA
1Sa 28: 4 and they encamped at **G**
1Sa 31: 1 and fell slain on Mount **G**
1Sa 31: 8 three sons fallen on Mount **G**
2Sa 1: 6 by chance to be on Mount **G**
2Sa 1:21 O mountains of **G**, let there
2Sa 21:12 had struck down Saul in **G**
1Ch 10: 1 and fell slain on Mount **G**
1Ch 10: 8 and his sons fallen on Mount **G**

GILEAD (*see* GILEADITE, GILEAD'S, JABESH GILEAD, RAMOTH GILEAD)
Gen 31:21 toward the mountains of **G**
Gen 31:23 him in the mountains of **G**
Gen 31:25 pitched in the mountains of **G**
Gen 37:25 coming from **G** with their
Num 26:29 and Machir begot **G**
Num 26:29 of **G**, the family of the
Num 26:30 These are the sons of **G**
Num 27: 1 son of Hepher, the son of **G**
Num 32: 1 of Jazer and the land of **G**
Num 32:26 be there in the cities of **G**
Num 32:29 the land of **G** as a possession
Num 32:39 the son of Manasseh went to **G**
Num 32:40 So Moses gave **G** to Machir the
Num 36: 1 of **G** the son of Machir, the
Deut 2:36 is in the ravine, as far as **G**
Deut 3:10 cities of the plain, all **G**
Deut 3:12 and half the mountains of **G**
Deut 3:13 The rest of **G**, and all Bashan,
Deut 3:15 And I gave **G** to Machir
Deut 3:16 the Gadites I gave from **G** as
Deut 4:43 Ramoth in **G** for the Gadites,
Deut 34: 1 the land of **G** as far as Dan
Josh 12: 2 in Heshbon and ruled half of **G**
Josh 12: 5 over half of **G** as far as the
Josh 13:11 **G**, and the border of the
Josh 13:25 Jazer, and all the cities of **G**
Josh 13:31 half of **G**, and Ashtaroth and

Josh 17: 1 of Manasseh, the father of **G**
Josh 17: 1 therefore he was given **G** and
Josh 17: 3 son of Hepher, the son of **G**
Josh 17: 5 besides the land of **G** and
Josh 17: 6 sons had the land of **G**
Josh 20: 8 tribe of Reuben, Ramoth in **G**
Josh 21:38 of Gad, Ramoth in **G** with its
Josh 22: 9 to go to the country of **G**
Josh 22:13 Manasseh, into the land of **G**
Josh 22:15 of Manasseh, to the land of **G**
Josh 22:32 from the land of **G** to the
Judg 5:17 **G** stayed beyond the Jordan,
Judg 7: 3 depart at once from Mount **G**
Judg 10: 4 which are in the land of **G**
Judg 10: 8 land of the Amorites, in **G**
Judg 10:17 together and encamped in **G**
Judg 10:18 the people, the leaders of **G**
Judg 10:18 over all the inhabitants of **G**
Judg 11: 1 and **G** begot Jephthah
Judg 11: 5 that the elders of **G** went to
Judg 11: 7 said to the elders of **G**
Judg 11: 8 And the elders of **G** said to
Judg 11: 8 over all the inhabitants of **G**
Judg 11: 9 said to the elders of **G**, "If
Judg 11:10 And the elders of **G** said to
Judg 11:11 went with the elders of **G**
Judg 11:29 and he passed through **G** and
Judg 11:29 and passed through Mizpah of **G**
Judg 11:29 from Mizpah of **G** he advanced
Judg 12: 4 together all the men of **G**
Judg 12: 4 the men of **G** defeated Ephraim
Judg 12: 5 the men of **G** would say to
Judg 12: 7 in one of the cities of **G**
Judg 20: 1 as well as from the land of **G**
1Sa 13: 7 to the land of Gad and **G**
2Sa 2: 9 and he made him king over **G**
2Sa 17:26 encamped in the land of **G**
2Sa 24: 6 Then they came to **G** and to the
1Ki 4:13 Ben-Geber, in Ramoth **G**
1Ki 4:13 the son of Manasseh, in **G**
1Ki 4:19 son of Uri, in the land of **G**
1Ki 17: 1 of the inhabitants of **G**,
1Ki 22: 3 know that Ramoth in **G** is ours
1Ki 22: 4 with me to fight at Ramoth **G**
1Ki 22: 6 go against Ramoth **G** to fight
1Ki 22:12 Go up to Ramoth **G** and
1Ki 22:15 we go to war against Ramoth **G**
1Ki 22:20 that he may fall at Ramoth **G**
1Ki 22:29 of Judah went up to Ramoth **G**
2Ki 8:28 king of Syria at Ramoth **G**
2Ki 9: 1 your hand, and go to Ramoth **G**
2Ki 9: 4 the prophet, went to Ramoth **G**
2Ki 9:14 had been defending Ramoth **G**
2Ki 10:33 all the land of **G**
2Ki 10:33 the River Arnon, including **G**
2Ki 15:25 with him were fifty men of **G**
2Ki 15:29 Janoah, Kedesh, Hazor, **G**
1Ch 2:21 of Machir the father of **G**
1Ch 2:22 cities in the land of **G**
1Ch 2:23 of Machir the father of **G**
1Ch 5: 9 multiplied in the land of **G**
1Ch 5:10 the entire area east of **G**
1Ch 5:14 son of Jaroah, the son of **G**
1Ch 5:16 And the Gadites dwelt in **G**
1Ch 6:80 Ramoth in **G** with its
1Ch 7:14 him Machir the father of **G**
1Ch 7:17 of **G** the son of Machir, the
1Ch 26:31 capable men at Jazer of **G**
1Ch 27:21 half-tribe of Manasseh in **G**
2Ch 18: 2 to go up with him to Ramoth **G**
2Ch 18: 3 go with me against Ramoth **G**
2Ch 18: 5 we go to war against Ramoth **G**
2Ch 18:11 Go up to Ramoth **G** and
2Ch 18:14 we go to war against Ramoth **G**
2Ch 18:19 that he may fall at Ramoth **G**
2Ch 18:28 of Judah went up to Ramoth **G**
2Ch 22: 5 king of Syria at Ramoth **G**
Ps 60: 7 **G** is Mine, and Manasseh is
Ps 108: 8 **G** is Mine; Manasseh is Mine
Song 4: 1 going down from Mount **G**
Song 6: 5 of goats going down from **G**
Jer 8:22 Is there no balm in **G**, is
Jer 22: 6 You are **G** to Me, the head of
Jer 46:11 Go up to **G** and take balm, O
Jer 50:19 on Mount Ephraim and **G**
Ezek 47:18 and Damascus, and between **G**
Hos 6: 8 **G** is a city of evildoers, and
Hos 12:11 Though **G** has idols
Amos 1: 3 **G** with implements of iron
Amos 1:13 the women with child in **G**
Obad 19 Benjamin shall possess **G**
Mic 7:14 let them feed in Bashan and **G**
Zech 10:10 bring them into the land of **G**

GILEADITE (*see* GILEAD, GILEADITES)
Judg 10: 3 After him arose Jair, a **G**
Judg 11: 1 Now Jephthah the **G** was a
Judg 11:40 daughter of Jephthah the **G**
Judg 12: 7 Then Jephthah the **G** died and
2Sa 17:27 Barzillai the **G** from Rogelim
2Sa 19:31 Barzillai the **G** came down
1Ki 2: 7 the sons of Barzillai the **G**
Ezra 2:61 daughters of Barzillai the **G**
Neh 7:63 daughters of Barzillai the **G**

GILEADITES (*see* GILEADITE)
Num 26:29 Gilead, the family of the **G**
Judg 12: 4 You **G** are fugitives of
Judg 12: 5 The **G** seized the fords of the

GILEAD'S (*see* GILEAD)
Judg 11: 2 **G** wife bore sons
1Ch 7:15 The name of **G** grandson was

GILGAL
Deut 11:30 dwell in the plain opposite **G**
Josh 4:19 they camped in **G** on the east
Josh 4:20 Jordan, Joshua set up in **G**
Josh 5: 9 place is called **G** to this day
Josh 5:10 of Israel camped in **G**, and
Josh 9: 6 to Joshua, to the camp at **G**
Josh 10: 6 to Joshua at the camp at **G**
Josh 10: 7 So Joshua ascended from **G**
Josh 10: 9 marched all night from **G**
Josh 10:15 with him, to the camp at **G**
Josh 10:43 with him, to the camp at **G**
Josh 12:23 the king of the people of **G**
Josh 14: 6 of Judah came to Joshua in **G**
Josh 15: 7 it turned northward toward **G**
Judg 2: 1 LORD came up from **G** to
Judg 3:19 stone images that were at **G**
1Sa 7:16 on a circuit to Bethel, **G**
1Sa 10: 8 shall go down before me to **G**
1Sa 11:14 Come, let us go to **G** and renew
1Sa 11:15 So all the people went to **G**
1Sa 11:15 king before the LORD in **G**
1Sa 13: 4 called together to Saul at **G**
1Sa 13: 7 for Saul, he was still in **G**
1Sa 13: 8 But Samuel did not come to **G**
1Sa 13:12 will now come down on me at **G**
1Sa 13:15 went up from **G** to Gibeah of
1Sa 15:12 passed by, and gone down to **G**
1Sa 15:21 to the LORD your God in **G**
1Sa 15:33 pieces before the LORD in **G**
2Sa 19:15 And Judah came to **G**, to go to
2Sa 19:40 Now the king went on to **G**
2Ki 2: 1 went with Elisha from **G**
2Ki 4:38 And Elisha returned to **G**, and
Neh 12:29 from the house of **G**, and from
Hos 4:15 Do not come up to **G**, nor go
Hos 9:15 All their wickedness is in **G**
Hos 12:11 they sacrifice bulls in **G**
Amos 4: 4 at **G** multiply transgression
Amos 5: 5 not seek Bethel, nor enter **G**
Amos 5: 5 for **G** shall surely go into
Mic 6: 5 him, from Acacia Grove to **G**

GILOH (*see* GILONITE)
Josh 15:51 Goshen, Holon, and **G**
2Sa 15:12 from his city, namely from **G**

GILONITE (*see* GILOH)
2Sa 15:12 sent for Ahithophel the **G**
2Sa 23:34 the son of Ahithophel the **G**

GIMZO
2Ch 28:18 and **G** with its villages

GINATH
1Ki 16:21 followed Tibni the son of **G**
1Ki 16:22 followed Tibni the son of **G**

GINNETHOI (*see* GINNETHON)
Neh 12: 4 Iddo, **G**, Abijah,

GINNETHON (*see* GINNETHOI)
Neh 10: 6 Daniel, **G**, Baruch,
Neh 12:16 of **G**, Meshullam

GIRD (*see* GIRDED, GIRDING, GIRDS)
Ex 29: 5 **g** him with the intricately
Ex 29: 9 you shall **g** them with sashes,
1Sa 25:13 Every man **g** on his sword
2Sa 3:31 **g** yourselves with sackcloth,
Ps 45: 3 **G** Your sword upon Your thigh,
Ps 76:10 of wrath You shall **g** Yourself
Is 8: 9 **G** yourselves, but be broken
Is 8: 9 **g** yourselves, but be broken
Is 32:11 **g** sackcloth on your waists
Is 45: 5 I will **g** you, though you have
Jer 49: 3 **g** yourselves with sackcloth
Lam 2:10 **g** themselves with sackcloth
Ezek 27:31 **g** themselves with sackcloth,
Joel 1:13 **G** yourselves and lament, you
Luke 12:37 to you that he will **g** himself
Luke 17: 8 **g** yourself and serve me till I
John 21:18 hands, and another will **g** you
Acts 12: 8 **G** yourself and tie on your
1Pe 1:13 Therefore **g** up the loins of

GIRDED (*see* GIRD)
Lev 8: 7 **g** him with the sash, clothed
Lev 8: 7 he **g** him with the intricately
Lev 8:13 **g** them with sashes, and put
Lev 16: 4 he shall be **g** with a linen
Deut 1:41 had **g** on his weapons of war
1Sa 2: 4 stumbled are **g** with strength
1Sa 25:13 So every man **g** on his sword
1Sa 25:13 David also **g** on his sword
1Ki 18:46 and he **g** up his loins and ran
Neh 4:18 **g** at his side as he built
Ps 93: 1 He has **g** Himself with
Ezek 7:18 will also be **g** with sackcloth
Ezek 23:15 **g** with belts around their
Dan 10: 5 whose waist was **g** with gold
Joel 1: 8 Lament like a virgin **g** with
Luke 12:35 Let your waist be **g** and your
John 13: 4 took a towel and **g** Himself
John 13: 5 the towel with which He was **g**
John 21:18 you **g** yourself and walked
Eph 6:14 having **g** your waist with
Rev 1:13 and **g** about the chest with a
Rev 15: 6 chests **g** with golden bands

GIRDING (*see* GIRD)
Is 3:24 a rich robe, a **g** of sackcloth
Is 22:12 and for **g** with sackcloth

GIRDS (*see* GIRD)
Ps 109:19 he **g** himself continually
Prov 31:17 She **g** herself with strength,

GIRGASHITE (*see* GIRGASHITES)
Gen 10:16 the Amorite, and the **G**
1Ch 1:14 the Amorite, and the **G**

GIRGASHITES (*see* GIRGASHITE)
Gen 15:21 the Canaanites, the **G**, and
Deut 7: 1 you, the Hittites and the **G**
Josh 3:10 and the Perizzites and the **G**
Josh 24:11 the Hittites, the **G**, the
Neh 9: 8 the Jebusites, and the **G**

GIRL (*see* GIRLS)
Judg 5:30 to every man a **g** or two
2Ki 5: 2 back captive a young **g** from
2Ki 5: 4 thus said the **g** who is from
Joel 3: 3 sold a **g** for wine, that they
Amos 2: 7 father go in to the same **g**
Matt 9:24 for the **g** is not dead, but
Matt 9:25 by the hand, and the **g** arose
Matt 14:11 a platter and given to the **g**
Matt 26:69 And a servant **g** came to him,
Matt 26:71 gateway, another **g** saw him
Mark 5:41 Little **g**, I say to you, arise
Mark 5:42 Immediately the **g** arose and
Mark 6:22 him, the king said to the **g**
Mark 6:28 platter, and gave it to the **g**
Mark 6:28 the **g** gave it to her mother
Mark 14:69 the servant **g** saw him again,
Luke 8:51 the father and mother of the **g**
Luke 8:54 Little **g**, arise
Luke 22:56 And a certain servant **g**,
John 18:17 Then the servant **g** who kept
Acts 12:13 gate, a **g** named Rhoda came to
Acts 16:16 that a certain slave **g**
Acts 16:17 This **g** followed Paul and us,

GIRLS (*see* GIRL)
Num 31:18 **g** who have not known a man
Zech 8: 5 and **g** playing in its streets
Mark 14:66 one of the servant **g** of the

GIRZITES
1Sa 27: 8 raided the Geshurites, the **G**

GISHPA
Neh 11:21 and **G** were over the Nethinim

Ruth 4:12 which the LORD will **g** you
1Sa 1: 4 he would **g** portions to
1Sa 1: 5 he would **g** a double portion
1Sa 1:11 but will **g** your maidservant a
1Sa 1:11 then I will **g** him to the LORD
1Sa 2:10 He will **g** strength to His
1Sa 2:15 **G** meat for roasting to the
1Sa 2:16 but you must **g** it to me now
1Sa 2:20 The LORD **g** you descendants
1Sa 2:28 did I not **g** to the house of
1Sa 6: 5 you shall **g** glory to the God
1Sa 8: 6 **G** us a king to judge us
1Sa 8:14 and **g** them to his servants
1Sa 8:15 and **g** it to his officers and
1Sa 9: 8 I will **g** that to the man of
1Sa 10: 4 **g** you two loaves of bread,
1Sa 14:41 of Israel, "**G** a perfect lot
1Sa 17:10 **g** me a man, that we may fight
1Sa 17:25 will **g** him his daughter, and
1Sa 17:25 and **g** his father's house
1Sa 17:44 I will **g** your flesh to the
1Sa 17:46 And this day I will **g** the
1Sa 17:47 He will **g** you into our hands
1Sa 18:17 I will **g** her to you as a wife
1Sa 18:21 I will **g** her to him, that she
1Sa 21: 3 **G** me five loaves of bread in
1Sa 21: 9 **g** it to me
1Sa 22: 7 Will the son of Jesse **g** every
1Sa 25: 8 Please **g** whatever comes to
1Sa 25:11 **g** it to men when I do not
1Sa 27: 5 let them **g** me a place in some
1Sa 30:22 we will not **g** them any of the
2Sa 3:14 **G** me my wife Michal, whom I
2Sa 4:10 **g** him a reward for his news
2Sa 12:11 **g** them to your neighbor, and
2Sa 13: 5 **g** me food, and prepare the
2Sa 14: 8 I will **g** orders concerning
2Sa 15: 4 then I would **g** him justice
2Sa 16:20 **G** counsel as to what we
2Sa 21: 6 king said, "I will **g** them."
2Sa 22:50 I will **g** thanks to You, O
2Sa 23:15 that someone would **g** me a
1Ki 1:12 let me now **g** you counsel,
1Ki 2:17 that he may **g** me Abishag the
1Ki 3: 5 What shall I **g** you
1Ki 3: 9 Therefore **g** to Your servant
1Ki 3:25 **g** half to one, and half to the
1Ki 3:26 **g** her the living child, and by
1Ki 3:27 **G** the first woman the living
1Ki 8:36 **g** rain on Your land which You
1Ki 8:39 **g** to everyone according to
1Ki 11:11 you and **g** it to your servant
1Ki 11:13 but I will **g** one tribe to
1Ki 11:31 and will **g** ten tribes to you
1Ki 11:35 his son's hand and **g** it to you
1Ki 11:36 to his son I will **g** one tribe
1Ki 11:38 and will **g** Israel to you
1Ki 12: 9 What counsel do you **g**
1Ki 13: 7 and I will **g** you a reward
1Ki 13: 8 If you were to **g** me half your
1Ki 14:16 He will **g** Israel up because
1Ki 17:19 said to her, "**G** me your son
1Ki 18:23 let them **g** us two bulls
1Ki 21: 2 **G** me your vineyard, that I
1Ki 21: 2 and for it I will **g** you a
1Ki 21: 2 I will **g** you its worth in
1Ki 21: 3 **g** the inheritance of my
1Ki 21: 4 said, "I will not **g** you the
1Ki 21: 6 **G** me your vineyard for money
1Ki 21: 6 I will **g** you another vineyard
1Ki 21: 6 I will not **g** you my vineyard
1Ki 21: 7 I will **g** you the vineyard of
1Ki 21:15 he refused to **g** you for money
2Ki 4:42 **G** it to the people, that they
2Ki 4:43 **G** it to the people, that they
2Ki 5:22 Please **g** them a talent of
2Ki 6:28 **G** your son, that we may eat
2Ki 6:29 **G** your son, that we may eat
2Ki 8:19 him to **g** a lamp to him and his
2Ki 10:15 If it is, **g** me your hand
2Ki 14: 9 **G** your daughter to my son as
2Ki 15:20 to **g** to the king of Assyria
2Ki 18:23 **g** a pledge to my master the
2Ki 18:23 I will **g** you two thousand
2Ki 22: 5 let them **g** it to those who
2Ki 23:35 to **g** money according to the
2Ki 23:35 to **g** it to Pharaoh Necho
1Ch 11:17 that someone would **g** me a
1Ch 16: 8 Oh, **g** thanks to the LORD
1Ch 16:18 To you I will **g** the land of
1Ch 16:28 **G** to the LORD, O kindreds of
1Ch 16:28 **g** to the LORD glory and
1Ch 16:29 **G** to the LORD the glory due
1Ch 16:34 **g** thanks to the LORD, for He
1Ch 16:35 to **g** thanks to Your holy name
1Ch 16:41 to **g** thanks to the LORD,
1Ch 21:23 I also **g** you the oxen for
1Ch 21:23 I **g** it all
1Ch 22: 9 I will **g** him rest from all
1Ch 22: 9 Solomon, for I will **g** peace
1Ch 22:12 may the LORD **g** you wisdom
1Ch 22:12 and **g** you charge concerning
1Ch 23:13 to **g** the blessing in His name
1Ch 25: 3 with a harp to **g** thanks and to
1Ch 29:12 great and to **g** strength to all
1Ch 29:19 And **g** my son Solomon a loyal
2Ch 1: 7 What shall I **g** you
2Ch 1:10 **g** me wisdom and knowledge
2Ch 1:12 I will **g** you riches and wealth
2Ch 2:10 And indeed I will **g** to your
2Ch 6:30 **g** to everyone according to
2Ch 10: 9 What advice do you **g**
2Ch 21: 7 promised to **g** a lamp to him
2Ch 25: 9 The LORD is able to **g** you
2Ch 25:18 **G** your daughter to my son as
2Ch 25:20 that He might **g** them into the
2Ch 30:12 **g** them singleness of heart to
2Ch 31: 2 to **g** thanks, and to praise in
2Ch 32:11 Hezekiah persuade you to **g**
2Ch 35:12 **g** them to the divisions of
Ezra 4:21 Now **g** the command to make
Ezra 9: 8 to **g** us a peg in His holy
Ezra 9: 8 **g** us a measure of revival in
Ezra 9: 9 to **g** us a wall in Judah and
Ezra 9:12 do not **g** your daughters as
Neh 2: 8 that he must **g** me timber to
Neh 4: 4 **g** them as plunder to a land
Neh 9: 8 **g** the land of the Canaanites
Neh 9: 8 to **g** it to his descendants
Neh 9:12 to **g** them light on the road
Neh 9:15 which You had sworn to **g** them
Neh 10:30 that we would not **g** our
Neh 12:24 **g** thanks, group alternating
Neh 13:25 You shall not **g** your
Esth 1:19 and let the king **g** her royal
Job 2: 4 has he will **g** for his life
Job 10: 1 I will **g** free course to my
Job 33:13 For He does not **g** an
Job 33:31 **G** ear, Job, listen to me
Job 34: 2 **g** ear to me, you who have
Job 35: 7 righteous, what do you **g** Him
Ps 2: 8 I will **g** You The nations for
Ps 5: 1 **G** ear to my words, O LORD,
Ps 5: 2 **G** heed to the voice of my cry
Ps 6: 5 grave who will **g** You thanks
Ps 17: 1 **G** ear to my prayer that is
Ps 18:49 I will **g** thanks to You, O
Ps 28: 4 **G** to them according to their
Ps 28: 4 **G** to them according to the
Ps 29: 1 **G** unto the LORD, O you mighty
Ps 29: 1 **G** unto the LORD glory and
Ps 29: 2 **G** unto the LORD the glory due
Ps 29: 9 LORD makes the deer **g** birth
Ps 29:11 The LORD will **g** strength to
Ps 30: 4 **g** thanks at the remembrance
Ps 30:12 God, I will **g** thanks to You
Ps 35:18 I will **g** You thanks in the
Ps 36: 8 You **g** them drink from the
Ps 37: 4 He shall **g** you the desires of
Ps 39:12 O LORD, And **g** ear to my cry
Ps 49: 1 **G** ear, all you inhabitants of
Ps 49: 7 Nor **g** to God a ransom for him
Ps 50:19 You **g** your mouth to evil, And
Ps 51:16 or else I would **g** it
Ps 54: 2 **G** ear to the words of my
Ps 55: 1 **G** ear to my prayer, O God, And
Ps 57: 7 I will sing and **g** praise
Ps 60:11 **G** us help from trouble, For
Ps 72: 1 **G** the king Your judgments, O
Ps 75: 1 We **g** thanks to You, O God, we
Ps 75: 1 to You, O God, we **g** thanks
Ps 78: 1 **G** ear, O my people, to my law
Ps 78:20 Can He **g** bread also
Ps 79:13 Will **g** You thanks forever
Ps 80: 1 **G** ear, O Shepherd of Israel,
Ps 84: 8 **G** ear, O God of Jacob
Ps 84:11 The LORD will **g** grace and
Ps 85:12 the LORD will **g** what is good
Ps 86: 6 **G** ear, O LORD, to my prayer
Ps 86:16 **G** Your strength to Your
Ps 91:11 For He shall **g** His angels
Ps 92: 1 It is good to **g** thanks to the
Ps 94:13 That You may **g** him rest from
Ps 96: 7 **G** to the LORD, O kindreds of
Ps 96: 7 **G** to the LORD glory and
Ps 96: 8 **G** to the LORD the glory due
Ps 97:12 **g** thanks at the remembrance
Ps 104:11 They **g** drink to every beast
Ps 104:27 That You may **g** them their
Ps 104:28 What You **g** them they gather
Ps 105: 1 Oh, **g** thanks to the LORD
Ps 105:11 To you I will **g** the land of
Ps 105:39 fire to **g** light in the night
Ps 106: 1 **g** thanks to the LORD, for He
Ps 106:47 To **g** thanks to Your holy name
Ps 107: 1 **g** thanks to the LORD, for He
Ps 107: 8 that men would **g** thanks to
Ps 107:15 that men would **g** thanks to
Ps 107:21 that men would **g** thanks to
Ps 107:31 that men would **g** thanks to
Ps 108: 1 **g** praise, even with my glory
Ps 108:12 **G** us help from trouble, For
Ps 109: 4 But I **g** myself to prayer
Ps 115: 1 us, But to Your name **g** glory
Ps 115:14 May the LORD **g** you increase
Ps 118: 1 **g** thanks to the LORD, for He
Ps 118:29 **g** thanks to the LORD, for He
Ps 119:34 **G** me understanding, and I
Ps 119:62 will rise to **g** thanks to You
Ps 119:73 **G** me understanding, that I
Ps 119:125 **G** me understanding, That I
Ps 119:144 **G** me understanding, and I
Ps 119:169 **G** me understanding according
Ps 122: 4 To **g** thanks to the name of
Ps 132: 4 I will not **g** sleep to my eyes
Ps 136: 1 **g** thanks to the LORD, for He
Ps 136: 2 **g** thanks to the God of gods
Ps 136: 3 **g** thanks to the Lord of lords
Ps 136:26 **g** thanks to the God of heaven
Ps 140:13 shall **g** thanks to Your name
Ps 141: 1 **G** ear to my voice when I cry
Ps 143: 1 **G** ear to my supplications
Ps 145:15 You **g** them their food in due
Prov 1: 4 to **g** prudence to the simple,
Prov 3:28 back, and tomorrow I will **g** it
Prov 4: 1 and **g** attention to know
Prov 4: 2 for I **g** you good doctrine
Prov 4:20 son, **g** attention to my words
Prov 5: 9 lest you **g** your honor to
Prov 6: 4 **G** no sleep to your eyes, nor
Prov 6:31 he may have to **g** up all the
Prov 6:35 though you **g** many gifts
Prov 9: 9 **G** instruction to a wise man,
Prov 23:26 **g** me your heart, and let your
Prov 25:21 is hungry, **g** him bread to eat
Prov 25:21 thirsty, **g** him water to drink
Prov 29:15 The rod and reproof **g** wisdom
Prov 29:17 son, and he will **g** you rest
Prov 29:17 he will **g** delight to your
Prov 30: 8 **g** me neither poverty nor
Prov 30:15 crying, "**G**! **G**!"
Prov 31: 3 Do not **g** your strength to
Prov 31: 6 **G** strong drink to him who is
Prov 31:31 **G** her of the fruit of her
Eccl 2:26 that he may **g** to him who is
Eccl 5: 1 to **g** the sacrifice of fools
Eccl 6: 2 yet God does not **g** him power
Eccl 10: 1 cause it to **g** off a foul odor
Eccl 11: 2 **G** a serving to seven, and also
Song 2:13 tender grapes **g** a good smell
Song 7:12 There I will **g** you my love
Song 7:13 The mandrakes **g** off a
Song 8: 7 If a man would **g** for love all
Is 1: 2 O heavens, and **g** ear, O earth
Is 1:10 **g** ear to the law of our God,
Is 3: 4 I will **g** children to be their
Is 7:14 Himself will **g** you a sign
Is 7:22 the abundance of milk they **g**
Is 8: 9 **G** ear, all you from far
Is 10: 6 My wrath I will **g** him charge
Is 13:10 will not **g** their light
Is 19: 4 the Egyptians I will **g** into
Is 19:11 counselors **g** foolish counsel
Is 28:23 **G** ear and hear my voice,
Is 30:23 Then He will **g** the rain for
Is 32: 9 daughters, **g** ear to my speech
Is 36: 8 **g** a pledge to my master the
Is 36: 8 I will **g** you two thousand
Is 41:27 I will **g** to Jerusalem one who
Is 42: 6 **g** You as a covenant to the

Is 42: 8 glory I will not **g** to another
Is 42:12 Let them **g** glory to the LORD,
Is 42:23 among you will **g** ear to this
Is 43: 4 I will **g** men for you, and
Is 43: 6 say to the north, '**G** them up
Is 43:20 because I **g** waters in the
Is 43:20 to **g** drink to My people, My
Is 43:28 I will **g** Jacob to the curse,
Is 45: 3 I will **g** you the treasures of
Is 48:11 And I will not **g** My glory to
Is 49: 6 I will also **g** You as a light
Is 49: 8 **g** You as a covenant to the
Is 49:20 **g** me a place where I may
Is 51: 4 and **g** ear to Me, O My nation
Is 55:10 that it may **g** seed to the
Is 56: 5 to them I will **g** in My house
Is 56: 5 I will **g** them an everlasting
Is 60:19 shall the moon **g** light to you
Is 61: 3 to **g** them beauty for ashes,
Is 62: 7 and **g** Him no rest till He
Is 62: 8 Surely I will no longer **g**
Is 66: 8 be made to **g** birth in one day
Jer 3:15 And I will **g** you shepherds
Jer 3:19 and **g** you a pleasant land, a
Jer 6:10 **g** warning, that they may hear
Jer 6:10 and they cannot **g** heed
Jer 8:10 Therefore I will **g** their
Jer 9:15 **g** them water of gall to drink
Jer 11: 5 to **g** them a land flowing with
Jer 13:15 Hear and **g** ear
Jer 13:16 **G** glory to the LORD your God
Jer 14:13 but I will **g** you assured
Jer 14:22 Or can the heavens **g** showers
Jer 15:13 your treasures I will **g** as
Jer 16: 7 nor shall men **g** them the cup
Jer 17: 3 I will **g** as plunder your
Jer 17:10 even to **g** every man according
Jer 18:18 let us not **g** heed to any of
Jer 18:19 **G** heed to me, O LORD, and
Jer 19: 7 their corpses I will **g** as
Jer 20: 4 I will **g** all Judah into the
Jer 20: 5 will **g** into the hand of their
Jer 22:25 I will **g** you into the hand of
Jer 24: 7 Then I will **g** them a heart
Jer 24: 8 so will I **g** up Zedekiah the
Jer 25:30 He will **g** a shout, as those
Jer 25:31 He will **g** those who are
Jer 26:24 so that they should not **g** him
Jer 29: 6 **g** your daughters to husbands,
Jer 29:11 to **g** you a future and a hope
Jer 31: 2 when I went to **g** him rest
Jer 31: 7 **g** praise, and say, 'O LORD,
Jer 32: 3 I will **g** this city into the
Jer 32:19 to **g** everyone according to
Jer 32:22 to their fathers to **g** them
Jer 32:28 I will **g** this city into the
Jer 32:39 then I will **g** them one heart
Jer 34: 2 I will **g** this city into the
Jer 34:18 I will **g** the men who have
Jer 34:20 I will **g** them into the hand
Jer 34:21 I will **g** Zedekiah king of
Jer 35: 2 and **g** them wine to drink
Jer 37:21 that they should **g** him daily
Jer 38:15 if I **g** you counsel, you will
Jer 38:16 nor will I **g** you into the
Jer 44:30 I will **g** Pharaoh Hophra king
Jer 45: 5 But I will **g** your life to you
Jer 48: 9 **G** wings to Moab, that she may
Jer 50:34 that He may **g** rest to the
Lam 2:18 **g** yourself no relief
Lam 2:18 **g** your eyes no rest
Lam 3:30 Let him **g** his cheek to the
Lam 3:65 **G** them a veiled heart
Ezek 2: 8 mouth and eat what I **g** you
Ezek 3: 3 with this scroll that I **g** you
Ezek 3:17 and **g** them warning from Me
Ezek 3:18 you **g** him no warning, nor
Ezek 3:20 you did not **g** him warning
Ezek 7:21 I will **g** it as plunder into
Ezek 11: 2 **g** wicked counsel in this city
Ezek 11:17 and I will **g** you the land of
Ezek 11:19 Then I will **g** them one heart,
Ezek 11:19 and **g** them a heart of flesh,
Ezek 15: 6 for fuel, so I will **g** up the
Ezek 16:39 I will also **g** you into their
Ezek 16:61 for I will **g** them to you for
Ezek 17:15 that they might **g** him horses
Ezek 20:28 My hand in an oath to **g** them
Ezek 20:42 an oath to **g** to your fathers
Ezek 21:27 it is, and I will **g** it to Him
Ezek 23:46 them, **g** them up to trouble and
Ezek 25: 7 and **g** you as plunder to the
Ezek 25:10 I will **g** it as a possession
Ezek 29:19 Surely I will **g** the land of
Ezek 32: 7 moon shall not **g** her light
Ezek 33:27 I will **g** to the beasts to be
Ezek 36:26 I will **g** you a new heart and
Ezek 36:26 and **g** you a heart of flesh
Ezek 39: 4 I will **g** you to birds of prey
Ezek 39:11 in that day that I will **g** Gog
Ezek 43:19 You shall **g** a young bull for
Ezek 44:28 You shall **g** them no
Ezek 44:30 also you shall **g** to the
Ezek 45: 8 but they shall **g** the rest of
Ezek 45:13 you shall **g** one-sixth of an
Ezek 45:16 shall **g** this offering for the
Ezek 45:17 part to **g** burnt offerings
Ezek 46: 5 as much as he wants to **g**
Ezek 46: 7 he wants to **g** for the lambs
Ezek 46:11 he wants to **g** for the lambs
Ezek 47:14 oath to **g** it to your fathers
Ezek 47:23 there you shall **g** him his
Dan 1:12 let them **g** us vegetables to
Dan 2: 4 we will **g** the interpretation
Dan 2: 7 we will **g** its interpretation
Dan 2: 9 can **g** me its interpretation
Dan 2:16 asked the king to **g** him time
Dan 5:12 he will **g** the interpretation
Dan 5:15 but they could not **g** the
Dan 5:16 heard of you, that you can **g**
Dan 5:17 **g** your rewards to another
Dan 6: 2 might **g** account to them, so
Dan 9:22 to **g** you skill to understand
Dan 11:17 he shall **g** him the daughter
Dan 11:21 not **g** the honor of royalty
Hos 2: 5 who **g** me my bread and my
Hos 2:15 I will **g** her her vineyards
Hos 5: 1 **G** ear, O house of the king
Hos 9:14 **G** them, O LORD
Hos 9:14 what will You **g**?
Hos 9:14 **G** them a miscarrying womb and
Hos 11: 8 How can I **g** you up, Ephraim
Hos 13:10 **G** me a king and princes'
Joel 1: 2 **g** ear, all you inhabitants of
Joel 2:17 do not **g** Your heritage to
Mic 1:14 Therefore you shall **g**
Mic 5: 3 Therefore He shall **g** them up
Mic 6: 7 Shall I **g** my firstborn for my
Mic 6:14 I will **g** over to the sword
Mic 7:20 You will **g** truth to Jacob and
Zeph 3:20 for I will **g** you fame and
Hag 2: 9 in this place I will **g** peace
Zech 3: 7 I will **g** you places to walk
Zech 8:12 the vine shall **g** its fruit
Zech 8:12 ground shall **g** her increase
Zech 8:12 the heavens shall **g** their dew
Zech 8:16 **g** judgment in your gates for
Zech 10: 1 he will **g** them showers of
Zech 11: 6 I will **g** everyone into his
Zech 11:12 to you, **g** me my wages
Mal 2: 2 to **g** glory to My name," says
Matt 4: 6 He shall **g** His angels charge
Matt 4: 9 All these things I will **g** You
Matt 5:31 let him **g** her a certificate
Matt 5:42 **G** to him who asks you, and
Matt 6:11 **G** us this day our daily bread
Matt 7: 6 Do not **g** what is holy to the
Matt 7: 9 for bread, will **g** him a stone
Matt 7:10 fish, will he **g** him a serpent
Matt 7:11 know how to **g** good gifts to
Matt 7:11 Father who is in heaven **g**
Matt 10: 8 you have received, freely **g**
Matt 11:28 laden, and I will **g** you rest
Matt 12:36 they will **g** account of it in
Matt 14: 7 **g** her whatever she might ask
Matt 14: 8 **G** me John the Baptist's head
Matt 14:16 You **g** them something to eat
Matt 16:19 I will **g** you the keys of the
Matt 16:26 Or what will a man **g** in
Matt 17:27 **g** it to them for Me and you
Matt 19: 7 to **g** a certificate of divorce
Matt 19:21 **g** to the poor, and you will
Matt 20: 4 is right I will **g** you
Matt 20: 8 **g** them their wages, beginning
Matt 20:14 I wish to **g** to this last man
Matt 20:23 on My left is not Mine to **g**
Matt 20:28 to **g** His life a ransom for
Matt 24:29 the moon will not **g** its light
Matt 24:45 to **g** them food in due season
Matt 25: 8 **G** us some of your oil, for
Matt 25:28 and **g** it to him who has ten
Matt 26:37 or thirsty and **g** You drink
Matt 26:15 What are you willing to **g** me
Mark 6:22 want, and I will **g** it to you
Mark 6:23 you ask me, I will **g** you, up
Mark 6:25 I want you to **g** me at once
Mark 6:37 You **g** them something to eat
Mark 6:37 and **g** them something to eat
Mark 8:37 Or what will a man **g** in
Mark 10:21 **g** to the poor, and you will
Mark 10:40 on My left is not Mine to **g**
Mark 10:45 to **g** His life a ransom for
Mark 12: 9 and **g** the vineyard to others
Mark 13:24 the moon will not **g** its light
Mark 14:11 and promised to **g** him money
Luke 1:32 the Lord God will **g** Him the
Luke 1:77 to **g** knowledge of salvation
Luke 1:79 to **g** light to those who sit
Luke 3:11 let him **g** to him who has none
Luke 4: 6 this authority I will **g** You
Luke 4: 6 I **g** it to whomever I wish
Luke 4:10 He shall **g** His angels charge
Luke 6:30 **G** to everyone who asks of you
Luke 6:38 **G**, and it will be given to you
Luke 9:13 You **g** them something to eat
Luke 10: 7 such things as they **g**, for
Luke 10:19 I **g** you the authority to
Luke 11: 3 **G** us day by day our daily
Luke 11: 7 I cannot rise and **g** to you'
Luke 11: 8 **g** to him because he is his
Luke 11: 8 **g** him as many as he needs
Luke 11:11 you, will he **g** him a stone
Luke 11:11 fish, will he **g** him a serpent
Luke 11:13 know how to **g** good gifts to
Luke 11:13 **g** the Holy Spirit to those
Luke 11:41 But rather **g** alms of such
Luke 12:32 pleasure to **g** you the kingdom
Luke 12:33 Sell what you have and **g** alms
Luke 12:42 to **g** them their portion of
Luke 12:51 I came to **g** peace on earth
Luke 14: 9 **G** place to this man,' and
Luke 14:12 When you **g** a dinner or a
Luke 14:13 But when you **g** a feast,
Luke 15:12 **g** me the portion of goods
Luke 16: 2 **G** an account of your
Luke 16:12 who will **g** you what is your
Luke 17:18 to **g** glory to God except this
Luke 18:12 I **g** tithes of all that I
Luke 19: 8 I **g** half of my goods to the
Luke 19:24 **g** it to him who has ten minas
Luke 20:10 that they might **g** him some of
Luke 20:16 and **g** the vineyard to others
Luke 21:15 for I will **g** you a mouth and
Luke 22: 5 and agreed to **g** him money
John 1:22 that we may **g** an answer to
John 3:34 for God does not **g** the Spirit
John 4: 7 said to her, "**G** Me a drink
John 4:10 **G** Me a drink,' you would
John 4:14 shall **g** him will never thirst
John 4:14 **g** him will become in him a
John 4:15 **g** me this water, that I may
John 6:27 the Son of Man will **g** you
John 6:32 Moses did not **g** you the bread
John 6:34 Lord, **g** us this bread always
John 6:51 that I shall **g** is My flesh
John 6:51 which I shall **g** for the life
John 6:52 How can this Man **g** us His
John 7:19 Did not Moses **g** you the law
John 9:24 to him, "**G** God the glory
John 10:28 I **g** them eternal life, and
John 11:22 ask of God, God will **g** You
John 13:26 **g** a piece of bread when I
John 13:29 feast," or that he should **g**
John 13:34 A new commandment I **g** to you
John 14:16 He will **g** you another Helper,
John 14:27 with you, My peace I **g** to you
John 14:27 the world gives do I **g** to you
John 15:16 in My name He may **g** you
John 16:23 in My name He will **g** you
John 17: 2 that He should **g** eternal life
Acts 3: 6 but what I do have I **g** you
Acts 5:31 to **g** repentance to Israel and
Acts 6: 4 but we will **g** ourselves
Acts 7: 5 He promised to **g** it to him
Acts 7:38 the living oracles to **g** to us
Acts 8:19 **G** me this power also, that
Acts 12:23 he did not **g** glory to God
Acts 13:34 I will **g** you the sure
Acts 19:40 we may **g** to account for this
Acts 20:32 **g** you an inheritance among

Acts 20:35 blessed to **g** than to receive
Rom 8:11 from the dead will also **g**
Rom 8:32 also freely **g** us all things
Rom 12:19 but rather **g** place to wrath
Rom 12:20 if he thirsts, **g** him a drink
Rom 14:12 So then each of us shall **g**
Rom 16: 4 to whom not only I **g** thanks
1Co 7: 5 that you may **g** yourselves to
1Co 7:25 yet I **g** judgment as one whom
1Co 7:38 but he who does not **g** her in
1Co 10:30 food over which I **g** thanks
1Co 10:32 **G** no offense, either to the
1Co 13: 3 and though I **g** my body to be
1Co 14:17 For you indeed **g** thanks well
2Co 4: 6 **g** the light of the knowledge
2Co 5:12 you, but **g** you opportunity to
2Co 6: 3 We **g** no offense in anything,
2Co 8:10 And in this I **g** my advice
2Co 9: 7 So let each one **g** as he
Eph 1:16 not cease to **g** thanks for you
Eph 1:17 may **g** to you the spirit of
Eph 4:27 nor **g** place to the devil
Eph 4:28 to **g** him who has need
Eph 5:14 and Christ will **g** you light
Col 1: 3 We **g** thanks to the God and
Col 4: 1 **g** your servants what is just
1Th 1: 2 We **g** thanks to God always for
1Th 5:18 in everything **g** thanks
2Th 1: 7 to **g** you who are troubled
2Th 2:13 But we are bound to **g** thanks
2Th 3:16 **g** you peace always in every
1Ti 1: 4 nor **g** heed to fables and
1Ti 4:13 **g** attention to reading, to
1Ti 4:15 **g** yourself entirely to them,
1Ti 5:14 **g** no opportunity to the
1Ti 6:18 in good works, ready to **g**
2Ti 2: 7 I say, and may the Lord **g** you
2Ti 4: 8 will **g** to me on that Day, and
Heb 2: 1 Therefore we must **g** the more
Heb 2:16 He does not **g** aid to angels
Heb 2:16 but He does **g** aid to the seed
Heb 4:13 Him to whom we must **g** account
Heb 13:17 as those who must **g** account
Jas 2:16 but you do not **g** them the
1Pe 3:15 and always be ready to **g** a
1Pe 4: 5 They will **g** an account to Him
1Jn 5:16 He will **g** him life for those
Rev 2: 7 **g** to eat from the tree of
Rev 2:10 I will **g** you the crown of
Rev 2:17 **g** some of the hidden manna to
Rev 2:17 I will **g** him a white stone,
Rev 2:23 I will **g** to each one of you
Rev 2:26 to him I will **g** power over
Rev 2:28 I will **g** him the morning star
Rev 4: 9 the living creatures **g** glory
Rev 10: 9 him, "**G** me the little book
Rev 11: 3 And I will **g** power to my two
Rev 11:17 We **g** You thanks, O Lord God
Rev 12: 2 labor and in pain to **g** birth
Rev 12: 4 who was ready to **g** birth, to
Rev 13:15 He was granted power to **g**
Rev 14: 7 **g** glory to Him, for the hour
Rev 16: 9 did not repent and **g** Him glory
Rev 16:19 to **g** her the cup of the wine
Rev 17:13 they will **g** their power and
Rev 17:17 to **g** their kingdom to the
Rev 18: 7 same measure **g** her torment
Rev 19: 7 **g** Him glory, for the marriage
Rev 21: 6 I will **g** of the fountain of
Rev 22:12 to **g** to every one according

GIVEN (*see* GIVE)
Gen 1:29 I have **g** you every herb that
Gen 1:30 I have **g** every green herb for
Gen 9: 2 They are **g** into your hand
Gen 9: 3 I have **g** you all things, even
Gen 15: 3 You have **g** me no offspring
Gen 15:18 I have **g** this land, from the
Gen 20:16 I have **g** your brother a
Gen 24:35 He has **g** him flocks and herds,
Gen 24:36 to him he has **g** all that he
Gen 27:37 I have **g** to him as servants
Gen 29:33 therefore **g** me this son also
Gen 30: 6 heard my voice and **g** me a son
Gen 30:18 God has **g** me my hire, because
Gen 30:18 because I have **g** my maid to
Gen 31: 9 your father and **g** them to me
Gen 33: 5 has graciously **g** your servant
Gen 38:14 she was not **g** to him as a
Gen 43:23 **g** you treasure in your sacks
Gen 48: 9 whom God has **g** me in this
Gen 48:22 Moreover I have **g** to you one
Ex 5:16 no straw **g** to your servants
Ex 5:18 for no straw shall be **g** you
Ex 12:36 the LORD had **g** the people
Ex 16:15 the LORD has **g** you to eat
Ex 16:29 LORD has **g** you the Sabbath
Ex 21: 4 his master has **g** him a wife
Lev 6:17 I have **g** it to them as their
Lev 7:34 I have **g** them to Aaron the
Lev 7:36 LORD commanded this to be **g**
Lev 10:14 due, which are **g** from the
Lev 10:17 God has **g** it to you to bear
Lev 17:11 I have **g** it to you upon the
Lev 19:20 redeemed nor **g** her freedom
Lev 20: 3 because he has **g** some of his
Num 3: 9 they are **g** entirely to him
Num 8:16 For they are wholly **g** to Me
Num 8:19 I have **g** the Levites as a
Num 16:14 nor **g** us inheritance of
Num 18: 6 **g** by the LORD, to do the work
Num 18: 8 I Myself have also **g** you
Num 18: 8 I have **g** them as a portion to
Num 18:11 I have **g** them to you, and your
Num 18:12 LORD, I have **g** them to you
Num 18:19 to the LORD, I have **g** to you
Num 18:21 I have **g** the children of Levi
Num 18:24 I have **g** to the Levites as an
Num 18:26 have **g** you from them as your
Num 20:12 the land which I have **g** them
Num 20:24 **g** to the children of Israel
Num 21:29 He has **g** his sons as
Num 26:54 Each shall be **g** its
Num 26:62 there was no inheritance **g** to
Num 27:12 **g** to the children of Israel
Num 32: 5 let this land be **g** to your
Num 32: 7 which the LORD has **g** them
Num 32: 9 which the LORD had **g** them
Num 33:53 for I have **g** you the land to
Deut 1: 3 to all that the LORD had **g**
Deut 2: 5 because I have **g** Mount Seir
Deut 2: 9 because I have **g** Ar to the
Deut 2:19 because I have **g** it to the
Deut 2:24 I have **g** into your hand Sihon
Deut 3:18 The LORD your God has **g** you
Deut 3:19 cities which I have **g** you
Deut 3:20 until the LORD has **g** rest to
Deut 3:20 possession which I have **g** you
Deut 4:19 **g** to all the peoples under
Deut 8:10 good land which He has **g** you
Deut 9:23 the land which I have **g** you
Deut 12:15 your God which He has **g** you
Deut 12:21 which the LORD has **g** you,
Deut 16:17 your God which He has **g** you
Deut 25:19 **g** you rest from your enemies
Deut 26: 9 place and has **g** us this land,
Deut 26:10 which you, O LORD, have **g** me
Deut 26:11 LORD your God has **g** to you
Deut 26:12 have **g** it to the Levite, the
Deut 26:13 and also have **g** them to the
Deut 26:14 nor **g** any of it for the dead
Deut 26:15 the land which You have **g** us
Deut 28:31 shall be **g** to your enemies
Deut 28:32 shall be **g** to another people
Deut 28:52 the LORD your God has **g** you
Deut 28:53 the LORD your God has **g** you
Deut 29: 4 Yet the LORD has not **g** you a
Deut 29:26 and that He had not **g** to them
Josh 1: 3 will tread upon I have **g** you
Josh 1:15 LORD has **g** your brethren rest
Josh 1:15 rest, as He has **g** you, and
Josh 2: 9 the LORD has **g** you the land
Josh 2:14 the LORD has **g** us the land
Josh 6: 2 I have **g** Jericho into your
Josh 6:16 the LORD has **g** you the city
Josh 8: 1 I have **g** into your hand the
Josh 12: 6 **g** it as a possession to the
Josh 13: 8 which Moses had **g** them,
Josh 13: 8 of the LORD had **g** them
Josh 13:14 Levi he had **g** no inheritance
Josh 13:15 Moses had **g** to the tribe of
Josh 13:24 Moses also had **g** an
Josh 13:33 Moses had **g** no inheritance
Josh 14: 3 For Moses had **g** the
Josh 14: 3 **g** no inheritance among them
Josh 15:19 since you have **g** me land in
Josh 17: 1 therefore he was **g** Gilead
Josh 17:14 Why have you **g** us but one lot
Josh 18: 3 God of your fathers has **g** you
Josh 22: 4 has **g** rest to your brethren
Josh 22: 7 had **g** a possession in Bashan
Josh 23: 1 had **g** rest to Israel from all
Josh 23:13 the LORD your God has **g** you
Josh 23:15 the LORD your God has **g** you
Josh 23:16 good land which He has **g** you
Josh 24:13 I have **g** you a land for
Josh 24:33 which was **g** to him in the
Judg 1:15 since you have **g** me land in
Judg 11:35 For I have **g** my word to the
Judg 11:36 if you have **g** your word to
Judg 14:20 wife was **g** to his companion
Judg 15: 6 and **g** her to his companion
Judg 15:18 said, "You have **g** this great
Judg 18:10 For God has **g** it into your
Judg 20:36 The men of Israel had **g**
Judg 21:22 is not as though you have **g**
Ruth 2:12 a full reward be **g** you by the
1Sa 15:28 has **g** it to a neighbor of
1Sa 18:19 should have been **g** to David
1Sa 18:19 that she was **g** to Adriel the
1Sa 22:13 in that you have **g** him bread
1Sa 25:27 let it be **g** to the young men
1Sa 25:44 But Saul had **g** Michal his
1Sa 28:17 **g** it to your neighbor, namely
1Sa 30:23 with what the LORD has **g** us
2Sa 2:27 all the people would have **g**
2Sa 7: 1 the LORD had **g** him rest from
2Sa 9: 9 I have **g** to your master's son
2Sa 12: 8 would have **g** you much more
2Sa 12:14 have **g** great occasion to the
2Sa 17: 7 **g** is not good at this time
2Sa 18:11 I would have **g** you ten
2Sa 19:42 Or has he **g** us any gift
2Sa 22:36 You have also **g** me the shield
2Sa 22:41 You have also **g** me the necks
2Sa 24:23 Araunah has **g** to the king
1Ki 1:48 who has **g** one to sit on my
1Ki 2:21 Abishag the Shunammite be **g**
1Ki 3: 6 You have **g** him a son to sit
1Ki 3:12 see, I have **g** you a wise and
1Ki 3:13 I have also **g** you what you
1Ki 3:18 third day after I had **g** birth
1Ki 5: 4 has **g** me rest on every side
1Ki 5: 7 for He has **g** David a wise son
1Ki 8:36 have **g** to Your people as an
1Ki 8:56 who has **g** rest to His people
1Ki 9: 7 the land which I have **g** them
1Ki 9:12 which Solomon had **g** him, but
1Ki 9:13 are these which you have **g** me
1Ki 9:16 had **g** it as a dowry to his
1Ki 10:13 besides what Solomon had **g**
1Ki 12:13 which the elders had **g** him
1Ki 13: 5 had **g** by the word of the LORD
1Ki 18:26 the bull which was **g** them
1Ki 20:27 **g** provisions, and they went
2Ki 5: 1 LORD had **g** victory to Syria
2Ki 5:17 be **g** two mule-loads of earth
2Ki 18:30 this city shall not be **g** into
2Ki 19:10 Jerusalem shall not be **g** into
2Ki 22:10 the priest has **g** me a book
2Ki 25:30 ration **g** him by the king, a
1Ch 5: 1 his birthright was **g** to the
1Ch 6:66 **g** cities as their territory
1Ch 6:71 **g** Golan in Bashan with its
1Ch 6:77 Merari were **g** Rimmon with its
1Ch 6:78 they were **g** from the tribe of
1Ch 22:18 And has He not **g** you rest on
1Ch 22:18 For He has **g** the inhabitants
1Ch 23:25 has **g** rest to His people,
1Ch 28: 5 my sons (for the LORD has **g**
1Ch 29: 3 I have **g** to the house of my
1Ch 29:14 and of Your own we have **g** You
2Ch 2:12 for He has **g** King David a
2Ch 2:14 plan which may be **g** to him
2Ch 6:27 have **g** to Your people as an
2Ch 7:20 My land which I have **g** them
2Ch 8: 2 which Hiram had **g** to Solomon
2Ch 10: 8 which the elders had **g** him
2Ch 14: 6 the LORD had **g** him rest
2Ch 14: 7 He has **g** us rest on every
2Ch 20:11 You have **g** us to inherit
2Ch 24:10 the chest until all had **g**
2Ch 25: 9 talents which I have **g** to the
2Ch 29: 8 He has **g** them up to trouble,
2Ch 32:29 for God had **g** him very much
2Ch 34:14 Law of the LORD **g** by Moses
2Ch 34:18 the priest has **g** me a book
2Ch 36:23 LORD God of heaven has **g** me
Ezra 1: 2 LORD God of heaven has **g** me
Ezra 4:21 until the command is **g** by me
Ezra 5:14 and they were **g** to one named

Ezra 6: 8 this is to be **g** immediately
Ezra 6: 9 let it be **g** them day by day
Ezra 7: 6 the LORD God of Israel had **g**
Ezra 7:19 **g** to you for the service of
Ezra 9:13 have **g** us such deliverance as
Neh 2: 7 let letters be **g** to me for
Neh 10:29 Law, which was **g** by Moses the
Neh 13: 5 to be **g** to the Levites and
Neh 13:10 Levites had not been **g** them
Esth 2: 3 beauty preparations be **g** them
Esth 2:13 and she was **g** whatever she
Esth 3:11 and the people are **g** to you
Esth 4: 8 which was **g** at Shushan, that
Esth 5: 3 It shall be **g** to you
Esth 7: 3 let my life be **g** me at my
Esth 8: 7 I have **g** Esther the house of
Job 3:20 Why is light **g** to him who is
Job 3:23 Why is light **g** to a man whose
Job 9:24 The earth is **g** into the hand
Job 15:19 to whom alone the land was **g**
Job 22: 7 You have not **g** the weary
Job 37:10 By the breath of God ice is **g**
Job 38:36 Or who has **g** understanding to
Job 39:19 Have you **g** the horse strength
Ps 16: 7 the LORD who has **g** me counsel
Ps 18:35 You have also **g** me the shield
Ps 18:40 You have also **g** me the necks
Ps 21: 2 You have **g** him his heart's
Ps 44:11 You have **g** us up like sheep
Ps 60: 4 You have **g** a banner to those
Ps 61: 5 You have **g** me the heritage of
Ps 71: 3 You have **g** the commandment
Ps 72:15 of Sheba will be **g** to Him
Ps 78:24 **g** them of the bread of heaven
Ps 78:63 were not **g** in marriage
Ps 79: 2 **g** as food for the birds of
Ps 80: 5 And **g** them tears to drink in
Ps 89:19 I have **g** help to one who is
Ps 111: 5 He has **g** food to those who
Ps 112: 9 abroad, He has **g** to the poor
Ps 115:16 But the earth He has **g** to the
Ps 118:18 But He has not **g** me over to
Ps 118:27 LORD, And He has **g** us light
Ps 119:50 For Your word has **g** me life
Ps 119:93 by them You have **g** me life
Ps 120: 3 What shall be **g** to you, Or
Ps 124: 6 Who has not **g** us as prey to
Prov 19:17 will pay back what he has **g**
Prov 23: 2 you are a man **g** to appetite
Prov 24:21 with those **g** to change
Eccl 1:13 God has **g** to the sons of man
Eccl 5:19 man to whom God has **g** riches
Eccl 5:19 **g** him power to eat of it, to
Eccl 6: 2 man to whom God has **g** riches
Eccl 8: 8 deliver those who are **g** to it
Eccl 9: 9 He has **g** you under the sun
Eccl 12:11 nails, **g** by one Shepherd
Is 3:11 of his hands shall be **g** him
Is 8:18 whom the LORD has **g** me
Is 9: 6 is born, unto us a Son is **g**
Is 23:11 the LORD has **g** a commandment
Is 33:16 bread will be **g** him, his
Is 34: 2 He has **g** them over to the
Is 35: 2 of Lebanon shall be **g** to it
Is 36:15 this city will not be **g** into
Is 37:10 Jerusalem will not be **g** into
Is 47: 6 and **g** them into your hand
Is 47: 8 you who are **g** to pleasures,
Is 50: 4 The Lord GOD has **g** Me the
Is 55: 4 Indeed I have **g** him as a
Jer 3: 8 and **g** her a certificate of
Jer 3:18 to the land that I have **g** as
Jer 6:13 everyone is **g** to covetousness
Jer 8:10 everyone is **g** to covetousness
Jer 8:13 and the things I have **g** them
Jer 8:14 **g** us water of gall to drink,
Jer 12: 7 I have **g** the dearly beloved
Jer 13:20 the flock that was **g** to you
Jer 21:10 It shall be **g** into the hand
Jer 25: 5 that the LORD has **g** to you
Jer 27: 5 have **g** it to whom it seemed
Jer 27: 6 now I have **g** all these lands
Jer 27: 6 have also **g** him to serve him
Jer 28:14 I have **g** him the beasts of
Jer 32:22 You have **g** them this land,
Jer 32:24 the city has been **g** into the
Jer 32:25 been **g** into the hand of the
Jer 32:43 it has been **g** into the hand
Jer 35:15 the land which I have **g** you
Jer 38: 3 **g** into the hand of the king
Jer 38:18 be **g** into the hand of the
Jer 39:17 you shall not be **g** into the
Jer 44:20 who had **g** him that answer
Jer 47: 7 has **g** it a charge against
Jer 50:15 she has **g** her hand, her
Jer 52:34 **g** him by the king of Babylon
Lam 1:11 they have **g** their valuables
Lam 2: 7 He has **g** up the walls of her
Lam 5: 6 We have **g** our hand to the
Ezek 11:15 this land has been **g** to us as
Ezek 15: 6 which I have **g** to the fire
Ezek 16:17 My silver, which I had **g** you
Ezek 16:34 but no payment was **g** you,
Ezek 18: 7 but has **g** his bread to the
Ezek 18:16 but has **g** his bread to the
Ezek 20:15 the land which I had **g** them
Ezek 21:11 He has **g** it to be polished,
Ezek 21:11 it is polished to be **g** into
Ezek 23: 8 She has never **g** up her
Ezek 29: 5 I have **g** you as food to the
Ezek 29:20 I have **g** him the land of
Ezek 33:24 the land has been **g** to us as
Ezek 35:12 they are **g** to us to consume
Ezek 37:25 I have **g** to Jacob My servant
Ezek 45:15 one lamb shall be **g** from a
Ezek 47:11 they will be **g** over to salt
Dan 2:23 you have **g** me wisdom and
Dan 2:37 of heaven has **g** you a kingdom
Dan 2:38 He has **g** them into your hand,
Dan 4:16 let him be **g** the heart of an
Dan 5:28 **g** to the Medes and Persians
Dan 7: 4 and a man's heart was **g** to it
Dan 7: 6 and dominion was **g** to it
Dan 7:11 and **g** to the burning flame
Dan 7:14 Then to Him was **g** dominion
Dan 7:25 be **g** into his hand for a time
Dan 7:27 shall be **g** to the people, the
Dan 8:12 an army was **g** over to the
Dan 9: 2 LORD, **g** through Jeremiah the
Dan 11: 6 but she shall be **g** up, with
Dan 11:11 **g** into the hand of his enemy
Hos 2: 9 **g** to cover her nakedness
Hos 2:12 that my lovers have **g** me
Hos 12:10 I have **g** symbols through the
Joel 2:23 for He has **g** you the former
Joel 3: 3 have **g** a boy in exchange for
Amos 9:15 from the land I have **g** them
Mic 5: 3 who is in labor has **g** birth
Nah 1:14 The LORD has **g** a command
Zech 6: 8 the north country have **g** rest
Matt 7: 7 Ask, and it will be **g** to you
Matt 9: 8 who had **g** such power to men
Matt 10:19 For it will be **g** to you in
Matt 12:39 and no sign will be **g** to it
Matt 13:11 has been **g** to you to know the
Matt 13:11 but to them it has not been **g**
Matt 13:12 has, to him more will be **g**
Matt 14: 9 commanded it to be **g** to her
Matt 14:11 **g** to the girl, and she brought
Matt 16: 4 and no sign shall be **g** to it
Matt 19:11 those to whom it has been **g**
Matt 21:43 **g** to a nation bearing the
Matt 22:30 marry nor are **g** in marriage
Matt 25:29 who has, more will be **g**, and
Matt 26: 9 for much and **g** to the poor
Matt 26:48 betrayer had **g** them a sign
Matt 27:58 the body to be **g** to him
Matt 28:18 has been **g** to Me in heaven
Mark 4:11 To you it has been **g** to know
Mark 4:24 you who hear, more will be **g**
Mark 4:25 has, to him more will be **g**
Mark 5:43 should be **g** her to eat
Mark 6: 2 is this which is **g** to Him
Mark 8:12 no sign shall be **g** to this
Mark 12:25 marry nor are **g** in marriage
Mark 12:43 who have **g** to the treasury
Mark 13:11 But whatever is **g** you in that
Mark 14: 5 denarii and **g** to the poor
Mark 14:23 when He had **g** thanks He gave
Mark 14:44 betrayer had **g** them a signal
Luke 2:21 the name **g** by the angel
Luke 6:38 Give, and it will be **g** to you
Luke 8:10 To you it has been **g** to know
Luke 8:10 the rest it is **g** in parables
Luke 8:18 has, to him more will be **g**
Luke 8:55 she be **g** something to eat
Luke 11: 9 ask, and it will be **g** to you
Luke 11:29 and no sign will be **g** to it
Luke 12:48 everyone to whom much is **g**
Luke 17:27 they were **g** in marriage,
Luke 19:15 to whom he had **g** the money
Luke 19:26 to everyone who has will be **g**
Luke 20:34 marry and are **g** in marriage
Luke 20:35 marry nor are **g** in marriage
Luke 22:19 is My body which is **g** for you
John 1:17 the law was **g** through Moses
John 3:27 has been **g** to him from heaven
John 3:35 has **g** all things into His
John 4:10 He would have **g** you living
John 5:27 and has **g** Him authority to
John 5:36 the Father has **g** Me to finish
John 6:11 and when He had **g** thanks He
John 6:23 after the Lord had **g** thanks
John 6:39 that of all He has **g** Me I
John 7:39 the Holy Spirit was not yet **g**
John 10:29 who has **g** them to Me, is
John 11:57 the Pharisees had **g** a command
John 12: 5 denarii and **g** to the poor
John 13: 3 **g** all things into His hands
John 13:15 For I have **g** you an example,
John 16:21 she has **g** birth to the child
John 17: 2 as You have **g** Him authority
John 17: 2 to as many as You have **g** Him
John 17: 4 which You have **g** Me to do
John 17: 6 have **g** Me out of the world
John 17: 7 You have **g** Me are from You
John 17: 8 For I have **g** to them the
John 17: 8 the words which You have **g** Me
John 17: 9 for those whom You have **g** Me
John 17:11 name those whom You have **g**
John 17:14 I have **g** them Your word
John 17:22 You gave Me I have **g** them
John 17:24 My glory which You have **g** Me
John 18:11 cup which My Father has **g** Me
John 19:11 it had been **g** you from above
Acts 1: 2 had **g** commandments to the
Acts 3:16 **g** him this perfect soundness
Acts 4:12 **g** among men by which we must
Acts 5:32 has **g** to those who obey Him
Acts 8:18 hands the Holy Spirit was **g**
Acts 17:16 the city was **g** over to idols
Acts 17:31 He has **g** assurance of this to
Acts 20:13 for so he had **g** orders,
Acts 21:40 when he had **g** him permission
Acts 24:26 money would be **g** him by Paul
Acts 27:20 be saved was finally **g** up
Rom 5: 5 Holy Spirit who was **g** to us
Rom 11: 8 God has **g** them a spirit of
Rom 11:35 Or who has first **g** to Him
Rom 12: 3 through the grace **g** to me
Rom 12: 6 to the grace that is **g** to us
Rom 12:13 the saints, **g** to hospitality
Rom 15:15 of the grace **g** to me by God
1Co 1: 4 was **g** to you by Christ Jesus
1Co 2:12 been freely **g** to us by God
1Co 3:10 of God which was **g** to me, as
1Co 11:15 for her hair is **g** to her for
1Co 11:24 and when He had **g** thanks, He
1Co 12: 7 of the Spirit is **g** to each
1Co 12: 8 for to one is **g** the word of
1Co 12:24 having **g** greater honor to
1Co 16: 1 as I have **g** orders to the
2Co 1:11 that thanks may be **g** by many
2Co 1:22 **g** us the Spirit in our hearts
2Co 5: 5 who also has **g** us the Spirit
2Co 5:18 and has **g** us the ministry of
2Co 9: 9 abroad, He has **g** to the poor
2Co 12: 7 in the flesh was **g** to me, a
2Co 13:10 Lord has **g** me for edification
Gal 2: 9 grace that had been **g** to me
Gal 3:21 **g** which could have **g** life
Gal 3:21 **g** which could have **g** life
Gal 3:22 be **g** to those who believe
Gal 4:15 your own eyes and **g** them to me
Eph 3: 2 God which was **g** to me for you
Eph 3: 7 God **g** to me by the effective
Eph 3: 8 the saints, this grace was **g**
Eph 4: 7 **g** according to the measure of
Eph 4:19 have **g** themselves over to
Eph 5: 2 **g** Himself for us, an offering
Eph 6:19 that utterance may be **g** to me
Phil 2: 9 **g** Him the name which is above
Col 1:25 God which was **g** to me for you
1Th 4: 8 who has also **g** us His Holy
2Th 2:16 **g** us everlasting consolation
1Ti 3: 3 not **g** to wine, not violent,
1Ti 3: 8 not **g** to much wine, not
1Ti 4:14 in you, which was **g** to you by
2Ti 1: 7 For God has not **g** us a spirit
2Ti 1: 9 grace which was **g** to us in

2Ti 3:16 All Scripture is **g** by
Tit 1: 7 not **g** to wine, not violent,
Tit 2: 3 not **g** to much wine, teachers
Heb 2:13 children whom God has **g** Me
Heb 4: 8 For if Joshua had **g** them rest
Jas 1: 5 and it will be **g** to him
2Pe 1: 3 has **g** to us all things that
2Pe 1: 4 by which have been **g** to us
2Pe 3:15 to the wisdom **g** to him, has
1Jn 3:24 the Spirit whom He has **g** us
1Jn 4:13 because He has **g** us of His
1Jn 5:10 that God has **g** of His Son
1Jn 5:11 that God has **g** us eternal
1Jn 5:20 has **g** us an understanding,
Jude 7 having **g** themselves over to
Rev 6: 2 and a crown was **g** to him, and
Rev 6: 4 there was **g** to him a great
Rev 6: 8 power was **g** to them over a
Rev 6:11 robe was **g** to each of them
Rev 8: 2 to them were **g** seven trumpets
Rev 8: 3 he was **g** much incense, that
Rev 9: 1 to him was **g** the key to the
Rev 9: 3 And to them was **g** power, as
Rev 9: 5 they were not **g** authority to
Rev 11: 1 Then I was **g** a reed like a
Rev 11: 2 it has been **g** to the Gentiles
Rev 12:14 But the woman was **g** two wings
Rev 13: 5 he was **g** a mouth speaking
Rev 13: 5 and he was **g** authority to
Rev 13: 7 And authority was **g** him over
Rev 16: 6 and You have **g** them blood to
Rev 16: 8 power was **g** to him to scorch

GIVER (*see* GIVE)
2Co 9: 7 for God loves a cheerful **g**

GIVES (*see* GIVE)
Gen 49:21 he **g** goodly words
Ex 13:11 your fathers, and **g** it to you,
Ex 16: 8 LORD **g** you meat to eat in the
Ex 16:29 therefore He **g** you on the
Ex 21:22 child, so that she **g** birth
Ex 25: 2 From everyone who **g** it
Lev 20: 2 who **g** any of his descendants
Lev 20: 4 man, when he **g** some of his
Lev 27: 9 all such that any man **g** to
Num 5:10 whatever any man **g** the priest
Deut 8:18 for it is He who **g** you power
Deut 12:10 when He **g** you rest from all
Deut 13: 1 he **g** you a sign or a wonder,
Deut 13:12 your God **g** you to dwell in
Deut 16: 5 which the LORD your God **g** you
Deut 16:18 which the LORD your God **g** you
Deut 17: 2 which the LORD your God **g** you
Deut 19: 8 and **g** you the land which He
Deut 20:14 which the LORD your God **g** you
Deut 20:16 God **g** you as an inheritance
Judg 11:24 your god **g** you to possess
Judg 21:18 one who **g** a wife to Benjamin
Job 5:10 He **g** rain on the earth, and
Job 19:16 servant, but he **g** no answer
Job 24:23 He **g** them security, and they
Job 32: 8 Almighty **g** him understanding
Job 33: 4 of the Almighty **g** me life
Job 34:29 When He **g** quietness, who then
Job 35:10 Who **g** songs in the night,
Job 36: 6 wicked, but **g** justice to the
Job 36:31 He **g** food in abundance
Job 38:29 of heaven, who **g** it birth
Job 39: 1 mark when the deer **g** birth
Ps 18:50 deliverance He **g** to His king
Ps 37:21 righteous shows mercy and **g**
Ps 68:35 Israel is He who **g** strength
Ps 119:130 of Your words **g** light
Ps 119:130 It **g** understanding to the
Ps 127: 2 For so He **g** His beloved sleep
Ps 136:25 Who **g** food to all flesh, For
Ps 144:10 The One who **g** salvation to
Ps 146: 7 Who **g** food to the hungry
Ps 146: 7 The LORD **g** freedom to the
Ps 147: 9 He **g** to the beast its food,
Ps 147:16 He **g** snow like wool
Prov 2: 6 For the LORD **g** wisdom
Prov 3:34 but **g** grace to the humble
Prov 17: 4 An evildoer **g** heed to false
Prov 19: 6 a friend to one who **g** gifts
Prov 21:26 day long, but the righteous **g**
Prov 22: 9 for he **g** of his bread to the
Prov 22:16 he who **g** to the rich, will
Prov 24:26 He who **g** a right answer
Prov 26: 8 is he who **g** honor to a fool
Prov 26:10 things **g** the fool his hire
Prov 28:27 He who **g** to the poor will not
Prov 29:13 the LORD **g** light to the eyes
Eccl 2:26 For God **g** wisdom and
Eccl 2:26 but to the sinner He **g** the
Eccl 5:18 of his life which God **g** him
Eccl 7:12 **g** life to those who have it
Eccl 8:15 which God **g** him under the sun
Is 14: 3 **g** you rest from your sorrow
Is 30:20 though the Lord **g** you the
Is 40:29 He **g** power to the weak, and to
Is 42: 5 Who **g** breath to the people on
Jer 5:24 Who **g** rain, both the former
Jer 22:13 **g** him nothing for his work,
Jer 31:35 Who **g** the sun for a light by
Ezek 33:15 **g** back what he has stolen, and
Ezek 46:16 If the prince **g** a gift of
Ezek 46:17 But if he **g** a gift of some of
Dan 2:21 He **g** wisdom to the wise And
Dan 4:17 **g** it to whomever He will, and
Dan 4:25 **g** it to whomever He chooses
Dan 4:32 **g** it to whomever He chooses
Joel 2:11 The LORD **g** voice before His
Amos 6:11 behold, the LORD **g** a command
Hab 2:15 Woe to him who **g** drink to his
Matt 5:15 it **g** light to all who are in
Matt 10:42 whoever **g** one of these little
Mark 9:41 For whoever **g** you a cup of
Luke 11:36 shining of a lamp **g** you light
John 1: 9 **g** light to every man who
John 5:21 **g** life to them, even so the
John 5:21 even so the Son **g** life to
John 6:32 but My Father **g** you the true
John 6:33 heaven and **g** life to the world
John 6:37 Father **g** Me will come to Me
John 6:63 It is the Spirit who **g** life
John 10:11 The good shepherd **g** His life
John 14:27 the world **g** do I give to you
Acts 17:25 since He **g** to all life,
Rom 4:17 who **g** life to the dead and
Rom 12: 8 he who **g**, with liberality
Rom 14: 6 the Lord, for he **g** God thanks
Rom 14: 6 does not eat, and **g** God thanks
1Co 3: 7 but God who **g** the increase
1Co 7:38 So then he who **g** her in
1Co 15:38 But God **g** it a body as He
1Co 15:57 who **g** us the victory through
2Co 3: 6 kills, but the Spirit **g** life
Gal 4:24 which **g** birth to bondage,
1Ti 6:13 God who **g** life to all things
1Ti 6:17 who **g** us richly all things to
Jas 1: 5 who **g** to all liberally and
Jas 1:15 conceived, it **g** birth to sin
Jas 4: 6 But He **g** more grace
Jas 4: 6 but **g** grace to the humble
1Pe 5: 5 but **g** grace to the humble
Rev 22: 5 for the Lord God **g** them light

GIVING (*see* GIVE)
Gen 24:19 had finished **g** him a drink
Gen 38:27 pass, at the time for **g** birth
Gen 38:28 it was, when she was **g** birth
Ex 20:12 the LORD your God is **g** you
Num 13: 2 which I am **g** to the children
Num 15: 2 inhabit, which I am **g** to you
Deut 1:20 the LORD our God is **g** us
Deut 1:25 the LORD our God is **g** us
Deut 1:36 his children I am **g** the land
Deut 2:29 the LORD our God is **g** us
Deut 3:20 is **g** them beyond the Jordan
Deut 4: 1 God of your fathers is **g** you
Deut 4:21 is **g** you as an inheritance
Deut 4:40 God is **g** you for all time
Deut 5:16 the LORD your God is **g** you
Deut 5:31 which I am **g** them to possess
Deut 9: 6 not **g** you this good land to
Deut 10:18 **g** him food and clothing
Deut 11:17 land which the LORD is **g** you
Deut 11:31 the LORD your God is **g** you
Deut 12: 1 fathers is **g** you to possess
Deut 12: 9 the LORD your God is **g** you
Deut 12:10 your God is **g** you to inherit
Deut 15: 4 God is **g** you to possess as an
Deut 15: 7 the LORD your God is **g** you
Deut 16:20 the LORD your God is **g** you
Deut 17:14 the LORD your God is **g** you
Deut 18: 9 the LORD your God is **g** you
Deut 19: 1 the LORD your God is **g** you
Deut 19: 2 your God is **g** you to possess
Deut 19: 3 your God is **g** you to inherit
Deut 19:10 is **g** you as an inheritance
Deut 19:14 your God is **g** you to possess
Deut 21: 1 your God is **g** you to possess
Deut 21:17 wife as the firstborn by **g**
Deut 21:23 is **g** you as an inheritance
Deut 24: 4 is **g** you as an inheritance
Deut 25:15 the LORD your God is **g** you
Deut 25:19 God is **g** you to possess as an
Deut 26: 1 is **g** you as an inheritance
Deut 26: 2 the LORD your God is **g** you
Deut 27: 2 the LORD your God is **g** you
Deut 27: 3 the LORD your God is **g** you
Deut 28: 8 the LORD your God is **g** you
Deut 32:52 into the land which I am **g** to
Josh 1: 2 the land which I am **g** to them
Josh 1:11 your God is **g** you to possess
Josh 1:13 LORD your God is **g** you rest
Josh 1:13 rest and is **g** you this land
Josh 1:15 the LORD your God is **g** them
Judg 9: 9 Should I cease **g** my oil
Ruth 1: 6 His people in **g** them bread
1Ki 5: 9 by **g** food for my household
1Ki 8:32 by **g** him according to his
1Ch 23: 5 said David, "for **g** praise
2Ch 6:23 by **g** him according to his
Ezra 3:11 and **g** thanks to the LORD
Ps 111: 6 In **g** them the heritage of the
Prov 25:14 boasts of **g** is like clouds
Ezek 4:15 I am **g** you cow dung instead
Dan 8:13 the **g** of both the sanctuary
Matt 24:38 **g** in marriage, until the day
Luke 17:16 at His feet, **g** Him thanks
Acts 15: 8 by **g** them the Holy Spirit
Rom 4:20 in faith, **g** glory to God,
Rom 9: 4 the **g** of the law, the service
Rom 12:10 in honor **g** preference to one
1Co 11:17 Now in **g** these instructions I
1Co 14:16 Amen" at your **g** of thanks
Eph 5: 4 but rather **g** of thanks
Eph 5:20 **g** thanks always for all
Eph 6: 9 **g** up threatening, knowing
Phil 4:15 shared with me concerning **g**
Col 1:12 **g** thanks to the Father who
Col 3:17 **g** thanks to God the Father
1Ti 2: 1 **g** of thanks be made for all
1Ti 4: 1 **g** heed to deceiving spirits
Tit 1:14 not **g** heed to Jewish fables
Heb 13:15 lips, **g** thanks to His name
1Pe 3: 7 **g** honor to the wife, as to
2Pe 1: 5 **g** all diligence, add to your

GIZONITE
1Ch 11:34 the sons of Hashem the **G**,

GLAD (*see* GLADLY, GLADNESS)
Ex 4:14 he will be **g** in his heart
Judg 18:20 So the priest's heart was **g**
Judg 19: 3 saw him, he was **g** to meet him
1Sa 11: 9 men of Jabesh, and they were **g**
1Ki 8:66 and **g** of heart for all the
1Ch 16:31 and let the earth be **g**
2Ch 7:10 **g** of heart for the goodness
Esth 5: 9 day joyful and with a **g** heart
Esth 8:15 of Shushan rejoiced and was **g**
Job 3:22 are **g** when they can find the
Job 22:19 The righteous see it and are **g**
Ps 9: 2 I will be **g** and rejoice in You
Ps 14: 7 Jacob rejoice and Israel be **g**
Ps 16: 9 Therefore my heart is **g**, and
Ps 21: 6 **g** with Your presence
Ps 31: 7 I will be **g** and rejoice in
Ps 32:11 Be **g** in the LORD and rejoice,
Ps 34: 2 shall hear of it and be **g**
Ps 35:27 them shout for joy and be **g**
Ps 40:16 You rejoice and be **g** in You
Ps 45: 8 by which they have made You **g**
Ps 46: 4 shall make **g** the city of God
Ps 48:11 the daughters of Judah be **g**
Ps 53: 6 Jacob rejoice and Israel be **g**
Ps 64:10 shall be **g** in the LORD, and
Ps 67: 4 Oh, let the nations be **g** and
Ps 68: 3 But let the righteous be **g**
Ps 69:32 humble shall see this and be **g**
Ps 70: 4 You rejoice and be **g** in You
Ps 90:14 rejoice and be **g** all our days
Ps 90:15 Make us **g** according to the
Ps 92: 4 have made me **g** through Your
Ps 96:11 and let the earth be **g**
Ps 97: 1 the multitude of isles be **g**
Ps 97: 8 Zion hears and is **g**, And the
Ps 104:15 wine that makes **g** the heart
Ps 104:34 I will be **g** in the LORD

Ps 105:38 Egypt was g when they
Ps 107:30 Then they are g because they
Ps 118:24 We will rejoice and be g in it
Ps 119:74 will be g when they see me
Ps 122: 1 I was g when they said to me,
Ps 126: 3 for us, Whereof we are g
Prov 10: 1 A wise son makes a g father
Prov 12:25 but a good word makes it g
Prov 15:20 A wise son makes a father g
Prov 17: 5 he who is g at calamity will
Prov 23:25 father and your mother be g
Prov 24:17 heart be g when he stumbles
Prov 27:11 be wise, and make my heart g
Song 1: 4 We will be g and rejoice
Is 25: 9 we will be g and rejoice in
Is 35: 1 wasteland shall be g for them
Is 52: 7 who brings g tidings of good
Is 65:18 But be g and rejoice forever
Is 66:10 be g with her, all you who
Jer 20:15 Making him very g
Jer 41:13 with him, that they were g
Jer 50:11 Because you were g, because
Lam 1:21 they are g that You have done
Lam 4:21 Rejoice and be g, O daughter
Dan 6:23 was exceedingly g for him
Hos 7: 3 They make a king g with their
Joel 2:21 be g and rejoice, for the LORD
Joel 2:23 Be g then, you children of
Hab 1:15 they rejoice and are g
Zeph 3:14 Be g and rejoice with all your
Zech 10: 7 children shall see it and be g
Matt 5:12 Rejoice and be exceedingly g
Mark 14:11 they heard it, they were g
Luke 1:19 and bring you these g tidings
Luke 8: 1 bringing the g tidings of the
Luke 15:32 we should make merry and be g
Luke 22: 5 And they were g, and agreed to
Luke 23: 8 Jesus, he was exceedingly g
John 8:56 My day, and he saw it and was g
John 11:15 I am g for your sakes that I
John 20:20 were g when they saw the Lord
Acts 2:26 rejoiced, and my tongue was g
Acts 11:23 the grace of God, he was g
Acts 13:32 we declare to you g tidings
Acts 13:48 heard this, they were g and
Rom 10:15 who bring g tidings of good
Rom 16:19 I am g on your behalf
1Co 16:17 I am g about the coming of
2Co 2: 2 me g but the one who is made
2Co 13: 9 For we are g when we are weak
Phil 2:17 service of your faith, I am g
Phil 2:18 the same reason you also be g
1Pe 4:13 you may also be g with
Rev 19: 7 Let us be g and rejoice and

GLADLY (*see* GLAD)
Judg 8:25 We will g give them
Mark 6:20 many things, and heard him g
Mark 12:37 common people heard Him g
Luke 15:16 he would g have filled his
Acts 2:41 Then those who g received his
Acts 21:17 the brethren received us g
2Co 11:19 For you put up with fools g
2Co 12: 9 Therefore most g I will
2Co 12:15 And I will very g spend and be

GLADNESS (*see* GLAD)
Num 10:10 Also in the day of your g
Deut 28:47 g of heart, for the abundance
2Sa 6:12 to the City of David with g
1Ch 16:27 and g are in His place
1Ch 29:22 LORD with great g on that day
2Ch 29:30 So they sang praises with g
2Ch 30:21 Bread seven days with great g
2Ch 30:23 it another seven days with g
Neh 8:17 And there was very great g
Neh 12:27 the dedication with g, both
Esth 8:16 The Jews had light and g, joy
Esth 8:17 came, the Jews had joy and g
Esth 9:17 it a day of feasting and g
Esth 9:18 it a day of feasting and g
Esth 9:19 month of Adar as a day of g
Ps 4: 7 You have put g in my heart
Ps 30:11 and clothed me with g,
Ps 45: 7 You With the oil of g more
Ps 45:15 With g and rejoicing they
Ps 51: 8 Make me to hear joy and g,
Ps 97:11 g for the upright in heart
Ps 100: 2 Serve the LORD with g
Ps 105:43 joy, His chosen ones with g
Ps 106: 5 in the g of Your nation, That
Prov 10:28 of the righteous will be g
Song 3:11 the day of the g of his heart
Is 16:10 G is taken away, and joy from
Is 22:13 But instead, joy and g,
Is 30:29 g of heart as when one goes
Is 35:10 They shall obtain joy and g
Is 51: 3 joy and g will be found in it,
Is 51:11 They shall obtain joy and g
Jer 7:34 of mirth and the voice of g
Jer 16: 9 of mirth and the voice of g
Jer 25:10 of mirth and the voice of g
Jer 31: 7 Sing with g for Jacob, and
Jer 33:11 of joy and the voice of g, the
Jer 48:33 Joy and g are taken from the
Joel 1:16 g from the house of our God
Zeph 3:17 will rejoice over you with g
Zech 8:19 the tenth, shall be joy and g
Mark 4:16 immediately receive it with g
Luke 1:14 And you will have joy and g
Acts 2:46 they ate their food with g
Acts 12:14 because of her g she did not
Acts 14:17 our hearts with food and g
Phil 2:29 in the Lord with all g, and
Heb 1: 9 You with the oil of g more

GLASS
Rev 4: 6 throne there was a sea of g
Rev 15: 2 a sea of g mingled with fire
Rev 15: 2 standing on the sea of g
Rev 21:18 was pure gold, like clear g
Rev 21:21 pure gold, like transparent g

GLAZED
1Ki 14: 4 for his eyes were g by reason

GLEAN (*see* GLEANED, GLEANING)
Lev 19:10 you shall not g your vineyard
Deut 24:21 you shall not g it afterward
Ruth 2: 2 g heads of grain after him in
Ruth 2: 7 And she said, 'Please let me g
Ruth 2: 8 Do not go to g in another
Ruth 2:15 And when she rose up to g,
Ruth 2:15 Let her g even among the
Ruth 2:16 leave it that she may g, and
Ruth 2:23 to g until the end of barley
Job 24: 6 and g in the vineyard of the
Jer 6: 9 They shall thoroughly g as a
Mic 7: 1 those who g vintage grapes

GLEANED (*see* GLEAN)
Ruth 2: 3 and g in the field after the
Ruth 2:17 So she g in the field until
Ruth 2:17 and beat out what she had g
Ruth 2:18 saw what she had g
Ruth 2:19 Where have you g today

GLEANING (*see* GLEAN, GLEANINGS)
Lev 23:22 any g from your harvest
Judg 8: 2 Is not the g of the grapes of
Is 17: 6 Yet g grapes will be left in
Is 24:13 like the g of grapes when the
Jer 49: 9 they not leave some g grapes

GLEANINGS (*see* GLEANING)
Lev 19: 9 gather the g of your harvest
Obad 5 they not have left some g

GLISTENING
1Ch 29: 2 g stones of various colors,
Luke 9:29 His robe became white and g

GLITTERING
Deut 32:41 If I whet My g sword, and My
Job 20:25 the g point comes out of his
Job 39:23 him, the g spear and javelin
Nah 3: 3 with bright sword and g spear
Hab 3:11 the shining of Your g spear

GLOOM (*see* GLOOMINESS)
Is 8:22 and darkness, g of anguish
Is 9: 1 Nevertheless the g will not
Jas 4: 9 to mourning and your joy to g
2Pe 2:17 to whom the g of darkness is

GLOOMINESS (*see* GLOOM)
Joel 2: 2 a day of darkness and g, a day
Zeph 1:15 a day of darkness and g, a

GLORIES (*see* GLORY)
Jer 9:24 let him who g glory in this
1Co 1:31 He who g, let him glory in
2Co 10:17 He who g, let him glory in
1Pe 1:11 and the g that would follow

GLORIFIED (*see* GLORIFY)
Lev 10: 3 all the people I must be g
Is 26:15 You are g
Is 44:23 Jacob, and g Himself in Israel
Is 49: 3 O Israel, in whom I will be g
Is 55: 5 For He has g you
Is 60: 9 Israel, because He has g you
Is 60:21 of My hands, that I may be g
Is 61: 3 of the LORD, that He may be g
Is 66: 5 said, 'Let the LORD be g
Ezek 28:22 I will be g in your midst
Ezek 39:13 for it on the day that I am g
Dan 5:23 all your ways, you have not g
Hag 1: 8 take pleasure in it and be g
Matt 9: 8 and g God who had given such
Matt 15:31 and they g the God of Israel
Mark 2:12 were amazed and g God, saying,
Luke 4:15 synagogues, being g by all
Luke 5:26 all amazed, and they g God
Luke 7:16 came upon all, and they g God
Luke 13:13 was made straight, and g God
Luke 17:15 and with a loud voice g God
Luke 23:47 happened, he g God, saying,
John 7:39 because Jesus was not yet g
John 11: 4 of God may be g through it
John 12:16 but when Jesus was g, then
John 12:23 the Son of Man should be g
John 12:28 I have both g it and will
John 13:31 Now the Son of Man is g
John 13:31 and God is g in Him
John 13:32 If God is g in Him, God will
John 14:13 Father may be g in the Son
John 15: 8 By this My Father is g, that
John 17: 4 I have g You on the earth
John 17:10 are Mine, and I am g in them
Acts 3:13 g His Servant Jesus, whom you
Acts 4:21 since they all g God for what
Acts 11:18 and they g God, saying, "Then
Acts 13:48 and g the word of the Lord
Acts 21:20 heard it, they g the Lord
Rom 8:17 we may also be g together
Rom 8:30 He justified, these He also g
Gal 1:24 And they g God in me
2Th 1:10 to be g in His saints and to
2Th 1:12 Jesus Christ may be g in you
2Th 3: 1 may have free course and be g
1Pe 4:11 may be g through Jesus Christ
1Pe 4:14 but on your part He is g
Rev 18: 7 measure that she g herself

GLORIFIES (*see* GLORIFY)
Ps 50:23 Whoever offers praise g Me

GLORIFY (*see* GLORIFIED, GLORIFIES, GLORIFYING, GLORY)
Ps 22:23 g Him, And fear Him, all you
Ps 50:15 you, and you shall g Me
Ps 86: 9 O Lord, And shall g Your name
Ps 86:12 heart, And I will g Your name
Is 24:15 Therefore g the LORD in the
Is 25: 3 the strong people will g You
Is 60: 7 and I will g the house of My
Jer 30:19 I will also g them, and they
Matt 5:16 and g your Father in heaven
John 12:28 Father, g Your name
John 12:28 it and will g it again
John 13:32 Him, God will also g Him in
John 13:32 and g Him immediately
John 16:14 He will g Me, for He will
John 17: 1 G Your Son, that Your Son
John 17: 1 that Your Son also may g You
John 17: 5 g Me together with Yourself,
John 21:19 by what death he would g God
Rom 1:21 they did not g Him as God
Rom 15: 6 mind and one mouth g the God
Rom 15: 9 might g God for His mercy
1Co 6:20 therefore g God in your body
2Co 9:13 they g God for the obedience
Heb 5: 5 not g Himself to become High
1Pe 2:12 observe, g God in the day of
1Pe 4:16 but let him g God in this
Rev 15: 4 You, O Lord, and g Your name

GLORIFYING (*see* GLORIFY)
Luke 2:20 the shepherds returned, g
Luke 5:25 to his own house, g God
Luke 18:43 sight, and followed Him, g God

GLORIOUS (*see* GLORIOUSLY, GLORY)
Ex 15: 6 O LORD, has become g in power
Ex 15:11 g in holiness, fearful in
Deut 28:58 that you may fear this g

2Sa 6:20 How **g** was the king of Israel
1Ch 22: 5 **g** throughout all countries
1Ch 29:13 You and praise Your **g** name
Neh 9: 5 Blessed be Your **g** name, which
Esth 1: 4 the riches of his **g** kingdom
Ps 45:13 is all **g** within the palace
Ps 66: 2 Make His praise **g**
Ps 72:19 blessed be His **g** name forever
Ps 76: 4 You are more **g** and excellent
Ps 87: 3 **G** things are spoken of you, O
Ps 111: 3 His work is honorable and **g**
Ps 145: 5 I will meditate on the **g**
Ps 145:12 the **g** majesty of His kingdom
Is 4: 2 LORD shall be beautiful and **g**
Is 11:10 His resting place shall be **g**
Is 22:18 there your **g** chariots shall
Is 22:23 he will become a **g** throne to
Is 28: 1 whose **g** beauty is a fading
Is 28: 4 and the **g** beauty is a fading
Is 30:30 cause His **g** voice to be heard
Is 49: 5 to Him (for I shall be **g** in
Is 60:13 make the place of My feet **g**
Is 63: 1 One who is **g** in His apparel
Is 63:12 hand of Moses, with His **g** arm
Is 63:14 to make Yourself a **g** name
Is 63:15 Your habitation, holy and **g**
Jer 17:12 A **g** high throne from the
Ezek 27:25 very **g** in the midst of the
Dan 8: 9 east, and toward the **G** Land
Dan 11:16 He shall stand in the **G** Land
Dan 11:20 taxes on the **g** kingdom
Dan 11:41 shall also enter the **G** Land
Dan 11:45 seas and the **g** holy mountain
Luke 13:17 rejoiced for all the **g** things
Rom 8:21 of corruption into the **g**
2Co 3: 7 and engraved on stones, was **g**
2Co 3: 8 of the Spirit not be more **g**
2Co 3:10 made **g** had no glory in this
2Co 3:11 if what is passing away was **g**
2Co 3:11 what remains is much more **g**
Eph 5:27 it to Himself a **g** church, not
Phil 3:21 be conformed to His **g** body
Col 1:11 according to His **g** power
1Ti 1:11 according to the **g** gospel of
Tit 2:13 **g** appearing of our great God

GLORIOUSLY (*see* GLORIOUS)
Ex 15: 1 LORD, for He has triumphed **g**
Ex 15:21 LORD, for He has triumphed **g**
Is 24:23 and before His elders, **g**

GLORY (*see* GLORIES, GLORIFY, GLORIOUS, GLORYING)
Gen 45:13 father of all my **g** in Egypt
Ex 16: 7 shall see the **g** of the LORD
Ex 16:10 the **g** of the LORD appeared in
Ex 24:16 Now the **g** of the LORD rested
Ex 24:17 The sight of the **g** of the
Ex 28: 2 for Aaron your brother, for **g**
Ex 28:40 make hats for them, for **g**
Ex 29:43 shall be sanctified by My **g**
Ex 33:18 Please, show me Your **g**
Ex 33:22 while My **g** passes by, that I
Ex 40:34 the **g** of the LORD filled the
Ex 40:35 the **g** of the LORD filled the
Lev 9: 6 the **g** of the LORD will appear
Lev 9:23 Then the **g** of the LORD
Num 14:10 Now the **g** of the LORD
Num 14:21 filled with the **g** of the LORD
Num 14:22 these men who have seen My **g**
Num 16:19 Then the **g** of the LORD
Num 16:42 the **g** of the LORD appeared
Num 20: 6 the **g** of the LORD appeared to
Deut 5:24 our God has shown us His **g**
Deut 33:17 His **g** is like a firstborn
Josh 7:19 give **g** to the LORD God of
Judg 4: 9 there will be no **g** for you in
Judg 7: 2 lest Israel claim **g** for
1Sa 2: 8 them inherit the throne of **g**
1Sa 4:21 The **g** has departed from
1Sa 4:22 The **g** has departed from
1Sa 6: 5 you shall give **g** to the God
1Ki 8:11 for the **g** of the LORD filled
2Ki 14:10 **G** in your success, and stay at
1Ch 16:10 **G** in His holy name
1Ch 16:24 Declare His **g** among the
1Ch 16:28 peoples, give to the LORD **g**
1Ch 16:29 the LORD the **g** due His name
1Ch 29:11 greatness, the power and the **g**
2Ch 5:14 for the **g** of the LORD filled
2Ch 7: 1 the **g** of the LORD filled the
2Ch 7: 2 because the **g** of the LORD had
2Ch 7: 3 and the **g** of the LORD on the
Job 19: 9 He has stripped me of my **g**
Job 29:20 My **g** is fresh within me, and
Job 40:10 and array yourself with **g**
Ps 3: 3 are a shield for me, My **g**
Ps 4: 2 Will you turn my **g** to shame
Ps 8: 1 You who set Your **g** above the
Ps 8: 5 You have crowned him with **g**
Ps 16: 9 is glad, and my **g** rejoices
Ps 19: 1 heavens declare the **g** of God
Ps 21: 5 His **g** is great in Your
Ps 24: 7 the King of **g** shall come in
Ps 24: 8 Who is this King of **g**
Ps 24: 9 the King of **g** shall come in
Ps 24:10 Who is this King of **g**
Ps 24:10 of hosts, He is the King of **g**
Ps 26: 8 the place where Your **g** dwells
Ps 29: 1 ones, Give unto the LORD **g**
Ps 29: 2 LORD the **g** due to His name
Ps 29: 3 The God of **g** thunders
Ps 29: 9 temple everyone says, "**G**!"
Ps 30:12 To the end that my **g** may sing
Ps 45: 3 O Mighty One, With Your **g**
Ps 49:16 When the **g** of his house is
Ps 49:17 His **g** shall not descend after
Ps 57: 5 Let Your **g** be above all the
Ps 57: 8 Awake, my **g**!
Ps 57:11 Let Your **g** be above all the
Ps 62: 7 God is my salvation and my **g**
Ps 63: 2 To see Your power and Your **g**
Ps 63:11 who swears by Him shall **g**
Ps 64:10 the upright in heart shall **g**
Ps 71: 8 And with Your **g** all the day
Ps 72:19 earth be filled with His **g**
Ps 73:24 And afterward receive me to **g**
Ps 78:61 His **g** into the enemy's hand
Ps 79: 9 For the **g** of Your name
Ps 84:11 The LORD will give grace and **g**
Ps 85: 9 That **g** may dwell in our land
Ps 89:17 For You are the **g** of their
Ps 89:44 You have made his **g** cease
Ps 90:16 And Your **g** to their children
Ps 96: 3 Declare His **g** among the
Ps 96: 7 peoples, Give to the LORD **g**
Ps 96: 8 the LORD the **g** due His name
Ps 97: 6 And all the peoples see His **g**
Ps 102:15 the kings of the earth Your **g**
Ps 102:16 He shall appear in His **g**
Ps 104:31 May the **g** of the LORD endure
Ps 105: 3 **G** in His holy name
Ps 106: 5 That I may **g** with Your
Ps 106:20 **g** Into the image of an ox
Ps 108: 1 give praise, even with my **g**
Ps 108: 5 Your **g** above all the earth
Ps 113: 4 And His **g** above the heavens
Ps 115: 1 us, But to Your name give **g**
Ps 138: 5 great is the **g** of the LORD
Ps 145:11 of the **g** of Your kingdom, And
Ps 148:13 His **g** is above the earth and
Ps 149: 5 Let the saints be joyful in **g**
Prov 3:35 The wise shall inherit **g**, but
Prov 4: 9 a crown of **g** she will deliver
Prov 16:31 head is a crown of **g**, if it
Prov 17: 6 the **g** of children is their
Prov 19:11 it is to his **g** to overlook a
Prov 20:29 The **g** of young men is their
Prov 25: 2 It is the **g** of God to conceal
Prov 25: 2 but the **g** of kings is to
Prov 25:27 seek one's own **g** is not **g**
Prov 28:12 rejoice, there is great **g**
Is 2:10 LORD and the **g** of His majesty
Is 2:19 the **g** of His majesty, when He
Is 2:21 the **g** of His majesty, when He
Is 3: 8 to provoke the eyes of His **g**
Is 4: 5 For over all the **g** there will
Is 5:14 their **g** and their multitude and
Is 6: 3 whole earth is full of His **g**
Is 8: 7 king of Assyria and all his **g**
Is 10: 3 where will you leave your **g**
Is 10:12 the **g** of his haughty looks
Is 10:16 under his **g** he will kindle a
Is 10:18 consume the **g** of his forest
Is 13:19 the **g** of kingdoms, the beauty
Is 14:18 all of them, sleep in **g**,
Is 16:14 man, the **g** of Moab will be
Is 17: 3 they will be as the **g** of the
Is 17: 4 that the **g** of Jacob will wane
Is 20: 5 expectation and Egypt their **g**
Is 21:16 all the **g** of Kedar will fail
Is 22:24 the **g** of his father's house
Is 23: 9 dishonor the pride of all **g**
Is 24:16 **G** to the righteous
Is 28: 5 will be for a crown of **g** and a
Is 35: 2 The **g** of Lebanon shall be
Is 35: 2 shall see the **g** of the LORD
Is 40: 5 the **g** of the LORD shall be
Is 41:16 **g** in the Holy One of Israel
Is 42: 8 and My **g** I will not give to
Is 42:12 Let them give **g** to the LORD
Is 43: 7 whom I have created for My **g**
Is 45:25 be justified, and shall **g**
Is 46:13 in Zion, for Israel My **g**
Is 48:11 will not give My **g** to another
Is 58: 8 the **g** of the LORD shall be
Is 59:19 His **g** from the rising of the
Is 60: 1 the **g** of the LORD is risen
Is 60: 2 His **g** will be seen upon you
Is 60: 7 glorify the house of My **g**
Is 60:13 The **g** of Lebanon shall come
Is 60:19 light, and your God your **g**
Is 61: 6 in their **g** you shall boast
Is 62: 2 and all kings your **g**
Is 62: 3 of **g** in the hand of the LORD
Is 66:11 with the abundance of her **g**
Is 66:12 the **g** of the Gentiles like a
Is 66:18 they shall come and see My **g**
Is 66:19 heard My fame nor seen My **g**
Is 66:19 My **g** among the Gentiles
Jer 2:11 **G** for what does not profit
Jer 4: 2 Him, and in Him they shall **g**
Jer 9:23 the wise man **g** in his wisdom
Jer 9:23 the mighty man **g** in his might
Jer 9:23 the rich man **g** in his riches
Jer 9:24 let him who glories **g** in this
Jer 13:11 renown, for praise, and for **g**
Jer 13:16 Give **g** to the LORD your God
Jer 13:18 collapse, the crown of your **g**
Jer 14:21 disgrace the throne of Your **g**
Jer 22:18 or 'Alas, his **g**!'
Jer 48:18 Dibon, come down from your **g**
Jer 49: 4 Why do you **g** in the valleys,
Ezek 1:28 likeness of the **g** of the LORD
Ezek 3:12 Blessed is the **g** of the LORD
Ezek 3:23 the **g** of the LORD stood there
Ezek 3:23 like the **g** which I saw by the
Ezek 8: 4 the **g** of the God of Israel
Ezek 9: 3 Now the **g** of the God of
Ezek 10: 4 Then the **g** of the LORD went
Ezek 10: 4 brightness of the LORD's **g**
Ezek 10:18 Then the **g** of the LORD
Ezek 10:19 the **g** of the God of Israel
Ezek 11:22 the **g** of the God of Israel
Ezek 11:23 the **g** of the LORD went up
Ezek 20: 6 and honey, the **g** of all lands
Ezek 20:15 and honey, the **g** of all lands,
Ezek 24:25 their joy and their **g**, the
Ezek 25: 9 the **g** of the country, Beth
Ezek 26:20 I shall establish **g** in the
Ezek 31:18 will you then be likened in **g**
Ezek 39:21 I will set My **g** among the
Ezek 43: 2 the **g** of the God of Israel
Ezek 43: 2 and the earth shone with His **g**
Ezek 43: 4 the **g** of the LORD came into
Ezek 43: 5 the **g** of the LORD filled the
Ezek 44: 4 the **g** of the LORD filled the
Dan 2:37 power, strength, and **g**
Dan 4:36 for the **g** of my kingdom, my
Dan 5:18 a kingdom and majesty, **g** and
Dan 5:20 and they took his **g** from him
Dan 7:14 Him was given dominion and **g**
Dan 11:39 acknowledge, and advance its **g**
Hos 4: 7 change their **g** into shame
Hos 9:11 their **g** shall fly away like a
Hos 10: 5 because its **g** has departed
Mic 1:15 the **g** of Israel shall come to
Mic 2: 9 have taken away My **g** forever
Hab 2:14 of the **g** of the LORD, as the
Hab 2:16 with shame instead of **g**
Hab 2:16 utter shame will be on your **g**
Hab 3: 3 Selah His **g** covered the
Hag 2: 3 this temple in its former **g**
Hag 2: 7 will fill this temple with **g**
Hag 2: 9 The **g** of this latter temple
Zech 2: 5 I will be the **g** in her midst
Zech 2: 8 He sent Me after **g**, to the
Zech 6:13 He shall bear the **g**, and shall
Zech 11: 3 for their **g** is in ruins
Zech 12: 7 so that the **g** of the house of
Zech 12: 7 the **g** of the inhabitants of

Mal 2: 2 to give **g** to My name," says
Matt 4: 8 of the world and their **g**
Matt 6: 2 that they may have **g** from men
Matt 6:13 and the power and the **g** forever
Matt 6:29 even Solomon in all his **g** was
Matt 16:27 the **g** of His Father with His
Matt 19:28 sits on the throne of His **g**
Matt 24:30 heaven with power and great **g**
Matt 25:31 the Son of Man comes in His **g**
Matt 25:31 sit on the throne of His **g**
Mark 8:38 when He comes in the **g** of His
Mark 10:37 other on Your left, in Your **g**
Mark 13:26 clouds with great power and **g**
Luke 2: 9 and the **g** of the Lord shone
Luke 2:14 **G** to God in the highest, and
Luke 2:32 the **g** of Your people Israel
Luke 4: 6 I will give You, and their **g**
Luke 9:26 when He comes in His own **g**
Luke 9:31 who appeared in **g** and spoke of
Luke 9:32 fully awake, they saw His **g**
Luke 12:27 even Solomon in all his **g** was
Luke 14:10 Then you will have **g** in the
Luke 17:18 to give **g** to God except this
Luke 19:38 in heaven and **g** in the highest
Luke 21:27 a cloud with power and great **g**
Luke 24:26 things and to enter into His **g**
John 1:14 among us, and we beheld His **g**
John 1:14 the **g** as of the only begotten
John 2:11 Galilee, and manifested His **g**
John 7:18 from himself seeks his own **g**
John 7:18 but He who seeks the **g** of the
John 8:50 And I do not seek My own **g**
John 9:24 Give God the **g**
John 11: 4 death, but for the **g** of God
John 11:40 you would see the **g** of God
John 12:41 Isaiah said when he saw His **g**
John 17: 5 with the **g** which I had with
John 17:22 the **g** which You gave Me I
John 17:24 My **g** which You have given Me
Acts 7: 2 The God of **g** appeared to our
Acts 7:55 heaven and saw the **g** of God
Acts 12:23 he did not give **g** to God
Acts 22:11 see for the **g** of that light
Rom 1:23 and changed the **g** of the
Rom 2: 7 in doing good seek for **g**,
Rom 2:10 but **g**, honor, and peace to
Rom 3: 7 through my lie to His **g**, why
Rom 3:23 and fall short of the **g** of God
Rom 4:20 in faith, giving **g** to God
Rom 5: 2 in hope of the **g** of God
Rom 5: 3 but we also **g** in tribulations
Rom 6: 4 dead by the **g** of the Father
Rom 8:18 to be compared with the **g**
Rom 9: 4 pertain the adoption, the **g**
Rom 9:23 His **g** on the vessels of mercy
Rom 9:23 had prepared beforehand for **g**
Rom 11:36 things, to whom be **g** forever
Rom 15: 7 received us, to the **g** of God
Rom 15:17 to **g** in Christ Jesus in the
Rom 16:27 be **g** through Jesus Christ
1Co 1:29 should **g** in His presence
1Co 1:31 let him **g** in the LORD
1Co 2: 7 before the ages for our **g**
1Co 2: 8 have crucified the Lord of **g**
1Co 3:21 Therefore let no one **g** in men
1Co 4: 7 why do you **g** as if you had
1Co 10:31 do, do all to the **g** of God
1Co 11: 7 he is the image and **g** of God
1Co 11: 7 but woman is the **g** of man
1Co 11:15 long hair, it is a **g** to her
1Co 15:40 but the **g** of the celestial is
1Co 15:40 the **g** of the terrestrial is
1Co 15:41 There is one **g** of the sun
1Co 15:41 another **g** of the moon, and
1Co 15:41 and another **g** of the stars
1Co 15:41 from another star in **g**
1Co 15:43 dishonor, it is raised in **g**
2Co 1:20 to the **g** of God through us
2Co 3: 7 of the **g** of his countenance
2Co 3: 7 which **g** was passing away,
2Co 3: 9 of condemnation had **g**, the
2Co 3: 9 exceeds much more in **g**
2Co 3:10 had no **g** in this respect,
2Co 3:10 because of the **g** that excels
2Co 3:18 in a mirror the **g** of the Lord
2Co 3:18 same image from **g** to **g**
2Co 4: 4 the gospel of the **g** of Christ
2Co 4: 6 of the knowledge of the **g** of
2Co 4:15 to abound to the **g** of God
2Co 4:17 and eternal weight of **g**,
2Co 5:12 to **g** on our behalf, that you
2Co 5:12 those who **g** in appearance
2Co 8:19 to the **g** of the Lord Himself
2Co 8:23 the churches, the **g** of Christ
2Co 10:17 let him **g** in the LORD
Gal 1: 5 to whom be **g** forever and ever
Gal 6:13 that they may **g** in your flesh
Gal 6:14 God forbid that I should **g**
Eph 1: 6 praise of the **g** of His grace
Eph 1:12 be to the praise of His **g**
Eph 1:14 to the praise of His **g**
Eph 1:17 Jesus Christ, the Father of **g**
Eph 1:18 **g** of His inheritance in the
Eph 3:13 for you, which is your **g**
Eph 3:16 to the riches of His **g**, to be
Eph 3:21 to Him be **g** in the church by
Phil 1:11 are by Jesus Christ, to the **g**
Phil 2:11 to the **g** of God the Father
Phil 3:19 whose **g** is in their shame
Phil 4:19 riches in **g** by Christ Jesus
Phil 4:20 God and Father be **g** forever
Col 1:27 **g** of this mystery among the
Col 1:27 Christ in you, the hope of **g**
Col 3: 4 will appear with Him in **g**
1Th 2: 6 Nor did we seek **g** from men
1Th 2:12 you into His own kingdom and **g**
1Th 2:20 For you are our **g** and joy
2Th 1: 9 and from the **g** of His power,
2Th 2:14 **g** of our Lord Jesus Christ
1Ti 1:17 be honor and **g** forever and ever
1Ti 3:16 the world, received up in **g**
2Ti 2:10 Christ Jesus with eternal **g**
2Ti 4:18 To Him be **g** forever and ever
Heb 1: 3 being the brightness of His **g**
Heb 2: 7 You crowned him with **g** and
Heb 2: 9 of death crowned with **g** and
Heb 2:10 in bringing many sons to **g**
Heb 3: 3 worthy of more **g** than Moses
Heb 9: 5 of **g** overshadowing the mercy
Heb 13:21 Christ, to whom be **g** forever
Jas 1: 9 brother **g** in his exaltation
Jas 2: 1 Jesus Christ, the Lord of **g**
1Pe 1: 7 **g** at the revelation of Jesus
1Pe 1: 8 inexpressible and full of **g**
1Pe 1:21 from the dead and gave Him **g**
1Pe 1:24 and all the **g** of man as the
1Pe 4:11 Christ, to whom belong the **g**
1Pe 4:13 that when His **g** is revealed
1Pe 4:14 are you, for the Spirit of **g**
1Pe 5: 1 the **g** that will be revealed
1Pe 5: 4 of **g** that does not fade away
1Pe 5:10 His eternal **g** by Christ Jesus
1Pe 5:11 To Him be the **g** and the
2Pe 1: 3 of Him who called us by **g**
2Pe 1:17 **g** when such a voice came to
2Pe 1:17 to Him from the Excellent **G**
2Pe 3:18 To Him be the **g** both now and
Jude 24 of His **g** with exceeding joy
Jude 25 who alone is wise, be **g** and
Rev 1: 6 God and Father, to Him be **g**
Rev 4: 9 the living creatures give **g**
Rev 4:11 worthy, O Lord, to receive **g**
Rev 5:12 and strength and honor and **g**
Rev 5:13 Blessing and honor and **g** and
Rev 7:12 Blessing and **g** and wisdom,
Rev 11:13 gave **g** to the God of heaven
Rev 14: 7 give **g** to Him, for the hour
Rev 15: 8 with smoke from the **g** of God
Rev 16: 9 did not repent and give Him **g**
Rev 18: 1 was illuminated with his **g**
Rev 19: 1 Salvation and **g** and honor and
Rev 19: 7 glad and rejoice and give Him **g**
Rev 21:11 having the **g** of God
Rev 21:23 for the **g** of God illuminated
Rev 21:24 of the earth bring their **g**
Rev 21:26 And they shall bring the **g**

GLORYING (*see* GLORY)
1Co 5: 6 Your **g** is not good

GLUTTON (*see* GLUTTONOUS, GLUTTONS)
Deut 21:20 he is a **g** and a drunkard
Prov 23:21 the **g** will come to poverty,
Luke 7:34 and you say, 'Look, a **g** and a

GLUTTONOUS (*see* GLUTTON)
Prov 23:20 or with **g** eaters of meat
Matt 11:19 a **g** man and a winebibber, a

GLUTTONS (*see* GLUTTON)
Prov 28: 7 of **g** shames his father
Tit 1:12 liars, evil beasts, lazy **g**

GNASH (*see* GNASHED, GNASHES, GNASHING)
Ps 112:10 He will **g** his teeth and melt
Lam 2:16 they hiss and **g** their teeth

GNASHED (*see* GNASH)
Ps 35:16 They **g** at me with their teeth
Acts 7:54 and they **g** at him with their

GNASHES (*see* GNASH)
Job 16: 9 He **g** at me with His teeth
Ps 37:12 And **g** at him with his teeth
Mark 9:18 **g** his teeth, and becomes rigid

GNASHING (*see* GNASH)
Matt 8:12 will be weeping and **g** of teeth
Matt 13:42 will be wailing and **g** of teeth
Matt 13:50 will be wailing and **g** of teeth
Matt 22:13 will be weeping and **g** of teeth
Matt 24:51 be weeping and **g** of teeth
Matt 25:30 will be weeping and **g** of teeth
Luke 13:28 and **g** of teeth, when you see

GNAT
Matt 23:24 guides, who strain out a **g**

GNAWED (*see* GNAWING)
Rev 16:10 they **g** their tongues because

GNAWING (*see* GNAWED)
Job 30:17 and my **g** pains take no rest

GO (*see* PREFACE)

GOAD (*see* GOADS)
Judg 3:31 the Philistines with an ox **g**

GOADS (*see* GOAD)
1Sa 13:21 and to set the points of the **g**
Eccl 12:11 words of the wise are like **g**
Acts 9: 5 for you to kick against the **g**
Acts 26:14 for you to kick against the **g**

GOAL
Phil 3:14 I press toward the **g** for the

GOAT (*see* GOATHERDS, GOATS, GOATSKINS)
Gen 15: 9 a three-year-old female **g**
Gen 38:17 you a young **g** from the flock
Gen 38:20 Judah sent the young **g** by the
Gen 38:23 for I sent this young **g** and
Ex 23:19 young **g** in its mother's milk
Ex 34:26 young **g** in its mother's milk
Lev 3:12 And if his offering is a **g**
Lev 4:24 his hand on the head of the **g**
Lev 7:23 any fat, of ox or sheep or **g**
Lev 9:15 offering, and took the **g**,
Lev 10:16 the **g** of the sin offering
Lev 16: 9 Aaron shall bring the **g** on
Lev 16:10 But the **g** on which the lot
Lev 16:15 the **g** of the sin offering
Lev 16:18 and some of the blood of the **g**
Lev 16:20 he shall bring the live **g**
Lev 16:21 on the head of the live **g**
Lev 16:21 them on the head of the **g**
Lev 16:22 The **g** shall bear on itself
Lev 16:22 the **g** in the wilderness
Lev 16:26 he who released the **g** as the
Lev 16:27 the **g** for the sin offering,
Lev 17: 3 ox or lamb or **g** in the camp
Lev 22:27 or a sheep or a **g** is born
Num 15:11 or for each lamb or young **g**
Num 15:27 he shall bring a female **g** in
Num 18:17 of a **g** you shall not redeem
Num 28:22 also one **g** as a sin offering
Num 29:22 also one **g** as a sin offering
Num 29:28 also one **g** as a sin offering
Num 29:31 also one **g** as a sin offering
Num 29:34 also one **g** as a sin offering
Num 29:38 also one **g** as a sin offering
Deut 14: 4 the ox, the sheep, the **g**,
Deut 14: 5 the wild **g**, the mountain **g**
Deut 14:21 young **g** in its mother's milk
Judg 6:19 went in and prepared a young **g**
Judg 13:15 prepare a young **g** for You
Judg 13:19 **g** with the grain offering
Judg 14: 6 have torn apart a young **g**
Judg 15: 1 his wife with a young **g**
1Sa 16:20 a skin of wine, and a young **g**
Prov 30:31 a greyhound, a male **g** also
Is 11: 6 lie down with the young **g**
Is 34:14 the wild **g** shall bleat to its
Ezek 43:25 a **g** for a sin offering

Dan 8: 5 suddenly a male **g** came from
Dan 8: 5 and the **g** had a notable horn
Dan 8: 8 the male **g** grew very great
Dan 8:21 the male **g** is the kingdom of
Luke 15:29 you never gave me a young **g**

GOATH
Jer 31:39 then it shall turn toward **G**

GOATHERDS (*see* GOAT)
Zech 10: 3 and I will punish the **g**

GOATS (*see* GOAT, GOATS')
Gen 27: 9 two choice kids of the **g**, and
Gen 27:16 kids of the **g** on his hands
Gen 30:32 and speckled among the **g**
Gen 30:33 and spotted among the **g**, and
Gen 30:35 the male **g** that were speckled
Gen 30:35 all the female **g** that were
Gen 31:38 and your female **g** have not
Gen 32:14 female **g** and twenty male **g**
Gen 37:31 tunic, killed a kid of the **g**
Ex 12: 5 from the sheep or from the **g**
Ex 35:23 **g**' hair, red skins of rams,
Lev 1:10 of the sheep or of the **g**
Lev 4:23 his offering a kid of the **g**
Lev 4:28 his offering a kid of the **g**
Lev 5: 6 of the **g** as a sin offering
Lev 9: 3 of the **g** as a sin offering
Lev 16: 5 of the **g** as a sin offering
Lev 16: 7 He shall take the two **g** and
Lev 16: 8 shall cast lots for the two **g**
Lev 22:19 from the sheep, or from the **g**
Lev 23:19 of the **g** as a sin offering
Num 7:16 one kid of the **g** as a sin
Num 7:17 oxen, five rams, five male **g**
Num 7:22 one kid of the **g** as a sin
Num 7:23 oxen, five rams, five male **g**
Num 7:28 one kid of the **g** as a sin
Num 7:29 oxen, five rams, five male **g**
Num 7:34 one kid of the **g** as a sin
Num 7:35 oxen, five rams, five male **g**
Num 7:40 one kid of the **g** as a sin
Num 7:41 oxen, five rams, five male **g**
Num 7:46 one kid of the **g** as a sin
Num 7:47 oxen, five rams, five male **g**
Num 7:52 one kid of the **g** as a sin
Num 7:53 oxen, five rams, five male **g**
Num 7:58 one kid of the **g** as a sin
Num 7:59 oxen, five rams, five male **g**
Num 7:64 one kid of the **g** as a sin
Num 7:65 oxen, five rams, five male **g**
Num 7:70 one kid of the **g** as a sin
Num 7:71 oxen, five rams, five male **g**
Num 7:76 one kid of the **g** as a sin
Num 7:77 oxen, five rams, five male **g**
Num 7:82 one kid of the **g** as a sin
Num 7:83 oxen, five rams, five male **g**
Num 7:87 the kids of the **g** as a sin
Num 7:88 rams sixty, the male **g** sixty
Num 15:24 one kid of the **g** as a sin
Num 28:15 Also one kid of the **g** as a
Num 28:30 also one kid of the **g**, to
Num 29: 5 of the **g** as a sin offering
Num 29:11 of the **g** as a sin offering
Num 29:16 of the **g** as a sin offering
Num 29:19 of the **g** as a sin offering
Num 29:25 of the **g** as a sin offering
Num 31:20 everything woven of **g**' hair
Deut 32:14 of the breed of Bashan, and **g**
1Sa 10: 3 one carrying three young **g**
1Sa 24: 2 on the Rocks of the Wild **G**
1Sa 25: 2 sheep and a thousand **g**
1Ki 20:27 like two little flocks of **g**
2Ch 17:11 thousand seven hundred male **g**
2Ch 29:21 and seven male **g** for a sin
2Ch 29:23 they brought out the male **g**
2Ch 35: 7 young **g** from the flock, all
Ezra 6:17 for all Israel twelve male **g**
Ezra 8:35 and twelve male **g** as a sin
Job 39: 1 wild mountain **g** bear young
Ps 50: 9 Nor **g** out of your folds
Ps 50:13 Or drink the blood of **g**
Ps 66:15 I will offer bulls with **g**
Ps 104:18 high hills are for the wild **g**
Prov 27:26 the **g** the price of a field
Song 1: 8 feed your little **g** beside the
Song 4: 1 hair is like a flock of **g**
Song 6: 5 of **g** going down from Gilead
Is 1:11 of bulls, or of lambs or **g**
Is 13:21 And wild **g** will caper there
Is 34: 6 with the blood of lambs and **g**
Jer 51:40 like rams with male **g**
Ezek 27:21 with you in lambs, rams, and **g**
Ezek 34:17 and sheep, between rams and **g**
Ezek 39:18 earth, of rams and lambs, of **g**
Ezek 43:22 shall offer a kid of the **g**
Ezek 45:23 a kid of the **g** daily for a
Matt 25:32 divides his sheep from the **g**
Matt 25:33 hand, but the **g** on the left
Heb 9:12 Not with the blood of **g** and
Heb 9:13 if the blood of bulls and **g**
Heb 9:19 took the blood of calves and **g**
Heb 10: 4 and **g** could take away sins

GOATS' (*see* GOATS)
Ex 25: 4 fine linen thread, and **g** hair
Ex 26: 7 also make curtains of **g** hair
Ex 35: 6 fine linen thread, and **g** hair
Ex 35:26 wisdom spun yarn of **g** hair
Ex 36:14 He made curtains of **g** hair
1Sa 19:13 put a cover of **g** hair for his
1Sa 19:16 with a cover of **g** hair for
Prov 27:27 enough **g** milk for your food

GOATSKINS (*see* GOAT)
Heb 11:37 about in sheepskins and **g**,

GOB
2Sa 21:18 with the Philistines at **G**
2Sa 21:19 in **G** with the Philistines

GOBLET
Song 7: 2 **g** which lacks no blended

GOD (*see* GOD-GIVEN, GODHEAD, GODLY, GOD'S, GOD-WHO-FORGIVES, YAH, YOU-ARE-THE-GOD-WHO-SEES)
Gen 1: 1 In the beginning **G** created
Gen 1: 2 the Spirit of **G** was hovering
Gen 1: 3 Then **G** said, "Let there be
Gen 1: 4 **G** saw the light, that it was
Gen 1: 4 **G** divided the light from the
Gen 1: 5 **G** called the light Day, and
Gen 1: 6 Then **G** said, "Let there be a
Gen 1: 7 Thus **G** made the firmament,
Gen 1: 8 **G** called the firmament Heaven
Gen 1: 9 Then **G** said, "Let the waters
Gen 1:10 **G** called the dry land Earth,
Gen 1:10 And **G** saw that it was good
Gen 1:11 Then **G** said, "Let the earth
Gen 1:12 And **G** saw that it was good
Gen 1:14 Then **G** said, "Let there be
Gen 1:16 Then **G** made two great lights
Gen 1:17 **G** set them in the firmament
Gen 1:18 And **G** saw that it was good
Gen 1:20 Then **G** said, "Let the waters
Gen 1:21 So **G** created great sea
Gen 1:21 And **G** saw that it was good
Gen 1:22 And **G** blessed them, saying,
Gen 1:24 Then **G** said, "Let the earth
Gen 1:25 **G** made the beast of the earth
Gen 1:25 And **G** saw that it was good
Gen 1:26 Then **G** said, "Let Us make
Gen 1:27 So **G** created man in His own
Gen 1:27 the image of **G** He created him
Gen 1:28 Then **G** blessed them
Gen 1:28 and **G** said to them
Gen 1:29 And **G** said, "See, I have
Gen 1:31 Then **G** saw everything that He
Gen 2: 2 on the seventh day **G** ended
Gen 2: 3 Then **G** blessed the seventh
Gen 2: 3 His work which **G** had created
Gen 2: 4 the LORD **G** made the earth
Gen 2: 5 For the LORD **G** had not caused
Gen 2: 7 the LORD **G** formed man of the
Gen 2: 8 The LORD **G** planted a garden
Gen 2: 9 **G** made every tree grow that
Gen 2:15 Then the LORD **G** took the man
Gen 2:16 the LORD **G** commanded the
Gen 2:18 And the LORD **G** said, "It is
Gen 2:19 **G** formed every beast of the
Gen 2:21 And the LORD **G** caused a deep
Gen 2:22 **G** had taken from man He made
Gen 3: 1 which the LORD **G** had made
Gen 3: 1 Has **G** indeed said, 'You shall
Gen 3: 3 **G** has said, 'You shall not
Gen 3: 5 For **G** knows that in the day
Gen 3: 5 opened, and you will be like **G**
Gen 3: 8 **G** walking in the garden in
Gen 3: 8 LORD **G** among the trees of the
Gen 3: 9 Then the LORD **G** called to
Gen 3:13 the LORD **G** said to the woman,
Gen 3:14 So the LORD **G** said to the
Gen 3:21 and his wife the LORD **G** made
Gen 3:22 Then the LORD **G** said
Gen 3:23 therefore the LORD **G** sent him
Gen 4:25 For **G** has appointed another
Gen 5: 1 In the day that **G** created man
Gen 5: 1 made him in the likeness of **G**
Gen 5:22 Enoch walked with **G** three
Gen 5:24 And Enoch walked with **G**
Gen 5:24 and he was not, for **G** took him
Gen 6: 2 that the sons of **G** saw the
Gen 6: 4 when the sons of **G** came in to
Gen 6: 9 Noah walked with **G**
Gen 6:11 also was corrupt before **G**
Gen 6:12 So **G** looked upon the earth,
Gen 6:13 And **G** said to Noah,
Gen 6:22 to all that **G** commanded him
Gen 7: 9 as **G** had commanded Noah
Gen 7:16 went in as **G** had commanded
Gen 8: 1 Then **G** remembered Noah, and
Gen 8: 1 **G** made a wind to pass over
Gen 8:15 Then **G** spoke to Noah, saying,
Gen 9: 1 So **G** blessed Noah and his sons
Gen 9: 6 in the image of **G** He made man
Gen 9: 8 Then **G** spoke to Noah and to
Gen 9:12 And **G** said: "This is the sign of
Gen 9:16 covenant between **G** and every
Gen 9:17 And **G** said to Noah,
Gen 9:26 the **G** of Shem, and may Canaan
Gen 9:27 May **G** enlarge Japheth, and
Gen 14:18 was the priest of **G** Most High
Gen 14:19 be Abram of **G** Most High,
Gen 14:20 And blessed be **G** Most High
Gen 14:22 **G** Most High, the Possessor of
Gen 15: 2 Lord **G**, what will You give me
Gen 15: 8 Lord **G**, how shall I know that
Gen 17: 1 I am Almighty **G**
Gen 17: 3 **G** talked with him, saying
Gen 17: 7 to be **G** to you and your
Gen 17: 8 and I will be their **G**
Gen 17: 9 And **G** said to Abraham
Gen 17:15 Then **G** said to Abraham, "As
Gen 17:18 And Abraham said to **G**, "Oh,
Gen 17:19 Then **G** said: "No, Sarah your
Gen 17:22 and **G** went up from Abraham
Gen 17:23 day, as **G** had said to him
Gen 19:29 when **G** destroyed the cities
Gen 19:29 that **G** remembered Abraham,
Gen 20: 3 But **G** came to Abimelech in a
Gen 20: 6 **G** said to him in a dream,
Gen 20:11 surely the fear of **G** is not
Gen 20:13 when **G** caused me to wander
Gen 20:17 So Abraham prayed to **G**
Gen 20:17 **G** healed Abimelech, his wife,
Gen 21: 2 of which **G** had spoken to him
Gen 21: 4 old, as **G** had commanded him
Gen 21: 6 **G** has made me laugh, so that
Gen 21:12 But **G** said to Abraham, "Do
Gen 21:17 **G** heard the voice of the lad
Gen 21:17 Then the angel of **G** called to
Gen 21:17 for **G** has heard the voice of
Gen 21:19 **G** opened her eyes, and she saw
Gen 21:20 So **G** was with the lad
Gen 21:22 **G** is with you in all that you
Gen 21:23 swear to me by **G** that you
Gen 21:33 the LORD, the Everlasting **G**
Gen 22: 1 things that **G** tested Abraham
Gen 22: 3 place of which **G** had told him
Gen 22: 8 **G** will provide for Himself
Gen 22: 9 place of which **G** had told him
Gen 22:12 now I know that you fear **G**
Gen 24: 3 the **G** of heaven and
Gen 24: 3 the **G** of the earth
Gen 24: 7 The LORD **G** of heaven, who
Gen 24:12 O LORD **G** of my master
Gen 24:27 Blessed be the LORD **G** of my
Gen 24:42 said, 'O LORD **G** of my master
Gen 24:48 and blessed the LORD **G** of my
Gen 25:11 that **G** blessed his son Isaac
Gen 26:24 I am the **G** of your father
Gen 27:20 LORD your **G** brought it to me
Gen 27:28 Therefore may **G** give you of
Gen 28: 3 May **G** Almighty bless you, and
Gen 28: 4 which **G** gave to Abraham
Gen 28:12 angels of **G** were ascending
Gen 28:13 I am the LORD **G** of Abraham
Gen 28:13 your father and the **G** of Isaac
Gen 28:17 other than the house of **G**
Gen 28:20 If **G** will be with me, and keep
Gen 28:21 then the LORD shall be my **G**
Gen 30: 2 Am I in the place of **G**, who
Gen 30: 6 said, "**G** has judged my case

Gen 30:17 **G** listened to Leah, and she
Gen 30:18 **G** has given me my hire,
Gen 30:20 **G** has endowed me with a good
Gen 30:22 Then **G** remembered Rachel,
Gen 30:22 **G** listened to her and opened
Gen 30:23 **G** has taken away my reproach
Gen 31: 5 but the **G** of my father has
Gen 31: 7 but **G** did not allow him to
Gen 31: 9 So **G** has taken away the
Gen 31:11 Then the Angel of **G** spoke to
Gen 31:13 I am the **G** of Bethel, where
Gen 31:16 **G** has taken from our father
Gen 31:16 whatever **G** has said to you,
Gen 31:24 But **G** had come to Laban the
Gen 31:29 but the **G** of your father
Gen 31:42 Unless the **G** of my father,
Gen 31:42 the **G** of Abraham and the Fear
Gen 31:42 **G** has seen my affliction and
Gen 31:50 **G** is witness between you and
Gen 31:53 The **G** of Abraham
Gen 31:53 the **G** of Nahor
Gen 31:53 the **G** of their father judge
Gen 32: 1 and the angels of **G** met him
Gen 32: 9 O **G** of my father Abraham and
Gen 32: 9 **G** of my father Isaac, the
Gen 32:28 for you have struggled with **G**
Gen 32:30 I have seen **G** face to face
Gen 33: 5 The children whom **G** has
Gen 33:10 I had seen the face of **G**, and
Gen 33:11 to you, because **G** has dealt
Gen 35: 1 Then **G** said to Jacob, "Arise
Gen 35: 1 and make an altar there to **G**
Gen 35: 3 will make an altar there to **G**
Gen 35: 5 the terror of **G** was upon the
Gen 35: 7 because there **G** appeared to
Gen 35: 9 Then **G** appeared to Jacob
Gen 35:10 And **G** said to him, "Your name
Gen 35:11 **G** said to him: "I am **G**
Gen 35:13 Then **G** went up from him in
Gen 35:15 place where **G** spoke with him
Gen 39: 9 wickedness, and sin against **G**
Gen 40: 8 interpretations belong to **G**
Gen 41:16 **G** will give Pharaoh an answer
Gen 41:25 **G** has shown Pharaoh what He
Gen 41:28 **G** has shown Pharaoh what He
Gen 41:32 the thing is established by **G**
Gen 41:32 **G** will shortly bring it to
Gen 41:38 in whom is the Spirit of **G**
Gen 41:39 Inasmuch as **G** has shown you
Gen 41:51 For **G** has made me forget all
Gen 41:52 For **G** has caused me to be
Gen 42:18 Do this and live, for I fear **G**
Gen 42:28 is this that **G** has done to us
Gen 43:14 may **G** Almighty give you mercy
Gen 43:23 **G** and the **G** of your father
Gen 43:29 **G** be gracious to you, my son
Gen 44:16 **G** has found out the iniquity
Gen 45: 5 for **G** sent me before you to
Gen 45: 7 And **G** sent me before you to
Gen 45: 8 you who sent me here, but **G**
Gen 45: 9 **G** has made me lord of all
Gen 46: 1 to the **G** of his father Isaac
Gen 46: 2 Then **G** spoke to Israel in the
Gen 46: 3 I am **G**, the **G** of your father
Gen 48: 3 **G** Almighty appeared to me at
Gen 48: 9 whom **G** has given me in this
Gen 48:11 **G** has also shown me your
Gen 48:15 **G**, before whom my fathers
Gen 48:15 the **G** who has fed me all my
Gen 48:20 May **G** make you as Ephraim
Gen 48:21 but **G** will be with you and
Gen 49:24 by the hands of the Mighty **G**
Gen 49:25 by the **G** of your father who
Gen 50:17 of the **G** of your father
Gen 50:19 for am I in the place of **G**
Gen 50:20 but **G** meant it for good, in
Gen 50:24 but **G** will surely visit you,
Gen 50:25 **G** will surely visit you, and
Ex 1:17 But the midwives feared **G**
Ex 1:20 Therefore **G** dealt well with
Ex 1:21 because the midwives feared **G**
Ex 2:23 and their cry came up to **G**
Ex 2:24 So **G** heard their groaning, and
Ex 2:24 **G** remembered His covenant
Ex 2:25 **G** looked upon the children of
Ex 2:25 and **G** acknowledged them
Ex 3: 1 to Horeb, the mountain of **G**
Ex 3: 4 **G** called to him from the
Ex 3: 6 I am the **G** of your father
Ex 3: 6 the **G** of Abraham

Ex 3: 6 the **G** of Isaac
Ex 3: 6 and the **G** of Jacob
Ex 3: 6 he was afraid to look upon **G**
Ex 3:11 But Moses said to **G**, "Who am
Ex 3:12 you shall serve **G** on this
Ex 3:13 Then Moses said to **G**
Ex 3:13 The **G** of your fathers has
Ex 3:14 And **G** said to Moses,
Ex 3:15 Moreover **G** said to Moses,
Ex 3:15 The LORD **G** of your fathers,
Ex 3:15 the **G** of Abraham
Ex 3:15 the **G** of Isaac
Ex 3:15 the **G** of Jacob, has sent me
Ex 3:16 The LORD **G** of your fathers,
Ex 3:16 the **G** of Abraham, of Isaac,
Ex 3:18 The LORD **G** of the Hebrews
Ex 3:18 sacrifice to the LORD our **G**
Ex 4: 5 the LORD **G** of their fathers
Ex 4: 5 the **G** of Abraham
Ex 4: 5 the **G** of Isaac
Ex 4: 5 the **G** of Jacob, has appeared
Ex 4:16 and you shall be to him as **G**
Ex 4:20 took the rod of **G** in his hand
Ex 4:27 met him on the mountain of **G**
Ex 5: 1 says the LORD **G** of Israel
Ex 5: 3 The **G** of the Hebrews has met
Ex 5: 3 sacrifice to the LORD our **G**
Ex 5: 8 us go and sacrifice to our **G**
Ex 6: 2 **G** spoke to Moses and said to
Ex 6: 3 as **G** Almighty, but by My name
Ex 6: 7 people, and I will be your **G**
Ex 6: 7 **G** who brings you out from
Ex 7: 1 have made you as **G** to Pharaoh
Ex 7:16 The LORD **G** of the Hebrews
Ex 8:10 is no one like the LORD our **G**
Ex 8:19 This is the finger of **G**
Ex 8:25 to your **G** in the land
Ex 8:26 Egyptians to the LORD our **G**
Ex 8:27 our **G** as He will command us
Ex 8:28 LORD your **G** in the wilderness
Ex 9: 1 the LORD **G** of the Hebrews
Ex 9:13 the LORD **G** of the Hebrews
Ex 9:30 will not yet fear the LORD **G**
Ex 10: 3 the LORD **G** of the Hebrews
Ex 10: 7 may serve the LORD their **G**
Ex 10: 8 Go, serve the LORD your **G**
Ex 10:16 against the LORD your **G** and
Ex 10:17 and entreat the LORD your **G**
Ex 10:25 sacrifice to the LORD our **G**
Ex 10:26 them to serve the LORD our **G**
Ex 13:17 that **G** did not lead them by
Ex 13:17 for **G** said, "Lest perhaps
Ex 13:18 So **G** led the people around by
Ex 13:19 **G** will surely visit you, and
Ex 14:19 And the Angel of **G**, who went
Ex 15: 2 He is my **G**, and I will praise
Ex 15: 2 my father's **G**, and I will
Ex 15:26 the voice of the LORD your **G**
Ex 16:12 that I am the LORD your **G**
Ex 17: 9 with the rod of **G** in my hand
Ex 18: 1 heard of all that **G** had done
Ex 18: 4 The **G** of my father was my
Ex 18: 5 encamped at the mountain of **G**
Ex 18:12 offering and sacrifices to **G**
Ex 18:12 Moses' father-in-law before **G**
Ex 18:15 come to me to inquire of **G**
Ex 18:16 make known the statutes of **G**
Ex 18:19 and **G** will be with you
Ex 18:19 Stand before **G** for the people
Ex 18:19 bring the difficulties to **G**
Ex 18:21 able men, such as fear **G**, men
Ex 18:23 **G** so commands you, then you
Ex 19: 3 And Moses went up to **G**, and
Ex 19:17 of the camp to meet with **G**
Ex 19:19 and **G** answered him by voice
Ex 20: 1 And **G** spoke all these words,
Ex 20: 2 I am the LORD your **G**, who
Ex 20: 5 For I, the LORD your **G**
Ex 20: 5 am a jealous **G**
Ex 20: 7 of the LORD your **G** in vain
Ex 20:10 Sabbath of the LORD your **G**
Ex 20:12 the LORD your **G** is giving you
Ex 20:19 but let not **G** speak with us,
Ex 20:20 for **G** has come to test you,
Ex 20:21 thick darkness where **G** was
Ex 21:13 but **G** delivered him into his
Ex 22:28 You shall not revile **G**, nor
Ex 23:17 appear before the Lord **G**
Ex 23:19 the house of the LORD your **G**
Ex 23:25 shall serve the LORD your **G**

Ex 24:10 and they saw the **G** of Israel
Ex 24:11 So they saw **G**, and they ate and
Ex 24:13 went up to the mountain of **G**
Ex 29:45 of Israel and will be their **G**
Ex 29:46 that I am the LORD their **G**
Ex 29:46 I am the LORD their **G**
Ex 31: 3 him with the Spirit of **G**, in
Ex 31:18 written with the finger of **G**
Ex 32:11 pleaded with the LORD his **G**
Ex 32:16 tablets were the work of **G**
Ex 32:16 of **G** engraved on the tablets
Ex 32:27 says the LORD **G** of Israel
Ex 34: 6 The LORD, the LORD **G**,
Ex 34:14 is Jealous, is a jealous **G**)
Ex 34:23 Lord, the LORD **G** of Israel
Ex 34:24 **G** three times in the year
Ex 34:26 the house of the LORD your **G**
Ex 35:31 him with the Spirit of **G**, in
Lev 2:13 **G** to be lacking from your
Lev 4:22 of the LORD his **G** in anything
Lev 10:17 **G** has given it to you to bear
Lev 11:44 For I am the LORD your **G**
Lev 11:45 land of Egypt, to be your **G**
Lev 18: 2 I am the LORD your **G**
Lev 18: 4 I am the LORD your **G**
Lev 18:21 profane the name of your **G**
Lev 18:30 I am the LORD your **G**
Lev 19: 2 for I the LORD your **G** am holy
Lev 19: 3 I am the LORD your **G**
Lev 19: 4 I am the LORD your **G**
Lev 19:10 I am the LORD your **G**
Lev 19:12 profane the name of your **G**
Lev 19:14 blind, but shall fear your **G**
Lev 19:25 I am the LORD your **G**
Lev 19:31 I am the LORD your **G**
Lev 19:32 of an old man, and fear your **G**
Lev 19:34 I am the LORD your **G**
Lev 19:36 I am the LORD your **G**, who
Lev 20: 7 for I am the LORD your **G**
Lev 20:24 I am the LORD your **G**, who
Lev 21: 6 They shall be holy to their **G**
Lev 21: 6 profane the name of their **G**
Lev 21: 6 fire, and the bread of their **G**
Lev 21: 7 the priest is holy to his **G**
Lev 21: 8 he offers the bread of your **G**
Lev 21:12 the sanctuary of his **G**
Lev 21:12 oil of his **G** is upon him
Lev 21:17 to offer the bread of his **G**
Lev 21:21 to offer the bread of his **G**
Lev 21:22 He may eat the bread of his **G**
Lev 22:25 these as the bread of your **G**
Lev 22:33 land of Egypt, to be your **G**
Lev 23:14 brought an offering to your **G**
Lev 23:22 I am the LORD your **G**
Lev 23:28 you before the LORD your **G**
Lev 23:40 LORD your **G** for seven days
Lev 23:43 I am the LORD your **G**
Lev 24:15 his **G** shall bear his sin
Lev 24:22 for I am the LORD your **G**
Lev 25:17 but you shall fear your **G**
Lev 25:17 for I am the LORD your **G**
Lev 25:36 but fear your **G**, that your
Lev 25:38 I am the LORD your **G**, who
Lev 25:38 of Canaan and to be your **G**
Lev 25:43 but you shall fear your **G**
Lev 25:55 I am the LORD your **G**
Lev 26: 1 for I am the LORD your **G**
Lev 26:12 walk among you and be your **G**
Lev 26:13 I am the LORD your **G**, who
Lev 26:44 for I am the LORD their **G**
Lev 26:45 that I might be their **G**
Num 6: 7 to **G** is on his head
Num 10: 9 before the LORD your **G**, and
Num 10:10 for you before your **G**
Num 10:10 I am the LORD your **G**
Num 12:13 Please heal her, O **G**, I pray
Num 15:40 and be holy for your **G**
Num 15:41 I am the LORD your **G**, who
Num 15:41 land of Egypt, to be your **G**
Num 15:41 I am the LORD your **G**
Num 16: 9 **G** of Israel has separated you
Num 16:22 O **G**, the **G** of the spirits
Num 21: 5 And the people spoke against **G**
Num 22: 9 Then **G** came to Balaam and
Num 22:10 And Balaam said to **G**, "Balak
Num 22:12 And **G** said to Balaam,
Num 22:18 the word of the LORD my **G**
Num 22:20 **G** came to Balaam at night and
Num 22:38 The word that **G** puts in my
Num 23: 4 **G** met Balaam, and he said to

Num 23: 8 I curse whom **G** has not cursed
Num 23:19 **G** is not a man, that He
Num 23:21 The LORD his **G** is with him
Num 23:22 **G** brings them out of Egypt
Num 23:23 Israel, 'Oh, what **G** has done
Num 23:27 perhaps it will please **G** that
Num 24: 2 the Spirit of **G** came upon him
Num 24: 4 him who hears the words of **G**
Num 24: 8 **G** brings him out of Egypt
Num 24:16 him who hears the words of **G**
Num 24:23 shall live when **G** does this
Num 25:13 he was zealous for his **G**, and
Num 27:16 the **G** of the spirits of all
Deut 1: 6 The LORD our **G** spoke to us in
Deut 1:10 The LORD your **G** has
Deut 1:11 May the LORD **G** of your
Deut 1:19 as the LORD our **G** had
Deut 1:20 the LORD our **G** is giving us
Deut 1:21 the LORD your **G** has set the
Deut 1:21 as the LORD **G** of your fathers
Deut 1:25 the LORD our **G** is giving us
Deut 1:26 command of the LORD your **G**
Deut 1:30 The LORD your **G**, who goes
Deut 1:31 the LORD your **G** carried you
Deut 1:32 not believe the LORD your **G**
Deut 1:41 the LORD our **G** commanded us
Deut 2: 7 For the LORD your **G** has
Deut 2: 7 LORD your **G** has been with you
Deut 2:29 the LORD our **G** is giving us
Deut 2:30 for the LORD your **G** hardened
Deut 2:33 the LORD our **G** delivered him
Deut 2:36 the LORD our **G** delivered all
Deut 2:37 LORD our **G** had forbidden us
Deut 3: 3 So the LORD our **G** also
Deut 3:18 The LORD your **G** has given
Deut 3:20 land which the LORD your **G** is
Deut 3:21 **G** has done to these two kings
Deut 3:22 for the LORD your **G** Himself
Deut 3:24 O Lord **G**, You have begun to
Deut 4: 1 the land which the LORD **G** of
Deut 4: 2 of the LORD your **G** which I
Deut 4: 3 for the LORD your **G** has
Deut 4: 4 LORD your **G** are alive today
Deut 4: 5 as the LORD my **G** commanded
Deut 4: 7 that has **G** so near to it, as
Deut 4: 7 as the LORD our **G** is to us
Deut 4:10 the LORD your **G** in Horeb,
Deut 4:19 which the LORD your **G** has
Deut 4:21 your **G** is giving you as an
Deut 4:23 your **G** which He made with you
Deut 4:23 LORD your **G** has forbidden you
Deut 4:24 For the LORD your **G** is a
Deut 4:24 a consuming fire, a jealous **G**
Deut 4:25 **G** to provoke Him to anger
Deut 4:29 you will seek the LORD your **G**
Deut 4:30 you turn to the LORD your **G**
Deut 4:31 your **G** is a merciful **G**)
Deut 4:32 since the day that **G** created
Deut 4:33 ever hear the voice of **G**
Deut 4:34 Or did **G** ever try to go and
Deut 4:34 to all that the LORD your **G**
Deut 4:35 that the LORD Himself is **G**
Deut 4:39 Himself is **G** in heaven above
Deut 4:40 land which the LORD your **G** is
Deut 5: 2 The LORD our **G** made a
Deut 5: 6 I am the LORD your **G** who
Deut 5: 9 For I, the LORD your **G**
Deut 5: 9 am a jealous **G**
Deut 5:11 of the LORD your **G** in vain
Deut 5:12 the LORD your **G** commanded
Deut 5:14 Sabbath of the LORD your **G**
Deut 5:15 that the LORD your **G** brought
Deut 5:15 therefore the LORD your **G**
Deut 5:16 as the LORD your **G** has
Deut 5:16 the LORD your **G** is giving you
Deut 5:24 Surely the LORD our **G** has
Deut 5:24 day that **G** speaks with man
Deut 5:25 of the LORD our **G** anymore
Deut 5:26 the voice of the living **G**
Deut 5:27 that the LORD our **G** may say
Deut 5:27 the LORD our **G** says to you
Deut 5:32 LORD your **G** has commanded
Deut 5:33 LORD your **G** has commanded
Deut 6: 1 which the LORD your **G** has
Deut 6: 2 you may fear the LORD your **G**
Deut 6: 3 LORD **G** of your fathers has
Deut 6: 4 The LORD our **G**, the LORD is
Deut 6: 5 your **G** with all your heart
Deut 6:10 when the LORD your **G** brings
Deut 6:13 shall fear the LORD your **G**
Deut 6:15 **G** is a jealous **G** among you)
Deut 6:15 your **G** be aroused against you
Deut 6:16 your **G** as you tempted Him in
Deut 6:17 of the LORD your **G**, His
Deut 6:20 LORD our **G** has commanded you
Deut 6:24 to fear the LORD our **G**, for
Deut 6:25 before the LORD our **G**, as He
Deut 7: 1 When the LORD your **G** brings
Deut 7: 2 when the LORD your **G** delivers
Deut 7: 6 people to the LORD your **G**
Deut 7: 6 the LORD your **G** has chosen
Deut 7: 9 the LORD your **G**, He is **G**
Deut 7: 9 the faithful **G** who keeps
Deut 7:12 that the LORD your **G** will
Deut 7:16 your **G** delivers over to you
Deut 7:18 LORD your **G** did to Pharaoh
Deut 7:19 LORD your **G** brought you out
Deut 7:19 So shall the LORD your **G** do
Deut 7:20 Moreover the LORD your **G** will
Deut 7:21 for the LORD your **G**
Deut 7:21 the great and awesome **G**
Deut 7:22 the LORD your **G** will drive
Deut 7:23 But the LORD your **G** will
Deut 7:25 to the LORD your **G**
Deut 8: 2 **G** led you all the way these
Deut 8: 5 the LORD your **G** chastens you
Deut 8: 6 of the LORD your **G**, to walk
Deut 8: 7 For the LORD your **G** is
Deut 8:10 shall bless the LORD your **G**
Deut 8:11 your **G** by not keeping His
Deut 8:14 you forget the LORD your **G**
Deut 8:18 remember the LORD your **G**, for
Deut 8:19 means forget the LORD your **G**
Deut 8:20 the voice of the LORD your **G**
Deut 9: 3 today that the LORD your **G** is
Deut 9: 4 after the LORD your **G** has
Deut 9: 5 nations that the LORD your **G**
Deut 9: 6 that the LORD your **G** is not
Deut 9: 7 **G** to wrath in the wilderness
Deut 9:10 written with the finger of **G**
Deut 9:16 against the LORD your **G**, and
Deut 9:23 of the LORD your **G**, and you
Deut 9:26 O Lord **G**, do not destroy
Deut 10: 9 the LORD your **G** promised him
Deut 10:12 LORD your **G** require of you
Deut 10:12 but to fear the LORD your **G**
Deut 10:12 your **G** with all your heart
Deut 10:14 belong to the LORD your **G**
Deut 10:17 LORD your **G** is **G** of gods
Deut 10:17 and Lord of lords, the great **G**
Deut 10:20 shall fear the LORD your **G**
Deut 10:21 your praise, and He is your **G**
Deut 10:22 now the LORD your **G** has made
Deut 11: 1 shall love the LORD your **G**
Deut 11: 2 chastening of the LORD your **G**
Deut 11:12 which the LORD your **G** cares
Deut 11:12 LORD your **G** are always on it
Deut 11:13 to love the LORD your **G** and
Deut 11:22 to love the LORD your **G**, to
Deut 11:25 the LORD your **G** will put the
Deut 11:27 of the LORD your **G** which I
Deut 11:28 of the LORD your **G**, but turn
Deut 11:29 be, when the LORD your **G** has
Deut 11:31 the LORD your **G** is giving you
Deut 12: 1 **G** of your fathers is giving
Deut 12: 4 LORD your **G** with such things
Deut 12: 5 where the LORD your **G** chooses
Deut 12: 7 eat before the LORD your **G**
Deut 12: 7 LORD your **G** has blessed you
Deut 12: 9 the LORD your **G** is giving you
Deut 12:10 **G** is giving you to inherit
Deut 12:11 **G** chooses to make His name
Deut 12:12 before the LORD your **G**, you
Deut 12:15 your **G** which He has given you
Deut 12:18 them before the LORD your **G**
Deut 12:18 which the LORD your **G** chooses
Deut 12:18 before the LORD your **G** in all
Deut 12:20 When the LORD your **G** enlarges
Deut 12:21 place where the LORD your **G**
Deut 12:27 the altar of the LORD your **G**
Deut 12:27 the altar of the LORD your **G**
Deut 12:28 the sight of the LORD your **G**
Deut 12:29 When the LORD your **G** cuts off
Deut 12:31 the LORD your **G** in that way
Deut 13: 3 for the LORD your **G** is
Deut 13: 3 your **G** with all your heart
Deut 13: 4 walk after the LORD your **G**
Deut 13: 5 you away from the LORD your **G**
Deut 13: 5 your **G** commanded you to walk
Deut 13:10 you away from the LORD your **G**
Deut 13:12 which the LORD your **G** gives
Deut 13:16 plunder, for the LORD your **G**
Deut 13:18 the voice of the LORD your **G**
Deut 13:18 the eyes of the LORD your **G**
Deut 14: 1 children of the LORD your **G**
Deut 14: 2 people to the LORD your **G**
Deut 14:21 people to the LORD your **G**
Deut 14:23 eat before the LORD your **G**
Deut 14:23 fear the LORD your **G** always
Deut 14:24 place where the LORD your **G**
Deut 14:24 LORD your **G** has blessed you
Deut 14:25 which the LORD your **G** chooses
Deut 14:26 there before the LORD your **G**
Deut 14:29 that the LORD your **G** may
Deut 15: 4 land which the LORD your **G** is
Deut 15: 5 the voice of the LORD your **G**
Deut 15: 6 For the LORD your **G** will
Deut 15: 7 the LORD your **G** is giving you
Deut 15:10 this thing the LORD your **G**
Deut 15:15 the LORD your **G** redeemed you
Deut 15:18 Then the LORD your **G** will
Deut 15:19 sanctify to the LORD your **G**
Deut 15:20 **G** year by year in the place
Deut 15:21 it to the LORD your **G**
Deut 16: 1 Passover to the LORD your **G**
Deut 16: 1 **G** brought you out of Egypt by
Deut 16: 2 Passover to the LORD your **G**
Deut 16: 5 the LORD your **G** gives you
Deut 16: 6 **G** chooses to make His name
Deut 16: 7 which the LORD your **G** chooses
Deut 16: 8 assembly to the LORD your **G**
Deut 16:10 your **G** with the tribute of a
Deut 16:10 the LORD your **G** blesses you
Deut 16:11 before the LORD your **G**, you
Deut 16:11 **G** chooses to make His name
Deut 16:15 feast to the LORD your **G** in
Deut 16:15 because the LORD your **G** will
Deut 16:16 your **G** in the place which He
Deut 16:17 your **G** which He has given you
Deut 16:18 the LORD your **G** gives you
Deut 16:20 the LORD your **G** is giving you
Deut 16:21 yourself to the LORD your **G**
Deut 16:22 which the LORD your **G** hates
Deut 17: 1 **G** a bull or sheep which has
Deut 17: 1 to the LORD your **G**
Deut 17: 2 the LORD your **G** gives you
Deut 17: 2 the sight of the LORD your **G**
Deut 17: 8 which the LORD your **G** chooses
Deut 17:12 there before the LORD your **G**
Deut 17:14 the LORD your **G** is giving you
Deut 17:15 whom the LORD your **G** chooses
Deut 17:19 learn to fear the LORD his **G**
Deut 18: 5 For the LORD your **G** has
Deut 18: 7 his **G** as all his brethren the
Deut 18: 9 the LORD your **G** is giving you
Deut 18:12 abominations the LORD your **G**
Deut 18:13 before the LORD your **G**
Deut 18:14 you, the LORD your **G** has not
Deut 18:15 The LORD your **G** will raise up
Deut 18:16 desired of the LORD your **G** in
Deut 18:16 the voice of the LORD my **G**
Deut 19: 1 When the LORD your **G** has cut
Deut 19: 1 the LORD your **G** is giving you
Deut 19: 2 **G** is giving you to possess
Deut 19: 3 **G** is giving you to inherit
Deut 19: 8 Now if the LORD your **G**
Deut 19: 9 to love the LORD your **G** and
Deut 19:10 your **G** is giving you as an
Deut 19:14 **G** is giving you to possess
Deut 20: 1 the LORD your **G** is with you
Deut 20: 4 for the LORD your **G** is He
Deut 20:13 when the LORD your **G** delivers
Deut 20:14 the LORD your **G** gives you
Deut 20:16 **G** gives you as an inheritance
Deut 20:17 LORD your **G** has commanded
Deut 20:18 sin against the LORD your **G**
Deut 21: 1 **G** is giving you to possess
Deut 21: 5 near, for the LORD your **G** has
Deut 21:10 the LORD your **G** delivers them
Deut 21:23 your **G** is giving you as an
Deut 21:23 is hanged is accursed of **G**
Deut 22: 5 to the LORD your **G**
Deut 23: 5 **G** would not listen to Balaam
Deut 23: 5 but the LORD your **G** turned
Deut 23: 5 the LORD your **G** loves you
Deut 23:14 For the LORD your **G** walks in
Deut 23:18 your **G** for any vowed offering
Deut 23:18 to the LORD your **G**
Deut 23:20 that the LORD your **G** may
Deut 23:21 make a vow to the LORD your **G**

Deut 23:21 for the LORD your G will
Deut 23:23 vowed to the LORD your G what
Deut 24: 4 your G is giving you as an
Deut 24: 9 G did to Miriam on the way
Deut 24:13 to you before the LORD your G
Deut 24:18 the LORD your G redeemed you
Deut 24:19 that the LORD your G may
Deut 25:15 the LORD your G is giving you
Deut 25:16 to the LORD your G
Deut 25:18 and he did not fear G
Deut 25:19 be, when the LORD your G has
Deut 25:19 land which the LORD your G is
Deut 26: 1 your G is giving you as an
Deut 26: 2 the LORD your G is giving you
Deut 26: 2 G chooses to make His name
Deut 26: 3 today to the LORD your G that
Deut 26: 4 the altar of the LORD your G
Deut 26: 5 and say before the LORD your G
Deut 26: 7 to the LORD G of our fathers
Deut 26:10 set it before the LORD your G
Deut 26:10 before the LORD your G
Deut 26:11 LORD your G has given to you
Deut 26:13 say before the LORD your G
Deut 26:14 the voice of the LORD my G
Deut 26:16 This day the LORD your G
Deut 26:17 the LORD to be your G, and
Deut 26:19 people to the LORD your G
Deut 27: 2 the LORD your G is giving you
Deut 27: 3 the LORD your G is giving you
Deut 27: 3 just as the LORD G of your
Deut 27: 5 an altar to the LORD your G
Deut 27: 6 the altar of the LORD your G
Deut 27: 6 on it to the LORD your G
Deut 27: 7 before the LORD your G
Deut 27: 9 the people of the LORD your G
Deut 27:10 the voice of the LORD your G
Deut 28: 1 the voice of the LORD your G
Deut 28: 1 that the LORD your G will set
Deut 28: 2 the voice of the LORD your G
Deut 28: 8 the LORD your G is giving you
Deut 28: 9 of the LORD your G and walk in
Deut 28:13 of the LORD your G, which I
Deut 28:15 the voice of the LORD your G
Deut 28:45 the voice of the LORD your G
Deut 28:47 the LORD your G with joy and
Deut 28:52 the LORD your G has given you
Deut 28:53 the LORD your G has given you
Deut 28:58 name, THE LORD YOUR G
Deut 28:62 the voice of the LORD your G
Deut 29: 6 that I am the LORD your G
Deut 29:10 today before the LORD your G
Deut 29:12 covenant with the LORD your G
Deut 29:12 which the LORD your G makes
Deut 29:13 and that He may be G to you
Deut 29:15 today before the LORD our G
Deut 29:18 today from the LORD our G
Deut 29:25 the LORD G of their fathers
Deut 29:29 belong to the LORD our G, but
Deut 30: 1 the LORD your G drives you
Deut 30: 2 you return to the LORD your G
Deut 30: 3 that the LORD your G will
Deut 30: 3 LORD your G has scattered you
Deut 30: 4 LORD your G will gather you
Deut 30: 5 Then the LORD your G will
Deut 30: 6 And the LORD your G will
Deut 30: 6 your G with all your heart
Deut 30: 7 Also the LORD your G will put
Deut 30: 9 The LORD your G will make you
Deut 30:10 the voice of the LORD your G
Deut 30:10 your G with all your heart
Deut 30:16 today to love the LORD your G
Deut 30:16 the LORD your G will bless
Deut 30:20 you may love the LORD your G
Deut 31: 3 The LORD your G Himself
Deut 31: 6 for the LORD your G, He is
Deut 31:11 your G in the place which He
Deut 31:12 learn to fear the LORD your G
Deut 31:13 G as long as you live in the
Deut 31:17 because our G is not among us
Deut 31:26 covenant of the LORD your G
Deut 32: 3 ascribe greatness to our G
Deut 32: 4 a G of truth and without
Deut 32:15 he forsook G who made him
Deut 32:17 to demons, not to G, to gods
Deut 32:18 the G who fathered you
Deut 32:21 to jealousy by what is not G
Deut 32:39 and there is no G besides Me
Deut 33: 1 of G blessed the children of
Deut 33:26 no one like the G of Jeshurun
Deut 33:27 The eternal G is your refuge,

Josh 1: 9 for the LORD your G is with
Josh 1:11 G is giving you to possess
Josh 1:13 The LORD your G is giving
Josh 1:15 LORD your G is giving them
Josh 1:17 the LORD your G be with you
Josh 2:11 of you, for the LORD your G
Josh 2:11 He is G in heaven above and on
Josh 3: 3 covenant of the LORD your G
Josh 3: 9 the words of the LORD your G
Josh 3:10 the living G is among you
Josh 4: 5 your G into the midst of the
Josh 4:23 for the LORD your G dried up
Josh 4:23 as the LORD your G did to the
Josh 4:24 fear the LORD your G forever
Josh 7: 7 Alas, Lord G, why have You
Josh 7:13 says the LORD G of Israel
Josh 7:19 glory to the LORD G of Israel
Josh 7:20 against the LORD G of Israel
Josh 8: 7 for the LORD your G will
Josh 8:30 G of Israel in Mount Ebal
Josh 9: 9 the name of the LORD your G
Josh 9:18 them by the LORD G of Israel
Josh 9:19 them by the LORD G of Israel
Josh 9:23 for the house of my G
Josh 9:24 G commanded His servant
Josh 10:19 for the LORD your G has
Josh 10:40 as the LORD G of Israel had
Josh 10:42 because the LORD G of Israel
Josh 13:14 G of Israel made by fire are
Josh 13:33 the LORD G of Israel was
Josh 14: 6 the man of G concerning you
Josh 14: 8 wholly followed the LORD my G
Josh 14: 9 wholly followed the LORD my G
Josh 14:14 followed the LORD G of Israel
Josh 18: 3 the land which the LORD G of
Josh 18: 6 here before the LORD our G
Josh 22: 3 of the LORD your G
Josh 22: 4 now the LORD your G has given
Josh 22: 5 you, to love the LORD your G
Josh 22:16 against the G of Israel, to
Josh 22:19 the altar of the LORD our G
Josh 22:22 The LORD G of gods, the LORD
Josh 22:22 of gods, the LORD G of gods
Josh 22:24 do with the LORD G of Israel
Josh 22:29 our G which is before His
Josh 22:33 children of Israel blessed G
Josh 22:34 between us that the LORD is G
Josh 23: 3 your G has done to all these
Josh 23: 3 for the LORD your G is He who
Josh 23: 5 the LORD your G will expel
Josh 23: 5 LORD your G has promised you
Josh 23: 8 hold fast to the LORD your G
Josh 23:10 for the LORD your G is He who
Josh 23:11 that you love the LORD your G
Josh 23:13 G will no longer drive out
Josh 23:13 the LORD your G has given you
Josh 23:14 your G spoke concerning you
Josh 23:15 the LORD your G promised you
Josh 23:15 the LORD your G has given you
Josh 23:16 covenant of the LORD your G
Josh 24: 1 presented themselves before G
Josh 24: 2 says the LORD G of Israel
Josh 24:17 for the LORD our G is He who
Josh 24:18 the LORD, for He is our G
Josh 24:19 the LORD, for He is a holy G
Josh 24:19 He is a jealous G
Josh 24:23 heart to the LORD G of Israel
Josh 24:24 The LORD our G we will serve,
Josh 24:26 in the Book of the Law of G
Josh 24:27 to you, lest you deny your G
Judg 1: 7 have done, so G has repaid me
Judg 2:12 the LORD G of their fathers
Judg 3: 7 They forgot the LORD their G
Judg 3:20 have a message from G for you
Judg 4: 6 Has not the LORD G of Israel
Judg 4:23 So on that day G subdued
Judg 5: 3 to the LORD G of Israel
Judg 5: 5 before the LORD G of Israel
Judg 6: 8 says the LORD G of Israel
Judg 6:10 I am the LORD your G
Judg 6:20 The Angel of G said to him
Judg 6:22 Alas, O Lord G!
Judg 6:26 an altar to the LORD your G
Judg 6:36 Then Gideon said to G, "If
Judg 6:39 Then Gideon said to G, "Do
Judg 6:40 And G did so that night
Judg 7:14 for into his hand G has
Judg 8: 3 G has delivered into your
Judg 8:34 not remember the LORD their G
Judg 9: 7 that G may listen to you

Judg 9: 9 oil, with which they honor G
Judg 9:13 new wine, which cheers both G
Judg 9:23 G sent a spirit of ill will
Judg 9:56 Thus G repaid the wickedness
Judg 9:57 evil of the men of Shechem G
Judg 10:10 we have both forsaken our G
Judg 11:21 And the LORD G of Israel
Judg 11:23 So now the LORD G of Israel
Judg 11:24 So whatever the LORD our G
Judg 13: 5 a Nazirite to G from the womb
Judg 13: 6 A Man of G came to me, and His
Judg 13: 6 countenance of the Angel of G
Judg 13: 7 shall be a Nazirite to G from
Judg 13: 8 please let the Man of G whom
Judg 13: 9 G listened to the voice of
Judg 13: 9 the Angel of G came to the
Judg 13:22 die, because we have seen G
Judg 15:19 So G split the hollow place
Judg 16:17 to G from my mother's womb
Judg 16:28 O Lord G, remember me, I pray
Judg 16:28 I pray, just this once, O G
Judg 18: 5 Please inquire of G, that we
Judg 18:10 For G has given it into your
Judg 18:31 the house of G was in Shiloh
Judg 20: 2 assembly of the people of G
Judg 20:18 of G to ask counsel of G
Judg 20:26 up and came to the house of G
Judg 20:27 of G was there in those days
Judg 21: 2 people came to the house of G
Judg 21: 2 there before G till evening
Judg 21: 3 O LORD G of Israel, why has
Ruth 1:16 my people, and your G, my G
Ruth 2:12 you by the LORD G of Israel
1Sa 1:17 the G of Israel grant your
1Sa 2: 2 is there any rock like our G
1Sa 2: 3 LORD is the G of knowledge
1Sa 2:25 another, G will judge him
1Sa 2:27 Then a man of G came to Eli
1Sa 2:30 the LORD G of Israel says
1Sa 2:32 good which G does for Israel
1Sa 3: 3 before the lamp of G went out
1Sa 3: 3 LORD where the ark of G was
1Sa 3:17 G do so to you, and more also,
1Sa 4: 4 the ark of the covenant of G
1Sa 4: 7 G has come into the camp
1Sa 4:11 the ark of G was captured
1Sa 4:13 trembled for the ark of G
1Sa 4:17 and the ark of G has been
1Sa 4:18 made mention of the ark of G
1Sa 4:19 the ark of G was captured
1Sa 4:21 ark of G had been captured
1Sa 4:22 for the ark of G has been
1Sa 5: 1 Philistines took the ark of G
1Sa 5: 2 Philistines took the ark of G
1Sa 5: 7 The ark of the G of Israel
1Sa 5: 8 the ark of the G of Israel
1Sa 5: 8 Let the ark of the G of
1Sa 5: 8 ark of the G of Israel away
1Sa 5:10 sent the ark of G to Ekron
1Sa 5:10 as the ark of G came to Ekron
1Sa 5:10 ark of the G of Israel to us
1Sa 5:11 the ark of the G of Israel
1Sa 5:11 the hand of G was very heavy
1Sa 6: 3 the ark of the G of Israel
1Sa 6: 5 give glory to the G of Israel
1Sa 6:20 stand before this holy LORD G
1Sa 7: 8 out to the LORD our G for us
1Sa 9: 6 is in this city a man of G
1Sa 9: 7 to bring to the man of G
1Sa 9: 8 give that to the man of G
1Sa 9: 9 a man went to inquire of G
1Sa 9:10 city where the man of G was
1Sa 9:27 announce to you the word of G
1Sa 10: 3 to G at Bethel will meet you
1Sa 10: 5 of G where the Philistine
1Sa 10: 7 for G is with you
1Sa 10: 9 that G gave him another heart
1Sa 10:10 the Spirit of G came upon him
1Sa 10:18 says the LORD G of Israel
1Sa 10:19 have today rejected your G
1Sa 10:26 whose hearts G had touched
1Sa 11: 6 Then the Spirit of G came
1Sa 12: 9 they forgot the LORD their G
1Sa 12:12 the LORD your G was your king
1Sa 12:14 following the LORD your G
1Sa 12:19 servants to the LORD your G
1Sa 13:13 of the LORD your G, which He
1Sa 14:18 Bring the ark of G here"
1Sa 14:18 of G was with the children of
1Sa 14:36 Let us draw near to G here

1Sa 14:37 So Saul asked counsel of **G**
1Sa 14:41 said to the LORD **G** of Israel
1Sa 14:44 **G** do so and more also
1Sa 14:45 he has worked with **G** this day
1Sa 15:15 sacrifice to the LORD your **G**
1Sa 15:21 to the LORD your **G** in Gilgal
1Sa 15:30 I may worship the LORD your **G**
1Sa 16:15 from **G** is troubling you
1Sa 16:16 spirit from **G** is upon you
1Sa 16:23 spirit from **G** was upon Saul
1Sa 17:26 the armies of the living **G**
1Sa 17:36 the armies of the living **G**
1Sa 17:45 the **G** of the armies of Israel
1Sa 17:46 that there is a **G** in Israel
1Sa 18:10 spirit from **G** came upon Saul
1Sa 19:20 the Spirit of **G** came upon the
1Sa 19:23 Spirit of **G** was upon him also
1Sa 20:12 The LORD **G** of Israel is
1Sa 22: 3 I know what **G** will do for me
1Sa 22:13 and have inquired of **G** for him
1Sa 22:15 begin to inquire of **G** for him
1Sa 23: 7 **G** has delivered him into my
1Sa 23:10 O LORD **G** of Israel, Your
1Sa 23:11 O LORD **G** of Israel, I pray,
1Sa 23:14 but **G** did not deliver him
1Sa 23:16 and strengthened his hand in **G**
1Sa 25:22 May **G** do so, and more also, to
1Sa 25:29 living with the LORD your **G**
1Sa 25:32 be the LORD **G** of Israel, who
1Sa 25:34 as the LORD **G** of Israel lives
1Sa 26: 8 **G** has delivered your enemy
1Sa 28:15 **G** has departed from me and
1Sa 29: 9 in my sight as an angel of **G**
1Sa 30: 6 himself in the LORD his **G**
1Sa 30:15 Swear to me by **G** that you
2Sa 2:27 As **G** lives, unless you had
2Sa 3: 9 May **G** do so to Abner, and
2Sa 3:35 **G** do so to me, and more also,
2Sa 5:10 the LORD **G** of hosts was with
2Sa 6: 2 up from there the ark of **G**
2Sa 6: 3 the ark of **G** on a new cart
2Sa 6: 4 accompanying the ark of **G**
2Sa 6: 6 out his hand to the ark of **G**
2Sa 6: 7 **G** struck him there for his
2Sa 6: 7 he died there by the ark of **G**
2Sa 6:12 him, because of the ark of **G**
2Sa 6:12 brought up the ark of **G** from
2Sa 7: 2 but the ark of **G** dwells
2Sa 7:18 Who am I, O Lord **G**
2Sa 7:19 thing in Your sight, O Lord **G**
2Sa 7:19 the manner of man, O Lord **G**
2Sa 7:20 For You, Lord **G**, know Your
2Sa 7:22 You are great, O Lord **G**
2Sa 7:22 is there any **G** besides You
2Sa 7:23 nation on the earth whom **G**
2Sa 7:24 LORD, have become their **G**
2Sa 7:25 And now, O LORD **G**, the word
2Sa 7:26 of hosts is the **G** over Israel
2Sa 7:27 **G** of Israel, have revealed
2Sa 7:28 And now, O Lord **G**, You are **G**
2Sa 7:29 for You, O Lord **G**, have
2Sa 9: 3 I may show the kindness of **G**
2Sa 10:12 and for the cities of our **G**
2Sa 12: 7 says the LORD **G** of Israel
2Sa 12:16 pleaded with **G** for the child
2Sa 14:11 king remember the LORD your **G**
2Sa 14:13 thing against the people of **G**
2Sa 14:14 Yet **G** does not take away a
2Sa 14:16 from the inheritance of **G**
2Sa 14:17 for as the angel of **G**, so is
2Sa 14:17 the LORD your **G** be with you
2Sa 14:20 the wisdom of the angel of **G**
2Sa 15:24 the ark of the covenant of **G**
2Sa 15:24 And they set down the ark of **G**
2Sa 15:25 Carry the ark of **G** back into
2Sa 15:29 ark of **G** back to Jerusalem
2Sa 15:32 where he worshiped **G**, that
2Sa 16:23 inquired at the oracle of **G**
2Sa 18:28 Blessed be the LORD your **G**
2Sa 19:13 **G** do so to me, and more also,
2Sa 19:27 king is like the angel of **G**
2Sa 21:14 And after that **G** heeded the
2Sa 22: 3 the **G** of my strength, in Him
2Sa 22: 7 the LORD, and cried to my **G**
2Sa 22:22 wickedly departed from my **G**
2Sa 22:30 by my **G** I can leap over a
2Sa 22:31 As for **G**, His way is perfect
2Sa 22:32 For who is **G**, except the LORD
2Sa 22:32 who is a rock, except our **G**
2Sa 22:33 **G** is my strength and power, and
2Sa 22:47 Let **G** be exalted, the Rock of
2Sa 22:48 It is **G** who avenges me, who
2Sa 23: 1 anointed of the **G** of Jacob
2Sa 23: 3 The **G** of Israel said, the
2Sa 23: 4 ruling in the fear of **G**
2Sa 23: 5 my house is not so with **G**
2Sa 24: 3 your **G** add to the people a
2Sa 24:23 the LORD your **G** accept you
2Sa 24:24 my **G** with that which costs me
1Ki 1:17 your **G** to your maidservant
1Ki 1:30 you by the LORD **G** of Israel
1Ki 1:36 May the LORD **G** of my lord the
1Ki 1:47 May **G** make the name of
1Ki 1:48 be the LORD **G** of Israel, who
1Ki 2: 3 the charge of the LORD your **G**
1Ki 2:23 May **G** do so to me, and more
1Ki 2:26 Lord **G** before my father David
1Ki 3: 5 and **G** said, "Ask!
1Ki 3: 7 Now, O LORD my **G**, You have
1Ki 3:11 Then **G** said to him
1Ki 3:28 of **G** was in him to administer
1Ki 4:29 And **G** gave Solomon wisdom
1Ki 5: 3 the name of the LORD his **G**
1Ki 5: 4 But now the LORD my **G** has
1Ki 5: 5 for the name of the LORD my **G**
1Ki 8:15 be the LORD **G** of Israel, who
1Ki 8:17 name of the LORD **G** of Israel
1Ki 8:20 name of the LORD **G** of Israel
1Ki 8:23 LORD **G** of Israel, there is no
1Ki 8:23 there is no **G** in heaven above
1Ki 8:25 LORD **G** of Israel, now keep
1Ki 8:26 O **G** of Israel, let Your word
1Ki 8:27 But will **G** indeed dwell on
1Ki 8:28 his supplication, O LORD my **G**
1Ki 8:53 out of Egypt, O Lord **G**
1Ki 8:57 May the LORD our **G** be with us
1Ki 8:59 be near the LORD our **G** day
1Ki 8:60 may know that the LORD is **G**
1Ki 8:61 be loyal to the LORD our **G**
1Ki 8:65 Egypt, before the LORD our **G**
1Ki 9: 9 they forsook the LORD their **G**
1Ki 10: 9 Blessed be the LORD your **G**
1Ki 10:24 which **G** had put in his heart
1Ki 11: 4 not loyal to the LORD his **G**
1Ki 11: 9 from the LORD **G** of Israel
1Ki 11:23 **G** raised up another adversary
1Ki 11:31 the LORD, the **G** of Israel
1Ki 12:22 But the word of **G** came to
1Ki 12:22 came to Shemaiah the man of **G**
1Ki 13: 1 a man of **G** went from Judah to
1Ki 13: 4 the saying of the man of **G**
1Ki 13: 5 of **G** had given by the word of
1Ki 13: 6 and said to the man of **G**
1Ki 13: 6 the favor of the LORD your **G**
1Ki 13: 6 So the man of **G** entreated
1Ki 13: 7 the king said to the man of **G**
1Ki 13: 8 But the man of **G** said to the
1Ki 13:11 the works that the man of **G**
1Ki 13:12 of **G** went who came from Judah
1Ki 13:14 and went after the man of **G**
1Ki 13:14 Are you the man of **G** who came
1Ki 13:21 man of **G** who came from Judah
1Ki 13:21 the LORD your **G** commanded
1Ki 13:26 It is the man of **G** who was
1Ki 13:29 up the corpse of the man of **G**
1Ki 13:31 where the man of **G** is buried
1Ki 14: 7 says the LORD **G** of Israel
1Ki 14:13 good toward the LORD **G** of
1Ki 15: 3 not loyal to the LORD his **G**
1Ki 15: 4 LORD his **G** gave him a lamp in
1Ki 15:30 the LORD **G** of Israel to anger
1Ki 16:13 in provoking the LORD **G** of
1Ki 16:26 sin, provoking the LORD **G** of
1Ki 16:33 more to provoke the LORD **G** of
1Ki 17: 1 As the LORD **G** of Israel lives
1Ki 17:12 As the LORD your **G** lives, I
1Ki 17:14 says the LORD **G** of Israel
1Ki 17:18 I to do with you, O man of **G**
1Ki 17:20 O LORD my **G**, have You also
1Ki 17:21 O LORD my **G**, I pray, let this
1Ki 17:24 know that you are a man of **G**
1Ki 18:10 As the LORD your **G** lives,
1Ki 18:21 If the LORD is **G**, follow Him
1Ki 18:24 the **G** who answers by fire, He
1Ki 18:24 who answers by fire, He is **G**
1Ki 18:36 LORD **G** of Abraham, Isaac, and
1Ki 18:36 day that You are **G** in Israel
1Ki 18:37 know that You are the LORD **G**
1Ki 18:39 The LORD, He is **G**
1Ki 18:39 The LORD, He is **G**
1Ki 19: 8 as Horeb, the mountain of **G**
1Ki 19:10 for the LORD **G** of hosts
1Ki 19:14 for the LORD **G** of hosts
1Ki 20:28 Then a man of **G** came and
1Ki 20:28 The LORD is **G** of the hills,
1Ki 20:28 hills, but He is not **G** of the
1Ki 21:10 You have blasphemed **G** and
1Ki 21:13 Naboth has blasphemed **G** and
1Ki 22:53 provoked the LORD **G** of Israel
2Ki 1: 3 no **G** in Israel that you are
2Ki 1: 6 no **G** in Israel that you are
2Ki 1: 9 Man of **G**, the king has said
2Ki 1:10 If I am a man of **G**, then let
2Ki 1:11 Man of **G**, thus has the king
2Ki 1:12 If I am a man of **G**, let fire
2Ki 1:12 the fire of **G** came down from
2Ki 1:13 Man of **G**, please let my life
2Ki 1:16 is it because there is no **G**
2Ki 2:14 Where is the LORD **G** of Elijah
2Ki 4: 7 she came and told the man of **G**
2Ki 4: 9 that this is a holy man of **G**
2Ki 4:16 Man of **G**, do not lie to your
2Ki 4:21 on the bed of the man of **G**
2Ki 4:22 I may run to the man of **G**
2Ki 4:25 the man of **G** at Mount Carmel
2Ki 4:25 when the man of **G** saw her
2Ki 4:27 to the man of **G** at the hill
2Ki 4:27 But the man of **G** said, "Let
2Ki 4:40 O man of **G**, there is death in
2Ki 4:42 brought the man of **G** bread of
2Ki 5: 7 Am I **G**, to kill and make alive
2Ki 5: 8 of **G** heard that the king of
2Ki 5:11 on the name of the LORD his **G**
2Ki 5:14 to the saying of the man of **G**
2Ki 5:15 he returned to the man of **G**
2Ki 5:15 is no **G** in all the earth,
2Ki 5:20 of Elisha the man of **G**, said,
2Ki 6: 6 And the man of **G** said, "Where
2Ki 6: 9 the man of **G** sent to the king
2Ki 6:10 the man of **G** had told him
2Ki 6:15 of the man of **G** arose early
2Ki 6:31 **G** do so to me and more also,
2Ki 7: 2 leaned answered the man of **G**
2Ki 7:17 just as the man of **G** had said
2Ki 7:18 of **G** had spoken to the king
2Ki 7:19 had answered the man of **G**
2Ki 8: 2 to the saying of the man of **G**
2Ki 8: 4 the servant of the man of **G**
2Ki 8: 7 The man of **G** has come here
2Ki 8: 8 and go to meet the man of **G**
2Ki 8:11 and the man of **G** wept
2Ki 9: 6 says the LORD **G** of Israel
2Ki 10:31 LORD **G** of Israel with all his
2Ki 13:19 the man of **G** was angry with
2Ki 14:25 word of the LORD **G** of Israel
2Ki 16: 2 the sight of the LORD his **G**
2Ki 17: 7 against the LORD their **G**, who
2Ki 17: 9 **G** things that were not right
2Ki 17:14 believe in the LORD their **G**
2Ki 17:16 of the LORD their **G**, made for
2Ki 17:19 of the LORD their **G**, but
2Ki 17:26 rituals of the **G** of the land
2Ki 17:26 rituals of the **G** of the land
2Ki 17:27 rituals of the **G** of the land
2Ki 17:39 LORD your **G** you shall fear
2Ki 18: 5 in the LORD **G** of Israel, so
2Ki 18:12 the voice of the LORD their **G**
2Ki 18:22 We trust in the LORD our **G**
2Ki 19: 4 may be that the LORD your **G**
2Ki 19: 4 sent to reproach the living **G**
2Ki 19: 4 the LORD your **G** has heard
2Ki 19:10 Do not let your **G** in whom
2Ki 19:15 O LORD **G** of Israel, the One
2Ki 19:15 the cherubim, You are **G**, You
2Ki 19:16 sent to reproach the living **G**
2Ki 19:19 Now therefore, O LORD our **G**
2Ki 19:19 know that You are the LORD **G**
2Ki 19:20 says the LORD **G** of Israel
2Ki 20: 5 the **G** of David your father
2Ki 21:12 says the LORD **G** of Israel
2Ki 21:22 the LORD **G** of his fathers
2Ki 22:15 says the LORD **G** of Israel
2Ki 22:18 says the LORD **G** of Israel
2Ki 23:16 which the man of **G** proclaimed
2Ki 23:17 man of **G** who came from Judah
2Ki 23:21 Passover to the LORD your **G**
1Ch 4:10 on the **G** of Israel saying
1Ch 4:10 So **G** granted him what he
1Ch 5:20 cried out to **G** in the battle
1Ch 5:25 to the **G** of their fathers

1Ch 5:25 whom **G** had destroyed before
1Ch 5:26 So the **G** of Israel stirred up
1Ch 6:48 tabernacle of the house of **G**
1Ch 6:49 servant of **G** had commanded
1Ch 9:11 officer over the house of **G**
1Ch 9:13 the service of the house of **G**
1Ch 9:26 treasuries of the house of **G**
1Ch 9:27 of **G** because they had the
1Ch 11: 2 the LORD your **G** said to you
1Ch 11:19 Far be it from me, O my **G**
1Ch 12:17 may the **G** of our fathers look
1Ch 12:18 For your **G** helps you
1Ch 12:22 army, like the army of **G**
1Ch 13: 2 and if it is of the LORD our **G**
1Ch 13: 3 the ark of our **G** back to us
1Ch 13: 5 ark of **G** from Kirjath Jearim
1Ch 13: 6 there the ark of **G** the LORD
1Ch 13: 7 of **G** on a new cart from the
1Ch 13: 8 before **G** with all their might
1Ch 13:10 and he died there before **G**
1Ch 13:12 was afraid of **G** that day,
1Ch 13:12 I bring the ark of **G** to me
1Ch 13:14 The ark of **G** remained with
1Ch 14:10 And David inquired of **G**,
1Ch 14:11 **G** has broken through my
1Ch 14:14 David inquired again of **G**
1Ch 14:14 and **G** said to him, "You shall
1Ch 14:15 for **G** has gone out before you
1Ch 14:16 David did as **G** commanded him
1Ch 15: 1 a place for the ark of **G**, and
1Ch 15: 2 the ark of **G** but the Levites
1Ch 15: 2 them to carry the ark of **G**
1Ch 15:12 up the ark of the LORD **G** of
1Ch 15:13 the LORD our **G** broke out
1Ch 15:14 ark of the LORD **G** of Israel
1Ch 15:15 ark of **G** on their shoulders
1Ch 15:24 trumpets before the ark of **G**
1Ch 15:26 when **G** helped the Levites who
1Ch 16: 1 So they brought the ark of **G**
1Ch 16: 1 and peace offerings before **G**
1Ch 16: 4 praise the LORD **G** of Israel
1Ch 16: 6 the ark of the covenant of **G**
1Ch 16:14 He is the LORD our **G**
1Ch 16:35 Save us, O **G** of our salvation
1Ch 16:36 Blessed be the LORD **G** of
1Ch 16:42 the musical instruments of **G**
1Ch 17: 2 your heart, for **G** is with you
1Ch 17: 3 the word of **G** came to Nathan
1Ch 17:16 Who am I, O LORD **G**
1Ch 17:17 thing in Your sight, O **G**
1Ch 17:17 man of high degree, O LORD **G**
1Ch 17:20 is there any **G** besides You
1Ch 17:21 nation on the earth whom **G**
1Ch 17:22 LORD, have become their **G**
1Ch 17:24 **G** of Israel, is Israel's **G**
1Ch 17:25 For You, O my **G**, have told
1Ch 17:26 And now, LORD, You are **G**, and
1Ch 19:13 and for the cities of our **G**
1Ch 21: 7 **G** was displeased with this
1Ch 21: 8 So David said to **G**, "I have
1Ch 21:15 **G** sent an angel to Jerusalem
1Ch 21:17 And David said to **G**, "Was it
1Ch 21:17 hand, I pray, O LORD my **G**
1Ch 21:30 go before it to inquire of **G**
1Ch 22: 1 is the house of the LORD **G**
1Ch 22: 2 to build the house of **G**
1Ch 22: 6 for the LORD **G** of Israel
1Ch 22: 7 to the name of the LORD my **G**
1Ch 22:11 the house of the LORD your **G**
1Ch 22:12 the law of the LORD your **G**
1Ch 22:18 not the LORD your **G** with you
1Ch 22:19 soul to seek the LORD your **G**
1Ch 22:19 the sanctuary of the LORD **G**
1Ch 22:19 the holy articles of **G** into
1Ch 23:14 sons of Moses the man of **G**
1Ch 23:25 The LORD **G** of Israel has
1Ch 23:28 the service of the house of **G**
1Ch 24: 5 officials of the house of **G**
1Ch 24:19 as the LORD **G** of Israel had
1Ch 25: 5 king's seer in the words of **G**
1Ch 25: 5 For **G** gave Heman fourteen
1Ch 25: 6 the service of the house of **G**
1Ch 26: 5 for **G** blessed him
1Ch 26:20 treasuries of the house of **G**
1Ch 26:32 every matter pertaining to **G**
1Ch 28: 2 and for the footstool of our **G**
1Ch 28: 3 But **G** said to me, 'You shall
1Ch 28: 4 However the LORD **G** of Israel
1Ch 28: 8 and in the hearing of our **G**
1Ch 28: 8 of the LORD your **G**, that you
1Ch 28: 9 know the **G** of your father, and
1Ch 28:12 treasuries of the house of **G**
1Ch 28:20 be dismayed, for the LORD **G**
1Ch 28:20 LORD **G**—my **G**—will be
1Ch 28:21 the service of the house of **G**
1Ch 29: 1 whom alone **G** has chosen, is
1Ch 29: 1 for man but for the LORD **G**
1Ch 29: 2 Now for the house of my **G** I
1Ch 29: 3 on the house of my **G**, I have
1Ch 29: 3 given to the house of my **G**
1Ch 29: 7 of **G** five thousand talents
1Ch 29:10 LORD **G** of Israel, our Father,
1Ch 29:13 Now therefore, our **G**, we
1Ch 29:16 O LORD our **G**, all this
1Ch 29:17 I know also, my **G**, that You
1Ch 29:18 O LORD **G** of Abraham, Isaac,
1Ch 29:20 Now bless the LORD your **G**
1Ch 29:20 the LORD **G** of their fathers
2Ch 1: 1 the LORD his **G** was with him
2Ch 1: 3 of meeting with **G** was there
2Ch 1: 4 had brought up the ark of **G**
2Ch 1: 7 On that night **G** appeared to
2Ch 1: 8 And Solomon said to **G**
2Ch 1: 9 Now, O LORD **G**, let Your
2Ch 1:11 And **G** said to Solomon
2Ch 2: 4 for the name of the LORD my **G**
2Ch 2: 4 set feasts of the LORD our **G**
2Ch 2: 5 for our **G** is greater than all
2Ch 2:12 be the LORD **G** of Israel, who
2Ch 3: 3 for building the house of **G**
2Ch 4:11 Solomon for the house of **G**
2Ch 4:19 made for the house of **G**
2Ch 5: 1 treasuries of the house of **G**
2Ch 5:14 LORD filled the house of **G**
2Ch 6: 4 be the LORD **G** of Israel, who
2Ch 6: 7 name of the LORD **G** of Israel
2Ch 6:10 name of the LORD **G** of Israel
2Ch 6:14 LORD **G** of Israel, there is no
2Ch 6:14 there is no **G** in heaven or on
2Ch 6:16 LORD **G** of Israel, now keep
2Ch 6:17 O LORD **G** of Israel, let Your
2Ch 6:18 But will **G** indeed dwell with
2Ch 6:19 his supplication, O LORD my **G**
2Ch 6:40 Now, my **G**, I pray, let Your
2Ch 6:41 therefore, arise, O LORD **G**
2Ch 6:41 Let Your priests, O LORD **G**
2Ch 6:42 O LORD **G**, do not turn away
2Ch 7: 5 dedicated the house of **G**
2Ch 7:22 the LORD **G** of their fathers
2Ch 8:14 the man of **G** had commanded
2Ch 9: 8 Blessed be the LORD your **G**
2Ch 9: 8 be king for the LORD your **G**
2Ch 9: 8 Because your **G** has loved
2Ch 9:23 which **G** had put in his heart
2Ch 10:15 turn of affairs was from **G**
2Ch 11: 2 came to Shemaiah the man of **G**
2Ch 11:16 to seek the LORD **G** of Israel
2Ch 11:16 the LORD **G** of their fathers
2Ch 13: 5 you not know that the LORD **G**
2Ch 13:10 as for us, the LORD is our **G**
2Ch 13:11 the command of the LORD our **G**
2Ch 13:12 **G** Himself is with us as our
2Ch 13:12 the LORD **G** of your fathers
2Ch 13:15 that **G** struck Jeroboam and all
2Ch 13:16 **G** delivered them into their
2Ch 13:18 the LORD **G** of their fathers
2Ch 14: 2 in the eyes of the LORD his **G**
2Ch 14: 4 the LORD **G** of their fathers
2Ch 14: 7 we have sought the LORD our **G**
2Ch 14:11 cried out to the LORD his **G**
2Ch 14:11 help us, O LORD our **G**, for we
2Ch 14:11 O LORD, You are our **G**
2Ch 15: 1 Now the Spirit of **G** came upon
2Ch 15: 3 has been without the true **G**
2Ch 15: 4 to the LORD **G** of Israel, and
2Ch 15: 6 for **G** troubled them with
2Ch 15: 9 the LORD his **G** was with him
2Ch 15:12 **G** of their fathers with all
2Ch 15:13 would not seek the LORD **G** of
2Ch 15:18 brought into the house of **G**
2Ch 16: 7 not relied on the LORD your **G**
2Ch 17: 4 sought the **G** of his father
2Ch 18: 5 for **G** will deliver it into
2Ch 18:13 lives, whatever my **G** says
2Ch 18:31 **G** moved them to turn away
2Ch 19: 3 prepared your heart to seek **G**
2Ch 19: 4 the LORD **G** of their fathers
2Ch 19: 7 iniquity with the LORD our **G**
2Ch 20: 6 O LORD **G** of our fathers, are
2Ch 20: 6 are You not **G** in heaven, and
2Ch 20: 7 Are You not our **G**, who drove
2Ch 20:12 O our **G**, will You not judge
2Ch 20:19 **G** of Israel with voices loud
2Ch 20:20 Believe in the LORD your **G**
2Ch 20:29 the fear of **G** was on all the
2Ch 20:30 for his **G** gave him rest all
2Ch 20:33 to the **G** of their fathers
2Ch 21:10 the LORD **G** of his fathers
2Ch 21:12 Thus says the LORD **G** of your
2Ch 22:12 the house of **G** for six years
2Ch 23: 3 the king in the house of **G**
2Ch 23: 9 that were in the temple of **G**
2Ch 24: 5 of your **G** from year to year
2Ch 24: 7 broken into the house of **G**
2Ch 24: 9 of **G** had imposed on Israel in
2Ch 24:13 **G** to its original condition
2Ch 24:16 good in Israel, both toward **G**
2Ch 24:18 the LORD **G** of their fathers
2Ch 24:20 Then the Spirit of **G** came
2Ch 24:20 Thus says **G**: 'Why do you
2Ch 24:24 the LORD **G** of their fathers
2Ch 24:27 repairing of the house of **G**
2Ch 25: 7 But a man of **G** came to him
2Ch 25: 8 **G** shall make you fall before
2Ch 25: 8 for **G** has power to help and to
2Ch 25: 9 Amaziah said to the man of **G**
2Ch 25: 9 And the man of **G** answered
2Ch 25:16 I know that **G** has determined
2Ch 25:20 not heed, for it came from **G**
2Ch 25:24 the house of **G** with Obed-Edom
2Ch 26: 5 He sought **G** in the days of
2Ch 26: 5 in the visions of **G**
2Ch 26: 5 the LORD, **G** made him prosper
2Ch 26: 7 **G** helped him against the
2Ch 26:16 against the LORD his **G** by
2Ch 26:18 have no honor from the LORD **G**
2Ch 27: 6 ways before the LORD his **G**
2Ch 28: 5 Therefore the LORD his **G**
2Ch 28: 6 the LORD **G** of their fathers
2Ch 28: 9 because the LORD **G** of your
2Ch 28:10 guilty before the LORD your **G**
2Ch 28:24 articles of the house of **G**
2Ch 28:24 articles of the house of **G**
2Ch 28:25 the LORD **G** of his fathers
2Ch 29: 5 of the LORD **G** of your fathers
2Ch 29: 6 in the eyes of the LORD our **G**
2Ch 29: 7 holy place to the **G** of Israel
2Ch 29:10 with the LORD **G** of Israel
2Ch 29:36 **G** had prepared the people
2Ch 30: 1 to the LORD **G** of Israel
2Ch 30: 5 LORD **G** of Israel at Jerusalem
2Ch 30: 6 to the LORD **G** of Abraham,
2Ch 30: 7 the LORD **G** of their fathers
2Ch 30: 8 and serve the LORD your **G**
2Ch 30: 9 the LORD your **G** is gracious
2Ch 30:12 Also the hand of **G** was on
2Ch 30:16 the Law of Moses the man of **G**
2Ch 30:19 prepares his heart to seek **G**
2Ch 30:19 the LORD **G** of his fathers,
2Ch 30:22 the LORD **G** of their fathers
2Ch 31: 6 to the LORD their **G** they laid
2Ch 31:13 the ruler of the house of **G**
2Ch 31:14 the freewill offerings to **G**
2Ch 31:20 and true before the LORD his **G**
2Ch 31:21 the service of the house of **G**
2Ch 31:21 commandment, to seek his **G**
2Ch 32: 8 but with us is the LORD our **G**
2Ch 32:11 The LORD our **G** will deliver
2Ch 32:14 that your **G** should be able to
2Ch 32:15 How much less will your **G**
2Ch 32:16 even more against the LORD **G**
2Ch 32:17 revile the LORD **G** of Israel
2Ch 32:17 so the **G** of Hezekiah will not
2Ch 32:19 against the **G** of Jerusalem
2Ch 32:29 for **G** had given him very much
2Ch 32:31 **G** withdrew from him, in order
2Ch 33: 7 had made, in the house of **G**
2Ch 33: 7 of which **G** had said to David
2Ch 33:12 he implored the LORD his **G**
2Ch 33:12 before the **G** of his fathers
2Ch 33:13 knew that the LORD was **G**
2Ch 33:16 to serve the LORD **G** of Israel
2Ch 33:17 but only to the LORD their **G**
2Ch 33:18 Manasseh, his prayer to his **G**
2Ch 33:18 name of the LORD **G** of Israel
2Ch 33:19 how **G** received his entreaty,
2Ch 34: 3 the **G** of his father David
2Ch 34: 8 the house of the LORD his **G**
2Ch 34: 9 brought into the house of **G**
2Ch 34:23 says the LORD **G** of Israel

2Ch 34:26 says the LORD **G** of Israel
2Ch 34:27 **G** when you heard His words
2Ch 34:32 to the covenant of **G**
2Ch 34:32 the **G** of their fathers
2Ch 34:33 serve the LORD their **G**
2Ch 34:33 the LORD **G** of their fathers
2Ch 35: 3 Now serve the LORD your **G**
2Ch 35: 8 rulers of the house of **G**
2Ch 35:21 for **G** commanded me to make
2Ch 35:21 Refrain from meddling with **G**
2Ch 35:22 of Necho from the mouth of **G**
2Ch 36: 5 the sight of the LORD his **G**
2Ch 36:12 the sight of the LORD his **G**
2Ch 36:13 made him swear an oath by **G**
2Ch 36:13 to the LORD **G** of Israel
2Ch 36:15 the LORD **G** of their fathers
2Ch 36:16 mocked the messengers of **G**
2Ch 36:18 articles from the house of **G**
2Ch 36:19 they burned the house of **G**
2Ch 36:23 of the earth the LORD **G** of
2Ch 36:23 the LORD his **G** be with him
Ezra 1: 2 of the earth the LORD **G** of
Ezra 1: 3 May his **G** be with him
Ezra 1: 3 LORD **G** of Israel (He is **G**)
Ezra 1: 4 of **G** which is in Jerusalem
Ezra 1: 5 whose spirits **G** had moved
Ezra 2:68 freely for the house of **G**
Ezra 3: 2 the altar of the **G** of Israel
Ezra 3: 2 the Law of Moses the man of **G**
Ezra 3: 8 the house of **G** at Jerusalem
Ezra 3: 9 working on the house of **G**
Ezra 4: 1 of the LORD **G** of Israel,
Ezra 4: 2 for we seek your **G** as you do
Ezra 4: 3 us to build a house for our **G**
Ezra 4: 3 build to the LORD **G** of Israel
Ezra 4:24 of **G** which is at Jerusalem
Ezra 5: 1 the name of the **G** of Israel
Ezra 5: 2 of **G** which is in Jerusalem
Ezra 5: 2 prophets of **G** were with them
Ezra 5: 5 But the eye of their **G** was
Ezra 5: 8 to the temple of the great **G**
Ezra 5:11 servants of the **G** of heaven
Ezra 5:12 the **G** of heaven to wrath, He
Ezra 5:13 to build this house of **G**
Ezra 5:14 articles of the house of **G**
Ezra 5:15 let the house of **G** be rebuilt
Ezra 5:16 of **G** which is in Jerusalem
Ezra 5:17 this house of **G** at Jerusalem
Ezra 6: 3 the house of **G** at Jerusalem
Ezra 6: 5 articles of the house of **G**
Ezra 6: 5 them in the house of **G**"
Ezra 6: 7 work of this house of **G** alone
Ezra 6: 7 this house of **G** on its site
Ezra 6: 8 building of this house of **G**
Ezra 6: 9 offerings of the **G** of heaven
Ezra 6:10 aroma to the **G** of heaven, and
Ezra 6:12 may the **G** who causes His name
Ezra 6:12 of **G** which is in Jerusalem
Ezra 6:14 of the **G** of Israel, and
Ezra 6:16 of this house of **G** with joy
Ezra 6:17 dedication of this house of **G**
Ezra 6:18 the service of **G** in Jerusalem
Ezra 6:21 to seek the LORD **G** of Israel
Ezra 6:22 in the work of the house of **G**
Ezra 6:22 house of **G**, the **G** of Israel
Ezra 7: 6 which the LORD **G** of Israel
Ezra 7: 6 of the LORD his **G** upon him
Ezra 7: 9 good hand of his **G** upon him
Ezra 7:12 of the Law of the **G** of heaven
Ezra 7:14 your **G** which is in your hand
Ezra 7:15 offered to the **G** of Israel
Ezra 7:16 house of their **G** in Jerusalem
Ezra 7:17 house of your **G** in Jerusalem
Ezra 7:18 to the will of your **G**
Ezra 7:19 of the house of your **G**,
Ezra 7:19 before the **G** of Jerusalem
Ezra 7:20 for the house of your **G**,
Ezra 7:21 of the Law of the **G** of heaven
Ezra 7:23 commanded by the **G** of heaven
Ezra 7:23 the house of the **G** of heaven
Ezra 7:24 servants of this house of **G**
Ezra 7:25 as know the laws of your **G**
Ezra 7:26 not observe the law of your **G**
Ezra 7:27 be the LORD **G** of our fathers
Ezra 7:28 of the LORD my **G** was upon me
Ezra 8:17 for the house of our **G**
Ezra 8:18 good hand of our **G** upon us
Ezra 8:21 humble ourselves before our **G**
Ezra 8:22 The hand of our **G** is upon all
Ezra 8:23 and entreated our **G** for this
Ezra 8:25 house of our **G** which the king
Ezra 8:28 to the LORD **G** of your fathers
Ezra 8:30 to the house of our **G**
Ezra 8:31 the hand of our **G** was upon us
Ezra 8:33 **G** by the hand of Meremoth the
Ezra 8:35 offerings to the **G** of Israel
Ezra 8:36 the people and the house of **G**
Ezra 9: 4 at the words of the **G** of
Ezra 9: 5 out my hands to the LORD my **G**
Ezra 9: 6 O my **G**: I am too ashamed
Ezra 9: 6 lift up my face to You, my **G**
Ezra 9: 8 shown from the LORD our **G**
Ezra 9: 8 that our **G** may enlighten our
Ezra 9: 9 Yet our **G** did not forsake us
Ezra 9: 9 to repair the house of our **G**
Ezra 9:10 And now, O our **G**, what shall
Ezra 9:13 since You our **G** have punished
Ezra 9:15 O LORD **G** of Israel, You are
Ezra 10: 1 down before the house of **G**
Ezra 10: 2 have trespassed against our **G**
Ezra 10: 3 **G** to put away all these wives
Ezra 10: 3 at the commandment of our **G**
Ezra 10: 6 up from before the house of **G**
Ezra 10: 9 open square of the house of **G**
Ezra 10:11 to the LORD **G** of your fathers
Ezra 10:14 the fierce wrath of our **G** is
Neh 1: 4 before the **G** of heaven
Neh 1: 5 LORD **G** of heaven, O great and
Neh 1: 5 heaven, O great and awesome **G**
Neh 2: 4 I prayed to the **G** of heaven
Neh 2: 8 the good hand of my **G** upon me
Neh 2:12 I told no one what my **G** had
Neh 2:18 **G** which had been good upon me
Neh 2:20 The **G** of heaven Himself will
Neh 4: 4 Hear, O our **G**, for we are
Neh 4: 9 we made our prayer to our **G**
Neh 4:15 and that **G** had brought their
Neh 4:20 Our **G** will fight for us
Neh 5: 9 **G** because of the reproach of
Neh 5:13 So may **G** shake out each man
Neh 5:15 so, because of the fear of **G**
Neh 5:19 Remember me, my **G**, for good,
Neh 6: 9 Now therefore, O **G**,
Neh 6:10 together in the house of **G**
Neh 6:12 Then I perceived that **G** had
Neh 6:14 My **G**, remember Tobiah and
Neh 6:16 this work was done by our **G**
Neh 7: 2 and feared **G** more than many
Neh 7: 5 Then my **G** put it into my
Neh 8: 6 blessed the LORD, the great **G**
Neh 8: 8 the book, in the Law of **G**
Neh 8: 9 is holy to the LORD your **G**
Neh 8:16 the courts of the house of **G**
Neh 8:18 from the Book of the Law of **G**
Neh 9: 3 **G** for one-fourth of the day
Neh 9: 3 and worshiped the LORD their **G**
Neh 9: 4 voice to the LORD their **G**
Neh 9: 5 bless the LORD your **G** forever
Neh 9: 7 You are the LORD **G**, Who chose
Neh 9:17 But You are **G**, ready to
Neh 9:18 This is your **g** that brought
Neh 9:31 for You are **G**, gracious and
Neh 9:32 Now therefore, our **G**, the
Neh 9:32 the mighty, and awesome **G**
Neh 10:28 of the lands to the Law of **G**
Neh 10:29 by Moses the servant of **G**
Neh 10:32 service of the house of our **G**
Neh 10:33 work of the house of our **G**
Neh 10:34 into the house of our **G**,
Neh 10:34 the altar of the LORD our **G**
Neh 10:36 flocks, to the house of our **G**
Neh 10:36 in the house of our **G**
Neh 10:37 of the house of our **G**
Neh 10:38 tithes to the house of our **G**
Neh 10:39 neglect the house of our **G**
Neh 11:11 the leader of the house of **G**
Neh 11:16 outside of the house of **G**
Neh 11:22 the service of the house of **G**
Neh 12:24 command of David the man of **G**
Neh 12:36 of David the man of **G**
Neh 12:40 stood in the house of **G**,
Neh 12:43 for **G** had made them rejoice
Neh 12:45 kept the charge of their **G**
Neh 12:46 praise and thanksgiving to **G**
Neh 13: 1 into the congregation of **G**
Neh 13: 2 our **G** turned the curse into a
Neh 13: 4 of the house of our **G**, was
Neh 13: 7 the courts of the house of **G**
Neh 13: 9 articles of the house of **G**
Neh 13:11 is the house of **G** forsaken
Neh 13:14 Remember me, O my **G**,
Neh 13:14 done for the house of my **G**
Neh 13:18 did not our **G** bring all this
Neh 13:22 Remember me, O my **G**,
Neh 13:25 hair, and made them swear by **G**
Neh 13:26 him, who was beloved of his **G**
Neh 13:26 and **G** made him king over all
Neh 13:27 our **G** by marrying pagan
Neh 13:29 Remember them, O my **G**,
Neh 13:31 Remember me, O my **G**, for
Job 1: 1 upright, and one who feared **G**
Job 1: 5 and cursed **G** in their hearts
Job 1: 6 **G** came to present themselves
Job 1: 8 upright man, one who fears **G**
Job 1: 9 Does Job fear **G** for nothing
Job 1:16 The fire of **G** fell from
Job 1:22 sin nor charge **G** with wrong
Job 2: 1 **G** came to present themselves
Job 2: 3 upright man, one who fears **G**
Job 2: 9 Curse **G** and die
Job 2:10 we indeed accept good from **G**
Job 3: 4 may **G** above not seek it, nor
Job 3:23 and whom **G** has hedged in
Job 4: 9 By the blast of **G** they perish
Job 4:17 be more righteous than **G**
Job 5: 8 But as for me, I would seek **G**
Job 5: 8 to **G** I would commit my cause
Job 5:17 is the man whom **G** corrects
Job 6: 4 the terrors of **G** are arrayed
Job 6: 8 that **G** would grant me the
Job 6: 9 it would please **G** to crush me
Job 8: 3 Does **G** subvert judgment
Job 8: 5 If you would earnestly seek **G**
Job 8:13 the paths of all who forget **G**
Job 8:20 **G** will not cast away the
Job 9: 2 a man be righteous before **G**
Job 9: 4 **G** is wise in heart and mighty
Job 9:13 **G** will not withdraw His anger
Job 10: 2 I will say to **G**, 'Do not
Job 11: 5 that **G** would speak, and open
Job 11: 6 Know therefore that **G** exacts
Job 11: 7 out the deep things of **G**
Job 12: 4 his friends, who called on **G**
Job 12: 6 who provoke **G** are secure
Job 12: 6 in what **G** provides by His
Job 13: 3 and I desire to reason with **G**
Job 13: 7 Will you speak wickedly for **G**
Job 13: 8 Will you contend for **G**
Job 15: 4 and restrain prayer before **G**
Job 15: 8 you heard the counsel of **G**
Job 15:11 of **G** too small for you, and
Job 15:13 turn your spirit against **G**
Job 15:15 If **G** puts no trust in His
Job 15:25 out his hand against **G**, and
Job 16:11 **G** has delivered me to the
Job 16:20 my eyes pour out tears to **G**
Job 16:21 might plead for a man with **G**
Job 18:21 of him who does not know **G**
Job 19: 6 then that **G** has wronged me
Job 19:21 the hand of **G** has struck me
Job 19:22 do you persecute me as **G** does
Job 19:26 in my flesh I shall see **G**
Job 20:15 **G** casts them out of his belly
Job 20:23 **G** will cast on him the fury
Job 20:29 from **G** for a wicked man, the
Job 20:29 appointed to him by **G**
Job 21: 9 is the rod of **G** upon them
Job 21:14 Yet they say to **G**, 'Depart
Job 21:17 the sorrows **G** distributes in
Job 21:19 **G** lays up one's iniquity for
Job 21:22 Can anyone teach **G** knowledge
Job 22: 2 Can a man be profitable to **G**
Job 22:12 Is not **G** in the height of
Job 22:13 And you say, 'What does **G**
Job 22:17 They said to **G**, 'Depart from
Job 22:26 and lift up your face to **G**
Job 23:16 For **G** made my heart weak, and
Job 24:12 yet **G** does not charge them
Job 24:22 But **G** draws the mighty away
Job 25: 4 can man be righteous before **G**
Job 27: 2 As **G** lives, who has taken
Job 27: 3 me, and the breath of **G** in my
Job 27: 8 if **G** takes away his life
Job 27: 9 Will **G** hear his cry when
Job 27:10 Will he always call on **G**
Job 27:11 teach you about the hand of **G**
Job 27:13 of a wicked man with **G**, and
Job 28:23 **G** understands its way, and He
Job 29: 2 days when **G** watched over me
Job 29: 4 counsel of **G** was over my tent

Job	31: 2	the allotment of **G** from above
Job	31: 6	that **G** may know my integrity
Job	31:14	shall I do when **G** rises up
Job	31:23	from **G** is a terror to me, and
Job	31:28	have denied **G** who is above
Job	32: 2	himself rather than **G**
Job	32:13	**G** will vanquish him, not man
Job	33: 4	The Spirit of **G** has made me
Job	33: 6	am as your spokesman before **G**
Job	33:12	for **G** is greater than man
Job	33:14	For **G** may speak in one way,
Job	33:26	He shall pray to **G**, and He
Job	33:29	**G** works all these things,
Job	34: 5	but **G** has taken away my
Job	34: 9	that he should delight in **G**
Job	34:10	far be it from **G** to do
Job	34:12	Surely **G** will never do
Job	34:23	go before **G** in judgment
Job	34:31	For has anyone said to **G**, 'I
Job	34:37	his words against **G**
Job	35:10	says, 'Where is **G** my Maker
Job	35:13	Surely **G** will not listen to
Job	36: 5	**G** is mighty, but despises no
Job	36:22	**G** is exalted by His power
Job	36:26	**G** is great, and we do not know
Job	37: 5	**G** thunders marvelously with
Job	37:10	the breath of **G** ice is given
Job	37:14	the wondrous works of **G**
Job	37:15	know when **G** dispatches them
Job	37:22	with **G** is awesome majesty
Job	38: 7	the sons of **G** shouted for joy
Job	38:41	when its young ones cry to **G**
Job	39:17	because **G** deprived her of
Job	40: 2	He who rebukes **G**, let him
Job	40: 9	Have you an arm like **G**
Job	40:19	is the first of the ways of **G**
Ps	3: 2	There is no help for him in **G**
Ps	3: 7	Save me, O my **G**
Ps	4: 1	call, O **G** of my righteousness
Ps	5: 2	of my cry, My King and my **G**
Ps	5: 4	For You are not a **G** who takes
Ps	5:10	Pronounce them guilty, O **G**
Ps	7: 1	O LORD my **G**, in You I put my
Ps	7: 3	O LORD my **G**, if I have done
Ps	7: 9	righteous **G** tests the hearts
Ps	7:10	My defense is of **G**, Who saves
Ps	7:11	**G** is a just judge
Ps	7:11	**G** is angry with the wicked
Ps	9:17	all the nations that forget **G**
Ps	10: 4	countenance does not seek **G**
Ps	10: 4	**G** is in none of his thoughts
Ps	10:11	his heart, "**G** has forgotten
Ps	10:12	O **G**, lift up Your hand
Ps	10:13	Why do the wicked renounce **G**
Ps	13: 3	and hear me, O LORD my **G**
Ps	14: 1	his heart, "There is no **G**."
Ps	14: 2	who understand, who seek **G**
Ps	14: 5	For **G** is with the generation
Ps	16: 1	Preserve me, O **G**, for in You
Ps	17: 6	for You will hear me, O **G**
Ps	18: 2	My **G**, my strength, in whom I
Ps	18: 6	LORD, And cried out to my **G**
Ps	18:21	wickedly departed from my **G**
Ps	18:28	The LORD my **G** will enlighten
Ps	18:29	by my **G** I can leap over a
Ps	18:30	As for **G**, His way is perfect
Ps	18:31	For who is **G**, except the LORD
Ps	18:31	who is a rock, except our **G**
Ps	18:32	It is **G** who arms me with
Ps	18:46	Let the **G** of my salvation be
Ps	18:47	It is **G** who avenges me, And
Ps	19: 1	declare the glory of **G**
Ps	20: 1	of the **G** of Jacob defend you
Ps	20: 5	in the name of our **G** we will
Ps	20: 7	the name of the LORD our **G**
Ps	22: 1	My **G**, My **G**, why have You
Ps	22: 2	O My **G**, I cry in the daytime,
Ps	22:10	womb You have been My **G**
Ps	24: 5	from the **G** of his salvation
Ps	25: 2	O my **G**, I trust in You
Ps	25: 5	You are the **G** of my salvation
Ps	25:22	Redeem Israel, O **G**, Out of
Ps	27: 9	me, O **G** of my salvation
Ps	29: 3	The **G** of glory thunders
Ps	30: 2	O LORD my **G**, I cried out to
Ps	30:12	O LORD my **G**, I will give
Ps	31: 5	me, O LORD **G** of truth
Ps	31:14	You are my **G**
Ps	33:12	nation whose **G** is the LORD
Ps	35:23	To my cause, my **G** and my Lord
Ps	35:24	Vindicate me, O LORD my **G**
Ps	36: 1	no fear of **G** before his eyes
Ps	36: 7	is Your lovingkindness, O **G**
Ps	37:31	The law of his **G** is in his
Ps	38:15	You will hear, O Lord my **G**
Ps	38:21	O my **G**, be not far from me
Ps	40: 3	Praise to our **G**
Ps	40: 5	Many, O LORD my **G**, are Your
Ps	40: 8	to do Your will, O my **G**, And
Ps	40:17	Do not delay, O my **G**
Ps	41:13	Blessed be the LORD **G** of
Ps	42: 1	So pants my soul for You, O **G**
Ps	42: 2	My soul thirsts for **G**
Ps	42: 2	for the living **G**
Ps	42: 2	I come and appear before **G**
Ps	42: 3	Where is your **G**
Ps	42: 4	with them to the house of **G**
Ps	42: 5	Hope in **G**, for I shall yet
Ps	42: 6	O my **G**, my soul is cast down
Ps	42: 8	A prayer to the **G** of my life
Ps	42: 9	I will say to **G** my Rock
Ps	42:10	Where is your **G**?"
Ps	42:11	Hope in **G**
Ps	42:11	of my countenance and my **G**
Ps	43: 1	Vindicate me, O **G**, And plead
Ps	43: 2	You are the **G** of my strength
Ps	43: 4	I will go to the altar of **G**
Ps	43: 4	To **G** my exceeding joy
Ps	43: 4	will praise You, O **G**, my **G**
Ps	43: 5	Hope in **G**
Ps	43: 5	of my countenance and my **G**
Ps	44: 1	have heard with our ears, O **G**
Ps	44: 4	You are my King, O **G**
Ps	44: 8	In **G** we boast all day long,
Ps	44:20	forgotten the name of our **G**
Ps	44:21	Would not **G** search this out
Ps	45: 2	Therefore **G** has blessed You
Ps	45: 6	Your throne, O **G**, is forever
Ps	45: 7	Therefore **G**, Your **G**, has
Ps	46: 1	**G** is our refuge and strength,
Ps	46: 4	shall make glad the city of **G**
Ps	46: 5	**G** is in the midst of her, she
Ps	46: 5	**G** shall help her, just at the
Ps	46: 7	The **G** of Jacob is our refuge
Ps	46:10	Be still, and know that I am **G**
Ps	46:11	The **G** of Jacob is our refuge
Ps	47: 1	Shout to **G** with the voice of
Ps	47: 5	**G** has gone up with a shout,
Ps	47: 6	Sing praises to **G**, sing
Ps	47: 7	For **G** is the King of all the
Ps	47: 8	**G** reigns over the nations
Ps	47: 8	**G** sits on His holy throne
Ps	47: 9	people of the **G** of Abraham
Ps	47: 9	of the earth belong to **G**
Ps	48: 1	praised In the city of our **G**
Ps	48: 3	**G** is in her palaces
Ps	48: 8	hosts, In the city of our **G**
Ps	48: 8	**G** will establish it forever
Ps	48: 9	We have thought, O **G**, on Your
Ps	48:10	According to Your name, O **G**
Ps	48:14	is **G**, Our **G** forever and ever
Ps	49: 7	Nor give to **G** a ransom for
Ps	49:15	But **G** will redeem my soul
Ps	50: 1	**G** the LORD, Has spoken and
Ps	50: 2	of beauty, **G** will shine forth
Ps	50: 3	Our **G** shall come, and shall
Ps	50: 6	For **G** Himself is Judge
Ps	50: 7	I am **G**, your **G**
Ps	50:14	Offer to **G** thanksgiving, And
Ps	50:16	But to the wicked **G** says
Ps	50:22	this, you who forget **G**, Lest
Ps	50:23	will show the salvation of **G**
Ps	51: 1	Have mercy upon me, O **G**,
Ps	51:10	in me a clean heart, O **G**, And
Ps	51:14	me from bloodguiltiness, O **G**
Ps	51:14	The **G** of my salvation, And my
Ps	51:17	The sacrifices of **G** are a
Ps	51:17	These, O **G**, You will not
Ps	52: 1	The goodness of **G** endures
Ps	52: 5	**G** shall likewise destroy you
Ps	52: 7	did not make **G** his strength
Ps	52: 8	olive tree in the house of **G**
Ps	52: 8	in the mercy of **G** forever
Ps	53: 1	There is no **G**
Ps	53: 2	**G** looks down from heaven upon
Ps	53: 2	who understand, who seek **G**
Ps	53: 4	bread, And do not call upon **G**
Ps	53: 5	For **G** has scattered the bones
Ps	53: 5	Because **G** has despised them
Ps	53: 6	When **G** brings back the
Ps	54: 1	Save me, O **G**, by Your name,
Ps	54: 2	Hear my prayer, O **G**
Ps	54: 3	have not set **G** before them
Ps	54: 4	Behold, **G** is my helper
Ps	55: 1	Give ear to my prayer, O **G**
Ps	55:14	the house of **G** in the throng
Ps	55:16	As for me, I will call upon **G**
Ps	55:19	**G** will hear, and afflict them,
Ps	55:19	Therefore they do not fear **G**
Ps	55:23	But You, O **G**, shall bring
Ps	56: 1	Be merciful to me, O **G**, for
Ps	56: 4	In **G** (I will praise His word)
Ps	56: 4	In **G** I have put my trust
Ps	56: 7	cast down the peoples, O **G**
Ps	56: 9	I know, because **G** is for me
Ps	56:10	In **G** (I will praise His word)
Ps	56:11	In **G** I have put my trust
Ps	56:12	You are binding upon me, O **G**
Ps	56:13	That I may walk before **G** In
Ps	57: 1	Be merciful to me, O **G**, be
Ps	57: 2	I will cry out to **G** Most High
Ps	57: 2	To **G** who performs all things
Ps	57: 3	Selah **G** shall send forth His
Ps	57: 5	Be exalted, O **G**, above the
Ps	57: 7	My heart is steadfast, O **G**
Ps	57:11	Be exalted, O **G**, above the
Ps	58: 6	teeth in their mouth, O **G**
Ps	58:11	Surely He is **G** who judges in
Ps	59: 1	me from my enemies, O my **G**
Ps	59: 5	O LORD **G** of hosts, the **G** of
Ps	59: 5	the **G** of Israel, Awake to
Ps	59: 9	For **G** is my defense
Ps	59:10	My merciful **G** shall come to
Ps	59:10	**G** shall let me see my desire
Ps	59:13	let them know that **G** rules in
Ps	59:17	For **G** is my defense
Ps	59:17	The **G** of my mercy
Ps	60: 1	O **G**, You have cast us off
Ps	60: 6	**G** has spoken in His holiness
Ps	60:10	Is it not You, O **G**, who cast
Ps	60:10	And You, O **G**, who did not go
Ps	60:12	Through **G** we will do
Ps	61: 1	Hear my cry, O **G**
Ps	61: 5	For You, O **G**, have heard my
Ps	61: 7	shall abide before **G** forever
Ps	62: 1	my soul silently waits for **G**
Ps	62: 5	wait silently for **G** alone
Ps	62: 7	In **G** is my salvation and my
Ps	62: 7	And my refuge, is in **G**
Ps	62: 8	**G** is a refuge for us
Ps	62:11	**G** has spoken once, Twice I
Ps	62:11	That power belongs to **G**
Ps	63: 1	O **G**, You are my **G**
Ps	63:11	the king shall rejoice in **G**
Ps	64: 1	Hear my voice, O **G**, in my
Ps	64: 7	But **G** shall shoot at them
Ps	64: 9	shall declare the work of **G**
Ps	65: 1	Praise is awaiting You, O **G**
Ps	65: 5	O **G** of our salvation, You who
Ps	65: 9	The river of **G** is full of
Ps	66: 1	Make a joyful shout to **G**, all
Ps	66: 3	Say to **G**, "How awesome are
Ps	66: 5	Come and see the works of **G**
Ps	66: 8	Oh, bless our **G**, you peoples
Ps	66:10	For You, O **G**, have proved us
Ps	66:16	and hear, all you who fear **G**
Ps	66:19	But certainly **G** has heard me
Ps	66:20	Blessed be **G**, Who has not
Ps	67: 1	**G** be merciful to us and bless
Ps	67: 3	the peoples praise You, O **G**
Ps	67: 5	the peoples praise You, O **G**
Ps	67: 6	**G**, our own **G**, shall bless
Ps	67: 7	**G** shall bless us, And all the
Ps	68: 1	Let **G** arise, Let His enemies
Ps	68: 2	perish at the presence of **G**
Ps	68: 3	Let them rejoice before **G**
Ps	68: 4	Sing to **G**, sing praises to
Ps	68: 5	Is **G** in His holy habitation
Ps	68: 6	**G** sets the solitary in
Ps	68: 7	O **G**, when You went out before
Ps	68: 8	rain at the presence of **G**
Ps	68: 8	moved at the presence of **G**
Ps	68: 8	the **G** of Israel
Ps	68: 9	You, O **G**, sent a plentiful
Ps	68:10	You, O **G**, provided from Your
Ps	68:15	A mountain of **G** is the
Ps	68:16	which **G** desires to dwell in
Ps	68:17	The chariots of **G** are twenty
Ps	68:18	That the LORD **G** might dwell
Ps	68:19	The **G** of our salvation

Ps 68:20 Our **G** is the **G** of salvation
Ps 68:20 to **G** the Lord belong escapes
Ps 68:21 But **G** will wound the head of
Ps 68:24 seen Your procession, O **G**
Ps 68:24 O **G**, The procession of my **G**
Ps 68:26 Bless **G** in the congregations,
Ps 68:28 Your **G** has commanded your
Ps 68:28 Strengthen, O **G**, what You
Ps 68:31 stretch out her hands to **G**
Ps 68:32 Sing to **G**, you kingdoms of
Ps 68:34 Ascribe strength to **G**
Ps 68:35 O **G**, You are more awesome
Ps 68:35 The **G** of Israel is He who
Ps 68:35 Blessed be **G**
Ps 69: 1 Save me, O **G**
Ps 69: 3 fail while I wait for my **G**
Ps 69: 5 O **G**, You know my foolishness
Ps 69: 6 O Lord **G** of hosts, be ashamed
Ps 69: 6 because of me, O **G** of Israel
Ps 69:13 O **G**, in the multitude of Your
Ps 69:29 Let Your salvation, O **G**, set
Ps 69:30 the name of **G** with a song
Ps 69:32 And you who seek **G**, your
Ps 69:35 For **G** will save Zion And build
Ps 70: 1 Make haste, O **G**, to deliver
Ps 70: 4 Let **G** be magnified
Ps 70: 5 Make haste to me, O **G**
Ps 71: 4 Deliver me, O my **G**, out of
Ps 71: 5 For You are my hope, O Lord **G**
Ps 71:11 Saying, "**G** has forsaken him
Ps 71:12 O **G**, do not be far from me
Ps 71:12 O my **G**, make haste to help me
Ps 71:16 in the strength of the Lord **G**
Ps 71:17 O **G**, You have taught me from
Ps 71:18 I am old and gray-headed, O **G**
Ps 71:19 Also Your righteousness, O **G**
Ps 71:19 O **G**, who is like You
Ps 71:22 And Your faithfulness, O my **G**
Ps 72: 1 the king Your judgments, O **G**
Ps 72:18 Blessed be the LORD **G**, the
Ps 72:18 the **G** of Israel, Who only
Ps 73: 1 Truly **G** is good to Israel, To
Ps 73:11 How does **G** know
Ps 73:17 went into the sanctuary of **G**
Ps 73:26 But **G** is the strength of my
Ps 73:28 good for me to draw near to **G**
Ps 73:28 put my trust in the Lord **G**
Ps 74: 1 O **G**, why have You cast us off
Ps 74: 8 places of **G** in the land
Ps 74:10 O **G**, how long will the
Ps 74:12 For **G** is my King from of old,
Ps 74:22 Arise, O **G**, plead Your own
Ps 75: 1 We give thanks to You, O **G**
Ps 75: 7 But **G** is the Judge
Ps 75: 9 praises to the **G** of Jacob
Ps 76: 1 In Judah **G** is known
Ps 76: 6 O **G** of Jacob, Both the
Ps 76: 9 When **G** arose to judgment, To
Ps 76:11 Make vows to the LORD your **G**
Ps 77: 1 cried out to **G** with my voice
Ps 77: 1 To **G** with my voice
Ps 77: 3 I remembered **G**, and was
Ps 77: 9 Has **G** forgotten to be
Ps 77:13 Your way, O **G**, is in the
Ps 77:13 is so great a **G** as our **G**
Ps 77:14 You are the **G** who does
Ps 77:16 The waters saw You, O **G**
Ps 78: 7 they may set their hope in **G**
Ps 78: 7 And not forget the works of **G**
Ps 78: 8 spirit was not faithful to **G**
Ps 78:10 not keep the covenant of **G**
Ps 78:18 they tested **G** in their heart
Ps 78:19 Yes, they spoke against **G**
Ps 78:19 Can **G** prepare a table in the
Ps 78:22 they did not believe in **G**
Ps 78:31 The wrath of **G** came against
Ps 78:34 and sought diligently for **G**
Ps 78:35 that **G** was their rock, And the
Ps 78:35 And the Most High **G** their
Ps 78:41 again and again they tempted **G**
Ps 78:56 and provoked the Most High **G**
Ps 78:59 When **G** heard this, He was
Ps 79: 1 O **G**, the nations have come
Ps 79: 9 O **G** of our salvation, For the
Ps 79:10 Where is their **G**?"
Ps 80: 3 Restore us, O **G**
Ps 80: 4 O LORD **G** of hosts, How long
Ps 80: 7 Restore us, O **G** of hosts
Ps 80:14 we beseech You, O **G** of hosts
Ps 80:19 Restore us, O LORD **G** of hosts

Ps 81: 1 Sing aloud to **G** our strength
Ps 81: 1 shout to the **G** of Jacob
Ps 81: 4 And a law of the **G** of Jacob
Ps 81:10 I am the LORD your **G**, Who
Ps 82: 1 **G** stands in the congregation
Ps 82: 8 Arise, O **G**, judge the earth
Ps 83: 1 Do not keep silent, O **G**
Ps 83: 1 And do not be still, O **G**
Ps 83:12 of **G** for a possession
Ps 83:13 O my **G**, make them like the
Ps 84: 2 cry out for the living **G**
Ps 84: 3 of hosts, My King and my **G**
Ps 84: 7 them appears before **G** in Zion
Ps 84: 8 O LORD **G** of hosts, hear my
Ps 84: 8 Give ear, O **G** of Jacob
Ps 84: 9 O **G**, behold our shield, And
Ps 84:10 in the house of my **G** Than
Ps 84:11 For the LORD **G** is a sun and
Ps 85: 4 us, O **G** of our salvation, And
Ps 85: 8 I will hear what **G** the LORD
Ps 86: 2 You are my **G**
Ps 86:10 You alone are **G**
Ps 86:12 will praise You, O Lord my **G**
Ps 86:14 O **G**, the proud have risen
Ps 86:15 are a **G** full of compassion,
Ps 87: 3 spoken of you, O city of **G**
Ps 88: 1 **G** of my salvation, I have
Ps 89: 7 **G** is greatly to be feared in
Ps 89: 8 O LORD **G** of hosts, Who is
Ps 89:26 Me, 'You are my Father, My **G**
Ps 90: 2 to everlasting, You are **G**
Ps 90:17 of the LORD our **G** be upon us
Ps 91: 2 My **G**, in Him I will trust
Ps 92:13 in the courts of our **G**
Ps 94: 1 O LORD **G**, to whom vengeance
Ps 94: 1 O **G**, to whom vengeance
Ps 94: 7 see, Nor does the **G** of Jacob
Ps 94:22 my **G** the rock of my refuge
Ps 94:23 The LORD our **G** shall cut them
Ps 95: 3 For the LORD is the great **G**
Ps 95: 7 For He is our **G**, And we are
Ps 98: 3 seen the salvation of our **G**
Ps 99: 5 Exalt the LORD our **G**, And
Ps 99: 8 answered them, O LORD our **G**
Ps 99: 9 Exalt the LORD our **G**, And
Ps 99: 9 For the LORD our **G** is holy
Ps 100: 3 Know that the LORD, He is **G**
Ps 102:24 O my **G**, Do not take me away
Ps 104: 1 O LORD my **G**, You are very
Ps 104:21 And seek their food from **G**
Ps 104:33 to my **G** while I have my being
Ps 105: 7 He is the LORD our **G**
Ps 106:14 And tested **G** in the desert
Ps 106:21 They forgot **G** their Savior,
Ps 106:47 Save us, O LORD our **G**, And
Ps 106:48 Blessed be the LORD **G** of
Ps 107:11 against the words of **G**, And
Ps 108: 1 O **G**, my heart is steadfast
Ps 108: 5 Be exalted, O **G**, above the
Ps 108: 7 **G** has spoken in His holiness
Ps 108:11 Is it not You, O **G**, who cast
Ps 108:11 And You, O **G**, who did not go
Ps 108:13 Through **G** we will do
Ps 109: 1 keep silent, O **G** of my praise
Ps 109:21 O **G** the Lord, Deal with me
Ps 109:26 Help me, O LORD my **G**
Ps 113: 5 Who is like the LORD our **G**
Ps 114: 7 presence of the **G** of Jacob
Ps 115: 2 Where now is their **G**
Ps 115: 3 But our **G** is in heaven
Ps 116: 5 Yes, our **G** is merciful
Ps 118:27 **G** is the LORD, And He has
Ps 118:28 You are my **G**, and I will
Ps 118:28 You are my **G**, I will exalt
Ps 119:115 the commandments of my **G**
Ps 122: 9 our **G** I will seek your good
Ps 123: 2 eyes look to the LORD our **G**
Ps 132: 2 to the Mighty **G** of Jacob
Ps 132: 5 for the Mighty **G** of Jacob
Ps 135: 2 courts of the house of our **G**
Ps 136: 2 give thanks to the **G** of gods
Ps 136:26 thanks to the **G** of heaven
Ps 139:17 are Your thoughts to me, O **G**
Ps 139:19 would slay the wicked, O **G**
Ps 139:23 Search me, O **G**, and know my
Ps 140: 6 You are my **G**
Ps 140: 7 O **G** the Lord, the strength of
Ps 141: 8 are upon You, O **G** the Lord
Ps 143:10 Your will, For You are my **G**
Ps 144: 9 sing a new song to You, O **G**

Ps 144:15 people whose **G** is the LORD
Ps 145: 1 I will extol You, my **G**, O
Ps 146: 2 to my **G** while I have my being
Ps 146: 5 the **G** of Jacob for his help
Ps 146: 5 hope is in the LORD his **G**
Ps 146:10 Your **G**, O Zion, to all
Ps 147: 1 good to sing praises to our **G**
Ps 147: 7 praises on the harp to our **G**
Ps 147:12 Praise your **G**, O Zion
Ps 149: 6 of **G** be in their mouth, And a
Ps 150: 1 Praise **G** in His sanctuary
Prov 2: 5 and find the knowledge of **G**
Prov 2:17 forgets the covenant of her **G**
Prov 3: 4 high esteem in the sight of **G**
Prov 21:12 The righteous **G** wisely
Prov 25: 2 It is the glory of **G** to
Prov 26:10 The great **G** who formed all
Prov 30: 5 Every word of **G** is pure
Prov 30: 9 and profane the name of my **G**
Eccl 1:13 this grievous task **G** has
Eccl 2:24 I saw, was from the hand of **G**
Eccl 2:26 For **G** gives wisdom and
Eccl 2:26 to him who is good before **G**
Eccl 3:11 **G** does from beginning to end
Eccl 3:13 it is the gift of **G**
Eccl 3:14 I know that whatever **G** does
Eccl 3:14 **G** does it, that men should
Eccl 3:15 **G** requires an account of what
Eccl 3:17 **G** shall judge the righteous
Eccl 3:18 **G** tests them, that they may
Eccl 5: 1 when you go to the house of **G**
Eccl 5: 2 anything hastily before **G**
Eccl 5: 2 For **G** is in heaven, and you on
Eccl 5: 4 When you make a vow to **G**, do
Eccl 5: 6 of **G** that it was an error
Eccl 5: 6 Why should **G** be angry at your
Eccl 5: 7 But fear **G**
Eccl 5:18 of his life which **G** gives him
Eccl 5:19 to whom **G** has given riches
Eccl 5:19 this is the gift of **G**
Eccl 5:20 because **G** keeps him busy with
Eccl 6: 2 A man to whom **G** has given
Eccl 6: 2 yet **G** does not give him power
Eccl 7:13 Consider the work of **G**
Eccl 7:14 Surely **G** has appointed the
Eccl 7:18 for he who fears **G** will
Eccl 7:26 He who pleases **G** shall escape
Eccl 7:29 that **G** made man upright, but
Eccl 8: 2 the sake of your oath to **G**
Eccl 8:12 be well with those who fear **G**
Eccl 8:13 he does not fear before **G**
Eccl 8:15 **G** gives him under the sun
Eccl 8:17 then I saw all the work of **G**
Eccl 9: 1 works are in the hand of **G**
Eccl 9: 7 for **G** has already accepted
Eccl 11: 5 of **G** who makes all things
Eccl 11: 9 these **G** will bring you into
Eccl 12: 7 will return to **G** who gave it
Eccl 12:13 Fear **G** and keep His
Eccl 12:14 For **G** will bring every work
Is 1:10 give ear to the law of our **G**
Is 2: 3 the house of the **G** of Jacob
Is 3:15 says the Lord **G** of hosts
Is 5:16 and **G** who is holy shall be
Is 7: 7 thus says the Lord **G**
Is 7:11 yourself from the LORD your **G**
Is 7:13 but will you weary my **G** also
Is 8:10 not stand, for **G** is with us
Is 8:19 not a people seek their **G**
Is 8:21 curse their king and their **G**
Is 9: 6 Counselor, Mighty **G**,
Is 10:21 of Jacob, to the Mighty **G**
Is 10:23 For the Lord **G** of hosts will
Is 10:24 thus says the Lord **G** of hosts
Is 12: 2 **G** is my salvation, I will
Is 13:19 be as when **G** overthrew Sodom
Is 14:13 throne above the stars of **G**
Is 17: 6 Says the LORD **G** of Israel
Is 17:10 the **G** of your salvation, and
Is 17:13 but **G** will rebuke them and
Is 21:10 the **G** of Israel, I have
Is 21:17 for the LORD **G** of Israel has
Is 22: 5 perplexity by the Lord **G** of
Is 22:12 in that day the Lord **G** of
Is 22:14 says the Lord **G** of hosts
Is 22:15 Thus says the Lord **G** of hosts
Is 24:15 the name of the LORD **G** of
Is 25: 1 O LORD, You are my **G**
Is 25: 8 the Lord **G** will wipe away
Is 25: 9 Behold, this is our **G**

Is 26: 1 **G** will appoint salvation for
Is 26:13 O LORD our **G**, other masters
Is 28:16 thus says the Lord **G**
Is 28:22 from the Lord **G** of hosts, a
Is 28:26 judgment, his **G** teaches him
Is 29:23 and fear the **G** of Israel
Is 30:15 For thus says the Lord **G**, the
Is 30:18 the LORD is a **G** of justice
Is 31: 3 Egyptians are men, and not **G**
Is 35: 2 LORD, the excellency of our **G**
Is 35: 4 Behold, your **G** will come with
Is 35: 4 with the recompense of **G**
Is 36: 7 We trust in the LORD our **G**
Is 37: 4 may be that the LORD your **G**
Is 37: 4 sent to reproach the living **G**
Is 37: 4 the LORD your **G** has heard
Is 37:10 Do not let your **G** in whom
Is 37:16 **G** of Israel, the One who
Is 37:16 the cherubim, You are **G**, You
Is 37:17 sent to reproach the living **G**
Is 37:20 Now therefore, O LORD our **G**
Is 37:21 says the LORD **G** of Israel
Is 38: 5 the **G** of David your father
Is 40: 1 My people!" says your **G**.
Is 40: 3 desert a highway for our **G**
Is 40: 8 word of our **G** stands forever
Is 40: 9 Behold your **G**!"
Is 40:10 the Lord **G** shall come with a
Is 40:18 To whom then will you liken **G**
Is 40:27 is passed over by my **G**"
Is 40:28 The everlasting **G**, the LORD,
Is 41:10 not dismayed, for I am your **G**
Is 41:13 For I, the LORD your **G**, will
Is 41:17 the **G** of Israel, will not
Is 42: 5 Thus says **G** the LORD, Who
Is 43: 3 For I am the LORD your **G**, the
Is 43:10 Me there was no **G** formed, nor
Is 43:12 says the LORD, "that I am **G**.
Is 44: 6 besides Me there is no **G**
Is 44: 8 Is there a **G** besides Me
Is 45: 3 your name, am the **G** of Israel
Is 45: 5 there is no **G** besides Me
Is 45:14 Surely **G** is in you, and there
Is 45:14 there is no other **G**
Is 45:15 Truly You are **G**, who hide
Is 45:15 O **G** of Israel, the Savior
Is 45:18 created the heavens, Who is **G**
Is 45:21 is no other **G** besides Me
Is 45:21 a just **G** and a Savior
Is 45:22 For I am **G**, and there is no
Is 46: 9 things of old, for I am **G**
Is 46: 9 I am **G**, and there is none like
Is 48: 1 mention of the **G** of Israel
Is 48: 2 and lean on the **G** of Israel
Is 48:16 And now the Lord **G** and His
Is 48:17 I am the LORD your **G**, Who
Is 49: 4 LORD, and my work with my **G**
Is 49: 5 My **G** shall be My strength),
Is 49:22 Thus says the Lord **G**
Is 50: 4 The Lord **G** has given Me the
Is 50: 5 The Lord **G** has opened My ear
Is 50: 7 For the Lord **G** will help Me
Is 50: 9 the Lord **G** will help Me
Is 50:10 the LORD and rely upon his **G**
Is 51:15 But I am the LORD your **G**, who
Is 51:20 LORD, the rebuke of your **G**
Is 51:22 your Lord, the LORD and your **G**
Is 52: 4 For thus says the Lord **G**
Is 52: 7 says to Zion, "Your **G** reigns
Is 52:10 see the salvation of our **G**
Is 52:12 the **G** of Israel will be your
Is 53: 4 Him stricken, smitten by **G**
Is 54: 5 He is called the **G** of the
Is 54: 6 were refused," says your **G**
Is 55: 5 because of the LORD your **G**
Is 55: 7 and to our **G**, for He will
Is 56: 8 The Lord **G**, who gathers the
Is 57:21 is no peace," says my **G**
Is 58: 2 the ordinance of their **G**
Is 58: 2 take delight in approaching **G**
Is 59: 2 separated you from your **G**
Is 59:13 LORD, and departing from our **G**
Is 60: 9 the name of the LORD your **G**
Is 60:19 light, and your **G** your glory
Is 61: 1 of the Lord **G** is upon Me,
Is 61: 2 the day of vengeance of our **G**
Is 61: 6 you the Servants of our **G**
Is 61:10 soul shall be joyful in my **G**
Is 61:11 so the Lord **G** will cause
Is 62: 3 diadem in the hand of your **G**
Is 62: 5 so shall your **G** rejoice over
Is 64: 4 eye seen any **G** besides You
Is 65:13 thus says the Lord **G**
Is 65:15 for the Lord **G** will slay you,
Is 65:16 himself in the **G** of truth
Is 65:16 shall swear by the **G** of truth
Is 66: 9 shut up the womb?" says your **G**
Jer 1: 6 Ah, Lord **G**! Behold, I cannot
Jer 2:17 **G** when He led you in the way
Jer 2:19 have forsaken the LORD your **G**
Jer 2:19 says the Lord **G** of hosts
Jer 2:22 before Me," says the Lord **G**
Jer 3:13 against the LORD your **G**, and
Jer 3:21 forgotten the LORD their **G**
Jer 3:22 for You are the LORD our **G**
Jer 3:23 in the LORD our **G** is the
Jer 3:25 sinned against the LORD our **G**
Jer 3:25 the voice of the LORD our **G**
Jer 4:10 Then I said, "Ah, Lord **G**!
Jer 5: 4 LORD, the judgment of their **G**
Jer 5: 5 LORD, the judgment of their **G**
Jer 5:14 thus says the LORD **G** of hosts
Jer 5:19 Why does the LORD our **G** do
Jer 5:24 us now fear the LORD our **G**
Jer 7: 3 of hosts, the **G** of Israel
Jer 7:20 thus says the Lord **G**
Jer 7:21 of hosts, the **G** of Israel
Jer 7:23 My voice, and I will be your **G**
Jer 7:28 **G** nor receive correction
Jer 8:14 For the LORD our **G** has put us
Jer 9:15 of hosts, the **G** of Israel
Jer 10:10 But the LORD is the true **G**
Jer 10:10 He is the living **G** and the
Jer 11: 3 says the LORD **G** of Israel
Jer 11: 4 people, and I will be your **G**
Jer 13:12 says the LORD **G** of Israel
Jer 13:16 **G** before He causes darkness
Jer 14:13 Then I said, "Ah, Lord **G**!
Jer 14:22 Are You not He, O LORD our **G**
Jer 15:16 Your name, O LORD **G** of hosts
Jer 16: 9 of hosts, the **G** of Israel
Jer 16:10 against the LORD our **G**
Jer 19: 3 of hosts, the **G** of Israel
Jer 19:15 of hosts, the **G** of Israel
Jer 21: 4 says the LORD **G** of Israel
Jer 22: 9 covenant of the LORD their **G**
Jer 23: 2 thus says the LORD **G** of
Jer 23:23 Am I a **G** near at hand," says
Jer 23:23 LORD, "And not a **G** afar off
Jer 23:36 the words of the living **G**
Jer 23:36 the LORD of hosts, our **G**
Jer 24: 5 the LORD, the **G** of Israel
Jer 24: 7 people, and I will be their **G**
Jer 25:15 the LORD **G** of Israel to me
Jer 25:27 of hosts, the **G** of Israel
Jer 26:13 the voice of the LORD your **G**
Jer 26:16 in the name of the LORD our **G**
Jer 27: 4 of hosts, the **G** of Israel
Jer 27:21 the **G** of Israel, concerning
Jer 28: 2 the **G** of Israel, saying
Jer 28:14 of hosts, the **G** of Israel
Jer 29: 4 the **G** of Israel, to all who
Jer 29: 8 of hosts, the **G** of Israel
Jer 29:21 the **G** of Israel, concerning
Jer 29:25 the **G** of Israel, saying
Jer 30: 2 speaks the LORD **G** of Israel
Jer 30: 9 shall serve the LORD their **G**
Jer 30:22 people, and I will be your **G**
Jer 31: 1 I will be the **G** of all the
Jer 31: 6 up to Zion, to the LORD our **G**
Jer 31:18 for You are the LORD my **G**
Jer 31:23 of hosts, the **G** of Israel
Jer 31:33 and I will be their **G**, and they
Jer 32:14 of hosts, the **G** of Israel
Jer 32:15 of hosts, the **G** of Israel
Jer 32:17 Ah, Lord **G**! Behold, You have
Jer 32:18 the Great, the Mighty **G**,
Jer 32:25 You have said to me, O Lord **G**
Jer 32:27 the LORD, the **G** of all flesh
Jer 32:36 the **G** of Israel, concerning
Jer 32:38 people, and I will be their **G**
Jer 33: 4 the **G** of Israel, concerning
Jer 34: 2 the LORD, the **G** of Israel
Jer 34:13 the LORD, the **G** of Israel
Jer 35: 4 son of Igdaliah, a man of **G**
Jer 35:13 of hosts, the **G** of Israel
Jer 35:17 **G** of hosts, the **G** of Israel
Jer 35:18 of hosts, the **G** of Israel
Jer 35:19 of hosts, the **G** of Israel
Jer 37: 3 now to the LORD our **G** for us
Jer 37: 7 the **G** of Israel, 'Thus you
Jer 38:17 **G** of hosts, the **G** of Israel
Jer 39:16 of hosts, the **G** of Israel
Jer 40: 2 The LORD your **G** has
Jer 42: 2 for us to the LORD your **G**
Jer 42: 3 that the LORD your **G** may show
Jer 42: 4 **G** according to your words
Jer 42: 5 LORD your **G** sends us by you
Jer 42: 6 our **G** to whom we send you
Jer 42: 6 the voice of the LORD our **G**
Jer 42: 9 the **G** of Israel, to whom you
Jer 42:13 the voice of the LORD your **G**
Jer 42:15 of hosts, the **G** of Israel
Jer 42:18 of hosts, the **G** of Israel
Jer 42:20 sent me to the LORD your **G**
Jer 42:20 Pray for us to the LORD our **G**
Jer 42:20 all that the LORD your **G** says
Jer 42:21 the voice of the LORD your **G**
Jer 43: 1 the words of the LORD their **G**
Jer 43: 1 their **G** had sent him to them
Jer 43: 2 The LORD our **G** has not sent
Jer 43:10 of hosts, the **G** of Israel
Jer 44: 2 of hosts, the **G** of Israel
Jer 44: 7 **G** of hosts, the **G** of Israel
Jer 44:11 of hosts, the **G** of Israel
Jer 44:25 the **G** of Israel, saying
Jer 44:26 The Lord **G** lives
Jer 45: 2 the **G** of Israel, to you, O
Jer 46:10 day of the Lord **G** of hosts
Jer 46:10 for the Lord **G** of hosts has a
Jer 46:25 hosts, the **G** of Israel, says
Jer 48: 1 of hosts, the **G** of Israel
Jer 49: 5 says the Lord **G** of hosts
Jer 50: 4 and seek the LORD their **G**
Jer 50:18 of hosts, the **G** of Israel
Jer 50:25 is the work of the Lord **G** of
Jer 50:28 vengeance of the LORD our **G**
Jer 50:31 says the Lord **G** of hosts
Jer 50:40 As **G** overthrew Sodom and
Jer 51: 5 forsaken, nor Judah, by his **G**
Jer 51:10 the work of the LORD our **G**
Jer 51:33 of hosts, the **G** of Israel
Jer 51:56 LORD is the **G** of recompense
Lam 3:28 because **G** has laid it on him
Lam 3:41 and hands to **G** in heaven
Ezek 1: 1 opened and I saw visions of **G**
Ezek 2: 4 them, 'Thus says the Lord **G**
Ezek 3:11 them, 'Thus says the Lord **G**
Ezek 3:27 them, 'Thus says the Lord **G**
Ezek 4:14 So I said, "Ah, Lord **G**!
Ezek 5: 5 Thus says the Lord **G**
Ezek 5: 7 thus says the Lord **G**
Ezek 5: 8 thus says the Lord **G**
Ezek 5:11 as I live,' says the Lord **G**
Ezek 6: 3 hear the word of the Lord **G**
Ezek 6: 3 the Lord **G** to the mountains
Ezek 6:11 Thus says the Lord **G**
Ezek 7: 2 thus says the Lord **G** to the
Ezek 7: 5 Thus says the Lord **G**
Ezek 8: 1 the Lord **G** fell upon me there
Ezek 8: 3 in visions of **G** to Jerusalem
Ezek 8: 4 the glory of the **G** of Israel
Ezek 9: 3 Now the glory of the **G** of
Ezek 9: 8 Ah, Lord **G**!
Ezek 10: 5 of Almighty **G** when He speaks
Ezek 10:19 the glory of the **G** of Israel
Ezek 10:20 the **G** of Israel by the River
Ezek 11: 7 thus says the Lord **G**
Ezek 11: 8 upon you," says the Lord **G**
Ezek 11:13 Ah, Lord **G**!
Ezek 11:16 say, 'Thus says the Lord **G**
Ezek 11:17 say, 'Thus says the Lord **G**
Ezek 11:20 people, and I will be their **G**
Ezek 11:21 own heads," says the Lord **G**
Ezek 11:22 the glory of the **G** of Israel
Ezek 11:24 the Spirit of **G** into Chaldea
Ezek 12:10 them, 'Thus says the Lord **G**
Ezek 12:19 Thus says the Lord **G** to the
Ezek 12:23 Thus says the Lord **G**
Ezek 12:25 perform it," says the Lord **G**
Ezek 12:28 them, 'Thus says the Lord **G**
Ezek 12:28 be done," says the Lord **G**
Ezek 13: 3 Thus says the Lord **G**
Ezek 13: 8 thus says the Lord **G**
Ezek 13: 8 you," says the Lord **G**
Ezek 13: 9 know that I am the Lord **G**
Ezek 13:13 thus says the Lord **G**
Ezek 13:16 no peace,'" says the Lord **G**
Ezek 13:18 and say, 'Thus says the Lord **G**
Ezek 13:20 thus says the Lord **G**

Hos 4: 6 forgotten the law of your **G**
Hos 4:12 the harlot against their **G**
Hos 5: 4 toward turning to their **G**
Hos 6: 6 the knowledge of **G** more than
Hos 7:10 return to the LORD their **G**
Hos 8: 2 Israel will cry to Me, 'My **G**
Hos 8: 6 made it, and it is not **G**
Hos 9: 1 the harlot against your **G**
Hos 9: 8 of Ephraim is with my **G**
Hos 9: 8 enmity in the house of his **G**
Hos 9:17 My **G** will cast them away,
Hos 11: 9 For I am **G**, and not man, the
Hos 11:12 but Judah still walks with **G**
Hos 12: 3 strength he struggled with **G**
Hos 12: 5 that is, the LORD **G** of hosts
Hos 12: 6 So you, by the help of your **G**
Hos 12: 6 and wait on your **G** continually
Hos 12: 9 But I am the LORD your **G**,
Hos 13: 4 your **G** ever since the land of
Hos 13: 4 and you shall know no **G** but Me
Hos 13:16 has rebelled against her **G**
Hos 14: 1 return to the LORD your **G**
Joel 1:13 you who minister to my **G**
Joel 1:13 from the house of your **G**
Joel 1:14 the house of the LORD your **G**
Joel 1:16 from the house of our **G**
Joel 2:13 return to the LORD your **G**
Joel 2:14 offering for the LORD your **G**
Joel 2:17 peoples, 'Where is their **G**
Joel 2:23 and rejoice in the LORD your **G**
Joel 2:26 the name of the LORD your **G**
Joel 2:27 and that I am the LORD your **G**
Joel 3:17 that I am the LORD your **G**
Amos 1: 8 perish," says the Lord **G**
Amos 3: 7 the Lord **G** does nothing,
Amos 3: 8 The Lord **G** has spoken
Amos 3:11 thus says the Lord **G**
Amos 3:13 of Jacob," says the Lord **G**
Amos 3:13 the Lord **G**, the **G** of hosts,
Amos 4: 2 The Lord **G** has sworn by His
Amos 4: 5 says the Lord **G**
Amos 4:11 you, as **G** overthrew Sodom and
Amos 4:12 you, prepare to meet your **G**
Amos 4:13 The LORD **G** of hosts is His
Amos 5: 3 For thus says the Lord **G**
Amos 5:14 so the LORD **G** of hosts will
Amos 5:15 It may be that the LORD **G** of
Amos 5:16 Therefore the LORD **G** of hosts
Amos 5:27 whose name is the **G** of hosts
Amos 6: 8 The Lord **G** has sworn by
Amos 6: 8 the LORD **G** of hosts says
Amos 6:14 says the LORD **G** of hosts
Amos 7: 1 Thus the Lord **G** showed me
Amos 7: 2 O Lord **G**, forgive, I pray
Amos 7: 4 Thus the Lord **G** showed me
Amos 7: 4 Behold, the Lord **G** called for
Amos 7: 5 O Lord **G**, cease, I pray
Amos 7: 6 not be," said the Lord **G**
Amos 8: 1 Thus the Lord **G** showed me
Amos 8: 3 that day," says the Lord **G**
Amos 8: 9 that day," says the Lord **G**
Amos 8:11 are coming," says the Lord **G**
Amos 9: 5 The Lord **G** of hosts, He who
Amos 9: 8 the eyes of the Lord **G** are on
Amos 9:15 them," says the LORD your **G**
Obad 1 Thus says the Lord **G**
Jon 1: 6 Arise, call on your **G**
Jon 1: 6 perhaps your **G** will consider
Jon 1: 9 the **G** of heaven, who made the
Jon 2: 1 his **G** from the fish's belly
Jon 2: 6 from the pit, O LORD, my **G**
Jon 3: 5 people of Nineveh believed **G**
Jon 3: 8 and cry mightily to **G**
Jon 3: 9 Who can tell if **G** will turn
Jon 3:10 Then **G** saw their works, that
Jon 3:10 **G** relented from the disaster
Jon 4: 2 are a gracious and merciful **G**
Jon 4: 6 the LORD **G** prepared a plant
Jon 4: 7 next day **G** prepared a worm
Jon 4: 8 that **G** prepared a vehement
Jon 4: 9 Then **G** said to Jonah, "Is it
Mic 1: 2 Let the Lord **G** be a witness
Mic 3: 7 for there is no answer from **G**
Mic 4: 2 the house of the **G** of Jacob
Mic 4: 5 of the LORD our **G** forever
Mic 5: 4 of the name of the LORD His **G**
Mic 6: 6 bow myself before the High **G**
Mic 6: 8 and to walk humbly with your **G**
Mic 7: 7 for the **G** of my salvation
Mic 7: 7 my **G** will hear me

Mic 7:10 Where is the LORD your **G**
Mic 7:17 be afraid of the LORD our **G**
Mic 7:18 Who is a **G** like You,
Nah 1: 2 **G** is jealous, and the LORD
Hab 1:12 from everlasting, O LORD my **G**
Hab 3: 3 **G** came from Teman, the Holy
Hab 3:18 joy in the **G** of my salvation
Hab 3:19 The LORD **G** is my strength
Zeph 1: 7 in the presence of the Lord **G**
Zeph 2: 7 for the LORD their **G** will
Zeph 2: 9 of hosts, the **G** of Israel,
Zeph 3: 2 has not drawn near to her **G**
Zeph 3:17 The LORD your **G** in your midst
Hag 1:12 the voice of the LORD their **G**
Hag 1:12 the LORD their **G** had sent him
Hag 1:14 of the LORD of hosts, their **G**
Zech 6:15 the voice of the LORD your **G**
Zech 7: 2 and his men, to the house of **G**
Zech 8: 8 people and I will be their **G**
Zech 8:23 have heard that **G** is with you
Zech 9: 7 even he shall be for our **G**
Zech 9:14 The Lord **G** will blow the
Zech 9:16 The LORD their **G** will save
Zech 10: 6 for I am the LORD their **G**
Zech 11: 4 Thus says the LORD my **G**
Zech 12: 5 in the LORD of hosts, their **G**
Zech 12: 8 of David shall be like **G**,
Zech 13: 9 will say, 'The LORD is my **G**
Zech 14: 5 Thus the LORD my **G** will come
Mal 2:10 Has not one **G** created us
Mal 2:16 For the LORD **G** of Israel says
Mal 2:17 Where is the **G** of justice
Mal 3: 8 Will a man rob **G**
Mal 3:14 said, 'It is vain to serve **G**
Mal 3:15 those who tempt **G** go free
Mal 3:18 between one who serves **G**
Matt 1:23 is translated, "**G** with us
Matt 2:22 being warned by **G** in a dream
Matt 3: 9 that **G** is able to raise up
Matt 3:16 and He saw the Spirit of **G**
Matt 4: 3 If You are the Son of **G**,
Matt 4: 4 proceeds from the mouth of **G**
Matt 4: 6 If You are the Son of **G**,
Matt 4: 7 not tempt the LORD your **G**
Matt 4:10 shall worship the LORD your **G**
Matt 5: 8 heart, for they shall see **G**
Matt 5: 9 shall be called sons of **G**
Matt 6:24 cannot serve **G** and mammon
Matt 6:30 Now if **G** so clothes the grass
Matt 6:33 seek first the kingdom of **G**
Matt 8:29 with You, Jesus, You Son of **G**
Matt 9: 8 glorified **G** who had given
Matt 12: 4 how he entered the house of **G**
Matt 12:28 out demons by the Spirit of **G**
Matt 12:28 of **G** has come upon you
Matt 14:33 Truly You are the Son of **G**
Matt 15: 3 the commandment of **G** because
Matt 15: 4 For **G** commanded, saying
Matt 15: 6 of **G** of no effect by your
Matt 15:31 glorified the **G** of Israel
Matt 16:16 the Son of the living **G**
Matt 16:23 mindful of the things of **G**
Matt 19: 6 Therefore what **G** has joined
Matt 19:17 is good but One, that is, **G**
Matt 19:24 man to enter the kingdom of **G**
Matt 19:26 but with **G** all things are
Matt 21:12 went into the temple of **G**
Matt 21:31 the kingdom of **G** before you
Matt 21:43 you, the kingdom of **G** will be
Matt 22:16 teach the way of **G** in truth
Matt 22:21 and to **G** the things that are
Matt 22:29 Scriptures nor the power of **G**
Matt 22:30 like angels of **G** in heaven
Matt 22:31 what was spoken to you by **G**
Matt 22:32 I am the **G** of Abraham
Matt 22:32 the **G** of Isaac
Matt 22:32 and the **G** of Jacob
Matt 22:32 **G** is not the **G** of the dead,
Matt 22:32 **G** is not the **G** of the dead
Matt 22:37 your **G** with all your heart
Matt 23:22 swears by the throne of **G**
Matt 26:61 to destroy the temple of **G**
Matt 26:63 I adjure You by the living **G**
Matt 26:63 are the Christ, the Son of **G**
Matt 27:40 If You are the Son of **G**, come
Matt 27:43 He trusted in **G**
Matt 27:43 He said, 'I am the Son of **G**
Matt 27:46 My **G**, My **G**, why have You
Matt 27:54 Truly this was the Son of **G**
Mark 1: 1 of Jesus Christ, the Son of **G**

Mark 1:14 gospel of the kingdom of **G**
Mark 1:15 the kingdom of **G** is at hand
Mark 1:24 the Holy One of **G**
Mark 2: 7 can forgive sins but **G** alone
Mark 2:12 were amazed and glorified **G**
Mark 2:26 he went into the house of **G**
Mark 3:11 You are the Son of **G**
Mark 3:35 the will of **G** is My brother
Mark 4:11 mystery of the kingdom of **G**
Mark 4:26 The kingdom of **G** is as if a
Mark 4:30 we liken the kingdom of **G**
Mark 5: 7 Jesus, Son of the Most High **G**
Mark 5: 7 I implore You by **G** that You
Mark 7: 8 aside the commandment of **G**
Mark 7: 9 reject the commandment of **G**
Mark 7:13 making the word of **G** of no
Mark 8:33 mindful of the things of **G**
Mark 9: 1 of **G** present with power
Mark 9:47 the kingdom of **G** with one eye
Mark 10: 6 **G** 'made them male and female
Mark 10: 9 Therefore what **G** has joined
Mark 10:14 of such is the kingdom of **G**
Mark 10:15 **G** as a little child will by
Mark 10:18 is good but One, that is, **G**
Mark 10:23 to enter the kingdom of **G**
Mark 10:24 to enter the kingdom of **G**
Mark 10:25 man to enter the kingdom of **G**
Mark 10:27 is impossible, but not with **G**
Mark 10:27 for with **G** all things are
Mark 11:22 Have faith in **G**
Mark 12:14 teach the way of **G** in truth
Mark 12:17 and to **G** the things that are
Mark 12:24 Scriptures nor the power of **G**
Mark 12:26 how **G** spoke to him, saying
Mark 12:26 I am the **G** of Abraham
Mark 12:26 the **G** of Isaac
Mark 12:26 and the **G** of Jacob
Mark 12:27 He is not the **G** of the dead
Mark 12:27 dead, but the **G** of the living
Mark 12:29 O Israel, the LORD our **G**
Mark 12:30 your **G** with all your heart
Mark 12:32 the truth, for there is one **G**
Mark 12:34 not far from the kingdom of **G**
Mark 13:19 **G** created until this time
Mark 14:25 it new in the kingdom of **G**
Mark 15:34 My **G**, My **G**, why have You
Mark 15:39 this Man was the Son of **G**
Mark 15:43 waiting for the kingdom of **G**
Mark 16:19 down at the right hand of **G**
Luke 1: 6 were both righteous before **G**
Luke 1: 8 before **G** in the order of his
Luke 1:16 of Israel to the Lord their **G**
Luke 1:19 stands in the presence of **G**
Luke 1:26 angel Gabriel was sent by **G**
Luke 1:30 you have found favor with **G**
Luke 1:32 the Lord **G** will give Him the
Luke 1:35 will be called the Son of **G**
Luke 1:37 For with **G** nothing will be
Luke 1:47 has rejoiced in **G** my Savior
Luke 1:64 and he spoke, praising **G**
Luke 1:68 is the Lord **G** of Israel, for
Luke 1:78 the tender mercy of our **G**
Luke 2:13 the heavenly host praising **G**
Luke 2:14 Glory to **G** in the highest, and
Luke 2:20 praising **G** for all the things
Luke 2:28 up in his arms and blessed **G**
Luke 2:37 but served **G** with fastings and
Luke 2:40 the grace of **G** was upon Him
Luke 2:52 stature, and in favor with **G**
Luke 3: 2 the word of **G** came to John
Luke 3: 6 shall see the salvation of **G**
Luke 3: 8 that **G** is able to raise up
Luke 3:38 the son of Adam, the son of **G**
Luke 4: 3 If You are the Son of **G**,
Luke 4: 4 alone, but by every word of **G**
Luke 4: 8 shall worship the LORD your **G**
Luke 4: 9 If You are the Son of **G**,
Luke 4:12 not tempt the LORD your **G**
Luke 4:34 the Holy One of **G**
Luke 4:41 are the Christ, the Son of **G**
Luke 4:43 of **G** to the other cities also
Luke 5: 1 Him to hear the word of **G**
Luke 5:21 can forgive sins but **G** alone
Luke 5:25 his own house, glorifying **G**
Luke 5:26 amazed, and they glorified **G**
Luke 6: 4 he went into the house of **G**
Luke 6:12 all night in prayer to **G**
Luke 6:20 for yours is the kingdom of **G**
Luke 7:16 upon all, and they glorified **G**
Luke 7:16 **G** has visited His people

Luke 7:28 of **G** is greater than he
Luke 7:29 tax collectors justified **G**
Luke 7:30 counsel of **G** for themselves
Luke 8: 1 tidings of the kingdom of **G**
Luke 8:10 mysteries of the kingdom of **G**
Luke 8:11 The seed is the word of **G**
Luke 8:21 these who hear the word of **G**
Luke 8:28 Jesus, Son of the Most High **G**
Luke 8:39 things **G** has done for you
Luke 9: 2 to preach the kingdom of **G**
Luke 9:11 them about the kingdom of **G**
Luke 9:20 and said, "The Christ of **G**."
Luke 9:27 they see the kingdom of **G**
Luke 9:43 amazed at the majesty of **G**
Luke 9:60 go and preach the kingdom of **G**
Luke 9:62 is fit for the kingdom of **G**
Luke 10: 9 The kingdom of **G** has come
Luke 10:11 of **G** has come near you
Luke 10:27 your **G** with all your heart
Luke 11:20 demons with the finger of **G**
Luke 11:20 of **G** has come upon you
Luke 11:28 those who hear the word of **G**
Luke 11:42 by justice and the love of **G**
Luke 11:49 the wisdom of **G** also said
Luke 12: 6 of them is forgotten before **G**
Luke 12: 8 before the angels of **G**
Luke 12: 9 denied before the angels of **G**
Luke 12:20 But **G** said to him, 'You fool
Luke 12:21 and is not rich toward **G**
Luke 12:24 and **G** feeds them
Luke 12:28 If then **G** so clothes the
Luke 12:31 But seek the kingdom of **G**
Luke 13:13 made straight, and glorified **G**
Luke 13:18 What is the kingdom of **G** like
Luke 13:20 I liken the kingdom of **G**
Luke 13:28 prophets in the kingdom of **G**
Luke 13:29 sit down in the kingdom of **G**
Luke 14:15 eat bread in the kingdom of **G**
Luke 15:10 presence of the angels of **G**
Luke 16:13 cannot serve **G** and mammon
Luke 16:15 men, but **G** knows your hearts
Luke 16:15 abomination in the sight of **G**
Luke 16:16 of **G** has been preached, and
Luke 17:15 with a loud voice glorified **G**
Luke 17:18 to **G** except this foreigner
Luke 17:20 the kingdom of **G** would come
Luke 17:20 The kingdom of **G** does not
Luke 17:21 kingdom of **G** is within you
Luke 18: 2 did not fear **G** nor regard man
Luke 18: 4 do not fear **G** nor regard man
Luke 18: 7 shall **G** not avenge His own
Luke 18:11 prayed thus with himself, '**G**
Luke 18:13 **G** be merciful to me a sinner
Luke 18:16 of such is the kingdom of **G**
Luke 18:17 **G** as a little child will by
Luke 18:19 is good but One, that is, **G**
Luke 18:24 to enter the kingdom of **G**
Luke 18:25 man to enter the kingdom of **G**
Luke 18:27 with men are possible with **G**
Luke 18:29 the sake of the kingdom of **G**
Luke 18:43 and followed Him, glorifying **G**
Luke 18:43 they saw it, gave praise to **G**
Luke 19:11 of **G** would appear immediately
Luke 19:37 praise **G** with a loud voice
Luke 20:21 but teach the way of **G** truly
Luke 20:25 and to **G** the things that are
Luke 20:36 the angels and are sons of **G**
Luke 20:37 the Lord 'the **G** of Abraham
Luke 20:37 the **G** of Isaac
Luke 20:37 and the **G** of Jacob
Luke 20:38 For He is not the **G** of the
Luke 21: 4 have put in offerings for **G**
Luke 21:31 that the kingdom of **G** is near
Luke 22:16 fulfilled in the kingdom of **G**
Luke 22:18 until the kingdom of **G** comes
Luke 22:69 right hand of the power of **G**
Luke 22:70 Are You then the Son of **G**
Luke 23:35 the Christ, the chosen of **G**
Luke 23:40 Do you not even fear **G**,
Luke 23:47 had happened, he glorified **G**
Luke 23:51 waiting for the kingdom of **G**
Luke 24:19 in deed and word before **G** and
Luke 24:53 temple praising and blessing **G**
John 1: 1 and the Word was with **G**
John 1: 1 and the Word was **G**
John 1: 2 was in the beginning with **G**
John 1: 6 There was a man sent from **G**
John 1:12 right to become children of **G**
John 1:13 of the will of man, but of **G**
John 1:18 No one has seen **G** at any time
John 1:29 The Lamb of **G** who takes away
John 1:34 that this is the Son of **G**
John 1:36 Behold the Lamb of **G**
John 1:49 Rabbi, You are the Son of **G**
John 1:51 and the angels of **G** ascending
John 3: 2 You are a teacher come from **G**
John 3: 2 You do unless **G** is with him
John 3: 3 cannot see the kingdom of **G**
John 3: 5 cannot enter the kingdom of **G**
John 3:16 For **G** so loved the world that
John 3:17 For **G** did not send His Son
John 3:18 of the only begotten Son of **G**
John 3:21 that they have been done in **G**
John 3:33 has certified that **G** is true
John 3:34 For He whom **G** has sent
John 3:34 speaks the words of **G**
John 3:34 for **G** does not give the
John 3:36 the wrath of **G** abides on him
John 4:10 If you knew the gift of **G**
John 4:24 **G** is Spirit, and those who
John 5:18 said that **G** was His Father
John 5:18 making Himself equal with **G**
John 5:25 the voice of the Son of **G**
John 5:42 not have the love of **G** in you
John 5:44 that comes from the only **G**
John 6:27 because **G** the Father has set
John 6:28 we may work the works of **G**
John 6:29 This is the work of **G**, that
John 6:33 For the bread of **G** is He who
John 6:45 they shall all be taught by **G**
John 6:46 except He who is from **G**
John 6:69 the Son of the living **G**
John 7:17 whether it is from **G** or
John 8:40 truth which I heard from **G**
John 8:41 we have one Father—**G**
John 8:42 If **G** were your Father, you
John 8:42 forth and came from **G**
John 8:47 He who is of **G** hears God's
John 8:47 because you are not of **G**
John 8:54 you say that He is your **G**
John 9: 3 but that the works of **G**
John 9:16 This Man is not from **G**,
John 9:24 to him, "Give **G** the glory
John 9:29 We know that **G** spoke to Moses
John 9:31 Now we know that **G** does not
John 9:31 if anyone is a worshiper of **G**
John 9:33 If this Man were not from **G**
John 9:35 you believe in the Son of **G**
John 10:33 being a Man, make Yourself **G**
John 10:35 to whom the word of **G** came
John 10:36 I said, 'I am the Son of **G**'
John 11: 4 but for the glory of **G**
John 11: 4 that the Son of **G** may be
John 11:22 ask of **G**, **G** will give You
John 11:27 are the Christ, the Son of **G**
John 11:40 you would see the glory of **G**
John 11:52 in one the children of **G** who
John 12:43 men more than the praise of **G**
John 13: 3 and that He had come from **G**
John 13: 3 and was going to **G**
John 13:31 and **G** is glorified in Him
John 13:32 If **G** is glorified in Him
John 13:32 **G** will also glorify Him in
John 14: 1 you believe in **G**, believe
John 16: 2 that he offers **G** service
John 16:27 that I came forth from **G**
John 16:30 that You came forth from **G**
John 17: 3 may know You, the only true **G**
John 19: 7 He made Himself the Son of **G**
John 20:17 and to My **G** and your **G**
John 20:28 My Lord and my **G**
John 20:31 is the Christ, the Son of **G**
John 21:19 what death he would glorify **G**
Acts 1: 3 to the kingdom of **G**
Acts 2:11 the wonderful works of **G**
Acts 2:17 pass in the last days, says **G**
Acts 2:22 a Man attested by **G** to you by
Acts 2:22 signs which **G** did through Him
Acts 2:23 counsel and foreknowledge of **G**
Acts 2:24 whom **G** raised up, having
Acts 2:30 knowing that **G** had sworn with
Acts 2:32 This Jesus **G** has raised up,
Acts 2:33 to the right hand of **G**, and
Acts 2:36 that **G** has made this Jesus
Acts 2:39 as the Lord our **G** will call
Acts 2:47 praising **G** and having favor
Acts 3: 8 leaping, and praising **G**
Acts 3: 9 saw him walking and praising **G**
Acts 3:13 The **G** of Abraham, Isaac, and
Acts 3:13 Jacob, the **G** of our fathers,
Acts 3:15 whom **G** raised from the dead,
Acts 3:18 But those things which **G**
Acts 3:21 which **G** has spoken by the
Acts 3:22 The LORD your **G** will raise
Acts 3:25 which **G** made with our fathers
Acts 3:26 To you first, **G**, having
Acts 4:10 whom **G** raised from the dead,
Acts 4:19 **G** to listen to you more than
Acts 4:19 listen to you more than to **G**
Acts 4:21 **G** for what had been done
Acts 4:24 voice to **G** with one accord
Acts 4:24 Lord, You are **G**, who made
Acts 4:31 the word of **G** with boldness
Acts 5: 4 have not lied to men but to **G**
Acts 5:29 to obey **G** rather than men
Acts 5:30 The **G** of our fathers raised
Acts 5:31 Him **G** has exalted to His
Acts 5:32 is the Holy Spirit whom **G** has
Acts 5:39 but if it is of **G**, you cannot
Acts 5:39 be found to fight against **G**
Acts 6: 2 we should leave the word of **G**
Acts 6: 7 And the word of **G** spread, and
Acts 6:11 words against Moses and **G**
Acts 7: 2 The **G** of glory appeared to
Acts 7: 5 **G** gave him no inheritance in
Acts 7: 6 But **G** spoke in this way
Acts 7: 7 bondage I will judge,' said **G**
Acts 7: 9 But **G** was with him
Acts 7:17 which **G** had sworn to Abraham
Acts 7:20 and was well pleasing to **G**
Acts 7:25 **G** would deliver them by his
Acts 7:32 I am the **G** of your fathers
Acts 7:32 the **G** of Abraham
Acts 7:32 the **G** of Isaac
Acts 7:32 and the **G** of Jacob
Acts 7:35 is the one **G** sent to be a
Acts 7:37 The LORD your **G** will raise
Acts 7:42 Then **G** turned and gave them
Acts 7:45 whom **G** drove out before the
Acts 7:46 who found favor before **G** and
Acts 7:46 a dwelling for the **G** of Jacob
Acts 7:55 heaven and saw the glory of **G**
Acts 7:55 at the right hand of **G**,
Acts 7:56 at the right hand of **G**
Acts 7:59 as he was calling on **G** and
Acts 8:10 man is the great power of **G**
Acts 8:12 concerning the kingdom of **G**
Acts 8:14 had received the word of **G**
Acts 8:20 of **G** could be purchased with
Acts 8:21 not right in the sight of **G**
Acts 8:22 pray **G** if perhaps the thought
Acts 8:37 Jesus Christ is the Son of **G**
Acts 9:20 that He is the Son of **G**
Acts 10: 2 one who feared **G** with all his
Acts 10: 2 people, and prayed to **G** always
Acts 10: 3 an angel of **G** coming in and
Acts 10: 4 up for a memorial before **G**
Acts 10:15 What **G** has cleansed you must
Acts 10:22 a just man, one who fears **G**
Acts 10:28 But **G** has shown me that I
Acts 10:31 remembered in the sight of **G**
Acts 10:33 we are all present before **G**
Acts 10:33 the things commanded you by **G**
Acts 10:34 that **G** shows no partiality
Acts 10:36 The word which **G** sent to the
Acts 10:38 how **G** anointed Jesus of
Acts 10:38 the devil, for **G** was with Him
Acts 10:40 Him **G** raised up on the third
Acts 10:41 witnesses chosen before by **G**
Acts 10:42 **G** to be Judge of the living
Acts 10:46 with tongues and magnify **G**
Acts 11: 1 also received the word of **G**
Acts 11: 9 What **G** has cleansed you must
Acts 11:17 If therefore **G** gave them the
Acts 11:17 I that I could withstand **G**
Acts 11:18 and they glorified **G**, saying,
Acts 11:18 Then **G** has also granted to
Acts 11:23 and had seen the grace of **G**
Acts 12: 5 to **G** for him by the church
Acts 12:23 he did not give glory to **G**
Acts 12:24 But the word of **G** grew and
Acts 13: 5 of **G** in the synagogues of the
Acts 13: 7 sought to hear the word of **G**
Acts 13:16 of Israel, and you who fear **G**
Acts 13:17 The **G** of this people Israel
Acts 13:21 so **G** gave them Saul the son
Acts 13:23 **G** raised up for Israel a
Acts 13:26 and those among you who fear **G**
Acts 13:30 But **G** raised Him from the
Acts 13:33 **G** has fulfilled this for us

Acts 13:36 generation by the will of **G**
Acts 13:37 but He whom **G** raised up saw
Acts 13:43 to continue in the grace of **G**
Acts 13:44 to hear the word of **G**
Acts 13:46 of **G** should be spoken to you
Acts 14:15 vain things to the living **G**
Acts 14:22 enter the kingdom of **G**
Acts 14:26 commended to the grace of **G**
Acts 14:27 all that **G** had done with them
Acts 15: 4 that **G** had done with them
Acts 15: 7 while ago **G** chose among us
Acts 15: 8 So **G**, who knows the heart,
Acts 15:10 why do you test **G** by putting
Acts 15:12 wonders **G** had worked through
Acts 15:14 Simon has declared how **G** at
Acts 15:18 Known to **G** from eternity are
Acts 15:19 Gentiles who are turning to **G**
Acts 15:40 brethren to the grace of **G**
Acts 16:14 of Thyatira, who worshiped **G**
Acts 16:17 servants of the Most High **G**
Acts 16:25 praying and singing hymns to **G**
Acts 16:34 having believed in **G** with all
Acts 17:13 of **G** was preached by Paul at
Acts 17:23 to the unknown **G**
Acts 17:24 **G**, who made the world and
Acts 17:29 we are the offspring of **G**
Acts 17:30 of ignorance **G** overlooked
Acts 18: 7 Justus, one who worshiped **G**
Acts 18:11 the word of **G** among them
Acts 18:13 worship **G** contrary to the law
Acts 18:21 again to you, **G** willing
Acts 18:26 the way of **G** more accurately
Acts 19: 8 things of the kingdom of **G**
Acts 19:11 Now **G** worked unusual miracles
Acts 20:21 Greeks, repentance toward **G**
Acts 20:24 the gospel of the grace of **G**
Acts 20:25 preaching the kingdom of **G**
Acts 20:27 to you the whole counsel of **G**
Acts 20:28 to shepherd the church of **G**
Acts 20:32 brethren, I commend you to **G**
Acts 21:19 detail those things which **G**
Acts 22: 3 was zealous toward **G** as you
Acts 22:14 The **G** of our fathers has
Acts 23: 1 before **G** until this day
Acts 23: 3 him, "**G** will strike you, you
Acts 23: 9 let us not fight against **G**
Acts 24:14 I worship the **G** of my fathers
Acts 24:15 I have hope in **G**, which they
Acts 24:16 without offense toward **G** and
Acts 26: 6 made by **G** to our fathers
Acts 26: 7 earnestly serving **G** night
Acts 26: 8 by you that **G** raises the dead
Acts 26:18 from the power of Satan to **G**
Acts 26:20 they should repent, turn to **G**
Acts 26:22 having obtained help from **G**
Acts 26:29 I would to **G** that not only
Acts 27:23 of the **G** to whom I belong
Acts 27:24 indeed **G** has granted you all
Acts 27:25 for I believe **G** that it will
Acts 27:35 and gave thanks to **G** in the
Acts 28:15 Paul saw them, he thanked **G**
Acts 28:23 testified of the kingdom of **G**
Acts 28:28 of **G** has been sent to the
Acts 28:31 preaching the kingdom of **G**
Rom 1: 1 separated to the gospel of **G**
Rom 1: 4 to be the Son of **G** with power
Rom 1: 7 who are in Rome, beloved of **G**
Rom 1: 7 and peace from **G** our Father
Rom 1: 8 I thank my **G** through Jesus
Rom 1: 9 For **G** is my witness, whom I
Rom 1:10 the will of **G** to come to you
Rom 1:16 for it is the power of **G** to
Rom 1:17 **G** is revealed from faith to
Rom 1:18 For the wrath of **G** is
Rom 1:19 of **G** is manifest in them, for
Rom 1:19 for **G** has shown it to them
Rom 1:21 because, although they knew **G**
Rom 1:21 they did not glorify Him as **G**
Rom 1:23 **G** into an image made like
Rom 1:24 Therefore **G** also gave them up
Rom 1:25 the truth of **G** for the lie
Rom 1:26 For this reason **G** gave them
Rom 1:28 retain **G** in their knowledge
Rom 1:28 **G** gave them over to a debased
Rom 1:30 backbiters, haters of **G**,
Rom 1:32 the righteous judgment of **G**
Rom 2: 2 of **G** is according to truth
Rom 2: 3 will escape the judgment of **G**
Rom 2: 4 that the goodness of **G** leads
Rom 2: 5 the righteous judgment of **G**
Rom 2:11 there is no partiality with **G**
Rom 2:13 are just in the sight of **G**
Rom 2:16 in the day when **G** will judge
Rom 2:17 law, and make your boast in **G**
Rom 2:23 do you dishonor **G** through
Rom 2:24 The name of **G** is blasphemed
Rom 2:29 is not from men but from **G**
Rom 3: 2 committed the oracles of **G**
Rom 3: 3 of **G** without effect
Rom 3: 4 let **G** be true but every man a
Rom 3: 5 the righteousness of **G**, what
Rom 3: 5 Is **G** unjust who inflicts
Rom 3: 6 how will **G** judge the world
Rom 3: 7 For if the truth of **G** has
Rom 3:11 is none who seeks after **G**
Rom 3:18 fear of **G** before their eyes
Rom 3:19 may become guilty before **G**
Rom 3:21 of **G** apart from the law is
Rom 3:22 **G** which is through faith in
Rom 3:23 fall short of the glory of **G**
Rom 3:25 whom **G** set forth to be a
Rom 3:25 **G** had passed over the sins
Rom 3:29 Or is He the **G** of the Jews
Rom 3:29 also the **G** of the Gentiles
Rom 3:30 since there is one **G** who will
Rom 4: 2 to boast, but not before **G**
Rom 4: 3 Abraham believed **G**, and it was
Rom 4: 6 of the man to whom **G** imputes
Rom 4:17 Him whom he believed, even **G**
Rom 4:20 promise of **G** through unbelief
Rom 4:20 in faith, giving glory to **G**
Rom 5: 1 we have peace with **G** through
Rom 5: 2 in hope of the glory of **G**
Rom 5: 5 because the love of **G** has
Rom 5: 8 But **G** demonstrates His own
Rom 5:10 we were reconciled to **G**
Rom 5:11 in **G** through our Lord Jesus
Rom 5:15 much more the grace of **G**
Rom 6:10 that He lives, He lives to **G**
Rom 6:11 sin, but alive to **G** in Christ
Rom 6:13 to **G** as being alive from the
Rom 6:13 of righteousness to **G**
Rom 6:17 But **G** be thanked that though
Rom 6:22 and having become slaves of **G**
Rom 6:23 but the gift of **G** is eternal
Rom 7: 4 we should bear fruit to **G**
Rom 7:22 **G** according to the inward man
Rom 7:25 I thank **G**—through Jesus
Rom 7:25 I myself serve the law of **G**
Rom 8: 3 **G** did by sending His own Son
Rom 8: 7 mind is enmity against **G**
Rom 8: 7 not subject to the law of **G**
Rom 8: 8 in the flesh cannot please **G**
Rom 8: 9 the Spirit of **G** dwells in you
Rom 8:14 as are led by the Spirit of **G**
Rom 8:14 these are sons of **G**
Rom 8:16 that we are children of **G**
Rom 8:17 heirs of **G** and joint heirs
Rom 8:19 revealing of the sons of **G**
Rom 8:21 liberty of the children of **G**
Rom 8:27 according to the will of **G**
Rom 8:28 for good to those who love **G**
Rom 8:31 If **G** is for us, who can be
Rom 8:33 It is **G** who justifies
Rom 8:34 even at the right hand of **G**
Rom 8:39 us from the love of **G** which
Rom 9: 4 of the law, the service of **G**
Rom 9: 5 all, the eternally blessed **G**
Rom 9: 6 word of **G** has taken no effect
Rom 9: 8 are not the children of **G**
Rom 9:11 evil, that the purpose of **G**
Rom 9:14 there unrighteousness with **G**
Rom 9:16 but of **G** who shows mercy
Rom 9:20 are you to reply against **G**
Rom 9:22 What if **G**, wanting to show
Rom 9:26 called sons of the living **G**
Rom 10: 1 prayer to **G** for Israel is
Rom 10: 2 that they have a zeal for **G**
Rom 10: 3 to the righteousness of **G**
Rom 10: 9 **G** has raised Him from the
Rom 10:17 and hearing by the word of **G**
Rom 11: 1 has **G** cast away His people
Rom 11: 2 **G** has not cast away His
Rom 11: 2 pleads with **G** against Israel
Rom 11: 8 **G** has given them a spirit of
Rom 11:21 For if **G** did not spare the
Rom 11:22 the goodness and severity of **G**
Rom 11:23 for **G** is able to graft them
Rom 11:29 gifts and the calling of **G** are
Rom 11:30 were once disobedient to **G**
Rom 11:32 For **G** has committed them all
Rom 11:33 the wisdom and knowledge of **G**
Rom 12: 1 brethren, by the mercies of **G**
Rom 12: 1 holy, acceptable to **G**, which
Rom 12: 2 and perfect will of **G**
Rom 12: 3 as **G** has dealt to each one a
Rom 13: 1 is no authority except from **G**
Rom 13: 1 that exist are appointed by **G**
Rom 13: 2 resists the ordinance of **G**
Rom 14: 3 for **G** has received him
Rom 14: 4 for **G** is able to make him
Rom 14: 6 Lord, for he gives **G** thanks
Rom 14: 6 not eat, and gives **G** thanks
Rom 14:11 tongue shall confess to **G**
Rom 14:12 give account of himself to **G**
Rom 14:17 the kingdom of **G** is not food
Rom 14:18 things is acceptable to **G**
Rom 14:20 of **G** for the sake of food
Rom 14:22 Have it to yourself before **G**
Rom 15: 5 Now may the **G** of patience
Rom 15: 6 and one mouth glorify the **G**
Rom 15: 7 us, to the glory of **G**
Rom 15: 8 for the truth of **G**, to
Rom 15: 9 might glorify **G** for His mercy
Rom 15:13 Now may the **G** of hope fill
Rom 15:15 of the grace given to me by **G**
Rom 15:16 ministering the gospel of **G**
Rom 15:17 the things which pertain to **G**
Rom 15:19 the power of the Spirit of **G**
Rom 15:30 in your prayers to **G** for me
Rom 15:32 you with joy by the will of **G**
Rom 15:33 Now the **G** of peace be with
Rom 16:20 the **G** of peace will crush
Rom 16:26 of the everlasting **G**, for
Rom 16:27 to **G**, alone wise, be glory
1Co 1: 1 Christ through the will of **G**
1Co 1: 2 To the church of **G** which is
1Co 1: 3 and peace from **G** our Father
1Co 1: 4 I thank my **G** always
1Co 1: 4 you for the grace of **G** which
1Co 1: 9 **G** is faithful, by whom you
1Co 1:14 I thank **G** that I baptized
1Co 1:18 saved it is the power of **G**
1Co 1:20 Has not **G** made foolish the
1Co 1:21 For since, in the wisdom of **G**
1Co 1:21 through wisdom did not know **G**
1Co 1:21 **G**, it pleased **G** through the
1Co 1:24 Greeks, Christ the power of **G**
1Co 1:24 and the wisdom of **G**
1Co 1:25 of **G** is wiser than men, and
1Co 1:25 the weakness of **G** is stronger
1Co 1:27 But **G** has chosen the foolish
1Co 1:27 **G** has chosen the weak things
1Co 1:28 are despised **G** has chosen
1Co 1:30 became for us wisdom from **G**
1Co 2: 1 to you the testimony of **G**
1Co 2: 5 of men but in the power of **G**
1Co 2: 7 the wisdom of **G** in a mystery
1Co 2: 7 the hidden wisdom which **G**
1Co 2: 9 of man the things which **G** has
1Co 2:10 But **G** has revealed them to us
1Co 2:10 yes, the deep things of **G**
1Co 2:11 of **G** except the Spirit of **G**
1Co 2:12 but the Spirit who is from **G**
1Co 2:12 been freely given to us by **G**
1Co 2:14 the things of the Spirit of **G**
1Co 3: 6 but **G** gave the increase
1Co 3: 7 but **G** who gives the increase
1Co 3:10 of **G** which was given to me
1Co 3:16 that you are the temple of **G**
1Co 3:16 the Spirit of **G** dwells in you
1Co 3:17 anyone defiles the temple of **G**
1Co 3:17 **G** will destroy him
1Co 3:17 For the temple of **G** is holy
1Co 3:19 world is foolishness with **G**
1Co 4: 1 of the mysteries of **G**
1Co 4: 5 one's praise will come from **G**
1Co 4: 9 think that **G** has displayed us
1Co 4:20 For the kingdom of **G** is not
1Co 5:13 who are outside **G** judges
1Co 6: 9 not inherit the kingdom of **G**
1Co 6:10 will inherit the kingdom of **G**
1Co 6:11 and by the Spirit of our **G**
1Co 6:13 but **G** will destroy both it and
1Co 6:14 **G** both raised up the Lord and
1Co 6:19 in you, whom you have from **G**
1Co 6:20 glorify **G** in your body and in
1Co 7: 7 one has his own gift from **G**
1Co 7:15 But **G** has called us to peace
1Co 7:17 But as **G** has distributed to

1Co 7:19 of **G** is what matters
1Co 7:24 let each one remain with **G** in
1Co 7:40 I also have the Spirit of **G**
1Co 8: 3 But if anyone loves **G**, this
1Co 8: 4 there is no other **G** but one
1Co 8: 6 for us there is only one **G**
1Co 8: 8 food does not commend us to **G**
1Co 9: 9 Is it oxen **G** is concerned
1Co 9:21 being without law toward **G**
1Co 10: 5 them **G** was not well pleased
1Co 10:13 but **G** is faithful, who will
1Co 10:20 to demons and not to **G**, and I
1Co 10:31 do, do all to the glory of **G**
1Co 10:32 Greeks or to the church of **G**
1Co 11: 3 and the head of Christ is **G**
1Co 11: 7 he is the image and glory of **G**
1Co 11:12 but all things are from **G**
1Co 11:13 for a woman to pray to **G** with
1Co 11:16 nor do the churches of **G**
1Co 11:22 you despise the church of **G**
1Co 12: 3 of **G** calls Jesus accursed
1Co 12: 6 but it is the same **G** who
1Co 12:18 But now **G** has set the members
1Co 12:24 But **G** composed the body,
1Co 12:28 **G** has appointed these in the
1Co 14: 2 not speak to men but to **G**
1Co 14:18 I thank my **G** I speak with
1Co 14:25 his face, he will worship **G**
1Co 14:25 report that **G** is truly among
1Co 14:28 him speak to himself and to **G**
1Co 14:33 For **G** is not the author of
1Co 14:36 Or did the word of **G** come
1Co 15: 9 I persecuted the church of **G**
1Co 15:10 the grace of **G** I am what I am
1Co 15:10 but the grace of **G** which was
1Co 15:15 found false witnesses of **G**
1Co 15:15 we have testified of **G** that
1Co 15:24 the kingdom to **G** the Father
1Co 15:28 Him, that **G** may be all in all
1Co 15:34 not have the knowledge of **G**
1Co 15:38 But **G** gives it a body as He
1Co 15:50 inherit the kingdom of **G**
1Co 15:57 But thanks be to **G**, who gives
2Co 1: 1 Jesus Christ by the will of **G**
2Co 1: 1 To the church of **G** which is
2Co 1: 2 and peace from **G** our Father
2Co 1: 3 Blessed be the **G** and Father of
2Co 1: 3 mercies and **G** of all comfort,
2Co 1: 4 ourselves are comforted by **G**
2Co 1: 9 but in **G** who raises the dead
2Co 1:12 wisdom but by the grace of **G**
2Co 1:18 But as **G** is faithful, our
2Co 1:19 For the Son of **G**, Jesus
2Co 1:20 promises of **G** in Him are Yes
2Co 1:20 to the glory of **G** through us
2Co 1:21 and has anointed us is **G**,
2Co 1:23 Moreover I call **G** as witness
2Co 2:14 Now thanks be to **G** who always
2Co 2:15 For we are to **G** the fragrance
2Co 2:17 many, peddling the word of **G**
2Co 2:17 of sincerity, but as from **G**
2Co 2:17 in the sight of **G** in Christ
2Co 3: 3 by the Spirit of the living **G**
2Co 3: 4 trust through Christ toward **G**
2Co 3: 5 but our sufficiency is from **G**
2Co 4: 2 the word of **G** deceitfully
2Co 4: 2 conscience in the sight of **G**
2Co 4: 4 Christ, who is the image of **G**
2Co 4: 6 For it is the **G** who commanded
2Co 4: 6 knowledge of the glory of **G**
2Co 4: 7 of the power may be of **G** and
2Co 4:15 to abound to the glory of **G**
2Co 5: 1 we have a building from **G**
2Co 5: 5 us for this very thing is **G**
2Co 5:11 but we are well-known to **G**
2Co 5:13 beside ourselves, it is for **G**
2Co 5:18 Now all things are of **G**, who
2Co 5:19 that is, that **G** was in Christ
2Co 5:20 as though **G** were pleading
2Co 5:20 behalf, be reconciled to **G**
2Co 5:21 the righteousness of **G** in Him
2Co 6: 1 the grace of **G** in vain
2Co 6: 4 ourselves as ministers of **G**
2Co 6: 7 of truth, by the power of **G**
2Co 6:16 the temple of **G** with idols
2Co 6:16 the temple of the living **G**
2Co 6:16 As **G** has said: "I will dwell
2Co 6:16 I will be their **G**, and they
2Co 7: 1 holiness in the fear of **G**
2Co 7: 6 Nevertheless **G**, who comforts
2Co 7:12 of **G** might appear to you
2Co 8: 1 known to you the grace of **G**
2Co 8: 5 then to us by the will of **G**
2Co 8:16 But thanks be to **G** who puts
2Co 9: 7 for **G** loves a cheerful giver
2Co 9: 8 **G** is able to make all grace
2Co 9:11 thanksgiving through us to **G**
2Co 9:12 many thanksgivings to **G**,
2Co 9:13 they glorify **G** for the
2Co 9:14 exceeding grace of **G** in you
2Co 9:15 Thanks be to **G** for His
2Co 10: 4 mighty in **G** for pulling down
2Co 10: 5 against the knowledge of **G**
2Co 10:13 sphere which **G** appointed us
2Co 11: 7 of **G** to you free of charge
2Co 11:11 I do not love you? **G** knows!
2Co 11:31 The **G** and Father of our Lord
2Co 12: 2 body I do not know, **G** knows
2Co 12: 3 body I do not know, **G** knows
2Co 12:19 We speak before **G** in Christ
2Co 12:21 my **G** will humble me among you
2Co 13: 4 He lives by the power of **G**
2Co 13: 4 by the power of **G** toward you
2Co 13: 7 Now I pray to **G** that you do
2Co 13:11 the **G** of love and peace will
2Co 13:14 Christ, and the love of **G**, and
Gal 1: 1 **G** the Father who raised Him
Gal 1: 3 and peace from **G** the Father
Gal 1: 4 to the will of our **G** and
Gal 1:10 do I now persuade men, or **G**
Gal 1:13 church of **G** beyond measure
Gal 1:15 But when it pleased **G**, who
Gal 1:20 to you, indeed, before **G**, I
Gal 1:24 And they glorified **G** in me
Gal 2: 6 **G** shows personal favoritism
Gal 2:19 law that I might live to **G**
Gal 2:20 live by faith in the Son of **G**
Gal 2:21 not set aside the grace of **G**
Gal 3: 6 believed **G**, and it was
Gal 3: 8 foreseeing that **G** would
Gal 3:11 in the sight of **G** is evident
Gal 3:17 before by **G** in Christ, that
Gal 3:18 but **G** gave it to Abraham by
Gal 3:20 for one only, but **G** is one
Gal 3:21 against the promises of **G**
Gal 3:26 of **G** through faith in Christ
Gal 4: 4 **G** sent forth His Son, born of
Gal 4: 6 **G** has sent forth the Spirit
Gal 4: 7 an heir of **G** through Christ
Gal 4: 8 when you did not know **G**, you
Gal 4: 9 now after you have known **G**
Gal 4: 9 **G**, or rather are known by **G**
Gal 4:14 received me as an angel of **G**
Gal 5:21 not inherit the kingdom of **G**
Gal 6: 7 be deceived, **G** is not mocked
Gal 6:14 But **G** forbid that I should
Gal 6:16 them, and upon the Israel of **G**
Eph 1: 1 Jesus Christ by the will of **G**
Eph 1: 2 and peace from **G** our Father
Eph 1: 3 Blessed be the **G** and Father of
Eph 1:17 that the **G** of our Lord Jesus
Eph 2: 4 But **G**, who is rich in mercy,
Eph 2: 8 it is the gift of **G**,
Eph 2:10 which **G** prepared beforehand
Eph 2:12 and without **G** in the world
Eph 2:16 reconcile them both to **G** in
Eph 2:19 members of the household of **G**
Eph 2:22 habitation of **G** in the Spirit
Eph 3: 2 of the grace of **G** which was
Eph 3: 7 grace of **G** given to me by the
Eph 3: 9 in **G** who created all things
Eph 3:10 **G** might be made known by the
Eph 3:19 with all the fullness of **G**
Eph 4: 6 one **G** and Father of all, who
Eph 4:13 the knowledge of the Son of **G**
Eph 4:18 alienated from the life of **G**
Eph 4:24 was created according to **G**
Eph 4:30 grieve the Holy Spirit of **G**
Eph 4:32 just as **G** in Christ also
Eph 5: 1 of **G** as dear children
Eph 5: 2 and a sacrifice to **G** for a
Eph 5: 5 in the kingdom of Christ and **G**
Eph 5: 6 of **G** comes upon the sons of
Eph 5:20 always for all things to **G**
Eph 5:21 one another in the fear of **G**
Eph 6: 6 the will of **G** from the heart
Eph 6:11 Put on the whole armor of **G**
Eph 6:13 take up the whole armor of **G**
Eph 6:17 which is the word of **G**
Eph 6:23 from **G** the Father and the Lord
Phil 1: 2 and peace from **G** our Father
Phil 1: 3 I thank my **G** upon every
Phil 1: 8 For **G** is my witness, how
Phil 1:11 to the glory and praise of **G**
Phil 1:28 of salvation, and that from **G**
Phil 2: 6 who, being in the form of **G**
Phil 2: 6 it robbery to be equal with **G**
Phil 2: 9 Therefore **G** also has highly
Phil 2:11 to the glory of **G** the Father
Phil 2:13 for it is **G** who works in you
Phil 2:15 children of **G** without fault
Phil 2:27 but **G** had mercy on him, and
Phil 3: 3 who worship **G** in the Spirit,
Phil 3: 9 which is from **G** by faith
Phil 3:14 call of **G** in Christ Jesus
Phil 3:15 **G** will reveal even this to
Phil 4: 6 requests be made known to **G**
Phil 4: 7 and the peace of **G**, which
Phil 4: 9 the **G** of peace will be with
Phil 4:18 sacrifice, well pleasing to **G**
Phil 4:19 my **G** shall supply all your
Phil 4:20 Now to our **G** and Father be
Col 1: 1 Jesus Christ by the will of **G**
Col 1: 2 and peace from **G** our Father
Col 1: 3 We give thanks to the **G** and
Col 1: 6 knew the grace of **G** in truth
Col 1:10 in the knowledge of **G**
Col 1:15 the image of the invisible **G**
Col 1:25 to the stewardship from **G**
Col 1:25 you, to fulfill the word of **G**
Col 1:27 To them **G** willed to make
Col 2: 2 knowledge of the mystery of **G**
Col 2:12 faith in the working of **G**
Col 2:19 the increase which is from **G**
Col 3: 1 at the right hand of **G**
Col 3: 3 is hidden with Christ in **G**
Col 3: 6 these things the wrath of **G**
Col 3:12 Therefore, as the elect of **G**
Col 3:15 let the peace of **G** rule in
Col 3:17 giving thanks to **G** the Father
Col 3:22 sincerity of heart, fearing **G**
Col 4: 3 that **G** would open to us a
Col 4:11 workers for the kingdom of **G**
Col 4:12 complete in all the will of **G**
1Th 1: 1 Thessalonians in **G** the Father
1Th 1: 1 and peace from **G** our Father
1Th 1: 2 We give thanks to **G** always
1Th 1: 3 Christ in the sight of our **G**
1Th 1: 4 brethren, your election by **G**
1Th 1: 8 faith toward **G** has gone out
1Th 1: 9 and how you turned to **G** from
1Th 1: 9 to serve the living and true **G**
1Th 2: 2 we were bold in our **G** to
1Th 2: 2 gospel of **G** in much conflict
1Th 2: 4 by **G** to be entrusted with the
1Th 2: 4 but **G** who tests our hearts
1Th 2: 5 **G** is witness.
1Th 2: 8 you not only the gospel of **G**
1Th 2: 9 to you the gospel of **G**
1Th 2:10 and **G** also, how devoutly and
1Th 2:12 **G** who calls you into His own
1Th 2:13 also thank **G** without ceasing
1Th 2:13 of **G** which you heard from us
1Th 2:13 it is in truth, the word of **G**
1Th 2:14 of the churches of **G** which
1Th 2:15 and they do not please **G** and
1Th 3: 2 our brother and minister of **G**
1Th 3: 9 can we render to **G** for you
1Th 3: 9 for your sake before our **G**
1Th 3:11 Now may our **G** and Father
1Th 3:13 in holiness before our **G** and
1Th 4: 1 ought to walk and to please **G**
1Th 4: 3 For this is the will of **G**
1Th 4: 5 Gentiles who do not know **G**
1Th 4: 7 For **G** did not call us to
1Th 4: 8 does not reject man, but **G**
1Th 4: 9 by **G** to love one another
1Th 4:14 even so **G** will bring with Him
1Th 4:16 and with the trumpet of **G**
1Th 5: 9 For **G** did not appoint us to
1Th 5:18 of **G** in Christ Jesus for you
1Th 5:23 Now may the **G** of peace
2Th 1: 1 Thessalonians in **G** our Father
2Th 1: 2 and peace from **G** our Father
2Th 1: 3 to thank **G** always for you
2Th 1: 4 of **G** for your patience and
2Th 1: 5 the righteous judgment of **G**
2Th 1: 5 worthy of the kingdom of **G**
2Th 1: 6 **G** to repay with tribulation
2Th 1: 8 on those who do not know **G**

2Th 1:11 always for you that our **G**
2Th 1:12 to the grace of our **G** and the
2Th 2: 4 called **G** or that is worshiped
2Th 2: 4 temple of **G**, showing himself
2Th 2: 4 showing himself that he is **G**
2Th 2:11 for this reason **G** will send
2Th 2:13 thanks to **G** always for you
2Th 2:13 because **G** from the beginning
2Th 2:16 Christ Himself, and our **G** and
2Th 3: 5 hearts into the love of **G**
1Ti 1: 1 commandment of **G** our Savior
1Ti 1: 2 and peace from **G** our Father
1Ti 1:11 gospel of the blessed **G** which
1Ti 1:17 to **G** who alone is wise, be
1Ti 2: 3 in the sight of **G** our Savior
1Ti 2: 5 For there is one **G**
1Ti 2: 5 and one Mediator between **G**
1Ti 3: 5 take care of the church of **G**
1Ti 3:15 yourself in the house of **G**
1Ti 3:15 is the church of the living **G**
1Ti 3:16 **G** was manifested in the flesh
1Ti 4: 3 **G** created to be received with
1Ti 4: 4 every creature of **G** is good
1Ti 4: 5 sanctified by the word of **G**
1Ti 4:10 we trust in the living **G**, who
1Ti 5: 4 good and acceptable before **G**
1Ti 5: 5 and left alone, trusts in **G**
1Ti 5:21 I charge you before **G** and the
1Ti 6: 1 honor, so that the name of **G**
1Ti 6:11 But you, O man of **G**, flee
1Ti 6:13 of **G** who gives life to all
1Ti 6:17 riches but in the living **G**
2Ti 1: 1 Jesus Christ by the will of **G**
2Ti 1: 2 and peace from **G** the Father
2Ti 1: 3 I thank **G**, whom I serve with
2Ti 1: 6 you to stir up the gift of **G**
2Ti 1: 7 For **G** has not given us a
2Ti 1: 8 according to the power of **G**
2Ti 2: 9 the word of **G** is not chained
2Ti 2:15 yourself approved to **G**, a
2Ti 2:19 solid foundation of **G** stands
2Ti 2:25 if **G** perhaps will grant them
2Ti 3: 4 rather than lovers of **G**,
2Ti 3:16 is given by inspiration of **G**
2Ti 3:17 the man of **G** may be complete
2Ti 4: 1 charge you therefore before **G**
Tit 1: 1 Paul, a servant of **G** and an
Tit 1: 2 hope of eternal life which **G**
Tit 1: 3 commandment of **G** our Savior
Tit 1: 4 and peace from **G** the Father
Tit 1: 7 blameless, as a steward of **G**
Tit 1:16 They profess to know **G**, but
Tit 2: 5 that the word of **G** may not be
Tit 2:10 of **G** our Savior in all things
Tit 2:11 For the grace of **G** that
Tit 2:13 appearing of our great **G** and
Tit 3: 4 and the love of **G** our Savior
Tit 3: 8 in **G** should be careful to
Phm 3 and peace from **G** our Father
Phm 4 I thank my **G**, making mention
Heb 1: 1 **G**, who at various times and in
Heb 1: 6 the angels of **G** worship Him
Heb 1: 8 Your throne, O **G**, is forever
Heb 1: 9 therefore **G**, Your **G**, has
Heb 2: 4 **G** also bearing witness both
Heb 2: 9 that He, by the grace of **G**
Heb 2:13 children whom **G** has given Me
Heb 2:17 in things pertaining to **G**
Heb 3: 4 He who built all things is **G**
Heb 3:12 departing from the living **G**
Heb 4: 4 **G** rested on the seventh day
Heb 4: 9 a rest for the people of **G**
Heb 4:10 his works as **G** did from His
Heb 4:12 For the word of **G** is living
Heb 4:14 heavens, Jesus the Son of **G**
Heb 5: 1 men in things pertaining to **G**
Heb 5: 4 but he who is called by **G**
Heb 5:10 called by **G** as High Priest
Heb 5:12 of the oracles of **G**
Heb 6: 1 works and of faith toward **G**
Heb 6: 3 this we will do if **G** permits
Heb 6: 5 tasted the good word of **G**
Heb 6: 6 for themselves the Son of **G**
Heb 6: 7 receives blessing from **G**
Heb 6:10 For **G** is not unjust to forget
Heb 6:13 For when **G** made a promise to
Heb 6:17 Thus **G**, determining to show
Heb 6:18 it is impossible for **G** to lie
Heb 7: 1 priest of the Most High **G**
Heb 7: 3 but made like the Son of **G**
Heb 7:19 which we draw near to **G**
Heb 7:25 who come to **G** through Him
Heb 8:10 and I will be their **G**, and they
Heb 9:14 Himself without spot to **G**
Heb 9:14 works to serve the living **G**
Heb 9:20 which **G** has commanded you
Heb 9:24 in the presence of **G** for us
Heb 10: 7 to do Your will, O **G**
Heb 10: 9 come to do Your will, O **G**
Heb 10:12 down at the right hand of **G**
Heb 10:21 Priest over the house of **G**
Heb 10:29 the Son of **G** underfoot,
Heb 10:31 the hands of the living **G**
Heb 10:36 you have done the will of **G**
Heb 11: 3 were framed by the word of **G**
Heb 11: 4 By faith Abel offered to **G** a
Heb 11: 4 **G** testifying of his gifts
Heb 11: 5 **G** had translated him"
Heb 11: 5 testimony, that he pleased **G**
Heb 11: 6 for he who comes to **G** must
Heb 11:10 whose builder and maker is **G**
Heb 11:16 Therefore **G** is not ashamed to
Heb 11:16 ashamed to be called their **G**
Heb 11:19 accounting that **G** was able to
Heb 11:25 with the people of **G** than to
Heb 11:40 **G** having provided something
Heb 12: 2 right hand of the throne of **G**
Heb 12: 7 **G** deals with you as with sons
Heb 12:15 fall short of the grace of **G**
Heb 12:22 to the city of the living **G**
Heb 12:23 to **G** the Judge of all, to the
Heb 12:28 by which we may serve **G**
Heb 12:29 For our **G** is a consuming fire
Heb 13: 4 and adulterers **G** will judge
Heb 13: 7 spoken the word of **G** to you
Heb 13:15 the sacrifice of praise to **G**
Heb 13:16 sacrifices **G** is well pleased
Heb 13:20 Now may the **G** of peace who
Jas 1: 1 James, a servant of **G** and of
Jas 1: 5 wisdom, let him ask of **G**, who
Jas 1:13 I am tempted by **G**"
Jas 1:13 for **G** cannot be tempted by
Jas 1:20 the righteousness of **G**
Jas 1:27 undefiled religion before **G**
Jas 2: 5 Has **G** not chosen the poor of
Jas 2:19 believe that there is one **G**
Jas 2:23 Abraham believed **G**, and it was
Jas 2:23 he was called the friend of **G**
Jas 3: 9 With it we bless our **G** and
Jas 3: 9 made in the similitude of **G**
Jas 4: 4 the world is enmity with **G**
Jas 4: 4 makes himself an enemy of **G**
Jas 4: 6 **G** resists the proud, but
Jas 4: 7 Therefore submit to **G**
Jas 4: 8 Draw near to **G** and He will
1Pe 1: 2 foreknowledge of **G** the Father
1Pe 1: 3 Blessed be the **G** and Father of
1Pe 1: 5 are kept by the power of **G**
1Pe 1:21 who through Him believe in **G**
1Pe 1:21 your faith and hope are in **G**
1Pe 1:23 the word of **G** which lives
1Pe 2: 4 by men, but chosen by **G** and
1Pe 2: 5 to **G** through Jesus Christ
1Pe 2:10 but are now the people of **G**
1Pe 2:12 glorify **G** in the day of
1Pe 2:15 For this is the will of **G**
1Pe 2:16 vice, but as servants of **G**
1Pe 2:17 Fear **G**. Honor the king.
1Pe 2:19 toward **G** one endures grief
1Pe 2:20 this is commendable before **G**
1Pe 3: 4 precious in the sight of **G**
1Pe 3: 5 in **G** also adorned themselves
1Pe 3:15 the Lord **G** in your hearts
1Pe 3:17 if it is the will of **G**, to
1Pe 3:18 that He might bring us to **G**
1Pe 3:20 once the longsuffering of **G**
1Pe 3:21 a good conscience toward **G**)
1Pe 3:22 and is at the right hand of **G**
1Pe 4: 2 of men, but for the will of **G**
1Pe 4: 6 according to **G** in the spirit
1Pe 4:10 of the manifold grace of **G**
1Pe 4:11 him speak as the oracles of **G**
1Pe 4:11 the ability which **G** supplies
1Pe 4:11 that in all things **G** may be
1Pe 4:14 glory and of **G** rests upon you
1Pe 4:16 him glorify **G** in this matter
1Pe 4:17 to begin at the house of **G**
1Pe 4:17 do not obey the gospel of **G**
1Pe 4:19 according to the will of **G**
1Pe 5: 2 flock of **G** which is among you
1Pe 5: 5 **G** resists the proud, but
1Pe 5: 6 under the mighty hand of **G**
1Pe 5:10 But may the **G** of all grace,
1Pe 5:12 grace of **G** in which you stand
2Pe 1: 1 by the righteousness of our **G**
2Pe 1: 2 to you in the knowledge of **G**
2Pe 1:17 from **G** the Father honor and
2Pe 1:21 but holy men of **G** spoke as
2Pe 2: 4 For if **G** did not spare the
2Pe 3: 5 that by the word of **G** the
2Pe 3:12 the coming of the day of **G**
1Jn 1: 5 that **G** is light and in Him is
1Jn 2: 5 word, truly the love of **G** is
1Jn 2:14 the word of **G** abides in you,
1Jn 2:17 the will of **G** abides forever
1Jn 3: 1 be called children of **G**
1Jn 3: 2 now we are children of **G**
1Jn 3: 8 the Son of **G** was manifested
1Jn 3: 9 been born of **G** does not sin
1Jn 3: 9 because he has been born of **G**
1Jn 3:10 In this the children of **G**
1Jn 3:10 righteousness is not of **G**
1Jn 3:17 the love of **G** abide in him
1Jn 3:20 **G** is greater than our heart,
1Jn 3:21 we have confidence toward **G**
1Jn 4: 1 whether they are of **G**
1Jn 4: 2 this you know the Spirit of **G**
1Jn 4: 2 has come in the flesh is of **G**
1Jn 4: 3 come in the flesh is not of **G**
1Jn 4: 4 You are of **G**, little children
1Jn 4: 6 We are of **G**
1Jn 4: 6 He who knows **G** hears us
1Jn 4: 6 is not of **G** does not hear us
1Jn 4: 7 one another, for love is of **G**
1Jn 4: 7 who loves is born of **G**
1Jn 4: 7 and knows **G**
1Jn 4: 8 does not love does not know **G**
1Jn 4: 8 for **G** is love
1Jn 4: 9 In this the love of **G** was
1Jn 4: 9 us, that **G** has sent His only
1Jn 4:10 is love, not that we loved **G**
1Jn 4:11 if **G** so loved us, we also
1Jn 4:12 No one has seen **G** at any time
1Jn 4:12 **G** abides in us, and His love
1Jn 4:15 that Jesus is the Son of **G**
1Jn 4:15 **G** abides in him, and he in **G**
1Jn 4:16 the love that **G** has for us
1Jn 4:16 **G** is love, and he who abides
1Jn 4:16 abides in love abides in **G**
1Jn 4:16 abides in **G**, and **G** in him
1Jn 4:20 I love **G**," and hates his
1Jn 4:20 how can he love **G** whom he has
1Jn 4:21 that he who loves **G** must love
1Jn 5: 1 is the Christ is born of **G**
1Jn 5: 2 we love the children of **G**
1Jn 5: 2 when we love **G** and keep His
1Jn 5: 3 For this is the love of **G**
1Jn 5: 4 born of **G** overcomes the world
1Jn 5: 5 that Jesus is the Son of **G**
1Jn 5: 9 the witness of **G** is greater
1Jn 5: 9 **G** which He has testified of
1Jn 5:10 **G** has the witness in himself
1Jn 5:10 believe **G** has made Him a liar
1Jn 5:10 that **G** has given of His Son
1Jn 5:11 that **G** has given us eternal
1Jn 5:12 Son of **G** does not have life
1Jn 5:13 in the name of the Son of **G**
1Jn 5:13 in the name of the Son of **G**
1Jn 5:18 is born of **G** does not sin
1Jn 5:18 been born of **G** keeps himself
1Jn 5:19 We know that we are of **G**, and
1Jn 5:20 that the Son of **G** has come
1Jn 5:20 This is the true **G** and eternal
2Jn 3 be with you from **G** the Father
2Jn 9 of Christ does not have **G**
3Jn 6 in a manner worthy of **G**, you
3Jn 11 He who does good is of **G**, but
3Jn 11 who does evil has not seen **G**
Jude 1 sanctified by **G** the Father
Jude 4 of our **G** into licentiousness
Jude 4 and deny the only Lord **G** and
Jude 21 yourselves in the love of **G**
Jude 25 to **G** our Savior, who alone is
Rev 1: 1 which **G** gave Him to show His
Rev 1: 2 bore witness to the word of **G**
Rev 1: 6 us kings and priests to His **G**
Rev 1: 9 Patmos for the word of **G** and
Rev 2: 7 midst of the Paradise of **G**
Rev 2:18 things says the Son of **G**, who
Rev 3: 1 has the seven Spirits of **G**

Rev 3: 2 your works perfect before **G**
Rev 3:12 pillar in the temple of My **G**
Rev 3:12 write on him the name of My **G**
Rev 3:12 the name of the city of My **G**
Rev 3:12 down out of heaven from My **G**
Rev 3:14 of the creation of **G**
Rev 4: 5 are the seven Spirits of **G**
Rev 4: 8 Lord **G** Almighty, Who was and
Rev 5: 6 are the seven Spirits of **G**
Rev 5: 9 have redeemed us to **G** by Your
Rev 5:10 us kings and priests to our **G**
Rev 6: 9 been slain for the word of **G**
Rev 7: 2 the seal of the living **G**
Rev 7: 3 of our **G** on their foreheads
Rev 7:10 our **G** who sits on the throne
Rev 7:11 the throne and worshiped **G**
Rev 7:12 and might, be to our **G** forever
Rev 7:15 are before the throne of **G**
Rev 7:17 **G** will wipe away every tear
Rev 8: 2 angels who stand before **G**
Rev 8: 4 ascended before **G** from the
Rev 9: 4 seal of **G** on their foreheads
Rev 9:13 altar which is before **G**,
Rev 10: 7 the mystery of **G** would be
Rev 11: 1 and measure the temple of **G**
Rev 11: 4 before the **G** of the earth
Rev 11:11 of life from **G** entered them
Rev 11:13 gave glory to the **G** of heaven
Rev 11:16 elders who sat before **G** on
Rev 11:16 on their faces and worshiped **G**
Rev 11:17 O Lord **G** Almighty, the One
Rev 11:19 Then the temple of **G** was
Rev 12: 5 her Child was caught up to **G**
Rev 12: 6 she has a place prepared by **G**
Rev 12:10 and the kingdom of our **G**, and
Rev 12:10 accused them before our **G** day
Rev 12:17 keep the commandments of **G**
Rev 13: 6 mouth in blasphemy against **G**
Rev 14: 4 men, being firstfruits to **G**
Rev 14: 5 fault before the throne of **G**
Rev 14: 7 Fear **G** and give glory to Him,
Rev 14:10 of the wine of the wrath of **G**
Rev 14:12 keep the commandments of **G**
Rev 14:19 winepress of the wrath of **G**
Rev 15: 1 the wrath of **G** is complete
Rev 15: 2 of glass, having harps of **G**
Rev 15: 3 of Moses, the servant of **G**
Rev 15: 3 Your works, Lord **G** Almighty
Rev 15: 7 wrath of **G** who lives forever
Rev 15: 8 smoke from the glory of **G**
Rev 16: 1 the wrath of **G** on the earth
Rev 16: 7 so, Lord **G** Almighty, true and
Rev 16: 9 of **G** who has power over these
Rev 16:11 And they blasphemed the **G** of
Rev 16:14 that great day of **G** Almighty
Rev 16:19 was remembered before **G**, to
Rev 16:21 men blasphemed **G** because of
Rev 17:17 For **G** has put it into their
Rev 17:17 the words of **G** are fulfilled
Rev 18: 5 and **G** has remembered her
Rev 18: 8 is the Lord **G** who judges her
Rev 18:20 for **G** has avenged you on her
Rev 19: 1 and power to the Lord our **G**
Rev 19: 4 worshiped **G** who sat on the
Rev 19: 5 Praise our **G**, all you His
Rev 19: 6 For the Lord **G** Omnipotent
Rev 19: 9 are the true sayings of **G**
Rev 19:10 Worship **G**!
Rev 19:13 name is called The Word of **G**
Rev 19:15 and wrath of Almighty **G**
Rev 19:17 for the supper of the great **G**
Rev 20: 4 to Jesus and for the word of **G**
Rev 20: 6 they shall be priests of **G**
Rev 20: 9 down from **G** out of heaven
Rev 20:12 and great, standing before **G**
Rev 21: 2 down out of heaven from **G**
Rev 21: 3 tabernacle of **G** is with men
Rev 21: 3 **G** Himself will be with them
Rev 21: 3 be with them and be their **G**
Rev 21: 4 **G** will wipe away every tear
Rev 21: 7 things, and I will be his **G**
Rev 21:10 out of heaven from **G**,
Rev 21:11 having the glory of **G**
Rev 21:22 it, for the Lord **G** Almighty
Rev 21:23 the glory of **G** illuminated it
Rev 22: 1 from the throne of **G** and of
Rev 22: 3 curse, but the throne of **G**
Rev 22: 5 for the Lord **G** gives them
Rev 22: 6 And the Lord **G** of the holy
Rev 22: 9 Worship **G**.
Rev 22:18 **G** will add to him the plagues
Rev 22:19 **G** shall take away his part

GOD* (*see* GODDESS, GODS)
Ex 22:20 He who sacrifices to any **g**
Ex 32: 4 This is your **g**, O Israel,
Ex 32: 8 it, and said, This is your **g**
Ex 32:31 for themselves a **g** of gold
Ex 34:14 you shall worship no other **g**
Deut 3:24 for what **g** is there in heaven
Deut 32:12 was no foreign **g** with him
Judg 6:31 If he is a **g**, let him plead
Judg 8:33 and made Baal-Berith their **g**
Judg 9:27 into the house of their **g**
Judg 9:46 of the temple of the **g** Berith
Judg 11:24 your **g** gives you to possess
Judg 16:23 sacrifice to Dagon their **g**
Judg 16:23 Our **g** has delivered into our
Judg 16:24 saw him, they praised their **g**
Judg 16:24 Our **g** has delivered into our
1Sa 5: 7 toward us and Dagon our **g**
1Ki 11:33 Chemosh the **g** of the Moabites
1Ki 11:33 Milcom the **g** of the people of
1Ki 18:25 and call on the name of your **g**
1Ki 18:27 Cry aloud, for he is a **g**
2Ki 1: 2 the **g** of Ekron, whether I
2Ki 1: 3 of Baal-Zebub, the **g** of Ekron
2Ki 1: 6 of Baal-Zebub, the **g** of Ekron
2Ki 1:16 the **g** of Ekron, is it because
2Ki 19:37 the temple of Nisroch his **g**
2Ch 32:15 for no **g** of any nation or
2Ch 32:21 gone into the temple of his **g**
Ps 16: 4 who hasten after another **g**
Ps 44:20 out our hands to a foreign **g**
Ps 81: 9 be no foreign **g** among you
Ps 81: 9 you worship any foreign **g**
Is 37:38 in the house of Nisroch his **g**
Is 43:12 was no foreign **g** among you
Is 44:10 Who would form a **g** or cast a
Is 44:15 indeed he makes a **g** and
Is 44:17 rest of it he makes into a **g**
Is 44:17 Deliver me, for you are my **g**
Is 45:20 pray to a **g** that cannot save
Is 46: 6 goldsmith, and he makes it a **g**
Ezek 28: 2 up, and you say, 'I am a **g**
Ezek 28: 2 yet you are a man, and not a **g**
Ezek 28: 2 heart as the heart of a **g**
Ezek 28: 6 heart as the heart of a **g**
Ezek 28: 9 him who slays you, 'I am a **g**'
Ezek 28: 9 shall be a man, and not a **g**
Dan 1: 2 Shinar to the house of his **g**
Dan 1: 2 the treasure house of his **g**
Dan 3:28 any **g** except their own God
Dan 4: 8 according to the name of my **g**
Dan 6: 7 any **g** or man for thirty days
Dan 6:12 **g** or man within thirty days
Dan 11:36 magnify himself above every **g**
Dan 11:37 of women, nor regard any **g**
Dan 11:38 shall honor a **g** of fortresses
Dan 11:38 a **g** which his fathers did not
Dan 11:39 fortresses with a foreign **g**
Amos 2: 8 in the house of their **g**
Amos 8:14 who say, 'As your **g** lives
Jon 1: 5 every man cried out to his **g**
Mic 4: 5 each in the name of his **g**
Hab 1:11 imputing this power to his **g**
Mal 2:11 the daughter of a foreign **g**
Acts 7:43 and the star of your **g** Remphan
Acts 12:22 The voice of a **g** and not of a
Acts 28: 6 minds and said that he was a **g**
2Co 4: 4 whose minds the **g** of this age
Phil 3:19 whose **g** is their belly, and

GODDESS (*see* GOD*)
1Ki 11: 5 the **g** of the Sidonians, and
1Ki 11:33 the **g** of the Sidonians,
Acts 19:27 great **g** Diana may be despised
Acts 19:35 guardian of the great **g** Diana
Acts 19:37 nor blasphemers of your **g**

GOD-GIVEN (*see* GOD)
Ezra 7:25 according to your **G** wisdom
Eccl 3:10 I have seen the **G** task with

GODHEAD (*see* GOD)
Rom 1:20 even His eternal power and **G**
Col 2: 9 the fullness of the **G** bodily

GODLINESS (*see* GODLY)
Acts 3:12 **g** we had made this man walk
1Ti 2: 2 and peaceable life in all **g**
1Ti 2:10 proper for women professing **g**
1Ti 3:16 great is the mystery of **g**
1Ti 4: 7 exercise yourself rather to **g**
1Ti 4: 8 but **g** is profitable for all
1Ti 6: 3 which is according to **g**,
1Ti 6: 5 who suppose that **g** is a means
1Ti 6: 6 But **g** with contentment is
1Ti 6:11 and pursue righteousness, **g**
2Ti 3: 5 having a form of **g** but
Tit 1: 1 truth which is according to **g**
2Pe 1: 3 that pertain to life and **g**
2Pe 1: 6 to perseverance **g**,
2Pe 1: 7 to **g** brotherly kindness, and
2Pe 3:11 to be in holy conduct and **g**

GODLY (*see* GOD, GODLINESS, UNGODLY)
Ps 4: 3 for Himself him who is **g**
Ps 12: 1 LORD, for the **g** man ceases
Ps 32: 6 this cause everyone who is **g**
Mal 2:15 He seeks **g** offspring
2Co 1:12 **g** sincerity, not with fleshly
2Co 7: 9 were made sorry in a **g** manner
2Co 7:10 For **g** sorrow produces
2Co 7:11 you sorrowed in a **g** manner
2Co 11: 2 for you with **g** jealousy
1Ti 1: 4 **g** edification which is in
2Ti 3:12 all who desire to live **g** in
Tit 2:12 and **g** in the present age,
Heb 5: 7 heard because of His **g** fear
Heb 11: 7 yet seen, moved with **g** fear
Heb 12:28 with reverence and **g** fear
2Pe 2: 9 the **g** out of temptations and

GOD'S (*see* GOD)
Gen 28:22 as a pillar shall be **G** house
Gen 32: 2 This is **G** camp
Num 22:22 Then **G** anger was aroused
Deut 1:17 for the judgment is **G**
1Ch 5:22 dead, because the war was **G**
2Ch 20:15 battle is not yours, but **G**
2Ch 22: 7 was **G** occasion for Ahaziah's
Neh 10:29 and an oath to walk in **G** Law
Job 35: 2 righteousness is more than **G**'
Job 36: 2 words to speak on **G** behalf
Mal 1: 9 But now entreat **G** favor, that
Matt 5:34 by heaven, for it is **G** throne
Matt 22:21 to God the things that are **G**
Mark 12:17 to God the things that are **G**
Luke 20:25 to God the things that are **G**
John 8:47 who is of God hears **G** words
Acts 23: 4 Do you revile **G** high priest
Rom 8:33 a charge against **G** elect
Rom 10: 3 ignorant of **G** righteousness
Rom 13: 4 For he is **G** minister to you
Rom 13: 4 for he is **G** minister, an
Rom 13: 6 for they are **G** ministers
1Co 3: 9 For we are **G** fellow workers
1Co 3: 9 you are **G** field, you are
1Co 3: 9 field, you are **G** building
1Co 3:23 are Christ's, and Christ is **G**
1Co 6:20 in your spirit, which are **G**
Tit 1: 1 to the faith of **G** elect and

GODS (*see* GOD*)
Gen 31:30 but why did you steal my **g**
Gen 31:32 With whomever you find your **g**
Gen 35: 2 foreign **g** that are among you
Gen 35: 4 **g** which were in their hands
Ex 12:12 against all the **g** of Egypt I
Ex 15:11 like You, O LORD, among the **g**
Ex 18:11 is greater than all the **g**
Ex 20: 3 have no other **g** before Me
Ex 20:23 **g** of silver or **g** of gold
Ex 20:23 **g** of silver or **g** of gold
Ex 23:13 of the name of other **g**, nor
Ex 23:24 shall not bow down to their **g**
Ex 23:32 with them, nor with their **g**
Ex 23:33 For if you serve their **g**, it
Ex 32: 1 Come, make us **g** that shall go
Ex 32:23 me, Make us **g** that shall go
Ex 34:15 play the harlot with their **g**
Ex 34:15 and make sacrifice to their **g**
Ex 34:16 play the harlot with their **g**
Ex 34:16 play the harlot with their **g**
Ex 34:17 no molded **g** for yourselves
Lev 19: 4 make for yourselves molded **g**
Num 25: 2 to the sacrifices of their **g**
Num 25: 2 ate and bowed down to their **g**
Num 33: 4 Also on their **g** the LORD had
Deut 4:28 And there you will serve **g**
Deut 5: 7 have no other **g** before Me
Deut 6:14 shall not go after other **g**
Deut 6:14 the **g** of the peoples who are
Deut 7: 4 Me, to serve other **g**

Deut 7:16 nor shall you serve their g
Deut 7:25 images of their g with fire
Deut 8:19 your God, and follow other g
Deut 10:17 the LORD your God is God of g
Deut 11:16 turn aside and serve other g
Deut 11:28 to go after other g which you
Deut 12: 2 dispossess served their g
Deut 12: 3 the carved images of their g
Deut 12:30 do not inquire after their g
Deut 12:30 these nations serve their g
Deut 12:31 they have done to their g
Deut 12:31 in the fire to their g
Deut 13: 2 Let us go after other g
Deut 13: 6 Let us go and serve other g
Deut 13: 7 of the g of the people which
Deut 13:13 Let us go and serve other g
Deut 13:13 g whom you have not known,'
Deut 17: 3 has gone and served other g
Deut 18:20 speaks in the name of other g
Deut 20:18 they have done for their g
Deut 28:14 after other g to serve them
Deut 28:36 there you shall serve other g
Deut 28:64 there you shall serve other g
Deut 29:18 serve the g of these nations,
Deut 29:26 they went and served other g
Deut 29:26 g that they did not know and
Deut 30:17 away, and worship other g and
Deut 31:16 g of the foreigners of the
Deut 31:18 they have turned to other g
Deut 31:20 they will turn to other g
Deut 32:16 to jealousy with foreign g
Deut 32:17 to g they did not know, to
Deut 32:17 they did not know, to new g
Deut 32:37 Where are their g, the rock
Josh 22:22 God of g, the LORD God of g
Josh 23: 7 of the name of their g, nor
Josh 23:16 have gone and served other g
Josh 24: 2 and they served other g
Josh 24:14 put away the g which your
Josh 24:15 whether the g which your
Josh 24:15 or the g of the Amorites, in
Josh 24:16 the LORD to serve other g
Josh 24:20 the LORD and serve foreign g
Josh 24:23 foreign g which are among you
Judg 2: 3 their g shall be a snare to
Judg 2:12 other g from among the g
Judg 2:17 the harlot with other g, and
Judg 2:19 fathers, by following other g
Judg 3: 6 and they served their g
Judg 5: 8 They chose new g
Judg 6:10 fear the g of the Amorites
Judg 10: 6 the g of Syria
Judg 10: 6 the g of Sidon
Judg 10: 6 the g of Moab
Judg 10: 6 the g of the people of Ammon,
Judg 10: 6 and the g of the Philistines
Judg 10:13 forsaken Me and served other g
Judg 10:14 cry out to the g which you
Judg 10:16 the foreign g from among them
Judg 18:24 taken away my g which I made
Ruth 1:15 to her people and to her g
1Sa 4: 8 the hand of these mighty g
1Sa 4: 8 These are the g who struck
1Sa 6: 5 hand from you, from your g
1Sa 7: 3 then put away the foreign g
1Sa 8: 8 forsaken Me and served other g
1Sa 17:43 cursed David by his g
1Sa 26:19 saying, 'Go, serve other g
2Sa 7:23 from the nations and their g
1Ki 9: 6 you, but go and serve other g
1Ki 9: 9 and have embraced other g
1Ki 11: 2 your hearts after their g
1Ki 11: 4 his heart after other g
1Ki 11: 8 and sacrificed to their g
1Ki 11:10 should not go after other g
1Ki 12:28 Here are your g, O Israel,
1Ki 14: 9 and made for yourself other g
1Ki 18:24 call on the name of your g
1Ki 19: 2 So let the g do to me, and
1Ki 20:10 The g do so to me, and more
1Ki 20:23 Their g are g of the hills
2Ki 5:17 or sacrifice to other g, but
2Ki 17: 7 and they had feared other g
2Ki 17:29 to make g of its own, and put
2Ki 17:31 the g of Sepharvaim
2Ki 17:33 LORD, yet served their own g
2Ki 17:35 You shall not fear other g
2Ki 17:37 you shall not fear other g
2Ki 17:38 nor shall you fear other g
2Ki 18:33 Has any of the g of the
2Ki 18:34 Where are the g of Hamath
2Ki 18:34 Where are the g of Sepharvaim
2Ki 18:35 Who among all the g of the
2Ki 19:12 Have the g of the nations
2Ki 19:18 cast their g into the fire
2Ki 19:18 for they were not g, but the
2Ki 22:17 and burned incense to other g
2Ki 23:24 spiritists, the household g
1Ch 5:25 g of the peoples of the land
1Ch 10:10 in the temple of their g, and
1Ch 14:12 when they left their g there
1Ch 16:25 also to be feared above all g
1Ch 16:26 For all the g of the peoples
2Ch 2: 5 our God is greater than all g
2Ch 7:19 you, and go and serve other g
2Ch 7:22 of Egypt, and embraced other g
2Ch 13: 8 Jeroboam made for you as g
2Ch 13: 9 of things that are not g
2Ch 14: 3 the altars of the foreign g
2Ch 25:14 that he brought the g of the
2Ch 25:14 Seir, set them up to be his g
2Ch 25:15 sought the g of the people
2Ch 25:20 they sought the g of Edom
2Ch 28:23 the g of Damascus which had
2Ch 28:23 Because the g of the kings of
2Ch 28:25 to burn incense to other g
2Ch 32:13 Were the g of the nations of
2Ch 32:14 g of those nations that my
2Ch 32:17 As the g of the nations of
2Ch 32:19 as against the g of the
2Ch 33:15 He took away the foreign g
2Ch 34:25 and burned incense to other g
Ezra 1: 7 and put in the temple of his g
Ps 82: 1 He judges among the g
Ps 82: 6 You are g, And all of you are
Ps 86: 8 Among the g there is none
Ps 95: 3 And the great King above all g
Ps 96: 4 is to be feared above all g
Ps 96: 5 For all the g of the peoples
Ps 97: 7 Worship Him, all you g
Ps 97: 9 are exalted far above all g
Ps 135: 5 And our Lord is above all g
Ps 136: 2 give thanks to the God of g
Ps 138: 1 Before the g I will sing
Is 21: 9 the carved images of her g he
Is 36:18 Has any one of the g of the
Is 36:19 Where are the g of Hamath
Is 36:19 Where are the g of Sepharvaim
Is 36:20 Who among all the g of these
Is 37:12 Have the g of the nations
Is 37:19 cast their g into the fire
Is 37:19 for they were not g, but the
Is 41:23 we may know that you are g
Is 42:17 molded images, 'You are our g
Is 57: 5 with g under every green tree
Jer 1:16 Me, burned incense to other g
Jer 2:11 Has a nation changed its g
Jer 2:11 its g, which are not g
Jer 2:28 But where are your g that you
Jer 2:28 of your cities are your g
Jer 5: 7 sworn by those that are not g
Jer 5:19 served foreign g in your land
Jer 7: 6 after other g to your hurt
Jer 7: 9 walk after other g whom you
Jer 7:18 drink offerings to other g
Jer 10:11 The g that have not made the
Jer 11:10 after other g to serve them
Jer 11:12 cry out to the g to whom they
Jer 11:13 of your cities were your g
Jer 13:10 after other g to serve them
Jer 16:11 have walked after other g
Jer 16:13 you shall serve other g day
Jer 16:20 Will a man make g for himself
Jer 16:20 for himself, which are not g
Jer 19: 4 to other g whom neither they
Jer 19:13 drink offerings to other g
Jer 22: 9 God, and worshiped other g
Jer 25: 6 after other g to serve them
Jer 32:29 drink offerings to other g
Jer 35:15 after other g to serve them
Jer 43:12 the houses of the g of Egypt
Jer 43:13 the houses of the g of the
Jer 44: 3 to serve other g whom they
Jer 44: 5 to burn no incense to other g
Jer 44: 8 burning incense to other g in
Jer 44:15 had burned incense to other g
Jer 46:25 and Egypt, with their g and
Jer 48:35 and burns incense to his g
Ezek 28: 2 a god, I sit in the seat of g
Dan 2:11 it to the king except the g
Dan 2:47 your God is the God of g, the
Dan 3:12 They do not serve your g or
Dan 3:14 that you do not serve my g or
Dan 3:18 that we do not serve your g
Dan 5: 4 and praised the g of gold
Dan 5:11 like the wisdom of the g
Dan 5:23 have praised the g of silver
Dan 11: 8 their g captive to Egypt,
Dan 11:36 against the God of g, and
Hos 3: 1 Israel, who look to other g
Hos 14: 3 of our hands, 'You are our g
Amos 5:26 idols, the star of your g
Nah 1:14 Out of the house of your g I
Zeph 2:11 all the g of the earth
John 10:34 I said, "You are g" '?
John 10:35 If He called them g, to whom
Acts 7:40 Make us g to go before us
Acts 14:11 The g have come down to us in
Acts 17:18 be a proclaimer of foreign g
Acts 19:26 saying that they are not g
1Co 8: 5 even if there are so-called g
1Co 8: 5 on earth (as there are many g
Gal 4: 8 which by nature are not g

GOD-WHO-FORGIVES (*see* GOD)
Ps 99: 8 You were to them G, Though

GOES (*see* PREFACE)

GOG (*see* HAMON GOG, MAGOG)
1Ch 5: 4 G his son, Shimei his son,
Ezek 38: 2 man, set your face against G
Ezek 38: 3 Behold, I am against you, O G
Ezek 38:14 of man, prophesy and say to G
Ezek 38:16 I am hallowed in you, O G
Ezek 38:18 when G comes against the land
Ezek 38:21 call for a sword against G
Ezek 39: 1 of man, prophesy against G
Ezek 39: 1 Behold, I am against you, O G
Ezek 39:11 G a burial place there in
Ezek 39:11 there they will bury G and all
Rev 20: 8 four corners of the earth, G

GOING (*see* PREFACE)

GOINGS (*see* PREFACE)

GOLAN
Deut 4:43 and G in Bashan for the
Josh 20: 8 G in Bashan, from the tribe
Josh 21:27 they gave G in Bashan with
1Ch 6:71 given G in Bashan with its

GOLD (*see* GOLDEN, GOLDSMITH)
Gen 2:11 of Havilah, where there is g
Gen 2:12 the g of that land is good
Gen 13: 2 livestock, in silver, and in g
Gen 24:22 weighing ten shekels of g
Gen 24:35 flocks and herds, silver and g
Gen 24:53 of silver, jewelry of g, and
Gen 41:42 put a g chain around his neck
Gen 44: 8 or g from your lord's house
Ex 3:22 of silver, articles of g, and
Ex 11: 2 of silver and articles of g
Ex 12:35 of silver, articles of g, and
Ex 20:23 of g you shall not make for
Ex 25: 3 g, silver, and bronze
Ex 25:11 shall overlay it with pure g
Ex 25:11 it a molding of g all around
Ex 25:12 cast four rings of g for it
Ex 25:13 wood, and overlay them with g
Ex 25:17 make a mercy seat of pure g
Ex 25:18 shall make two cherubim of g
Ex 25:24 shall overlay it with pure g
Ex 25:24 a molding of g all around
Ex 25:25 you shall make a g molding
Ex 25:26 make for it four rings of g
Ex 25:28 wood, and overlay them with g
Ex 25:29 You shall make them of pure g
Ex 25:31 make a lampstand of pure g
Ex 25:36 one hammered piece of pure g
Ex 25:38 trays shall be of pure g
Ex 25:39 be made of a talent of pure g
Ex 26: 6 shall make fifty clasps of g
Ex 26:29 overlay the boards with g
Ex 26:29 make their rings of g as
Ex 26:29 and overlay the bars with g
Ex 26:32 acacia wood overlaid with g
Ex 26:32 Their hooks shall be of g
Ex 26:37 wood, and overlay them with g
Ex 26:37 their hooks shall be of g
Ex 28: 5 They shall take the g and blue
Ex 28: 6 shall make the ephod of g
Ex 28: 8 same workmanship, woven of g

Ex 28:11 set them in settings of **g**
Ex 28:13 shall also make settings of **g**
Ex 28:14 of pure **g** like braided cords
Ex 28:15 of **g** and blue and purple and
Ex 28:20 shall be set in **g** settings
Ex 28:22 like braided cords of pure **g**
Ex 28:23 of **g** for the breastplate, and
Ex 28:24 the two braided chains of **g**
Ex 28:26 You shall make two rings of **g**
Ex 28:27 rings of **g** you shall make
Ex 28:33 bells of **g** between them all
Ex 28:36 also make a plate of pure **g**
Ex 30: 3 and its horns with pure **g**
Ex 30: 3 it a molding of **g** all around
Ex 30: 4 Two **g** rings you shall make
Ex 30: 5 wood, and overlay them with **g**
Ex 31: 4 artistic works, to work in **g**
Ex 32: 4 the **g** from their hand, and he
Ex 32:24 to them, 'Whoever has any **g**
Ex 32:31 for themselves a god of **g**
Ex 35: 5 **g**, silver, and bronze
Ex 35:22 necklaces, all jewelry of **g**
Ex 35:22 an offering of **g** to the LORD
Ex 35:32 artistic works, to work in **g**
Ex 36:13 And he made fifty clasps of **g**
Ex 36:34 He overlaid the boards with **g**
Ex 36:34 made their rings of **g** to be
Ex 36:34 and overlaid the bars with **g**
Ex 36:36 wood, and overlaid them with **g**
Ex 36:36 with their hooks of **g**
Ex 36:38 and their rings with **g**, but
Ex 37: 2 it with pure **g** inside and
Ex 37: 2 a molding of **g** all around it
Ex 37: 3 of **g** to be set in its four
Ex 37: 4 wood, and overlaid them with **g**
Ex 37: 6 made the mercy seat of pure **g**
Ex 37: 7 made two cherubim of beaten **g**
Ex 37:11 And he overlaid it with pure **g**
Ex 37:11 a molding of **g** all around it
Ex 37:12 made a molding of **g** for the
Ex 37:13 cast for it four rings of **g**
Ex 37:15 and overlaid them with **g**
Ex 37:16 He made of pure **g** the
Ex 37:17 made the lampstand of pure **g**
Ex 37:22 one hammered piece of pure **g**
Ex 37:23 and its trays of pure **g**
Ex 37:24 a talent of pure **g** he made it
Ex 37:26 And he overlaid it with pure **g**
Ex 37:26 a molding of **g** all around it
Ex 37:27 He made two rings of **g** for it
Ex 37:28 wood, and overlaid them with **g**
Ex 38:24 All the **g** that was used in
Ex 38:24 the **g** of the offering, was
Ex 39: 2 He made the ephod of **g** and
Ex 39: 3 they beat the **g** into thin
Ex 39: 5 same workmanship, woven of **g**
Ex 39: 6 enclosed in settings of **g**
Ex 39: 8 of the ephod, of **g** and blue and
Ex 39:13 of **g** in their mountings
Ex 39:15 like braided cords of pure **g**
Ex 39:16 also made two settings of **g**
Ex 39:16 two **g** rings, and put the two
Ex 39:17 of **g** in the two rings on the
Ex 39:19 And they made two rings of **g**
Ex 39:20 They made two other **g** rings
Ex 39:25 And they made bells of pure **g**
Ex 39:30 of the holy crown of pure **g**
Ex 39:38 the **g** altar, the anointing
Ex 40: 5 **g** for the incense before the
Ex 40:26 He put the **g** altar in the
Lev 24: 4 of the lamps on the pure **g**
Num 7:14 one **g** pan of ten shekels,
Num 7:20 one **g** pan of ten shekels,
Num 7:26 one **g** pan of ten shekels,
Num 7:32 one **g** pan of ten shekels,
Num 7:38 one **g** pan of ten shekels,
Num 7:44 one **g** pan of ten shekels,
Num 7:50 one **g** pan of ten shekels,
Num 7:56 one **g** pan of ten shekels,
Num 7:62 one **g** pan of ten shekels,
Num 7:68 one **g** pan of ten shekels,
Num 7:74 one **g** pan of ten shekels,
Num 7:80 one **g** pan of ten shekels,
Num 7:84 bowls, and twelve **g** pans
Num 7:86 The twelve **g** pans full of
Num 7:86 all the **g** of the pans weighed
Num 8: 4 lampstand was of hammered **g**
Num 22:18 his house full of silver and **g**
Num 24:13 his house full of silver and **g**
Num 31:22 Only the **g**, the silver, the
Num 31:50 man found of ornaments of **g**
Num 31:51 received the **g** from them, all
Num 31:52 all the **g** of the offering
Num 31:54 the **g** from the captains of
Deut 7:25 silver or **g** that is on them
Deut 8:13 your **g** are multiplied, and all
Deut 17:17 silver and **g** for himself
Deut 29:17 wood and stone and silver and **g**)
Josh 6:19 But all the silver and **g**, and
Josh 6:24 Only the silver and **g**, and the
Josh 7:21 a wedge of **g** weighing fifty
Josh 7:24 the garment, the wedge of **g**
Josh 22: 8 with silver, with **g**, with
Judg 8:24 For they had **g** earrings
Judg 8:26 Now the weight of the **g**
Judg 8:26 seven hundred shekels of **g**
1Sa 6: 8 put the articles of **g** which
1Sa 6:11 and the chest with the **g** rats
1Sa 6:15 which were the articles of **g**
1Sa 6:17 are the **g** tumors which the
1Sa 6:18 the **g** rats, according to the
2Sa 1:24 of **g** on your apparel
2Sa 8: 7 of **g** that had belonged to the
2Sa 8:10 of silver, articles of **g**, and
2Sa 8:11 **g** that he had dedicated from
2Sa 12:30 Its weight was a talent of **g**
2Sa 21: 4 We will have no silver or **g**
1Ki 6:20 He overlaid it with pure **g**
1Ki 6:21 of the temple with pure **g**
1Ki 6:21 He stretched **g** chains across
1Ki 6:21 and he overlaid it with **g**
1Ki 6:22 temple he overlaid with **g**
1Ki 6:22 also he overlaid with **g** the
1Ki 6:28 overlaid the cherubim with **g**
1Ki 6:30 the temple he overlaid with **g**
1Ki 6:32 and overlaid them with **g**
1Ki 6:32 he spread **g** on the cherubim
1Ki 6:35 overlaid them with **g** applied
1Ki 7:48 the altar of **g**, and the table
1Ki 7:48 the table of **g** on which was
1Ki 7:49 the lampstands of pure **g**,
1Ki 7:49 and the wick-trimmers of **g**
1Ki 7:50 and the censers of pure **g**
1Ki 7:50 and the hinges of **g**, both for
1Ki 7:51 the silver and the **g** and the
1Ki 9:11 with cedar and cypress and **g**
1Ki 9:14 and twenty talents of **g**
1Ki 9:28 talents of **g** from there, and
1Ki 10: 2 that bore spices, very much **g**
1Ki 10:10 and twenty talents of **g**,
1Ki 10:11 which brought **g** from Ophir
1Ki 10:14 The weight of **g** that came to
1Ki 10:14 and sixty-six talents of **g**
1Ki 10:16 large shields of hammered **g**
1Ki 10:16 of **g** went into each shield
1Ki 10:17 hundred shields of hammered **g**
1Ki 10:17 three minas of **g** went into
1Ki 10:18 and overlaid it with pure **g**
1Ki 10:21 drinking vessels were of **g**
1Ki 10:21 of Lebanon were of pure **g**
1Ki 10:22 ships came bringing **g**, silver
1Ki 10:25 articles of silver and **g**,
1Ki 12:28 and made two calves of **g**, and
1Ki 14:26 **g** shields which Solomon had
1Ki 15:15 silver and **g** and utensils
1Ki 15:18 and **g** that was left in the
1Ki 15:19 you a present of silver and **g**
1Ki 20: 3 silver and your **g** are mine
1Ki 20: 5 to me your silver and your **g**
1Ki 20: 7 children, my silver, and my **g**
1Ki 22:48 ships to go to Ophir for **g**
2Ki 5: 5 six thousand shekels of **g**
2Ki 7: 8 carried from it silver and **g**
2Ki 12:13 trumpets, any articles of **g**
2Ki 12:18 and all the **g** found in the
2Ki 14:14 And he took all the **g** and
2Ki 16: 8 **g** that was found in the house
2Ki 18:14 silver and thirty talents of **g**
2Ki 18:16 the **g** from the doors of the
2Ki 20:13 the silver and **g**, the spices
2Ki 23:33 of silver and a talent of **g**
2Ki 23:35 the silver and **g** to Pharaoh
2Ki 23:35 **g** from the people of the land
2Ki 24:13 of **g** which Solomon king of
2Ki 25:15 the things made of solid **g**
1Ch 18: 7 **g** that were on the servants
1Ch 18:10 all kinds of articles of **g**
1Ch 18:11 **g** that he had brought from
1Ch 20: 2 it to weigh a talent of **g**
1Ch 21:25 six hundred shekels of **g** by
1Ch 22:14 hundred thousand talents of **g**
1Ch 22:16 Of **g** and silver and bronze and
1Ch 28:14 He gave **g** by weight for
1Ch 28:14 by weight for things of **g**
1Ch 28:15 for the lampstands of **g**, and
1Ch 28:15 of **g**, and their lamps of **g**
1Ch 28:16 by weight he gave **g** for the
1Ch 28:17 also pure **g** for the forks,
1Ch 28:17 the pitchers of pure **g**, and
1Ch 28:17 he gave **g** by weight for every
1Ch 28:18 refined **g** by weight for the
1Ch 28:18 the **g** cherubim that spread
1Ch 29: 2 **g** for things to be made of
1Ch 29: 2 for things to be made of **g**
1Ch 29: 3 my own special treasure of **g**
1Ch 29: 4 three thousand talents of **g**
1Ch 29: 4 of the **g** of Ophir, and seven
1Ch 29: 5 the **g** for things of **g** and
1Ch 29: 7 and ten thousand darics of **g**
2Ch 1:15 **g** as common in Jerusalem as
2Ch 2: 7 a man skillful to work in **g**
2Ch 2:14 Tyre), skilled to work in **g**
2Ch 3: 4 the inside with pure **g**
2Ch 3: 5 which he overlaid with fine **g**
2Ch 3: 6 the **g** was **g** from Parvaim
2Ch 3: 7 its walls and doors—with **g**
2Ch 3: 8 six hundred talents of fine **g**
2Ch 3: 9 nails was fifty shekels of **g**
2Ch 3: 9 the upper area with **g**
2Ch 3:10 and overlaid them with **g**
2Ch 4: 7 **g** according to their design
2Ch 4: 8 made one hundred bowls of **g**
2Ch 4:19 the altar of **g** and the tables
2Ch 4:20 with their lamps of pure **g**
2Ch 4:21 and the wick-trimmers of **g**
2Ch 4:21 of purest **g**
2Ch 4:22 and the censers of pure **g**
2Ch 4:22 hall of the temple, were of **g**
2Ch 5: 1 the silver and the **g** and all
2Ch 8:18 fifty talents of **g** from there
2Ch 9: 1 **g** in abundance, and precious
2Ch 9: 9 and twenty talents of **g**,
2Ch 9:10 who brought **g** from Ophir
2Ch 9:13 The weight of **g** that came to
2Ch 9:13 and sixty-six talents of **g**
2Ch 9:14 of the country brought **g** and
2Ch 9:15 large shields of hammered **g**
2Ch 9:15 **g** went into each shield
2Ch 9:16 hundred shields of hammered **g**
2Ch 9:16 of **g** went into each shield
2Ch 9:17 and overlaid it with pure **g**
2Ch 9:18 steps, with a footstool of **g**
2Ch 9:20 drinking vessels were of **g**
2Ch 9:20 of Lebanon were of pure **g**
2Ch 9:21 ships came, bringing **g**,
2Ch 9:24 articles of silver and **g**,
2Ch 12: 9 He also carried away the **g**
2Ch 13: 8 with you are the **g** calves
2Ch 13:11 the lampstand of **g** with its
2Ch 15:18 silver and **g** and utensils
2Ch 16: 2 **g** from the treasuries of the
2Ch 16: 3 I have sent you silver and **g**
2Ch 21: 3 great gifts of silver and **g**
2Ch 24:14 spoons and vessels of **g** and
2Ch 25:24 And he took all the **g** and
2Ch 32:27 treasuries for silver, for **g**
2Ch 36: 3 of silver and a talent of **g**
Ezra 1: 4 help him with silver and **g**
Ezra 1: 6 with articles of silver and **g**
Ezra 1: 9 thirty **g** platters, one
Ezra 1:10 thirty **g** basins, four hundred
Ezra 1:11 All the articles of **g** and
Ezra 2:69 sixty-one thousand **g** drachmas
Ezra 5:14 Also, the **g** and silver
Ezra 6: 5 Also let the **g** and silver
Ezra 7:15 and **g** which the king and his
Ezra 7:16 **g** that you may find in all
Ezra 7:18 rest of the silver and the **g**
Ezra 8:25 out to them the silver, the **g**
Ezra 8:26 one hundred talents of **g**
Ezra 8:27 twenty **g** basins worth a
Ezra 8:27 bronze, precious as **g**
Ezra 8:28 the **g** are a freewill offering
Ezra 8:30 received the silver and the **g**
Ezra 8:33 day the silver and the **g** and
Neh 7:70 one thousand **g** drachmas,
Neh 7:71 twenty thousand **g** drachmas
Neh 7:72 twenty thousand **g** drachmas
Esth 1: 6 and the couches were of **g** and
Esth 8:15 with a great crown of **g** and a

Job 3:15 or with princes who had g
Job 22:24 will lay your g in the dust
Job 22:24 and the g of Ophir among the
Job 22:25 the Almighty will be your g
Job 23:10 me, I shall come forth as g
Job 28: 1 and a place where g is refined
Job 28: 6 and it contains g dust
Job 28:15 It cannot be purchased for g
Job 28:16 be valued in the g of Ophir
Job 28:17 Neither g nor crystal can
Job 28:17 for jewelry of fine g
Job 28:19 can it be valued in pure g
Job 31:24 If I have made g my hope, or
Job 31:24 my hope, or said to fine g
Job 42:11 of silver and each a ring of g
Ps 19:10 to be desired are they than g
Ps 19:10 Yea, than much fine g
Ps 21: 3 crown of pure g upon his head
Ps 45: 9 the queen in g from Ophir
Ps 45:13 Her clothing is woven with g
Ps 68:13 And her feathers with yellow g
Ps 72:15 the g of Sheba will be given
Ps 105:37 them out with silver and g
Ps 115: 4 Their idols are silver and g
Ps 119:72 thousands of shekels of g
Ps 119:127 More than g
Ps 119:127 yes, than fine g
Ps 135:15 the nations are silver and g
Prov 3:14 and her gain than fine g
Prov 8:10 rather than choice g
Prov 8:19 My fruit is better than g
Prov 8:19 yes, than fine g
Prov 11:22 As a ring of g in a swine's
Prov 16:16 it is to get wisdom than g
Prov 17: 3 silver and the furnace for g
Prov 20:15 There is g and a multitude of
Prov 22: 1 favor rather than silver and g
Prov 25:11 of g in settings of silver
Prov 25:12 Like an earring of g and an
Prov 25:12 an ornament of fine g is a
Prov 27:21 silver and the furnace for g
Eccl 2: 8 for myself silver and g and the
Song 1:10 your neck with chains of g
Song 1:11 of g with studs of silver
Song 3:10 of silver, its support of g
Song 5:11 His head is like the finest g
Song 5:14 are rods of g set with beryl
Song 5:15 marble set on bases of fine g
Is 2: 7 is also full of silver and g
Is 2:20 of silver and his idols of g
Is 13:12 mortal more rare than fine g
Is 13:17 and as for g, they will not
Is 30:22 of your molded images of g
Is 31: 7 of silver and his idols of g
Is 39: 2 the silver and g, the spices
Is 40:19 overspreads it with g, and the
Is 46: 6 They lavish g out of the bag,
Is 60: 6 they shall bring g and incense
Is 60: 9 their g with them, to the
Is 60:17 of bronze I will bring g,
Jer 4:30 yourself with ornaments of g
Jer 10: 4 decorate it with silver and g
Jer 10: 9 g from Uphaz, the work of the
Jer 52:19 cups, whatever was of solid g
Lam 4: 1 How the g has become dim
Lam 4: 1 How changed the fine g
Lam 4: 2 of Zion, valuable as fine g
Ezek 7:19 their g will be like refuse
Ezek 7:19 their g will not be able to
Ezek 16:13 Thus you were adorned with g
Ezek 16:17 beautiful jewelry from My g
Ezek 27:22 of precious stones, and g
Ezek 28: 4 for yourself, and gathered g
Ezek 28:13 turquoise, and emerald with g
Ezek 38:13 to carry away silver and g
Dan 2:32 image's head was of fine g
Dan 2:35 the g were crushed together,
Dan 2:38 you are this head of g
Dan 2:45 clay, the silver, and the g
Dan 3: 1 the king made an image of g
Dan 3: 5 worship the g image that King
Dan 3: 7 worshiped the g image which
Dan 3:10 down and worship the g image
Dan 3:12 your gods or worship the g
Dan 3:14 my gods or worship the g
Dan 3:18 nor will we worship the g
Dan 5: 2 the command to bring the g
Dan 5: 3 Then they brought the g
Dan 5: 4 and praised the gods of g
Dan 5: 7 a chain of g around his neck
Dan 5:16 have a chain of g around your
Dan 5:23 the gods of silver and g,
Dan 5:29 put a chain of g around his
Dan 10: 5 was girded with g of Uphaz
Dan 11: 8 articles of silver and g
Dan 11:38 know he shall honor with g
Dan 11:43 power over the treasures of g
Hos 2: 8 and multiplied her silver and g
Hos 8: 4 and g they made idols for
Joel 3: 5 have taken My silver and My g
Nah 2: 9 Take spoil of g
Hab 2:19 Behold, it is overlaid with g
Zeph 1:18 their silver nor their g
Hag 2: 8 the g is Mine,' says the LORD
Zech 4: 2 is a lampstand of solid g
Zech 4:12 the receptacles of the two g
Zech 6:11 Take the silver and g, make an
Zech 9: 3 and g like the mire of the
Zech 13: 9 and test them as g is tested
Zech 14:14 g, silver, and apparel in
Mal 3: 3 of Levi, and purge them as g
Matt 2:11 g, frankincense, and myrrh
Matt 10: 9 Provide neither g nor silver
Matt 23:16 swears by the g of the temple
Matt 23:17 the g or the temple that
Matt 23:17 temple that sanctifies the g
Acts 3: 6 g I do not have, but what I
Acts 17:29 is like g or silver or stone
Acts 20:33 one's silver or g or apparel
1Co 3:12 on this foundation with g
1Ti 2: 9 hair or g or pearls or costly
2Ti 2:20 are not only vessels of g
Heb 9: 4 overlaid on all sides with g
Jas 2: 2 assembly a man with g rings
Jas 5: 3 Your g and silver are corroded
1Pe 1: 7 precious than g that perishes
1Pe 1:18 things, like silver or g,
1Pe 3: 3 the hair, of wearing g, or of
Rev 3:18 from Me g refined in the fire
Rev 4: 4 crowns of g on their heads
Rev 9: 7 crowns of something like g
Rev 9:20 worship demons, and idols of g
Rev 17: 4 and scarlet, and adorned with g
Rev 18:12 merchandise of g and silver,
Rev 18:16 and scarlet, and adorned with g
Rev 21:15 a g reed to measure the city
Rev 21:18 and the city was pure g, like
Rev 21:21 street of the city was pure g

GOLDEN (*see* GOLD)
Gen 24:22 that the man took a g nose
Ex 28:34 a g bell and a pomegranate, a
Ex 28:34 a g bell and a pomegranate,
Ex 32: 2 Break off the g earrings
Ex 32: 3 the g earrings which were in
Lev 8: 9 its front, he put the g plate
Num 4:11 Over the g altar they shall
1Sa 6: 4 Five g tumors and five g rats
2Ki 10:29 from the g calves that were
1Ch 28:17 of pure gold, and the g bowls
Esth 1: 7 served drinks in g vessels
Esth 4:11 king holds out the g scepter
Esth 5: 2 the g scepter that was in his
Esth 8: 4 the g scepter toward Esther
Job 37:22 from the north as g splendor
Eccl 12: 6 or the g bowl is broken, or
Is 13:12 than the g wedge of Ophir
Is 14: 4 has ceased, the g city ceased
Jer 51: 7 Babylon was a g cup in the
Zech 4:12 from which the g oil drains
Heb 9: 4 which had the g altar of
Heb 9: 4 in which were the g pot that
Rev 1:12 I saw seven g lampstands,
Rev 1:13 about the chest with a g band
Rev 1:20 and the seven g lampstands
Rev 2: 1 of the seven g lampstands
Rev 5: 8 and g bowls full of incense,
Rev 8: 3 angel, having a g censer,
Rev 8: 3 g altar which was before the
Rev 9:13 g altar which is before God
Rev 14:14 having on His head a g crown
Rev 15: 6 chests girded with g bands
Rev 15: 7 to the seven angels seven g
Rev 17: 4 having in her hand a g cup

GOLDSMITH (*see* GOLD, GOLDSMITHS)
Is 40:19 the g overspreads it with
Is 41: 7 craftsman encouraged the g
Is 46: 6 they hire a g, and he makes it

GOLDSMITHS (*see* GOLDSMITH)
Neh 3: 8 son of Harhaiah, one of the g
Neh 3:31 him Malchijah, one of the g
Neh 3:32 far as the Sheep Gate, the g

GOLGOTHA (*see* CALVARY)
Matt 27:33 had come to a place called G
Mark 15:22 brought Him to the place G
John 19:17 which is called in Hebrew, G

GOLIATH
1Sa 17: 4 of the Philistines, named G
1Sa 17:23 G by name, coming up from the
1Sa 21: 9 The sword of G the Philistine
1Sa 22:10 the sword of G the Philistine
2Sa 21:19 the brother of G the Gittite
1Ch 20: 5 the brother of G the Gittite

GOMER
Gen 10: 2 The sons of Japheth were G
Gen 10: 3 The sons of G were Ashkenaz,
1Ch 1: 5 The sons of Japheth were G
1Ch 1: 6 The sons of G were Ashkenaz,
Ezek 38: 6 G and all its troops
Hos 1: 3 and took G the daughter of

GOMORRAH
Gen 10:19 as you go toward Sodom, G
Gen 13:10 G) like the garden of the
Gen 14: 2 of Sodom, Birsha king of G
Gen 14: 8 king of Sodom, the king of G
Gen 14:10 the kings of Sodom and G fled
Gen 14:11 all the goods of Sodom and G
Gen 18:20 G is great, and because their
Gen 19:24 and fire on Sodom and G, from
Gen 19:28 he looked toward Sodom and G
Deut 29:23 the overthrow of Sodom and G
Deut 32:32 Sodom and of the fields of G
Is 1: 9 would have been made like G
Is 1:10 of our God, you people of G
Is 13:19 overthrew Sodom and G
Jer 23:14 Me, and her inhabitants like G
Jer 49:18 the overthrow of Sodom and G
Jer 50:40 God overthrew Sodom and G
Amos 4:11 as God overthrew Sodom and G
Zeph 2: 9 and the people of Ammon like G
Matt 10:15 G in the day of judgment than
Mark 6:11 G in the day of judgment than
Rom 9:29 would have been made like G
2Pe 2: 6 G into ashes, condemned them
Jude 7 as Sodom and G, and the cities

GONE (*see* PREFACE)

GOOD (*see* GOOD-LOOKING, GOODLY, GOODNESS)
Gen 1: 4 saw the light, that it was g
Gen 1:10 And God saw that it was g
Gen 1:12 And God saw that it was g
Gen 1:18 And God saw that it was g
Gen 1:21 And God saw that it was g
Gen 1:25 And God saw that it was g
Gen 1:31 made, and indeed it was very g
Gen 2: 9 to the sight and g for food
Gen 2: 9 tree of the knowledge of g
Gen 2:12 And the gold of that land is g
Gen 2:17 tree of the knowledge of g
Gen 2:18 It is not g that man should
Gen 3: 5 will be like God, knowing g
Gen 3: 6 that the tree was g for food
Gen 3:22 like one of Us, to know g
Gen 15:15 be buried at a g old age
Gen 18: 7 g calf, gave it to a young
Gen 24:50 speak to you either bad or g
Gen 25: 8 last and died in a g old age
Gen 26:29 done nothing to you but g
Gen 27:46 what g will my life be to me
Gen 30:20 endowed me with a g
Gen 31:24 to Jacob neither g nor bad
Gen 31:29 to Jacob neither g nor bad
Gen 40:16 that the interpretation was g
Gen 41: 5 up on one stalk, plump and g
Gen 41:22 up on one stalk, full and g
Gen 41:24 devoured the seven g heads
Gen 41:26 The seven g cows are seven
Gen 41:26 the seven g heads are seven
Gen 41:35 those g years that are coming
Gen 41:37 So the advice was g in the
Gen 43:28 our father is in g health
Gen 44: 4 have you repaid evil for g
Gen 45:23 with the g things of Egypt
Gen 46:29 and wept on his neck a g while
Gen 49:15 he saw that rest was g, and

Gen 50:20 but God meant it for **g**, in
Ex 3: 8 them up from that land to a **g**
Ex 18: 9 **g** which the LORD had done for
Ex 18:17 thing that you do is not **g**
Ex 21:34 of the pit shall make it **g**
Ex 22:11 and he shall not make it **g**
Ex 22:13 not make **g** what was torn
Ex 22:14 it, he shall surely make it **g**
Ex 22:15 it, he shall not make it **g**
Lev 5: 4 lips to do evil or to do **g**
Lev 24:18 an animal shall make it **g**
Lev 27:10 **g** for bad or bad for **g**
Lev 27:12 it, whether it is **g** or bad
Lev 27:14 it, whether it is **g** or bad
Lev 27:33 whether it is **g** or bad, nor
Num 10:29 promised **g** things to Israel
Num 10:32 that whatever **g** the LORD will
Num 13:19 they dwell in is **g** or bad
Num 13:20 Be of **g** courage
Num 14: 7 out is an exceedingly **g** land
Num 23:19 and will He not make it **g**
Num 24:13 to do either **g** or bad of my
Deut 1:14 you have told us to do is **g**
Deut 1:25 It is a **g** land which the
Deut 1:35 **g** land of which I swore to
Deut 1:39 today have no knowledge of **g**
Deut 3:25 see the **g** land beyond the
Deut 4:21 **g** land which the LORD your
Deut 4:22 over and possess that **g** land
Deut 6:11 houses full of all **g** things
Deut 6:18 **g** in the sight of the LORD,
Deut 6:18 possess the **g** land of which
Deut 6:24 our God, for our **g** always
Deut 8: 7 is bringing you into a **g** land
Deut 8:10 the LORD your God for the **g**
Deut 8:16 you, to do you **g** in the end
Deut 9: 6 **g** land to possess because of
Deut 10:13 command you today for your **g**
Deut 11:17 the **g** land which the LORD is
Deut 12:28 when you do what is **g** and
Deut 18:17 What they have spoken is **g**
Deut 26:11 **g** thing which the LORD your
Deut 28:12 open to you His **g** treasure
Deut 28:63 rejoiced over you to do you **g**
Deut 30: 9 produce of your land for **g**
Deut 30: 9 **g** as He rejoiced over your
Deut 30:15 before you today life and **g**
Deut 31: 6 of **g** courage, do not fear nor
Deut 31: 7 of **g** courage, for you must go
Deut 31:23 Be strong and of **g** courage
Josh 1: 6 of **g** courage, for to this
Josh 1: 8 then you will have **g** success
Josh 1: 9 Be strong and of **g** courage
Josh 1:18 be strong and of **g** courage
Josh 9:25 do with us as it seems **g** and
Josh 10:25 of **g** courage, for thus the
Josh 21:45 **g** thing which the LORD had
Josh 23:13 **g** land which the LORD your
Josh 23:14 **g** things which the LORD your
Josh 23:15 that as all the **g** things have
Josh 23:15 **g** land which the LORD your
Josh 23:16 perish quickly from the **g**
Josh 24:20 you, after He has done you **g**
Judg 8:32 of Joash died at a **g** old age
Judg 8:35 the **g** he had done for Israel
Judg 9:11 my **g** fruit, and go to sway
Judg 17:13 that the LORD will be **g** to me
Judg 18: 9 land, and indeed it is very **g**
Judg 18:22 When they were a **g** way from
Ruth 2:22 It is **g**, my daughter, that
Ruth 3:13 of a near kinsman for you—**g**
1Sa 2:24 For it is not a **g** report that
1Sa 2:32 despite all the **g** which God
1Sa 3:18 Him do what seems **g** to Him
1Sa 11:10 us whatever seems **g** to you
1Sa 12:23 but I will teach you the **g**
1Sa 14:36 Do whatever seems **g** to you
1Sa 14:40 Do what seems **g** to you
1Sa 15: 9 the lambs, and all that was **g**
1Sa 19: 4 have been very **g** toward you
1Sa 20:12 there is **g** toward David, and I
1Sa 24: 4 to him as it seems **g** to you
1Sa 24:17 you have rewarded me with **g**
1Sa 24:19 the LORD reward you with **g**
1Sa 25: 3 a woman of **g** understanding
1Sa 25:15 But the men were very **g** to us
1Sa 25:21 he has repaid me evil for **g**
1Sa 25:30 all the **g** that He has spoken
1Sa 26:16 that you have done is not **g**
1Sa 29: 6 in the army is **g** in my sight
1Sa 29: 9 I know that you are as **g** in
2Sa 3:13 **G**, I will make a covenant
2Sa 3:19 all that seemed **g** to Israel
2Sa 4:10 to have brought **g** news, I
2Sa 10:12 Be of **g** courage, and let us be
2Sa 10:12 LORD do what seems **g** to Him
2Sa 13:22 Amnon neither **g** nor bad
2Sa 14:17 lord the king in discerning **g**
2Sa 14:25 as Absalom for his **g** looks
2Sa 15: 3 Look, your case is **g** and right
2Sa 15:26 do to me as seems **g** to Him
2Sa 16:12 **g** for his cursing this day
2Sa 17: 7 given is not **g** at this time
2Sa 17:14 the **g** counsel of Ahithophel
2Sa 18:27 He is a **g** man, and comes with
2Sa 18:27 man, and comes with **g** news
2Sa 18:31 There is **g** news, my lord the
2Sa 19:18 and to do what he thought **g**
2Sa 19:27 do what is **g** in your eyes
2Sa 19:35 Can I discern between the **g**
2Sa 19:37 for him what seems **g** to you
2Sa 19:38 for him what seems **g** to you
2Sa 24:22 up whatever seems **g** to him
1Ki 1:42 man, and bring **g** tidings
1Ki 2:38 The saying is **g**
1Ki 2:42 The word I have heard is **g**
1Ki 3: 9 that I may discern between **g**
1Ki 8:36 **g** way in which they should
1Ki 8:56 one word of all His **g** promise
1Ki 12: 7 speak **g** words to them, then
1Ki 14:13 **g** toward the LORD God of
1Ki 14:15 uproot Israel from this **g**
1Ki 21: 2 Or, if it seems **g** to you, I
1Ki 22: 8 not prophesy **g** concerning me
1Ki 22:18 not prophesy **g** concerning me
2Ki 3:19 shall cut down every **g** tree
2Ki 3:19 ruin every **g** piece of land
2Ki 3:25 on every **g** piece of land and
2Ki 3:25 and cut down all the **g** trees
2Ki 7: 9 This day is a day of **g** news
2Ki 8: 9 of every **g** thing of Damascus,
2Ki 10: 5 Do what is **g** in your sight
2Ki 20: 3 done what was **g** in Your sight
2Ki 20:19 which you have spoken is **g**
1Ch 4:40 **g** pasture, and the land was
1Ch 13: 2 If it seems **g** to you, and if
1Ch 16:23 proclaim the **g** news of His
1Ch 16:34 to the LORD, for He is **g**
1Ch 19:13 Be of **g** courage, and let us be
1Ch 19:13 do what is **g** in His sight
1Ch 21:23 king do what is **g** in his eyes
1Ch 22:13 Be strong and of **g** courage
1Ch 28: 8 you may possess this **g** land
1Ch 28:20 and of **g** courage, and do it
1Ch 29:28 So he died in a **g** old age
2Ch 5:13 For He is **g**, for His mercy
2Ch 6:27 **g** way in which they should
2Ch 7: 3 For He is **g**, for His mercy
2Ch 10: 7 speak **g** words to them, they
2Ch 14: 2 Asa did what was **g** and right
2Ch 18: 7 prophesies **g** concerning me
2Ch 18:17 not prophesy **g** concerning me
2Ch 19: 3 Nevertheless **g** things are
2Ch 19:11 the LORD will be with the **g**
2Ch 24:16 he had done **g** in Israel, both
2Ch 30:18 May the **g** LORD provide
2Ch 30:22 the **g** knowledge of the LORD
2Ch 31:20 Judah, and he did what was **g**
Ezra 3:11 For He is **g**, For His mercy
Ezra 5:17 if it seems **g** to the king
Ezra 7: 9 according to the **g** hand of
Ezra 7:18 And whatever seems **g** to you
Ezra 8:18 by the **g** hand of our God upon
Ezra 8:22 all those for **g** who seek Him
Ezra 9:12 eat the **g** of the land, and
Ezra 10: 4 Be of **g** courage, and do it
Neh 2: 8 the **g** hand of my God upon me
Neh 2:18 God which had been **g** upon me
Neh 2:18 their hands to do this **g** work
Neh 5: 9 What you are doing is not **g**
Neh 5:19 Remember me, my God, for **g**
Neh 6:19 his **g** deeds before me, and
Neh 9:13 **g** statutes and commandments
Neh 9:20 You also gave Your **g** Spirit
Neh 9:35 or in the many **g** things that
Neh 9:36 its **g** things, here we are,
Neh 13:14 do not wipe out my **g** deeds
Neh 13:31 Remember me, O my God, for **g**
Esth 3:11 with them as seems **g** to you
Esth 7: 9 who spoke **g** on the king's
Esth 10: 3 seeking the **g** of his people
Job 2:10 we indeed accept **g** from God
Job 7: 7 My eye will never again see **g**
Job 9:25 they flee away, they see no **g**
Job 10: 3 Does it seem **g** to You that
Job 15: 3 with which he can do no **g**
Job 22:18 their houses with **g** things
Job 22:21 thereby **g** will come to you
Job 24:21 and does no **g** for the widow
Job 30:26 But when I looked for **g**, evil
Job 34: 4 among ourselves what is **g**
Ps 4: 6 Who will show us any **g**
Ps 14: 1 There is none who does **g**
Ps 14: 3 There is none who does **g**, No,
Ps 16: 6 Yes, I have a **g** inheritance
Ps 25: 8 **G** and upright is the LORD
Ps 27:14 Be of **g** courage, And He shall
Ps 31:24 Be of **g** courage, And He shall
Ps 34: 8 and see that the LORD is **g**
Ps 34:10 shall not lack any **g** thing
Ps 34:12 many days, that he may see **g**
Ps 34:14 Depart from evil, and do **g**
Ps 35:12 They reward me evil for **g**
Ps 36: 3 ceased to be wise and to do **g**
Ps 36: 4 in a way that is not **g**
Ps 37: 3 Trust in the LORD, and do **g**
Ps 37:23 The steps of a **g** man are
Ps 37:27 Depart from evil, and do **g**
Ps 38:20 also who render evil for **g**
Ps 38:20 because I follow what is **g**
Ps 39: 2 I held my peace even from **g**
Ps 40: 9 I have proclaimed the **g** news
Ps 45: 1 is overflowing with a **g** theme
Ps 51:18 Do **g** in Your **g** pleasure to
Ps 52: 3 You love evil more than **g**
Ps 52: 9 on Your name, for it is **g**
Ps 53: 1 There is none who does **g**
Ps 53: 3 There is none who does **g**, No,
Ps 54: 6 name, O LORD, for it is **g**
Ps 69:16 for Your lovingkindness is **g**
Ps 73: 1 Truly God is **g** to Israel, To
Ps 73:28 But it is **g** for me to draw
Ps 84:11 No **g** thing will He withhold
Ps 85:12 the LORD will give what is **g**
Ps 86: 5 For You, Lord, are **g**, and
Ps 86:17 Show me a sign for **g**, That
Ps 92: 1 It is **g** to give thanks to the
Ps 96: 2 Proclaim the **g** news of His
Ps 100: 5 For the LORD is **g**
Ps 103: 5 your mouth with **g** things, So
Ps 104:28 hand, they are filled with **g**
Ps 106: 1 to the LORD, for He is **g**
Ps 107: 1 to the LORD, for He is **g**
Ps 109: 5 have rewarded me evil for **g**
Ps 109:21 Because Your mercy is **g**,
Ps 111:10 A **g** understanding have all
Ps 112: 5 A **g** man deals graciously and
Ps 118: 1 to the LORD, for He is **g**
Ps 118:29 to the LORD, for He is **g**
Ps 119:39 For Your judgments are **g**
Ps 119:66 Teach me **g** judgment and
Ps 119:68 You are **g**, and do **g**
Ps 119:71 It is **g** for me that I have
Ps 119:122 surety for Your servant for **g**
Ps 122: 9 our God I will seek your **g**
Ps 125: 4 Do **g**, O LORD, to those who
Ps 125: 4 O LORD, to those who are **g**
Ps 128: 5 Zion, And may you see the **g** of
Ps 133: 1 Behold, how **g** and how pleasant
Ps 135: 3 the LORD, for the LORD is **g**
Ps 136: 1 to the LORD, for He is **g**
Ps 143:10 Your Spirit is **g**
Ps 145: 9 The LORD is **g** to all, And His
Ps 147: 1 For it is **g** to sing praises
Prov 2: 9 equity and every **g** path
Prov 3:27 Do not withhold **g** from those
Prov 4: 2 for I give you **g** doctrine
Prov 11:17 man does **g** for his own soul
Prov 11:23 of the righteous is only **g**
Prov 11:27 seeks **g** finds favor, but
Prov 12: 2 A **g** man obtains favor from
Prov 12:14 **g** by the fruit of his mouth
Prov 12:25 but a **g** word makes it glad
Prov 13:15 **G** understanding gains favor,
Prov 13:21 righteous, **g** shall be repaid
Prov 13:22 A **g** man leaves an inheritance
Prov 14:14 but a **g** man will be satisfied
Prov 14:19 evil will bow before the **g**
Prov 14:22 belong to those who devise **g**
Prov 15: 3 watch on the evil and the **g**

Prov 15:23 in due season, how **g** it is
Prov 15:30 a **g** report makes the bones
Prov 16:20 the word wisely will find **g**
Prov 16:29 him in a way that is not **g**
Prov 17:13 Whoever rewards evil for **g**
Prov 17:20 a deceitful heart finds no **g**
Prov 17:22 A merry heart does **g**, like
Prov 17:26 punish the righteous is not **g**
Prov 18: 5 It is not **g** to show
Prov 18:22 finds a wife finds a **g** thing
Prov 19: 2 Also it is not **g** for a soul
Prov 19: 8 understanding will find **g**
Prov 20:14 It is **g** for nothing," cries
Prov 20:23 and a false balance is not **g**
Prov 22: 1 A **g** name is to be chosen
Prov 24:13 eat honey because it is **g**
Prov 24:23 It is not **g** to show
Prov 24:25 a **g** blessing will come upon
Prov 25:25 soul, so is **g** news from a far
Prov 25:27 It is not **g** to eat much honey
Prov 28:10 will inherit **g** things
Prov 28:21 To show partiality is not **g**
Prov 31:12 She does him **g** and not evil
Prov 31:18 that her merchandise is **g**
Eccl 2: 3 **g** for the sons of men to do
Eccl 2:24 should enjoy **g** in his labor
Eccl 2:26 a man who is **g** in His sight
Eccl 2:26 to him who is **g** before God
Eccl 3:12 and to do **g** in their lives,
Eccl 3:13 enjoy the **g** of all his labor
Eccl 4: 8 I toil and deprive myself of **g**
Eccl 4: 9 because they have a **g** reward
Eccl 5:18 It is **g** and fitting for one to
Eccl 5:18 to enjoy the **g** of all his
Eccl 6:12 what is **g** for man in life
Eccl 7: 1 A **g** name is better than
Eccl 7:11 Wisdom is **g** with an
Eccl 7:18 It is **g** that you grasp this,
Eccl 7:20 just man on earth who does **g**
Eccl 9: 2 to the **g**, the clean, and the
Eccl 9: 2 As is the **g**, so is the sinner
Eccl 9:18 one sinner destroys much **g**
Eccl 11: 6 whether both alike will be **g**
Eccl 12:14 whether it is **g** or whether it
Song 1: 3 fragrance of your **g** ointments
Song 2:13 tender grapes give a **g** smell
Is 1:17 learn to do **g**
Is 1:19 shall eat the **g** of the land
Is 5: 2 it to bring forth **g** grapes
Is 5: 4 it to bring forth **g** grapes
Is 5:20 who call evil **g**, and **g** evil
Is 7:15 the evil and choose the **g**
Is 7:16 the evil and choose the **g**, the
Is 38: 3 done what is **g** in Your sight
Is 39: 8 which you have spoken is **g**
Is 40: 9 Zion, you who bring **g** tidings
Is 40: 9 you who bring **g** tidings,
Is 41: 6 brother, Be of **g** courage
Is 41:23 do **g** or do evil, that we may
Is 41:27 one who brings **g** tidings
Is 52: 7 feet of him who brings **g** news
Is 52: 7 glad tidings of **g** things, who
Is 55: 2 to Me, and eat what is **g**, and
Is 61: 1 preach **g** tidings to the poor
Is 65: 2 walk in a way that is not **g**
Jer 4:22 but to do **g** they have no
Jer 5:25 withheld **g** things from you
Jer 6:16 old paths, where the **g** way is
Jer 8:15 for peace, but no **g** came
Jer 10: 5 evil, nor can they do any **g**
Jer 11:16 Tree, Lovely and of **G** Fruit
Jer 13:23 Then may you also do **g** who
Jer 14:11 for this people, for their **g**
Jer 14:19 for peace, but there was no **g**
Jer 17: 6 and shall not see when **g** comes
Jer 18: 4 as it seemed **g** to the potter
Jer 18:10 **g** with which I said I would
Jer 18:11 your ways and your doings **g**
Jer 18:20 Shall evil be repaid for **g**
Jer 18:20 You to speak **g** for them, and
Jer 21:10 for adversity and not for **g**
Jer 24: 2 One basket had very **g** figs
Jer 24: 3 Figs, the **g** figs, very **g**
Jer 24: 5 Like these **g** figs, so will I
Jer 24: 5 of this place for their own **g**
Jer 24: 6 set My eyes on them for **g**
Jer 26:14 do with me as seems **g** and
Jer 29:10 perform My **g** word toward you,
Jer 29:32 nor shall he see the **g** that I
Jer 32:39 Me forever, for the **g** of them

Jer 32:40 turn away from doing them **g**
Jer 32:41 over them to do them **g**, and I
Jer 32:42 **g** that I have promised them
Jer 33: 9 all the **g** that I do to them
Jer 33:11 of hosts, for the LORD is **g**
Jer 33:14 that I will perform that **g**
Jer 39:16 for adversity and not for **g**
Jer 40: 4 If it seems **g** to you to come
Jer 40: 4 wherever it seems **g** and
Jer 44:27 for adversity and not for **g**
Lam 3:25 The LORD is **g** to those who
Lam 3:26 It is **g** that one should hope
Lam 3:27 It is **g** for a man to bear the
Ezek 17: 8 It was planted in **g** soil by
Ezek 18:18 did what is not **g** among his
Ezek 20:25 to statutes that were not **g**
Ezek 24: 4 of meat in it, every **g** piece
Ezek 34:14 I will feed them in **g** pasture
Ezek 34:14 shall lie down in a **g** fold
Ezek 34:18 have eaten up the **g** pasture
Ezek 36:31 and your deeds that were not **g**
Dan 1: 9 **g** will of the chief of the
Dan 3:15 image which I have made, **g**
Dan 4: 2 I thought it **g** to declare the
Hos 4:13 because their shade is **g**
Hos 8: 3 Israel has cast off the **g**
Amos 5:14 Seek **g** and not evil, that you
Amos 5:15 Hate evil, love **g**
Amos 5:18 For what **g** is the day of the
Amos 9: 4 on them for harm and not for **g**
Mic 1:12 of Maroth pined for **g**, but
Mic 2: 7 Do not My words do **g** to him
Mic 3: 2 You who hate **g** and love evil
Mic 6: 8 shown you, O man, what is **g**
Nah 1: 7 The LORD is **g**, a stronghold
Nah 1:15 of him who brings **g** tidings
Zeph 1:12 The LORD will not do **g**, nor
Zech 1:13 who talked to me, with **g** and
Zech 8:15 to do **g** to Jerusalem and to
Mal 2:13 nor receive it with **g** will
Mal 2:17 is **g** in the sight of the LORD
Matt 3:10 not bear **g** fruit is cut down
Matt 5:13 It is then **g** for nothing but
Matt 5:16 they may see your **g** works
Matt 5:44 do **g** to those who hate you,
Matt 5:45 rise on the evil and on the **g**
Matt 6:22 If therefore your eye is **g**
Matt 7:11 know how to give **g** gifts to
Matt 7:11 who is in heaven give **g**
Matt 7:17 every **g** tree bears **g** fruit
Matt 7:18 A **g** tree cannot bear bad
Matt 7:18 can a bad tree bear **g** fruit
Matt 7:19 not bear **g** fruit is cut down
Matt 8:30 Now a **g** way off from them
Matt 9: 2 Son, be of **g** cheer
Matt 9:22 Be of **g** cheer, daughter
Matt 11:26 so it seemed **g** in Your sight
Matt 12:12 lawful to do **g** on the Sabbath
Matt 12:33 the tree **g** and its fruit **g**
Matt 12:34 being evil, speak **g** things
Matt 12:35 **g** man out of the **g** treasure
Matt 12:35 heart brings forth **g** things
Matt 13: 8 But others fell on **g** ground
Matt 13:23 **g** ground is he who hears the
Matt 13:24 who sowed **g** seed in his field
Matt 13:27 did you not sow **g** seed in
Matt 13:37 He who sows the **g** seed is the
Matt 13:38 the **g** seeds are the sons of
Matt 13:48 gathered the **g** into vessels
Matt 14:27 Be of **g** cheer
Matt 15:26 It is not **g** to take the
Matt 17: 4 it is **g** for us to be here
Matt 19:16 **G** Teacher, what **g** thing
Matt 19:17 Why do you call Me **g**
Matt 19:17 No one is **g** but One, that is,
Matt 20:15 your eye evil because I am **g**
Matt 22:10 they found, both bad and **g**
Matt 25:21 said to him, 'Well done, **g**
Matt 25:23 said to him, 'Well done, **g**
Matt 26:10 she has done a **g** work for Me
Matt 26:24 It would have been **g** for that
Mark 3: 4 Sabbath to do **g** or to do evil
Mark 4: 8 other seed fell on **g** ground
Mark 4:20 are the ones sown on **g** ground
Mark 6:50 Be of **g** cheer
Mark 7:27 for it is not **g** to take the
Mark 9: 5 it is **g** for us to be here
Mark 9:50 Salt is **g**, but if the salt
Mark 10:17 **G** Teacher, what shall I do
Mark 10:18 Why do you call Me **g**

Mark 10:18 No one is **g** but One, that is,
Mark 10:49 Be of **g** cheer
Mark 14: 6 She has done a **g** work for Me
Mark 14: 7 you wish you may do them **g**
Mark 14:21 It would have been **g** for that
Luke 1: 3 it seemed **g** to me also,
Luke 1:53 the hungry with **g** things, and
Luke 2:10 I bring you **g** tidings of
Luke 2:14 peace, **g** will toward men
Luke 3: 9 not bear **g** fruit is cut down
Luke 6: 9 Sabbath to do **g** or to do evil
Luke 6:27 do **g** to those who hate you,
Luke 6:33 if you do **g** to those who do **g**
Luke 6:35 But love your enemies, do **g**
Luke 6:38 **g** measure, pressed down,
Luke 6:43 For a **g** tree does not bear
Luke 6:43 does a bad tree bear **g** fruit
Luke 6:45 A **g** man out of the **g**
Luke 6:45 of his heart brings forth **g**
Luke 8: 8 But others fell on **g** ground
Luke 8:15 on the **g** ground are those who
Luke 8:15 and **g** heart, keep it and bear
Luke 8:48 Daughter, be of **g** cheer
Luke 9:33 it is **g** for us to be here
Luke 10:21 so it seemed **g** in Your sight
Luke 10:42 Mary has chosen that **g** part
Luke 11:13 know how to give **g** gifts to
Luke 11:34 Therefore, when your eye is **g**
Luke 12:32 for it is your Father's **g**
Luke 14:34 Salt is **g**
Luke 16:25 you received your **g** things
Luke 18:18 **G** Teacher, what shall I do to
Luke 18:19 Why do you call Me **g**
Luke 18:19 No one is **g** but One, that is,
Luke 19:17 to him, 'Well done, **g** servant
Luke 23:50 Joseph, a council member, a **g**
John 1:46 Can anything **g** come out of
John 2:10 beginning sets out the **g** wine
John 2:10 kept the **g** wine until now
John 5:29 those who have done **g**, to the
John 7:12 Some said, "He is **g**"
John 10:11 I am the **g** shepherd
John 10:11 The **g** shepherd gives His life
John 10:14 I am the **g** shepherd
John 10:32 Many **g** works I have shown you
John 10:33 For a **g** work we do not stone
John 16:33 but be of **g** cheer, I have
Acts 4: 9 a **g** deed done to the helpless
Acts 6: 3 you seven men of **g** reputation
Acts 9:36 woman was full of **g** works
Acts 10:22 has a **g** reputation among all
Acts 10:38 power, who went about doing **g**
Acts 11:24 For he was a **g** man, full of
Acts 14:17 witness, in that He did **g**
Acts 15: 7 you know that a **g** while ago
Acts 15:25 it seemed **g** to us, being
Acts 15:28 For it seemed **g** to the Holy
Acts 15:34 it seemed **g** to Silas to
Acts 18:18 Paul still remained a **g** while
Acts 22:12 having a **g** testimony with all
Acts 23: 1 I have lived in all **g**
Acts 23:11 Be of **g** cheer, Paul
Rom 2: 7 in doing **g** seek for glory
Rom 2:10 everyone who works what is **g**
Rom 3: 8 us do evil that **g** may come"
Rom 3:12 there is none who does **g**, no,
Rom 5: 7 yet perhaps for a **g** man
Rom 7:12 holy and just and **g**
Rom 7:13 Has then what is **g** become
Rom 7:13 death in me through what is **g**
Rom 7:16 with the law that it is **g**
Rom 7:18 in my flesh) nothing **g** dwells
Rom 7:18 what is **g** I do not find
Rom 7:19 For the **g** that I will to do,
Rom 7:21 me, the one who wills to do **g**
Rom 8:28 for **g** to those who love God
Rom 9:11 nor having done any **g** or evil
Rom 10:15 glad tidings of **g** things
Rom 11:24 to nature into a **g** olive tree
Rom 12: 2 you may prove what is that **g**
Rom 12: 9 Cling to what is **g**
Rom 12:17 Have regard for **g** things in
Rom 12:21 but overcome evil with **g**
Rom 13: 3 are not a terror to **g** works
Rom 13: 3 Do what is **g**, and you will
Rom 13: 4 God's minister to you for **g**
Rom 14:16 your **g** be spoken of as evil
Rom 14:21 It is **g** neither to eat meat
Rom 15: 2 please his neighbor for his **g**
Rom 16:19 you to be wise in what is **g**

1Co 5: 6 Your glorying is not **g**
1Co 7: 1 It is **g** for a man not to
1Co 7: 8 It is **g** for them if they
1Co 7:26 is **g** because of the present
1Co 7:26 that it is **g** for a man to
1Co 15:33 company corrupts **g** habits
2Co 5:10 he has done, whether **g** or bad
2Co 6: 8 by evil report and **g** report
2Co 9: 8 an abundance for every **g** work
2Co 13:11 Be of **g** comfort, be of one
Gal 4:17 court you, but for no **g**
Gal 4:18 But it is **g** to be zealous in
Gal 4:18 zealous in a **g** thing always
Gal 6: 6 the word share in all **g**
Gal 6: 9 not grow weary while doing **g**
Gal 6:10 let us do **g** to all,
Gal 6:12 make a **g** showing in the flesh
Eph 1: 5 according to the **g** pleasure
Eph 1: 9 according to His **g** pleasure
Eph 2:10 in Christ Jesus for **g** works
Eph 4:28 with his hands what is **g**,
Eph 4:29 but what is **g** for necessary
Eph 6: 7 with **g** will doing service, as
Eph 6: 8 that whatever **g** anyone does
Phil 1: 6 that He who has begun a **g**
Phil 1:15 and some also from **g** will
Phil 2:13 and to do for His **g** pleasure
Phil 4: 8 things are of **g** report, if
Col 1:10 fruitful in every **g** work and
Col 2: 5 rejoicing to see your **g** order
1Th 3: 1 we thought it **g** to be left in
1Th 3: 6 brought us **g** news of your
1Th 3: 6 have **g** remembrance of us,
1Th 5:15 what is **g** both for yourselves
1Th 5:21 hold fast what is **g**
2Th 1:11 fulfill all the **g** pleasure of
2Th 2:16 and **g** hope by grace,
2Th 2:17 establish you in every **g** word
2Th 3:13 do not grow weary in doing **g**
1Ti 1: 5 from a **g** conscience, and from
1Ti 1: 8 is **g** if one uses it lawfully
1Ti 1:18 you may wage the **g** warfare
1Ti 1:19 a **g** conscience, which some
1Ti 2: 3 For this is **g** and acceptable
1Ti 2:10 godliness, with **g** works
1Ti 3: 1 a bishop, he desires a **g** work
1Ti 3: 2 of **g** behavior, hospitable,
1Ti 3: 7 Moreover he must have a **g**
1Ti 3:13 for themselves a **g** standing
1Ti 4: 4 every creature of God is **g**
1Ti 4: 6 you will be a **g** minister of
1Ti 4: 6 of the **g** doctrine which you
1Ti 5: 4 for this is **g** and acceptable
1Ti 5:10 well reported for **g** works
1Ti 5:10 followed every **g** work
1Ti 5:25 the **g** works of some are
1Ti 6:12 Fight the **g** fight of faith,
1Ti 6:12 and have confessed the **g**
1Ti 6:13 Jesus who witnessed the **g**
1Ti 6:18 Let them do **g**, that they be
1Ti 6:18 that they be rich in **g** works
1Ti 6:19 **g** foundation for the time to
2Ti 1:14 That **g** thing which was
2Ti 2: 3 a **g** soldier of Jesus Christ
2Ti 2:21 prepared for every **g** work
2Ti 3: 3 brutal, despisers of **g**,
2Ti 3:17 equipped for every **g** work
2Ti 4: 7 I have fought the **g** fight
Tit 1: 8 a lover of what is **g**,
Tit 1:16 disqualified for every **g** work
Tit 2: 3 wine, teachers of **g** things
Tit 2: 5 chaste, homemakers, **g**,
Tit 2: 7 to be a pattern of **g** works
Tit 2:10 but showing all **g** fidelity
Tit 2:14 people, zealous for **g** works
Tit 3: 1 to be ready for every **g** work
Tit 3: 8 careful to maintain **g** works
Tit 3: 8 These things are **g** and
Tit 3:14 learn to maintain **g** works
Phm 6 **g** thing which is in you in
Phm 14 that your **g** deed might not be
Heb 5:14 exercised to discern both **g**
Heb 6: 5 have tasted the **g** word of God
Heb 9:11 of the **g** things to come, with
Heb 10: 1 of the **g** things to come, and
Heb 10:24 to stir up love and **g** works,
Heb 11: 2 elders obtained a **g** testimony
Heb 11:12 him as **g** as dead, were born
Heb 11:39 having obtained a **g** testimony
Heb 13: 9 For it is **g** that the heart be
Heb 13:16 But do not forget to do **g**
Heb 13:18 that we have a **g** conscience
Heb 13:21 every **g** work to do His will
Jas 1:17 Every **g** gift and every perfect
Jas 2: 3 You sit here in a **g** place
Jas 3:13 Let him show by **g** conduct
Jas 3:17 **g** fruits, without partiality
Jas 4:17 to him who knows to do **g**
1Pe 2:12 by your **g** works which they
1Pe 2:14 the praise of those who do **g**
1Pe 2:15 that by doing **g** you may put
1Pe 2:18 all fear, not only to the **g**
1Pe 2:20 But when you do **g** and suffer
1Pe 3: 6 daughters you are if you do **g**
1Pe 3:10 see **g** days, let him refrain
1Pe 3:11 turn away from evil and do **g**
1Pe 3:13 become followers of what is **g**
1Pe 3:16 having a **g** conscience, that
1Pe 3:16 those who revile your **g**
1Pe 3:17 doing **g** than for doing evil
1Pe 3:21 flesh, but the answer of a **g**
1Pe 4:10 as **g** stewards of the manifold
1Pe 4:19 their souls to Him in doing **g**
3Jn 11 what is evil, but what is **g**
3Jn 11 He who does **g** is of God, but
3Jn 12 Demetrius has a **g** testimony

GOOD-LOOKING (*see* GOOD)
1Sa 16:12 ruddy, with bright eyes, and **g**
1Sa 17:42 was but a youth, ruddy and **g**
1Ki 1: 6 He was also a very **g** man
Dan 1: 4 there was no blemish, but **g**

GOODLY (*see* GOOD)
Gen 49:21 he gives **g** words

GOODNESS (*see* GOOD, GOODNESS')
Ex 33:19 make all My **g** pass before you
Ex 34: 6 and abounding in **g** and truth,
2Sa 7:28 this **g** to Your servant
1Ki 8:66 glad of heart for all the **g**
1Ch 17:26 this **g** to Your servant
2Ch 6:41 let Your saints rejoice in **g**
2Ch 7:10 glad of heart for the **g** that
2Ch 32:32 acts of Hezekiah, and his **g**
2Ch 35:26 the acts of Josiah and his **g**
Neh 9:25 themselves in Your great **g**
Ps 16: 2 My **g** is nothing apart from
Ps 21: 3 him with the blessings of **g**
Ps 23: 6 Surely **g** and mercy shall
Ps 27:13 That I would see the **g** of the
Ps 31:19 Oh, how great is Your **g**,
Ps 33: 5 is full of the **g** of the LORD
Ps 52: 1 The **g** of God endures
Ps 65: 4 with the **g** of Your house, Of
Ps 65:11 crown the year with Your **g**
Ps 68:10 from Your **g** for the poor
Ps 107: 8 thanks to the LORD for His **g**
Ps 107: 9 fills the hungry soul with **g**
Ps 107:15 thanks to the LORD for His **g**
Ps 107:21 thanks to the LORD for His **g**
Ps 107:31 thanks to the LORD for His **g**
Ps 145: 7 the memory of Your great **g**
Prov 2:20 you may walk in the way of **g**
Prov 20: 6 will proclaim each his own **g**
Eccl 6: 3 soul is not satisfied with **g**
Eccl 6: 6 but has not seen **g**
Is 63: 7 the great **g** toward the house
Jer 2: 7 to eat its fruit and its **g**
Jer 31:12 to the **g** of the LORD
Jer 31:14 shall be satisfied with My **g**
Jer 33: 9 fear and tremble for all the **g**
Hos 3: 5 and His **g** in the latter days
Zech 9:17 for how great is their **g** And
Rom 2: 4 despise the riches of His **g**
Rom 2: 4 the **g** of God leads you to
Rom 11:22 Therefore consider the **g** and
Rom 11:22 but toward you, **g**, if you
Rom 11:22 if you continue in His **g**
Rom 15:14 that you also are full of **g**
Gal 5:22 longsuffering, kindness, **g**
Eph 5: 9 of the Spirit is in all **g**
2Th 1:11 the good pleasure of His **g**

GOODNESS' (*see* GOODNESS)
Ps 25: 7 remember me, For Your **g** sake

GOODS
Gen 14:11 they took all the **g** of Sodom
Gen 14:12 who dwelt in Sodom, and his **g**
Gen 14:16 So he brought back all the **g**
Gen 14:16 back his brother Lot and his **g**
Gen 14:21 and take the **g** for yourself
Gen 24:10 master's **g** were in his hand
Gen 36: 6 all his **g** which he had gained
Gen 40:17 kinds of baked **g** for Pharaoh
Gen 45:20 not be concerned about your **g**
Gen 46: 6 their livestock and their **g**
Ex 22: 8 hand into his neighbor's **g**
Ex 22:11 hand into his neighbor's **g**
Num 16:32 with Korah, with all their **g**
Num 31: 9 their flocks, and all their **g**
Deut 28:11 will grant you plenty of **g**
Judg 18:21 and the **g** in front of them
Ezra 1: 4 with silver and gold, with **g**
Ezra 1: 6 of silver and gold, with **g**
Ezra 7:26 or confiscation of **g**, or
Neh 9:25 houses full of all **g**,
Neh 13: 8 **g** of Tobiah out of the room
Neh 13:16 in fish and all kinds of **g**
Job 20:28 his **g** will flow away in the
Eccl 5:11 When **g** increase, they
Ezek 27:12 because of your many luxury **g**
Ezek 27:12 iron, tin, and lead for your **g**
Ezek 27:16 the abundance of **g** you made
Ezek 27:18 the abundance of **g** you made
Ezek 27:33 earth with your many luxury **g**
Ezek 38:12 have acquired livestock and **g**
Ezek 38:13 to take away livestock and **g**
Zeph 1:13 Therefore their **g** shall
Matt 12:29 man's house and plunder his **g**
Matt 24:47 make him ruler over all his **g**
Matt 25:14 and delivered his **g** to them
Mark 3:27 man's house and plunder his **g**
Luke 6:30 your **g** do not ask them back
Luke 11:21 palace, his **g** are in peace
Luke 12:18 store all my crops and my **g**
Luke 12:19 you have many **g** laid up for
Luke 15:12 portion of **g** that falls to me
Luke 16: 1 this man was wasting his **g**
Luke 17:31 his **g** are in the house, let
Luke 19: 8 give half of my **g** to the poor
Acts 2:45 sold their possessions and **g**
1Co 13: 3 all my **g** to feed the poor
Heb 10:34 the plundering of your **g**,
1Jn 3:17 whoever has this world's **g**

GOPHERWOOD
Gen 6:14 Make yourself an ark of **g**

GORE (*see* GORED, GORES)
1Ki 22:11 With these you shall **g** the
2Ch 18:10 With these you shall **g** the

GORED (*see* GORE)
Ex 21:31 has **g** a son or **g** a daughter

GORES (*see* GORE)
Ex 21:28 If an ox **g** a man or a woman
Ex 21:32 If the ox **g** a manservant or a

GORGEOUS (*see* GORGEOUSLY)
Luke 23:11 Him, arrayed Him in a **g** robe

GORGEOUSLY (*see* GORGEOUS)
Ezek 23:12 and rulers, clothed most **g**
Luke 7:25 those who are **g** appareled

GOSHEN (*see* EGYPT)
Gen 45:10 shall dwell in the land of **G**
Gen 46:28 out before him the way to **G**
Gen 46:28 And they came to the land of **G**
Gen 46:29 and went up to **G** to meet his
Gen 46:34 may dwell in the land of **G**
Gen 47: 1 they are in the land of **G**
Gen 47: 4 dwell in the land of **G**
Gen 47: 6 them dwell in the land of **G**
Gen 47:27 of Egypt, in the country of **G**
Gen 50: 8 they left in the land of **G**
Ex 8:22 will set apart the land of **G**
Ex 9:26 Only in the land of **G**, where
Josh 10:41 Gaza, and all the country of **G**
Josh 11:16 the South, all the land of **G**
Josh 15:51 **G**, Holon, and Giloh

GOSPEL (*see* GOSPEL'S)
Matt 4:23 preaching the **g** of the
Matt 9:35 preaching the **g** of the
Matt 11: 5 have the **g** preached to them
Matt 24:14 this **g** of the kingdom will be
Matt 26:13 wherever this **g** is preached
Mark 1: 1 of the **g** of Jesus Christ, the
Mark 1:14 preaching the **g** of the
Mark 1:15 Repent, and believe in the **g**
Mark 13:10 the **g** must first be preached
Mark 14: 9 wherever this **g** is preached
Mark 16:15 and preach the **g** to every

Luke 4:18 to preach the g to the poor
Luke 7:22 have the g preached to them
Luke 9: 6 the towns, preaching the g
Luke 20: 1 the temple and preached the g
Acts 8:25 preaching the g in many
Acts 14: 7 were preaching the g there
Acts 14:21 preached the g to that city
Acts 15: 7 should hear the word of the g
Acts 16:10 us to preach the g to them
Acts 20:24 to testify to the g of the
Rom 1: 1 separated to the g of God
Rom 1: 9 my spirit in the g of His Son
Rom 1:15 I am ready to preach the g to
Rom 1:16 ashamed of the g of Christ
Rom 2:16 Christ, according to my g
Rom 10:15 who preach the g of peace
Rom 10:16 have not all obeyed the g
Rom 11:28 Concerning the g they are
Rom 15:16 ministering the g of God
Rom 15:19 preached the g of Christ
Rom 15:20 it my aim to preach the g
Rom 15:29 blessing of the g of Christ
Rom 16:25 you according to my g and the
1Co 1:17 baptize, but to preach the g
1Co 4:15 begotten you through the g
1Co 9:12 we hinder the g of Christ
1Co 9:14 that those who preach the g
1Co 9:14 should live from the g
1Co 9:16 For if I preach the g, I have
1Co 9:16 me if I do not preach the g
1Co 9:18 That when I preach the g, I
1Co 9:18 I may present the g of Christ
1Co 9:18 abuse my authority in the g
1Co 15: 1 I declare to you the g which
2Co 2:12 to Troas to preach Christ's g
2Co 4: 3 But even if our g is veiled
2Co 4: 4 lest the light of the g of
2Co 8:18 whose praise is in the g
2Co 9:13 confession to the g of Christ
2Co 10:14 we came with the g of Christ
2Co 10:16 to preach the g in the
2Co 11: 4 or a different g which you
2Co 11: 7 the g of God to you free of
Gal 1: 6 of Christ, to a different g
Gal 1: 7 to pervert the g of Christ
Gal 1: 8 preach any other g to you
Gal 1: 9 g to you than what you have
Gal 1:11 that the g which was preached
Gal 2: 2 g which I preach among the
Gal 2: 5 that the truth of the g might
Gal 2: 7 when they saw that the g for
Gal 2: 7 as the g for the circumcised
Gal 2:14 about the truth of the g, I
Gal 3: 8 preached the g to Abraham
Gal 4:13 the g to you at the first
Eph 1:13 the g of your salvation
Eph 3: 6 in Christ through the g,
Eph 6:15 preparation of the g of peace
Eph 6:19 known the mystery of the g
Phil 1: 5 g from the first day until
Phil 1: 7 and confirmation of the g, you
Phil 1:12 for the furtherance of the g
Phil 1:17 for the defense of the g
Phil 1:27 be worthy of the g of Christ
Phil 1:27 for the faith of the g,
Phil 2:22 he served with me in the g
Phil 4: 3 who labored with me in the g
Phil 4:15 in the beginning of the g
Col 1: 5 word of the truth of the g
Col 1:23 hope of the g which you heard
1Th 1: 5 For our g did not come to you
1Th 2: 2 the g of God in much conflict
1Th 2: 4 to be entrusted with the g
1Th 2: 8 to you not only the g of God
1Th 2: 9 preached to you the g of God
1Th 3: 2 laborer in the g of Christ
2Th 1: 8 g of our Lord Jesus Christ
2Th 2:14 which He called you by our g
1Ti 1:11 g of the blessed God which
2Ti 1: 8 g according to the power of
2Ti 1:10 to light through the g,
2Ti 2: 8 the dead according to my g
Phm 13 to me in my chains for the g
Heb 4: 2 For indeed the g was preached
1Pe 1:12 g to you by the Holy Spirit
1Pe 1:25 by the g was preached to you
1Pe 4: 6 For this reason the g was
1Pe 4:17 who do not obey the g of God
Rev 14: 6 g to preach to those who

GOSPEL'S (*see* GOSPEL)
Mark 8:35 My sake and the g will save it
Mark 10:29 lands, for My sake and the g
1Co 9:23 Now this I do for the g sake

GOSSIPS
1Ti 5:13 and not only idle but also g

GOT (*see* GET)
Gen 27:14 g them and brought them to his
Num 16:27 So they g away from around
Judg 7: 6 g down on their knees to
Judg 19:28 and the man g up and went to
1Sa 24: 7 Saul g up from the cave and
1Sa 26:12 Saul's head, and they g away
2Sa 13:29 each one g on his mule and
1Ki 20:12 they g ready to attack the
1Ki 21:16 was dead, that Ahab g up and
2Ki 5:21 he g down from the chariot to
Jer 13: 2 So I g a sash according to
Matt 8:23 Now when He g into a boat
Matt 9: 1 So He g into a boat, crossed
Matt 13: 2 so that He g into a boat and
Matt 14:32 when they g into the boat,
Matt 15:39 g into the boat, and came to
Mark 4: 1 so that He g into a boat and
Mark 5:18 when He g into the boat, he
Mark 8:10 immediately He g into the
Luke 5: 3 Then He g into one of the
Luke 8:22 that He g into a boat with
Luke 8:37 And He g into the boat and
John 4:52 the hour when he g better
John 6:17 g into the boat, and went over
John 6:24 they also g into boats and
John 21: 3 immediately g into the boat,

GOTTEN (*see* PREFACE)

GOURDS
2Ki 4:39 from it a lap full of wild g

GOVERN (*see* GOVERNED, GOVERNING, GOVERNMENT, GOVERNS)
Job 34:17 one who hates justice g
Ps 67: 4 And g the nations on earth

GOVERNED (*see* GOVERN)
1Ch 26: 6 who g their fathers' houses

GOVERNING (*see* GOVERN)
1Ch 23:31 to the ordinance g them,
Luke 2: 2 while Quirinius was g Syria
Rom 13: 1 subject to the g authorities

GOVERNMENT (*see* GOVERN)
Is 9: 6 and the g will be upon His
Is 9: 7 Of the increase of His g and

GOVERNOR (*see* GOVERNOR'S, GOVERNORS)
Gen 42: 6 Joseph was g over the land
Gen 45:26 he is g over all the land of
1Ki 4:19 he was the only g who was in
1Ki 22:26 him to Amon the g of the city
2Ki 23: 8 of Joshua the g of the city
2Ki 25:22 g over the people who
2Ki 25:23 Babylon had made Gedaliah g
2Ch 18:25 him to Amon the g of the city
2Ch 34: 8 Maaseiah the g of the city
Ezra 2:63 the g said to them that they
Ezra 5: 3 g of the region beyond the
Ezra 5: 6 The g of the region beyond
Ezra 5:14 whom he had made g
Ezra 6: 6 g of the region beyond the
Ezra 6: 7 let the g of the Jews and the
Ezra 6:13 g of the region beyond the
Neh 3: 7 the residence of the g of the
Neh 5:14 their g in the land of Judah
Neh 7:65 the g said to them that they
Neh 7:70 The g gave to the treasury
Neh 8: 9 And Nehemiah, who was the g
Neh 10: 1 Nehemiah the g, the son of
Neh 12:26 in the days of Nehemiah the g
Jer 20: 1 g in the house of the LORD
Jer 30:21 their g shall come from their
Jer 40: 5 g over the cities of Judah
Jer 40: 7 son of Ahikam g in the land
Jer 41: 2 had made g over the land
Jer 41:18 had made g in the land
Hag 1: 1 g of Judah, and to Joshua the
Hag 1:14 g of Judah, and the spirit of
Hag 2: 2 g of Judah, and to Joshua the
Hag 2:21 g of Judah, saying
Mal 1: 8 Offer it then to your g
Matt 27: 2 Him to Pontius Pilate the g
Matt 27:11 Now Jesus stood before the g
Matt 27:11 And the g asked Him, saying,
Matt 27:14 word, so that the g marveled
Matt 27:15 Now at the feast the g was
Matt 27:21 The g answered and said to
Matt 27:23 Then the g said, Why, what
Matt 27:27 of the g took Jesus into the
Luke 3: 1 Pilate being g of Judea,
Luke 20:20 and the authority of the g
Acts 7:10 and he made him g over Egypt
Acts 23:24 him safely to Felix the g
Acts 23:26 to the most excellent g Felix
Acts 23:33 delivered the letter to the g
Acts 23:34 when the g had read it, he
Acts 24: 1 to the g against Paul
Acts 24:10 after the g had nodded to him
Acts 26:30 stood up, as well as the g
2Co 11:32 In Damascus the g, under

GOVERNOR'S (*see* GOVERNOR)
Neh 5:14 brothers ate the g provisions
Neh 5:18 not demand the g provisions
Matt 28:14 if this comes to the g ears

GOVERNORS (*see* GOVERNOR)
1Ki 4: 7 had twelve g over all Israel
1Ki 4:27 And these g, each man in his
1Ki 10:15 from the g of the country
2Ch 9:14 g of the country brought gold
2Ch 23:20 the g of the people, and all
Ezra 8:36 the g in the region beyond
Neh 2: 7 be given to me for the g of
Neh 2: 9 Then I went to the g in the
Neh 5:15 But the former g who had been
Esth 3:12 to the g who were over each
Esth 8: 9 the Jews, the satraps, the g
Esth 9: 3 provinces, the satraps, the g
Jer 51:23 you I will break in pieces g
Jer 51:28 the kings of the Medes, its g
Jer 51:57 princes and wise men, her g
Ezek 23:23 them desirable young men, g
Dan 3: 2 the administrators, the g
Dan 3: 3 the administrators, the g
Dan 3:27 satraps, administrators, g
Dan 6: 2 and over these, three g, of
Dan 6: 3 himself above the g and
Dan 6: 4 So the g and satraps sought to
Dan 6: 6 So these g and satraps
Dan 6: 7 All the g of the kingdom, the
Zech 12: 5 the g of Judah shall say in
Zech 12: 6 g of Judah like a firepan in
Matt 10:18 you will be brought before g
1Pe 2:14 or to g, as to those who are

GOVERNS (*see* GOVERN)
Luke 22:26 he who g as he who serves

GOZAN
2Ki 17: 6 by the Habor, the River of G
2Ki 18:11 by the Habor, the River of G
2Ki 19:12 my fathers have destroyed, G
1Ch 5:26 and the river of G to this day
Is 37:12 my fathers have destroyed, G

GRACE (*see* GRACEFUL, GRACIOUS)
Gen 6: 8 But Noah found g in the eyes
Ex 33:12 have also found g in My sight
Ex 33:13 I have found g in Your sight
Ex 33:13 I may find g in Your sight
Ex 33:16 I have found g in Your sight,
Ex 33:17 you have found g in My sight
Ex 34: 9 I have found g in Your sight
Ezra 9: 8 now for a little while g has
Esth 2:17 women, and she obtained g and
Ps 45: 2 G is poured upon Your lips
Ps 84:11 The LORD will give g and glory
Prov 3:22 your soul and g to your neck
Prov 3:34 but gives g to the humble
Prov 4: 9 on your head an ornament of g
Prov 22:11 has g on his lips, the king
Is 26:10 Let g be shown to the wicked,
Jer 31: 2 found g in the wilderness
Zech 4: 7 shouts of "G, g to it
Zech 12:10 of Jerusalem the Spirit of g
Luke 2:40 the g of God was upon Him
John 1:14 of the Father, full of g and
John 1:16 all received, and g for g
John 1:17 given through Moses, but g
Acts 4:33 great g was upon them all
Acts 11:23 came and had seen the g of God
Acts 13:43 to continue in the g of God
Acts 14: 3 witness to the word of His g
Acts 14:26 g of God for the work which
Acts 15:11 g of the Lord Jesus Christ we

Acts 15:40 the brethren to the **g** of God
Acts 18:27 who had believed through **g**
Acts 20:24 to the gospel of the **g** of God
Acts 20:32 God and to the word of His **g**
Rom 1: 5 whom we have received **g** and
Rom 1: 7 **G** to you and peace from God
Rom 3:24 justified freely by His **g**
Rom 4: 4 not counted as **g** but as debt
Rom 4:16 it might be according to **g**
Rom 5: 2 into this **g** in which we stand
Rom 5:15 died, much more the **g** of God
Rom 5:15 gift by the **g** of the one Man
Rom 5:17 who receive abundance of **g**
Rom 5:20 **g** abounded much more,
Rom 5:21 even so **g** might reign through
Rom 6: 1 in sin that **g** may abound
Rom 6:14 are not under law but under **g**
Rom 6:15 are not under law but under **g**
Rom 11: 5 to the election of **g**
Rom 11: 6 And if by **g**, then it is no
Rom 11: 6 otherwise **g** is no longer **g**
Rom 11: 6 of works, it is no longer **g**
Rom 12: 3 through the **g** given to me
Rom 12: 6 to the **g** that is given to us
Rom 15:15 because of the **g** given to me
Rom 16:20 The **g** of our Lord Jesus
Rom 16:24 The **g** of our Lord Jesus
1Co 1: 3 **G** to you and peace from God
1Co 1: 4 concerning you for the **g** of
1Co 3:10 According to the **g** of God
1Co 15:10 But by the **g** of God I am what
1Co 15:10 His **g** toward me was not in
1Co 15:10 but the **g** of God which was
1Co 16:23 The **g** of our Lord Jesus
2Co 1: 2 **G** to you and peace from God
2Co 1:12 wisdom but by the **g** of God
2Co 4:15 are for your sakes, that **g**
2Co 6: 1 receive the **g** of God in vain
2Co 8: 1 the **g** of God bestowed on the
2Co 8: 6 this **g** in you as well
2Co 8: 7 you abound in this **g** also
2Co 8: 9 For you know the **g** of our
2Co 9: 8 make all **g** abound toward you
2Co 9:14 the exceeding **g** of God in you
2Co 12: 9 My **g** is sufficient for you,
2Co 13:14 The **g** of the Lord Jesus
Gal 1: 3 **G** to you and peace from God
Gal 1: 6 called you in the **g** of Christ
Gal 1:15 and called me through His **g**
Gal 2: 9 perceived the **g** that had been
Gal 2:21 do not set aside the **g** of God
Gal 5: 4 you have fallen from **g**
Gal 6:18 the **g** of our Lord Jesus
Eph 1: 2 **G** to you and peace from God
Eph 1: 6 praise of the glory of His **g**
Eph 1: 7 to the riches of His **g**
Eph 2: 5 (by **g** you have been saved)
Eph 2: 7 **g** in His kindness toward us
Eph 2: 8 For by **g** you have been saved
Eph 3: 2 **g** of God which was given to
Eph 3: 7 to the gift of the **g** of God
Eph 3: 8 this **g** was given, that I
Eph 4: 7 But to each one of us **g** was
Eph 4:29 may impart **g** to the hearers
Eph 6:24 **G** be with all those who love
Phil 1: 2 **G** to you and peace from God
Phil 1: 7 are partakers with me of **g**
Phil 4:23 The **g** of our Lord Jesus
Col 1: 2 **G** to you and peace from God
Col 1: 6 knew the **g** of God in truth
Col 3:16 singing with **g** in your hearts
Col 4: 6 your speech always be with **g**
Col 4:18 **G** be with you
1Th 1: 1 **G** to you and peace from God
1Th 5:28 The **g** of our Lord Jesus
2Th 1: 2 **G** to you and peace from God
2Th 1:12 according to the **g** of our God
2Th 2:16 consolation and good hope by **g**
2Th 3:18 The **g** of our Lord Jesus
1Ti 1: 2 **G**, mercy, and peace from God
1Ti 1:14 And the **g** of our Lord was
1Ti 6:21 **G** be with you
2Ti 1: 2 **G**, mercy, and peace from God
2Ti 1: 9 **g** which was given to us in
2Ti 2: 1 be strong in the **g** that is in
2Ti 4:22 **G** be with you
Tit 1: 4 **G**, mercy, and peace from God
Tit 2:11 For the **g** of God that brings
Tit 3: 7 been justified by His **g** we
Tit 3:15 **G** be with you all
Phm 3 **G** to you and peace from God
Phm 25 The **g** of our Lord Jesus
Heb 2: 9 that He, by the **g** of God
Heb 4:16 boldly to the throne of **g**
Heb 4:16 find **g** to help in time of
Heb 10:29 and insulted the Spirit of **g**
Heb 12:15 fall short of the **g** of God
Heb 12:28 be shaken, let us have **g**, by
Heb 13: 9 the heart be established by **g**
Heb 13:25 **G** be with you all
Jas 4: 6 But He gives more **g**
Jas 4: 6 but gives **g** to the humble
1Pe 1: 2 **G** to you and peace be
1Pe 1:10 who prophesied of the **g** that
1Pe 1:13 **g** that is to be brought to
1Pe 3: 7 together of the **g** of life
1Pe 4:10 of the manifold **g** of God
1Pe 5: 5 but gives **g** to the humble
1Pe 5:10 But may the God of all **g**, who
1Pe 5:12 that this is the true **g** of
2Pe 1: 2 **G** and peace be multiplied to
2Pe 3:18 but grow in the **g** and
2Jn 3 **G**, mercy, and peace will be
Jude 4 who turn the **g** of our God
Rev 1: 4 **G** to you and peace from Him
Rev 22:21 The **g** of our Lord Jesus

GRACEFUL (*see* GRACE)
Job 41:12 power, or his **g** proportions
Prov 1: 9 for they will be **g** ornaments
Prov 5:19 and a **g** doe, let her breasts

GRACIOUS (*see* GRACE, GRACIOUSLY)
Gen 43:29 God be **g** to you, my son
Ex 22:27 Me, I will hear, for I am **g**
Ex 33:19 will be **g** to whom I will be **g**
Ex 34: 6 the LORD God, merciful and **g**
Num 6:25 upon you, and be **g** to you
2Sa 12:22 the LORD will be **g** to me,
2Ki 13:23 But the LORD was **g** to them
2Ch 30: 9 for the LORD your God is **g**
Neh 9:17 are God, ready to pardon, **g**
Neh 9:31 for You are God, **g** and
Job 33:24 then He is **g** to him, and says,
Ps 77: 9 Has God forgotten to be **g**
Ps 86:15 God full of compassion, and **g**
Ps 103: 8 The LORD is merciful and **g**
Ps 111: 4 The LORD is **g** and full of
Ps 112: 4 He is **g**, and full of
Ps 116: 5 **G** is the LORD, and righteous
Ps 145: 8 The LORD is **g** and full of
Ps 145:17 His ways, **G** in all His works
Prov 11:16 A **g** woman retains honor, but
Eccl 10:12 of a wise man's mouth are **g**
Is 30:18 wait, that He may be **g** to you
Is 30:19 He will be very **g** to you at
Is 33: 2 O LORD, be **g** to us
Jer 22:23 how **g** will you be when pangs
Joel 2:13 LORD your God, for He is **g**
Amos 5:15 be **g** to the remnant of Joseph
Jon 4: 2 for I know that You are a **g**
Mal 1: 9 favor, that He may be **g** to us
Luke 4:22 marveled at the **g** words which
1Pe 2: 3 tasted that the Lord is **g**

GRACIOUSLY (*see* GRACIOUS)
Gen 33: 5 God has **g** given your servant
Gen 33:11 God has dealt **g** with me, and
Ps 112: 5 A good man deals **g** and lends
Ps 119:29 lying, And grant me Your law **g**
Hos 14: 2 receive us **g**, for we will

GRAFT (*see* GRAFTED)
Rom 11:23 is able to **g** them in again

GRAFTED (*see* GRAFT)
Rom 11:17 were **g** in among them, and with
Rom 11:19 off that I might be **g** in
Rom 11:23 in unbelief, will be **g** in
Rom 11:24 were **g** contrary to nature
Rom 11:24 be **g** into their own olive

GRAIN (*see* GRAINFIELDS, GRAINS)
Gen 27:28 of the earth, and plenty of **g**
Gen 27:37 with **g** and wine I have
Gen 41: 5 of **g** came up on one stalk
Gen 41:35 and store up **g** under the
Gen 41:49 Joseph gathered very much **g**
Gen 41:57 to Joseph in Egypt to buy **g**
Gen 42: 1 saw that there was **g** in Egypt
Gen 42: 2 that there is **g** in Egypt
Gen 42: 3 went down to buy **g** in Egypt
Gen 42: 5 **g** among those who journeyed
Gen 42:19 carry **g** for the famine of
Gen 42:25 to fill their sacks with **g**
Gen 42:26 their donkeys with the **g** and
Gen 43: 2 when they had eaten up the **g**
Gen 44: 2 the youngest, and his **g** money
Gen 45:23 female donkeys loaded with **g**
Gen 47:14 for the **g** which they bought
Ex 22: 6 in thorns, so that stacked **g**
Ex 22: 6 stacked **g**, standing **g**
Ex 29:41 offer with it the **g** offering
Ex 40:29 the **g** offering, as the LORD
Lev 2: 1 a **g** offering to the LORD, his
Lev 2: 3 The rest of the **g** offering
Lev 2: 4 **g** offering baked in the oven
Lev 2: 5 a **g** offering baked in a pan
Lev 2: 6 it is a **g** offering
Lev 2: 7 And if your offering is a **g**
Lev 2: 8 You shall bring the **g**
Lev 2: 9 priest shall take from the **g**
Lev 2:10 And what is left of the **g**
Lev 2:11 No **g** offering which you
Lev 2:13 And every offering of your **g**
Lev 2:13 lacking from your **g** offering
Lev 2:14 If you offer a **g** offering of
Lev 2:14 for the **g** offering of your
Lev 2:14 of **g** roasted on the fire,
Lev 2:14 **g** beaten from full heads
Lev 2:15 It is a **g** offering
Lev 2:16 part of its beaten **g** and part
Lev 5:13 the priest's as a **g** offering
Lev 6:14 is the law of the **g** offering
Lev 6:15 fine flour of the **g** offering
Lev 6:15 which is on the **g** offering
Lev 6:20 flour as a daily **g** offering
Lev 6:21 the baked pieces of the **g**
Lev 6:23 For every **g** offering for the
Lev 7: 9 Also every **g** offering that
Lev 7:10 Every **g** offering mixed with
Lev 7:37 the **g** offering, the sin
Lev 9: 4 a **g** offering mixed with oil
Lev 9:17 he brought the **g** offering
Lev 10:12 Take the **g** offering that
Lev 14:10 with oil as a **g** offering, and
Lev 14:20 the **g** offering on the altar
Lev 14:21 with oil as a **g** offering, a
Lev 14:31 offering, with the **g** offering
Lev 23:13 Its **g** offering shall be
Lev 23:14 **g** nor fresh **g** until the
Lev 23:16 a new **g** offering to the LORD
Lev 23:18 LORD, with their **g** offering
Lev 23:37 a **g** offering, a sacrifice and
Num 4:16 incense, the daily **g** offering
Num 5:15 because it is a **g** offering of
Num 5:18 which is the **g** offering of
Num 5:25 **g** offering of jealousy from
Num 6:15 their **g** offering with their
Num 6:17 also offer its **g** offering
Num 7:13 with oil as a **g** offering
Num 7:19 with oil as a **g** offering
Num 7:25 with oil as a **g** offering
Num 7:31 with oil as a **g** offering
Num 7:37 with oil as a **g** offering
Num 7:43 with oil as a **g** offering
Num 7:49 with oil as a **g** offering
Num 7:55 with oil as a **g** offering
Num 7:61 with oil as a **g** offering
Num 7:67 with oil as a **g** offering
Num 7:73 with oil as a **g** offering
Num 7:79 with oil as a **g** offering
Num 7:87 twelve, with their **g** offering
Num 8: 8 its **g** offering of fine flour
Num 15: 4 to the LORD shall bring a **g**
Num 15: 6 a **g** offering two-tenths of an
Num 15: 9 with the young bull a **g**
Num 15:24 the LORD, with its **g** offering
Num 18: 9 every **g** offering and every sin
Num 18:12 best of the new wine and the **g**
Num 18:27 the **g** of the threshing floor
Num 20: 5 of **g** or figs or vines or
Num 28: 5 as a **g** offering mixed with
Num 28: 8 as the morning **g** offering
Num 28: 9 of fine flour as a **g** offering
Num 28:12 of fine flour as a **g** offering
Num 28:12 of fine flour as a **g** offering
Num 28:13 as a **g** offering for each lamb
Num 28:20 Their **g** offering shall be of
Num 28:26 when you bring a new **g**
Num 28:28 with their **g** offering of
Num 28:31 offering with its **g** offering
Num 29: 3 Their **g** offering shall be

Num 29: 6 **g** offering for the New Moon
Num 29: 6 offering with its **g** offering
Num 29: 9 Their **g** offering shall be of
Num 29:11 offering with its **g** offering
Num 29:14 Their **g** offering shall be of
Num 29:16 its **g** offering, and its drink
Num 29:18 their **g** offering and their
Num 29:19 offering with its **g** offering
Num 29:21 their **g** offering and their
Num 29:22 its **g** offering, and its drink
Num 29:24 their **g** offering and their
Num 29:25 its **g** offering, and its drink
Num 29:27 their **g** offering and their
Num 29:28 its **g** offering, and its drink
Num 29:30 their **g** offering and their
Num 29:31 its **g** offering, and its drink
Num 29:33 their **g** offering and their
Num 29:34 its **g** offering, and its drink
Num 29:37 their **g** offering and their
Num 29:38 its **g** offering, and its drink
Num 29:39 your **g** offerings, as your
Deut 7:13 fruit of your land, your **g**
Deut 11:14 that you may gather in your **g**
Deut 12:17 gates the tithe of your **g** or
Deut 14:22 **g** that the field produces
Deut 14:23 abide, the tithe of your **g**
Deut 16: 9 to put the sickle to the **g**
Deut 18: 4 The firstfruits of your **g**
Deut 23:25 your neighbor's standing **g**
Deut 23:25 on your neighbor's standing **g**
Deut 25: 4 ox while it treads out the **g**
Deut 28:51 you **g** or new wine or oil, or
Deut 33:28 Jacob alone, in a land of **g**
Josh 5:11 parched **g** on the very same
Josh 22:23 offerings or **g** offerings, or
Josh 22:29 for **g** offerings, or for
Judg 13:19 goat with the **g** offering, and
Judg 13:23 a **g** offering from our hands,
Judg 15: 5 standing **g** of the Philistines
Judg 15: 5 the shocks and the standing **g**
Ruth 2: 2 glean heads of **g** after him in
Ruth 2:14 and he passed parched **g** to her
Ruth 2:16 Also let some **g** from the
Ruth 3: 7 at the end of the heap of **g**
1Sa 8:15 will take a tenth of your **g**
1Sa 17:17 an ephah of this dried **g** and
1Sa 25:18 five seahs of roasted **g**, one
2Sa 17:19 and spread ground **g** on it
2Sa 17:28 barley and flour, parched **g**
1Ki 8:64 **g** offerings, and the fat of
1Ki 8:64 the **g** offerings, and the fat
2Ki 3:20 when the **g** offering was
2Ki 4:42 and newly ripened **g** in his
2Ki 16:13 offering and his **g** offering
2Ki 16:15 the evening **g** offering, the
2Ki 16:15 and his **g** offering, with the
2Ki 16:15 their **g** offering, and their
2Ki 18:32 your own land, a land of **g**
2Ki 19:26 **g** blighted before it is grown
1Ch 21:23 the wheat for the **g** offering
1Ch 23:29 fine flour for the **g** offering
2Ch 7: 7 the **g** offerings, and the fat
2Ch 31: 5 the firstfruits of **g** and wine,
2Ch 32:28 for the harvest of **g**, wine,
Ezra 7:17 lambs, with their **g** offerings
Neh 5: 2 let us get **g** for them, that
Neh 5: 3 that we might buy **g** because
Neh 5:10 am lending them money and **g**
Neh 5:11 part of the money and the **g**
Neh 10:31 **g** to sell on the Sabbath day
Neh 10:33 for the regular **g** offering
Neh 10:39 bring the offering of the **g**
Neh 13: 5 had stored the **g** offerings
Neh 13: 5 the articles, the tithes of **g**
Neh 13: 9 of God, with the **g** offering
Neh 13:12 brought the tithe of the **g**
Job 5:26 as a sheaf of **g** ripens in its
Job 24:24 dry out like the heads of **g**
Job 39: 4 they grow strong with **g**
Job 39:12 him to bring home your **g**, and
Ps 4: 7 in the season that their **g**
Ps 65: 9 You provide their **g**, For so
Ps 65:13 also are covered with **g**
Ps 72:16 abundance of **g** in the earth
Prov 11:26 curse him who withholds **g**
Prov 27:22 a pestle along with crushed **g**
Is 17: 5 the harvester gathers the **g**
Is 17: 5 of **g** in the Valley of Rephaim
Is 21:10 and the **g** of my floor
Is 23: 3 great waters the **g** of Shihor
Is 36:17 your own land, a land of **g**
Is 37:27 as **g** blighted before it is
Is 43:23 you to serve with **g** offerings
Is 57: 6 you have offered a **g** offering
Is 62: 8 I will no longer give your **g**
Is 66: 3 he who offers a **g** offering
Jer 14:12 **g** offering, I will not accept
Jer 17:26 **g** offerings and incense,
Jer 33:18 Me, to kindle **g** offerings
Jer 50:11 fat like a heifer threshing **g**
Lam 2:12 Where is **g** and wine
Ezek 36:29 I will call for the **g** and
Ezek 42:13 the **g** offering, the sin
Ezek 44:29 They shall eat the **g** offering
Ezek 45:15 shall be for **g** offerings,
Ezek 45:17 **g** offerings, and drink
Ezek 45:17 the **g** offering, the burnt
Ezek 45:24 he shall prepare a **g** offering
Ezek 45:25 the **g** offering, and the oil
Ezek 46: 5 the **g** offering shall be one
Ezek 46: 5 the **g** offering for the lambs,
Ezek 46: 7 He shall prepare a **g** offering
Ezek 46:11 appointed feast days the **g**
Ezek 46:14 And you shall prepare a **g**
Ezek 46:14 This **g** offering is a
Ezek 46:15 the **g** offering, and the oil,
Ezek 46:20 shall bake the **g** offering
Hos 2: 8 not know that I gave her **g**
Hos 2: 9 and take away my **g** in its time
Hos 2:22 The earth shall answer With **g**
Hos 7:14 They assemble together for **g**
Hos 10:11 heifer that loves to thresh **g**
Hos 14: 7 they shall be revived like **g**
Joel 1: 9 The **g** offering and the drink
Joel 1:10 for the **g** is ruined, the new
Joel 1:13 for the **g** offering and the
Joel 1:17 The seed **g** shrivels under the
Joel 1:17 down, for the **g** has withered
Joel 2:14 a **g** offering and a drink
Joel 2:19 Behold, I will send you **g**
Amos 5:11 take **g** taxes from him, though
Amos 5:22 your **g** offerings, I will not
Amos 8: 5 be past, that we may sell **g**
Amos 9: 9 as **g** is sifted in a sieve
Amos 9: 9 yet not the smallest **g** shall
Hag 1:11 and the mountains, on the **g**
Zech 9:17 **G** shall make the young men
Matt 12: 1 and began to pluck heads of **g**
Matt 13:26 But when the **g** had sprouted
Mark 2:23 began to pluck the heads of **g**
Mark 4:28 that the full **g** in the head
Mark 4:29 But when the **g** ripens,
Luke 6: 1 plucked the heads of **g** and ate
John 12:24 unless a **g** of wheat falls
John 12:24 it dies, it produces much **g**
Acts 7:12 that there was **g** in Egypt
1Co 9: 9 ox while it treads out the **g**
1Co 15:37 that shall be, but mere **g**
1Co 15:37 perhaps wheat or some other **g**
1Ti 5:18 ox while it treads out the **g**

GRAINFIELDS (*see* GRAIN)
Matt 12: 1 through the **g** on the Sabbath
Mark 2:23 through the **g** on the Sabbath
Luke 6: 1 that He went through the **g**

GRAINS (*see* GRAIN)
Is 48:19 your body like the **g** of sand

GRANDCHILDREN (*see* CHILDREN)
Deut 4: 9 to your children and your **g**
Deut 4:25 When you beget children and **g**
Job 42:16 and **g** for four generations
1Ti 5: 4 any widow has children or **g**

GRANDDAUGHTER (*see* DAUGHTER)
1Ki 15: 2 Maachah the **g** of Abishalom
1Ki 15:10 Maachah the **g** of Abishalom
2Ki 8:26 was Athaliah the **g** of Omri
2Ch 11:20 took Maachah the **g** of Absalom
2Ch 11:21 **g** of Absalom more than all
2Ch 22: 2 was Athaliah the **g** of Omri

GRANDFATHER (*see* FATHER)
2Sa 9: 7 all the land of Saul your **g**

GRANDMOTHER (*see* GRANDMOTHER'S, MOTHER)
1Ki 15:13 his **g** from being queen mother
2Ti 1: 5 dwelt first in your **g** Lois

GRANDMOTHER'S (*see* GRANDMOTHER)
1Ki 15:10 His **g** name was Maachah the

GRANDSON (*see* GRANDSONS, SON)
Gen 11:31 his son Abram and his **g** Lot
Deut 6: 2 you and your son and your **g**
Judg 8:22 and your son, and your **g** also
1Ch 7:15 of Gilead's **g** was Zelophehad

GRANDSONS (*see* GRANDSON)
Judg 12:14 He had forty sons and thirty **g**
1Ch 8:40 They had many sons and **g**, one

GRANT (*see* GRANTED, GRANTING, GRANTS)
Lev 25:24 **g** redemption of the land
Deut 15: 1 shall **g** a release of debts
Deut 28:11 the LORD will **g** you plenty of
Ruth 1: 9 The LORD **g** that you may find
1Sa 1:17 and the God of Israel **g** your
1Ki 8:50 and **g** them compassion before
1Ch 21:22 **G** me the place of this
1Ch 21:22 You shall **g** it to me at the
2Ch 12: 7 them, but I will **g** them some
Neh 1:11 **g** him mercy in the sight of
Esth 5: 8 the king to **g** my petition
Job 6: 8 that God would **g** me the thing
Ps 20: 4 May He **g** you according to
Ps 85: 7 LORD, And **g** us Your salvation
Ps 119:29 And **g** me Your law graciously
Ps 140: 8 Do not **g**, O LORD, the desires
Matt 20:21 **G** that these two sons of mine
Mark 10:37 **G** us that we may sit, one on
Luke 1:74 to **g** us that we, Being
Acts 4:29 **g** to Your servants that with
Rom 15: 5 and comfort **g** you to be
Eph 3:16 that He would **g** you,
2Ti 1:16 The Lord **g** mercy to the
2Ti 1:18 The Lord **g** to him that he may
2Ti 2:25 will **g** them repentance, so
Rev 3:21 **g** to sit with Me on My throne

GRANTED (*see* GRANT)
Gen 25:21 and the LORD **g** his plea, and
Ex 12:36 so that they **g** them what they
1Sa 1:27 the LORD has **g** me my petition
2Sa 14:21 right, I have **g** this thing
1Ch 4:10 So God **g** him what he
2Ch 1:12 and knowledge are **g** to you
Ezra 7: 6 The king **g** him all his
Neh 2: 8 And the king **g** them to me
Esth 5: 6 It shall be **g** you
Esth 7: 2 It shall be **g** you
Esth 9:12 It shall be **g** to you
Esth 9:13 let it be **g** to the Jews who
Job 10:12 You have **g** me life and favor,
Prov 10:24 of the righteous will be **g**
Mark 15:45 he **g** the body to Joseph
Luke 1:43 But why is this **g** to me, that
John 5:26 so He has **g** the Son to have
John 6:65 been **g** to him by My Father
Acts 3:14 for a murderer to be **g** to you
Acts 11:18 Then God has also **g** to the
Acts 27:24 and indeed God has **g** you all
2Co 1:11 the gift **g** to us through many
Phil 1:29 been **g** on behalf of Christ
Phm 22 prayers I shall be **g** to you
Rev 6: 4 it was **g** to the one who sat
Rev 7: 2 it was **g** to harm the earth
Rev 13: 7 it was **g** to him to make war
Rev 13:14 **g** to do in the sight of the
Rev 13:15 He was **g** power to give breath
Rev 19: 8 to her it was **g** to be arrayed

GRANTING (*see* GRANT)
Acts 14: 3 **g** signs and wonders to be done

GRANTS (*see* GRANT)
Ps 113: 9 He **g** the barren woman a home,

GRAPE (*see* GRAPE-GATHERER, GRAPES, GRAPEVINE)
Lev 19:10 every **g** of your vineyard
Num 6: 3 shall he drink any **g** juice
Job 15:33 off his unripe **g** like a vine
Song 7:12 whether the **g** blossoms are
Is 18: 5 the sour **g** is ripening in the

GRAPE-GATHERER (*see* GRAPE, GRAPE-GATHERERS)
Jer 6: 9 as a **g**, put your hand back

GRAPE-GATHERERS (*see* GRAPE-GATHERER)
Jer 49: 9 If **g** came to you, would they
Obad 5 If **g** had come to you, would

GRAPES (*see* GRAPE)
Gen 40:10 clusters brought forth ripe **g**
Gen 40:11 and I took the **g** and pressed
Gen 49:11 his clothes in the blood of **g**
Lev 25: 5 nor gather the **g** of your
Lev 25:11 nor gather the **g** of your
Num 6: 3 nor eat fresh **g** or raisins
Num 13:20 season of the first ripe **g**
Num 13:23 branch with one cluster of **g**
Deut 23:24 fill of **g** at your pleasure
Deut 24:21 gather the **g** of your vineyard
Deut 28:30 but shall not gather its **g**
Deut 28:39 of the wine nor gather the **g**
Deut 32:14 wine, the blood of the **g**
Deut 32:32 their **g** are **g** of gall,
Judg 8: 2 **g** of Ephraim better than the
Judg 9:27 and gathered **g** from their
Neh 13:15 loading donkeys with wine, **g**
Song 2:13 tender **g** give a good smell
Song 2:15 for our vines have tender **g**
Is 5: 2 it to bring forth good **g**, but
Is 5: 2 but it brought forth wild **g**
Is 5: 4 it to bring forth good **g**, did
Is 5: 4 did it bring forth wild **g**
Is 17: 6 Yet gleaning **g** will be left
Is 24:13 like the gleaning of **g** when
Jer 8:13 shall be no **g** on the vine
Jer 25:30 as those who tread the **g**
Jer 31:29 The fathers have eaten sour **g**
Jer 31:30 every man who eats the sour **g**
Jer 49: 9 not leave some gleaning **g**
Ezek 18: 2 The fathers have eaten sour **g**
Hos 9:10 like **g** in the wilderness
Amos 9:13 the treader of **g** him who sows
Mic 7: 1 those who glean vintage **g**
Matt 7:16 Do men gather **g** from
Luke 6:44 nor do they gather **g** from a
Rev 14:18 for her **g** are fully ripe

GRAPEVINE (*see* GRAPE, VINE)
Num 6: 4 that is produced by the **g**
Jas 3:12 bear olives, or a **g** bear figs

GRASP (*see* GRASPED, GRASPING, GRASPS)
Eccl 7:18 It is good that you **g** this
Zech 8:23 of the nations shall **g** the

GRASPED (*see* GRASP)
2Sa 2:16 each one **g** his opponent by
1Ki 20:33 they quickly **g** at this word
Ezek 21:15 it is **g** for slaughter

GRASPING (*see* GRASP)
Eccl 1:14 is vanity and **g** for the wind
Eccl 1:17 this also is **g** for the wind
Eccl 2:11 was vanity and **g** for the wind
Eccl 2:17 is vanity and **g** for the wind
Eccl 2:26 is vanity and **g** for the wind
Eccl 4: 4 is vanity and **g** for the wind
Eccl 4: 6 with toil and **g** for the wind
Eccl 4:16 is vanity and **g** for the wind
Eccl 6: 9 is vanity and **g** for the wind

GRASPS (*see* GRASP)
Prov 27:16 **g** oil with his right hand
Prov 30:28 skillfully **g** with its hands

GRASS (*see* GRASSHOPPER)
Gen 1:11 Let the earth bring forth **g**
Gen 1:12 And the earth brought forth **g**
Num 22: 4 licks up the **g** of the field
Deut 11:15 I will send **g** in your fields
Deut 29:23 nor does any **g** grow there
Deut 32: 2 herb, and as showers on the **g**
2Sa 23: 4 Like the tender **g** springing
1Ki 18: 5 may find **g** to keep the horses
2Ki 19:26 were as the **g** of the field
2Ki 19:26 as the **g** on the housetops and
Job 5:25 like the **g** of the earth
Job 6: 5 donkey bray when it has **g**
Job 38:27 forth the growth of tender **g**
Job 40:15 he eats **g** like an ox
Ps 37: 2 soon be cut down like the **g**
Ps 72: 6 like rain upon the mown **g**
Ps 72:16 flourish like **g** of the earth
Ps 90: 5 are like **g** which grows up
Ps 92: 7 the wicked spring up like **g**
Ps 102: 4 stricken and withered like **g**
Ps 102:11 And I wither away like **g**
Ps 103:15 for man, his days are like **g**
Ps 104:14 He causes the **g** to grow for
Ps 106:20 image of an ox that eats **g**
Ps 129: 6 be as the **g** on the housetops
Ps 147: 8 Who makes **g** to grow on the
Prov 19:12 favor is like dew on the **g**
Prov 27:25 the tender **g** shows itself, and
Is 15: 6 For the green **g** has withered
Is 15: 6 the **g** fails, there is nothing
Is 35: 7 there shall be **g** with reeds
Is 37:27 were as the **g** of the field
Is 37:27 as the **g** on the housetops and
Is 40: 6 All flesh is **g**, and all its
Is 40: 7 The **g** withers, the flower
Is 40: 7 surely the people are **g**
Is 40: 8 The **g** withers, the flower
Is 44: 4 the **g** like willows by the
Is 51:12 a man who will be made like **g**
Is 66:14 bones shall flourish like **g**
Jer 14: 5 left because there was no **g**
Jer 14: 6 failed because there was no **g**
Dan 4:15 in the tender **g** of the field
Dan 4:15 beasts on the **g** of the earth
Dan 4:23 in the tender **g** of the field
Dan 4:25 make you eat **g** like oxen
Dan 4:32 make you eat **g** like oxen
Dan 4:33 from men and ate **g** like oxen
Dan 5:21 They fed him with **g** like oxen
Amos 7: 2 eating the **g** of the land,
Mic 5: 7 LORD, like showers on the **g**
Zech 10: 1 **g** in the field for everyone
Matt 6:30 so clothes the **g** of the field
Matt 14:19 to sit down on the **g**
Mark 6:39 down in groups on the green **g**
Luke 12:28 If then God so clothes the **g**
John 6:10 there was much **g** in the place
Jas 1:11 heat than it withers the **g**
1Pe 1:24 All flesh is as **g**, and all the
1Pe 1:24 of man as the flower of the **g**
1Pe 1:24 The **g** withers, and its flower
Rev 8: 7 all green **g** was burned up
Rev 9: 4 to harm the **g** of the earth

GRASSHOPPER (*see* GRASS, GRASSHOPPERS)
Lev 11:22 kind, and the **g** after its kind
Eccl 12: 5 the **g** is a burden, and desire

GRASSHOPPERS (*see* GRASSHOPPER)
Num 13:33 we were like **g** in our own
1Ki 8:37 or mildew, locusts or **g**
2Ch 6:28 or mildew, locusts or **g**
Is 40:22 and its inhabitants are like **g**
Jer 46:23 and more numerous than **g**
Nah 3:17 and your captains like great **g**

GRATE (*see* GRATING)
Ex 27: 4 You shall make a **g** for it
Ex 38: 4 he made a **g** of bronze network
Ex 39:39 its **g** of bronze, its poles,

GRATEFUL
Jon 4: 6 was very **g** for the plant

GRATIFY
Eccl 2: 3 how to **g** my flesh with wine
Mark 15:15 wanting to **g** the crowd,

GRATING (*see* GRATE)
Ex 35:16 offering with its bronze **g**
Ex 38: 5 four corners of the bronze **g**
Ex 38:30 altar, the bronze **g** for it

GRAVE (*see* GRAVECLOTHES, GRAVES, GRAVESTONE)
Gen 35:20 Jacob set a pillar on her **g**
Gen 35:20 of Rachel's **g** to this day
Gen 37:35 the **g** to my son in mourning
Gen 42:38 hair with sorrow to the **g**
Gen 44:29 hair with sorrow to the **g**
Gen 44:31 father with sorrow to the **g**
Gen 50: 5 in my **g** which I dug for
Ex 33: 4 people heard these **g** tidings
Num 19:16 or a bone of a man, or a **g**
Num 19:18 the slain, the dead, or a **g**
Deut 34: 6 one knows his **g** to this day
1Sa 2: 6 He brings down to the **g** and
2Sa 3:32 and wept at the **g** of Abner
2Sa 19:37 buried by the **g** of my father
1Ki 2: 6 go down to the **g** in peace
1Ki 2: 9 hair down to the **g** with blood
1Ki 14:13 who shall come to the **g**,
2Ki 22:20 gathered to your **g** in peace
2Ch 34:28 gathered to your **g** in peace
Job 3:22 glad when they can find the **g**
Job 5:26 come to the **g** at a full age
Job 7: 9 to the **g** does not come up
Job 10:19 from the womb to the **g**
Job 14:13 You would hide me in the **g**
Job 17: 1 the **g** is ready for me
Job 17:13 I wait for the **g** as my house
Job 21:13 in a moment go down to the **g**
Job 21:32 he shall be brought to the **g**
Job 24:19 so should the **g** those who
Ps 6: 5 In the **g** who will give You
Ps 30: 3 brought my soul up from the **g**
Ps 31:17 Let them be silent in the **g**
Ps 49:14 sheep they are laid in the **g**
Ps 49:14 shall be consumed in the **g**
Ps 49:15 soul from the power of the **g**
Ps 88: 3 my life draws near to the **g**
Ps 88: 5 the slain who lie in the **g**
Ps 88:11 be declared in the **g**
Ps 89:48 life from the power of the **g**
Ps 141: 7 at the mouth of the **g**, As
Prov 12:21 No **g** trouble will overtake
Prov 30:16 The **g**, the barren womb, the
Eccl 4: 8 is vanity and a **g** misfortune
Eccl 9:10 in the **g** where you are going
Song 8: 6 jealousy as cruel as the **g**
Is 14:19 you are cast out of your **g**
Is 53: 9 And they made His **g** with the
Jer 20:17 mother might have been my **g**
Ezek 32:23 company is all around her **g**
Ezek 32:24 multitude, all around her **g**
Hos 13:14 them from the power of the **g**
Hos 13:14 O **G**, I will be your
Nah 1:14 I will dig your **g**, for you

GRAVECLOTHES (*see* GRAVE)
John 11:44 out bound hand and foot with **g**

GRAVEL
Prov 20:17 mouth will be filled with **g**
Lam 3:16 also broken my teeth with **g**

GRAVEN
Judg 18:18 house and took the **g** image
Is 30:22 of your **g** images of silver
Is 40:19 The workman molds a **g** image
Is 42: 8 nor My praise to **g** images
Is 44: 9 Those who make a **g** image, all
Is 44:10 a **g** image that profits him
Jer 10:14 put to shame by the **g** image

GRAVES (*see* GRAVE)
Ex 14:11 there were no **g** in Egypt,
2Ki 23: 6 on the **g** of the common people
2Ch 34: 4 and scattered it on the **g** of
Is 65: 4 Who sit among the **g**, and spend
Jer 8: 1 of Jerusalem, out of their **g**
Jer 26:23 the **g** of the common people
Ezek 32:22 with their **g** all around her,
Ezek 32:23 Her **g** are set in the recesses
Ezek 32:25 with her **g** all around it, all
Ezek 32:26 with all their **g** around it
Ezek 37:12 My people, I will open your **g**
Ezek 37:12 you to come up from your **g**
Ezek 37:13 when I have opened your **g**
Ezek 37:13 and brought you up from your **g**
Matt 27:52 and the **g** were opened
Matt 27:53 coming out of the **g** after His
Luke 11:44 For you are like **g** which are
John 5:28 in the **g** will hear His voice
Rev 11: 9 dead bodies to be put into **g**

GRAVESTONE (*see* GRAVE)
2Ki 23:17 What **g** is this that I see

GRAY (*see* GRAY-HAIRED, GRAYHEADED, GRAY-SPOTTED)
Gen 42:38 my **g** hair with sorrow to the
Gen 44:29 my **g** hair with sorrow to the
Gen 44:31 will bring down the **g** hair of
Lev 19:32 rise before the **g** headed and
Deut 32:25 child with the man of **g** hairs
1Ki 2: 6 do not let his **g** hair go down
1Ki 2: 9 but bring his **g** hair down to
Prov 20:29 of old men is their **g** head
Is 46: 4 even to **g** hairs I will carry
Hos 7: 9 **g** hairs are here and there on

GRAY-HAIRED (*see* GRAY)
Job 15:10 Both the **g** and the aged are

GRAYHEADED (*see* GRAY)
1Sa 12: 2 and I am old and **g**, and look, my
Ps 71:18 Now also when I am old and **g**

GRAY-SPOTTED (*see* GRAY)
Gen 31:10 were streaked, speckled, and **g**
Gen 31:12 are streaked, speckled, and **g**

GRAZE (*see* GRAZED)
Is 11: 7 The cow and the bear shall **g**
Dan 4:15 let him **g** with the beasts on
Dan 4:23 let him **g** with the beasts of

GRAZED (*see* GRAZE)
Ex 22: 5 a field or vineyard to be **g**

GREASE
Ps 119:70 Their heart is as fat as **g**

GREAT (*see* GREATER, GREATEST, GREATLY, GREATNESS)
Gen 1:16 Then God made two **g** lights
Gen 1:21 God created **g** sea creatures
Gen 6: 5 of man was **g** in the earth
Gen 7:11 of the **g** deep were broken up
Gen 12: 2 I will make you a **g** nation
Gen 12: 2 bless you and make your name **g**
Gen 12:17 and his house with **g** plagues
Gen 13: 6 **g** that they could not dwell
Gen 15: 1 your exceedingly **g** reward
Gen 15:12 and **g** darkness fell upon him
Gen 15:14 come out with **g** possessions
Gen 15:18 river of Egypt to the **g** river
Gen 17:20 and I will make him a **g** nation
Gen 18:18 shall surely become a **g** and
Gen 18:20 Sodom and Gomorrah is **g**, and
Gen 19:11 blindness, both small and **g**
Gen 19:13 against them has grown **g**
Gen 20: 9 me and on my kingdom a **g** sin
Gen 21: 8 Abraham made a **g** feast on the
Gen 21:18 I will make him a **g** nation
Gen 24:35 greatly, and he has become **g**
Gen 26:14 and a **g** number of servants
Gen 27:34 cried with an exceedingly **g**
Gen 30: 8 With **g** wrestlings I have
Gen 30:30 now increased to a **g** amount
Gen 36: 7 **g** for them to dwell together
Gen 39: 9 can I do this **g** wickedness
Gen 41:29 Indeed seven years of **g**
Gen 45: 7 your lives by a **g** deliverance
Gen 46: 3 make of you a **g** nation there
Gen 48:19 people, and he also shall be **g**
Gen 50: 9 and it was a very **g** gathering
Gen 50:10 they mourned there with a **g**
Ex 3: 3 aside and see this **g** sight
Ex 6: 6 arm and with **g** judgments
Ex 7: 4 land of Egypt by **g** judgments
Ex 11: 3 very **g** in the land of Egypt
Ex 11: 6 Then there shall be a **g** cry
Ex 11: 8 out from Pharaoh in **g** anger
Ex 12:30 there was a **g** cry in Egypt,
Ex 12:38 a **g** deal of livestock
Ex 14:31 Thus Israel saw the **g** work
Ex 18:22 **g** matter they shall bring to
Ex 32:10 I will make of you a **g** nation
Ex 32:11 land of Egypt with **g** power
Ex 32:21 brought so **g** a sin upon them
Ex 32:30 You have sinned a **g** sin
Ex 32:31 people have sinned a **g** sin
Num 11:33 people with a very **g** plague
Num 13:32 in it are men of **g** stature
Num 14:17 let the power of my LORD be **g**
Num 32: 1 very **g** multitude of livestock
Num 34: 6 have the **G** Sea for a border
Num 34: 7 From the **G** Sea you shall mark
Deut 1: 7 as far as the **g** river, the
Deut 1:17 the small as well as the **g**
Deut 1:19 and went through all that **g**
Deut 1:28 the cities are **g** and fortified
Deut 2: 7 through this **g** wilderness
Deut 2:10 in times past, a people as **g**
Deut 2:21 a people as **g** and numerous and
Deut 3: 5 besides a **g** many rural towns
Deut 4: 6 Surely this **g** nation is a
Deut 4: 7 For what **g** nation is there
Deut 4: 8 what **g** nation is there that
Deut 4:32 whether any **g** thing like this
Deut 4:34 by **g** terrors, according to
Deut 4:36 He showed you His **g** fire, and
Deut 5:25 For this **g** fire will consume
Deut 6:22 and wonders before our eyes, **g**
Deut 7:19 the **g** trials which your eyes
Deut 7:21 for the LORD your God, the **g**
Deut 8:15 who led you through that **g**
Deut 9: 1 than yourself, cities **g** and
Deut 9: 2 a people **g** and tall, the
Deut 10:17 and Lord of lords, the **g** God
Deut 10:21 who has done for you these **g**
Deut 11: 7 **g** act of the LORD which He
Deut 18:16 me see this **g** fire anymore
Deut 26: 5 there he became a nation, **g**
Deut 26: 8 with **g** terror and with signs
Deut 28:59 **g** and prolonged plagues
Deut 29: 3 the **g** trials which your eyes
Deut 29: 3 the signs, and those **g** wonders
Deut 29:24 the heat of this **g** anger mean
Deut 29:28 in **g** indignation, and cast
Deut 34:12 all the **g** terror which Moses
Josh 1: 4 Lebanon as far as the **g** river
Josh 1: 4 to the **G** Sea toward the going
Josh 6: 5 shall shout with a **g** shout
Josh 6:20 people shouted with a **g** shout
Josh 7: 9 will You do for Your **g** name
Josh 7:26 over him a **g** heap of stones
Josh 8:29 raise over it a **g** heap of
Josh 9: 1 of the **G** Sea toward Lebanon
Josh 10: 2 because Gibeon was a **g** city
Josh 10:10 Israel, killed them with a **g**
Josh 10:20 them with a very **g** slaughter
Josh 14:12 and that the cities were **g**
Josh 15:12 the coastline of the **G** Sea
Josh 15:47 the **G** Sea with its coastline
Josh 17:14 since we are a **g** people,
Josh 17:15 If you are a **g** people, then
Josh 17:17 **g** people and have **g** power
Josh 22:10 a **g**, impressive altar
Josh 23: 4 as far as the **G** Sea westward
Josh 23: 9 driven out from before you **g**
Josh 24:17 who did those **g** signs in our
Judg 2: 7 who had seen all the **g** works
Judg 5:15 were **g** resolves of heart
Judg 5:16 have **g** searchings of heart
Judg 11:33 with a very **g** slaughter
Judg 12: 2 I were in a **g** struggle with
Judg 15: 8 and thigh with a **g** slaughter
Judg 15:18 said, "You have given this **g**
Judg 16: 5 out where his **g** strength lies
Judg 16: 6 me where your **g** strength lies
Judg 16:15 me where your **g** strength lies
Judg 16:23 together to offer a **g**
Judg 20:38 was that they would make a **g**
Judg 21: 5 For they had made a **g** oath
Ruth 2: 1 husband's, a man of **g** wealth
1Sa 2:17 was very **g** before the LORD
1Sa 4: 6 **g** shout in the camp of the
1Sa 4:10 There was a very **g** slaughter
1Sa 4:17 there has been a **g** slaughter
1Sa 5: 9 with a very **g** destruction
1Sa 5: 9 of the city, both small and **g**
1Sa 6: 9 He has done us this **g** evil
1Sa 6:19 the people with a **g** slaughter
1Sa 12:16 see this **g** thing which the
1Sa 12:17 see that your wickedness is **g**
1Sa 12:22 for His **g** name's sake,
1Sa 12:24 for consider what **g** things He
1Sa 14:15 it was a very **g** trembling
1Sa 14:20 and there was very **g** confusion
1Sa 14:45 this **g** salvation in Israel
1Sa 15:22 Has the LORD as **g** delight in
1Sa 17:25 will enrich with **g** riches
1Sa 19: 5 a **g** salvation for all Israel
1Sa 19:22 came to the **g** well that is at
1Sa 20: 2 **g** or small without first
1Sa 26:13 a **g** distance being between
1Sa 26:25 You shall both do **g** things
1Sa 30: 2 were there, from small to **g**
1Sa 30:16 because of all the **g** spoil
1Sa 30:19 lacking, either small or **g**
2Sa 3:38 a **g** man has fallen this day
2Sa 5:10 So David went on and became **g**
2Sa 7: 9 and have made you a **g** name
2Sa 7: 9 like the name of the **g** men
2Sa 7:19 house for a **g** while to come
2Sa 7:21 have done all these **g** things
2Sa 7:22 Therefore You are **g**, O Lord
2Sa 7:23 for You **g** and awesome
2Sa 12:14 **g** occasion to the enemies of
2Sa 12:30 of the city in **g** abundance
2Sa 18: 7 and a **g** slaughter of twenty
2Sa 18: 9 boughs of a **g** terebinth tree
2Sa 18:29 servant, I saw a **g** tumult
2Sa 21:20 there was a man of **g** stature
2Sa 22:36 Your gentleness has made me **g**
2Sa 23:10 about a **g** victory that day
2Sa 23:12 brought about a **g** victory
2Sa 24:14 to Gad, "I am in **g** distress
2Sa 24:14 LORD, for His mercies are **g**
1Ki 1:40 flutes and rejoiced with **g** joy
1Ki 3: 4 for that was the **g** high place
1Ki 3: 6 You have shown **g** mercy to
1Ki 3: 6 this **g** kindness for him, and
1Ki 3: 8 a **g** people, too numerous to
1Ki 3: 9 judge this **g** people of Yours
1Ki 4:29 exceedingly **g** understanding,
1Ki 5: 7 a wise son over this **g** people
1Ki 7: 9 on the outside to the **g** court
1Ki 7:12 The **g** court was enclosed with
1Ki 8:42 they will hear of Your **g** name
1Ki 8:65 a **g** congregation from the
1Ki 10: 2 with a very **g** retinue, with
1Ki 10:10 gold, spices in **g** abundance
1Ki 10:11 brought **g** quantities of almug
1Ki 10:18 king made a **g** throne of ivory
1Ki 11:19 Hadad found **g** favor in the
1Ki 19: 7 the journey is too **g** for you
1Ki 19:11 the LORD passed by, and a **g**
1Ki 20:13 you seen all this **g** multitude
1Ki 20:21 Syrians with a **g** slaughter
1Ki 20:28 I will deliver all this **g**
1Ki 22:31 Fight with no one small or **g**
2Ki 3:27 and there was **g** indignation
2Ki 5: 1 of the king of Syria, was a **g**
2Ki 5:13 told you to do something **g**
2Ki 6:14 a **g** army there, and they came
2Ki 6:23 prepared a **g** feast for them
2Ki 6:25 And there was a **g** famine in
2Ki 7: 6 the noise of a **g** army
2Ki 8: 4 all the **g** things Elisha has
2Ki 10: 6 were with the **g** men of the
2Ki 10:11 in Jezreel, and all his **g** men
2Ki 10:19 for I have a **g** sacrifice to
2Ki 16:15 On the **g** new altar burn the
2Ki 17:21 and made them commit a **g** sin
2Ki 17:36 land of Egypt with **g** power
2Ki 18:17 with a **g** army against
2Ki 18:19 Thus says the **g** king, the
2Ki 18:28 Hear the word of the **g** king
2Ki 22:13 for **g** is the wrath of the
2Ki 23: 2 the people, both small and **g**
2Ki 23:26 the fierceness of His **g** wrath
2Ki 25: 9 all the houses of the **g** men
2Ki 25:26 And all the people, small and **g**
1Ch 11: 9 David went on and became **g**
1Ch 11:14 saved them by a **g** deliverance
1Ch 11:23 Egyptian, a man of **g** height
1Ch 12:22 him, until it was a **g** army
1Ch 16:25 For the LORD is **g** and greatly
1Ch 17: 8 **g** men who are on the earth
1Ch 17:17 house for a **g** while to come
1Ch 17:19 known all these **g** things
1Ch 17:21 make for Yourself a name by **g**
1Ch 20: 2 of the city in **g** abundance
1Ch 20: 6 there was a man of **g** stature
1Ch 21:13 to Gad, "I am in **g** distress
1Ch 21:13 for His mercies are very **g**
1Ch 22: 8 blood and have made **g** wars
1Ch 25: 8 the small as well as the **g**
1Ch 26: 6 they were men of **g** ability
1Ch 26:13 the small as well as the **g**
1Ch 29: 1 and the work is **g**, because the
1Ch 29:12 in Your hand it is to make **g**
1Ch 29:22 with **g** gladness on that day
2Ch 1: 8 You have shown **g** mercy to
2Ch 1:10 judge this **g** people of Yours
2Ch 2: 5 which I build will be **g**, for
2Ch 2: 9 am about to build shall be **g**
2Ch 4: 9 the **g** court and doors for the
2Ch 4:18 **g** abundance that the weight
2Ch 6:32 for the sake of Your **g** name
2Ch 7: 8 a very **g** congregation from
2Ch 9: 1 having a very **g** retinue,
2Ch 9: 9 gold, spices in **g** abundance
2Ch 9:17 king made a **g** throne of ivory
2Ch 13: 8 and you are a **g** multitude, and
2Ch 13:17 them with a **g** slaughter
2Ch 15: 5 but **g** turmoil was on all the
2Ch 15: 9 in **g** numbers from Israel when
2Ch 15:13 to death, whether small or **g**
2Ch 16:14 made a very **g** burning for him
2Ch 18:30 Fight with no one small or **g**
2Ch 20: 2 A **g** multitude is coming
2Ch 20:12 **g** multitude that is coming
2Ch 20:15 because of this **g** multitude
2Ch 21: 3 gave them **g** gifts of silver
2Ch 24:24 a very **g** army into their hand
2Ch 25:10 they returned home in **g** anger

2Ch 28: 5 carried away a **g** multitude of
2Ch 28: 5 him with a **g** slaughter
2Ch 28:13 for our guilt is **g**, and there
2Ch 30:13 a very **g** congregation,
2Ch 30:21 seven days with **g** gladness
2Ch 30:24 and a **g** number of priests
2Ch 30:26 So there was **g** joy in
2Ch 31:10 is left is this **g** abundance
2Ch 31:15 to the **g** as well as the small
2Ch 32:27 Hezekiah had very **g** riches
2Ch 33:14 raised it to a very **g** height
2Ch 34:21 for **g** is the wrath of the
2Ch 34:30 Levites, and all the people, **g**
2Ch 36:18 from the house of God, **g** and
Ezra 3:11 people shouted with a **g** shout
Ezra 4:10 of the nations whom the **g**
Ezra 5: 8 to the temple of the **g** God
Ezra 5:11 ago, which a **g** king of Israel
Ezra 9:13 evil deeds and for our **g** guilt
Neh 1: 3 are there in **g** distress and
Neh 1: 5 pray, LORD God of heaven, O **g**
Neh 1:10 have redeemed by Your **g** power
Neh 3:27 next to the **g** projecting
Neh 4:14 Remember the Lord, **g** and
Neh 4:19 The work is **g** and extensive,
Neh 5: 1 there was a **g** outcry of the
Neh 5: 7 So I called a **g** assembly
Neh 6: 3 I am doing a **g** work, so that
Neh 8: 6 blessed the LORD, the **g** God
Neh 8:17 And there was very **g** gladness
Neh 9:18 and worked **g** provocations,
Neh 9:25 themselves in Your **g** goodness
Neh 9:26 they worked **g** provocations
Neh 9:31 Nevertheless in Your **g** mercy
Neh 9:32 Now therefore, our God, the **g**
Neh 9:37 And we are in **g** distress
Neh 11:14 the son of one of the **g** men
Neh 12:43 day they offered **g** sacrifices
Neh 12:43 made them rejoice with **g** joy
Neh 13:27 of your doing all this **g** evil
Esth 1: 5 from **g** to small, in the court
Esth 1:20 all his empire (for it is **g**)
Esth 1:20 honor their husbands, both **g**
Esth 2:18 Then the king made a **g** feast
Esth 4: 3 there was **g** mourning among
Esth 5:11 told them of his **g** riches
Esth 8:15 with a **g** crown of gold and a
Esth 9: 4 For Mordecai was **g** in the
Esth 10: 3 and was **g** among the Jews and
Job 1:19 suddenly a **g** wind came from
Job 2:13 saw that his grief was very **g**
Job 3:19 **g** are there, and the servant
Job 5: 9 Who does **g** things, and
Job 9:10 He does **g** things past finding
Job 12:23 He makes nations **g**, and
Job 22: 5 Is not your wickedness **g**, And
Job 23: 6 with me in His **g** power
Job 30:18 By **g** force my garment is
Job 31:25 because my wealth was **g**, and
Job 31:34 I feared the **g** multitude, and
Job 32: 9 **G** men are not always wise,
Job 36:26 Behold, God is **g**, and we do
Job 37: 5 He does **g** things which we
Job 38:21 the number of your days is **g**
Job 38:32 the **G** Bear with its cubs
Job 39:11 him because his strength is **g**
Ps 14: 5 There they are in **g** fear, For
Ps 18:35 Your gentleness has made me **g**
Ps 18:50 **G** deliverance He gives to His
Ps 19:11 them there is **g** reward
Ps 19:13 innocent of **g** transgression
Ps 21: 5 His glory is **g** in Your
Ps 22:25 of You in the **g** congregation
Ps 25:11 my iniquity, for it is **g**
Ps 31:19 how **g** is Your goodness, Which
Ps 32: 6 Surely in a flood of **g** waters
Ps 33:16 not delivered by **g** strength
Ps 33:17 deliver any by its **g** strength
Ps 35:18 thanks in the **g** congregation
Ps 36: 6 is like the **g** mountains
Ps 36: 6 Your judgments are a **g** deep
Ps 37:35 seen the wicked in **g** power
Ps 40: 9 In the **g** congregation
Ps 40:10 truth From the **g** congregation
Ps 47: 2 He is a **g** King over all the
Ps 48: 1 **G** is the LORD, and greatly to
Ps 48: 2 north, The city of the **g** King
Ps 53: 5 There they are in **g** fear
Ps 68:11 **G** was the company of those
Ps 71:19 You who have done **g** things
Ps 71:20 You, who have shown me **g** and
Ps 76: 1 His name is **g** in Israel
Ps 77:13 Who is so **g** a God as our God
Ps 77:19 Your path in the **g** waters
Ps 80: 5 tears to drink in **g** measure
Ps 86:10 For You are **g**, and do wondrous
Ps 86:13 For **g** is Your mercy toward me
Ps 92: 5 O LORD, how **g** are Your works
Ps 95: 3 For the LORD is the **g** God
Ps 95: 3 the **g** King above all gods
Ps 96: 4 For the LORD is **g** and greatly
Ps 99: 2 The LORD is **g** in Zion, And He
Ps 99: 3 Let them praise Your **g** and
Ps 103:11 So **g** is His mercy toward
Ps 104: 1 O LORD my God, You are very **g**
Ps 104:25 This **g** and wide sea, In which
Ps 104:25 Living things both small and **g**
Ps 106:21 Who had done **g** things in
Ps 107:23 Who do business on **g** waters
Ps 108: 4 mercy is **g** above the heavens
Ps 111: 2 The works of the LORD are **g**
Ps 115:13 the LORD, Both small and **g**
Ps 117: 2 kindness is **g** toward us, And
Ps 119:51 proud have me in **g** derision
Ps 119:156 **G** are Your tender mercies, O
Ps 119:162 As one who finds **g** treasure
Ps 119:165 **G** peace have those who love
Ps 126: 2 has done **g** things for them
Ps 126: 3 LORD has done **g** things for us
Ps 131: 1 concern myself with **g** matters
Ps 135: 5 For I know that the LORD is **g**
Ps 136: 4 Him who alone does **g** wonders
Ps 136: 7 To Him who made **g** lights, For
Ps 136:17 Him who struck down **g** kings
Ps 138: 5 For **g** is the glory of the
Ps 139:17 How **g** is the sum of them
Ps 144: 7 and deliver me out of **g** waters
Ps 145: 3 **G** is the LORD, and greatly to
Ps 145: 7 the memory of Your **g** goodness
Ps 145: 8 Slow to anger and **g** in mercy
Ps 147: 5 **G** is our Lord, and mighty in
Ps 148: 7 You **g** sea creatures and all
Prov 13: 7 poor, yet has **g** riches
Prov 14:29 to wrath has **g** understanding
Prov 15:16 than **g** treasure with trouble
Prov 18: 9 to him who is a **g** destroyer
Prov 18:16 and brings him before **g** men
Prov 19:19 A man of **g** wrath will suffer
Prov 22: 1 chosen rather than **g** riches
Prov 25: 6 stand in the place of **g** men
Prov 26:10 The **g** God who formed all
Prov 28:12 rejoice, there is **g** glory
Prov 28:16 is a **g** oppressor, but he who
Eccl 1:16 heart has understood **g** wisdom
Eccl 2: 4 I made my works **g**, I built
Eccl 2: 9 So I became **g** and excelled
Eccl 2:21 also is vanity and a **g** evil
Eccl 9:13 the sun, and it seemed **g** to me
Eccl 9:14 a **g** king came against it,
Eccl 9:14 and built **g** snares around it
Eccl 10: 4 pacifies **g** offenses
Eccl 10: 6 folly is set in **g** dignity
Song 2: 3 in his shade with **g** delight
Is 5: 9 houses shall be desolate, **g**
Is 9: 2 darkness have seen a **g** light
Is 12: 6 for **g** is the Holy One of
Is 16:14 with all that **g** multitude
Is 21: 7 diligently with **g** care
Is 22: 9 city of David, that it was **g**
Is 23: 3 And on **g** waters the grain of
Is 27: 1 LORD with His severe sword, **g**
Is 27:13 that the **g** trumpet will be
Is 29: 6 and **g** noise, with storm and
Is 30:25 in the day of the **g** slaughter
Is 32: 2 as the shadow of a **g** rock in
Is 33:23 Then the prey of **g** plunder is
Is 34: 6 a **g** slaughter in the land of
Is 36: 2 a **g** army from Lachish to King
Is 36: 4 Thus says the **g** king, the
Is 36:13 Hear the words of the **g** king
Is 38:17 peace that I had **g** bitterness
Is 47: 9 for the **g** abundance of your
Is 51:10 sea, the waters of the **g** deep
Is 53:12 Him a portion with the **g**, and
Is 54: 7 but with **g** mercies I will
Is 54:13 **g** shall be the peace of your
Is 63: 7 the **g** goodness toward the
Jer 4: 6 the north, and **g** destruction
Jer 5: 5 I will go to the **g** men and
Jer 5:27 Therefore they have become **g**
Jer 6: 1 the north, and **g** destruction
Jer 6:22 a **g** nation will be raised
Jer 10: 6 like You, O LORD (You are **g**
Jer 10: 6 and Your name is **g** in might)
Jer 10:22 and a **g** commotion out of the
Jer 11:16 With the noise of a **g** tumult
Jer 13: 9 and the **g** pride of Jerusalem
Jer 16: 6 Both the **g** and the small shall
Jer 16:10 this **g** disaster against us
Jer 21: 5 in anger and fury and **g** wrath
Jer 21: 6 shall die of a **g** pestilence
Jer 22: 8 LORD done so to this **g** city
Jer 25:14 **g** kings shall be served by
Jer 25:32 a **g** whirlwind shall be raised
Jer 26:19 But we are doing **g** evil
Jer 27: 5 on the ground, by My **g** power
Jer 27: 7 **g** kings shall make him serve
Jer 28: 8 many countries and **g** kingdoms
Jer 30: 7 For that day is **g**, so that
Jer 31: 8 a **g** throng shall return there
Jer 32:17 and the earth by Your **g** power
Jer 32:18 the **G**, the Mighty God, whose
Jer 32:19 You are **g** in counsel and
Jer 32:21 arm, and with **g** terror
Jer 32:37 in My fury, and in **g** wrath
Jer 32:42 **g** calamity on this people
Jer 33: 3 answer you, and show you **g**
Jer 36: 7 For **g** is the anger and the
Jer 41:12 they found him by the **g** pool
Jer 44: 7 **g** evil against yourselves
Jer 44:15 a **g** multitude, and all the
Jer 44:26 I have sworn by My **g** name
Jer 45: 5 And do you seek **g** things for
Jer 48: 3 Plundering and **g** destruction
Jer 50: 9 of **g** nations from the north
Jer 50:22 the land, and of **g** destruction
Jer 50:41 and a **g** nation and many kings
Jer 51:54 **g** destruction from the land
Jer 51:55 her waves roar like **g** waters
Jer 52:13 all the houses of the **g** men
Lam 1: 1 Who was **g** among the nations
Lam 3:23 **g** is Your faithfulness
Ezek 1: 4 a **g** cloud with raging fire
Ezek 3:12 me a **g** thunderous voice
Ezek 3:13 them, and a **g** thunderous noise
Ezek 8: 6 the **g** abominations that the
Ezek 9: 9 and Judah is exceedingly **g**
Ezek 13:11 O **g** hailstones, shall fall
Ezek 13:13 and **g** hailstones in fury to
Ezek 17: 3 A **g** eagle with large wings and
Ezek 17: 7 But there was another **g** eagle
Ezek 17: 9 no **g** power or many people
Ezek 17:17 **g** company do anything in the
Ezek 21:14 sword that slays the **g** men
Ezek 24: 9 I too will make the pyre **g**
Ezek 24:12 her **g** scum has not gone from
Ezek 25:17 I will execute **g** vengeance on
Ezek 26:19 you, and **g** waters cover you,
Ezek 28: 5 by your **g** wisdom in trade you
Ezek 29: 3 O **g** monster who lies in the
Ezek 30: 4 and **g** anguish shall be in
Ezek 30: 9 **g** anguish shall come upon
Ezek 30:16 Sin shall have **g** pain, no
Ezek 31: 6 in its shadow all **g** nations
Ezek 31:15 the **g** waters were held back
Ezek 32:13 from beside its **g** waters
Ezek 36:23 And I will sanctify My **g** name
Ezek 37:10 feet, an exceedingly **g** army
Ezek 38: 4 a **g** company with bucklers and
Ezek 38:13 and goods, to take **g** plunder
Ezek 38:15 a **g** company and a mighty army
Ezek 38:19 a **g** earthquake in the land of
Ezek 38:22 rain, **g** hailstones, fire, and
Ezek 39:17 A **g** sacrificial meal on the
Ezek 47: 9 be a very **g** multitude of fish
Ezek 47:10 as the fish of the **G** Sea,
Ezek 47:15 from the **G** Sea, by the road
Ezek 47:19 along the brook to the **G** Sea
Ezek 47:20 west side shall be the **G** Sea
Ezek 48:28 along the brook to the **G** Sea
Dan 2: 6 me gifts, rewards, and **g** honor
Dan 2:31 and behold, a **g** image
Dan 2:31 This **g** image, whose splendor
Dan 2:35 the image became a **g** mountain
Dan 2:45 the **g** God has made known to
Dan 2:48 and gave him many **g** gifts
Dan 4: 3 How **g** are His signs, and how
Dan 4:10 earth, and its height was **g**
Dan 4:30 Is not this **g** Babylon, that I
Dan 5: 1 Belshazzar the king made a **g**

Dan 7: 2 were stirring up the **G** Sea
Dan 7: 3 four **g** beasts came up from
Dan 7:17 Those **g** beasts, which are
Dan 8: 4 to his will and became **g**
Dan 8: 8 the male goat grew very **g**
Dan 8: 9 **g** toward the south, toward
Dan 9: 4 O Lord, **g** and awesome God,
Dan 9:12 bringing upon us a **g** disaster
Dan 9:18 but because of Your **g** mercies
Dan 10: 4 by the side of the **g** river
Dan 10: 7 but a **g** terror fell upon them
Dan 10: 8 when I saw this **g** vision, and
Dan 11: 3 shall rule with **g** dominion
Dan 11: 5 shall be a **g** dominion
Dan 11:10 a multitude of **g** forces
Dan 11:11 shall muster a **g** multitude
Dan 11:13 of some years with a **g** army
Dan 11:25 of the South with a **g** army
Dan 11:25 up to battle with a very **g**
Dan 11:28 to his land with **g** riches
Dan 11:32 and carry out **g** exploits
Dan 11:44 go out with **g** fury to destroy
Dan 12: 1 the **g** prince who stands watch
Hos 1: 2 **g** harlotry by departing from
Hos 1:11 for **g** will be the day of
Hos 8:12 him the **g** things of My law
Hos 9: 7 of your iniquity and **g** enmity
Hos 10:15 because of your **g** wickedness
Hos 13: 5 in the land of **g** drought
Joel 2: 2 a people come, **g** and strong,
Joel 2:11 army, for His camp is very **g**
Joel 2:11 For the day of the LORD is **g**
Joel 2:13 to anger, and of **g** kindness
Joel 2:25 my **g** army which I sent among
Joel 2:31 before the coming of the **g**
Joel 3:13 for their wickedness is **g**
Amos 3: 9 see **g** tumults in her midst,
Amos 3:15 the **g** houses shall have an
Amos 6: 2 from there go to Hamath the **g**
Amos 6:11 break the **g** house into bits
Amos 7: 4 and it consumed the **g** deep
Jon 1: 2 go to Nineveh, that **g** city
Jon 1: 4 sent out a **g** wind on the sea
Jon 1:12 For I know that this **g**
Jon 1:17 a **g** fish to swallow Jonah
Jon 3: 2 go to Nineveh, that **g** city
Jon 3: 3 was an exceedingly **g** city
Jon 4:11 not pity Nineveh, that **g** city
Mic 5: 4 for now He shall be **g** to the
Mic 7: 3 the **g** man utters his evil
Nah 1: 3 **g** in power, and will not at
Nah 3: 3 slain, a **g** number of bodies,
Nah 3:10 all her **g** men were bound in
Nah 3:17 captains like **g** grasshoppers
Hab 3:15 through the heap of **g** waters
Zeph 1:14 The **g** day of the LORD is near
Zech 1:14 and for Zion with **g** zeal
Zech 4: 7 Who are you, O **g** mountain
Zech 7:12 Thus **g** wrath came from the
Zech 8: 2 zealous for Zion with **g** zeal
Zech 8: 2 with **g** fervor I am zealous
Zech 8: 4 in his hand because of **g** age
Zech 9:17 for how **g** is their goodness
Zech 9:17 And how **g** their beauty
Zech 12:11 be a **g** mourning in Jerusalem
Zech 14:13 to pass in that day that a **g**
Zech 14:14 and apparel in **g** abundance
Mal 1:11 my name shall be **g** among the
Mal 1:11 shall be **g** among the nations
Mal 1:14 for I am a **g** King," says the
Mal 4: 5 before the coming of the **g**
Matt 2:10 with exceedingly **g** joy
Matt 2:18 **g** mourning, Rachel weeping
Matt 4:16 sat in darkness saw a **g** light
Matt 4:25 **g** multitudes followed Him
Matt 5:12 glad, for **g** is your reward in
Matt 5:19 he shall be called **g** in the
Matt 5:35 it is the city of the **g** King
Matt 6:23 how **g** is that darkness
Matt 7:27 And **g** was its fall
Matt 8: 1 **g** multitudes followed Him
Matt 8:10 I have not found such **g** faith
Matt 8:18 Now when Jesus saw **g**
Matt 8:24 suddenly a **g** tempest arose on
Matt 8:26 And there was a **g** calm
Matt 12:15 **g** multitudes followed Him, and
Matt 12:40 in the belly of the **g** fish
Matt 13: 2 **g** multitudes were gathered
Matt 13:46 found one pearl of **g** price
Matt 14:14 went out He saw a **g** multitude
Matt 15:28 O woman, **g** is your faith
Matt 15:30 Then **g** multitudes came to Him
Matt 15:33 to fill such a **g** multitude
Matt 19: 2 **g** multitudes followed Him, and
Matt 19:22 for he had **g** possessions
Matt 20:25 and those who are **g** exercise
Matt 20:26 desires to become **g** among you
Matt 20:29 a **g** multitude followed Him
Matt 21: 8 a very **g** multitude spread
Matt 22:36 which is the **g** commandment in
Matt 22:38 is the first and **g** commandment
Matt 24:21 there will be **g** tribulation
Matt 24:24 show **g** signs and wonders, so
Matt 24:30 heaven with power and **g** glory
Matt 24:31 with a **g** sound of a trumpet
Matt 26:47 with a **g** multitude with
Matt 28: 2 there was a **g** earthquake
Matt 28: 8 **g** joy, and ran to bring His
Mark 3: 7 a **g** multitude from Galilee
Mark 3: 8 a **g** multitude, when they
Mark 4: 1 a **g** multitude was gathered to
Mark 4:37 a **g** windstorm arose, and the
Mark 4:39 ceased and there was a **g** calm
Mark 5:19 tell them what **g** things the
Mark 5:21 a **g** multitude gathered to Him
Mark 5:24 a **g** multitude followed Him and
Mark 5:42 overcome with **g** amazement
Mark 6:34 out, saw a **g** multitude and was
Mark 8: 1 the multitude being very **g**
Mark 9:14 He saw a **g** multitude around
Mark 10:22 for he had **g** possessions
Mark 10:42 and their **g** ones exercise
Mark 10:43 **g** among you shall be your
Mark 10:46 and a **g** multitude, blind
Mark 13: 2 Do you see these **g** buildings
Mark 13:26 in the clouds with **g** power
Mark 14:43 with a **g** multitude with
Luke 1:15 For he will be **g** in the sight
Luke 1:32 He will be **g**, and will be
Luke 1:49 has done **g** things for me, and
Luke 1:58 Lord had shown **g** mercy to her
Luke 2:10 of **g** joy which will be to all
Luke 2:36 She was of a **g** age, and had
Luke 4:25 and there was a **g** famine
Luke 5: 6 they caught a **g** number of
Luke 5:15 **g** multitudes came together to
Luke 5:29 Then Levi gave Him a **g** feast
Luke 5:29 there were a **g** number of tax
Luke 6:17 a **g** multitude of people from
Luke 6:23 your reward is **g** in heaven
Luke 6:35 and your reward will be **g**, and
Luke 6:49 the ruin of that house was **g**
Luke 7: 9 I have not found such **g** faith
Luke 7:16 A **g** prophet has risen up
Luke 8: 4 And when a **g** multitude had
Luke 8:37 they were seized with **g** fear
Luke 8:39 tell what **g** things God has
Luke 8:39 the whole city what **g** things
Luke 9:37 that a **g** multitude met Him
Luke 9:39 from him with **g** difficulty
Luke 9:48 least among you all will be **g**
Luke 10: 2 The harvest truly is **g**, but
Luke 10:13 have repented a **g** while ago
Luke 14:16 A certain man gave a **g** supper
Luke 14:25 **g** multitudes went with Him
Luke 14:32 other is still a **g** way off
Luke 15:20 when he was still a **g** way off
Luke 16:26 you there is a **g** gulf fixed
Luke 21:11 there will be **g** earthquakes
Luke 21:11 sights and **g** signs from heaven
Luke 21:23 For there will be **g** distress
Luke 21:27 a cloud with power and **g** glory
Luke 22:44 His sweat became like **g** drops
Luke 23:27 a **g** multitude of the people
Luke 24:52 to Jerusalem with **g** joy,
John 5: 3 In these lay a **g** multitude of
John 6: 2 Then a **g** multitude followed
John 6: 5 seeing a **g** multitude coming
John 6:18 because a **g** wind was blowing
John 7:37 day, that **g** day of the feast,
John 12: 9 Then a **g** many of the Jews
John 12:12 The next day a **g** multitude
Acts 2:20 before the coming of the **g**
Acts 4:33 with **g** power the apostles
Acts 4:33 **g** grace was upon them all
Acts 5: 5 So **g** fear came upon all those
Acts 5:11 So **g** fear came upon all the
Acts 6: 7 a **g** many of the priests were
Acts 6: 8 did **g** wonders and signs among
Acts 7:11 **g** trouble came over all the
Acts 8: 1 At that time a **g** persecution
Acts 8: 2 made **g** lamentation over him
Acts 8: 8 there was **g** joy in that city
Acts 8: 9 that he was someone **g**,
Acts 8:10 man is the **g** power of God
Acts 8:27 a eunuch of **g** authority under
Acts 10:11 and an object like a **g** sheet
Acts 11: 5 descending like a **g** sheet
Acts 11:21 a **g** number believed and turned
Acts 11:24 a **g** many people were added to
Acts 11:26 and taught a **g** many people
Acts 11:28 there was going to be a **g**
Acts 14: 1 so spoke that a **g** multitude
Acts 15: 3 they caused **g** joy to all the
Acts 16:26 there was a **g** earthquake, so
Acts 17: 4 a **g** multitude of the devout
Acts 19:23 a **g** commotion about the Way
Acts 19:27 of the **g** goddess Diana may be
Acts 19:28 **G** is Diana of the Ephesians
Acts 19:34 **G** is Diana of the Ephesians
Acts 19:35 of the **g** goddess Diana, and of
Acts 21:40 And when there was a **g** silence
Acts 22: 6 noon, suddenly a **g** light from
Acts 23:10 there arose a **g** dissension
Acts 23:14 a **g** oath that we will eat
Acts 24: 2 through you we enjoy **g** peace
Acts 24: 7 with **g** violence took him out
Acts 25:23 Bernice had come with **g** pomp
Acts 26:22 witnessing both to small and **g**
Acts 28:29 and had a **g** dispute among
Rom 9: 2 that I have **g** sorrow and
Rom 15:23 having a **g** desire these many
1Co 9:11 is it a **g** thing if we reap
1Co 16: 9 For a **g** and effective door has
2Co 1:10 us from so **g** a death, and does
2Co 3:12 we use **g** boldness of speech
2Co 7: 4 **G** is my boldness of speech
2Co 7: 4 you, **g** is my boasting on your
2Co 8: 2 that in a **g** trial of
2Co 8:22 because of the **g** confidence
2Co 11:15 Therefore it is no **g** thing if
Eph 2: 4 because of His **g** love with
Eph 5:32 This is a **g** mystery, but I
Col 2: 1 a **g** conflict I have for you
Col 4:13 that he has a **g** zeal for you
1Th 2:17 see your face with **g** desire
1Ti 3:13 **g** boldness in the faith which
1Ti 3:16 without controversy **g** is the
1Ti 6: 6 with contentment is **g** gain
2Ti 2:20 But in a **g** house there are
Tit 2:13 appearing of our **g** God and
Phm 7 For we have **g** joy and
Heb 2: 3 we neglect so **g** a salvation
Heb 4:14 **g** High Priest who has passed
Heb 7: 4 consider how **g** this man was
Heb 10:32 you endured a **g** struggle with
Heb 10:35 which has **g** reward
Heb 12: 1 by so **g** a cloud of witnesses
Heb 13:20 that **g** Shepherd of the sheep,
Jas 3: 5 member and boasts **g** things
Jas 3: 5 See how **g** a forest a little
2Pe 1: 4 given to us exceedingly **g**
2Pe 2:18 For when they speak **g**
2Pe 3:10 will pass away with a **g** noise
Jude 6 for the judgment of the **g** day
Jude 16 they mouth **g** swelling words,
Rev 2:22 with her into **g** tribulation
Rev 6: 4 was given to him a **g** sword
Rev 6:12 there was a **g** earthquake
Rev 6:15 kings of the earth, the **g** men
Rev 6:17 For the **g** day of His wrath
Rev 7: 9 a **g** multitude which no one
Rev 7:14 come out of the **g** tribulation
Rev 8: 8 something like a **g** mountain
Rev 8:10 a **g** star fell from heaven,
Rev 9: 2 like the smoke of a **g** furnace
Rev 9:14 at the **g** river Euphrates
Rev 11: 8 lie in the street of the **g**
Rev 11:11 **g** fear fell on those who saw
Rev 11:13 hour there was a **g** earthquake
Rev 11:17 You have taken Your **g** power
Rev 11:18 fear Your name, small and **g**
Rev 11:19 an earthquake, and **g** hail
Rev 12: 1 Now a **g** sign appeared in
Rev 12: 3 behold, a **g**, fiery red dragon
Rev 12: 9 So the **g** dragon was cast out,
Rev 12:12 down to you, having **g** wrath
Rev 12:14 given two wings of a **g** eagle
Rev 13: 2 his throne, and **g** authority
Rev 13: 5 a mouth speaking **g** things

Rev 13:13 He performs g signs, so that
Rev 13:16 causes all, both small and g
Rev 14: 8 is fallen, that g city,
Rev 14:19 threw it into the g winepress
Rev 15: 1 saw another sign in heaven, g
Rev 15: 3 G and marvelous are Your
Rev 16: 9 men were scorched with g heat
Rev 16:12 bowl on the g river Euphrates
Rev 16:14 of that g day of God Almighty
Rev 16:18 and there was a g earthquake
Rev 16:18 and g earthquake as had not
Rev 16:19 Now the g city was divided
Rev 16:19 g Babylon was remembered
Rev 16:21 g hail from heaven fell upon
Rev 16:21 that plague was exceedingly g
Rev 17: 1 the g harlot who sits on many
Rev 17: 5 BABYLON THE G, THE
Rev 17: 6 I marveled with g amazement
Rev 17:18 g city which reigns over the
Rev 18: 1 having g authority, and the
Rev 18: 2 Babylon the g is fallen, is
Rev 18:10 that g city Babylon, that
Rev 18:16 that g city that was clothed
Rev 18:17 For in one hour such g
Rev 18:18 What is like this g city
Rev 18:19 Alas, alas, that g city
Rev 18:21 up a stone like a g millstone
Rev 18:21 the g city Babylon shall be
Rev 18:23 were the g men of the earth
Rev 19: 1 of a g multitude in heaven
Rev 19: 2 g harlot who corrupted the
Rev 19: 5 who fear Him, both small and g
Rev 19: 6 the voice of a g multitude
Rev 19:17 for the supper of the g God
Rev 19:18 and slave, both small and g
Rev 20: 1 pit and a g chain in his hand
Rev 20:11 Then I saw a g white throne
Rev 20:12 And I saw the dead, small and g
Rev 21:10 me away in the Spirit to a g
Rev 21:10 and showed me the g city, the
Rev 21:12 Also she had a g and high wall
Rev 21:16 length is as g as its breadth

GREATER (*see* GREAT)
Gen 1:16 the g light to rule the day,
Gen 4:13 is g than I can bear
Gen 39: 9 There is no one g in this
Gen 41:40 throne will I be g than you
Gen 48:19 brother shall be g than he
Ex 18:11 LORD is g than all the gods
Num 14:12 I will make of you a nation g
Deut 1:28 The people are g and taller
Deut 4:38 out from before you nations g
Deut 7: 1 Jebusites, seven nations g
Deut 7:17 These nations are g than I
Deut 9: 1 go in to dispossess nations g
Deut 9:14 mightier and g than they
Deut 11:23 you, and you will dispossess g
Josh 10: 2 and because it was g than Ai
Josh 11: 8 and chased them to G Sidon
Josh 19:28 and Kanah, as far as G Sidon
1Sa 14:30 a much g slaughter among the
2Sa 13:15 g than the love with which he
1Ki 1:37 make his throne g than the
1Ki 1:47 his throne g than your throne
2Ch 2: 5 our God is g than all gods
Job 33:12 you, for God is g than man
Eccl 2: 7 I had g possessions of herds
Lam 4: 6 daughter of my people is g
Ezek 8: 6 you will see g abominations
Ezek 8:13 you will see g abominations
Ezek 8:15 you will see g abominations
Dan 7:20 was g than his fellows
Dan 11:13 a multitude g than the former
Amos 6: 2 g than your territory
Hag 2: 9 shall be g than the former
Zech 12: 7 become g than that of Judah
Matt 11:11 one g than John the Baptist
Matt 11:11 of heaven is g than he
Matt 12: 6 is One g than the temple
Matt 12:41 indeed a g than Jonah is here
Matt 12:42 indeed a g than Solomon is
Matt 13:32 grown it is g than the herbs
Matt 23:14 will receive g condemnation
Matt 23:17 For which is g, the gold or
Matt 23:19 For which is g, the gift or
Mark 4:32 becomes g than all herbs, and
Mark 12:31 commandment g than these
Mark 12:40 will receive g condemnation
Luke 7:28 not a g prophet than John the
Luke 7:28 kingdom of God is g than he
Luke 11:31 indeed a g than Solomon is
Luke 11:32 indeed a g than Jonah is here
Luke 12:18 pull down my barns and build g
Luke 20:47 will receive g condemnation
Luke 22:27 For who is g, he who sits at
John 1:50 You will see g things than
John 4:12 Are You g than our father
John 5:20 show Him g works than these
John 5:36 But I have a g witness than
John 8:53 Are You g than our father
John 10:29 them to Me, is g than all
John 13:16 is not g than his master
John 13:16 sent g than he who sent him
John 14:12 g works than these he will do
John 14:28 for My Father is g than I
John 15:13 G love has no one than this,
John 15:20 is not g than his master
John 19:11 Me to you has the g sin
Acts 15:28 to lay upon you no g burden
1Co 12:23 on these we bestow g honor
1Co 12:23 parts have g modesty,
1Co 12:24 having given g honor to that
1Co 14: 5 is g than he who speaks with
1Co 15: 6 of whom the g part remain to
2Co 7:15 his affections are g for you
Heb 6:13 He could swear by no one g
Heb 6:16 For men indeed swear by the g
Heb 9:11 things to come, with the g
Heb 11:26 the reproach of Christ g
2Pe 2:11 who are g in power and might,
1Jn 3:20 God is g than our heart, and
1Jn 4: 4 g than he who is in the world
1Jn 5: 9 men, the witness of God is g
3Jn 4 I have no g joy than to hear

GREATEST (*see* GREAT)
Josh 14:15 for Arba was the g man among
1Ch 12:14 the g was over a thousand
1Ch 12:29 thousand (until then the g
Jer 6:13 of them even to the g of them
Jer 8:10 to the g everyone is given to
Jer 31:34 of them to the g of them,"
Jer 42: 1 from the least to the g,
Jer 42: 8 from the least even to the g
Jer 44:12 die, from the least to the g
Jon 3: 5 from the g to the least of
Matt 18: 1 Who then is g in the kingdom
Matt 18: 4 g in the kingdom of heaven
Matt 23:11 But he who is g among you
Mark 9:34 themselves who would be the g
Luke 9:46 to which of them would be g
Luke 22:24 should be considered the g
Luke 22:26 he who is g among you, let
Acts 8:10 heed, from the least to the g
1Co 13:13 but the g of these is love
Heb 8:11 of them to the g of them

GREATLY (*see* GREAT)
Gen 3:16 I will g multiply your sorrow
Gen 7:18 g increased on the earth, and
Gen 24:35 LORD has blessed my master g
Gen 31:30 you g long for your father's
Gen 32: 7 So Jacob was g afraid and
Ex 19:18 the whole mountain quaked g
Num 11:10 of the LORD was g aroused
Num 14:39 and the people mourned g
Num 22:17 I will certainly honor you g
Num 24:11 I said I would g honor you
Deut 6: 3 that you may multiply g as
Deut 15: 4 for the LORD will g bless you
Deut 17:17 nor shall he g multiply
Josh 10: 2 that they feared g, because
Judg 2:15 And they were g distressed
Judg 6: 6 So Israel was g impoverished
1Sa 11: 6 and his anger was g aroused
1Sa 11:15 the men of Israel rejoiced g
1Sa 12:18 all the people g feared the
1Sa 15:11 I g regret that I have set up
1Sa 16:21 And he loved him g, and he
1Sa 17:11 were dismayed and g afraid
1Sa 28: 5 and his heart trembled g
1Sa 30: 6 Then David was g distressed
1Sa 31: 4 not, for he was g afraid
2Sa 10: 5 the men were g ashamed
2Sa 12: 5 Then David's anger was g
2Sa 24:10 I have sinned g in what I
1Ki 5: 7 Solomon, that he rejoiced g
1Ki 18: 3 Now Obadiah feared the LORD g
2Ki 6:11 was g troubled by this thing
1Ch 4:38 father's house increased g
1Ch 10: 4 not, for he was g afraid
1Ch 16:25 is great and g to be praised
1Ch 19: 5 the men were g ashamed
1Ch 21: 8 I have sinned g, because I
1Ch 29: 9 and King David also rejoiced g
2Ch 25:10 was g aroused against Judah
2Ch 33:12 humbled himself g before the
Neh 8:12 to send portions and rejoice g
Job 3:25 For the thing I g feared has
Ps 6: 3 My soul also is g troubled
Ps 6:10 be ashamed and g troubled
Ps 21: 1 how g shall he rejoice
Ps 28: 7 Therefore my heart g rejoices
Ps 38: 6 troubled, I am bowed down g
Ps 45:11 So the King will g desire
Ps 47: 9 He is g exalted
Ps 48: 1 g to be praised In the city
Ps 62: 2 I shall not be g moved
Ps 65: 9 and water it, You g enrich it
Ps 71:23 My lips shall g rejoice when
Ps 78:59 And g abhorred Israel,
Ps 89: 7 God is g to be feared in the
Ps 96: 4 is great and g to be praised
Ps 105:24 And He increased His people g
Ps 107:38 them, and they multiply g
Ps 109:30 I will g praise the LORD with
Ps 112: 1 LORD, Who delights g in His
Ps 116:10 I spoke, "I am g afflicted
Ps 145: 3 the LORD, and g to be praised
Prov 23:24 the righteous will g rejoice
Eccl 8: 6 the misery of man increases g
Is 42:17 back, they shall be g ashamed
Is 61:10 I will g rejoice in the LORD,
Jer 3: 1 not that land be g polluted
Jer 4:10 Surely You have g deceived
Jer 9:19 We are g ashamed, because we
Jer 20:11 They will be g ashamed, for
Ezek 20:13 they g defiled My Sabbaths
Ezek 25:12 has g offended by avenging
Ezek 27:35 their kings will be g afraid
Dan 5: 9 Belshazzar was g troubled
Dan 6:14 was g displeased with himself
Dan 7:28 my thoughts g troubled me
Dan 9:23 you, for you are g beloved
Dan 10:11 man g beloved, understand the
Dan 10:19 O man g beloved, fear not
Obad 2 you shall be g despised
Zech 9: 9 Rejoice g, O daughter of Zion
Matt 17: 6 their faces and were g afraid
Matt 27:14 that the governor marveled g
Matt 27:54 had happened, they feared g
Mark 6:51 And they were g amazed in
Mark 9: 6 say, for they were g afraid
Mark 9:15 all the people were g amazed
Mark 9:26 cried out, convulsed him g
Mark 10:14 He was g displeased and said
Mark 10:41 they began to be g displeased
Mark 12:27 You are therefore g mistaken
Luke 2: 9 them, and they were g afraid
Luke 24: 4 as they were g perplexed
John 3:29 rejoices g because of the
Acts 3:11 is called Solomon's, g amazed
Acts 4: 2 being g disturbed that they
Acts 6: 7 multiplied g in Jerusalem
Acts 16:18 g annoyed, turned and said to
Acts 18:27 he g helped those who had
2Co 10:15 we shall be g enlarged by you
Phil 1: 8 how g I long for you all with
Phil 4:10 g that now at last your care
1Th 3: 6 g desiring to see us, as we
2Ti 1: 4 g desiring to see you, being
2Ti 4:15 for he has g resisted our
1Pe 1: 6 In this you g rejoice, though
2Jn 4 I rejoiced g that I have
3Jn 3 For I rejoiced g when

GREATNESS (*see* GREAT)
Ex 15: 7 in the g of Your excellence
Ex 15:16 by the g of Your arm they
Num 14:19 to the g of Your mercy, just
Deut 3:24 to show Your servant Your g
Deut 5:24 shown us His glory and His g
Deut 9:26 have redeemed through Your g
Deut 11: 2 of the LORD your God, His g
Deut 32: 3 ascribe g to our God
1Ch 17:19 You have done all this g
1Ch 29:11 Yours, O LORD, is the g, the
2Ch 9: 6 the half of the g of your
Neh 13:22 to the g of Your mercy
Esth 10: 2 account of the g of Mordecai
Ps 66: 3 Through the g of Your power
Ps 71:21 You shall increase my g, And

Ps 79:11 According to the **g** of Your
Ps 145: 3 And His **g** is unsearchable
Ps 145: 6 And I will declare Your **g**
Ps 150: 2 according to His excellent **g**
Prov 5:23 and in the **g** of his folly he
Eccl 1:16 Look, I have attained **g**, and
Is 40:26 by the **g** of His might and the
Is 63: 1 in the **g** of His strength
Jer 13:22 For the **g** of your iniquity
Ezek 31: 2 Whom are you like in your **g**
Ezek 31: 7 Thus it was beautiful in **g**
Ezek 31:18 then be likened in glory and **g**
Dan 4:22 for your **g** has grown and
Dan 7:27 the **g** of the kingdoms under
Hos 9: 7 Because of the **g** of your
Eph 1:19 what is the exceeding **g** of

GREAVES
1Sa 17: 6 he had bronze **g** on his legs

GREECE (*see* GREEK)
Dan 8:21 male goat is the kingdom of **G**
Dan 10:20 the prince of **G** will come
Dan 11: 2 up all against the realm of **G**
Zech 9:13 Zion, against your sons, O **G**
Acts 20: 2 with many words, he came to **G**

GREED (*see* GREEDILY, GREEDY)
Luke 11:39 your inward part is full of **g**

GREEDILY (*see* GREED)
Prov 21:26 He covets **g** all day long, but
Jude 11 have run **g** in the error of

GREEDINESS (*see* GREEDY)
Eph 4:19 work all uncleanness with **g**
1Ti 6:10 from the faith in their **g**

GREEDY (*see* GREED, GREEDINESS)
Ps 10: 3 He blesses the **g** and renounces
Prov 1:19 of everyone who is **g** for gain
Prov 15:27 He who is **g** for gain troubles
Is 56:11 they are **g** dogs which never
1Ti 3: 3 not **g** for money, but gentle,
1Ti 3: 8 much wine, not **g** for money,
Tit 1: 7 not violent, not **g** for money,

GREEK (*see* GREECE, GREEKS)
Mark 7:26 The woman was a **G**, a
Luke 23:38 over Him in letters of **G**,
John 19:20 it was written in Hebrew, **G**
Acts 16: 1 but his father was **G**
Acts 16: 3 knew that his father was **G**
Acts 21:37 Can you speak **G**
Rom 1:16 Jew first and also for the **G**
Rom 2: 9 Jew first and also of the **G**
Rom 2:10 Jew first and also to the **G**
Rom 10:12 distinction between Jew and **G**
Gal 2: 3 who was with me, being a **G**
Gal 3:28 There is neither Jew nor **G**
Col 3:11 there is neither **G** nor Jew
Rev 9:11 but in **G** he has the name

GREEKS (*see* GREEK)
Joel 3: 6 You have sold to the **G**, that
John 7:35 to the Dispersion among the **G**
John 7:35 the **G** and teach the **G**
John 12:20 Now there were certain **G**
Acts 14: 1 the Jews and of the **G** believed
Acts 17: 4 multitude of the devout **G**
Acts 17:12 and also not a few of the **G**
Acts 18: 4 and persuaded both Jews and **G**
Acts 18:17 Then all the **G** took Sosthenes
Acts 19:10 Lord Jesus, both Jews and **G**
Acts 19:17 Jews and **G** dwelling in Ephesus
Acts 20:21 to Jews, and also to **G**,
Acts 21:28 brought **G** into the temple
Rom 1:14 I am a debtor both to **G** and to
Rom 3: 9 **G** that they are all under sin
1Co 1:22 sign, and **G** seek after wisdom
1Co 1:23 and to the **G** foolishness,
1Co 1:24 are called, both Jews and **G**
1Co 10:32 to the Jews or to the **G** or to
1Co 12:13 whether Jews or **G**, whether

GREEN (*see* GREENISH)
Gen 1:30 given every **g** herb for food"
Gen 9: 3 things, even as the **g** herbs
Gen 30:37 for himself rods of **g** poplar
Ex 10:15 **g** on the trees or on the
Lev 2:14 of your firstfruits **g** heads
Deut 12: 2 hills and under every **g** tree
1Ki 14:23 hill and under every **g** tree
2Ki 16: 4 hills, and under every **g** tree
2Ki 17:10 hill and under every **g** tree
2Ki 19:26 the **g** herb, as the grass on
2Ch 28: 4 hills, and under every **g** tree
Job 8:12 While it is yet **g** and not cut
Job 8:16 He grows **g** in the sun, and his
Job 15:32 and his branch will not be **g**
Job 39: 8 searches after every **g** thing
Ps 23: 2 me to lie down in **g** pastures
Ps 37: 2 And wither as the **g** herb
Ps 37:35 himself like a native **g** tree
Ps 52: 8 But I am like a **g** olive tree
Song 1:16 Also our bed is **g**
Song 2:13 tree puts forth her **g** figs
Is 15: 6 For the **g** grass has withered
Is 15: 6 fails, there is nothing **g**
Is 37:27 of the field and as the **g** herb
Is 57: 5 with gods under every **g** tree
Jer 2:20 under every **g** tree you lay
Jer 3: 6 and under every **g** tree, and
Jer 3:13 deities under every **g** tree
Jer 11:16 **g** Olive Tree, Lovely and of
Jer 17: 2 the **g** trees on the high hills
Jer 17: 8 but her leaf will be **g**, and
Ezek 6:13 under every **g** tree, and under
Ezek 17:24 low tree, dried up the **g** tree
Ezek 20:47 it shall devour every **g** tree
Hos 14: 8 I am like a **g** cypress tree
Mark 6:39 down in groups on the **g** grass
Luke 23:31 do these things in the **g** wood
Rev 8: 7 all **g** grass was burned up
Rev 9: 4 of the earth, or any **g** thing

GREENISH (*see* GREEN)
Lev 13:49 if the plague is **g** or reddish
Lev 14:37 **g** or reddish, which appear to

GREET (*see* GREETED, GREETING, GREETS)
1Sa 10: 4 And they will **g** you and give
1Sa 13:10 meet him, that he might **g** him
1Sa 25: 5 to Nabal, and **g** him in my name
1Sa 25:14 wilderness to **g** our master
2Sa 8:10 David, to **g** him and bless him,
2Ki 4:29 you meet anyone, do not **g** him
2Ki 10:13 to **g** the sons of the king
1Ch 18:10 David, to **g** him and bless him,
Matt 5:47 if you **g** your brethren only,
Matt 10:12 you go into a household, **g** it
Luke 10: 4 and **g** no one along the road
Acts 25:13 came to Caesarea to **g** Festus
Rom 16: 3 **G** Priscilla and Aquila, my
Rom 16: 5 Likewise **g** the church that is
Rom 16: 5 **G** my beloved Epaenetus, who
Rom 16: 6 **G** Mary, who labored much for
Rom 16: 7 **G** Andronicus and Junia, my
Rom 16: 8 **G** Amplias, my beloved in the
Rom 16: 9 **G** Urbanus, our fellow worker
Rom 16:10 **G** Apelles, approved in Christ
Rom 16:10 **G** those who are of the
Rom 16:11 **G** Herodion, my kinsman
Rom 16:11 **G** those who are of the
Rom 16:12 **G** Tryphena and Tryphosa, who
Rom 16:12 **G** the beloved Persis, who
Rom 16:13 **G** Rufus, chosen in the Lord,
Rom 16:14 **G** Asyncritus, Phlegon, Hermas
Rom 16:15 **G** Philologus and Julia, Nereus
Rom 16:16 **G** one another with a holy
Rom 16:16 The churches of Christ **g** you
Rom 16:21 Sosipater, my kinsmen, **g** you
Rom 16:22 epistle, **g** you in the Lord
1Co 16:19 The churches of Asia **g** you
1Co 16:19 Priscilla **g** you heartily in
1Co 16:20 All the brethren **g** you
1Co 16:20 **G** one another with a holy
2Co 13:12 **G** one another with a holy
2Co 13:13 All the saints **g** you
Phil 4:21 **G** every saint in Christ Jesus
Phil 4:21 who are with me **g** you
Phil 4:22 All the saints **g** you, but
Col 4:14 physician and Demas **g** you
Col 4:15 **G** the brethren who are in
1Th 5:26 **G** all the brethren with a
2Ti 4:19 **G** Prisca and Aquila, and the
Tit 3:15 All who are with me **g** you
Tit 3:15 **G** those who love us in the
Heb 13:24 **G** all those who rule over you
Heb 13:24 Those from Italy **g** you
1Pe 5:14 **G** one another with a kiss of
2Jn 10 him into your house nor **g** him
2Jn 13 of your elect sister **g** you
3Jn 14 Our friends **g** you
3Jn 14 **G** the friends by name

GREETED (*see* GREET)
Judg 18:15 the house of Micah, and **g** him
1Sa 17:22 and came and **g** his brothers
1Sa 30:21 near the people, he **g** them
2Ki 10:15 and he **g** him and said to him,
Mark 9:15 and running to Him, **g** Him
Luke 1:40 of Zacharias and **g** Elizabeth
Acts 18:22 **g** the church, he went down to
Acts 21: 7 **g** the brethren, and stayed
Acts 21:19 When he had **g** them, he told

GREETING (*see* GREET, GREETINGS)
Luke 1:29 what manner of **g** this was
Luke 1:41 Elizabeth heard the **g** of Mary
Luke 1:44 of your **g** sounded in my ears

GREETINGS (*see* GREETING)
Matt 23: 7 **g** in the marketplaces, and to
Matt 26:49 **G**, Rabbi!" and kissed Him.
Mark 12:38 love **g** in the marketplaces,
Luke 11:43 and **g** in the marketplaces
Luke 20:46 love **g** in the marketplaces,
Acts 15:23 Syria, and Cilicia: **G**.
Acts 15:33 **g** from the brethren to the
Acts 23:26 governor Felix: **G**.
Jas 1: 1 are scattered abroad: **G**.

GREETS (*see* GREET)
2Ki 4:29 and if anyone **g** you, do not
Rom 16:23 of the whole church, **g** you
Rom 16:23 **g** you, and Quartus, a brother
Col 4:10 my fellow prisoner **g** you,
Col 4:12 **g** you, always laboring
2Ti 4:21 Eubulus **g** you, as well as
Phm 23 in Christ Jesus, **g** you,
1Pe 5:13 together with you, **g** you
2Jn 11 for he who **g** him shares in

GREW (*see* GROW)
Gen 19:25 and what **g** on the ground
Gen 21: 8 So the child **g** and was weaned
Gen 21:20 and he **g** and dwelt in the
Gen 25:27 So the boys **g**
Gen 47:27 had possessions there and **g**
Ex 1: 7 and **g** exceedingly mighty
Ex 1:12 the more they multiplied and **g**
Ex 1:20 multiplied and **g** very mighty
Ex 2:10 And the child **g**, and she
Ex 7:13 And Pharaoh's heart **g** hard
Ex 7:22 and Pharaoh's heart **g** hard
Ex 8:19 But Pharaoh's heart **g** hard
Deut 32:15 But Jeshurun **g** fat and kicked
Deut 32:15 you **g** fat, you **g** thick,
Josh 17:13 children of Israel **g** strong
Judg 4:24 children of Israel **g** stronger
Judg 11: 2 and when his wife's sons **g** up
Judg 13:24 and the child **g**, and the LORD
1Sa 2:21 Samuel **g** before the LORD
1Sa 2:26 the child Samuel **g** in stature
1Sa 3:19 So Samuel **g**, and the LORD was
2Sa 3: 1 But David **g** stronger and
2Sa 3: 1 and the house of Saul **g** weaker
2Sa 12: 3 it **g** up together with him and
2Sa 15:12 And the conspiracy **g** strong
2Sa 21:15 and David **g** faint
2Ki 4:18 So the child **g**
2Ch 13:21 But Abijah **g** mighty, married
2Ch 24:15 But Jehoiada **g** old and was
Neh 9:25 filled and **g** fat, and delighted
Ps 32: 3 my bones **g** old Through my
Ezek 16: 7 and you **g**, matured, and became
Ezek 16: 7 were formed, your hair **g**, but
Ezek 17: 6 And it **g** and became a spreading
Ezek 17:10 the garden terrace where it **g**
Dan 4:11 The tree **g** and became strong
Dan 4:20 tree that you saw, which **g**
Dan 8: 8 the male goat **g** very great
Dan 8: 9 **g** exceedingly great toward
Dan 8:10 it **g** up to the host of heaven
Jon 4: 8 head, so that he **g** faint
Mark 4: 7 and the thorns **g** up and choked
Mark 5:26 no better, but rather **g** worse
Luke 1:80 So the child **g** and became
Luke 2:40 And the Child **g** and became
Luke 13:19 and it **g** and became a large
Acts 7:17 to Abraham, the people **g** and
Acts 12:24 But the word of God **g** and
Acts 13:46 Then Paul and Barnabas **g** bold
Acts 19:20 word of the Lord **g** mightily

GREYHOUND
Prov 30:31 a **g**, a male goat also, and a

GRIEF (*see* GRIEFS, GRIEVE)
Gen 26:35 And they were a **g** of mind to
1Sa 1:16 **g** I have spoken until now
1Sa 25:31 that this will be no **g** to you
2Ch 6:29 his own burden and his own **g**
Job 2:13 saw that his **g** was very great
Job 6: 2 that my **g** were fully weighed,
Job 16: 5 my lips would relieve your **g**
Job 16: 6 I speak, my **g** is not relieved
Ps 6: 7 eye wastes away because of **g**
Ps 10:14 for You observe trouble and **g**
Ps 31: 9 My eye wastes away with **g**
Ps 31:10 For my life is spent with **g**
Ps 69:26 talk of the **g** of those You
Prov 10: 1 son is the **g** of his mother
Prov 14:13 and the end of mirth may be **g**
Prov 17:25 son is a **g** to his father, and
Eccl 1:18 For in much wisdom is much **g**
Is 17:11 heap of ruins in the day of **g**
Is 53: 3 sorrows and acquainted with **g**
Is 53:10 He has put Him to **g**
Is 65:14 and wail for **g** of spirit
Jer 6: 7 Before Me continually are **g**
Jer 45: 3 LORD has added **g** to my sorrow
Lam 3:32 Though He causes **g**, yet He
Rom 9: 2 and continual **g** in my heart
2Co 2: 5 But if anyone has caused **g**
Heb 13:17 do so with joy and not with **g**
1Pe 2:19 toward God one endures **g**,

GRIEFS (*see* GRIEF)
Is 53: 4 Surely He has borne our **g**

GRIEVE (*see* GRIEF, GRIEVED, GRIEVES, GRIEVOUS)
1Sa 2:33 your eyes and **g** your heart
Lam 3:33 nor **g** the children of men
Zech 12:10 **g** for Him as one grieves for
Eph 4:30 do not **g** the Holy Spirit of

GRIEVED (*see* GRIEVE)
Gen 6: 6 and He was **g** in His heart
Gen 34: 7 and the men were **g** and very
Gen 45: 5 do not therefore be **g** nor
Gen 49:23 archers have bitterly **g** him
Deut 15:10 not be **g** when you give to him
Judg 21: 6 the children of Israel **g** for
Judg 21:15 the people **g** for Benjamin,
1Sa 1: 8 And why is your heart **g**
1Sa 15:11 it **g** Samuel, and he cried out
1Sa 20: 3 know this, lest he be **g**
1Sa 20:34 month, for he was **g** for David
1Sa 30: 6 soul of all the people was **g**
2Sa 19: 2 The king is **g** for his son
Neh 8:11 do not be **g**
Neh 13: 8 And it **g** me bitterly
Job 30:25 not my soul **g** for the poor
Ps 73:21 Thus my heart was **g**, And I was
Ps 78:40 And **g** Him in the desert
Ps 95:10 I was **g** with that generation
Ps 112:10 wicked will see it and be **g**
Is 54: 6 **g** in spirit, like a youthful
Is 57:10 therefore you were not **g**
Is 63:10 rebelled and **g** His Holy Spirit
Jer 5: 3 them, but they have not **g**
Dan 7:15 was **g** in my spirit within my
Dan 11:30 therefore he shall be **g**, and
Amos 6: 6 but are not **g** for the
Matt 18:31 been done, they were very **g**
Mark 3: 5 being **g** by the hardness of
Mark 10:22 at this word, and went away **g**
John 21:17 Peter was **g** because He said
Rom 14:15 is **g** because of your food
2Co 2: 4 not that you should be **g**
2Co 2: 5 caused grief, he has not **g** me
1Pe 1: 6 you have been **g** by various

GRIEVES (*see* GRIEVE)
Ruth 1:13 for it **g** me very much for
Zech 12:10 Him as one **g** for a firstborn

GRIEVOUS (*see* GRIEVE, GRIEVOUSLY)
Gen 18:20 because their sin is very **g**
Gen 50:11 This is a **g** mourning of the
Eccl 1:13 this **g** task God has given to
Eccl 2:17 under the sun was **g** to me
Eccl 2:23 are sorrowful, and his work **g**
Heb 12:11 joyful for the present, but **g**

GRIEVOUSLY (*see* GRIEVOUS)
Lam 1: 8 Jerusalem has sinned **g**,

GRIND (*see* GRINDER, GRINDING)
Job 31:10 let my wife **g** for another
Prov 27:22 Though you **g** a fool in a
Is 47: 2 Take the millstones and **g** meal
Matt 21:44 it will **g** him to powder
Luke 20:18 it will **g** him to powder

GRINDER (*see* GRIND, GRINDERS)
Judg 16:21 he became a **g** in the prison

GRINDERS (*see* GRINDER)
Eccl 12: 3 when the **g** cease because they

GRINDING (*see* GRIND)
Eccl 12: 4 and the sound of **g** is low
Is 3:15 and **g** the faces of the poor
Matt 24:41 women will be **g** at the mill
Luke 17:35 Two women will be **g** together

GRIP
Jer 15:21 from the **g** of the terrible

GROAN (*see* GROANED, GROANING, GROANS)
Job 24:12 The dying **g** in the city, and
Ps 38: 8 I **g** because of the turmoil of
Prov 29: 2 man rules, the people **g**
Jer 51:52 her land the wounded shall **g**
Ezek 30:24 he will **g** before him with the
Joel 1:18 How the beasts **g**
Rom 8:23 ourselves **g** within ourselves
2Co 5: 2 For in this we **g**, earnestly
2Co 5: 4 For we who are in this tent **g**

GROANED (*see* GROAN)
Ex 2:23 **g** because of the bondage, and
John 11:33 He **g** in the spirit and was

GROANING (*see* GROAN, GROANINGS)
Ex 2:24 So God heard their **g**, and God
Ex 6: 5 I have also heard the **g** of
Judg 2:18 their **g** because of those who
Job 23: 2 is listless because of my **g**
Ps 6: 6 I am weary with my **g**
Ps 22: 1 Me, And from the words of My **g**
Ps 32: 3 Through my **g** all the day long
Ps 79:11 Let the **g** of the prisoner
Ps 102: 5 **g** My bones cling to my skin
Ps 102:20 To hear the **g** of the prisoner
John 11:38 again **g** in Himself, came to
Acts 7:34 I have heard their **g** and have

GROANINGS (*see* GROANING)
Job 3:24 and my **g** pour out like water
Ezek 30:24 **g** of a mortally wounded man
Rom 8:26 **g** which cannot be uttered

GROANS (*see* GROAN)
Rom 8:22 that the whole creation **g**

GROPE (*see* GROPES)
Deut 28:29 you shall **g** at noonday, as a
Job 5:14 **g** at noontime as in the night
Job 12:25 They **g** in the dark without
Is 59:10 We **g** for the wall like the
Is 59:10 we **g** as if we had no eyes
Acts 17:27 that they might **g** for Him

GROPES (*see* GROPE)
Deut 28:29 as a blind man **g** in darkness

GROSS
2Ki 8:13 he should do this **g** thing

GROUND (*see* GROUNDED)
Gen 2: 5 was no man to till the **g**
Gen 2: 6 the whole face of the **g**
Gen 2: 7 man of the dust of the **g**, and
Gen 2: 9 out of the **g** the LORD God
Gen 2:19 Out of the **g** the LORD God
Gen 3:17 Cursed is the **g** for your sake
Gen 3:19 till you return to the **g**, for
Gen 3:23 the **g** from which he was taken
Gen 4: 2 Cain was a tiller of the **g**
Gen 4: 3 fruit of the **g** to the LORD
Gen 4:10 cries out to Me from the **g**
Gen 4:12 When you till the **g**, it shall
Gen 4:14 day from the face of the **g**
Gen 5:29 because of the **g** which the
Gen 7:23 were on the face of the **g**
Gen 8: 8 abated from the face of the **g**
Gen 8:13 the surface of the **g** was dry
Gen 8:21 curse the **g** for man's sake
Gen 18: 2 and bowed himself to the **g**
Gen 19: 1 with his face toward the **g**
Gen 19:25 cities, and what grew on the **g**
Gen 33: 3 himself to the **g** seven times
Gen 38: 9 that he emitted on the **g**
Gen 41:47 **g** brought forth abundantly
Gen 44:11 let down his sack to the **g**
Gen 44:14 they fell before him on the **g**
Ex 3: 5 where you stand is holy **g**
Ex 4: 3 Cast it on the **g**
Ex 4: 3 So he cast it on the **g**, and
Ex 8:21 and also the **g** on which they
Ex 9:23 hail, and fire darted to the **g**
Ex 14:16 **g** through the midst of the
Ex 14:22 midst of the sea on the dry **g**
Ex 16:14 as fine as frost on the **g**
Ex 32:20 the fire, and **g** it to powder
Lev 20:25 thing that creeps on the **g**
Num 11: 8 **g** it on millstones or beat it
Num 11:31 above the surface of the **g**
Num 15:20 **g** meal as a heave offering
Num 15:21 Of the first of your **g** meal
Num 16:31 that the **g** split apart under
Deut 4:18 **g** or the likeness of any fish
Deut 9:21 **g** it very small, until it was
Deut 15:23 pour it on the **g** like water
Deut 22: 6 way, in any tree or on the **g**
Deut 26: 2 of all the produce of the **g**
Deut 28: 4 body, the produce of your **g**
Deut 28:11 and in the produce of your **g**
Deut 28:56 **g** because of her delicateness
Josh 3:17 **g** in the midst of the Jordan
Josh 3:17 Israel crossed over on dry **g**
Josh 24:32 in the plot of **g** which Jacob
Judg 4:21 and it went down into the **g**
Judg 6:37 and it is dry on all the **g**
Judg 6:39 but on all the **g** let there be
Judg 6:40 there was dew on all the **g**
Judg 13:20 fell on their faces to the **g**
Judg 20:21 **g** twenty-two thousand men of
Judg 20:25 cut down to the **g** eighteen
Judg 20:36 had given **g** to the Benjamites
Ruth 2:10 her face, bowed down to the **g**
1Sa 3:19 of his words fall to the **g**
1Sa 5: 4 fallen on its face to the **g**
1Sa 8:12 will set some to plow his **g**
1Sa 14:25 and there was honey on the **g**
1Sa 14:32 and slaughtered them on the **g**
1Sa 14:45 his head shall fall to the **g**
1Sa 20:41 fell on his face to the **g**
1Sa 25:23 David, and bowed down to the **g**
1Sa 26: 7 stuck in the **g** by his head
1Sa 28:14 with his face to the **g** and
1Sa 28:20 fell full length on the **g**
1Sa 28:23 So he arose from the **g** and sat
2Sa 1: 2 David, that he fell to the **g**
2Sa 2:22 should I strike you to the **g**
2Sa 8: 2 Forcing them down to the **g**
2Sa 12:16 in and lay all night on the **g**
2Sa 12:17 to raise him up from the **g**
2Sa 12:20 So David arose from the **g**
2Sa 13:31 his garments and lay on the **g**
2Sa 14: 4 she fell on her face to the **g**
2Sa 14:11 your son shall fall to the **g**
2Sa 14:14 like water spilled on the **g**
2Sa 14:22 fell to the **g** on his face
2Sa 14:33 face to the **g** before the king
2Sa 17:12 him as the dew falls on the **g**
2Sa 17:19 and spread **g** grain on it
2Sa 18:11 not strike him there to the **g**
2Sa 20:10 entrails poured out on the **g**
2Sa 23:11 a piece of **g** full of lentils
2Sa 24:20 king with his face to the **g**
1Ki 1:23 king with his face to the **g**
1Ki 18:42 then he bowed down on the **g**
2Ki 2: 8 of them crossed over on dry **g**
2Ki 2:15 and bowed to the **g** before him
2Ki 2:19 water is bad, and the **g** barren
2Ki 4:37 his feet, and bowed to the **g**
2Ki 9:26 and throw him on the plot of **g**
2Ki 9:36 On the plot of **g** at Jezreel
2Ki 13:18 Strike the **g**"
2Ki 23: 6 **g** it to ashes, and threw its
1Ch 11:13 a piece of **g** full of barley
1Ch 21:21 David with his face to the **g**
1Ch 27:26 the field for tilling the **g**
2Ch 2:10 thousand kors of **g** wheat,
2Ch 7: 3 to the **g** on the pavement, and
2Ch 20:18 head with his face to the **g**
Neh 8: 6 with their faces to the **g**
Neh 10:35 the firstfruits of our **g** and
Job 1:20 his head, and he fell to the **g**

Job 2:13 with him on the **g** seven days
Job 5: 6 trouble spring from the **g**
Job 14: 8 and its stump may die in the **g**
Job 16:13 He pours out my gall on the **g**
Job 18:10 is hidden for him on the **g**
Job 39:14 she leaves her eggs on the **g**
Ps 44:25 Our body clings to the **g**
Ps 74: 7 place of Your name to the **g**
Ps 89:39 crown by casting it to the **g**
Ps 89:44 cast his throne down to the **g**
Ps 105:35 devoured the fruit of their **g**
Ps 107:33 the watersprings into dry **g**
Ps 143: 3 has crushed my life to the **g**
Ps 147: 6 the wicked down to the **g**
Prov 13:23 in the fallow **g** of the poor
Eccl 10: 7 walk on the **g** like servants
Is 3:26 desolate shall sit on the **g**
Is 14:12 How you are cut down to the **g**
Is 21: 9 gods he has broken to the **g**
Is 25:12 lay low, and bring to the **g**
Is 26: 5 low, He lays it low to the **g**
Is 28:28 Bread flour must be **g**
Is 29: 4 you shall speak out of the **g**
Is 29: 4 like a medium's, out of the **g**
Is 30:23 seed with which you sow the **g**
Is 30:24 the **g** will eat cured fodder
Is 35: 7 The parched **g** shall become a
Is 44: 3 and floods on the dry **g**
Is 47: 1 sit on the **g** without a throne
Is 51:23 laid your body like the **g**
Is 53: 2 and as a root out of dry **g**
Jer 4: 3 Break up your fallow **g**, and do
Jer 7:20 and on the fruit of the **g**
Jer 14: 4 Because the **g** is parched, for
Jer 25:33 shall become refuse on the **g**
Jer 27: 5 the beast that are on the **g**
Lam 2: 2 brought them down to the **g**
Lam 2: 9 gates have sunk into the **g**
Lam 2:10 daughter of Zion sit on the **g**
Lam 2:10 bow their heads to the **g**
Lam 2:11 my bile is poured on the **g**
Lam 2:21 lie on the **g** in the streets
Lam 5:13 Young men **g** at the millstones
Ezek 12: 6 so that you cannot see the **g**
Ezek 12:12 see the **g** with his eyes
Ezek 13:14 and bring it down to the **g**
Ezek 19:12 she was cast down to the **g**
Ezek 24: 7 she did not pour it on the **g**
Ezek 26:11 pillars will fall to the **g**
Ezek 26:16 they will sit on the **g**,
Ezek 28:17 I cast you to the **g**, I laid
Ezek 38:20 wall shall fall to the **g**
Ezek 39:14 bodies remaining on the **g**
Ezek 41:16 from the **g** to the windows
Ezek 42: 6 middle levels from the **g** up
Ezek 43:14 on the **g** to the lower ledge
Ezek 44:30 the first of your **g** meal, to
Dan 8: 5 earth, without touching the **g**
Dan 8: 7 but he cast him down to the **g**
Dan 8:10 and some of the stars to the **g**
Dan 8:12 he cast truth down to the **g**
Dan 8:18 sleep with my face to the **g**
Dan 10: 9 face, with my face to the **g**
Dan 10:15 I turned my face toward the **g**
Hos 2:18 the creeping things of the **g**
Hos 10:12 break up your fallow **g**, for
Amos 3:14 be cut off and fall to the **g**
Amos 9: 9 grain shall fall to the **g**
Obad 3 will bring me down to the **g**
Hag 1:11 whatever the **g** brings forth
Zech 8:12 the **g** shall give her increase
Mal 3:11 destroy the fruit of your **g**
Matt 10:29 **g** apart from your Father's
Matt 13: 8 But others fell on good **g**
Matt 13:23 **g** is he who hears the word
Matt 15:35 to sit down on the **g**
Matt 25:18 one went and dug in the **g**, and
Matt 25:25 and hid your talent in the **g**
Mark 4: 5 Some fell on stony **g**, where
Mark 4: 8 But other seed fell on good **g**
Mark 4:16 the ones sown on stony **g** who
Mark 4:20 are the ones sown on good **g**
Mark 4:26 should scatter seed on the **g**
Mark 4:31 when it is sown on the **g**
Mark 8: 6 to sit down on the **g**
Mark 9:20 him, and he fell on the **g** and
Mark 14:35 farther, and fell on the **g**
Luke 8: 8 But others fell on good **g**
Luke 8:15 on the good **g** are those who
Luke 12:16 The **g** of a certain rich man
Luke 13: 7 why does it use up the **g**
Luke 14:18 I have bought a piece of **g**
Luke 19:44 children within you, to the **g**
Luke 22:44 blood falling down to the **g**
John 4: 5 near the plot of **g** that Jacob
John 8: 6 and wrote on the **g** with His
John 8: 8 down and wrote on the **g**
John 9: 6 things, He spat on the **g** and
John 12:24 of wheat falls into the **g**
John 18: 6 drew back and fell to the **g**
Acts 7:33 where you stand is holy **g**
Acts 9: 4 Then he fell to the **g**, and
Acts 9: 8 Then Saul arose from the **g**
Acts 22: 7 And I fell to the **g** and heard a
Acts 26:14 we all had fallen to the **g**
1Ti 3:15 the pillar and **g** of the truth

GROUNDED (*see* GROUND)
Eph 3:17 being rooted and **g** in love,
Col 1:23 you continue in the faith, **g**

GROUP (*see* GROUPS)
1Sa 10: 5 that you will meet a **g** of
1Sa 10:10 there was a **g** of prophets to
1Sa 19:20 And when they saw the **g** of
1Ch 24: 5 one **g** as another, for there
Neh 12:24 **g** alternating with **g**,

GROUPS (*see* GROUP)
Mark 6:39 down in **g** on the green grass
Luke 9:14 them sit down in **g** of fifty

GROVE (*see* GROVES)
Ex 23:11 your vineyard and your olive **g**
Num 25: 1 Israel remained in Acacia **G**
Josh 2: 1 from Acacia **G** to spy secretly
Josh 3: 1 and they set out from Acacia **G**
Eccl 2: 6 the growing trees of the **g**
Mic 6: 5 him, from Acacia **G** to Gilgal

GROVES (*see* GROVE)
Josh 24:13 olive **g** which you did not
Judg 15: 5 as the vineyards and olive **g**
1Sa 8:14 vineyards, and your olive **g**
2Ki 5:26 to receive clothing, olive **g**
2Ki 18:32 vineyards, a land of olive **g**
Neh 5:11 vineyards, their olive **g**, and
Neh 9:25 dug, vineyards, olive **g**, and

GROW (*see* FULL-GROWN, GREW, GROWING, GROWN, GROWS, GROWTH)
Gen 2: 9 **g** that is pleasant to the
Gen 48:16 let them **g** into a multitude
Num 6: 5 of the hair of his head **g**
Deut 29:23 nor does any grass **g** there
Judg 16:22 to **g** again after it had been
1Sa 3: 2 to **g** so dim that he could not
Job 8:11 Can the papyrus **g** up without
Job 8:19 of the earth others will **g**
Job 14: 8 root may **g** old in the earth
Job 31:40 thistles **g** instead of wheat
Job 39: 4 they **g** strong with grain
Ps 92:12 He shall **g** like a cedar in
Ps 102:26 all of them will **g** old like a
Ps 104:14 the grass to **g** for the cattle
Ps 132:17 will make the horn of David **g**
Ps 147: 8 grass to **g** on the mountains
Eccl 11: 5 or how the bones **g** in the
Eccl 12: 3 through the windows **g** dim
Is 11: 1 a Branch shall **g** out of his
Is 17: 4 fatness of his flesh **g** lean
Is 17:11 you will make your plant to **g**
Is 29:22 nor shall his face now **g** pale
Is 50: 9 will all **g** old like a garment
Is 51: 6 the earth will **g** old like a
Is 53: 2 For He shall **g** up before Him
Jer 6:24 our hands **g** feeble
Jer 12: 2 they **g**, yes, they bear fruit
Jer 33:15 to **g** up to David a Branch of
Jer 50:43 them, and his hands **g** feeble
Lam 5:17 these things our eyes **g** dim
Ezek 31: 4 The waters made it **g**
Ezek 44:20 nor let their hair **g** long
Ezek 47:12 will **g** all kinds of trees
Hos 10: 8 and thistle shall **g** on their
Hos 14: 5 He shall **g** like the lily, and
Hos 14: 7 grain, and **g** like the vine
Joel 2:10 the sun and moon **g** dark, and
Joel 3:15 The sun and moon will **g** dark
Jon 1:13 to **g** more tempestuous against
Jon 4:10 not labored, nor made it **g**
Mal 4: 2 **g** fat like stall-fed calves
Matt 6:28 of the field, how they **g**
Matt 13:30 Let both **g** together until
Matt 21:19 Let no fruit **g** on you ever
Matt 24:12 the love of many will **g** cold
Mark 4:27 the seed should sprout and **g**
Luke 12:27 the lilies, how they **g**
Luke 12:33 money bags which do not **g** old
Gal 6: 9 And let us not **g** weary while
Eph 4:15 may **g** up in all things into
2Th 3:13 do not **g** weary in doing good
1Ti 5:11 to **g** wanton against Christ
2Ti 3:13 men and impostors will **g** worse
Heb 1:11 they will all **g** old like a
1Pe 2: 2 word, that you may **g** thereby
2Pe 3:18 but **g** in the grace and

GROWING (*see* GROW)
Eccl 2: 6 the **g** trees of the grove
Jon 1:11 for the sea was **g** more
Heb 8:13 **g** old is ready to vanish away

GROWL (*see* GROWLED)
Ps 59: 6 They **g** like a dog, And go all
Ps 59:14 They **g** like a dog, And go all
Is 59:11 We all **g** like bears, and moan
Jer 51:38 they shall **g** like lions'

GROWLED (*see* GROWL)
Jer 2:15 lions roared at him, and **g**

GROWN (*see* GROW)
Gen 2: 5 any herb of the field had **g**
Gen 18:12 After I have **g** old, shall I
Gen 19:13 **g** great before the face of
Gen 38:11 house till my son Shelah is **g**
Gen 38:14 for she saw that Shelah was **g**
Ex 2:11 those days, when Moses was **g**
Lev 13:37 is black hair **g** up in it, the
Deut 4:25 have **g** old in the land, act
Deut 31:20 **g** fat, then they will turn to
Ruth 1:13 for them till they were **g**
2Sa 10: 5 until your beards have **g**, and
1Ki 12: 8 men who had **g** up with him
1Ki 12:10 **g** up with him spoke to him
2Ki 19:26 grain blighted before it is **g**
1Ch 19: 5 until your beards have **g**, and
2Ch 10: 8 men who had **g** up with him
2Ch 10:10 **g** up with him spoke to him
Ezra 9: 6 our guilt has **g** up to the
Job 17: 7 My eye has also **g** dim because
Ps 144:12 as plants **g** up in their youth
Is 37:27 grain blighted before it is **g**
Jer 5:27 have become great and **g** rich
Jer 5:28 They have **g** fat, they are
Jer 49:24 Damascus has **g** feeble And
Jer 50:11 because you have **g** fat like a
Ezek 23:43 who had **g** old in adulteries
Dan 4:22 it is you, O king, who have **g**
Dan 4:22 for your greatness has **g** and
Dan 4:33 had **g** like eagles' feathers
Matt 13:15 of this people has **g** dull
Matt 13:32 but when it is **g** it is
Acts 28:27 of this people has **g** dull

GROWS (*see* GROW)
Ex 10: 5 shall eat every tree which **g**
Lev 13:39 white spot that **g** on the skin
Lev 25: 5 What **g** of its own accord of
Lev 25:11 reap what **g** of its own accord
2Ki 19:29 this year such as **g** of itself
Job 8:16 He **g** green in the sun, and his
Job 30:30 My skin **g** black and falls from
Ps 6: 7 It **g** old because of all my
Ps 90: 5 are like grass which **g** up
Ps 90: 6 morning it flourishes and **g** up
Ps 129: 6 Which withers before it **g** up
Is 37:30 this year such as **g** of itself
Mark 4:32 but when it is sown, it **g** up
Eph 2:21 **g** into a holy temple in the
Eph 4:22 the old man which **g** corrupt
Col 2:19 **g** with the increase which is
2Th 1: 3 your faith **g** exceedingly, and

GROWTH (*see* GROW)
Job 38:27 forth the **g** of tender grass
Ps 65:10 with showers, You bless its **g**
Eph 4:16 causes **g** of the body for the

GRUDGE (*see* GRUDGING, GRUDGINGLY)
Lev 19:18 nor bear any **g** against the

GRUDGING (*see* GRUDGE, GRUDGINGLY)
2Co 9: 5 and not as a **g** obligation

GRUDGINGLY (*see* GRUDGE, GRUDGING)
2Co 9: 7 heart, not **g** or of necessity

GRUESOME
Jer 16: 4 They shall die **g** deaths

GRUMBLE (*see* GRUMBLING)
Jas 5: 9 Do not **g** against one another,

GRUMBLING (*see* GRUMBLE)
1Pe 4: 9 to one another without **g**

GUARANTEE
2Co 5: 5 given us the Spirit as a **g**
Eph 1:14 who is the **g** of our

GUARD (*see* GUARDED, GUARDIAN, GUARDING, GUARDROOM, GUARDS)
Gen 3:24 to **g** the way to the tree of
Gen 37:36 Pharaoh and captain of the **g**
Gen 39: 1 of Pharaoh, captain of the **g**
Gen 40: 3 house of the captain of the **g**
Gen 40: 4 the captain of the **g** charged
Gen 41:10 house of the captain of the **g**
Gen 41:12 of the captain of the **g**
Num 10:25 the rear **g** of all the camps
Num 15:34 They put him under **g**, because
Josh 6: 9 the rear **g** came after the ark
Josh 6:13 But the rear **g** came after the
Josh 8:13 its rear **g** on the west of the
Josh 10:18 and set men by it to **g** them
1Sa 2: 9 He will **g** the feet of His
1Sa 19: 2 be on your **g** until morning
2Sa 23:23 appointed him over his **g**
1Ki 14:28 them back into the **g** chamber
1Ki 20:39 to me, and said, '**G** this man
2Ki 10:25 that Jehu said to the **g** and
2Ki 11:15 Take her outside under **g**, and
2Ki 25: 8 the captain of the **g**, a
2Ki 25:10 the **g** broke down the walls of
2Ki 25:11 the captain of the **g** carried
2Ki 25:12 But the captain of the **g** left
2Ki 25:15 captain of the **g** took away
2Ki 25:18 the captain of the **g** took
2Ki 25:20 Nebuzaradan, captain of the **g**
1Ch 11:25 appointed him over his **g**
2Ch 12:10 of the captains of the **g**, who
2Ch 12:11 the **g** would go and bring them
2Ch 23:14 Take her outside under **g**, and
Neh 4:22 they may be our **g** by night
Neh 4:23 nor the men of the **g** who
Neh 7: 3 and while they stand **g**, let
Neh 13:22 **g** the gates, to sanctify the
Job 7:12 that You set a **g** over me
Ps 39: 1 I will **g** my ways, Lest I sin
Ps 141: 3 Set a **g**, O LORD, over my
Is 52:12 of Israel will be your rear **g**
Is 58: 8 the LORD shall be your rear **g**
Jer 37:13 a captain of the **g** was there
Jer 39: 9 the captain of the **g** carried
Jer 39:10 the captain of the **g** left in
Jer 39:11 the captain of the **g**, saying,
Jer 39:13 of the **g** sent Nebushasban
Jer 40: 1 the captain of the **g** had let
Jer 40: 2 of the **g** took Jeremiah and
Jer 40: 5 of the **g** gave him rations
Jer 41:10 the captain of the **g** had
Jer 43: 6 the captain of the **g** had left
Jer 51:12 make the **g** strong, set up the
Jer 52:12 the captain of the **g**, who
Jer 52:14 with the captain of the **g**
Jer 52:15 the captain of the **g** carried
Jer 52:16 the captain of the **g** left
Jer 52:19 captain of the **g** took away
Jer 52:24 The captain of the **g** took
Jer 52:26 captain of the **g** took these
Jer 52:30 the captain of the **g** carried
Ezek 38: 7 and be a **g** for them
Dan 2:14 the captain of the king's **g**
Mic 7: 5 **G** the doors of your mouth
Matt 27:65 said to them, "You have a **g**
Matt 27:66 the stone and setting the **g**
Matt 28:11 some of the **g** came into the
Luke 8:29 him, and he was kept under **g**
Acts 12:10 first and the second **g** posts
Acts 28:16 to the captain of the **g**
Gal 3:23 were kept under **g** by the law
Phil 1:13 evident to the whole palace **g**
Phil 4: 7 will **g** your hearts and minds
2Th 3: 3 and **g** you from the evil one
1Ti 6:20 **G** what was committed to your

GUARDED (*see* GUARD)
1Sa 26:15 you not **g** your lord the king
1Sa 26:16 you have not **g** your master
1Ki 14:27 who **g** the doorway of the
2Ch 12:10 who **g** the entrance of the
Acts 28:16 with the soldier who **g** him

GUARDIAN (*see* GUARD, GUARDIANS)
Num 11:12 as a **g** carries a nursing
Acts 19:35 **g** of the great goddess Diana

GUARDIANS (*see* GUARDIAN)
1Sa 28: 2 you one of my chief **g** forever
Gal 4: 2 but is under **g** and stewards

GUARDING (*see* GUARD)
Matt 27:54 with him, who were **g** Jesus
Acts 22:20 **g** the clothes of those who
2Co 11:32 king, was **g** the city of the

GUARDROOM (*see* GUARD)
2Ch 12:11 take them back into the **g**

GUARDS (*see* GUARD)
1Sa 22:17 to the **g** who stood about him
1Ki 14:27 of the captains of the **g**, who
1Ki 14:28 that the **g** carried them, then
2Ki 10:25 then the **g** and the officers
Neh 7: 3 and appoint **g** from among the
Ps 34:20 He **g** all his bones
Ps 127: 1 Unless the LORD **g** the city
Prov 2: 8 He **g** the paths of justice, and
Prov 13: 3 He who **g** his mouth preserves
Prov 21:23 Whoever **g** his mouth and
Prov 22: 5 he who **g** his soul will be far
Matt 28: 4 the **g** shook for fear of him,
Luke 11:21 **g** his own palace, his goods
Acts 5:23 the **g** standing outside before
Acts 12: 6 the **g** before the door were
Acts 12:19 found him, he examined the **g**

GUDGODAH (*see* HOR HAGIDGAD)
Deut 10: 7 there they journeyed to **G**
Deut 10: 7 from **G** to Jotbathah, a land

GUEST (*see* GUESTS)
Mark 14:14 Where is the **g** room in which
Luke 19: 7 He has gone to be a **g** with a
Luke 22:11 Where is the **g** room in which
Phm 22 also prepare a **g** room for me

GUESTS (*see* GUEST)
1Ki 1:41 all the **g** who were with him
1Ki 1:49 Then all the **g** who were with
Prov 9:18 that her **g** are in the depths
Zeph 1: 7 He has invited His **g**
Matt 22:10 hall was filled with **g**
Matt 22:11 the king came in to see the **g**
John 2:10 when the **g** have well drunk,

GUIDANCE (*see* GUIDE)
1Ch 10:13 he consulted a medium for **g**
Job 37:12 about, being turned by His **g**
Is 28:29 in counsel and excellent in **g**

GUIDE (*see* GUIDANCE, GUIDED, GUIDES, GUIDING)
Job 38:32 or can you **g** the Great Bear
Ps 31: 3 name's sake, Lead me and **g** me
Ps 32: 8 I will **g** you with My eye
Ps 48:14 will be our **g** Even to death
Ps 73:24 You will **g** me with Your
Ps 112: 5 He will **g** his affairs with
Prov 11: 3 of the upright will **g** them
Prov 23:19 and **g** your heart in the way
Is 49:10 of water He will **g** them
Is 51:18 There is no one to **g** her
Is 58:11 The LORD will **g** you
Jer 3: 4 You are the **g** of my youth
Luke 1:79 to **g** our feet into the way of
John 16:13 He will **g** you into all truth
Acts 1:16 who became a **g** to those who
Rom 2:19 yourself are a **g** to the blind

GUIDED (*see* GUIDE)
Ex 15:13 you have **g** them in Your
2Ch 32:22 and **g** them on every side
Job 31:18 mother's womb I **g** the widow)
Ps 78:52 **g** them in the wilderness like
Ps 78:72 **g** them by the skillfulness of

GUIDES (*see* GUIDE)
Job 12:23 enlarges nations, and **g** them
Ps 25: 9 The humble He **g** in justice
Ps 107:30 So He **g** them to their desired
Matt 23:16 Woe to you, blind **g**, who say,
Matt 23:24 Blind **g**, who strain out a
Acts 8:31 can I, unless someone **g** me

GUIDING (*see* GUIDE)
Gen 48:14 **g** his hands knowingly, for
Eccl 2: 3 while **g** my heart with wisdom,

GUILE
Ex 21:14 neighbor, to kill him with **g**
Ps 32: 2 in whose spirit there is no **g**
Ps 34:13 And your lips from speaking **g**
Ps 55:11 and **g** do not depart from its
John 1:47 indeed, in whom is no **g**
2Co 12:16 crafty, I caught you with **g**
1Th 2: 3 uncleanness, nor was it in **g**
1Pe 2: 1 aside all malice, all **g**,
1Pe 2:22 nor was **g** found in His mouth
1Pe 3:10 and his lips from speaking **g**
Rev 14: 5 in their mouth was found no **g**

GUILT (*see* GUILTLESS, GUILTY)
Gen 26:10 would have brought **g** on us
Ex 22: 2 be no **g** for his bloodshed
Ex 22: 3 him, there shall be **g** for his
Lev 4: 3 bringing **g** on the people,
Lev 5: 1 does not tell it, he bears **g**
Lev 7:18 who eats of it shall bear **g**
Lev 10:17 the **g** of the congregation
Lev 17:16 then he shall bear his **g**
Lev 20:17 He shall bear his **g**
Lev 20:19 They shall bear their **g**
Lev 22:16 **g** of trespass when they eat
Lev 26:41 and they accept their **g**
Lev 26:43 they will accept their **g**,
Num 5:31 that woman shall bear her **g**
Num 14:34 shall bear your **g** one year
Num 15:31 his **g** shall be upon him
Num 30:15 then he shall bear her **g**
Deut 19:13 the **g** of innocent blood from
Deut 21: 9 the **g** of innocent blood from
Deut 25: 2 presence, according to his **g**
1Ch 21: 3 he be a cause of **g** in Israel
2Ch 28:13 add to our sins and to our **g**
2Ch 28:13 for our **g** is great, and there
Ezra 9: 6 our **g** has grown up to the
Ezra 9:13 evil deeds and for our great **g**
Ezra 9:15 we are before You, in our **g**
Ezra 10: 6 he mourned because of the **g**
Ezra 10:10 adding to the **g** of Israel
Ezek 18:19 not bear the **g** of the father
Ezek 18:20 not bear the **g** of the father
Ezek 18:20 father bear the **g** of the son
Zech 11: 5 slaughter them and feel no **g**
Matt 23:32 measure of your fathers' **g**

GUILTLESS (*see* GUILT)
Ex 20: 7 **g** who takes His name in vain
Deut 5:11 **g** who takes His name in vain
Josh 2:19 his own head, and we will be **g**
1Sa 26: 9 the LORD's anointed, and be **g**
2Sa 3:28 and I are **g** before the LORD
2Sa 14: 9 the king and his throne be **g**
1Ki 2: 9 therefore, do not hold him **g**
Matt 12: 7 not have condemned the **g**

GUILTY (*see* GUILT)
Gen 42:21 We are truly **g** concerning our
Ex 34: 7 by no means clearing the **g**
Lev 4:13 should not be done, and are **g**
Lev 4:22 should not be done, and is **g**
Lev 4:27 ought not to be done, and is **g**
Lev 5: 2 he also shall be unclean and **g**
Lev 5: 3 it, then he shall be **g**
Lev 5: 4 then he shall be **g** in any of
Lev 5: 5 when he is **g** in any of these
Lev 5:17 does not know it, yet he is **g**
Lev 6: 4 because he has sinned and is **g**
Num 5: 6 the LORD, and that person is **g**
Num 14:18 He by no means clears the **g**
Num 35:27 he shall not be **g** of blood
Num 35:31 a murderer who is **g** of death
Judg 21:22 yourselves **g** of your oath
2Sa 14:13 this thing as one who is **g**
2Ch 19:10 Do this, and you will not be **g**
2Ch 28:10 but are you not also **g** before
Ezra 9: 7 this day we have been very **g**
Ezra 10:19 and being **g**, they presented a
Ps 5:10 Pronounce them **g**, O God
Ps 109: 7 is judged, let him be found **g**
Prov 21: 8 The way of a **g** man is
Prov 30:10 curse you, and you be found **g**
Ezek 18:24 of which he is **g** and the sin
Ezek 22: 4 You have become **g** by the

Hos 10: 2 now they are held **g**
Hos 13:16 Samaria is held **g**, for she
Rom 3:19 world may become **g** before God
1Co 11:27 manner will be **g** of the body
Jas 2:10 in one point, he is **g** of all

GULF
Luke 16:26 you there is a great **g** fixed

GULLIBLE
2Ti 3: 6 and make captives of **g** women

GUNI (*see* GUNITES)
Gen 46:24 of Naphtali were Jahzeel, **G**
Num 26:48 of **G**, the family of the
1Ch 5:15 son of Abdiel, the son of **G**
1Ch 7:13 of Naphtali were Jahziel, **G**

GUNITES (*see* GUNI)
Num 26:48 of Guni, the family of the **G**

GUR
2Ki 9:27 did so at the ascent to **G**

GUR BAAL
2Ch 26: 7 the Arabians who lived in **G**

GUSH (*see* GUSHED, GUSHES)
Jer 9:18 and our eyelids **g** with water

GUSHED (*see* GUSH)
Judg 5: 5 the mountains **g** before the
1Ki 18:28 until the blood **g** out on them
Ps 78:20 So that the waters **g** out
Ps 105:41 the rock, and water **g** out
Is 48:21 the rock, and the waters **g** out
Acts 1:18 and all his entrails **g** out

GUSHES (*see* GUSH)
Job 40:23 the Jordan **g** into his mouth

GUTTERS
Gen 30:38 before the flocks in the **g**
Gen 30:41 of the livestock in the **g**

H

HAAHASHTARI
1Ch 4: 6 Hepher, Temeni, and **H**

HABAIAH
Ezra 2:61 the sons of **H**, the sons of
Neh 7:63 the children of **H**, the

HABAKKUK
Hab 1: 1 which the prophet **H** saw
Hab 3: 1 A prayer of **H** the prophet

HABAZZINIAH
Jer 35: 3 son of Jeremiah, the son of **H**

HABITATION (*see* HABITATIONS)
Gen 49: 5 of cruelty are in their **h**
Ex 15:13 Your strength to Your holy **h**
Lev 13:46 his **h** shall be outside the
Deut 12: 5 to put His name for His **h**
Deut 26:15 Look down from Your holy **h**
1Sa 2:29 I have commanded in My **h**, and
1Sa 2:32 you will see an enemy in My **h**
2Sa 15:25 and show me both it and His **h**
2Ch 29: 6 away from the **h** of the LORD
Job 5: 3 but suddenly I cursed his **h**
Job 5:24 You shall visit your **h** and
Job 8: 6 and prosper your rightful **h**
Job 18:15 is scattered on his **h**
Ps 26: 8 loved the **h** of Your house
Ps 33:14 of His **h** He looks On all the
Ps 68: 5 widows, Is God in His holy **h**
Ps 69:25 Let their **h** be desolate
Ps 71: 3 Be my strong **h**, To which I
Ps 91: 9 Even the Most High, your **h**
Ps 104:12 of the heavens have their **h**
Ps 107: 7 they might go to a city for **h**
Ps 107:36 may establish a city for **h**
Ps 132:13 He has desired it for His **h**
Prov 3:33 He blesses the **h** of the just
Is 27:10 the **h** forsaken and left like a
Is 32:18 will dwell in a peaceful **h**
Is 33:20 will see Jerusalem, a quiet **h**
Is 34:13 it shall be a **h** of jackals
Is 35: 7 in the **h** of jackals, where
Is 63:15 heaven, and see from Your **h**
Jer 9: 6 Your **h** is in the midst of
Jer 10:25 him, and made his **h** desolate
Jer 25:30 His voice from His holy **h**
Jer 31:23 O **h** of justice, and mountain
Jer 33:12 there shall again be a **h** of
Jer 41:17 and dwelt in the **h** of Chimham
Jer 49:19 Against the **h** of the strong
Jer 50: 7 the **h** of justice, the LORD,
Jer 50:19 bring back Israel to his **h**
Jer 50:44 against the **h** of the strong
Jer 50:45 their **h** desolate with them
Dan 4:21 of the heaven had their **h**
Obad 3 of the rock, whose **h** is high
Hab 3:11 moon stood still in their **h**
Zech 2:13 He is aroused from His holy **h**
Acts 1:20 Let his **h** be desolate, and
Acts 17:26 and the boundaries of their **h**
2Co 5: 2 our **h** which is from heaven
Eph 2:22 for a **h** of God in the Spirit
Jude 6 domain, but left their own **h**
Rev 18: 2 and has become a **h** of demons

HABITATIONS (*see* HABITATION)
Gen 36:43 according to their **h** in the
Ex 12:20 in all your **h** you shall eat
Ex 35: 3 your **h** on the Sabbath day
Lev 23:17 your **h** two wave loaves of
1Ch 4:33 These were their **h**, and they
1Ch 7:28 **h** were Bethel and its towns
Ps 74:20 are full of the **h** of cruelty
Ps 78:28 camp, All around their **h**
Is 54: 2 out the curtains of your **h**
Jer 9:10 for the **h** of the wilderness a
Jer 21:13 Or who shall enter our **h**
Jer 25:37 the peaceful **h** are cut down
Jer 49:20 their **h** desolate with them
Lam 2: 2 not pitied all the **h** of Jacob
Ezek 6:14 toward Diblah, in all their **h**
Luke 16: 9 you into everlasting **h**

HABITS
1Co 15:33 Evil company corrupts good **h**

HABOR
2Ki 17: 6 them in Halah and by the **H**
2Ki 18:11 put them in Halah and by the **H**
1Ch 5:26 He took them to Halah, **H**,

HACALIAH
Neh 10: 1 the governor, the son of **H**

HACHALIAH
Neh 1: 1 of Nehemiah the son of **H**

HACHILAH
1Sa 23:19 the woods, in the hill of **H**
1Sa 26: 1 not hiding in the hill of **H**
1Sa 26: 3 encamped in the hill of **H**

HACHMONI (*see* HACHMONITE)
1Ch 27:32 Jehiel the son of **H** was with

HACHMONITE (*see* HACHMONI, TACHMONITE)
1Ch 11:11 Jashobeam the son of a **H**,

HACKED
1Sa 15:33 And Samuel **h** Agag in pieces

HAD (*see* PREFACE)

HADAD (*see* BEN-HADAD, HADAR)
Gen 36:35 died, **H** the son of Bedad, who
Gen 36:36 When **H** died, Samlah of
1Ki 11:14 Solomon, **H** the Edomite
1Ki 11:17 that **H** fled to go to Egypt,
1Ki 11:17 **H** was still a little child
1Ki 11:19 **H** found great favor in the
1Ki 11:21 Now when **H** heard in Egypt
1Ki 11:21 was dead, **H** said to Pharaoh,
1Ki 11:25 the trouble that **H** caused)
1Ch 1:30 Mishma, Dumah, Massa, **H**,
1Ch 1:46 died, **H** the son of Bedad, who
1Ch 1:47 When **H** died, Samlah of
1Ch 1:50 died, **H** reigned in his place
1Ch 1:51 **H** died also

HADADEZER (*see* HADADEZER'S)
2Sa 8: 3 defeated **H** the son of Rehob
2Sa 8: 5 came to help **H** king of Zobah
2Sa 8: 7 belonged to the servants of **H**
2Sa 8: 8 and from Berothai, cities of **H**
2Sa 8: 9 defeated all the army of **H**
2Sa 8:10 he had fought against **H** and
2Sa 8:10 for **H** had wars with Toi
2Sa 8:12 spoil of **H** the son of Rehob
2Sa 10:16 Then **H** sent and brought out
2Sa 10:19 kings who were servants to **H**
1Ki 11:23 his lord, **H** king of Zobah
1Ch 18: 3 And David defeated **H** king of
1Ch 18: 5 came to help **H** king of Zobah
1Ch 18: 7 were on the servants of **H**
1Ch 18: 8 and from Chun, cities of **H**
1Ch 18: 9 the army of **H** king of Zobah
1Ch 18:10 he had fought against **H** and
1Ch 18:10 defeated him (for **H** had been
1Ch 19:19 when the servants of **H** saw

HADADEZER'S (*see* HADADEZER)
2Sa 10:16 of **H** army went before them
1Ch 19:16 of **H** army went before them

HADAD RIMMON
Zech 12:11 like the mourning at **H** in the

HADAR (*see* HADAD)
Gen 25:15 **H**, Tema, Jetur, Naphish, and
Gen 36:39 died, **H** reigned in his place

HADASHAH
Josh 15:37 Zenan, **H**, Migdal Gad,

HADASSAH (*see* ESTHER)
Esth 2: 7 Mordecai had brought up **H**

HADATTAH
Josh 15:25 Hazor, **H**, Kerioth, Hezron

HADES
Matt 11:23 will be brought down to **H**
Matt 16:18 and the gates of **H** shall not
Luke 10:15 will be thrust down to **H**
Luke 16:23 And being in torments in **H**
Acts 2:27 will not leave my soul in **H**
Acts 2:31 His soul was not left in **H**
1Co 15:55 O **H**, where is your victory
Rev 1:18 And I have the keys of **H** and of
Rev 6: 8 Death, and **H** followed with him
Rev 20:13 **H** delivered up the dead who
Rev 20:14 **H** were cast into the lake of

HADID
Ezra 2:33 the people of Lod, **H**, and Ono,
Neh 7:37 the children of Lod, **H**, and
Neh 11:34 in **H**, Zeboim, Neballat

HADLAI
2Ch 28:12 and Amasa the son of **H**, stood

HADORAM (*see* JEHORAM)
Gen 10:27 **H**, Uzal, Diklah,
1Ch 1:21 **H**, Uzal, Diklah,
1Ch 18:10 he sent **H** his son to King
1Ch 18:10 **H** brought with him all kinds
2Ch 10:18 Then King Rehoboam sent **H**

HADRACH
Zech 9: 1 LORD against the land of **H**

HAGAB (*see* HAGABA, HAGABAH)
Ezra 2:46 the sons of **H**, the sons of

HAGABA (*see* HAGAB)
Neh 7:48 of Lebana, the children of **H**

HAGABAH (*see* HAGAB)
Ezra 2:45 of Lebanah, the sons of **H**

HAGAR (*see* HAGERITE)
Gen 16: 1 maidservant whose name was **H**
Gen 16: 3 took **H** her maid, the Egyptian
Gen 16: 4 So he went in to **H**, and she
Gen 16: 8 **H**, Sarai's maid, where have
Gen 16:15 So **H** bore Abram a son
Gen 16:15 named his son, whom **H** bore
Gen 16:16 when **H** bore Ishmael to Abram
Gen 21: 9 saw the son of **H** the Egyptian
Gen 21:14 he gave it and the boy to **H**
Gen 21:17 God called to **H** out of heaven
Gen 21:17 What ails you, **H**
Gen 25:12 whom **H** the Egyptian, Sarah's
Gal 4:24 birth to bondage, which is **H**
Gal 4:25 for this **H** is Mount Sinai in

HAGARITES (*see* HAGERITE)
Ps 83: 6 Moab and the **H**

HAGERITE (*see* HAGAR, HAGARITES)
1Ch 27:31 and Jaziz the **H** was over the

HAGGAI
Ezra 5: 1 Then the prophet **H** and
Ezra 6:14 prophesying of **H** the prophet
Hag 1: 1 word of the LORD came by **H**
Hag 1: 3 LORD came by **H** the prophet
Hag 1:12 and the words of **H** the prophet

Hag 1:13 Then **H**, the LORD's messenger,
Hag 2: 1 LORD came by **H** the prophet
Hag 2:10 LORD came by **H** the prophet
Hag 2:13 And **H** said, "If one who is
Hag 2:14 Then **H** answered and said,
Hag 2:20 word of the LORD came to **H** on

HAGGI (*see* HAGGITES)
Gen 46:16 sons of Gad were Ziphion, **H**
Num 26:15 of **H**, the family of the

HAGGIAH
1Ch 6:30 **H** his son, and Asaiah his son

HAGGITES (*see* HAGGI)
Num 26:15 of Haggi, the family of the **H**

HAGGITH
2Sa 3: 4 fourth, Adonijah the son of **H**
1Ki 1: 5 the son of **H** exalted himself
1Ki 1:11 the son of **H** has become king
1Ki 2:13 of **H** came to Bathsheba the
1Ch 3: 2 fourth, Adonijah the son of **H**

HAGRI (*see* HAGRITES)
1Ch 11:38 Nathan, Mibhar the son of **H**

HAGRITES (*see* HAGRI)
1Ch 5:10 Saul they made war with the **H**
1Ch 5:19 They made war with the **H**,
1Ch 5:20 the **H** were delivered into

HAHIROTH (*see* PI HAHIROTH)
Num 33: 8 They departed from before **H**

HAIL (*see* HAILSTONE)
Ex 9:18 very heavy **h** to rain down
Ex 9:19 for the **h** shall come down on
Ex 9:22 that there may be **h** in all
Ex 9:23 and the LORD sent thunder and **h**
Ex 9:23 the LORD rained **h** on the land
Ex 9:24 So there was **h**, and fire
Ex 9:24 and fire mingled with the **h**
Ex 9:25 the **h** struck throughout the
Ex 9:25 the **h** struck every herb of
Ex 9:26 Israel were, there was no **h**
Ex 9:28 more mighty thundering and **h**
Ex 9:29 and there will be no more **h**
Ex 9:33 the **h** ceased, and the rain was
Ex 9:34 saw that the rain, the **h**, and
Ex 10: 5 remains to you from the **h**
Ex 10:12 all that the **h** has left
Ex 10:15 trees which the **h** had left
Job 38:22 you seen the treasury of **h**
Ps 78:47 destroyed their vines with **h**
Ps 78:48 gave up their cattle to the **h**
Ps 105:32 He gave them **h** for rain, And
Ps 147:17 casts out His **h** like morsels
Ps 148: 8 Fire and **h**, snow and clouds
Is 28: 2 one, like a tempest of **h** and a
Is 28:17 the **h** will sweep away the
Is 32:19 Though **h** comes down on the
Hag 2:17 **h** in all the labors of your
Matt 27:29 **H**, King of the Jews
Mark 15:18 **H**, King of the Jews
John 19: 3 **H**, King of the Jews
Rev 8: 7 And **h** and fire followed,
Rev 11:19 an earthquake, and great **h**
Rev 16:21 great **h** from heaven fell upon
Rev 16:21 of the plague of the **h**, since

HAILSTONE (*see* HAIL, HAILSTONES)
Rev 16:21 every **h** about the weight of a

HAILSTONES (*see* HAILSTONE)
Josh 10:11 the LORD cast down large **h**
Josh 10:11 the **h** than those whom the
Ps 18:12 thick clouds passed with **h**
Ps 18:13 High uttered His voice, **H**
Is 30:30 scattering, tempest, and **h**
Ezek 13:11 rain, and you, O great **h**,
Ezek 13:13 great **h** in fury to consume it
Ezek 38:22 him, flooding rain, great **h**

HAIR (*see* HAIR'S, HAIRS, HAIRY)
Gen 42:38 **h** with sorrow to the grave
Gen 44:29 **h** with sorrow to the grave
Gen 44:31 will bring down the gray **h** of
Ex 25: 4 linen thread, and goats' **h**
Ex 26: 7 make curtains of goats' **h**
Ex 35: 6 linen thread, and goats' **h**
Ex 35:23 scarlet, fine linen, goats' **h**
Ex 35:26 wisdom spun yarn of goats' **h**
Ex 36:14 **h** for the tent over the
Lev 13: 3 and if the **h** on the sore has
Lev 13: 4 its **h** has not turned white,
Lev 13:10 and it has turned the **h** white
Lev 13:20 its **h** has turned white, the
Lev 13:25 indeed if the **h** of the bright
Lev 13:30 there is in it thin yellow **h**
Lev 13:31 and there is no black **h** in it
Lev 13:32 and there is no yellow **h** in it
Lev 13:36 need not seek for yellow **h**
Lev 13:37 is black **h** grown up in it
Lev 13:40 As for the man whose **h** has
Lev 13:41 He whose **h** has fallen from
Lev 14: 8 clothes, shave off all his **h**
Lev 14: 9 shave all the **h** off his head
Lev 14: 9 all his **h** he shall shave off
Num 6: 5 of the **h** of his head grow
Num 6:18 shall take the **h** from his
Num 6:19 has shaved his consecrated **h**
Num 31:20 everything woven of goats' **h**
Judg 16:22 the **h** of his head began to
1Sa 14:45 not one **h** of his head shall
1Sa 19:13 of goats' **h** for his head, and
1Sa 19:16 of goats' **h** for his head
2Sa 14:11 not one **h** of your son shall
2Sa 14:26 when he cut the **h** of his head
2Sa 14:26 he weighed the **h** of his head
1Ki 1:52 not one **h** of him shall fall
1Ki 2: 6 do not let his gray **h** go down
1Ki 2: 9 but bring his gray **h** down to
Ezra 9: 3 out some of the **h** of my head
Neh 13:25 of them and pulled out their **h**
Job 4:15 the **h** on my body stood up
Job 41:32 think the deep had white **h**
Song 4: 1 Your **h** is like a flock of
Song 6: 5 Your **h** is like a flock of
Song 7: 5 the **h** of your head is like
Is 3:24 instead of well-set **h**,
Is 7:20 the **h** of the legs, and will
Jer 7:29 Cut off your **h** and cast it
Ezek 5: 1 to weigh and divide the **h**
Ezek 8: 3 and took me by a lock of my **h**
Ezek 16: 7 were formed, your **h** grew, but
Ezek 44:20 nor let their **h** grow long
Ezek 44:20 keep their **h** well trimmed
Dan 3:27 the **h** of their head was not
Dan 4:33 his **h** had grown like eagles'
Dan 7: 9 the **h** of His head was like
Mic 1:16 bald and cut off your **h**,
Zech 13: 4 a robe of coarse **h** to deceive
Matt 3: 4 was clothed in camel's **h**,
Matt 5:36 make one **h** white or black
Mark 1: 6 was clothed with camel's **h**
Luke 7:38 them with the **h** of her head
Luke 7:44 them with the **h** of her head
Luke 21:18 But not a **h** of your head
John 11: 2 and wiped His feet with her **h**
John 12: 3 and wiped His feet with her **h**
Acts 18:18 He had his **h** cut off at
Acts 27:34 since not a **h** will fall from
1Co 11:14 you that if a man has long **h**
1Co 11:15 But if a woman has long **h**
1Co 11:15 for her **h** is given to her for
1Ti 2: 9 not with braided **h** or gold or
1Pe 3: 3 adorning of arranging the **h**
Rev 1:14 His **h** were white like wool,
Rev 6:12 black as sackcloth of **h**, and
Rev 9: 8 They had **h** like women's **h**,
Rev 9: 8 They had **h** like women's **h**

HAIR'S (*see* HAIR)
Judg 20:16 sling a stone at a **h** breadth

HAIRS (*see* HAIR)
Lev 13:21 there are no white **h** in it
Lev 13:26 no white **h** in the bright spot
Deut 32:25 child with the man of gray **h**
Ps 40:12 more than the **h** of my head
Ps 69: 4 more than the **h** of my head
Is 46: 4 even to gray **h** I will carry
Hos 7: 9 gray **h** are here and there on
Matt 10:30 But the very **h** of your head
Luke 12: 7 But the very **h** of your head

HAIRY (*see* HAIR)
Gen 25:25 He was like a **h** garment all
Gen 27:11 Esau my brother is a **h** man
Gen 27:23 because his hands were **h** like
2Ki 1: 8 He was a **h** man, and wore a
Ps 68:21 The **h** scalp of the one who

HAKKATAN
Ezra 8:12 Azgad, Johanan the son of **H**

HAKKOZ (*see* KOZ)
1Ch 24:10 the seventh to **H**, the eighth

HAKUPHA
Ezra 2:51 sons of Bakbuk, the sons of **H**
Neh 7:53 of Bakbuk, the children of **H**

HALAH
2Ki 17: 6 Assyria, and placed them in **H**
2Ki 18:11 to Assyria, and put them in **H**
1Ch 5:26 He took them to **H**, Habor,

HALAK
Josh 11:17 from Mount **H** and the ascent to
Josh 12: 7 of Lebanon as far as Mount **H**

HALF
Gen 24:22 nose ring weighing **h** a shekel
Ex 24: 6 And Moses took **h** the blood
Ex 24: 6 **h** the blood he sprinkled on
Ex 25:10 and a **h** cubits shall be its
Ex 25:10 a **h** its width, and a cubit and
Ex 25:10 and a cubit and a **h** its height
Ex 25:17 and a **h** cubits shall be its
Ex 25:17 and a cubit and a **h** its width
Ex 25:23 and a cubit and a **h** its height
Ex 26:12 the **h** curtain that remains,
Ex 26:16 a **h** shall be the width of
Ex 30:13 **h** a shekel according to the
Ex 30:15 not give less than **h** a shekel
Ex 30:23 **h** as much sweet-smelling
Ex 36:21 of each board a cubit and a **h**
Ex 37: 1 a **h** cubits was its length, a
Ex 37: 1 a **h** its width, and a cubit and
Ex 37: 1 and a cubit and a **h** its height
Ex 37: 6 a **h** cubits was its length and
Ex 37: 6 and a cubit and a **h** its width
Ex 37:10 and a cubit and a **h** its height
Ex 38:26 **h** a shekel, according to the
Lev 6:20 **h** of it in the morning and
Lev 6:20 morning and **h** of it at night
Num 12:12 whose flesh is **h** consumed
Num 15: 9 mixed with **h** a hin of oil
Num 15:10 **h** a hin of wine as an
Num 28:14 drink offering shall be **h** a
Num 31:29 take it from their **h**, and give
Num 31:30 the children of Israel's **h**
Num 31:36 And the **h**, the portion for
Num 31:42 the children of Israel's **h**
Num 31:43 now the **h** belonging to the
Num 31:47 **h** Moses took one of every
Num 32:33 to **h** the tribe of Manasseh
Deut 3:12 **h** the mountains of Gilead and
Deut 3:13 Og, I gave to **h** the tribe of
Deut 29: 8 to **h** the tribe of Manasseh
Josh 1:12 and **h** the tribe of Manasseh
Josh 4:12 and **h** the tribe of Manasseh
Josh 8:33 **H** of them were in front of
Josh 8:33 **h** of them in front of Mount
Josh 12: 2 ruled **h** of Gilead, from Aroer
Josh 12: 5 over **h** of Gilead as far as
Josh 12: 6 and **h** the tribe of Manasseh
Josh 13: 7 and **h** the tribe of Manasseh
Josh 13: 8 With the other **h** tribe the
Josh 13:25 **h** the land of the Ammonites
Josh 13:29 to **h** the tribe of Manasseh
Josh 13:29 it was for **h** the tribe of the
Josh 13:31 **h** of Gilead, and Ashtaroth and
Josh 13:31 for **h** of the children of
Josh 18: 7 **h** the tribe of Manasseh have
Josh 22: 1 and **h** the tribe of Manasseh,
Josh 22: 7 Now to **h** the tribe of
Josh 22: 7 but to the other **h** of it
Josh 22: 9 and **h** the tribe of Manasseh
Josh 22:10 **h** the tribe of Manasseh built
Josh 22:11 **h** the tribe of Manasseh have
Josh 22:13 to **h** the tribe of Manasseh,
Josh 22:15 to **h** the tribe of Manasseh,
Josh 22:21 and **h** the tribe of Manasseh
1Sa 14:14 about **h** an acre of land
2Sa 10: 4 shaved off **h** of their beards,
2Sa 18: 3 nor if **h** of us die, will they
2Sa 19:40 also **h** the people of Israel
1Ki 3:25 give **h** to one, and **h** to the
1Ki 3:25 to one, and **h** to the other
1Ki 7:31 one and a **h** cubits in outside
1Ki 7:32 a wheel was one and a **h** cubits
1Ki 7:35 at the height of **h** a cubit
1Ki 10: 7 indeed the **h** was not told me
1Ki 13: 8 were to give me **h** your house
1Ki 16: 9 commander of **h** his chariots
1Ki 16:21 **h** of the people followed

1Ki 16:21 him king, and **h** followed Omri
1Ch 2:52 **h** of the families of Manuhoth
1Ch 2:54 **h** of the Manahethites, and the
1Ch 5:18 **h** the tribe of Manasseh had
1Ch 6:61 from **h** the tribe of Manasseh
2Ch 9: 6 the **h** of the greatness of
Neh 3: 9 leader of **h** the district of
Neh 3:12 leader of **h** the district of
Neh 3:16 leader of **h** the district of
Neh 3:17 leader of **h** the district of
Neh 3:18 leader of the other **h** of the
Neh 4: 6 together up to **h** its height
Neh 4:16 that **h** of my servants worked
Neh 4:16 the other **h** held the spears
Neh 4:21 **h** of the men held the spears
Neh 12:32 **h** of the leaders of Judah,
Neh 12:38 I was behind them with **h** of
Neh 12:40 the **h** of the rulers with me
Neh 13:24 **h** of their children spoke the
Esth 5: 3 up to **h** my kingdom
Esth 5: 6 request, up to **h** my kingdom
Esth 7: 2 request, up to **h** my kingdom
Job 21:21 of his months is cut in **h**
Ps 55:23 not live out **h** their days
Is 44:16 He burns **h** of it in the fire
Is 44:16 with this **h** he eats meat
Is 44:19 I have burned **h** of it in the
Ezek 16:51 did not commit **h** of your sins
Ezek 40:42 a **h** long, one cubit and a **h**
Ezek 40:42 a **h** wide, and one cubit high
Ezek 43:17 with a rim of **h** a cubit
Dan 7:25 a time and times and **h** a time
Dan 12: 7 a time, times, and **h** a time
Zech 14: 2 **H** of the city shall go into
Zech 14: 4 **h** of the mountain shall move
Zech 14: 4 and **h** of it toward the south
Zech 14: 8 **h** of them toward the eastern
Zech 14: 8 **h** of them toward the western
Mark 6:23 you, up to **h** of my kingdom
Luke 10:30 departed, leaving him **h** dead
Luke 19: 8 I give **h** of my goods to the
Rev 8: 1 in heaven for about **h** an hour
Rev 11: 9 a **h** days, and not allow their
Rev 11:11 a **h** days the breath of life
Rev 12:14 **h** a time, from the presence

HALF-SHEKEL
Ex 30:13 The **h** shall be an offering to

HALF-TRIBE
Num 34:13 the nine tribes and to the **h**
Num 34:14 and the **h** of Manasseh has
Num 34:15 the **h** have received their
Josh 14: 2 for the nine tribes and the **h**
Josh 14: 3 the **h** on the other side of
Josh 21: 5 and from the **h** of Manasseh
Josh 21: 6 from the **h** of Manasseh in
Josh 21:25 and from the **h** of Manasseh,
Josh 21:27 from the other **h** of Manasseh
1Ch 5:23 So the children of the **h** of
1Ch 5:26 and the **h** of Manasseh into
1Ch 6:70 And from the **h** of Manasseh
1Ch 6:71 From the family of the **h** of
1Ch 12:31 of the **h** of Manasseh eighteen
1Ch 12:37 the **h** of Manasseh, from the
1Ch 26:32 the **h** of Manasseh, for every
1Ch 27:20 over the **h** of Manasseh, Joel
1Ch 27:21 over the **h** of Manasseh in

HALHUL
Josh 15:58 **H**, Beth Zur, Gedor,

HALI
Josh 19:25 territory included Helkath, **H**

HALL
1Sa 9:22 and brought them into the **h**
1Ki 7: 6 He also made the **H** of Pillars
1Ki 7: 7 he made a **h** for the throne
1Ki 7: 7 the **H** of Judgment, where he
1Ki 7: 8 another court inside the **h**
1Ki 7: 8 this **h** for Pharaoh's daughter
1Ki 7:19 top of the pillars in the **h**
1Ki 7:50 of the main **h** of the temple
2Ch 4:22 of the main **h** of the temple
Dan 5:10 lords, came to the banquet **h**
Matt 22:10 the wedding **h** was filled with
Mark 15:16 into the **h** called Praetorium

HALLOHESH
Neh 3:12 him was Shallum the son of **H**
Neh 10:24 **H**, Pilha, Shobek,

HALLOW (*see* HALLOWED)
Ex 28:38 the children of Israel **h** in
Ex 29: 1 you shall do to them to **h**
Ex 40: 9 and you shall **h** it and all its
Num 20:12 to **h** Me in the eyes of the
Num 27:14 against My command to **h** Me at
Deut 32:51 because you did not **h** Me in
Is 8:13 of hosts, Him you shall **h**
Is 29:23 midst, they will **h** My name
Is 29:23 **h** the Holy One of Jacob, and
Jer 17:22 but **h** the Sabbath day, as I
Jer 17:24 but **h** the Sabbath day, to do
Jer 17:27 heed Me to **h** the Sabbath day
Ezek 20:20 **h** My Sabbaths, and they will
Ezek 44:24 and they shall **h** My Sabbaths

HALLOWED (*see* HALLOW)
Ex 20:11 the Sabbath day and **h** it
Ex 29:21 he and his garments shall be **h**
Lev 12: 4 shall not touch any **h** thing
Lev 19: 8 the **h** offering of the LORD
Lev 22:32 but I will be **h** among the
Num 20:13 LORD, and He was **h** among
Is 5:16 shall be **h** in righteousness
Ezek 20:41 I will be **h** in you before the
Ezek 28:22 in her and am **h** in her
Ezek 28:25 am **h** in them in the sight of
Ezek 36:23 when I am **h** in you before
Ezek 38:16 know Me, when I am **h** in you
Ezek 39:27 I am **h** in them in the sight
Matt 6: 9 in heaven, **h** be Your name
Luke 11: 2 in heaven, **h** be Your name

HALT (*see* HALTED)
Is 13:11 I will **h** the arrogance of the
Nah 2: 8 **H**! **H**!" they cry

HALTED (*see* HALT)
1Sa 23:13 so he **h** the expedition
2Sa 20:12 everyone who came upon him **h**

HAM (*see* HAMITES)
Gen 5:32 old, and Noah begot Shem, **H**
Gen 6:10 Shem, **H**, and Japheth
Gen 7:13 Noah and Noah's sons, Shem, **H**
Gen 9:18 out of the ark were Shem, **H**
Gen 9:18 **H** was the father of Canaan
Gen 9:22 And **H**, the father of Canaan,
Gen 10: 1 Shem, **H**, and Japheth
Gen 10: 6 The sons of **H** were Cush,
Gen 10:20 These were the sons of **H**,
Gen 14: 5 Karnaim, the Zuzim in **H**, the
1Ch 1: 4 Noah, Shem, **H**, and Japheth
1Ch 1: 8 The sons of **H** were Cush,
Ps 78:51 strength in the tents of **H**
Ps 105:23 sojourned in the land of **H**
Ps 105:27 And wonders in the land of **H**
Ps 106:22 works in the land of **H**,

HAMAN (*see* HAMAN'S)
Esth 3: 1 King Ahasuerus promoted **H**
Esth 3: 2 bowed and paid homage to **H**
Esth 3: 4 them, that they told it to **H**
Esth 3: 5 When **H** saw that Mordecai did
Esth 3: 5 **H** was filled with wrath
Esth 3: 6 **H** sought to destroy all the
Esth 3: 7 before **H** to determine the day
Esth 3: 8 Then **H** said to King Ahasuerus
Esth 3:10 from his hand and gave it to **H**
Esth 3:11 And the king said to **H**, "The
Esth 3:12 to all that **H** commanded
Esth 3:15 **H** sat down to drink, but the
Esth 4: 7 the sum of money that **H** had
Esth 5: 4 **H** come today to the banquet
Esth 5: 5 Bring **H** quickly, that he may
Esth 5: 5 **H** went to the banquet that
Esth 5: 8 **H** come to the banquet which I
Esth 5: 9 So **H** went out that day joyful
Esth 5: 9 but when **H** saw Mordecai in
Esth 5:10 Nevertheless **H** restrained
Esth 5:11 Then **H** told them of his great
Esth 5:12 Moreover **H** said, "Besides,
Esth 5:14 And the thing pleased **H**
Esth 6: 4 Now **H** had just entered the
Esth 6: 5 **H** is there, standing in the
Esth 6: 6 So **H** came in, and the king
Esth 6: 6 Now **H** thought in his heart,
Esth 6: 7 And **H** answered the king,
Esth 6:10 Then the king said to **H**
Esth 6:11 So **H** took the robe and the
Esth 6:12 But **H** hastened to his house,
Esth 6:13 When **H** told his wife Zeresh
Esth 6:14 hastened to bring **H** to the
Esth 7: 1 **H** went to dine with Queen
Esth 7: 6 and enemy is this wicked **H**
Esth 7: 6 So **H** was terrified before
Esth 7: 7 but **H** stood before Queen
Esth 7: 8 **H** had fallen across the couch
Esth 7: 9 which **H** made for Mordecai,
Esth 7: 9 is standing at the house of **H**
Esth 7:10 So they hanged **H** on the
Esth 8: 1 Queen Esther the house of **H**
Esth 8: 2 which he had taken from **H**
Esth 8: 2 Mordecai over the house of **H**
Esth 8: 3 evil plot of **H** the Agagite
Esth 8: 5 the letters devised by **H**, the
Esth 8: 7 given Esther the house of **H**
Esth 9:10 the ten sons of **H** the son of
Esth 9:12 citadel, and the ten sons of **H**
Esth 9:24 because **H**, the son of
Esth 9:25 **H** had devised against the

HAMAN'S (*see* HAMAN)
Esth 7: 8 mouth, they covered **H** face
Esth 9:13 let **H** ten sons be hanged on
Esth 9:14 and they hanged **H** ten sons

HAMATH (*see* HAMATHITE)
Num 13:21 Rehob, near the entrance of **H**
Num 34: 8 border to the entrance of **H**
Josh 13: 5 as far as the entrance to **H**
Judg 3: 3 Hermon to the entrance of **H**
2Sa 8: 9 When Toi king of **H** heard that
1Ki 8:65 from the entrance of **H** to the
2Ki 14:25 of **H** to the Sea of the Arabah
2Ki 14:28 Israel, from Damascus and **H**
2Ki 17:24 from Babylon, Cuthah, Ava, **H**
2Ki 17:30 the men of **H** made Ashima,
2Ki 18:34 Where are the gods of **H** and
2Ki 19:13 Where is the king of **H**, the
2Ki 23:33 at Riblah in the land of **H**
2Ki 25:21 at Riblah in the land of **H**
1Ch 13: 5 as far as the entrance of **H**
1Ch 18: 3 king of Zobah as far as **H**
1Ch 18: 9 When Tou king of **H** heard that
2Ch 7: 8 from the entrance of **H** to the
2Ch 8: 4 cities which he built in **H**
Is 10: 9 Is not **H** like Arpad
Is 11:11 from Elam and Shinar, from **H**
Is 36:19 Where are the gods of **H** and
Is 37:13 Where is the king of **H**, the
Jer 39: 5 to Riblah in the land of **H**
Jer 49:23 **H** and Arpad are shamed, for
Jer 52: 9 at Riblah in the land of **H**
Jer 52:27 at Riblah in the land of **H**
Ezek 47:16 **H**, Berothah, Sibraim (which
Ezek 47:16 Damascus and the border of **H**)
Ezek 47:17 it is the border of **H**
Ezek 47:20 comes to a point opposite **H**
Ezek 48: 1 Hethlon at the entrance of **H**
Ezek 48: 1 in the direction of **H**, there
Amos 6: 2 from there go to **H** the great
Amos 6:14 you from the entrance of **H** to
Zech 9: 2 also against **H**, which borders

HAMATHITE (*see* HAMATH)
Gen 10:18 the Zemarite, and the **H**
1Ch 1:16 the Zemarite, and the **H**

HAMATH ZOBAH (*see* ZOBAH)
2Ch 8: 3 And Solomon went to **H** and

HAMITES (*see* HAM)
1Ch 4:40 for some **H** formerly lived

HAMMATH
Josh 19:35 cities are Ziddim, Zer, **H**
1Ch 2:55 the Kenites who came from **H**

HAMMEDATHA
Esth 3: 1 the son of **H** the Agagite, and
Esth 3:10 the son of **H** the Agagite, the
Esth 8: 5 the son of **H** the Agagite,
Esth 9:10 sons of Haman the son of **H**
Esth 9:24 the son of **H** the Agagite, the

HAMMER (*see* HAMMERED, HAMMERS)
Judg 4:21 took a **h** in her hand, and went
Judg 5:26 right hand to the workmen's **h**
1Ki 6: 7 so that no **h** or chisel or any
Is 41: 7 he who smooths with the **h**
Jer 23:29 like a **h** that breaks the rock
Jer 50:23 How the **h** of the whole earth

HAMMERED (*see* HAMMER)
Ex 25:18 of **h** work you shall make them
Ex 25:31 lampstand shall be of **h** work
Ex 25:36 be one **h** piece of pure gold

Ex 37:17 of **h** work he made the
Ex 37:22 all of it was one **h** piece of
Num 8: 4 the lampstand was of **h** gold
Num 8: 4 to its flowers it was **h** work
Num 10: 2 you shall make them of **h** work
Num 16:38 let them be made into **h**
Num 16:39 they were **h** out as a covering
1Ki 10:16 large shields of **h** gold
1Ki 10:17 hundred shields of **h** gold
2Ch 9:15 large shields of **h** gold
2Ch 9:15 six hundred shekels of **h** gold
2Ch 9:16 hundred shields of **h** gold

HAMMERS (*see* HAMMER)
Ps 74: 6 all at once, With axes and **h**
Is 44:12 the coals, fashions it with **h**
Jer 10: 4 **h** so that it will not topple

HAMMOLEKETH
1Ch 7:18 His sister **H** bore Ishhod,

HAMMON
Josh 19:28 including Ebron, Rehob, **H**
1Ch 6:76 **H** with its common-lands, and

HAMMOTH DOR
Josh 21:32 **H** with its common-land, and

HAMONAH
Ezek 39:16 of the city will also be **H**

HAMON GOG (*see* GOG)
Ezek 39:11 will call it the Valley of **H**
Ezek 39:15 buried it in the Valley of **H**

HAMOR (*see* HAMOR'S)
Gen 33:19 tent, from the children of **H**
Gen 34: 2 the son of **H** the Hivite,
Gen 34: 4 Shechem spoke to his father **H**
Gen 34: 6 Then **H** the father of Shechem
Gen 34: 8 But **H** spoke with them, saying
Gen 34:13 and **H** his father, and spoke
Gen 34:18 And their words pleased **H** and
Gen 34:20 And **H** and Shechem his son
Gen 34:24 the gate of his city heeded **H**
Gen 34:26 And they killed **H** and Shechem
Josh 24:32 **H** the father of Shechem for
Judg 9:28 Serve the men of **H** the father
Acts 7:16 of money from the sons of **H**

HAMOR'S (*see* HAMOR)
Gen 34:18 Hamor and Shechem, **H** son

HAMRAN
1Ch 1:41 The sons of Dishon were **H**

HAMSTRING (*see* HAMSTRUNG)
Josh 11: 6 You shall **h** their horses and

HAMSTRUNG (*see* HAMSTRING)
Gen 49: 6 their self-will they **h** an ox
Josh 11: 9 he **h** their horses and burned
2Sa 8: 4 Also David **h** all the chariot
1Ch 18: 4 David also **h** all the chariot

HAMUEL
1Ch 4:26 sons of Mishma were **H** his son

HAMUL (*see* HAMULITES)
Gen 46:12 of Perez were Hezron and **H**
Num 26:21 of **H**, the family of the
1Ch 2: 5 of Perez were Hezron and **H**

HAMULITES (*see* HAMUL)
Num 26:21 of Hamul, the family of the **H**

HAMUTAL
2Ki 23:31 His mother's name was **H** the
2Ki 24:18 His mother's name was **H** the
Jer 52: 1 His mother's name was **H** the

HANAMEEL
Jer 32: 7 **H** the son of Shallum your
Jer 32: 8 Then **H** my uncle's son came to
Jer 32: 9 So I bought the field from **H**
Jer 32:12 presence of **H** my uncle's son

HANAN (*see* BAAL-HANAN, BEN-HANAN, ELON BETH HANAN)
1Ch 8:23 Abdon, Zichri, **H**,
1Ch 8:38 Sheariah, Obadiah, and **H**
1Ch 9:44 Sheariah, Obadiah, and **H**
1Ch 11:43 **H** the son of Maachah,
Ezra 2:46 of Shalmai, the sons of **H**
Neh 7:49 the children of **H**, the
Neh 8: 7 Kelita, Azariah, Jozabad, **H**
Neh 10:10 Hodijah, Kelita, Pelaiah, **H**
Neh 10:22 Pelatiah, **H**, Anaiah,
Neh 10:26 Ahijah, **H**, Anan,
Neh 13:13 next to them was **H** the son of
Jer 35: 4 sons of **H** the son of Igdaliah

HANANEAL
Neh 12:39 the Fish Gate, the Tower of **H**

HANANEEL
Neh 3: 1 then as far as the Tower of **H**
Jer 31:38 Tower of **H** to the Corner Gate
Zech 14:10 from the Tower of **H** to the

HANANI
1Ki 16: 1 came to Jehu the son of **H**
1Ki 16: 7 the son of **H** against Baasha
1Ch 25: 4 Jerimoth, Hananiah, **H**,
1Ch 25:25 the eighteenth for **H**, his
2Ch 16: 7 at that time **H** the seer came
2Ch 19: 2 Jehu the son of **H** the seer
2Ch 20:34 the book of Jehu the son of **H**
Ezra 10:20 of Immer: **H** and Zebadiah
Neh 1: 2 that **H** one of my brethren
Neh 7: 2 of Jerusalem to my brother **H**
Neh 12:36 Maai, Nethaneal, Judah, and **H**

HANANIAH (*see* SHADRACH)
1Ch 3:19 Zerubbabel were Meshullam, **H**
1Ch 3:21 The sons of **H** were Pelatiah
1Ch 8:24 **H**, Elam, Antothijah,
1Ch 25: 4 Uzziel, Shebuel, Jerimoth, **H**
1Ch 25:23 the sixteenth for **H**, his sons
2Ch 26:11 officer, under the hand of **H**
Ezra 10:28 Jehohanan, **H**, Zabbai, and
Neh 3: 8 Also next to him **H**, one of
Neh 3:30 After him **H** the son of
Neh 7: 2 **H** the leader of the citadel,
Neh 10:23 Hoshea, **H**, Hasshub,
Neh 12:12 of Jeremiah, **H**
Neh 12:41 Elioenai, Zechariah, and **H**
Jer 28: 1 that **H** the son of Azur the
Jer 28: 5 spoke to the prophet **H** in the
Jer 28:10 Then **H** the prophet took the
Jer 28:11 **H** spoke in the presence of
Jer 28:12 after **H** the prophet had
Jer 28:13 Go and tell **H**, saying, 'Thus
Jer 28:15 said to **H** the prophet, "Hear
Jer 28:15 Hear now, **H**, the LORD has not
Jer 28:17 So **H** the prophet died the
Jer 36:12 Zedekiah the son of **H**, and
Jer 37:13 of Shelemiah, the son of **H**
Dan 1: 6 sons of Judah were Daniel, **H**
Dan 1: 7 to **H**, Shadrach
Dan 1:11 had set over Daniel, **H**,
Dan 1:19 none was found like Daniel, **H**
Dan 2:17 made the decision known to **H**

HAND (*see* HANDED, HANDFUL, HANDIWORK, HANDS)
Gen 3:22 And now, lest he put out his **h**
Gen 4:11 brother's blood from your **h**
Gen 8: 9 So he put out his **h** and took
Gen 9: 2 They are given into your **h**
Gen 9: 5 from the **h** of every beast I
Gen 9: 5 it, and from the **h** of man
Gen 9: 5 From the **h** of every man's
Gen 14:20 your enemies into your **h**
Gen 14:22 have lifted my **h** to the LORD
Gen 16: 6 Indeed your maid is in your **h**
Gen 16: 9 submit yourself under her **h**
Gen 16:12 his **h** shall be against every
Gen 16:12 and every man's **h** against him
Gen 19:16 of his **h**, his wife's **h**
Gen 21:18 lad and hold him with your **h**
Gen 21:30 seven ewe lambs from my **h**
Gen 22: 6 and he took the fire in his **h**
Gen 22:10 Abraham stretched out his **h**
Gen 22:12 Do not lay your **h** on the lad
Gen 24: 2 put your **h** under my thigh,
Gen 24: 9 So the servant put his **h**
Gen 24:10 master's goods were in his **h**
Gen 24:18 let her pitcher down to her **h**
Gen 24:49 to the right **h** or to the left
Gen 25:26 his **h** took hold of Esau's
Gen 27:17 into the **h** of her son Jacob
Gen 27:41 for my father are at **h**
Gen 30:35 them into the **h** of his sons
Gen 31:39 You required it from my **h**
Gen 32:11 from the **h** of my brother,
Gen 32:11 brother, from the **h** of Esau
Gen 32:13 took what came to his **h** as a
Gen 32:16 them to the **h** of his servants
Gen 33:10 receive my present from my **h**
Gen 37:22 and do not lay a **h** on him"
Gen 37:27 and let not our **h** be upon him
Gen 38:18 your staff that is in your **h**
Gen 38:20 by the **h** of his friend the
Gen 38:20 his pledge from the woman's **h**
Gen 38:28 that the one put out his **h**
Gen 38:28 thread and bound it on his **h**
Gen 38:29 as he drew back his **h**, that
Gen 38:30 the scarlet thread on his **h**
Gen 39: 3 he did to prosper in his **h**
Gen 39: 4 that he had he put in his **h**
Gen 39: 6 all that he had in Joseph's **h**
Gen 39: 8 all that he has to my **h**
Gen 39:12 he left his garment in her **h**
Gen 39:13 had left his garment in her **h**
Gen 39:22 committed to Joseph's **h** all
Gen 39:23 that was under Joseph's **h**
Gen 40:11 Pharaoh's cup was in my **h**
Gen 40:11 placed the cup in Pharaoh's **h**
Gen 40:13 his **h** according to the former
Gen 40:21 placed the cup in Pharaoh's **h**
Gen 41:42 his signet ring off his **h**
Gen 41:42 **h** and put it on Joseph's **h**
Gen 41:44 **h** or foot in all the land of
Gen 43: 9 from my **h** you shall require
Gen 43:12 Take double money in your **h**
Gen 43:12 take back in your **h** the money
Gen 43:15 took double money in their **h**
Gen 43:21 have brought it back in our **h**
Gen 43:26 was in their **h** into the house
Gen 44:17 in whose **h** the cup was found
Gen 46: 4 will put his **h** on your eyes
Gen 47:29 put your **h** under my thigh
Gen 48:13 right **h** toward Israel's left **h**
Gen 48:13 and Manasseh with his left **h**
Gen 48:13 **h** toward Israel's right **h**
Gen 48:14 stretched out his right **h**
Gen 48:14 his left **h** on Manasseh's head
Gen 48:17 **h** on the head of Ephraim, it
Gen 48:17 took hold of his father's **h**
Gen 48:18 put your right **h** on his head
Gen 48:22 which I took from the **h** of
Gen 49: 8 your **h** shall be on the neck
Ex 2:19 from the **h** of the shepherds
Ex 3: 8 out of the **h** of the Egyptians
Ex 3:19 no, not even by a mighty **h**
Ex 3:20 So I will stretch out My **h**
Ex 4: 2 What is that in your **h**
Ex 4: 4 Reach out your **h** and take it
Ex 4: 4 (and he reached out his **h**
Ex 4: 4 and it became a rod in his **h**)
Ex 4: 6 Now put your **h** in your bosom
Ex 4: 6 he put his **h** in his bosom, and
Ex 4: 6 his **h** was leprous, like snow
Ex 4: 7 Put your **h** in your bosom
Ex 4: 7 So he put his **h** in his
Ex 4:13 Lord, please send by the **h** of
Ex 4:17 shall take this rod in your **h**
Ex 4:20 took the rod of God in his **h**
Ex 4:21 which I have put in your **h**
Ex 5:21 a sword in their **h** to kill us
Ex 6: 1 For with a strong **h** he will
Ex 6: 1 with a strong **h** he will drive
Ex 7: 4 that I may lay My **h** on Egypt
Ex 7: 5 I stretch out My **h** on Egypt
Ex 7:15 you shall take in your **h**
Ex 7:17 with the rod that is in my **h**
Ex 7:19 stretch out your **h** over the
Ex 8: 5 Stretch out your **h** with your
Ex 8: 6 **h** over the waters of Egypt
Ex 8:17 out his **h** with his rod and
Ex 9: 3 the **h** of the LORD will be on
Ex 9:15 if I had stretched out My **h**
Ex 9:22 out your **h** toward heaven,
Ex 10:12 Stretch out your **h** over the
Ex 10:21 out your **h** toward heaven,
Ex 10:22 out his **h** toward heaven, and
Ex 12:11 feet, and your staff in your **h**
Ex 13: 3 for by strength of **h** the LORD
Ex 13: 9 be as a sign to you on your **h**
Ex 13: 9 for with a strong **h** the LORD
Ex 13:14 By strength of **h** the LORD
Ex 13:16 shall be as a sign on your **h**
Ex 13:16 for by strength of **h** the LORD
Ex 14:16 out your **h** over the sea and
Ex 14:21 out his **h** over the sea
Ex 14:22 wall to them on their right **h**
Ex 14:26 out your **h** over the sea, that
Ex 14:27 out his **h** over the sea
Ex 14:29 wall to them on their right **h**
Ex 14:30 out of the **h** of the Egyptians
Ex 15: 6 Your right **h**, O LORD, has

Ex 15: 6 Your right **h**, O LORD, has
Ex 15: 9 my **h** shall destroy them
Ex 15:12 stretched out Your right **h**
Ex 15:20 took the timbrel in her **h**
Ex 16: 3 that we had died by the **h** of
Ex 17: 5 Also take in your **h** your rod
Ex 17: 9 with the rod of God in my **h**
Ex 17:11 was, when Moses held up his **h**
Ex 17:11 and when he let down his **h**
Ex 18: 9 out of the **h** of the Egyptians
Ex 18:10 out of the **h** of the Egyptians
Ex 18:10 and out of the **h** of Pharaoh
Ex 18:10 under the **h** of the Egyptians
Ex 19:13 Not a **h** shall touch him, but
Ex 21:13 God delivered him into his **h**
Ex 21:16 or if he is found in his **h**
Ex 21:20 so that he dies under his **h**
Ex 21:24 tooth for tooth, **h** for **h**
Ex 22: 4 found alive in his **h**, whether
Ex 22: 8 **h** into his neighbor's goods
Ex 22:11 that he has not put his **h**
Ex 23: 1 Do not put your **h** with the
Ex 23:31 of the land into your **h**, and
Ex 24:11 Israel He did not lay His **h**
Ex 29:20 on the thumb of their right **h**
Ex 32: 4 the gold from their **h**, and he
Ex 32:11 power and with a mighty **h**
Ex 32:15 the Testimony were in his **h**
Ex 33:22 you with My **h** while I pass by
Ex 33:23 Then I will take away My **h**
Ex 34: 4 and he took in his **h** the two
Ex 34:29 Testimony were in Moses' **h**
Ex 35:29 LORD, by the **h** of Moses, had
Ex 38:21 by the **h** of Ithamar, son of
Lev 1: 4 Then he shall put his **h** on
Lev 3: 2 he shall lay his **h** on the
Lev 3: 8 he shall lay his **h** on the
Lev 3:13 shall lay his **h** on its head
Lev 4: 4 lay his **h** on the bull's head,
Lev 4:24 he shall lay his **h** on the
Lev 4:29 he shall lay his **h** on the
Lev 4:33 his **h** on the head of the sin
Lev 8:23 on the thumb of his right **h**
Lev 8:36 commanded by the **h** of Moses
Lev 9:22 his **h** toward the people,
Lev 10:11 to them by the **h** of Moses
Lev 14:14 on the thumb of his right **h**
Lev 14:15 the palm of his own left **h**
Lev 14:16 the oil that is in his left **h**
Lev 14:17 the rest of the oil in his **h**
Lev 14:17 on the thumb of his right **h**
Lev 14:18 **h** he shall put on the head of
Lev 14:25 on the thumb of his right **h**
Lev 14:26 the palm of his own left **h**
Lev 14:27 **h** seven times before the LORD
Lev 14:28 of the oil that is in his **h**
Lev 14:28 on the thumb of the right **h**
Lev 14:29 **h** he shall put on the head of
Lev 16:21 by the **h** of a suitable man
Lev 21:19 has a broken foot or broken **h**
Lev 22:25 **h** shall you offer any of
Lev 25:14 or buy from your neighbor's **h**
Lev 25:28 sold shall remain in the **h** of
Lev 26:25 into the **h** of the enemy
Lev 26:46 on Mount Sinai by the **h** of
Num 4:28 duties shall be under the **h**
Num 4:33 under the **h** of Ithamar the
Num 4:37 of the LORD by the **h** of Moses
Num 4:45 of the LORD by the **h** of Moses
Num 4:49 numbered by the **h** of Moses
Num 5:18 his **h** the bitter water that
Num 5:25 jealousy from the woman's **h**
Num 6:21 whatever else his **h** is able
Num 7: 8 under the **h** of Ithamar the
Num 9:23 of the LORD by the **h** of Moses
Num 10:13 of the LORD by the **h** of Moses
Num 15:23 you by the **h** of Moses, from
Num 20:11 Then Moses lifted his **h** and
Num 20:17 **h** or to the left until we
Num 20:20 many men and with a strong **h**
Num 21: 2 deliver this people into my **h**
Num 21:26 his **h** as far as the Arnon
Num 21:34 delivered him into your **h**
Num 22: 7 the diviner's fee in their **h**
Num 22:23 with His drawn sword in His **h**
Num 22:26 to the right **h** or to the left
Num 22:29 there were a sword in my **h**
Num 22:31 with His drawn sword in His **h**
Num 25: 7 and took a javelin in his **h**
Num 27:18 Spirit, and lay your **h** on him
Num 27:23 commanded by the **h** of Moses
Num 31: 6 the signal trumpets in his **h**
Num 33: 1 armies under the **h** of Moses
Num 35:17 him with a stone in the **h**
Num 35:18 him with a wooden **h** weapon
Num 35:21 with his **h** so that he dies
Num 35:25 the manslayer from the **h** of
Num 36:13 **h** of Moses in the plains of
Deut 1:27 us into the **h** of the Amorites
Deut 2: 7 you in all the work of your **h**
Deut 2:15 For indeed the **h** of the LORD
Deut 2:24 into your **h** Sihon the Amorite
Deut 2:30 might deliver him into your **h**
Deut 3: 2 and his land into your **h**
Deut 3: 8 the **h** of the two kings of the
Deut 3:24 greatness and Your mighty **h**
Deut 4:34 by war, by a mighty **h** and an
Deut 5:15 out from there by a mighty **h**
Deut 5:32 to the right **h** or to the left
Deut 6: 8 bind them as a sign on your **h**
Deut 6:21 out of Egypt with a mighty **h**
Deut 7: 8 you out with a mighty **h**, and
Deut 7: 8 from the **h** of Pharaoh king of
Deut 7:19 and the wonders, the mighty **h**
Deut 7:24 their kings into your **h**, and
Deut 8:17 the might of my **h** have gained
Deut 9:26 out of Egypt with a mighty **h**
Deut 10: 3 the two tablets in my **h**
Deut 11: 2 His greatness and His mighty **h**
Deut 11:18 bind them as a sign on your **h**
Deut 12: 6 the heave offerings of your **h**
Deut 12: 7 to which you have put your **h**
Deut 12:11 the heave offerings of your **h**
Deut 12:17 the heave offering of your **h**
Deut 13: 9 your **h** shall be first against
Deut 13: 9 afterward the **h** of all the
Deut 13:17 things shall remain in your **h**
Deut 14:25 take the money in your **h**
Deut 14:29 work of your **h** which you do
Deut 15: 3 but your **h** shall release what
Deut 15: 7 your **h** from your poor brother
Deut 15: 8 shall open your **h** wide to him
Deut 15: 9 the year of release, is at **h**
Deut 15:10 all to which you put your **h**
Deut 15:11 your **h** wide to your brother
Deut 16:10 freewill offering from your **h**
Deut 17:11 **h** or to the left from the
Deut 17:20 to the right **h** or to the left
Deut 19: 5 his **h** swings a stroke with
Deut 19:12 the **h** of the avenger of blood
Deut 19:21 tooth for tooth, **h** for **h**
Deut 21:10 God delivers them into your **h**
Deut 23:20 **h** in the land which you are
Deut 23:25 pluck the heads with your **h**
Deut 24: 1 of divorce, puts it in her **h**
Deut 24: 3 of divorce, puts it in her **h**
Deut 25:11 **h** of the one attacking him
Deut 25:11 him, and puts out her **h** and
Deut 25:12 then you shall cut off her **h**
Deut 26: 4 take the basket out of your **h**
Deut 26: 8 out of Egypt with a mighty **h**
Deut 28: 8 all to which you set your **h**
Deut 28:12 bless all the work of your **h**
Deut 28:14 to the right **h** or to the left
Deut 28:20 all that you set your **h** to do
Deut 28:32 be no strength in your **h**
Deut 30: 9 in all the work of your **h**
Deut 32:27 should say, 'Our **h** is high
Deut 32:35 day of their calamity is at **h**
Deut 32:39 any who can deliver from My **h**
Deut 32:40 For I lift My **h** to heaven
Deut 32:41 My **h** takes hold on judgment,
Deut 33: 2 from His right **h** came a fiery
Deut 33: 3 all His saints are in Your **h**
Josh 1: 7 to the right **h** or to the left
Josh 2:19 head if a **h** is laid on him
Josh 4:24 may know the **h** of the LORD
Josh 5:13 with His sword drawn in His **h**
Josh 6: 2 given Jericho into your **h**
Josh 7: 7 us into the **h** of the Amorites
Josh 8: 1 into your **h** the king of Ai
Josh 8: 7 will deliver it into your **h**
Josh 8:18 that is in your **h** toward Ai
Josh 8:18 I will give it into your **h**
Josh 8:18 had in his **h** toward the city
Josh 8:19 as he had stretched out his **h**
Josh 8:26 did not draw back his **h**, with
Josh 9:26 **h** of the children of Israel
Josh 10: 8 delivered them into your **h**
Josh 10:19 delivered them into your **h**
Josh 10:30 its king into the **h** of Israel
Josh 10:32 Lachish into the **h** of Israel
Josh 11: 8 them into the **h** of Israel
Josh 14: 2 commanded by the **h** of Moses
Josh 20: 5 deliver the slayer into his **h**
Josh 20: 9 and not die by the **h** of the
Josh 21: 8 commanded by the **h** of Moses
Josh 21:44 their enemies into their **h**
Josh 22: 9 of the LORD by the **h** of Moses
Josh 22:31 out of the **h** of the LORD
Josh 23: 6 to the right **h** or to the left
Josh 24: 8 But I gave them into your **h**
Josh 24:10 I delivered you out of his **h**
Josh 24:11 I delivered them into your **h**
Judg 1: 2 delivered the land into his **h**
Judg 1: 4 the Perizzites into their **h**
Judg 1:35 yet when the **h** of the house
Judg 2:15 the **h** of the LORD was against
Judg 2:16 delivered them out of the **h**
Judg 2:18 **h** of their enemies all the
Judg 2:23 them into the **h** of Joshua
Judg 3: 4 fathers by the **h** of Moses
Judg 3: 8 He sold them into the **h** of
Judg 3:10 of Mesopotamia into his **h**
Judg 3:10 and his **h** prevailed over
Judg 3:21 Ehud reached with his left **h**
Judg 3:28 the Moabites into your **h**
Judg 3:30 day under the **h** of Israel
Judg 4: 2 the **h** of Jabin king of Canaan
Judg 4: 7 will deliver him into your **h**'
Judg 4: 9 Sisera into the **h** of a woman
Judg 4:14 delivered Sisera into your **h**
Judg 4:21 peg and took a hammer in her **h**
Judg 4:24 And the **h** of the children of
Judg 5:26 her **h** to the tent peg, her
Judg 5:26 her right **h** to the workmen's
Judg 6: 1 delivered them into the **h** of
Judg 6: 2 the **h** of Midian prevailed
Judg 6: 9 out of the **h** of the Egyptians
Judg 6: 9 and out of the **h** of all who
Judg 6:14 from the **h** of the Midianites
Judg 6:21 the staff that was in His **h**
Judg 6:36 by my **h** as You have said
Judg 6:37 You will save Israel by my **h**
Judg 7: 2 My own **h** has saved me
Judg 7: 6 putting their **h** to their
Judg 7: 7 the Midianites into your **h**
Judg 7: 9 have delivered it into your **h**
Judg 7:14 for into his **h** God has
Judg 7:15 camp of Midian into your **h**
Judg 7:16 a trumpet into every man's **h**
Judg 8: 6 and Zalmunna now in your **h**
Judg 8: 7 Zebah and Zalmunna into my **h**
Judg 8:15 and Zalmunna now in your **h**
Judg 8:22 us from the **h** of Midian
Judg 9:17 you out of the **h** of Midian
Judg 9:29 this people were under my **h**
Judg 9:48 Abimelech took an ax in his **h**
Judg 10:12 I delivered you from their **h**
Judg 11:21 people into the **h** of Israel
Judg 12: 3 LORD delivered them into my **h**
Judg 13: 1 the **h** of the Philistines for
Judg 13: 5 of the **h** of the Philistines
Judg 14: 6 he had nothing in his **h**
Judg 15:12 into the **h** of the Philistines
Judg 15:13 and deliver you into their **h**
Judg 15:15 a donkey, reached out his **h**
Judg 15:17 threw the jawbone from his **h**
Judg 15:18 by the **h** of Your servant
Judg 15:18 and fall into the **h** of the
Judg 16:18 brought the money in their **h**
Judg 16:26 the lad who held him by the **h**
Judg 17: 3 the silver from my **h** to the
Judg 18:19 put your **h** over your mouth,
Judg 20:28 will deliver them into your **h**
Ruth 1:13 for your sakes that the **h** of
Ruth 4: 5 the field from the **h** of Naomi
Ruth 4: 9 Mahlon's, from the **h** of Naomi
1Sa 2:13 fleshhook in his **h** while the
1Sa 4: 3 us from the **h** of our enemies
1Sa 4: 8 the **h** of these mighty gods
1Sa 5: 6 But the **h** of the LORD was
1Sa 5: 7 for His **h** is harsh toward us
1Sa 5: 9 that the **h** of the LORD was
1Sa 5:11 the **h** of God was very heavy
1Sa 6: 3 His **h** is not removed from you
1Sa 6: 5 will lighten His **h** from you
1Sa 6: 9 is not His **h** that struck us
1Sa 6:12 to the right **h** or the left
1Sa 7: 3 from the **h** of the Philistines

1Sa 7: 8 from the **h** of the Philistines
1Sa 7:13 the **h** of the LORD was against
1Sa 9: 8 I have here at **h** one fourth
1Sa 9:16 from the **h** of the Philistines
1Sa 10:18 from the **h** of the Egyptians
1Sa 10:18 from the **h** of all kingdoms and
1Sa 12: 3 or from whose **h** have I
1Sa 12: 4 anything from any man's **h**
1Sa 12: 5 not found anything in my **h**
1Sa 12: 9 them into the **h** of Sisera
1Sa 12: 9 into the **h** of the Philistines
1Sa 12: 9 into the **h** of the king of
1Sa 12:10 us from the **h** of our enemies
1Sa 12:11 **h** of your enemies on every
1Sa 12:15 then the **h** of the LORD will
1Sa 13:22 nor spear found in the **h** of
1Sa 14:10 has delivered them into our **h**
1Sa 14:12 them into the **h** of Israel
1Sa 14:19 Withdraw your **h**
1Sa 14:26 no one put his **h** to his mouth
1Sa 14:27 of the rod that was in his **h**
1Sa 14:27 and put his **h** to his mouth
1Sa 14:37 them into the **h** of Israel
1Sa 14:43 of the rod that was in my **h**
1Sa 16:16 he will play it with his **h**
1Sa 16:23 a harp and play it with his **h**
1Sa 17:22 in the **h** of the supply keeper
1Sa 17:37 from the **h** of this Philistine
1Sa 17:40 he took his staff in his **h**
1Sa 17:40 and his sling was in his **h**
1Sa 17:46 will deliver you into my **h**
1Sa 17:49 David put his **h** in his bag
1Sa 17:50 no sword in the **h** of David
1Sa 17:57 of the Philistine in his **h**
1Sa 18:10 David played music with his **h**
1Sa 18:10 there was a spear in Saul's **h**
1Sa 18:17 Let my **h** not be against him,
1Sa 18:17 him, but let the **h** of the
1Sa 18:21 that the **h** of the Philistines
1Sa 18:25 by the **h** of the Philistines
1Sa 19: 9 house with his spear in his **h**
1Sa 19: 9 was playing music with his **h**
1Sa 20:16 at the **h** of David's enemies
1Sa 21: 3 therefore, what have you on **h**
1Sa 21: 3 five loaves of bread in my **h**
1Sa 21: 4 There is no common bread on **h**
1Sa 21: 8 here on **h** a spear or a sword
1Sa 22: 6 with his spear in his **h**, and
1Sa 22:17 because their **h** also is with
1Sa 23: 4 the Philistines into your **h**
1Sa 23: 6 down with an ephod in his **h**
1Sa 23: 7 has delivered him into my **h**
1Sa 23:11 Keilah deliver me into his **h**
1Sa 23:12 and my men into the **h** of Saul
1Sa 23:14 not deliver him into his **h**
1Sa 23:16 and strengthened his **h** in God
1Sa 23:17 for the **h** of Saul my father
1Sa 23:20 deliver him into the king's **h**
1Sa 24: 4 your enemy into your **h**, that
1Sa 24: 6 stretch out my **h** against him
1Sa 24:10 today into my **h** in the cave
1Sa 24:10 out my **h** against my lord, for
1Sa 24:11 corner of your robe in my **h**
1Sa 24:11 evil nor rebellion in my **h**
1Sa 24:12 But my **h** shall not be against
1Sa 24:13 But my **h** shall not be
1Sa 24:15 and deliver me out of your **h**
1Sa 24:18 LORD delivered me into your **h**
1Sa 24:20 be established in your **h**
1Sa 25: 8 to your **h** to your servants
1Sa 25:26 yourself with your own **h**, now
1Sa 25:33 avenging myself with my own **h**
1Sa 25:35 **h** what she had brought him
1Sa 25:39 reproach from the **h** of Nabal
1Sa 26: 8 enemy into your **h** this day
1Sa 26: 9 **h** against the LORD's anointed
1Sa 26:11 I should stretch out my **h**
1Sa 26:18 done, or what evil is in my **h**
1Sa 26:23 delivered you into my **h** today
1Sa 26:23 I would not stretch out my **h**
1Sa 27: 1 someday by the **h** of Saul
1Sa 27: 1 I shall escape out of his **h**
1Sa 28:17 the kingdom out of your **h**
1Sa 28:19 into the **h** of the Philistines
1Sa 28:19 into the **h** of the Philistines
1Sa 30:23 and delivered into our **h** the
2Sa 1:14 your **h** to destroy the LORD's
2Sa 2:19 right **h** or to the left from
2Sa 2:21 your right **h** or to your left
2Sa 3: 8 you into the **h** of David
2Sa 3:12 indeed my **h** shall be with you
2Sa 3:18 By the **h** of My servant David
2Sa 3:18 from the **h** of the Philistines
2Sa 3:18 the **h** of all their enemies
2Sa 4:11 require his blood at your **h**
2Sa 5:19 You deliver them into my **h**
2Sa 5:19 the Philistines into your **h**
2Sa 6: 6 out his **h** to the ark of God
2Sa 8: 1 from the **h** of the Philistines
2Sa 10: 2 So David sent by the **h** of
2Sa 11:14 and sent it by the **h** of Uriah
2Sa 12: 7 you from the **h** of Saul
2Sa 12:25 And He sent word by the **h** of
2Sa 13: 5 see it and eat it from her **h**
2Sa 13: 6 that I may eat from her **h**
2Sa 13:10 that I may eat from your **h**
2Sa 13:19 laid her **h** on her head and
2Sa 14:16 the **h** of the man who would
2Sa 14:19 Is the **h** of Joab with you in
2Sa 14:19 right **h** or to the left from
2Sa 15: 5 that he would put out his **h**
2Sa 16: 6 men were on his right **h** and on
2Sa 16: 8 the **h** of Absalom your son
2Sa 18: 2 people under the **h** of Joab
2Sa 18: 2 one third under the **h** of
2Sa 18: 2 and one third under the **h** of
2Sa 18:12 shekels of silver in my **h**
2Sa 18:12 **h**, I would not raise my **h**
2Sa 18:14 he took three spears in his **h**
2Sa 18:28 **h** against my lord the king
2Sa 19: 9 us from the **h** of our enemies
2Sa 19: 9 from the **h** of the Philistines
2Sa 20: 9 with his right **h** to kiss him
2Sa 20:10 sword that was in Joab's **h**
2Sa 20:21 has raised his **h** against the
2Sa 21:20 who had six fingers on each **h**
2Sa 21:22 and fell by the **h** of David
2Sa 21:22 and by the **h** of his servants
2Sa 22: 1 from the **h** of all his enemies
2Sa 22: 1 and from the **h** of Saul
2Sa 23:10 until his **h** was weary, and his
2Sa 23:10 and his **h** stuck to the sword
2Sa 23:21 Egyptian had a spear in his **h**
2Sa 23:21 spear out of the Egyptian's **h**
2Sa 24:14 fall into the **h** of the LORD
2Sa 24:14 let me fall into the **h** of man
2Sa 24:16 **h** over Jerusalem to destroy
2Sa 24:16 now restrain Your **h**
2Sa 24:17 Let Your **h**, I pray, be
1Ki 2:19 so she sat at his right **h**
1Ki 2:25 the **h** of Benaiah the son of
1Ki 2:46 in the **h** of Solomon
1Ki 8:15 with His **h** has fulfilled it,
1Ki 8:24 and fulfilled it with Your **h**
1Ki 8:42 great name and Your strong **h**
1Ki 8:53 as You spoke by the **h** of Your
1Ki 11:12 it out of the **h** of your son
1Ki 11:31 out of the **h** of Solomon and
1Ki 11:34 whole kingdom out of his **h**
1Ki 11:35 kingdom out of his son's **h**
1Ki 13: 4 out his **h** from the altar,
1Ki 13: 4 Then his **h**, which he
1Ki 13: 6 that my **h** may be restored to
1Ki 13: 6 the king's **h** was restored to
1Ki 15:18 into the **h** of his servants
1Ki 17:11 a morsel of bread in your **h**
1Ki 18: 9 servant into the **h** of Ahab
1Ki 18:44 cloud, as small as a man's **h**
1Ki 18:46 Then the **h** of the LORD came
1Ki 20:13 deliver it into your **h** today
1Ki 20:28 great multitude into your **h**
1Ki 20:42 **h** a man whom I appointed to
1Ki 22: 3 of the **h** of the king of Syria
1Ki 22: 6 it into the **h** of the king
1Ki 22:12 deliver it into the king's **h**
1Ki 22:15 it into the **h** of the king
1Ki 22:19 standing by, on His right **h**
2Ki 3:10 them into the **h** of Moab
2Ki 3:13 them into the **h** of Moab
2Ki 3:15 that the **h** of the LORD came
2Ki 3:18 the Moabites into your **h**
2Ki 4:29 and take my staff in your **h**
2Ki 5:11 wave his **h** over the place, and
2Ki 5:18 there, and he leans on my **h**
2Ki 5:24 he took them from their **h**
2Ki 6: 7 So he reached out his **h**
2Ki 7: 2 So an officer on whose **h** the
2Ki 7:17 the officer on whose **h** he
2Ki 8: 8 Take a present in your **h**, and
2Ki 9: 1 this flask of oil in your **h**
2Ki 9: 7 the LORD, at the **h** of Jezebel
2Ki 10:15 If it is, give me your **h**
2Ki 10:15 So he gave him his **h**, and he
2Ki 11: 8 man with his weapons in his **h**
2Ki 11:11 man with his weapons in his **h**
2Ki 12:15 from the men into whose **h**
2Ki 13: 3 the **h** of Hazael king of Syria
2Ki 13: 3 into the **h** of Ben-Hadad the
2Ki 13: 5 under the **h** of the Syrians
2Ki 13:16 Put your **h** on the bow
2Ki 13:16 So he put his **h** on it, and
2Ki 13:25 from the **h** of Ben-Hadad, the
2Ki 13:25 he had taken out of the **h** of
2Ki 14: 5 was established in his **h**,
2Ki 14:27 the **h** of Jeroboam the son of
2Ki 15:19 that his **h** might be with him
2Ki 15:19 the kingdom in his **h**
2Ki 16: 7 save me from the **h** of the
2Ki 16: 7 from the **h** of the king of
2Ki 17: 7 from under the **h** of Pharaoh
2Ki 17:20 them into the **h** of plunderers
2Ki 17:39 the **h** of all your enemies
2Ki 18:21 leans, it will go into his **h**
2Ki 18:29 to deliver you from his **h**
2Ki 18:30 the **h** of the king of Assyria
2Ki 18:33 the **h** of the king of Assyria
2Ki 18:34 delivered Samaria from my **h**
2Ki 18:35 their countries from my **h**
2Ki 18:35 deliver Jerusalem from my **h**
2Ki 19:10 the **h** of the king of Assyria
2Ki 19:14 from the **h** of the messengers
2Ki 19:19 I pray, save us from his **h**
2Ki 20: 6 this city from the **h** of the
2Ki 21:14 into the **h** of their enemies
2Ki 22: 2 to the right **h** or to the left
2Ki 22: 5 the **h** of those doing the work
2Ki 22: 7 money delivered into their **h**
2Ki 22: 9 **h** of those who do the work
1Ch 4:10 that Your **h** would be with me,
1Ch 5:10 Hagrites, who fell by their **h**
1Ch 5:20 were delivered into their **h**
1Ch 6:15 by the **h** of Nebuchadnezzar
1Ch 6:39 who stood at his right **h**
1Ch 6:44 sons of Merari, on the left **h**
1Ch 11:23 In the Egyptian's **h** there had
1Ch 11:23 spear out of the Egyptian's **h**
1Ch 12: 2 bows, using both the right **h**
1Ch 13: 9 put out his **h** to hold the ark
1Ch 13:10 he put his **h** to the ark
1Ch 14:10 You deliver them into my **h**
1Ch 14:10 will deliver them into your **h**
1Ch 14:11 my **h** like a breakthrough of
1Ch 16: 7 psalm into the **h** of Asaph
1Ch 18: 1 from the **h** of the Philistines
1Ch 20: 6 and toes, six on each **h** and six
1Ch 20: 8 they fell by the **h** of David
1Ch 20: 8 and by the **h** of his servants
1Ch 21:13 fall into the **h** of the LORD
1Ch 21:13 let me fall into the **h** of man
1Ch 21:15 now restrain your **h**
1Ch 21:16 having in his **h** a drawn sword
1Ch 21:17 Let Your **h**, I pray, O LORD my
1Ch 22:18 of the land into my **h**, and the
1Ch 24:19 the **h** of Aaron their father
1Ch 26:28 was under the **h** of Shelomith
1Ch 28:19 by His **h** upon me, all the
1Ch 29: 8 into the **h** of Jehiel the
1Ch 29:12 In Your **h** is power and might
1Ch 29:12 in Your **h** it is to make great
1Ch 29:16 Your holy name is from Your **h**
2Ch 3:17 temple, one on the right **h**
2Ch 3:17 the one on the right **h** Jachin
2Ch 6:15 and fulfilled it with Your **h**
2Ch 6:32 great name and Your mighty **h**
2Ch 8:18 by the **h** of his servants, and
2Ch 10:15 **h** of Ahijah the Shilonite to
2Ch 12: 5 left you in the **h** of Shishak
2Ch 12: 7 Jerusalem by the **h** of Shishak
2Ch 13: 8 which is in the **h** of the sons
2Ch 13:16 delivered them into their **h**
2Ch 16: 7 Syria has escaped from your **h**
2Ch 16: 8 He delivered them into your **h**
2Ch 17: 5 the kingdom in his **h**
2Ch 18: 5 deliver it into the king's **h**
2Ch 18:11 deliver it into the king's **h**
2Ch 18:14 be delivered into your **h**
2Ch 18:18 standing on His right **h** and on
2Ch 20: 6 in Your **h** is there not power
2Ch 23: 7 man with his weapons in his **h**
2Ch 23:10 man with his weapon in his **h**

2Ch 23:18 LORD to the **h** of the priests
2Ch 24:11 by the **h** of the Levites, and
2Ch 24:24 very great army into their **h**
2Ch 25:15 their own people from your **h**
2Ch 25:20 into the **h** of their enemies
2Ch 26:11 under the **h** of Hananiah, one
2Ch 26:13 under their **h** was an army of
2Ch 26:19 in his **h** to burn incense
2Ch 28: 5 the **h** of the king of Syria
2Ch 28: 5 the **h** of the king of Israel
2Ch 28: 9 delivered them into your **h**
2Ch 30: 6 the **h** of the kings of Assyria
2Ch 30:12 Also the **h** of God was on
2Ch 30:16 from the **h** of the Levites
2Ch 31:13 under the **h** of Cononiah and
2Ch 32:11 **h** of the king of Assyria"
2Ch 32:13 their lands out of my **h**
2Ch 32:14 deliver his people from my **h**
2Ch 32:14 able to deliver you from my **h**
2Ch 32:15 **h** or the **h** of my fathers
2Ch 32:15 God deliver you from my **h**
2Ch 32:17 their people from my **h**, so
2Ch 32:17 deliver His people from my **h**
2Ch 32:22 of Jerusalem from the **h** of
2Ch 32:22 from the **h** of all others, and
2Ch 33: 8 ordinances by the **h** of Moses
2Ch 34: 2 to the right **h** or to the left
2Ch 34: 9 from the **h** of Manasseh and
2Ch 34:10 Then they put it in the **h** of
2Ch 34:17 into the **h** of the overseers
2Ch 35: 6 of the LORD by the **h** of Moses
2Ch 36:17 He gave them all into his **h**
Ezra 1: 8 brought them out by the **h** of
Ezra 5:12 He gave them into the **h** of
Ezra 6:12 who put their **h** to alter it
Ezra 7: 6 according to the **h** of the
Ezra 7: 9 good **h** of his God upon him
Ezra 7:14 your God which is in your **h**
Ezra 7:28 as the **h** of the LORD my God
Ezra 8:18 by the good **h** of our God upon
Ezra 8:22 The **h** of our God is upon all
Ezra 8:26 into their **h** six hundred and
Ezra 8:31 the **h** of our God was upon us,
Ezra 8:31 us from the **h** of the enemy
Ezra 8:33 the **h** of Meremoth the son of
Ezra 9: 2 the **h** of the leaders and
Ezra 9: 7 been delivered into the **h** of
Neh 1:10 power, and by Your strong **h**
Neh 2: 8 the good **h** of my God upon me
Neh 2:18 I told them of the **h** of my
Neh 4:17 **h** they worked at construction
Neh 6: 5 with an open letter in his **h**
Neh 8: 4 and beside him, at his right **h**
Neh 8: 4 and at his left **h** Pedaiah,
Neh 9:14 laws, by the **h** of Moses Your
Neh 9:27 into the **h** of their enemies
Neh 9:27 from the **h** of their enemies
Neh 9:28 in the **h** of their enemies
Neh 9:30 You gave them into the **h** of
Neh 12:31 **h** on the wall toward the
Esth 3:10 his signet ring from his **h**
Esth 5: 2 scepter that was in his **h**
Esth 6: 9 **h** of one of the king's most
Esth 8: 7 to lay his **h** on the Jews
Esth 9:10 not lay a **h** on the plunder
Esth 9:15 not lay a **h** on the plunder
Esth 9:16 not lay a **h** on the plunder
Job 1:11 But now, stretch out Your **h**
Job 1:12 do not lay a **h** on his person
Job 2: 5 But stretch out Your **h** now
Job 2: 6 Behold, he is in your **h**, but
Job 5:15 the mighty, and from their **h**
Job 6: 9 me, that He would loose his **h**
Job 6:23 me from the enemy's **h**'
Job 6:23 me from the **h** of oppressors'
Job 9:24 into the **h** of the wicked
Job 9:33 who may lay his **h** on us both
Job 10: 7 who can deliver from Your **h**
Job 11:14 if iniquity were in your **h**
Job 12: 6 in what God provides by His **h**
Job 12: 9 does not know that the **h** of
Job 12:10 In whose **h** is the life of
Job 13:21 Withdraw Your **h** far from me
Job 15:23 of darkness is ready at his **h**
Job 15:25 out his **h** against God, and
Job 19:21 For the **h** of God has struck
Job 20:22 every **h** of misery will come
Job 21: 5 put your **h** over your mouth
Job 21:16 prosperity is not in their **h**
Job 23: 2 my **h** is listless because of
Job 23: 9 when He works on the left **h**
Job 23: 9 when He turns to the right **h**
Job 26:13 His **h** pierced the fleeing
Job 27:11 teach you about the **h** of God
Job 28: 9 He puts his **h** on the flint
Job 29: 9 put their **h** on their mouth
Job 29:20 and my bow is renewed in my **h**
Job 30:12 At my right **h** the rabble
Job 30:21 of Your **h** You oppose me
Job 30:24 His **h** against a heap of ruins
Job 31:21 if I have raised my **h** against
Job 31:25 because my **h** had gained much
Job 31:27 and my mouth has kissed my **h**
Job 33: 7 nor will my **h** be heavy on you
Job 34:20 are taken away without a **h**
Job 35: 7 does He receive from your **h**
Job 37: 7 He seals the **h** of every man
Job 40: 4 I lay my **h** over my mouth
Job 40:14 your own right **h** can save you
Job 41: 8 Lay your **h** on him
Ps 10:12 O God, lift up Your **h**
Ps 10:14 grief, To repay it by Your **h**
Ps 16: 8 right **h** I shall not be moved
Ps 16:11 At Your right **h** are pleasures
Ps 17: 7 by Your right **h**, O You who
Ps 17:14 With Your **h** from men, O LORD,
Ps 18:35 Your right **h** has held me up,
Ps 20: 6 strength of His right **h**
Ps 21: 8 Your **h** will find all Your
Ps 21: 8 Your right **h** will find those
Ps 26:10 And whose right **h** is full of
Ps 31: 5 Into Your **h** I commit my
Ps 31: 8 me up into the **h** of the enemy
Ps 31:15 My times are in Your **h**
Ps 31:15 me from the **h** of my enemies
Ps 32: 4 night Your **h** was heavy upon
Ps 36:11 let not the **h** of the wicked
Ps 37:24 LORD upholds him with His **h**
Ps 37:33 will not leave him in his **h**
Ps 38: 2 And Your **h** presses me down
Ps 39:10 by the blow of Your **h**
Ps 44: 2 out the nations with Your **h**
Ps 44: 3 But it was Your right **h**, Your
Ps 45: 4 Your right **h** shall teach You
Ps 45: 9 At Your right **h** stands the
Ps 48:10 Your right **h** is full of
Ps 60: 5 Save with Your right **h**, and
Ps 63: 8 Your right **h** upholds me
Ps 71: 4 out of the **h** of the wicked,
Ps 71: 4 wicked, Out of the **h** of the
Ps 73:23 You hold me by my right **h**
Ps 74:11 Your **h**, even Your right **h**
Ps 75: 8 For in the **h** of the LORD
Ps 77: 2 My **h** was stretched out in the
Ps 77:10 the right **h** of the Most High
Ps 77:20 a flock By the **h** of Moses
Ps 78:54 His right **h** had acquired
Ps 78:61 His glory into the enemy's **h**
Ps 80:15 Your right **h** has planted, And
Ps 80:17 Let Your **h** be upon the man of
Ps 80:17 upon the man of Your right **h**
Ps 81:14 And turn My **h** against their
Ps 82: 4 them from the **h** of the wicked
Ps 88: 5 who are cut off from Your **h**
Ps 89:13 Strong is Your **h**
Ps 89:13 and high is Your right **h**
Ps 89:21 With whom My **h** shall be
Ps 89:25 I will set his **h** over the sea
Ps 89:25 his right **h** over the rivers
Ps 89:42 right **h** of his adversaries
Ps 91: 7 ten thousand at your right **h**
Ps 95: 4 In His **h** are the deep places
Ps 95: 7 And the sheep of His **h**
Ps 97:10 out of the **h** of the wicked
Ps 98: 1 His right **h** and His holy arm
Ps 104:28 You open Your **h**, they are
Ps 106:10 the **h** of him who hated them
Ps 106:10 them from the **h** of the enemy
Ps 106:26 His **h** in an oath against them
Ps 106:41 into the **h** of the Gentiles
Ps 106:42 into subjection under their **h**
Ps 107: 2 from the **h** of the enemy,
Ps 108: 6 Save with Your right **h**, and
Ps 109: 6 accuser stand at his right **h**
Ps 109:27 may know that this is Your **h**
Ps 109:31 at the right **h** of the poor
Ps 110: 1 Sit at My right **h**, Till I
Ps 110: 5 The Lord is at Your right **h**
Ps 118:15 The right **h** of the LORD does
Ps 118:16 The right **h** of the LORD is
Ps 118:16 The right **h** of the LORD does
Ps 119:109 life is continually in my **h**
Ps 119:173 Let Your **h** become my help,
Ps 121: 5 is your shade at your right **h**
Ps 123: 2 to the **h** of their masters
Ps 123: 2 maid to the **h** of her mistress
Ps 127: 4 arrows in the **h** of a warrior
Ps 129: 7 reaper does not fill his **h**
Ps 136:12 With a strong **h**, and with an
Ps 137: 5 Let my right **h** forget her
Ps 138: 7 **h** Against the wrath of my
Ps 138: 7 Your right **h** will save me
Ps 139: 5 And laid Your **h** upon me
Ps 139:10 there Your **h** shall lead me
Ps 139:10 Your right **h** shall hold me
Ps 142: 4 Look on my right **h** and see,
Ps 144: 7 Stretch out Your **h** from above
Ps 144: 7 From the **h** of foreigners,
Ps 144: 8 whose right **h** is a right **h**
Ps 144:11 me from the **h** of foreigners
Ps 144:11 whose right **h** is a right **h**
Ps 145:16 You open Your **h** And satisfy
Ps 149: 6 a two-edged sword in their **h**
Prov 1:24 I have stretched out my **h**
Prov 3:16 of days is in her right **h**
Prov 3:16 **h**, in her left **h** riches
Prov 3:27 the power of your **h** to do so
Prov 6: 3 into the **h** of your friend
Prov 6: 5 from the **h** of the hunter, and
Prov 6: 5 bird from the **h** of the fowler
Prov 10: 4 with a slack **h** becomes poor
Prov 10: 4 but the **h** of the diligent
Prov 12:24 The **h** of the diligent will
Prov 17:16 Why is there in the **h** of a
Prov 19:24 man buries his **h** in the bowl
Prov 21: 1 heart is in the **h** of the LORD
Prov 26: 6 **h** of a fool cuts off his own
Prov 26: 9 **h** of a drunkard is a proverb
Prov 26:15 man buries his **h** in the bowl
Prov 27:16 grasps oil with his right **h**
Prov 30:32 put your **h** on your mouth
Prov 31:19 and her **h** holds the spindle
Prov 31:20 She extends her **h** to the poor
Eccl 2:24 I saw, was from the **h** of God
Eccl 5:14 there is nothing in his **h**
Eccl 5:15 he may carry away in his **h**
Eccl 7:18 remove your **h** from the other
Eccl 9: 1 works are in the **h** of God
Eccl 9:10 Whatever your **h** finds to do
Eccl 10: 2 man's heart is at his right **h**
Eccl 11: 6 do not withhold your **h**
Song 2: 6 His left **h** is under my head,
Song 2: 6 and his right **h** embraces me
Song 5: 4 my beloved put his **h** by the
Song 8: 3 His left **h** is under my head,
Song 8: 3 and his right **h** embraces me
Is 1:12 has required this from your **h**
Is 1:25 I will turn My **h** against you
Is 3: 6 these ruins be under your **h**
Is 5:25 out His **h** against them and
Is 5:25 but His **h** is stretched out
Is 6: 6 having in his **h** a live coal
Is 8:11 thus to me with a strong **h**
Is 9:12 but His **h** is stretched out
Is 9:17 but His **h** is stretched out
Is 9:20 shall snatch on the right **h**
Is 9:20 He shall devour on the left **h**
Is 9:21 but His **h** is stretched out
Is 10: 4 but His **h** is stretched out
Is 10: 5 in whose **h** is My indignation
Is 10:10 As my **h** has found the
Is 10:13 of my **h** I have done it, and by
Is 10:14 My **h** has found like a nest
Is 11: 8 put his **h** in the viper's den
Is 11:11 **h** again the second time to
Is 11:14 shall lay their **h** on Edom
Is 13: 2 wave your **h**, that they may
Is 13: 6 the day of the LORD is at **h**
Is 14:26 and this is the **h** that is
Is 14:27 His **h** is stretched out, and
Is 19: 4 into the **h** of a cruel master
Is 19:16 of the **h** of the LORD of hosts
Is 22:21 responsibility into his **h**
Is 23:11 out His **h** over the sea, He
Is 25:10 the **h** of the LORD will rest
Is 26:11 when Your **h** is lifted up,
Is 28: 2 down to the earth with His **h**
Is 28: 4 up while it is still in his **h**
Is 30:21 you turn to the right **h** or
Is 31: 3 the LORD stretches out His **h**

Is 34:17 His **h** has divided it among
Is 36: 6 leans, it will go into his **h**
Is 36:15 the **h** of the king of Assyria
Is 36:18 the **h** of the king of Assyria
Is 36:19 delivered Samaria from my **h**
Is 36:20 their countries from my **h**
Is 36:20 deliver Jerusalem from my **h**
Is 37:10 the **h** of the king of Assyria
Is 37:14 from the **h** of the messengers
Is 37:20 our God, save us from his **h**
Is 38: 6 this city from the **h** of the
Is 40: 2 **h** double for all her sins
Is 40:10 shall come with a strong **h**
Is 40:12 waters in the hollow of his **h**
Is 41:10 you with My righteous right **h**
Is 41:13 God, will hold your right **h**
Is 41:20 that the **h** of the LORD has
Is 42: 6 and will hold Your **h**
Is 43:13 who can deliver out of My **h**
Is 44: 5 another will write with his **h**
Is 44:20 there not a lie in my right **h**
Is 45: 1 whose right **h** I have held
Is 47: 6 and given them into your **h**
Is 48:13 Indeed My **h** has laid the
Is 48:13 My right **h** has stretched out
Is 49: 2 of His **h** He has hidden Me
Is 49:22 I will lift My **h** in an oath
Is 50: 2 Is My **h** shortened at all that
Is 50:11 this you shall have from My **h**
Is 51:16 you with the shadow of My **h**
Is 51:17 you who have drunk at the **h**
Is 51:18 any who takes her by the **h**
Is 51:22 your **h** the cup of trembling
Is 51:23 **h** of those who afflict you
Is 53:10 LORD shall prosper in His **h**
Is 56: 2 keeps his **h** from doing any
Is 57: 8 bed, where you saw their **h**
Is 57:10 have found the life of your **h**
Is 59: 1 the LORD's **h** is not shortened
Is 62: 3 of glory in the **h** of the LORD
Is 62: 3 diadem in the **h** of your God
Is 62: 8 LORD has sworn by His right **h**
Is 63:12 them by the right **h** of Moses
Is 64: 8 all we are the work of Your **h**
Is 66: 2 those things My **h** has made
Is 66:14 the **h** of the LORD shall be
Jer 1: 9 Then the LORD put forth His **h**
Jer 6: 9 put your **h** back into the
Jer 6:12 for I will stretch out My **h**
Jer 11:21 LORD, lest you die by our **h**'
Jer 12: 7 into the **h** of her enemies
Jer 15: 4 I will **h** them over to trouble
Jer 15: 6 stretch out My **h** against you
Jer 15:17 I sat alone because of Your **h**
Jer 15:21 you from the **h** of the wicked
Jer 16:21 will cause them to know My **h**
Jer 18: 4 marred in the **h** of the potter
Jer 18: 6 the clay is in the potter's **h**
Jer 18: 6 so are you in My **h**,
Jer 20: 4 the **h** of the king of Babylon
Jer 20: 5 into the **h** of their enemies
Jer 20:13 poor from the **h** of evildoers
Jer 21: 5 you with an outstretched **h**
Jer 21: 7 into the **h** of Nebuchadnezzar
Jer 21: 7 into the **h** of their enemies,
Jer 21: 7 into the **h** of those who seek
Jer 21:10 the **h** of the king of Babylon
Jer 21:12 out of the **h** of the oppressor
Jer 22: 3 out of the **h** of the oppressor
Jer 22:24 were the signet on My right **h**
Jer 22:25 I will give you into the **h** of
Jer 22:25 into the **h** of those whose
Jer 22:25 the **h** of Nebuchadnezzar king
Jer 22:25 and the **h** of the Chaldeans
Jer 23:23 Am I a God near at **h**," says
Jer 25:15 wine cup of fury from My **h**
Jer 25:17 the cup from the LORD's **h**
Jer 25:28 the cup from your **h** to drink
Jer 26:14 for me, here I am, in your **h**
Jer 26:24 Nevertheless the **h** of Ahikam
Jer 26:24 not give him into the **h** of
Jer 27: 3 by the **h** of the messengers
Jer 27: 6 all these lands into the **h** of
Jer 27: 8 I have consumed them by his **h**
Jer 29: 3 by the **h** of Elasah the son of
Jer 29:21 **h** of Nebuchadnezzar king of
Jer 31:11 ransomed him from the **h** of
Jer 31:32 **h** to bring them out of the
Jer 32: 3 the **h** of the king of Babylon
Jer 32: 4 from the **h** of the Chaldeans
Jer 32: 4 be delivered into the **h** of
Jer 32:21 and wonders, with a strong **h**
Jer 32:24 has been given into the **h** of
Jer 32:25 into the **h** of the Chaldeans
Jer 32:28 into the **h** of the Chaldeans
Jer 32:28 into the **h** of Nebuchadnezzar
Jer 32:36 **h** of the king of Babylon by
Jer 32:43 into the **h** of the Chaldeans
Jer 34: 2 the **h** of the king of Babylon
Jer 34: 3 shall not escape from his **h**
Jer 34: 3 taken and delivered into his **h**
Jer 34:20 into the **h** of their enemies
Jer 34:20 into the **h** of those who seek
Jer 34:21 into the **h** of their enemies
Jer 34:21 into the **h** of those who seek
Jer 34:21 into the **h** of the king of
Jer 36:14 Take in your **h** the scroll
Jer 36:14 took the scroll in his **h** and
Jer 37:17 the **h** of the king of Babylon
Jer 38: 3 **h** of the king of Babylon's
Jer 38: 5 Look, he is in your **h**
Jer 38:16 will I give you into the **h** of
Jer 38:18 into the **h** of the Chaldeans
Jer 38:18 shall not escape from their **h**
Jer 38:19 they deliver me into their **h**
Jer 38:23 shall not escape from their **h**
Jer 38:23 the **h** of the king of Babylon
Jer 39:17 **h** of the men of whom you are
Jer 40: 4 chains that were on your **h**
Jer 41: 5 and incense in their **h**, to
Jer 42:11 you and deliver you from his **h**
Jer 43: 3 into the **h** of the Chaldeans
Jer 43: 9 Take large stones in your **h**
Jer 44:30 into the **h** of his enemies
Jer 44:30 into the **h** of those who seek
Jer 44:30 king of Judah into the **h** of
Jer 46:24 **h** of the people of the north
Jer 46:26 the **h** of those who seek their
Jer 46:26 into the **h** of Nebuchadnezzar
Jer 46:26 and the **h** of his servants
Jer 48:16 calamity of Moab is near at **h**
Jer 50:15 she has given her **h**, her
Jer 51: 7 a golden cup in the LORD's **h**
Jer 51:25 stretch out My **h** against you
Lam 1: 7 fell into the **h** of the enemy
Lam 1:10 his **h** over all her pleasant
Lam 2: 3 right **h** from before the enemy
Lam 2: 4 with His right **h**, like an
Lam 2: 7 into the **h** of the enemy
Lam 2: 8 His **h** from destroying
Lam 3: 3 turned His **h** against me time
Lam 4: 6 moment, with no **h** to help her
Lam 5: 6 given our **h** to the Egyptians
Lam 5: 8 to deliver us from their **h**
Ezek 1: 3 the **h** of the LORD was upon
Ezek 2: 9 there was a **h** stretched out
Ezek 3:14 but the **h** of the LORD was
Ezek 3:18 I will require at your **h**
Ezek 3:20 I will require at your **h**
Ezek 3:22 Then the **h** of the LORD was
Ezek 6:14 stretch out My **h** against them
Ezek 7:17 Every **h** will be feeble, and
Ezek 8: 1 that the **h** of the Lord GOD
Ezek 8: 3 stretched out the form of a **h**
Ezek 8:11 man had a censer in his **h**
Ezek 9: 1 with a deadly weapon in his **h**
Ezek 9: 2 with his battle-ax in his **h**
Ezek 10: 7 cherub stretched out his **h**
Ezek 10: 8 a man's **h** under their wings
Ezek 12: 7 through the wall with my **h**
Ezek 12:23 The days are at **h**, and the
Ezek 13: 9 My **h** will be against the
Ezek 13:21 My people out of your **h**, and
Ezek 13:21 longer be as prey in your **h**
Ezek 13:23 My people out of your **h**, and
Ezek 14: 9 stretch out My **h** against him
Ezek 14:13 stretch out My **h** against it
Ezek 16:27 out My **h** against you,
Ezek 16:39 also give you into their **h**
Ezek 16:49 strengthen the **h** of the poor
Ezek 17:18 and in fact gave his **h** and
Ezek 18: 8 withdrawn his **h** from iniquity
Ezek 18:17 withdrawn his **h** from the poor
Ezek 20: 5 lifted My **h** in an oath to the
Ezek 20: 5 I lifted My **h** in an oath to
Ezek 20: 6 My **h** in an oath to them, to
Ezek 20:15 So I also lifted My **h** in an
Ezek 20:22 Nevertheless I withdrew My **h**
Ezek 20:23 Also I lifted My **h** in an oath
Ezek 20:28 My **h** in an oath to give them
Ezek 20:33 surely with a mighty **h**, with
Ezek 20:34 scattered, with a mighty **h**
Ezek 20:42 for which I lifted My **h** in an
Ezek 21:11 into the **h** of the slayer
Ezek 21:22 In his right **h** is the
Ezek 21:24 you shall be taken in **h**
Ezek 23: 9 her into the **h** of her lovers
Ezek 23: 9 into the **h** of the Assyrians,
Ezek 23:28 the **h** of those whom you hate
Ezek 23:28 into the **h** of those from whom
Ezek 23:31 I will put her cup in your **h**
Ezek 25: 7 stretch out My **h** against you
Ezek 25:13 stretch out My **h** against Edom
Ezek 25:14 by the **h** of My people Israel
Ezek 25:16 I will stretch out My **h**
Ezek 27:15 were the market of your **h**
Ezek 28: 9 in the **h** of him who slays you
Ezek 28:10 by the **h** of aliens
Ezek 29: 7 took hold of you with the **h**
Ezek 30:10 of Egypt to cease by the **h** of
Ezek 30:12 land into the **h** of the wicked
Ezek 30:12 is in it, by the **h** of aliens
Ezek 30:22 the sword fall out of his **h**
Ezek 30:24 and put My sword in his **h**
Ezek 30:25 the **h** of the king of Babylon
Ezek 31:11 **h** of the mighty one of the
Ezek 33: 6 require at the watchman's **h**
Ezek 33: 8 I will require at your **h**
Ezek 33:22 Now the **h** of the LORD had
Ezek 34:10 require My flock at their **h**
Ezek 34:27 delivered them from the **h** of
Ezek 35: 3 stretch out My **h** against you
Ezek 36: 7 I have lifted My **h** in an oath
Ezek 37: 1 The **h** of the LORD came upon
Ezek 37:17 will become one in your **h**
Ezek 37:19 which is in the **h** of Ephraim
Ezek 37:19 and they will be one in My **h**
Ezek 37:20 in your **h** before their eyes
Ezek 38:12 to stretch out your **h** against
Ezek 39: 3 the bow out of your left **h**
Ezek 39: 3 to fall out of your right **h**
Ezek 39:21 My **h** which I have laid on
Ezek 39:23 into the **h** of their enemies
Ezek 40: 1 the **h** of the LORD was upon me
Ezek 40: 3 and a measuring rod in his **h**
Ezek 40: 5 In the man's **h** was a
Ezek 44:12 My **h** in an oath against them
Ezek 47: 3 east with the line in his **h**
Ezek 47:14 for I lifted My **h** in an oath
Dan 1: 2 king of Judah into his **h**,
Dan 2:38 He has given them into your **h**
Dan 3:17 will deliver us from your **h**
Dan 4:35 restrain His **h** or say to Him
Dan 5: 5 fingers of a man's **h** appeared
Dan 5: 5 the part of the **h** that wrote
Dan 5:23 holds your breath in His **h**
Dan 5:24 of the **h** were sent from Him
Dan 7:25 given into his **h** for a time
Dan 8: 4 that could deliver from his **h**
Dan 8: 7 deliver the ram from his **h**
Dan 8:25 deceit to prosper under his **h**
Dan 8:25 be broken without human **h**
Dan 9:15 land of Egypt with a mighty **h**
Dan 10:10 a **h** touched me, which made me
Dan 11:11 given into the **h** of his enemy
Dan 11:41 these shall escape from his **h**
Dan 11:42 his **h** against the countries
Dan 12: 7 when he held up his right **h**
Dan 12: 7 and his left **h** to heaven, and
Hos 2:10 shall deliver her from My **h**
Hos 7: 5 out his **h** with scoffers
Hos 11: 8 How can I **h** you over, Israel
Hos 12: 7 deceitful scales are in his **h**
Joel 1:15 the day of the LORD is at **h**
Joel 2: 1 is coming, for it is at **h**
Joel 3: 8 the **h** of the people of Judah
Amos 1: 8 will turn My **h** against Ekron
Amos 5:19 leaned his **h** on the wall, and
Amos 7: 7 with a plumb line in His **h**
Amos 9: 2 from there my **h** shall take
Jon 4:11 discern between their right **h**
Mic 2: 1 it is in the power of their **h**
Mic 4:10 from the **h** of your enemies
Mic 5: 9 Your **h** shall be lifted
Mic 5:12 cut off sorceries from your **h**
Mic 7:16 put their **h** over their mouth
Hab 2:16 **h** will be turned against you
Hab 3: 4 had rays flashing from His **h**
Zeph 1: 4 out My **h** against Judah, and
Zeph 1: 7 the day of the LORD is at **h**

Zeph 2:13 out His **h** against the north
Zech 2: 1 a measuring line in his **h**
Zech 2: 9 will shake My **h** against them
Zech 3: 1 at his right **h** to oppose him
Zech 4:10 line in the **h** of Zerubbabel
Zech 8: 4 in his **h** because of great age
Zech 11: 6 into his neighbor's **h** and into
Zech 11: 6 and into the **h** of his king
Zech 11: 6 not deliver them from their **h**
Zech 12: 6 peoples on the right **h** and on
Zech 13: 7 then I will turn My **h** against
Zech 14:13 seize the **h** of his neighbor
Zech 14:13 **h** against his neighbor's **h**
Mal 1:13 I accept this from your **h**
Matt 3: 2 the kingdom of heaven is at **h**
Matt 3:12 His winnowing fan is in His **h**
Matt 4:17 the kingdom of heaven is at **h**
Matt 5:25 the judge **h** you over to the
Matt 5:30 if your right **h** causes you to
Matt 6: 3 do not let your left **h** know
Matt 6: 3 what your right **h** is doing
Matt 8: 3 Then Jesus put out His **h** and
Matt 8:15 And He touched her **h**, and the
Matt 9:18 but come and lay Your **h** on her
Matt 9:25 went in and took her by the **h**
Matt 10: 7 The kingdom of heaven is at **h**
Matt 12:10 a man who had a withered **h**
Matt 12:13 Stretch out your **h**
Matt 12:49 His **h** toward His disciples
Matt 14:31 Jesus stretched out His **h**
Matt 18: 8 if your **h** or foot causes you
Matt 20:21 may sit, one on Your right **h**
Matt 20:23 but to sit on My right **h** and
Matt 22:13 to the servants, 'Bind him **h**
Matt 22:44 Sit at My right **h**, till I
Matt 25:33 set the sheep on His right **h**
Matt 25:34 say to those on His right **h**
Matt 25:41 say to those on the left **h**
Matt 26:18 My time is at **h**
Matt 26:23 He who dipped his **h** with Me
Matt 26:45 Behold, the hour is at **h**, and
Matt 26:46 he who betrays Me is at **h**
Matt 26:51 Jesus stretched out his **h**
Matt 26:64 at the right **h** of the Power
Matt 27:29 and a reed in His right **h**
Mark 1:15 and the kingdom of God is at **h**
Mark 1:31 He came and took her by the **h**
Mark 1:41 compassion, put out His **h**
Mark 3: 1 there who had a withered **h**
Mark 3: 3 man who had the withered **h**
Mark 3: 5 Stretch out your **h**
Mark 3: 5 his **h** was restored as whole
Mark 5:41 He took the child by the **h**
Mark 7:32 Him to put His **h** on him
Mark 8:23 took the blind man by the **h**
Mark 9:27 But Jesus took him by the **h**
Mark 9:43 if your **h** makes you sin, cut
Mark 10:37 may sit, one on Your right **h**
Mark 10:40 but to sit on My right **h** and
Mark 12:36 Sit at My right **h**, till I
Mark 14:42 See, My betrayer is at **h**
Mark 14:62 at the right **h** of the Power
Mark 16:19 down at the right **h** of God
Luke 1: 1 as many have taken in **h** to
Luke 1:66 the **h** of the Lord was with
Luke 1:71 from the **h** of all who hate us
Luke 1:74 from the **h** of our enemies
Luke 3:17 His winnowing fan is in His **h**
Luke 5:13 Then He put out His **h** and
Luke 6: 6 whose right **h** was withered
Luke 6: 8 man who had the withered **h**
Luke 6:10 Stretch out your **h**
Luke 6:10 his **h** was restored as whole
Luke 8:54 all out, took her by the **h**
Luke 9:62 having put his **h** to the plow
Luke 15:22 him, and put a ring on his **h**
Luke 20:42 sit at My right **h**,
Luke 22:21 the **h** of My betrayer is with
Luke 22:69 right **h** of the power of God
Luke 23:33 criminals, one on the right **h**
John 2:13 Passover of the Jews was at **h**
John 3:35 given all things into His **h**
John 7: 2 Feast of Tabernacles was at **h**
John 7:30 but no one laid a **h** on Him
John 10:28 snatch them out of My **h**
John 10:29 them out of My Father's **h**
John 10:39 but He escaped out of their **h**
John 11:44 who had died came out bound **h**
John 18:22 Jesus with the palm of his **h**
John 20:25 put my **h** into His side, I
John 20:27 and reach your **h** here, and put
Acts 2:25 face, for He is at my right **h**
Acts 2:33 exalted to the right **h** of God
Acts 2:34 Sit at My right **h**,
Acts 3: 7 And he took him by the right **h**
Acts 4:28 to do whatever Your **h** and Your
Acts 4:30 stretching out Your **h** to heal
Acts 5:31 to His right **h** to be Prince
Acts 7:25 would deliver them by his **h**
Acts 7:35 a deliverer by the **h** of the
Acts 7:50 Has My **h** not made all these
Acts 7:55 at the right **h** of God,
Acts 7:56 at the right **h** of God
Acts 9: 8 But they led him by the **h**
Acts 9:12 in and putting his **h** on him
Acts 9:41 Then he gave her his **h** and
Acts 11:21 the **h** of the Lord was with
Acts 12: 1 his **h** to harass some from the
Acts 12:11 me from the **h** of Herod and
Acts 12:17 with his **h** to keep silent
Acts 13:11 the **h** of the Lord is upon you
Acts 13:11 someone to lead him by the **h**
Acts 13:16 and motioning with his **h** said
Acts 19:33 Alexander motioned with his **h**
Acts 21:40 with his **h** to the people
Acts 22:11 being led by the **h** of those
Acts 23:19 commander took him by the **h**
Acts 26: 1 So Paul stretched out his **h**
Acts 28: 3 heat, and fastened on his **h**
Acts 28: 4 creature hanging from his **h**
Rom 8:34 is even at the right **h** of God
Rom 13:12 is far spent, the day is at **h**
1Co 12:15 Because I am not a **h**, I am
1Co 12:21 the eye cannot say to the **h**
1Co 16:21 The salutation with my own **h**
2Co 6: 7 righteousness on the right **h**
Gal 2: 9 the right **h** of fellowship
Gal 3:19 angels by the **h** of a mediator
Gal 6:11 written to you with my own **h**
Eph 1:20 **h** in the heavenly places,
Phil 4: 5 The Lord is at **h**
Col 3: 1 sitting at the right **h** of God
Col 4:18 This salutation by my own **h**
2Th 3:17 of Paul with my own **h**, which
2Ti 4: 6 time of my departure is at **h**
Phm 19 am writing with my own **h**
Heb 1: 3 sat down at the right **h** of
Heb 1:13 Sit at My right **h**, Till I
Heb 7:18 For on the one **h** there is an
Heb 7:19 on the other **h**, there is the
Heb 8: 1 right **h** of the throne of the
Heb 8: 9 the **h** to lead them out of the
Heb 10:12 down at the right **h** of God
Heb 12: 2 right **h** of the throne of God
Jas 5: 8 coming of the Lord is at **h**
1Pe 3:22 and is at the right **h** of God
1Pe 4: 7 the end of all things is at **h**
1Pe 5: 6 under the mighty **h** of God
Rev 1:16 in His right **h** seven stars
Rev 1:17 But He laid His right **h** on me
Rev 1:20 which you saw in My right **h**
Rev 2: 1 seven stars in His right **h**
Rev 5: 1 I saw in the right **h** of Him
Rev 5: 7 right **h** of Him who sat on the
Rev 6: 5 had a pair of scales in his **h**
Rev 8: 4 before God from the angel's **h**
Rev 10: 2 a little book open in his **h**
Rev 10: 5 lifted up his **h** to heaven
Rev 10: 8 book which is open in the **h**
Rev 10:10 book out of the angel's **h**
Rev 13:16 right **h** or on their foreheads
Rev 14: 9 on his forehead or on his **h**
Rev 14:14 and in His **h** a sharp sickle
Rev 17: 4 having in her **h** a golden cup
Rev 20: 1 pit and a great chain in his **h**
Rev 22:10 book, for the time is at **h**

HANDBREADTH (*see* HANDBREADTHS)
Ex 25:25 it a frame of a **h** all around
Ex 37:12 a frame of a **h** all around it
1Ki 7:26 It was a **h** thick
2Ch 4: 5 It was a **h** thick
Ezek 40: 5 each being a cubit and a **h**
Ezek 40:43 a **h** wide, fastened all around
Ezek 43:13 cubit is one cubit and a **h**)

HANDBREADTHS (*see* HANDBREADTH)
Ps 39: 5 You have made my days as **h**

HANDED (*see* HAND)
2Ki 5:23 **h** them to two of his servants
Mark 7:13 which you have **h** down
Mark 15:10 **h** Him over because of envy
Luke 4:17 And He was **h** the book of the

HANDFUL (*see* HAND, HANDFULS)
Lev 2: 2 from it his **h** of fine flour
Lev 5:12 the priest shall take his **h**
Lev 6:15 **h** of the fine flour of the
Lev 9:17 offering, took a **h** of it, and
Num 5:26 take a **h** of the offering, as
1Ki 17:12 only a **h** of flour in a bin,
1Ki 20:10 is left of Samaria for a **h**
Eccl 4: 6 Better is a **h** with quietness

HANDFULS (*see* HANDFUL)
Ex 9: 8 Take for yourselves **h** of
Ezek 13:19 My people for **h** of barley

HANDIWORK (*see* HAND)
Ps 19: 1 And the firmament shows His **h**
Is 45: 9 Or shall your **h** say, 'He has

HANDKERCHIEF (*see* HANDKERCHIEFS)
Luke 19:20 I have kept put away in a **h**
John 20: 7 the **h** that had been around

HANDKERCHIEFS (*see* HANDKERCHIEF)
Acts 19:12 so that even **h** or aprons were

HANDLE (*see* HANDLED, HANDLES, HANDLING)
Deut 19: 5 and the head slips from the **h**
1Ch 12: 8 battle, who could **h** shield
2Ch 25: 5 go to war, who could **h** spear
Ps 115: 7 have hands, but they do not **h**
Jer 2: 8 those who **h** the law did not
Jer 46: 9 the Libyans who **h** the shield
Jer 46: 9 shield, and the Lydians who **h**
Ezek 27:29 All who **h** the oar, the
Zeph 1:11 all those who **h** money are cut
Luke 24:39 **H** Me and see, for a spirit
Col 2:21 touch, do not taste, do not **h**

HANDLED (*see* HANDLE)
Ezek 21:11 be polished, that it may be **h**
1Jn 1: 1 upon, and our hands have **h**

HANDLES (*see* HANDLE)
Song 5: 5 myrrh, on the **h** of the lock
Jer 50:16 and him who **h** the sickle at
Amos 2:15 shall not stand who **h** the bow

HANDLING (*see* HANDLE)
Ezek 38: 4 shields, all of them **h** swords
2Co 4: 2 walking in craftiness nor **h**

HANDMILL
Ex 11: 5 who is behind the **h**, and all

HANDS (*see* HAND)
Gen 5:29 our work and the toil of our **h**
Gen 19:10 the men reached out their **h**
Gen 19:16 the **h** of his two daughters,
Gen 20: 5 innocence of my **h** I have done
Gen 27:16 kids of the goats on his **h**
Gen 27:22 but the **h** are the **h** of
Gen 27:22 the **h** are the **h** of Esau
Gen 27:23 because his **h** were hairy like
Gen 27:23 like his brother Esau's **h**
Gen 31:42 and the labor of my **h**, and
Gen 35: 4 gods which were in their **h**
Gen 37:21 delivered him out of their **h**
Gen 37:22 deliver him out of their **h**
Gen 42:37 put him in my **h**, and I will
Gen 43:22 money in our **h** to buy food
Gen 48:14 head, guiding his **h** knowingly
Gen 49:24 the arms of his **h** were made
Gen 49:24 were made strong by the **h** of
Ex 9:29 spread out my **h** to the LORD
Ex 9:33 spread out his **h** to the LORD
Ex 15:17 which Your **h** have established
Ex 17:12 But Moses' **h** became heavy
Ex 17:12 Aaron and Hur supported his **h**
Ex 17:12 his **h** were steady until the
Ex 29:10 **h** on the head of the bull
Ex 29:15 **h** on the head of the ram
Ex 29:19 **h** on the head of the ram
Ex 29:24 all these in the **h** of Aaron
Ex 29:24 in the **h** of his sons, and you
Ex 29:25 them back from their **h** and
Ex 30:19 his sons shall wash their **h**
Ex 30:21 So they shall wash their **h**
Ex 32:19 cast the tablets out of his **h**
Ex 35:25 spun yarn with their **h**, and

Ex 40:31 and his sons washed their **h**
Lev 4:15 shall lay their **h** on the head
Lev 7:30 His own **h** shall bring the
Lev 8:14 his sons laid their **h** on the
Lev 8:18 his sons laid their **h** on the
Lev 8:22 his sons laid their **h** on the
Lev 8:24 the thumbs of their right **h**
Lev 8:27 he put all these in Aaron's **h**
Lev 8:27 and in his sons' **h**, and
Lev 8:28 Moses took them from their **h**
Lev 15:11 has not rinsed his **h** in water
Lev 16:12 with his **h** full of sweet
Lev 16:21 his **h** on the head of the live
Lev 24:14 him lay their **h** on his head
Num 5:18 for remembering in her **h**,
Num 6:19 put them upon the **h** of the
Num 8:10 lay their **h** on the Levites
Num 8:12 **h** on the heads of the young
Num 24:10 and he struck his **h** together
Num 27:23 And he laid his **h** on him and
Num 36: 7 change **h** from tribe to tribe
Num 36: 9 **h** from one tribe to another
Deut 1:25 fruit of the land in their **h**
Deut 3: 3 into our **h** Og king of Bashan
Deut 4:28 gods, the work of men's **h**
Deut 9:15 the covenant were in my two **h**
Deut 9:17 and threw them out of my two **h**
Deut 12:18 all to which you put your **h**
Deut 16:15 and in all the work of your **h**
Deut 17: 7 The **h** of the witnesses shall
Deut 17: 7 afterward the **h** of all the
Deut 20:13 God delivers it into your **h**
Deut 21: 6 **h** over the heifer whose neck
Deut 21: 7 Our **h** have not shed this
Deut 24:19 you in all the work of your **h**
Deut 27:15 the work of the **h** of the
Deut 31:29 through the work of your **h**
Deut 33: 7 let his **h** be sufficient for
Deut 33:11 and accept the work of his **h**
Deut 34: 9 Moses had laid his **h** on him
Josh 2:24 all the land into our **h**, for
Josh 9:25 now, here we are, in your **h**
Judg 2:14 He delivered them into the **h**
Judg 2:14 He sold them into the **h** of
Judg 6:13 into the **h** of the Midianites
Judg 7: 2 the Midianites into their **h**
Judg 7: 8 and their trumpets in their **h**
Judg 7:11 afterward your **h** shall be
Judg 7:19 pitchers that were in their **h**
Judg 7:20 the torches in their left **h**
Judg 7:20 in their right **h** for blowing
Judg 8: 3 your **h** the princes of Midian
Judg 8: 6 said, "Are the **h** of Zebah and
Judg 8:15 saying, 'Are the **h** of Zebah
Judg 8:34 the **h** of all their enemies on
Judg 10: 7 into the **h** of the Philistines
Judg 10: 7 into the **h** of the people of
Judg 11:30 the people of Ammon into my **h**
Judg 11:32 delivered them into his **h**
Judg 12: 2 not deliver me out of their **h**
Judg 12: 3 me, I took my life in my **h**
Judg 13:23 a grain offering from our **h**
Judg 14: 9 He took some of it in his **h**
Judg 15:14 bonds broke loose from his **h**
Judg 16:23 into our **h** Samson our enemy
Judg 16:24 into our **h** our enemy, the
Judg 18:10 God has given it into your **h**
Judg 19:27 with her **h** on the threshold
1Sa 5: 4 both the palms of its **h** were
1Sa 7:14 from the **h** of the Philistines
1Sa 10: 4 shall receive from their **h**
1Sa 11: 7 Israel by the **h** of messengers
1Sa 14:13 Jonathan climbed up on his **h**
1Sa 14:48 delivered Israel from the **h**
1Sa 17:47 He will give you into our **h**
1Sa 19: 5 For he took his life in his **h**
1Sa 21:13 feigned madness in their **h**
1Sa 22:17 **h** to strike the priests of
1Sa 28:21 and I have put my life in my **h**
1Sa 30:15 me into the **h** of my master
2Sa 2: 7 let your **h** be strengthened,
2Sa 3:34 Your **h** were not bound nor
2Sa 4:12 them, cut off their **h** and feet
2Sa 16:21 Then the **h** of all who are
2Sa 21: 9 into the **h** of the Gibeonites
2Sa 22:21 of my **h** He has recompensed me
2Sa 22:35 He teaches my **h** to make war
2Sa 23: 6 they cannot be taken with **h**
1Ki 8:22 out his **h** toward heaven
1Ki 8:38 spreads out his **h** toward this
1Ki 8:54 his **h** spread up to heaven
1Ki 14:27 committed them to the **h** of
1Ki 16: 7 anger with the work of his **h**
1Ki 20: 6 they shall put in their **h**
2Ki 3:11 water on the **h** of Elijah
2Ki 4:34 eyes, and his **h** on his **h**
2Ki 4:34 eyes, and his **h** on his **h**
2Ki 5:20 from his **h** what he brought
2Ki 9:35 feet and the palms of her **h**
2Ki 10:24 brought into your **h** escapes
2Ki 11:12 him, and they clapped their **h**
2Ki 12:11 into the **h** of those who did
2Ki 13:16 and Elisha put his **h** on the
2Ki 13:16 put his **h** on the king's **h**
2Ki 19:18 gods, but the work of men's **h**
2Ki 22:17 with all the works of their **h**
1Ch 12:17 there is no wrong in my **h**
1Ch 29: 5 be done by the **h** of craftsmen
2Ch 6: 4 His **h** what He spoke with His
2Ch 6:12 Israel, and spread out his **h**
2Ch 6:13 out his **h** toward heaven),
2Ch 6:29 out his **h** to this house
2Ch 12:10 committed them to the **h** of
2Ch 15: 7 and do not let your **h** be weak
2Ch 29:23 and they laid their **h** on them
2Ch 32:19 the work of men's **h**
2Ch 34:25 with all the works of their **h**
2Ch 35:11 the blood with their **h**, while
Ezra 5: 8 and prospers in their **h**
Ezra 6:22 to strengthen their **h** in the
Ezra 9: 5 spread out my **h** to the LORD
Neh 2:18 their **h** to do this good work
Neh 6: 9 Their **h** will be weakened in
Neh 6: 9 O God, strengthen my **h**
Neh 8: 6 while lifting up their **h**
Neh 9:24 and gave them into their **h**
Neh 13:21 so again, I will lay **h** on you
Esth 2:21 and sought to lay **h** on King
Esth 3: 6 to lay **h** on Mordecai alone
Esth 3: 9 **h** of those who do the work
Esth 6: 2 to lay **h** on King Ahasuerus
Esth 9: 2 of King Ahasuerus to lay **h** on
Job 1:10 blessed the work of his **h**
Job 4: 3 you have strengthened weak **h**
Job 5:12 so that their **h** cannot carry
Job 5:18 wounds, but His **h** make whole
Job 9:30 and cleanse my **h** with soap
Job 10: 3 despise the work of Your **h**
Job 10: 8 Your **h** have made me and
Job 11:13 stretch out your **h** toward Him
Job 13:14 teeth, and put my life in my **h**
Job 14:15 desire the work of Your **h**
Job 16:11 over to the **h** of the wicked
Job 16:17 no violence is in my **h**, and my
Job 17: 3 he who will shake **h** with me
Job 17: 9 has clean **h** will be stronger
Job 20:10 his **h** will restore his wealth
Job 22:30 by the purity of your **h**
Job 27:23 Men shall clap their **h** at him
Job 30: 2 the strength of their **h** to me
Job 31: 7 if any spot adheres to my **h**
Job 34:19 are all the work of His **h**
Job 34:37 he claps his **h** among us, and
Job 36:32 He covers His **h** with
Ps 7: 3 If there is iniquity in my **h**
Ps 8: 6 over the works of Your **h**
Ps 9:16 in the work of his own **h**
Ps 18:20 of my **h** He has recompensed me
Ps 18:24 of my **h** in His sight
Ps 18:34 He teaches my **h** to make war
Ps 22:16 They pierced My **h** and My feet
Ps 24: 4 He who has clean **h** and a pure
Ps 26: 6 I will wash my **h** in innocence
Ps 26:10 In whose **h** is a sinister
Ps 28: 2 When I lift up my **h** toward
Ps 28: 4 to the work of their **h**
Ps 28: 5 Nor the operation of His **h**
Ps 44:20 out our **h** to a foreign god
Ps 47: 1 Oh, clap your **h**, all you
Ps 55:20 He has put forth his **h**
Ps 58: 2 of your **h** in the earth
Ps 63: 4 lift up my **h** in Your name
Ps 68:31 stretch out her **h** to God
Ps 73:13 And washed my **h** in innocence
Ps 76: 5 have found the use of their **h**
Ps 78:72 by the skillfulness of his **h**
Ps 81: 6 His **h** were freed from the
Ps 88: 9 stretched out my **h** to You
Ps 90:17 the work of our **h** for us
Ps 90:17 establish the work of our **h**
Ps 91:12 shall bear you up in their **h**
Ps 92: 4 in the works of Your **h**
Ps 95: 5 His **h** formed the dry land
Ps 98: 8 Let the rivers clap their **h**
Ps 102:25 are the work of Your **h**
Ps 111: 7 The works of His **h** are verity
Ps 115: 4 and gold, The work of men's **h**
Ps 115: 7 They have **h**, but they do not
Ps 119:48 My **h** also I will lift up to
Ps 119:73 Your **h** have made me and
Ps 125: 3 reach out their **h** to iniquity
Ps 128: 2 you eat the labor of your **h**
Ps 134: 2 Lift up your **h** in the
Ps 135:15 and gold, The work of men's **h**
Ps 138: 8 forsake the works of Your **h**
Ps 140: 4 from the **h** of the wicked
Ps 141: 2 The lifting up of my **h** as the
Ps 143: 5 I muse on the work of Your **h**
Ps 143: 6 I spread out my **h** to You
Ps 144: 1 Rock, Who trains my **h** for war
Prov 6: 1 if you have shaken **h** in
Prov 6:10 folding of the **h** to sleep
Prov 6:17 **h** that shed innocent blood,
Prov 12:14 **h** will be rendered to him
Prov 14: 1 pulls it down with her **h**
Prov 17:18 shakes **h** in a pledge, and
Prov 21:25 for his **h** refuse to labor
Prov 22:26 who shakes **h** in a pledge, one
Prov 24:33 folding of the **h** to rest
Prov 30:28 skillfully grasps with its **h**
Prov 31:13 and willingly works with her **h**
Prov 31:19 out her **h** to the distaff, and
Prov 31:20 out her **h** to the needy
Prov 31:31 her of the fruit of her **h**
Eccl 2:11 the works that my **h** had done
Eccl 4: 5 The fool folds his **h** and
Eccl 4: 6 quietness than both **h** full
Eccl 5: 6 and destroy the work of your **h**
Eccl 7:26 and nets, whose **h** are fetters
Eccl 10:18 idleness of **h** the house leaks
Song 5: 5 my **h** dripped with myrrh, My
Song 5:14 His **h** are rods of gold set
Song 7: 1 the work of the **h** of a
Is 1:15 When you spread out your **h**
Is 1:15 Your **h** are full of blood
Is 2: 8 the work of their own **h**, that
Is 3:11 of his **h** shall be given him
Is 5:12 the operation of His **h**
Is 13: 7 Therefore all **h** will be limp
Is 17: 8 the altars, the work of his **h**
Is 19:25 and Assyria the work of My **h**
Is 25:11 He will spread out His **h** in
Is 25:11 spreads out his **h** to swim
Is 25:11 with the trickery of their **h**
Is 29:23 children, the work of My **h**
Is 31: 7 which your own **h** have made
Is 33:15 who gestures with his **h**,
Is 35: 3 Strengthen the weak **h**, and
Is 37:19 gods, but the work of men's **h**
Is 45: 9 handiwork say, 'He has no **h**'
Is 45:11 concerning the work of My **h**
Is 45:12 My **h** that stretched out the
Is 49:16 you on the palms of My **h**
Is 55:12 the field shall clap their **h**
Is 59: 3 For your **h** are defiled with
Is 59: 6 act of violence is in their **h**
Is 60:21 My planting, the work of My **h**
Is 65: 2 out My **h** all day long to a
Is 65:22 enjoy the work of their **h**
Jer 1:16 the works of their own **h**
Jer 2:37 him with your **h** on your head
Jer 4:31 herself, who spreads her **h**
Jer 6:24 our **h** grow feeble
Jer 10: 3 work of the **h** of the workman
Jer 10: 9 of the **h** of the metalsmith
Jer 19: 7 by the **h** of those who seek
Jer 21: 4 of war that are in your **h**
Jer 23:14 strengthen the **h** of evildoers
Jer 25: 6 with the works of your **h**
Jer 25: 7 of your **h** to your own hurt
Jer 25:14 to the works of their own **h**
Jer 30: 6 **h** on his loins like a woman
Jer 32:30 with the work of their **h**,"
Jer 33:13 the **h** of him who counts them
Jer 38: 4 the **h** of the men of war who
Jer 38: 4 the **h** of all the people, by
Jer 44: 8 with the works of your **h**,
Jer 44:25 and fulfilled with your **h**,
Jer 48:37 on all the **h** shall be cuts,
Jer 50:43 them, and his **h** grow feeble

Lam 1:14 were woven together by His **h**
Lam 1:14 Lord delivered me into the **h**
Lam 1:17 Zion spreads out her **h**, but
Lam 2:15 pass by clap their **h** at you
Lam 2:19 Lift your **h** toward Him for
Lam 3:41 hearts and **h** to God in heaven
Lam 3:64 to the work of their **h**
Lam 4: 2 work of the **h** of the potter
Lam 4:10 The **h** of the compassionate
Lam 5:12 were hung up by their **h**, and
Ezek 1: 8 They had the **h** of a man under
Ezek 7:21 into the **h** of strangers, and
Ezek 7:27 the **h** of the common people
Ezek 10: 2 fill your **h** with coals of
Ezek 10: 7 put it into the **h** of the man
Ezek 10:12 with their back, their **h**
Ezek 10:21 the likeness of the **h** of a
Ezek 11: 9 you into the **h** of strangers
Ezek 13:22 the **h** of the wicked, so that
Ezek 21: 7 all **h** will be feeble, every
Ezek 21:14 and strike your **h** together
Ezek 21:31 deliver you into the **h** of
Ezek 22:14 or can your **h** remain strong,
Ezek 23:37 and blood is on their **h**
Ezek 23:45 and blood is on their **h**
Ezek 25: 6 Because you clapped your **h**
Dan 2:34 a stone was cut out without **h**
Dan 2:45 out of the mountain without **h**
Dan 3:15 will deliver you from my **h**
Dan 10:10 knees and on the palms of my **h**
Hos 14: 3 anymore to the work of our **h**
Obad 13 nor laid **h** on their substance
Jon 3: 8 the violence that is in his **h**
Mic 5:13 worship the work of your **h**
Mic 7: 3 do evil with both **h**
Nah 3:19 will clap their **h** over you
Hab 3:10 and lifted its **h** on high
Zeph 3:16 Zion, let not your **h** be weak
Hag 1:11 and on all the labor of your **h**
Hag 2:14 so is every work of their **h**
Hag 2:17 in all the labors of your **h**
Zech 4: 9 The **h** of Zerubbabel have laid
Zech 4: 9 his **h** shall also finish it
Zech 8: 9 Let your **h** be strong, you
Zech 8:13 fear, let your **h** be strong
Zech 13: 6 are these wounds in your **h**
Mal 1: 9 this is being done by your **h**
Mal 1:10 an offering from your **h**
Mal 2:13 it with good will from your **h**
Matt 4: 6 In their **h** they shall bear
Matt 15: 2 their **h** when they eat bread
Matt 15:20 **h** does not defile a man
Matt 17:12 about to suffer at their **h**
Matt 17:22 be betrayed into the **h** of men
Matt 18: 8 than having two **h** or two feet
Matt 18:28 and he laid **h** on him and took
Matt 19:13 He might put His **h** on them
Matt 19:15 And He laid His **h** on them and
Matt 21:46 they sought to lay **h** on Him
Matt 26:45 into the **h** of sinners
Matt 26:50 laid **h** on Jesus and took Him
Matt 26:67 Him with the palms of their **h**
Matt 27:24 and washed his **h** before the
Mark 5:23 Come and lay Your **h** on her
Mark 6: 2 works are performed by His **h**
Mark 6: 5 His **h** on a few sick people
Mark 7: 2 that is, with unwashed **h**
Mark 7: 3 wash their **h** in a special way
Mark 7: 5 but eat bread with unwashed **h**
Mark 8:23 his eyes and put His **h** on him
Mark 8:25 Then He put His **h** on his eyes
Mark 9:31 delivered into the **h** of men
Mark 9:43 maimed, than having two **h**
Mark 10:16 His arms, put His **h** on them
Mark 14:41 into the **h** of sinners
Mark 14:46 Then they laid their **h** on Him
Mark 14:58 temple that is made with **h**
Mark 14:58 build another made without **h**
Mark 14:65 Him with the palms of their **h**
Mark 16:18 they will lay **h** on the sick
Luke 4:11 In their **h** they shall bear
Luke 4:40 He laid His **h** on every one of
Luke 6: 1 them, rubbing them in their **h**
Luke 9:44 delivered into the **h** of men
Luke 13:13 And He laid His **h** on her, and
Luke 20:19 hour sought to lay **h** on Him
Luke 21:12 they will lay their **h** on you
Luke 23:46 into Your **h** I commend My
Luke 24: 7 into the **h** of sinful men, and
Luke 24:39 Behold My **h** and My feet, that
Luke 24:40 this, He showed them His **h**
Luke 24:50 and He lifted up His **h** and
John 7:44 Him, but no one laid **h** on Him
John 8:20 and no one laid **h** on Him, for
John 13: 3 given all things into His **h**
John 13: 9 my feet only, but also my **h**
John 19: 3 they struck Him with their **h**
John 20:20 this, He showed them His **h**
John 20:25 Unless I see in His **h** the
John 20:27 finger here, and look at My **h**
John 21:18 you will stretch out your **h**
Acts 2:23 you have taken by lawless **h**
Acts 4: 3 And they laid **h** on them, and
Acts 5:12 through the **h** of the apostles
Acts 5:18 laid their **h** on the apostles
Acts 6: 6 prayed, they laid **h** on them
Acts 7:41 in the works of their own **h**
Acts 7:48 dwell in temples made with **h**
Acts 8:17 Then they laid **h** on them, and
Acts 8:18 **h** the Holy Spirit was given
Acts 8:19 that anyone on whom I lay **h**
Acts 9:17 laying his **h** on him he said,
Acts 11:30 elders by the **h** of Barnabas
Acts 12: 7 And his chains fell off his **h**
Acts 13: 3 laid **h** on them, they sent
Acts 14: 3 wonders to be done by their **h**
Acts 17:24 dwell in temples made with **h**
Acts 17:25 is He worshiped with men's **h**
Acts 19: 6 when Paul had laid **h** on them
Acts 19:11 miracles by the **h** of Paul
Acts 19:26 gods which are made with **h**
Acts 20:34 these **h** have provided for my
Acts 21:11 Paul's belt, bound his own **h**
Acts 21:11 into the **h** of the Gentiles
Acts 21:27 whole crowd and laid **h** on him,
Acts 24: 7 took him out of our **h**,
Acts 27:19 overboard with our own **h**
Acts 28: 8 and he laid his **h** on him and
Acts 28:17 into the **h** of the Romans,
Rom 10:21 out My **h** to a disobedient
1Co 4:12 labor, working with our own **h**
2Co 5: 1 God, a house not made with **h**
2Co 11:33 wall, and escaped from his **h**
Eph 2:11 made in the flesh by **h**
Eph 4:28 with his **h** what is good, that
Col 2:11 circumcision made without **h**
1Th 4:11 and to work with your own **h**
1Ti 2: 8 everywhere, lifting up holy **h**
1Ti 4:14 on of the **h** of the presbytery
1Ti 5:22 Do not lay **h** on anyone
2Ti 1: 6 through the laying on of my **h**
Heb 1:10 are the work of Your **h**
Heb 2: 7 him over the works of Your **h**
Heb 6: 2 baptisms, of laying on of **h**
Heb 9:11 tabernacle not made with **h**
Heb 9:24 the holy places made with **h**
Heb 10:31 into the **h** of the living God
Heb 12:12 the **h** which hang down, and the
Jas 4: 8 Cleanse your **h**, you sinners
1Jn 1: 1 upon, and our **h** have handled,
Rev 7: 9 with palm branches in their **h**
Rev 9:20 of the works of their **h**, that
Rev 20: 4 their foreheads or on their **h**

HANDSOME
Gen 39: 6 And Joseph was **h** in form and
1Sa 9: 2 Saul, a choice and **h** young man
1Sa 9: 2 There was not a more **h** person
1Sa 16:18 in speech, and a **h** person
Song 1:16 Behold, you are **h**, my beloved

HANDWRITING
Col 2:14 having wiped out the **h** of

HANES
Is 30: 4 and his ambassadors came to **H**

HANG (*see* HANGED, HANGING, HANGS, HUNG)
Gen 40:19 from you and **h** you on a tree
Ex 26:12 shall **h** over the back of the
Ex 26:13 shall **h** over the sides of the
Ex 26:32 You shall **h** it upon the four
Ex 26:33 you shall **h** the veil from the
Ex 40: 8 **h** up the screen at the court
Num 25: 4 **h** the offenders before the
Deut 21:22 and you **h** him on a tree,
Deut 28:66 Your life shall **h** in doubt
2Sa 21: 6 we will **h** them before the
Esth 6: 4 **h** Mordecai on the gallows
Esth 7: 9 the king said, "**H** him on it
Job 28: 4 feet they **h** far away from men
Prov 26: 7 **h** limp is a proverb in the
Song 4: 4 armory, on which **h** a thousand
Is 22:24 They will **h** on him all the
Ezek 15: 3 from it to **h** any vessel on
Matt 22:40 commandments **h** all the Law
Heb 12:12 the hands which **h** down, and

HANGED (*see* HANG)
Gen 40:22 But he **h** the chief baker, as
Gen 41:13 me to my office, and he **h** him
Deut 21:23 for he who is **h** is accursed
Josh 8:29 the king of Ai he **h** on a tree
Josh 10:26 them, and **h** them on five trees
2Sa 4:12 **h** them by the pool in Hebron
2Sa 17:23 order, and **h** himself, and died
2Sa 21: 9 and they **h** them on the hill
2Sa 21:13 bones of those who had been **h**
Ezra 6:11 and let him be **h** on it
Esth 2:23 and both were **h** on a gallows
Esth 5:14 king that Mordecai be **h** on it
Esth 7:10 So they **h** Haman on the
Esth 8: 7 and they have **h** him on the
Esth 9:13 ten sons be **h** on the gallows
Esth 9:14 and they **h** Haman's ten sons
Esth 9:25 should be **h** on the gallows
Matt 27: 5 and went and **h** himself
Luke 23:39 who were **h** blasphemed Him

HANGING (*see* HANG, HANGINGS)
Josh 10:26 and they were **h** on the trees
2Sa 18: 9 he was left **h** between heaven
2Sa 18:10 I just saw Absalom **h** in a
Acts 5:30 you murdered by **h** on a tree
Acts 10:39 they killed by **h** on a tree
Acts 28: 4 the creature **h** from his hand

HANGINGS (*see* HANGING)
Ex 27: 9 south side there shall be **h**
Ex 27:11 be **h** one hundred cubits long
Ex 27:12 shall be **h** of fifty cubits
Ex 27:14 The **h** on one side of the gate
Ex 27:15 shall be **h** of fifteen cubits
Ex 35:17 the **h** of the court, its
Ex 38: 9 the **h** of the court were woven
Ex 38:11 On the north side the **h** were
Ex 38:12 there were **h** of fifty cubits
Ex 38:13 side the **h** were fifty cubits
Ex 38:14 The **h** of one side of the gate
Ex 38:15 that were **h** of fifteen cubits
Ex 38:16 All the **h** of the court all
Ex 38:18 to the **h** of the court
Ex 39:40 the **h** of the court, its
Num 3:26 the **h** of the court which are
Num 4:26 the **h** of the court which are
2Ki 23: 7 wove **h** for the wooden image

HANGS (*see* HANG)
Job 26: 7 he **h** the earth on nothing
Gal 3:13 everyone who **h** on a tree")

HANIEL (*see* HANNIEL)
1Ch 7:39 The sons of Ulla were Arah, **H**

HANNAH
1Sa 1: 2 the name of one was **H**, and the
1Sa 1: 2 but **H** had no children
1Sa 1: 5 But to **H** he would give a
1Sa 1: 5 portion, for he loved **H**,
1Sa 1: 8 **H**, why do you weep
1Sa 1: 9 So **H** arose after they had
1Sa 1:13 Now **H** spoke in her heart
1Sa 1:15 And **H** answered and said,
1Sa 1:19 And Elkanah knew **H** his wife
1Sa 1:20 of time that **H** conceived and
1Sa 1:22 But **H** did not go up, for she
1Sa 2: 1 And **H** prayed and said
1Sa 2:21 And the LORD visited **H**, so

HANNATHON
Josh 19:14 it on the north side of **H**

HANNIEL (*see* HANIEL)
Num 34:23 Manasseh, **H** the son of Ephod,

HANOCH (*see* HANOCHITES)
Gen 25: 4 Midian were Ephah, Epher, **H**
Gen 46: 9 The sons of Reuben were **H**
Ex 6:14 firstborn of Israel, were **H**
Num 26: 5 of **H**, the family of the
1Ch 1:33 Midian were Ephah, Epher, **H**
1Ch 5: 3 firstborn of Israel were **H**

HANOCHITES (*see* HANOCH)
Num 26: 5 Hanoch, the family of the H

HANUN
2Sa 10: 1 and H his son reigned in his
2Sa 10: 2 to H the son of Nahash, as
2Sa 10: 3 of Ammon said to H their lord
2Sa 10: 4 Therefore H took David's
1Ch 19: 2 to H the son of Nahash,
1Ch 19: 2 H in the land of the people
1Ch 19: 3 the people of Ammon said to H
1Ch 19: 4 Therefore H took David's
1Ch 19: 6 repulsive to David, H and the
Neh 3:13 H and the inhabitants of
Neh 3:30 the son of Shelemiah, and H

HAPHRAIM
Josh 19:19 H, Shion, Anaharath,

HAPPEN (*see* PREFACE)

HAPPENED (*see* PREFACE)

HAPPENING (*see* PREFACE)

HAPPENS (*see* PREFACE)

HAPPIER (*see* HAPPY)
1Co 7:40 But she is h if she remains

HAPPINESS (*see* HAPPY)
Deut 24: 5 bring h to his wife whom he

HAPPIZZEZ
1Ch 24:15 to Hezir, the eighteenth to H

HAPPY (*see* HAPPINESS, HAPPIER)
Gen 30:13 I am h, for the daughters
Deut 33:29 H are you, O Israel
1Ki 10: 8 H are your men
1Ki 10: 8 h are these your servants,
2Ch 9: 7 H are your men and h are
2Ch 9: 7 h are these your servants,
Job 5:17 Behold, h is the man whom God
Ps 127: 5 H is the man who has his
Ps 128: 2 of your hands, You shall be h
Ps 137: 8 H shall he be who repays you
Ps 137: 9 H shall he be who takes and
Ps 144:15 H are the people who are in
Ps 144:15 H are the people whose God is
Ps 146: 5 H is he who has the God of
Prov 3:13 H is the man who finds wisdom
Prov 3:18 and h are all who retain her
Prov 14:21 mercy on the poor, h is he
Prov 16:20 trusts in the LORD, h is he
Prov 28:14 H is the man who is always
Prov 29:18 but h is he who keeps the law
Is 32:13 on all the h homes in the
Jer 12: 1 Why are those h who deal so
John 13:17 h are you if you do them
Acts 26: 2 I think myself h, King
Rom 14:22 H is he who does not condemn

HARA
1Ch 5:26 took them to Halah, Habor, H

HARADAH
Num 33:24 Shepher and camped at H
Num 33:25 They moved from H and

HARAN (*see* BETH HARAN)
Gen 11:26 and begot Abram, Nahor, and H
Gen 11:27 begot Abram, Nahor, and H
Gen 11:27 H begot Lot
Gen 11:28 And H died before his father
Gen 11:29 the daughter of H the father
Gen 11:31 grandson Lot, the son of H
Gen 11:31 and they came to H and dwelt
Gen 11:32 years, and Terah died in H
Gen 12: 4 old when he departed from H
Gen 12: 5 whom they had acquired in H
Gen 27:43 flee to my brother Laban in H
Gen 28:10 Beersheba and went toward H
Gen 29: 4 We are from H
2Ki 19:12 have destroyed, Gozan and H
1Ch 2:46 Caleb's concubine, bore H
1Ch 2:46 and H begot Gazez
1Ch 23: 9 Shelomith, Haziel, and H
Is 37:12 have destroyed, Gozan and H
Ezek 27:23 H, Canneh, Eden, the
Acts 7: 2 before he dwelt in H,
Acts 7: 4 the Chaldeans and dwelt in H

HARARITE
2Sa 23:11 Shammah the son of Agee the H
2Sa 23:33 Shammah the H, Ahiam the son
2Sa 23:33 Ahiam the son of Sharar the H
1Ch 11:34 the son of Shageh the H,
1Ch 11:35 Ahiam the son of Sacar the H

HARASS (*see* HARASSED)
Num 25:17 H the Midianites, and attack
Num 33:55 they shall h you in the land
Deut 2: 9 said to me, 'Do not h Moab
Deut 2:19 do not h them or meddle with
Is 11:13 and Judah shall not h Ephraim
Acts 12: 1 to h some from the church

HARASSED (*see* HARASS)
Num 25:18 for they h you with their
Judg 2:18 who oppressed them and h them
Judg 10: 8 From that year they h and
1Sa 14:47 Wherever he turned, he h them

HARBONA (*see* HARBONAH)
Esth 1:10 Mehuman, Biztha, H

HARBONAH (*see* HARBONA)
Esth 7: 9 Now H, one of the eunuchs,

HARBOR (*see* HARBORED)
Is 23: 1 that there is no house, no h
Acts 27:12 And because the h was not
Acts 27:12 a h of Crete opening toward

HARBORED (*see* HARBOR)
Acts 17: 7 Jason has h them, and these

HARD (*see* HARDEN, HARDER, HARDNESS, HARDSHIP)
Gen 18:14 anything too h for the LORD
Gen 19: 9 So they pressed h against
Gen 33:13 should drive them h one day
Gen 35:16 and she had h labor
Gen 35:17 pass, when she was in h labor
Ex 1:14 lives bitter with h bondage
Ex 7:13 And Pharaoh's heart grew h
Ex 7:14 Pharaoh's heart is h
Ex 7:22 and Pharaoh's heart grew h
Ex 8:19 But Pharaoh's heart grew h
Ex 9: 7 the heart of Pharaoh became h
Ex 9:35 So the heart of Pharaoh was h
Ex 18:26 the h cases they brought to
Deut 1:17 case that is too h for you
Deut 15:18 It shall not seem h to you
Deut 17: 8 is too h for you to judge
Deut 26: 6 us, and laid h bondage on us
1Sa 14:22 they also followed h after
1Sa 31: 2 followed h after Saul and his
2Sa 1: 6 horsemen followed h after him
1Ki 10: 1 to test him with h questions
2Ki 2:10 You have asked a h thing
1Ch 10: 2 followed h after Saul and his
2Ch 9: 1 test Solomon with h questions
Job 7: 1 Is there not a time of h
Job 14:14 All the days of my h service
Job 41:24 His heart is as h as stone
Job 41:24 stone, even as h as the lower
Ps 60: 3 shown Your people h things
Prov 13:15 way of the unfaithful is h
Is 8:21 pass through it h pressed
Is 14: 3 the h bondage in which you
Jer 32:17 is nothing too h for You
Jer 32:27 there anything too h for Me
Lam 1: 3 affliction and h servitude
Ezek 3: 5 of h language, but to the
Ezek 3: 6 of h language, whose words
Jon 1:13 h to bring the ship to land
Matt 13:15 Their ears are h of hearing
Matt 19:23 I say to you that it is h for
Matt 23: 4 h to bear, and lay them on
Matt 25:24 I knew you to be a h man
Mark 10:23 How h it is for those who
Mark 10:24 how h it is for those who
Luke 11:46 men with burdens h to bear
Luke 18:24 How h it is for those who
John 6:60 This is a h saying
Acts 9: 5 It is h for you to kick
Acts 26:14 It is h for you to kick
Acts 28:27 their ears are h of hearing
2Co 4: 8 We are h pressed on every
Phil 1:23 For I am h pressed between
Heb 5:11 h to explain, since you have
2Pe 3:16 some things h to understand

HARDEN (*see* HARD, HARDENED, HARDENING, HARDENS)
Ex 4:21 But I will h his heart, so
Ex 7: 3 I will h Pharaoh's heart, and
Ex 14: 4 Then I will h Pharaoh's heart
Ex 14:17 I indeed will h the hearts of
Deut 15: 7 you shall not h your heart
Josh 11:20 of the LORD to h their hearts
1Sa 6: 6 Why then do you h your hearts
Job 38:30 The waters h like stone, and
Ps 95: 8 Do not h your hearts, as in
Heb 3: 8 do not h your hearts as in
Heb 3:15 do not h your hearts as in
Heb 4: 7 voice, do not h your hearts

HARDENED (*see* HARDEN)
Ex 8:15 he h his heart and did not
Ex 8:32 But Pharaoh h his heart at
Ex 9:12 But the LORD h the heart of
Ex 9:34 he h his heart, he and his
Ex 10: 1 for I have h his heart and the
Ex 10:20 But the LORD h Pharaoh's
Ex 10:27 But the LORD h Pharaoh's
Ex 11:10 the LORD h Pharaoh's heart,
Ex 14: 8 And the LORD h the heart of
Deut 2:30 LORD your God h his spirit
1Sa 6: 6 and Pharaoh h their hearts
2Ch 36:13 h his heart against turning
Neh 9:16 h their necks, and did not
Neh 9:17 But they h their necks, and in
Job 9: 4 Who has h himself against Him
Is 63:17 h our heart from Your fear
Dan 5:20 and his spirit was h in pride
Mark 6:52 because their heart was h
Mark 8:17 Is your heart still h
John 12:40 and h their heart, lest they
Acts 19: 9 But when some were h and did
Rom 11: 7 it, and the rest were h
2Co 3:14 But their minds were h
Heb 3:13 Today," lest any of you be h

HARDENING (*see* HARDEN)
Rom 11:25 that h in part has happened
Eph 4:18 of the h of their heart

HARDENS (*see* HARDEN)
Job 38:38 when the dust h in clumps
Prov 21:29 A wicked man h his face, but
Prov 28:14 but he who h his heart will
Prov 29: 1 h his neck, will suddenly be
Rom 9:18 wills, and whom He wills He h

HARDER (*see* HARD)
Prov 18:19 A brother offended is h to
Jer 5: 3 made their faces h than rock
Ezek 3: 9 h than flint, I have made

HARD-HEARTED
Ezek 3: 7 of Israel are impudent and h

HARDNESS (*see* HARD)
Matt 19: 8 of the h of your hearts,
Mark 3: 5 by the h of their hearts, He
Mark 10: 5 Because of the h of your
Mark 16:14 h of heart, because they did
Rom 2: 5 But in accordance with your h

HARDSHIP (*see* HARD)
Ex 18: 8 all the h that had come upon
Num 20:14 You know all the h that has
2Ti 2: 3 You therefore must endure h

HARD-WORKING
2Ti 2: 6 The h farmer must be first to

HARE
Lev 11: 6 the h, because it chews the
Deut 14: 7 the camel, the h, and the rock

HAREPH
1Ch 2:51 H the father of Beth Gader

HARHAIAH
Neh 3: 8 to him Uzziel the son of H

HARHAS (*see* HASRAH)
2Ki 22:14 son of Tikvah, the son of H

HARHUR
Ezra 2:51 of Hakupha, the sons of H
Neh 7:53 of Hakupha, the children of H

HARIM
1Ch 24: 8 the third to H, the fourth to
Ezra 2:32 the people of H, three
Ezra 2:39 the sons of H, one thousand
Ezra 10:21 of the sons of H
Ezra 10:31 of the sons of H
Neh 3:11 Malchijah the son of H and
Neh 7:35 the children of H, three
Neh 7:42 the children of H, one
Neh 10: 5 H, Meremoth, Obadiah,
Neh 10:27 Malluch, H, and Baanah

Neh 12:15 of **H**, Adna

HARIPH (*see* JORAH)
Neh 7:24 the children of **H**, one
Neh 10:19 **H**, Anathoth, Nebai,

HARLOT (*see* HARLOTRY, HARLOT'S, HARLOTS)
Gen 34:31 he treat our sister like a **h**
Gen 38:15 her, he thought she was a **h**
Gen 38:21 Where is the **h** who was openly
Gen 38:21 There was no **h** in this place
Gen 38:22 there was no **h** in this place
Gen 38:24 has played the **h**
Ex 34:15 they play the **h** with their
Ex 34:16 play the **h** with their gods
Ex 34:16 play the **h** with their gods
Lev 17: 7 whom they have played the **h**
Lev 19:29 to cause her to be a **h**, lest
Lev 21: 7 who is a **h** or a defiled woman
Lev 21: 9 herself by playing the **h**, she
Lev 21:14 or a defiled woman or a **h**
Deut 22:21 to play the **h** in her father's
Deut 23:17 There shall be no ritual **h** of
Deut 23:18 not bring the hire of a **h** or
Deut 31:16 play the **h** with the gods of
Josh 2: 1 the house of a **h** named Rahab
Josh 6:17 Only Rahab the **h** shall live
Josh 6:25 And Joshua spared Rahab the **h**
Judg 2:17 played the **h** with other gods
Judg 8:27 played the **h** with it there
Judg 8:33 played the **h** with the Baals
Judg 11: 1 but he was the son of a **h**
Judg 16: 1 went to Gaza and saw a **h** there
Judg 19: 2 played the **h** against him, and
1Ch 5:25 played the **h** after the gods
2Ch 21:13 **h** like the harlotry of the
Ps 106:39 played the **h** by their own
Prov 6:26 For by means of a **h** a man is
Prov 7:10 him, with the attire of a **h**
Prov 23:27 For a **h** is a deep pit, and a
Is 1:21 faithful city has become a **h**
Is 23:15 Tyre as in the song of the **h**
Is 23:16 the city, you forgotten **h**
Is 57: 3 of the adulterer and the **h**
Jer 2:20 you lay down, playing the **h**
Jer 3: 1 played the **h** with many lovers
Jer 3: 6 tree, and there played the **h**
Jer 3: 8 but went and played the **h** also
Ezek 6: 9 play the **h** after their idols
Ezek 16:15 played the **h** because of your
Ezek 16:16 and played the **h** on them
Ezek 16:17 and played the **h** with them
Ezek 16:28 the **h** with the Assyrians,
Ezek 16:28 you played the **h** with them
Ezek 16:30 the deeds of a brazen **h**
Ezek 16:31 Yet you were not like a **h**
Ezek 16:34 one solicited you to be a **h**
Ezek 16:35 Now then, O **h**, hear the word
Ezek 16:41 make you cease playing the **h**
Ezek 23: 5 Oholah played the **h** even
Ezek 23:19 the **h** in the land of Egypt
Ezek 23:30 as a **h** after the Gentiles
Ezek 23:44 in to a woman who plays the **h**
Hos 2: 5 their mother has played the **h**
Hos 3: 3 you shall not play the **h**, nor
Hos 4:12 the **h** against their God
Hos 4:14 sacrifices with a ritual **h**
Hos 4:15 you, Israel, play the **h**, let
Hos 9: 1 played the **h** against your God
Joel 3: 3 a boy in exchange for a **h**
Amos 7:17 wife shall be a **h** in the city
Mic 1: 7 all her pay as a **h** shall be
Mic 1: 7 it from the pay of a **h**, and
Mic 1: 7 return to the pay of a **h**
Nah 3: 4 harlotries of the seductive **h**
1Co 6:15 and make them members of a **h**
1Co 6:16 to a **h** is one body with her
Heb 11:31 By faith the **h** Rahab did not
Jas 2:25 was not Rahab the **h** also
Rev 17: 1 **h** who sits on many waters
Rev 17:15 you saw, where the **h** sits
Rev 17:16 beast, these will hate the **h**
Rev 19: 2 **h** who corrupted the earth

HARLOTRIES (*see* HARLOTRY)
2Ki 9:22 as long as the **h** of your
Jer 3: 2 polluted the land with your **h**
Hos 2: 2 put away her **h** from her sight
Nah 3: 4 of **h** of the seductive harlot
Nah 3: 4 sells nations through her **h**

HARLOTRY (*see* HARLOT, HARLOTRIES)
Gen 38:24 she is with child by **h**
Lev 19:29 lest the land fall into **h**
Lev 20: 5 him to commit **h** with Molech
Num 15:39 the **h** to which your own heart
Num 25: 1 **h** with the women of Moab
2Ch 21:11 of Jerusalem to commit **h**, and
2Ch 21:13 the **h** of the house of Ahab
Ps 73:27 those who desert You for **h**
Jer 3: 9 to pass, through her casual **h**
Jer 13:27 the lewdness of your **h**, your
Ezek 16:15 poured out your **h** on everyone
Ezek 16:20 your acts of **h** a small matter
Ezek 16:22 and acts of **h** you did not
Ezek 16:25 and multiplied your acts of **h**
Ezek 16:26 **h** with the Egyptians, your
Ezek 16:26 of **h** to provoke Me to anger
Ezek 16:29 **h** as far as the land of the
Ezek 16:33 from all around for your **h**
Ezek 16:34 of other women in your **h**,
Ezek 16:36 in your **h** with your lovers
Ezek 20:30 committing **h** according to
Ezek 23: 3 They committed **h** in Egypt
Ezek 23: 3 committed **h** in their youth
Ezek 23: 7 she committed her **h** with them
Ezek 23: 8 up her **h** brought from Egypt
Ezek 23:11 in her **h** more corrupt than
Ezek 23:11 corrupt than her sister's **h**
Ezek 23:14 But she increased her **h**
Ezek 23:18 She revealed her **h** and
Ezek 23:19 Yet she multiplied her **h** in
Ezek 23:27 your **h** brought from the land
Ezek 23:29 of your **h** shall be uncovered
Ezek 23:29 both your lewdness and your **h**
Ezek 23:35 of your lewdness and your **h**
Ezek 23:43 they commit **h** with her now
Ezek 43: 7 kings, by their **h** or with the
Ezek 43: 9 Now let them put their **h** and
Hos 1: 2 Go, take yourself a wife of **h**
Hos 1: 2 and children of **h**
Hos 1: 2 land has committed great **h** by
Hos 2: 4 they are the children of **h**
Hos 4:10 they shall commit **h**, but not
Hos 4:11 **H**, wine, and new wine enslave
Hos 4:12 For the spirit of **h** has
Hos 4:13 your daughters commit **h**, and
Hos 4:14 daughters when they commit **h**
Hos 4:18 they commit **h** continually
Hos 5: 3 now, O Ephraim, you commit **h**
Hos 5: 4 spirit of **h** is in their midst
Hos 6:10 there is the **h** of Ephraim

HARLOT'S (*see* HARLOT)
Josh 6:22 Go into the **h** house, and from
Jer 3: 3 You have had a **h** forehead

HARLOTS (*see* HARLOT)
1Ki 3:16 who were **h** came to the king
1Ki 22:38 his blood while the **h** bathed
Prov 29: 3 of **h** wastes his wealth
Jer 5: 7 by troops in the **h**' houses
Ezek 16:33 Men make payment to all **h**
Hos 4:14 themselves go apart with **h**
Matt 21:31 **h** enter the kingdom of God
Matt 21:32 collectors and **h** believed him
Luke 15:30 your livelihood with **h**, you
Rev 17: 5 THE MOTHER OF **H**

HARM (*see* HARMFUL, HARMLESS)
Gen 26:29 that you will do us no **h**
Gen 31:29 It is in my power to do you **h**
Gen 31:52 and this pillar to me, for **h**
Ex 21:22 yet no lasting **h** follows
Ex 21:23 But if any lasting **h** follows
Ex 32:12 He brought them out to **h** them
Ex 32:12 from this **h** to Your people
Ex 32:14 **h** which He said He would do
Lev 5:16 make restitution for the **h**
Num 35:23 his enemy or seeking his **h**
Josh 24:20 then He will turn and do you **h**
Judg 15: 3 the Philistines if I **h** them
1Sa 20:21 is safety for you and no **h**
1Sa 24: 9 Indeed David seeks your **h**'
1Sa 25:17 for **h** is determined against
1Sa 25:26 those who seek **h** for my lord
1Sa 26:21 For I will **h** you no more,
2Sa 12:18 He may do some **h**
2Sa 18:32 rise against you to do you **h**
2Sa 20: 6 do us more **h** than Absalom
1Ch 16:22 ones, and do My prophets no **h**
Neh 6: 2 But they thought to do me **h**
Esth 9: 2 on those who sought their **h**
Ps 37: 8 it only causes **h**
Ps 105:15 ones, And do My prophets no **h**
Prov 3:30 if he has done you no **h**
Jer 24: 9 of the earth, for their **h**
Jer 25: 6 and I will not **h** you
Jer 38: 4 of this people, but their **h**
Jer 39:12 after him, and do him no **h**
Joel 2:13 and He relents from doing **h**
Amos 9: 4 set My eyes on them for **h**
Jon 4: 2 One who relents from doing **h**
Mic 3:11 No **h** can come upon us
Acts 9:13 how much **h** he has done to
Acts 16:28 Do yourself no **h**, for we are
Acts 28: 5 the fire and suffered no **h**
Acts 28: 6 saw no **h** come to him, they
Rom 13:10 Love does no **h** to a neighbor
2Ti 4:14 the coppersmith did me much **h**
1Pe 3:13 who is he who will **h** you if
Rev 6: 6 do not **h** the oil and the wine
Rev 7: 2 it was granted to **h** the earth
Rev 7: 3 Do not **h** the earth, the sea,
Rev 9: 4 to **h** the grass of the earth
Rev 9:19 and with them they do **h**
Rev 11: 5 And if anyone wants to **h** them
Rev 11: 5 And if anyone wants to **h** them

HARMFUL (*see* HARM)
Josh 23:15 bring upon you all **h** things
2Ki 4:41 was nothing **h** in the pot
Ezra 4:15 **h** to kings and provinces, and
Eccl 8: 5 will experience nothing **h**
1Ti 6: 9 **h** lusts which drown men in

HARMLESS (*see* HARM)
Matt 10:16 as serpents and **h** as doves
Phil 2:15 may become blameless and **h**
Heb 7:26 for us, who is holy, **h**,

HARMON
Amos 4: 3 and you will be cast into **H**

HARMONIOUS
Ps 92: 3 And on the harp, With **h** sound

HARNEPHER
1Ch 7:36 sons of Zophah were Suah, **H**

HARNESS (*see* HARNESSED)
Jer 46: 4 **H** the horses, and mount up,
Mic 1:13 **h** the chariot to the swift

HARNESSED (*see* HARNESS)
Ps 32: 9 Which must be **h** with bit
Hos 10:11 but I **h** her fair neck, I will

HAROD (*see* HARODITE)
Judg 7: 1 encamped beside the well of **H**

HARODITE (*see* HAROD, HARORITE)
2Sa 23:25 Shammah the **H**, Elika the **H**

HAROEH (*see* REAIAH)
1Ch 2:52 **H**, and half of the families of

HARORITE (*see* HARODITE)
1Ch 11:27 Shammoth the **H**, Helez the

HAROSHETH HAGOYIM
Judg 4: 2 was Sisera, who dwelt in **H**
Judg 4:13 from **H** to the River Kishon
Judg 4:16 and the army as far as **H**, and

HARP (*see* HARPISTS, HARPS)
Gen 4:21 of all those who play the **h**
Gen 31:27 and songs, with timbrel and **h**
1Sa 10: 5 a flute, and a **h** before them
1Sa 16:16 is a skillful player on the **h**
1Sa 16:23 that David would take a **h**
1Ch 25: 3 with a **h** to give thanks and to
Job 21:12 sing to the tambourine and **h**
Job 30:31 My **h** is turned to mourning,
Ps 33: 2 Praise the LORD with the **h**
Ps 43: 4 on the **h** I will praise You, O
Ps 49: 4 my dark saying on the **h**
Ps 57: 8 Awake, lute and **h**
Ps 71:22 To You I will sing with the **h**
Ps 81: 2 The pleasant **h** with the lute
Ps 92: 3 On the lute, And on the **h**
Ps 98: 5 Sing to the LORD with the **h**
Ps 98: 5 With the **h** and the sound
Ps 108: 2 Awake, lute and **h**
Ps 144: 9 On a **h** of ten strings I will
Ps 147: 7 praises on the **h** to our God
Ps 149: 3 to Him with the timbrel and **h**
Ps 150: 3 Praise Him with the lute and **h**
Is 5:12 The **h** and the strings, the
Is 16:11 resound like a **h** for Moab

Is 23:16 Take a **h**, go about the city,
Is 24: 8 ends, the joy of the **h** ceases
Dan 3: 5 sound of the horn, flute, **h**
Dan 3: 7 sound of the horn, flute, **h**
Dan 3:10 sound of the horn, flute, **h**
Dan 3:15 sound of the horn, flute, **h**
1Co 14: 7 life, whether flute or **h**,
Rev 5: 8 the Lamb, each having a **h**

HARPISTS (*see* HARP)
Rev 14: 2 of **h** playing their harps
Rev 18:22 The sound of **h**, musicians,

HARPOONS
Job 41: 7 Can you fill his skin with **h**

HARPS (*see* HARP)
2Sa 6: 5 made of fir wood, on **h**, on
1Ki 10:12 for the king's house, also **h**
1Ch 13: 8 might, with singing, on **h**
1Ch 15:16 stringed instruments, **h**, and
1Ch 15:21 to direct with **h** on the
1Ch 15:28 stringed instruments and **h**
1Ch 16: 5 stringed instruments and **h**
1Ch 25: 1 who should prophesy with **h**
1Ch 25: 6 stringed instruments, and **h**
2Ch 5:12 stringed instruments and **h**
2Ch 9:11 for the king's house, also **h**
2Ch 20:28 stringed instruments and **h**
2Ch 29:25 instruments, and with **h**,
Neh 12:27 and stringed instruments and **h**
Ps 137: 2 We hung our **h** Upon the
Is 30:32 will be with tambourines and **h**
Ezek 26:13 the sound of your **h** shall be
Rev 14: 2 of harpists playing their **h**
Rev 15: 2 sea of glass, having **h** of God

HARSH (*see* HARSHLY)
1Sa 5: 7 for His hand is **h** toward us
1Sa 25: 3 but the man was **h** and evil in
2Sa 3:39 of Zeruiah, are too **h** for me
Prov 15: 1 but a **h** word stirs up anger
Prov 15:10 **H** correction is for him who
Mal 3:13 words have been **h** against Me
1Pe 2:18 and gentle, but also to the **h**
Jude 15 of all the **h** things which

HARSHA
Ezra 2:52 sons of Mehida, the sons of **H**
Neh 7:54 of Mehida, the children of **H**

HARSHLY (*see* HARSH)
Gen 16: 6 when Sarai dealt **h** with her
Judg 4: 3 and for twenty years he **h**
Job 39:16 She treats her young **h**, as

HARUM
1Ch 4: 8 of Aharhel the son of **H**

HARUMAPH
Neh 3:10 of **H** made repairs in front of

HARUPHITE
1Ch 12: 5 and Shephatiah the **H**

HARUZ
2Ki 21:19 the daughter of **H** of Jotbah

HARVEST (*see* HARVESTER, HARVESTING)
Gen 8:22 earth remains, seedtime and **h**
Gen 30:14 went in the days of wheat **h**
Gen 47:24 in the **h** that you shall give
Ex 23:16 and the Feast of **H**, the
Ex 34:21 time and in **h** you shall rest
Ex 34:22 of the firstfruits of wheat **h**
Lev 19: 9 you reap the **h** of your land
Lev 19: 9 the gleanings of your **h**
Lev 23:10 I give to you, and reap its **h**
Lev 23:10 of your **h** to the priest
Lev 23:22 you reap the **h** of your land
Lev 23:22 any gleaning from your **h**
Lev 25: 5 of your **h** you shall not reap
Lev 25:22 you shall eat of the old **h**
Lev 26:10 You shall eat the old **h**, and
Deut 24:19 you reap your **h** in your field
Josh 3:15 during the whole time of **h**)
Judg 15: 1 while, in the time of wheat **h**
Ruth 1:22 at the beginning of barley **h**
Ruth 2:21 they have finished all my **h**
Ruth 2:23 of barley **h** and wheat **h**
1Sa 6:13 their wheat **h** in the valley
1Sa 8:12 plow his ground and reap his **h**
1Sa 12:17 Is today not the wheat **h**
2Sa 9:10 and you shall bring in the **h**
2Sa 21: 9 put to death in the days of **h**
2Sa 21: 9 in the beginning of barley **h**
2Sa 21:10 from the beginning of **h** until
2Sa 23:13 chief men went down at **h** time
2Ch 32:28 for the **h** of grain, wine, and
Job 5: 5 the hungry eat up his **h**,
Job 31: 8 yes, let my **h** be rooted out
Ps 107:37 they may yield a fruitful **h**
Prov 6: 8 and gathers her food in the **h**
Prov 10: 5 but he who sleeps in **h** is a
Prov 20: 4 he will beg during the **h** and
Prov 25:13 **h** is a faithful messenger to
Prov 26: 1 snow in summer and rain in **h**
Is 9: 3 You According to the joy of **h**
Is 16: 9 your summer fruits and your **h**
Is 17:11 but the **h** will be a heap of
Is 18: 4 cloud of dew in the heat of **h**
Is 18: 5 For before the **h**, when the
Is 23: 3 the **h** of the River, is her
Jer 5:17 And they shall eat up your **h**
Jer 5:24 the appointed weeks of the **h**
Jer 8:20 The **h** is past, the summer is
Jer 12:13 But be ashamed of your **h**
Jer 50:16 handles the sickle at **h** time
Jer 51:33 the time of her **h** will come
Hos 6:11 a **h** is appointed for you,
Joel 1:11 because the **h** of the field
Joel 3:13 the sickle, for the **h** is ripe
Amos 4: 7 still three months to the **h**
Matt 9:37 The **h** truly is plentiful, but
Matt 9:38 pray the Lord of the **h** to
Matt 9:38 send out laborers into His **h**
Matt 13:30 grow together until the **h**
Matt 13:30 at the time of **h** I will say
Matt 13:39 the **h** is the end of the age,
Mark 4:29 because the **h** has come
Luke 10: 2 The **h** truly is great, but the
Luke 10: 2 pray the Lord of the **h** to
Luke 10: 2 send out laborers into His **h**
John 4:35 months and then comes the **h**'
John 4:35 they are already white for **h**
Rev 14:15 for the **h** of the earth is

HARVESTER (*see* HARVEST)
Is 17: 5 when the **h** gathers the grain
Jer 9:22 like cuttings after the **h**

HARVESTING (*see* HARVEST)
Gen 45: 6 will be neither plowing nor **h**

HAS (*see* PREFACE)

HASADIAH
1Ch 3:20 Hashubah, Ohel, Berechiah, **H**

HASHABIAH
1Ch 6:45 the son of **H**, the son of
1Ch 9:14 son of Azrikam, the son of **H**
1Ch 25: 3 Zeri, Jeshaiah, Shimei, **H**
1Ch 25:19 the twelfth for **H**, his sons
1Ch 26:30 Of the Hebronites, **H** and his
1Ch 27:17 Levites, **H** the son of Kemuel
2Ch 35: 9 Shemaiah and Nethaneel, and **H**
Ezra 8:19 and **H**, and with him Jeshaiah of
Ezra 8:24 Sherebiah, **H**, and ten of their
Neh 3:17 Next to him **H**, leader of half
Neh 10:11 Micha, Rehob, **H**,
Neh 11:15 son of Azrikam, the son of **H**
Neh 11:22 the son of Bani, the son of **H**
Neh 12:21 of Hilkiah, **H**
Neh 12:24 heads of the Levites were **H**

HASHABNAH
Neh 10:25 Rehum, **H**, Maaseiah,

HASHABNIAH
Neh 3:10 the son of **H** made repairs
Neh 9: 5 Jeshua, Kadmiel, Bani, **H**

HASHBADANA
Neh 8: 4 Mishael, Malchijah, Hashum, **H**

HASHEM (*see* JASHEN)
1Ch 11:34 the sons of **H** the Gizonite,

HASHMONAH
Num 33:29 from Mithkah and camped at **H**
Num 33:30 They departed from **H** and

HASHUB (*see* HASSHUB)
Neh 3:11 and **H** the son of Pahath-Moab

HASHUBAH
1Ch 3:20 and **H**, Ohel, Berechiah,

HASHUM
Ezra 2:19 the people of **H**, two hundred
Ezra 10:33 of the sons of **H**
Neh 7:22 the children of **H**, three
Neh 8: 4 Mishael, Malchijah, **H**,
Neh 10:18 Hodijah, **H**, Bezai,

HASRAH (*see* HARHAS)
2Ch 34:22 son of Tokhath, the son of **H**

HASSENAAH (*see* SENAAH)
Neh 3: 3 Also the sons of **H** built the

HASSENUAH (*see* SENUAH)
1Ch 9: 7 son of Hodaviah, the son of **H**

HASSHUB (*see* HASHUB)
1Ch 9:14 Shemaiah the son of **H**, the
Neh 3:23 **H** made repairs opposite their
Neh 10:23 Hoshea, Hananiah, **H**,
Neh 11:15 Shemaiah the son of **H**, the

HASTE (*see* HASTEN, HASTILY, HASTY)
Gen 24:46 And she made **h** and let her
Gen 43:30 so Joseph made **h** and sought
Ex 10:16 for Moses and Aaron in **h**, and
Ex 12:11 So you shall eat it in **h**
Ex 12:33 them out of the land in **h**
Ex 34: 8 So Moses made **h** and bowed his
Deut 16: 3 of the land of Egypt in **h**)
Judg 9:48 you have seen me do, make **h**
Judg 13:10 Then the woman ran in **h** and
1Sa 20:38 Make **h**, hurry, do not delay
1Sa 21: 8 king's business required **h**
1Sa 23:26 So David made **h** to get away
1Sa 25:18 Then Abigail made **h** and took
1Sa 25:42 So Abigail rose in **h** and rode
2Sa 4: 4 as she made **h** to flee, that
2Sa 15:14 Make **h** to depart, lest he
1Ki 12:18 in **h** to flee to Jerusalem
2Ki 7:15 had thrown away in their **h**
2Ch 10:18 in **h** to flee to Jerusalem
2Ch 35:21 God commanded me to make **h**
Ezra 4:23 they went up in **h** to
Ps 31:22 For I said in my **h**, 'I am
Ps 38:22 Make **h** to help me, O Lord, my
Ps 40:13 O LORD, make **h** to help me
Ps 70: 1 Make **h**, O God, to deliver me
Ps 70: 1 Make **h** to help me, O LORD
Ps 70: 5 Make **h** to me, O God
Ps 71:12 O my God, make **h** to help me
Ps 116:11 I said in my **h**, "All men are
Ps 119:60 I made **h**, and did not delay To
Ps 141: 1 Make **h** to me
Prov 1:16 they make **h** to shed blood
Song 8:14 Make **h**, my beloved, and be
Is 49:17 Your sons shall make **h**
Is 52:12 you shall not go out with **h**
Is 59: 7 they make **h** to shed innocent
Jer 9:18 Let them make **h** and take up a
Dan 3:24 and he rose in **h** and spoke,
Dan 6:19 went in **h** to the den of lions
Nah 2: 5 they make **h** to her walls, and
Mark 6:25 came in with **h** to the king
Luke 1:39 into the hill country with **h**
Luke 2:16 And they came with **h** and found
Luke 19: 5 Zacchaeus, make **h** and come
Luke 19: 6 So he made **h** and came down,
Acts 22:18 saw Him saying to me, 'Make **h**
Tit 3:13 on their journey with **h**, that

HASTEN (*see* HASTE, HASTENED, HASTENING, HASTENS)
Gen 45: 9 **H** and go up to my father, and
Gen 45:13 and you shall **h** and bring my
Deut 32:35 things to come **h** upon them
Josh 10:13 and did not **h** to go down for
1Sa 23:27 **H** and come, for the
Esth 6:10 **H**, take the robe and the horse
Ps 16: 4 who **h** after another god
Ps 22:19 O My Strength, **h** to help Me
Ps 55: 8 I would **h** my escape From the
Eccl 7: 9 Do not **h** in your spirit to be
Is 5:19 **h** His work, that we may see
Is 60:22 LORD, will **h** it in its time

HASTENED (*see* HASTEN)
Gen 18: 6 So Abraham **h** into the tent to
Gen 18: 7 man, and he **h** to prepare it
Gen 24:18 Then she **h** and let her
Gen 24:20 Then she **h** and emptied her
Josh 4:10 and the people **h** and crossed
Josh 8:14 that the men of the city **h**
Josh 8:19 **h** to set the city on fire
1Sa 17:48 to meet David, that David **h**
1Sa 25:23 she **h** to dismount from the
1Sa 25:34 hurting you, unless you had **h**
1Sa 28:24 house, and she **h** to kill it

HATS
Ex 28:40 And you shall make **h** for them
Ex 29: 9 sons, and put the **h** on them
Ex 39:28 exquisite **h** of fine linen,
Lev 8:13 put **h** on them, as the LORD

HATTIL
Ezra 2:57 of Shephatiah, the sons of **H**
Neh 7:59 Shephatiah, the children of **H**

HATTUSH
1Ch 3:22 The sons of Shemaiah were **H**
Ezra 8: 2 of the sons of David, **H**
Neh 3:10 And next to him **H** the son of
Neh 10: 4 **H**, Shebaniah, Malluch,
Neh 12: 2 Amariah, Malluch, **H**,

HAUGHTILY (*see* HAUGHTY)
Mic 2: 3 nor shall you walk **h**, for

HAUGHTINESS (*see* HAUGHTY)
Job 20: 6 Though his **h** mounts up to the
Is 2:11 the **h** of men shall be bowed
Is 2:17 the **h** of men shall be brought
Is 13:11 lay low the **h** of the terrible
Is 16: 6 of his **h** and his pride and his
Jer 48:29 and of the **h** of his heart

HAUGHTY (*see* HAUGHTILY, HAUGHTINESS)
2Sa 22:28 but Your eyes are on the **h**
Ps 18:27 But will bring down **h** looks
Ps 101: 5 The one who has a **h** look and a
Ps 131: 1 Lord, my heart is not **h**, Nor
Prov 16:18 and a **h** spirit before a fall
Prov 18:12 the heart of a man is **h**, and
Prov 21: 4 A **h** look, a proud heart, and
Prov 21:24 A proud and **h** man
Is 3:16 the daughters of Zion are **h**
Is 10:12 and the glory of his **h** looks
Is 10:33 and the **h** will be humbled
Is 24: 4 the **h** people of the earth
Ezek 16:50 And they were **h** and committed
Zeph 3:11 be **h** In My holy mountain
Rom 11:20 Do not be **h**, but fear
1Ti 6:17 this present age not to be **h**
2Ti 3: 4 traitors, headstrong, **h**,

HAURAN
Ezek 47:16 (which is on the border of **H**)
Ezek 47:18 out the border from between **H**

HAVE (*see* PREFACE)

HAVEN (*see* HAVENS)
Gen 49:13 dwell by the **h** of the sea
Gen 49:13 he shall become a **h** for ships
Ps 107:30 them to their desired **h**

HAVENS (*see* HAVEN)
Acts 27: 8 came to a place called Fair **H**

HAVILAH
Gen 2:11 the whole land of **H**, where
Gen 10: 7 The sons of Cush were Seba, **H**
Gen 10:29 Ophir, **H**, and Jobab
Gen 25:18 dwelt from **H** as far as Shur
1Sa 15: 7 from **H** all the way to Shur,
1Ch 1: 9 The sons of Cush were Seba, **H**
1Ch 1:23 Ophir, **H**, and Jobab

HAVING (*see* PREFACE)

HAVOC
Acts 8: 3 he made **h** of the church,

HAVOTH JAIR (*see* JAIR)
Num 32:41 small towns, and called them **H**
Deut 3:14 Bashan after his own name, **H**
Judg 10: 4 are called **H**" to this day

HAWK (*see* HAWKS)
Lev 11:16 and the **h** after its kind
Deut 14:15 and the **h** after their kinds
Job 39:26 Does the **h** fly by your wisdom

HAWKS (*see* HAWK)
Is 34:15 also shall the **h** be gathered

HAY
Prov 27:25 When the **h** is removed, and the
1Co 3:12 precious stones, wood, **h**

HAZAEL
1Ki 19:15 anoint **H** as king over Syria
1Ki 19:17 escapes the sword of **H**, Jehu
2Ki 8: 8 And the king said to **H**, "Take
2Ki 8: 9 So **H** went to meet him and took
2Ki 8:12 And **H** said, "Why is my
2Ki 8:13 So **H** said, "But what is your
2Ki 8:15 and **H** reigned in his place
2Ki 8:28 **H** king of Syria at Ramoth
2Ki 8:29 against **H** king of Syria
2Ki 9:14 against **H** king of Syria
2Ki 9:15 fought with **H** king of Syria
2Ki 10:32 **H** conquered them in all the
2Ki 12:17 Now **H** king of Syria went up
2Ki 12:17 so **H** set his face to go up to
2Ki 12:18 sent them to **H** king of Syria
2Ki 13: 3 the hand of **H** king of Syria
2Ki 13: 3 of Ben-Hadad the son of **H**
2Ki 13:22 **H** king of Syria oppressed
2Ki 13:24 Now **H** king of Syria died
2Ki 13:25 of Ben-Hadad, the son of **H**
2Ch 22: 5 **H** king of Syria at Ramoth
2Ch 22: 6 against **H** king of Syria
Amos 1: 4 a fire into the house of **H**

HAZAIAH
Neh 11: 5 of Col-Hozeh, the son of **H**

HAZAR ADDAR
Num 34: 4 then it shall go on to **H**, and

HAZAR ENAN
Num 34: 9 Ziphron, and it shall end at **H**
Num 34:10 border from **H** to Shepham
Ezek 47:17 shall be from the Sea to **H**
Ezek 48: 1 the entrance of Hamath, to **H**

HAZAR GADDAH
Josh 15:27 **H**, Heshmon, Beth Pelet,

HAZAR HATTICON
Ezek 47:16 to **H** (which is on the border

HAZARMAVETH
Gen 10:26 begot Almodad, Sheleph, **H**
1Ch 1:20 begot Almodad, Sheleph, **H**

HAZAR SHUAL (*see* SHUAL)
Josh 15:28 **H**, Beersheba, Bizjothjah,
Josh 19: 3 **H**, Balah, Ezem,
1Ch 4:28 at Beersheba, Moladah, **H**,
Neh 11:27 **H**, and Beersheba and its

HAZAR SUSAH (*see* HAZAR SUSIM)
Josh 19: 5 Ziklag, Beth Marcaboth, **H**

HAZAR SUSIM (*see* HAZAR SUSAH)
1Ch 4:31 Beth Marcaboth, **H**, Beth Biri,

HAZAZON TAMAR (*see* EN GEDI, TAMAR)
2Ch 20: 2 they are in **H**" (which is En

HAZELELPONI
1Ch 4: 3 name of their sister was **H**

HAZEROTH
Num 11:35 the people moved to **H**, and
Num 11:35 to **H**, and camped at **H**
Num 12:16 the people moved from **H** and
Num 33:17 Hattaavah and camped at **H**
Num 33:18 They departed from **H** and
Deut 1: 1 Paran, Tophel, Laban, **H**, and

HAZEZON TAMAR (*see* EN GEDI)
Gen 14: 7 the Amorites who dwelt in **H**

HAZIEL
1Ch 23: 9 Shelomith, **H**, and Haran

HAZO
Gen 22:22 Chesed, **H**, Pildash, Jidlaph,

HAZOR (*see* BAAL HAZOR, HEZRON)
Josh 11: 1 king of **H** heard these things
Josh 11:10 back at that time and took **H**
Josh 11:10 for **H** was formerly the head
Josh 11:11 Then he burned **H** with fire
Josh 11:13 none of them, except **H** only
Josh 12:19 the king of **H**, one
Josh 15:23 Kedesh, **H**, Ithnan,
Josh 15:25 **H**, Hadattah, Kerioth, Hezron
Josh 15:25 Kerioth, Hezron (which is **H**)
Josh 19:36 Adamah, Ramah, **H**,
Judg 4: 2 of Canaan, who reigned in **H**
Judg 4:17 peace between Jabin king of **H**
1Sa 12: 9 commander of the army of **H**
1Ki 9:15 the wall of Jerusalem, **H**
2Ki 15:29 Maachah, Janoah, Kedesh, **H**
Neh 11:33 in **H**, Ramah, Gittaim
Jer 49:28 and against the kingdoms of **H**
Jer 49:30 depths, O inhabitants of **H**
Jer 49:33 **H** shall be a dwelling for

HE (*see* PREFACE)

HEAD (*see* HEADED, HEADS)
Gen 3:15 He shall bruise your **h**, and
Gen 24:26 Then the man bowed down his **h**
Gen 24:48 And I bowed my **h** and
Gen 28:11 that place and put it at his **h**
Gen 28:18 that he had put at his **h**, set
Gen 40:13 Pharaoh will lift up your **h**
Gen 40:16 three white baskets on my **h**
Gen 40:17 out of the basket on my **h**
Gen 40:19 will lift off your **h** from you
Gen 40:20 he lifted up the **h** of the
Gen 47:31 himself on the **h** of the bed
Gen 48:14 and laid it on Ephraim's **h**
Gen 48:14 his left hand on Manasseh's **h**
Gen 48:17 hand on the **h** of Ephraim, it
Gen 48:17 Ephraim's **h** to Manasseh's **h**
Gen 48:18 put your right hand on his **h**
Gen 49:26 shall be on the **h** of Joseph
Gen 49:26 on the crown of the **h** of him
Ex 9:31 for the barley was in the **h**
Ex 12: 9 its **h** with its legs and its
Ex 28:32 for his **h** in the middle of it
Ex 29: 6 shall put the turban on his **h**
Ex 29: 7 oil, pour it on his **h**, and
Ex 29:10 hands on the **h** of the bull
Ex 29:15 hands on the **h** of the ram
Ex 29:17 with its pieces and with its **h**
Ex 29:19 hands on the **h** of the ram
Ex 34: 8 bowed his **h** toward the earth,
Lev 1: 4 the **h** of the burnt offering
Lev 1: 8 shall lay the parts, the **h**
Lev 1:12 into its pieces, with its **h**
Lev 1:15 to the altar, wring off its **h**
Lev 3: 2 hand on the **h** of his offering
Lev 3: 8 hand on the **h** of his offering
Lev 3:13 shall lay his hand on its **h**
Lev 4: 4 lay his hand on the bull's **h**
Lev 4:11 and all its flesh, with its **h**
Lev 4:15 lay their hands on the **h** of
Lev 4:24 his hand on the **h** of the goat
Lev 4:29 on the **h** of the sin offering
Lev 4:33 on the **h** of the sin offering
Lev 5: 8 wring off its **h** from its neck
Lev 8: 9 And he put the turban on his **h**
Lev 8:12 anointing oil on Aaron's **h**
Lev 8:14 the **h** of the bull for the sin
Lev 8:18 hands on the **h** of the ram
Lev 8:20 and Moses burned the **h**, the
Lev 8:22 hands on the **h** of the ram
Lev 9:13 to him, with its pieces and **h**
Lev 13:12 sore, from his **h** to his foot,
Lev 13:29 a sore on the **h** or the beard
Lev 13:30 a leprosy of the **h** or beard
Lev 13:40 hair has fallen from his **h**
Lev 13:42 the bald **h** or bald forehead a
Lev 13:42 bald **h** or his bald forehead
Lev 13:43 **h** or on his bald forehead
Lev 13:44 his sore is on his **h**
Lev 13:45 shall be torn and his **h** bare
Lev 14: 9 shave all the hair off his **h**
Lev 14:18 on the **h** of him who is to be
Lev 14:29 on the **h** of him who is to be
Lev 16:21 on the **h** of the live goat
Lev 16:21 them on the **h** of the goat
Lev 19:27 around the sides of your **h**
Lev 21:10 on whose **h** the anointing oil
Lev 21:10 his **h** nor tear his clothes
Lev 24:14 him lay their hands on his **h**
Num 1: 4 tribe, each one the **h** of his
Num 5:18 LORD, uncover the woman's **h**
Num 6: 5 razor shall come upon his **h**
Num 6: 5 of the hair of his **h** grow
Num 6: 7 separation to God is on his **h**
Num 6: 9 he defiles his consecrated **h**
Num 6: 9 then he shall shave his **h** on
Num 6:11 sanctify his **h** that same day
Num 6:18 **h** at the door of the
Num 6:18 hair from his consecrated **h**
Num 17: 3 the **h** of each father's house
Num 22:31 and he bowed his **h** and fell
Num 25:15 he was **h** of the people of a
Deut 14: 1 front of your **h** for the dead
Deut 19: 5 the **h** slips from the handle
Deut 21:12 and she shall shave her **h**
Deut 28:13 the LORD will make you the **h**
Deut 28:23 over your **h** shall be bronze
Deut 28:35 foot to the top of your **h**
Deut 28:44 he shall be the **h**, and you
Deut 33:16 come 'on the **h** of Joseph, and

Deut 33:16 on the crown of the **h** of him
Deut 33:20 the arm and the crown of his **h**
Josh 2:19 blood shall be on his own **h**
Josh 2:19 **h** if a hand is laid on him
Josh 11:10 the **h** of all those kingdoms
Josh 22:14 each one was the **h** of the
Judg 5:26 Sisera, she pierced his **h**
Judg 9:53 millstone on Abimelech's **h**
Judg 10:18 He shall be **h** over all the
Judg 11: 8 and be our **h** over all the
Judg 11: 9 them to me, shall I be your **h**
Judg 11:11 and the people made him **h**
Judg 13: 5 razor shall come upon his **h**
Judg 16:13 **h** into the web of the loom"
Judg 16:17 razor has ever come upon my **h**
Judg 16:19 off the seven locks of his **h**
Judg 16:22 the hair of his **h** began to
1Sa 1:11 razor shall come upon his **h**
1Sa 4:12 clothes torn and dirt on his **h**
1Sa 5: 4 The **h** of Dagon and both the
1Sa 10: 1 of oil and poured it on his **h**
1Sa 14:45 not one hair of his **h** shall
1Sa 15:17 were you not **h** of the tribes
1Sa 17: 5 had a bronze helmet on his **h**
1Sa 17:38 put a bronze helmet on his **h**
1Sa 17:46 you and take your **h** from you
1Sa 17:51 him, and cut off his **h** with it
1Sa 17:54 And David took the **h** of the
1Sa 17:57 **h** of the Philistine in his
1Sa 19:13 of goats' hair for his **h**, and
1Sa 19:16 of goats' hair for his **h**
1Sa 25:39 of Nabal on his own **h**
1Sa 26: 7 stuck in the ground by his **h**
1Sa 26:11 of water that are by his **h**
1Sa 26:12 the jug of water by Saul's **h**
1Sa 26:16 of water that was by his **h**
1Sa 31: 9 And they cut off his **h** and
2Sa 1: 2 clothes torn and dust on his **h**
2Sa 1:10 the crown that was on his **h**
2Sa 1:16 Your blood is on your own **h**
2Sa 2:16 grasped his opponent by the **h**
2Sa 3: 8 Am I a dog's **h** that belongs
2Sa 3:29 Let it rest on the **h** of Joab
2Sa 4: 7 beheaded him and took his **h**
2Sa 4: 8 And they brought the **h** of
2Sa 4: 8 Here is the **h** of Ishbosheth,
2Sa 4:12 they took the **h** of Ishbosheth
2Sa 12:30 their king's crown from his **h**
2Sa 12:30 And it was set on David's **h**
2Sa 13:19 Then Tamar put ashes on her **h**
2Sa 13:19 and laid her hand on her **h**
2Sa 14:25 foot to the crown of his **h**
2Sa 14:26 when he cut the hair of his **h**
2Sa 14:26 his **h** at two hundred shekels
2Sa 15:30 and he had his **h** covered and
2Sa 15:32 robe torn and dust on his **h**
2Sa 16: 9 me go over and take off his **h**
2Sa 18: 9 his **h** caught in the terebinth
2Sa 20:21 his **h** will be thrown to you
2Sa 20:22 they cut off the **h** of Sheba
2Sa 22:44 me as the **h** of the nations
1Ki 2:32 return his blood on his **h**
1Ki 2:33 return upon the **h** of Joab
1Ki 2:33 upon the **h** of his descendants
1Ki 2:37 blood shall be on your own **h**
1Ki 2:44 your wickedness on your own **h**
1Ki 8:32 bringing his way on his **h**
1Ki 19: 6 there by his **h** was a cake
2Ki 4:19 My **h**, my **h**!"
2Ki 6: 5 the iron ax **h** fell into the
2Ki 6:25 it until a donkey's **h** was
2Ki 6:31 if the **h** of Elisha the son of
2Ki 6:32 someone to take away my **h**
2Ki 9: 3 of oil, and pour it on his **h**
2Ki 9: 6 And he poured the oil on his **h**
2Ki 9:30 on her eyes and adorned her **h**
2Ki 19:21 shaken her **h** behind your back
1Ch 10: 9 stripped him and took his **h**
1Ch 10:10 fastened his **h** in the temple
1Ch 20: 2 their king's crown from his **h**
1Ch 20: 2 And it was set on David's **h**
1Ch 26:31 Jerijah was **h** of the
1Ch 29:11 You are exalted as **h** over all
2Ch 6:23 bringing his way on his own **h**
2Ch 13:12 Himself is with us as our **h**
2Ch 20:18 Jehoshaphat bowed his **h** with
Ezra 9: 3 out some of the hair of my **h**
Esth 2:17 the royal crown upon her **h**
Esth 6: 8 a royal crest placed on its **h**
Esth 6:12 and with his **h** covered
Esth 9:25 should return on his own **h**
Job 1:20 tore his robe and shaved his **h**
Job 2: 7 foot to the crown of his **h**
Job 2:12 dust on his **h** toward heaven
Job 10:15 I cannot lift up my **h**
Job 10:16 If my **h** is exalted, you hunt
Job 16: 4 you, and shake my **h** at you
Job 16:15 and laid my **h** in the dust
Job 19: 9 and taken the crown from my **h**
Job 20: 6 his **h** reaches to the clouds,
Job 29: 3 when His lamp shone upon my **h**
Job 41: 7 or his **h** with fishing spears
Ps 3: 3 and the One who lifts up my **h**
Ps 7:16 shall return upon his own **h**
Ps 18:43 made me the **h** of the nations
Ps 21: 3 crown of pure gold upon his **h**
Ps 22: 7 out the lip, they shake the **h**
Ps 23: 5 You anoint my **h** with oil
Ps 27: 6 now my **h** shall be lifted up
Ps 38: 4 have gone over my **h**
Ps 40:12 more than the hairs of my **h**
Ps 44:14 A shaking of the **h** among the
Ps 60: 7 also is the helmet for My **h**
Ps 68:21 wound the **h** of His enemies
Ps 69: 4 more than the hairs of my **h**
Ps 83: 2 You have lifted up their **h**
Ps 108: 8 also is the helmet for My **h**
Ps 110: 7 He shall lift up the **h**
Ps 133: 2 the precious oil upon the **h**
Ps 140: 7 You have covered my **h** in the
Ps 140: 9 As for the **h** of those who
Ps 141: 5 Let my **h** not refuse it
Prov 1: 9 graceful ornaments on your **h**
Prov 4: 9 your **h** an ornament of grace
Prov 10: 6 are on the **h** of the righteous
Prov 11:26 on the **h** of him who sells it
Prov 16:31 The silver-haired **h** is a
Prov 20:29 of old men is their gray **h**
Prov 25:22 heap coals of fire on his **h**
Eccl 2:14 wise man's eyes are in his **h**
Eccl 9: 8 and let your **h** lack no oil
Song 2: 6 His left hand is under my **h**
Song 5: 2 for my **h** is covered with dew,
Song 5:11 His **h** is like the finest gold
Song 7: 5 Your **h** crowns you like Mount
Song 7: 5 hair of your **h** is like purple
Song 8: 3 His left hand is under my **h**
Is 1: 5 The whole **h** is sick, and the
Is 1: 6 of the foot even to the **h**
Is 3:17 a scab the crown of the **h** of
Is 7: 8 For the **h** of Syria is
Is 7: 8 the **h** of Damascus is Rezin
Is 7: 9 The **h** of Ephraim is Samaria,
Is 7: 9 and the **h** of Samaria is
Is 7:20 the king of Assyria, the **h**
Is 9:14 the LORD will cut off **h** and
Is 9:15 and honorable, he is the **h**
Is 19:15 Egypt, which the **h** or tail
Is 28: 1 the **h** of the verdant valleys
Is 28: 4 the **h** of the verdant valley
Is 37:22 shaken her **h** behind your back
Is 51:20 they lie at the **h** of all the
Is 58: 5 bow down his **h** like a bulrush
Is 59:17 helmet of salvation on His **h**
Jer 2:16 broken the crown of your **h**
Jer 2:37 him with your hands on your **h**
Jer 9: 1 that my **h** were waters, and my
Jer 13:21 chieftains, to be **h** over you
Jer 18:16 be astonished and shake his **h**
Jer 22: 6 to Me, the **h** of Lebanon
Jer 23:19 on the **h** of the wicked
Jer 30:23 on the **h** of the wicked
Jer 48:27 You shake your **h** in scorn
Jer 48:37 For every **h** shall be bald, and
Jer 48:45 The crown of the **h** of the
Jer 52:31 lifted up the **h** of Jehoiachin
Lam 2:19 at the **h** of every street
Lam 3:54 The waters flowed over my **h**
Lam 4: 1 at the **h** of every street
Lam 5:16 crown has fallen from our **h**
Ezek 5: 1 razor, and pass it over your **h**
Ezek 9:10 their deeds on their own **h**
Ezek 10: 1 above the **h** of the cherubim
Ezek 10:11 direction the **h** was facing
Ezek 16:12 a beautiful crown on your **h**
Ezek 16:25 places at the **h** of every road
Ezek 16:31 shrine at the **h** of every road
Ezek 16:43 your deeds on your own **h**,"
Ezek 17:19 will recompense on his own **h**
Ezek 21:19 put it at the **h** of the road
Ezek 24:17 bind your turban on your **h**
Ezek 29:18 every **h** was made bald, and
Ezek 33: 4 blood shall be on his own **h**
Dan 1:10 endanger my **h** before the king
Dan 2:28 of your **h** upon your bed, were
Dan 2:32 This image's **h** was of fine
Dan 2:38 you are this **h** of gold
Dan 3:27 the hair of their **h** was not
Dan 4: 5 visions of my **h** troubled me
Dan 4:10 of my **h** while on my bed
Dan 4:13 of my **h** while on my bed, and
Dan 7: 1 visions of his **h** while on his
Dan 7: 9 the hair of His **h** was like
Dan 7:15 visions of my **h** troubled me
Dan 7:20 ten horns that were on its **h**
Hos 1:11 appoint for themselves one **h**
Joel 3: 4 retaliation upon your own **h**
Joel 3: 7 retaliation upon your own **h**
Amos 2: 7 which is on the **h** of the poor
Amos 8:10 waist, and baldness on every **h**
Obad 15 shall return upon your own **h**
Jon 2: 5 were wrapped around my **h**
Jon 4: 6 his **h** to deliver him from his
Jon 4: 8 and the sun beat on Jonah's **h**
Mic 2:13 with the LORD at their **h**
Nah 3:10 at the **h** of every street
Hab 3:13 You struck the **h** from the
Hab 3:14 arrows the **h** of his villages
Zech 1:21 no one could lift up his **h**
Zech 3: 5 put a clean turban on his **h**
Zech 3: 5 put a clean turban on his **h**
Zech 6:11 set it on the **h** of Joshua the
Matt 5:36 Nor shall you swear by your **h**
Matt 6:17 when you fast, anoint your **h**
Matt 8:20 Man has nowhere to lay His **h**
Matt 10:30 of your **h** are all numbered
Matt 14: 8 Baptist's **h** here on a platter
Matt 14:11 And his **h** was brought on a
Matt 26: 7 she poured it on His **h** as He
Matt 27:29 thorns, they put it on His **h**
Matt 27:30 reed and struck Him on the **h**
Matt 27:37 they put up over His **h** the
Mark 4:28 first the blade, then the **h**
Mark 4:28 that the full grain in the **h**
Mark 6:24 The **h** of John the Baptist
Mark 6:25 **h** of John the Baptist on a
Mark 6:27 commanded his **h** to be brought
Mark 6:28 brought his **h** on a platter,
Mark 12: 4 stones, wounded him in the **h**
Mark 14: 3 flask and poured it on His **h**
Mark 15:17 of thorns, put it on His **h**
Mark 15:19 Him on the **h** with a reed and
Luke 7:38 them with the hair of her **h**
Luke 7:44 them with the hair of her **h**
Luke 7:46 did not anoint My **h** with oil
Luke 9:58 Man has nowhere to lay His **h**
Luke 12: 7 of your **h** are all numbered
Luke 21:18 hair of your **h** shall be lost
John 13: 9 but also my hands and my **h**
John 19: 2 of thorns and put it on His **h**
John 19:30 And bowing His **h**, He gave up
John 20: 7 that had been around His **h**
John 20:12 white sitting, one at the **h**
Acts 27:14 a tempestuous **h** wind arose
Acts 27:15 could not **h** into the wind, we
Acts 27:34 fall from the **h** of any of you
Rom 12:20 heap coals of fire on his **h**
1Co 11: 3 the **h** of every man is Christ
1Co 11: 3 the **h** of woman is man, and the
1Co 11: 3 and the **h** of Christ is God
1Co 11: 4 **h** covered, dishonors his **h**
1Co 11: 5 or prophesies with her **h**
1Co 11: 5 uncovered dishonors her **h**
1Co 11: 5 same as if her **h** were shaved
1Co 11: 7 ought not to cover his **h**,
1Co 11:10 symbol of authority on her **h**
1Co 11:13 to God with her **h** uncovered
1Co 12:21 nor again the **h** to the feet
Eph 1:22 gave Him to be **h** over all
Eph 4:15 things into Him who is the **h**
Eph 5:23 the husband is **h** of the wife
Eph 5:23 Christ is **h** of the church
Col 1:18 He is the **h** of the body, the
Col 2:10 in Him, who is the **h** of all
Col 2:19 and not holding fast to the **H**
Rev 1:14 His **h** and His hair were white
Rev 10: 1 And a rainbow was on his **h**
Rev 12: 1 on her **h** a garland of twelve
Rev 14:14 Man, having on His **h** a golden
Rev 19:12 on His **h** were many crowns

HEADBANDS
Is 3:20 the leg ornaments, and the **h**

HEADDRESSES
Is 3:20 the **h**, the leg ornaments, and

HEADED (*see* HEAD)
Gen 31:21 **h** toward the mountains of
Lev 19:32 shall rise before the gray **h**
1Sa 6:12 Then the cows **h** straight for

HEADLONG
Jer 49: 5 be driven out, everyone **h**
Acts 1:18 and falling **h**, he burst open

HEADS (*see* HEAD)
Gen 41: 5 suddenly seven **h** of grain
Gen 41: 6 Then behold, seven thin **h**
Gen 41: 7 the seven thin **h** devoured the
Gen 41: 7 the seven plump and full **h**
Gen 41:22 suddenly seven **h** came up on
Gen 41:23 Then behold, seven **h**,
Gen 41:24 the thin **h** devoured the seven
Gen 41:24 devoured the seven good **h**
Gen 41:26 the seven good **h** are seven
Gen 41:27 the seven empty **h** blighted by
Gen 43:28 And they bowed their **h** down
Ex 4:31 then they bowed their **h** and
Ex 6:14 These are the **h** of their
Ex 6:25 These are the **h** of the
Ex 12:27 So the people bowed their **h**
Ex 18:25 made them **h** over the people
Lev 2:14 **h** of grain roasted on the
Lev 2:14 grain beaten from full **h**
Lev 10: 6 Do not uncover your **h** nor
Lev 21: 5 any bald place on their **h**
Num 1:16 **h** of the divisions in Israel
Num 7: 2 the **h** of their fathers'
Num 8:12 on the **h** of the young bulls
Num 10: 4 the **h** of the divisions of
Num 13: 3 all of them men who were **h** of
Num 30: 1 Then Moses spoke to the **h** of
Deut 1:13 I will make them **h** over you
Deut 1:15 So I took the **h** of your
Deut 1:15 men, and made them **h** over you
Deut 5:23 all the **h** of your tribes and
Deut 23:25 pluck the **h** with your hand
Deut 32:42 from the **h** of the leaders of
Deut 33:21 came with the **h** of the people
Josh 7: 6 and they put dust on their **h**
Josh 14: 1 the **h** of the fathers of the
Josh 19:51 the **h** of the fathers of the
Josh 21: 1 Now the **h** of the fathers of
Josh 21: 1 to the **h** of the fathers of
Josh 22:21 and said to the **h** of the
Josh 22:30 the **h** of the divisions of
Josh 23: 2 for their elders, for their **h**
Josh 24: 1 elders of Israel, for their **h**
Judg 7:25 and brought the **h** of Oreb and
Judg 8:28 they lifted their **h** no more
Judg 9:57 God returned on their own **h**
Ruth 2: 2 glean **h** of grain after him in
1Sa 29: 4 not with the **h** of these men
2Sa 15:30 were with him covered their **h**
1Ki 8: 1 all the **h** of the tribes, the
1Ki 20:31 waists and ropes around our **h**
1Ki 20:32 and put ropes around their **h**
2Ki 10: 6 take the **h** of the men, your
2Ki 10: 7 put their **h** in baskets and
2Ki 10: 8 the **h** of the king's sons
1Ch 5:24 These were the **h** of their
1Ch 5:24 **h** of their fathers' houses
1Ch 7: 2 **h** of their father's house
1Ch 7: 7 They were **h** of their fathers'
1Ch 7: 9 **h** of their fathers' houses,
1Ch 7:11 **h** of their fathers' houses
1Ch 7:40 **h** of their fathers' houses,
1Ch 8: 6 Ehud, who were the **h** of the
1Ch 8:10 **h** of their fathers' houses
1Ch 8:13 who were **h** of their fathers'
1Ch 8:28 These were **h** of the fathers'
1Ch 9: 9 All these men were **h** of a
1Ch 9:13 **h** of their fathers' houses
1Ch 9:33 **h** of the fathers' houses of
1Ch 9:34 These **h** of the fathers'
1Ch 9:34 were **h** throughout their
1Ch 11:10 Now these were the **h** of the
1Ch 12:19 master Saul and endanger our **h**
1Ch 15:12 You are the **h** of the fathers'
1Ch 23: 9 These were the **h** of the
1Ch 23:24 the **h** of the fathers' houses
1Ch 24: 4 **h** of their fathers' houses
1Ch 24: 4 eight **h** of their fathers'
1Ch 24: 6 the **h** of the fathers' houses
1Ch 24:31 the **h** of the fathers' houses
1Ch 26:21 **h** of their fathers' houses,
1Ch 26:26 the **h** of fathers' houses, the
1Ch 26:32 **h** of fathers' houses, whom
1Ch 27: 1 the **h** of fathers' houses, the
1Ch 29:20 fathers, and bowed their **h**
2Ch 1: 2 the **h** of the fathers' houses
2Ch 5: 2 all the **h** of the tribes, the
2Ch 28:12 Then some of the **h** of the
2Ch 29:30 and they bowed their **h** and
Ezra 1: 5 Then the **h** of the fathers'
Ezra 2:68 Some of the **h** of the fathers'
Ezra 3:12 **h** of the fathers' houses, who
Ezra 4: 2 the **h** of the fathers' houses,
Ezra 4: 3 and the rest of the **h** of the
Ezra 8: 1 These are the **h** of their
Ezra 8:29 **h** of the fathers' houses of
Ezra 9: 6 have risen higher than our **h**
Ezra 10:16 priest, with certain **h** of the
Neh 4: 4 their reproach on their own **h**
Neh 7:70 some of the **h** of the fathers'
Neh 7:71 Some of the **h** of the fathers'
Neh 8: 6 And they bowed their **h** and
Neh 8:13 **h** of the fathers' houses of
Neh 9: 1 and with dust on their **h**
Neh 11: 3 Now these are the **h** of the
Neh 11:13 **h** of the fathers' houses,
Neh 11:16 of the **h** of the Levites, had
Neh 12: 7 were the **h** of the priests
Neh 12:12 the **h** of the fathers' houses
Neh 12:22 priests who had been **h** of
Neh 12:23 the **h** of the fathers' houses
Neh 12:24 the **h** of the Levites were
Job 24:24 dry out like the **h** of grain
Ps 24: 7 Lift up your **h**, O you gates
Ps 24: 9 Lift up your **h**, O you gates
Ps 66:12 caused men to ride over our **h**
Ps 74:13 You broke the **h** of the sea
Ps 74:14 You broke the **h** of Leviathan
Ps 109:25 at me, they shake their **h**
Ps 110: 6 the **h** of many countries
Is 15: 2 on all their **h** will be
Is 17: 5 and reaps the **h** with his arm
Is 17: 5 **h** of grain in the Valley of
Is 29:10 and He has covered your **h**,
Is 35:10 everlasting joy on their **h**
Is 51:11 everlasting joy on their **h**
Jer 14: 3 confounded and covered their **h**
Jer 14: 4 they covered their **h**
Lam 2:10 they throw dust on their **h**
Lam 2:10 bow their **h** to the ground
Lam 2:15 shake their **h** at the daughter
Ezek 1:22 of the firmament above the **h**
Ezek 1:22 stretched out over their **h**
Ezek 1:25 that was over their **h**
Ezek 1:26 their **h** was the likeness of a
Ezek 7:18 face, baldness on all their **h**
Ezek 11:21 their deeds on their own **h**
Ezek 13:18 and make veils for the **h** of
Ezek 22:31 their deeds on their own **h**
Ezek 23:15 flowing turbans on their **h**
Ezek 23:42 beautiful crowns on their **h**
Ezek 24:23 turbans shall be on your **h**
Ezek 27:30 and cast dust on their **h**
Ezek 32:27 their swords under their **h**
Ezek 44:18 have linen turbans on their **h**
Ezek 44:20 Nor shall they shave their **h**
Dan 7: 6 The beast also had four **h**
Amos 9: 1 them on the **h** of them all
Mic 3: 1 O **h** of Jacob, and you rulers
Mic 3: 9 you **h** of the house of Jacob
Mic 3:11 her **h** judge for a bribe, her
Matt 12: 1 and began to pluck **h** of grain
Matt 27:39 Him, wagging their **h**
Mark 2:23 began to pluck the **h** of grain
Mark 15:29 Him, wagging their **h** and
Luke 6: 1 plucked the **h** of grain and ate
Luke 21:28 look up and lift up your **h**
Acts 18: 6 Your blood be upon your own **h**
Acts 21:24 that they may shave their **h**
Rev 4: 4 had crowns of gold on their **h**
Rev 9: 7 on their **h** were crowns of
Rev 9:17 the **h** of the horses were like
Rev 9:17 were like the **h** of lions
Rev 9:19 are like serpents, having **h**
Rev 12: 3 red dragon having seven **h**
Rev 12: 3 and seven diadems on his **h**
Rev 13: 1 of the sea, having seven **h**
Rev 13: 1 on his **h** a blasphemous name
Rev 13: 3 I saw one of his **h** as if it
Rev 17: 3 of blasphemy, having seven **h**
Rev 17: 7 her, which has the seven **h**
Rev 17: 9 The seven **h** are seven
Rev 18:19 And they threw dust on their **h**

HEADSTRONG
2Ti 3: 4 traitors, **h**, haughty, lovers

HEAL (*see* HEALED, HEALING, HEALS)
Num 12:13 Please **h** her, O God, I pray
Deut 32:39 I wound and I **h**
2Ki 5: 3 For he would **h** him of his
2Ki 5: 6 that you may **h** him of his
2Ki 5: 7 to me to **h** him of his leprosy
2Ki 5:11 the place, and **h** the leprosy
2Ki 20: 5 surely I will **h** you
2Ki 20: 8 sign that the LORD will **h** me
2Ch 7:14 their sin and **h** their land
Ps 6: 2 LORD, **h** me, for my bones are
Ps 41: 4 **H** my soul, for I have sinned
Ps 60: 2 **H** its breaches, for it is
Eccl 3: 3 time to kill, and a time to **h**
Is 19:22 Egypt, He will strike and **h** it
Is 19:22 entreated by them and **h** them
Is 57:18 seen his ways, and will **h** him
Is 57:19 And I will **h** him
Is 61: 1 Me to **h** the brokenhearted
Jer 3:22 I will **h** your backslidings
Jer 17:14 **H** me, O LORD, and I shall be
Jer 30:17 **h** you of your wounds,' says
Jer 33: 6 I will **h** them and reveal to
Lam 2:13 who can **h** you
Hos 5:13 you, nor **h** you of your wound
Hos 6: 1 He has torn, but He will **h** us
Hos 14: 4 I will **h** their backsliding, I
Zech 11:16 nor **h** those that are broken,
Matt 8: 7 him, "I will come and **h** him
Matt 10: 1 to **h** all kinds of sickness and
Matt 10: 8 **H** the sick, cleanse the
Matt 12:10 it lawful to **h** on the Sabbath
Matt 13:15 turn, so that I should **h** them
Mark 3: 2 whether He would **h** him on the
Mark 3:15 to have power to **h** sicknesses
Luke 4:18 Me to **h** the brokenhearted
Luke 4:23 to Me, 'Physician, **h** yourself
Luke 5:17 Lord was present to **h** them
Luke 6: 7 He would **h** on the Sabbath
Luke 7: 3 Him to come and **h** his servant
Luke 9: 2 of God and to **h** the sick
Luke 10: 9 **h** the sick who are there, and
Luke 14: 3 it lawful to **h** on the Sabbath
John 4:47 **h** his son, for he was at the
John 12:40 turn, so that I should **h** them
Acts 4:30 stretching out Your hand to **h**
Acts 28:27 turn, so that I should **h** them

HEALED (*see* HEAL)
Gen 20:17 God **h** Abimelech, his wife, and
Ex 21:19 for him to be thoroughly **h**
Lev 13:18 boil in the skin, and it is **h**
Lev 13:37 up in it, the scall has **h**
Lev 14: 3 the leprosy is **h** in the leper
Lev 14:48 because the plague is **h**
Deut 28:27 from which you cannot be **h**
Deut 28:35 boils which cannot be **h**, and
Josh 5: 8 in the camp till they were **h**
1Sa 6: 3 Then you will be **h**, and it
2Ki 2:21 I have **h** this water
2Ki 2:22 water remains **h** to this day
2Ch 30:20 to Hezekiah and **h** the people
Ps 30: 2 out to You, And You have **h** me
Ps 107:20 **h** them, And delivered them
Is 6:10 heart, and return and be **h**
Is 53: 5 and by His stripes we are **h**
Jer 6:14 They have also **h** the hurt of
Jer 8:11 For they have **h** the hurt of
Jer 15:18 which refuses to be **h**
Jer 17:14 me, O LORD, and I shall be **h**
Jer 51: 8 perhaps she may be **h**
Jer 51: 9 We would have **h** Babylon, but
Jer 51: 9 Babylon, but she is not **h**
Ezek 34: 4 nor have you **h** those who were
Ezek 47: 8 the sea, its waters are **h**
Ezek 47: 9 for they will be **h**, and
Ezek 47:11 and marshes will not be **h**
Hos 7: 1 When I would have **h** Israel
Hos 11: 3 did not know that I **h** them
Matt 4:24 and He **h** them
Matt 8: 8 word, and my servant will be **h**
Matt 8:13 servant was **h** that same hour

Matt 8:16 word, and **h** all who were sick,
Matt 12:15 Him, and He **h** them all
Matt 12:22 He **h** him, so that the blind
Matt 14:14 for them, and **h** their sick
Matt 15:28 her daughter was **h** from that
Matt 15:30 at Jesus' feet, and He **h** them
Matt 19: 2 Him, and He **h** them there
Matt 21:14 in the temple, and He **h** them
Mark 1:34 Then He **h** many who were sick
Mark 3:10 For He **h** many, so that as
Mark 5:23 on her, that she may be **h**
Mark 5:29 she was **h** of the affliction
Mark 5:34 and be **h** of your affliction
Mark 6: 5 a few sick people and **h** them
Mark 6:13 many who were sick, and **h** them
Luke 4:40 every one of them and **h** them
Luke 5:15 and to be **h** by Him of their
Luke 6:17 and be **h** of their diseases,
Luke 6:18 And they were **h**
Luke 6:19 out from Him and **h** them all
Luke 7: 7 word, and my servant will be **h**
Luke 8: 2 had been **h** of evil spirits
Luke 8:36 been demon-possessed was **h**
Luke 8:43 and could not be **h** by any,
Luke 8:47 and how she was **h** immediately
Luke 9:11 and **h** those who had need of
Luke 9:42 **h** the child, and gave him back
Luke 13:14 Jesus had **h** on the Sabbath
Luke 13:14 be **h** on them, and not on the
Luke 14: 4 him and **h** him, and let him go
Luke 17:15 when he saw that he was **h**
Luke 22:51 He touched his ear and **h** him
John 5:13 But the one who was **h** did not
Acts 3:11 who was **h** held on to Peter
Acts 4:14 had been **h** standing with them
Acts 5:16 spirits, and they were all **h**
Acts 8: 7 were paralyzed and lame were **h**
Acts 14: 9 that he had faith to be **h**
Acts 28: 8 his hands on him and **h** him
Acts 28: 9 diseases also came and were **h**
Heb 12:13 dislocated, but rather be **h**
Jas 5:16 another, that you may be **h**
1Pe 2:24 by whose stripes you were **h**
Rev 13: 3 and his deadly wound was **h**
Rev 13:12 whose deadly wound was **h**

HEALING (*see* HEAL, HEALINGS)
Is 58: 8 your **h** shall spring forth
Jer 14:19 so that there is no **h** for us
Jer 14:19 and for the time of **h**, and
Jer 30:13 you have no **h** medicines
Jer 33: 6 I will bring it health and **h**
Ezek 30:21 has not been bandaged for **h**
Nah 3:19 Your injury has no **h**, your
Mal 4: 2 arise with **h** in His wings
Matt 4:23 **h** all kinds of sickness and
Matt 9:35 **h** every sickness and every
Luke 9: 6 the gospel and **h** everywhere
Luke 9:11 those who had need of **h**
Acts 4:22 of **h** had been performed
Acts 10:38 **h** all who were oppressed by
Rev 22: 2 were for the **h** of the nations

HEALINGS (*see* HEALING)
1Co 12: 9 gifts of **h** by the same Spirit
1Co 12:28 miracles, then gifts of **h**
1Co 12:30 Do all have gifts of **h**

HEALS (*see* HEAL)
Ex 15:26 For I am the LORD who **h** you
Ps 103: 3 Who **h** all your diseases,
Ps 147: 3 He **h** the broken-hearted And
Is 30:26 **h** the stroke of their wound
Acts 9:34 Jesus the Christ **h** you

HEALTH (*see* HEALTHY)
Gen 43:28 our father is in good **h**
2Sa 20: 9 Are you in **h**, my brother
Ps 38: 3 Nor is there any **h** in my
Prov 3: 8 It will be **h** to your flesh,
Prov 4:22 them, and **h** to all their flesh
Prov 12:18 tongue of the wise promotes **h**
Prov 13:17 faithful ambassador brings **h**
Prov 16:24 to the soul and **h** to the bones
Jer 8:15 and for a time of **h**, and there
Jer 8:22 the **h** of the daughter of my
Jer 30:17 For I will restore **h** to you
Jer 33: 6 Behold, I will bring it **h**
3Jn 2 in all things and be in **h**,

HEALTHY (*see* HEALTH)
Job 39: 4 Their young ones are **h**, they
Prov 15:30 good report makes the bones **h**

HEAP (*see* HEAPED, HEAPS)
Gen 31:46 they took stones and made a **h**
Gen 31:46 and they ate there on the **h**
Gen 31:48 This **h** is a witness between
Gen 31:51 Here is this **h** and here is
Gen 31:52 This **h** is a witness, and this
Gen 31:52 not pass beyond this **h** to you
Gen 31:52 will not pass beyond this **h**
Ex 15: 8 floods stood upright like a **h**
Deut 13:16 and it shall be a **h** forever
Deut 32:23 I will **h** disasters upon them
Josh 3:13 and they shall stand as a **h**
Josh 3:16 rose in a **h** very far away at
Josh 7:26 over him a great **h** of stones
Josh 8:28 Ai and made it a **h** forever
Josh 8:29 raise over it a great **h** of
Ruth 3: 7 at the end of the **h** of grain
1Sa 2: 8 the beggar from the ash **h**
2Sa 18:17 laid a very large **h** of stones
Ezra 6:11 a refuse **h** because of this
Job 8:17 roots wrap around the rock **h**
Job 16: 4 I could **h** up words against
Job 30:24 His hand against a **h** of ruins
Ps 33: 7 of the sea together as a **h**
Ps 78:13 the waters stand up like a **h**
Ps 113: 7 the needy out of the ash **h**
Prov 25:22 For so you will **h** coals of
Song 7: 2 Your waist is a **h** of wheat
Is 17: 1 and it will be a ruinous **h**
Is 17:11 be a **h** of ruins in the day of
Is 25:10 down for the refuse **h**
Is 57:14 **H** it up! **H** it up!
Jer 9:11 make Jerusalem a **h** of ruins
Jer 51:37 Babylon shall become a **h**, a
Ezek 4: 2 and **h** up a mound against it
Ezek 17:17 when they **h** up a siege mound
Ezek 21:22 to **h** up a siege mound, and to
Ezek 24:10 **H** on the wood, kindle the
Ezek 26: 8 he will **h** up a siege mound
Dan 2: 5 houses shall be made an ash **h**
Dan 3:29 houses shall be made an ash **h**
Mic 1: 6 a **h** of ruins in the field
Hab 1:10 for they **h** up mounds of earth
Hab 3:15 through the **h** of great waters
Hag 2:16 came to a **h** of twenty ephahs
Rom 12:20 for in so doing you will **h**
2Ti 4: 3 they will **h** up for themselves

HEAPED (*see* HEAP)
Zech 9: 3 **h** up silver like the dust, and
Jas 5: 3 You have **h** up treasure in the

HEAPS (*see* HEAP)
Ex 8:14 gathered them together in **h**
Judg 15:16 of a donkey, **h** upon **h**
2Ki 10: 8 Lay them in two **h** at the
2Ki 19:25 cities into **h** of ruins
2Ch 31: 6 LORD their God they laid in **h**
2Ch 31: 7 they began laying them in **h**
2Ch 31: 8 the leaders came and saw the **h**
2Ch 31: 9 the Levites concerning the **h**
Neh 4: 2 stones from the **h** of rubbish
Job 27:16 Though he **h** up silver like
Ps 39: 6 He **h** up riches, And does not
Ps 79: 1 They have laid Jerusalem in **h**
Is 37:26 cities into **h** of ruins
Jer 26:18 shall become **h** of ruins, and
Jer 50:26 cast her up as **h** of ruins
Lam 4: 5 up in scarlet embrace ash **h**
Hos 12:11 their altars shall be **h** in
Mic 3:12 shall become **h** of ruins, and
Hab 2: 5 **h** up for himself all peoples

HEAR (*see* HEARD, HEARER, HEARING, HEARS, UNHEARD)
Gen 4:23 Adah and Zillah, **h** my voice
Gen 21: 6 so that all who **h** will laugh
Gen 23: 6 **H** us, my lord
Gen 23: 8 **h** me, and meet with Ephron the
Gen 23:11 No, my lord, **h** me
Gen 23:13 you will give it, please **h** me
Gen 37: 6 Please **h** this dream which I
Gen 42:21 with us, and we would not **h**
Gen 49: 2 Gather together and **h**, you
Ex 7:16 until now you would not **h**
Ex 15:14 The people will **h** and be
Ex 19: 9 that the people may **h** when I
Ex 20:19 speak with us, and we will **h**
Ex 22:23 Me, I will surely **h** their cry
Ex 22:27 when he cries to Me, I will **h**
Ex 32:18 of those who sing that I **h**
Num 9: 8 that I may **h** what the LORD
Num 12: 6 He said, "**H** now My words
Num 14:13 Then the Egyptians will **h** it
Num 16: 8 **H** now, you sons of Levi
Num 20:10 to them, "**H** now, you rebels
Num 23:18 Rise up, Balak, and **h**
Deut 1:16 **H** the cases between your
Deut 1:17 you shall **h** the small as well
Deut 1:17 it to me, and I will **h** it
Deut 2:25 who shall **h** the report of you
Deut 4: 6 who will **h** all these statutes
Deut 4:10 and I will let them **h** My words
Deut 4:28 see nor **h** nor eat nor smell
Deut 4:33 Did any people ever **h** the
Deut 4:36 heaven He let you **h** His voice
Deut 5: 1 **H**, O Israel, the statutes and
Deut 5:25 if we **h** the voice of the LORD
Deut 5:27 **h** all that the LORD our God
Deut 5:27 God says to you, and we will **h**
Deut 6: 3 Therefore **h**, O Israel, and be
Deut 6: 4 **H**, O Israel: The LORD our God
Deut 9: 1 **H**, O Israel
Deut 13:11 So all Israel shall **h** and fear
Deut 13:12 If you **h** someone in one of
Deut 17: 4 you **h** of it, then you shall
Deut 17:13 And all the people shall **h**
Deut 18:15 Him you shall **h**,
Deut 18:16 Let me not **h** again the voice
Deut 18:19 whoever will not **h** My words
Deut 19:20 And those who remain shall **h**
Deut 20: 3 And he shall say to them, '**H**
Deut 21:21 you, and all Israel shall **h**
Deut 29: 4 and eyes to see and ears to **h**
Deut 30:12 it to us, that we may **h** it
Deut 30:13 it to us, that we may **h** it
Deut 30:17 away so that you do not **h**
Deut 31:12 your gates, that they may **h**
Deut 31:13 who have not known it, may **h**
Deut 32: 1 and **h**, O earth, the words of
Deut 33: 7 **H**, LORD, the voice of Judah,
Josh 3: 9 **h** the words of the LORD your
Josh 6: 5 when you **h** the sound of the
Josh 7: 9 of the land will **h** of it, and
Judg 5: 3 **H**, O kings
Judg 5:16 to **h** the pipings for the
Judg 7:11 you shall **h** what they say
Judg 14:13 your riddle, that we may **h** it
1Sa 2:23 For I **h** of your evil dealings
1Sa 2:24 is not a good report that I **h**
1Sa 8:18 will not **h** you in that day
1Sa 13: 3 Let the Hebrews **h**
1Sa 15:14 lowing of the oxen which I **h**
1Sa 22: 7 him, "**H** now, you Benjamites
1Sa 22:12 said, "**H** now, son of Ahitub
1Sa 25:24 ears, and **h** the words of your
1Sa 26:19 let my lord the king **h** the
2Sa 5:24 be, when you **h** the sound of
2Sa 14:16 For the king will **h** and
2Sa 15: 3 deputy of the king to **h** you
2Sa 15:10 As soon as you **h** the sound of
2Sa 15:35 you **h** from the king's house
2Sa 15:36 send me everything you **h**
2Sa 16:21 all Israel will **h** that you
2Sa 17: 5 let us **h** what he says too
2Sa 19:35 Can I **h** any longer the voice
2Sa 20:16 **H**, **H**! Please say to Joab
2Sa 20:17 to him, "**H** the words of your
2Sa 22:45 as soon as they **h**, they obey
1Ki 4:34 came to **h** the wisdom of
1Ki 8:29 that You may **h** the prayer
1Ki 8:30 may You **h** the supplication of
1Ki 8:30 place, then **h** in heaven Your
1Ki 8:30 and when You **h**, forgive
1Ki 8:32 then **h** in heaven, and act and
1Ki 8:34 then **h** in heaven, and forgive
1Ki 8:36 then **h** in heaven, and forgive
1Ki 8:39 then **h** in heaven Your
1Ki 8:42 (for they will **h** of Your
1Ki 8:43 **h** in heaven Your dwelling
1Ki 8:45 then **h** in heaven their prayer
1Ki 8:49 then **h** in heaven Your
1Ki 10: 8 before you and **h** your wisdom
1Ki 10:24 of Solomon to **h** his wisdom
1Ki 18:26 noon, saying, "O Baal, **h** us
1Ki 18:37 **H** me, O LORD, **h** me, that
1Ki 22:19 Therefore **h** the word of the
2Ki 7: 1 **H** the word of the LORD

2Ki 7: 6 to **h** the noise of chariots
2Ki 17:14 Nevertheless they would not **h**
2Ki 18:12 would neither **h** nor do them
2Ki 18:28 **H** the word of the great king,
2Ki 19: 4 will **h** all the words of the
2Ki 19: 7 him, and he shall **h** a rumor
2Ki 19:16 Your ear, O LORD, and **h**
2Ki 19:16 **h** the words of Sennacherib,
2Ki 19:25 Did you not **h** long ago how I
2Ki 20:16 **H** the word of the LORD
1Ch 14:15 be, when you **h** a sound of
1Ch 28: 2 **H** me, my brethren and my
2Ch 6:20 that You may **h** the prayer
2Ch 6:21 may You **h** the supplications
2Ch 6:21 **h** from Your dwelling place,
2Ch 6:21 and when You **h**, forgive
2Ch 6:23 then **h** from heaven, and act,
2Ch 6:25 then **h** from heaven and forgive
2Ch 6:27 then **h** in heaven, and forgive
2Ch 6:30 then **h** from heaven Your
2Ch 6:33 then **h** from heaven Your
2Ch 6:35 then **h** from heaven their
2Ch 6:39 then **h** from heaven Your
2Ch 7:14 then I will **h** from heaven
2Ch 9: 7 before you and **h** your wisdom
2Ch 9:23 of Solomon to **h** his wisdom
2Ch 13: 4 **H** me, Jeroboam and all Israel
2Ch 15: 2 **H** me, Asa, and all Judah and
2Ch 18:18 Therefore **h** the word of the
2Ch 20: 9 our affliction, and You will **h**
2Ch 20:20 said, "**H** me, O Judah and you
2Ch 28:11 Now **h** me, therefore, and
2Ch 29: 5 **H** me, Levites
Neh 1: 6 that You may **h** the prayer of
Neh 4: 4 **H**, O our God, for we are
Neh 4:20 wherever you **h** the sound of
Neh 8: 2 women and all who could **h** with
Neh 9:29 their necks, and would not **h**
Neh 13:27 Should we then **h** of your
Job 3:18 they do not **h** the voice of
Job 5:27 **H** it, and know for yourself
Job 13: 6 Now **h** my reasoning, and heed
Job 15:17 I will tell you, **h** me
Job 22:27 prayer to Him, He will **h** you
Job 26:14 small a whisper we **h** of Him
Job 27: 9 Will God **h** his cry when
Job 31:35 Oh, that I had one to **h** me
Job 33: 1 **h** my speech, and listen to all
Job 34: 2 **H** my words, you wise men
Job 34:16 have understanding, **h** this
Job 37: 2 **H** attentively the thunder of
Ps 4: 1 **H** me when I call, O God of my
Ps 4: 1 mercy on me, and **h** my prayer
Ps 4: 3 The LORD will **h** when I call
Ps 5: 3 You shall **h** in the morning
Ps 10:17 You will cause Your ear to **h**
Ps 13: 3 and **h** me, O LORD my God
Ps 17: 1 **H** a just cause, O LORD,
Ps 17: 6 upon You, for You will **h** me
Ps 17: 6 ear to me, and **h** my speech
Ps 18:44 As soon as they **h** of me they
Ps 22: 2 the daytime, but You do not **h**
Ps 27: 7 **H**, O LORD, when I cry with my
Ps 28: 2 **H** the voice of my
Ps 30:10 **H**, O LORD, and have mercy on
Ps 31:13 For I **h** the slander of many
Ps 34: 2 The humble shall **h** of it and
Ps 38:13 I, like a deaf man, do not **h**
Ps 38:14 am like a man who does not **h**
Ps 38:15 You will **h**, O Lord my God
Ps 38:16 **H** me, lest they rejoice over
Ps 39:12 **H** my prayer, O LORD, And give
Ps 49: 1 **H** this, all you peoples
Ps 50: 7 **H**, O My people, and I will
Ps 51: 8 Make me to **h** joy and gladness,
Ps 54: 2 **H** my prayer, O God
Ps 55: 2 Attend to me, and **h** me
Ps 55:17 aloud, And He shall **h** my voice
Ps 55:19 God will **h**, and afflict them,
Ps 60: 5 with Your right hand, and **h** me
Ps 61: 1 **H** my cry, O God
Ps 64: 1 **H** my voice, O God, in my
Ps 65: 2 O You who **h** prayer, To You
Ps 66:16 Come and **h**, all you who fear
Ps 66:18 my heart, The Lord will not **h**
Ps 69:13 **H** me in the truth of Your
Ps 69:16 **H** me, O LORD, for Your
Ps 69:17 **H** me speedily
Ps 81: 8 **H**, O My people, and I will
Ps 84: 8 God of hosts, **h** my prayer
Ps 85: 8 I will **h** what God the LORD
Ps 86: 1 down Your ear, O LORD, **h** me
Ps 92:11 My ears **h** my desire on the
Ps 94: 9 the ear, shall He not **h**
Ps 95: 7 if you will **h** His voice
Ps 102: 1 **H** my prayer, O LORD, And let
Ps 102:20 To **h** the groaning of the
Ps 108: 6 with Your right hand, and **h** me
Ps 115: 6 have ears, but they do not **h**
Ps 119:145 **H** me, O LORD
Ps 119:149 **H** my voice according to Your
Ps 130: 2 Lord, **h** my voice
Ps 135:17 have ears, but they do not **h**
Ps 138: 4 When they **h** the words of Your
Ps 140: 6 **H** the voice of my
Ps 141: 6 they **h** my words, for they are
Ps 143: 1 **H** my prayer, O LORD, Give ear
Ps 143: 8 Cause me to **h** Your
Ps 145:19 He also will **h** their cry and
Prov 1: 5 A wise man will **h** and increase
Prov 1: 8 **h** the instruction of your
Prov 4: 1 **H**, my children, the
Prov 4:10 **H**, my son, and receive my
Prov 5: 7 Therefore **h** me now, my
Prov 8:33 **H** instruction and be wise, and
Prov 13: 8 the poor does not **h** rebuke
Prov 22:17 **h** the words of the wise, and
Prov 23:19 **H**, my son, and be wise
Eccl 5: 1 draw near to **h** rather than to
Eccl 7: 5 It is better to **h** the rebuke
Eccl 7: 5 a man to **h** the song of fools
Eccl 7:21 say, lest you **h** your servant
Eccl 12:13 Let us **h** the conclusion of
Song 2:14 let me **h** your voice
Song 8:13 let me **h** it
Is 1: 2 **H**, O heavens, and give ear, O
Is 1:10 **H** the word of the LORD, you
Is 1:15 many prayers, I will not **h**
Is 6:10 and **h** with their ears, and
Is 7:13 **H** now, O house of David
Is 18: 3 he blows a trumpet, you **h** it
Is 28:12 yet they would not **h**
Is 28:14 Therefore **h** the word of the
Is 28:23 **h** my voice, listen and **h** my
Is 28:23 voice, listen and **h** my speech
Is 29:18 shall **h** the words of the book
Is 30: 9 not **h** the law of the LORD
Is 30:21 Your ears shall **h** a word
Is 32: 3 of those who **h** will listen
Is 32: 9 who are at ease, **h** my voice
Is 33:13 **H**, you who are afar off, what
Is 34: 1 Come near, you nations, to **h**
Is 34: 1 Let the earth **h**, and all that
Is 36:13 **H** the words of the great king
Is 37: 4 **h** the words of the Rabshakeh
Is 37: 7 him, and he shall **h** a rumor
Is 37:17 Your ear, O LORD, and **h**
Is 37:17 and **h** all the words of
Is 37:26 Did you not **h** long ago how I
Is 39: 5 **H** the word of the LORD of
Is 41:17 I, the LORD, will **h** them
Is 42:18 **H**, you deaf
Is 42:20 the ears, but he does not **h**
Is 42:23 and **h** for the time to come
Is 43: 9 or let them **h** and say, "It is
Is 44: 1 Yet **h** now, O Jacob My servant
Is 47: 8 Therefore **h** this now, you who
Is 48: 1 **H** this, O house of Jacob, who
Is 48: 3 and I caused them to **h** it
Is 48: 6 I have made you **h** new things
Is 48: 8 Surely you did not **h**, surely
Is 48:14 assemble yourselves, and **h**
Is 48:16 Come near to Me, **h** this
Is 50: 4 My ear to **h** as the learned
Is 51:21 Therefore please **h** this, you
Is 55: 3 **H**, and your soul shall live
Is 59: 1 ear heavy, that it cannot **h**
Is 59: 2 you, so that He will not **h**
Is 65:12 when I spoke, you did not **h**
Is 65:24 are still speaking, I will **h**
Is 66: 4 when I spoke they did not **h**
Is 66: 5 **H** the word of the LORD, you
Jer 2: 4 **H** the word of the LORD, O
Jer 4:21 **h** the sound of the trumpet
Jer 5:21 **H** this now, O foolish people
Jer 5:21 and who have ears and **h** not
Jer 6:10 give warning, that they may **h**
Jer 6:18 Therefore **h**, you nations, and
Jer 6:19 **H**, O earth!
Jer 7: 2 **H** the word of the LORD, all
Jer 7:13 speaking, but you did not **h**
Jer 7:16 for I will not **h** you
Jer 9:10 nor can men **h** the voice of
Jer 9:20 Yet **h** the word of the LORD, O
Jer 10: 1 **H** the word which the LORD
Jer 11: 2 **H** the words of this covenant,
Jer 11: 6 **H** the words of this covenant
Jer 11:10 who refused to **h** My words
Jer 11:14 for I will not **h** them in the
Jer 13:10 who refuse to **h** My words
Jer 13:11 but they would not **h**
Jer 13:15 **H** and give ear
Jer 13:17 But if you will not **h** it, my
Jer 14:12 fast, I will not **h** their cry
Jer 17:20 **H** the word of the LORD, you
Jer 17:23 that they might not **h** nor
Jer 18: 2 will cause you to **h** My words
Jer 19: 3 **H** the word of the LORD, O
Jer 19:15 they might not **h** My words
Jer 20:16 Let him **h** the cry in the
Jer 21:11 say, '**H** the word of the LORD,
Jer 22: 2 **H** the word of the LORD, O
Jer 22: 5 if you will not **h** these words
Jer 22:21 but you said, 'I will not **h**
Jer 22:29 earth, **h** the word of the LORD
Jer 23:22 My people to **h** My words, then
Jer 25: 4 nor inclined your ear to **h**
Jer 28: 7 Nevertheless **h** now this word
Jer 28:15 **H** now, Hananiah, the LORD has
Jer 29:20 Therefore **h** the word of the
Jer 31:10 **H** the word of the LORD, O
Jer 33: 9 who shall **h** all the good that
Jer 34: 4 Yet **h** the word of the LORD, O
Jer 36: 3 the house of Judah will **h** all
Jer 37:20 Therefore please **h** now, O my
Jer 38:25 But if the princes **h** that I
Jer 42:14 war, nor **h** the sound of the
Jer 42:15 Then **h** now the word of the
Jer 44:24 **H** the word of the LORD, all
Jer 44:26 Therefore **h** the word of the
Jer 49:20 Therefore **h** the counsel of
Jer 50:45 Therefore **h** the counsel of
Lam 1:18 **H** now, all peoples, and behold
Ezek 2: 5 whether they **h** or whether
Ezek 2: 7 whether they **h** or whether
Ezek 2: 8 of man, **h** what I say to you
Ezek 3:10 to you, and **h** with your ears
Ezek 3:11 the Lord GOD,' whether they **h**
Ezek 3:17 therefore **h** a word from My
Ezek 3:27 He who hears, let him **h**
Ezek 6: 3 **h** the word of the Lord GOD
Ezek 8:18 loud voice, I will not **h** them
Ezek 12: 2 ears to **h** but does not **h**
Ezek 13: 2 **H** the word of the LORD
Ezek 16:35 **h** the word of the LORD
Ezek 18:25 **H** now, O house of Israel, is
Ezek 20:47 **H** the word of the LORD
Ezek 24:26 let you **h** it with your ears
Ezek 25: 3 **H** the word of the Lord GOD
Ezek 33: 7 therefore you shall **h** a word
Ezek 33:30 **h** what the word is that comes
Ezek 33:31 they **h** your words, but they
Ezek 33:32 for they **h** your words, but
Ezek 34: 7 **h** the word of the LORD
Ezek 34: 9 **h** the word of the LORD
Ezek 36: 1 **h** the word of the LORD
Ezek 36: 4 **h** the word of the Lord GOD
Ezek 36:15 Nor will I let you **h** the
Ezek 37: 4 bones, **h** the word of the LORD
Ezek 40: 4 **h** with your ears, and fix your
Ezek 44: 5 **h** with your ears, all that I
Dan 3: 5 that at the time you **h** the
Dan 3:15 you **h** the sound of the horn
Dan 5:23 which do not see or **h** or know
Dan 9:17 **h** the prayer of Your servant,
Dan 9:18 my God, incline Your ear and **h**
Dan 9:19 O Lord, **h**!
Hos 4: 1 **H** the word of the LORD, you
Hos 5: 1 **H** this, O priests
Joel 1: 2 **H** this, you elders, and give
Amos 3: 1 **H** this word that the LORD has
Amos 3:13 **H** and testify against the
Amos 4: 1 **H** this word, you cows of
Amos 5: 1 **H** this word which I take up
Amos 5:23 for I will not **h** the melody
Amos 7:16 **h** the word of the LORD
Amos 8: 4 **H** this, you who swallow up
Mic 1: 2 **H**, all you peoples
Mic 3: 1 **H** now, O heads of Jacob, and
Mic 3: 4 LORD, but He will not **h** them

Mic 3: 9 Now **h** this, you heads of the
Mic 6: 1 **H** now what the LORD says
Mic 6: 1 and let the hills **h** your voice
Mic 6: 2 **H**, O you mountains, the
Mic 6: 9 **H** the Rod!
Mic 7: 7 my God will **h** me
Nah 3:19 All who **h** news of you will
Hab 1: 2 I cry, and You will not **h**
Zech 1: 4 they did not **h** nor heed Me
Zech 3: 8 **H**, O Joshua, the high priest
Zech 7:11 ears so that they could not **h**
Zech 7:12 flint, refusing to **h** the law
Zech 7:13 and they would not **h**, so they
Zech 10: 6 their God, and I will **h** them
Mal 2: 2 If you will not **h**, and if you
Matt 10:14 receive you nor **h** your words
Matt 10:27 what you **h** in the ear, preach
Matt 11: 4 John the things which you **h**
Matt 11: 5 are cleansed and the deaf **h**
Matt 11:15 has ears to **h**, let him **h**
Matt 12:19 nor will anyone **h** His voice
Matt 12:42 to **h** the wisdom of Solomon
Matt 13: 9 has ears to **h**, let him **h**
Matt 13:13 see, and hearing they do not **h**
Matt 13:14 Hearing you will **h** and shall
Matt 13:15 **h** with their ears, lest they
Matt 13:16 see, and your ears for they **h**
Matt 13:17 see it, and to **h** what you **h**
Matt 13:17 and did not **h** it
Matt 13:18 Therefore **h** the parable of
Matt 13:43 has ears to **h**, let him **h**
Matt 15:10 **H** and understand
Matt 17: 5 **H** Him!
Matt 18:16 But if he will not **h** you,
Matt 18:17 And if he refuses to **h** them
Matt 18:17 refuses even to **h** the church
Matt 21:16 Do You **h** what these are
Matt 21:33 **H** another parable
Matt 24: 6 And you will **h** of wars and
Matt 27:13 Do You not **h** how many things
Mark 4: 9 has ears to **h**, let him **h**
Mark 4:12 and hearing they may **h** and not
Mark 4:15 And when they **h**, Satan comes
Mark 4:16 who, when they **h** the word
Mark 4:18 are the ones who **h** the word
Mark 4:20 ground, those who **h** the word
Mark 4:23 has ears to **h**, let him **h**
Mark 4:24 Take heed what you **h**
Mark 4:24 and to you who **h**, more will be
Mark 4:33 as they were able to **h** it
Mark 6:11 not receive you nor **h** you
Mark 7:14 **H** Me, everyone, and
Mark 7:16 has ears to **h**, let him **h**
Mark 7:37 He makes both the deaf to **h**
Mark 8:18 And having ears, do you not **h**
Mark 9: 7 **H** Him!
Mark 12:29 **H**, O Israel, the LORD our
Mark 13: 7 And when you **h** of wars and
Luke 5: 1 Him to **h** the word of God,
Luke 5:15 multitudes came together to **h**
Luke 6:17 and Sidon, who came to **h** Him
Luke 6:27 But I say to you who **h**
Luke 7:22 are cleansed, the deaf **h**, the
Luke 8: 8 has ears to **h**, let him **h**
Luke 8:12 wayside are the ones who **h**
Luke 8:13 are those who, when they **h**
Luke 8:18 Therefore take heed how you **h**
Luke 8:21 these who **h** the word of God
Luke 9: 9 this of whom I **h** such things
Luke 9:35 **H** Him!
Luke 10:24 to **h** what you **h**, and have
Luke 11:28 those who **h** the word of God
Luke 11:31 to **h** the wisdom of Solomon
Luke 14:35 has ears to **h**, let him **h**
Luke 15: 1 drew near to Him to **h** Him
Luke 16: 2 What is this I **h** about you
Luke 16:29 let them **h** them
Luke 16:31 him, 'If they do not **h** Moses
Luke 18: 6 **H** what the unjust judge said
Luke 19:48 were very attentive to **h** Him
Luke 21: 9 But when you **h** of wars and
Luke 21:38 to Him in the temple to **h** Him
John 3: 8 you **h** the sound of it, but
John 5:25 is, when the dead will **h** the
John 5:25 and those who **h** will live
John 5:28 the graves will **h** His voice
John 5:30 As I **h**, I judge
John 8: 6 as though He did not **h**
John 8:47 therefore you do not **h**,
John 9:27 Why do you want to **h** it again
John 9:31 that God does not **h** sinners
John 10: 3 and the sheep **h** his voice
John 10: 8 but the sheep did not **h** them
John 10:16 and they will **h** My voice
John 10:27 My sheep **h** My voice, and I
John 11:42 I know that You always **h** Me
John 14:24 the word which you **h** is not
Acts 2: 8 And how is it that we **h**, each
Acts 2:11 we **h** them speaking in our own
Acts 2:22 Men of Israel, **h** these words
Acts 2:33 this which you now see and **h**
Acts 3:22 Him you shall **h** in all things
Acts 3:23 not **h** that Prophet shall be
Acts 7:37 Him you shall **h**
Acts 10:22 house, and to **h** words from you
Acts 10:33 to **h** all the things commanded
Acts 13: 7 sought to **h** the word of God
Acts 13:44 together to **h** the word of God
Acts 15: 7 **h** the word of the gospel and
Acts 17:21 tell or to **h** some new thing
Acts 17:32 We will **h** you again on this
Acts 19:26 **h** that not only at Ephesus,
Acts 21:22 for they will **h** that you have
Acts 22: 1 **h** my defense before you now
Acts 22: 9 but they did not **h** the voice
Acts 22:14 and **h** the voice of His mouth
Acts 23:35 I will **h** you when your
Acts 24: 4 any further, I beg you to **h**
Acts 25:22 like to **h** the man myself
Acts 25:22 you shall **h** him
Acts 26: 3 I beg you to **h** me patiently
Acts 26:29 but also all who **h** me today
Acts 28:22 But we desire to **h** from you
Acts 28:26 Hearing you will **h**, and shall
Acts 28:27 **h** with their ears, lest they
Acts 28:28 Gentiles, and they will **h** it
Rom 10:14 how shall they **h** without a
Rom 11: 8 ears that they should not **h**
1Co 11:18 I **h** that there are divisions
1Co 14:21 all that, they will not **h** Me
Gal 4:21 the law, do you not **h** the law
Phil 1:27 I may **h** of your affairs, that
Phil 1:30 saw in me and now **h** is in me
2Th 3:11 For we **h** that there are some
1Ti 4:16 yourself and those who **h** you
2Ti 4:17 that all the Gentiles might **h**
Heb 3: 7 if you will **h** His voice,
Heb 3:15 if you will **h** His voice, do
Heb 4: 7 if you will **h** His voice, do
Jas 1:19 let every man be swift to **h**
1Jn 4: 6 is not of God does not **h** us
3Jn 4 to **h** that my children walk in
Rev 1: 3 those who **h** the words of this
Rev 2: 7 let him **h** what the Spirit
Rev 2:11 let him **h** what the Spirit
Rev 2:17 let him **h** what the Spirit
Rev 2:29 let him **h** what the Spirit
Rev 3: 6 let him **h** what the Spirit
Rev 3:13 let him **h** what the Spirit
Rev 3:22 let him **h** what the Spirit
Rev 9:20 neither see nor **h** nor walk
Rev 13: 9 anyone has an ear, let him **h**

HEARD (*see* HEAR)

Gen 3: 8 they **h** the sound of the LORD
Gen 3:10 I **h** Your voice in the garden,
Gen 14:14 Now when Abram **h** that his
Gen 16:11 LORD has **h** your affliction
Gen 17:20 as for Ishmael, I have **h** you
Gen 21:17 God **h** the voice of the lad
Gen 21:17 for God has **h** the voice of
Gen 21:26 nor had I **h** of it until today
Gen 24:30 when he **h** the words of his
Gen 24:52 servant **h** their words, that
Gen 27: 6 Indeed I **h** your father speak
Gen 27:34 When Esau **h** the words of his
Gen 29:13 when Laban **h** the report about
Gen 29:33 LORD has **h** that I am unloved
Gen 30: 6 and He has also **h** my voice
Gen 31: 1 Now Jacob **h** the words of
Gen 34: 5 Jacob **h** that he had defiled
Gen 34: 7 from the field when they **h** it
Gen 35:22 and Israel **h** about it
Gen 37:17 for I **h** them say, 'Let us go
Gen 37:21 But Reuben **h** it, and he
Gen 39:15 when he **h** that I lifted my
Gen 39:19 when his master **h** the words
Gen 41:15 But I have **h** it said of you
Gen 42: 2 Indeed I have **h** that there is
Gen 43:25 for they **h** that they would
Gen 45: 2 and the house of Pharaoh **h** it
Gen 45:16 it was **h** in Pharaoh's house
Ex 2:15 When Pharaoh **h** of this matter
Ex 2:24 So God **h** their groaning, and
Ex 3: 7 have **h** their cry because of
Ex 4:31 when they **h** that the LORD had
Ex 6: 5 I have also **h** the groaning of
Ex 16: 9 for He has **h** your murmurings
Ex 16:12 I have **h** the murmurings of
Ex 18: 1 **h** of all that God had done
Ex 23:13 nor let it be **h** from your
Ex 28:35 its sound will be **h** when he
Ex 32:17 when Joshua **h** the noise of
Ex 33: 4 when the people **h** these grave
Lev 10:20 So when Moses **h** that, he was
Lev 24:14 then let all who **h** him lay
Num 7:89 Him, he **h** the voice of One
Num 11: 1 for the LORD **h** it, and His
Num 11:10 Now Moses **h** the people
Num 12: 2 And the LORD **h** it
Num 14:14 They have **h** that You, LORD,
Num 14:15 **h** of Your fame will speak
Num 14:27 I have **h** the murmurings which
Num 16: 4 So when Moses **h** it, he fell
Num 20:16 He **h** our voice and sent the
Num 21: 1 **h** that Israel was coming on
Num 22:36 Now when Balak **h** that Balaam
Num 30:11 and her husband **h** it, and made
Num 30:12 void on the day he **h** them
Num 30:14 her on the day that he **h** them
Num 30:15 them void after he has **h** them
Num 33:40 **h** of the coming of the
Deut 1:34 the LORD **h** the sound of your
Deut 4:12 You **h** the sound of the words,
Deut 4:12 you only **h** a voice
Deut 4:32 anything like it has been **h**
Deut 4:33 of the fire, as you have **h**
Deut 4:36 you **h** His words out of the
Deut 5:23 when you **h** the voice from the
Deut 5:24 we have **h** His voice from the
Deut 5:26 there of all flesh who has **h**
Deut 5:28 Then the LORD **h** the voice of
Deut 5:28 I have **h** the voice of the
Deut 9: 2 and of whom you **h** it said
Deut 10:10 the LORD also **h** me at that
Deut 26: 7 and the LORD **h** our voice and
Josh 2:10 For we have **h** how the LORD
Josh 2:11 as soon as we **h** these things
Josh 5: 1 **h** that the LORD had dried up
Josh 6:20 **h** the sound of the trumpet
Josh 9: 1 and the Jebusite—**h** of it
Josh 9: 3 **h** what Joshua had done to
Josh 9: 9 for we have **h** of His fame
Josh 9:16 that they **h** that they were
Josh 10: 1 king of Jerusalem **h** how
Josh 11: 1 king of Hazor **h** these things
Josh 14:12 for you **h** in that day how the
Josh 22:11 of Israel **h** someone say
Josh 22:12 children of Israel **h** of it
Josh 22:30 **h** the words that the children
Josh 24:27 for it has **h** all the words of
Judg 7:15 when Gideon **h** the telling of
Judg 9:30 **h** the words of Gaal the son
Judg 9:46 tower of Shechem had **h** that
Judg 18:25 let your voice be **h** among us
Judg 20: 3 the children of Benjamin **h**
Ruth 1: 6 for she had **h** in the country
1Sa 1:13 but her voice was not **h**
1Sa 2:22 he **h** everything his sons did
1Sa 4: 6 **h** the noise of the shout,
1Sa 4:14 When Eli **h** the noise of the
1Sa 4:19 when she **h** the news that the
1Sa 7: 7 Now when the Philistines **h**
1Sa 7: 7 children of Israel **h** of it
1Sa 8:21 Samuel **h** all the words of the
1Sa 11: 6 upon Saul when he **h** this news
1Sa 13: 3 and the Philistines **h** of it
1Sa 13: 4 Now all Israel **h** it said that
1Sa 14:22 Ephraim, when they **h** that the
1Sa 14:27 But Jonathan had not **h** his
1Sa 17:11 all Israel **h** these words of
1Sa 17:23 So David **h** them
1Sa 17:28 **h** when he spoke to the men
1Sa 17:31 which David spoke were **h**,
1Sa 22: 1 all his father's house **h** it
1Sa 22: 6 When Saul **h** that David and the
1Sa 23:10 **h** that Saul seeks to come to
1Sa 23:11 down, as Your servant has **h**
1Sa 23:25 And when Saul **h** that, he
1Sa 25: 4 When David **h** in the
1Sa 25: 7 Now I have **h** that you have

1Sa 25:39 So when David **h** that Nabal
1Sa 31:11 of Jabesh Gilead **h** what the
2Sa 3:28 And afterward, when David **h** it
2Sa 4: 1 when Saul's son **h** that Abner
2Sa 5:17 **h** that they had anointed
2Sa 5:17 And David **h** of it and went
2Sa 7:22 that we have **h** with our ears
2Sa 8: 9 When Toi king of Hamath **h**
2Sa 10: 7 Now when David **h** of it, he
2Sa 11:26 When the wife of Uriah **h** that
2Sa 13:21 David **h** of all these things
2Sa 18: 5 all the people **h** when the
2Sa 19: 2 For the people **h** it said that
2Sa 22: 7 He **h** my voice from His temple
1Ki 1:11 Have you not **h** that Adonijah
1Ki 1:41 guests who were with him **h** it
1Ki 1:41 when Joab **h** the sound of the
1Ki 1:45 is the noise that you have **h**
1Ki 2:42 The word I have **h** is good
1Ki 3:28 all Israel **h** of the judgment
1Ki 4:34 earth who had **h** of his wisdom
1Ki 5: 1 because he **h** that they had
1Ki 5: 7 when Hiram **h** the words of
1Ki 6: 7 **h** in the temple while it was
1Ki 9: 3 I have **h** your prayer and your
1Ki 10: 1 **h** of the fame of Solomon
1Ki 10: 6 I **h** in my own land about your
1Ki 10: 7 exceed the fame of which I **h**
1Ki 11:21 Now when Hadad **h** in Egypt
1Ki 12: 2 **h** it (he was still in Egypt
1Ki 12:20 to pass when all Israel **h**
1Ki 13: 4 **h** the saying of the man of
1Ki 13:26 him back from the way **h** it
1Ki 14: 6 when Ahijah **h** the sound of
1Ki 15:21 it happened, when Baasha **h** it
1Ki 16:16 who were encamped **h** it said
1Ki 17:22 Then the LORD **h** the voice of
1Ki 19:13 So it was, when Elijah **h** it
1Ki 20:12 when Ben-Hadad **h** this message
1Ki 20:31 we have **h** that the kings of
1Ki 21:15 when Jezebel **h** that Naboth
1Ki 21:16 when Ahab **h** that Naboth was
1Ki 21:27 when Ahab **h** those words, that
2Ki 3:21 when all the Moabites **h** that
2Ki 5: 8 when Elisha the man of God **h**
2Ki 6:30 when the king **h** the words of
2Ki 9:30 to Jezreel, Jezebel **h** of it
2Ki 11:13 Now when Athaliah **h** the noise
2Ki 19: 1 was, when King Hezekiah **h** it
2Ki 19: 4 which the LORD your God has **h**
2Ki 19: 6 of the words which you have **h**
2Ki 19: 8 for he **h** that he had departed
2Ki 19: 9 And the king **h** concerning
2Ki 19:11 You have **h** what the kings of
2Ki 19:20 king of Assyria I have **h**
2Ki 20: 5 I have **h** your prayer, I have
2Ki 20:12 for he **h** that Hezekiah had
2Ki 22:11 when the king **h** the words of
2Ki 22:18 the words which you have **h**
2Ki 22:19 before the LORD when you **h**
2Ki 22:19 before Me, I also have **h** you
2Ki 25:23 **h** that the king of Babylon
1Ch 10:11 when all Jabesh Gilead **h** all
1Ch 14: 8 **h** that David had been
1Ch 14: 8 And David **h** of it and went out
1Ch 17:20 that we have **h** with our ears
1Ch 18: 9 When Tou king of Hamath **h**
1Ch 19: 8 And when David **h** of it, he
2Ch 5:13 one sound to be **h** in praising
2Ch 7:12 I have **h** your prayer, and have
2Ch 9: 1 **h** of the fame of Solomon, she
2Ch 9: 5 I **h** in my own land about your
2Ch 9: 6 exceed the fame of which I **h**
2Ch 10: 2 Nebat **h** it (he was in Egypt
2Ch 15: 8 when Asa **h** these words and the
2Ch 16: 5 it happened, when Baasha **h** it
2Ch 20:29 **h** that the LORD had fought
2Ch 23:12 Now when Athaliah **h** the noise
2Ch 30:27 people, and their voice was **h**
2Ch 33:13 **h** his supplication, and
2Ch 34:19 when the king **h** the words of
2Ch 34:26 the words which you have **h**
2Ch 34:27 before God when you **h** His
2Ch 34:27 before Me, I also have **h** you
Ezra 3:13 and the sound was **h** afar off
Ezra 4: 1 Judah and Benjamin **h** that the
Ezra 9: 3 So when I **h** this thing, I
Neh 1: 4 when I **h** these words, that I
Neh 2:10 the Ammonite official **h** of it
Neh 2:19 and Geshem the Arab **h** of it

Neh 4: 1 when Sanballat **h** that we were
Neh 4: 7 the Ashdodites **h** that the
Neh 4:15 when our enemies **h** that it
Neh 5: 6 angry when I **h** their outcry
Neh 6: 1 the rest of our enemies **h**
Neh 6:16 when all our enemies **h** of it
Neh 8: 9 when they **h** the words of the
Neh 9: 9 **h** their cry by the Red Sea
Neh 9:27 to You, You **h** from heaven
Neh 9:28 out to You, You **h** from heaven
Neh 12:43 of Jerusalem was **h** afar off
Neh 13: 3 was, when they had **h** the Law
Esth 1:18 have **h** of the behavior of the
Esth 2: 8 command and decree were **h**,
Job 2:11 when Job's three friends **h** of
Job 4:16 then I **h** a voice saying
Job 13: 1 seen all this, My ear has **h**
Job 15: 8 Have you **h** the counsel of God
Job 16: 2 I have **h** many such things
Job 19: 7 concerning wrong, I am not **h**
Job 20: 3 I have **h** the reproof that
Job 28:22 We have **h** a report about it
Job 29:11 When the ear **h**, then it
Job 33: 8 I have **h** the sound of your
Job 37: 4 them when His voice is **h**
Job 42: 5 I have **h** of You by the
Ps 3: 4 He **h** me from His holy hill
Ps 6: 8 For the LORD has **h** the voice
Ps 6: 9 The LORD has **h** my
Ps 10:17 You have **h** the desire of the
Ps 18: 6 He **h** my voice from His temple
Ps 19: 3 Where their voice is not **h**
Ps 22:24 when He cried to Him, He **h**
Ps 28: 6 Because He has **h** the voice of
Ps 31:22 You **h** the voice of my
Ps 34: 4 I sought the LORD, and He **h** me
Ps 34: 6 cried out, and the LORD **h** him
Ps 40: 1 inclined to me, And **h** my cry
Ps 44: 1 We have **h** with our ears, O
Ps 48: 8 As we have **h**, So we have seen
Ps 61: 5 You, O God, have **h** my vows
Ps 62:11 once, Twice I have **h** this
Ps 66: 8 voice of His praise to be **h**
Ps 66:19 But certainly God has **h** me
Ps 76: 8 judgment to be **h** from heaven
Ps 78: 3 Which we have **h** and known,
Ps 78:21 Therefore the LORD **h** this
Ps 78:59 When God **h** this, He was
Ps 81: 5 Where I **h** a language that I
Ps 106:44 When He **h** their cry
Ps 116: 1 because He has **h** My voice
Ps 120: 1 cried to the LORD, And He **h** me
Ps 132: 6 we **h** of it in Ephrathah
Prov 21:13 also cry himself and not be **h**
Eccl 9:16 and his words are not **h**
Eccl 9:17 should be **h** rather than the
Song 2:12 turtledove is **h** in our land
Is 6: 8 Also I **h** the voice of the
Is 10:30 Cause it to be **h** as far as
Is 15: 4 shall be **h** as far as Jahaz
Is 16: 6 We have **h** of the pride of
Is 21: 3 I was distressed when I **h** it
Is 21:10 That which I have **h** from the
Is 24:16 of the earth we have **h** songs
Is 28:22 for I have **h** from the Lord
Is 30:30 His glorious voice to be **h**
Is 37: 1 was, when King Hezekiah **h** it
Is 37: 4 which the LORD your God has **h**
Is 37: 6 of the words which you have **h**
Is 37: 8 for he had **h** that he had
Is 37: 9 And the king **h** concerning
Is 37: 9 So when he **h** it, he sent
Is 37:11 You have **h** what the kings of
Is 38: 5 I have **h** your prayer, I have
Is 39: 1 for he **h** that he had been
Is 40:21 Have you not **h**
Is 40:28 Have you not **h**
Is 42: 2 voice to be **h** in the street
Is 48: 6 You have **h**; see all this.
Is 48: 7 this day you have not **h** them
Is 49: 8 acceptable time I have **h** You
Is 52:15 and what they had not **h** they
Is 58: 4 to make your voice **h** on high
Is 60:18 no longer be **h** in your land
Is 64: 4 **h** nor perceived by the ear
Is 65:19 shall no longer be **h** in her
Is 66: 8 Who has **h** such a thing
Is 66:19 afar off who have not **h** My
Jer 3:21 A voice was **h** on the desolate
Jer 4:19 my peace, because you have **h**

Jer 4:31 For I have **h** a voice as of a
Jer 6: 7 and plundering are **h** in her
Jer 6:24 We have **h** the report of it
Jer 8: 6 I listened and **h**, but they do
Jer 8:16 of His horses was **h** from Dan
Jer 9:19 of wailing is **h** from Zion
Jer 18:13 who has **h** such things
Jer 18:22 Let a cry be **h** from their
Jer 20: 1 **h** that Jeremiah prophesied
Jer 20:10 For I **h** many mocking
Jer 23:18 has perceived and **h** His word
Jer 23:18 has marked His word and **h** it
Jer 23:25 I have **h** what the prophets
Jer 25: 8 you have not **h** My words,
Jer 25:36 to the flock will be **h**
Jer 26: 7 all the people **h** Jeremiah
Jer 26:10 of Judah **h** these things, they
Jer 26:11 as you have **h** with your ears
Jer 26:12 all the words that you have **h**
Jer 26:21 **h** his words, the king sought
Jer 26:21 but when Urijah **h** it, he was
Jer 30: 5 We have **h** a voice of
Jer 31:15 A voice was **h** in Ramah,
Jer 31:18 I have surely **h** Ephraim
Jer 33:10 shall be **h** in this place
Jer 34:10 **h** that everyone should set
Jer 35:17 to them but they have not **h**
Jer 36:11 **h** all the words of the LORD
Jer 36:13 **h** when Baruch read the book
Jer 36:16 when they had **h** all the words
Jer 36:24 who **h** all these words
Jer 37: 5 Jerusalem **h** news of them,
Jer 38: 1 **h** the words that Jeremiah had
Jer 38: 7 **h** that they had put Jeremiah
Jer 38:27 conversation had not been **h**
Jer 40: 7 **h** that the king of Babylon
Jer 40:11 **h** that the king of Babylon
Jer 41:11 him **h** of all the evil that
Jer 42: 4 I have **h**.
Jer 46:12 nations have **h** of your shame
Jer 48: 4 have caused a cry to be **h**
Jer 48: 5 have **h** a cry of destruction
Jer 48:29 We have **h** the pride of Moab
Jer 49: 2 That I will cause to be **h** an
Jer 49:14 I have **h** a message from the
Jer 49:21 its noise is **h** at the Red Sea
Jer 49:23 for they have **h** bad news
Jer 50:43 has **h** the report about them
Jer 50:46 and the cry is **h** among the
Jer 51:46 **h** in the land (a rumor will
Jer 51:51 because we have **h** reproach
Lam 1:21 They have **h** that I sigh, with
Lam 1:21 enemies have **h** of my trouble
Lam 3:56 You have **h** my voice
Lam 3:61 You have **h** their reproach, O
Ezek 1:24 I **h** the noise of their wings,
Ezek 1:28 I **h** a voice of One speaking
Ezek 2: 2 and I **h** Him who spoke to me
Ezek 3:12 up, and I **h** behind me a great
Ezek 3:13 I also **h** the noise of the
Ezek 10: 5 was **h** even in the outer court
Ezek 19: 4 The nations also **h** of him
Ezek 19: 9 voice should no longer be **h**
Ezek 26:13 your harps shall be **h** no more
Ezek 27:30 their voice **h** because of you
Ezek 33: 5 He **h** the sound of the
Ezek 35:12 I have **h** all your blasphemies
Ezek 35:13 I have **h** them
Ezek 43: 6 Then I **h** Him speaking to me
Dan 3: 7 when all the people **h** the
Dan 5:14 I have **h** of you, that the
Dan 5:16 And I have **h** of you, that you
Dan 6:14 when he **h** these words, was
Dan 8:13 Then I **h** a holy one speaking
Dan 8:16 I **h** a man's voice between the
Dan 10: 9 Yet I **h** the sound of his
Dan 10: 9 while I **h** the sound of his
Dan 10:12 your God, your words were **h**
Dan 12: 7 Then I **h** the man clothed in
Dan 12: 8 Although I **h**, I did not
Hos 7:12 what their congregation has **h**
Hos 14: 8 I have **h** and observed him
Obad 1 have **h** a report from the LORD
Jon 2: 2 I cried, and You **h** my voice
Mic 5:15 the nations that have not **h**
Nah 2:13 messengers shall be **h** no more
Hab 3: 2 I have **h** your speech and was
Hab 3:16 When I **h**, my body trembled
Zeph 2: 8 I have **h** the reproach of Moab
Zech 8:23 for we have **h** that God is

Mal 3:16 the LORD listened and **h** them
Matt 2: 3 Herod the king **h** these things
Matt 2: 9 When they **h** the king, they
Matt 2:18 A voice was **h** in Ramah,
Matt 2:22 But when he **h** that Archelaus
Matt 4:12 Now when Jesus **h** that John
Matt 5:21 You have **h** that it was said
Matt 5:27 You have **h** that it was said
Matt 5:33 Again you have **h** that it was
Matt 5:38 You have **h** that it was said
Matt 5:43 You have **h** that it was said
Matt 6: 7 be **h** for their many words
Matt 8:10 When Jesus **h** it, He marveled,
Matt 9:12 But when Jesus **h** that, He
Matt 11: 2 when John had **h** in prison
Matt 12:24 the Pharisees **h** it they said
Matt 14: 1 **h** the report about Jesus
Matt 14:13 When Jesus **h** it, He departed
Matt 14:13 But when the multitudes **h** it
Matt 15:12 when they **h** this saying
Matt 17: 6 And when the disciples **h** it
Matt 19:22 the young man **h** that saying
Matt 19:25 When His disciples **h** it, they
Matt 20:24 And when the ten **h** it, they
Matt 20:30 when they **h** that Jesus was
Matt 21:45 Pharisees **h** His parables,
Matt 22: 7 But when the king **h** about it
Matt 22:22 When they had **h** these words
Matt 22:33 And when the multitudes **h** this
Matt 22:34 But when the Pharisees **h** that
Matt 25: 6 And at midnight a cry was **h**
Matt 26:65 now you have **h** His blasphemy
Matt 27:47 stood there, when they **h** that
Mark 2: 1 it was **h** that He was in the
Mark 2:17 When Jesus **h** it, He said to
Mark 3: 8 when they **h** how many things
Mark 3:21 His own people **h** about this
Mark 5:27 When she **h** about Jesus, she
Mark 5:36 As soon as Jesus **h** the word
Mark 6:14 Now King Herod **h** of Him, for
Mark 6:16 But when Herod **h**, he said
Mark 6:20 And when he **h** him, he did
Mark 6:20 many things, and **h** him gladly
Mark 6:29 And when his disciples **h** of it
Mark 6:55 to wherever they **h** He was
Mark 7:25 an unclean spirit **h** about Him
Mark 10:41 And when the ten **h** it, they
Mark 10:47 when he **h** that it was Jesus
Mark 11:14 And His disciples **h** it
Mark 11:18 scribes and chief priests **h** it
Mark 12:28 and having **h** them reasoning
Mark 12:37 common people **h** Him gladly
Mark 14:11 So when they **h** it, they were
Mark 14:58 We **h** Him say, 'I will destroy
Mark 14:64 You have **h** the blasphemy
Mark 15:35 who stood by, when they **h** it
Mark 16:11 when they **h** that He was alive
Luke 1:13 for your prayer is **h**
Luke 1:41 when Elizabeth **h** the greeting
Luke 1:58 relatives **h** how the Lord had
Luke 1:66 all those who **h** them kept
Luke 2:18 all those who **h** it marveled
Luke 2:20 the things that they had **h**
Luke 2:47 all who **h** Him were astonished
Luke 4:23 Whatever we have **h** done in
Luke 4:28 when they **h** these things,
Luke 6:49 But he who **h** and did nothing
Luke 7: 3 So when he **h** about Jesus, he
Luke 7: 9 When Jesus **h** these things, He
Luke 7:22 the things you have seen and **h**
Luke 7:29 And when all the people **h** Him
Luke 8:14 those who, when they have **h**
Luke 8:15 who, having **h** the word with a
Luke 8:50 But when Jesus **h** it, He
Luke 9: 7 Now Herod the tetrarch **h** of
Luke 10:24 you hear, and have not **h** it
Luke 10:39 at Jesus' feet and **h** His word
Luke 12: 3 dark will be **h** in the light
Luke 14:15 table with Him **h** these things
Luke 15:25 house, he **h** music and dancing
Luke 16:14 also **h** all these things, and
Luke 18:22 So when Jesus **h** these things
Luke 18:23 But when he **h** this, he became
Luke 18:26 And those who **h** it said, "Who
Luke 19:11 Now as they **h** these things,
Luke 20:16 when they **h** it they said,
Luke 22:71 For we have **h** it ourselves
Luke 23: 6 When Pilate **h** of Galilee, he
Luke 23: 8 because he had **h** many things
John 1:37 The two disciples **h** him speak
John 1:40 of the two who **h** John speak
John 3:32 And what He has seen and **h**,
John 4: 1 had **h** that Jesus made and
John 4:42 for we have **h** for ourselves
John 4:47 When he **h** that Jesus had come
John 5:37 You have neither **h** His voice
John 6:45 Therefore everyone who has **h**
John 6:60 disciples, when they **h** this
John 7:32 The Pharisees **h** the crowd
John 7:40 when they **h** this saying, said
John 8: 9 Then those who **h** it, being
John 8:26 things which I **h** from Him
John 8:40 the truth which I **h** from God
John 9:35 Jesus **h** that they had cast
John 9:40 were with Him **h** these words
John 11: 4 When Jesus **h** that, He said
John 11: 6 when He **h** that he was sick,
John 11:20 as soon as she **h** that Jesus
John 11:29 As soon as she **h** that, she
John 11:41 thank You that You have **h** Me
John 12:12 when they **h** that Jesus was
John 12:18 because they **h** that He had
John 12:29 by and **h** it said that it had
John 12:34 We have **h** from the law that
John 14:28 You have **h** Me say to you, 'I
John 15:15 for all things that I **h** from
John 18:21 Ask those who have **h** Me what
John 19: 8 when Pilate **h** that saying
John 19:13 therefore **h** that saying, he
John 21: 7 Peter **h** that it was the Lord
Acts 1: 4 you have **h** from Me
Acts 2: 6 because everyone **h** them speak
Acts 2:37 Now when they **h** this, they
Acts 4: 4 those who **h** the word believed
Acts 4:20 which we have seen and **h**
Acts 4:24 So when they **h** that, they
Acts 5: 5 all those who **h** these things
Acts 5:11 upon all who **h** these things
Acts 5:21 And when they **h** that, they
Acts 5:24 chief priests **h** these things
Acts 5:33 When they **h** this, they were
Acts 6:11 to say, We have **h** him speak
Acts 6:14 for we have **h** him say that
Acts 7:12 But when Jacob **h** that there
Acts 7:34 I have **h** their groaning and
Acts 7:54 When they **h** these things they
Acts 8:14 who were at Jerusalem **h** that
Acts 8:30 **h** him reading the prophet
Acts 9: 4 and **h** a voice saying to him,
Acts 9:13 I have **h** from many about this
Acts 9:21 Then all who **h** were amazed
Acts 9:38 and the disciples had **h** that
Acts 10:31 your prayer has been **h**, and
Acts 10:44 upon all those who **h** the word
Acts 10:46 For they **h** them speak with
Acts 11: 1 **h** that the Gentiles had also
Acts 11: 7 I **h** a voice saying to me
Acts 11:18 When they **h** these things they
Acts 13:48 Now when the Gentiles **h** this
Acts 14: 9 This man **h** Paul speaking
Acts 14:14 Barnabas and Paul **h** this, they
Acts 15:24 Since we have **h** that some who
Acts 16:14 woman named Lydia **h** us
Acts 16:38 they **h** that they were Romans
Acts 17: 8 city when they **h** these things
Acts 17:32 And when they **h** of the
Acts 18:26 Aquila and Priscilla **h** him
Acts 19: 2 We have not so much as **h**
Acts 19: 5 When they **h** this, they were
Acts 19:10 **h** the word of the Lord Jesus
Acts 19:28 And when they **h** this, they
Acts 21:12 when we **h** these things, both
Acts 21:20 And when they **h** it, they
Acts 22: 2 when they **h** that he spoke to
Acts 22: 7 **h** a voice saying to me, 'Saul
Acts 22:15 of what you have seen and **h**
Acts 22:26 When the centurion **h** that
Acts 23:16 son **h** of their ambush, he
Acts 24:22 But when Felix **h** these things
Acts 24:24 **h** him concerning the faith in
Acts 26:14 I **h** a voice speaking to me and
Acts 28:15 when the brethren **h** about us
Rom 10:14 Him of whom they have not **h**
Rom 10:18 But I say, have they not **h**
Rom 15:21 have not **h** shall understand
1Co 2: 9 Eye has not seen, nor ear **h**
2Co 6: 2 acceptable time I have **h** you
2Co 12: 4 **h** inexpressible words, which
Gal 1:13 For you have **h** of my former
Eph 1:13 after you **h** the word of truth
Eph 1:15 after I **h** of your faith in
Eph 3: 2 if indeed you have **h** of the
Eph 4:21 if indeed you have **h** Him and
Phil 2:26 you had **h** that he was sick
Phil 4: 9 you learned and received and **h**
Col 1: 4 since we **h** of your faith in
Col 1: 5 of which you **h** before in the
Col 1: 6 among you since the day you **h**
Col 1: 9 also, since the day we **h** it
Col 1:23 of the gospel which you **h**
1Th 2:13 of God which you **h** from us
2Ti 1:13 which you have **h** from me, in
2Ti 2: 2 you have **h** from me among
Heb 2: 1 heed to the things we have **h**
Heb 2: 3 to us by those who **h** Him,
Heb 3:16 For who, having **h**, rebelled
Heb 4: 2 they **h** did not profit them
Heb 4: 2 with faith in those who **h** it
Heb 5: 7 was **h** because of His godly
Heb 12:19 so that those who **h** it begged
Jas 5:11 You have **h** of the
2Pe 1:18 we **h** this voice which came
1Jn 1: 1 beginning, which we have **h**
1Jn 1: 3 **h** we declare to you, that you
1Jn 1: 5 which we have **h** from Him and
1Jn 2: 7 you **h** from the beginning
1Jn 2:18 and as you have **h** that the
1Jn 2:24 you **h** from the beginning
1Jn 2:24 If what you **h** from the
1Jn 3:11 that you **h** from the beginning
1Jn 4: 3 which you have **h** was coming
2Jn 6 that as you have **h** from the
Rev 1:10 I **h** behind me a loud voice,
Rev 3: 3 how you have received and **h**
Rev 4: 1 the first voice which I **h** was
Rev 5:11 I **h** the voice of many angels
Rev 5:13 that are in them, I **h** saying
Rev 6: 1 I **h** one of the four living
Rev 6: 3 seal, I **h** the second living
Rev 6: 5 I **h** the third living creature
Rev 6: 6 I **h** a voice in the midst of
Rev 6: 7 I **h** the voice of the fourth
Rev 7: 4 I **h** the number of those who
Rev 8:13 I **h** an angel flying through
Rev 9:13 I **h** a voice from the four
Rev 9:16 and I **h** the number of them
Rev 10: 4 but I **h** a voice from heaven
Rev 10: 8 Then the voice which I **h** from
Rev 11:12 And they **h** a loud voice from
Rev 12:10 Then I **h** a loud voice saying
Rev 14: 2 I **h** a voice from heaven, like
Rev 14: 2 I **h** the sound of harpists
Rev 14:13 Then I **h** a voice from heaven
Rev 16: 1 Then I **h** a loud voice from
Rev 16: 5 I **h** the angel of the waters
Rev 16: 7 I **h** another from the altar
Rev 18: 4 I **h** another voice from heaven
Rev 18:22 shall not be **h** in you anymore
Rev 18:22 shall not be **h** in you anymore
Rev 18:23 shall not be **h** in you anymore
Rev 19: 1 After these things I **h** a loud
Rev 19: 6 And I **h**, as it were, the voice
Rev 21: 3 I **h** a loud voice from heaven
Rev 22: 8 John, saw and **h** these things
Rev 22: 8 And when I **h** and saw, I fell

HEARER (*see* HEAR, HEARERS)
Jas 1:23 if anyone is a **h** of the word
Jas 1:25 is not a forgetful **h** but a

HEARERS (*see* HEARER)
Rom 2:13 (for not the **h** of the law are
Eph 4:29 it may impart grace to the **h**
2Ti 2:14 profit, to the ruin of the **h**
Jas 1:22 and not **h** only, deceiving

HEARING (*see* HEAR)
Gen 20: 8 all these things in their **h**
Gen 23:13 **h** of the people of the land
Gen 23:16 in the **h** of the sons of Heth
Gen 44:18 speak a word in my lord's **h**
Gen 50: 4 speak in the **h** of Pharaoh
Ex 10: 2 may tell in the **h** of your son
Ex 11: 2 now in the **h** of the people
Ex 17:14 recount it in the **h** of Joshua
Ex 24: 7 read in the **h** of the people
Lev 5: 1 If a person sins in **h** the
Num 11:18 wept in the **h** of the LORD
Num 14:28 as you have spoken in My **h**
Deut 5: 1 which I speak in your **h** today
Deut 31:11 before all Israel in their **h**
Deut 31:28 speak these words in their **h**

Deut 31:30 Then Moses spoke in the **h** of
Deut 32:44 song in the **h** of the people
Josh 20: 4 declares his case in the **h** of
Judg 7: 3 in the **h** of the people,
Judg 9: 2 Please speak in the **h** of all
Judg 9: 3 **h** of all the men of Shechem
1Sa 8:21 them in the **h** of the LORD
1Sa 11: 4 news in the **h** of the people
1Sa 18:23 those words in the **h** of David
2Sa 3:19 spoke in the **h** of Benjamin
2Sa 3:19 also went to speak in the **h**
2Sa 18:12 For in our **h** the king
2Ki 4:31 there was neither voice nor **h**
2Ki 18:26 to us in Hebrew in the **h** of
2Ki 23: 2 he read in their **h** all the
1Ch 28: 8 and in the **h** of our God, be
2Ch 34:30 he read in their **h** all the
Neh 13: 1 Moses in the **h** of the people
Job 33: 8 you have spoken in my **h**, and I
Job 42: 5 of You by the **h** of the ear
Prov 20:12 The **h** ear and the seeing eye,
Prov 23: 9 not speak in the **h** of a fool
Prov 28: 9 away his ear from **h** the law
Eccl 1: 8 nor the ear filled with **h**
Is 5: 9 In my **h** the LORD of hosts
Is 6: 9 Keep on **h**, but do not
Is 11: 3 decide by the **h** of His ears
Is 22:14 in my **h** by the LORD of hosts
Is 33:15 his ears from **h** of bloodshed
Is 36:11 to us in Hebrew in the **h** of
Jer 2: 2 cry in the **h** of Jerusalem,
Jer 26:15 all these words in your **h**
Jer 28: 7 word that I speak in your **h**
Jer 28: 7 in the **h** of all the people
Jer 29:29 the **h** of Jeremiah the prophet
Jer 36: 6 in the **h** of the people in the
Jer 36: 6 **h** of all Judah who come from
Jer 36:10 in the **h** of all the people
Jer 36:13 book in the **h** of the people
Jer 36:14 read in the **h** of the people
Jer 36:15 down now, and read it in our **h**
Jer 36:15 So Baruch read it in their **h**
Jer 36:20 words in the **h** of the king
Jer 36:21 read it in the **h** of the king
Jer 36:21 in the **h** of all the princes
Ezek 9: 1 out in my **h** with a loud voice
Ezek 9: 5 To the others He said in my **h**
Ezek 10:13 they were called in my **h**
Amos 8:11 but of **h** the words of the
Zech 8: 9 you who have been **h** in these
Matt 13:13 **h** they do not hear, nor do
Matt 13:14 **H** you will hear and shall not
Matt 13:15 Their ears are hard of **h**, and
Mark 4:12 and **h** they may hear and not
Mark 6: 2 many **h** Him were astonished,
Luke 4:21 is fulfilled in your **h**
Luke 7: 1 in the **h** of the people, He
Luke 8:10 **h** they may not understand
Luke 18:36 **h** a multitude passing by, he
Luke 20:45 in the **h** of all the people,
Acts 5: 5 **h** these words, fell down and
Acts 8: 6 things spoken by Philip, **h**
Acts 9: 7 **h** a voice but seeing no one
Acts 18: 8 And many of the Corinthians, **h**
Acts 28:26 **H** you will hear, and shall not
Acts 28:27 their ears are hard of **h**, and
Rom 10:17 So then faith comes by **h**, and
Rom 10:17 and **h** by the word of God
1Co 12:17 an eye, where would be the **h**
1Co 12:17 If the whole were **h**, where
Gal 1:23 But they were **h** only, "He
Gal 3: 2 the law, or by the **h** of faith
Gal 3: 5 the law, or by the **h** of faith
Phm 5 **h** of your love and faith which
Heb 5:11 you have become dull of **h**
2Pe 2: 8 and **h** their lawless deeds)

HEARS (*see* HEAR)
Ex 16: 7 for He **h** your murmurings
Ex 16: 8 for the LORD **h** your
Num 24: 4 of him who **h** the words of God
Num 24:16 of him who **h** the words of God
Num 30: 4 and her father **h** her vow and
Num 30: 5 her on the day that he **h**,
Num 30: 7 and her husband **h** it, and makes
Num 30: 7 to her on the day that he **h**
Num 30: 8 her on the day that he **h** it
Deut 29:19 when he **h** the words of this
1Sa 3: 9 LORD, for Your servant **h**
1Sa 3:10 Speak, for Your servant **h**
1Sa 3:11 everyone who **h** it will tingle
1Sa 16: 2 If Saul **h** it, he will kill me
2Sa 17: 9 that whoever **h** it will say
2Ki 21:12 Judah, that whoever **h** of it
Job 34:28 for He **h** the cry of the
Ps 34:17 cry out, and the LORD **h**, And
Ps 59: 7 Who **h**?"
Ps 69:33 For the LORD **h** the poor, And
Ps 97: 8 Zion **h** and is glad, And the
Prov 15:29 but He **h** the prayer of the
Prov 15:31 The ear that **h** the reproof of
Prov 18:13 a matter before he **h** it, it
Prov 21:28 but the man who **h** him will
Prov 25:10 lest he who **h** it expose your
Is 30:19 when He **h** it, He will answer
Is 41:26 is no one who **h** your words
Jer 19: 3 place, that whoever **h** of it
Ezek 3:27 He who **h**, let him hear
Ezek 33: 4 then whoever **h** the sound of
Dan 3:10 who **h** the sound of the horn
Matt 7:24 Therefore whoever **h** these
Matt 7:26 Now everyone who **h** these
Matt 13:19 When anyone **h** the word of the
Matt 13:20 this is he who **h** the word
Matt 13:22 thorns is he who **h** the word
Matt 13:23 ground is he who **h** the word
Matt 18:15 If he **h** you, you have gained
Luke 6:47 **h** My sayings and does them, I
Luke 10:16 He who **h** you **h** Me, he who
John 3:29 and **h** him, rejoices greatly
John 5:24 he who **h** My word and believes
John 7:51 judge a man before it **h** him
John 8:47 who is of God **h** God's words
John 9:31 and does His will, He **h** him
John 12:47 And if anyone **h** My words and
John 16:13 whatever He **h** He will speak
John 18:37 is of the truth **h** My voice
2Co 12: 6 he sees me to be or **h** from me
1Jn 4: 5 world, and the world **h** them
1Jn 4: 6 He who knows God **h** us
1Jn 5:14 to His will, He **h** us
1Jn 5:15 And if we know that He **h** us
Rev 3:20 If anyone **h** My voice and opens
Rev 22:17 And let him who **h** say
Rev 22:18 **h** the words of the prophecy

HEART (*see* BROKEN-HEARTED, BROKENHEARTED, HEART'S, HEARTS, WHOLE-HEARTED)
Gen 6: 5 of the thoughts of his **h** was
Gen 6: 6 and He was grieved in His **h**
Gen 8:21 Then the LORD said in His **h**
Gen 8:21 **h** is evil from his youth
Gen 17:17 and laughed, and said in his **h**
Gen 20: 5 In the integrity of my **h**
Gen 20: 6 in the integrity of your **h**
Gen 24:45 had finished speaking in my **h**
Gen 27:41 him, and Esau said in his **h**
Gen 43:30 Now his **h** yearned for his
Gen 45:26 And Jacob's **h** stood still,
Ex 4:14 you, he will be glad in his **h**
Ex 4:21 But I will harden his **h**, so
Ex 7: 3 And I will harden Pharaoh's **h**
Ex 7:13 And Pharaoh's **h** grew hard, and
Ex 7:14 Pharaoh's **h** is hard
Ex 7:22 and Pharaoh's **h** grew hard, and
Ex 7:23 was his **h** moved by this
Ex 8:15 was relief, he hardened his **h**
Ex 8:19 But Pharaoh's **h** grew hard
Ex 8:32 his **h** at this time also
Ex 9: 7 But the **h** of Pharaoh became
Ex 9:12 hardened the **h** of Pharaoh
Ex 9:14 all My plagues to your very **h**
Ex 9:34 and he hardened his **h**, he and
Ex 9:35 So the **h** of Pharaoh was hard
Ex 10: 1 for I have hardened his **h**
Ex 10:20 the LORD hardened Pharaoh's **h**
Ex 10:27 the LORD hardened Pharaoh's **h**
Ex 11:10 the LORD hardened Pharaoh's **h**
Ex 14: 4 I will harden Pharaoh's **h**
Ex 14: 5 and the **h** of Pharaoh and his
Ex 14: 8 the LORD hardened the **h** of
Ex 15: 8 congealed in the **h** of the sea
Ex 23: 9 you know the **h** of a stranger
Ex 25: 2 **h** you shall take My offering
Ex 28:29 of judgment over his **h**, when
Ex 28:30 **h** when he goes in before the
Ex 28:30 **h** before the LORD continually
Ex 35: 5 Whoever is of a willing **h**
Ex 35:21 came whose **h** was stirred, and
Ex 35:22 as many as had a willing **h**
Ex 35:26 all the women whose **h** stirred
Ex 35:34 And He has put in his **h** the
Ex 36: 2 **h** the LORD had put wisdom
Ex 36: 2 everyone whose **h** was stirred
Lev 19:17 hate your brother in your **h**
Lev 26:16 the eyes and cause sorrow of **h**
Num 15:39 harlotry to which your own **h**
Num 32: 7 **h** of the children of Israel
Num 32: 9 they discouraged the **h** of the
Deut 2:30 made his **h** obstinate, that He
Deut 4: 9 **h** all the days of your life
Deut 4:29 you seek Him with all your **h**
Deut 4:39 day, and consider it in your **h**
Deut 5:29 that they had such a **h** in
Deut 6: 5 LORD your God with all your **h**
Deut 6: 6 you today shall be in your **h**
Deut 7:17 If you should say in your **h**
Deut 8: 2 to know what was in your **h**
Deut 8: 5 **h** that as a man chastens his
Deut 8:14 when your **h** is lifted up, and
Deut 8:17 then you say in your **h**, 'My
Deut 9: 4 Do not think in your **h**, after
Deut 9: 5 **h** that you go in to possess
Deut 10:12 LORD your God with all your **h**
Deut 10:16 the foreskin of your **h**, and be
Deut 11:13 and serve Him with all your **h**
Deut 11:16 lest your **h** be deceived, and
Deut 11:18 these words of mine in your **h**
Deut 12:15 whatever your **h** desires,
Deut 12:20 much meat as your **h** desires
Deut 12:21 as much as your **h** desires
Deut 13: 3 LORD your God with all your **h**
Deut 14:26 for whatever your **h** desires
Deut 14:26 for whatever your **h** desires
Deut 15: 7 **h** nor shut your hand from
Deut 15: 9 be a wicked thought in your **h**
Deut 15:10 your **h** should not be grieved
Deut 17:17 himself, lest his **h** turn away
Deut 17:20 that his **h** may not be lifted
Deut 18:21 And if you say in your **h**, 'How
Deut 20: 3 do not let your **h** faint, do
Deut 20: 8 lest the **h** of his brethren
Deut 20: 8 his brethren faint like his **h**
Deut 24:15 poor and has set his **h** on it
Deut 26:16 observe them with all your **h**
Deut 28:28 blindness and confusion of **h**
Deut 28:47 God with joy and gladness of **h**
Deut 28:65 will give you a trembling **h**
Deut 28:67 fear which terrifies your **h**
Deut 29: 4 not given you a **h** to perceive
Deut 29:18 whose **h** turns away today from
Deut 29:19 he blesses himself in his **h**
Deut 29:19 in the imagination of my **h**'
Deut 30: 2 children, with all your **h**
Deut 30: 6 God will circumcise your **h**
Deut 30: 6 the **h** of your descendants, to
Deut 30: 6 LORD your God with all your **h**
Deut 30:10 LORD your God with all your **h**
Deut 30:14 in your mouth and in your **h**
Deut 30:17 But if your **h** turns away so
Josh 5: 1 over, that their **h** melted
Josh 14: 7 word to him as it was in my **h**
Josh 14: 8 made the **h** of the people melt
Josh 22: 5 to serve Him with all your **h**
Josh 24:23 incline your **h** to the LORD
Judg 5: 9 My **h** is with the rulers of
Judg 5:15 were great resolves of **h**
Judg 5:16 have great searchings of **h**
Judg 9: 3 and their **h** was inclined to
Judg 16:15 when your **h** is not with me
Judg 16:17 that he told her all his **h**
Judg 16:18 he had told her all his **h**
Judg 16:18 for he has told me all his **h**
Judg 18:20 So the priest's **h** was glad
Judg 19: 5 Refresh your **h** with a morsel
Judg 19: 6 night, and let your **h** be merry
Judg 19: 8 Please refresh your **h**
Judg 19: 9 that your **h** may be merry
Ruth 3: 7 his **h** was cheerful, he went
1Sa 1: 8 And why is your **h** grieved
1Sa 1:13 Now Hannah spoke in her **h**
1Sa 2: 1 My **h** rejoices in the LORD
1Sa 2:16 as much as your **h** desires
1Sa 2:33 your eyes and grieve your **h**
1Sa 2:35 according to what is in My **h**
1Sa 4:13 for his **h** trembled for the
1Sa 9:19 you all that is in your **h**
1Sa 10: 9 that God gave him another **h**
1Sa 12:20 the LORD with all your **h**
1Sa 12:24 Him in truth with all your **h**
1Sa 13:14 Himself a man after His own **h**

1Sa 14: 7 Do all that is in your **h**
1Sa 14: 7 with you, according to your **h**
1Sa 16: 7 but the LORD looks at the **h**
1Sa 17:28 and the insolence of your **h**
1Sa 17:32 Let no man's **h** fail because
1Sa 21:12 David took these words to **h**
1Sa 24: 5 afterward that David's **h**
1Sa 25:31 nor offense of **h** to my lord
1Sa 25:36 Nabal's **h** was merry within
1Sa 25:37 that his **h** died within him,
1Sa 27: 1 And David said in his **h**, "Now
1Sa 28: 5 and his **h** trembled greatly
2Sa 3:21 over all that your **h** desires
2Sa 4: 1 had died in Hebron, he lost **h**
2Sa 6:16 and she despised him in her **h**
2Sa 7: 3 Go, do all that is in your **h**
2Sa 7:21 and according to Your own **h**
2Sa 7:27 servant found it in his **h** to
2Sa 13:20 do not take this thing to **h**
2Sa 13:28 when Amnon's **h** is merry with
2Sa 13:33 king take the thing to his **h**
2Sa 14: 1 perceived that the king's **h**
2Sa 17:10 **h** is like the **h** of a lion
2Sa 18:14 them through Absalom's **h**,
2Sa 19:14 just as the **h** of one man
2Sa 19:19 the king should take it to **h**
2Sa 24:10 David's **h** condemned him after
1Ki 2: 4 Me in truth with all their **h**
1Ki 2:44 as your **h** acknowledges, all
1Ki 3: 6 in uprightness of **h** with You
1Ki 3: 9 **h** to judge Your people, that
1Ki 3:12 you a wise and understanding **h**
1Ki 4:29 largeness of **h** like the sand
1Ki 8:17 Now it was in the **h** of my
1Ki 8:18 **h** to build a house for My
1Ki 8:18 well that it was in your **h**
1Ki 8:23 before You with all their **h**
1Ki 8:38 knows the plague of his own **h**
1Ki 8:39 whose **h** You know (for You,
1Ki 8:48 to You with all their **h** and
1Ki 8:61 Let your **h** therefore be loyal
1Ki 8:66 and glad of **h** for all the
1Ki 9: 3 My eyes and My **h** will be there
1Ki 9: 4 walked, in integrity of **h**
1Ki 10: 2 about all that was in her **h**
1Ki 10:24 which God had put in his **h**
1Ki 11: 3 his wives turned away his **h**
1Ki 11: 4 turned his **h** after other gods
1Ki 11: 4 his **h** was not loyal to the
1Ki 11: 4 as was the **h** of his father
1Ki 11: 9 because his **h** had turned from
1Ki 11:37 reign over all your **h** desires
1Ki 12:26 And Jeroboam said in his **h**
1Ki 12:27 then the **h** of this people
1Ki 12:33 he had devised in his own **h**
1Ki 14: 8 followed Me with all his **h**
1Ki 15: 3 his **h** was not loyal to the
1Ki 15: 3 as was the **h** of his father
1Ki 15:14 Nevertheless Asa's **h** was
1Ki 21: 7 and let your **h** be cheerful
2Ki 5:26 Did not my **h** go with you when
2Ki 6:11 Therefore the **h** of the king
2Ki 9:24 the arrow came out at his **h**
2Ki 10:15 Is your **h** right
2Ki 10:15 as my **h** is toward your **h**
2Ki 10:30 of Ahab all that was in My **h**
2Ki 10:31 God of Israel with all his **h**
2Ki 12: 4 **h** to bring into the house of
2Ki 14:10 and your **h** has lifted you up
2Ki 20: 3 in truth and with a loyal **h**
2Ki 22:19 because your **h** was tender
2Ki 23: 3 His statutes, with all his **h**
2Ki 23:25 to the LORD with all his **h**
1Ch 12:17 my **h** will be united with you
1Ch 12:38 came to Hebron with a loyal **h**
1Ch 15:29 and she despised him in her **h**
1Ch 17: 2 Do all that is in your **h**, for
1Ch 17:19 and according to Your own **h**
1Ch 17:25 in his **h** to pray before You
1Ch 22:19 Now set your **h** and your soul
1Ch 28: 2 I had it in my **h** to build a
1Ch 28: 9 and serve Him with a loyal **h**
1Ch 29: 9 because with a loyal **h** they
1Ch 29:17 my God, that You test the **h**
1Ch 29:17 my **h** I have willingly offered
1Ch 29:18 of the **h** of Your people, and
1Ch 29:18 and fix their **h** toward You
1Ch 29:19 **h** to keep Your commandments
2Ch 1:11 Because this was in your **h**
2Ch 6: 7 Now it was in the **h** of my
2Ch 6: 8 Whereas it was in your **h** to
2Ch 6: 8 well in that it was in your **h**
2Ch 6:30 whose **h** You know (for You
2Ch 6:38 to You with all their **h** and
2Ch 7:10 glad of **h** for the goodness
2Ch 7:11 all that came into his **h** to
2Ch 7:16 My eyes and My **h** will be there
2Ch 9: 1 about all that was in her **h**
2Ch 9:23 which God had put in his **h**
2Ch 11:16 such as set their **h** to seek
2Ch 12:14 his **h** to seek the LORD
2Ch 15:12 fathers with all their **h** and
2Ch 15:15 had sworn with all their **h**
2Ch 15:17 Nevertheless the **h** of Asa was
2Ch 16: 9 those whose **h** is loyal to Him
2Ch 17: 6 his **h** took delight in the
2Ch 19: 3 prepared your **h** to seek God
2Ch 19: 9 faithfully and with a loyal **h**
2Ch 22: 9 the LORD with all his **h**
2Ch 24: 4 this that Joash set his **h** on
2Ch 25: 2 LORD, but not with a loyal **h**
2Ch 25:19 your **h** is lifted up to boast
2Ch 26:16 strong his **h** was lifted up
2Ch 29:10 Now it is in my **h** to make a
2Ch 29:31 **h** brought burnt offerings
2Ch 30:12 of **h** to do the commandment of
2Ch 30:19 prepares his **h** to seek God
2Ch 31:21 God, he did it with all his **h**
2Ch 32:25 him, for his **h** was lifted up
2Ch 32:26 for the pride of his **h**, he and
2Ch 32:31 know all that was in his **h**
2Ch 34:27 because your **h** was tender
2Ch 34:31 His statutes with all his **h**
2Ch 36:13 and hardened his **h** against
Ezra 6:22 turned the **h** of the king of
Ezra 7:10 For Ezra had prepared his **h**
Ezra 7:27 thing as this in the king's **h**
Neh 2: 2 is nothing but sorrow of **h**
Neh 2:12 in my **h** to do at Jerusalem
Neh 6: 8 you invent them in your own **h**
Neh 7: 5 my **h** to gather the nobles
Neh 9: 8 You found his **h** faithful
Esth 1:10 when the **h** of the king was
Esth 4:13 Do not think in your **h** that
Esth 5: 9 day joyful and with a glad **h**
Esth 6: 6 Now Haman thought in his **h**
Esth 7: 5 in his **h** to do such a thing
Job 7:17 You should set Your **h** on him
Job 8:10 and utter words from their **h**
Job 9: 4 God is wise in **h** and mighty in
Job 10:13 You have hidden in Your **h**
Job 11:13 If you would prepare your **h**
Job 15:12 Why does your **h** carry you
Job 16:13 He pierces my **h** and does not
Job 17: 4 their **h** from understanding
Job 17:11 even the thoughts of my **h**
Job 19:27 How my **h** yearns within me
Job 20:20 knows no quietness in his **h**
Job 22:22 and lay up His words in your **h**
Job 23:16 For God made my **h** weak, and
Job 27: 6 my **h** shall not reproach me as
Job 29:13 the widow's **h** to sing for joy
Job 30:27 My **h** is in turmoil and cannot
Job 31: 7 or my **h** walked after my eyes,
Job 31: 9 If my **h** has been enticed by a
Job 31:20 if his **h** has not blessed me,
Job 31:27 so that my **h** has been
Job 33: 3 words come from my upright **h**
Job 34:14 If He should set His **h** on it
Job 36:13 in **h** store up wrath
Job 37: 1 At this also my **h** trembles
Job 37:24 to any who are wise of **h**
Job 38:36 given understanding to the **h**
Job 41:24 His **h** is as hard as stone,
Ps 4: 4 within your **h** on your bed
Ps 4: 7 You have put gladness in my **h**
Ps 7:10 Who saves the upright in **h**
Ps 9: 1 You, O LORD, with my whole **h**
Ps 10: 6 He has said in his **h**, "I
Ps 10:11 He has said in his **h**, "God
Ps 10:13 He has said in his **h**, "You
Ps 10:17 You will prepare their **h**
Ps 11: 2 secretly at the upright in **h**
Ps 12: 2 lips and a double **h** they speak
Ps 13: 2 Having sorrow in my **h** daily
Ps 13: 5 My **h** shall rejoice in Your
Ps 14: 1 The fool has said in his **h**
Ps 15: 2 And speaks the truth in his **h**
Ps 16: 7 My **h** also instructs me in the
Ps 16: 9 Therefore my **h** is glad, and my
Ps 17: 3 You have tested my **h**
Ps 19: 8 are right, rejoicing the **h**
Ps 19:14 the meditation of my **h** Be
Ps 22:14 My **h** is like wax
Ps 22:26 Let your **h** live forever
Ps 24: 4 has clean hands and a pure **h**
Ps 25:17 of my **h** have enlarged
Ps 26: 2 Try my mind and my **h**
Ps 27: 3 me, My **h** shall not fear
Ps 27: 8 My face," My **h** said to You,
Ps 27:13 I would have lost **h**, unless I
Ps 27:14 And He shall strengthen your **h**
Ps 28: 7 My **h** trusted in Him, and I am
Ps 28: 7 Therefore my **h** greatly
Ps 31:24 And He shall strengthen your **h**
Ps 32:11 for joy, all you upright in **h**
Ps 33:11 The plans of His **h** to all
Ps 33:21 For our **h** shall rejoice in
Ps 34:18 to those who have a broken **h**
Ps 35:13 would return to my own **h**
Ps 36: 1 within my **h** concerning the
Ps 36:10 to the upright in **h**
Ps 37: 4 you the desires of your **h**
Ps 37:15 sword shall enter their own **h**
Ps 37:31 law of his God is in his **h**
Ps 38: 8 of the turmoil of my **h**
Ps 38:10 My **h** pants, my strength fails
Ps 39: 3 My **h** was hot within me
Ps 40: 8 And Your law is within my **h**
Ps 40:10 righteousness within my **h**
Ps 40:12 Therefore my **h** fails me
Ps 41: 6 His **h** gathers iniquity to
Ps 44:18 Our **h** has not turned back,
Ps 44:21 He knows the secrets of the **h**
Ps 45: 1 My **h** is overflowing with a
Ps 45: 5 the **h** of the King's enemies
Ps 49: 3 the meditation of my **h** shall
Ps 51:10 Create in me a clean **h**, O God
Ps 51:17 A broken and a contrite **h**
Ps 53: 1 The fool has said in his **h**
Ps 55: 4 My **h** is severely pained
Ps 55:21 butter, But war was in his **h**
Ps 57: 7 My **h** is steadfast, O God, my
Ps 57: 7 O God, my **h** is steadfast
Ps 58: 2 No, in **h** you work wickedness
Ps 61: 2 my **h** is overwhelmed
Ps 62: 8 Pour out your **h** before Him
Ps 62:10 Do not set your **h** on them
Ps 64: 6 and the **h** of man are deep
Ps 64:10 the upright in **h** shall glory
Ps 66:18 If I regard iniquity in my **h**
Ps 69:20 Reproach has broken my **h**, And
Ps 73: 1 To such as are pure in **h**
Ps 73: 7 have more than **h** could wish
Ps 73:13 I have cleansed my **h** in vain
Ps 73:21 Thus my **h** was grieved, And I
Ps 73:26 My flesh and my **h** fail
Ps 73:26 God is the strength of my **h**
Ps 77: 6 I meditate within my **h**, And my
Ps 78: 8 that did not set its **h** aright
Ps 78:18 they tested God in their **h** By
Ps 78:37 For their **h** was not steadfast
Ps 78:72 to the integrity of his **h**
Ps 81:12 over to their own stubborn **h**
Ps 84: 2 My **h** and my flesh cry out for
Ps 84: 5 Whose **h** is set on pilgrimage
Ps 86:11 Unite my **h** to fear Your name
Ps 86:12 O Lord my God, with all my **h**
Ps 90:12 we may gain a **h** of wisdom
Ps 94:15 upright in **h** will follow it
Ps 97:11 gladness for the upright in **h**
Ps 101: 2 my house with a perfect **h**
Ps 101: 4 A perverse **h** shall depart
Ps 101: 5 a haughty look and a proud **h**
Ps 102: 4 My **h** is stricken and withered
Ps 104:15 that makes glad the **h** of man
Ps 104:15 which strengthens man's **h**
Ps 105:25 He turned their **h** to hate His
Ps 107:12 down their **h** with labor
Ps 108: 1 O God, my **h** is steadfast
Ps 109:16 even slay the broken in **h**
Ps 109:22 my **h** is wounded within me
Ps 111: 1 the LORD with my whole **h**, In
Ps 112: 7 His **h** is steadfast, trusting
Ps 112: 8 His **h** is established
Ps 119: 2 Who seek Him with the whole **h**
Ps 119: 7 You with uprightness of **h**
Ps 119:10 With my whole **h** I have sought
Ps 119:11 word I have hidden in my **h**
Ps 119:32 For You shall enlarge my **h**

Ps 119:34 observe it with my whole **h**
Ps 119:36 Incline my **h** to Your
Ps 119:58 Your favor with my whole **h**
Ps 119:69 Your precepts with my whole **h**
Ps 119:70 Their **h** is as fat as grease,
Ps 119:80 Let my **h** be blameless
Ps 119:111 are the rejoicing of my **h**
Ps 119:112 I have inclined my **h** to
Ps 119:145 I cry out with my whole **h**
Ps 119:161 But my **h** stands in awe of
Ps 128: 3 In the very **h** of your house
Ps 131: 1 my **h** is not haughty, Nor my
Ps 138: 1 praise You with my whole **h**
Ps 139:23 me, O God, and know my **h**
Ps 141: 4 my **h** to any evil thing, To
Ps 143: 4 My **h** within me is distressed
Prov 2: 2 apply your **h** to understanding
Prov 2:10 When wisdom enters your **h**
Prov 3: 1 law, but let your **h** keep my
Prov 3: 3 them on the tablet of your **h**
Prov 3: 5 in the LORD with all your **h**
Prov 4: 4 Let your **h** retain my words
Prov 4:21 them in the midst of your **h**
Prov 4:23 Keep your **h** with all
Prov 5:12 And my **h** despised reproof
Prov 6:14 perversity is in his **h**, he
Prov 6:18 a **h** that devises wicked plans
Prov 6:21 them continually upon your **h**
Prov 6:25 after her beauty in your **h**
Prov 7: 3 them on the tablet of your **h**
Prov 7:10 of a harlot, and a crafty **h**
Prov 7:25 Do not let your **h** turn aside
Prov 8: 5 be of an understanding **h**
Prov 10: 8 The wise in **h** will receive
Prov 10:20 the **h** of the wicked is worth
Prov 11:20 **h** are an abomination to the
Prov 11:29 be servant to the wise of **h**
Prov 12: 8 a perverse **h** will be despised
Prov 12:20 Deceit is in the **h** of those
Prov 12:23 but the **h** of fools proclaims
Prov 12:25 Anxiety in the **h** of man
Prov 13:12 deferred makes the **h** sick
Prov 14:10 The **h** knows its own
Prov 14:13 in laughter the **h** may sorrow
Prov 14:14 The backslider in **h** will be
Prov 14:30 A sound **h** is life to the body
Prov 14:33 in the **h** of him who has
Prov 14:33 but what is in the **h** of fools
Prov 15: 7 but the **h** of the fool does
Prov 15:13 A merry **h** makes a cheerful
Prov 15:13 of the **h** the spirit is broken
Prov 15:14 The **h** of him who has
Prov 15:15 merry **h** has a continual feast
Prov 15:28 The **h** of the righteous
Prov 15:30 of the eyes rejoices the **h**
Prov 16: 1 of the **h** belong to man, but
Prov 16: 5 in **h** is an abomination to the
Prov 16: 9 A man's **h** plans his way, but
Prov 16:21 The wise in **h** will be called
Prov 16:23 The **h** of the wise teaches his
Prov 17:16 since he has no **h** for it
Prov 17:20 a deceitful **h** finds no good
Prov 17:22 A merry **h** does good, like
Prov 18: 2 but in expressing his own **h**
Prov 18:12 the **h** of a man is haughty
Prov 18:15 The **h** of the prudent acquires
Prov 19: 3 his **h** frets against the LORD
Prov 19:18 and do not set your **h** on his
Prov 19:21 are many plans in a man's **h**
Prov 20: 5 Counsel in the **h** of man is
Prov 20: 9 I have made my **h** clean, I am
Prov 20:27 all the inner depths of his **h**
Prov 20:30 the inner depths of the **h**
Prov 21: 1 The king's **h** is in the hand
Prov 21: 4 A haughty look, a proud **h**
Prov 22:11 He who loves purity of **h** and
Prov 22:15 bound up in the **h** of a child
Prov 22:17 apply your **h** to my knowledge
Prov 23: 7 for as he thinks in his **h**
Prov 23: 7 but his **h** is not with you
Prov 23:12 Apply your **h** to instruction,
Prov 23:15 My son, if your **h** is wise
Prov 23:15 is wise, my **h** will rejoice
Prov 23:17 not let your **h** envy sinners
Prov 23:19 and guide your **h** in the way
Prov 23:26 My son, give me your **h**, and
Prov 23:33 your **h** will utter perverse
Prov 24: 2 for their **h** devises violence,
Prov 24:17 do not let your **h** be glad
Prov 25: 3 depth, so the **h** of kings is
Prov 25:20 who sings songs to a heavy **h**
Prov 26:23 wicked **h** are like earthenware
Prov 26:25 seven abominations in his **h**
Prov 27: 9 and perfume delight the **h**, and
Prov 27:11 be wise, and make my **h** glad
Prov 27:19 so a man's **h** reveals the man
Prov 28:14 but he who hardens his **h** will
Prov 28:25 of a proud **h** stirs up strife
Prov 28:26 trusts in his own **h** is a fool
Prov 31: 6 to those who are bitter of **h**
Prov 31:11 The **h** of her husband safely
Eccl 1:13 And I set my **h** to seek and
Eccl 1:16 I communed with my **h**, saying,
Eccl 1:16 My **h** has understood great
Eccl 1:17 I set my **h** to know wisdom and
Eccl 2: 1 I said in my **h**, Come now, I
Eccl 2: 3 I searched in my **h** how to
Eccl 2: 3 guiding my **h** with wisdom, and
Eccl 2:10 my **h** from any pleasure, for
Eccl 2:10 for my **h** rejoiced in all my
Eccl 2:15 So I said in my **h**, As it
Eccl 2:15 Then I said in my **h**, This
Eccl 2:20 Therefore I turned my **h** and
Eccl 2:22 for the striving of his **h**
Eccl 2:23 the night his **h** takes no rest
Eccl 3:17 I said in my **h**, God shall
Eccl 3:18 I said in my **h**, Concerning
Eccl 5: 2 let not your **h** utter anything
Eccl 5:20 busy with the joy of his **h**
Eccl 7: 2 the living will take it to **h**
Eccl 7: 3 the **h** is made better
Eccl 7: 4 The **h** of the wise is in the
Eccl 7: 4 but the **h** of fools is in the
Eccl 7: 7 and a bribe debases the **h**
Eccl 7:21 Also do not take to **h**
Eccl 7:22 your own **h** has known that
Eccl 7:25 I applied my **h** to know, to
Eccl 7:26 the woman whose **h** is snares
Eccl 8: 5 a wise man's **h** discerns both
Eccl 8: 9 applied my **h** to every work
Eccl 8:11 therefore the **h** of the sons
Eccl 8:16 I applied my **h** to know wisdom
Eccl 9: 1 I considered all this in my **h**
Eccl 9: 7 your wine with a merry **h**
Eccl 10: 2 A wise man's **h** is at his
Eccl 10: 2 but a fool's **h** at his left
Eccl 11: 9 let your **h** cheer you in the
Eccl 11: 9 walk in the ways of your **h**
Eccl 11:10 remove sorrow from your **h**
Song 3:11 day of the gladness of his **h**
Song 4: 9 You have ravished my **h**, my
Song 4: 9 you have ravished my **h** with
Song 5: 2 I sleep, but my **h** is awake
Song 5: 4 door, and my **h** yearned for him
Song 5: 6 My **h** went out to him when he
Song 8: 6 Set me as a seal upon your **h**
Is 1: 5 sick, and the whole **h** faints
Is 6:10 Make the **h** of this people
Is 6:10 and understand with their **h**
Is 7: 2 So his **h** and the **h** of
Is 7: 2 and the **h** of his people were
Is 9: 9 in pride and arrogance of **h**
Is 10: 7 so, nor does his **h** think so
Is 10: 7 but it is in his **h** to destroy
Is 10:12 **h** of the king of Assyria, and
Is 13: 7 limp, every man's **h** will melt
Is 14:13 For you have said in your **h**
Is 15: 5 My **h** will cry out for Moab
Is 16:11 Therefore my **h** shall resound
Is 19: 1 the **h** of Egypt will melt in
Is 21: 4 My **h** wavered, fearfulness
Is 30:29 gladness of **h** as when one
Is 32: 4 Also the **h** of the rash will
Is 32: 6 and his **h** will work iniquity
Is 33:18 Your **h** will meditate on
Is 38: 3 in truth and with a loyal **h**
Is 42:25 yet he did not take it to **h**
Is 44:19 And no one considers in his **h**
Is 44:20 a deceived **h** has turned him
Is 47: 7 not take these things to **h**
Is 47: 8 securely, who say in your **h**
Is 47:10 and you have said in your **h**
Is 49:21 Then you will say in your **h**
Is 51: 7 people in whose **h** is My law
Is 57: 1 and no man takes it to **h**
Is 57:11 Me, nor taken it to your **h**
Is 57:15 and to revive the **h** of the
Is 57:17 in the way of his **h**
Is 59:13 uttering from the **h** words of
Is 60: 5 your **h** shall swell with joy
Is 63: 4 day of vengeance is in My **h**
Is 63:15 the yearning of Your **h** and
Is 63:17 hardened our **h** from Your fear
Is 65:14 shall sing for joy of **h**, but
Is 65:14 you shall cry for sorrow of **h**
Is 66:14 your **h** shall rejoice, and your
Jer 3:10 turned to Me with her whole **h**
Jer 3:15 shepherds according to My **h**
Jer 3:17 stubbornness of their evil **h**
Jer 4: 9 That the **h** of the king shall
Jer 4: 9 and the **h** of the princes
Jer 4:10 the sword reaches to the **h**
Jer 4:14 wash your **h** from wickedness,
Jer 4:18 because it reaches to your **h**
Jer 4:19 I am pained in my very **h**
Jer 4:19 My **h** makes a noise in me
Jer 5:23 has a defiant and rebellious **h**
Jer 5:24 They do not say in their **h**
Jer 7:24 imagination of their evil **h**
Jer 7:31 nor did it come into My **h**
Jer 8:18 my **h** is faint in me
Jer 9: 8 but in his **h** he lies in wait
Jer 9:14 imagination of their own **h**
Jer 9:26 are uncircumcised in the **h**
Jer 11: 8 the imagination of his evil **h**
Jer 11:20 testing the mind and the **h**
Jer 12: 3 have tested my **h** toward You
Jer 12:11 because no one takes it to **h**
Jer 13:10 in the imagination of their **h**
Jer 13:22 And if you say in your **h**
Jer 14:14 and the deceit of their **h**
Jer 15:16 the joy and rejoicing of my **h**
Jer 16:12 imagination of his own evil **h**
Jer 17: 1 on the tablet of their **h**, and
Jer 17: 5 whose **h** departs from the LORD
Jer 17: 9 The **h** is deceitful above all
Jer 17:10 I, the LORD, search the **h**
Jer 18:12 the imagination of his evil **h**
Jer 20: 9 But His word was in my **h**
Jer 20:12 and see the mind and **h**, let me
Jer 22:17 your **h** are for nothing but
Jer 23: 9 My **h** within me is broken
Jer 23:16 speak a vision of their own **h**
Jer 23:17 the imagination of his own **h**
Jer 23:20 the thoughts of His **h**
Jer 23:26 in the **h** of the prophets who
Jer 23:26 of the deceit of their own **h**
Jer 24: 7 will give them a **h** to know Me
Jer 24: 7 to Me with their whole **h**
Jer 29:13 search for Me with all your **h**
Jer 30:21 pledged his **h** to approach Me
Jer 30:24 the intents of His **h**
Jer 31:20 therefore My **h** yearns for him
Jer 31:21 set your **h** toward the highway
Jer 32:39 then I will give them one **h**
Jer 32:41 in this land, with all My **h**
Jer 48:29 of the haughtiness of his **h**
Jer 48:36 Therefore My **h** shall wail
Jer 48:36 like flutes My **h** shall wail
Jer 48:41 **h** of a woman in birth pangs
Jer 49:16 you, the pride of your **h**, O
Jer 49:22 The **h** of the mighty men of
Jer 49:22 **h** of a woman in birth pangs
Jer 51:46 And lest your **h** faint, and you
Lam 1:20 my **h** is overturned within me,
Lam 1:22 are many, and my **h** is faint
Lam 2:11 with tears, my **h** is troubled
Lam 2:18 Their **h** cried out to the Lord
Lam 2:19 pour out your **h** like water
Lam 3:65 Give them a veiled **h**
Lam 5:15 The joy of our **h** has ceased
Lam 5:17 of this our **h** is faint
Ezek 3:10 receive into your **h** all My
Ezek 6: 9 **h** which has departed from Me
Ezek 11:19 Then I will give them one **h**
Ezek 11:19 take the stony **h** out of their
Ezek 11:19 and give them a **h** of flesh
Ezek 11:21 **h** of their detestable things
Ezek 13: 2 prophesy out of their own **h**
Ezek 13:17 prophesy out of their own **h**
Ezek 13:22 the **h** of the righteous sad
Ezek 14: 4 sets up his idols in his **h**
Ezek 14: 5 house of Israel by their **h**
Ezek 14: 7 and sets up his idols in his **h**
Ezek 16:30 How degenerate is your **h**
Ezek 18:31 and get yourselves a new **h**
Ezek 20:16 for their **h** went after their
Ezek 21: 6 son of man, with a breaking **h**
Ezek 21: 7 every **h** will melt, all hands
Ezek 21:15 gates, that the **h** may melt

Ezek 22:14 Can your **h** endure, or can
Ezek 25: 6 rejoiced in **h** with all your
Ezek 25:15 vengeance with a spiteful **h**
Ezek 27:31 for you with bitterness of **h**
Ezek 28: 2 Because your **h** is lifted up
Ezek 28: 2 your **h** as the **h** of a god
Ezek 28: 5 your **h** is lifted up because
Ezek 28: 6 your **h** as the **h** of a god
Ezek 28:17 Your **h** was lifted up because
Ezek 31:10 its **h** was lifted up in its
Ezek 36:26 I will give you a new **h** and
Ezek 36:26 I will take the **h** of stone
Ezek 36:26 and give you a **h** of flesh
Ezek 44: 7 uncircumcised in **h** and
Ezek 44: 9 uncircumcised in **h** or
Dan 1: 8 **h** that he would not defile
Dan 2:30 know the thoughts of your **h**
Dan 4:16 Let his **h** be changed from
Dan 4:16 be given the **h** of an animal
Dan 5:20 But when his **h** was lifted up,
Dan 5:21 men, his **h** was made like the
Dan 5:22 have not humbled your **h**,
Dan 6:14 and set his **h** on Daniel to
Dan 7: 4 a man's **h** was given to it
Dan 7:28 but I kept the matter in my **h**
Dan 8:25 magnify himself in his **h**
Dan 10:12 you set your **h** to understand
Dan 11:12 his **h** will be lifted up
Dan 11:28 his **h** shall be moved against
Hos 4: 8 they set their **h** on their
Hos 4:11 and new wine enslave the **h**
Hos 7: 6 prepare their **h** like an oven
Hos 7:14 cry out to Me with their **h**
Hos 10: 2 Their **h** is divided
Hos 11: 8 My **h** churns within Me
Hos 13: 6 filled and their **h** was exalted
Joel 2:12 Turn to me with all your **h**
Joel 2:13 So rend your **h**, and not your
Obad 3 of your **h** has deceived you
Obad 3 you who say in your **h**, 'Who
Jon 2: 3 into the **h** of the seas, and
Nah 2:10 The **h** melts, and the knees
Zeph 1:12 who say in their **h**, 'The
Zeph 2:15 securely, that said in her **h**
Zeph 3:14 and rejoice with all your **h**
Zech 7:10 in his **h** against his brother
Zech 8:17 your **h** against your neighbor
Zech 10: 7 their **h** shall rejoice as if
Zech 10: 7 their **h** shall rejoice in the
Zech 12: 5 of Judah shall say in their **h**
Mal 2: 2 if you will not take it to **h**
Mal 2: 2 you do not take it to **h**
Matt 5: 8 Blessed are the pure in **h**
Matt 5:28 adultery with her in his **h**
Matt 6:21 there your **h** will be also
Matt 11:29 for I am gentle and lowly in **h**
Matt 12:34 of the **h** the mouth speaks
Matt 12:35 **h** brings forth good things
Matt 12:40 nights in the **h** of the earth
Matt 13:15 for the **h** of this people has
Matt 13:15 understand with their **h** and
Matt 13:19 away what was sown in his **h**
Matt 15: 8 but their **h** is far from Me
Matt 15:18 of the mouth come from the **h**
Matt 15:19 For out of the **h** proceed evil
Matt 18:35 if each of you, from his **h**
Matt 22:37 LORD your God with all your **h**
Matt 24:48 evil servant says in his **h**
Mark 6:52 because their **h** was hardened
Mark 7: 6 but their **h** is far from Me
Mark 7:19 enter his **h** but his stomach
Mark 7:21 within, out of the **h** of men
Mark 8:17 Is your **h** still hardened
Mark 10: 5 of the hardness of your **h** he
Mark 11:23 and does not doubt in his **h**
Mark 12:30 LORD your God with all your **h**
Mark 12:33 And to love Him with all the **h**
Mark 16:14 unbelief and hardness of **h**
Luke 2:19 and pondered them in her **h**
Luke 2:51 all these things in her **h**
Luke 6:45 of his **h** brings forth good
Luke 6:45 of his **h** brings forth evil
Luke 6:45 of the **h** his mouth speaks
Luke 8:15 word with a noble and good **h**
Luke 9:47 the thought of their **h**, took
Luke 10:27 LORD your God with all your **h**
Luke 12:34 there your **h** will be also
Luke 12:45 if that servant says in his **h**
Luke 18: 1 ought to pray and not lose **h**
Luke 24:25 slow of **h** to believe in all
Luke 24:32 Did not our **h** burn within us
John 7:38 out of his **h** will flow rivers
John 12:40 eyes and hardened their **h**,
John 12:40 and understand with their **h**
John 13: 2 into the **h** of Judas Iscariot
John 14: 1 Let not your **h** be troubled
John 14:27 Let not your **h** be troubled
John 16: 6 you, sorrow has filled your **h**
John 16:22 your **h** will rejoice, and your
Acts 2:26 therefore my **h** rejoiced, and
Acts 2:37 this, they were cut to the **h**
Acts 2:46 gladness and simplicity of **h**
Acts 4:32 who believed were of one **h**
Acts 5: 3 **h** to lie to the Holy Spirit
Acts 5: 4 this thing in your **h**
Acts 7:23 it came into his **h** to visit
Acts 7:51 and uncircumcised in **h** and ears
Acts 7:54 things they were cut to the **h**
Acts 8:21 for your **h** is not right in
Acts 8:22 of your **h** may be forgiven you
Acts 8:37 you believe with all your **h**
Acts 11:23 all that with purpose of **h**
Acts 13:22 Jesse, a man after My own **h**
Acts 15: 8 So God, who knows the **h**,
Acts 16:14 The Lord opened her **h** to heed
Acts 21:13 by weeping and breaking my **h**
Acts 27:22 And now I urge you to take **h**
Acts 27:25 Therefore take **h**, men, for I
Acts 28:27 For the **h** of this people has
Acts 28:27 understand with their **h** and
Rom 2: 5 your impenitent **h** you are
Rom 2:29 circumcision is that of the **h**
Rom 6:17 yet you obeyed from the **h**
Rom 9: 2 and continual grief in my **h**
Rom 10: 6 Do not say in your **h**, Who
Rom 10: 8 in your **h**" (that is, the
Rom 10: 9 believe in your **h** that God
Rom 10:10 For with the **h** one believes
1Co 2: 9 nor have entered into the **h**
1Co 7:37 who stands steadfast in his **h**
1Co 7:37 his **h** that he will keep his
1Co 14:25 secrets of his **h** are revealed
2Co 2: 4 anguish of **h** I wrote to you,
2Co 3: 3 of flesh, that is, of the **h**
2Co 3:15 read, a veil lies on their **h**
2Co 4: 1 mercy, we do not lose **h**
2Co 4:16 Therefore we do not lose **h**
2Co 5:12 in appearance and not in **h**
2Co 6:11 to you, our **h** is wide open
2Co 8:16 for you into the **h** of Titus
2Co 9: 7 give as he purposes in his **h**
Gal 6: 9 reap if we do not lose **h**
Eph 3:13 **h** at my tribulations for you
Eph 4:18 of the hardening of their **h**
Eph 5:19 melody in your **h** to the Lord
Eph 6: 5 trembling, in sincerity of **h**
Eph 6: 6 the will of God from the **h**
Phil 1: 7 because I have you in my **h**
Col 3:22 but in sincerity of **h**,
1Th 2:17 time in presence, not in **h**
1Ti 1: 5 is love from a pure **h**, from a
2Ti 2:22 on the Lord out of a pure **h**
Phm 12 him, that is, my own **h**,
Phm 20 refresh my **h** in the Lord
Heb 3:10 always go astray in their **h**
Heb 3:12 **h** of unbelief in departing
Heb 4:12 thoughts and intents of the **h**
Heb 10:22 us draw near with a true **h** in
Heb 13: 9 the **h** be established by grace
Jas 1:26 tongue but deceives his own **h**
1Pe 1:22 fervently with a pure **h**,
1Pe 3: 4 be the hidden person of the **h**
2Pe 2:14 They have a **h** trained in
1Jn 3:17 and shuts up his **h** from him
1Jn 3:20 For if our **h** condemns us, God
1Jn 3:20 us, God is greater than our **h**
1Jn 3:21 if our **h** does not condemn us,
Rev 18: 7 for she says in her **h**, 'I sit

HEARTH
Lev 6: 9 **h** upon the altar all night
Ps 102: 3 my bones are burned like a **h**
Is 30:14 shard to take fire from the **h**
Jer 36:22 burning on the **h** before him
Jer 36:23 the fire that was on the **h**
Jer 36:23 in the fire that was on the **h**
Ezek 43:15 The altar **h** is four cubits
Ezek 43:15 extending upward from the **h**
Ezek 43:16 The altar **h** is twelve cubits

HEARTHS
Ezek 46:23 cooking **h** were made under the

HEARTILY (*see* HEARTY)
1Co 16:19 greet you **h** in the Lord, with
Col 3:23 And whatever you do, do it **h**

HEART'S (*see* HEART)
Ps 10: 3 wicked boasts of his **h** desire
Ps 20: 4 according to your **h** desire
Ps 21: 2 have given him his **h** desire
Rom 10: 1 my **h** desire and prayer to God

HEARTS (*see* HEART)
Gen 18: 5 that you may refresh your **h**
Gen 42:28 Then their **h** failed them
Ex 10: 1 the **h** of his servants, that I
Ex 14:17 harden the **h** of the Egyptians
Ex 31: 6 the **h** of all who are gifted
Ex 35:29 women whose **h** were willing to
Lev 26:36 their **h** in the lands of their
Lev 26:41 uncircumcised **h** are humbled
Deut 1:28 have discouraged our **h**,
Deut 32:46 Set your **h** on all the words
Josh 2:11 these things, our **h** melted
Josh 7: 5 therefore the **h** of the people
Josh 11:20 of the LORD to harden their **h**
Josh 23:14 And you know in all your **h**
Judg 16:25 when their **h** were merry,
1Sa 6: 6 your **h** as the Egyptians and
1Sa 6: 6 and Pharaoh hardened their **h**
1Sa 7: 3 to the LORD with all your **h**
1Sa 7: 3 prepare your **h** for the LORD
1Sa 10:26 him, whose **h** God had touched
2Sa 15: 6 the **h** of the men of Israel
2Sa 15:13 The **h** of the men of Israel
2Sa 19:14 So he swayed the **h** of all the
1Ki 8:39 know the **h** of all the sons of
1Ki 8:58 may incline our **h** to Himself
1Ki 11: 2 away your **h** after their gods
1Ki 18:37 their **h** back to You again
1Ch 16:10 let the **h** of those rejoice
1Ch 28: 9 for the LORD searches all **h**
2Ch 6:14 before You with all their **h**
2Ch 6:30 the **h** of the sons of men)
2Ch 20:33 had not directed their **h** to
Job 1: 5 and cursed God in their **h**
Ps 7: 9 the righteous God tests the **h**
Ps 17:10 have closed up their fat **h**
Ps 28: 3 But evil is in their **h**
Ps 33:15 fashions their **h** individually
Ps 35:25 Let them not say in their **h**
Ps 69:32 seek God, your **h** shall live
Ps 74: 8 They said in their **h**, "Let
Ps 95: 8 Do not harden your **h**, as in
Ps 95:10 who go astray in their **h**, And
Ps 105: 3 Let the **h** of those rejoice
Ps 125: 4 who are upright in their **h**
Ps 140: 2 plan evil things in their **h**
Prov 15:11 more the **h** of the sons of men
Prov 17: 3 but the LORD tests the **h**
Prov 21: 2 but the LORD weighs the **h**
Prov 24:12 who weighs the **h** consider it
Eccl 3:11 has put eternity in their **h**
Eccl 9: 3 Truly the **h** of the sons of
Eccl 9: 3 is in their **h** while they live
Is 29:13 removed their **h** far from Me
Is 44:18 they cannot see, and their **h**
Jer 4: 4 away the foreskins of your **h**
Jer 31:33 minds, and write it on their **h**
Jer 32:40 their **h** so that they will not
Jer 42:20 **h** when you sent me to the
Jer 48:41 the mighty men's **h** in Moab on
Lam 3:41 let us lift our **h** and hands to
Ezek 11:21 But as for those whose **h** walk
Ezek 14: 3 set up their idols in their **h**
Ezek 32: 9 trouble the **h** of many peoples
Ezek 33:31 but their **h** pursue their own
Dan 11:27 Both these kings' **h** shall be
Hos 7: 2 do not consider in their **h**
Zech 7:12 they made their **h** like flint
Mal 4: 6 he will turn the **h** of the
Mal 4: 6 and the **h** of the children to
Matt 9: 4 do you think evil in your **h**
Matt 19: 8 of the hardness of your **h**
Mark 2: 6 there and reasoning in their **h**
Mark 2: 8 about these things in your **h**
Mark 3: 5 by the hardness of their **h**
Mark 4:15 word that was sown in their **h**
Luke 1:17 to turn the **h** of the fathers
Luke 1:51 in the imagination of their **h**
Luke 1:66 them kept them in their **h**

Luke 2:35 of many **h** may be revealed
Luke 3:15 in their **h** about John,
Luke 5:22 are you reasoning in your **h**
Luke 8:12 away the word out of their **h**
Luke 16:15 men, but God knows your **h**
Luke 21:14 **h** not to meditate beforehand
Luke 21:26 men's **h** failing them from
Luke 21:34 lest your **h** be weighed down
Luke 24:38 why do doubts arise in your **h**
Acts 1:24 O Lord, who know the **h** of all
Acts 7:39 in their **h** they turned back
Acts 14:17 filling our **h** with food and
Acts 15: 9 purifying their **h** by faith
Rom 1:21 their foolish **h** were darkened
Rom 1:24 in the lusts of their **h**, to
Rom 2:15 of the law written in their **h**
Rom 5: 5 **h** by the Holy Spirit who was
Rom 8:27 Now He who searches the **h**
Rom 16:18 deceive the **h** of the simple
1Co 4: 5 reveal the counsels of the **h**
2Co 1:22 Spirit in our **h** as a deposit
2Co 3: 2 our epistle written in our **h**
2Co 4: 6 who has shone in our **h** to
2Co 7: 2 Open your **h** to us
2Co 7: 3 before that you are in our **h**
Gal 4: 6 Spirit of His Son into your **h**
Eph 3:17 dwell in your **h** through faith
Eph 6:22 and that he may comfort your **h**
Phil 4: 7 will guard your **h** and minds
Col 2: 2 that their **h** may be
Col 3:15 peace of God rule in your **h**
Col 3:16 grace in your **h** to the Lord
Col 4: 8 and comfort your **h**,
1Th 2: 4 men, but God who tests our **h**
1Th 3:13 your **h** blameless in holiness
2Th 2:17 comfort your **h** and establish
2Th 3: 5 your **h** into the love of God
Phm 7 because the **h** of the saints
Heb 3: 8 do not harden your **h** as in
Heb 3:15 do not harden your **h** as in
Heb 4: 7 voice, do not harden your **h**
Heb 8:10 mind and write them on their **h**
Heb 10:16 will put My laws into their **h**
Heb 10:22 having our **h** sprinkled from
Jas 3:14 and self-seeking in your **h**
Jas 4: 8 and purify your **h**, you
Jas 5: 5 you have fattened your **h** as
Jas 5: 8 Establish your **h**, for the
1Pe 3:15 the Lord God in your **h**, and
2Pe 1:19 morning star rises in your **h**
1Jn 3:19 shall assure our **h** before Him
Rev 2:23 who searches the minds and **h**
Rev 17:17 **h** to fulfill His purpose, to

HEARTY (*see* HEARTILY)
Prov 27: 9 friend does so by **h** counsel

HEAT (*see* HEATED)
Gen 8:22 and harvest, and cold and **h**, and
Gen 18: 1 tent door in the **h** of the day
Deut 29:24 What does the **h** of this great
1Sa 11:11 until the **h** of the day
2Sa 4: 5 came at about the **h** of the
Job 24:19 **h** consume the snow waters, so
Ps 19: 6 is nothing hidden from its **h**
Is 4: 6 in the daytime from the **h**
Is 18: 4 like clear **h** in sunshine,
Is 18: 4 of dew in the **h** of harvest
Is 25: 4 the storm, a shade from the **h**
Is 25: 5 aliens, as **h** in a dry place
Is 25: 5 as **h** in the shadow of a cloud
Is 49:10 neither **h** nor sun shall
Jer 17: 8 and will not fear when **h** comes
Jer 36:30 cast out to the **h** of the day
Ezek 3:14 in the **h** of my spirit
Dan 3:19 commanded that they **h** the
Matt 20:12 burden and the **h** of the day
Acts 28: 3 came out because of the **h**
Jas 1:11 sun risen with a burning **h**
2Pe 3:10 will melt with fervent **h**
2Pe 3:12 will melt with fervent **h**
Rev 7:16 not strike them, nor any **h**
Rev 16: 9 were scorched with great **h**

HEATED (*see* HEAT)
Dan 3:19 more than it was usually **h**
Hos 7: 4 like an oven **h** by a baker

HEATHEN
Matt 6: 7 vain repetitions as the **h** do
Matt 18:17 let him be to you like a **h**

HEAVE (*see* HEAVES)
Ex 29:27 the thigh of the **h** offering
Ex 29:28 For it is a **h** offering
Ex 29:28 it shall be a **h** offering from
Ex 29:28 their **h** offering to the LORD
Lev 7:14 as a **h** offering to the LORD
Lev 7:32 as a **h** offering from the
Lev 7:34 the thigh of the **h** offering I
Lev 10:14 the thigh of the **h** offering
Lev 10:15 The thigh of the **h** offering
Num 6:20 the thigh of the **h** offering
Num 15:19 up a **h** offering to the LORD
Num 15:20 ground meal as a **h** offering
Num 15:20 as a **h** offering of the
Num 15:21 a **h** offering throughout your
Num 18: 8 you charge of My **h** offerings
Num 18:11 the **h** offering of their gift,
Num 18:19 All the **h** offerings of the
Num 18:24 as a **h** offering to the LORD
Num 18:26 then you shall offer up a **h**
Num 18:27 And your **h** offering shall be
Num 18:28 a **h** offering to the LORD from
Num 18:28 **h** offering from it to Aaron
Num 18:29 **h** offering due to the LORD
Num 31:29 as a **h** offering to the LORD
Num 31:41 which was the LORD's **h**
Deut 12: 6 the **h** offerings of your hand,
Deut 12:11 the **h** offerings of your hand,
Deut 12:17 or of the **h** offering of your
Amos 8: 8 shall swell like the River, **h**
Zech 12: 3 all who would **h** it away will

HEAVEN (*see* HEAVENLY, HEAVEN'S, HEAVENS)
Gen 1: 8 God called the firmament **H**
Gen 6:17 to destroy from under **h** all
Gen 7:11 the windows of **h** were opened
Gen 7:19 the whole **h** were covered
Gen 8: 2 the windows of **h** were also
Gen 8: 2 and the rain from **h** was
Gen 14:19 God Most High, Possessor of **h**
Gen 14:22 Most High, the Possessor of **h**
Gen 15: 5 Look now toward **h**, and count
Gen 21:17 God called to Hagar out of **h**
Gen 22:11 the LORD called to him from **h**
Gen 22:15 a second time out of **h**,
Gen 22:17 as the stars of the **h** and as
Gen 24: 3 by the LORD, the God of **h**
Gen 24: 7 The LORD God of **h**, who took
Gen 26: 4 multiply as the stars of **h**
Gen 27:28 God give you of the dew of **h**
Gen 27:39 and of the dew of **h** from above
Gen 28:12 and its top reached to **h**
Gen 28:17 God, and this is the gate of **h**
Gen 49:25 you with blessings of **h** above
Ex 9:10 Moses scattered them toward **h**
Ex 9:22 out your hand toward **h**, that
Ex 9:23 out his rod toward **h**
Ex 10:21 out your hand toward **h**, that
Ex 10:22 out his hand toward **h**, and
Ex 16: 4 rain bread from **h** for you
Ex 17:14 of Amalek from under **h**
Ex 20: 4 anything that is in **h** above
Ex 20:22 I have talked with you from **h**
Ex 32:13 descendants as the stars of **h**
Deut 1:10 the stars of **h** in multitude
Deut 1:28 great and fortified up to **h**
Deut 2:25 the nations under the whole **h**
Deut 3:24 in **h** or on earth who can do
Deut 4:11 with fire to the midst of **h**
Deut 4:19 lest you lift your eyes to **h**
Deut 4:19 the stars, all the host of **h**
Deut 4:19 the whole **h** as a heritage
Deut 4:26 I call **h** and earth to witness
Deut 4:32 one end of **h** to the other
Deut 4:36 Out of **h** He let you hear His
Deut 4:39 Himself is God in **h** above
Deut 5: 8 anything that is in **h** above
Deut 7:24 their name from under **h**
Deut 9: 1 great and fortified up to **h**
Deut 9:14 out their name from under **h**
Deut 10:14 Indeed **h** and the highest
Deut 10:22 the stars of **h** in multitude
Deut 11:11 water from the rain of **h**,
Deut 17: 3 moon or any of the host of **h**
Deut 25:19 of Amalek from under **h**
Deut 26:15 Your holy habitation, from **h**
Deut 28:24 from the **h** it shall come down
Deut 28:62 the stars of **h** in multitude
Deut 29:20 out his name from under **h**
Deut 30: 4 to the farthest parts under **h**
Deut 30:12 It is not in **h**, that you
Deut 30:12 Who will ascend into **h** for us
Deut 30:19 I call **h** and earth as
Deut 31:28 in their hearing and call **h**
Deut 32:40 For I lift My hand to **h**, and
Deut 33:13 with the precious things of **h**
Josh 2:11 God, He is God in **h** above
Josh 8:20 of the city ascended to **h**
Josh 10:11 **h** on them as far as Azekah
Josh 10:13 stood still in the midst of **h**
Judg 13:20 up toward **h** from the altar
Judg 20:40 city going up in smoke to **h**
1Sa 2:10 from **h** He will thunder
1Sa 5:12 cry of the city went up to **h**
2Sa 18: 9 he was left hanging between **h**
2Sa 21:10 rains poured on them from **h**
2Sa 22: 8 the foundations of **h** moved
2Sa 22:14 The LORD thundered from **h**
1Ki 8:22 spread out his hands toward **h**
1Ki 8:23 there is no God in **h** above or
1Ki 8:27 Behold, **h** and the **h** of
1Ki 8:30 then hear in **h** Your dwelling
1Ki 8:32 then hear in **h**, and act and
1Ki 8:34 then hear in **h**, and forgive
1Ki 8:36 then hear in **h**, and forgive
1Ki 8:39 then hear in **h** Your dwelling
1Ki 8:43 hear in **h** Your dwelling place
1Ki 8:45 then hear in **h** their prayer
1Ki 8:49 then hear in **h** Your dwelling
1Ki 8:54 with his hands spread up to **h**
1Ki 22:19 all the host of **h** standing by
2Ki 1:10 let fire come down from **h**
2Ki 1:10 And fire came down from **h**
2Ki 1:12 let fire come down from **h**
2Ki 1:12 fire of God came down from **h**
2Ki 1:14 fire has come down from **h**
2Ki 2: 1 Elijah into **h** by a whirlwind
2Ki 2:11 went up by a whirlwind into **h**
2Ki 7: 2 LORD would make windows in **h**
2Ki 7:19 LORD would make windows in **h**
2Ki 14:27 name of Israel from under **h**
2Ki 17:16 worshiped all the host of **h**
2Ki 19:15 You have made **h** and earth
2Ki 21: 3 worshiped all the host of **h**
2Ki 21: 5 of **h** in the two courts of the
2Ki 23: 4 and for all the host of **h**
2Ki 23: 5 and to all the host of **h**
1Ch 21:16 standing between earth and **h**
1Ch 21:26 He answered him from **h** by
1Ch 29:11 for all that is in **h** and in
2Ch 2: 6 build Him a temple, since **h**
2Ch 2: 6 and the **h** of heavens cannot
2Ch 2:12 God of Israel, who made **h**
2Ch 6:13 out his hands toward **h**),
2Ch 6:14 there is no God in **h** or on
2Ch 6:18 Behold, **h** and the **h** of
2Ch 6:21 Your dwelling place, in **h**
2Ch 6:23 then hear from **h**, and act, and
2Ch 6:25 then hear from **h** and forgive
2Ch 6:26 When **h** is shut up and there is
2Ch 6:27 then hear in **h**, and forgive
2Ch 6:30 then hear from **h** Your
2Ch 6:33 then hear from **h** Your
2Ch 6:35 then hear from **h** their prayer
2Ch 6:39 then hear from **h** Your
2Ch 7: 1 fire came down from **h** and
2Ch 7:13 When I shut up **h** and there is
2Ch 7:14 ways, then I will hear from **h**
2Ch 18:18 all the host of **h** standing on
2Ch 20: 6 fathers, are You not God in **h**
2Ch 28: 9 a rage that reaches up to **h**
2Ch 30:27 His holy dwelling place, to **h**
2Ch 32:20 prayed and cried out to **h**
2Ch 33: 3 worshiped all the host of **h**
2Ch 33: 5 of **h** in the two courts of the
2Ch 36:23 LORD God of **h** has given me
Ezra 1: 2 LORD God of **h** has given me
Ezra 5:11 the servants of the God of **h**
Ezra 5:12 the God of **h** to wrath, He
Ezra 6: 9 offerings of the God of **h**
Ezra 6:10 sweet aroma to the God of **h**
Ezra 7:12 of the Law of the God of **h**
Ezra 7:21 of the Law of the God of **h**
Ezra 7:23 is commanded by the God of **h**
Ezra 7:23 for the house of the God of **h**
Neh 1: 4 praying before the God of **h**
Neh 1: 5 I pray, LORD God of **h**, O
Neh 2: 4 So I prayed to the God of **h**
Neh 2:20 The God of **h** Himself will
Neh 9: 6 made **h**, the **h** of heavens

Neh 9: 6 the host of **h** worships You
Neh 9:13 and spoke with them from **h**
Neh 9:15 bread from **h** for their hunger
Neh 9:23 children as the stars of **h**
Neh 9:27 to You, You heard from **h**
Neh 9:28 out to You, You heard from **h**
Job 1:16 The fire of God fell from **h**
Job 2:12 dust on his head toward **h**
Job 11: 8 They are higher than **h**
Job 16:19 even now my witness is in **h**
Job 22:12 Is not God in the height of **h**
Job 22:14 walks above the circle of **h**
Job 26:11 The pillars of **h** tremble, and
Job 35:11 us wiser than the birds of **h**
Job 37: 3 it forth under the whole **h**
Job 38:29 and the frost of **h**, who gives
Job 38:37 can pour out the bottles of **h**
Job 41:11 Everything under **h** is Mine
Ps 11: 4 The LORD's throne is in **h**
Ps 14: 2 **h** upon the children of men
Ps 19: 6 rising is from one end of **h**
Ps 20: 6 answer him from His holy **h**
Ps 33:13 The LORD looks from **h**
Ps 53: 2 God looks down from **h** upon
Ps 57: 3 He shall send from **h** and save
Ps 68:33 who rides on the **h** of heavens
Ps 69:34 Let **h** and earth praise Him,
Ps 73:25 Whom have I in **h** but You
Ps 76: 8 judgment to be heard from **h**
Ps 78:23 And opened the doors of **h**
Ps 78:24 given them of the bread of **h**
Ps 80:14 Look down from **h** and see, And
Ps 85:11 shall look down from **h**
Ps 89:29 his throne as the days of **h**
Ps 102:19 From **h** the LORD viewed the
Ps 103:19 established His throne in **h**
Ps 105:40 them with the bread of **h**
Ps 115: 3 But our God is in **h**
Ps 115:15 by the LORD, Who made **h** and
Ps 115:16 The **h**, even the heavens, are
Ps 119:89 Your word is settled in **h**
Ps 121: 2 from the LORD, Who made **h**
Ps 124: 8 name of the LORD, Who made **h**
Ps 134: 3 The LORD who made **h** and earth
Ps 135: 6 LORD pleases He does, In **h**
Ps 136:26 give thanks to the God of **h**
Ps 139: 8 If I ascend into **h**, You are
Ps 146: 6 Who made **h** and earth, The sea,
Ps 148:13 glory is above the earth and **h**
Prov 23: 5 away like an eagle toward **h**
Prov 30: 4 Who has ascended into **h**, or
Eccl 1:13 all that is done under **h**
Eccl 2: 3 **h** all the days of their lives
Eccl 3: 1 for every purpose under **h**
Eccl 5: 2 For God is in **h**, and you on
Is 13: 5 country, from the end of **h**
Is 13:10 For the stars of **h** and their
Is 14:12 How you are fallen from **h**
Is 14:13 I will ascend into **h**, I will
Is 34: 4 All the host of **h** shall be
Is 34: 5 My sword shall be bathed in **h**
Is 37:16 You have made **h** and earth
Is 40:12 measured **h** with a span and
Is 55:10 down, and the snow from **h**, and
Is 63:15 Look down from **h**, and see from
Is 66: 1 **H** is My throne, and earth is
Jer 7:18 make cakes for the queen of **h**
Jer 7:33 food for the birds of the **h**
Jer 8: 2 the moon and all the host of **h**
Jer 10: 2 be dismayed at the signs of **h**
Jer 16: 4 be meat for the birds of **h**
Jer 19: 7 meat for the birds of the **h**
Jer 19:13 incense to all the host of **h**
Jer 23:24 do I not fill **h** and earth
Jer 31:37 If **h** above can be measured,
Jer 33:22 As the host of **h** cannot be
Jer 33:25 appointed the ordinances of **h**
Jer 34:20 meat for the birds of the **h**
Jer 44:17 incense to the queen of **h**
Jer 44:18 incense to the queen of **h**
Jer 44:19 incense to the queen of **h**
Jer 44:25 incense to the queen of **h**
Jer 49:36 from the four quarters of **h**
Jer 51: 9 for her judgment reaches to **h**
Jer 51:15 stretched out the **h** by His
Jer 51:53 Babylon were to mount up to **h**
Lam 2: 1 He cast down from **h** to the
Lam 3:41 hearts and hands to God in **h**
Lam 3:50 the LORD from **h** looks down
Ezek 8: 3 me up between earth and **h**, and

Dan 2:18 of **h** concerning this secret
Dan 2:19 Daniel blessed the God of **h**
Dan 2:28 God in **h** who reveals secrets
Dan 2:37 For the God of **h** has given
Dan 2:38 field and the birds of the **h**
Dan 2:44 of these kings the God of **h**
Dan 4:13 holy one, coming down from **h**
Dan 4:15 it be wet with the dew of **h**
Dan 4:21 of the **h** had their habitation
Dan 4:23 holy one, coming down from **h**
Dan 4:23 it be wet with the dew of **h**
Dan 4:25 wet you with the dew of **h**
Dan 4:26 you come to know that **H** rules
Dan 4:31 mouth, a voice fell from **h**
Dan 4:33 of **h** till his hair had grown
Dan 4:34 lifted my eyes to **h**, and my
Dan 4:35 to His will in the army of **h**
Dan 4:37 extol and honor the King of **h**
Dan 5:21 was wet with the dew of **h**
Dan 5:23 up against the Lord of **h**
Dan 6:27 works signs and wonders in **h**
Dan 7: 2 the four winds of **h** were
Dan 7:13 coming with the clouds of **h**
Dan 7:27 kingdoms under the whole **h**
Dan 8: 8 up toward the four winds of **h**
Dan 8:10 it grew up to the host of **h**
Dan 9:12 for under the whole **h** such
Dan 11: 4 toward the four winds of **h**
Dan 12: 7 hand and his left hand to **h**
Amos 9: 2 though they climb up to **h**
Jon 1: 9 I fear the LORD, the God of **h**
Nah 3:16 more than the stars of **h**
Zeph 1: 5 host of **h** on the housetops
Hag 2: 6 little while) I will shake **h**
Hag 2:21 I will shake **h** and earth
Zech 2: 6 like the four winds of **h**,"
Zech 5: 9 the basket between earth and **h**
Zech 6: 5 These are four spirits of **h**
Mal 3:10 open for you the windows of **h**
Matt 3: 2 the kingdom of **h** is at hand
Matt 3:17 suddenly a voice came from **h**
Matt 4:17 the kingdom of **h** is at hand
Matt 5: 3 theirs is the kingdom of **h**
Matt 5:10 theirs is the kingdom of **h**
Matt 5:12 for great is your reward in **h**
Matt 5:16 and glorify your Father in **h**
Matt 5:18 I say to you, till **h** and
Matt 5:19 least in the kingdom of **h**
Matt 5:19 great in the kingdom of **h**
Matt 5:20 means enter the kingdom of **h**
Matt 5:34 neither by **h**, for it is God's
Matt 5:45 be sons of your Father in **h**
Matt 5:48 your Father in **h** is perfect
Matt 6: 1 reward from your Father in **h**
Matt 6: 9 Our Father in **h**, hallowed be
Matt 6:10 done on earth as it is in **h**
Matt 6:20 for yourselves treasures in **h**
Matt 7:11 **h** give good things to those
Matt 7:21 shall enter the kingdom of **h**
Matt 7:21 the will of My Father in **h**
Matt 8:11 and Jacob in the kingdom of **h**
Matt 10: 7 The kingdom of **h** is at hand
Matt 10:32 before My Father who is in **h**
Matt 10:33 before My Father who is in **h**
Matt 11:11 of **h** is greater than he
Matt 11:12 kingdom of **h** suffers violence
Matt 11:23 who are exalted to **h**, will
Matt 11:25 thank You, Father, Lord of **h**
Matt 12:50 My Father in **h** is My brother
Matt 13:11 mysteries of the kingdom of **h**
Matt 13:24 The kingdom of **h** is like a
Matt 13:31 The kingdom of **h** is like a
Matt 13:33 kingdom of **h** is like leaven
Matt 13:44 the kingdom of **h** is like
Matt 13:45 the kingdom of **h** is like a
Matt 13:47 the kingdom of **h** is like a
Matt 13:52 **h** is like a householder who
Matt 14:19 two fish, and looking up to **h**
Matt 16: 1 would show them a sign from **h**
Matt 16:17 but My Father who is in **h**
Matt 16:19 the keys of the kingdom of **h**
Matt 16:19 on earth will be bound in **h**
Matt 16:19 on earth will be loosed in **h**
Matt 18: 1 greatest in the kingdom of **h**
Matt 18: 3 means enter the kingdom of **h**
Matt 18: 4 greatest in the kingdom of **h**
Matt 18:10 for I say to you that in **h**
Matt 18:10 face of My Father who is in **h**
Matt 18:14 in **h** that one of these little
Matt 18:18 on earth will be bound in **h**

Matt 18:18 on earth will be loosed in **h**
Matt 18:19 for them by My Father in **h**
Matt 18:23 Therefore the kingdom of **h** is
Matt 19:14 of such is the kingdom of **h**
Matt 19:21 you will have treasure in **h**
Matt 19:23 man to enter the kingdom of **h**
Matt 20: 1 For the kingdom of **h** is like
Matt 21:25 From **h** or from men
Matt 21:25 If we say, From **h**,' He will
Matt 22: 2 The kingdom of **h** is like a
Matt 22:30 are like angels of God in **h**
Matt 23: 9 your Father, He who is in **h**
Matt 23:13 the kingdom of **h** against men
Matt 23:22 And he who swears by **h**, swears
Matt 24:29 the stars will fall from **h**
Matt 24:30 Son of Man will appear in **h**
Matt 24:30 on the clouds of **h** with power
Matt 24:31 one end of **h** to the other
Matt 24:35 **H** and earth will pass away,
Matt 24:36 no, not even the angels of **h**
Matt 25: 1 Then the kingdom of **h** shall
Matt 25:14 For the kingdom of **h** is like
Matt 26:64 and coming on the clouds of **h**
Matt 28: 2 of the Lord descended from **h**
Matt 28:18 has been given to Me in **h**
Mark 1:11 Then a voice came from **h**
Mark 6:41 two fish, He looked up to **h**
Mark 7:34 Then, looking up to **h**, He
Mark 8:11 from Him a sign from **h**,
Mark 10:21 you will have treasure in **h**
Mark 11:25 that your Father in **h** may
Mark 11:26 in **h** forgive your trespasses
Mark 11:30 was it from **h** or from men
Mark 11:31 If we say, 'From **h**,' He will
Mark 12:25 but are like angels in **h**
Mark 13:25 the stars of **h** will fall, and
Mark 13:25 and the powers in **h** will be
Mark 13:27 to the farthest part of **h**
Mark 13:31 **H** and earth will pass away,
Mark 13:32 neither the angels in **h**, nor
Mark 14:62 coming with the clouds of **h**
Mark 16:19 He was received up into **h**
Luke 2:15 gone away from them into **h**
Luke 3:21 He prayed, the **h** was opened
Luke 3:22 voice came from **h** which said
Luke 4:25 when the **h** was shut up three
Luke 6:23 your reward is great in **h**
Luke 9:16 two fish, and looking up to **h**
Luke 9:54 fire to come down from **h** and
Luke 10:15 who are exalted to **h**, will
Luke 10:18 fall like lightning from **h**
Luke 10:20 your names are written in **h**
Luke 10:21 praise You, Father, Lord of **h**
Luke 11: 2 Our Father in **h**, hallowed be
Luke 11: 2 done On earth as it is in **h**
Luke 11:16 sought from Him a sign from **h**
Luke 15: 7 there will be more joy in **h**
Luke 15:18 I have sinned against **h** and
Luke 15:21 I have sinned against **h** and
Luke 16:17 And it is easier for **h** and
Luke 17:24 out of one part under **h**
Luke 17:24 to the other part under **h**
Luke 17:29 fire and brimstone from **h** and
Luke 18:13 much as raise his eyes to **h**
Luke 18:22 you will have treasure in **h**
Luke 19:38 Peace in **h** and glory in the
Luke 20: 4 was it from **h** or from men
Luke 20: 5 If we say, 'From **h**,' He will
Luke 21:11 sights and great signs from **h**
Luke 21:26 powers of **h** will be shaken
Luke 21:33 **H** and earth will pass away,
Luke 22:43 angel appeared to Him from **h**
Luke 24:51 them and carried up into **h**
John 1:32 descending from **h** like a dove
John 1:51 you shall see **h** open, and the
John 3:13 No one has ascended to **h** but
John 3:13 but He who came down from **h**
John 3:13 the Son of Man who is in **h**
John 3:27 has been given to him from **h**
John 3:31 who comes from **h** is above all
John 6:31 gave them bread from **h** to eat
John 6:32 not give you the bread from **h**
John 6:32 you the true bread from **h**
John 6:33 is He who comes down from **h**
John 6:38 For I have come down from **h**
John 6:41 bread which came down from **h**
John 6:42 I have come down from **h**'
John 6:50 bread which comes down from **h**
John 6:51 bread which came down from **h**
John 6:58 bread which came down from **h**

John 12:28 Then a voice came from **h**
John 17: 1 lifted up His eyes to **h**, and
Acts 1:10 toward **h** as He went up,
Acts 1:11 do you stand gazing up into **h**
Acts 1:11 was taken up from you into **h**
Acts 1:11 as you saw Him go into **h**
Acts 2: 2 there came a sound from **h**
Acts 2: 5 from every nation under **h**
Acts 2:19 will show wonders in **h** above
Acts 3:21 whom **h** must receive until the
Acts 4:12 is no other name under **h**
Acts 4:24 Lord, You are God, who made **h**
Acts 7:42 up to worship the host of **h**
Acts 7:49 **H** is My throne, and earth is
Acts 7:55 the Holy Spirit, gazed into **h**
Acts 9: 3 light shone around him from **h**
Acts 10:11 saw **h** opened and an object
Acts 10:16 was taken up into **h** again
Acts 11: 5 let down from **h** by four
Acts 11: 9 answered me again from **h**
Acts 11:10 were drawn up again into **h**
Acts 14:15 living God, who made the **h**
Acts 14:17 did good, gave us rain from **h**
Acts 17:24 in it, since He is Lord of **h**
Acts 22: 6 light from **h** shone around me
Acts 26:13 the road I saw a light from **h**
Rom 1:18 **h** against all ungodliness
Rom 10: 6 Who will ascend into **h**
1Co 8: 5 whether in **h** or on earth (as
1Co 15:47 second Man is the Lord from **h**
2Co 5: 2 habitation which is from **h**
2Co 12: 2 was caught up to the third **h**
Gal 1: 8 if we, or an angel from **h**
Eph 1:10 Christ, both which are in **h**
Eph 3:15 whom the whole family in **h**
Eph 6: 9 your own Master also is in **h**
Phil 2:10 should bow, of those in **h**
Phil 3:20 For our citizenship is in **h**
Col 1: 5 which is laid up for you in **h**
Col 1:16 were created that are in **h**
Col 1:20 on earth or things in **h**,
Col 1:23 to every creature under **h**
Col 4: 1 you also have a Master in **h**
1Th 1:10 and to wait for His Son from **h**
1Th 4:16 descend from **h** with a shout
2Th 1: 7 from **h** with His mighty angels
Heb 9:24 the true, but into **h** itself
Heb 10:34 for yourselves in **h**
Heb 12:23 who are registered in **h**, to
Heb 12:25 from Him who speaks from **h**
Heb 12:26 only the earth, but also **h**
Jas 5:12 either by **h** or by earth or
Jas 5:18 the **h** gave rain, and the earth
1Pe 1: 4 away, reserved in **h** for you
1Pe 1:12 the Holy Spirit sent from **h**
1Pe 3:22 who has gone into **h** and is at
2Pe 1:18 **h** when we were with Him on
1Jn 5: 7 three who bear witness in **h**
Rev 3:12 down out of **h** from My God
Rev 4: 1 a door standing open in **h**
Rev 4: 2 and behold, a throne set in **h**
Rev 5: 3 no one in **h** or on the earth
Rev 5:13 every creature which is in **h**
Rev 6:13 the stars of **h** fell to the
Rev 8: 1 there was silence in **h** for
Rev 8:10 And a great star fell from **h**
Rev 8:13 flying through the midst of **h**
Rev 9: 1 fallen from **h** to the earth
Rev 10: 1 angel coming down from **h**,
Rev 10: 4 a voice from **h** saying to me
Rev 10: 5 land lifted up his hand to **h**
Rev 10: 6 and ever, who created **h** and the
Rev 10: 8 from **h** spoke to me again and
Rev 11: 6 These have power to shut **h**
Rev 11:12 voice from **h** saying to them
Rev 11:12 they ascended to **h** in a cloud
Rev 11:13 and gave glory to the God of **h**
Rev 11:15 there were loud voices in **h**
Rev 11:19 temple of God was opened in **h**
Rev 12: 1 a great sign appeared in **h**
Rev 12: 3 And another sign appeared in **h**
Rev 12: 4 a third of the stars of **h**
Rev 12: 7 And war broke out in **h**
Rev 12: 8 for them in **h** any longer
Rev 12:10 a loud voice saying in **h**
Rev 13: 6 and those who dwell in **h**
Rev 13:13 **h** on the earth in the sight
Rev 14: 2 And I heard a voice from **h**
Rev 14: 6 flying in the midst of **h**,
Rev 14: 7 and worship Him who made **h**
Rev 14:13 a voice from **h** saying to me
Rev 14:17 of the temple which is in **h**
Rev 15: 1 Then I saw another sign in **h**
Rev 15: 5 the testimony in **h** was opened
Rev 16:11 of **h** because of their pains
Rev 16:17 came out of the temple of **h**
Rev 16:21 hail from **h** fell upon men
Rev 18: 1 angel coming down from **h**,
Rev 18: 4 another voice from **h** saying
Rev 18: 5 her sins have reached to **h**
Rev 18:20 Rejoice over her, O **h**, and you
Rev 19: 1 of a great multitude in **h**
Rev 19:11 Then I saw **h** opened, and
Rev 19:14 And the armies in **h**, clothed
Rev 19:17 that fly in the midst of **h**
Rev 20: 1 an angel coming down from **h**
Rev 20: 9 came down from God out of **h**
Rev 20:11 the earth and the **h** fled away
Rev 21: 1 And I saw a new **h** and a new
Rev 21: 1 a new earth, for the first **h**
Rev 21: 2 coming down out of **h** from God
Rev 21: 3 a loud voice from **h** saying
Rev 21:10 descending out of **h** from God

HEAVENLY (*see* HEAVEN)
Matt 6:14 your **h** Father will also
Matt 6:26 yet your **h** Father feeds them
Matt 6:32 For your **h** Father knows that
Matt 15:13 Every plant which My **h** Father
Matt 18:35 So My **h** Father also will do
Luke 2:13 of the **h** host praising God
Luke 11:13 how much more will your **h**
John 3:12 if I tell you **h** things
Acts 26:19 disobedient to the **h** vision
1Co 15:48 and as is the **h** Man, so also
1Co 15:48 so also are those who are **h**
1Co 15:49 bear the image of the **h** Man
Eph 1: 3 in the **h** places in Christ
Eph 1:20 right hand in the **h** places
Eph 2: 6 the **h** places in Christ Jesus
Eph 3:10 and powers in the **h** places
Eph 6:12 of wickedness in the **h** places
2Ti 4:18 preserve me for His **h** kingdom
Heb 3: 1 partakers of the **h** calling
Heb 6: 4 and have tasted the **h** gift
Heb 8: 5 and shadow of the **h** things
Heb 9:23 but the **h** things themselves
Heb 11:16 better, that is, a **h** country
Heb 12:22 God, the **h** Jerusalem, to an

HEAVEN'S (*see* HEAVEN)
Matt 19:12 for the kingdom of **h** sake

HEAVENS (*see* HEAVEN)
Gen 1: 1 beginning God created the **h**
Gen 1: 9 Let the waters under the **h** be
Gen 1:14 in the firmament of the **h** to
Gen 1:15 in the firmament of the **h** to
Gen 1:17 in the firmament of the **h** to
Gen 1:20 of the firmament of the **h**
Gen 2: 1 Thus the **h** and the earth, and
Gen 2: 4 This is the history of the **h**
Gen 2: 4 God made the earth and the **h**
Gen 11: 4 a tower whose top is in the **h**
Gen 19:24 from the LORD out of the **h**
Ex 9: 8 the **h** in the sight of Pharaoh
Ex 20:11 six days the LORD made the **h**
Ex 24:10 the very **h** in its clarity
Ex 31:17 six days the LORD made the **h**
Lev 26:19 I will make your **h** like iron
Deut 10:14 the highest **h** belong to the
Deut 11:17 and He shut up the **h** so that
Deut 11:21 days of the **h** above the earth
Deut 28:12 you His good treasure, the **h**
Deut 28:23 your **h** which are over your
Deut 32: 1 Give ear, O **h**, and I will
Deut 33:26 Who rides the **h** to help you
Deut 33:28 His **H** shall also drop dew
Judg 5: 4 the **h** poured, the clouds also
Judg 5:20 They fought from the **h**
2Sa 22:10 He bowed the **h** also, and came
1Ki 8:27 and the heaven of **h** cannot
1Ki 8:35 When the **h** are shut up and
1Ch 16:26 but the LORD made the **h**
1Ch 16:31 Let the **h** rejoice, and let the
1Ch 27:23 like the stars of the **h**
2Ch 2: 6 and the heaven of **h** cannot
2Ch 6:18 and the heaven of **h** cannot
Ezra 9: 6 guilt has grown up to the **h**
Neh 1: 9 to the farthest part of the **h**
Neh 9: 6 made heaven, the heaven of **h**
Job 9: 8 He alone spreads out the **h**
Job 14:12 Till the **h** are no more, they
Job 15:15 the **h** are not pure in His
Job 20: 6 mounts up to the **h**, and his
Job 20:27 The **h** will reveal his
Job 26:13 His Spirit He adorned the **h**
Job 28:24 and sees under the whole **h**
Job 35: 5 Look to the **h**, and see
Job 38:33 know the ordinances of the **h**
Ps 2: 4 who sits in the **h** shall laugh
Ps 8: 1 set Your glory above the **h**
Ps 8: 3 When I consider Your **h**, the
Ps 18: 9 He bowed the **h** also, and came
Ps 18:13 LORD also thundered in the **h**
Ps 19: 1 The **h** declare the glory of
Ps 33: 6 of the LORD the **h** were made
Ps 36: 5 mercy, O LORD, is in the **h**
Ps 50: 4 call to the **h** from above, And
Ps 50: 6 Let the **h** declare His
Ps 57: 5 exalted, O God, above the **h**
Ps 57:10 Your mercy reaches unto the **h**
Ps 57:11 exalted, O God, above the **h**
Ps 68: 8 The **h** also dropped rain at
Ps 68:33 who rides on the heaven of **h**
Ps 73: 9 set their mouth against the **h**
Ps 78:26 an east wind to blow in the **h**
Ps 79: 2 food for the birds of the **h**
Ps 89: 2 shall establish in the very **h**
Ps 89: 5 And the **h** will praise Your
Ps 89: 6 For who in the **h** can be
Ps 89:11 The **h** are Yours, the earth
Ps 96: 5 But the LORD made the **h**
Ps 96:11 Let the **h** rejoice, and let the
Ps 97: 6 The **h** declare His
Ps 102:25 the **h** are the work of Your
Ps 103:11 For as the **h** are high above
Ps 104: 2 out the **h** like a curtain
Ps 104:12 the **h** have their habitation
Ps 107:26 They mount up to the **h**, They
Ps 108: 4 mercy is great above the **h**
Ps 108: 5 exalted, O God, above the **h**
Ps 113: 4 And His glory above the **h**
Ps 113: 6 The things that are in the **h**
Ps 115:16 The heaven, even the **h**, are
Ps 123: 1 O You who dwell in the **h**
Ps 136: 5 Him who by wisdom made the **h**
Ps 144: 5 Bow down Your **h**, O LORD, and
Ps 147: 8 Who covers the **h** with clouds
Ps 148: 1 Praise the LORD from the **h**
Ps 148: 4 Praise Him, you **h** of **h**
Ps 148: 4 And you waters above the **h**
Prov 3:19 He established the **h**
Prov 8:27 When He prepared the **h**, I was
Prov 25: 3 As the **h** for height and the
Is 1: 2 Hear, O **h**, and give ear, O
Is 13:13 Therefore I will shake the **h**
Is 34: 4 the **h** shall be rolled up like
Is 40:22 out the **h** like a curtain, and
Is 42: 5 the LORD, Who created the **h**
Is 44:23 Sing, O **h**, for the LORD has
Is 44:24 stretches out the **h** all alone
Is 45: 8 Rain down, you **h**, from above,
Is 45:12 that stretched out the **h**, and
Is 45:18 the LORD, Who created the **h**
Is 48:13 hand has stretched out the **h**
Is 49:13 Sing, O **h**!
Is 50: 3 I clothe the **h** with blackness
Is 51: 6 Lift up your eyes to the **h**
Is 51: 6 For the **h** will vanish away
Is 51:13 Who stretched out the **h** and
Is 51:16 hand, that I may plant the **h**
Is 55: 9 For as the **h** are higher than
Is 64: 1 Oh, that You would rend the **h**
Is 65:17 For behold, I create new **h**
Is 66:22 For as the new **h** and the new
Jer 2:12 Be astonished, O **h**, at this,
Jer 4:23 and the **h**, they had no light
Jer 4:25 the birds of the **h** had fled
Jer 4:28 the **h** above be black, because
Jer 8: 7 Even the stork in the **h** knows
Jer 9:10 Both the birds of the **h** and
Jer 10:11 gods that have not made the **h**
Jer 10:11 earth and from under these **h**
Jer 10:12 out the **h** at His discretion
Jer 10:13 multitude of waters in the **h**
Jer 14:22 Or can the **h** give showers
Jer 15: 3 to drag, the birds of the **h**
Jer 32:17 Behold, You have made the **h**
Jer 51:16 multitude of waters in the **h**
Jer 51:48 Then the **h** and the earth and
Lam 3:66 from under the **h** of the LORD

Lam 4:19 than the eagles of the **h**
Ezek 1: 1 that the **h** were opened and I
Ezek 29: 5 and to the birds of the **h**
Ezek 31: 6 All the birds of the **h** made
Ezek 31:13 remain all the birds of the **h**
Ezek 32: 4 on you all the birds of the **h**
Ezek 32: 7 light, I will cover the **h**
Ezek 32: 8 the bright lights of the **h** I
Ezek 38:20 the sea, the birds of the **h**
Dan 4:11 its height reached to the **h**
Dan 4:12 the birds of the **h** dwelt in
Dan 4:20 whose height reached to the **h**
Dan 4:22 has grown and reaches to the **h**
Hos 2:21 I will answer the **h**, and they
Joel 2:10 before them, the **h** tremble
Joel 2:30 I will show wonders in the **h**
Joel 3:16 the **h** and earth will shake
Hab 3: 3 Selah His glory covered the **h**
Zeph 1: 3 consume the birds of the **h**
Hag 1:10 Therefore the **h** above you
Zech 8:12 the **h** shall give their dew
Zech 12: 1 LORD, who stretches out the **h**
Matt 3:16 the **h** were opened to Him, and
Matt 24:29 of the **h** will be shaken
Mark 1:10 water, He saw the **h** parting
Luke 12:33 a treasure in the **h** that does
Acts 2:34 did not ascend into the **h**
Acts 7:56 I see the **h** opened and the Son
2Co 5: 1 with hands, eternal in the **h**
Eph 4:10 ascended far above all the **h**
Heb 1:10 the **h** are the work of Your
Heb 4:14 who has passed through the **h**
Heb 7:26 has become higher than the **h**
Heb 8: 1 of the Majesty in the **h**,
Heb 9:23 the **h** should be purified with
2Pe 3: 5 word of God the **h** were of old
2Pe 3: 7 But the **h** and the earth which
2Pe 3:10 in which the **h** will pass away
2Pe 3:12 because of which the **h** will
2Pe 3:13 His promise, look for new **h**
Rev 12:12 Therefore rejoice, O **h**, and

HEAVES (*see* HEAVE)
Nah 1: 5 the earth **h** at His presence,

HEAVIER (*see* HEAVY)
Job 6: 3 For then it would be **h** than
Prov 27: 3 wrath is **h** than both of them

HEAVILY (*see* HEAVY)
Ps 35:14 I bowed down **h**, as one who
Is 9: 1 more **h** oppressed her, by the
Is 46: 1 Your carriages were **h** loaded
Is 47: 6 you laid your yoke very **h**

HEAVINESS (*see* HEAVY)
Ps 69:20 my heart, And I am full of **h**
Ps 119:28 My soul melts from **h**
Is 29: 2 there shall be **h** and sorrow,
Is 61: 3 of praise for the spirit of **h**

HEAVY (*see* HEAVIER, HEAVILY, HEAVINESS)
Ex 9:18 very **h** hail to rain down,
Ex 9:24 so very **h** that there was none
Ex 17:12 But Moses' hands became **h**
Num 11:14 the burden is too **h** for me
Deut 25:13 bag differing weights, a **h**
1Sa 4:18 for the man was old and **h**
1Sa 5: 6 was **h** on the people of Ashdod
1Sa 5:11 hand of God was very **h** there
2Sa 14:26 it because it was **h** on him
1Ki 12: 4 Your father made our yoke **h**
1Ki 12: 4 his **h** yoke which he put on us
1Ki 12:10 Your father made our yoke **h**
1Ki 12:11 father laid a **h** yoke on you
1Ki 12:14 My father made your yoke **h**
1Ki 18:45 wind, and there was a **h** rain
2Ch 10: 4 Your father made our yoke **h**
2Ch 10: 4 his **h** yoke which he put on us
2Ch 10:10 Your father made our yoke **h**
2Ch 10:11 my father put a **h** yoke on you
2Ch 10:14 My father made your yoke **h**
Ezra 5: 8 is being built with **h** stones
Ezra 6: 4 with three rows of **h** stones
Ezra 10: 9 matter and because of **h** rain
Ezra 10:13 it is the season for **h** rain
Neh 5:18 bondage was **h** on this people
Job 15:27 and made his waist **h** with fat
Job 33: 7 nor will my hand be **h** on you
Job 37: 6 the **h** rain of His strength
Ps 32: 4 night Your hand was **h** upon me
Ps 38: 4 Like a **h** burden they are too
Ps 38: 4 burden they are too **h** for me
Ps 88: 7 Your wrath lies **h** upon me
Prov 25:20 who sings songs to a **h** heart
Prov 27: 3 A stone is **h** and sand is
Is 6:10 people dull, and their ears **h**
Is 24:20 shall be **h** upon it, and it
Is 30:27 His anger, and His burden is **h**
Is 58: 6 to undo the **h** burdens, to
Is 59: 1 nor His ear **h**, that it cannot
Lam 3: 7 he has made my chain **h**
Zech 12: 3 very **h** stone for all peoples
Matt 11:28 are **h** laden, and I will give
Matt 23: 4 For they bind **h** burdens, hard
Matt 26:43 again, for their eyes were **h**
Mark 14:40 again, for their eyes were **h**
Luke 9:32 with him were **h** with sleep

HEBER (*see* EBER, HEBERITES, HEBER'S)
Gen 46:17 And the sons of Beriah were **H**
Num 26:45 of **H**, the family of the
Judg 4:11 Now **H** the Kenite, of the
Judg 4:17 the wife of **H** the Kenite
Judg 4:17 and the house of **H** the Kenite
Judg 5:24 the wife of **H** the Kenite
1Ch 4:18 **H** the father of Sochoh, and
1Ch 5:13 Jorai, Jachan, Zia, and **H**
1Ch 7:31 The sons of Beriah were **H**
1Ch 7:32 And **H** begot Japhlet, Shomer,
1Ch 8:17 Zebadiah, Meshullam, Hizki, **H**

HEBERITES (*see* HEBER)
Num 26:45 of Heber, the family of the **H**

HEBER'S (*see* HEBER)
Judg 4:21 **H** wife, took a tent peg and

HEBREW (*see* HEBREWS)
Gen 14:13 came and told Abram the **H**, for
Gen 39:14 in to us a **H** to mock us
Gen 39:17 The **H** servant whom you
Gen 41:12 a young **H** man with us there
Ex 1:15 Egypt spoke to the **H** midwives
Ex 1:16 of a midwife for the **H** women
Ex 1:19 Because the **H** women are not
Ex 2: 7 for you from the **H** women,
Ex 2:11 saw an Egyptian beating a **H**
Ex 2:13 two **H** men were fighting, and
Ex 21: 2 If you buy a **H** servant, he
Deut 15:12 a **H** man, or a **H** woman,
2Ki 18:26 us in **H** in the hearing of the
2Ki 18:28 out with a loud voice in **H**
2Ch 32:18 out with a loud voice in **H** to
Is 36:11 us in **H** in the hearing of the
Is 36:13 out with a loud voice in **H**
Jer 34: 9 a **H** man or woman
Jer 34:14 man set free his **H** brother
Jon 1: 9 I am a **H**
Luke 23:38 letters of Greek, Latin, and **H**
John 5: 2 a pool, which is called in **H**
John 19:13 called The Pavement, but in **H**
John 19:17 a Skull, which is called in **H**
John 19:20 and it was written in **H**, Greek
Acts 21:40 to them in the **H** language
Acts 22: 2 to them in the **H** language
Acts 26:14 and saying in the **H** language
Phil 3: 5 Benjamin, a **H** of the Hebrews
Rev 9:11 whose name in **H** is Abaddon
Rev 16:16 to the place called in **H**,

HEBREWS (*see* HEBREW)
Gen 40:15 away from the land of the **H**
Gen 43:32 could not eat food with the **H**
Ex 2: 6 is one of the **H**' children
Ex 3:18 God of the **H** has met with us
Ex 5: 3 The God of the **H** has met with
Ex 7:16 of the **H** has sent me to you
Ex 9: 1 says the LORD God of the **H**
Ex 9:13 says the LORD God of the **H**
Ex 10: 3 says the LORD God of the **H**
1Sa 4: 6 in the camp of the **H** mean
1Sa 4: 9 not become servants of the **H**
1Sa 13: 3 Let the **H** hear
1Sa 13: 7 some of the **H** crossed over
1Sa 13:19 Lest the **H** make swords or
1Sa 14:11 the **H** are coming out of the
1Sa 14:21 Moreover the **H** who were with
1Sa 29: 3 What are these **H** doing here
Acts 6: 1 the **H** by the Hellenists,
2Co 11:22 Are they **H**?
Phil 3: 5 Benjamin, a Hebrew of the **H**

HEBRON (*see* HEBRONITES, KIRJATH ARBA)
Gen 13:18 of Mamre, which are in **H**, and
Gen 23: 2 **H**) in the land of Canaan, and
Gen 23:19 is, **H**) in the land of Canaan
Gen 35:27 **H**), where Abraham and Isaac
Gen 37:14 him out of the Valley of **H**
Ex 6:18 Kohath were Amram, Izhar, **H**
Num 3:19 Amram, Izehar, **H**, and Uzziel
Num 13:22 the South and came to **H**
Num 13:22 (Now **H** was built seven years
Josh 10: 3 sent to Hoham king of **H**,
Josh 10: 5 of Jerusalem, the king of **H**
Josh 10:23 of Jerusalem, the king of **H**
Josh 10:36 and all Israel with him, to **H**
Josh 10:39 as he had done to **H**, so he
Josh 11:21 from **H**, from Debir, from Anab
Josh 12:10 the king of **H**, one
Josh 14:13 gave **H** to Caleb the son of
Josh 14:14 **H** therefore became the
Josh 14:15 the name of **H** formerly was
Josh 15:13 which is **H** (Arba was the
Josh 15:54 Kirjath Arba (which is **H**)
Josh 20: 7 Kirjath Arba (which is **H**) in
Josh 21:11 father of Anak), which is **H**
Josh 21:13 **H** with its common-land (a
Judg 1:10 the Canaanites who dwelt in **H**
Judg 1:10 (Now the name of **H** was
Judg 1:20 And they gave **H** to Caleb, as
Judg 16: 3 top of the hill that faces **H**
1Sa 30:31 those who were in **H**, and to
2Sa 2: 1 And He said, "To **H**."
2Sa 2: 3 they dwelt in the cities of **H**
2Sa 2:11 **H** over the house of Judah was
2Sa 2:32 and they came to **H** at daybreak
2Sa 3: 2 Sons were born to David in **H**
2Sa 3: 5 These were born to David in **H**
2Sa 3:19 in **H** all that seemed good to
2Sa 3:20 with him came to David at **H**
2Sa 3:22 Abner was not with David in **H**
2Sa 3:27 when Abner had returned to **H**
2Sa 3:32 So they buried Abner in **H**
2Sa 4: 1 that Abner had died in **H**, he
2Sa 4: 8 of Ishbosheth to David at **H**
2Sa 4:12 hanged them by the pool in **H**
2Sa 4:12 it in the tomb of Abner in **H**
2Sa 5: 1 of Israel came to David at **H**
2Sa 5: 3 Israel came to the king at **H**
2Sa 5: 3 them at **H** before the LORD
2Sa 5: 5 In **H** he reigned over Judah
2Sa 5:13 after he had come from **H**
2Sa 15: 7 Please, let me go to **H** and pay
2Sa 15: 9 So he arose and went to **H**
2Sa 15:10 say, Absalom reigns in **H**
1Ki 2:11 seven years he reigned in **H**
1Ch 2:42 of Mareshah the father of **H**
1Ch 2:43 The sons of **H** were Korah,
1Ch 3: 1 who were born to him in **H**
1Ch 3: 4 six were born to him in **H**
1Ch 6: 2 Kohath were Amram, Izhar, **H**
1Ch 6:18 Kohath were Amram, Izhar, **H**
1Ch 6:55 They gave them **H** in the land
1Ch 6:57 of the cities of refuge, **H**
1Ch 11: 1 came together to David at **H**
1Ch 11: 3 Israel came to the king at **H**
1Ch 11: 3 them at **H** before the LORD
1Ch 12:23 came to David at **H** to turn
1Ch 12:38 came to **H** with a loyal heart,
1Ch 15: 9 of the sons of **H**, Eliel the
1Ch 23:12 Amram, Izhar, **H**, and Uzziel
1Ch 23:19 Of the sons of **H**, Jeriah was
1Ch 24:23 Of the sons of **H**, Jeriah was
1Ch 29:27 seven years he reigned in **H**
2Ch 11:10 Zorah, Aijalon, and **H**, which

HEBRONITES (*see* HEBRON)
Num 3:27 the family of the **H**, and the
Num 26:58 Libnites, the family of the **H**
1Ch 26:23 the Izharites, the **H**, and the
1Ch 26:30 Of the **H**, Hashabiah and his
1Ch 26:31 Among the **H**, Jerijah was head
1Ch 26:31 Jerijah was head of the **H**

HEDGE (*see* HEDGED, HEDGES)
Job 1:10 You not made a **h** around him
Prov 15:19 man is like a **h** of thorns
Is 5: 5 I will take away its **h**, and it
Hos 2: 6 I will **h** up your way with
Mic 7: 4 is sharper than a thorn **h**
Matt 21:33 and set a **h** around it, dug a
Mark 12: 1 and set a **h** around it, dug a

HEDGED (*see* HEDGE)
Job 3:23 hidden, and whom God has **h** in
Ps 139: 5 You have **h** me behind and
Lam 3: 7 He has **h** me in so that I

HEDGES (*see* HEDGE)
Ps 80:12 have You broken down her **h**
Ps 89:40 have broken down all his **h**
Nah 3:17 camp in the **h** on a cold day
Luke 14:23 Go out into the highways and **h**

HEED (*see* HEEDED, HEEDING, HEEDS)
Gen 34:17 But if you will not **h** us and
Gen 39:10 by day, that he did not **h** her
Ex 3:18 Then they will **h** your voice
Ex 4: 8 you, nor **h** the message of the
Ex 6: 9 but they would not **h** Moses
Ex 6:12 How then shall Pharaoh **h** me
Ex 6:30 and how shall Pharaoh **h** me
Ex 7: 4 But Pharaoh will not **h** you
Ex 7:13 hard, and he did not **h** them
Ex 7:22 hard, and he did not **h** them
Ex 8:15 his heart and did not **h** them
Ex 8:19 hard, and he did not **h** them
Ex 9:12 and he did not **h** them, just as
Ex 10:28 Take **h** to yourself and see my
Ex 11: 9 Pharaoh will not **h** you, so
Ex 15:26 If you diligently **h** the voice
Ex 16:20 they did not **h** Moses
Ex 19:12 Take **h** to yourselves that
Ex 34:12 Take **h** to yourself, lest you
Num 23:12 Must I not take **h** to speak
Deut 4: 9 Only take **h** to yourself, and
Deut 4:15 Take careful **h** to yourselves,
Deut 4:19 And take **h**, lest you lift your
Deut 4:23 Take **h** to yourselves, lest
Deut 11:16 Take **h** to yourselves, lest
Deut 12:13 Take **h** to yourself that you
Deut 12:19 Take **h** to yourself that you
Deut 12:30 take **h** to yourself that you
Deut 17:12 will not **h** the priest who
Deut 21:18 him, will not **h** them,
Deut 24: 8 Take **h** in an outbreak of
Deut 27: 9 Take **h** and listen, O Israel
Deut 28:13 if you **h** the commandments of
Josh 1:17 all things, so we will **h** you
Josh 1:18 does not **h** your words, in all
Josh 22: 5 But take diligent **h** to do the
Josh 23:11 take diligent **h** to yourselves
Judg 11:17 the king of Edom would not **h**
Judg 11:28 **h** the words which Jephthah
Judg 19:25 But the men would not **h** him
1Sa 2:25 **h** the voice of their father
1Sa 8: 7 **H** the voice of the people in
1Sa 8: 9 Now therefore, **h** their voice
1Sa 8:22 **H** their voice, and make them a
1Sa 15: 1 **h** the voice of the words of
1Sa 15:22 to **h** than the fat of rams
1Sa 28:22 **h** also the voice of your
1Sa 30:24 For who will **h** you in this
2Sa 12:18 and he would not **h** our voice
2Sa 13:14 he would not **h** her voice
1Ki 2: 4 your sons take **h** to their way
1Ki 8:25 your sons take **h** to their way
1Ki 11:38 if you **h** all that I command
1Ki 22:28 Take **h**, all you people
2Ki 10:31 But Jehu took no **h** to walk in
2Ki 14:11 But Amaziah would not **h**
2Ch 6:16 your sons take **h** to their way
2Ch 18:27 Take **h**, all you people
2Ch 19: 6 Take **h** to what you are doing,
2Ch 25:20 But Amaziah would not **h**, for
2Ch 35:22 did not **h** the words of Necho
Ezra 4:22 Take **h** now that you do not
Neh 9:16 did not **h** Your commandments
Neh 9:29 did not **h** Your commandments,
Job 13: 6 **h** the pleadings of my lips
Job 36:21 Take **h**, do not turn to
Job 39: 7 he does not **h** the shouts of
Ps 5: 2 Give **h** to the voice of my cry
Ps 58: 5 Which will not **h** the voice of
Ps 81:11 people would not **h** My voice
Ps 106:25 did not **h** the voice of the
Ps 119: 9 By taking **h** according to Your
Prov 17: 4 gives **h** to false lips
Is 7: 4 Take **h**, and be quiet
Is 34: 1 and **h**, you people!
Is 49: 1 coastlands, to Me, and take **h**
Jer 6:10 and they cannot give **h**
Jer 9: 4 Everyone take **h** to his
Jer 17:21 Take **h** to yourselves, and bear
Jer 17:24 be, if you diligently **h** Me
Jer 17:27 But if you will not **h** Me to
Jer 18:18 let us not give **h** to any of
Jer 18:19 Give **h** to me, O LORD, and
Jer 26: 5 to **h** the words of My servants
Jer 29:19 neither would you **h**, says the
Jer 36:31 but they did not **h**
Jer 37: 2 **h** to the words of the LORD
Hos 5: 1 Take **h**, O house of Israel
Zech 1: 4 they did not hear nor **h** Me
Zech 7:11 But they refused to **h**,
Mal 2:15 take **h** to your spirit, and let
Mal 2:16 take **h** to your spirit, that
Matt 6: 1 Take **h** that you do not do
Matt 16: 6 Take **h** and beware of the
Matt 18:10 Take **h** that you do not
Matt 24: 4 Take **h** that no one deceives
Mark 4:24 them, "Take **h** what you hear
Mark 8:15 Take **h**, beware of the leaven
Mark 13: 5 Take **h** that no one deceives
Mark 13:23 But take **h**
Mark 13:33 Take **h**, watch and pray
Luke 8:18 Therefore take **h** how you hear
Luke 11:35 Therefore take **h** that the
Luke 12:15 Take **h** and beware of
Luke 17: 3 Take **h** to yourselves
Luke 21: 8 Take **h** that you not be
Luke 21:34 But take **h** to yourselves,
Acts 2:14 known to you, and **h** my words
Acts 5:35 take **h** to yourselves what you
Acts 8:10 to whom they all gave **h**, from
Acts 16:14 Lord opened her heart to **h**
Acts 20:28 take **h** to yourselves and to
1Co 3:10 take **h** how he builds on it
1Co 10:12 he stands take **h** lest he fall
Col 4:17 Take **h** to the ministry which
1Ti 1: 4 nor give **h** to fables and
1Ti 4: 1 giving **h** to deceiving spirits
1Ti 4:16 Take **h** to yourself and to the
Tit 1:14 not giving **h** to Jewish fables
Heb 2: 1 must give the more earnest **h**
2Pe 1:19 which you do well to **h** as a

HEEDED (*see* HEED)
Gen 3:17 Because you have **h** the voice
Gen 16: 2 Abram **h** the voice of Sarai
Gen 34:24 the gate of his city **h** Hamor
Ex 6:12 of Israel have not **h** me
Ex 18:24 So Moses **h** the voice of his
Num 14:22 times, and have not **h** My voice
Deut 34: 9 the children of Israel **h** him
Josh 1:17 Just as we **h** Moses in all
Josh 10:14 that the LORD **h** the voice of
Judg 2:20 and has not **h** My voice,
1Sa 12: 1 Indeed I have **h** your voice in
1Sa 19: 6 So Saul **h** the voice of
1Sa 25:35 See, I have **h** your voice and
1Sa 28:21 **h** the words which you spoke
1Sa 28:23 and he **h** their voice
2Sa 21:14 after that God **h** the prayer
2Sa 24:25 So the LORD **h** the prayers for
1Ki 15:20 So Ben-Hadad **h** King Asa, and
2Ki 16: 9 So the king of Assyria **h** him
1Ch 5:20 He **h** their prayer, because
2Ch 16: 4 So Ben-Hadad **h** King Asa, and
2Ch 25:16 this and have not **h** my counsel
Neh 9:34 nor **h** Your commandments and
Is 48:18 Oh, that you had **h** My
Jer 6:19 they have not **h** My words, nor
Jer 26: 5 them (but you have not **h**)
Jer 29:19 they have not **h** My words,
Dan 9: 6 Neither have we **h** Your
Acts 8: 6 multitudes with one accord **h**
Acts 8:11 they **h** him because he had

HEEDING (*see* HEED)
Ps 103:20 word, **H** the voice of His word

HEEDS (*see* HEED)
Prov 12:15 but he who **h** counsel is wise
Prov 13: 1 A wise son **h** his father's
Prov 15:32 but he who **h** reproof gets
Prov 16:20 He who **h** the word wisely will

HEEL (*see* HEELS)
Gen 3:15 and you shall bruise His **h**
Gen 25:26 hand took hold of Esau's **h**
Job 18: 9 The net takes him by the **h**
Ps 41: 9 lifted up his **h** against me
Hos 12: 3 brother by the **h** in the womb
John 13:18 lifted up his **h** against Me

HEELS (*see* HEEL)
Gen 49:17 that bites the horse's **h** so
1Sa 25:12 young men turned on their **h**
Ps 49: 5 iniquity at my **h** surrounds me
Jer 13:22 uncovered, your **h** made bare
Lam 5: 5 They pursue at our **h**
Dan 11:43 shall follow at his **h**

HEGAI
Esth 2: 3 of **H** the king's eunuch,
Esth 2: 8 under the custody of **H**, that
Esth 2: 8 into the care of **H** the
Esth 2:15 but what **H** the king's eunuch

HEIFER (*see* HEIFER'S)
Gen 15: 9 Bring Me a three-year-old **h**
Num 19: 2 you a red **h** without blemish
Num 19: 5 Then the **h** shall be burned
Num 19: 6 of the fire burning the **h**
Num 19: 9 gather up the ashes of the **h**
Num 19:10 the **h** shall wash his clothes
Num 19:17 some of the ashes of the **h**
Deut 21: 3 a **h** which has not been worked
Deut 21: 4 the **h** down to a valley with
Deut 21: 6 **h** whose neck was broken in
Judg 14:18 you had not plowed with my **h**
1Sa 16: 2 Take a **h** with you, and say, 'I
Is 15: 5 Zoar, like a three-year-old **h**
Jer 46:20 Egypt is like a very pretty **h**
Jer 48:34 like a three-year-old **h**
Jer 50:11 fat like a **h** threshing grain
Hos 10:11 Ephraim is a trained **h** that
Heb 9:13 and goats and the ashes of a **h**

HEIFER'S (*see* HEIFER)
Deut 21: 4 they shall break the **h** neck

HEIGHT (*see* HEIGHTS)
Gen 6:15 and its **h** thirty cubits
Ex 25:10 and a cubit and a half its **h**
Ex 25:23 and a cubit and a half its **h**
Ex 27: 1 its **h** shall be three cubits
Ex 27:18 the **h** five cubits, woven of
Ex 30: 2 and two cubits shall be its **h**
Ex 37: 1 and a cubit and a half its **h**
Ex 37:10 and a cubit and a half its **h**
Ex 37:25 and two cubits was its **h**
Ex 38: 1 and its **h** was three cubits
Ex 38:18 the **h** along its width was
Num 23: 3 So he went to a desolate **h**
1Sa 16: 7 or at the **h** of his stature
1Sa 17: 4 whose **h** was six cubits and a
1Ki 6: 2 and its **h** thirty cubits
1Ki 6:26 The **h** of one cherub was ten
1Ki 7: 2 its **h** thirty cubits, with
1Ki 7:16 The **h** of one capital was five
1Ki 7:16 the **h** of the other capital
1Ki 7:23 Its **h** was five cubits, and a
1Ki 7:27 width, and three cubits its **h**
1Ki 7:32 The **h** of a wheel was one and a
1Ki 7:35 at the **h** of half a cubit, it
2Ki 19:23 up to the **h** of the mountains
2Ki 25:17 The **h** of one pillar was
2Ki 25:17 The **h** of the capital was
1Ch 11:23 an Egyptian, a man of great **h**
2Ch 3: 4 and the **h** was one hundred and
2Ch 4: 1 width, and ten cubits its **h**
2Ch 4: 2 Its **h** was five cubits, and a
2Ch 33:14 raised it to a very great **h**
Ezra 6: 3 its **h** sixty cubits and its
Neh 4: 6 together up to half its **h**
Job 22:12 Is not God in the **h** of heaven
Ps 102:19 from the **h** of His sanctuary
Prov 25: 3 As the heavens for **h** and the
Eccl 12: 5 when they are afraid of **h**
Is 7:11 the depth or in the **h** above
Is 37:24 up to the **h** of the mountains
Is 37:24 I will enter its farthest **h**
Jer 31:12 come and sing in the **h** of Zion
Jer 49:16 Who hold the **h** of the hill
Jer 51:53 fortify the **h** of her strength
Jer 52:21 the **h** of one pillar was
Jer 52:22 the **h** of one capital was five
Ezek 13:18 of every **h** to hunt souls
Ezek 17:23 On the mountain **h** of Israel I
Ezek 19:11 was seen in her **h** amid the
Ezek 20:40 on the mountain **h** of Israel
Ezek 31: 4 underground waters gave it **h**
Ezek 31: 5 Therefore its **h** was exalted
Ezek 31:10 you have increased in **h**, and
Ezek 31:10 heart was lifted up in its **h**
Ezek 31:14 exalt themselves for their **h**

Ezek 40: 5 and the **h**, one rod
Ezek 43:13 This is the **h** of the altar
Dan 3: 1 whose **h** was sixty cubits and
Dan 4:10 the earth, and its **h** was great
Dan 4:11 its **h** reached to the heavens,
Dan 4:20 whose **h** reached to the
Amos 2: 9 whose **h** was like the **h**
Rom 8:39 nor **h** nor depth, nor any
Eph 3:18 and length and depth and **h**
Rev 21:16 breadth, and **h** are equal

HEIGHTS (*see* HEIGHT)
Num 21:28 lords of the **h** of the Arnon
Deut 32:13 ride in the **h** of the earth
Josh 11: 2 in the **h** of Dor on the west,
Josh 12:23 king of Dor in the **h** of Dor
Judg 5:18 on the **h** of the battlefield
Ps 42: 6 from the **h** of Hermon, From
Ps 78:69 His sanctuary like the **h**,
Ps 95: 4 The **h** of the hills are His
Ps 148: 1 Praise Him in the **h**
Is 14:14 above the **h** of the clouds
Is 41:18 open rivers in desolate **h**
Is 49: 9 shall be on all desolate **h**
Jer 3: 2 your eyes to the desolate **h**
Jer 3:21 was heard on the desolate **h**
Jer 4:11 **h** blows in the wilderness
Jer 7:29 lamentation on the desolate **h**
Jer 12:12 desolate **h** in the wilderness
Jer 14: 6 stood in the desolate **h**
Ezek 36: 2 The ancient **h** have become our

HEIR (*see* HEIRS)
Gen 15: 2 the **h** of my house is Eliezer
Gen 15: 3 one born in my house is my **h**
Gen 15: 4 This one shall not be your **h**
Gen 15: 4 your own body shall be your **h**
Gen 21:10 shall not be **h** with my son
Gen 38: 8 raise up an **h** to your brother
Gen 38: 9 that the **h** would not be his
Gen 38: 9 give an **h** to his brother
2Sa 14: 7 and we will destroy the **h** also
Is 65: 9 and from Judah an **h** of My
Jer 49: 1 Has he no **h**?
Mic 1:15 I will yet bring an **h** to you
Matt 21:38 themselves, 'This is the **h**
Mark 12: 7 themselves, 'This is the **h**
Luke 20:14 saying, 'This is the **h**
Rom 4:13 that he would be the **h** of the
Gal 4: 1 Now I say that the **h**, as long
Gal 4: 7 son, then an **h** of God through
Gal 4:30 not be **h** with the son of the
Heb 1: 2 has appointed **h** of all things
Heb 11: 7 became **h** of the righteousness

HEIRS (*see* HEIR)
2Ki 11: 1 and destroyed all the royal **h**
2Ch 22:10 royal **h** of the house of Judah
Rom 4:14 who are of the law are **h**,
Rom 8:17 if children, then **h**—**h** of God
Rom 8:17 and joint **h** with Christ, if
Gal 3:29 **h** according to the promise
Eph 3: 6 Gentiles should be fellow **h**
Tit 3: 7 **h** according to the hope of
Heb 6:17 **h** of promise the immutability
Heb 11: 9 the **h** with him of the same
Jas 2: 5 **h** of the kingdom which He
1Pe 3: 7 as being **h** together of the

HELAH
1Ch 4: 5 of Tekoa had two wives, **H**
1Ch 4: 7 The sons of **H** were Zereth

HELAM
2Sa 10:16 the River, and they came to **H**
2Sa 10:17 over the Jordan, and came to **H**

HELBAH
Judg 1:31 Sidon, or of Ahlab, Achzib, **H**

HELBON
Ezek 27:18 items, with the wine of **H**

HELD (*see* HOLD)
Gen 34: 5 so Jacob **h** his peace until
Ex 17:11 when Moses **h** up his hand,
Ex 36:12 the loops **h** one curtain to
Lev 10: 3 So Aaron **h** his peace
Deut 4: 4 But you who **h** fast to the
Judg 7:20 they **h** the torches in their
Judg 16:26 the lad who **h** him by the hand
Ruth 3:15 And when she **h** it, he
1Sa 10:27 But he **h** his peace
1Sa 25:26 since the LORD has **h** you back
2Sa 6:22 by them I will be **h** in honor
2Sa 18:16 For Joab **h** back the people
1Ki 8:65 that time Solomon **h** a feast
2Ki 18: 6 For he **h** fast to the LORD
2Ki 18:36 But the people **h** their peace
2Ki 23:22 been **h** since the days of the
2Ki 23:23 was **h** before the LORD in
2Ch 7: 9 day they **h** a sacred assembly
Neh 4:16 the other half **h** the spears
Neh 4:17 and with the other **h** a weapon
Neh 4:21 half of the men **h** the spears
Esth 5: 2 the king **h** out to Esther the
Esth 7: 4 I would have **h** my tongue
Esth 8: 4 the king **h** out the golden
Job 23:11 My foot has **h** fast to His
Job 36: 8 **h** in the cords of affliction,
Ps 18:35 Your right hand has **h** me up
Ps 39: 2 I **h** my peace even from good
Ps 89: 7 to be **h** in reverence by all
Song 3: 4 I **h** him and would not let him
Song 7: 5 the king is **h** captive by its
Is 36:21 But they **h** their peace and
Is 42:14 I have **h** My peace a long time
Is 45: 1 whose right hand I have **h**
Is 57:11 Is it not because I have **h** My
Jer 50:33 them captive have **h** them fast
Ezek 23:32 to scorn and **h** in derision
Ezek 31:15 the great waters were **h** back
Dan 12: 7 when he **h** up his right hand
Hos 10: 2 now they are **h** guilty
Hos 13:16 Samaria is **h** guilty, for she
Matt 28: 9 came and **h** Him by the feet and
Mark 6:19 Herodias **h** it against him
Mark 15: 1 the chief priests **h** a
Luke 22:63 Now the men who **h** Jesus
Acts 2:24 that He should be **h** by it
Acts 3:11 who was healed **h** on to Peter
Acts 5:34 a teacher of the law **h** in
Rom 7: 6 died to what we were **h** by
Rev 6: 9 the testimony which they **h**

HELDAI (*see* HELED, HELEM)
1Ch 27:15 month was **H** the Netophathite
Zech 6:10 from **H**, Tobijah, and Jedaiah,

HELEB (*see* HELED)
2Sa 23:29 **H** the son of Baanah (the

HELED (*see* HELDAI, HELEB)
1Ch 11:30 **H** the son of Baanah the

HELEK (*see* HELEKITES)
Num 26:30 of **H**, the family of the
Josh 17: 2 of Abiezer, the children of **H**

HELEKITES (*see* HELEK)
Num 26:30 of Helek, the family of the **H**

HELEM (*see* HELDAI)
1Ch 7:35 of his brother **H** were Zophah
Zech 6:14 the temple of the LORD for **H**

HELEPH
Josh 19:33 And their border began at **H**
Josh 19:34 From **H** the border extended

HELEZ
2Sa 23:26 **H** the Paltite, Ira the son of
1Ch 2:39 Azariah begot **H**
1Ch 2:39 and **H** begot Eleasah
1Ch 11:27 the Harorite, **H** the Pelonite,
1Ch 27:10 month was **H** the Pelonite, of

HELI
Luke 3:23 son of Joseph, the son of **H**

HELKAI (*see* HILKIAH)
Neh 12:15 of Meraioth, **H**

HELKATH (*see* HUKKOK)
Josh 19:25 And their territory included **H**
Josh 21:31 **H** with its common-land, and

HELL
Deut 32:22 and shall burn to the lowest **h**
Ps 9:17 wicked shall be turned into **h**
Ps 55:15 Let them go down alive into **h**
Ps 139: 8 If I make my bed in **h**, behold
Prov 5: 5 her steps lay hold of **h**
Prov 7:27 Her house is the way to **h**
Prov 9:18 guests are in the depths of **h**
Prov 15:11 **H** and Destruction are before
Prov 15:24 he may turn away from **h** below
Prov 23:14 and deliver his soul from **h**
Prov 27:20 **H** and Destruction are never
Is 14: 9 **H** from beneath is excited
Ezek 31:15 day when it went down to **h**
Ezek 31:16 when I cast it down to **h**
Ezek 31:17 also went down to **h** with it
Ezek 32:21 of **h** with those who help him
Ezek 32:27 who have gone down to **h** with
Amos 9: 2 Though they dig into **h**, from
Hab 2: 5 he enlarges his desire as **h**
Matt 5:22 shall be in danger of **h** fire
Matt 5:29 whole body to be cast into **h**
Matt 5:30 whole body to be cast into **h**
Matt 10:28 both soul and body in **h**
Matt 18: 9 eyes, to be cast into **h** fire
Matt 23:15 much a son of **h** as yourselves
Matt 23:33 escape the condemnation of **h**
Mark 9:43 having two hands, to go to **h**
Mark 9:45 two feet, to be cast into **h**
Mark 9:47 eyes, to be cast into **h** fire
Luke 12: 5 has power to cast into **h**
Jas 3: 6 and it is set on fire by **h**
2Pe 2: 4 but cast them down to **h** and

HELLENISTS
Acts 6: 1 against the Hebrews by the **H**
Acts 9:29 and disputed against the **H**
Acts 11:20 to Antioch, spoke to the **H**

HELMET (*see* HELMETS)
1Sa 17: 5 He had a bronze **h** on his head
1Sa 17:38 he put a bronze **h** on his head
Ps 60: 7 also is the **h** for My head
Ps 108: 8 also is the **h** for My head
Is 59:17 a **h** of salvation on His head
Ezek 23:24 shield, and **h** all around
Ezek 27:10 they hung shield and **h** in you
Ezek 38: 5 all of them with shield and **h**
Eph 6:17 take the **h** of salvation, and
1Th 5: 8 as a **h** the hope of salvation

HELMETS (*see* HELMET)
2Ch 26:14 army, shields, spears, **h**,
Jer 46: 4 Stand forth with your **h**,

HELMSMAN
Acts 27:11 was more persuaded by the **h**

HELON
Num 1: 9 Zebulun, Eliab the son of **H**
Num 2: 7 Eliab the son of **H** shall be
Num 7:24 third day Eliab the son of **H**
Num 7:29 of Eliab the son of **H**
Num 10:16 was Eliab the son of **H**

HELP (*see* HELPED, HELPER, HELPFUL, HELPING, HELPLESS, HELPS)
Gen 49:25 of your father who will **h** you
Ex 18: 4 The God of my father was my **h**
Ex 23: 5 shall surely **h** him with it
Lev 25:35 you, then you shall **h** him
Deut 22: 4 you shall surely **h** him lift
Deut 32:38 and **h** you, and be your refuge
Deut 33: 7 may You be a **h** against his
Deut 33:26 rides the heavens to **h** you
Deut 33:29 LORD, the shield of your **h**
Josh 1:14 men of valor, and **h** them,
Josh 10: 4 and **h** me, that we may attack
Josh 10: 6 **h** us, for all the kings of
Josh 10:33 of Gezer came up to **h** Lachish
Judg 5:23 not come to the **h** of the LORD
Judg 5:23 to the **h** of the LORD against
1Sa 11: 9 sun is hot, you shall have **h**
2Sa 8: 5 to **h** Hadadezer king of Zobah
2Sa 10:11 for me, then you shall **h** me
2Sa 10:11 then I will come and **h** you
2Sa 10:19 the Syrians were afraid to **h**
2Sa 14: 4 **H**, O king!"
2Sa 18: 3 now more **h** to us in the city
2Ki 6:26 **H**, my lord, O king
2Ki 6:27 If the LORD does not **h** you
2Ki 6:27 where can I find **h** for you
1Ch 12:17 come peaceably to me to **h** me
1Ch 12:19 but they did not **h** them, for
1Ch 12:22 to David day by day to **h** him
1Ch 18: 5 to **h** Hadadezer king of Zobah
1Ch 19:12 for me, then you shall **h** me
1Ch 19:12 for you, then I will **h** you
1Ch 19:19 **h** the people of Ammon
1Ch 22:17 Israel to **h** Solomon his son
1Ch 23:28 to **h** the sons of Aaron in the
2Ch 14:11 it is nothing for You to **h**
2Ch 14:11 **h** us, O LORD our God, for we
2Ch 19: 2 Should you **h** the wicked and
2Ch 20: 4 to ask **h** from the LORD
2Ch 25: 8 for God has power to **h** and to

2Ch 26:13 to **h** the king against the
2Ch 28:16 the kings of Assyria to **h** him
2Ch 28:21 but he did not **h** him
2Ch 28:23 of the kings of Syria **h** them
2Ch 28:23 to them that they may **h** me
2Ch 32: 8 is the LORD our God, to **h** us
Ezra 1: 4 his place **h** him with silver
Ezra 8:22 horsemen to **h** us against the
Job 6:13 Is my **h** not within me
Job 30:28 congregation and cry out for **h**
Job 31:21 I saw I had **h** in the gate
Job 35: 9 they cry out for **h** because of
Job 36:13 cry for **h** when He binds them
Job 36:18 would not **h** you avoid it
Ps 3: 2 There is no **h** for him in God
Ps 12: 1 **H**, LORD, for the godly man
Ps 20: 2 May He send you **h** from the
Ps 22:11 For there is none to **h**
Ps 22:19 O My Strength, hasten to **h** Me
Ps 27: 9 You have been my **h**
Ps 33:20 He is our **h** and our shield
Ps 35: 2 buckler, And stand up for my **h**
Ps 37:40 And the LORD shall **h** them and
Ps 38:22 Make haste to **h** me, O Lord,
Ps 40:13 O LORD, make haste to **h** me
Ps 40:17 You are my **h** and my deliverer
Ps 42: 5 For the **h** of His countenance
Ps 42:11 The **h** of my countenance and
Ps 43: 5 The **h** of my countenance and
Ps 44:26 Arise for our **h**, And redeem us
Ps 46: 1 A very present **h** in trouble
Ps 46: 5 God shall **h** her, just at the
Ps 59: 4 Awake to **h** me, and behold
Ps 60:11 Give us **h** from trouble, For
Ps 60:11 For vain is the **h** of man
Ps 63: 7 Because You have been my **h**
Ps 70: 1 Make haste to **h** me, O LORD
Ps 70: 5 You are my **h** and my deliverer
Ps 71:12 O my God, make haste to **h** me
Ps 79: 9 **H** us, O God of our salvation,
Ps 89:19 I have given **h** to one who is
Ps 94:17 Unless the LORD had been my **h**
Ps 107:12 down, and there was none to **h**
Ps 108:12 Give us **h** from trouble, For
Ps 108:12 For vain is the **h** of man
Ps 109:26 **H** me, O LORD my God
Ps 115: 9 He is their **h** and their shield
Ps 115:10 He is their **h** and their shield
Ps 115:11 He is their **h** and their shield
Ps 118: 7 for me among those who **h** me
Ps 119:86 **H** me!
Ps 119:147 of the morning, And cry for **h**
Ps 119:173 Let Your hand become my **h**
Ps 119:175 And let Your judgments **h** me
Ps 121: 1 From whence comes my **h**
Ps 121: 2 My **h** comes from the LORD,
Ps 124: 8 Our **h** is in the name of the
Ps 146: 3 of man, in whom there is no **h**
Ps 146: 5 the God of Jacob for his **h**
Prov 28:17 let no one **h** him
Eccl 4:10 for he has no one to **h** him up
Is 10: 3 To whom will you flee for **h**
Is 20: 6 wherever we flee for **h** to be
Is 30: 5 or be **h** or benefit, but a
Is 30: 7 the Egyptians shall **h** in vain
Is 31: 1 who go down to Egypt for **h**
Is 31: 2 against the **h** of those who
Is 41:10 you, yes, I will **h** you, I
Is 41:13 you, 'Fear not, I will **h** you
Is 41:14 I will **h** you," says the LORD
Is 44: 2 from the womb, who will **h** you
Is 50: 7 For the Lord GOD will **h** Me
Is 50: 9 Surely the Lord GOD will **h** Me
Is 63: 5 but there was no one to **h**
Jer 37: 7 to **h** you will return to Egypt
Lam 1: 7 enemy, with no one to **h** her
Lam 3:56 my sighing, from my cry for **h**
Lam 4: 6 moment, with no hand to **h** her
Lam 4:17 us, watching vainly for our **h**
Ezek 12:14 who are around him to **h** him
Ezek 32:21 of hell with those who **h** him
Ezek 39:14 with the **h** of a search party,
Dan 10:13 chief princes, came to **h** me
Dan 11:34 be aided with a little **h**
Dan 11:45 his end, and no one will **h** him
Hos 12: 6 by the **h** of your God, return
Hos 13: 9 but your **h** is from Me
Matt 15:25 Him, saying, "Lord, **h** me
Mark 9:22 have compassion on us and **h** us
Mark 9:24 I believe; **h** my unbelief!
Luke 5: 7 other boat to come and **h** them
Luke 10:40 Therefore tell her to **h** me
Acts 16: 9 over to Macedonia and **h** us
Acts 21:28 Men of Israel, **h**!
Acts 26:22 having obtained **h** from God
Phil 4: 3 **h** these women who labored
Heb 4:16 find grace to **h** in time of

HELPED (*see* HELP)
Ex 2:17 and **h** them, and watered their
1Sa 7:12 Thus far the LORD has **h** us
1Ki 1: 7 they followed and **h** Adonijah
1Ch 5:20 they were **h** against them, and
1Ch 12:21 And they **h** David against the
1Ch 15:26 when God **h** the Levites who
2Ch 18:31 cried out, and the LORD **h** him
2Ch 20:23 they **h** to destroy one another
2Ch 26: 7 God **h** him against the
2Ch 26:15 **h** till he became strong
2Ch 29:34 **h** them until the work was
2Ch 32: 3 and they **h** him
Neh 8: 7 **h** the people to understand
Neh 8: 8 and **h** them to understand the
Esth 9: 3 **h** the Jews, because the fear
Job 26: 2 How have you **h** him who is
Ps 28: 7 trusted in Him, and I am **h**
Ps 83: 8 They have **h** the children of
Ps 86:17 Because You, LORD, have **h** me
Ps 118:13 might fall, But the LORD **h** me
Is 31: 3 he who is **h** will fall down
Is 41: 6 Everyone **h** his neighbor, and
Is 49: 8 day of salvation I have **h** You
Zech 1:15 was a little angry, and they **h**
Luke 1:54 He has **h** His servant Israel,
Acts 18:27 he greatly **h** those who had
Rom 15:24 to be **h** on my way there by
2Co 1:16 and be **h** by you on my way to
2Co 6: 2 day of salvation I have **h** you
Rev 12:16 But the earth **h** the woman

HELPER (*see* HELP, HELPERS)
Gen 2:18 him a **h** comparable to him
Gen 2:20 found a **h** comparable to him
2Ki 14:26 there was no **h** for Israel
Job 29:12 fatherless and he who had no **h**
Job 30:13 they have no **h**
Ps 10:14 You are the **h** of the
Ps 30:10 LORD, be my **h**
Ps 54: 4 Behold, God is my **h**
Ps 72:12 also, and him who has no **h**
Jer 47: 4 and Sidon every **h** who remains
John 14:16 and He will give you another **H**
John 14:26 But the **H**, the Holy Spirit,
John 15:26 But when the **H** comes, whom I
John 16: 7 the **H** will not come to you
Rom 16: 2 she has been a **h** of many and
Heb 13: 6 The LORD is my **h**

HELPERS (*see* HELPER)
1Ch 12: 1 the mighty men, **h** in the war,
1Ch 12:18 to you, and peace to your **h**
Ezek 30: 8 and all her **h** are destroyed
Nah 3: 9 Put and Lubim were your **h**

HELPFUL (*see* HELP)
Acts 20:20 kept back nothing that was **h**
1Co 6:12 me, but all things are not **h**
1Co 10:23 me, but all things are not **h**

HELPING (*see* HELP)
Ex 23: 5 you would refrain from **h** it
1Ki 20:16 the thirty-two kings **h** him
Ezra 5: 2 of God were with them, **h** them
Ps 22: 1 Why are You so far from **h** Me
2Co 1:11 you also **h** together in prayer

HELPLESS (*see* HELP)
Ps 10: 8 are secretly fixed on the **h**
Ps 10:10 That the **h** may fall by his
Ps 10:14 The **h** commits himself to You
Acts 4: 9 a good deed done to the **h** man

HELPS (*see* HELP)
1Ch 12:18 For your God **h** you
Is 31: 3 hand, both he who **h** will fall
Rom 8:26 also **h** in our weaknesses
1Co 12:28 then gifts of healings, **h**

HEM
Ex 28:33 upon its **h** you shall make
Ex 28:33 yarn, all around its **h**, and
Ex 28:34 upon the **h** of the robe all
Ex 39:24 They made on the **h** of the
Ex 39:25 the **h** of the robe all around
Ex 39:26 all around the **h** of the robe
Matt 9:20 touched the **h** of His garment
Matt 14:36 touch the **h** of His garment

HEMAM (*see* HOMAM)
Gen 36:22 sons of Lotan were Hori and **H**

HEMAN
1Ki 4:31 than Ethan the Ezrahite, and **H**
1Ch 2: 6 of Zerah were Zimri, Ethan, **H**
1Ch 6:33 Kohathites were **H** the singer
1Ch 15:17 appointed **H** the son of Joel
1Ch 15:19 the singers, **H**, Asaph, and
1Ch 16:41 and with them **H** and Jeduthun
1Ch 16:42 and with them **H** and Jeduthun,
1Ch 25: 1 of the sons of Asaph, of **H**
1Ch 25: 4 Of **H**, the sons of **H**
1Ch 25: 5 of **H** the king's seer in the
1Ch 25: 5 For God gave **H** fourteen sons
1Ch 25: 6 **H** were under the authority of
2Ch 5:12 all those of Asaph and **H** and
2Ch 29:14 of the sons of **H**, Jehiel and
2Ch 35:15 command of David, Asaph, **H**

HEMDAN (*see* AMRAM)
Gen 36:26 **H**, Eshban, Ithran, and Cheran

HEMLOCK
Hos 10: 4 judgment springs up like **h** in

HEN
Matt 23:37 as a **h** gathers her chicks
Luke 13:34 as a **h** gathers her brood

HEN*
Zech 6:14 and **H** the son of Zephaniah

HENA
2Ki 18:34 the gods of Sepharvaim and **H**
2Ki 19:13 of the city of Sepharvaim, **H**
Is 37:13 of the city of Sepharvaim, **H**

HENADAD
Ezra 3: 9 the sons of **H** with their sons
Neh 3:18 under Bavai the son of **H**
Neh 3:24 of **H** repaired another section
Neh 10: 9 Binnui of the sons of **H**, and

HENCEFORTH
Luke 1:48 **h** all generations will call

HENNA
Song 1:14 is to me a cluster of **h**
Song 4:13 fragrant **h** with spikenard,

HEPHER (*see* HEPHERITES)
Num 26:32 of **H**, the family of the
Num 26:33 the son of **H** had no sons, but
Num 27: 1 of Zelophehad the son of **H**
Josh 12:17 the king of **H**, one
Josh 17: 2 of Shechem, the children of **H**
Josh 17: 3 But Zelophehad the son of **H**
1Ki 4:10 Sochoh and all the land of **H**
1Ch 4: 6 Naarah bore him Ahuzzam, **H**
1Ch 11:36 **H** the Mecherathite, Ahijah

HEPHERITES (*see* HEPHER)
Num 26:32 Hepher, the family of the **H**

HEPHZIBAH
2Ki 21: 1 His mother's name was **H**
Is 62: 4 But you shall be called **H**

HER (*see* PREFACE)

HERALD
Dan 3: 4 Then a **h** cried aloud

HERB (*see* HERBS)
Gen 1:11 the **h** that yields seed, and
Gen 1:12 grass, the **h** that yields seed
Gen 1:29 I have given you every **h** that
Gen 1:30 every green **h** for food"
Gen 2: 5 before any **h** of the field had
Gen 3:18 shall eat the **h** of the field
Ex 9:22 and on every **h** of the field,
Ex 9:25 struck every **h** of the field
Ex 10:12 and eat every **h** of the land
Ex 10:15 they ate every **h** of the land
Deut 32: 2 as raindrops on the tender **h**
2Ki 19:26 of the field and the green **h**
Ps 37: 2 And wither as the green **h**
Is 37:27 the field and as the green **h**

HERBS (*see* HERB)
Gen 9: 3 things, even as the green **h**
Ex 12: 8 with bitter **h** they shall eat
Num 9:11 unleavened bread and bitter **h**
2Ki 4:39 into the field to gather **h**

Prov 15:17 a dinner of **h** where love is
Prov 27:25 the **h** of the mountains are
Song 5:13 like banks of scented **h**
Is 26:19 your dew is like the dew of **h**
Jer 12: 4 the **h** of every field wither
Matt 13:32 it is greater than the **h** and
Mark 4:32 and becomes greater than all **h**
Luke 11:42 and rue and all manner of **h**
Heb 6: 7 bears **h** useful for those by

HERD (*see* HERDS, HERDSMAN)
Gen 18: 7 And Abraham ran to the **h**, took
Lev 1: 2 of the **h** and of the flock
Lev 1: 3 is a burnt sacrifice of the **h**
Lev 3: 1 if he offers it of the **h**
Lev 27:32 tithe of the **h** or the flock
Num 15: 3 from the **h** or the flock,
Deut 12:17 of your **h** or your flock, of
Deut 12:21 you may slaughter from your **h**
Deut 15:19 males that come from your **h**
Deut 15:19 with the firstborn of your **h**
Deut 16: 2 God, from the flock and the **h**
1Sa 11: 5 behind the **h** from the field
2Sa 12: 4 from his own **h** to prepare one
2Sa 17:29 sheep and cheese of the **h**
Ps 68:30 The **h** of bulls with the
Jer 31:12 young of the flock and the **h**
Jon 3: 7 **h** nor flock, taste anything
Hab 3:17 there be no **h** in the stalls
Matt 8:30 was a **h** of many swine feeding
Matt 8:31 go away into the **h** of swine
Matt 8:32 they went into the **h** of swine
Matt 8:32 suddenly the whole **h** of swine
Mark 5:11 Now a large **h** of swine was
Mark 5:13 the **h** ran violently down the
Luke 8:32 Now a **h** of many swine was
Luke 8:33 the **h** ran violently down the

HERDS (*see* HERD)
Gen 13: 5 with Abram, had flocks and **h**
Gen 24:35 He has given him flocks and **h**
Gen 26:14 of flocks and possessions of **h**
Gen 32: 7 with him, and the flocks and **h**
Gen 33:13 **h** which are nursing are with
Gen 45:10 your flocks and your **h**, and
Gen 46:32 brought their flocks, their **h**
Gen 47: 1 their flocks and their **h** and
Gen 47:17 flocks, the cattle of the **h**
Gen 47:18 also has our **h** of livestock
Gen 50: 8 their **h** they left in the land
Ex 10: 9 our **h** we will go, for we must
Ex 10:24 flocks and your **h** be kept back
Ex 12:32 take your flocks and your **h**
Ex 12:38 them also, and flocks and **h**
Ex 34: 3 let neither flocks nor **h** feed
Num 11:22 **h** be slaughtered for them, to
Num 35: 3 for their cattle, for their **h**
Deut 8:13 and when your **h** and your flocks
Deut 12: 6 and the firstlings of your **h**
Deut 14:23 of the firstlings of your **h**
Deut 28: 4 and the increase of your **h**
1Sa 30:20 and **h** which they had driven
2Sa 12: 2 exceedingly many flocks and **h**
1Ch 27:29 over the **h** that fed in Sharon
1Ch 27:29 **h** that were in the valleys
2Ch 32:29 of flocks and **h** in abundance
Neh 10:36 and the firstlings of our **h**
Prov 27:23 flocks, and attend to your **h**
Eccl 2: 7 had greater possessions of **h**
Is 65:10 a place for **h** to lie down
Jer 3:24 their flocks and their **h**,
Jer 5:17 eat up your flocks and your **h**
Hos 5: 6 **h** they shall go to seek the
Joel 1:18 The **h** of cattle are restless,
Zeph 2:14 The **h** shall lie down in her

HERDSMAN (*see* HERD, HERDSMEN)
Amos 7:14 of a prophet, but I was a **h**

HERDSMEN (*see* HERDSMAN)
Gen 13: 7 the **h** of Abram's livestock
Gen 13: 7 and the **h** of Lot's livestock
Gen 13: 8 between my **h** and your **h**
Gen 26:20 But the **h** of Gerar quarreled
Gen 26:20 quarreled with Isaac's **h**,
Gen 47: 6 chief **h** over my livestock
1Sa 21: 7 the chief of the **h** who
Amos 1: 1 who was among the **h** of Tekoa

HERE (*see* PREFACE)

HEREAFTER (*see* PREFACE)

HERES (*see* TIMNATH HERES)
Judg 1:35 to dwell in Mount **H**, in
Judg 8:13 battle, from the Ascent of **H**
Is 16:11 and my inner being for Kir **H**
Jer 48:31 mourn for the men of Kir **H**
Jer 48:36 wail for the men of Kir **H**

HERESH
1Ch 9:15 Bakbakkar, **H**, Galal, and

HERESIES
Gal 5:20 ambitions, dissensions, **h**
2Pe 2: 1 bring in destructive **h**, even

HERETH
1Sa 22: 5 and went into the forest of **H**

HERITAGE (*see* HERITAGES)
Ex 6: 8 I will give it to you as a **h**
Deut 4:19 under the whole heaven as a **h**
Deut 33: 4 a **h** of the congregation of
Neh 2:20 but you have no **h** or right or
Job 20:29 the **h** appointed to him by God
Job 27:13 the **h** of oppressors, received
Ps 61: 5 You have given me the **h** of
Ps 94: 5 O LORD, And afflict Your **h**
Ps 111: 6 them the **h** of the nations
Ps 119:111 I have taken as a **h** forever
Ps 127: 3 are a **h** from the LORD, The
Ps 135:12 And gave their land as a **h**
Ps 135:12 A **h** to Israel His people
Ps 136:21 And gave their land as a **h**
Ps 136:22 A **h** to Israel His servant,
Eccl 2:21 his **h** to a man who has not
Eccl 3:22 own works, for that is his **h**
Eccl 5:18 for it is his **h**
Eccl 5:19 eat of it, to receive his **h**
Is 54:17 This is the **h** of the servants
Is 58:14 feed you with the **h** of Jacob
Jer 2: 7 and made My **h** an abomination
Jer 3:19 a beautiful **h** of the hosts of
Jer 12: 7 My house, I have left My **h**
Jer 12: 8 My **h** is to Me like a lion in
Jer 12: 9 My **h** is to Me like a speckled
Jer 12:15 them back, everyone to his **h**
Jer 17: 4 go of your **h** which I gave you
Jer 50:11 you destroyers of My **h**,
Hos 5: 7 shall devour them and their **h**
Joel 2:17 not give Your **h** to reproach
Joel 3: 2 My **h** Israel, whom they have
Mic 2: 4 changed the **h** of my people
Mic 7:14 staff, the flock of Your **h**
Mic 7:18 of the remnant of His **h**
Mal 1: 3 his **h** for the jackals of the

HERITAGES (*see* HERITAGE)
Is 49: 8 to inherit the desolate **h**

HERMAS
Rom 16:14 Greet Asyncritus, Phlegon, **H**

HERMES
Acts 14:12 they called Zeus, and Paul, **H**
Rom 16:14 Phlegon, Hermas, Patrobas, **H**

HERMOGENES
2Ti 1:15 whom are Phygellus and **H**

HERMON (*see* BAAL HERMON, SIRION)
Deut 3: 8 the River Arnon to Mount **H**
Deut 3: 9 (the Sidonians call **H** Sirion
Deut 4:48 to Mount Sion (that is, **H**),
Josh 11: 3 the Hivite below **H** in the
Josh 11:17 of Lebanon below Mount **H**
Josh 12: 1 the River Arnon to Mount **H**
Josh 12: 5 and reigned over Mount **H**, over
Josh 13: 5 **H** as far as the entrance to
Josh 13:11 and Maachathites, all Mount **H**
1Ch 5:23 that is, to Senir, or Mount **H**
Ps 42: 6 And from the heights of **H**
Ps 89:12 and **H** rejoice in Your name
Ps 133: 3 It is like the dew of **H**,
Song 4: 8 from the top of Senir and **H**

HEROD (*see* HERODIANS, HEROD'S)
Matt 2: 1 in the days of **H** the king
Matt 2: 3 When **H** the king heard these
Matt 2: 7 Then **H**, when he had secretly
Matt 2:12 they should not return to **H**
Matt 2:13 for **H** will seek the young
Matt 2:15 there until the death of **H**
Matt 2:16 Then **H**, when he saw that he
Matt 2:19 But when **H** was dead, behold,
Matt 2:22 Judea instead of his father **H**
Matt 14: 1 At that time **H** the tetrarch
Matt 14: 3 For **H** had laid hold of John
Matt 14: 6 before them and pleased **H**
Mark 6:14 Now King **H** heard of Him, for
Mark 6:16 But when **H** heard, he said
Mark 6:17 For **H** himself had sent and
Mark 6:18 For John had said to **H**, "It
Mark 6:20 for **H** feared John, knowing
Mark 6:21 when **H** on his birthday gave a
Mark 6:22 in and danced, and pleased **H**
Mark 8:15 Pharisees and the leaven of **H**
Luke 1: 5 There was in the days of **H**
Luke 3: 1 **H** being tetrarch of Galilee,
Luke 3:19 But **H** the tetrarch, being
Luke 3:19 the evils which **H** had done
Luke 9: 7 Now **H** the tetrarch heard of
Luke 9: 9 And **H** said, "John I have
Luke 13:31 here, for **H** wants to kill You
Luke 23: 7 he sent Him to **H**, who was
Luke 23: 8 Now when **H** saw Jesus, he was
Luke 23:11 Then **H**, with his men of war,
Luke 23:12 **H** became friends with each
Luke 23:15 no, neither did **H**, for I sent
Acts 4:27 whom You anointed, both **H**
Acts 12: 1 Now about that time **H** the
Acts 12: 6 when **H** was about to bring him
Acts 12:11 me from the hand of **H** and from
Acts 12:19 But when **H** had searched for
Acts 12:20 Now **H** had been very angry
Acts 12:21 So on a set day **H**, arrayed in
Acts 13: 1 up with **H** the tetrarch, and

HERODIANS (*see* HEROD)
Matt 22:16 their disciples with the **H**
Mark 3: 6 with the **H** against Him, how
Mark 12:13 of the Pharisees and the **H**

HERODIAS
Matt 14: 3 in prison for the sake of **H**
Matt 14: 6 the daughter of **H** danced
Mark 6:17 in prison for the sake of **H**
Mark 6:19 Therefore **H** held it against
Mark 6:22 when **H**' daughter herself came
Luke 3:19 rebuked by him concerning **H**

HERODION
Rom 16:11 Greet **H**, my kinsman

HEROD'S (*see* HEROD)
Matt 14: 6 But when **H** birthday was
Luke 8: 3 **H** steward, and Susanna, and
Luke 23: 7 He belonged to **H** jurisdiction
Acts 23:35 to be kept in **H** Praetorium

HEROES
2Sa 23:20 two lion-like **h** of Moab
1Ch 11:22 two lion-like **h** of Moab

HERON
Lev 11:19 the **h** after its kind, the
Deut 14:18 the **h** after its kind, and the

HERS (*see* PREFACE)

HERSELF (*see* PREFACE)

HESHBON
Num 21:25 cities of the Amorites, in **H**
Num 21:26 For **H** was the city of Sihon
Num 21:27 Come to **H**, let it be built
Num 21:28 For fire went out from **H**, a
Num 21:30 **H** has perished as far as
Num 21:34 the Amorites, who dwelt at **H**
Num 32: 3 Dibon, Jazer, Nimrah, **H**,
Num 32:37 children of Reuben built **H**
Deut 1: 4 the Amorites, who dwelt in **H**
Deut 2:24 Sihon the Amorite, king of **H**
Deut 2:26 Kedemoth to Sihon king of **H**
Deut 2:30 But Sihon king of **H** would not
Deut 3: 2 the Amorites, who dwelt at **H**
Deut 3: 6 as we did to Sihon king of **H**
Deut 4:46 the Amorites, who dwelt at **H**
Deut 29: 7 this place, Sihon king of **H**
Josh 9:10 to Sihon king of **H**, and Og
Josh 12: 2 the Amorites, who dwelt in **H**
Josh 12: 5 the border of Sihon king of **H**
Josh 13:10 Amorites, who reigned in **H**
Josh 13:17 **H** and all its cities that are
Josh 13:21 Amorites, who reigned in **H**
Josh 13:26 from **H** to Ramath Mizpah and
Josh 13:27 kingdom of Sihon king of **H**
Josh 21:39 **H** with its common-land, and
Judg 11:19 of the Amorites, king of **H**
Judg 11:26 While Israel dwelt in **H** and
1Ch 6:81 **H** with its common-lands, and

Neh 9:22 the land of the king of **H**
Song 7: 4 **H** by the gate of Bath Rabbim
Is 15: 4 **H** and Elealeh will cry out,
Is 16: 8 For the fields of **H** languish
Is 16: 9 drench you with my tears, O **H**
Jer 48: 2 In **H** they have devised evil
Jer 48:34 From the cry of **H** to Elealeh
Jer 48:45 of **H** because of exhaustion
Jer 48:45 a fire shall come out of **H**
Jer 49: 3 Wail, O **H**, for Ai is

HESHMON (*see* AZMON)
Josh 15:27 Hazar Gaddah, **H**, Beth Pelet,

HESITATE
Judg 18: 9 Do not **h** to go, that you may
1Ki 22: 3 but we **h** to take it out of
Job 30:10 they do not **h** to spit in my

HETH
Gen 10:15 Sidon his firstborn, and **H**
Gen 23: 3 and spoke to the sons of **H**
Gen 23: 5 And the sons of **H** answered
Gen 23: 7 of the land, the sons of **H**
Gen 23:10 dwelt among the sons of **H**
Gen 23:10 the presence of the sons of **H**
Gen 23:16 the hearing of the sons of **H**
Gen 23:18 the presence of the sons of **H**
Gen 23:20 of **H** as property for a burial
Gen 25:10 purchased from the sons of **H**
Gen 27:46 because of the daughters of **H**
Gen 27:46 a wife of the daughters of **H**
Gen 49:32 purchased from the sons of **H**
1Ch 1:13 Sidon, his firstborn, and **H**

HETHLON
Ezek 47:15 Great Sea, by the road to **H**
Ezek 48: 1 border along the road to **H** at

HEW (*see* HEWED, HEWERS, HEWN, HEWS)
Deut 10: 1 **H** for yourself two tablets
Jer 6: 6 **H** down trees, and build a

HEWED (*see* HEW)
Deut 10: 3 **h** two tablets of stone like

HEWERS (*see* HEW)
1Ch 22:15 **h** and workers of stone and
2Ch 2:10 the **h** who cut timber, twenty
2Ch 2:18 eighty thousand **h** of stone in

HEWN (*see* HEW, HEWN-OUT)
Ex 20:25 shall not build it of **h** stone
1Ki 5:17 and **h** stones, to lay the
1Ki 6:36 with three rows of **h** stone
1Ki 7: 9 of costly stones **h** to size
1Ki 7:11 **h** to size, and cedar wood
1Ki 7:12 with three rows of **h** stones
2Ki 12:12 **h** stone, to repair the damage
2Ki 22: 6 **h** stone to repair the house
1Ch 22: 2 **h** stones to build the house
2Ch 34:11 and builders to buy **h** stone
Prov 9: 1 she has **h** out her seven
Is 9:10 we will rebuild with **h** stones
Is 10:33 high stature will be **h** down
Is 22:16 that you have **h** a sepulcher
Is 51: 1 rock from which you were **h**
Jer 2:13 and **h** themselves cisterns
Lam 3: 9 blocked my ways with **h** stone
Ezek 40:42 of **h** stone for the burnt
Hos 6: 5 Therefore I have **h** them by
Amos 5:11 have built houses of **h** stone
Matt 27:60 he had **h** out of the rock
Mark 15:46 had been **h** out of the rock
Luke 23:53 that was **h** out of the rock

HEWN-OUT (*see* HEWN)
Deut 6:11 **h** wells which you did not dig

HEWS (*see* HEW)
Is 22:16 here, as he who **h** himself a
Is 44:14 He **h** down cedars for himself,

HEZEKIAH (*see* JEHIZKIAH)
2Ki 16:20 Then **H** his son reigned in his
2Ki 18: 1 that **H** the son of Ahaz, king
2Ki 18: 9 in the fourth year of King **H**
2Ki 18:10 In the sixth year of **H**, that
2Ki 18:13 the fourteenth year of King **H**
2Ki 18:14 Then **H** king of Judah sent to
2Ki 18:14 king of Assyria assessed **H**
2Ki 18:15 So **H** gave him all the silver
2Ki 18:16 At that time **H** stripped the
2Ki 18:16 from the pillars which **H** king
2Ki 18:17 against Jerusalem, to King **H**
2Ki 18:19 Say now to **H**, 'Thus says the
2Ki 18:22 whose altars **H** has taken away
2Ki 18:29 Do not let **H** deceive you
2Ki 18:30 nor let **H** make you trust in
2Ki 18:31 Do not listen to **H**
2Ki 18:32 But do not listen to **H**, lest
2Ki 18:37 came to **H** with their clothes
2Ki 19: 1 it was, when King **H** heard it
2Ki 19: 3 Thus says **H**: 'This day is
2Ki 19: 5 of King **H** came to Isaiah
2Ki 19: 9 he again sent messengers to **H**
2Ki 19:10 speak to **H** king of Judah,
2Ki 19:14 **H** received the letter from
2Ki 19:14 **H** went up to the house of the
2Ki 19:15 Then **H** prayed before the LORD
2Ki 19:20 the son of Amoz sent to **H**
2Ki 20: 1 In those days **H** was sick and
2Ki 20: 3 And **H** wept bitterly
2Ki 20: 5 and tell **H** the leader of My
2Ki 20: 8 And **H** said to Isaiah,
2Ki 20:10 And **H** answered, "It is an easy
2Ki 20:12 letters and a present to **H**
2Ki 20:12 he heard that **H** had been sick
2Ki 20:13 **H** was attentive to them, and
2Ki 20:13 that **H** did not show them
2Ki 20:14 the prophet went to King **H**
2Ki 20:14 And **H** said, "They came from
2Ki 20:15 So **H** answered, "They have
2Ki 20:16 Then Isaiah said to **H**, "Hear
2Ki 20:19 Then **H** said to Isaiah, "The
2Ki 20:20 Now the rest of the acts of **H**
2Ki 20:21 So **H** rested with his fathers
2Ki 21: 3 the high places which **H** his
1Ch 3:13 **H** his son, Manasseh his son,
1Ch 3:23 of Neariah were Elioenai, **H**
1Ch 4:41 the days of **H** king of Judah
2Ch 28:27 Then **H** his son reigned in his
2Ch 29: 1 **H** became king when he was
2Ch 29:18 Then they went in to King **H**
2Ch 29:20 Then King **H** rose early,
2Ch 29:27 Then **H** commanded them to
2Ch 29:30 Moreover King **H** and the
2Ch 29:31 Then **H** answered and said
2Ch 29:36 Then **H** and all the people
2Ch 30: 1 **H** sent to all Israel and Judah
2Ch 30:18 But **H** prayed for them, saying
2Ch 30:20 And the LORD listened to **H**
2Ch 30:22 **H** gave encouragement to all
2Ch 30:24 For **H** king of Judah gave to
2Ch 31: 2 **H** appointed the divisions of
2Ch 31: 8 And when **H** and the leaders
2Ch 31: 9 Then **H** questioned the priests
2Ch 31:11 Now **H** commanded them to
2Ch 31:13 the commandment of **H** the king
2Ch 31:20 Thus **H** did throughout all
2Ch 32: 2 when **H** saw that Sennacherib
2Ch 32: 8 the words of **H** king of Judah
2Ch 32: 9 to **H** king of Judah, and to all
2Ch 32:11 Does not **H** persuade you to
2Ch 32:12 Has not the same **H** taken
2Ch 32:15 do not let **H** deceive you or
2Ch 32:16 God and against His servant **H**
2Ch 32:17 so the God of **H** will not
2Ch 32:20 Now for this cause King **H**
2Ch 32:22 Thus the LORD saved **H** and the
2Ch 32:23 presents to **H** king of Judah,
2Ch 32:24 In those days **H** was sick and
2Ch 32:25 But **H** did not repay according
2Ch 32:26 Then **H** humbled himself for
2Ch 32:26 upon them in the days of **H**
2Ch 32:27 **H** had very great riches and
2Ch 32:30 This same **H** also stopped the
2Ch 32:30 **H** prospered in all his works
2Ch 32:32 Now the rest of the acts of **H**
2Ch 32:33 So **H** rested with his fathers,
2Ch 33: 3 the high places which **H** his
Ezra 2:16 the people of Ater of **H**,
Neh 7:21 the children of Ater of **H**
Neh 10:17 Ater, **H**, Azzur,
Prov 25: 1 men of **H** king of Judah copied
Is 1: 1 of Uzziah, Jotham, Ahaz, and **H**
Is 36: 1 **H** that Sennacherib king of
Is 36: 2 to King **H** at Jerusalem
Is 36: 4 Say now to **H**, 'Thus says the
Is 36: 7 whose altars **H** has taken away
Is 36:14 Do not let **H** deceive you
Is 36:15 nor let **H** make you trust in
Is 36:16 Do not listen to **H**
Is 36:18 Beware lest **H** persuade you
Is 36:22 came to **H** with their clothes
Is 37: 1 it was, when King **H** heard it
Is 37: 3 Thus says **H**: 'This day is
Is 37: 5 of King **H** came to Isaiah
Is 37: 9 it, he sent messengers to **H**
Is 37:10 speak to **H** king of Judah,
Is 37:14 **H** received the letter from
Is 37:14 **H** went up to the house of the
Is 37:15 Then **H** prayed to the LORD,
Is 37:21 the son of Amoz sent to **H**
Is 38: 1 In those days **H** was sick and
Is 38: 2 Then **H** turned his face toward
Is 38: 3 And **H** wept bitterly
Is 38: 5 Go and say to **H**, 'Thus says
Is 38: 9 writing of **H** king of Judah
Is 38:22 And **H** had said, "What is the
Is 39: 1 letters and a present to **H**
Is 39: 2 **H** was pleased with them, and
Is 39: 2 that **H** did not show them
Is 39: 3 the prophet went to King **H**
Is 39: 3 And **H** said, "They came to me
Is 39: 4 So **H** answered, "They have
Is 39: 5 Then Isaiah said to **H**, "Hear
Is 39: 8 Then **H** said to Isaiah, "The
Jer 15: 4 of Manasseh the son of **H**,
Jer 26:18 the days of **H** king of Judah
Jer 26:19 Did **H** king of Judah and all
Hos 1: 1 of Uzziah, Jotham, Ahaz, and **H**
Mic 1: 1 days of Jotham, Ahaz, and **H**
Zeph 1: 1 son of Amariah, the son of **H**
Matt 1: 9 begot Ahaz, and Ahaz begot **H**
Matt 1:10 **H** begot Manasseh, Manasseh

HEZION
1Ki 15:18 of Tabrimmon, the son of **H**

HEZIR
1Ch 24:15 the seventeenth to **H**, the
Neh 10:20 Magpiash, Meshullam, **H**,

HEZRAI (*see* HEZRO)
2Sa 23:35 **H** the Carmelite, Paarai the

HEZRO (*see* HEZRAI)
1Ch 11:37 **H** the Carmelite, Naarai the

HEZRON (*see* HAZOR, HEZRONITES, HEZRON'S)
Gen 46: 9 Reuben were Hanoch, Pallu, **H**
Gen 46:12 The sons of Perez were **H** and
Ex 6:14 Israel, were Hanoch, Pallu, **H**
Num 26: 6 of **H**, the family of the
Num 26:21 of **H**, the family of the
Josh 15: 3 Barnea, passed along to **H**
Josh 15:25 Kerioth, **H** (which is Hazor),
Ruth 4:18 Perez begot **H**
Ruth 4:19 **H** begot Ram, and Ram begot
1Ch 2: 5 The sons of Perez were **H** and
1Ch 2: 9 Also the sons of **H** who were
1Ch 2:18 Caleb the son of **H** begot
1Ch 2:21 Now afterward **H** went in to
1Ch 2:24 After **H** died in Caleb
1Ch 2:25 Jerahmeel, the firstborn of **H**
1Ch 4: 1 sons of Judah were Perez, **H**
1Ch 5: 3 Israel were Hanoch, Pallu, **H**
Matt 1: 3 Zerah by Tamar, Perez begot **H**
Matt 1: 3 and **H** begot Ram
Luke 3:33 the son of Ram, the son of **H**

HEZRONITES (*see* HEZRON)
Num 26: 6 Hezron, the family of the **H**
Num 26:21 Hezron, the family of the **H**

HEZRON'S (*see* HEZRON)
1Ch 2:24 **H** wife Abijah bore him Ashhur

HID (*see* HIDE)
Gen 3: 8 his wife **h** themselves from
Gen 3:10 and I **h** myself
Gen 35: 4 and Jacob **h** them under the
Ex 2: 2 child, she **h** him three months
Ex 2:12 Egyptian and **h** him in the sand
Ex 3: 6 Moses **h** his face, for he was
Josh 2: 4 took the two men and **h** them
Josh 6:17 because she **h** the messengers
Josh 6:25 because she **h** the messengers
Judg 9: 5 left, because he **h** himself
1Sa 3:18 and **h** nothing from him
1Sa 13: 6 then the people **h** in caves
1Sa 20:19 you **h** on the day of the deed
1Sa 20:24 So David **h** in the field
1Ki 18:13 how I **h** one hundred men of
2Ki 7: 8 clothing, and went and **h** them
2Ki 7: 8 there also, and went and **h** it
2Ki 11: 2 and they **h** him and his nurse in
1Ch 21:20 were with him **h** themselves

2Ch 22:11 **h** him from Athaliah so that
Job 29: 8 the young men saw me and **h**
Ps 9:15 In the net which they **h**,
Ps 30: 7 You **h** Your face, and I was
Is 53: 3 And we **h**, as it were, our
Is 54: 8 With a little wrath I **h** My
Is 57:17 I **h** and was angry, and he went
Jer 13: 5 **h** it by the Euphrates, as the
Jer 36:26 prophet, but the LORD **h** them
Ezek 39:23 therefore I **h** My face from
Matt 13:33 **h** in three measures of meai
Matt 13:44 field, which a man found and **h**
Matt 25:18 ground, and **h** his lord's money
Matt 25:25 **h** your talent in the ground
Luke 1:24 she **h** herself five months,
Luke 13:21 **h** in three measures of meal
John 8:59 but Jesus **h** Himself and went
Rev 6:15 **h** themselves in the caves and

HIDDAI (*see* HURAI)
2Sa 23:30 **H** from the brooks of Gaash,

HIDDEKEL
Gen 2:14 name of the third river is **H**

HIDDEN (*see* HIDE)
Gen 4:14 I shall be **h** from Your face
Lev 4:13 the thing is **h** from the eyes
Lev 5: 2 it is **h** from him, he also
Lev 5: 3 defiled, and it is **h** from him
Lev 5: 4 an oath, and it is **h** from him
Num 5:13 it is **h** from the eyes of her
Deut 33:19 and of treasures **h** in the sand
Josh 2: 6 **h** them with the stalks of
Josh 7:21 **h** in the earth in the midst
Josh 7:22 was, **h** in his tent, with the
Josh 10:16 **h** themselves in a cave at
Josh 10:17 **h** in the cave at Makkedah
Josh 10:27 cave where they had been **h**
1Sa 10:22 he is, **h** among the equipment
1Sa 14:11 the holes where they have **h**
1Sa 14:22 the men of Israel who had **h**
2Sa 17: 9 by now he is **h** in some pit
2Sa 18:13 is nothing **h** from the king
1Ki 18: 4 **h** them, fifty to a cave, and
2Ki 4:27 and the LORD has **h** it from me
2Ki 6:29 but she has **h** her son
2Ki 11: 3 So he was **h** with her in the
2Ch 22:12 he was **h** with them in the
Job 3:16 or why was I not **h** like a
Job 3:21 for it more than **h** treasures
Job 3:23 given to a man whose way is **h**
Job 5:21 You shall be **h** from the
Job 10:13 You have **h** in Your heart
Job 15:20 years is **h** from the oppressor
Job 17: 4 For You have **h** their heart
Job 18:10 A noose is **h** for him on the
Job 24: 1 are not **h** from the Almighty
Job 28:11 what is **h** he brings forth to
Job 28:21 It is **h** from the eyes of all
Job 40:13 their faces in **h** darkness
Ps 17:14 You fill with Your **h** treasure
Ps 19: 6 is nothing **h** from its heat
Ps 22:24 Nor has He **h** His face from
Ps 32: 5 And my iniquity I have not **h**
Ps 35: 7 **h** their net for me in a pit
Ps 35: 8 that he has **h** catch himself
Ps 38: 9 my sighing is not **h** from You
Ps 40:10 I have not **h** Your
Ps 51: 6 in the **h** part You will make
Ps 69: 5 And my sins are not **h** from You
Ps 119:11 word I have **h** in my heart
Ps 139:15 My frame was not **h** from You
Ps 140: 5 proud have **h** a snare for me
Prov 2: 4 for her as for **h** treasures
Is 28:15 falsehood we have **h** ourselves
Is 29:14 their prudent men shall be **h**
Is 40:27 My way is **h** from the LORD, and
Is 42:22 they are **h** in prison houses
Is 45: 3 **h** riches of secret places,
Is 48: 6 even **h** things, and you did not
Is 49: 2 of His hand He has **h** Me, and
Is 49: 2 in His quiver He has **h** Me
Is 59: 2 your sins have **h** His face
Is 64: 7 for You have **h** Your face from
Is 65:16 they are **h** from My eyes
Jer 13: 7 the place where I had **h** it
Jer 16:17 they are not **h** from My face
Jer 16:17 their iniquity **h** from My eyes
Jer 18:22 me, and **h** snares for my feet
Jer 33: 5 have **h** My face from this city
Jer 43:10 these stones that I have **h**
Ezek 22:26 they have **h** their eyes from
Ezek 28: 3 secret that can be **h** from you
Ezek 39:24 them, and **h** My face from them
Hos 5: 3 and Israel is not **h** from Me
Hos 13:14 Pity is **h** from My eyes
Obad 6 How his **h** treasures shall be
Nah 3:11 you will be **h**
Hab 3: 4 and there His power was **h**
Zeph 2: 3 be **h** in the day of the LORD's
Matt 5:14 is set on a hill cannot be **h**
Matt 10:26 and **h** that will not be known
Matt 11:25 because You have **h** these
Matt 13:44 is like treasure **h** in a field
Mark 4:22 For there is nothing **h** which
Mark 7:24 it, but He could not be **h**
Luke 8:17 nor anything **h** that will not
Luke 8:47 woman saw that she was not **h**
Luke 9:45 it was **h** from them so that
Luke 10:21 that You have **h** these things
Luke 12: 2 nor **h** that will not be known
Luke 18:34 this saying was **h** from them
Luke 19:42 now they are **h** from your eyes
John 12:36 departed, and was **h** from them
1Co 2: 7 the **h** wisdom which God
1Co 4: 5 the **h** things of darkness and
2Co 4: 2 the **h** things of shame, not
Eph 3: 9 of the ages has been **h** in God
Col 1:26 which has been **h** from ages
Col 2: 3 in whom are **h** all the
Col 3: 3 your life is **h** with Christ in
1Ti 5:25 are otherwise cannot be **h**
Heb 4:13 no creature **h** from His sight
Heb 11:23 was **h** three months by his
1Pe 3: 4 but let it be the **h** person of
Rev 2:17 some of the **h** manna to eat

HIDE (*see* HID, HIDDEN, HIDEOUT, HIDES, HIDING)
Gen 18:17 Shall I **h** from Abraham what I
Gen 47:18 We will not **h** from my lord
Ex 2: 3 she could no longer **h** him
Lev 4:11 But the bull's **h** and all its
Lev 8:17 But the bull, its **h**, its
Lev 9:11 the **h** he burned with fire
Lev 20: 4 way **h** their eyes from the man
Num 19: 5 its **h**, its flesh, its blood,
Deut 7:20 who **h** themselves from you,
Deut 22: 1 and **h** yourself from them
Deut 22: 3 you must not **h** yourself
Deut 22: 4 road, and **h** yourself from them
Deut 31:17 I will **h** My face from them,
Deut 31:18 I will surely **h** My face in
Deut 32:20 I will **h** My face from them,
Josh 2:16 **H** there three days, until the
Josh 7:19 do not **h** it from me
Judg 6:11 in order to **h** it from the
1Sa 3:17 Please do not **h** it from me
1Sa 3:17 if you **h** anything from me of
1Sa 19: 2 stay in a secret place and **h**
1Sa 20: 2 father **h** this thing from me
1Sa 20: 5 that I may **h** in the field
2Sa 14:18 Please do not **h** from me
1Ki 17: 3 **h** by the Brook Cherith, which
1Ki 22:25 go into an inner chamber to **h**
2Ki 7:12 to **h** themselves in the field
2Ch 18:24 go into an inner chamber to **h**
Job 3:10 nor **h** sorrow from my eyes
Job 13:20 I will not **h** myself from You
Job 13:24 Why do You **h** Your face, and
Job 14:13 that You would **h** me in the
Job 23:17 He did not **h** deep darkness
Job 24: 4 of the land are forced to **h**
Job 34:22 of iniquity may **h** themselves
Job 40:13 **H** them in the dust together,
Ps 10: 1 Why do You **h** Yourself in
Ps 13: 1 will You **h** Your face from me
Ps 17: 8 **H** me under the shadow of Your
Ps 27: 5 He shall **h** me in His pavilion
Ps 27: 5 His tabernacle He shall **h** me
Ps 27: 9 Do not **h** Your face from me
Ps 31:20 You shall **h** them in the
Ps 44:24 Why do You **h** Your face, And
Ps 51: 9 **H** Your face from my sins, And
Ps 55: 1 do not **h** Yourself from my
Ps 55:12 Then I could **h** from him
Ps 56: 6 They gather together, They **h**
Ps 64: 2 **H** me from the secret counsel
Ps 69:17 do not **h** Your face from Your
Ps 78: 4 We will not **h** them from their
Ps 88:14 Why do You **h** Your face from
Ps 89:46 Will You **h** Yourself forever
Ps 102: 2 Do not **h** Your face from me in
Ps 104:29 You **h** Your face, they are
Ps 119:19 Do not **h** Your commandments
Ps 139:12 darkness shall not **h** from You
Ps 143: 7 Do not **h** Your face from me,
Prov 28:12 arise, men **h** themselves
Prov 28:28 arise, men **h** themselves
Is 1:15 I will **h** My eyes from you
Is 2:10 and **h** in the dust, from the
Is 3: 9 they do not **h** it
Is 16: 3 **h** the outcasts, do not betray
Is 26:20 **h** yourself, as it were, for a
Is 29:15 to those who seek deep to **h**
Is 45:15 God, who **h** Yourself, O God of
Is 50: 6 I did not **h** My face from
Is 58: 7 not **h** yourself from your own
Jer 13: 4 **h** it there in a hole in the
Jer 13: 6 I commanded you to **h** there
Jer 23:24 Can anyone **h** himself in
Jer 36:19 Go and **h**, you and Jeremiah
Jer 38:14 **H** nothing from me
Jer 38:25 do not **h** it from us, and we
Jer 43: 9 **h** them in the sight of the
Jer 49:10 not be able to **h** himself
Lam 3:56 Do not **h** Your ear from my
Ezek 31: 8 garden of God could not **h** it
Ezek 39:29 I will not **h** My face from
Dan 10: 7 they fled to **h** themselves
Amos 9: 3 though they **h** themselves on
Amos 9: 3 though they **h** from My sight
Mic 3: 4 He will even **h** His face from
Rev 6:16 **h** us from the face of Him who

HIDEOUT (*see* HIDE, HIDEOUTS)
1Sa 23:22 see the place where his **h** is

HIDEOUTS (*see* HIDEOUT)
2Sa 22:46 come frightened from their **h**
Ps 18:45 come frightened from their **h**

HIDES (*see* HIDE)
1Sa 23:23 the lurking places where he **h**
Job 20:12 he **h** it under his tongue,
Job 34:29 when He **h** His face, who then
Job 42: 3 Who is this who **h** counsel
Ps 10:11 He **h** His face
Prov 10:18 Whoever **h** hatred has lying
Prov 22: 3 **h** himself, but the simple
Prov 27:12 foresees evil and **h** himself
Prov 28:27 but he who **h** his eyes will
Is 8:17 Who **h** His face from the house

HIDING (*see* HIDE)
1Sa 23:19 Is David not **h** with us in
1Sa 26: 1 Is David not **h** in the hill of
2Ch 22: 9 him (he was **h** in Samaria)
Job 15:18 not **h** anything received from
Job 31:33 by **h** my iniquity in my bosom,
Ps 32: 7 You are my **h** place
Ps 119:114 You are my **h** place and my
Is 28:17 will overflow the **h** place
Is 32: 2 A man will be as a **h** place

HIEL
1Ki 16:34 In his days **H** of Bethel built

HIERAPOLIS
Col 4:13 in Laodicea, and those in **H**

HIGH (*see* HIGHER, HIGHEST, HIGHLY)
Gen 7:17 it rose **h** above the earth
Gen 7:19 all the **h** hills under the
Gen 14:18 was the priest of God Most **H**
Gen 14:19 be Abram of God Most **H**,
Gen 14:20 And blessed be God Most **H**,
Gen 14:22 hand to the LORD, God Most **H**
Gen 29: 7 Look, it is still **h** day
Lev 21:10 he who is the **h** priest among
Lev 26:30 I will destroy your **h** places
Num 22:41 up to the **h** places of Baal
Num 24:16 the knowledge of the Most **H**
Num 33:52 demolish all their **h** places
Num 35:25 until the death of the **h**
Num 35:28 the death of the **h** priest
Num 35:28 **h** priest the manslayer may
Deut 3: 5 were fortified with **h** walls
Deut 12: 2 on the **h** mountains and on the
Deut 26:19 that He will set you **h** above
Deut 28: 1 **h** above all nations of the
Deut 28:52 all your gates until your **h**
Deut 32: 8 when the Most **H** divided their
Deut 32:27 Our hand is **h**
Deut 33:29 tread down their **h** places
Josh 20: 6 who is **h** priest in those days

1Sa 9:12 people today on the **h** place
1Sa 9:13 goes up to the **h** place to eat
1Sa 9:14 on his way up to the **h** place
1Sa 9:19 up before me to the **h** place
1Sa 9:25 the **h** place into the city
1Sa 10: 5 coming down from the **h** place
1Sa 10:13 he went to the **h** place
2Sa 1:19 is slain on your **h** places
2Sa 1:25 was slain in your **h** places
2Sa 22:14 the Most **H** uttered His voice
2Sa 22:34 and sets me on my **h** places
2Sa 23: 1 says the man raised up on **h**
1Ki 3: 2 sacrificed at the **h** places
1Ki 3: 3 incense at the **h** places
1Ki 3: 4 that was the great **h** place
1Ki 6:10 temple, each five cubits **h**
1Ki 6:20 wide, and twenty cubits **h**
1Ki 6:23 olive wood, each ten cubits **h**
1Ki 7:15 each one eighteen cubits **h**
1Ki 11: 7 Then Solomon built a **h** place
1Ki 12:31 made shrines on the **h** places
1Ki 12:32 the priests of the **h** places
1Ki 13: 2 the priests of the **h** places
1Ki 13:32 all the shrines on the **h**
1Ki 13:33 of people for the **h** places
1Ki 13:33 the priests of the **h** places
1Ki 14:23 built for themselves **h** places
1Ki 14:23 wooden images on every **h** hill
1Ki 15:14 But the **h** places were not
1Ki 21: 9 and seat Naboth with **h** honor
1Ki 21:12 seated Naboth with **h** honor
1Ki 22:43 Nevertheless the **h** places
1Ki 22:43 incense on the **h** places
2Ki 12: 3 But the **h** places were not
2Ki 12: 3 incense on the **h** places
2Ki 12:10 the **h** priest came up and put
2Ki 14: 4 However the **h** places were not
2Ki 14: 4 incense on the **h** places
2Ki 15: 4 except that the **h** places were
2Ki 15: 4 incense on the **h** places
2Ki 15:35 However the **h** places were not
2Ki 15:35 incense on the **h** places
2Ki 16: 4 incense on the **h** places, on
2Ki 17: 9 they built for themselves **h**
2Ki 17:10 wooden images on every **h** hill
2Ki 17:11 incense on all the **h** places
2Ki 17:29 them in the houses of the **h**
2Ki 17:32 priests of the **h** places, who
2Ki 17:32 the shrines of the **h** places
2Ki 18: 4 He removed the **h** places and
2Ki 18:22 is it not He whose **h** places
2Ki 19:22 and lifted up your eyes on **h**
2Ki 21: 3 For he rebuilt the **h** places
2Ki 22: 4 Go up to Hilkiah the **h** priest
2Ki 22: 8 Then Hilkiah the **h** priest
2Ki 23: 4 Hilkiah the **h** priest, the
2Ki 23: 5 to burn incense on the **h**
2Ki 23: 8 defiled the **h** places where
2Ki 23: 8 also he broke down the **h**
2Ki 23: 9 the priests of the **h** places
2Ki 23:13 **h** places that were east of
2Ki 23:15 the **h** place which Jeroboam
2Ki 23:15 the **h** place he broke down
2Ki 23:15 and he burned the **h** place and
2Ki 23:19 the **h** places that were in the
2Ki 23:20 all the priests of the **h**
1Ch 16:39 of the LORD at the **h** place
1Ch 17:17 estate of a man of **h** degree
1Ch 21:29 time at the **h** place in Gibeon
2Ch 1: 3 went to the **h** place that was
2Ch 1:13 **h** place that was at Gibeon
2Ch 3:15 pillars thirty-five cubits **h**
2Ch 6:13 broad, and three cubits **h**, and
2Ch 11:15 priests for the **h** places, for
2Ch 14: 3 the **h** places, and broke down
2Ch 14: 5 He also removed the **h** places
2Ch 15:17 But the **h** places were not
2Ch 17: 6 he removed the **h** places and
2Ch 20:19 Israel with voices loud and **h**
2Ch 20:33 Nevertheless the **h** places
2Ch 21:11 Moreover he made **h** places in
2Ch 24:11 the **h** priest's officer came
2Ch 28: 4 incense on the **h** places, on
2Ch 28:25 city of Judah he made **h**
2Ch 31: 1 and threw down the **h** places
2Ch 32:12 taken away His **h** places and
2Ch 33: 3 For he rebuilt the **h** places
2Ch 33:17 sacrificed on the **h** places
2Ch 33:19 sites where he built **h** places
2Ch 34: 3 and Jerusalem of the **h** places
2Ch 34: 9 came to Hilkiah the **h** priest
Neh 3: 1 Then Eliashib the **h** priest
Neh 3:20 of Eliashib the **h** priest
Neh 13:28 son of Eliashib the **h** priest
Esth 5:14 be made, fifty cubits **h**, and
Esth 7: 9 The gallows, fifty cubits **h**
Job 5:11 He sets on **h** those who are
Job 16:19 and my evidence is on **h**
Job 21:22 He judges those who are on **h**
Job 25: 2 makes peace in His **h** places
Job 31: 2 of the Almighty from on **h**
Job 39:18 When she lifts herself on **h**
Job 39:27 and make its nest on **h**
Job 41:34 He beholds every **h** thing
Ps 7: 7 sakes, therefore, return on **h**
Ps 7:17 the name of the LORD Most **H**
Ps 9: 2 praise to Your name, O Most **H**
Ps 18:13 the Most **H** uttered His voice,
Ps 18:33 And sets me on my **h** places
Ps 21: 7 Most **H** he shall not be moved
Ps 27: 5 He shall set me **h** upon a rock
Ps 46: 4 the tabernacle of the Most **H**
Ps 47: 2 the LORD Most **H** is awesome
Ps 49: 2 Both low and **h**, Rich and poor
Ps 50:14 pay your vows to the Most **H**
Ps 56: 2 fight against me, O Most **H**
Ps 57: 2 I will cry out to God Most **H**
Ps 62: 4 him down from his **h** position
Ps 62: 9 Men of **h** degree are a lie
Ps 68:18 You have ascended on **h**, You
Ps 69:29 O God, set me up on **h**
Ps 71:19 O God, is very **h**, You who
Ps 73:11 there knowledge in the Most **H**
Ps 75: 5 Do not lift up your horn on **h**
Ps 77:10 the right hand of the Most **H**
Ps 78:17 the Most **H** in the wilderness
Ps 78:35 the Most **H** God their redeemer
Ps 78:56 and provoked the Most **H** God
Ps 78:58 to anger with their **h** places
Ps 82: 6 are children of the Most **H**
Ps 83:18 Are the Most **H** over all the
Ps 87: 5 And the Most **H** Himself shall
Ps 89:13 hand, and **h** is Your right hand
Ps 91: 1 Most **H** Shall abide under the
Ps 91: 9 is my refuge, Even the Most **H**
Ps 91:14 I will set him on **h**, because
Ps 92: 1 to Your name, O Most **H**
Ps 92: 8 LORD, are on **h** forevermore
Ps 93: 4 The LORD on **h** is mightier
Ps 97: 9 are most **h** above all the
Ps 99: 2 He is **h** above all the peoples
Ps 103:11 heavens are **h** above the earth
Ps 104:18 The **h** hills are for the wild
Ps 107:11 the counsel of the Most **H**
Ps 107:41 Yet He sets the poor on **h**
Ps 113: 4 The LORD is **h** above all
Ps 113: 5 LORD our God, Who dwells on **h**
Ps 138: 6 Though the LORD is on **h**, Yet
Ps 139: 6 It is **h**, I cannot attain it
Ps 144: 2 My **h** tower and my deliverer,
Ps 149: 6 Let the **h** praises of God be
Ps 150: 5 Praise Him with **h** sounding
Prov 3: 4 **h** esteem in the sight of God
Prov 8: 2 on the top of the **h** hill,
Prov 18:11 and like a **h** wall in his own
Eccl 5: 8 for **h** official watches over
Eccl 5: 8 watches over **h** official, and
Is 2:13 cedars of Lebanon that are **h**
Is 2:14 upon all the **h** mountains, and
Is 2:15 upon every **h** tower, and upon
Is 6: 1 Lord sitting on a throne, **h**
Is 10:33 those of **h** stature will be
Is 13: 2 up a banner on the **h** mountain
Is 14:14 I will be like the Most **H**
Is 15: 2 to the **h** places to weep
Is 16:12 Moab is weary on the **h** place
Is 22:16 hews himself a sepulcher on **h**
Is 24:18 windows from on **h** are open
Is 24:21 the LORD will punish on **h** the
Is 25:12 The fortress of the **h** fort of
Is 26: 5 down those who dwell on **h**
Is 30:13 to fall, a bulge in a **h** wall
Is 30:25 will be on every **h** mountain
Is 30:25 on every **h** hill rivers and
Is 32:15 is poured upon us from on **h**
Is 33: 5 exalted, for He dwells on **h**
Is 33:16 he will dwell on **h**
Is 36: 7 is it not He whose **h** places
Is 37:23 and lifted up your eyes on **h**
Is 40: 9 get up into the **h** mountain
Is 40:26 Lift up your eyes on **h**, and
Is 52:13 and extolled and be very **h**
Is 57: 7 **h** mountain you have set your
Is 57:15 For thus says the **H** and Lofty
Is 57:15 I dwell in the **h** and holy
Is 58: 4 to make your voice heard on **h**
Is 58:14 on the **h** hills of the earth
Jer 2:20 when on every **h** hill and
Jer 3: 6 gone up on every **h** mountain
Jer 7:31 built the **h** places of Tophet
Jer 17: 2 green trees on the **h** hills
Jer 17: 3 your **h** places of sin within
Jer 17:12 A glorious **h** throne from the
Jer 19: 5 built the **h** places of Baal
Jer 20: 2 in the **h** gate of Benjamin
Jer 25:30 The LORD will roar from on **h**
Jer 32:35 they built the **h** places of
Jer 48: 1 the **h** stronghold is shamed and
Jer 48:35 sacrifices in the **h** places
Jer 49:16 your nest as **h** as the eagle
Jer 51:58 her **h** gates shall be burned
Lam 3:35 before the face of the Most **H**
Lam 3:38 mouth of the Most **H** that woe
Ezek 1:18 they were so **h** they were
Ezek 1:26 of a man **h** above it
Ezek 6: 3 I will destroy your **h** places
Ezek 6: 6 and the **h** places shall be
Ezek 6:13 their altars, on every **h** hill
Ezek 11:22 of Israel was **h** above them
Ezek 16:16 **h** places for yourself, and
Ezek 16:24 made a **h** place for yourself
Ezek 16:25 You built your **h** places at
Ezek 16:31 built your **h** place in every
Ezek 16:39 and break down your **h** places
Ezek 17:22 branches of the **h** cedar and
Ezek 17:22 one, and will plant it on a **h**
Ezek 17:24 have brought down the **h** tree
Ezek 20:28 and they saw all the **h** hills
Ezek 20:29 What is this **h** place to
Ezek 31: 3 the forest, and of **h** stature
Ezek 31:14 drinks water may ever be **h**
Ezek 34: 6 mountains, and on every **h** hill
Ezek 34:14 on the **h** mountains of Israel
Ezek 40: 2 set me on a very **h** mountain
Ezek 40:14 the gateposts, sixty cubits **h**
Ezek 40:42 a half wide, and one cubit **h**
Ezek 41: 3 and the entrance, six cubits **h**
Ezek 41: 8 rod, that is, six cubits **h**
Ezek 41:22 was of wood, three cubits **h**
Ezek 43: 7 their kings on their **h** places
Ezek 43:13 the base one cubit **h** and one
Ezek 43:15 altar hearth is four cubits **h**
Dan 3:26 servants of the Most **H** God
Dan 4: 2 Most **H** God has worked for me
Dan 4:17 may know that the Most **H**
Dan 4:24 is the decree of the Most **H**
Dan 4:25 **H** rules in the kingdom of men
Dan 4:32 you know that the Most **H**
Dan 4:34 and I blessed the Most **H** and
Dan 5:18 O king, the Most **H** God gave
Dan 5:21 till he knew that the Most **H**
Dan 7:18 **H** shall receive the kingdom
Dan 7:22 of the saints of the Most **H**
Dan 7:25 words against the Most **H**,
Dan 7:25 the saints of the Most **H**, and
Dan 7:27 the saints of the Most **H**
Dan 8: 3 and the two horns were **h**
Dan 8:11 **h** as the Prince of the host
Hos 7:16 return, but not to the Most **H**
Hos 10: 8 Also the **h** places of Aven,
Hos 11: 7 they call to the Most **H**, none
Amos 4:13 who treads the **h** places of
Amos 7: 9 The **h** places of Isaac shall
Obad 3 rock, whose habitation is **h**
Obad 4 yourself as **h** as the eagle
Mic 1: 3 tread on the **h** places of the
Mic 1: 5 And what are the **h** places of
Mic 6: 6 bow myself before the **H** God
Hab 2: 9 that he may set his nest on **h**
Hab 3:10 and lifted its hands on **h**
Hab 3:19 make me walk on my **h** hills
Zeph 1:16 and against the **h** towers
Hag 1: 1 the **h** priest, saying,
Hag 1:12 the **h** priest, with all the
Hag 1:14 the **h** priest, and the spirit
Hag 2: 2 the **h** priest, and to the
Hag 2: 4 of Jehozadak, the **h** priest
Zech 3: 1 he showed me Joshua the **h**
Zech 3: 8 the **h** priest, you and your
Zech 6:11 of Jehozadak, the **h** priest

Matt 4: 8 on an exceedingly **h** mountain
Matt 17: 1 brought them up on a **h**
Matt 26: 3 at the palace of the **h** priest
Matt 26:51 the servant of the **h** priest
Matt 26:57 away to Caiaphas the **h** priest
Matt 26:58 to the **h** priest's courtyard
Matt 26:62 the **h** priest arose and said to
Matt 26:63 the **h** priest answered and said
Matt 26:65 Then the **h** priest tore his
Mark 2:26 days of Abiathar the **h** priest
Mark 5: 7 Jesus, Son of the Most **H** God
Mark 6:21 the **h** officers, and the chief
Mark 9: 2 led them up on a **h** mountain
Mark 14:47 the servant of the **h** priest
Mark 14:53 Jesus away to the **h** priest
Mark 14:54 the courtyard of the **h** priest
Mark 14:60 the **h** priest stood up in the
Mark 14:61 Again the **h** priest asked Him,
Mark 14:63 Then the **h** priest tore his
Mark 14:66 girls of the **h** priest came
Luke 1:78 from on **h** has visited us
Luke 3: 2 and Caiaphas being **h** priests
Luke 4: 5 taking Him up on a **h** mountain
Luke 4:38 was sick with a **h** fever, and
Luke 8:28 Jesus, Son of the Most **H** God
Luke 22:50 the servant of the **h** priest
Luke 22:54 Him into the **h** priest's house
Luke 24:49 endued with power from on **h**
John 11:49 being **h** priest that year,
John 11:51 but being **h** priest that year
John 18:10 struck the **h** priest's servant
John 18:13 who was **h** priest that year
John 18:15 was known to the **h** priest
John 18:15 the courtyard of the **h** priest
John 18:16 who was known to the **h** priest
John 18:19 The **h** priest then asked Jesus
John 18:22 answer the **h** priest like that
John 18:24 to Caiaphas the **h** priest
John 18:26 the servants of the **h** priest
John 19:31 for that Sabbath was a **h** day)
Acts 4: 6 as well as Annas the **h** priest
Acts 4: 6 of the family of the **h** priest
Acts 5:17 Then the **h** priest rose up, and
Acts 5:21 But the **h** priest and those
Acts 5:24 Now when the **h** priest, the
Acts 5:27 And the **h** priest asked them,
Acts 7: 1 Then the **h** priest said, "Are
Acts 7:48 the Most **H** does not dwell in
Acts 9: 1 Lord, went to the **h** priest
Acts 16:17 servants of the Most **H** God
Acts 22: 5 as also the **h** priest bears me
Acts 23: 2 And the **h** priest Ananias
Acts 23: 4 Do you revile God's **h** priest
Acts 23: 5 that he was the **h** priest
Acts 24: 1 **h** priest came down with the
Acts 25: 2 Then the **h** priest and the
Rom 12:16 not set your mind on **h** things
Rom 13:11 that now it is **h** time to
2Co 10: 5 every **h** thing that exalts
Eph 4: 8 When He ascended on **h**, He led
Heb 1: 3 hand of the Majesty on **h**,
Heb 2:17 faithful **H** Priest in things
Heb 3: 1 **H** Priest of our confession,
Heb 4:14 great **H** Priest who has passed
Heb 4:15 have a **H** Priest who cannot
Heb 5: 5 Himself to become **H** Priest
Heb 5:10 called by God as **H** Priest
Heb 6:20 Jesus, having become **H** Priest
Heb 7: 1 priest of the Most **H** God
Heb 7:26 For such a **H** Priest was
Heb 7:27 daily, as those **h** priests
Heb 7:28 as **h** priests men who have
Heb 8: 1 We have such a **H** Priest, who
Heb 8: 3 For every **h** priest is
Heb 9: 7 **h** priest went alone once a
Heb 9:11 But Christ came as **H** Priest
Heb 9:25 as the **h** priest enters the
Heb 10:21 having a **H** Priest over the
Heb 13:11 by the **h** priest for sin, are
Rev 21:10 **h** mountain, and showed me the
Rev 21:12 **h** wall with twelve gates, and

HIGHER (*see* HIGH)
Num 24: 7 His king shall be **h** than Agag
Deut 28:43 who is among you shall rise **h**
Deut 28:43 **h** above you, and you shall
Ezra 9: 6 have risen **h** than our heads
Job 11: 8 They are **h** than heaven
Job 35: 5 clouds which are **h** than you
Ps 61: 2 to the rock that is **h** than I
Eccl 5: 8 **h** officials are over them
Is 55: 9 heavens are **h** than the earth
Is 55: 9 are My ways **h** than your ways
Dan 8: 3 but one was **h** than the other,
Dan 8: 3 and the **h** one came up last
Luke 14:10 say to you, 'Friend, go up **h**
Heb 7:26 has become **h** than the heavens

HIGHEST (*see* HIGH)
Deut 10:14 the **h** heavens belong to the
Esth 1:14 who ranked **h** in the kingdom)
Job 22:12 And see the **h** stars, how lofty
Ps 89:27 The **h** of the kings of the
Prov 9: 3 from the **h** places of the city
Prov 9:14 on a seat by the **h** places of
Jer 2:21 vine, a seed of **h** quality
Ezek 17: 3 from the cedar the **h** branch
Ezek 17:22 **h** branches of the high cedar
Ezek 41: 7 the lowest story to the **h** by
Matt 21: 9 Hosanna in the **h**!
Mark 11:10 Hosanna in the **h**!
Luke 1:32 be called the Son of the **H**
Luke 1:35 and the power of the **H** will
Luke 1:76 called the prophet of the **H**
Luke 2:14 Glory to God in the **h**, and on
Luke 6:35 and you will be sons of the **H**
Luke 19:38 in heaven and glory in the **h**

HIGHLY (*see* HIGH)
1Sa 18:30 his name became **h** esteemed
1Ch 14: 2 for his kingdom was **h** exalted
Luke 1:28 **h** favored one, the Lord is
Luke 16:15 For what is **h** esteemed among
Acts 5:13 the people esteemed them **h**
Rom 12: 3 more **h** than he ought to think
Phil 2: 9 God also has **h** exalted Him
1Th 5:13 to esteem them very **h** in love

HIGHWAY (*see* HIGHWAYS)
Num 20:17 we will go along the King's **H**
Num 20:19 We will go by the **H**, and if I
Num 21:22 King's **H** until we have passed
Judg 21:19 on the east side of the **h**
1Sa 6:12 Shemesh, and went along the **h**
2Sa 20:12 blood in the middle of the **h**
2Sa 20:12 Amasa from the **h** to the field
2Sa 20:13 he was removed from the **h**
2Ki 18:17 which was on the **h** to the
1Ch 26:16 Gate on the ascending **h**
1Ch 26:18 there were four on the **h**
Prov 15:19 the way of the upright is a **h**
Prov 16:17 The **h** of the upright is to
Is 7: 3 on the **h** to the Fuller's
Is 11:16 There will be a **h** for the
Is 19:23 be a **h** from Egypt to Assyria
Is 35: 8 A **h** shall be there, and a road
Is 35: 8 be called the **H** of Holiness
Is 36: 2 on the **h** to the Fuller's
Is 40: 3 in the desert a **h** for our God
Is 62:10 build up, build up the **h**
Jer 18:15 in pathways and not on a **h**
Jer 31:21 set your heart toward the **h**

HIGHWAYS (*see* HIGHWAY)
Lev 26:22 and your **h** shall be desolate
Judg 5: 6 the **h** were deserted, and the
Judg 20:31 in the **h** (one of which goes
Judg 20:32 away from the city to the **h**
Judg 20:45 thousand of them on the **h**
Is 33: 8 The **h** lie waste, the
Is 49:11 and My **h** shall be elevated
Amos 5:16 they shall say in all the **h**
Matt 22: 9 Therefore go into the **h**, and
Matt 22:10 servants went out into the **h**
Luke 14:23 servant, 'Go out into the **h**

HILEN (*see* HOLON)
1Ch 6:58 **H** with its common-lands,

HILKIAH (*see* HELKAI)
2Ki 18:18 king, Eliakim the son of **H**
2Ki 18:26 Then Eliakim the son of **H**
2Ki 18:37 Then Eliakim the son of **H**
2Ki 22: 4 Go up to **H** the high priest,
2Ki 22: 8 Then **H** the high priest said
2Ki 22: 8 **H** gave the book to Shaphan,
2Ki 22:10 **H** the priest has given me a
2Ki 22:12 king commanded **H** the priest
2Ki 22:14 So **H** the priest, Ahikam,
2Ki 23: 4 commanded **H** the high priest
2Ki 23:24 **H** the priest found in the
1Ch 6:13 Shallum begot **H**
1Ch 6:13 and **H** begot Azariah
1Ch 6:45 son of Amaziah, the son of **H**
1Ch 9:11 Azariah the son of **H**, the son
1Ch 26:11 **H** the second, Tebaliah the
2Ch 34: 9 came to **H** the high priest
2Ch 34:14 **H** the priest found the Book
2Ch 34:15 Then **H** answered and said to
2Ch 34:15 **H** gave the book to Shaphan
2Ch 34:18 **H** the priest has given me a
2Ch 34:20 Then the king commanded **H**
2Ch 34:22 So **H** and those whom the king
2Ch 35: 8 **H**, Zechariah, and Jehiel,
Ezra 7: 1 son of Azariah, the son of **H**
Neh 8: 4 Shema, Anaiah, Urijah, **H**
Neh 11:11 Seraiah the son of **H**, the son
Neh 12: 7 Sallu, Amok, **H**, and Jedaiah
Neh 12:21 of **H**, Hashabiah
Is 22:20 servant Eliakim the son of **H**
Is 36: 3 And Eliakim the son of **H**, who
Is 36:22 Then Eliakim the son of **H**
Jer 1: 1 of Jeremiah the son of **H**, of
Jer 29: 3 and Gemariah the son of **H**

HILL (*see* HILLS, HILLSIDE, HILLY)
Ex 17: 9 stand on the top of the **h**
Ex 17:10 went up to the top of the **h**
Josh 5: 3 at the **h** of the foreskins
Josh 15: 9 the **h** to the fountain of the
Josh 18:13 near the **h** that lies on the
Josh 18:14 from the **h** that lies before
Josh 24:33 they buried him in a **h** that
Judg 7: 1 the **h** of Moreh in the valley
Judg 16: 3 of the **h** that faces Hebron
1Sa 7: 1 house of Abinadab on the **h**
1Sa 9:11 went up the **h** to the city
1Sa 10: 5 that you shall come to the **h**
1Sa 10:10 When they came there to the **h**
1Sa 23:19 in the **h** of Hachilah, which
1Sa 25:20 down under cover of the **h**
1Sa 26: 1 hiding in the **h** of Hachilah
1Sa 26: 3 encamped in the **h** of Hachilah
1Sa 26:13 on the top of a **h** afar off
2Sa 2:24 they came to the **h** of Ammah
2Sa 2:25 their stand on top of a **h**
2Sa 6: 3 Abinadab, which was on the **h**
2Sa 6: 4 Abinadab, which was on the **h**
2Sa 21: 9 them on the **h** before the LORD
1Ki 11: 7 on the **h** that is east of
1Ki 14:23 wooden images on every high **h**
1Ki 16:24 he bought the **h** of Samaria
1Ki 16:24 then he built on the **h**, and
1Ki 16:24 of Shemer, owner of the **h**
2Ki 1: 9 sitting on the top of a **h**
2Ki 4:27 to the man of God at the **h**
2Ki 17:10 wooden images on every high **h**
Ps 2: 6 My King On My holy **h** of Zion
Ps 3: 4 He heard me from His holy **h**
Ps 15: 1 Who may dwell in Your holy **h**
Ps 24: 3 ascend into the **h** of the LORD
Ps 42: 6 of Hermon, From the **H** Mizar
Ps 43: 3 them bring me to Your holy **h**
Ps 99: 9 God, And worship at His holy **h**
Prov 8: 2 on the top of the high **h**,
Song 4: 6 and to the **h** of frankincense
Is 5: 1 vineyard On a very fruitful **h**
Is 7:25 to any **h** which could be dug
Is 10:32 of Zion, the **h** of Jerusalem
Is 30:17 and as a banner on a **h**
Is 30:25 and on every high **h** rivers
Is 31: 4 for Mount Zion and for its **h**
Is 40: 4 and **h** shall be made low
Jer 2:20 when on every high **h** and
Jer 16:16 every mountain and every **h**
Jer 31:39 forward over the **h** Gareb
Jer 49:16 Who hold the height of the **h**
Jer 50: 6 have gone from mountain to **h**
Ezek 6:13 their altars, on every high **h**
Ezek 34: 6 mountains, and on every high **h**
Ezek 34:26 all around My **h** a blessing
Matt 5:14 set on a **h** cannot be hidden
Luke 1:39 went into the **h** country with
Luke 1:65 all the **h** country of Judea
Luke 3: 5 mountain and **h** brought low
Luke 4:29 the **h** on which their city was

HILLEL
Judg 12:13 him, Abdon the son of **H** the
Judg 12:15 son of **H** the Pirathonite died

HILLS (*see* HILL)
Gen 7:19 and all the high **h** under the
Gen 49:26 bound of the everlasting **h**
Num 23: 9 and from the **h** I behold him
Deut 8: 7 that flow out of valleys and **h**

Deut 8: 9 out of whose **h** you can dig
Deut 11:11 to possess is a land of **h**
Deut 12: 2 high mountains and on the **h**
Deut 33:15 things of the everlasting **h**
Josh 9: 1 side of the Jordan, in the **h**
1Ki 20:23 Their gods are gods of the **h**
1Ki 20:28 The LORD is God of the **h**, but
2Ki 16: 4 on the high places, on the **h**
2Ch 28: 4 on the high places, on the **h**
Job 15: 7 Or were you made before the **h**
Ps 18: 7 of the **h** also quaked and were
Ps 50:10 And the cattle on a thousand **h**
Ps 65:12 the little **h** rejoice on every
Ps 72: 3 the people, And the little **h**
Ps 80:10 The **h** were covered with its
Ps 95: 4 heights of the **h** are His also
Ps 98: 8 Let the **h** be joyful together
Ps 104:10 Which flow among the **h**
Ps 104:13 He waters the **h** from His
Ps 104:18 The high **h** are for the wild
Ps 104:32 He touches the **h**, and they
Ps 114: 4 rams, The little **h** like lambs
Ps 114: 6 O little **h**, like lambs
Ps 121: 1 will lift up my eyes to the **h**
Ps 148: 9 Mountains and all **h**
Prov 8:25 were settled, before the **h**
Song 2: 8 skipping upon the **h**
Is 2: 2 shall be exalted above the **h**
Is 2:14 and upon all the **h** that are
Is 5:25 them, and the **h** trembled
Is 40:12 scales and the **h** in a balance
Is 41:15 and make the **h** like chaff
Is 42:15 lay waste the mountains and **h**
Is 54:10 and the **h** be removed, but My
Is 55:12 the **h** shall break forth into
Is 58:14 on the high **h** of the earth
Is 65: 7 and blasphemed Me on the **h**
Jer 3:23 hoped for from the **h**, and from
Jer 4:24 all the **h** moved back and forth
Jer 13:27 on the **h** in the fields
Jer 17: 2 the green trees on the high **h**
Jer 26:18 like the bare **h** of the forest
Ezek 6: 3 to the mountains, to the **h**
Ezek 20:28 and they saw all the high **h**
Ezek 35: 8 on your **h** and in your valleys
Ezek 36: 4 GOD to the mountains, the **h**
Ezek 36: 6 say to the mountains, the **h**
Hos 4:13 and burn incense on the **h**
Hos 10: 8 And to the **h**, "Fall on us
Joel 3:18 the **h** shall flow with milk,
Amos 9:13 all the **h** shall flow with it
Mic 3:12 like the bare **h** of the forest
Mic 4: 1 shall be exalted above the **h**
Mic 6: 1 let the **h** hear your voice
Nah 1: 5 Him, the **h** melt, and the earth
Hab 3: 6 the perpetual **h** bowed
Hab 3:19 make me walk on my high **h**
Zeph 1:10 and a loud crashing from the **h**
Luke 23:30 and to the **h**, "Cover us

HILLSIDE (*see* HILL)
2Sa 13:34 the road on the **h** behind him
2Sa 16:13 went along the **h** opposite him

HILLY (*see* HILL)
Josh 17:11 three **h** regions

HILT
Judg 3:22 Even the **h** went in after the

HIM (*see* PREFACE)

HIMSELF (*see* PREFACE)

HIN
Ex 29:40 of a **h** of pressed oil, and
Ex 29:40 one-fourth of a **h** of wine as
Ex 30:24 and a **h** of olive oil
Lev 19:36 a just ephah, and a just **h**
Lev 23:13 be of wine, one-fourth of a **h**
Num 15: 4 with one-fourth of a **h** of oil
Num 15: 5 one-fourth of a **h** of wine as
Num 15: 6 with one-third of a **h** of oil
Num 15: 7 shall offer one-third of a **h**
Num 15: 9 mixed with half a **h** of oil
Num 15:10 the drink offering half a **h**
Num 28: 5 of a **h** of pressed oil
Num 28: 7 of a **h** for each lamb
Num 28:14 half a **h** of wine for a bull
Num 28:14 one-third of a **h** for a ram
Num 28:14 one-fourth of a **h** for a lamb
Ezek 4:11 by measure, one-sixth of a **h**
Ezek 45:24 together with a **h** of oil for
Ezek 46: 5 as well as a **h** of oil with
Ezek 46: 7 a **h** of oil with every ephah
Ezek 46:11 a **h** of oil with every ephah
Ezek 46:14 and a third of a **h** of oil to

HINDER (*see* HINDERED, HINDERS)
Gen 24:56 Do not **h** me, since the LORD
Num 22:16 Please let nothing **h** you
Job 9:12 He takes away, who can **h** Him
Job 11:10 judgment, then who can **h** Him
1Co 9:12 we **h** the gospel of Christ

HINDERED (*see* HINDER)
Ezra 6: 8 men, so that they are not **h**
Prov 4:12 your steps will not be **h**
Luke 11:52 who were entering in you **h**
Rom 1:13 to you (but was **h** until now)
Rom 15:22 much **h** from coming to you
Gal 5: 7 Who **h** you from obeying the
1Th 2:18 but Satan **h** us
1Pe 3: 7 your prayers may not be **h**

HINDERS (*see* HINDER)
Is 14: 6 is persecuted and no one **h**
Acts 8:36 What **h** me from being baptized

HINGES
1Ki 7:50 the **h** of gold, both for the
Prov 26:14 As a door turns on its **h**, so

HINNOM
Josh 15: 8 of **H** to the southern slope of
Josh 15: 8 the Valley of **H** westward,
Josh 18:16 the Valley of the Son of **H**
Josh 18:16 descended to the Valley of **H**
2Ki 23:10 in the Valley of the Son of **H**
2Ch 28: 3 in the Valley of the Son of **H**
2Ch 33: 6 in the Valley of the Son of **H**
Neh 11:30 Beersheba to the Valley of **H**
Jer 7:31 in the Valley of the Son of **H**
Jer 7:32 or the Valley of the Son of **H**
Jer 19: 2 to the Valley of the Son of **H**
Jer 19: 6 or the Valley of the Son of **H**
Jer 32:35 in the Valley of the Son of **H**

HIP (*see* HIPS)
Gen 32:25 touched the socket of his **h**
Gen 32:25 the socket of Jacob's **h** was
Gen 32:31 on him, and he limped on his **h**
Gen 32:32 which is on the **h** socket
Gen 32:32 the socket of Jacob's **h** in
Judg 15: 8 So he attacked them **h** and

HIPS (*see* HIP)
2Sa 20: 8 in its sheath at his **h**
Job 40:16 now, his strength is in his **h**
Dan 5: 6 joints of his **h** were loosened

HIRAH
Gen 38: 1 Adullamite whose name was **H**
Gen 38:12 his friend **H** the Adullamite

HIRAM (*see* HIRAM'S, HURAM)
2Sa 5:11 Then **H** king of Tyre sent
1Ki 5: 1 Now **H** king of Tyre sent his
1Ki 5: 1 for **H** had always loved David
1Ki 5: 2 Then Solomon sent to **H**,
1Ki 5: 7 when **H** heard the words of
1Ki 5: 8 Then **H** sent to Solomon,
1Ki 5:10 So **H** gave Solomon cedar and
1Ki 5:11 And Solomon gave **H** twenty
1Ki 5:11 gave to **H** year by year
1Ki 5:12 and there was peace between **H**
1Ki 7:13 sent and brought **H** from Tyre
1Ki 7:40 **H** made the lavers and the
1Ki 7:40 So **H** finished doing all the
1Ki 7:45 All these articles which **H**
1Ki 9:11 (**H** the king of Tyre had
1Ki 9:11 **H** twenty cities in the land
1Ki 9:12 Then **H** went from Tyre to see
1Ki 9:14 Then **H** sent the king one
1Ki 9:27 Then **H** sent his servants with
1Ki 10:11 Also, the ships of **H**, which
1Ki 10:22 at sea with the fleet of **H**
1Ch 14: 1 Now **H** king of Tyre sent
2Ch 2: 3 sent to **H** king of Tyre,
2Ch 2:11 Then **H** king of Tyre answered
2Ch 2:12 **H** also said: Blessed be
2Ch 8: 2 which **H** had given to Solomon
2Ch 8:18 **H** sent him ships by the hand
2Ch 9:10 Also, the servants of **H** and

HIRAM'S (*see* HIRAM)
1Ki 5:18 **H** builders, and the Gebalites

HIRE (*see* HIRED, HIRELING)
Gen 30:18 God has given me my **h**,
Ex 22:15 was hired, it came for its **h**
Deut 23:18 You shall not bring the **h** of
1Ch 19: 6 talents of silver to **h** for
Prov 26:10 things gives the fool his **h**
Is 46: 6 they **h** a goldsmith, and he
Ezek 16:41 you shall no longer **h** lovers
Zech 8:10 for man nor any **h** for beast
Matt 20: 1 **h** laborers for his vineyard

HIRED (*see* HIRE)
Gen 30:16 for I have surely **h** you with
Ex 12:45 a **h** servant shall not eat it
Ex 22:15 if it was **h**, it came for its
Lev 19:13 The wages of him who is **h**
Lev 22:10 or a **h** servant, shall not eat
Lev 25: 6 and your **h** servant, for the
Lev 25:40 But as a **h** servant and a
Lev 25:50 time of a **h** servant for him
Lev 25:53 him as a yearly **h** servant
Deut 15:18 **h** servant in serving you six
Deut 23: 4 because they **h** against you
Deut 24:14 a **h** servant who is poor and
Judg 9: 4 which Abimelech **h** worthless
Judg 18: 4 He has **h** me, and I have become
1Sa 2: 5 **h** themselves out for bread
2Sa 10: 6 **h** the Syrians of Beth Rehob
2Ki 7: 6 the king of Israel has **h**
1Ch 19: 7 So they **h** for themselves
2Ch 24:12 they **h** masons and carpenters
2Ch 25: 6 He also **h** one hundred
Ezra 4: 5 **h** counselors against them to
Neh 6:12 Tobiah and Sanballat had **h** him
Neh 6:13 For this reason he was **h**,
Neh 13: 2 but **h** Balaam against them to
Job 7: 1 also like the days of a **h** man
Job 7: 2 and like a **h** man who eagerly
Job 14: 6 till like a **h** man he finishes
Is 7:20 will shave with a **h** razor
Is 16:14 as the years of a **h** man, the
Is 21:16 to the year of a **h** man, all
Ezek 16:33 **h** them to come to you from
Hos 8: 9 Ephraim has **h** lovers
Hos 8:10 though they have **h** among the
Matt 20: 7 to him, 'Because no one **h** us
Matt 20: 9 **h** about the eleventh hour
Mark 1:20 the boat with the **h** servants
Luke 15:17 How many of my father's **h**
Luke 15:19 like one of your **h** servants

HIRELING (*see* HIRE)
John 10:12 But he who is a **h** and not the
John 10:13 The **h** flees because he is a
John 10:13 flees because he is a **h** and

HIS (*see* PREFACE)

HISS (*see* HISSING)
1Ki 9: 8 will be astonished and will **h**
Job 27:23 shall **h** him out of his place
Jer 19: 8 **h** because of all its plagues
Jer 49:17 will **h** at all its plagues
Jer 50:13 and **h** at all her plagues
Lam 2:15 they **h** and shake their heads
Lam 2:16 they **h** and gnash their teeth
Ezek 27:36 the peoples will **h** at you
Zeph 2:15 who passes by her shall **h**

HISSING (*see* HISS)
Jer 18:16 desolate and a perpetual **h**
Jer 19: 8 this city desolate and a **h**
Jer 25: 9 them an astonishment, a **h**
Jer 25:18 an astonishment, a **h**, and a
Jer 29:18 a curse, an astonishment, a **h**
Jer 51:37 an astonishment and a **h**,
Mic 6:16 and your inhabitants a **h**

HISTORY
Gen 2: 4 This is the **h** of the heavens

HIT
1Sa 31: 3 and the archers **h** him, and he
1Ch 10: 3 and the archers **h** him, and he

HITCH (*see* HITCHED)
1Sa 6: 7 and **h** the cows to the cart

HITCHED (*see* HITCH)
1Sa 6:10 **h** them to the cart, and shut

HITTITE (*see* HITTITES)
Gen 23:10 Ephron the **H** answered
Gen 25: 9 Ephron the son of Zohar the **H**
Gen 26:34 the daughter of Beeri the **H**
Gen 26:34 the daughter of Elon the **H**
Gen 36: 2 the daughter of Elon the **H**
Gen 49:29 in the field of Ephron the **H**
Gen 49:30 the **H** as a possession for a
Gen 50:13 **H** as property for a burial
Ex 23:28 and the **H** from before you
Ex 33: 2 and the Amorite and the **H** and
Ex 34:11 and the Canaanite and the **H**
Deut 20:17 the **H** and the Amorite and the
Josh 9: 1 the **H**, the Amorite, the
Josh 11: 3 the west, the Amorite, the **H**
1Sa 26: 6 and said to Ahimelech the **H**
2Sa 11: 3 the wife of Uriah the **H**
2Sa 11: 6 Send me Uriah the **H**
2Sa 11:17 and Uriah the **H** died also
2Sa 11:21 Uriah the **H** is dead also
2Sa 11:24 Uriah the **H** is dead also
2Sa 12: 9 Uriah the **H** with the sword
2Sa 12:10 Uriah the **H** to be your wife
2Sa 23:39 and Uriah the **H**
1Ki 15: 5 in the matter of Uriah the **H**
1Ch 11:41 Uriah the **H**, Zabad the son of
Ezek 16: 3 an Amorite and your mother a **H**
Ezek 16:45 your mother was a **H** and your

HITTITES (*see* HITTITE)
Gen 15:20 the **H**, the Perizzites, and the
Ex 3: 8 of the Canaanites and the **H**
Ex 3:17 of the Canaanites and the **H**
Ex 13: 5 of the Canaanites and the **H**
Ex 23:23 in to the Amorites and the **H**
Num 13:29 the **H**, the Jebusites, and the
Deut 7: 1 nations before you, the **H**
Josh 1: 4 all the land of the **H**, and to
Josh 3:10 you the Canaanites and the **H**
Josh 12: 8 the **H**, the Amorites, the
Josh 24:11 the Canaanites, the **H**, the
Judg 1:26 man went to the land of the **H**
Judg 3: 5 among the Canaanites, the **H**
1Ki 9:20 were left of the Amorites, **H**
1Ki 10:29 to all the kings of the **H**
1Ki 11: 1 Edomites, Sidonians, and **H**
2Ki 7: 6 against us the kings of the **H**
2Ch 1:17 to all the kings of the **H**
2Ch 8: 7 people who were left of the **H**
Ezra 9: 1 of the Canaanites, the **H**, the
Neh 9: 8 land of the Canaanites, the **H**

HIVITE (*see* HIVITES)
Gen 10:17 the **H**, the Arkite, and the
Gen 34: 2 the son of Hamor the **H**,
Gen 36: 2 the daughter of Zibeon the **H**
Ex 23:28 which shall drive out the **H**
Ex 33: 2 and the Perizzite and the **H**
Ex 34:11 and the Perizzite and the **H**
Deut 20:17 and the Perizzite and the **H**
Josh 9: 1 the Perizzite, the **H**, and the
Josh 11: 3 the **H** below Hermon in the
1Ch 1:15 the **H**, the Arkite, and the

HIVITES (*see* HIVITE)
Ex 3: 8 and the Perizzites and the **H**
Ex 3:17 and the Perizzites and the **H**
Ex 13: 5 and the Amorites and the **H** and
Ex 23:23 and the Canaanites and the **H**
Deut 7: 1 and the Perizzites and the **H**
Josh 3:10 and the Hittites and the **H** and
Josh 9: 7 men of Israel said to the **H**
Josh 11:19 of Israel, except the **H**, the
Josh 12: 8 the Perizzites, the **H**, and
Josh 24:11 the Girgashites, the **H**, and
Judg 3: 3 and the **H** who dwelt in Mount
Judg 3: 5 the Perizzites, the **H**, and
2Sa 24: 7 and to all the cities of the **H**
1Ki 9:20 Hittites, Perizzites, **H**, and
2Ch 8: 7 Amorites, Perizzites, **H**, and

HIZKI
1Ch 8:17 Zebadiah, Meshullam, **H**,

HO
Is 55: 1 **H**! Everyone who thirsts,

HOBAB (*see* JETHER, JETHRO)
Num 10:29 Now Moses said to **H** the son
Judg 4:11 of the children of **H** the

HOBAH
Gen 14:15 and pursued them as far as **H**

HOD
1Ch 7:37 Bezer, **H**, Shamma, Shilshah,

HODAVIAH (*see* HODEVAH)
1Ch 3:24 The sons of Elioenai were **H**
1Ch 5:24 Eliel, Azriel, Jeremiah, **H**
1Ch 9: 7 of Meshullam, the son of **H**
Ezra 2:40 and Kadmiel, of the sons of **H**

HODESH
1Ch 8: 9 By **H** his wife he begot Jobab,

HODEVAH (*see* HODAVIAH)
Neh 7:43 and of the children of **H**,

HODIAH'S (*see* HODIJAH)
1Ch 4:19 The sons of **H** wife, the

HODIJAH (*see* HODIAH'S)
Neh 8: 7 Jamin, Akkub, Shabbethai, **H**
Neh 9: 5 Hashabniah, Sherebiah, **H**
Neh 10:10 Shebaniah, **H**, Kelita, Pelaiah
Neh 10:13 **H**, Bani, and Beninu
Neh 10:18 **H**, Hashum, Bezai,

HOE
Is 7:25 which could be dug with the **h**

HOGLAH (*see* BETH HOGLAH)
Num 26:33 were Mahlah, Noah, **H**, Milcah,
Num 27: 1 Mahlah, Noah, **H**, Milcah, and
Num 36:11 for Mahlah, Tirzah, **H**, Milcah
Josh 17: 3 Mahlah, Noah, **H**, Milcah, and

HOHAM
Josh 10: 3 sent to **H** king of Hebron,

HOISTED
Acts 27:40 they **h** the mainsail to the

HOLD (*see* HELD, HOLDERS, HOLDING, HOLDS)
Gen 19:16 the men took **h** of his hand
Gen 21:18 **h** him with your hand, for I
Gen 25:26 his hand took **h** of Esau's
Gen 48:17 so he took **h** of his father's
Ex 5: 1 that they may **h** a feast to Me
Ex 9: 2 let them go, and still **h** them
Ex 10: 9 for we must **h** a feast to the
Ex 14:14 and you shall **h** your peace
Ex 15:14 sorrow will take **h** of the
Ex 15:15 trembling will take **h** of them
Ex 20: 7 for the LORD will not **h** him
Deut 5:11 for the LORD will not **h** him
Deut 10:20 and to Him you shall **h** fast
Deut 11:22 His ways, and to **h** fast to Him
Deut 13: 4 serve Him and **h** fast to Him
Deut 21:19 mother shall take **h** of him
Deut 32:41 My hand takes **h** on judgment
Josh 22: 5 to **h** fast to Him, and to serve
Josh 23: 8 but you shall **h** fast to the
Judg 16: 3 took **h** of the doors of the
Judg 16:29 And Samson took **h** of the two
Judg 19:29 laid **h** of his concubine, and
Judg 20: 6 So I took **h** of my concubine,
Ruth 3:15 shawl that is on you and **h** it
1Sa 11: 3 **H** off for seven days, that we
2Sa 1:11 Then David took **h** of his own
2Sa 2:21 lay **h** on one of the young men
2Sa 3: 6 his **h** on the house of Saul
2Sa 6: 6 took **h** of it, for the oxen
2Sa 13:11 him to eat, he took **h** of her
2Sa 13:20 But now **h** your peace, my
1Ki 1:50 took **h** of the horns of the
1Ki 1:51 he has taken **h** of the horns
1Ki 2: 9 do not **h** him guiltless, for
1Ki 2:28 took **h** of the horns of the
1Ki 11:30 Then Ahijah took **h** of the new
1Ki 18:32 enough to **h** two seahs of seed
2Ki 2:12 he took **h** of his own clothes
2Ki 6:32 and **h** him fast at the door
1Ch 13: 9 put out his hand to **h** the ark
Job 2: 9 him, "Do you still **h** to your
Job 6:24 me, and I will **h** my tongue
Job 9:28 You will not **h** me innocent
Job 11: 3 talk make men **h** their peace
Job 13:13 **H** your peace with me, and let
Job 13:19 If now I **h** my tongue, I
Job 17: 9 righteous will **h** to his way
Job 18: 9 and a snare lays **h** of him
Job 21: 6 trembling takes **h** of my flesh
Job 27: 6 My righteousness I **h** fast
Job 30:16 of affliction take **h** of me
Job 33:31 **h** your peace, and I will speak
Job 33:33 **h** your peace, and I will teach
Job 36:17 and justice take **h** of you
Job 38:13 that it might take **h** of the
Ps 2: 4 The LORD shall **h** them in
Ps 35: 2 Take **h** of shield and buckler,
Ps 48: 6 Fear took **h** of them there, And
Ps 69:24 wrathful anger take **h** of them
Ps 73:23 You **h** me by my right hand
Ps 77: 4 You **h** my eyelids open
Ps 83: 1 Do not **h** Your peace, And do
Ps 94:18 mercy, O LORD, will **h** me up
Ps 116: 3 pangs of Sheol laid **h** of me
Ps 119:53 Indignation has taken **h** of me
Ps 119:117 **H** me up, and I shall be safe,
Ps 139:10 And Your right hand shall **h** me
Prov 3:18 to those who take **h** of her
Prov 4:13 Take firm **h** of instruction,
Prov 5: 5 her steps lay **h** of hell
Prov 20:16 **h** it as a pledge when it is
Prov 24:11 **h** back those stumbling to the
Prov 27:13 **h** it in pledge when he is
Eccl 2: 3 and how to lay **h** on folly
Song 3: 8 They all **h** swords, being
Song 7: 8 I will take **h** of its branches
Is 3: 6 When a man takes **h** of his
Is 4: 1 women shall take **h** of one man
Is 5:29 roar and lay **h** of the prey
Is 13: 8 sorrows will take **h** of them
Is 21: 3 pangs have taken **h** of me,
Is 27: 5 let him take **h** of My strength
Is 41:13 God, will **h** your right hand,
Is 42: 6 and will **h** Your hand
Is 56: 2 son of man who lays **h** on it
Is 56: 4 Me, and **h** fast My covenant,
Is 62: 1 sake I will not **h** My peace
Is 62: 6 who shall never **h** their peace
Is 64: 7 himself up to take **h** of You
Is 64:12 Will You **h** Your peace, and
Jer 2:13 cisterns that can **h** no water
Jer 4:19 I cannot **h** my peace, because
Jer 6:23 They will lay **h** on bow and
Jer 6:24 Anguish has taken **h** of us
Jer 8: 5 They **h** fast to deceit, they
Jer 8:21 has taken **h** of me
Jer 49:16 Who **h** the height of the hill
Jer 50:42 They shall **h** the bow and the
Jer 50:43 anguish has taken **h** of him
Ezek 24:14 I will not **h** back, nor will I
Ezek 29: 7 When they took **h** of you with
Ezek 30:21 it strong enough to **h** a sword
Amos 6:10 he will say, "**H** your tongue
Hab 1:13 **h** Your tongue when the wicked
Matt 12:11 Sabbath, will not lay **h** of it
Matt 14: 3 For Herod had laid **h** of John
Matt 26:57 those who had laid **h** of Jesus
Mark 3:21 they went out to lay **h** of Him
Mark 6:17 laid **h** of John, and bound him
Mark 7: 4 which they have received and **h**
Mark 7: 8 you **h** the tradition of men
Mark 12:12 they sought to lay **h** of Him
Mark 14:51 the young men laid **h** of him
Luke 23:26 they laid **h** of a certain man,
1Co 15: 2 if you **h** fast that word which
Phil 2:29 and **h** such men in esteem
Phil 3:12 that I may lay **h** of that for
Phil 3:12 Jesus has also laid **h** of me
1Th 5:21 **h** fast what is good
2Th 2:15 **h** the traditions which you
1Ti 6:12 lay **h** on eternal life, to
1Ti 6:19 may lay **h** on eternal life
2Ti 1:13 **H** fast the pattern of sound
Heb 3: 6 if we **h** fast the confidence
Heb 3:14 if we **h** the beginning of our
Heb 4:14 let us **h** fast our confession
Heb 6:18 **h** of the hope set before us
Heb 10:23 Let us **h** fast the confession
Jas 2: 1 do not **h** the faith of our
Rev 2:13 you **h** fast to My name, and did
Rev 2:14 who **h** the doctrine of Balaam
Rev 2:15 who **h** the doctrine of the
Rev 2:25 But **h** fast what you have till
Rev 3: 3 **h** fast and repent
Rev 3:11 **H** fast what you have, that no
Rev 20: 2 He laid **h** of the dragon, that

HOLDERS (*see* HOLD)
Ex 25:27 as **h** for the poles to bear
Ex 26:29 of gold as **h** for the bars
Ex 30: 4 they will be **h** for the poles
Ex 36:34 of gold to be **h** for the bars
Ex 37:14 as **h** for the poles to bear

Ex 37:27 as **h** for the poles with which
Ex 38: 5 grating, as **h** for the poles

HOLDING (*see* HOLD)
1Sa 25:36 **h** a feast in his house, like
Jer 6:11 I am weary of **h** it in
Jer 20: 9 I was weary of **h** it back, and
Mark 7: 3 **h** the tradition of the elders
Phil 2:16 **h** fast the word of life, so
Col 2:19 not **h** fast to the Head, from
1Ti 3: 9 **h** the mystery of the faith
Tit 1: 9 **h** fast the faithful word as
Rev 7: 1 **h** the four winds of the earth

HOLDS (*see* HOLD)
Num 30: 4 and her father **h** his peace
Esth 4:11 king **h** out the golden scepter
Job 2: 3 And still he **h** fast to his
Job 8:15 He **h** it fast, but it does not
Prov 11:12 of understanding **h** his peace
Prov 17:28 wise when he **h** his peace
Prov 29:11 but a wise man **h** them back
Prov 31:19 and her hand **h** the spindle
Is 56: 6 and **h** fast My covenant
Dan 5:23 the God who **h** your breath in
Amos 1: 5 the one who **h** the scepter
Amos 1: 8 the one who **h** the scepter
Rev 2: 1 who **h** the seven stars in His

HOLE (*see* HOLES)
2Ki 12: 9 bored a **h** in its lid, and set
Is 11: 8 shall play by the cobra's **h**
Is 51: 1 and to the **h** of the pit from
Jer 13: 4 it there in a **h** in the rock
Ezek 8: 7 there was a **h** in the wall

HOLES (*see* HOLE)
1Sa 13: 6 in thickets, in rocks, in **h**
1Sa 14:11 are coming out of the **h** where
Is 2:19 go into the **h** of the rocks
Is 42:22 all of them are snared in **h**
Jer 16:16 out of the **h** of the rocks
Mic 7:17 **h** like snakes of the earth
Hag 1: 6 to put into a bag with **h**
Matt 8:20 Foxes have **h** and birds of the
Luke 9:58 Foxes have **h** and birds of the

HOLIDAY
Esth 2:18 and he proclaimed a **h** in the
Esth 8:17 and gladness, a feast and a **h**
Esth 9:19 gladness and feasting, as a **h**
Esth 9:22 them, and from mourning to a **h**

HOLIER (*see* HOLY)
Is 65: 5 near me, for I am **h** than you

HOLIEST (*see* HOLY)
Heb 9: 3 which is called the **H** of All
Heb 9: 8 that the way into the **H** of
Heb 10:19 the **H** by the blood of Jesus

HOLINESS (*see* HOLY)
Ex 15:11 is like You, glorious in **h**
Ex 28:36 **H** TO THE LORD
Ex 39:30 **H** TO THE LORD
1Ch 16:29 the LORD in the beauty of **h**
2Ch 20:21 should praise the beauty of **h**
2Ch 31:18 sanctified themselves in **h**
Ps 29: 2 the LORD in the beauty of **h**
Ps 60: 6 God has spoken in His **h**
Ps 89:35 Once I have sworn by My **h**
Ps 93: 5 **H** adorns Your house, O LORD,
Ps 96: 9 the LORD in the beauty of **h**
Ps 108: 7 God has spoken in His **h**
Ps 110: 3 In the beauties of **h**, from
Eccl 8:10 and gone from the place of **h**
Is 35: 8 be called the Highway of **H**
Jer 2: 3 Israel was **h** to the LORD, the
Jer 31:23 of justice, and mountain of **h**
Amos 4: 2 Lord GOD has sworn by His **h**
Obad 17 and there shall be **h**
Zech 14:20 **H** TO THE LORD" shall be
Zech 14:21 Judah shall be **h** to the LORD
Luke 1:75 in **h** and righteousness before
Rom 1: 4 according to the Spirit of **h**
Rom 6:19 slaves of righteousness for **h**
Rom 6:22 God, you have your fruit to **h**
2Co 7: 1 perfecting **h** in the fear of
Eph 4:24 in righteousness and true **h**
1Th 3:13 blameless in **h** before our God
1Th 4: 7 us to uncleanness, but in **h**
1Ti 2:15 continue in faith, love, and **h**
Heb 12:10 we may be partakers of His **h**
Heb 12:14 peace with all men, and **h**,

HOLLOW
Ex 27: 8 shall make it **h** with boards
Ex 38: 7 made the altar **h** with boards
Judg 15:19 So God split the **h** place that
Is 40:12 waters in the **h** of his hand
Jer 52:21 it was **h**
Zech 1: 8 the myrtle trees in the **h**

HOLON (*see* HILEN, HORONAIM)
Josh 15:51 Goshen, **H**, and Giloh
Josh 21:15 **H** with its common-land, Debir
Jer 48:21 on **H** and Jahzah and Mephaath,

HOLY (*see* HOLIER, HOLIEST, HOLINESS, SPIRIT, UNHOLY)
Ex 3: 5 where you stand is **h** ground
Ex 12:16 shall be a **h** convocation, and
Ex 12:16 be a **h** convocation for you
Ex 15:13 strength to Your **h** habitation
Ex 16:23 rest, a **h** Sabbath to the LORD
Ex 19: 6 of priests and a **h** nation
Ex 20: 8 the Sabbath day, to keep it **h**
Ex 22:31 And you shall be **h** men to Me
Ex 26:33 the **h** place and the Most **H**
Ex 26:34 the Testimony in the Most **H**
Ex 28: 2 you shall make **h** garments for
Ex 28: 4 So they shall make **h** garments
Ex 28:29 when he goes into the **h** place
Ex 28:35 the **h** place before the LORD
Ex 28:38 bear the iniquity of the **h**
Ex 28:38 hallow in all their **h** gifts
Ex 28:43 to minister in the **h** place
Ex 29: 6 put the **h** crown on the turban
Ex 29:29 the **h** garments of Aaron shall
Ex 29:30 to minister in the **h** place
Ex 29:31 boil its flesh in the **h** place
Ex 29:33 eat them, because they are **h**
Ex 29:34 not be eaten, because it is **h**
Ex 29:37 And the altar shall be most **h**
Ex 29:37 touches the altar must be **h**
Ex 30:10 It is most **h** to the LORD
Ex 30:25 from these a **h** anointing oil
Ex 30:25 It shall be a **h** anointing oil
Ex 30:29 them, that they may be most **h**
Ex 30:29 touches them must be **h**
Ex 30:31 This shall be a **h** anointing
Ex 30:32 It is **h**, and it shall be **h**
Ex 30:35 perfumer, salted, pure, and **h**
Ex 30:36 It shall be most **h** to you
Ex 30:37 be to you **h** for the LORD
Ex 31:10 the **h** garments for Aaron the
Ex 31:11 sweet incense for the **h** place
Ex 31:14 therefore, for it is **h** to you
Ex 31:15 of rest, **h** to the LORD
Ex 35: 2 day shall be a **h** day for you
Ex 35:19 ministering in the **h** place
Ex 35:19 the **h** garments for Aaron the
Ex 35:21 and for the **h** garments
Ex 37:29 also made the **h** anointing oil
Ex 38:24 all the work of the **h** place
Ex 39: 1 ministering in the **h** place
Ex 39: 1 made the **h** garments for Aaron
Ex 39:30 of the **h** crown of pure gold
Ex 39:41 to minister in the **h** place
Ex 39:41 the **h** garments for Aaron the
Ex 40: 9 utensils, and it shall be **h**
Ex 40:10 The altar shall be most **h**
Ex 40:13 put the **h** garments on Aaron
Lev 2: 3 It is a most **h** offering of
Lev 2:10 It is a most **h** offering of
Lev 5:15 in regard to the **h** things of
Lev 5:16 done in regard to the **h** thing
Lev 6:16 shall be eaten in a **h** place
Lev 6:17 it is most **h**, like the sin
Lev 6:18 who touches them must be **h**
Lev 6:25 It is most **h**
Lev 6:26 In a **h** place it shall be
Lev 6:27 touches its flesh must be **h**
Lev 6:27 was sprinkled, in a **h** place
Lev 6:29 It is most **h**
Lev 6:30 make atonement in the **h** place
Lev 7: 1 offering (it is most **h**)
Lev 7: 6 shall be eaten in a **h** place
Lev 7: 6 It is most **h**
Lev 8: 9 the **h** crown, as the LORD had
Lev 10: 3 Me I must be regarded as **h**
Lev 10:10 you may distinguish between **h**
Lev 10:12 for it is most **h**
Lev 10:13 you shall eat it in a **h** place
Lev 10:17 the sin offering in a **h** place
Lev 10:17 place, since it is most **h**
Lev 10:18 brought inside the **h** place
Lev 10:18 have eaten it in a **h** place
Lev 11:44 you shall be **h**; for I am **h**
Lev 11:45 You shall therefore be **h**, for
Lev 11:45 therefore be **h**, for I am **h**
Lev 14:13 burnt offering, in a **h** place
Lev 14:13 It is most **h**
Lev 16: 2 the **H** Place inside the veil
Lev 16: 3 shall come into the **H** Place
Lev 16: 4 shall put the **h** linen tunic
Lev 16: 4 These are **h** garments
Lev 16:16 atonement for the **H** Place
Lev 16:17 make atonement in the **H** Place
Lev 16:20 of atoning for the **H** Place
Lev 16:23 when he went into the **H** Place
Lev 16:24 body with water in a **h** place
Lev 16:27 make atonement in the **H** Place
Lev 16:32 linen clothes, the **h** garments
Lev 16:33 atonement for the **H** Sanctuary
Lev 19: 2 You shall be **h**, for I the
Lev 19: 2 for I the LORD your God am **h**
Lev 19:24 year all its fruit shall be **h**
Lev 20: 3 and profane My **h** name
Lev 20: 7 yourselves therefore, and be **h**
Lev 20:26 And you shall be **h** to Me, for
Lev 20:26 to Me, for I the LORD am **h**
Lev 21: 6 They shall be **h** to their God
Lev 21: 6 therefore they shall be **h**
Lev 21: 7 the priest is **h** to his God
Lev 21: 8 He shall be **h** to you, for I
Lev 21: 8 LORD, who sanctify you, am **h**
Lev 21:22 both the most **h** and the **h**
Lev 22: 2 themselves from the **h** things
Lev 22: 2 **h** name in those things which
Lev 22: 3 who goes near the **h** things
Lev 22: 4 shall not eat the **h** offerings
Lev 22: 6 shall not eat the **h** offerings
Lev 22: 7 he may eat the **h** offerings
Lev 22:10 shall eat the **h** offering
Lev 22:10 shall not eat the **h** thing
Lev 22:12 not eat of the **h** offerings
Lev 22:14 if a man eats the **h** offering
Lev 22:14 a **h** offering to the priest
Lev 22:15 **h** offerings of the children
Lev 22:16 they eat their **h** offerings
Lev 22:32 shall not profane My **h** name
Lev 23: 2 proclaim to be **h** convocations
Lev 23: 3 solemn rest, a **h** convocation
Lev 23: 4 **h** convocations which you
Lev 23: 7 shall have a **h** convocation
Lev 23: 8 day shall be a **h** convocation
Lev 23:20 They shall be **h** to the LORD
Lev 23:21 it is a **h** convocation to you
Lev 23:24 of trumpets, a **h** convocation
Lev 23:27 It shall be a **h** convocation
Lev 23:35 shall be a **h** convocation
Lev 23:36 shall have a **h** convocation
Lev 23:37 proclaim to be **h** convocations
Lev 24: 9 shall eat it in a **h** place
Lev 24: 9 for it is most **h** to him from
Lev 25:12 it shall be **h** to you
Lev 27: 9 gives to the LORD shall be **h**
Lev 27:10 exchanged for it shall be **h**
Lev 27:14 his house to be **h** to the LORD
Lev 27:21 shall be **h** to the LORD, as a
Lev 27:23 as a **h** offering to the LORD
Lev 27:28 is most **h** to the LORD
Lev 27:30 It is **h** to the LORD
Lev 27:32 one shall be **h** to the LORD
Lev 27:33 exchanged for it shall be **h**
Num 4: 4 relating to the most **h** things
Num 4:15 shall not touch any **h** thing
Num 4:19 approach the most **h** things
Num 4:20 **h** things are being covered
Num 5: 9 **h** things of the children of
Num 5:10 every man's **h** things shall be
Num 5:17 The priest shall take **h**
Num 6: 5 to the LORD, he shall be **h**
Num 6: 8 he shall be **h** to the LORD
Num 6:20 they are **h** for the priest,
Num 7: 9 the service of the **h** things
Num 10:21 out, carrying the **h** things
Num 15:40 and be **h** for your God
Num 16: 3 for all the congregation is **h**
Num 16: 5 show who is His and who is **h**
Num 16: 7 chooses shall be the **h** one
Num 16:37 of the blaze, for they are **h**
Num 16:38 LORD, therefore they are **h**
Num 18: 8 all the **h** gifts of the
Num 18: 9 **h** things reserved from the

Num 18: 9 Me, shall be most **h** for you
Num 18:10 In a most **h** place you shall
Num 18:10 It shall be **h** to you
Num 18:17 they are **h**
Num 18:19 offerings of the **h** things
Num 18:32 **h** gifts of the children of
Num 28: 7 in a **h** place you shall pour
Num 28:18 shall have a **h** convocation
Num 28:25 shall have a **h** convocation
Num 28:26 shall have a **h** convocation
Num 29: 1 shall have a **h** convocation
Num 29: 7 shall have a **h** convocation
Num 29:12 shall have a **h** convocation
Num 31: 6 priest, with the **h** articles
Num 35:25 was anointed with the **h** oil
Deut 5:12 the Sabbath day, to keep it **h**
Deut 7: 6 For you are a **h** people to the
Deut 12:26 Only the **h** things which you
Deut 14: 2 For you are a **h** people to the
Deut 14:21 for you are a **h** people to the
Deut 23:14 your camp shall be **h**, that He
Deut 26:13 the **h** tithe from my house
Deut 26:15 down from Your **h** habitation
Deut 26:19 that you may be a **h** people to
Deut 28: 9 you as a **h** people to Himself
Deut 33: 8 Your Urim be with Your **h** one
Josh 5:15 place where you stand is **h**
Josh 24:19 the LORD, for He is a **h** God
1Sa 2: 2 There is none **h** like the LORD
1Sa 6:20 stand before this **h** LORD God
1Sa 21: 4 but there is **h** bread, if the
1Sa 21: 5 of the young men are **h**, and
1Sa 21: 6 the priest gave him **h** bread
1Ki 6:16 as the Most **H** Place
1Ki 7:50 inner room (the Most **H** Place)
1Ki 8: 4 all the **h** furnishings that
1Ki 8: 6 temple, to the Most **H** Place
1Ki 8: 8 be seen from the **h** place, in
1Ki 8:10 came out of the **h** place, that
2Ki 4: 9 that this is a **h** man of God
2Ki 19:22 Against the **H** One of Israel
1Ch 6:49 the work of the Most **H** Place
1Ch 16:10 Glory in His **h** name
1Ch 16:35 to give thanks to Your **h** name
1Ch 22:19 the **h** articles of God into
1Ch 23:13 sanctify the most **h** things
1Ch 23:28 the purifying of all **h** things
1Ch 23:32 the needs of the **h** place
1Ch 29: 3 have prepared for the **h** house
1Ch 29:16 Your **h** name is from Your hand
2Ch 3: 8 And he made the Most **H** Place
2Ch 3:10 In the Most **H** Place he made
2Ch 4:22 doors to the Most **H** Place
2Ch 5: 5 all the **h** furnishings that
2Ch 5: 7 temple, to the Most **H** Place
2Ch 5: 9 be seen from the **h** place, in
2Ch 5:11 came out of the Most **H** Place
2Ch 8:11 of the LORD has come are **h**
2Ch 23: 6 may go in, for they are **h**
2Ch 29: 5 the rubbish from the **h** place
2Ch 29: 7 burnt offerings in the **h**
2Ch 30:27 up to His **h** dwelling place
2Ch 31: 6 tithe of **h** things which were
2Ch 31:14 the LORD and the most **h** things
2Ch 35: 3 who were **h** to the LORD
2Ch 35: 3 Put the **h** ark in the house
2Ch 35: 5 And stand in the **h** place
2Ch 35:13 but the other **h** offerings
Ezra 2:63 **h** things till a priest could
Ezra 8:28 them, "You are **h** to the LORD
Ezra 8:28 the articles are **h** also
Ezra 9: 2 sons, so that the **h** seed is
Ezra 9: 8 give us a peg in His **h** place
Neh 7:65 **h** things till a priest could
Neh 8: 9 This day is **h** to the LORD
Neh 8:10 for this day is **h** to our LORD
Neh 8:11 Be still, for the day is **h**
Neh 9:14 known to them Your **h** Sabbath
Neh 10:31 on the Sabbath, or on a **h** day
Neh 10:33 for the **h** things, for the sin
Neh 11: 1 the **h** city, and nine-tenths
Neh 11:18 the **h** city were two hundred
Neh 12:47 They also consecrated **h**
Job 5: 1 to which of the **h** ones will
Job 6:10 the words of the **H** One
Ps 2: 6 My King On My **h** hill of Zion
Ps 3: 4 He heard me from His **h** hill
Ps 5: 7 worship toward Your **h** temple
Ps 11: 4 The LORD is in His **h** temple
Ps 15: 1 Who may dwell in Your **h** hill
Ps 16:10 Your **H** One to see corruption
Ps 20: 6 His **h** heaven With the saving
Ps 22: 3 But You are **h**, Who inhabit
Ps 24: 3 who may stand in His **h** place
Ps 28: 2 hands toward Your **h** sanctuary
Ps 30: 4 the remembrance of His **h** name
Ps 33:21 we have trusted in His **h** name
Ps 43: 3 them bring me to Your **h** hill
Ps 46: 4 The **h** place of the tabernacle
Ps 47: 8 God sits on His **h** throne
Ps 48: 1 of our God, In His **h** mountain
Ps 51:11 take Your **H** Spirit from me
Ps 65: 4 Your house, Of Your **h** temple
Ps 68: 5 Is God in His **h** habitation
Ps 68:17 as in Sinai, in the **H** Place
Ps 68:35 awesome than Your **h** places
Ps 71:22 the harp, O **H** One of Israel
Ps 78:41 limited the **H** One of Israel
Ps 78:54 brought them to His **h** border
Ps 79: 1 Your **h** temple they have
Ps 86: 2 Preserve my life, for I am **h**
Ps 87: 1 is in the **h** mountains
Ps 89:18 king to the **H** One of Israel
Ps 89:19 in a vision to Your **h** one
Ps 89:20 With My **h** oil I have anointed
Ps 97:12 the remembrance of His **h** name
Ps 98: 1 His **h** arm have gained Him the
Ps 99: 3 He is **h**
Ps 99: 5 For He is **h**
Ps 99: 9 God, And worship at His **h** hill
Ps 99: 9 For the LORD our God is **h**
Ps 103: 1 within me, bless His **h** name
Ps 105: 3 Glory in His **h** name
Ps 105:42 He remembered His **h** promise
Ps 106:47 To give thanks to Your **h** name
Ps 111: 9 **H** and awesome is His name
Ps 138: 2 worship toward Your **h** temple
Ps 145:21 bless His **h** name Forever and
Prov 9:10 of the **H** One is understanding
Prov 20:25 devote rashly something as **h**
Prov 30: 3 have knowledge of the **H** One
Is 1: 4 to anger the **H** One of Israel
Is 4: 3 in Jerusalem will be called **h**
Is 5:16 and God who is **h** shall be
Is 5:19 let the counsel of the **H** One
Is 5:24 word of the **H** One of Israel
Is 6: 3 **H**, **h**, **h** is the LORD of hosts
Is 6:13 So the **h** seed shall be its
Is 10:17 and his **H** One for a flame
Is 10:20 the **H** One of Israel, in truth
Is 11: 9 destroy in all My **h** mountain
Is 12: 6 for great is the **H** One of
Is 17: 7 for the **H** One of Israel
Is 27:13 in the **h** mount at Jerusalem
Is 29:19 In the **H** One of Israel
Is 29:23 hallow the **H** One of Jacob, and
Is 30:11 cause the **H** One of Israel to
Is 30:12 thus says the **H** One of Israel
Is 30:15 Lord GOD, the **H** One of Israel
Is 30:29 when a **h** festival is kept
Is 31: 1 look to the **H** One of Israel
Is 37:23 Against the **H** One of Israel
Is 40:25 I be equal?" says the **H** One
Is 41:14 Redeemer, the **H** One of Israel
Is 41:16 glory in the **H** One of Israel
Is 41:20 and the **H** One of Israel has
Is 43: 3 the **H** One of Israel, your
Is 43:14 Redeemer, the **H** One of Israel
Is 43:15 I am the LORD, your **H** One
Is 45:11 the **H** One of Israel, and his
Is 47: 4 His name, the **H** One of Israel
Is 48: 2 themselves after the **h** city
Is 48:17 Redeemer, the **H** One of Israel
Is 49: 7 of Israel, their **H** One, to
Is 49: 7 faithful, the **H** One of Israel
Is 52: 1 O Jerusalem, the **h** city
Is 52:10 **h** arm in the eyes of all the
Is 54: 5 is the **H** One of Israel
Is 55: 5 God, and the **H** One of Israel
Is 56: 7 I will bring to My **h** mountain
Is 57:13 shall inherit My **h** mountain
Is 57:15 eternity, whose name is **H**
Is 57:15 **h** place, with him who has a
Is 58:13 your pleasure on My **h** day
Is 58:13 the **h** day of the LORD
Is 60: 9 and to the **H** One of Israel,
Is 60:14 Zion of the **H** One of Israel
Is 62: 9 shall drink it in My **h** courts
Is 62:12 shall call them The **H** People
Is 63:10 and grieved His **H** Spirit
Is 63:11 put His **H** Spirit within them
Is 63:15 see from Your habitation, **h**
Is 63:18 Your **h** people have possessed
Is 64:10 Your **h** cities are a
Is 64:11 Our **h** and beautiful temple,
Is 65:11 who forget My **h** mountain
Is 65:25 destroy in all My **h** mountain
Is 66:20 to My **h** mountain Jerusalem,"
Jer 11:15 the **h** flesh has passed from
Jer 23: 9 and because of His **h** words
Jer 25:30 voice from His **h** habitation
Jer 31:40 east, shall be **h** to the LORD
Jer 50:29 against the **H** One of Israel
Jer 51: 5 against the **H** One of Israel
Ezek 7:24 and their **h** places shall be
Ezek 20:39 but profane My **h** name no more
Ezek 20:40 For on My **h** mountain, on the
Ezek 20:40 with all your **h** things
Ezek 21: 2 preach against the **h** places
Ezek 22: 8 You have despised My **h** things
Ezek 22:26 law and profaned My **h** things
Ezek 22:26 distinguished between the **h**
Ezek 28:14 were on the **h** mountain of God
Ezek 36:20 went, they profaned My **h** name
Ezek 36:21 I had concern for My **h** name
Ezek 36:22 but for My **h** name's sake,
Ezek 36:38 flock offered as **h** sacrifices
Ezek 39: 7 So I will make My **h** name
Ezek 39: 7 profane My **h** name anymore
Ezek 39: 7 the LORD, the **H** One in Israel
Ezek 39:25 will be jealous for My **h** name
Ezek 41: 4 This is the Most **H** Place
Ezek 42:13 are the **h** chambers where the
Ezek 42:13 eat the most **h** offerings
Ezek 42:13 lay the most **h** offerings
Ezek 42:13 for the place is **h**
Ezek 42:14 the **h** chamber into the outer
Ezek 42:14 they minister, for they are **h**
Ezek 42:20 to separate the **h** areas from
Ezek 43: 7 of Israel defile My **h** name
Ezek 43: 8 they defiled My **h** name by the
Ezek 43:12 mountaintop shall be most **h**
Ezek 44: 8 kept charge of My **h** things
Ezek 44:13 come near any of My **h** things
Ezek 44:13 nor into the Most **H** Place
Ezek 44:19 leave them in the **h** chambers
Ezek 44:19 and in their **h** garments they
Ezek 44:23 the difference between the **h**
Ezek 45: 1 LORD, a **h** portion of the land
Ezek 45: 1 It shall be **h** throughout its
Ezek 45: 3 sanctuary, the Most **H** Place
Ezek 45: 4 It shall be a **h** portion of
Ezek 45: 4 a **h** place for the sanctuary
Ezek 45: 6 the district of the **h** portion
Ezek 45: 7 the other of the **h** district
Ezek 45: 7 bordering on the **h** district
Ezek 46:19 into the **h** chambers of the
Ezek 48:10 shall this **h** district belong
Ezek 48:12 most **h** by the border of the
Ezek 48:14 land, for it is **h** to the LORD
Ezek 48:18 the district of the **h** portion
Ezek 48:18 the district of the **h** portion
Ezek 48:20 You shall set apart the **h**
Ezek 48:21 the other of the **h** district
Ezek 48:21 the **h** district as far as the
Ezek 48:21 It shall be the **h** district
Dan 4: 8 is the Spirit of the **H** God)
Dan 4: 9 Spirit of the **H** God is in you
Dan 4:13 a **h** one, coming down from
Dan 4:17 by the word of the **h** ones
Dan 4:18 Spirit of the **H** God is in you
Dan 4:23 a **h** one, coming down from
Dan 5:11 is the Spirit of the **H** God
Dan 8:13 Then I heard a **h** one speaking
Dan 8:13 another **h** one said to that
Dan 8:24 mighty, and also the **h** people
Dan 9:16 Jerusalem, Your **h** mountain
Dan 9:20 for the **h** mountain of my God
Dan 9:24 people and for your **h** city
Dan 9:24 and to anoint the Most **H**
Dan 11:28 moved against the **h** covenant
Dan 11:30 rage against the **h** covenant
Dan 11:30 who forsake the **h** covenant
Dan 11:45 and the glorious **h** mountain
Dan 12: 7 and when the power of the **h**
Hos 11: 9 man, the **H** One in your midst
Hos 11:12 even with the **H** One who is
Joel 2: 1 an alarm in My **h** mountain
Joel 3:17 in Zion My **h** mountain
Joel 3:17 then Jerusalem shall be **h**

Amos 2: 7 girl, to defile My **h** name
Obad 16 as you drank on my **h** mountain
Jon 2: 4 again toward Your **h** temple
Jon 2: 7 up to You, into Your **h** temple
Mic 1: 2 the Lord from His **h** temple
Hab 1:12 O LORD my God, my **H** One
Hab 2:20 the LORD is in His **h** temple
Hab 3: 3 the **H** One from Mount Paran
Zeph 3:11 be haughty In My **h** mountain
Hag 2:12 If one carries **h** meat in the
Hag 2:12 or any food, will it become **h**
Zech 2:12 His inheritance in the **H** Land
Zech 2:13 aroused from His **h** habitation
Zech 8: 3 LORD of hosts, the **H** Mountain
Mal 2:11 has profaned the LORD's **h**
Matt 1:18 with child of the **H** Spirit
Matt 1:20 in her is of the **H** Spirit
Matt 3:11 baptize you with the **H** Spirit
Matt 4: 5 took Him up into the **h** city
Matt 7: 6 give what is **h** to the dogs
Matt 12:32 speaks against the **H** Spirit
Matt 24:15 standing in the **h** place"
Matt 25:31 all the **h** angels with Him,
Matt 27:53 they went into the **h** city
Matt 28:19 of the Son and of the **H** Spirit
Mark 1: 8 baptize you with the **H** Spirit
Mark 1:24 You are—the **H** One of God!
Mark 3:29 the **H** Spirit never has
Mark 6:20 **h** man, and he protected him
Mark 8:38 His Father with the **h** angels
Mark 12:36 himself said by the **H** Spirit
Mark 13:11 who speak, but the **H** Spirit
Luke 1:15 be filled with the **H** Spirit
Luke 1:35 The **H** Spirit will come upon
Luke 1:35 that **H** One who is to be born
Luke 1:41 was filled with the **H** Spirit
Luke 1:49 for me, and **h** is His name
Luke 1:67 was filled with the **H** Spirit
Luke 1:70 the mouth of His **h** prophets
Luke 1:72 and to remember His **h** covenant
Luke 2:23 be called **h** to the LORD")
Luke 2:25 the **H** Spirit was upon him
Luke 2:26 **H** Spirit that he would not
Luke 3:16 baptize you with the **H** Spirit
Luke 3:22 the **H** Spirit descended in
Luke 4: 1 filled with the **H** Spirit,
Luke 4:34 You are—the **H** One of God!
Luke 9:26 Father's, and of the **h** angels
Luke 11:13 heavenly Father give the **H**
Luke 12:10 against the **H** Spirit, it will
Luke 12:12 For the **H** Spirit will teach
John 1:33 baptizes with the **H** Spirit
John 7:39 for the **H** Spirit was not yet
John 14:26 the **H** Spirit, whom the Father
John 17:11 **H** Father, keep through Your
John 20:22 Receive the **H** Spirit
Acts 1: 2 the **H** Spirit had given
Acts 1: 5 **H** Spirit not many days from
Acts 1: 8 receive power when the **H**
Acts 1:16 which the **H** Spirit spoke
Acts 2: 4 all filled with the **H** Spirit
Acts 2:27 Your **H** One to see corruption
Acts 2:33 the promise of the **H** Spirit
Acts 2:38 the gift of the **H** Spirit
Acts 3:14 But you denied the **H** One and
Acts 3:21 by the mouth of all His **h**
Acts 4: 8 filled with the **H** Spirit
Acts 4:27 against Your **h** Servant Jesus
Acts 4:30 name of Your **h** Servant Jesus
Acts 4:31 all filled with the **H** Spirit
Acts 5: 3 heart to lie to the **H** Spirit
Acts 5:32 so also is the **H** Spirit whom
Acts 6: 3 full of the **H** Spirit and
Acts 6: 5 and the **H** Spirit, and Philip,
Acts 6:13 words against this **h** place
Acts 7:33 where you stand is **h** ground
Acts 7:51 always resist the **H** Spirit
Acts 7:55 being full of the **H** Spirit
Acts 8:15 might receive the **H** Spirit
Acts 8:17 and they received the **H** Spirit
Acts 8:18 hands the **H** Spirit was given
Acts 8:19 may receive the **H** Spirit
Acts 9:17 be filled with the **H** Spirit
Acts 9:31 the comfort of the **H** Spirit
Acts 10:22 divinely instructed by a **h**
Acts 10:38 of Nazareth with the **H** Spirit
Acts 10:44 the **H** Spirit fell upon all
Acts 10:45 because the gift of the **H**
Acts 10:47 who have received the **H**
Acts 11:15 the **H** Spirit fell upon them,
Acts 11:16 be baptized with the **H** Spirit
Acts 11:24 man, full of the **H** Spirit
Acts 13: 2 and fasted, the **H** Spirit said,
Acts 13: 4 sent out by the **H** Spirit,
Acts 13: 9 filled with the **H** Spirit
Acts 13:35 Your **H** One to see corruption
Acts 13:52 with joy and with the **H** Spirit
Acts 15: 8 by giving them the **H** Spirit
Acts 15:28 seemed good to the **H** Spirit
Acts 16: 6 **H** Spirit to preach the word
Acts 19: 2 Did you receive the **H** Spirit
Acts 19: 2 whether there is a **H** Spirit
Acts 19: 6 the **H** Spirit came upon them,
Acts 20:23 except that the **H** Spirit
Acts 20:28 among which the **H** Spirit has
Acts 21:11 Thus says the **H** Spirit, 'So
Acts 21:28 and has defiled this **h** place
Acts 28:25 The **H** Spirit spoke rightly
Rom 1: 2 prophets in the **H** Scriptures
Rom 5: 5 out in our hearts by the **H**
Rom 7:12 Therefore the law is **h**
Rom 7:12 and the commandment **h** and
Rom 9: 1 me witness in the **H** Spirit
Rom 11:16 For if the firstfruit is **h**
Rom 11:16 the lump is also **h**
Rom 11:16 and if the root is **h**, so are
Rom 12: 1 bodies a living sacrifice, **h**
Rom 14:17 peace and joy in the **H** Spirit
Rom 15:13 by the power of the **H** Spirit
Rom 15:16 sanctified by the **H** Spirit
Rom 16:16 one another with a **h** kiss
1Co 2:13 which the **H** Spirit teaches
1Co 3:17 For the temple of God is **h**
1Co 6:19 of the **H** Spirit who is in you
1Co 7:14 unclean, but now they are **h**
1Co 7:34 she may be **h** both in body
1Co 9:13 **h** things eat of the things of
1Co 12: 3 Lord except by the **H** Spirit
1Co 16:20 one another with a **h** kiss
2Co 6: 6 by kindness, by the **H** Spirit
2Co 13:12 one another with a **h** kiss
2Co 13:14 the communion of the **H** Spirit
Eph 1: 4 world, that we should be **h**
Eph 1:13 with the **H** Spirit of promise
Eph 2:21 grows into a **h** temple in the
Eph 3: 5 the Spirit to His **h** apostles
Eph 4:30 grieve the **H** Spirit of God
Eph 5:27 but that it should be **h** and
Col 1:22 death, to present you **h**, and
Col 3:12 as the elect of God, **h** and
1Th 1: 5 in power, and in the **H** Spirit
1Th 1: 6 with joy of the **H** Spirit
1Th 4: 8 also given us His **H** Spirit
1Th 5:26 the brethren with a **h** kiss
1Th 5:27 be read to all the **h** brethren
1Ti 2: 8 lifting up **h** hands, without
2Ti 1: 9 and called us with a **h** calling
2Ti 1:14 you, keep by the **H** Spirit who
2Ti 3:15 have known the **H** Scriptures
Tit 1: 8 good, sober-minded, just, **h**
Tit 3: 5 and renewing of the **H** Spirit
Heb 2: 4 and gifts of the **H** Spirit
Heb 3: 1 **h** brethren, partakers of the
Heb 3: 7 as the **H** Spirit says
Heb 6: 4 partakers of the **H** Spirit
Heb 7:26 was fitting for us, who is **h**
Heb 9: 8 the **H** Spirit indicating this,
Heb 9:12 the Most **H** Place once for all
Heb 9:24 the **h** places made with hands
Heb 9:25 **H** Place every year with blood
Heb 10:15 the **H** Spirit also witnesses
1Pe 1:12 the **H** Spirit sent from heaven
1Pe 1:15 but as He who called you is **h**
1Pe 1:15 you also be **h** in all your
1Pe 1:16 Be **h**, for I am **h**
1Pe 2: 5 a **h** priesthood, to offer up
1Pe 2: 9 a **h** nation, His own special
1Pe 3: 5 the **h** women who trusted in
2Pe 1:18 with Him on the **h** mountain
2Pe 1:21 but **h** men of God spoke as
2Pe 1:21 were moved by the **H** Spirit
2Pe 2:21 known it, to turn from the **h**
2Pe 3: 2 before by the **h** prophets, and
2Pe 3:11 ought you to be in **h** conduct
1Jn 2:20 an anointing from the **H** One
1Jn 5: 7 the Word, and the **H** Spirit
Jude 20 up on your most **h** faith,
Jude 20 praying in the **H** Spirit,
Rev 3: 7 These things says He who is **h**
Rev 4: 8 **H**, **h**, **h**, Lord God
Rev 6:10 How long, O Lord, **h** and true,
Rev 11: 2 the **h** city under foot for
Rev 14:10 the presence of the **h** angels
Rev 15: 4 For You alone are **h**
Rev 18:20 you **h** apostles and prophets,
Rev 20: 6 **h** is he who has part in the
Rev 21: 2 Then I, John, saw the **h** city
Rev 21:10 the **h** Jerusalem, descending
Rev 22: 6 And the Lord God of the **h**
Rev 22:11 he who is **h**, let him be **h**
Rev 22:19 Book of Life, from the **h** city

HOMAGE
1Ki 1:16 bowed and did **h** to the king
1Ki 1:31 did **h** to the king, and said,
Esth 3: 2 paid **h** to Haman, for so the
Esth 3: 2 would not bow or pay **h**
Esth 3: 5 did not bow or pay him **h**,

HOMAM (*see* HEMAM)
1Ch 1:39 sons of Lotan were Hori and **H**

HOME (*see* HOMEBORN, HOMELAND, HOMELESS, HOMEMAKERS, HOMES)
Gen 39:16 her until his master came **h**
Gen 43:16 Take these men to my **h**, and
Gen 43:26 And when Joseph came **h**, they
Ex 9:19 the field and is not brought **h**
Lev 18: 9 born at **h** or elsewhere, their
Deut 21:12 bring her **h** to your house
Deut 24: 5 shall be free at **h** one year
Josh 2:18 household to your own **h**
Judg 11: 9 If you take me back **h** to
Judg 19: 9 early, so that you may get **h**
Ruth 1:21 has brought me **h** again empty
1Sa 2:20 they would go to their own **h**
1Sa 6: 7 and take their calves **h**, away
1Sa 6:10 and shut up their calves at **h**
1Sa 7:17 to Ramah, for his **h** was there
1Sa 10:26 And Saul also went **h** to Gibeah
1Sa 18: 2 would not let him go **h** to his
1Sa 18: 6 as they were coming **h**, when
1Sa 24:22 And Saul went **h**, but David and
1Sa 25: 1 buried him at his **h** in Ramah
2Sa 13: 7 And David sent **h** to Tamar,
2Sa 14:13 his banished one **h** again
2Sa 17:23 went **h** to his house, to his
1Ki 5:14 in Lebanon and two months at **h**
1Ki 13: 7 Come **h** with me and refresh
1Ki 13:15 Come **h** with me and eat bread
2Ki 14:10 in your success, and stay at **h**
2Ki 19:36 and went away, returned **h**, and
2Ch 25:10 from Ephraim, to go back **h**
2Ch 25:10 and they returned **h** in great
2Ch 25:19 Stay at **h** now
Esth 5:10 restrained himself and went **h**
Job 38:20 may know the paths to its **h**
Job 39: 6 Whose **h** I have made the
Job 39:12 him to bring **h** your grain
Ps 68:12 at **h** divides the spoil
Ps 84: 3 the sparrow has found a **h**
Ps 104:17 has her **h** in the fir trees
Ps 113: 9 grants the barren woman a **h**
Prov 7:11 her feet would not stay at **h**
Prov 7:19 For my husband is not at **h**
Prov 7:20 will come **h** on the appointed
Eccl 12: 5 For man goes to his eternal **h**
Is 37:37 and went away, returned **h**, and
Jer 39:14 that he should take him **h**
Lam 1:20 at **h** it is like death
Ezek 31: 6 great nations made their **h**
Dan 6:10 writing was signed, he went **h**
Hab 2: 5 man, and he does not stay at **h**
Hag 1: 9 and when you brought it **h**, I
Matt 8: 6 is lying at **h** paralyzed,
Mark 5:19 Go **h** to your friends, and tell
Luke 15: 6 And when he comes **h**, he calls
John 14:23 to him and make Our **h** with him
John 19:27 took her to his own **h**
Acts 21: 6 the ship, and they returned **h**
1Co 11:34 is hungry, let him eat at **h**
1Co 14:35 ask their own husbands at **h**
2Co 5: 6 that while we are at **h** in the
1Ti 5: 4 learn to show piety at **h** and

HOMEBORN (*see* HOME)
Jer 2:14 is he a **h** slave

HOMELAND (*see* HOME)
Heb 11:14 plainly that they seek a **h**

HOMELESS (*see* HOME)
1Co 4:11 clothed, and beaten, and **h**

HOMEMAKERS (*see* HOME)
Tit 2: 5 to be discreet, chaste, **h**

HOMER (*see* HOMERS)
Lev 27:16 A **h** of barley seed shall be
Is 5:10 a **h** of seed shall yield one
Ezek 45:11 contains one-tenth of a **h**
Ezek 45:11 and the ephah one-tenth of a **h**
Ezek 45:11 shall be according to the **h**
Ezek 45:13 of an ephah from a **h** of wheat
Ezek 45:13 an ephah from a **h** of barley
Ezek 45:14 A kor is a **h** or ten baths,
Ezek 45:14 baths, for ten baths are a **h**

HOMERS (*see* HOMER)
Num 11:32 least gathered ten **h**)
Hos 3: 2 one and one-half **h** of barley

HOMES (*see* HOME)
Num 32:18 our **h** until every one of the
Prov 30:26 make their **h** in the crags
Is 32:13 on all the happy **h** in the
John 20:10 away again to their own **h**

HOMOSEXUALS
1Co 6: 9 nor adulterers, nor **h**, nor

HONEST
Gen 42:11 we are **h** men
Gen 42:19 If you are **h** men, let one of
Gen 42:31 we said to him, 'We are **h** men
Gen 42:33 will know that you are **h** men
Gen 42:34 spies, but that you are **h** men

HONEY (*see* HONEYCOMB)
Gen 43:11 a little balm and a little **h**
Ex 3: 8 a land flowing with milk and **h**
Ex 3:17 a land flowing with milk and **h**
Ex 13: 5 a land flowing with milk and **h**
Ex 16:31 was like wafers made with **h**
Ex 33: 3 a land flowing with milk and **h**
Lev 2:11 burn no leaven nor any **h** in
Lev 20:24 a land flowing with milk and **h**
Num 13:27 It truly flows with milk and **h**
Num 14: 8 which flows with milk and **h**
Num 16:13 a land flowing with milk and **h**
Num 16:14 a land flowing with milk and **h**
Deut 6: 3 a land flowing with milk and **h**
Deut 8: 8 a land of olive oil and **h**
Deut 11: 9 a land flowing with milk and **h**
Deut 26: 9 land flowing with milk and **h**"
Deut 26:15 a land flowing with milk and **h**
Deut 27: 3 a land flowing with milk and **h**
Deut 31:20 land flowing with milk and **h**
Deut 32:13 him to draw **h** from the rock
Josh 5: 6 a land flowing with milk and **h**
Judg 14: 8 **h** were in the carcass of the
Judg 14: 9 **h** out of the carcass of the
Judg 14:18 What is sweeter than **h**
1Sa 14:25 there was **h** on the ground
1Sa 14:26 the woods, there was the **h**
1Sa 14:29 I tasted a little of this **h**
1Sa 14:43 I only tasted a little **h** with
2Sa 17:29 **h** and curds, sheep and cheese
1Ki 14: 3 some cakes, and a jar of **h**
2Ki 18:32 a land of olive groves and **h**
2Ch 31: 5 of grain and wine, oil and **h**
Job 20:17 the rivers flowing with **h**
Ps 19:10 Sweeter also than **h** and the
Ps 81:16 with **h** from the rock I would
Ps 119:103 sweeter than **h** to my mouth
Prov 5: 3 of an immoral woman drip **h**
Prov 24:13 eat **h** because it is good, and
Prov 25:16 Have you found **h**
Prov 25:27 It is not good to eat much **h**
Song 4:11 **h** and milk are under your
Song 5: 1 eaten my honeycomb with my **h**
Is 7:15 **h** He shall eat, that He may
Is 7:22 **h** everyone will eat who is
Jer 11: 5 a land flowing with milk and **h**
Jer 32:22 a land flowing with milk and **h**
Jer 41: 8 oil, and **h** in the field
Ezek 3: 3 my mouth like **h** in sweetness
Ezek 16:13 ate pastry of fine flour, **h**
Ezek 16:19 oil, and **h** which I fed you
Ezek 20: 6 them, flowing with milk and **h**
Ezek 20:15 them, flowing with milk and **h**
Ezek 27:17 wheat of Minnith, millet, **h**
Matt 3: 4 food was locusts and wild **h**
Mark 1: 6 and he ate locusts and wild **h**
Rev 10: 9 as sweet as **h** in your mouth
Rev 10:10 was as sweet as **h** in my mouth

HONEYCOMB (*see* HONEY)
1Sa 14:27 his hand and dipped it in a **h**
Ps 19:10 also than honey and the **h**
Prov 16:24 Pleasant words are like a **h**
Prov 24:13 the **h** which is sweet to your
Prov 27: 7 satisfied soul loathes the **h**
Song 4:11 O my spouse, drip as the **h**
Song 5: 1 have eaten my **h** with my honey
Luke 24:42 of a broiled fish and some **h**

HONOR (*see* HONORABLE, HONORED, HONORING, HONORS)
Gen 49: 6 let not my **h** be united to
Ex 8: 9 Accept the **h** of saying when I
Ex 14: 4 I will gain **h** over Pharaoh and
Ex 14:17 So I will gain **h** over Pharaoh
Ex 14:18 when I have gained **h** for
Ex 20:12 **H** your father and your mother,
Lev 19:15 poor, nor **h** the person of the
Lev 19:32 **h** the presence of an old man,
Num 22:17 will certainly **h** you greatly
Num 22:37 Am I not able to **h** you
Num 24:11 I said I would greatly **h** you
Num 24:11 LORD has kept you back from **h**
Deut 5:16 **H** your father and your mother
Deut 26:19 in praise, in name, and in **h**
Judg 9: 9 my oil, with which they **h** God
Judg 13:17 come to pass we may **h** You
1Sa 2:29 **h** your sons more than Me, to
1Sa 2:30 those who **h** Me I will **h**
1Sa 9:22 of **h** among those who were
1Sa 15:30 yet **h** me now, please, before
2Sa 6:22 by them I will be held in **h**
1Ki 3:13 both riches and **h**, so that
1Ki 21: 9 with high **h** among the people
1Ki 21:12 with high **h** among the people
1Ch 16:27 **H** and majesty are before Him
1Ch 17:18 You for the **h** of Your servant
1Ch 29:12 **h** come from You, and You
1Ch 29:28 full of days and riches and **h**
2Ch 1:11 asked riches or wealth or **h**
2Ch 1:12 you riches and wealth and **h**
2Ch 17: 5 had riches and **h** in abundance
2Ch 18: 1 had riches and **h** in abundance
2Ch 26:18 have no **h** from the LORD God
2Ch 32:27 had very great riches and **h**
Esth 1:20 wives will **h** their husbands
Esth 6: 3 What **h** or dignity has been
Esth 6: 6 whom the king delights to **h**
Esth 6: 6 delight to **h** more than me
Esth 6: 7 whom the king delights to **h**
Esth 6: 9 whom the king delights to **h**
Esth 6: 9 whom the king delights to **h**
Esth 6:11 man the king delights to **h**
Esth 8:16 light and gladness, joy and **h**
Job 14:21 His sons come to **h**, and he
Job 30:15 they pursue my **h** as the wind
Ps 7: 5 And lay my **h** in the dust
Ps 8: 5 crowned him with glory and **h**
Ps 21: 5 **H** and majesty You have placed
Ps 49:12 Nevertheless man, though in **h**
Ps 49:20 Man who is in **h**, yet does not
Ps 66: 2 Sing out the **h** of His name
Ps 91:15 I will deliver him and **h** him
Ps 96: 6 **H** and majesty are before Him
Ps 104: 1 You are clothed with **h** and
Ps 112: 9 horn will be exalted with **h**
Ps 149: 9 This **h** have all His saints
Prov 3: 9 **H** the LORD with your
Prov 3:16 in her left hand riches and **h**
Prov 4: 8 she will bring you **h**, when
Prov 5: 9 you give your **h** to others
Prov 8:18 and **h** are with me, enduring
Prov 11:16 A gracious woman retains **h**
Prov 14:28 of people is a king's **h**, but
Prov 15:33 and before **h** is humility
Prov 18:12 and before **h** is humility
Prov 21:21 life, righteousness and **h**
Prov 22: 4 of the LORD are riches and **h**
Prov 26: 1 so **h** is not fitting for a
Prov 26: 8 is he who gives **h** to a fool
Prov 29:23 in spirit will retain **h**
Prov 31:25 and **h** are her clothing
Eccl 6: 2 given riches and wealth and **h**
Eccl 10: 1 one respected for wisdom and **h**
Is 29:13 **h** Me with their lips, but
Is 43:20 beast of the field will **h** Me
Is 58:13 honorable, and shall **h** Him
Is 61: 7 shame you shall have double **h**
Jer 33: 9 an **h** before all nations of
Dan 2: 6 me gifts, rewards, and great **h**
Dan 4:30 and for the **h** of my majesty
Dan 4:36 the glory of my kingdom, my **h**
Dan 4:37 **h** the King of heaven, all of
Dan 5:18 and majesty, glory and **h**
Dan 11:21 not give the **h** of royalty
Dan 11:38 shall **h** a god of fortresses
Dan 11:38 not know he shall **h** with gold
Mal 1: 6 am the Father, where is My **h**
Matt 13:57 A prophet is not without **h**
Matt 15: 4 **H** your father and your mother
Matt 15: 8 **h** Me with their lips, but
Matt 19:19 **H** your father and your mother
Mark 6: 4 A prophet is not without **h**
Mark 7:10 **H** your father and your mother
Mark 10:19 **H** your father and your
Luke 18:20 **H** your father and your
John 4:44 has no **h** in his own country
John 5:23 that all should **h** the Son
John 5:23 just as they **h** the Father
John 5:23 He who does not **h** the Son
John 5:23 does not **h** the Father who sent
John 5:41 I do not receive **h** from men
John 5:44 who receive **h** from one
John 5:44 do not seek the **h** that comes
John 8:49 but I **h** My Father, and you
John 8:54 If I **h** Myself, My **h** is
John 12:26 Me, him My Father will **h**
Rom 2: 7 doing good seek for glory, **h**
Rom 2:10 but glory, **h**, and peace to
Rom 9:21 lump to make one vessel for **h**
Rom 12:10 in **h** giving preference to one
Rom 13: 7 to whom fear, **h** to whom **h**
1Co 12:23 on these we bestow greater **h**
1Co 12:24 having given greater **h** to
2Co 6: 8 by **h** and dishonor, by evil
Eph 6: 2 **H** your father and mother,"
1Th 4: 4 vessel in sanctification and **h**
1Ti 1:17 God who alone is wise, be **h**
1Ti 5: 3 **H** widows who are really
1Ti 5:17 be counted worthy of double **h**
1Ti 6: 1 own masters worthy of all **h**
1Ti 6:16 seen or can see, to whom be **h**
2Ti 2:20 of wood and clay, some for **h**
2Ti 2:21 he will be a vessel for **h**
Heb 2: 7 crowned him with glory and **h**
Heb 2: 9 death crowned with glory and **h**
Heb 3: 3 has more **h** than the house
Heb 5: 4 man takes this **h** to himself
1Pe 1: 7 may be found to praise, **h**
1Pe 2:17 **H** all people.
1Pe 2:17 **H** the king.
1Pe 3: 7 giving **h** to the wife, as to
2Pe 1:17 from God the Father **h** and
Rev 4: 9 creatures give glory and **h**
Rev 4:11 O Lord, to receive glory and **h**
Rev 5:12 and wisdom, and strength and **h**
Rev 5:13 Blessing and **h** and glory and
Rev 7:12 and wisdom, thanksgiving and **h**
Rev 19: 1 Salvation and glory and **h** and
Rev 21:24 their glory and **h** into it
Rev 21:26 the **h** of the nations into it

HONORABLE (*see* HONOR, HONORABLY)
Gen 34:19 He was more **h** than all the
Num 22:15 numerous and more **h** than they
1Sa 9: 6 man of God, and he is an **h** man
1Sa 22:14 and is **h** in your house
2Ki 5: 1 and **h** man in the eyes of his
1Ch 4: 9 was more **h** than his brothers
Job 22: 8 and the **h** man dwelt in it
Ps 45: 9 are among Your **h** women
Ps 111: 3 His work is **h** and glorious, And
Prov 20: 3 It is **h** for a man to stop
Is 3: 3 captain of fifty and the **h** man
Is 3: 5 and the base toward the **h**
Is 5:13 their **h** men are famished, and
Is 9:15 The elder and **h**, he is the
Is 23: 8 are the **h** of the earth
Is 23: 9 all the **h** of the earth
Is 42:21 magnify the law and make it **h**
Is 58:13 the holy day of the LORD **h**
Nah 3:10 they cast lots for her **h** men
Luke 14: 8 lest one more **h** than you be
1Co 12:23 which we think to be less **h**
2Co 8:21 providing **h** things, not only
2Co 13: 7 that you should do what is **h**
Heb 13: 4 Marriage is **h** among all, and
1Pe 2:12 conduct **h** among the Gentiles

HONORABLY (*see* HONORABLE)
Heb 13:18 all things desiring to live **h**

HONORED (*see* HONOR)
2Sa 23:19 he not the most **h** of three
2Sa 23:23 He was more **h** than the thirty
1Ch 11:21 more **h** than the other two men
1Ch 11:25 he was more **h** than the thirty
2Ch 32:33 Jerusalem **h** him at his death
Prov 13:18 who regards reproof will be **h**
Prov 27:18 waits on his master will be **h**
Is 43: 4 in My sight, you have been **h**
Is 43:23 nor have you **h** Me with your
Lam 1: 8 All who **h** her despise her
Dan 4:34 and **h** Him who lives forever
Acts 28:10 They also **h** us in many ways
1Co 12:26 or if one member is **h**, all

HONORING (*see* HONOR)
Matt 15: 6 is released from **h** his

HONORS (*see* HONOR)
2Sa 10: 3 **h** your father because he has
1Ch 19: 3 **h** your father because he has
Ps 15: 4 But he **h** those who fear the
Prov 12: 9 than he who **h** himself but
Prov 14:31 but he who **h** Him has mercy on
Mal 1: 6 A son **h** his father, and a
Mark 7: 6 This people **h** Me with their
John 8:54 It is My Father who **h** Me, of

HOOF (*see* HOOVES)
Ex 10:26 not a **h** shall be left behind
Lev 11: 3 whatever divides the **h**,
Lev 11: 7 though it divides the **h**,
Deut 14: 6 having the **h** split into two

HOOK (*see* HOOKS)
2Ki 19:28 I will put My **h** in your nose
Job 41: 1 draw out Leviathan with a **h**
Job 41: 2 or pierce his jaw with a **h**
Is 37:29 I will put My **h** in your nose
Hab 1:15 take up all of them with a **h**
Matt 17:27 go to the sea, cast in a **h**

HOOKS (*see* HOOK)
Ex 26:32 Their **h** shall be of gold,
Ex 26:37 their **h** shall be of gold, and
Ex 27:10 The **h** of the pillars and their
Ex 27:11 the **h** of the pillars and their
Ex 27:17 their **h** shall be of silver and
Ex 36:36 gold, with their **h** of gold
Ex 36:38 its five pillars with their **h**
Ex 38:10 The **h** of the pillars and their
Ex 38:11 The **h** of the pillars and their
Ex 38:12 The **h** of the pillars and their
Ex 38:17 the **h** of the pillars and their
Ex 38:19 their **h** were of silver, and
Ex 38:28 he made **h** for the pillars
2Ch 33:11 who took Manasseh with **h**
Is 2: 4 their spears into pruning **h**
Is 18: 5 off the sprigs with pruning **h**
Is 19: 8 who cast **h** into the River
Ezek 29: 4 But I will put **h** in your jaws
Ezek 38: 4 put **h** into your jaws, and lead
Ezek 40:43 Inside were **h**, a handbreadth
Mic 4: 3 their spears into pruning **h**

HOOPOE
Lev 11:19 heron after its kind, the **h**
Deut 14:18 after its kind, and the **h** and

HOOVES (*see* HOOF)
Lev 11: 3 the hoof, having cloven **h**
Lev 11: 4 or those that have cloven **h**
Lev 11: 4 but does not have cloven **h**
Lev 11: 5 but does not have cloven **h**
Lev 11: 6 but does not have cloven **h**
Lev 11: 7 the hoof, having cloven **h**
Deut 14: 6 every animal with cloven **h**
Deut 14: 7 chew the cud or have cloven **h**
Deut 14: 7 cud but do not have cloven **h**
Deut 14: 8 you, because it has cloven **h**
Judg 5:22 Then the horses' **h** pounded
Ps 69:31 or bull, Which has horns and **h**
Is 5:28 their horses' **h** will seem
Jer 47: 3 **h** of his strong horses, at
Ezek 26:11 With the **h** of his horses he
Ezek 32:13 nor shall the **h** of beasts
Mic 4:13 and I will make your **h** bronze
Zech 11:16 fat and tear their **h** in pieces

HOPE (*see* HOPED, HOPELESS, HOPE'S, HOPES, HOPING)
Ruth 1:12 If I should say I have **h**,
1Ch 29:15 are as a shadow, and without **h**
Ezra 10: 2 yet now there is **h** in Israel
Job 4: 6 integrity of your ways your **h**
Job 5:16 So the poor have **h**, and
Job 6:11 do I have, that I should **h**
Job 6:19 travelers of Sheba **h** for them
Job 7: 6 and are spent without **h**
Job 8:13 the **h** of the hypocrite shall
Job 11:18 be secure, because there is **h**
Job 11:20 shall not escape, and their **h**
Job 14: 7 For there is **h** for a tree
Job 14:19 so You destroy the **h** of man
Job 17:15 where then is my **h**
Job 17:15 As for my **h**, who can see it
Job 19:10 My **h** He has uprooted like a
Job 27: 8 For what is the **h** of the
Job 31:24 If I have made gold my **h**, or
Job 41: 9 any **h** of overcoming him is
Ps 16: 9 My flesh also will rest in **h**
Ps 31:24 All you who **h** in the LORD
Ps 33:17 horse is a vain **h** for safety
Ps 33:18 On those who **h** in His mercy
Ps 33:22 upon us, Just as we **h** in You
Ps 38:15 For in You, O LORD, I **h**
Ps 39: 7 My **h** is in You
Ps 42: 5 **H** in God, for I shall yet
Ps 42:11 **H** in God
Ps 43: 5 **H** in God
Ps 62:10 Nor vainly **h** in robbery
Ps 71: 5 For You are my **h**, O Lord GOD
Ps 71:14 But I will **h** continually, And
Ps 78: 7 they may set their **h** in God
Ps 119:49 which You have caused me to **h**
Ps 119:81 But I **h** in Your word
Ps 119:114 I **h** in Your word
Ps 119:116 not let me be ashamed of my **h**
Ps 119:147 I **h** in Your word
Ps 119:166 I **h** for Your salvation, And I
Ps 130: 5 waits, And in His word I do **h**
Ps 130: 7 O Israel, **h** in the LORD
Ps 131: 3 **h** in the LORD From this time
Ps 146: 5 Whose **h** is in the LORD his
Ps 147:11 In those who **h** in His mercy
Prov 10:28 The **h** of the righteous will
Prov 11: 7 the **h** of the unjust perishes
Prov 13:12 **H** deferred makes the heart
Prov 19:18 your son while there is **h**
Prov 23:18 your **h** will not be cut off
Prov 24:14 your **h** will not be cut off
Prov 26:12 There is more **h** for a fool
Prov 29:20 There is more **h** for a fool
Eccl 9: 4 to all the living there is **h**
Is 8:17 and I will **h** in Him
Is 38:18 pit cannot **h** for Your truth
Is 57:10 did not say, 'There is no **h**
Jer 2:25 But you said, 'There is no **h**
Jer 14: 8 O the **H** of Israel, his Savior
Jer 17: 7 LORD, and whose **h** is the LORD
Jer 17:13 the **h** of Israel, all who
Jer 17:17 You are my **h** in the day of
Jer 29:11 to give you a future and a **h**
Jer 31:17 There is **h** in your future,"
Jer 50: 7 LORD, the **h** of their fathers
Lam 3:18 my **h** Have perished from the
Lam 3:21 my mind, therefore I have **h**
Lam 3:24 Therefore I **h** in Him
Lam 3:26 It is good that one should **h**
Lam 3:29 there may yet be **h**
Ezek 13: 6 yet they **h** that the word may
Ezek 19: 5 waited, that her **h** was lost
Ezek 37:11 are dry, our **h** is lost, and we
Hos 2:15 of Achor as a door of **h**
Zech 9:12 you prisoners of **h**
Luke 6:34 whom you **h** to receive back
Acts 2:26 my flesh will also rest in **h**
Acts 16:19 their **h** of profit was gone
Acts 17:27 in the **h** that they might
Acts 23: 6 concerning the **h** and
Acts 24:15 I have **h** in God, which they
Acts 26: 6 am judged for the **h** of the
Acts 26: 7 God night and day, **h** to attain
Acts 27:20 all **h** that we would be saved
Acts 28:20 because for the **h** of Israel I
Rom 4:18 contrary to **h**, in **h** believed
Rom 5: 2 rejoice in **h** of the glory of
Rom 5: 4 and character, **h**.
Rom 5: 5 Now **h** does not disappoint,
Rom 8:20 of Him who subjected it in **h**
Rom 8:24 For we were saved in this **h**
Rom 8:24 **h** that is seen is not **h**
Rom 8:24 one still **h** for what he sees
Rom 8:25 But if we **h** for what we do
Rom 12:12 rejoicing in **h**, patient in
Rom 15: 4 the Scriptures might have **h**
Rom 15:12 in Him the Gentiles shall **h**
Rom 15:13 Now may the God of **h** fill you
Rom 15:13 that you may abound in **h** by
Rom 15:24 For I **h** to see you on my
1Co 9:10 he who plows should plow in **h**
1Co 9:10 he who threshes in **h** should
1Co 9:10 should be partaker of his **h**
1Co 13:13 And now abide faith, **h**, love,
1Co 15:19 life only we have **h** in Christ
1Co 16: 7 but I **h** to stay a while with
2Co 1: 7 our **h** for you is steadfast,
2Co 3:12 since we have such **h**, we use
2Co 10:15 men's labors, but having **h**
Gal 5: 5 **h** of righteousness by faith
Eph 1:18 what is the **h** of His calling
Eph 2:12 of promise, having no **h** and
Eph 4: 4 in one **h** of your calling
Phil 1:20 **h** that in nothing I shall be
Phil 2:23 Therefore I **h** to send him at
Col 1: 5 because of the **h** which is
Col 1:23 the **h** of the gospel which you
Col 1:27 Christ in you, the **h** of glory
1Th 1: 3 patience of **h** in our Lord
1Th 2:19 For what is our **h**, or joy, or
1Th 4:13 as others who have no **h**
1Th 5: 8 a helmet the **h** of salvation
2Th 2:16 and good **h** by grace,
1Ti 1: 1 the Lord Jesus Christ, our **h**
1Ti 3:14 though I **h** to come to you
Tit 1: 2 in **h** of eternal life which
Tit 2:13 looking for the blessed **h**
Tit 3: 7 to the **h** of eternal life
Heb 3: 6 of the **h** firm to the end
Heb 6:11 assurance of **h** until the end
Heb 6:18 hold of the **h** set before us
Heb 6:19 This **h** we have as an anchor
Heb 7:19 the bringing in of a better **h**
Heb 10:23 of our **h** without wavering
1Pe 1: 3 us again to a living **h**
1Pe 1:13 rest your **h** fully upon the
1Pe 1:21 your faith and **h** are in God
1Pe 3:15 for the **h** that is in you,
1Jn 3: 3 everyone who has this **h** in
2Jn 12 but I **h** to come to you and
3Jn 14 but I **h** to see you shortly,

HOPED (*see* HOPE)
Esth 9: 1 Jews had **h** to overpower them
Ps 119:43 mouth, For I have **h** in Your
Ps 119:74 Because I have **h** in Your word
Jer 3:23 **h** for from the hills, and from
Luke 23: 8 he **h** to see some miracle done
Acts 24:26 Meanwhile he also **h** that
2Co 8: 5 they did, not as we had **h**
Heb 11: 1 the substance of things **h** for

HOPELESS (*see* HOPE)
Jer 18:12 they said, "That is **h**!

HOPE'S (*see* HOPE)
Acts 26: 7 For this **h** sake, King Agrippa

HOPES (*see* HOPE)
1Co 13: 7 **h** all things, endures all

HOPHNI
1Sa 1: 3 Also the two sons of Eli, **H**
1Sa 2:34 come upon your two sons, on **H**
1Sa 4: 4 And the two sons of Eli, **H**
1Sa 4:11 and the two sons of Eli, **H**
1Sa 4:17 Also your two sons, **H** and

HOPHRA (*see* PHARAOH)
Jer 44:30 I will give Pharaoh **H** king of

HOPING (*see* HOPE)
Luke 6:35 lend, **h** for nothing in return
Luke 24:21 But we were **h** that it was He

HOR
Num 20:22 Kadesh and came to Mount **H**
Num 20:23 and Aaron in Mount **H** by the
Num 20:25 and bring them up to Mount **H**
Num 20:27 they went up to Mount **H** in
Num 21: 4 **H** by the Way of the Red Sea
Num 33:37 Kadesh and camped at Mount **H**
Num 33:38 **H** at the command of the LORD

Num 33:39 old when he died on Mount **H**
Num 33:41 So they departed from Mount **H**
Num 34: 7 your border line to Mount **H**
Num 34: 8 from Mount **H** you shall mark
Deut 32:50 your brother died on Mount **H**

HORAM
Josh 10:33 Then **H** king of Gezer came up

HORDE
Ezek 23:24 With a **h** of people

HOREB (*see* SINAI)
Ex 3: 1 of the desert, and came to **H**
Ex 17: 6 you there on the rock in **H**
Ex 33: 6 of their ornaments by Mount **H**
Deut 1: 2 **H** by way of Mount Seir to
Deut 1: 6 LORD our God spoke to us in **H**
Deut 1:19 So we departed from **H**, and
Deut 4:10 before the LORD your God in **H**
Deut 4:15 at **H** out of the midst of the
Deut 5: 2 made a covenant with us in **H**
Deut 9: 8 Also in **H** you provoked the
Deut 18:16 of the LORD your God in **H** in
Deut 29: 1 which He made with them in **H**
1Ki 8: 9 which Moses put there at **H**
1Ki 19: 8 and forty nights as far as **H**
2Ch 5:10 which Moses put there at **H**
Ps 106:19 They made a calf in **H**, And
Mal 4: 4 him in **H** for all Israel, with

HOREM
Josh 19:38 Iron, Migdal El, **H**, Beth

HOR HAGIDGAD (*see* GUDGODAH)
Num 33:32 Bene Jaakan and camped at **H**
Num 33:33 They went from **H** and camped

HORI (*see* HORITE)
Gen 36:22 And the sons of Lotan were **H**
Num 13: 5 Simeon, Shaphat the son of **H**
1Ch 1:39 And the sons of Lotan were **H**

HORITE (*see* HORI, HORITES)
Gen 36:20 the **H** who inhabited the land

HORITES (*see* HORITE)
Gen 14: 6 the **H** in their mountain of
Gen 36:21 were the chiefs of the **H**, the
Gen 36:29 were the chiefs of the **H**
Gen 36:30 were the chiefs of the **H**,
Deut 2:12 The **H** formerly dwelt in Seir,
Deut 2:22 the **H** from before them

HORIZON
Job 26:10 He drew a circular **h** on the

HORMAH (*see* ZEPHATH)
Num 14:45 drove them back as far as **H**
Num 21: 3 of that place was called **H**
Deut 1:44 drove you back from Seir to **H**
Josh 12:14 the king of **H**, one
Josh 15:30 Eltolad, Chesil, **H**,
Josh 19: 4 Eltolad, Bethul, **H**,
Judg 1:17 name of the city was called **H**
1Sa 30:30 those who were in **H**, those
1Ch 4:30 Bethuel, **H**, Ziklag,

HORN (*see* HORNS)
Ex 21:29 with its **h** in times past, and
Josh 6: 5 a long blast with the ram's **h**
1Sa 2: 1 my **h** is exalted in the LORD
1Sa 2:10 exalt the **h** of His anointed
1Sa 16: 1 Fill your **h** with oil, and go
1Sa 16:13 Then Samuel took the **h** of oil
2Sa 22: 3 the **h** of my salvation, my
1Ki 1:34 and blow the **h**, and say, 'Long
1Ki 1:39 Zadok the priest took a **h** of
1Ki 1:39 And they blew the **h**, and all
1Ki 1:41 Joab heard the sound of the **h**
1Ch 15:28 and with the sound of the **h**
1Ch 25: 5 words of God, to exalt his **h**
Ps 18: 2 the **h** of my salvation, my
Ps 75: 4 wicked, 'Do not lift up the **h**
Ps 75: 5 Do not lift up your **h** on high
Ps 89:17 Your favor our **h** is exalted
Ps 89:24 in My name his **h** shall be
Ps 92:10 But my **h** You have exalted
Ps 98: 6 trumpets and the sound of a **h**
Ps 112: 9 His **h** will be exalted with
Ps 132:17 will make the **h** of David grow
Ps 148:14 exalted the **h** of His people
Jer 48:25 The **h** of Moab is cut off, and
Lam 2: 3 anger every **h** of Israel
Lam 2:17 He has exalted the **h** of your
Ezek 29:21 **h** of the house of Israel to
Dan 3: 5 you hear the sound of the **h**
Dan 3: 7 heard the sound of the **h**,
Dan 3:10 who hears the sound of the **h**
Dan 3:15 you hear the sound of the **h**
Dan 7: 8 horns, and there was another **h**
Dan 7: 8 And there, in this **h**, were
Dan 7:11 which the **h** was speaking
Dan 7:20 the other **h** which came up
Dan 7:20 that **h** which had eyes and a
Dan 7:21 the same **h** was making war
Dan 8: 5 a notable **h** between his eyes
Dan 8: 8 the large **h** was broken, and in
Dan 8: 9 **h** which grew exceedingly
Dan 8:12 to the **h** to oppose the daily
Dan 8:21 The large **h** that is between
Dan 8:22 As for the broken **h** and the
Hos 5: 8 Blow the ram's **h** in Gibeah
Mic 4:13 for I will make your **h** iron
Zech 1:21 that lifted up their **h**
Luke 1:69 and has raised up a **h** of

HORNET (*see* HORNETS)
Deut 7:20 **h** among them until those who
Josh 24:12 I sent the **h** before you

HORNETS (*see* HORNET)
Ex 23:28 And I will send **h** before you

HORNS (*see* HORN)
Gen 22:13 caught in a thicket by its **h**
Ex 27: 2 You shall make its **h** on its
Ex 27: 2 its **h** shall be of one piece
Ex 29:12 put it on the **h** of the altar
Ex 30: 2 Its **h** shall be of one piece
Ex 30: 3 and its **h** with pure gold
Ex 30:10 make atonement upon its **h**
Ex 37:25 Its **h** were of one piece with
Ex 37:26 sides all around, and its **h**
Ex 38: 2 He made its **h** on its four
Ex 38: 2 the **h** were of one piece with
Lev 4: 7 the **h** of the altar of sweet
Lev 4:18 the **h** of the altar which is
Lev 4:25 put it on the **h** of the altar
Lev 4:30 put it on the **h** of the altar
Lev 4:34 put it on the **h** of the altar
Lev 8:15 and put some on the **h** of the
Lev 9: 9 put it on the **h** of the altar
Lev 16:18 put it on the **h** of the altar
Deut 33:17 his **h** are like the **h** of
Deut 33:17 are like the **h** of the wild ox
Josh 6: 4 of rams' **h** before the ark
Josh 6: 6 seven trumpets of rams' **h**
Josh 6: 8 **h** before the LORD advanced
Josh 6:13 seven trumpets of rams' **h**
1Ki 1:50 hold of the **h** of the altar
1Ki 1:51 hold of the **h** of the altar
1Ki 2:28 hold of the **h** of the altar
1Ki 22:11 made **h** of iron for himself
2Ch 15:14 and trumpets and rams' **h**
2Ch 18:10 made **h** of iron for himself
Ps 22:21 from the **h** of the wild oxen
Ps 69:31 an ox or bull, Which has **h**
Ps 75:10 All the **h** of the wicked I
Ps 75:10 But the **h** of the righteous
Ps 118:27 cords to the **h** of the altar
Jer 17: 1 and on the **h** of your altars,
Ezek 34:21 all the weak ones with your **h**
Ezek 43:15 with four **h** extending upward
Ezek 43:20 it on the four **h** of the altar
Dan 7: 7 before it, and it had ten **h**
Dan 7: 8 I was considering the **h**, and
Dan 7: 8 **h** were plucked out by the
Dan 7:20 about the ten **h** that were on
Dan 7:24 The ten **h** are ten kings who
Dan 8: 3 was a ram which had two **h**
Dan 8: 3 and the two **h** were high
Dan 8: 6 to the ram that had two **h**
Dan 8: 7 the ram, and broke his two **h**
Dan 8:20 you saw, having the two **h**
Amos 3:14 the **h** of the altar shall be
Zech 1:18 looked, and there were four **h**
Zech 1:19 These are the **h** that have
Zech 1:21 said, "These are the **h** that
Zech 1:21 to cast out the **h** of the
Rev 5: 6 been slain, having seven **h**
Rev 9:13 **h** of the golden altar which
Rev 12: 3 having seven heads and ten **h**
Rev 13: 1 having seven heads and ten **h**
Rev 13: 1 on his **h** ten crowns, and on
Rev 13:11 he had two **h** like a lamb and
Rev 17: 3 having seven heads and ten **h**
Rev 17: 7 the seven heads and the ten **h**
Rev 17:12 the ten **h** which you saw are
Rev 17:16 the ten **h** which you saw on

HORONAIM (*see* HOLON)
Is 15: 5 for in the way of **H** they will
Jer 48: 3 of crying shall be from **H**
Jer 48: 5 for in the descent of **H** the
Jer 48:34 their voice, from Zoar to **H**

HORONITE
Neh 2:10 When Sanballat the **H** and
Neh 2:19 But when Sanballat the **H**,
Neh 13:28 son-in-law of Sanballat the **H**

HORRIBLE (*see* HORRIBLY, HORROR)
Ps 40: 2 brought me up out of a **h** pit
Jer 5:30 **h** thing has been committed in
Jer 18:13 has done a very **h** thing
Jer 23:14 Also I have seen a **h** thing in
Hos 6:10 I have seen a **h** thing in the

HORRIBLY (*see* HORRIBLE)
Jer 2:12 at this, and be **h** afraid
Ezek 32:10 be **h** afraid of you when I

HORRIFIED (*see* HORROR)
Jer 50:13 goes by Babylon shall be **h**

HORROR (*see* HORRIBLE, HORRIFIED)
Gen 15:12 and behold, **h** and great
Ps 55: 5 me, And **h** has overwhelmed me
Ezek 7:18 **h** will cover them
Ezek 23:33 and sorrow, the cup of **h** and
Ezek 27:36 you will become a **h**, and be no
Ezek 28:19 you have become a **h**, and shall

HORSE (*see* HORSEBACK, HORSEMAN, HORSE'S, HORSES, WAR-HORSES)
Ex 15: 1 The **h** and its rider He has
Ex 15:21 The **h** and its rider He has
1Ki 10:29 and a **h** one hundred and fifty
1Ki 20:20 on a **h** with the cavalry
1Ki 20:25 you have lost, **h** for **h**
2Ch 1:17 a **h** for one hundred and fifty
2Ch 23:15 **H** Gate into the king's house
Neh 3:28 Beyond the **H** Gate the priests
Esth 6: 8 a **h** on which the king has
Esth 6: 9 **h** be delivered to the hand of
Esth 6:10 take the robe and the **h**, as
Esth 6:11 Haman took the robe and the **h**
Job 39:18 on high, she scorns the **h**
Job 39:19 Have you given the **h** strength
Ps 32: 9 like the **h** or like the mule
Ps 33:17 A **h** is a vain hope for safety
Ps 76: 6 **h** were cast into a dead sleep
Ps 147:10 in the strength of the **h**
Prov 21:31 The **h** is prepared for the day
Prov 26: 3 A whip for the **h**, a bridle
Is 43:17 brings forth the chariot and **h**
Is 63:13 as a **h** in the wilderness,
Jer 8: 6 as the **h** rushes into the
Jer 31:40 of the **H** Gate toward the east
Jer 51:21 I will break in pieces the **h**
Amos 2:15 who rides a **h** deliver himself
Zech 1: 8 a man riding on a red **h**, and
Zech 9:10 and the **h** from Jerusalem
Zech 10: 3 as His royal **h** in the battle
Zech 12: 4 strike every **h** with confusion
Zech 12: 4 will strike every **h** of the
Zech 14:15 shall be the plague on the **h**
Rev 6: 2 looked, and behold, a white **h**
Rev 6: 4 And another **h**, fiery red, went
Rev 6: 5 looked, and behold, a black **h**
Rev 6: 8 I looked, and behold, a pale **h**
Rev 19:11 opened, and behold, a white **h**
Rev 19:19 against Him who sat on the **h**
Rev 19:21 mouth of Him who sat on the **h**

HORSEBACK (*see* HORSE)
Esth 6: 9 Then parade him on **h** through
Esth 6:11 led him on **h** through the city
Esth 8:10 sent letters by couriers on **h**

HORSEMAN (*see* HORSE, HORSEMEN)
2Ki 9:17 Get a **h** and send him to meet
2Ki 9:18 So the **h** went to meet him, and
2Ki 9:19 a second **h** who came to them

HORSEMEN (*see* HORSEMAN)
Gen 50: 9 with him both chariots and **h**
Ex 14: 9 and chariots of Pharaoh, his **h**
Ex 14:17 army, his chariots, and his **h**
Ex 14:18 his chariots, and his **h**
Ex 14:23 his chariots, and his **h**
Ex 14:26 their chariots, and on their **h**

Ex 14:28 covered the chariots, the **h**
Ex 15:19 his **h** into the sea, and the
Josh 24: 6 chariots and **h** to the Red Sea
1Sa 8:11 own chariots and to be his **h**
1Sa 13: 5 chariots and six thousand **h**
2Sa 1: 6 **h** followed hard after him
2Sa 8: 4 chariots, seven hundred **h**
2Sa 10:18 thousand **h** of the Syrians
1Ki 1: 5 for himself chariots and **h**
1Ki 4:26 and twelve thousand **h**
1Ki 10:26 gathered chariots and **h**
1Ki 10:26 chariots and twelve thousand **h**
2Ki 2:12 chariot of Israel and its **h**
2Ki 13: 7 army of Jehoahaz only fifty **h**
2Ki 13:14 chariots of Israel and their **h**
2Ki 18:24 in Egypt for chariots and **h**
1Ch 18: 4 chariots, seven thousand **h**
1Ch 19: 6 and **h** from Mesopotamia, from
2Ch 1:14 gathered chariots and **h**
2Ch 1:14 chariots and twelve thousand **h**
2Ch 9:25 twelve thousand **h** whom he
2Ch 12: 3 chariots, sixty thousand **h**
2Ch 16: 8 with very many chariots and **h**
Ezra 8:22 and **h** to help us against the
Neh 2: 9 of the army and **h** with me
Is 21: 7 a chariot with a pair of **h**
Is 21: 9 of men with a pair of **h**
Is 22: 6 with chariots of men and **h**
Is 22: 7 the **h** shall set themselves in
Is 28:28 or crush it with his **h**
Is 31: 1 in **h** because they are very
Is 36: 9 in Egypt for chariots and **h**
Jer 4:29 flee from the noise of the **h**
Jer 46: 4 horses, and mount up, you **h**
Ezek 23: 6 young men, **h** riding on horses
Ezek 23:12 **h** riding on horses, all of
Ezek 26: 7 with chariots, and with **h**
Ezek 26:10 shake at the noise of the **h**
Ezek 38: 4 all your army, horses, and **h**
Dan 11:40 a whirlwind, with chariots, **h**
Hos 1: 7 or battle, by horses or **h**
Nah 3: 3 **H** charge with bright sword and
Acts 23:23 hundred soldiers, seventy **h**
Acts 23:32 left the **h** to go on with him
Rev 9:16 the **h** was two hundred million

HORSE'S (*see* HORSE)
Gen 49:17 that bites the **h** heels so

HORSES (*see* HORSE)
Gen 47:17 bread in exchange for the **h**
Ex 9: 3 cattle in the field, on the **h**
Ex 14: 9 pursued them, all the **h** and
Ex 14:23 of the sea, all Pharaoh's **h**
Ex 15:19 For the **h** of Pharaoh went
Deut 11: 4 the army of Egypt, to their **h**
Deut 17:16 not multiply **h** for himself
Deut 17:16 return to Egypt to multiply **h**
Deut 20: 1 your enemies, and see **h** and
Josh 11: 4 multitude, with very many **h**
Josh 11: 6 You shall hamstring their **h**
Josh 11: 9 he hamstrung their **h** and
Judg 5:22 Then the **h'** hooves pounded,
2Sa 8: 4 hamstrung all the chariot **h**
2Sa 15: 1 himself with chariots and **h**
1Ki 4:26 stalls of **h** for his chariots
1Ki 4:28 the proper place, for the **h**
1Ki 10:25 garments, armor, spices, **h**
1Ki 10:28 Solomon had **h** imported from
1Ki 18: 5 may find grass to keep the **h**
1Ki 20: 1 kings with him, with **h** and
1Ki 20:21 went out and attacked the **h**
1Ki 22: 4 people, my **h** as your **h**
2Ki 2:11 fire appeared with **h** of fire
2Ki 3: 7 people, my **h** as your **h**
2Ki 5: 9 Then Naaman went with his **h**
2Ki 6:14 Therefore he sent **h** and
2Ki 6:15 surrounding the city with **h**
2Ki 6:17 the mountain was full of **h**
2Ki 7: 6 of chariots and the noise of **h**
2Ki 7: 7 their tents, their **h**, and
2Ki 7:10 only **h** and donkeys tied, and
2Ki 7:13 **h** which are left in the city
2Ki 7:14 they took two chariots with **h**
2Ki 9:33 on the wall and on the **h**
2Ki 10: 2 and you have chariots and **h**
2Ki 11:16 she went by way of the **h'**
2Ki 14:20 Then they brought him on **h**
2Ki 18:23 will give you two thousand **h**
2Ki 23:11 Then he removed the **h** that
1Ch 18: 4 hamstrung all the chariot **h**
2Ch 1:16 Solomon had **h** imported from
2Ch 9:24 garments, armor, spices, **h**
2Ch 9:25 four thousand stalls for **h**
2Ch 9:28 they brought **h** to Solomon
2Ch 25:28 Then they brought him on **h**
Ezra 2:66 Their **h** were seven hundred and
Neh 7:68 Their **h** were seven hundred and
Esth 8:10 riding on royal **h** bred from
Esth 8:14 who rode on royal **h** went out
Ps 20: 7 in chariots, and some in **h**
Eccl 10: 7 I have seen servants on **h**
Is 2: 7 their land is also full of **h**
Is 5:28 their **h'** hooves will seem
Is 30:16 No, for we will flee on **h**"
Is 30:16 We will ride on swift **h**"
Is 31: 1 Egypt for help, and rely on **h**
Is 31: 3 their **h** are flesh, and not
Is 36: 8 will give you two thousand **h**
Is 66:20 LORD out of all nations, on **h**
Jer 4:13 His **h** are swifter than eagles
Jer 6:23 and they ride on **h**, as men of
Jer 8:16 of His **h** was heard from Dan
Jer 12: 5 how can you contend with **h**
Jer 17:25 riding in chariots and on **h**
Jer 22: 4 of this house, riding on **h**
Jer 46: 4 Harness the **h**, and mount up,
Jer 46: 9 Come up, O **h**, and rage, O
Jer 47: 3 hooves of his strong **h**, at
Jer 50:37 A sword is against their **h**
Jer 50:42 They shall ride on **h**, set in
Jer 51:27 cause the **h** to come up like
Ezek 17:15 that they might give him **h**
Ezek 23: 6 men, horsemen riding on **h**
Ezek 23:12 horsemen riding on **h**, all of
Ezek 23:20 issue is like the issue of **h**
Ezek 23:23 all of them riding on **h**
Ezek 26: 7 king of kings, with **h**, with
Ezek 26:10 of the abundance of his **h**
Ezek 26:11 With the hooves of his **h** he
Ezek 27:14 traded for your wares with **h**
Ezek 38: 4 out, with all your army, **h**
Ezek 38:15 you, all of them riding on **h**
Ezek 39:20 be filled at My table with **h**
Hos 1: 7 or battle, by **h** or horsemen
Hos 14: 3 us, we will not ride on **h**
Joel 2: 4 is like the appearance of **h**
Amos 4:10 along with your captive **h**
Amos 6:12 Do **h** run on rocks
Mic 5:10 off your **h** from your midst
Nah 3: 2 wheels, of galloping **h**, of
Hab 1: 8 Their **h** also are swifter than
Hab 3: 8 sea, that You rode on Your **h**
Hab 3:15 through the sea with Your **h**
Hag 2:22 the **h** and their riders shall
Zech 1: 8 and behind him were **h**
Zech 6: 2 the first chariot were red **h**
Zech 6: 2 the second chariot black **h**
Zech 6: 3 the third chariot white **h**
Zech 6: 3 the fourth chariot dappled **h**
Zech 6: 6 black **h** is going to the north
Zech 10: 5 the riders on **h** shall be put
Zech 14:20 on the bells of the **h**
Jas 3: 3 we put bits in **h'** mouths that
Rev 9: 7 like **h** prepared for battle
Rev 9: 9 many **h** running into battle
Rev 9:17 I saw the **h** in the vision
Rev 9:17 the heads of the **h** were like
Rev 14:20 up to the **h'** bridles, for
Rev 18:13 and wheat, cattle and sheep, **h**
Rev 19:14 followed Him on white **h**
Rev 19:18 of mighty men, the flesh of **h**

HOSAH
Josh 19:29 then the border turned to **H**
1Ch 16:38 the son of Jeduthun, and **H**
1Ch 26:10 Also **H**, of the children of
1Ch 26:11 brethren of **H** were thirteen
1Ch 26:16 **H** the lot came out for the

HOSANNA
Matt 21: 9 **H** to the Son of David
Matt 21: 9 **H** in the highest
Matt 21:15 **H** to the Son of David
Mark 11: 9 **H**! 'Blessed is He who comes
Mark 11:10 **H** in the highest
John 12:13 **H**! 'Blessed is He who comes

HOSEA (*see* HOSHEA, JOSHUA)
Hos 1: 1 came to **H** the son of Beeri
Hos 1: 2 the LORD began to speak by **H**
Hos 1: 2 the LORD said to **H**
Rom 9:25 As He says also in **H**

HOSHAIAH
Neh 12:32 after them went **H** and half of
Jer 42: 1 Kareah, Jezaniah the son of **H**
Jer 43: 2 that Azariah the son of **H**

HOSHAMA
1Ch 3:18 Shenazzar, Jecamiah, **H**, and

HOSHEA (*see* HOSEA, JOSHUA)
Num 13: 8 of Ephraim, **H** the son of Nun
Num 13:16 Moses called **H** the son of Nun
2Ki 15:30 Then **H** the son of Elah led a
2Ki 17: 1 **H** the son of Elah became king
2Ki 17: 3 **H** became his vassal, and paid
2Ki 17: 4 uncovered a conspiracy by **H**
2Ki 17: 6 In the ninth year of **H**, the
2Ki 18: 1 year of **H** the son of Elah
2Ki 18: 9 year of **H** the son of Elah
2Ki 18:10 year of **H** king of Israel,
1Ch 27:20 Ephraim, **H** the son of Azaziah
Neh 10:23 **H**, Hananiah, Hasshub,

HOSPITABLE (*see* HOSPITALITY)
1Ti 3: 2 of good behavior, **h**, able to
Tit 1: 8 but **h**, a lover of what is
1Pe 4: 9 Be **h** to one another without

HOSPITALITY (*see* HOSPITABLE)
Rom 12:13 of the saints, given to **h**

HOST (*see* HOSTS)
Gen 2: 1 earth, and all the **h** of them
Deut 4:19 all the **h** of heaven, you feel
Deut 17: 3 or any of the **h** of heaven
1Ki 22:19 all the **h** of heaven standing
2Ki 17:16 worshiped all the **h** of heaven
2Ki 21: 3 worshiped all the **h** of heaven
2Ki 21: 5 **h** of heaven in the two courts
2Ki 23: 4 and for all the **h** of heaven
2Ki 23: 5 and to all the **h** of heaven
2Ch 18:18 all the **h** of heaven standing
2Ch 33: 3 worshiped all the **h** of heaven
2Ch 33: 5 **h** of heaven in the two courts
Neh 9: 6 of heavens, with all their **h**
Neh 9: 6 the **h** of heaven worships You
Ps 33: 6 And all the **h** of them by the
Is 24:21 on high the **h** of exalted ones
Is 34: 4 All the **h** of heaven shall be
Is 34: 4 all their **h** shall fall down
Is 40:26 brings out their **h** by number
Is 45:12 all their **h** I have commanded
Jer 8: 2 all the **h** of heaven, which
Jer 19:13 to all the **h** of heaven, and
Jer 33:22 As the **h** of heaven cannot be
Dan 8:10 it grew up to the **h** of heaven
Dan 8:10 and it cast down some of the **h**
Dan 8:11 high as the Prince of the **h**
Dan 8:13 the **h** to be trampled under
Obad 20 the captives of this **h** of the
Zeph 1: 5 those who worship the **h** of
Luke 2:13 the heavenly **h** praising God
Acts 7:42 up to worship the **h** of heaven
Rom 16:23 Gaius, my **h** and the **h** of

HOSTAGES
2Ki 14:14 of the king's house, and **h**
2Ch 25:24 of the king's house, and **h**

HOSTILE (*see* HOSTILITY)
Deut 28:54 will be **h** toward his brother

HOSTILITY (*see* HOSTILE)
Heb 12: 3 such **h** from sinners against

HOSTS (*see* HOST)
1Sa 1: 3 to the LORD of **h** in Shiloh
1Sa 1:11 O LORD of **h**, if You will
1Sa 4: 4 the covenant of the LORD of **h**
1Sa 15: 2 Thus says the LORD of **h**
1Sa 17:45 in the name of the LORD of **h**
2Sa 5:10 LORD God of **h** was with him
2Sa 6: 2 by the Name, the LORD of **H**
2Sa 6:18 in the name of the LORD of **h**
2Sa 7: 8 Thus says the LORD of **h**
2Sa 7:26 The LORD of **h** is the God
2Sa 7:27 For You, O LORD of **h**, God of
1Ki 18:15 As the LORD of **h** lives,
1Ki 19:10 zealous for the LORD God of **h**
1Ki 19:14 zealous for the LORD God of **h**
2Ki 3:14 As the LORD of **h** lives,
2Ki 19:31 the LORD of **h** shall do this
1Ch 11: 9 the LORD of **h** was with him
1Ch 17: 7 Thus says the LORD of **h**
1Ch 17:24 saying, 'The LORD of **h**, the
Ps 24:10 The LORD of **h**, He is the King

Ps 46: 7 The LORD of **h** is with us
Ps 46:11 The LORD of **h** is with us
Ps 48: 8 In the city of the LORD of **h**
Ps 59: 5 therefore, O LORD God of **h**
Ps 69: 6 wait for You, O Lord GOD of **h**
Ps 80: 4 O LORD God of **h**, How long
Ps 80: 7 Restore us, O God of **h**
Ps 80:14 we beseech You, O God of **h**
Ps 80:19 Restore us, O LORD God of **h**
Ps 84: 1 Your tabernacle, O LORD of **h**
Ps 84: 3 Even Your altars, O LORD of **h**
Ps 84: 8 O LORD God of **h**, hear my
Ps 84:12 O LORD of **h**, Blessed is the
Ps 89: 8 O LORD God of **h**, Who is
Ps 103:21 Bless the LORD, all you His **h**
Ps 148: 2 Praise Him, all His **h**
Is 1: 9 Unless the LORD of **h** had left
Is 1:24 the Lord says, the LORD of **h**
Is 2:12 **h** shall come upon everything
Is 3: 1 the Lord, the LORD of **h**,
Is 3:15 says the Lord GOD of **h**
Is 5: 7 of **h** is the house of Israel
Is 5: 9 my hearing the LORD of **h** said
Is 5:16 But the LORD of **h** shall be
Is 5:24 the law of the LORD of **h**, and
Is 6: 3 holy, holy is the LORD of **h**
Is 6: 5 seen the King, the LORD of **h**
Is 8:13 The LORD of **h**, Him you shall
Is 8:18 in Israel From the LORD of **h**
Is 9: 7 LORD of **h** will perform this
Is 9:13 do they seek the LORD of **h**
Is 9:19 of **h** the land is burned up
Is 10:16 the Lord, the Lord of **h**, will
Is 10:23 For the Lord GOD of **h** will
Is 10:24 thus says the Lord GOD of **h**
Is 10:26 the LORD of **h** will stir up a
Is 10:33 the Lord, the LORD of **h**,
Is 13: 4 The LORD of **h** musters the
Is 13:13 in the wrath of the LORD of **h**
Is 14:22 them," says the LORD of **h**
Is 14:23 says the LORD of **h**
Is 14:24 The LORD of **h** has sworn,
Is 14:27 the LORD of **h** has purposed
Is 17: 3 Israel," says the LORD of **h**
Is 18: 7 LORD of **h** from a people tall
Is 18: 7 of the name of the LORD of **h**
Is 19: 4 says the Lord, the LORD of **h**
Is 19:12 **h** has purposed against Egypt
Is 19:16 of the hand of the LORD of **h**
Is 19:17 of **h** which He has determined
Is 19:18 and swear by the LORD of **h**
Is 19:20 of **h** in the land of Egypt
Is 19:25 the LORD of **h** shall bless
Is 21:10 have heard from the LORD of **h**
Is 22: 5 by the Lord GOD of **h** in the
Is 22:12 GOD of **h** called for weeping
Is 22:14 my hearing by the LORD of **h**
Is 22:14 says the Lord GOD of **h**
Is 22:15 Thus says the Lord GOD of **h**
Is 22:25 that day,' says the LORD of **h**
Is 23: 9 The LORD of **h** has purposed it
Is 24:23 for the LORD of **h** will reign
Is 25: 6 this mountain the LORD of **h**
Is 28: 5 of **h** will be for a crown of
Is 28:22 heard from the Lord GOD of **h**
Is 28:29 also comes from the LORD of **h**
Is 29: 6 by the LORD of **h** with thunder
Is 31: 4 so the LORD of **h** will come
Is 31: 5 LORD of **h** defend Jerusalem
Is 37:16 O LORD of **h**, God of Israel,
Is 37:32 of the LORD of **h** will do this
Is 39: 5 the word of the LORD of **h**
Is 44: 6 his Redeemer, the LORD of **h**
Is 45:13 reward," says the LORD of **h**
Is 47: 4 the LORD of **h** is His name
Is 48: 2 the LORD of **h** is His name
Is 51:15 the LORD of **h** is His name
Is 54: 5 the LORD of **h** is His name
Jer 2:19 you," says the Lord GOD of **h**
Jer 3:19 heritage of the **h** of nations
Jer 5:14 thus says the LORD God of **h**
Jer 6: 6 thus has the LORD of **h** said
Jer 6: 9 Thus says the LORD of **h**
Jer 7: 3 Thus says the LORD of **h**, the
Jer 7:21 Thus says the LORD of **h**, the
Jer 8: 3 them," says the LORD of **h**
Jer 9: 7 thus says the LORD of **h**
Jer 9:15 thus says the LORD of **h**, the
Jer 9:17 Thus says the LORD of **h**
Jer 10:16 the LORD of **h** is His name
Jer 11:17 For the LORD of **h**, who
Jer 11:20 But, O LORD of **h**, you who
Jer 11:22 thus says the LORD of **h**
Jer 15:16 by Your name, O LORD God of **h**
Jer 16: 9 For thus says the LORD of **h**
Jer 19: 3 Thus says the LORD of **h**, the
Jer 19:11 Thus says the LORD of **h**
Jer 19:15 Thus says the LORD of **h**, the
Jer 20:12 But, O LORD of **h**, You who
Jer 23:15 thus says the LORD of **h**
Jer 23:16 Thus says the LORD of **h**
Jer 23:36 the living God, the LORD of **h**
Jer 25: 8 thus says the LORD of **h**
Jer 25:27 Thus says the LORD of **h**
Jer 25:28 Thus says the LORD of **h**
Jer 25:29 earth," says the LORD of **h**
Jer 25:32 Thus says the LORD of **h**
Jer 26:18 Thus says the LORD of **h**
Jer 27: 4 Thus says the LORD of **h**, the
Jer 27:18 intercession to the LORD of **h**
Jer 27:19 of **h** concerning the pillars
Jer 27:21 yes, thus says the LORD of **h**
Jer 28: 2 Thus speaks the LORD of **h**
Jer 28:14 For thus says the LORD of **h**
Jer 29: 4 Thus says the LORD of **h**, the
Jer 29: 8 For thus says the LORD of **h**
Jer 29:17 thus says the LORD of **h**
Jer 29:21 Thus says the LORD of **h**, the
Jer 29:25 Thus speaks the LORD of **h**
Jer 30: 8 that day,' says the LORD of **h**
Jer 31:23 Thus says the LORD of **h**, the
Jer 31:35 (the LORD of **h** is His name)
Jer 32:14 Thus says the LORD of **h**, the
Jer 32:15 For thus says the LORD of **h**
Jer 32:18 whose name is the LORD of **h**
Jer 33:11 Praise the LORD of **h**, for the
Jer 33:12 Thus says the LORD of **h**
Jer 35:13 Thus says the LORD of **h**, the
Jer 35:17 thus says the LORD God of **h**
Jer 35:18 Thus says the LORD of **h**, the
Jer 35:19 thus says the LORD of **h**, the
Jer 38:17 says the LORD, the God of **h**
Jer 39:16 Thus says the LORD of **h**
Jer 42:15 Thus says the LORD of **h**, the
Jer 42:18 For thus says the LORD of **h**
Jer 43:10 Thus says the LORD of **h**
Jer 44: 2 Thus says the LORD of **h**, the
Jer 44: 7 says the LORD, the God of **h**
Jer 44:11 thus says the LORD of **h**, the
Jer 44:25 Thus says the LORD of **h**, the
Jer 46:10 the day of the Lord GOD of **h**
Jer 46:10 for the Lord GOD of **h** has a
Jer 46:18 whose name is the LORD of **h**
Jer 46:25 The LORD of **h**, the God of
Jer 48: 1 Thus says the LORD of **h**, the
Jer 48:15 Whose name is the LORD of **h**
Jer 49: 5 you," says the Lord GOD of **h**
Jer 49: 7 Thus says the LORD of **h**
Jer 49:26 day," says the LORD of **h**
Jer 49:35 Thus says the LORD of **h**
Jer 50:18 thus says the LORD of **h**, the
Jer 50:25 God of **h** in the land of the
Jer 50:31 says the Lord GOD of **h**
Jer 50:33 Thus says the LORD of **h**
Jer 50:34 the LORD of **h** is His name
Jer 51: 5 by his God, the LORD of **h**
Jer 51:14 The LORD of **h** has sworn by
Jer 51:19 The LORD of **h** is His name
Jer 51:33 For thus says the LORD of **h**
Jer 51:57 Whose name is the LORD of **h**
Jer 51:58 Thus says the LORD of **h**
Hos 12: 5 that is, the LORD God of **h**
Amos 3:13 the Lord GOD, the God of **h**
Amos 4:13 The LORD God of **h** is His name
Amos 5:14 God of **h** will be with you
Amos 5:15 of **h** will be gracious to the
Amos 5:16 Therefore the LORD God of **h**
Amos 5:27 whose name is the God of **h**
Amos 6: 8 the LORD God of **h** says
Amos 6:14 says the LORD God of **h**
Amos 9: 5 The Lord GOD of **h**, He who
Mic 4: 4 of the LORD of **h** has spoken
Nah 2:13 you," says the LORD of **h**
Nah 3: 5 you," says the LORD of **h**
Hab 2:13 is it not of the LORD of **h**
Zeph 2: 9 I live," says the LORD of **h**
Zeph 2:10 the people of the LORD of **h**
Hag 1: 2 Thus speaks the LORD of **h**
Hag 1: 5 thus says the LORD of **h**
Hag 1: 7 Thus says the LORD of **h**
Hag 1: 9 says the LORD of **h**
Hag 1:14 on the house of the LORD of **h**
Hag 2: 4 with you,' says the LORD of **h**
Hag 2: 6 For thus says the LORD of **h**
Hag 2: 7 glory,' says the LORD of **h**
Hag 2: 8 is Mine,' says the LORD of **h**
Hag 2: 9 former,' says the LORD of **h**
Hag 2: 9 peace,' says the LORD of **h**
Hag 2:11 Thus says the LORD of **h**
Hag 2:23 that day,' says the LORD of **h**
Hag 2:23 you,' says the LORD of **h**
Zech 1: 3 Thus says the LORD of **h**
Zech 1: 3 to Me," says the LORD of **h**
Zech 1: 3 to you," says the LORD of **h**
Zech 1: 4 Thus says the LORD of **h**
Zech 1: 6 Just as the LORD of **h**
Zech 1:12 O LORD of **h**, how long will
Zech 1:14 Thus says the LORD of **h**
Zech 1:16 in it," says the LORD of **h**
Zech 1:17 Thus says the LORD of **h**
Zech 2: 8 For thus says the LORD of **h**
Zech 2: 9 the LORD of **h** has sent Me
Zech 2:11 LORD of **h** has sent Me to you
Zech 3: 7 Thus says the LORD of **h**
Zech 3: 9 says the LORD of **h**, 'And I
Zech 3:10 that day,' says the LORD of **h**
Zech 4: 6 Spirit,' says the LORD of **h**
Zech 4: 9 LORD of **h** has sent Me to you
Zech 5: 4 curse," says the LORD of **h**
Zech 6:12 Thus says the LORD of **h**
Zech 6:15 LORD of **h** has sent Me to you
Zech 7: 3 in the house of the LORD of **h**
Zech 7: 4 of the LORD of **h** came to me
Zech 7: 9 Thus says the LORD of **h**
Zech 7:12 of **h** had sent by His Spirit
Zech 7:12 wrath came from the LORD of **h**
Zech 7:13 listen," says the LORD of **h**
Zech 8: 1 word of the LORD of **h** came
Zech 8: 2 Thus says the LORD of **h**
Zech 8: 3 the Mountain of the LORD of **h**
Zech 8: 4 Thus says the LORD of **h**
Zech 8: 6 Thus says the LORD of **h**
Zech 8: 6 says the LORD of **h**
Zech 8: 7 Thus says the LORD of **h**
Zech 8: 9 Thus says the LORD of **h**
Zech 8: 9 the house of the LORD of **h**
Zech 8:11 days,' says the LORD of **h**
Zech 8:14 For thus says the LORD of **h**
Zech 8:14 to wrath,' says the LORD of **h**
Zech 8:18 of the LORD of **h** came to me
Zech 8:19 Thus says the LORD of **h**
Zech 8:20 Thus says the LORD of **h**
Zech 8:21 LORD, and seek the LORD of **h**
Zech 8:22 the LORD of **h** in Jerusalem
Zech 8:23 Thus says the LORD of **h**
Zech 9:15 The LORD of **h** will defend
Zech 10: 3 For the LORD of **h** will visit
Zech 12: 5 my strength in the LORD of **h**
Zech 13: 2 day," says the LORD of **h**
Zech 13: 7 says the LORD of **h**
Zech 14:16 the King, the LORD of **h**, and
Zech 14:17 the King, the LORD of **h**, on
Zech 14:21 be holiness to the LORD of **h**
Zech 14:21 in the house of the LORD of **h**
Mal 1: 4 Thus says the LORD of **h**
Mal 1: 6 Says the LORD of **h** to you
Mal 1: 8 says the LORD of **h**
Mal 1: 9 says the LORD of **h**
Mal 1:10 in you," Says the LORD of **h**
Mal 1:11 nations," says the LORD of **h**
Mal 1:13 at it," says the LORD of **h**
Mal 1:14 King," says the LORD of **h**
Mal 2: 2 My name," says the LORD of **h**
Mal 2: 4 says the LORD of **h**
Mal 2: 7 messenger of the LORD of **h**
Mal 2: 8 of Levi," says the LORD of **h**
Mal 2:12 an offering to the LORD of **h**
Mal 2:16 says the LORD of **h**
Mal 3: 1 coming," says the LORD of **h**
Mal 3: 5 fear Me," says the LORD of **h**
Mal 3: 7 to you," says the LORD of **h**
Mal 3:10 in this," says the LORD of **h**
Mal 3:11 field," says the LORD of **h**
Mal 3:12 land," says the LORD of **h**
Mal 3:14 mourners before the LORD of **h**
Mal 3:17 be Mine," says the LORD of **h**
Mal 4: 1 them up," says the LORD of **h**
Mal 4: 3 do this," says the LORD of **h**
Eph 6:12 age, against spiritual **h** of

HOT (*see* HOTLY, HOTTEST)
Ex 16:21 And when the sun became **h**, it
Ex 22:24 and My wrath will become **h**
Ex 32:10 wrath may burn **h** against them
Ex 32:11 **h** against Your people whom
Ex 32:19 So Moses' anger became **h**, and
Ex 32:22 the anger of my lord become **h**
Deut 9:19 **h** displeasure with which the
Deut 19: 6 blood, while his anger is **h**
Josh 9:12 **h** for our provision from our
Judg 2:14 the LORD was **h** against Israel
Judg 2:20 the LORD was **h** against Israel
Judg 3: 8 the LORD was **h** against Israel
Judg 10: 7 the LORD was **h** against Israel
1Sa 11: 9 by the time the sun is **h**
1Sa 21: 6 in order to put **h** bread in
Neh 7: 3 be opened until the sun is **h**
Job 6:17 when it is **h**, they vanish
Job 37:17 Why are your garments **h**, when
Ps 6: 1 me in Your **h** displeasure
Ps 38: 1 me in Your **h** displeasure
Ps 39: 3 My heart was **h** within me
Prov 6:28 Can one walk on **h** coals, and
Lam 5:10 Our skin is **h** as an oven,
Ezek 24:11 coals, that it may become **h**
Dan 3:22 and the furnace exceedingly **h**
Hos 7: 7 They are all **h**, like an oven,
Luke 12:55 There will be **h** weather'
1Ti 4: 2 seared with a **h** iron,
Rev 3:15 you are neither cold nor **h**
Rev 3:15 could wish you were cold or **h**
Rev 3:16 and neither cold nor **h**, I

HOTHAM
1Ch 7:32 begot Japhlet, Shomer, **H**, and
1Ch 11:44 the sons of **H** the Aroerite

HOTHIR
1Ch 25: 4 Joshbekashah, Mallothi, **H**
1Ch 25:28 the twenty-first for **H**, his

HOTLY (*see* HOT)
Gen 31:36 that you have so **h** pursued me

HOTTEST (*see* HOT)
2Sa 11:15 the forefront of the **h** battle

HOUND
Ps 56: 2 My enemies would **h** me all day

HOUR (*see* HOURS)
Dan 4:33 That very **h** the word was
Dan 5: 5 In the same **h** the fingers of
Matt 8:13 was healed that same **h**
Matt 9:22 was made well from that **h**
Matt 10:19 that **h** what you should speak
Matt 14:15 and the **h** is already late
Matt 15:28 was healed from that very **h**
Matt 17:18 was cured from that very **h**
Matt 20: 3 he went out about the third **h**
Matt 20: 5 the sixth and the ninth **h**, and
Matt 20: 6 the eleventh **h** he went out
Matt 20: 9 hired about the eleventh **h**
Matt 20:12 men have worked only one **h**
Matt 24:36 **h** no one knows, no, not even
Matt 24:42 what **h** your Lord is coming
Matt 24:43 what **h** the thief would come
Matt 24:44 **h** when you do not expect Him
Matt 24:50 at an **h** that he is not aware
Matt 25:13 neither the day nor the **h** in
Matt 26:40 you not watch with Me one **h**
Matt 26:45 the **h** is at hand, and the Son
Matt 26:55 In that **h** Jesus said to the
Matt 27:45 sixth **h** until the ninth **h**
Matt 27:46 about the ninth **h** Jesus cried
Mark 6:35 and already the **h** is late
Mark 11:11 as the **h** was already late, He
Mark 13:11 is given you in that **h**, speak
Mark 13:32 **h** no one knows, neither the
Mark 14:35 the **h** might pass from Him
Mark 14:37 Could you not watch one **h**
Mark 14:41 The **h** has come
Mark 15:25 Now it was the third **h**, and
Mark 15:33 Now when the sixth **h** had come
Mark 15:33 whole land until the ninth **h**
Mark 15:34 at the ninth **h** Jesus cried
Luke 1:10 outside at the **h** of incense
Luke 7:21 that very **h** He cured many
Luke 10:21 In that **h** Jesus rejoiced in
Luke 12:12 very **h** what you ought to say
Luke 12:39 what **h** the thief would come
Luke 12:40 at an **h** you do not expect
Luke 12:46 at an **h** when he is not aware
Luke 20:19 and the scribes that very **h**
Luke 22:14 And when the **h** had come, He
Luke 22:53 But this is your **h**, and the
Luke 22:59 after about an **h** had passed
Luke 23:44 And it was about the sixth **h**
Luke 23:44 the earth until the ninth **h**
Luke 24:33 So they rose up that very **h**
John 1:39 now it was about the tenth **h**)
John 2: 4 My **h** has not yet come
John 4: 6 It was about the sixth **h**
John 4:21 the **h** is coming when you will
John 4:23 But the **h** is coming, and now
John 4:52 them the **h** when he got better
John 4:52 seventh **h** the fever left him
John 4:53 that it was at the same **h** in
John 5:25 the **h** is coming, and now is,
John 5:28 for the **h** is coming in which
John 7:30 because His **h** had not yet
John 8:20 for His **h** had not yet come
John 12:23 The **h** has come that the Son
John 12:27 Father, save Me from this **h**'
John 12:27 this purpose I came to this **h**
John 13: 1 His **h** had come that He should
John 16:21 sorrow because her **h** has come
John 16:32 Indeed the **h** is coming, yes,
John 17: 1 Father, the **h** has come
John 19:14 and about the sixth **h**
John 19:27 from that **h** that disciple
Acts 2:15 only the third **h** of the day
Acts 3: 1 the temple at the **h** of prayer
Acts 3: 1 **h** of prayer, the ninth **h**
Acts 10: 3 About the ninth **h** of the day
Acts 10: 9 to pray, about the sixth **h**
Acts 10:30 I was fasting until this **h**
Acts 10:30 at the ninth **h** I prayed in my
Acts 16:18 And he came out that very **h**
Acts 16:33 them the same **h** of the night
Acts 22:13 at that same **h** I looked up at
Acts 23:23 at the third **h** of the night
1Co 4:11 the present **h** we both hunger
1Co 15:30 we stand in jeopardy every **h**
Gal 2: 5 submission even for an **h**,
1Jn 2:18 children, it is the last **h**
1Jn 2:18 we know that it is the last **h**
Rev 3: 3 what **h** I will come upon you
Rev 3:10 **h** of trial which shall come
Rev 8: 1 in heaven for about half an **h**
Rev 9:15 had been prepared for the **h**
Rev 11:13 In the same **h** there was a
Rev 14: 7 for the **h** of His judgment has
Rev 17:12 one **h** as kings with the beast
Rev 18:10 For in one **h** your judgment
Rev 18:17 For in one **h** such great
Rev 18:19 For in one **h** she is made

HOURS (*see* HOUR)
John 11: 9 there not twelve **h** in the day
Acts 5: 7 Now it was about three **h**
Acts 19:34 cried out for about two **h**

HOUSE (*see* HOUSEHOLD, HOUSES, HOUSETOP)
Gen 12: 1 and from your father's **h**, to a
Gen 12:15 was taken to Pharaoh's **h**
Gen 12:17 and his **h** with great plagues
Gen 14:14 who were born in his own **h**
Gen 15: 2 the heir of my **h** is Eliezer
Gen 15: 3 one born in my **h** is my heir
Gen 17:12 he who is born in your **h** or
Gen 17:13 He who is born in your **h** and
Gen 17:23 all who were born in his **h**
Gen 17:23 among the men of Abraham's **h**
Gen 17:27 and all the men of his **h**, born
Gen 17:27 born in the **h** or bought with
Gen 19: 2 turn in to your servant's **h**
Gen 19: 3 in to him and entered his **h**
Gen 19: 4 quarter, surrounded the **h**
Gen 19:10 Lot into the **h** with them, and
Gen 19:11 of the **h** with blindness, both
Gen 20:13 to wander from my father's **h**
Gen 20:18 the **h** of Abimelech because of
Gen 24: 2 the oldest servant of his **h**
Gen 24: 7 took me from my father's **h**
Gen 24:23 father's **h** for us to lodge
Gen 24:27 the LORD led me to the **h** of
Gen 24:28 her mother's **h** these things
Gen 24:31 For I have prepared the **h**
Gen 24:32 Then the man came to the **h**
Gen 24:38 you shall go to my father's **h**
Gen 24:40 kindred and from my father's **h**
Gen 27:15 which were with her in the **h**
Gen 28: 2 to the **h** of Bethuel your
Gen 28:17 none other than the **h** of God
Gen 28:21 to my father's **h** in peace
Gen 28:22 as a pillar shall be God's **h**
Gen 29:13 him, and brought him to his **h**
Gen 30:30 I also provide for my own **h**
Gen 31:14 for us in our father's **h**
Gen 31:30 long for your father's **h**, but
Gen 31:41 been in your **h** twenty years
Gen 33:17 to Succoth, built himself a **h**
Gen 34:26 took Dinah from Shechem's **h**
Gen 38:11 a widow in your father's **h**
Gen 38:11 and dwelt in her father's **h**
Gen 39: 2 he was in the **h** of his master
Gen 39: 4 he made him overseer of his **h**
Gen 39: 5 made him overseer of his **h**
Gen 39: 5 **h** for Joseph's sake
Gen 39: 5 on all that he had in the **h**
Gen 39: 8 know what is with me in the **h**
Gen 39: 9 one greater in this **h** than I
Gen 39:11 into the **h** to do his work
Gen 39:11 the men of the **h** was inside
Gen 39:14 called to the men of her **h**
Gen 40: 3 put them in custody in the **h**
Gen 40: 7 the custody of his lord's **h**
Gen 40:14 and get me out of this **h**
Gen 41:10 put me in custody in the **h** of
Gen 41:40 You shall be over my **h**, and
Gen 41:51 my toil and all my father's **h**
Gen 42:19 be confined to your prison **h**
Gen 43:16 said to the steward of his **h**
Gen 43:17 the men into Joseph's **h**
Gen 43:18 were brought into Joseph's **h**
Gen 43:19 to the steward of Joseph's **h**
Gen 43:19 with him at the door of the **h**
Gen 43:24 the men into Joseph's **h** and
Gen 43:26 was in their hand into the **h**
Gen 44: 1 the steward of his **h**, saying,
Gen 44: 8 or gold from your lord's **h**
Gen 44:14 brothers came to Joseph's **h**
Gen 45: 2 the **h** of Pharaoh heard it
Gen 45: 8 Pharaoh, and lord of all his **h**
Gen 45:16 it was heard in Pharaoh's **h**
Gen 46:27 All the persons of the **h** of
Gen 46:31 and those of my father's **h**
Gen 47:14 the money into Pharaoh's **h**
Gen 50: 7 Pharaoh, the elders of his **h**
Gen 50: 8 well as all the **h** of Joseph
Gen 50: 8 brothers, and his father's **h**
Ex 2: 1 a man of the **h** of Levi went
Ex 3:22 of her who dwells near her **h**
Ex 7:23 turned and went into his **h**
Ex 8: 3 go up and come into your **h**
Ex 8:24 came into the **h** of Pharaoh
Ex 12: 3 to the **h** of his father, a
Ex 12: 4 **h** take it according to the
Ex 12:22 door of his **h** until morning
Ex 12:30 for there was not a **h** where
Ex 12:46 In one **h** it shall be eaten
Ex 12:46 of the flesh outside the **h**
Ex 13: 3 out of the **h** of bondage
Ex 13:14 out of the **h** of bondage
Ex 16:31 the **h** of Israel called its
Ex 19: 3 shall say to the **h** of Jacob
Ex 20: 2 out of the **h** of bondage
Ex 20:17 not covet your neighbor's **h**
Ex 22: 7 is stolen out of the man's **h**
Ex 22: 8 then the master of the **h**
Ex 23:19 the **h** of the LORD your God
Ex 34:26 to the **h** of the LORD your God
Ex 40:38 sight of all the **h** of Israel
Lev 10: 6 the whole **h** of Israel,
Lev 14:34 in a **h** in the land of your
Lev 14:35 and he who owns the **h** comes
Lev 14:35 there is some plague in the **h**
Lev 14:36 command that they empty the **h**
Lev 14:36 the **h** may not be made unclean
Lev 14:36 shall go in to look at the **h**
Lev 14:37 the **h** with ingrained streaks
Lev 14:38 priest shall go out of the **h**
Lev 14:38 to the door of the **h**
Lev 14:38 and shut up the **h** seven days
Lev 14:39 spread on the walls of the **h**
Lev 14:41 he shall cause the **h** to be
Lev 14:42 other mortar and plaster the **h**
Lev 14:43 back and breaks out in the **h**
Lev 14:43 after he has scraped the **h**
Lev 14:44 plague has spread in the **h**
Lev 14:44 is an active leprosy in the **h**
Lev 14:45 And he shall break down the **h**
Lev 14:45 and all the plaster of the **h**

Lev 14:46 he who goes into the **h** at all
Lev 14:47 the **h** shall wash his clothes
Lev 14:47 he who eats in the **h** shall
Lev 14:48 in the **h** after the **h** was
Lev 14:48 shall pronounce the **h** clean
Lev 14:49 shall take, to cleanse the **h**
Lev 14:51 and sprinkle the **h** seven times
Lev 14:52 he shall cleanse the **h** with
Lev 14:53 and make atonement for the **h**
Lev 14:55 of a garment and of a **h**,
Lev 16: 6 for himself and for his **h**
Lev 16:11 for himself and for his **h**, and
Lev 17: 3 man of the **h** of Israel, kills
Lev 17: 8 man of the **h** of Israel, or of
Lev 17:10 man of the **h** of Israel, or of
Lev 22:11 in his **h** may eat his food
Lev 22:13 father's **h** as in her youth
Lev 22:18 man of the **h** of Israel, or of
Lev 25:29 sells a **h** in a walled city
Lev 25:30 then the **h** in the walled city
Lev 25:33 a **h** from the Levites, then
Lev 25:33 then the **h** that was sold in
Lev 27:14 his **h** to be holy to the LORD
Lev 27:15 it wants to redeem his **h**,
Num 1: 4 the head of his father's **h**
Num 1:20 families, by their fathers' **h**
Num 1:22 families, by their fathers' **h**
Num 1:24 families, by their fathers' **h**
Num 1:26 families, by their fathers' **h**
Num 1:28 families, by their fathers' **h**
Num 1:30 families, by their fathers' **h**
Num 1:32 families, by their fathers' **h**
Num 1:34 families, by their fathers' **h**
Num 1:36 families, by their fathers' **h**
Num 1:38 families, by their fathers' **h**
Num 1:40 families, by their fathers' **h**
Num 1:42 families, by their fathers' **h**
Num 1:44 representing his father's **h**
Num 2: 2 the emblems of his father's **h**
Num 3:24 **h** of the Gershonites was
Num 3:30 **h** of the families of the
Num 3:35 **h** of the families of Merari
Num 4: 2 families, by their fathers' **h**
Num 4:22 Gershon, by their fathers' **h**
Num 4:29 and by their fathers' **h**
Num 4:34 and by their fathers' **h**,
Num 4:38 and by their fathers' **h**,
Num 4:40 families, by their fathers' **h**
Num 4:42 families, by their fathers' **h**
Num 12: 7 he is faithful in all My **h**
Num 17: 2 a rod from each father's **h**
Num 17: 3 the head of each father's **h**
Num 17: 8 Aaron, of the **h** of Levi, had
Num 18: 1 and your father's **h** with you
Num 18:11 is clean in your **h** may eat it
Num 18:13 is clean in your **h** may eat it
Num 20:29 all the **h** of Israel mourned
Num 22:18 give me his **h** full of silver
Num 24:13 give me his **h** full of silver
Num 25:14 **h** among the Simeonites
Num 25:15 of a father's **h** in Midian
Num 30: 3 her father's **h** in her youth
Num 30:10 she vowed in her husband's **h**
Num 30:16 her youth in her father's **h**
Num 34:14 to the **h** of their fathers
Num 34:14 to the **h** of their fathers
Deut 5: 6 out of the **h** of bondage
Deut 5:21 not desire your neighbor's **h**
Deut 6: 7 them when you sit in your **h**
Deut 6: 9 on the doorposts of your **h**
Deut 6:12 Egypt, from the **h** of bondage
Deut 7: 8 you from the **h** of bondage
Deut 7:26 an abomination into your **h**
Deut 8:14 Egypt, from the **h** of bondage
Deut 11:19 them when you sit in your **h**
Deut 11:20 on the doorposts of your **h**
Deut 13: 5 you from the **h** of bondage
Deut 13:10 Egypt, from the **h** of bondage
Deut 15:16 he loves you and your **h**, since
Deut 20: 5 there who has built a new **h**
Deut 20: 5 Let him go and return to his **h**
Deut 20: 6 also go and return to his **h**
Deut 20: 7 Let him go and return to his **h**
Deut 20: 8 Let him go and return to his **h**
Deut 21:12 bring her home to your **h**, and
Deut 21:13 captivity, remain in your **h**
Deut 22: 2 shall bring it to your own **h**
Deut 22: 8 When you build a new **h**, then
Deut 22: 8 **h** if anyone falls from it
Deut 22:21 to the door of her father's **h**
Deut 22:21 the harlot in her father's **h**
Deut 23:18 **h** of the LORD your God for
Deut 24: 1 and sends her out of his **h**
Deut 24: 2 she has departed from his **h**
Deut 24: 3 and sends her out of his **h**
Deut 24:10 into his **h** to get his pledge
Deut 25: 9 not build up his brother's **h**
Deut 25:10 The **h** of him who had his
Deut 25:14 in your **h** differing measures
Deut 26:11 has given to you and your **h**
Deut 26:13 the holy tithe from my **h**, and
Deut 28:30 you shall build a **h**, but you
Josh 2: 1 came to the **h** of a harlot
Josh 2: 3 you, who have entered your **h**
Josh 2:12 kindness to my father's **h**
Josh 2:15 for her **h** was on the city
Josh 2:19 of your **h** into the street
Josh 2:19 whoever is with you in the **h**
Josh 6:17 all who are with her in the **h**
Josh 6:22 Go into the harlot's **h**, and
Josh 6:24 treasury of the **h** of the LORD
Josh 9:23 carriers for the **h** of my God
Josh 17:17 spoke to the **h** of Joseph
Josh 18: 5 the **h** of Joseph shall remain
Josh 20: 6 to his own city and his own **h**
Josh 21:45 had spoken to the **h** of Israel
Josh 22:14 **h** of every tribe of Israel
Josh 22:14 the **h** of his father among the
Josh 24:15 But as for me and my **h**, we
Josh 24:17 from the **h** of bondage, who
Judg 1:22 the **h** of Joseph also went up
Judg 1:23 So the **h** of Joseph sent men
Judg 1:35 yet when the hand of the **h** of
Judg 4:17 the **h** of Heber the Kenite
Judg 6: 8 you out of the **h** of bondage
Judg 6:15 am the least in my father's **h**
Judg 8:27 a snare to Gideon and to his **h**
Judg 8:29 went and dwelt in his own **h**
Judg 8:35 the **h** of Jerubbaal (that is
Judg 9: 1 the **h** of his mother's father
Judg 9: 5 to his father's **h** at Ophrah
Judg 9:16 well with Jerubbaal and his **h**
Judg 9:18 my father's **h** this day, and
Judg 9:19 and with his **h** this day, then
Judg 9:27 went into the **h** of their god
Judg 10: 9 and against the **h** of Ephraim
Judg 11: 2 inheritance in our father's **h**
Judg 11: 7 expel me from my father's **h**
Judg 11:31 the doors of my **h** to meet me
Judg 11:34 came to his **h** at Mizpah,
Judg 12: 1 We will burn your **h** down on
Judg 14:15 and your father's **h** with fire
Judg 14:19 back up to his father's **h**
Judg 17: 4 they were in the **h** of Micah
Judg 17: 8 to the **h** of Micah, as he
Judg 17:12 and lived in the **h** of Micah
Judg 18: 2 to the **h** of Micah, and lodged
Judg 18: 3 they were at the **h** of Micah
Judg 18:13 and came to the **h** of Micah
Judg 18:15 came to the **h** of the young
Judg 18:15 to the **h** of Micah, and greeted
Judg 18:18 these went into Micah's **h**
Judg 18:22 good way from the **h** of Micah
Judg 18:22 Micah's **h** gathered together
Judg 18:26 turned and went back to his **h**
Judg 18:31 the **h** of God was in Shiloh
Judg 19: 2 **h** at Bethlehem in Judah, and
Judg 19: 3 him into her father's **h**
Judg 19:15 into his **h** to spend the night
Judg 19:18 am going to the **h** of the LORD
Judg 19:18 who will take me into his **h**
Judg 19:21 So he brought him into his **h**
Judg 19:22 men, surrounded the **h** and beat
Judg 19:22 spoke to the master of the **h**
Judg 19:22 the man who came to your **h**
Judg 19:23 the man, the master of the **h**
Judg 19:23 this man has come into my **h**
Judg 19:26 man's **h** where her master was
Judg 19:27 and opened the doors of the **h**
Judg 19:27 the **h** with her hands on the
Judg 19:29 entered his **h** he took a knife
Judg 20: 5 surrounded the **h** at night
Judg 20: 8 any of us turn back to his **h**
Judg 20:18 went up to the **h** of God to
Judg 20:26 up and came to the **h** of God
Judg 21: 2 people came to the **h** of God
Ruth 1: 8 return each to her mother's **h**
Ruth 1: 9 each in the **h** of her husband
Ruth 2: 7 she rested a little in the **h**
Ruth 4:11 coming to your **h** like Rachel
Ruth 4:11 two who built the **h** of Israel
Ruth 4:12 May your **h** be like the **h**
1Sa 1: 7 went up to the **h** of the LORD
1Sa 1:19 and came to their **h** at Ramah
1Sa 1:21 all his **h** went up to offer to
1Sa 1:24 brought him to the **h** of the
1Sa 2:11 went to his **h** at Ramah
1Sa 2:27 reveal Myself to the **h** of
1Sa 2:27 were in Egypt in Pharaoh's **h**
1Sa 2:28 did I not give to the **h** of
1Sa 2:30 I said indeed that your **h**
1Sa 2:30 the **h** of your father would
1Sa 2:31 and the arm of your father's **h**
1Sa 2:31 not be an old man in your **h**
1Sa 2:32 an old man in your **h** forever
1Sa 2:33 **h** shall die in the flower of
1Sa 2:35 I will build him a sure **h**
1Sa 2:36 is left in your **h** will come
1Sa 3:12 have spoken concerning his **h**
1Sa 3:13 **h** forever for the iniquity
1Sa 3:14 I have sworn to the **h** of Eli
1Sa 3:14 **h** shall not be atoned for by
1Sa 3:15 doors of the **h** of the LORD
1Sa 7: 1 and brought it into the **h** of
1Sa 7: 2 all the **h** of Israel lamented
1Sa 7: 3 spoke to all the **h** of Israel
1Sa 9:18 me, where is the seer's **h**
1Sa 9:20 you and on all your father's **h**
1Sa 9:25 with Saul on the top of the **h**
1Sa 9:26 to Saul on the top of the **h**
1Sa 10:25 away, every man to his **h**
1Sa 15:34 up to his **h** at Gibeah of Saul
1Sa 17:25 give his father's **h** exemption
1Sa 18: 2 to his father's **h** anymore
1Sa 18:10 and he prophesied inside the **h**
1Sa 19: 9 **h** with his spear in his hand
1Sa 19:11 to David's **h** to watch him
1Sa 20:15 kindness from my **h** forever
1Sa 20:16 covenant with the **h** of David
1Sa 21:15 this fellow come into my **h**
1Sa 22: 1 all his father's **h** heard it
1Sa 22:11 Ahitub, and all his father's **h**
1Sa 22:14 and is honorable in your **h**
1Sa 22:15 to any in the **h** of my father
1Sa 22:16 you and all your father's **h**
1Sa 22:22 persons of your father's **h**
1Sa 23:18 and Jonathan went to his own **h**
1Sa 24:21 my name from my father's **h**
1Sa 25: 3 And he was of the **h** of Caleb
1Sa 25: 6 be to you, peace to your **h**
1Sa 25:28 for my lord an enduring **h**
1Sa 25:35 Go up in peace to your **h**
1Sa 25:36 was, holding a feast in his **h**
1Sa 28:24 had a fatted calf in the **h**
2Sa 1:12 for the **h** of Israel, because
2Sa 2: 4 king over the **h** of Judah
2Sa 2: 7 and also the **h** of Judah has
2Sa 2:10 Only the **h** of Judah followed
2Sa 2:11 **h** of Judah was seven years
2Sa 3: 1 war between the **h** of Saul
2Sa 3: 1 of Saul and the **h** of David
2Sa 3: 1 the **h** of Saul grew weaker and
2Sa 3: 6 was war between the **h** of Saul
2Sa 3: 6 the **h** of David, that Abner
2Sa 3: 6 his hold on the **h** of Saul
2Sa 3: 8 to the **h** of Saul your father
2Sa 3:10 kingdom from the **h** of Saul
2Sa 3:19 and the whole **h** of Benjamin
2Sa 3:29 Joab and on all his father's **h**
2Sa 3:29 the **h** of Joab one who has a
2Sa 4: 5 day to the **h** of Ishbosheth
2Sa 4: 6 there, all the way into the **h**
2Sa 4: 7 For when they came into the **h**
2Sa 4:11 in his own **h** on his bed
2Sa 5: 8 shall not come into the **h**
2Sa 5:11 And they built David a **h**
2Sa 6: 3 it out of the **h** of Abinadab
2Sa 6: 4 it out of the **h** of Abinadab
2Sa 6: 5 all the **h** of Israel played
2Sa 6:10 took it aside into the **h** of
2Sa 6:11 **h** of Obed-Edom the Gittite
2Sa 6:12 blessed the **h** of Obed-Edom
2Sa 6:12 up the ark of God from the **h**
2Sa 6:15 all the **h** of Israel brought
2Sa 6:19 departed, everyone to his **h**
2Sa 6:21 of your father and all his **h**
2Sa 7: 1 king was dwelling in his **h**
2Sa 7: 2 now, I dwell in a **h** of cedar
2Sa 7: 5 Would you build a **h** for Me to
2Sa 7: 6 in a **h** since the time that I

2Sa 7: 7 you not built Me a **h** of cedar
2Sa 7:11 you that He will make you a **h**
2Sa 7:13 shall build a **h** for My name
2Sa 7:16 And your **h** and your kingdom
2Sa 7:18 And what is my **h**, that You
2Sa 7:19 spoken of Your servant's **h**
2Sa 7:25 servant and concerning his **h**
2Sa 7:26 let the **h** of Your servant
2Sa 7:27 saying, 'I will build you a **h**
2Sa 7:29 bless the **h** of Your servant
2Sa 7:29 **h** of Your servant be blessed
2Sa 9: 1 who is left of the **h** of Saul
2Sa 9: 2 there was a servant of the **h**
2Sa 9: 3 someone of the **h** of Saul, to
2Sa 9: 4 Indeed he is in the **h** of
2Sa 9: 5 brought him out of the **h** of
2Sa 9: 9 to Saul and to all his **h**
2Sa 9:12 all who dwelt in the **h** of
2Sa 11: 2 on the roof of the king's **h**
2Sa 11: 4 and she returned to her **h**
2Sa 11: 8 Go down to your **h** and wash
2Sa 11: 8 departed from the king's **h**
2Sa 11: 9 **h** with all the servants of
2Sa 11: 9 and did not go down to his **h**
2Sa 11:10 did not go down to his **h**,"
2Sa 11:10 did you not go down to your **h**
2Sa 11:11 I then go to my **h** to eat and
2Sa 11:13 he did not go down to his **h**
2Sa 11:27 sent and brought her to his **h**
2Sa 12: 8 I gave you your master's **h**
2Sa 12: 8 and gave you the **h** of Israel
2Sa 12:10 never depart from your **h**,
2Sa 12:11 against you from your own **h**
2Sa 12:15 Then Nathan departed to his **h**
2Sa 12:17 So the elders of his **h** arose
2Sa 12:20 went into the **h** of the LORD
2Sa 12:20 Then he went to his own **h**
2Sa 13: 7 go to your brother Amnon's **h**
2Sa 13: 8 went to her brother Amnon's **h**
2Sa 13:20 in her brother Absalom's **h**
2Sa 14: 8 Go to your **h**, and I will give
2Sa 14: 9 be on me and on my father's **h**
2Sa 14:24 Let him return to his own **h**
2Sa 14:24 Absalom returned to his own **h**
2Sa 14:31 arose and came to Absalom's **h**
2Sa 15:16 concubines, to keep the **h**
2Sa 15:35 you hear from the king's **h**
2Sa 16: 3 Today the **h** of Israel will
2Sa 16: 5 the family of the **h** of Saul
2Sa 16: 8 the blood of the **h** of Saul
2Sa 16:21 he has left to keep the **h**
2Sa 16:22 Absalom on the top of the **h**
2Sa 17:18 came to a man's **h** in Bahurim
2Sa 17:20 came to the woman at the **h**
2Sa 17:23 arose and went home to his **h**
2Sa 19: 5 came into the **h** to the king
2Sa 19:11 bring the king back to his **h**
2Sa 19:11 to the king, even to his **h**
2Sa 19:17 the servant of the **h** of Saul
2Sa 19:20 the **h** of Joseph to go down to
2Sa 19:28 For all of my father's **h** were
2Sa 19:30 back in peace to his own **h**
2Sa 20: 3 came to his **h** at Jerusalem
2Sa 20: 3 he had left to keep the **h**
2Sa 21: 1 of Saul and his bloodthirsty **h**
2Sa 21: 4 gold from Saul or from his **h**
2Sa 23: 5 Although my **h** is not so with
2Sa 24:17 me and against my father's **h**
1Ki 1:53 Go to your **h**
1Ki 2:24 and who has made me a **h**, as
1Ki 2:27 the **h** of Eli at Shiloh
1Ki 2:31 from the **h** of my father the
1Ki 2:33 his descendants, upon his **h**
1Ki 2:34 his own **h** in the wilderness
1Ki 2:36 yourself a **h** in Jerusalem
1Ki 3: 1 finished building his own **h**
1Ki 3: 1 the **h** of the LORD, and the
1Ki 3: 2 because there was no **h** built
1Ki 3:17 and I dwell in the same **h**
1Ki 3:17 birth while she was in the **h**
1Ki 3:18 was no one with us in the **h**
1Ki 3:18 except the two of us in the **h**
1Ki 5: 3 David could not build a **h** for
1Ki 5: 5 I propose to build a **h** for
1Ki 5: 5 shall build the **h** for My name
1Ki 6: 1 to build the **h** of the LORD
1Ki 6: 2 Now the **h** which King Solomon
1Ki 6: 3 the **h** was twenty cubits long
1Ki 6: 3 across the breadth of the **h**
1Ki 6: 3 from the front of the **h**
1Ki 6: 4 he made for the **h** windows
1Ki 6:37 of the **h** of the LORD was laid
1Ki 6:38 the **h** was finished in all its
1Ki 7: 1 years to build his own **h**
1Ki 7: 1 so he finished all his **h**
1Ki 7: 2 He also built the **H** of the
1Ki 7: 8 And the **h** where he dwelt had
1Ki 7: 8 made a **h** like this hall for
1Ki 7:12 court of the **h** of the LORD
1Ki 7:39 on the right side of the **h**
1Ki 7:39 on the left side of the **h**
1Ki 7:39 of the **h** toward the southeast
1Ki 7:40 Solomon on the **h** of the LORD
1Ki 7:45 for the **h** of the LORD were of
1Ki 7:48 made for the **h** of the LORD
1Ki 7:51 **h** of the LORD was finished
1Ki 7:51 of the **h** of the LORD
1Ki 8:10 filled the **h** of the LORD,
1Ki 8:11 LORD filled the **h** of the LORD
1Ki 8:13 surely built You an exalted **h**
1Ki 8:16 Israel in which to build a **h**
1Ki 8:17 a **h** for the name of the LORD
1Ki 8:18 to build a **h** for My name, you
1Ki 8:19 you shall not build the **h**
1Ki 8:19 shall build the **h** for My name
1Ki 8:20 I have built a **h** for the name
1Ki 8:63 dedicated the **h** of the LORD
1Ki 8:64 in front of the **h** of the LORD
1Ki 9: 1 building the **h** of the LORD
1Ki 9: 1 of the LORD and the king's **h**
1Ki 9: 3 I have sanctified this **h**
1Ki 9: 7 and this **h** which I have
1Ki 9: 8 And this **h** will be exalted
1Ki 9: 8 to this land and to this **h**
1Ki 9:10 the **h** of the LORD and the
1Ki 9:10 of the LORD and the king's **h**
1Ki 9:15 to build the **h** of the LORD
1Ki 9:15 **h** of the LORD, his own **h**
1Ki 9:24 the City of David to her **h**
1Ki 10: 4 the **h** that he had built,
1Ki 10: 5 went up to the **h** of the LORD
1Ki 10:12 wood for the **h** of the LORD
1Ki 10:12 the LORD and for the king's **h**
1Ki 10:17 **H** of the Forest of Lebanon
1Ki 10:21 all the vessels of the **H** of
1Ki 11:18 of Egypt, who gave him a **h**
1Ki 11:20 weaned in Pharaoh's **h**
1Ki 11:28 force of the **h** of Joseph
1Ki 11:38 build for you an enduring **h**
1Ki 12:16 Now, see to your own **h**, O
1Ki 12:19 the **h** of David to this day
1Ki 12:20 who followed the **h** of David
1Ki 12:21 he assembled all the **h** of
1Ki 12:21 fight against the **h** of Israel
1Ki 12:23 Judah, to all the **h** of Judah
1Ki 12:24 Let every man return to his **h**
1Ki 12:26 may return to the **h** of David
1Ki 12:27 **h** of the LORD at Jerusalem
1Ki 13: 2 be born to the **h** of David
1Ki 13: 8 were to give me half your **h**
1Ki 13:18 him back with you to your **h**
1Ki 13:19 him, and ate bread in his **h**
1Ki 13:34 the sin of the **h** of Jeroboam
1Ki 14: 4 and came to the **h** of Ahijah
1Ki 14: 8 away from the **h** of David, and
1Ki 14:10 disaster on the **h** of Jeroboam
1Ki 14:10 remnant of the **h** of Jeroboam
1Ki 14:12 therefore, go to your own **h**
1Ki 14:13 Israel in the **h** of Jeroboam
1Ki 14:14 cut off the **h** of Jeroboam
1Ki 14:17 to the threshold of the **h**
1Ki 14:26 of the **h** of the LORD and the
1Ki 14:26 the treasures of the king's **h**
1Ki 14:27 the doorway of the king's **h**
1Ki 14:28 went into the **h** of the LORD
1Ki 15:15 the **h** of the LORD the things
1Ki 15:18 of the **h** of the LORD and the
1Ki 15:18 treasuries of the king's **h**
1Ki 15:27 Ahijah, of the **h** of Issachar,
1Ki 15:29 killed all the **h** of Jeroboam
1Ki 16: 3 and the posterity of his **h**
1Ki 16: 3 I will make your **h** like the
1Ki 16: 3 the **h** of Jeroboam the son of
1Ki 16: 7 against Baasha and his **h**,
1Ki 16: 7 being like the **h** of Jeroboam
1Ki 16: 9 drunk in the **h** of Arza,
1Ki 16: 9 steward of his **h** in Tirzah
1Ki 16:18 the citadel of the king's **h**
1Ki 16:18 burned the king's **h** down upon
1Ki 17:17 who owned the **h** became sick
1Ki 17:23 the upper room into the **h**
1Ki 18: 3 who was in charge of his **h**
1Ki 18:18 you and your father's **h** have
1Ki 20: 6 and they shall search your **h**
1Ki 20:31 the **h** of Israel are merciful
1Ki 20:43 Israel went to his **h** sullen
1Ki 21: 2 it is near, next to my **h**
1Ki 21: 4 Ahab went into his **h** sullen
1Ki 21:22 I will make your **h** like the
1Ki 21:22 the **h** of Jeroboam the son of
1Ki 21:22 like the **h** of Baasha the son
1Ki 21:29 bring the calamity on his **h**
1Ki 22:17 each return to his **h** in peace
1Ki 22:39 the ivory **h** which he built and
2Ki 4: 2 me, what do you have in the **h**
2Ki 4: 2 in the **h** but a jar of oil
2Ki 4:32 when Elisha came into the **h**
2Ki 4:35 walked back and forth in the **h**
2Ki 5: 9 the door of the **h** of Elisha
2Ki 5:24 and stored them away in the **h**
2Ki 6:32 Elisha was sitting in his **h**
2Ki 8: 3 appeal to the king for her **h**
2Ki 8: 5 to the king for her **h** and for
2Ki 8:18 just as the **h** of Ahab had
2Ki 8:27 in the way of the **h** of Ahab
2Ki 8:27 as the **h** of Ahab had done,
2Ki 8:27 son-in-law of the **h** of Ahab
2Ki 9: 6 he arose and went into the **h**
2Ki 9: 7 the **h** of Ahab your master
2Ki 9: 8 For the whole **h** of Ahab
2Ki 9: 9 So I will make the **h** of Ahab
2Ki 9: 9 the **h** of Jeroboam the son of
2Ki 9: 9 like the **h** of Baasha the son
2Ki 10: 3 and fight for your master's **h**
2Ki 10: 5 he who was in charge of the **h**
2Ki 10:10 concerning the **h** of Ahab
2Ki 10:11 of the **h** of Ahab in Jezreel
2Ki 10:30 have done to the **h** of Ahab
2Ki 11: 3 **h** of the LORD for six years
2Ki 11: 4 into the **h** of the LORD to him
2Ki 11: 4 them in the **h** of the LORD
2Ki 11: 5 watch over the king's **h**,
2Ki 11: 6 shall keep the watch of the **h**
2Ki 11: 7 **h** of the LORD for the king
2Ki 11:15 killed in the **h** of the LORD
2Ki 11:16 entrance to the king's **h**
2Ki 11:18 over the **h** of the LORD
2Ki 11:19 down from the **h** of the LORD
2Ki 11:19 the escorts to the king's **h**
2Ki 11:20 the sword in the king's **h**
2Ki 12: 4 into the **h** of the LORD
2Ki 12: 4 bring into the **h** of the LORD
2Ki 12: 9 comes into the **h** of the LORD
2Ki 12: 9 into the **h** of the LORD
2Ki 12:10 found in the **h** of the LORD
2Ki 12:11 of the **h** of the LORD
2Ki 12:11 worked on the **h** of the LORD
2Ki 12:12 damage of the **h** of the LORD
2Ki 12:13 the **h** of the LORD basins of
2Ki 12:13 into the **h** of the LORD
2Ki 12:14 they repaired the **h** of the
2Ki 12:16 into the **h** of the LORD
2Ki 12:18 of the **h** of the LORD and in
2Ki 12:18 the LORD and in the king's **h**
2Ki 12:20 Joash in the **h** of the Millo
2Ki 13: 6 the sins of the **h** of Jeroboam
2Ki 14:14 found in the **h** of the LORD
2Ki 14:14 treasuries of the king's **h**
2Ki 15: 5 so he dwelt in an isolated **h**
2Ki 15: 5 son was over the royal **h**,
2Ki 15:25 the citadel of the king's **h**
2Ki 15:35 Gate of the **h** of the LORD
2Ki 16: 8 found in the **h** of the LORD
2Ki 16: 8 treasuries of the king's **h**
2Ki 16:14 altar and the **h** of the LORD
2Ki 16:18 from the **h** of the LORD, on
2Ki 17:21 Israel from the **h** of David
2Ki 18:15 found in the **h** of the LORD
2Ki 18:15 treasuries of the king's **h**
2Ki 19: 1 went into the **h** of the LORD
2Ki 19:14 went up to the **h** of the LORD
2Ki 19:30 who have escaped of the **h** of
2Ki 20: 1 Set your **h** in order, for you
2Ki 20: 5 go up to the **h** of the LORD
2Ki 20: 8 **h** of the LORD the third day
2Ki 20:13 all the **h** of his treasures
2Ki 20:13 There was nothing in his **h** or
2Ki 20:15 What have they seen in your **h**
2Ki 20:15 have seen all that is in my **h**
2Ki 20:17 when all that is in your **h**

2Ki 21: 4 altars in the **h** of the LORD
2Ki 21: 5 courts of the **h** of the LORD
2Ki 21: 7 in the **h** of which the LORD
2Ki 21: 7 In this **h** and in Jerusalem,
2Ki 21:13 the plummet of the **h** of Ahab
2Ki 21:18 in the garden of his own **h**
2Ki 21:23 killed the king in his own **h**
2Ki 22: 3 to the **h** of the LORD, saying
2Ki 22: 4 into the **h** of the LORD, which
2Ki 22: 5 in the **h** of the LORD
2Ki 22: 5 **h** of the LORD doing the work
2Ki 22: 5 repair the damages of the **h**
2Ki 22: 6 and hewn stone to repair the **h**
2Ki 22: 8 the Law in the **h** of the LORD
2Ki 22: 9 money that was found in the **h**
2Ki 22: 9 who oversee the **h** of the LORD
2Ki 23: 2 the king went up to the **h** of
2Ki 23: 2 found in the **h** of the LORD
2Ki 23: 6 image from the **h** of the LORD
2Ki 23: 7 were in the **h** of the LORD
2Ki 23:11 entrance to the **h** of the LORD
2Ki 23:12 courts of the **h** of the LORD
2Ki 23:24 found in the **h** of the LORD
2Ki 23:27 the **h** of which I said, 'My
2Ki 24:13 of the **h** of the LORD and the
2Ki 24:13 the treasures of the king's **h**
2Ki 25: 9 He burned the **h** of the LORD
2Ki 25: 9 of the LORD and the king's **h**
2Ki 25:13 were in the **h** of the LORD
2Ki 25:13 were in the **h** of the LORD
2Ki 25:16 made for the **h** of the LORD
1Ch 2:55 the father of the **h** of Rechab
1Ch 4:21 the families of the **h** of the
1Ch 4:21 workers of the **h** of Ashbea
1Ch 4:38 their father's **h** increased
1Ch 5:13 brethren of their father's **h**
1Ch 5:15 was chief of their father's **h**
1Ch 6:31 of song in the **h** of the LORD
1Ch 6:32 **h** of the LORD in Jerusalem
1Ch 6:48 tabernacle of the **h** of God
1Ch 7: 2 heads of their father's **h**
1Ch 7:23 tragedy had come upon his **h**
1Ch 9: 9 **h** in their fathers' houses
1Ch 9:11 the officer over the **h** of God
1Ch 9:13 the service of the **h** of God
1Ch 9:19 brethren, from his father's **h**
1Ch 9:23 gates of the **h** of the LORD
1Ch 9:23 the **h** of the tabernacle, by
1Ch 9:26 and treasuries of the **h** of God
1Ch 9:27 they lodged all around the **h**
1Ch 10: 6 and all his **h** died together
1Ch 12:28 and from his father's **h**
1Ch 12:29 loyal to the **h** of Saul)
1Ch 12:30 throughout their father's **h**
1Ch 13: 7 cart from the **h** of Abinadab
1Ch 13:13 **h** of Obed-Edom the Gittite
1Ch 13:14 in his **h** three months
1Ch 13:14 blessed the **h** of Obed-Edom
1Ch 14: 1 carpenters, to build him a **h**
1Ch 15:25 of the LORD from the **h** of
1Ch 16:43 departed, every man to his **h**
1Ch 16:43 David returned to bless his **h**
1Ch 17: 1 David was dwelling in his **h**
1Ch 17: 1 now, I dwell in a **h** of cedar
1Ch 17: 4 not build Me a **h** to dwell in
1Ch 17: 5 in a **h** since the time that I
1Ch 17: 6 you not built Me a **h** of cedar
1Ch 17:10 the LORD will build you a **h**
1Ch 17:12 He shall build Me a **h**, and I
1Ch 17:14 I will establish him in My **h**
1Ch 17:16 And what is my **h**, that You
1Ch 17:17 spoken of Your servant's **h**
1Ch 17:23 servant and concerning his **h**
1Ch 17:24 let the **h** of Your servant
1Ch 17:25 that You will build him a **h**
1Ch 17:27 bless the **h** of Your servant
1Ch 21:17 against me and my father's **h**
1Ch 22: 1 This is the **h** of the LORD God
1Ch 22: 2 stones to build the **h** of God
1Ch 22: 5 the **h** that is to be built for
1Ch 22: 6 charged him to build a **h** for
1Ch 22: 7 was in my mind to build a **h**
1Ch 22: 8 not build a **h** for My name
1Ch 22:10 shall build a **h** for My name
1Ch 22:11 build the **h** of the LORD your
1Ch 22:14 the **h** of the LORD one hundred
1Ch 22:19 articles of God into the **h**
1Ch 23: 4 the work of the **h** of the LORD
1Ch 23:11 assigned as one father's **h**
1Ch 23:24 service of the **h** of the LORD

1Ch 23:28 service of the **h** of the LORD
1Ch 23:28 the service of the **h** of God
1Ch 23:32 the work of the **h** of the LORD
1Ch 24: 5 and officials of the **h** of God
1Ch 24: 6 one father's **h** taken for
1Ch 24:19 **h** of the LORD according to
1Ch 25: 6 music in the **h** of the LORD
1Ch 25: 6 the service of the **h** of God
1Ch 26:12 to serve in the **h** of the LORD
1Ch 26:13 according to their father's **h**
1Ch 26:20 treasuries of the **h** of God
1Ch 26:22 of the **h** of the LORD
1Ch 26:27 to maintain the **h** of the LORD
1Ch 28: 2 it in my heart to build a **h**
1Ch 28: 3 not build a **h** for My name
1Ch 28: 4 above all the **h** of my father
1Ch 28: 4 **h** of Judah, the **h** of my father
1Ch 28: 6 Solomon who shall build My **h**
1Ch 28:10 build a **h** for the sanctuary
1Ch 28:12 courts of the **h** of the LORD
1Ch 28:12 treasuries of the **h** of God
1Ch 28:13 service of the **h** of the LORD
1Ch 28:13 service in the **h** of the LORD
1Ch 28:20 service of the **h** of the LORD
1Ch 28:21 the service of the **h** of God
1Ch 29: 2 Now for the **h** of my God I
1Ch 29: 3 affection on the **h** of my God
1Ch 29: 3 have given to the **h** of my God
1Ch 29: 3 have prepared for the holy **h**
1Ch 29: 7 of the **h** of God five thousand
1Ch 29: 8 treasury of the **h** of the LORD
1Ch 29:16 prepared to build You a **h** for
2Ch 2: 1 and a royal **h** for himself
2Ch 2: 3 build himself a **h** to dwell in
2Ch 2:12 LORD and a royal **h** for himself
2Ch 3: 1 Solomon began to build the **h**
2Ch 3: 3 for building the **h** of God
2Ch 3: 4 across the width of the **h**
2Ch 3: 6 And he decorated the **h** with
2Ch 3: 7 He also overlaid the **h**
2Ch 3: 8 to the width of the **h**, twenty
2Ch 4:11 King Solomon for the **h** of God
2Ch 4:16 Solomon for the **h** of the LORD
2Ch 4:19 made for the **h** of God
2Ch 5: 1 **h** of the LORD was finished
2Ch 5: 1 treasuries of the **h** of God
2Ch 5:13 endures forever," that the **h**
2Ch 5:13 the **h** of the LORD, was filled
2Ch 5:14 the LORD filled the **h** of God
2Ch 6: 2 I have built You an exalted **h**
2Ch 6: 5 Israel in which to build a **h**
2Ch 6: 9 you shall not build the **h**
2Ch 6:29 out his hands to this **h**
2Ch 7: 2 not enter the **h** of the LORD
2Ch 7: 2 LORD had filled the LORD's **h**
2Ch 7: 5 people dedicated the **h** of God
2Ch 7: 7 in front of the **h** of the LORD
2Ch 7:11 finished the **h** of the LORD
2Ch 7:11 of the LORD and the king's **h**
2Ch 7:11 to make in the **h** of the LORD
2Ch 7:11 of the LORD and in his own **h**
2Ch 7:12 Myself as a **h** of sacrifice
2Ch 7:16 chosen and sanctified this **h**
2Ch 7:20 and this **h** which I have
2Ch 7:21 And as for this **h**, which is
2Ch 7:21 thus to this land and this **h**
2Ch 8: 1 had built the **h** of the LORD
2Ch 8: 1 of the LORD and his own **h**,
2Ch 8:11 to the **h** he had built for her
2Ch 8:11 the **h** of David king of Israel
2Ch 8:16 **h** of the LORD until it was
2Ch 8:16 So the **h** of the LORD was
2Ch 9: 3 the **h** that he had built,
2Ch 9: 4 went up to the **h** of the LORD
2Ch 9:11 wood for the **h** of the LORD
2Ch 9:11 the LORD and for the king's **h**
2Ch 9:16 **H** of the Forest of Lebanon
2Ch 9:20 all the vessels of the **H** of
2Ch 10:16 Now see to your own **h**, O
2Ch 10:19 the **h** of David to this day
2Ch 11: 1 assembled from the **h** of Judah
2Ch 11: 4 Let every man return to his **h**
2Ch 12: 9 of the **h** of the LORD and the
2Ch 12: 9 the treasures of the king's **h**
2Ch 12:10 the entrance of the king's **h**
2Ch 12:11 entered the **h** of the LORD
2Ch 15:18 He also brought into the **h** of
2Ch 16: 2 of the **h** of the LORD and of
2Ch 16: 2 the LORD and of the king's **h**
2Ch 18:16 each return to his **h** in peace

2Ch 19: 1 safely to his **h** in Jerusalem
2Ch 19:11 the ruler of the **h** of Judah
2Ch 20: 5 in the **h** of the LORD, before
2Ch 20:28 to the **h** of the LORD
2Ch 21: 6 just as the **h** of Ahab had
2Ch 21: 7 not destroy the **h** of David
2Ch 21:13 the harlotry of the **h** of Ahab
2Ch 21:17 were found in the king's **h**
2Ch 22: 3 in the ways of the **h** of Ahab
2Ch 22: 4 the LORD, like the **h** of Ahab
2Ch 22: 7 to cut off the **h** of Ahab
2Ch 22: 8 judgment on the **h** of Ahab
2Ch 22: 9 So the **h** of Ahaziah had no
2Ch 22:10 royal heirs of the **h** of Judah
2Ch 22:12 in the **h** of God for six years
2Ch 23: 3 with the king in the **h** of God
2Ch 23: 5 shall be at the king's **h**
2Ch 23: 5 courts of the **h** of the LORD
2Ch 23: 6 the **h** of the LORD except the
2Ch 23: 7 and whoever comes into the **h**
2Ch 23:14 kill her in the **h** of the LORD
2Ch 23:15 Horse Gate into the king's **h**
2Ch 23:18 the oversight of the **h** of the
2Ch 23:18 assigned in the **h** of the LORD
2Ch 23:19 gates of the **h** of the LORD
2Ch 23:20 down from the **h** of the LORD
2Ch 23:20 Upper Gate to the king's **h**
2Ch 24: 4 repairing the **h** of the LORD
2Ch 24: 5 **h** of your God from year to
2Ch 24: 7 had broken into the **h** of God
2Ch 24: 7 **h** of the LORD to the Baals
2Ch 24: 8 the gate of the **h** of the LORD
2Ch 24:12 service of the **h** of the LORD
2Ch 24:12 to repair the **h** of the LORD
2Ch 24:12 to restore the **h** of the LORD
2Ch 24:13 they restored the **h** of God to
2Ch 24:14 for the **h** of the LORD,
2Ch 24:14 burnt offerings in the **h** of
2Ch 24:16 both toward God and His **h**
2Ch 24:18 Therefore they left the **h** of
2Ch 24:21 court of the **h** of the LORD
2Ch 24:27 the repairing of the **h** of God
2Ch 25:24 the **h** of God with Obed-Edom
2Ch 25:24 the treasures of the king's **h**
2Ch 26:19 priests in the **h** of the LORD
2Ch 26:21 He dwelt in an isolated **h**
2Ch 26:21 off from the **h** of the LORD
2Ch 26:21 his son was over the king's **h**
2Ch 27: 3 Gate of the **h** of the LORD
2Ch 28: 7 the officer over the **h**, and
2Ch 28:21 from the **h** of the LORD, from
2Ch 28:21 from the **h** of the king, and
2Ch 28:24 the articles of the **h** of God
2Ch 28:24 the articles of the **h** of God
2Ch 28:24 doors of the **h** of the LORD
2Ch 29: 3 doors of the **h** of the LORD
2Ch 29: 5 sanctify the **h** of the LORD
2Ch 29:15 to cleanse the **h** of the LORD
2Ch 29:16 **h** of the LORD to cleanse it
2Ch 29:16 court of the **h** of the LORD
2Ch 29:17 Then they sanctified the **h** of
2Ch 29:18 all the **h** of the LORD, the
2Ch 29:20 went up to the **h** of the LORD
2Ch 29:25 the Levites in the **h** of the
2Ch 29:31 into the **h** of the LORD
2Ch 29:35 So the service of the **h** of
2Ch 30: 1 they should come to the **h** of
2Ch 30:15 to the **h** of the LORD
2Ch 31:10 priest, from the **h** of Zadok
2Ch 31:10 into the **h** of the LORD, we
2Ch 31:11 rooms in the **h** of the LORD
2Ch 31:13 the ruler of the **h** of God
2Ch 31:16 the **h** of the LORD his daily
2Ch 31:17 according to their father's **h**
2Ch 31:21 the service of the **h** of God
2Ch 33: 4 altars in the **h** of the LORD
2Ch 33: 5 courts of the **h** of the LORD
2Ch 33: 7 he had made, in the **h** of God
2Ch 33: 7 In this **h** and in Jerusalem,
2Ch 33:15 idol from the **h** of the LORD
2Ch 33:15 mount of the **h** of the LORD
2Ch 33:20 they buried him in his own **h**
2Ch 33:24 and killed him in his own **h**
2Ch 34: 8 to repair the **h** of the LORD
2Ch 34: 9 was brought into the **h** of God
2Ch 34:10 of the **h** of the LORD
2Ch 34:10 worked in the **h** of the LORD
2Ch 34:10 to repair and restore the **h**
2Ch 34:14 into the **h** of the LORD,
2Ch 34:15 the Law in the **h** of the LORD

2Ch 34:17 found in the **h** of the LORD
2Ch 34:30 went up to the **h** of the LORD
2Ch 34:30 found in the **h** of the LORD
2Ch 35: 2 service of the **h** of the LORD
2Ch 35: 3 Put the holy ark in the **h**
2Ch 35: 5 the father's **h** of the Levites
2Ch 35: 8 rulers of the **h** of God, gave
2Ch 35:21 but against the **h** with which
2Ch 36: 7 the **h** of the LORD to Babylon
2Ch 36:10 from the **h** of the LORD, and
2Ch 36:14 defiled the **h** of the LORD
2Ch 36:17 in the **h** of their sanctuary
2Ch 36:18 articles from the **h** of God
2Ch 36:18 of the **h** of the LORD, and the
2Ch 36:19 Then they burned the **h** of God
2Ch 36:23 a **h** at Jerusalem which is in
Ezra 1: 2 a **h** at Jerusalem which is in
Ezra 1: 3 build the **h** of the LORD God
Ezra 1: 4 for the **h** of God which is in
Ezra 1: 5 build the **h** of the LORD which
Ezra 1: 7 articles of the **h** of the LORD
Ezra 2:36 of the **h** of Jeshua, nine
Ezra 2:59 father's **h** or their genealogy
Ezra 2:68 when they came to the **h** of
Ezra 2:68 freely for the **h** of God, to
Ezra 3: 8 to the **h** of God at Jerusalem
Ezra 3: 8 the work of the **h** of the LORD
Ezra 3: 9 those working on the **h** of God
Ezra 3:11 of the **h** of the LORD was laid
Ezra 4: 3 us to build a **h** for our God
Ezra 4:24 of the **h** of God which is at
Ezra 5: 2 the **h** of God which is in
Ezra 5:13 decree to build this **h** of God
Ezra 5:14 articles of the **h** of God,
Ezra 5:15 let the **h** of God be rebuilt
Ezra 5:16 of the **h** of God which is in
Ezra 5:17 made in the king's treasure **h**
Ezra 5:17 this **h** of God at Jerusalem
Ezra 6: 3 the **h** of God at Jerusalem
Ezra 6: 3 Let the **h** be rebuilt, the
Ezra 6: 5 articles of the **h** of God,
Ezra 6: 5 them in the **h** of God"
Ezra 6: 7 work of this **h** of God alone
Ezra 6: 7 this **h** of God on its site
Ezra 6: 8 the building of this **h** of God
Ezra 6:11 a timber be pulled from his **h**
Ezra 6:11 let his **h** be made a refuse
Ezra 6:12 this **h** of God which is in
Ezra 6:16 of this **h** of God with joy
Ezra 6:17 dedication of this **h** of God
Ezra 6:22 in the work of the **h** of God
Ezra 7:16 **h** of their God in Jerusalem
Ezra 7:17 **h** of your God in Jerusalem
Ezra 7:19 service of the **h** of your God
Ezra 7:20 needed for the **h** of your God
Ezra 7:23 the **h** of the God of heaven
Ezra 7:24 or servants of this **h** of God
Ezra 7:27 to beautify the **h** of the LORD
Ezra 8:17 servants for the **h** of our God
Ezra 8:25 the offering for the **h** of our
Ezra 8:29 chambers of the **h** of the LORD
Ezra 8:30 Jerusalem to the **h** of our God
Ezra 8:33 were weighed in the **h** of our
Ezra 8:36 to the people and the **h** of God
Ezra 9: 9 to repair the **h** of our God
Ezra 10: 1 down before the **h** of God, a
Ezra 10: 6 up from before the **h** of God
Ezra 10: 9 open square of the **h** of God
Neh 1: 6 Both my father's **h** and I have
Neh 2: 8 for the **h** that I will occupy
Neh 3:10 repairs in front of his **h**
Neh 3:16 as far as the **H** of the Mighty
Neh 3:20 **h** of Eliashib the high priest
Neh 3:21 from the door of the **h** of
Neh 3:21 the end of the **h** of Eliashib
Neh 3:23 made repairs opposite their **h**
Neh 3:23 made repairs by his **h**
Neh 3:24 from the **h** of Azariah to the
Neh 3:25 from the king's upper **h** that
Neh 3:28 each in front of his own **h**
Neh 3:29 repairs in front of his own **h**
Neh 3:31 far as the **h** of the Nethinim
Neh 4:16 behind all the **h** of Judah
Neh 5:13 shake out each man from his **h**
Neh 6:10 the **h** of Shemaiah the son of
Neh 6:10 meet together in the **h** of God
Neh 7: 3 another in front of his own **h**
Neh 7:39 of the **h** of Jeshua, nine
Neh 7:61 father's **h** nor their lineage
Neh 8:16 each one on the roof of his **h**
Neh 8:16 or the courts of the **h** of God
Neh 10:32 service of the **h** of our God
Neh 10:33 the work of the **h** of our God
Neh 10:34 into the **h** of our God,
Neh 10:35 by year, to the **h** of the LORD
Neh 10:36 to the **h** of our God, to the
Neh 10:36 minister in the **h** of our God
Neh 10:37 of the **h** of our God
Neh 10:38 tithes to the **h** of our God
Neh 10:39 not neglect the **h** of our God
Neh 11:11 the leader of the **h** of God
Neh 11:12 of the **h** were eight hundred
Neh 11:16 outside of the **h** of God
Neh 11:22 the service of the **h** of God
Neh 12:29 from the **h** of Gilgal, and from
Neh 12:37 wall, beyond the **h** of David
Neh 12:40 choirs stood in the **h** of God
Neh 13: 4 of the **h** of our God, was
Neh 13: 7 in the courts of the **h** of God
Neh 13: 9 the articles of the **h** of God
Neh 13:11 Why is the **h** of God forsaken
Neh 13:14 have done for the **h** of my God
Esth 1:22 should be master in his own **h**
Esth 2: 9 place in the **h** of the women
Esth 2:14 to the second **h** of the women
Esth 4:14 your father's **h** will perish
Esth 5: 1 across from the king's **h**
Esth 5: 1 royal throne in the royal **h**
Esth 5: 1 facing the entrance of the **h**
Esth 6:12 But Haman hastened to his **h**
Esth 7: 8 the queen while I am in the **h**
Esth 7: 9 is standing at the **h** of Haman
Esth 8: 1 Queen Esther the **h** of Haman
Esth 8: 2 Mordecai over the **h** of Haman
Esth 8: 7 given Esther the **h** of Haman
Job 1:13 in their oldest brother's **h**
Job 1:18 in their oldest brother's **h**
Job 1:19 the four corners of the **h**
Job 7:10 shall never return to his **h**
Job 8:15 He leans on his **h**, but it
Job 17:13 I wait for the grave as my **h**
Job 19:15 Those who dwell in my **h**, and
Job 20:19 a **h** which he did not build
Job 20:28 increase of his **h** will depart
Job 21:28 Where is the **h** of the prince
Job 27:18 He builds his **h** like a moth
Job 30:23 to the **h** appointed for all
Job 42:11 and ate food with him in his **h**
Ps 5: 7 I will come into Your **h** in
Ps 23: 6 in the **h** of the LORD Forever
Ps 26: 8 the habitation of Your **h**, And
Ps 27: 4 That I may dwell in the **h** of
Ps 36: 8 with the fullness of Your **h**
Ps 42: 4 with them to the **h** of God
Ps 45:10 also, and your father's **h**
Ps 49:16 glory of his **h** is increased
Ps 50: 9 not take a bull from your **h**
Ps 52: 8 olive tree in the **h** of God
Ps 55:14 walked to the **h** of God in the
Ps 65: 4 with the goodness of Your **h**
Ps 66:13 I will go into Your **h** with
Ps 69: 9 for Your **h** has eaten me up
Ps 84: 4 are those who dwell in Your **h**
Ps 84:10 be a doorkeeper in the **h** of
Ps 92:13 who are planted in the **h** of
Ps 93: 5 Holiness adorns Your **h**, O
Ps 98: 3 to the **h** of Israel
Ps 101: 2 my **h** with a perfect heart
Ps 101: 7 shall not dwell within my **h**
Ps 105:21 He made him lord of his **h**
Ps 112: 3 and riches will be in his **h**
Ps 114: 1 The **h** of Jacob from a people
Ps 115:10 O **h** of Aaron, trust in the
Ps 115:12 He will bless the **h** of Israel
Ps 115:12 He will bless the **h** of Aaron
Ps 116:19 In the courts of the LORD's **h**
Ps 118: 3 Let the **h** of Aaron now say,
Ps 118:26 you from the **h** of the LORD
Ps 119:54 In the **h** of my pilgrimage
Ps 122: 1 us go into the **h** of the LORD
Ps 122: 5 The thrones of the **h** of David
Ps 122: 9 Because of the **h** of the LORD
Ps 127: 1 Unless the LORD builds the **h**
Ps 128: 3 In the very heart of your **h**
Ps 132: 3 go into the chamber of my **h**
Ps 134: 1 stand in the **h** of the LORD
Ps 135: 2 stand in the **h** of the LORD
Ps 135: 2 courts of the **h** of our God
Ps 135:19 Bless the LORD, O **h** of Israel
Ps 135:19 Bless the LORD, O **h** of Aaron
Ps 135:20 Bless the LORD, O **h** of Levi
Prov 2:18 for her **h** leads down to death
Prov 3:33 is on the **h** of the wicked
Prov 5: 8 not go near the door of her **h**
Prov 5:10 go to the **h** of a foreigner
Prov 6:31 up all the substance of his **h**
Prov 7: 6 For at the window of my **h** I
Prov 7: 8 and he took the path to her **h**
Prov 7:27 Her **h** is the way to hell,
Prov 9: 1 Wisdom has built her **h**, she
Prov 9:14 she sits at the door of her **h**
Prov 11:29 own **h** will inherit the wind
Prov 12: 7 but the **h** of the righteous
Prov 14: 1 Every wise woman builds her **h**
Prov 14:11 The **h** of the wicked will be
Prov 15: 6 In the **h** of the righteous
Prov 15:25 destroy the **h** of the proud
Prov 15:27 for gain troubles his own **h**
Prov 17: 1 than a **h** full of feasting
Prov 17:13 will not depart from his **h**
Prov 21: 9 than in a **h** shared with a
Prov 21:12 considers the **h** of the wicked
Prov 24: 3 Through wisdom a **h** is built
Prov 24:27 and afterward build your **h**
Prov 25:17 set foot in your neighbor's **h**
Prov 25:24 than in a **h** shared with a
Prov 27:10 nor go to your brother's **h** in
Eccl 2: 7 and had servants born in my **h**
Eccl 5: 1 when you go to the **h** of God
Eccl 7: 2 **h** of mourning than to go to
Eccl 7: 2 to go to the **h** of feasting
Eccl 7: 4 wise is in the **h** of mourning
Eccl 7: 4 of fools is in the **h** of mirth
Eccl 10:18 idleness of hands the **h** leaks
Eccl 12: 3 the keepers of the **h** tremble
Song 2: 4 me to the banqueting **h**, and
Song 3: 4 him to the **h** of my mother
Song 8: 2 you into the **h** of my mother
Song 8: 7 love all the wealth of his **h**
Is 2: 2 the mountain of the LORD's **h**
Is 2: 3 to the **h** of the God of Jacob
Is 2: 5 O **h** of Jacob, come and let us
Is 2: 6 the **h** of Jacob, because they
Is 3: 6 In the **h** of his father,
Is 3: 7 for in my **h** is neither food
Is 5: 7 of hosts is the **h** of Israel
Is 5: 8 to those who join **h** to **h**
Is 6: 4 the **h** was filled with smoke
Is 7: 2 it was told to the **h** of David
Is 7:13 Hear now, O **h** of David
Is 7:17 people and your father's **h**
Is 8:17 His face from the **h** of Jacob
Is 10:20 escaped of the **h** of Jacob
Is 14: 1 will cling to the **h** of Jacob
Is 14: 2 the **h** of Israel will possess
Is 14:17 open the **h** of his prisoners
Is 14:18 glory, everyone in his own **h**
Is 22: 8 armor of the **H** of the Forest
Is 22:15 to Shebna, who is over the **h**
Is 22:18 the shame of your master's **h**
Is 22:21 and to the **h** of Judah
Is 22:22 The key of the **h** of David I
Is 22:23 throne to his father's **h**
Is 22:24 the glory of his father's **h**
Is 23: 1 waste, so that there is no **h**
Is 24:10 every **h** is shut up, so that
Is 29:22 concerning the **h** of Jacob
Is 31: 2 against the **h** of evildoers
Is 37: 1 went into the **h** of the LORD
Is 37:14 went up to the **h** of the LORD
Is 37:31 who have escaped of the **h** of
Is 37:38 in the **h** of Nisroch his god
Is 38: 1 Set your **h** in order, for you
Is 38:20 life, in the **h** of the LORD
Is 38:22 go up to the **h** of the LORD
Is 39: 2 and showed them the **h** of his
Is 39: 2 There was nothing in his **h** or
Is 39: 4 What have they seen in your **h**
Is 39: 4 have seen all that is in my **h**
Is 39: 6 when all that is in your **h**
Is 42: 7 in darkness from the prison **h**
Is 44:13 that it may remain in the **h**
Is 46: 3 Me, O **h** of Jacob, and all the
Is 46: 3 remnant of the **h** of Israel
Is 48: 1 O **h** of Jacob, who are called
Is 56: 5 to them I will give in My **h**
Is 56: 7 them joyful in My **h** of prayer
Is 56: 7 for My **h** shall be called a
Is 56: 7 a **h** of prayer for all nations
Is 58: 1 the **h** of Jacob their sins

Is 58: 7 that you bring to your **h** the
Is 60: 7 glorify the **h** of My glory
Is 63: 7 toward the **h** of Israel, which
Is 66: 1 Where is the **h** that you will
Is 66:20 vessel into the **h** of the LORD
Jer 2: 4 LORD, O **h** of Jacob and all the
Jer 2: 4 families of the **h** of Israel
Jer 2:26 so is the **h** of Israel ashamed
Jer 3:18 In those days the **h** of Judah
Jer 3:18 walk with the **h** of Israel
Jer 3:20 O **h** of Israel," says the
Jer 5:11 For the **h** of Israel and the
Jer 5:11 the **h** of Judah have dealt
Jer 5:15 O **h** of Israel," says the
Jer 5:20 this in the **h** of Jacob and
Jer 7: 2 in the gate of the LORD's **h**
Jer 7:10 stand before Me in this **h**
Jer 7:11 Has this **h**, which is called
Jer 7:14 **h** which is called by My name
Jer 7:30 their abominations in the **h**
Jer 9:26 and all the **h** of Israel are
Jer 10: 1 speaks to you, O **h** of Israel
Jer 11:10 **h** of Israel and the **h** of Judah
Jer 11:15 has My beloved to do in My **h**
Jer 11:17 the evil of the **h** of Israel
Jer 11:17 of the **h** of Judah, which they
Jer 12: 6 the **h** of your father, even
Jer 12: 7 I have forsaken My **h**, I have
Jer 12:14 pluck out the **h** of Judah from
Jer 13:11 caused the whole **h** of Israel
Jer 13:11 the whole **h** of Judah to cling
Jer 16: 5 not enter the **h** of mourning
Jer 16: 8 the **h** of feasting to sit with
Jer 17:26 praise to the **h** of the LORD
Jer 18: 2 and go down to the potter's **h**
Jer 18: 3 I went down to the potter's **h**
Jer 18: 6 O **h** of Israel, can I not do
Jer 18: 6 you in My hand, O **h** of Israel
Jer 19:14 in the court of the Lord's **h**
Jer 20: 1 governor in the **h** of the LORD
Jer 20: 2 was by the **h** of the LORD
Jer 20: 6 and all who dwell in your **h**
Jer 21:11 concerning the **h** of the king
Jer 21:12 O **h** of David
Jer 22: 1 Go down to the **h** of the king
Jer 22: 4 enter the gates of this **h**
Jer 22: 5 that this **h** shall become a
Jer 22: 6 to the **h** of the king of Judah
Jer 22:13 his **h** by unrighteousness and
Jer 22:14 wide **h** with spacious chambers
Jer 23: 8 **h** of Israel from the north
Jer 23:11 in My **h** I have found their
Jer 23:34 even punish that man and his **h**
Jer 26: 2 in the court of the LORD's **h**
Jer 26: 2 to worship in the LORD's **h**
Jer 26: 6 will make this **h** like Shiloh
Jer 26: 7 words in the **h** of the LORD
Jer 26: 9 This **h** shall be like Shiloh,
Jer 26: 9 Jeremiah in the **h** of the LORD
Jer 26:10 came up from the king's **h**
Jer 26:10 to the **h** of the LORD
Jer 26:10 the new gate of the LORD's **h**
Jer 26:12 me to prophesy against this **h**
Jer 27:16 the vessels of the LORD's **h**
Jer 27:18 are left in the **h** of the LORD
Jer 27:18 in the **h** of the king of Judah
Jer 27:21 remain in the **h** of the LORD
Jer 27:21 in the **h** of the king of Judah
Jer 28: 1 spoke to me in the **h** of the
Jer 28: 3 the vessels of the LORD's **h**
Jer 28: 5 stood in the **h** of the LORD
Jer 28: 6 the vessels of the LORD's **h**
Jer 29:26 should be officers in the **h**
Jer 31:27 I will sow the **h** of Israel
Jer 31:27 the **h** of Judah with the seed
Jer 31:31 covenant with the **h** of Israel
Jer 31:31 Israel and with the **h** of Judah
Jer 31:33 make with the **h** of Israel
Jer 32: 2 was in the king of Judah's **h**
Jer 32:34 their abominations in the **h**
Jer 33:11 praise into the **h** of the LORD
Jer 33:14 promised to the **h** of Israel
Jer 33:14 Israel and to the **h** of Judah
Jer 33:17 the throne of the **h** of Israel
Jer 34:13 out of the **h** of bondage,
Jer 34:15 **h** which is called by My name
Jer 35: 2 Go to the **h** of the Rechabites
Jer 35: 2 them into the **h** of the LORD
Jer 35: 3 the whole **h** of the Rechabites
Jer 35: 4 them into the **h** of the LORD
Jer 35: 5 the **h** of the Rechabites bowls
Jer 35: 7 You shall not build a **h**, sow
Jer 35:18 to the **h** of the Rechabites
Jer 36: 3 It may be that the **h** of Judah
Jer 36: 5 go into the **h** of the LORD
Jer 36: 6 **h** on the day of fasting
Jer 36: 8 of the LORD in the LORD's **h**
Jer 36:10 Jeremiah in the **h** of the LORD
Jer 36:10 the New Gate of the LORD's **h**
Jer 36:12 went down to the king's **h**
Jer 36:22 winter **h** in the ninth month
Jer 37:15 the **h** of Jonathan the scribe
Jer 37:17 asked him secretly in his **h**
Jer 37:20 the **h** of Jonathan the scribe
Jer 38: 7 who was in the king's **h**,
Jer 38: 8 went out of the king's **h** and
Jer 38:11 went into the **h** of the king
Jer 38:14 entrance of the **h** of the LORD
Jer 38:17 and you and your **h** shall live
Jer 38:22 **h** shall be surrendered to the
Jer 38:26 to Jonathan's **h** to die there
Jer 39: 8 Chaldeans burned the king's **h**
Jer 41: 5 them to the **h** of the LORD
Jer 43: 9 to Pharaoh's **h** in Tahpanhes
Jer 48:13 as the **h** of Israel was
Jer 51:51 sanctuaries of the LORD's **h**
Jer 52:13 He burned the **h** of the LORD
Jer 52:13 of the LORD and the king's **h**
Jer 52:17 were in the **h** of the LORD
Jer 52:17 were in the **h** of the LORD
Jer 52:20 made for the **h** of the LORD
Lam 2: 7 have made a noise in the **h** of
Ezek 2: 5 for they are a rebellious **h**
Ezek 2: 6 they are a rebellious **h**
Ezek 2: 8 like that rebellious **h**
Ezek 3: 1 go, speak to the **h** of Israel
Ezek 3: 4 of man, go to the **h** of Israel
Ezek 3: 5 but to the **h** of Israel,
Ezek 3: 7 But the **h** of Israel will not
Ezek 3: 7 for all the **h** of Israel are
Ezek 3: 9 they are a rebellious **h**
Ezek 3:17 watchman for the **h** of Israel
Ezek 3:24 shut yourself inside your **h**
Ezek 3:26 for they are a rebellious **h**
Ezek 3:27 for they are a rebellious **h**
Ezek 4: 3 be a sign to the **h** of Israel
Ezek 4: 4 of the **h** of Israel upon it
Ezek 4: 5 iniquity of the **h** of Israel
Ezek 4: 6 of the **h** of Judah forty days
Ezek 5: 4 out into all the **h** of Israel
Ezek 6:11 of the **h** of Israel
Ezek 8: 1 as I sat in my **h** with the
Ezek 8: 6 the **h** of Israel commits here
Ezek 8:10 the idols of the **h** of Israel
Ezek 8:11 the elders of the **h** of Israel
Ezek 8:12 **h** of Israel do in the dark
Ezek 8:14 north gate of the LORD's **h**
Ezek 8:16 inner court of the LORD's **h**
Ezek 8:17 the **h** of Judah to commit the
Ezek 9: 9 iniquity of the **h** of Israel
Ezek 10: 4 the **h** was filled with the
Ezek 10:19 the east gate of the LORD's **h**
Ezek 11: 1 the east gate of the LORD's **h**
Ezek 11: 5 you have said, O **h** of Israel
Ezek 11:15 all the **h** of Israel in its
Ezek 12: 2 the midst of a rebellious **h**
Ezek 12: 2 for they are a rebellious **h**
Ezek 12: 3 they are a rebellious **h**
Ezek 12: 6 you a sign to the **h** of Israel
Ezek 12: 9 man, has not the **h** of Israel
Ezek 12: 9 of Israel, the rebellious **h**
Ezek 12:10 all the **h** of Israel who are
Ezek 12:24 within the **h** of Israel
Ezek 12:25 in your days, O rebellious **h**
Ezek 12:27 the **h** of Israel is saying
Ezek 13: 5 the **h** of Israel to stand in
Ezek 13: 9 the record of the **h** of Israel
Ezek 14: 4 Everyone of the **h** of Israel
Ezek 14: 5 that I may seize the **h** of
Ezek 14: 6 say to the **h** of Israel, 'Thus
Ezek 14: 7 For anyone of the **h** of Israel
Ezek 14:11 that the **h** of Israel may no
Ezek 17: 2 a parable to the **h** of Israel
Ezek 17:12 Say now to the rebellious **h**
Ezek 18: 6 the idols of the **h** of Israel
Ezek 18:15 the idols of the **h** of Israel
Ezek 18:25 O **h** of Israel, is it not My
Ezek 18:29 Yet the **h** of Israel says
Ezek 18:29 O **h** of Israel, is it not My
Ezek 18:30 you, O **h** of Israel, every one
Ezek 18:31 should you die, O **h** of Israel
Ezek 20: 5 descendants of the **h** of Jacob
Ezek 20:13 Yet the **h** of Israel rebelled
Ezek 20:27 man, speak to the **h** of Israel
Ezek 20:30 say to the **h** of Israel, 'Thus
Ezek 20:31 of by you, O **h** of Israel
Ezek 20:39 O **h** of Israel," thus says
Ezek 20:40 there all the **h** of Israel
Ezek 20:44 O **h** of Israel," says the
Ezek 22:18 the **h** of Israel has become
Ezek 23:39 done in the midst of My **h**
Ezek 24: 3 a parable to the rebellious **h**
Ezek 24:21 Speak to the **h** of Israel
Ezek 25: 3 against the **h** of Judah when
Ezek 25: 8 The **h** of Judah is like all
Ezek 25:12 the **h** of Judah by taking
Ezek 27:14 Those from the **h** of Togarmah
Ezek 28:24 **h** of Israel from among all
Ezek 28:25 When I have gathered the **h** of
Ezek 29: 6 of reed to the **h** of Israel
Ezek 29:16 confidence of the **h** of Israel
Ezek 29:21 **h** of Israel to spring forth
Ezek 33: 7 watchman for the **h** of Israel
Ezek 33:10 man, say to the **h** of Israel
Ezek 33:11 should you die, O **h** of Israel
Ezek 33:20 O **h** of Israel, I will judge
Ezek 34:30 they, the **h** of Israel, are My
Ezek 35:15 the **h** of Israel was desolate
Ezek 36:10 all the **h** of Israel, all of
Ezek 36:17 when the **h** of Israel dwelt in
Ezek 36:21 which the **h** of Israel had
Ezek 36:22 say to the **h** of Israel, 'Thus
Ezek 36:22 O **h** of Israel, but for My
Ezek 36:32 your own ways, O **h** of Israel
Ezek 36:37 I will also let the **h** of
Ezek 37:11 are the whole **h** of Israel
Ezek 37:16 and for all the **h** of Israel
Ezek 38: 6 the **h** of Togarmah from the
Ezek 39:12 For seven months the **h** of
Ezek 39:22 So the **h** of Israel shall know
Ezek 39:23 the **h** of Israel went into
Ezek 39:25 on the whole **h** of Israel
Ezek 39:29 My Spirit on the **h** of Israel
Ezek 40: 4 Declare to the **h** of Israel
Ezek 43: 7 No more shall the **h** of Israel
Ezek 43:10 the temple to the **h** of Israel
Ezek 44: 4 LORD filled the **h** of the LORD
Ezek 44: 5 of the **h** of the LORD and all
Ezek 44: 5 Mark well who may enter the **h**
Ezek 44: 6 to the **h** of Israel, 'Thus
Ezek 44: 6 O **h** of Israel, let us have no
Ezek 44: 7 sanctuary to defile it—My **h**
Ezek 44:11 as gatekeepers of the **h** and
Ezek 44:11 and ministers of the **h**
Ezek 44:12 caused the **h** of Israel to
Ezek 44:17 inner court or within the **h**
Ezek 44:22 of the **h** of Israel, or widows
Ezek 44:30 a blessing to rest on your **h**
Ezek 45: 6 to the whole **h** of Israel
Ezek 45: 8 the land to the **h** of Israel
Ezek 45:17 seasons of the **h** of Israel
Ezek 45:17 atonement for the **h** of Israel
Dan 1: 2 the articles of the **h** of God
Dan 1: 2 of Shinar to the **h** of his god
Dan 1: 2 the treasure **h** of his god
Dan 2:17 Then Daniel went to his **h**
Dan 4: 4 was at rest in my **h**, and
Dan 5: 3 from the temple of the **h** of
Dan 5:23 vessels of His **h** before you
Hos 1: 4 of Jezreel on the **h** of Jehu
Hos 1: 4 kingdom of the **h** of Israel
Hos 1: 6 have mercy on the **h** of Israel
Hos 1: 7 have mercy on the **h** of Judah
Hos 5: 1 Take heed, O **h** of Israel
Hos 5: 1 Give ear, O **h** of the king
Hos 5:12 and to the **h** of Judah like
Hos 5:14 young lion to the **h** of Judah
Hos 6:10 thing in the **h** of Israel
Hos 8: 1 against the **h** of the LORD
Hos 9: 4 come into the **h** of the LORD
Hos 9: 8 and enmity in the **h** of his God
Hos 9:15 I will drive them from My **h**
Hos 11:12 the **h** of Israel with deceit
Joel 1: 9 off from the **h** of the LORD
Joel 1:13 from the **h** of your God
Joel 1:14 the **h** of the LORD your God
Joel 1:16 from the **h** of our God
Joel 3:18 flow from the **h** of the LORD
Amos 1: 4 a fire into the **h** of Hazael
Amos 2: 8 in the **h** of their god

Amos 3:13 against the **h** of Jacob,"
Amos 3:15 I will destroy the winter **h**
Amos 3:15 along with the summer **h**
Amos 5: 1 lamentation, O **h** of Israel
Amos 5: 3 ten left to the **h** of Israel
Amos 5: 4 the LORD to the **h** of Israel
Amos 5: 6 like fire in the **h** of Joseph
Amos 5:19 as though he went into the **h**
Amos 5:25 forty years, O **h** of Israel
Amos 6: 1 to whom the **h** of Israel comes
Amos 6: 9 if ten men remain in one **h**
Amos 6:10 to take them out of the **h**
Amos 6:10 will say to one inside the **h**
Amos 6:11 break the great **h** into bits
Amos 6:11 and the little **h** into pieces
Amos 6:14 O **h** of Israel," says the
Amos 7: 9 against the **h** of Jeroboam
Amos 7:10 the midst of the **h** of Israel
Amos 7:16 spout against the **h** of Isaac
Amos 9: 8 destroy the **h** of Jacob,"
Amos 9: 9 will sift the **h** of Israel
Obad 17 the **h** of Jacob shall possess
Obad 18 The **h** of Jacob shall be a
Obad 18 and the **h** of Joseph a flame
Obad 18 but the **h** of Esau shall be
Obad 18 shall remain of the **h** of Esau
Mic 1: 5 the sins of the **h** of Israel
Mic 2: 2 they oppress a man and his **h**
Mic 2: 7 who are named the **h** of Jacob
Mic 3: 1 you rulers of the **h** of Israel
Mic 3: 9 you heads of the **h** of Jacob
Mic 3: 9 and rulers of the **h** of Israel
Mic 4: 1 the mountain of the LORD's **h**
Mic 4: 2 to the **h** of the God of Jacob
Mic 6: 4 you from the **h** of bondage
Mic 6:10 in the **h** of the wicked, and
Mic 6:16 works of Ahab's **h** are done
Mic 7: 6 are the men of his own **h**
Nah 1:14 Out of the **h** of your gods I
Hab 2: 9 covets evil gain for his **h**
Hab 2:10 shameful counsel to your **h**
Hab 3:13 head from the **h** of the wicked
Zeph 2: 7 the remnant of the **h** of Judah
Hag 1: 2 the LORD's **h** should be built
Hag 1: 9 Because of My **h** that is in
Hag 1: 9 one of you runs to his own **h**
Hag 1:14 worked on the **h** of the LORD
Zech 1:16 my **h** shall be built in it,"
Zech 3: 7 you shall also judge My **h**
Zech 5: 4 enter the **h** of the thief and
Zech 5: 4 the **h** of the one who swears
Zech 5: 4 remain in the midst of his **h**
Zech 5:11 To build a **h** for it in the
Zech 6:10 enter the **h** of Josiah the son
Zech 7: 2 and his men, to the **h** of God
Zech 7: 3 in the **h** of the LORD of hosts
Zech 8: 9 the **h** of the LORD of hosts
Zech 8:13 **h** of Judah and **h** of Israel
Zech 8:15 and to the **h** of Judah
Zech 8:19 feasts for the **h** of Judah
Zech 9: 8 My **h** because of the army,
Zech 10: 3 the **h** of Judah, and will make
Zech 10: 6 strengthen the **h** of Judah
Zech 10: 6 I will save the **h** of Joseph
Zech 11:13 threw them into the **h** of the
Zech 12: 4 My eyes on the **h** of Judah
Zech 12: 7 the glory of the **h** of David
Zech 12: 8 the **h** of David shall be like
Zech 12:10 I will pour on the **h** of David
Zech 12:12 the family of the **h** of David
Zech 12:12 the family of the **h** of Nathan
Zech 12:13 of the **h** of Levi by itself
Zech 13: 1 be opened for the **h** of David
Zech 13: 6 in the **h** of my friends
Zech 14:20 The pots in the LORD's **h**
Zech 14:21 in the **h** of the LORD of hosts
Mal 3:10 there may be food in My **h**
Matt 2:11 when they had come into the **h**
Matt 5:15 light to all who are in the **h**
Matt 7:24 who built his **h** on the rock
Matt 7:25 winds blew and beat on that **h**
Matt 7:26 who built his **h** on the sand
Matt 7:27 winds blew and beat on that **h**
Matt 8:14 Jesus had come into Peter's **h**
Matt 9: 6 up your bed, and go to your **h**
Matt 9: 7 he arose and departed to his **h**
Matt 9:10 sat at the table in the **h**
Matt 9:23 Jesus came into the ruler's **h**
Matt 9:28 when He had come into the **h**
Matt 10: 6 lost sheep of the **h** of Israel
Matt 10:14 depart from that **h** or city
Matt 10:25 the master of the **h** Beelzebub
Matt 12: 4 how he entered the **h** of God
Matt 12:25 and every city or **h** divided
Matt 12:29 one enter a strong man's **h**
Matt 12:29 And then he will plunder his **h**
Matt 12:44 to my **h** from which I came
Matt 13: 1 day Jesus went out of the **h**
Matt 13:36 away and went into the **h**
Matt 13:57 own country and in his own **h**
Matt 15:24 lost sheep of the **h** of Israel
Matt 17:25 when he had come into the **h**
Matt 21:13 My **h** shall be called a **h**
Matt 23:38 Your **h** is left to you
Matt 24:17 to take anything out of his **h**
Matt 24:43 the **h** had known what hour the
Matt 24:43 and not allowed his **h** to be
Matt 26: 6 at the **h** of Simon the leper
Matt 26:18 at your **h** with My disciples
Mark 1:29 they entered the **h** of Simon
Mark 2: 1 heard that He was in the **h**
Mark 2:11 bed, and go your way to your **h**
Mark 2:15 as He was dining in Levi's **h**
Mark 2:26 how he went into the **h** of God
Mark 3:19 And they went into a **h**
Mark 3:25 if a **h** is divided against
Mark 3:25 itself, that **h** cannot stand
Mark 3:27 can enter a strong man's **h**
Mark 3:27 and then he will plunder his **h**
Mark 5:35 of the synagogue's **h** who said
Mark 5:38 to the **h** of the ruler of the
Mark 6: 4 relatives, and in his own **h**
Mark 6:10 whatever place you enter a **h**
Mark 7:17 a **h** away from the crowd, His
Mark 7:24 And He entered a **h** and wanted
Mark 7:30 And when she had come to her **h**
Mark 8:26 And He sent him away to his **h**
Mark 9:28 when He had come into the **h**
Mark 9:33 He was in the **h** He asked them
Mark 10:10 in the **h** His disciples asked
Mark 10:29 is no one who has left **h** or
Mark 11:17 My **h** shall be called a **h**
Mark 13:15 not go down into the **h**, nor
Mark 13:15 to take anything out of his **h**
Mark 13:34 a far country, who left his **h**
Mark 13:35 the master of the **h** is coming
Mark 14: 3 at the **h** of Simon the leper
Mark 14:14 say to the master of the **h**
Luke 1:23 that he departed to his own **h**
Luke 1:27 was Joseph, of the **h** of David
Luke 1:33 over the **h** of Jacob forever
Luke 1:40 entered the **h** of Zacharias and
Luke 1:56 months, and returned to her **h**
Luke 1:69 in the **h** of His servant David
Luke 2: 4 because he was of the **h** and
Luke 4:38 and entered Simon's **h**
Luke 5:24 up your bed, and go to your **h**
Luke 5:25 on, and departed to his own **h**
Luke 5:29 a great feast in his own **h**
Luke 6: 4 how he went into the **h** of God
Luke 6:48 He is like a man building a **h**
Luke 6:48 vehemently against that **h**
Luke 6:49 a **h** on the earth without a
Luke 6:49 the ruin of that **h** was great
Luke 7: 6 already not far from the **h**
Luke 7:10 were sent, returning to the **h**
Luke 7:36 He went to the Pharisee's **h**
Luke 7:37 the table in the Pharisee's **h**
Luke 7:44 I entered your **h**
Luke 8:27 live in a **h** but in the tombs
Luke 8:39 Return to your own **h**, and tell
Luke 8:41 begged Him to come to his **h**
Luke 8:49 ruler of the synagogue's **h**
Luke 8:51 When He came into the **h**, He
Luke 9: 4 Whatever **h** you enter, stay
Luke 9:61 them farewell who are at my **h**
Luke 10: 5 But whatever **h** you enter,
Luke 10: 5 first say, 'Peace to this **h**
Luke 10: 7 And remain in the same **h**,
Luke 10: 7 Do not go from **h** to **h**
Luke 10:38 welcomed Him into her **h**
Luke 11:17 a **h** divided against a **h**
Luke 11:17 divided against a **h** falls
Luke 11:24 to my **h** from which I came
Luke 12:39 the **h** had known what hour the
Luke 12:39 and not allowed his **h** to be
Luke 12:52 five in one **h** will be divided
Luke 13:25 Master of the **h** has risen up
Luke 13:35 Your **h** is left to you
Luke 14: 1 as He went into the **h** of one
Luke 14:21 Then the master of the **h**,
Luke 14:23 in, that my **h** may be filled
Luke 15: 8 not light a lamp, sweep the **h**
Luke 15:25 he came and drew near to the **h**
Luke 16:27 send him to my father's **h**
Luke 17:31 and his goods are in the **h**
Luke 18:14 **h** justified rather than the
Luke 18:29 is no one who has left **h** or
Luke 19: 5 today I must stay at your **h**
Luke 19: 9 salvation has come to this **h**
Luke 19:46 My **h** is a **h** of prayer,'
Luke 22:10 into the **h** which he enters
Luke 22:11 say to the master of the **h**
Luke 22:54 Him into the high priest's **h**
John 2:16 Father's **h** a **h** of merchandise
John 2:17 Zeal for Your **h** has eaten Me
John 7:53 And everyone went to his own **h**
John 8:35 not abide in the **h** forever
John 11:20 but Mary was sitting in the **h**
John 11:31 who were with her in the **h**
John 12: 3 the **h** was filled with the
John 14: 2 In My Father's **h** are many
Acts 2: 2 it filled the whole **h** where
Acts 2:36 Therefore let all the **h** of
Acts 2:46 bread from **h** to **h**, they
Acts 5:42 in the temple, and in every **h**
Acts 7:10 over Egypt and all his **h**
Acts 7:20 father's **h** for three months
Acts 7:42 the wilderness, O **h** of Israel
Acts 7:47 But Solomon built Him a **h**
Acts 7:49 What **h** will you build for Me
Acts 8: 3 the church, entering every **h**
Acts 9:11 inquire at the **h** of Judas for
Acts 9:17 went his way and entered the **h**
Acts 10: 6 tanner, whose **h** is by the sea
Acts 10:17 made inquiry for Simon's **h**
Acts 10:22 angel to summon you to his **h**
Acts 10:30 ninth hour I prayed in my **h**
Acts 10:32 is lodging in the **h** of Simon
Acts 11:11 before the **h** where I was,
Acts 11:12 me, and we entered the man's **h**
Acts 11:13 an angel standing in his **h**
Acts 12:12 he came to the **h** of Mary
Acts 16:15 to the Lord, come to my **h**
Acts 16:32 and to all who were in his **h**
Acts 16:34 had brought them into his **h**
Acts 16:40 and entered the **h** of Lydia
Acts 17: 5 and attacked the **h** of Jason
Acts 18: 7 entered the **h** of a certain
Acts 18: 7 whose **h** was next door to the
Acts 19:16 they fled out of that **h** naked
Acts 20:20 publicly and from **h** to **h**,
Acts 21: 8 entered the **h** of Philip the
Acts 28:30 years in his own rented **h**
Rom 16: 5 the church that is in their **h**
1Co 16:19 the church that is in their **h**
2Co 5: 1 we know that if our earthly **h**
2Co 5: 1 God, a **h** not made with hands,
Col 4:15 the church that is in his **h**
1Ti 3: 4 one who rules his own **h** well
1Ti 3: 5 know how to rule his own **h**
1Ti 3:15 yourself in the **h** of God,
1Ti 5:13 about from **h** to **h**, and not
1Ti 5:14 bear children, manage the **h**
2Ti 2:20 But in a great **h** there are
Phm 2 and to the church in your **h**
Heb 3: 2 was faithful in all His **h**
Heb 3: 3 as He who built the **h** has
Heb 3: 3 has more honor than the **h**
Heb 3: 4 For every **h** is built by
Heb 3: 5 in all His **h** as a servant
Heb 3: 6 as a Son over His own **h**,
Heb 3: 6 whose **h** we are if we hold
Heb 8: 8 covenant with the **h** of Israel
Heb 8: 8 Israel and with the **h** of Judah
Heb 8:10 make with the **h** of Israel
Heb 10:21 High Priest over the **h** of God
1Pe 2: 5 being built up a spiritual **h**
1Pe 4:17 to begin at the **h** of God
2Jn 10 him into your **h** nor greet him

HOUSEHOLD (*see* HOUSE, HOUSEHOLDER, HOUSEHOLDS)
Gen 7: 1 the ark, you and all your **h**
Gen 18:19 his **h** after him, that they
Gen 31:19 the **h** idols that were her
Gen 31:34 Rachel had taken the **h** idols
Gen 31:35 but did not find the **h** idols
Gen 31:37 what part of your **h** things
Gen 34:19 than all the **h** of his father
Gen 34:30 I shall be destroyed, my **h**

Gen 35: 2 And Jacob said to his **h** and to
Gen 36: 6 and all the persons of his **h**
Gen 45:11 for you, lest you and your **h**
Gen 46:31 brothers and to his father's **h**
Gen 47:12 all his father's **h** with bread
Gen 50: 4 to the **h** of Pharaoh saying
Gen 50:22 Egypt, he and his father's **h**
Ex 1: 1 man and his **h** came with Jacob
Ex 12: 3 of his father, a lamb for a **h**
Ex 12: 4 if the **h** is too small for the
Lev 16:17 for himself, for his **h**, and
Deut 6:22 Egypt, Pharaoh, and all his **h**
Deut 14:26 shall rejoice, you and your **h**
Deut 15:20 your **h** shall eat it before
Josh 2:18 father's **h** to your own home
Josh 6:25 the harlot, her father's **h**
Josh 7:14 the **h** which the LORD takes
Josh 7:18 he brought his **h** man by man
Judg 6:27 he feared his father's **h** and
Judg 16:31 all his father's **h** came down
Judg 17: 5 and made an ephod and **h** idols
Judg 18:14 **h** idols, a carved image, and a
Judg 18:17 the **h** idols, and the molded
Judg 18:18 the **h** idols, and the molded
Judg 18:19 a priest to the **h** of one man
Judg 18:20 the **h** idols, and the carved
Judg 18:25 with the lives of your **h**
1Sa 25:17 master and against all his **h**
1Sa 27: 3 his men, each man with his **h**
2Sa 2: 3 him, every man with his **h**
2Sa 6:11 Obed-Edom and all his **h**
2Sa 6:20 David returned to bless his **h**
2Sa 15:16 out with all his **h** after him
2Sa 16: 2 for the king's **h** to ride on
2Sa 17:23 Then he put his **h** in order
2Sa 19:18 to carry over the king's **h**
2Sa 19:41 and brought the king, his **h**
1Ki 4: 6 Ahishar, over the **h**
1Ki 4: 7 food for the king and his **h**
1Ki 5: 9 by giving food for my **h**
1Ki 5:11 of wheat as food for his **h**
1Ki 11:20 **h** among the sons of Pharaoh
1Ki 16:11 he killed all the **h** of Baasha
1Ki 16:12 destroyed all the **h** of Baasha
1Ki 17:15 he and her **h** ate for many days
2Ki 7: 9 us go and tell the king's **h**
2Ki 7:11 it to the king's **h** inside
2Ki 8: 1 Arise and go, you and your **h**
2Ki 8: 2 God, and she went with her **h**
2Ki 18:18 Hilkiah, who was over the **h**
2Ki 18:37 Hilkiah, who was over the **h**
2Ki 19: 2 Eliakim, who was over the **h**
2Ki 23:24 the **h** gods and idols, all the
2Ch 21:13 those of your father's **h**
Neh 13: 8 therefore I threw all the **h**
Esth 1: 8 all the officers of his **h**
Job 1:10 around him, around his **h**, and
Job 21:21 he care about his **h** after him
Prov 27:27 food, for the food of your **h**
Prov 31:15 and provides food for her **h**
Prov 31:21 not afraid of snow for her **h**
Prov 31:21 for all her **h** is clothed with
Prov 31:27 over the ways of her **h**, and
Is 36: 3 Hilkiah, who was over the **h**
Is 36:22 Hilkiah, who was over the **h**
Is 37: 2 Eliakim, who was over the **h**
Matt 10:12 And when you go into a **h**,
Matt 10:13 If the **h** is worthy, let your
Matt 10:25 will they call those of his **h**
Matt 10:36 will be those of his own **h**
Matt 24:45 master made ruler over his **h**
Luke 12:42 will make ruler over his **h**
John 4:53 believed, and his whole **h**
Acts 10: 2 who feared God with all his **h**
Acts 10: 7 called two of his **h** servants
Acts 11:14 and all your **h** will be saved
Acts 16:15 and her **h** were baptized, she
Acts 16:31 will be saved, you and your **h**
Acts 16:34 in God with all his **h**
Acts 18: 8 on the Lord with all his **h**
Rom 16:10 are of the **h** of Aristobulus
Rom 16:11 Greet those who are of the **h**
1Co 1:11 by those of Chloe's **h**, that
1Co 1:16 baptized the **h** of Stephanas
1Co 16:15 you know the **h** of Stephanas
Gal 6:10 who are of the **h** of faith
Eph 2:19 and members of the **h** of God
Phil 4:22 those who are of Caesar's **h**
1Ti 5: 8 especially for those of his **h**
2Ti 1:16 mercy to the **h** of Onesiphorus
2Ti 4:19 and the **h** of Onesiphorus
Heb 11: 7 ark for the saving of his **h**

HOUSEHOLDER (*see* HOUSEHOLD)
Matt 13:52 a **h** who brings out of his

HOUSEHOLDS (*see* HOUSEHOLD)
Gen 42:33 food for the famine of your **h**
Gen 45:18 Bring your father and your **h**
Gen 47:24 food, for those of your **h**
Ex 1:21 that He provided **h** for them
Ex 12:27 Egyptians and delivered our **h**
Num 16:32 them up, with their **h** and all
Num 18:31 in any place, you and your **h**
Deut 11: 6 and swallowed them up, their **h**
Deut 12: 7 put your hand, you and your **h**
Josh 7:14 LORD takes shall come by **h**
Ezra 10:16 heads of the fathers' **h**, were
Ezra 10:16 set apart by the fathers' **h**
2Ti 3: 6 are those who creep into **h**
Tit 1:11 stopped, who subvert whole **h**

HOUSES (*see* HOUSE)
Gen 34:29 even all that was in the **h**
Gen 42:19 for the famine of your **h**
Ex 6:14 the heads of their fathers' **h**
Ex 8: 3 into the **h** of your servants,
Ex 8: 9 the frogs from you and your **h**
Ex 8:11 depart from you, from your **h**
Ex 8:13 the frogs died out of the **h**
Ex 8:21 on your people and into your **h**
Ex 8:21 The **h** of the Egyptians shall
Ex 8:24 Pharaoh, into his servants' **h**
Ex 9:20 his livestock flee to the **h**
Ex 10: 6 They shall fill your **h**, the
Ex 10: 6 the **h** of all your servants,
Ex 10: 6 the **h** of all the Egyptians
Ex 12: 7 of the **h** where they eat it
Ex 12:13 you on the **h** where you are
Ex 12:15 remove leaven from your **h**
Ex 12:19 shall be found in your **h**,
Ex 12:23 into your **h** to strike you
Ex 12:27 who passed over the **h** of the
Lev 25:31 However the **h** of villages
Lev 25:32 the **h** in the cities of their
Lev 25:33 for the **h** in the cities of
Num 1: 2 families, by their fathers' **h**
Num 1:18 families, by their fathers' **h**
Num 1:45 Israel, by their fathers' **h**
Num 2:32 of Israel by their fathers' **h**
Num 2:34 according to their fathers' **h**
Num 3:15 of Levi by their fathers' **h**
Num 3:20 Levites by their fathers' **h**
Num 4:46 and by their fathers' **h**,
Num 7: 2 the heads of their fathers' **h**
Num 17: 2 according to their fathers' **h**
Num 17: 6 according to their fathers' **h**
Num 26: 2 and above, by their fathers' **h**
Deut 6:11 **h** full of all good things,
Deut 8:12 and have built beautiful **h**
Deut 19: 1 in their cities and in their **h**
Josh 9:12 **h** on the day we departed to
Judg 18:14 there are in these **h** an ephod
Judg 18:22 the men who were in the **h**
1Ki 9:10 Solomon had built the two **h**
1Ki 20: 6 and the **h** of your servants
2Ki 17:29 put them in the **h** of the high
2Ki 25: 9 all the **h** of Jerusalem, that
2Ki 25: 9 all the **h** of the great men,
1Ch 5:24 the heads of their fathers' **h**
1Ch 5:24 and heads of their fathers' **h**
1Ch 7: 4 according to their fathers' **h**
1Ch 7: 7 heads of their fathers' **h**
1Ch 7: 9 heads of their fathers' **h**
1Ch 7:11 heads of their fathers' **h**
1Ch 7:40 heads of their fathers' **h**
1Ch 8: 6 the heads of the fathers' **h**
1Ch 8:10 heads of their fathers' **h**
1Ch 8:13 **h** of the inhabitants of
1Ch 8:28 **h** by their generations, chief
1Ch 9: 9 house in their fathers' **h**
1Ch 9:13 heads of their fathers' **h**
1Ch 9:33 the fathers' **h** of the Levites
1Ch 9:34 **h** of the Levites were heads
1Ch 15: 1 David built **h** for himself in
1Ch 15:12 the fathers' **h** of the Levites
1Ch 23: 9 of the fathers' **h** of Laadan
1Ch 23:24 of Levi by their fathers' **h**
1Ch 23:24 **h** as they were counted
1Ch 24: 4 heads of their fathers' **h**
1Ch 24: 4 heads of their fathers' **h**
1Ch 24: 6 the fathers' **h** of the priests
1Ch 24:30 according to their fathers' **h**
1Ch 24:31 the fathers' **h** of the priests
1Ch 26: 6 who governed their fathers' **h**
1Ch 26:21 heads of their fathers' **h**
1Ch 26:26 and the heads of fathers' **h**
1Ch 26:32 able men, heads of fathers' **h**
1Ch 27: 1 the heads of fathers' **h**, the
1Ch 28:11 for the vestibule, its **h**, its
1Ch 29: 4 to overlay the walls of the **h**
1Ch 29: 6 the leaders of the fathers' **h**
2Ch 1: 2 the heads of the fathers' **h**
2Ch 17:14 according to their fathers' **h**
2Ch 25: 5 according to their fathers' **h**
2Ch 34:11 and to floor the **h** which the
2Ch 35: 4 according to your fathers' **h**
2Ch 35: 5 **h** of your brethren the lay
2Ch 35:12 fathers' **h** of the lay people
Ezra 1: 5 of the fathers' **h** of Judah
Ezra 2:68 the heads of the fathers' **h**
Ezra 3:12 and heads of the fathers' **h**
Ezra 4: 2 the heads of the fathers' **h**
Ezra 4: 3 **h** of Israel said to them
Ezra 8: 1 the heads of their fathers' **h**
Ezra 8:29 heads of the fathers' **h** of
Neh 4:14 your wives, and your **h**
Neh 5: 3 our lands and vineyards and **h**
Neh 5:11 olive groves, and their **h**,
Neh 7: 4 and the **h** were not rebuilt
Neh 7:70 fathers' **h** gave to the work
Neh 7:71 the heads of the fathers' **h**
Neh 8:13 fathers' **h** of all the people
Neh 9:25 possessed **h** full of all goods
Neh 10:34 according to our fathers' **h**
Neh 11:13 heads of the fathers' **h**,
Neh 12:12 heads of the fathers' **h** were
Neh 12:22 **h** in the days of Eliashib
Neh 12:23 **h** until the days of Johanan
Job 1: 4 would go and feast in their **h**
Job 3:15 filled their **h** with silver
Job 4:19 those who dwell in **h** of clay
Job 15:28 in **h** which no one inhabits,
Job 21: 9 Their **h** are safe from fear,
Job 22:18 their **h** with good things
Job 24:16 into **h** which they marked for
Ps 49:11 their **h** will continue forever
Prov 1:13 shall fill our **h** with spoil
Prov 19:14 **H** and riches are an
Eccl 2: 4 works great, I built myself **h**
Song 1:17 The beams of our **h** are cedar
Is 3:14 of the poor is in your **h**
Is 5: 9 many **h** shall be desolate,
Is 6:11 the **h** are without a man, the
Is 8:14 to both the **h** of Israel, as a
Is 13:16 their **h** will be plundered and
Is 13:21 their **h** will be full of owls
Is 15: 3 on the tops of their **h** and in
Is 22:10 numbered the **h** of Jerusalem
Is 22:10 and the **h** you broke down to
Is 42:22 they are hidden in prison **h**
Is 65:21 They shall build **h** and inhabit
Jer 5: 7 by troops in the harlots' **h**
Jer 5:27 so their **h** are full of deceit
Jer 6:12 their **h** shall be turned over
Jer 17:22 of your **h** on the Sabbath day
Jer 18:22 a cry be heard from their **h**
Jer 19:13 the **h** of Jerusalem and the
Jer 19:13 the **h** of the kings of Judah
Jer 19:13 because of all the **h** on whose
Jer 29: 5 Build **h** and dwell in them
Jer 29:28 build **h** and dwell in them, and
Jer 32:15 **H** and fields and vineyards
Jer 32:29 with the **h** on whose roofs
Jer 33: 4 concerning the **h** of this city
Jer 33: 4 the **h** of the kings of Judah,
Jer 35: 9 build ourselves **h** to dwell in
Jer 39: 8 the **h** of the people with fire
Jer 43:12 in the **h** of the gods of Egypt
Jer 43:13 and the **h** of the gods of the
Jer 52:13 all the **h** of Jerusalem, that
Jer 52:13 all the **h** of the great men,
Lam 5: 2 and our **h** to foreigners
Ezek 7:24 and they will possess their **h**
Ezek 11: 3 time is not near to build **h**
Ezek 16:41 shall burn your **h** with fire
Ezek 23:47 and burn their **h** with fire
Ezek 26:12 and destroy your pleasant **h**
Ezek 28:26 dwell safely there, build **h**
Ezek 33:30 and in the doors of the **h**
Ezek 45: 4 shall be a place for their **h**
Dan 2: 5 your **h** shall be made an ash

Dan 3:29 their **h** shall be made an ash
Hos 11:11 let them dwell in their **h**
Joel 2: 9 they climb into the **h**, they
Amos 3:15 the **h** of ivory shall perish,
Amos 3:15 the great **h** shall have an end
Amos 5:11 have built **h** of hewn stone
Mic 1:14 the **h** of Achzib shall be a
Mic 2: 2 take them by violence, also **h**
Mic 2: 9 out from their pleasant **h**
Zeph 1: 9 masters' **h** with violence and
Zeph 1:13 and their **h** a desolation
Zeph 1:13 They shall build **h**, but not
Zeph 2: 7 in the **h** of Ashkelon they
Hag 1: 4 to dwell in your paneled **h**
Zech 14: 2 the **h** rifled, and the women
Matt 11: 8 soft clothing are in kings' **h**
Matt 19:29 everyone who has left **h** or
Matt 23:14 For you devour widows' **h**, and
Mark 8: 3 away hungry to their own **h**
Mark 10:30 **h** and brothers and sisters and
Mark 12:40 who devour widows' **h**, and for
Luke 16: 4 may receive me into their **h**
Luke 20:47 who devour widows' **h**, and for
Acts 4:34 of lands or **h** sold them, and
1Co 11:22 Do you not have **h** to eat and
1Ti 3:12 children and their own **h** well

HOUSETOP (*see* HOUSE, HOUSETOPS)
Ps 102: 7 like a sparrow alone on the **h**
Prov 21: 9 to dwell in a corner of a **h**
Prov 25:24 to dwell in a corner of a **h**
Matt 24:17 the **h** not come down to take
Mark 13:15 let him who is on the **h** not
Luke 5:19 crowd, they went up on the **h**
Luke 17:31 that day, he who is on the **h**
Acts 10: 9 went up on the **h** to pray,

HOUSETOPS (*see* HOUSETOP)
2Ki 19:26 herb, as the grass on the **h**
Ps 129: 6 them be as the grass on the **h**
Is 22: 1 you have all gone up to the **h**
Is 37:27 herb, as the grass on the **h**
Jer 48:38 on all the **h** of Moab, and in
Zeph 1: 5 the host of heaven on the **h**
Matt 10:27 in the ear, preach on the **h**
Luke 12: 3 will be proclaimed on the **h**

HOVERING (*see* HOVERS)
Gen 1: 2 the Spirit of God was **h** over

HOVERS (*see* HOVERING)
Deut 32:11 **h** over its young, spreading

HOW (*see* PREFACE)

HOWEVER (*see* PREFACE)

HOWL (*see* HOWLING)
Ps 59:15 **h** if they are not satisfied
Is 13:22 The hyenas will **h** in their
Mic 1: 8 Therefore I will wail and **h**
Jas 5: 1 **h** for your miseries that are

HOWLING (*see* HOWL)
Deut 32:10 the wasteland, a **h** wilderness

HOZAI
2Ch 33:19 among the sayings of **H**

HUBS
1Ki 7:33 and their **h** were all of cast

HUDDLE
Job 24: 8 **h** around the rock for want of

HUGE
2Ch 16: 8 the Lubim not a **h** army with
Dan 7: 7 It had **h** iron teeth

HUKKOK (*see* HELKATH, HUKOK)
Josh 19:34 went out from there toward **H**

HUKOK (*see* HUKKOK)
1Ch 6:75 **H** with its common-lands, and

HUL
Gen 10:23 The sons of Aram were Uz, **H**
1Ch 1:17 Arphaxad, Lud, Aram, Uz, **H**

HULDAH
2Ki 22:14 went to **H** the prophetess, the
2Ch 34:22 went to **H** the prophetess, the

HUMAN
Lev 5: 3 if he touches **h** uncleanness
Lev 7:21 such as **h** uncleanness, any
2Ki 7:10 one was there, not a **h** sound
Ezek 4:12 of **h** waste in their sight
Ezek 4:15 cow dung instead of **h** waste
Ezek 27:13 They bartered **h** lives and
Dan 8:25 be broken without **h** hand
Hos 5:11 willingly walked by **h** precept
John 16:21 for joy that a **h** being has
Rom 6:19 I speak in **h** terms because of
1Co 2: 4 persuasive words of **h** wisdom
1Co 4: 3 judged by you or by a **h** court
Heb 12: 9 we have had **h** fathers who

HUMBLE (*see* HUMBLED, HUMBLENESS, HUMBLES, HUMBLY)
Ex 10: 3 to **h** yourself before Me
Num 12: 3 (Now the man Moses was very **h**
Deut 8: 2 to **h** you and test you, to know
Deut 8:16 not know, that He might **h** you
Judg 19:24 **H** them, and do with them as
2Sa 6:22 will be **h** in my own sight
2Sa 22:28 You will save the **h** people
2Ch 7:14 by My name will **h** themselves
2Ch 33:23 he did not **h** himself before
2Ch 36:12 and did not **h** himself before
Ezra 8:21 that we might **h** ourselves
Job 22:29 He will save the **h** person
Job 40:11 who is proud, and **h** him
Ps 9:12 not forget the cry of the **h**
Ps 10:12 Do not forget the **h**
Ps 10:17 heard the desire of the **h**
Ps 18:27 You will save the **h** people
Ps 25: 9 The **h** He guides in justice,
Ps 25: 9 And the **h** He teaches His way
Ps 34: 2 The **h** shall hear of it and be
Ps 69:32 The **h** shall see this and be
Ps 147: 6 The LORD lifts up the **h**
Ps 149: 4 beautify the **h** with salvation
Prov 3:34 but gives grace to the **h**
Prov 6: 3 go and **h** yourself
Prov 11: 2 but with the **h** is wisdom
Prov 16:19 Better to be of a **h** spirit
Prov 29:23 low, but the **h** in spirit will
Is 29:19 The **h** also shall increase
Is 57:15 and **h** spirit, to revive the
Is 57:15 to revive the spirit of the **h**
Jer 13:18 queen mother, "**H** yourselves
Dan 10:12 to **h** yourself before your God
Amos 2: 7 and pervert the way of the **h**
Zeph 3:12 **h** people, and they shall trust
Rom 12:16 but associate with the **h**
2Co 12:21 my God will **h** me among you,
Jas 4: 6 but gives grace to the **h**
Jas 4:10 **H** yourselves in the sight of
1Pe 5: 5 but gives grace to the **h**
1Pe 5: 6 Therefore **h** yourselves under

HUMBLED (*see* HUMBLE)
Lev 26:41 uncircumcised hearts are **h**
Deut 8: 3 So He **h** you, allowed you to
Deut 21:14 because you have **h** her
Deut 22:24 and the man because he **h** his
Deut 22:29 his wife because he has **h** her
1Ki 21:29 See how Ahab has **h** himself
1Ki 21:29 Because he has **h** himself
2Ki 22:19 you **h** yourself before the
2Ch 12: 6 and the king **h** themselves
2Ch 12: 7 saw that they **h** themselves
2Ch 12: 7 They have **h** themselves
2Ch 12:12 When he **h** himself, the wrath
2Ch 30:11 Zebulun **h** themselves and came
2Ch 32:26 Then Hezekiah **h** himself for
2Ch 33:12 **h** himself greatly before the
2Ch 33:19 images, before he was **h**,
2Ch 33:23 father Manasseh had **h** himself
2Ch 34:27 you **h** yourself before God
2Ch 34:27 you **h** yourself before Me, and
Ps 35:13 I **h** myself with fasting
Is 2:11 lofty looks of man shall be **h**
Is 5:15 down, Each man shall be **h**
Is 5:15 eyes of the lofty shall be **h**
Is 10:33 and the haughty will be **h**
Jer 44:10 They have not been **h**, to
Dan 5:22 have not **h** your heart,
Phil 2: 8 a man, He **h** Himself and

HUMBLENESS (*see* HUMBLE)
Col 3:12 **h** of mind, meekness,

HUMBLES (*see* HUMBLE)
Ps 113: 6 Who **h** Himself to behold The
Is 2: 9 down, and each man **h** himself
Matt 18: 4 Therefore whoever **h** himself
Matt 23:12 and he who **h** himself will be
Luke 14:11 and he who **h** himself will be
Luke 18:14 and he who **h** himself will be

HUMBLY (*see* HUMBLE)
2Sa 16: 4 I **h** bow before you, that I
Mic 6: 8 and to walk **h** with your God

HUMILIATED (*see* HUMILIATION, HUMILITY)
Deut 25: 3 brother be **h** in your sight
Ezra 9: 6 **h** to lift up my face to You,
Jer 22:22 **h** for all your wickedness
Jer 31:19 I was ashamed, yes, even **h**
Jer 50: 2 her idols are **h**, her images

HUMILIATION (*see* HUMILIATED)
Ezra 9: 7 to plunder, and to **h**, as it
Is 30: 3 of Egypt shall be your **h**
Is 32:19 the city is brought low in **h**
Acts 8:33 In His **h** His justice was
Jas 1:10 but the rich in his **h**,

HUMILITY (*see* HUMILIATED)
Ps 45: 4 because of truth, **h**, and
Prov 15:33 wisdom, and before honor is **h**
Prov 18:12 haughty, and before honor is **h**
Prov 22: 4 By **h** and the fear of the LORD
Zeph 2: 3 Seek righteousness, seek **h**
Acts 20:19 serving the Lord with all **h**
Col 2:18 taking delight in false **h**
Col 2:23 religion, false **h**, and neglect
2Ti 2:25 in **h** correcting those who are
Tit 3: 2 showing all **h** to all men
1Pe 5: 5 another, and be clothed with **h**

HUMPS
Is 30: 6 treasures on the **h** of camels

HUMTAH
Josh 15:54 **H**, Kirjath Arba (which is

HUNCHBACK
Lev 21:20 or is a **h** or a dwarf, or a

HUNDRED (*see* HUNDREDFOLD, HUNDREDS, HUNDREDTH)
Gen 5: 3 And Adam lived one **h** and
Gen 5: 4 of Adam were eight **h** years
Gen 5: 5 that Adam lived were nine **h**
Gen 5: 6 Seth lived one **h** and five
Gen 5: 7 Enosh, Seth lived eight **h**
Gen 5: 8 the days of Seth were nine **h**
Gen 5:10 Cainan, Enosh lived eight **h**
Gen 5:11 the days of Enosh were nine **h**
Gen 5:13 Cainan lived eight **h** and
Gen 5:14 days of Cainan were nine **h**
Gen 5:16 Mahalaleel lived eight **h**
Gen 5:17 of Mahalaleel were eight **h**
Gen 5:18 Jared lived one **h** and
Gen 5:19 Jared lived eight **h** years
Gen 5:20 the days of Jared were nine **h**
Gen 5:22 walked with God three **h** years
Gen 5:23 days of Enoch were three **h**
Gen 5:25 Methuselah lived one **h** and
Gen 5:26 Methuselah lived seven **h**
Gen 5:27 of Methuselah were nine **h**
Gen 5:28 Lamech lived one **h** and
Gen 5:30 Noah, Lamech lived five **h**
Gen 5:31 days of Lamech were seven **h**
Gen 5:32 And Noah was five **h** years old
Gen 6: 3 yet his days shall be one **h**
Gen 6:15 ark shall be three **h** cubits
Gen 7: 6 Noah was six **h** years old when
Gen 7:24 prevailed on the earth one **h**
Gen 8: 3 At the end of the **h** and fifty
Gen 8:13 it came to pass in the six **h**
Gen 9:28 lived after the flood three **h**
Gen 9:29 the days of Noah were nine **h**
Gen 11:10 Shem was one **h** years old, and
Gen 11:11 Shem lived five **h** years, and
Gen 11:13 Salah, Arphaxad lived four **h**
Gen 11:15 Eber, Salah lived four **h** and
Gen 11:17 Peleg, Eber lived four **h** and
Gen 11:19 begot Reu, Peleg lived two **h**
Gen 11:21 begot Serug, Reu lived two **h**
Gen 11:23 Serug lived two **h** years, and
Gen 11:25 Terah, Nahor lived one **h** and
Gen 11:32 the days of Terah were two **h**
Gen 14:14 captive, he armed his three **h**
Gen 15:13 afflict them four **h** years
Gen 17:17 a man who is one **h** years old
Gen 21: 5 Now Abraham was one **h** years
Gen 23: 1 Sarah lived one **h** and
Gen 23:15 four **h** shekels of silver
Gen 23:16 four **h** shekels of silver,
Gen 25: 7 one **h** and seventy-five years
Gen 25:17 one **h** and thirty-seven years
Gen 32: 6 and four **h** men are with him

1Ch 21: 5 **h** thousand men who drew the
1Ch 21: 5 sword, and Judah had four **h**
1Ch 21:25 So David gave Ornan six **h**
1Ch 22:14 **h** thousand talents of gold
1Ch 25: 7 who were skillful, was two **h**
1Ch 26:30 one thousand seven **h** able men
1Ch 26:32 two thousand seven **h** able men
1Ch 29: 7 one **h** thousand talents of
2Ch 1:14 one thousand four **h** chariots
2Ch 1:17 for six **h** shekels of silver
2Ch 1:17 silver, and a horse for one **h**
2Ch 2: 2 six **h** to oversee them
2Ch 2:17 there were found to be one **h**
2Ch 2:17 and fifty-three thousand six **h**
2Ch 2:18 and three thousand six **h**
2Ch 3: 4 and the height was one **h** and
2Ch 3: 8 six **h** talents of fine gold
2Ch 3:16 he made one **h** pomegranates,
2Ch 4: 8 he made one **h** bowls of gold
2Ch 4:13 four **h** pomegranates for the
2Ch 5:12 and harps, and with them one **h**
2Ch 7: 5 thousand bulls and one **h** and
2Ch 8:10 two **h** and fifty, who ruled
2Ch 8:18 to Ophir, and acquired four **h**
2Ch 9: 9 Then she gave the king one **h**
2Ch 9:13 to Solomon yearly was six **h**
2Ch 9:15 King Solomon made two **h** large
2Ch 9:15 six **h** shekels of hammered
2Ch 9:16 He also made three **h** shields
2Ch 9:16 three **h** shekels of gold went
2Ch 11: 1 of Judah and Benjamin one **h**
2Ch 12: 3 with twelve **h** chariots, sixty
2Ch 13: 3 four **h** thousand choice men
2Ch 13: 3 eight **h** thousand choice men
2Ch 13:17 so five **h** thousand choice men
2Ch 14: 8 Asa had an army of three **h**
2Ch 14: 8 and from Benjamin two **h** and
2Ch 14: 9 three **h** chariots, and he came
2Ch 15:11 at that time seven **h** bulls
2Ch 17:11 seven thousand seven **h** rams
2Ch 17:11 thousand seven **h** male goats
2Ch 17:14 with him three **h** thousand
2Ch 17:15 captain, and with him two **h**
2Ch 17:16 and with him two **h** thousand
2Ch 17:17 with him two **h** thousand men
2Ch 17:18 Jehozabad, and with him one **h**
2Ch 18: 5 prophets together, four **h** men
2Ch 24:15 he was one **h** and thirty years
2Ch 25: 5 three **h** thousand choice men
2Ch 25: 6 He also hired one **h** thousand
2Ch 25: 6 for one **h** talents of silver
2Ch 25: 9 **h** talents which I have given
2Ch 25:23 Corner Gate—four **h** cubits.
2Ch 26:12 valor was two thousand six **h**
2Ch 26:13 hand was an army of three **h**
2Ch 26:13 and seven thousand five **h**,
2Ch 27: 5 year one **h** talents of silver
2Ch 28: 6 son of Remaliah killed one **h**
2Ch 28: 8 brethren two **h** thousand women
2Ch 29:32 one **h** rams, and two **h** lambs
2Ch 29:33 things were six **h** bulls and
2Ch 35: 8 thousand six **h** from the flock
2Ch 35: 8 the flock, and three **h** cattle
2Ch 35: 9 the flock and five **h** cattle
2Ch 36: 3 of one **h** talents of silver
Ezra 1:10 thirty gold basins, four **h**
Ezra 1:11 were five thousand four **h**
Ezra 2: 3 of Parosh, two thousand one **h**
Ezra 2: 4 people of Shephatiah, three **h**
Ezra 2: 5 the people of Arah, seven **h**
Ezra 2: 6 and Joab, two thousand eight **h**
Ezra 2: 7 of Elam, one thousand two **h**
Ezra 2: 8 the people of Zattu, nine **h**
Ezra 2: 9 the people of Zaccai, seven **h**
Ezra 2:10 the people of Bani, six **h**
Ezra 2:11 the people of Bebai, six **h**
Ezra 2:12 of Azgad, one thousand two **h**
Ezra 2:13 the people of Adonikam, six **h**
Ezra 2:15 the people of Adin, four **h**
Ezra 2:17 the people of Bezai, three **h**
Ezra 2:18 the people of Jorah, one **h**
Ezra 2:19 the people of Hashum, two **h**
Ezra 2:21 people of Bethlehem, one **h**
Ezra 2:23 the men of Anathoth, one **h**
Ezra 2:25 and Beeroth, seven **h** and
Ezra 2:26 of Ramah and Geba, six **h** and
Ezra 2:27 the men of Michmas, one **h**
Ezra 2:28 men of Bethel and Ai, two **h**
Ezra 2:30 the people of Magbish, one **h**
Ezra 2:31 Elam, one thousand two **h** and
Ezra 2:32 the people of Harim, three **h**
Ezra 2:33 Lod, Hadid, and Ono, seven **h**
Ezra 2:34 people of Jericho, three **h**
Ezra 2:35 Senaah, three thousand six **h**
Ezra 2:36 the house of Jeshua, nine **h**
Ezra 2:38 Pashhur, one thousand two **h**
Ezra 2:41 the sons of Asaph, one **h** and
Ezra 2:42 and the sons of Shobai, one **h**
Ezra 2:58 servants were three **h** and
Ezra 2:60 and the sons of Nekoda, six **h**
Ezra 2:64 forty-two thousand three **h**
Ezra 2:65 were seven thousand three **h**
Ezra 2:65 and they had two **h** men and
Ezra 2:66 Their horses were seven **h**
Ezra 2:66 thirty-six, their mules two **h**
Ezra 2:67 their camels four **h** and
Ezra 2:67 donkeys six thousand seven **h**
Ezra 2:69 and one **h** priestly garments
Ezra 6:17 one **h** bulls, two **h** rams
Ezra 6:17 four **h** lambs, and as a sin
Ezra 7:22 up to one **h** talents of silver
Ezra 7:22 one **h** kors of wheat, one
Ezra 7:22 one **h** baths of wine, one
Ezra 7:22 one **h** baths of oil, and salt
Ezra 8: 3 with him were one **h** and fifty
Ezra 8: 4 and with him two **h** males
Ezra 8: 5 and with him three **h** males
Ezra 8: 9 of Jehiel, and with him two **h**
Ezra 8:10 and with him one **h** and sixty
Ezra 8:12 Hakkatan, and with him one **h**
Ezra 8:20 service of the Levites, two **h**
Ezra 8:26 weighed into their hand six **h**
Ezra 8:26 weighing one **h** talents, one
Ezra 8:26 one **h** talents of gold,
Neh 3: 1 as far as the Tower of the **H**
Neh 5:17 there were at my table one **h**
Neh 7: 8 of Parosh, two thousand one **h**
Neh 7: 9 of Shephatiah, three **h** and
Neh 7:10 the children of Arah, six **h**
Neh 7:11 and Joab, two thousand eight **h**
Neh 7:12 of Elam, one thousand two **h**
Neh 7:13 children of Zattu, eight **h**
Neh 7:14 children of Zaccai, seven **h**
Neh 7:15 the children of Binnui, six **h**
Neh 7:16 the children of Bebai, six **h**
Neh 7:17 Azgad, two thousand three **h**
Neh 7:18 children of Adonikam, six **h**
Neh 7:20 the children of Adin, six **h**
Neh 7:22 children of Hashum, three **h**
Neh 7:23 children of Bezai, three **h**
Neh 7:24 the children of Hariph, one **h**
Neh 7:26 and Netophah, one **h**
Neh 7:27 the men of Anathoth, one **h**
Neh 7:29 and Beeroth, seven **h** and
Neh 7:30 men of Ramah and Geba, six **h**
Neh 7:31 the men of Michmas, one **h**
Neh 7:32 men of Bethel and Ai, one **h**
Neh 7:34 Elam, one thousand two **h** and
Neh 7:35 children of Harim, three **h**
Neh 7:36 children of Jericho, three **h**
Neh 7:37 Lod, Hadid, and Ono, seven **h**
Neh 7:38 Senaah, three thousand nine **h**
Neh 7:39 the house of Jeshua, nine **h**
Neh 7:41 Pashhur, one thousand two **h**
Neh 7:44 the children of Asaph, one **h**
Neh 7:45 the children of Shobai, one **h**
Neh 7:60 servants, were three **h** and
Neh 7:62 the children of Nekoda, six **h**
Neh 7:66 forty-two thousand three **h**
Neh 7:67 were seven thousand three **h**
Neh 7:67 and they had two **h** and
Neh 7:68 Their horses were seven **h**
Neh 7:68 thirty-six, their mules two **h**
Neh 7:69 their camels four **h** and
Neh 7:69 donkeys six thousand seven **h**
Neh 7:70 fifty basins, and five **h** and
Neh 7:71 thousand two **h** silver minas
Neh 11: 6 at Jerusalem were four **h** and
Neh 11: 8 him Gabbai and Sallai, nine **h**
Neh 11:12 of the house were eight **h**
Neh 11:13 fathers' houses, were two **h**
Neh 11:14 men of valor, were one **h** and
Neh 11:18 in the holy city were two **h**
Neh 11:19 kept the gates, were one **h**
Neh 12:39 Hananeal, the Tower of the **H**
Esth 1: 1 India to Ethiopia, over one **h**
Esth 1: 4 majesty for many days, one **h**
Esth 8: 9 from India to Ethiopia, one **h**
Esth 9: 6 and destroyed five **h** men
Esth 9:12 and destroyed five **h** men in
Esth 9:15 killed three **h** men at Shushan
Esth 9:30 to all the Jews, to the one **h**
Job 42:16 After this Job lived one **h**
Prov 17:10 man than a **h** blows on a fool
Eccl 6: 3 If a man begets a **h** children
Eccl 8:12 a sinner does evil a **h** times
Song 8:12 who keep its fruit two **h**
Is 37:36 camp of the Assyrians one **h**
Is 65:20 shall die one **h** years old
Is 65:20 but the sinner being one **h**
Jer 52:23 on the network, were one **h**
Jer 52:29 from Jerusalem eight **h** and
Jer 52:30 captive of the Jews seven **h**
Jer 52:30 were four thousand six **h**
Ezek 4: 5 number of the days, three **h**
Ezek 4: 9 you lie on your side, three **h**
Ezek 40:19 one **h** cubits toward the east
Ezek 40:23 to gateway, one **h** cubits
Ezek 40:27 the south, one **h** cubits
Ezek 40:47 one **h** cubits long and one
Ezek 40:47 one **h** cubits wide, foursquare
Ezek 41:13 the temple, one **h** cubits long
Ezek 41:13 walls was one **h** cubits long
Ezek 41:14 courtyard, was one **h** cubits
Ezek 41:15 one **h** cubits, as well as the
Ezek 42: 2 which was one **h** cubits (the
Ezek 42: 8 the temple was one **h** cubits
Ezek 42:16 five **h** rods by the measuring
Ezek 42:17 five **h** rods by the measuring
Ezek 42:18 five **h** rods by the measuring
Ezek 42:19 measured five **h** rods by the
Ezek 42:20 five **h** cubits long and five
Ezek 42:20 cubits long and five **h** wide
Ezek 45: 2 five **h** by five **h** rods,
Ezek 45:15 given from a flock of two **h**
Ezek 48:16 four thousand five **h** cubits
Ezek 48:16 side four thousand five **h**
Ezek 48:16 side four thousand five **h**
Ezek 48:16 side four thousand five **h**
Ezek 48:17 to the north two **h** and fifty
Ezek 48:17 cubits, to the south two **h**
Ezek 48:17 and fifty, to the east two **h**
Ezek 48:17 fifty, and to the west two **h**
Ezek 48:30 four thousand five **h** cubits
Ezek 48:32 four thousand five **h** cubits
Ezek 48:33 four thousand five **h** cubits
Ezek 48:34 four thousand five **h** cubits
Dan 6: 1 to set over the kingdom one **h**
Dan 8:14 For two thousand three **h** days
Dan 12:11 shall be one thousand two **h**
Dan 12:12 to the one thousand three **h**
Amos 5: 3 thousand shall have a **h** left
Amos 5: 3 that which goes out by a **h**
Jon 4:11 in which are more than one **h**
Matt 18:12 If a man has a **h** sheep, and
Matt 18:28 who owed him a **h** denarii
Mark 4: 8 some sixty, and some a **h**
Mark 4:20 some sixty, and some a **h**
Mark 6:37 buy two **h** denarii worth of
Mark 14: 5 for more than three **h** denarii
Luke 7:41 One owed five **h** denarii, and
Luke 15: 4 man of you, having a **h** sheep
Luke 16: 6 he said, 'A **h** measures of oil
Luke 16: 7 said, 'A **h** measures of wheat
John 6: 7 Two **h** denarii worth of bread
John 12: 5 not sold for three **h** denarii
John 19:39 and aloes, about a **h** pounds
John 21: 8 land, but about two **h** cubits)
John 21:11 full of large fish, one **h**
Acts 1:15 number of names was about a **h**
Acts 5:36 A number of men, about four **h**
Acts 7: 6 and oppress them four **h** years
Acts 13:20 them judges for about four **h**
Acts 23:23 Prepare two **h** soldiers,
Acts 23:23 and two **h** spearmen to go to
Acts 27:37 And in all we were two **h** and
Rom 4:19 he was about a **h** years old)
1Co 15: 6 over five **h** brethren at once
Gal 3:17 the law, which was four **h**
Rev 7: 4 One **h** and forty-four thousand
Rev 9:16 horsemen was two **h** million
Rev 11: 3 prophesy one thousand two **h**
Rev 12: 6 her there one thousand two **h**
Rev 14: 1 Zion, and with Him one **h**
Rev 14: 3 learn that song except the **h**
Rev 14:20 one thousand six **h** furlongs
Rev 21:17 one **h** and forty-four cubits,

HUNDREDFOLD (*see* HUNDRED)
Gen 26:12 reaped in the same year a **h**
2Sa 24: 3 a **h** more than there are, and
Matt 13: 8 some a **h**, some sixty, some
Matt 13:23 some a **h**, some sixty, some
Matt 19:29 sake, shall receive a **h**, and
Mark 10:30 receive a **h** now in this time
Luke 8: 8 up, and yielded a crop a **h**

HUNDREDS (*see* HUNDRED)
Ex 18:21 of thousands, rulers of **h**
Ex 18:25 of thousands, rulers of **h**
Num 31:14 thousands and captains over **h**
Num 31:48 of thousands and captains of **h**
Num 31:52 of thousands and captains of **h**
Num 31:54 captains of thousands and of **h**
Deut 1:15 of thousands, leaders of **h**
1Sa 22: 7 of thousands and captains of **h**
1Sa 29: 2 passed in review by **h** and by
2Sa 18: 1 and captains of **h** over them
2Sa 18: 4 all the people went out by **h**
2Ki 11: 4 and brought the captains of **h**
2Ki 11: 9 So the captains of the **h** did
2Ki 11:10 the captains of **h** the spears
2Ki 11:15 the captains of the **h**, the
2Ki 11:19 he took the captains of **h**
1Ch 13: 1 captains of thousands and **h**
1Ch 26:26 captains over thousands and **h**
1Ch 27: 1 captains of thousands and **h**
1Ch 28: 1 thousands and captains over **h**
1Ch 29: 6 captains of thousands and of **h**
2Ch 1: 2 captains of thousands and of **h**
2Ch 23: 1 with the captains of **h**
2Ch 23: 9 the captains of **h** the spears
2Ch 23:14 **h** who were set over the army
2Ch 23:20 he took the captains of **h**
2Ch 25: 5 of thousands and captains of **h**
Mark 6:40 they sat down in ranks, in **h**

HUNDREDTH (*see* HUNDRED)
Gen 7:11 In the six **h** year of Noah's
Neh 5:11 also the **h** part of the money

HUNG (*see* HANG)
Ex 40:21 **h** up the veil of the covering
Ex 40:28 He **h** up the screen at the
Ex 40:33 **h** up the screen of the court
2Sa 21:12 the Philistines had **h** them up
Neh 3: 1 consecrated it and **h** its doors
Neh 3: 3 **h** its doors with its bolts and
Neh 3: 6 **h** its doors, with its bolts
Neh 3:13 **h** its doors with its bolts and
Neh 3:14 **h** its doors with its bolts and
Neh 3:15 **h** its doors with its bolts and
Neh 6: 1 at that time I had not **h** the
Neh 7: 1 I had **h** the doors, when the
Ps 137: 2 We **h** our harps Upon the
Lam 5:12 Princes were **h** up by their
Ezek 27:10 they **h** shield and helmet in
Ezek 27:11 they **h** their shields on your
Matt 18: 6 were **h** around his neck, and he
Mark 9:42 were **h** around his neck, and he
Luke 17: 2 were **h** around his neck, and he

HUNGER (*see* HUNGERS, HUNGRY)
Ex 16: 3 this whole assembly with **h**
Deut 8: 3 humbled you, allowed you to **h**
Deut 28:48 will send against you, in **h**
Deut 32:24 They shall be wasted with **h**
1Sa 2: 5 were hungry have ceased to **h**
Neh 9:15 bread from heaven for their **h**
Ps 34:10 young lions lack and suffer **h**
Prov 19:15 an idle person will suffer **h**
Is 49:10 shall neither **h** nor thirst
Jer 38: 9 **h** in the place where he is
Lam 2:19 who faint from **h** at the head
Lam 4: 9 off than those who die of **h**
Ezek 34:29 consumed with **h** in the land
Mic 6:14 **h** shall be in your midst
Matt 5: 6 Blessed are those who **h** and
Luke 6:21 Blessed are you who **h** now
Luke 6:25 who are full, For you shall **h**
Luke 15:17 to spare, and I perish with **h**
John 6:35 who comes to Me shall never **h**
1Co 4:11 to the present hour we both **h**
2Co 11:27 in sleeplessness often, in **h**
Rev 6: 8 to kill with sword, with **h**
Rev 7:16 They shall neither **h** anymore

HUNGERS (*see* HUNGER)
Rom 12:20 Therefore if your enemy **h**

HUNGRY (*see* HUNGER)
1Sa 2: 5 those who were **h** have ceased
2Sa 17:29 The people are **h** and weary and
2Ki 7:12 They know that we are **h**
Job 5: 5 Because the **h** eat up his
Job 22: 7 withheld bread from the **h**
Job 24:10 away the sheaves from the **h**
Ps 50:12 If I were **h**, I would not tell
Ps 107: 5 **H** and thirsty, Their soul
Ps 107: 9 And fills the **h** soul with
Ps 107:36 There He makes the **h** dwell
Ps 146: 7 Who gives food to the **h**
Prov 16:26 for his **h** mouth drives him on
Prov 25:21 If your enemy is **h**, give him
Prov 27: 7 but to a **h** soul every bitter
Is 8:21 through it hard pressed and **h**
Is 8:21 shall happen, when they are **h**
Is 9:20 on the right hand and be **h**
Is 29: 8 be as when a **h** man dreams
Is 32: 6 to keep the **h** unsatisfied
Is 44:12 even so, he is **h**, and his
Is 58: 7 share your bread with the **h**
Is 58:10 you extend your soul to the **h**
Is 65:13 shall eat, but you shall be **h**
Jer 42:14 nor be **h** for bread, and there
Ezek 18: 7 has given his bread to the **h**
Ezek 18:16 has given his bread to the **h**
Matt 4: 2 nights, afterward He was **h**
Matt 12: 1 And His disciples were **h**, and
Matt 12: 3 what David did when he was **h**
Matt 15:32 not want to send them away **h**
Matt 21:18 to the city, He was **h**
Matt 25:35 for I was **h** and you gave Me
Matt 25:37 Lord, when did we see You **h**
Matt 25:42 for I was **h** and you gave Me
Matt 25:44 when did we see You **h** or
Mark 2:25 did when he was in need and **h**
Mark 8: 3 away **h** to their own houses
Mark 11:12 out from Bethany, He was **h**
Luke 1:53 filled the **h** with good things
Luke 4: 2 when they had ended, He was **h**
Luke 6: 3 what David did when he was **h**
Acts 10:10 Then he became very **h** and
1Co 11:21 and one is **h** and another is
1Co 11:34 But if anyone is **h**, let him
Phil 4:12 both to be full and to be **h**

HUNT (*see* HUNTED, HUNTER, HUNTING, HUNTS)
Gen 27: 3 to the field and **h** game for me
Gen 27: 5 went to the field to **h** game
1Sa 24:11 Yet you **h** my life to take it
1Ki 18:10 not sent someone to **h** for you
Job 10:16 you **h** me like a fierce lion,
Job 38:39 Can you **h** the prey for the
Ps 140:11 Let evil **h** the violent man to
Jer 16:16 they shall **h** them from every
Ezek 13:18 of every height to **h** souls
Ezek 13:18 Will you **h** the souls of My
Ezek 13:20 you **h** souls there like birds
Ezek 13:20 the souls you **h** like birds

HUNTED (*see* HUNT)
Gen 27:33 Where is the one who **h** game
Is 13:14 It shall be as the **h** gazelle
Lam 3:52 cause **h** me down like a bird

HUNTER (*see* HUNT, HUNTERS)
Gen 10: 9 a mighty **h** before the LORD
Gen 10: 9 the mighty **h** before the LORD
Gen 25:27 And Esau was a skillful **h**, a
Prov 6: 5 from the hand of the **h**, and

HUNTERS (*see* HUNTER)
Jer 16:16 I will send for many **h**, and

HUNTING (*see* HUNT)
Gen 27:30 brother came in from his **h**
Prov 12:27 not roast what he took in **h**

HUNTS (*see* HUNT)
Lev 17:13 who sojourn among you, who **h**
1Sa 26:20 as when one **h** a partridge in
Mic 7: 2 every man **h** his brother with

HUPHAM (*see* HUPHAMITES, HUPPIM)
Num 26:39 of **H**, the family of the

HUPHAMITES (*see* HUPHAM)
Num 26:39 Hupham, the family of the **H**

HUPPAH
1Ch 24:13 the thirteenth to **H**, the

HUPPIM (*see* HUPHAM)
Gen 46:21 Ehi, Rosh, Muppim, **H**
1Ch 7:12 **H** were the sons of Ir, and
1Ch 7:15 as his wife the sister of **H**

HUR
Ex 17:10 **H** went up to the top of the
Ex 17:12 **H** supported his hands, one on
Ex 24:14 Aaron and **H** are with you
Ex 31: 2 the son of Uri, the son of **H**
Ex 35:30 the son of Uri, the son of **H**
Ex 38:22 the son of Uri, the son of **H**
Num 31: 8 Evi, Rekem, Zur, **H**, and Reba,
Josh 13:21 Evi, Rekem, Zur, **H**, and Reba,
1Ch 2:19 as his wife, who bore him **H**
1Ch 2:20 **H** begot Uri, and Uri begot
1Ch 2:50 The sons of **H**, the firstborn
1Ch 4: 1 were Perez, Hezron, Carmi, **H**
1Ch 4: 4 These were the sons of **H**, the
2Ch 1: 5 the son of Uri, the son of **H**
Neh 3: 9 to them Rephaiah the son of **H**

HURAI (*see* HIDDAI)
1Ch 11:32 **H** of the brooks of Gaash,

HURAM (*see* HIRAM)
1Ch 8: 5 Gera, Shephuphan, and **H**
2Ch 2:13 **H** my master craftsman
2Ch 4:11 Then **H** made the pots and the
2Ch 4:11 So **H** finished doing the work
2Ch 4:16 and all their articles **H** his
2Ch 9:21 with the servants of **H**

HURI
1Ch 5:14 of Abihail the son of **H**, the

HURLING (*see* HURLS)
1Ch 12: 2 hand and the left in **h** stones

HURLS (*see* HURLING)
Num 35:20 **h** something at him so that he
Job 27:22 It **h** against him and does not

HURRIED (*see* HURRY)
2Ch 26:20 Indeed he also **h** to get out
Jer 17:16 I have not **h** away from being

HURRY (*see* HURRIED, HURRYING)
Gen 19:15 the angels urged Lot to **h**
Gen 19:22 **H**, escape there.
Ex 5:13 taskmasters forced them to **h**
1Sa 9:12 **H** now; for today he came
1Sa 20:38 Make haste, **h**, do not delay

HURRYING (*see* HURRY)
Acts 20:16 for he was **h** to be at

HURT (*see* HURTING, HURTS)
Gen 31: 7 God did not allow him to **h** me
Ex 21:22 **h** a woman with child, so that
Ex 22:10 to keep, and it dies, is **h**
Num 16:15 nor have I **h** one of them
1Sa 25: 7 with us, and we did not **h** them
1Sa 25:15 good to us, and we were not **h**
Ezra 4:22 to the **h** of the kings
Ps 15: 4 He who swears to his own **h**
Ps 35: 4 to confusion Who plot my **h**
Ps 35:26 confusion Who rejoice at my **h**
Ps 38:12 Those who seek my **h** speak of
Ps 41: 7 Against me they devise my **h**
Ps 70: 2 and confused Who desire my **h**
Ps 71:13 and dishonor Who seek my **h**
Ps 71:24 to shame Who seek my **h**
Ps 105:18 They **h** his feet with fetters,
Prov 20:30 Blows that **h** cleanse away
Prov 23:35 struck me, but I was not **h**
Eccl 5:13 kept for their owner to his **h**
Eccl 8: 9 over another to his own **h**
Eccl 10: 9 stones may be **h** by them, and
Is 11: 9 They shall not **h** nor destroy
Is 27: 3 lest any **h** it, I keep it
Is 65:25 They shall not **h** nor destroy
Jer 6:14 the **h** of My people slightly
Jer 7: 6 after other gods to your **h**
Jer 8:11 the **h** of the daughter of My
Jer 8:21 For the **h** of the daughter of
Jer 8:21 daughter of my people I am **h**
Jer 10:19 Woe is me for my **h**
Jer 25: 7 of your hands to your own **h**
Dan 3:25 and they are not **h**, and the
Dan 6:22 so that they have not **h** me
Mark 16:18 it will by no means **h** them
Luke 4:35 out of him and did not **h** him
Luke 10:19 shall by any means **h** you
Acts 18:10 one will attack you to **h** you

Rev 2:11 not be **h** by the second death
Rev 9:10 was to **h** men five months

HURTING (*see* HURT)
Gen 4:23 me, even a young man for **h** me
1Sa 25:34 has kept me back from **h** you

HURTS (*see* HURT)
Ex 21:35 if one man's ox **h** another's

HUSBAND (*see* HUSBAND'S, HUSBANDS)
Gen 3: 6 also gave to her **h** with her
Gen 3:16 desire shall be for your **h**
Gen 16: 3 gave her to her **h** Abram to be
Gen 29:32 therefore, my **h** will love me
Gen 29:34 Now this time my **h** will
Gen 30:15 that you have taken away my **h**
Gen 30:18 I have given my maid to my **h**
Gen 30:20 now my **h** will dwell with me,
Ex 4:25 you are a **h** of blood to me
Ex 4:26 You are a **h** of blood
Ex 21:22 the woman's **h** imposes on him
Lev 21: 3 near to him, who has had no **h**
Lev 21: 7 a woman divorced from her **h**
Num 5:13 hidden from the eyes of her **h**
Num 5:20 your **h** has lain with you"
Num 5:27 unfaithfully toward her **h**
Num 30: 6 But if indeed she takes a **h**
Num 30: 7 her **h** hears it, and makes no
Num 30: 8 But if her **h** overrules her on
Num 30:11 her **h** heard it, and made no
Num 30:12 But if her **h** truly made them
Num 30:12 her **h** has made them void, and
Num 30:13 her **h** may confirm it, or her
Num 30:13 or her **h** may make it void
Num 30:14 But if her **h** makes no
Deut 21:13 may go in to her and be her **h**
Deut 22:22 with a woman married to a **h**
Deut 22:23 a virgin is betrothed to a **h**
Deut 24: 3 if the latter **h** detests her
Deut 24: 3 or if the latter **h** dies who
Deut 24: 4 then her former **h** who
Deut 25:11 **h** from the hand of the one
Deut 28:56 refuse to the **h** of her bosom
Judg 13: 6 the woman came and told her **h**
Judg 13: 9 but Manoah her **h** was not with
Judg 13:10 ran in haste and told her **h**
Judg 14:15 Entice your **h**, that he may
Judg 19: 3 Then her **h** arose and went
Judg 20: 4 the **h** of the woman who was
Ruth 1: 3 Then Elimelech, Naomi's **h**
Ruth 1: 5 her two sons and her **h**
Ruth 1: 9 each in the house of her **h**
Ruth 1:12 for I am too old to have a **h**
Ruth 1:12 if I should have a **h** tonight
Ruth 2:11 since the death of your **h**
1Sa 1: 8 Elkanah her **h** said to her
1Sa 1:22 go up, for she said to her **h**
1Sa 1:23 And Elkanah her **h** said to her
1Sa 2:19 her **h** to offer the yearly
1Sa 4:19 her **h** were dead, she bowed
1Sa 4:21 of her father-in-law and her **h**
1Sa 25:19 she did not tell her **h** Nabal
2Sa 3:15 sent and took her from her **h**
2Sa 3:16 Then her **h** went along with
2Sa 11:26 that Uriah her **h** was dead
2Sa 11:26 dead, she mourned for her **h**
2Sa 14: 5 I am a widow, my **h** is dead
2Sa 14: 7 leave to my **h** neither name
2Ki 4: 1 Your servant my **h** is dead
2Ki 4: 9 And she said to her **h**, "Look
2Ki 4:14 has no son, and her **h** is old
2Ki 4:22 Then she called to her **h**, and
2Ki 4:26 Is it well with your **h**
Prov 7:19 For my **h** is not at home
Prov 12: 4 wife is the crown of her **h**
Prov 31:11 The heart of her **h** safely
Prov 31:23 Her **h** is known in the gates,
Prov 31:28 her **h** also, and he praises her
Is 54: 5 For your Maker is your **h**, the
Jer 3:20 departs from her **h**, so have
Jer 6:11 for even the **h** shall be taken
Jer 31:32 though I was a **h** to them
Ezek 16:32 strangers instead of her **h**
Ezek 16:45 mother's daughter, loathing **h**
Hos 2: 2 not My wife, nor am I her **H**
Hos 2: 7 go and return to my first **h**
Hos 2:16 That you will call Me "My **H**
Joel 1: 8 for the **h** of her youth
Matt 1:16 begot Joseph the **h** of Mary
Matt 1:19 Then Joseph her **h**, being a
Mark 10:12 And if a woman divorces her **h**
Luke 2:36 and had lived with a **h** seven
Luke 16:18 from her **h** commits adultery
John 4:16 Go, call your **h**, and come here
John 4:17 I have no **h**
John 4:17 have well said, 'I have no **h**
John 4:18 you now have is not your **h**
Acts 5: 9 buried your **h** are at the door
Acts 5:10 her out, buried her by her **h**
Rom 7: 2 For the woman who has a **h** is
Rom 7: 2 to her **h** as long as he lives
Rom 7: 2 But if the **h** dies, she is
Rom 7: 2 from the law of her **h**
Rom 7: 3 So then if, while her **h** lives
Rom 7: 3 but if her **h** dies, she is
1Co 7: 2 let each woman have her own **h**
1Co 7: 3 Let the **h** render to his wife
1Co 7: 3 also the wife to her **h**
1Co 7: 4 her own body, but the **h** does
1Co 7: 4 likewise the **h** does not have
1Co 7:10 is not to depart from her **h**
1Co 7:11 or be reconciled to her **h**
1Co 7:11 a **h** is not to divorce his
1Co 7:13 a woman who has a **h** who does
1Co 7:14 For the unbelieving **h** is
1Co 7:14 wife is sanctified by the **h**
1Co 7:16 whether you will save your **h**
1Co 7:16 Or how do you know, O **h**,
1Co 7:34 how she may please her **h**
1Co 7:39 by law as long as her **h** lives
1Co 7:39 but if her **h** dies, she is at
2Co 11: 2 I have betrothed you to one **h**
Gal 4:27 children than she who has a **h**
Eph 5:23 For the **h** is head of the wife
Eph 5:33 see that she respects her **h**
1Ti 3: 2 the **h** of one wife, temperate,
Tit 1: 6 the **h** of one wife, having
Rev 21: 2 as a bride adorned for her **h**

HUSBAND'S (*see* HUSBAND)
Num 5:19 while under your **h** authority
Num 5:20 while under your **h** authority
Num 5:29 while under her **h** authority
Num 30:10 If she vowed in her **h** house
Deut 25: 5 her **h** brother shall go in to
Deut 25: 5 duty of a **h** brother to her
Deut 25: 7 say, 'My **h** brother refuses to
Deut 25: 7 the duty of my **h** brother
Ruth 2: 1 Naomi had a kinsman of her **h**
Prov 6:34 For jealousy is a **h** fury

HUSBANDS (*see* HUSBAND, HUSBANDS')
Ruth 1:11 womb, that they may be your **h**
Ruth 1:13 yourselves from having **h**
Esth 1:17 despise their **h** in their eyes
Esth 1:20 all wives will honor their **h**
Jer 29: 6 and give your daughters to **h**
Ezek 16:45 sisters, who loathed their **h**
Amos 4: 1 the needy, who say to your **h**
John 4:18 for you have had five **h**, and
1Co 14:35 them ask their own **h** at home
Eph 5:22 Wives, submit to your own **h**
Eph 5:24 to their own **h** in everything
Eph 5:25 **H**, love your wives, just as
Eph 5:28 So **h** ought to love their own
Col 3:18 Wives, submit to your own **h**
Col 3:19 **H**, love your wives and do not
1Ti 3:12 deacons be the **h** of one wife
Tit 2: 4 young women to love their **h**
Tit 2: 5 good, obedient to their own **h**
1Pe 3: 1 be submissive to your own **h**
1Pe 3: 5 submissive to their own **h**
1Pe 3: 7 Likewise you **h**, dwell with

HUSBANDS' (*see* HUSBANDS)
Jer 44:19 her without our **h** permission

HUSHAH (*see* SHUAH)
1Ch 4: 4 and Ezer was the father of **H**

HUSHAI
2Sa 15:32 that there was **H** the Archite
2Sa 15:37 So **H**, David's friend, went
2Sa 16:16 when **H** the Archite, David's
2Sa 16:16 that **H** said to Absalom,
2Sa 16:17 So Absalom said to **H**, "Is
2Sa 16:18 And **H** said to Absalom,
2Sa 17: 5 Now call **H** the Archite also,
2Sa 17: 6 And when **H** came to Absalom,
2Sa 17: 7 So **H** said to Absalom
2Sa 17: 8 For," said **H**, "you know
2Sa 17:14 The counsel of **H** the Archite
2Sa 17:15 Then **H** said to Zadok and
1Ki 4:16 Baanah the son of **H**, in Asher
1Ch 27:33 **H** the Archite was the king's

HUSHAM
Gen 36:34 died, **H** of the land of the
Gen 36:35 And when **H** died, Hadad the
1Ch 1:45 died, **H** of the land of the
1Ch 1:46 And when **H** died, Hadad the

HUSHATHITE
2Sa 21:18 Sibbechai the **H** killed Saph
2Sa 23:27 Anathothite, Mebunnai the **H**
1Ch 11:29 Sibbechai the **H**, Ilai the
1Ch 20: 4 Sibbechai the **H** killed Sippai
1Ch 27:11 month was Sibbechai the **H**

HUSHED
Job 29:10 the voice of nobles was **h**

HUSHIM (*see* SHUHAM)
Gen 46:23 The son of Dan was **H**
1Ch 7:12 Ir, and **H** was the son of Aher
1Ch 8: 8 after he had sent away **H**
1Ch 8:11 And by **H** he begot Abitub and

HUT
Is 1: 8 as a **h** in a garden of
Is 24:20 and shall totter like a **h**

HUZ
Gen 22:21 **H** his firstborn, Buz his

HYACINTH
Rev 9:17 red, **h** blue, and sulfur yellow

HYENAS
Is 13:22 The **h** will howl in their

HYMENAEUS
1Ti 1:20 of whom are **H** and Alexander,
2Ti 2:17 **H** and Philetus are of this

HYMN (*see* HYMNS)
Matt 26:30 And when they had sung a **h**
Mark 14:26 And when they had sung a **h**

HYMNS (*see* HYMN)
Acts 16:25 praying and singing **h** to God
Eph 5:19 to one another in psalms and **h**
Col 3:16 one another in psalms and **h**

HYPOCRISY (*see* HYPOCRITE)
Matt 23:28 but inside you are full of **h**
Mark 12:15 But He, knowing their **h**
Luke 12: 1 of the Pharisees, which is **h**
Rom 12: 9 Let love be without **h**
Gal 2:13 was carried away with their **h**
1Ti 4: 2 speaking lies in **h**, having
Jas 3:17 partiality and without **h**
1Pe 2: 1 all malice, all guile, **h**,

HYPOCRITE (*see* HYPOCRISY, HYPOCRITES)
Job 8:13 hope of the **h** shall perish
Job 13:16 for a **h** could not come before
Job 17: 8 himself up against the **h**
Job 20: 5 the joy of the **h** is but for a
Job 27: 8 For what is the hope of the **h**
Job 34:30 that the **h** should not reign,
Prov 11: 9 The **h** with his mouth destroys
Is 9:17 for everyone is a **h** and an
Matt 7: 5 **H**! First remove the plank
Luke 6:42 **H**! First remove the plank
Luke 13:15 **H**! Does not each one
Gal 2:13 also played the **h** with him

HYPOCRITES (*see* HYPOCRITE)
Job 15:34 company of **h** will be barren
Job 36:13 But the **h** in heart store up
Ps 26: 4 Nor will I go in with **h**
Is 33:14 fearfulness has seized the **h**
Jer 42:20 For you were **h** in your hearts
Matt 6: 2 as the **h** do in the synagogues
Matt 6: 5 you shall not be like the **h**
Matt 6:16 fast, do not be like the **h**
Matt 15: 7 **H**! Well did Isaiah
Matt 16: 3 **H**! You know how to discern
Matt 22:18 Why do you test Me, you **h**
Matt 23:13 you, scribes and Pharisees, **h**
Matt 23:14 you, scribes and Pharisees, **h**
Matt 23:15 you, scribes and Pharisees, **h**
Matt 23:23 you, scribes and Pharisees, **h**
Matt 23:25 you, scribes and Pharisees, **h**
Matt 23:27 you, scribes and Pharisees, **h**
Matt 23:29 you, scribes and Pharisees, **h**
Matt 24:51 him his portion with the **h**
Mark 7: 6 did Isaiah prophesy of you **h**
Luke 11:44 you, scribes and Pharisees, **h**
Luke 12:56 **H**! You can discern

HYRAX
Lev 11: 5 the rock h, because it chews
Deut 14: 7 the hare, and the rock h

HYSSOP
Ex 12:22 you shall take a bunch of h
Lev 14: 4 cedar wood, scarlet, and h
Lev 14: 6 wood and the scarlet and the h
Lev 14:49 cedar wood, scarlet, and h
Lev 14:51 take the cedar wood, the h
Lev 14:52 with the cedar wood, the h
Num 19: 6 shall take cedar wood and h
Num 19:18 A clean person shall take h
1Ki 4:33 the h that springs out of the
Ps 51: 7 Purge me with h, and I shall
John 19:29 with sour wine, put it on h
Heb 9:19 water, scarlet wool, and h

I

I (*see* PREFACE)

IBHAR
2Sa 5:15 I, Elishua, Nepheg, Japhia,
1Ch 3: 6 Also there were I, Elishama,
1Ch 14: 5 I, Elishua, Elpelet,

IBLEAM (*see* BILEAM)
Josh 17:11 Beth Shean and its towns, I
Judg 1:27 or the inhabitants of I and
2Ki 9:27 ascent to Gur, which is by I

IBNEIAH
1Ch 9: 8 I the son of Jeroham

IBNIJAH
1Ch 9: 8 son of Reuel, the son of I

IBRI
1Ch 24:27 Beno, Shoham, Zaccur, and I

IBZAN
Judg 12: 8 I of Bethlehem judged Israel
Judg 12:10 Then I died and was buried at

ICE
Job 6:16 are dark because of the i
Job 37:10 the breath of God i is given
Job 38:29 From whose womb comes the i

ICHABOD (*see* ICHABOD'S)
1Sa 4:21 Then she named the child I

ICHABOD'S (*see* ICHABOD)
1Sa 14: 3 Ahitub, I brother, the son of

ICONIUM
Acts 13:51 against them, and came to I
Acts 14: 1 Now it happened in I that
Acts 14:19 from Antioch and I came there
Acts 14:21 they returned to Lystra, I
Acts 16: 2 who were at Lystra and I
2Ti 3:11 to me at Antioch, at I, at

IDALAH
Josh 19:15 Kattath, Nahallal, Shimron, I

IDBASH
1Ch 4: 3 Jezreel, Ishma, and I

IDDO
1Ki 4:14 Ahinadab the son of I, in
1Ch 6:21 I his son, Zerah his son, and
1Ch 27:21 I the son of Zechariah
2Ch 9:29 in the visions of I the seer
2Ch 12:15 and of I the seer concerning
2Ch 13:22 the annals of the prophet I
Ezra 5: 1 and Zechariah the son of I
Ezra 6:14 and Zechariah the son of I
Ezra 8:17 I gave them a command for I
Ezra 8:17 what they should say to I
Neh 12: 4 I, Ginnethoi, Abijah,
Neh 12:16 of I, Zechariah
Zech 1: 1 the son of I the prophet,
Zech 1: 7 the son of I the prophet

IDENTIFY
Gen 31:32 i what I have of yours and
Ezra 2:59 but they could not i their
Neh 7:61 but they could not i their

IDLE (*see* IDLENESS, IDLY)
Ex 5: 8 For they are i
Ex 5:17 You are i! You are i!
Prov 14:23 but i chatter leads only to
Prov 19:15 and an i person will suffer
Matt 12:36 every i word men may speak
Matt 20: 3 standing i in the marketplace
Matt 20: 6 and found others standing i
Matt 20: 6 been standing here i all day
Luke 24:11 seemed to them like i tales
1Ti 1: 6 have turned aside to i talk
1Ti 5:13 And besides they learn to be i
1Ti 5:13 not only i but also gossips
Tit 1:10 both i talkers and deceivers,
2Pe 2: 3 their judgment has not been i

IDLENESS (*see* IDLE)
Prov 31:27 does not eat the bread of i
Eccl 10:18 through i of hands the house
Ezek 16:49 of food, and abundance of i

IDLY (*see* IDLE)
Ps 12: 2 They speak i everyone with

IDOL (*see* IDOLATER, IDOLATRY, IDOL'S, IDOLS)
2Ch 33: 7 the i which he had made, in
2Ch 33:15 the i from the house of the
Ps 24: 4 lifted up his soul to an i
Is 48: 5 My i has done them, and my
Is 66: 3 as if he blesses an i
Is 66:17 after an i in the midst,
Jer 10: 8 a wooden i is a worthless
Jer 22:28 Coniah a despised, broken i
Hos 10: 6 The i also shall be carried
Acts 7:41 offered sacrifices to the i
1Co 8: 4 we know that an i is nothing
1Co 8: 7 with consciousness of the i
1Co 8: 7 it as a thing offered to an i
1Co 10:19 That an i is anything, or

IDOLATER (*see* IDOL, IDOLATERS)
1Co 5:11 or covetous, or an i, or a
Eph 5: 5 nor covetous man, who is an i

IDOLATERS (*see* IDOLATER)
2Ki 17:15 they followed idols, became i
Jer 2: 5 idols, and have become i
1Co 5:10 or extortioners, or i, since
1Co 6: 9 Neither fornicators, nor i
1Co 10: 7 do not become i as were some
Rev 21: 8 immoral, sorcerers, i, and all
Rev 22:15 immoral and murderers and i

IDOLATRIES (*see* IDOLATRY)
1Pe 4: 3 parties, and abominable i

IDOLATROUS (*see* IDOLATRY)
2Ki 23: 5 Then he removed the i priests
Ps 26: 4 I have not sat with i mortals
Ezek 23:49 you shall pay for your i sins
Zeph 1: 4 the names of the i priests

IDOLATRY (*see* IDOL, IDOLATRIES, IDOLATROUS)
1Sa 15:23 is as iniquity and i
1Co 10:14 my beloved, flee from i
Gal 5:20 i, sorcery, hatred,
Col 3: 5 and covetousness, which is i

IDOL'S (*see* IDOL)
1Co 8:10 eating in an i temple, will

IDOLS (*see* IDOL)
Gen 31:19 i that were her father's
Gen 31:34 had taken the household i
Gen 31:35 did not find the household i
Lev 19: 4 Do not turn to i, nor make
Lev 26: 1 not make i for yourselves
Lev 26:30 the lifeless forms of your i
Deut 29:17 their i which were among them
Deut 32:21 to anger by their foolish i
Judg 17: 5 made an ephod and household i
Judg 18:14 houses an ephod, household i
Judg 18:17 the ephod, the household i
Judg 18:18 the ephod, the household i
Judg 18:20 the ephod, the household i
1Sa 31: 9 it in the temple of their i
1Ki 15:12 removed all the i that his
1Ki 16:13 Israel to anger with their i
1Ki 16:26 Israel to anger with their i
1Ki 21:26 abominably in following i
2Ki 17:12 for they served i, of which
2Ki 17:15 they followed i, became
2Ki 21:11 made Judah sin with his i)
2Ki 21:21 and he served the i that his
2Ki 23:24 the household gods and i, all
1Ch 10: 9 news in the temple of their i
1Ch 16:26 the gods of the peoples are i
2Ch 11:15 the calf i which he had made
2Ch 15: 8 removed the abominable i from
2Ch 24:18 and served wooden images and i
Ps 31: 6 hated those who regard vain i
Ps 96: 5 the gods of the peoples are i
Ps 97: 7 carved images, Who boast of i
Ps 106:36 They served their i, Which
Ps 106:38 sacrificed to the i of Canaan
Ps 115: 4 Their i are silver and gold,
Ps 135:15 The i of the nations are
Is 2: 8 Their land is also full of i
Is 2:18 but the i He shall utterly
Is 2:20 cast away his i of silver
Is 2:20 his i of gold, which they
Is 10:10 found the kingdoms of the i
Is 10:11 have done to Samaria and her i
Is 10:11 do also to Jerusalem and her i
Is 19: 1 the i of Egypt will totter at
Is 19: 3 and they will consult the i
Is 31: 7 throw away his i of silver
Is 31: 7 of silver and his i of gold
Is 45:16 together, who are makers of i
Is 46: 1 their i were on the beasts and
Is 57:13 collection of i deliver you
Jer 2: 5 far from Me, have followed i
Jer 8:19 images, and with foreign i
Jer 14:22 the i of the nations that can
Jer 16:18 detestable and abominable i
Jer 18:15 burned incense to worthless i
Jer 50: 2 her i are humiliated, her
Jer 50:38 they are insane with their i
Ezek 6: 4 your slain men before your i
Ezek 6: 5 of Israel before their i, and
Ezek 6: 6 your i may be broken and made
Ezek 6: 9 play the harlot after their i
Ezek 6:13 i all around their altars
Ezek 6:13 sweet incense to all their i
Ezek 8:10 all the i of the house of
Ezek 8:12 man in the room of his i
Ezek 14: 3 up their i in their hearts
Ezek 14: 4 sets up his i in his heart
Ezek 14: 4 to the multitude of his i
Ezek 14: 5 estranged from Me by their i
Ezek 14: 6 Repent, turn away from your i
Ezek 14: 7 sets up his i in his heart and
Ezek 16:36 and with all your abominable i
Ezek 18: 6 the i of the house of Israel
Ezek 18:12 lifted his eyes to the i
Ezek 18:15 the i of the house of Israel
Ezek 20: 7 with the i of Egypt
Ezek 20: 8 they forsake the i of Egypt
Ezek 20:16 heart went after their i
Ezek 20:18 yourselves with their i
Ezek 20:24 fixed on their fathers' i
Ezek 20:31 yourselves with all your i
Ezek 20:39 serve every one of you his i
Ezek 20:39 with your gifts and your i
Ezek 22: 3 she makes i within herself to
Ezek 22: 4 the i which you have made
Ezek 23: 7 she lusted, with all their i
Ezek 23:30 become defiled by their i
Ezek 23:37 adultery with their i, and
Ezek 23:39 their children for their i
Ezek 30:13 I will also destroy the i
Ezek 33:25 up your eyes toward your i
Ezek 36:18 for their i with which they
Ezek 36:25 filthiness and from all your i
Ezek 37:23 anymore with their i, nor
Ezek 44:10 away from Me after their i
Ezek 44:12 to them before their i and
Hos 4:12 counsel from their wooden i
Hos 4:17 Ephraim is joined to i, let
Hos 8: 4 they made i for themselves
Hos 12:11 Though Gilead has i
Hos 13: 2 i of their silver, according
Hos 14: 8 have I to do anymore with i
Amos 5:26 your king and Chiun, your i
Jon 2: 8 i forsake their own Mercy
Mic 1: 7 all her i I will lay desolate
Hab 2:18 trust in it, to make mute i
Zech 10: 2 For the i speak delusion
Zech 13: 2 names of the i from the land
Acts 15:20 from things polluted by i
Acts 15:29 from things offered to i,
Acts 17:16 the city was given over to i
Acts 21:25 from things offered to i,
Rom 2:22 You who abhor i, do you rob

1Co 8: 1 things offered to **i**
1Co 8: 4 eating of things offered to **i**
1Co 8:10 eat those things offered to **i**
1Co 10:19 is offered to **i** is anything
1Co 10:28 This was offered to **i**," do
1Co 12: 2 carried away to these dumb **i**
2Co 6:16 has the temple of God with **i**
1Th 1: 9 from **i** to serve the living
1Jn 5:21 keep yourselves from **i**
Rev 2:14 to eat things sacrificed to **i**
Rev 2:20 to eat things sacrificed to **i**
Rev 9:20 **i** of gold, silver, brass,

IDUMEA (*see* EDOM)
Mark 3: 8 and Jerusalem and **I** and beyond

IF (*see* PREFACE)

IGAL
Num 13: 7 Issachar, **I** the son of Joseph
2Sa 23:36 **I** the son of Nathan of Zobah,
1Ch 3:22 of Shemaiah were Hattush, **I**

IGDALIAH
Jer 35: 4 sons of Hanan the son of **I**

IGNORANCE (*see* IGNORANT)
Lev 5:18 his **i** in which he erred and
Ezek 45:20 unintentionally or in **i**
Acts 3:17 I know that you did it in **i**
Acts 17:30 times of **i** God overlooked
Eph 4:18 because of the **i** that is in
Heb 9: 7 people's sins committed in **i**
1Pe 1:14 former lusts, as in your **i**
1Pe 2:15 silence the **i** of foolish men

IGNORANT (*see* IGNORANCE, IGNORANTLY)
Ps 73:22 I was so foolish and **i**
Is 56:10 are blind, they are all **i**
Is 63:16 though Abraham was **i** of us
Rom 10: 3 For they being **i** of God's
Rom 11:25 should be **i** of this mystery
1Co 12: 1 I do not want you to be **i**
1Co 14:38 if anyone is **i**, let him be **i**
2Co 1: 8 we do not want you to be **i**
2Co 2:11 we are not **i** of his devices
1Th 4:13 But I do not want you to be **i**
2Ti 2:23 **i** disputes, knowing that they
Heb 5: 2 compassion on those who are **i**

IGNORANTLY (*see* IGNORANT)
1Ti 1:13 I did it **i** in unbelief

IJE ABARIM
Num 21:11 from Oboth and camped at **I**
Num 33:44 from Oboth and camped at **I**

IJIM
Num 33:45 They departed from **I** and
Josh 15:29 Baalah, **I**, Ezem,

IJON
1Ki 15:20 He attacked **I**, Dan, Abel Beth
2Ki 15:29 of Assyria came and took **I**
2Ch 16: 4 They attacked **I**, Dan, Abel

IKKESH
2Sa 23:26 Ira the son of **I** the Tekoite
1Ch 11:28 Ira the son of **I** the Tekoite
1Ch 27: 9 Ira the son of **I** the Tekoite

ILAI (*see* SALMON, ZALMON)
1Ch 11:29 Hushathite, **I** the Ahohite,

ILL (*see* ILLNESS, ILLS)
Judg 9:23 God sent a spirit of **i** will
2Sa 12:15 to David, and it became very **i**
2Sa 13: 5 your bed and pretend to be **i**
2Sa 13: 6 lay down and pretended to be **i**
Job 20:26 it shall go **i** with him who is
Ps 106:32 So that it went **i** with Moses
Is 3:11 It shall be **i** with him, for

ILLEGITIMATE
Deut 23: 2 One of **i** birth shall not
Heb 12: 8 partakers, then you are **i**

ILLITERATE
Is 29:12 is delivered to one who is **i**

ILLNESS (*see* ILL)
2Ki 13:14 the **i** of which he would die
Ps 41: 3 him on his bed of **i**

ILLS (*see* ILL)
Is 3: 7 I cannot cure your **i**, for in

ILLUMINATED
Heb 10:32 in which, after you were **i**
Rev 18: 1 and the earth was **i** with his
Rev 21:23 it, for the glory of God **i** it

ILLUSTRATION
John 10: 6 Jesus used this **i**, but they

ILLYRICUM
Rom 15:19 round about to **I** I have fully

IMAGE (*see* IMAGE'S, IMAGES)
Gen 1:26 Let Us make man in Our **i**,
Gen 1:27 God created man in His own **i**
Gen 1:27 in the **i** of God He created
Gen 5: 3 his own likeness, after his **i**
Gen 9: 6 for in the **i** of God He made
Ex 20: 4 for yourself any carved **i**
Lev 26: 1 neither a carved **i** nor a
Deut 4:16 for yourselves a carved **i** in
Deut 4:23 **i** in the form of anything
Deut 4:25 make a carved **i** in the form
Deut 5: 8 for yourself any carved **i**
Deut 9:12 made themselves a molded **i**
Deut 16:21 any tree, as a wooden **i**, near
Deut 27:15 makes any carved or molded **i**
Judg 6:25 wooden **i** that is beside it
Judg 6:26 with the wood of the **i** which
Judg 6:28 the wooden **i** that was beside
Judg 6:30 wooden **i** that was beside it
Judg 17: 3 a carved **i** and a molded **i**
Judg 17: 4 a carved **i** and a molded **i**
Judg 18:14 a carved **i**, and a molded **i**
Judg 18:17 there, they took the carved **i**
Judg 18:17 idols, and the molded **i**
Judg 18:18 house and took the graven **i**
Judg 18:18 idols, and the molded **i**, the
Judg 18:20 idols, and the carved **i**, and
Judg 18:30 for themselves the carved **i**
Judg 18:31 carved **i** which he made, all
1Sa 19:13 And Michal took an **i** and laid
1Sa 19:16 there was the **i** in the bed
1Ki 15:13 made an obscene **i** of Asherah
1Ki 15:13 And Asa cut down her obscene **i**
1Ki 16:33 And Ahab made a wooden **i**
2Ki 17:16 for themselves a molded **i**
2Ki 17:16 two calves, made a wooden **i**
2Ki 21: 3 for Baal, and made a wooden **i**
2Ki 21: 7 He even set a carved **i** of
2Ki 23: 6 he brought out the wooden **i**
2Ki 23: 7 hangings for the wooden **i**
2Ki 23:15 and burned the wooden **i**
2Ch 15:16 made an obscene **i** of Asherah
2Ch 15:16 and Asa cut down her obscene **i**
2Ch 33: 7 He even set a carved **i**, the
Ps 73:20 You shall despise their **i**
Ps 106:19 And worshiped the molded **i**
Ps 106:20 their glory Into the **i** of an
Is 40:19 The workman molds a graven **i**
Is 40:20 carved **i** that will not totter
Is 44: 9 Those who make a graven **i**
Is 44:10 **i** that profits him nothing
Is 44:15 he makes it a carved **i**, and
Is 44:17 into a god, his carved **i**
Is 45:20 the wood of their carved **i**
Is 48: 5 has done them, and my carved **i**
Is 48: 5 my molded **i** have commanded
Jer 10:14 put to shame by the graven **i**
Jer 10:14 for his molded **i** is falsehood
Jer 51:17 put to shame by the carved **i**
Jer 51:17 for his molded **i** is falsehood
Ezek 8: 3 seat of the **i** of jealousy was
Ezek 8: 5 was this **i** of jealousy in the
Dan 2:31 and behold, a great **i**
Dan 2:31 This great **i**, whose splendor
Dan 2:34 which struck the **i** on its
Dan 2:35 the **i** became a great mountain
Dan 3: 1 the king made an **i** of gold
Dan 3: 2 to the dedication of the **i**
Dan 3: 3 **i** that King Nebuchadnezzar
Dan 3: 3 they stood before the **i** that
Dan 3: 5 worship the gold **i** that King
Dan 3: 7 worshiped the gold **i** which
Dan 3:10 down and worship the gold **i**
Dan 3:12 gold **i** which you have set up
Dan 3:14 gold **i** which I have set up
Dan 3:15 worship the **i** which I have
Dan 3:18 gold **i** which you have set up
Nah 1:14 I will cut off the carved **i**
Nah 1:14 carved **i** and the molded **i**
Hab 2:18 What profit is the **i**, that
Hab 2:18 should carve it, the molded **i**
Matt 22:20 Whose **i** and inscription is
Mark 12:16 Whose **i** and inscription is
Luke 20:24 Whose **i** and inscription does
Acts 19:35 of the **i** which fell down from
Rom 1:23 **i** made like corruptible man
Rom 8:29 conformed to the **i** of His Son
1Co 11: 7 his head, since he is the **i**
1Co 15:49 the **i** of the man of dust, we
1Co 15:49 the **i** of the heavenly Man
2Co 3:18 same **i** from glory to glory
2Co 4: 4 Christ, who is the **i** of God
Col 1:15 He is the **i** of the invisible
Col 3:10 the **i** of Him who created him
Heb 1: 3 the express **i** of His person,
Heb 10: 1 not the very **i** of the things,
Rev 13:14 an **i** to the beast who was
Rev 13:15 breath to the **i** of the beast
Rev 13:15 that the **i** of the beast
Rev 13:15 as would not worship the **i** of
Rev 14: 9 worships the beast and his **i**
Rev 14:11 worship the beast and his **i**
Rev 15: 2 over the beast, over his **i**
Rev 16: 2 and those who worshiped his **i**
Rev 19:20 and those who worshiped his **i**
Rev 20: 4 worshiped the beast or his **i**

IMAGE'S (*see* IMAGE)
Dan 2:32 This **i** head was of fine gold,

IMAGES (*see* IMAGE)
Ex 34:13 and cut down their wooden **i**
Num 33:52 destroy all their molded **i**
Deut 7: 5 and cut down their wooden **i**
Deut 7: 5 burn their carved **i** with fire
Deut 7:25 **i** of their gods with fire
Deut 12: 3 burn their wooden **i** with fire
Deut 12: 3 the carved **i** of their gods
Judg 3:19 stone **i** that were at Gilgal
Judg 3:26 and passed beyond the stone **i**
1Sa 6: 5 shall make **i** of your tumors
1Sa 6: 5 **i** of your rats that ravage
1Sa 6:11 rats and the **i** of their tumors
2Sa 5:21 And they left their **i** there
1Ki 14: 9 molded **i** to provoke Me to
1Ki 14:15 they have made their wooden **i**
1Ki 14:23 wooden **i** on every high hill
2Ki 11:18 in pieces its altars and **i**
2Ki 13: 6 the wooden **i** also remained in
2Ki 17:10 wooden **i** on every high hill
2Ki 17:41 yet served their carved **i**
2Ki 18: 4 cut down the wooden **i** and
2Ki 23:14 and cut down the wooden **i**, and
2Ch 14: 3 and cut down the wooden **i**
2Ch 17: 6 places and wooden **i** from Judah
2Ch 19: 3 the wooden **i** from the land
2Ch 23:17 in pieces its altars and **i**
2Ch 24:18 fathers, and served wooden **i**
2Ch 28: 2 made molded **i** for the Baals
2Ch 31: 1 pieces, cut down the wooden **i**
2Ch 33: 3 the Baals, and made wooden **i**
2Ch 33:19 up wooden **i** and carved **i**
2Ch 33:22 to all the carved **i** which his
2Ch 34: 3 carved **i**, and the molded **i**
2Ch 34: 4 and the wooden **i**, the carved **i**
2Ch 34: 4 and the molded **i** he broke in
2Ch 34: 7 the altars and the wooden **i**
2Ch 34: 7 the carved **i** into powder, and
Ps 78:58 jealousy with their carved **i**
Ps 97: 7 to shame who serve carved **i**
Is 10:10 whose carved **i** excelled those
Is 17: 8 nor the wooden **i** nor the
Is 21: 9 all the carved **i** of her gods
Is 27: 9 beaten to dust, when wooden **i**
Is 30:22 of your graven **i** of silver
Is 30:22 of your molded **i** of gold
Is 41:29 their molded **i** are wind and
Is 42: 8 nor My praise to graven **i**
Is 42:17 who trust in carved **i**, who
Is 42:17 who say to the molded **i**
Jer 8:19 to anger with their carved **i**
Jer 17: 2 their wooden **i** by the green
Jer 50: 2 her **i** are broken in pieces
Jer 50:38 it is the land of carved **i**
Jer 51:47 on the carved **i** of Babylon
Jer 51:52 judgment on her carved **i**, and
Ezek 7:20 the **i** of their abominations
Ezek 16:17 and made for yourself male **i**
Ezek 21:21 the arrows, he consults the **i**
Ezek 23:14 **i** of Chaldeans portrayed in
Ezek 30:13 cause the **i** to cease from
Hos 11: 2 and burned incense to carved **i**

Hos 13: 2 made for themselves molded i
Mic 1: 7 All her carved i shall be
Mic 5:13 Your carved i I will also cut
Mic 5:14 your wooden i from your midst
Acts 7:43 i which you made to worship

IMAGINATION
Gen 8:21 although the i of man's heart
Deut 29:19 I walk in the i of my heart'
Jer 7:24 in the i of their evil heart,
Jer 9:14 to the i of their own heart
Jer 11: 8 in the i of his evil heart
Jer 13:10 walk in the i of their heart
Jer 16:12 the i of his own evil heart
Jer 18:12 do the i of his evil heart
Jer 23:17 to the i of his own heart
Luke 1:51 in the i of their hearts

IMITATE (*see* IMITATORS)
1Co 4:16 Therefore I urge you, i me
1Co 11: 1 I me, just as I also i Christ
Heb 6:12 but i those who through faith
3Jn 11 do not i what is evil, but

IMITATORS (*see* IMITATE)
1Th 2:14 became i of the churches of

IMLA (*see* IMLAH)
2Ch 18: 7 He is Micaiah the son of I
2Ch 18: 8 Micaiah the son of I quickly

IMLAH (*see* IMLA)
1Ki 22: 8 one man, Micaiah the son of I
1Ki 22: 9 Micaiah the son of I quickly

IMMANUEL
Is 7:14 Son, and shall call His name I
Is 8: 8 the breadth of Your land, O I
Matt 1:23 and they shall call His name I

IMMEDIATELY
Judg 2:23 without driving them out i
1Sa 28:20 Then i Saul fell full length
1Ki 1:13 Go i to King David and say to
Ezra 6: 8 is to be given i to these men
Prov 7:22 I he went after her, as an ox
Dan 3: 6 worship shall be cast i into
Dan 3:15 you shall be cast i into the
Matt 3:16 came up i from the water
Matt 4:20 Then they i left their nets
Matt 4:22 i they left the boat and their
Matt 8: 3 i his leprosy was cleansed
Matt 13: 5 they i sprang up because they
Matt 13:20 and i receives it with joy
Matt 13:21 of the word, i he stumbles
Matt 14:22 I Jesus made His disciples
Matt 14:27 But i Jesus spoke to them,
Matt 14:31 i Jesus stretched out His
Matt 20:34 i their eyes received sight,
Matt 21: 2 i you will find a donkey tied
Matt 21: 3 them,' and i he will send them
Matt 21:19 i the fig tree withered away
Matt 24:29 I after the tribulation of
Matt 25:15 and i he went on a journey
Matt 26:49 Then i he went up to Jesus and
Matt 26:74 And i a rooster crowed
Matt 27:48 I one of them ran and took a
Mark 1:10 And i, coming up from the
Mark 1:12 i the Spirit drove Him into
Mark 1:18 i they left their nets and
Mark 1:20 i He called them, and they
Mark 1:21 i on the Sabbath He entered
Mark 1:28 i His fame spread throughout
Mark 1:31 up, and i the fever left her
Mark 1:42 i the leprosy left him, and he
Mark 2: 2 I many gathered together, so
Mark 2: 8 And i, when Jesus perceived in
Mark 2:12 i he arose, took up the bed,
Mark 3: 6 i plotted with the Herodians
Mark 4: 5 i it sprang up because it had
Mark 4:15 when they hear, Satan comes i
Mark 4:16 i receive it with gladness
Mark 4:17 word's sake, i they stumble
Mark 4:29 i he puts in the sickle,
Mark 5: 2 i there met Him out of the
Mark 5:29 I the fountain of her blood
Mark 5:30 i knowing in Himself that
Mark 5:42 I the girl arose and walked,
Mark 6:25 I she came in with haste to
Mark 6:27 And i the king sent an
Mark 6:45 I He made His disciples get
Mark 6:50 i He talked with them and said
Mark 6:54 i the people recognized Him,
Mark 7:35 I his ears were opened, and
Mark 8:10 i He got into the boat with
Mark 9:15 I, when they saw Him, all the
Mark 9:20 i the spirit convulsed him,
Mark 9:24 I the father of the child
Mark 10:52 i he received his sight and
Mark 11: 3 and i he will send it here
Mark 14:43 And i, while He was still
Mark 14:45 i he went up to Him and said
Mark 15: 1 I, in the morning, the chief
Luke 1:64 I his mouth was opened and his
Luke 4:39 i she arose and served them
Luke 5:13 And i the leprosy left him
Luke 5:25 I he rose up before them,
Luke 5:39 drunk old wine, i desires new
Luke 6:49 and i it fell
Luke 8:44 i her flow of blood stopped
Luke 8:47 Him and how she was healed i
Luke 8:55 returned, and she arose i
Luke 12:36 knocks they may open to him i
Luke 12:54 west, i you say, 'A shower is
Luke 13:13 i she was made straight, and
Luke 14: 5 will not i pull him out on
Luke 18:43 i he received his sight, and
Luke 19:11 kingdom of God would appear i
Luke 19:40 the stones would i cry out
Luke 21: 9 but the end will not come i
Luke 22:60 And i, while he was still
John 5: 9 i the man was made well, took
John 6:21 i the boat was at the land
John 13:30 of bread, he then went out i
John 13:32 in Himself, and glorify Him i
John 18:27 and i a rooster crowed
John 19:34 i blood and water came out
John 21: 3 i got into the boat, and that
Acts 3: 7 i his feet and ankle bones
Acts 5:10 Then i she fell down at his
Acts 9:18 I there fell from his eyes
Acts 9:20 I he preached the Christ in
Acts 9:34 Then he arose i
Acts 10:33 So I sent to you i, and you
Acts 12:10 i the angel departed from him
Acts 12:23 Then i an angel of the Lord
Acts 13:11 i a dark mist fell on him, and
Acts 16:10 vision, i we sought to go to
Acts 16:26 i all the doors were opened
Acts 16:33 i he and all his family were
Acts 17:10 Then the brethren i sent Paul
Acts 17:14 Then i the brethren sent Paul
Acts 21:30 and i the doors were shut
Acts 21:32 He i took soldiers and
Acts 22:29 Then i those who were about
Acts 23:30 the man, I sent him i to you
Gal 1:16 I did not i confer with flesh
Jas 1:24 i forgets what kind of man he
Rev 4: 2 I I was in the Spirit

IMMER
1Ch 9:12 of Meshillemith, the son of I
1Ch 24:14 to Bilgah, the sixteenth to I
Ezra 2:37 the sons of I, one thousand
Ezra 2:59 Harsha, Cherub, Addan, and I
Ezra 10:20 Also of the sons of I
Neh 3:29 of I made repairs in front of
Neh 7:40 the children of I, one
Neh 7:61 Harsha, Cherub, Addon, and I
Neh 11:13 of Meshillemoth, the son of I
Jer 20: 1 Now Pashhur the son of I, the

IMMORAL (*see* IMMORALITY)
Prov 2:16 deliver you from the i woman
Prov 5: 3 lips of an i woman drip honey
Prov 5:20 be enraptured by an i woman
Prov 7: 5 may keep you from the i woman
Prov 22:14 The mouth of an i woman is a
1Co 5: 9 with sexually i people
1Co 5:10 i people of this world, or
Rev 21: 8 murderers, sexually i,
Rev 22:15 and sorcerers and sexually i

IMMORALITY (*see* IMMORAL)
Ezek 23: 8 poured out their i upon her
Ezek 23:17 they defiled her with their i
Matt 5:32 sexual i causes her to commit
Matt 19: 9 his wife, except for sexual i
Acts 15:20 by idols, from sexual i, from
Acts 15:29 strangled, and from sexual i
Acts 21:25 strangled, and from sexual i
Rom 1:29 all unrighteousness, sexual i
1Co 5: 1 there is sexual i among you
1Co 5: 1 such sexual i as is not even
1Co 6:13 for sexual i but for the Lord
1Co 6:18 Flee sexual i
1Co 6:18 i sins against his own body
1Co 7: 2 because of sexual i, let
1Co 10: 8 Nor let us commit sexual i
1Th 4: 3 should abstain from sexual i
Jude 7 themselves over to sexual i
Rev 2:14 idols, and to commit sexual i
Rev 2:20 servants to commit sexual i
Rev 2:21 to repent of her sexual i
Rev 9:21 sexual i or their thefts

IMMORTAL (*see* IMMORTALITY)
1Ti 1:17 Now to the King eternal, i

IMMORTALITY (*see* IMMORTAL)
Rom 2: 7 seek for glory, honor, and i
1Co 15:53 and this mortal must put on i
1Co 15:54 and this mortal has put on i
1Ti 6:16 who alone has i, dwelling in
2Ti 1:10 i to light through the gospel

IMMOVABLE
Acts 27:41 prow stuck fast and remained i
1Co 15:58 brethren, be steadfast, i

IMMUTABILITY (*see* IMMUTABLE)
Heb 6:17 promise the i of His counsel

IMMUTABLE (*see* IMMUTABILITY)
Heb 6:18 that by two i things, in

IMNA (*see* IMNAH, JIMNA)
1Ch 7:35 brother Helem were Zophah, I

IMNAH (*see* IMNA, JIMNAH)
1Ch 7:30 The sons of Asher were I,
2Ch 31:14 Kore the son of I the Levite

IMPART
Rom 1:11 you, that I may i to you some
Eph 4:29 that it may i grace to the
1Th 2: 8 we were well pleased to i to

IMPATIENT
Job 21: 4 were, why should I not be i

IMPEDIMENT
Mark 7:32 had an i in his speech, and
Mark 7:35 and the i of his tongue was

IMPENITENT
Rom 2: 5 and your i heart you are

IMPERISHABLE
1Co 9:25 crown, but we for an i crown

IMPLANTED
Jas 1:21 with meekness the i word,

IMPLEMENT (*see* IMPLEMENTS)
Num 35:16 he strikes him with an iron i
Deut 23:13 you shall have an i among

IMPLEMENTS (*see* IMPLEMENT)
Num 4:14 shall put on it all its i
2Sa 24:22 sacrifice, and threshing i
1Ch 9:29 and over all the i of the
1Ch 21:23 the threshing i for wood
Amos 1: 3 Gilead with i of iron
Zech 11:15 the i of a foolish shepherd

IMPLORE (*see* IMPLORED, IMPLORING)
Ps 116: 4 I i You, deliver my soul
Mark 5: 7 I i You by God that You do
Luke 9:38 I i You, look on my son, for
Acts 21:39 I i you, permit me to speak
2Co 5:20 we i you on Christ's behalf,
Phil 4: 2 I i Euodia and I i
Phil 4: 2 I i Syntyche to be of the

IMPLORED (*see* IMPLORE)
2Ch 33:12 he i the LORD his God, and
Esth 8: 3 feet, and i him with tears to
Jer 36:25 Gemariah i the king not to
Luke 5:12 on his face and i Him, saying,
Luke 9:40 So I i Your disciples to cast
John 4:47 i Him to come down and heal
Acts 27:33 Paul i them all to take food,

IMPLORING (*see* IMPLORE)
Mark 1:40 i Him, kneeling down to Him
Acts 9:38 i him not to delay in coming
2Co 8: 4 i us with much urgency that

IMPORTED
1Ki 10:28 had horses i from Egypt and
1Ki 10:29 Now a chariot that was i from
2Ch 1:16 had horses i from Egypt and
2Ch 1:17 i from Egypt a chariot for

IMPOSE (*see* IMPOSED, IMPOSES)
2Ki 18:14 whatever you **i** on me I will
Ezra 7:24 shall not be lawful to **i** tax

IMPOSED (*see* IMPOSE)
Ex 21:30 If there is **i** on him a sum of
Ex 21:30 life, whatever is **i** on him
2Ki 23:33 he **i** on the land a tribute of
2Ch 24: 9 the servant of God had **i** on
2Ch 36: 3 he **i** on the land a tribute of
Esth 9:27 **i** it upon themselves and their
Esth 10: 1 King Ahasuerus **i** tribute on
Heb 9:10 **i** until the time of

IMPOSES (*see* IMPOSE)
Ex 21:22 the woman's husband **i** on him
Dan 11:20 who **i** taxes on the glorious

IMPOSSIBLE
Matt 17:20 and nothing will be **i** for you
Matt 19:26 With men this is **i**, but with
Mark 10:27 With men it is **i**, but not
Luke 1:37 with God nothing will be **i**
Luke 17: 1 It is **i** that no offenses
Luke 18:27 The things which are **i** with
Heb 6: 4 For it is **i** for those who
Heb 6:18 which it is **i** for God to lie
Heb 11: 6 faith it is **i** to please Him

IMPOSTORS
2Ti 3:13 **i** will grow worse and worse,

IMPOVERISHED
Judg 6: 6 So Israel was greatly **i**
Is 40:20 Whoever is too **i** for such a
Mal 1: 4 We have been **i**, but we will

IMPRESSIVE
Josh 22:10 a great, **i** altar

IMPRISONED (*see* IMPRISONMENT, IMPRISONS)
Acts 22:19 that in every synagogue I **i**

IMPRISONMENT (*see* IMPRISONED, IMPRISONMENTS)
Ezra 7:26 confiscation of goods, or **i**
Heb 11:36 yes, and of chains and **i**

IMPRISONMENTS (*see* IMPRISONMENT)
2Co 6: 5 in stripes, in **i**, in tumults,

IMPRISONS (*see* IMPRISONED)
Job 11:10 If He passes by, **i**, and
Job 12:14 if He **i** a man, there can be

IMPROPER (*see* IMPROPERLY)
2Sa 13: 2 And it was **i** for Amnon to do

IMPROPERLY (*see* IMPROPER)
1Co 7:36 behaving **i** toward his virgin

IMPUDENT
Prov 7:13 with an **i** face she said to
Ezek 2: 4 For they are **i** and stubborn
Ezek 3: 7 all the house of Israel are **i**

IMPULSIVE
Prov 14:29 but he who is **i** exalts folly

IMPURITY
Lev 12: 2 **i** she shall be unclean
Lev 12: 5 weeks, as in her customary **i**
Lev 15:20 during her **i** shall be unclean
Lev 15:24 all, so that her **i** is on him
Lev 15:25 the time of her customary **i**
Lev 15:25 beyond her usual time of **i**
Lev 15:25 the days of her customary **i**
Lev 15:26 be to her as the bed of her **i**
Lev 15:26 as the uncleanness of her **i**
Lev 15:33 because of her customary **i**
Lev 18:19 as she is in her customary **i**
2Sa 11: 4 she was cleansed from her **i**
Ezra 9:11 end to another with their **i**
Ezek 18: 6 a woman during her **i**
Ezek 22:10 are set apart during their **i**
Ezek 36:17 of a woman in her customary **i**

IMPUTE (*see* IMPUTED, IMPUTES, IMPUTING)
1Sa 22:15 Let not the king **i** anything
2Sa 19:19 let my lord **i** iniquity to me
Ps 32: 2 the LORD does not **i** iniquity
Rom 4: 8 whom the LORD shall not **i** sin

IMPUTED (*see* IMPUTE)
Lev 7:18 nor shall it be **i** to him
Lev 17: 4 shall be **i** to that man
Rom 4:11 might be **i** to them also,
Rom 4:23 alone that it was **i** to him
Rom 4:24 It shall be **i** to us who
Rom 5:13 but sin is not **i** when there

IMPUTES (*see* IMPUTE)
Rom 4: 6 of the man to whom God **i**

IMPUTING (*see* IMPUTE)
Hab 1:11 **i** this power to his god
2Co 5:19 not **i** their trespasses to

IMRAH
1Ch 7:36 Harnepher, Shual, Beri, **I**

IMRI
1Ch 9: 4 the son of Omri, the son of **I**
Neh 3: 2 Zaccur the son of **I** built

IN (*see* PREFACE)

INASMUCH (*see* PREFACE)

INAUGURATE (*see* INAUGURATED)
Num 27:19 and **i** him in their sight
Deut 31:14 of meeting, that I may **i** him

INAUGURATED (*see* INAUGURATE)
Num 27:23 and **i** him, just as the LORD
Deut 31:23 Then He **i** Joshua the son of

INCENSE
Ex 25: 6 oil and for the sweet **i**
Ex 30: 1 make an altar to burn **i** on
Ex 30: 7 on it sweet **i** every morning
Ex 30: 7 lamps, he shall burn **i** on it
Ex 30: 8 he shall burn **i** on it, a
Ex 30: 8 a perpetual **i** before the LORD
Ex 30: 9 not offer strange **i** on it
Ex 30:27 utensils, and the altar of **i**
Ex 30:35 You shall make of these an **i**
Ex 30:37 But as for the **i** which you
Ex 31: 8 its utensils, the altar of **i**
Ex 31:11 sweet **i** for the holy place
Ex 35: 8 oil and for the sweet **i**
Ex 35:15 the **i** altar, its poles, the
Ex 35:15 anointing oil, the sweet **i**
Ex 35:28 oil, and for the sweet **i**
Ex 37:25 He made the **i** altar of acacia
Ex 37:29 the pure **i** of sweet spices,
Ex 39:38 anointing oil, and the sweet **i**
Ex 40: 5 the **i** before the ark of the
Ex 40:27 and he burned sweet **i** on it
Lev 4: 7 of sweet **i** before the LORD
Lev 10: 1 it, put **i** on it, and offered
Lev 16:12 full of sweet **i** beaten fine
Lev 16:13 he shall put the **i** on the
Lev 16:13 that the cloud of **i** may cover
Lev 26:30 cut down your **i** altars, and
Num 4:16 for the light, the sweet **i**
Num 7:14 pan of ten shekels, full of **i**
Num 7:20 pan of ten shekels, full of **i**
Num 7:26 pan of ten shekels, full of **i**
Num 7:32 pan of ten shekels, full of **i**
Num 7:38 pan of ten shekels, full of **i**
Num 7:44 pan of ten shekels, full of **i**
Num 7:50 pan of ten shekels, full of **i**
Num 7:56 pan of ten shekels, full of **i**
Num 7:62 pan of ten shekels, full of **i**
Num 7:68 pan of ten shekels, full of **i**
Num 7:74 pan of ten shekels, full of **i**
Num 7:80 pan of ten shekels, full of **i**
Num 7:86 twelve gold pans full of **i**
Num 16: 7 put **i** in them before the LORD
Num 16:17 put **i** in it, and each of you
Num 16:18 laid **i** on it, and stood at the
Num 16:35 fifty men who were offering **i**
Num 16:40 to offer **i** before the LORD
Num 16:46 put **i** on it, and take it
Num 16:47 So he put in the **i** and made
Deut 33:10 They shall put **i** before You
1Sa 2:28 upon My altar, to burn **i**, and
1Ki 3: 3 burned **i** at the high places
1Ki 9:25 he burned **i** with them on the
1Ki 11: 8 foreign wives, who burned **i**
1Ki 12:33 on the altar and burned **i**
1Ki 13: 1 stood by the altar to burn **i**
1Ki 13: 2 high places who burn **i** on you
1Ki 22:43 burned **i** on the high places
2Ki 12: 3 burned **i** on the high places
2Ki 14: 4 burned **i** on the high places
2Ki 15: 4 burned **i** on the high places
2Ki 15:35 burned **i** on the high places
2Ki 16: 4 burned **i** on the high places,
2Ki 17:11 there they burned **i** on all
2Ki 18: 4 of Israel burned **i** to it, and
2Ki 22:17 burned **i** to other gods, that
2Ki 23: 5 **i** on the high places in the
2Ki 23: 5 and those who burned **i** to Baal
2Ki 23: 8 the priests had burned **i**,
1Ch 6:49 offering and on the altar of **i**
1Ch 9:29 the wine and the oil and the **i**
1Ch 23:13 to burn **i** before the LORD, to
1Ch 28:18 by weight for the altar of **i**
2Ch 2: 4 to burn before Him sweet **i**
2Ch 13:11 burnt sacrifices and sweet **i**
2Ch 14: 5 the **i** altars from all the
2Ch 25:14 them and burned **i** to them
2Ch 26:16 burn **i** on the altar of **i**.
2Ch 26:18 to burn **i** to the LORD, but
2Ch 26:18 who are consecrated to burn **i**
2Ch 26:19 censer in his hand to burn **i**
2Ch 26:19 the LORD, beside the **i** altar
2Ch 28: 3 He burned **i** in the Valley of
2Ch 28: 4 burned **i** on the high places,
2Ch 28:25 to burn **i** to other gods, and
2Ch 29: 7 have not burned **i** or offered
2Ch 29:11 minister to Him and burn **i**
2Ch 30:14 took away all the **i** altars
2Ch 32:12 one altar and burn **i** on it"
2Ch 34: 4 the **i** altars which were above
2Ch 34: 7 cut down all the **i** altars
2Ch 34:25 burned **i** to other gods, that
Ps 141: 2 prayer be set before You as **i**
Is 1:13 **i** is an abomination to Me
Is 17: 8 images nor the **i** altars
Is 27: 9 and **i** altars do not stand up
Is 43:23 nor wearied you with **i**
Is 60: 6 they shall bring gold and **i**
Is 65: 3 burn **i** on altars of brick
Is 65: 7 Who have burned **i** on the
Is 66: 3 he who burns **i**, as if he
Jer 1:16 burned **i** to other gods, and
Jer 7: 9 burn **i** to Baal, and walk after
Jer 11:12 the gods to whom they offer **i**
Jer 11:13 altars to burn **i** to Baal
Jer 11:17 anger in offering **i** to Baal
Jer 17:26 grain offerings and **i**,
Jer 18:15 Me, they have burned **i** to
Jer 19: 4 **i** in it to other gods whom
Jer 19:13 roofs they have burned **i** to
Jer 32:29 they have offered **i** to Baal
Jer 34: 5 so they shall burn **i** for you
Jer 41: 5 **i** in their hand, to bring
Jer 44: 3 in that they went to burn **i**
Jer 44: 5 to burn no **i** to other gods
Jer 44: 8 burning **i** to other gods in
Jer 44:15 had burned **i** to other gods
Jer 44:17 to burn **i** to the queen of
Jer 44:18 **i** to the queen of heaven and
Jer 44:19 when we burned **i** to the queen
Jer 44:21 The **i** that you burned in the
Jer 44:23 Because you have burned **i**
Jer 44:25 to burn **i** to the queen of
Jer 48:35 places and burns **i** to his gods
Ezek 6: 4 your **i** altars shall be broken
Ezek 6: 6 your **i** altars may be cut down
Ezek 6:13 sweet **i** to all their idols
Ezek 8:11 and a thick cloud of **i** went up
Ezek 16:18 My oil and My **i** before them
Ezek 16:19 set it before them as sweet **i**
Ezek 23:41 it, on which you had set My **i**
Dan 2:46 an offering and **i** to him
Hos 2:13 Baals to which she burned **i**
Hos 4:13 burn **i** on the hills, under
Hos 11: 2 burned **i** to carved images
Hab 1:16 and burn **i** to their dragnet
Mal 1:11 In every place **i** shall be
Luke 1: 9 his lot fell to burn **i** when
Luke 1:10 outside at the hour of **i**
Luke 1:11 right side of the altar of **i**
Heb 9: 4 had the golden altar of **i**
Rev 5: 8 and golden bowls full of **i**
Rev 8: 3 And he was given much **i**, that
Rev 8: 4 And the smoke of the **i**, with
Rev 18:13 and cinnamon and **i**, fragrant

INCENSED
Is 41:11 all those who were **i** against
Is 45:24 ashamed who are **i** against Him

INCIDENT
Num 16:49 those who died in the Korah **i**
Num 31:16 the LORD in the **i** of Peor

INCITED (*see* INCITING)
Ezra 4:15 that they have **i** sedition
Job 2: 3 although you **i** Me against him

INCITING (*see* INCITED)
Acts 24:12 with anyone nor **i** the crowd

INCLINATION (*see* INCLINE)
Deut 31:21 for I know the **i** of their

INCLINE (*see* INCLINATION, INCLINED)
Josh 24:23 **i** your heart to the LORD God
1Ki 8:58 that He may **i** our hearts to
2Ki 19:16 **I** Your ear, O LORD, and hear
Ps 17: 6 **I** Your ear to me, and hear my
Ps 45:10 Consider and **i** your ear
Ps 49: 4 I will **i** my ear to a proverb
Ps 71: 2 **I** Your ear to me, and save me
Ps 78: 1 **I** your ears to the words of
Ps 88: 2 **I** Your ear to my cry
Ps 102: 2 **I** Your ear to me
Ps 119:36 **I** my heart to Your
Ps 141: 4 Do not **i** my heart to any evil
Prov 2: 2 so that you **i** your ear to
Prov 4:20 **i** your ear to my sayings
Prov 22:17 **I** your ear and hear the words
Is 37:17 **I** Your ear, O LORD, and hear
Is 55: 3 **I** your ear, and come to Me
Jer 7:24 did not obey or **i** their ear
Jer 7:26 not obey Me or **i** their ear
Jer 11: 8 did not obey or **i** their ear
Jer 17:23 did not obey nor **i** their ear
Jer 34:14 not obey Me nor **i** their ear
Jer 44: 5 or **i** their ear to turn from
Dan 9:18 O my God, **i** Your ear and hear

INCLINED (*see* INCLINE)
Num 15:39 heart and your own eyes are **i**
Judg 9: 3 their heart was **i** to follow
Ps 40: 1 He **i** to me, And heard my cry
Ps 116: 2 He has **i** His ear to me,
Ps 119:112 I have **i** my heart to perform
Prov 5:13 nor **i** my ear to those who
Jer 25: 4 nor **i** your ear to hear
Jer 35:15 But you have not **i** your ear

INCLUDED (*see* INCLUDES)
Ex 30:14 Everyone **i** among those who
Ex 38:26 for everyone **i** in the
Num 3:25 of meeting **i** the tabernacle
Num 3:31 Their duty **i** the ark, the
Num 3:36 of Merari **i** the boards of the
Deut 29:19 could be **i** with the sober
Josh 19: 9 was **i** in the portion of the
Josh 19:15 **I** were Kattath, Nahallal,
Josh 19:18 and **i** Chesulloth, Shunem,
Josh 19:25 And their territory **i** Helkath
Josh 19:30 Aphek, and Rehob were **i**
Job 3: 6 may it not be **i** among the

INCLUDES (*see* INCLUDED, INCLUDING)
2Co 10:13 sphere which especially **i** you

INCLUDING (*see* INCLUDES)
Josh 19:28 **i** Ebron, Rehob, Hammon, and
Josh 24: 2 **i** Terah, the father of
Judg 21:10 **i** the women and children
2Ki 10:33 Arnon, **i** Gilead and Bashan
1Ch 16:38 **i** Obed-Edom the son of
Eccl 12:14 **i** every secret thing, whether
Ezek 21:12 Terrors **i** the sword will be
Ezek 41:14 **i** the separating courtyard,
Ezek 44: 9 **i** any foreigner who is among
Matt 8:33 **i** what had happened to the

INCOME
1Ki 10:15 from the **i** of traders, from

INCORRUPTIBILITY (*see* INCORRUPTIBLE)
Tit 2: 7 integrity, reverence, **i**,

INCORRUPTIBLE (*see* INCORRUPTIBILITY, INCORRUPTION)
Rom 1:23 changed the glory of the **i**
1Co 15:52 and the dead will be raised **i**
1Pe 1: 4 to an inheritance **i** and
1Pe 1:23 not of corruptible seed but **i**
1Pe 3: 4 with the **i** ornament of a

INCORRUPTION (*see* INCORRUPTIBLE)
1Co 15:42 corruption, it is raised in **i**
1Co 15:50 nor does corruption inherit **i**
1Co 15:53 corruptible must put on **i**
1Co 15:54 this corruptible has put on **i**

INCREASE (*see* INCREASED, INCREASES, INCREASING)
Lev 19:25 it may yield to you its **i**
Lev 25:16 years you shall **i** its price
Num 32:14 to **i** still more the fierce
Deut 7:13 the **i** of your cattle and the
Deut 14:22 the **i** of your grain that the
Deut 26:12 of your **i** in the third year
Deut 28: 4 and the **i** of your herds, the
Deut 28: 4 the **i** of your cattle and the
Deut 28:11 in the **i** of your livestock,
Deut 28:18 the **i** of your cattle and the
Deut 28:51 eat the **i** of your livestock
Deut 28:51 or the **i** of your cattle or
Deut 30: 9 in the **i** of your livestock,
Deut 32:22 consume the earth with her **i**
Judg 9:29 **I** your army and come out
1Sa 14:19 Philistines continued to **i**
2Sa 23: 5 will He not make it **i**
Ezra 4:22 Why should damage **i** to the
Neh 9:37 it yields much **i** to the kings
Job 8: 7 latter end would **i** abundantly
Job 10:17 **i** Your indignation toward me
Job 20:28 The **i** of his house will
Job 31:12 and would root out all my **i**
Ps 62:10 If riches **i**, Do not set your
Ps 67: 6 the earth shall yield her **i**
Ps 71:21 You shall **i** my greatness, And
Ps 73:12 They **i** in riches
Ps 85:12 And our land will yield its **i**
Ps 115:14 May the LORD give you **i** more
Prov 1: 5 and **i** learning, and a man of
Prov 3: 9 the firstfruits of all your **i**
Prov 9: 9 man, and he will **i** in learning
Prov 13:11 who gathers by labor will **i**
Prov 14: 4 but much **i** comes by the
Prov 22:16 the poor to **i** his riches, and
Prov 28:28 they perish, the righteous **i**
Eccl 5:10 who loves abundance, with **i**
Eccl 5:11 When goods **i**, they **i** who eat
Eccl 6:11 are many things that **i** vanity
Is 9: 7 Of the **i** of His government and
Is 29:19 shall **i** their joy in the LORD
Is 30:23 bread of the **i** of the earth
Jer 2: 3 the firstfruits of His **i**
Jer 23: 3 they shall be fruitful and **i**
Ezek 5:16 I will **i** the famine upon you
Ezek 18: 8 exacted usury nor taken any **i**
Ezek 18:13 has exacted usury or taken **i**
Ezek 18:17 and not received usury or **i**
Ezek 22:12 you take usury and **i**
Ezek 34:27 the earth shall yield her **i**
Ezek 36:11 and they shall **i** and bear young
Ezek 36:30 the **i** of your fields, so that
Ezek 36:37 I will **i** their men like a
Dan 12: 4 and fro, and knowledge shall **i**
Hos 4:10 commit harlotry, but not **i**
Zech 8:12 the ground shall give her **i**
Zech 10: 8 they shall **i** as they once
Luke 17: 5 to the Lord, "**I** our faith
John 3:30 He must **i**, but I must
1Co 3: 6 watered, but God gave the **i**
1Co 3: 7 but God who gives the **i**
2Co 9:10 sown and **i** the fruits of your
Col 2:19 grows with the **i** which is
1Th 3:12 And may the Lord make you **i**
1Th 4:10 brethren, that you **i** more
2Ti 2:16 for they will **i** to more

INCREASED (*see* INCREASE)
Gen 7:17 The waters **i** and lifted up the
Gen 7:18 greatly **i** on the earth, and
Gen 19:19 you have **i** your mercy which
Gen 30:30 it is now **i** to a great amount
Ex 1: 7 **i** abundantly, multiplied and
Ex 23:30 before you, until you have **i**
2Sa 15:12 continually **i** in number
1Ki 22:35 The battle **i** that day
1Ch 4:38 father's house **i** greatly
1Ch 5:23 Their numbers **i** from Bashan
2Ch 18:34 The battle **i** that day, and the
Job 1:10 have **i** in the land
Ps 3: 1 how they have **i** who trouble
Ps 4: 7 that their grain and wine **i**
Ps 49:16 the glory of his house is **i**
Ps 105:24 He **i** His people greatly, And
Is 9: 3 the nation and **i** its joy
Is 26:15 You have **i** the nation, O LORD
Is 26:15 O LORD, you have **i** the nation
Is 51: 2 and blessed him and **i** him
Is 57: 9 ointment, and **i** your perfumes
Jer 3:16 **i** in the land in those days,
Jer 5: 6 their backslidings have **i**
Jer 15: 8 Their widows will be **i** to Me
Jer 29: 6 that you may be **i** there, and
Jer 30:14 because your sins have **i**
Jer 30:15 because your sins have **i**
Lam 2: 5 has **i** mourning and lamentation
Ezek 16:26 **i** your acts of harlotry to
Ezek 23:14 But she **i** her harlotry
Ezek 28: 5 trade you have **i** your riches
Ezek 31:10 Because you have **i** in height
Ezek 41: 7 **i** as one went up from the
Hos 4: 7 The more they **i**, the more
Hos 10: 1 his fruit he has **i** the altars
Amos 4: 9 When your gardens **i**, your
Zech 10: 8 shall increase as they once **i**
Mark 4: 8 a crop that sprang up, **i** and
Luke 2:52 Jesus **i** in wisdom and stature,
Acts 9:22 But Saul **i** all the more in
Acts 16: 5 faith, and **i** in number daily
Rom 3: 7 **i** through my lie to His glory
2Co 10:15 hope, that as your faith is **i**

INCREASES (*see* INCREASE)
Ps 74:23 up against You **i** continually
Prov 11:24 one who scatters, yet **i** more
Prov 16:21 of the lips **i** learning
Prov 23:28 **i** the unfaithful among men
Prov 24: 5 a man of knowledge **i** strength
Prov 28: 8 One who **i** his possessions by
Prov 29:16 multiplied, transgression **i**
Eccl 1:18 he who **i** knowledge **i** sorrow
Eccl 8: 6 the misery of man **i** greatly
Is 40:29 have no might He **i** strength
Hos 12: 1 He daily **i** lies and desolation
Hab 2: 6 to him who **i** what is not his

INCREASING (*see* INCREASE, INCREASINGLY)
Col 1:10 **i** in the knowledge of God

INCREASINGLY (*see* INCREASING)
2Ch 17:12 Jehoshaphat became **i** powerful
2Ch 28:22 **i** unfaithful to the LORD
Esth 9: 4 Mordecai became **i** prominent
Acts 5:14 believers were **i** added to the

INCREDIBLE
Acts 26: 8 Why should it be thought **i** by

INCUR (*see* INCURRED)
Ex 28:43 that they do not **i** iniquity

INCURABLE
2Ch 21:18 intestines with an **i** disease
Job 34: 6 My wound is **i**, though I am
Jer 15:18 pain perpetual and my wound **i**
Jer 30:12 Your affliction is **i**, your
Jer 30:15 Your sorrow is **i**
Mic 1: 9 For her wounds are **i**

INCURRED (*see* INCUR)
Acts 27:21 and **i** this disaster and loss

INDEBTED
Luke 11: 4 everyone who is **i** to us

INDEED (*see* PREFACE)

INDEPENDENT
1Co 11:11 neither is man **i** of woman
1Co 11:11 of woman, nor woman **i** of man

INDESCRIBABLE
2Co 9:15 be to God for His **i** gift

INDIA
Esth 1: 1 reigned from **I** to Ethiopia
Esth 8: 9 provinces from **I** to Ethiopia

INDICATE (*see* INDICATED, INDICATES, INDICATING)
1Ki 5: 9 sea to the place you **i** to me

INDICATED (*see* INDICATE)
Luke 24:28 He **i** that He would have gone

INDICATES (*see* INDICATE)
Heb 12:27 **i** the removal of those

INDICATING (*see* INDICATE)
Heb 9: 8 the Holy Spirit **i** this, that
1Pe 1:11 them was **i** when He testified

INDIGNANT (*see* INDIGNATION)
Neh 4: 1 that he was furious and very **i**
Matt 21:15 they were **i**
Matt 26: 8 disciples saw it, they were **i**
Mark 14: 4 who were **i** among themselves

INDIGNATION (*see* INDIGNANT)
Deut 29:28 in wrath, and in great **i**, and
2Ki 3:27 was great **i** against Israel
Esth 5: 9 with **i** against Mordecai
Job 10:17 and increase Your **i** toward me

Ps 69:24 Pour out Your i upon them
Ps 78:49 of His anger, Wrath, i, and
Ps 102:10 Because of Your i and Your
Ps 119:53 I has taken hold of me
Is 10: 5 staff in whose hand is My i
Is 10:25 the i will cease, as will My
Is 13: 5 the LORD and His weapons of i
Is 26:20 moment, until the i is past
Is 30:27 His lips are full of i, and
Is 30:30 with the i of His anger and
Is 34: 2 For the i of the LORD is
Is 66:14 and His i to His enemies
Jer 10:10 not be able to abide His i
Jer 15:17 for You have filled me with i
Jer 50:25 out the weapons of His i
Lam 2: 6 In His burning i He has
Ezek 21:31 I will pour out My i on you
Ezek 22:24 or rained on in the day of i
Ezek 22:31 have poured out My i on them
Dan 8:19 in the latter time of the i
Mic 7: 9 I will bear the i of the LORD
Nah 1: 6 Who can stand before His i
Hab 3:12 marched through the land in i
Zeph 3: 8 to pour on them My i, All my
Mal 1: 4 the LORD will have i forever
Matt 20:24 it, they were moved with i
Luke 13:14 the synagogue answered with i
Acts 5:17 and they were filled with i
Rom 2: 8 unrighteousness—i and wrath,
2Co 7:11 of yourselves, what i, what
2Co 11:29 and I do not burn with i
Heb 10:27 fiery i which will devour the
Rev 14:10 into the cup of His i

INDISPOSED
Lev 15:33 for her who is i because of

INDIVIDUAL (*see* INDIVIDUALLY)
1Ch 23: 3 the number of i males was
Rev 21:21 each i gate was of one pearl

INDIVIDUALLY (*see* INDIVIDUAL)
Num 1: 2 number of names, every male i
Num 1:18 old and above, each one i
Num 1:20 number of names, every male i
Num 1:22 number of names, every male i
Num 3:47 five shekels for each one i
1Ch 23:24 i by the number of their
Ps 33:15 He fashions their hearts i
Rom 12: 5 and i members of one another
1Co 12:11 to each one i as He wills
1Co 12:27 body of Christ, and members i

INDUCED
Jer 20: 7 O LORD, You i me, and I was
Jer 20:10 Perhaps he can be i
Ezek 14: 9 is i to speak anything, I the
Ezek 14: 9 the LORD have i that prophet
Acts 6:11 they secretly i men to say

INDULGENCE
Col 2:23 against the i of the flesh

INDUSTRIOUS
1Ki 11:28 that the young man was i,

INEXCUSABLE
Rom 2: 1 Therefore you are i, O man,

INEXPERIENCED
1Ch 22: 5 Solomon my son is young and i
1Ch 29: 1 God has chosen, is young and i
2Ch 13: 7 Rehoboam was young and i

INEXPRESSIBLE
2Co 12: 4 Paradise and heard i words
1Pe 1: 8 you rejoice with joy i and

INFALLIBLE
Acts 1: 3 suffering by many i proofs

INFAMOUS
Ezek 22: 5 from you will mock you as i

INFANT (*see* INFANTS)
1Sa 15: 3 But kill both man and woman, i
Is 65:20 No more shall an i from there
Jer 44: 7 you man and woman, child and i
Lam 4: 4 The tongue of the i clings to

INFANTS (*see* INFANT)
1Sa 22:19 women, children and nursing i
Job 3:16 like i who never saw light
Ps 8: 2 i You have ordained strength,
Lam 2:11 the i faint in the streets of
Hos 13:16 their i shall be dashed in
Matt 21:16 nursing i You have perfected
Luke 18:15 Then they also brought i to

INFERIOR
Job 12: 3 I am not i to you
Job 13: 2 I am not i to you
Dan 2:39 another kingdom i to yours
John 2:10 drunk, then that which is i
2Co 11: 5 at all i to the most eminent
2Co 12:13 you were i to other churches

INFIDELITY
Num 14:33 and bear the brunt of your i

INFINITE
Ps 147: 5 His understanding is i

INFIRMITIES (*see* INFIRMITY)
Matt 8:17 He Himself took our i and bore
Luke 5:15 be healed by Him of their i
Luke 7:21 cured many people of their i
Luke 8: 2 healed of evil spirits and i
2Co 12: 5 not boast, except in my i
2Co 12: 9 I will rather boast in my i
2Co 12:10 I take pleasure in i, in
1Ti 5:23 sake and your frequent i

INFIRMITY (*see* INFIRMITIES)
Jer 10:19 Truly this is an i, and I must
Luke 13:11 a spirit of i eighteen years
Luke 13:12 you are loosed from your i
John 5: 5 had an i thirty-eight years
2Co 11:30 the things which concern my i
Gal 4:13 i I preached the gospel to

INFLAMED (*see* INFLAMES)
Hos 7: 5 made him sick, i with wine

INFLAMES (*see* INFLAMED, INFLAMING, INFLAMMATION)
Is 5:11 until night, till wine i them

INFLAMING (*see* INFLAMES)
Is 57: 5 i yourselves with gods under

INFLAMMATION (*see* INFLAMES)
Deut 28:22 with fever, with i, with
Ps 38: 7 For my loins are full of i

INFLICT (*see* INFLICTED, INFLICTING, INFLICTS)
Deut 7:23 will i defeat upon them until

INFLICTED (*see* INFLICT)
2Ki 8:29 Syrians had i on him at Ramah
2Ki 9:15 which the Syrians had i on
Lam 1:12 which the LORD has i on me in
2Co 2: 6 was i by the majority is

INFLICTING (*see* INFLICT)
1Ki 20:37 the man struck him, i a wound

INFLICTS (*see* INFLICT)
Rom 3: 5 Is God unjust who i wrath

INFORM (*see* INFORMED, INFORMER, INFORMS)
Ruth 4: 4 And I thought to i you, saying
1Sa 27:11 Lest they should i on us,
2Sa 15:28 word comes from you to i me
Ezra 4:16 We i the king that if this
Ezra 5:10 them their names to i you
Ezra 7:24 Also we i you that it shall

INFORMED (*see* INFORM)
Ezra 4:14 we have sent and i the king,
Esth 2:22 and Esther i the king in
Dan 9:22 And he i me, and talked with me
Acts 21:21 but they have been i about
Acts 21:24 things of which they were i
Acts 25: 2 the Jews i him against Paul
Acts 25:15 the elders of the Jews i me

INFORMER (*see* INFORM)
Neh 6:10 who was a secret i

INFORMS (*see* INFORM)
Hos 4:12 idols, and their staff i them

INGATHERING
Ex 23:16 and the Feast of I, which is
Ex 34:22 the Feast of I at the year's

INGRAINED
Lev 14:37 of the house with i streaks

INGREDIENTS
2Ch 16:14 and various i prepared in a

INHABIT (*see* INHABITANT, INHABITED, INHABITING, INHABITS, UNINHABITED)
Num 13:19 they i are like camps or
Num 15: 2 into the land you are to i
Num 35:34 defile the land which you i
Ps 22: 3 Who i the praises of Israel
Prov 10:30 wicked will not i the earth
Is 65:21 shall build houses and i them
Is 65:22 shall not build and another i
Jer 17: 6 but shall i the parched
Ezek 33:24 they who i those ruins in the
Amos 9:14 the waste cities and i them
Zeph 1:13 build houses, but not i them

INHABITANT (*see* INHABIT, INHABITANTS)
Is 5: 9 and beautiful ones, without i
Is 6:11 are laid waste and without i
Is 9: 9 Ephraim and the i of Samaria
Is 12: 6 O i of Zion, for great is the
Is 20: 6 the i of this territory will
Is 24:17 upon you, O i of the earth
Is 33:24 And the i will not say,
Jer 2:15 cities are burned, without i
Jer 4: 7 will be laid waste, without i
Jer 9:11 Judah desolate, without an i
Jer 10:17 the land, O i of the fortress
Jer 21:13 O i of the valley, and rock of
Jer 22:23 O i of Lebanon, making your
Jer 26: 9 be desolate, without an i
Jer 33:10 without man and without i
Jer 34:22 Judah a desolation without i
Jer 44:22 a curse, and without an i
Jer 46:19 and be desolate, without i
Jer 48:19 O i of Aroer, stand by the
Jer 48:43 O i of Moab," says the LORD
Jer 51:29 a desolation without i
Jer 51:35 the i of Zion will say
Jer 51:37 and a hissing, without an i
Amos 1: 5 cut off the i from the Valley
Amos 1: 8 cut off the i from Ashdod
Mic 1:11 naked shame, you i of Shaphir
Mic 1:11 the i of Zaanan does not go
Mic 1:12 For the i of Maroth pined for
Mic 1:13 O i of Lachish, harness the
Mic 1:15 heir to you, O i of Mareshah
Zeph 2: 5 so there shall be no i
Zeph 3: 6 there is no one, no i

INHABITANTS (*see* INHABITANT)
Gen 19:25 all the i of the cities, and
Gen 34:30 among the i of the land,
Gen 50:11 when the i of the land, the
Ex 15:14 hold of the i of Palestina
Ex 15:15 all the i of Canaan will melt
Ex 23:31 For I will deliver the i of
Ex 34:12 make a covenant with the i of
Ex 34:15 with the i of the land, and
Lev 18:25 and the land vomits out its i
Lev 25:10 all the land to all its i
Num 13:32 is a land that devours its i
Num 14:14 tell it to the i of this land
Num 32:17 because of the i of the land
Num 33:52 i of the land from before you
Num 33:53 dispossess the i of the land
Num 33:55 i of the land from before you
Deut 13:13 enticed the i of their city,
Deut 13:15 i of that city with the edge
Josh 2: 9 that all the i of the land
Josh 2:24 all the i of the country are
Josh 7: 9 all the i of the land will
Josh 8:24 all the i of Ai in the field
Josh 8:26 destroyed all the i of Ai
Josh 9: 3 But when the i of Gibeon
Josh 9:11 and all the i of our country
Josh 9:24 to destroy all the i of the
Josh 10: 1 how the i of Gibeon had made
Josh 11:19 the Hivites, the i of Gibeon
Josh 13: 6 all the i of the mountains
Josh 15:15 went up from there to the i
Josh 15:63 the i of Jerusalem, the
Josh 17: 7 south to the i of En Tappuah
Josh 17:11 the i of Dor and its towns,
Josh 17:11 the i of En Dor and its towns,
Josh 17:11 the i of Taanach and its towns
Josh 17:11 the i of Megiddo and its towns
Josh 17:12 out the i of those cities
Judg 1:11 went against the i of Debir
Judg 1:19 out the i of the mountains
Judg 1:19 out the i of the lowland,
Judg 1:27 drive out the i of Beth Shean
Judg 1:27 its villages, or the i of Dor
Judg 1:27 or the i of Ibleam and its
Judg 1:27 or the i of Megiddo and its
Judg 1:30 out the i of Kitron or the
Judg 1:30 of Kitron or the i of Nahalol

Judg 1:31 i of Acco or the i of Sidon
Judg 1:32 Canaanites, the i of the land
Judg 1:33 the i of Beth Shemesh or the
Judg 1:33 or the i of Beth Anath
Judg 1:33 Canaanites, the i of the land
Judg 1:33 the i of Beth Shemesh and Beth
Judg 2: 2 with the i of this land
Judg 5:23 LORD, curse its i bitterly
Judg 10:18 head over all the i of Gilead
Judg 11: 8 head over all the i of Gilead
Judg 20:15 besides the i of Gibeah, who
Judg 21: 9 not one of the i of Jabesh
Judg 21:10 strike the i of Jabesh Gilead
Judg 21:12 the i of Jabesh Gilead four
Ruth 4: 4 back in the presence of the i
1Sa 6:21 to the i of Kirjath Jearim
1Sa 23: 5 David saved the i of Keilah
1Sa 27: 8 the i of the land from of old
1Sa 31:11 when the i of Jabesh Gilead
2Sa 5: 6 the i of the land, who spoke
1Ki 17: 1 of the i of Gilead, said to
1Ki 21:11 nobles who were i of his city
2Ki 19:26 Therefore their i had little
2Ki 22:16 on this place and on its i
2Ki 22:19 this place and against its i
2Ki 23: 2 him all the i of Jerusalem
1Ch 8: 6 houses of the i of Geba, and
1Ch 8:13 houses of the i of Aijalon
1Ch 8:13 who drove out the i of Gath
1Ch 9: 2 And the first i who dwelt in
1Ch 11: 4 were, the i of the land
1Ch 11: 5 Then the i of Jebus said to
1Ch 22:18 For He has given the i of the
2Ch 15: 5 was on all the i of the lands
2Ch 20: 7 who drove out the i of this
2Ch 20:15 you i of Jerusalem, and you,
2Ch 20:18 and the i of Jerusalem bowed
2Ch 20:20 O Judah and you i of Jerusalem
2Ch 20:23 i of Mount Seir to utterly
2Ch 20:23 made an end of the i of Seir
2Ch 21:11 caused the i of Jerusalem to
2Ch 21:13 the i of Jerusalem to play
2Ch 22: 1 Then the i of Jerusalem made
2Ch 32:22 the i of Jerusalem from the
2Ch 32:26 the i of Jerusalem, so that
2Ch 32:33 the i of Jerusalem honored
2Ch 33: 9 the i of Jerusalem to do more
2Ch 34:24 on this place and on its i
2Ch 34:27 this place and against its i
2Ch 34:28 bring on this place and its i
2Ch 34:30 Judah and the i of Jerusalem
2Ch 34:32 So the i of Jerusalem did
2Ch 35:18 and the i of Jerusalem
Ezra 4: 6 against the i of Judah and
Neh 3:13 the i of Zanoah repaired the
Neh 7: 3 from among the i of Jerusalem
Neh 9:24 before them the i of the land
Ps 33: 8 Let all the i of the world
Ps 33:14 On all the i of the earth
Ps 49: 1 ear, all you i of the world,
Ps 75: 3 and all its i are dissolved
Ps 83: 7 Philistia with the i of Tyre
Is 5: 3 O i of Jerusalem and men of
Is 8:14 a snare to the i of Jerusalem
Is 10:13 down the i like a valiant man
Is 10:31 the i of Gebim seek refuge
Is 18: 3 All i of the world and
Is 21:14 O i of the land of Tema,
Is 22:21 father to the i of Jerusalem
Is 23: 2 you i of the coastland, you
Is 23: 6 wail, you i of the coastland
Is 24: 1 and scatters abroad its i
Is 24: 5 is also defiled under its i
Is 24: 6 Therefore the i of the earth
Is 26: 9 the i of the world will learn
Is 26:18 nor have the i of the world
Is 26:21 the i of the earth for their
Is 37:27 Therefore their i had little
Is 38:11 more among the i of the world
Is 40:22 its i are like grasshoppers,
Is 42:10 coastlands and you i of them
Is 42:11 Let the i of Sela sing, let
Is 49:19 now be too small for the i
Jer 1:14 on all the i of the land
Jer 4: 4 i of Jerusalem, lest My fury
Jer 6:12 against the i of the land
Jer 8: 1 bones of the i of Jerusalem
Jer 10:18 this time the i of the land
Jer 11: 2 and to the i of Jerusalem
Jer 11: 9 and among the i of Jerusalem
Jer 11:12 the i of Jerusalem will go and
Jer 13:13 fill all the i of this land
Jer 13:13 and all the i of Jerusalem
Jer 17:20 all the i of Jerusalem, who
Jer 17:25 Judah and the i of Jerusalem
Jer 18:11 to the i of Jerusalem, saying
Jer 19: 3 of Judah and i of Jerusalem
Jer 19:12 and to its i, and make this
Jer 21: 6 strike the i of this city
Jer 23:14 to Me, and her i like Gomorrah
Jer 25: 2 to all the i of Jerusalem,
Jer 25: 9 this land, against its i, and
Jer 25:29 on all the i of the earth
Jer 25:30 all the i of the earth
Jer 26:15 on this city, and on its i
Jer 32:32 Judah, and the i of Jerusalem
Jer 35:13 Judah and the i of Jerusalem,
Jer 35:17 on all the i of Jerusalem all
Jer 36:31 on the i of Jerusalem, and on
Jer 42:18 out on the i of Jerusalem
Jer 46: 8 destroy the city and its i
Jer 47: 2 all the i of the land shall
Jer 49: 8 in the depths, O i of Dedan
Jer 49:20 against the i of Teman
Jer 49:30 in the depths, O i of Hazor
Jer 50:21 it, and against the i of Pekod
Jer 50:34 and disquiet the i of Babylon
Jer 50:35 Against the i of Babylon, and
Jer 51:12 against the i of Babylon
Jer 51:24 all the i of Chaldea for all
Jer 51:35 be upon the i of Chaldea
Lam 4:12 all i of the world, would not
Ezek 11:15 the i of Jerusalem have said
Ezek 12:19 GOD to the i of Jerusalem
Ezek 15: 6 give up the i of Jerusalem
Ezek 26:17 strong at sea, she and her i
Ezek 26:17 terror to be on all her i
Ezek 27: 8 I of Sidon and Arvad were your
Ezek 27:35 All the i of the isles will
Ezek 29: 6 Then all the i of Egypt shall
Dan 4:35 All the i of the earth are
Dan 4:35 and among the i of the earth
Dan 9: 7 to the i of Jerusalem and all
Hos 4: 1 against the i of the land
Hos 10: 5 The i of Samaria fear because
Joel 1: 2 ear, all you i of the land
Joel 1:14 all the i of the land into
Joel 2: 1 Let all the i of the land
Obad 19 The i of the South shall
Obad 19 and the i of the Philistine
Mic 6:12 her i have spoken lies, and
Mic 6:16 and your i a hissing
Zeph 1: 4 all the i of Jerusalem
Zeph 1:11 Wail, you i of Maktesh
Zeph 2: 5 Woe to the i of the seacoast,
Zech 8:20 yet come, i of many cities
Zech 8:21 the i of one city shall go to
Zech 11: 6 longer pity the i of the land
Zech 12: 5 The i of Jerusalem are my
Zech 12: 7 and the glory of the i of
Zech 12: 8 defend the i of Jerusalem
Zech 12:10 on the i of Jerusalem the
Zech 13: 1 for the i of Jerusalem, for
Rev 8:13 woe to the i of the earth,
Rev 12:12 Woe to the i of the earth and
Rev 17: 2 the i of the earth were made

INHABITED (*see* INHABIT)
Gen 36:20 the Horite who i the land
Ex 16:35 until they came to an i land
Judg 1:17 the Canaanites who i Zephath
Judg 1:21 the Jebusites who i Jerusalem
Judg 11:21 Amorites, who i that country
Prov 8:31 rejoicing in His i world, and
Is 13:20 It will never be i, nor will
Is 44:26 to Jerusalem, 'You shall be i
Is 45:18 vain, Who formed it to be i
Is 54: 3 and make the desolate cities i
Jer 6: 8 you desolate, a land not i
Jer 17: 6 in a salt land which is not i
Jer 22: 6 and cities which are not i
Jer 46:26 be i as in the days of old
Jer 50:13 the LORD she shall not be i
Jer 50:39 It shall be i no more forever
Ezek 12:20 are i shall be laid waste
Ezek 26:17 O one i by seafaring men, O
Ezek 26:19 like cities that are not i
Ezek 26:20 so that you may never be i
Ezek 34:13 in all the i places of the
Ezek 36:10 and the cities shall be i and
Ezek 36:11 I will make you i as in
Ezek 36:35 cities are now fortified and i
Ezek 38:12 waste places that are again i
Zech 2: 4 Jerusalem shall be i as
Zech 7: 7 the cities around it were i
Zech 7: 7 South and the Lowland were i
Zech 9: 5 and Ashkelon shall not be i
Zech 12: 6 be i again in her own place
Zech 14:10 up and i in her place from
Zech 14:11 Jerusalem shall be safely i

INHABITING (*see* INHABIT)
Job 26: 5 the waters and those i them
Ps 74:14 the people i the wilderness
Jer 48:18 O daughter i Dibon, come down

INHABITS (*see* INHABIT)
Job 15:28 in houses which no one i
Is 42:11 the villages that Kedar i
Is 57:15 and Lofty One Who i eternity

INHERIT (*see* INHERITANCE, INHERITED, INHERITS)
Gen 15: 7 to give you this land to i it
Gen 15: 8 shall I know that I will i it
Gen 28: 4 that you may i the land in
Ex 23:30 increased, and you i the land
Ex 32:13 and they shall i it forever
Lev 20:24 You shall i their land, and I
Lev 25:46 to i them as a possession
Num 14:24 and his descendants shall i it
Num 26:55 they shall i according to the
Num 32:19 For we will not i with them
Num 33:54 You shall i according to the
Num 34:13 land which you shall i by lot
Deut 1:38 he shall cause Israel to i it
Deut 2:31 it, that you may i his land
Deut 3:28 he shall cause them to i the
Deut 12:10 your God is giving you to i
Deut 16:20 i the land which the LORD
Deut 19: 3 your God is giving you to i
Deut 19:14 i in the land that the LORD
Deut 31: 7 you shall cause them to i it
Josh 17:14 one lot and one portion to i
1Sa 2: 8 make them i the throne of
2Ch 20:11 which You have given us to i
Job 13:26 make me i the iniquities of
Ps 25:13 descendants shall i the earth
Ps 37: 9 LORD, They shall i the earth
Ps 37:11 the meek shall i the earth
Ps 37:22 by Him shall i the earth, But
Ps 37:29 righteous shall i the land
Ps 37:34 shall exalt you to i the land
Ps 69:36 of His servants shall i it
Ps 82: 8 For You shall i all nations
Prov 3:35 The wise shall i glory, but
Prov 8:21 those who love me to i wealth
Prov 11:29 his own house will i the wind
Prov 14:18 The simple i folly, but the
Prov 28:10 blameless will i good things
Is 49: 8 earth, to cause them to i the
Is 54: 3 will i the nations, and make
Is 57:13 and shall i My holy mountain
Is 60:21 they shall i the land forever
Is 65: 9 My elect shall i it, and My
Jer 8:10 to those who will i them
Jer 12:14 caused My people Israel to i
Jer 49: 1 Why then does Milcham i Gad
Ezek 47:14 You shall i it equally with
Matt 5: 5 for they shall i the earth
Matt 19:29 and i everlasting life
Matt 25:34 i the kingdom prepared for
Mark 10:17 do that I may i eternal life
Luke 10:25 shall I do to i eternal life
Luke 18:18 shall I do to i eternal life
1Co 6: 9 will not i the kingdom of God
1Co 6:10 will i the kingdom of God
1Co 15:50 blood cannot i the kingdom of
1Co 15:50 corruption i incorruption
Gal 5:21 will not i the kingdom of God
Heb 1:14 those who will i salvation
Heb 6:12 and patience i the promises
Heb 12:17 he wanted to i the blessing
1Pe 3: 9 that you may i a blessing
Rev 21: 7 overcomes shall i all things

INHERITANCE (*see* INHERIT, INHERITANCES)
Gen 31:14 or i for us in our father's
Gen 48: 6 of their brothers in their i
Ex 15:17 in the mountain of Your i
Ex 34: 9 our sin, and take us as Your i
Lev 25:46 you may take them as an i for
Num 16:14 nor given us i of fields

Num 18:20 shall have no i in their land
Num 18:20 your i among the children of
Num 18:21 an i in return for the work
Num 18:23 Israel they shall have no i
Num 18:24 given to the Levites as an i
Num 18:24 Israel they shall have no i
Num 18:26 given you from them as your i
Num 26:53 land shall be divided as an i
Num 26:54 you shall give a larger i
Num 26:54 you shall give a smaller i
Num 26:54 Each shall be given its i
Num 26:56 i shall be divided between
Num 26:62 because there was no i given
Num 27: 7 of i among their father's
Num 27: 7 cause the i of their father
Num 27: 8 his i to pass to his daughter
Num 27: 9 give his i to his brothers
Num 27:10 then you shall give his i to
Num 27:11 then you shall give his i to
Num 32:18 of Israel has received his i
Num 32:19 because our i has fallen to
Num 32:32 our i shall remain with us on
Num 33:54 as an i among your families
Num 33:54 you shall give a larger i
Num 33:54 you shall give a smaller i
Num 33:54 there everyone's i shall be
Num 34: 2 shall fall to you as an i
Num 34:14 have received their i
Num 34:14 Manasseh has received its i
Num 34:15 have received their i on this
Num 34:17 the land among you as an i
Num 34:18 to divide the land for the i
Num 34:29 the i among the children of
Num 35: 2 the i of their possession
Num 35: 8 to the i that each inherits
Num 36: 2 to give the land as an i by
Num 36: 2 by the LORD to give the i of
Num 36: 3 then their i will be taken
Num 36: 3 from the i of our fathers
Num 36: 3 the i of the tribe into which
Num 36: 3 taken from the lot of our i
Num 36: 4 then their i will be added to
Num 36: 4 will be added to the i of the
Num 36: 4 so their i will be taken away
Num 36: 4 i of the tribe of our fathers
Num 36: 7 So the i of the children of
Num 36: 7 of Israel shall keep the i of
Num 36: 8 an i in any tribe of the
Num 36: 8 possess the i of his fathers
Num 36: 9 Thus no i shall change hands
Num 36: 9 Israel shall keep its own i
Num 36:12 their i remained in the tribe
Deut 4:20 to be His people, His i, as
Deut 4:21 God is giving you as an i
Deut 4:38 give you their land as an i
Deut 9:26 Your i whom You have
Deut 9:29 are Your people and Your i
Deut 10: 9 nor i with his brethren
Deut 10: 9 the LORD is his i, just as
Deut 12: 9 the i which the LORD your God
Deut 12:12 has no portion nor i with you
Deut 14:27 he has no part nor i with you
Deut 14:29 has no portion nor i with you
Deut 15: 4 giving you to possess as an i
Deut 18: 1 no part nor i with Israel
Deut 18: 2 they shall have no i among
Deut 18: 2 the LORD is their i, as He
Deut 18: 8 comes from the sale of his i
Deut 19:10 God is giving you as an i
Deut 19:14 set, in your i which you will
Deut 20:16 your God gives you as an i
Deut 21:23 God is giving you as an i
Deut 24: 4 God is giving you as an i
Deut 25:19 giving you to possess as an i
Deut 26: 1 God is giving you as an i
Deut 29: 8 and gave it as an i to the
Deut 32: 8 their i to the nations, when
Deut 32: 9 Jacob is the place of His i
Josh 1: 6 you shall divide as an i the
Josh 11:23 Joshua gave it as an i to
Josh 13: 6 it by lot to Israel as an i
Josh 13: 7 as an i to the nine tribes
Josh 13: 8 the Gadites received their i
Josh 13:14 of Levi he had given no i
Josh 13:14 made by fire are their i, as
Josh 13:15 the children of Reuben an i
Josh 13:23 This was the i of the
Josh 13:24 an i to the tribe of Gad, to
Josh 13:28 This is the i of the children
Josh 13:29 Moses also gave an i to half
Josh 13:32 an i in the plains of Moab on
Josh 13:33 of Levi Moses had given no i
Josh 13:33 God of Israel was their i
Josh 14: 1 distributed as an i to them
Josh 14: 2 Their i was by lot, as the
Josh 14: 3 given the i of the two tribes
Josh 14: 3 he had given no i among them
Josh 14: 9 has trodden shall be your i
Josh 14:13 the son of Jephunneh as an i
Josh 14:14 the i of Caleb the son of
Josh 15:20 This was the i of the tribe
Josh 16: 4 and Ephraim, took their i
Josh 16: 5 The border of their i on the
Josh 16: 8 This was the i of the tribe
Josh 16: 9 of Ephraim were among the i
Josh 17: 4 us an i among our brothers
Josh 17: 4 he gave them an i among their
Josh 17: 6 received an i among his sons
Josh 18: 2 had not yet received their i
Josh 18: 4 it according to their i, and
Josh 18: 7 of the LORD is their i
Josh 18: 7 have received their i beyond
Josh 18:20 This was the i of the
Josh 18:28 This was the i of the
Josh 19: 1 And their i was within the
Josh 19: 1 i of the children of Judah
Josh 19: 2 in their i Beersheba (Sheba)
Josh 19: 8 This was the i of the tribe
Josh 19: 9 The i of the children of
Josh 19: 9 of Simeon had their i within
Josh 19: 9 within the i of that people
Josh 19:10 their i was as far as Sarid
Josh 19:16 This was the i of the
Josh 19:23 This was the i of the tribe
Josh 19:31 This was the i of the tribe
Josh 19:39 This was the i of the tribe
Josh 19:41 of their i was Zorah, Eshtaol
Josh 19:48 This is the i of the tribe of
Josh 19:49 i according to their borders
Josh 19:49 an i among them to Joshua the
Josh 19:51 of Israel divided as an i by
Josh 21: 3 to the Levites from their i
Josh 23: 4 to be an i for your tribes,
Josh 24:28 depart, each to his own i
Josh 24:30 of his i at Timnath Serah
Josh 24:32 which had become an i of the
Judg 2: 6 his own i to possess the land
Judg 2: 9 of his i at Timnath Heres
Judg 11: 2 You shall have no i in our
Judg 18: 1 an i for itself to dwell in
Judg 18: 1 i among the tribes of Israel
Judg 20: 6 territory of the i of Israel
Judg 21:17 There must be an i for the
Judg 21:23 went and returned to their i
Judg 21:24 there, every man to his i
Ruth 4: 5 the name of the dead on his i
Ruth 4: 6 myself, lest I ruin my own i
Ruth 4:10 the name of the dead on his i
1Sa 10: 1 you commander over His i
1Sa 26:19 abiding in the i of the LORD
2Sa 14:16 together from the i of God
2Sa 20: 1 nor do we have i in the son
2Sa 20:19 swallow up the i of the LORD
2Sa 21: 3 may bless the i of the LORD
1Ki 8:36 given to Your people as an i
1Ki 8:51 are Your people and Your i
1Ki 8:53 of the earth to be Your i
1Ki 12:16 We have no i in the son of
1Ki 21: 3 the i of my fathers to you
1Ki 21: 4 give you the i of my fathers
2Ki 21:14 forsake the remnant of My i
1Ch 16:18 as the allotment of your i
1Ch 28: 8 leave it as an i for your
2Ch 6:27 given to Your people as an i
2Ch 10:16 We have no i in the son of
Ezra 9:12 and leave it as an i to your
Neh 11:20 Judah, everyone in his own i
Job 31: 2 the i of the Almighty from on
Job 42:15 an i among their brothers
Ps 2: 8 You The nations for Your i
Ps 16: 5 LORD, are the portion of my i
Ps 16: 6 Yes, I have a good i
Ps 28: 9 Your people, And bless Your i
Ps 33:12 He has chosen as His own i
Ps 37:18 And their i shall be forever
Ps 47: 4 He will choose our i for us
Ps 68: 9 Whereby You confirmed Your i
Ps 74: 2 of old, The tribe of Your i
Ps 78:55 Allotted them an i by survey
Ps 78:62 And was furious with His i
Ps 78:71 His people, And Israel His i
Ps 79: 1 nations have come into Your i
Ps 94:14 Nor will He forsake His i
Ps 105:11 As the allotment of your i
Ps 106: 5 That I may glory with Your i
Ps 106:40 So that He abhorred His own i
Prov 13:22 A good man leaves an i to his
Prov 17: 2 will share an i among the
Prov 19:14 riches are an i from fathers
Prov 20:21 An i gained hastily at the
Eccl 7:11 Wisdom is good with an i, and
Is 19:25 of My hands, and Israel My i
Is 47: 6 I have profaned My i, and
Is 63:17 sake, the tribes of Your i
Jer 3:18 given as an i to your fathers
Jer 10:16 Israel is the tribe of His i
Jer 12:14 the i which I have caused My
Jer 16:18 they have filled My i with
Jer 32: 8 for the right of i is yours
Jer 49: 2 take possession of his i,"
Jer 51:19 Israel is the tribe of His i
Lam 5: 2 Our i has been turned over to
Ezek 35:15 i of the house of Israel was
Ezek 36:12 you, and you shall be their i
Ezek 44:28 be, in regard to their i,
Ezek 44:28 that I am their i
Ezek 45: 1 divide the land by lot into i
Ezek 46:16 of his i to any of his sons
Ezek 46:16 it is their possession by i
Ezek 46:17 his i to one of his servants
Ezek 46:17 But his i shall belong to his
Ezek 46:18 take any of the people's i by
Ezek 46:18 he shall provide an i for his
Ezek 47:13 i among the twelve tribes of
Ezek 47:14 shall fall to you as your i
Ezek 47:22 by lot as an i for yourselves
Ezek 47:22 they shall have an i with you
Ezek 47:23 you shall give him his i,"
Ezek 48:29 shall divide by lot as an i
Dan 12:13 will arise to your i at the
Mic 2: 2 and his house, a man and his i
Zech 2:12 as His i in the Holy Land
Matt 21:38 us kill him and seize his i
Mark 12: 7 him, and the i will be ours
Luke 12:13 to divide the i with me
Luke 20:14 him, that the i may be ours
Acts 7: 5 And God gave him no i in it
Acts 20:32 give you an i among all those
Acts 26:18 and an i among those who are
Gal 3:18 For if the i is of the law,
Eph 1:11 also we have obtained an i
Eph 1:14 i until the redemption of the
Eph 1:18 glory of His i in the saints
Eph 5: 5 has any i in the kingdom of
Col 1:12 us to be partakers of the i
Col 3:24 receive the reward of the i
Heb 1: 4 as He has by i obtained a
Heb 9:15 the promise of the eternal i
Heb 11: 8 afterward receive as an i
1Pe 1: 4 to an i incorruptible and

INHERITANCES (*see* INHERITANCE)
Josh 19:51 These were the i which

INHERITED (*see* INHERIT)
Josh 14: 1 i in the land of Canaan,
Ps 105:44 And they i the labor of the
Jer 16:19 our fathers have i lies,
Ezek 33:24 only one, and he i the land

INHERITS (*see* INHERIT)
Num 35: 8 the inheritance that each i

INIQUITIES (*see* INIQUITY)
Lev 16:21 confess over it all the i of
Lev 16:22 i to an uninhabited land
Lev 26:39 also in their fathers' i,
Ezra 9: 6 for our i have risen higher
Ezra 9: 7 very guilty, and for our i we
Ezra 9:13 us less than our i deserve
Neh 9: 2 and the i of their fathers
Job 13:23 How many are my i and sins
Job 13:26 me inherit the i of my youth
Ps 38: 4 For my i have gone over my
Ps 40:12 My i have overtaken me, so
Ps 51: 9 my sins, And blot out all my i
Ps 64: 6 They devise i
Ps 65: 3 I prevail against me
Ps 79: 8 remember former i against us
Ps 90: 8 You have set our i before You
Ps 103: 3 Who forgives all your i, Who
Ps 103:10 us according to our i

Ps 107:17 And because of their i, were
Ps 130: 3 If You, LORD, should mark i
Ps 130: 8 redeem Israel From all his i
Prov 5:22 His own i entrap the wicked
Is 43:24 have wearied Me with your i
Is 50: 1 For your i you have sold
Is 53: 5 He was bruised for our i
Is 53:11 for He shall bear their i
Is 59: 2 But your i have separated you
Is 59:12 are with us, and as for our i
Is 64: 6 all fade as a leaf, and our i
Is 64: 7 consumed us because of our i
Is 65: 7 your i and the i of
Jer 5:25 Your i have turned these
Jer 11:10 have turned back to the i of
Jer 14: 7 though our i testify against
Jer 30:14 for the multitude of your i
Jer 30:15 of the multitude of your i
Jer 33: 8 I will pardon all their i by
Lam 4:13 the i of her priests, who
Lam 5: 7 no more, but we bear their i
Ezek 24:23 you shall pine away in your i
Ezek 28:18 by the multitude of your i
Ezek 32:27 but their i will be on their
Ezek 36:31 in your own sight, for your i
Ezek 36:33 I cleanse you from all your i
Ezek 43:10 may be ashamed of their i
Dan 4:27 your i by showing mercy to
Dan 9:13 that we might turn from our i
Dan 9:16 for the i of our fathers,
Amos 3: 2 punish you for all your i
Mic 7:19 on us, and will subdue our i
Acts 3:26 every one of you from your i
Rev 18: 5 and God has remembered her i

INIQUITY (*see* INIQUITIES)
Gen 15:16 for the i of the Amorites is
Gen 44:16 out the i of your servants
Ex 20: 5 visiting the i of the fathers
Ex 28:38 that Aaron may bear the i of
Ex 28:43 that they do not incur i
Ex 34: 7 for thousands, forgiving i
Ex 34: 7 visiting the i of the fathers
Ex 34: 9 and pardon our i and our sin,
Lev 5:17 is guilty and shall bear his i
Lev 18:25 punishment of its i upon it
Lev 19: 8 who eats it shall bear his i
Lev 26:39 i in your enemies' lands
Lev 26:40 But if they confess their i
Lev 26:40 the i of their fathers, with
Num 5:15 for bringing i to remembrance
Num 5:31 the man shall be free from i
Num 14:18 in mercy, forgiving i and
Num 14:18 visiting the i of the fathers
Num 14:19 Pardon the i of this people,
Num 18: 1 with you shall bear the i
Num 18: 1 the i associated with your
Num 18:23 and they shall bear their i
Num 23:21 has not observed i in Jacob
Deut 5: 9 visiting the i of the fathers
Deut 19:15 a man concerning any i or any
Josh 22:17 Is the i of Peor not enough
Josh 22:20 did not perish alone in his i
1Sa 3:13 for the i which he knows,
1Sa 3:14 the house of Eli that the i
1Sa 15:23 and stubbornness is as i and
1Sa 20: 1 What is my i, and what is my
1Sa 20: 8 if there is i in me, kill me
1Sa 25:24 my lord, on me let this i be
2Sa 7:14 If he commits i, I will
2Sa 14: 9 let the i be on me and on my
2Sa 14:32 but if there is any i in me
2Sa 19:19 let my lord impute i to me
2Sa 22:24 and I kept myself from my i
2Sa 24:10 LORD, take away the i of Your
1Ch 21: 8 pray, take away the i of Your
2Ch 19: 7 for there is no i with the
Neh 4: 5 Do not cover their i, and do
Job 4: 8 I have seen, those who plow i
Job 7:21 and take away my i
Job 10: 6 that You should seek for my i
Job 10:14 and will not acquit me of my i
Job 11: 6 you less than your i deserves
Job 11:14 if i were in your hand, and
Job 14:17 in a bag, and You cover my i
Job 15: 5 For your i teaches your mouth
Job 15:16 Who drinks i like water
Job 20:27 The heavens will reveal his i
Job 21:19 up one's i for his children'
Job 22: 5 great, And your i without end
Job 22:23 you will remove i far from
Job 31: 3 disaster for the workers of i
Job 31:11 yes, it would be i worthy of
Job 31:28 be an i worthy of judgment
Job 31:33 by hiding my i in my bosom
Job 33: 9 and there is no i in me
Job 34: 8 company with the workers of i
Job 34:10 from the Almighty to commit i
Job 34:22 of i may hide themselves
Job 34:32 if I have done i, I will do
Job 36:10 that they turn from i
Job 36:21 Take heed, do not turn to i
Ps 5: 5 You hate all workers of i
Ps 6: 8 from me, all you workers of i
Ps 7: 3 If there is i in my hands
Ps 7:14 the wicked travails with i
Ps 10: 7 his tongue is trouble and i
Ps 14: 4 the workers of i no knowledge
Ps 18:23 And I kept myself from my i
Ps 25:11 sake, O LORD, Pardon my i
Ps 28: 3 And with the workers of i, Who
Ps 31:10 fails because of my i, And my
Ps 32: 2 the LORD does not impute i
Ps 32: 5 And my i I have not hidden
Ps 32: 5 You forgave the i of my sin
Ps 36: 2 eyes, When he finds out his i
Ps 36:12 the workers of i have fallen
Ps 37: 1 envious of the workers of i
Ps 38:18 For I will declare my i
Ps 39:11 rebukes You correct man for i
Ps 41: 6 His heart gathers i to itself
Ps 49: 5 evil, When the i at my heels
Ps 51: 2 Wash me thoroughly from my i
Ps 51: 5 I was brought forth in i
Ps 53: 1 and have done abominable i
Ps 53: 4 the workers of i no knowledge
Ps 55:10 I and trouble are also in the
Ps 56: 7 Shall they escape by i
Ps 59: 2 me from the workers of i, And
Ps 64: 2 of the workers of i,
Ps 66:18 If I regard i in my heart
Ps 69:27 Add i to their i, And
Ps 78:38 compassion, forgave their i
Ps 85: 2 forgiven the i of Your people
Ps 89:32 rod, And their i with stripes
Ps 92: 7 all the workers of i flourish
Ps 92: 9 of i shall be scattered
Ps 94: 4 All the workers of i boast in
Ps 94:16 me against the workers of i
Ps 94:20 Shall the throne of i, which
Ps 94:23 brought on them their own i
Ps 106: 6 fathers, We have committed i
Ps 106:43 were brought low for their i
Ps 107:42 And all i stops its mouth
Ps 109:14 Let the i of his fathers be
Ps 119: 3 They also do no i
Ps 119:133 let no i have dominion over
Ps 125: 3 reach out their hands to i
Ps 125: 5 away With the workers of i
Ps 141: 4 works With men who work i
Ps 141: 9 the traps of the workers of i
Prov 10:29 will come to the workers of i
Prov 16: 6 atonement is provided for i
Prov 19:28 mouth of the wicked devours i
Prov 21:15 will come to the workers of i
Prov 22: 8 He who sows i will reap
Eccl 3:16 of righteousness, i was there
Is 1: 4 nation, a people laden with i
Is 1:13 I cannot endure i and the
Is 5:18 draw i with cords of vanity
Is 6: 7 your i is taken away, and your
Is 13:11 and the wicked for their i
Is 14:21 of the i of their fathers
Is 22:14 Surely for this i there will
Is 26:21 of the earth for their i
Is 27: 9 Therefore by this the i of
Is 29:20 who watch for i are cut off
Is 30:13 therefore this i shall be to
Is 31: 2 the help of those who work i
Is 32: 6 and his heart will work i
Is 33:24 it will be forgiven their i
Is 40: 2 ended, that her i is pardoned
Is 53: 6 laid on Him the i of us all
Is 57:17 For the i of his covetousness
Is 59: 3 blood, and your fingers with i
Is 59: 4 evil and bring forth i
Is 59: 6 their works are works of i
Is 59: 7 thoughts are thoughts of i
Is 64: 9 LORD, nor remember i forever
Jer 2:22 yet your i is marked before
Jer 3:13 Only acknowledge your i, that
Jer 9: 5 weary themselves to commit i
Jer 13:22 your i your skirts have been
Jer 14:10 He will remember their i now
Jer 14:20 the i of our fathers, for we
Jer 16:10 Or what is our i
Jer 16:17 nor is their i hidden from My
Jer 16:18 will repay double for their i
Jer 18:23 no atonement for their i, nor
Jer 25:12 of the Chaldeans, for their i
Jer 31:30 one shall die for his own i
Jer 31:34 For I will forgive their i
Jer 32:18 repay the i of the fathers
Jer 33: 8 i by which they have sinned
Jer 36: 3 that I may forgive their i
Jer 36:31 and his servants for their i
Jer 50:20 The i of Israel shall be
Jer 51: 6 Do not be cut off in her i
Lam 2:14 have not uncovered your i
Lam 4: 6 the i of the daughter of my
Lam 4:22 of your i is accomplished
Lam 4:22 He will punish your i
Ezek 3:18 wicked man shall die in his i
Ezek 3:19 way, he shall die in his i
Ezek 3:20 righteousness and commits i
Ezek 4: 4 lay the i of the house of
Ezek 4: 4 on it, you shall bear their i
Ezek 4: 5 on you the years of their i
Ezek 4: 5 so you shall bear the i of
Ezek 4: 6 then you shall bear the i of
Ezek 4:17 waste away because of their i
Ezek 7:13 himself who lives in i
Ezek 7:16 them mourning, Each for his i
Ezek 7:19 their stumbling block of i
Ezek 9: 9 The i of the house of Israel
Ezek 11: 2 are the men who devise i and
Ezek 14: 3 causes them to stumble into i
Ezek 14: 4 causes him to stumble into i
Ezek 14: 7 causes him to stumble into i
Ezek 14:10 And they shall bear their i
Ezek 16:49 this was the i of your sister
Ezek 18: 8 has withdrawn his hand from i
Ezek 18:17 die for the i of his father
Ezek 18:18 he shall die for his i
Ezek 18:24 righteousness and commits i
Ezek 18:26 his righteousness, commits i
Ezek 18:26 it is because of the i which
Ezek 18:30 so that i will not be your
Ezek 21:23 bring their i to remembrance
Ezek 21:24 made your i to be remembered
Ezek 21:25 has come, whose i shall end,
Ezek 21:29 has come, whose i shall end
Ezek 28:15 till i was found in you
Ezek 28:18 by the i of your trading
Ezek 29:16 will remind them of their i
Ezek 33: 6 he is taken away in his i
Ezek 33: 8 wicked man shall die in his i
Ezek 33: 9 way, he shall die in his i
Ezek 33:13 righteousness and commits i
Ezek 33:13 but because of the i that he
Ezek 33:15 of life without committing i
Ezek 33:18 righteousness and commits i
Ezek 35: 5 when their i came to an end,
Ezek 39:23 into captivity for their i
Ezek 44:10 they shall bear their i
Ezek 44:12 of Israel to fall into i,
Ezek 44:12 that they shall bear their i
Dan 9: 5 we have sinned and committed i
Dan 9:24 to make reconciliation for i
Hos 4: 8 set their heart on their i
Hos 5: 5 and Ephraim stumble in their i
Hos 7: 1 then the i of Ephraim was
Hos 8:13 Now He will remember their i
Hos 9: 7 of the greatness of your i
Hos 9: 9 He will remember their i
Hos 10: 9 of i did not overtake them
Hos 10:13 you have reaped i
Hos 12: 8 find in me no i that is sin
Hos 13:12 The i of Ephraim is bound up
Hos 14: 1 stumbled because of your i
Hos 14: 2 Take away all i
Mic 2: 1 Woe to those who devise i
Mic 3:10 bloodshed and Jerusalem with i
Mic 7:18 a God like You, pardoning i
Hab 1: 3 Why do You show me i, and
Hab 2:12 who establishes a city by i
Zech 3: 4 have removed your i from you
Zech 3: 9 I will remove the i of that
Mal 2: 6 and turned many away from i
Luke 13:27 from Me, all you workers of i
Acts 1:18 a field with the wages of i

Acts 8:23 by bitterness and bound by **i**
1Co 13: 6 does not rejoice in **i**, but
2Ti 2:19 name of Christ depart from **i**
Jas 3: 6 is a fire, a world of **i**
2Pe 2:16 but he was rebuked for his **i**

INJURED (*see* INJURY)
Ex 22:14 and it becomes **i** or dies, the
2Ki 1: 2 room in Samaria, and was **i**
Gal 4:12 You have not **i** me at all

INJURY (*see* INJURED)
2Ki 1: 2 I shall recover from this **i**
Dan 6:23 no **i** whatever was found on
Nah 3:19 Your **i** has no healing, your

INJUSTICE
Lev 19:15 You shall do no **i** in judgment
Lev 19:35 You shall do no **i** in judgment
Deut 32: 4 a God of truth and without **i**
Job 5:16 hope, and **i** shuts her mouth
Job 6:29 Turn now, let there be no **i**
Job 6:30 Is there **i** on my tongue
Jer 2: 5 What **i** have your fathers
Jer 22:13 and his chambers by **i**, who
Mal 2: 6 **i** was not found on his lips

INK (*see* INKHORN)
Jer 36:18 wrote them with **i** in the book
2Co 3: 3 written not with **i** but by the
2Jn 12 wish to do so with paper and **i**
3Jn 13 to write to you with pen and **i**

INKHORN (*see* INK)
Ezek 9: 2 had a writer's **i** at his side
Ezek 9: 3 the writer's **i** at his side
Ezek 9:11 who had the **i** at his side

INLAID
Song 5:14 carved ivory **i** with sapphires
Ezek 27: 6 company of Ashurites have **i**

INLETS
Judg 5:17 seashore, and stayed by his **i**

INMOST
Prov 18: 8 they go down into the **i** body
Prov 23:16 my **i** being will rejoice when
Prov 26:22 they go down into the **i** body

INN (*see* INNKEEPER, INNS)
Luke 2: 7 was no room for them in the **i**
Luke 10:34 animal, brought him to an **i**

INNER
Ex 28:26 which is on the **i** side of the
1Ki 6: 5 sanctuary and the **i** sanctuary
1Ki 6:16 it inside as the **i** sanctuary
1Ki 6:19 he prepared the **i** sanctuary
1Ki 6:20 The **i** sanctuary was twenty
1Ki 6:21 the front of the **i** sanctuary
1Ki 6:22 that was by the **i** sanctuary
1Ki 6:23 Inside the **i** sanctuary he
1Ki 6:27 cherubim inside the **i** room
1Ki 6:29 temple all around, both the **i**
1Ki 6:30 with gold, both the **i** and
1Ki 6:31 For the entrance of the **i**
1Ki 6:36 he built the **i** court with
1Ki 7:12 So were the **i** court of the
1Ki 7:49 in front of the **i** sanctuary
1Ki 7:50 both for the doors of the **i**
1Ki 8: 6 into the **i** sanctuary of the
1Ki 8: 8 in front of the **i** sanctuary
1Ki 20:30 the city, into an **i** chamber
1Ki 22:25 go into an **i** chamber to hide
2Ki 9: 2 and take him to an **i** room
2Ki 10:25 went into the **i** room of the
1Ch 28:11 its **i** chambers, and the place
2Ch 3:16 as in the **i** sanctuary, and
2Ch 4:20 in front of the **i** sanctuary
2Ch 4:22 its **i** doors to the Most Holy
2Ch 5: 7 into the **i** sanctuary of the
2Ch 5: 9 in front of the **i** sanctuary
2Ch 18:24 go into an **i** chamber to hide
2Ch 29:16 **i** part of the house of the
Esth 4:11 into the **i** court to the king
Esth 5: 1 stood in the **i** court of the
Ps 49:11 Their **i** thought is that their
Prov 20:27 searching all the **i** depths of
Prov 20:30 as do stripes the **i** depths of
Is 16:11 and my **i** being for Kir Heres
Ezek 8: 3 the north gate of the **i** court
Ezek 8:16 **i** court of the LORD's house
Ezek 10: 3 the cloud filled the **i** court
Ezek 40:15 the **i** gate was fifty cubits
Ezek 40:19 front of the **i** court exterior
Ezek 40:23 A gate of the **i** court was
Ezek 40:27 also a gateway on the **i** court
Ezek 40:28 Then he brought me to the **i**
Ezek 40:32 into the **i** court facing east
Ezek 40:44 Outside the **i** gate were the
Ezek 40:44 the singers in the **i** court
Ezek 41:15 as well as the **i** temple and
Ezek 41:17 the door, even to the **i** room
Ezek 42: 3 Opposite the **i** court of
Ezek 42:15 measuring the **i** temple, he
Ezek 43: 5 brought me into the **i** court
Ezek 44:17 the gates of the **i** court,
Ezek 44:17 within the gates of the **i**
Ezek 44:21 when he enters the **i** court
Ezek 44:27 sin offering in the **i** court
Ezek 45:19 of the gate of the **i** court
Ezek 46: 1 The gateway of the **i** court
Matt 24:26 Look, He is in the **i** rooms
Luke 12: 3 have spoken in the ear in **i**
Acts 16:24 he put them into the **i** prison
Eph 3:16 His Spirit in the **i** man,

INNKEEPER (*see* INN)
Luke 10:35 denarii, gave them to the **i**

INNOCENCE (*see* INNOCENT)
Gen 20: 5 **i** of my hands I have done
Ps 26: 6 I will wash my hands in **i**
Ps 73:13 vain, And washed my hands in **i**
Hos 8: 5 it be until they attain to **i**

INNOCENT (*see* INNOCENCE, INNOCENTLY, INNOCENTS)
Ex 23: 7 do not kill the **i** and
Deut 19:10 lest **i** blood be shed in the
Deut 19:13 guilt of **i** blood from Israel
Deut 21: 8 do not lay **i** blood to the
Deut 21: 9 **i** blood from among you when
Deut 27:25 a bribe to slay an **i** person
1Sa 19: 5 will you sin against **i** blood
1Ki 2:31 the **i** blood which Joab shed
2Ki 21:16 shed very much **i** blood, till
2Ki 24: 4 also because of the **i** blood
2Ki 24: 4 filled Jerusalem with **i** blood
Job 4: 7 who ever perished being **i**
Job 9:23 laughs at the plight of the **i**
Job 9:28 that You will not hold me **i**
Job 17: 8 and the **i** stirs himself up
Job 22:19 the **i** laugh them to scorn
Job 22:30 even deliver one who is not **i**
Job 27:17 the **i** will divide the silver
Job 33: 9 I am **i**, and there is no
Ps 10: 8 places he murders the **i**
Ps 15: 5 he take a bribe against the **i**
Ps 19:13 And I shall be **i** of great
Ps 94:21 righteous, And condemn **i** blood
Ps 106:38 shed **i** blood, Even the blood
Prov 1:11 for the **i** without cause
Prov 6:17 hands that shed **i** blood,
Prov 6:29 touches her shall not be **i**
Is 59: 7 make haste to shed **i** blood
Jer 2:35 Yet you say, 'Because I am **i**
Jer 7: 6 do not shed **i** blood in this
Jer 22: 3 nor shed **i** blood in this
Jer 22:17 for shedding **i** blood, and
Jer 26:15 bring **i** blood on yourselves
Dan 6:22 I was found **i** before Him
Joel 3:19 for they have shed **i** blood in
Jon 1:14 do not charge us with **i** blood
Matt 27: 4 sinned by betraying **i** blood
Matt 27:24 I am **i** of the blood of this
Acts 20:26 am **i** of the blood of all men

INNOCENTLY (*see* INNOCENT)
2Sa 15:11 invited, and they went along **i**

INNOCENTS (*see* INNOCENT)
Jer 2:34 of the lives of the poor **i**
Jer 19: 4 place with the blood of the **i**

INNS (*see* INN)
Acts 28:15 far as Appii Forum and Three **I**

INNUMERABLE
Ps 40:12 For **i** evils have surrounded
Ps 104:25 In which are **i** teeming things
Jer 46:23 searched, because they are **i**
Luke 12: 1 when an **i** multitude of people
Heb 11:12 **i** as the sand which is by the
Heb 12:22 to an **i** company of angels,

INORDINATE
Ezek 23:11 in her **i** love than she, and in

INQUIRE (*see* INQUIRED, INQUIRES, INQUIRING, INQUIRY)
Gen 25:22 So she went to **i** of the LORD
Ex 18:15 people come to me to **i** of God
Lev 27:33 He shall not **i** whether it is
Num 27:21 who shall **i** before the LORD
Deut 12:30 that you do not **i** after their
Deut 13:14 then you shall **i**, search out,
Deut 17: 4 then you shall **i** diligently
Deut 17: 9 in those days, and **i** of them
Judg 18: 5 Please **i** of God, that we may
1Sa 9: 9 when a man went to **i** of God
1Sa 17:56 **I** whose son this young man is
1Sa 22:15 begin to **i** of God for him
1Sa 28: 7 I may go to her and **i** of her
1Ki 22: 5 Please **i** for the word of the
1Ki 22: 7 here, that we may **i** of Him
1Ki 22: 8 by whom we may **i** of the LORD
2Ki 1: 2 **i** of Baal-Zebub, the god of
2Ki 1: 3 are going to **i** of Baal-Zebub
2Ki 1: 6 sending to **i** of Baal-Zebub
2Ki 1:16 messengers to **i** of Baal-Zebub
2Ki 1:16 in Israel to **i** of His word
2Ki 3:11 that we may **i** of the LORD by
2Ki 8: 8 **i** of the LORD by him, saying,
2Ki 16:15 altar shall be for me to **i** by
2Ki 22:13 **i** of the LORD for me, for the
2Ki 22:18 who sent you to **i** of the LORD
1Ch 10:14 But he did not **i** of the LORD
1Ch 21:30 not go before it to **i** of God
2Ch 18: 4 Please **i** for the word of the
2Ch 18: 6 here, that we may **i** of Him
2Ch 18: 7 by whom we may **i** of the LORD
2Ch 32:31 whom they sent to him to **i**
2Ch 34:21 **i** of the LORD for me, and for
2Ch 34:26 who sent you to **i** of the LORD
Ezra 7:14 to **i** concerning Judah and
Job 8: 8 For **i**, please, of the former
Ps 27: 4 LORD, And to **i** in His temple
Eccl 7:10 For you do not **i** wisely
Is 21:12 If you will **i**, **i**
Jer 21: 2 Please **i** of the LORD for us,
Jer 37: 7 who sent you to Me to **i** of Me
Ezek 14: 7 to **i** of him concerning Me
Ezek 20: 1 Israel came to **i** of the LORD
Ezek 20: 3 Have you come to **i** of Me
Ezek 36:37 let the house of Israel **i** of
Matt 10:11 **i** who in it is worthy, and
Acts 9:11 **i** at the house of Judas for
Acts 23:20 to **i** more fully about him

INQUIRED (*see* INQUIRE)
Judg 6:29 And when they had **i** and asked
Judg 20:27 So the children of Israel **i**
1Sa 10:22 Therefore they **i** of the LORD
1Sa 22:10 he **i** of the LORD for him,
1Sa 22:13 have **i** of God for him, that
1Sa 23: 2 Therefore David **i** of the LORD
1Sa 23: 4 Then David **i** of the LORD once
1Sa 28: 6 when Saul **i** of the LORD, the
1Sa 30: 8 So David **i** of the LORD,
2Sa 2: 1 this that David **i** of the LORD
2Sa 5:19 David **i** of the LORD, saying,
2Sa 5:23 when David **i** of the LORD, He
2Sa 11: 3 sent and **i** about the woman
2Sa 16:23 was as if one had **i** at the
2Sa 21: 1 and David **i** of the LORD
1Ch 13: 3 for we have not **i** at it since
1Ch 14:10 And David **i** of God, saying,
1Ch 14:14 David **i** again of God, and God
Ezek 14: 3 Myself be **i** of at all by them
Ezek 14:10 punishment of the one who **i**
Ezek 20: 3 I will not be **i** of by you
Ezek 20:31 So shall I be **i** of by you
Ezek 20:31 I will not be **i** of by you
Zeph 1: 6 sought the LORD, nor **i** of Him
Matt 2: 4 he **i** of them where the Christ
John 4:52 Then he **i** of them the hour
2Co 8:23 if our brethren are **i** about
1Pe 1:10 salvation the prophets have **i**

INQUIRES (*see* INQUIRE)
Judg 4:20 **i** of you, and says, 'Is there
2Co 8:23 If anyone **i** about Titus, he

INQUIRIES (*see* INQUIRY)
Acts 23:15 make further **i** concerning him

INQUIRING (*see* INQUIRE)
John 16:19 Are you **i** among yourselves

INQUIRY (*see* INQUIRE, INQUIRIES)
Lev 10:16 **i** about the goat of the sin
Deut 19:18 judges shall make diligent **i**
Esth 2:23 when an **i** was made into the
Job 34:24 pieces mighty men without **i**
Acts 10:17 had made **i** for Simon's house
Acts 19:39 you have any other **i** to make

INSANE
1Sa 21:14 Look, you see the man is **i**
Jer 50:38 they are **i** with their idols
Hos 9: 7 fool, the spiritual man is **i**

INSATIABLE
Ezek 16:28 Assyrians, because you were **i**

INSCRIBED (*see* INSCRIPTION)
1Ch 9: 1 they were **i** in the book of
Job 19:23 that they were **i** in a book
Is 49:16 I have **i** you on the palms of

INSCRIPTION (*see* INSCRIBED)
Ex 39:30 wrote on it an **i** like the
Dan 5:25 And this is the **i** that was
Zech 3: 9 Behold, I will engrave its **i**
Matt 22:20 Whose image and **i** is this
Mark 12:16 Whose image and **i** is this
Mark 15:26 the **i** of His accusation was
Luke 20:24 Whose image and **i** does it have
Luke 23:38 an **i** also was written over
Acts 17:23 found an altar with this **i**

INSECT (*see* INSECTS)
Lev 11:21 **i** that creeps on all fours

INSECTS (*see* INSECT)
Lev 11:20 All flying **i** that creep on
Lev 11:23 But all other flying **i** which

INSERT (*see* INSERTED)
Num 4: 6 and they shall **i** its poles
Num 4: 8 and they shall **i** its poles
Num 4:11 and they shall **i** its poles
Num 4:14 badger skins, and **i** its poles

INSERTED (*see* INSERT)
Ex 40:20 **i** the poles through the rings

INSIDE (*see* PREFACE)

INSISTED (*see* INSISTENT, INSISTING)
Gen 19: 3 But he **i** strongly
Acts 15:38 But Paul **i** that they should

INSISTENT (*see* INSISTED)
Luke 23:23 But they were **i**, demanding

INSISTING (*see* INSISTED)
Acts 12:15 Yet she kept **i** that it was so

INSOLENCE (*see* INSOLENT)
1Sa 17:28 the **i** of your heart, for you

INSOLENT (*see* INSOLENCE)
Ps 31:18 Which speak **i** things proudly
Ps 94: 4 speech, and speak **i** things
Is 3: 5 will be **i** toward the elder
Zeph 3: 4 Her prophets are **i**,
1Ti 1:13 a persecutor, and an **i** man

INSPIRATION (*see* INSPIRED)
2Ti 3:16 is given by **i** of God, and is

INSPIRED (*see* INSPIRATION)
Is 41: 7 **i** him who strikes the anvil

INSTALLED
1Ki 12:32 at Bethel he **i** the priests of

INSTANT
Is 29: 5 yes, it shall be in an **i**,
Is 30:13 comes suddenly, in an **i**
Jer 18: 7 The **i** I speak concerning a
Jer 18: 9 the **i** I speak concerning a
Luke 2:38 coming in that **i** she gave

INSTEAD (*see* PREFACE)

INSTITUTION
Mal 2:11 LORD's holy **i** which He loves

INSTRUCT (*see* INSTRUCTED, INSTRUCTING, INSTRUCTION, INSTRUCTOR, INSTRUCTS)
Deut 4:36 voice, that He might **i** you
Deut 17:11 the law in which they **i** you
Neh 9:20 Your good Spirit to **i** them
Ps 32: 8 I will **i** you and teach you in
Ps 94:12 Blessed is the man whom You **i**
Song 8: 2 mother, she who used to **i** me
Dan 11:33 who understand shall **i** many
1Co 2:16 of the LORD that he may **i** Him
1Ti 4: 6 If you **i** the brethren in

INSTRUCTED (*see* INSTRUCT)
Deut 32:10 He **i** him, He kept him as the
Judg 21:20 Therefore they **i** the children
Ruth 3: 6 that her mother-in-law **i** her
2Ki 12: 2 Jehoiada the priest **i** him
1Ch 25: 7 their brethren who were **i** in
Job 4: 3 Surely you have **i** many, and
Ps 2:10 Be **i**, you judges of the earth
Prov 5:13 my ear to those who **i** me
Prov 21:11 but when the wise is **i**, he
Prov 22:19 I have **i** you today, even you
Is 8:11 **i** me that I should not walk
Is 40:14 He take counsel, and who **i** Him
Jer 6: 8 Be **i**, O Jerusalem, lest My
Jer 31:19 and after I was **i**, I struck
Dan 1: 3 Then the king **i** Ashpenaz, the
Matt 13:52 Therefore every scribe **i**
Matt 28:15 money and did as they were **i**
Luke 1: 4 things in which you were **i**
Acts 10:22 was divinely **i** by a holy
Acts 18:25 This man had been **i** in the
Rom 2:18 being **i** out of the law,
Heb 8: 5 as Moses was divinely **i** when

INSTRUCTING (*see* INSTRUCT)
Acts 7:44 **i** Moses to make it according

INSTRUCTION (*see* INSTRUCT, INSTRUCTIONS)
2Ch 35: 4 following the written **i** of
2Ch 35: 4 the written **i** of Solomon his
Job 22:22 **i** from His mouth, and lay up
Job 33:16 ears of men, and seals their **i**
Job 36:10 He also opens their ear to **i**
Ps 50:17 Seeing you hate **i** And cast My
Prov 1: 2 To know wisdom and **i**, to
Prov 1: 3 to receive the **i** of wisdom
Prov 1: 7 but fools despise wisdom and **i**
Prov 1: 8 hear the **i** of your father, and
Prov 4: 1 the **i** of a father, and give
Prov 4:13 Take firm hold of **i**, do not
Prov 5:12 How I have hated **i**, And my
Prov 5:23 He shall die for lack of **i**
Prov 6:23 reproofs of **i** are the way of
Prov 8:10 Receive my **i**, and not silver,
Prov 8:33 Hear **i** and be wise, and do not
Prov 9: 9 Give **i** to a wise man, and he
Prov 10:17 He who keeps **i** is in the way
Prov 12: 1 Whoever loves **i** loves
Prov 13: 1 wise son heeds his father's **i**
Prov 15: 5 fool despises his father's **i**
Prov 15:32 He who disdains **i** despises
Prov 15:33 the LORD is the **i** of wisdom
Prov 19:20 to counsel and receive **i**, that
Prov 19:27 Cease listening to **i**, my son,
Prov 23:12 Apply your heart to **i**, and
Prov 23:23 not sell it, also wisdom and **i**
Prov 24:32 I looked on it and received **i**
Jer 17:23 might not hear nor receive **i**
Jer 32:33 not listened to receive **i**
Jer 35:13 receive **i** to obey My words
Jer 36: 4 at the **i** of Jeremiah, all the
Jer 36: 6 you have written at my **i**, the
Jer 36:17 all these words—at his **i**?
Jer 36:27 written at the **i** of Jeremiah
Jer 36:32 who wrote on it at the **i** of
Jer 45: 1 a book at the **i** of Jeremiah
Zeph 3: 7 fear Me, you will receive **i**'
2Ti 3:16 for **i** in righteousness,

INSTRUCTIONS (*see* INSTRUCTION)
Esth 9:27 according to the written **i**
1Co 11:17 these **i** I do not praise you
Col 4:10 (about whom you received **i**
Heb 11:22 gave **i** concerning his bones

INSTRUCTOR (*see* INSTRUCT, INSTRUCTORS)
Gen 4:22 an **i** of every craftsman in
1Ch 15:22 was **i** in charge of the music,
Rom 2:20 an **i** of the foolish, a

INSTRUCTORS (*see* INSTRUCTOR)
1Co 4:15 have ten thousand **i** in Christ

INSTRUCTS (*see* INSTRUCT)
Ps 16: 7 My heart also **i** me in the
Ps 94:10 He who **i** the nations, shall
Is 28:26 For He **i** him in right

INSTRUMENT (*see* INSTRUMENTS)
1Sa 10: 5 high place with a stringed **i**
Ps 33: 2 Him with an **i** of ten strings
Ps 92: 3 On an **i** of ten strings, On
Is 54:16 forth an **i** for his work
Ezek 33:32 and can play well on an **i**

INSTRUMENTS (*see* INSTRUMENT)
Gen 49: 5 **i** of cruelty are in their
1Sa 18: 6 with joy, and with musical **i**
2Sa 6: 5 kinds of **i** made of fir wood
2Sa 6: 5 wood, on harps, on stringed **i**
1Ki 10:12 and stringed **i** for singers
1Ch 13: 8 on harps, on stringed **i**, on
1Ch 15:16 accompanied by **i** of music
1Ch 15:16 of music, stringed **i**, harps,
1Ch 15:28 making music with stringed **i**
1Ch 16: 5 Jeiel with stringed **i** and
1Ch 16:42 and the musical **i** of God
1Ch 23: 5 the LORD with musical **i**
1Ch 25: 1 with harps, stringed **i**, and
1Ch 25: 6 with cymbals, stringed **i**
2Ch 5:12 having cymbals, stringed **i**
2Ch 5:13 **i** of music, and praised the
2Ch 7: 6 the Levites also with **i** of
2Ch 9:11 and stringed **i** for singers
2Ch 20:28 to Jerusalem, with stringed **i**
2Ch 23:13 the singers with **i** of music
2Ch 29:25 with cymbals, with stringed **i**
2Ch 29:26 stood with the **i** of David
2Ch 29:27 with the **i** of David king of
2Ch 30:21 LORD, accompanied by loud **i**
2Ch 34:12 were skillful with **i** of music
Neh 12:27 with cymbals and stringed **i**
Neh 12:36 with the musical **i** of David
Ps 7:13 for Himself **i** of death
Ps 68:25 players on **i** followed after
Ps 87: 7 and the players on **i** say
Ps 150: 4 Praise Him with stringed **i**
Eccl 2: 8 and musical **i** of all kinds
Is 14:11 the sound of your stringed **i**
Is 38:20 **i** all the days of our life
Ezek 40:42 on these they laid the **i** with
Amos 5:23 the melody of your stringed **i**
Amos 6: 5 to the sound of stringed **i**
Amos 6: 5 musical **i** like David
Hab 3:19 With my stringed **i**
Rom 6:13 **i** of unrighteousness to sin
Rom 6:13 dead, and your members as **i** of

INSUBORDINATE (*see* INSUBORDINATION)
1Ti 1: 9 but for the lawless and **i**
Tit 1:10 For there are many **i**, both

INSUBORDINATION (*see* INSUBORDINATE)
Tit 1: 6 accused of dissipation or **i**

INSULT (*see* INSULTED)
Mic 2: 6 shall not return **i** for **i**

INSULTED (*see* INSULT)
Luke 18:32 and will be mocked and **i** and
Heb 10:29 and **i** the Spirit of grace

INSURRECTION (*see* INSURRECTIONISTS)
Ezra 4:19 has made **i** against kings, and
Ps 64: 2 From the **i** of the workers of
Mark 15: 7 had committed murder in the **i**
Luke 23:19 a certain **i** made in the city
Luke 23:25 one they requested, who for **i**
Acts 21:38 who some time ago raised an **i**

INSURRECTIONISTS (*see* INSURRECTION)
Mark 15: 7 was chained with his fellow **i**

INTACT
2Ki 3:25 except that they left **i** the
2Ki 7: 7 twilight, and left the camp **i**
2Ki 7:10 donkeys tied, and the tents **i**

INTEGRITY
Gen 20: 5 In the **i** of my heart and
Gen 20: 6 this in the **i** of your heart
1Ki 9: 4 walked, in **i** of heart and in
Job 2: 3 still he holds fast to his **i**
Job 2: 9 Do you still hold to your **i**
Job 4: 6 the **i** of your ways your hope
Job 27: 5 not put away my **i** from me
Job 31: 6 that God may know my **i**
Ps 7: 8 according to my **i** within me
Ps 25:21 Let **i** and uprightness preserve
Ps 26: 1 For I have walked in my **i**
Ps 26:11 for me, I will walk in my **i**
Ps 41:12 for me, You uphold me in my **i**
Ps 78:72 to the **i** of his heart, And

Prov 10: 9 walks with **i** walks securely
Prov 11: 3 The **i** of the upright will
Prov 19: 1 the poor who walks in his **i**
Prov 20: 7 righteous man walks in his **i**
Prov 28: 6 **i** than one perverse in his
Tit 2: 7 in doctrine showing **i**,

INTELLIGENT
Acts 13: 7 Sergius Paulus, an **i** man

INTEND (*see* INTENDED, INTENDING, UNINTENDED)
Ex 2:14 Do you **i** to kill me as you
2Ch 28:13 You **i** to add to our sins and
Job 6:26 Do you **i** to reprove my words,
Dan 7:25 shall **i** to change times and
John 7:35 Where does He **i** to go that we
John 7:35 Does He **i** to go to the
Acts 5:28 **i** to bring this Man's blood
Acts 5:35 **i** to do regarding these men
2Co 10: 2 I **i** to be bold against some

INTENDED (*see* INTEND)
Gen 31:20 tell him that he **i** to flee
Judg 20: 5 They **i** to kill me, but
2Ch 11:22 for he **i** to make him king
Ps 21:11 For they **i** evil against You
Ps 44:11 us up like sheep **i** for food
2Co 1:15 in this confidence I **i** to
Jas 5:11 and seen the end **i** by the Lord

INTENDING (*see* INTEND)
Gen 27:42 you by **i** to kill you
Luke 14:28 **i** to build a tower, does not
Acts 12: 4 **i** to bring him before the
Acts 14:13 **i** to sacrifice with the
Acts 20:13 there **i** to take Paul on board
Acts 20:13 **i** himself to go on foot

INTENSE
Num 11: 4 them yielded to **i** craving
1Sa 31: 3 battle became **i** against Saul
2Ki 3:26 the battle was too **i** for him
1Ch 10: 3 battle became **i** against Saul

INTENT (*see* INTENTIONS, INTENTLY, INTENTS)
Gen 6: 5 that every **i** of the thoughts
2Sa 3:37 **i** to kill Abner the son of
2Sa 17:14 to the **i** that the LORD might
2Ki 10:19 with the **i** of destroying the
1Ch 28: 9 all the **i** of the thoughts
1Ch 29:18 the **i** of the thoughts of the
Prov 21:27 he brings it with wicked **i**
Zech 1:15 but with evil **i**
1Co 10: 6 to the **i** that we should not
Eph 3:10 to the **i** that now the

INTENTIONS (*see* INTENT)
Prov 14:17 and a man of wicked **i** is hated

INTENTLY (*see* INTENT)
Luke 22:56 by the fire, looked **i** at him
Acts 3:12 Or why look so **i** at us, as
Acts 11: 6 When I observed it **i** and
Acts 13: 9 Holy Spirit, looked **i** at him
Acts 14: 9 Paul, observing him **i** and

INTENTS (*see* INTENT)
Jer 30:24 performed the **i** of His heart
Heb 4:12 thoughts and **i** of the heart

INTERCEDE (*see* INTERCESSION, INTERCESSOR)
Ex 8: 9 saying when I shall **i** for you
Ex 8:28 not go very far away. **I** for me.
1Sa 2:25 the LORD, who will **i** for him
Jer 15:11 to **i** with you in the time of

INTERCESSION (*see* INTERCEDE, INTERCESSIONS)
Is 53:12 made **i** for the transgressors
Jer 7:16 for them, nor make **i** to Me
Jer 27:18 let them now make **i** to the
Rom 8:26 the Spirit Himself makes **i**
Rom 8:27 because He makes **i** for the
Rom 8:34 God, who also makes **i** for us
Heb 7:25 ever lives to make **i** for them

INTERCESSIONS (*see* INTERCESSION)
1Ti 2: 1 supplications, prayers, **i**

INTERCESSOR (*see* INTERCEDE)
Is 59:16 wondered that there was no **i**

INTEREST (*see* INTERESTS)
Ex 22:25 you shall not charge him **i**
Lev 25:36 Take no usury or **i** from him
Deut 23:19 not charge **i** to your brother
Deut 23:19 **i** on money or food or
Deut 23:19 that is lent out at **i**
Deut 23:20 a foreigner you may charge **i**
Deut 23:20 you shall not charge **i**, that
Jer 15:10 I have neither lent for **i**
Jer 15:10 nor have men lent to me for **i**
Matt 25:27 received back my own with **i**
Luke 19:23 have collected it with **i**

INTERESTS (*see* INTEREST)
Phil 2: 4 out not only for his own **i**
Phil 2: 4 but also for the **i** of others

INTERIOR
Song 3:10 its **i** paved with love by the

INTERMARRY
1Ki 11: 2 You shall not **i** with them

INTERMINGLED
Ezra 9: 2 so that the holy seed is **i**

INTERPRET (*see* INTERPRETATION, INTERPRETED, INTERPRETER, INTERPRETING, INTERPRETS)
Gen 41: 8 who could **i** them for Pharaoh
Gen 41:15 there is no one who can **i** it
Gen 41:15 understand a dream, to **i** it
1Co 12:30 speak with tongues? Do all **i**?
1Co 14:13 a tongue pray that he may **i**
1Co 14:27 each in turn, and let one **i**

INTERPRETATION (*see* INTERPRET, INTERPRETATIONS)
Gen 40: 5 man's dream with its own **i**
Gen 40:12 This is the **i** of it
Gen 40:16 baker saw that the **i** was good
Gen 40:18 This is the **i** of it
Gen 41:11 to the **i** of his own dream
Judg 7:15 telling of the dream and its **i**
Eccl 8: 1 and who knows the **i** of a thing
Dan 2: 4 dream, and we will give the **i**
Dan 2: 5 the dream to me, and its **i**
Dan 2: 6 you tell the dream and its **i**
Dan 2: 6 tell me the dream and its **i**
Dan 2: 7 dream, and we will give its **i**
Dan 2: 9 that you can give me its **i**
Dan 2:16 he might tell the king the **i**
Dan 2:24 and I will tell the king the **i**
Dan 2:25 make known to the king the **i**
Dan 2:26 which I have seen, and its **i**
Dan 2:30 make known the **i** to the king
Dan 2:36 Now we will tell the **i** of it
Dan 2:45 is certain, and its **i** is sure
Dan 4: 6 to me the **i** of the dream
Dan 4: 7 not make known to me its **i**
Dan 4: 9 that I have seen, and its **i**
Dan 4:18 Belteshazzar, declare its **i**
Dan 4:18 to make known to me the **i**
Dan 4:19 dream or its **i** trouble you
Dan 4:19 its **i** concern your enemies
Dan 4:24 this is the **i**, O king, and
Dan 5: 7 writing, and tells me its **i**
Dan 5: 8 make known to the king its **i**
Dan 5:12 called, and he will give the **i**
Dan 5:15 and make known to me its **i**
Dan 5:15 not give the **i** of the thing
Dan 5:16 and make known to me its **i**
Dan 5:17 and make known to him the **i**
Dan 5:26 This is the **i** of each word
Dan 7:16 to me the **i** of these things
1Co 12:10 to another the **i** of tongues
1Co 14:26 has a revelation, has an **i**
2Pe 1:20 Scripture is of any private **i**

INTERPRETATIONS (*see* INTERPRETATION)
Gen 40: 8 Do not **i** belong to God
Dan 5:16 of you, that you can give **i**

INTERPRETED (*see* INTERPRET)
Gen 40:22 as Joseph had **i** to them
Gen 41:12 and he **i** our dreams for us
Gen 41:12 to each man he **i** according to
Gen 41:13 to pass just as he **i** for us

INTERPRETER (*see* INTERPRET)
Gen 40: 8 dream, and there is no **i** of it
Gen 42:23 he spoke to them through an **i**
1Co 14:28 But if there is no **i**, let him

INTERPRETING (*see* INTERPRET)
Dan 5:12 **i** dreams, solving riddles, and

INTERPRETS (*see* INTERPRET)
Deut 18:10 or one who **i** omens, or a
1Co 14: 5 tongues, unless indeed he **i**

INTERROGATED
Judg 8:14 the men of Succoth and **i** him

INTERRUPTION
Lam 3:49 and do not cease, without **i**

INTERVENE (*see* INTERVENED, INTERVENING)
Zeph 2: 7 their God will **i** for them

INTERVENED (*see* INTERVENE)
Ps 106:30 Then Phinehas stood up and **i**

INTERVENING (*see* INTERVENE)
Ezek 40:16 in their **i** archways on the

INTERVIEWED
Dan 1:19 Then the king **i** them, and

INTESTINES
2Ch 21:15 sick with a disease of your **i**
2Ch 21:15 until your **i** come out by
2Ch 21:18 **i** with an incurable disease
2Ch 21:19 that his **i** came out because

INTIMATELY
Num 31:17 woman who has known a man **i**
Num 31:18 who have not known a man **i**
Num 31:35 who had not known a man **i**
Judg 21:11 woman who has known a man **i**
Judg 21:12 who had not known a man **i**

INTIMIDATE
Luke 3:14 Do not **i** anyone or accuse

INTO (*see* PREFACE)

INTOXICATING
Lev 10: 9 Do not drink wine or **i** drink
1Sa 1:15 neither wine nor **i** drink, but
Prov 20: 1 **i** drink arouses brawling, and
Prov 31: 4 wine, nor for princes **i** drink
Is 5:11 that they may follow **i** drink
Is 5:22 valiant for mixing **i** drink
Is 28: 7 through **i** drink are out of
Is 28: 7 have erred through **i** drink
Is 28: 7 of the way through **i** drink
Is 29: 9 stagger, but not with **i** drink
Is 56:12 fill ourselves with **i** drink

INTRICATE (*see* INTRICATELY)
Job 10: 8 and fashioned me, an **i** unity

INTRICATELY (*see* INTRICATE)
Ex 28: 8 the **i** woven band of the ephod
Ex 28:27 the **i** woven band of the ephod
Ex 28:28 the **i** woven band of the ephod
Ex 29: 5 gird him with the **i** woven
Ex 39: 5 the **i** woven band of his ephod
Ex 39:20 the **i** woven band of the ephod
Ex 39:21 the **i** woven band of the ephod
Lev 8: 7 and he girded him with the **i**

INTRIGUE
Dan 11:21 and seize the kingdom by **i**
Dan 11:34 shall join with them by **i**

INTRUDING
Col 2:18 **i** into those things which he

INVADE (*see* INVADED, INVASION)
2Ch 20:10 You would not let Israel **i**
Hab 3:16 He will **i** them with his

INVADED (*see* INVADE)
1Sa 23:27 Philistines have **i** the land
1Sa 30: 1 Amalekites had **i** the South
2Ki 13:20 **i** the land in the spring of
2Ch 21:17 **i** it, and carried away all the
2Ch 28:18 The Philistines also had **i**

INVASION (*see* INVADE)
1Sa 30:14 We made an **i** of the southern

INVENT (*see* INVENTED, INVENTORS)
Neh 6: 8 but you **i** them in your own
Amos 6: 5 and **i** for yourselves musical

INVENTED (*see* INVENT)
2Ch 26:15 **i** by skillful men, to be on

INVENTORS (*see* INVENT)
Rom 1:30 **i** of evil things, disobedient

INVENTORY
Ex 38:21 This is the i of the

INVISIBLE
Rom 1:20 creation of the world His i
Col 1:15 He is the image of the i God
Col 1:16 are on earth, visible and i
1Ti 1:17 the King eternal, immortal, i
Heb 11:27 as seeing Him who is i

INVITE (*see* INVITED, INVITES)
1Sa 16: 3 Then i Jesse to the sacrifice
1Ki 1:10 But he did not i Nathan the
Job 1: 4 i their three sisters to eat
Zech 3:10 Everyone will i his neighbor
Matt 22: 9 as you find, i to the wedding
Luke 14:12 lest they also i you back
Luke 14:13 i the poor, the maimed, the

INVITED (*see* INVITE)
Num 25: 2 They i the people to the
Judg 14:15 Have you i us in order to
1Sa 9:13 those who are i will eat
1Sa 9:22 honor among those who were i
1Sa 9:24 since I said I i the people
1Sa 16: 5 and i them to the sacrifice
2Sa 13:23 so Absalom i all the king's
2Sa 15:11 men from Jerusalem who were i
1Ki 1: 9 he also i all his brothers,
1Ki 1:19 has i all the sons of the
1Ki 1:19 your servant he has not i
1Ki 1:25 has i all the king's sons, and
1Ki 1:26 But he has not i me, even me
Esth 5:12 Queen Esther i no one but me
Esth 5:12 tomorrow I am again i by her
Lam 2:22 You have i as to a feast day
Zeph 1: 7 He has i His guests
Matt 22: 3 who were i to the wedding
Matt 22: 4 saying, 'Tell those who are i
Matt 22: 8 who were i were not worthy
Luke 7:39 who had i Him saw this, he
Luke 14: 7 a parable to those who were i
Luke 14: 8 When you are i by anyone to a
Luke 14: 8 than you be i by him
Luke 14: 9 and he who i you and him come
Luke 14:10 But when you are i, go and sit
Luke 14:10 so that when he who i you
Luke 14:12 He also said to him who i Him
Luke 14:16 a great supper and i many,
Luke 14:17 to say to those who were i
Luke 14:24 were i shall taste my supper
John 2: 2 were i to the wedding
Acts 10:23 Then he i them in and lodged
Acts 28:14 and were i to stay with them

INVITES (*see* INVITE)
Ex 34:15 gods, and one of them i you
1Co 10:27 not believe i you to dinner

INVOLVED (*see* INVOLVES)
Hos 5: 2 are deeply i in slaughter

INVOLVES (*see* INVOLVED)
1Jn 4:18 fear, because fear i torment

INWARD (*see* INWARDLY)
Ex 39:19 which was on the i side of
2Sa 5: 9 around from the Millo and i
1Ki 7:25 their back parts pointed i
2Ch 3:13 their feet, and they faced i
2Ch 4: 4 their back parts pointed i
Ps 5: 9 Their i part is destruction
Ps 51: 6 desire truth in the i parts
Ps 64: 6 Both the i thought and the
Ps 139:13 You have formed my i parts
Luke 11:39 but your i part is full of
Rom 7:22 of God according to the i man
2Co 4:16 yet the i man is being

INWARDLY (*see* INWARD)
Ps 62: 4 their mouth, But they curse i
Matt 7:15 but i they are ravenous
Rom 2:29 but he is a Jew who is one i

IPHDEIAH
1Ch 8:25 I, and Penuel were the sons of

IR
1Ch 7:12 and Huppim were the sons of I

IRA
2Sa 20:26 I the Jairite was a chief
2Sa 23:26 I the son of Ikkesh the
2Sa 23:38 I the Ithrite, Gareb the
1Ch 11:28 I the son of Ikkesh the
1Ch 11:40 I the Ithrite, Gareb the
1Ch 27: 9 was I the son of Ikkesh the

IRAD
Gen 4:18 To Enoch was born I
Gen 4:18 I begot Mehujael, and Mehujael

IRAM
Gen 36:43 Chief Magdiel, and Chief I
1Ch 1:54 Chief Magdiel, and Chief I

IRI
1Ch 7: 7 Uzzi, Uzziel, Jerimoth, and I

IRIJAH
Jer 37:13 was I the son of Shelemiah
Jer 37:14 So I seized Jeremiah and

IR-NAHASH (*see* NAHASH)
1Ch 4:12 and Tehinnah the father of I

IRON (*see* IRONS)
Gen 4:22 craftsman in bronze and i
Lev 26:19 will make your heavens like i
Num 31:22 the silver, the bronze, the i
Num 35:16 him with an i implement, so
Deut 3:11 bedstead was an i bedstead
Deut 4:20 you out of the i furnace, out
Deut 8: 9 a land whose stones are i
Deut 27: 5 not use any i tool on them
Deut 28:23 which is under you shall be i
Deut 28:48 He will put a yoke of i on
Deut 33:25 Your sandals shall be i and
Josh 6:19 and vessels of bronze and i
Josh 6:24 and the vessels of bronze and i
Josh 8:31 no man has wielded any i tool
Josh 17:16 the valley have chariots of i
Josh 17:18 though they have i chariots
Josh 22: 8 gold, with bronze, with i
Judg 1:19 they had chariots of i
Judg 4: 3 nine hundred chariots of i
Judg 4:13 nine hundred chariots of i
1Sa 17: 7 his i spearhead weighed six
2Sa 12:31 i picks and i axes, and made
2Sa 12:31 i axes, and made them cross
2Sa 23: 7 them must be armed with i
1Ki 6: 7 any i tool was heard in the
1Ki 8:51 Egypt, out of the i furnace)
1Ki 22:11 made horns of i for himself
2Ki 6: 5 the i ax head fell into the
2Ki 6: 6 and he made the i float
1Ch 20: 3 with i picks, and with axes
1Ch 22: 3 David prepared i in abundance
1Ch 22:14 i beyond measure, for it is
1Ch 22:16 bronze and i there is no limit
1Ch 29: 2 i for things of i, wood
1Ch 29: 7 hundred thousand talents of i
2Ch 2: 7 and silver, in bronze and i
2Ch 2:14 gold and silver, bronze and i
2Ch 18:10 made horns of i for himself
2Ch 24:12 and also those who worked in i
Job 19:24 on a rock with an i pen and
Job 20:24 will flee from the i weapon
Job 28: 2 I is taken from the earth, and
Job 40:18 his ribs like bars of i
Job 41:27 He regards i as straw, and
Ps 2: 9 break them with a rod of i
Ps 107:16 And cut the bars of i in two
Ps 149: 8 nobles with fetters of i
Prov 27:17 As i sharpens i, so a man
Is 10:34 thickets of the forest with i
Is 45: 2 bronze and cut the bars of i
Is 48: 4 and your neck was an i sinew
Is 60:17 instead of i I will bring
Is 60:17 and instead of stones, i
Jer 1:18 an i pillar, and bronze walls
Jer 6:28 They are bronze and i, they
Jer 11: 4 of Egypt, from the i furnace
Jer 15:12 break i, the northern i
Jer 17: 1 is written with a pen of i
Jer 28:13 in their place yokes of i
Jer 28:14 I have put a yoke of i on the
Ezek 4: 3 take for yourself an i plate
Ezek 4: 3 set it as an i wall between
Ezek 22:18 they are all bronze, tin, i
Ezek 22:20 men gather silver, bronze, i
Ezek 27:12 They gave you silver, i, tin,
Ezek 27:19 Wrought i, cassia, and cane
Dan 2:33 its legs of i,
Dan 2:33 its feet partly of i
Dan 2:34 the image on its feet of i
Dan 2:35 Then the i, the clay, the
Dan 2:40 shall be as strong as i,
Dan 2:40 as i breaks in pieces
Dan 2:40 like i that crushes, that
Dan 2:41 potter's clay and partly of i
Dan 2:41 of the i shall be in it, just
Dan 2:41 just as you saw the i mixed
Dan 2:42 of the feet were partly of i
Dan 2:43 As you saw i mixed with
Dan 2:43 just as i does not mix with
Dan 2:45 that it broke in pieces the i
Dan 4:15 earth, bound with a band of i
Dan 4:23 earth, bound with a band of i
Dan 5: 4 gold and silver, bronze and i
Dan 5:23 silver and gold, bronze and i
Dan 7: 7 It had huge i teeth
Dan 7:19 dreadful, with its teeth of i
Amos 1: 3 Gilead with implements of i
Mic 4:13 for I will make your horn i
Acts 12:10 they came to the i gate that
1Ti 4: 2 seared with a hot i,
Rev 2:27 rule them with a rod of i
Rev 9: 9 like breastplates of i, and
Rev 12: 5 all nations with a rod of i
Rev 18:12 most precious wood, bronze, i
Rev 19:15 rule them with a rod of i

IRON*
Josh 19:38 I, Migdal El, Horem, Beth

IRONS (*see* IRON)
Ps 105:18 fetters, He was laid in i
Ps 107:10 Bound in affliction and i

IRPEEL
Josh 18:27 Rekem, I, Taralah,

IRREPROACHABLE
Col 1:22 blameless, and i in His sight

IRREVOCABLE
Rom 11:29 and the calling of God are i

IRRITANTS
Num 33:55 shall be i in your eyes and

IR SHEMESH
Josh 19:41 was Zorah, Eshtaol, I,

IRU
1Ch 4:15 the son of Jephunneh were I

IS (*see* PREFACE)

ISAAC (*see* ISAAC'S)
Gen 17:19 and you shall call his name I
Gen 17:21 I will establish with I, whom
Gen 21: 3 whom Sarah bore to him—I.
Gen 21: 4 I when he was eight days old
Gen 21: 5 his son I was born to him
Gen 21: 8 same day that I was weaned
Gen 21:10 with my son, namely with I
Gen 21:12 for in I your seed shall be
Gen 22: 2 now your son, your only son I
Gen 22: 3 men with him, and I his son
Gen 22: 6 and laid it on I his son
Gen 22: 7 But I spoke to Abraham his
Gen 22: 9 and he bound I his son and laid
Gen 24: 4 and take a wife for my son I
Gen 24:14 appointed for Your servant I
Gen 24:62 Now I came from the way of
Gen 24:63 I went out to meditate in the
Gen 24:64 when she saw I she dismounted
Gen 24:66 the servant told I all the
Gen 24:67 Then I brought her into his
Gen 24:67 So I was comforted after his
Gen 25: 5 gave all that he had to I
Gen 25: 6 eastward, away from I his son
Gen 25: 9 And his sons I and Ishmael
Gen 25:11 that God blessed his son I
Gen 25:11 I dwelt at Beer Lahai Roi
Gen 25:19 This is the genealogy of I
Gen 25:19 Abraham begot I
Gen 25:20 I was forty years old when he
Gen 25:21 Now I pleaded with the LORD
Gen 25:26 I was sixty years old when
Gen 25:28 I loved Esau because he ate
Gen 26: 1 I went to Abimelech king of
Gen 26: 6 So I dwelt in Gerar
Gen 26: 8 and saw, and there was I,
Gen 26: 9 Then Abimelech called I and
Gen 26: 9 And I said to him,
Gen 26:12 Then I sowed in that land, and
Gen 26:16 And Abimelech said to I, Go
Gen 26:17 Then I departed from there and
Gen 26:18 And I dug again the wells of
Gen 26:27 And I said to them,
Gen 26:31 I sent them away, and they

Gen 26:35 were a grief of mind to **I**
Gen 27: 1 when **I** was old and his eyes
Gen 27: 5 when **I** spoke to Esau his son
Gen 27:20 But **I** said to his son, "How
Gen 27:21 Then **I** said to Jacob
Gen 27:22 went near to **I** his father
Gen 27:26 Then his father **I** said to him
Gen 27:30 as soon as **I** had finished
Gen 27:30 the presence of **I** his father
Gen 27:32 his father **I** said to him,
Gen 27:33 Then **I** trembled exceedingly,
Gen 27:37 Then **I** answered and said to
Gen 27:39 Then **I** his father answered and
Gen 27:46 And Rebekah said to **I**, "I am
Gen 28: 1 Then **I** called Jacob and
Gen 28: 5 So **I** sent Jacob away, and he
Gen 28: 6 Esau saw that **I** had blessed
Gen 28: 8 did not please his father **I**
Gen 28:13 your father and the God of **I**
Gen 31:18 to go to his father **I** in the
Gen 31:42 of Abraham and the Fear of **I**
Gen 31:53 by the Fear of his father **I**
Gen 32: 9 and God of my father **I**
Gen 35:12 Abraham and **I** I give to you
Gen 35:27 came to his father **I** at Mamre
Gen 35:27 Abraham and **I** had sojourned
Gen 35:28 Now the days of **I** were one
Gen 35:29 So **I** breathed his last and
Gen 46: 1 to the God of his father **I**
Gen 48:15 **I** walked, the God who has fed
Gen 48:16 of my fathers Abraham and **I**
Gen 49:31 his wife, there they buried **I**
Gen 50:24 He swore to Abraham, to **I**
Ex 2:24 covenant with Abraham, with **I**
Ex 3: 6 God of Abraham, the God of **I**
Ex 3:15 God of Abraham, the God of **I**
Ex 3:16 the God of Abraham, of **I**
Ex 4: 5 God of Abraham, the God of **I**
Ex 6: 3 I appeared to Abraham, to **I**
Ex 6: 8 I swore to give to Abraham, **I**
Ex 32:13 Remember Abraham, **I**, and
Ex 33: 1 which I swore to Abraham, **I**
Lev 26:42 Jacob, and My covenant with **I**
Num 32:11 which I swore to Abraham, **I**
Deut 1: 8 to Abraham, **I**, and Jacob
Deut 6:10 your fathers, to Abraham, **I**
Deut 9: 5 your fathers, to Abraham, **I**
Deut 9:27 Your servants, Abraham, **I**
Deut 29:13 your fathers, to Abraham, **I**
Deut 30:20 your fathers, to Abraham, **I**
Deut 34: 4 I swore to give Abraham, **I**
Josh 24: 3 his descendants and gave him **I**
Josh 24: 4 To **I** I gave Jacob and Esau
1Ki 18:36 LORD God of Abraham, **I**, and
2Ki 13:23 His covenant with Abraham, **I**
1Ch 1:28 The sons of Abraham were **I**
1Ch 1:34 And Abraham begot **I**
1Ch 1:34 The sons of **I** were Esau and
1Ch 16:16 Abraham, and His oath to **I**
1Ch 29:18 O LORD God of Abraham, **I**, and
2Ch 30: 6 to the LORD God of Abraham, **I**
Ps 105: 9 Abraham, And His oath to **I**
Jer 33:26 the descendants of Abraham, **I**
Amos 7: 9 places of **I** shall be desolate
Amos 7:16 spout against the house of **I**
Matt 1: 2 Abraham begot **I**
Matt 1: 2 **I** begot Jacob
Matt 8:11 and sit down with Abraham, **I**
Matt 22:32 God of Abraham, the God of **I**
Mark 12:26 God of Abraham, the God of **I**
Luke 3:34 son of Jacob, the son of **I**
Luke 13:28 when you see Abraham and **I**
Luke 20:37 God of Abraham, the God of **I**
Acts 3:13 The God of Abraham, **I**, and
Acts 7: 8 and so Abraham begot **I** and
Acts 7: 8 **I** begot Jacob, and Jacob begot
Acts 7:32 God of Abraham, the God of **I**
Rom 9: 7 In **I** your seed shall be
Rom 9:10 one man, even by our father **I**
Gal 4:28 as **I** was, are children of
Heb 11: 9 dwelling in tents with **I**
Heb 11:17 he was tested, offered up **I**
Heb 11:18 In **I** your seed shall be
Heb 11:20 By faith **I** blessed Jacob and
Jas 2:21 **I** his son on the altar

ISAAC'S (*see* ISAAC)
Gen 26:19 Also **I** servants dug in the
Gen 26:20 quarreled with **I** herdsmen
Gen 26:25 there **I** servants dug a well
Gen 26:32 same day that **I** servants came

ISAIAH (*see* ISSHIAH)
2Ki 19: 2 to **I** the prophet, the son of
2Ki 19: 5 of King Hezekiah came to **I**
2Ki 19: 6 And **I** said to them,
2Ki 19:20 Then **I** the son of Amoz sent
2Ki 20: 1 **I** the prophet, the son of
2Ki 20: 4 before **I** had gone out into
2Ki 20: 7 Then **I** said, "Take a lump of
2Ki 20: 8 And Hezekiah said to **I**, "What
2Ki 20: 9 Then **I** said, "This is the
2Ki 20:11 So **I** the prophet cried out to
2Ki 20:14 Then **I** the prophet went to
2Ki 20:16 Then **I** said to Hezekiah
2Ki 20:19 Then Hezekiah said to **I**
2Ch 26:22 the prophet **I** the son of Amoz
2Ch 32:20 Hezekiah and the prophet **I**
2Ch 32:32 the vision of **I** the prophet
Is 1: 1 The vision of **I** the son of
Is 2: 1 The word that **I** the son of
Is 7: 3 Then the LORD said to **I**, "Go
Is 13: 1 which **I** the son of Amoz saw
Is 20: 2 spoke by **I** the son of Amoz
Is 20: 3 My servant **I** has walked naked
Is 37: 2 to **I** the prophet, the son of
Is 37: 5 of King Hezekiah came to **I**
Is 37: 6 And **I** said to them,
Is 37:21 Then **I** the son of Amoz sent
Is 38: 1 **I** the prophet, the son of
Is 38: 4 word of the LORD came to **I**
Is 38:21 Now **I** had said, "Let them
Is 39: 3 Then **I** the prophet went to
Is 39: 5 Then **I** said to Hezekiah
Is 39: 8 Then Hezekiah said to **I**
Matt 3: 3 spoken of by the prophet **I**
Matt 4:14 was spoken by **I** the prophet
Matt 8:17 was spoken by **I** the prophet
Matt 12:17 was spoken by **I** the prophet
Matt 13:14 prophecy of **I** is fulfilled
Matt 15: 7 Well did **I** prophesy about you
Mark 7: 6 Well did **I** prophesy of you
Luke 3: 4 of the words of **I** the prophet
Luke 4:17 the book of the prophet **I**
John 1:23 as the prophet **I** said
John 12:38 that the word of **I** the
John 12:39 believe, because **I** said again
John 12:41 These things **I** said when he
Acts 8:28 he was reading **I** the prophet
Acts 8:30 him reading the prophet **I**
Acts 28:25 spoke rightly through **I** the
Rom 9:27 **I** also cries out concerning
Rom 9:29 And as **I** said before
Rom 10:16 For **I** says, "Lord, who has
Rom 10:20 But **I** is very bold and says
Rom 15:12 **I** says: "There shall be

ISCAH (*see* SARAH)
Gen 11:29 of Milcah and the father of **I**

ISCARIOT (*see* JUDAS)
Matt 10: 4 the Canaanite, and Judas **I**
Matt 26:14 of the twelve, called Judas **I**
Mark 3:19 and Judas **I**, who also betrayed
Mark 14:10 Then Judas **I**, one of the
Luke 6:16 Judas **I** who also became a
Luke 22: 3 entered Judas, surnamed **I**
John 6:71 He spoke of Judas **I**, the son
John 12: 4 one of His disciples, Judas **I**
John 13: 2 it into the heart of Judas **I**
John 13:26 bread, He gave it to Judas **I**
John 14:22 Judas (not **I**) said to Him,

ISHBAH (*see* NAHAM)
1Ch 4:17 and **I** the father of Eshtemoa

ISHBAK
Gen 25: 2 Jokshan, Medan, Midian, **I**
1Ch 1:32 Jokshan, Medan, Midian, **I**

ISHBI-BENOB
2Sa 21:16 Then **I**, who was one of the

ISHBOSHETH (*see* ESH-BAAL)
2Sa 2: 8 took **I** the son of Saul and
2Sa 2:10 **I**, Saul's son, was forty
2Sa 2:12 servants of **I** the son of Saul
2Sa 2:15 followers of **I** the son of
2Sa 3: 7 So **I** said to Abner,
2Sa 3: 8 very angry at the words of **I**
2Sa 3:14 So David sent messengers to **I**
2Sa 3:15 **I** sent and took her from her
2Sa 4: 5 of the day to the house of **I**
2Sa 4: 8 head of **I** to David at Hebron
2Sa 4: 8 Here is the head of **I**, the
2Sa 4:12 But they took the head of **I**

ISHHOD
1Ch 7:18 His sister Hammoleketh bore **I**

ISHI
1Ch 2:31 The son of Appaim was **I**, the
1Ch 2:31 the son of **I** was Sheshan, and
1Ch 4:20 And the sons of **I** were Zoheth
1Ch 4:42 and Uzziel, the sons of **I**
1Ch 5:24 Epher, **I**, Eliel, Azriel,

ISHIAH
1Ch 7: 3 Michael, Obadiah, Joel, and **I**

ISHIJAH
Ezra 10:31 Eliezer, **I**, Malchijah,

ISHMA
1Ch 4: 3 Jezreel, **I**, and Idbash

ISHMAEL (*see* ISHMAELITE, ISHMAEL'S)
Gen 16:11 You shall call his name **I**
Gen 16:15 his son, whom Hagar bore, **I**
Gen 16:16 when Hagar bore **I** to Abram
Gen 17:18 that **I** might live before You
Gen 17:20 And as for **I**, I have heard you
Gen 17:23 So Abraham took **I** his son
Gen 17:25 **I** his son was thirteen years
Gen 17:26 was circumcised, and his son **I**
Gen 25: 9 **I** buried him in the cave of
Gen 25:12 this is the genealogy of **I**
Gen 25:13 the names of the sons of **I**
Gen 25:13 The firstborn of **I**, Nebajoth
Gen 25:16 These were the sons of **I** and
Gen 25:17 the years of the life of **I**
Gen 28: 9 So Esau went to **I** and took
Gen 28: 9 Mahalath the daughter of **I**
2Ki 25:23 **I** the son of Nethaniah,
2Ki 25:25 that **I** the son of Nethaniah
1Ch 1:28 of Abraham were Isaac and **I**
1Ch 1:29 firstborn of **I** was Nabajoth
1Ch 1:31 These were the sons of **I**
1Ch 8:38 Azrikam, Bocheru, **I**, Sheariah
1Ch 9:44 Azrikam, Bocheru, **I**, Sheariah
2Ch 19:11 and Zebadiah the son of **I**, the
2Ch 23: 1 **I** the son of Jehohanan,
Ezra 10:22 Elioenai, Maaseiah, **I**,
Jer 40: 8 **I** the son of Nethaniah,
Jer 40:14 **I** the son of Nethaniah to
Jer 40:15 and I will kill **I** the son of
Jer 40:16 speak falsely concerning **I**
Jer 41: 1 that **I** the son of Nethaniah
Jer 41: 2 Then **I** the son of Nethaniah,
Jer 41: 3 **I** also struck down all the
Jer 41: 6 Now **I** the son of Nethaniah
Jer 41: 7 that **I** the son of Nethaniah
Jer 41: 8 among them who said to **I**
Jer 41: 9 which **I** had cast all the dead
Jer 41: 9 **I** the son of Nethaniah filled
Jer 41:10 Then **I** carried away captive
Jer 41:10 And **I** the son of Nethaniah
Jer 41:11 **I** the son of Nethaniah had
Jer 41:12 went to fight with **I** the son
Jer 41:13 with **I** saw Johanan the son of
Jer 41:14 **I** had carried away captive
Jer 41:15 But **I** the son of Nethaniah
Jer 41:16 **I** the son of Nethaniah after
Jer 41:18 of them, because **I** the son of

ISHMAELITE (*see* ISHMAEL, ISHMAELITES)
1Ch 2:17 of Amasa was Jether the **I**
1Ch 27:30 Obil the **I** was over the

ISHMAELITES (*see* ISHMAELITE)
Gen 37:25 and there was a company of **I**
Gen 37:27 and let us sell him to the **I**
Gen 37:28 sold him to the **I** for twenty
Gen 39: 1 bought him from the **I** who had
Judg 8:24 earrings, because they were **I**
Ps 83: 6 The tents of Edom and the **I**

ISHMAEL'S (*see* ISHMAEL)
Gen 36: 3 **I** daughter, sister of

ISHMAIAH
1Ch 12: 4 **I** the Gibeonite, a mighty man
1Ch 27:19 Zebulun, **I** the son of Obadiah

ISHMERAI
1Ch 8:18 **I**, Jizliah, and Jobab were the

ISHPAN
1Ch 8:22 **I**, Eber, Eliel,

ISH-TOB (*see* TOB)
2Sa 10: 6 from I twelve thousand men
2Sa 10: 8 the Syrians of Zoba, Rehob, I

ISHUAH
Gen 46:17 sons of Asher were Jimnah, I

ISHVAH
1Ch 7:30 sons of Asher were Imnah, I

ISHVI
1Ch 7:30 Asher were Imnah, Ishvah, I

ISLAND (*see* ISLANDS, ISLES)
Acts 13: 6 gone through the i to Paphos
Acts 27:16 shelter of an i called Clauda
Acts 27:26 run aground on a certain i
Acts 28: 1 that the i was called Malta
Acts 28: 7 the leading citizen of the i
Acts 28: 9 the rest of those on the i
Acts 28:11 which had wintered at the i
Rev 1: 9 was on the i that is called
Rev 6:14 i was moved out of its place
Rev 16:20 Then every i fled away, and

ISLANDS (*see* ISLAND)
Esth 10: 1 land and on the i of the sea
Is 11:11 Hamath and the i of the sea

ISLES (*see* ISLAND)
Ps 72:10 of the i Will bring presents
Ps 97: 1 the multitude of i be glad
Is 40:15 He lifts up the i as a very
Jer 31:10 declare it in the i afar off
Ezek 27:15 many i were the market of
Ezek 27:35 i will be astonished at you

ISMACHIAH
2Ch 31:13 Jerimoth, Jozabad, Eliel, I

ISOLATE (*see* ISOLATED, ISOLATES)
Lev 13: 4 then the priest shall i the
Lev 13: 5 then the priest shall i him
Lev 13:11 unclean, and shall not i him
Lev 13:21 priest shall i him seven days
Lev 13:26 priest shall i him seven days
Lev 13:31 then the priest shall i the
Lev 13:33 the priest shall i the one
Lev 13:50 i that which has the plague
Lev 13:54 he shall i it another seven

ISOLATED (*see* ISOLATE)
2Ki 15: 5 so he dwelt in an i house
2Ch 26:21 He dwelt in an i house,

ISOLATES (*see* ISOLATE)
Prov 18: 1 A man who i himself seeks his

ISPAH
1Ch 8:16 Michael, I, and Joha were the

ISRAEL (*see* ISRAELITE, ISRAEL'S, JACOB)
Gen 32:28 longer be called Jacob, but I
Gen 32:32 I do not eat the muscle that
Gen 34: 7 in I by lying with Jacob's
Gen 35:10 but I shall be your name
Gen 35:10 So He called his name I
Gen 35:21 Then I journeyed and pitched
Gen 35:22 when I dwelt in that land,
Gen 35:22 and I heard about it
Gen 36:31 over the children of I
Gen 37: 3 Now I loved Joseph more than
Gen 37:13 And I said to Joseph,
Gen 42: 5 the sons of I went to buy
Gen 43: 6 And I said, "Why did you
Gen 43: 8 Judah said to I his father
Gen 43:11 their father I said to them
Gen 45:21 Then the sons of I did so
Gen 45:28 Then I said, "It is enough
Gen 46: 1 So I took his journey with
Gen 46: 2 Then God spoke to I in the
Gen 46: 5 the sons of I carried their
Gen 46: 8 names of the children of I
Gen 46:29 Goshen to meet his father I
Gen 46:30 And I said to Joseph,
Gen 47:27 So I dwelt in the land of
Gen 47:29 drew near that I must die
Gen 47:31 So I bowed himself on the
Gen 48: 2 I strengthened himself and sat
Gen 48: 8 Then I saw Joseph's sons, and
Gen 48:10 Now the eyes of I were dim
Gen 48:11 And I said to Joseph,
Gen 48:14 Then I stretched out his
Gen 48:20 By you I will bless, saying
Gen 48:21 Then I said to Joseph
Gen 49: 2 and listen to I your father
Gen 49: 7 in Jacob and scatter them in I
Gen 49:16 as one of the tribes of I
Gen 49:24 the Shepherd, the Stone of I)
Gen 49:28 are the twelve tribes of I
Gen 50: 2 So the physicians embalmed I
Gen 50:25 oath from the children of I
Ex 1: 1 of I who came to Egypt
Ex 1: 7 children of I were fruitful
Ex 1: 9 of the children of I are more
Ex 1:12 in dread of the children of I
Ex 1:13 of I serve with rigor
Ex 2:23 Then the children of I
Ex 2:25 looked upon the children of I
Ex 3: 9 children of I has come to Me
Ex 3:10 My people, the children of I
Ex 3:11 children of I out of Egypt
Ex 3:13 I come to the children of I
Ex 3:14 say to the children of I, 'I
Ex 3:15 say to the children of I
Ex 3:16 the elders of I together, and
Ex 3:18 come, you and the elders of I
Ex 4:22 I is My son, My firstborn
Ex 4:29 elders of the children of I
Ex 4:31 had visited the children of I
Ex 5: 1 Thus says the LORD God of I
Ex 5: 2 obey His voice to let I go
Ex 5: 2 the LORD, nor will I let I go
Ex 5:14 officers of the children of I
Ex 5:15 of the children of I came
Ex 5:19 of I saw that they were in
Ex 6: 5 I whom the Egyptians keep in
Ex 6: 6 say to the children of I
Ex 6: 9 thus to the children of I
Ex 6:11 of I go out of his land
Ex 6:12 The children of I have not
Ex 6:13 command for the children of I
Ex 6:13 of I out of the land of Egypt
Ex 6:14 of Reuben, the firstborn of I
Ex 6:26 of I from the land of Egypt
Ex 6:27 the children of I from Egypt
Ex 7: 2 children of I out of his land
Ex 7: 4 My people, the children of I
Ex 7: 5 children of I from among them
Ex 9: 4 between the livestock of I
Ex 9: 4 belongs to the children of I
Ex 9: 6 of the children of I, not one
Ex 9:26 where the children of I were
Ex 9:35 he let the children of I go
Ex 10:20 not let the children of I go
Ex 10:23 of I had light in their
Ex 11: 7 none of the children of I
Ex 11: 7 between the Egyptians and I
Ex 11:10 of I go out of his land
Ex 12: 3 to all the congregation of I
Ex 12: 6 of the congregation of I
Ex 12:15 shall be cut off from I
Ex 12:19 from the congregation of I
Ex 12:21 for all the elders of I and
Ex 12:27 houses of the children of I
Ex 12:28 the children of I went away
Ex 12:31 both you and the children of I
Ex 12:35 Now the children of I had
Ex 12:37 Then the children of I
Ex 12:40 sojourn of the children of I
Ex 12:42 of I throughout their
Ex 12:47 of I shall keep it
Ex 12:50 all the children of I did
Ex 12:51 brought the children of I out
Ex 13: 2 womb among the children of I
Ex 13:18 the children of I went up in
Ex 13:19 of I under solemn oath,
Ex 14: 2 Speak to the children of I
Ex 14: 3 will say of the children of I
Ex 14: 5 that we have let I go from
Ex 14: 8 he pursued the children of I
Ex 14: 8 the children of I went out
Ex 14:10 the children of I lifted
Ex 14:10 the children of I cried out
Ex 14:15 children of I to go forward
Ex 14:16 the children of I shall go on
Ex 14:19 who went before the camp of I
Ex 14:20 Egyptians and the camp of I
Ex 14:22 So the children of I went
Ex 14:25 us flee from the face of I
Ex 14:29 But the children of I had
Ex 14:30 So the LORD saved I that day
Ex 14:30 I saw the Egyptians dead on
Ex 14:31 Thus I saw the great work
Ex 15: 1 the children of I sang this
Ex 15:19 But the children of I went on
Ex 15:22 brought I from the Red Sea
Ex 16: 1 of the children of I came to
Ex 16: 2 of the children of I murmured
Ex 16: 3 children of I said to them
Ex 16: 6 said to all the children of I
Ex 16: 9 of the children of I, Come
Ex 16:10 of the children of I, that
Ex 16:12 of the children of I
Ex 16:15 when the children of I saw it
Ex 16:17 And the children of I did so
Ex 16:31 the house of I called its
Ex 16:35 the children of I ate manna
Ex 17: 1 of the children of I set out
Ex 17: 5 you some of the elders of I
Ex 17: 6 the sight of the elders of I
Ex 17: 7 of the children of I, and
Ex 17: 8 and fought with I in Rephidim
Ex 17:11 up his hand, that I prevailed
Ex 18: 1 for Moses and for I His people
Ex 18: 1 had brought I out of Egypt
Ex 18: 9 which the LORD had done for I
Ex 18:12 of I to eat bread with Moses'
Ex 18:25 chose able men out of all I
Ex 19: 1 I had gone out of the land of
Ex 19: 2 So I camped there before the
Ex 19: 3 and tell the children of I
Ex 19: 6 speak to the children of I
Ex 20:22 say to the children of I
Ex 24: 1 and seventy of the elders of I
Ex 24: 4 to the twelve tribes of I
Ex 24: 5 men of the children of I, who
Ex 24: 9 and seventy of the elders of I
Ex 24:10 and they saw the God of I
Ex 24:11 of I He did not lay His hand
Ex 24:17 the eyes of the children of I
Ex 25: 2 Speak to the children of I
Ex 25:22 to the children of I
Ex 27:20 command the children of I
Ex 27:21 behalf of the children of I
Ex 28: 1 from among the children of I
Ex 28: 9 the names of the sons of I
Ex 28:11 the names of the sons of I
Ex 28:12 stones for the sons of I
Ex 28:21 the names of the sons of I
Ex 28:29 of I on the breastplate of
Ex 28:30 I over his heart before the
Ex 28:38 which the children of I
Ex 29:28 the children of I for Aaron
Ex 29:28 from the children of I from
Ex 29:43 meet with the children of I
Ex 29:45 dwell among the children of I
Ex 30:12 of I for their number, then
Ex 30:16 money of the children of I
Ex 30:16 children of I before the LORD
Ex 30:31 speak to the children of I
Ex 31:13 also to the children of I
Ex 31:16 of I shall keep the Sabbath
Ex 31:17 and the children of I forever
Ex 32: 4 This is your god, O I, that
Ex 32: 8 said, 'This is your god, O I
Ex 32:13 Abraham, Isaac, and I
Ex 32:20 the children of I drink it
Ex 32:27 Thus says the LORD God of I
Ex 33: 5 Say to the children of I
Ex 33: 6 So the children of I stripped
Ex 34:23 the Lord, the LORD God of I
Ex 34:27 a covenant with you and with I
Ex 34:30 the children of I saw Moses
Ex 34:32 the children of I came near
Ex 34:34 of I whatever he had been
Ex 34:35 of I saw the face of Moses
Ex 35: 1 of the children of I together
Ex 35: 4 of the children of I, saying,
Ex 35:20 of the children of I departed
Ex 35:29 The children of I brought a
Ex 35:30 said to the children of I
Ex 36: 3 which the children of I had
Ex 39: 6 the names of the sons of I
Ex 39: 7 a memorial for the sons of I
Ex 39:14 to the names of the sons of I
Ex 39:32 And the children of I did
Ex 39:42 of I did all the work
Ex 40:36 the children of I went onward
Ex 40:38 sight of all the house of I
Lev 1: 2 Speak to the children of I
Lev 4: 2 Speak to the children of I
Lev 4:13 of I sins unintentionally
Lev 7:23 Speak to the children of I
Lev 7:29 Speak to the children of I
Lev 7:34 taken from the children of I

Lev 7:34 of I by a statute forever
Lev 7:36 to them by the children of I
Lev 7:38 commanded the children of I
Lev 9: 1 his sons and the elders of I
Lev 9: 3 children of I you shall speak
Lev 10: 6 the whole house of I, bewail
Lev 10:11 may teach the children of I
Lev 10:14 of the children of I
Lev 11: 2 Speak to the children of I
Lev 12: 2 Speak to the children of I
Lev 15: 2 Speak to the children of I
Lev 15:31 of I from their uncleanness
Lev 16: 5 of the children of I two kids
Lev 16:16 of the children of I, and
Lev 16:17 for all the congregation of I
Lev 16:19 of the children of I
Lev 16:21 of the children of I, and all
Lev 16:34 for the children of I, for
Lev 17: 2 and to all the children of I
Lev 17: 3 man of the house of I, kills
Lev 17: 5 end that the children of I
Lev 17: 8 man of the house of I, or of
Lev 17:10 man of the house of I, or of
Lev 17:12 I said to the children of I
Lev 17:13 man of the children of I, or
Lev 17:14 I said to the children of I
Lev 18: 2 Speak to the children of I
Lev 19: 2 of the children of I, and say
Lev 20: 2 say to the children of I
Lev 20: 2 Whoever of the children of I
Lev 20: 2 strangers who sojourn in I
Lev 21:24 and to all the children of I
Lev 22: 2 things of the children of I
Lev 22: 3 of I sanctify to the LORD
Lev 22:15 of the children of I, which
Lev 22:18 and to all the children of I
Lev 22:18 man of the house of I, or of
Lev 22:18 or of the strangers in I
Lev 22:32 among the children of I
Lev 23: 2 Speak to the children of I
Lev 23:10 Speak to the children of I
Lev 23:24 Speak to the children of I
Lev 23:34 Speak to the children of I
Lev 23:43 of I dwell in booths when I
Lev 23:44 of I the feasts of the LORD
Lev 24: 2 Command the children of I
Lev 24: 8 I by an everlasting covenant
Lev 24:10 out among the children of I
Lev 24:10 a man of I fought each other
Lev 24:15 speak to the children of I
Lev 24:23 spoke to the children of I
Lev 24:23 So the children of I did as
Lev 25: 2 Speak to the children of I
Lev 25:33 among the children of I
Lev 25:46 brethren, the children of I
Lev 25:55 of I are servants to Me
Lev 26:46 the children of I on Mount
Lev 27: 2 Speak to the children of I
Lev 27:34 children of I on Mount Sinai
Num 1: 2 of the children of I, by
Num 1: 3 are able to go to war in I
Num 1:16 heads of the divisions in I
Num 1:44 with the leaders of I,
Num 1:45 numbered of the children of I
Num 1:45 were able to go to war in I
Num 1:49 them among the children of I
Num 1:52 The children of I shall pitch
Num 1:53 of the children of I
Num 1:54 Thus the children of I did
Num 2: 2 of I shall camp by his own
Num 2:32 of I by their fathers' houses
Num 2:33 among the children of I, just
Num 2:34 Thus the children of I did
Num 3: 8 needs of the children of I
Num 3: 9 from among the children of I
Num 3:12 I instead of every firstborn
Num 3:12 womb among the children of I
Num 3:13 Myself all the firstborn in I
Num 3:38 needs of the children of I
Num 3:40 of I from a month old and
Num 3:41 among the children of I, and
Num 3:41 of the children of I
Num 3:42 among the children of I, as
Num 3:45 among the children of I, and
Num 3:46 of the children of I, who are
Num 3:50 of I he took the money, one
Num 4:46 and the leaders of I numbered
Num 5: 2 Command the children of I
Num 5: 4 And the children of I did so
Num 5: 4 so the children of I did
Num 5: 6 Speak to the children of I
Num 5: 9 things of the children of I
Num 5:12 Speak to the children of I
Num 6: 2 Speak to the children of I
Num 6:23 shall bless the children of I
Num 6:27 My name on the children of I
Num 7: 2 Then the leaders of I, the
Num 7:84 altar from the leaders of I
Num 8: 6 from among the children of I
Num 8: 9 assembly of the children of I
Num 8:10 the children of I shall lay
Num 8:11 from the children of I, that
Num 8:14 from among the children of I
Num 8:16 from among the children of I
Num 8:16 of all the children of I
Num 8:17 the children of I are Mine
Num 8:18 of the children of I
Num 8:19 from among the children of I
Num 8:19 of I in the tabernacle of
Num 8:19 for the children of I, that
Num 8:19 among the children of I when
Num 8:19 of I come near the sanctuary
Num 8:20 of I did to the Levites
Num 8:20 the children of I did to them
Num 9: 2 Let the children of I keep
Num 9: 4 I that they should keep the
Num 9: 5 so the children of I did
Num 9: 7 time among the children of I
Num 9:10 Speak to the children of I
Num 9:17 children of I would journey
Num 9:17 there the children of I would
Num 9:18 children of I would journey
Num 9:19 the children of I kept the
Num 9:22 the children of I would
Num 10: 4 heads of the divisions of I
Num 10:12 the children of I set out
Num 10:28 of march of the children of I
Num 10:29 has promised good things to I
Num 10:36 to the many thousands of I
Num 11: 4 children of I also wept again
Num 11:16 men of the elders of I, whom
Num 11:30 both he and the elders of I
Num 13: 2 giving to the children of I
Num 13: 3 heads of the children of I
Num 13:24 the men of I cut down there
Num 13:26 of the children of I in the
Num 13:32 of I a bad report of the land
Num 14: 2 And all the children of I
Num 14: 5 of the children of I
Num 14: 7 of the children of I, saying
Num 14:10 before all the children of I
Num 14:27 of I murmur against Me
Num 14:39 to all the children of I, and
Num 15: 2 Speak to the children of I
Num 15:18 Speak to the children of I
Num 15:25 of the children of I, and it
Num 15:26 of the children of I and the
Num 15:29 among the children of I and
Num 15:32 of I were in the wilderness
Num 15:38 Speak to the children of I
Num 16: 2 some of the children of I
Num 16: 9 to you that the God of I has
Num 16: 9 from the congregation of I
Num 16:25 the elders of I followed him
Num 16:34 Then all I who were around
Num 16:38 a sign to the children of I
Num 16:40 of I that no outsider, who is
Num 16:41 of the children of I murmured
Num 17: 2 Speak to the children of I
Num 17: 5 of the children of I, which
Num 17: 6 spoke to the children of I
Num 17: 9 LORD to all the children of I
Num 17:12 children of I spoke to Moses
Num 18: 5 wrath on the children of I
Num 18: 6 from among the children of I
Num 18: 8 gifts of the children of I
Num 18:11 of the children of I
Num 18:14 thing in I shall be yours
Num 18:19 of I offer to the LORD, I
Num 18:20 among the children of I
Num 18:21 of Levi all the tithes in I
Num 18:22 of I shall not come near the
Num 18:23 of I they shall have no
Num 18:24 tithes of the children of I
Num 18:24 of I they shall have no
Num 18:26 of I the tithes which I have
Num 18:28 from the children of I, and
Num 18:32 gifts of the children of I
Num 19: 2 Speak to the children of I
Num 19: 9 of I for the water of
Num 19:10 forever to the children of I
Num 19:13 shall be cut off from I
Num 20: 1 Then the children of I, the
Num 20:12 the eyes of the children of I
Num 20:13 of I contended with the LORD
Num 20:14 Thus says your brother I
Num 20:19 the children of I said to him
Num 20:21 to give I passage through his
Num 20:21 so I turned away from him
Num 20:22 Then the children of I, the
Num 20:24 given to the children of I
Num 20:29 all the house of I mourned
Num 21: 1 heard that I was coming on
Num 21: 1 then he fought against I
Num 21: 2 So I made a vow to the LORD,
Num 21: 3 listened to the voice of I
Num 21: 6 many of the people of I died
Num 21:10 the children of I moved on
Num 21:17 Then I sang this song
Num 21:21 Then I sent messengers to
Num 21:23 allow I to pass through his
Num 21:23 went out against I in the
Num 21:23 to Jahaz and fought against I
Num 21:24 Then I defeated him with the
Num 21:25 So I took all these cities,
Num 21:25 I dwelt in all the cities of
Num 21:31 Thus I dwelt in the land of
Num 22: 1 Then the children of I moved
Num 22: 2 I had done to the Amorites
Num 22: 3 because of the children of I
Num 23: 7 for me, and come, denounce I
Num 23:10 or number one-fourth of I
Num 23:21 has He seen wickedness in I
Num 23:23 any divination against I
Num 23:23 must be said of Jacob and of I
Num 24: 1 pleased the LORD to bless I
Num 24: 2 saw I encamped according to
Num 24: 5 your dwellings, O I
Num 24:17 A Scepter shall rise out of I
Num 24:18 while I does valiantly
Num 25: 1 Then I remained in Acacia
Num 25: 3 So I was joined to Baal of
Num 25: 3 LORD was aroused against I
Num 25: 4 the LORD may turn away from I
Num 25: 5 Moses said to the judges of I
Num 25: 6 one of the children of I came
Num 25: 6 of the children of I, who
Num 25: 8 the man of I into the tent
Num 25: 8 of them through, the man of I
Num 25: 8 among the children of I
Num 25:11 wrath from the children of I
Num 25:11 the children of I in My zeal
Num 25:13 for the children of I
Num 26: 2 of the children of I from
Num 26: 2 are able to go to war in I
Num 26: 4 the children of I who came
Num 26: 5 Reuben was the firstborn of I
Num 26:51 numbered of the children of I
Num 26:62 among the other children of I
Num 26:62 them among the children of I
Num 26:63 of I in the plains of Moab by
Num 26:64 numbered the children of I in
Num 27: 8 speak to the children of I
Num 27:11 of I a statute of judgment
Num 27:12 given to the children of I
Num 27:20 children of I may be obedient
Num 27:21 the children of I with him
Num 28: 2 Command the children of I
Num 29:40 the children of I everything
Num 30: 1 concerning the children of I
Num 31: 2 of I on the Midianites
Num 31: 4 I you shall send to the war
Num 31: 5 from the divisions of I one
Num 31: 9 the children of I took all
Num 31:12 of the children of I, to the
Num 31:16 caused the children of I,
Num 31:54 children of I before the LORD
Num 32: 4 before the congregation of I
Num 32: 7 of I from going over into the
Num 32: 9 heart of the children of I
Num 32:13 anger was aroused against I
Num 32:14 anger of the LORD against I
Num 32:17 go before the children of I
Num 32:18 of I has received his
Num 32:22 before the LORD and before I
Num 32:28 tribes of the children of I
Num 33: 1 journeys of the children of I
Num 33: 3 Passover the children of I
Num 33: 5 of I moved from Rameses and
Num 33:38 year after the children of I

Num 33:40 coming of the children of I
Num 33:51 Speak to the children of I
Num 34: 2 Command the children of I
Num 34:13 commanded the children of I
Num 34:29 of I in the land of Canaan
Num 35: 2 Command the children of I
Num 35: 8 of the children of I
Num 35:10 Speak to the children of I
Num 35:15 refuge for the children of I
Num 35:34 dwell among the children of I
Num 36: 1 fathers of the children of I
Num 36: 2 by lot to the children of I
Num 36: 3 tribes of the children of I
Num 36: 4 of the children of I comes
Num 36: 5 of I according to the word of
Num 36: 7 of the children of I shall
Num 36: 7 one of the children of I
Num 36: 8 tribe of the children of I
Num 36: 8 of I each may possess the
Num 36: 9 of I shall keep its own
Num 36:13 commanded the children of I
Deut 1: 1 which Moses spoke to all I on
Deut 1: 3 spoke to the children of I
Deut 1:38 shall cause I to inherit it
Deut 2:12 just as I did to the land of
Deut 3:18 brethren, the children of I
Deut 4: 1 Now, O I, listen to the
Deut 4:44 set before the children of I
Deut 4:45 of I after they came out of
Deut 4:46 the children of I defeated
Deut 5: 1 And Moses called all I, and
Deut 5: 1 Hear, O I, the statutes and
Deut 6: 3 Therefore hear, O I, and be
Deut 6: 4 Hear, O I: The LORD our
Deut 9: 1 Hear, O I: You are
Deut 10: 6 (Now the children of I
Deut 10:12 And now, I, what does the LORD
Deut 11: 6 in the midst of all I
Deut 13:11 So all I shall hear and fear,
Deut 17: 4 has been committed in I,
Deut 17:12 away the evil person from I
Deut 17:20 children in the midst of I
Deut 18: 1 part nor inheritance with I
Deut 18: 6 where he sojourns among all I
Deut 19:13 of innocent blood from I,
Deut 20: 3 shall say to them, 'Hear, O I
Deut 21: 8 O LORD, for Your people I
Deut 21: 8 the charge of Your people I
Deut 21:21 and all I shall hear and fear
Deut 22:19 a bad name on a virgin of I
Deut 22:21 done a disgraceful thing in I
Deut 22:22 away the evil person from I
Deut 23:17 harlot of the daughters of I
Deut 23:17 one of the sons of I
Deut 24: 7 brethren of the children of I
Deut 25: 6 may not be blotted out of I
Deut 25: 7 up a name to his brother in I
Deut 25:10 his name shall be called in I
Deut 26:15 and bless Your people I and
Deut 27: 1 Moses, with the elders of I
Deut 27: 9 the Levites, spoke to all I
Deut 27: 9 Take heed and listen, O I
Deut 27:14 and say to all the men of I
Deut 29: 1 of I in the land of Moab,
Deut 29: 2 Now Moses called all I and
Deut 29:10 officers, all the men of I
Deut 29:21 the tribes of I for adversity
Deut 31: 1 and spoke these words to all I
Deut 31: 7 to him in the sight of all I
Deut 31: 9 and to all the elders of I
Deut 31:11 when all I comes to appear
Deut 31:11 before all I in their hearing
Deut 31:19 teach it to the children of I
Deut 31:19 Me against the children of I
Deut 31:22 it to the children of I
Deut 31:23 of I into the land of which I
Deut 31:30 of I the words of this song
Deut 32: 8 number of the children of I
Deut 32:45 all these words to all I,
Deut 32:49 children of I as a possession
Deut 32:51 of I at the waters of Meribah
Deut 32:51 midst of the children of I
Deut 32:52 giving to the children of I
Deut 33: 1 of I before his death
Deut 33: 5 all the tribes of I together
Deut 33:10 Your judgments, and I Your law
Deut 33:21 LORD, and His judgments with I
Deut 33:28 Then I shall dwell in safety,
Deut 33:29 Happy are you, O I
Deut 34: 8 the children of I wept for
Deut 34: 9 the children of I heeded him
Deut 34:10 in I a prophet like Moses
Deut 34:12 in the sight of all I
Josh 1: 2 the children of I
Josh 2: 2 from the children of I to
Josh 3: 1 he and all the children of I
Josh 3: 7 you in the sight of all I
Josh 3: 9 said to the children of I
Josh 3:12 men from the tribes of I, one
Josh 3:17 all I crossed over on dry
Josh 4: 4 from the children of I, one
Josh 4: 5 tribes of the children of I
Josh 4: 7 to the children of I forever
Josh 4: 8 And the children of I did so
Josh 4: 8 tribes of the children of I
Josh 4:12 before the children of I, as
Josh 4:14 Joshua in the sight of all I
Josh 4:21 he spoke to the children of I
Josh 4:22 I crossed over this Jordan
Josh 5: 1 I until we had crossed over
Josh 5: 1 because of the children of I
Josh 5: 2 of I again the second time
Josh 5: 3 sons of I at the hill of the
Josh 5: 6 For the children of I walked
Josh 5:10 of I camped in Gilgal, and
Josh 5:12 the children of I no longer
Josh 6: 1 because of the children of I
Josh 6:18 and make the camp of I a curse
Josh 6:23 them outside the camp of I
Josh 6:25 she dwells in I to this day
Josh 7: 1 But the children of I
Josh 7: 1 against the children of I
Josh 7: 6 both he and the elders of I
Josh 7: 8 what shall I say when I turns
Josh 7:11 I has sinned, and they have
Josh 7:12 of I could not stand before
Josh 7:13 thus says the LORD God of I
Josh 7:13 thing in your midst, O I
Josh 7:15 done a disgraceful thing in I
Josh 7:16 brought I by their tribes, and
Josh 7:19 glory to the LORD God of I
Josh 7:20 against the LORD God of I
Josh 7:23 and to all the children of I
Josh 7:24 all I with him, took Achan
Josh 7:25 So all I stoned him with
Josh 8:10 up, he and the elders of I
Josh 8:14 went out against I to battle
Josh 8:15 all I made as if they were
Josh 8:17 who did not go out after I
Josh 8:17 the city open and pursued I
Josh 8:21 all I saw that the ambush had
Josh 8:22 were caught in the midst of I
Josh 8:24 it came to pass when I had
Josh 8:27 that city I took as booty for
Josh 8:30 LORD God of I in Mount Ebal
Josh 8:31 commanded the children of I
Josh 8:32 presence of the children of I
Josh 8:33 Then all I, with their elders
Josh 8:33 should bless the people of I
Josh 8:35 all the congregation of I
Josh 9: 2 Joshua and I with one accord
Josh 9: 6 to him and to the men of I
Josh 9: 7 But the men of I said to the
Josh 9:14 Then the men of I took some
Josh 9:17 the children of I journeyed
Josh 9:18 of I did not attack them,
Josh 9:18 to them by the LORD God of I
Josh 9:19 to them by the LORD God of I
Josh 9:26 the hand of the children of I
Josh 10: 1 Gibeon had made peace with I
Josh 10: 4 and with the children of I
Josh 10:10 the LORD routed them before I
Josh 10:11 as they fled before I and
Josh 10:11 of I killed with the sword
Josh 10:12 before the children of I, and
Josh 10:12 and he said in the sight of I
Josh 10:14 for the LORD fought for I
Josh 10:15 all I with him, to the camp
Josh 10:20 the children of I made an end
Josh 10:21 any of the children of I
Josh 10:24 called for all the men of I
Josh 10:29 all I with him, to Libnah
Josh 10:30 its king into the hand of I
Josh 10:31 all I with him, to Lachish
Josh 10:32 Lachish into the hand of I
Josh 10:34 to Eglon, and all I with him
Josh 10:36 all I with him, to Hebron
Josh 10:38 and all I with him, to Debir
Josh 10:40 LORD God of I had commanded
Josh 10:42 God of I fought for I
Josh 10:43 all I with him, to the camp
Josh 11: 5 of Merom to fight against I
Josh 11: 6 all of them slain before I
Josh 11: 8 them into the hand of I, who
Josh 11:13 I burned none of them, except
Josh 11:14 the children of I took as
Josh 11:16 the mountains of I and its
Josh 11:19 peace with the children of I
Josh 11:20 come against I in battle,
Josh 11:21 from all the mountains of I
Josh 11:22 the land of the children of I
Josh 11:23 to I according to their
Josh 12: 1 the children of I defeated
Josh 12: 6 children of I had conquered
Josh 12: 7 the children of I conquered
Josh 12: 7 gave to the tribes of I as a
Josh 13: 6 from before the children of I
Josh 13: 6 by lot to I as an inheritance
Josh 13:13 the children of I did not
Josh 13:14 of the LORD God of I made by
Josh 13:22 The children of I also killed
Josh 13:33 the LORD God of I was their
Josh 14: 1 of I inherited in the land of
Josh 14: 1 of I distributed as an
Josh 14: 5 so the children of I did
Josh 14:10 this word to Moses while I
Josh 14:14 followed the LORD God of I
Josh 17:13 the children of I grew strong
Josh 18: 1 of the children of I
Josh 18: 2 among the children of I seven
Josh 18: 3 said to the children of I
Josh 18:10 of I according to their
Josh 19:49 the children of I gave an
Josh 19:51 I divided as an inheritance
Josh 20: 2 Speak to the children of I
Josh 20: 9 for all the children of I
Josh 21: 1 tribes of the children of I
Josh 21: 3 So the children of I gave to
Josh 21: 8 the children of I gave these
Josh 21:41 of the children of I were
Josh 21:43 So the LORD gave to I all the
Josh 21:45 had spoken to the house of I
Josh 22: 9 the children of I at Shiloh
Josh 22:11 of I heard someone say
Josh 22:11 occupied by the children of I
Josh 22:12 the children of I heard of it
Josh 22:12 of the children of I gathered
Josh 22:13 Then the children of I sent
Josh 22:14 house of every tribe of I
Josh 22:14 among the divisions of I
Josh 22:16 against the God of I, to turn
Josh 22:18 the whole congregation of I
Josh 22:20 on all the congregation of I
Josh 22:21 heads of the divisions of I
Josh 22:22 knows, and let I itself know
Josh 22:24 to do with the LORD God of I
Josh 22:30 of I who were with him, heard
Josh 22:31 delivered the children of I
Josh 22:32 Canaan, to the children of I
Josh 22:33 pleased the children of I
Josh 22:33 the children of I blessed God
Josh 23: 1 to I from all their enemies
Josh 23: 2 And Joshua called for all I
Josh 24: 1 the tribes of I to Shechem
Josh 24: 1 and called for the elders of I
Josh 24: 2 Thus says the LORD God of I
Josh 24: 9 arose to make war against I
Josh 24:23 heart to the LORD God of I
Josh 24:31 I served the LORD all the
Josh 24:31 LORD which He had done for I
Josh 24:32 which the children of I had
Judg 1: 1 children of I asked the LORD
Judg 1:28 when I was strong, that they
Judg 2: 4 to all the children of I,
Judg 2: 6 the children of I went each
Judg 2: 7 LORD which He had done for I
Judg 2:10 work which He had done for I
Judg 2:11 Then the children of I did
Judg 2:14 of the LORD was hot against I
Judg 2:20 of the LORD was hot against I
Judg 2:22 through them I may test I
Judg 3: 1 that He might test I by them
Judg 3: 2 of the children of I might be
Judg 3: 4 that He might test I by them
Judg 3: 5 So the children of I dwelt
Judg 3: 7 So the children of I did evil
Judg 3: 8 of the LORD was hot against I
Judg 3: 8 and the children of I served
Judg 3: 9 When the children of I cried
Judg 3: 9 for the children of I, who

Judg 3:10 came upon him, and he judged I
Judg 3:12 the children of I again did
Judg 3:12 Eglon king of Moab against I
Judg 3:13 Amalek, went and defeated I
Judg 3:14 So the children of I served
Judg 3:15 when the children of I cried
Judg 3:15 By him the children of I sent
Judg 3:27 the children of I went down
Judg 3:30 that day under the hand of I
Judg 3:31 and he also delivered I
Judg 4: 1 the children of I again did
Judg 4: 3 the children of I cried out
Judg 4: 3 oppressed the children of I
Judg 4: 4 was judging I at that time
Judg 4: 5 the children of I came up to
Judg 4: 6 the LORD God of I commanded
Judg 4:23 presence of the children of I
Judg 4:24 children of I grew stronger
Judg 5: 2 When leaders lead in I, when
Judg 5: 3 praise to the LORD God of I
Judg 5: 5 before the LORD God of I
Judg 5: 7 life ceased, it ceased in I
Judg 5: 7 arose, arose a mother in I
Judg 5: 8 among forty thousand in I
Judg 5: 9 of I who offered themselves
Judg 5:11 acts for His villagers in I
Judg 6: 1 the children of I did evil in
Judg 6: 2 of Midian prevailed against I
Judg 6: 2 the children of I made for
Judg 6: 3 it was, whenever I had sown
Judg 6: 4 and leave no sustenance for I
Judg 6: 6 So I was greatly impoverished
Judg 6: 6 the children of I cried out
Judg 6: 7 when the children of I cried
Judg 6: 8 prophet to the children of I
Judg 6: 8 Thus says the LORD God of I
Judg 6:14 you shall save I from the
Judg 6:15 O my Lord, how can I save I
Judg 6:36 If You will save I by my hand
Judg 6:37 You will save I by my hand
Judg 7: 2 lest I claim glory for itself
Judg 7: 8 sent away all the rest of I
Judg 7:14 the son of Joash, a man of I
Judg 7:15 He returned to the camp of I
Judg 7:23 And the men of I gathered
Judg 8:22 the men of I said to Gideon
Judg 8:27 all I played the harlot with
Judg 8:28 before the children of I, so
Judg 8:33 that the children of I again
Judg 8:34 Thus the children of I did
Judg 8:35 the good he had done for I
Judg 9:22 reigned over I three years
Judg 9:55 when the men of I saw that
Judg 10: 1 there arose to save I Tola
Judg 10: 2 He judged I twenty-three
Judg 10: 3 he judged I twenty-two years
Judg 10: 6 Then the children of I again
Judg 10: 7 of the LORD was hot against I
Judg 10: 8 of I for eighteen years
Judg 10: 8 all the children of I who
Judg 10: 9 so that I was severely
Judg 10:10 the children of I cried out
Judg 10:11 said to the children of I
Judg 10:15 of I said to the LORD, "We
Judg 10:16 longer endure the misery of I
Judg 10:17 the children of I assembled
Judg 11: 4 of Ammon made war against I
Judg 11: 5 of Ammon made war against I
Judg 11:13 Because I took away my land
Judg 11:15 I did not take away the land
Judg 11:16 for when I came up from
Judg 11:17 Then I sent messengers to
Judg 11:17 So I remained in Kadesh
Judg 11:19 Then I sent messengers to
Judg 11:19 and I said to him,
Judg 11:20 trust I to pass through his
Judg 11:20 in Jahaz, and fought against I
Judg 11:21 LORD God of I delivered Sihon
Judg 11:21 his people into the hand of I
Judg 11:21 Thus I gained possession of
Judg 11:23 God of I has dispossessed the
Judg 11:23 from before His people I
Judg 11:25 Did he ever strive against I
Judg 11:26 While I dwelt in Heshbon and
Judg 11:27 day between the children of I
Judg 11:33 before the children of I
Judg 11:39 And it became a custom in I
Judg 11:40 that the daughters of I went
Judg 12: 7 Jephthah judged I six years
Judg 12: 8 Ibzan of Bethlehem judged I
Judg 12: 9 He judged I seven years
Judg 12:11 Elon the Zebulunite judged I
Judg 12:11 He judged I ten years
Judg 12:13 the Pirathonite judged I
Judg 12:14 He judged I eight years
Judg 13: 1 Again the children of I did
Judg 13: 5 I out of the hand of the
Judg 14: 4 had dominion over I
Judg 15:20 he judged I twenty years in
Judg 16:31 He had judged I twenty years
Judg 17: 6 days there was no king in I
Judg 18: 1 days there was no king in I
Judg 18: 1 among the tribes of I had not
Judg 18:19 to a tribe and a family in I
Judg 18:29 father, who was born to I
Judg 19: 1 when there was no king in I
Judg 19:12 are not of the children of I
Judg 19:29 all the territory of I
Judg 19:30 of I came up from the land of
Judg 20: 1 the children of I came out
Judg 20: 2 people, all the tribes of I
Judg 20: 3 of I had gone up to Mizpah
Judg 20: 3 Then the children of I said
Judg 20: 6 of the inheritance of I,
Judg 20: 6 lewdness and outrage in I
Judg 20: 7 All of you are children of I
Judg 20:10 all the tribes of I, a
Judg 20:10 that they have done in I
Judg 20:11 So all the men of I were
Judg 20:12 Then the tribes of I sent men
Judg 20:13 and remove the evil from I
Judg 20:13 brethren, the children of I
Judg 20:14 against the children of I
Judg 20:17 the men of I numbered four
Judg 20:18 And the children of I arose
Judg 20:19 So the children of I rose in
Judg 20:20 And the men of I went out to
Judg 20:20 the men of I put themselves
Judg 20:22 people, that is, the men of I
Judg 20:23 the children of I went up
Judg 20:24 So the children of I
Judg 20:25 more of the children of I
Judg 20:26 Then all the children of I
Judg 20:27 So the children of I inquired
Judg 20:29 Then I set men in ambush all
Judg 20:30 the children of I went up
Judg 20:31 field, about thirty men of I
Judg 20:32 But the children of I said
Judg 20:33 So all the men of I rose from
Judg 20:34 all I came against Gibeah
Judg 20:35 defeated Benjamin before I
Judg 20:35 the children of I destroyed
Judg 20:36 The men of I had given ground
Judg 20:38 signal between the men of I
Judg 20:39 men of I would turn in battle
Judg 20:39 about thirty of the men of I
Judg 20:41 when the men of I turned back
Judg 20:42 of I in the direction of the
Judg 20:48 And the men of I turned back
Judg 21: 1 Now the men of I had sworn an
Judg 21: 3 O LORD God of I, why has this
Judg 21: 3 has this come to pass in I
Judg 21: 3 be one tribe missing in I
Judg 21: 5 The children of I said, "Who
Judg 21: 5 among all the tribes of I who
Judg 21: 6 the children of I grieved for
Judg 21: 6 tribe is cut off from I today
Judg 21: 8 of I who did not come up to
Judg 21:15 a void in the tribes of I
Judg 21:17 may not be destroyed from I
Judg 21:18 of I have sworn an oath,
Judg 21:24 So the children of I departed
Judg 21:25 days there was no king in I
Ruth 2:12 you by the LORD God of I,
Ruth 4: 7 in I concerning redeeming
Ruth 4: 7 this was an attestation in I
Ruth 4:11 two who built the house of I
Ruth 4:14 may his name be famous in I
1Sa 1:17 and the God of I grant your
1Sa 2:22 his sons did to all I, and how
1Sa 2:28 tribes of I to be My priest
1Sa 2:28 children of I made by fire
1Sa 2:29 the offerings of I My people
1Sa 2:30 the LORD God of I says
1Sa 2:32 the good which God does for I
1Sa 3:11 in I at which both ears of
1Sa 3:20 all I from Dan to Beersheba
1Sa 4: 1 word of Samuel came to all I
1Sa 4: 1 now I went out to battle
1Sa 4: 2 in battle array against I
1Sa 4: 2 battle, I was defeated by the
1Sa 4: 3 camp, the elders of I said
1Sa 4: 5 all I shouted so loudly that
1Sa 4:10 I was defeated, and every man
1Sa 4:10 and there fell of I thirty
1Sa 4:17 said, "I has fled before the
1Sa 4:18 he had judged I forty years
1Sa 4:21 The glory has departed from I
1Sa 4:22 The glory has departed from I
1Sa 5: 7 The ark of the God of I must
1Sa 5: 8 with the ark of the God of I
1Sa 5: 8 of I be carried away to Gath
1Sa 5: 8 the ark of the God of I away
1Sa 5:10 the ark of the God of I to us
1Sa 5:11 away the ark of the God of I
1Sa 6: 3 away the ark of the God of I
1Sa 6: 5 give glory to the God of I
1Sa 7: 2 all the house of I lamented
1Sa 7: 3 spoke to all the house of I
1Sa 7: 4 of I put away the Baals and
1Sa 7: 5 Gather all I to Mizpah, and I
1Sa 7: 6 the children of I at Mizpah
1Sa 7: 7 of I had gathered together at
1Sa 7: 7 Philistines went up against I
1Sa 7: 7 the children of I heard of it
1Sa 7: 8 children of I said to Samuel
1Sa 7: 9 cried out to the LORD for I
1Sa 7:10 drew near to battle against I
1Sa 7:10 they were overcome before I
1Sa 7:11 And the men of I went out of
1Sa 7:13 into the territory of I
1Sa 7:14 I were restored to I
1Sa 7:14 I recovered its territory
1Sa 7:14 there was peace between I
1Sa 7:15 So Samuel judged I all the
1Sa 7:16 judged I in all those places
1Sa 7:17 There he judged I, and there
1Sa 8: 1 made his sons judges over I
1Sa 8: 4 elders of I gathered together
1Sa 8:22 Samuel said to the men of I
1Sa 9: 2 he among the children of I
1Sa 9: 9 (Formerly in I, when a man
1Sa 9:16 commander over My people I
1Sa 9:20 whom is all the desire of I
1Sa 9:21 smallest of the tribes of I
1Sa 10:18 and said to the children of I
1Sa 10:18 Thus says the LORD God of I
1Sa 10:18 I brought up I out of Egypt
1Sa 10:20 the tribes of I to come near
1Sa 11: 2 and bring reproach on all I
1Sa 11: 3 to all the territory of I
1Sa 11: 7 all the territory of I by the
1Sa 11: 8 the children of I were three
1Sa 11:13 accomplished salvation in I
1Sa 11:15 all the men of I rejoiced
1Sa 12: 1 Now Samuel said to all I
1Sa 13: 1 had reigned two years over I
1Sa 13: 2 three thousand men of I
1Sa 13: 4 Now all I heard it said that
1Sa 13: 4 that I had also become an
1Sa 13: 5 together to fight with I,
1Sa 13: 6 When the men of I saw that
1Sa 13:13 your kingdom over I forever
1Sa 13:19 throughout all the land of I
1Sa 14:12 them into the hand of I
1Sa 14:18 was with the children of I)
1Sa 14:22 of I who had hidden in the
1Sa 14:23 So the LORD saved I that day
1Sa 14:24 the men of I were distressed
1Sa 14:37 them into the hand of I
1Sa 14:39 the LORD lives, who saves I
1Sa 14:40 Then he said to all I, "You
1Sa 14:41 said to the LORD God of I
1Sa 14:45 this great salvation in I
1Sa 14:47 his sovereignty over I, and
1Sa 14:48 delivered I from the hands of
1Sa 15: 1 king over His people, over I
1Sa 15: 2 punish what Amalek did to I
1Sa 15: 6 to all the children of I when
1Sa 15:17 not head of the tribes of I
1Sa 15:17 LORD anoint you king over I
1Sa 15:26 you from being king over I
1Sa 15:28 kingdom of I from you today
1Sa 15:29 also the Strength of I will
1Sa 15:30 of my people and before I, and
1Sa 15:35 He had made Saul king over I
1Sa 16: 1 him from reigning over I
1Sa 17: 2 the men of I were gathered
1Sa 17: 3 I stood on a mountain on the
1Sa 17: 8 cried out to the armies of I

1Sa 17:10 defy the armies of I this day
1Sa 17:11 all I heard these words of
1Sa 17:19 all the men of I were in the
1Sa 17:21 For I and the Philistines had
1Sa 17:24 And all the men of I, when
1Sa 17:25 So the men of I said, "Have
1Sa 17:25 he has come up to defy I
1Sa 17:25 father's house exemption in I
1Sa 17:26 away the reproach from I
1Sa 17:45 the God of the armies of I
1Sa 17:46 know that there is a God in I
1Sa 17:52 Now the men of I and Judah
1Sa 17:53 Then the children of I
1Sa 18: 6 out of all the cities of I
1Sa 18:16 But all I and Judah loved
1Sa 18:18 or my father's family in I
1Sa 19: 5 a great salvation for all I
1Sa 20:12 The LORD God of I is witness
1Sa 23:10 O LORD God of I, Your servant
1Sa 23:11 O LORD God of I, I pray, tell
1Sa 23:17 You shall be king over I, and
1Sa 24: 2 chosen men from all I, and
1Sa 24:14 has the king of I come out
1Sa 24:20 that the kingdom of I shall
1Sa 25:30 appointed you ruler over I
1Sa 25:32 Blessed be the LORD God of I
1Sa 25:34 as the LORD God of I lives
1Sa 26: 2 chosen men of I with him, to
1Sa 26:15 And who is like you in I
1Sa 26:20 For the king of I has come
1Sa 27: 1 me anymore in any part of I
1Sa 27:12 people I utterly abhor him
1Sa 28: 1 for war, to fight with I
1Sa 28: 3 all I had lamented for him and
1Sa 28: 4 Saul gathered all I together
1Sa 28:19 I with you into the hand of
1Sa 28:19 of I into the hand of the
1Sa 29: 3 the servant of Saul king of I
1Sa 30:25 ordinance for I to this day
1Sa 31: 1 Philistines fought against I
1Sa 31: 1 the men of I fled from before
1Sa 31: 7 when the men of I who were on
1Sa 31: 7 that the men of I had fled
2Sa 1: 3 escaped from the camp of I
2Sa 1:12 LORD and for the house of I
2Sa 1:19 The beauty of I is slain on
2Sa 1:24 O daughters of I, weep over
2Sa 2: 9 over Benjamin, and over all I
2Sa 2:10 when he began to reign over I
2Sa 2:17 and the men of I were beaten
2Sa 2:28 and did not pursue I anymore
2Sa 3:10 up the throne of David over I
2Sa 3:12 you to bring all I to you
2Sa 3:17 with the elders of I, saying,
2Sa 3:18 people I from the hand of the
2Sa 3:19 all that seemed good to I
2Sa 3:21 gather all I to my lord the
2Sa 3:37 all I understood that day
2Sa 3:38 man has fallen this day in I
2Sa 4: 1 heart, and all I was troubled
2Sa 5: 1 Then all the tribes of I came
2Sa 5: 2 were the one who led I out
2Sa 5: 2 shall shepherd My people I
2Sa 5: 2 and be ruler over I.
2Sa 5: 3 So all the elders of I came
2Sa 5: 3 anointed David king over I
2Sa 5: 5 thirty-three years over all I
2Sa 5:12 him as king over I, and that
2Sa 5:17 anointed David king over I
2Sa 6: 1 all the choice men of I,
2Sa 6: 5 all the house of I played
2Sa 6:15 all the house of I brought up
2Sa 6:19 the whole multitude of I,
2Sa 6:20 was the king of I today,
2Sa 6:21 people of the LORD, over I
2Sa 7: 6 children of I up from Egypt
2Sa 7: 7 with all the children of I
2Sa 7: 7 anyone from the tribes of I
2Sa 7: 7 to shepherd My people I,
2Sa 7: 8 ruler over My people, over I
2Sa 7:10 a place for My people I, and
2Sa 7:11 judges to be over My people I
2Sa 7:23 is like Your people, like I
2Sa 7:24 people I Your very own people
2Sa 7:26 of hosts is the God over I
2Sa 7:27 O LORD of hosts, God of I
2Sa 8:15 So David reigned over all I
2Sa 10: 9 some of the choice men of I
2Sa 10:15 had been defeated before I
2Sa 10:17 told David, he gathered all I
2Sa 10:18 the Syrians fled before I
2Sa 10:19 that they were defeated by I
2Sa 10:19 they made peace with I and
2Sa 11: 1 servants with him, and all I
2Sa 11:11 The ark and I and Judah are
2Sa 12: 7 Thus says the LORD God of I
2Sa 12: 7 I anointed you king over I
2Sa 12: 8 and gave you the house of I
2Sa 12:12 do this thing before all I
2Sa 13:12 thing should be done in I
2Sa 13:13 be like one of the fools in I
2Sa 14:25 Now in all I there was no one
2Sa 15: 2 such and such a tribe of I
2Sa 15: 6 I who came to the king for
2Sa 15: 6 the hearts of the men of I
2Sa 15:10 all the tribes of I, saying,
2Sa 15:13 the men of I are with Absalom
2Sa 16: 3 Today the house of I will
2Sa 16:15 all the people, the men of I
2Sa 16:18 and all the men of I choose
2Sa 16:21 all I will hear that you are
2Sa 16:22 in the sight of all I
2Sa 17: 4 and all the elders of I
2Sa 17:10 For all I knows that your
2Sa 17:11 I counsel that all I be fully
2Sa 17:13 then all I shall bring ropes
2Sa 17:14 and all the men of I said
2Sa 17:15 Absalom and the elders of I
2Sa 17:24 and all the men of I with him
2Sa 17:26 So I and Absalom encamped in
2Sa 18: 6 the field of battle against I
2Sa 18: 7 The people of I were
2Sa 18:16 returned from pursuing I
2Sa 18:17 Then all I fled, everyone to
2Sa 19: 8 For everyone of I had fled to
2Sa 19: 9 all the tribes of I, saying,
2Sa 19:11 all I have come to the king
2Sa 19:22 be put to death today in I
2Sa 19:22 that today I am king over I
2Sa 19:40 and also half the people of I
2Sa 19:41 the men of I came to the king
2Sa 19:42 Judah answered the men of I
2Sa 19:43 the men of I answered the men
2Sa 19:43 the words of the men of I
2Sa 20: 1 every man to his tents, O I
2Sa 20: 2 every man of I deserted David
2Sa 20:14 all the tribes of I to Abel
2Sa 20:19 peaceable and faithful in I
2Sa 20:19 a city and a mother in I
2Sa 20:23 was over all the army of I
2Sa 21: 2 were not of the children of I
2Sa 21: 2 the children of I had sworn
2Sa 21: 2 zeal for the children of I
2Sa 21: 4 you kill any man in I for us
2Sa 21: 5 any of the territories of I
2Sa 21:15 were at war again with I,
2Sa 21:17 lest you quench the lamp of I
2Sa 21:21 So when he defied I, Jonathan
2Sa 23: 1 and the sweet psalmist of I
2Sa 23: 3 The God of I said, the Rock
2Sa 23: 3 the Rock of I spoke to me
2Sa 23: 9 the men of I had retreated
2Sa 24: 1 LORD was aroused against I
2Sa 24: 1 Go, number I and Judah
2Sa 24: 2 all the tribes of I, from Dan
2Sa 24: 4 king to count the people of I
2Sa 24: 9 there were in I eight hundred
2Sa 24:15 I from the morning till the
2Sa 24:25 plague was withdrawn from I
1Ki 1: 3 all the territory of I, and
1Ki 1:20 the eyes of all I are on you
1Ki 1:30 to you by the LORD God of I
1Ki 1:34 anoint him king over I
1Ki 1:35 him to be ruler over I and
1Ki 1:48 Blessed be the LORD God of I
1Ki 2: 4 lack a man on the throne of I
1Ki 2: 5 commanders of the armies of I
1Ki 2:11 over I was forty years
1Ki 2:15 mine, and all I had set their
1Ki 2:32 commander of the army of I
1Ki 3:28 all I heard of the judgment
1Ki 4: 1 Solomon was king over all I
1Ki 4: 7 twelve governors over all I
1Ki 4:20 I were as numerous as the
1Ki 4:25 and I dwelt safely, each man
1Ki 5:13 up a labor force out of all I
1Ki 6: 1 year after the children of I
1Ki 6: 1 of Solomon's reign over I
1Ki 6:13 dwell among the children of I
1Ki 6:13 will not forsake My people I
1Ki 8: 1 assembled the elders of I
1Ki 8: 1 fathers of the children of I
1Ki 8: 2 all the men of I assembled to
1Ki 8: 3 Then all the elders of I came
1Ki 8: 5 all the congregation of I who
1Ki 8: 9 with the children of I, when
1Ki 8:14 the whole congregation of I
1Ki 8:14 of I was standing
1Ki 8:15 Blessed be the LORD God of I
1Ki 8:16 My people I out of Egypt, I
1Ki 8:16 I in which to build a house
1Ki 8:16 David to be over My people I
1Ki 8:17 the name of the LORD God of I
1Ki 8:20 and sit on the throne of I
1Ki 8:20 the name of the LORD God of I
1Ki 8:22 of all the congregation of I
1Ki 8:23 LORD God of I, there is no
1Ki 8:25 Therefore, LORD God of I, now
1Ki 8:25 before Me on the throne of I
1Ki 8:26 And now I pray, O God of I
1Ki 8:30 servant and of Your people I
1Ki 8:33 When Your people I are
1Ki 8:34 the sin of Your people I, and
1Ki 8:36 Your servants, Your people I
1Ki 8:38 or by all Your people I,
1Ki 8:41 who is not of Your people I
1Ki 8:43 fear You, as do Your people I
1Ki 8:52 supplication of Your people I
1Ki 8:55 of I with a loud voice,
1Ki 8:56 given rest to His people I
1Ki 8:59 and the cause of His people I
1Ki 8:62 and all I with him offered
1Ki 8:63 king and all the children of I
1Ki 8:65 and all I with him, a great
1Ki 8:66 David, and for I His people
1Ki 9: 5 your kingdom over I forever
1Ki 9: 5 have a man on the throne of I
1Ki 9: 7 then I will cut off I from
1Ki 9: 7 I will be a proverb and a
1Ki 9:20 were not of the children of I
1Ki 9:21 of I had not been able to
1Ki 9:22 of I Solomon made no forced
1Ki 10: 9 you on the throne of I
1Ki 10: 9 the LORD has loved I forever
1Ki 11: 2 had said to the children of I
1Ki 11: 9 turned from the LORD God of I
1Ki 11:16 remained there with all I
1Ki 11:25 He was an adversary of I all
1Ki 11:25 and he abhorred I, and reigned
1Ki 11:31 says the LORD, the God of I
1Ki 11:32 out of all the tribes of I)
1Ki 11:37 and you shall be king over I
1Ki 11:38 David, and will give I to you
1Ki 11:42 over all I was forty years
1Ki 12: 1 for all I had gone to Shechem
1Ki 12: 3 whole congregation of I came
1Ki 12:16 Now when all I saw that the
1Ki 12:16 To your tents, O I
1Ki 12:16 So I departed to their
1Ki 12:17 over the children of I who
1Ki 12:18 but all I stoned him with
1Ki 12:19 So I has been in rebellion
1Ki 12:20 all I heard that Jeroboam had
1Ki 12:20 and made him king over all I
1Ki 12:21 fight against the house of I
1Ki 12:24 brethren the children of I
1Ki 12:28 Here are your gods, O I,
1Ki 12:33 a feast for the children of I
1Ki 14: 7 Thus says the LORD God of I
1Ki 14: 7 you ruler over My people I
1Ki 14:10 from Jeroboam every male in I
1Ki 14:13 all I shall mourn for him and
1Ki 14:13 of I in the house of Jeroboam
1Ki 14:14 up for Himself a king over I
1Ki 14:15 For the LORD will strike I
1Ki 14:15 He will uproot I from this
1Ki 14:16 He will give I up because of
1Ki 14:16 who sinned and who made I sin
1Ki 14:18 and all I mourned for him,
1Ki 14:19 chronicles of the kings of I
1Ki 14:21 out of all the tribes of I
1Ki 14:24 out before the children of I
1Ki 15: 9 year of Jeroboam king of I
1Ki 15:16 king of I all their days
1Ki 15:17 And Baasha king of I came up
1Ki 15:19 treaty with Baasha king of I
1Ki 15:20 against the cities of I
1Ki 15:25 I in the second year of Asa
1Ki 15:25 he reigned over I two years
1Ki 15:26 by which he had made I sin

1Ki 15:27 all I laid siege to Gibbethon
1Ki 15:30 and by which he had made I sin
1Ki 15:30 the LORD God of I to anger
1Ki 15:31 chronicles of the kings of I
1Ki 15:32 king of I all their days
1Ki 15:33 king over all I in Tirzah
1Ki 15:34 by which he had made I sin
1Ki 16: 2 you ruler over My people I
1Ki 16: 2 and have made My people I sin
1Ki 16: 5 chronicles of the kings of I
1Ki 16: 8 of Baasha became king over I
1Ki 16:13 by which they had made I sin
1Ki 16:13 I to anger with their idols
1Ki 16:14 chronicles of the kings of I
1Ki 16:16 So all I made Omri, the
1Ki 16:16 king over I that day in the
1Ki 16:17 all I with him went up from
1Ki 16:19 had committed to make I sin
1Ki 16:20 chronicles of the kings of I
1Ki 16:21 Then the people of I were
1Ki 16:23 Omri became king over I, and
1Ki 16:26 by which he had made I sin
1Ki 16:26 I to anger with their idols
1Ki 16:27 chronicles of the kings of I
1Ki 16:29 of Omri became king over I
1Ki 16:29 son of Omri reigned over I in
1Ki 16:33 to provoke the LORD God of I
1Ki 16:33 of I who were before him
1Ki 17: 1 As the LORD God of I lives
1Ki 17:14 thus says the LORD God of I
1Ki 18:17 Is that you, O troubler of I
1Ki 18:18 I have not troubled I, but
1Ki 18:19 gather all I to me on Mount
1Ki 18:20 for all the children of I
1Ki 18:31 I shall be your name
1Ki 18:36 God of Abraham, Isaac, and I
1Ki 18:36 day that You are God in I
1Ki 19:10 for the children of I have
1Ki 19:14 because the children of I
1Ki 19:16 son of Nimshi as king over I
1Ki 19:18 reserved seven thousand in I
1Ki 20: 2 the city to Ahab king of I
1Ki 20: 4 And the king of I answered
1Ki 20: 7 Then the king of I called all
1Ki 20:11 So the king of I answered
1Ki 20:13 approached Ahab king of I
1Ki 20:15 people, all the children of I
1Ki 20:20 fled, and I pursued them
1Ki 20:21 Then the king of I went out
1Ki 20:22 prophet came to the king of I
1Ki 20:26 to Aphek to fight against I
1Ki 20:27 children of I were mustered
1Ki 20:27 Now the children of I
1Ki 20:28 and spoke to the king of I
1Ki 20:29 the children of I killed one
1Ki 20:31 house of I are merciful kings
1Ki 20:31 and go out to the king of I
1Ki 20:32 and came to the king of I
1Ki 20:40 And the king of I said to him
1Ki 20:41 the king of I recognized him
1Ki 20:43 So the king of I went to his
1Ki 21: 7 now exercise authority over I
1Ki 21:18 down to meet Ahab king of I
1Ki 21:21 off from Ahab every male in I
1Ki 21:22 Me to anger, and made I sin
1Ki 21:26 out before the children of I
1Ki 22: 1 war between Syria and I
1Ki 22: 2 down to visit the king of I
1Ki 22: 3 the king of I said to his
1Ki 22: 4 said to the king of I, "I am
1Ki 22: 5 said to the king of I
1Ki 22: 6 Then the king of I gathered
1Ki 22: 8 So the king of I said to
1Ki 22: 9 Then the king of I called an
1Ki 22:10 The king of I and Jehoshaphat
1Ki 22:17 I saw all I scattered on the
1Ki 22:18 And the king of I said to
1Ki 22:26 Then the king of I said
1Ki 22:29 So the king of I and
1Ki 22:30 And the king of I said to
1Ki 22:30 So the king of I disguised
1Ki 22:31 but only with the king of I
1Ki 22:32 Surely it is the king of I
1Ki 22:33 that it was not the king of I
1Ki 22:34 struck the king of I between
1Ki 22:39 chronicles of the kings of I
1Ki 22:41 fourth year of Ahab king of I
1Ki 22:44 made peace with the king of I
1Ki 22:51 king over I in Samaria in the
1Ki 22:51 and reigned two years over I
1Ki 22:52 of Nebat, who had made I sin
1Ki 22:53 the LORD God of I to anger
2Ki 1: 1 Moab rebelled against I after
2Ki 1: 3 in I that you are going to
2Ki 1: 6 in I that you are sending to
2Ki 1:16 in I to inquire of His word
2Ki 1:18 chronicles of the kings of I
2Ki 2:12 my father, the chariot of I
2Ki 3: 1 king over I at Samaria in the
2Ki 3: 3 of Nebat, who had made I sin
2Ki 3: 4 I one hundred thousand lambs
2Ki 3: 5 against the king of I
2Ki 3: 6 that time and mustered all I
2Ki 3: 9 So the king of I went with
2Ki 3:10 And the king of I said, "Alas
2Ki 3:11 of the king of I answered
2Ki 3:12 So the king of I and
2Ki 3:13 Elisha said to the king of I
2Ki 3:13 And the king of I said to him
2Ki 3:24 they came to the camp of I
2Ki 3:24 I rose up and attacked the
2Ki 3:27 great indignation against I
2Ki 5: 2 young girl from the land of I
2Ki 5: 4 who is from the land of I
2Ki 5: 5 a letter to the king of I
2Ki 5: 6 the letter to the king of I
2Ki 5: 7 the king of I read the letter
2Ki 5: 8 of I had torn his clothes
2Ki 5: 8 that there is a prophet in I
2Ki 5:12 than all the waters of I
2Ki 5:15 in all the earth, except in I
2Ki 6: 8 was making war against I
2Ki 6: 9 of God sent to the king of I
2Ki 6:10 Then the king of I sent
2Ki 6:11 of us is for the king of I
2Ki 6:12 the prophet who is in I,
2Ki 6:12 tells the king of I the words
2Ki 6:21 when the king of I saw them
2Ki 6:23 no more into the land of I
2Ki 6:26 as the king of I was passing
2Ki 7: 6 Look, the king of I has hired
2Ki 7:13 of I that are left in it
2Ki 7:13 of I left from those who are
2Ki 8:12 will do to the children of I
2Ki 8:16 the son of Ahab, king of I
2Ki 8:18 in the way of the kings of I
2Ki 8:25 the son of Ahab, king of I
2Ki 8:26 of Omri, king of I
2Ki 9: 3 have anointed you king over I
2Ki 9: 6 Thus says the LORD God of I
2Ki 9: 6 people of the LORD, over I
2Ki 9: 8 from Ahab all the males in I
2Ki 9:12 have anointed you king over I
2Ki 9:14 Ramoth Gilead, he and all I
2Ki 9:21 Then Joram king of I and
2Ki 10:21 Jehu sent throughout all I
2Ki 10:28 Jehu destroyed Baal from I
2Ki 10:29 of Nebat, who had made I sin
2Ki 10:30 of I to the fourth generation
2Ki 10:31 God of I with all his heart
2Ki 10:31 Jeroboam, who had made I sin
2Ki 10:32 began to cut off parts of I
2Ki 10:32 in all the territory of I
2Ki 10:34 chronicles of the kings of I
2Ki 10:36 that Jehu reigned over I in
2Ki 13: 1 became king over I in Samaria
2Ki 13: 2 of Nebat, who had made I sin
2Ki 13: 3 LORD was aroused against I
2Ki 13: 4 He saw the oppression of I
2Ki 13: 5 the LORD gave I a deliverer
2Ki 13: 5 the children of I dwelt in
2Ki 13: 6 Jeroboam, who had made I sin
2Ki 13: 8 chronicles of the kings of I
2Ki 13:10 became king over I in Samaria
2Ki 13:11 of Nebat, who had made I sin
2Ki 13:12 chronicles of the kings of I
2Ki 13:13 Samaria with the kings of I
2Ki 13:14 king of I came down to him
2Ki 13:14 my father, the chariots of I
2Ki 13:16 Then he said to the king of I
2Ki 13:18 And he said to the king of I
2Ki 13:22 king of Syria oppressed I all
2Ki 13:25 and recaptured the cities of I
2Ki 14: 1 son of Jehoahaz, king of I
2Ki 14: 8 the son of Jehu, king of I
2Ki 14: 9 Jehoash king of I sent to
2Ki 14:11 Jehoash king of I went out
2Ki 14:12 And Judah was defeated by I
2Ki 14:13 Then Jehoash king of I
2Ki 14:15 chronicles of the kings of I
2Ki 14:16 Samaria with the kings of I
2Ki 14:17 son of Jehoahaz, king of I
2Ki 14:23 the son of Joash, king of I
2Ki 14:24 of Nebat, who had made I sin
2Ki 14:25 restored the territory of I
2Ki 14:25 the word of the LORD God of I
2Ki 14:26 of I was very bitter
2Ki 14:26 there was no helper for I
2Ki 14:27 name of I from under heaven
2Ki 14:28 and how he recaptured for I
2Ki 14:28 chronicles of the kings of I
2Ki 14:29 his fathers, the kings of I
2Ki 15: 1 year of Jeroboam king of I
2Ki 15: 8 over I in Samaria six months
2Ki 15: 9 of Nebat, who had made I sin
2Ki 15:11 chronicles of the kings of I
2Ki 15:12 of I to the fourth generation
2Ki 15:15 chronicles of the kings of I
2Ki 15:17 of Gadi became king over I
2Ki 15:18 of Nebat, who had made I sin
2Ki 15:20 exacted the money from I,
2Ki 15:21 chronicles of the kings of I
2Ki 15:23 became king over I in Samaria
2Ki 15:24 of Nebat, who had made I sin
2Ki 15:26 chronicles of the kings of I
2Ki 15:27 became king over I in Samaria
2Ki 15:28 of Nebat, who had made I sin
2Ki 15:29 the days of Pekah king of I
2Ki 15:31 chronicles of the kings of I
2Ki 15:32 son of Remaliah, king of I
2Ki 16: 3 in the way of the kings of I
2Ki 16: 3 from before the children of I
2Ki 16: 5 son of Remaliah, king of I
2Ki 16: 7 the hand of the king of I
2Ki 17: 1 became king of I in Samaria
2Ki 17: 2 of I who were before him
2Ki 17: 6 carried I away to Assyria, and
2Ki 17: 7 I had sinned against the LORD
2Ki 17: 8 from before the children of I
2Ki 17: 8 and of the kings of I
2Ki 17: 9 Also the children of I
2Ki 17:13 the LORD testified against I
2Ki 17:18 LORD was very angry with I
2Ki 17:19 statutes of I which they made
2Ki 17:20 all the descendants of I,
2Ki 17:21 For He tore I from the house
2Ki 17:21 Then Jeroboam drove I from
2Ki 17:22 For the children of I walked
2Ki 17:23 removed I out of His sight
2Ki 17:23 So I was carried away from
2Ki 17:24 instead of the children of I
2Ki 17:34 of Jacob, whom He named I
2Ki 18: 1 the son of Elah, king of I
2Ki 18: 4 of I burned incense to it
2Ki 18: 5 trusted in the LORD God of I
2Ki 18: 9 the son of Elah, king of I
2Ki 18:10 year of Hoshea king of I,
2Ki 18:11 I away captive to Assyria
2Ki 19:15 O LORD God of I, the One who
2Ki 19:20 Thus says the LORD God of I
2Ki 19:22 Against the Holy One of I
2Ki 21: 2 out before the children of I
2Ki 21: 3 as Ahab king of I had done
2Ki 21: 7 out of all the tribes of I
2Ki 21: 8 of I wander anymore from the
2Ki 21: 9 before the children of I
2Ki 21:12 thus says the LORD God of I
2Ki 22:15 Thus says the LORD God of I
2Ki 22:18 Thus says the LORD God of I
2Ki 23:13 which Solomon king of I had
2Ki 23:15 son of Nebat, who made I sin
2Ki 23:19 which the kings of I had made
2Ki 23:22 of the judges who judged I
2Ki 23:22 the days of the kings of I
2Ki 23:27 My sight, as I have removed I
2Ki 24:13 I had made in the temple of
1Ch 1:34 sons of Isaac were Esau and I
1Ch 1:43 over the children of I
1Ch 2: 1 These were the sons of I
1Ch 2: 7 was Achar, the troubler of I
1Ch 4:10 called on the God of I saying
1Ch 5: 1 of Reuben the firstborn of I
1Ch 5: 1 sons of Joseph, the son of I
1Ch 5: 3 firstborn of I were Hanoch
1Ch 5:17 days of Jeroboam king of I
1Ch 5:26 So the God of I stirred up
1Ch 6:38 the son of Levi, the son of I
1Ch 6:49 and to make atonement for I
1Ch 6:64 So the children of I gave
1Ch 7:29 of Joseph, the son of I

2Ch 34:26 Thus says the LORD God of I
2Ch 34:33 belonged to the children of I
2Ch 34:33 all who were present in I
2Ch 35: 3 the Levites who taught all I
2Ch 35: 3 the son of David, king of I
2Ch 35: 3 LORD your God and His people I
2Ch 35: 4 of David king of I and the
2Ch 35:17 the children of I who were
2Ch 35:18 been no Passover kept in I
2Ch 35:18 none of the kings of I had
2Ch 35:18 I who were present, and the
2Ch 35:25 They made it a custom in I
2Ch 35:27 in the book of the kings of I
2Ch 36: 8 in the book of the kings of I
2Ch 36:13 turning to the LORD God of I
Ezra 1: 3 the LORD God of I (He is God)
Ezra 2: 2 of the men of the people of I
Ezra 2:59 whether they were of I
Ezra 2:70 and all I in their cities
Ezra 3: 1 the children of I were in the
Ezra 3: 2 the altar of the God of I
Ezra 3:10 ordinance of David king of I
Ezra 3:11 endures forever toward I
Ezra 4: 1 temple of the LORD God of I
Ezra 4: 3 houses of I said to them
Ezra 4: 3 build to the LORD God of I
Ezra 5: 1 in the name of the God of I
Ezra 5:11 which a great king of I built
Ezra 6:14 commandment of the God of I
Ezra 6:16 Then the children of I, the
Ezra 6:17 for all I twelve male goats
Ezra 6:17 the number of the tribes of I
Ezra 6:21 Then the children of I who
Ezra 6:21 to seek the LORD God of I
Ezra 6:22 house of God, the God of I
Ezra 7: 6 the LORD God of I had given
Ezra 7: 7 Some of the children of I
Ezra 7:10 statutes and ordinances in I
Ezra 7:11 LORD, and of His statutes to I
Ezra 7:13 all those of the people of I
Ezra 7:15 offered to the God of I,
Ezra 7:28 men of I to go up with me
Ezra 8:18 the son of Levi, the son of I
Ezra 8:25 all I who were present, had
Ezra 8:29 houses of I in Jerusalem, in
Ezra 8:35 offerings to the God of I
Ezra 8:35 twelve bulls for all I,
Ezra 9: 1 The people of I and the
Ezra 9: 4 the God of I assembled to me
Ezra 9:15 O LORD God of I, You are
Ezra 10: 1 assembled to him from I
Ezra 10: 2 is hope in I in spite of this
Ezra 10: 5 all I swear an oath that they
Ezra 10:10 adding to the guilt of I
Ezra 10:25 And others of I
Neh 1: 6 children of I Your servants
Neh 1: 6 of I which we have sinned
Neh 2:10 of the children of I
Neh 7: 7 of the men of the people of I
Neh 7:61 whether they were of I
Neh 7:73 all I dwelt in their cities
Neh 7:73 the children of I were in
Neh 8: 1 the LORD had commanded I
Neh 8:14 that the children of I should
Neh 8:17 children of I had not done so
Neh 9: 1 this month the children of I
Neh 10:33 to make atonement for I, and
Neh 10:39 For the children of I and the
Neh 11:20 And the rest of I, of the
Neh 12:47 I gave the portions for the
Neh 13: 2 the children of I with bread
Neh 13: 3 the mixed multitude from I
Neh 13:18 on I by profaning the Sabbath
Neh 13:26 king of I sin by these things
Neh 13:26 God made him king over all I
Ps 14: 7 that the salvation of I would
Ps 14: 7 Jacob rejoice and I be glad
Ps 22: 3 Who inhabit the praises of I
Ps 22:23 Him, all you offspring of I
Ps 25:22 Redeem I, O God, Out of all
Ps 41:13 God of I From everlasting to
Ps 50: 7 people, and I will speak, O I
Ps 53: 6 that the salvation of I would
Ps 53: 6 Jacob rejoice and I be glad
Ps 59: 5 God of hosts, the God of I
Ps 68: 8 presence of God, the God of I
Ps 68:26 Lord, from the fountain of I
Ps 68:34 His excellence is over I, And
Ps 68:35 The God of I is He who gives
Ps 69: 6 because of me, O God of I
Ps 71:22 the harp, O Holy One of I
Ps 72:18 be the LORD God, the God of I
Ps 73: 1 Truly God is good to I, To
Ps 76: 1 His name is great in I
Ps 78: 5 And appointed a law in I,
Ps 78:21 anger also came up against I
Ps 78:31 down the choice men of I
Ps 78:41 And limited the Holy One of I
Ps 78:55 made the tribes of I dwell in
Ps 78:59 And greatly abhorred I,
Ps 78:71 people, And I His inheritance
Ps 80: 1 Give ear, O Shepherd of I
Ps 81: 4 For this is a statute for I
Ps 81: 8 O I, if you will listen to Me
Ps 81:11 And I would have none of Me
Ps 81:13 That I would walk in My ways
Ps 83: 4 That the name of I may be
Ps 89:18 our king to the Holy One of I
Ps 98: 3 to the house of I
Ps 103: 7 His acts to the children of I
Ps 105:10 To I for an everlasting
Ps 105:23 I also came into Egypt, And
Ps 106:48 God of I From everlasting to
Ps 114: 1 When I went out of Egypt, The
Ps 114: 2 sanctuary, And I His dominion
Ps 115: 9 O I, trust in the LORD
Ps 115:12 He will bless the house of I
Ps 118: 2 Let I now say, "His mercy
Ps 121: 4 He who keeps I Shall neither
Ps 122: 4 LORD, To the Testimony of I
Ps 124: 1 on our side," Let I now say
Ps 125: 5 Peace be upon I
Ps 128: 6 Peace be upon I
Ps 129: 1 my youth," Let I now say
Ps 130: 7 O I, hope in the LORD
Ps 130: 8 He shall redeem I From all
Ps 131: 3 O I, hope in the LORD From
Ps 135: 4 I for His special treasure
Ps 135:12 A heritage to I His people
Ps 135:19 Bless the LORD, O house of I
Ps 136:11 brought out I from among them
Ps 136:14 made I pass through the midst
Ps 136:22 A heritage to I His servant
Ps 147: 2 together the outcasts of I
Ps 147:19 and His judgments to I
Ps 148:14 Of the children of I, A
Ps 149: 2 Let I rejoice in their Maker
Prov 1: 1 the son of David, king of I
Eccl 1:12 was king over I in Jerusalem
Song 3: 7 it, of the valiant of I
Is 1: 3 but I does not know, My
Is 1: 4 to anger the Holy One of I
Is 1:24 of hosts, the Mighty One of I
Is 4: 2 those of I who have escaped
Is 5: 7 of hosts is the house of I
Is 5:19 the Holy One of I draw near
Is 5:24 the word of the Holy One of I
Is 7: 1 son of Remaliah, king of I
Is 8:14 to both the houses of I, as a
Is 8:18 wonders in I From the LORD of
Is 9: 8 Jacob, and it has fallen on I
Is 9:12 they shall devour I with an
Is 9:14 cut off head and tail from I
Is 10:17 So the Light of I will be for
Is 10:20 day that the remnant of I
Is 10:20 the LORD, the Holy One of I
Is 10:22 For though your people, O I
Is 11:12 assemble the outcasts of I
Is 11:16 as it was for I in the day
Is 12: 6 Holy One of I in your midst
Is 14: 1 Jacob, and will still choose I
Is 14: 2 the house of I will possess
Is 17: 3 glory of the children of I
Is 17: 6 Says the LORD God of I
Is 17: 7 respect for the Holy One of I
Is 17: 9 because of the children of I
Is 19:24 In that day I will be one of
Is 19:25 My hands, and I My inheritance
Is 21:10 LORD of hosts, the God of I
Is 21:17 LORD God of I has spoken it
Is 24:15 of I in the coastlands of the
Is 27: 6 I shall blossom and bud, and
Is 27: 7 Has He struck I as He struck
Is 27:12 by one, O you children of I
Is 29:19 rejoice In the Holy One of I
Is 29:23 Jacob, and fear the God of I
Is 30:11 cause the Holy One of I to
Is 30:12 thus says the Holy One of I
Is 30:15 Lord GOD, the Holy One of I
Is 30:29 LORD, to the Mighty One of I
Is 31: 1 not look to the Holy One of I
Is 31: 6 of I have deeply revolted
Is 37:16 O LORD of hosts, God of I
Is 37:21 Thus says the LORD God of I
Is 37:23 Against the Holy One of I
Is 40:27 say, O Jacob, and speak, O I
Is 41: 8 But you, I, are My servant,
Is 41:14 you worm Jacob, you men of I
Is 41:14 Redeemer, the Holy One of I
Is 41:16 and glory in the Holy One of I
Is 41:17 I, the God of I, will not
Is 41:20 Holy One of I has created it
Is 42:24 plunder, and I to the robbers
Is 43: 1 and He who formed you, O I
Is 43: 3 your God, the Holy One of I
Is 43:14 Redeemer, the Holy One of I
Is 43:15 Holy One, the Creator of I
Is 43:22 have been weary of Me, O I
Is 43:28 the curse, and I to reproaches
Is 44: 1 and I whom I have chosen
Is 44: 5 name himself by the name of I
Is 44: 6 says the LORD, the King of I
Is 44:21 these, O Jacob, And I
Is 44:21 O I, you will not be
Is 44:23 and glorified Himself in I
Is 45: 3 by your name, am the God of I
Is 45: 4 and I My elect, I have even
Is 45:11 the LORD, the Holy One of I
Is 45:15 who hide Yourself, O God of I
Is 45:17 But I shall be saved by the
Is 45:25 of I shall be justified, and
Is 46: 3 the remnant of the house of I
Is 46:13 in Zion, for I My glory
Is 47: 4 His name, the Holy One of I
Is 48: 1 are called by the name of I
Is 48: 1 make mention of the God of I
Is 48: 2 city, and lean on the God of I
Is 48:12 Listen to Me, O Jacob, and I
Is 48:17 Redeemer, the Holy One of I
Is 49: 3 me, 'You are My servant, O I
Is 49: 5 so that I is gathered to Him
Is 49: 6 the preserved ones of I
Is 49: 7 the LORD, the Redeemer of I
Is 49: 7 faithful, the Holy One of I
Is 52:12 the God of I will be your
Is 54: 5 Redeemer is the Holy One of I
Is 55: 5 God, and the Holy One of I
Is 56: 8 who gathers the outcasts of I
Is 60: 9 God, and to the Holy One of I
Is 60:14 Zion of the Holy One of I
Is 63: 7 toward the house of I, which
Is 63:16 I does not acknowledge us
Is 66:20 as the children of I bring an
Jer 2: 3 I was holiness to the LORD,
Jer 2: 4 families of the house of I
Jer 2:14 Is I a servant?
Jer 2:26 so is the house of I ashamed
Jer 2:31 Have I been a wilderness to I
Jer 3: 6 what backsliding I has done
Jer 3: 8 for which backsliding I had
Jer 3:11 me, "Backsliding I has shown
Jer 3:12 Return, backsliding I,' says
Jer 3:18 walk with the house of I, and
Jer 3:20 with Me, O house of I," says
Jer 3:21 of the children of I
Jer 3:23 our God is the salvation of I
Jer 4: 1 If you will return, O I,"
Jer 5:11 For the house of I and the
Jer 5:15 you from afar, O house of I
Jer 6: 9 as a vine the remnant of I
Jer 7: 3 LORD of hosts, the God of I
Jer 7:12 the wickedness of My people I
Jer 7:21 LORD of hosts, the God of I
Jer 9:15 LORD of hosts, the God of I
Jer 9:26 and all the house of I are
Jer 10: 1 speaks to you, O house of I
Jer 10:16 and I is the tribe of His
Jer 11: 3 Thus says the LORD God of I
Jer 11:10 the house of I and the house
Jer 11:17 the evil of the house of I
Jer 12:14 caused My people I to inherit
Jer 13:11 caused the whole house of I
Jer 13:12 Thus says the LORD God of I
Jer 14: 8 O the Hope of I, his Savior
Jer 16: 9 LORD of hosts, the God of I
Jer 16:14 of I from the land of Egypt
Jer 16:15 I from the land of the north
Jer 17:13 O LORD, the hope of I, all
Jer 18: 6 O house of I, can I not do
Jer 18: 6 you in My hand, O house of I

Ezek 47:18 Gilead and the land of I,
Ezek 47:21 according to the tribes of I
Ezek 47:22 among the children of I
Ezek 47:22 you among the tribes of I
Ezek 48:11 the children of I went astray
Ezek 48:19 from all the tribes of I
Ezek 48:29 among the tribes of I, and
Ezek 48:31 named after the tribes of I)
Dan 1: 3 some of the children of I
Dan 9: 7 of Jerusalem and all I, those
Dan 9:11 all I has transgressed Your
Dan 9:20 sin and the sin of my people I
Hos 1: 1 the son of Joash, king of I
Hos 1: 4 the kingdom of the house of I
Hos 1: 5 I will break the bow of I in
Hos 1: 6 have mercy on the house of I
Hos 1:10 number of the children of I
Hos 1:11 the children of I shall be
Hos 3: 1 LORD for the children of I
Hos 3: 4 For the children of I shall
Hos 3: 5 children of I shall return
Hos 4: 1 the LORD, you children of I
Hos 4:15 Though you, I, play the
Hos 4:16 For I is stubborn like a
Hos 5: 1 Take heed, O house of I
Hos 5: 3 and I is not hidden from Me
Hos 5: 3 I is defiled.
Hos 5: 5 The pride of I testifies to
Hos 5: 5 therefore I and Ephraim
Hos 5: 9 among the tribes of I I make
Hos 6:10 thing in the house of I
Hos 6:10 I is defiled.
Hos 7: 1 When I would have healed I
Hos 7:10 the pride of I testifies to
Hos 8: 2 I will cry to Me, 'My God, we
Hos 8: 3 I has cast off the good
Hos 8: 6 For from I is even this
Hos 8: 8 I is swallowed up
Hos 8:14 For I has forgotten his Maker
Hos 9: 1 Do not rejoice, O I, with joy
Hos 9: 7 I knows!
Hos 9:10 I found I like grapes in the
Hos 10: 1 I empties his vine
Hos 10: 6 I shall be ashamed of his own
Hos 10: 8 places of Aven, the sin of I
Hos 10: 9 O I, you have sinned from the
Hos 10:15 of I shall be cut off utterly
Hos 11: 1 When I was a child, I loved
Hos 11: 8 How can I hand you over, I
Hos 11:12 and the house of I with deceit
Hos 12:12 I served for a spouse, and for
Hos 12:13 LORD brought I out of Egypt
Hos 13: 1 he exalted himself in I
Hos 13: 9 O I, you are destroyed, but
Hos 14: 1 O I, return to the LORD your
Hos 14: 5 I will be like the dew to I
Joel 2:27 that I am in the midst of I
Joel 3: 2 of My people, My heritage I
Joel 3:16 strength of the children of I
Amos 1: 1 which he saw concerning I in
Amos 1: 1 the son of Joash, king of I
Amos 2: 6 For three transgressions of I
Amos 2:11 not so, O you children of I
Amos 3: 1 against you, O children of I
Amos 3:12 so shall the children of I be
Amos 3:14 I for their transgressions
Amos 4: 5 you love, you children of I
Amos 4:12 thus will I do to you, O I
Amos 4:12 prepare to meet your God, O I
Amos 5: 1 lamentation, O house of I
Amos 5: 2 The virgin of I has fallen
Amos 5: 3 ten left to the house of I
Amos 5: 4 the LORD to the house of I
Amos 5:25 forty years, O house of I
Amos 6: 1 to whom the house of I comes
Amos 6:14 against you, O house of I
Amos 7: 8 in the midst of My people I
Amos 7: 9 the sanctuaries of I shall be
Amos 7:10 sent to Jeroboam king of I
Amos 7:10 the midst of the house of I
Amos 7:11 I shall surely be led away
Amos 7:15 Go, prophesy to My people I
Amos 7:16 Do not prophesy against I
Amos 7:17 I shall surely be led away
Amos 8: 2 end has come upon my people I
Amos 9: 7 to Me, O children of I
Amos 9: 7 Did I not bring up I from the
Amos 9: 9 house of I among all nations
Amos 9:14 the captives of My people I
Obad 20 host of the children of I

Mic 1: 5 the sins of the house of I
Mic 1:13 of I were found in you
Mic 1:14 be a lie to the kings of I
Mic 1:15 the glory of I shall come to
Mic 2:12 gather the remnant of I
Mic 3: 1 you rulers of the house of I
Mic 3: 8 transgression and to I his sin
Mic 3: 9 and rulers of the house of I
Mic 5: 1 of I with a rod on the cheek
Mic 5: 2 Me the One to be ruler in I
Mic 5: 3 return to the children of I
Mic 6: 2 and He will contend with I
Nah 2: 2 like the excellence of I, for
Zeph 2: 9 LORD of hosts, the God of I
Zeph 3:13 The remnant of I shall do no
Zeph 3:14 Shout, O I!
Zeph 3:15 the King of I, the LORD, is
Zech 1:19 that have scattered Judah, I
Zech 8:13 house of Judah and house of I
Zech 9: 1 tribes of I are on the LORD)
Zech 11:14 between Judah and I
Zech 12: 1 word of the LORD against I
Mal 1: 1 of the LORD to I by Malachi
Mal 1: 5 beyond the border of I
Mal 2:11 has been committed in I and in
Mal 2:16 For the LORD God of I says
Mal 4: 4 him in Horeb for all I, with
Matt 2: 6 who will shepherd My people I
Matt 2:20 and go to the land of I, for
Matt 2:21 and came into the land of I
Matt 8:10 great faith, not even in I
Matt 9:33 was never seen like this in I
Matt 10: 6 lost sheep of the house of I
Matt 10:23 gone through the cities of I
Matt 15:24 lost sheep of the house of I
Matt 15:31 they glorified the God of I
Matt 19:28 the twelve tribes of I
Matt 27: 9 of the children of I priced
Matt 27:42 If He is the King of I, let
Mark 12:29 Hear, O I, the LORD our God,
Mark 15:32 Let the Christ, the King of I
Luke 1:16 of I to the Lord their God
Luke 1:54 He has helped His servant I
Luke 1:68 Blessed is the Lord God of I
Luke 1:80 day of his manifestation to I
Luke 2:25 for the Consolation of I, and
Luke 2:32 and the glory of Your people I
Luke 2:34 fall and rising of many in I
Luke 4:25 many widows were in I in the
Luke 4:27 many lepers were in I in the
Luke 7: 9 great faith, not even in I
Luke 22:30 the twelve tribes of I
Luke 24:21 He who was going to redeem I
John 1:31 He should be revealed to I
John 1:49 You are the King of I
John 3:10 Are you the teacher of I, and
John 12:13 The King of I!
Acts 1: 6 time restore the kingdom to I
Acts 2:22 Men of I, hear these words
Acts 2:36 let all the house of I know
Acts 3:12 Men of I, why do you marvel
Acts 4: 8 of the people and elders of I
Acts 4:10 and to all the people of I
Acts 4:27 Gentiles and the people of I
Acts 5:21 elders of the children of I
Acts 5:31 to give repentance to I and
Acts 5:35 Men of I, take heed to
Acts 7:23 brethren, the children of I
Acts 7:37 who said to the children of I
Acts 7:42 the wilderness, O house of I
Acts 9:15 kings, and the children of I
Acts 10:36 God sent to the children of I
Acts 13:16 Men of I, and you who fear God
Acts 13:17 people I chose our fathers
Acts 13:23 God raised up for I a Savior
Acts 13:24 to all the people of I
Acts 21:28 Men of I, help!
Acts 28:20 because for the hope of I I
Rom 9: 6 not all I who are of I
Rom 9: 6 not all I who are of I
Rom 9:27 also cries out concerning I
Rom 9:27 I be as the sand of the sea
Rom 9:31 but I, pursuing the law of
Rom 10: 1 prayer to God for I is that
Rom 10:19 But I say, did I not know
Rom 10:21 to I he says: "All day long
Rom 11: 2 he pleads with God against I
Rom 11: 7 I has not obtained what it
Rom 11:25 in part has happened to I
Rom 11:26 so all I will be saved, as it

1Co 10:18 Observe I after the flesh
2Co 3: 7 so that the children of I
2Co 3:13 so that the children of I
Gal 6:16 them, and upon the I of God
Eph 2:12 from the commonwealth of I
Phil 3: 5 eighth day, of the stock of I
Heb 8: 8 covenant with the house of I
Heb 8:10 will make with the house of I
Heb 11:22 of the children of I, and gave
Rev 2:14 before the children of I, to
Rev 7: 4 the children of I were sealed
Rev 21:12 tribes of the children of I

ISRAELITE (*see* ISRAEL, ISRAELITES)
Lev 24:10 Now the son of an I woman
Lev 24:10 this I woman's son and a man
Lev 24:11 the I woman's son blasphemed
Num 25:14 name of the I who was killed
2Sa 17:25 whose name was Jithra, an I
Neh 9: 2 Then those of I lineage
John 1:47 an I indeed, in whom is no
Rom 11: 1 For I also am an I, of the

ISRAELITES (*see* ISRAELITE)
Ex 9: 7 livestock of the I was dead
Lev 23:42 All who are native I shall
Josh 8:24 that all the I returned to Ai
Josh 13:13 among the I until this day
Judg 20:21 thousand men of the I
1Sa 2:14 to all the I who came there
1Sa 13:20 But all the I would go down
1Sa 14:21 the I who were with Saul and
1Sa 25: 1 the I gathered together and
1Sa 29: 1 the I encamped by a fountain
1Ch 9: 2 in their cities were I,
Neh 11: 3 I, priests, Levites, Nethinim
Rom 9: 4 who are I, to whom pertain
2Co 11:22 Are they I? So am I.

ISRAEL'S (*see* ISRAEL)
Gen 48:13 right hand toward I left hand
Gen 48:13 left hand toward I right hand
Ex 18: 8 to the Egyptians for I sake
Num 1:20 Reuben, I oldest son, their
Num 31:30 from the children of I half
Num 31:42 from the children of I half
Num 31:47 from the children of I half
Judg 20:33 Then I men in ambush burst
2Sa 5:12 kingdom for His people I sake
1Ch 17:24 the God of Israel, is I God

ISSACHAR
Gen 30:18 So she called his name I
Gen 35:23 and Simeon, Levi, Judah, I
Gen 46:13 The sons of I were Tola,
Gen 49:14 I is a strong donkey, lying
Ex 1: 3 I, Zebulun, and Benjamin
Num 1: 8 from I, Nethaneel the son of
Num 1:28 From the children of I, their
Num 1:29 of I were fifty-four thousand
Num 2: 5 him shall be the tribe of I
Num 2: 5 leader of the children of I
Num 7:18 the son of Zuar, leader of I
Num 10:15 of I was Nethaneel the son of
Num 13: 7 from the tribe of I, Igal the
Num 26:23 The sons of I according to
Num 26:25 These are the families of I
Num 34:26 tribe of the children of I
Deut 27:12 Simeon, Levi, Judah, I,
Deut 33:18 going out, and I in your tents
Josh 17:10 on the north and I on the east
Josh 17:11 And in I and in Asher,
Josh 19:17 The fourth lot came out to I
Josh 19:17 for the children of I
Josh 19:23 tribe of the children of I
Josh 21: 6 families of the tribe of I
Josh 21:28 and from the tribe of I,
Judg 5:15 the princes of I were with
Judg 5:15 as I, so was Barak sent into
Judg 10: 1 the son of Dodo, a man of I
1Ki 4:17 the son of Paruah, in I
1Ki 15:27 of Ahijah, of the house of I
1Ch 2: 1 Simeon, Levi, Judah, I,
1Ch 6:62 cities from the tribe of I
1Ch 6:72 And from the tribe of I
1Ch 7: 1 The sons of I were Tola, Puah
1Ch 7: 5 of I were mighty men of valor
1Ch 12:32 of the children of I who had
1Ch 12:40 them, from as far away as I
1Ch 26: 5 I the seventh, Peulthai the
1Ch 27:18 over I, Omri the son of
2Ch 30:18 from Ephraim, Manasseh, I

Ezek 48:25 I shall have one portion
Ezek 48:26 by the border of I, from the
Ezek 48:33 for Simeon, one gate for I
Rev 7: 7 of the tribe of I twelve

ISSHIAH (*see* ISAIAH)
1Ch 24:21 of Rehabiah, the first was I
1Ch 24:25 The brother of Michah, I
1Ch 24:25 of the sons of I, Zechariah

ISSUE (*see* ISSUED, ISSUES)
Ezra 6: 8 Moreover I i a decree as to
Ezra 6:11 Also I i a decree that
Ezra 6:12 I Darius i the decree
Ezra 7:13 I i a decree that all those
Ezra 7:21 do i a decree to all the
Is 22:24 house, the offspring and the i
Ezek 23:20 i is like the i of horses

ISSUED (*see* ISSUE)
Ezra 5:13 King Cyrus i a decree to
Ezra 5:17 it is so that a decree was i
Ezra 6: 1 Then King Darius i a decree
Ezra 6: 3 Cyrus, King Cyrus i a decree
Ezra 10: 7 And they i a proclamation
Esth 3:14 be i as law in every province
Esth 8:13 to be i as a decree in every
Esth 8:14 the decree was i in Shushan
Esth 9:14 the decree was i in Shushan
Job 38: 8 forth and i from the womb
Dan 4: 6 Therefore I i a decree to
Dan 7:10 A fiery stream i and came
Zeph 2: 2 before the decree is i,

ISSUES (*see* ISSUE)
Prov 4:23 of it spring the i of life

ISUI
Gen 46:17 Asher were Jimnah, Ishuah, I

IT (*see* PREFACE)

ITALIAN (*see* ITALY)
Acts 10: 1 was called the I Regiment

ITALY (*see* ITALIAN)
Acts 18: 2 I with his wife Priscilla
Acts 27: 1 that we should sail to I,
Acts 27: 6 Alexandrian ship sailing to I
Heb 13:24 Those from I greet you

ITCH (*see* ITCHING)
Deut 28:27 with the scab, and with the i

ITCHING (*see* ITCH)
2Ti 4: 3 because they have i ears

ITEM (*see* ITEMS)
Lev 11:32 whether it is any i of wood
Lev 11:32 or sack, whatever i it is

ITEMS (*see* ITEM)
Num 4:32 by name the i he must carry
2Ch 32:27 for all kinds of desirable i
Ezek 27:18 because of your many luxury i
Ezek 27:24 your merchants in choice i

ITHAI (*see* ITTAI)
1Ch 11:31 I the son of Ribai of Gibeah,

ITHAMAR
Ex 6:23 Nadab, Abihu, Eleazar, and I
Ex 28: 1 Nadab, Abihu, Eleazar, and I
Ex 38:21 the Levites, by the hand of I
Lev 10: 6 to Aaron, and to Eleazar and I
Lev 10:12 to Aaron, and to Eleazar and I
Lev 10:16 was angry with Eleazar and I
Num 3: 2 and Abihu, Eleazar, and I
Num 3: 4 I ministered as priests under
Num 4:28 shall be under the hand of I
Num 4:33 under the hand of I the son
Num 7: 8 under the hand of I the son
Num 26:60 Nadab and Abihu, Eleazar and I
1Ch 6: 3 Nadab, Abihu, Eleazar, and I
1Ch 24: 1 Nadab, Abihu, Eleazar, and I
1Ch 24: 2 and I ministered as priests
1Ch 24: 3 and Ahimelech of the sons of I
1Ch 24: 4 Eleazar than of the sons of I
1Ch 24: 4 houses among the sons of I
1Ch 24: 5 Eleazar and from the sons of I
1Ch 24: 6 for Eleazar and one for I
Ezra 8: 2 of the sons of I, Daniel

ITHIEL
Neh 11: 7 son of Maaseiah, the son of I
Prov 30: 1 This man declared to I
Prov 30: 1 to I and Ucal

ITHMAH
1Ch 11:46 of Elnaam, I the Moabite,

ITHNAN
Josh 15:23 Kedesh, Hazor, I,

ITHRAN
Gen 36:26 Hemdan, Eshban, I, and
1Ch 1:41 were Hamran, Eshban, I

ITHREAM
2Sa 3: 5 and the sixth, I, by David's
1Ch 3: 3 the sixth, I, by his wife

ITHRITE (*see* ITHRITES)
2Sa 23:38 Ira the I, Gareb the I,
1Ch 11:40 Ira the I, Gareb the I,

ITHRITES (*see* ITHRITE)
1Ch 2:53 of Kirjath Jearim were the I

ITINERANT
Acts 19:13 Then some of the i Jewish

ITS (*see* PREFACE)

ITSELF (*see* PREFACE)

ITTAI (*see* ITHAI)
2Sa 15:19 king said to I the Gittite
2Sa 15:21 I answered the king and said,
2Sa 15:22 So David said to I, "Go, and
2Sa 15:22 Then I the Gittite and all
2Sa 18: 2 the hand of I the Gittite
2Sa 18: 5 Joab, Abishai, and I
2Sa 18:12 you and Abishai and I
2Sa 23:29 I the son of Ribai from

ITUREA
Luke 3: 1 brother Philip tetrarch of I

IVAH (*see* AHAVA, AVA)
2Ki 18:34 of Sepharvaim and Hena and I
2Ki 19:13 of Sepharvaim, Hena, and I
Is 37:13 of Sepharvaim, Hena, and I

IVORY
1Ki 10:18 king made a great throne of i
1Ki 10:22 came bringing gold, silver, i
1Ki 22:39 the i house which he built and
2Ch 9:17 king made a great throne of i
2Ch 9:21 bringing gold, silver, i
Ps 45: 8 cassia, Out of the i palaces
Song 5:14 His body is carved i inlaid
Song 7: 4 Your neck is like an i tower
Ezek 27: 6 inlaid your planks with i
Ezek 27:15 They brought you i tusks and
Amos 3:15 the houses of i shall perish
Amos 6: 4 who lie on beds of i, stretch
Rev 18:12 every kind of object of i

IZEHAR (*see* IZHAR)
Num 3:19 Amram, I, Hebron, and Uzziel

IZHAR (*see* IZEHAR, IZHARITES)
Ex 6:18 sons of Kohath were Amram, I
Ex 6:21 The sons of I were Korah,
Num 16: 1 Now Korah the son of I, the
1Ch 6: 2 sons of Kohath were Amram, I
1Ch 6:18 sons of Kohath were Amram, I
1Ch 6:38 the son of I, the son of
1Ch 23:12 Amram, I, Hebron, and Uzziel
1Ch 23:18 Of the sons of I, Shelomith

IZHARITES (*see* IZHAR)
Num 3:27 the family of the I, the
1Ch 24:22 Of the I, Shelomoth
1Ch 26:23 Of the Amramites, the I, the
1Ch 26:29 Of the I, Chenaniah and his

IZRAHIAH (*see* IZRAHITE, JEZRAHIAH)
1Ch 7: 3 The son of Uzzi was I, and the
1Ch 7: 3 the sons of I were Michael,

IZRAHITE (*see* EZRAHITE, IZRAHIAH)
1Ch 27: 8 month was Shamhuth the I

J

JAAKAN (*see* AKAN)
1Ch 1:42 were Bilhan, Zaavan, and J

JAAKOBAH
1Ch 4:36 Elioenai, J, Jeshohaiah,

JAALA
Ezra 2:56 the sons of J, the sons of
Neh 7:58 the children of J, the

JAALAM
Gen 36: 5 And Aholibamah bore Jeush, J
Gen 36:14 Jeush, J, and Korah
Gen 36:18 Chief Jeush, Chief J, and
1Ch 1:35 were Eliphaz, Reuel, Jeush, J

JAANAI
1Ch 5:12 Shapham the next, then J

JAARE-OREGIM (*see* JAIR)
2Sa 21:19 where Elhanan the son of J

JAARESHIAH
1Ch 8:27 J, Elijah, and Zichri were the

JAASAI
Ezra 10:37 Mattaniah, Mattenai, J,

JAASIEL
1Ch 11:47 Obed, and J the Mezobaite
1Ch 27:21 Benjamin, J the son of Abner

JAAZANIAH (*see* JEZANIAH)
2Ki 25:23 J the son of a Maachathite,
Jer 35: 3 Then I took J the son of
Ezek 8:11 stood J the son of Shaphan
Ezek 11: 1 whom I saw J the son of Azzur

JAAZIAH
1Ch 24:26 the son of J, Beno
1Ch 24:27 sons of Merari by J were Beno

JAAZIEL
1Ch 15:18 Zechariah, Ben, J,

JABAL
Gen 4:20 And Adah bore J

JABBOK
Gen 32:22 and crossed over the ford of J
Num 21:24 land from the Arnon to the J
Deut 2:37 or anywhere along the River J
Deut 3:16 border, as far as the River J
Josh 12: 2 even as far as the River J
Judg 11:13 the Arnon as far as the J
Judg 11:22 from the Arnon to the J and

JABESH (*see* JABESH GILEAD)
1Sa 11: 1 the men of J said to Nahash
1Sa 11: 3 the elders of J said to him
1Sa 11: 5 him the words of the men of J
1Sa 11: 9 reported it to the men of J
1Sa 11:10 Therefore the men of J said
1Sa 31:12 and they came to J and burned
1Sa 31:13 under the tamarisk tree at J
2Ki 15:10 of J conspired against him
2Ki 15:13 son of J became king in the
2Ki 15:14 the son of J in Samaria and
1Ch 10:12 and they brought them to J
1Ch 10:12 under the tamarisk tree at J

JABESH GILEAD (*see* GILEAD, JABESH)
Judg 21: 8 camp from J to the assembly
Judg 21: 9 inhabitants of J was there
Judg 21:10 strike the inhabitants of J
Judg 21:12 among the inhabitants of J
Judg 21:14 saved alive of the women of J
1Sa 11: 1 came up and encamped against J
1Sa 11: 9 you shall say to the men of J
1Sa 31:11 when the inhabitants of J
2Sa 2: 4 The men of J were the ones
2Sa 2: 5 messengers to the men of J
2Sa 21:12 from the men of J who had
1Ch 10:11 when all J heard all that the

JABEZ
1Ch 2:55 at J were the Tirathites, the
1Ch 4: 9 Now J was more honorable than
1Ch 4: 9 his mother called his name J
1Ch 4:10 J called on the God of Israel

JABIN (*see* JABIN'S)
Josh 11: 1 when J king of Hazor heard
Judg 4: 2 the hand of J king of Canaan
Judg 4: 3 for J had nine hundred
Judg 4:17 peace between J king of Hazor
Judg 4:23 J king of Canaan in the
Judg 4:24 against J king of Canaan,
Judg 4:24 destroyed J king of Canaan
Ps 83: 9 As with J at the Brook Kishon

JABIN'S (*see* JABIN)
Judg 4: 7 the commander of **J** army,

JABNEEL (*see* JABNEH)
Josh 15:11 Baalah, and extended to **J**
Josh 19:33 Adami Nekeb, and **J**

JABNEH (*see* JABNEEL)
2Ch 26: 6 wall of Gath, the wall of **J**

JACHAN (*see* AKAN)
1Ch 5:13 Meshullam, Sheba, Jorai, **J**

JACHIN (*see* JACHINITES, JARIB)
Gen 46:10 were Jemuel, Jamin, Ohad, **J**
Ex 6:15 were Jemuel, Jamin, Ohad, **J**
Num 26:12 of **J**, the family of the
1Ki 7:21 right and called its name **J**
1Ch 9:10 Jedaiah, Jehoiarib, and **J**
1Ch 24:17 the twenty-first to **J**, the
2Ch 3:17 the one on the right hand **J**
Neh 11:10 the son of Joiarib, and **J**

JACHINITES (*see* JACHIN)
Num 26:12 Jachin, the family of the **J**

JACINTH
Ex 28:19 the third row, a **j**, an agate,
Ex 39:12 the third row, a **j**, an agate,
Rev 21:20 chrysoprase, the eleventh **j**

JACKALS
Job 30:29 I am a brother of **j**, and a
Ps 44:19 broken us in the place of **j**
Ps 63:10 They shall be a portion for **j**
Is 13:22 **j** in their pleasant palaces
Is 34:13 it shall be a habitation of **j**
Is 34:14 shall also meet with the **j**
Is 35: 7 in the habitation of **j**, where
Is 43:20 field will honor Me, the **j**
Jer 9:11 a heap of ruins and a den of **j**
Jer 10:22 of Judah desolate, a den of **j**
Jer 14: 6 sniffed at the wind like **j**
Jer 49:33 shall be a dwelling for **j**
Jer 50:39 shall dwell there with the **j**
Jer 51:37 heap, a dwelling place for **j**
Lam 4: 3 Even the **j** present their
Mic 1: 8 make a wailing like the **j**
Mal 1: 3 for the **j** of the wilderness

JACKDAW
Lev 11:18 the white owl, the **j**, and the
Deut 14:17 the **j**, the carrion vulture,

JACOB (*see* ISRAEL, JACOB'S, JAMES)
Gen 25:26 so his name was called **J**
Gen 25:27 but **J** was a mild man,
Gen 25:28 his game, but Rebekah loved **J**
Gen 25:29 Now **J** cooked a stew
Gen 25:30 And Esau said to **J**, "Please
Gen 25:31 But **J** said, "Sell me your
Gen 25:33 Then **J** said, "Swear to me as
Gen 25:33 and sold his birthright to **J**
Gen 25:34 **J** gave Esau bread and stew of
Gen 27: 6 So Rebekah spoke to **J** her son
Gen 27:11 **J** said to Rebekah his mother,
Gen 27:15 put them on **J** her younger son
Gen 27:17 into the hand of her son **J**
Gen 27:19 And **J** said to his father,
Gen 27:21 Then Isaac said to **J**
Gen 27:22 So **J** went near to Isaac his
Gen 27:30 Isaac had finished blessing **J**
Gen 27:30 **J** had scarcely gone out from
Gen 27:36 Is he not rightly named **J**
Gen 27:41 So Esau hated **J** because of
Gen 27:41 then I will kill my brother **J**
Gen 27:42 called **J** her younger son, and
Gen 27:46 if **J** takes a wife of the
Gen 28: 1 Then Isaac called **J** and
Gen 28: 5 So Isaac sent **J** away, and he
Gen 28: 5 of Rebekah, the mother of **J**
Gen 28: 6 saw that Isaac had blessed **J**
Gen 28: 7 that **J** had obeyed his father
Gen 28:10 Now **J** went out from Beersheba
Gen 28:16 Then **J** awoke from his sleep
Gen 28:18 Then **J** rose early in the
Gen 28:20 Then **J** made a vow, saying,
Gen 29: 1 So **J** went on his journey and
Gen 29: 4 And **J** said to them,
Gen 29:10 pass, when **J** saw Rachel the
Gen 29:10 that **J** went near and rolled
Gen 29:11 Then **J** kissed Rachel, and
Gen 29:12 **J** told Rachel that he was her
Gen 29:13 about **J** his sister's son,
Gen 29:15 Then Laban said to **J**
Gen 29:18 Now **J** loved Rachel
Gen 29:20 So **J** served seven years for
Gen 29:21 Then **J** said to Laban, "Give
Gen 29:23 daughter and brought her to **J**
Gen 29:28 Then **J** did so and fulfilled
Gen 29:30 Then **J** also went in to Rachel
Gen 30: 1 that she bore **J** no children
Gen 30: 1 her sister, and said to **J**
Gen 30: 4 as wife, and **J** went in to her
Gen 30: 5 conceived and bore **J** a son
Gen 30: 7 again and bore **J** a second son
Gen 30: 9 maid and gave her to **J** as wife
Gen 30:10 maid Zilpah bore **J** a son
Gen 30:12 Zilpah bore **J** a second son
Gen 30:16 When **J** came out of the field
Gen 30:17 and bore **J** a fifth son
Gen 30:19 again and bore **J** a sixth son
Gen 30:25 Joseph, that **J** said to Laban,
Gen 30:29 And **J** said to him, "You know
Gen 30:31 And **J** said, "You shall not
Gen 30:36 journey between himself and **J**
Gen 30:36 **J** fed the rest of Laban's
Gen 30:37 Now **J** took for himself rods
Gen 30:40 Then **J** separated the lambs,
Gen 30:41 that **J** placed the rods before
Gen 31: 1 Now **J** heard the words of
Gen 31: 1 **J** has taken away all that was
Gen 31: 2 And **J** saw the countenance of
Gen 31: 3 Then the LORD said to **J**
Gen 31: 4 So **J** sent and called Rachel and
Gen 31:11 to me in a dream, saying, "**J**
Gen 31:17 Then **J** rose and set his sons
Gen 31:20 And **J** stole away, unknown to
Gen 31:22 the third day that **J** had fled
Gen 31:24 to **J** neither good nor bad
Gen 31:25 So Laban overtook **J**
Gen 31:25 Now **J** had pitched his tent in
Gen 31:26 And Laban said to **J**
Gen 31:29 to **J** neither good nor bad
Gen 31:31 Then **J** answered and said to
Gen 31:32 For **J** did not know that
Gen 31:36 Then **J** was angry and rebuked
Gen 31:36 **J** answered and said to Laban
Gen 31:43 Laban answered and said to **J**
Gen 31:45 So **J** took a stone and set it
Gen 31:46 Then **J** said to his brethren,
Gen 31:47 but **J** called it Galeed
Gen 31:51 Then Laban said to **J**, "Here
Gen 31:53 **J** swore by the Fear of his
Gen 31:54 Then **J** offered a sacrifice on
Gen 32: 1 So **J** went on his way, and the
Gen 32: 2 When **J** saw them, he said,
Gen 32: 3 Then **J** sent messengers before
Gen 32: 4 Thus your servant **J** says
Gen 32: 6 the messengers returned to **J**
Gen 32: 7 So **J** was greatly afraid and
Gen 32: 9 Then **J** said, "O God of my
Gen 32:20 your servant **J** is behind us
Gen 32:24 Then **J** was left alone
Gen 32:27 And he said, "**J**."
Gen 32:28 shall no longer be called **J**
Gen 32:29 Then **J** asked Him, saying,
Gen 32:30 And **J** called the name of the
Gen 33: 1 Now **J** lifted his eyes and
Gen 33:10 And **J** said, "No, please, if I
Gen 33:13 But **J** said to him, "My lord
Gen 33:17 **J** journeyed to Succoth, built
Gen 33:18 Then **J** came safely to the
Gen 34: 1 Leah, whom she had borne to **J**
Gen 34: 3 to Dinah the daughter of **J**
Gen 34: 5 **J** heard that he had defiled
Gen 34: 5 so **J** held his peace until
Gen 34: 6 out to **J** to speak with him
Gen 34: 7 the sons of **J** came in from
Gen 34:13 But the sons of **J** answered
Gen 34:25 that two of the sons of **J**
Gen 34:27 The sons of **J** came upon the
Gen 34:30 Then **J** said to Simeon and Levi
Gen 35: 1 Then God said to **J**, "Arise,
Gen 35: 2 **J** said to his household and to
Gen 35: 4 So they gave **J** all the
Gen 35: 4 and **J** hid them under the
Gen 35: 5 did not pursue the sons of **J**
Gen 35: 6 So **J** came to Luz (that is,
Gen 35: 9 Then God appeared to **J** again
Gen 35:10 Your name is **J**
Gen 35:10 shall not be called **J** anymore
Gen 35:14 So **J** set up a pillar in the
Gen 35:15 And **J** called the name of the
Gen 35:20 **J** set a pillar on her grave,
Gen 35:22 Now the sons of **J** were twelve
Gen 35:26 These were the sons of **J** who
Gen 35:27 Then **J** came to his father
Gen 35:29 his sons Esau and **J** buried him
Gen 36: 6 the presence of his brother **J**
Gen 37: 1 Now **J** dwelt in the land where
Gen 37: 2 This is the genealogy of **J**
Gen 37:34 Then **J** tore his clothes, put
Gen 42: 1 When **J** saw that there was
Gen 42: 1 in Egypt, **J** said to his sons,
Gen 42: 4 But **J** did not send Joseph's
Gen 42:29 Then they went to **J** their
Gen 42:36 **J** their father said to them,
Gen 45:25 of Canaan to **J** their father
Gen 45:27 the spirit of **J** their father
Gen 46: 2 the night, and said, "**J**, **J**!"
Gen 46: 5 Then **J** arose from Beersheba
Gen 46: 5 Israel carried their father **J**
Gen 46: 6 Canaan, and went to Egypt, **J**
Gen 46: 8 of the children of Israel, **J**
Gen 46:15 she bore to **J** in Padan Aram
Gen 46:18 and these she bore to **J**
Gen 46:22 of Rachel, who were born to **J**
Gen 46:25 and she bore these to **J**
Gen 46:26 who went with **J** to Egypt, who
Gen 46:27 of **J** who went to Egypt were
Gen 47: 7 brought in his father **J** and
Gen 47: 7 and **J** blessed Pharaoh
Gen 47: 8 Pharaoh said to **J**, "How old
Gen 47: 9 And **J** said to Pharaoh,
Gen 47:10 So **J** blessed Pharaoh, and went
Gen 47:28 **J** lived in the land of Egypt
Gen 48: 2 **J** was told, "Look, your son
Gen 48: 3 Then **J** said to Joseph
Gen 49: 1 **J** called his sons and said,
Gen 49: 2 and hear, you sons of **J**, and
Gen 49: 7 I will divide them in **J** and
Gen 49:24 hands of the Mighty God of **J**
Gen 49:33 And when **J** had finished
Gen 50:24 to Abraham, to Isaac, and to **J**
Ex 1: 1 and his household came with **J**
Ex 1: 5 who were descendants of **J**
Ex 2:24 with Isaac, and with **J**
Ex 3: 6 God of Isaac, and the God of **J**
Ex 3:15 God of Isaac, and the God of **J**
Ex 3:16 of Abraham, of Isaac, and of **J**
Ex 4: 5 God of Isaac, and the God of **J**
Ex 6: 3 to Abraham, to Isaac, and to **J**
Ex 6: 8 give to Abraham, Isaac, and **J**
Ex 19: 3 shall say to the house of **J**
Ex 33: 1 swore to Abraham, Isaac, and **J**
Lev 26:42 remember My covenant with **J**
Num 23: 7 curse **J** for me, and come,
Num 23:10 Who can count the dust of **J**
Num 23:21 not observed iniquity in **J**
Num 23:23 there is no sorcery against **J**
Num 23:23 It now must be said of **J** and
Num 24: 5 lovely are your tents, O **J**
Num 24:17 A Star shall come out of **J**
Num 24:19 Out of **J** One shall have
Num 32:11 swore to Abraham, Isaac, and **J**
Deut 1: 8 to Abraham, Isaac, and **J**
Deut 6:10 to Abraham, Isaac, and **J**, to
Deut 9: 5 to Abraham, Isaac, and **J**
Deut 9:27 Abraham, Isaac, and **J**
Deut 29:13 to Abraham, Isaac, and **J**
Deut 30:20 to Abraham, Isaac, and **J**, to
Deut 32: 9 **J** is the place of His
Deut 33: 4 of the congregation of **J**
Deut 33:10 shall teach **J** Your judgments
Deut 33:28 the fountain of **J** alone, in
Deut 34: 4 to give Abraham, Isaac, and **J**
Josh 24: 4 To Isaac I gave **J** and Esau
Josh 24: 4 of Seir to possess, but **J**
Josh 24:32 **J** had bought from the sons of
1Sa 12: 8 When **J** had gone into Egypt,
2Sa 23: 1 the anointed of the God of **J**
1Ki 18:31 the tribes of the sons of **J**
2Ki 13:23 with Abraham, Isaac, and **J**
2Ki 17:34 commanded the children of **J**
1Ch 16:13 servant, you children of **J**
1Ch 16:17 it to **J** for a statute, to
Ps 14: 7 Let **J** rejoice and Israel be
Ps 20: 1 of the God of **J** defend you
Ps 22:23 All you descendants of **J**,
Ps 24: 6 This is **J**, the generation of
Ps 44: 4 Command victories for **J**
Ps 46: 7 The God of **J** is our refuge
Ps 46:11 The God of **J** is our refuge
Ps 47: 4 excellence of **J** whom He loves

Ps 53: 6 Let J rejoice and Israel be
Ps 59:13 in J To the ends of the earth
Ps 75: 9 sing praises to the God of J
Ps 76: 6 At Your rebuke, O God of J
Ps 77:15 Your people, The sons of J
Ps 78: 5 established a testimony in J
Ps 78:21 a fire was kindled against J
Ps 78:71 him, To shepherd J His people
Ps 79: 7 For they have devoured J, And
Ps 81: 1 joyful shout to the God of J
Ps 81: 4 And a law of the God of J
Ps 84: 8 Give ear, O God of J
Ps 85: 1 back the captivity of J
Ps 87: 2 than all the dwellings of J
Ps 94: 7 does the God of J understand
Ps 99: 4 justice and righteousness in J
Ps 105: 6 servant, You children of J
Ps 105:10 it to J for a statute, To
Ps 105:23 J sojourned in the land of
Ps 114: 1 The house of J from a people
Ps 114: 7 the presence of the God of J
Ps 132: 2 vowed to the Mighty God of J
Ps 132: 5 place for the Mighty God of J
Ps 135: 4 LORD has chosen J for Himself
Ps 146: 5 has the God of J for his help
Ps 147:19 He declares His word to J
Is 2: 3 to the house of the God of J
Is 2: 5 O house of J, come and let us
Is 2: 6 Your people, the house of J
Is 8:17 His face from the house of J
Is 9: 8 LORD sent a word against J
Is 10:20 escaped of the house of J
Is 10:21 will return, the remnant of J
Is 14: 1 the LORD will have mercy on J
Is 14: 1 will cling to the house of J
Is 17: 4 that the glory of J will wane
Is 27: 6 shall cause to take root in J
Is 27: 9 iniquity of J will be covered
Is 29:22 concerning the house of J
Is 29:22 J shall not now be ashamed,
Is 29:23 and hallow the Holy One of J
Is 40:27 Why do you say, O J, and speak
Is 41: 8 Israel, are My servant, J
Is 41:14 Fear not, you worm J, you men
Is 41:21 reasons," says the King of J
Is 42:24 Who gave J for plunder, and
Is 43: 1 LORD, who created you, O J
Is 43:22 have not called upon Me, O J
Is 43:28 I will give J to the curse,
Is 44: 1 O J My servant, and Israel
Is 44: 2 Fear not, O J My servant
Is 44: 5 call himself by the name of J
Is 44:21 Remember these, O J, And
Is 44:23 for the LORD has redeemed J
Is 45: 4 For J My servant's sake, and
Is 45:19 did not say to the seed of J
Is 46: 3 Listen to Me, O house of J
Is 48: 1 Hear this, O house of J, who
Is 48:12 Listen to Me, O J, and Israel,
Is 48:20 has redeemed His servant J
Is 49: 5 to bring J back to Him, so
Is 49: 6 to raise up the tribes of J
Is 49:26 Redeemer, the Mighty One of J
Is 58: 1 and the house of J their sins
Is 58:14 the heritage of J your father
Is 59:20 turn from transgression in J
Is 60:16 Redeemer, the Mighty One of J
Is 65: 9 forth descendants from J, and
Jer 2: 4 of the LORD, O house of J
Jer 5:20 this in the house of J and
Jer 10:16 The Portion of J is not like
Jer 10:25 for they have eaten up J,
Jer 30:10 do not fear, O My servant J
Jer 30:10 J shall return, have rest and
Jer 31: 7 Sing with gladness for J, and
Jer 31:11 For the LORD has redeemed J
Jer 33:26 away the descendants of J
Jer 33:26 of Abraham, Isaac, and J
Jer 46:27 do not fear, O My servant J
Jer 46:27 J shall return, have rest and
Jer 46:28 O J My servant," says the
Jer 51:19 The Portion of J is not like
Lam 1:17 J that those around him
Lam 2: 2 all the habitations of J
Lam 2: 3 He has blazed against J like
Ezek 20: 5 descendants of the house of J
Ezek 28:25 which I gave to My servant J
Ezek 37:25 I have given to J My servant
Ezek 39:25 bring back the captives of J
Hos 10:11 J shall break his clods
Hos 12: 2 will punish J according to
Hos 12:12 J fled to the country of
Amos 3:13 against the house of J,"
Amos 6: 8 I abhor the pride of J, and
Amos 7: 2 that J may stand, for he is
Amos 7: 5 that J may stand, for he is
Amos 8: 7 has sworn by the pride of J
Amos 9: 8 destroy the house of J,"
Obad 10 against your brother J, shame
Obad 17 the house of J shall possess
Obad 18 The house of J shall be a
Mic 1: 5 is for the transgression of J
Mic 1: 5 is the transgression of J
Mic 2: 7 who are named the house of J
Mic 2:12 assemble all of you, O J, I
Mic 3: 1 Hear now, O heads of J, and
Mic 3: 8 and might, to declare to J his
Mic 3: 9 you heads of the house of J
Mic 4: 2 to the house of the God of J
Mic 5: 7 Then the remnant of J shall
Mic 5: 8 the remnant of J shall be
Mic 7:20 You will give truth to J and
Nah 2: 2 of J like the excellence of
Mal 1: 2 Yet J I have loved
Mal 2:12 of J the man who does this
Mal 3: 6 are not consumed, O sons of J
Matt 1: 2 begot Isaac, Isaac begot J
Matt 1: 2 J begot Judah and his brothers
Matt 1:15 Matthan, and Matthan begot J
Matt 1:16 J begot Joseph the husband of
Matt 8:11 J in the kingdom of heaven
Matt 22:32 of Isaac, and the God of J'
Mark 12:26 of Isaac, and the God of J'
Luke 1:33 over the house of J forever
Luke 3:34 the son of J, the son of
Luke 13:28 see Abraham and Isaac and J
Luke 20:37 God of Isaac, and the God of J
John 4: 5 that J gave to his son Joseph
John 4:12 You greater than our father J
Acts 3:13 God of Abraham, Isaac, and J
Acts 7: 8 and Isaac begot J
Acts 7: 8 J begot the twelve patriarchs
Acts 7:12 But when J heard that there
Acts 7:14 sent and called his father J
Acts 7:15 So J went down to Egypt
Acts 7:32 God of Isaac, and the God of J
Acts 7:46 a dwelling for the God of J
Rom 9:13 J I have loved, but Esau I
Rom 11:26 turn away ungodliness from J
Heb 11: 9 in tents with Isaac and J, the
Heb 11:20 By faith Isaac blessed J and
Heb 11:21 By faith J, when he was dying

JACOB'S (*see* JACOB)
Gen 27:22 The voice is J voice, but the
Gen 30: 2 J anger was aroused against
Gen 30:42 Laban's and the stronger J
Gen 31:33 And Laban went into J tent
Gen 32:18 say, "They are your servant J
Gen 32:25 the socket of J hip was out
Gen 32:32 of J hip in the muscle that
Gen 34: 7 by lying with J daughter, a
Gen 34:19 he delighted in J daughter
Gen 35:23 J firstborn, and Simeon, Levi,
Gen 45:26 J heart stood still, because
Gen 46: 8 Reuben was J firstborn
Gen 46:19 J wife, were Joseph and
Gen 46:26 besides J sons' wives, were
Gen 47:28 So the length of J life was
Jer 30: 7 it is the time of J trouble
Jer 30:18 back the captivity of J tents
Mal 1: 2 Was not Esau J brother
John 4: 6 Now J well was there

JADA
1Ch 2:28 of Onam were Shammai and J
1Ch 2:32 The sons of J, the brother of

JADDAI
Ezra 10:43 Mattithiah, Zabad, Zebina, J

JADDUA
Neh 10:21 Meshezabeel, Zadok, J,
Neh 12:11 Jonathan, and Jonathan begot J
Neh 12:22 Joiada, Johanan, and J

JADON
Neh 3: 7 J the Meronothite, the men of

JAEL
Judg 4:17 away on foot to the tent of J
Judg 4:18 J went out to meet Sisera, and
Judg 4:21 Then J, Heber's wife, took a
Judg 4:22 J came out to meet him, and
Judg 5: 6 of Anath, in the days of J
Judg 5:24 Most blessed among women is J

JAGUR
Josh 15:21 South, were Kabzeel, Eder, J

JAHALELEEL
1Ch 4:16 The sons of J were Ziph,

JAHATH
1Ch 4: 2 the son of Shobal begot J
1Ch 4: 2 and J begot Ahumai and Lahad
1Ch 6:20 J his son, Zimmah his son,
1Ch 6:43 the son of J, the son of
1Ch 23:10 J, Zina, Jeush, and Beriah
1Ch 23:11 J was the first and Zizah the
1Ch 24:22 of the sons of Shelomoth, J
2Ch 34:12 Their overseers were J and

JAHAZ (*see* JAHAZA, JAHZAH)
Num 21:23 wilderness, and he came to J
Deut 2:32 out against us to fight at J
Josh 21:36 J with its common-land,
Judg 11:20 together, encamped in J, and
Is 15: 4 shall be heard as far as J
Jer 48:34 to J they have uttered their

JAHAZA (*see* JAHAZ)
Josh 13:18 J, Kedemoth, Mephaath,

JAHAZIAH
Ezra 10:15 J the son of Tikvah opposed

JAHAZIEL
1Ch 12: 4 Jeremiah, J, Johanan, and
1Ch 16: 6 J the priests regularly blew
1Ch 23:19 J the third, and Jekameam the
1Ch 24:23 J the third, and Jekameam the
2Ch 20:14 upon J the son of Zechariah

JAHDAI
1Ch 2:47 And the sons of J were Regem

JAHDIEL
1Ch 5:24 Jeremiah, Hodaviah, and J

JAHDO
1Ch 5:14 of Jeshishai, the son of J

JAHLEEL (*see* JAHLEELITES)
Gen 46:14 were Sered, Elon, and J
Num 26:26 of J, the family of the

JAHLEELITES (*see* JAHLEEL)
Num 26:26 Jahleel, the family of the J

JAHMAI
1Ch 7: 2 Uzzi, Rephaiah, Jeriel, J

JAHZAH (*see* JAHAZ)
1Ch 6:78 J with its common-lands,
Jer 48:21 on Holon and J and Mephaath,

JAHZEEL (*see* JAHZEELITES, JAHZIEL)
Gen 46:24 The sons of Naphtali were J
Num 26:48 of J, the family of the

JAHZEELITES (*see* JAHZEEL)
Num 26:48 Jahzeel, the family of the J

JAHZERAH
1Ch 9:12 son of Adiel, the son of J

JAHZIEL (*see* JAHZEEL)
1Ch 7:13 The sons of Naphtali were J

JAILER
Acts 16:23 commanding the j to keep them

JAIR (*see* HAVOTH JAIR, JAARE-OREGIM, JAIRITE)
Num 32:41 Also J the son of Manasseh
Deut 3:14 J the son of Manasseh took
Josh 13:30 all the towns of J which are
Judg 10: 3 After him arose J, a
Judg 10: 5 J died and was buried in Camon
1Ki 4:13 of J the son of Manasseh, in
1Ch 2:22 Segub begot J, who had
1Ch 2:23 took from them the towns of J
1Ch 20: 5 Elhanan the son of J killed
Esth 2: 5 was Mordecai the son of J

JAIRITE (*see* JAIR)
2Sa 20:26 and Ira the J was a chief

JAIRUS
Mark 5:22 the synagogue came, J by name
Luke 8:41 there came a man named J

JAKEH
Prov 30: 1 words of Agur the son of J

JAKIM
1Ch 8:19 J, Zichri, Zabdi,
1Ch 24:12 to Eliashib, the twelfth to J

JALON
1Ch 4:17 Jether, Mered, Epher, and J

JAMBRES
2Ti 3: 8 J resisted Moses, so do these

JAMES (*see* JACOB)
Matt 4:21 J the son of Zebedee, and John
Matt 10: 2 J the son of Zebedee, and John
Matt 10: 3 J the son of Alphaeus, and
Matt 13:55 And His brothers J, Joses,
Matt 17: 1 six days Jesus took Peter, J
Matt 27:56 Mary the mother of J and
Mark 1:19 He saw J the son of Zebedee,
Mark 1:29 of Simon and Andrew, with J
Mark 3:17 J the son of Zebedee and John
Mark 3:17 and John the brother of J, to
Mark 3:18 J the son of Alphaeus,
Mark 5:37 to follow Him except Peter, J
Mark 5:37 and John the brother of J
Mark 6: 3 Son of Mary, and brother of J
Mark 9: 2 six days Jesus took Peter, J
Mark 10:35 Then J and John, the sons of
Mark 10:41 be greatly displeased with J
Mark 13: 3 opposite the temple, Peter, J
Mark 14:33 And He took Peter, J, and John
Mark 15:40 Mary the mother of J the Less
Mark 16: 1 Mary the mother of J, and
Luke 5:10 and so also were J and John,
Luke 6:14 J and John
Luke 6:15 J the son of Alphaeus, and
Luke 6:16 Judas the son of J, and Judas
Luke 8:51 one to go in except Peter, J
Luke 9:28 He took Peter, John, and J
Luke 9:54 And when His disciples J and
Luke 24:10 Joanna, Mary the mother of J
Acts 1:13 Peter, J, John, and Andrew
Acts 1:13 J the son of Alphaeus and
Acts 1:13 and Judas the son of J
Acts 12: 2 Then he killed J the brother
Acts 12:17 Go, tell these things to J
Acts 15:13 silent, J answered, saying,
Acts 21:18 day Paul went in with us to J
1Co 15: 7 After that He was seen by J
Gal 1:19 the other apostles except J
Gal 2: 9 and when J, Cephas, and John,
Gal 2:12 certain men came from J, he
Jas 1: 1 J, a servant of God and of the
Jude 1 Jesus Christ, and brother of J

JAMIN (*see* JAMINITES)
Gen 46:10 sons of Simeon were Jemuel, J
Ex 6:15 sons of Simeon were Jemuel, J
Num 26:12 of J, the family of the
1Ch 2:27 of Jerahmeel, were Maaz, J
1Ch 4:24 sons of Simeon were Nemuel, J
Neh 8: 7 Jeshua, Bani, Sherebiah, J

JAMINITES (*see* JAMIN)
Num 26:12 of Jamin, the family of the J

JAMLECH
1Ch 4:34 Meshobab, J, and Joshah the

JANNA
Luke 3:24 son of Melchi, the son of J

JANNES
2Ti 3: 8 Now as J and Jambres resisted

JANOAH (*see* JANOHAH)
2Ki 15:29 Ijon, Abel Beth Maachah, J

JANOHAH (*see* JANOAH)
Josh 16: 6 passed by it on the east of J
Josh 16: 7 went down from J to Ataroth

JANUM
Josh 15:53 J, Beth Tappuah, Aphekah,

JAPHETH
Gen 5:32 begot Shem, Ham, and J
Gen 6:10 Shem, Ham, and J
Gen 7:13 Noah's sons, Shem, Ham, and J
Gen 9:18 the ark were Shem, Ham, and J
Gen 9:23 J took a garment, laid it on
Gen 9:27 May God enlarge J, and may he
Gen 10: 1 Shem, Ham, and J
Gen 10: 2 The sons of J were Gomer,
Gen 10:21 the brother of J the elder
1Ch 1: 4 Noah, Shem, Ham, and J
1Ch 1: 5 The sons of J were Gomer,

JAPHIA
Josh 10: 3 J king of Lachish, and Debir
Josh 19:12 toward Daberath, bypassing J
2Sa 5:15 Ibhar, Elishua, Nepheg, J
1Ch 3: 7 Nogah, Nepheg, J,
1Ch 14: 6 Nogah, Nepheg, J,

JAPHLET (*see* JAPHLETITES)
1Ch 7:32 And Heber begot J, Shomer,
1Ch 7:33 The sons of J were Pasach
1Ch 7:33 These were the children of J

JAPHLETITES (*see* JAPHLET)
Josh 16: 3 to the boundary of the J, as

JAR
1Ki 14: 3 a j of honey, and go to him
1Ki 17:12 a bin, and a little oil in a j
1Ki 17:14 nor shall the j of oil run
1Ki 17:16 nor did the j of oil run dry,
1Ki 19: 6 on coals, and a j of water
2Ki 4: 2 in the house but a j of oil

JARAH
1Ch 9:42 Ahaz begot J; J begot Alemeth

JAREB
Hos 5:13 to Assyria and sent to King J
Hos 10: 6 as a present for King J

JARED (*see* JERED)
Gen 5:15 sixty-five years, and begot J
Gen 5:16 After he begot J, Mahalaleel
Gen 5:18 J lived one hundred and
Gen 5:19 J lived eight hundred years,
Gen 5:20 days of J were nine hundred
1Ch 1: 2 Cainan, Mahalaleel, J,
Luke 3:37 son of Enoch, the son of J

JARHA
1Ch 2:34 servant whose name was J
1Ch 2:35 to J his servant as wife, and

JARIB (*see* JACHIN)
1Ch 4:24 Simeon were Nemuel, Jamin, J
Ezra 8:16 Ariel, Shemaiah, Elnathan, J
Ezra 10:18 Maaseiah, Eliezer, J, and

JARMUTH (*see* RAMOTH, REMETH)
Josh 10: 3 of Hebron, Piram king of J
Josh 10: 5 king of Hebron, the king of J
Josh 10:23 king of Hebron, the king of J
Josh 12:11 the king of J, one
Josh 15:35 J, Adullam, Socoh, Azekah,
Josh 21:29 J with its common-land, and En
Neh 11:29 in En Rimmon, Zorah, J,

JAROAH
1Ch 5:14 the son of Huri, the son of J

JASHEN (*see* HASHEM)
2Sa 23:32 (of the sons of J), Jonathan,

JASHER
Josh 10:13 not written in the Book of J
2Sa 1:18 is written in the Book of J

JASHOBEAM
1Ch 11:11 J the son of a Hachmonite,
1Ch 12: 6 Azareel, Joezer, and J, the
1Ch 27: 2 was J the son of Zabdiel, and

JASHUB (*see* JASHUBI-LEHEM, JASHUBITES, JOB, SHEAR-JASHUB)
Num 26:24 of J, the family of the
1Ch 7: 1 Issachar were Tola, Puah, J
Ezra 10:29 Meshullam, Malluch, Adaiah, J

JASHUBI-LEHEM (*see* JASHUB)
1Ch 4:22 who ruled in Moab, and J

JASHUBITES (*see* JASHUB)
Num 26:24 Jashub, the family of the J

JASON
Acts 17: 5 and attacked the house of J
Acts 17: 6 not find them, they dragged J
Acts 17: 7 J has harbored them, and these
Acts 17: 9 had taken security from J
Rom 16:21 fellow worker, and Lucius, J

JASPER
Ex 28:20 row, a beryl, an onyx, and a j
Ex 39:13 row, a beryl, an onyx, and a j
Ezek 28:13 and diamond, beryl, onyx, and j
Rev 4: 3 He who sat there was like a j
Rev 21:11 stone, like a j stone, clear
Rev 21:18 of its wall was of j
Rev 21:19 the first foundation was j

JATHNIEL
1Ch 26: 2 the third, J the fourth,

JATTIR
Josh 15:48 Shamir, J, Sochoh,
Josh 21:14 J with its common-land,
1Sa 30:27 South, those who were in J
1Ch 6:57 with its common-lands, J,

JAVAN
Gen 10: 2 were Gomer, Magog, Madai, J
Gen 10: 4 The sons of J were Elishah,
1Ch 1: 5 were Gomer, Magog, Madai, J
1Ch 1: 7 The sons of J were Elishah,
Is 66:19 draw the bow, and Tubal and J
Ezek 27:13 J, Tubal, and Meshech were
Ezek 27:19 Dan and J paid for your wares,

JAVELIN (*see* JAVELINS)
Num 25: 7 and took a j in his hand
1Sa 17: 6 and a bronze j between his
1Sa 17:45 with a spear, and with a j
Job 39:23 the glittering spear and j
Job 41:26 nor does spear, dart, or j

JAVELINS (*see* JAVELIN)
Job 41:29 he laughs at the threat of j
Ezek 39: 9 the bows and arrows, the j

JAW (*see* JAWBONE, JAWS)
Job 41: 2 or pierce his j with a hook

JAWBONE (*see* JAW)
Judg 15:15 found a fresh j of a donkey
Judg 15:16 With the j of a donkey, heaps
Judg 15:16 with the j of a donkey I have
Judg 15:17 he threw the j from his hand

JAWS (*see* JAW)
Ps 22:15 And My tongue clings to My j
Is 30:28 bridle in the j of the people
Ezek 29: 4 I will put hooks in your j
Ezek 38: 4 around, put hooks into your j

JAZER
Num 21:32 Then Moses sent to spy out J
Num 32: 1 when they saw the land of J
Num 32: 3 Ataroth, Dibon, J, Nimrah,
Num 32:35 Atroth and Shophan and J and
Josh 13:25 Their territory was J, and all
Josh 21:39 and J with its common-land
2Sa 24: 5 ravine of Gad, and toward J
1Ch 6:81 and J with its common-lands
1Ch 26:31 capable men at J of Gilead
Is 16: 8 which have reached to J and
Is 16: 9 Sibmah, with the weeping of J
Jer 48:32 for you with the weeping of J
Jer 48:32 they reach to the sea of J

JAZIZ
1Ch 27:31 J the Hagerite was over the

JEALOUS (*see* JEALOUSLY, JEALOUSY)
Ex 20: 5 the LORD your God, am a j God
Ex 34:14 whose name is J, is a j God
Num 5:14 he becomes j of his wife, who
Num 5:14 he becomes j of his wife,
Num 5:30 and he becomes j of his wife
Deut 4:24 is a consuming fire, a j God
Deut 5: 9 the LORD your God, am a j God
Deut 6:15 God is a j God among you)
Josh 24:19 He is a j God
Ezek 39:25 I will be j for My holy name
Nah 1: 2 God is j, and the LORD avenges
2Co 11: 2 For I am j for you with godly

JEALOUSIES (*see* JEALOUSY)
2Co 12:20 lest there be contentions, j
Gal 5:20 hatred, contentions, j,

JEALOUSLY (*see* JEALOUS)
Jas 4: 5 who dwells in us yearns j"

JEALOUSY (*see* JEALOUS, JEALOUSIES)
Num 5:14 spirit of j comes upon him
Num 5:14 spirit of j comes upon him
Num 5:15 it is a grain offering of j
Num 5:18 is the grain offering of j
Num 5:25 of j from the woman's hand
Num 5:29 This is the law of j, when a
Num 5:30 spirit of j comes upon a man
Deut 29:20 His j would burn against that
Deut 32:16 Him to j with foreign gods
Deut 32:21 Me to j by what is not God

1Ki 1:44 prophet, Benaiah the son of **J**
1Ki 2:25 hand of Benaiah the son of **J**
1Ki 2:29 sent Benaiah the son of **J**
1Ki 2:34 Benaiah the son of **J** went up
1Ki 2:35 **J** in his place over the army
1Ki 2:46 Benaiah the son of **J**
1Ki 4: 4 Benaiah the son of **J**, over
2Ki 11: 4 In the seventh year **J** sent
2Ki 11: 9 that **J** the priest commanded
2Ki 11: 9 and came to **J** the priest
2Ki 11:15 Then **J** the priest commanded
2Ki 11:17 Then **J** made a covenant
2Ki 12: 2 **J** the priest instructed him
2Ki 12: 7 Jehoash called **J** the priest
2Ki 12: 9 Then **J** the priest took a
1Ch 11:22 Benaiah was the son of **J**, the
1Ch 11:24 Benaiah the son of **J** had done
1Ch 12:27 **J**, the leader of the
1Ch 18:17 Benaiah the son of **J** was over
1Ch 27: 5 the son of **J** the priest, who
1Ch 27:34 was **J** the son of Benaiah,
2Ch 22:11 the wife of **J** the priest (for
2Ch 23: 1 In the seventh year **J**
2Ch 23: 8 that **J** the priest commanded
2Ch 23: 8 for **J** the priest had not
2Ch 23: 9 And **J** the priest gave to the
2Ch 23:11 Then **J** and his sons anointed
2Ch 23:14 Then **J** the priest brought out
2Ch 23:16 Then **J** made a covenant
2Ch 23:18 Also **J** appointed the
2Ch 24: 2 all the days of **J** the priest
2Ch 24: 3 **J** took for him two wives, and
2Ch 24: 6 called **J** the chief priest
2Ch 24:12 **J** gave it to those who did
2Ch 24:14 money before the king and **J**
2Ch 24:14 continually all the days of **J**
2Ch 24:15 But **J** grew old and was full of
2Ch 24:17 Now after the death of **J** the
2Ch 24:20 the son of **J** the priest, who
2Ch 24:22 **J** his father had done to him
2Ch 24:25 of the sons of **J** the priest
Neh 3: 6 Moreover **J** the son of Paseah
Jer 29:26 instead of **J** the priest, so

JEHOIAKIM (*see* ELIAKIM, JEHOIAKIM'S, JOIAKIM)
2Ki 23:34 and changed his name to **J**
2Ki 23:35 So **J** gave the silver and gold
2Ki 23:36 **J** was twenty-five years old
2Ki 24: 1 **J** became his vassal for three
2Ki 24: 5 Now the rest of the acts of **J**
2Ki 24: 6 So **J** rested with his fathers
2Ki 24:19 to all that **J** had done
1Ch 3:15 the firstborn, the second **J**
1Ch 3:16 The sons of **J** were Jeconiah
2Ch 36: 4 and changed his name to **J**
2Ch 36: 5 **J** was twenty-five years old
2Ch 36: 8 Now the rest of the acts of **J**
Jer 1: 3 days of **J** the son of Josiah
Jer 22:18 **J** the son of Josiah, king of
Jer 22:24 though Coniah the son of **J**
Jer 24: 1 captive Jeconiah the son of **J**
Jer 25: 1 year of **J** the son of Josiah
Jer 26: 1 reign of **J** the son of Josiah
Jer 26:21 when **J** the king, with all his
Jer 26:22 Then **J** the king sent men to
Jer 26:23 and brought him to **J** the king
Jer 27: 1 reign of **J** the son of Josiah
Jer 27:20 captive Jeconiah the son of **J**
Jer 28: 4 place Jeconiah the son of **J**
Jer 35: 1 days of **J** the son of Josiah
Jer 36: 1 year of **J** the son of Josiah
Jer 36: 9 year of **J** the son of Josiah
Jer 36:28 which **J** the king of Judah has
Jer 36:29 shall say to **J** king of Judah
Jer 36:30 concerning **J** king of Judah
Jer 36:32 **J** king of Judah had burned in
Jer 37: 1 of Coniah the son of **J**, whom
Jer 45: 1 year of **J** the son of Josiah
Jer 46: 2 year of **J** the son of Josiah
Jer 52: 2 to all that **J** had done
Dan 1: 1 the reign of **J** king of Judah
Dan 1: 2 the Lord gave **J** king of Judah

JEHOIAKIM'S (*see* JEHOIAKIM)
2Ch 36:10 **J** brother, king over Judah and

JEHOIARIB (*see* JOIARIB)
1Ch 9:10 Jedaiah, **J**, and Jachin
1Ch 24: 7 Now the first lot fell to **J**

JEHONADAB (*see* JONADAB)
2Ki 10:15 he met **J** the son of Rechab,
2Ki 10:15 And **J** answered, "It is."
2Ki 10:23 **J** the son of Rechab went into

JEHONATHAN (*see* JOHN, JONATHAN)
1Ch 27:25 **J** the son of Uzziah was over
1Ch 27:32 Also **J**, David's uncle, was a
2Ch 17: 8 Asahel, Shemiramoth, **J**,
Neh 12:18 of Shemaiah, **J**

JEHORAM (*see* HADORAM, JORAM)
1Ki 22:50 Then **J** his son reigned in his
2Ki 1:17 **J** became king in his place,
2Ki 1:17 in the second year of **J** the
2Ki 3: 1 Now **J** the son of Ahab became
2Ki 3: 6 So King **J** went out of Samaria
2Ki 8:16 **J** the son of Jehoshaphat
2Ki 8:25 Israel, Ahaziah the son of **J**
2Ki 8:29 And Ahaziah the son of **J**, king
2Ki 9:24 and shot **J** between his arms
2Ki 12:18 his fathers, Jehoshaphat and **J**
2Ch 17: 8 and with them Elishama and **J**
2Ch 21: 1 Then **J** his son reigned in his
2Ch 21: 3 but he gave the kingdom to **J**
2Ch 21: 4 Now when **J** was established
2Ch 21: 5 **J** was thirty-two years old
2Ch 21: 9 So **J** went out with his
2Ch 21:16 against **J** the spirit of the
2Ch 22: 1 So Ahaziah the son of **J**, king
2Ch 22: 5 went with **J** the son of Ahab
2Ch 22: 6 And Azariah the son of **J**, king
2Ch 22: 6 went down to see **J** the son of
2Ch 22: 7 he went out with **J** against
2Ch 22:11 the daughter of King **J**, the

JEHOSHABEATH (*see* JEHOSHEBA)
2Ch 22:11 But **J**, the daughter of the
2Ch 22:11 So **J**, the daughter of King

JEHOSHAPHAT (*see* JOSHAPHAT)
2Sa 8:16 **J** the son of Ahilud was
2Sa 20:24 **J** the son of Ahilud was
1Ki 4: 3 **J** the son of Ahilud, the
1Ki 4:17 **J** the son of Paruah, in
1Ki 15:24 Then **J** his son reigned in his
1Ki 22: 2 that **J** the king of Judah went
1Ki 22: 4 So he said to **J**, "Will you
1Ki 22: 4 **J** said to the king of Israel,
1Ki 22: 5 **J** said to the king of Israel,
1Ki 22: 7 And **J** said, "Is there not
1Ki 22: 8 the king of Israel said to **J**
1Ki 22: 8 And **J** said, "Let not the king
1Ki 22:10 **J** the king of Judah, having
1Ki 22:18 the king of Israel said to **J**
1Ki 22:29 **J** the king of Judah went up
1Ki 22:30 the king of Israel said to **J**
1Ki 22:32 of the chariots saw **J**, that
1Ki 22:32 against him, and **J** cried out
1Ki 22:41 Now **J** the son of Asa had
1Ki 22:42 **J** was thirty-five years old
1Ki 22:44 Also **J** made peace with the
1Ki 22:45 Now the rest of the acts of **J**
1Ki 22:48 **J** made merchant ships to go
1Ki 22:49 the son of Ahab said to **J**
1Ki 22:49 But **J** would not.
1Ki 22:50 **J** rested with his fathers, and
1Ki 22:51 year of **J** king of Judah, and
2Ki 1:17 year of Jehoram the son of **J**
2Ki 3: 1 year of **J** king of Judah, and
2Ki 3: 7 and sent to **J** king of Judah,
2Ki 3:11 But **J** said, "Is there no
2Ki 3:12 And **J** said, "The word of
2Ki 3:12 So the king of Israel and **J**
2Ki 3:14 presence of **J** king of Judah
2Ki 8:16 **J** having been king of Judah,
2Ki 8:16 Jehoram the son of **J** began to
2Ki 9: 2 there for Jehu the son of **J**
2Ki 9:14 So Jehu the son of **J**, the son
2Ki 12:18 things that his fathers, **J**
1Ch 3:10 son, Asa his son, **J** his son,
1Ch 18:15 **J** the son of Ahilud was
2Ch 17: 1 Then **J** his son reigned in his
2Ch 17: 3 Now the LORD was with **J**,
2Ch 17: 5 all Judah gave presents to **J**
2Ch 17:10 did not make war against **J**
2Ch 17:11 brought **J** presents and silver
2Ch 17:12 So **J** became increasingly
2Ch 18: 1 **J** had riches and honor in
2Ch 18: 3 said to **J** king of Judah
2Ch 18: 4 **J** said to the king of Israel,
2Ch 18: 6 But **J** said, "Is there not
2Ch 18: 7 the king of Israel said to **J**
2Ch 18: 7 And **J** said, "Let not the king
2Ch 18: 9 **J** king of Judah, clothed in
2Ch 18:17 the king of Israel said to **J**
2Ch 18:28 **J** the king of Judah went up
2Ch 18:29 the king of Israel said to **J**
2Ch 18:31 of the chariots saw **J**, that
2Ch 18:31 but **J** cried out, and the LORD
2Ch 19: 1 Then **J** the king of Judah
2Ch 19: 2 meet him, and said to King **J**
2Ch 19: 4 So **J** dwelt at Jerusalem
2Ch 19: 8 **J** appointed some of the
2Ch 20: 1 came to battle against **J**
2Ch 20: 2 Then some came and told **J**,
2Ch 20: 3 **J** feared, and set himself to
2Ch 20: 5 Then **J** stood in the
2Ch 20:15 of Jerusalem, and you, King **J**
2Ch 20:18 **J** bowed his head with his
2Ch 20:20 went out, **J** stood and said,
2Ch 20:25 When **J** and his people came to
2Ch 20:27 with **J** in front of them, to
2Ch 20:30 Then the realm of **J** was quiet
2Ch 20:31 So **J** was king over Judah
2Ch 20:34 Now the rest of the acts of **J**
2Ch 20:35 After this **J** king of Judah
2Ch 20:37 Mareshah prophesied against **J**
2Ch 21: 1 **J** rested with his fathers, and
2Ch 21: 2 had brothers, the sons of **J**
2Ch 21: 2 the sons of **J** king of Israel
2Ch 21:12 in the ways of **J** your father
2Ch 22: 9 he is the son of **J**, who
Joel 3: 2 them down to the Valley of **J**
Joel 3:12 and come up to the Valley of **J**
Matt 1: 8 Asa begot **J**, **J** begot Joram

JEHOSHEBA (*see* JEHOSHABEATH)
2Ki 11: 2 But **J**, the daughter of King

JEHOZABAD (*see* JOZABAD)
2Ki 12:21 and **J** the son of Shomer, his
1Ch 26: 4 **J** the second, Joah the third,
2Ch 17:18 and next to him was **J**, and with
2Ch 24:26 **J** the son of Shimrith the

JEHOZADAK (*see* JOZADAK)
1Ch 6:14 Seraiah, and Seraiah begot **J**
1Ch 6:15 **J** went into captivity when
Hag 1: 1 and to Joshua the son of **J**
Hag 1:12 and Joshua the son of **J**, the
Hag 1:14 spirit of Joshua the son of **J**
Hag 2: 2 and to Joshua the son of **J**
Hag 2: 4 be strong, Joshua, son of **J**
Zech 6:11 head of Joshua the son of **J**

JEHU
1Ki 16: 1 came to **J** the son of Hanani
1Ki 16: 7 LORD came by the prophet **J**
1Ki 16:12 Baasha by **J** the prophet,
1Ki 19:16 Also you shall anoint **J** the
1Ki 19:17 sword of Hazael, **J** will kill
1Ki 19:17 escapes from the sword of **J**
2Ki 9: 2 look there for **J** the son of
2Ki 9: 5 And **J** said,
2Ki 9:11 Then **J** came out to the
2Ki 9:13 trumpets, saying, "**J** is king
2Ki 9:14 So **J** the son of Jehoshaphat,
2Ki 9:15 **J** said, "If you are so minded
2Ki 9:16 So **J** rode in a chariot and
2Ki 9:17 the company of **J** as he came
2Ki 9:18 And **J** said, "What have you
2Ki 9:19 **J** answered, "What have you
2Ki 9:20 of **J** the son of Nimshi, for
2Ki 9:21 and they went out to meet **J**
2Ki 9:22 it happened, when Joram saw **J**
2Ki 9:22 Is it peace, **J**
2Ki 9:24 Now **J** drew his bow with full
2Ki 9:25 Then **J** said to Bidkar his
2Ki 9:27 So **J** pursued him, and said,
2Ki 9:30 when **J** had come to Jezreel,
2Ki 9:31 as **J** entered at the gate, she
2Ki 10: 1 **J** wrote letters and sent them
2Ki 10: 5 reared the sons, sent to **J**
2Ki 10:11 So **J** killed all who remained
2Ki 10:13 **J** met with the brothers of
2Ki 10:15 **J** said, "If it is, give me
2Ki 10:18 Then **J** gathered all the
2Ki 10:18 but **J** will serve him much
2Ki 10:19 But **J** acted deceptively,
2Ki 10:20 And **J** said, "Proclaim
2Ki 10:21 Then **J** sent throughout all
2Ki 10:23 Then **J** and Jehonadab the son
2Ki 10:24 Now **J** had appointed for

2Ki 10:25 that J said to the guard and
2Ki 10:28 Thus J destroyed Baal from
2Ki 10:29 However J did not turn away
2Ki 10:30 And the LORD said to J
2Ki 10:31 But J took no heed to walk in
2Ki 10:34 Now the rest of the acts of J
2Ki 10:35 So J rested with his fathers,
2Ki 10:36 the period that J reigned
2Ki 12: 1 In the seventh year of J,
2Ki 13: 1 Jehoahaz the son of J became
2Ki 14: 8 son of Jehoahaz, the son of J
2Ki 15:12 the LORD which He spoke to J
1Ch 2:38 Obed begot J
1Ch 2:38 and J begot Azariah
1Ch 4:35 J the son of Joshibiah, the
1Ch 12: 3 and J the Anathothite
2Ch 19: 2 J the son of Hanani the seer
2Ch 20:34 book of J the son of Hanani
2Ch 22: 7 against J the son of Nimshi
2Ch 22: 8 when J was executing judgment
2Ch 22: 9 Samaria), and brought him to J
2Ch 25:17 son of Jehoahaz, the son of J
Hos 1: 4 of Jezreel on the house of J

JEHUBBAH
1Ch 7:34 of Shemer were Ahi, Rohgah, J

JEHUCAL (*see* JUCAL)
Jer 37: 3 sent J the son of Shelemiah

JEHUD
Josh 19:45 J, Bene Berak, Gath Rimmon,

JEHUDI
Jer 36:14 sent J the son of Nethaniah
Jer 36:21 So the king sent J to bring
Jer 36:21 J read it in the hearing of
Jer 36:23 when J had read three or four

JEHUDIJAH
1Ch 4:18 (His wife J bore Jered the

JEIEL (*see* JEHIEL, JEUEL)
1Ch 5: 7 the chief, J, and Zechariah,
1Ch 9:35 J the father of Gibeon, whose
1Ch 11:44 and J the sons of Hotham the
1Ch 15:18 Mikneiah, Obed-Edom, and J
1Ch 15:21 Mikneiah, Obed-Edom, J, and
1Ch 16: 5 next to him Zechariah, then J
1Ch 16: 5 J with stringed instruments
2Ch 20:14 son of Benaiah, the son of J
2Ch 26:11 as prepared by J the scribe
2Ch 29:13 of Elizaphan, Shimri and J
2Ch 35: 9 and Hashabiah and J
Ezra 8:13 Eliphelet, J, and Shemaiah
Ezra 10:43 J, Mattithiah, Zabad, Zebina,

JEKABZEEL (*see* KABZEEL)
Neh 11:25 Dibon and its villages, J

JEKAMEAM
1Ch 23:19 the third, and J the fourth
1Ch 24:23 the third, and J the fourth

JEKAMIAH (*see* JECAMIAH)
1Ch 2:41 Shallum begot J
1Ch 2:41 and J begot Elishama

JEKUTHIEL
1Ch 4:18 and J the father of Zanoah

JEMIMAH
Job 42:14 the name of the first J, the

JEMUEL (*see* NEMUEL)
Gen 46:10 The sons of Simeon were J
Ex 6:15 And the sons of Simeon were J

JEOPARDIZED (*see* JEOPARDY)
Judg 5:18 Zebulun is a people who j

JEOPARDY (*see* JEOPARDIZED)
2Sa 23:17 who went in j of their lives
1Ch 11:19 who have put their lives in j
Luke 8:23 with water, and were in j
1Co 15:30 do we stand in j every hour

JEPHTHAH (*see* JIPHTHAH EL)
Judg 11: 1 Now J the Gileadite was a
Judg 11: 1 and Gilead begot J
Judg 11: 2 grew up, they drove J out
Judg 11: 3 Then J fled from his brothers
Judg 11: 3 men banded together with J
Judg 11: 5 to get J from the land of Tob
Judg 11: 6 Then they said to J, "Come
Judg 11: 7 So J said to the elders of
Judg 11: 8 elders of Gilead said to J
Judg 11: 9 So J said to the elders of
Judg 11:10 elders of Gilead said to J
Judg 11:11 Then J went with the elders
Judg 11:11 J spoke all his words before
Judg 11:12 Now J sent messengers to the
Judg 11:13 answered the messengers of J
Judg 11:14 So J again sent messengers to
Judg 11:15 Thus says J: 'Israel did not
Judg 11:28 the words which J sent him
Judg 11:29 of the LORD came upon J, and
Judg 11:30 J made a vow to the LORD, and
Judg 11:32 So J advanced toward the
Judg 11:34 When J came to his house at
Judg 11:40 daughter of J the Gileadite
Judg 12: 1 toward Zaphon, and said to J
Judg 12: 2 J said to them, "My people
Judg 12: 4 Now J gathered together all
Judg 12: 7 J judged Israel six years
Judg 12: 7 Then J the Gileadite died and
1Sa 12:11 LORD sent Jerubbaal, Bedan, J
Heb 11:32 and Barak and Samson and J,

JEPHUNNEH
Num 13: 6 of Judah, Caleb the son of J
Num 14: 6 of Nun and Caleb the son of J
Num 14:30 Except for Caleb the son of J
Num 14:38 the son of J remained alive
Num 26:65 except Caleb the son of J
Num 32:12 except Caleb the son of J
Num 34:19 of Judah, Caleb the son of J
Deut 1:36 except Caleb the son of J
Josh 14: 6 And Caleb the son of J the
Josh 14:13 son of J as an inheritance
Josh 14:14 of Caleb the son of J the
Josh 15:13 Now to Caleb the son of J he
Josh 21:12 son of J as his possession
1Ch 4:15 Caleb the son of J were Iru
1Ch 6:56 gave to Caleb the son of J
1Ch 7:38 The sons of Jether were J

JERAH
Gen 10:26 Sheleph, Hazarmaveth, J,
1Ch 1:20 Sheleph, Hazarmaveth, J,

JERAHMEEL (*see* JERAHMEELITES)
1Ch 2: 9 who were born to him were J
1Ch 2:25 The sons of J, the firstborn
1Ch 2:26 J had another wife, whose
1Ch 2:27 of Ram, the firstborn of J
1Ch 2:33 These were the sons of J
1Ch 2:42 the brother of J were Mesha
1Ch 24:29 the son of Kish, J
Jer 36:26 commanded J the king's son

JERAHMEELITES (*see* JERAHMEEL)
1Sa 27:10 the southern area of the J
1Sa 30:29 were in the cities of the J

JERED (*see* JARED)
1Ch 4:18 bore J the father of Gedor

JEREMAI
Ezra 10:33 Zabad, Eliphelet, J,

JEREMIAH (*see* JEREMIAH'S)
2Ki 23:31 the daughter of J of Libnah
2Ki 24:18 the daughter of J of Libnah
1Ch 5:24 Epher, Ishi, Eliel, Azriel, J
1Ch 12: 4 J, Jahaziel, Johanan, and
1Ch 12:10 the fourth, J the fifth,
1Ch 12:13 J the tenth, and Machbanai the
2Ch 35:25 J also lamented for Josiah
2Ch 36:12 himself before J the prophet
2Ch 36:21 of the LORD by the mouth of J
2Ch 36:22 mouth of J might be fulfilled
Ezra 1: 1 mouth of J might be fulfilled
Neh 10: 2 Seraiah, Azariah, J,
Neh 12: 1 Seraiah, J, Ezra,
Neh 12:12 of J, Hananiah
Neh 12:34 Judah, Benjamin, Shemaiah, J
Jer 1: 1 The words of J the son of
Jer 1:11 J, what do you see
Jer 7: 1 that came to J from the LORD
Jer 11: 1 that came to J from the LORD
Jer 14: 1 to J concerning the droughts
Jer 18: 1 which came to J from the LORD
Jer 18:18 let us devise plans against J
Jer 19:14 Then J came from Tophet,
Jer 20: 1 heard that J prophesied these
Jer 20: 2 Pashhur struck J the prophet
Jer 20: 3 brought J out of the stocks
Jer 20: 3 Then J said to him,
Jer 21: 1 The word which came to J from
Jer 21: 3 Then J said to them, "Thus
Jer 24: 3 What do you see, J
Jer 25: 1 The word that came to J
Jer 25: 2 which J the prophet spoke to
Jer 25:13 book, which J has prophesied
Jer 26: 7 and all the people heard J
Jer 26: 8 when J had made an end of
Jer 26: 9 were gathered against J in
Jer 26:12 Then J spoke to all the
Jer 26:20 to all the words of J
Jer 26:24 the son of Shaphan was with J
Jer 27: 1 word came to J from the LORD
Jer 28: 5 Then the prophet J spoke to
Jer 28: 6 and the prophet J said, "Amen
Jer 28:11 the prophet J went his way
Jer 28:12 word of the LORD came to J
Jer 28:12 the neck of the prophet J
Jer 28:15 Then the prophet J said to
Jer 29: 1 that J the prophet sent from
Jer 29:27 J of Anathoth who makes
Jer 29:29 the hearing of J the prophet
Jer 29:30 word of the LORD came to J
Jer 30: 1 that came to J from the LORD
Jer 32: 1 The word that came to J from
Jer 32: 2 J the prophet was shut up in
Jer 32: 6 And J said, "The word of
Jer 32:26 word of the LORD came to J
Jer 33: 1 LORD came to J a second time
Jer 33:19 word of the LORD came to J
Jer 33:23 word of the LORD came to J
Jer 34: 1 which came to J from the LORD
Jer 34: 6 Then J the prophet spoke all
Jer 34: 8 that came to J from the LORD
Jer 34:12 LORD came to J from the LORD
Jer 35: 1 The word which came to J from
Jer 35: 3 I took Jaazaniah the son of J
Jer 35:12 the word of the LORD to J
Jer 35:18 J said to the house of the
Jer 36: 1 word came to J from the LORD
Jer 36: 4 Then J called Baruch the son
Jer 36: 4 book, at the instruction of J
Jer 36: 5 J commanded Baruch, saying,
Jer 36: 8 J the prophet commanded him
Jer 36:10 of J in the house of the LORD
Jer 36:19 Go and hide, you and J
Jer 36:26 J the prophet, but the LORD
Jer 36:27 at the instruction of J, the
Jer 36:27 word of the LORD came to J
Jer 36:32 Then J took another scroll and
Jer 36:32 J all the words of the book
Jer 37: 2 He spoke by the prophet J
Jer 37: 3 the priest, to the prophet J
Jer 37: 4 Now J was coming and going
Jer 37: 6 LORD came to the prophet J
Jer 37:12 that J went out of Jerusalem
Jer 37:13 and he seized J the prophet,
Jer 37:14 Then J said, "It is false
Jer 37:14 So Irijah seized J and brought
Jer 37:15 the princes were angry with J
Jer 37:16 When J entered the dungeon
Jer 37:16 J had remained there many
Jer 37:17 And J said, "There is."
Jer 37:18 Moreover J said to King
Jer 37:21 that they should commit J to
Jer 37:21 Thus J remained in the court
Jer 38: 1 heard the words that J had
Jer 38: 6 So they took J and cast him
Jer 38: 6 they let J down with ropes
Jer 38: 6 So J sank in the mire
Jer 38: 7 they had put J in the dungeon
Jer 38: 9 have done to J the prophet
Jer 38:10 lift J the prophet out of the
Jer 38:11 ropes into the dungeon to J
Jer 38:12 the Ethiopian said to J
Jer 38:12 And J did so.
Jer 38:13 they pulled J up with ropes
Jer 38:13 J remained in the court of
Jer 38:14 had J the prophet brought to
Jer 38:14 And the king said to J, "I
Jer 38:15 Then J said to Zedekiah, "If
Jer 38:16 the king swore secretly to J
Jer 38:17 Then J said to Zedekiah
Jer 38:19 Zedekiah the king said to J
Jer 38:20 But J said, "They shall not
Jer 38:24 Then Zedekiah said to J
Jer 38:27 all the princes came to J
Jer 38:28 Now J remained in the court
Jer 39:11 gave charge concerning J to
Jer 39:14 take J from the court of the
Jer 39:15 of the LORD had come to J
Jer 40: 1 came to J from the LORD after
Jer 40: 2 captain of the guard took J

Jer 40: 5 Now while J had not yet gone
Jer 40: 6 Then J went to Gedaliah the
Jer 42: 2 and said to J the prophet,
Jer 42: 4 Then J the prophet said to
Jer 42: 5 Then they said to J, "Let
Jer 42: 7 word of the LORD came to J
Jer 43: 1 when J had stopped speaking
Jer 43: 2 proud men spoke, saying to J
Jer 43: 6 J the prophet and Baruch the
Jer 43: 8 LORD came to J in Tahpanhes
Jer 44: 1 The word that came to J
Jer 44:15 Egypt, in Pathros, answered J
Jer 44:20 Then J spoke to all the
Jer 44:24 Moreover J said to all the
Jer 45: 1 The word that J the prophet
Jer 45: 1 book at the instruction of J
Jer 46: 1 to J the prophet against the
Jer 46:13 LORD spoke to J the prophet
Jer 47: 1 to J the prophet against the
Jer 49:34 to J the prophet against Elam
Jer 50: 1 Chaldeans by J the prophet
Jer 51:59 The word which J the prophet
Jer 51:60 So J wrote in a book all the
Jer 51:61 And J said to Seraiah,
Jer 51:64 Thus far are the words of J
Jer 52: 1 the daughter of J of Libnah
Dan 9: 2 given through J the prophet
Matt 2:17 was spoken by J the prophet
Matt 16:14 and others J or one of the
Matt 27: 9 was spoken by J the prophet

JEREMIAH'S (*see* JEREMIAH)
Jer 28:10 yoke off the prophet J neck

JEREMOTH (*see* JERIMOTH)
1Ch 8:14 Ahio, Shashak, J,
1Ch 23:23 Mushi were Mahli, Eder, and J
1Ch 25:22 the fifteenth for J, his sons
Ezra 10:26 Zechariah, Jehiel, Abdi, J
Ezra 10:27 Eliashib, Mattaniah, J,

JERIAH (*see* JERIJAH)
1Ch 23:19 J was the first, Amariah the
1Ch 24:23 J was the first, Amariah the

JERIBAI
1Ch 11:46 Eliel the Mahavite, J and

JERICHO
Num 22: 1 of the Jordan across from J
Num 26: 3 by the Jordan, across from J
Num 26:63 by the Jordan, across from J
Num 31:12 by the Jordan, across from J
Num 33:48 by the Jordan, across from J
Num 33:50 by the Jordan, across from J
Num 34:15 across from J eastward,
Num 35: 1 by the Jordan across from J
Num 36:13 by the Jordan, across from J
Deut 32:49 land of Moab, across from J
Deut 34: 1 which is across from J
Deut 34: 3 the plain of the Valley of J
Josh 2: 1 view the land, especially J
Josh 2: 2 And it was told the king of J
Josh 2: 3 the king of J sent to Rahab
Josh 3:16 crossed over opposite J
Josh 4:13 battle, to the plains of J
Josh 4:19 on the east border of J
Josh 5:10 twilight on the plains of J
Josh 5:13 to pass, when Joshua was by J
Josh 6: 1 Now J was securely shut up
Josh 6: 2 I have given J into your hand
Josh 6:25 whom Joshua sent to spy out J
Josh 6:26 up and builds this city J
Josh 7: 2 Joshua sent men from J to Ai
Josh 8: 2 and its king as you did to J
Josh 9: 3 what Joshua had done to J
Josh 10: 1 as he had done to J and its
Josh 10:28 he had done to the king of J
Josh 10:30 he had done to the king of J
Josh 12: 9 the king of J, one
Josh 13:32 of the Jordan, by J eastward
Josh 16: 1 Joseph from the Jordan, by J
Josh 16: 1 the waters of J on the east
Josh 16: 1 that goes up from J through
Josh 16: 7 and Naarah, reached to J, and
Josh 18:12 to the side of J on the north
Josh 18:21 to their families, were J
Josh 20: 8 by J eastward, they assigned
Josh 24:11 over the Jordan and came to J
Josh 24:11 the men of J fought against
2Sa 10: 5 Wait at J until your beards
1Ki 16:34 days Hiel of Bethel built J
2Ki 2: 4 the LORD has sent me on to J
2Ki 2: 4 So they came to J
2Ki 2: 5 who were at J came to Elisha
2Ki 2:15 who were from J saw him, they
2Ki 2:18 him, for he had stayed in J
2Ki 25: 5 him in the plains of J
1Ch 6:78 of the Jordan, across from J
1Ch 19: 5 Wait at J until your beards
2Ch 28:15 them to their brethren at J
Ezra 2:34 the people of J, three
Neh 3: 2 Eliashib the men of J built
Neh 7:36 the children of J, three
Jer 39: 5 Zedekiah in the plains of J
Jer 52: 8 Zedekiah in the plains of J
Matt 20:29 Now as they departed from J
Mark 10:46 Then they came to J
Mark 10:46 as He went out of J with His
Luke 10:30 went down from Jerusalem to J
Luke 18:35 that as He was coming near J
Luke 19: 1 entered and passed through J
Heb 11:30 By faith the walls of J fell

JERIEL
1Ch 7: 2 Tola were Uzzi, Rephaiah, J

JERIJAH (*see* JERIAH)
1Ch 26:31 J was head of the Hebronites

JERIMOTH (*see* JEREMOTH)
1Ch 7: 7 were Ezbon, Uzzi, Uzziel, J
1Ch 7: 8 Eliezer, Elioenai, Omri, J
1Ch 12: 5 Eluzai, J, Bealiah, Shemariah
1Ch 24:30 Mushi were Mahli, Eder, and J
1Ch 25: 4 Mattaniah, Uzziel, Shebuel, J
1Ch 27:19 Naphtali, J the son of Azriel
2Ch 11:18 of J the son of David, and of
2Ch 31:13 Azaziah, Nahath, Asahel, J

JERIOTH
1Ch 2:18 by Azubah, his wife, and by J

JEROBOAM (*see* JEROBOAM'S)
1Ki 11:26 J the son of Nebat, an
1Ki 11:28 The man J was a mighty man of
1Ki 11:29 when J went out of Jerusalem,
1Ki 11:31 And he said to J, "Take for
1Ki 11:40 therefore sought to kill J
1Ki 11:40 But J arose and fled to Egypt,
1Ki 12: 2 when J the son of Nebat heard
1Ki 12: 3 Then J and the whole
1Ki 12:12 So J and all the people came
1Ki 12:15 to J the son of Nebat
1Ki 12:20 heard that J had come back
1Ki 12:25 Then J built Shechem in the
1Ki 12:26 And J said in his heart,
1Ki 12:32 J ordained a feast on the
1Ki 13: 1 J stood by the altar to burn
1Ki 13: 4 it came to pass when King J
1Ki 13:33 After this event J did not
1Ki 13:34 was the sin of the house of J
1Ki 14: 1 the son of J became sick
1Ki 14: 2 And J said to his wife,
1Ki 14: 2 you as the wife of J, and go
1Ki 14: 5 Here is the wife of J, coming
1Ki 14: 6 Come in, wife of J
1Ki 14: 7 Go, tell J, 'Thus says the
1Ki 14:10 disaster on the house of J
1Ki 14:10 will cut off from J every
1Ki 14:10 the remnant of the house of J
1Ki 14:11 eat whoever belongs to J and
1Ki 14:13 for he is the only one of J
1Ki 14:13 of Israel in the house of J
1Ki 14:14 shall cut off the house of J
1Ki 14:16 up because of the sins of J
1Ki 14:19 Now the rest of the acts of J
1Ki 14:20 The period that J reigned was
1Ki 14:30 Rehoboam and J all their days
1Ki 15: 1 of King J the son of Nebat
1Ki 15: 6 J all the days of his life
1Ki 15: 7 was war between Abijam and J
1Ki 15: 9 year of J king of Israel, Asa
1Ki 15:25 Now Nadab the son of J became
1Ki 15:29 he killed all the house of J
1Ki 15:29 He did not leave to J anyone
1Ki 15:30 because of the sins of J,
1Ki 15:34 and walked in the way of J
1Ki 16: 2 have walked in the way of J
1Ki 16: 3 house of J the son of Nebat
1Ki 16: 7 in being like the house of J
1Ki 16:19 in walking in the way of J
1Ki 16:26 ways of J the son of Nebat
1Ki 16:31 sins of J the son of Nebat
1Ki 21:22 house of J the son of Nebat
1Ki 22:52 in the way of J the son of
2Ki 3: 3 sins of J the son of Nebat
2Ki 9: 9 house of J the son of Nebat
2Ki 10:29 sins of J the son of Nebat
2Ki 10:31 not depart from the sins of J
2Ki 13: 2 sins of J the son of Nebat
2Ki 13: 6 the sins of the house of J
2Ki 13:11 sins of J the son of Nebat
2Ki 13:13 Then J sat on his throne
2Ki 14:16 Then J his son reigned in his
2Ki 14:23 J the son of Joash, king of
2Ki 14:24 sins of J the son of Nebat
2Ki 14:27 hand of J the son of Joash
2Ki 14:28 Now the rest of the acts of J
2Ki 14:29 So J rested with his fathers,
2Ki 15: 1 year of J king of Israel,
2Ki 15: 8 Judah, Zechariah the son of J
2Ki 15: 9 sins of J the son of Nebat
2Ki 15:18 sins of J the son of Nebat
2Ki 15:24 sins of J the son of Nebat
2Ki 15:28 sins of J the son of Nebat
2Ki 17:21 they made J the son of Nebat
2Ki 17:21 Then J drove Israel from
2Ki 17:22 the sins of J which he did
2Ki 23:15 which J the son of Nebat, who
1Ch 5:17 the days of J king of Israel
2Ch 9:29 concerning J the son of Nebat
2Ch 10: 2 So it happened when J the son
2Ch 10: 2 that J returned from Egypt
2Ch 10: 3 And J and all Israel came and
2Ch 10:12 So J and all the people came
2Ch 10:15 to J the son of Nebat
2Ch 11: 4 turned back from attacking J
2Ch 11:14 to Judah and Jerusalem, for J
2Ch 12:15 Rehoboam and J all their days
2Ch 13: 1 the eighteenth year of King J
2Ch 13: 2 was war between Abijah and J
2Ch 13: 3 J also drew up in battle
2Ch 13: 4 Hear me, J and all Israel
2Ch 13: 6 Yet J the son of Nebat, the
2Ch 13: 8 which J made for you as gods
2Ch 13:13 But J caused an ambush to go
2Ch 13:15 it happened that God struck J
2Ch 13:19 And Abijah pursued J and took
2Ch 13:20 So J did not recover strength
Hos 1: 1 in the days of J the son of
Amos 1: 1 in the days of J the son of
Amos 7: 9 sword against the house of J
Amos 7:10 sent to J king of Israel,
Amos 7:11 J shall die by the sword, and

JEROBOAM'S (*see* JEROBOAM)
1Ki 14: 4 And J wife did so
1Ki 14:17 Then J wife arose and departed

JEROHAM
1Sa 1: 1 name was Elkanah the son of J
1Ch 6:27 J his son, and Elkanah his son
1Ch 6:34 son of Elkanah, the son of J
1Ch 8:27 and Zichri were the sons of J
1Ch 9: 8 Ibneiah the son of J
1Ch 9:12 Adaiah the son of J, the son
1Ch 12: 7 the sons of J of Gedor
1Ch 27:22 over Dan, Azarel the son of J
2Ch 23: 1 Azariah the son of J, Ishmael
Neh 11:12 and Adaiah the son of J, the

JERUBBAAL (*see* GIDEON, JERUBBESHETH)
Judg 6:32 on that day he called him J
Judg 7: 1 Then J (that is, Gideon) and
Judg 8:29 Then J the son of Joash went
Judg 8:35 to the house of J (that is
Judg 9: 1 the son of J went to Shechem
Judg 9: 2 the sons of J reign over you
Judg 9: 5 the seventy sons of J, on
Judg 9: 5 youngest son of J was left
Judg 9:16 if you have dealt well with J
Judg 9:19 in truth and sincerity with J
Judg 9:24 sons of J might be settled
Judg 9:28 Is he not the son of J, and is
Judg 9:57 curse of Jotham the son of J
1Sa 12:11 And the LORD sent J, Bedan,

JERUBBESHETH (*see* JERUBBAAL)
2Sa 11:21 struck Abimelech the son of J

JERUEL
2Ch 20:16 before the Wilderness of J

JERUSALEM (*see* ARIEL, JEBUS, JERUSALEM'S, SALEM)
Josh 10: 1 when Adoni-Zedek king of J
Josh 10: 3 Adoni-Zedek king of J sent to
Josh 10: 5 the Amorites, the king of J

Josh 10:23 the king of J, the king of
Josh 12:10 the king of J, one
Josh 15: 8 Jebusite city (which is J)
Josh 15:63 the inhabitants of J, the
Josh 15:63 of Judah at J to this day
Josh 18:28 Eleph, Jebus (which is J)
Judg 1: 7 Then they brought him to J
Judg 1: 8 of Judah fought against J
Judg 1:21 the Jebusites who inhabited J
Judg 1:21 of Benjamin in J to this day
Judg 19:10 opposite Jebus (that is, J)
1Sa 17:54 Philistine and brought it to J
2Sa 5: 5 in J he reigned thirty-three
2Sa 5: 6 his men went to J against the
2Sa 5:13 concubines and wives from J
2Sa 5:14 who were born to him in J
2Sa 8: 7 and brought them to J
2Sa 9:13 So Mephibosheth dwelt in J
2Sa 10:14 people of Ammon and went to J
2Sa 11: 1 But David remained at J
2Sa 11:12 Uriah remained in J that day
2Sa 12:31 all the people returned to J
2Sa 14:23 and brought Absalom to J
2Sa 14:28 dwelt two full years in J
2Sa 15: 8 indeed brings me back to J
2Sa 15:11 men from J who were invited
2Sa 15:14 who were with him at J
2Sa 15:29 the ark of God back to J
2Sa 15:37 And Absalom came into J
2Sa 16: 3 Indeed he is staying in J
2Sa 16:15 the men of Israel, came to J
2Sa 17:20 find them, they returned to J
2Sa 19:19 that my lord the king left J
2Sa 19:25 come to J to meet the king
2Sa 19:33 while you are with me in J
2Sa 19:34 go up with the king to J
2Sa 20: 2 from the Jordan as far as J
2Sa 20: 3 David came to his house at J
2Sa 20: 7 they went out of J to pursue
2Sa 20:22 returned to the king at J
2Sa 24: 8 they came to J at the end of
2Sa 24:16 His hand over J to destroy it
1Ki 2:11 in J he reigned thirty-three
1Ki 2:36 Build yourself a house in J
1Ki 2:38 Shimei dwelt in J many days
1Ki 2:41 had gone from J to Gath and
1Ki 3: 1 and the wall all around J
1Ki 3:15 And he came to J and stood
1Ki 8: 1 Israel, to King Solomon in J
1Ki 9:15 the Millo, the wall of J
1Ki 9:19 Solomon desired to build in J
1Ki 10: 2 She came to J with a very
1Ki 10:26 cities and with the king in J
1Ki 10:27 as common in J as stones, and
1Ki 11: 7 on the hill that is east of J
1Ki 11:13 for the sake of J which I
1Ki 11:29 when Jeroboam went out of J
1Ki 11:32 David, and for the sake of J
1Ki 11:36 have a lamp before Me in J
1Ki 11:42 that Solomon reigned in J
1Ki 12:18 chariot in haste to flee to J
1Ki 12:21 And when Rehoboam came to J
1Ki 12:27 in the house of the LORD at J
1Ki 12:28 much for you to go up to J
1Ki 14:21 reigned seventeen years in J
1Ki 14:25 of Egypt came up against J
1Ki 15: 2 He reigned three years in J
1Ki 15: 4 his God gave him a lamp in J
1Ki 15: 4 him and by establishing J
1Ki 15:10 reigned forty-one years in J
1Ki 22:42 twenty-five years in J
2Ki 8:17 he reigned eight years in J
2Ki 8:26 and he reigned one year in J
2Ki 9:28 him in the chariot to J, and
2Ki 12: 1 he reigned forty years in J
2Ki 12:17 set his face to go up to J
2Ki 12:18 Then he went away from J
2Ki 14: 2 twenty-nine years in J
2Ki 14: 2 name was Jehoaddan of J
2Ki 14:13 and he went to J, and broke
2Ki 14:13 broke down the wall of J from
2Ki 14:19 a conspiracy against him in J
2Ki 14:20 he was buried at J with his
2Ki 15: 2 reigned fifty-two years in J
2Ki 15: 2 name was Jecholiah of J
2Ki 15:33 he reigned sixteen years in J
2Ki 16: 2 he reigned sixteen years in J
2Ki 16: 5 came up to J to make war
2Ki 18: 2 twenty-nine years in J
2Ki 18:17 with a great army against J
2Ki 18:17 And they went up and came to J
2Ki 18:22 away, and said to Judah and J
2Ki 18:22 before this altar in J'
2Ki 18:35 should deliver J from my hand
2Ki 19:10 J shall not be given into the
2Ki 19:21 the daughter of J has shaken
2Ki 19:31 For out of J shall go a
2Ki 21: 1 reigned fifty-five years in J
2Ki 21: 4 In J I will put My name
2Ki 21: 7 In this house and in J, which
2Ki 21:12 bringing such calamity upon J
2Ki 21:13 I will stretch over J the
2Ki 21:13 I will wipe J as one wipes a
2Ki 21:16 till he had filled J from one
2Ki 21:19 and he reigned two years in J
2Ki 22: 1 reigned thirty-one years in J
2Ki 22:14 (She dwelt in J in the Second
2Ki 23: 1 elders of Judah and J to him
2Ki 23: 2 him all the inhabitants of J
2Ki 23: 4 he burned them outside J in
2Ki 23: 5 and in the places all around J
2Ki 23: 6 to the Brook Kidron outside J
2Ki 23: 9 to the altar of the LORD in J
2Ki 23:13 places that were east of J
2Ki 23:20 and he returned to J
2Ki 23:23 was held before the LORD in J
2Ki 23:24 in the land of Judah and in J
2Ki 23:27 city J which I have chosen
2Ki 23:30 Megiddo, brought him to J
2Ki 23:31 he reigned three months in J
2Ki 23:33 that he might not reign in J
2Ki 23:36 he reigned eleven years in J
2Ki 24: 4 for he had filled J with
2Ki 24: 8 he reigned in J three months
2Ki 24: 8 the daughter of Elnathan of J
2Ki 24:10 of Babylon came up against J
2Ki 24:14 carried into captivity all J
2Ki 24:15 captivity from J to Babylon
2Ki 24:18 he reigned eleven years in J
2Ki 24:20 the LORD this happened in J
2Ki 25: 1 all his army came against J
2Ki 25: 8 king of Babylon, came to J
2Ki 25: 9 all the houses of J, that is,
2Ki 25:10 the walls of J all around
1Ch 3: 4 in J he reigned thirty-three
1Ch 3: 5 these were born to him in J
1Ch 6:10 that Solomon built in J)
1Ch 6:15 J into captivity by the hand
1Ch 6:32 the house of the LORD in J
1Ch 8:28 These dwelt in J
1Ch 8:32 their relatives in J, with
1Ch 9: 3 Now in J the children of
1Ch 9:34 They dwelt at J
1Ch 9:38 their relatives in J, with
1Ch 11: 4 David and all Israel went to J
1Ch 14: 3 David took more wives in J
1Ch 14: 4 his children whom he had in J
1Ch 15: 3 all Israel together at J, to
1Ch 18: 7 and brought them to J
1Ch 19:15 So Joab went to J
1Ch 20: 1 But David stayed at J
1Ch 20: 3 all the people returned to J
1Ch 21: 4 all Israel and came to J
1Ch 21:15 an angel to J to destroy it
1Ch 21:16 sword stretched out over J
1Ch 23:25 they may dwell in J forever"
1Ch 26:29 judges over Israel outside J
1Ch 28: 1 Now David assembled at J all
1Ch 29:27 years he reigned in J
2Ch 1: 4 pitched a tent for it at J
2Ch 1:13 So Solomon came to J from the
2Ch 1:14 cities and with the king in J
2Ch 1:15 gold as common in J as stones
2Ch 2: 7 who are with me in Judah and J
2Ch 2:16 and you will carry it up to J
2Ch 3: 1 the LORD at J on Mount Moriah
2Ch 5: 2 the children of Israel, in J
2Ch 6: 6 but I have chosen J, that My
2Ch 8: 6 Solomon desired to build in J
2Ch 9: 1 she came to J to test Solomon
2Ch 9:25 cities and with the king at J
2Ch 9:27 as common in J as stones, and
2Ch 9:30 Solomon reigned in J over all
2Ch 10:18 chariot in haste to flee to J
2Ch 11: 1 Now when Rehoboam came to J
2Ch 11: 5 So Rehoboam dwelt in J, and
2Ch 11:14 and came to Judah and J, for
2Ch 11:16 came to J to sacrifice to the
2Ch 12: 2 of Egypt came up against J
2Ch 12: 4 cities of Judah and came to J
2Ch 12: 5 in J because of Shishak, and
2Ch 12: 7 on J by the hand of Shishak
2Ch 12: 9 of Egypt came up against J
2Ch 12:13 strengthened himself in J
2Ch 12:13 reigned seventeen years in J
2Ch 13: 2 He reigned three years in J
2Ch 14:15 abundance, and returned to J
2Ch 15:10 at J in the third month, in
2Ch 17:13 men of valor, were in J
2Ch 19: 1 safely to his house in J
2Ch 19: 4 So Jehoshaphat dwelt at J
2Ch 19: 8 Moreover in J, for the
2Ch 19: 8 when they returned to J
2Ch 20: 5 congregation of Judah and J
2Ch 20:15 Judah and you inhabitants of J
2Ch 20:17 who is with you, O Judah and J
2Ch 20:18 the inhabitants of J bowed
2Ch 20:20 Judah and you inhabitants of J
2Ch 20:27 every man of Judah and J,
2Ch 20:27 to go back to J with joy
2Ch 20:28 So they came to J, with
2Ch 20:31 twenty-five years in J
2Ch 21: 5 he reigned eight years in J
2Ch 21:11 of J to commit harlotry, and
2Ch 21:13 the inhabitants of J to play
2Ch 21:20 He reigned in J eight years
2Ch 22: 1 Then the inhabitants of J
2Ch 22: 2 and he reigned one year in J
2Ch 23: 2 of Israel, and they came to J
2Ch 24: 1 he reigned forty years in J
2Ch 24: 6 and from J the collection,
2Ch 24: 9 J to bring to the LORD the
2Ch 24:18 J because of their trespass
2Ch 24:23 and they came to Judah and J
2Ch 25: 1 twenty-nine years in J
2Ch 25: 1 name was Jehoaddan of J
2Ch 25:23 and he brought him to J, and
2Ch 25:23 broke down the wall of J from
2Ch 25:27 a conspiracy against him in J
2Ch 26: 3 reigned fifty-two years in J
2Ch 26: 3 name was Jecholiah of J
2Ch 26: 9 in J at the Corner Gate, at
2Ch 26:15 And he made devices in J,
2Ch 27: 1 he reigned sixteen years in J
2Ch 27: 8 he reigned sixteen years in J
2Ch 28: 1 he reigned sixteen years in J
2Ch 28:10 J to be your male and female
2Ch 28:24 altars in every corner of J
2Ch 28:27 buried him in the city, in J
2Ch 29: 1 twenty-nine years in J
2Ch 29: 8 the LORD fell upon Judah and J
2Ch 30: 1 to the house of the LORD at J
2Ch 30: 2 in J had agreed to keep the
2Ch 30: 3 people gathered together at J
2Ch 30: 5 the LORD God of Israel at J
2Ch 30:11 themselves and came to J
2Ch 30:13 assembled at J to keep the
2Ch 30:14 the altars that were in J
2Ch 30:21 at J kept the Feast of
2Ch 30:26 So there was great joy in J
2Ch 30:26 been nothing like this in J
2Ch 31: 4 the people who dwelt in J to
2Ch 32: 2 was to make war against J
2Ch 32: 9 servants to J (but he himself
2Ch 32: 9 and to all Judah who were in J
2Ch 32:10 you remain under siege in J
2Ch 32:12 and commanded Judah and J,
2Ch 32:18 of J who were on the wall
2Ch 32:19 spoke against the God of J
2Ch 32:22 of J from the hand of
2Ch 32:23 gifts to the LORD at J, and
2Ch 32:25 over him and over Judah and J
2Ch 32:26 he and the inhabitants of J
2Ch 32:33 the inhabitants of J honored
2Ch 33: 1 reigned fifty-five years in J
2Ch 33: 4 In J shall My name be forever
2Ch 33: 7 In this house and in J, which
2Ch 33: 9 the inhabitants of J to do
2Ch 33:13 back to J into his kingdom
2Ch 33:15 the house of the LORD and in J
2Ch 33:21 and he reigned two years in J
2Ch 34: 1 reigned thirty-one years in J
2Ch 34: 3 J of the high places, the
2Ch 34: 5 and cleansed Judah and J
2Ch 34: 7 of Israel, he returned to J
2Ch 34: 9 they had brought back to J
2Ch 34:22 (She dwelt in J in the Second
2Ch 34:29 all the elders of Judah and J
2Ch 34:30 Judah and the inhabitants of J
2Ch 34:32 all who were present in J

2Ch 34:32 of **J** did according to the
2Ch 35: 1 a Passover to the LORD in **J**
2Ch 35:18 and the inhabitants of **J**
2Ch 35:24 had, and they brought him to **J**
2Ch 35:24 Judah and **J** mourned for Josiah
2Ch 36: 1 in his father's place in **J**
2Ch 36: 2 he reigned three months in **J**
2Ch 36: 3 of Egypt deposed him at **J**
2Ch 36: 4 Eliakim king over Judah and **J**
2Ch 36: 5 he reigned eleven years in **J**
2Ch 36: 9 he reigned in **J** three months
2Ch 36:10 brother, king over Judah and **J**
2Ch 36:11 he reigned eleven years in **J**
2Ch 36:14 which He had consecrated in **J**
2Ch 36:19 God, broke down the wall of **J**
2Ch 36:23 house at **J** which is in Judah
Ezra 1: 2 house at **J** which is in Judah
Ezra 1: 3 Now let him go up to **J**, which
Ezra 1: 3 (He is God), which is in **J**
Ezra 1: 4 house of God which is in **J**
Ezra 1: 5 of the LORD which is in **J**
Ezra 1: 7 had taken from **J** and put in
Ezra 1:11 brought from Babylon to **J**
Ezra 2: 1 Babylon, and who returned to **J**
Ezra 2:68 of the LORD which is in **J**
Ezra 3: 1 together as one man to **J**
Ezra 3: 8 to the house of God at **J**,
Ezra 3: 8 out of the captivity to **J**
Ezra 4: 6 the inhabitants of Judah and **J**
Ezra 4: 8 wrote a letter against **J** to
Ezra 4:12 from you have come to us at **J**
Ezra 4:20 also been mighty kings over **J**
Ezra 4:23 haste to **J** against the Jews
Ezra 4:24 of God which is at **J** ceased
Ezra 5: 1 Jews who were in Judah and **J**
Ezra 5: 2 house of God which is in **J**
Ezra 5:14 from the temple that was in **J**
Ezra 5:15 the temple site that is in **J**
Ezra 5:16 house of God which is in **J**
Ezra 5:17 build this house of God at **J**
Ezra 6: 3 the house of God at **J**
Ezra 6: 5 from the temple which is in **J**
Ezra 6: 5 to the temple which is in **J**
Ezra 6: 9 of the priests who are in **J**
Ezra 6:12 house of God which is in **J**
Ezra 6:18 over the service of God in **J**
Ezra 7: 7 the Nethinim came up to **J** in
Ezra 7: 8 Ezra came to **J** in the fifth
Ezra 7: 9 the fifth month he came to **J**
Ezra 7:13 who volunteer to go up to **J**
Ezra 7:14 inquire concerning Judah and **J**
Ezra 7:15 whose dwelling is in **J**
Ezra 7:16 the house of their God in **J**
Ezra 7:17 of the house of your God in **J**
Ezra 7:19 in full before the God of **J**
Ezra 7:27 of the LORD which is in **J**
Ezra 8:29 houses of Israel in **J**, in the
Ezra 8:30 to bring them to **J** to the
Ezra 8:31 the first month, to go to **J**
Ezra 8:32 So we came to **J**, and stayed
Ezra 9: 9 give us a wall in Judah and **J**
Ezra 10: 7 **J** to all the descendants of
Ezra 10: 7 that they must gather at **J**
Ezra 10: 9 at **J** within three days
Neh 1: 2 captivity, and concerning **J**
Neh 1: 3 The wall of **J** is also broken
Neh 2:11 So I came to **J** and was there
Neh 2:12 put in my heart to do at **J**
Neh 2:13 viewed the walls of **J** which
Neh 2:17 in, how **J** lies waste, and its
Neh 2:17 and let us build the wall of **J**
Neh 2:20 or right or memorial in **J**
Neh 3: 8 they fortified **J** as far as
Neh 3: 9 of half the district of **J**
Neh 3:12 of half the district of **J**
Neh 4: 7 of **J** were being restored and
Neh 4: 8 together to come and attack **J**
Neh 4:22 servant stay at night in **J**
Neh 6: 7 proclaim concerning you at **J**
Neh 7: 2 of **J** to my brother Hanani
Neh 7: 3 Do not let the gates of **J** be
Neh 7: 3 among the inhabitants of **J**
Neh 7: 6 captive, and who returned to **J**
Neh 8:15 in all their cities and in **J**
Neh 11: 1 of the people dwelt at **J**
Neh 11: 1 one out of ten to dwell in **J**
Neh 11: 2 themselves to dwell at **J**
Neh 11: 3 the province who dwelt in **J**
Neh 11: 4 Also in **J** dwelt certain of
Neh 11: 6 dwelt at **J** were four hundred
Neh 11:22 at **J** was Uzzi the son of Bani
Neh 12:27 dedication of the wall of **J**
Neh 12:27 places, to bring them to **J** to
Neh 12:28 from the countryside around **J**
Neh 12:29 villages all around **J**
Neh 12:43 joy of **J** was heard afar off
Neh 13: 6 all this I was not in **J**, for
Neh 13: 7 and I came to **J** and discovered
Neh 13:15 into **J** on the Sabbath day
Neh 13:16 children of Judah, and in **J**
Neh 13:19 So it was, at the gates of **J**
Neh 13:20 outside **J** once or twice
Esth 2: 6 **J** with the captives who had
Ps 51:18 Build the walls of **J**
Ps 68:29 Because of Your temple at **J**
Ps 79: 1 They have laid **J** in heaps
Ps 79: 3 shed like water all around **J**
Ps 102:21 in Zion, And His praise in **J**
Ps 116:19 In the midst of you, O **J**
Ps 122: 2 Within your gates, O **J**
Ps 122: 3 **J** is built As a city that is
Ps 122: 6 Pray for the peace of **J**
Ps 125: 2 As the mountains surround **J**
Ps 128: 5 may you see the good of **J** All
Ps 135:21 out of Zion, Who dwells in **J**
Ps 137: 5 If I forget you, O **J**, Let my
Ps 137: 6 If I do not exalt **J** Above my
Ps 137: 7 the sons of Edom The day of **J**
Ps 147: 2 The LORD builds up **J**
Ps 147:12 Praise the LORD, O **J**
Eccl 1: 1 the son of David, king in **J**
Eccl 1:12 was king over Israel in **J**
Eccl 1:16 all who were before me in **J**
Eccl 2: 7 all who were in **J** before me
Eccl 2: 9 all who were before me in **J**
Song 1: 5 but lovely, O daughters of **J**
Song 3:10 love by the daughters of **J**
Song 5: 8 charge you, O daughters of **J**
Song 5:16 my friend, O daughters of **J**
Song 6: 4 as Tirzah, lovely as **J**,
Song 8: 4 charge you, O daughters of **J**
Is 1: 1 and **J** in the days of Uzziah,
Is 2: 1 saw concerning Judah and **J**
Is 2: 3 the word of the LORD from **J**
Is 3: 1 of hosts, takes away from **J**
Is 3: 8 For **J** stumbled, and Judah is
Is 4: 3 he who remains in **J** will be
Is 4: 3 among the living in **J**
Is 4: 4 the blood of **J** from her midst
Is 5: 3 And now, O inhabitants of **J**
Is 7: 1 went up to **J** to make war
Is 8:14 snare to the inhabitants of **J**
Is 10:10 images excelled those of **J**
Is 10:11 shall I not do also to **J**
Is 10:12 work on Mount Zion and on **J**
Is 10:32 of Zion, the hill of **J**
Is 22:10 You numbered the houses of **J**
Is 22:21 to the inhabitants of **J** and to
Is 24:23 reign on Mount Zion and in **J**
Is 27:13 LORD in the holy mount at **J**
Is 28:14 rule this people who are in **J**
Is 30:19 shall dwell in Zion at **J**
Is 31: 5 the LORD of hosts defend **J**
Is 31: 9 Zion and whose furnace is in **J**
Is 33:20 your eyes will see **J**, a quiet
Is 36: 2 Lachish to King Hezekiah at **J**
Is 36: 7 away, and said to Judah and **J**
Is 36:20 should deliver **J** from my hand
Is 37:10 **J** will not be given into the
Is 37:22 the daughter of **J** has shaken
Is 37:32 For out of **J** shall go a
Is 40: 2 Speak comfort to **J**, and cry
Is 40: 9 O **J**, you who bring good
Is 41:27 and I will give to **J** one who
Is 44:26 Who says to **J**, "You shall be
Is 44:28 My pleasure, even saying to **J**
Is 51:17 Stand up, O **J**, you who have
Is 52: 1 your beautiful garments, O **J**
Is 52: 2 dust, arise, and sit down, O **J**
Is 52: 9 you waste places of **J**
Is 52: 9 His people, He has redeemed **J**
Is 62: 6 watchmen on your walls, O **J**
Is 62: 7 till He makes **J** a praise in
Is 64:10 a wilderness, **J** a desolation
Is 65:18 I create **J** as a rejoicing, and
Is 65:19 I will rejoice in **J**, and joy
Is 66:10 Rejoice with **J**, and be glad
Is 66:13 you shall be comforted in **J**
Is 66:20 camels, to My holy mountain **J**
Jer 1: 3 **J** captive in the fifth month
Jer 1:15 entrance of the gates of **J**
Jer 2: 2 Go and cry in the hearing of **J**
Jer 3:17 At that time **J** shall be
Jer 3:17 to the name of the LORD, to **J**
Jer 4: 3 LORD to the men of Judah and **J**
Jer 4: 4 of Judah and inhabitants of **J**
Jer 4: 5 in Judah and proclaim in **J**
Jer 4:10 deceived this people and **J**
Jer 4:11 said to this people and to **J**
Jer 4:14 O **J**, wash your heart from
Jer 4:16 yes, proclaim against **J**,
Jer 5: 1 fro through the streets of **J**
Jer 6: 1 to flee from the midst of **J**
Jer 6: 6 and build a mound against **J**
Jer 6: 8 Be instructed, O **J**, lest My
Jer 7:17 Judah and in the streets of **J**
Jer 7:34 of **J** the voice of mirth and
Jer 8: 1 bones of the inhabitants of **J**
Jer 8: 5 this people slidden back, **J**
Jer 9:11 I will make **J** a heap of ruins
Jer 11: 2 and to the inhabitants of **J**
Jer 11: 6 Judah and in the streets of **J**
Jer 11: 9 and among the inhabitants of **J**
Jer 11:12 the inhabitants of **J** will go
Jer 11:13 number of the streets of **J**
Jer 13: 9 Judah and the great pride of **J**
Jer 13:13 and all the inhabitants of **J**
Jer 13:27 Woe to you, O **J**
Jer 14: 2 and the cry of **J** has gone up
Jer 14:16 of **J** because of the famine
Jer 15: 4 Judah, for what he did in **J**
Jer 15: 5 will have pity on you, O **J**
Jer 17:19 out, and in all the gates of **J**
Jer 17:20 and all the inhabitants of **J**
Jer 17:21 bring it in by the gates of **J**
Jer 17:25 Judah and the inhabitants of **J**
Jer 17:26 and from the places around **J**
Jer 17:27 gates of **J** on the Sabbath day
Jer 17:27 shall devour the palaces of **J**
Jer 18:11 and to the inhabitants of **J**
Jer 19: 3 of Judah and inhabitants of **J**
Jer 19: 7 **J** in this place, and I will
Jer 19:13 And the houses of **J** and the
Jer 22:19 out beyond the gates of **J**
Jer 23:14 thing in the prophets of **J**
Jer 23:15 of **J** profaneness has gone out
Jer 24: 1 craftsmen and smiths, from **J**
Jer 24: 8 the residue of **J** who remain
Jer 25: 2 to all the inhabitants of **J**
Jer 25:18 **J** and the cities of Judah, its
Jer 26:18 **J** shall become heaps of ruins
Jer 27: 3 **J** to Zedekiah king of Judah
Jer 27:18 of the king of Judah, and at **J**
Jer 27:20 from **J** to Babylon, and all the
Jer 27:20 all the nobles of Judah and **J**
Jer 27:21 of the king of Judah and of **J**
Jer 29: 1 the prophet sent from **J** to
Jer 29: 1 captive from **J** to Babylon
Jer 29: 2 the princes of Judah and **J**
Jer 29: 2 smiths had departed from **J**
Jer 29: 4 away from **J** to Babylon
Jer 29:20 I have sent from **J** to Babylon
Jer 29:25 all the people who are at **J**
Jer 32: 2 of Babylon's army besieged **J**
Jer 32:32 and the inhabitants of **J**
Jer 32:44 in the places around **J**, in
Jer 33:10 of **J** that are desolate,
Jer 33:13 in the places around **J**, and
Jer 33:16 saved, and **J** will dwell safely
Jer 34: 1 the people, fought against **J**
Jer 34: 6 Zedekiah king of Judah in **J**
Jer 34: 7 army fought against **J** and all
Jer 34: 8 all the people who were at **J**
Jer 34:19 of Judah, the princes of **J**
Jer 35:11 let us go to **J** for fear of
Jer 35:11 So we dwell at **J**
Jer 35:13 Judah and the inhabitants of **J**
Jer 35:17 of **J** all the doom that I have
Jer 36: 9 LORD to all the people in **J**
Jer 36: 9 from the cities of Judah to **J**
Jer 36:31 them, on the inhabitants of **J**
Jer 37: 5 **J** heard news of them, they
Jer 37: 5 of them, they departed from **J**
Jer 37:11 **J** for fear of Pharaoh's army
Jer 37:12 of **J** to go into the land of
Jer 38:28 the day that **J** was taken
Jer 38:28 he was there when **J** was taken
Jer 39: 1 all his army came against **J**
Jer 39: 8 and broke down the walls of **J**
Jer 40: 1 carried away captive from **J**

Jer 42:18 out on the inhabitants of J
Jer 44: 2 that I have brought on J and
Jer 44: 6 Judah and in the streets of J
Jer 44: 9 Judah and in the streets of J
Jer 44:13 Egypt, as I have punished J
Jer 44:17 Judah and in the streets of J
Jer 44:21 Judah and in the streets of J
Jer 51:35 J will say.
Jer 51:50 and let J come to your mind
Jer 52: 1 he reigned eleven years in J
Jer 52: 3 the LORD this happened in J
Jer 52: 4 all his army came against J
Jer 52:12 king of Babylon, came to J
Jer 52:13 all the houses of J, that is,
Jer 52:14 all the walls of J all around
Jer 52:29 captive from J eight hundred
Lam 1: 7 J remembers all her pleasant
Lam 1: 8 J has sinned grievously,
Lam 1:17 J has become an unclean thing
Lam 2:10 The virgins of J bow their
Lam 2:13 I liken you, O daughter of J
Lam 2:15 heads at the daughter of J
Lam 4:12 could enter the gates of J
Ezek 4: 1 and portray on it a city, J
Ezek 4: 7 face toward the siege of J
Ezek 4:16 off the supply of bread in J
Ezek 5: 5 says the Lord GOD: 'This is J
Ezek 8: 3 me in visions of God to J
Ezek 9: 4 city, through the midst of J
Ezek 9: 8 in pouring out Your fury on J
Ezek 11:15 inhabitants of J have said
Ezek 12:10 concerns the prince in J and
Ezek 12:19 GOD to the inhabitants of J
Ezek 13:16 who prophesy concerning J
Ezek 14:21 My four severe judgments on J
Ezek 14:22 that I have brought upon J
Ezek 15: 6 give up the inhabitants of J
Ezek 16: 2 of man, cause J to know her
Ezek 16: 3 Thus says the Lord GOD to J
Ezek 17:12 the king of Babylon went to J
Ezek 21: 2 man, set your face toward J
Ezek 21:20 and to Judah, into fortified J
Ezek 21:22 hand is the divination for J
Ezek 22:19 you into the midst of J
Ezek 23: 4 is Oholah, and J is Oholibah
Ezek 24: 2 siege against J this very day
Ezek 26: 2 Tyre has said against J, 'Aha
Ezek 33:21 had escaped from J came to me
Ezek 36:38 flock at J on its feast days
Dan 1: 1 king of Babylon came to J
Dan 5: 2 temple which had been in J
Dan 5: 3 of God which had been in J
Dan 6:10 his windows open toward J
Dan 9: 2 years in the desolations of J
Dan 9: 7 to the inhabitants of J and
Dan 9:12 as what has been done to J
Dan 9:16 turned away from Your city J
Dan 9:16 iniquities of our fathers, J
Dan 9:25 build J until Messiah the
Joel 2:32 Zion and in J there shall be
Joel 3: 1 the captives of Judah and J
Joel 3: 6 the people of J You have sold
Joel 3:16 and utter His voice from J
Joel 3:17 then J shall be holy, and no
Joel 3:20 and J from generation to
Amos 1: 2 and utters His voice from J
Amos 2: 5 shall devour the palaces of J
Obad 11 his gates and cast lots for J
Obad 20 The captives of J who are in
Mic 1: 1 saw concerning Samaria and J
Mic 1: 5 Are they not J?
Mic 1: 9 gate of My people, even to J
Mic 1:12 the LORD to the gate of J
Mic 3:10 bloodshed and J with iniquity
Mic 3:12 J shall become heaps of ruins
Mic 4: 2 the word of the LORD from J
Mic 4: 8 kingdom of the daughter of J
Zeph 1: 4 all the inhabitants of J
Zeph 1:12 I will search J with lamps
Zeph 3:14 your heart, O daughter of J
Zeph 3:16 day it shall be said to J
Zech 1:12 will You not have mercy on J
Zech 1:14 I am zealous for J and for
Zech 1:16 am returning to J with mercy
Zech 1:16 shall be stretched out over J
Zech 1:17 Zion, and will again choose J
Zech 1:19 scattered Judah, Israel, and J
Zech 2: 2 To measure J, to see what is
Zech 2: 4 J shall be inhabited as
Zech 2:12 Land, and will again choose J
Zech 3: 2 who has chosen J rebuke you
Zech 7: 7 the former prophets when J
Zech 8: 3 and dwell in the midst of J
Zech 8: 3 J shall be called the City of
Zech 8: 4 again sit in the streets of J
Zech 8: 8 shall dwell in the midst of J
Zech 8:15 am determined to do good to J
Zech 8:22 seek the LORD of hosts in J
Zech 9: 9 Shout, O daughter of J
Zech 9:10 Ephraim and the horse from J
Zech 12: 2 I will make J a cup of
Zech 12: 2 lay siege against Judah and J
Zech 12: 3 that day that I will make J a
Zech 12: 5 The inhabitants of J are my
Zech 12: 6 but J shall be inhabited
Zech 12: 6 again in her own place—J.
Zech 12: 7 of J shall not become greater
Zech 12: 8 defend the inhabitants of J
Zech 12: 9 nations that come against J
Zech 12:10 of J the Spirit of grace and
Zech 12:11 be a great mourning in J,
Zech 13: 1 and for the inhabitants of J
Zech 14: 2 nations to battle against J
Zech 14: 4 which faces J on the east
Zech 14: 8 waters shall flow from J,
Zech 14:10 Geba to Rimmon south of J
Zech 14:10 J shall be raised up and
Zech 14:11 but J shall be safely
Zech 14:12 people who fought against J
Zech 14:14 Judah also will fight at J
Zech 14:16 J shall go up from year to
Zech 14:17 up to J to worship the King
Zech 14:21 Yes, every pot in J and Judah
Mal 2:11 committed in Israel and in J
Mal 3: 4 J will be pleasant to the
Matt 2: 1 men from the East came to J
Matt 2: 3 troubled, and all J with him
Matt 3: 5 Then J, all Judea, and all the
Matt 4:25 Galilee, and from Decapolis, J
Matt 5:35 nor by J, for it is the city
Matt 15: 1 who were from J came to Jesus
Matt 16:21 that He must go to J, and
Matt 20:17 Then Jesus, going up to J
Matt 20:18 Behold, we are going up to J
Matt 21: 1 Now when they drew near to J
Matt 21:10 And when He had come into J
Matt 23:37 O J, J, the one who
Mark 1: 5 of Judea, and those from J
Mark 3: 8 and J and Idumea and beyond
Mark 3:22 who came down from J said
Mark 7: 1 to Him, having come from J
Mark 10:32 on the road, going up to J
Mark 10:33 Behold, we are going up to J
Mark 11: 1 Now when they came near J
Mark 11:11 And Jesus went into J and into
Mark 11:15 So they came to J
Mark 11:27 Then they came again to J
Mark 15:41 who came up with Him to J
Luke 2:22 they brought Him to J to
Luke 2:25 there was a man in J whose
Luke 2:38 looked for redemption in J
Luke 2:41 His parents went to J every
Luke 2:42 they went up to J according
Luke 2:43 Jesus lingered behind in J
Luke 2:45 find Him, they returned to J
Luke 4: 9 Then he brought Him to J, set
Luke 5:17 town of Galilee, Judea, and J
Luke 6:17 of people from all Judea and J
Luke 9:31 was about to accomplish at J
Luke 9:51 set His face to go to J,
Luke 9:53 was set for the journey to J
Luke 10:30 went down from J to Jericho
Luke 13: 4 all other men who dwelt in J
Luke 13:22 and journeying toward J
Luke 13:33 should perish outside of J
Luke 13:34 O J, J, the one who
Luke 17:11 it happened as He went to J
Luke 18:31 Behold, we are going up to J
Luke 19:11 because He was near J and
Luke 19:28 went on ahead, going up to J
Luke 21:20 But when you see J surrounded
Luke 21:24 And J will be trampled by
Luke 23: 7 was also in J at that time
Luke 23:28 Daughters of J, do not weep
Luke 24:13 was about seven miles from J
Luke 24:18 You the only stranger in J
Luke 24:33 very hour and returned to J
Luke 24:47 all nations, beginning at J
Luke 24:49 but tarry in the city of J
Luke 24:52 returned to J with great joy,
John 1:19 and Levites from J to ask him
John 2:13 hand, and Jesus went up to J
John 2:23 He was in J at the Passover
John 4:20 you Jews say that in J is the
John 4:21 on this mountain, nor in J
John 4:45 He did in J at the feast
John 5: 1 Jews, and Jesus went up to J
John 5: 2 Now there is in J by the
John 7:25 Then some of them from J said
John 10:22 the Feast of Dedication in J
John 11:18 Now Bethany was near J, about
John 11:55 up to J before the Passover
John 12:12 that Jesus was coming to J
Acts 1: 4 them not to depart from J
Acts 1: 8 shall be witnesses to Me in J
Acts 1:12 to J from the Mount called
Acts 1:12 Olivet, which is near J, a
Acts 1:19 to all those dwelling in J
Acts 2: 5 there were dwelling in J Jews
Acts 2:14 Judea and all who dwell in J
Acts 4: 6 were gathered together at J
Acts 4:16 evident to all who dwell in J
Acts 5:16 the surrounding cities to J
Acts 5:28 you have filled J with your
Acts 6: 7 multiplied greatly in J, and a
Acts 8: 1 the church which was at J
Acts 8:14 at J heard that Samaria had
Acts 8:25 the Lord, they returned to J
Acts 8:26 goes down from J to Gaza
Acts 8:27 and had come to J to worship
Acts 9: 2 might bring them bound to J
Acts 9:13 has done to Your saints in J
Acts 9:21 who called on this name in J
Acts 9:26 And when Saul had come to J
Acts 9:28 So he was with them at J,
Acts 10:39 the land of the Jews and in J
Acts 11: 2 And when Peter came up to J
Acts 11:22 the ears of the church in J
Acts 11:27 came from J to Antioch
Acts 12:25 Saul returned from J when
Acts 13:13 from them, returned to J
Acts 13:27 For those who dwell in J, and
Acts 13:31 up with Him from Galilee to J
Acts 15: 2 of them should go up to J
Acts 15: 4 And when they had come to J
Acts 16: 4 the apostles and elders at J
Acts 18:21 keep this coming feast in J
Acts 19:21 and Achaia, to go to J, saying
Acts 20:16 he was hurrying to be at J
Acts 20:22 I go bound in the spirit to J
Acts 21: 4 the Spirit not to go up to J
Acts 21:11 So shall the Jews at J bind
Acts 21:12 with him not to go up to J
Acts 21:13 but also to die at J for the
Acts 21:15 we packed and went up to J
Acts 21:17 And when we had come to J, the
Acts 21:31 that all J was in an uproar
Acts 22: 5 there to J to be punished
Acts 22:17 when I returned to J and was
Acts 22:18 haste and get out of J quickly
Acts 23:11 have testified for Me in J
Acts 24:11 I went up to J to worship
Acts 25: 1 he went up from Caesarea to J
Acts 25: 3 that he would summon him to J
Acts 25: 7 come down from J stood about
Acts 25: 9 Are you willing to go up to J
Acts 25:15 informed me, when I was in J
Acts 25:20 he was willing to go to J
Acts 25:24 Jews petitioned me, both at J
Acts 26: 4 among my own nation at J, all
Acts 26:10 This I also did in J, and many
Acts 26:20 to those in Damascus and in J
Acts 28:17 as a prisoner from J into the
Rom 15:19 Spirit of God, so that from J
Rom 15:25 But now I am going to J to
Rom 15:26 among the saints who are in J
Rom 15:31 that my service for J may be
1Co 16: 3 send to bear your gift to J
Gal 1:17 nor did I go up to J to those
Gal 1:18 I went up to J to see Peter
Gal 2: 1 up again to J with Barnabas
Gal 4:25 corresponds to J which now is
Gal 4:26 but the J above is free,
Heb 12:22 living God, the heavenly J
Rev 3:12 the city of My God, the New J
Rev 21: 2 saw the holy city, New J
Rev 21:10 me the great city, the holy J

JERUSALEM'S (*see* JERUSALEM)
Is 62: 1 for J sake I will not rest,

JERUSHA (*see* JERUSHAH)
2Ki 15:33 was J the daughter of Zadok

JERUSHAH (*see* JERUSHA)
2Ch 27: 1 was J the daughter of Zadok

JESHAIAH
1Ch 3:21 Hananiah were Pelatiah and J
1Ch 25: 3 Gedaliah, Zeri, J, Shimei,
1Ch 25:15 the eighth for J, his sons and
1Ch 26:25 J his son, Joram his son,
Ezra 8: 7 J the son of Athaliah, and
Ezra 8:19 with him J of the sons of
Neh 11: 7 son of Ithiel, the son of J

JESHANAH
2Ch 13:19 J with its villages, and

JESHARELAH
1Ch 25:14 the seventh for J, his sons

JESHEBEAB
1Ch 24:13 Huppah, the fourteenth to J

JESHER
1Ch 2:18 J, Shobab, and Ardon

JESHIMON
1Sa 23:19 which is on the south of J
1Sa 23:24 the plain on the south of J
1Sa 26: 1 Hachilah, which is opposite J
1Sa 26: 3 Hachilah, which is opposite J

JESHISHAI
1Ch 5:14 son of Michael, the son of J

JESHOHAIAH
1Ch 4:36 Elioenai, Jaakobah, J, Asaiah

JESHUA (*see* JOSHUA)
1Ch 24:11 the ninth to J, the tenth to
2Ch 31:15 him were Eden, Miniamin, J
Ezra 2: 2 came with Zerubbabel were J
Ezra 2: 6 of the people of J and Joab,
Ezra 2:36 of Jedaiah, of the house of J
Ezra 2:40 the sons of J and Kadmiel, of
Ezra 3: 2 Then J the son of Jozadak and
Ezra 3: 8 J the son of Jozadak, and the
Ezra 3: 9 Then J with his sons and
Ezra 4: 3 But Zerubbabel and J and the
Ezra 5: 2 J the son of Jozadak rose up
Ezra 8:33 Levites, Jozabad the son of J
Ezra 10:18 sons of J the son of Jozadak
Neh 3:19 next to him Ezer the son of J
Neh 7: 7 came with Zerubbabel were J
Neh 7:11 of the children of J and Joab
Neh 7:39 of Jedaiah, of the house of J
Neh 7:43 the children of J, of Kadmiel
Neh 8: 7 Also J, Bani, Sherebiah,
Neh 9: 4 Then J, Bani, Kadmiel,
Neh 9: 5 Then the Levites, J, Kadmiel,
Neh 10: 9 J the son of Azaniah, Binnui
Neh 11:26 in J, Moladah, Beth Pelet,
Neh 12: 1 the son of Shealtiel, and J
Neh 12: 7 brethren in the days of J
Neh 12: 8 Moreover the Levites were J
Neh 12:10 J begot Joiakim, Joiakim
Neh 12:24 J the son of Kadmiel, with
Neh 12:26 days of Joiakim the son of J

JESHURUN
Deut 32:15 But J grew fat and kicked
Deut 33: 5 And He was King in J, when the
Deut 33:26 is no one like the God of J
Is 44: 2 and you, J, whom I have chosen

JESIMIEL
1Ch 4:36 Jeshohaiah, Asaiah, Adiel, J

JESIMOTH
Num 33:49 from Beth J as far as the

JESSE
Ruth 4:17 He is the father of J, the
Ruth 4:22 Obed begot J
Ruth 4:22 and J begot David
1Sa 16: 1 you to J the Bethlehemite
1Sa 16: 3 Then invite J to the
1Sa 16: 5 Then he sanctified J and his
1Sa 16: 8 So J called Abinadab, and made
1Sa 16: 9 Then J made Shammah pass by
1Sa 16:10 Thus J made seven of his sons
1Sa 16:10 And Samuel said to J, "The
1Sa 16:11 And Samuel said to J, "Are
1Sa 16:11 And Samuel said to J, "Send
1Sa 16:18 a son of J the Bethlehemite
1Sa 16:19 Saul sent messengers to J
1Sa 16:20 J took a donkey loaded with
1Sa 16:22 Then Saul sent to J, saying,
1Sa 17:12 Judah, whose name was J, and
1Sa 17:13 The three oldest sons of J
1Sa 17:17 Then J said to his son David,
1Sa 17:20 went as J had commanded him
1Sa 17:58 servant J the Bethlehemite
1Sa 20:27 the son of J not come to eat
1Sa 20:30 son of J to your own shame
1Sa 20:31 son of J lives on the earth
1Sa 22: 7 Will the son of J give every
1Sa 22: 8 a covenant with the son of J
1Sa 22: 9 saw the son of J going to Nob
1Sa 22:13 me, you and the son of J, in
1Sa 25:10 David, and who is the son of J
2Sa 20: 1 inheritance in the son of J
2Sa 23: 1 Thus says David the son of J
1Ki 12:16 inheritance in the son of J
1Ch 2:12 begot Obed, and Obed begot J
1Ch 2:13 J begot Eliab his firstborn,
1Ch 10:14 over to David the son of J
1Ch 12:18 are on your side, O son of J
1Ch 29:26 Thus David the son of J
2Ch 10:16 inheritance in the son of J
2Ch 11:18 of Eliah the son of J
Ps 72:20 David the son of J are ended
Is 11: 1 a Rod from the stem of J, and
Is 11:10 there shall be a Root of J
Matt 1: 5 Obed by Ruth, Obed begot J
Matt 1: 6 and J begot David the king
Luke 3:32 the son of J, the son of Obed
Acts 13:22 have found David the son of J
Rom 15:12 There shall be a root of J

JESSHIAH
1Ch 23:20 was the first and J the second

JESTING
Eph 5: 4 foolish talking, nor coarse j

JESUI
Num 26:44 of J, the family of the

JESUITES
Num 26:44 of Jesui, the family of the J

JESUS (*see* CHRIST, JESUS', JUSTUS)
Matt 1: 1 of the genealogy of J Christ
Matt 1:16 of whom was born J who is
Matt 1:18 Now the birth of J Christ was
Matt 1:21 and you shall call His name J
Matt 1:25 And he called His name J
Matt 2: 1 Now after J was born in
Matt 3:13 Then J came from Galilee to
Matt 3:15 But J answered and said to him
Matt 3:16 Then J, when He had been
Matt 4: 1 Then J was led up by the
Matt 4: 7 J said to him, "It is
Matt 4:10 Then J said to him, "Away
Matt 4:12 Now when J heard that John
Matt 4:17 From that time J began to
Matt 4:18 Now J, walking by the Sea of
Matt 4:23 Now J went about all Galilee,
Matt 7:28 was, when J had ended these
Matt 8: 3 Then J put out His hand and
Matt 8: 4 And J said to him, "See that you
Matt 8: 5 Now when J had entered
Matt 8: 7 And J said to him,
Matt 8:10 When J heard it, He marveled,
Matt 8:13 Then J said to the centurion,
Matt 8:14 Now when J had come into
Matt 8:18 Now when J saw great
Matt 8:20 And J said to him, "Foxes have
Matt 8:22 But J said to him, "Follow
Matt 8:29 have we to do with You, J
Matt 8:34 whole city came out to meet J
Matt 9: 2 And J, seeing their faith,
Matt 9: 4 But J, knowing their thoughts
Matt 9: 9 Then as J passed on from
Matt 9:10 as J sat at the table in the
Matt 9:12 But when J heard that, He
Matt 9:15 And J said to them, "Can the
Matt 9:19 So J arose and followed him,
Matt 9:22 But J turned around, and when
Matt 9:23 when J came into the ruler's
Matt 9:27 When J departed from there,
Matt 9:28 And J said to them,
Matt 9:30 J sternly warned them, saying
Matt 9:35 J went about all the cities
Matt 10: 5 These twelve J sent out and
Matt 11: 1 when J finished commanding
Matt 11: 4 J answered and said to them
Matt 11: 7 J began to say to the
Matt 11:25 At that time J answered and
Matt 12: 1 At that time J went through
Matt 12:15 But when J knew it, He
Matt 12:25 But J knew their thoughts, and
Matt 13: 1 On the same day J went out of
Matt 13:34 All these things J spoke to
Matt 13:36 Then J sent the multitude
Matt 13:51 J said to them, "Have you
Matt 13:53 when J had finished these
Matt 13:57 J said to them, "A prophet is
Matt 14: 1 heard the report about J
Matt 14:12 buried it, and went and told J
Matt 14:13 When J heard it, He departed
Matt 14:14 And when J went out He saw a
Matt 14:16 But J said to them, "They do
Matt 14:22 Immediately J made His
Matt 14:25 of the night J went to them
Matt 14:27 immediately J spoke to them
Matt 14:29 on the water to go to J
Matt 14:31 immediately J stretched out
Matt 15: 1 were from Jerusalem came to J
Matt 15:16 So J said, "Are you also
Matt 15:21 Then J went out from there and
Matt 15:28 Then J answered and said to
Matt 15:29 And J departed from there,
Matt 15:32 Then J called His disciples
Matt 15:34 J said to them, "How many
Matt 16: 6 Then J said to them, "Take
Matt 16: 8 But when J perceived it, He
Matt 16:13 When J came into the region
Matt 16:17 J answered and said to him
Matt 16:20 one that He was J the Christ
Matt 16:21 From that time J began to
Matt 16:24 Then J said to His disciples,
Matt 17: 1 after six days J took Peter
Matt 17: 4 Peter answered and said to J
Matt 17: 7 But J came and touched them
Matt 17: 8 they saw no one but J only
Matt 17: 9 J commanded them, saying,
Matt 17:11 Then J answered and said to
Matt 17:17 Then J answered and said, "O
Matt 17:18 J rebuked the demon, and he
Matt 17:19 disciples came to J privately
Matt 17:20 So J said to them, "Because
Matt 17:22 in Galilee, J said to them,
Matt 17:25 J anticipated him, saying,
Matt 17:26 J said to him, "Then the sons are
Matt 18: 1 time the disciples came to J
Matt 18: 2 J called a little child to
Matt 18:22 J said to him, "I do not say
Matt 19: 1 when J had finished these
Matt 19:14 But J said, "Let the little
Matt 19:18 J said, "You shall not murder,
Matt 19:21 J said to him, "If you want
Matt 19:23 Then J said to His disciples,
Matt 19:26 But J looked at them and said
Matt 19:28 So J said to them, "Assuredly I
Matt 20:17 Then J, going up to Jerusalem
Matt 20:22 But J answered and said, "You
Matt 20:25 But J called them to Himself
Matt 20:30 heard that J was passing by
Matt 20:32 So J stood still and called
Matt 20:34 So J had compassion and
Matt 21: 1 then J sent two disciples,
Matt 21: 6 and did as J commanded them
Matt 21:11 This is J, the prophet from
Matt 21:12 Then J went into the temple
Matt 21:16 And J said to them, "Yes. Have
Matt 21:21 So J answered and said to them
Matt 21:24 But J answered and said to
Matt 21:27 So they answered J and said
Matt 21:31 J said to them, "Assuredly, I
Matt 21:42 J said to them, "Did you
Matt 22: 1 J answered and spoke to them
Matt 22:18 But J perceived their
Matt 22:29 J answered and said to them
Matt 22:37 J said to him, "You shall
Matt 22:41 together, J asked them,
Matt 23: 1 Then J spoke to the
Matt 24: 1 Then J went out and departed
Matt 24: 2 J said to them, "Do you not see
Matt 24: 4 J answered and said to them
Matt 26: 1 when J had finished all these
Matt 26: 4 plotted to take J by trickery
Matt 26: 6 when J was in Bethany at the
Matt 26:10 But when J was aware of it,
Matt 26:17 Bread the disciples came to J
Matt 26:19 did as J had directed them

Matt 26:26 J took bread, blessed it and
Matt 26:31 Then J said to them, "All of
Matt 26:34 J said to him, "Assuredly, I
Matt 26:36 Then J came with them to a
Matt 26:49 immediately he went up to J
Matt 26:50 And J said to him, "Friend,
Matt 26:50 they came and laid hands on J
Matt 26:51 with J stretched out his hand
Matt 26:52 Then J said to him, "Put
Matt 26:55 In that hour J said to the
Matt 26:57 of J led Him away to Caiaphas
Matt 26:59 against J to put Him to death
Matt 26:63 But J kept silent
Matt 26:64 J said to him, "It is as you
Matt 26:69 also were with J of Galilee
Matt 26:71 also was with J of Nazareth
Matt 26:75 word of J who had said to him
Matt 27: 1 against J to put Him to death
Matt 27:11 Now J stood before the
Matt 27:11 So J said to him, "It is as you
Matt 27:17 or J who is called Christ
Matt 27:20 ask for Barabbas and destroy J
Matt 27:22 with J who is called Christ
Matt 27:26 and when he had scourged J
Matt 27:27 took J into the Praetorium
Matt 27:37 THIS IS J THE KING OF THE
Matt 27:46 about the ninth hour J cried
Matt 27:50 J, when He had cried out
Matt 27:54 with him, who were guarding J
Matt 27:55 who followed J from Galilee
Matt 27:57 also become a disciple of J
Matt 27:58 and asked for the body of J
Matt 28: 5 you seek J who was crucified
Matt 28: 9 behold, J met them, saying,
Matt 28:10 Then J said to them, "Do not
Matt 28:16 to the mountain which J had
Matt 28:18 Then J came and spoke to them,
Mark 1: 1 of the gospel of J Christ
Mark 1: 9 that J came from Nazareth of
Mark 1:14 J came to Galilee, preaching
Mark 1:17 Then J said to them, "Come
Mark 1:24 to do with You, J of Nazareth
Mark 1:25 But J rebuked him, saying,
Mark 1:41 And J, moved with compassion,
Mark 1:45 so that J could no longer
Mark 2: 5 When J saw their faith, He
Mark 2: 8 when J perceived in His
Mark 2:15 also sat together with J and
Mark 2:17 When J heard it, He said to
Mark 2:19 So J said to them, "Can the
Mark 3: 7 But J withdrew with His
Mark 5: 6 But when he saw J from afar
Mark 5: 7 What have I to do with You, J
Mark 5:13 And at once J gave them
Mark 5:15 Then they came to J, and saw
Mark 5:19 J did not permit him, but
Mark 5:20 all that J had done for him
Mark 5:21 Now when J had crossed over
Mark 5:24 So J went with him, and a
Mark 5:27 When she heard about J, she
Mark 5:30 And J, immediately knowing in
Mark 5:36 As soon as J heard the word
Mark 6: 4 But J said to them, "A
Mark 6:30 the apostles gathered to J
Mark 6:34 And J, when He came out, saw a
Mark 7:27 But J said to her, "Let the
Mark 8: 1 J called His disciples to Him
Mark 8:17 And J, being aware of it, said
Mark 8:27 Now J and His disciples went
Mark 9: 2 after six days J took Peter
Mark 9: 4 and they were talking with J
Mark 9: 5 Peter answered and said to J
Mark 9: 8 but only J with themselves
Mark 9:23 J said to him, "If you can
Mark 9:25 When J saw that the people
Mark 9:27 But J took him by the hand and
Mark 9:39 But J said, "Do not forbid
Mark 10: 5 J answered and said to them,
Mark 10:14 But when J saw it, He was
Mark 10:18 So J said to him, "Why do
Mark 10:21 Then J, looking at him, loved
Mark 10:23 Then J looked around and said
Mark 10:24 But J answered again and said
Mark 10:27 But looking at them, J said,
Mark 10:29 So J answered and said
Mark 10:32 and J was going before them
Mark 10:38 But J said to them, "You do
Mark 10:39 J said to them, "You will
Mark 10:42 But J called them to Himself
Mark 10:47 that it was J of Nazareth
Mark 10:47 J, Son of David, have mercy
Mark 10:49 So J stood still and commanded
Mark 10:50 garment, he rose and came to J
Mark 10:51 J answered and said to him,
Mark 10:52 Then J said to him, "Go your
Mark 10:52 and followed J on the road
Mark 11: 6 them just as J had commanded
Mark 11: 7 they brought the colt to J
Mark 11:11 J went into Jerusalem and into
Mark 11:14 In response J said to it
Mark 11:15 J went into the temple and
Mark 11:22 So J answered and said to them
Mark 11:29 But J answered and said to
Mark 11:33 So they answered and said to J
Mark 11:33 J answered and said to them,
Mark 12:17 Then J answered and said to
Mark 12:24 J answered and said to them
Mark 12:29 J answered him, "The first
Mark 12:34 So when J saw that he
Mark 12:35 Then J answered and said,
Mark 12:41 Now J sat opposite the
Mark 13: 2 J answered and said to him,
Mark 13: 5 And J, answering them, began
Mark 14: 6 But J said, "Let her alone
Mark 14:18 as they sat and ate, J said,
Mark 14:22 J took bread, blessed it and
Mark 14:27 Then J said to them, "All of
Mark 14:30 And J said to him, "Assuredly,
Mark 14:48 Then J answered and said to
Mark 14:53 they led J away to the high
Mark 14:55 against J to put Him to death
Mark 14:60 up in the midst and asked J
Mark 14:62 J said, "I am. And you will
Mark 14:67 also were with J of Nazareth
Mark 14:72 word that J had said to him
Mark 15: 1 and they bound J, led Him away
Mark 15: 5 But J still answered nothing,
Mark 15:15 and he delivered J, after he
Mark 15:34 at the ninth hour J cried out
Mark 15:37 J cried out with a loud voice
Mark 15:43 and asked for the body of J
Mark 16: 6 You seek J of Nazareth, who
Luke 1:31 Son, and shall call His name J
Luke 2:21 Child, His name was called J
Luke 2:27 brought in the Child J, to do
Luke 2:43 the Boy J lingered behind in
Luke 2:52 And J increased in wisdom and
Luke 3:21 pass that J also was baptized
Luke 3:23 Now J Himself began His
Luke 4: 1 Then J, being filled with the
Luke 4: 4 But J answered him, saying,
Luke 4: 8 J answered and said to him,
Luke 4:12 J answered and said to him,
Luke 4:14 Then J returned in the power
Luke 4:34 to do with You, J of Nazareth
Luke 4:35 But J rebuked him, saying,
Luke 5:10 And J said to Simon,
Luke 5:12 who was full of leprosy saw J
Luke 5:19 into the midst before J
Luke 5:22 But when J perceived their
Luke 5:31 J answered and said to them,
Luke 6: 3 But J answering them said,
Luke 6: 9 Then J said to them, "I will
Luke 6:11 what they might do to J
Luke 7: 3 So when he heard about J, he
Luke 7: 4 And when they came to J, they
Luke 7: 6 Then J went with them
Luke 7: 9 When J heard these things, He
Luke 7:19 to him, sent them to J,
Luke 7:22 Then J answered and said to
Luke 7:37 when she knew that J sat at
Luke 7:40 J answered and said to him,
Luke 8:28 When he saw J, he cried out,
Luke 8:28 What have I to do with You, J
Luke 8:30 J asked him, saying, "What
Luke 8:35 had happened, and came to J
Luke 8:35 sitting at the feet of J
Luke 8:38 But J sent him away, saying,
Luke 8:39 things J had done for him
Luke 8:40 when J returned, that the
Luke 8:45 And J said, "Who touched
Luke 8:46 But J said, "Somebody
Luke 8:50 But when J heard it, He
Luke 9:33 Him, that Peter said to J
Luke 9:36 had ceased, J was found alone
Luke 9:41 Then J answered and said, "O
Luke 9:42 Then J rebuked the unclean
Luke 9:43 at all the things which J did
Luke 9:47 And J, perceiving the thought
Luke 9:50 But J said to him, "Do not
Luke 9:58 And J said to him, "Foxes have
Luke 9:60 J said to him, "Let the dead
Luke 9:62 But J said to him, "No one,
Luke 10:21 In that hour J rejoiced in
Luke 10:29 to justify himself, said to J
Luke 10:30 Then J answered and said
Luke 10:37 Then J said to him, "Go and do
Luke 10:41 J answered and said to her,
Luke 13: 2 J answered and said to them,
Luke 13:12 But when J saw her, He called
Luke 13:14 because J had healed on the
Luke 14: 3 And J, answering, spoke to the
Luke 17:13 J, Master, have mercy on us
Luke 17:17 So J answered and said, "Were
Luke 18:16 But J called them to Him and
Luke 18:19 So J said to him, "Why do
Luke 18:22 So when J heard these things,
Luke 18:24 when J saw that he became
Luke 18:37 So they told him that J of
Luke 18:38 J, Son of David, have mercy
Luke 18:40 So J stood still and commanded
Luke 18:42 Then J said to him, "Receive
Luke 19: 1 Then J entered and passed
Luke 19: 3 And he sought to see who J was
Luke 19: 5 when J came to the place, He
Luke 19: 9 And J said to him, "Today
Luke 19:35 Then they brought him to J
Luke 19:35 colt, and they set J on him
Luke 20: 8 J said to them, "Neither will
Luke 20:34 J answered and said to them,
Luke 22:47 and drew near to J to kiss Him
Luke 22:48 But J said to him, "Judas,
Luke 22:51 But J answered and said
Luke 22:52 Then J said to the chief
Luke 22:63 the men who held J mocked
Luke 23: 8 Now when Herod saw J, he was
Luke 23:20 wishing to release J, again
Luke 23:25 he delivered J to their will
Luke 23:26 that he might bear it after J
Luke 23:28 But J, turning to them, said,
Luke 23:34 Then J said, "Father,
Luke 23:42 Then he said to J, "Lord,
Luke 23:43 And J said to him, "Assuredly,
Luke 23:46 when J had cried out with a
Luke 23:52 and asked for the body of J
Luke 24: 3 find the body of the Lord J
Luke 24:15 that J Himself drew near and
Luke 24:19 concerning J of Nazareth, who
Luke 24:36 J Himself stood in the midst
John 1:17 truth came through J Christ
John 1:29 John saw J coming toward him
John 1:36 looking at J as He walked, he
John 1:37 him speak, and they followed J
John 1:38 Then J turned, and seeing them
John 1:42 And he brought him to J
John 1:42 Now when J looked at him, He
John 1:43 The following day J wanted to
John 1:45 J of Nazareth, the son of
John 1:47 J saw Nathanael coming toward
John 1:48 J answered and said to him,
John 1:50 J answered and said to him
John 2: 1 and the mother of J was there
John 2: 2 Now both J and His disciples
John 2: 3 the mother of J said to Him
John 2: 4 J said to her, "Woman, what
John 2: 7 J said to them, "Fill the
John 2:11 J did in Cana of Galilee, and
John 2:13 and J went up to Jerusalem
John 2:19 J answered and said to them
John 2:22 and the word which J had said
John 2:24 But J did not commit Himself
John 3: 2 This man came to J by night
John 3: 3 J answered and said to him
John 3: 5 J answered, "Most assuredly,
John 3:10 J answered and said to him
John 3:22 After these things J and His
John 4: 1 had heard that J made and
John 4: 2 (though J Himself did not
John 4: 6 J therefore, being wearied
John 4: 7 J said to her, "Give Me a
John 4:10 J answered and said to her
John 4:13 J answered and said to her
John 4:16 J said to her, "Go, call
John 4:17 J said to her, "You have
John 4:21 J said to her, "Woman,
John 4:26 J said to her, "I who speak
John 4:34 J said to them, "My food is
John 4:44 For J Himself testified that
John 4:46 So J came again to Cana of
John 4:47 When he heard that J had come

Acts 20:21 toward our Lord J Christ
Acts 20:24 I received from the Lord J
Acts 20:35 the words of the Lord J, that
Acts 21:13 for the name of the Lord J
Acts 22: 8 I am J of Nazareth, whom you
Acts 25:19 own religion and about one, J
Acts 26: 9 to the name of J of Nazareth
Acts 26:15 And He said, 'I am J, whom
Acts 28:23 J from both the Law of Moses
Acts 28:31 which concern the Lord J
Rom 1: 1 Paul, a servant of J Christ
Rom 1: 3 His Son J Christ our Lord
Rom 1: 6 are the called of J Christ
Rom 1: 7 Father and the Lord J Christ
Rom 1: 8 through J Christ for you all
Rom 2:16 secrets of men by J Christ
Rom 3:22 faith in J Christ to all and
Rom 3:24 that is in Christ J,
Rom 3:26 of the one who has faith in J
Rom 4:24 in Him who raised up J our
Rom 5: 1 God through our Lord J Christ
Rom 5:11 God through our Lord J Christ
Rom 5:15 J Christ, abounded to many
Rom 5:17 through the One, J Christ
Rom 5:21 through J Christ our Lord
Rom 6: 3 J were baptized into His
Rom 6:11 to God in Christ J our Lord
Rom 6:23 life in Christ J our Lord
Rom 7:25 through J Christ our Lord
Rom 8: 1 to those who are in Christ J
Rom 8: 2 Spirit of life in Christ J
Rom 8:11 Spirit of Him who raised J
Rom 8:39 which is in Christ J our Lord
Rom 10: 9 with your mouth the Lord J
Rom 13:14 But put on the Lord J Christ
Rom 14:14 Lord J that there is nothing
Rom 15: 5 according to Christ J,
Rom 15: 6 Father of our Lord J Christ
Rom 15: 8 Now I say that J Christ has
Rom 15:16 of J Christ to the Gentiles
Rom 15:17 reason to glory in Christ J
Rom 15:30 through the Lord J Christ
Rom 16: 3 my fellow workers in Christ J
Rom 16:18 not serve our Lord J Christ
Rom 16:20 our Lord J Christ be with you
Rom 16:24 The grace of our Lord J
Rom 16:25 and the preaching of J Christ
Rom 16:27 through J Christ forever
1Co 1: 1 J Christ through the will of
1Co 1: 2 are sanctified in Christ J
1Co 1: 2 the name of J Christ our Lord
1Co 1: 3 Father and the Lord J Christ
1Co 1: 4 was given to you by Christ J
1Co 1: 7 of our Lord J Christ,
1Co 1: 8 the day of our Lord J Christ
1Co 1: 9 of His Son, J Christ our Lord
1Co 1:10 the name of our Lord J Christ
1Co 1:30 of Him you are in Christ J
1Co 2: 2 among you except J Christ
1Co 3:11 is laid, which is J Christ
1Co 4:15 for in Christ J I have
1Co 5: 4 the name of our Lord J Christ
1Co 5: 4 power of our Lord J Christ
1Co 5: 5 in the day of the Lord J
1Co 6:11 in the name of the Lord J
1Co 8: 6 and one Lord J Christ, through
1Co 9: 1 I not seen J Christ our Lord
1Co 11:23 that the Lord J on the same
1Co 12: 3 of God calls J accursed, and
1Co 12: 3 no one can say that J is Lord
1Co 15:31 I have in Christ J our Lord
1Co 15:57 through our Lord J Christ
1Co 16:22 not love the Lord J Christ
1Co 16:23 our Lord J Christ be with you
1Co 16:24 be with you all in Christ J
2Co 1: 1 an apostle of J Christ by the
2Co 1: 2 Father and the Lord J Christ
2Co 1: 3 Father of our Lord J Christ
2Co 1:14 in the day of the Lord J
2Co 1:19 J Christ, who was preached
2Co 4: 5 but Christ J the Lord, and
2Co 4: 6 God in the face of J Christ
2Co 4:10 body the dying of the Lord J
2Co 4:10 that the life of J also may
2Co 4:11 that the life of J also may
2Co 4:14 He who raised up the Lord J
2Co 4:14 will also raise us up with J
2Co 5:18 to Himself through J Christ
2Co 8: 9 grace of our Lord J Christ
2Co 11: 4 J whom we have not preached
2Co 11:31 Father of our Lord J Christ
2Co 13: 5 that J Christ is in you
2Co 13:14 grace of the Lord J Christ
Gal 1: 1 man, but through J Christ
Gal 1: 3 Father and our Lord J Christ
Gal 1:12 the revelation of J Christ
Gal 2: 4 which we have in Christ J
Gal 2:16 law but by faith in J Christ
Gal 2:16 we have believed in Christ J
Gal 3: 1 before whose eyes J Christ
Gal 3:14 upon the Gentiles in Christ J
Gal 3:22 the promise by faith in J
Gal 3:26 God through faith in Christ J
Gal 3:28 you are all one in Christ J
Gal 4:14 of God, even as Christ J
Gal 5: 6 For in Christ J neither
Gal 6:14 cross of our Lord J Christ
Gal 6:15 For in Christ J neither
Gal 6:17 body the marks of the Lord J
Gal 6:18 the grace of our Lord J
Eph 1: 1 an apostle of J Christ by the
Eph 1: 1 and faithful in Christ J
Eph 1: 2 Father and the Lord J Christ
Eph 1: 3 Father of our Lord J Christ
Eph 1: 5 sons by J Christ to Himself
Eph 1:15 of your faith in the Lord J
Eph 1:17 the God of our Lord J Christ
Eph 2: 6 heavenly places in Christ J
Eph 2: 7 toward us in Christ J
Eph 2:10 in Christ J for good works
Eph 2:13 But now in Christ J you who
Eph 2:20 J Christ Himself being the
Eph 3: 1 the prisoner of J Christ for
Eph 3: 9 all things through J Christ
Eph 3:11 in Christ J our Lord,
Eph 3:14 Father of our Lord J Christ
Eph 3:21 Christ J throughout all ages
Eph 4:21 by Him, as the truth is in J
Eph 5:20 the name of our Lord J Christ
Eph 6:23 Father and the Lord J Christ
Eph 6:24 Lord J Christ in sincerity
Phil 1: 1 Timothy, servants of J Christ
Phil 1: 1 Christ J who are in Philippi
Phil 1: 2 Father and the Lord J Christ
Phil 1: 6 it until the day of J Christ
Phil 1: 8 the affection of J Christ
Phil 1:11 which are by J Christ, to the
Phil 1:19 of the Spirit of J Christ
Phil 1:26 J Christ by my coming to you
Phil 2: 5 which was also in Christ J
Phil 2:10 that at the name of J every
Phil 2:11 confess that J Christ is Lord
Phil 2:19 Lord J to send Timothy to you
Phil 2:21 things which are of Christ J
Phil 3: 3 Spirit, rejoice in Christ J
Phil 3: 8 knowledge of Christ J my Lord
Phil 3:12 J has also laid hold of me
Phil 3:14 call of God in Christ J
Phil 3:20 the Savior, the Lord J Christ
Phil 4: 7 and minds through Christ J
Phil 4:19 riches in glory by Christ J
Phil 4:21 Greet every saint in Christ J
Phil 4:23 The grace of our Lord J
Col 1: 1 an apostle of J Christ by the
Col 1: 2 Father and the Lord J Christ
Col 1: 3 Father of our Lord J Christ
Col 1: 4 of your faith in Christ J
Col 1:28 every man perfect in Christ J
Col 2: 6 received Christ J the Lord
Col 3:17 all in the name of the Lord J
Col 4:11 and J who is called Justus
1Th 1: 1 Father and the Lord J Christ
1Th 1: 1 Father and the Lord J Christ
1Th 1: 3 of hope in our Lord J Christ
1Th 1:10 even J who delivers us from
1Th 2:14 are in Judea in Christ J
1Th 2:15 who killed both the Lord J
1Th 2:19 Lord J Christ at His coming
1Th 3:11 Himself, and our Lord J Christ
1Th 3:13 at the coming of our Lord J
1Th 4: 1 exhort in the Lord J that you
1Th 4: 2 gave you through the Lord J
1Th 4:14 For if we believe that J died
1Th 4:14 with Him those who sleep in J
1Th 5: 9 through our Lord J Christ
1Th 5:18 of God in Christ J for you
1Th 5:23 coming of our Lord J Christ
1Th 5:28 our Lord J Christ be with you
2Th 1: 1 Father and the Lord J Christ
2Th 1: 2 Father and the Lord J Christ
2Th 1: 7 J is revealed from heaven
2Th 1: 8 gospel of our Lord J Christ
2Th 1:12 that the name of our Lord J
2Th 1:12 our God and the Lord J Christ
2Th 2: 1 coming of our Lord J Christ
2Th 2:14 glory of our Lord J Christ
2Th 2:16 may our Lord J Christ Himself
2Th 3: 6 the name of our Lord J Christ
2Th 3:12 exhort through our Lord J
2Th 3:18 The grace of our Lord J
1Ti 1: 1 Paul, an apostle of J Christ
1Ti 1: 1 Savior and the Lord J Christ
1Ti 1: 2 Father and J Christ our Lord
1Ti 1:12 I thank Christ J our Lord who
1Ti 1:14 and love which are in Christ J
1Ti 1:15 that Christ J came into the
1Ti 1:16 that in me first J Christ
1Ti 2: 5 God and men, the Man Christ J
1Ti 3:13 faith which is in Christ J
1Ti 4: 6 a good minister of J Christ
1Ti 5:21 God and the Lord J Christ and
1Ti 6: 3 words of our Lord J Christ
1Ti 6:13 before Christ J who witnessed
1Ti 6:14 our Lord J Christ's appearing
2Ti 1: 1 an apostle of J Christ by the
2Ti 1: 1 of life which is in Christ J
2Ti 1: 2 Father and Christ J our Lord
2Ti 1: 9 in Christ J before time began
2Ti 1:10 of our Savior J Christ, who
2Ti 1:13 and love which are in Christ J
2Ti 2: 1 the grace that is in Christ J
2Ti 2: 3 as a good soldier of J Christ
2Ti 2: 8 Remember that J Christ, of
2Ti 2:10 Christ J with eternal glory
2Ti 3:12 J will suffer persecution
2Ti 3:15 faith which is in Christ J
2Ti 4: 1 God and the Lord J Christ, who
2Ti 4:22 The Lord J Christ be with
Tit 1: 1 God and an apostle of J Christ
Tit 1: 4 the Lord J Christ our Savior
Tit 2:13 great God and Savior J Christ
Tit 3: 6 through J Christ our Savior
Phm 1 Paul, a prisoner of Christ J
Phm 3 Father and the Lord J Christ
Phm 5 you have toward the Lord J
Phm 6 which is in you in Christ J
Phm 9 also a prisoner of J Christ
Phm 23 fellow prisoner in Christ J
Phm 25 The grace of our Lord J
Heb 2: 9 But we see J, who was made a
Heb 3: 1 of our confession, Christ J
Heb 4:14 J the Son of God, let us hold
Heb 6:20 has entered for us, even J
Heb 7:22 by so much more J has become
Heb 10:10 body of J Christ once for all
Heb 10:19 the Holiest by the blood of J
Heb 12: 2 looking unto J, the author and
Heb 12:24 to J the Mediator of the new
Heb 13: 8 J Christ is the same
Heb 13:12 Therefore J also, that He
Heb 13:20 up our Lord J from the dead
Heb 13:21 His sight, through J Christ
Jas 1: 1 God and of the Lord J Christ
Jas 2: 1 faith of our Lord J Christ
1Pe 1: 1 Peter, an apostle of J Christ
1Pe 1: 2 of the blood of J Christ
1Pe 1: 3 Father of our Lord J Christ
1Pe 1: 3 of J Christ from the dead
1Pe 1: 7 at the revelation of J Christ
1Pe 1:13 at the revelation of J Christ
1Pe 2: 5 to God through J Christ
1Pe 3:21 the resurrection of J Christ
1Pe 4:11 be glorified through J Christ
1Pe 5:10 His eternal glory by Christ J
1Pe 5:14 you all who are in Christ J
2Pe 1: 1 and apostle of J Christ, To
2Pe 1: 1 of our God and Savior J Christ
2Pe 1: 2 of God and of J our Lord,
2Pe 1: 8 of our Lord J Christ
2Pe 1:11 our Lord and Savior J Christ
2Pe 1:14 our Lord J Christ showed me
2Pe 1:16 coming of our Lord J Christ
2Pe 2:20 the Lord and Savior J Christ
2Pe 3:18 our Lord and Savior J Christ
1Jn 1: 3 and with His Son J Christ
1Jn 1: 7 the blood of J Christ His Son
1Jn 2: 1 J Christ the righteous
1Jn 2:22 denies that J is the Christ
1Jn 3:23 the name of His Son J Christ
1Jn 4: 2 that J Christ has come in the

1Jn 4: 3 that J Christ has come in the
1Jn 4:15 that J is the Son of God, God
1Jn 5: 1 Whoever believes that J is
1Jn 5: 5 that J is the Son of God
1Jn 5: 6 by water and blood—J Christ
1Jn 5:20 is true, in His Son J Christ
2Jn 3 and from the Lord J Christ
2Jn 7 J Christ as coming in the
Jude 1 Jude, a servant of J Christ
Jude 1 and preserved in J Christ
Jude 4 Lord God and our Lord J Christ
Jude 17 apostles of our Lord J Christ
Jude 21 J Christ unto eternal life
Rev 1: 1 The Revelation of J Christ
Rev 1: 2 to the testimony of J Christ
Rev 1: 5 from J Christ, the faithful
Rev 1: 9 and patience of J Christ, was
Rev 1: 9 for the testimony of J Christ
Rev 12:17 the testimony of J Christ
Rev 14:12 of God and the faith of J
Rev 17: 6 the blood of the martyrs of J
Rev 19:10 who have the testimony of J
Rev 19:10 For the testimony of J is the
Rev 20: 4 for their witness to J and for
Rev 22:16 I, J, have sent My angel to
Rev 22:20 Even so, come, Lord J
Rev 22:21 The grace of our Lord J

JESUS' (*see* JESUS)
Matt 15:30 they laid them down at J feet
Luke 5: 8 it, he fell down at J knees
Luke 8:41 And he fell down at J feet
Luke 10:39 Mary, who also sat at J feet
John 12: 9 not for J sake only, but that
John 13:23 Now there was leaning on J
John 13:25 leaning back on J breast
2Co 4: 5 your servants for J sake
2Co 4:11 delivered to death for J sake

JETHER (*see* HOBAB, JETHRO)
Judg 8:20 he said to J his firstborn,
1Ki 2: 5 of Ner and Amasa the son of J
1Ki 2:32 Israel, and Amasa the son of J
1Ch 2:17 of Amasa was J the Ishmaelite
1Ch 2:32 brother of Shammai, were J
1Ch 2:32 J died without children
1Ch 4:17 The sons of Ezrah were J,
1Ch 7:38 The sons of J were Jephunneh,

JETHETH
Gen 36:40 Timnah, Chief Alvah, Chief J
1Ch 1:51 Timnah, Chief Aliah, Chief J

JETHLAH
Josh 19:42 Shaalabbin, Aijalon, J,

JETHRO (*see* HOBAB, JETHER, REUEL)
Ex 3: 1 flock of J his father-in-law
Ex 4:18 went and returned to J his
Ex 4:18 And J said to Moses,
Ex 18: 1 And J, the priest of Midian,
Ex 18: 2 Then J, Moses' father-in-law,
Ex 18: 5 and J, Moses' father-in-law,
Ex 18: 6 I, your father-in-law J, am
Ex 18: 9 Then J rejoiced for all the
Ex 18:10 J said, "Blessed be the LORD
Ex 18:12 Then J, Moses' father-in-law,

JETUR
Gen 25:15 Hadar, Tema, J, Naphish, and
1Ch 1:31 J, Naphish, and Kedemah
1Ch 5:19 made war with the Hagrites, J

JEUEL (*see* JEIEL)
1Ch 9: 6 J, and their brethren

JEUSH
Gen 36: 5 And Aholibamah bore J,
Gen 36:14 J, Jaalam, and Korah
Gen 36:18 Chief J, Chief Jaalam, and
1Ch 1:35 Esau were Eliphaz, Reuel, J
1Ch 7:10 and the sons of Bilhan were J
1Ch 8:39 J the second, and Eliphelet
1Ch 23:10 Jahath, Zina, J, and Beriah
1Ch 23:11 But J and Beriah did not have
2Ch 11:19 J, Shamariah, and Zaham

JEUZ
1Ch 8:10 J, Sachiah, and Mirmah

JEW (*see* JEWISH, JEWS, JUDAISM)
Esth 2: 5 J whose name was Mordecai the
Esth 3: 4 had told them that he was a J
Esth 5:13 J sitting at the king's gate
Esth 6:10 do so for Mordecai the J who
Esth 8: 7 Esther and Mordecai the J
Esth 9:29 Abihail, with Mordecai the J
Esth 9:31 time, as Mordecai the J and
Esth 10: 3 For Mordecai the J was second
John 4: 9 How is it that You, being a J
John 18:35 Am I a J?
Acts 13: 6 a J whose name was Bar-Jesus,
Acts 18: 2 a certain J named Aquila,
Acts 18:24 Now a certain J named Apollos
Acts 19:34 found out that he was a J
Acts 21:39 I am a J from Tarsus, in
Acts 22: 3 I am indeed a J, born in
Rom 1:16 who believes, for the J first
Rom 2: 9 who does evil, of the J first
Rom 2:10 what is good, to the J first
Rom 2:17 Indeed you are called a J
Rom 2:28 For he is not a J who is one
Rom 2:29 but he is a J who is one
Rom 3: 1 What advantage then has the J
Rom 10:12 is no distinction between J
1Co 9:20 to the Jews I became as a J
Gal 2:14 If you, being a J, live in
Gal 3:28 There is neither J nor Greek
Col 3:11 there is neither Greek nor J

JEWEL (*see* JEWELRY, JEWELS)
Prov 20:15 of knowledge are a precious j
Ezek 16:12 And I put a j in your nose,

JEWELRY (*see* JEWEL)
Gen 24:53 brought out j of silver,
Gen 24:53 j of gold, and clothing, and
Ex 35:22 all j of gold, that is, every
2Ch 20:25 dead bodies, and precious j
Job 28:17 exchanged for j of fine gold
Prov 25: 4 go to the silversmith for j
Ezek 16:17 your beautiful j from My gold
Ezek 16:39 take your beautiful j, and
Ezek 23:26 and take away your beautiful j
Hos 2:13 with her earrings and j, And

JEWELS (*see* JEWEL)
Ex 31: 5 in cutting j for setting, in
Ex 35:33 in cutting j for setting, in
Song 7: 1 of your thighs are like j
Is 3:21 and the rings; the nose j
Is 61:10 adorns herself with her j
Zech 9:16 be like the j of a crown,
Mal 3:17 the day that I make them My j

JEWISH (*see* JEW)
Neh 5: 1 against their J brethren
Neh 5: 8 we have redeemed our J
Esth 6:13 is of J descent, you will not
Jer 34: 9 keep a J brother in bondage
Zech 8:23 grasp the sleeve of a J man
Acts 10:28 how unlawful it is for a J
Acts 12:11 expectation of the J people
Acts 16: 1 certain J woman who believed
Acts 19:13 J exorcists took it upon
Acts 19:14 a J chief priest, who did so
Acts 24:24 his wife Drusilla, who was J
Acts 26:17 deliver you from the J people
Acts 26:23 light to the J people and to
Tit 1:14 not giving heed to J fables

JEWS (*see* JEW, JEWS')
2Ki 25:25 and killed Gedaliah, the J
Ezra 4:12 J who came up from you have
Ezra 4:23 to Jerusalem against the J
Ezra 5: 1 to the J who were in Judah
Ezra 5: 5 was upon the elders of the J
Ezra 6: 7 let the governor of the J
Ezra 6: 7 the elders of the J build
Ezra 6: 8 do for the elders of these J
Ezra 6:14 So the elders of the J built
Neh 1: 2 the J who had escaped, who
Neh 2:16 I had not yet told the J, the
Neh 4: 1 indignant, and mocked the J
Neh 4: 2 What are these feeble J doing
Neh 4:12 when the J who dwelt near
Neh 5:17 table one hundred and fifty J
Neh 6: 6 you and the J plan to rebel
Neh 13:23 J who had married women of
Esth 3: 6 the J who were throughout the
Esth 3:10 Agagite, the enemy of the J
Esth 3:13 and to annihilate all the J
Esth 4: 3 great mourning among the J
Esth 4: 7 treasuries to destroy the J
Esth 4:13 any more than all the other J
Esth 4:14 for the J from another place
Esth 4:16 Go, gather all the J who are
Esth 8: 1 of Haman, the enemy of the J
Esth 8: 3 he had devised against the J
Esth 8: 5 J who are in all the king's
Esth 8: 7 to lay his hand on the J
Esth 8: 8 write a decree for the J, as
Esth 8: 9 Mordecai commanded, to the J
Esth 8: 9 to the J in their own script
Esth 8:11 the king permitted the J who
Esth 8:13 so that the J would be ready
Esth 8:16 The J had light and gladness,
Esth 8:17 the J had joy and gladness, a
Esth 8:17 people of the land became J
Esth 8:17 fear of the J fell upon them
Esth 9: 1 J had hoped to overpower them
Esth 9: 1 in that the J themselves
Esth 9: 2 The J gathered together in
Esth 9: 3 the king's work, helped the J
Esth 9: 5 Thus the J defeated all their
Esth 9: 6 the citadel the J killed and
Esth 9:10 the enemy of the J
Esth 9:12 The J have killed and
Esth 9:13 J who are in Shushan to do
Esth 9:15 the J who were in Shushan
Esth 9:16 The remainder of the J in the
Esth 9:18 But the J who were at Shushan
Esth 9:19 Therefore the J of the
Esth 9:20 all the J who were in all the
Esth 9:22 as the days on which the J
Esth 9:23 So the J accepted the custom
Esth 9:24 the enemy of all the J, had
Esth 9:24 the J to annihilate them, and
Esth 9:25 had devised against the J
Esth 9:27 the J established and imposed
Esth 9:28 to be observed among the J
Esth 9:30 sent letters to all the J
Esth 10: 3 and was great among the J
Jer 32:12 before all the J who sat in
Jer 38:19 I am afraid of the J who have
Jer 40:11 when all the J who were in
Jer 40:12 then all the J returned out
Jer 40:15 so that all the J who are
Jer 41: 3 all the J who were with him
Jer 44: 1 J who dwell in the land of
Jer 52:28 thousand and twenty-three J
Jer 52:30 of the J seven hundred and
Dan 3: 8 came forward and accused the J
Dan 3:12 There are certain J whom you
Matt 2: 2 has been born King of the J
Matt 27:11 Are You the King of the J
Matt 27:29 Hail, King of the J
Matt 27:37 JESUS THE KING OF THE J
Matt 28:15 among the J until this day
Mark 7: 3 all the J do not eat unless
Mark 15: 2 Are You the King of the J
Mark 15: 9 to you the King of the J
Mark 15:12 you call the King of the J
Mark 15:18 Hail, King of the J
Mark 15:26 THE KING OF THE J
Luke 7: 3 sent elders of the J to Him
Luke 23: 3 Are You the King of the J
Luke 23:37 If You are the King of the J
Luke 23:38 THIS IS THE KING OF THE J
Luke 23:51 Arimathea, a city of the J
John 1:19 when the J sent priests and
John 2: 6 of purification of the J,
John 2:13 Passover of the J was at hand
John 2:18 So the J answered and said to
John 2:20 Then the J said, "It has
John 3: 1 Nicodemus, a ruler of the J
John 3:25 and the J about purification
John 4: 9 For J have no dealings with
John 4:20 you J say that in Jerusalem
John 4:22 for salvation is of the J
John 5: 1 there was a feast of the J
John 5:10 The J therefore said to him
John 5:15 told the J that it was Jesus
John 5:16 reason the J persecuted Jesus
John 5:18 Therefore the J sought all
John 6: 4 Passover, a feast of the J
John 6:41 The J then murmured against
John 6:52 The J therefore quarreled
John 7: 1 because the J sought to kill
John 7:11 Then the J sought Him at the
John 7:13 of Him for fear of the J
John 7:15 And the J marveled, saying,
John 7:35 Then the J said among
John 8:22 So the J said, "Will He kill
John 8:31 to those J who believed Him
John 8:48 Then the J answered and said
John 8:52 Then the J said to Him, "Now
John 8:57 Then the J said to Him, "You

John 9:18 But the **J** did not believe
John 9:22 because they feared the **J**
John 9:22 for the **J** had agreed already
John 10:19 **J** because of these sayings
John 10:24 Then the **J** surrounded Him and
John 10:31 Then the **J** took up stones
John 10:33 The **J** answered Him, saying,
John 11: 8 lately the **J** sought to stone
John 11:19 many of the **J** had joined the
John 11:31 Then the **J** who were with her
John 11:33 and the **J** who came with her
John 11:36 Then the **J** said, "See how He
John 11:45 Then many of the **J** who had
John 11:54 walked openly among the **J**
John 11:55 Passover of the **J** was near
John 12: 9 the **J** knew that He was there
John 12:11 him many of the **J** went away
John 13:33 and as I said to the **J**, "Where
John 18:12 of the **J** arrested Jesus and
John 18:14 who gave counsel to the **J**
John 18:20 where the **J** always meet, and
John 18:31 Therefore the **J** said to him
John 18:33 Are You the King of the **J**
John 18:36 not be delivered to the **J**
John 18:38 he went out again to the **J**
John 18:39 to you the King of the **J**
John 19: 3 Hail, King of the **J**
John 19: 7 The **J** answered him, "We have
John 19:12 but the **J** cried out, saying,
John 19:14 And he said to the **J**, "Behold
John 19:19 Nazareth, The King of the **J**
John 19:20 many of the **J** read this title
John 19:21 of the **J** said to Pilate, "Do
John 19:21 not write, "The King of the **J**
John 19:21 I am the King of the **J**
John 19:31 the **J** asked Pilate that their
John 19:38 secretly, for fear of the **J**
John 19:40 custom of the **J** is to bury
John 20:19 assembled, for fear of the **J**
Acts 2: 5 were dwelling in Jerusalem **J**
Acts 2:10 visitors from Rome, both **J**
Acts 9:22 confounded the **J** who dwelt in
Acts 9:23 the **J** plotted to kill him
Acts 10:22 among all the nation of the **J**
Acts 10:39 did both in the land of the **J**
Acts 11:19 word to no one but the **J** only
Acts 12: 3 he saw that it pleased the **J**
Acts 13: 5 in the synagogues of the **J**
Acts 13:42 when the **J** went out of the
Acts 13:43 had broken up, many of the **J**
Acts 13:45 But when the **J** saw the
Acts 13:50 But the **J** stirred up the
Acts 14: 1 to the synagogue of the **J**
Acts 14: 1 great multitude both of the **J**
Acts 14: 2 But the unbelieving **J** stirred
Acts 14: 4 part sided with the **J**, and
Acts 14: 5 by both the Gentiles and **J**
Acts 14:19 Then **J** from Antioch and
Acts 16: 3 him because of the **J** who were
Acts 16:20 These men, being **J**,
Acts 17: 1 was a synagogue of the **J**
Acts 17: 5 But the **J** who were not
Acts 17:10 into the synagogue of the **J**
Acts 17:13 But when the **J** from
Acts 17:17 in the synagogue with the **J**
Acts 18: 2 the **J** to depart from Rome)
Acts 18: 4 Sabbath, and persuaded both **J**
Acts 18: 5 testified to the **J** that Jesus
Acts 18:12 the **J** with one accord rose up
Acts 18:14 mouth, Gallio said to the **J**
Acts 18:14 or wicked crimes, O **J**, there
Acts 18:19 and reasoned with the **J**
Acts 18:28 refuted the **J** publicly,
Acts 19:10 of the Lord Jesus, both **J**
Acts 19:17 became known both to all **J**
Acts 19:33 the **J** putting him forward
Acts 20: 3 when the **J** plotted against
Acts 20:19 me by the plotting of the **J**
Acts 20:21 testifying to **J**, and also to
Acts 21:11 So shall the **J** at Jerusalem
Acts 21:20 how many myriads of **J** there
Acts 21:21 **J** who are among the Gentiles
Acts 21:27 the **J** from Asia, seeing him
Acts 22:12 all the **J** who dwelt there
Acts 22:30 why he was accused by the **J**
Acts 23:12 some of the **J** banded together
Acts 23:20 The **J** have agreed to ask that
Acts 23:27 This man was seized by the **J**
Acts 23:30 the **J** lay in wait for the man
Acts 24: 5 the **J** throughout the world
Acts 24: 9 And the **J** also assented,
Acts 24:18 in the midst of which some **J**
Acts 24:27 wanting to do the **J** a favor
Acts 25: 2 and the chief men of the **J**
Acts 25: 7 the **J** who had come down from
Acts 25: 8 against the law of the **J**, nor
Acts 25: 9 wanting to do the **J** a favor
Acts 25:10 To the **J** I have done no wrong
Acts 25:15 elders of the **J** informed me
Acts 25:24 of the **J** petitioned me, both
Acts 26: 2 which I am accused by the **J**
Acts 26: 3 which have to do with the **J**
Acts 26: 4 at Jerusalem, all the **J** know
Acts 26: 7 I am accused by the **J**
Acts 26:21 For these reasons the **J**
Acts 28:17 the leaders of the **J** together
Acts 28:19 But when the **J** spoke against
Acts 28:29 the **J** departed and had a great
Rom 3: 9 previously charged both **J**
Rom 3:29 is He the God of the **J** only
Rom 9:24 He called, not of the **J** only
1Co 1:22 For **J** request a sign, and
1Co 1:23 to the **J** a stumbling block and
1Co 1:24 those who are called, both **J**
1Co 9:20 to the **J** I became as a Jew,
1Co 9:20 as a Jew, that I might win **J**
1Co 10:32 to the **J** or to the Greeks
1Co 12:13 whether **J** or Greeks, whether
2Co 11:24 From the **J** five times I
Gal 2:13 the rest of the **J** also played
Gal 2:14 of Gentiles and not as the **J**
Gal 2:14 compel Gentiles to live as **J**
Gal 2:15 We who are **J** by nature, and
1Th 2:14 just as they did from the **J**
Rev 2: 9 of those who say they are **J**
Rev 3: 9 of Satan, who say they are **J**

JEWS' (*see* JEWS)
John 7: 2 Now the **J** Feast of
John 19:42 because of the **J** Preparation

JEZANIAH (*see* JAAZANIAH)
Jer 40: 8 **J** the son of a Maachathite,
Jer 42: 1 **J** the son of Hoshaiah, and all

JEZEBEL (*see* JEZEBEL'S)
1Ki 16:31 that he took as wife **J** the
1Ki 18: 4 it was, while **J** massacred the
1Ki 18:13 **J** killed the prophets of the
1Ki 19: 1 Ahab told **J** all that Elijah
1Ki 19: 2 Then **J** sent a messenger to
1Ki 21: 5 But **J** his wife came to him,
1Ki 21: 7 Then **J** his wife said to him,
1Ki 21:11 did as **J** had sent to them, as
1Ki 21:14 Then they sent to **J**, saying,
1Ki 21:15 when **J** heard that Naboth had
1Ki 21:15 dead, that **J** said to Ahab,
1Ki 21:23 concerning **J** the LORD also
1Ki 21:23 The dogs shall eat **J** by the
1Ki 21:25 because **J** his wife stirred
2Ki 9: 7 of the LORD, at the hand of **J**
2Ki 9:10 The dogs shall eat **J** in the
2Ki 9:22 harlotries of your mother **J**
2Ki 9:30 to Jezreel, **J** heard of it
2Ki 9:36 dogs shall eat the flesh of **J**
2Ki 9:37 the corpse of **J** shall be as
2Ki 9:37 Here lies **J**."
Rev 2:20 you allow that woman **J**, who

JEZEBEL'S (*see* JEZEBEL)
1Ki 18:19 Asherah, who eat at **J** table

JEZER (*see* JEZERITES)
Gen 46:24 were Jahzeel, Guni, **J**, and
Num 26:49 of **J**, the family of the
1Ch 7:13 were Jahziel, Guni, **J**, and

JEZERITES (*see* JEZER)
Num 26:49 of Jezer, the family of the **J**

JEZIAH
Ezra 10:25 Ramiah, **J**, Malchiah, Mijamin,

JEZIEL
1Ch 12: 3 **J** and Pelet the sons of

JEZRAHIAH (*see* IZRAHIAH)
Neh 12:42 with **J** as their director

JEZREEL (*see* JEZREELITE)
Josh 15:56 **J**, Jokdeam, Zanoah,
Josh 17:16 who are of the Valley of **J**
Josh 19:18 And their territory went to **J**
Judg 6:33 encamped in the Valley of **J**
1Sa 25:43 David also took Ahinoam of **J**
1Sa 29: 1 by a fountain which is in **J**
1Sa 29:11 the Philistines went up to **J**
2Sa 2: 9 over the Ashurites, over **J**
2Sa 4: 4 Saul and Jonathan came from **J**
1Ki 4:12 is beside Zaretan below **J**
1Ki 18:45 Ahab rode away and went to **J**
1Ki 18:46 of Ahab to the entrance of **J**
1Ki 21: 1 had a vineyard which was in **J**
1Ki 21:23 eat Jezebel by the wall of **J**
2Ki 8:29 King Joram went back to **J** to
2Ki 8:29 Joram the son of Ahab in **J**
2Ki 9:10 Jezebel in the vicinity of **J**
2Ki 9:15 **J** to recover from the wounds
2Ki 9:15 city to go and tell it in **J**
2Ki 9:16 in a chariot and went to **J**
2Ki 9:17 stood on the tower in **J**, and
2Ki 9:30 And when Jehu had come to **J**
2Ki 9:36 On the plot of ground at **J**
2Ki 9:37 the field, in the plot at **J**
2Ki 10: 1 Samaria, to the rulers of **J**
2Ki 10: 6 come to me at **J** by this time
2Ki 10: 7 and sent them to him at **J**
2Ki 10:11 of the house of Ahab in **J**
1Ch 4: 3 **J**, Ishma, and Idbash
2Ch 22: 6 Then he returned to **J** to
2Ch 22: 6 Jehoram the son of Ahab in **J**
Hos 1: 4 Call his name **J**, for in a
Hos 1: 4 of **J** on the house of Jehu
Hos 1: 5 of Israel in the Valley of **J**
Hos 1:11 great will be the day of **J**
Hos 2:22 they shall answer **J**

JEZREELITE (*see* JEZREEL)
1Ki 21: 1 things that Naboth the **J** had
1Ki 21: 4 the **J** had spoken to him
1Ki 21: 6 I spoke to Naboth the **J**, and
1Ki 21: 7 the vineyard of Naboth the **J**
1Ki 21:15 the vineyard of Naboth the **J**
1Ki 21:16 the vineyard of Naboth the **J**
2Ki 9:21 the property of Naboth the **J**
2Ki 9:25 of the field of Naboth the **J**

JEZREELITESS
1Sa 27: 3 his two wives, Ahinoam the **J**
1Sa 30: 5 two wives, Ahinoam the **J**, and
2Sa 2: 2 two wives also, Ahinoam the **J**
2Sa 3: 2 was Amnon by Ahinoam the **J**
1Ch 3: 1 was Amnon, by Ahinoam the **J**

JIBSAM
1Ch 7: 2 Rephaiah, Jeriel, Jahmai, **J**

JIDLAPH
Gen 22:22 Chesed, Hazo, Pildash, **J**, and

JIMNA (*see* IMNA, JIMNAH, JIMNITES)
Num 26:44 of **J**, the family of the

JIMNAH (*see* IMNAH, JIMNA)
Gen 46:17 The sons of Asher were **J**,

JIMNITES (*see* JIMNA)
Num 26:44 of Jimna, the family of the **J**

JINGLING
Is 3:16 making a **j** with their feet,
Is 3:18 the **j** anklets, the scarves,

JIPHTAH
Josh 15:43 **J**, Ashnah, Nezib,

JIPHTHAH EL (*see* JEPHTHAH, JIPHTHAH)
Josh 19:14 it ended in the Valley of **J**
Josh 19:27 Zebulun and to the Valley of **J**

JISHUI
1Sa 14:49 of Saul were Jonathan and **J**

JISSHIAH
1Ch 12: 6 Elkanah, **J**, Azareel, Joezer,

JITHRA
2Sa 17:25 son of a man whose name was **J**

JITHRAN
1Ch 7:37 Hod, Shamma, Shilshah, **J**

JIZLIAH
1Ch 8:18 Ishmerai, **J**, and Jobab were

JIZRI
1Ch 25:11 the fourth for **J**, his sons and

JOAB (*see* ATAROTH, JOAB'S)
1Sa 26: 6 son of Zeruiah, brother of **J**
2Sa 2:13 **J** the son of Zeruiah, and the
2Sa 2:14 Then Abner said to **J**, Let
2Sa 2:14 **J** said, Let them arise."
2Sa 2:18 **J** and Abishai and Asahel

2Sa 2:22 could I face your brother J
2Sa 2:24 J and Abishai also pursued
2Sa 2:26 Then Abner called to J and
2Sa 2:27 And J said, "As God lives,
2Sa 2:28 So J blew a trumpet
2Sa 2:30 So J returned from pursuing
2Sa 2:32 And J and his men went all
2Sa 3:22 J came from a raid and brought
2Sa 3:23 When J and all the troops that
2Sa 3:23 him had come, they told J
2Sa 3:24 Then J came to the king and
2Sa 3:26 when J had gone from David's
2Sa 3:27 J took him aside in the gate
2Sa 3:29 Let it rest on the head of J
2Sa 3:29 J one who has a discharge or
2Sa 3:30 So J and Abishai his brother
2Sa 3:31 Then David said to J and to
2Sa 8:16 J the son of Zeruiah was over
2Sa 10: 7 David heard of it, he sent J
2Sa 10: 9 When J saw that the battle
2Sa 10:13 So J and the people who were
2Sa 10:14 So J returned from the people
2Sa 11: 1 to battle, that David sent J
2Sa 11: 6 Then David sent to J, saying,
2Sa 11: 6 And J sent Uriah to David
2Sa 11: 7 David asked how J was doing
2Sa 11:11 in tents, and my lord J and the
2Sa 11:14 David wrote a letter to J
2Sa 11:16 while J besieged the city,
2Sa 11:17 came out and fought with J
2Sa 11:18 Then J sent and told David all
2Sa 11:22 all that J had sent by him
2Sa 11:25 Thus you shall say to J
2Sa 12:26 Now J fought against Rabbah
2Sa 12:27 J sent messengers to David,
2Sa 14: 1 So J the son of Zeruiah
2Sa 14: 2 J sent to Tekoa and brought
2Sa 14: 3 So J put the words in her
2Sa 14:19 Is the hand of J with you in
2Sa 14:19 your servant J commanded me
2Sa 14:20 servant J has done this thing
2Sa 14:21 And the king said to J, "All
2Sa 14:22 Then J fell to the ground on
2Sa 14:22 J said, "Today your servant
2Sa 14:23 So J arose and went to Geshur,
2Sa 14:29 Therefore Absalom sent for J
2Sa 14:31 Then J arose and came to
2Sa 14:32 And Absalom answered J,
2Sa 14:33 So J went to the king and told
2Sa 17:25 of the army instead of J
2Sa 18: 2 people under the hand of J
2Sa 18: 5 Now the king had commanded J
2Sa 18:10 certain man saw it and told J
2Sa 18:11 So J said to the man who told
2Sa 18:12 But the man said to J
2Sa 18:14 Then J said, "I cannot
2Sa 18:16 Then J blew the trumpet, and
2Sa 18:16 For J held back the people
2Sa 18:20 And J said to him,
2Sa 18:21 Then J said to the Cushite,
2Sa 18:21 Cushite bowed himself to J
2Sa 18:22 son of Zadok said again to J
2Sa 18:22 J said, "Why will you run
2Sa 18:29 When J sent the king's
2Sa 19: 1 And J was told,
2Sa 19: 5 Then J came into the house to
2Sa 19:13 me continually in place of J
2Sa 20: 8 Now J was dressed in battle
2Sa 20: 9 Then J said to Amasa, "Are
2Sa 20: 9 J took Amasa by the beard
2Sa 20:10 Then J and Abishai his brother
2Sa 20:11 Whoever favors J and whoever
2Sa 20:11 for David, let him follow J
2Sa 20:13 the people went on after J to
2Sa 20:15 the people who were with J
2Sa 20:16 Please say to J, "Come nearby
2Sa 20:17 woman said, "Are you J?"
2Sa 20:20 And J answered and said,
2Sa 20:21 And the woman said to J
2Sa 20:22 Bichri, and threw it out to J
2Sa 20:22 So J returned to the king at
2Sa 20:23 J was over all the army of
2Sa 23:18 Now Abishai the brother of J
2Sa 23:24 of J was one of the thirty
2Sa 23:37 of J the son of Zeruiah),
2Sa 24: 2 So the king said to J the
2Sa 24: 3 And J said to the king,
2Sa 24: 4 word prevailed against J and
2Sa 24: 4 So J and the captains of the
2Sa 24: 9 Then J gave the sum of the
1Ki 1: 7 with J the son of Zeruiah
1Ki 1:19 J the commander of the army
1Ki 1:41 when J heard the sound of the
1Ki 2: 5 J the son of Zeruiah did to
1Ki 2:22 and for J the son of Zeruiah
1Ki 2:28 Then news came to J
1Ki 2:28 J had defected to Adonijah
1Ki 2:28 So J fled to the tabernacle
1Ki 2:29 J has fled to the tabernacle
1Ki 2:30 Thus said J, and thus he
1Ki 2:31 innocent blood which J shed
1Ki 2:33 return upon the head of J
1Ki 11:15 J the commander of the army
1Ki 11:16 J remained there with all
1Ki 11:21 that J the commander of the
1Ch 2:16 of Zeruiah were Abishai, J
1Ch 4:14 Seraiah begot J the father of
1Ch 11: 6 J the son of Zeruiah went up
1Ch 11: 8 J repaired the rest of the
1Ch 11:20 J was chief of another three
1Ch 11:26 were Asahel the brother of J
1Ch 11:39 of J the son of Zeruiah),
1Ch 18:15 J the son of Zeruiah was over
1Ch 19: 8 David heard of it, he sent J
1Ch 19:10 When J saw that the battle
1Ch 19:14 So J and the people who were
1Ch 19:15 So J went to Jerusalem
1Ch 20: 1 that J led out the armed
1Ch 20: 1 And J defeated Rabbah and
1Ch 21: 2 So David said to J and to the
1Ch 21: 3 And J answered, "May the
1Ch 21: 4 word prevailed against J
1Ch 21: 4 Therefore J departed and went
1Ch 21: 5 Then J gave the sum of the
1Ch 21: 6 word was abominable to J
1Ch 26:28 and J the son of Zeruiah had
1Ch 27: 7 was Asahel the brother of J
1Ch 27:24 J the son of Zeruiah began a
1Ch 27:34 of the king's army was J
Ezra 2: 6 of the people of Jeshua and J
Ezra 8: 9 of the sons of J, Obadiah the
Neh 7:11 the children of Jeshua and J

JOAB'S (*see* JOAB)
2Sa 14:30 J field is near mine, and he
2Sa 17:25 sister of Zeruiah, J mother
2Sa 18: 2 J brother, and one third under
2Sa 18:15 And ten young men who bore J
2Sa 20: 7 So J men, with the
2Sa 20:10 the sword that was in J hand
2Sa 20:11 Meanwhile one of J men stood

JOAH (*see* ETHAN)
2Ki 18:18 and J the son of Asaph, the
2Ki 18:26 and J said to the Rabshakeh,
2Ki 18:37 and J the son of Asaph, the
1Ch 6:21 J his son, Iddo his son,
1Ch 26: 4 J the third, Sacar the fourth
2Ch 29:12 J the son of Zimmah and Eden
2Ch 29:12 Zimmah and Eden the son of J
2Ch 34: 8 and J the son of Joahaz the
Is 36: 3 and J the son of Asaph, the
Is 36:11 and J said to the Rabshakeh,
Is 36:22 and J the son of Asaph, the

JOAHAZ (*see* JEHOAHAZ)
2Ch 34: 8 the son of J the recorder

JOANNA
Luke 8: 3 J the wife of Chuza, Herod's
Luke 24:10 It was Mary Magdalene, J,

JOANNAS
Luke 3:27 the son of J, the son of

JOASH (*see* JEHOASH)
Judg 6:11 belonged to J the Abiezrite
Judg 6:29 Gideon the son of J has done
Judg 6:30 the men of the city said to J
Judg 6:31 And J said to all who stood
Judg 7:14 sword of Gideon the son of J
Judg 8:13 son of J returned from battle
Judg 8:29 Jerubbaal the son of J went
Judg 8:32 Now Gideon the son of J died
Judg 8:32 in the tomb of J his father
1Ki 22:26 city and to J the king's son
2Ki 11: 2 took J the son of Ahaziah, and
2Ki 12:19 Now the rest of the acts of J
2Ki 12:20 killed J in the house of the
2Ki 13: 1 year of J the son of Ahaziah
2Ki 13: 9 Then J his son reigned in his
2Ki 13:10 year of J king of Judah,
2Ki 13:12 Now the rest of the acts of J
2Ki 13:13 So J rested with his fathers
2Ki 13:13 J was buried in Samaria with
2Ki 13:14 Then J the king of Israel
2Ki 13:25 Three times J defeated him and
2Ki 14: 1 year of J the son of Jehoahaz
2Ki 14: 1 Israel, Amaziah the son of J
2Ki 14: 3 as his father J had done
2Ki 14:17 Amaziah the son of J, king of
2Ki 14:23 year of Amaziah the son of J
2Ki 14:23 Judah, Jeroboam the son of J
2Ki 14:27 hand of Jeroboam the son of J
1Ch 3:11 Ahaziah his son, J his son,
1Ch 4:22 the men of Chozeba, and J
1Ch 7: 8 of Becher were Zemirah, J
1Ch 12: 3 The chief was Ahiezer, then J
1Ch 27:28 J was over the store of oil
2Ch 18:25 city and to J the king's son
2Ch 22:11 took J the son of Ahaziah, and
2Ch 24: 1 J was seven years old when he
2Ch 24: 2 J did what was right in the
2Ch 24: 4 J set his heart on repairing
2Ch 24:22 Thus J the king did not
2Ch 24:24 executed judgment against J
2Ch 25:17 sent to J the son of Jehoahaz
2Ch 25:18 And J king of Israel sent to
2Ch 25:21 So J king of Israel went out
2Ch 25:23 Then J the king of Israel
2Ch 25:23 king of Judah, the son of J
2Ch 25:25 Amaziah the son of J, king of
2Ch 25:25 of J the son of Jehoahaz,
Hos 1: 1 days of Jeroboam the son of J
Amos 1: 1 days of Jeroboam the son of J

JOB (*see* JASHUB, JOB'S)
Gen 46:13 Issachar were Tola, Puvah, J
Job 1: 1 land of Uz, whose name was J
Job 1: 5 that J would send and sanctify
Job 1: 5 For J said, "It may be that
Job 1: 5 Thus J did regularly
Job 1: 8 you considered My servant J
Job 1: 9 Does J fear God for nothing
Job 1:14 and a messenger came to J and
Job 1:20 Then J arose and tore his robe
Job 1:22 In all this J did not sin nor
Job 2: 3 you considered My servant J
Job 2: 7 struck J with painful boils
Job 2:10 In all this J did not sin
Job 3: 1 After this J opened his mouth
Job 3: 2 And J spoke, and said
Job 6: 1 Then J answered and said
Job 9: 1 Then J answered and said
Job 12: 1 Then J answered and said
Job 16: 1 Then J answered and said
Job 19: 1 Then J answered and said
Job 21: 1 Then J answered and said
Job 23: 1 Then J answered and said
Job 26: 1 But J answered and said
Job 27: 1 Moreover J continued his
Job 29: 1 J further continued his
Job 31:40 The words of J are ended
Job 32: 1 three men ceased answering J
Job 32: 2 of Ram, was aroused against J
Job 32: 3 and yet had condemned J
Job 32: 4 had waited to speak to J
Job 32:12 not one of you convinced J
Job 33: 1 But please, J, hear my speech
Job 33:31 Give ear, J, listen to me
Job 34: 5 For J has said, 'I am
Job 34: 7 What man is like J, who
Job 34:35 J speaks without knowledge,
Job 34:36 Oh, that J were tried to the
Job 35:16 Therefore J opens his mouth
Job 37:14 Listen to this, O J
Job 38: 1 J out of the whirlwind, and
Job 40: 1 Moreover the LORD answered J
Job 40: 3 Then J answered the LORD and
Job 40: 6 J out of the whirlwind, and
Job 42: 1 Then J answered the LORD and
Job 42: 7 had spoken these words to J
Job 42: 7 is right, as My servant J has
Job 42: 8 rams, go to My servant J, and
Job 42: 8 My servant J shall pray for
Job 42: 8 is right, as My servant J has
Job 42: 9 for the LORD had accepted J
Job 42:10 Indeed the LORD gave J twice
Job 42:12 of J more than his beginning
Job 42:15 as the daughters of J
Job 42:16 After this J lived one
Job 42:17 So J died, old and full of
Ezek 14:14 three men, Noah, Daniel, and J
Ezek 14:20 J were in it, as I live,"

Jas 5:11 of the perseverance of J and

JOBAB
Gen 10:29 Ophir, Havilah, and J
Gen 36:33 J the son of Zerah of Bozrah
Gen 36:34 When J died, Husham of the
Josh 11: 1 he sent to J king of Madon
1Ch 1:23 Ophir, Havilah, and J
1Ch 1:44 J the son of Zerah of Bozrah
1Ch 1:45 When J died, Husham of the
1Ch 8: 9 By Hodesh his wife he begot J
1Ch 8:18 J were the sons of Elpaal

JOB'S (*see* JOB)
Job 2:11 Now when J three friends
Job 42:10 the LORD restored J losses

JOCHEBED
Ex 6:20 Now Amram took for himself J
Num 26:59 was J the daughter of Levi

JOED
Neh 11: 7 of Meshullam, the son of J

JOEL
1Sa 8: 2 name of his firstborn was J
1Ch 4:35 J, and Jehu the son of
1Ch 5: 4 The sons of J were Shemaiah
1Ch 5: 8 son of Shema, the son of J
1Ch 5:12 J was the chief, Shapham the
1Ch 6:28 Samuel were J the firstborn
1Ch 6:33 the singer, the son of J, the
1Ch 6:36 son of Elkanah, the son of J
1Ch 7: 3 were Michael, Obadiah, J, and
1Ch 11:38 J the brother of Nathan,
1Ch 15: 7 J the chief, and one hundred
1Ch 15:11 for Uriel, Asaiah, J,
1Ch 15:17 appointed Heman the son of J
1Ch 23: 8 Jehiel, then Zetham and J
1Ch 26:22 J his brother, were over the
1Ch 27:20 J the son of Pedaiah
2Ch 29:12 J the son of Azariah, of the
Ezra 10:43 Zabad, Zebina, Jaddai, J
Neh 11: 9 J the son of Zichri was their
Joel 1: 1 came to J the son of Pethuel
Acts 2:16 was spoken by the prophet J

JOELAH
1Ch 12: 7 and J and Zebadiah the sons of

JOEZER
1Ch 12: 6 Elkanah, Jisshiah, Azareel, J

JOGBEHAH
Num 32:35 and Shophan and Jazer and J,
Judg 8:11 on the east of Nobah and J

JOGLI
Num 34:22 of Dan, Bukki the son of J

JOHA
1Ch 8:16 J were the sons of Beriah
1Ch 11:45 J his brother, the Tizite,

JOHANAN (*see* JEHOHANAN)
2Ki 25:23 J the son of Careah, Seraiah
1Ch 3:15 Josiah were J the firstborn
1Ch 3:24 Eliashib, Pelaiah, Akkub, J
1Ch 6: 9 Azariah, and Azariah begot J
1Ch 6:10 J begot Azariah (it was he
1Ch 12: 4 Jeremiah, Jahaziel, J, and
1Ch 12:12 J the eighth, Elzabad the
2Ch 28:12 Ephraim, Azariah the son of J
Ezra 8:12 J the son of Hakkatan, and
Neh 12:22 days of Eliashib, Joiada, J
Neh 12:23 days of J the son of Eliashib
Jer 40: 8 the son of Nethaniah, J and
Jer 40:13 Moreover J the son of Kareah
Jer 40:15 Then J the son of Kareah
Jer 40:16 said to J the son of Kareah
Jer 41:11 But when J the son of Kareah
Jer 41:13 saw J the son of Kareah, and
Jer 41:14 went to J the son of Kareah
Jer 41:15 escaped from J with eight men
Jer 41:16 Then J the son of Kareah, and
Jer 42: 1 J the son of Kareah, Jezaniah
Jer 42: 8 Then he called J the son of
Jer 43: 2 J the son of Kareah, and all
Jer 43: 4 So J the son of Kareah, all
Jer 43: 5 But J the son of Kareah and

JOHN (*see* BAPTIST, JEHOHANAN, JEHONATHAN, JOHN'S, MARK*)
Matt 3: 1 In those days J the Baptist
Matt 3: 4 And J himself was clothed in
Matt 3:13 to J at the Jordan to be
Matt 3:14 And J tried to prevent Him,
Matt 4:12 that J had been put in prison
Matt 4:21 J his brother, in the boat
Matt 9:14 disciples of J came to Him
Matt 10: 2 of Zebedee, and J his brother
Matt 11: 2 when J had heard in prison
Matt 11: 4 tell J the things which you
Matt 11: 7 the multitudes concerning J
Matt 11:11 greater than J the Baptist
Matt 11:12 And from the days of J the
Matt 11:13 and the law prophesied until J
Matt 11:18 For J came neither eating nor
Matt 14: 2 This is J the Baptist
Matt 14: 3 For Herod had laid hold of J
Matt 14: 4 For J had said to him, "It
Matt 14: 8 Give me J the Baptist's head
Matt 14:10 and had J beheaded in prison
Matt 16:14 Some say J the Baptist, some
Matt 17: 1 J his brother, brought them
Matt 17:13 to them of J the Baptist
Matt 21:25 The baptism of J, where was
Matt 21:26 for all count J as a prophet
Matt 21:32 For J came to you in the way
Mark 1: 4 J came baptizing in the
Mark 1: 6 Now J was clothed with
Mark 1: 9 baptized by J in the Jordan
Mark 1:14 Now after J was put in prison
Mark 1:19 J his brother, who also were
Mark 1:29 and Andrew, with James and J
Mark 2:18 And the disciples of J and of
Mark 2:18 Why do the disciples of J
Mark 3:17 J the brother of James, to
Mark 5:37 and J the brother of James
Mark 6:14 J the Baptist is risen from
Mark 6:16 This is J, whom I beheaded
Mark 6:17 had sent and laid hold of J
Mark 6:18 For J had said to Herod, "It
Mark 6:20 for Herod feared J, knowing
Mark 6:24 The head of J the Baptist
Mark 6:25 of J the Baptist on a platter
Mark 8:28 answered, "J the Baptist
Mark 9: 2 Jesus took Peter, James, and J
Mark 9:38 Now J answered Him, saying,
Mark 10:35 Then James and J, the sons of
Mark 10:41 displeased with James and J
Mark 11:30 The baptism of J
Mark 11:32 for all counted J to have
Mark 13: 3 the temple, Peter, James, J
Mark 14:33 J with Him, and He began to be
Luke 1:13 and you shall call his name J
Luke 1:60 he shall be called J
Luke 1:63 His name is J
Luke 3: 2 the word of God came to J the
Luke 3:15 in their hearts about J,
Luke 3:16 J answered, saying to them
Luke 3:20 that he shut J up in prison
Luke 5:10 and so also were James and J
Luke 5:33 the disciples of J fast often
Luke 6:14 James and J
Luke 7:18 Then the disciples of J
Luke 7:19 And J, calling two of his
Luke 7:20 J the Baptist has sent us to
Luke 7:22 tell J the things you have
Luke 7:24 messengers of J had departed
Luke 7:24 the multitudes concerning J
Luke 7:28 prophet than J the Baptist
Luke 7:29 with the baptism of J
Luke 7:33 For J the Baptist came
Luke 8:51 in except Peter, James, and J
Luke 9: 7 J had risen from the dead
Luke 9: 9 J I have beheaded, but who is
Luke 9:19 J the Baptist, but some say
Luke 9:28 that He took Peter, J, and
Luke 9:49 Then J answered and said
Luke 9:54 and J saw this, they said,
Luke 11: 1 to pray, as J also taught his
Luke 16:16 and the prophets were until J
Luke 20: 4 The baptism of J
Luke 20: 6 that J was a prophet
Luke 22: 8 And He sent Peter and J, saying
John 1: 6 from God, whose name was J
John 1:15 J bore witness of Him and
John 1:19 this is the testimony of J
John 1:26 J answered them, saying, "I
John 1:28 Jordan, where J was baptizing
John 1:29 The next day J saw Jesus
John 1:32 And J bore witness, saying,
John 1:35 day, J stood with two of his
John 1:40 of the two who heard J speak
John 3:23 Now J also was baptizing in
John 3:24 For J had not yet been thrown
John 3:26 And they came to J and said to
John 3:27 J answered and said, "A man
John 4: 1 more disciples than J
John 5:33 You have sent to J, and he has
John 10:40 J was baptizing at first, and
John 10:41 J performed no sign, but all
John 10:41 but all the things that J
Acts 1: 5 for J truly baptized with
Acts 1:13 Peter, James, J, and Andrew
Acts 1:22 from the baptism of J to that
Acts 3: 1 J went up together to the
Acts 3: 3 J about to go into the temple
Acts 3: 4 his eyes on him, with J,
Acts 3:11 healed held on to Peter and J
Acts 4: 6 the high priest, Caiaphas, J
Acts 4:13 the boldness of Peter and J
Acts 4:19 J answered and said to them,
Acts 8:14 they sent Peter and J to them,
Acts 10:37 the baptism which J preached
Acts 11:16 J indeed baptized with water
Acts 12: 2 brother of J with the sword
Acts 12:12 the mother of J whose surname
Acts 12:25 J whose surname was Mark
Acts 13: 5 They also had J as their
Acts 13:13 and J, departing from them,
Acts 13:24 after J had first preached,
Acts 13:25 as J was finishing his course
Acts 15:37 take with them J called Mark
Acts 18:25 he knew only the baptism of J
Acts 19: 4 J indeed baptized with a
Gal 2: 9 and when James, Cephas, and J
Rev 1: 1 by His angel to His servant J
Rev 1: 4 J, to the seven churches
Rev 1: 9 I, J, both your brother and
Rev 21: 2 Then I, J, saw the holy city,
Rev 22: 8 Now I, J, saw and heard these

JOHN'S (*see* JOHN)
John 3:25 between some of J disciples
John 5:36 have a greater witness than J
Acts 19: 3 they said, "Into J baptism

JOIADA (*see* JEHOIADA)
Neh 12:10 Eliashib, Eliashib begot J
Neh 12:11 J begot Jonathan, and Jonathan
Neh 12:22 in the days of Eliashib, J
Neh 13:28 And one of the sons of J, the

JOIAKIM (*see* JEHOIAKIM)
Neh 12:10 Jeshua begot J
Neh 12:10 J begot Eliashib
Neh 12:12 Now in the days of J, the
Neh 12:26 days of J the son of Jeshua

JOIARIB (*see* JEHOIARIB)
Ezra 8:16 also for J and Elnathan, men
Neh 11: 5 son of Adaiah, the son of J
Neh 11:10 Jedaiah the son of J, and
Neh 12: 6 Shemaiah, J, Jedaiah,
Neh 12:19 of J, Mattenai

JOIN (*see* JOINED)
Ex 1:10 that they also j our enemies
Ezra 9:14 j in marriage with the people
Esth 9:27 and all who should j them,
Prov 11:21 Though they j forces, the
Prov 16: 5 though they j forces, none
Is 5: 8 to those who j house to house
Is 56: 6 who j themselves to the LORD
Jer 50: 5 let us j ourselves to the
Ezek 37:17 Then j them one to another
Ezek 37:19 I will j them with it, with
Dan 11: 6 years they shall j forces
Dan 11:34 but many shall j with them by
Acts 5:13 none of the rest dared j them
Acts 9:26 he tried to j the disciples
Phil 3:17 j in following my example, and

JOINED (*see* JOIN)
Gen 2:24 be j to his wife, and they
Gen 14: 3 All these j together in the
Gen 14: 8 j together in battle in the
Ex 28: 7 straps j at its two edges
Ex 28: 7 and so it shall be j together
Num 18: 2 that they may be j with you
Num 18: 4 They shall be j with you and
Num 25: 3 So Israel was j to Baal of
Num 25: 5 who were j to Baal of Peor
1Sa 4: 2 And when they j battle, Israel
1Sa 14:21 they also j the Israelites
1Ki 7:32 the wheels were j to the cart
1Ki 20:29 seventh day the battle was j

1Ch 12: 8 Some Gadites **j** David at the
Neh 4: 6 and the entire wall was **j**
Neh 10:29 they **j** with their brethren,
Job 41:17 They are **j** one to another,
Job 41:23 of his flesh are **j** together
Ps 83: 8 Assyria also has **j** with them
Ps 106:28 They **j** themselves also to
Eccl 9: 4 But for him who is **j** to all
Is 14: 1 strangers will be **j** with them
Is 14:20 You will not be **j** with them
Is 56: 3 of the foreigner who has **j**
Hos 4:17 Ephraim is **j** to idols, let
Zech 2:11 Many nations shall be **j** to
Matt 19: 5 be **j** to his wife, and the two
Matt 19: 6 what God has **j** together, let
Mark 10: 7 mother and be **j** to his wife,
Mark 10: 9 what God has **j** together, let
Luke 9:18 that His disciples **j** Him
Luke 15:15 **j** himself to a citizen of
John 11:19 many of the Jews had **j** the
Acts 5:36 about four hundred, **j** him
Acts 17: 4 women, **j** Paul and Silas
Acts 17:34 However, some men **j** him and
Acts 20: 6 in five days **j** them at Troas,
1Co 1:10 **j** together in the same mind
1Co 6:16 is **j** to a harlot is one body
1Co 6:17 But he who is **j** to the Lord
Eph 2:21 being **j** together, grows into
Eph 4:16 from whom the whole body, **j**
Eph 5:31 be **j** to his wife, and the two

JOINT (*see* JOINTED, JOINTS)
Gen 32:25 of **j** as He wrestled with him
Ps 22:14 And all My bones are out of **j**
Prov 25:19 bad tooth and a foot out of **j**
Rom 8:17 and **j** heirs with Christ, if
Eph 4:16 by what every **j** supplies,

JOINTED (*see* JOINT)
Lev 11:21 those which have **j** legs above

JOINTS (*see* JOINT)
1Ki 22:34 between the **j** of his armor
1Ch 22: 3 of the gates and for the **j**
2Ch 18:33 between the **j** of his armor
Dan 5: 6 so that the **j** of his hips
Col 2:19 and knit together by **j** and
Heb 4:12 of soul and spirit, and of **j**

JOKDEAM
Josh 15:56 Jezreel, **J**, Zanoah,

JOKIM
1Ch 4:22 also **J**, the men of Chozeba,

JOKING
Gen 19:14 sons-in-law he seemed to be **j**
Prov 26:19 I was only **j**

JOKMEAM (*see* JOKNEAM, KIBZAIM)
1Ch 6:68 **J** with its common-lands, Beth

JOKNEAM (*see* JOKMEAM)
Josh 12:22 the king of **J** in Carmel, one
Josh 19:11 the brook that is east of **J**
Josh 21:34 **J** with its common-land,
1Ki 4:12 as far as the other side of **J**

JOKSHAN
Gen 25: 2 And she bore him Zimran, **J**
Gen 25: 3 **J** begot Sheba and Dedan
1Ch 1:32 concubine, were Zimran, **J**
1Ch 1:32 The sons of **J** were Sheba and

JOKTAN
Gen 10:25 and his brother's name was **J**
Gen 10:26 **J** begot Almodad, Sheleph,
Gen 10:29 All these were the sons of **J**
1Ch 1:19 and his brother's name was **J**
1Ch 1:20 **J** begot Almodad, Sheleph,
1Ch 1:23 All these were the sons of **J**

JOKTHEEL
Josh 15:38 Dilean, Mizpah, **J**,
2Ki 14: 7 called its name **J** to this day

JONADAB (*see* JEHONADAB)
2Sa 13: 3 name was **J** the son of Shimeah
2Sa 13: 3 Now **J** was a very crafty man
2Sa 13: 5 So **J** said to him, "Lie down
2Sa 13:32 Then **J** the son of Shimeah,
2Sa 13:35 And **J** said to the king,
Jer 35: 6 for **J** the son of Rechab, our
Jer 35: 8 voice of **J** the son of Rechab
Jer 35:10 **J** our father commanded us
Jer 35:14 The words of **J** the son of
Jer 35:16 Surely the sons of **J** the son
Jer 35:18 commandment of **J** your father
Jer 35:19 **J** the son of Rechab shall not

JONAH (*see* JONAH'S)
2Ki 14:25 servant **J** the son of Amittai
Jon 1: 1 came to **J** the son of Amittai
Jon 1: 3 But **J** arose to flee to
Jon 1: 5 But **J** had gone down into the
Jon 1: 7 lots, and the lot fell on **J**
Jon 1:15 So they picked up **J** and threw
Jon 1:17 a great fish to swallow **J**
Jon 1:17 **J** was in the belly of the
Jon 2: 1 Then **J** prayed to the LORD his
Jon 2:10 it vomited **J** onto dry land
Jon 3: 1 came to **J** the second time
Jon 3: 3 So **J** arose and went to Nineveh
Jon 3: 4 **J** began to enter the city on
Jon 4: 1 it displeased **J** exceedingly
Jon 4: 5 So **J** went out of the city and
Jon 4: 6 and made it come up over **J**
Jon 4: 6 So **J** was very grateful for
Jon 4: 9 Then God said to **J**, "Is it
Matt 12:39 the sign of the prophet **J**
Matt 12:40 For as **J** was three days and
Matt 12:41 at the preaching of **J**
Matt 12:41 a greater than **J** is here
Matt 16: 4 the sign of the prophet **J**
Luke 11:29 the sign of **J** the prophet
Luke 11:30 For as **J** became a sign to the
Luke 11:32 at the preaching of **J**
Luke 11:32 a greater than **J** is here
John 1:42 You are Simon the son of **J**
John 21:15 Simon, son of **J**, do you love
John 21:16 Simon, son of **J**, do you love
John 21:17 Simon, son of **J**, do you love

JONAH'S (*see* JONAH)
Jon 4: 8 and the sun beat on **J** head

JONAN
Luke 3:30 son of Joseph, the son of **J**

JONATHAN (*see* JEHONATHAN, JONATHAN'S)
Judg 18:30 **J** the son of Gershom, the son
1Sa 13: 2 a thousand were with **J** in
1Sa 13: 3 **J** attacked the garrison of
1Sa 13:16 **J** his son, and the people who
1Sa 13:22 who were with Saul and **J**
1Sa 13:22 found with Saul and **J** his son
1Sa 14: 1 it happened one day that **J**
1Sa 14: 3 did not know that **J** had gone
1Sa 14: 4 by which **J** sought to go over
1Sa 14: 6 Then **J** said to the young man
1Sa 14: 8 Then **J** said, "Very well, let
1Sa 14:12 of the garrison called to **J**
1Sa 14:12 **J** said to his armorbearer
1Sa 14:13 **J** climbed up on his hands and
1Sa 14:13 and they fell before **J**
1Sa 14:14 That first slaughter which **J**
1Sa 14:17 the roll, surprisingly, **J**
1Sa 14:21 who were with Saul and **J**
1Sa 14:27 But **J** had not heard his
1Sa 14:29 But **J** said, "My father has
1Sa 14:39 though it be in **J** my son
1Sa 14:40 be on one side, and my son **J**
1Sa 14:41 **J** were taken, but the people
1Sa 14:42 Cast lots between my son **J**
1Sa 14:42 So **J** was taken
1Sa 14:43 Then Saul said to **J**, "Tell
1Sa 14:43 And **J** told him, and said,
1Sa 14:44 for you shall surely die, **J**
1Sa 14:45 Shall **J** die, who has
1Sa 14:45 So the people rescued **J**
1Sa 14:49 Now the sons of Saul were **J**
1Sa 18: 1 that the soul of **J** was knit
1Sa 18: 1 **J** loved him as his own soul
1Sa 18: 3 Then **J** and David made a
1Sa 18: 4 **J** took off the robe that was
1Sa 19: 1 Now Saul spoke to **J** his son
1Sa 19: 1 but **J**, Saul's son, delighted
1Sa 19: 2 So **J** told David, saying, "My
1Sa 19: 4 Now **J** spoke well of David to
1Sa 19: 6 So Saul heeded the voice of **J**
1Sa 19: 7 Then **J** called David, and
1Sa 19: 7 **J** told him all these things
1Sa 19: 7 So **J** brought David to Saul,
1Sa 20: 1 Ramah, and went and said to **J**
1Sa 20: 2 So **J** said to him, "By no
1Sa 20: 3 says, 'Do not let **J** know this
1Sa 20: 4 So **J** said to David
1Sa 20: 5 And David said to **J**, 'Indeed
1Sa 20: 9 **J** said, "Far be it from you!
1Sa 20:10 Then David said to **J**, "Who
1Sa 20:11 And **J** said to David,
1Sa 20:12 Then **J** said to David
1Sa 20:13 LORD do so and much more to **J**
1Sa 20:16 So **J** made a covenant with the
1Sa 20:17 **J** again caused David to vow,
1Sa 20:18 Then **J** said to David
1Sa 20:25 And **J** arose, and Abner sat by
1Sa 20:27 And Saul said to **J** his son
1Sa 20:28 So **J** answered Saul, "David
1Sa 20:30 anger was aroused against **J**
1Sa 20:32 **J** answered Saul his father,
1Sa 20:33 by which **J** knew that it was
1Sa 20:34 So **J** arose from the table in
1Sa 20:35 that **J** went out into the
1Sa 20:37 arrow was which **J** had shot
1Sa 20:37 **J** cried out after the lad and
1Sa 20:38 **J** cried out after the lad,
1Sa 20:39 Only **J** and David knew of the
1Sa 20:40 Then **J** gave his weapons to
1Sa 20:42 Then **J** said to David, "Go in
1Sa 20:42 and **J** went into the city
1Sa 23:16 Then **J**, Saul's son, arose and
1Sa 23:18 and **J** went to his own house
1Sa 31: 2 And the Philistines killed **J**
2Sa 1: 4 and **J** his son are dead also
2Sa 1: 5 Saul and **J** his son are dead
2Sa 1:12 for **J** his son, for the people
2Sa 1:17 over Saul and over **J** his son,
2Sa 1:22 the bow of **J** did not turn
2Sa 1:23 **J** were beloved and pleasant in
2Sa 1:25 **J** was slain in your high
2Sa 1:26 for you, my brother **J**
2Sa 4: 4 **J**, Saul's son, had a son who
2Sa 4: 4 Saul and **J** came from Jezreel
2Sa 9: 3 of **J** who is lame in his feet
2Sa 9: 6 Mephibosheth the son of **J**
2Sa 9: 7 for **J** your father's sake, and
2Sa 15:27 son, and **J** the son of Abiathar
2Sa 15:36 Ahimaaz, Zadok's son, and **J**
2Sa 17:17 Now **J** and Ahimaaz stayed at
2Sa 17:20 Where are Ahimaaz and **J**
2Sa 21: 7 Mephibosheth the son of **J**
2Sa 21: 7 David and **J** the son of Saul
2Sa 21:12 and the bones of **J** his son
2Sa 21:13 the bones of **J** his son from
2Sa 21:14 **J** his son in the country of
2Sa 21:21 **J** the son of Shimeah, the
2Sa 23:32 (of the sons of Jashen), **J**
1Ki 1:42 still speaking, there came **J**
1Ki 1:43 Then **J** answered and said to
1Ch 2:32 of Shammai, were Jether and **J**
1Ch 2:33 The sons of **J** were Peleth
1Ch 8:33 begot Saul, and Saul begot **J**
1Ch 8:34 The son of **J** was Merib-Baal,
1Ch 9:39 begot Saul, and Saul begot **J**
1Ch 9:40 The son of **J** was Merib-Baal,
1Ch 10: 2 And the Philistines killed **J**
1Ch 11:34 **J** the son of Shageh the
1Ch 20: 7 **J** the son of Shimea, David's
Ezra 8: 6 of Adin, Ebed the son of **J**
Ezra 10:15 Only **J** the son of Asahel and
Neh 12:11 Joiada begot **J**, and **J**
Neh 12:11 **J**, and **J** begot Jaddua
Neh 12:14 of Melichu, **J**
Neh 12:35 Zechariah the son of **J**, the
Jer 37:15 in the house of **J** the scribe
Jer 37:20 to the house of **J** the scribe
Jer 40: 8 **J** the sons of Kareah, Seraiah

JONATHAN'S (*see* JONATHAN)
1Sa 20:38 So **J** lad gathered up the
2Sa 9: 1 show him kindness for **J** sake
Jer 38:26 to **J** house to die there

JOPPA
Josh 19:46 with the region near **J**
2Ch 2:16 to you in rafts by sea to **J**
Ezra 3: 7 from Lebanon to the sea at **J**
Jon 1: 3 He went down to **J**, and found a
Acts 9:36 At **J** there was a certain
Acts 9:38 And since Lydda was near **J**
Acts 9:42 became known throughout all **J**
Acts 9:43 many days in **J** with Simon
Acts 10: 5 Now send men to **J**, and send
Acts 10: 8 to them, he sent them to **J**
Acts 10:23 from **J** accompanied him
Acts 10:32 Send therefore to **J** and call
Acts 11: 5 was in the city of **J** praying
Acts 11:13 said to him, 'Send men to **J**

JORAH (*see* HARIPH)
Ezra 2:18 the people of J, one hundred

JORAI
1Ch 5:13 Michael, Meshullam, Sheba, J

JORAM (*see* JEHORAM)
2Sa 8:10 then Toi sent J his son to
2Sa 8:10 J brought with him articles
2Ki 8:16 year of J the son of Ahab
2Ki 8:21 So J went to Zair, and all his
2Ki 8:23 Now the rest of the acts of J
2Ki 8:24 So J rested with his fathers,
2Ki 8:25 year of J the son of Ahab
2Ki 8:28 Now he went with J the son of
2Ki 8:28 and the Syrians wounded J
2Ki 8:29 Then King J went back to
2Ki 8:29 went down to see J the son of
2Ki 9:14 Nimshi, conspired against J
2Ki 9:14 (Now J had been defending
2Ki 9:15 But King J had returned to
2Ki 9:16 for J was laid up there
2Ki 9:16 Judah had come down to see J
2Ki 9:17 And J said, "Get a horseman
2Ki 9:21 So J said, "Make ready
2Ki 9:21 Then J king of Israel and
2Ki 9:22 when J saw Jehu, that he said
2Ki 9:23 Then J turned around and fled,
2Ki 9:29 year of J the son of Ahab
2Ki 11: 2 the daughter of King J,
1Ch 3:11 J his son, Ahaziah his son,
1Ch 26:25 J his son, Zichri his son, and
2Ch 22: 5 and the Syrians wounded J
2Ch 22: 7 His going to J was God's
Matt 1: 8 Jehoshaphat begot J
Matt 1: 8 and J begot Uzziah

JORDAN
Gen 13:10 and saw all the plain of J
Gen 13:11 himself all the plain of J
Gen 32:10 over this J with my staff
Gen 50:10 Atad, which is beyond the J
Gen 50:11 which is beyond the J
Num 13:29 and along the banks of the J
Num 22: 1 of the J across from Jericho
Num 26: 3 the plains of Moab by the J
Num 26:63 the plains of Moab by the J
Num 31:12 the plains of Moab by the J
Num 32: 5 and do not take us over the J
Num 32:19 on the other side of the J
Num 32:19 on this eastern side of the J
Num 32:21 J before the LORD until He
Num 32:29 cross over the J with you
Num 32:32 with us on this side of the J
Num 33:48 the plains of Moab by the J
Num 33:49 They camped by the J, from
Num 33:50 the plains of Moab by the J
Num 33:51 the J into the land of Canaan
Num 34:12 shall go down along the J
Num 34:15 on this side of the J, across
Num 35: 1 by the J across from Jericho
Num 35:10 When you cross the J into
Num 35:14 cities on this side of the J
Num 36:13 the plains of Moab by the J
Deut 1: 1 of the J in the wilderness
Deut 1: 5 of the J in the land of Moab
Deut 2:29 until I cross the J to the
Deut 3: 8 were on this side of the J
Deut 3:17 with the J as the border,
Deut 3:20 is giving them beyond the J
Deut 3:25 the good land beyond the J
Deut 3:27 shall not cross over this J
Deut 4:21 I would not cross over the J
Deut 4:22 I must not cross over the J
Deut 4:26 cross over the J to possess
Deut 4:41 cities on this side of the J
Deut 4:46 on this side of the J, in the
Deut 4:47 were on this side of the J
Deut 4:49 on the east side of the J as
Deut 9: 1 are to cross over the J today
Deut 11:30 on the other side of the J
Deut 11:31 For you will cross over the J
Deut 12:10 But when you cross over the J
Deut 27: 2 J to the land which the LORD
Deut 27: 4 you have crossed over the J
Deut 27:12 you have crossed over the J
Deut 30:18 you cross over the J to go in
Deut 31: 2 shall not cross over this J
Deut 31:13 you cross the J to possess
Deut 32:47 cross over the J to possess
Josh 1: 2 arise, go over this J, you
Josh 1:11 you will cross over this J
Josh 1:14 you on this side of the J
Josh 1:15 of the J toward the sunrise
Josh 2: 7 them by the road to the J
Josh 2:10 on the other side of the J
Josh 3: 1 Acacia Grove and came to the J
Josh 3: 8 edge of the water of the J
Josh 3: 8 you shall stand in the J
Josh 3:11 over before you into the J
Josh 3:13 rest in the waters of the J
Josh 3:13 of the J shall be cut off
Josh 3:14 camp to cross over the J,
Josh 3:15 bore the ark came to the J
Josh 3:15 the J overflows all its banks
Josh 3:17 ground in the midst of the J
Josh 3:17 crossed completely over the J
Josh 4: 1 completely crossed over the J
Josh 4: 3 out of the midst of the J
Josh 4: 5 God into the midst of the J
Josh 4: 7 J were cut off before the ark
Josh 4: 7 when it crossed over the J
Josh 4: 7 waters of the J were cut off
Josh 4: 8 from the midst of the J, as
Josh 4: 9 stones in the midst of the J
Josh 4:10 of the J until everything was
Josh 4:16 to come up from the J
Josh 4:17 Come up from the J
Josh 4:18 come from the midst of the J
Josh 4:18 that the waters of the J
Josh 4:19 the J on the tenth day of the
Josh 4:20 which they took out of the J
Josh 4:22 over this J on dry land'
Josh 4:23 J before you until you had
Josh 5: 1 on the west side of the J
Josh 5: 1 dried up the waters of the J
Josh 7: 7 this people over the J at all
Josh 7: 7 on the other side of the J
Josh 9: 1 were on this side of the J
Josh 9:10 who were beyond the J
Josh 11:16 the lowland, and the J plain
Josh 12: 1 J toward the rising of the
Josh 12: 1 and all the eastern J plain
Josh 12: 3 the eastern J plain from the
Josh 12: 7 on this side of the J, on the
Josh 12: 8 the lowlands, in the J plain
Josh 13: 8 them, beyond the J eastward
Josh 13:23 Reuben was the bank of the J
Josh 13:27 with the J as its border, as
Josh 13:27 other side of the J eastward
Josh 13:32 on the other side of the J
Josh 14: 3 on the other side of the J
Josh 15: 5 as far as the mouth of the J
Josh 15: 5 the sea at the mouth of the J
Josh 16: 1 children of Joseph from the J
Josh 16: 7 Jericho, and came out at the J
Josh 17: 5 on the other side of the J
Josh 18: 7 beyond the J on the east,
Josh 18:12 the north side began at the J
Josh 18:19 at the south end of the J
Josh 18:20 The J was its border on the
Josh 19:22 their border ended at the J
Josh 19:33 it ended at the J
Josh 19:34 by the J toward the sunrise
Josh 20: 8 And on the other side of the J
Josh 22: 4 on the other side of the J
Josh 22: 7 on this side of the J,
Josh 22:10 the J which is in the land of
Josh 22:10 built an altar there by the J
Josh 22:11 in the region of the J, on
Josh 22:25 the J a border between you
Josh 23: 4 for your tribes, from the J
Josh 24: 8 on the other side of the J
Josh 24:11 Then you went over the J
Judg 3:28 of the J leading to Moab, and
Judg 5:17 Gilead stayed beyond the J
Judg 7:24 as far as Beth Barah and the J
Judg 7:24 as far as Beth Barah and the J
Judg 7:25 on the other side of the J
Judg 8: 4 When Gideon came to the J
Judg 10: 8 on the other side of the J in
Judg 10: 9 of Ammon crossed over the J
Judg 11:13 as the Jabbok, and to the J
Judg 11:22 from the wilderness to the J
Judg 12: 5 the J before the Ephraimites
Judg 12: 6 him at the fords of the J
1Sa 13: 7 over the J to the land of Gad
1Sa 31: 7 on the other side of the J
2Sa 2:29 the plain, crossed over the J
2Sa 10:17 Israel, crossed over the J
2Sa 17:22 arose and crossed over the J
2Sa 17:22 who had not gone over the J
2Sa 17:24 And Absalom crossed over the J
2Sa 19:15 returned and came to the J
2Sa 19:15 escort the king across the J
2Sa 19:17 over the J before the king
2Sa 19:18 when he had crossed the J
2Sa 19:31 across the J with the king
2Sa 19:31 to escort him across the J
2Sa 19:36 across the J with the king
2Sa 19:39 the people went over the J
2Sa 19:41 men with him across the J
2Sa 20: 2 Judah, from the J as far as
2Sa 24: 5 And they crossed over the J
1Ki 2: 8 came down to meet me at the J
1Ki 7:46 In the plain of J the king
1Ki 17: 3 which flows into the J
1Ki 17: 5 which flows into the J
2Ki 2: 6 LORD has sent me on to the J
2Ki 2: 7 two of them stood by the J
2Ki 2:13 and stood by the bank of the J
2Ki 5:10 and wash in the J seven times
2Ki 5:14 dipped seven times in the J
2Ki 6: 2 Please, let us go to the J
2Ki 6: 4 And when they came to the J
2Ki 7:15 they went after them to the J
2Ki 10:33 from the J eastward
1Ch 6:78 And on the other side of the J
1Ch 6:78 on the east side of the J
1Ch 12:15 the J in the first month,
1Ch 12:37 from the other side of the J
1Ch 19:17 Israel, crossed over the J
1Ch 26:30 on the west side of the J for
2Ch 4:17 In the plain of J the king
Job 40:23 though the J gushes into his
Ps 42: 6 You from the land of the J
Ps 114: 3 J turned back
Ps 114: 5 O J, that you turned back
Is 9: 1 way of the sea, beyond the J
Jer 12: 5 do in the flooding of the J
Jer 49:19 from the flooding of the J
Jer 50:44 from the flooding of the J
Ezek 47:18 land of Israel, along the J
Zech 11: 3 pride of the J is in ruins
Matt 3: 5 around the J went out to him
Matt 3: 6 were baptized by him in the J
Matt 3:13 the J to be baptized by him
Matt 4:15 way of the sea, beyond the J
Matt 4:25 Judea, and beyond the J
Matt 19: 1 region of Judea beyond the J
Mark 1: 5 by him in the J River,
Mark 1: 9 was baptized by John in the J
Mark 3: 8 and Idumea and beyond the J
Mark 10: 1 by the other side of the J
Luke 3: 3 all the region around the J
Luke 4: 1 Spirit, returned from the J
John 1:28 in Bethabara beyond the J
John 3:26 who was with you beyond the J
John 10:40 went away again beyond the J

JORIM
Luke 3:29 son of Eliezer, the son of J

JORKOAM
1Ch 2:44 begot Raham the father of J

JOSE (*see* JOSES)
Luke 3:29 the son of J, the son of

JOSEPH (*see* BARSABAS, JOSEPH'S)
Gen 30:24 So she called his name J, and
Gen 30:25 pass, when Rachel had borne J
Gen 33: 2 behind, and Rachel and J last
Gen 33: 7 Afterward J and Rachel came
Gen 35:24 the sons of Rachel were J
Gen 37: 2 J, being seventeen years old,
Gen 37: 2 J brought a bad report of
Gen 37: 3 Now Israel loved J more than
Gen 37: 5 Now J dreamed a dream, and he
Gen 37:13 And Israel said to J, "Are
Gen 37:17 So J went after his
Gen 37:23 pass, when J had come to his
Gen 37:23 they stripped J of his tunic
Gen 37:28 so the brothers pulled J up
Gen 37:28 And they took J to Egypt
Gen 37:29 indeed J was not in the pit
Gen 37:33 Without doubt J is torn to
Gen 39: 1 Now J had been taken down to
Gen 39: 2 The LORD was with J, and he
Gen 39: 4 So J found favor in his sight
Gen 39: 6 J was handsome in form and
Gen 39: 7 wife cast longing eyes on J
Gen 39:10 as she spoke to J day by day
Gen 39:11 when J went into the house to

Num 32:28 to J the son of Nun, and to
Num 34:17 priest and J the son of Nun
Deut 1:38 but J the son of Nun, who
Deut 3:21 I commanded J at that time,
Deut 3:28 But command J, and encourage
Deut 31: 3 J himself crosses over before
Deut 31: 7 Then Moses called J and said
Deut 31:14 call J, and present yourselves
Deut 31:14 Moses and J went and presented
Deut 31:23 inaugurated J the son of Nun
Deut 32:44 came with J the son of Nun
Deut 34: 9 Now J the son of Nun was full
Josh 1: 1 spoke to J the son of Nun
Josh 1:10 Then J commanded the officers
Josh 1:12 the tribe of Manasseh J spoke
Josh 1:16 And they answered J, saying
Josh 2: 1 Now J the son of Nun sent out
Josh 2:23 they came to J the son of Nun
Josh 2:24 And they said to J, "Truly
Josh 3: 1 Then J rose early in the
Josh 3: 5 And J said to the people,
Josh 3: 6 Then J spoke to the priests,
Josh 3: 7 And the LORD said to J, "This
Josh 3: 9 So J said to the children of
Josh 3:10 And J said, "By this you
Josh 4: 1 that the LORD spoke to J
Josh 4: 4 Then J called the twelve men
Josh 4: 5 and J said to them
Josh 4: 8 just as J commanded, and took
Josh 4: 8 as the LORD had spoken to J
Josh 4: 9 Then J set up twelve stones
Josh 4:10 J to speak to the people,
Josh 4:10 that Moses had commanded J
Josh 4:14 J in the sight of all Israel
Josh 4:15 Then the LORD spoke to J,
Josh 4:17 J therefore commanded the
Josh 4:20 Jordan, J set up in Gilgal
Josh 5: 2 that time the LORD said to J
Josh 5: 3 So J made flint knives for
Josh 5: 4 reason why J circumcised them
Josh 5: 7 So J circumcised their sons
Josh 5: 9 Then the LORD said to J
Josh 5:13 when J was by Jericho, that
Josh 5:13 J went to Him and said to Him,
Josh 5:14 J fell on his face to the
Josh 5:15 of the LORD's army said to J
Josh 5:15 And J did so
Josh 6: 2 And the LORD said to J
Josh 6: 6 So J the son of Nun called
Josh 6: 8 was, when J had spoken to the
Josh 6:10 Now J had commanded the
Josh 6:12 J rose early in the morning,
Josh 6:16 that J said to the people
Josh 6:22 But J had said to the two men
Josh 6:25 J spared Rahab the harlot,
Josh 6:25 J sent to spy out Jericho
Josh 6:26 Then J charged them at that
Josh 6:27 So the LORD was with J, and
Josh 7: 2 Now J sent men from Jericho
Josh 7: 3 And they returned to J and said
Josh 7: 6 Then J tore his clothes, and
Josh 7: 7 And J said, "Alas, Lord GOD,
Josh 7:10 So the LORD said to J
Josh 7:16 So J rose early in the
Josh 7:19 So J said to Achan, "My son,
Josh 7:20 And Achan answered J and
Josh 7:22 So J sent messengers, and they
Josh 7:23 the tent, brought them to J
Josh 7:24 Then J, and all Israel with
Josh 7:25 And J said, "Why have you
Josh 8: 1 Then the LORD said to J
Josh 8: 3 So J arose, and all the people
Josh 8: 3 and J chose thirty thousand
Josh 8: 9 J therefore sent them out
Josh 8: 9 but J lodged that night among
Josh 8:10 Then J rose up early in the
Josh 8:13 J went that night into the
Josh 8:15 And J and all Israel made as if
Josh 8:16 And they pursued J and were
Josh 8:18 Then the LORD said to J
Josh 8:18 J stretched out the spear
Josh 8:21 Now when J and all Israel saw
Josh 8:23 alive, and brought him to J
Josh 8:26 For J did not draw back his
Josh 8:27 He had commanded J
Josh 8:28 So J burned Ai and made it a
Josh 8:29 J commanded that they should
Josh 8:30 Now J built an altar to the
Josh 8:35 Moses had commanded which J
Josh 9: 2 together to fight with J and
Josh 9: 3 what J had done to Jericho
Josh 9: 6 And they went to J, to the
Josh 9: 8 And they said to J, "We are
Josh 9: 8 And J said to them,
Josh 9:15 So J made peace with them, and
Josh 9:22 Then J called for them, and he
Josh 9:24 So they answered J and said
Josh 9:27 And that day J made them
Josh 10: 1 heard how J had taken Ai and
Josh 10: 4 for it has made peace with J
Josh 10: 6 to J at the camp at Gilgal
Josh 10: 7 So J ascended from Gilgal, he
Josh 10: 8 And the LORD said to J, "Do
Josh 10: 9 J therefore came upon them
Josh 10:12 Then J spoke to the LORD in
Josh 10:15 Then J returned, and all
Josh 10:17 And it was told J, saying
Josh 10:18 So J said, "Roll large
Josh 10:20 Then it happened, while J
Josh 10:21 to J at Makkedah, in peace
Josh 10:22 Then J said, "Open the mouth
Josh 10:24 brought out those kings to J
Josh 10:24 that J called for all the men
Josh 10:25 Then J said to them, "Do not
Josh 10:26 afterward J struck them and
Josh 10:27 of the sun that J commanded
Josh 10:28 On that day J took Makkedah,
Josh 10:29 Then J passed from Makkedah,
Josh 10:31 Then J passed from Libnah, and
Josh 10:33 J struck him and his people,
Josh 10:34 From Lachish J passed to
Josh 10:36 Then J went up from Eglon, and
Josh 10:38 Then J returned, and all
Josh 10:40 So J conquered all the land
Josh 10:41 J conquered them from Kadesh
Josh 10:42 their land J took at one time
Josh 10:43 Then J returned, and all
Josh 11: 6 But the LORD said to J, "Do
Josh 11: 7 So J and all the people of war
Josh 11: 9 So J did to them as the LORD
Josh 11:10 J turned back at that time and
Josh 11:12 J took and struck with the
Josh 11:13 Hazor only, which J burned
Josh 11:15 commanded J, and so J did
Josh 11:16 So J took all this land
Josh 11:18 J made war a long time with
Josh 11:21 And at that time J came and cut
Josh 11:21 J utterly destroyed them with
Josh 11:23 So J took the whole land,
Josh 11:23 J gave it as an inheritance
Josh 12: 7 kings of the country which J
Josh 12: 7 which J gave to the tribes of
Josh 13: 1 Now J was old, advanced in
Josh 14: 1 J the son of Nun, and the
Josh 14: 6 of Judah came to J in Gilgal
Josh 14:13 J blessed him, and gave Hebron
Josh 15:13 commandment of the LORD to J
Josh 17: 4 before J the son of Nun, and
Josh 17:14 children of Joseph spoke to J
Josh 17:15 So J answered them, "If you
Josh 17:17 And J spoke to the house of
Josh 18: 3 Then J said to the children
Josh 18: 8 J charged those who went to
Josh 18: 9 they came to J at the camp in
Josh 18:10 Then J cast lots for them in
Josh 18:10 there J divided the land to
Josh 19:49 them to J the son of Nun
Josh 19:51 J the son of Nun, and the
Josh 20: 1 The LORD also spoke to J,
Josh 21: 1 to J the son of Nun, and to
Josh 22: 1 Then J called the Reubenites,
Josh 22: 6 So J blessed them and sent
Josh 22: 7 it J gave a possession among
Josh 22: 7 when J sent them away to
Josh 23: 1 that J was old, advanced in
Josh 23: 2 J called for all Israel, for
Josh 24: 1 Then J gathered all the
Josh 24: 2 J said to all the people,
Josh 24:19 But J said to the people,
Josh 24:21 And the people said to J, "No
Josh 24:22 So J said to the people
Josh 24:24 And the people said to J
Josh 24:25 So J made a covenant with the
Josh 24:26 Then J wrote these words in
Josh 24:27 J said to all the people,
Josh 24:28 So J let the people depart,
Josh 24:29 things that J the son of Nun
Josh 24:31 the LORD all the days of J
Josh 24:31 of the elders who outlived J
Judg 1: 1 Now after the death of J it
Judg 2: 6 And when J had dismissed the
Judg 2: 7 the LORD all the days of J
Judg 2: 7 of the elders who outlived J
Judg 2: 8 Now J the son of Nun, the
Judg 2:21 which J left when he died
Judg 2:23 them into the hand of J
1Sa 6:14 field of J of Beth Shemesh
1Sa 6:18 field of J of Beth Shemesh
1Ki 16:34 through J the son of Nun
2Ki 23: 8 of J the governor of the city
1Ch 7:27 Nun his son, and J his son
Neh 8:17 for since the days of J the
Hag 1: 1 to J the son of Jehozadak,
Hag 1:12 J the son of Jehozadak, the
Hag 1:14 the spirit of J the son of
Hag 2: 2 to J the son of Jehozadak,
Hag 2: 4 and be strong, J, son of
Zech 3: 1 Then he showed me J the high
Zech 3: 3 Now J was clothed with filthy
Zech 3: 6 of the LORD admonished J,
Zech 3: 8 Hear, O J, the high priest,
Zech 3: 9 that I have laid before J
Zech 6:11 of J the son of Jehozadak
Acts 7:45 also brought with J into the
Heb 4: 8 For if J had given them rest,

JOSIAH

1Ki 13: 2 J by name, shall be born to
2Ki 21:24 his son J king in his place
2Ki 21:26 Then J his son reigned in his
2Ki 22: 1 J was eight years old when he
2Ki 22: 3 the eighteenth year of King J
2Ki 23:16 As J turned, he saw the tombs
2Ki 23:19 Then J also took away all the
2Ki 23:23 King J this Passover was held
2Ki 23:24 Moreover J put away those who
2Ki 23:28 Now the rest of the acts of J
2Ki 23:29 and King J went against him
2Ki 23:30 took Jehoahaz the son of J
2Ki 23:34 made Eliakim the son of J
2Ki 23:34 king in place of his father J
1Ch 3:14 Amon his son, and J his son
1Ch 3:15 The sons of J were Johanan
2Ch 33:25 his son J king in his place
2Ch 34: 1 J was eight years old when he
2Ch 34:33 Thus J removed all the
2Ch 35: 1 Now J kept a Passover to the
2Ch 35: 7 Then J gave the lay people
2Ch 35:16 to the command of King J
2Ch 35:18 such a Passover as J kept
2Ch 35:19 year of the reign of J this
2Ch 35:20 this, when J had prepared the
2Ch 35:20 and J went out against him
2Ch 35:22 Nevertheless J would not turn
2Ch 35:23 And the archers shot King J
2Ch 35:24 and Jerusalem mourned for J
2Ch 35:25 Jeremiah also lamented for J
2Ch 35:25 of J in their lamentations
2Ch 35:26 Now the rest of the acts of J
2Ch 36: 1 took Jehoahaz the son of J
Jer 1: 2 the days of J the son of Amon
Jer 1: 3 of Jehoiakim the son of J
Jer 1: 3 year of Zedekiah the son of J
Jer 3: 6 me in the days of J the king
Jer 22:11 Shallum the son of J, king of
Jer 22:11 instead of J his father, who
Jer 22:18 Jehoiakim the son of J, king
Jer 25: 1 of Jehoiakim the son of J
Jer 25: 3 year of J the son of Amon
Jer 26: 1 of Jehoiakim the son of J
Jer 27: 1 of Jehoiakim the son of J
Jer 35: 1 of Jehoiakim the son of J
Jer 36: 1 of Jehoiakim the son of J
Jer 36: 2 days of J even to this day
Jer 36: 9 of Jehoiakim the son of J
Jer 37: 1 King Zedekiah the son of J
Jer 45: 1 of Jehoiakim the son of J
Jer 46: 2 of Jehoiakim the son of J
Zeph 1: 1 in the days of J the son of
Zech 6:10 enter the house of J the son
Matt 1:10 begot Amon, and Amon begot J
Matt 1:11 J begot Jeconiah and his

JOSTLE

Nah 2: 4 they j one another in the

JOT

Matt 5:18 one j or one tittle will by

JOTBAH (*see* JOTBATHAH)
2Ki 21:19 the daughter of Haruz of **J**

JOTBATHAH (*see* JOTBAH)
Num 33:33 Hor Hagidgad and camped at **J**
Num 33:34 They moved from **J** and camped
Deut 10: 7 and from Gudgodah to **J**, a

JOTHAM
Judg 9: 5 But **J** the youngest son of
Judg 9: 7 Now when they told it to **J**
Judg 9:21 And **J** ran away and fled
Judg 9:57 of **J** the son of Jerubbaal
2Ki 15: 5 **J** the king's son was over the
2Ki 15: 7 Then **J** his son reigned in his
2Ki 15:30 year of **J** the son of Uzziah
2Ki 15:32 **J** the son of Uzziah, king of
2Ki 15:36 Now the rest of the acts of **J**
2Ki 15:38 So **J** rested with his fathers,
2Ki 16: 1 Remaliah, Ahaz the son of **J**
1Ch 2:47 sons of Jahdai were Regem, **J**
1Ch 3:12 Azariah his son, **J** his son,
1Ch 5:17 the days of **J** king of Judah
2Ch 26:21 Then **J** his son was over the
2Ch 26:23 Then **J** his son reigned in
2Ch 27: 1 **J** was twenty-five years old
2Ch 27: 6 So **J** became mighty, because
2Ch 27: 7 Now the rest of the acts of **J**
2Ch 27: 9 So **J** rested with his fathers,
Is 1: 1 in the days of Uzziah, **J**,
Is 7: 1 the days of Ahaz the son of **J**
Hos 1: 1 in the days of Uzziah, **J**
Mic 1: 1 of Moresheth in the days of **J**
Matt 1: 9 Uzziah begot **J**, **J** begot Ahaz

JOURNEY (*see* JOURNEYED, JOURNEYING, JOURNEYS)
Gen 13: 3 he went on his **j** from the
Gen 24:21 made his **j** prosperous or not
Gen 29: 1 So Jacob went on his **j** and
Gen 30:36 three days' **j** between himself
Gen 31:23 pursued him for seven days' **j**
Gen 33:12 Let us take our **j**
Gen 42:25 them provisions for the **j**
Gen 45:21 them provisions for the **j**
Gen 45:23 food for his father for the **j**
Gen 46: 1 So Israel took his **j** with all
Ex 3:18 days' **j** into the wilderness
Ex 5: 3 three days' **j** into the desert
Ex 8:27 days' **j** into the wilderness
Ex 13:20 took their **j** from Succoth
Ex 17: 1 **j** from the Wilderness of Sin
Ex 40:37 then they did not **j** till the
Num 4: 5 When the camp prepares to **j**
Num 9:10 body, or is far away on a **j**
Num 9:13 who is clean and is not on a **j**
Num 9:17 children of Israel would **j**
Num 9:18 children of Israel would **j**
Num 9:19 of the LORD and did not **j**
Num 9:20 of the LORD they would **j**
Num 9:21 morning, then they would **j**
Num 9:21 was taken up, they would **j**
Num 9:22 remain encamped and not **j**
Num 9:22 it was taken up, they would **j**
Num 10: 5 side shall then begin their **j**
Num 10: 6 side shall begin their **j**
Num 10:28 when they began their **j**
Num 10:33 the LORD on a **j** of three days
Num 10:33 them for the three days' **j**
Num 11:31 about a day's **j** on this side
Num 11:31 about a day's **j** on the other
Num 12:15 the people did not **j** on till
Num 33: 8 went three days' **j** in the
Deut 1: 2 It is eleven days' **j** from
Deut 1: 7 Turn and take your **j**, and go
Deut 1:40 turn and take your **j** into the
Deut 2:24 Rise, take your **j**, and cross
Deut 10:11 begin your **j** before the
Deut 14:24 But if the **j** is too long for
Josh 9:11 provisions with you for the **j**
Josh 9:13 because of the very long **j**
Judg 4: 9 you in the **j** you are taking
Judg 18: 5 the **j** on which we go will be
2Sa 11:10 Did you not come from a **j**
1Ki 18:27 he is busy, or he is on a **j**
1Ki 19: 4 a day's **j** into the wilderness
1Ki 19: 7 because the **j** is too great
Ezra 7: 9 he began his **j** from Babylon
Neh 2: 6 How long will your **j** be
Prov 7:19 he has gone on a long **j**
Jon 3: 3 city, a three-day **j** in extent
Matt 10:10 nor bag for your **j**, nor two
Matt 25:15 and immediately he went on a **j**
Mark 6: 8 for the **j** except a staff
Luke 2:44 company, they went a day's **j**
Luke 9: 3 Take nothing for the **j**,
Luke 9:53 set for the **j** to Jerusalem
Luke 11: 6 mine has come to me on his **j**
Luke 13:33 Nevertheless I must **j** today
John 4: 6 being wearied from His **j**
Acts 1:12 Jerusalem, a Sabbath day's **j**
Acts 10: 9 day, as they went on their **j**
Rom 15:24 whenever I **j** to Spain, I
Rom 15:24 For I hope to see you on my **j**
1Co 16: 6 that you may send me on my **j**
1Co 16:11 send him on his **j** in peace
Tit 3:13 Apollos on their **j** with haste
3Jn 6 **j** in a manner worthy of God

JOURNEYED (*see* JOURNEY)
Gen 11: 2 as they **j** from the east, that
Gen 12: 9 So Abram **j**, going on still
Gen 13:11 of Jordan, and Lot **j** east
Gen 20: 1 Abraham **j** from there to the
Gen 33:17 Jacob **j** to Succoth, built
Gen 35: 5 And they **j**, and the terror of
Gen 35:16 Then they **j** from Bethel
Gen 35:21 Then Israel **j** and pitched his
Gen 42: 5 buy grain among those who **j**
Ex 12:37 **j** from Rameses to Succoth
Ex 16: 1 they **j** from Elim, and all the
Num 9:23 command of the LORD they **j**
Num 20:22 **j** from Kadesh and came to
Num 21: 4 Then they **j** from Mount Hor by
Num 21:11 they **j** from Oboth and camped
Num 33:12 They **j** from the Wilderness of
Num 33:22 They **j** from Rissah and camped
Deut 2: 1 **j** into the wilderness of the
Deut 10: 6 **j** from the wells of Bene
Deut 10: 7 From there they **j** to Gudgodah
Josh 9:17 Then the children of Israel **j**
Judg 17: 8 the house of Micah, as he **j**
Luke 9:57 as they **j** on the road, that
Luke 10:33 a certain Samaritan, as he **j**
Luke 15:13 **j** to a far country, and there
Acts 9: 3 as he **j** he came near Damascus
Acts 9: 7 the men who **j** with him stood
Acts 22: 6 Now it happened, as I **j** and
Acts 26:12 as I **j** to Damascus with
Acts 26:13 me and those who **j** with me

JOURNEYING (*see* JOURNEY)
Luke 13:22 and **j** toward Jerusalem

JOURNEYS (*see* JOURNEY)
Ex 40:36 went onward in all their **j**
Ex 40:38 throughout all their **j**
Num 10: 6 for them to begin their **j**
Num 10:12 of Sinai on their **j**
Num 33: 1 These are the **j** of the
Num 33: 2 starting points of their **j** at
Num 33: 2 these are their **j** according
2Co 11:26 in **j** often, in perils of

JOY (*see* JOYFUL, JOYOUS)
Gen 31:27 have sent you away with **j**
Deut 28:47 the LORD your God with **j** and
1Sa 18: 6 with tambourines, with **j**
1Ki 1:40 and rejoiced with great **j**, so
1Ch 12:40 for there was **j** in Israel
1Ch 15:16 the voice with resounding **j**
1Ch 15:25 the house of Obed-Edom with **j**
1Ch 29:17 now with **j** I have seen Your
2Ch 20:27 go back to Jerusalem with **j**
2Ch 30:26 was great **j** in Jerusalem, for
Ezra 3:12 yet many shouted aloud for **j**
Ezra 3:13 of **j** from the noise of the
Ezra 6:16 of this house of God with **j**
Ezra 6:22 Bread seven days with **j**
Neh 8:10 for the **j** of the LORD is your
Neh 12:43 them rejoice with great **j**
Neh 12:43 so that the **j** of Jerusalem
Esth 8:16 Jews had light and gladness, **j**
Esth 8:17 decree came, the Jews had **j**
Esth 9:22 from sorrow to **j** for them
Esth 9:22 them days of feasting and **j**
Job 8:19 this is the **j** of His way
Job 20: 5 the **j** of the hypocrite is but
Job 29:13 widow's heart to sing for **j**
Job 33:26 He shall see His face with **j**
Job 38: 7 the sons of God shouted for **j**
Ps 5:11 Let them ever shout for **j**
Ps 16:11 presence is fullness of **j**
Ps 21: 1 shall have **j** in Your strength
Ps 27: 6 of **j** in His tabernacle
Ps 30: 5 But **j** comes in the morning
Ps 32:11 And shout for **j**, all you
Ps 33: 3 skillfully with a shout of **j**
Ps 35:27 Let them shout for **j** and be
Ps 42: 4 of God, With the voice of **j**
Ps 43: 4 of God, To God my exceeding **j**
Ps 48: 2 The **j** of the whole earth, Is
Ps 51: 8 Make me to hear **j** and gladness
Ps 51:12 to me the **j** of Your salvation
Ps 65:13 They shout for **j**, they also
Ps 67: 4 nations be glad and sing for **j**
Ps 105:43 brought out His people with **j**
Ps 126: 5 sow in tears Shall reap in **j**
Ps 132: 9 let Your saints shout for **j**
Ps 132:16 shall shout aloud for **j**
Ps 137: 6 Jerusalem Above my chief **j**
Prov 12:20 counselors of peace have **j**
Prov 14:10 stranger does not share its **j**
Prov 15:21 Folly is **j** to him who is
Prov 15:23 A man has **j** by the answer of
Prov 17:21 the father of a fool has no **j**
Prov 21:15 It is a **j** for the just to do
Eccl 2:26 **j** to a man who is good in His
Eccl 5:20 busy with the **j** of his heart
Eccl 9: 7 Go, eat your bread with **j**
Is 9: 3 the nation and increased its **j**
Is 9: 3 According to the **j** of harvest
Is 9:17 have no **j** in their young men
Is 12: 3 Therefore with **j** you will
Is 16:10 **j** from the plentiful field
Is 22:13 But instead, **j** and gladness,
Is 24: 8 the **j** of the harp ceases
Is 24:11 all **j** is darkened, the mirth
Is 29:19 increase their **j** in the LORD
Is 32:14 a **j** of wild donkeys, a
Is 35: 2 and rejoice, even with **j** and
Is 35:10 everlasting **j** on their heads
Is 35:10 They shall obtain **j** and
Is 51: 3 **j** and gladness will be found
Is 51:11 everlasting **j** on their heads
Is 51:11 They shall obtain **j** and
Is 52: 9 Break forth into **j**, sing
Is 55:12 For you shall go out with **j**
Is 60: 5 your heart shall swell with **j**
Is 60:15 a **j** of many generations
Is 61: 3 the oil of **j** for mourning,
Is 61: 7 everlasting **j** shall be theirs
Is 65:14 shall sing for **j** of heart
Is 65:18 rejoicing, and her people a **j**
Is 65:19 Jerusalem, and **j** in My people
Is 66: 5 that we may see your **j**
Is 66:10 rejoice for **j** with her, all
Jer 15:16 and Your word was to me the **j**
Jer 31:13 will turn their mourning to **j**
Jer 33: 9 it shall be to Me a name of **j**
Jer 33:11 the voice of **j** and the voice
Jer 48:33 **J** and gladness are taken from
Jer 49:25 deserted, the city of My **j**
Lam 2:15 the **j** of the whole earth'
Lam 5:15 The **j** of our heart has ceased
Ezek 24:25 their stronghold, their **j**
Ezek 36: 5 with whole-hearted **j** and
Hos 9: 1 with **j** like other peoples,
Joel 1:12 surely **j** has withered away
Joel 1:16 cut off before our eyes, **j**
Hab 3:18 I will **j** in the God of my
Zech 8:19 fast of the tenth, shall be **j**
Matt 2:10 with exceedingly great **j**
Matt 13:20 receives it with **j**
Matt 13:44 and for **j** over it he goes and
Matt 25:21 Enter into the **j** of your lord
Matt 25:23 Enter into the **j** of your lord
Matt 28: 8 the tomb with fear and great **j**
Luke 1:14 And you will have **j** and
Luke 1:44 babe leaped in my womb for **j**
Luke 2:10 you good tidings of great **j**
Luke 6:23 in that day and leap for **j**
Luke 8:13 hear, receive the word with **j**
Luke 10:17 the seventy returned with **j**
Luke 15: 7 **j** in heaven over one sinner
Luke 15:10 there is **j** in the presence of
Luke 24:41 still did not believe for **j**
Luke 24:52 to Jerusalem with great **j**
John 3:29 Therefore this **j** of mine is
John 15:11 that My **j** may remain in you,
John 15:11 and that your **j** may be full
John 16:20 sorrow will be turned into **j**
John 16:21 for **j** that a human being has
John 16:22 your **j** no one will take from

John 16:24 that your j may be full
John 17:13 that they may have My j
Acts 2:28 me full of j in Your presence
Acts 8: 8 was great j in that city
Acts 13:52 disciples were filled with j
Acts 15: 3 they caused great j to all
Acts 20:24 I may finish my race with j
Rom 14:17 peace and j in the Holy Spirit
Rom 15:13 of hope fill you with all j
Rom 15:32 you with j by the will of God
2Co 1:24 are fellow workers for your j
2Co 2: 3 from whom I ought to have j
2Co 2: 3 my j is the j of you all
2Co 7:13 more for the j of Titus,
2Co 8: 2 the abundance of their j and
Gal 5:22 of the Spirit is love, j,
Phil 1: 4 request for you all with j
Phil 1:25 your progress and j of faith,
Phil 2: 2 fulfill my j by being
Phil 4: 1 and longed-for brethren, my j
Col 1:11 and longsuffering with j
1Th 1: 6 with j of the Holy Spirit,
1Th 2:19 For what is our hope, or j
1Th 2:20 For you are our glory and j
1Th 3: 9 for all the j with which we
2Ti 1: 4 that I may be filled with j
Phm 7 For we have great j and
Phm 20 let me have j from you in the
Heb 12: 2 who for the j that was set
Heb 13:17 Let them do so with j and not
Jas 1: 2 count it all j when you fall
Jas 4: 9 mourning and your j to gloom
1Pe 1: 8 rejoice with j inexpressible
1Pe 4:13 also be glad with exceeding j
1Jn 1: 4 you that your j may be full
2Jn 12 face, that our j may be full
3Jn 4 I have no greater j than to
Jude 24 of His glory with exceeding j

JOYFUL (*see* JOY, JOYFULLY)
1Ki 8:66 and went to their tents j
2Ch 7:10 people away to their tents, j
Ezra 6:22 for the LORD made them j, and
Esth 5: 9 So Haman went out that day j
Job 3: 7 May no j shout come into it
Ps 5:11 love Your name Be j in You
Ps 35: 9 soul shall be j in the LORD
Ps 63: 5 shall praise You with j lips
Ps 66: 1 Make a j shout to God, all
Ps 81: 1 Make a j shout to the God of
Ps 89:15 people who know the j sound
Ps 96:12 Let the field be j, and all
Ps 98: 8 Let the hills be j together
Ps 100: 1 Make a j shout to the LORD,
Ps 113: 9 Like a j mother of children
Ps 149: 2 of Zion be j in their King
Ps 149: 5 Let the saints be j in glory
Eccl 7:14 In the day of prosperity be j
Is 49:13 Be j, O earth
Is 56: 7 make them j in My house of
Is 61:10 my soul shall be j in my God
2Co 7: 4 I am exceedingly j in all our
Heb 12:11 seems to be j for the present

JOYFULLY (*see* JOYFUL)
Ps 95: 1 Let us shout j to the Rock of
Ps 95: 2 Let us shout j to Him with
Ps 98: 4 Shout j to the LORD, all the
Ps 98: 6 Shout j before the LORD, the
Eccl 9: 9 Live j with the wife whom you
Luke 19: 6 came down, and received Him j
Heb 10:34 j accepted the plundering of

JOYOUS (*see* JOY, JOYOUSLY)
Is 22: 2 a tumultuous city, a j city
Is 23: 7 Is this your j city, whose
Is 32:13 the happy homes in the j city
Jer 48:33 will tread with j shouting
Jer 48:33 not j shouting

JOYOUSLY (*see* JOYOUS)
Jer 51:48 shall sing j over Babylon

JOZABAD (*see* JEHOZABAD)
1Ch 12: 4 Johanan, and J the Gederathite
1Ch 12:20 J, Jediael, Michael, J
2Ch 31:13 Nahath, Asahel, Jerimoth, J
2Ch 35: 9 and Hashabiah and Jeiel and J
Ezra 8:33 J the son of Jeshua and
Ezra 10:22 Ishmael, Nethaneel, J, and
Ezra 10:23 J, Shimei, Kelaiah (the same
Neh 8: 7 Maaseiah, Kelita, Azariah, J
Neh 11:16 Shabbethai and J, of the heads

JOZACHAR
2Ki 12:21 For J the son of Shimeath and

JOZADAK (*see* JEHOZADAK)
Ezra 3: 2 Then Jeshua the son of J and
Ezra 3: 8 Jeshua the son of J, and the
Ezra 5: 2 Jeshua the son of J rose up
Ezra 10:18 sons of Jeshua the son of J
Neh 12:26 son of Jeshua, the son of J

JUBAL
Gen 4:21 His brother's name was J

JUBILANT (*see* JUBILEE)
Is 5:14 and their pomp, and he who is j
Is 24: 8 the noise of the j ends, the

JUBILEE (*see* JUBILANT)
Lev 25: 9 cause the trumpet of the J to
Lev 25:10 It shall be a J for you
Lev 25:11 year shall be a J to you
Lev 25:12 For it is the J
Lev 25:13 In this Year of J, each of
Lev 25:15 the J you shall buy from your
Lev 25:28 bought it until the Year of J
Lev 25:28 in the J it shall be released
Lev 25:30 not be released in the J
Lev 25:31 shall be released in the J
Lev 25:33 be released in the Year of J
Lev 25:40 serve you until the Year of J
Lev 25:50 to him until the Year of J
Lev 25:52 few years until the Year of J
Lev 25:54 be released in the Year of J
Lev 27:17 his field from the Year of J
Lev 27:18 his field after the J, then
Lev 27:18 remain till the Year of J
Lev 27:21 when it is released in the J
Lev 27:23 up to the Year of J, and he
Lev 27:24 In the Year of J the field
Num 36: 4 when the J of the children of

JUCAL (*see* JEHUCAL)
Jer 38: 1 J the son of Shelemiah, and

JUDAH (*see* JUDAH'S, JUDEA)
Gen 29:35 she called his name J
Gen 35:23 firstborn, and Simeon, Levi, J
Gen 37:26 So J said to his brothers,
Gen 38: 1 to pass at that time that J
Gen 38: 2 J saw there a daughter of a
Gen 38: 6 Then J took a wife for Er his
Gen 38: 8 And J said to Onan,
Gen 38:11 Then J said to Tamar his
Gen 38:12 J was comforted, and went up
Gen 38:15 When J saw her, he thought
Gen 38:20 J sent the young goat by the
Gen 38:22 And he returned to J and said,
Gen 38:23 Then J said, "Let her take
Gen 38:24 that J was told, saying,
Gen 38:24 So J said, "Bring her out
Gen 38:26 So J acknowledged them and
Gen 43: 3 But J spoke to him, saying,
Gen 43: 8 Then J said to Israel his
Gen 44:14 So J and his brothers came to
Gen 44:16 Then J said, "What shall we
Gen 44:18 Then J came near to him and
Gen 46:12 The sons of J were Er, Onan,
Gen 46:28 Then he sent J before him to
Gen 49: 8 J, you are he whom your
Gen 49: 9 J is a lion's whelp
Gen 49:10 shall not depart from J, nor
Ex 1: 2 Reuben, Simeon, Levi, and J
Ex 31: 2 son of Hur, of the tribe of J
Ex 35:30 son of Hur, of the tribe of J
Ex 38:22 son of Hur, of the tribe of J
Num 1: 7 from J, Nahshon the son of
Num 1:26 From the children of J, their
Num 1:27 numbered of the tribe of J
Num 2: 3 J shall camp according to
Num 2: 3 leader of the children of J
Num 2: 9 armies of the forces with J
Num 7:12 from the tribe of J
Num 10:14 J set out first according to
Num 13: 6 from the tribe of J, Caleb
Num 26:19 The sons of J were Er and Onan
Num 26:20 the sons of J according to
Num 26:22 These are the families of J
Num 34:19 from the tribe of J, Caleb
Deut 27:12 Simeon, Levi, J, Issachar,
Deut 33: 7 And this he said of J
Deut 33: 7 Hear, LORD, the voice of J
Deut 34: 2 all the land of J as far as
Josh 7: 1 of Zerah, of the tribe of J
Josh 7:16 and the tribe of J was taken
Josh 7:17 and he brought the clan of J
Josh 7:18 of Zerah, of the tribe of J
Josh 11:21 from all the mountains of J
Josh 14: 6 Then the children of J came
Josh 15: 1 tribe of the children of J
Josh 15:12 of J all around according to
Josh 15:13 among the children of J,
Josh 15:20 tribe of the children of J
Josh 15:21 tribe of the children of J
Josh 15:63 the children of J could not
Josh 15:63 of J at Jerusalem to this day
Josh 18: 5 J shall remain in their
Josh 18:11 out between the children of J
Josh 18:14 a city of the children of J
Josh 19: 1 of the children of J
Josh 19: 9 portion of the children of J
Josh 19: 9 of J was too much for them
Josh 19:34 and ended at J by the Jordan
Josh 20: 7 Hebron) in the mountains of J
Josh 21: 4 by lot from the tribe of J
Josh 21: 9 tribe of the children of J
Josh 21:11 Hebron, in the mountains of J
Judg 1: 2 LORD said, "J shall go up
Judg 1: 3 So J said to Simeon his
Judg 1: 4 Then J went up, and the LORD
Judg 1: 8 Now the children of J fought
Judg 1: 9 afterward the children of J
Judg 1:10 Then J went against the
Judg 1:16 of J into the Wilderness of
Judg 1:16 into the Wilderness of J,
Judg 1:17 And J went with his brother
Judg 1:18 Also J took Gaza with its
Judg 1:19 So the LORD was with J
Judg 10: 9 to fight against J also,
Judg 15: 9 went up, encamped in J, and
Judg 15:10 And the men of J said, "Why
Judg 15:11 J went down to the cleft of
Judg 17: 7 young man from Bethlehem in J
Judg 17: 7 of the family of J
Judg 17: 8 in J to sojourn wherever he
Judg 17: 9 a Levite from Bethlehem in J
Judg 18:12 in Kirjath Jearim in J
Judg 19: 1 concubine from Bethlehem in J
Judg 19: 2 house at Bethlehem in J, and
Judg 19:18 passing from Bethlehem in J
Judg 19:18 I went to Bethlehem in J, and
Judg 20:18 said, "J shall go up first
Ruth 1: 1 a certain man of Bethlehem, J
Ruth 1: 2 Ephrathites of Bethlehem, J
Ruth 1: 7 to return to the land of J
Ruth 4:12 Perez, whom Tamar bore to J
1Sa 11: 8 the men of J thirty thousand
1Sa 15: 4 and ten thousand men of J
1Sa 17: 1 at Sochoh, which belongs to J
1Sa 17:12 Ephrathite of Bethlehem J
1Sa 17:52 and J arose and shouted, and
1Sa 18:16 J loved David, because he
1Sa 22: 5 and go to the land of J
1Sa 23: 3 Look, we are afraid here in J
1Sa 23:23 throughout all the clans of J
1Sa 27: 6 to the kings of J to this day
1Sa 27:10 the southern area of J, or
1Sa 30:14 territory which belongs to J
1Sa 30:16 and from the land of J
1Sa 30:26 the spoil to the elders of J
2Sa 1:18 of J the Song of the Bow
2Sa 2: 1 up to any of the cities of J
2Sa 2: 4 Then the men of J came, and
2Sa 2: 4 king over the house of J
2Sa 2: 7 and also the house of J has
2Sa 2:10 the house of J followed David
2Sa 2:11 house of J was seven years
2Sa 3: 8 dog's head that belongs to J
2Sa 3:10 David over Israel and over J
2Sa 5: 5 he reigned over J seven years
2Sa 5: 5 years over all Israel and J
2Sa 11:11 J are dwelling in tents, and
2Sa 12: 8 you the house of Israel and J
2Sa 19:11 Speak to the elders of J,
2Sa 19:14 hearts of all the men of J
2Sa 19:15 J came to Gilgal, to go to
2Sa 19:16 men of J to meet King David
2Sa 19:40 people of J escorted the king
2Sa 19:41 our brethren, the men of J
2Sa 19:42 So all the men of J answered
2Sa 19:43 Israel answered the men of J
2Sa 19:43 J were fiercer than the words
2Sa 20: 2 But the men of J, from the
2Sa 20: 4 Assemble the men of J for me

2Sa 20: 5 went to assemble the men of J
2Sa 21: 2 the children of Israel and J
2Sa 24: 1 Go, number Israel and J
2Sa 24: 7 South J as far as Beersheba
2Sa 24: 9 and the men of J were five
1Ki 1: 9 sons, and all the men of J
1Ki 1:35 to be ruler over Israel and J
1Ki 2:32 commander of the army of J
1Ki 4:20 J and Israel were as numerous
1Ki 4:25 And J and Israel dwelt safely,
1Ki 9:18 wilderness, in the land of J
1Ki 12:17 who dwelt in the cities of J
1Ki 12:20 but the tribe of J only
1Ki 12:21 J with the tribe of Benjamin
1Ki 12:23 the son of Solomon, king of J
1Ki 12:23 to all the house of J
1Ki 12:27 lord, Rehoboam king of J, and
1Ki 12:27 go back to Rehoboam king of J
1Ki 12:32 like the feast that was in J
1Ki 13: 1 a man of God went from J to
1Ki 13:12 of God went who came from J
1Ki 13:14 man of God who came from J
1Ki 13:21 man of God who came from J
1Ki 14:21 son of Solomon reigned in J
1Ki 14:22 Now J did evil in the sight
1Ki 14:29 chronicles of the kings of J
1Ki 15: 1 Abijam became king over J
1Ki 15: 7 chronicles of the kings of J
1Ki 15: 9 Asa became king over J
1Ki 15:17 of Israel came up against J
1Ki 15:17 or come in to Asa king of J
1Ki 15:22 proclamation throughout all J
1Ki 15:23 chronicles of the kings of J
1Ki 15:25 second year of Asa king of J
1Ki 15:28 third year of Asa king of J
1Ki 15:33 third year of Asa king of J
1Ki 16: 8 year of Asa king of J, Elah
1Ki 16:10 year of Asa king of J, and
1Ki 16:15 year of Asa king of J, Zimri
1Ki 16:23 year of Asa king of J, Omri
1Ki 16:29 year of Asa king of J, Ahab
1Ki 19: 3 Beersheba, which belongs to J
1Ki 22: 2 Jehoshaphat the king of J
1Ki 22:10 and Jehoshaphat the king of J
1Ki 22:29 Jehoshaphat the king of J
1Ki 22:41 J in the fourth year of Ahab
1Ki 22:45 chronicles of the kings of J
1Ki 22:51 year of Jehoshaphat king of J
2Ki 1:17 son of Jehoshaphat, king of J
2Ki 3: 1 year of Jehoshaphat king of J
2Ki 3: 7 sent to Jehoshaphat king of J
2Ki 3: 9 went with the king of J and
2Ki 3:14 of Jehoshaphat king of J, I
2Ki 8:16 having been king of J,
2Ki 8:16 began to reign as king of J
2Ki 8:19 the LORD would not destroy J
2Ki 8:23 chronicles of the kings of J
2Ki 8:25 the son of Jehoram, king of J
2Ki 8:29 the son of Jehoram, king of J
2Ki 9:16 Ahaziah king of J had come
2Ki 9:21 and Ahaziah king of J went out
2Ki 9:27 Ahaziah king of J saw this
2Ki 9:29 had become king over J
2Ki 10:13 brothers of Ahaziah king of J
2Ki 12:18 Jehoash king of J took all
2Ki 12:18 and Ahaziah, kings of J, had
2Ki 12:19 chronicles of the kings of J
2Ki 13: 1 the son of Ahaziah, king of J
2Ki 13:10 year of Joash king of J,
2Ki 13:12 against Amaziah king of J
2Ki 14: 1 the son of Joash, king of J
2Ki 14: 9 sent to Amaziah king of J
2Ki 14:10 you and J with you
2Ki 14:11 Amaziah king of J faced one
2Ki 14:11 Shemesh, which belongs to J
2Ki 14:12 J was defeated by Israel, and
2Ki 14:13 captured Amaziah king of J
2Ki 14:15 fought with Amaziah king of J
2Ki 14:17 the son of Joash, king of J
2Ki 14:18 chronicles of the kings of J
2Ki 14:21 the people of J took Azariah
2Ki 14:22 Elath and restored it to J
2Ki 14:23 the son of Joash, king of J
2Ki 14:28 what had belonged to J
2Ki 15: 1 the son of Amaziah, king of J
2Ki 15: 6 chronicles of the kings of J
2Ki 15: 8 year of Azariah king of J
2Ki 15:13 year of Uzziah king of J
2Ki 15:17 year of Azariah king of J
2Ki 15:23 year of Azariah king of J
2Ki 15:27 year of Azariah king of J
2Ki 15:32 the son of Uzziah, king of J
2Ki 15:36 chronicles of the kings of J
2Ki 15:37 the son of Remaliah against J
2Ki 16: 1 the son of Jotham, king of J
2Ki 16: 6 drove the men of J from Elath
2Ki 16:19 chronicles of the kings of J
2Ki 17: 1 year of Ahaz king of J,
2Ki 17:13 against Israel and against J
2Ki 17:18 left but the tribe of J alone
2Ki 17:19 Also J did not keep the
2Ki 18: 1 the son of Ahaz, king of J
2Ki 18: 5 him among all the kings of J
2Ki 18:13 all the fortified cities of J
2Ki 18:14 Then Hezekiah king of J sent
2Ki 18:14 of J three hundred talents of
2Ki 18:16 king of J had overlaid, and
2Ki 18:22 has taken away, and said to J
2Ki 19:10 speak to Hezekiah king of J
2Ki 19:30 of J shall again take root
2Ki 20:20 chronicles of the kings of J
2Ki 21:11 Because Manasseh king of J
2Ki 21:11 has also made J sin with his
2Ki 21:12 calamity upon Jerusalem and J
2Ki 21:16 sin with which he made J sin
2Ki 21:17 chronicles of the kings of J
2Ki 21:25 chronicles of the kings of J
2Ki 22:13 for the people and for all J
2Ki 22:16 which the king of J has read
2Ki 22:18 But to the king of J, who
2Ki 23: 1 to gather all the elders of J
2Ki 23: 2 LORD with all the men of J
2Ki 23: 5 of J had ordained to burn
2Ki 23: 5 places in the cities of J
2Ki 23: 8 priests from the cities of J
2Ki 23:11 of J had dedicated to the sun
2Ki 23:12 which the kings of J had made
2Ki 23:17 man of God who came from J
2Ki 23:22 of Israel and the kings of J
2Ki 23:24 were seen in the land of J
2Ki 23:26 anger was aroused against J
2Ki 23:27 also remove J from My sight
2Ki 23:28 chronicles of the kings of J
2Ki 24: 2 them against J to destroy it
2Ki 24: 3 of the LORD this came upon J
2Ki 24: 5 chronicles of the kings of J
2Ki 24:12 Then Jehoiachin king of J
2Ki 24:20 happened in Jerusalem and J
2Ki 25:21 Thus J was carried away
2Ki 25:22 who remained in the land of J
2Ki 25:27 of Jehoiachin king of J, in
2Ki 25:27 king of J from prison
1Ch 2: 1 Reuben, Simeon, Levi, J,
1Ch 2: 3 The sons of J were Er, Onan,
1Ch 2: 3 Er, the firstborn of J, was
1Ch 2: 4 All the sons of J were five
1Ch 2:10 leader of the children of J
1Ch 4: 1 The sons of J were Perez,
1Ch 4:21 sons of Shelah the son of J
1Ch 4:27 as much as the children of J
1Ch 4:41 days of Hezekiah king of J
1Ch 5: 2 yet J prevailed over his
1Ch 5:17 the days of Jotham king of J
1Ch 6:15 when the LORD carried J and
1Ch 6:55 them Hebron in the land of J
1Ch 6:65 tribe of the children of J
1Ch 9: 1 But J was carried away
1Ch 9: 3 the children of J dwelt, and
1Ch 9: 4 of Perez, the son of J
1Ch 12:16 and J came to David at the
1Ch 12:24 children of J bearing shield
1Ch 13: 6 Jearim, which belonged to J
1Ch 21: 5 J had four hundred and seventy
1Ch 27:18 over J, Elihu, one of David's
1Ch 28: 4 has chosen J to be the ruler
1Ch 28: 4 and of the house of J, the
2Ch 2: 7 men who are with me in J and
2Ch 9:11 seen before in the land of J
2Ch 10:17 who dwelt in the cities of J
2Ch 11: 1 assembled from the house of J
2Ch 11: 3 the son of Solomon, king of J
2Ch 11: 3 J, and to all Israel in J
2Ch 11: 5 built cities for defense in J
2Ch 11:10 and Hebron, which are in J
2Ch 11:12 them very strong, having J
2Ch 11:14 possessions and came to J and
2Ch 11:17 strengthened the kingdom of J
2Ch 11:23 all the territories of J and
2Ch 12: 4 the fortified cities of J
2Ch 12: 5 Rehoboam and the leaders of J
2Ch 12:12 and things also went well in J
2Ch 13: 1 Abijah became king over J
2Ch 13:13 so they were in front of J
2Ch 13:14 And when J looked around, to
2Ch 13:15 the men of J gave a shout
2Ch 13:15 and as the men of J shouted
2Ch 13:15 all Israel before Abijah and J
2Ch 13:16 of Israel fled before J, and
2Ch 13:18 the children of J prevailed
2Ch 14: 4 He commanded J to seek the
2Ch 14: 5 from all the cities of J, and
2Ch 14: 6 built fortified cities in J
2Ch 14: 7 Therefore he said to J, "Let
2Ch 14: 8 from J who carried shields
2Ch 14:12 Ethiopians before Asa and J
2Ch 15: 2 Hear me, Asa, and all J and
2Ch 15: 8 idols from all the land of J
2Ch 15: 9 Then he gathered all J and
2Ch 15:15 all J rejoiced at the oath,
2Ch 16: 1 of Israel came up against J
2Ch 16: 1 or come in to Asa king of J
2Ch 16: 6 Then King Asa took all J, and
2Ch 16: 7 seer came to Asa king of J
2Ch 16:11 in the book of the kings of J
2Ch 17: 2 all the fortified cities of J
2Ch 17: 2 garrisons in the land of J
2Ch 17: 5 and all J gave presents to
2Ch 17: 6 and wooden images from J
2Ch 17: 7 to teach in the cities of J
2Ch 17: 9 So they taught in J, and had
2Ch 17: 9 all the cities of J and taught
2Ch 17:10 the lands that were around J
2Ch 17:12 and storage cities in J
2Ch 17:13 property in the cities of J
2Ch 17:14 Of J, the captains of
2Ch 17:19 cities throughout all J
2Ch 18: 3 said to Jehoshaphat king of J
2Ch 18: 9 and Jehoshaphat king of J,
2Ch 18:28 Jehoshaphat the king of J
2Ch 19: 1 of J returned safely to his
2Ch 19: 5 all the fortified cities of J
2Ch 19:11 the ruler of the house of J
2Ch 20: 3 a fast throughout all J
2Ch 20: 4 So J gathered together to ask
2Ch 20: 4 from all the cities of J they
2Ch 20: 5 in the congregation of J and
2Ch 20:13 Now all J, with their little
2Ch 20:15 Listen, all you of J and you
2Ch 20:17 LORD, who is with you, O J
2Ch 20:18 face to the ground, and all J
2Ch 20:20 Hear me, O J and you
2Ch 20:22 Seir, who had come against J
2Ch 20:24 So when J came to a place
2Ch 20:27 they returned, every man of J
2Ch 20:31 Jehoshaphat was king over J
2Ch 20:35 this Jehoshaphat king of J
2Ch 21: 3 with fortified cities in J
2Ch 21:11 places in the mountains of J
2Ch 21:11 harlotry, and led J astray
2Ch 21:12 in the ways of Asa king of J
2Ch 21:13 of Israel, and have made J
2Ch 21:17 And they came up into J and
2Ch 22: 1 the son of Jehoram, king of J
2Ch 22: 6 the son of Jehoram, king of J
2Ch 22: 8 and found the princes of J
2Ch 22:10 royal heirs of the house of J
2Ch 23: 2 And they went throughout J
2Ch 23: 2 from all the cities of J, and
2Ch 23: 8 all J did according to all
2Ch 24: 5 Go out to the cities of J
2Ch 24: 6 Levites to bring in from J
2Ch 24: 9 a proclamation throughout J
2Ch 24:17 the leaders of J came and
2Ch 24:18 and wrath came upon J and
2Ch 24:23 and they came to J and
2Ch 25: 5 Amaziah gathered J together
2Ch 25: 5 houses, throughout all J and
2Ch 25:10 was greatly aroused against J
2Ch 25:12 And the children of J took
2Ch 25:13 they raided the cities of J
2Ch 25:17 king of J took counsel and
2Ch 25:18 sent to Amaziah king of J
2Ch 25:19 you and J with you
2Ch 25:21 Amaziah king of J faced one
2Ch 25:21 Shemesh, which belongs to J
2Ch 25:22 J was defeated by Israel, and
2Ch 25:23 captured Amaziah king of J
2Ch 25:25 the son of Joash, king of J
2Ch 25:26 in the book of the kings of J
2Ch 25:28 his fathers in the City of J

2Ch 26: 1 the people of J took Uzziah
2Ch 26: 2 Elath and restored it to J
2Ch 27: 4 cities in the mountains of J
2Ch 27: 7 of the kings of Israel and J
2Ch 28: 6 thousand in J in one day, all
2Ch 28: 9 your fathers was angry with J
2Ch 28:10 to force the children of J
2Ch 28:17 Edomites had come, attacked J
2Ch 28:18 lowland and of the South of J
2Ch 28:19 For the LORD brought J low
2Ch 28:19 encouraged moral decline in J
2Ch 28:25 in every single city of J he
2Ch 28:26 in the book of the kings of J
2Ch 29: 8 wrath of the LORD fell upon J
2Ch 29:21 for the sanctuary, and for J
2Ch 30: 1 sent to all Israel and J, and
2Ch 30: 6 J with the letters from the
2Ch 30:12 J to give them singleness of
2Ch 30:24 For Hezekiah king of J gave
2Ch 30:25 congregation of J rejoiced
2Ch 30:25 and those who dwelt in J
2Ch 31: 1 went out to the cities of J
2Ch 31: 1 from all J, Benjamin, Ephraim
2Ch 31: 6 the children of Israel and J
2Ch 31: 6 who dwelt in the cities of J
2Ch 31:20 Hezekiah did throughout all J
2Ch 32: 1 of Assyria came and entered J
2Ch 32: 8 words of Hezekiah king of J
2Ch 32: 9 to Hezekiah king of J, and
2Ch 32: 9 and to all J who were in
2Ch 32:12 His altars, and commanded J
2Ch 32:23 to Hezekiah king of J, so
2Ch 32:25 looming over him and over J
2Ch 32:32 in the book of the kings of J
2Ch 32:33 and all J and the inhabitants
2Ch 33: 9 So Manasseh seduced J and the
2Ch 33:14 all the fortified cities of J
2Ch 33:16 commanded J to serve the LORD
2Ch 34: 3 year he began to purge J and
2Ch 34: 5 their altars, and cleansed J
2Ch 34: 9 remnant of Israel, from all J
2Ch 34:11 the kings of J had destroyed
2Ch 34:21 who are left in Israel and J
2Ch 34:24 read before the king of J
2Ch 34:26 And as for the king of J, who
2Ch 34:29 gathered all the elders of J
2Ch 34:30 LORD, with all the men of J
2Ch 35:18 priests and the Levites, all J
2Ch 35:21 I to do with you, king of J
2Ch 35:24 J and Jerusalem mourned
2Ch 35:27 of the kings of Israel and J
2Ch 36: 4 brother Eliakim king over J
2Ch 36: 8 of the kings of Israel and J
2Ch 36:10 brother, king over J and
2Ch 36:23 at Jerusalem which is in J
Ezra 1: 2 at Jerusalem which is in J
Ezra 1: 3 to Jerusalem, which is in J
Ezra 1: 5 of the fathers' houses of J
Ezra 1: 8 Sheshbazzar the prince of J
Ezra 2: 1 returned to Jerusalem and J
Ezra 3: 9 his sons, and the sons of J
Ezra 4: 1 Now when the adversaries of J
Ezra 4: 4 to discourage the people of J
Ezra 4: 6 against the inhabitants of J
Ezra 5: 1 to the Jews who were in J
Ezra 7:14 to inquire concerning J and
Ezra 9: 9 and to give us a wall in J
Ezra 10: 7 a proclamation throughout J
Ezra 10: 9 So all the men of J and
Ezra 10:23 same is Kelita), Pethahiah, J
Neh 1: 2 brethren came with men from J
Neh 2: 5 I ask that you send me to J
Neh 2: 7 pass through till I come to J
Neh 4:10 Then J said, "The strength
Neh 4:16 behind all the house of J
Neh 5:14 governor in the land of J
Neh 6: 7 saying, "There is a king in J
Neh 6:17 J sent many letters to Tobiah
Neh 6:18 For many in J were pledged to
Neh 7: 6 returned to Jerusalem and J
Neh 11: 3 (But in the cities of J
Neh 11: 4 certain of the children of J
Neh 11: 4 The children of J
Neh 11: 9 and J the son of Senuah was
Neh 11:20 were in all the cities of J
Neh 11:24 of Zerah the son of J, was
Neh 11:25 of J dwelt in Kirjath Arba
Neh 12: 8 Binnui, Kadmiel, Sherebiah, J
Neh 12:31 leaders of J up on the wall
Neh 12:32 and half of the leaders of J
Neh 12:34 J, Benjamin, Shemaiah,
Neh 12:36 Gilalai, Maai, Nethaneal, J
Neh 12:44 for J rejoiced over the
Neh 13:12 Then all J brought the tithe
Neh 13:15 In those days I saw in J some
Neh 13:16 Sabbath to the children of J
Neh 13:17 with the nobles of J, and said
Neh 13:24 not speak the language of J
Esth 2: 6 with Jeconiah king of J, whom
Ps 48:11 the daughters of J be glad
Ps 60: 7 J is My lawgiver
Ps 68:27 leader, The princes of J and
Ps 69:35 Zion And build the cities of J
Ps 76: 1 In J God is known
Ps 78:68 But chose the tribe of J,
Ps 97: 8 the daughters of J rejoice
Ps 108: 8 J is My lawgiver
Ps 114: 2 J became His sanctuary, And
Prov 25: 1 of Hezekiah king of J copied
Is 1: 1 which he saw concerning J
Is 1: 1 Ahaz, and Hezekiah, kings of J
Is 2: 1 son of Amoz saw concerning J
Is 3: 1 from J the stock and the store
Is 3: 8 J is fallen, because their
Is 5: 3 of Jerusalem and men of J,
Is 5: 7 the men of J are His pleasant
Is 7: 1 the son of Uzziah, king of J
Is 7: 6 Let us go up against J and
Is 7:17 that Ephraim departed from J
Is 8: 8 He will pass through J, he
Is 9:21 together shall be against J
Is 11:12 of J from the four corners of
Is 11:13 of J shall be cut off
Is 11:13 Ephraim shall not envy J, and
Is 11:13 J shall not harass Ephraim
Is 19:17 And the land of J will be a
Is 22: 8 removed the protection of J
Is 22:21 and to the house of J
Is 26: 1 will be sung in the land of J
Is 36: 1 all the fortified cities of J
Is 36: 7 has taken away, and said to J
Is 37:10 speak to Hezekiah king of J
Is 37:31 of J shall again take root
Is 38: 9 writing of Hezekiah king of J
Is 40: 9 say to the cities of J
Is 44:26 to the cities of J, 'You
Is 48: 1 from the wellsprings of J
Is 65: 9 and from J an heir of My
Jer 1: 2 the son of Amon, king of J
Jer 1: 3 the son of Josiah, king of J
Jer 1: 3 the son of Josiah, king of J
Jer 1:15 against all the cities of J
Jer 1:18 against the kings of J,
Jer 2:28 cities are your gods, O J
Jer 3: 7 treacherous sister J saw it
Jer 3: 8 sister J did not fear, but
Jer 3:10 J has not turned to Me with
Jer 3:11 righteous than treacherous J
Jer 3:18 J shall walk with the house
Jer 4: 3 says the LORD to the men of J
Jer 4: 4 of your hearts, you men of J
Jer 4: 5 Declare in J and proclaim in
Jer 4:16 voice against the cities of J
Jer 5:11 the house of J have dealt
Jer 5:20 of Jacob and proclaim it in J
Jer 7: 2 all you of J who enter in at
Jer 7:17 they do in the cities of J
Jer 7:30 For the children of J have
Jer 7:34 to cease from the cities of J
Jer 8: 1 the bones of the kings of J
Jer 9:11 make the cities of J desolate
Jer 9:26 Egypt, J, Edom, the people of
Jer 10:22 make the cities of J desolate
Jer 11: 2 and speak to the men of J
Jer 11: 6 words in the cities of J and
Jer 11: 9 been found among the men of J
Jer 11:10 the house of J have broken My
Jer 11:12 Then the cities of J and the
Jer 11:13 cities were your gods, O J
Jer 11:17 Israel and of the house of J
Jer 12:14 house of J from among them
Jer 13: 9 I will ruin the pride of J
Jer 13:11 house of J to cling to Me
Jer 13:19 J shall be carried away
Jer 14: 2 J mourns, and her gates
Jer 14:19 Have You utterly rejected J
Jer 15: 4 son of Hezekiah, king of J
Jer 17: 1 The sin of J is written with
Jer 17:19 which the kings of J come in
Jer 17:20 of the LORD, you kings of J
Jer 17:20 you kings of J, and all J
Jer 17:25 accompanied by the men of J
Jer 17:26 come from the cities of J
Jer 18:11 speak to the men of J and to
Jer 19: 3 of the LORD, O kings of J
Jer 19: 4 nor the kings of J have known
Jer 19: 7 make void the counsel of J
Jer 19:13 J shall be defiled like the
Jer 20: 4 I will give all J into the
Jer 20: 5 J I will give into the hand
Jer 21: 7 deliver Zedekiah king of J
Jer 21:11 the house of the king of J
Jer 22: 1 to the house of the king of J
Jer 22: 2 word of the LORD, O king of J
Jer 22: 6 to the house of the king of J
Jer 22:11 the son of Josiah, king of J
Jer 22:18 the son of Josiah, king of J
Jer 22:24 son of Jehoiakim, king of J
Jer 22:30 David, and ruling anymore in J
Jer 23: 6 In His days J will be saved,
Jer 24: 1 son of Jehoiakim, king of J
Jer 24: 1 the princes of J with the
Jer 24: 5 carried away captive from J
Jer 24: 8 up Zedekiah the king of J
Jer 25: 1 all the people of J, in the
Jer 25: 1 king of J (which was the
Jer 25: 2 spoke to all the people of J
Jer 25: 3 the son of Amon, king of J
Jer 25:18 Jerusalem and the cities of J
Jer 26: 1 the son of Josiah, king of J
Jer 26: 2 speak to all the cities of J
Jer 26:10 of J heard these things, they
Jer 26:18 days of Hezekiah king of J
Jer 26:18 spoke to all the people of J
Jer 26:19 Did Hezekiah king of J and all
Jer 26:19 all J ever put him to death
Jer 27: 1 the son of Josiah, king of J
Jer 27: 3 to Zedekiah king of J
Jer 27:12 of J according to all these
Jer 27:18 in the house of the king of J
Jer 27:20 son of Jehoiakim, king of J
Jer 27:20 and all the nobles of J and
Jer 27:21 in the house of the king of J
Jer 28: 1 reign of Zedekiah king of J
Jer 28: 4 son of Jehoiakim, king of J
Jer 28: 4 of J who went to Babylon,'
Jer 29: 2 the eunuchs, the princes of J
Jer 29: 3 king of J sent to Babylon
Jer 29:22 of J who are in Babylon,
Jer 30: 3 My people Israel and J,' says
Jer 30: 4 spoke concerning Israel and J
Jer 31:23 this speech in the land of J
Jer 31:24 there shall dwell in J itself
Jer 31:27 the house of J with the seed
Jer 31:31 Israel and with the house of J
Jer 32: 1 year of Zedekiah king of J
Jer 32: 3 king of J had shut him up
Jer 32: 4 Zedekiah king of J shall not
Jer 32:30 the children of J have done
Jer 32:32 Israel and the children of J
Jer 32:32 their prophets, the men of J
Jer 32:35 to cause J to sin
Jer 32:44 Jerusalem, in the cities of J
Jer 33: 4 the houses of the kings of J
Jer 33: 7 will cause the captives of J
Jer 33:10 in the cities of J, in the
Jer 33:13 and in the cities of J, the
Jer 33:14 Israel and to the house of J
Jer 33:16 In those days J will be saved
Jer 34: 2 speak to Zedekiah king of J
Jer 34: 4 LORD, O Zedekiah king of J
Jer 34: 6 king of J in Jerusalem,
Jer 34: 7 cities of J that were left
Jer 34: 7 remained of the cities of J
Jer 34:19 the princes of J, the
Jer 34:21 will give Zedekiah king of J
Jer 34:22 of J a desolation without
Jer 35: 1 the son of Josiah, king of J
Jer 35:13 Go and tell the men of J and
Jer 35:17 Behold, I will bring on J
Jer 36: 1 the son of Josiah, king of J
Jer 36: 2 you against Israel, against J
Jer 36: 3 house of J will hear all the
Jer 36: 6 J who come from their cities
Jer 36: 9 the son of Josiah, king of J
Jer 36: 9 the cities of J to Jerusalem
Jer 36:28 the king of J has burned
Jer 36:29 say to Jehoiakim king of J
Jer 36:30 Jehoiakim king of J
Jer 36:31 on the men of J all the doom

Jer 36:32 of J had burned in the fire
Jer 37: 1 made king in the land of J
Jer 37: 7 shall say to the king of J
Jer 39: 1 year of Zedekiah king of J
Jer 39: 4 when Zedekiah the king of J
Jer 39: 6 killed all the nobles of J
Jer 39:10 the land of J the poor people
Jer 40: 1 captive from Jerusalem and J
Jer 40: 5 governor over the cities of J
Jer 40:11 had left a remnant of J, and
Jer 40:12 and came to the land of J
Jer 40:15 and the remnant in J perish
Jer 42:15 of the LORD, O remnant of J
Jer 42:19 you, O remnant of J, 'Do not
Jer 43: 4 to remain in the land of J
Jer 43: 5 took all the remnant of J who
Jer 43: 5 to dwell in the land of J
Jer 43: 9 in the sight of the men of J
Jer 44: 2 and on all the cities of J
Jer 44: 6 and kindled in the cities of J
Jer 44: 7 child and infant, out of J
Jer 44: 9 wickedness of the kings of J
Jer 44: 9 committed in the land of J
Jer 44:11 and for cutting off all J
Jer 44:12 I will take the remnant of J
Jer 44:14 J who have gone into the land
Jer 44:14 they return to the land of J
Jer 44:17 princes, in the cities of J
Jer 44:21 you burned in the cities of J
Jer 44:24 all J who are in the land of
Jer 44:26 all J who dwell in the land
Jer 44:26 of J in all the land of Egypt
Jer 44:27 all the men of J who are in
Jer 44:28 of Egypt to the land of J
Jer 44:28 and all the remnant of J, who
Jer 44:30 king of J into the hand of
Jer 45: 1 the son of Josiah, king of J
Jer 46: 2 the son of Josiah, king of J
Jer 49:34 reign of Zedekiah king of J
Jer 50: 4 and the children of J together
Jer 50:20 and the sins of J, but they
Jer 50:33 along with the children of J
Jer 51: 5 Israel is not forsaken, nor J
Jer 51:59 of J to Babylon in the fourth
Jer 52: 3 happened in Jerusalem and J
Jer 52:10 the princes of J in Riblah
Jer 52:27 Thus J was carried away
Jer 52:31 of Jehoiachin king of J, in
Jer 52:31 head of Jehoiachin king of J
Lam 1: 3 J has gone into captivity,
Lam 1:15 the virgin daughter of J
Lam 2: 2 of the daughter of J
Lam 2: 5 in the daughter of J
Lam 5:11 maidens in the cities of J
Ezek 4: 6 of the house of J forty days
Ezek 8: 1 elders of J sitting before me
Ezek 8:17 thing to the house of J to
Ezek 9: 9 J is exceedingly great, and
Ezek 21:20 of the Ammonites, and to J
Ezek 25: 3 of J when they went into
Ezek 25: 8 The house of J is like all
Ezek 25:12 of J by taking vengeance, and
Ezek 27:17 J and the land of Israel were
Ezek 37:16 For J and for the children of
Ezek 37:19 with it, with the stick of J
Ezek 48: 7 the west, one portion for J
Ezek 48: 8 by the border of J, from the
Ezek 48:22 area between the border of J
Ezek 48:31 for Reuben, one gate for J
Dan 1: 1 reign of Jehoiakim king of J
Dan 1: 2 king of J into his hand, with
Dan 1: 6 of the sons of J were Daniel
Dan 2:25 a man of the captives of J
Dan 5:13 is one of the captives from J
Dan 5:13 the king brought from J
Dan 6:13 is one of the captives from J
Dan 9: 7 to the men of J, to the
Hos 1: 1 Ahaz, and Hezekiah, kings of J
Hos 1: 7 have mercy on the house of J
Hos 1:11 Then the children of J and the
Hos 4:15 the harlot, let not J offend
Hos 5: 5 J also stumbles with them
Hos 5:10 The princes of J are like
Hos 5:12 house of J like rottenness
Hos 5:13 J saw his wound, then Ephraim
Hos 5:14 young lion to the house of J
Hos 6: 4 O J, what shall I do to you
Hos 6:11 Also, O J, a harvest is
Hos 8:14 J also has multiplied
Hos 10:11 J shall plow
Hos 11:12 but J still walks with God,
Hos 12: 2 brings a charge against J
Joel 3: 1 bring back the captives of J
Joel 3: 6 Also the people of J and the
Joel 3: 8 the hand of the people of J
Joel 3:18 all the brooks of J shall be
Joel 3:19 against the people of J, for
Joel 3:20 But J shall abide forever, and
Amos 1: 1 the days of Uzziah king of J
Amos 2: 4 For three transgressions of J
Amos 2: 5 but I will send a fire upon J
Amos 7:12 Flee to the land of J
Obad 12 of J in the day of their
Mic 1: 1 Ahaz, and Hezekiah, kings of J
Mic 1: 5 what are the high places of J
Mic 1: 9 for it has come to J
Mic 5: 2 among the thousands of J, yet
Nah 1:15 O J, keep your appointed
Zeph 1: 1 the son of Amon, king of J
Zeph 1: 4 stretch out My hand against J
Zeph 2: 7 the remnant of the house of J
Hag 1: 1 of Shealtiel, governor of J
Hag 1:14 of Shealtiel, governor of J
Hag 2: 2 of Shealtiel, governor of J
Hag 2:21 to Zerubbabel, governor of J
Zech 1:12 and on the cities of J,
Zech 1:19 horns that have scattered J
Zech 1:21 the horns that scattered J
Zech 1:21 the land of J to scatter it
Zech 2:12 will take possession of J as
Zech 8:13 the nations, O house of J
Zech 8:15 and to the house of J
Zech 8:19 feasts for the house of J
Zech 9: 7 shall be like a leader in J
Zech 9:13 For I have bent J, My bow,
Zech 10: 3 His flock, the house of J
Zech 10: 6 strengthen the house of J
Zech 11:14 the brotherhood between J
Zech 12: 2 when they lay siege against J
Zech 12: 4 My eyes on the house of J
Zech 12: 5 the governors of J shall say
Zech 12: 6 of J like a firepan in the
Zech 12: 7 save the tents of J first
Zech 12: 7 become greater than that of J
Zech 14: 5 the days of Uzziah king of J
Zech 14:14 J also will fight at
Zech 14:21 J shall be holiness to the
Mal 2:11 J has dealt treacherously, and
Mal 2:11 for J has profaned the LORD's
Mal 3: 4 Then the offering of J and
Matt 1: 2 begot Jacob, and Jacob begot J
Matt 1: 3 J begot Perez and Zerah by
Matt 2: 6 Bethlehem, in the land of J
Matt 2: 6 least among the rulers of J
Luke 1:39 with haste, to a city of J
Luke 3:26 son of Joseph, the son of J
Luke 3:30 son of Simeon, the son of J
Luke 3:33 son of Perez, the son of J
Heb 7:14 that our Lord arose from J
Heb 8: 8 Israel and with the house of J
Rev 5: 5 the Lion of the tribe of J
Rev 7: 5 of the tribe of J twelve

JUDAH'S (*see* JUDAH)
Gen 38: 7 J firstborn, was wicked in
Gen 38:12 of Shua, J wife, died
2Ki 8:20 revolted against J authority
2Ki 8:22 J authority to this day
2Ch 21: 8 revolted against J authority
2Ch 21:10 J authority to this day
Jer 32: 2 was in the king of J house
Jer 38:22 J house shall be surrendered

JUDAISM (*see* JEW)
Gal 1:13 of my former conduct in J
Gal 1:14 I advanced in J beyond many

JUDAS (*see* BARSABAS, ISCARIOT, JUDE, LEBBAEUS, THADDAEUS)
Matt 10: 4 J Iscariot, who also betrayed
Matt 13:55 James, Joses, Simon, and J
Matt 26:14 called J Iscariot, went to
Matt 26:25 Then J, who was betraying Him
Matt 26:47 was still speaking, behold, J
Matt 27: 3 Then J, His betrayer, seeing
Mark 3:19 J Iscariot, who also betrayed
Mark 6: 3 and brother of James, Joses, J
Mark 14:10 Then J Iscariot, one of the
Mark 14:43 He was still speaking, J, one
Luke 6:16 J the son of James, and J
Luke 6:16 J Iscariot who also became a
Luke 22: 3 Then Satan entered J,
Luke 22:47 and he who was called J, one
Luke 22:48 J, are you betraying the Son
John 6:71 He spoke of J Iscariot, the
John 12: 4 J Iscariot, Simon's son, who
John 13: 2 into the heart of J Iscariot
John 13:26 He gave it to J Iscariot
John 13:29 because J had the money box,
John 14:22 J (not Iscariot) said to Him,
John 18: 2 And J, who betrayed Him, also
John 18: 3 Then J, having received a
John 18: 5 And J, who betrayed Him,
Acts 1:13 and J the son of James
Acts 1:16 mouth of David concerning J
Acts 1:25 which J by transgression fell
Acts 5:37 J of Galilee rose up in the
Acts 9:11 of J for one called Saul of
Acts 15:22 J who was also named Barsabas
Acts 15:27 We have therefore sent J and
Acts 15:32 Now J and Silas, themselves

JUDE (*see* JUDAS)
Jude 1 J, a servant of Jesus Christ,

JUDEA (*see* JUDAH, JUDEAN)
Ezra 5: 8 went into the province of J
Matt 2: 1 of J in the days of Herod the
Matt 2: 5 In Bethlehem of J, for thus
Matt 2:22 J instead of his father Herod
Matt 3: 1 in the wilderness of J,
Matt 3: 5 Then Jerusalem, all J, and all
Matt 4:25 from Decapolis, Jerusalem, J
Matt 19: 1 region of J beyond the Jordan
Matt 24:16 in J flee to the mountains
Mark 1: 5 And all the land of J, and
Mark 3: 7 followed Him, and from J
Mark 10: 1 came to the region of J by
Mark 13:14 in J flee to the mountains
Luke 1: 5 days of Herod, the king of J
Luke 1:65 all the hill country of J
Luke 2: 4 the city of Nazareth, into J
Luke 3: 1 Pilate being governor of J
Luke 5:17 of every town of Galilee, J
Luke 6:17 of people from all J and
Luke 7:17 Him went throughout all J
Luke 21:21 Then let those in J flee to
Luke 23: 5 teaching throughout all J
John 3:22 came into the land of J, and
John 4: 3 He left J and departed again
John 4:47 come out of J into Galilee
John 4:54 come out of J into Galilee
John 7: 1 He did not want to walk in J
John 7: 3 Depart from here and go into J
John 11: 7 Let us go to J again
Acts 1: 8 Me in Jerusalem, and in all J
Acts 2: 9 dwelling in Mesopotamia, J
Acts 2:14 Men of J and all who dwell in
Acts 8: 1 throughout the regions of J
Acts 9:31 the churches throughout all J
Acts 10:37 proclaimed throughout all J
Acts 11: 1 brethren who were in J heard
Acts 11:29 to the brethren dwelling in J
Acts 12:19 went down from J to Caesarea
Acts 15: 1 certain men came down from J
Acts 21:10 Agabus came down from J
Acts 26:20 all the region of J, and then
Acts 28:21 letters from J concerning you
Rom 15:31 those in J who do not believe
2Co 1:16 helped by you on my way to J
Gal 1:22 of J which were in Christ
1Th 2:14 are in J in Christ Jesus

JUDEAN (*see* JUDEA)
Neh 11:36 Some of the J divisions of

JUDGE (*see* JUDGED, JUDGES, JUDGING, JUDGMENT)
Gen 15:14 whom they serve I will j
Gen 16: 5 The LORD j between you and me
Gen 18:25 Shall not the J of all the
Gen 19: 9 and he keeps acting as a j
Gen 31:37 that they may j between us
Gen 31:53 of their father j between us
Gen 49:16 Dan shall j his people as one
Ex 2:14 you a prince and a j over us
Ex 5:21 Let the LORD look on you and j
Ex 18:13 Moses sat to j the people
Ex 18:16 I j between one and another
Ex 18:22 let them j the people at all
Ex 18:22 they themselves shall j
Lev 19:15 you shall j your neighbor
Num 35:24 shall j between the manslayer
Deut 1:16 j righteously between a man

Deut 16:18 they shall **j** the people with
Deut 17: 8 is too hard for you to **j**,
Deut 17: 9 to the **j** there in those days,
Deut 17:12 the LORD your God, or the **j**
Deut 25: 1 that the judges may **j** them
Deut 25: 2 that the **j** will cause him to
Deut 32:36 the LORD will **j** His people
Judg 2:18 them, the LORD was with the **j**
Judg 2:18 enemies all the days of the **j**
Judg 2:19 to pass, when the **j** was dead
Judg 11:27 May the LORD, the **J**, render
1Sa 2:10 The LORD will **j** the ends of
1Sa 2:25 another, God will **j** him
1Sa 3:13 **j** his house forever for the
1Sa 8: 5 to **j** us like all the nations
1Sa 8: 6 Give us a king to **j** us
1Sa 8:20 and that our king may **j** us
1Sa 24:12 Let the LORD **j** between you
1Sa 24:15 Therefore let the LORD be **j**
1Sa 24:15 **j** between you and me, and see
2Sa 15: 4 I were made **j** in the land
1Ki 3: 9 heart to **j** Your people, that
1Ki 3: 9 For who is able to **j** this
1Ki 7: 7 of Judgment, where he might **j**
1Ki 8:32 **j** Your servants, condemning
1Ch 16:33 He is coming to **j** the earth
2Ch 1:10 for who can **j** this great
2Ch 1:11 that you may **j** My people over
2Ch 6:23 **j** Your servants, bringing
2Ch 19: 6 for you do not **j** for man but
2Ch 20:12 our God, will You not **j** them
Ezra 7:25 and judges who may **j** all the
Job 9:15 I would beg mercy of my **J**
Job 22:13 Can He **j** through the deep
Job 23: 7 delivered forever from my **J**
Ps 7: 8 The LORD shall **j** the peoples
Ps 7: 8 **J** me, O LORD, according to my
Ps 7:11 God is a just **j**, And God is
Ps 9: 8 He shall **j** the world in
Ps 50: 4 that He may **j** His people
Ps 50: 6 For God Himself is **J**
Ps 51: 4 And blameless when You **j**
Ps 58: 1 Do you **j** uprightly, you sons
Ps 67: 4 For You shall **j** the people
Ps 72: 2 He will **j** Your people with
Ps 75: 2 time, I will **j** uprightly
Ps 75: 7 But God is the **J**
Ps 82: 2 How long will you **j** unjustly
Ps 82: 8 Arise, O God, **j** the earth
Ps 94: 2 Rise up, O **J** of the earth
Ps 96:10 He shall **j** the peoples
Ps 96:13 He is coming to **j** the earth
Ps 96:13 He shall **j** the world with
Ps 98: 9 He is coming to **j** the earth
Ps 98: 9 He shall **j** the world, And the
Ps 110: 6 He shall **j** among the nations,
Ps 135:14 the LORD will **j** His people
Prov 31: 9 **j** righteously, and plead the
Eccl 3:17 God shall **j** the righteous and
Is 2: 4 He shall **j** between the
Is 3: 2 man and the man of war, the **j**
Is 3:13 and stands to **j** the people
Is 5: 3 Jerusalem and men of Judah, **j**
Is 11: 3 He shall not **j** by the sight
Is 11: 4 He shall **j** the poor, and
Is 33:22 (for the LORD is our **J**, the
Is 51: 5 and My arms will **j** the peoples
Is 66:16 the LORD will **j** all flesh
Jer 11:20 hosts, you who **j** righteously,
Lam 3:59 I am wronged; **j** my case.
Ezek 7: 3 I will **j** you according to
Ezek 7: 8 I will **j** you according to
Ezek 7:27 they deserve I will **j** them
Ezek 11:10 I will **j** you at the border of
Ezek 11:11 I will **j** you at the border of
Ezek 16:38 I will **j** you as women who
Ezek 18:30 Therefore I will **j** you, O
Ezek 20: 4 Will you **j** them, son of man,
Ezek 20: 4 son of man, will you **j** them
Ezek 21:30 I will **j** you in the place
Ezek 22: 2 Now, son of man, will you **j**
Ezek 22: 2 will you **j** the bloody city
Ezek 23:24 they shall **j** you according to
Ezek 23:36 Son of man, will you **j** Oholah
Ezek 23:45 But righteous men will **j** them
Ezek 24:14 to your deeds they will **j** you
Ezek 33:20 I will **j** every one of you
Ezek 34:17 I shall **j** between sheep and
Ezek 34:20 I Myself will **j** between the
Ezek 34:22 I will **j** between sheep and
Ezek 35:11 known among them when I **j** you
Ezek 44:24 and **j** it according to My
Joel 3:12 for there I will sit to **j** all
Amos 2: 3 cut off the **j** from its midst
Obad 21 to **j** the mountains of Esau
Mic 3:11 her heads **j** for a bribe, her
Mic 4: 3 He shall **j** between many
Mic 5: 1 they will strike the **j** of
Mic 7: 3 the **j** seeks a bribe, and the
Zech 3: 7 you shall also **j** My house
Matt 5:25 deliver you to the **j**, the
Matt 5:25 the **j** hand you over to the
Matt 7: 1 **J** not, that you be not judged
Matt 7: 2 For with what judgment you **j**
Luke 6:37 **J** not, and you shall not be
Luke 12:14 Man, who made Me a **j** or an
Luke 12:57 do you not **j** what is right
Luke 12:58 lest he drag you to the **j**
Luke 12:58 the **j** deliver you to the
Luke 18: 2 was in a certain city a **j** who
Luke 18: 6 Hear what the unjust **j** said
Luke 19:22 your own mouth I will **j** you
John 5:30 As I hear, I **j**
John 7:24 Do not **j** according to
John 7:24 but **j** with righteous judgment
John 7:51 Does our law **j** a man before
John 8:15 You **j** according to the flesh
John 8:15 I **j** no one
John 8:16 And yet if I do **j**, My judgment
John 8:26 to **j** concerning you, but He
John 12:47 not believe, I do not **j** him
John 12:47 for I did not come to **j** the
John 12:48 will **j** him in the last day
John 18:31 **j** Him according to your law
Acts 4:19 you more than to God, you **j**
Acts 7: 7 will be in bondage I will **j**
Acts 7:27 you a ruler and a **j** over us
Acts 7:35 Who made you a ruler and a **j**
Acts 10:42 by God to be **J** of the living
Acts 13:46 and **j** yourselves unworthy of
Acts 15:19 Therefore I **j** that we should
Acts 17:31 a day on which He will **j** the
Acts 18:15 to be a **j** of such matters
Acts 23: 3 For you sit to **j** me according
Acts 24: 6 wanted to **j** him according to
Acts 24:10 many years a **j** of this nation
Rom 2: 1 O man, whoever you are who **j**
Rom 2: 1 you **j** another you condemn
Rom 2: 1 for you who **j** practice the
Rom 2: 3 you who **j** those practicing
Rom 2:16 in the day when God will **j**
Rom 2:27 **j** you who, even with your
Rom 3: 6 then how will God **j** the world
Rom 14: 3 does not eat **j** him who eats
Rom 14: 4 Who are you to **j** another's
Rom 14:10 But why do you **j** your brother
Rom 14:13 us not **j** one another anymore
1Co 4: 3 fact, I do not even **j** myself
1Co 4: 5 Therefore **j** nothing before
1Co 5:12 Do you not **j** those who are
1Co 6: 2 the saints will **j** the world
1Co 6: 2 are you unworthy to **j** the
1Co 6: 3 know that we shall **j** angels
1Co 6: 4 esteemed by the church to **j**
1Co 6: 5 who will be able to **j** between
1Co 10:15 **j** for yourselves what I say
1Co 11:13 **J** among yourselves
1Co 11:31 For if we would **j** ourselves
1Co 14:29 speak, and let the others **j**
2Co 5:14 us, because we **j** thus
Col 2:16 Therefore let no one **j** you in
2Ti 4: 1 who will **j** the living and the
2Ti 4: 8 the Lord, the righteous **J**
Heb 10:30 The LORD will **j** His people
Heb 12:23 heaven, to God the **J** of all
Heb 13: 4 and adulterers God will **j**
Jas 4:11 But if you **j** the law, you are
Jas 4:11 not a doer of the law but a **j**
Jas 4:12 Who are you to **j** another
Jas 5: 9 the **J** is standing at the door
1Pe 4: 5 who is ready to **j** the living
Rev 6:10 holy and true, until You **j**

JUDGED (*see* JUDGE)
Gen 30: 6 God has **j** my case
Ex 18:26 So they **j** the people at all
Ex 18:26 but they **j** every small case
Judg 3:10 came upon him, and he **j** Israel
Judg 10: 2 He **j** Israel twenty-three
Judg 10: 3 he **j** Israel twenty-two years
Judg 12: 7 Jephthah **j** Israel six years
Judg 12: 8 Ibzan of Bethlehem **j** Israel
Judg 12: 9 He **j** Israel seven years
Judg 12:11 Elon the Zebulunite **j** Israel
Judg 12:11 He **j** Israel ten years
Judg 12:13 the Pirathonite **j** Israel
Judg 12:14 He **j** Israel eight years
Judg 15:20 he **j** Israel twenty years in
Judg 16:31 He had **j** Israel twenty years
1Sa 4:18 he had **j** Israel forty years
1Sa 7: 6 And Samuel **j** the children of
1Sa 7:15 So Samuel **j** Israel all the
1Sa 7:16 **j** Israel in all those places
1Sa 7:17 There he **j** Israel, and there
2Ki 23:22 of the judges who **j** Israel
Ps 9:19 nations be **j** in Your sight
Ps 37:33 Nor condemn him when he is **j**
Ps 109: 7 When he is **j**, let him be
Jer 22:16 He **j** the cause of the poor and
Ezek 16:38 wedlock or shed blood are **j**
Ezek 16:52 You who **j** your sisters, bear
Ezek 28:23 the wounded shall be **j** in her
Ezek 36:19 I **j** them according to their
Dan 9:12 against our judges who **j** us
Matt 7: 1 Judge not, that you be not **j**
Matt 7: 2 you judge, you will be **j**
Luke 6:37 not, and you shall not be **j**
Luke 7:43 You have rightly **j**
John 16:11 the ruler of this world is **j**
Acts 4: 9 If we this day are **j** for a
Acts 16:15 If you have **j** me to be
Acts 23: 6 of the dead I am being **j**
Acts 24:21 I am being **j** by you this day
Acts 25: 9 and there be **j** before me
Acts 25:10 seat, where I ought to be **j**
Acts 25:20 there be **j** concerning these
Acts 26: 6 and am **j** for the hope of the
Rom 2:12 the law will be **j** by the law
Rom 3: 4 may overcome when You are **j**
Rom 3: 7 am I also still **j** as a sinner
1Co 2:15 is rightly **j** by no one
1Co 4: 3 thing that I should be **j** by
1Co 5: 3 in spirit, have already **j**
1Co 6: 2 if the world will be **j** by you
1Co 10:29 For why is my liberty **j** by
1Co 11:31 ourselves, we would not be **j**
1Co 11:32 But when we are **j**, we are
1Co 14:24 by all, he is **j** by all
Heb 11:11 because she **j** Him faithful
Jas 2:12 be **j** by the law of liberty
1Pe 4: 6 dead, that they might be **j**
Rev 11:18 dead, that they should be **j**
Rev 16: 5 You have **j** these things
Rev 19: 2 because He has **j** the great
Rev 20:12 the dead were **j** according to
Rev 20:13 And they were **j**, each one

JUDGES (*see* JUDGE, JUDGES')
Ex 21: 6 shall bring him to the **j**
Ex 21:22 shall pay as the **j** determine
Ex 22: 8 shall be brought to the **j** to
Ex 22: 9 shall come before the **j**
Ex 22: 9 whomever the **j** condemn shall
Num 25: 5 Moses said to the **j** of Israel
Deut 1:16 commanded your **j** at that time
Deut 16:18 You shall appoint **j** and
Deut 19:17 the **j** who serve in those days
Deut 19:18 the **j** shall make diligent
Deut 21: 2 your **j** shall go out, and they
Deut 25: 1 that the **j** may judge them, and
Deut 32:31 enemies themselves being **j**
Josh 8:33 their elders and officers and **j**
Josh 23: 2 for their heads, for their **j**
Josh 24: 1 for their heads, for their **j**
Judg 2:16 Then the LORD raised up **j** who
Judg 2:17 would not listen to their **j**
Judg 2:18 the LORD raised up **j** for them
Ruth 1: 1 in the days when the **j** ruled
1Sa 8: 1 made his sons **j** over Israel
1Sa 8: 2 they were **j** in Beersheba
2Sa 7:11 the time that I commanded **j**
2Ki 23:22 of the **j** who judged Israel
1Ch 17: 6 to any of the **j** of Israel
1Ch 17:10 the time that I commanded **j**
1Ch 23: 4 thousand were officers and **j**
1Ch 26:29 and **j** over Israel outside
2Ch 1: 2 and of hundreds, to the **j**, and
2Ch 19: 5 Then he set **j** in the land
2Ch 19: 6 and said to the **j**, "Take heed
Ezra 7:25 and **j** who may judge all the
Ezra 10:14 **j** of their cities, until the
Job 9:24 He covers the faces of its **j**

Job 12:17 and makes fools of the j
Job 21:22 since He j those who are on
Job 36:31 For by these He j the peoples
Ps 2:10 you j of the earth
Ps 58:11 He is God who j in the earth
Ps 82: 1 He j among the gods
Ps 141: 6 Their j are overthrown by the
Ps 148:11 Princes and all j of the earth
Prov 8:16 all the j of the earth
Prov 29:14 The king who j the poor with
Is 1:26 your j as at the first, and
Is 40:23 He makes the j of the earth
Ezek 44:24 they shall stand as j, and
Dan 3: 2 the treasurers, the j, the
Dan 3: 3 the treasurers, the j, the
Dan 9:12 against our j who judged us,
Hos 7: 7 and have devoured their j
Hos 13:10 your j to whom you said
Zeph 3: 3 her j are evening wolves that
Matt 12:27 they shall be your j
Luke 11:19 Therefore they will be your j
John 5:22 For the Father j no one, but
John 8:50 there is One who seeks and j
John 12:48 words, has that which j him
Acts 13:20 them j for about four hundred
1Co 2:15 who is spiritual j all things
1Co 4: 4 but He who j me is the Lord
1Co 5:13 those who are outside God j
Jas 2: 4 become j with evil thoughts
Jas 4:11 j his brother, speaks evil of
Jas 4:11 evil of the law and j the law
1Pe 1:17 who without partiality j
1Pe 2:23 to Him who j righteously
Rev 18: 8 is the Lord God who j her
Rev 19:11 and in righteousness He j

JUDGES' (*see* JUDGES)
Judg 5:10 donkeys, who sit in j attire

JUDGING (*see* JUDGE)
Judg 4: 4 was j Israel at that time
2Ki 15: 5 j the people of the land
2Ch 26:21 j the people of the land
Ps 9: 4 the throne j in righteousness
Is 16: 5 in the tabernacle of David, j
Matt 19:28 j the twelve tribes of Israel
Luke 22:30 sit on thrones j the twelve
1Co 5:12 j those also who are outside

JUDGMENT (*see* JUDGE, JUDGMENTS)
Ex 12:12 of Egypt I will execute j
Ex 21:31 according to this j it shall
Ex 23: 6 You shall not pervert the j
Ex 28:15 make the breastplate of j
Ex 28:29 of j over his heart, when he
Ex 28:30 the breastplate of j the Urim
Ex 28:30 So Aaron shall bear the j of
Lev 19:15 shall do no injustice in j
Lev 19:35 shall do no injustice in j
Num 27:11 of Israel a statute of j,
Num 27:21 for him by the j of the Urim
Num 35:12 before the congregation in j
Num 35:29 shall be a statute of j to
Deut 1:17 not show partiality in j
Deut 1:17 presence, for the j is God's
Deut 16:18 judge the people with just j
Deut 17: 8 between one j or another
Deut 17: 9 upon you the sentence of j
Deut 17:11 according to the j which they
Deut 32:41 and My hand takes hold on j
Josh 20: 6 before the congregation for j
Judg 4: 5 Israel came up to her for j
Judg 11:27 render j this day between the
2Sa 8:15 and David administered j and
2Sa 15: 6 who came to the king for j
1Ki 3:28 all Israel heard of the j
1Ki 7: 7 for the throne, the Hall of J
1Ki 20:40 So shall your j be
2Ki 25: 6 and they pronounced j on him
1Ch 12:17 our fathers look and bring j
1Ch 18:14 all Israel, and administered j
2Ch 19: 6 who is with you in the j
2Ch 19: 8 for the j of the LORD and for
2Ch 20: 9 upon us, such as the sword, j
2Ch 22: 8 j on the house of Ahab, and
2Ch 24:24 they executed j against Joash
Ezra 7:26 let j be executed speedily on
Job 8: 3 Does God subvert j
Job 11:10 imprisons, and gathers to j
Job 14: 3 bring me to j with Yourself
Job 19:29 you may know there is a j
Job 22: 4 and enters into j with you
Job 31:11 would be iniquity worthy of j
Job 31:28 be an iniquity worthy of j
Job 34:23 he should go before God in j
Job 36:17 with the j due the wicked
Job 36:17 j and justice take hold of you
Job 37:23 is excellent in power, in j
Job 40: 8 Would you indeed annul My j
Ps 1: 5 shall not stand in the j, Nor
Ps 7: 6 to the j You have commanded
Ps 9: 7 has prepared His throne for j
Ps 9: 8 j for the peoples in
Ps 9:16 is known by the j He executes
Ps 76: 8 You caused j to be heard from
Ps 76: 9 When God arose to j, To
Ps 94:15 But j will return to
Ps 119:66 Teach me good j and
Ps 119:84 When will You execute j on
Ps 122: 5 thrones are set there for j
Ps 143: 2 into j with Your servant, For
Ps 149: 9 execute on them the written j
Prov 1: 3 of wisdom, Justice, j, and
Prov 16:10 must not transgress in j
Prov 18: 1 he rages against all wise j
Prov 18: 5 overthrow the righteous in j
Prov 20: 8 who sits on the throne of j
Prov 24:23 good to show partiality in j
Eccl 3:16 In the place of j, wickedness
Eccl 8: 5 heart discerns both time and j
Eccl 8: 6 matter there is a time and j
Eccl 11: 9 God will bring you into j
Eccl 12:14 will bring every work into j
Is 3:14 into j with the elders of His
Is 4: 4 her midst, by the spirit of j
Is 5:16 hosts shall be exalted in j
Is 9: 7 it and establish it with j
Is 16: 3 Take counsel, execute j
Is 28: 6 justice to him who sits in j
Is 28: 7 in vision, they stumble in j
Is 28:26 He instructs him in right j
Is 34: 5 the people of My curse, for j
Is 41: 1 us come near together for j
Is 53: 8 taken from prison and from j
Is 54:17 you in j you shall condemn
Jer 4: 2 LORD lives,' in truth, in j
Jer 4:12 also speak j against them
Jer 5: 1 is anyone who executes j, who
Jer 5: 4 the LORD, the j of their God
Jer 5: 5 the LORD, the j of their God
Jer 7: 5 execute j between a man and
Jer 8: 7 do not know the j of the LORD
Jer 9:24 exercising lovingkindness, j
Jer 21:12 Execute j in the morning
Jer 22: 3 Execute j and righteousness,
Jer 23: 5 and prosper, and execute j and
Jer 33:15 He shall execute j and
Jer 39: 5 where he pronounced j on him
Jer 48:21 And j has come on the plain
Jer 48:47 Thus far is the j of Moab
Jer 49:12 those whose j was not to
Jer 51: 9 for her j reaches to heaven
Jer 51:47 j on the carved images of
Jer 51:52 That I will bring j on her
Jer 52: 9 and he pronounced j on him
Ezek 18: 8 executed true j between man
Ezek 23:10 they had executed j on her
Ezek 23:24 I will delegate j to them
Ezek 34:16 the strong, and feed them in j
Ezek 38:22 him to j with pestilence and
Ezek 39:21 My j which I have executed
Dan 7:22 a j was made in favor of the
Hos 5: 1 For yours is the j, because
Hos 5:11 is oppressed and broken in j
Hos 10: 4 Thus j springs up like
Joel 3: 2 I will enter into j with them
Hab 1: 4 therefore perverse j proceeds
Hab 1: 7 Their j and their dignity
Hab 1:12 You have appointed them for j
Zech 8:16 give j in your gates for
Mal 3: 5 And I will come near you for j
Matt 5:21 will be in danger of the j
Matt 5:22 shall be in danger of the j
Matt 7: 2 For with what j you judge
Matt 10:15 day of j than for that city
Matt 11:22 in the day of j than for you
Matt 11:24 in the day of j than for you
Matt 12:36 account of it in the day of j
Matt 12:41 in the j with this generation
Matt 12:42 in the j with this generation
Matt 27:19 he was sitting on the j seat
Mark 6:11 day of j than for that city
Luke 10:14 Sidon at the j than for you
Luke 11:31 in the j with the men of this
Luke 11:32 in the j with this generation
John 5:22 committed all j to the Son
John 5:24 and shall not come into j
John 5:27 authority to execute j also
John 5:30 My j is righteous, because I
John 7:24 but judge with righteous j
John 8:16 if I do judge, My j is true
John 9:39 For j I have come into this
John 12:31 Now is the j of this world
John 16: 8 and of righteousness, and of j
John 16:11 of j, because the ruler of
John 19:13 sat down in the j seat in a
Acts 18:12 and brought him to the j seat
Acts 18:16 he drove them from the j seat
Acts 18:17 and beat him before the j seat
Acts 24:25 and the j to come, Felix was
Acts 25: 6 day, sitting on the j seat
Acts 25:10 I stand at Caesar's j seat
Acts 25:15 asking for a j against him
Acts 25:17 next day I sat on the j seat
Rom 1:32 the righteous j of God, that
Rom 2: 2 But we know that the j of God
Rom 2: 3 you will escape the j of God
Rom 2: 5 of the righteous j of God
Rom 5:16 For the j which came from one
Rom 5:18 offense j came to all men
Rom 13: 2 will bring j on themselves
Rom 14:10 before the j seat of Christ
1Co 1:10 same mind and in the same j
1Co 7:25 yet I give j as one whom the
1Co 7:40 as she is, according to my j
1Co 11:29 and drinks j to himself, not
1Co 11:34 lest you come together for j
2Co 5:10 before the j seat of Christ
Gal 5:10 troubles you shall bear his j
2Th 1: 5 of the righteous j of God
1Ti 5:24 evident, preceding them to j
Heb 6: 2 of the dead, and of eternal j
Heb 9:27 once, but after this the j
Heb 10:27 fearful expectation of j, and
Jas 2:13 For j is without mercy to the
Jas 2:13 Mercy triumphs over j
Jas 3: 1 we shall receive a stricter j
Jas 5:12 No," lest you fall into j
1Pe 4:17 j to begin at the house of
2Pe 2: 3 their j has not been idle
2Pe 2: 4 to be reserved for j
2Pe 2: 9 punishment for the day of j
2Pe 3: 7 for fire until the day of j
1Jn 4:17 have boldness in the day of j
Jude 6 for the j of the great day
Jude 15 to execute j on all, to
Rev 14: 7 the hour of His j has come
Rev 17: 1 I will show you the j of the
Rev 18:10 in one hour your j has come
Rev 20: 4 and j was committed to them

JUDGMENTS (*see* JUDGMENT)
Ex 6: 6 arm and with great j
Ex 7: 4 the land of Egypt by great j
Ex 21: 1 Now these are the j which you
Ex 24: 3 of the LORD and all the j
Lev 18: 4 You shall observe My j and
Lev 18: 5 keep My statutes and My j,
Lev 18:26 keep My statutes and My j, and
Lev 19:37 all My statutes and all My j
Lev 20:22 all My statutes and all My j
Lev 25:18 My statutes and keep My j, and
Lev 26:15 or if your soul abhors My j
Lev 26:43 because they despised My j
Lev 26:46 These are the statutes and j
Num 33: 4 gods the LORD had executed j
Num 35:24 of blood according to these j
Num 36:13 and the j which the LORD
Deut 4: 1 the j which I teach you to
Deut 4: 5 have taught you statutes and j
Deut 4: 8 righteous j as are in all
Deut 4:14 to teach you statutes and j
Deut 4:45 the j which Moses spoke to
Deut 5: 1 and j which I speak in your
Deut 5:31 the j which you shall teach
Deut 6: 1 j which the LORD your God has
Deut 6:20 the j which the LORD our God
Deut 7:11 the j which I command you
Deut 7:12 because you listen to these j
Deut 8:11 His commandments, His j, and
Deut 11: 1 charge, His statutes, His j
Deut 11:32 and j which I set before you
Deut 12: 1 j which you shall be careful

Deut 26:16 observe these statutes and **j**
Deut 26:17 His commandments, and His **j**
Deut 30:16 His statutes, and His **j**, that
Deut 33:10 They shall teach Jacob Your **j**
Deut 33:21 LORD, and His **j** with Israel
2Sa 22:23 For all His **j** were before me
1Ki 2: 3 His commandments, His **j**, and
1Ki 6:12 in My statutes, execute My **j**
1Ki 8:58 and His statutes and His **j**,
1Ki 9: 4 you keep My statutes and My **j**
1Ki 11:33 and keep My statutes and My **j**
1Ch 16:12 and the **j** of His mouth,
1Ch 16:14 His **j** are in all the earth
1Ch 22:13 **j** with which the LORD charged
1Ch 28: 7 My commandments and My **j**, as
2Ch 7:17 you keep My statutes and My **j**
Neh 9:29 but sinned against Your **j**
Ps 10: 5 Your **j** are far above, out of
Ps 18:22 For all His **j** were before me,
Ps 19: 9 The **j** of the LORD are true and
Ps 36: 6 Your **j** are a great deep
Ps 48:11 be glad, Because of Your **j**
Ps 72: 1 Give the king Your **j**, O God,
Ps 89:30 My law And do not walk in My **j**
Ps 97: 8 rejoice Because of Your **j**
Ps 105: 5 and the **j** of His mouth,
Ps 105: 7 His **j** are in all the earth
Ps 119: 7 When I learn Your righteous **j**
Ps 119:13 All the **j** of Your mouth
Ps 119:20 For Your **j** at all times
Ps 119:30 Your **j** I have laid before me
Ps 119:39 I dread, For Your **j** are good
Ps 119:52 I remembered Your **j** of old
Ps 119:62 Because of Your righteous **j**
Ps 119:75 O LORD, that Your **j** are right
Ps 119:102 have not departed from Your **j**
Ps 119:106 I will keep Your righteous **j**
Ps 119:108 O LORD, And teach me Your **j**
Ps 119:120 You, And I am afraid of Your **j**
Ps 119:137 O LORD, And upright are Your **j**
Ps 119:156 Revive me according to Your **j**
Ps 119:160 righteous **j** endures forever
Ps 119:164 Because of Your righteous **j**
Ps 119:175 And let Your **j** help me
Ps 147:19 statutes and His **j** to Israel
Ps 147:20 And as for His **j**, they have
Prov 19:29 **J** are prepared for scoffers,
Is 26: 8 Yes, in the way of Your **j**
Is 26: 9 for when Your **j** are in the
Jer 1:16 I will utter My **j** against
Jer 12: 1 me talk with You about Your **j**
Ezek 5: 6 My **j** by doing wickedness more
Ezek 5: 6 for they have refused My **j**
Ezek 5: 7 in My statutes, nor kept My **j**
Ezek 5: 7 even done according to the **j**
Ezek 5: 8 will execute **j** in your midst
Ezek 5:10 and I will execute **j** among you
Ezek 5:15 when I execute **j** among you in
Ezek 11: 9 and execute **j** on you
Ezek 11:12 My statutes nor executed My **j**
Ezek 11:20 in My statutes and keep My **j**
Ezek 14:21 My four severe **j** on Jerusalem
Ezek 16:41 execute **j** on you in the sight
Ezek 18: 9 and kept My **j** faithfully
Ezek 18:17 but has executed My **j** and
Ezek 20:11 statutes and showed them My **j**
Ezek 20:13 they despised My **j**, which, if
Ezek 20:16 because they despised My **j**
Ezek 20:18 fathers, nor observe their **j**
Ezek 20:19 in My statutes, keep My **j**
Ezek 20:21 not careful to observe My **j**
Ezek 20:24 they had not executed My **j**
Ezek 20:25 **j** by which they could not
Ezek 23:24 you according to their **j**
Ezek 25:11 And I will execute **j** upon Moab
Ezek 28:22 LORD, when I execute **j** in her
Ezek 28:26 when I execute **j** on all those
Ezek 30:14 to Zoan, and execute **j** in No
Ezek 30:19 I will execute **j** on Egypt
Ezek 36:27 and you will keep My **j** and do
Ezek 37:24 they shall also walk in My **j**
Ezek 44:24 and judge it according to My **j**
Dan 9: 5 from Your precepts and Your **j**
Hos 6: 5 your **j** are like light that
Zeph 3:15 LORD has taken away your **j**
Mal 4: 4 with the statutes and **j**
Rom 11:33 How unsearchable are His **j**
1Co 6: 4 If then you have **j** concerning
Rev 15: 4 You, for Your **j** have been
Rev 16: 7 true and righteous are Your **j**
Rev 19: 2 true and righteous are His **j**

JUDITH
Gen 26:34 old, he took as wives **J** the

JUG
Judg 4:19 So she opened a **j** of milk
1Sa 26:11 the **j** of water that are by
1Sa 26:12 the **j** of water by Saul's head
1Sa 26:16 the **j** of water that was by

JUICE (*see* JUICES)
Num 6: 3 shall he drink any grape **j**
Song 8: 2 of the **j** of my pomegranate

JUICES (*see* JUICE)
Ex 22:29 your ripe produce and your **j**

JULIA
Rom 16:15 Greet Philologus and **J**, Nereus

JULIUS
Acts 27: 1 prisoners to one named **J**, a
Acts 27: 3 **J** treated Paul kindly and gave

JUMP
Acts 27:43 swim should **j** overboard first

JUNIA
Rom 16: 7 Greet Andronicus and **J**, my

JUNIPER
Jer 48: 6 And be like the **j** in the

JURISDICTION
Luke 23: 7 that He belonged to Herod's **j**

JUSHAB-HESED
1Ch 3:20 Berechiah, Hasadiah, and **J**

JUST (*see* JUSTICE, JUSTIFY, JUSTLY, UNJUST)
Gen 6: 9 Noah was a **j** man, perfect in
Gen 27:19 I have done **j** as you told me
Gen 32:31 **J** as he crossed over Penuel
Gen 41:13 And it came to pass **j** as he
Gen 41:21 for they were **j** as ugly as at
Gen 50:12 So his sons did for him **j** as
Ex 7: 6 **j** as the LORD commanded them,
Ex 7:10 so, **j** as the LORD commanded
Ex 7:20 so, **j** as the LORD commanded
Ex 8:19 them, **j** as the LORD had said
Ex 9:12 **j** as the LORD had spoken to
Ex 12:25 **j** as He promised, that you
Ex 12:28 **j** as the LORD had commanded
Ex 25: 9 **j** so you shall make it
Ex 39:43 **j** so they had done it
Lev 19:36 You shall have **j** balances
Lev 19:36 **j** weights, a **j** ephah, and a
Lev 19:36 a **j** ephah, and a **j** hin
Num 2:33 **j** as the LORD commanded
Num 14:17 **j** as You have spoken, saying,
Num 14:19 **j** as You have forgiven this
Num 14:28 **j** as you have spoken in My
Num 15:14 **j** as you do, so shall he do
Num 16:40 **j** as the LORD had said to him
Num 17:11 **j** as the LORD had commanded
Num 18:18 **j** as the wave breast and the
Num 20:27 So Moses did **j** as the LORD
Num 23: 2 Balak did **j** as Balaam had
Num 26: 4 **j** as the LORD commanded
Num 27:11 **j** as the LORD commanded
Num 27:23 **j** as the LORD commanded by
Num 29:40 **j** as the LORD commanded
Num 31: 7 **j** as the LORD commanded
Num 32:27 to battle, **j** as my lord says
Num 36:10 **J** as the LORD commanded
Deut 1:41 fight, **j** as the LORD our God
Deut 2:12 **j** as Israel did to the land
Deut 2:14 **j** as the LORD had sworn to
Deut 2:22 **j** as He had done for the
Deut 2:29 **j** as the descendants of Esau
Deut 4: 5 **j** as the LORD my God
Deut 10: 5 **j** as the LORD commanded me
Deut 10: 9 **j** as the LORD your God
Deut 11:25 **j** as He has said to you
Deut 12:21 **j** as I have commanded you, and
Deut 12:22 **J** as the gazelle and the deer
Deut 13:17 **j** as He swore to your fathers
Deut 15: 6 you **j** as He promised you
Deut 16:18 the people with **j** judgment
Deut 16:20 follow what is altogether **j**
Deut 20:17 **j** as the LORD your God has
Deut 22:26 for **j** as when a man rises
Deut 24: 8 **j** as I commanded them, so you
Deut 25:15 have a perfect and **j** weight
Deut 25:15 a perfect and **j** measure
Deut 26:15 **j** as You swore to our fathers
Deut 26:18 **j** as He has promised you,
Deut 26:19 your God, **j** as He has spoken
Deut 27: 3 **j** as the LORD God of your
Deut 28: 9 **j** as He has sworn to you, if
Deut 28:63 that **j** as the LORD rejoiced
Deut 29:13 **j** as He has spoken to you, and
Deut 29:13 **j** as He has sworn to your
Deut 31: 3 you, **j** as the LORD has said
Deut 32:50 **j** as Aaron your brother died
Josh 1:17 **J** as we heeded Moses in all
Josh 4: 8 **j** as Joshua commanded, and
Josh 14:11 **j** as my strength was then, so
Judg 6:39 and let me speak **j** once more
Judg 6:39 **j** once more with the fleece
Judg 7:13 said, "I have **j** had a dream
Judg 7:17 camp you shall do **j** as I do
Judg 7:19 **j** as they had posted the
Judg 13:10 the Man has **j** now appeared to
Judg 16:28 **j** this once, O God, that I
Judg 19:16 **J** then an old man came in
Judg 21:21 and **j** when the daughters of
1Sa 9:12 there he is, **j** ahead of you
2Sa 15:34 **j** as I have been your
2Sa 18:10 I **j** saw Absalom hanging in a
2Sa 18:11 who told him, "You **j** saw him
2Sa 18:31 **J** then the Cushite came, and
2Sa 19:14 **j** as the heart of one man, so
2Sa 19:41 **J** then all the men of Israel
2Sa 23: 3 who rules over men must be **j**
1Ki 1:22 **j** then, while she was still
1Ki 1:30 **j** as I swore to you by the
1Ki 20: 4 **j** as you say, I and all that I
2Ki 4: 3 do not gather **j** a few
2Ki 5:22 **j** now two young men of the
2Ki 6:10 there, not **j** once or twice
2Ki 7:17 **j** as the man of God had said,
2Ki 7:18 So it happened **j** as the man
2Ki 8:18 **j** as the house of Ahab had
1Ch 24:31 These also cast lots **j** as
1Ch 24:31 The chief fathers did **j** as
1Ch 26:12 having duties **j** like their
2Ch 21: 6 **j** as the house of Ahab had
Neh 9:13 gave them **j** ordinances and
Neh 9:33 However You are **j** in all that
Esth 2:20 **j** as Mordecai had charged her
Esth 6: 4 Now Haman had **j** entered the
Job 12: 4 and He answered him, the **j**
Job 27:17 but the **j** will wear it, and
Job 29: 4 **j** as I was in the days of my
Job 31: 6 me be weighed in a **j** balance
Job 34:17 you condemn Him who is most **j**
Job 34:33 **j** because you disavow it
Ps 7: 9 an end, But establish the **j**
Ps 7:11 God is a **j** judge, And God is
Ps 17: 1 Hear a **j** cause, O LORD,
Ps 33:22 upon us, **J** as we hope in You
Ps 37:12 wicked plots against the **j**
Ps 46: 5 her, **j** at the break of dawn
Ps 51: 4 may be found **j** when You speak
Prov 3:12 **j** as a father the son in whom
Prov 3:33 the habitation of the **j**
Prov 4:18 But the path of the **j** is like
Prov 9: 9 teach a **j** man, and he will
Prov 11: 1 but a **j** weight is His delight
Prov 16:11 A **j** weight and balance are the
Prov 17:15 and he who condemns the **j**
Prov 21:15 a joy for the **j** to do justice
Prov 24:29 I will do to him **j** as he has
Prov 29:10 but the **j** seek his well-being
Eccl 5:16 That **j** exactly as he came, so
Eccl 7:15 There is a **j** man who perishes
Eccl 7:20 For there is not a **j** man on
Eccl 8:14 that there are **j** men to whom
Is 20: 3 **J** as My servant Isaiah has
Is 26: 7 way of the **j** is uprightness
Is 26: 7 You weigh the path of the **j**
Is 28: 9 Those **j** weaned from milk
Is 28: 9 Those **j** drawn from the
Is 28:19 it will be a terror **j** to
Is 29:21 turn aside the **j** for a thing
Is 40:27 my **j** claim is passed over by
Is 45:21 Me, a **j** God and a Savior
Is 49: 4 yet surely my **j** reward is
Is 52:14 **J** as many were astonished at
Is 66: 3 **J** as they have chosen their
Jer 5:19 **J** as you have forsaken Me and
Jer 13:10 shall be **j** like this sash
Jer 32:42 **J** as I have brought all this
Jer 39:12 but do to him **j** as he says to

Jer 40: 3 it, and has done **j** as He said
Lam 4:13 her midst the blood of the **j**
Ezek 9:11 **J** then, the man clothed with
Ezek 18: 5 But if a man is **j** and does
Ezek 18: 9 he is **j**
Ezek 20:36 **J** as I pleaded My case with
Ezek 40:23 **j** as the eastern gateway
Ezek 41:25 **j** as they were carved on the
Ezek 45:10 You shall have **j** balances
Ezek 45:10 a **j** ephah, and a **j** bath
Dan 2:41 **j** as you saw the iron mixed
Dan 2:43 **j** as iron does not mix with
Hos 3: 1 **j** like the love of the LORD
Hos 9:13 **J** as I saw Ephraim like Tyre,
Amos 5:12 You afflict the **j** and take
Hab 2: 4 but the **j** shall live by his
Zech 1: 6 **J** as the LORD of hosts
Zech 7:13 that **j** as He proclaimed and
Zech 8:13 **j** as you were a curse among
Zech 8:14 **J** as I determined to punish
Zech 9: 9 He is **j** and having salvation,
Matt 1:19 her husband, being a **j** man
Matt 5:45 good, and sends rain on the **j**
Matt 5:48 **j** as your Father in heaven is
Matt 9:18 My daughter has **j** died, but
Matt 13:49 the wicked from among the **j**
Matt 18:33 **j** as I had pity on you
Matt 19: 3 his wife for **j** any reason
Matt 20:28 **j** as the Son of Man did not
Matt 27:19 nothing to do with that **j** Man
Matt 27:24 of the blood of this **j** Person
Mark 6:20 John, knowing that he was a **j**
Mark 6:56 **j** touch the border of His
Mark 11: 6 So they spoke to them **j** as
Mark 14:16 found it **j** as He had said to
Mark 14:21 **j** as it is written of Him
Mark 15: 8 began to ask him to do **j** as
Luke 1: 2 **j** as those who from the
Luke 1:17 to the wisdom of the **j**, to
Luke 2:25 was Simeon, and this man was **j**
Luke 5:14 to them, **j** as Moses commanded
Luke 6:31 **j** as you want men to do to
Luke 6:36 **j** as your Father also is
Luke 9:54 consume them, **j** as Elijah did
Luke 14:14 at the resurrection of the **j**
Luke 15: 7 **j** persons who need no
Luke 19:32 found it **j** as He had said to
Luke 22:29 **j** as My Father bestowed one
Luke 23:50 member, a good and **j** man
Luke 24:24 found it **j** as the women had
John 5:23 **j** as they honor the Father
John 8:25 **J** what I have been saying to
John 12:50 **j** as the Father has told Me,
John 15:10 **j** as I have kept My Father's
John 17:14 **j** as I am not of the world
John 17:16 **j** as I am not of the world
John 17:22 may be one **j** as We are one
John 21:10 fish which you have **j** caught
Acts 3:14 denied the Holy One and the **J**
Acts 7:52 the coming of the **J** One, of
Acts 10:22 a **j** man, one who fears God and
Acts 10:47 the Holy Spirit **j** as we have
Acts 15: 8 Holy Spirit **j** as He did to us
Acts 15:15 agree, **j** as it is written
Acts 22:14 His will, and see the **J** One
Acts 24:15 of the dead, both of the **j**
Acts 27:25 will be **j** as it was told me
Rom 1:13 **j** as among the other Gentiles
Rom 1:17 The **j** shall live by faith
Rom 2:13 law are **j** in the sight of God
Rom 3: 8 Their condemnation is **j**
Rom 3:26 that He might be **j** and the
Rom 4: 6 **j** as David also describes the
Rom 5:12 **j** as through one man sin
Rom 6: 4 that **j** as Christ was raised
Rom 6:19 For **j** as you presented your
Rom 7:12 the commandment holy and **j**
Rom 11: 8 **J** as it is written
Rom 15: 7 **j** as Christ also received us,
1Co 10:33 **j** as I also please all men in
1Co 11: 1 **j** as I also imitate Christ
1Co 12:18 in the body **j** as He pleased
1Co 13:12 know **j** as I also am known
2Co 3:18 **j** as by the Spirit of the
2Co 10: 7 that **j** as he is Christ's,
2Co 11:12 **j** as we are in the things of
Gal 3: 6 **j** as Abraham "believed God,
Gal 3:11 The **j** shall live by faith
Gal 5:21 **j** as I also told you in time
Eph 1: 4 **j** as He chose us in Him
Eph 2: 3 of wrath, **j** as the others
Eph 4: 4 **j** as you were called in one
Eph 4:32 **j** as God in Christ also
Eph 5:24 **j** as the church is subject to
Eph 5:25 **j** as Christ also loved the
Eph 5:29 **j** as the Lord does the church
Phil 1: 7 **j** as it is right for me to
Phil 4: 8 noble, whatever things are **j**
Col 4: 1 give your servants what is **j**
1Th 2: 7 you, **j** as a nursing mother
1Th 2:14 **j** as they did from the Jews,
1Th 3: 4 **j** as it happened, and you know
1Th 3:12 and to all, **j** as we do to you,
1Th 4: 1 **j** as you received from us how
1Th 5:11 **j** as you also are doing
2Th 3: 1 **j** as it is with you,
Tit 1: 8 what is good, sober-minded, **j**
Heb 2: 2 received a **j** reward,
Heb 5: 4 called by God, **j** as Aaron was
Heb 10:38 Now the **j** shall live by faith
Heb 12:23 spirits of **j** men made perfect
Jas 5: 6 you have murdered the **j**
1Pe 3:18 the **j** for the unjust, that He
2Pe 1:14 **j** as our Lord Jesus Christ
1Jn 1: 9 **j** to forgive us our sins and
1Jn 2: 6 also to walk **j** as He walked
1Jn 2:27 **j** as it has taught you, you
1Jn 3: 3 himself, **j** as He is pure
1Jn 3: 7 **j** as He is righteous
3Jn 2 **j** as your soul prospers
3Jn 3 **j** as you walk in the truth
Rev 15: 3 **J** and true are Your ways
Rev 16: 6 for it is their **j** due
Rev 18: 6 Render to her **j** as she

JUSTICE (*see* JUST)
Gen 18:19 to do righteousness and **j**
Ex 23: 2 aside after many to pervert **j**
Deut 10:18 He administers **j** for the
Deut 16:19 You shall not pervert **j**
Deut 24:17 You shall not pervert **j** due
Deut 27:19 the **j** due the stranger, the
Deut 32: 4 for all His ways are **j**, a God
Deut 33:21 the **j** of the LORD, and His
1Sa 8: 3 took bribes, and perverted **j**
2Sa 8:15 and **j** to all his people
2Sa 15: 4 then I would give him **j**
1Ki 3:11 understanding to discern **j**
1Ki 3:28 was in him to administer **j**
1Ki 10: 9 He made you king, to do **j**
1Ch 18:14 and **j** to all his people
2Ch 9: 8 you king over them, to do **j**
Esth 1:13 toward all who knew law and **j**
Job 8: 3 does the Almighty pervert **j**
Job 9:19 and if of **j**, who will appoint
Job 19: 7 If I cry aloud, there is no **j**
Job 27: 2 who has taken away my **j**, and
Job 29:14 my **j** was like a robe and a
Job 32: 9 the aged always understand **j**
Job 34: 4 Let us choose **j** for ourselves
Job 34: 5 but God has taken away my **j**
Job 34:12 will the Almighty pervert **j**
Job 34:17 Should one who hates **j** govern
Job 35:14 yet **j** is before Him, and you
Job 36: 6 but gives **j** to the oppressed
Job 36:17 and **j** take hold of you
Job 37:23 in judgment and abundant **j**
Ps 10:18 To do **j** to the fatherless and
Ps 25: 9 The humble He guides in **j**
Ps 33: 5 He loves righteousness and **j**
Ps 37: 6 And your **j** as the noonday
Ps 37:28 For the LORD loves **j**, And does
Ps 37:30 And his tongue talks of **j**
Ps 72: 2 And Your poor with **j**
Ps 72: 4 He will bring **j** to the poor
Ps 82: 3 Do **j** to the afflicted and
Ps 89:14 **j** are the foundation of Your
Ps 97: 2 **j** are the foundation of His
Ps 99: 4 King's strength also loves **j**
Ps 99: 4 You have executed **j** and
Ps 101: 1 I will sing of mercy and **j**
Ps 103: 6 **j** for all who are oppressed
Ps 106: 3 Blessed are those who keep **j**
Ps 111: 7 of His hands are verity and **j**
Ps 119:121 I have done **j** and
Ps 119:149 revive me according to Your **j**
Ps 140:12 afflicted, And **j** for the poor
Ps 146: 7 Who executes **j** for the
Prov 1: 3 the instruction of wisdom, **J**
Prov 2: 8 He guards the paths of **j**, and
Prov 2: 9 understand righteousness and **j**
Prov 8:15 reign, and rulers decree **j**
Prov 8:20 the midst of the paths of **j**
Prov 13:23 for lack of **j** there is waste
Prov 16: 8 than vast revenues without **j**
Prov 17:23 back to pervert the ways of **j**
Prov 19:28 disreputable witness scorns **j**
Prov 21: 3 **j** is more acceptable to the
Prov 21: 7 because they refuse to do **j**
Prov 21:15 is a joy for the just to do **j**
Prov 28: 5 Evil men do not understand **j**
Prov 29: 4 establishes the land by **j**
Prov 29:26 but **j** for man comes from the
Prov 31: 5 and pervert the **j** of all the
Eccl 5: 8 the violent perversion of **j**
Is 1:17 seek **j**, reprove the oppressor
Is 1:21 It was full of **j**
Is 1:27 Zion shall be redeemed with **j**
Is 5: 7 He looked for **j**, but behold,
Is 5:23 and take away **j** from the
Is 9: 7 **j** from that time forward,
Is 10: 2 to rob the needy of **j**, and to
Is 16: 5 David, judging and seeking **j**
Is 28: 6 for a spirit of **j** to him who
Is 28:17 Also I will make **j** the
Is 30:18 For the LORD is a God of **j**
Is 32: 1 and princes will rule with **j**
Is 32: 7 even when the needy speaks **j**
Is 32:16 Then **j** will dwell in the
Is 33: 5 He has filled Zion with **j**
Is 40:14 taught Him in the path of **j**
Is 42: 1 bring forth **j** to the Gentiles
Is 42: 3 will bring forth **j** for truth
Is 42: 4 established **j** in the earth
Is 51: 4 I will make My **j** rest as a
Is 56: 1 Keep **j**, and do righteousness,
Is 58: 2 ask of Me the ordinances of **j**
Is 59: 4 No one calls for **j**, nor does
Is 59: 8 there is no **j** in their ways
Is 59: 9 Therefore **j** is far from us,
Is 59:11 we look for **j**, but there is
Is 59:14 **J** is turned back, and
Is 59:15 Him that there was no **j**
Is 61: 8 For I, the LORD, love **j**
Jer 10:24 LORD, correct me, but with **j**
Jer 22:15 father eat and drink, and do **j**
Jer 30:11 But I will correct you in **j**
Jer 31:23 bless you, O habitation of **j**
Jer 50: 7 the LORD, the habitation of **j**
Lam 3:35 to turn aside the **j** due a man
Ezek 45: 9 and plundering, execute **j** and
Dan 4:37 are truth, and His ways **j**
Hos 2:19 to Me in righteousness and **j**
Hos 12: 6 observe mercy and **j**, and wait
Amos 5: 7 you who turn **j** to wormwood
Amos 5:12 the poor from **j** at the gate
Amos 5:15 establish **j** in the gate
Amos 5:24 But let **j** run down like water
Amos 6:12 you have turned **j** into gall
Mic 3: 1 Is it not for you to know **j**
Mic 3: 8 Spirit of the LORD, and of **j**
Mic 3: 9 house of Israel, who abhor **j**
Mic 7: 9 my case and executes **j** for me
Hab 1: 4 and **j** never goes forth
Zeph 2: 3 earth, who have upheld His **j**
Zeph 3: 5 He brings His **j** to light
Zech 7: 9 Execute true **j**, show mercy
Zech 8:16 in your gates for truth, **j**
Mal 2:17 Where is the God of **j**
Matt 12:18 declare **j** to the Gentiles
Matt 12:20 He sends forth **j** to victory
Matt 23:23 **j** and mercy and faith
Luke 11:42 manner of herbs, and pass by **j**
Acts 8:33 His **j** was taken away
Acts 28: 4 yet **j** does not allow to live

JUSTIFICATION (*see* JUSTIFY)
Rom 4:25 was raised because of our **j**
Rom 5:16 many offenses resulted in **j**
Rom 5:18 men, resulting in **j** of life

JUSTIFIED (*see* JUSTIFY)
Job 32: 2 was aroused because he **j**
Job 40: 8 condemn Me that you may be **j**
Is 43: 9 witnesses, that they may be **j**
Is 45:25 of Israel shall be **j**, and
Ezek 16:51 have **j** your sisters by all
Ezek 16:52 because you **j** your sisters
Matt 11:19 But wisdom is **j** by her
Matt 12:37 by your words you will be **j**
Luke 7:29 even the tax collectors **j** God
Luke 7:35 But wisdom is **j** by all her

Luke 18:14 house **j** rather than the other
Acts 13:39 everyone who believes is **j**
Acts 13:39 not be **j** by the law of Moses
Rom 2:13 doers of the law will be **j**
Rom 3: 4 You may be **j** in Your words
Rom 3:20 flesh will be **j** in His sight
Rom 3:24 being **j** freely by His grace
Rom 3:28 is **j** by faith apart from the
Rom 4: 2 For if Abraham was **j** by works
Rom 5: 1 having been **j** by faith, we
Rom 5: 9 now been **j** by His blood, we
Rom 8:30 He called, these He also **j**
Rom 8:30 and whom He **j**, these He also
1Co 4: 4 yet I am not **j** by this
1Co 6:11 but you were **j** in the name of
Gal 2:16 knowing that a man is not **j**
Gal 2:16 that we might be **j** by faith
Gal 2:16 the law no flesh shall be **j**
Gal 2:17 we seek to be **j** by Christ
Gal 3:11 But that no one is **j** by the
Gal 3:24 that we might be **j** by faith
Gal 5: 4 who attempt to be **j** by law
1Ti 3:16 **j** in the Spirit, seen by
Tit 3: 7 that having been **j** by His
Jas 2:21 **j** by works when he offered
Jas 2:24 then that a man is **j** by works
Jas 2:25 not Rahab the harlot also **j**

JUSTIFIER (*see* JUSTIFY)
Rom 3:26 and the **j** of the one who has

JUSTIFIES (*see* JUSTIFY)
Prov 17:15 He who **j** the wicked, and he
Is 50: 8 He is near who **j** Me
Rom 4: 5 on Him who **j** the ungodly, his
Rom 8:33 It is God who **j**

JUSTIFY (*see* JUST, JUSTIFICATION, JUSTIFIED, JUSTIFIER, JUSTIFIES, JUSTIFYING)
Ex 23: 7 For I will not **j** the wicked
Deut 25: 1 and they **j** the righteous and
Job 33:32 speak, for I desire to **j** you
Is 5:23 who **j** the wicked for a bribe,
Is 53:11 Servant shall **j** many, for He
Luke 10:29 But he, wanting to **j** himself
Luke 16:15 them, You are those who **j**
Rom 3:30 **j** the circumcised by faith
Gal 3: 8 would **j** the nations by faith

JUSTIFYING (*see* JUSTIFY)
1Ki 8:32 **j** the righteous by giving him
2Ch 6:23 **j** the righteous by giving him

JUSTLY (*see* JUST)
Mic 6: 8 require of you but to do **j**
Luke 23:41 And we indeed **j**, for we
1Th 2:10 God also, how devoutly and **j**

JUSTUS (*see* BARSABAS, JESUS)
Acts 1:23 Barsabas, who was surnamed **J**
Acts 18: 7 of a certain man named **J**, one
Col 4:11 and Jesus who is called **J**

JUTTAH
Josh 15:55 Maon, Carmel, Ziph, **J**,
Josh 21:16 **J** with its common-land, and

K

KAB
2Ki 6:25 one-fourth of a **k** of dove

KABZEEL (*see* JEKABZEEL)
Josh 15:21 of Edom in the South, were **K**
2Sa 23:20 son of a valiant man from **K**
1Ch 11:22 son of a valiant man from **K**

KADESH (*see* EN MISHPAT, KADESH BARNEA, KEDESH)
Gen 14: 7 is, **K**), and attacked all the
Gen 16:14 observe, it is between **K** and
Gen 20: 1 the South, and dwelt between **K**
Num 13:26 the Wilderness of Paran, at **K**
Num 20: 1 and the people stayed in **K**
Num 20:14 from **K** to the king of Edom
Num 20:16 now here we are in **K**, a city
Num 20:22 journeyed from **K** and came to
Num 27:14 at **K** in the Wilderness of Zin
Num 33:36 Wilderness of Zin, which is **K**
Num 33:37 They moved from **K** and
Deut 1:46 you remained in **K** many days
Deut 32:51 at the waters of Meribah **K**
Judg 11:16 as the Red Sea and came to **K**
Judg 11:17 So Israel remained in **K**
Ps 29: 8 shakes the Wilderness of **K**
Ezek 47:19 to the waters of Meribah by **K**
Ezek 48:28 to the waters of Meribah by **K**

KADESH BARNEA (*see* KADESH)
Num 32: 8 away from **K** to see the land
Num 34: 4 Zin, and be on the south of **K**
Deut 1: 2 by way of Mount Seir to **K**
Deut 1:19 Then we came to **K**
Deut 2:14 **K** until we crossed over the
Deut 9:23 when the LORD sent you from **K**
Josh 10:41 them from **K** as far as Gaza
Josh 14: 6 concerning you and me in **K**
Josh 14: 7 me from **K** to spy out the land
Josh 15: 3 on the south side of **K**,

KADMIEL
Ezra 2:40 the sons of Jeshua and **K**, of
Ezra 3: 9 **K** with his sons, and the sons
Neh 7:43 the children of Jeshua, of **K**
Neh 9: 4 Then Jeshua, Bani, **K**,
Neh 9: 5 Then the Levites, Jeshua, **K**
Neh 10: 9 of the sons of Henadad, and **K**
Neh 12: 8 were Jeshua, Binnui, **K**,
Neh 12:24 and Jeshua the son of **K**, with

KADMONITES
Gen 15:19 the Kenezzites, and the **K**

KAIN
Num 24:22 nevertheless **K** shall be
Josh 15:57 **K**, Gibeah, and Timnah

KALLAI
Neh 12:20 of Sallai, **K**

KANAH
Josh 16: 8 westward to the Brook **K**, and
Josh 17: 9 descended to the Brook **K**,
Josh 19:28 Rehob, Hammon, and **K**

KAREAH (*see* CAREAH)
Jer 40: 8 and Jonathan the sons of **K**
Jer 40:13 Moreover Johanan the son of **K**
Jer 40:15 Then Johanan the son of **K**
Jer 40:16 said to Johanan the son of **K**
Jer 41:11 But when Johanan the son of **K**
Jer 41:13 saw Johanan the son of **K**, and
Jer 41:14 went to Johanan the son of **K**
Jer 41:16 Then Johanan the son of **K**
Jer 42: 1 forces, Johanan the son of **K**
Jer 42: 8 called Johanan the son of **K**
Jer 43: 2 Johanan the son of **K**, and all
Jer 43: 4 So Johanan the son of **K**, all
Jer 43: 5 But Johanan the son of **K** and

KARKAA
Josh 15: 3 to Adar, and went around to **K**

KARKOR
Judg 8:10 Zebah and Zalmunna were at **K**

KARNAIM (*see* ASHTEROTH)
Gen 14: 5 the Rephaim in Ashteroth **K**
Amos 6:13 Have we not taken **K** for

KARTAH (*see* KATTATH)
Josh 21:34 **K** with its common-land,

KARTAN (*see* KIRIATHAIM)
Josh 21:32 and **K** with its common-land

KATTATH (*see* KARTAH, KITRON)
Josh 19:15 Included were **K**, Nahallal,

KEDAR
Gen 25:13 then **K**, Adbeel, Mibsam,
1Ch 1:29 then **K**, Adbeel, Mibsam,
Ps 120: 5 I dwell among the tents of **K**
Song 1: 5 like the tents of **K**, like
Is 21:16 all the glory of **K** will fail
Is 21:17 mighty men of the people of **K**
Is 42:11 the villages that **K** inhabits
Is 60: 7 All the flocks of **K** shall be
Jer 2:10 of Cyprus and see, send to **K**
Jer 49:28 Against **K** and against the
Jer 49:28 Arise, go up to **K**, and
Ezek 27:21 all the princes of **K** were

KEDEMAH
Gen 25:15 Tema, Jetur, Naphish, and **K**
1Ch 1:31 Jetur, Naphish, and **K**

KEDEMOTH
Deut 2:26 from the Wilderness of **K** to
Josh 13:18 Jahaza, **K**, Mephaath,
Josh 21:37 **K** with its common-land, and
1Ch 6:79 **K** with its common-lands, and

KEDESH (*see* KADESH, KISHION)
Josh 12:22 the king of **K**, one
Josh 15:23 **K**, Hazor, Ithnan,
Josh 19:37 **K**, Edrei, En Hazor,
Josh 20: 7 they appointed **K** in Galilee
Josh 21:32 **K** in Galilee with its
Judg 4: 6 of Abinoam from **K** in Naphtali
Judg 4: 9 arose and went with Barak to **K**
Judg 4:10 Zebulun and Naphtali to **K**
Judg 4:11 at Zaanaim, which is beside **K**
2Ki 15:29 Abel Beth Maachah, Janoah, **K**
1Ch 6:72 **K** with its common-lands,
1Ch 6:76 **K** in Galilee with its

KEEP (*see* KEEPER, KEEPING, KEEPS, KEPT)
Gen 2:15 of Eden to tend and **k** it
Gen 6:19 ark, to **k** them alive with you
Gen 6:20 come to you to **k** them alive
Gen 7: 3 to **k** the species alive on the
Gen 17: 9 you shall **k** My covenant, you
Gen 17:10 My covenant which you shall **k**
Gen 18:19 that they **k** the way of the
Gen 28:15 will **k** you wherever you go,
Gen 28:20 **k** me in this way that I am
Gen 30:31 again feed and **k** your flocks
Gen 33: 9 **k** what you have for yourself
Gen 41:35 let them **k** food in the cities
Ex 6: 5 the Egyptians **k** in bondage
Ex 12: 6 Now you shall **k** it until the
Ex 12:14 you shall **k** it as a feast to
Ex 12:14 You shall **k** it as a feast by
Ex 12:25 that you shall **k** this service
Ex 12:47 of Israel shall **k** it
Ex 12:48 wants to **k** the Passover to
Ex 12:48 let him come near and **k** it
Ex 13: 5 that you shall **k** this service
Ex 13:10 You shall therefore **k** this
Ex 15:26 **k** all His statutes, I will
Ex 16:28 refuse to **k** My commandments
Ex 19: 5 **k** My covenant, then you shall
Ex 20: 6 **k** My commandments
Ex 20: 8 the Sabbath day, to **k** it holy
Ex 22: 7 money or articles to **k**, and it
Ex 22:10 a sheep, or any beast to **k**
Ex 23: 7 **K** yourself far from a false
Ex 23:14 Three times you shall **k** a
Ex 23:15 You shall **k** the Feast of
Ex 23:20 you to **k** you in the way and to
Ex 31:13 My Sabbaths you shall **k**, for
Ex 31:14 You shall **k** the Sabbath,
Ex 31:16 of Israel shall **k** the Sabbath
Ex 34:18 Unleavened Bread you shall **k**
Lev 8:35 **k** the charge of the LORD, so
Lev 18: 4 **k** My ordinances, to walk in
Lev 18: 5 shall therefore **k** My statutes
Lev 18:26 shall therefore **k** My statutes
Lev 18:30 you shall **k** My ordinance, so
Lev 19: 3 his father, and **k** My Sabbaths
Lev 19:19 You shall **k** My statutes
Lev 19:30 You shall **k** My Sabbaths and
Lev 20: 8 you shall **k** My statutes, and
Lev 20:22 therefore **k** all My statutes
Lev 22: 9 therefore **k** My ordinance,
Lev 22:31 you shall **k** My commandments
Lev 23:39 you shall **k** the feast of the
Lev 23:41 You shall **k** it as a feast to
Lev 25: 2 you, then the land shall **k** a
Lev 25:18 **k** My judgments, and perform
Lev 26: 2 You shall **k** My Sabbaths and
Lev 26: 3 **k** My commandments,
Num 1:53 the Levites shall **k** charge of
Num 6:24 The LORD bless you and **k** you
Num 9: 2 Israel **k** the Passover at its
Num 9: 3 you shall **k** it at its
Num 9: 3 and ceremonies you shall **k** it
Num 9: 4 they should **k** the Passover
Num 9: 6 so that they could not **k** the
Num 9:10 he may still **k** the LORD's
Num 9:11 at twilight, they may **k** it
Num 9:12 the Passover they shall **k** it
Num 9:13 ceases to **k** the Passover,
Num 9:14 would **k** the LORD's Passover,
Num 16:13 that you should **k** acting like
Num 29:12 you shall **k** a feast to the
Num 31:18 But **k** alive for yourselves

Num 31:30 them to the Levites who **k**
Num 36: 7 **k** the inheritance of the
Num 36: 9 shall **k** its own inheritance
Deut 2:27 I will **k** strictly to the road
Deut 4: 2 from it, that you may **k** the
Deut 4: 9 and diligently **k** yourself
Deut 4:40 therefore **k** His statutes and
Deut 5:10 **k** My commandments
Deut 5:12 to **k** it holy, as the LORD
Deut 5:15 you to **k** the Sabbath day
Deut 5:29 always **k** all My commandments,
Deut 6: 2 to **k** all His statutes and His
Deut 6:17 You shall diligently **k** the
Deut 7: 8 because He would **k** the oath
Deut 7: 9 Him and **k** His commandments
Deut 7:11 you shall **k** the commandment
Deut 7:12 to these judgments, and **k** and
Deut 7:12 will **k** with you the covenant
Deut 8: 2 whether you would **k** His
Deut 8: 6 Therefore you shall **k** the
Deut 10:13 to **k** the commandments of the
Deut 11: 1 **k** His charge, His statutes,
Deut 11: 8 Therefore you shall **k** every
Deut 11:22 For if you carefully **k** all
Deut 13: 4 **k** His commandments and obey
Deut 13:18 to **k** all His commandments
Deut 16: 1 **k** the Passover to the LORD
Deut 16:10 Then you shall **k** the Feast of
Deut 16:15 Seven days you shall **k** a
Deut 19: 9 and if you **k** all these
Deut 23: 9 then **k** yourself from every
Deut 23:23 from your lips you shall **k**
Deut 24:12 you shall not **k** his pledge
Deut 26:17 ways and **k** His statutes, His
Deut 26:18 that you should **k** all His
Deut 27: 1 **K** all the commandments which
Deut 28: 9 if you **k** the commandments of
Deut 28:45 to **k** His commandments and His
Deut 29: 9 Therefore **k** the words of this
Deut 30:10 to **k** His commandments and His
Deut 30:16 to **k** His commandments, His
Josh 6:18 by all means **k** yourselves
Josh 22: 5 to **k** His commandments, to
Josh 23: 6 be very courageous to **k** and to
Judg 2:22 whether they will **k** the ways
Judg 3:19 He said, "**K** silence
1Sa 7: 1 Eleazar his son to **k** the ark
1Sa 17:34 used to **k** his father's sheep
2Sa 15:16 concubines, to **k** the house
2Sa 16:21 he has left to **k** the house
2Sa 18:18 I have no son to **k** my name in
2Sa 20: 3 he had left to **k** the house
1Ki 2: 3 **k** the charge of the LORD your
1Ki 2: 3 ways, to **k** His statutes, His
1Ki 3:14 ways, to **k** My statutes and My
1Ki 6:12 **k** all My commandments, and
1Ki 8:23 who **k** Your covenant and mercy
1Ki 8:25 now **k** what You promised Your
1Ki 8:58 to **k** His commandments and His
1Ki 8:61 **k** His commandments, as at
1Ki 9: 4 if you **k** My statutes and My
1Ki 9: 6 do not **k** My commandments
1Ki 11:10 but he did not **k** what the
1Ki 11:33 **k** My statutes and My judgments
1Ki 11:38 sight, to **k** My statutes and My
1Ki 18: 5 find grass to **k** the horses
2Ki 2: 3 Yes, I know; **k** silent!"
2Ki 2: 5 Yes, I know; **k** silent!"
2Ki 7: 4 If they **k** us alive, we shall
2Ki 11: 6 You shall **k** the watch of the
2Ki 11: 7 **k** the watch of the house of
2Ki 17:13 and **k** My commandments and
2Ki 17:19 Also Judah did not **k** the
2Ki 23: 3 to **k** His commandments and His
2Ki 23:21 **K** the Passover to the LORD
1Ch 4:10 that You would **k** me from evil
1Ch 10:13 because he did not **k** the word
1Ch 12:33 men who could **k** ranks
1Ch 12:35 who could **k** battle formation
1Ch 12:36 able to **k** battle formation,
1Ch 12:38 men of war, who could **k** ranks
1Ch 22:12 that you may **k** the law of the
1Ch 29:18 **k** this forever in the intent
1Ch 29:19 heart to **k** Your commandments
2Ch 6:14 who **k** Your covenant and mercy
2Ch 6:16 now **k** what You promised Your
2Ch 7:17 if you **k** My statutes and My
2Ch 13:11 for we **k** the command of the
2Ch 23: 6 shall **k** the watch of the LORD
2Ch 30: 1 to **k** the Passover to the LORD
2Ch 30: 2 **k** the Passover in the second
2Ch 30: 3 could not **k** it at that time
2Ch 30: 5 to **k** the Passover to the LORD
2Ch 30:13 to **k** the Feast of Unleavened
2Ch 30:23 to **k** the feast another seven
2Ch 34:31 to **k** His commandments and His
2Ch 35:16 to **k** the Passover and to offer
Ezra 6: 6 **k** yourselves far from there
Ezra 8:29 **k** them until you weigh them
Neh 1: 5 You who **k** Your covenant and
Neh 1: 9 **k** My commandments and do
Esth 3: 8 they do not **k** the king's laws
Job 21: 3 I have spoken, **k** mocking
Job 22:15 Will you **k** to the old way
Job 30:10 abhor me, they **k** far from me
Job 36:19 forces, **k** you from distress
Ps 12: 7 You shall **k** them, O LORD, You
Ps 17: 8 **K** me as the apple of Your eye
Ps 19:13 **K** back Your servant also from
Ps 22:29 he who cannot **k** himself alive
Ps 25:10 To such as **k** His covenant and
Ps 25:20 Oh, **k** my soul, and deliver me
Ps 31:20 You shall **k** them secretly in
Ps 33:19 to **k** them alive in famine
Ps 34:13 **K** your tongue from evil, And
Ps 35:22 Do not **k** silence
Ps 37:34 **k** His way, And He shall exalt
Ps 41: 2 **k** him alive, And he will be
Ps 50: 3 come, and shall not **k** silent
Ps 78: 7 God, But **k** His commandments
Ps 78:10 They did not **k** the covenant
Ps 78:56 did not **k** His testimonies,
Ps 83: 1 Do not **k** silent, O God
Ps 89:28 I will **k** for him forever, And
Ps 89:31 do not **k** My commandments,
Ps 91:11 To **k** you in all your ways
Ps 103: 9 us, Nor will He **k** His anger
Ps 103:18 To such as **k** His covenant, And
Ps 105:45 His statutes And **k** His laws
Ps 106: 3 are those who **k** justice, And
Ps 109: 1 Do not **k** silent, O God of my
Ps 119: 2 those who **k** His testimonies
Ps 119: 4 To **k** Your precepts diligently
Ps 119: 5 directed To **k** Your statutes
Ps 119: 8 I will **k** Your statutes
Ps 119:17 I may live and **k** Your word
Ps 119:33 And I shall **k** it to the end
Ps 119:34 and I shall **k** Your law
Ps 119:44 So shall I **k** Your law
Ps 119:55 O LORD, And I **k** Your law
Ps 119:57 that I would **k** Your words
Ps 119:60 and did not delay To **k** Your
Ps 119:63 of those who **k** Your precepts
Ps 119:67 astray, But now I **k** Your word
Ps 119:69 But I will **k** Your precepts
Ps 119:88 So that I may **k** the testimony
Ps 119:100 Because I **k** Your precepts
Ps 119:101 way, That I may **k** Your word
Ps 119:106 confirmed That I will **k** Your
Ps 119:115 For I will **k** the commandments
Ps 119:134 That I may **k** Your precepts
Ps 119:136 Because men do not **k** Your law
Ps 119:145 I will **k** Your statutes
Ps 119:146 I will **k** Your testimonies
Ps 119:158 they do not **k** Your word
Ps 119:168 I **k** Your precepts and Your
Ps 132:12 your sons will **k** My covenant
Ps 140: 4 **K** me, O LORD, from the hands
Ps 141: 3 **K** watch over the door of my
Ps 141: 9 **K** me from the snares which
Prov 1:15 **k** your foot from their path
Prov 2:11 Understanding will **k** you,
Prov 2:20 and **k** to the paths of
Prov 3: 1 let your heart **k** my commands
Prov 3:21 **k** sound wisdom and discretion
Prov 3:26 will **k** your foot from being
Prov 4: 4 **k** my commands, and live
Prov 4: 6 love her, and she will **k** you
Prov 4:13 **k** her, for she is your life
Prov 4:21 **k** them in the midst of your
Prov 4:23 **K** your heart with all
Prov 5: 2 your lips may **k** knowledge
Prov 6:20 **k** your father's command, and
Prov 6:22 you sleep, they will **k** you
Prov 6:24 to **k** you from the evil woman,
Prov 7: 1 **k** my words, and treasure my
Prov 7: 2 **K** my commands and live, and
Prov 7: 5 that they may **k** you from the
Prov 8:32 are those who **k** my ways
Prov 22:18 if you **k** them within you
Prov 28: 4 but such as **k** the law contend
Eccl 2:10 desired I did not **k** from them
Eccl 3: 6 a time to **k**, and a time to
Eccl 3: 7 a time to **k** silence, and a
Eccl 4:11 together, they will **k** warm
Eccl 8: 2 **K** the king's commandment for
Eccl 12:13 **k** His commandments, for this
Song 8:12 those who **k** its fruit two
Is 6: 9 **K** on hearing, but do not
Is 6: 9 **k** on seeing, but do not
Is 7:21 man will **k** alive a young cow
Is 26: 3 You will **k** him in perfect
Is 27: 3 **k** it, I water it every moment
Is 27: 3 hurt it, I **k** it night and day
Is 28:24 Does the plowman **k** plowing
Is 28:24 Does he **k** turning his soil and
Is 32: 6 to **k** the hungry unsatisfied,
Is 41: 1 **K** silence before Me, O
Is 42: 6 I will **k** You and give You as a
Is 43: 6 south, Do not **k** them back
Is 56: 1 **K** justice, and do
Is 56: 4 the eunuchs who **k** My Sabbaths
Is 62: 6 of the LORD, do not **k** silent
Is 65: 5 **K** to yourself, do not come
Is 65: 6 I will not **k** silence, but
Jer 3: 5 Will He **k** it to the end
Jer 31:10 **k** him as a shepherd does his
Jer 34: 9 that no one should **k** a Jewish
Jer 34:10 that no one should **k** them in
Jer 42: 4 I will **k** nothing back from
Lam 2:10 on the ground and **k** silence
Lam 3:28 **k** silent, because God has
Ezek 11:20 **k** My judgments and do them
Ezek 13:18 people, and **k** yourselves alive
Ezek 20:19 **k** My judgments, and do them
Ezek 36:27 you will **k** My judgments and do
Ezek 43:11 they may **k** its whole design
Ezek 44: 8 **k** charge of My sanctuary for
Ezek 44:14 I will make them **k** charge of
Ezek 44:16 Me, and they shall **k** My charge
Ezek 44:20 but they shall **k** their hair
Ezek 44:24 They shall **k** My laws and My
Dan 9: 4 Him, and with those who **k** His
Amos 5:13 prudent **k** silent at that time
Nah 1:15 **k** your appointed feasts,
Hab 2:20 Let all the earth **k** silence
Zech 3: 7 and if you will **k** My command
Zech 13: 5 me to **k** cattle from my youth
Zech 14:16 to **k** the Feast of Tabernacles
Zech 14:18 who do not come up to **k** the
Zech 14:19 that do not come up to **k** the
Mal 2: 7 a priest should **k** knowledge
Matt 19:17 into life, **k** the commandments
Matt 26:18 I will **k** the Passover at your
Mark 7: 9 that you may **k** your tradition
Luke 4:10 charge over You, to **k** You,'
Luke 4:42 tried to **k** Him from leaving
Luke 8:15 **k** it and bear fruit with
Luke 11:28 hear the word of God and **k** it
Luke 19:40 that if these should **k** silent
John 8:55 I do know Him and **k** His word
John 9:16 He does not **k** the Sabbath
John 10:24 How long do You **k** us in doubt
John 12:25 will **k** it for eternal life
John 14:15 love Me, **k** My commandments
John 14:23 loves Me, he will **k** My word
John 14:24 love Me does not **k** My words
John 15:10 If you **k** My commandments,
John 15:20 word, they will **k** yours also
John 17:11 **k** through Your name those
John 17:15 but that You should **k** them
Acts 5: 3 **k** back part of the price of
Acts 5:38 **k** away from these men and let
Acts 10:28 **k** company with or go to one
Acts 12: 4 squads of soldiers to **k** him
Acts 12:17 with his hand to **k** silent
Acts 15: 5 them to **k** the law of Moses
Acts 15:24 be circumcised and **k** the law'
Acts 15:29 If you **k** yourselves from
Acts 16: 4 to them the decrees to **k**,
Acts 16:23 the jailer to **k** them securely
Acts 18: 9 but speak, and do not **k** silent
Acts 18:21 I must by all means **k** this
Acts 21:24 walk orderly and **k** the law
Acts 21:25 **k** themselves from things
Acts 24:23 the centurion to **k** Paul and to
Rom 2:25 profitable if you **k** the law
1Co 5: 8 Therefore let us **k** the feast
1Co 5: 9 to **k** company with sexually
1Co 5:11 have written to you not to **k**

1Co 7:37 that he will **k** his virgin
1Co 11: 2 and **k** the traditions as I
1Co 14:28 let him **k** silent in church,
1Co 14:30 by, let the first **k** silent
1Co 14:34 Let your women **k** silent in
2Co 11: 9 to you, and so I will **k** myself
Gal 5: 3 a debtor to **k** the whole law
Gal 6:13 who are circumcised **k** the law
Eph 4: 3 endeavoring to **k** the unity of
2Th 3:14 do not **k** company with him,
1Ti 5:22 **k** yourself pure
1Ti 6:14 that you **k** this commandment
2Ti 1:12 that He is able to **k** what I
2Ti 1:14 you, **k** by the Holy Spirit who
Phm 13 whom I wished to **k** with me
Jas 1:27 to **k** oneself unspotted from
Jas 2:10 whoever shall **k** the whole law
1Jn 2: 3 if we **k** His commandments
1Jn 2: 4 does not **k** His commandments,
1Jn 3:22 we **k** His commandments
1Jn 5: 2 God and **k** His commandments
1Jn 5: 3 that we **k** His commandments
1Jn 5:21 **k** yourselves from idols
Jude 6 did not **k** their proper domain
Jude 21 **k** yourselves in the love of
Jude 24 able to **k** you from stumbling
Rev 1: 3 and **k** those things which are
Rev 3:10 I also will **k** you from the
Rev 12:17 **k** the commandments of God
Rev 14:12 here are those who **k** the
Rev 22: 9 of those who **k** the words of

KEEPER (*see* KEEP, KEEPERS)
Gen 4: 2 Now Abel was a **k** of sheep
Gen 4: 9 Am I my brother's **k**
Gen 39:21 sight of the **k** of the prison
Gen 39:22 the **k** of the prison committed
Gen 39:23 The **k** of the prison did not
1Sa 17:20 left the sheep with a **k**, and
1Sa 17:22 in the hand of the supply **k**
2Ki 22:14 of Harhas, **k** of the wardrobe
1Ch 9:21 was **k** of the door of the
2Ch 31:14 the **k** of the East Gate, was
2Ch 34:22 of Hasrah, **k** of the wardrobe
Neh 2: 8 the **k** of the king's forest
Neh 3:29 the **k** of the East Gate, made
Ps 121: 5 The LORD is your **k**
Song 1: 6 me the **k** of the vineyards
Jer 35: 4 of Shallum, the **k** of the door
Luke 13: 7 said to the **k** of his vineyard
Acts 16:27 the **k** of the prison, awaking
Acts 16:36 So the **k** of the prison

KEEPERS (*see* KEEPER)
1Ch 9:19 Their fathers had been **k** of
Eccl 12: 3 in the day when the **k** of the
Song 5: 7 the **k** of the walls took my
Song 8:11 he leased the vineyard to **k**
Jer 4:17 Like **k** of a field they are

KEEPING (*see* KEEP)
Ex 34: 7 **k** mercy for thousands,
Num 3:28 **k** charge of the sanctuary
Num 3:38 **k** charge of the sanctuary, to
Deut 8:11 **k** His commandments
1Sa 16:11 and there he is, **k** the sheep
1Sa 25:16 we were with them **k** the sheep
2Sa 12: 8 master's wives into your **k**
2Sa 13:34 was **k** watch lifted his eyes
2Ki 11: 5 on the Sabbath shall be **k**
2Ch 5:11 without **k** to their divisions)
2Ch 23: 4 shall be **k** watch over the
Neh 12:25 Akkub were gatekeepers **k** the
Ps 19:11 And in **k** them there is great
Prov 15: 3 **k** watch on the evil and the
Ezek 13:19 **k** people alive who should not
Ezek 17:14 but that by **k** his covenant it
Luke 2: 8 **k** watch over their flock by
Acts 12: 6 the door were **k** the prison
1Co 7:19 **k** the commandments of God

KEEPS (*see* KEEP)
Gen 19: 9 and he **k** acting as a judge
Deut 7: 9 faithful God who **k** covenant
Neh 9:32 God, Who **k** covenant and
Job 20:13 but still **k** it in his mouth,
Job 33:18 He **k** back his soul from the
Ps 66: 9 Who **k** our soul among the
Ps 119:129 Therefore my soul **k** them
Ps 119:167 My soul **k** Your testimonies,
Ps 121: 3 He who **k** you will not slumber
Ps 121: 4 He who **k** Israel Shall neither
Ps 146: 6 Who **k** truth forever,
Prov 10:17 He who **k** instruction is in
Prov 13: 6 Righteousness **k** him whose way
Prov 16:17 he who **k** his way preserves
Prov 18:18 cease, and **k** the mighty apart
Prov 19: 8 he who **k** understanding will
Prov 19:16 He who **k** the commandment
Prov 19:16 the commandment **k** his soul
Prov 21:23 and tongue **k** his soul from
Prov 24:12 he who **k** your soul, does He
Prov 27:18 Whoever **k** the fig tree will
Prov 28: 7 Whoever **k** the law is a
Prov 29:18 but happy is he who **k** the law
Eccl 5:20 because God **k** him busy with
Eccl 8: 5 He who **k** his command will
Is 26: 2 **k** the truth may enter in
Is 56: 2 who **k** from defiling the
Is 56: 2 **k** his hand from doing any
Is 56: 6 everyone who **k** from defiling
Jer 48:10 cursed is he who **k** back his
Ezek 18:21 **k** all My statutes, and does
Dan 9: 4 who **k** His covenant and mercy
John 7:19 and yet none of you **k** the law
John 8:51 if anyone **k** My word he shall
John 8:52 If anyone **k** My word he shall
John 14:21 **k** them, it is he who loves Me
Rom 2:26 if an uncircumcised man **k** the
1Jn 2: 5 But whoever **k** His word, truly
1Jn 3:24 Now he who **k** His
1Jn 5:18 been born of God **k** himself
Rev 2:26 **k** My works until the end, to
Rev 16:15 **k** his garments, lest he walk
Rev 22: 7 Blessed is he who **k** the words

KEHELATHAH
Num 33:22 from Rissah and camped at **K**
Num 33:23 They went from **K** and camped

KEILAH
Josh 15:44 **K**, Achzib, and Mareshah
1Sa 23: 1 are fighting against **K**, and
1Sa 23: 2 the Philistines, and save **K**
1Sa 23: 3 **K** against the armies of the
1Sa 23: 4 Arise, go down to **K**
1Sa 23: 5 David and his men went to **K**
1Sa 23: 5 saved the inhabitants of **K**
1Sa 23: 6 Ahimelech fled to David at **K**
1Sa 23: 7 told that David had gone to **K**
1Sa 23: 8 to go down to **K** to besiege
1Sa 23:10 **K** to destroy the city for my
1Sa 23:11 Will the men of **K** deliver me
1Sa 23:12 Will the men of **K** deliver me
1Sa 23:13 arose and departed from **K**
1Sa 23:13 that David had escaped from **K**
1Ch 4:19 the fathers of **K** the Garmite
Neh 3:17 of half the district of **K**
Neh 3:18 half of the district of **K**

KELAIAH (*see* KELITA)
Ezra 10:23 **K** (the same is Kelita),

KELITA (*see* KELAIAH)
Ezra 10:23 Kelaiah (the same is **K**),
Neh 8: 7 Hodijah, Maaseiah, **K**,
Neh 10:10 Shebaniah, Hodijah, **K**,

KEMUEL
Gen 22:21 **K** the father of Aram,
Num 34:24 **K** the son of Shiphtan
1Ch 27:17 Hashabiah the son of **K**

KENATH (*see* NOBAH)
Num 32:42 Then Nobah went and took **K**
1Ch 2:23 the towns of Jair, with **K**

KENAZ (*see* KENEZZITES)
Gen 36:11 Omar, Zepho, Gatam, and **K**
Gen 36:15 Omar, Chief Zepho, Chief **K**
Gen 36:42 Chief **K**, Chief Teman, Chief
Josh 15:17 So Othniel the son of **K**, the
Judg 1:13 And Othniel the son of **K**,
Judg 3: 9 Othniel the son of **K**, Caleb's
Judg 3:11 Othniel the son of **K** died
1Ch 1:36 Omar, Zephi, Gatam, and **K**
1Ch 1:53 Chief **K**, Chief Teman, Chief
1Ch 4:13 The sons of **K** were Othniel and
1Ch 4:15 The son of Elah was **K**

KENEZZITES (*see* KENAZ)
Gen 15:19 the Kenites, the **K**, and the

KENITE (*see* KENITES)
Judg 1:16 Now the children of the **K**
Judg 4:11 Now Heber the **K**, of the
Judg 4:17 Jael, the wife of Heber the **K**
Judg 4:17 and the house of Heber the **K**
Judg 5:24 Jael, the wife of Heber the **K**

KENITES (*see* KENITE, MIDIANITES)
Gen 15:19 the **K**, the Kenezzites, and the
Num 24:21 Then he looked on the **K**, and
Judg 4:11 separated himself from the **K**
1Sa 15: 6 Then Saul said to the **K**, Go
1Sa 15: 6 So the **K** departed from
1Sa 27:10 the southern area of the **K**
1Sa 30:29 were in the cities of the **K**
1Ch 2:55 These were the **K** who came

KENIZZITE
Num 32:12 the son of Jephunneh, the **K**
Josh 14: 6 Jephunneh the **K** said to him
Josh 14:14 Jephunneh the **K** to this day

KEPT (*see* KEEP)
Gen 8: 7 which **k** going to and fro until
Gen 26: 5 **k** My charge, My
Gen 37:11 but his father **k** the matter
Gen 39: 9 nor has he **k** back anything
Gen 39:16 So she **k** his garment with her
Gen 42:16 and you shall be **k** in prison
Ex 3: 1 Now Moses **k** the flock of
Ex 10:24 and your herds be **k** back
Ex 16:23 to be **k** until morning
Ex 16:32 to be **k** for your generations,
Ex 16:33 to be **k** for your generations
Ex 16:34 before the Testimony, to be **k**
Ex 21:29 he has not **k** it confined, so
Ex 21:36 owner has not **k** it confined
Lev 6: 9 shall be **k** burning on it
Lev 6:12 shall be **k** burning on it
Num 3:32 who **k** charge of the sanctuary
Num 9: 5 they **k** the Passover on the
Num 9: 7 Why are we **k** from presenting
Num 9:19 **k** the charge of the LORD and
Num 9:23 they **k** the charge of the LORD
Num 17:10 to be **k** as a sign against the
Num 19: 9 and they shall be **k** for the
Num 24:11 the LORD has **k** you back from
Num 31:15 Have you **k** all the women
Num 31:47 Levites, who **k** charge of the
Deut 9:25 forty nights I **k** prostrating
Deut 32:10 He **k** him as the apple of His
Deut 33: 9 Your word and **k** Your covenant
Josh 5:10 and **k** the Passover on the
Josh 14:10 the LORD has **k** me alive, as
Josh 22: 2 You have **k** all that Moses the
Josh 22: 3 but have **k** the charge of the
Judg 2:22 them as their fathers **k** them
Ruth 2:14 was satisfied, and **k** some back
Ruth 2:18 had **k** back after she had been
1Sa 9:24 Here it is, what was **k** back
1Sa 9:24 time it has been **k** for you
1Sa 13:13 You have not **k** the
1Sa 13:14 because you have not **k** what
1Sa 21: 4 least **k** themselves from women
1Sa 21: 5 women have been **k** from us
1Sa 25:33 because you have **k** me this
1Sa 25:34 lives, who has **k** me back from
1Sa 25:39 has **k** His servant from evil
2Sa 8: 2 full line those to be **k** alive
2Sa 22:22 For I have **k** the ways of the
2Sa 22:24 I **k** myself from my iniquity
2Sa 22:44 you have **k** me as the head of
1Ki 2:43 not **k** the oath of the LORD
1Ki 8:24 You have **k** what You promised
1Ki 11:11 have not **k** My covenant and My
1Ki 11:34 because he **k** My
1Ki 13:21 have not **k** the commandment
1Ki 14: 8 who **k** My commandments and
2Ki 12: 9 the priests who **k** the door
2Ki 18: 6 but **k** His commandments,
2Ch 6:15 You have **k** what You promised
2Ch 7: 8 **k** the feast seven days, and
2Ch 30:21 **k** the Feast of Unleavened
2Ch 30:23 they **k** it another seven days
2Ch 34: 9 which the Levites who **k** the
2Ch 34:21 not **k** the word of the LORD
2Ch 35: 1 Now Josiah **k** a Passover to
2Ch 35:17 **k** the Passover at that time
2Ch 35:18 **k** in Israel like that since
2Ch 35:18 **k** such a Passover as Josiah
2Ch 35:18 such a Passover as Josiah **k**
2Ch 35:19 of Josiah this Passover was **k**
2Ch 36:21 lay desolate she **k** Sabbath
Ezra 3: 4 They also **k** the Feast of
Ezra 6:19 of the captivity **k** the
Ezra 6:22 And they **k** the Feast of

Neh 1: 7 have not **k** the commandments,
Neh 8:18 they **k** the feast seven days
Neh 9:34 have **k** Your law, nor heeded
Neh 11:19 brethren who **k** the gates,
Neh 12:22 was also **k** of the Levites
Neh 12:45 the gatekeepers **k** the charge
Esth 2:14 eunuch who **k** the concubines
Esth 9:28 **k** throughout every generation
Job 21:32 and a vigil **k** over the tomb
Job 23:11 I have **k** His way and not
Job 29:21 and **k** silence for my counsel
Job 31:16 If I have **k** the poor from
Job 31:34 families, so that I **k** silence
Ps 17: 4 I have **k** myself from the
Ps 18:21 For I have **k** the ways of the
Ps 18:23 I **k** myself from my iniquity
Ps 30: 3 You have **k** me alive, that I
Ps 32: 3 When I **k** silent, my bones
Ps 42: 4 that **k** a pilgrim feast
Ps 50:21 you have done, and I **k** silent
Ps 99: 7 They **k** His testimonies and the
Ps 119:22 For I have **k** Your testimonies
Ps 119:56 Because I **k** Your precepts
Eccl 5:13 riches **k** for their owner to
Song 1: 6 my own vineyard I have not **k**
Is 30:29 when a holy festival is **k**
Jer 16:11 forsaken Me and not **k** My law
Jer 35:18 **k** all his precepts and done
Ezek 5: 7 nor **k** My judgments, nor even
Ezek 18: 9 **k** My judgments faithfully
Ezek 18:19 has **k** all My statutes and done
Ezek 44: 8 you have not **k** charge of My
Ezek 44:15 who **k** charge of My sanctuary
Ezek 48:11 who have **k** My charge, who did
Dan 5:19 he wished, he **k** alive
Dan 7:28 but I **k** the matter in my
Dan 9:14 has **k** the disaster in mind
Amos 1:11 and he **k** his wrath forever
Amos 2: 4 have not **k** His commandments
Mic 6:16 the statutes of Omri are **k**
Mal 2: 9 because you have not **k** My
Mal 3: 7 ordinances and have not **k** them
Mal 3:14 that we have **k** His ordinance
Matt 8:33 Then those who **k** them fled
Matt 13:35 things which have been **k**
Matt 19:20 things I have **k** from my youth
Matt 26:63 But Jesus **k** silent
Matt 27:36 they **k** watch over Him there
Mark 3: 4 But they **k** silent
Mark 3: 9 be **k** ready for Him because of
Mark 4:22 nor has anything been **k**
Mark 7:26 she **k** asking Him to cast the
Mark 9:10 So they **k** this word to
Mark 9:34 But they **k** silent, for on the
Mark 14:61 But He **k** silent and answered
Luke 1:66 them **k** them in their hearts
Luke 2:19 But Mary **k** all these things
Luke 2:51 but His mother **k** all these
Luke 8:29 he was **k** under guard, bound
Luke 9:36 But they **k** quiet, and told no
Luke 14: 4 But they **k** silent
Luke 18:21 these I have **k** from my youth
Luke 19:20 which I have **k** put away in a
Luke 20:26 at His answer and **k** silent
John 2:10 but you have **k** the good wine
John 11:37 also have **k** this man from
John 12: 7 she has **k** this for the day of
John 15:10 just as I have **k** My Father's
John 15:20 If they **k** My word, they will
John 17: 6 Me, and they have **k** Your word
John 17:12 world, I **k** them in Your name
John 17:12 whom You gave Me I have **k**
John 18:16 spoke to her who **k** the door
John 18:17 who **k** the door said to Peter
Acts 5: 2 And he **k** back part of the
Acts 7:53 of angels and have not **k** it
Acts 12: 5 was therefore **k** in prison
Acts 12:15 Yet she **k** insisting that it
Acts 12:22 And the people **k** shouting
Acts 15:12 all the multitude **k** silent
Acts 20:20 how I **k** back nothing that was
Acts 22: 2 they **k** all the more silent
Acts 23:35 to be **k** in Herod's Praetorium
Acts 25: 4 Paul should be **k** at Caesarea
Acts 25:21 I commanded him to be **k** till
Acts 27:43 **k** them from their purpose, and
Rom 16:25 was **k** secret since the world
2Co 11: 9 in everything I **k** myself from
Gal 3:23 we were **k** under guard by the
Gal 3:23 **k** for the faith which would
2Ti 4: 7 the race, I have **k** the faith
Heb 11:28 By faith he **k** the Passover and
Jas 5: 4 which you **k** back by fraud,
1Pe 1: 5 who are **k** by the power of God
2Pe 3: 7 **k** in store by the same word
Rev 3: 8 have **k** My word, and have not
Rev 3:10 Because you have **k** My

KEREN-HAPPUCH
Job 42:14 and the name of the third **K**

KERIOTH
Josh 15:25 Hazor, Hadattah, **K**, Hezron
Jer 48:24 on **K** and Bozrah, on all the
Jer 48:41 **K** is taken, and the
Amos 2: 2 shall devour the palaces of **K**

KEROS
Ezra 2:44 the sons of **K**, the sons of
Neh 7:47 the children of **K**, the

KETTLE
1Sa 2:14 thrust it into the pan, or **k**

KETURAH
Gen 25: 1 a wife, and her name was **K**
Gen 25: 4 these were the children of **K**
1Ch 1:32 Now the sons born to **K**,
1Ch 1:33 these were the children of **K**

KEVEH
1Ki 10:28 imported from Egypt and **K**
1Ki 10:28 in **K** at the current price
2Ch 1:16 imported from Egypt and **K**
2Ch 1:16 in **K** at the current price

KEY (*see* KEYS)
Judg 3:25 Therefore they took the **k**
Is 22:22 The **k** of the house of David I
Luke 11:52 taken away the **k** of knowledge
Rev 3: 7 He who has the **k** of David
Rev 9: 1 to him was given the **k** to the
Rev 20: 1 heaven, having the **k** to the

KEYS (*see* KEY)
Matt 16:19 I will give you the **k** of the
Rev 1:18 And I have the **k** of Hades and

KEZIAH
Job 42:14 the name of the second **K**

KIBROTH HATTAAVAH
Num 11:34 the name of that place **K**,
Num 11:35 From **K** the people moved to
Num 33:16 of Sinai and camped at **K**
Num 33:17 They departed from **K** and
Deut 9:22 **K** you provoked the LORD to

KIBZAIM (*see* JOKMEAM)
Josh 21:22 **K** with its common-land, and

KICK (*see* KICKED)
1Sa 2:29 Why do you **k** at My sacrifice
Acts 9: 5 you to **k** against the goads
Acts 26:14 you to **k** against the goads

KICKED (*see* KICK)
Deut 32:15 But Jeshurun grew fat and **k**
2Sa 16:13 stones at him and **k** up dust

KID (*see* KIDS)
Gen 37:31 killed a **k** of the goats, and
Lev 4:23 his offering a **k** of the goats
Lev 4:28 his offering a **k** of the goats
Lev 5: 6 a lamb or a **k** of the goats as
Lev 9: 3 Take a **k** of the goats as a
Lev 23:19 one **k** of the goats as a sin
Num 7:16 one **k** of the goats as a sin
Num 7:22 one **k** of the goats as a sin
Num 7:28 one **k** of the goats as a sin
Num 7:34 one **k** of the goats as a sin
Num 7:40 one **k** of the goats as a sin
Num 7:46 one **k** of the goats as a sin
Num 7:52 one **k** of the goats as a sin
Num 7:58 one **k** of the goats as a sin
Num 7:64 one **k** of the goats as a sin
Num 7:70 one **k** of the goats as a sin
Num 7:76 one **k** of the goats as a sin
Num 7:82 one **k** of the goats as a sin
Num 15:24 one **k** of the goats as a sin
Num 28:15 Also one **k** of the goats as a
Num 28:30 also one **k** of the goats, to
Num 29: 5 also one **k** of the goats as a
Num 29:11 also one **k** of the goats as a
Num 29:16 also one **k** of the goats as a
Num 29:19 also one **k** of the goats as a
Num 29:25 also one **k** of the goats as a
Ezek 43:22 a **k** of the goats without
Ezek 45:23 a **k** of the goats daily for a

KIDNAPPER (*see* KIDNAPPERS, KIDNAPS)
Deut 24: 7 him, then that **k** shall die

KIDNAPPERS (*see* KIDNAPPER)
1Ti 1:10 for sodomites, for **k**, for

KIDNAPPING (*see* KIDNAPS)
Deut 24: 7 If a man is found **k** any of

KIDNAPS (*see* KIDNAPPER, KIDNAPPING)
Ex 21:16 He who **k** a man and sells him,

KIDNEYS
Ex 29:13 to the liver, and the two **k**
Ex 29:22 to the liver, the two **k** and
Lev 3: 4 the two **k** and the fat that is
Lev 3: 4 to the liver above the **k**, he
Lev 3:10 the two **k** and the fat that is
Lev 3:10 to the liver above the **k**, he
Lev 3:15 the two **k** and the fat that is
Lev 3:15 to the liver above the **k**, he
Lev 4: 9 the two **k** and the fat that is
Lev 4: 9 to the liver above the **k**, he
Lev 7: 4 the two **k** and the fat that is
Lev 7: 4 to the liver above the **k**, he
Lev 8:16 the two **k** with their fat, and
Lev 8:25 to the liver, the two **k** and
Lev 9:10 But the fat, the **k**, and the
Lev 9:19 covers the entrails and the **k**
Is 34: 6 with the fat of the **k** of rams

KIDRON
2Sa 15:23 also crossed over the Brook **K**
1Ki 2:37 go out and cross the Brook **K**
1Ki 15:13 and burned it by the Brook **K**
2Ki 23: 4 Jerusalem in the fields of **K**
2Ki 23: 6 LORD, to the Brook **K** outside
2Ki 23: 6 burned it at the Brook **K**
2Ki 23:12 their dust into the Brook **K**
2Ch 15:16 and burned it by the Brook **K**
2Ch 29:16 and carried it to the Brook **K**
2Ch 30:14 and cast them into the Brook **K**
Jer 31:40 fields as far as the Brook **K**
John 18: 1 disciples over the Brook **K**

KIDS (*see* KID)
Gen 27: 9 two choice **k** of the goats
Gen 27:16 she put the skins of the **k** of
Lev 16: 5 two **k** of the goats as a sin
Num 7:87 the **k** of the goats as a sin

KILL (*see* KILLED, KILLING, KILLS)
Gen 4:14 anyone who finds me will **k** me
Gen 4:15 finding him should **k** him
Gen 12:12 and they will **k** me, but they
Gen 20:11 they will **k** me on account of
Gen 26: 7 place should **k** me for Rebekah
Gen 27:41 then I will **k** my brother
Gen 27:42 you by intending to **k** you
Gen 34:30 together against me and **k** me
Gen 37:18 against him to **k** him
Gen 37:20 therefore, let us now **k** him
Gen 37:21 Let us not **k** him
Gen 37:26 is there if we **k** our brother
Gen 42:37 **K** my two sons if I do not
Ex 1:16 a son, then you shall **k** him
Ex 2:14 Do you intend to **k** me as you
Ex 2:15 matter, he sought to **k** Moses
Ex 4:23 go, indeed I will **k** your son
Ex 4:24 met him and sought to **k** him
Ex 5:21 a sword in their hand to **k** us
Ex 12: 6 Israel shall **k** it at twilight
Ex 12:21 and **k** the Passover lamb
Ex 16: 3 to **k** this whole assembly with
Ex 17: 3 us up out of Egypt, to **k** us
Ex 21:14 to **k** him with guile, you
Ex 22:24 I will **k** you with the sword
Ex 23: 7 do not **k** the innocent and
Ex 29:11 Then you shall **k** the bull
Ex 29:16 and you shall **k** the ram, and
Ex 29:20 Then you shall **k** the ram, and
Ex 32:12 to **k** them in the mountains,
Ex 32:27 let every man **k** his brother
Lev 1: 5 He shall **k** the bull before
Lev 1:11 He shall **k** it on the north
Lev 3: 2 and **k** it at the door of the
Lev 3: 8 **k** it before the tabernacle of
Lev 3:13 **k** it before the tabernacle of
Lev 4: 4 **k** the bull before the LORD
Lev 4:24 **k** it at the place where they
Lev 4:24 **k** the burnt offering before

Lev 4:29 **k** the sin offering in the
Lev 4:33 they **k** the burnt offering
Lev 7: 2 shall **k** the trespass offering
Lev 14:13 Then he shall **k** the lamb in
Lev 14:19 he shall **k** the burnt offering
Lev 14:25 Then he shall **k** the lamb of
Lev 14:50 Then he shall **k** one of the
Lev 16:11 shall **k** the bull as the sin
Lev 16:15 Then he shall **k** the goat of
Lev 20: 4 Molech, and they do not **k** him
Lev 20:15 and you shall **k** the beast
Lev 20:16 it, you shall **k** the woman
Lev 22:28 ewe, do not **k** both her and her
Num 11:15 this, please **k** me here and now
Num 14:15 Now if You **k** these people as
Num 16:13 to **k** us in the wilderness,
Num 22:29 hand, for now I would **k** you
Num 25: 5 Every one of you **k** his men
Num 31:17 **k** every male among the little
Num 31:17 **k** every woman who has known a
Deut 9:28 to **k** them in the wilderness
Deut 13: 9 but you shall surely **k** him
Deut 19: 6 and **k** him, though he was not
Deut 32:39 I **k** and I make alive
Josh 9:26 so that they did not **k** them
Judg 8:19 them live, I would not **k** you
Judg 8:20 his firstborn, Rise, **k** them
Judg 8:21 Rise yourself, and **k** us
Judg 9:54 **k** me, lest men say of me, A
Judg 12: 6 **k** him at the fords of the
Judg 13:23 the LORD had desired to **k** us
Judg 15:12 you will not **k** me yourselves
Judg 15:13 but we will surely not **k** you
Judg 16: 2 it is daylight, we will **k** him
Judg 20: 5 They intended to **k** me, but
Judg 20:31 **k** some of the people, as at
Judg 20:39 **k** about thirty of the men of
1Sa 2:25 the LORD desired to **k** them
1Sa 5:10 God of Israel to us, to **k** us
1Sa 5:11 so that it does not **k** us
1Sa 15: 3 But **k** both man and woman,
1Sa 16: 2 Saul hears it, he will **k** me
1Sa 17: 9 **k** me, then we will be your
1Sa 17: 9 **k** him, then you shall be our
1Sa 19: 1 that they should **k** David
1Sa 19: 2 My father Saul seeks to **k** you
1Sa 19: 5 to **k** David without a cause
1Sa 19:11 and to **k** him in the morning
1Sa 19:15 in the bed, that I may **k** him
1Sa 19:17 Why should I **k** you
1Sa 20: 8 **k** me yourself, for why should
1Sa 20:33 cast a spear at him to **k** him
1Sa 20:33 by his father to **k** David
1Sa 22:17 **k** the priests of the LORD,
1Sa 22:18 You turn and **k** the priests
1Sa 24:10 and someone urged me to **k** you
1Sa 24:11 your robe, and did not **k** you
1Sa 24:18 your hand, you did not **k** me
1Sa 28:24 and she hastened to **k** it
1Sa 30: 2 they did not **k** anyone, but
1Sa 30:15 God that you will neither **k**
2Sa 1: 9 **k** me, for anguish has come
2Sa 3:37 to **k** Abner the son of Ner
2Sa 13:28 Strike Amnon!' then **k** him.
2Sa 21: 2 but Saul had sought to **k** them
2Sa 21: 4 nor shall you **k** any man in
2Sa 21:16 thought he could **k** David
1Ki 3:26 child, and by no means **k** him
1Ki 3:27 child, and by no means **k** him
1Ki 11:40 sought to **k** Jeroboam
1Ki 12:27 of Judah, and they will **k** me
1Ki 17:18 remembrance, and to **k** my son
1Ki 18: 5 not have to **k** any livestock
1Ki 18: 9 the hand of Ahab, to **k** me
1Ki 18:12 cannot find you, he will **k** me
1Ki 18:14 and he will **k** me
1Ki 19:17 sword of Hazael, Jehu will **k**
1Ki 19:17 sword of Jehu, Elisha will **k**
1Ki 20:36 from me, a lion shall **k** you
2Ki 5: 7 Am I God, to **k** and make alive,
2Ki 6:21 My father, shall I **k** them
2Ki 6:21 Shall I **k** them
2Ki 6:22 You shall not **k** them
2Ki 6:22 Would you **k** those whom you
2Ki 7: 4 and if they **k** us, we shall but
2Ki 8:12 men you will **k** with the sword
2Ki 10:25 captains, Go in and **k** them
2Ch 20:23 of Mount Seir to utterly **k**
2Ch 22:11 so that she did not **k** him
2Ch 23:14 Do not **k** her in the house of
Neh 4:11 **k** them and cause the work to
Neh 6:10 for they are coming to **k** you
Neh 6:10 night they will come to **k** you
Esth 3:13 provinces, to destroy, to **k**
Esth 8:11 to destroy, **k**, and annihilate
Eccl 3: 3 a time to **k**, and a time to
Is 14:30 I will **k** your roots with
Jer 9:21 to **k** off the children
Jer 20:17 he did not **k** me from the womb
Jer 40:15 I will **k** Ishmael the son of
Jer 41: 8 Do not **k** us, for we have
Jer 41: 8 did not **k** them among their
Ezek 9: 5 him through the city and **k**
Dan 2:13 and his companions, to **k** them
Dan 2:14 who had gone out to **k** the
Hos 9:16 I would **k** the beloved fruit
Matt 10:28 do not fear those who **k** the
Matt 10:28 body but cannot **k** the soul
Matt 17:23 and they will **k** Him, and the
Matt 21:38 Come, let us **k** him and seize
Matt 23:34 some of them you will **k** and
Matt 24: 9 **k** you, and you will be hated
Matt 26: 4 Jesus by trickery and **k** Him
Mark 3: 4 do evil, to save life or to **k**
Mark 6:19 him and wanted to **k** him, but
Mark 9:31 of men, and they will **k** Him
Mark 10:34 and spit on Him, and **k** Him
Mark 12: 7 Come, let us **k** him, and the
Luke 11:49 and some of them they will **k**
Luke 12: 4 of those who **k** the body, and
Luke 13:31 for Herod wants to **k** You
Luke 15:23 **k** it, and let us eat and be
Luke 20:14 Come, let us **k** him, that the
Luke 22: 2 sought how they might **k** Him
John 5:16 Jesus, and sought to **k** Him
John 5:18 sought all the more to **k** Him
John 7: 1 the Jews sought to **k** Him
John 7:19 Why do you seek to **k** Me
John 7:20 Who is seeking to **k** You
John 7:25 not He whom they seek to **k**
John 8:22 Will He **k** Himself, because He
John 8:37 but you seek to **k** Me,
John 8:40 But now you seek to **k** Me, a
John 10:10 come except to steal, and to **k**
Acts 5:33 and took counsel to **k** them
Acts 7:28 Do you want to **k** me as you
Acts 9:23 the Jews plotted to **k** him
Acts 9:24 gates day and night, to **k** him
Acts 9:29 but they attempted to **k** him
Acts 10:13 Rise, Peter; **k** and eat."
Acts 11: 7 Rise, Peter; **k** and eat.'
Acts 16:27 and was about to **k** himself
Acts 21:31 as they were seeking to **k** him
Acts 23:15 but we are ready to **k** him
Acts 25: 3 along the road to **k** him
Acts 26:21 the temple and tried to **k** me
Acts 27:42 plan was to **k** the prisoners
Rev 2:23 I will **k** her children with
Rev 6: 4 people should **k** one another
Rev 6: 8 to **k** with sword, with hunger,
Rev 9: 5 not given authority to **k** them
Rev 9:15 were released to **k** a third of
Rev 11: 7 overcome them, and **k** them

KILLED (*see* KILL)
Gen 4: 8 Abel his brother and **k** him
Gen 4:23 For I have **k** a man for
Gen 4:25 instead of Abel, whom Cain **k**
Gen 34:25 the city and **k** all the males
Gen 34:26 they **k** Hamor and Shechem his
Gen 37:31 **k** a kid of the goats, and
Gen 38: 7 the LORD, and the LORD **k** him
Gen 38:10 therefore He **k** him also
Ex 2:12 he **k** the Egyptian and hid him
Ex 2:14 kill me as you **k** the Egyptian
Ex 13:15 go, that the LORD **k** all the
Ex 21:29 so that it has **k** a man or a
Lev 4:15 shall be **k** before the LORD
Lev 6:25 where the burnt offering is **k**
Lev 6:25 shall be **k** before the LORD
Lev 7: 2 **k** the burnt offering they
Lev 8:15 and Moses **k** it
Lev 8:19 and Moses **k** it
Lev 8:23 and Moses **k** it
Lev 9: 8 and **k** the calf of the sin
Lev 9:12 And he **k** the burnt offering
Lev 9:15 **k** it and offered it for sin,
Lev 9:18 He also **k** the bull and the ram
Lev 14: 5 that one of the birds be **k** in
Lev 14: 6 was **k** over the running water
Num 14:16 therefore He **k** them in the
Num 16:41 You have **k** the people of the
Num 22:33 would also have **k** you by now
Num 25:14 of the Israelite who was **k**
Num 25:14 who was **k** with the Midianite
Num 25:15 **k** was Cozbi the daughter of
Num 25:18 who was **k** in the day of the
Num 31: 7 and they **k** all the males
Num 31: 8 They **k** the kings of Midian
Num 31: 8 the rest of those who were **k**
Num 31: 8 they also **k** with the sword
Num 31:19 whoever has **k** any person, and
Num 33: 4 the LORD had **k** among them
Deut 1: 4 after he had **k** Sihon king of
Deut 21: 1 and it is not known who **k** him
Josh 10:10 **k** them with a great slaughter
Josh 10:11 of Israel **k** with the sword
Josh 10:26 **k** them, and hanged them on
Josh 11:17 and struck them down and **k**
Josh 13:22 **k** with the sword Balaam the
Josh 13:22 those who were **k** by them
Josh 20: 9 that whoever **k** any person
Judg 1: 4 they **k** ten thousand men at
Judg 1:10 they **k** Sheshai, Ahiman, and
Judg 3:29 at that time they **k** about ten
Judg 3:31 who **k** six hundred men of the
Judg 7:25 They **k** Oreb at the rock of
Judg 7:25 Zeeb they **k** at the winepress
Judg 8:17 and **k** the men of the city
Judg 8:18 were they whom you **k** at Tabor
Judg 8:21 **k** Zebah and Zalmunna, and
Judg 9: 5 **k** his brothers, the seventy
Judg 9:18 **k** his seventy sons on one
Judg 9:24 who **k** them, and on the men of
Judg 9:44 were in the fields and **k** them
Judg 9:45 **k** the people who were in it
Judg 9:54 men say of me, 'A woman **k** him
Judg 14:19 **k** thirty of their men, took
Judg 15:15 and **k** a thousand men with it
Judg 16:30 So the dead that he **k** at his
Judg 16:30 than he had **k** in his life
Judg 20:45 and **k** two thousand of them
1Sa 4: 2 who **k** about four thousand men
1Sa 11:11 **k** Ammonites until the heat of
1Sa 14:13 him, his armorbearer **k** them
1Sa 17:35 its beard, and struck and **k** it
1Sa 17:36 Your servant has **k** both lion
1Sa 17:50 the Philistine and **k** him
1Sa 17:51 **k** him, and cut off his head
1Sa 18:27 and **k** two hundred men of the
1Sa 19: 5 **k** the Philistine, and the LORD
1Sa 19: 6 LORD lives, he shall not be **k**
1Sa 19:11 tomorrow you will be **k**
1Sa 20:32 Why should he be **k**
1Sa 21: 9 whom you **k** in the Valley of
1Sa 22:18 **k** on that day eighty-five men
1Sa 22:21 Saul had **k** the LORD's priests
1Sa 25:11 that I have **k** for my shearers
1Sa 31: 2 And the Philistines **k** Jonathan
2Sa 1:10 **k** him, because I was sure
2Sa 1:16 I have **k** the LORD's anointed
2Sa 3:30 Abishai his brother **k** Abner
2Sa 3:30 Abner, because he had **k** their
2Sa 4: 7 **k** him, beheaded him and took
2Sa 4:11 when wicked men have **k** a
2Sa 8: 5 David **k** twenty-two thousand
2Sa 10:18 and David **k** seven hundred
2Sa 12: 9 You have **k** Uriah the Hittite
2Sa 12: 9 have **k** him with the sword of
2Sa 13:30 Absalom has **k** all the king's
2Sa 13:32 they have **k** all the young men
2Sa 14: 6 one struck the other and **k** him
2Sa 14: 7 life of his brother whom he **k**
2Sa 18:15 Absalom, and struck and **k** him
2Sa 21: 1 because he **k** the Gibeonites
2Sa 21:17 the Philistine and **k** him
2Sa 21:18 the Hushathite **k** Saph, who
2Sa 21:19 the Bethlehemite **k** the
2Sa 21:21 the brother of David, **k** him
2Sa 23: 8 because he had **k** eight
2Sa 23:12 it, and **k** the Philistines
2Sa 23:18 **k** them, and won a name among
2Sa 23:20 He had **k** two lion-like heroes
2Sa 23:20 **k** a lion in the midst of a
2Sa 23:21 And he **k** an Egyptian, a
2Sa 23:21 and **k** him with his own spear
1Ki 2: 5 the son of Jether, whom he **k**
1Ki 2:32 he, and **k** them with the sword
1Ki 2:34 went up and struck and **k** him
1Ki 9:16 had **k** the Canaanites who
1Ki 11:15 after he had **k** every male in

1Ki 11:24 when David **k** those of Zobah
1Ki 13:24 met him on the road and **k** him
1Ki 13:26 **k** him, according to the word
1Ki 15:27 Baasha **k** him at Gibbethon,
1Ki 15:28 Baasha **k** him in the third
1Ki 15:29 that he **k** all the house of
1Ki 16: 7 and because he **k** them
1Ki 16:10 **k** him in the twenty-seventh
1Ki 16:11 that he **k** all the household
1Ki 16:16 and also has **k** the king
1Ki 18:13 what I did when Jezebel **k** the
1Ki 19:10 and **k** Your prophets with the
1Ki 19:14 and **k** Your prophets with the
1Ki 20:20 And each one **k** his man
1Ki 20:21 **k** the Syrians with a great
1Ki 20:29 the children of Israel **k** one
1Ki 20:36 a lion found him and **k** him
2Ki 3:23 swords and have **k** one another
2Ki 10: 9 against my master and **k** him
2Ki 10: 9 but who **k** all these
2Ki 10:11 So Jehu **k** all who remained of
2Ki 10:14 **k** them at the well of Beth
2Ki 10:17 he **k** all who remained to Ahab
2Ki 10:25 they **k** them with the edge of
2Ki 11: 2 so that he was not **k**
2Ki 11:15 Do not let her be **k** in the
2Ki 11:16 house, and there she was **k**
2Ki 11:18 **k** Mattan the priest of Baal
2Ki 12:20 **k** Joash in the house of the
2Ki 14: 7 He **k** ten thousand Edomites in
2Ki 14:19 him to Lachish and **k** him there
2Ki 15:10 **k** him in front of the people
2Ki 15:14 of Jabesh in Samaria and **k** him
2Ki 15:25 and **k** him in Samaria, in the
2Ki 15:25 He **k** him and reigned in his
2Ki 15:30 Remaliah, and struck and **k** him
2Ki 16: 9 captive to Kir, and **k** Rezin
2Ki 17:25 them, which **k** some of them
2Ki 19:35 out, and **k** in the camp of the
2Ki 21:23 **k** the king in his own house
2Ki 23:29 And Pharaoh Necho **k** him at
2Ki 25: 7 Then they **k** the sons of
2Ki 25:25 **k** Gedaliah, the Jews, and the
1Ch 2: 3 and He **k** him
1Ch 7:21 who were born in that land **k**
1Ch 10: 2 And the Philistines **k** Jonathan
1Ch 10:14 therefore He **k** him, and turned
1Ch 11:11 hundred, **k** by him at one time
1Ch 11:14 it, and **k** the Philistines
1Ch 11:20 **k** them, and won a name among
1Ch 11:22 He had **k** two lion-like heroes
1Ch 11:22 **k** a lion in the midst of a
1Ch 11:23 he **k** an Egyptian, a man of
1Ch 11:23 and **k** him with his own spear
1Ch 18: 5 David **k** twenty-two thousand
1Ch 18:12 **k** eighteen thousand Edomites
1Ch 19:18 and David **k** seven thousand
1Ch 19:18 **k** Shophach the commander of
1Ch 20: 4 the Hushathite **k** Sippai, who
1Ch 20: 5 Jair **k** Lahmi the brother of
1Ch 20: 7 David's brother, **k** him
2Ch 18: 2 and Ahab **k** sheep and oxen in
2Ch 21: 4 **k** all his brothers with the
2Ch 21:13 also have **k** your brothers,
2Ch 22: 1 camp had **k** all the older sons
2Ch 22: 8 Ahaziah, that he **k** them
2Ch 22: 9 When they had **k** him, they
2Ch 23:15 house, and they **k** her there
2Ch 23:17 **k** Mattan the priest of Baal
2Ch 24:22 done to him, but **k** his son
2Ch 24:25 priest, and **k** him on his bed
2Ch 25:11 **k** ten thousand of the people
2Ch 25:13 **k** three thousand in them, and
2Ch 25:16 Why should you be **k**
2Ch 25:27 him to Lachish and **k** him there
2Ch 28: 6 son of Remaliah **k** one hundred
2Ch 28: 7 **k** Maaseiah the king's son,
2Ch 28: 9 but you have **k** them in a rage
2Ch 29:22 So they **k** the bulls, and the
2Ch 29:22 Likewise they **k** the rams and
2Ch 29:22 They also **k** the lambs and
2Ch 29:24 And the priests **k** them
2Ch 33:24 and **k** him in his own house
2Ch 36:17 who **k** their young men with
Neh 9:26 backs and **k** Your prophets, who
Esth 7: 4 I, to be destroyed, to be **k**
Esth 9: 6 the citadel the Jews **k** and
Esth 9:10 the enemy of the Jews—they **k**
Esth 9:11 number of those who were **k** in
Esth 9:12 The Jews have **k** and destroyed
Esth 9:15 and **k** three hundred men at
Esth 9:16 **k** seventy-five thousand of
Job 1:15 indeed they have **k** the
Job 1:17 **k** the servants with the edge
Ps 44:22 sake we are **k** all day long
Ps 105:29 into blood, And **k** their fish
Is 37:36 out, and **k** in the camp of the
Jer 26:23 who **k** him with the sword and
Jer 39: 6 Then the king of Babylon **k**
Jer 39: 6 **k** all the nobles of Judah
Jer 41: 2 and **k** him whom the king of
Jer 41: 4 day after he had **k** Gedaliah
Jer 41: 7 the son of Nethaniah **k** them
Jer 52:10 Then the king of Babylon **k**
Jer 52:10 he **k** all the princes of Judah
Ezek 9: 7 went out and **k** in the city
Dan 3:22 fire **k** those men who took up
Amos 4:10 young men I **k** with a sword
Nah 2:12 **k** for his lionesses, filled
Matt 16:21 priests and scribes, and be **k**
Matt 21:35 one, **k** one, and stoned another
Matt 21:39 out of the vineyard, and **k** him
Matt 22: 4 oxen and fatted cattle are **k**
Matt 22: 6 them spitefully, and **k** them
Mark 8:31 priests and scribes, and be **k**
Mark 9:31 And after He is **k**, He will
Mark 12: 5 sent another, and him they **k**
Mark 12: 8 **k** him and cast him out of the
Mark 14:12 when they **k** the Passover lamb
Luke 9:22 priests and scribes, and be **k**
Luke 11:47 and your fathers **k** them
Luke 11:48 for they indeed **k** them, and
Luke 12: 5 Fear Him who, after He has **k**
Luke 13: 4 **k** them, do you think that
Luke 15:27 father has **k** the fatted calf
Luke 15:30 you **k** the fatted calf for him
Luke 20:15 out of the vineyard and **k** him
Luke 22: 7 when the Passover must be **k**
Acts 3:15 **k** the Prince of life, whom
Acts 7:52 they **k** those who foretold the
Acts 10:39 whom they **k** by hanging on a
Acts 12: 2 Then he **k** James the brother
Acts 23:12 drink till they had **k** Paul
Acts 23:14 nothing until we have **k** Paul
Acts 23:21 drink till they have **k** him
Acts 23:27 and was about to be **k** by them
Rom 7:11 deceived me, and by it **k** me
Rom 8:36 sake we are **k** all day long
Rom 11: 3 they have **k** Your prophets and
2Co 6: 9 as chastened, and yet not **k**
1Th 2:15 who **k** both the Lord Jesus and
Rev 2:13 who was **k** among you, where
Rev 6:11 who would be **k** as they were
Rev 9:18 a third of mankind was **k**
Rev 9:20 who were not **k** by these
Rev 11: 5 he must be **k** in this manner
Rev 11:13 seven thousand men were **k**
Rev 13:10 must be **k** with the sword
Rev 13:15 image of the beast to be **k**
Rev 19:21 And the rest were **k** with the

KILLING (*see* KILL)
Judg 9:24 him in the **k** of his brothers
Judg 9:56 by **k** his seventy brothers
2Sa 8:13 **k** eighteen thousand Syrians
1Ki 17:20 whom I lodge, by **k** her son
2Ki 3:24 their land, **k** the Moabites
2Ki 17:26 they are **k** them because they
Is 22:13 and **k** sheep, eating meat and
Ezek 9: 8 that while they were **k** them
Ezek 13:19 **k** people who should not die,
Dan 2:13 they began **k** the wise men
Hos 4: 2 By swearing and lying, **k** and
Mark 12: 5 beating some and **k** some
Acts 22:20 of those who were **k** him

KILLS (*see* KILL)
Gen 4:15 Therefore, whoever **k** Cain
Lev 14:13 where he **k** the sin offering
Lev 17: 3 **k** an ox or lamb or goat in
Lev 17: 3 or who **k** it outside the camp,
Lev 24:17 Whoever **k** any man shall
Lev 24:18 Whoever **k** an animal shall
Lev 24:21 whoever **k** an animal shall
Lev 24:21 but whoever **k** a man shall be
Num 35:11 that the manslayer who **k** any
Num 35:15 that anyone who **k** a person
Num 35:27 of blood **k** the manslayer, he
Num 35:30 Whoever **k** a person, the
Deut 4:42 there, who **k** his neighbor
Deut 19: 4 Whoever **k** his neighbor
Deut 22:26 **k** him, even so is this matter
Josh 20: 3 that the slayer who **k** any
1Sa 2: 6 The LORD **k** and makes alive
1Sa 17:25 **k** him the king will enrich
1Sa 17:26 the man who **k** this Philistine
1Sa 17:27 be done for the man who **k** him
Job 5: 2 For wrath **k** a foolish man, and
Job 24:14 he **k** the poor and needy
Prov 21:25 desire of the slothful **k** him
Is 66: 3 He who **k** a bull is as if he
Matt 23:37 the one who **k** the prophets and
Luke 13:34 the one who **k** the prophets and
John 16: 2 **k** you will think that he
2Co 3: 6 for the letter **k**, but the
Rev 13:10 he who **k** with the sword must

KILN
Nah 3:14 Make strong the brick **k**

KIN (*see* KINDRED, KINSMAN)
Lev 18: 6 who is near of **k** to him, to
Lev 18:12 is near of **k** to your father
Lev 18:13 is near of **k** to your mother
Lev 18:17 They are near of **k** to her
Lev 20:19 would uncover his near of **k**
Lev 25:49 of **k** to him in his family may
Prov 7: 4 understanding your nearest **k**

KINAH
Josh 15:22 **K**, Dimonah, Adadah,

KIND (*see* KINDLY, KINDNESS, KINDS)
Gen 1:11 fruit according to its **k**,
Gen 1:12 seed according to its **k**, and
Gen 1:12 in itself according to its **k**
Gen 1:21 according to their **k**, and
Gen 1:21 bird according to its **k**
Gen 1:24 creature according to its **k**
Gen 1:24 each according to its **k**"
Gen 1:25 the earth according to its **k**
Gen 1:25 cattle according to its **k**
Gen 1:25 the earth according to its **k**
Gen 6:20 Of the birds after their **k**
Gen 6:20 of animals after their **k**
Gen 6:20 of the earth after its **k**, two
Gen 6:20 two of every **k** will come to
Gen 7:14 and every beast after its **k**
Gen 7:14 all cattle after their **k**
Gen 7:14 on the earth after its **k**, and
Gen 7:14 and every bird after its **k**
Ex 22: 9 For any **k** of trespass,
Ex 22: 9 or for any **k** of lost thing
Lev 11:14 and the falcon after its **k**
Lev 11:15 every raven after its **k**,
Lev 11:16 and the hawk after its **k**
Lev 11:19 stork, the heron after its **k**
Lev 11:22 the locust after its **k**, the
Lev 11:22 destroying locust after its **k**
Lev 11:22 the cricket after its **k**
Lev 11:22 the grasshopper after its **k**
Lev 11:29 the large lizard after its **k**
Lev 19:19 breed with another **k**
Lev 20:25 or by any **k** of living thing
Deut 14:14 every raven after its **k**
Deut 14:18 stork, the heron after its **k**
Deut 27:21 who lies with any **k** of animal
Judg 8:18 What **k** of men were they whom
Judg 21:22 Be **k** to them for our sakes,
1Ki 9:13 What **k** of cities are these
2Ki 1: 7 What **k** of man was it who came
1Ch 6:48 to every **k** of service of the
1Ch 12:37 with every **k** of weapon of war
1Ch 22:15 men for every **k** of work
1Ch 28:14 used in every **k** of service
1Ch 28:14 used in every **k** of service
1Ch 28:21 for every **k** of service
2Ch 10: 7 If you are **k** to these people,
2Ch 34:13 did work in any **k** of service
Ezra 1:10 silver basins of a similar **k**
Ezek 44:30 of all firstfruits of any **k**
Ezek 44:30 every sacrifice of any **k** from
Matt 13:47 and gathered some of every **k**
Matt 17:21 this **k** does not go out except
Mark 9:29 This **k** can come out by
Luke 1:66 What **k** of child will this be
Luke 6:35 For He is **k** to the unthankful
Luke 24:17 What **k** of conversation is
1Co 13: 4 Love suffers long and is **k**
1Co 15:39 is one **k** of flesh of men,
Eph 4:32 And be **k** to one another,
1Th 1: 5 as you know what **k** of men we
Jas 1:18 that we might be a **k** of

Jas 1:24 forgets what **k** of man he was
Jas 3: 7 For every **k** of beast and bird,
Rev 18:12 every **k** of citron wood, every
Rev 18:12 every **k** of object of ivory,
Rev 18:12 every **k** of object of most

KINDLE (*see* KINDLED, KINDLES)
Ex 35: 3 You shall **k** no fire
Prov 26:21 a contentious man to **k** strife
Is 9:18 and **k** in the thickets of the
Is 10:16 under his glory he will **k** a
Is 50:11 Look, all you who **k** a fire
Jer 7:18 wood, the fathers **k** the fire
Jer 17:27 then I will **k** a fire in its
Jer 21:14 I will **k** a fire in its forest
Jer 33:18 to **k** grain offerings, and to
Jer 43:12 I will **k** a fire in the houses
Jer 49:27 I will **k** a fire in the wall
Jer 50:32 I will **k** a fire in his cities
Ezek 20:47 I will **k** a fire in you, and it
Ezek 24:10 Heap on the wood, **k** the fire
Amos 1:14 But I will **k** a fire in the
Obad 18 they shall **k** them and devour
Mal 1:10 So that you would not **k** fire

KINDLED (*see* KINDLE)
Ex 4:14 the LORD was **k** against Moses
Ex 22: 6 he who **k** the fire shall
Lev 10: 6 burning which the LORD has **k**
Deut 32:22 For a fire is **k** in My anger
2Sa 22: 9 coals were **k** by it
2Sa 22:13 Him coals of fire were **k**
Job 19:11 He has also **k** His wrath
Ps 2:12 His wrath is **k** but a little
Ps 18: 8 Coals were **k** by it
Ps 78:21 So a fire was **k** against Jacob
Ps 106:18 A fire was **k** in their company
Ps 106:40 LORD was **k** against His people
Ps 124: 3 their wrath was **k** against us
Is 50:11 and in the sparks you have **k**
Jer 11:16 tumult He has **k** fire on it
Jer 15:14 for a fire is **k** in My anger
Jer 17: 4 for you have **k** a fire in My
Jer 44: 6 **k** in the cities of Judah and
Lam 4:11 He **k** a fire in Zion, and it
Ezek 20:48 that I, the LORD, have **k** it
Zech 10: 3 My anger is **k** against the
Luke 12:49 how I wish it were already **k**
Luke 22:55 Now when they had **k** a fire in
Acts 28: 2 for they **k** a fire and made us

KINDLES (*see* KINDLE)
Job 41:21 His breath **k** coals, and a
Is 30:33 a stream of brimstone, **k** it
Is 44:15 yes, he **k** it and bakes bread
Jas 3: 5 a forest a little fire **k**

KINDLY (*see* KIND)
Gen 24:49 Now if you will deal **k** and
Gen 34: 3 spoke **k** to the young woman
Gen 47:29 under my thigh, and deal **k**
Gen 50:21 them and spoke **k** to them
Josh 2:14 the land, that we will deal **k**
Judg 19: 3 after her, to speak **k** to her
Ruth 1: 8 The LORD deal **k** with you, as
Ruth 2:13 me, and have spoken **k** to your
1Sa 20: 8 deal **k** with your servant, for
2Sa 13:24 **K** note, your servant has
2Ki 25:28 He spoke **k** to him, and gave
Job 39:13 and pinions like the **k** stork's
Prov 26:25 when he speaks **k**, do not
Jer 52:32 And he spoke **k** to him and gave
Acts 27: 3 And Julius treated Paul **k** and
Rom 12:10 Be **k** affectionate to one

KINDNESS (*see* KIND)
Gen 20:13 her, 'This is your **k** that you
Gen 21:23 the **k** that I have done to you
Gen 24:12 show **k** to my master Abraham
Gen 24:14 You have shown **k** to my master
Gen 40:14 you, and please show **k** to me
Josh 2:12 since I have shown you **k**
Josh 2:12 show **k** to my father's house
Judg 8:35 nor did they show **k** to the
Ruth 2:20 forsaken His **k** to the living
Ruth 3:10 more **k** at the end than at the
1Sa 15: 6 For you showed **k** to all the
1Sa 20:14 **k** of the LORD while I still
1Sa 20:15 your **k** from my house forever
2Sa 2: 5 shown this **k** to your lord
2Sa 2: 6 And now may the LORD show **k**
2Sa 2: 6 I also will repay you this **k**
2Sa 9: 1 him **k** for Jonathan's sake
2Sa 9: 3 whom I may show the **k** of God
2Sa 9: 7 **k** for Jonathan your father's
2Sa 10: 2 I will show **k** to Hanun the
2Sa 10: 2 as his father showed **k** to me
1Ki 2: 7 But show **k** to the sons of
1Ki 3: 6 this great **k** for him, and You
1Ch 19: 2 I will show **k** to Hanun the
1Ch 19: 2 his father showed **k** to me
2Ch 24:22 **k** which Jehoiada his father
Neh 9:17 slow to anger, abundant in **k**
Job 6:14 **k** should be shown by his
Ps 31:21 marvelous **k** in a strong city
Ps 117: 2 For His merciful **k** is great
Ps 119:76 Your merciful **k** be for my
Ps 141: 5 It shall be a **k**
Prov 19:22 What is desired in a man is **k**
Prov 31:26 on her tongue is the law of **k**
Is 54: 8 but with everlasting **k** I will
Is 54:10 but My **k** shall not depart
Jer 2: 2 the **k** of your youth, the love
Joel 2:13 slow to anger, and of great **k**
Acts 28: 2 natives showed us unusual **k**
2Co 6: 6 by longsuffering, by **k**, by
Gal 5:22 joy, peace, longsuffering, **k**
Eph 2: 7 **k** toward us in Christ Jesus
Col 3:12 put on tender mercies, **k**
Tit 3: 4 But when the **k** and the love of
2Pe 1: 7 to godliness brotherly **k**, and
2Pe 1: 7 and to brotherly **k** love

KINDRED (*see* KIN, KINDREDS)
Gen 12: 1 of your country, from your **k**
Gen 24: 4 go to my country and to my **k**
Gen 24: 7 and from the land of my **k**, and
Gen 24:38 my father's house and to my **k**
Gen 24:40 a wife for my son from my **k**
Gen 24:41 when you arrive among my **k**
Gen 31: 3 of your fathers and to your **k**
Gen 31:13 return to the land of your **k**
Gen 32: 9 to your country and to your **k**
Gen 43: 7 about ourselves and our **k**,
Esth 2:10 not revealed her people or **k**
Esth 2:20 had not yet revealed her **k**
Esth 8: 6 see the destruction of my **k**
Esth 10: 3 speaking peace to all his **k**

KINDREDS (*see* KINDRED)
1Ch 16:28 O **k** of the peoples, give to
Ps 96: 7 O **k** of the peoples, Give to

KINDS (*see* KIND)
Gen 40:17 basket there were all **k** of
Ex 35:29 all **k** of work which the LORD
Lev 11:27 among all **k** of animals that
Lev 19:23 have planted all **k** of trees
Deut 14:13 and the kite after their **k**
Deut 14:15 and the hawk after their **k**
Deut 22: 9 with different **k** of seed,
2Sa 6: 5 before the LORD on all **k** of
1Ki 7:14 with all **k** of bronze work
1Ch 18:10 him all **k** of articles of gold
1Ch 23:29 with all **k** of measures and
1Ch 29: 2 all **k** of precious stones, and
1Ch 29: 5 for all **k** of work to be done
2Ch 32:27 for all **k** of desirable items
2Ch 32:28 stalls for all **k** of livestock
Neh 5:18 an abundance of all **k** of wine
Neh 10:37 the fruit from all **k** of trees
Neh 13:15 all **k** of burdens, which they
Neh 13:16 all **k** of goods, and sold them
Neh 13:20 sellers of all **k** of wares
Ps 144:13 Supplying all **k** of produce
Prov 1:13 we shall find all **k** of
Eccl 2: 5 and I planted all **k** of fruit
Eccl 2: 8 musical instruments of all **k**
Ezek 27:22 all **k** of precious stones, and
Ezek 47:10 **k** as the fish of the Great
Ezek 47:12 will grow all **k** of trees used
Dan 3: 5 symphony with all **k** of music
Dan 3: 7 symphony with all **k** of music
Dan 3:10 symphony with all **k** of music
Dan 3:15 symphony with all **k** of music
Matt 4:23 and healing all **k** of sickness
Matt 4:23 all **k** of disease among the
Matt 5:11 say all **k** of evil against you
Matt 10: 1 and to heal all **k** of sickness
Matt 10: 1 sickness and all **k** of disease
Acts 10:12 In it were all **k** of
1Co 12:10 different **k** of tongues, to
1Co 14:10 so many **k** of languages in the
1Ti 6:10 is a root of all **k** of evil
Rev 21:19 with all **k** of precious stones

KING (*see* KINGLY, KING'S, KINGS)
Gen 14: 1 days of Amraphel **k** of Shinar
Gen 14: 1 Shinar, Arioch **k** of Ellasar,
Gen 14: 1 Chedorlaomer **k** of Elam, and
Gen 14: 1 Elam, and Tidal **k** of nations,
Gen 14: 2 made war with Bera **k** of Sodom
Gen 14: 2 Birsha **k** of Gomorrah, Shinab
Gen 14: 2 Shinab **k** of Admah, Shemeber
Gen 14: 2 Shemeber **k** of Zeboiim, and the
Gen 14: 2 the **k** of Bela (that is, Zoar)
Gen 14: 8 **k** of Sodom, the **k** of Gomorrah
Gen 14: 8 **k** of Admah, the **k** of Zeboiim
Gen 14: 8 the **k** of Bela (that is, Zoar)
Gen 14: 9 Chedorlaomer **k** of Elam, Tidal
Gen 14: 9 Tidal **k** of nations, Amraphel
Gen 14: 9 Amraphel **k** of Shinar, and
Gen 14: 9 and Arioch **k** of Ellasar
Gen 14:17 the **k** of Sodom went out to
Gen 14:18 Then Melchizedek **k** of Salem
Gen 14:21 Now the **k** of Sodom said to
Gen 14:22 Abram said to the **k** of Sodom
Gen 20: 2 Abimelech **k** of Gerar sent and
Gen 26: 1 **k** of the Philistines, in
Gen 26: 8 time, that Abimelech **k** of the
Gen 36:31 **k** reigned over the children
Gen 40: 1 the baker of the **k** of Egypt
Gen 40: 1 their lord, the **k** of Egypt
Gen 40: 5 the baker of the **k** of Egypt
Gen 41:46 before Pharaoh **k** of Egypt
Ex 1: 8 arose a new **k** over Egypt, who
Ex 1:15 Then the **k** of Egypt spoke to
Ex 1:17 did not do as the **k** of Egypt
Ex 1:18 So the **k** of Egypt called for
Ex 2:23 time that the **k** of Egypt died
Ex 3:18 of Israel, to the **k** of Egypt
Ex 3:19 But I am sure that the **k** of
Ex 5: 4 Then the **k** of Egypt said to
Ex 6:11 speak to Pharaoh **k** of Egypt
Ex 6:13 and for Pharaoh **k** of Egypt
Ex 6:27 spoke to Pharaoh **k** of Egypt
Ex 6:29 Speak to Pharaoh **k** of Egypt
Ex 14: 5 Now it was told the **k** of
Ex 14: 8 heart of Pharaoh **k** of Egypt
Num 20:14 from Kadesh to the **k** of Edom
Num 21: 1 When the **k** of Arad, the
Num 21:21 to Sihon **k** of the Amorites
Num 21:26 of Sihon **k** of the Amorites
Num 21:26 against the former **k** of Moab
Num 21:29 to Sihon **k** of the Amorites
Num 21:33 So Og **k** of Bashan went out
Num 21:34 to Sihon **k** of the Amorites
Num 22: 4 was **k** of the Moabites at that
Num 22:10 **k** of Moab, has sent to me,
Num 23: 7 Balak the **k** of Moab has
Num 23:21 shout of a **K** is among them
Num 24: 7 His **k** shall be higher than
Num 32:33 of Sihon **k** of the Amorites
Num 32:33 the kingdom of Og **k** of Bashan
Num 33:40 Now the **k** of Arad, the
Deut 1: 4 Sihon **k** of the Amorites, who
Deut 1: 4 Og **k** of Bashan, who dwelt at
Deut 2:24 **k** of Heshbon, and his land
Deut 2:26 to Sihon **k** of Heshbon, with
Deut 2:30 But Sihon **k** of Heshbon would
Deut 3: 1 and Og **k** of Bashan came out
Deut 3: 2 to Sihon **k** of the Amorites
Deut 3: 3 into our hands Og **k** of Bashan
Deut 3: 6 we did to Sihon **k** of Heshbon
Deut 3:11 For only Og **k** of Bashan
Deut 4:46 of Sihon **k** of the Amorites
Deut 4:47 and the land of Og **k** of Bashan
Deut 7: 8 hand of Pharaoh **k** of Egypt
Deut 11: 3 Egypt, to Pharaoh **k** of Egypt
Deut 17:14 I will set a **k** over me like
Deut 17:15 you shall surely set a **k** over
Deut 17:15 you shall set as **k** over you
Deut 28:36 the **k** whom you set over you
Deut 29: 7 Sihon **k** of Heshbon
Deut 29: 7 and Og **k** of Bashan came out
Deut 33: 5 He was **K** in Jeshurun, when
Josh 2: 2 it was told the **k** of Jericho
Josh 2: 3 So the **k** of Jericho sent to
Josh 6: 2 Jericho into your hand, its **k**
Josh 8: 1 into your hand the **k** of Ai
Josh 8: 2 its **k** as you did to Jericho
Josh 8: 2 you did to Jericho and its **k**
Josh 8:14 when the **k** of Ai saw it, that
Josh 8:23 But the **k** of Ai they took
Josh 8:29 the **k** of Ai he hanged on a
Josh 9:10 to Sihon **k** of Heshbon, and Og

Josh 9:10 Og **k** of Bashan, who was at
Josh 10: 1 **k** of Jerusalem heard how
Josh 10: 1 had done to Jericho and its **k**
Josh 10: 1 so he had done to Ai and its **k**
Josh 10: 3 Therefore Adoni-Zedek **k** of
Josh 10: 3 sent to Hoham **k** of Hebron
Josh 10: 3 Piram **k** of Jarmuth, Japhia
Josh 10: 3 Japhia **k** of Lachish, and Debir
Josh 10: 3 Debir **k** of Eglon, saying,
Josh 10: 5 the **k** of Jerusalem
Josh 10: 5 the **k** of Hebron
Josh 10: 5 the **k** of Jarmuth
Josh 10: 5 the **k** of Lachish
Josh 10: 5 and the **k** of Eglon, gathered
Josh 10:23 the **k** of Jerusalem
Josh 10:23 the **k** of Hebron
Josh 10:23 the **k** of Jarmuth
Josh 10:23 the **k** of Lachish
Josh 10:23 and the **k** of Eglon
Josh 10:28 its **k** with the edge of the
Josh 10:28 He also did to the **k** of
Josh 10:28 had done to the **k** of Jericho
Josh 10:30 its **k** into the hand of Israel
Josh 10:30 but did to its **k** as he had
Josh 10:30 had done to the **k** of Jericho
Josh 10:33 Then Horam **k** of Gezer came
Josh 10:37 its **k**, all its cities, and all
Josh 10:39 And he took it and its **k** and all
Josh 10:39 so he did to Debir and its **k**
Josh 10:39 done also to Libnah and its **k**
Josh 11: 1 when Jabin **k** of Hazor heard
Josh 11: 1 he sent to Jobab **k** of Madon
Josh 11: 1 to the **k** of Shimron, to the
Josh 11: 1 to the **k** of Achshaph,
Josh 11:10 struck its **k** with the sword
Josh 12: 2 Sihon **k** of the Amorites, who
Josh 12: 4 Og **k** of Bashan and his
Josh 12: 5 border of Sihon **k** of Heshbon
Josh 12: 9 the **k** of Jericho, one
Josh 12: 9 the **k** of Ai, which is beside
Josh 12:10 the **k** of Jerusalem, one
Josh 12:10 the **k** of Hebron, one
Josh 12:11 the **k** of Jarmuth, one
Josh 12:11 the **k** of Lachish, one
Josh 12:12 the **k** of Eglon, one
Josh 12:12 the **k** of Gezer, one
Josh 12:13 the **k** of Debir, one
Josh 12:13 the **k** of Geder, one
Josh 12:14 the **k** of Hormah, one
Josh 12:14 the **k** of Arad, one
Josh 12:15 the **k** of Libnah, one
Josh 12:15 the **k** of Adullam, one
Josh 12:16 the **k** of Makkedah, one
Josh 12:16 the **k** of Bethel, one
Josh 12:17 the **k** of Tappuah, one
Josh 12:17 the **k** of Hepher, one
Josh 12:18 the **k** of Aphek, one
Josh 12:18 the **k** of Lasharon, one
Josh 12:19 the **k** of Madon, one
Josh 12:19 the **k** of Hazor, one
Josh 12:20 the **k** of Shimron Meron, one
Josh 12:20 the **k** of Achshaph, one
Josh 12:21 the **k** of Taanach, one
Josh 12:21 the **k** of Megiddo, one
Josh 12:22 the **k** of Kedesh, one
Josh 12:22 the **k** of Jokneam in Carmel,
Josh 12:23 the **k** of Dor in the heights
Josh 12:23 the **k** of the people of Gilgal
Josh 12:24 the **k** of Tirzah, one
Josh 13:10 of Sihon **k** of the Amorites
Josh 13:21 of Sihon **k** of the Amorites
Josh 13:27 kingdom of Sihon **k** of Heshbon
Josh 13:30 the kingdom of Og **k** of Bashan
Josh 24: 9 **k** of Moab, arose to make war
Judg 3: 8 **k** of Mesopotamia
Judg 3:10 **k** of Mesopotamia into his
Judg 3:12 **k** of Moab against Israel,
Judg 3:14 **k** of Moab eighteen years
Judg 3:15 tribute to Eglon **k** of Moab
Judg 3:17 tribute to Eglon **k** of Moab
Judg 3:19 a secret message for you, O **k**
Judg 4: 2 the hand of Jabin **k** of Canaan
Judg 4:17 between Jabin **k** of Hazor and
Judg 4:23 **k** of Canaan in the presence
Judg 4:24 against Jabin **k** of Canaan
Judg 4:24 destroyed Jabin **k** of Canaan
Judg 8:18 one resembled the son of a **k**
Judg 9: 6 made Abimelech **k** beside the
Judg 9: 8 forth to anoint a **k** over them
Judg 9:15 you anoint me as **k** over you
Judg 9:16 in making Abimelech **k**, and if
Judg 9:18 **k** over the men of Shechem,
Judg 11:12 the **k** of the people of Ammon
Judg 11:13 the **k** of the people of Ammon
Judg 11:14 the **k** of the people of Ammon
Judg 11:17 messengers to the **k** of Edom
Judg 11:17 But the **k** of Edom would not
Judg 11:17 they sent to the **k** of Moab
Judg 11:19 to Sihon **k** of the Amorites
Judg 11:19 of the Amorites, **k** of Heshbon
Judg 11:25 the son of Zippor, **k** of Moab
Judg 11:28 the **k** of the people of Ammon
Judg 17: 6 days there was no **k** in Israel
Judg 18: 1 days there was no **k** in Israel
Judg 19: 1 when there was no **k** in Israel
Judg 21:25 days there was no **k** in Israel
1Sa 2:10 will give strength to His **k**
1Sa 8: 5 Now make for us a **k** to judge
1Sa 8: 6 Give us a **k** to judge us
1Sa 8: 9 **k** who will reign over them
1Sa 8:10 people who asked him for a **k**
1Sa 8:11 the **k** who will reign over you
1Sa 8:18 **k** whom you have chosen for
1Sa 8:19 but we will have a **k** over us
1Sa 8:20 that our **k** may judge us and go
1Sa 8:22 their voice, and make them a **k**
1Sa 10:19 Him, 'No, but set a **k** over us
1Sa 10:24 Long live the **k**
1Sa 11:15 there they made Saul **k** before
1Sa 12: 1 me, and have made a **k** over you
1Sa 12: 2 And now here is the **k**, walking
1Sa 12: 9 the hand of the **k** of Moab
1Sa 12:12 **k** of the Ammonites came
1Sa 12:12 but a **k** shall reign over us,'
1Sa 12:12 the LORD your God was your **k**
1Sa 12:13 here is the **k** whom you have
1Sa 12:13 the LORD has set a **k** over you
1Sa 12:14 the **k** who reigns over you
1Sa 12:17 in asking a **k** for yourselves
1Sa 12:19 of asking a **k** for ourselves
1Sa 12:25 away, both you and your **k**
1Sa 15: 1 anoint you **k** over His people
1Sa 15: 8 He also took Agag **k** of the
1Sa 15:11 that I have set up Saul as **k**
1Sa 15:17 LORD anoint you **k** over Israel
1Sa 15:20 brought back Agag **k** of Amalek
1Sa 15:23 has rejected you from being **k**
1Sa 15:26 you from being **k** over Israel
1Sa 15:32 said, "Bring Agag **k** of the
1Sa 15:35 had made Saul **k** over Israel
1Sa 16: 1 Myself a **k** among his sons
1Sa 17:25 the **k** will enrich with great
1Sa 17:55 As your soul lives, O **k**, I do
1Sa 17:56 the **k** said, "Inquire whose
1Sa 18: 6 and dancing, to meet **K** Saul
1Sa 18:18 should be son-in-law to the **k**
1Sa 18:22 the **k** has delight in you, and
1Sa 18:25 The **k** does not desire any
1Sa 18:27 them in full count to the **k**
1Sa 19: 4 Let not the **k** sin against his
1Sa 20: 5 fail to sit with the **k** to eat
1Sa 20:24 the **k** sat down to eat the
1Sa 20:25 Now the **k** sat on his seat, as
1Sa 21: 2 The **k** has ordered me on some
1Sa 21:10 went to Achish the **k** of Gath
1Sa 21:11 not David the **k** of the land
1Sa 21:12 of Achish the **k** of Gath
1Sa 22: 3 and he said to the **k** of Moab
1Sa 22: 4 them before the **k** of Moab
1Sa 22:11 Then the **k** sent to call
1Sa 22:11 And they all came to the **k**
1Sa 22:14 So Ahimelech answered the **k**
1Sa 22:15 Let not the **k** impute anything
1Sa 22:16 the **k** said, "You shall
1Sa 22:17 Then the **k** said to the guards
1Sa 22:17 But the servants of the **k**
1Sa 22:18 And the **k** said to Doeg,
1Sa 23:17 You shall be **k** over Israel
1Sa 23:20 Now therefore, O **k**, come down
1Sa 24: 8 saying, "My lord the **k**!"
1Sa 24:14 has the **k** of Israel come out
1Sa 24:20 that you shall surely be **k**
1Sa 25:36 house, like the feast of a **k**
1Sa 26:14 are you, calling out to the **k**
1Sa 26:15 not guarded your lord the **k**
1Sa 26:15 in to destroy your lord the **k**
1Sa 26:17 It is my voice, my lord, O **k**
1Sa 26:19 let my lord the **k** hear the
1Sa 26:20 For the **k** of Israel has come
1Sa 27: 2 the son of Maoch, **k** of Gath
1Sa 28:13 And the **k** said to her,
1Sa 29: 3 servant of Saul **k** of Israel
1Sa 29: 8 the enemies of my lord the **k**
2Sa 2: 4 **k** over the house of Judah
2Sa 2: 7 has anointed me **k** over them
2Sa 2: 9 and he made him **k** over Gilead
2Sa 2:11 the time that David was **k** in
2Sa 3: 3 of Talmai, **k** of Geshur
2Sa 3:17 for David to be **k** over you
2Sa 3:21 all Israel to my lord the **k**
2Sa 3:23 the son of Ner came to the **k**
2Sa 3:24 Then Joab came to the **k** and
2Sa 3:31 **K** David followed the coffin
2Sa 3:32 the **k** lifted up his voice and
2Sa 3:33 And the **k** sang a lament over
2Sa 3:36 since whatever the **k** did
2Sa 3:38 Then the **k** said to his
2Sa 3:39 weak today, though anointed **k**
2Sa 4: 8 at Hebron, and said to the **k**
2Sa 4: 8 lord the **k** this day of Saul
2Sa 5: 2 past, when Saul was **k** over us
2Sa 5: 3 came to the **k** at Hebron, and
2Sa 5: 3 **K** David made a covenant with
2Sa 5: 3 anointed David **k** over Israel
2Sa 5: 6 And the **k** and his men went to
2Sa 5:11 Then Hiram **k** of Tyre sent
2Sa 5:12 him as **k** over Israel, and that
2Sa 5:17 anointed David **k** over Israel
2Sa 6:12 And it was told **K** David,
2Sa 6:16 and saw **K** David leaping and
2Sa 6:20 was the **k** of Israel today
2Sa 7: 1 it came to pass when the **k**
2Sa 7: 2 that the **k** said to Nathan the
2Sa 7: 3 Then Nathan said to the **k**
2Sa 7:18 Then **K** David went in and sat
2Sa 8: 3 **k** of Zobah, as he went to
2Sa 8: 5 to help Hadadezer **k** of Zobah
2Sa 8: 8 **K** David took a large amount
2Sa 8: 9 When Toi **k** of Hamath heard
2Sa 8:10 sent Joram his son to **K** David
2Sa 8:11 **K** David dedicated these to
2Sa 8:12 the son of Rehob, **k** of Zobah
2Sa 9: 2 to David, the **k** said to him,
2Sa 9: 3 Then the **k** said, "Is there
2Sa 9: 3 And Ziba said to the **k**
2Sa 9: 4 So the **k** said to him, "Where
2Sa 9: 4 And Ziba said to the **k**
2Sa 9: 5 Then **K** David sent and brought
2Sa 9: 9 the **k** called to Ziba, Saul's
2Sa 9:11 Then Ziba said to the **k**
2Sa 9:11 to all that my lord the **k** has
2Sa 9:11 Mephibosheth," said the **k**
2Sa 10: 1 after this that the **k** of the
2Sa 10: 5 the **k** said, "Wait at
2Sa 10: 6 from **K** Maacah one thousand
2Sa 11: 8 food from the **k** followed him
2Sa 11:19 matters of the war to the **k**
2Sa 12: 7 I anointed you **k** over Israel
2Sa 13: 6 when the **k** came to see him,
2Sa 13: 6 see him, Amnon said to the **k**
2Sa 13:13 please speak to the **k**
2Sa 13:21 But when **K** David heard of all
2Sa 13:24 Then Absalom came to the **k**
2Sa 13:24 please, let the **k** and his
2Sa 13:25 But the **k** said to Absalom,
2Sa 13:26 And the **k** said to him,
2Sa 13:31 So the **k** arose and tore his
2Sa 13:33 let not my lord the **k** take
2Sa 13:35 And Jonadab said to the **k**
2Sa 13:36 Also the **k** and all his
2Sa 13:37 son of Ammihud, **k** of Geshur
2Sa 13:39 And **K** David longed to go to
2Sa 14: 3 Go to the **k** and speak to him
2Sa 14: 4 woman of Tekoa spoke to the **k**
2Sa 14: 4 and said, "Help, O **k**!"
2Sa 14: 5 Then the **k** said to her
2Sa 14: 8 Then the **k** said to the woman,
2Sa 14: 9 woman of Tekoa said to the **k**
2Sa 14: 9 My lord, O **k**, let the
2Sa 14: 9 my father's house, and the **k**
2Sa 14:10 So the **k** said, "Whoever says
2Sa 14:11 Please let the **k** remember the
2Sa 14:12 another word to my lord the **k**
2Sa 14:13 For the **k** speaks this thing
2Sa 14:13 in that the **k** does not bring
2Sa 14:15 the **k** because the people have
2Sa 14:15 I will now speak to the **k**
2Sa 14:15 it may be that the **k** will
2Sa 14:16 For the **k** will hear and
2Sa 14:17 the **k** will now be comforting

1Ki 7:13 Now **K** Solomon sent and
1Ki 7:14 So he came to **K** Solomon and
1Ki 7:40 work that he was to do for **K**
1Ki 7:45 which Hiram made for **K**
1Ki 7:46 In the plain of Jordan the **k**
1Ki 7:51 Thus all the work that **K**
1Ki 8: 1 to **K** Solomon in Jerusalem,
1Ki 8: 2 men of Israel assembled to **K**
1Ki 8: 5 Also **K** Solomon, and all the
1Ki 8:14 And the **k** turned around and
1Ki 8:62 Then the **k** and all Israel with
1Ki 8:63 So the **k** and all the children
1Ki 8:64 On the same day the **k**
1Ki 8:66 and they blessed the **k**, and
1Ki 9:11 (Hiram the **k** of Tyre had
1Ki 9:11 that **K** Solomon then gave
1Ki 9:14 Hiram sent the **k** one hundred
1Ki 9:15 force which **K** Solomon raised
1Ki 9:16 (Pharaoh **k** of Egypt had gone
1Ki 9:26 **K** Solomon also built a fleet
1Ki 9:28 and brought it to **K** Solomon
1Ki 10: 3 so difficult for the **k** that
1Ki 10: 6 Then she said to the **k**
1Ki 10: 9 therefore He made you **k**, to
1Ki 10:10 she gave the **k** one hundred
1Ki 10:10 of Sheba gave to **K** Solomon
1Ki 10:12 the **k** made steps of the almug
1Ki 10:13 **K** Solomon gave the queen of
1Ki 10:16 **K** Solomon made two hundred
1Ki 10:17 the **k** put them in the House
1Ki 10:18 Moreover the **k** made a great
1Ki 10:21 All **K** Solomon's drinking
1Ki 10:22 For the **k** had merchant ships
1Ki 10:23 So **K** Solomon surpassed all
1Ki 10:26 and with the **k** in Jerusalem
1Ki 10:27 The **k** made silver as common
1Ki 11: 1 But **K** Solomon loved many
1Ki 11:14 a descendant of the **k** in Edom
1Ki 11:18 Egypt, to Pharaoh **k** of Egypt
1Ki 11:23 lord, Hadadezer **k** of Zobah
1Ki 11:26 also rebelled against the **k**
1Ki 11:27 him to rebel against the **k**
1Ki 11:37 and you shall be **k** over Israel
1Ki 11:40 Egypt, to Shishak **k** of Egypt
1Ki 12: 1 gone to Shechem to make him **k**
1Ki 12: 2 the presence of **K** Solomon
1Ki 12: 6 Then **K** Rehoboam consulted
1Ki 12:12 as the **k** directed, saying,
1Ki 12:13 Then the **k** answered the
1Ki 12:15 So the **k** did not listen to
1Ki 12:16 the **k** did not listen to them
1Ki 12:16 the people answered the **k**
1Ki 12:18 Then **K** Rehoboam sent
1Ki 12:18 Therefore **K** Rehoboam
1Ki 12:20 made him **k** over all Israel
1Ki 12:23 **k** of Judah, to all the house
1Ki 12:27 lord, Rehoboam **k** of Judah
1Ki 12:27 back to Rehoboam **k** of Judah
1Ki 12:28 Therefore the **k** took counsel
1Ki 13: 4 So it came to pass when **K**
1Ki 13: 6 Then the **k** answered and said
1Ki 13: 7 Then the **k** said to the man of
1Ki 13: 8 the man of God said to the **k**
1Ki 13:11 which he had spoken to the **k**
1Ki 14: 2 I would be **k** over this people
1Ki 14:14 a **k** over Israel who shall cut
1Ki 14:21 years old when he became **k**
1Ki 14:25 the fifth year of **K** Rehoboam
1Ki 14:25 that Shishak **k** of Egypt came
1Ki 14:27 Then **K** Rehoboam made
1Ki 14:28 whenever the **k** went into the
1Ki 15: 1 **K** Jeroboam the son of Nebat
1Ki 15: 1 Abijam became **k** over Judah
1Ki 15: 9 year of Jeroboam **k** of Israel
1Ki 15: 9 Asa became **k** over Judah
1Ki 15:16 Baasha **k** of Israel all their
1Ki 15:17 Baasha **k** of Israel came up
1Ki 15:17 or come in to Asa **k** of Judah
1Ki 15:18 **K** Asa sent them to Ben-Hadad
1Ki 15:18 **k** of Syria, who dwelt in
1Ki 15:19 with Baasha **k** of Israel, so
1Ki 15:20 So Ben-Hadad heeded **K** Asa
1Ki 15:22 Then **K** Asa made a
1Ki 15:22 with them **K** Asa built Geba of
1Ki 15:25 **k** over Israel in the second
1Ki 15:25 second year of Asa **k** of Judah
1Ki 15:28 third year of Asa **k** of Judah
1Ki 15:29 it was so, when he became **k**
1Ki 15:32 Baasha **k** of Israel all their
1Ki 15:33 third year of Asa **k** of Judah
1Ki 15:33 the son of Ahijah became **k**
1Ki 16: 8 year of Asa **k** of Judah, Elah
1Ki 16: 8 Baasha became **k** over Israel
1Ki 16:10 year of Asa **k** of Judah, and
1Ki 16:15 year of Asa **k** of Judah, Zimri
1Ki 16:16 and also has killed the **k**
1Ki 16:16 **k** over Israel that day in the
1Ki 16:21 son of Ginath, to make him **k**
1Ki 16:23 year of Asa **k** of Judah, Omri
1Ki 16:23 Omri became **k** over Israel
1Ki 16:29 year of Asa **k** of Judah, Ahab
1Ki 16:29 of Omri became **k** over Israel
1Ki 16:31 Ethbaal, **k** of the Sidonians
1Ki 19:15 anoint Hazael as **k** over Syria
1Ki 19:16 of Nimshi as **k** over Israel
1Ki 20: 1 Now Ben-Hadad the **k** of Syria
1Ki 20: 2 the city to Ahab **k** of Israel
1Ki 20: 4 the **k** of Israel answered and
1Ki 20: 4 My lord, O **k**, just as you say
1Ki 20: 7 Then the **k** of Israel called
1Ki 20: 9 Tell my lord the **k**, 'All that
1Ki 20:11 So the **k** of Israel answered
1Ki 20:13 approached Ahab **k** of Israel
1Ki 20:20 and Ben-Hadad the **k** of Syria
1Ki 20:21 Then the **k** of Israel went out
1Ki 20:22 came to the **k** of Israel and
1Ki 20:22 the **k** of Syria will come up
1Ki 20:23 of the **k** of Syria said to him
1Ki 20:28 and spoke to the **k** of Israel
1Ki 20:31 and go out to the **k** of Israel
1Ki 20:32 and came to the **k** of Israel
1Ki 20:38 waited for the **k** by the road
1Ki 20:39 Now as the **k** passed by, he
1Ki 20:39 by, he cried out to the **k**
1Ki 20:40 the **k** of Israel said to him,
1Ki 20:41 the **k** of Israel recognized
1Ki 20:43 So the **k** of Israel went to
1Ki 21: 1 palace of Ahab **k** of Samaria
1Ki 21:10 have blasphemed God and the **k**
1Ki 21:13 has blasphemed God and the **k**
1Ki 21:18 down to meet Ahab **k** of Israel
1Ki 22: 2 that Jehoshaphat the **k** of
1Ki 22: 2 down to visit the **k** of Israel
1Ki 22: 3 the **k** of Israel said to his
1Ki 22: 3 of the hand of the **k** of Syria
1Ki 22: 4 said to the **k** of Israel, "I
1Ki 22: 5 said to the **k** of Israel
1Ki 22: 6 Then the **k** of Israel gathered
1Ki 22: 6 it into the hand of the **k**
1Ki 22: 8 So the **k** of Israel said to
1Ki 22: 8 Let not the **k** say such things
1Ki 22: 9 Then the **k** of Israel called
1Ki 22:10 The **k** of Israel and
1Ki 22:10 and Jehoshaphat the **k** of Judah
1Ki 22:13 one accord encourage the **k**
1Ki 22:15 Then he came to the **k**
1Ki 22:15 and the **k** said to him,
1Ki 22:15 it into the hand of the **k**
1Ki 22:16 So the **k** said to him, "How
1Ki 22:18 And the **k** of Israel said to
1Ki 22:26 Then the **k** of Israel said,
1Ki 22:27 and say, 'Thus says the **k**
1Ki 22:29 So the **k** of Israel and
1Ki 22:29 Jehoshaphat the **k** of Judah
1Ki 22:30 And the **k** of Israel said to
1Ki 22:30 So the **k** of Israel
1Ki 22:31 Now the **k** of Syria had
1Ki 22:31 but only with the **k** of Israel
1Ki 22:32 Surely it is the **k** of Israel
1Ki 22:33 it was not the **k** of Israel
1Ki 22:34 and struck the **k** of Israel
1Ki 22:35 the **k** was propped up in his
1Ki 22:37 So the **k** died, and was brought
1Ki 22:37 they buried the **k** in Samaria
1Ki 22:41 **k** over Judah in the fourth
1Ki 22:41 year of Ahab **k** of Israel
1Ki 22:42 years old when he became **k**
1Ki 22:44 peace with the **k** of Israel
1Ki 22:47 There was then no **k** in Edom
1Ki 22:47 Edom, only a deputy of the **k**
1Ki 22:51 the son of Ahab became **k** over
1Ki 22:51 of Jehoshaphat **k** of Judah
2Ki 1: 3 of the **k** of Samaria, and say
2Ki 1: 6 return to the **k** who sent you
2Ki 1: 9 Then the **k** sent to him a
2Ki 1: 9 the **k** has said, 'Come down
2Ki 1:11 of God, thus has the **k** said
2Ki 1:15 went down with him to the **k**
2Ki 1:17 Jehoram became **k** in his place
2Ki 1:17 of Jehoshaphat, **k** of Judah
2Ki 3: 1 the son of Ahab became **k** over
2Ki 3: 1 of Jehoshaphat **k** of Judah
2Ki 3: 4 Now Mesha **k** of Moab was a
2Ki 3: 4 the **k** of Israel one hundred
2Ki 3: 5 that the **k** of Moab rebelled
2Ki 3: 5 against the **k** of Israel
2Ki 3: 6 So **K** Jehoram went out of
2Ki 3: 7 to Jehoshaphat **k** of Judah
2Ki 3: 7 The **k** of Moab has rebelled
2Ki 3: 9 So the **k** of Israel went with
2Ki 3: 9 went with the **k** of Judah and
2Ki 3: 9 and the **k** of Edom, and they
2Ki 3:10 And the **k** of Israel said,
2Ki 3:11 of the **k** of Israel answered
2Ki 3:12 So the **k** of Israel and
2Ki 3:12 the **k** of Edom went down to
2Ki 3:13 said to the **k** of Israel
2Ki 3:13 the **k** of Israel said to him,
2Ki 3:14 of Jehoshaphat **k** of Judah
2Ki 3:26 when the **k** of Moab saw that
2Ki 3:26 through to the **k** of Edom, but
2Ki 4:13 **k** or to the commander of the
2Ki 5: 1 of the army of the **k** of Syria
2Ki 5: 5 So the **k** of Syria said, "Go
2Ki 5: 5 a letter to the **k** of Israel
2Ki 5: 6 the letter to the **k** of Israel
2Ki 5: 7 when the **k** of Israel read the
2Ki 5: 8 the **k** of Israel had torn his
2Ki 5: 8 that he sent to the **k**,
2Ki 6: 8 Now the **k** of Syria was making
2Ki 6: 9 God sent to the **k** of Israel
2Ki 6:10 Then the **k** of Israel sent
2Ki 6:11 of the **k** of Syria was greatly
2Ki 6:11 of us is for the **k** of Israel
2Ki 6:12 None, my lord, O **k**
2Ki 6:12 tells the **k** of Israel the
2Ki 6:21 Now when the **k** of Israel saw
2Ki 6:24 **k** of Syria gathered all his
2Ki 6:26 Then, as the **k** of Israel was
2Ki 6:26 Help, my lord, O **k**
2Ki 6:28 Then the **k** said to her
2Ki 6:30 when the **k** heard the words of
2Ki 6:32 the **k** sent a man ahead of him
2Ki 7: 2 officer on whose hand the **k**
2Ki 7: 6 the **k** of Israel has hired
2Ki 7:12 Then the **k** arose in the night
2Ki 7:14 and the **k** sent them in the
2Ki 7:15 returned and told the **k**
2Ki 7:17 Now the **k** had appointed the
2Ki 7:17 when the **k** came down to him
2Ki 7:18 of God had spoken to the **k**
2Ki 8: 3 appeal to the **k** for her house
2Ki 8: 4 Then the **k** talked with Gehazi
2Ki 8: 5 as he was telling the **k** how
2Ki 8: 5 to the **k** for her house and for
2Ki 8: 5 My lord, O **k**, this is the
2Ki 8: 6 when the **k** asked the woman,
2Ki 8: 6 So the **k** appointed a certain
2Ki 8: 7 Ben-Hadad **k** of Syria was sick
2Ki 8: 8 And the **k** said to Hazael,
2Ki 8: 9 Your son Ben-Hadad **k** of Syria
2Ki 8:13 you will become **k** over Syria
2Ki 8:16 **k** of Israel, Jehoshaphat
2Ki 8:16 having been **k** of Judah,
2Ki 8:16 began to reign as **k** of Judah
2Ki 8:17 years old when he became **k**
2Ki 8:20 and made a **k** over themselves
2Ki 8:25 **k** of Israel, Ahaziah the son
2Ki 8:25 **k** of Judah, began to reign
2Ki 8:26 years old when he became **k**
2Ki 8:26 of Omri, **k** of Israel
2Ki 8:28 **k** of Syria at Ramoth Gilead
2Ki 8:29 Then **K** Joram went back to
2Ki 8:29 against Hazael **k** of Syria
2Ki 8:29 **k** of Judah, went down to see
2Ki 9: 3 anointed you **k** over Israel
2Ki 9: 6 I have anointed you **k** over
2Ki 9:12 anointed you **k** over Israel
2Ki 9:13 saying, "Jehu is **k**!"
2Ki 9:14 against Hazael **k** of Syria
2Ki 9:15 But **K** Joram had returned to
2Ki 9:15 fought with Hazael **k** of Syria
2Ki 9:16 Ahaziah **k** of Judah had come
2Ki 9:18 says the **k**: 'Is it peace?'
2Ki 9:19 says the **k**: 'Is it peace?'
2Ki 9:21 Then Joram **k** of Israel and
2Ki 9:21 Ahaziah **k** of Judah went out,
2Ki 9:27 But when Ahaziah **k** of Judah
2Ki 9:29 had become **k** over Judah
2Ki 10: 5 but we will not make anyone **k**

2Ki 10:13 of Ahaziah **k** of Judah, and
2Ki 10:13 to greet the sons of the **k**
2Ki 11: 2 the daughter of **K** Joram,
2Ki 11: 7 house of the LORD for the **k**
2Ki 11: 8 surround the **k** on all sides
2Ki 11: 8 be with the **k** as he goes out
2Ki 11:10 which had belonged to **K** David
2Ki 11:11 in his hand, all around the **k**
2Ki 11:12 they made him **k** and anointed
2Ki 11:12 Long live the **k**
2Ki 11:14 she looked, there was the **k**
2Ki 11:14 the trumpeters were by the **k**
2Ki 11:17 between the LORD, the **k**, and
2Ki 11:17 people, and also between the **k**
2Ki 11:19 they brought the **k** down from
2Ki 11:21 years old when he became **k**
2Ki 12: 1 of Jehu, Jehoash became **k**
2Ki 12: 6 year of **K** Jehoash, that the
2Ki 12: 7 So **K** Jehoash called Jehoiada
2Ki 12:17 Now Hazael **k** of Syria went up
2Ki 12:18 Jehoash **k** of Judah took all
2Ki 12:18 them to Hazael **k** of Syria
2Ki 13: 1 **k** of Judah, Jehoahaz the son
2Ki 13: 1 **k** over Israel in Samaria, and
2Ki 13: 3 the hand of Hazael **k** of Syria
2Ki 13: 4 because the **k** of Syria
2Ki 13: 7 for the **k** of Syria had
2Ki 13:10 year of Joash **k** of Judah,
2Ki 13:10 **k** over Israel in Samaria, and
2Ki 13:12 against Amaziah **k** of Judah
2Ki 13:14 Then Joash the **k** of Israel
2Ki 13:16 he said to the **k** of Israel
2Ki 13:18 And he said to the **k** of Israel
2Ki 13:22 Hazael **k** of Syria oppressed
2Ki 13:24 Now Hazael **k** of Syria died
2Ki 14: 1 **k** of Israel, Amaziah the son
2Ki 14: 1 **k** of Judah, became **k**
2Ki 14: 2 years old when he became **k**
2Ki 14: 5 had murdered his father the **k**
2Ki 14: 8 of Jehu, **k** of Israel, saying,
2Ki 14: 9 Jehoash **k** of Israel sent to
2Ki 14: 9 sent to Amaziah **k** of Judah
2Ki 14:11 Therefore Jehoash **k** of Israel
2Ki 14:11 Amaziah **k** of Judah faced one
2Ki 14:13 Then Jehoash **k** of Israel
2Ki 14:13 captured Amaziah **k** of Judah
2Ki 14:15 with Amaziah **k** of Judah
2Ki 14:17 **k** of Judah, lived fifteen
2Ki 14:17 son of Jehoahaz, **k** of Israel
2Ki 14:21 made him **k** instead of his
2Ki 14:22 after the **k** rested with his
2Ki 14:23 **k** of Judah, Jeroboam the son
2Ki 14:23 **k** of Israel, became **k** in
2Ki 14:23 became **k** in Samaria, and
2Ki 15: 1 year of Jeroboam **k** of Israel
2Ki 15: 1 **k** of Judah, became **k**
2Ki 15: 2 years old when he became **k**
2Ki 15: 5 Then the LORD struck the **k**
2Ki 15: 8 year of Azariah **k** of Judah
2Ki 15:13 the son of Jabesh became **k** in
2Ki 15:13 year of Uzziah **k** of Judah
2Ki 15:17 year of Azariah **k** of Judah
2Ki 15:17 of Gadi became **k** over Israel
2Ki 15:19 Pul **k** of Assyria came against
2Ki 15:20 to give to the **k** of Assyria
2Ki 15:20 So the **k** of Assyria turned
2Ki 15:23 year of Azariah **k** of Judah
2Ki 15:23 **k** over Israel in Samaria, and
2Ki 15:27 year of Azariah **k** of Judah
2Ki 15:27 **k** over Israel in Samaria, and
2Ki 15:29 the days of Pekah **k** of Israel
2Ki 15:29 **k** of Assyria came and took
2Ki 15:32 **k** of Israel, Jotham the son
2Ki 15:32 **k** of Judah, began to reign
2Ki 15:33 years old when he became **k**
2Ki 15:37 to send Rezin **k** of Syria and
2Ki 16: 1 **k** of Judah, began to reign
2Ki 16: 2 years old when he became **k**
2Ki 16: 5 Then Rezin **k** of Syria and
2Ki 16: 5 **k** of Israel, came up to
2Ki 16: 6 At that time Rezin **k** of Syria
2Ki 16: 7 Tiglath-Pileser **k** of Assyria
2Ki 16: 7 the hand of the **k** of Syria
2Ki 16: 7 the hand of the **k** of Israel
2Ki 16: 8 a present to the **k** of Assyria
2Ki 16: 9 So the **k** of Assyria heeded
2Ki 16: 9 for the **k** of Assyria went up
2Ki 16:10 Now **K** Ahaz went to Damascus
2Ki 16:10 Tiglath-Pileser **k** of Assyria
2Ki 16:10 **K** Ahaz sent to Urijah the
2Ki 16:11 **K** Ahaz had sent from
2Ki 16:11 **K** Ahaz came from Damascus
2Ki 16:12 **k** came from Damascus
2Ki 16:12 Damascus, the **k** saw the altar
2Ki 16:12 the **k** approached the altar and
2Ki 16:15 Then **K** Ahaz commanded
2Ki 16:16 to all that **K** Ahaz commanded
2Ki 16:17 **K** Ahaz cut off the panels of
2Ki 16:18 account of the **k** of Assyria
2Ki 17: 1 year of Ahaz **k** of Judah,
2Ki 17: 1 became **k** of Israel in Samaria
2Ki 17: 3 Shalmaneser **k** of Assyria came
2Ki 17: 4 the **k** of Assyria uncovered a
2Ki 17: 4 **k** of Egypt, and brought no
2Ki 17: 4 tribute to the **k** of Assyria
2Ki 17: 4 Therefore the **k** of Assyria
2Ki 17: 5 Now the **k** of Assyria went
2Ki 17: 6 the **k** of Assyria took Samaria
2Ki 17: 7 hand of Pharaoh **k** of Egypt
2Ki 17:21 Jeroboam the son of Nebat **k**
2Ki 17:24 Then the **k** of Assyria brought
2Ki 17:26 spoke to the **k** of Assyria
2Ki 17:27 Then the **k** of Assyria
2Ki 18: 1 **k** of Israel, that Hezekiah
2Ki 18: 1 **k** of Judah, began to reign
2Ki 18: 2 years old when he became **k**
2Ki 18: 7 against the **k** of Assyria and
2Ki 18: 9 the fourth year of **K** Hezekiah
2Ki 18: 9 **k** of Israel, that Shalmaneser
2Ki 18: 9 that Shalmaneser **k** of Assyria
2Ki 18:10 year of Hoshea **k** of Israel
2Ki 18:11 Then the **k** of Assyria carried
2Ki 18:13 fourteenth year of **K** Hezekiah
2Ki 18:13 Sennacherib **k** of Assyria came
2Ki 18:14 Then Hezekiah **k** of Judah sent
2Ki 18:14 the **k** of Assyria at Lachish
2Ki 18:14 the **k** of Assyria assessed
2Ki 18:14 **k** of Judah three hundred
2Ki 18:16 **k** of Judah had overlaid, and
2Ki 18:16 gave it to the **k** of Assyria
2Ki 18:17 Then the **k** of Assyria sent
2Ki 18:17 Jerusalem, to **K** Hezekiah
2Ki 18:18 when they had called to the **k**
2Ki 18:19 great **k**, the **k** of Assyria
2Ki 18:21 So is Pharaoh **k** of Egypt to
2Ki 18:23 to my master the **k** of Assyria
2Ki 18:28 great **k**, the **k** of Assyria
2Ki 18:29 Thus says the **k**
2Ki 18:30 the hand of the **k** of Assyria
2Ki 18:31 thus says the **k** of Assyria
2Ki 18:33 the hand of the **k** of Assyria
2Ki 19: 1 when **K** Hezekiah heard it,
2Ki 19: 4 whom his master the **k** of
2Ki 19: 5 So the servants of **K** Hezekiah
2Ki 19: 6 which the servants of the **k**
2Ki 19: 8 and found the **k** of Assyria
2Ki 19: 9 And the **k** heard concerning
2Ki 19: 9 Tirhakah **k** of Ethiopia
2Ki 19:10 speak to Hezekiah **k** of Judah
2Ki 19:10 the hand of the **k** of Assyria
2Ki 19:13 Where is the **k** of Hamath
2Ki 19:13 the **k** of Arpad
2Ki 19:13 and the **k** of the city of
2Ki 19:20 **k** of Assyria I have heard
2Ki 19:32 concerning the **k** of Assyria
2Ki 19:36 So Sennacherib **k** of Assyria
2Ki 20: 6 the hand of the **k** of Assyria
2Ki 20:12 **k** of Babylon, sent letters and
2Ki 20:14 prophet went to **K** Hezekiah
2Ki 20:18 palace of the **k** of Babylon
2Ki 21: 1 years old when he became **k**
2Ki 21: 3 as Ahab **k** of Israel had done
2Ki 21:11 Because Manasseh **k** of Judah
2Ki 21:19 years old when he became **k**
2Ki 21:23 killed the **k** in his own house
2Ki 21:24 had conspired against **K** Amon
2Ki 21:24 his son Josiah **k** in his place
2Ki 22: 1 years old when he became **k**
2Ki 22: 3 eighteenth year of **K** Josiah
2Ki 22: 3 that the **k** sent Shaphan the
2Ki 22: 9 the scribe went to the **k**,
2Ki 22: 9 bringing the **k** word
2Ki 22:10 the scribe showed the **k**,
2Ki 22:10 Shaphan read it before the **k**
2Ki 22:11 when the **k** heard the words of
2Ki 22:12 Then the **k** commanded Hilkiah
2Ki 22:12 and Asaiah a servant of the **k**
2Ki 22:16 which the **k** of Judah has read
2Ki 22:18 But to the **k** of Judah, who
2Ki 22:20 So they brought word to the **k**
2Ki 23: 1 Then the **k** sent them to
2Ki 23: 2 the **k** went up to the house of
2Ki 23: 3 Then the **k** stood by a pillar
2Ki 23: 4 the **k** commanded Hilkiah the
2Ki 23:12 the LORD, the **k** broke down and
2Ki 23:13 Then the **k** defiled the high
2Ki 23:13 which Solomon **k** of Israel had
2Ki 23:21 Then the **k** commanded all the
2Ki 23:23 of **K** Josiah this Passover was
2Ki 23:25 him there was no **k** like him
2Ki 23:29 In his days Pharaoh Necho **k**
2Ki 23:29 the aid of the **k** of Assyria
2Ki 23:29 **K** Josiah went against him
2Ki 23:30 made him **k** in his father's
2Ki 23:31 years old when he became **k**
2Ki 23:34 **k** in place of his father
2Ki 23:36 years old when he became **k**
2Ki 24: 1 **k** of Babylon came up, and
2Ki 24: 7 the **k** of Egypt did not come
2Ki 24: 7 for the **k** of Babylon had
2Ki 24: 7 all that belonged to the **k** of
2Ki 24: 8 years old when he became **k**
2Ki 24:10 **k** of Babylon came up against
2Ki 24:11 Nebuchadnezzar **k** of Babylon
2Ki 24:12 Then Jehoiachin **k** of Judah
2Ki 24:12 went out to the **k** of Babylon
2Ki 24:12 and the **k** of Babylon, in the
2Ki 24:13 of gold which Solomon **k** of
2Ki 24:16 war, these the **k** of Babylon
2Ki 24:17 Then the **k** of Babylon made
2Ki 24:17 **k** in his place, and changed
2Ki 24:18 years old when he became **k**
2Ki 24:20 against the **k** of Babylon
2Ki 25: 1 Nebuchadnezzar **k** of Babylon
2Ki 25: 2 eleventh year of **K** Zedekiah
2Ki 25: 4 And the **k** went by way of the
2Ki 25: 5 the Chaldeans pursued the **k**
2Ki 25: 6 So they took the **k** and brought
2Ki 25: 6 to the **k** of Babylon at Riblah
2Ki 25: 8 **K** Nebuchadnezzar **k** of Babylon
2Ki 25: 8 a servant of the **k** of Babylon
2Ki 25:11 deserted to the **k** of Babylon
2Ki 25:20 and brought them to the **k** of
2Ki 25:21 Then the **k** of Babylon struck
2Ki 25:22 **k** of Babylon had left
2Ki 25:23 heard that the **k** of Babylon
2Ki 25:24 serve the **k** of Babylon, and it
2Ki 25:27 of Jehoiachin **k** of Judah, in
2Ki 25:27 Evil-Merodach **k** of Babylon
2Ki 25:27 released Jehoiachin **k** of
2Ki 25:29 **k** all the days of his life
2Ki 25:30 ration given him by the **k**
1Ch 1:43 **k** reigned over the children
1Ch 3: 2 of Talmai, **k** of Geshur
1Ch 4:23 dwelt with the **k** for his work
1Ch 4:41 days of Hezekiah **k** of Judah
1Ch 5: 6 whom Tiglath-Pileser **k** of
1Ch 5:17 the days of Jotham **k** of Judah
1Ch 5:17 days of Jeroboam **k** of Israel
1Ch 5:26 spirit of Pul **k** of Assyria
1Ch 5:26 Tiglath-Pileser **k** of Assyria
1Ch 11: 2 past, even when Saul was **k**
1Ch 11: 3 came to the **k** at Hebron, and
1Ch 11: 3 anointed David **k** over Israel
1Ch 11:10 all Israel, to make him **k**
1Ch 12:31 name to come and make David **k**
1Ch 12:38 to make David **k** over all
1Ch 12:38 of one mind to make David **k**
1Ch 14: 1 Now Hiram **k** of Tyre sent
1Ch 14: 2 him as **k** over Israel, for his
1Ch 14: 8 anointed **k** over all Israel
1Ch 15:29 saw **K** David whirling and
1Ch 17:16 Then **K** David went in and sat
1Ch 18: 3 David defeated Hadadezer **k** of
1Ch 18: 5 to help Hadadezer **k** of Zobah
1Ch 18: 9 When Tou **k** of Hamath heard
1Ch 18: 9 army of Hadadezer **k** of Zobah
1Ch 18:10 Hadoram his son to **K** David
1Ch 18:11 **K** David also dedicated these
1Ch 19: 1 after this that Nahash the **k**
1Ch 19: 5 the **k** said, "Wait at Jericho
1Ch 19: 7 with the **k** of Maachah and his
1Ch 21: 3 But, my lord the **k**, are they
1Ch 21:23 let my lord the **k** do what is
1Ch 21:24 Then **K** David said to Ornan,
1Ch 23: 1 his son Solomon **k** over Israel
1Ch 24: 6 wrote them down before the **k**
1Ch 24:31 in the presence of **K** David
1Ch 25: 2 to the order of the **k**
1Ch 25: 6 under the authority of the **k**

1Ch 26:26 things which **K** David and the
1Ch 26:30 and in the service of the **k**
1Ch 26:32 whom **K** David made officials
1Ch 26:32 God and the affairs of the **k**
1Ch 27: 1 served the **k** in every matter
1Ch 27:24 of the chronicles of **K** David
1Ch 27:31 over **K** David's property
1Ch 28: 1 divisions who served the **k**
1Ch 28: 1 and possessions of the **k** and of
1Ch 28: 2 Then **K** David rose to his feet
1Ch 28: 4 to be **k** over Israel forever
1Ch 28: 4 to make me **k** over all Israel
1Ch 29: 1 Furthermore **K** David said to
1Ch 29: 9 **K** David also rejoiced greatly
1Ch 29:20 before the LORD and the **k**
1Ch 29:22 of David **k** the second time
1Ch 29:23 the throne of the LORD as **k**
1Ch 29:24 also all the sons of **K** David
1Ch 29:24 themselves to **K** Solomon
1Ch 29:25 on any **k** before him in Israel
1Ch 29:29 Now the acts of **K** David,
2Ch 1: 8 have made me **k** in his place
2Ch 1: 9 for You have made me **k** over a
2Ch 1:11 over whom I have made you **k**
2Ch 1:14 and with the **k** in Jerusalem
2Ch 1:15 Also the **k** made silver and
2Ch 2: 3 sent to Hiram **k** of Tyre,
2Ch 2:11 Then Hiram **k** of Tyre answered
2Ch 2:11 He has made you **k** over them
2Ch 2:12 has given **K** David a wise son
2Ch 4:11 **K** Solomon for the house of
2Ch 4:16 of burnished bronze for **K**
2Ch 4:17 In the plain of Jordan the **k**
2Ch 5: 3 with the **k** at the feast,
2Ch 5: 6 Also **K** Solomon, and all the
2Ch 6: 3 Then the **k** turned around and
2Ch 7: 4 Then the **k** and all the people
2Ch 7: 5 **K** Solomon offered a sacrifice
2Ch 7: 5 So the **k** and all the people
2Ch 7: 6 which **K** David had made to
2Ch 8:10 of the officials of **K** Solomon
2Ch 8:11 house of David **k** of Israel
2Ch 8:15 of the **k** to the priests and
2Ch 8:18 and brought it to **K** Solomon
2Ch 9: 5 Then she said to the **k**
2Ch 9: 8 to be **k** for the LORD your God
2Ch 9: 8 He made you **k** over them, to
2Ch 9: 9 she gave the **k** one hundred
2Ch 9: 9 of Sheba gave to **K** Solomon
2Ch 9:11 the **k** made walkways of the
2Ch 9:12 Now **K** Solomon gave to the
2Ch 9:12 than she had brought to the **k**
2Ch 9:15 **K** Solomon made two hundred
2Ch 9:16 The **k** put them in the House
2Ch 9:17 Moreover the **k** made a great
2Ch 9:20 All **K** Solomon's drinking
2Ch 9:22 So **K** Solomon surpassed all
2Ch 9:25 and with the **k** at Jerusalem
2Ch 9:27 The **k** made silver as common
2Ch 10: 1 gone to Shechem to make him **k**
2Ch 10: 2 presence of Solomon the **k**)
2Ch 10: 6 Then **K** Rehoboam consulted
2Ch 10:12 day, as the **k** had appointed,
2Ch 10:13 Then the **k** answered them
2Ch 10:13 **K** Rehoboam rejected the
2Ch 10:15 So the **k** did not listen to
2Ch 10:16 the **k** did not listen to them
2Ch 10:16 the people answered the **k**
2Ch 10:18 Then **K** Rehoboam sent,
2Ch 10:18 **K** Rehoboam mounted
2Ch 11: 3 **k** of Judah, and to all Israel
2Ch 11:22 for he intended to make him **k**
2Ch 12: 2 the fifth year of **K** Rehoboam
2Ch 12: 2 that Shishak **k** of Egypt came
2Ch 12: 6 and the **k** humbled themselves
2Ch 12: 9 So Shishak **k** of Egypt came up
2Ch 12:10 In their place **K** Rehoboam
2Ch 12:11 whenever the **k** entered the
2Ch 12:13 So **K** Rehoboam strengthened
2Ch 12:13 years old when he became **k**
2Ch 13: 1 eighteenth year of **K** Jeroboam
2Ch 13: 1 Abijah became **k** over Judah
2Ch 15:16 the mother of Asa the **k**,
2Ch 16: 1 Baasha **k** of Israel came up
2Ch 16: 1 or come in to Asa **k** of Judah
2Ch 16: 2 sent to Ben-Hadad **k** of Syria
2Ch 16: 3 with Baasha **k** of Israel, so
2Ch 16: 4 So Ben-Hadad heeded **K** Asa
2Ch 16: 6 Then **K** Asa took all Judah, and
2Ch 16: 7 seer came to Asa **k** of Judah
2Ch 16: 7 have relied on the **k** of Syria
2Ch 16: 7 **k** of Syria has escaped from
2Ch 17:19 These served the **k**, besides
2Ch 17:19 besides those whom the **k** put
2Ch 18: 3 So Ahab **k** of Israel said to
2Ch 18: 3 to Jehoshaphat **k** of Judah
2Ch 18: 4 said to the **k** of Israel
2Ch 18: 5 Then the **k** of Israel gathered
2Ch 18: 7 So the **k** of Israel said to
2Ch 18: 7 Let not the **k** say such things
2Ch 18: 8 Then the **k** of Israel called
2Ch 18: 9 And the **k** of Israel and
2Ch 18: 9 and Jehoshaphat **k** of Judah
2Ch 18:12 one accord encourage the **k**
2Ch 18:14 Then he came to the **k**
2Ch 18:14 and the **k** said to him,
2Ch 18:15 So the **k** said to him, "How
2Ch 18:17 And the **k** of Israel said to
2Ch 18:19 Ahab **k** of Israel to go up
2Ch 18:25 Then the **k** of Israel said,
2Ch 18:26 and say, 'Thus says the **k**
2Ch 18:28 So the **k** of Israel and
2Ch 18:28 Jehoshaphat the **k** of Judah
2Ch 18:29 And the **k** of Israel said to
2Ch 18:29 So the **k** of Israel
2Ch 18:30 Now the **k** of Syria had
2Ch 18:30 but only with the **k** of Israel
2Ch 18:31 It is the **k** of Israel
2Ch 18:32 it was not the **k** of Israel
2Ch 18:33 and struck the **k** of Israel
2Ch 18:34 and the **k** of Israel propped
2Ch 19: 1 Then Jehoshaphat the **k** of
2Ch 19: 2 and said to **K** Jehoshaphat,
2Ch 20:15 and you, **K** Jehoshaphat
2Ch 20:31 Jehoshaphat was **k** over Judah
2Ch 20:31 years old when he became **k**
2Ch 20:35 After this Jehoshaphat **k** of
2Ch 20:35 with Ahaziah **k** of Israel, who
2Ch 21: 2 of Jehoshaphat **k** of Israel
2Ch 21: 5 years old when he became **k**
2Ch 21: 8 and made a **k** over themselves
2Ch 21:12 in the ways of Asa **k** of Judah
2Ch 21:20 years old when he became **k**
2Ch 22: 1 youngest son **k** in his place
2Ch 22: 1 Jehoram, **k** of Judah, reigned
2Ch 22: 2 years old when he became **k**
2Ch 22: 5 Ahab **k** of Israel to make war
2Ch 22: 5 **k** of Syria at Ramoth Gilead
2Ch 22: 6 against Hazael **k** of Syria
2Ch 22: 6 **k** of Judah, went down to see
2Ch 22:11 the daughter of the **k**, took
2Ch 22:11 the daughter of **K** Jehoram
2Ch 23: 3 the **k** in the house of God
2Ch 23: 7 surround the **k** on all sides
2Ch 23: 7 with the **k** when he comes in
2Ch 23: 9 which had been **K** David's,
2Ch 23:10 the temple, all around the **k**
2Ch 23:11 the Testimony, and made him **k**
2Ch 23:11 Long live the **k**
2Ch 23:12 running and praising the **k**
2Ch 23:13 there was the **k** standing by
2Ch 23:13 the trumpeters were by the **k**
2Ch 23:16 himself, the people, and the **k**
2Ch 23:20 brought the **k** down from the
2Ch 23:20 set the **k** on the throne of
2Ch 24: 1 years old when he became **k**
2Ch 24: 6 So the **k** called Jehoiada the
2Ch 24:12 Then the **k** and Jehoiada gave
2Ch 24:14 of the money before the **k**
2Ch 24:17 came and bowed down to the **k**
2Ch 24:17 And the **k** listened to them
2Ch 24:21 at the commandment of the **k**
2Ch 24:22 Thus Joash the **k** did not
2Ch 24:23 spoil to the **k** of Damascus
2Ch 25: 1 years old when he became **k**
2Ch 25: 3 had murdered his father the **k**
2Ch 25: 7 O **k**, do not let the army of
2Ch 25:16 him, that the **k** said to him,
2Ch 25:17 Then Amaziah **k** of Judah took
2Ch 25:17 of Jehu, **k** of Israel, saying,
2Ch 25:18 Joash **k** of Israel sent to
2Ch 25:18 sent to Amaziah **k** of Judah
2Ch 25:21 So Joash **k** of Israel went out
2Ch 25:21 Amaziah **k** of Judah faced one
2Ch 25:23 Then Joash the **k** of Israel
2Ch 25:23 captured Amaziah **k** of Judah
2Ch 25:25 **k** of Judah, lived fifteen
2Ch 25:25 son of Jehoahaz, **k** of Israel
2Ch 26: 1 made him **k** instead of his
2Ch 26: 2 after the **k** rested with his
2Ch 26: 3 years old when he became **k**
2Ch 26:13 to help the **k** against the
2Ch 26:18 And they withstood **K** Uzziah
2Ch 26:21 **K** Uzziah was a leper until
2Ch 27: 1 years old when he became **k**
2Ch 27: 5 with the **k** of the Ammonites
2Ch 27: 8 years old when he became **k**
2Ch 28: 1 years old when he became **k**
2Ch 28: 5 the hand of the **k** of Syria
2Ch 28: 5 the hand of the **k** of Israel
2Ch 28: 7 who was second to the **k**
2Ch 28:16 At the same time **K** Ahaz sent
2Ch 28:19 because of Ahaz **k** of Israel
2Ch 28:20 Also Tiglath-Pileser **k** of
2Ch 28:21 LORD, from the house of the **k**
2Ch 28:21 gave it to the **k** of Assyria
2Ch 28:22 **K** Ahaz became increasingly
2Ch 28:22 This is that **K** Ahaz
2Ch 29: 1 Hezekiah became **k** when he
2Ch 29:15 to the commandment of the **k**
2Ch 29:18 they went in to **K** Hezekiah
2Ch 29:19 all the articles which **K** Ahaz
2Ch 29:20 Then **K** Hezekiah rose early,
2Ch 29:23 the sin offering before the **k**
2Ch 29:24 for the **k** commanded that the
2Ch 29:27 of David **k** of Israel
2Ch 29:29 had finished offering, the **k**
2Ch 29:30 Moreover **K** Hezekiah and the
2Ch 30: 2 For the **k** and his leaders and
2Ch 30: 4 And the matter pleased the **k**
2Ch 30: 6 with the letters from the **k**
2Ch 30: 6 to the commandment of the **k**
2Ch 30:12 do the commandment of the **k**
2Ch 30:24 For Hezekiah **k** of Judah gave
2Ch 30:26 **k** of Israel, there had been
2Ch 31: 3 The **k** also appointed a
2Ch 31:13 of Hezekiah the **k**
2Ch 32: 1 Sennacherib **k** of Assyria came
2Ch 32: 7 before the **k** of Assyria, nor
2Ch 32: 8 words of Hezekiah **k** of Judah
2Ch 32: 9 **k** of Assyria sent his
2Ch 32: 9 to Hezekiah **k** of Judah
2Ch 32:10 says Sennacherib **k** of Assyria
2Ch 32:11 hand of the **k** of Assyria"
2Ch 32:20 Now for this cause **K** Hezekiah
2Ch 32:21 the camp of the **k** of Assyria
2Ch 32:22 Sennacherib the **k** of Assyria
2Ch 32:23 to Hezekiah **k** of Judah, so
2Ch 33: 1 years old when he became **k**
2Ch 33:11 the army of the **k** of Assyria
2Ch 33:21 years old when he became **k**
2Ch 33:25 had conspired against **K** Amon
2Ch 33:25 his son Josiah **k** in his place
2Ch 34: 1 years old when he became **k**
2Ch 34:16 carried the book to the **k**
2Ch 34:16 bringing the **k** word, saying,
2Ch 34:18 Shaphan the scribe told the **k**
2Ch 34:18 Shaphan read it before the **k**
2Ch 34:19 when the **k** heard the words of
2Ch 34:20 Then the **k** commanded Hilkiah,
2Ch 34:20 and Asaiah a servant of the **k**
2Ch 34:22 and those whom the **k** had
2Ch 34:24 read before the **k** of Judah
2Ch 34:26 And as for the **k** of Judah, who
2Ch 34:28 brought back word to the **k**
2Ch 34:29 Then the **k** sent and gathered
2Ch 34:30 the **k** went up to the house of
2Ch 34:31 Then the **k** stood in his place
2Ch 35: 3 of David, **k** of Israel, built
2Ch 35: 4 of David **k** of Israel and the
2Ch 35:16 to the command of **K** Josiah
2Ch 35:20 Necho **k** of Egypt came up to
2Ch 35:21 I to do with you, **k** of Judah
2Ch 35:23 And the archers shot **K** Josiah
2Ch 35:23 the **k** said to his servants,
2Ch 36: 1 made him **k** in his father's
2Ch 36: 2 years old when he became **k**
2Ch 36: 3 Now the **k** of Egypt deposed
2Ch 36: 4 Then the **k** of Egypt made his
2Ch 36: 4 brother Eliakim **k** over Judah
2Ch 36: 5 years old when he became **k**
2Ch 36: 6 Nebuchadnezzar **k** of Babylon
2Ch 36: 9 years old when he became **k**
2Ch 36:10 At the turn of the year **K**
2Ch 36:10 **k** over Judah and Jerusalem
2Ch 36:11 years old when he became **k**
2Ch 36:13 against **K** Nebuchadnezzar, who
2Ch 36:17 them the **k** of the Chaldeans
2Ch 36:18 and the treasures of the **k**
2Ch 36:22 year of Cyrus **k** of Persia

2Ch 36:22 spirit of Cyrus **k** of Persia
2Ch 36:23 Thus says Cyrus **k** of Persia
Ezra 1: 1 year of Cyrus **k** of Persia
Ezra 1: 1 spirit of Cyrus **k** of Persia
Ezra 1: 2 Thus says Cyrus **k** of Persia
Ezra 1: 7 **K** Cyrus also brought out the
Ezra 1: 8 Cyrus **k** of Persia brought
Ezra 2: 1 whom Nebuchadnezzar the **k** of
Ezra 3: 7 had from Cyrus **k** of Persia
Ezra 3:10 of David **k** of Israel
Ezra 4: 2 of Esarhaddon **k** of Assyria
Ezra 4: 3 as **K** Cyrus the **k** of Persia
Ezra 4: 5 the days of Cyrus **k** of Persia
Ezra 4: 5 reign of Darius **k** of Persia
Ezra 4: 7 to Artaxerxes **k** of Persia
Ezra 4: 8 **K** Artaxerxes in this fashion
Ezra 4:11 To **K** Artaxerxes from your
Ezra 4:12 Let it be known to the **k** that
Ezra 4:13 it now be known to the **k** that
Ezra 4:14 have sent and informed the **k**
Ezra 4:16 We inform the **k** that if this
Ezra 4:17 Then the **k** sent an answer
Ezra 4:23 Now when the copy of **K**
Ezra 4:24 reign of Darius **k** of Persia
Ezra 5: 6 the River, to Darius the **k**
Ezra 5: 7 To Darius the **k**
Ezra 5: 8 the **k** that we went into the
Ezra 5:11 which a great **k** of Israel
Ezra 5:12 Nebuchadnezzar **k** of Babylon
Ezra 5:13 year of Cyrus **k** of Babylon
Ezra 5:13 **K** Cyrus issued a decree to
Ezra 5:14 those **K** Cyrus took from the
Ezra 5:17 if it seems good to the **k**
Ezra 5:17 **K** Cyrus to build this house
Ezra 5:17 and let the **k** send us his
Ezra 6: 1 Then **K** Darius issued a decree
Ezra 6: 3 In the first year of **K** Cyrus
Ezra 6: 3 **K** Cyrus issued a decree
Ezra 6:10 and pray for the life of the **k**
Ezra 6:12 any **k** or people who put their
Ezra 6:13 to what **K** Darius had sent
Ezra 6:14 and Artaxerxes **k** of Persia
Ezra 6:15 year of the reign of **K** Darius
Ezra 6:22 the **k** of Assyria toward them
Ezra 7: 1 of Artaxerxes **k** of Persia
Ezra 7: 6 The **k** granted him all his
Ezra 7: 7 seventh year of **K** Artaxerxes
Ezra 7: 8 in the seventh year of the **k**
Ezra 7:11 **K** Artaxerxes gave Ezra the
Ezra 7:12 **k** of kings, To Ezra the
Ezra 7:14 you are being sent by the **k**
Ezra 7:15 silver and gold which the **k**
Ezra 7:21 I, even I, Artaxerxes the **k**
Ezra 7:23 against the realm of the **k**
Ezra 7:26 your God and the law of the **k**
Ezra 7:28 mercy to me before the **k** and
Ezra 8: 1 in the reign of **K** Artaxerxes
Ezra 8:22 the **k** an escort of soldiers
Ezra 8:22 we had spoken to the **k**,
Ezra 8:25 house of our God which the **k**
Neh 2: 1 year of **K** Artaxerxes, when
Neh 2: 1 the wine and gave it to the **k**
Neh 2: 2 Therefore the **k** said to me
Neh 2: 3 and said to the **k**, "May the
Neh 2: 3 May the **k** live forever
Neh 2: 4 Then the **k** said to me, "What
Neh 2: 5 And I said to the **k**, If it
Neh 2: 5 If it pleases the **k**, and if
Neh 2: 6 So the **k** said to me (the
Neh 2: 6 it pleased the **k** to send me
Neh 2: 7 Furthermore I said to the **k**
Neh 2: 7 If it pleases the **k**, let
Neh 2: 8 And the **k** granted them to me
Neh 2: 9 Now the **k** had sent captains
Neh 2:19 Will you rebel against the **k**
Neh 5:14 year of **K** Artaxerxes, twelve
Neh 6: 6 wall, that you may be their **k**
Neh 6: 7 There is a **k** in Judah
Neh 6: 7 will be reported to the **k**
Neh 7: 6 whom Nebuchadnezzar the **k** of
Neh 9:22 the land of the **k** of Heshbon
Neh 9:22 and the land of Og **k** of Bashan
Neh 13: 6 year of Artaxerxes **k** of
Neh 13: 6 I had returned to the **k**
Neh 13: 6 I obtained leave from the **k**
Neh 13:26 Did not Solomon **k** of Israel
Neh 13:26 there was no **k** like him, who
Neh 13:26 and God made him **k** over all
Esth 1: 2 in those days when **K**
Esth 1: 5 the **k** made a feast lasting
Esth 1: 7 to the generosity of the **k**
Esth 1: 8 for so the **k** had ordered all
Esth 1: 9 which belonged to **K** Ahasuerus
Esth 1:10 of the **k** was merry with wine
Esth 1:10 the presence of **K** Ahasuerus
Esth 1:11 Queen Vashti before the **k**
Esth 1:12 therefore the **k** was furious
Esth 1:13 Then the **k** said to the wise
Esth 1:15 **K** Ahasuerus brought to her by
Esth 1:16 answered before the **k**
Esth 1:16 has not only wronged the **k**
Esth 1:16 the provinces of **K** Ahasuerus
Esth 1:17 **K** Ahasuerus commanded
Esth 1:19 If it pleases the **k**, let a
Esth 1:19 no more before **K** Ahasuerus
Esth 1:19 and let the **k** give her royal
Esth 1:21 And the reply pleased the **k**
Esth 1:21 the **k** did according to the
Esth 2: 1 when the wrath of **K** Ahasuerus
Esth 2: 2 virgins be sought for the **k**
Esth 2: 3 let the **k** appoint officers in
Esth 2: 4 **k** be queen instead of Vashti
Esth 2: 4 This thing pleased the **k**
Esth 2: 6 with Jeconiah **k** of Judah,
Esth 2: 6 whom Nebuchadnezzar the **k** of
Esth 2:12 turn came to go in to **K**
Esth 2:13 young woman went to the **k**
Esth 2:14 the **k** again unless the **k**
Esth 2:14 unless the **k** delighted in her
Esth 2:15 daughter, to go in to the **k**
Esth 2:16 was taken to **K** Ahasuerus,
Esth 2:17 The **k** loved Esther more than
Esth 2:18 Then the **k** made a great feast
Esth 2:18 to the generosity of a **k**
Esth 2:21 to lay hands on **K** Ahasuerus
Esth 2:22 the **k** in Mordecai's name
Esth 2:23 in the presence of the **k**
Esth 3: 1 After these things **K**
Esth 3: 2 for so the **k** had commanded
Esth 3: 7 twelfth year of **K** Ahasuerus
Esth 3: 8 Haman said to **K** Ahasuerus
Esth 3: 8 for the **k** to let them remain
Esth 3: 9 If it pleases the **k**, let a
Esth 3:10 So the **k** took his signet ring
Esth 3:11 And the **k** said to Haman,
Esth 3:12 In the name of **K** Ahasuerus it
Esth 3:15 So the **k** and Haman sat down to
Esth 4: 8 **k** to make supplication to him
Esth 4:11 into the inner court to the **k**
Esth 4:11 the **k** holds out the golden
Esth 4:11 in to the **k** these thirty days
Esth 4:16 And so I will go to the **k**,
Esth 5: 1 while the **k** sat on his royal
Esth 5: 2 when the **k** saw Queen Esther
Esth 5: 2 the **k** held out to Esther the
Esth 5: 3 And the **k** said to her,
Esth 5: 4 If it pleases the **k**, let the **k**
Esth 5: 5 Then the **k** said, "Bring
Esth 5: 5 So the **k** and Haman went to
Esth 5: 6 of wine the **k** said to Esther
Esth 5: 8 favor in the sight of the **k**
Esth 5: 8 if it pleases the **k** to grant
Esth 5: 8 my request, then let the **k**
Esth 5: 8 I will do as the **k** has said
Esth 5:11 which the **k** had promoted him
Esth 5:11 and servants of the **k**
Esth 5:12 the **k** to the banquet that she
Esth 5:12 by her, along with the **k**
Esth 5:14 **k** that Mordecai be hanged on
Esth 5:14 with the **k** to the banquet
Esth 6: 1 That night the **k** could not
Esth 6: 1 they were read before the **k**
Esth 6: 2 to lay hands on **K** Ahasuerus
Esth 6: 3 Then the **k** said, "What honor
Esth 6: 4 And the **k** said, "Who is in
Esth 6: 4 the **k** hang Mordecai on the
Esth 6: 5 the **k** said, "Let him come in."
Esth 6: 6 came in, and the **k** asked him,
Esth 6: 6 whom the **k** delights to honor
Esth 6: 6 Whom would the **k** delight to
Esth 6: 7 And Haman answered the **k**
Esth 6: 7 whom the **k** delights to honor
Esth 6: 8 brought which the **k** has worn
Esth 6: 8 on which the **k** has ridden
Esth 6: 9 whom the **k** delights to honor
Esth 6: 9 whom the **k** delights to honor
Esth 6:10 Then the **k** said to Haman,
Esth 6:11 man the **k** delights to honor
Esth 7: 1 So the **k** and Haman went to
Esth 7: 2 the **k** again said to Esther,
Esth 7: 3 favor in your sight, O **k**, and
Esth 7: 3 O **k**, and if it pleases the **k**
Esth 7: 5 Then **K** Ahasuerus answered
Esth 7: 6 was terrified before the **k**
Esth 7: 7 Then the **k** arose in his wrath
Esth 7: 7 against him by the **k**
Esth 7: 8 When the **k** returned from the
Esth 7: 8 Then the **k** said, "Will he
Esth 7: 9 of the eunuchs, said to the **k**
Esth 7: 9 Then the **k** said, "Hang him
Esth 8: 1 On that day **K** Ahasuerus gave
Esth 8: 1 Mordecai came before the **k**
Esth 8: 2 So the **k** took off his signet
Esth 8: 3 Esther spoke again to the **k**
Esth 8: 4 the **k** held out the golden
Esth 8: 4 arose and stood before the **k**
Esth 8: 5 If it pleases the **k**, and if I
Esth 8: 5 thing seems right to the **k**
Esth 8: 7 Then **K** Ahasuerus said to
Esth 8:10 in the name of **K** Ahasuerus
Esth 8:11 By these letters the **k**
Esth 8:12 the provinces of **K** Ahasuerus
Esth 8:15 **k** in royal apparel of blue
Esth 9: 2 all the provinces of **K**
Esth 9:11 citadel was brought to the **k**
Esth 9:12 the **k** said to Queen Esther,
Esth 9:13 If it pleases the **k**, let it
Esth 9:14 So the **k** commanded this to be
Esth 9:20 the provinces of **K** Ahasuerus
Esth 9:25 when Esther came before the **k**
Esth 10: 1 **K** Ahasuerus imposed tribute
Esth 10: 2 to which the **k** advanced him
Esth 10: 3 Jew was second to **K** Ahasuerus
Job 15:24 like a **k** ready for battle
Job 18:14 him before the **k** of terrors
Job 29:25 so I dwelt as a **k** in the army
Job 34:18 Is it fitting to say to a **k**
Job 41:34 he is **k** over all the children
Ps 2: 6 Yet I have set My **K** On My
Ps 5: 2 to the voice of my cry, My **K**
Ps 10:16 The LORD is **K** forever and ever
Ps 18:50 deliverance He gives to His **k**
Ps 20: 9 May the **K** answer us when we
Ps 21: 1 The **k** shall have joy in Your
Ps 21: 7 For the **k** trusts in the LORD,
Ps 24: 7 the **K** of glory shall come in
Ps 24: 8 Who is this **K** of glory
Ps 24: 9 the **K** of glory shall come in
Ps 24:10 Who is this **K** of glory
Ps 24:10 hosts, He is the **K** of glory
Ps 29:10 And the LORD sits as **K** forever
Ps 33:16 No **k** is saved by the
Ps 44: 4 You are my **K**, O God
Ps 45: 1 composition concerning the **K**
Ps 45:11 So the **K** will greatly desire
Ps 45:14 the **K** in robes of many colors
Ps 47: 2 He is a great **K** over all the
Ps 47: 6 Sing praises to our **K**, sing
Ps 47: 7 For God is the **K** of all the
Ps 48: 2 The city of the great **K**
Ps 63:11 But the **k** shall rejoice in
Ps 68:24 procession of my God, my **K**
Ps 72: 1 Give the **k** Your judgments, O
Ps 74:12 For God is my **K** from of old
Ps 84: 3 altars, O LORD of hosts, My **K**
Ps 89:18 And our **k** to the Holy One of
Ps 95: 3 the great **K** above all gods
Ps 98: 6 before the LORD, the **K**
Ps 105:20 The **k** sent and released him,
Ps 135:11 Sihon **k** of the Amorites, Og
Ps 135:11 Og **k** of Bashan, And all the
Ps 136:19 Sihon **k** of the Amorites, For
Ps 136:20 Og **k** of Bashan, For His mercy
Ps 145: 1 I will extol You, my God, O **K**
Ps 149: 2 of Zion be joyful in their **K**
Prov 1: 1 the son of David, **k** of Israel
Prov 16:10 is on the lips of the **k**, his
Prov 20: 2 The wrath of a **k** is like the
Prov 20: 8 A **k** who sits on the throne of
Prov 20:26 A wise **k** sifts out the wicked
Prov 20:28 Mercy and truth preserve the **k**
Prov 22:11 the **k** will be his friend
Prov 24:21 son, fear the LORD and the **k**
Prov 25: 1 of Hezekiah **k** of Judah copied
Prov 25: 5 the wicked from before the **k**
Prov 25: 6 in the presence of the **k**, and
Prov 29: 4 The **k** establishes the land by
Prov 29:14 The **k** who judges the poor
Prov 30:27 the locusts have no **k**, yet
Prov 30:31 a **k** whose troops are with him

Prov 31: 1 The words of **K** Lemuel, the
Eccl 1: 1 son of David, **k** in Jerusalem
Eccl 1:12 was **k** over Israel in
Eccl 2:12 the man do who succeeds the **k**
Eccl 4:13 old and foolish **k** who will be
Eccl 4:14 comes out of prison to be **k**
Eccl 4:16 over whom he was made **k**
Eccl 5: 9 the **k** himself is served from
Eccl 8: 4 Where the word of a **k** is,
Eccl 9:14 a great **k** came against it,
Eccl 10:16 when your **k** is a child, and
Eccl 10:17 when your **k** is the son of
Eccl 10:20 Do not curse the **k**, even in
Song 1: 4 The **k** has brought me
Song 1:12 While the **k** is at his table,
Song 3: 9 **K** made himself a palanquin
Song 3:11 see **K** Solomon with the crown
Song 7: 5 the **k** is held captive by its
Is 6: 1 the year that **K** Uzziah died
Is 6: 5 for my eyes have seen the **K**
Is 7: 1 **k** of Judah, that Rezin **k**
Is 7: 1 **k** of Israel, went up to
Is 7: 6 set a **k** over them, the son of
Is 7:17 the **k** of Assyria upon you
Is 7:20 with the **k** of Assyria, the
Is 8: 4 away before the **k** of Assyria
Is 8: 7 the **k** of Assyria and all his
Is 8:21 be enraged and curse their **k**
Is 10:12 heart of the **k** of Assyria
Is 14: 4 against the **k** of Babylon, and
Is 14:28 in the year that **K** Ahaz died
Is 19: 4 a fierce **k** will rule over
Is 20: 1 when Sargon the **k** of Assyria
Is 20: 4 so shall the **k** of Assyria
Is 20: 6 from the **k** of Assyria
Is 23:15 to the days of one **k**
Is 30:33 yes, for the **k** it is prepared
Is 32: 1 Behold, a **k** will reign in
Is 33:17 will see the **K** in His beauty
Is 33:22 Lawgiver, the LORD is our **K**
Is 36: 1 **K** Hezekiah that Sennacherib
Is 36: 1 Hezekiah that Sennacherib **k**
Is 36: 2 Then the **k** of Assyria sent
Is 36: 2 to **K** Hezekiah at Jerusalem
Is 36: 4 great **k**, the **k** of Assyria
Is 36: 6 So is Pharaoh **k** of Egypt to
Is 36: 8 to my master the **k** of Assyria
Is 36:13 great **k**, the **k** of Assyria
Is 36:14 Thus says the **k**: 'Do not let
Is 36:15 the hand of the **k** of Assyria
Is 36:16 thus says the **k** of Assyria
Is 36:18 the hand of the **k** of Assyria
Is 37: 1 when **K** Hezekiah heard it,
Is 37: 4 whom his master the **k** of
Is 37: 5 So the servants of **K** Hezekiah
Is 37: 6 which the servants of the **k**
Is 37: 8 and found the **k** of Assyria
Is 37: 9 And the **k** heard concerning
Is 37: 9 Tirhakah **k** of Ethiopia, "He
Is 37:10 speak to Hezekiah **k** of Judah
Is 37:10 the hand of the **k** of Assyria
Is 37:13 Where is the **k** of Hamath
Is 37:13 the **k** of Arpad
Is 37:13 and the **k** of the city of
Is 37:21 Sennacherib **k** of Assyria,
Is 37:33 concerning the **k** of Assyria
Is 37:37 So Sennacherib **k** of Assyria
Is 38: 6 the hand of the **k** of Assyria
Is 38: 9 of Hezekiah **k** of Judah, when
Is 39: 1 **k** of Babylon, sent letters and
Is 39: 3 prophet went to **K** Hezekiah
Is 39: 7 palace of the **k** of Babylon
Is 41:21 says the **K** of Jacob
Is 43:15 the Creator of Israel, your **K**
Is 44: 6 LORD, the **K** of Israel, and his
Is 57: 9 went to the **k** with ointment
Jer 1: 2 **k** of Judah, in the thirteenth
Jer 1: 3 **k** of Judah, until the end of
Jer 1: 3 Josiah, **k** of Judah, until the
Jer 3: 6 in the days of Josiah the **k**
Jer 4: 9 heart of the **k** shall perish
Jer 8:19 Is not her **K** in her
Jer 10: 7 fear You, O **K** of the nations
Jer 10:10 God and the everlasting **K**
Jer 13:18 Say to the **k** and to the queen
Jer 15: 4 **k** of Judah, for what he did
Jer 20: 4 the hand of the **k** of Babylon
Jer 21: 1 when **K** Zedekiah sent to him
Jer 21: 2 us, for Nebuchadnezzar **k** of
Jer 21: 2 that the **k** may go away from
Jer 21: 4 against the **k** of Babylon and
Jer 21: 7 deliver Zedekiah **k** of Judah
Jer 21: 7 Nebuchadnezzar **k** of Babylon
Jer 21:10 the hand of the **k** of Babylon
Jer 21:11 the house of the **k** of Judah
Jer 22: 1 the house of the **k** of Judah
Jer 22: 2 O **k** of Judah, you who sit on
Jer 22: 6 the house of the **k** of Judah
Jer 22:11 **k** of Judah, who reigned
Jer 22:18 the son of Josiah, **k** of Judah
Jer 22:24 **k** of Judah, were the signet
Jer 22:25 Nebuchadnezzar **k** of Babylon
Jer 23: 5 a **K** shall reign and prosper,
Jer 24: 1 after Nebuchadnezzar **k** of
Jer 24: 1 **k** of Judah, and the princes of
Jer 24: 8 up Zedekiah the **k** of Judah
Jer 25: 1 **k** of Judah (which was the
Jer 25: 1 Nebuchadnezzar **k** of Babylon)
Jer 25: 3 **k** of Judah, even to this day,
Jer 25: 9 the **k** of Babylon, My servant,
Jer 25:11 nations shall serve the **k** of
Jer 25:12 will punish the **k** of Babylon
Jer 25:19 Pharaoh **k** of Egypt, his
Jer 25:26 Also the **k** of Sheshach shall
Jer 26: 1 **k** of Judah, this word came
Jer 26:18 days of Hezekiah **k** of Judah
Jer 26:19 Did Hezekiah **k** of Judah and
Jer 26:21 And when Jehoiakim the **k**, with
Jer 26:21 the **k** sought to put him to
Jer 26:22 the **k** sent men to Egypt
Jer 26:23 him to Jehoiakim the **k**, who
Jer 27: 1 **k** of Judah, this word came to
Jer 27: 3 and send them to the **k** of Edom
Jer 27: 3 the **k** of Moab
Jer 27: 3 the **k** of the Ammonites
Jer 27: 3 the **k** of Tyre
Jer 27: 3 the **k** of Sidon
Jer 27: 3 to Zedekiah **k** of Judah
Jer 27: 6 the **k** of Babylon, My servant
Jer 27: 8 the **k** of Babylon, and which
Jer 27: 8 the yoke of the **k** of Babylon
Jer 27: 9 not serve the **k** of Babylon
Jer 27:11 the yoke of the **k** of Babylon
Jer 27:12 I also spoke to Zedekiah **k** of
Jer 27:12 the yoke of the **k** of Babylon
Jer 27:13 not serve the **k** of Babylon
Jer 27:14 not serve the **k** of Babylon
Jer 27:17 serve the **k** of Babylon, and
Jer 27:18 the house of the **k** of Judah
Jer 27:20 which Nebuchadnezzar **k** of
Jer 27:20 **k** of Judah, from Jerusalem to
Jer 27:21 the house of the **k** of Judah
Jer 28: 1 reign of Zedekiah **k** of Judah
Jer 28: 2 the yoke of the **k** of Babylon
Jer 28: 3 that Nebuchadnezzar **k** of
Jer 28: 4 **k** of Judah, with all the
Jer 28: 4 the yoke of the **k** of Babylon
Jer 28:11 the yoke of Nebuchadnezzar **k**
Jer 28:14 Nebuchadnezzar **k** of Babylon
Jer 29: 2 happened after Jeconiah the **k**
Jer 29: 3 whom Zedekiah **k** of Judah sent
Jer 29: 3 Nebuchadnezzar **k** of Babylon
Jer 29:16 the LORD concerning the **k** who
Jer 29:21 Nebuchadnezzar **k** of Babylon
Jer 29:22 whom the **k** of Babylon roasted
Jer 30: 9 their God, and David their **k**
Jer 32: 1 year of Zedekiah **k** of Judah
Jer 32: 2 For then the **k** of Babylon's
Jer 32: 2 was in the **k** of Judah's house
Jer 32: 3 For Zedekiah **k** of Judah had
Jer 32: 3 the hand of the **k** of Babylon
Jer 32: 4 Zedekiah **k** of Judah shall not
Jer 32: 4 the hand of the **k** of Babylon
Jer 32:28 Nebuchadnezzar **k** of Babylon
Jer 32:36 into the hand of the **k** of
Jer 34: 1 Nebuchadnezzar **k** of Babylon
Jer 34: 2 speak to Zedekiah **k** of Judah
Jer 34: 2 the hand of the **k** of Babylon
Jer 34: 3 the eyes of the **k** of Babylon
Jer 34: 4 LORD, O Zedekiah **k** of Judah
Jer 34: 6 **k** of Judah in Jerusalem,
Jer 34: 7 when the **k** of Babylon's army
Jer 34: 8 after **K** Zedekiah had made a
Jer 34:21 will give Zedekiah **k** of Judah
Jer 34:21 into the hand of the **k** of
Jer 35: 1 Josiah, **k** of Judah, saying,
Jer 35:11 when Nebuchadnezzar **k** of
Jer 36: 1 **k** of Judah, that this word
Jer 36: 9 **k** of Judah, in the ninth
Jer 36:16 tell the **k** of all these words
Jer 36:20 And they went to the **k**, into
Jer 36:20 words in the hearing of the **k**
Jer 36:21 So the **k** sent Jehudi to bring
Jer 36:21 it in the hearing of the **k**
Jer 36:21 who stood beside the **k**
Jer 36:22 Now the **k** was sitting in the
Jer 36:23 that the **k** cut it with the
Jer 36:24 the **k** nor any of his servants
Jer 36:25 Gemariah implored the **k** not
Jer 36:26 the **k** commanded Jerahmeel the
Jer 36:27 Now after the **k** had burned
Jer 36:28 the **k** of Judah has burned
Jer 36:29 say to Jehoiakim **k** of Judah
Jer 36:29 **k** of Babylon will certainly
Jer 36:30 Jehoiakim **k** of Judah
Jer 36:32 **k** of Judah had burned in the
Jer 37: 1 Then **K** Zedekiah the son of
Jer 37: 1 whom Nebuchadnezzar **k** of
Jer 37: 1 made **k** in the land of Judah
Jer 37: 3 Zedekiah the **k** sent Jehucal
Jer 37: 7 shall say to the **k** of Judah
Jer 37:17 then Zedekiah the **k** sent and
Jer 37:17 The **k** asked him secretly in
Jer 37:17 the hand of the **k** of Babylon
Jer 37:18 Jeremiah said to **K** Zedekiah
Jer 37:19 The **k** of Babylon will not
Jer 37:20 hear now, O my lord the **k**
Jer 37:21 Then Zedekiah the **k**
Jer 38: 3 of the **k** of Babylon's army
Jer 38: 4 the princes said to the **k**
Jer 38: 5 Then Zedekiah the **k** said
Jer 38: 5 For the **k** can do nothing
Jer 38: 7 When the **k** was sitting at the
Jer 38: 8 house and spoke to the **k**,
Jer 38: 9 My lord the **k**, these men have
Jer 38:10 Then the **k** commanded
Jer 38:11 of the **k** under the treasury
Jer 38:14 Then Zedekiah the **k** sent and
Jer 38:14 And the **k** said to Jeremiah,
Jer 38:16 So Zedekiah the **k** swore
Jer 38:17 to the **k** of Babylon's princes
Jer 38:18 to the **k** of Babylon's princes
Jer 38:19 And Zedekiah the **k** said to
Jer 38:22 **k** of Judah's house shall be
Jer 38:22 to the **k** of Babylon's princes
Jer 38:23 the hand of the **k** of Babylon
Jer 38:25 what you have said to the **k**
Jer 38:25 also what the **k** said to you
Jer 38:26 my request before the **k**, that
Jer 38:27 that the **k** had commanded
Jer 39: 1 year of Zedekiah **k** of Judah
Jer 39: 1 Nebuchadnezzar **k** of Babylon
Jer 39: 3 of the **k** of Babylon came in
Jer 39: 3 princes of the **k** of Babylon
Jer 39: 4 when Zedekiah the **k** of Judah
Jer 39: 5 Nebuchadnezzar **k** of Babylon
Jer 39: 6 Then the **k** of Babylon killed
Jer 39: 6 the **k** of Babylon also killed
Jer 39:11 Now Nebuchadnezzar **k** of
Jer 39:13 all the **k** of Babylon's chief
Jer 40: 5 whom the **k** of Babylon has
Jer 40: 7 heard that the **k** of Babylon
Jer 40: 9 serve the **k** of Babylon, and it
Jer 40:11 heard that the **k** of Babylon
Jer 40:14 know that Baalis the **k** of the
Jer 41: 1 and of the officers of the **k**
Jer 41: 2 the **k** of Babylon had made
Jer 41: 9 was the same one Asa the **k**
Jer 41: 9 fear of Baasha **k** of Israel
Jer 41:18 whom the **k** of Babylon had
Jer 42:11 be afraid of the **k** of Babylon
Jer 43:10 the **k** of Babylon, My servant,
Jer 44:30 **k** of Egypt into the hand of
Jer 44:30 as I gave Zedekiah **k** of Judah
Jer 44:30 Nebuchadnezzar **k** of Babylon
Jer 45: 1 Josiah, **k** of Judah, saying,
Jer 46: 2 **k** of Egypt, which was by the
Jer 46: 2 which Nebuchadnezzar **k** of
Jer 46: 2 the son of Josiah, **k** of Judah
Jer 46:13 how Nebuchadnezzar **k** of
Jer 46:17 **k** of Egypt, is but a noise
Jer 46:18 As I live," says the **K**,
Jer 46:26 Nebuchadnezzar **k** of Babylon
Jer 48:15 the slaughter," says the **K**
Jer 49:28 which Nebuchadnezzar **k** of
Jer 49:30 For Nebuchadnezzar **k** of
Jer 49:34 reign of Zedekiah **k** of Judah
Jer 49:38 will destroy from there the **k**
Jer 50:17 First the **k** of Assyria
Jer 50:17 **k** of Babylon has broken his

Jer 50:18 will punish the **k** of Babylon
Jer 50:18 punished the **k** of Assyria
Jer 50:43 The **k** of Babylon has heard
Jer 51:31 to show the **k** of Babylon that
Jer 51:34 Nebuchadnezzar the **k** of
Jer 51:57 and not awake," says the **K**
Jer 51:59 he went with Zedekiah the **k**
Jer 52: 1 years old when he became **k**
Jer 52: 3 against the **k** of Babylon
Jer 52: 4 Nebuchadnezzar **k** of Babylon
Jer 52: 5 eleventh year of **K** Zedekiah
Jer 52: 8 the Chaldeans pursued the **k**
Jer 52: 9 So they took the **k** and brought
Jer 52: 9 brought him up to the **k** of
Jer 52:10 Then the **k** of Babylon killed
Jer 52:11 the **k** of Babylon bound him in
Jer 52:12 **K** Nebuchadnezzar **k** of Babylon
Jer 52:12 who served the **k** of Babylon
Jer 52:15 deserted to the **k** of Babylon
Jer 52:20 which **K** Solomon had made for
Jer 52:26 and brought them to the **k** of
Jer 52:27 Then the **k** of Babylon struck
Jer 52:31 of Jehoiachin **k** of Judah, in
Jer 52:31 Evil-Merodach **k** of Babylon
Jer 52:31 head of Jehoiachin **k** of Judah
Jer 52:33 **k** all the days of his life
Jer 52:34 given him by the **k** of Babylon
Lam 2: 6 He has spurned the **k** and the
Lam 2: 9 Her **k** and her princes are
Ezek 1: 2 of **K** Jehoiachin's captivity
Ezek 7:27 The **k** will mourn, the prince
Ezek 17:12 Indeed the **k** of Babylon went
Ezek 17:12 to Jerusalem and took its **k**
Ezek 17:16 **k** dwells who made him **k**
Ezek 19: 9 him to the **k** of Babylon
Ezek 21:19 of the **k** of Babylon to go
Ezek 21:21 For the **k** of Babylon stands
Ezek 24: 2 the **k** of Babylon started his
Ezek 26: 7 Nebuchadnezzar **k** of Babylon
Ezek 26: 7 **k** of kings, with horses, with
Ezek 28:12 lamentation for the **k** of Tyre
Ezek 29: 2 against Pharaoh **k** of Egypt
Ezek 29: 3 you, O Pharaoh **k** of Egypt
Ezek 29:18 Nebuchadnezzar **k** of Babylon
Ezek 29:19 Nebuchadnezzar **k** of Babylon
Ezek 30:10 Nebuchadnezzar **k** of Babylon
Ezek 30:21 the arm of Pharaoh **k** of Egypt
Ezek 30:22 am against Pharaoh **k** of Egypt
Ezek 30:24 the arms of the **k** of Babylon
Ezek 30:25 the arms of the **k** of Babylon
Ezek 30:25 the hand of the **k** of Babylon
Ezek 31: 2 say to Pharaoh **k** of Egypt
Ezek 32: 2 for Pharaoh **k** of Egypt, and
Ezek 32:11 The sword of the **k** of
Ezek 37:22 one **k** shall be **k** over them
Ezek 37:24 servant shall be **k** over them
Dan 1: 1 reign of Jehoiakim **k** of Judah
Dan 1: 1 Nebuchadnezzar **k** of Babylon
Dan 1: 2 **k** of Judah into his hand,
Dan 1: 3 Then the **k** instructed
Dan 1: 5 the **k** appointed for them a
Dan 1: 5 they might serve before the **k**
Dan 1:10 I fear my lord the **k**, who has
Dan 1:10 endanger my head before the **k**
Dan 1:18 when the **k** had said that they
Dan 1:19 Then the **k** interviewed them,
Dan 1:19 they served before the **k**
Dan 1:20 which the **k** examined them
Dan 1:21 the first year of **K** Cyrus
Dan 2: 2 Then the **k** gave the command
Dan 2: 2 to tell the **k** his dreams
Dan 2: 2 came and stood before the **k**
Dan 2: 3 And the **k** said to them,
Dan 2: 4 spoke to the **k** in Aramaic
Dan 2: 4 O **k**, live forever
Dan 2: 5 But the **k** answered and said to
Dan 2: 7 Let the **k** tell his servants
Dan 2: 8 The **k** answered and said, "I
Dan 2:10 The Chaldeans answered the **k**
Dan 2:10 therefore no **k**, lord, or
Dan 2:11 thing that the **k** requires
Dan 2:11 it to the **k** except the gods
Dan 2:12 this reason the **k** was angry
Dan 2:15 decree from the **k** so urgent
Dan 2:16 asked the **k** to give him time,
Dan 2:16 tell the **k** the interpretation
Dan 2:24 whom the **k** had appointed to
Dan 2:24 take me before the **k**, and I
Dan 2:24 and I will tell the **k** the
Dan 2:25 brought Daniel before the **k**
Dan 2:25 to the **k** the interpretation
Dan 2:26 The **k** answered and said to
Dan 2:27 in the presence of the **k**, and
Dan 2:27 which the **k** has demanded, the
Dan 2:27 cannot declare to the **k**
Dan 2:28 and He has made known to **K**
Dan 2:29 As for you, O **k**, thoughts
Dan 2:30 the interpretation to the **k**
Dan 2:31 You, O **k**, were watching
Dan 2:36 of it before the **k**
Dan 2:37 You, O **k**, are a **k** of kings
Dan 2:45 the **k** what will come to pass
Dan 2:46 Then **K** Nebuchadnezzar fell on
Dan 2:47 The **k** answered Daniel, and
Dan 2:48 Then the **k** promoted Daniel
Dan 2:49 Also Daniel petitioned the **k**
Dan 2:49 sat in the gate of the **k**
Dan 3: 1 Nebuchadnezzar the **k** made an
Dan 3: 2 **K** Nebuchadnezzar sent word to
Dan 3: 2 of the image which **K**
Dan 3: 3 of the image that **K**
Dan 3: 5 **K** Nebuchadnezzar has set up
Dan 3: 7 the gold image which **K**
Dan 3: 9 said to **K** Nebuchadnezzar,
Dan 3: 9 O **k**, live forever
Dan 3:10 You, O **k**, have made a decree
Dan 3:12 these men, O **k**, have not paid
Dan 3:13 these men before the **k**
Dan 3:16 answered and said to the **k**
Dan 3:17 us from your hand, O **k**
Dan 3:18 let it be known to you, O **k**
Dan 3:24 Then **K** Nebuchadnezzar was
Dan 3:24 said to the **k**, "True, O **k**."
Dan 3:30 Then the **k** promoted Shadrach,
Dan 4: 1 Nebuchadnezzar the **k**, To all
Dan 4:18 **K** Nebuchadnezzar, have seen
Dan 4:19 So the **k** spoke, and said
Dan 4:22 it is you, O **k**, who have
Dan 4:23 as the **k** saw a watcher, a
Dan 4:24 is the interpretation, O **k**
Dan 4:24 has come upon my lord the **k**
Dan 4:27 Therefore, O **k**, let my
Dan 4:28 came upon **K** Nebuchadnezzar
Dan 4:30 The **k** spoke, saying, "Is not
Dan 4:31 **K** Nebuchadnezzar, to you it
Dan 4:37 and honor the **K** of heaven, all
Dan 5: 1 Belshazzar the **k** made a great
Dan 5: 2 been in Jerusalem, that the **k**
Dan 5: 3 and the **k** and his lords, his
Dan 5: 5 the **k** saw the part of the
Dan 5: 7 The **k** cried aloud to bring in
Dan 5: 7 the **k** spoke, saying to the
Dan 5: 8 to the **k** its interpretation
Dan 5: 9 Then **K** Belshazzar was greatly
Dan 5:10 because of the words of the **k**
Dan 5:10 O **k**, live forever
Dan 5:11 **K** Nebuchadnezzar your father
Dan 5:11 your father the **k**
Dan 5:12 whom the **k** named Belteshazzar
Dan 5:13 was brought in before the **k**
Dan 5:13 And the **k** spoke, and said to
Dan 5:13 the **k** brought from Judah
Dan 5:17 and said before the **k**, "Let
Dan 5:17 read the writing to the **k**
Dan 5:18 O **k**, the Most High God gave
Dan 5:30 **k** of the Chaldeans, was slain
Dan 6: 2 so that the **k** would suffer no
Dan 6: 3 the **k** gave thought to setting
Dan 6: 6 satraps thronged before the **k**
Dan 6: 6 **K** Darius, live forever
Dan 6: 7 thirty days, except you, O **k**
Dan 6: 8 Now, O **k**, establish the
Dan 6: 9 Therefore **K** Darius signed the
Dan 6:12 And they went before the **k**
Dan 6:12 thirty days, except you, O **k**
Dan 6:12 The **k** answered and said,
Dan 6:13 answered and said before the **k**
Dan 6:13 show due regard for you, O **k**
Dan 6:14 And the **k**, when he heard these
Dan 6:15 these men approached the **k**
Dan 6:15 and said to the **k**
Dan 6:15 Know, O **k**, that it is the law
Dan 6:15 **k** establishes may be changed
Dan 6:16 So the **k** gave the command, and
Dan 6:16 But the **k** spoke, saying to
Dan 6:17 the **k** sealed it with his own
Dan 6:18 Now the **k** went to his palace
Dan 6:19 Then the **k** arose very early
Dan 6:20 The **k** spoke, saying to Daniel
Dan 6:21 Then Daniel said to the **k**
Dan 6:21 O **k**, live forever
Dan 6:22 and also, O **k**, I have done no
Dan 6:23 Then the **k** was exceedingly
Dan 6:24 the **k** gave the command, and
Dan 6:25 Then **K** Darius wrote
Dan 7: 1 of Belshazzar **k** of Babylon
Dan 8: 1 of **K** Belshazzar a vision
Dan 8:21 its eyes is the first **k**
Dan 8:23 a **k** shall arise, having
Dan 9: 1 who was made **k** over the realm
Dan 10: 1 **k** of Persia a message was
Dan 11: 3 Then a mighty **k** shall arise
Dan 11: 5 Then the **k** of the South shall
Dan 11: 6 for the daughter of the **k** of
Dan 11: 6 the **k** of the North to make an
Dan 11: 7 of the **k** of the North, and
Dan 11: 8 years than the **k** of the North
Dan 11: 9 Then the **k** of the North shall
Dan 11: 9 kingdom of the **k** of the South
Dan 11:11 the **k** of the South shall be
Dan 11:11 with the **k** of the North, who
Dan 11:13 For the **k** of the North will
Dan 11:14 up against the **k** of the South
Dan 11:15 So the **k** of the North shall
Dan 11:25 his courage against the **k** of
Dan 11:25 the **k** of the South shall be
Dan 11:36 Then the **k** shall do according
Dan 11:40 **k** of the South shall attack
Dan 11:40 the **k** of the North shall come
Hos 1: 1 the son of Joash, **k** of Israel
Hos 3: 4 many days without **k** or prince
Hos 3: 5 their God and David their **k**
Hos 5: 1 Give ear, O house of the **k**
Hos 5:13 to Assyria and sent to **K** Jareb
Hos 7: 3 They make a **k** glad with their
Hos 7: 5 In the day of our **k** princes
Hos 8:10 burden of the **k** of princes
Hos 10: 3 We have no **k**, Because we did
Hos 10: 3 and as for a **k**, what would he
Hos 10: 6 as a present for **K** Jareb
Hos 10: 7 her **k** is cut off like a twig
Hos 10:15 In a morning the **k** of Israel
Hos 11: 5 the Assyrian shall be his **k**
Hos 13:10 I will be your **K**
Hos 13:10 whom you said, 'Give me a **k**
Hos 13:11 I gave you a **k** in My anger
Amos 1: 1 the days of Uzziah **k** of Judah
Amos 1: 1 **k** of Israel, two years before
Amos 1:15 Their **k** shall go into
Amos 2: 1 of the **k** of Edom to lime
Amos 5:26 also carried Sikkuth your **k**
Amos 7:10 sent to Jeroboam **k** of Israel
Jon 3: 6 word came to the **k** of Nineveh
Jon 3: 7 by the decree of the **k** and his
Mic 2:13 their **k** will pass before them
Mic 4: 9 Is there no **k** in your midst
Mic 6: 5 Balak **k** of Moab counseled
Nah 3:18 slumber, O **k** of Assyria
Zeph 1: 1 the son of Amon, **k** of Judah
Zeph 3:15 the **K** of Israel, the LORD, is
Hag 1: 1 the second year of **K** Darius
Hag 1:15 the second year of **K** Darius
Zech 7: 1 Now in the fourth year of **K**
Zech 9: 5 The **k** shall perish from Gaza,
Zech 9: 9 your **K** is coming to you
Zech 11: 6 and into the hand of his **k**
Zech 14: 5 the days of Uzziah **k** of Judah
Zech 14: 9 the LORD shall be **K** over all
Zech 14:16 year to year to worship the **K**
Zech 14:17 to Jerusalem to worship the **K**
Mal 1:14 for I am a great **K**," says
Matt 1: 6 and Jesse begot David the **k**
Matt 1: 6 David the **k** begot Solomon by
Matt 2: 1 in the days of Herod the **k**
Matt 2: 2 has been born **K** of the Jews
Matt 2: 3 When Herod the **k** heard these
Matt 2: 9 When they heard the **k**, they
Matt 5:35 it is the city of the great **K**
Matt 14: 9 And the **k** was sorry
Matt 18:23 **k** who wanted to settle
Matt 21: 5 your **K** is coming to you,
Matt 22: 2 **k** who arranged a marriage for
Matt 22: 7 But when the **k** heard about it
Matt 22:11 But when the **k** came in to see
Matt 22:13 Then the **k** said to the
Matt 25:34 Then the **K** will say to those
Matt 25:40 the **K** will answer and say to
Matt 27:11 Are You the **K** of the Jews
Matt 27:29 saying, "Hail, **K** of the Jews
Matt 27:37 IS JESUS THE **K** OF THE

Matt 27:42 If He is the **K** of Israel, let
Mark 6:14 Now **K** Herod heard of Him, for
Mark 6:22 him, the **k** said to the girl,
Mark 6:25 came in with haste to the **k**
Mark 6:26 the **k** was exceedingly sorry
Mark 6:27 immediately the **k** sent an
Mark 15: 2 Are You the **K** of the Jews
Mark 15: 9 to you the **K** of the Jews
Mark 15:12 you call the **K** of the Jews
Mark 15:18 Him, "Hail, **K** of the Jews
Mark 15:26 THE **K** OF THE JEWS
Mark 15:32 the **K** of Israel, descend now
Luke 1: 5 the **k** of Judea, a certain
Luke 14:31 Or what **k**, going to make war
Luke 14:31 to make war against another **k**
Luke 19:38 Blessed is the **K** who comes
Luke 23: 2 He Himself is Christ, a **K**
Luke 23: 3 Are You the **K** of the Jews
Luke 23:37 If You are the **K** of the Jews
Luke 23:38 THIS IS THE **K** OF THE JEWS
John 1:49 You are the **K** of Israel
John 6:15 Him by force to make Him **k**
John 12:13 The **K** of Israel
John 12:15 your **K** is coming, sitting on
John 18:33 Are You the **K** of the Jews
John 18:37 Are You a **k** then
John 18:37 You say rightly that I am a **k**
John 18:39 to you the **K** of the Jews
John 19: 3 said, "Hail, **K** of the Jews
John 19:12 a **k** speaks against Caesar
John 19:14 to the Jews, "Behold your **K**!"
John 19:15 Shall I crucify your **K**
John 19:15 We have no **k** but Caesar
John 19:19 Nazareth, The **K** of the Jews
John 19:21 The **K** of the Jews,' but, 'He
John 19:21 I am the **K** of the Jews
Acts 7:10 of Pharaoh, **k** of Egypt
Acts 7:18 till another **k** arose who did
Acts 12: 1 **k** stretched out his hand to
Acts 13:21 afterward they asked for a **k**
Acts 13:22 raised up for them David as **k**
Acts 17: 7 saying there is another **k**
Acts 25:13 And after some days **K** Agrippa
Acts 25:14 laid Paul's case before the **k**
Acts 25:24 **K** Agrippa and all the men who
Acts 25:26 **K** Agrippa, so that after the
Acts 26: 2 **K** Agrippa, because today I
Acts 26: 7 **K** Agrippa, I am accused by
Acts 26:13 at midday, O **k**, along the
Acts 26:19 **K** Agrippa, I was not
Acts 26:26 For the **k**, before whom I also
Acts 26:27 **K** Agrippa, do you believe the
Acts 26:30 the **k** stood up, as well as
2Co 11:32 governor, under Aretas the **k**
1Ti 1:17 Now to the **K** eternal,
1Ti 6:15 the **K** of kings and Lord of
Heb 7: 1 **k** of Salem, priest of the
Heb 7: 2 **k** of righteousness," and then
Heb 7: 2 and then also **k** of Salem
Heb 7: 2 meaning "**k** of peace,"
Heb 11:27 fearing the wrath of the **k**
1Pe 2:13 whether to the **k** as supreme
1Pe 2:17 Fear God. Honor the **k**.
Rev 9:11 they had as **k** over them the
Rev 15: 3 Your ways, O **K** of the saints
Rev 17:14 Lord of lords and **K** of kings
Rev 19:16 **K** OF KINGS AND LORD OF

KINGDOM (*see* KINGDOMS)
Gen 10:10 beginning of his **k** was Babel
Gen 20: 9 on me and on my **k** a great sin
Ex 19: 6 shall be to Me a **k** of priests
Num 24: 7 and his **k** shall be exalted
Num 32:33 the **k** of Sihon king of the
Num 32:33 the **k** of Og king of Bashan,
Deut 3: 4 Argob, the **k** of Og in Bashan
Deut 3:10 cities of the **k** of Og in
Deut 3:13 the **k** of Og, I gave to half
Deut 17:18 sits on the throne of his **k**
Deut 17:20 may prolong his days in his **k**
Josh 13:12 all the **k** of Og in Bashan,
Josh 13:21 all the **k** of Sihon king of
Josh 13:27 the rest of the **k** of Sihon
Josh 13:30 all the **k** of Og king of
Josh 13:31 cities of the **k** of Og in
1Sa 10:16 But about the matter of the **k**
1Sa 11:14 Gilgal and renew the **k** there
1Sa 13:13 your **k** over Israel forever
1Sa 13:14 But now your **k** shall not
1Sa 15:28 The LORD has torn the **k** of
1Sa 18: 8 more can he have but the **k**
1Sa 20:31 be established, nor your **k**
1Sa 24:20 that the **k** of Israel shall be
1Sa 28:17 torn the **k** out of your hand
2Sa 3:10 to transfer the **k** from the
2Sa 3:28 My **k** and I are guiltless
2Sa 5:12 His **k** for His people Israel's
2Sa 7:12 and I will establish his **k**
2Sa 7:13 the throne of his **k** forever
2Sa 7:16 your **k** shall be established
2Sa 16: 3 the **k** of my father to me
2Sa 16: 8 **k** into the hand of Absalom
1Ki 1:46 sits on the throne of the **k**
1Ki 2:12 his **k** was firmly established
1Ki 2:15 You know that the **k** was mine
1Ki 2:15 the **k** has been turned over,
1Ki 2:22 Ask for him the **k** also
1Ki 2:46 Thus the **k** was established in
1Ki 9: 5 the throne of your **k** over
1Ki 10:20 had been made for any other **k**
1Ki 11:11 tear the **k** away from you and
1Ki 11:13 not tear away the whole **k**
1Ki 11:31 I will tear the **k** out of the
1Ki 11:34 the whole **k** out of his hand
1Ki 11:35 But I will take the **k** out of
1Ki 12:21 the **k** to Rehoboam the son of
1Ki 12:26 Now the **k** may return to the
1Ki 14: 8 and tore the **k** away from the
1Ki 18:10 there is no nation or **k** where
1Ki 18:10 **k** or nation that they could
2Ki 14: 5 as soon as the **k** was
2Ki 15:19 strengthen the **k** in his hand
1Ch 10:14 turned the **k** over to David
1Ch 11:10 themselves with him in his **k**
1Ch 12:23 over the **k** of Saul to him
1Ch 14: 2 for his **k** was highly exalted
1Ch 16:20 from one **k** to another people,
1Ch 17:11 and I will establish his **k**
1Ch 17:14 My house and in My **k** forever
1Ch 22:10 of his **k** over Israel forever
1Ch 28: 5 the **k** of the LORD over Israel
1Ch 28: 7 will establish his **k** forever
1Ch 29:11 Yours is the **k**, O LORD, and
2Ch 1: 1 was strengthened in his **k**
2Ch 7:18 the throne of your **k**, as I
2Ch 9:19 had been made for any other **k**
2Ch 11: 1 restore the **k** to Rehoboam
2Ch 11:17 strengthened the **k** of Judah
2Ch 12: 1 had established the **k** and had
2Ch 13: 8 withstand the **k** of the LORD
2Ch 14: 5 the **k** was quiet under him
2Ch 17: 5 established the **k** in his hand
2Ch 21: 3 but he gave the **k** to Jehoram
2Ch 21: 4 over the **k** of his father, he
2Ch 22: 9 to assume power over the **k**
2Ch 23:20 king on the throne of the **k**
2Ch 25: 3 when the **k** was established
2Ch 29:21 for a sin offering for the **k**
2Ch 32:15 or **k** was able to deliver his
2Ch 33:13 back to Jerusalem into his **k**
2Ch 36:20 the reign of the **k** of Persia
2Ch 36:22 throughout all his **k**, and also
Ezra 1: 1 throughout all his **k**, and also
Neh 9:35 not served You in their **k**
Esth 1: 2 sat on the throne of his **k**
Esth 1: 4 the riches of his glorious **k**
Esth 1:14 who ranked highest in the **k**)
Esth 2: 3 in all the provinces of his **k**
Esth 3: 6 the whole **k** of Ahasuerus
Esth 3: 8 all the provinces of your **k**
Esth 4:14 you have come to the **k** for
Esth 5: 3 given to you—up to half my **k**!
Esth 5: 6 your request, up to half my **k**
Esth 7: 2 your request, up to half my **k**
Esth 9:30 of the **k** of Ahasuerus, with
Ps 22:28 For the **k** is the LORD's, And
Ps 45: 6 is the scepter of Your **k**
Ps 103:19 And His **k** rules over all
Ps 105:13 From one **k** to another people,
Ps 145:11 speak of the glory of Your **k**
Ps 145:12 the glorious majesty of His **k**
Ps 145:13 Your **k** is an everlasting **k**
Eccl 4:14 he was born poor in his **k**
Is 9: 7 throne of David and over His **k**
Is 17: 3 the **k** from Damascus, and the
Is 19: 2 city, **k** against **k**
Is 34:12 call its nobles to the **k**, but
Is 60:12 **k** which will not serve you
Jer 18: 7 a nation and concerning a **k**
Jer 18: 9 a nation and concerning a **k**
Jer 27: 8 and **k** which will not serve
Lam 2: 2 He has profaned the **k** and its
Ezek 17:14 that the **k** might be abased
Ezek 29:14 there they shall be a lowly **k**
Dan 2:37 of heaven has given you a **k**
Dan 2:39 another **k** inferior to yours
Dan 2:39 a third **k** of bronze, which
Dan 2:40 And the fourth **k** shall be as
Dan 2:40 that **k** will break in pieces
Dan 2:41 iron, the **k** shall be divided
Dan 2:42 so the **k** shall be partly
Dan 2:44 up a **k** which shall never be
Dan 2:44 the **k** shall not be left to
Dan 4: 3 His **k** is an everlasting
Dan 4: 3 **k** is an everlasting **k**
Dan 4:17 High rules in the **k** of men
Dan 4:18 all the wise men of my **k** are
Dan 4:25 High rules in the **k** of men
Dan 4:26 your **k** shall be assured to
Dan 4:31 the **k** has departed from you
Dan 4:32 High rules in the **k** of men
Dan 4:34 His **k** is from generation to
Dan 4:36 me, and for the glory of my **k**
Dan 4:36 to me, I was restored to my **k**
Dan 5: 7 be the third ruler in the **k**
Dan 5:11 There is a man in your **k** in
Dan 5:16 be the third ruler in the **k**
Dan 5:18 your father a **k** and majesty,
Dan 5:21 God rules in the **k** of men
Dan 5:26 God has numbered your **k**, and
Dan 5:28 Your **k** has been divided, and
Dan 5:29 be the third ruler in the **k**
Dan 5:31 the Mede received the **k**,
Dan 6: 1 to set over the **k** one hundred
Dan 6: 1 to be over the whole **k**
Dan 6: 4 Daniel concerning the **k**
Dan 6: 7 All the governors of the **k**
Dan 6:26 of my **k** men must tremble and
Dan 6:26 His **k** is the one which shall
Dan 7:14 dominion and glory and a **k**,
Dan 7:14 His **k** the one which shall not
Dan 7:18 Most High shall receive the **k**
Dan 7:18 and possess the **k** forever
Dan 7:22 the saints to possess the **k**
Dan 7:23 shall be a fourth **k** on earth
Dan 7:24 who shall arise from this **k**
Dan 7:27 Then the **k** and dominion, and
Dan 7:27 His **k** is an everlasting **k**
Dan 8:21 male goat is the **k** of Greece
Dan 8:23 in the latter time of their **k**
Dan 10:13 But the prince of the **k** of
Dan 11: 4 his **k** shall be broken up and
Dan 11: 4 for his **k** shall be uprooted,
Dan 11: 9 **k** of the king of the South
Dan 11:17 the strength of his whole **k**
Dan 11:20 taxes on the glorious **k**
Dan 11:21 and seize the **k** by intrigue
Hos 1: 4 bring an end to the **k** of the
Amos 9: 8 Lord GOD are on the sinful **k**
Obad 21 the **k** shall be the LORD's
Mic 4: 8 the **k** of the daughter of
Matt 3: 2 for the **k** of heaven is at
Matt 4:17 for the **k** of heaven is at
Matt 4:23 preaching the gospel of the **k**
Matt 5: 3 for theirs is the **k** of heaven
Matt 5:10 for theirs is the **k** of heaven
Matt 5:19 least in the **k** of heaven
Matt 5:19 great in the **k** of heaven
Matt 5:20 means enter the **k** of heaven
Matt 6:10 Your **k** come. Your will be done
Matt 6:13 for Yours is the **k** and the
Matt 6:33 But seek first the **k** of God
Matt 7:21 shall enter the **k** of heaven
Matt 8:11 and Jacob in the **k** of heaven
Matt 8:12 But the sons of the **k** will be
Matt 9:35 preaching the gospel of the **k**
Matt 10: 7 The **k** of heaven is at hand
Matt 11:11 **k** of heaven is greater than
Matt 11:12 the Baptist until now the **k**
Matt 12:25 Every **k** divided against
Matt 12:26 How then will his **k** stand
Matt 12:28 surely the **k** of God has come
Matt 13:11 mysteries of the **k** of heaven
Matt 13:19 hears the word of the **k**, and
Matt 13:24 The **k** of heaven is like a man
Matt 13:31 The **k** of heaven is like a
Matt 13:33 The **k** of heaven is like
Matt 13:38 seeds are the sons of the **k**
Matt 13:41 His **k** all things that offend
Matt 13:43 sun in the **k** of their Father
Matt 13:44 the **k** of heaven is like

Matt 13:45 the **k** of heaven is like a
Matt 13:47 the **k** of heaven is like a
Matt 13:52 the **k** of heaven is like a
Matt 16:19 the keys of the **k** of heaven
Matt 16:28 Son of Man coming in His **k**
Matt 18: 1 greatest in the **k** of heaven
Matt 18: 3 means enter the **k** of heaven
Matt 18: 4 greatest in the **k** of heaven
Matt 18:23 Therefore the **k** of heaven is
Matt 19:12 for the **k** of heaven's sake
Matt 19:14 of such is the **k** of heaven
Matt 19:23 man to enter the **k** of heaven
Matt 19:24 man to enter the **k** of God
Matt 20: 1 For the **k** of heaven is like a
Matt 20:21 other on the left, in Your **k**
Matt 21:31 enter the **k** of God before you
Matt 21:43 the **k** of God will be taken
Matt 22: 2 The **k** of heaven is like a
Matt 23:13 For you shut up the **k** of
Matt 24: 7 nation, and **k** against **k**
Matt 24:14 this gospel of the **k** will be
Matt 25: 1 Then the **k** of heaven shall be
Matt 25:14 For the **k** of heaven is like a
Matt 25:34 inherit the **k** prepared for
Matt 26:29 new with you in My Father's **k**
Mark 1:14 the gospel of the **k** of God
Mark 1:15 and the **k** of God is at hand
Mark 3:24 If a **k** is divided against
Mark 3:24 itself, that **k** cannot stand
Mark 4:11 the mystery of the **k** of God
Mark 4:26 The **k** of God is as if a man
Mark 4:30 shall we liken the **k** of God
Mark 6:23 give you, up to half of my **k**
Mark 9: 1 death till they see the **k** of
Mark 9:47 the **k** of God with one eye
Mark 10:14 for of such is the **k** of God
Mark 10:15 does not receive the **k** of God
Mark 10:23 riches to enter the **k** of God
Mark 10:24 riches to enter the **k** of God
Mark 10:25 man to enter the **k** of God
Mark 11:10 Blessed is the **k** of our
Mark 12:34 are not far from the **k** of God
Mark 13: 8 nation, and **k** against **k**
Mark 14:25 drink it new in the **k** of God
Mark 15:43 waiting for the **k** of God,
Luke 1:33 of His **k** there will be no end
Luke 4:43 I must preach the **k** of God to
Luke 6:20 for yours is the **k** of God
Luke 7:28 **k** of God is greater than he
Luke 8: 1 glad tidings of the **k** of God
Luke 8:10 the mysteries of the **k** of God
Luke 9: 2 them to preach the **k** of God
Luke 9:11 to them about the **k** of God
Luke 9:27 till they see the **k** of God
Luke 9:60 you go and preach the **k** of God
Luke 9:62 back, is fit for the **k** of God
Luke 10: 9 The **k** of God has come near
Luke 10:11 that the **k** of God has come
Luke 11: 2 Your **k** come. Your will be done
Luke 11:17 Every **k** divided against
Luke 11:18 himself, how will his **k** stand
Luke 11:20 surely the **k** of God has come
Luke 12:31 But seek the **k** of God, and all
Luke 12:32 pleasure to give you the **k**
Luke 13:18 What is the **k** of God like
Luke 13:20 shall I liken the **k** of God
Luke 13:28 the prophets in the **k** of God
Luke 13:29 and sit down in the **k** of God
Luke 14:15 eat bread in the **k** of God
Luke 16:16 Since that time the **k** of God
Luke 17:20 when the **k** of God would come
Luke 17:20 The **k** of God does not come
Luke 17:21 the **k** of God is within you
Luke 18:16 for of such is the **k** of God
Luke 18:17 does not receive the **k** of God
Luke 18:24 riches to enter the **k** of God
Luke 18:25 man to enter the **k** of God
Luke 18:29 for the sake of the **k** of God
Luke 19:11 the **k** of God would appear
Luke 19:12 to receive for himself a **k**
Luke 19:15 having received the **k**, he
Luke 21:10 nation, and **k** against **k**
Luke 21:31 know that the **k** of God is
Luke 22:16 is fulfilled in the **k** of God
Luke 22:18 vine until the **k** of God comes
Luke 22:29 And I bestow upon you a **k**,
Luke 22:30 and drink at My table in My **k**
Luke 23:42 me when You come into Your **k**
Luke 23:51 also waiting for the **k** of God
John 3: 3 he cannot see the **k** of God
John 3: 5 he cannot enter the **k** of God
John 18:36 My **k** is not of this world
John 18:36 If My **k** were of this world,
John 18:36 but now My **k** is not from here
Acts 1: 3 pertaining to the **k** of God
Acts 1: 6 time restore the **k** to Israel
Acts 8:12 concerning the **k** of God and
Acts 14:22 enter the **k** of God
Acts 19: 8 the things of the **k** of God
Acts 20:25 gone preaching the **k** of God
Acts 28:23 testified of the **k** of God
Acts 28:31 preaching the **k** of God and
Rom 14:17 for the **k** of God is not food
1Co 4:20 For the **k** of God is not in
1Co 6: 9 will not inherit the **k** of God
1Co 6:10 will inherit the **k** of God
1Co 15:24 the **k** to God the Father, when
1Co 15:50 cannot inherit the **k** of God
Gal 5:21 will not inherit the **k** of God
Eph 5: 5 in the **k** of Christ and God
Col 1:13 the **k** of the Son of His love
Col 4:11 the **k** of God who are of the
1Th 2:12 who calls you into His own **k**
2Th 1: 5 worthy of the **k** of God, for
2Ti 4: 1 at His appearing and His **k**
2Ti 4:18 me for His heavenly **k**
Heb 1: 8 is the scepter of Your **K**
Heb 12:28 a **k** which cannot be shaken
Jas 2: 5 and heirs of the **k** which He
2Pe 1:11 the everlasting **k** of our Lord
Rev 1: 9 in tribulation, and in the **k**
Rev 12:10 and the **k** of our God, and the
Rev 16:10 his **k** became full of darkness
Rev 17:12 who have received no **k** as yet
Rev 17:17 to give their **k** to the beast

KINGDOMS (*see* KINGDOM)
Deut 3:21 the **k** through which you pass
Deut 28:25 to all the **k** of the earth
Josh 11:10 the head of all those **k**
1Sa 10:18 and from the hand of all **k**
1Ki 4:21 **k** from the River to the land
2Ki 19:15 of all the **k** of the earth
2Ki 19:19 that all the **k** of the earth
1Ch 29:30 to all the **k** of the lands
2Ch 12: 8 of the **k** of the nations
2Ch 17:10 the **k** of the lands that were
2Ch 20: 6 over all the **k** of the nations
2Ch 20:29 the **k** of those countries when
2Ch 36:23 All the **k** of the earth the
Ezra 1: 2 All the **k** of the earth the
Neh 9:22 Moreover You gave them **k** and
Ps 46: 6 raged, the **k** were moved
Ps 68:32 to God, you **k** of the earth
Ps 79: 6 on the **k** that do not call on
Ps 102:22 gathered together, And the **k**
Ps 135:11 And all the **k** of Canaan
Is 10:10 has found the **k** of the idols
Is 13: 4 of the **k** of nations gathered
Is 13:19 And Babylon, the glory of **k**
Is 14:16 earth tremble, who shook **k**
Is 23:11 over the sea, He shook the **k**
Is 23:17 fornication with all the **k** of
Is 37:16 of all the **k** of the earth
Is 37:20 that all the **k** of the earth
Is 47: 5 be called the Lady of **K**
Jer 1:10 the nations and over the **k**
Jer 1:15 of the **k** of the north," says
Jer 10: 7 nations, and in all their **k**
Jer 15: 4 to all **k** of the earth,
Jer 24: 9 into all the **k** of the earth
Jer 25:26 all the **k** of the world which
Jer 28: 8 many countries and great **k**
Jer 29:18 among all the **k** of the earth
Jer 34: 1 all the **k** of the earth under
Jer 34:17 among all the **k** of the earth
Jer 49:28 and against the **k** of Hazor
Jer 51:20 with you I will destroy **k**
Jer 51:27 call the **k** together against
Ezek 29:15 It shall be the lowliest of **k**
Ezek 37:22 be divided into two **k** again
Dan 2:44 pieces and consume all these **k**
Dan 7:23 be different from all other **k**
Dan 7:27 the greatness of the **k** under
Dan 8:22 four **k** shall arise out of
Amos 6: 2 Are you better than these **k**
Nah 3: 5 and the **k** your shame
Zeph 3: 8 nations to My assembly of **k**
Hag 2:22 overthrow the throne of **k**
Hag 2:22 the strength of the Gentile **k**
Matt 4: 8 Him all the **k** of the world
Luke 4: 5 showed Him all the **k** of the
Heb 11:33 who through faith subdued **k**
Rev 11:15 The **k** of this world have
Rev 11:15 have become the **k** of our Lord

KINGLY (*see* KING)
Dan 5:20 was deposed from his **k** throne

KING'S (*see* KING)
Gen 14:17 is, the **K** Valley), after his
Gen 39:20 a place where the **k** prisoners
Num 20:17 will go along the **K** Highway
Num 21:22 the **K** Highway until we have
1Sa 18:22 become the **k** son-in-law
1Sa 18:23 thing to be a **k** son-in-law
1Sa 18:25 vengeance on the **k** enemies
1Sa 18:26 to become the **k** son-in-law
1Sa 18:27 might become the **k** son-in-law
1Sa 20:29 has not come to the **k** table
1Sa 21: 8 me, because the **k** business
1Sa 22:14 who is the **k** son-in-law, who
1Sa 23:20 deliver him into the **k** hand
1Sa 26:16 now see where the **k** spear is
1Sa 26:22 Here is the **k** spear
2Sa 3:37 **k** intent to kill Abner the
2Sa 9:11 table like one of the **k** sons
2Sa 9:13 continually at the **k** table
2Sa 11: 2 on the roof of the **k** house
2Sa 11: 8 departed from the **k** house
2Sa 11: 9 slept at the door of the **k**
2Sa 11:20 that the **k** wrath rises, and he
2Sa 11:24 some of the **k** servants are
2Sa 12:30 Then he took their **k** crown
2Sa 13: 4 Why are you, the **k** son,
2Sa 13:18 for the **k** virgin daughters
2Sa 13:23 invited all the **k** sons
2Sa 13:27 all the **k** sons go with him
2Sa 13:29 Then all the **k** sons arose
2Sa 13:30 has killed all the **k** sons
2Sa 13:32 the **k** sons, for only Amnon is
2Sa 13:33 that all the **k** sons are dead
2Sa 13:35 Look, the **k** sons are coming
2Sa 13:36 that the **k** sons indeed came,
2Sa 14: 1 **k** heart was concerned about
2Sa 14:24 but did not see the **k** face
2Sa 14:26 according to the **k** standard
2Sa 14:28 but did not see the **k** face
2Sa 14:32 let me see the **k** face
2Sa 15:15 the **k** servants said to the
2Sa 15:35 you hear from the **k** house
2Sa 16: 2 the **k** household to ride on
2Sa 18:12 my hand against the **k** son
2Sa 18:18 which is in the **K** Valley
2Sa 18:20 because the **k** son is dead
2Sa 18:29 When Joab sent the **k** servant
2Sa 19:18 to carry over the **k** household
2Sa 19:42 ever eaten at the **k** expense
2Sa 24: 4 Nevertheless the **k** word
1Ki 1: 9 the **k** sons, and all the men of
1Ki 1: 9 men of Judah, the **k** servants
1Ki 1:25 and has invited all the **k** sons
1Ki 1:28 she came into the **k** presence
1Ki 1:44 made him ride on the **k** mule
1Ki 1:47 moreover the **k** servants have
1Ki 2:19 a throne set for the **k** mother
1Ki 4: 5 a priest and the **k** friend
1Ki 9: 1 the **k** house, and all Solomon's
1Ki 9:10 of the LORD and the **k** house
1Ki 10:12 the LORD and for the **k** house
1Ki 10:28 the **k** merchants bought them
1Ki 13: 6 the **k** hand was restored to
1Ki 14:26 the treasures of the **k** house
1Ki 14:27 the doorway of the **k** house
1Ki 15:18 the treasuries of the **k** house
1Ki 16:18 the citadel of the **k** house
1Ki 16:18 burned the **k** house down upon
1Ki 22:12 deliver it into the **k** hand
1Ki 22:26 city and to Joash the **k** son
2Ki 7: 9 us go and tell the **k** household
2Ki 7:11 it to the **k** household inside
2Ki 9:34 her, for she was a **k** daughter
2Ki 10: 6 Now the **k** sons, seventy
2Ki 10: 7 that they took the **k** sons
2Ki 10: 8 the heads of the **k** sons
2Ki 11: 2 the **k** sons who were being
2Ki 11: 4 and showed them the **k** son
2Ki 11: 5 watch over the **k** house,
2Ki 11:12 And he brought out the **k** son
2Ki 11:16 entrance to the **k** house, and
2Ki 11:19 of the escorts to the **k** house
2Ki 11:20 with the sword in the **k** house

2Ki 12:10 the chest, that the **k** scribe
2Ki 12:18 of the LORD and in the **k** house
2Ki 13:16 put his hands on the **k** hands
2Ki 14:14 the treasuries of the **k** house
2Ki 15: 5 Jotham the **k** son was over the
2Ki 15:25 in the citadel of the **k** house
2Ki 16: 8 the treasuries of the **k** house
2Ki 16:15 the **k** burnt sacrifice, and his
2Ki 16:18 and he removed the **k** outer
2Ki 18:15 the treasuries of the **k** house
2Ki 18:36 for the **k** commandment was,
2Ki 24:13 the treasures of the **k** house
2Ki 24:15 The **k** mother, the **k** wives
2Ki 25: 4 which was by the **k** garden
2Ki 25: 9 of the LORD and the **k** house
2Ki 25:19 war, five men of the **k** close
1Ch 9:18 at the **K** Gate on the east
1Ch 18:17 chief ministers at the **k** side
1Ch 20: 2 their **k** crown from his head
1Ch 21: 4 Nevertheless the **k** word
1Ch 21: 6 for the **k** word was abominable
1Ch 25: 5 **k** seer in the words of God
1Ch 27:25 was over the **k** treasuries
1Ch 27:32 Hachmoni was with the **k** sons
1Ch 27:33 was the **k** counselor, and
1Ch 27:33 Archite was the **k** companion
1Ch 27:34 of the **k** army was Joab
1Ch 29: 6 the officers over the **k** work
2Ch 1:16 the **k** merchants bought them
2Ch 7:11 of the LORD and the **k** house
2Ch 9:11 the LORD and for the **k** house
2Ch 9:21 For the **k** ships went to
2Ch 12: 9 the treasures of the **k** house
2Ch 12:10 the entrance of the **k** house
2Ch 16: 2 of the LORD and of the **k** house
2Ch 18: 5 deliver it into the **k** hand
2Ch 18:11 deliver it into the **k** hand
2Ch 18:25 city and to Joash the **k** son
2Ch 19:11 Judah, for all the **k** matters
2Ch 21:17 were found in the **k** house
2Ch 22:11 the **k** sons who were being
2Ch 23: 3 the **k** son shall reign, as the
2Ch 23: 5 shall be at the **k** house
2Ch 23:11 And they brought out the **k** son
2Ch 23:15 Horse Gate into the **k** house
2Ch 23:20 the Upper Gate to the **k** house
2Ch 24: 8 Then at the **k** commandment
2Ch 24:11 chest was brought to the **k**
2Ch 24:11 much money, that the **k** scribe
2Ch 25:16 we made you the **k** counsel
2Ch 25:24 the treasures of the **k** house
2Ch 26:11 one of the **k** captains
2Ch 26:21 his son was over the **k** house
2Ch 28: 7 killed Maaseiah the **k** son
2Ch 29:25 of David, of Gad the **k** seer
2Ch 35: 7 were from the **k** possessions
2Ch 35:10 according to the **k** command
2Ch 35:15 Heman, and Jeduthun the **k** seer
Ezra 4:13 and the **k** treasury will be
Ezra 4:14 for us to see the **k** dishonor
Ezra 5:17 made in the **k** treasure house
Ezra 6: 4 be paid from the **k** treasury
Ezra 6: 8 **k** expense from taxes on the
Ezra 7:20 for it from the **k** treasury
Ezra 7:27 thing as this in the **k** heart
Ezra 7:28 all the **k** mighty princes
Ezra 8:36 they delivered the **k** orders
Ezra 8:36 orders to the **k** satraps and
Neh 1:11 For I was the **k** cupbearer
Neh 2: 8 the keeper of the **k** forest
Neh 2: 9 and gave them the **k** letters
Neh 2:14 Gate and to the **K** Pool, but
Neh 2:18 also of the **k** words that he
Neh 3:15 of Shelah by the **K** Garden
Neh 3:25 which projects from the **k**
Neh 5: 4 for the **k** tax on our lands
Neh 11:23 For it was the **k** command
Neh 11:24 was the **k** deputy in all
Esth 1: 5 of the garden of the **k** palace
Esth 1:12 the **k** command brought by his
Esth 1:13 **k** manner toward all who knew
Esth 1:14 had access to the **k** presence
Esth 1:18 **k** officials that they have
Esth 1:20 When the **k** decree which he
Esth 1:22 to all the **k** provinces, to
Esth 2: 2 Then the **k** servants who
Esth 2: 3 custody of Hegai the **k** eunuch
Esth 2: 8 So it was, when the **k** command
Esth 2: 8 was taken to the **k** palace
Esth 2: 9 for her from the **k** palace

Esth 2:13 quarters to the **k** palace
Esth 2:14 the **k** eunuch who kept the
Esth 2:15 but what Hegai the **k** eunuch
Esth 2:19 sat within the **k** gate
Esth 2:21 sat within the **k** gate, two of
Esth 2:21 gate, two of the **k** eunuchs
Esth 3: 2 all the **k** servants who were
Esth 3: 2 were within the **k** gate bowed
Esth 3: 3 Then the **k** servants who were
Esth 3: 3 who were within the **k** gate
Esth 3: 3 you transgress the **k** command
Esth 3: 8 they do not keep the **k** laws
Esth 3: 9 it into the **k** treasuries
Esth 3:12 Then the **k** scribes were
Esth 3:12 to the **k** satraps, to the
Esth 3:12 sealed with the **k** signet ring
Esth 3:13 into all the **k** provinces, to
Esth 3:15 hastened by the **k** command
Esth 4: 2 square in front of the **k** gate
Esth 4: 2 for no one might enter the **k**
Esth 4: 3 province where the **k** command
Esth 4: 5 one of the **k** eunuchs whom he
Esth 4: 6 was in front of the **k** gate
Esth 4: 7 promised to pay into the **k**
Esth 4:11 All the **k** servants and the
Esth 4:11 the people of the **k** provinces
Esth 4:13 **k** palace any more than all
Esth 5: 1 inner court of the **k** palace
Esth 5: 1 across from the **k** house,
Esth 5: 9 saw Mordecai in the **k** gate
Esth 5:13 the Jew sitting at the **k** gate
Esth 6: 2 Teresh, two of the **k** eunuchs
Esth 6: 3 the **k** servants who attended
Esth 6: 4 the outer court of the **k**
Esth 6: 5 The **k** servants said to him,
Esth 6: 9 of the **k** most noble princes
Esth 6:10 who sits within the **k** gate
Esth 6:12 went back to the **k** gate
Esth 6:14 him, the **k** eunuchs came, and
Esth 7: 4 compensate for the **k** loss
Esth 7: 8 As the word left the **k** mouth
Esth 7: 9 spoke good on the **k** behalf
Esth 7:10 Then the **k** wrath subsided
Esth 8: 5 are in all the **k** provinces
Esth 8: 8 as you please, in the **k** name
Esth 8: 8 it with the **k** signet ring
Esth 8: 8 is written in the **k** name and
Esth 8: 8 sealed with the **k** signet ring
Esth 8: 9 So the **k** scribes were called
Esth 8:10 it with the **k** signet ring
Esth 8:14 pressed on by the **k** command
Esth 8:17 city, wherever the **k** command
Esth 9: 1 time came for the **k** command
Esth 9: 3 and all those doing the **k** work
Esth 9: 4 was great in the **k** palace
Esth 9:12 the rest of the **k** provinces
Esth 9:16 of the Jews in the **k**
Ps 45: 5 in the heart of the **K** enemies
Ps 45:15 They shall enter the **K** palace
Ps 61: 6 You will prolong the **k** life
Ps 72: 1 righteousness to the **k** Son
Ps 99: 4 The **K** strength also loves
Prov 14:28 of people is a **k** honor, but
Prov 14:35 The **k** favor is toward a wise
Prov 16:14 of death is the **k** wrath, but
Prov 16:15 light of the **k** face is life
Prov 19:12 The **k** wrath is like the
Prov 21: 1 The **k** heart is in the hand of
Eccl 8: 2 Keep the **k** commandment for
Is 36:21 for the **k** commandment was,
Jer 26:10 they came up from the **k** house
Jer 36:12 then went down to the **k** house
Jer 36:26 commanded Jerahmeel the **k**
Jer 38: 6 dungeon of Malchiah the **k** son
Jer 38: 7 who was in the **k** house,
Jer 38: 8 went out of the **k** house and
Jer 39: 4 night, by way of the **k** garden
Jer 39: 8 Chaldeans burned the **k** house
Jer 41:10 the **k** daughters and all the
Jer 43: 6 the **k** daughters, and every
Jer 52: 7 which was by the **k** garden
Jer 52:13 of the LORD and the **k** house
Jer 52:25 war, seven men of the **k** close
Ezek 17:13 And he took the **k** offspring
Dan 1: 3 and some of the **k** descendants
Dan 1: 4 to serve in the **k** palace, and
Dan 1: 5 provision of the **k** delicacies
Dan 1: 8 portion of the **k** delicacies
Dan 1:13 portion of the **k** delicacies
Dan 1:15 portion of the **k** delicacies

Dan 2:10 who can tell the **k** matter
Dan 2:14 the captain of the **k** guard
Dan 2:15 said to Arioch the **k** captain
Dan 2:23 made known to us the **k** demand
Dan 3:22 because the **k** command was
Dan 3:27 the **k** counselors gathered
Dan 3:28 have frustrated the **k** word
Dan 4:31 word was still in the **k** mouth
Dan 5: 5 of the wall of the **k** palace
Dan 5: 6 Then the **k** countenance
Dan 5: 8 Now all the **k** wise men came,
Dan 6:12 spoke concerning the **k** decree
Dan 8:27 and went about the **k** business
Amos 7: 1 late crop after the **k** mowings
Amos 7:13 for it is the **k** sanctuary
Zeph 1: 8 the **k** children, and all such
Zech 14:10 Hananeel to the **k** winepresses
Acts 12:20 having made Blastus the **k**
Acts 12:20 with food by the **k** country
Heb 11:23 not afraid of the **k** command

KINGS (*see* KING, KINGS')
Gen 14: 5 the **k** that were with him came
Gen 14: 9 four **k** against five
Gen 14:10 the **k** of Sodom and Gomorrah
Gen 14:17 and the **k** who were with him
Gen 17: 6 you, and **k** shall come from you
Gen 17:16 **k** of peoples shall be from
Gen 35:11 **k** shall come from your body
Gen 36:31 Now these were the **k** who
Num 31: 8 They killed the **k** of Midian
Num 31: 8 and Reba, the five **k** of Midian
Deut 3: 8 from the hand of the two **k** of
Deut 3:21 God has done to these two **k**
Deut 4:47 two **k** of the Amorites, who
Deut 7:24 their **k** into your hand, and
Deut 31: 4 Og, the **k** of the Amorites and
Josh 2:10 what you did to the two **k** of
Josh 5: 1 it was, when all the **k** of the
Josh 5: 1 all the **k** of the Canaanites
Josh 9: 1 **k** who were on this side of
Josh 9:10 **k** of the Amorites who were
Josh 10: 5 the five **k** of the Amorites
Josh 10: 6 for all the **k** of the Amorites
Josh 10:16 But these five **k** had fled
Josh 10:17 The five **k** have been found
Josh 10:22 five **k** to me from the cave
Josh 10:23 five **k** to him from the cave
Josh 10:24 brought out those **k** to Joshua
Josh 10:24 feet on the necks of these **k**
Josh 10:40 slopes, and all their **k**
Josh 10:42 All these **k** and their land
Josh 11: 2 to the **k** who were from the
Josh 11: 5 And when all these **k** had met
Josh 11:12 So all the cities of those **k**
Josh 11:12 and all their **k**
Josh 11:17 He captured all their **k**, and
Josh 11:18 a long time with all those **k**
Josh 12: 1 These are the **k** of the land
Josh 12: 7 And these are the **k** of the
Josh 12:24 all the **k**, thirty-one
Josh 24:12 you, also the two **k** of the
Judg 1: 7 Seventy **k** with their thumbs
Judg 5: 3 Hear, O **k**! Give ear,
Judg 5:19 The **k** came and fought, then
Judg 5:19 then the **k** of Canaan fought
Judg 8: 5 and Zalmunna, **k** of Midian
Judg 8:12 he took the two **k** of Midian
Judg 8:26 which were on the **k** of Midian
1Sa 14:47 Edom, against the **k** of Zobah
1Sa 27: 6 to the **k** of Judah to this day
2Sa 10:19 And when all the **k** who were
2Sa 11: 1 time when **k** go out to battle
1Ki 3:13 you among the **k** all your days
1Ki 4:24 namely over all the **k** on this
1Ki 4:34 from all the **k** of the earth
1Ki 10:15 from all the **k** of Arabia
1Ki 10:23 the **k** of the earth in riches
1Ki 10:29 to all the **k** of the Hittites
1Ki 10:29 Hittites and the **k** of Syria
1Ki 14:19 chronicles of the **k** of Israel
1Ki 14:29 chronicles of the **k** of Judah
1Ki 15: 7 chronicles of the **k** of Judah
1Ki 15:23 chronicles of the **k** of Judah
1Ki 15:31 chronicles of the **k** of Israel
1Ki 16: 5 chronicles of the **k** of Israel
1Ki 16:14 chronicles of the **k** of Israel
1Ki 16:20 chronicles of the **k** of Israel
1Ki 16:27 chronicles of the **k** of Israel
1Ki 16:33 to anger than all the **k** of
1Ki 20: 1 were thirty-two **k** with him

1Ki 20:12 the **k** were drinking at the
1Ki 20:16 the thirty-two **k** helping him
1Ki 20:24 Dismiss the **k**, each from his
1Ki 20:31 we have heard that the **k** of
1Ki 20:31 of Israel are merciful **k**
1Ki 22:39 chronicles of the **k** of Israel
1Ki 22:45 chronicles of the **k** of Judah
2Ki 1:18 chronicles of the **k** of Israel
2Ki 3:10 **k** together to deliver them
2Ki 3:13 **k** together to deliver them
2Ki 3:21 the **k** had come up to fight
2Ki 3:23 the **k** have surely struck
2Ki 7: 6 us the **k** of the Hittites and
2Ki 7: 6 the **k** of the Egyptians to
2Ki 8:18 in the way of the **k** of Israel
2Ki 8:23 chronicles of the **k** of Judah
2Ki 10: 4 two **k** could not stand up to
2Ki 10:34 chronicles of the **k** of Israel
2Ki 11:19 he sat on the throne of the **k**
2Ki 12:18 **k** of Judah, had dedicated, and
2Ki 12:19 chronicles of the **k** of Judah
2Ki 13: 8 chronicles of the **k** of Israel
2Ki 13:12 chronicles of the **k** of Israel
2Ki 13:13 Samaria with the **k** of Israel
2Ki 14:15 chronicles of the **k** of Israel
2Ki 14:16 Samaria with the **k** of Israel
2Ki 14:18 chronicles of the **k** of Judah
2Ki 14:28 chronicles of the **k** of Israel
2Ki 14:29 his fathers, the **k** of Israel
2Ki 15: 6 chronicles of the **k** of Judah
2Ki 15:11 chronicles of the **k** of Israel
2Ki 15:15 chronicles of the **k** of Israel
2Ki 15:21 chronicles of the **k** of Israel
2Ki 15:26 chronicles of the **k** of Israel
2Ki 15:31 chronicles of the **k** of Israel
2Ki 15:36 chronicles of the **k** of Judah
2Ki 16: 3 in the way of the **k** of Israel
2Ki 16:19 chronicles of the **k** of Judah
2Ki 17: 2 but not as the **k** of Israel
2Ki 17: 8 of the **k** of Israel, which
2Ki 18: 5 him among all the **k** of Judah
2Ki 19:11 You have heard what the **k** of
2Ki 19:17 the **k** of Assyria have laid
2Ki 20:20 chronicles of the **k** of Judah
2Ki 21:17 chronicles of the **k** of Judah
2Ki 21:25 chronicles of the **k** of Judah
2Ki 23: 5 **k** of Judah had ordained to
2Ki 23:11 **k** of Judah had dedicated to
2Ki 23:12 which the **k** of Judah had made
2Ki 23:19 which the **k** of Israel had
2Ki 23:22 the days of the **k** of Israel
2Ki 23:22 of Israel and the **k** of Judah
2Ki 23:28 chronicles of the **k** of Judah
2Ki 24: 5 chronicles of the **k** of Judah
2Ki 25:28 of the **k** who were with him in
1Ch 1:43 Now these were the **k** who
1Ch 9: 1 the book of the **k** of Israel
1Ch 16:21 He reproved **k** for their sakes
1Ch 19: 9 the **k** who had come were by
1Ch 20: 1 year, at the time **k** go out to
2Ch 1:12 such as none of the **k** have
2Ch 1:17 to all the **k** of the Hittites
2Ch 1:17 Hittites and the **k** of Syria
2Ch 9:14 And all the **k** of Arabia and
2Ch 9:22 the **k** of the earth in riches
2Ch 9:23 all the **k** of the earth sought
2Ch 9:26 **k** from the River to the land
2Ch 16:11 in the book of the **k** of Judah
2Ch 20:34 the book of the **k** of Israel
2Ch 21: 6 in the way of the **k** of Israel
2Ch 21:13 in the way of the **k** of Israel
2Ch 21:20 but not in the tombs of the **k**
2Ch 24:16 the City of David among the **k**
2Ch 24:25 him in the tombs of the **k**
2Ch 24:27 annals of the book of the **k**
2Ch 25:26 in the book of the **k** of Judah
2Ch 26:23 which belonged to the **k**, for
2Ch 27: 7 the book of the **k** of Israel
2Ch 28: 2 the ways of the **k** of Israel
2Ch 28:16 the **k** of Assyria to help him
2Ch 28:23 of the **k** of Syria help them
2Ch 28:26 in the book of the **k** of Judah
2Ch 28:27 the tombs the **k** of Israel
2Ch 30: 6 the hand of the **k** of Assyria
2Ch 32: 4 Why should the **k** of Assyria
2Ch 32:32 in the book of the **k** of Judah
2Ch 33:18 the book of the **k** of Israel
2Ch 34:11 the **k** of Judah had destroyed
2Ch 35:18 none of the **k** of Israel had
2Ch 35:27 the book of the **k** of Israel
2Ch 36: 8 the book of the **k** of Israel
Ezra 4:15 rebellious city, harmful to **k**
Ezra 4:19 made insurrection against **k**
Ezra 4:20 been mighty **k** over Jerusalem
Ezra 4:22 increase to the hurt of the **k**
Ezra 7:12 Artaxerxes, king of **k**, To
Ezra 9: 7 for our iniquities we, our **k**
Ezra 9: 7 hand of the **k** of the lands
Ezra 9: 9 the sight of the **k** of Persia
Neh 9:24 their hands, with their **k**
Neh 9:32 that has come upon us, our **k**
Neh 9:32 from the days of the **k** of
Neh 9:34 Neither our **k** nor our princes
Neh 9:37 to the **k** You have set over us
Esth 10: 2 chronicles of the **k** of Media
Job 3:14 with **k** and counselors of the
Job 12:18 He loosens the bonds of **k**
Job 36: 7 they are on the throne with **k**
Ps 2: 2 The **k** of the earth set
Ps 2:10 Now therefore, be wise, O **k**
Ps 45: 9 **K** daughters are among Your
Ps 48: 4 the **k** assembled, They passed
Ps 68:12 **K** of armies flee, they flee,
Ps 68:14 Almighty scattered **k** in it
Ps 68:29 **K** will bring presents to You
Ps 72:10 The **k** of Tarshish and of the
Ps 72:10 The **k** of Sheba and Seba Will
Ps 72:11 all **k** shall fall down before
Ps 76:12 awesome to the **k** of the earth
Ps 89:27 highest of the **k** of the earth
Ps 102:15 all the **k** of the earth Your
Ps 105:14 He reproved **k** for their sakes
Ps 105:30 in the chambers of their **k**
Ps 110: 5 He shall execute **k** in the day
Ps 119:46 testimonies also before **k**
Ps 135:10 many nations And slew mighty **k**
Ps 136:17 Him who struck down great **k**
Ps 136:18 And slew famous **k**, For His
Ps 138: 4 All the **k** of the earth shall
Ps 144:10 One who gives salvation to **k**
Ps 148:11 **K** of the earth and all peoples
Ps 149: 8 To bind their **k** with chains
Prov 8:15 By me **k** reign, and rulers
Prov 16:12 for **k** to commit wickedness
Prov 16:13 lips are the delight of **k**
Prov 22:29 He will stand before **k**
Prov 25: 2 but the glory of **k** is to
Prov 25: 3 heart of **k** is unsearchable
Prov 31: 3 ways to that which destroys **k**
Prov 31: 4 It is not for **k**, O Lemuel, it
Prov 31: 4 it is not for **k** to drink wine
Eccl 2: 8 and the special treasures of **k**
Is 1: 1 Ahaz, and Hezekiah, **k** of Judah
Is 7:16 be forsaken by both her **k**
Is 10: 8 not my princes altogether **k**
Is 14: 9 all the **k** of the nations
Is 14:18 All the **k** of the nations, all
Is 19:11 wise, the son of ancient **k**
Is 24:21 the earth the **k** of the earth
Is 37:11 You have heard what the **k** of
Is 37:18 the **k** of Assyria have laid
Is 41: 2 him, and made him rule over **k**
Is 45: 1 him and loose the armor of **k**
Is 49: 7 **K** shall see and arise, princes
Is 49:23 **K** shall be your foster
Is 52:15 **K** shall shut their mouths at
Is 60: 3 **k** to the brightness of your
Is 60:10 their **k** shall minister to you
Is 60:11 and their **k** in procession
Is 60:16 and shall milk the breast of **k**
Is 62: 2 and all **k** your glory
Jer 1:18 against the **k** of Judah,
Jer 2:26 they and their **k** and their
Jer 8: 1 the bones of the **k** of Judah
Jer 13:13 even the **k** who sit on David's
Jer 17:19 by which the **k** of Judah come
Jer 17:20 you **k** of Judah, and all Judah,
Jer 17:25 the gates of this city **k** and
Jer 19: 3 O **k** of Judah and inhabitants
Jer 19: 4 nor the **k** of Judah have known
Jer 19:13 the houses of the **k** of Judah
Jer 20: 5 all the treasures of the **k** of
Jer 22: 4 **k** who sit on the throne of
Jer 25:14 great **k** shall be served by
Jer 25:18 and the cities of Judah, its **k**
Jer 25:20 all the **k** of the land of Uz,
Jer 25:20 all the **k** of the land of the
Jer 25:22 all the **k** of Tyre, all the
Jer 25:22 all the **k** of Sidon, and the
Jer 25:22 the **k** of the coastlands which
Jer 25:24 all the **k** of Arabia and all
Jer 25:24 and all the **k** of the mixed
Jer 25:25 all the **k** of Zimri, all the
Jer 25:25 of Zimri, all the **k** of Elam
Jer 25:25 and all the **k** of the Medes
Jer 25:26 all the **k** of the north, far
Jer 27: 7 great **k** shall make him serve
Jer 32:32 they, their **k**, their princes,
Jer 33: 4 the houses of the **k** of Judah
Jer 34: 5 the former **k** who were before
Jer 44: 9 wickedness of the **k** of Judah
Jer 44:17 we and our fathers, our **k**
Jer 44:21 you and your fathers, your **k**
Jer 46:25 with their gods and their **k**
Jer 50:41 many **k** shall be raised up
Jer 51:11 spirit of the **k** of the Medes
Jer 51:28 with the **k** of the Medes, its
Jer 52:32 of the **k** who were with him in
Lam 4:12 The **k** of the earth, and all
Ezek 26: 7 king of Babylon, king of **k**
Ezek 27:33 you enriched the **k** of the
Ezek 27:35 their **k** will be greatly
Ezek 28:17 ground, I laid you before **k**
Ezek 32:10 their **k** shall be horribly
Ezek 32:29 There is Edom, her **k** and all
Ezek 43: 7 holy name, they nor their **k**
Ezek 43: 7 their **k** on their high places
Ezek 43: 9 of their **k** far away from Me
Dan 2:21 He removes **k** and raises up **k**
Dan 2:37 You, O king, are a king of **k**
Dan 2:44 in the days of these **k** the
Dan 2:47 God of gods, the Lord of **k**
Dan 7:17 are four **k** which arise out of
Dan 7:24 The ten horns are ten **k** who
Dan 7:24 ones, and shall subdue three **k**
Dan 8:20 they are the **k** of Media and
Dan 9: 6 spoke in Your name to our **k**
Dan 9: 8 shame of face, to our **k**, our
Dan 10:13 there with the **k** of Persia
Dan 11: 2 three more **k** will arise in
Hos 1: 1 **k** of Judah, and in the days of
Hos 7: 7 All their **k** have fallen
Hos 8: 4 They set up **k**, but not by Me
Mic 1: 1 **k** of Judah, which he saw
Mic 1:14 be a lie to the **k** of Israel
Hab 1:10 They scoff at **k**, and princes
Matt 10:18 **k** for My sake, as a testimony
Matt 17:25 From whom do the **k** of the
Mark 13: 9 and **k** for My sake, for a
Luke 10:24 **k** have desired to see what
Luke 21:12 you will be brought before **k**
Luke 22:25 them, "The **k** of the Gentiles
Acts 4:26 the **k** of the earth took their
Acts 9:15 My name before Gentiles, **k**
1Co 4: 8 have reigned as **k** without us
1Ti 2: 2 for **k** and all who are in
1Ti 6:15 only Potentate, the King of **k**
Heb 7: 1 from the slaughter of the **k**
Rev 1: 5 ruler over the **k** of the earth
Rev 1: 6 and has made us **k** and priests
Rev 5:10 and have made us **k** and priests
Rev 6:15 the **k** of the earth, the great
Rev 10:11 nations, tongues, and **k**
Rev 16:12 the **k** from the east might be
Rev 16:14 go out to the **k** of the earth
Rev 17: 2 with whom the **k** of the earth
Rev 17:10 There are also seven **k**
Rev 17:12 ten **k** who have received no
Rev 17:12 one hour as **k** with the beast
Rev 17:14 is Lord of lords and King of **k**
Rev 17:18 over the **k** of the earth
Rev 18: 3 the **k** of the earth have
Rev 18: 9 And the **k** of the earth who
Rev 19:16 KING OF **K** AND LORD OF
Rev 19:18 you may eat the flesh of **k**
Rev 19:19 the **k** of the earth, and their
Rev 21:24 and the **k** of the earth bring

KINGS' (*see* KINGS)
Prov 30:28 hands, and it is in **k** palaces
Dan 11:27 Both these **k** hearts shall be
Matt 11: 8 soft clothing are in **k** houses
Luke 7:25 in luxury are in **k** courts

KINSMAN (*see* KIN, KINSMAN-REDEEMER, KINSMEN)
Num 5: 8 But if the man has no **k** to
Num 27:11 **k** nearest him in his family
Ruth 2: 1 And Naomi had a **k** of her
Ruth 3: 2 were with, is he not our **k**
Ruth 3: 9 wing, for you are a near **k**

Ruth 3:12 is true that I am your near **k**
Ruth 3:12 there is a **k** nearer than I
Ruth 3:13 the duty of a near **k** for you
Ruth 4: 1 the near **k** of whom Boaz had
Ruth 4: 3 Then he said to the near **k**
Ruth 4: 6 And the near **k** said, I
Ruth 4: 8 the near **k** said to Boaz
Ruth 4:14 you this day without a near **k**
Amos 6:10 when a **k** of the dead, with
Rom 16:11 Greet Herodion, my **k**

KINSMAN-REDEEMER (*see* KINSMAN)
Lev 25:25 if his **k** comes to redeem it,

KINSMEN (*see* KINSMAN)
Num 10:30 to my own land and to my **k**
Ruth 2:20 of ours, one of our near **k**
1Ki 16:11 neither of his **k** nor of his
1Ch 12:29 **k** of Saul, three thousand
Ps 38:11 And my **k** stand afar off
Ezek 11:15 your relatives, your **k**, and
Rom 9: 3 my **k** according to the flesh,
Rom 16: 7 Andronicus and Junia, my **k**
Rom 16:21 Jason, and Sosipater, my **k**

KIR
2Ki 16: 9 its people captive to **K**, and
Is 15: 1 because in the night **K** of
Is 16:11 and my inner being for **K** Heres
Is 22: 6 and **K** uncovered the shield
Jer 48:31 mourn for the men of **K** Heres
Jer 48:36 wail for the men of **K** Heres
Amos 1: 5 Syria shall go captive to **K**
Amos 9: 7 and the Syrians from **K**

KIR HARASETH (*see* KIR HARESETH)
2Ki 3:25 left intact the stones of **K**

KIR HARESETH (*see* KIR HARASETH)
Is 16: 7 of **K** you shall mourn

KIRJATH (*see* SANNAH)
Josh 18:28 is Jerusalem), Gibeath, and **K**

KIRJATHAIM (*see* KIRIATHAIM)
Num 32:37 Heshbon and Elealeh and **K**
Josh 13:19 **K**, Sibmah, Zereth Shahar on
1Ch 6:76 and **K** with its common-lands
Jer 48: 1 **K** is shamed and taken
Jer 48:23 on **K** and Beth Gamul and Beth
Ezek 25: 9 Jeshimoth, Baal Meon, and **K**

KIRJATH ARBA (*see* HEBRON)
Gen 23: 2 So Sarah died in **K** (that is
Gen 35:27 or **K** (that is, Hebron), where
Josh 14:15 name of Hebron formerly was **K**
Josh 15:13 the LORD to Joshua, namely, **K**
Josh 15:54 **K** (which is Hebron), and Zior
Josh 20: 7 **K** (which is Hebron) in the
Josh 21:11 they gave them **K** (Arba being
Judg 1:10 name of Hebron was formerly **K**
Neh 11:25 children of Judah dwelt in **K**

KIRJATH ARIM (*see* KIRJATH JEARIM)
Ezra 2:25 the people of **K**, Chephirah,

KIRJATH BAAL (*see* BAALAH, KIRJATH JEARIM)
Josh 15:60 **K** (which is Kirjath Jearim)
Josh 18:14 and it ended at **K** (which is

KIRJATH HUZOTH
Num 22:39 with Balak, and they came to **K**

KIRJATH JEARIM (*see* JEARIM, KIRJATH ARIM, KIRJATH BAAL)
Josh 9:17 Chephirah, Beeroth, and **K**
Josh 15: 9 around to Baalah (which is **K**)
Josh 15:60 Kirjath Baal (which is **K**)
Josh 18:14 at Kirjath Baal (which is **K**)
Josh 18:15 side began at the end of **K**
Judg 18:12 up and encamped in **K** in Judah
Judg 18:12 There it is, west of **K**
1Sa 6:21 to the inhabitants of **K**,
1Sa 7: 1 Then the men of **K** came and
1Sa 7: 2 ark remained in **K** a long time
1Ch 2:50 were Shobal the father of **K**
1Ch 2:52 father of **K** had descendants
1Ch 2:53 The families of **K** were the
1Ch 13: 5 bring the ark of God from **K**
1Ch 13: 6 went up to Baalah, to **K**,
2Ch 1: 4 from **K** to the place David had
Neh 7:29 the men of **K**, Chephirah, and
Jer 26:20 the son of Shemaiah of **K**, who

KIRJATH SANNAH (*see* DEBIR, KIRJATH SEPHER, SANSANNAH)
Josh 15:49 Dannah, **K** (which is Debir),

KIRJATH SEPHER (*see* DEBIR, KIRJATH SANNAH)
Josh 15:15 the name of Debir was **K**)
Josh 15:16 He who attacks **K** and takes it,
Judg 1:11 name of Debir was formerly **K**
Judg 1:12 He who attacks **K** and takes it,

KISH
1Sa 9: 1 name was **K** the son of Abiel
1Sa 9: 3 Now the donkeys of **K**, Saul's
1Sa 9: 3 And **K** said to his son Saul,
1Sa 10:11 has come upon the son of **K**
1Sa 10:21 Saul the son of **K** was chosen
1Sa 14:51 **K** was the father of Saul, and
2Sa 21:14 in the tomb of **K** his father
1Ch 8:30 son was Abdon, then Zur, **K**
1Ch 8:33 Ner begot **K**, **K** begot Saul,
1Ch 9:36 son was Abdon, then Zur, **K**
1Ch 9:39 Ner begot **K**, **K** begot Saul,
1Ch 12: 1 from Saul the son of **K**
1Ch 23:21 of Mahli were Eleazar and **K**
1Ch 23:22 their brethren, the sons of **K**
1Ch 24:29 Of **K**: the son of **K**, Jerahmeel
1Ch 26:28 the seer, Saul the son of **K**
2Ch 29:12 **K** the son of Abdi and Azariah
Esth 2: 5 son of Shimei, the son of **K**
Esth 2: 6 **K** had been carried away from
Acts 13:21 gave them Saul the son of **K**

KISHI (*see* KUSHAIAH)
1Ch 6:44 hand, were Ethan the son of **K**

KISHION (*see* KEDESH, KISHON)
Josh 19:20 Rabbith, **K**, Abez,
Josh 21:28 **K** with its common-land,

KISHON (*see* KISHION)
Judg 4: 7 his multitude at the River **K**
Judg 4:13 Hagoyim to the River **K**
Judg 5:21 The torrent of **K** swept them
Judg 5:21 torrent, the torrent of **K**
1Ki 18:40 them down to the Brook **K** and
Ps 83: 9 As with Jabin at the Brook **K**

KISS (*see* KISSED, KISSES)
Gen 27:26 Come near now and **k** me, my
Gen 31:28 did not allow me to **k** my sons
2Sa 15: 5 his hand and take him and **k** him
2Sa 20: 9 with his right hand to **k** him
1Ki 19:20 Please let me **k** my father
Ps 2:12 **K** the Son, lest He be angry,
Song 1: 2 Let him **k** me with the kisses
Song 8: 1 you outside, I would **k** you
Hos 13: 2 who sacrifice **k** the calves
Matt 26:48 Whomever I **k**, He is the One
Mark 14:44 Whomever I **k**, He is the One
Luke 7:45 You gave Me no **k**, but this
Luke 7:45 woman has not ceased to **k** My
Luke 22:47 drew near to Jesus to **k** Him
Luke 22:48 the Son of Man with a **k**
Rom 16:16 one another with a holy **k**
1Co 16:20 one another with a holy **k**
2Co 13:12 one another with a holy **k**
1Th 5:26 the brethren with a holy **k**
1Pe 5:14 one another with a **k** of love

KISSED (*see* KISS)
Gen 27:27 And he came near and **k** him
Gen 29:11 Then Jacob **k** Rachel, and
Gen 29:13 **k** him, and brought him to his
Gen 31:55 **k** his sons and daughters and
Gen 33: 4 neck and **k** him, and they wept
Gen 45:15 Moreover he **k** all his
Gen 48:10 he **k** them and embraced them
Gen 50: 1 and wept over him, and **k** him
Ex 4:27 the mountain of God, and **k** him
Ex 18: 7 bowed down, and **k** him
Ruth 1: 9 Then she **k** them, and they
Ruth 1:14 Orpah **k** her mother-in-law,
1Sa 10: 1 on his head, and **k** him and said
1Sa 20:41 And they **k** one another
2Sa 14:33 Then the king **k** Absalom
2Sa 19:39 over, the king **k** Barzillai and
1Ki 19:18 mouth that has not **k** him
Job 31:27 and my mouth has **k** my hand
Ps 85:10 and peace have **k** each other
Prov 7:13 So she caught him and **k** him
Matt 26:49 and **k** Him
Mark 14:45 and **k** Him
Luke 7:38 she **k** His feet and anointed
Luke 15:20 and fell on his neck and **k** him
Acts 20:37 fell on Paul's neck and **k** him,

KISSES (*see* KISS)
Prov 24:26 a right answer **k** the lips
Prov 27: 6 but the **k** of an enemy are
Song 1: 2 me with the **k** of his mouth

KITCHENS
Ezek 46:24 These are the **k** where the

KITE
Lev 11:14 the **k**, and the falcon after
Deut 14:13 the red **k**, the falcon, and the
Deut 14:13 and the **k** after their kinds

KITHLISH
Josh 15:40 Cabbon, Lahmas, **K**,

KITRON (*see* KATTATH)
Judg 1:30 of **K** or the inhabitants of

KITTIM
Gen 10: 4 were Elishah, Tarshish, **K**
1Ch 1: 7 were Elishah, Tarshishah, **K**

KNAPSACK
2Ki 4:42 newly ripened grain in his **k**

KNEAD (*see* KNEADED, KNEADING)
Gen 18: 6 **k** it and make cakes
Jer 7:18 the women **k** their dough, to

KNEADED (*see* KNEAD)
1Sa 28:24 **k** it, and baked unleavened
2Sa 13: 8 **k** it, made cakes in his sight

KNEADING (*see* KNEAD)
Ex 8: 3 ovens, and into your **k** bowls
Ex 12:34 having their **k** bowls bound up
Deut 28: 5 be your basket and your **k** bowl
Deut 28:17 be your basket and your **k** bowl
Hos 7: 4 the fire after **k** the dough

KNEE (*see* KNEES)
Gen 41:43 Bow the **k**!
Is 45:23 that to Me every **k** shall bow
Ezek 7:17 every **k** will be as weak as
Matt 27:29 they bowed the **k** before Him
Mark 15:19 and bowing the **k**, they
Rom 11: 4 have not bowed the **k** to Baal
Rom 14:11 every **k** shall bow to Me, and
Phil 2:10 of Jesus every **k** should bow

KNEEL (*see* KNEELING, KNELT)
Gen 24:11 he made his camels **k** down
Ps 95: 6 Let us **k** before the LORD our

KNEELING (*see* KNEEL)
1Ki 8:54 from **k** on his knees with his
Matt 17:14 Him, **k** down to Him and saying,
Matt 20:20 **k** down and asking something
Mark 1:40 **k** down to Him and saying to

KNEES (*see* KNEE)
Gen 30: 3 she will bear a child on my **k**
Gen 48:12 them from beside his **k**, and he
Gen 50:23 also brought up on Joseph's **k**
Deut 28:35 LORD will strike you in the **k**
Judg 7: 5 gets down on his **k** to drink
Judg 7: 6 on their **k** to drink water
Judg 16:19 lulled him to sleep on her **k**
1Sa 14:13 **k** with his armorbearer after
1Ki 8:54 from kneeling on his **k** with
1Ki 18:42 and put his face between his **k**
1Ki 19:18 all whose **k** have not bowed to
2Ki 1:13 fell on his **k** before Elijah,
2Ki 4:20 he sat on her **k** till noon
2Ch 6:13 knelt down on his **k** before
Ezra 9: 5 and my robe, I fell on my **k**
Job 3:12 Why did the **k** receive me
Job 4: 4 strengthened the feeble **k**
Ps 109:24 My **k** are weak through fasting
Is 35: 3 and make firm the feeble **k**
Is 66:12 and be dandled on her **k**
Ezek 21: 7 all **k** will be weak as water
Ezek 47: 4 the water came up to my **k**
Dan 5: 6 his **k** knocked against each
Dan 6:10 on his **k** three times that day
Dan 10:10 which made me tremble on my **k**
Nah 2:10 heart melts, and the **k** shake
Luke 5: 8 it, he fell down at Jesus' **k**
Eph 3:14 For this reason I bow my **k** to
Heb 12:12 hang down, and the feeble **k**

KNELT (*see* KNEEL)
2Ch 6:13 **k** down on his knees before
Dan 6:10 he **k** down on his knees three
Mark 10:17 **k** before Him, and asked Him,
Luke 22:41 and He **k** down and prayed,
Acts 7:60 Then he **k** down and cried out
Acts 9:40 all out, and **k** down and prayed
Acts 20:36 he **k** down and prayed with them
Acts 21: 5 we **k** down on the shore and

KNEW (*see* KNOW)
Gen 3: 7 they **k** that they were naked
Gen 4: 1 Now Adam **k** Eve his wife, and
Gen 4:17 And Cain **k** his wife, and she
Gen 4:25 Adam **k** his wife again, and she
Gen 8:11 Noah **k** that the waters had
Gen 9:24 **k** what his younger son had
Gen 38: 9 But Onan **k** that the heir
Gen 38:26 And he never **k** her again
Deut 9:24 from the day that I **k** you
Deut 34:10 whom the LORD **k** face to face
Judg 11:39 She **k** no man
Judg 13:21 then Manoah **k** that He was the
Judg 19:25 And they **k** her and abused her
1Sa 1:19 Elkanah **k** Hannah his wife, and
1Sa 3:20 **k** that Samuel had been
1Sa 10:11 when all who **k** him formerly
1Sa 18:28 and **k** that the LORD was with
1Sa 20: 9 For if I **k** certainly that
1Sa 20:33 by which Jonathan **k** that it
1Sa 20:39 and David **k** of the matter
1Sa 22:15 For your servant **k** nothing of
1Sa 22:17 because they **k** when he fled
1Sa 22:22 I **k** that day, when Doeg the
1Sa 23: 9 When David **k** that Saul
1Sa 26:12 man saw it or **k** it or awoke
1Sa 26:17 Then Saul **k** David's voice, and
2Sa 5:12 So David **k** that the LORD had
2Sa 11:16 he **k** there were valiant men
1Ki 9:27 fleet, seamen who **k** the sea
2Ch 8:18 and servants who **k** the sea
2Ch 33:13 Then Manasseh **k** that the LORD
Neh 9:10 For You **k** that they acted
Esth 1:13 manner toward all who **k** law
Job 23: 3 that I **k** where I might find
Ps 142: 3 within me, Then You **k** my path
Is 48: 4 Because I **k** that you were
Is 48: 7 say, 'Of course I **k** them
Is 48: 8 For I **k** that you would deal
Jer 1: 5 you in the womb I **k** you
Jer 32: 8 Then I **k** that this was the
Jer 41: 4 when as yet no one **k** it,
Jer 44:15 Then all the men who **k** that
Ezek 10:20 and I **k** they were cherubim
Ezek 19: 7 He **k** their desolate places,
Ezek 28:19 All who **k** you among the
Dan 5:21 till he **k** that the Most High
Dan 5:22 although you **k** all this
Dan 6:10 Now when Daniel **k** that the
Hos 13: 5 I **k** you in the wilderness, in
Jon 1:10 For the men **k** that he fled
Zech 11:11 **k** that it was the word of the
Matt 7:23 to them, 'I never **k** you
Matt 12:15 But when Jesus **k** it, He
Matt 12:25 But Jesus **k** their thoughts,
Matt 25:24 I **k** you to be a hard man,
Matt 25:26 you **k** that I reap where I
Matt 27:18 For he **k** that because of envy
Mark 1:34 to speak, because they **k** Him
Mark 6:33 them departing, and many **k**
Mark 12:12 for they **k** He had spoken the
Mark 15:10 For he **k** that the chief
Luke 4:41 for they **k** that He was the
Luke 6: 8 But He **k** their thoughts, and
Luke 7:37 when she **k** that Jesus sat at
Luke 9:11 But when the multitudes **k** it
Luke 12:47 And that servant who **k** his
Luke 19:22 You **k** that I was an austere
Luke 20:19 for they **k** that He had spoken
Luke 23: 7 And as soon as he **k** that He
Luke 24:31 were opened and they **k** Him
John 2: 9 who had drawn the water **k**)
John 2:24 to them, because He **k** all men
John 2:25 man, for He **k** what was in man
John 4: 1 when the Lord **k** that the
John 4:10 If you **k** the gift of God, and
John 4:53 So the father **k** that it was
John 5: 6 **k** that he already had been in
John 6: 6 him, for He Himself **k** what He
John 6:61 When Jesus **k** in Himself that
John 6:64 For Jesus **k** from the
John 11:57 that if anyone **k** where He was
John 12: 9 the Jews **k** that He was there
John 13: 1 when Jesus **k** that His hour
John 13:11 For He **k** who would betray Him
John 13:28 **k** for what reason He said
John 16:19 Now Jesus **k** that they desired
John 18: 2 Him, also **k** the place
Acts 3:10 Then they **k** that it was he
Acts 16: 3 for they all **k** that his
Acts 18:25 though he **k** only the baptism
Acts 26: 5 They **k** me from the first, if
Rom 1:21 because, although they **k** God
1Co 2: 8 of the rulers of this age **k**
2Co 5:21 For He made Him who **k** no sin
Col 1: 6 **k** the grace of God in truth
Jude 5 you, though you once **k** this
Rev 19:12 that no one **k** except Himself

KNIFE (*see* KNIVES)
Gen 22: 6 the fire in his hand, and a **k**
Gen 22:10 took the **k** to slay his son
Judg 19:29 entered his house he took a **k**
Prov 23: 2 put a **k** to your throat if you
Jer 36:23 cut it with the scribe's **k**

KNIT
1Sa 18: 1 was **k** to the soul of David
Job 10:11 **k** me together with bones and
Job 40:17 of his thighs are tightly **k**
Eph 4:16 and **k** together by what every
Col 2: 2 being **k** together in love, and
Col 2:19 and **k** together by joints and

KNIVES (*see* KNIFE)
Josh 5: 2 Make flint **k** for yourself, and
Josh 5: 3 made flint **k** for himself, and
1Ki 18:28 as was their custom, with **k**
Ezra 1: 9 platters, twenty-nine **k**,
Prov 30:14 and whose fangs are like **k**

KNOB (*see* KNOBS)
Ex 25:33 branch, with an ornamental **k**
Ex 25:33 branch, with an ornamental **k**
Ex 25:34 each with its ornamental **k**
Ex 25:35 there shall be a **k** under the
Ex 25:35 a **k** under the second two
Ex 25:35 and a **k** under the third two
Ex 37:19 branch, with an ornamental **k**
Ex 37:19 branch, with an ornamental **k**
Ex 37:20 each with its ornamental **k**
Ex 37:21 There was a **k** under the first
Ex 37:21 a **k** under the second two
Ex 37:21 and a **k** under the third two

KNOBS (*see* KNOB)
Ex 25:31 its bowls, its ornamental **k**
Ex 25:36 Their **k** and their branches
Ex 37:17 its bowls, its ornamental **k**
Ex 37:22 Their **k** and their branches

KNOCK (*see* KNOCKED, KNOCKING, KNOCKS)
Ezek 39: 3 Then I will **k** the bow out of
Matt 7: 7 **k**, and it will be opened to
Luke 11: 9 **k**, and it will be opened to
Luke 13:25 **k** at the door, saying, Lord,
Rev 3:20 I stand at the door and **k**

KNOCKED (*see* KNOCK)
Dan 5: 6 and his knees **k** against each
Acts 12:13 as Peter **k** at the door of the

KNOCKING (*see* KNOCK)
Acts 12:16 Now Peter continued **k**

KNOCKS (*see* KNOCK)
Ex 21:27 if he **k** out his servant's
Song 5: 2 He **k**, saying, "Open for me,
Matt 7: 8 and to him who **k** it will be
Luke 11:10 and to him who **k** it will be
Luke 12:36 and **k** they may open to him

KNOW (*see* KNEW, KNOWING, KNOWLEDGE, KNOWN, KNOWS, UNKNOWN, WELL-KNOWN)
Gen 3:22 one of Us, to **k** good and evil
Gen 4: 9 I do not **k**
Gen 12:11 Indeed I **k** that you are a
Gen 15: 8 how shall I **k** that I will
Gen 15:13 **K** certainly that your
Gen 18:21 and if not, I will **k**
Gen 19: 5 that we may **k** them carnally
Gen 19:33 he did not **k** when she lay
Gen 19:35 he did not **k** when she lay
Gen 20: 6 I **k** that you did this in the
Gen 20: 7 **k** that you shall surely die,
Gen 21:26 I do not **k** who has done this
Gen 22:12 for now I **k** that you fear God
Gen 24:14 by this I will **k** that You
Gen 24:21 remained silent so as to **k**
Gen 27: 2 I do not **k** the day of my
Gen 28:16 this place, and I did not **k** it
Gen 29: 5 Do you **k** Laban the son of
Gen 29: 5 And they said, "We **k** him
Gen 30:26 for you **k** my service which I
Gen 30:29 You **k** how I have served you
Gen 31: 6 you **k** that with all my might
Gen 31:32 For Jacob did not **k** that
Gen 37:32 Do you **k** whether it is your
Gen 38:16 for he did not **k** that she was
Gen 39: 6 and he did not **k** what he had
Gen 39: 8 my master does not **k** what is
Gen 42:23 But they did not **k** that
Gen 42:33 By this I will **k** that you
Gen 42:34 so I shall **k** that you are not
Gen 43:22 We do not **k** who put our money
Gen 44:15 Did you not **k** that such a man
Gen 44:27 You **k** that my wife bore me
Gen 47: 6 if you **k** any competent men
Gen 48:19 I **k**, my son, I **k**
Ex 1: 8 Egypt, who did not **k** Joseph
Ex 2: 4 to **k** what would be done to
Ex 3: 7 for I **k** their sorrows
Ex 4:14 I **k** that he can speak well
Ex 5: 2 I do not **k** the LORD, nor will
Ex 6: 7 Then you shall **k** that I am
Ex 7: 5 shall **k** that I am the LORD
Ex 7:17 By this you shall **k** that I am
Ex 8:10 that you may **k** that there is
Ex 8:22 in order that you may **k** that
Ex 9:14 that you may **k** that there is
Ex 9:29 that you may **k** that the earth
Ex 9:30 I **k** that you will not yet
Ex 10: 2 that you may **k** that I am the
Ex 10: 7 Do you not yet **k** that Egypt
Ex 10:26 even we do not **k** with what we
Ex 11: 7 that you may **k** that the LORD
Ex 14: 4 may **k** that I am the LORD
Ex 14:18 shall **k** that I am the LORD
Ex 16: 6 At evening you shall **k** that
Ex 16:12 you shall **k** that I am the
Ex 16:15 they did not **k** what it was
Ex 18:11 Now I **k** that the LORD is
Ex 23: 9 for you **k** the heart of a
Ex 29:46 they shall **k** that I am the
Ex 31:13 that you may **k** that I am the
Ex 32: 1 we do not **k** what has become
Ex 32:22 You **k** the people, that they
Ex 32:23 we do not **k** what has become
Ex 33: 5 that I may **k** what to do to
Ex 33:12 But You have not let me **k**
Ex 33:12 I **k** you by name, and you have
Ex 33:13 Your way, that I may **k** You
Ex 33:17 My sight, and I **k** you by name
Ex 34:29 that Moses did not **k** that the
Ex 36: 1 to **k** how to do all manner of
Lev 5:17 LORD, though he does not **k** it
Lev 5:18 he erred and did not **k** it, and
Lev 23:43 that your generations may **k**
Num 10:31 inasmuch as you **k** how we are
Num 11:16 whom you **k** to be the elders
Num 14:31 they shall **k** the land which
Num 14:34 and you shall **k** My rejection
Num 16:28 By this you shall **k** that the
Num 20:14 You **k** all the hardship that
Num 22: 6 for I **k** that he whom you
Num 22:19 that I may **k** what more the
Num 22:34 for I did not **k** You stood in
Deut 3:19 your livestock (I **k** that you
Deut 4:35 that you might **k** that the
Deut 4:39 Therefore **k** this day, and
Deut 7: 9 Therefore **k** that the LORD
Deut 8: 2 to **k** what was in your heart,
Deut 8: 3 manna which you did not **k** nor
Deut 8: 3 **k** nor did your fathers **k**
Deut 8: 3 that He might make you **k** that
Deut 8: 5 So you should **k** in your heart
Deut 8:16 which your fathers did not **k**
Deut 9: 2 of the Anakim, whom you **k**
Deut 11: 2 **K** today that I do not speak
Deut 13: 3 **k** whether you love the LORD
Deut 18:21 How shall we **k** the word
Deut 20:20 Only the trees which you **k**
Deut 22: 2 you, or if you do not **k** him
Deut 29: 6 that you may **k** that I am the
Deut 29:16 (for you **k** that we dwelt in
Deut 29:26 gods that they did not **k**

Deut 31:21 for I **k** the inclination of
Deut 31:27 for I **k** your rebellion and
Deut 31:29 For I **k** that after my death
Deut 32:17 God, to gods they did not **k**
Deut 33: 9 Or **k** his own children
Josh 2: 4 but I did not **k** where they
Josh 2: 5 Where the men went I do not **k**
Josh 2: 9 I **k** that the LORD has given
Josh 3: 4 that you may **k** the way by
Josh 3: 7 Israel, that they may **k** that
Josh 3:10 By this you shall **k** that the
Josh 4:22 you shall let your children **k**
Josh 4:24 may **k** the hand of the LORD
Josh 8:14 But he did not **k** that there
Josh 14: 6 You **k** the word which the LORD
Josh 22:22 knows, and let Israel itself **k**
Josh 23:13 **k** for certain that the LORD
Josh 23:14 you **k** in all your hearts and
Judg 2:10 after them who did not **k** the
Judg 3: 2 might be taught to **k** war, at
Judg 3: 4 to **k** whether they would obey
Judg 6:37 then I shall **k** that You will
Judg 13:16 (For Manoah did not **k** He
Judg 14: 4 mother did not **k** that it was
Judg 15:11 Do you not **k** that the
Judg 16:20 But he did not **k** that the
Judg 17:13 Now I **k** that the LORD will be
Judg 18: 5 that we may **k** whether the
Judg 18:14 Do you **k** that there are in
Judg 19:22 that we may **k** him carnally
Judg 20:34 But the Benjamites did not **k**
Ruth 2:11 whom you did not **k** before
Ruth 3:11 **k** that you are a virtuous
Ruth 3:18 until you **k** how the matter
Ruth 4: 4 then tell me, that I may **k**
1Sa 2:12 they did not **k** the LORD
1Sa 3: 7 Samuel did not yet **k** the LORD
1Sa 6: 9 then we shall **k** that it is
1Sa 14: 3 not **k** that Jonathan had gone
1Sa 14:38 chiefs of the people, and **k**
1Sa 17:28 I **k** your pride and the
1Sa 17:46 may **k** that there is a God in
1Sa 17:47 all this assembly shall **k**
1Sa 17:55 lives, O king, I do not **k**
1Sa 20: 3 Do not let Jonathan **k** this
1Sa 20:30 Do I not **k** that you have
1Sa 20:39 the lad did not **k** anything
1Sa 21: 2 Do not let anyone **k** anything
1Sa 22: 3 till I **k** what God will do for
1Sa 24:11 robe, and did not kill you, **k**
1Sa 24:20 now I **k** indeed that you shall
1Sa 25:11 do not **k** where they are from
1Sa 25:17 Now therefore, **k** and consider
1Sa 28: 1 You assuredly **k** that you will
1Sa 28: 2 Surely you **k** what your
1Sa 28: 9 you **k** what Saul has done, how
1Sa 29: 9 I **k** that you are as good in
2Sa 1: 5 How do you **k** that Saul and
2Sa 2:26 Do you not **k** that it will be
2Sa 3:25 to **k** your going out and your
2Sa 3:25 to **k** all that you are doing
2Sa 3:26 But David did not **k** it
2Sa 3:38 Do you not **k** that a prince and
2Sa 7:20 You, Lord GOD, **k** Your servant
2Sa 7:21 to make Your servant **k** them
2Sa 11:20 Did you not **k** that they would
2Sa 14:20 to **k** all things that are in
2Sa 15:11 and did not **k** anything
2Sa 15:20 since I go I **k** not where
2Sa 17: 8 you **k** your father and his men,
2Sa 18:29 but I did not **k** what it was
2Sa 19:20 servant, **k** that I have sinned
2Sa 19:22 For do I not **k** that today I
2Sa 24: 2 that I may **k** the number of
1Ki 1: 4 but the king did not **k** her
1Ki 1:11 David our lord does not **k** it
1Ki 1:18 king, you do not **k** about it
1Ki 2: 5 Moreover you **k** also what Joab
1Ki 2: 9 **k** what you ought to do to him
1Ki 2:15 You **k** that the kingdom was
1Ki 2:32 my father David did not **k** it
1Ki 2:37 **k** for certain you shall
1Ki 2:42 **K** for certain that on the
1Ki 2:44 You **k**, as your heart
1Ki 3: 7 I do not **k** how to go out or
1Ki 5: 3 You **k** how my father David
1Ki 5: 6 For you **k** there is none among
1Ki 8:39 whose heart You **k** (for You
1Ki 8:39 **k** the hearts of all the sons
1Ki 8:43 of the earth may **k** Your name
1Ki 8:43 that they may **k** that this
1Ki 8:60 may **k** that the LORD is God
1Ki 17:24 Now by this I **k** that you are
1Ki 18:12 you to a place I do not **k**
1Ki 18:37 that this people may **k** that
1Ki 20:13 you shall **k** that I am the
1Ki 20:28 you shall **k** that I am the
1Ki 22: 3 Do you **k** that Ramoth in
2Ki 2: 3 Do you **k** that the LORD will
2Ki 2: 3 Yes, I **k**; keep silent!"
2Ki 2: 5 Do you **k** that the LORD will
2Ki 2: 5 Yes, I **k**; keep silent!"
2Ki 4: 1 and you **k** that your servant
2Ki 4: 9 I **k** that this is a holy man
2Ki 4:39 they did not **k** what they were
2Ki 5: 8 he shall **k** that there is a
2Ki 5:15 now I **k** that there is no God
2Ki 7:12 They **k** that we are hungry
2Ki 8:12 Because I **k** the evil that you
2Ki 9:11 You **k** the man and his babble
2Ki 10:10 **K** now that nothing shall fall
2Ki 17:26 cities of Samaria do not **k**
2Ki 17:26 them because they do not **k**
2Ki 19:19 **k** that You are the LORD God
2Ki 19:27 But I **k** your dwelling place,
1Ch 12:32 to **k** what Israel ought to do,
1Ch 17:18 For You **k** Your servant
1Ch 21: 2 of them to me that I may **k** it
1Ch 28: 9 **k** the God of your father, and
1Ch 29:17 I **k** also, my God, that You
2Ch 2: 8 for I **k** that your servants
2Ch 6:30 You **k** (for You alone **k** the
2Ch 6:33 of the earth may **k** Your name
2Ch 6:33 that they may **k** that this
2Ch 13: 5 Should you not **k** that the
2Ch 20:12 nor do we **k** what to do, but
2Ch 25:16 I **k** that God has determined
2Ch 32:13 Do you not **k** what I and my
2Ch 32:31 that He might **k** all that was
Ezra 4:15 and **k** that this city is a
Ezra 7:25 all such as **k** the laws of
Ezra 7:25 teach those who do not **k** them
Neh 2:16 the officials did not **k** where
Neh 4:11 neither **k** nor see anything
Esth 4:11 of the king's provinces **k**
Job 5:24 You shall **k** that your tent is
Job 5:25 You shall also **k** that your
Job 5:27 Hear it, and **k** for yourself
Job 7:10 shall his place **k** him anymore
Job 8: 9 **k** nothing, because our days
Job 9: 2 Truly I **k** it is so, but how
Job 9: 5 and they do not **k** when He
Job 9:21 yet I do not **k** myself
Job 9:28 I **k** that You will not hold me
Job 10: 7 although You **k** that I am not
Job 10:13 I **k** that this was with You
Job 11: 6 **K** therefore that God exacts
Job 11: 8 what can you **k**?
Job 12: 3 who does not **k** such things as
Job 12: 9 among all these does not **k**
Job 13: 2 What you **k**, I also **k**
Job 13:18 my case, I **k** that I shall be
Job 13:23 Make me **k** my transgression
Job 14:21 to honor, and he does not **k** it
Job 15: 9 What do you **k** that we do not
Job 18:21 of him who does not **k** God
Job 19: 6 **K** then that God has wronged
Job 19:25 For I **k** that my Redeemer
Job 19:26 skin is destroyed, this I **k**
Job 19:29 that you may **k** there is a
Job 20: 4 Do you not **k** this of old,
Job 21:19 him, that he may **k** it
Job 21:27 I **k** your thoughts, and the
Job 21:29 And do you not **k** their signs
Job 22:13 And you say, 'What does God **k**
Job 23: 5 I would **k** the words which He
Job 24: 1 Why do those who **k** Him see
Job 24:13 they do not **k** its ways nor
Job 24:16 they do not **k** the light
Job 28:13 Man does not **k** its value, Nor
Job 29:16 out the case that I did not **k**
Job 30:23 For I **k** that You will bring
Job 31: 6 that God may **k** my integrity
Job 32:22 For I do not **k** how to flatter
Job 34: 4 let us **k** among ourselves what
Job 34:33 therefore speak what you **k**
Job 36:26 is great, and we do not **k** Him
Job 37: 7 that all men may **k** His work
Job 37:15 Do you **k** when God dispatches
Job 37:16 Do you **k** the balance of
Job 38: 5 Surely you **k**!
Job 38:12 the dawn to **k** its place,
Job 38:18 Tell Me, if you **k** all this
Job 38:20 that you may **k** the paths to
Job 38:21 Do you **k** it, because you were
Job 38:33 Do you **k** the ordinances of
Job 39: 1 Do you **k** the time when the
Job 39: 2 Or do you **k** the time when
Job 42: 2 I **k** that You can do
Job 42: 3 for me, which I did not **k**
Ps 4: 3 But **k** that the LORD has set
Ps 9:10 those who **k** Your name will
Ps 9:20 LORD, That the nations may **k**
Ps 20: 6 Now I **k** that the LORD saves
Ps 35:11 ask me things that I do not **k**
Ps 35:15 against me, And I did not **k** it
Ps 36:10 to those who **k** You, And Your
Ps 39: 4 LORD, make me to **k** my end
Ps 39: 4 That I may **k** how frail I am
Ps 39: 6 does not **k** who will gather
Ps 40: 9 lips, O LORD, You Yourself **k**
Ps 41:11 By this I **k** that You are well
Ps 46:10 Be still, and **k** that I am God
Ps 50:11 I **k** all the birds of the
Ps 51: 6 You will make me to **k** wisdom
Ps 56: 9 This I **k**, because God is for
Ps 59:13 let them **k** that God rules in
Ps 69: 5 O God, You **k** my foolishness
Ps 69:19 You **k** my reproach, my shame,
Ps 71:15 For I do not **k** their limits
Ps 73:11 How does God **k**
Ps 78: 6 to come might **k** them, The
Ps 79: 6 the nations that do not **k** You
Ps 82: 5 They do not **k**, nor do they
Ps 83:18 That men may **k** that You,
Ps 87: 4 and Babylon to those who **k** Me
Ps 89:15 people who **k** the joyful sound
Ps 92: 6 A senseless man does not **k**
Ps 95:10 And they do not **k** My ways
Ps 100: 3 **K** that the LORD, He is God
Ps 101: 4 I will not **k** wickedness
Ps 109:27 That they may **k** that this is
Ps 119:75 I **k**, O LORD, that Your
Ps 119:79 Those who **k** Your testimonies
Ps 119:125 That I may **k** Your testimonies
Ps 135: 5 For I **k** that the LORD is
Ps 139: 2 You **k** my sitting down and my
Ps 139: 4 O LORD, You **k** it altogether
Ps 139:23 me, O God, and **k** my heart
Ps 139:23 Try me, and **k** my anxieties
Ps 140:12 I **k** that the LORD will
Ps 143: 8 Cause me to **k** the way in
Prov 1: 2 To **k** wisdom and instruction,
Prov 4: 1 attention to **k** understanding
Prov 4:19 They do not **k** what makes them
Prov 5: 6 you do not **k** them
Prov 7:23 he did not **k** it would take
Prov 9:18 But he does not **k** that the
Prov 10:32 **k** what is acceptable, but the
Prov 22:21 That I may make you **k** the
Prov 24:12 Surely we did not **k** this,"
Prov 24:12 your soul, does He not **k** it
Prov 27: 1 for you do not **k** what a day
Prov 27:23 Be diligent to **k** the state of
Prov 30: 4 is His Son's name, if you **k**
Eccl 1:17 And I set my heart to **k** wisdom
Eccl 1:17 and to **k** madness and folly
Eccl 3:12 I **k** that there is nothing
Eccl 3:14 I **k** that whatever God does,
Eccl 5: 1 for they do not **k** that they
Eccl 7:25 I applied my heart to **k**, to
Eccl 7:25 to **k** the wickedness of folly,
Eccl 8: 7 For he does not **k** what will
Eccl 8:12 yet I surely **k** that it will
Eccl 8:16 applied my heart to **k** wisdom
Eccl 8:17 a wise man attempts to **k** it
Eccl 9: 1 People **k** neither love nor
Eccl 9: 5 For the living **k** that they
Eccl 9: 5 but the dead **k** nothing, and
Eccl 9:12 man also does not **k** his time
Eccl 10:15 for they do not even **k** how to
Eccl 11: 2 for you do not **k** what evil
Eccl 11: 5 As you do not **k** what is the
Eccl 11: 5 so you do not **k** the works of
Eccl 11: 6 for you do not **k** which will
Eccl 11: 9 but **k** that for all these God
Song 1: 8 If you do not **k**, O fairest
Is 1: 3 but Israel does not **k**, My
Is 5:19 and come, that we may **k** it
Is 7:15 that He may **k** to refuse the

Is 7:16 shall **k** to refuse the evil
Is 9: 9 All the people will **k**
Is 19:12 let them **k** what the LORD of
Is 19:21 the Egyptians will **k** the LORD
Is 37:20 may **k** that You are the LORD
Is 37:28 But I **k** your dwelling place,
Is 41:20 That they may see and **k**, and
Is 41:22 and **k** the latter end of them
Is 41:23 that we may **k** that you are
Is 41:26 the beginning, that we may **k**
Is 42:16 blind by a way they did not **k**
Is 42:25 all around, yet he did not **k**
Is 43:10 I have chosen, that you may **k**
Is 43:19 shall you not **k** it
Is 44: 8 I **k** not one
Is 44: 9 they neither see nor **k**, that
Is 44:18 They do not **k** nor understand
Is 45: 3 places, That you may **k** that I
Is 45: 6 That they may **k** from the
Is 47: 8 nor shall I **k** the loss of
Is 47:11 you shall not **k** from where it
Is 47:11 which you shall not **k**
Is 48: 6 things, and you did not **k** them
Is 48: 8 hear, surely you did not **k**
Is 49:23 Then you will **k** that I am the
Is 49:26 All flesh shall **k** that I, the
Is 50: 4 that I should **k** how to speak
Is 50: 7 and I **k** that I will not be
Is 51: 7 you who **k** righteousness, you
Is 52: 6 My people shall **k** My name
Is 52: 6 therefore they shall **k** in
Is 55: 5 call a nation you do not **k**
Is 55: 5 and nations who do not **k** you
Is 58: 2 and delight to **k** My ways, as
Is 59: 8 that way shall not **k** peace
Is 59:12 for our iniquities, we **k** them
Is 60:16 you shall **k** that I, the LORD,
Is 66:18 For I **k** their works and their
Jer 2: 8 handle the law did not **k** Me
Jer 2:19 **K** therefore and see that it is
Jer 2:23 **k** what you have done
Jer 5: 1 see now and **k**
Jer 5: 4 for they do not **k** the way of
Jer 5:15 whose language you do not **k**
Jer 6:15 nor did they **k** how to blush
Jer 6:18 hear, you nations, and **k**, O
Jer 6:27 My people, that you may **k**
Jer 7: 9 other gods whom you do not **k**
Jer 8: 7 But My people do not **k** the
Jer 8:12 nor did they **k** how to blush
Jer 9: 3 to evil, and they do not **k** Me
Jer 9: 6 deceit they refuse to **k** Me
Jer 10:23 I **k** the way of man is not in
Jer 10:25 Gentiles, who do not **k** You
Jer 11:18 me knowledge of it, and I **k** it
Jer 11:19 I did not **k** that they had
Jer 12: 3 But You, O LORD, **k** me
Jer 13:12 Do we not certainly **k** that
Jer 14:18 about in a land they do not **k**
Jer 15:14 a land which you do not **k**
Jer 15:15 O LORD, You **k**
Jer 15:15 **K** that for Your sake I have
Jer 16:13 into a land that you do not **k**
Jer 16:21 this once cause them to **k**
Jer 16:21 will cause them to **k** My hand
Jer 16:21 they shall **k** that My name is
Jer 17: 4 the land which you do not **k**
Jer 17: 9 Who can **k** it?
Jer 17:16 You **k** what came out of my
Jer 18:23 You **k** all their counsel which
Jer 22:28 a land which they do not **k**
Jer 24: 7 give them a heart to **k** Me
Jer 26:15 But **k** for certain that if you
Jer 29:11 For I **k** the thoughts that I
Jer 29:23 Indeed I **k**, and am a witness,
Jer 31:34 **K** the LORD,' for they all
Jer 31:34 for they all shall **k** Me
Jer 33: 3 things, which you do not **k**
Jer 36:19 let no one **k** where you are
Jer 38:24 Let no one **k** of these words,
Jer 40:14 Do you certainly **k** that
Jer 40:15 and no one will **k** it
Jer 42:19 **K** certainly that I have
Jer 42:22 **k** certainly that you shall
Jer 44: 3 gods whom they did not **k**,
Jer 44:28 shall **k** whose words will
Jer 44:29 that you may **k** that My words
Jer 48:17 and all you who **k** his name
Jer 48:30 I **k** his wrath," says the
Ezek 2: 5 yet they will **k** that a
Ezek 5:13 and they shall **k** that I, the
Ezek 6: 7 you shall **k** that I am the
Ezek 6:10 they shall **k** that I am the
Ezek 6:13 Then you shall **k** that I am
Ezek 6:14 Then they shall **k** that I am
Ezek 7: 4 then you shall **k** that I am
Ezek 7: 9 Then you will **k** that I am the
Ezek 7:27 then they shall **k** that I am
Ezek 11: 5 for I **k** the things that come
Ezek 11:10 Then you shall **k** that I am
Ezek 11:12 you shall **k** that I am the
Ezek 12:15 Then they shall **k** that I am
Ezek 12:16 Then they shall **k** that I am
Ezek 12:20 you shall **k** that I am the
Ezek 13: 9 Then you shall **k** that I am
Ezek 13:14 Then you shall **k** that I am
Ezek 13:21 Then you shall **k** that I am
Ezek 13:23 you shall **k** that I am the
Ezek 14: 8 Then you shall **k** that I am
Ezek 14:23 you shall **k** that I have done
Ezek 15: 7 Then you shall **k** that I am
Ezek 16: 2 to **k** her abominations,
Ezek 16:62 Then you shall **k** that I am
Ezek 17:12 Do you not **k** what these
Ezek 17:21 and you shall **k** that I, the
Ezek 17:24 of the field shall **k** that I
Ezek 20:12 that they might **k** that I am
Ezek 20:20 that you may **k** that I am the
Ezek 20:26 that they might **k** that I am
Ezek 20:38 Then you will **k** that I am the
Ezek 20:42 Then you shall **k** that I am
Ezek 20:44 Then you shall **k** that I am
Ezek 21: 5 that all flesh may **k** that I
Ezek 22:16 then you shall **k** that I am
Ezek 22:22 then you shall **k** that I, the
Ezek 23:49 Then you shall **k** that I am
Ezek 24:24 you shall **k** that I am the
Ezek 24:27 they will **k** that I am the
Ezek 25: 5 Then you shall **k** that I am
Ezek 25: 7 you shall **k** that I am the
Ezek 25:11 they shall **k** that I am the
Ezek 25:14 they shall **k** My vengeance,"
Ezek 25:17 they shall **k** that I am the
Ezek 26: 6 Then they shall **k** that I am
Ezek 28:22 they shall **k** that I am the
Ezek 28:23 then they shall **k** that I am
Ezek 28:24 Then they shall **k** that I am
Ezek 28:26 Then they shall **k** that I am
Ezek 29: 6 shall **k** that I am the LORD
Ezek 29: 9 then they will **k** that I am
Ezek 29:16 Then they shall **k** that I am
Ezek 29:21 Then they shall **k** that I am
Ezek 30: 8 Then they will **k** that I am
Ezek 30:19 then they shall **k** that I am
Ezek 30:25 they shall **k** that I am the
Ezek 30:26 Then they shall **k** that I am
Ezek 32:15 then they shall **k** that I am
Ezek 33:29 Then they shall **k** that I am
Ezek 33:33 then they will **k** that a
Ezek 34:27 they shall **k** that I am the
Ezek 34:30 Thus they shall **k** that I, the
Ezek 35: 4 Then you shall **k** that I am
Ezek 35: 9 then you shall **k** that I am
Ezek 35:12 Then you shall **k** that I am
Ezek 35:15 Then they shall **k** that I am
Ezek 36:11 Then you shall **k** that I am
Ezek 36:23 the nations shall **k** that I am
Ezek 36:36 all around you shall **k** that I
Ezek 36:38 Then they shall **k** that I am
Ezek 37: 3 O Lord GOD, You **k**
Ezek 37: 6 Then you shall **k** that I am
Ezek 37:13 Then you shall **k** that I am
Ezek 37:14 Then you shall **k** that I, the
Ezek 37:28 nations also will **k** that I
Ezek 38:14 safely, will you not **k** it
Ezek 38:16 so that the nations may **k** Me
Ezek 38:23 Then they shall **k** that I am
Ezek 39: 6 Then they shall **k** that I am
Ezek 39: 7 shall **k** that I am the LORD
Ezek 39:22 **k** that I am the LORD their
Ezek 39:23 The Gentiles shall **k** that the
Ezek 39:28 then they shall **k** that I am
Dan 2: 3 is anxious to **k** the dream
Dan 2: 8 I **k** for certain that you
Dan 2: 9 I shall **k** that you can give
Dan 2:30 that you may **k** the thoughts
Dan 4: 9 because I **k** that the Spirit
Dan 4:17 order that the living may **k**
Dan 4:25 till you **k** that the Most High
Dan 4:26 come to **k** that Heaven rules
Dan 4:32 until you **k** that the Most
Dan 5:23 which do not see or hear or **k**
Dan 6:15 **K**, O king, that it is the law
Dan 7:19 Then I wished to **k** the truth
Dan 9:25 **K** therefore and understand,
Dan 10:20 Do you **k** why I have come to
Dan 11:32 but the people who **k** their
Dan 11:38 **k** he shall honor with gold
Hos 2: 8 For she did not **k** that I gave
Hos 2:20 and you shall **k** the LORD
Hos 5: 3 I **k** Ephraim, and Israel is not
Hos 5: 4 and they do not **k** the LORD
Hos 6: 3 Let us **k**, let us pursue the
Hos 7: 9 but he does not **k** it
Hos 7: 9 on him, yet he does not **k** it
Hos 8: 2 cry to Me, 'My God, we **k** You
Hos 11: 3 but they did not **k** that I
Hos 13: 4 you shall **k** no God but Me
Hos 14: 9 Let him **k** them
Joel 2:27 Then you shall **k** that I am in
Joel 3:17 So you shall **k** that I am the
Amos 3:10 For they do not **k** to do right
Amos 5:12 For I **k** your manifold
Jon 1: 7 that we may **k** for whose cause
Jon 1:12 For I **k** that this great
Jon 4: 2 for I **k** that You are a
Mic 3: 1 it not for you to **k** justice
Mic 4:12 But they do not **k** the
Mic 6: 5 to Gilgal, that you may **k** the
Zech 2: 9 Then you will **k** that the LORD
Zech 2:11 Then you will **k** that the LORD
Zech 4: 5 Do you not **k** what these are
Zech 4: 9 Then you will **k** that the LORD
Zech 4:13 Do you not **k** what these are
Zech 6:15 Then you shall **k** that the
Mal 2: 4 Then you shall **k** that I have
Matt 1:25 did not **k** her till she had
Matt 6: 3 **k** what your right hand is
Matt 7:11 **k** how to give good gifts to
Matt 7:16 You will **k** them by their
Matt 7:20 their fruits you will **k** them
Matt 9: 6 But that you may **k** that the
Matt 11:27 Nor does anyone **k** the Father
Matt 13:11 you to **k** the mysteries of the
Matt 15:12 Do You **k** that the Pharisees
Matt 16: 3 You **k** how to discern the face
Matt 17:12 they did not **k** him but did to
Matt 20:22 You do not **k** what you ask
Matt 20:25 You **k** that the rulers of the
Matt 21:27 We do not **k**
Matt 22:16 we **k** that You are true, and
Matt 24:32 you **k** that summer is near
Matt 24:33 **k** that it is near, at the
Matt 24:39 did not **k** until the flood
Matt 24:42 for you do not **k** what hour
Matt 24:43 But **k** this, that if the
Matt 25:12 I say to you, I do not **k** you
Matt 25:13 for you **k** neither the day nor
Matt 26: 2 You **k** that after two days is
Matt 26:70 I do not **k** what you are
Matt 26:72 I do not **k** the Man
Matt 26:74 I do not **k** the Man
Matt 27:65 it as secure as you **k** how
Matt 28: 5 for I **k** that you seek Jesus
Mark 1:24 I **k** who You are
Mark 2:10 But that you may **k** that the
Mark 4:11 **k** the mystery of the kingdom
Mark 4:27 he himself does not **k** how
Mark 5:43 that no one should **k** it, and
Mark 7:24 and wanted no one to **k** it, but
Mark 9: 6 he did not **k** what to say, for
Mark 9:30 did not want anyone to **k** it
Mark 10:19 You **k** the commandments
Mark 10:38 You do not **k** what you ask
Mark 10:42 You **k** that those who are
Mark 11:33 We do not **k**
Mark 12:14 we **k** that You are true, and
Mark 12:24 because you do not **k** the
Mark 13:28 you **k** that summer is near
Mark 13:29 **k** that it is near, at the
Mark 13:33 for you do not **k** when the
Mark 13:35 for you do not **k** when the
Mark 14:40 they did not **k** what to answer
Mark 14:68 I neither **k** nor understand
Mark 14:71 I do not **k** this Man of whom
Luke 1: 4 that you may **k** the certainty
Luke 1:18 How shall I **k** this
Luke 1:34 be, since I do not **k** a man
Luke 2:43 and His mother did not **k** it
Luke 2:49 Did you not **k** that I must be

Luke 4:34 I **k** You, who You are
Luke 5:24 But that you may **k** that the
Luke 7:39 were a prophet, would **k** who
Luke 8:10 to **k** the mysteries of the
Luke 9:55 You do not **k** what manner of
Luke 10:11 Nevertheless **k** this, that the
Luke 11:13 **k** how to give good gifts to
Luke 12:39 But **k** this, that if the
Luke 12:48 But he who did not **k**, yet
Luke 13:25 say to you, 'I do not **k** you
Luke 13:27 I tell you I do not **k** you
Luke 18:20 You **k** the commandments
Luke 18:34 they did not **k** the things
Luke 19:15 him, that he might **k** how much
Luke 19:44 because you did not **k** the
Luke 20: 7 did not **k** where it was from
Luke 20:21 we **k** that You say and teach
Luke 21:20 then **k** that its desolation is
Luke 21:30 **k** for yourselves that summer
Luke 21:31 **k** that the kingdom of God is
Luke 22:34 three times that you **k** Me
Luke 22:57 Woman, I do not **k** Him
Luke 22:60 Man, I do not **k** what you are
Luke 23:34 they do not **k** what they do
Luke 24:16 so that they did not **k** Him
John 1:10 and the world did not **k** Him
John 1:26 among you whom you do not **k**
John 1:31 I did not **k** Him
John 1:33 I did not **k** Him, but He who
John 1:48 How do You **k** me
John 2: 9 did not **k** where it came from
John 3: 2 we **k** that You are a teacher
John 3:10 and do not **k** these things
John 3:11 to you, We speak what We **k**
John 4:22 You worship what you do not **k**
John 4:22 we **k** what we worship, for
John 4:25 I **k** that Messiah is coming"
John 4:32 to eat of which you do not **k**
John 4:42 **k** that this is indeed the
John 5:13 healed did not **k** who it was
John 5:32 I **k** that the witness which He
John 5:42 But I **k** you, that you do not
John 6:42 whose father and mother we **k**
John 6:69 **k** that You are the Christ,
John 7:15 How does this Man **k** letters
John 7:17 he shall **k** concerning the
John 7:26 Do the rulers **k** indeed that
John 7:27 we **k** where this Man is from
John 7:28 both **k** Me, and you **k** where
John 7:28 Me is true, whom you do not **k**
John 7:29 But I **k** Him, for I am from
John 7:49 not **k** the law is accursed
John 8:14 for I **k** where I came from and
John 8:14 but you do not **k** where I come
John 8:19 You **k** neither Me nor My
John 8:28 then you will **k** that I am He
John 8:32 And you shall **k** the truth, and
John 8:37 I **k** that you are Abraham's
John 8:52 Now we **k** that You have a
John 8:55 not known Him, but I **k** Him
John 8:55 And if I say, 'I do not **k** Him
John 8:55 but I do **k** Him and keep His
John 9:12 I do not **k**
John 9:20 We **k** that this is our son, and
John 9:21 means he now sees we do not **k**
John 9:21 opened his eyes we do not **k**
John 9:24 We **k** that this Man is a
John 9:25 is a sinner or not I do not **k**
John 9:25 One thing I **k**
John 9:29 We **k** that God spoke to Moses
John 9:29 we do not **k** where He is from
John 9:30 that you do not **k** where He is
John 9:31 Now we **k** that God does not
John 10: 4 him, for they **k** his voice
John 10: 5 for they do not **k** the voice
John 10:14 I **k** My sheep, and am known by
John 10:15 Me, even so I **k** the Father
John 10:27 I **k** them, and they follow Me
John 10:38 the works, that you may **k**
John 11:22 But even now I **k** that
John 11:24 I **k** that he will rise again
John 11:42 I **k** that You always hear Me,
John 11:49 them, "You **k** nothing at all,
John 12:35 does not **k** where he is going
John 12:50 And I **k** that His command is
John 13: 7 but you will **k** after this
John 13:12 Do you **k** what I have done to
John 13:17 If you **k** these things, happy
John 13:18 I **k** whom I have chosen
John 13:35 By this all will **k** that you
John 14: 4 And where I go you **k**
John 14: 4 and the way you **k**
John 14: 5 we do not **k** where You are
John 14: 5 and how can we **k** the way
John 14: 7 and from now on you **k** Him and
John 14:17 but you **k** Him, for He dwells
John 14:20 At that day you will **k** that I
John 14:31 may **k** that I love the Father
John 15:15 for a servant does not **k** what
John 15:18 you **k** that it hated Me before
John 15:21 they do not **k** Him who sent Me
John 16:18 We do not **k** what He is saying
John 16:30 sure that You **k** all things
John 17: 3 life, that they may **k** You
John 17:23 that the world may **k** that You
John 18:21 Indeed they **k** what I said
John 19: 4 that you may **k** that I find no
John 19:10 Do You not **k** that I have
John 20: 2 we do not **k** where they have
John 20: 9 they did not **k** the Scripture
John 20:13 I do not **k** where they have
John 20:14 did not **k** that it was Jesus
John 21: 4 did not **k** that it was Jesus
John 21:15 You **k** that I love You
John 21:16 You **k** that I love You
John 21:17 Him, "Lord, You **k** all things
John 21:17 You **k** that I love You
John 21:24 we **k** that his testimony is
Acts 1: 7 It is not for you to **k** times
Acts 1:24 who **k** the hearts of all, show
Acts 2:22 as you yourselves also **k**
Acts 2:36 **k** assuredly that God has made
Acts 3:16 man strong, whom you see and **k**
Acts 3:17 I **k** that you did it in
Acts 7:18 arose who did not **k** Joseph
Acts 7:40 we do not **k** what has become
Acts 10:28 You **k** how unlawful it is for
Acts 10:37 that word you **k**, which was
Acts 12: 9 did not **k** that what was done
Acts 12:11 Now I **k** for certain that the
Acts 13:27 because they did not **k** Him
Acts 15: 7 you **k** that a good while ago
Acts 17:19 May we **k** what this new
Acts 17:20 Therefore we want to **k** what
Acts 19:15 Jesus I **k**, and Paul I **k**
Acts 19:25 Men, you **k** that we have our
Acts 19:32 most of them did not **k** why
Acts 19:35 not **k** that the city of the
Acts 20:18 You **k**, from the first day
Acts 20:25 now I **k** that you all, among
Acts 20:29 For I **k** this, that after my
Acts 20:34 you yourselves **k** that these
Acts 21:24 that all may **k** that those
Acts 22:14 that you should **k** His will
Acts 22:19 Lord, they **k** that in every
Acts 22:24 so that he might **k** why they
Acts 22:30 because he wanted to **k** for
Acts 23: 5 I did not **k**, brethren, that
Acts 23:28 when I wanted to **k** the reason
Acts 24:10 Inasmuch as I **k** that you have
Acts 25:10 no wrong, as you very well **k**
Acts 26: 4 at Jerusalem, all the Jews **k**
Acts 26:27 I **k** that you do believe
Acts 28:22 sect, we **k** that it is spoken
Rom 2: 2 But we **k** that the judgment of
Rom 2:18 **k** His will, and approve the
Rom 3:19 Now we **k** that whatever the
Rom 6: 3 Or do you not **k** that as many
Rom 6:16 Do you not **k** that to whom you
Rom 7: 1 Or do you not **k**, brethren
Rom 7: 1 speak to those who **k** the law)
Rom 7:14 For we **k** that the law is
Rom 7:18 For I **k** that in me (that is,
Rom 8:22 For we **k** that the whole
Rom 8:26 For we do not **k** what we
Rom 8:28 we **k** that all things work
Rom 10:19 But I say, did Israel not **k**
Rom 11: 2 Or do you not **k** what the
Rom 14:14 I **k** and am convinced by the
Rom 15:29 But I **k** that when I come to
1Co 1:16 I do not **k** whether I baptized
1Co 1:21 through wisdom did not **k** God
1Co 2: 2 For I determined not to **k**
1Co 2:12 that we might **k** the things
1Co 2:14 nor can he **k** them, because
1Co 3:16 Do you not **k** that you are the
1Co 4: 4 For I **k** nothing against
1Co 4:19 the Lord wills, and I will **k**
1Co 5: 6 Do you not **k** that a little
1Co 6: 2 Do you not **k** that the saints
1Co 6: 3 Do you not **k** that we shall
1Co 6: 9 Do you not **k** that the
1Co 6:15 Do you not **k** that your bodies
1Co 6:16 Or do you not **k** that he who
1Co 6:19 Or do you not **k** that your
1Co 7:16 For how do you **k**, O wife,
1Co 7:16 Or how do you **k**, O husband,
1Co 8: 1 We **k** that we all have
1Co 8: 2 nothing yet as he ought to **k**
1Co 8: 4 we **k** that an idol is nothing
1Co 9:13 Do you not **k** that those who
1Co 9:24 Do you not **k** that those who
1Co 11: 3 But I want you to **k** that the
1Co 12: 2 You **k** that you were Gentiles,
1Co 13: 9 For we **k** in part and we
1Co 13:12 Now I **k** in part, but then I
1Co 13:12 but then I shall **k** just as I
1Co 14:11 if I do not **k** the meaning of
1Co 16:15 you **k** the household of
2Co 1: 7 because we **k** that as you are
2Co 2: 4 but that you might **k** the love
2Co 5: 1 For we **k** that if our earthly
2Co 5:16 yet now we **k** Him thus no
2Co 8: 9 For you **k** the grace of our
2Co 9: 2 for I **k** your willingness,
2Co 12: 2 I **k** a man in Christ who
2Co 12: 2 in the body I do not **k**, or
2Co 12: 2 out of the body I do not **k**
2Co 12: 3 And I **k** such a man
2Co 12: 3 or out of the body I do not **k**
2Co 13: 5 Do you not **k** yourselves, that
2Co 13: 6 you will **k** that we are not
Gal 3: 7 Therefore **k** that only those
Gal 4: 8 when you did not **k** God, you
Gal 4:13 You **k** that because of
Eph 1:18 that you may **k** what is the
Eph 3:19 to **k** the love of Christ which
Eph 5: 5 For this you **k**, that no
Eph 6:21 you also may **k** my affairs
Eph 6:22 that you may **k** our affairs
Phil 1:12 But I want you to **k**, brethren
Phil 1:19 For I **k** that this will turn
Phil 1:25 I **k** that I shall remain and
Phil 2:19 when I **k** your state
Phil 2:22 But you **k** his proven
Phil 3:10 that I may **k** Him and the power
Phil 4:12 I **k** how to be abased, and I
Phil 4:12 abased, and I **k** how to abound
Phil 4:15 Now you Philippians **k** also
Col 2: 1 For I want you to **k** what a
Col 4: 6 that you may **k** how you ought
Col 4: 8 purpose, that he may **k** your
1Th 1: 5 as you **k** what kind of men we
1Th 2: 1 For you yourselves **k**,
1Th 2: 2 treated at Philippi, as you **k**
1Th 2: 5 flattering words, as you **k**
1Th 2:11 as you **k** how we exhorted, and
1Th 3: 3 for you yourselves **k** that we
1Th 3: 4 just as it happened, and you **k**
1Th 3: 5 I sent to **k** your faith, lest
1Th 4: 2 for you **k** what commandments
1Th 4: 4 **k** how to possess his own
1Th 4: 5 the Gentiles who do not **k** God
1Th 5: 2 For you yourselves **k**
2Th 1: 8 on those who do not **k** God
2Th 2: 6 now you **k** what is restraining
2Th 3: 7 For you yourselves **k** how you
1Ti 1: 8 But we **k** that the law is good
1Ti 3: 5 (for if a man does not **k** how
1Ti 3:15 I write so that you may **k** how
1Ti 4: 3 who believe and **k** the truth
2Ti 1:12 for I **k** whom I have believed
2Ti 1:15 This you **k**, that all those in
2Ti 1:18 you **k** very well how many ways
2Ti 2:25 so that they may **k** the truth
2Ti 3: 1 But **k** this, that in the last
Tit 1:16 They profess to **k** God, but in
Heb 8:11 **K** the LORD,' for all shall
Heb 8:11 the LORD,' for all shall **k** Me
Heb 10:30 For we **k** Him who said
Heb 12:17 For you **k** that afterward,
Heb 13:23 **K** that our brother Timothy
Jas 2:20 But do you want to **k**, O
Jas 4: 4 Do you not **k** that friendship
Jas 4:14 whereas you do not **k** what
Jas 5:20 let him **k** that he who turns a
2Pe 1:12 things, though you **k** them
2Pe 3:17 since you **k** these things
1Jn 2: 3 by this we **k** that we **k** Him
1Jn 2: 4 I **k** Him," and does not keep

1Jn 2: 5 By this we **k** that we are in
1Jn 2:11 does not **k** where he is going,
1Jn 2:18 by which we **k** that it is the
1Jn 2:20 Holy One, and you **k** all things
1Jn 2:21 you do not **k** the truth, but
1Jn 2:21 truth, but because you **k** it
1Jn 2:29 If you **k** that He is righteous
1Jn 2:29 you **k** that everyone who
1Jn 3: 1 the world does not **k** us,
1Jn 3: 1 us, because it did not **k** Him
1Jn 3: 2 be, but we **k** that when He is
1Jn 3: 5 you **k** that He was manifested
1Jn 3:14 We **k** that we have passed from
1Jn 3:15 you **k** that no murderer has
1Jn 3:16 By this we **k** love, because He
1Jn 3:19 by this we **k** that we are of
1Jn 3:24 by this we **k** that He abides
1Jn 4: 2 By this you **k** the Spirit of
1Jn 4: 6 By this we **k** the spirit of
1Jn 4: 8 does not love does not **k** God
1Jn 4:13 By this we **k** that we abide in
1Jn 5: 2 By this we **k** that we love the
1Jn 5:13 that you may **k** that you have
1Jn 5:15 if we **k** that He hears us,
1Jn 5:15 we ask, we **k** that we have the
1Jn 5:18 We **k** that whoever is born of
1Jn 5:19 We **k** that we are of God, and
1Jn 5:20 we **k** that the Son of God has
1Jn 5:20 that we may **k** Him who is true
3Jn 12 you **k** that our testimony is
Jude 10 of whatever they do not **k**
Jude 10 and whatever they **k** naturally
Rev 2: 2 I **k** your works, your labor,
Rev 2: 9 I **k** your works, tribulation,
Rev 2: 9 I **k** the blasphemy of those
Rev 2:13 I **k** your works, and where you
Rev 2:19 I **k** your works, love, service
Rev 2:23 all the churches shall **k** that
Rev 3: 1 I **k** your works, that you
Rev 3: 3 you will not **k** what hour I
Rev 3: 8 I **k** your works
Rev 3: 9 to **k** that I have loved you
Rev 3:15 I **k** your works, that you are
Rev 3:17 and do not **k** that you are
Rev 7:14 Sir, you **k**

KNOWING (*see* KNOW, KNOWINGLY)
Gen 3: 5 be like God, **k** good and evil
Jer 22:16 Was not this **k** Me
Matt 9: 4 **k** their thoughts, said,
Matt 22:29 not **k** the Scriptures nor the
Mark 5:30 immediately **k** in Himself that
Mark 5:33 **k** what had happened to her,
Mark 6:20 **k** that he was a just and holy
Mark 12:15 **k** their hypocrisy, said to
Luke 8:53 to scorn, **k** that she was dead
Luke 9:33 not **k** what he said
Luke 11:17 **k** their thoughts, said to
John 13: 3 **k** that the Father had given
John 18: 4 **k** all things that would come
John 19:28 **k** that all things were now
John 21:12 **k** that it was the Lord
Acts 2:30 **k** that God had sworn with an
Acts 5: 7 in, not **k** what had happened
Acts 17:23 whom you worship without **k**
Acts 20:22 not **k** the things that will
Rom 1:32 **k** the righteous judgment of
Rom 2: 4 not **k** that the goodness of
Rom 5: 3 **k** that tribulation produces
Rom 6: 6 **k** this, that our old man was
Rom 6: 9 **k** that Christ, having been
Rom 13:11 **k** the time, that now it is
1Co 15:58 **k** that your labor is not in
2Co 4:14 **k** that He who raised up the
2Co 5: 6 **k** that while we are at home
2Co 5:11 **K**, therefore, the terror of
Gal 2:16 **k** that a man is not justified
Eph 6: 8 **k** that whatever good anyone
Eph 6: 9 **k** that your own Master also
Phil 1:17 **k** that I am appointed for the
Col 3:24 **k** that from the Lord you will
Col 4: 1 **k** that you also have a Master
1Th 1: 4 **k**, beloved brethren, your
1Ti 1: 9 **k** this: that the law is not
1Ti 6: 4 **k** nothing, but is obsessed
2Ti 2:23 **k** that they generate strife
2Ti 3:14 **k** from whom you have learned
Tit 3:11 **k** that such a person is
Phm 21 **k** that you will do even more
Heb 10:34 **k** that you have a better and
Heb 11: 8 out, not **k** where he was going
Jas 1: 3 **k** that the testing of your
Jas 3: 1 **k** that we shall receive a
1Pe 1:18 **k** that you were not redeemed
1Pe 3: 9 **k** that you were called to
1Pe 5: 9 **k** that the same sufferings
2Pe 1:14 **k** that shortly I must put off
2Pe 1:20 **k** this first, that no
2Pe 3: 3 **k** this first: that scoffers

KNOWINGLY (*see* KNOWING)
Gen 48:14 head, guiding his hands **k**

KNOWLEDGE (*see* KNOW, KNOWLEDGEABLE)
Gen 2: 9 and the tree of the **k** of good
Gen 2:17 of the tree of the **k** of good
Ex 31: 3 in understanding, in **k**, and
Ex 35:31 wisdom and understanding, in **k**
Lev 4:23 he has sinned comes to his **k**
Lev 4:28 he has sinned comes to his **k**
Num 15:24 without the **k** of the
Num 24:16 knows the **k** of the Most High,
Deut 1:39 who today have no **k** of good
1Sa 2: 3 for the LORD is the God of **k**
1Sa 23:23 take **k** of all the lurking
2Ch 1:10 Now give me wisdom and **k**, that
2Ch 1:11 **k** for yourself, that you may
2Ch 1:12 and **k** are granted to you
2Ch 30:22 taught the good **k** of the LORD
Neh 10:28 daughters, everyone who had **k**
Job 15: 2 wise man answer with empty **k**
Job 21:14 not desire the **k** of Your ways
Job 21:22 Can anyone teach God **k**, since
Job 33: 3 my lips utter pure **k**
Job 34: 2 ear to me, you who have **k**
Job 34:35 Job speaks without **k**, his
Job 35:16 he multiplies words without **k**
Job 36: 3 I will fetch my **k** from afar
Job 36: 4 is perfect in **k** is with you
Job 36:12 and they shall die without **k**
Job 37:16 of Him who is perfect in **k**
Job 38: 2 counsel by words without **k**
Job 42: 3 who hides counsel without **k**
Ps 14: 4 the workers of iniquity no **k**
Ps 19: 2 And night unto night reveals **k**
Ps 53: 4 the workers of iniquity no **k**
Ps 73:11 is there **k** in the Most High
Ps 94:10 correct, He who teaches man **k**
Ps 119:66 Teach me good judgment and **k**
Ps 139: 6 Such **k** is too wonderful for
Ps 144: 3 man, that You take **k** of him
Prov 1: 4 simple, to the young man **k**
Prov 1: 7 LORD is the beginning of **k**
Prov 1:22 scorning, and fools hate **k**
Prov 1:29 Because they hated **k** and did
Prov 2: 5 LORD, and find the **k** of God
Prov 2: 6 from His mouth come **k** and
Prov 2:10 **k** is pleasant to your soul,
Prov 3:20 by His **k** the depths were
Prov 5: 2 and that your lips may keep **k**
Prov 8: 9 and right to those who find **k**
Prov 8:10 **k** rather than choice gold
Prov 8:12 with prudence, and find out **k**
Prov 9:10 and the **k** of the Holy One is
Prov 10:14 Wise people store up **k**, but
Prov 11: 9 but through **k** the righteous
Prov 12: 1 loves instruction loves **k**
Prov 12:23 A prudent man conceals **k**, but
Prov 13:16 Every prudent man acts with **k**
Prov 14: 6 it, but **k** is easy to him who
Prov 14: 7 perceive in him the lips of **k**
Prov 14:18 prudent are crowned with **k**
Prov 15: 2 of the wise uses **k** rightly
Prov 15: 7 lips of the wise disperse **k**
Prov 15:14 who has understanding seeks **k**
Prov 17:27 He who has **k** spares his words
Prov 18:15 of the prudent acquires **k**
Prov 18:15 the ear of the wise seeks **k**
Prov 19: 2 for a soul to be without **k**
Prov 19:25 and he will discern **k**
Prov 19:27 stray from the words of **k**
Prov 20:15 but the lips of **k** are a
Prov 21:11 is instructed, he receives **k**
Prov 22:12 eyes of the LORD preserve **k**
Prov 22:17 and apply your heart to my **k**
Prov 22:20 things of counsels and **k**,
Prov 23:12 and your ears to words of **k**
Prov 24: 4 by **k** the rooms are filled
Prov 24: 5 a man of **k** increases strength
Prov 24:14 so shall the **k** of wisdom be
Prov 28: 2 **k** right will be prolonged
Prov 29: 7 does not understand such **k**
Prov 30: 3 nor have **k** of the Holy One
Eccl 1:16 understood great wisdom and **k**
Eccl 1:18 increases **k** increases sorrow
Eccl 2:21 whose labor is with wisdom, **k**
Eccl 2:26 For God gives wisdom and **k**
Eccl 7:12 but the excellence of **k** is
Eccl 9:10 or **k** or wisdom in the grave
Eccl 12: 9 he still taught the people **k**
Is 5:13 because they have no **k**
Is 8: 4 have **k** to cry 'My father'
Is 11: 2 and might, the Spirit of **k**
Is 11: 9 **k** of the LORD as the waters
Is 28: 9 Whom will he teach **k**
Is 32: 4 of the rash will understand **k**
Is 33: 6 **k** will be the stability of
Is 40:14 Who taught Him **k**, and showed
Is 44:19 his heart, nor is there **k** nor
Is 44:25 and makes their **k** foolishness
Is 45:20 They have no **k**, who carry the
Is 47:10 and your **k** have warped you
Is 53:11 by His **k** My righteous Servant
Jer 3:15 who will feed you with **k**
Jer 4:22 but to do good they have no **k**
Jer 10:14 is dull-hearted, without **k**
Jer 11:18 Now the LORD gave me **k** of it
Jer 51:17 is dull-hearted, without **k**
Dan 1: 4 in all wisdom, possessing **k**
Dan 1:17 young men, God gave them **k**
Dan 2:21 wise And **k** to those who have
Dan 5:12 as an excellent spirit, **k**
Dan 12: 4 and fro, and **k** shall increase
Hos 4: 1 mercy or **k** of God in the land
Hos 4: 6 are destroyed for lack of **k**
Hos 4: 6 Because you have rejected **k**
Hos 6: 3 us pursue the **k** of the LORD
Hos 6: 6 the **k** of God more than burnt
Hab 2:14 will be filled with the **k** of
Mal 2: 7 of a priest should keep **k**
Luke 1:77 to give **k** of salvation to His
Luke 11:52 have taken away the key of **k**
Acts 24:22 more accurate **k** of the Way
Rom 1:28 like to retain God in their **k**
Rom 2:20 babes, having the form of **k**
Rom 3:20 by the law is the **k** of sin
Rom 10: 2 God, but not according to **k**
Rom 11:33 of the wisdom and **k** of God
Rom 15:14 goodness, filled with all **k**
1Co 1: 5 Him in all utterance and all **k**
1Co 8: 1 We know that we all have **k**
1Co 8: 1 **K** puffs up, but love edifies
1Co 8: 7 is not in everyone that **k**
1Co 8:10 **k** eating in an idol's temple
1Co 8:11 because of your **k** shall the
1Co 12: 8 to another the word of **k**
1Co 13: 2 all mysteries and all **k**, and
1Co 13: 8 whether there is **k**, it will
1Co 14: 6 either by revelation, by **k**
1Co 15:34 some do not have the **k** of God
2Co 2:14 of His **k** in every place
2Co 4: 6 to give the light of the **k** of
2Co 6: 6 by purity, by **k**, by
2Co 8: 7 in faith, in speech, in **k**
2Co 10: 5 itself against the **k** of God
2Co 11: 6 in speech, yet I am not in **k**
Eph 1:17 and revelation in the **k** of Him
Eph 3: 4 you may understand my **k** in
Eph 3:19 love of Christ which passes **k**
Eph 4:13 the **k** of the Son of God, to a
Phil 1: 9 still more and more in **k** and
Phil 3: 8 the **k** of Christ Jesus my Lord
Col 1: 9 **k** of His will in all wisdom
Col 1:10 and increasing in the **k** of God
Col 2: 2 to the **k** of the mystery of
Col 2: 3 the treasures of wisdom and **k**
Col 3:10 **k** according to the image of
1Ti 2: 4 to come to the **k** of the truth
1Ti 6:20 of what is falsely called **k**
2Ti 3: 7 to come to the **k** of the truth
Heb 10:26 received the **k** of the truth
2Pe 1: 2 to you in the **k** of God and of
2Pe 1: 3 through the **k** of Him who
2Pe 1: 5 faith virtue, to virtue **k**
2Pe 1: 6 to **k** self-control, to
2Pe 1: 8 nor unfruitful in the **k** of
2Pe 2:20 through the **k** of the Lord
2Pe 3:18 **k** of our Lord and Savior Jesus

KNOWLEDGEABLE (*see* KNOWLEDGE)
Deut 1:13 **k** men from among your tribes,
Deut 1:15 **k** men, and made them heads

KNOWN (*see* KNOW, WELL-KNOWN)
Gen 18:19 For I have **k** him, in order
Gen 19: 8 who have not **k** a man
Gen 24:16 no man had **k** her
Gen 41:21 no one would have **k** that they
Gen 41:31 So the plenty will not be **k**
Gen 43: 7 have **k** that he would say
Gen 45: 1 himself **k** to his brothers
Ex 2:14 Surely this thing is **k**
Ex 6: 3 LORD, I was not **k** to them
Ex 18:16 I make **k** the statutes of God
Ex 21:29 has been made **k** to his owner
Ex 21:36 Or if it was **k** that the ox
Ex 33:16 will it be **k** that Your people
Lev 4:14 they have sinned becomes **k**
Lev 5: 1 has seen or **k** of the matter
Num 12: 6 make Myself **k** to him in a
Num 31:17 who has **k** a man intimately
Num 31:18 have not **k** a man intimately
Num 31:35 had not **k** a man intimately
Deut 7:15 of Egypt which you have **k**
Deut 11: 2 your children, who have not **k**
Deut 11:28 gods which you have not **k**
Deut 13: 2 gods which you have not **k**
Deut 13: 6 gods,' which you have not **k**
Deut 13:13 gods whom you have not **k**
Deut 21: 1 it is not **k** who killed him,
Deut 28:33 A nation whom you have not **k**
Deut 28:36 you nor your fathers have **k**
Deut 28:64 you nor your fathers have **k**
Deut 31:13 children, who have not **k** it
Josh 24:31 who had **k** all the works of
Judg 3: 1 all who had not **k** any of the
Judg 3: 2 who had not formerly **k** it)
Judg 16: 9 of his strength was not **k**
Judg 21:11 who has **k** a man intimately
Judg 21:12 had not **k** a man intimately
Ruth 3: 3 **k** to the man until he has
Ruth 3:14 Do not let it be **k** that the
1Sa 6: 3 it will be **k** to you why His
2Sa 17:19 and the thing was not **k**
2Sa 22:44 I have not **k** shall serve me
1Ki 18:36 let it be **k** this day that You
1Ch 16: 8 make **k** His deeds among the
1Ch 17:19 in making **k** all these great
Ezra 4:12 Let it be **k** to the king that
Ezra 4:13 Let it now be **k** to the king
Ezra 5: 8 Let it be **k** to the king that
Neh 4:15 heard that it was **k** to us
Neh 9:14 You made **k** to them Your holy
Esth 1:17 will become **k** to all women
Esth 2:22 matter became **k** to Mordecai
Ps 9:16 The LORD is **k** by the judgment
Ps 18:43 I have not **k** shall serve me
Ps 31: 7 You have **k** my soul in
Ps 48: 3 He is **k** as her refuge
Ps 67: 2 Your way may be **k** on earth
Ps 76: 1 In Judah God is **k**
Ps 77:19 And Your footsteps were not **k**
Ps 78: 3 Which we have heard and **k**,
Ps 78: 5 make them **k** to their children
Ps 79:10 Let there be **k** among the
Ps 88:12 Your wonders be **k** in the dark
Ps 89: 1 **k** Your faithfulness to all
Ps 91:14 because he has **k** My name
Ps 98: 2 LORD has made **k** His salvation
Ps 103: 7 He made **k** His ways to Moses,
Ps 105: 1 Make **k** His deeds among the
Ps 106: 8 might make His mighty power **k**
Ps 119:152 I have **k** of old that You have
Ps 139: 1 You have searched me and **k** me
Ps 145:12 To make **k** to the sons of men
Ps 147:20 they have not **k** them
Prov 1:23 I will make my words **k** to you
Prov 10: 9 his ways will become **k**
Prov 12:16 A fool's wrath is **k** at once
Prov 14:33 the heart of fools is made **k**
Prov 20:11 a child is **k** by his deeds
Prov 31:23 Her husband is **k** in the gates
Eccl 5: 3 voice is **k** by his many words
Eccl 6: 5 seen the sun or **k** anything
Eccl 6:10 for it is **k** that he is man
Eccl 7:22 your own heart has **k** that
Is 12: 5 this is **k** in all the earth
Is 19:21 the LORD will be **k** to Egypt
Is 38:19 the father shall make **k** Your
Is 40:21 Have you not **k**?
Is 40:28 Have you not **k**?
Is 42:16 them in paths they have not **k**
Is 45: 4 you, though you have not **k** Me
Is 45: 5 you, though you have not **k** Me
Is 59: 8 way of peace they have not **k**
Is 61: 9 shall be **k** among the Gentiles
Is 64: 2 to make Your name **k** to Your
Is 66:14 shall be **k** to His servants
Jer 4:22 foolish, they have not **k** Me
Jer 5: 5 for they have **k** the way of
Jer 9:16 they nor their fathers have **k**
Jer 19: 4 nor the kings of Judah have **k**
Jer 28: 9 the prophet will be **k** as one
Ezek 20: 4 Then make **k** to them the
Ezek 20: 5 made Myself **k** to them in the
Ezek 20: 9 I had made Myself **k** to them
Ezek 22:26 nor have they made **k** the
Ezek 32: 9 which you have not **k**
Ezek 35:11 I will make Myself **k** among
Ezek 36:32 let it be **k** to you
Ezek 38:23 I will be **k** in the eyes of
Ezek 39: 7 **k** in the midst of My people
Ezek 43:11 make **k** to them the design of
Dan 2: 5 do not make **k** the dream to me
Dan 2: 9 do not make **k** the dream to me
Dan 2:15 made the decision **k** to Daniel
Dan 2:17 the decision **k** to Hananiah
Dan 2:23 have now made **k** to me what we
Dan 2:23 for You have made **k** to us the
Dan 2:25 who will make **k** to the king
Dan 2:26 Are you able to make **k** to me
Dan 2:28 and He has made **k** to King
Dan 2:29 made **k** to you what will be
Dan 2:30 **k** the interpretation to the
Dan 2:45 the great God has made **k** to
Dan 3:18 if not, let it be **k** to you
Dan 4: 6 that they might make **k** to me
Dan 4: 7 but they did not make **k** to me
Dan 4:18 are not able to make **k** to me
Dan 5: 8 or make **k** to the king its
Dan 5:15 writing and make **k** to me its
Dan 5:16 writing and make **k** to me its
Dan 5:17 king, and make **k** to him the
Dan 7:16 told me and made **k** to me the
Dan 8:19 I am making **k** to you what
Hos 5: 9 Israel I make **k** what is sure
Amos 3: 2 You only have I **k** of all the
Nah 3:17 place where they are is not **k**
Hab 3: 2 midst of the years make it **k**
Zech 7:14 nations which they had not **k**
Zech 14: 7 day which is **k** to the LORD
Matt 10:26 and hidden that will not be **k**
Matt 12: 7 But if you had **k** what this
Matt 12:16 warned them not to make Him **k**
Matt 12:33 for a tree is **k** by its fruit
Matt 24:43 **k** what hour the thief would
Mark 3:12 they should not make Him **k**
Luke 2:15 the Lord has made **k** to us
Luke 2:17 they made widely **k** the saying
Luke 6:44 tree is **k** by its own fruit
Luke 8:17 hidden that will not be **k**
Luke 12: 2 nor hidden that will not be **k**
Luke 12:39 **k** what hour the thief would
Luke 19:42 If you had **k**, even you,
Luke 24:18 have You not **k** the things
Luke 24:35 how He was **k** to them in the
John 7: 4 himself seeks to be **k** openly
John 8:19 If you had **k** Me, you would
John 8:19 would have **k** My Father also
John 8:55 Yet you have not **k** Him, but I
John 10:14 My sheep, and am **k** by My own
John 14: 7 If you had **k** Me, you would
John 14: 7 would have **k** My Father also
John 14: 9 and yet you have not **k** Me
John 15:15 Father I have made **k** to you
John 16: 3 have not **k** the Father nor Me
John 17: 7 Now they have **k** that all
John 17: 8 have **k** surely that I came
John 17:25 The world has not **k** You
John 17:25 but I have **k** You
John 17:25 these have **k** that You sent Me
John 18:15 was **k** to the high priest, and
John 18:16 who was **k** to the high priest,
Acts 1:19 And it became **k** to all those
Acts 2:14 let this be **k** to you, and
Acts 2:28 You have made **k** to me the
Acts 4:10 let it be **k** to you all, and to
Acts 7:13 was made **k** to his brothers
Acts 7:13 became **k** to the Pharaoh
Acts 9:24 their plot became **k** to Saul
Acts 9:42 it became **k** throughout all
Acts 13:38 Therefore let it be **k** to you
Acts 15:18 **K** to God from eternity are
Acts 19:17 This became **k** both to all
Acts 28:28 Therefore let it be **k** to you
Rom 1:19 because what may be **k** of God
Rom 3:17 way of peace they have not **k**
Rom 7: 7 I would not have **k** sin except
Rom 7: 7 For I would not have **k**
Rom 9:22 wrath and to make His power **k**
Rom 9:23 and that He might make **k** the
Rom 11:34 For who has **k** the mind of the
Rom 16:19 obedience has become **k** to all
Rom 16:26 been made **k** to all nations
1Co 2: 8 for had they **k**, they would
1Co 2:16 Who has **k** the mind of the
1Co 8: 3 God, this one is **k** by Him
1Co 12: 3 Therefore I make **k** to you
1Co 13:12 know just as I also am **k**
1Co 14: 7 how will it be **k** what is
1Co 14: 9 will it be **k** what is spoken
2Co 3: 2 written in our hearts, **k** and
2Co 5:16 Even though we have **k** Christ
2Co 8: 1 we make **k** to you the grace of
Gal 1:11 But I make **k** to you, brethren
Gal 4: 9 But now after you have **k** God
Gal 4: 9 God, or rather are **k** by God
Eph 1: 9 having made **k** to us the
Eph 3: 3 **k** to me the mystery (as I
Eph 3: 5 not made **k** to the sons of men
Eph 3:10 made **k** by the church to the
Eph 6:19 my mouth boldly to make **k** the
Eph 6:21 will make all things **k** to you
Phil 4: 5 gentleness be **k** to all men
Phil 4: 6 requests be made **k** to God
Col 1:27 **k** what are the riches of the
Col 4: 9 They will make **k** to you all
2Ti 3:15 have **k** the Holy Scriptures
Heb 3:10 and they have not **k** My ways
2Pe 1:16 we made **k** to you the power
2Pe 2:21 **k** the way of righteousness
2Pe 2:21 than having **k** it, to turn
1Jn 2:13 because you have **k** Him who is
1Jn 2:13 because you have **k** the Father
1Jn 2:14 because you have **k** Him who is
1Jn 3: 6 neither seen Him nor **k** Him
1Jn 4:16 And we have **k** and believed the
2Jn 1 those who have **k** the truth
Rev 2:24 who have not **k** the depths of

KNOWS (*see* KNOW)
Gen 3: 5 For God **k** that in the day you
Gen 33:13 My lord **k** that the children
Num 24:16 **k** the knowledge of the Most
Deut 2: 7 He **k** your trudging through
Deut 34: 6 but no one **k** his grave to
Josh 22:22 the LORD God of gods, He **k**
1Sa 3:13 for the iniquity which he **k**
1Sa 20: 3 Your father certainly **k** that
1Sa 23:17 Even my father Saul **k** that
2Sa 14:22 Today your servant **k** that I
2Sa 17:10 For all Israel **k** that your
1Ki 8:38 when each one **k** the plague of
2Ch 6:29 when each one **k** his own
Esth 4:14 Yet who **k** whether you have
Job 11:11 For He **k** deceitful men
Job 15:23 He **k** that a day of darkness
Job 20:20 Because he **k** no quietness in
Job 23:10 But He **k** the way that I take
Job 28: 7 That path no bird **k**, nor has
Job 28:23 its way, and He **k** its place
Job 34:25 Therefore he **k** their works
Ps 1: 6 For the LORD **k** the way of the
Ps 37:18 The LORD **k** the days of the
Ps 44:21 For He **k** the secrets of the
Ps 74: 9 any among us who **k** how long
Ps 90:11 Who **k** the power of Your anger
Ps 94:11 The LORD **k** the thoughts of
Ps 103:14 For He **k** our frame
Ps 104:19 The sun **k** its going down
Ps 138: 6 But the proud He **k** from afar
Ps 139:14 And that my soul **k** very well
Prov 9:13 she is simple, and **k** nothing
Prov 14:10 The heart **k** its own
Prov 24:22 who **k** the ruin those two can
Eccl 2:19 who **k** whether he will be a
Eccl 3:21 Who **k** the spirit of the sons
Eccl 6: 8 who **k** how to walk before the
Eccl 6:12 For who **k** what is good for
Eccl 8: 1 who **k** the interpretation of a
Eccl 10:14 No man **k** what is to be

Is 1: 3 the ox **k** its owner And the
Is 29:15 Who **k** us?
Jer 8: 7 heavens **k** her appointed times
Jer 9:24 **k** Me, that I am the LORD,
Dan 2:22 He **k** what is in the darkness,
Hos 9: 7 Israel **k**!
Joel 2:14 Who **k** if He will turn and
Nah 1: 7 He **k** those who trust in Him
Zeph 3: 5 But the unjust **k** no shame
Matt 6: 8 For your Father **k** the things
Matt 6:32 **k** that you need all these
Matt 9:30 See that no one **k** it
Matt 11:27 no one **k** the Son except the
Matt 24:36 of that day and hour no one **k**
Mark 13:32 of that day and hour no one **k**
Luke 10:22 no one **k** who the Son is but
Luke 12:30 your Father **k** that you need
Luke 16:15 men, but God **k** your hearts
John 7:27 no one **k** where He is from
John 7:51 him and **k** what he is doing
John 10:15 As the Father **k** Me, even so I
John 14:17 it neither sees Him nor **k** Him
John 19:35 he **k** that he is telling the
Acts 15: 8 who **k** the heart, acknowledged
Acts 26:26 speak freely, **k** these things
Rom 8:27 He who searches the hearts **k**
1Co 2:11 For what man **k** the things of
1Co 2:11 Even so no one **k** the things
1Co 3:20 The LORD **k** the thoughts of
1Co 8: 2 thinks that he **k** anything
1Co 8: 2 he **k** nothing yet as he ought
2Co 11:11 God **k**!
2Co 11:31 **k** that I am not lying
2Co 12: 2 the body I do not know, God **k**
2Co 12: 3 the body I do not know, God **k**
2Ti 2:19 The Lord **k** those who are His,
Jas 4:17 to him who **k** to do good and
2Pe 2: 9 then the Lord **k** how to
1Jn 3:20 our heart, and **k** all things
1Jn 4: 6 He who **k** God hears us
1Jn 4: 7 loves is born of God and **k** God
Rev 2:17 name written which no one **k**
Rev 12:12 because he **k** that he has a

KOA
Ezek 23:23 the Chaldeans, Pekod, Shoa, **K**

KOHATH (*see* KOHATHITES)
Gen 46:11 sons of Levi were Gershon, **K**
Ex 6:16 Gershon, **K**, and Merari
Ex 6:18 And the sons of **K** were Amram
Ex 6:18 life of **K** were one hundred
Num 3:17 Gershon, **K**, and Merari
Num 3:19 And the sons of **K** by their
Num 3:27 From **K** came the family of the
Num 3:29 **K** were to camp on the south
Num 4: 2 a census of the sons of **K**
Num 4: 4 of **K** in the tabernacle of
Num 4:15 then the sons of **K** shall come
Num 4:15 the sons of **K** are to carry
Num 7: 9 to the sons of **K** he gave none
Num 16: 1 son of Izhar, the son of **K**
Num 26:57 of **K**, the family of the
Num 26:58 And **K** begot Amram
Josh 21: 5 **K** had ten cities by lot from
Josh 21:20 families of the children of **K**
Josh 21:20 the rest of the children of **K**
Josh 21:26 families of the children of **K**
1Ch 6: 1 sons of Levi were Gershon, **K**
1Ch 6: 2 The sons of **K** were Amram,
1Ch 6:16 sons of Levi were Gershon, **K**
1Ch 6:18 The sons of **K** were Amram,
1Ch 6:22 The sons of **K** were Amminadab
1Ch 6:38 son of Izhar, the son of **K**
1Ch 6:66 **K** were given cities as their
1Ch 6:70 the family of the sons of **K**
1Ch 15: 5 of the sons of **K**, Uriel the
1Ch 23: 6 Gershon, **K**, and Merari
1Ch 23:12 The sons of **K**

KOHATHITES (*see* KOHATH)
Num 3:27 were the families of the **K**
Num 3:30 of the families of the **K** was
Num 4:18 the **K** from among the Levites
Num 4:34 of the **K** by their families
Num 4:37 of the families of the **K**, all
Num 10:21 Then the **K** set out, carrying
Num 26:57 Kohath, the family of the **K**
Josh 21: 4 out for the families of the **K**
Josh 21:10 one of the families of the **K**
1Ch 6:33 Of the sons of the **K** were
1Ch 6:54 Aaron, of the family of the **K**
1Ch 6:61 family of the tribe of the **K**
1Ch 9:32 **K** were in charge of preparing
2Ch 20:19 of the children of the **K** and
2Ch 29:12 Azariah, of the sons of the **K**
2Ch 34:12 of the sons of the **K**, to

KOLAIAH
Neh 11: 7 son of Pedaiah, the son of **K**
Jer 29:21 concerning Ahab the son of **K**

KOR (*see* KORS)
Ezek 45:14 one-tenth of a bath from a **k**
Ezek 45:14 A **k** is a homer or ten baths,

KORAH (*see* KORAHITE, KORE)
Gen 36: 5 bore Jeush, Jaalam, and **K**
Gen 36:14 Jeush, Jaalam, and **K**
Gen 36:16 Chief **K**, Chief Gatam, and
Gen 36:18 Chief Jaalam, and Chief **K**
Ex 6:21 The sons of Izhar were **K**,
Ex 6:24 And the sons of **K** were Assir
Num 16: 1 Now **K** the son of Izhar, the
Num 16: 5 and he spoke to **K** and all his
Num 16: 6 Take censers, **K** and all your
Num 16: 8 Then Moses said to **K**, "Hear
Num 16:16 And Moses said to **K**
Num 16:19 And **K** gathered all the
Num 16:24 Get away from the tents of **K**
Num 16:27 from around the tents of **K**
Num 16:32 and all the men with **K**, with
Num 16:40 he might not become like **K**
Num 16:49 who died in the **K** incident
Num 26: 9 and Aaron in the company of **K**
Num 26:10 them up together with **K** when
Num 26:11 the children of **K** did not die
Num 27: 3 the LORD, in company with **K**
1Ch 1:35 Reuel, Jeush, Jaalam, and **K**
1Ch 2:43 The sons of Hebron were **K**
1Ch 6:22 **K** his son, Assir his son,
1Ch 6:37 son of Ebiasaph, the son of **K**
1Ch 9:19 son of Ebiasaph, the son of **K**
1Ch 26:19 among the sons of **K** and among
Jude 11 in the rebellion of **K**

KORAHITE (*see* KORAH, KORAHITES, KORE)
1Ch 9:31 firstborn of Shallum the **K**

KORAHITES (*see* KORAHITE)
Ex 6:24 are the families of the **K**
1Ch 9:19 his father's house, the **K**
1Ch 12: 6 Joezer, and Jashobeam, the **K**
1Ch 26: 1 of the **K**, Meshelemiah the son
2Ch 20:19 and of the children of the **K**

KORATHITES
Num 26:58 and the family of the **K**

KORE (*see* KORAH, KORAHITE)
1Ch 9:19 Shallum the son of **K**, the son
1Ch 26: 1 Meshelemiah the son of **K**
2Ch 31:14 **K** the son of Imnah the Levite

KORS (*see* KOR)
1Ki 4:22 was thirty **k** of fine flour
1Ki 4:22 fine flour, sixty **k** of meal,
1Ki 5:11 **k** of wheat as food for his
1Ki 5:11 and twenty **k** of pressed oil
2Ch 2:10 thousand **k** of ground wheat
2Ch 2:10 twenty thousand **k** of barley
2Ch 27: 5 ten thousand **k** of wheat, and
Ezra 7:22 one hundred **k** of wheat, one

KOZ (*see* HAKKOZ)
1Ch 4: 8 **K** begot Anub, Zobebah, and
Ezra 2:61 of Habaiah, the sons of **K**
Neh 3: 4 son of Urijah, the son of **K**
Neh 3:21 son of Urijah, the son of **K**
Neh 7:63 of Habaiah, the children of **K**

KUSHAIAH (*see* KISHI)
1Ch 15:17 of Merari, Ethan the son of **K**

L

LAADAH
1Ch 4:21 **L** the father of Mareshah, and

LAADAN (*see* LIBNI)
1Ch 7:26 **L** his son, Ammihud his son,
1Ch 23: 7 **L** and Shimei
1Ch 23: 8 The sons of **L**
1Ch 23: 9 of the fathers' houses of **L**
1Ch 26:21 The sons of **L**, the
1Ch 26:21 of the Gershonites of **L**,
1Ch 26:21 houses, of **L** the Gershonite

LABAN (*see* LABAN'S, LIBNAH)
Gen 24:29 a brother whose name was **L**
Gen 24:29 **L** ran out to the man by the
Gen 24:50 Then **L** and Bethuel answered
Gen 25:20 the sister of **L** the Syrian
Gen 27:43 flee to my brother **L** in Haran
Gen 28: 2 of **L** your mother's brother
Gen 28: 5 to **L** the son of Bethuel the
Gen 29: 5 Do you know **L** the son of
Gen 29:10 of **L** his mother's brother
Gen 29:10 the sheep of **L** his mother's
Gen 29:10 of **L** his mother's brother
Gen 29:13 when **L** heard the report about
Gen 29:13 So he told **L** all these things
Gen 29:14 **L** said to him, Surely you
Gen 29:15 Then **L** said to Jacob
Gen 29:16 Now **L** had two daughters
Gen 29:19 **L** said, "It is better
Gen 29:21 Then Jacob said to **L**, "Give
Gen 29:22 **L** gathered together all the
Gen 29:24 **L** gave his maid Zilpah to his
Gen 29:25 And he said to **L**, "What is
Gen 29:26 **L** said, "It must not be done
Gen 29:29 **L** gave his maid Bilhah to his
Gen 29:30 And he served with **L** still
Gen 30:25 Joseph, that Jacob said to **L**
Gen 30:27 **L** said to him, "Please stay,
Gen 30:34 **L** said, "Oh, that it were
Gen 30:40 the brown in the flock of **L**
Gen 31: 2 saw the countenance of **L**, and
Gen 31:12 all that **L** is doing to you
Gen 31:19 Now **L** had gone to shear his
Gen 31:20 away, unknown to **L** the Syrian
Gen 31:22 **L** was told on the third day
Gen 31:24 But God had come to **L** the
Gen 31:25 So **L** overtook Jacob
Gen 31:25 **L** with his brethren pitched
Gen 31:26 And **L** said to Jacob
Gen 31:31 Jacob answered and said to **L**
Gen 31:33 **L** went into Jacob's tent,
Gen 31:34 **L** searched all about the tent
Gen 31:36 Jacob was angry and rebuked **L**
Gen 31:36 Jacob answered and said to **L**
Gen 31:43 **L** answered and said to Jacob,
Gen 31:47 **L** called it Jegar Sahadutha,
Gen 31:48 And **L** said, "This heap is
Gen 31:51 Then **L** said to Jacob, "Here
Gen 31:55 early in the morning **L** arose
Gen 31:55 Then **L** departed and returned
Gen 32: 4 I have sojourned with **L** and
Gen 46:18 whom **L** gave to Leah his
Gen 46:25 whom **L** gave to Rachel his
Deut 1: 1 between Paran, Tophel, **L**

LABAN'S (*see* LABAN)
Gen 30:36 fed the rest of **L** flocks
Gen 30:40 did not put them with **L** flock
Gen 30:42 so the feebler were **L** and the
Gen 31: 1 heard the words of **L** sons

LABOR (*see* LABORED, LABORER, LABORING, LABORS)
Gen 31:42 the **l** of my hands, and rebuked
Gen 35:16 childbirth, and she had hard **l**
Gen 35:17 pass, when she was in hard **l**
Ex 5: 4 Get back to your **l**
Ex 5: 5 make them rest from their **l**
Ex 5: 9 men, that they may **l** in it
Ex 20: 9 Six days you shall **l** and do
Deut 5:13 Six days you shall **l** and do
Deut 26: 7 on our affliction and our **l**
Deut 28:33 land and the produce of your **l**
Josh 17:13 the Canaanites to forced **l**
Josh 24:13 land for which you did not **l**
1Sa 4:19 for her **l** pains came upon her
1Ki 4: 6 son of Abda, over the **l** force
1Ki 5:13 a **l** force out of all Israel
1Ki 5:13 and the **l** force was thirty
1Ki 5:14 was in charge of the **l** force
1Ki 9:15 **l** force which King Solomon
1Ki 9:21 these Solomon raised forced **l**
1Ki 11:28 the **l** force of the house of
2Ch 8: 8 these Solomon raised forced **l**
Job 9:29 why then do I **l** in vain
Job 39:11 will you leave your **l** to him
Job 39:16 her **l** is in vain, without
Ps 78:46 And their **l** to the locust
Ps 90:10 Yet their boast is only **l**

Ps 104:23 to his l until the evening
Ps 105:44 the l of the nations,
Ps 107:12 down their heart with l
Ps 109:11 let strangers plunder his l
Ps 127: 1 They l in vain who build it
Ps 128: 2 you eat the l of your hands
Prov 10:16 The l of the righteous leads
Prov 12:24 will be put to forced l
Prov 13:11 gathers by l will increase
Prov 14:23 In all l there is profit, but
Prov 21:25 for his hands refuse to l
Eccl 1: 3 has a man from all his l in
Eccl 1: 8 All things are full of l
Eccl 2:10 my heart rejoiced in all my l
Eccl 2:10 was my reward from all my l
Eccl 2:11 and on the l in which I had
Eccl 2:18 Then I hated all my l in
Eccl 2:19 all my l in which I toiled
Eccl 2:20 despaired of all the l in
Eccl 2:21 a man whose l is with wisdom
Eccl 2:22 what has man for all his l
Eccl 2:24 should enjoy good in his l
Eccl 3:13 enjoy the good of all his l
Eccl 4: 9 a good reward for their l
Eccl 5:15 l which he may carry away in
Eccl 5:18 enjoy the good of all his l
Eccl 5:19 heritage and rejoice in his l
Eccl 6: 7 All the l of man is for his
Eccl 8:15 l for the days of his life
Eccl 9: 9 in the l which you perform
Eccl 10:15 The l of fools wearies them,
Is 21: 3 the pangs of a woman in l
Is 22: 4 do not l to comfort me
Is 23: 4 I do not l, nor bring forth
Is 31: 8 men shall become forced l
Is 42:14 I will cry like a woman in l
Is 45:14 The l of Egypt and merchandise
Is 65:23 They shall not l in vain, nor
Jer 3:24 the l of our fathers from our
Jer 4:31 a voice as of a woman in l
Jer 6:24 us, pain as of a woman in l
Jer 13:21 seize you, like a woman in l
Jer 20:18 forth from the womb to see l
Jer 22:23 like the pain of a woman in l
Jer 30: 6 a man is ever in l with child
Jer 30: 6 his loins like a woman in l
Jer 49:24 taken her like a woman in l
Jer 51:58 the people will l in vain
Lam 5: 5 we l and have no rest
Ezek 29:18 to l strenuously against Tyre
Ezek 29:18 for the l which they expended
Ezek 29:20 the land of Egypt for his l
Mic 4: 9 seized you like a woman in l
Mic 4:10 l to bring forth, O daughter
Mic 5: 3 who is in l has given birth
Hab 2:13 peoples l to feed the fire
Hab 3:17 though the l of the olive may
Hag 1:11 on all the l of your hands
Matt 11:28 Come to Me, all you who l
John 6:27 Do not l for the food which
John 16:21 A woman, when she is in l
1Co 3: 8 reward according to his own l
1Co 4:12 And we l, working with our own
1Co 15:58 knowing that your l is not in
Gal 4:19 for whom I l in birth again
Eph 4:28 longer, but rather let him l
Phil 1:22 will mean fruit from my l
Col 1:29 To this end I also l,
1Th 1: 3 l of love, and patience of
1Th 2: 9 you remember, brethren, our l
1Th 3: 5 and our l might be in vain
1Th 5: 3 as l pains upon a pregnant
1Th 5:12 those who l among you, and are
2Th 3: 8 of charge, but worked with l
1Ti 4:10 For to this end we both l
1Ti 5:17 those who l in the word and
Heb 6:10 and l of love which you have
Rev 2: 2 I know your works, your l
Rev 12: 2 child, she cried out in l

LABORED (*see* LABOR)
1Ki 5:16 the people who l in the work
2Ch 24:13 So the workmen l, and the work
Neh 4:21 So we l in the work, and half
Job 20:18 restore that for which he l
Eccl 2:21 to a man who has not l for it
Eccl 5:16 has he who has l for the wind
Is 47:12 you have l from your youth
Is 47:15 to you with whom you have l
Is 49: 4 I said, 'I have l in vain
Is 62: 8 wine, for which you have l
Dan 6:14 he l till the going down of
Jon 4:10 for which you have not l, nor
John 4:38 that for which you have not l
John 4:38 others have l, and you have
Rom 16: 6 Greet Mary, who l much for us
Rom 16:12 who have l in the Lord
Rom 16:12 who l much in the Lord
1Co 15:10 but I l more abundantly than
Gal 4:11 lest I have l for you in vain
Phil 2:16 not run in vain or l in vain
Phil 4: 3 help these women who l with
Rev 2: 3 have l for My name's sake and

LABORER (*see* LABOR, LABORERS)
Luke 10: 7 for the l is worthy of his
1Th 3: 2 our fellow l in the gospel of
1Ti 5:18 The l is worthy of his wages
Phm 1 beloved friend and fellow l

LABORERS (*see* LABORER)
Josh 16:10 day and have become forced l
1Ki 9:22 Solomon made no forced l,
Neh 4:10 strength of the l is failing
Is 58: 3 and exploit all your l
Matt 9:37 plentiful, but the l are few
Matt 9:38 send out l into His harvest
Matt 20: 1 to hire l for his vineyard
Matt 20: 2 the l for a denarius a day
Matt 20: 8 to his steward, 'Call the l
Luke 10: 2 is great, but the l are few
Luke 10: 2 send out l into His harvest
Phm 24 Demas, Luke, my fellow l
Jas 5: 4 the l who mowed your fields

LABORING (*see* LABOR)
Eccl 5:12 The sleep of a l man is sweet
Acts 20:35 by l like this, that you must
Col 4:12 always l fervently for you in
1Th 2: 9 for l night and day, that we

LABORS (*see* LABOR)
Ex 23:16 the firstfruits of your l
Ex 23:16 of your l from the field
Prov 5:10 your l go to the house of a
Prov 16:26 The person who l, l for
Prov 16:26 l for himself, for his hungry
Eccl 3: 9 from that in which he l
Eccl 4: 8 there is no end to all his l
Eccl 8:17 though a man l to discover it
Jer 31: 8 and the one who l with child
Hos 12: 8 in all my l they shall find
Hag 2:17 in all the l of your hands
John 4:38 you have entered into their l
Rom 8:22 l with birth pangs together
1Co 16:16 who works and l with us
2Co 6: 5 in tumults, in l, in
2Co 10:15 that is, in other men's l
2Co 11:23 in l more abundant, in
Rev 14:13 they may rest from their l

LACHISH
Josh 10: 3 of Jarmuth, Japhia king of L
Josh 10: 5 of Jarmuth, the king of L
Josh 10:23 of Jarmuth, the king of L
Josh 10:31 and all Israel with him, to L
Josh 10:32 the LORD delivered L into the
Josh 10:33 of Gezer came up to help L
Josh 10:34 From L Joshua passed to Eglon
Josh 10:35 to all that he had done to L
Josh 12:11 the king of L, one
Josh 15:39 L, Bozkath, Eglon,
2Ki 14:19 in Jerusalem, and he fled to L
2Ki 14:19 but they sent after him to L
2Ki 18:14 to the king of Assyria at L
2Ki 18:17 and the Rabshakeh from L,
2Ki 19: 8 that he had departed from L
2Ch 11: 9 Adoraim, L, Azekah,
2Ch 25:27 in Jerusalem, and he fled to L
2Ch 25:27 but they sent after him to L
2Ch 32: 9 him, laid siege against L)
Neh 11:30 in L and its fields
Is 36: 2 from L to King Hezekiah at
Is 37: 8 that he had departed from L
Jer 34: 7 that were left, against L
Mic 1:13 O inhabitant of L, harness

LACK (*see* LACKED, LACKING, LACKS)
Gen 18:28 all of the city for l of five
Ex 16:18 who gathered little had no l
Deut 8: 9 in which you will l nothing
Deut 28:57 l of all things in the siege
Judg 18:10 a place where there is no l
Judg 19:19 there is no l of anything
1Ki 2: 4 you shall not l a man on the
1Ki 4:27 There was no l in their
Job 4:11 lion perishes for l of prey
Job 31:19 perish for l of clothing, or
Job 38:41 and wander about for l of food
Ps 34:10 The young lions l and suffer
Ps 34:10 shall not l any good thing
Ps 109:24 is feeble from l of fatness
Prov 5:23 die for l of instruction, and
Prov 10:21 but fools die for l of wisdom
Prov 13:23 for l of justice there is
Prov 14:28 but in the l of people is the
Prov 28:27 gives to the poor will not l
Prov 31:11 so he will have no l of gain
Eccl 9: 8 and let your head l no oil
Is 34:16 not one shall l her mate
Jer 33:17 David shall never l a man to
Jer 33:18 l a man to offer burnt
Jer 35:19 l a man to stand before Me
Lam 4: 9 stricken for l of the fruits
Ezek 4:17 that they may l bread and
Hos 4: 6 destroyed for l of knowledge
Amos 4: 6 l of bread in all your places
Matt 19:20 What do I still l
Mark 10:21 One thing you l
Luke 18:22 You still l one thing
Luke 22:35 sandals, did you l anything
1Co 7: 5 of your l of self-control
2Co 8:14 abundance may supply their l
2Co 8:14 also may supply your l
2Co 8:15 who gathered little had no l
1Th 4:12 and that you may l nothing
Tit 3:13 that they may l nothing

LACKED (*see* LACK)
Deut 2: 7 you have l nothing
1Ki 11:22 But what have you l with me
Neh 9:21 so that they l nothing
Jer 44:18 we have l everything and have
Luke 8: 6 away because it l moisture
Acts 4:34 there anyone among them who l
Phil 4:10 care, but you l opportunity

LACKING (*see* LACK)
Lev 2:13 be l from your grain offering
1Sa 30:19 And nothing of theirs was l
Prov 10:19 of words sin is not l, but he
Eccl 1:15 what is l cannot be numbered
Jer 23: 4 dismayed, nor shall they be l
Jer 47: 3 their children, l courage,
1Co 16:17 for what was l on your part
2Co 11: 9 one, for what was l to me the
Phil 2:30 to supply what was l in your
Col 1:24 is l in the afflictions of
1Th 3:10 what is l in your faith
Tit 1: 5 order the things that are l
Jas 1: 4 and complete, l nothing

LACKS (*see* LACK)
2Sa 3:29 by the sword, or who l bread
Prov 6:32 with a woman l understanding
Prov 9: 4 for him who l understanding
Prov 9:16 for him who l understanding
Prov 11:22 lovely woman who l discretion
Prov 12: 9 honors himself but l bread
Prov 28:16 A ruler who l understanding
Eccl 6: 2 so that he l nothing for
Eccl 10: 3 way, he l wisdom, and he shows
Song 7: 2 which l no blended beverage
1Co 12:24 honor to that part which l it
Jas 1: 5 If any of you l wisdom, let
2Pe 1: 9 For he who l these things is

LAD (*see* LAD'S, LADS)
Gen 21:12 of the l or because of your
Gen 21:17 God heard the voice of the l
Gen 21:17 voice of the l where he is
Gen 21:18 Arise, lift up the l and hold
Gen 21:19 water, and gave the l a drink
Gen 21:20 So God was with the l
Gen 22: 5 the l and I will go yonder and
Gen 22:12 Do not lay your hand on the l
Gen 37: 2 the l was with the sons of
Gen 37:30 and said, "The l is no more
Gen 43: 8 Send the l with me, and we
Gen 44:22 lord, 'The l cannot leave his
Gen 44:30 the l is not with us, since
Gen 44:31 that the l is not with us
Gen 44:32 surety for the l to my father
Gen 44:33 the l as a slave to my lord
Gen 44:33 and let the l go up with his
Gen 44:34 if the l is not with me, lest

Judg 16:26 Then Samson said to the l who
1Sa 20:21 and there I will send a l,
1Sa 20:35 and a little l was with him
1Sa 20:36 Then he said to his l, "Now
1Sa 20:36 As the l ran, he shot an
1Sa 20:37 When the l had come to the
1Sa 20:37 cried out after the l and said
1Sa 20:38 cried out after the l, "Make
1Sa 20:38 So Jonathan's l gathered up
1Sa 20:39 But the l did not know
1Sa 20:40 gave his weapons to his l
1Sa 20:41 Now as soon as the l had gone
2Sa 17:18 Nevertheless a l saw them
John 6: 9 There is a l here who has

LADDER
Gen 28:12 a l was set up on the earth,

LADEN (*see* WELL-LADEN)
Is 1: 4 a people l with iniquity, a
Matt 11:28 you who labor and are heavy l

LADIES (*see* LADY)
Judg 5:29 Her wisest l answered her,
Esth 1:18 day the noble l of Persia

LADLES
1Ki 7:50 trimmers, the bowls, the l
2Ch 4:22 trimmers, the bowls, the l

LAD'S (*see* LAD)
Gen 44:30 is bound up in the l life

LADS (*see* LAD)
Gen 48:16 me from all evil, bless the l
Jer 14: 3 have sent their l for water

LADY (*see* LADIES)
Is 47: 5 be called the L of Kingdoms
Is 47: 7 said, I shall be a l forever
2Jn 1 THE ELDER, To the elect l
2Jn 5 And now I plead with you, l

LAEL
Num 3:24 was Eliasaph the son of L

LAGGING
Rom 12:11 not l in diligence, fervent

LAHAD
1Ch 4: 2 and Jahath begot Ahumai and L

LAHAI ROI (*see* BEER LAHAI ROI)
Gen 16:14 the well was called Beer L
Gen 24:62 came from the way of Beer L
Gen 25:11 And Isaac dwelt at Beer L

LAHMAS
Josh 15:40 Cabbon, L, Kithlish,

LAHMI (*see* BETHLEHEMITE)
1Ch 20: 5 the son of Jair killed L the

LAID (*see* LAY)
Gen 9:23 l it on both their shoulders,
Gen 22: 6 and l it on Isaac his son
Gen 22: 9 l him on the altar, upon the
Gen 38:19 l aside her veil and put on
Gen 41:48 l up the food in the cities
Gen 41:48 he l up in every city the
Gen 48:14 l it on Ephraim's head, who
Gen 48:17 l his right hand on the head
Ex 2: 3 and l it in the reeds by the
Ex 5: 9 Let more work be l on the men
Ex 16:24 So they l it up till morning,
Ex 16:34 so Aaron l it up before the
Ex 19: 7 l before them all these words
Lev 8:14 his sons l their hands on the
Lev 8:18 his sons l their hands on the
Lev 8:22 his sons l their hands on the
Num 11:11 that You have l the burden of
Num 16:18 l incense on it, and stood at
Num 21:30 Then we l waste as far as
Num 27:23 And he l his hands on him and
Deut 26: 6 us, and l hard bondage on us
Deut 29:22 which the LORD has l on it
Deut 32:34 Is this not l up in store
Deut 34: 9 for Moses had l his hands on
Josh 2: 6 which she had l in order on
Josh 2:19 head if a hand is l on him
Josh 4: 8 lodged, and l them down there
Josh 7:23 l them out before the LORD
Josh 10:27 l large stones against the
Judg 9:24 their blood be l on Abimelech
Judg 9:34 l in wait against Shechem in
Judg 9:43 and l in wait in the field
Judg 9:48 it and l it on his shoulder
Judg 19:29 l hold of his concubine, and
Ruth 3:15 of barley, and l it on her
Ruth 4:16 l him on her bosom, and became
1Sa 10:25 and l it up before the LORD
1Sa 15: 2 how he l wait for him on the
1Sa 19:13 l it in the bed, put a cover
2Sa 13:19 l her hand on her head and
2Sa 18:17 l a very large heap of stones
1Ki 3:20 l him in her bosom
1Ki 3:20 l her dead child in my bosom
1Ki 6:37 the house of the LORD was l
1Ki 12:11 whereas my father l a heavy
1Ki 13:29 God, l it on the donkey, and
1Ki 13:30 Then he l the corpse in his
1Ki 15:27 and all Israel l siege to
1Ki 16:34 He l its foundation with
1Ki 17:19 and l him on his own bed
1Ki 18:33 l it on the wood, and said,
2Ki 4:21 l him on the bed of the man
2Ki 4:31 l the staff on the face of
2Ki 9:16 for Joram was l up there
2Ki 9:25 that the LORD l this burden
2Ki 19:17 have l waste the nations and
2Ki 20: 7 and l it on the boil, and he
2Ch 3: 3 foundation which Solomon l
2Ch 16:14 they l him in the bed which
2Ch 29:23 they l their hands on them
2Ch 31: 6 their God they l in heaps
2Ch 32: 9 l siege against Lachish), to
Ezra 3: 6 the LORD had not yet been l
Ezra 3:10 When the builders l the
Ezra 3:11 the house of the LORD was l
Ezra 3:12 was l before their eyes
Ezra 5: 8 is being l in the walls
Ezra 5:16 l the foundation of the house
Ezra 6: 3 foundations of it be firmly l
Neh 3: 3 they l its beams and hung its
Neh 3: 6 they l its beams and hung its
Neh 5:15 me l burdens on the people
Job 6: 2 my calamity l with it in the
Job 14:10 But man dies and is l away
Job 16:15 and l my head in the dust
Job 38: 4 Where were you when I l the
Job 38: 6 Or who l its cornerstone,
Ps 31: 4 they have secretly l for me
Ps 31:19 Which You have l up for those
Ps 49:14 sheep they are l in the grave
Ps 66:11 You l affliction on our backs
Ps 79: 1 They have l Jerusalem in
Ps 79: 7 l waste his dwelling place
Ps 88: 6 You have l me in the lowest
Ps 102:25 Of old You l the foundation
Ps 104: 5 You who l the foundations of
Ps 105:18 fetters, He was l in irons
Ps 116: 3 pangs of Sheol l hold of me
Ps 119:30 judgments I have l before me
Ps 119:110 wicked have l a snare for me
Ps 136: 6 To Him who l out the earth
Ps 139: 5 And l Your hand upon me
Ps 141: 9 which they have l for me, And
Song 7:13 which I have l up for you
Is 6:11 Until the cities are l waste
Is 15: 1 night Ar of Moab is l waste
Is 15: 1 night Kir of Moab is l waste
Is 15: 7 and what they have l up, they
Is 23: 1 For it is l waste, so that
Is 23:14 for your strength is l waste
Is 23:18 not be treasured nor l up
Is 37:18 have l waste all the nations
Is 44:28 Your foundation shall be l
Is 47: 6 on the elderly you l your
Is 48:13 Indeed My hand has l the
Is 49:17 those who l you waste shall
Is 51:13 and l the foundations of the
Is 51:23 you have l your body like the
Is 53: 6 the LORD has l on Him the
Is 64:11 pleasant things are l waste
Jer 4: 7 Your cities will be l waste
Jer 27:17 should this city be l waste
Jer 50:23 I have l a snare for you
Lam 3:28 because God has l it on him
Ezek 4: 5 For I have l on you the years
Ezek 4: 6 I have l on you a day for
Ezek 6: 6 the cities shall be l waste
Ezek 6: 6 your altars may be l waste
Ezek 11: 7 whom you have l in its midst
Ezek 12:20 inhabited shall be l waste
Ezek 19: 7 and l waste their cities
Ezek 26: 2 she is l waste
Ezek 28:17 I l you before kings, that
Ezek 29:12 the cities that are l waste
Ezek 30: 7 the cities that are l waste
Ezek 32:27 they have l their swords
Ezek 32:29 l beside those who were slain
Ezek 39:21 hand which I have l on them
Ezek 40:42 on these they l the
Dan 6:17 l on the mouth of the den, and
Joel 1: 7 He has l waste My vine, and
Amos 7: 9 of Israel shall be l waste
Obad 13 nor l hands on their
Jon 3: 6 l aside his robe, covered
Mic 5: 1 He has l siege against us
Nah 3: 7 and say, Nineveh is l waste
Hag 2:15 from before stone was l upon
Hag 2:18 of the LORD's temple was l
Zech 3: 9 that I have l before Joshua
Zech 4: 9 have l the foundation of this
Zech 8: 9 l for the house of the LORD
Mal 1: 3 l waste his mountains and his
Matt 3:10 even now the ax is l to the
Matt 14: 3 For Herod had l hold of John
Matt 15:30 they l them down at Jesus'
Matt 18:28 he l hands on him and took him
Matt 19:15 He l His hands on them and
Matt 21: 7 l their clothes on them, and
Matt 26:50 l hands on Jesus and took Him
Matt 26:57 those who had l hold of Jesus
Matt 27:60 l it in his new tomb which he
Mark 6: 5 except that He l His hands on
Mark 6:17 l hold of John, and bound him
Mark 6:29 his corpse and l it in a tomb
Mark 6:56 they l the sick in the
Mark 14:46 Then they l their hands on
Mark 14:51 the young men l hold of him
Mark 15:46 he l Him in a tomb which had
Mark 15:47 Joses observed where He was l
Mark 16: 6 the place where they l Him
Luke 2: 7 l Him in a manger, because
Luke 3: 9 even now the ax is l to the
Luke 4:40 He l His hands on every one
Luke 6:48 l the foundation on the rock
Luke 12:19 goods l up for many years
Luke 13:13 He l His hands on her, and
Luke 14:29 after he has l the foundation
Luke 16:20 sores, who was l at his gate,
Luke 23:26 they l hold of a certain man,
Luke 23:26 on him they l the cross that
Luke 23:53 l it in a tomb that was hewn
Luke 23:55 tomb and how His body was l
John 7:30 but no one l a hand on Him,
John 7:44 but no one l hands on Him
John 8:20 no one l hands on Him, for
John 11:34 Where have you l him
John 13: 4 l aside His garments, took a
John 19:41 which no one had yet been l
John 19:42 So there they l Jesus,
John 20: 2 know where they have l Him
John 20:13 know where they have l Him
John 20:15 tell me where You have l Him
John 21: 9 and fish l on it, and bread
Acts 3: 2 whom they l daily at the gate
Acts 4: 3 they l hands on them, and put
Acts 4:35 l them at the apostles' feet
Acts 4:37 l it at the apostles' feet
Acts 5: 2 l it at the apostles' feet
Acts 5:15 l them on beds and couches,
Acts 5:18 l their hands on the apostles
Acts 6: 6 prayed, they l hands on them
Acts 7:16 l in the tomb that Abraham
Acts 7:58 the witnesses l down their
Acts 8:17 Then they l hands on them, and
Acts 9:37 they l her in an upper room
Acts 13: 3 l hands on them, they sent
Acts 13:29 the tree and l Him in a tomb
Acts 16:23 when they had l many stripes
Acts 19: 6 when Paul had l hands on them
Acts 21:27 crowd and l hands on him,
Acts 25: 7 l many serious complaints
Acts 25:14 Festus l Paul's case before
Acts 28: 3 l them on the fire, a viper
Acts 28: 8 and he l his hands on him and
1Co 3:10 I have l the foundation, and
1Co 3:11 lay than that which is l,
1Co 9:16 for necessity is l upon me
Phil 3:12 Jesus has also l hold of me
Col 1: 5 is l up for you in heaven
2Ti 4: 8 there is l up for me the
Heb 1:10 LORD, in the beginning l the
1Jn 3:16 because He l down His life
Rev 1:17 But He l His right hand on me

Rev 20: 2 He l hold of the dragon, that
Rev 21:16 the city is l out as a square

LAIN (*see* LIE)
Gen 26:10 soon have l with your wife
Num 5:19 If no man has l with you, and
Num 5:20 your husband has l with you"
Job 3:13 For now I would have l still
Jer 3: 2 where have you not l with men
Ezek 23: 8 her youth they had l with her
Jon 1: 5 ship, had l down, and was fast
Luke 23:53 no one had ever l before
John 20:12 where the body of Jesus had l

LAIR (*see* LAIRS)
Jer 25:38 has left his l like the lion

LAIRS (*see* LAIR)
Job 37: 8 dens, and remain in their l
Job 38:40 in their l to lie in wait
Is 32:14 towers will become l forever

LAISH (*see* DAN, LESHEM)
Judg 18: 7 men departed and went to L
Judg 18:14 out the country of L answered
Judg 18:27 belonged to him, and went to L
Judg 18:29 of the city formerly was L
1Sa 25:44 wife, to Palti the son of L
2Sa 3:15 from Paltiel the son of L
Is 10:30 it to be heard as far as L

LAKE
Luke 5: 1 stood by the L of Gennesaret
Luke 5: 2 two boats standing by the l
Luke 8:22 to the other side of the l
Luke 8:23 windstorm came down on the l
Luke 8:33 the steep place into the l
Rev 19:20 the l of fire burning with
Rev 20:10 was cast into the l of fire
Rev 20:14 were cast into the l of fire
Rev 20:15 was cast into the l of fire
Rev 21: 8 the l which burns with fire

LAKKUM
Josh 19:33 and Jabneel, as far as L

LAMA
Matt 27:46 Eli, Eli, l sabachthani
Mark 15:34 Eloi, Eloi, l sabachthani

LAMB (*see* LAMB'S, LAMBS)
Gen 22: 7 but where is the l for a
Gen 22: 8 the l for a burnt offering
Ex 12: 3 shall take for himself a l
Ex 12: 3 father, a l for a household
Ex 12: 4 is too small for the l, let
Ex 12: 4 make your count for the l
Ex 12: 5 Your l shall be without
Ex 12:21 and kill the Passover l
Ex 13:13 you shall redeem with a l
Ex 29:39 One l you shall offer in the
Ex 29:39 the other l you shall offer
Ex 29:40 With the one l shall be
Ex 29:41 the other l you shall offer
Ex 34:20 you shall redeem with a l
Lev 3: 7 he offers a l as his offering
Lev 4:32 If he brings a l as his sin
Lev 4:35 fat, as the fat of the l is
Lev 5: 6 a l or a kid of the goats as
Lev 5: 7 he is not able to bring a l
Lev 9: 3 offering, and a calf and a l
Lev 12: 6 a l of the first year as a
Lev 12: 8 she is not able to bring a l
Lev 14:10 one ewe l of the first year
Lev 14:12 priest shall take one male l
Lev 14:13 Then he shall kill the l in
Lev 14:21 l as a trespass offering to
Lev 14:24 l of the trespass offering
Lev 14:25 Then he shall kill the l of
Lev 17: 3 kills an ox or l or goat in
Lev 22:23 Either a bull or a l that
Lev 23:12 a male l of the first year,
Num 6:12 bring a male l in its first
Num 6:14 one male l in its first year
Num 6:14 one ewe l in its first year
Num 7:15 one male l in its first year,
Num 7:21 one male l in its first year,
Num 7:27 one male l in its first year,
Num 7:33 one male l in its first year,
Num 7:39 one male l in its first year,
Num 7:45 one male l in its first year,
Num 7:51 one male l in its first year,
Num 7:57 one male l in its first year,
Num 7:63 one male l in its first year,
Num 7:69 one male l in its first year,
Num 7:75 one male l in its first year,
Num 7:81 one male l in its first year,
Num 15: 5 or the sacrifice, for each l
Num 15:11 or for each l or young goat
Num 28: 4 The one l you shall offer in
Num 28: 4 the other l you shall offer
Num 28: 7 of a hin for each l
Num 28: 8 The other l you shall offer
Num 28:13 a grain offering for each l
Num 28:14 one-fourth of a hin for a l
1Sa 7: 9 And Samuel took a suckling l
1Sa 17:34 took a l out of the flock,
1Sa 17:35 and delivered the l from its
2Sa 12: 3 ewe l which he had bought
2Sa 12: 4 but he took the poor man's l
2Sa 12: 6 restore fourfold for the l
Is 11: 6 also shall dwell with the l
Is 16: 1 Send the l to the ruler of
Is 53: 7 He was led as a l to the
Is 65:25 the l shall feed together,
Is 66: 3 he who sacrifices a l, as if
Jer 11:19 But I was like a docile l
Ezek 45:15 one l shall be given from a
Ezek 46:13 a l of the first year without
Ezek 46:15 Thus they shall prepare the l
Hos 4:16 like a l in open country
Mark 14:12 they killed the Passover l
John 1:29 The L of God who takes away
John 1:36 Behold the L of God
Acts 8:32 like a l silent before its
1Pe 1:19 as of a l without blemish and
Rev 5: 6 stood a L as though it had
Rev 5: 8 elders fell down before the L
Rev 5:12 Worthy is the L who was slain
Rev 5:13 on the throne, and to the L
Rev 6: 1 Now I saw when the L opened
Rev 6:16 and from the wrath of the L
Rev 7: 9 the throne and before the L
Rev 7:10 on the throne, and to the L
Rev 7:14 white in the blood of the L
Rev 7:17 for the L who is in the midst
Rev 12:11 him by the blood of the L
Rev 13: 8 L slain from the foundation
Rev 13:11 and he had two horns like a l
Rev 14: 1 a L standing on Mount Zion,
Rev 14: 4 follow the L wherever He goes
Rev 14: 4 to God and to the L
Rev 14:10 and in the presence of the L
Rev 15: 3 of God, and the song of the L
Rev 17:14 will make war with the L, and
Rev 17:14 the L will overcome them, for
Rev 19: 7 marriage of the L has come
Rev 19: 9 the marriage supper of the L
Rev 21:14 the twelve apostles of the L
Rev 21:22 and the L are its temple
Rev 21:23 it, and the L is its light
Rev 22: 1 the throne of God and of the L
Rev 22: 3 of the L shall be in it, and

LAMB'S (*see* LAMB)
Rev 21: 9 you the bride, the L wife
Rev 21:27 written in the L Book of Life

LAMBS (*see* LAMB)
Gen 21:28 Abraham set seven ewe l of
Gen 21:29 ewe l which you have set by
Gen 21:30 seven ewe l from my hand,
Gen 30:32 the brown ones among the l
Gen 30:33 goats, and brown among the l
Gen 30:35 the brown ones among the l
Gen 30:40 Then Jacob separated the l
Ex 12:21 out and take l for yourselves
Ex 29:38 two l of the first year, day
Lev 14:10 two male l without blemish
Lev 23:18 seven l of the first year
Lev 23:19 two male l of the first year
Lev 23:20 the LORD, with the two l
Num 7:17 five male l in their first
Num 7:23 five male l in their first
Num 7:29 five male l in their first
Num 7:35 five male l in their first
Num 7:41 five male l in their first
Num 7:47 five male l in their first
Num 7:53 five male l in their first
Num 7:59 five male l in their first
Num 7:65 five male l in their first
Num 7:71 five male l in their first
Num 7:77 five male l in their first
Num 7:83 five male l in their first
Num 7:87 the male l in their first
Num 7:88 the l in their first year
Num 28: 3 two male l in their first
Num 28: 9 day two l in their first year
Num 28:11 seven l in their first year,
Num 28:19 seven l in their first year
Num 28:21 ephah for each of the seven l
Num 28:27 seven l in their first year,
Num 28:29 for each of the seven l
Num 29: 2 seven l in their first year,
Num 29: 4 for each of the seven l
Num 29: 8 seven l in their first year
Num 29:10 for each of the seven l
Num 29:13 fourteen l in their first
Num 29:15 for each of the fourteen l
Num 29:17 fourteen l in their first
Num 29:18 for the rams, and for the l
Num 29:20 fourteen l in their first
Num 29:21 for the rams, and for the l
Num 29:23 fourteen l in their first
Num 29:24 for the rams, and for the l
Num 29:26 fourteen l in their first
Num 29:27 for the rams, and for the l
Num 29:29 fourteen l in their first
Num 29:30 for the rams, and for the l
Num 29:32 fourteen l in their first
Num 29:33 for the rams, and for the l
Num 29:36 seven l in their first year
Num 29:37 for the ram, and for the l
Deut 32:14 of the flock, with fat of l
1Sa 15: 9 the oxen, the fatlings, the l
2Ki 3: 4 Israel one hundred thousand l
1Ch 29:21 a thousand rams, a thousand l
2Ch 29:21 bulls, seven rams, seven l
2Ch 29:22 They also killed the l and
2Ch 29:32 rams, and two hundred l
2Ch 30:15 l on the fourteenth day of
2Ch 30:17 l for everyone who was not
2Ch 35: 1 l on the fourteenth day of
2Ch 35: 7 Josiah gave the lay people l
Ezra 6: 9 l for the burnt offerings of
Ezra 6:17 hundred rams, four hundred l
Ezra 6:20 slaughtered the Passover l
Ezra 7:17 this money bulls, rams, and l
Ezra 8:35 rams, seventy-seven l, and
Ps 114: 4 rams, The little hills like l
Ps 114: 6 O little hills, like l
Prov 27:26 the l will provide your
Is 1:11 of bulls, or of l or goats
Is 5:17 Then the l shall feed in
Is 34: 6 and with the blood of l and
Is 40:11 gather the l with His arm
Jer 51:40 down like l to the slaughter
Ezek 27:21 They traded with you in l
Ezek 39:18 of the earth, of rams and l
Ezek 46: 4 be six l without blemish, and
Ezek 46: 5 the grain offering for the l
Ezek 46: 6 bull without blemish, six l
Ezek 46: 7 as he wants to give for the l
Ezek 46:11 as he wants to give for the l
Amos 6: 4 eat l from the flock and
Luke 10: 3 you out as l among wolves
John 21:15 Feed My l

LAME
Lev 21:18 a man blind or l, who has a
Deut 15:21 if it is l or blind or has
2Sa 4: 4 a son who was l in his feet
2Sa 4: 4 that he fell and became l
2Sa 5: 6 and the l will repel you,"
2Sa 5: 8 defeats the Jebusites (the l
2Sa 5: 8 the l shall not come into the
2Sa 9: 3 Jonathan who is l in his feet
2Sa 9:13 he was l in both his feet
2Sa 19:26 because your servant is l
Job 29:15 blind, and I was feet to the l
Prov 26: 7 Like the legs of the l that
Is 33:23 the l take the prey
Is 35: 6 Then the l shall leap like a
Jer 31: 8 among them the blind and the l
Mic 4: 6 I will assemble the l, I will
Mic 4: 7 I will make the l a remnant
Zeph 3:19 I will save the l, and gather
Mal 1: 8 And when you offer the l and
Mal 1:13 you bring the stolen, the l
Matt 11: 5 their sight and the l walk
Matt 15:30 with them those who were l
Matt 15:31 the l walking, and the blind
Matt 18: 8 enter into life l or maimed
Matt 21:14 and the l came to Him in the
Mark 9:45 for you to enter life l, than
Luke 7:22 the l walk, the lepers are

Luke 14:13 the poor, the maimed, the l
Luke 14:21 poor and the maimed and the l
John 5: 3 of sick people, blind, l,
Acts 3: 2 And a certain man l from his
Acts 3:11 Now as the l man who was
Acts 8: 7 paralyzed and l were healed
Heb 12:13 so that what is l may not be

LAMECH
Gen 4:18 and Methushael begot L
Gen 4:19 Then L took for himself two
Gen 4:23 Then L said to his wives
Gen 4:23 O wives of L, listen to my
Gen 4:24 then L seventy-sevenfold
Gen 5:25 years, and begot L
Gen 5:26 After he begot L, Methuselah
Gen 5:28 L lived one hundred and
Gen 5:30 Noah, L lived five hundred and
Gen 5:31 days of L were seven hundred
1Ch 1: 3 Enoch, Methuselah, L,
Luke 3:36 the son of Noah, the son of L

LAMENT (*see* LAMENTATION, LAMENTED, LAMENTERS, LAMENTING, LAMENTS)
Judg 11:40 to l the daughter of Jephthah
2Sa 3:33 the king sang a l over Abner
Is 3:26 Her gates shall l and mourn,
Is 19: 8 all those will l who cast
Jer 4: 8 yourself with sackcloth, l
Jer 16: 5 nor go to l or bemoan them
Jer 16: 6 neither shall men l for them
Jer 22:18 They shall not l for him,
Jer 22:18 They shall not l for him
Jer 34: 5 for you and l for you, saying,
Jer 49: 3 L and run to and fro by the
Lam 2: 8 the rampart and wall to l
Ezek 27:32 l for you, 'What city is like
Ezek 32:16 with which they shall l her
Ezek 32:16 of the nations shall l her
Ezek 32:16 they shall l for her, for
Joel 1: 8 L like a virgin girded with
Joel 1:13 Gird yourselves and l, you
Mic 2: 4 l with a bitter lamentation,
Matt 11:17 to you, And you did not l
John 16:20 you that you will weep and l
Jas 4: 9 L and mourn and weep
Rev 18: 9 l for her, when they see the

LAMENTATION (*see* LAMENT, LAMENTATIONS)
Gen 50:10 with a great and very solemn l
2Sa 1:17 with this l over Saul and over
Ps 78:64 And their widows made no l
Jer 6:26 an only son, most bitter l
Jer 7:29 take up a l on the desolate
Jer 9:10 of the wilderness a l,
Jer 9:20 and everyone her neighbor a l
Jer 31:15 A voice was heard in Ramah, l
Jer 48:38 A general l on all the
Lam 2: 5 l in the daughter of Judah
Ezek 19: 1 Moreover take up a l for the
Ezek 19:14 This is a l, and has become
Ezek 19:14 and has become a l
Ezek 26:17 they will take up a l for you
Ezek 27: 2 of man, take up a l for Tyre
Ezek 27:32 for you they will take up a l
Ezek 28:12 take up a l for the king of
Ezek 32: 2 take up a l for Pharaoh king
Ezek 32:16 This is the l with which
Amos 5: 1 I take up against you, this l
Amos 8:10 and all your songs into l
Mic 2: 4 and lament with a bitter l
Matt 2:18 A voice was heard in Ramah, l
Acts 8: 2 and made great l over him

LAMENTATIONS (*see* LAMENTATION)
2Ch 35:25 speak of Josiah in their l
Ezek 2:10 and written on it were l and

LAMENTED (*see* LAMENT)
1Sa 6:19 the people l because the LORD
1Sa 7: 2 of Israel l after the LORD
1Sa 25: 1 l for him, and buried him at
1Sa 28: 3 and all Israel had l for him
2Sa 1:17 Then David l with this
2Ch 35:25 Jeremiah also l for Josiah
Jer 16: 4 they shall not be l nor shall
Jer 25:33 They shall not be l, or
Luke 23:27 who also mourned and l Him

LAMENTERS (*see* LAMENT)
Amos 5:16 and skillful l to wailing

LAMENTING (*see* LAMENT)
Esth 9:31 matters of their fasting and l
Dan 6:20 out with a l voice to Daniel

LAMENTS (*see* LAMENT)
2Ch 35:25 they are written in the L

LAMP (*see* LAMPS, LAMPSTAND)
Ex 27:20 light, to cause the l to burn
1Sa 3: 3 before the l of God went out
2Sa 21:17 you quench the l of Israel
2Sa 22:29 For You are my l, O LORD
1Ki 11:36 a l before Me in Jerusalem
1Ki 15: 4 God gave him a l in Jerusalem
2Ki 8:19 him to give a l to him and his
2Ch 21: 7 promised to give a l to him
Job 12: 5 A l is despised in the
Job 18: 6 his l beside him is put out
Job 21:17 How often is the l of the
Job 29: 3 when His l shone upon my head
Ps 18:28 For You will light my l
Ps 119:105 Your word is a l to my feet
Ps 132:17 prepare a l for My Anointed
Prov 6:23 For the commandment is a l
Prov 13: 9 but the l of the wicked will
Prov 20:20 his l will be put out in deep
Prov 20:27 of a man is the l of the LORD
Prov 24:20 the l of the wicked will be
Prov 31:18 and her l does not go out by
Is 62: 1 salvation as a l that burns
Jer 25:10 and the light of the l
Matt 5:15 Nor do they light a l and put
Matt 6:22 The l of the body is the eye
Mark 4:21 Is a l brought to be put
Luke 8:16 No one, when he has lit a l
Luke 11:33 No one, when he has lit a l
Luke 11:34 The l of the body is the eye
Luke 11:36 of a l gives you light
Luke 15: 8 one coin, does not light a l
John 5:35 was the burning and shining l
Rev 18:23 the light of a l shall not
Rev 22: 5 They need no l nor light of

LAMPS (*see* LAMP)
Ex 25:37 You shall make seven l for it
Ex 25:37 they shall arrange its l so
Ex 30: 7 when he tends the l, he shall
Ex 30: 8 lights the l at twilight, he
Ex 35:14 light, its utensils, its l
Ex 37:23 And he made its seven l, its
Ex 39:37 l (the l set in order)
Ex 40: 4 the lampstand and light its l
Ex 40:25 he lit the l before the LORD,
Lev 24: 2 the light, to make the l burn
Lev 24: 4 shall be in charge of the l
Num 4: 9 of the light, with its l, its
Num 8: 2 him, 'When you arrange the l
Num 8: 2 the seven l shall give light
Num 8: 3 he arranged the l to face
1Ki 7:49 with the flowers and the l
1Ch 28:15 their l of gold, by weight
1Ch 28:15 for each lampstand and its l
1Ch 28:15 for the lampstand and its l
2Ch 4:20 with their l of pure gold
2Ch 4:21 with the flowers and the l
2Ch 13:11 its l to burn every evening
2Ch 29: 7 the vestibule, put out the l
Zeph 1:12 will search Jerusalem with l
Zech 4: 2 on the stand seven l with
Zech 4: 2 seven pipes to the seven l
Matt 25: 1 ten virgins who took their l
Matt 25: 3 who were foolish took their l
Matt 25: 4 in their vessels with their l
Matt 25: 7 arose and trimmed their l
Matt 25: 8 oil, for our l are going out
Luke 12:35 be girded and your l burning
Acts 20: 8 There were many l in the
Rev 4: 5 there were seven l of fire

LAMPSTAND (*see* LAMP, LAMPSTANDS)
Ex 25:31 also make a l of pure gold
Ex 25:31 the l shall be of hammered
Ex 25:32 of the l out of one side, and
Ex 25:32 the l out of the other side
Ex 25:33 that come out of the l
Ex 25:34 On the l itself four bowls
Ex 25:35 that extend from the l
Ex 26:35 the l across from the table
Ex 30:27 and all its utensils, the l
Ex 31: 8 the pure l with all its
Ex 35:14 also the l for the light,
Ex 37:17 also made the l of pure gold
Ex 37:17 hammered work he made the l
Ex 37:18 of the l out of one side, and
Ex 37:18 the l out of the other side
Ex 37:19 branches coming out of the l
Ex 37:20 on the l itself were four
Ex 39:37 the pure l with its lamps
Ex 40: 4 and you shall bring in the l
Ex 40:24 He put the l in the
Lev 24: 4 the lamps on the pure gold l
Num 3:31 the ark, the table, the l
Num 4: 9 cover the l of the light,
Num 8: 2 give light in front of the l
Num 8: 3 toward the front of the l
Num 8: 4 of the l was of hammered gold
Num 8: 4 shown Moses, so he made the l
2Ki 4:10 and a table and a chair and a l
1Ch 28:15 of gold, by weight for each l
1Ch 28:15 silver by weight, for the l
1Ch 28:15 to the use of each l
2Ch 13:11 the l of gold with its lamps
Dan 5: 5 wrote opposite the l on the
Zech 4: 2 there is a l of solid gold
Zech 4:11 one at the right of the l
Matt 5:15 it under a basket, but on a l
Mark 4:21 Is it not to be set on a l
Luke 8:16 a bed, but sets it on a l
Luke 11:33 or under a basket, but on a l
Heb 9: 2 part, in which was the l, the
Rev 2: 5 remove your l from its place

LAMPSTANDS (*see* LAMPSTAND)
1Ki 7:49 the l of pure gold, five on
1Ch 28:15 the weight for the l of gold
1Ch 28:15 for the l of silver by weight
2Ch 4: 7 And he made ten l of gold
2Ch 4:20 the l with their lamps of
Jer 52:19 the bowls, the pots, the l
Rev 1:12 turned I saw seven golden l
Rev 1:13 l One like the Son of Man
Rev 1:20 hand, and the seven golden l
Rev 1:20 the seven l which you saw are
Rev 2: 1 midst of the seven golden l
Rev 11: 4 the two l standing before the

LANCE (*see* LANCES)
Jer 50:42 shall hold the bow and the l

LANCES (*see* LANCE)
1Ki 18:28 custom, with knives and l,

LAND (*see* LANDED, LANDING, LANDMARK, LANDOWNER, LANDS)
Gen 1: 9 and let the dry l appear"
Gen 1:10 And God called the dry l Earth
Gen 2:11 the whole l of Havilah, where
Gen 2:12 And the gold of that l is good
Gen 2:13 the whole l of Cush
Gen 4:16 dwelt in the l of Nod on the
Gen 7:22 all that was on the dry l
Gen 10:10 and Calneh, in the l of Shinar
Gen 10:11 From that l he went to
Gen 11: 2 a plain in the l of Shinar
Gen 11:28 father Terah in his native l
Gen 11:31 to go to the l of Canaan
Gen 12: 1 to a l that I will show you
Gen 12: 5 to go to the l of Canaan
Gen 12: 5 they came to the l of Canaan
Gen 12: 6 the l to the place of Shechem
Gen 12: 6 Canaanites were then in the l
Gen 12: 7 I will give this l
Gen 12:10 there was a famine in the l
Gen 12:10 famine was severe in the l
Gen 13: 6 Now the l was not able to
Gen 13: 7 then dwelt in the l
Gen 13: 9 Is not the whole l before you
Gen 13:10 like the l of Egypt as you go
Gen 13:12 dwelt in the l of Canaan, and
Gen 13:15 for all the l which you see I
Gen 13:17 walk in the l through its
Gen 15: 7 give you this l to inherit it
Gen 15:13 in a l that is not theirs
Gen 15:18 I have given this l, from the
Gen 16: 3 ten years in the l of Canaan
Gen 17: 8 descendants after you the l
Gen 17: 8 all the l of Canaan, as an
Gen 19:28 toward all the l of the plain
Gen 19:28 the smoke of the l which went
Gen 20:15 See, my l is before you
Gen 21:21 for him from the l of Egypt
Gen 21:23 to the l in which you have

Gen 21:32 to the l of the Philistines
Gen 21:34 the l of the Philistines many
Gen 22: 2 and go to the l of Moriah
Gen 23: 2 Hebron) in the l of Canaan
Gen 23: 7 to the people of the l, the
Gen 23:12 before the people of the l
Gen 23:13 of the people of the l,
Gen 23:15 the l is worth four hundred
Gen 23:19 Hebron) in the l of Canaan
Gen 24: 5 to follow me to this l
Gen 24: 5 to the l from which you came
Gen 24: 7 from the l of my kindred, and
Gen 24: 7 descendants I give this l
Gen 24:37 in whose l I dwell
Gen 26: 1 There was a famine in the l
Gen 26: 2 dwell in the l of which I
Gen 26: 3 Sojourn in this l, and I will
Gen 26:12 Then Isaac sowed in that l
Gen 26:22 we shall be fruitful in the l
Gen 27:46 are the daughters of the l
Gen 28: 4 that you may inherit the l in
Gen 28:13 the l on which you lie I will
Gen 28:15 will bring you back to this l
Gen 29: 1 came to the l of the people
Gen 31: 3 Return to the l of your
Gen 31:13 Now arise, get out of this l
Gen 31:13 and return to the l of your
Gen 31:18 Isaac in the l of Canaan
Gen 32: 3 his brother in the l of Seir
Gen 33:18 which is in the l of Canaan
Gen 33:19 And he bought the parcel of l
Gen 34: 1 to see the daughters of the l
Gen 34:10 the l shall be before you
Gen 34:21 let them dwell in the l and
Gen 34:21 For indeed the l is large
Gen 34:30 the inhabitants of the l,
Gen 35: 6 which is in the l of Canaan
Gen 35:12 The l which I gave Abraham and
Gen 35:12 after you I give this l
Gen 35:22 when Israel dwelt in that l
Gen 36: 5 to him in the l of Canaan
Gen 36: 6 had gained in the l of Canaan
Gen 36: 7 and the l where they were
Gen 36:16 of Eliphaz in the l of Edom
Gen 36:17 of Reuel in the l of Edom
Gen 36:20 Horite who inhabited the l
Gen 36:21 of Seir, in the l of Edom
Gen 36:30 their chiefs in the l of Seir
Gen 36:31 the l of Edom before any king
Gen 36:34 died, Husham of the l of the
Gen 36:43 in the l of their possession
Gen 37: 1 the l where his father was a
Gen 37: 1 stranger, in the l of Canaan
Gen 40:15 from the l of the Hebrews
Gen 41:19 seen in all the l of Egypt
Gen 41:29 throughout all the l of Egypt
Gen 41:30 forgotten in the l of Egypt
Gen 41:30 the famine will deplete the l
Gen 41:31 the l because of the famine
Gen 41:33 set him over the l of Egypt
Gen 41:34 appoint officers over the l
Gen 41:34 the l of Egypt in the seven
Gen 41:36 the l for the seven years of
Gen 41:36 shall be in the l of Egypt
Gen 41:36 that the l may not perish
Gen 41:41 you over all the l of Egypt
Gen 41:43 him over all the l of Egypt
Gen 41:44 or foot in all the l of Egypt
Gen 41:45 out over all the l of Egypt
Gen 41:46 throughout all the l of Egypt
Gen 41:48 which were in the l of Egypt
Gen 41:52 in the l of my affliction
Gen 41:53 were in the l of Egypt ended
Gen 41:54 but in all the l of Egypt
Gen 41:55 So when all the l of Egypt
Gen 41:56 severe in the l of Egypt
Gen 42: 5 famine was in the l of Canaan
Gen 42: 6 was governor over the l
Gen 42: 6 to all the people of the l
Gen 42: 7 From the l of Canaan to buy
Gen 42: 9 to see the nakedness of the l
Gen 42:12 to see the nakedness of the l
Gen 42:13 of one man in the l of Canaan
Gen 42:29 father in the l of Canaan
Gen 42:30 of the l spoke roughly to us
Gen 42:32 this day in the l of Canaan
Gen 42:34 and you may trade in the l
Gen 43: 1 famine was severe in the l
Gen 43:11 of the l in your vessels and
Gen 44: 8 back to you from the l of
Gen 45: 6 the famine has been in the l
Gen 45: 8 throughout all the l of Egypt
Gen 45:10 dwell in the l of Goshen, and
Gen 45:17 go to the l of Canaan
Gen 45:18 the best of the l of Egypt
Gen 45:18 you will eat the fat of the l
Gen 45:19 Take carts out of the l of
Gen 45:20 all the l of Egypt is yours
Gen 45:25 came to the l of Canaan to
Gen 45:26 over all the l of Egypt
Gen 46: 6 acquired in the l of Canaan
Gen 46:12 Onan died in the l of Canaan)
Gen 46:20 to Joseph in the l of Egypt
Gen 46:28 they came to the l of Goshen
Gen 46:31 who were in the l of Canaan
Gen 46:34 may dwell in the l of Goshen
Gen 47: 1 come from the l of Canaan
Gen 47: 1 they are in the l of Goshen
Gen 47: 4 have come to sojourn in the l
Gen 47: 4 is severe in the l of Canaan
Gen 47: 4 dwell in the l of Goshen
Gen 47: 6 The l of Egypt is before you
Gen 47: 6 dwell in the best of the l
Gen 47: 6 them dwell in the l of Goshen
Gen 47:11 possession in the l of Egypt
Gen 47:11 Egypt, in the best of the l
Gen 47:11 in the l of Rameses
Gen 47:13 was no bread in all the l
Gen 47:13 so that the l of Egypt and
Gen 47:13 Egypt and all the l of Canaan
Gen 47:14 was found in the l of Egypt
Gen 47:14 in the l of Canaan, for the
Gen 47:15 failed in the l of Egypt and
Gen 47:15 in the l of Canaan, all the
Gen 47:19 your eyes, both we and our l
Gen 47:19 our l for bread, and we and our
Gen 47:19 our l will be servants of
Gen 47:19 die, that the l may not be
Gen 47:20 the l of Egypt for Pharaoh
Gen 47:20 So the l became Pharaoh's
Gen 47:22 Only the l of the priests he
Gen 47:23 your l this day for Pharaoh
Gen 47:23 you, and you shall sow the l
Gen 47:26 the l of Egypt to this day
Gen 47:26 except for the l of the
Gen 47:27 dwelt in the l of Egypt, in
Gen 47:28 Jacob lived in the l of Egypt
Gen 48: 3 me at Luz in the l of Canaan
Gen 48: 4 and give this l to your
Gen 48: 5 l of Egypt before I came to
Gen 48: 7 in the l of Canaan on the way
Gen 48:21 back to the l of your fathers
Gen 49:15 and that the l was pleasant
Gen 49:30 Mamre in the l of Canaan,
Gen 50: 5 for myself in the l of Canaan
Gen 50: 7 the elders of the l of Egypt
Gen 50: 8 they left in the l of Goshen
Gen 50:11 when the inhabitants of the l
Gen 50:13 him to the l of Canaan, and
Gen 50:24 bring you out of this l to
Gen 50:24 to the l of which He swore to
Ex 1: 7 the l was filled with them
Ex 1:10 us, and so go up out of the l
Ex 2:15 and dwelt in the l of Midian
Ex 2:22 a stranger in a foreign l
Ex 3: 8 that l to a good and large l
Ex 3: 8 to a l flowing with milk and
Ex 3:17 to the l of the Canaanites
Ex 3:17 to a l flowing with milk and
Ex 4: 9 river and pour it on the dry l
Ex 4: 9 become blood on the dry l
Ex 4:20 he returned to the l of Egypt
Ex 5: 5 people of the l are many now
Ex 5:12 abroad throughout all the l
Ex 6: 1 will drive them out of his l
Ex 6: 4 to give them the l of Canaan
Ex 6: 4 the l of their pilgrimage, in
Ex 6: 8 l which I swore to give to
Ex 6:11 of Israel go out of his l
Ex 6:13 Israel out of the l of Egypt
Ex 6:26 l of Egypt according to their
Ex 6:28 to Moses in the l of Egypt
Ex 7: 2 of Israel out of his l
Ex 7: 3 My wonders in the l of Egypt
Ex 7: 4 out of the l of Egypt by
Ex 7:19 throughout all the l of Egypt
Ex 7:21 throughout all the l of Egypt
Ex 8: 5 to come up on the l of Egypt
Ex 8: 6 up and covered the l of Egypt
Ex 8: 7 up frogs on the l of Egypt
Ex 8:14 in heaps, and the l stank
Ex 8:16 and strike the dust of the l
Ex 8:16 throughout all the l of Egypt
Ex 8:17 All the dust of the l became
Ex 8:17 throughout all the l of Egypt
Ex 8:22 set apart the l of Goshen
Ex 8:22 LORD in the midst of the l
Ex 8:24 and into all the l of Egypt
Ex 8:24 The l was corrupted because
Ex 8:25 to your God in the l
Ex 9: 5 will do this thing in the l
Ex 9: 9 dust in all the l of Egypt
Ex 9: 9 throughout all the l of Egypt
Ex 9:22 be hail in all the l of Egypt
Ex 9:22 throughout the l of Egypt
Ex 9:23 rained hail on the l of Egypt
Ex 9:24 l of Egypt since it became a
Ex 9:25 the whole l of Egypt, all
Ex 9:26 Only in the l of Goshen,
Ex 10:12 out your hand over the l of
Ex 10:12 may come upon the l of Egypt
Ex 10:12 and eat every herb of the l
Ex 10:13 his rod over the l of Egypt
Ex 10:13 wind on the l all that day
Ex 10:14 up over all the l of Egypt
Ex 10:15 so that the l was darkened
Ex 10:15 they ate every herb of the l
Ex 10:15 throughout all the l of Egypt
Ex 10:21 darkness over the l of Egypt
Ex 10:22 all the l of Egypt three days
Ex 11: 3 very great in the l of Egypt
Ex 11: 5 in the l of Egypt shall die
Ex 11: 6 throughout all the l of Egypt
Ex 11: 9 multiplied in the l of Egypt
Ex 11:10 of Israel go out of his l
Ex 12: 1 and Aaron in the l of Egypt
Ex 12:12 the l of Egypt on that night
Ex 12:12 firstborn in the l of Egypt
Ex 12:13 when I strike the l of Egypt
Ex 12:17 armies out of the l of Egypt
Ex 12:19 stranger or a native of the l
Ex 12:25 l which the LORD will give
Ex 12:29 firstborn in the l of Egypt
Ex 12:33 them out of the l in haste
Ex 12:41 went out from the l of Egypt
Ex 12:42 them out of the l of Egypt
Ex 12:48 shall be as a native of the l
Ex 12:51 of Israel out of the l of
Ex 13: 5 into the l of the Canaanites
Ex 13: 5 you, a l flowing with milk and
Ex 13:11 into the l of the Canaanites
Ex 13:15 firstborn in the l of Egypt
Ex 13:17 of the l of the Philistines
Ex 13:18 ranks out of the l of Egypt
Ex 14: 3 They are bewildered by the l
Ex 14:21 and made the sea into dry l
Ex 14:29 dry l in the midst of the sea
Ex 15:19 of Israel went on dry l in
Ex 16: 1 departed from the l of Egypt
Ex 16: 3 of the LORD in the l of Egypt
Ex 16: 6 you out of the l of Egypt
Ex 16:32 you out of the l of Egypt
Ex 16:35 they came to an inhabited l
Ex 16:35 the border of the l of Canaan
Ex 18: 3 a stranger in a foreign l")
Ex 18:27 he went his way to his own l
Ex 19: 1 gone out of the l of Egypt
Ex 20: 2 you out of the l of Egypt
Ex 20:12 days may be long upon the l
Ex 22:21 strangers in the l of Egypt
Ex 23: 9 strangers in the l of Egypt
Ex 23:10 years you shall sow your l
Ex 23:19 l you shall bring into the
Ex 23:26 or be barren in your l
Ex 23:29 lest the l become desolate and
Ex 23:30 and you inherit the l
Ex 23:31 of the l into your hand, and
Ex 23:33 shall not dwell in your l
Ex 29:46 them up out of the l of Egypt
Ex 32: 1 us up out of the l of Egypt
Ex 32: 4 you out of the l of Egypt
Ex 32: 7 the l of Egypt have corrupted
Ex 32: 8 you out of the l of Egypt
Ex 32:11 l of Egypt with great power
Ex 32:13 all this l that I have spoken
Ex 32:23 us out of the l of Egypt, we
Ex 33: 1 brought out of the l of Egypt
Ex 33: 1 to the l of which I swore to
Ex 33: 3 Go up to a l flowing with
Ex 34:12 of the l where you are going

Ex 34:15 with the inhabitants of the l
Ex 34:24 will any man covet your l
Ex 34:26 your l you shall bring to the
Lev 11:45 you up out of the l of Egypt
Lev 14:34 come into the l of Canaan
Lev 14:34 in the l of your possession
Lev 16:22 to an uninhabited l
Lev 18: 3 the doings of the l of Egypt
Lev 18: 3 the doings of the l of Canaan
Lev 18:25 For the l is defiled
Lev 18:25 it, and the l vomits out its
Lev 18:27 the men of the l have done
Lev 18:27 and thus the l is defiled),
Lev 18:28 lest the l vomit you out
Lev 19: 9 reap the harvest of your l
Lev 19:23 When you come into the l
Lev 19:29 lest the l fall into harlotry
Lev 19:29 and the l become full of
Lev 19:33 sojourns with you in your l
Lev 19:34 strangers in the l of Egypt
Lev 19:36 you out of the l of Egypt
Lev 20: 2 The people of the l shall
Lev 20: 4 if the people of the l should
Lev 20:22 them, that the l where I am
Lev 20:24 You shall inherit their l
Lev 20:24 a l flowing with milk and
Lev 22:24 offering of them in your l
Lev 22:33 you out of the l of Egypt
Lev 23:10 the l which I give to you
Lev 23:22 reap the harvest of your l
Lev 23:39 in the fruit of the l, you
Lev 23:43 them out of the l of Egypt
Lev 24:16 as him who is born in the l
Lev 25: 2 into the l which I give you
Lev 25: 2 you, then the l shall keep a
Lev 25: 4 of solemn rest for the l, a
Lev 25: 5 is a year of rest for the l
Lev 25: 6 the l shall be food for you
Lev 25: 7 animals that are in your l
Lev 25: 9 sound throughout all your l
Lev 25:10 the l to all its inhabitants
Lev 25:18 will dwell in the l in safety
Lev 25:19 Then the l will yield its
Lev 25:23 The l shall not be sold
Lev 25:23 for the l is Mine
Lev 25:24 And in all the l of your
Lev 25:24 grant redemption of the l
Lev 25:38 you out of the l of Egypt
Lev 25:38 to give you the l of Canaan
Lev 25:42 brought out of the l of Egypt
Lev 25:45 which they beget in your l
Lev 25:55 brought out of the l of Egypt
Lev 26: 1 an engraved stone in your l
Lev 26: 4 the l shall yield its produce
Lev 26: 5 and dwell in your l safely
Lev 26: 6 I will give peace in the l
Lev 26: 6 will rid the l of evil beasts
Lev 26: 6 will not go through your l
Lev 26:13 you out of the l of Egypt
Lev 26:20 for your l shall not yield
Lev 26:20 of the l yield their fruit
Lev 26:32 bring the l to desolation
Lev 26:33 your l shall be desolate and
Lev 26:34 Then the l shall enjoy its
Lev 26:34 and you are in your enemies' l
Lev 26:34 then the l shall rest and
Lev 26:38 the l of your enemies shall
Lev 26:41 into the l of their enemies
Lev 26:42 I will remember the l
Lev 26:43 The l also shall be left
Lev 26:44 are in the l of their enemies
Lev 26:45 l of Egypt in the sight of
Lev 27:24 owned the l as a possession
Lev 27:30 And all the tithe of the l
Lev 27:30 whether of the seed of the l
Num 1: 1 come out of the l of Egypt
Num 3:13 firstborn in the l of Egypt
Num 8:17 all the firstborn in the l of
Num 9: 1 come out of the l of Egypt
Num 9:14 and the native of the l
Num 10: 9 your l against the enemy who
Num 10:30 but I will depart to my own l
Num 11:12 to the l which You swore to
Num 13: 2 to spy out the l of Canaan
Num 13:16 Moses sent to spy out the l
Num 13:17 to spy out the l of Canaan
Num 13:18 and see what the l is like
Num 13:19 whether the l they dwell in
Num 13:20 whether the l is rich or poor
Num 13:20 some of the fruit of the l
Num 13:21 and spied out the l from the
Num 13:25 out the l after forty days
Num 13:26 them the fruit of the l
Num 13:27 We went to the l where you
Num 13:28 who dwell in the l are strong
Num 13:29 dwell in the l of the South
Num 13:32 l which they had spied out
Num 13:32 The l through which we have
Num 13:32 spies is a l that devours its
Num 14: 2 we had died in the l of Egypt
Num 14: 3 this l to fall by the sword
Num 14: 6 those who had spied out the l
Num 14: 7 The l we passed through to
Num 14: 7 out is an exceedingly good l
Num 14: 8 He will bring us into this l
Num 14: 8 a l which flows with milk and
Num 14: 9 nor fear the people of the l
Num 14:14 to the inhabitants of this l
Num 14:16 l which He swore to give them
Num 14:23 l of which I swore to their
Num 14:24 into the l where he went, and
Num 14:30 l which I swore I would make
Num 14:31 they shall know the l which
Num 14:34 in which you spied out the l
Num 14:36 Moses sent to spy out the l
Num 14:36 a bad report of the l,
Num 14:37 the evil report about the l
Num 14:38 men who went to spy out the l
Num 15: 2 into the l you are to inhabit
Num 15:18 the l to which I bring you
Num 15:19 you eat of the bread of the l
Num 15:41 you out of the l of Egypt
Num 16:13 out of a l flowing with milk
Num 16:14 us into a l flowing with milk
Num 18:13 ripe fruit is in their l,
Num 18:20 no inheritance in their l
Num 20:12 the l which I have given them
Num 20:18 shall not pass through my l
Num 20:23 the border of the l of Edom
Num 20:24 l which I have given to the
Num 21: 4 to go around the l of Edom
Num 21:22 Let me pass through your l
Num 21:24 his l from the Arnon to the
Num 21:26 had taken all his l from his
Num 21:31 in the l of the Amorites
Num 21:34 with all his people and his l
Num 21:35 they took possession of his l
Num 22: 5 is near the River in the l of
Num 22: 6 and drive them out of the l
Num 22:13 Go back to your l, for the
Num 26: 4 came out of the l of Egypt
Num 26:19 Onan died in the l of Canaan
Num 26:53 To these the l shall be
Num 26:55 But the l shall be divided by
Num 27:12 see the l which I have given
Num 32: 1 when they saw the l of Jazer
Num 32: 1 the l of Gilead, that indeed
Num 32: 4 is a l for livestock, and your
Num 32: 5 let this l be given to your
Num 32: 7 l which the LORD has given
Num 32: 8 Kadesh Barnea to see the l
Num 32: 9 Valley of Eshcol and saw the l
Num 32: 9 l which the LORD had given
Num 32:11 shall see the l of which I
Num 32:17 of the inhabitants of the l
Num 32:22 the l is subdued before the
Num 32:22 and this l shall be your
Num 32:29 the l is subdued before you,
Num 32:29 you shall give them the l of
Num 32:30 among you in the l of Canaan
Num 32:32 the LORD into the l of Canaan
Num 32:33 the l with its cities within
Num 33: 1 who went out of the l of
Num 33:37 the boundary of the l of Edom
Num 33:38 come out of the l of Egypt
Num 33:40 the South in the l of Canaan
Num 33:51 Jordan into the l of Canaan
Num 33:52 of the l from before you,
Num 33:53 the inhabitants of the l and
Num 33:53 given you the l to possess
Num 33:54 you shall divide the l by lot
Num 33:55 of the l from before you,
Num 33:55 you in the l where you dwell
Num 34: 2 you come into the l of Canaan
Num 34: 2 this is the l that shall fall
Num 34: 2 the l of Canaan to its
Num 34:12 This shall be your l with its
Num 34:13 This is the l which you shall
Num 34:17 men who shall divide the l
Num 34:18 the l for the inheritance
Num 34:29 of Israel in the l of Canaan
Num 35:10 Jordan into the l of Canaan
Num 35:14 appoint in the l of Canaan
Num 35:28 to the l of his possession
Num 35:32 the l before the death of the
Num 35:33 pollute the l where you are
Num 35:33 for blood defiles the l, and
Num 35:33 can be made for the l, for
Num 35:34 the l which you inhabit, in
Num 36: 2 my lord Moses to give the l
Deut 1: 5 the Jordan in the l of Moab
Deut 1: 7 to the l of the Canaanites and
Deut 1: 8 I have set the l before you
Deut 1: 8 possess the l which the LORD
Deut 1:21 God has set the l before you
Deut 1:22 them search out the l for us
Deut 1:25 fruit of the l in their hands
Deut 1:25 It is a good l which the
Deut 1:27 has brought us out of the l
Deut 1:35 shall see that good l of
Deut 1:36 the l on which he walked,
Deut 2: 5 not give you any of their l
Deut 2: 9 of their l as a possession
Deut 2:12 l of their possession which
Deut 2:19 not give you any of the l of
Deut 2:20 regarded as a l of giants
Deut 2:24 king of Heshbon, and his l
Deut 2:27 Let me pass through your l
Deut 2:29 l which the LORD our God is
Deut 2:31 Sihon and his l over to you
Deut 2:31 that you may inherit his l
Deut 2:37 the l of the people of Ammon
Deut 3: 2 and his l into your hand
Deut 3: 8 l from the hand of the two
Deut 3:12 And this l, which we possessed
Deut 3:13 called the l of the giants
Deut 3:18 given you this l to possess
Deut 3:20 they also possess the l which
Deut 3:25 see the good l beyond the
Deut 3:28 the l which you will see
Deut 4: 1 possess the l which the LORD
Deut 4: 5 the l which you go to possess
Deut 4:14 the l which you cross over to
Deut 4:21 l which the LORD your God is
Deut 4:22 But I must die in this l, I
Deut 4:22 over and possess that good l
Deut 4:25 and have grown old in the l
Deut 4:26 utterly perish from the l
Deut 4:38 you their l as an inheritance
Deut 4:40 prolong your days in the l
Deut 4:46 in the l of Sihon king of the
Deut 4:47 they took possession of his l
Deut 4:47 the l of Og king of Bashan,
Deut 5: 6 you out of the l of Egypt
Deut 5:15 a slave in the l of Egypt
Deut 5:16 l which the LORD your God is
Deut 5:31 may observe them in the l
Deut 5:33 the l which you shall possess
Deut 6: 1 l which you are crossing over
Deut 6: 3 a l flowing with milk and
Deut 6:10 God brings you into the l of
Deut 6:12 you out of the l of Egypt
Deut 6:18 possess the good l of which
Deut 6:23 to give us the l of which He
Deut 7: 1 the l which you go to possess
Deut 7:13 womb and the fruit of your l
Deut 7:13 in the l of which He swore to
Deut 8: 1 possess the l of which the
Deut 8: 7 is bringing you into a good l
Deut 8: 7 a l of brooks of water, of
Deut 8: 8 a l of wheat and barley, of
Deut 8: 8 a l of olive oil and honey
Deut 8: 9 a l in which you will eat
Deut 8: 9 a l whose stones are iron and
Deut 8:10 good l which He has given you
Deut 8:14 you out of the l of Egypt
Deut 8:15 thirsty l where there was no
Deut 9: 4 me in to possess this l'
Deut 9: 5 you go in to possess their l
Deut 9: 6 l to possess because of your
Deut 9: 7 l of Egypt until you came to
Deut 9:23 possess the l which I have
Deut 9:28 lest the l from which You
Deut 9:28 the l which He promised them
Deut 10: 7 a l of rivers of water
Deut 10:11 possess the l which I swore
Deut 10:19 strangers in the l of Egypt
Deut 11: 3 of Egypt, and to all his l
Deut 11: 8 possess the l which you cross
Deut 11: 9 the l which the LORD swore to

Deut 11: 9 a l flowing with milk and
Deut 11:10 For the l which you go to
Deut 11:10 the l of Egypt from which you
Deut 11:11 but the l which you cross
Deut 11:11 to possess is a l of hills
Deut 11:12 a l for which the LORD your
Deut 11:14 rain for your l in its season
Deut 11:17 the l yield no produce, and
Deut 11:17 quickly from the good l which
Deut 11:21 may be multiplied in the l of
Deut 11:25 all the l where you tread
Deut 11:29 the l which you go to possess
Deut 11:30 in the l of the Canaanites
Deut 11:31 go in to possess the l which
Deut 12: 1 careful to observe in the l
Deut 12:10 dwell in the l which the LORD
Deut 12:19 as long as you live in your l
Deut 12:29 them and dwell in their l,
Deut 13: 5 you out of the l of Egypt
Deut 13:10 you out of the l of Egypt
Deut 15: 4 greatly bless you in the l
Deut 15: 7 any of the gates in your l
Deut 15:11 will never cease from the l
Deut 15:11 poor and your needy, in your l
Deut 15:15 a slave in the l of Egypt
Deut 16: 3 of the l of Egypt in haste)
Deut 16: 3 l of Egypt all the days of
Deut 16:20 inherit the l which the LORD
Deut 17:14 When you come to the l which
Deut 18: 9 When you come into the l
Deut 19: 1 cut off the nations whose l
Deut 19: 2 in the midst of your l which
Deut 19: 3 l which the LORD your God is
Deut 19: 8 and gives you the l which He
Deut 19:10 shed in the midst of your l
Deut 19:14 you will inherit in the l
Deut 20: 1 you up from the l of Egypt
Deut 21: 1 lying in the field in the l
Deut 21:23 l which the LORD your God is
Deut 23: 7 you were an alien in his l
Deut 23:20 you set your hand in the l
Deut 24: 4 l which the LORD your God is
Deut 24:14 in your l within your gates
Deut 24:22 a slave in the l of Egypt
Deut 25:15 may be lengthened in the l
Deut 25:19 in the l which the LORD your
Deut 26: 1 be, when you come into the l
Deut 26: 2 l that the LORD your God is
Deut 26: 9 place and has given us this l
Deut 26: 9 a l flowing with milk and
Deut 26:10 of the l which You, O LORD,
Deut 26:15 the l which You have given us
Deut 26:15 a l flowing with milk and
Deut 27: 2 over the Jordan to the l
Deut 27: 3 that you may enter the l
Deut 27: 3 a l flowing with milk and
Deut 28: 8 He will bless you in the l
Deut 28:11 in the l of which the LORD
Deut 28:12 rain to your l in its season
Deut 28:18 body and the produce of your l
Deut 28:21 the l which you are going to
Deut 28:24 the rain of your l to powder
Deut 28:33 shall eat the fruit of your l
Deut 28:42 and the produce of your l
Deut 28:51 and the produce of your l,
Deut 28:52 down throughout all your l
Deut 28:52 gates throughout all your l
Deut 28:63 the l which you go to possess
Deut 29: 1 of Israel in the l of Moab
Deut 29: 2 your eyes in the l of Egypt
Deut 29: 2 his servants and to all his l
Deut 29: 8 We took their l and gave it as
Deut 29:16 we dwelt in the l of Egypt
Deut 29:22 who comes from a far l, would
Deut 29:22 see the plagues of that l
Deut 29:23 The whole l is brimstone,
Deut 29:24 the LORD done so to this l
Deut 29:25 them out of the l of Egypt
Deut 29:27 was aroused against this l
Deut 29:28 them from their l in anger
Deut 29:28 and cast them into another l
Deut 30: 5 to the l which your fathers
Deut 30: 9 produce of your l for good
Deut 30:16 the l which you go to possess
Deut 30:18 l which you cross over the
Deut 30:20 the l which the LORD swore to
Deut 31: 4 of the Amorites and their l
Deut 31: 7 go with this people to the l
Deut 31:13 l which you cross the Jordan
Deut 31:16 of the foreigners of the l
Deut 31:20 to the l flowing with milk
Deut 31:21 l of which I swore to give
Deut 31:23 l of which I swore to them
Deut 32:10 He found him in a desert l
Deut 32:43 provide atonement for His l
Deut 32:47 l which you cross over the
Deut 32:49 which is in the l of Moab
Deut 32:49 view the l of Canaan, which I
Deut 32:52 shall see the l before you
Deut 32:52 into the l which I am giving
Deut 33:13 Blessed of the LORD is his l
Deut 33:28 in a l of grain and new wine
Deut 34: 1 the l of Gilead as far as Dan
Deut 34: 2 the l of Ephraim and Manasseh,
Deut 34: 2 all the l of Judah as far as
Deut 34: 4 This is the l of which I
Deut 34: 5 died there in the l of Moab
Deut 34: 6 in a valley in the l of Moab
Deut 34:11 him to do in the l of Egypt
Deut 34:11 his servants, and in all his l
Josh 1: 2 to the l which I am giving to
Josh 1: 4 all the l of the Hittites, and
Josh 1: 6 as an inheritance the l which
Josh 1:11 to go in to possess the l
Josh 1:13 rest and is giving you this l
Josh 1:14 shall remain in the l which
Josh 1:15 taken possession of the l
Josh 1:15 to the l of your possession
Josh 2: 1 Go, view the l, especially
Josh 2: 9 the LORD has given you the l
Josh 2: 9 all the inhabitants of the l
Josh 2:14 the LORD has given us the l
Josh 2:18 when we come into the l, you
Josh 2:24 all the l into our hands, for
Josh 4:18 feet touched the dry l, that
Josh 4:22 over this Jordan on dry l'
Josh 5: 6 He would not show them the l
Josh 5: 6 a l flowing with milk and
Josh 5:11 of the l on the day after the
Josh 5:12 eaten the produce of the l
Josh 5:12 of the l of Canaan that year
Josh 7: 9 of the l will hear of it, and
Josh 8: 1 people, his city, and his l
Josh 9:24 Moses to give you all the l
Josh 9:24 of the l from before you
Josh 10:40 So Joshua conquered all the l
Josh 10:42 their l Joshua took at one
Josh 11: 3 Hermon in the l of Mizpah
Josh 11:16 So Joshua took all this l
Josh 11:16 all the l of Goshen, the
Josh 11:22 l of the children of Israel
Josh 11:23 So Joshua took the whole l
Josh 11:23 Then the l rested from war
Josh 12: 1 These are the kings of the l
Josh 12: 1 whose l they possessed on the
Josh 13: 1 much l yet to be possessed
Josh 13: 2 This is the l that yet
Josh 13: 4 all the l of the Canaanites,
Josh 13: 5 the l of the Gebalites, and
Josh 13: 7 divide this l as an
Josh 13:25 half the l of the Ammonites
Josh 14: 1 inherited in the l of Canaan
Josh 14: 4 part to the Levites in the l
Josh 14: 5 and they divided the l
Josh 14: 7 Barnea to spy out the l, and I
Josh 14: 9 Surely the l where your foot
Josh 14:15 Then the l had rest from war
Josh 15:19 have given me l in the South
Josh 17: 5 besides the l of Gilead and
Josh 17: 6 sons had the l of Gilead
Josh 17: 8 Manasseh had the l of Tappuah
Josh 17:12 determined to dwell in that l
Josh 17:15 in the l of the Perizzites
Josh 17:16 l of the valley have chariots
Josh 18: 1 the l was subdued before them
Josh 18: 3 possess the l which the LORD
Josh 18: 4 rise and go through the l,
Josh 18: 6 survey the l in seven parts
Josh 18: 8 who went to survey the l,
Josh 18: 8 Go, walk through the l,
Josh 18: 9 went, passed through the l
Josh 18:10 there Joshua divided the l to
Josh 19:49 l as an inheritance according
Josh 21: 2 at Shiloh in the l of Canaan
Josh 21:43 l of which He had sworn to
Josh 22: 4 to the l of your possession,
Josh 22: 9 which is in the l of Canaan
Josh 22: 9 to the l of their possession,
Josh 22:10 which is in the l of Canaan
Josh 22:11 frontier of the l of Canaan
Josh 22:13 into the l of Gilead,
Josh 22:15 to the l of Gilead, and they
Josh 22:19 if the l of your possession
Josh 22:19 then cross over to the l of
Josh 22:32 from the l of Gilead to the
Josh 22:32 of Gilead to the l of Canaan
Josh 22:33 to destroy the l where the
Josh 23: 5 So you shall possess their l
Josh 23:13 you perish from this good l
Josh 23:15 you from this good l which
Josh 23:16 quickly from the good l which
Josh 24: 3 all the l of Canaan, and
Josh 24: 8 into the l of the Amorites
Josh 24: 8 you might possess their l
Josh 24:13 I have given you a l for
Josh 24:15 in whose l you dwell
Josh 24:17 up out of the l of Egypt,
Josh 24:18 Amorites who dwelt in the l
Judg 1: 2 delivered the l into his hand
Judg 1:15 have given me l in the South
Judg 1:26 went to the l of the Hittites
Judg 1:27 determined to dwell in that l
Judg 1:32 the inhabitants of the l
Judg 1:33 the inhabitants of the l
Judg 2: 1 brought you to the l of which
Judg 2: 2 the inhabitants of this l
Judg 2: 6 inheritance to possess the l
Judg 2:12 them out of the l of Egypt
Judg 3:11 So the l had rest for forty
Judg 3:30 the l had rest for eighty
Judg 5:31 So the l had rest for forty
Judg 6: 5 enter the l to destroy it
Judg 6: 9 you and gave you their l
Judg 6:10 in whose l you dwell
Judg 9:37 down from the center of the l
Judg 10: 4 which are in the l of Gilead
Judg 10: 8 in the l of the Amorites, in
Judg 11: 3 and dwelt in the l of Tob
Judg 11: 5 Jephthah from the l of Tob
Judg 11:12 to fight against me in my l
Judg 11:13 my l when they came up out of
Judg 11:15 not take away the l of Moab
Judg 11:15 nor the l of the people of
Judg 11:17 let me pass through your l
Judg 11:18 and bypassed the l of Edom
Judg 11:18 the l of Moab, came to the
Judg 11:18 east side of the l of Moab
Judg 11:19 through your l into our place
Judg 11:21 of all the l of the Amorites
Judg 12:15 Pirathon in the l of Ephraim
Judg 16:24 enemy, the destroyer of our l
Judg 18: 2 and Eshtaol, to spy out the l
Judg 18: 2 Go, search the l
Judg 18: 7 l who might put them to shame
Judg 18: 9 For we have seen the l, and
Judg 18: 9 may enter to possess the l
Judg 18:10 a secure people and a large l
Judg 18:17 gone to spy out the l went up
Judg 18:30 day of the captivity of the l
Judg 19:30 the l of Egypt until this day
Judg 20: 1 well as from the l of Gilead
Judg 21:12 which is in the l of Canaan
Judg 21:21 then go to the l of Benjamin
Ruth 1: 1 there was a famine in the l
Ruth 1: 7 to return to the l of Judah
Ruth 2:11 the l of your birth, and have
Ruth 4: 3 sold the piece of l which
1Sa 6: 5 your rats that ravage the l
1Sa 6: 5 your gods, and from your l
1Sa 9: 4 and through the l of Shalisha
1Sa 9: 4 through the l of Shaalim, and
1Sa 9: 4 the l of the Benjamites, but
1Sa 9: 5 had come to the l of Zuph
1Sa 9:16 a man from the l of Benjamin
1Sa 12: 6 up from the l of Egypt
1Sa 13: 3 trumpet throughout all the l
1Sa 13: 7 the Jordan to the l of Gad
1Sa 13:17 to Ophrah, to the l of Shual,
1Sa 13:19 all the l of Israel, for the
1Sa 14:14 about half an acre of l
1Sa 14:25 of the l came to a forest
1Sa 14:29 My father has troubled the l
1Sa 21:11 not David the king of the l
1Sa 22: 5 and go to the l of Judah
1Sa 23:23 shall be, if he is in the l
1Sa 23:27 have invaded the l
1Sa 27: 1 to the l of the Philistines
1Sa 27: 8 of the l from of old, as you
1Sa 27: 8 even as far as the l of Egypt
1Sa 27: 9 Whenever David attacked the l

1Sa 28: 3 the spiritists out of the l
1Sa 28: 9 and the spiritists from the l
1Sa 29:11 to return to the l of the
1Sa 30:16 spread out over all the l
1Sa 30:16 from the l of the Philistines
1Sa 30:16 and from the l of Judah
1Sa 31: 9 the l of the Philistines, to
2Sa 3:12 Whose is the l?
2Sa 5: 6 the inhabitants of the l
2Sa 7:23 and awesome deeds for Your l
2Sa 9: 7 l of Saul your grandfather
2Sa 9:10 shall work the l for him
2Sa 10: 2 the l of the people of Ammon
2Sa 15: 4 I were made judge in the l
2Sa 17:26 encamped in the l of Gilead
2Sa 19: 9 from the l because of Absalom
2Sa 19:29 You and Ziba divide the l
2Sa 21:14 heeded the prayer for the l
2Sa 24: 6 to the l of Tahtim Hodshi
2Sa 24: 8 had gone through all the l
2Sa 24:13 famine come to you in your l
2Sa 24:13 three days' plague in your l
2Sa 24:25 heeded the prayers for the l
1Ki 4:10 Sochoh and all the l of Hepher
1Ki 4:19 in the l of Gilead, in the
1Ki 4:19 governor who was in the l
1Ki 4:21 to the l of the Philistines
1Ki 6: 1 come out of the l of Egypt
1Ki 8: 9 came out of the l of Egypt
1Ki 8:21 them out of the l of Egypt
1Ki 8:34 and bring them back to the l
1Ki 8:36 give rain on Your l which You
1Ki 8:37 When there is famine in the l
1Ki 8:37 them in the l of their cities
1Ki 8:40 the l which You gave to our
1Ki 8:46 captive to the l of the enemy
1Ki 8:47 the l where they were carried
1Ki 8:47 the l of those who took them
1Ki 8:48 l of their enemies who led
1Ki 8:48 l which You gave to their
1Ki 9: 7 the l which I have given them
1Ki 9: 8 the LORD done thus to this l
1Ki 9: 9 fathers out of the l of Egypt
1Ki 9:11 cities in the l of Galilee
1Ki 9:13 he called them the l of Cabul
1Ki 9:18 in the l of Judah,
1Ki 9:19 in all the l of his dominion
1Ki 9:21 were left in the l after them
1Ki 9:26 the Red Sea, in the l of Edom
1Ki 10: 6 in my own l about your words
1Ki 11:18 food for him, and gave him l
1Ki 12:28 you up from the l of Egypt
1Ki 14:15 Israel from this good l which
1Ki 14:24 perverted persons in the l
1Ki 15:12 perverted persons from the l
1Ki 15:20 with all the l of Naphtali
1Ki 17: 7 had been no rain in the l
1Ki 18: 5 Go into the l to all the
1Ki 18: 6 So they divided the l between
1Ki 20: 7 all the elders of the l, and
1Ki 22:46 Asa, he banished from the l
2Ki 3:19 good piece of l with stones
2Ki 3:20 the l was filled with water
2Ki 3:24 and they entered their l,
2Ki 3:25 on every good piece of l and
2Ki 3:27 and returned to their own l
2Ki 4:38 there was a famine in the l
2Ki 5: 2 girl from the l of Israel
2Ki 5: 4 who is from the l of Israel
2Ki 6:23 no more into the l of Israel
2Ki 8: 1 upon the l for seven years
2Ki 8: 2 sojourned in the l of the
2Ki 8: 3 from the l of the Philistines
2Ki 8: 3 for her house and for her l
2Ki 8: 5 for her house and for her l
2Ki 8: 6 that she left the l until now
2Ki 10:33 all the l of Gilead
2Ki 11: 3 Athaliah reigned over the l
2Ki 11:14 of the l were rejoicing and
2Ki 11:18 all the people of the l went
2Ki 11:19 and all the people of the l
2Ki 11:20 the people of the l rejoiced
2Ki 13:20 l in the spring of the year
2Ki 15: 5 judging the people of the l
2Ki 15:19 of Assyria came against the l
2Ki 15:20 did not stay there in the l
2Ki 15:29 all the l of Naphtali
2Ki 16:15 of all the people of the l
2Ki 17: 5 went throughout all the l
2Ki 17: 7 them up out of the l of Egypt
2Ki 17:23 from their own l to Assyria
2Ki 17:26 rituals of the God of the l
2Ki 17:26 rituals of the God of the l
2Ki 17:27 rituals of the God of the l
2Ki 17:36 l of Egypt with great power
2Ki 18:25 to me, Go up against this l
2Ki 18:32 to a l like your own l
2Ki 18:32 a l of grain and new wine, a
2Ki 18:32 a l of bread and vineyards, a
2Ki 18:32 a l of olive groves and honey,
2Ki 18:33 at all delivered its l from
2Ki 19: 7 rumor and return to his own l
2Ki 19: 7 by the sword in his own l
2Ki 19:37 escaped into the l of Ararat
2Ki 21: 8 wander anymore from the l
2Ki 21:24 But the people of the l
2Ki 21:24 Then the people of the l made
2Ki 23:24 were seen in the l of Judah
2Ki 23:30 And the people of the l took
2Ki 23:33 at Riblah in the l of Hamath
2Ki 23:33 he imposed on the l a tribute
2Ki 23:35 but he taxed the l to give
2Ki 23:35 gold from the people of the l
2Ki 24: 7 not come out of his l anymore
2Ki 24:14 the poorest people of the l
2Ki 24:15 and the mighty of the l he
2Ki 25: 3 food for the people of the l
2Ki 25:12 poor of the l as vinedressers
2Ki 25:19 mustered the people of the l
2Ki 25:19 men of the people of the l
2Ki 25:21 at Riblah in the l of Hamath
2Ki 25:21 away captive from its own l
2Ki 25:22 remained in the l of Judah
2Ki 25:24 Dwell in the l and serve the
1Ch 1:43 the l of Edom before any king
1Ch 1:45 died, Husham of the l of the
1Ch 2:22 cities in the l of Gilead
1Ch 4:40 the l was broad, quiet, and
1Ch 5: 9 multiplied in the l of Gilead
1Ch 5:11 dwelt next to them in the l
1Ch 5:23 of Manasseh dwelt in the l
1Ch 5:25 gods of the peoples of the l
1Ch 6:55 them Hebron in the l of Judah
1Ch 7:21 l killed them because they
1Ch 10: 9 the l of the Philistines to
1Ch 11: 4 the inhabitants of the l
1Ch 13: 2 left in all the l of Israel
1Ch 16:18 To you I will give the l of
1Ch 19: 2 l of the people of Ammon to
1Ch 19: 3 overthrow and to spy out the l
1Ch 21:12 the plague in the l, with the
1Ch 22: 2 who were in the l of Israel
1Ch 22:18 of the l into my hand, and the
1Ch 22:18 the l is subdued before the
1Ch 28: 8 you may possess this good l
2Ch 2:17 who were in the l of Israel
2Ch 6: 5 people out of the l of Egypt
2Ch 6:25 the l which You gave to them
2Ch 6:27 send rain on Your l which You
2Ch 6:28 When there is famine in the l
2Ch 6:28 them in the l of their cities
2Ch 6:31 the l which You gave to our
2Ch 6:36 captive to a l far or near
2Ch 6:37 the l where they were carried
2Ch 6:37 in the l of their captivity
2Ch 6:38 in the l of their captivity
2Ch 6:38 pray toward their l which You
2Ch 7:13 the locusts to devour the l
2Ch 7:14 their sin and heal their l
2Ch 7:20 My l which I have given them
2Ch 7:21 the LORD done thus to this l
2Ch 7:22 them out of the l of Egypt
2Ch 8: 6 all the l of his dominion
2Ch 8: 8 were left in the l after them
2Ch 8:17 seacoast, in the l of Edom
2Ch 9: 5 in my own l about your words
2Ch 9:11 seen before in the l of Judah
2Ch 9:26 to the l of the Philistines
2Ch 14: 1 In his days the l was quiet
2Ch 14: 6 in Judah, for the l had rest
2Ch 14: 7 while the l is yet before us,
2Ch 15: 8 idols from all the l of Judah
2Ch 17: 2 garrisons in the l of Judah
2Ch 19: 3 the wooden images from the l
2Ch 19: 5 in the l throughout all the
2Ch 20: 7 l before Your people Israel
2Ch 20:10 came out of the l of Egypt
2Ch 22:12 Athaliah reigned over the l
2Ch 23:13 were all the people of the l
2Ch 23:20 and all the people of the l
2Ch 23:21 the people of the l rejoiced
2Ch 26:21 judging the people of the l
2Ch 30: 9 they may come back to this l
2Ch 30:25 who came from the l of Israel
2Ch 32: 4 brook that ran through the l
2Ch 32:21 shamefaced to his own l
2Ch 32:31 wonder that was done in the l
2Ch 33: 8 l which I have appointed for
2Ch 33:25 But the people of the l
2Ch 33:25 Then the people of the l made
2Ch 34: 7 all the l of Israel, he
2Ch 34: 8 when he had purged the l
2Ch 36: 1 Then the people of the l took
2Ch 36: 3 he imposed on the l a tribute
2Ch 36:21 until the l had enjoyed her
Ezra 4: 4 Then the people of the l
Ezra 6:21 l in order to seek the LORD
Ezra 9:11 The l which you are entering
Ezra 9:11 to possess is an unclean l
Ezra 9:12 and eat the good of the l, and
Ezra 10: 2 from the peoples of the l
Ezra 10:11 from the peoples of the l
Neh 4: 4 plunder to a l of captivity
Neh 5:14 governor in the l of Judah
Neh 5:16 wall, and we did not buy any l
Neh 9: 8 give the l of the Canaanites
Neh 9:10 all the people of his l
Neh 9:11 midst of the sea on the dry l
Neh 9:15 to go in to possess the l
Neh 9:22 possession of the l of Sihon
Neh 9:22 the l of the king of Heshbon,
Neh 9:22 the l of Og king of Bashan
Neh 9:23 brought them into the l which
Neh 9:24 went in and possessed the l
Neh 9:24 them the inhabitants of the l
Neh 9:24 kings and the people of the l
Neh 9:25 strong cities and a rich l
Neh 9:35 rich l which You set before
Neh 9:36 the l that You gave to our
Neh 10:30 wives to the peoples of the l
Neh 10:31 that if the peoples of the l
Neh 10:37 of our l to the Levites, for
Esth 8:17 people of the l became Jews
Esth 10: 1 imposed tribute on the l and
Job 1: 1 was a man in the l of Uz,
Job 1:10 have increased in the l
Job 10:21 to the l of darkness and the
Job 10:22 a l as dark as darkness
Job 15:19 to whom alone the l was given
Job 22: 8 mighty man possessed the l
Job 24: 4 of the l are forced to hide
Job 28:13 found in the l of the living
Job 30: 8 they were scourged from the l
Job 31:38 If my l cries out against me,
Job 37:13 for correction, or for His l
Job 38:26 on a l where there is no one
Job 39: 6 the barren l his dwelling
Job 42:15 In all the l were found no
Ps 10:16 have perished out of His l
Ps 27:13 LORD In the l of the living
Ps 35:20 those who are quiet in the l
Ps 37: 3 Dwell in the l, and feed on
Ps 37:29 righteous shall inherit the l
Ps 37:34 exalt you to inherit the l
Ps 42: 6 You from the l of the Jordan
Ps 44: 3 of the l by their own sword
Ps 52: 5 you from the l of the living
Ps 63: 1 thirsty l Where there is no
Ps 66: 6 He turned the sea into dry l
Ps 68: 6 rebellious dwell in a dry l
Ps 74: 8 places of God in the l
Ps 78:12 In the l of Egypt, in the
Ps 80: 9 deep root, And it filled the l
Ps 81: 5 throughout the l of Egypt
Ps 81:10 you out of the l of Egypt
Ps 85: 1 have been favorable to Your l
Ps 85: 9 That glory may dwell in our l
Ps 85:12 our l will yield its increase
Ps 88:12 in the l of forgetfulness
Ps 95: 5 And His hands formed the dry l
Ps 101: 6 be on the faithful of the l
Ps 101: 8 all the wicked of the l, That
Ps 105:11 To you I will give the l of
Ps 105:16 called for a famine in the l
Ps 105:23 sojourned in the l of Ham
Ps 105:27 And wonders in the l of Ham
Ps 105:30 Their l abounded with frogs,
Ps 105:32 And flaming fire in their l
Ps 105:35 all the vegetation in their l
Ps 105:36 all the firstborn in their l

Ps 106:22 works in the l of Ham,
Ps 106:24 they despised the pleasant l
Ps 106:38 the l was polluted with blood
Ps 107:34 A fruitful l into barrenness,
Ps 107:35 And dry l into watersprings
Ps 116: 9 LORD In the l of the living
Ps 125: 3 shall not rest On the l
Ps 135:12 gave their l as a heritage, A
Ps 136:21 gave their l as a heritage,
Ps 137: 4 LORD's song In a foreign l
Ps 142: 5 in the l of the living
Ps 143: 6 for You like a thirsty l
Ps 143:10 me in the l of uprightness
Prov 2:21 upright will dwell in the l
Prov 12:11 He who tills his l will be
Prov 28: 2 of the transgression of a l
Prov 28:19 He who tills his l will have
Prov 29: 4 establishes the l by justice
Prov 31:23 among the elders of the l
Eccl 5: 9 profit of the l is for all
Eccl 10:16 Woe to you, O l, when your
Eccl 10:17 Blessed are you, O l, when
Song 2:12 turtledove is heard in our l
Is 1: 7 your l in your presence
Is 1:19 shall eat the good of the l
Is 2: 7 Their l is also full of
Is 2: 7 their l is also full of
Is 2: 8 Their l is also full of idols
Is 5: 8 alone in the midst of the l
Is 5:30 And if one looks to the l,
Is 6:11 the l is utterly desolate,
Is 6:12 many in the midst of the l
Is 7:16 the l that you dread will be
Is 7:18 that is in the l of Assyria
Is 7:22 will eat who is left in the l
Is 7:24 because all the l will become
Is 8: 8 fill the breadth of Your l
Is 9: 1 esteemed the l of Zebulun
Is 9: 1 and the l of Naphtali, and
Is 9: 2 the l of the shadow of death
Is 9:19 of hosts the l is burned up
Is 10:23 end in the midst of all the l
Is 11:16 came up from the l of Egypt
Is 13: 5 to destroy the whole l
Is 13: 9 anger, to lay the l desolate
Is 13:14 will flee to his own l
Is 14: 1 and settle them in their own l
Is 14: 2 and maids in the l of the LORD
Is 14:20 you have destroyed your l
Is 14:21 they rise up and possess the l
Is 14:25 break the Assyrian in My l
Is 15: 9 and on the remnant of the l
Is 16: 1 lamb to the ruler of the l
Is 16: 4 are consumed out of the l
Is 18: 1 Woe to the l shadowed with
Is 18: 2 whose l the rivers divide
Is 18: 7 whose l the rivers divide
Is 19:17 And the l of Judah will be a
Is 19:18 the l of Egypt will speak the
Is 19:19 the midst of the l of Egypt
Is 19:20 of hosts in the l of Egypt
Is 19:24 in the midst of the l,
Is 21: 1 the desert, from a terrible l
Is 21:14 inhabitants of the l of Tema
Is 23: 1 from the l of Cyprus it is
Is 23:10 through your l like the River
Is 23:13 the l of the Chaldeans, this
Is 24: 3 The l shall be entirely
Is 24:11 the mirth of the l is gone
Is 24:13 of the l among the people
Is 26: 1 be sung in the l of Judah
Is 26:10 in the l of uprightness he
Is 26:15 all the borders of the l
Is 27:13 to perish in the l of Assyria
Is 27:13 outcasts in the l of Egypt
Is 30: 6 Through a l of trouble and
Is 32: 2 of a great rock in a weary l
Is 32:13 On the l of my people will
Is 33:17 they will see the l that is
Is 34: 6 slaughter in the l of Edom
Is 34: 7 their l shall be soaked with
Is 34: 9 its l shall become burning
Is 35: 7 and the thirsty l springs of
Is 36:10 against this l to destroy it
Is 36:10 to me, Go up against this l
Is 36:17 to a l like your own l
Is 36:17 a l of grain and new wine, a
Is 36:17 a l of bread and vineyards
Is 36:18 l from the hand of the king
Is 37: 7 rumor and return to his own l
Is 37: 7 by the sword in his own l
Is 37:38 escaped into the l of Ararat
Is 38:11 LORD in the l of the living
Is 41:18 the dry l springs of water
Is 49:12 and these from the l of Sinim
Is 49:19 the l of your destruction,
Is 53: 8 off from the l of the living
Is 57:13 in Me shall possess the l
Is 60: 6 of camels shall cover your l
Is 60:18 no longer be heard in your l
Is 60:21 shall inherit the l forever
Is 61: 7 Therefore in their l they
Is 62: 4 nor shall your l any more be
Is 62: 4 Hephzibah, and your l Beulah
Is 62: 4 and your l shall be married
Jer 1: 1 Anathoth in the l of Benjamin
Jer 1:14 all the inhabitants of the l
Jer 1:18 walls against the whole l
Jer 1:18 against the people of the l
Jer 2: 2 in a l that was not sown
Jer 2: 6 us up out of the l of Egypt
Jer 2: 6 through a l of deserts and
Jer 2: 6 through a l of drought and the
Jer 2: 6 through a l that no one
Jer 2: 7 you entered, you defiled My l
Jer 2:15 they made his l waste
Jer 2:31 to Israel, Or a l of darkness
Jer 3: 1 Would not that l be greatly
Jer 3: 2 the l with your harlotries
Jer 3: 9 that she defiled the l and
Jer 3:16 in the l in those days
Jer 3:18 l of the north to the l
Jer 3:19 and give you a pleasant l, a
Jer 4: 5 Blow the trumpet in the l
Jer 4: 7 place to make your l desolate
Jer 4:20 for the whole l is plundered
Jer 4:26 fruitful l was a wilderness
Jer 4:27 The whole l shall be desolate
Jer 5:19 served foreign gods in your l
Jer 5:19 in a l that is not yours
Jer 5:30 has been committed in the l
Jer 6: 8 desolate, a l not inhabited
Jer 6:12 the inhabitants of the l,"
Jer 7: 7 in the l that I gave to your
Jer 7:22 them out of the l of Egypt
Jer 7:25 the l of Egypt until this day
Jer 7:34 For the l shall be desolate
Jer 8:16 The whole l trembled at the
Jer 8:16 have come and devoured the l
Jer 9:12 Why does the l perish and burn
Jer 9:19 we have forsaken the l,
Jer 10:17 up your wares from the l, O
Jer 10:18 time the inhabitants of the l
Jer 11: 4 them out of the l of Egypt
Jer 11: 5 to give them a l flowing with
Jer 11: 7 them up out of the l of Egypt
Jer 11:19 off from the l of the living
Jer 12: 4 How long will the l mourn
Jer 12: 5 And if in the l of peace, in
Jer 12:11 the whole l is made desolate,
Jer 12:12 the l to the other end of the
Jer 12:12 to the other end of the l
Jer 12:14 pluck them out of their l
Jer 12:15 heritage and everyone to his l
Jer 13:13 all the inhabitants of this l
Jer 14: 2 they mourn for the l, and the
Jer 14: 4 there was no rain in the l
Jer 14: 8 be like a stranger in the l
Jer 14:15 shall not be in this l'
Jer 14:18 about in a l they do not know
Jer 15: 7 fan in the gates of the l
Jer 15:14 a l which you do not know
Jer 16: 3 who begot them in this l
Jer 16: 6 the small shall die in this l
Jer 16:13 l into a l that you do not
Jer 16:14 of Israel from the l of Egypt
Jer 16:15 from the l of the north and
Jer 16:15 their l which I gave to their
Jer 16:18 they have defiled My l
Jer 17: 4 the l which you do not know
Jer 17: 6 in a salt l which is not
Jer 17:26 from the l of Benjamin and
Jer 18:16 to make their l desolate and a
Jer 22:12 and shall see this l no more
Jer 22:27 But to the l to which they
Jer 22:28 cast into a l which they do
Jer 23: 7 of Israel from the l of Egypt
Jer 23: 8 shall dwell in their own l
Jer 23:10 For the l is full of
Jer 23:10 of a curse the l mourns
Jer 23:15 has gone out into all the l
Jer 24: 5 into the l of the Chaldeans
Jer 24: 6 bring them back to this l
Jer 24: 8 who remain in this l, and
Jer 24: 8 who dwell in the l of Egypt
Jer 24:10 the l that I gave to them
Jer 25: 5 dwell in the l that the LORD
Jer 25: 9 bring them against this l
Jer 25:11 And this whole l shall be a
Jer 25:12 the l of the Chaldeans, for
Jer 25:13 So I will bring on that l
Jer 25:20 all the kings of the l of Uz
Jer 25:20 all the kings of the l of the
Jer 25:38 for their l is desolate
Jer 26:17 the elders of the l rose up
Jer 26:20 against this l according to
Jer 27: 7 until the time of his l comes
Jer 27:10 to remove you far from your l
Jer 27:11 them remain in their own l
Jer 30: 3 to the l that I gave to their
Jer 30:10 from the l of their captivity
Jer 31:16 back from the l of the enemy
Jer 31:23 this speech in the l of Judah
Jer 31:32 them out of the l of Egypt
Jer 32:15 be possessed again in this l
Jer 32:20 and wonders in the l of Egypt
Jer 32:21 of the l of Egypt with signs
Jer 32:22 You have given them this l
Jer 32:22 a l flowing with milk and
Jer 32:41 plant them in this l, with
Jer 32:43 in this l of which you say
Jer 32:44 in the l of Benjamin, in the
Jer 33:11 l to return as at the first
Jer 33:13 in the l of Benjamin, in the
Jer 34:13 them out of the l of Egypt
Jer 34:19 all the people of the l who
Jer 35: 7 l where you are sojourners
Jer 35:11 of Babylon came up into the l
Jer 35:15 the l which I have given you
Jer 36:29 come and destroy this l, and
Jer 37: 1 made king in the l of Judah
Jer 37: 2 nor the people of the l gave
Jer 37: 7 to Egypt, to their own l
Jer 37:12 l of Benjamin to claim his
Jer 37:19 against you or against this l
Jer 39: 5 to Riblah in the l of Hamath
Jer 39:10 l of Judah the poor people
Jer 40: 4 See, all the l is before you
Jer 40: 6 people who were left in the l
Jer 40: 7 of Ahikam governor in the l
Jer 40: 7 the poorest of the l who had
Jer 40: 9 Dwell in the l and serve the
Jer 40:12 and came to the l of Judah
Jer 41: 2 had made governor over the l
Jer 41:18 had made governor in the l
Jer 42:10 will still abide in this l
Jer 42:12 you to return to your own l
Jer 42:13 We will not dwell in this l
Jer 42:14 but we will go to the l of
Jer 42:16 you there in the l of Egypt
Jer 43: 4 to remain in the l of Judah
Jer 43: 5 to dwell in the l of Judah
Jer 43: 7 they went to the l of Egypt
Jer 43:11 shall strike the l of Egypt
Jer 43:12 himself with the l of Egypt
Jer 43:13 that are in the l of Egypt
Jer 44: 1 who dwell in the l of Egypt
Jer 44: 8 to other gods in the l of
Jer 44: 9 committed in the l of Judah
Jer 44:12 l of Egypt to sojourn there
Jer 44:12 and fall in the l of Egypt
Jer 44:13 who dwell in the l of Egypt
Jer 44:14 who have gone into the l of
Jer 44:14 they return to the l of Judah
Jer 44:15 who dwelt in the l of Egypt
Jer 44:21 and the people of the l, did
Jer 44:22 Therefore your l is a
Jer 44:24 who are in the l of Egypt
Jer 44:26 who dwell in the l of Egypt
Jer 44:26 Judah in all the l of Egypt
Jer 44:27 l of Egypt shall be consumed
Jer 44:28 the l of Egypt to the l of
Jer 44:28 of Egypt to the l of Judah
Jer 44:28 who have gone to the l of
Jer 45: 4 up, that is, this whole l
Jer 46:12 and your cry has filled the l
Jer 46:13 come and strike the l of Egypt
Jer 46:16 to the l of our nativity from
Jer 46:27 from the l of their captivity
Jer 47: 2 They shall overflow the l

Jer 47: 2 of the l shall wail
Jer 48:24 the cities of the l of Moab
Jer 48:33 field and from the l of Moab
Jer 50: 1 and against the l of the
Jer 50: 3 shall make her l desolate
Jer 50: 8 go out of the l of the
Jer 50:12 be a wilderness, a dry l and a
Jer 50:16 shall flee to his own l
Jer 50:18 the king of Babylon and his l
Jer 50:21 up against the l of Merathaim
Jer 50:22 A sound of battle is in the l
Jer 50:25 in the l of the Chaldeans
Jer 50:28 escape from the l of Babylon
Jer 50:34 He may give rest to the l
Jer 50:38 For it is the l of carved
Jer 50:45 the l of the Chaldeans
Jer 51: 2 winnow her and empty her l
Jer 51: 4 in the l of the Chaldeans
Jer 51: 5 though their l was filled
Jer 51:27 Set up a banner in the l,
Jer 51:28 All the l of his dominion
Jer 51:29 the l will tremble and sorrow
Jer 51:29 to make the l of Babylon a
Jer 51:43 are a desolation, a dry l
Jer 51:43 a l where no one dwells,
Jer 51:46 that will be heard in the l
Jer 51:46 come, and violence in the l
Jer 51:47 her whole l shall be ashamed,
Jer 51:52 and throughout all her l the
Jer 51:54 from the l of the Chaldeans
Jer 52: 6 food for the people of the l
Jer 52: 9 at Riblah in the l of Hamath
Jer 52:16 poor of the l as vinedressers
Jer 52:25 mustered the people of the l
Jer 52:25 men of the people of the l
Jer 52:27 at Riblah in the l of Hamath
Jer 52:27 away captive from its own l
Lam 4:21 you who dwell in the l of Uz
Ezek 1: 3 in the l of the Chaldeans by
Ezek 6:14 them and make the l desolate
Ezek 7: 2 Lord GOD to the l of Israel
Ezek 7: 2 the four corners of the l
Ezek 7: 7 you, you who dwell in the l
Ezek 7:23 for the l is filled with
Ezek 8:12 the LORD has forsaken the l
Ezek 8:17 filled the l with violence
Ezek 9: 9 the l is full of bloodshed,
Ezek 9: 9 The LORD has forsaken the l
Ezek 11:15 this l has been given to us
Ezek 11:17 will give you the l of Israel
Ezek 12:13 to the l of the Chaldeans
Ezek 12:19 And say to the people of the l
Ezek 12:19 and to the l of Israel
Ezek 12:19 so that her l may be emptied
Ezek 12:20 the l shall become desolate
Ezek 12:22 have about the l of Israel
Ezek 13: 9 enter into the l of Israel
Ezek 14:13 when a l sins against Me by
Ezek 14:15 beasts to pass through the l
Ezek 14:16 and the l would be desolate
Ezek 14:17 if I bring a sword on that l
Ezek 14:17 say, 'Sword, go through the l
Ezek 14:19 send a pestilence into that l
Ezek 15: 8 I will make the l desolate
Ezek 16: 3 are from the l of Canaan
Ezek 16:29 as far as the l of the trader
Ezek 17: 4 and carried it to a l of trade
Ezek 17: 5 some of the seed of the l
Ezek 17:13 took away the mighty of the l
Ezek 18: 2 concerning the l of Israel
Ezek 19: 4 with chains to the l of Egypt
Ezek 19: 7 the l with its fullness was
Ezek 19:13 in a dry and thirsty l
Ezek 20: 5 to them in the l of Egypt
Ezek 20: 6 to bring them out of the l of
Ezek 20: 6 l that I had searched out for
Ezek 20: 8 the midst of the l of Egypt
Ezek 20: 9 them out of the l of Egypt
Ezek 20:10 them go out of the l of Egypt
Ezek 20:15 the l which I had given them
Ezek 20:28 I brought them into the l for
Ezek 20:36 wilderness of the l of Egypt
Ezek 20:38 not enter the l of Israel
Ezek 20:40 Israel, all of them in the l
Ezek 20:42 you into the l of Israel,
Ezek 20:46 prophesy against the forest l
Ezek 21: 2 against the l of Israel
Ezek 21: 3 and say to the l of Israel
Ezek 21:19 them shall go from the same l
Ezek 21:30 in the l of your nativity
Ezek 21:32 be in the midst of the l
Ezek 22:24 You are a l that is not
Ezek 22:29 The people of the l have used
Ezek 22:30 before Me on behalf of the l
Ezek 23:15 the l of their nativity
Ezek 23:19 the harlot in the l of Egypt
Ezek 23:27 brought from the l of Egypt
Ezek 23:48 lewdness to cease from the l
Ezek 25: 3 against the l of Israel when
Ezek 25: 6 disdain for the l of Israel
Ezek 26:20 glory in the l of the living
Ezek 27:17 the l of Israel were your
Ezek 28:25 will dwell in their own l
Ezek 29: 9 the l of Egypt shall become
Ezek 29:10 I will make the l of Egypt
Ezek 29:12 I will make the l of Egypt
Ezek 29:14 to return to the l of Pathros
Ezek 29:14 to the l of their origin, and
Ezek 29:19 Surely I will give the l of
Ezek 29:20 I have given him the l of
Ezek 30:11 be brought to destroy the l
Ezek 30:11 fill the l with the slain
Ezek 30:12 sell the l into the hand of
Ezek 30:12 I will make the l waste, and
Ezek 30:13 princes from the l of Egypt
Ezek 30:13 put fear in the l of Egypt
Ezek 30:25 it out against the l of Egypt
Ezek 31:12 by all the rivers of the l
Ezek 32: 4 I will leave you on the l
Ezek 32: 6 I will also water the l with
Ezek 32: 8 and bring darkness upon your l
Ezek 32:15 When I make the l of Egypt
Ezek 32:23 terror in the l of the living
Ezek 32:24 terror in the l of the living
Ezek 32:25 caused in the l of the living
Ezek 32:26 terror in the l of the living
Ezek 32:27 mighty in the l of the living
Ezek 32:32 terror in the l of the living
Ezek 33: 2 I bring the sword upon a l
Ezek 33: 2 the people of the l take a
Ezek 33: 3 the sword coming upon the l
Ezek 33:24 in the l of Israel are saying
Ezek 33:24 one, and he inherited the l
Ezek 33:24 the l has been given to us as
Ezek 33:25 Should you then possess the l
Ezek 33:26 Should you then possess the l
Ezek 33:28 will make the l most desolate
Ezek 33:29 when I have made the l most
Ezek 34:13 bring them to their own l
Ezek 34:25 beasts to cease from the l
Ezek 34:27 They shall be safe in their l
Ezek 34:28 beasts of the l devour them
Ezek 34:29 consumed with hunger in the l
Ezek 36: 5 who gave My l to themselves
Ezek 36: 6 concerning the l of Israel
Ezek 36:17 Israel dwelt in their own l
Ezek 36:18 blood they had shed on the l
Ezek 36:20 they have gone out of His l
Ezek 36:24 and bring you into your own l
Ezek 36:28 l that I gave to your fathers
Ezek 36:34 The desolate l shall be
Ezek 36:35 This l that was desolate has
Ezek 37:12 you into the l of Israel
Ezek 37:14 will place you in your own l
Ezek 37:21 bring them into their own l
Ezek 37:22 make them one nation in the l
Ezek 37:25 they shall dwell in the l
Ezek 38: 2 of the l of Magog, the prince
Ezek 38: 8 you will come into the l of
Ezek 38: 9 covering the l like a cloud
Ezek 38:11 a l of unwalled villages
Ezek 38:12 dwell in the midst of the l
Ezek 38:16 like a cloud, to cover the l
Ezek 38:16 I will bring you against My l
Ezek 38:18 comes against the l of Israel
Ezek 38:19 earthquake in the l of Israel
Ezek 39:12 in order to cleanse the l
Ezek 39:13 of the l will be burying them
Ezek 39:14 party, to pass through the l
Ezek 39:15 party will pass through the l
Ezek 39:16 Thus they shall cleanse the l
Ezek 39:26 dwelt safely in their own l
Ezek 39:28 them back to their own l, and
Ezek 40: 2 took me into the l of Israel
Ezek 45: 1 when you divide the l by lot
Ezek 45: 1 LORD, a holy portion of the l
Ezek 45: 4 be a holy portion of the l
Ezek 45: 8 The l shall be his possession
Ezek 45: 8 the l to the house of Israel
Ezek 45:16 All the people of the l shall
Ezek 45:22 l a bull for a sin offering
Ezek 46: 3 of the l shall worship at the
Ezek 46: 9 But when the people of the l
Ezek 47:13 which you shall divide the l
Ezek 47:14 this l shall fall to you as
Ezek 47:15 border of the l on the north
Ezek 47:18 the l of Israel, along the
Ezek 47:21 l among yourselves according
Ezek 48:12 this district of l that is
Ezek 48:14 this best part of the l, for
Ezek 48:29 This is the l which you shall
Dan 1: 2 l of Shinar to the house of
Dan 8: 9 and toward the Glorious L
Dan 9: 6 and all the people of the l
Dan 9:15 Your people out of the l of
Dan 11: 9 but shall return to his own l
Dan 11:16 L with destruction in his
Dan 11:19 the fortress of his own l
Dan 11:28 to his l with great riches
Dan 11:28 damage and return to his own l
Dan 11:39 and divide the l for gain
Dan 11:41 also enter the Glorious L
Dan 11:42 and the l of Egypt shall not
Hos 1: 2 for the l has committed great
Hos 1:11 shall come up out of the l
Hos 2: 3 and set her like a dry l, and
Hos 2:15 came up from the l of Egypt
Hos 4: 1 the inhabitants of the l
Hos 4: 1 or knowledge of God in the l
Hos 4: 3 Therefore the l will mourn
Hos 7:16 derision in the l of Egypt
Hos 9: 3 not dwell in the LORD's l
Hos 10: 1 to the bounty of his l they
Hos 11: 5 not return to the l of Egypt
Hos 11:11 a dove from the l of Assyria
Hos 12: 9 ever since the l of Egypt
Hos 13: 4 God ever since the l of Egypt
Hos 13: 5 in the l of great drought
Joel 1: 2 all you inhabitants of the l
Joel 1: 6 has come up against My l,
Joel 1:10 field is wasted, the l mourns
Joel 1:14 l into the house of the LORD
Joel 2: 1 inhabitants of the l tremble
Joel 2: 3 the l is like the Garden of
Joel 2:18 will be zealous for His l
Joel 2:20 into a barren and desolate l
Joel 2:21 Fear not, O l
Joel 3: 2 have also divided up My l
Joel 3:19 innocent blood in their l
Amos 2:10 you up from the l of Egypt
Amos 2:10 possess the l of the Amorite
Amos 3: 1 up from the l of Egypt,
Amos 3: 9 the palaces in the l of Egypt
Amos 3:11 shall be all around the l
Amos 5: 2 She lies forsaken on her l
Amos 7: 2 eating the grass of the l
Amos 7:10 The l is not able to bear all
Amos 7:11 away captive from their own l
Amos 7:12 Flee to the l of Judah
Amos 7:17 your l shall be divided by
Amos 7:17 you shall die in a defiled l
Amos 7:17 away captive from his own l
Amos 8: 4 make the poor of the l fail
Amos 8: 8 Shall the l not tremble for
Amos 8:11 I will send a famine on the l
Amos 9: 7 up Israel from the l of Egypt
Amos 9:15 I will plant them in their l
Amos 9:15 from the l I have given them
Obad 20 l of the Canaanites as far as
Jon 1: 9 who made the sea and the dry l
Jon 1:13 hard to bring the ship to l
Jon 2:10 it vomited Jonah onto dry l
Mic 5: 5 the Assyrian comes into our l
Mic 5: 6 the sword the l of Assyria
Mic 5: 6 and the l of Nimrod at its
Mic 5: 6 when he comes into our l
Mic 5:11 cut off the cities of your l
Mic 6: 4 you up from the l of Egypt
Mic 7:13 Yet the l shall be desolate
Mic 7:15 came out of the l of Egypt
Nah 3:13 The gates of your l are wide
Hab 2: 8 and the violence of the l and
Hab 2:17 and the violence of the l and
Hab 3: 7 of the l of Midian trembled
Hab 3:12 through the l in indignation
Zeph 1: 2 things from the face of the l
Zeph 1: 3 man from the face of the l
Zeph 1:18 but the whole l shall be
Zeph 1:18 all those who dwell in the l
Zeph 2: 5 Canaan, l of the Philistines

Zeph 3:19 fame in every l where they
Hag 1:11 called for a drought on the l
Hag 2: 4 all you people of the l,'
Hag 2: 6 and earth, the sea and dry l
Zech 1:21 the l of Judah to scatter it
Zech 2: 6 Flee from the l of the north
Zech 2:12 His inheritance in the Holy L
Zech 3: 9 iniquity of that l in one day
Zech 5:11 for it in the l of Shinar
Zech 7: 5 to all the people of the l
Zech 7:14 Thus the l became desolate
Zech 7:14 made the pleasant l desolate
Zech 8: 7 people from the l of the east
Zech 8: 7 and from the l of the west
Zech 9: 1 LORD against the l of Hadrach
Zech 9:16 like a banner over His l
Zech 10:10 them back from the l of Egypt
Zech 10:10 them into the l of Gilead
Zech 11: 6 pity the inhabitants of the l
Zech 11: 6 They shall attack the l, and I
Zech 11:16 raise up a shepherd in the l
Zech 12:12 And the l shall mourn, every
Zech 13: 2 names of the idols from the l
Zech 13: 2 spirit to depart from the l
Zech 13: 8 come to pass in all the l
Zech 14:10 All the l shall be turned
Mal 3:12 you will be a delightful l
Matt 2: 6 in the l of Judah, are not
Matt 2:20 and go to the l of Israel
Matt 2:21 and came into the l of Israel
Matt 4:15 The l of Zebulun and the l
Matt 4:15 the l of Naphtali, the way of
Matt 9:26 this went out into all that l
Matt 10:15 tolerable for the l of Sodom
Matt 11:24 the l of Sodom in the day of
Matt 14:34 came to the l of Gennesaret
Matt 23:15 For you travel l and sea to
Matt 27:45 was darkness over all the l
Mark 1: 5 all the l of Judea, and those
Mark 4: 1 was on the l facing the sea
Mark 6:47 and He was alone on the l
Mark 6:53 came to the l of Gennesaret
Mark 15:33 whole l until the ninth hour
Luke 4:25 famine throughout all the l
Luke 5: 3 put out a little from the l
Luke 5:11 had brought their boats to l
Luke 8:27 when He stepped out on the l
Luke 14:35 the l nor for the dunghill
Luke 15:14 a severe famine in that l
Luke 21:23 be great distress in the l
John 3:22 came into the l of Judea, and
John 6:21 the boat was at the l where
John 21: 8 (for they were not far from l
John 21: 9 as soon as they had come to l
John 21:11 up and dragged the net to l
Acts 4:37 having l, sold it, and brought
Acts 5: 3 price of the l for yourself
Acts 5: 8 you sold the l for so much
Acts 7: 3 come to a l that I will show
Acts 7: 4 out of the l of the Chaldeans
Acts 7: 4 He moved him to this l in
Acts 7: 6 would sojourn in a foreign l
Acts 7:11 came over all the l of Egypt
Acts 7:29 sojourner in the l of Midian
Acts 7:36 and signs in the l of Egypt
Acts 7:40 us out of the l of Egypt, we
Acts 7:45 with Joshua into the l
Acts 10:39 did both in the l of the Jews
Acts 13:17 strangers in the l of Egypt
Acts 13:19 nations in the l of Canaan
Acts 13:19 their l to them by allotment
Acts 27:27 they were drawing near some l
Acts 27:39 they did not recognize the l
Acts 27:43 overboard first and get to l
Acts 27:44 they all escaped safely to l
Heb 8: 9 them out of the l of Egypt
Heb 11: 9 faith he sojourned in the l
Heb 11:29 the Red Sea as by dry l,
Jas 5:17 rain on the l for three years
Jude 5 people out of the l of Egypt
Rev 10: 2 sea and his left foot on the l
Rev 10: 5 on the l lifted up his hand

LANDED (*see* LAND)
Acts 18:22 And when he had l at Caesarea
Acts 21: 3 sailed to Syria, and l at Tyre
Acts 27: 3 And the next day we l at Sidon

LANDING (*see* LAND)
Acts 28:12 And l at Syracuse, we stayed

LANDMARK (*see* LAND, LANDMARKS)
Deut 19:14 not remove your neighbor's l
Deut 27:17 who moves his neighbor's l
Prov 22:28 Do not remove the ancient l
Prov 23:10 Do not remove the ancient l
Hos 5:10 are like those who remove a l

LANDMARKS (*see* LANDMARK)
Job 24: 2 Some remove l
Jer 31:21 Set up signposts, make l

LANDOWNER (*see* LAND)
Matt 20: 1 a l who went out early in the
Matt 20:11 they murmured against the l
Matt 21:33 There was a certain l who

LANDS (*see* LAND)
Gen 10: 5 were separated into their l
Gen 10:20 their languages, in their l
Gen 10:31 their languages, in their l
Gen 26: 3 I give all these l, and I will
Gen 26: 4 your descendants all these l
Gen 41:54 The famine was in all l, but
Gen 41:57 famine was severe in all l
Gen 47:18 lord but our bodies and our l
Gen 47:22 they did not sell their l
Lev 26:36 in the l of their enemies
Lev 26:39 iniquity in your enemies' l
Judg 11:13 restore those l peaceably
2Ki 18:35 of the l have delivered their
2Ki 19:11 l by utterly destroying them
2Ki 19:17 waste the nations and their l
1Ch 14:17 of David went out into all l
1Ch 29:30 to all the kingdoms of the l
2Ch 9:28 from Egypt and from all l
2Ch 13: 9 like the peoples of other l
2Ch 15: 5 all the inhabitants of the l
2Ch 17:10 the l that were around Judah
2Ch 32:13 to all the peoples of other l
2Ch 32:13 of the nations of those l in
2Ch 32:13 their l out of my hand
2Ch 32:17 of the nations of other l
Ezra 9: 1 from the peoples of the l
Ezra 9: 2 with the peoples of those l
Ezra 9: 7 hand of the kings of the l
Ezra 9:11 of the peoples of the l, with
Neh 5: 3 We have mortgaged our l and
Neh 5: 4 for the king's tax on our l
Neh 5: 5 for other men have our l
Neh 5:11 them, even this day, their l
Neh 9:30 hand of the peoples of the l
Neh 10:28 of the l to the Law of God
Ps 49:11 They call their l after their
Ps 100: 1 shout to the LORD, all you l
Ps 105:44 them the l of the Gentiles
Ps 106:27 And to scatter them in the l
Ps 107: 3 And gathered out of the l,
Is 36:20 these l have delivered their
Is 37:11 l by utterly destroying them
Is 37:18 all the nations and their l
Jer 16:15 from all the l where He had
Jer 27: 6 all these l into the hand of
Ezek 20: 6 and honey, the glory of all l
Ezek 20:15 and honey, the glory of all l
Ezek 30: 5 men of the l who are allied
Ezek 39:27 them out of their enemies' l
Matt 19:29 or wife or children or l, for
Mark 10:29 or wife or children or l, for
Mark 10:30 and mothers and children and l
Acts 4:34 of l or houses sold them, and

LANES
Luke 14:21 l of the city, and bring in

LANGUAGE (*see* LANGUAGES)
Gen 10: 5 according to his own l,
Gen 11: 1 Now the whole earth had one l
Gen 11: 6 one and they all have one l
Gen 11: 7 down and there confuse their l
Gen 11: 9 the l of all the earth
Deut 28:49 a nation whose l you will not
2Ki 18:26 servants in the Aramaic l
Ezra 4: 7 translated into the Aramaic l
Neh 13:24 spoke the l of Ashdod, and
Neh 13:24 not speak the l of Judah, but
Neh 13:24 l of one or the other people
Esth 1:22 every people in their own l
Esth 1:22 speak in the l of his own
Esth 3:12 and to every people in their l
Esth 8: 9 every people in their own l
Esth 8: 9 Jews in their own script and l
Ps 19: 3 There is no speech nor l
Ps 81: 5 Where I heard a l that I did
Ps 114: 1 from a people of strange l
Is 19:18 will speak the l of Canaan
Is 36:11 servants in the Aramaic l
Jer 5:15 a nation whose l you do not
Ezek 3: 5 speech and of hard l, but to
Ezek 3: 6 speech and of hard l, whose
Dan 1: 4 whom they might teach the l
Dan 3:29 or l which speaks anything
Zeph 3: 9 to the peoples a pure l, that
Zech 8:23 days ten men from every l of
John 16:25 spoken to you in figurative l
John 16:25 speak to you in figurative l
Acts 1:19 is called in their own l,
Acts 2: 6 heard them speak in his own l
Acts 2: 8 each in our own l in which we
Acts 14:11 saying in the Lycaonian l
Acts 21:40 spoke to them in the Hebrew l
Acts 22: 2 spoke to them in the Hebrew l
Acts 26:14 me and saying in the Hebrew l
1Co 14:11 not know the meaning of the l
Col 3: 8 filthy l out of your mouth

LANGUAGES (*see* LANGUAGE)
Gen 10:20 according to their l, in
Gen 10:31 according to their l, in
Dan 3: 4 O peoples, nations, and l
Dan 3: 7 l fell down and worshiped the
Dan 4: 1 l that dwell in all the earth
Dan 5:19 l trembled and feared before
Dan 6:25 l that dwell in all the earth
Dan 7:14 and l should serve Him
1Co 14:10 many kinds of l in the world

LANGUISH (*see* LANGUISHED, LANGUISHES)
Is 16: 8 For the fields of Heshbon l
Is 19: 8 they will l who spread nets
Is 24: 4 haughty people of the earth l
Jer 14: 2 Judah mourns, and her gates l

LANGUISHED (*see* LANGUISH)
Gen 47:13 l because of the famine
Lam 2: 8 they l together

LANGUISHES (*see* LANGUISH)
Is 24: 4 and fades away, the world l
Is 24: 7 new wine fails, the vine l
Is 33: 9 The earth mourns and l,
Jer 15: 9 She l who has borne seven

LANTERNS
John 18: 3 Pharisees, came there with l

LAODICEA (*see* LAODICEANS)
Col 2: 1 I have for you and those in L
Col 4:13 you, and those who are in L
Col 4:15 the brethren who are in L
Col 4:16 read the epistle from L
Rev 1:11 to Philadelphia, and to L

LAODICEANS (*see* LAODICEA)
Col 4:16 also in the church of the L
Rev 3:14 of the church of the L write

LAP (*see* LAPPED, LAPS)
2Ki 4:39 gathered from it a l full of
Prov 16:33 The lot is cast into the l

LAPIDOTH
Judg 4: 4 a prophetess, the wife of L

LAPPED (*see* LAP)
Judg 7: 6 And the number of those who l
Judg 7: 7 men who l I will save you

LAPS (*see* LAP)
Judg 7: 5 Everyone who l from the water
Judg 7: 5 with his tongue, as a dog l

LARGE (*see* PREFACE)

LARGENESS (*see* PREFACE)

LARGER (*see* PREFACE)

LASEA
Acts 27: 8 Havens, near the city of L

LASHA
Gen 10:19 Admah, and Zeboim, as far as L

LASHARON
Josh 12:18 the king of L, one

LAST (*see* LASTED, LASTING)
Gen 19:34 I lay with my father l night
Gen 25: 8 Then Abraham breathed his l
Gen 25:17 and he breathed his l and died,
Gen 31:29 father spoke to me l night
Gen 31:42 hands, and rebuked you l night
Gen 33: 2 behind, and Rachel and Joseph l
Gen 35:29 So Isaac breathed his l and
Gen 49: 1 befall you in the l days
Gen 49:19 but he shall triumph at l
Gen 49:33 the bed and breathed his l
Lev 26: 5 Your threshing shall l till
Lev 26: 5 the vintage shall l till the
Num 2:31 they shall break camp l, with
Num 24:20 But shall be l until he
1Sa 15:16 the LORD said to me l night
2Sa 19:11 Why are you the l to bring
2Sa 19:12 Why then are you the l to
2Sa 23: 1 are the l words of David
1Ch 23:27 For by the l words of David
1Ch 29:29 of King David, first and l
2Ch 9:29 acts of Solomon, first and l
2Ch 12:15 acts of Rehoboam, first and l
2Ch 16:11 the acts of Asa, first and l
2Ch 20:34 of Jehoshaphat, first and l
2Ch 25:26 of Amaziah, from first to l
2Ch 26:22 of Uzziah, from first to l
2Ch 28:26 all his ways, from first to l
2Ch 35:27 and his deeds from first to l
Ezra 8:13 of the l sons of Adonikam,
Neh 8:18 the first day until the l day
Job 14:10 indeed he breathes his l And
Job 19:25 shall stand at l on the earth
Job 20:21 his well-being will not l
Prov 5:11 and you mourn at l, when your
Prov 23:32 at the l it bites like a
Is 41: 4 and with the l I am He
Is 44: 6 I am the First and I am the L
Is 48:12 am the First, I am also the L
Jer 15: 9 she has breathed her l
Jer 32:14 that they may l many days
Jer 50:17 now at l this Nebuchadnezzar
Lam 1:19 breathed their l in the city
Dan 4: 8 But at l Daniel came before
Dan 8: 3 and the higher one came up l
Hos 9:12 bereave them to the l man
Amos 9: 1 I will slay the l of them
Matt 5:26 you have paid the l penny
Matt 12:45 the l state of that man is
Matt 19:30 many who are first will be l
Matt 19:30 and the l first
Matt 20: 8 with the l to the first
Matt 20:12 These l men have worked only
Matt 20:14 this l man the same as to you
Matt 20:16 So the l will be first, and
Matt 20:16 will be first, and the first l
Matt 21:37 Then l of all he sent his son
Matt 22:27 l of all the woman died also
Matt 26:60 But at l two false witnesses
Matt 27:64 So the l deception will be
Mark 9:35 first, he shall be l of all
Mark 10:31 many who are first will be l
Mark 10:31 and the l first
Mark 12: 6 he also sent him to them l
Mark 12:22 L of all the woman died also
Mark 15:37 loud voice, and breathed His l
Mark 15:39 like this and breathed His l
Luke 11:26 the l state of that man is
Luke 12:59 you have paid the very l mite
Luke 13:30 indeed there are l who will
Luke 13:30 there are first who will be l
Luke 20:32 L of all the woman died also
Luke 23:46 said this, He breathed His l
John 6:39 raise it up at the l day
John 6:40 raise him up at the l day
John 6:44 raise him up at the l day
John 6:54 raise him up at the l day
John 7:37 On the l day, that great day
John 8: 9 with the oldest even to the l
John 11:24 the resurrection at the l day
John 12:48 will judge him in the l day
Acts 2:17 come to pass in the l days
Acts 5: 5 fell down and breathed his l
Acts 5:10 at his feet and breathed her l
Rom 1:10 now at l I may find a way in
1Co 4: 9 displayed us, the apostles, l
1Co 15: 8 Then l of all He was seen by
1Co 15:26 The l enemy that will be
1Co 15:45 The l Adam became a
1Co 15:52 of an eye, at the l trumpet
Phil 4:10 now at l your care for me has
2Ti 3: 1 that in the l days perilous
Heb 1: 2 has in these l days spoken to
Jas 5: 3 up treasure in the l days
1Pe 1: 5 to be revealed in the l time
1Pe 1:20 in these l times for you
2Pe 3: 3 will come in the l days,
1Jn 2:18 children, it is the l hour
1Jn 2:18 we know that it is the l hour
Jude 18 in the l time who would walk
Rev 1:11 the Omega, the First and the L
Rev 1:17 I am the First and the L
Rev 2: 8 says the First and the L, who
Rev 2:19 the l are more than the first
Rev 15: 1 having the seven l plagues
Rev 21: 9 seven l plagues came to me
Rev 22:13 the End, the First and the L

LASTED (*see* LAST)
Judg 14:17 days while their feast l

LASTING (*see* LAST)
Ex 21:22 yet no l harm follows, he
Ex 21:23 But if any l harm follows,
Esth 1: 5 the king made a feast l seven

LATCH
Song 5: 4 his hand by the l of the door

LATE (*see* LATELY, LATER)
Ex 9:32 struck, for they are l crops
2Sa 21:10 of harvest until the l rains
Job 30: 3 fleeing l to the wilderness,
Ps 127: 2 to rise up early, To sit up l
Amos 7: 1 the beginning of the l crop
Amos 7: 1 indeed it was the l crop
Matt 14:15 and the hour is already l
Mark 6:35 and already the hour is l
Mark 11:11 as the hour was already l
Jude 12 l autumn trees without fruit,
Rev 6:13 as a fig tree drops its l

LATELY (*see* LATE)
Mic 2: 8 L My people have risen up as
John 11: 8 l the Jews sought to stone

LATER (*see* LATE)
Deut 10: 6 the place where Aaron died l
Mark 14:70 a little l those who stood by
Acts 5: 7 hours l when his wife came in
Gal 3:17 hundred and thirty years l
1Ti 5:24 those of some men follow l

LATIN
Luke 23:38 Him in letters of Greek, L
John 19:20 in Hebrew, Greek, and L

LATTER
Ex 4: 8 the message of the l sign
Num 24:14 to your people in the l days
Deut 4:30 come upon you in the l days
Deut 11:14 and the l rain, that you may
Deut 24: 3 if the l husband detests her
Deut 24: 3 or if the l husband dies who
Deut 31:29 will befall you in the l days
Deut 32:29 would consider their l end
2Sa 2:26 will be bitter in the l end
Job 8: 7 yet your l end would increase
Job 42:12 Now the LORD blessed the l
Prov 16:15 is like a cloud of the l rain
Prov 19:20 may be wise in your l days
Is 2: 2 l days that the mountain of
Is 41:22 and know the l end of them
Is 47: 7 remember the l end of them
Jer 3: 3 and there has been no l rain
Jer 5:24 both the former and the l
Jer 23:20 In the l days you will
Jer 30:24 In the l days you will
Jer 48:47 of Moab in the l days," says
Jer 49:39 come to pass in the l days
Ezek 38: 8 In the l years you will come
Ezek 38:16 It will be in the l days that
Dan 2:28 what will be in the l days
Dan 8:19 the l time of the indignation
Dan 8:23 And in the l time of their
Dan 10:14 to your people in the l days
Dan 11:29 be like the former or the l
Hos 3: 5 and His goodness in the l days
Hos 6: 3 us like the rain, like the l
Joel 2:23 the l rain in the first month
Mic 4: 1 l days That the mountain of
Hag 2: 9 The glory of this l temple
Zech 10: 1 in the time of the l rain
Phil 1:17 but the l out of love,
1Ti 4: 1 expressly says that in l
2Ti 2:21 cleanses himself from the l
Jas 5: 7 receives the early and l rain
2Pe 2:20 the l end is worse for them

LATTICE
Judg 5:28 and cried out through the l
1Ki 7:17 He made a l network, with
2Ki 1: 2 the l of his upper room in
Prov 7: 6 house I looked through my l
Song 2: 9 windows, gazing through the l

LAUD
Ps 117: 1 L Him, all you peoples
Rom 15:11 l Him, all you peoples

LAUGH (*see* LAUGHED, LAUGHING, LAUGHS, LAUGHTER)
Gen 18:13 Why did Sarah l, saying
Gen 18:15 I did not l," for she was
Gen 18:15 No, but you did l
Gen 21: 6 God has made me l, so that
Gen 21: 6 all who hear will l with me
Job 5:22 You shall l at destruction and
Job 22:19 the innocent l them to scorn
Ps 2: 4 sits in the heavens shall l
Ps 22: 7 who see Me l Me to scorn
Ps 52: 6 And shall l at him, saying,
Ps 59: 8 You, O LORD, shall l at them
Ps 80: 6 And our enemies l among
Prov 1:26 I also will l at your
Eccl 3: 4 time to weep, and a time to l
Luke 6:21 who weep now, for you shall l
Luke 6:25 Woe to you who l now, For you

LAUGHED (*see* LAUGH)
Gen 17:17 Abraham fell on his face and l
Gen 18:12 Sarah l within herself,
2Ki 19:21 despised you, l you to scorn
2Ch 30:10 but they l them to scorn and
Neh 2:19 of it, they l us to scorn and
Job 12: 4 blameless who is l to scorn
Is 37:22 despised you, l you to scorn
Ezek 23:32 you shall be l to scorn and
Matt 9:24 And they l Him to scorn
Mark 5:40 And they l Him to scorn
Luke 8:53 they l Him to scorn, knowing

LAUGHING (*see* LAUGH)
Job 8:21 yet fill your mouth with l

LAUGHS (*see* LAUGH)
Job 9:23 He l at the plight of the
Job 41:29 he l at the threat of
Ps 37:13 The Lord l at him, For He
Prov 29: 9 whether the fool rages or l

LAUGHTER (*see* LAUGH)
Ps 126: 2 our mouth was filled with l
Prov 14:13 Even in l the heart may
Eccl 2: 2 I said of l, "It is madness
Eccl 7: 3 Sorrow is better than l, for
Eccl 7: 6 pot, so is the l of the fool
Eccl 10:19 A feast is made for l, and
Jas 4: 9 Let your l be turned to

LAUNCH (*see* LAUNCHED)
Luke 5: 4 L out into the deep and let

LAUNCHED (*see* LAUNCH)
Luke 8:22 And they l out

LAUNDERER
Mark 9: 3 such as no l on earth can

LAVER (*see* LAVERS)
Ex 30:18 shall also make a l of bronze
Ex 30:28 all its utensils, and the l
Ex 31: 9 all its utensils, and the l
Ex 35:16 all its utensils, and the l
Ex 38: 8 He made the l of bronze and
Ex 39:39 the l with its base
Ex 40: 7 you shall set the l between
Ex 40:11 And you shall anoint the l
Ex 40:30 He set the l between the
Lev 8:11 and all its utensils, and the l
1Ki 7:30 Under the l were supports of
1Ki 7:38 each l contained forty baths,
1Ki 7:38 and each l was four cubits
1Ki 7:38 each of the ten carts was a l

LAVERS (*see* LAVER)
1Ki 7:38 Then he made ten l of bronze
1Ki 7:40 Hiram made the l and the
1Ki 7:43 carts, and ten l on the carts
2Ki 16:17 and removed the l from them

2Ch 4: 6 He also made ten l, and put
2Ch 4:14 carts and the l on the carts

LAVISH

Is 46: 6 They l gold out of the bag,
2Co 8:20 should blame us in this l

LAW (*see* LAWFUL, LAWGIVER, LAWLESS, LAWS, LAWSUIT, LAWYER)

Gen 47:26 Joseph made it a l over the
Ex 12:49 One l shall be for the
Ex 13: 9 that the LORD's l may be in
Ex 16: 4 they will walk in My l or not
Ex 24:12 tablets of stone, and the l
Lev 6: 9 This is the l of the burnt
Lev 6:14 This is the l of the grain
Lev 6:25 This is the l of the sin
Lev 7: 1 Likewise this is the l of
Lev 7: 7 there is one l for them both
Lev 7:11 This is the l of the
Lev 7:37 This is the l of the burnt
Lev 11:46 This is the l of the beasts
Lev 12: 7 This is the l for her who has
Lev 13:59 This is the l of the leprous
Lev 14: 2 This shall be the l of the
Lev 14:32 This is the l for one who had
Lev 14:54 This is the l for any leprous
Lev 14:57 This is the l of leprosy
Lev 15:32 This is the l for one who
Lev 24:22 the same l for the stranger
Num 5:29 This is the l of jealousy
Num 5:30 execute all this l upon her
Num 6:13 this is the l of the Nazirite
Num 6:21 This is the l of the Nazirite
Num 6:21 to the l of his separation
Num 15:16 One l and one custom shall be
Num 15:29 have one l for him who sins
Num 19: 2 of the l which the LORD has
Num 19:14 This is the l when a man
Num 31:21 is the ordinance of the l
Deut 1: 5 Moses began to explain this l
Deut 4: 8 as are in all this l which I
Deut 4:44 this is the l which Moses set
Deut 17:11 to the sentence of the l in
Deut 17:18 a copy of this l in a book
Deut 17:19 all the words of this l and
Deut 27: 3 them all the words of this l
Deut 27: 8 all the words of this l
Deut 27:26 all the words of this l
Deut 28:58 all the words of this l that
Deut 28:61 written in the book of this l
Deut 29:21 written in this Book of the L
Deut 29:29 do all the words of this l
Deut 30:10 written in this Book of the L
Deut 31: 9 So Moses wrote this l and
Deut 31:11 you shall read this l before
Deut 31:12 all the words of this l,
Deut 31:24 the words of this l in a book
Deut 31:26 Take this Book of the L, and
Deut 32:46 all the words of this l
Deut 33: 2 hand came a fiery l for them
Deut 33: 4 Moses commanded a l for us
Deut 33:10 judgments, and Israel Your l
Josh 1: 7 the l which Moses My servant
Josh 1: 8 This Book of the L shall not
Josh 8:31 in the Book of the L of Moses
Josh 8:32 a copy of the l of Moses,
Josh 8:34 read all the words of the l
Josh 8:34 written in the Book of the L
Josh 22: 5 the l which Moses the servant
Josh 23: 6 in the Book of the L of Moses
Josh 24:26 in the Book of the L of God
1Ki 2: 3 is written in the L of Moses
2Ki 10:31 l of the LORD God of Israel
2Ki 14: 6 in the Book of the L of Moses
2Ki 17:13 according to all the l which
2Ki 17:34 or their ordinances, or the l
2Ki 17:37 the ordinances, the l, and
2Ki 21: 8 according to all the l that
2Ki 22: 8 L in the house of the LORD
2Ki 22:11 words of the Book of the L
2Ki 23:24 perform the words of the l
2Ki 23:25 to all the L of Moses
1Ch 16:40 in the L of the LORD which He
1Ch 22:12 the l of the LORD your God
2Ch 6:16 to walk in My l as you have
2Ch 12: 1 he forsook the l of the LORD
2Ch 14: 4 fathers, and to observe the l
2Ch 15: 3 teaching priest, and without l
2Ch 17: 9 had the Book of the L of the
2Ch 19:10 against l or commandment,
2Ch 23:18 is written in the L of Moses
2Ch 25: 4 in the L in the Book of Moses
2Ch 30:16 according to the L of Moses
2Ch 31: 3 written in the L of the LORD
2Ch 31: 4 to the L of the LORD
2Ch 31:21 of the house of God, in the l
2Ch 33: 8 according to the whole l
2Ch 34:14 found the Book of the L of
2Ch 34:15 L in the house of the LORD
2Ch 34:19 king heard the words of the L
2Ch 35:26 written in the L of the LORD
Ezra 3: 2 the L of Moses the man of God
Ezra 7: 6 scribe in the L of Moses,
Ezra 7:10 to seek the L of the LORD
Ezra 7:12 a scribe of the L of the God
Ezra 7:14 with regard to the L of your
Ezra 7:21 the scribe of the L of the
Ezra 7:26 not observe the l of your God
Ezra 7:26 God and the l of the king, let
Ezra 10: 3 it be done according to the l
Neh 8: 1 the Book of the L of Moses
Neh 8: 2 the L before the congregation
Neh 8: 3 to the Book of the L
Neh 8: 7 people to understand the L
Neh 8: 8 the book, in the L of God
Neh 8: 9 they heard the words of the L
Neh 8:13 understand the words of the L
Neh 8:14 they found written in the L
Neh 8:18 from the Book of the L of God
Neh 9: 3 L of the LORD their God for
Neh 9:26 You, cast Your l behind their
Neh 9:29 bring them back to Your l
Neh 9:34 our fathers, have kept Your l
Neh 10:28 of the lands to the L of God
Neh 10:29 and an oath to walk in God's L
Neh 10:34 God as it is written in the L
Neh 10:36 as it is written in the L
Neh 12:44 by the L for the priests and
Neh 13: 3 when they had heard the L
Esth 1: 8 In accordance with the l, the
Esth 1:13 manner toward all who knew l
Esth 1:15 Queen Vashti, according to l
Esth 3:14 issued as l in every province
Esth 4:11 been called, he has but one l
Esth 4:16 king, which is against the l
Job 28:26 When He made a l for the rain
Ps 1: 2 is in the l of the LORD, And
Ps 1: 2 in His l he meditates day and
Ps 19: 7 The l of the LORD is perfect,
Ps 37:31 The l of his God is in his
Ps 40: 8 Your l is within my heart
Ps 78: 1 ear, O my people, to my l
Ps 78: 5 And appointed a l in Israel
Ps 78:10 They refused to walk in His l
Ps 81: 4 And a l of the God of Jacob
Ps 89:30 If his sons forsake My l And
Ps 94:12 LORD, And teach out of Your l
Ps 94:20 which devises evil by l,
Ps 119: 1 Who walk in the l of the LORD
Ps 119:18 Wondrous things from Your l
Ps 119:29 And grant me Your l graciously
Ps 119:34 and I shall keep Your l
Ps 119:44 I keep Your l continually
Ps 119:51 do not turn aside from Your l
Ps 119:53 wicked, who forsake Your l
Ps 119:55 O LORD, And I keep Your l
Ps 119:61 I have not forgotten Your l
Ps 119:70 But I delight in Your l
Ps 119:72 The l of Your mouth is better
Ps 119:77 For Your l is my delight
Ps 119:85 is not according to Your l
Ps 119:92 Unless Your l had been my
Ps 119:97 Oh, how I love Your l
Ps 119:109 Yet I do not forget Your l
Ps 119:113 But I love Your l
Ps 119:126 have regarded Your l as void
Ps 119:136 men do not keep Your l
Ps 119:142 And Your l is truth
Ps 119:150 They are far from Your l
Ps 119:153 For I do not forget Your l
Ps 119:163 lying, But I love Your l
Ps 119:165 have those who love Your l
Ps 119:174 LORD, And Your l is my delight
Prov 1: 8 forsake the l of your mother
Prov 3: 1 My son, do not forget my l
Prov 4: 2 do not forsake my l
Prov 6:20 forsake the l of your mother
Prov 6:23 is a lamp, and the l is light
Prov 7: 2 my l as the apple of your eye
Prov 13:14 The l of the wise is a
Prov 28: 4 the l praise the wicked, but
Prov 28: 4 keep the l contend with them
Prov 28: 7 Whoever keeps the l is a
Prov 28: 9 his ear from hearing the l
Prov 29:18 happy is he who keeps the l
Prov 31: 5 they drink and forget the l
Prov 31:26 tongue is the l of kindness
Is 1:10 give ear to the l of our God
Is 2: 3 of Zion shall go forth the l
Is 5:24 the l of the LORD of hosts
Is 8:16 Seal the l among my disciples
Is 8:20 To the l and to the testimony
Is 30: 9 not hear the l of the LORD
Is 42: 4 shall wait for His l
Is 42:21 He will magnify the l and make
Is 42:24 were they obedient to His l
Is 51: 4 for l will proceed from Me,
Is 51: 7 people in whose heart is My l
Jer 2: 8 handle the l did not know Me
Jer 6:19 not heeded My words, nor My l
Jer 8: 8 the l of the LORD is with us'
Jer 9:13 they have forsaken My l which
Jer 16:11 forsaken Me and not kept My l
Jer 18:18 for the l shall not perish
Jer 26: 4 to walk in My l which I have
Jer 31:33 I will put My l in their
Jer 32:11 was sealed according to the l
Jer 32:23 voice or walked in Your l
Jer 44:10 My l or in My statutes that I
Jer 44:23 the LORD or walked in His l
Lam 2: 9 the L is no more, and her
Ezek 7:26 but the l will perish from
Ezek 22:26 priests have violated My l
Ezek 43:12 This is the l of the temple
Ezek 43:12 this is the l of the temple
Dan 6: 5 concerning the l of his God
Dan 6: 8 to the l of the Medes and
Dan 6:12 to the l of the Medes and
Dan 6:15 that it is the l of the Medes
Dan 7:25 intend to change times and l
Dan 9:11 has transgressed Your l, and
Dan 9:11 the oath written in the L of
Dan 9:13 is written in the L of Moses
Hos 4: 6 forgotten the l of your God
Hos 8: 1 and rebelled against My l
Hos 8:12 him the great things of My l
Amos 2: 4 despised the l of the LORD
Mic 4: 2 of Zion the l shall go forth
Hab 1: 4 Therefore the l is powerless
Zeph 3: 4 have done violence to the l
Hag 2:11 the priests concerning the l
Zech 7:12 flint, refusing to hear the l
Mal 2: 6 The l of truth was in his
Mal 2: 7 seek the l from his mouth
Mal 2: 8 many to stumble at the l
Mal 2: 9 shown partiality in the l
Mal 4: 4 Remember the L of Moses, My
Matt 5:17 destroy the L or the Prophets
Matt 5:18 the l till all is fulfilled
Matt 7:12 to them, for this is the L
Matt 11:13 the l prophesied until John
Matt 12: 5 the l that on the Sabbath the
Matt 22:36 great commandment in the l
Matt 22:40 commandments hang all the L
Matt 23:23 weightier matters of the l
Luke 2:22 according to the l of Moses
Luke 2:23 written in the l of the Lord
Luke 2:24 is said in the l of the Lord
Luke 2:27 to the custom of the l,
Luke 2:39 to the l of the Lord, they
Luke 5:17 teachers of the l sitting by
Luke 10:26 What is written in the l
Luke 16:16 The l and the prophets were
Luke 16:17 one tittle of the l to fail
Luke 24:44 written in the L of Moses
John 1:17 For the l was given through
John 1:45 Him of whom Moses in the l
John 7:19 Did not Moses give you the l
John 7:19 yet none of you keeps the l
John 7:23 so that the l of Moses should
John 7:49 not know the l is accursed
John 7:51 Does our l judge a man before
John 8: 5 Now Moses, in the l,
John 8:17 l that the testimony of two
John 10:34 Is it not written in your l
John 12:34 We have heard from the l that
John 15:25 which is written in their l
John 18:31 judge Him according to your l
John 19: 7 We have a l, and according to
John 19: 7 to our l He ought to die,

Acts 5:34 a teacher of the l held in
Acts 6:13 this holy place and the l
Acts 7:53 who have received the l by
Acts 13:15 And after the reading of the L
Acts 13:39 justified by the l of Moses
Acts 15: 5 them to keep the l of Moses
Acts 15:24 be circumcised and keep the l'
Acts 18:13 worship God contrary to the l
Acts 18:15 words and names and your own l
Acts 21:20 are all zealous for the l
Acts 21:24 walk orderly and keep the l
Acts 21:28 against the people, the l
Acts 22: 3 strictness of our fathers' l
Acts 22:12 devout man according to the l
Acts 23: 3 judge me according to the l
Acts 23: 3 be struck contrary to the l
Acts 23:29 questions of their l, but had
Acts 24: 6 judge him according to our l
Acts 24:14 which are written in the L
Acts 25: 8 against the l of the Jews
Acts 28:23 from both the L of Moses and
Rom 2:12 l will also perish without
Rom 2:12 will also perish without l
Rom 2:12 l will be judged by the l
Rom 2:13 l are just in the sight of
Rom 2:13 of the l will be justified
Rom 2:14 who do not have the l, by
Rom 2:14 the things contained in the l
Rom 2:14 although not having the l
Rom 2:14 are a l to themselves
Rom 2:15 the l written in their hearts
Rom 2:17 a Jew, and rest on the l, and
Rom 2:18 being instructed out of the l
Rom 2:20 knowledge and truth in the l
Rom 2:23 who make your boast in the l
Rom 2:23 God through breaking the l
Rom 2:25 profitable if you keep the l
Rom 2:25 if you are a breaker of the l
Rom 2:26 requirements of the l, will
Rom 2:27 if he fulfills the l, judge
Rom 2:27 are a transgressor of the l
Rom 3:19 know that whatever the l says
Rom 3:19 to those who are under the l
Rom 3:20 by the deeds of the l no
Rom 3:20 for by the l is the knowledge
Rom 3:21 apart from the l is revealed
Rom 3:21 being witnessed by the L
Rom 3:27 By what l? Of works?
Rom 3:27 No, but by the l of faith
Rom 3:28 apart from the deeds of the l
Rom 3:31 make void the l through faith
Rom 3:31 contrary, we establish the l
Rom 4:13 or to his seed through the l
Rom 4:14 who are of the l are heirs
Rom 4:15 because the l brings about
Rom 4:15 for where there is no l there
Rom 4:16 to those who are of the l
Rom 5:13 (For until the l sin was in
Rom 5:13 imputed when there is no l
Rom 5:20 Moreover the l entered that
Rom 6:14 not under l but under grace
Rom 6:15 not under l but under grace
Rom 7: 1 to those who know the l),
Rom 7: 1 that the l has dominion over
Rom 7: 2 l to her husband as long as
Rom 7: 2 from the l of her husband
Rom 7: 3 dies, she is free from that l
Rom 7: 4 have become dead to the l
Rom 7: 5 which were aroused by the l
Rom 7: 6 been delivered from the l
Rom 7: 7 Is the l sin
Rom 7: 7 sin except through the l
Rom 7: 7 unless the l had said, "You
Rom 7: 8 apart from the l sin was dead
Rom 7: 9 was alive once without the l
Rom 7:12 Therefore the l is holy, and
Rom 7:14 know that the l is spiritual
Rom 7:16 with the l that it is good
Rom 7:21 I find then a l, that evil is
Rom 7:22 For I delight in the l of God
Rom 7:23 I see another l in my members
Rom 7:23 against the l of my mind, and
Rom 7:23 the l of sin which is in my
Rom 7:25 I myself serve the l of God
Rom 7:25 with the flesh the l of sin
Rom 8: 2 For the l of the Spirit of
Rom 8: 2 me free from the l of sin
Rom 8: 3 For what the l could not do
Rom 8: 4 requirement of the l might be
Rom 8: 7 not subject to the l of God
Rom 9: 4 the giving of the l, the
Rom 9:31 but Israel, pursuing the l of
Rom 9:31 to the l of righteousness
Rom 9:32 were, by the works of the l
Rom 10: 4 of the l for righteousness to
Rom 10: 5 which is of the l, The man
Rom 13: 8 another has fulfilled the l
Rom 13:10 is the fulfillment of the l
1Co 6: 1 another, go to l before the
1Co 6: 6 goes to l against brother
1Co 6: 7 go to l against one another
1Co 7:39 A wife is bound by l as long
1Co 9: 8 Or does not the l say the
1Co 9: 9 is written in the l of Moses
1Co 9:20 to those who are under the l
1Co 9:20 as under the l
1Co 9:20 win those who are under the l
1Co 9:21 to those who are without l
1Co 9:21 as without l (not being
1Co 9:21 being without l toward God
1Co 9:21 but under l toward Christ),
1Co 9:21 win those who are without l
1Co 14:21 In the l it is written
1Co 14:34 as the l also says
1Co 15:56 the strength of sin is the l
Gal 2:16 by the works of the l but by
Gal 2:16 and not by the works of the l
Gal 2:16 for by the works of the l no
Gal 2:19 For I through the l died to
Gal 2:19 l that I might live to God
Gal 2:21 comes through the l, then
Gal 3: 2 Spirit by the works of the l
Gal 3: 5 do it by the works of the l
Gal 3:10 of the l are under the curse
Gal 3:10 written in the book of the l
Gal 3:11 the l in the sight of God is
Gal 3:12 Yet the l is not of faith,
Gal 3:13 us from the curse of the l
Gal 3:17 And this I say, that the l
Gal 3:18 the inheritance is of the l
Gal 3:19 purpose then does the l serve
Gal 3:21 Is the l then against the
Gal 3:21 a l given which could have
Gal 3:21 would have been by the l
Gal 3:23 kept under guard by the l
Gal 3:24 Therefore the l was our tutor
Gal 4: 4 of a woman, born under the l
Gal 4: 5 those who were under the l
Gal 4:21 who desire to be under the l
Gal 4:21 do you not hear the l?
Gal 5: 3 a debtor to keep the whole l
Gal 5: 4 attempt to be justified by l
Gal 5:14 For all the l is fulfilled in
Gal 5:18 you are not under the l
Gal 5:23 Against such there is no l
Gal 6: 2 and so fulfill the l of Christ
Gal 6:13 are circumcised keep the l
Eph 2:15 is, the l of commandments
Phil 3: 5 concerning the l, a Pharisee
Phil 3: 6 which is in the l, blameless
Phil 3: 9 which is from the l, but
1Ti 1: 7 to be teachers of the l,
1Ti 1: 8 But we know that the l is
1Ti 1: 9 that the l is not made for a
Tit 3: 9 and strivings about the l
Heb 7: 5 the people according to the l
Heb 7:11 it the people received the l)
Heb 7:12 is also a change of the l
Heb 7:16 not according to the l of a
Heb 7:19 for the l made nothing
Heb 7:28 For the l appoints as high
Heb 7:28 oath, which came after the l
Heb 8: 4 the gifts according to the l
Heb 9:19 the people according to the l
Heb 9:22 according to the l almost all
Heb 10: 1 For the l, having a shadow of
Heb 10: 8 offered according to the l)
Heb 10:28 who has rejected Moses' l
Jas 1:25 into the perfect l of liberty
Jas 2: 8 really fulfill the royal l
Jas 2: 9 by the l as transgressors
Jas 2:10 shall keep the whole l, and
Jas 2:11 a transgressor of the l
Jas 2:12 be judged by the l of liberty
Jas 4:11 brother, speaks evil of the l
Jas 4:11 and judges the l
Jas 4:11 But if you judge the l, you
Jas 4:11 a doer of the l but a judge

LAWFUL (*see* LAW, LAWFULLY, UNLAWFUL)
Ezra 7:24 shall not be l to impose tax
Ezek 18: 5 man is just and does what is l
Ezek 18:19 the son has done what is l
Ezek 18:21 statutes, and does what is l
Ezek 18:27 committed, and does what is l
Ezek 33:14 his sin and does what is l
Ezek 33:16 he has done what is l and
Ezek 33:19 wickedness and does what is l
Matt 12: 2 is not l to do on the Sabbath
Matt 12: 4 was not l for him to eat, nor
Matt 12:10 Is it l to heal on the
Matt 12:12 Therefore it is l to do good
Matt 14: 4 It is not l for you to have
Matt 19: 3 Is it l for a man to divorce
Matt 20:15 Is it not l for me to do
Matt 22:17 Is it l to pay taxes to
Matt 27: 6 It is not l to put them into
Mark 2:24 what is not l on the Sabbath
Mark 2:26 which is not l to eat,
Mark 3: 4 Is it l on the Sabbath to do
Mark 6:18 It is not l for you to have
Mark 10: 2 Is it l for a man to divorce
Mark 12:14 Is it l to pay taxes to
Luke 6: 2 is not l to do on the Sabbath
Luke 6: 4 which is not l for any but
Luke 6: 9 Is it l on the Sabbath to do
Luke 14: 3 Is it l to heal on the
Luke 20:22 Is it l for us to pay taxes
John 5:10 it is not l for you to carry
John 18:31 It is not l for us to put
Acts 16:21 which are not l for us, being
Acts 19:39 determined in the l assembly
Acts 22:25 Is it l for you to scourge a
1Co 6:12 All things are l for me, but
1Co 6:12 All things are l for me, but
1Co 10:23 All things are l for me, but
1Co 10:23 all things are l for me, but
2Co 12: 4 which it is not l for a man

LAWFULLY (*see* LAWFUL)
1Ti 1: 8 law is good if one uses it l

LAWGIVER (*see* LAW, LAWGIVER'S)
Gen 49:10 nor a l from between his feet
Num 21:18 the nation's nobles, by the l
Ps 60: 7 Judah is My l
Ps 108: 8 Judah is My l
Is 33:22 our Judge, the LORD is our L
Jas 4:12 There is one L, who is able

LAWGIVER'S (*see* LAWGIVER)
Deut 33:21 because a l portion was

LAWLESS (*see* LAW, LAWLESSNESS)
Acts 2:23 you have taken by l hands
Rom 4: 7 whose l deeds are forgiven
2Th 2: 8 And then the l one will be
2Th 2: 9 The coming of the l one is
1Ti 1: 9 person, but for the l and
Tit 2:14 redeem us from every l deed
Heb 8:12 their l deeds I will remember
Heb 10:17 their l deeds I will remember
2Pe 2: 8 and hearing their l deeds)

LAWLESSNESS (*see* LAWLESS)
Matt 7:23 from Me, you who practice l
Matt 13:41 and those who practice l,
Matt 23:28 are full of hypocrisy and l
Matt 24:12 because l will abound, the
Rom 6:19 l leading to more l
2Co 6:14 has righteousness with l
2Th 2: 7 of l is already at work
Heb 1: 9 righteousness and hated l
1Jn 3: 4 also commits l, and sin is l

LAWS (*see* LAW)
Gen 26: 5 My statutes, and My l
Ex 16:28 My commandments and My l
Ex 18:16 the statutes of God and His l
Ex 18:20 them the statutes and the l
Lev 26:46 l which the LORD made between
Ezra 7:25 as know the l of your God
Neh 9:13 just ordinances and true l
Neh 9:14 them precepts, statutes and l
Esth 1:19 in the l of the Persians and
Esth 3: 8 their l are different from
Esth 3: 8 they do not keep the king's l
Ps 105:45 His statutes And keep His l
Is 24: 5 they have transgressed the l
Ezek 43:11 all its forms and all its l
Ezek 44: 5 of the LORD and all its l
Ezek 44:24 They shall keep My l and My

Dan 9:10 our God, to walk in His l
Heb 8:10 I will put My l in their mind
Heb 10:16 I will put My l into their

LAWSUIT (*see* LAW)
2Sa 15: 2 a l came to the king for a

LAWYER (*see* LAW, LAWYERS)
Matt 22:35 Then one of them, a l, asked
Luke 10:25 behold, a certain l stood up
Tit 3:13 Send Zenas the l and Apollos

LAWYERS (*see* LAWYER)
Luke 7:30 l rejected the counsel of God
Luke 11:45 Then one of the l answered
Luke 11:46 Woe to you also, you l
Luke 11:52 Woe to you l
Luke 14: 3 answering, spoke to the l

LAY (*see* LAID, LAYING, LAYS, LIE)
Gen 19: 4 Now before they l down, the
Gen 19:33 l with her father, and he did
Gen 19:33 she l down or when she arose
Gen 19:34 Indeed I l with my father
Gen 19:35 l with him, and he did not
Gen 19:35 she l down or when she arose
Gen 22:12 Do not l your hand on the lad
Gen 28:11 he l down in that place to
Gen 30:16 And he l with her that night
Gen 34: 2 l with her, and violated her
Gen 35:22 l with Bilhah his father's
Gen 37:22 and do not l a hand on him"
Ex 5: 8 you shall l on them the quota
Ex 7: 4 so that I may l My hand on
Ex 16:13 the dew l all around the camp
Ex 16:23 l up for yourselves all that
Ex 16:33 l it up before the LORD, to
Ex 24:11 Israel He did not l His hand
Lev 1: 7 l the wood in order on the
Lev 1: 8 shall l the parts, the head,
Lev 1:12 the priest shall l them in
Lev 2:15 it, and l frankincense on it
Lev 3: 2 he shall l his hand on the
Lev 3: 8 he shall l his hand on the
Lev 3:13 He shall l his hand on its
Lev 4: 4 l his hand on the bull's head
Lev 4:15 of the congregation shall l
Lev 4:24 he shall l his hand on the
Lev 4:29 he shall l his hand on the
Lev 4:33 Then he shall l his hand on
Lev 6:12 l the burnt offering in order
Lev 16:21 Aaron shall l both his hands
Lev 24:14 him l their hands on his head
Lev 26:31 I will l your cities waste and
Num 8:10 children of Israel shall l
Num 8:12 Then the Levites shall l
Num 12:11 Please do not l this sin on
Num 22:27 LORD, she l down under Balaam
Num 27:18 Spirit, and l your hand on him
Deut 7:15 but will l them on all those
Deut 11:18 Therefore you shall l up
Deut 21: 8 do not l innocent blood to
Deut 22:22 the man that l with the woman
Deut 22:25 man who l with her shall die
Deut 22:29 then the man who l with her
Josh 2: 8 So before they l down, she
Josh 6:26 he shall l its foundation
Josh 8: 2 L an ambush for the city
Josh 15:46 all that l near Ashdod, with
Judg 4:22 there l Sisera, dead with the
Judg 5:27 he sank, he fell, he l still
Judg 6:20 l them on this rock, and pour
Judg 16: 2 l in wait for him all night
Judg 16: 3 Samson l low till midnight
Ruth 3: 7 uncovered his feet, and l down
Ruth 3:14 So she l at his feet until
1Sa 2:22 how they l with the women who
1Sa 3: 5 And he went and l down
1Sa 3: 9 went and l down in his place
1Sa 3:15 So Samuel l down until
1Sa 15: 5 and l in wait in the valley
1Sa 19:24 l down naked all that day and
1Sa 26: 5 saw the place where Saul l
1Sa 26: 5 Now Saul l within the camp,
1Sa 26: 7 there Saul l sleeping within
1Sa 26: 7 the people l all around him
1Sa 28: 9 Why then do you l a snare for
2Sa 2:21 l hold on one of the young
2Sa 11: 4 he l with her, for she was
2Sa 12: 3 his own cup and l in his bosom
2Sa 12:16 l all night on the ground
2Sa 12:24 went in to her and l with her
2Sa 13: 6 Then Amnon l down and
2Sa 13:14 he forced her and l with her
2Sa 13:31 l on the ground, and all his
1Ki 3:19 night, because she l on him
1Ki 5:17 to l the foundation of the
1Ki 13:31 l my bones beside his bones
1Ki 18:23 l it on the wood, but put no
1Ki 18:23 l it on the wood, but put no
1Ki 19: 5 Then as he l and slept under a
1Ki 19: 6 ate and drank, and l down again
1Ki 21: 4 And he l down on his bed, and
1Ki 21:27 l in sackcloth, and went about
2Ki 4:11 upper room and l down there
2Ki 4:29 but l my staff on the face of
2Ki 4:34 l on the child, and put his
2Ki 10: 8 L them in two heaps at the
2Ch 35: 5 of your brethren the l people
2Ch 35: 7 gave the l people lambs and
2Ch 35:12 houses of the l people, to
2Ch 35:13 among all the l people
2Ch 36:21 As long as she l desolate she
Neh 13:21 again, I will l hands on you
Esth 2:21 sought to l hands on King
Esth 3: 6 But he disdained to l hands
Esth 4: 3 many l in sackcloth and ashes
Esth 6: 2 who had sought to l hands on
Esth 8: 7 to l his hand on the Jews
Esth 9: 2 of King Ahasuerus to l hands
Esth 9:10 but they did not l a hand on
Esth 9:15 but they did not l a hand on
Esth 9:16 but they did not l a hand on
Job 1:12 only do not l a hand on his
Job 9:33 who may l his hand on us both
Job 22:22 l up His words in your heart
Job 22:24 Then you will l your gold in
Job 40: 4 I l my hand over my mouth
Job 41: 8 L your hand on him
Ps 3: 5 I l down and slept
Ps 7: 5 And l my honor in the dust
Ps 38:12 seek my life l snares for me
Ps 84: 3 Where she may l her young
Prov 5: 5 her steps l hold of hell
Eccl 2: 3 how to l hold on folly, till
Is 5: 6 I will l it waste
Is 5:29 roar and l hold of the prey
Is 11:14 they shall l their hand on
Is 13: 9 anger, to l the land desolate
Is 13:11 will l low the haughtiness of
Is 22:22 I will l on his shoulder
Is 25:12 l low, and bring to the ground
Is 28:16 I l in Zion a stone for a
Is 29: 3 I will l siege against you
Is 29:21 and l a snare for him who
Is 34:15 l eggs and hatch, and gather
Is 35: 7 of jackals, where each l,
Is 42:15 I will l waste the mountains
Is 51:16 l the foundations of the
Is 54:11 I will l your stones with
Is 54:11 and l your foundations with
Jer 2:20 every green tree you l down
Jer 6:21 I will l stumbling blocks
Jer 6:23 They will l hold on bow and
Lam 4:19 and l in wait for us in the
Ezek 3:20 I l a stumbling block before
Ezek 4: 1 l it before you, and portray
Ezek 4: 2 L siege against it, build a
Ezek 4: 3 you shall l siege against it
Ezek 4: 4 l the iniquity of the house
Ezek 6: 5 I will l the corpses of the
Ezek 12:23 I will l this proverb to rest
Ezek 16:42 So I will l to rest My fury
Ezek 19: 2 she l down among the lions
Ezek 25:14 I will l My vengeance on Edom
Ezek 25:17 when I l My vengeance upon
Ezek 26:12 they will l your stones, your
Ezek 26:16 l aside their robes, and take
Ezek 32: 5 I will l your flesh on the
Ezek 35: 4 I shall l your cities waste,
Ezek 42:13 There they shall l the most
Amos 5: 7 l righteousness to rest in
Obad 7 bread shall l a trap for you
Mic 1: 7 her idols I will l desolate
Zeph 2:14 for He will l bare the cedar
Zech 12: 2 when they l siege against
Matt 6:19 Do not l up for yourselves
Matt 6:20 but l up for yourselves
Matt 8:20 Man has nowhere to l His head
Matt 9:18 l Your hand on her and she
Matt 12:11 will not l hold of it and lift
Matt 21:46 they sought to l hands on Him
Matt 23: 4 l them on men's shoulders
Matt 28: 6 the place where the Lord l
Mark 1:30 mother l sick with a fever
Mark 3:21 went out to l hold of Him
Mark 5:23 l Your hands on her, that she
Mark 12:12 they sought to l hold of Him
Mark 16:18 they will l hands on the sick
Luke 5:18 him in and l him before Him
Luke 9:58 Man has nowhere to l His head
Luke 20:19 hour sought to l hands on Him
Luke 21:12 they will l their hands on
John 5: 3 In these l a great multitude
John 10:15 and I l down My life for the
John 10:17 because I l down My life that
John 10:18 but I l it down of Myself
John 10:18 I have power to l it down
John 11:38 cave, and a stone l against it
John 13:37 I will l down my life for
John 13:38 Will you l down your life for
John 15:13 than to l down one's life for
Acts 8:19 that anyone on whom I l hands
Acts 15:28 us, to l upon you no greater
Acts 23:30 Jews l in wait for the man
Acts 25: 3 while they l in ambush along
Acts 28: 8 of Publius l sick of a fever
Rom 9:33 I l in Zion a stumbling stone
1Co 3:11 l than that which is laid
1Co 16: 2 one of you l something aside
2Co 12:14 not to l up for the parents
Phil 3:12 that I may l hold of that for
1Ti 5:22 Do not l hands on anyone
1Ti 6:12 l hold on eternal life, to
1Ti 6:19 come, that they may l hold on
Heb 6:18 l hold of the hope set before
Heb 12: 1 let us l aside every weight,
Jas 1:21 Therefore l aside all
1Pe 2: 6 Behold, I l in Zion a chief
1Jn 3:16 we also ought to l down our

LAYER (*see* LAYERS)
Ex 16:14 when the l of dew lifted,

LAYERS (*see* LAYER)
Amos 9: 6 who builds His l in the sky

LAYING (*see* LAY)
Deut 26:12 When you have finished l
2Ch 31: 7 they began l them in heaps
Ps 64: 5 They talk of l snares
Hab 3:13 by l bare from foundation to
Mark 7: 8 For l aside the commandment
Acts 8:18 l on of the apostles' hands
Acts 9:17 l his hands on him he said,
1Ti 4:14 the l on of the hands of the
2Ti 1: 6 through the l on of my hands
Heb 6: 1 not l again the foundation of
Heb 6: 2 of l on of hands, of
1Pe 2: 1 l aside all malice, all guile

LAYS (*see* LAY)
Job 18: 9 and a snare l hold of him
Job 21:19 God l up one's iniquity for
Ps 33: 7 He l up the deep in
Ps 91: 6 that l waste at noonday
Ps 104: 3 He l the beams of His upper
Prov 13:16 but a fool l open his folly
Prov 26:24 l up deceit within himself
Is 26: 5 He l it low, He l it low
Is 26: 5 He l it low to the ground, He
Is 30:32 which the LORD l on him, it
Is 56: 2 son of man who l hold on it
Zech 12: 1 l the foundation of the earth
Luke 12:21 So is he who l up treasure
Luke 15: 5 he l it on his shoulders,

LAZARUS
Luke 16:20 was a certain beggar named **L**
Luke 16:23 afar off, and **L** in his bosom
Luke 16:24 send **L** that he may dip the
Luke 16:25 and likewise **L** evil things
John 11: 1 **L** of Bethany, the town of
John 11: 2 whose brother **L** was sick
John 11: 5 Martha and her sister and **L**
John 11:11 Our friend **L** sleeps, but I go
John 11:14 to them plainly, "**L** is dead
John 11:43 **L**, come forth!
John 12: 1 where **L** was who had been dead
John 12: 2 but **L** was one of those who
John 12: 9 that they might also see **L**
John 12:10 might also put **L** to death
John 12:17 He called **L** out of his tomb

LAZINESS (*see* LAZY)
Eccl 10:18 Because of l the building

LAZY (*see* LAZINESS)
Matt 25:26 l servant, you knew that I
Tit 1:12 evil beasts, l gluttons

LEAD (*see* LEADER, LEADING, LEADS, LED)
Gen 33:14 I will l on slowly at a pace
Ex 13:17 that God did not l them by
Ex 13:21 pillar of cloud to l the way
Ex 15:10 they sank like l in the
Ex 32:34 l the people to the place of
Num 27:17 who may l them out and bring
Num 31:22 the iron, the tin, and the l
Deut 20: 9 of the armies to l the people
Deut 28:37 where the LORD will l you
Judg 5: 2 When leaders l in Israel,
Judg 5:12 l your captives away, O son
1Sa 30:22 that they may l them away
2Ch 30: 9 by those who l them captive
Neh 9:19 by day, to l them on the road
Job 19:24 a rock with an iron pen and l
Ps 5: 8 L me, O LORD, in Your
Ps 25: 5 L me in Your truth and teach
Ps 27:11 And l me in a smooth path,
Ps 31: 3 name's sake, L me and guide me
Ps 43: 3 Let them l me
Ps 60: 9 Who will l me to Edom
Ps 61: 2 L me to the rock that is
Ps 80: 1 You who l Joseph like a flock
Ps 108:10 Who will l me to Edom
Ps 125: 5 The LORD shall l them away
Ps 139:10 there Your hand shall l me
Ps 139:24 l me in the way everlasting
Ps 143:10 L me in the land of
Prov 6:22 you roam, they will l you
Prov 21: 5 diligent l surely to plenty
Song 1: 4 L me away!
Song 8: 2 I would l you and bring you
Is 3:12 Those who l you cause you to
Is 11: 6 a little child shall l them
Is 20: 4 l away the Egyptians as
Is 40:11 gently l those who are with
Is 42:16 I will l them in paths they
Is 49:10 has mercy on them will l them
Is 57:18 I will also l him, and restore
Is 63:14 so You l Your people, to make
Jer 6:29 the l is consumed by the fire
Jer 31: 9 supplications I will l them
Jer 32: 5 then he shall l Zedekiah to
Ezek 22:18 all bronze, tin, iron, and l
Ezek 22:20 silver, bronze, iron, l, and
Ezek 27:12 tin, and l for your goods
Ezek 38: 4 l you out, with all your army
Ezek 39: 2 l you on, bringing you up
Amos 2: 4 their lies l them astray,
Nah 2: 7 her maidservants shall l her
Zech 5: 7 Here is a l disc lifted up,
Zech 5: 8 threw the l cover over its
Matt 6:13 do not l us into temptation,
Mark 14:44 take Him and l Him away safely
Luke 6:39 Can the blind l the blind
Luke 11: 4 do not l us into temptation,
Luke 13:15 and l it away to water it
Acts 13:11 someone to l him by the hand
1Th 4:11 also aspire to l a quiet life
1Ti 2: 2 that we may l a quiet and
Heb 8: 9 to l them out of the land of
1Jn 5:16 sin which does not l to death
Rev 7:17 l them to living fountains of

LEADER (*see* LEAD, LEADERS)
Num 2: 3 l of the children of Judah
Num 2: 5 son of Zuar shall be the l of
Num 2: 7 son of Helon shall be the l
Num 2:10 and the l of the children of
Num 2:12 and the l of the children of
Num 2:14 the l of the children of Gad
Num 2:18 and the l of the children of
Num 2:20 and the l of the children of
Num 2:22 and the l of the children of
Num 2:25 the l of the children of Dan
Num 2:27 and the l of the children of
Num 2:29 and the l of the children of
Num 3:24 the l of the fathers' house
Num 3:30 the l of the fathers' house
Num 3:35 The l of the fathers' house
Num 7:11 one l each day, for the
Num 7:18 l of Issachar, presented an
Num 7:24 l of the children of Zebulun,
Num 7:30 l of the children of Reuben,
Num 7:36 l of the children of Simeon,
Num 7:42 l of the children of Gad,
Num 7:48 l of the children of Ephraim,
Num 7:54 l of the children of Manasseh
Num 7:60 l of the children of Benjamin
Num 7:66 l of the children of Dan,
Num 7:72 l of the children of Asher,
Num 7:78 l of the children of Naphtali
Num 13: 2 man, every one a l among them
Num 14: 4 Let us select a l and return
Num 17: 6 for each l according to their
Num 25:14 a l of a father's house among
Num 25:18 the daughter of a l of Midian
Num 34:18 you shall take one l of every
Num 34:22 a l from the tribe of the
Num 34:23 a l from the tribe of the
Num 34:24 a l from the tribe of the
Num 34:25 a l from the tribe of the
Num 34:26 a l from the tribe of the
Num 34:27 a l from the tribe of the
Num 34:28 a l from the tribe of the
1Sa 19:20 standing as l over them, the
2Ki 20: 5 Hezekiah the l of My people
1Ch 2:10 l of the children of Judah
1Ch 5: 6 He was l of the Reubenites
1Ch 12:27 the l of the Aaronites, and
1Ch 13: 1 and hundreds, and with every l
1Ch 15:22 l of the Levites, was
1Ch 27: 4 Mikloth also was the l
1Ch 29:22 before the LORD to be the l
2Ch 1: 2 to every l in all Israel, the
2Ch 11:22 to be l among his brothers
2Ch 32:21 every mighty man of valor, l
Neh 3: 9 l of half the district of
Neh 3:12 l of half the district of
Neh 3:14 l of the district of Beth
Neh 3:15 l of the district of Mizpah,
Neh 3:16 l of half the district of
Neh 3:17 l of half the district of
Neh 3:18 l of the other half of the
Neh 3:19 the l of Mizpah, repaired
Neh 7: 2 Hananiah the l of the citadel
Neh 9:17 l to return to their bondage
Neh 11:11 was the l of the house of God
Neh 11:17 who was the l who began the
Ps 68:27 is little Benjamin, their l
Is 55: 4 a witness to the people, a l
Zech 9: 7 and shall be like a l in Judah

LEADERS (*see* LEADER)
Num 1:16 l of their fathers' tribes,
Num 1:44 with the l of Israel, twelve
Num 3:32 over the l of the Levites
Num 4:34 the l of the congregation
Num 4:46 the l of Israel numbered, by
Num 7: 2 Then the l of Israel, the
Num 7: 2 who were the l of the tribes
Num 7: 3 a cart for every two of the l
Num 7:10 Now the l offered the
Num 7:10 so the l offered their
Num 7:84 altar from the l of Israel
Num 10: 4 blow only one, then the l
Num 16: 2 fifty l of the congregation,
Num 17: 2 all their l according to
Num 17: 6 each of their l gave him a
Num 21:18 the well the l sank, dug by
Num 25: 4 Take all the l of the people
Num 27: 2 the priest, and before the l
Num 31:13 all the l of the congregation
Num 32: 2 to the l of the congregation,
Num 36: 1 before Moses and before the l
Deut 1:15 l of thousands, l of hundreds
Deut 1:15 l of fifties, l of tens
Deut 29:10 your l and your tribes and your
Deut 32:42 heads of the l of the enemy
Deut 33: 5 when the l of the people were
Judg 5: 2 When l lead in Israel, when
Judg 8: 6 And the l of Succoth said,
Judg 8:14 down for him the l of Succoth
Judg 10:18 the l of Gilead, said to one
Judg 20: 2 the l of all the people, all
1Ki 20:14 By the young l of the
1Ki 20:15 the young l of the provinces
1Ki 20:17 The young l of the provinces
1Ki 20:19 Then these young l of the
2Ki 11:14 and the l and the trumpeters
1Ch 4:38 name were l in their families
1Ch 7:40 mighty men of valor, chief l
1Ch 15:16 Then David spoke to the l of
1Ch 21: 2 and to the l of the people,
1Ch 22:17 also commanded all the l of
1Ch 23: 2 together all the l of Israel
1Ch 24: 4 Now there were more l found
1Ch 24: 6 down before the king, the l
1Ch 27:22 These were the l of the
1Ch 28: 1 Jerusalem all the l of Israel
1Ch 28:21 also the l and all the people
1Ch 29: 6 Then the l of the fathers'
1Ch 29: 6 l of the tribes of Israel,
1Ch 29:24 All the l and the mighty men,
2Ch 12: 5 and the l of Judah, who were
2Ch 12: 6 So the l of Israel and the
2Ch 17: 7 of his reign he sent his l
2Ch 23:13 and the l and the trumpeters
2Ch 24:10 Then all the l and all the
2Ch 24:17 Jehoiada the l of Judah came
2Ch 24:23 destroyed all the l of the
2Ch 28:14 and the spoil before the l
2Ch 28:21 of the king, and from the l
2Ch 29:30 the l commanded the Levites
2Ch 30: 2 For the king and his l and all
2Ch 30: 6 from the king and his l, and
2Ch 30:12 of the king and the l, at the
2Ch 30:24 sheep, and the l gave to the
2Ch 31: 8 the l came and saw the heaps,
2Ch 32: 3 he took counsel with his l
2Ch 35: 8 his l gave willingly to the
2Ch 36:14 all the l of the priests and
2Ch 36:18 of the king and of his l, all
Ezra 8:16 Zechariah, and Meshullam, l
Ezra 8:20 the l had appointed for the
Ezra 8:24 of the l of the priests
Ezra 8:29 before the l of the priests
Ezra 9: 1 the l came to me, saying,
Ezra 9: 2 Indeed, the hand of the l
Ezra 10: 5 made the l of the priests,
Ezra 10: 8 to the counsel of the l and
Ezra 10:14 let the l of our entire
Neh 4:14 said to the nobles, to the l
Neh 4:16 the l were behind all the
Neh 9:38 and our l and our Levites and
Neh 10:14 The l of the people
Neh 11: 1 Now the l of the people dwelt
Neh 12:31 So I brought the l of Judah
Neh 12:32 and half of the l of Judah
Is 9:16 For the l of this people
Jer 25:34 the ashes, you l of the flock
Jer 25:35 nor the l of the flock to
Jer 25:36 a wailing of the l to the
Matt 15:14 They are blind l of the blind
Luke 19:47 the l of the people sought to
Acts 28:17 the l of the Jews together

LEADING (*see* LEAD)
Judg 3:28 fords of the Jordan l to Moab
Judg 9:39 out, l the men of Shechem, and
2Ch 25:11 l his people, he went to the
Acts 15:22 l men among the brethren
Acts 17: 4 and not a few of the l women
Acts 28: 7 the l citizen of the island
Rom 6:19 and of lawlessness l to more
Rom 15: 2 his good, l to edification
1Jn 5:16 who commit sin not l to death
1Jn 5:16 There is sin l to death
1Jn 5:17 there is sin not l to death

LEADS (*see* LEAD)
1Sa 13:17 to the road that l to Ophrah
Job 12:17 He l counselors away
Job 12:19 He l princes away plundered,
Ps 23: 2 He l me beside the still
Ps 23: 3 He l me in the paths of
Prov 2:18 for her house l down to death
Prov 10:16 of the righteous l to life
Prov 11:19 As righteousness l to life
Prov 11:24 is right, but it l to poverty
Prov 12:26 of the wicked l them astray
Prov 14:23 chatter l only to poverty
Prov 16:29 l him in a way that is not
Prov 19:23 fear of the LORD l to life
Is 48:17 Who l you by the way you
Matt 7:13 the way that l to destruction
Matt 7:14 is the way which l to life
Matt 15:14 And if the blind l the blind
John 10: 3 sheep by name and l them out
Acts 12:10 iron gate that l to the city
Rom 2: 4 of God l you to repentance
Rom 12: 8 he who l, with diligence
2Co 2:14 l us in triumph in Christ
Rev 13:10 He who l into captivity shall

LEAF (*see* LEAVES*)
Gen 8:11 olive **l** was in her mouth
Lev 26:36 the sound of a shaken **l** shall
Job 13:25 You frighten a **l** driven to
Ps 1: 3 Whose **l** also shall not wither
Is 1:30 as a terebinth whose **l** fades
Is 34: 4 as the **l** falls from the vine
Is 64: 6 we all fade as a **l**, and our
Jer 8:13 fig tree, and the **l** shall fade
Jer 17: 8 but her **l** will be green, and

LEAFY
Lev 23:40 trees, the boughs of **l** trees
Neh 8:15 and branches of **l** trees, to
Mark 11: 8 others cut down **l** branches

LEAGUE
Dan 11:23 after the **l** is made with him

LEAH (*see* LEAH'S)
Gen 29:16 the name of the elder was **L**
Gen 29:23 that he took **L** his daughter
Gen 29:24 to his daughter **L** as a maid
Gen 29:25 that behold, it was **L**
Gen 29:30 also loved Rachel more than **L**
Gen 29:31 LORD saw that **L** was unloved
Gen 29:32 So **L** conceived and bore a son,
Gen 30: 9 When **L** saw that she had
Gen 30:11 Then **L** said, A troop comes
Gen 30:13 Then **L** said, "I am happy,
Gen 30:14 brought them to his mother **L**
Gen 30:14 Then Rachel said to **L**
Gen 30:16 **L** went out to meet him and
Gen 30:17 And God listened to **L**, and she
Gen 30:18 **L** said, "God has given me my
Gen 30:19 Then **L** conceived again and
Gen 30:20 And **L** said, "God has endowed
Gen 31: 4 **L** to the field, to his flock,
Gen 31:14 **L** answered and said to him,
Gen 33: 1 divided the children among **L**
Gen 33: 2 and their children in front, **L**
Gen 33: 7 **L** also came near with her
Gen 34: 1 Now Dinah the daughter of **L**
Gen 35:23 the sons of **L** were Reuben
Gen 46:15 These were the sons of **L**,
Gen 46:18 Laban gave to **L** his daughter
Gen 49:31 his wife, and there I buried **L**
Ruth 4:11 your house like Rachel and **L**

LEAH'S (*see* LEAH)
Gen 29:17 **L** eyes were delicate, but
Gen 30:10 **L** maid Zilpah bore Jacob a
Gen 30:12 **L** maid Zilpah bore Jacob a
Gen 31:33 Jacob's tent, into **L** tent
Gen 31:33 Then he went out of **L** tent
Gen 35:26 **L** maidservant, were Gad and

LEAKS
Eccl 10:18 idleness of hands the house **l**

LEAN (*see* LEANED, LEANING, LEANNESS, LEANS)
Judg 16:26 so that I can **l** on them
Prov 3: 5 heart, and **l** not on your own
Is 17: 4 fatness of his flesh grow **l**
Is 48: 2 and **l** on the God of Israel
Ezek 34:20 the fat and the **l** sheep
Mic 3:11 yet they **l** on the LORD, and

LEANED (*see* LEAN)
2Ki 7: 2 on whose hand the king **l**
2Ki 7:17 officer on whose hand he **l** to
Ezek 29: 7 when they **l** on you, you broke
Amos 5:19 **l** his hand on the wall, and a
John 21:20 who also had **l** on His breast

LEANING (*see* LEAN)
2Sa 1: 6 was Saul, **l** on his spear
Ps 62: 3 all of you, Like a **l** wall
Song 8: 5 **l** upon her beloved
John 13:23 Now there was **l** on Jesus'
John 13:25 **l** back on Jesus' breast, he
Heb 11:21 **l** on the top of his staff

LEANNESS (*see* LEAN)
Job 16: 8 my **l** rises up against me and
Ps 106:15 But sent **l** into their soul
Is 10:16 will send **l** among his fat

LEANS (*see* LEAN)
2Sa 3:29 who **l** on a staff or falls by
2Ki 5:18 he **l** on my hand, and I bow
2Ki 18:21 Egypt, on which if a man **l**
Job 8:15 He **l** on his house, but it
Is 36: 6 Egypt, on which if a man **l**

LEAP (*see* LEAPED, LEAPING, LEAPS)
Gen 31:12 all the rams which **l** on the
Lev 11:21 with which to **l** on the earth
Deut 33:22 he shall **l** from Bashan
2Sa 22:30 by my God I can **l** over a wall
Ps 18:29 by my God I can **l** over a wall
Is 35: 6 the lame shall **l** like a deer
Joel 2: 5 over mountaintops they **l**,
Zeph 1: 9 who **l** over the threshold, who
Luke 6:23 in that day and **l** for joy

LEAPED (*see* LEAP)
Gen 31:10 the rams which **l** upon the
1Ki 18:26 they **l** about the altar which
Luke 1:41 that the babe **l** in her womb
Luke 1:44 the babe **l** in my womb for joy
Acts 14:10 And he **l** and walked
Acts 19:16 the evil spirit was **l** on them

LEAPING (*see* LEAP)
2Sa 6:16 a window and saw King David **l**
Song 2: 8 he comes **l** upon the mountains
Acts 3: 8 he, **l** up, stood and walked and
Acts 3: 8 walking, **l**, and praising God

LEAPS (*see* LEAP)
Job 37: 1 trembles, and **l** from its place

LEARN (*see* LEARNED, LEARNING)
Deut 4:10 that they may **l** to fear Me
Deut 5: 1 today, that you may **l** them
Deut 14:23 that you may **l** to fear the
Deut 17:19 that he may **l** to fear the
Deut 18: 9 you shall not **l** to follow the
Deut 31:12 that they may **l** to fear the
Deut 31:13 **l** to fear the LORD your God
Esth 2:11 to **l** of Esther's welfare and
Esth 4: 5 to **l** what and why this was
Ps 119: 7 When I **l** Your righteous
Ps 119:71 That I may **l** Your statutes
Ps 119:73 that I may **l** Your
Prov 22:25 lest you **l** his ways and set a
Is 1:17 **l** to do good
Is 2: 4 shall they **l** war anymore
Is 26: 9 world will **l** righteousness
Is 26:10 he will not **l** righteousness
Is 29:24 who murmured will **l** doctrine
Jer 10: 2 Do not **l** the way of the
Jer 12:16 **l** the ways of My people, to
Mic 4: 3 shall they **l** war any more
Matt 9:13 But go and **l** what this means
Matt 11:29 **l** from Me, for I am gentle and
Matt 24:32 Now **l** this parable from the
Mark 13:28 Now **l** this parable from the
1Co 4: 6 that you may **l** in us not to
1Co 14:31 one by one, that all may **l**
1Co 14:35 if they want to **l** something
Gal 3: 2 only I want to **l** from you
1Ti 1:20 they may **l** not to blaspheme
1Ti 2:11 Let a woman **l** in silence with
1Ti 5: 4 let them first **l** to show
1Ti 5:13 And besides they **l** to be idle
Tit 3:14 And let our people also **l** to
Rev 14: 3 and no one could **l** that song

LEARNED (*see* LEARN)
Gen 30:27 for I have **l** by experience
Esth 4: 1 When Mordecai **l** all that had
Ps 106:35 the Gentiles And **l** their works
Prov 30: 3 I neither **l** wisdom nor have
Is 50: 4 given Me the tongue of the **l**
Is 50: 4 My ear to hear as the **l**
Ezek 19: 3 he **l** to catch prey, and he
Ezek 19: 6 he **l** to catch prey
John 6:45 **l** from the Father comes to Me
Acts 7:22 Moses was **l** in all the wisdom
Acts 17:13 **l** that the word of God was
Acts 23:27 having **l** that he was a Roman
Rom 16:17 to the doctrine which you **l**
Eph 4:20 But you have not so **l** Christ
Phil 4: 9 The things which you **l** and
Phil 4:11 for I have **l** in whatever
Phil 4:12 I have **l** both to be full and
Col 1: 7 as you also **l** from Epaphras,
2Ti 3:14 the things which you have **l**
2Ti 3:14 from whom you have **l** them
Heb 5: 8 yet He **l** obedience by the

LEARNING (*see* LEARN)
Prov 1: 5 man will hear and increase **l**
Prov 9: 9 man, and he will increase in **l**
Prov 16:21 of the lips increases **l**
Prov 16:23 mouth, and adds **l** to his lips
Acts 26:24 Much **l** is driving you mad
Rom 15: 4 before were written for our **l**
2Ti 3: 7 always **l** and never able to

LEASE (*see* LEASED)
Matt 21:41 and **l** his vineyard to other

LEASED (*see* LEASE)
Song 8:11 he **l** the vineyard to keepers
Matt 21:33 he **l** it to vinedressers and
Mark 12: 1 he **l** it to vinedressers and
Luke 20: 9 **l** it to vinedressers, and went

LEASH
Job 41: 5 or will you **l** him for your
1Co 7:35 not that I may put a **l** on you

LEAST (*see* PREFACE)

LEATHER
Lev 13:48 whether in **l** or in anything
Lev 13:48 or in anything made of **l**,
Lev 13:49 in the garment or in the **l**
Lev 13:49 or in anything made of **l**
Lev 13:51 in the **l** or in anything made
Lev 13:51 or in anything made of **l**, the
Lev 13:52 or in linen, or anything of **l**
Lev 13:53 or in anything made of **l**
Lev 13:56 of the woof, or out of the **l**
Lev 13:57 or in anything made of **l**
Lev 13:58 or whatever is made of **l**
Lev 13:59 or in anything made of **l**
Lev 15:17 any **l** on which there is semen
Num 31:20 garment, everything made of **l**
2Ki 1: 8 and wore a **l** belt around his
Matt 3: 4 with a **l** belt around his
Mark 1: 6 and with a **l** belt around his

LEAVE (*see* PREFACE)

LEAVEN (*see* LEAVENED, LEAVENS, UNLEAVENED)
Ex 12:15 remove **l** from your houses
Ex 12:19 For seven days no **l** shall be
Ex 13: 7 nor shall **l** be seen among you
Ex 34:25 blood of My sacrifice with **l**
Lev 2:11 the LORD shall be made with **l**
Lev 2:11 no **l** nor any honey in any
Lev 6:17 It shall not be baked with **l**
Lev 10:12 eat it without **l** beside the
Lev 23:17 they shall be baked with **l**
Deut 16: 4 no **l** shall be seen among you
Amos 4: 5 of thanksgiving with **l**,
Matt 13:33 kingdom of heaven is like **l**
Matt 16: 6 and beware of the **l** of the
Matt 16:11 of the **l** of the Pharisees
Matt 16:12 to beware of the **l** of bread
Mark 8:15 heed, beware of the **l** of the
Mark 8:15 Pharisees and the **l** of Herod
Luke 12: 1 all, "Beware of the **l** of the
Luke 13:21 It is like **l**, which a woman
1Co 5: 6 **l** leavens the whole lump
1Co 5: 7 Therefore purge out the old **l**
1Co 5: 8 the feast, not with old **l**
1Co 5: 8 nor with the **l** of malice
Gal 5: 9 A little **l** leavens the whole

LEAVENED (*see* LEAVEN)
Ex 12:15 For whoever eats **l** bread from
Ex 12:19 since whoever eats what is **l**
Ex 12:20 You shall eat nothing **l**
Ex 12:34 their dough before it was **l**
Ex 12:39 for it was not **l**, because
Ex 13: 3 No **l** bread shall be eaten
Ex 13: 7 And no **l** bread shall be seen
Ex 23:18 of My sacrifice with **l** bread
Lev 7:13 **l** bread with the sacrifice of
Deut 16: 3 shall eat no **l** bread with it
Hos 7: 4 the dough, until it is **l**
Matt 13:33 of meal till it was all **l**
Luke 13:21 of meal till it was all **l**

LEAVENS (*see* LEAVEN)
1Co 5: 6 leaven **l** the whole lump
Gal 5: 9 leaven **l** the whole lump

LEAVES (*see* PREFACE)

LEAVES* (*see* LEAF)
Gen 3: 7 and they sewed fig **l** together
Ezek 17: 9 of its spring **l** will wither
Ezek 47:12 their **l** will not wither, and
Ezek 47:12 food, and their **l** for medicine
Dan 4:12 Its **l** were lovely, its fruit
Dan 4:14 its branches, strip off its **l**
Dan 4:21 whose **l** were lovely and its

Matt 21:19 and found nothing on it but l
Matt 24:32 become tender and puts forth l
Mark 11:13 from afar a fig tree having l
Mark 11:13 to it, He found nothing but l
Mark 13:28 tender, and puts forth l, you
Rev 22: 2 the l of the tree were for

LEAVING (*see* PREFACE)

LEBANA (*see* LEBANAH)
Neh 7:48 the children of **L**, the

LEBANAH (*see* LEBANA)
Ezra 2:45 the sons of **L**, the sons of

LEBANON
Deut 1: 7 of the Canaanites and to **L**
Deut 3:25 pleasant mountains, and **L**
Deut 11:24 from the wilderness and **L**,
Josh 1: 4 this **L** as far as the great
Josh 9: 1 of the Great Sea toward **L**
Josh 11:17 of **L** below Mount Hermon
Josh 12: 7 of **L** as far as Mount Halak
Josh 13: 5 of the Gebalites, and all **L**
Josh 13: 6 from **L** as far as the Brook
Judg 3: 3 Hivites who dwelt in Mount **L**
Judg 9:15 and devour the cedars of **L**
1Ki 4:33 from the cedar tree of **L** even
1Ki 5: 6 cut down cedars for me from **L**
1Ki 5: 9 them down from **L** to the sea
1Ki 5:14 And he sent them to **L**, ten
1Ki 5:14 they were one month in **L** and
1Ki 7: 2 the House of the Forest of **L**
1Ki 9:19 to build in Jerusalem, in **L**
1Ki 10:17 the House of the Forest of **L**
1Ki 10:21 Forest of **L** were of pure gold
2Ki 14: 9 The thistle that was in **L**
2Ki 14: 9 to the cedar that was in **L**
2Ki 14: 9 beast that was in **L** passed by
2Ki 19:23 mountains, to the limits of **L**
2Ch 2: 8 cypress and algum logs from **L**
2Ch 2: 8 have skill to cut timber in **L**
2Ch 2:16 And we will cut wood from **L**
2Ch 8: 6 to build in Jerusalem, in **L**
2Ch 9:16 the House of the Forest of **L**
2Ch 9:20 Forest of **L** were of pure gold
2Ch 25:18 The thistle that was in **L**
2Ch 25:18 to the cedar that was in **L**
2Ch 25:18 beast that was in **L** passed by
Ezra 3: 7 from **L** to the sea at Joppa
Ps 29: 5 splinters the cedars of **L**
Ps 29: 6 them also skip like a calf, **L**
Ps 72:16 Its fruit shall wave like **L**
Ps 92:12 shall grow like a cedar in **L**
Ps 104:16 sap, The cedars of **L** which He
Song 3: 9 Of the wood of **L** Solomon the
Song 4: 8 Come with me from **L**, my
Song 4: 8 my spouse, with me from **L**
Song 4:11 is like the fragrance of **L**
Song 4:15 waters, and streams from **L**
Song 5:15 His countenance is like **L**
Song 7: 4 nose is like the tower of **L**
Is 2:13 the cedars of **L** that are high
Is 10:34 **L** will fall by the Mighty One
Is 14: 8 over you, and the cedars of **L**
Is 29:17 till **L** shall be turned into a
Is 33: 9 **L** is shamed and shriveled
Is 35: 2 The glory of **L** shall be given
Is 37:24 mountains, to the limits of **L**
Is 40:16 **L** is not sufficient to burn,
Is 60:13 The glory of **L** shall come to
Jer 18:14 man leave the snow-water of **L**
Jer 22: 6 Gilead to Me, the head of **L**
Jer 22:20 Go up to **L**, and cry out, and
Jer 22:23 O inhabitant of **L**, making
Ezek 17: 3 of various colors, came to **L**
Ezek 27: 5 from **L** to make you a mast
Ezek 31: 3 Assyria was a cedar in **L**,
Ezek 31:15 I caused **L** to mourn for it,
Ezek 31:16 Eden, the choice and best of **L**
Hos 14: 5 and lengthen his roots like **L**
Hos 14: 6 tree, and his fragrance like **L**
Hos 14: 7 shall be like the wine of **L**
Nah 1: 4 and the flower of **L** wilts
Hab 2:17 done to **L** will cover you, and
Zech 10:10 into the land of Gilead and **L**
Zech 11: 1 Open your doors, O **L**, that

LEBAOTH (*see* BETH LEBAOTH)
Josh 15:32 **L**, Shilhim, Ain, and Rimmon

LEBBAEUS (*see* JUDAS, THADDAEUS)
Matt 10: 3 the son of Alphaeus, and **L**

LEB KAMAI
Jer 51: 1 against those who dwell in **L**

LEBONAH
Judg 21:19 to Shechem, and south of **L**

LECAH
1Ch 4:21 Judah were Er the father of **L**

LED (*see* LEAD)
Gen 24:27 the LORD l me to the house of
Gen 24:48 who had l me in the way of
Ex 3: 1 he l the flock to the back of
Ex 13:18 So God l the people around by
Ex 15:13 You in Your mercy have l
Deut 8: 2 that the LORD your God l you
Deut 8:15 who l you through that great
Deut 29: 5 I have l you forty years in
Deut 32:12 so the LORD alone l him, and
Josh 24: 3 l him throughout all the land
Judg 2: 1 I l you up from Egypt and
Judg 3:27 and he l them
2Sa 5: 2 were the one who l Israel out
1Ki 8:48 who l them away captive, and
2Ki 6:19 But he l them to Samaria
2Ki 15:15 and the conspiracy which he l
2Ki 15:30 l a conspiracy against Pekah
1Ch 11: 2 were the one who l Israel out
1Ch 20: 1 that Joab l out the armed
2Ch 21:11 harlotry, and l Judah astray
2Ch 23:13 and those who l in praise
Neh 9:12 Moreover You l them by day
Neh 12: 8 Judah, and Mattaniah who l the
Esth 6:11 l him on horseback through
Ps 68:18 You have l captivity captive
Ps 77:20 You l Your people like a
Ps 78:14 also He l them with the cloud
Ps 78:53 He l them on safely, so that
Ps 106: 9 So He l them through the
Ps 107: 7 He l them forth by the right
Ps 136:16 To Him who l His people
Prov 4:11 I have l you in right paths
Prov 20: 1 whoever is l astray by it is
Is 9:16 those who are l by them are
Is 48:21 He l them through the deserts
Is 53: 7 He was l as a lamb to the
Is 55:12 joy, and be l out with peace
Is 63:12 Who l them by the right hand
Is 63:13 Who l them through the deep,
Jer 2: 6 Egypt, Who l us through the
Jer 2:17 God when He l you in the way
Jer 22:12 where they have l him captive
Jer 23: 8 and l the descendants of the
Jer 50: 6 shepherds have l them astray
Lam 3: 2 He has l me and made me walk
Ezek 17:12 l them with him to Babylon
Ezek 40:26 Seven steps l up to it, and
Ezek 40:49 by the steps which l up to it
Ezek 47: 2 l me around on the outside to
Amos 2:10 l you forty years through the
Amos 7:11 Israel shall surely be l away
Amos 7:17 Israel shall surely be l away
Nah 2: 7 she shall be l away captive
Matt 4: 1 Then Jesus was l up by the
Matt 26:57 l Him away to Caiaphas the
Matt 27: 2 they l Him away and delivered
Matt 27:31 l Him away to be crucified
Mark 8:23 hand and l him out of the town
Mark 9: 2 l them up on a high mountain
Mark 14:53 they l Jesus away to the high
Mark 15: 1 l Him away, and delivered Him
Mark 15:16 Then the soldiers l Him away
Mark 15:20 and l Him out to crucify Him
Luke 4: 1 was l by the Spirit into the
Luke 4:29 they l Him to the brow of the
Luke 21:24 be l away captive into all
Luke 22:54 arrested Him, they l Him and
Luke 22:66 l Him into their council,
Luke 23: 1 them arose and l Him to Pilate
Luke 23:26 Now as they l Him away, they
Luke 23:32 l with Him to be put to death
Luke 24:50 And He l them out as far as
John 18:13 And they l Him away to Annas
John 18:28 Then they l Jesus from
John 19:16 they took Jesus and l Him away
Acts 8:32 He was l as a sheep to the
Acts 9: 8 But they l him by the hand and
Acts 21:37 to be l into the barracks
Acts 21:38 l the four thousand assassins
Acts 22:11 being l by the hand of those
Rom 8:14 For as many as are l by the
1Co 12: 2 idols, however you were l
2Co 7: 9 your sorrow l to repentance
Gal 5:18 if you are l by the Spirit
Eph 4: 8 He l captivity captive, and
2Ti 3: 6 l away by various lusts,
Heb 3:16 came out of Egypt, l by Moses
2Pe 3:17 being l away with the error

LEDGE (*see* LEDGES)
Ezek 43:14 on the ground to the lower l
Ezek 43:14 the width of the l, one cubit
Ezek 43:14 smaller l to the larger l
Ezek 43:14 and the width of the l, one
Ezek 43:17 the l, fourteen cubits long
Ezek 43:20 on the four corners of the l
Ezek 45:19 corners of the l of the altar

LEDGES (*see* LEDGE)
1Ki 6: 6 for he made narrow l around
Ezek 41: 6 they rested on l which were
Ezek 41: 7 because their supporting l in

LEECH
Prov 30:15 The l has two daughters,

LEEKS
Num 11: 5 cucumbers, the melons, the l

LEES
Is 25: 6 a feast of wines on the l
Is 25: 6 well-refined wines on the l

LEFT (*see* PREFACE)

LEFT* (*see* LEFT-HANDED)
Gen 13: 9 If you take the l, then I
Gen 13: 9 then I will go to the l
Gen 24:49 to the right hand or to the l
Gen 48:13 hand toward Israel's l hand
Gen 48:13 and Manasseh with his l hand
Gen 48:14 his l hand on Manasseh's head
Ex 14:22 right hand and on their l
Lev 14:15 the palm of his own l hand
Lev 14:16 the oil that is in his l hand
Lev 14:26 the palm of his own l hand
Lev 14:27 of the oil that is in his l
Num 20:17 to the l until we have passed
Num 22:26 to the right hand or to the l
Deut 2:27 to the right nor to the l
Deut 5:32 to the right hand or to the l
Deut 17:11 the l from the sentence which
Deut 17:20 to the right hand or to the l
Deut 28:14 to the right hand or to the l
Josh 1: 7 to the right hand or to the l
Josh 19:27 Cabul which was on the l,
Josh 23: 6 to the right hand or to the l
Judg 3:21 Ehud reached with his l hand
Judg 7:20 the torches in their l hands
Judg 16:29 right and the other on his l
1Sa 6:12 to the right hand or the l
2Sa 2:19 to the l from following Abner
2Sa 2:21 your right hand or to your l
2Sa 14:19 l from anything that my lord
2Sa 16: 6 on his right hand and on his l
1Ki 7:21 he set up the pillar on the l
1Ki 7:39 five on the l side of the
1Ki 7:49 five on the l in front of the
1Ki 22:19 on His right hand and on His l
2Ki 11:11 to the l side of the temple
2Ki 22: 2 to the right hand or to the l
2Ki 23: 8 to the l of the city gate
1Ch 6:44 sons of Merari, on the l hand
1Ch 12: 2 the l in hurling stones and
2Ch 3:17 hand and the other on the l
2Ch 3:17 name of the one on the l Boaz
2Ch 4: 6 right side and five on the l
2Ch 4: 7 right side and five on the l
2Ch 4: 8 right side and five on the l
2Ch 18:18 on His right hand and on His l
2Ch 23:10 to the l side of the temple
2Ch 34: 2 to the right hand or to the l
Neh 8: 4 and at his l hand Pedaiah,
Job 23: 9 when He works on the l hand
Prov 3:16 in her l hand riches and honor
Prov 4:27 turn to the right or the l
Eccl 10: 2 but a fool's heart at his l
Song 2: 6 His l hand is under my head,
Song 8: 3 His l hand is under my head,
Is 9:20 He shall devour on the l hand
Is 54: 3 to the right and to the l, and
Ezek 1:10 face of an ox on the l side
Ezek 4: 4 Lie also on your l side, and

Ezek 21:16 Set your blade! Thrust l—
Ezek 39: 3 the bow out of your l hand
Dan 12: 7 and his l hand to heaven, and
Jon 4:11 their right hand and their l
Zech 4: 3 bowl and the other at its l
Zech 4:11 and the other at its l
Zech 12: 6 on the right hand and on the l
Matt 6: 3 do not let your l hand know
Matt 20:21 hand and the other on the l
Matt 20:23 on My l is not Mine to give,
Matt 25:33 hand, but the goats on the l
Matt 25:41 say to those on the l hand
Matt 27:38 the right and another on the l
Mark 10:37 hand and the other on Your l
Mark 10:40 on My l is not Mine to give,
Mark 15:27 right and the other on His l
Luke 23:33 hand and the other on the l
Acts 21: 3 Cyprus, we passed it on the l
2Co 6: 7 on the right hand and on the l
Rev 10: 2 and his l foot on the land,

LEFT-HANDED (*see* LEFT*)
Judg 3:15 Gera, the Benjamite, a l man
Judg 20:16 hundred select men who were l

LEFTOVER
Mark 8: 8 large baskets of l fragments
Luke 9:17 and twelve baskets of the l

LEG (*see* LEGS)
Is 3:20 the l ornaments, and the

LEGACY
Prov 3:35 shame shall be the l of fools

LEGION (*see* LEGIONS)
Mark 5: 9 My name is **L**
Mark 5:15 demon-possessed and had the l
Luke 8:30 **L**," because many demons had

LEGIONS (*see* LEGION)
Matt 26:53 more than twelve l of angels

LEGS (*see* LEG)
Ex 12: 9 its head with its l and its
Ex 25:26 that are at its four l
Ex 29:17 wash its entrails and its l
Ex 37:13 that were at its four l
Lev 1: 9 entrails and its l with water
Lev 1:13 entrails and the l with water
Lev 4:11 its flesh, with its head and l
Lev 8:21 entrails and the l in water
Lev 9:14 washed the entrails and the l
Lev 11:21 those which have jointed l
Deut 28:35 on the l with severe boils
1Sa 17: 6 had bronze greaves on his l
Ps 147:10 no pleasure in the l of a man
Prov 26: 7 Like the l of the lame that
Song 5:15 His l are pillars of marble
Is 7:20 the head and the hair of the l
Ezek 1: 7 Their l were straight, and the
Dan 2:33 its l of iron, its feet
Amos 3:12 two l or a piece of an ear
John 19:31 that their l might be broken
John 19:32 broke the l of the first and
John 19:33 they did not break His l

LEHABIM (*see* LIBYA, LUBIM)
Gen 10:13 begot Ludim, Anamim, **L**,
1Ch 1:11 begot Ludim, Anamim, **L**,

LEHI (*see* RAMATH LEHI)
Judg 15: 9 deployed themselves against **L**
Judg 15:14 When he came to **L**, the
Judg 15:17 and called that place Ramath **L**
Judg 15:19 the hollow place that is in **L**
Judg 15:19 which is in **L** to this day

LEMUEL
Prov 31: 1 The words of King **L**, the
Prov 31: 4 It is not for kings, O **L**, it

LEND (*see* LENDER, LENDING, LENDS, LENT, LOAN)
Ex 22:25 If you l money to any of My
Lev 25:37 You shall not l him your
Lev 25:37 nor l him your food at a
Deut 15: 6 you shall l to many nations,
Deut 15: 8 willingly l him sufficient
Deut 24:10 When you l your brother
Deut 24:11 the man to whom you l shall
Deut 28:12 You shall l to many nations,
Deut 28:44 He shall l to you, but you
Deut 28:44 but you shall not l to him
Prov 5: 1 l your ear to my
Luke 6:34 if you l to those from whom
Luke 6:34 For even sinners l to sinners
Luke 6:35 your enemies, do good, and l
Luke 11: 5 Friend, l me three loaves

LENDER (*see* LEND)
Prov 22: 7 borrower is servant to the l
Is 24: 2 as with the l, so with the

LENDING (*see* LEND)
Neh 5:10 am l them money and grain

LENDS (*see* LEND)
Ps 37:26 He is ever merciful, and l
Ps 112: 5 man deals graciously and l
Prov 19:17 on the poor l to the LORD

LENGTH (*see* LENGTHEN)
Gen 6:15 The l of the ark shall be
Gen 13:17 in the land through its l
Gen 47:28 So the l of Jacob's life was
Ex 25:10 a half cubits shall be its l
Ex 25:17 a half cubits shall be its l
Ex 25:23 two cubits shall be its l
Ex 26: 2 The l of each curtain shall
Ex 26: 8 The l of each curtain shall
Ex 26:13 of what remains of the l of
Ex 26:16 shall be the l of a board
Ex 27:11 Likewise along the l of the
Ex 27:18 The l of the court shall be
Ex 28:16 a span shall be its l, and a
Ex 30: 2 A cubit shall be its l and a
Ex 36: 9 The l of each curtain was
Ex 36:15 The l of each curtain was
Ex 36:21 The l of each board was ten
Ex 37: 1 and a half cubits was its l
Ex 37: 6 and a half cubits was its l
Ex 37:10 two cubits was its l, a cubit
Ex 37:25 Its l was a cubit and its
Ex 38: 1 five cubits was its l and five
Ex 38:18 The l was twenty cubits, and
Ex 39: 9 a span was its l and a span
Lev 19:35 judgment, in measurement of l
Deut 3:11 Nine cubits is its l and four
Deut 30:20 life and the l of your days
Judg 3:16 double-edged and a cubit in l)
1Sa 28:20 fell full l on the ground
1Ki 6: 2 its l was sixty cubits, its
1Ki 7: 2 its l was one hundred cubits,
1Ki 7: 6 its l was fifty cubits, and
1Ki 7:27 cubits was the l of each cart
2Ch 3: 3 The l was sixty cubits (by
2Ch 3: 8 Its l was according to the
2Ch 3:11 twenty cubits in overall l
2Ch 4: 1 twenty cubits was its l,
Job 12:12 with l of days, understanding
Ps 21: 4 **L** of days forever and ever
Prov 3: 2 for l of days and long life and
Prov 3:16 **L** of days is in her right
Is 57:10 wearied in the l of your way
Ezek 31: 7 in the l of its branches,
Ezek 40:11 the l of the gate, thirteen
Ezek 40:18 to the l of the gateways
Ezek 40:20 north, and he measured its l
Ezek 40:21 its l was fifty cubits and its
Ezek 40:25 its l was fifty cubits and its
Ezek 40:36 its l was fifty cubits and its
Ezek 40:49 The l of the vestibule was
Ezek 41: 2 and he measured its l, forty
Ezek 41: 4 He measured the l, twenty
Ezek 41:12 and its l ninety cubits
Ezek 41:15 He measured the l of the
Ezek 41:22 high, and its l two cubits
Ezek 41:22 Its corners, its l, and its
Ezek 42: 2 Facing the l, which was one
Ezek 42: 7 its l was fifty cubits
Ezek 42: 8 The l of the chambers toward
Ezek 45: 1 its l shall be twenty-five
Ezek 45: 7 the l shall be side by side
Ezek 48: 8 in l the same as one of the
Ezek 48: 9 thousand cubits in l and ten
Ezek 48:10 thousand cubits in l, on the
Ezek 48:10 twenty-five thousand in l
Ezek 48:13 thousand cubits in l and ten
Ezek 48:13 its entire l shall be
Ezek 48:18 The rest of the l, alongside
Zech 2: 2 is its width and what is its l
Zech 5: 2 Its l is twenty cubits and its
Eph 3:18 saints what is the width and l
Rev 21:16 and its l is as great as its
Rev 21:16 Its l, breadth, and height are

LENGTHEN (*see* LENGTH, LENGTHENED, LENGTHENING, LENGTHENS)
1Ki 3:14 then I will l your days
Is 54: 2 l your cords, and strengthen
Hos 14: 5 and l his roots like Lebanon

LENGTHENED (*see* LENGTHEN)
Deut 25:15 that your days may be l in

LENGTHENING (*see* LENGTHEN)
Jer 6: 4 shadows of the evening are l
Dan 4:27 may be a l of your prosperity

LENGTHENS (*see* LENGTHEN)
Ps 102:11 days are like a shadow that l
Ps 109:23 gone like a shadow when it l

LENT (*see* LEND)
Deut 15: 2 Every creditor who has l
Deut 23:19 that is l out at interest
1Sa 1:28 I also have l him to the LORD
1Sa 1:28 he shall be l to the LORD
1Sa 2:20 loan that was l to the LORD
Jer 15:10 I have neither l for interest
Jer 15:10 nor have men l to me for

LENTILS
Gen 25:34 gave Esau bread and stew of l
2Sa 17:28 parched grain and beans, l
2Sa 23:11 a piece of ground full of l
Ezek 4: 9 wheat, barley, beans, l,

LEOPARD (*see* LEOPARDS)
Is 11: 6 the l shall lie down with the
Jer 5: 6 a l will watch over their
Jer 13:23 his skin or the l its spots
Dan 7: 6 there was another, like a l
Hos 13: 7 like a l by the road I will
Rev 13: 2 which I saw was like a l, his

LEOPARDS (*see* LEOPARD)
Song 4: 8 from the mountains of the l
Hab 1: 8 also are swifter than l, and

LEPER (*see* LEPERS, LEPROSY)
Lev 13:45 Now the l on whom the sore is
Lev 14: 2 of the l for the day of his
Lev 14: 3 leprosy is healed in the l
Lev 22: 4 who is a l or has a discharge
Num 5: 2 put out of the camp every l
Num 12:10 Miriam, and there she was, a l
2Sa 3:29 who has a discharge or is a l
2Ki 5: 1 man of valor, but he was a l
2Ki 15: 5 so that he was a l until the
2Ch 26:21 King Uzziah was a l until the
2Ch 26:21 house, because he was a l
2Ch 26:23 He is a l
Matt 8: 2 a l came and worshiped Him,
Matt 26: 6 at the house of Simon the l
Mark 1:40 Then a l came to Him,
Mark 14: 3 at the house of Simon the l

LEPERS (*see* LEPER)
2Ki 7: 8 And when these l came to the
Matt 10: 8 Heal the sick, cleanse the l
Matt 11: 5 the l are cleansed and the
Luke 4:27 many l were in Israel in the
Luke 7:22 the l are cleansed, the deaf
Luke 17:12 met Him ten men who were l

LEPROSY (*see* LEPER, LEPROUS)
Lev 13: 8 It is l
Lev 13:11 it is an old l on the skin of
Lev 13:12 if l breaks out all over the
Lev 13:12 the l covers all the skin of
Lev 13:13 indeed if the l has covered
Lev 13:15 It is l
Lev 13:25 it is l broken out in the
Lev 13:30 a l of the head or beard
Lev 13:42 it is l breaking out on his
Lev 13:43 as the appearance of l on the
Lev 13:51 the plague is an active l
Lev 13:52 for it is an active l
Lev 14: 3 if the l is healed in the
Lev 14: 7 is to be cleansed from the l
Lev 14:44 is an active l in the house
Lev 14:55 for the l of a garment and of
Lev 14:57 This is the law of l
Deut 24: 8 Take heed in an outbreak of l
2Ki 5: 3 he would heal him of his l
2Ki 5: 6 you may heal him of his l
2Ki 5: 7 to me to heal him of his l
2Ki 5:11 over the place, and heal the l
2Ki 5:27 Therefore the l of Naaman
2Ch 26:19 l broke out on his forehead,

Matt 8: 3 his l was cleansed
Mark 1:42 immediately the l left him
Luke 5:12 who was full of l saw Jesus
Luke 5:13 And immediately the l left him

LEPROUS (*see* LEPROSY)
Ex 4: 6 out, behold, his hand was l
Lev 13: 2 of his body like a l sore
Lev 13: 3 of his body, it is a l sore
Lev 13: 9 When the l sore is on a
Lev 13:20 It is a l sore which has
Lev 13:22 It is a l sore
Lev 13:25 It is a l sore
Lev 13:27 It is a l sore
Lev 13:44 he is a l man
Lev 13:47 garment has a l plague in it
Lev 13:49 of leather, it is a l plague
Lev 13:59 This is the law of the l
Lev 14:32 law for one who had a l sore
Lev 14:34 I put the l plague in a house
Lev 14:54 is the law for any l sore
Num 12:10 suddenly Miriam became l
2Ki 5:27 went out from his presence l
2Ki 7: 3 Now there were four l men at
2Ch 26:20 on his forehead, he was l

LESHEM (*see* LAISH)
Josh 19:47 went up to fight against L
Josh 19:47 They called L, Dan, after the

LESS (*see* PREFACE)

LESSER (*see* PREFACE)

LESSON
Ezek 5:15 be a reproach, a taunt, a l

LEST (*see* PREFACE)

LET (*see* PREFACE)

LETS (*see* PREFACE)

LETTER (*see* LETTERS)
2Sa 11:14 that David wrote a l to Joab
2Sa 11:15 And he wrote in the l, saying,
2Ki 5: 5 I will send a l to the king
2Ki 5: 6 Then he brought the l to the
2Ki 5: 6 when this l comes to you,
2Ki 5: 7 the king of Israel read the l
2Ki 10: 2 soon as this l comes to you
2Ki 10: 6 he wrote a second l to them
2Ki 10: 7 when the l came to them, that
2Ki 19:14 the l from the hand of the
2Ch 21:12 a l came to him from Elijah
Ezra 4: 7 the l was written in Aramaic
Ezra 4: 8 a l against Jerusalem to King
Ezra 4:11 of the l that they sent him
Ezra 4:18 The l which you sent to us
Ezra 4:23 l was read before Rehum,
Ezra 5: 6 of the l that Tattenai sent
Ezra 5: 7 They sent a l to him, in
Ezra 7:11 l that King Artaxerxes gave
Neh 2: 8 a l to Asaph the keeper of
Neh 6: 5 with an open l in his hand
Esth 8: 8 for a l which is written in
Esth 9:25 he commanded by l that this
Esth 9:26 of all the words of this l
Esth 9:29 this second l about Purim
Is 37:14 the l from the hand of the
Jer 29: 1 l that Jeremiah the prophet
Jer 29: 3 The l was sent by the hand of
Jer 29:29 the priest read this l in the
Acts 15:23 They wrote this l by them
Acts 15:30 they delivered the l
Acts 23:25 He wrote a l in the following
Acts 23:33 the l to the governor, they
Rom 2:29 the Spirit, and not in the l
Rom 7: 6 not in the oldness of the l
2Co 3: 6 not of the l but of the
2Co 3: 6 for the l kills, but the
2Co 7: 8 if I made you sorry with my l
2Th 2: 2 by spirit or by word or by l

LETTERS (*see* LETTER)
1Ki 21: 8 So she wrote l in Ahab's name
1Ki 21: 8 sent the l to the elders and
1Ki 21: 9 And she wrote in the l, saying
1Ki 21:11 as it was written in the l
2Ki 10: 1 And Jehu wrote l and sent them
2Ki 20:12 king of Babylon, sent l and a
2Ch 30: 1 and also wrote l to Ephraim
2Ch 30: 6 with the l from the king and
2Ch 32:17 He also wrote l to revile the
Neh 2: 7 let l be given to me for the
Neh 2: 9 and gave them the king's l
Neh 6:17 Judah sent many l to Tobiah
Neh 6:17 the l of Tobiah came to them
Neh 6:19 Tobiah sent l to frighten me
Esth 1:22 Then he sent l to all the
Esth 3:13 the l were sent by couriers
Esth 8: 5 revoke the l devised by Haman
Esth 8:10 and sent l by couriers on
Esth 8:11 By these l the king permitted
Esth 9:20 sent l to all the Jews who
Esth 9:30 Mordecai sent l to all the
Is 39: 1 king of Babylon, sent l and a
Jer 29:25 You have sent l in your name
Luke 23:38 over Him in l of Greek, Latin
John 7:15 How does this Man know l,
Acts 9: 2 and asked l from him to the
Acts 22: 5 received l to the brethren
Acts 28:21 We neither received l from
1Co 16: 3 you approve by your l, I will
2Co 3: 1 or l of commendation from you
2Co 10: 9 I seem to terrify you by l
2Co 10:10 For his l," they say, "are
2Co 10:11 word by l when we are absent
Gal 6:11 See with what large l I have

LETTING (*see* PREFACE)

LETUSHIM
Gen 25: 3 of Dedan were Asshurim, L

LEUMMIM
Gen 25: 3 Asshurim, Letushim, and L

LEVEL (*see* LEVELED, LEVELS)
Ezek 42: 6 therefore the upper l was
Luke 6:17 stood on a l place with a
Luke 19:44 and l you, and your children

LEVELED (*see* LEVEL)
Is 28:25 When he has l its surface

LEVELS (*see* LEVEL)
Ezek 42: 6 middle l from the ground up

LEVI (*see* LEVI'S, LEVITE, MATTHEW)
Gen 29:34 his name was called L
Gen 34:25 sons of Jacob, Simeon and L
Gen 34:30 Jacob said to Simeon and L
Gen 35:23 firstborn, and Simeon, L,
Gen 46:11 The sons of L were Gershon,
Gen 49: 5 Simeon and L are brothers
Ex 1: 2 Reuben, Simeon, L, and Judah
Ex 2: 1 a man of the house of L went
Ex 2: 1 took as wife a daughter of L
Ex 6:16 sons of L according to their
Ex 6:16 life of L were one hundred
Ex 6:19 of L according to their
Ex 32:26 all the sons of L gathered
Ex 32:28 So the sons of L did
Num 1:49 Only the tribe of L you shall
Num 3: 6 Bring the tribe of L near
Num 3:15 Number the children of L by
Num 3:17 the sons of L by their names
Num 4: 2 from among the children of L
Num 16: 1 son of Kohath, the son of L
Num 16: 7 yourselves, you sons of L
Num 16: 8 Hear now, you sons of L
Num 16:10 your brethren, the sons of L
Num 17: 3 Aaron's name on the rod of L
Num 17: 8 of Aaron, of the house of L
Num 18: 2 brethren of the tribe of L
Num 18:21 have given the children of L
Num 26:59 Jochebed the daughter of L
Num 26:59 who was born to L in Egypt
Deut 10: 8 of L to bear the ark of the
Deut 10: 9 Therefore L has no portion
Deut 18: 1 indeed all the tribe of L
Deut 21: 5 the priests, the sons of L
Deut 27:12 Simeon, L, Judah, Issachar,
Deut 31: 9 to the priests, the sons of L
Deut 33: 8 And of L he said: "Let Your
Josh 13:14 Only to the tribe of L he had
Josh 13:33 tribe of L Moses had given no
Josh 21:10 who were of the children of L
1Ki 12:31 who were not of the sons of L
1Ch 2: 1 Reuben, Simeon, L, Judah,
1Ch 6: 1 The sons of L were Gershon,
1Ch 6:16 The sons of L were Gershon,
1Ch 6:38 son of Kohath, the son of L
1Ch 6:43 son of Gershon, the son of L
1Ch 6:47 son of Merari, the son of L
1Ch 9:18 camps of the children of L at
1Ch 12:26 of the children of L four
1Ch 21: 6 But he did not count L and
1Ch 23: 6 divisions among the sons of L
1Ch 23:14 reckoned to the tribe of L
1Ch 23:24 These were the sons of L by
1Ch 24:20 Now the rest of the sons of L
Ezra 8:15 none of the sons of L there
Ezra 8:18 sons of Mahli the son of L
Neh 10:39 the children of L shall bring
Neh 12:23 The sons of L, the heads of
Ps 135:20 Bless the LORD, O house of L
Ezek 40:46 of Zadok, from the sons of L
Ezek 48:31 for Judah, and one gate for L
Zech 12:13 of the house of L by itself
Mal 2: 4 covenant with L may continue
Mal 2: 8 corrupted the covenant of L
Mal 3: 3 He will purify the sons of L
Mark 2:14 He saw L the son of Alphaeus
Luke 3:24 son of Matthat, the son of L
Luke 3:29 son of Matthat, the son of L
Luke 5:27 saw a tax collector named L
Luke 5:29 Then L gave Him a great feast
Heb 7: 5 who are of the sons of L, who
Heb 7: 9 Even L, who receives tithes,
Rev 7: 7 of the tribe of L twelve

LEVIATHAN
Job 3: 8 who are ready to arouse L
Job 41: 1 you draw out L with a hook
Ps 74:14 the heads of L in pieces, And
Ps 104:26 there is that L Which You
Is 27: 1 will punish L the fleeing
Is 27: 1 L that twisted serpent

LEVI'S (*see* LEVI)
Mark 2:15 as He was dining in L house

LEVITE (*see* LEVI, LEVITES, LEVITICAL)
Ex 4:14 not Aaron the L your brother
Deut 12:12 and the L who is within your
Deut 12:18 and the L who is within your
Deut 12:19 L as long as you live in your
Deut 14:27 L who is within your gates
Deut 14:29 And the L, because he has no
Deut 16:11 the L who is within your
Deut 16:14 and your maidservant and the L
Deut 18: 6 if a L comes from any of your
Deut 26:11 and your house, you and the L
Deut 26:12 and have given it to the L
Deut 26:13 also have given them to the L
Judg 17: 7 he was a L, and was sojourning
Judg 17: 9 I am a L from Bethlehem in
Judg 17:10 So the L went in
Judg 17:11 Then the L was content to
Judg 17:12 So Micah consecrated the L
Judg 17:13 since I have a L as priest
Judg 18: 3 the voice of the young L
Judg 18:15 the house of the young L man
Judg 19: 1 L sojourning in the remote
Judg 20: 4 So the L, the husband of the
2Ch 20:14 a L of the sons of Asaph, in
2Ch 31:12 Cononiah the L was ruler over
2Ch 31:14 Kore the son of Imnah the L
Ezra 10:15 Shabbethai the L gave them
Luke 10:32 Likewise a L, when he arrived
Acts 4:36 a L of the country of Cyprus,

LEVITES (*see* LEVITE)
Ex 6:25 L according to their families
Ex 38:21 for the service of the L
Lev 25:32 the cities of the L, and the
Lev 25:32 the L may redeem at any time
Lev 25:33 purchases a house from the L
Lev 25:33 L are their possession among
Num 1:47 But the L were not numbered
Num 1:50 but you shall appoint the L
Num 1:51 the L shall take it down
Num 1:51 set up, the L shall set it up
Num 1:53 but the L shall camp around
Num 1:53 the L shall keep charge of
Num 2:17 out with the camp of the L in
Num 2:33 But the L were not numbered
Num 3: 9 you shall give the L to Aaron
Num 3:12 I Myself have taken the L
Num 3:12 Therefore the L shall be Mine
Num 3:20 are the families of the L by
Num 3:32 over the leaders of the L
Num 3:39 who were numbered of the L
Num 3:41 you shall take the L for Me
Num 3:41 of the L instead of all the
Num 3:45 Take the L instead of all the
Num 3:45 and the livestock of the L
Num 3:45 The L shall be Mine
Num 3:46 more than the number of the L

Num 3:49 who were redeemed by the L
Num 4:18 Kohathites from among the L
Num 4:46 who were numbered of the L
Num 7: 5 you shall give them to the L
Num 7: 6 oxen, and gave them to the L
Num 8: 6 Take the L from among the
Num 8: 9 you shall bring the L before
Num 8:10 bring the L before the LORD
Num 8:10 lay their hands on the L
Num 8:11 offer the L before the LORD
Num 8:12 Then the L shall lay their
Num 8:12 to make atonement for the L
Num 8:13 stand the L before Aaron and
Num 8:14 L from among the children of
Num 8:14 and the L shall be Mine
Num 8:15 After that the L shall go in
Num 8:18 I have taken the L instead of
Num 8:19 I have given the L as a gift
Num 8:20 of Israel did to the L
Num 8:20 Moses concerning the L, so
Num 8:21 the L purified themselves and
Num 8:22 After that the L went in to
Num 8:22 Moses concerning the L, so
Num 8:24 is what pertains to the L
Num 8:26 the L regarding their duties
Num 18: 6 taken your brethren the L
Num 18:23 But the L shall perform the
Num 18:24 to the L as an inheritance
Num 18:26 Speak thus to the L, and say
Num 18:30 the L as the produce of the
Num 26:57 who were numbered of the L
Num 26:58 are the families of the L
Num 31:30 give them to the L who keep
Num 31:47 beast, and gave them to the L
Num 35: 2 Israel that they give the L
Num 35: 2 the L common-land around the
Num 35: 4 which you shall give the L
Num 35: 6 the L you shall appoint six
Num 35: 7 to the L shall be forty-eight
Num 35: 8 some of its cities to the L
Deut 17: 9 come to the priests, the L
Deut 17:18 one before the priests, the L
Deut 18: 1 The priests, the L, indeed
Deut 18: 7 as all his brethren the L do
Deut 24: 8 all that the priests, the L
Deut 27: 9 Moses and the priests, the L
Deut 27:14 the L shall speak with a loud
Deut 31:25 that Moses commanded the L
Josh 3: 3 God, and the priests, the L
Josh 8:33 ark before the priests, the L
Josh 14: 3 but to the L he had given no
Josh 14: 4 no part to the L in the land
Josh 18: 7 But the L have no part among
Josh 21: 1 L came near to Eleazar the
Josh 21: 3 of Israel gave to the L from
Josh 21: 4 the priest, who were of the L
Josh 21: 8 common-lands by lot to the L
Josh 21:20 the children of Kohath, the L
Josh 21:27 of the families of the L
Josh 21:34 of Merari, the rest of the L
Josh 21:40 rest of the families of the L
Josh 21:41 All the cities of the L
1Sa 6:15 The L took down the ark of
2Sa 15:24 all the L with him, bearing
1Ki 8: 4 and the L brought them up
1Ch 6:19 are the families of the L
1Ch 6:48 And their brethren, the L,
1Ch 6:64 their common-lands to the L
1Ch 9: 2 were Israelites, priests, L
1Ch 9:14 Of the L: Shemaiah
1Ch 9:26 they were L
1Ch 9:31 Mattithiah of the L, the
1Ch 9:33 the fathers' houses of the L
1Ch 9:34 the fathers' houses of the L
1Ch 13: 2 L who are in their cities and
1Ch 15: 2 the ark of God but the L, for
1Ch 15: 4 children of Aaron and the L
1Ch 15:11 the priests, and for the L
1Ch 15:12 the fathers' houses of the L
1Ch 15:14 the L sanctified themselves
1Ch 15:15 the children of the L bore
1Ch 15:16 L to appoint their brethren
1Ch 15:17 So the L appointed Heman the
1Ch 15:22 Chenaniah, leader of the L
1Ch 15:26 when God helped the L who
1Ch 15:27 as were all the L who bore
1Ch 16: 4 he appointed some of the L to
1Ch 23: 2 with the priests and the L
1Ch 23: 3 Now the L were numbered from
1Ch 23:26 and also to the L, They
1Ch 23:27 L were numbered from twenty
1Ch 24: 6 of Nethaneel, one of the L
1Ch 24: 6 houses of the priests and L
1Ch 24:30 These were the sons of the L
1Ch 24:31 houses of the priests and L
1Ch 26:17 On the east were six L, on
1Ch 26:20 Of the L, Ahijah was over the
1Ch 27:17 over the L, Hashabiah the son
1Ch 28:13 of the priests and the L, for
1Ch 28:21 the L for all the service of
2Ch 5: 4 and the L took up the ark
2Ch 5: 5 and the L brought them up
2Ch 5:12 the L who were the singers,
2Ch 7: 6 the L also with instruments
2Ch 8:14 the L for their duties (to
2Ch 8:15 L concerning any matter or
2Ch 11:13 the L who were in all Israel
2Ch 11:14 For the L left their
2Ch 11:16 And after the L left, those
2Ch 13: 9 the sons of Aaron, and the L
2Ch 13:10 the L attend to their duties
2Ch 17: 8 And with them he sent L
2Ch 17: 8 the L; and with them
2Ch 19: 8 appointed some of the L and
2Ch 19:11 also the L will be officials
2Ch 20:19 Then the L of the children of
2Ch 23: 2 gathered the L from all the
2Ch 23: 4 of the priests and the L,
2Ch 23: 6 and those of the L who serve
2Ch 23: 7 the L shall surround the king
2Ch 23: 8 So the L and all Judah did
2Ch 23:18 hand of the priests, the L
2Ch 24: 5 gathered the priests and the L
2Ch 24: 5 However the L did not do it
2Ch 24: 6 the L to bring in from Judah
2Ch 24:11 official by the hand of the L
2Ch 29: 4 in the priests and the L, and
2Ch 29: 5 Hear me, L! Now sanctify
2Ch 29:12 Then these L arose
2Ch 29:16 the L took it out and carried
2Ch 29:25 Then he stationed the L in
2Ch 29:26 The L stood with the
2Ch 29:30 the leaders commanded the L
2Ch 29:34 their brethren the L helped
2Ch 29:34 for the L were more diligent
2Ch 30:15 and the L were ashamed, and
2Ch 30:16 from the hand of the L
2Ch 30:17 therefore the L had charge of
2Ch 30:21 and the L and the priests
2Ch 30:22 all the L who taught the good
2Ch 30:25 also the priests and L, all
2Ch 30:27 Then the priests, the L,
2Ch 31: 2 and the L according to their
2Ch 31: 2 and L for burnt offerings and
2Ch 31: 4 for the priests and the L,
2Ch 31: 9 the L concerning the heaps
2Ch 31:17 to the L from twenty years
2Ch 31:19 by genealogies among the L
2Ch 34: 9 God, which the L who kept the
2Ch 34:12 were Jahath and Obadiah the L
2Ch 34:12 Others of the L, all of whom
2Ch 34:13 some of the L were scribes,
2Ch 34:30 the priests and the L, and all
2Ch 35: 3 Then he said to the L who
2Ch 35: 5 the father's house of the L
2Ch 35: 8 to the priests, and to the L
2Ch 35: 9 and Jozabad, chief of the L
2Ch 35: 9 gave to the L for Passover
2Ch 35:10 the L in their divisions,
2Ch 35:11 while the L skinned the
2Ch 35:14 therefore the L prepared
2Ch 35:15 L prepared portions for them
2Ch 35:18 with the priests and the L
Ezra 1: 5 and the priests and the L,
Ezra 2:40 The L: the sons of
Ezra 2:70 So the priests and the L, some
Ezra 3: 8 brethren the priests and the L
Ezra 3: 8 appointed the L from twenty
Ezra 3: 9 sons and their brethren the L
Ezra 3:10 with trumpets, and the L, the
Ezra 3:12 But many of the priests and L
Ezra 6:16 Israel, the priests and the L
Ezra 6:18 the L to their divisions,
Ezra 6:20 the L had purified themselves
Ezra 7: 7 of Israel, the priests, the L
Ezra 7:13 L in my realm, who volunteer
Ezra 7:24 on any of the priests, L,
Ezra 8:20 for the service of the L, two
Ezra 8:29 of the priests and the L and
Ezra 8:30 the L received the silver and
Ezra 8:33 with them were the L, Jozabad
Ezra 9: 1 and the L have not separated
Ezra 10: 5 leaders of the priests, the L
Ezra 10:23 Also of the L: Jozabad
Neh 3:17 After him the L, under Rehum
Neh 7: 1 the L had been appointed,
Neh 7:43 The L: the children of
Neh 7:73 So the priests, the L, the
Neh 8: 7 Hanan, Pelaiah, and the L
Neh 8: 9 the L who taught the people
Neh 8:11 So the L quieted all the
Neh 8:13 people, with the priests and L
Neh 9: 4 stood on the stairs of the L
Neh 9: 5 Then the L, Jeshua, Kadmiel,
Neh 9:38 and our leaders and our L and
Neh 10: 9 The L: Jeshua the son of
Neh 10:28 people (the priests, the L
Neh 10:34 lots among the priests, the L
Neh 10:37 tithes of our land to the L
Neh 10:37 for the L should receive the
Neh 10:38 shall be with the L when the
Neh 10:38 when the L receive tithes
Neh 10:38 the L shall bring up a tenth
Neh 11: 3 Israelites, priests, L,
Neh 11:15 Also of the L: Shemaiah
Neh 11:16 of the heads of the L, had
Neh 11:18 All the L in the holy city
Neh 11:20 Israel, of the priests and L
Neh 11:22 Also the overseer of the L at
Neh 11:36 of L were in Benjamin
Neh 12: 1 and the L who came up with
Neh 12: 8 Moreover the L were Jeshua
Neh 12:22 record was also kept of the L
Neh 12:24 heads of the L were Hashabiah
Neh 12:27 out the L in all their places
Neh 12:30 L purified themselves, and
Neh 12:44 the Law for the priests and L
Neh 12:44 priests and L who ministered
Neh 12:47 holy things for the L, and the
Neh 12:47 the L consecrated them for
Neh 13: 5 to be given to the L and
Neh 13:10 the L had not been given them
Neh 13:10 for each of the L and the
Neh 13:13 Zadok the scribe, and of the L
Neh 13:22 I commanded the L that they
Neh 13:29 of the priesthood and the L
Neh 13:30 to the priests and the L, each
Is 66:21 some of them for priests and L
Jer 33:18 nor shall the priests, the L
Jer 33:21 on his throne, and with the L
Jer 33:22 and the L who minister to Me
Ezek 43:19 to the priests, the L, who
Ezek 44:10 the L who went far from Me,
Ezek 44:15 But the priests, the L, the
Ezek 45: 5 wide shall belong to the L
Ezek 48:11 astray, as the L went astray
Ezek 48:12 holy by the border of the L
Ezek 48:13 the L shall have an area
Ezek 48:22 from the possession of the L
John 1:19 L from Jerusalem to ask him,

LEVITICAL (*see* LEVITE)
Heb 7:11 L priesthood (for under it

LEVY
Num 31:28 l a tribute for the LORD on

LEWD (*see* LEWDLY, LEWDNESS)
Jer 11:15 having done l deeds with many
Ezek 16:27 ashamed of your l behavior
Ezek 23:44 and Oholibah, the l women

LEWDLY (*see* LEWD)
Ezek 22:11 another l defiles his

LEWDNESS (*see* LEWD)
Judg 20: 6 because they committed l
Jer 13:27 the l of your harlotry, your
Ezek 16:43 you shall not commit l in
Ezek 16:58 You have paid for your l and
Ezek 22: 9 in your midst they commit l
Ezek 23:21 the l of your youth, when the
Ezek 23:27 I will make you cease your l
Ezek 23:29 be uncovered, both your l
Ezek 23:35 bear the penalty of your l
Ezek 23:48 Thus I will cause l to cease
Ezek 23:48 taught not to practice your l
Ezek 23:49 shall repay you for your l
Ezek 24:13 In your filthiness is l
Hos 2:10 Now I will uncover her l in
Hos 6: 9 surely they commit l
Rom 13:13 not in licentiousness and l

LIAR (*see* LIARS, LIE)
Job 24:25 not so, who will prove me a l
Prov 17: 4 a l listens eagerly to a
Prov 19:22 a poor man is better than a l
Prov 30: 6 you, and you be found a l
John 8:44 own resources, for he is a l
John 8:55 Him,' I shall be a l like you
Rom 3: 4 God be true but every man a l
1Jn 1:10 not sinned, we make Him a l
1Jn 2: 4 keep His commandments, is a l
1Jn 2:22 Who is a l but he who denies
1Jn 4:20 hates his brother, he is a l
1Jn 5:10 believe God has made Him a l

LIARS (*see* LIAR)
Ps 116:11 All men are l
1Ti 1:10 for kidnappers, for l, for
Tit 1:12 Cretans are always l, evil
Rev 2: 2 are not, and have found them l
Rev 21: 8 all l shall have their part

LIBERAL (*see* LIBERALITY, LIBERALLY)
2Co 9:13 for your l sharing with them

LIBERALITY (*see* LIBERAL)
Rom 12: 8 he who gives, with l
2Co 8: 2 in the riches of their l
2Co 9:11 in everything for all l,

LIBERALLY (*see* LIBERAL)
Deut 15:14 supply him l from your flock
Jas 1: 5 of God, who gives to all l

LIBERTY
Lev 25:10 proclaim l throughout all the
Ps 119:45 And I will walk at l, For I
Is 61: 1 to proclaim l to the captives
Jer 34: 8 to proclaim l to them
Jer 34:15 proclaiming l to his neighbor
Jer 34:16 slaves, whom he had set at l
Jer 34:17 obeyed Me in proclaiming l
Jer 34:17 Behold, I proclaim l to you
Ezek 46:17 be his until the year of l
Luke 4:18 to set at l those who are
Acts 24:23 Paul and to let him have l
Acts 27: 3 and gave him l to go to his
Rom 8:21 into the glorious l of the
1Co 7:39 she is at l to be married to
1Co 8: 9 beware lest somehow this l of
1Co 10:29 For why is my l judged by
2Co 3:17 of the Lord is, there is l
Gal 2: 4 our l which we have in Christ
Gal 5: 1 l by which Christ has made us
Gal 5:13 have been called to l
Gal 5:13 only do not use l as an
Jas 1:25 into the perfect law of l
Jas 2:12 be judged by the law of l
1Pe 2:16 yet not using your l as a
2Pe 2:19 While they promise them l

LIBNAH (*see* LABAN)
Num 33:20 Rimmon Perez and camped at L
Num 33:21 They moved from L and camped
Josh 10:29 and all Israel with him, to L
Josh 10:29 and they fought against L
Josh 10:31 Then Joshua passed from L
Josh 10:32 to all that he had done to L
Josh 10:39 as he had done also to L
Josh 12:15 the king of L, one
Josh 15:42 L, Ether, Ashan,
Josh 21:13 L with its common-land,
2Ki 8:22 And L revolted at that time
2Ki 19: 8 of Assyria warring against L
2Ki 23:31 the daughter of Jeremiah of L
2Ki 24:18 the daughter of Jeremiah of L
1Ch 6:57 also L with its common-lands,
2Ch 21:10 At that time L revolted
Is 37: 8 of Assyria warring against L
Jer 52: 1 the daughter of Jeremiah of L

LIBNI (*see* LAADAN, LIBNITES)
Ex 6:17 The sons of Gershon were L
Num 3:18 L and Shimei
1Ch 6:17 L and Shimei
1Ch 6:20 Of Gershon were L his son
1Ch 6:29 L his son, Shimei his son,

LIBNITES (*see* LIBNI)
Num 3:21 came the family of the L and
Num 26:58 the family of the L, the

LIBYA (*see* LEHABIM, LIBYANS)
Ezek 27:10 L were in your army as men of
Ezek 30: 5 Ethiopia, L, Lydia, all the
Ezek 38: 5 L are with them, all of them
Acts 2:10 and the parts of L adjoining

LIBYANS (*see* LIBYA)
Jer 46: 9 the L who handle the shield,
Dan 11:43 also the L and Ethiopians

LICE
Ex 8:16 land, so that it may become l
Ex 8:17 earth, and it became l on man
Ex 8:17 l throughout all the land of
Ex 8:18 enchantments to bring forth l
Ex 8:18 So there were l on man and
Ps 105:31 And l in all their territory

LICENTIOUSNESS
Mark 7:22 wickedness, deceit, l, an
Rom 13:13 and drunkenness, not in l and
2Co 12:21 l which they have practiced
Gal 5:19 fornication, uncleanness, l
Eph 4:19 given themselves over to l
1Pe 4: 3 when we walked in l, lusts,
2Pe 2:18 lusts of the flesh, through l
Jude 4 the grace of our God into l

LICK (*see* LICKED, LICKS)
Num 22: 4 Now this company will l up
1Ki 21:19 dogs shall l your blood,
Ps 72: 9 His enemies will l the dust
Is 49:23 l up the dust of your feet
Mic 7:17 They shall l the dust like a

LICKED (*see* LICK)
1Ki 18:38 it l up the water that was in
1Ki 21:19 dogs l the blood of Naboth
1Ki 22:38 the dogs l up his blood while
Luke 16:21 the dogs came and l his sores

LICKS (*see* LICK)
Num 22: 4 as an ox l up the grass of

LID
2Ki 12: 9 chest, bored a hole in its l

LIE (*see* LAIN, LAY, LIAR, LIED, LIES, LYING)
Gen 19:32 we will l with him, that we
Gen 19:34 in and l with him, that we may
Gen 28:13 you l I will give to you and
Gen 30:15 Therefore he will l with you
Gen 39: 7 and she said, L with me
Gen 39:10 to l with her or to be with
Gen 39:12 garment, saying, L with me
Gen 39:14 He came in to me to l with me
Gen 47:30 but let me l with my fathers
Ex 21:13 But if he did not l in wait
Ex 23:11 l fallow, that the poor of
Lev 18:20 not l carnally with your
Lev 18:22 You shall not l with a male
Lev 19:11 falsely, nor l to one another
Lev 26: 6 the land, and you shall l down
Num 10: 5 the camps that l on the east
Num 10: 6 then the camps that l on the
Num 23:19 not a man, that He should l
Num 23:24 it shall not l down until it
Deut 6: 7 by the way, when you l down
Deut 11:19 by the way, when you l down
Deut 25: 2 will cause him to l down and
Deut 28:30 another man shall l with her
Josh 7:10 Why do you l thus on your
Josh 8: 4 you shall l in ambush against
Josh 8: 9 and they went to l in ambush
Judg 9:32 and l in wait in the field
Judg 21:20 l in wait in the vineyards,
Ruth 3: 4 uncover his feet, and l down
Ruth 3: 7 he went to l down at the end
Ruth 3:13 L down until morning
1Sa 3: 5 l down again
1Sa 3: 6 l down again
1Sa 3: 9 said to Samuel, "Go, l down
1Sa 15:29 Israel will not l nor relent
1Sa 22: 8 to l in wait, as it is this
1Sa 22:13 to l in wait, as it is this
2Sa 11:11 drink, and to l with my wife
2Sa 11:13 out to l on his bed with the
2Sa 12:11 he shall l with your wives in
2Sa 13: 5 L down on your bed and pretend
2Sa 13:11 Come, l with me, my sister
1Ki 1: 2 let her l in your bosom, that
2Ki 4:16 do not l to your maidservant
2Ki 9:12 And they said, "A l!
Job 6:28 I would never l to your face
Job 7: 4 When I l down, I say, 'When
Job 7:21 For now I will l down in the
Job 9:13 proud l prostrate beneath Him
Job 11:19 You would also l down, and no
Job 20:11 but it will l down with him
Job 21:26 They l down alike in the dust
Job 27:19 The rich man will l down, but
Job 34: 6 Should I l concerning my
Job 38:40 in their lairs to l in wait
Ps 4: 8 I will both l down in peace,
Ps 23: 2 He makes me to l down in
Ps 56: 6 When they l in wait for my
Ps 57: 4 I l among the sons of men Who
Ps 59: 3 they l in wait for my life
Ps 62: 9 Men of high degree are a l
Ps 68:13 Though you l down among the
Ps 71:10 those who l in wait for my
Ps 88: 5 the slain who l in the grave
Ps 89:35 I will not l to David
Ps 102: 7 I l awake, And am like a
Ps 104:22 And l down in their dens
Ps 119:69 have forged a l against me
Prov 1:11 us, let us l in wait to shed
Prov 1:18 but they l in wait for their
Prov 3:24 When you l down, you will not
Prov 3:24 yes, you will l down and your
Prov 12: 6 L in wait for blood," but
Prov 14: 5 A faithful witness does not l
Prov 24:15 Do not l in wait, O wicked
Eccl 4:11 if two l down together, they
Eccl 11: 3 tree falls, there it shall l
Is 11: 6 the leopard shall l down with
Is 11: 7 ones shall l down together
Is 13:21 of the desert will l there
Is 14:30 needy will l down in safety
Is 17: 2 be for flocks which l down
Is 27:10 feed, and there it will l down
Is 33: 8 The highways l waste, the
Is 34:10 generation it shall l waste
Is 43:17 (they shall l down together
Is 44:20 Is there not a l in my right
Is 50:11 you shall l down in torment
Is 51:20 they l at the head of all the
Is 51:23 L down, that we may walk
Is 63: 8 children who will not l
Is 65:10 a place for herds to l down
Jer 3:25 We l down in our shame, and
Jer 5:26 they l in wait as one who
Jer 27:10 For they prophesy a l to you
Jer 27:14 for they prophesy a l to you
Jer 27:15 they prophesy a l in My name
Jer 27:16 for they prophesy a l to you
Jer 28:15 make this people trust in a l
Jer 29:21 who prophesy a l to you in My
Jer 29:31 caused you to trust in a l
Jer 33:12 their flocks to l down
Lam 2:21 old l on the ground in the
Ezek 4: 4 L also on your left side, and
Ezek 4: 4 of the days that you l on it
Ezek 4: 6 l again on your right side
Ezek 4: 9 days that you l on your side
Ezek 21:29 while they divine a l to you
Ezek 31:12 its boughs l broken by all
Ezek 31:18 you shall l in the midst of
Ezek 32:21 they l with the uncircumcised
Ezek 32:27 They do not l with the mighty
Ezek 32:28 l with those slain by the
Ezek 32:29 they shall l with the
Ezek 32:30 they l uncircumcised with
Ezek 33:10 and our sins l upon us, and we
Ezek 34:14 There they shall l down in a
Ezek 34:15 and I will make them l down
Hos 2:18 to make them l down safely
Hos 6: 9 robbers l in wait for a man
Hos 7: 6 an oven, while they l in wait
Joel 1:13 l all night in sackcloth, you
Amos 2: 8 They l down by every altar on
Amos 6: 4 who l on beds of ivory,
Mic 1:14 be a l to the kings of Israel
Mic 2:11 a false spirit and speak a l
Mic 7: 2 They all l in wait for blood
Hab 2: 3 will speak, and it will not l
Zeph 2: 7 they shall l down at evening
Zeph 2:14 The herds shall l down in her
Zeph 2:15 a place for beasts to l down
Zeph 3:13 l down, and no one shall make
Hag 1: 4 and this temple to l in ruins
John 8:44 When he speaks a l, he speaks
Acts 5: 3 heart to l to the Holy Spirit
Acts 23:21 of them l in wait for him
Rom 1:25 the truth of God for the l
Rom 3: 7 through my l to His glory
Gal 1:20 before God, I do not l

Eph 4:14 they l in wait to deceive
Col 3: 9 Do not l to one another,
2Th 2:11 they should believe the l
Tit 1: 2 life which God, who cannot l
Heb 6:18 it is impossible for God to l
Jas 3:14 boast and l against the truth
1Jn 1: 6 and walk in darkness, we l
1Jn 2:21 that no l is of the truth
1Jn 2:27 and is true, and is not a l
Rev 3: 9 are Jews and are not, but l
Rev 11: 8 their dead bodies will l in
Rev 21:27 causes an abomination or a l
Rev 22:15 loves and practices a l

LIED (*see* LIE)
1Ki 13:18 But he l to him
Ps 78:36 And they l to Him with their
Is 57:11 or feared, that you have l
Jer 5:12 They have l about the LORD,
Acts 5: 4 You have not l to men but to

LIES (*see* LIE)
Gen 4: 7 do well, sin l at the door
Gen 49: 9 down, he l down as a lion
Gen 49:25 of the deep that l beneath
Ex 22:16 l with her, he shall surely
Ex 22:19 Whoever l with a beast shall
Lev 6: 3 l concerning it, and swears
Lev 14:47 he who l down in the house
Lev 15: 4 he who has the discharge l
Lev 15:18 when a woman l with a man
Lev 15:20 Everything that she l on
Lev 15:24 if any man l with her at all,
Lev 15:24 which he l shall be unclean
Lev 15:26 she l all the days of her
Lev 15:33 for him who l with her who is
Lev 19:20 Whoever l carnally with a
Lev 20:11 The man who l with his
Lev 20:12 If a man l with his
Lev 20:13 If a man l with a male as he
Lev 20:13 a male as he l with a woman
Lev 20:18 If a man l with a woman
Lev 20:20 If a man l with his uncle's
Lev 26:34 as long as it l desolate and
Lev 26:35 As long as it l desolate it
Lev 26:43 it l desolate without them
Num 5:13 a man l with her carnally, and
Num 21:15 and l on the border of Moab
Num 24: 9 down, he l down as a lion
Deut 19:11 l in wait for him, rises
Deut 22:23 in the city and l with her,
Deut 22:25 l with her, then only the man
Deut 22:28 l with her, and they are found
Deut 27:20 who l with his father's wife
Deut 27:21 Cursed is the one who l with
Deut 27:22 the one who l with his sister
Deut 27:23 who l with his mother-in-law
Josh 15: 8 top of the mountain that l
Josh 17: 7 that l east of Shechem
Josh 18:13 near the hill that l on the
Josh 18:14 from the hill that l before
Josh 18:16 l before the Valley of the
Judg 1:16 which l in the South near
Judg 16: 5 where his great strength l
Judg 16: 6 where your great strength l
Judg 16:10 have mocked me and told me l
Judg 16:13 have mocked me and told me l
Judg 16:15 where your great strength l
Ruth 3: 4 it shall be, when he l down
Ruth 3: 4 notice the place where he l
2Ki 9:37 not say, "Here l Jezebel
Neh 2: 3 l waste, and its gates are
Neh 2:17 are in, how Jerusalem l waste
Job 13: 4 But you forgers of l, you are
Job 14:12 so man l down and does not
Job 29:19 the dew l all night on my
Job 40:21 He l under the lotus trees,
Ps 10: 9 He l in wait secretly, as a
Ps 10: 9 He l in wait to catch the
Ps 10:10 he l low, That the helpless
Ps 40: 4 nor such as turn aside to l
Ps 41: 8 And now that he l down, he
Ps 58: 3 as they are born, speaking l
Ps 62: 4 They delight in l
Ps 63:11 who speak l shall be stopped
Ps 88: 7 Your wrath l heavy upon me,
Ps 101: 7 He who tells l shall not
Prov 6:19 a false witness who speaks l
Prov 14: 5 a false witness will utter l
Prov 14:25 a deceitful witness speaks l
Prov 19: 5 and he who speaks l will not
Prov 19: 9 he who speaks l shall perish
Prov 23:28 She also l in wait as for a
Prov 23:34 l down in the midst of the
Prov 23:34 or like one who l at the top
Prov 29:12 a ruler pays attention to l
Prov 30: 8 falsehood and l far from me
Song 1:13 that l all night between my
Is 9:15 the prophet who teaches l
Is 16: 6 but his l shall not be so
Is 28:15 for we have made l our refuge
Is 28:17 sweep away the refuge of l
Is 59: 3 your lips have spoken l, your
Is 59: 4 in empty words and speak l
Jer 9: 3 have bent their tongues for l
Jer 9: 5 their tongue to speak l, and
Jer 9: 8 but in his heart he l in wait
Jer 14:14 prophesy l in My name
Jer 16:19 our fathers have inherited l
Jer 20: 6 to whom you have prophesied l
Jer 23:14 commit adultery and walk in l
Jer 23:25 who prophesy l in My name
Jer 23:26 the prophets who prophesy l
Jer 23:32 My people to err by their l
Jer 48:30 his l have made nothing right
Ezek 13: 8 nonsense and envisioned l,
Ezek 13: 9 futility and who divine l
Ezek 13:19 to My people who listen to l
Ezek 13:22 Because with l you have made
Ezek 22:28 and divining l for them,
Ezek 24:12 has wearied herself with l
Ezek 29: 3 O great monster who l in the
Dan 11:27 they shall speak l at the
Hos 7: 3 and princes with their l
Hos 7:13 they have spoken l against Me
Hos 10:13 You have eaten the fruit of l
Hos 11:12 has encompassed Me with l
Hos 12: 1 He daily increases l and
Amos 2: 4 their l lead them astray,
Amos 2: 4 l after which their fathers
Amos 5: 2 She l forsaken on her land
Mic 6:12 her inhabitants have spoken l
Mic 7: 5 from her who l in your bosom
Nah 3: 1 It is all full of l and
Hab 2:18 molded image, a teacher of l
Zeph 3:13 unrighteousness and speak no l
Zech 10: 2 the diviners envision l, and
Zech 13: 3 l in the name of the LORD
Mark 5:23 My little daughter l at the
2Co 3:15 read, a veil l on their heart
1Ti 4: 2 speaking l in hypocrisy,
1Jn 5:19 the whole world l under the

LIFE (*see* LIFEBLOOD, LIFE-GIVING, LIFELESS, LIFETIME, LIVE)
Gen 1:30 earth, in which there is l
Gen 2: 7 his nostrils the breath of l
Gen 2: 9 The tree of l was also in the
Gen 3:14 dust all the days of your l
Gen 3:17 of it all the days of your l
Gen 3:22 and take also of the tree of l
Gen 3:24 the way to the tree of l
Gen 6:17 in which is the breath of l
Gen 7:11 hundredth year of Noah's l
Gen 7:15 in which is the breath of l
Gen 7:22 the breath of the spirit of l
Gen 9: 4 not eat flesh with its l,
Gen 9: 5 I will require the l of man
Gen 18:10 according to the time of l
Gen 18:14 according to the time of l
Gen 19:17 Escape for your l
Gen 19:19 have shown me by saving my l
Gen 23: 1 the years of the l of Sarah
Gen 25: 7 of Abraham's l which he lived
Gen 25:17 the years of the l of Ishmael
Gen 27:46 I am weary of my l because of
Gen 27:46 what good will my l be to me
Gen 32:30 to face, and my l is preserved
Gen 42:15 By the l of Pharaoh, you
Gen 42:16 by the l of Pharaoh, surely
Gen 44:30 since his l is bound up in
Gen 44:30 is bound up in the lad's l
Gen 45: 5 me before you to preserve l
Gen 47: 9 the days of the years of my l
Gen 47: 9 days of the years of the l of
Gen 47:28 of Jacob's l was one hundred
Gen 48:15 me all my l long to this day
Ex 4:19 are dead who sought your l
Ex 6:16 the years of the l of Levi
Ex 6:18 the years of the l of Kohath
Ex 6:20 the years of the l of Amram
Ex 21:23 you shall give l for l
Ex 21:30 he shall pay to redeem his l
Lev 17:11 For the l of the flesh is in
Lev 17:14 for it is the l of all flesh
Lev 17:14 Its blood sustains its l
Lev 17:14 for the l of all flesh is its
Lev 19:16 the l of your neighbor
Num 35:31 take no ransom for the l of a
Deut 4: 9 heart all the days of your l
Deut 6: 2 all the days of your l, and
Deut 12:23 blood, for the blood is the l
Deut 12:23 not eat the l with the meat
Deut 16: 3 Egypt all the days of your l
Deut 17:19 read it all the days of his l
Deut 19:21 but l shall be for l, eye
Deut 28:66 Your l shall hang in doubt
Deut 28:66 and have no assurance of l
Deut 30:15 I have set before you today l
Deut 30:19 that I have set before you l
Deut 30:19 therefore choose l, that both
Deut 30:20 to Him, for He is your l and
Deut 32:47 for you, because it is your l
Josh 1: 5 you all the days of your l
Josh 4:14 Moses, all the days of his l
Judg 5: 7 Village l ceased, it ceased
Judg 9:17 fought for you, risked his l
Judg 12: 3 I took my l in my hands and
Judg 13:12 will be the boy's rule of l
Judg 16:30 than he had killed in his l
Judg 18:25 upon you, and you lose your l
Ruth 4:15 he be to you a restorer of l
1Sa 1:11 LORD all the days of his l
1Sa 7:15 Israel all the days of his l
1Sa 18:18 what is my l or my father's
1Sa 19: 5 he took his l in his hands
1Sa 19:11 do not save your l tonight
1Sa 20: 1 father, that he seeks my l
1Sa 22:23 seeks my l seeks your l
1Sa 23:15 had come out to seek his l
1Sa 24:11 Yet you hunt my l to take it
1Sa 25:29 to pursue you and seek your l
1Sa 25:29 but the l of my lord shall be
1Sa 26:21 because my l was precious in
1Sa 26:24 as your l was valued much
1Sa 26:24 so let my l be valued much in
1Sa 28: 9 do you lay a snare for my l
1Sa 28:21 I have put my l in my hands
2Sa 1: 9 but my l still remains in me
2Sa 4: 8 your enemy, who sought your l
2Sa 4: 9 my l from all adversity,
2Sa 14: 7 the l of his brother whom he
2Sa 14:14 God does not take away a l
2Sa 15:21 be, whether in death or l
2Sa 16:11 from my own body seeks my l
2Sa 18:13 falsely against my own l
2Sa 19: 5 who today have saved your l
1Ki 1:12 that you may save your own l
1Ki 1:12 the l of your son Solomon
1Ki 1:29 my l from every distress,
1Ki 2:23 this word against his own l
1Ki 3:11 not asked long l for yourself
1Ki 3:11 asked the l of your enemies
1Ki 4:21 Solomon all the days of his l
1Ki 11:34 ruler all the days of his l
1Ki 15: 5 him all the days of his l
1Ki 15: 6 all the days of his l
1Ki 19: 2 not make your l as the l
1Ki 19: 3 he arose and ran for his l
1Ki 19: 4 Now, LORD, take my l, for I
1Ki 19:10 and they seek to take my l
1Ki 19:14 and they seek to take my l
1Ki 20:31 perhaps he will spare your l
1Ki 20:39 your l shall be for his l,
1Ki 20:42 your l shall go for his l
2Ki 1:13 Man of God, please let my l
2Ki 1:13 the l of these fifty servants
2Ki 1:14 But let my l now be precious
2Ki 8: 1 son he had restored to l,
2Ki 8: 5 he had restored the dead to l
2Ki 8: 5 son he had restored to l,
2Ki 8: 5 son whom Elisha restored to l
2Ki 10:24 l for the l of the other
2Ki 25:29 king all the days of his l
2Ki 25:30 day, all the days of his l
2Ch 1:11 or the l of your enemies, nor
2Ch 1:11 nor have you asked long l
Ezra 6:10 and pray for the l of the king
Neh 6:11 into the temple to save his l
Esth 7: 3 let my l be given me at my
Esth 7: 7 Esther, pleading for his l
Job 2: 4 has he will give for his l

Job 2: 6 in your hand, but spare his l
Job 3:20 and l to the bitter of soul,
Job 6:11 that I should prolong my l
Job 7: 7 that my l is a breath
Job 7:16 I loathe my l
Job 9:21 I despise my l
Job 10: 1 My soul loathes l
Job 10:12 You have granted me l and
Job 11:17 your l would be brighter than
Job 11:20 and their hope—loss of l!
Job 12:10 In whose hand is the l of
Job 13:14 and put my l in my hands
Job 24:22 up, but no man is sure of l
Job 27: 8 much, if God takes away his l
Job 33: 4 of the Almighty gives me l
Job 33:18 his l from perishing by the
Job 33:20 So that his l abhors bread,
Job 33:22 his l to the executioners
Job 33:28 his l shall see the light
Job 33:30 with the light of l
Job 36: 6 preserve the l of the wicked
Job 36:14 and their l ends among the
Ps 7: 5 him trample my l to the earth
Ps 16:11 will show me the path of l
Ps 17:13 Deliver my l from the wicked
Ps 17:14 have their portion in this l
Ps 21: 4 He asked l from You, and You
Ps 22:20 My precious l from the power
Ps 23: 6 me All the days of my l
Ps 26: 9 Nor my l with bloodthirsty
Ps 27: 1 LORD is the strength of my l
Ps 27: 4 the LORD All the days of my l
Ps 30: 5 a moment, His favor is for l
Ps 31:10 For my l is spent with grief,
Ps 31:13 They scheme to take away my l
Ps 34:12 Who is the man who desires l
Ps 35: 4 dishonor Who seek after my l
Ps 35: 7 dug without cause for my l
Ps 35:17 My precious l from the lions
Ps 36: 9 with You is the fountain of l
Ps 38:12 seek my l lay snares for me
Ps 40:14 Who seek to destroy my l
Ps 42: 8 A prayer to the God of my l
Ps 54: 3 have sought after my l
Ps 54: 4 is with those who uphold my l
Ps 56: 6 they lie in wait for my l
Ps 59: 3 they lie in wait for my l
Ps 61: 6 You will prolong the king's l
Ps 63: 3 is better than l, My lips
Ps 63: 9 But those who seek my l, to
Ps 64: 1 Preserve my l from fear of
Ps 70: 2 and confounded Who seek my l
Ps 71:10 my l take counsel together
Ps 71:13 Who are adversaries of my l
Ps 72:14 their l from oppression and
Ps 74:19 do not deliver the l of Your
Ps 74:19 Do not forget the l of Your
Ps 78:50 But gave their l over to the
Ps 86: 2 Preserve my l, for I am holy
Ps 86:14 violent men have sought my l
Ps 88: 3 my l draws near to the grave
Ps 89:48 Can he deliver his l from the
Ps 91:16 With long l I will satisfy
Ps 94:21 the l of the righteous, And
Ps 103: 4 your l from destruction, Who
Ps 119:50 For Your word has given me l
Ps 119:93 by them You have given me l
Ps 119:109 My l is continually in my
Ps 128: 5 All the days of your l
Ps 133: 3 the blessing—L forevermore.
Ps 143: 3 crushed my l to the ground
Prov 1:19 away the l of its owners
Prov 2:19 do they regain the paths of l
Prov 3: 2 for length of days and long l
Prov 3:18 She is a tree of l to those
Prov 3:22 they will be l to your soul
Prov 4:10 years of your l will be many
Prov 4:13 keep her, for she is your l
Prov 4:22 For they are l to those who
Prov 4:23 of it spring the issues of l
Prov 5: 6 Lest you ponder her path of l
Prov 6:23 instruction are the way of l
Prov 6:26 will prey upon his precious l
Prov 7:23 not know it would take his l
Prov 8:35 For whoever finds me finds l
Prov 9:11 years of l will be added to
Prov 10:11 the righteous is a well of l
Prov 10:16 of the righteous leads to l
Prov 10:17 is in the way of l, but he
Prov 11:19 As righteousness leads to l
Prov 11:30 the righteous is a tree of l
Prov 12:10 regards the l of his animal
Prov 12:28 the way of righteousness is l
Prov 13: 3 his mouth preserves his l
Prov 13: 8 of a man's l is his riches
Prov 13:12 comes, it is a tree of l
Prov 13:14 the wise is a fountain of l
Prov 14:27 the LORD is a fountain of l
Prov 14:30 sound heart is l to the body
Prov 15: 4 tongue is a tree of l, but
Prov 15:24 The way of l winds upward for
Prov 15:31 l will abide among the wise
Prov 16:15 light of the king's face is l
Prov 16:22 of l to him who has it
Prov 18:21 l are in the power of the
Prov 19:23 fear of the LORD leads to l
Prov 20: 2 anger sins against his own l
Prov 21:21 and mercy finds l,
Prov 22: 4 LORD are riches and honor and l
Prov 29:24 with a thief hates his own l
Prov 31:12 evil all the days of her l
Eccl 2:17 Therefore I hated l because
Eccl 5:18 of his l which God gives him
Eccl 5:20 unduly on the days of his l
Eccl 6:12 what is good for man in l
Eccl 6:12 vain l which he passes like a
Eccl 7:12 gives l to those who have it
Eccl 7:15 his l in his wickedness
Eccl 8:15 l which God gives him under
Eccl 9: 9 vain l which He has given you
Eccl 9: 9 for that is your portion in l
Is 15: 4 his l will be burdensome to
Is 38:10 In the prime of my l I shall
Is 38:12 My l span is gone, taken from
Is 38:12 cut off my l like a weaver
Is 38:16 things is the l of my spirit
Is 38:20 all the days of our l, in the
Is 43: 4 for you, and people for your l
Is 57:10 have found the l of your hand
Jer 4:30 they will seek your l
Jer 8: 3 l by all the residue of those
Jer 11:21 of Anathoth who seek your l
Jer 18:20 they have dug a pit for my l
Jer 20:13 For He has delivered the l of
Jer 21: 7 of those who seek their l
Jer 21: 8 I set before you the way of l
Jer 21: 9 his l shall be as a prize to
Jer 22:25 hand of those who seek your l
Jer 23:10 Their course of l is evil
Jer 34:20 of those who seek their l
Jer 34:21 of those who seek their l
Jer 38: 2 his l shall be as a prize to
Jer 38:16 of these men who seek your l
Jer 39:18 but your l shall be as a
Jer 44:30 hand of those who seek his l
Jer 44:30 his enemy who sought his l
Jer 45: 5 But I will give your l to you
Jer 49:37 before those who seek their l
Jer 51: 6 and every one save his l
Jer 52:33 king all the days of his l
Jer 52:34 death, all the days of his l
Lam 1:11 for food to restore l
Lam 1:16 who should restore my l, is
Lam 1:19 food to restore their l
Lam 2:12 as their l is poured out in
Lam 2:19 the l of your young children
Lam 3:53 They silenced my l in the pit
Lam 3:58 You have redeemed my l
Ezek 3:18 his wicked way, to save his l
Ezek 13:22 his wicked way to save his l
Ezek 32:10 every man for his own l, in
Ezek 33: 5 takes warning will save his l
Ezek 33:15 walks in the statutes of l
Dan 12: 2 awake, some to everlasting l
Hos 9: 4 bread shall be for their l
Jon 1:14 us perish for this man's l
Jon 2: 6 brought up my l from the pit
Jon 4: 3 please take my l from me
Mal 2: 5 was with him, one of l and
Matt 2:20 the young Child's l are dead
Matt 6:25 do not worry about your l
Matt 6:25 Is not l more than food and
Matt 7:14 is the way which leads to l
Matt 10:39 who finds his l will lose it
Matt 10:39 he who loses his l for My
Matt 16:25 to save his l will lose it
Matt 16:25 whoever loses his l for My
Matt 18: 8 enter into l lame or maimed
Matt 18: 9 to enter into l with one eye
Matt 19:16 do that I may have eternal l
Matt 19:17 if you want to enter into l
Matt 19:29 and inherit everlasting l
Matt 20:28 to give His l a ransom for
Matt 25:46 the righteous into eternal l
Mark 3: 4 do evil, to save l or to kill
Mark 8:35 to save his l will lose it
Mark 8:35 loses his l for My sake and
Mark 9:43 you to enter into l maimed
Mark 9:45 for you to enter l lame, than
Mark 10:17 that I may inherit eternal l
Mark 10:30 in the age to come, eternal l
Mark 10:45 to give His l a ransom for
Luke 1:75 Him all the days of our l
Luke 6: 9 to save l or to destroy it
Luke 8:14 riches, and pleasures of l
Luke 9:24 to save his l will lose it
Luke 9:24 but whoever loses his l for
Luke 10:25 I do to inherit eternal l
Luke 12:15 for one's l does not consist
Luke 12:22 do not worry about your l
Luke 12:23 L is more than food, and the
Luke 14:26 yes, and his own l also, he
Luke 17:33 to save his l will lose it
Luke 17:33 loses his l will preserve it
Luke 18:18 I do to inherit eternal l
Luke 18:30 the age to come everlasting l
Luke 21:34 and cares of this l, and that
John 1: 4 In Him was l
John 1: 4 the l was the light of men
John 3:15 not perish but have eternal l
John 3:16 perish but have everlasting l
John 3:36 in the Son has everlasting l
John 3:36 the Son shall not see l, but
John 4:14 up into everlasting l
John 4:36 gathers fruit for eternal l
John 5:21 gives l to them, even so the
John 5:21 Son gives l to whom He will
John 5:24 who sent Me has everlasting l
John 5:24 has passed from death into l
John 5:26 the Father has l in Himself
John 5:26 the Son to have l in Himself
John 5:29 to the resurrection of l
John 5:39 you think you have eternal l
John 5:40 to Me that you may have l
John 6:27 endures to everlasting l,
John 6:33 and gives l to the world
John 6:35 I am the bread of l
John 6:40 in Him may have everlasting l
John 6:47 in Me has everlasting l
John 6:48 I am the bread of l
John 6:51 give for the l of the world
John 6:53 blood, you have no l in you
John 6:54 drinks My blood has eternal l
John 6:63 It is the Spirit who gives l
John 6:63 you are spirit, and they are l
John 6:68 have the words of eternal l
John 8:12 but have the light of l
John 10:10 come that they may have l
John 10:11 gives His l for the sheep
John 10:15 I lay down My l for the sheep
John 10:17 because I lay down My l that
John 10:28 And I give them eternal l, and
John 11:25 am the resurrection and the l
John 12:25 who loves his l will lose it
John 12:25 he who hates his l in this
John 12:25 will keep it for eternal l
John 12:50 His command is everlasting l
John 13:37 lay down my l for Your sake
John 13:38 lay down your l for My sake
John 14: 6 the way, the truth, and the l
John 15:13 down one's l for his friends
John 17: 2 l to as many as You have
John 17: 3 And this is eternal l, that
John 20:31 you may have l in His name
Acts 2:28 known to me the ways of l
Acts 3:15 and killed the Prince of l
Acts 5:20 all the words of this l
Acts 8:33 For His l is taken from the
Acts 11:18 the Gentiles repentance to l
Acts 13:46 unworthy of everlasting l
Acts 13:48 to eternal l believed
Acts 17:25 since He gives to all l,
Acts 20:10 for his l is in him
Acts 20:24 I count my l dear to myself
Acts 26: 4 My manner of l from my youth,
Acts 27:22 be no loss of l among you
Rom 2: 7 eternal l to those who by
Rom 4:17 who gives l to the dead and
Rom 5:10 we shall be saved by His l
Rom 5:17 reign in l through the One

Rom 5:18 in justification of l
Rom 5:21 l through Jesus Christ our
Rom 6: 4 should walk in newness of l
Rom 6:10 but the l that He lives, He
Rom 6:22 and the end, everlasting l
Rom 6:23 l in Christ Jesus our Lord
Rom 7:10 which was to bring l, I
Rom 8: 2 the law of the Spirit of l in
Rom 8: 6 to be spiritually minded is l
Rom 8:10 but the Spirit is l because
Rom 8:11 give l to your mortal bodies
Rom 8:38 that neither death nor l, nor
Rom 11: 3 am left, and they seek my l"
Rom 11:15 be but l from the dead
Rom 16: 4 their own necks for my l, to
1Co 3:22 or the world or l or death
1Co 6: 3 things that pertain to this l
1Co 6: 4 things pertaining to this l
1Co 14: 7 Even things without l,
1Co 15:19 If in this l only we have
2Co 1: 8 that we despaired even of l
2Co 2:16 other the aroma of l to l
2Co 3: 6 kills, but the Spirit gives l
2Co 4:10 that the l of Jesus also may
2Co 4:11 that the l of Jesus also may
2Co 4:12 working in us, but l in you
2Co 5: 4 may be swallowed up by l
Gal 2:20 the l which I now live in the
Gal 3:21 which could have given l,
Gal 6: 8 the Spirit reap everlasting l
Eph 4:18 alienated from the l of God
Phil 1:20 whether by l or by death
Phil 2:16 holding fast the word of l
Phil 2:30 to death, not regarding his l
Phil 4: 3 names are in the Book of L
Col 3: 3 your l is hidden with Christ
Col 3: 4 Christ who is our l appears
1Th 4:11 also aspire to lead a quiet l
1Ti 1:16 on Him for everlasting l
1Ti 2: 2 peaceable l in all godliness
1Ti 4: 8 promise of the l that now is
1Ti 6:12 faith, lay hold on eternal l
1Ti 6:13 God who gives l to all things
1Ti 6:19 may lay hold on eternal l
2Ti 1: 1 of l which is in Christ Jesus
2Ti 1:10 abolished death and brought l
2Ti 2: 4 with the affairs of this l
2Ti 3:10 my doctrine, manner of l,
Tit 1: 2 hope of eternal l which God
Tit 3: 7 to the hope of eternal l
Heb 7: 3 of days nor end of l, but
Heb 7:16 to the power of an endless l
Heb 11:35 their dead raised to l again
Jas 1:12 will receive the crown of l
Jas 4:14 For what is your l
1Pe 3: 7 together of the grace of l
1Pe 3:10 He who would love l and see
2Pe 1: 3 all things that pertain to l
1Jn 1: 1 concerning the Word of l
1Jn 1: 2 the l was manifested, and we
1Jn 1: 2 l which was with the Father
1Jn 2:16 the eyes, and the pride of l
1Jn 2:25 He has promised us—eternal l
1Jn 3:14 have passed from death to l
1Jn 3:15 has eternal l abiding in him
1Jn 3:16 He laid down His l for us
1Jn 5:11 God has given us eternal l
1Jn 5:11 and this l is in His Son
1Jn 5:12 He who has the Son has l
1Jn 5:12 Son of God does not have l
1Jn 5:13 know that you have eternal l
1Jn 5:16 He will give him l for those
1Jn 5:20 is the true God and eternal l
Jude 21 Jesus Christ unto eternal l
Rev 2: 7 to eat from the tree of l
Rev 2: 8 who was dead, and came to l
Rev 2:10 will give you the crown of l
Rev 3: 5 his name from the Book of L
Rev 11:11 of l from God entered them
Rev 13: 8 L of the Lamb slain from the
Rev 17: 8 L from the foundation of the
Rev 20:12 which is the Book of L
Rev 20:15 written in the Book of L was
Rev 21: 6 fountain of the water of l
Rev 21:27 in the Lamb's Book of L
Rev 22: 1 me a pure river of water of l
Rev 22: 2 the river, was the tree of l
Rev 22:14 the right to the tree of l
Rev 22:17 take the water of l freely
Rev 22:19 his part from the Book of L

LIFEBLOOD (*see* BLOOD, LIFE)
Gen 9: 5 Surely for your l I will

LIFE-GIVING (*see* LIFE)
1Co 15:45 last Adam became a l spirit

LIFELESS (*see* LIFE)
Lev 26:30 on the l forms of your idols

LIFETIME (*see* LIFE)
2Sa 18:18 Absalom in his l had taken
Luke 16:25 remember that in your l you
Heb 2:15 their l subject to bondage
1Pe 4: 3 l in doing the will of the

LIFT (*see* LIFTED, LIFTING, LIFTS, UNLIFTED, UPLIFTED)
Gen 13:14 L your eyes now and look from
Gen 21:18 l up the lad and hold him with
Gen 31:12 L your eyes now and see, all
Gen 40:13 Pharaoh will l up your head
Gen 40:19 will l off your head from you
Gen 41:44 your consent no man may l his
Ex 14:16 But l up your rod, and stretch
Num 6:26 the LORD l up His countenance
Deut 3:27 l your eyes toward the west,
Deut 4:19 heed, lest you l your eyes to
Deut 22: 4 help him l them up again
Deut 32:40 For I l My hand to heaven, and
1Sa 22:17 of the king would not l their
2Sa 22:49 You also l me above those who
2Ki 19: 4 Therefore l up your prayer
Ezra 9: 6 humiliated to l up my face to
Job 10:15 I cannot l up my head
Job 11:15 then surely you could l up
Job 22:26 and l up your face to God
Job 30:22 You l me up to the wind and
Job 38:34 Can you l up your voice to
Ps 4: 6 LORD, l up the light of Your
Ps 7: 6 L Yourself up because of the
Ps 9:13 me, You who l me up from the
Ps 10:12 O God, l up Your hand
Ps 18:48 You also l me up above those
Ps 24: 7 L up your heads, O you gates
Ps 24: 9 L up your heads, O you gates
Ps 24: 9 l them up, you everlasting
Ps 25: 1 You, O LORD, I l up my soul
Ps 28: 2 When I l up my hands toward
Ps 63: 4 I will l up my hands in Your
Ps 74: 3 L up Your feet to the
Ps 74: 5 They seem like men who l up
Ps 75: 4 wicked, 'Do not l up the horn
Ps 75: 5 Do not l up your horn on high
Ps 86: 4 You, O Lord, I l up my soul
Ps 93: 3 The floods l up their waves
Ps 110: 7 He shall l up the head
Ps 119:48 My hands also I will l up to
Ps 121: 1 I will l up my eyes to the
Ps 123: 1 Unto You I l up my eyes, O
Ps 134: 2 L up your hands in the
Ps 143: 8 For I l up my soul to You
Prov 2: 3 and l up your voice for
Prov 8: 1 understanding l up her voice
Eccl 4:10 one will l up his companion
Is 2: 4 Nation shall not l up sword
Is 5:26 He will l up a banner to the
Is 10:15 against those who l it up
Is 10:15 or as if a staff could l up
Is 10:24 l up his staff against you,
Is 10:26 so will He l it up in the
Is 10:30 L up your voice, O daughter
Is 13: 2 L up a banner on the high
Is 24:14 They shall l up their voice,
Is 33: 3 when You l Yourself up, the
Is 33:10 now I will l Myself up
Is 37: 4 Therefore l up your prayer
Is 40: 9 l up your voice with strength
Is 40: 9 l it up, be not afraid
Is 40:26 L up your eyes on high, and
Is 42:11 its cities l up their voice,
Is 49:18 L up your eyes, look around
Is 49:22 I will l My hand in an oath
Is 51: 6 L up your eyes to the heavens
Is 52: 8 shall l up their voices, with
Is 58: 1 l up your voice like a
Is 59:19 l up a standard against him
Is 60: 4 L up your eyes all around, and
Is 62:10 l up a banner for the peoples
Jer 3: 2 L up your eyes to the
Jer 7:16 nor l up a cry or prayer for
Jer 11:14 or l up a cry or prayer for
Jer 13:20 L up your eyes and see those
Jer 22:20 l up your voice in Bashan
Jer 38:10 l Jeremiah the prophet out of
Jer 51: 3 l himself up against her in
Jer 51:14 and they shall l up a shout
Lam 2:19 L your hands toward Him for
Lam 3:41 let us l our hearts and hands
Ezek 8: 5 l your eyes now toward the
Ezek 17:14 not l itself up, but that by
Ezek 21:22 to l the voice with shouting,
Ezek 23:27 will not l your eyes to them
Ezek 33:25 you l up your eyes toward
Mic 4: 3 Nation shall not l up sword
Nah 3: 5 I will l your skirts over
Zech 1:21 no one could l up his head
Zech 5: 5 L your eyes now, and see what
Matt 12:11 lay hold of it and l it out
Luke 21:28 l up your heads, because your
John 4:35 l up your eyes and look at the
John 8:28 When you l up the Son of Man,
Jas 4:10 the Lord, and He will l you up

LIFTED (*see* LIFT)
Gen 7:17 l up the ark, and it rose high
Gen 13:10 Lot l his eyes and saw all the
Gen 14:22 I have l my hand to the LORD,
Gen 18: 2 So he l his eyes and looked,
Gen 21:16 him, and l her voice and wept
Gen 22: 4 third day Abraham l his eyes
Gen 22:13 Then Abraham l his eyes and
Gen 24:63 he l his eyes and looked, and
Gen 24:64 Then Rebekah l her eyes, and
Gen 27:38 Esau l up his voice and wept
Gen 29:11 and l up his voice and wept
Gen 31:10 that I l my eyes and saw in a
Gen 33: 1 Now Jacob l his eyes and
Gen 33: 5 And he l his eyes and saw the
Gen 37:25 Then they l their eyes and
Gen 37:28 l him out of the pit, and sold
Gen 39:15 he heard that I l my voice
Gen 39:18 as I l my voice and cried out,
Gen 40:20 he l up the head of the chief
Gen 43:29 Then he l his eyes and saw his
Ex 7:20 So he l up the rod and struck
Ex 14:10 of Israel l their eyes, and
Ex 16:14 And when the layer of dew l
Lev 9:22 Then Aaron l his hand toward
Num 14: 1 l up their voices and cried,
Num 18:30 When you have l up the best
Num 18:32 when you have l up the best
Num 20:11 Then Moses l his hand and
Deut 8:14 when your heart is l up, and
Deut 17:20 not be l above his brethren
Josh 5:13 that he l his eyes and looked,
Judg 2: 4 the people l up their voice
Judg 8:28 so that they l their heads no
Judg 9: 7 l his voice and cried out, and
Judg 19:28 So the man l her onto the
Judg 21: 2 They l up their voices and
Ruth 1: 9 they l up their voices and
Ruth 1:14 Then they l up their voices
1Sa 6:13 they l their eyes and saw the
1Sa 11: 4 all the people l up their
1Sa 24:16 And Saul l his voice and wept
1Sa 30: 4 with him l up their voices
2Sa 3:32 the king l up his voice and
2Sa 13:34 was keeping watch l his eyes
2Sa 13:36 they l up their voice and wept
2Sa 18:24 l his eyes and looked, and
2Sa 23:18 He l his spear against three
1Ki 16: 2 Inasmuch as I l you out of
2Ki 14:10 and your heart has l you up
2Ki 19:22 and l up your eyes on high
1Ch 11:11 he had l up his spear against
1Ch 11:20 He had l up his spear against
1Ch 21:16 Then David l his eyes and saw
2Ch 5:13 when they l up their voice
2Ch 25:19 your heart is l up to boast
2Ch 26:16 was strong his heart was l up
2Ch 32:25 him, for his heart was l up
Job 2:12 they l their voices and wept
Job 5:11 who mourn are l to safety
Job 31:29 me, or l myself up when evil
Ps 24: 4 Who has not l up his soul to
Ps 24: 7 And be l up, you everlasting
Ps 27: 6 now my head shall be l up
Ps 30: 1 O LORD, for You have l me up
Ps 41: 9 Has l up his heel against me
Ps 83: 2 hate You have l up their head
Ps 93: 3 The floods have l up, O LORD,
Ps 93: 3 floods have l up their voice
Ps 102:10 For You have l me up and cast

Ps 106:26 Therefore He l up His hand in
Prov 30:13 And their eyelids are l up
Is 2:12 lofty, upon everything l up
Is 2:13 l up, and upon all the oaks of
Is 2:14 all the hills that are l up
Is 6: 1 l up, and the train of His
Is 26:11 LORD, when Your hand is l up
Is 37:23 and l up your eyes on high
Jer 38:13 and l him out of the dungeon
Jer 51: 9 and is l up to the skies
Jer 52:31 l up the head of Jehoiachin
Ezek 1:19 were l up from the earth, the
Ezek 1:19 earth, the wheels were l up
Ezek 1:20 the wheels were l together
Ezek 1:21 when those were l up from the
Ezek 1:21 the wheels were l up together
Ezek 3:12 Then the Spirit l me up, and I
Ezek 3:14 So the Spirit l me up and took
Ezek 8: 3 the Spirit l me up between
Ezek 8: 5 So I l my eyes toward the
Ezek 10:15 And the cherubim were l up
Ezek 10:16 when the cherubim l their
Ezek 10:17 still, and when one was l up
Ezek 10:17 up, the other l itself up
Ezek 10:19 And the cherubim l their wings
Ezek 11: 1 Then the Spirit l me up and
Ezek 11:22 the cherubim l up their wings
Ezek 18: 6 nor l up his eyes to the
Ezek 18:12 l his eyes to the idols, or
Ezek 18:15 nor l his eyes to the idols
Ezek 20: 5 l My hand in an oath to the
Ezek 20: 5 I l My hand in an oath to
Ezek 20: 6 On that day I l My hand in an
Ezek 20:15 So I also l My hand in an
Ezek 20:23 Also I l My hand in an oath
Ezek 20:28 the land for which I had l My
Ezek 20:42 the country for which I l My
Ezek 28: 2 Because your heart is l up
Ezek 28: 5 your heart is l up because of
Ezek 28:17 Your heart was l up because
Ezek 31:10 its heart was l up in its
Ezek 36: 7 I have l My hand in an oath
Ezek 43: 5 The Spirit l me up and brought
Ezek 44:12 therefore I have l My hand in
Ezek 47:14 for I l My hand in an oath to
Dan 4:34 l my eyes to heaven, and my
Dan 5:20 But when his heart was l up
Dan 5:23 And you have l yourself up
Dan 7: 4 it was l up from the earth and
Dan 8: 3 Then I l my eyes and saw, and
Dan 10: 5 I l my eyes and looked, and
Dan 11:12 his heart will be l up
Mic 5: 9 Your hand shall be l against
Hab 3:10 voice, and l its hands on high
Zech 1:21 l up their horn against the
Zech 5: 7 Here is a lead disc l up, and
Zech 5: 9 they l up the basket between
Zech 9:16 l like a banner over His land
Matt 17: 8 when they had l up their eyes
Mark 1:31 l her up, and immediately the
Mark 9:27 hand and l him up, and he arose
Luke 6:20 Then He l up His eyes toward
Luke 16:23 he l up his eyes and saw
Luke 17:13 they l up their voices and
Luke 24:50 He l up His hands and blessed
John 3:14 as Moses l up the serpent in
John 3:14 must the Son of Man be l up
John 6: 5 Then Jesus l up His eyes, and
John 11:41 Jesus l up His eyes and said,
John 12:32 if I am l up from the earth,
John 12:34 The Son of Man must be l up'
John 13:18 has l up his heel against Me
John 17: 1 l up His eyes to heaven, and
Acts 3: 7 l him up, and immediately his
Acts 9:41 gave her his hand and l her up
Acts 10:26 But Peter l him up, saying
Rev 10: 5 on the land l up his hand to

LIFTING (*see* LIFT)
Neh 8: 6 while l up their hands
Ps 141: 2 The l up of my hands as the
1Ti 2: 8 l up holy hands, without

LIFTS (*see* LIFT)
Num 23:24 And l itself up like a lion
1Sa 2: 7 He brings low and l up
1Sa 2: 8 l the beggar from the ash
Job 39:18 When she l herself on high,
Ps 3: 3 and the One who l up my head
Ps 107:25 Which l up the waves of the
Ps 113: 7 l the needy out of the ash
Ps 147: 6 The LORD l up the humble
Is 18: 3 when he l up a banner on the
Is 40:15 He l up the isles as a very

LIGAMENTS
Col 2:19 knit together by joints and l

LIGHT (*see* LIGHTEN, LIGHTER, LIGHTLY, LIGHTS, LIT)
Gen 1: 3 Let there be l"
Gen 1: 3 and there was l
Gen 1: 4 And God saw the l, that it was
Gen 1: 4 God divided the l from the
Gen 1: 5 God called the l Day, and the
Gen 1:15 to give l on the earth"
Gen 1:16 the greater l to rule the day
Gen 1:16 and the lesser l to rule the
Gen 1:17 to give l on the earth,
Gen 1:18 and to divide the l from the
Ex 10:23 had l in their dwellings
Ex 13:21 pillar of fire to give them l
Ex 14:20 it gave l by night to the
Ex 25: 6 oil for the l, and spices for
Ex 25:37 they give l in front of it
Ex 27:20 of pressed olives for the l
Ex 35: 8 oil for the l, and spices for
Ex 35:14 also the lampstand for the l
Ex 35:14 lamps, and the oil for the l
Ex 35:28 and spices and oil for the l
Ex 39:37 utensils, and the oil for l
Ex 40: 4 the lampstand and l its lamps
Lev 24: 2 of pressed olives for the l
Num 4: 9 cover the lampstand of the l
Num 4:16 priest is the oil for the l
Num 8: 2 l in front of the lampstand
Deut 25:13 weights, a heavy and a l
Judg 19:26 her master was, till it was l
1Sa 14:36 them until the morning l
1Sa 18:23 you a l thing to be a king's
1Sa 25:22 belong to him by morning l
1Sa 25:34 surely by morning l no males
1Sa 25:36 or much, until morning l
1Sa 29:10 in the morning and have l,
2Sa 17:22 By morning l not one of them
2Sa 23: 4 he shall be like the l of the
2Ki 7: 9 If we wait until morning l
Neh 9:12 to give them l on the road
Neh 9:19 fire by night, to show them l
Esth 8:16 The Jews had l and gladness,
Job 3: 4 it, nor the l shine upon it
Job 3: 9 may it look for l, but have
Job 3:16 like infants who never saw l
Job 3:20 Why is l given to him who is
Job 3:23 Why is l given to a man whose
Job 10:22 where even the l is like
Job 12:22 the shadow of death to l
Job 12:25 grope in the dark without l
Job 17:12 The l is near,' they say, in
Job 18: 5 The l of the wicked indeed
Job 18: 6 The l is dark in his tent, and
Job 18:18 driven from l into darkness
Job 22:28 so l will shine on your ways
Job 24:13 those who rebel against the l
Job 24:14 The murderer rises with the l
Job 24:16 they do not know the l
Job 25: 3 Upon whom does His l not rise
Job 26:10 waters, at the boundary of l
Job 28:11 hidden he brings forth to l
Job 29: 3 and when by His l I walked
Job 29:24 the l of my countenance they
Job 30:26 and when I waited for l, then
Job 33:28 And his life shall see the l
Job 33:30 with the l of life
Job 36:30 He scatters his l upon it
Job 37:15 causes the l of His cloud to
Job 37:21 l when it is bright in the
Job 38:15 wicked their l is withheld
Job 38:19 the way to the dwelling of l
Job 38:24 By what way is l diffused
Job 41:18 His sneezings flash forth l
Ps 4: 6 LORD, lift up the l of Your
Ps 18:28 For You will l my lamp
Ps 27: 1 The LORD is my l and my
Ps 36: 9 In Your l we see l
Ps 37: 6 your righteousness as the l
Ps 38:10 As for the l of my eyes, it
Ps 43: 3 Oh, send out Your l and Your
Ps 44: 3 the l of Your countenance,
Ps 49:19 They shall never see l
Ps 56:13 God In the l of the living
Ps 74:16 You have prepared the l and
Ps 78:14 the night with a l of fire
Ps 89:15 in the l of Your countenance
Ps 90: 8 in the l of Your countenance
Ps 97: 4 His lightnings l the world
Ps 97:11 L is sown for the righteous,
Ps 104: 2 with l as with a garment, Who
Ps 105:39 fire to give l in the night
Ps 112: 4 arises l in the darkness
Ps 118:27 LORD, And He has given us l
Ps 119:105 to my feet And a l to my path
Ps 119:130 of Your words gives l
Ps 139:11 the night shall be l about me
Ps 139:12 the l are both alike to You
Ps 148: 3 Him, all you stars of l
Prov 6:23 is a lamp, and the law is l
Prov 13: 9 The l of the righteous
Prov 15:30 The l of the eyes rejoices
Prov 16:15 In the l of the king's face
Prov 29:13 the LORD gives l to the eyes
Eccl 2:13 folly as l excels darkness
Eccl 11: 7 Truly the l is sweet, and it
Eccl 12: 2 while the sun and the l, the
Is 2: 5 us walk in the l of the LORD
Is 5:20 who put darkness for l
Is 5:20 and l for darkness
Is 5:30 and the l is darkened by the
Is 8:20 because there is no l in them
Is 9: 2 darkness have seen a great l
Is 9: 2 upon them a l has shined
Is 10:17 So the L of Israel will be
Is 13:10 will not give their l
Is 13:10 will not cause its l to shine
Is 24:15 the LORD in the dawning l
Is 30:26 Moreover the l of the moon
Is 30:26 will be as the l of the sun
Is 30:26 and the l of the sun will be
Is 30:26 as the l of seven days, in
Is 42: 6 as a l to the Gentiles,
Is 42:16 make darkness l before them
Is 45: 7 I form the l and create
Is 49: 6 You as a l to the Gentiles
Is 50:10 walks in darkness and has no l
Is 50:11 walk in the l of your fire and
Is 51: 4 rest as a l of the peoples
Is 58: 8 Then your l shall break forth
Is 58:10 then your l shall dawn in the
Is 59: 9 we look for l, but there is
Is 60: 1 For your l has come
Is 60: 3 Gentiles shall come to your l
Is 60:19 no longer be your l by day
Is 60:19 shall the moon give l to you
Is 60:19 be to you an everlasting l
Is 60:20 will be your everlasting l
Jer 4:23 and the heavens, they had no l
Jer 13:16 while you are looking for l
Jer 25:10 and the l of the lamp
Jer 31:35 gives the sun for a l by day
Jer 31:35 and the stars for a l by night
Lam 3: 2 walk in darkness and not in l
Ezek 22: 7 they have made l of father
Ezek 32: 7 When I put out your l, I will
Ezek 32: 7 the moon shall not give her l
Dan 2:22 and l dwells with Him
Dan 5:11 in the days of your father, l
Dan 5:14 of God is in you, and that l
Hos 6: 5 are like l that goes forth
Amos 5:18 It will be darkness, and not l
Amos 5:20 the LORD darkness, and not l
Mic 2: 1 At morning l they practice it
Mic 7: 8 the LORD will be a l to me
Mic 7: 9 will bring me forth to the l
Hab 3: 4 His brightness was like the l
Hab 3:11 at the l of Your arrows they
Zeph 3: 5 He brings His justice to l
Zech 14: 6 day that there will be no l
Zech 14: 7 happen that it will be l
Matt 4:16 sat in darkness saw a great l
Matt 4:16 shadow of death l has dawned
Matt 5:14 You are the l of the world
Matt 5:15 Nor do they l a lamp and put
Matt 5:15 it gives l to all who are in
Matt 5:16 Let your l so shine before
Matt 6:22 whole body will be full of l
Matt 6:23 If therefore the l that is in
Matt 10:27 in the dark, speak in the l
Matt 11:30 is easy and My burden is l
Matt 17: 2 became as white as the l
Matt 22: 5 But they made l of it and went
Matt 24:29 the moon will not give its l
Mark 4:22 but that it should come to l

Mark 13:24 the moon will not give its l
Luke 1:79 to give l to those who sit in
Luke 2:32 a l to bring revelation to
Luke 8:16 those who enter may see the l
Luke 8:17 not be known and come to l
Luke 11:33 who come in may see the l
Luke 11:34 whole body also is full of l
Luke 11:35 take heed that the l which is
Luke 11:36 your whole body is full of l
Luke 11:36 whole body will be full of l
Luke 11:36 shining of a lamp gives you l
Luke 12: 3 dark will be heard in the l
Luke 15: 8 one coin, does not l a lamp
Luke 16: 8 generation than the sons of l
John 1: 4 and the life was the l of men
John 1: 5 the l shines in the darkness,
John 1: 7 to bear witness of the L
John 1: 8 He was not that L, but was
John 1: 8 to bear witness of that L
John 1: 9 the true L which gives l
John 3:19 that the l has come into the
John 3:19 loved darkness rather than l
John 3:20 practicing evil hates the l
John 3:20 and does not come to the l
John 3:21 does the truth comes to the l
John 5:35 a time to rejoice in his l
John 8:12 I am the l of the world
John 8:12 but have the l of life
John 9: 5 I am the l of the world
John 11: 9 he sees the l of this world
John 11:10 because the l is not in him
John 12:35 longer the l is with you
John 12:35 Walk while you have the l
John 12:36 have the l, believe in the l
John 12:36 that you may become sons of l
John 12:46 come as a l into the world
Acts 9: 3 suddenly a l shone around him
Acts 12: 7 and a l shone in the prison
Acts 13:47 you to be a l to the Gentiles
Acts 16:29 Then he called for a l, ran
Acts 22: 6 noon, suddenly a great l from
Acts 22: 9 were with me indeed saw the l
Acts 22:11 see for the glory of that l
Acts 26:13 road I saw a l from heaven
Acts 26:18 turn them from darkness to l
Acts 26:23 and would proclaim l to the
Rom 2:19 a l to those who are in
Rom 13:12 let us put on the armor of l
1Co 4: 5 to l the hidden things of
2Co 4: 4 lest the l of the gospel of
2Co 4: 6 l to shine out of darkness
2Co 4: 6 the l of the knowledge of the
2Co 4:17 For our l affliction, which
2Co 6:14 communion has l with darkness
2Co 11:14 himself into an angel of l
Eph 5: 8 but now you are l in the Lord
Eph 5: 8 Walk as children of l
Eph 5:13 are made manifest by the l
Eph 5:13 whatever makes manifest is l
Eph 5:14 and Christ will give you l
Col 1:12 of the saints in the l
1Th 5: 5 You are all sons of l and sons
1Ti 6:16 dwelling in unapproachable l
2Ti 1:10 immortality to l through the
1Pe 2: 9 darkness into His marvelous l
2Pe 1:19 you do well to heed as a l
1Jn 1: 5 declare to you, that God is l
1Jn 1: 7 the l as He is in the l
1Jn 2: 8 the true l is already shining
1Jn 2: 9 He who says he is in the l
1Jn 2:10 his brother abides in the l
Rev 18:23 the l of a lamp shall not
Rev 21:11 And her l was like a most
Rev 21:23 it, and the Lamb is its l
Rev 21:24 are saved shall walk in its l
Rev 22: 5 need no lamp nor l of the sun
Rev 22: 5 for the Lord God gives them l

LIGHTEN (*see* LIGHT, LIGHTENED)
1Sa 6: 5 perhaps He will l His hand
1Ki 12: 4 l the burdensome service of
1Ki 12: 9 L the yoke which your father
2Ch 10: 4 l the burdensome service of
2Ch 10: 9 L the yoke which your father
Jon 1: 5 into the sea, to l the load

LIGHTENED (*see* LIGHTEN)
Acts 27:18 the next day they l the ship
Acts 27:38 they l the ship and threw out

LIGHTER (*see* LIGHT)
1Ki 12:10 but you make it l on us'
2Ch 10:10 but you make it l on us'
Ps 62: 9 are altogether l than vapor

LIGHTLY (*see* LIGHT)
1Sa 2:30 Me shall be l esteemed
1Sa 18:23 I am a poor and l esteemed man
Is 9: 1 as when at first He l
2Co 1:17 planning this, did I do it l

LIGHTNING (*see* LIGHTNINGS)
Ex 20:18 the l flashes, the sound of
2Sa 22:15 l bolts, and He vanquished
Job 36:32 He covers His hands with l
Job 37: 3 His l to the ends of the
Ps 78:48 And their flocks to fiery l
Ps 135: 7 He makes l for the rain
Ps 144: 6 Flash forth l and scatter them
Jer 10:13 He makes l for the rain, He
Ezek 1:13 and out of the fire went l
Ezek 1:14 appearance like a flash of l
Ezek 21:10 polished to flash like l
Dan 10: 6 face like the appearance of l
Nah 2: 4 like torches, they run like l
Zech 9:14 arrow will go forth like l
Matt 24:27 For as the l comes from the
Matt 28: 3 His countenance was like l
Luke 10:18 Satan fall like l from heaven
Luke 17:24 For as the l that flashes out

LIGHTNINGS (*see* LIGHTNING)
Ex 19:16 there were thunderings and l
Job 38:35 Can you send out l, that they
Ps 18:14 foe, L in abundance, and He
Ps 77:18 The l lit up the world
Ps 97: 4 His l light the world
Jer 51:16 He makes l for the rain
Rev 4: 5 from the throne proceeded l
Rev 8: 5 were noises, thunderings, l
Rev 11:19 And there were l, noises,
Rev 16:18 noises and thunderings and l

LIGHTS (*see* LIGHT)
Gen 1:14 said, "Let there be l in the
Gen 1:15 and let them be for l in the
Gen 1:16 Then God made two great l
Ex 30: 8 when Aaron l the lamps at
Job 41:19 Out of his mouth go burning l
Ps 136: 7 To Him who made great l, For
Ezek 32: 8 All the bright l of the
Zech 14: 6 the l will diminish
Phil 2:15 you shine as l in the world
Jas 1:17 down from the Father of l

LIKE (*see* PREFACE, UNLIKE)

LIKELY
Jer 38: 9 he is l to die from hunger in

LIKE-MINDED
Rom 15: 5 to be l toward one another
Phil 2: 2 fulfill my joy by being l
Phil 2:20 For I have no one l, who will

LIKEN (*see* LIKENED, LIKENESS)
Is 40:18 To whom then will you l God
Is 40:25 To whom then will you l Me
Is 46: 5 To whom will you l Me, and
Lam 2:13 To what shall I l you, O
Matt 7:24 I will l him to a wise man
Matt 11:16 shall I l this generation
Mark 4:30 To what shall we l the
Luke 7:31 To what then shall I l the
Luke 13:20 To what shall I l the kingdom

LIKENED (*see* LIKEN)
Ps 89: 6 mighty can be l to the LORD
Jer 6: 2 I have l the daughter of Zion
Ezek 31:18 will you then be l in glory
Matt 25: 1 be l to ten virgins who took

LIKENESS (*see* LIKEN)
Gen 1:26 Our image, according to Our l
Gen 5: 1 He made him in the l of God
Gen 5: 3 and begot a son in his own l
Ex 20: 4 or any l of anything that is
Deut 4:16 the l of male or female,
Deut 4:17 the l of any beast that is on
Deut 4:17 the l of any winged bird that
Deut 4:18 the l of anything that creeps
Deut 4:18 l of any fish that is in the
Deut 5: 8 or any l of anything that is
2Ch 4: 3 under it was the l of oxen
Ps 17:15 when I awake in Your l
Is 40:18 Or what l will you compare to
Ezek 1: 5 from within it came the l of
Ezek 1: 5 they had the l of a man
Ezek 1:10 As for the l of their faces,
Ezek 1:13 As for the l of the living
Ezek 1:16 and all four had the same l
Ezek 1:22 The l of the firmament above
Ezek 1:26 heads was the l of a throne
Ezek 1:26 on the l of the throne was a
Ezek 1:26 of the throne was a l with
Ezek 1:28 l of the glory of the LORD
Ezek 8: 2 I looked, and there was a l
Ezek 10: 1 of the l of a throne
Ezek 10:21 the l of the hands of a man
Ezek 10:22 the l of their faces was the
Dan 10:16 one having the l of the sons
Dan 10:18 the one having the l of a man
Acts 14:11 down to us in the l of men
Rom 5:14 the l of the transgression of
Rom 6: 5 in the l of His death,
Rom 6: 5 in the l of His resurrection
Rom 8: 3 Son in the l of sinful flesh
Phil 2: 7 and coming in the l of men
Heb 7:15 if, in the l of Melchizedek,

LIKEWISE (*see* PREFACE)

LIKHI
1Ch 7:19 were Ahian, Shechem, L, and

LILIES (*see* LILY)
1Ki 7:19 hall were in the shape of l
1Ki 7:22 were in the shape of l
Song 2:16 feeds his flock among the l
Song 4: 5 which feed among the l
Song 5:13 His lips are l, dripping
Song 6: 2 the gardens, and to gather l
Song 6: 3 feeds his flock among the l
Song 7: 2 of wheat set about with l
Matt 6:28 Consider the l of the field
Luke 12:27 Consider the l, how they grow

LILY (*see* LILIES)
1Ki 7:26 of a cup, like a l blossom
2Ch 4: 5 of a cup, like a l blossom
Song 2: 1 and the l of the valleys
Song 2: 2 Like a l among thorns, so is
Hos 14: 5 He shall grow like the l, and

LIMB (*see* LIMBS)
Lev 21:18 marred face or any l too long
Lev 22:23 l too long or too short you
Judg 19:29 into twelve pieces, l by l

LIMBS (*see* LIMB)
Job 18:13 of death devours his l
Job 41:12 I will not conceal his l, his

LIME
Deut 27: 2 and whitewash them with l
Deut 27: 4 shall whitewash them with l
Is 33:12 be like the burnings of l
Amos 2: 1 of the king of Edom to l

LIMIT (*see* LIMITED, LIMITS)
1Ch 22:16 bronze and iron there is no l
Ezra 7:22 and salt without prescribed l
Job 13:27 You set a l for the soles of
Job 15: 8 Do you l wisdom to yourself
Job 38:10 when I fixed My l for it, and
Prov 8:29 He assigned to the sea its l

LIMITED (*see* LIMIT)
Ps 78:41 And l the Holy One of Israel

LIMITS (*see* LIMIT)
Num 35:26 any time goes outside the l
Num 35:27 the l of his city of refuge
Josh 15:21 The cities at the l of the
2Ki 19:23 to the l of Lebanon
Job 11: 7 out the l of the Almighty
Job 14: 5 You have appointed his l, so
Ps 71:15 For I do not know their l
Is 37:24 to the l of Lebanon
2Co 10:13 but within the l of the

LIMP (*see* LIMPED)
Prov 26: 7 l is a proverb in the mouth
Is 13: 7 Therefore all hands will be l

LIMPED (*see* LIMP)
Gen 32:31 on him, and he l on his hip

LINE (*see* LINEAGE, LINES)
Num 34: 7 your border l to Mount Hor
Josh 2:18 you bind this l of scarlet
Judg 20:22 again formed the battle l at

1Sa 4:12 the battle l the same day
1Sa 4:16 fled today from the battle l
1Sa 17: 8 come out to l up for battle
2Sa 8: 2 he measured them off with a l
2Sa 8: 2 with one full l those to be
2Sa 10: 9 l was against him before and
1Ki 7:15 a l of twelve cubits measured
1Ki 7:23 a l of thirty cubits measured
2Ki 21:13 the measuring l of Samaria
1Ch 19:10 Joab saw that the battle l
2Ch 4: 2 a l of thirty cubits measured
2Ch 13:14 battle l was at both front
Job 38: 5 who stretched the l upon it
Job 41: 1 with a l which you lower
Ps 19: 4 Their l has gone out through
Is 28:10 upon precept, l upon l
Is 28:10 l upon l, here a little,
Is 28:13 upon precept, l upon l
Is 28:13 l upon l, here a little,
Is 28:17 make justice the measuring l
Is 34:11 over it the l of confusion
Is 34:17 among them with a measuring l
Jer 31:39 The surveyor's l shall again
Jer 52:21 a measuring l of twelve
Lam 2: 8 He has stretched out a l
Ezek 40: 3 He had a l of flax and a
Ezek 47: 3 east with the l in his hand
Amos 7: 7 on a wall made with a plumb l
Amos 7: 7 with a plumb l in His hand
Amos 7: 8 And I said, "A plumb l."
Amos 7: 8 I am setting a plumb l in the
Amos 7:17 shall be divided by survey l
Zech 1:16 and a surveyor's l shall be
Zech 2: 1 a measuring l in his hand
Zech 4:10 rejoice to see the plumb l in

LINEAGE (*see* LINE)
Gen 19:32 preserve the l of our father
Gen 19:34 preserve the l of our father
Neh 7:61 father's house nor their l
Neh 9: 2 Then those of Israelite l
Dan 9: 1 of the l of the Medes, who
Luke 2: 4 of the house and l of David,

LINEN
Gen 41:42 him in garments of fine l
Ex 25: 4 fine l thread, and goats' hair
Ex 26: 1 woven of fine l thread, and
Ex 26:31 yarn, and fine l thread
Ex 26:36 and fine l thread, made by a
Ex 27: 9 court woven of fine l thread
Ex 27:16 and fine l thread, made by a
Ex 27:18 woven of fine l thread, and
Ex 28: 5 and scarlet thread, and fine l
Ex 28: 6 fine l thread, artistically
Ex 28: 8 thread, and fine l thread
Ex 28:15 thread, and of fine l thread
Ex 28:39 the tunic of fine l thread
Ex 28:39 make the turban of fine l
Ex 28:42 l trousers to cover their
Ex 35: 6 fine l thread, and goats' hair
Ex 35:23 and purple and scarlet, fine l
Ex 35:25 purple and scarlet, and fine l
Ex 35:35 purple and scarlet and fine l
Ex 36: 8 woven of fine l thread, and
Ex 36:35 yarn, and fine l thread
Ex 36:37 and fine l thread, made by a
Ex 38: 9 court were woven of fine l
Ex 38:16 around were woven of fine l
Ex 38:18 yarn, and fine l thread
Ex 38:23 yarn, and fine l thread
Ex 39: 2 thread, and of fine l thread
Ex 39: 3 fine l thread, into artistic
Ex 39: 5 fine l thread, as the LORD
Ex 39: 8 thread, and fine l thread
Ex 39:24 and scarlet and fine l thread
Ex 39:27 artistically woven of fine l
Ex 39:28 a turban of fine l, exquisite
Ex 39:28 exquisite hats of fine l
Ex 39:28 short trousers of fine l
Ex 39:29 and a sash of fine l and blue
Lev 6:10 shall put on his l garment
Lev 6:10 his l trousers he shall put
Lev 13:47 woolen garment or a l garment
Lev 13:48 the warp or woof of l or wool
Lev 13:52 warp or woof, in wool or in l
Lev 13:59 in a garment of wool or l
Lev 16: 4 He shall put the holy l tunic
Lev 16: 4 the l trousers on his body
Lev 16: 4 shall be girded with a l sash
Lev 16: 4 with the l turban he shall be
Lev 16:23 shall take off the l garments
Lev 16:32 and put on the l clothes, the
Lev 19:19 shall a garment of mixed l
Deut 22:11 as wool and l mixed together
Judg 14:12 give you thirty l garments
Judg 14:13 give me thirty l garments
1Sa 2:18 as a child, wearing a l ephod
1Sa 22:18 men who wore a l ephod
2Sa 6:14 David was wearing a l ephod
1Ch 4:21 of the house of the l workers
1Ch 15:27 clothed with a robe of fine l
1Ch 15:27 David also wore a l ephod
2Ch 2:14 wood, purple and blue, fine l
2Ch 3:14 purple and crimson and fine l
2Ch 5:12 the altar, clothed in white l
Esth 1: 6 blue l curtains fastened with
Esth 1: 6 fastened with cords of fine l
Esth 8:15 gold and a garment of fine l
Prov 7:16 coverings of Egyptian l
Prov 31:22 her clothing is fine l and
Prov 31:24 She makes l garments and sells
Is 3:23 the fine l, the turbans, and
Jer 13: 1 Go and get yourself a l sash
Ezek 9: 2 among them was clothed with l
Ezek 9: 3 to the man clothed with l
Ezek 9:11 then, the man clothed with l
Ezek 10: 2 to the man clothed with l
Ezek 10: 6 the man clothed in l, saying,
Ezek 10: 7 of the man clothed with l
Ezek 16:10 I clothed you with fine l
Ezek 16:13 your clothing was of fine l
Ezek 27: 7 Fine embroidered l from Egypt
Ezek 27:16 purple, embroidery, fine l
Ezek 44:17 they shall put on l garments
Ezek 44:18 They shall have l turbans on
Ezek 44:18 l trousers on their bodies
Dan 10: 5 a certain man clothed in l
Dan 12: 6 said to the man clothed in l
Dan 12: 7 I heard the man clothed in l
Hos 2: 5 and my water, my wool and my l
Hos 2: 9 take back My wool and My l
Matt 27:59 wrapped it in a clean l cloth
Mark 14:51 Him, having a l cloth thrown
Mark 14:52 and he left the l cloth and
Mark 15:46 Then he bought fine l, took
Mark 15:46 down, and wrapped Him in the l
Luke 16:19 clothed in purple and fine l
Luke 23:53 took it down, wrapped it in l
Luke 24:12 he saw the l cloths lying by
John 19:40 strips of l with the spices
John 20: 5 saw the l cloths lying there
John 20: 6 he saw the l cloths lying
John 20: 7 not lying with the l cloths
Rev 15: 6 clothed in pure bright l
Rev 18:12 stones and pearls, fine l and
Rev 18:16 that was clothed in fine l
Rev 19: 8 to be arrayed in fine l,
Rev 19: 8 bright, for the fine l is the
Rev 19:14 in heaven, clothed in fine l

LINES (*see* LINE)
2Sa 8: 2 With two l he measured off
Ps 16: 6 The l have fallen to me in

LINGER (*see* LINGERED)
2Sa 18:14 I cannot l with you
Prov 23:30 Those who l long at the wine,
Is 46:13 My salvation shall not l

LINGERED (*see* LINGER)
Gen 19:16 And while he l, the men took
Gen 43:10 For if we had not l, surely
Luke 1:21 marveled that he l so long in
Luke 2:43 the Boy Jesus l behind in

LINK
Song 4: 9 with one l of your necklace

LINTEL
Ex 12: 7 on the l of the houses where
Ex 12:22 in the basin, and strike the l
Ex 12:23 He sees the blood on the l
1Ki 6:31 the l and doorposts were

LINUS
2Ti 4:21 you, as well as Pudens, L

LION (*see* LIONESS, LION-LIKE, LION'S, LIONS)
Gen 49: 9 down, he lies down as a l
Gen 49: 9 and as a l, who shall rouse
Num 23:24 And lifts itself up like a l
Num 24: 9 down, he lies down as a l
Num 24: 9 and as a l, who will rouse him
Deut 33:20 He dwells as a l, and tears
Judg 14: 5 a young l came roaring
Judg 14: 6 he tore the l apart as one
Judg 14: 8 to see the carcass of the l
Judg 14: 8 were in the carcass of the l
Judg 14: 9 out of the carcass of the l
Judg 14:18 and what is stronger than a l
1Sa 17:34 when a l or a bear came and
1Sa 17:36 servant has killed both l
1Sa 17:37 me from the paw of the l and
2Sa 17:10 is like the heart of a l,
2Sa 23:20 killed a l in the midst of a
1Ki 13:24 a l met him on the road and
1Ki 13:24 the l also stood by the
1Ki 13:25 the l standing by the corpse
1Ki 13:26 has delivered him to the l
1Ki 13:28 the l standing by the corpse
1Ki 13:28 The l had not eaten the
1Ki 20:36 from me, a l shall kill you
1Ki 20:36 a l found him and killed him
1Ch 11:22 killed a l in the midst of a
Job 4:10 The roaring of the l, the
Job 4:10 the voice of the fierce l
Job 4:11 The old l perishes for lack
Job 10:16 you hunt me like a fierce l
Job 28: 8 the fierce l passed over it
Job 38:39 you hunt the prey for the l
Ps 7: 2 Lest they tear me like a l
Ps 10: 9 secretly, as a l in his den
Ps 17:12 Like a l that is eager to
Ps 17:12 And as a young l lurking in
Ps 22:13 As a raging and roaring l
Ps 91:13 You shall tread upon the l
Ps 91:13 and the cobra, The young l
Prov 19:12 is like the roaring of a l
Prov 20: 2 is like the roaring of a l
Prov 22:13 There is a l outside
Prov 26:13 There is a l in the road
Prov 26:13 A fierce l is in the streets
Prov 28: 1 the righteous are bold as a l
Prov 28:15 Like a roaring l and a
Prov 30:30 a l, which is mighty among
Eccl 9: 4 dog is better than a dead l
Is 5:29 roaring will be like a l,
Is 11: 6 goat, the calf and the young l
Is 11: 7 the l shall eat straw like
Is 21: 8 A l, my Lord
Is 30: 6 which came the lioness and l
Is 31: 4 As a l roars, and a young l
Is 35: 9 No l shall be there, nor
Is 38:13 like a l, so He breaks all my
Is 65:25 the l shall eat straw like
Jer 2:30 prophets like a destroying l
Jer 4: 7 The l has come up from his
Jer 5: 6 Therefore a l from the forest
Jer 12: 8 to Me like a l in the forest
Jer 25:38 has left his lair like the l
Jer 49:19 he shall come up like a l
Jer 50:44 he shall come up like a l
Lam 3:10 in wait, like a l in ambush
Ezek 1:10 face of a l on the right side
Ezek 10:14 the third the face of a l
Ezek 19: 3 cubs, and he became a young l
Ezek 19: 5 cubs and made him a young l
Ezek 19: 6 lions, and became a young l
Ezek 22:25 a roaring l tearing the prey
Ezek 32: 2 a young l among the nations
Ezek 41:19 the face of a young l toward
Dan 7: 4 The first was like a l, and
Hos 5:14 I will be like a l to Ephraim
Hos 5:14 like a young l to the house
Hos 11:10 He will roar like a l
Hos 13: 7 So I will be to them like a l
Hos 13: 8 I will devour them like a l
Joel 1: 6 teeth are the teeth of a l
Joel 1: 6 has the fangs of a fierce l
Amos 3: 4 Will a l roar in the forest,
Amos 3: 4 Will a young l cry out of his
Amos 3: 8 A l has roared
Amos 3:12 a l two legs or a piece of an
Amos 5:19 as though a man fled from a l
Mic 5: 8 like a l among the beasts of
Mic 5: 8 like a young l among flocks
Nah 2:11 lions, where the l walked
Nah 2:12 The l tore in pieces enough
2Ti 4:17 out of the mouth of the l
1Pe 5: 8 walks about like a roaring l
Rev 4: 7 living creature was like a l
Rev 5: 5 the L of the tribe of Judah,
Rev 10: 3 loud voice, as when a l roars
Rev 13: 2 mouth like the mouth of a l

LIONESS (*see* LION, LIONESSES)
Num 23:24 Look, a people rises like a **l**
Job 4:11 cubs of the **l** are scattered
Is 30: 6 from which came the **l** and
Ezek 19: 2 A **l**: she lay down
Nah 2:11 where the lion walked, the **l**

LIONESSES (*see* LIONESS)
Nah 2:12 his cubs, killed for his **l**

LION-LIKE (*see* LION)
2Sa 23:20 killed two **l** heroes of Moab
1Ch 11:22 killed two **l** heroes of Moab

LION'S (*see* LION)
Gen 49: 9 Judah is a **l** whelp
Deut 33:22 Dan is a **l** whelp
Ps 22:21 Save Me from the **l** mouth And
Nah 2:11 **l** cub, and no one made them

LIONS (*see* LION, LIONS')
2Sa 1:23 they were stronger than **l**
1Ki 7:29 between the frames were **l**
1Ki 7:29 Below the **l** and oxen were
1Ki 7:36 he engraved cherubim, **l**, and
1Ki 10:19 and two **l** stood beside the
1Ki 10:20 Twelve **l** stood there, one on
2Ki 17:25 the LORD sent **l** among them
2Ki 17:26 He has sent **l** among them, and
1Ch 12: 8 were like the faces of **l**, and
2Ch 9:18 and two **l** stood beside the
2Ch 9:19 Twelve **l** stood there, one on
Job 4:10 of the young **l** are broken
Job 28: 8 The proud **l** have not trodden
Job 38:39 the appetite of the young **l**
Ps 34:10 The young **l** lack and suffer
Ps 35:17 My precious life from the **l**
Ps 57: 4 My soul is among **l**
Ps 58: 6 out the fangs of the young **l**
Ps 104:21 The young **l** roar after their
Is 5:29 they will roar like young **l**
Is 15: 9 **l** upon him who escapes from
Jer 2:15 The young **l** roared at him, and
Jer 50:17 the **l** have driven him away
Jer 51:38 shall roar together like **l**
Ezek 19: 2 she lay down among the **l**
Ezek 19: 2 among the young **l** she
Ezek 19: 6 He roved among the **l**, and
Ezek 38:13 their young **l** will say to you
Dan 6: 7 be cast into the den of **l**
Dan 6:12 be cast into the den of **l**
Dan 6:16 and cast him into the den of **l**
Dan 6:19 went in haste to the den of **l**
Dan 6:20 to deliver you from the **l**
Dan 6:24 cast them into the den of **l**
Dan 6:24 the **l** overpowered them, and
Dan 6:27 from the power of the **l**
Nah 2:11 is the dwelling of the **l**, and
Nah 2:11 feeding place of the young **l**
Nah 2:13 shall devour your young **l**
Zeph 3: 3 in her midst are roaring **l**
Zech 11: 3 is the sound of roaring **l**
Heb 11:33 stopped the mouths of **l**,
Rev 9:17 were like the heads of **l**

LIONS' (*see* LIONS)
Song 4: 8 and Hermon, from the **l** dens
Jer 51:38 shall growl like **l** whelps
Dan 6:22 angel and shut the **l** mouths
Rev 9: 8 their teeth were like **l** teeth

LIP (*see* LIPS)
Ps 22: 7 They shoot out the **l**, they
Prov 12:19 The truthful **l** shall be

LIPS (*see* LIP)
Ex 6:12 for I am of uncircumcised **l**
Ex 6:30 I am of uncircumcised **l**, and
Lev 5: 4 thoughtlessly with his **l** to
Num 30: 6 a rash utterance from her **l**
Num 30: 8 what she uttered with her **l**
Num 30:12 her **l** concerning her vows or
Deut 23:23 from your **l** you shall keep
1Sa 1:13 only her **l** moved, but her
2Ki 19:28 nose and My bridle in your **l**
Job 2:10 Job did not sin with his **l**
Job 8:21 and your **l** with rejoicing
Job 11: 5 and open His **l** against you,
Job 13: 6 and heed the pleadings of my **l**
Job 15: 6 your own **l** testify against
Job 16: 5 the comfort of my **l** would
Job 23:12 from the commandment of His **l**
Job 27: 4 my **l** will not speak
Job 32:20 I must open my **l** and answer
Job 33: 3 my **l** utter pure knowledge
Ps 12: 2 With flattering **l** and a double
Ps 12: 3 LORD cut off all flattering **l**
Ps 12: 4 Our **l** are our own
Ps 16: 4 take up their names on my **l**
Ps 17: 1 that is not from deceitful **l**
Ps 17: 4 of men, By the word of Your **l**
Ps 21: 2 withheld the request of his **l**
Ps 31:18 Let the lying **l** be put to
Ps 34:13 your **l** from speaking guile
Ps 40: 9 I do not restrain my **l**, O
Ps 45: 2 Grace is poured upon Your **l**
Ps 51:15 O Lord, open my **l**, And my
Ps 59: 7 Swords are in their **l**
Ps 59:12 mouth and the words of their **l**
Ps 63: 3 life, My **l** shall praise You
Ps 63: 5 praise You with joyful **l**
Ps 66:14 Which my **l** have uttered And
Ps 71:23 My **l** shall greatly rejoice
Ps 89:34 that has gone out of My **l**
Ps 106:33 he spoke rashly with his **l**
Ps 119:13 With my **l** I have declared All
Ps 119:171 My **l** shall utter praise, For
Ps 120: 2 my soul, O LORD, from lying **l**
Ps 140: 3 of asps is under their **l**
Ps 140: 9 evil of their **l** cover them
Ps 141: 3 watch over the door of my **l**
Prov 4:24 put perverse **l** far from you
Prov 5: 2 and that your **l** may keep
Prov 5: 3 For the **l** of an immoral woman
Prov 7:21 flattering **l** she seduced him
Prov 8: 6 my **l** will come right things
Prov 8: 7 is an abomination to my **l**
Prov 10:13 found on the **l** of him who has
Prov 10:18 hides hatred has lying **l**, and
Prov 10:19 who restrains his **l** is wise
Prov 10:21 The **l** of the righteous feed
Prov 10:32 The **l** of the righteous know
Prov 12:13 by the transgression of his **l**
Prov 12:22 Lying **l** are an abomination to
Prov 13: 3 his **l** shall have destruction
Prov 14: 3 but the **l** of the wise will
Prov 14: 7 in him the **l** of knowledge
Prov 15: 7 The **l** of the wise disperse
Prov 16:10 is on the **l** of the king, his
Prov 16:13 Righteous **l** are the delight
Prov 16:21 sweetness of the **l** increases
Prov 16:23 and adds learning to his **l**
Prov 16:27 it is on his **l** like a burning
Prov 16:30 he purses his **l** and brings
Prov 17: 4 gives heed to false **l**
Prov 17: 7 much less lying **l** to a prince
Prov 17:28 when he shuts his **l**, he is
Prov 18: 6 A fool's **l** enter into
Prov 18: 7 his **l** are the snare of his
Prov 18:20 of his **l** he shall be filled
Prov 19: 1 one who is perverse in his **l**
Prov 20:15 but the **l** of knowledge are a
Prov 20:19 one who flatters with his **l**
Prov 22:11 heart and has grace on his **l**
Prov 22:18 them all be fixed upon your **l**
Prov 23:16 your **l** speak right things
Prov 24: 2 their **l** talk of troublemaking
Prov 24:26 a right answer kisses the **l**
Prov 24:28 would you deceive with your **l**
Prov 26:23 Fervent **l** with a wicked heart
Prov 26:24 disguises it with his **l**, and
Prov 27: 2 a stranger, and not your own **l**
Eccl 10:12 but the **l** of a fool shall
Song 4: 3 Your **l** are like a strand of
Song 4:11 Your **l**, O my spouse, drip as
Song 5:13 His **l** are lilies, dripping
Song 7: 9 gently the **l** of sleepers
Is 6: 5 I am a man of unclean **l**, and I
Is 6: 5 of a people of unclean **l**
Is 6: 7 this has touched your **l**
Is 11: 4 with the breath of His **l** He
Is 28:11 For with stammering **l** and
Is 29:13 and honor Me with their **l**, but
Is 30:27 His **l** are full of indignation
Is 37:29 nose and My bridle in your **l**
Is 57:19 I create the fruit of the **l**
Is 59: 3 your **l** have spoken lies, your
Jer 17:16 know what came out of my **l**
Lam 3:62 The **l** of my enemies and their
Ezek 24:17 do not cover your **l**, and do
Ezek 24:22 your **l** nor eat man's bread of
Ezek 36: 3 taken up by the **l** of talkers
Dan 10:16 the sons of men touched my **l**
Hos 14: 2 offer the sacrifices of our **l**
Mic 3: 7 they shall all cover their **l**
Hab 3:16 my **l** quivered at the voice
Mal 2: 6 was not found on his **l**
Mal 2: 7 For the **l** of a priest should
Matt 15: 8 and honor Me with their **l**
Mark 7: 6 people honors Me with their **l**
Rom 3:13 of asps is under their **l**"
1Co 14:21 other **l** I will speak to this
Heb 13:15 that is, the fruit of our **l**
1Pe 3:10 his **l** from speaking guile

LIQUID
Ex 30:23 hundred shekels of **l** myrrh
Song 5: 5 My fingers with **l** myrrh, on
Song 5:13 are lilies, dripping **l** myrrh

LISTED
Num 11:26 Now they were among those **l**
1Ch 5: 1 that the genealogy is not **l**
1Ch 7: 5 **l** by their genealogies,
1Ch 7: 7 and they were **l** by their
2Ch 31:19 and to all who were **l** by

LISTEN (*see* LISTENED, LISTENING, LISTENS)
Gen 4:23 of Lamech, **l** to my speech
Gen 21:12 said to you, **l** to her voice
Gen 23:15 My lord, **l** to me
Gen 42:22 and you would not **l**
Gen 49: 2 and **l** to Israel your father
Ex 4: 1 believe me or **l** to my voice
Ex 4: 9 or **l** to your voice, that you
Ex 18:19 **L** now to my voice
Num 23:18 **L** to me, son of Zippor
Deut 1:43 yet you would not **l**, but
Deut 1:45 but the LORD would not **l** to
Deut 3:26 account, and would not **l** to me
Deut 4: 1 **l** to the statutes and the
Deut 7:12 pass, because you **l** to these
Deut 13: 3 you shall not **l** to the words
Deut 13: 8 consent to him or **l** to him
Deut 23: 5 God would not **l** to Balaam
Deut 27: 9 Take heed and **l**, O Israel
Josh 24:10 But I would not **l** to Balaam
Judg 2:17 would not **l** to their judges
Judg 9: 7 **L** to me, you men of Shechem,
Judg 9: 7 that God may **l** to you
Judg 20:13 not **l** to the voice of their
Ruth 2: 8 You will **l**, my daughter, will
1Sa 24: 9 Why do you **l** to the words of
2Sa 13:16 But he would not **l** to her
1Ki 8:28 **l** to the cry and the prayer
1Ki 8:52 to **l** to them whenever they
1Ki 12:15 king did not **l** to the people
1Ki 12:16 the king did not **l** to them
1Ki 20: 8 to him, "Do not **l** or consent
1Ki 22:13 Now **l**, the words of the
2Ki 18:31 Do not **l** to Hezekiah
2Ki 18:32 But do not **l** to Hezekiah,
2Ch 6:19 **l** to the cry and to the prayer
2Ch 10:15 king did not **l** to the people
2Ch 10:16 the king did not **l** to them
2Ch 18:12 Now **l**, the words of the
2Ch 20:15 **L**, all you of Judah and you
2Ch 24:19 them, but they would not **l**
2Ch 33:10 people, but they would not **l**
Neh 9:30 Yet they would not **l**
Esth 3: 4 and he would not **l** to them
Job 13:17 **L** diligently to my speech, and
Job 21: 2 **L** carefully to my speech, and
Job 32:10 **L** to me, I also will declare
Job 33: 1 speech, and **l** to all my words
Job 33:31 Give ear, Job, **l** to me
Job 33:33 If not, **l** to me
Job 34:10 Therefore **l** to me, you men of
Job 34:16 **l** to the sound of my words
Job 34:34 to me, wise men who **l** to me
Job 35:13 God will not **l** to empty talk
Job 37:14 **L** to this, O Job
Job 42: 4 **L**, please, and let me speak
Ps 34:11 Come, you children, **l** to me
Ps 45:10 **L**, O daughter, Consider and
Ps 81: 8 O Israel, if you will **l** to Me
Ps 81:13 that My people would **l** to Me
Prov 7:24 **l** to me, my children
Prov 8: 6 **L**, for I will speak of
Prov 8:32 **l** to me, my children, for
Prov 13: 1 scoffer does not **l** to rebuke
Prov 19:20 **L** to counsel and receive
Prov 23:22 **L** to your father who begot
Song 8:13 companions **l** for your voice
Is 28:23 Give ear and hear my voice, **l**
Is 32: 3 ears of those who hear will **l**

Is 36:16 Do not l to Hezekiah
Is 42:23 Who will l and hear for the
Is 46: 3 L to Me, O house of Jacob, and
Is 46:12 L to Me, you stubborn-hearted
Is 48:12 L to Me, O Jacob, and Israel,
Is 49: 1 L, O coastlands, to Me, and
Is 51: 1 L to Me, you who follow after
Is 51: 4 L to Me, My people
Is 51: 7 L to Me, you who know
Is 55: 2 L diligently to Me, and eat
Jer 6:17 l to the sound of the
Jer 6:17 But they said, 'We will not l
Jer 8:19 L! The voice, the cry of
Jer 11:11 to Me, I will not l to them
Jer 18:19 l to the voice of those who
Jer 23:16 Do not l to the words of the
Jer 26: 3 Perhaps everyone will l and
Jer 26: 4 If you will not l to Me, to
Jer 27: 9 do not l to your prophets
Jer 27:14 Therefore do not l to the
Jer 27:16 Do not l to the words of
Jer 27:17 Do not l to them
Jer 29: 8 nor l to your dreams which
Jer 29:12 to Me, and I will l to you
Jer 36:25 but he would not l to them
Jer 37:14 But he did not l to him
Jer 38:15 counsel, you will not l to me
Jer 44: 5 But they did not l or
Jer 44:16 LORD, we will not l to you
Ezek 3: 7 of Israel will not l to you
Ezek 3: 7 because they will not l to Me
Ezek 13:19 to My people who l to lies
Dan 9:19 O Lord, l and act
Mic 1: 2 l, O earth, and all that is in
Zech 7:13 called out and I would not l
Mark 4: 3 L! Behold, a sower went out
John 8:43 are not able to l to My word
John 9:27 you already, and you did not l
John 10:20 Why do you l to Him
Acts 4:19 in the sight of God to l to
Acts 7: 2 Men and brethren and fathers, l
Acts 13:16 and you who fear God, l
Acts 15:13 Men and brethren, l to me
Jas 2: 5 L, my beloved brethren

LISTENED (*see* LISTEN)
Gen 23:16 And Abraham l to Ephron
Gen 30:17 And God l to Leah, and she
Gen 30:22 God l to her and opened her
Gen 37:27 And his brothers l
Num 21: 3 the LORD l to the voice of
Deut 9:19 But the LORD l to me at that
Deut 13:18 because you have l to the
Deut 18:14 dispossess l to soothsayers
Judg 13: 9 God l to the voice of Manoah,
1Ki 20:25 he l to their voice and did so
2Ki 13: 4 LORD, and the LORD l to him
2Ch 24:17 And the king l to them
2Ch 30:20 the LORD l to Hezekiah and
Job 29:21 Men l to me and waited, and
Job 32:11 I l to your reasonings, while
Is 21: 7 he l diligently with great
Jer 8: 6 I l and heard, but they do not
Jer 25: 3 speaking, but you have not l
Jer 25: 4 them, but you have not l nor
Jer 25: 7 Yet you have not l to Me,"
Jer 32:33 them, yet they have not l to
Ezek 3: 6 they would have l to you
Mal 3:16 to one another, and the LORD l
Acts 15:12 and l to Barnabas and Paul
Acts 22:22 they l to him until this word
Acts 27:21 Men, you should have l to me

LISTENING (*see* LISTEN)
Gen 18:10 Sarah was l in the tent door
Gen 27: 5 Now Rebekah was l when Isaac
2Sa 20:17 And he answered, "I am l."
Job 9:16 that He was l to my voice
Prov 19:27 Cease l to instruction, my
Luke 2:46 both l to them and asking them
Acts 16:25 the prisoners were l to them

LISTENS (*see* LISTEN)
Prov 1:33 but whoever l to me will
Prov 8:34 is the man who l to me,
Prov 17: 4 a liar l eagerly to a
Jer 16:12 heart, so that no one l to Me

LISTING
Ezra 2:62 These sought their l among
Neh 7:64 These sought their l among

LISTLESS
Job 23: 2 my hand is l because of my

LIT (*see* LIGHT)
Ex 40:25 he l the lamps before the
Ps 77:18 The lightnings l up the world
Luke 8:16 No one, when he has l a lamp
Luke 11:33 No one, when he has l a lamp

LITERATE
Is 29:11 men deliver to one who is l
Is 29:12 and he says, I am not l."

LITERATURE
Dan 1: 4 and l of the Chaldeans
Dan 1:17 knowledge and skill in all l

LITTERS
Is 66:20 horses and in chariots and in l

LITTLE
Gen 18: 4 Please let a l water be
Gen 19:20 to flee to, and it is a l one
Gen 19:20 there (is it not a l one
Gen 24:17 Please let me drink a l water
Gen 24:43 Please give me a l water from
Gen 30:30 you had before I came was l
Gen 34:29 All their l ones and their
Gen 35:16 And when there was but a l
Gen 43: 2 Go back, buy us a l food
Gen 43: 8 we and you and also our l ones
Gen 43:11 a l balm and a l honey,
Gen 44:25 Go back and buy us a l food
Gen 45:19 land of Egypt for your l ones
Gen 46: 5 father Jacob, their l ones
Gen 47:24 and as food for your l ones
Gen 48: 7 way, when there was but a l
Gen 50: 8 Only their l ones, their
Gen 50:21 for you and your l ones
Ex 10:10 I let you and your l ones go
Ex 10:24 Let your l ones also go with
Ex 16:18 he who gathered l had no lack
Ex 23:30 L by l I will drive them
Lev 11:17 the l owl, the fisher owl,
Num 14:31 But your l ones, whom you
Num 16:27 sons, and their l children
Num 31: 9 captive, with their l ones
Num 31:17 every male among the l ones
Num 32:16 and cities for our l ones
Num 32:17 our l ones will dwell in the
Num 32:24 Build cities for your l ones
Num 32:26 Our l ones, our wives, our
Deut 1:39 Moreover your l ones and your
Deut 2:34 and l ones of every city
Deut 3:19 But your wives, your l ones
Deut 7:22 before you l by l
Deut 14:16 the l owl, the screech owl,
Deut 20:14 the l ones, the livestock, and
Deut 28:38 the field and gather but l in
Deut 29:11 your l ones and your wives
Deut 31:12 l ones, and the stranger who
Josh 1:14 Your wives, your l ones, and
Josh 8:35 the l ones, and the strangers
Judg 4:19 give me a l water to drink
Judg 18:21 departed, and put the l ones
Ruth 2: 7 she rested a l in the house
1Sa 2:19 used to make him a l robe
1Sa 14:29 I tasted a l of this honey
1Sa 14:43 I only tasted a l honey with
1Sa 15:17 When you were l in your own
1Sa 20:35 and a l lad was with him
1Sa 22:15 of all this, l or much
1Sa 25:36 l or much, until morning
2Sa 12: 3 except one l ewe lamb which
2Sa 12: 8 And if that had been too l
2Sa 15:22 all the l ones who were with
2Sa 16: 1 When David was a l past the
2Sa 19:36 Your servant will go a l way
1Ki 3: 7 David, but I am a l child
1Ki 11:17 Hadad was still a l child
1Ki 12:10 My l finger shall be thicker
1Ki 17:10 bring me a l water in a cup
1Ki 17:12 in a bin, and a l oil in a jar
1Ki 20:27 like two l flocks of goats
2Ki 5:14 like the flesh of a l child
2Ki 10:18 Ahab served Baal a l, but
2Ki 19:26 their inhabitants had l power
2Ch 10:10 My l finger shall be thicker
2Ch 20:13 all Judah, with their l ones
2Ch 31:18 their l ones and their wives,
Ezra 8:21 us and our l ones and all our
Ezra 9: 8 now for a l while grace has
Esth 3:13 l children and women, in one
Esth 8:11 both l children and women, and
Job 10:20 that I may take a l comfort
Job 21:11 their l ones like a flock
Job 24:24 are exalted for a l while
Job 36: 2 Bear with me a l, and I will
Ps 2:12 His wrath is kindled but a l
Ps 8: 5 him a l lower than the angels
Ps 37:10 For yet a l while and the
Ps 37:16 A l that a righteous man has
Ps 65:12 the l hills rejoice on every
Ps 68:27 There is l Benjamin, their
Ps 72: 3 the l hills, by righteousness
Ps 114: 4 rams, The l hills like lambs
Ps 114: 6 O l hills, like lambs
Ps 137: 9 dashes Your l ones against
Prov 6:10 A l sleep, a l slumber,
Prov 6:10 a l folding of the hands to
Prov 10:20 of the wicked is worth l
Prov 15:16 Better is a l with the fear
Prov 16: 8 Better is a l with
Prov 24:33 a l sleep, a l slumber,
Prov 24:33 a l folding of the hands to
Prov 30:24 which are l on the earth, but
Eccl 5:12 whether he eats l or much
Eccl 9:14 There was a l city with few
Eccl 10: 1 so does a l folly to one
Song 1: 8 feed your l goats beside the
Song 2:15 the l foxes that spoil the
Song 8: 8 We have a l sister, and she
Is 10:25 For yet a very l while and the
Is 11: 6 a l child shall lead them
Is 26:20 for a l moment, until the
Is 28:10 here a l, there a l
Is 28:13 here a l, there a l
Is 29:17 Is it not yet a very l while
Is 37:27 their inhabitants had l power
Is 40:15 the isles as a very l thing
Is 54: 8 With a l wrath I hid My face
Is 60:22 A l one shall become a
Is 63:18 possessed it but a l while
Jer 48: 4 her l ones have caused a cry
Jer 51:33 yet a l while and the time of
Ezek 9: 6 and l children and women
Ezek 11:16 yet I shall be a l sanctuary
Ezek 16:47 but, as if that were too l
Ezek 34:18 Is it too l for you to have
Dan 7: 8 a l one, coming up among them
Dan 8: 9 out of one of them came a l
Dan 11:34 shall be aided with a l help
Hos 1: 4 for in a l while I will
Hos 8:10 and they shall sorrow a l,
Amos 6:11 and the l house into pieces
Mic 5: 2 though you are l among the
Hag 1: 6 have sown much, and bring in l
Hag 1: 9 much, but indeed it came to l
Hag 2: 6 Once more (it is a l while) I
Zech 1:15 for I was a l angry, and they
Zech 13: 7 My hand against the l ones
Matt 6:30 clothe you, O you of l faith
Matt 8:26 you fearful, O you of l faith
Matt 10:42 l ones only a cup of cold
Matt 14:31 O you of l faith, why did you
Matt 15:26 and throw it to the l dogs
Matt 15:27 yet even the l dogs eat the
Matt 15:34 Seven, and a few l fish
Matt 16: 8 O you of l faith, why do you
Matt 18: 2 Jesus called a l child to Him
Matt 18: 3 and become as l children, you
Matt 18: 4 humbles himself as this l
Matt 18: 5 whoever receives one l child
Matt 18: 6 l ones who believe in Me to
Matt 18:10 despise one of these l ones
Matt 18:14 of these l ones should perish
Matt 19:13 Then l children were brought
Matt 19:14 Let the l children come to Me
Matt 26:39 He went a l farther and fell
Mark 1:19 gone a l farther from there
Mark 4:36 other l boats were also with
Mark 5:23 My l daughter lies at the
Mark 5:41 L girl, I say to you, arise
Mark 7:27 and throw it to the l dogs
Mark 7:28 yet even the l dogs under the
Mark 9:36 Then He took a l child and set
Mark 9:37 these l children in My name
Mark 9:42 l ones who believe in Me to
Mark 10:14 Let the l children come to Me
Mark 10:15 as a l child will by no means
Mark 14:35 He went a l farther, and fell
Mark 14:70 a l later those who stood by
Luke 5: 3 to put out a l from the land

Luke 7:47 But to whom l is forgiven
Luke 7:47 is forgiven, the same loves l
Luke 8:54 saying, "L girl, arise
Luke 9:47 their heart, took a l child
Luke 9:48 Whoever receives this l child
Luke 12:28 clothe you, O you of l faith
Luke 12:32 fear, l flock, for it is your
Luke 17: 2 offend one of these l ones
Luke 18:16 Let the l children come to Me
Luke 18:17 as a l child will by no means
Luke 19:17 you were faithful in a very l
Luke 22:58 after a l while another saw
John 6: 7 one of them may have a l
John 7:33 be with you a l while longer
John 12:35 A l while longer the light is
John 13:33 L children, I shall be with
John 13:33 be with you a l while longer
John 14:19 A l while longer and the world
John 16:16 A l while, and you will not
John 16:16 and again a l while, and you
John 16:17 A l while, and you will not
John 16:17 and again a l while, and you
John 16:18 that He says, 'A l while'
John 16:19 A l while, and you will not
John 16:19 and again a l while, and you
John 21: 8 l boat (for they were not far
Acts 5:34 outside for a l while
Acts 20:12 they were not a l comforted
Acts 27:28 they had gone a l farther
1Co 5: 6 Do you not know that a l
2Co 8:15 he who gathered l had no lack
2Co 11: 1 bear with me in a l folly
2Co 11:16 that I also may boast a l
Gal 4:19 My l children, for whom I
Gal 5: 9 A l leaven leavens the whole
1Ti 4: 8 bodily exercise profits a l
1Ti 5:23 but use a l wine for your
Heb 2: 7 You made him a l lower than
Heb 2: 9 who was made a l lower than
Heb 10:37 For yet a l while, And He who
Jas 3: 5 so the tongue is a l member
Jas 3: 5 a forest a l fire kindles
Jas 4:14 that appears for a l time
1Pe 1: 6 though now for a l while
1Jn 2: 1 My l children, these things I
1Jn 2:12 l children, because your sins
1Jn 2:13 l children, because you have
1Jn 2:18 L children, it is the last
1Jn 2:28 l children, abide in Him,
1Jn 3: 7 L children, let no one
1Jn 3:18 My l children, let us not
1Jn 4: 4 l children, and have overcome
1Jn 5:21 L children, keep yourselves
Rev 3: 8 for you have a l strength
Rev 6:11 should rest a l while longer
Rev 10: 2 he had a l book open in his
Rev 10: 8 take the l book which is open
Rev 10: 9 Give me the l book
Rev 10:10 I took the l book out of the
Rev 20: 3 be released for a l while

LIVE (*see* LIFE, LIVED, LIVES, LIVING)
Gen 3:22 life, and eat, and l forever"
Gen 12:12 me, but they will let you l
Gen 12:13 that I may l because of you
Gen 17:18 Ishmael might l before You
Gen 19:20 and my soul shall l
Gen 20: 7 pray for you and you shall l
Gen 27:40 By your sword you shall l
Gen 31:32 your gods, do not let him l
Gen 42: 2 for us there, that we may l
Gen 42:18 Do this and l, for I fear God
Gen 43: 8 arise and go, that we may l
Gen 45: 3 does my father still l
Gen 47:19 give us seed, that we may l
Ex 1:16 a daughter, then she shall l
Ex 2:21 was content to l with the man
Ex 19:13 man or beast, he shall not l
Ex 21:35 then they shall sell the l ox
Ex 22:18 not permit a sorceress to l
Ex 33:20 for no man shall see Me, and l
Lev 16:20 he shall bring the l goat
Lev 16:21 on the head of the l goat
Lev 18: 5 man does, he shall l by them
Lev 25:35 that he may l with you
Lev 25:36 your brother may l with you
Num 4:19 to them, that they may l and
Num 14:21 but truly, as I l, all the
Num 14:28 Say to them, 'As I l,' says
Num 21: 8 when he looks at it, shall l
Num 22:33 you by now, and let her l
Num 24:23 Who shall l when God does
Deut 2: 4 of Esau, who l in Seir
Deut 4: 1 to observe, that you may l
Deut 4:10 the days they l on the earth
Deut 4:33 fire, as you have heard, and l
Deut 4:42 of these cities he might l
Deut 5:33 commanded you, that you may l
Deut 8: 1 to observe, that you may l
Deut 8: 3 shall not l by bread alone
Deut 12: 1 days that you l on the earth
Deut 12:19 as long as you l in your land
Deut 16:20 just, that you may l and
Deut 19: 4 flees there, that he may l
Deut 19: 5 to one of these cities and l
Deut 30: 6 all your soul, that you may l
Deut 30:16 His judgments, that you may l
Deut 30:19 you and your descendants may l
Deut 31:13 your God as long as you l in
Deut 32:40 and say, "As I l forever,
Deut 33: 6 Let Reuben l, and not die, nor
Josh 6:17 Only Rahab the harlot shall l
Josh 9:15 with them to let them l
Josh 9:20 We will let them l, lest
Josh 9:21 Let them l, but let them be
Judg 8:19 lives, if you had let them l
1Sa 10:24 and said, Long l the king
1Sa 20:14 of the LORD while I still l
2Sa 1:10 not l after he had fallen
2Sa 11:11 As you l, and as your soul
2Sa 12:22 to me, that the child may l
2Sa 15:21 As you l, my lord the king,
2Sa 16:16 to Absalom, "Long l the king
2Sa 16:16 Long l the king
2Sa 19:34 How long have I to l, that I
1Ki 1:25 say, 'Long l King Adonijah
1Ki 1:31 my lord King David l forever
1Ki 1:34 and say, 'Long l King Solomon
1Ki 1:39 said, "Long l King Solomon
1Ki 8:40 l in the land which You gave
1Ki 20:32 says, 'Please let me l
2Ki 4: 7 and your sons l on the rest
2Ki 7: 4 keep us alive, we shall l
2Ki 10:19 is missing shall not l
2Ki 11:12 and said, "Long l the king
2Ki 18:32 and honey, that you may l and
2Ki 20: 1 for you shall die, and not l
2Ch 6:31 Your ways as long as they l
2Ch 23:11 and said, "Long l the king
Neh 2: 3 May the king l forever
Neh 5: 2 them, that we may eat and l
Neh 9:29 man does, he shall l by them
Esth 4:11 golden scepter, that he may l
Job 7:16 I would not l forever
Job 14:14 a man dies, shall he l again
Job 21: 7 Why do the wicked l and
Job 27: 6 reproach me as long as I l
Job 30: 6 They had to l in the clefts
Ps 22:26 Let your heart l forever
Ps 49: 9 continue to l eternally, And
Ps 55:23 not l out half their days
Ps 63: 4 I will bless You while I l
Ps 69:32 seek God, your hearts shall l
Ps 72:15 And He shall l
Ps 89:48 What man can l and not see
Ps 104:33 to the LORD as long as I l
Ps 116: 2 call upon Him as long as I l
Ps 118:17 I shall not die, but l, And
Ps 119:17 Your servant, That I may l
Ps 119:77 come to me, that I may l
Ps 119:116 to Your word, that I may l
Ps 119:144 understanding, and I shall l
Ps 119:175 Let my soul l, and it shall
Ps 146: 2 While I l I will praise the
Prov 4: 4 keep my commands, and l
Prov 7: 2 Keep my commands and l, and
Prov 9: 6 Forsake foolishness and l, and
Prov 15:27 he who hates bribes will l
Eccl 9: 3 in their hearts while they l
Eccl 9: 9 L joyfully with the wife whom
Is 6: 6 having in his hand a l coal
Is 26:14 are dead, they will not l
Is 26:19 Your dead shall l
Is 38: 1 for you shall die and not l
Is 38:16 O LORD, by these things men l
Is 38:16 will restore me and make me l
Is 49:18 As I l," says the LORD
Is 55: 3 Hear, and your soul shall l
Is 65:20 from there l but a few days
Jer 21: 9 who besiege you, he shall l
Jer 22:24 As I l," says the LORD
Jer 27:12 serve him and his people, and l
Jer 27:17 the king of Babylon, and l
Jer 35: 7 that you may l many days in
Jer 38: 2 over to the Chaldeans shall l
Jer 38: 2 a prize to him, and he shall l
Jer 38:17 then your soul shall l
Jer 38:17 and you and your house shall l
Jer 38:20 you, and your soul shall l
Jer 46:18 As I l," says the King,
Lam 4:20 we shall l among the nations
Ezek 3:21 he shall surely l because he
Ezek 5:11 Therefore, as I l,' says the
Ezek 13:19 people alive who should not l
Ezek 14:16 three men were in it, as I l
Ezek 14:18 three men were in it, as I l
Ezek 14:20 and Job were in it, as I l
Ezek 16: 6 said to you in your blood, 'L
Ezek 16: 6 said to you in your blood, 'L
Ezek 16:48 As I l," says the Lord GOD,
Ezek 17:16 As I l,' says the Lord GOD
Ezek 17:19 As I l, surely My oath which
Ezek 18: 3 As I l," says the Lord GOD,
Ezek 18: 9 he shall surely l
Ezek 18:13 shall he then l
Ezek 18:13 He shall not l
Ezek 18:17 he shall surely l
Ezek 18:19 done them, he shall surely l
Ezek 18:21 and right, he shall surely l
Ezek 18:22 which he has done, he shall l
Ezek 18:23 turn from his ways and l
Ezek 18:24 wicked man does, shall he l
Ezek 18:28 committed, he shall surely l
Ezek 18:32 Therefore turn and l
Ezek 20: 3 As I l," says the Lord GOD,
Ezek 20:11 man does, he shall l by them
Ezek 20:13 man does, he shall l by them
Ezek 20:21 man does, he shall l by them'
Ezek 20:25 by which they could not l
Ezek 20:31 As I l," says the Lord GOD,
Ezek 20:33 As I l," says the Lord GOD,
Ezek 33:10 in them, how can we then l
Ezek 33:11 As I l,' says the Lord GOD
Ezek 33:11 wicked turn from his way and l
Ezek 33:12 be able to l because of his
Ezek 33:13 that he shall surely l, but
Ezek 33:15 iniquity, he shall surely l
Ezek 33:16 he shall surely l
Ezek 33:19 he shall l because of it
Ezek 33:27 As I l, surely those who are
Ezek 34: 8 as I l," says the Lord GOD,
Ezek 35: 6 therefore, as I l," says the
Ezek 35:11 therefore, as I l," says the
Ezek 37: 3 Son of man, can these bones l
Ezek 37: 5 into you, and you shall l
Ezek 37: 6 and you shall l
Ezek 37: 9 these slain, that they may l
Ezek 37:14 Spirit in you, and you shall l
Ezek 39: 6 on those who l in security in
Ezek 47: 9 the rivers go, will l
Ezek 47: 9 everything will l wherever
Dan 2: 4 Aramaic, "O king, l forever
Dan 3: 9 O king, l forever
Dan 5:10 saying, "O king, l forever
Dan 6: 6 King Darius, l forever
Dan 6:21 the king, "O king, l forever
Hos 6: 2 that we may l in His sight
Amos 5: 4 Seek Me and l
Amos 5: 6 Seek the LORD and l, lest He
Amos 5:14 and not evil, that you may l
Jon 4: 3 for me to die than to l
Jon 4: 8 for me to die than to l
Hab 2: 4 the just shall l by his faith
Zeph 2: 9 Therefore, as I l," says the
Zech 1: 5 prophets, do they l forever
Zech 10: 9 they shall l, together with
Zech 13: 3 say to him, 'You shall not l
Matt 4: 4 shall not l by bread alone
Matt 9:18 hand on her and she will l
Mark 5:23 may be healed, and she will l
Luke 4: 4 shall not l by bread alone
Luke 7:25 l in luxury are in kings'
Luke 8:27 nor did he l in a house but
Luke 10:28 do this and you will l
Luke 20:38 the living, for all l to Him
John 5:25 and those who hear will l
John 6:51 this bread, he will l forever
John 6:57 I l because of the Father, so
John 6:57 on Me will l because of Me
John 6:58 this bread will l forever
John 11:25 though he may die, he shall l

John 14:19 Because I l, you will l
Acts 1:20 and let no one l in it'
Acts 7:19 so that they might not l
Acts 17:28 for in Him we l and move and
Acts 22:22 earth, for he is not fit to l
Acts 25:24 was not fit to l any longer
Acts 28: 4 justice does not allow to l
Rom 1:17 The just shall l by faith
Rom 6: 2 to sin l any longer in it
Rom 6: 8 that we shall also l with Him
Rom 8: 5 For those who l according to
Rom 8: 5 but those who l according to
Rom 8:12 to l according to the flesh
Rom 8:13 For if you l according to the
Rom 8:13 deeds of the body, you will l
Rom 10: 5 those things shall l by them
Rom 12:18 you, l peaceably with all men
Rom 14: 8 if we l, we l to the Lord
Rom 14: 8 whether we l or die, we are
Rom 14:11 As I l, says the LORD, every
1Co 7:12 she is willing to l with him
1Co 7:13 he is willing to l with her
1Co 8: 6 things, and through whom we l
1Co 9:14 should l from the gospel
2Co 4:11 For we who l are always
2Co 5:15 who l should l no longer for
2Co 6: 9 as dying, and behold we l
2Co 7: 3 die together and to l together
2Co 13: 4 but we shall l with Him by
2Co 13:11 be of one mind, l in peace
Gal 2:14 l in the manner of Gentiles
Gal 2:14 compel Gentiles to l as Jews
Gal 2:19 the law that I might l to God
Gal 2:20 it is no longer I who l, but
Gal 2:20 the life which I now l in the
Gal 2:20 I now l in the flesh I l
Gal 3:11 The just shall l by faith
Gal 3:12 who does them shall l by them
Gal 5:25 If we l in the Spirit, let us
Eph 6: 3 you may l long on the earth
Phil 1:21 to l is Christ, and to die is
Phil 1:22 But if I l on in the flesh,
1Th 3: 8 For now we l, if you stand
1Th 5:10 we should l together with Him
2Ti 2:11 Him, we shall also l with Him
2Ti 3:12 all who desire to l godly in
Tit 2:12 lusts, we should l soberly
Heb 10:38 Now the just shall l by faith
Heb 12: 9 to the Father of spirits and l
Heb 13:18 desiring to l honorably
Jas 4:15 If the Lord wills, we shall l
1Pe 2:24 might l for righteousness
1Pe 4: 2 that he no longer should l
1Pe 4: 6 but l according to God in the
2Pe 2: 6 who afterward would l ungodly
2Pe 2:18 from those who l in error
1Jn 4: 9 that we might l through Him
Rev 20: 5 l again until the thousand

LIVED (*see* LIVE)
Gen 5: 3 Adam l one hundred and thirty
Gen 5: 5 that Adam l were nine hundred
Gen 5: 6 Seth l one hundred and five
Gen 5: 7 Seth l eight hundred and seven
Gen 5: 9 Enosh l ninety years, and
Gen 5:10 Enosh l eight hundred and
Gen 5:12 Cainan l seventy years, and
Gen 5:13 Cainan l eight hundred and
Gen 5:15 Mahalaleel l sixty-five years
Gen 5:16 Mahalaleel l eight hundred and
Gen 5:18 Jared l one hundred and
Gen 5:19 Jared l eight hundred years,
Gen 5:21 Enoch l sixty-five years, and
Gen 5:25 Methuselah l one hundred and
Gen 5:26 Methuselah l seven hundred and
Gen 5:28 Lamech l one hundred and
Gen 5:30 Lamech l five hundred and
Gen 9:28 Noah l after the flood three
Gen 11:11 Shem l five hundred years, and
Gen 11:12 Arphaxad l thirty-five years,
Gen 11:13 Arphaxad l four hundred and
Gen 11:14 Salah l thirty years, and
Gen 11:15 Salah l four hundred and three
Gen 11:16 Eber l thirty-four years, and
Gen 11:17 Eber l four hundred and thirty
Gen 11:18 Peleg l thirty years, and
Gen 11:19 Peleg l two hundred and nine
Gen 11:20 Reu l thirty-two years, and
Gen 11:21 Reu l two hundred and seven
Gen 11:22 Serug l thirty years, and
Gen 11:23 Serug l two hundred years, and
Gen 11:24 Nahor l twenty-nine years, and
Gen 11:25 Terah, Nahor l one hundred and
Gen 11:26 Now Terah l seventy years, and
Gen 23: 1 Sarah l one hundred and
Gen 25: 7 of Abraham's life which he l
Gen 47:28 Jacob l in the land of Egypt
Gen 50:22 Joseph l one hundred and ten
Ex 12:40 l in Egypt was four hundred
Num 21: 9 at the bronze serpent, he l
Deut 5:26 of the fire, as we have, and l
Judg 17:12 and l in the house of Micah
2Sa 19: 6 that if Absalom had l and all
1Ki 12: 6 Solomon while he still l, and
2Ki 14:17 l fifteen years after the
1Ch 4:40 some Hamites formerly l there
1Ch 9:16 who l in the villages of the
2Ch 10: 6 Solomon while he still l,
2Ch 25:25 l fifteen years after the
2Ch 26: 7 Arabians who l in Gur Baal
Neh 12:26 These l in the days of
Job 42:16 After this Job l one hundred
Ezek 37:10 came into them, and they l
Matt 23:30 If we had l in the days of
Luke 2:36 had l with a husband seven
Acts 20:18 manner I always l among you
Acts 23: 1 I have l in all good
Acts 26: 5 our religion I l a Pharisee
Rom 14: 9 l again, that He might be
Col 3: 7 walked when you l in them
Jas 5: 5 You have l on the earth in
Rev 13:14 was wounded by the sword and l
Rev 18: 7 l luxuriously, in the same
Rev 18: 9 l luxuriously with her will
Rev 20: 4 And they l and reigned with

LIVELIHOOD
Mark 12:44 all that she had, her whole l
Luke 8:43 spent all her l on physicians
Luke 15:12 So he divided to them his l
Luke 15:30 devoured your l with harlots
Luke 21: 4 put in all the l that she had

LIVELY
Ex 1:19 for they are l and give birth

LIVER
Ex 29:13 fatty lobe attached to the l
Ex 29:22 fatty lobe attached to the l
Lev 3: 4 to the l above the kidneys
Lev 3:10 to the l above the kidneys
Lev 3:15 to the l above the kidneys
Lev 4: 9 to the l above the kidneys
Lev 7: 4 to the l above the kidneys
Lev 8:16 fatty lobe attached to the l
Lev 8:25 fatty lobe attached to the l
Lev 9:10 the l of the sin offering he
Lev 9:19 fatty lobe attached to the l
Prov 7:23 till an arrow struck his l
Ezek 21:21 the images, he looks at the l

LIVES (*see* LIVE)
Gen 9: 3 that l shall be food for you
Gen 45: 7 to save your l by a great
Gen 47:25 You have saved our l
Ex 1:14 they made their l bitter with
Deut 5:24 yet he still l
Deut 8: 3 but man l by every word that
Josh 2:13 and deliver our l from death
Josh 2:14 Our l for yours, if none of
Josh 9:24 for our l because of you, and
Judg 5:18 their l to the point of death
Judg 8:19 As the LORD l, if you had let
Judg 18:25 with the l of your household
Ruth 3:13 duty for you, as the LORD l
1Sa 1:26 As your soul l, my lord, I am
1Sa 1:28 as long as he l he shall be
1Sa 14:39 For as the LORD l, who saves
1Sa 14:45 As the LORD l, not one hair
1Sa 17:55 As your soul l, O king, I do
1Sa 19: 6 As the LORD l, he shall not
1Sa 20: 3 the LORD l and as your soul l
1Sa 20:21 then, as the LORD l, there is
1Sa 20:31 son of Jesse l on the earth
1Sa 25: 6 to him who l in prosperity
1Sa 25:26 my lord, as the LORD l and as
1Sa 25:26 LORD l and as your soul l
1Sa 25:29 and the l of your enemies He
1Sa 25:34 as the LORD God of Israel l
1Sa 26:10 As the LORD l, the LORD shall
1Sa 26:16 As the LORD l, you are worthy
1Sa 28:10 As the LORD l, no punishment
1Sa 29: 6 Surely, as the LORD l, you
2Sa 1:23 and pleasant in their l, and in
2Sa 2:27 As God l, unless you had
2Sa 4: 9 As the LORD l, who has
2Sa 11:11 you live, and as your soul l
2Sa 12: 5 As the LORD l, the man who
2Sa 14:11 As the LORD l, not one hair
2Sa 15:21 As the LORD l, and as my lord
2Sa 15:21 and as my lord the king l
2Sa 19: 5 life, the l of your sons and
2Sa 19: 5 the l of your wives and the
2Sa 19: 5 the l of your concubines,
2Sa 22:47 The LORD l!
2Sa 23:17 went in jeopardy of their l
1Ki 1:29 As the LORD l, who has
1Ki 2:24 Now therefore, as the LORD l
1Ki 3:23 says, 'This is my son, who l
1Ki 17: 1 As the LORD God of Israel l
1Ki 17:12 As the LORD your God l, I do
1Ki 17:23 See, your son l
1Ki 18:10 As the LORD your God l, there
1Ki 18:15 As the LORD of hosts l,
1Ki 21:18 of Israel, who l in Samaria
1Ki 22:14 As the LORD l, whatever the
2Ki 2: 2 LORD l, and as your soul l
2Ki 2: 4 LORD l, and as your soul l
2Ki 2: 6 LORD l, and as your soul l
2Ki 3:14 As the LORD of hosts l,
2Ki 4:30 the LORD l, and as your soul l
2Ki 5:16 As the LORD l, before whom I
2Ki 5:20 but as the LORD l, I will run
2Ki 7: 7 and they fled for their l
1Ch 11:19 have put their l in jeopardy
1Ch 11:19 of their l they brought it
2Ch 18:13 As the LORD l, whatever my
Esth 8:11 together and protect their l
Esth 9:16 together and protected their l
Job 19:25 For I know that my Redeemer l
Job 27: 2 As God l, who has taken away
Job 31:39 its owners to lose their l
Ps 18:46 The LORD l
Ps 49:18 Though while he l he blesses
Ps 90:10 The days of our l are seventy
Prov 1:18 lurk secretly for their own l
Eccl 2: 3 all the days of their l
Eccl 3:12 and to do good in their l
Eccl 6: 3 l many years, so that the
Eccl 6: 6 even if he l a thousand years
Eccl 11: 8 But if a man l many years
Jer 2:34 the l of the poor innocents
Jer 4: 2 you shall swear, 'The LORD l
Jer 5: 2 they say, 'As the LORD l,'
Jer 12:16 by My name, 'As the LORD l
Jer 16:14 The LORD l who brought up
Jer 16:15 The LORD l who brought up
Jer 19: 7 of those who seek their l
Jer 19: 9 those who seek their l shall
Jer 23: 7 As the LORD l who brought up
Jer 23: 8 As the LORD l who brought up
Jer 38:16 As the LORD l, who made our
Jer 44:26 The Lord GOD l
Jer 46:26 of those who seek their l
Jer 48: 6 Flee, save your l
Lam 5: 9 bread at the risk of our l
Ezek 7:13 himself who l in iniquity
Ezek 27:13 They bartered human l and
Dan 4:34 and honored Him who l forever
Dan 7:12 yet their l were prolonged
Dan 12: 7 and swore by Him who l forever
Hos 4:15 oath, saying, 'As the LORD l'
Amos 8:14 who say, 'As your god l, O
Amos 8:14 As the way of Beersheba l
Luke 9:56 men's l but to save them
John 4:50 Go your way; your son l."
John 4:51 Your son l
John 4:53 Your son l
John 11:26 And whoever l and believes in
Acts 15:26 l for the name of our Lord
Acts 27:10 cargo and ship, but also our l
Rom 6:10 l, He l to God.
Rom 7: 1 over a man as long as he l
Rom 7: 2 her husband as long as he l
Rom 7: 3 then if, while her husband l
Rom 14: 7 For none of us l to himself
1Co 7:39 law as long as her husband l
2Co 13: 4 yet He l by the power of God
Gal 2:20 who live, but Christ l in me
1Th 2: 8 of God, but also our own l
1Ti 5: 6 But she who l in pleasure is
1Ti 5: 6 pleasure is dead while she l
Heb 7: 8 it is witnessed that he l

Heb 7:25 Him, since He ever l to make
Heb 9:17 at all while the testator l
1Pe 1:23 the word of God which l and
1Jn 3:16 down our l for the brethren
Rev 1:18 I am He who l, and was dead,
Rev 4: 9 who l forever and ever,
Rev 4:10 and worship Him who l forever
Rev 5:14 worshiped Him who l forever
Rev 10: 6 and swore by Him who l forever
Rev 12:11 not love their l to the death
Rev 15: 7 wrath of God who l forever

LIVESTOCK
Gen 4:20 who dwell in tents and have l
Gen 13: 2 Abram was very rich in l, in
Gen 13: 7 the herdsmen of Abram's l
Gen 13: 7 and the herdsmen of Lot's l
Gen 30:29 how your l has been with me
Gen 30:41 the stronger l conceived,
Gen 30:41 eyes of the l in the gutters
Gen 31: 9 away the l of your father
Gen 31:18 And he carried away all his l
Gen 31:18 his acquired l which he had
Gen 33:14 which the l that go before me
Gen 33:17 and made booths for his l
Gen 34: 5 were with his l in the field
Gen 34:23 Will not their l, their
Gen 36: 7 them because of their l
Gen 46: 6 So they took their l and their
Gen 46:32 occupation has been to feed l
Gen 46:34 l from our youth even till
Gen 47: 6 them chief herdsmen over my l
Gen 47:16 Give your l, and I will give
Gen 47:16 give you bread for your l
Gen 47:17 brought their l to Joseph
Gen 47:17 for all their l that year
Gen 47:18 lord also has our herds of l
Ex 9: 4 between the l of Israel and
Ex 9: 4 of Israel and the l of Egypt
Ex 9: 6 and all the l of Egypt died
Ex 9: 6 but of the l of the children
Ex 9: 7 not even one of the l of the
Ex 9:19 send now and gather your l
Ex 9:20 and his l flee to the houses
Ex 9:21 and his l in the field
Ex 10:26 Our l also shall go with us
Ex 12:29 and all the firstborn of l
Ex 12:38 a great deal of l
Ex 17: 3 children and our l with thirst
Ex 34:19 male firstling among your l
Lev 1: 2 bring your offering of the l
Lev 5: 2 or the carcass of unclean l
Lev 19:19 You shall not let your l
Lev 25: 7 for your l and the animals
Lev 26:22 your children, destroy your l
Num 3:41 the l of the Levites instead
Num 3:41 l of the children of Israel
Num 3:45 the l of the Levites instead
Num 3:45 Levites instead of their l
Num 20:19 if I or my l drink any of
Num 31:30 and the sheep, from all the l
Num 32: 1 a very great multitude of l
Num 32: 1 the region was a place for l
Num 32: 4 of Israel, is a land for l
Num 32: 4 and your servants have l
Num 32:16 sheepfolds here for our l
Num 32:26 all our l will be there in
Deut 2:35 We took only the l as plunder
Deut 3: 7 But all the l and the spoil of
Deut 3:19 your l (I know that you have
Deut 3:19 l) shall stay in your cities
Deut 7:14 among you or among your l
Deut 11:15 in your fields for your l
Deut 13:15 all that is in it and its l
Deut 20:14 women, the little ones, the l
Deut 28:11 in the increase of your l
Deut 28:51 eat the increase of your l
Deut 30: 9 in the increase of your l
Josh 1:14 your l shall remain in the
Josh 8:27 Only the l and the spoil of
Josh 11:14 of these cities and the l, the
Josh 14: 4 common-lands for their l and
Josh 21: 2 their common-lands for our l
Josh 22: 8 your tents, with very much l
Judg 6: 5 would come up with their l
Judg 18:21 and put the little ones, the l
1Sa 23: 5 blow, and took away their l
1Sa 30:20 driven before those other l
1Ki 18: 5 will not have to kill any l
1Ch 5:21 Then they took away their l
2Ch 14:15 attacked the l enclosures
2Ch 26:10 many wells, for he had much l
2Ch 32:28 and stalls for all kinds of l
Ezra 1: 4 and gold, with goods and l,
Ezra 1: 6 and gold, with goods and l, and
Ezek 38:12 nations, who have acquired l
Ezek 38:13 and gold, to take away l and
Jon 4:11 and their left, and also much l
Hag 1:11 brings forth, on men and l
Zech 2: 4 multitude of men and l in it
John 4:12 as well as his sons and his l

LIVING (*see* LIVE)
Gen 1:20 an abundance of l creatures
Gen 1:21 every l thing that moves,
Gen 1:24 l creature according to its
Gen 1:28 over every l thing that moves
Gen 2: 7 and man became a l being
Gen 2:19 Adam called each l creature
Gen 3:20 she was the mother of all l
Gen 6:19 of every l thing of all flesh
Gen 7: 4 all l things that I have made
Gen 7:23 So He destroyed all l things
Gen 8: 1 Noah, and every l thing, and
Gen 8:17 Bring out with you every l
Gen 8:21 every l thing as I have done
Gen 9:10 with every l creature that is
Gen 9:12 every l creature that is with
Gen 9:15 every l creature of all flesh
Gen 9:16 every l creature of all flesh
Gen 25: 6 while he was still l he sent
Lev 11:10 move in the water or any l
Lev 11:46 every l creature that moves
Lev 14: 4 who is to be cleansed two l
Lev 14: 6 As for the l bird, he shall
Lev 14: 6 the l bird in the blood of
Lev 14: 7 shall let the l bird loose in
Lev 14:51 the l bird, and dip them in
Lev 14:52 the l bird, with the cedar
Lev 14:53 Then he shall let the l bird
Lev 20:25 or by any kind of l thing
Num 16:48 between the dead and the l
Deut 5:26 has heard the voice of the l
Deut 24: 6 he takes one's l in pledge
Josh 3:10 that the l God is among you
Josh 8:35 who were l among them
Ruth 2:20 His kindness to the l and the
1Sa 17:26 defy the armies of the l God
1Sa 17:36 the armies of the l God
1Sa 25:29 the l with the LORD your God
2Sa 20: 3 their death, l in widowhood
1Ki 3:22 But the l one is my son, and
1Ki 3:22 son, and the l one is my son
1Ki 3:23 one, and my son is the l one
1Ki 3:25 Divide the l child in two, and
1Ki 3:26 son was l spoke to the king
1Ki 3:26 my lord, give her the l child
1Ki 3:27 the first woman the l child
2Ki 19: 4 sent to reproach the l God
2Ki 19:16 sent to reproach the l God
Job 12:10 is the life of every l thing
Job 28:13 it found in the land of the l
Job 28:21 hidden from the eyes of all l
Job 30:23 the house appointed for all l
Ps 27:13 the LORD In the land of the l
Ps 42: 2 for God, for the l God
Ps 52: 5 you from the land of the l
Ps 56:13 God In the light of the l
Ps 58: 9 with a whirlwind, As in His l
Ps 66: 9 keeps our soul among the l
Ps 69:28 out of the book of the l, And
Ps 84: 2 flesh cry out for the l God
Ps 104:25 L things both small and great
Ps 116: 9 the LORD In the land of the l
Ps 142: 5 portion in the land of the l
Ps 143: 2 sight no one l is righteous
Ps 145:16 the desire of every l thing
Eccl 4: 2 more than the l who are still
Eccl 4:15 I saw all the l who walk
Eccl 6: 8 how to walk before the l
Eccl 7: 2 the l will take it to heart
Eccl 9: 4 to all the l there is hope
Eccl 9: 4 for a l dog is better than a
Eccl 9: 5 For the l know that they will
Song 4:15 gardens, a well of l waters
Is 4: 3 among the l in Jerusalem
Is 8:19 the dead on behalf of the l
Is 37: 4 sent to reproach the l God
Is 37:17 sent to reproach the l God
Is 38:11 the LORD in the land of the l
Is 38:19 The l, the l man, he
Is 53: 8 off from the land of the l
Jer 2:13 Me, the fountain of l waters
Jer 10:10 He is the l God and the
Jer 11:19 off from the land of the l
Jer 17:13 the fountain of l waters
Jer 23:36 the words of the l God, the
Lam 3:39 Why should a l man complain
Ezek 1: 5 likeness of four l creatures
Ezek 1:13 likeness of the l creatures
Ezek 1:13 forth among the l creatures
Ezek 1:14 the l creatures ran back and
Ezek 1:15 I looked at the l creatures
Ezek 1:15 each l creature with its four
Ezek 1:19 When the l creatures went,
Ezek 1:19 when the l creatures were
Ezek 1:20 them, for the spirit of the l
Ezek 1:21 them, for the spirit of the l
Ezek 1:22 the l creatures was like the
Ezek 3:13 noise of the wings of the l
Ezek 10:15 This was the l creature I saw
Ezek 10:17 of the l creature was in them
Ezek 10:20 This is the l creature I saw
Ezek 26:20 glory in the land of the l
Ezek 32:23 terror in the land of the l
Ezek 32:24 terror in the land of the l
Ezek 32:25 caused in the land of the l
Ezek 32:26 terror in the land of the l
Ezek 32:27 mighty in the land of the l
Ezek 32:32 terror in the land of the l
Ezek 47: 9 that every l thing that moves
Dan 2:30 more wisdom than anyone l
Dan 4:17 in order that the l may know
Dan 6:20 Daniel, servant of the l God
Dan 6:26 For He is the l God, and
Hos 1:10 You are the sons of the l God
Zech 14: 8 that l waters shall flow from
Matt 16:16 Christ, the Son of the l God
Matt 22:32 God of the dead, but of the l
Matt 26:63 I adjure You by the l God
Mark 12:27 dead, but the God of the l
Luke 2: 8 shepherds l out in the fields
Luke 15:13 possessions with prodigal l
Luke 20:38 God of the dead but of the l
Luke 24: 5 you seek the l among the dead
John 4:10 would have given you l water
John 4:11 then do You get that l water
John 6:51 I am the l bread which came
John 6:57 As the l Father sent Me, and I
John 6:69 Christ, the Son of the l God
John 7:38 will flow rivers of l water
Acts 7:38 the l oracles to give to us
Acts 10:42 by God to be Judge of the l
Acts 14:15 vain things to the l God, who
Rom 9:26 be called sons of the l God
Rom 12: 1 your bodies a l sacrifice
Rom 14: 9 of both the dead and the l
1Co 15:45 man Adam became a l being
2Co 3: 3 by the Spirit of the l God
2Co 6:16 are the temple of the l God
Col 2:20 as though l in the world, do
1Th 1: 9 God from idols to serve the l
1Ti 3:15 is the church of the l God
1Ti 4:10 because we trust in the l God
1Ti 6:17 riches but in the l God, who
2Ti 4: 1 Christ, who will judge the l
Tit 3: 3 l in malice and envy, hateful
Heb 3:12 in departing from the l God
Heb 4:12 For the word of God is l and
Heb 9:14 dead works to serve the l God
Heb 10:20 l way which He consecrated
Heb 10:31 into the hands of the l God
Heb 12:22 and to the city of the l God
1Pe 1: 3 again to a l hope through the
1Pe 2: 4 Coming to Him as to a l stone
1Pe 2: 5 as l stones, are being built
1Pe 4: 5 who is ready to judge the l
Rev 4: 6 were four l creatures full of
Rev 4: 7 The first l creature was like
Rev 4: 7 the second l creature like a
Rev 4: 7 the third l creature had a
Rev 4: 7 the fourth l creature was
Rev 4: 8 the four l creatures, each
Rev 4: 9 Whenever the l creatures give
Rev 5: 6 and of the four l creatures
Rev 5: 8 the four l creatures and the
Rev 5:11 the l creatures, and the
Rev 5:14 Then the four l creatures
Rev 6: 1 l creatures saying with a
Rev 6: 3 the second l creature saying
Rev 6: 5 the third l creature say
Rev 6: 6 the four l creatures saying

Rev 6: 7 the fourth l creature saying
Rev 7: 2 having the seal of the l God
Rev 7:11 the four l creatures, and fell
Rev 7:17 lead them to l fountains of
Rev 8: 9 a third of the l creatures in
Rev 14: 3 before the four l creatures
Rev 15: 7 Then one of the four l
Rev 16: 3 every l creature in the sea
Rev 19: 4 the four l creatures fell

LIZARD
Lev 11:29 the large l after its kind
Lev 11:30 the gecko, the monitor l
Lev 11:30 the sand reptile, the sand l

LO
Song 2:11 For l, the winter is past,
Matt 28:20 and l, I am with you always,
Luke 15:29 and said to his father, L

LOAD (*see* LOADED, LOADING, LOADS, UNLOAD)
Gen 45:17 L your beasts and depart
Jon 1: 5 the sea, to lighten the l
Luke 11:46 For you l men with burdens
Gal 6: 5 each one shall bear his own l

LOADED (*see* LOAD)
Gen 42:26 So they l their donkeys with
Gen 44:13 and each man l his donkey and
Gen 45:23 ten donkeys l with the good
Gen 45:23 female donkeys l with grain
1Sa 16:20 took a donkey l with bread
1Sa 25:18 of figs, and l them on donkeys
Neh 4:17 l themselves so that with one
Is 46: 1 Your carriages were heavily l
2Ti 3: 6 women l down with sins, led

LOADING (*see* LOAD)
Neh 13:15 l donkeys with wine, grapes,

LOADS (*see* LOAD)
Ps 68:19 Who daily l us with benefits,
Lam 5:13 staggered under l of wood
Hab 2: 6 to him who l himself with

LOAF (*see* LOAVES)
Ex 29:23 one l of bread, one cake made
Judg 7:13 a l of barley bread tumbled
2Sa 6:19 men, to everyone a l of bread
1Ch 16: 3 to everyone a l of bread
Mark 8:14 one l with them in the boat

LO-AMMI
Hos 1: 9 Call his name L, for you are

LOAN (*see* LEND)
1Sa 2:20 from this woman for the l

LOATHE (*see* LOATHED, LOATHES, LOATHING, LOATHSOME)
Ex 7:18 the Egyptians will l to drink
Job 7:16 I l my life
Ps 139:21 do I not l those who rise up
Ezek 6: 9 they will l themselves for
Ezek 20:43 you shall l yourselves in
Ezek 36:31 you will l yourselves in your

LOATHED (*see* LOATHE)
Jer 14:19 Has Your soul l Zion
Ezek 16: 5 when you yourself were l on
Ezek 16:45 who l their husbands and
Zech 11: 8 My soul l them, and their soul

LOATHES (*see* LOATHE)
Num 21: 5 our soul l this worthless
Job 10: 1 My soul l life
Prov 27: 7 soul l the honeycomb, but to

LOATHING (*see* LOATHE)
Ezek 16:45 l husband and children

LOATHSOME (*see* LOATHE)
Num 11:20 nostrils and becomes l to you
Job 6: 7 they are as l food to me
Prov 13: 5 lying, but a wicked man is l
Rev 16: 2 l sore came upon the men who

LOAVES (*see* LOAF)
Lev 23:17 l of two-tenths of an ephah
Judg 8: 5 Please give l of bread to the
1Sa 10: 3 carrying three l of bread
1Sa 10: 4 and give you two l of bread
1Sa 17:17 dried grain and these ten l
1Sa 21: 3 Give me five l of bread in my
1Sa 25:18 took two hundred l of bread
2Sa 16: 1 them two hundred l of bread
1Ki 14: 3 Also take with you ten l,
2Ki 4:42 twenty l of barley bread, and
Matt 14:17 We have here only five l and
Matt 14:19 And He took the five l and the
Matt 14:19 gave the l to the disciples
Matt 15:34 How many l do you have
Matt 15:36 And He took the seven l and the
Matt 16: 9 five l of the five thousand
Matt 16:10 Nor the seven l of the four
Mark 6:38 How many l do you have
Mark 6:41 when He had taken the five l
Mark 6:41 blessed and broke the l, and
Mark 6:44 l were about five thousand
Mark 6:52 not understood about the l
Mark 8: 5 How many l do you have
Mark 8: 6 And He took the seven l and
Mark 8:19 five l for the five thousand
Luke 9:13 We have no more than five l
Luke 9:16 Then He took the five l and
Luke 11: 5 him, 'Friend, lend me three l
John 6: 9 here who has five barley l
John 6:11 And Jesus took the l, and when
John 6:13 of the five barley l which
John 6:26 but because you ate of the l

LOBE
Ex 29:13 the fatty l attached to the
Ex 29:22 the fatty l attached to the
Lev 3: 4 the fatty l attached to the
Lev 3:10 the fatty l attached to the
Lev 3:15 the fatty l attached to the
Lev 4: 9 the fatty l attached to the
Lev 7: 4 the fatty l attached to the
Lev 8:16 the fatty l attached to the
Lev 8:25 the fatty l attached to the
Lev 9:10 the fatty l from the liver of
Lev 9:19 the fatty l attached to the

LOCK (*see* LOCKED, LOCKS)
Song 5: 5 on the handles of the l
Ezek 8: 3 and took me by a l of my hair

LOCKED (*see* LOCK)
Judg 3:23 room behind him and l them
Judg 3:24 of the upper room were l

LOCKS (*see* LOCK)
Num 6: 5 Then he shall let the l of
Judg 16:13 If you weave the seven l of
Judg 16:19 off the seven l of his head
Song 5: 2 my l with the drops of the
Song 5:11 his l are wavy, and black as a

LOCUST (*see* LOCUSTS)
Ex 10:19 There remained not one l in
Lev 11:22 the l after its kind, the
Lev 11:22 destroying l after its kind
Deut 28:38 for the l shall consume it
Job 39:20 Can you frighten him like a l
Ps 78:46 And their labor to the l
Ps 109:23 I am shaken off like a l
Joel 1: 4 What the chewing l left, the
Joel 1: 4 the swarming l has eaten
Joel 1: 4 what the swarming l left, the
Joel 1: 4 the crawling l has eaten
Joel 1: 4 and what the crawling l left
Joel 1: 4 the consuming l has eaten
Joel 2:25 that the swarming l has eaten
Joel 2:25 crawling l, the consuming l
Joel 2:25 and the chewing l
Amos 4: 9 trees, The l devoured them
Amos 7: 1 He formed l swarms at the
Nah 3:15 it will eat you up like a l
Nah 3:15 yourself many—like the l!
Nah 3:16 The l plunders and flies away

LOCUSTS (*see* LOCUST)
Ex 10: 4 bring l into your territory
Ex 10:12 the land of Egypt for the l
Ex 10:13 the east wind brought the l
Ex 10:14 the l went up over all the
Ex 10:14 had been no such l as they
Ex 10:19 wind, which took the l away
Deut 28:42 L shall consume all your
Judg 6: 5 coming in as numerous as l
Judg 7:12 the valley as numerous as l
1Ki 8:37 or mildew, l or grasshoppers
2Ch 6:28 or mildew, l or grasshoppers
2Ch 7:13 or command the l to devour
Ps 105:34 l came, Young l without
Prov 30:27 the l have no king, yet they
Is 33: 4 as the running to and fro of l
Jer 51:14 fill you with men, as with l
Jer 51:27 come up like the bristling l
Nah 3:15 like the swarming l
Nah 3:17 are like swarming l, and your
Matt 3: 4 and his food was l and wild
Mark 1: 6 around his waist, and he ate l
Rev 9: 3 smoke l came upon the earth
Rev 9: 7 the shape of the l was like

LOD (*see* LYDDA)
1Ch 8:12 built Ono and L with its towns
Ezra 2:33 the people of L, Hadid, and
Neh 7:37 the children of L, Hadid, and
Neh 11:35 in L, Ono, and the Valley of

LO DEBAR
2Sa 9: 4 the son of Ammiel, in L
2Sa 9: 5 the son of Ammiel, from L
2Sa 17:27 the son of Ammiel from L, and
Amos 6:13 you who rejoice over L, who

LODGE (*see* LODGED, LODGING)
Gen 24:23 father's house for us to l
Gen 24:25 and feed enough, and room to l
Num 22: 8 L here tonight, and I will
Josh 4: 3 place where you l tonight
Judg 19: 9 l here, that your heart may
Judg 19:11 of the Jebusites and l in it
Judg 19:15 there to go in to l in Gibeah
Ruth 1:16 wherever you l, I will l
1Ki 17:20 on the widow with whom I l
Job 31:32 had to l in the street, for I
Song 7:11 let us l in the villages
Is 21:13 forest in Arabia you will l
Jer 4:14 evil thoughts l within you
Zeph 2:14 the bittern shall l on the
Luke 9:12 towns and country, and l and get
Acts 21:16 with whom we were to l

LODGED (*see* LODGE)
Gen 32:13 So he l there that same night
Gen 32:21 but he himself l that night
Josh 2: 1 named Rahab, and l there
Josh 3: 1 l there before they crossed
Josh 4: 8 to the place where they l
Josh 6:11 the camp and l in the camp
Josh 8: 9 but Joshua l that night among
Judg 18: 2 house of Micah, and l there
Judg 19: 4 they ate and drank and l there
Judg 19: 7 so he l there again
1Ch 9:27 they l all around the house
1Ch 9:33 who l in the chambers, and
Neh 13:20 of all kinds of wares l
Is 1:21 righteousness l in it, but
Matt 21:17 to Bethany, and He l there
Acts 10:23 he invited them in and l them
1Ti 5:10 if she has l strangers, if

LODGING (*see* LODGE)
Josh 4: 3 leave them in the l place
Is 10:29 they have taken up l at Geba
Jer 9: 2 a l place for wayfaring men
Acts 10: 6 He is l with Simon, a tanner,
Acts 10:18 was Peter, was l there
Acts 10:32 He is l in the house of Simon
Acts 28:23 many came to him at his l

LOFTILY (*see* LOFTY)
Ps 73: 8 They speak l

LOFTINESS (*see* LOFTY)
Is 2:17 The l of man shall be bowed
Jer 48:29 exceedingly proud), of his l

LOFTY (*see* LOFTILY, LOFTINESS)
Job 22:12 highest stars, how l they are
Ps 131: 1 is not haughty, Nor my eyes l
Prov 24: 7 Wisdom is too l for a fool
Prov 30:13 oh, how l are their eyes
Is 2:11 The l looks of man shall be
Is 2:12 upon everything proud and l
Is 5:15 the eyes of the l shall be
Is 26: 5 who dwell on high, the l city
Is 57: 7 On a l and high mountain you
Is 57:15 L One Who inhabits eternity,

LOG (*see* LOGS)
Lev 14:10 offering, and one l of oil
Lev 14:12 the l of oil, and wave them as
Lev 14:15 take some of the l of oil
Lev 14:21 a grain offering, a l of oil,
Lev 14:24 the l of oil, and the priest

LOGS (*see* LOG)
1Ki 5: 8 the cedar and cypress l
1Ki 5:10 cypress l according to all
2Ch 2: 8 algum l from Lebanon, for I

Ezra 3: 7 Tyre to bring cedar l from

LOINS
Deut 33:11 strike the l of those who
1Ki 8:19 who shall come from your l
1Ki 18:46 and he girded up his l and ran
2Ch 6: 9 come forth from your own l
Ps 38: 7 For my l are full of
Ps 69:23 And make their l shake
Is 5:27 the belt on their l be loosed
Is 11: 5 shall be the belt of His l
Is 21: 3 Therefore my l are filled
Jer 30: 6 his l like a woman in labor
Jer 48:37 cuts, and on the l sackcloth
Lam 3:13 of His quiver to pierce my l
Ezek 29: 7 and made all their l shake
Heb 7: 5 come from the l of Abraham
Heb 7:10 in the l of his father when
1Pe 1:13 gird up the l of your mind

LOIS
2Ti 1: 5 first in your grandmother **L**

LONELY
Lam 1: 1 How l sits the city that was

LONG (*see* LONGED, LONGED-FOR, LONGER, LONGING, LONGS)
Gen 26: 8 he had been there a l time
Gen 31:30 l for your father's house
Gen 48:15 me all my life l to this day
Ex 10: 3 How l will you refuse to
Ex 10: 7 How l shall this man be a
Ex 16:28 How l do you refuse to keep
Ex 19:13 When the trumpet sounds l
Ex 19:19 of the trumpet sounded l and
Ex 20:12 that your days may be l upon
Ex 27: 1 of acacia wood, five cubits l
Ex 27: 9 hundred cubits l for one side
Ex 27:11 hangings one hundred cubits l
Ex 27:16 be a screen twenty cubits l
Ex 38: 9 linen, one hundred cubits l
Ex 38:11 were one hundred cubits l
Ex 38:14 gate were fifteen cubits l
Lev 18:19 l as she is in her customary
Lev 21:18 marred face or any limb too l
Lev 22:23 l or too short you may offer
Lev 26:34 as l as it lies desolate and
Lev 26:35 As l as it lies desolate it
Num 9:18 as l as the cloud stayed
Num 9:19 when the cloud continued l
Num 14:11 How l will these people
Num 14:11 how l will they not believe
Num 14:27 How l shall I bear with this
Num 20:15 and we dwelt in Egypt a l time
Num 24:22 How l until Asshur carries
Deut 1: 6 You have dwelt l enough at
Deut 2: 3 this mountain l enough
Deut 5:16 you, that your days may be l
Deut 12:19 as l as you live in your land
Deut 12:20 because you l to eat meat
Deut 14:24 the journey is too l for you
Deut 19: 6 him, because the way is l
Deut 20:19 besiege a city for a l time
Deut 28:32 longing for them all day l
Deut 31:13 as l as you live in the land
Deut 33:12 shelters him all the day l
Josh 6: 5 when they make a l blast with
Josh 9:13 because of the very l journey
Josh 11:18 Joshua made war a l time with
Josh 18: 3 How l will you neglect to go
Josh 23: 1 a l time after the LORD had
Josh 24: 7 in the wilderness a l time
Judg 5:28 is his chariot so l in coming
1Sa 1:14 How l will you be drunk
1Sa 1:28 as l as he lives he shall be
1Sa 7: 2 in Kirjath Jearim a l time
1Sa 10:24 and said, "L live the king
1Sa 16: 1 How l will you mourn for Saul
1Sa 20:31 For as l as the son of Jesse
1Sa 25:15 as l as we accompanied them
1Sa 29: 8 as l as I have been with you
2Sa 2:26 How l will it be then until
2Sa 3: 1 Now there was a l war between
2Sa 14: 2 a l time for the dead
2Sa 16:16 to Absalom, "L live the king
2Sa 19:34 How l have I to live, that I
1Ki 1:25 say, "L live King Adonijah
1Ki 1:34 and say, "L live King Solomon
1Ki 1:39 said, "L live King Solomon
1Ki 3:11 have not asked l life for
1Ki 6: 3 l across the breadth of the
1Ki 6:17 sanctuary was forty cubits l
1Ki 6:20 sanctuary was twenty cubits l
1Ki 18:21 How l will you falter between
2Ki 9:22 as l as the harlotries of
2Ki 11:12 and said, "L live the king
2Ki 19:25 not hear l ago how I made it
2Ch 1:11 nor have you asked l life
2Ch 3: 4 l across the width of the
2Ch 6:13 bronze platform five cubits l
2Ch 6:31 to walk in Your ways as l as
2Ch 15: 3 For a l time Israel has been
2Ch 23:11 and said, "L live the king
2Ch 26: 5 as l as he sought the LORD,
2Ch 30: 5 a l time in the prescribed
2Ch 36:21 As l as she lay desolate she
Neh 2: 6 How l will your journey be
Esth 5:13 so l as I see Mordecai the
Job 3:21 who l for death, but it does
Job 6: 8 me the thing that I l for
Job 7:19 How l? Will You not look
Job 8: 2 How l will you speak these
Job 18: 2 How l till you put an end to
Job 19: 2 How l will you torment my
Job 27: 3 as l as my breath is in me,
Job 27: 6 reproach me as l as I live
Ps 4: 2 How l, O you sons of men,
Ps 4: 2 How l will you love
Ps 6: 3 But You, O LORD—how l?
Ps 13: 1 How l, O LORD
Ps 13: 1 How l will You hide Your face
Ps 13: 2 How l shall I take counsel in
Ps 13: 2 How l will my enemy be
Ps 32: 3 my groaning all the day l
Ps 35:17 Lord, how l will You look on
Ps 35:28 of Your praise all the day l
Ps 38: 6 I go mourning all the day l
Ps 38:12 plan deception all the day l
Ps 42:10 they say to me all day l
Ps 44: 8 In God we boast all day l
Ps 44:22 sake we are killed all day l
Ps 62: 3 How l will you attack a man
Ps 71:24 righteousness all the day l
Ps 72: 5 fear You As l as the sun and
Ps 72:17 continue as l as the sun
Ps 73:14 For all day l I have been
Ps 74: 9 any among us who knows how l
Ps 74:10 God, how l will the adversary
Ps 79: 5 How l, LORD? Will You be
Ps 80: 4 How l will You be angry
Ps 82: 2 How l will you judge unjustly
Ps 86: 3 For I cry to You all day l
Ps 88:17 me all day l like water
Ps 89:16 name they rejoice all day l
Ps 89:46 How l, LORD? Will You hide
Ps 90:13 Return, O LORD! How l?
Ps 91:16 With l life I will satisfy
Ps 94: 3 how l will the wicked, How
Ps 94: 3 How l will the wicked triumph
Ps 102: 8 enemies reproach me all day l
Ps 104:33 to the LORD as l as I live
Ps 116: 2 call upon Him as l as I live
Ps 119:40 Behold, I l for Your precepts
Ps 119:174 I l for Your salvation, O
Ps 120: 6 My soul has dwelt too l With
Ps 129: 3 They made their furrows l
Ps 143: 3 those who have l been dead
Prov 1:22 How l, you simple ones, will
Prov 3: 2 l life and peace they will add
Prov 6: 9 How l will you slumber, O
Prov 7:19 he has gone on a l journey
Prov 21:26 He covets greedily all day l
Prov 23:17 the LORD continue all day l
Prov 23:30 who linger l at the wine,
Prov 25:15 By l forbearance a ruler is
Is 6:11 Then I said, "Lord, how l?"
Is 22:11 Him who fashioned it l ago
Is 37:26 Did you not hear l ago how I
Is 42:14 I have held My peace a l time
Is 48: 8 surely from l ago your ear
Is 65: 2 out My hands all day l to a
Is 65:22 My elect shall l enjoy the
Jer 4:14 How l shall your evil
Jer 4:21 How l will I see the standard
Jer 12: 4 How l will the land mourn, and
Jer 23:26 How l will this be in the
Jer 29:28 saying, 'This captivity is l
Jer 31:22 How l will you gad about, O
Jer 47: 5 How l will you cut yourself
Jer 47: 6 how l until you are quiet
Lam 3: 6 places like the dead of l ago
Lam 5:20 and forsake us for so l a time
Ezek 17: 3 l pinions, full of feathers
Ezek 31: 5 its branches became l because
Ezek 38: 8 which had l been desolate
Ezek 40: 5 a measuring rod six cubits l
Ezek 40: 7 gate chamber was one rod l
Ezek 40:29 it was fifty cubits l and
Ezek 40:30 around, twenty-five cubits l
Ezek 40:33 it was fifty cubits l and
Ezek 40:42 one cubit and a half l, one
Ezek 40:47 court, one hundred cubits l
Ezek 41:13 temple, one hundred cubits l
Ezek 41:13 was one hundred cubits l
Ezek 42:11 they were as l and as wide as
Ezek 42:20 around, five hundred cubits l
Ezek 43:16 hearth is twelve cubits l
Ezek 43:17 the ledge, fourteen cubits l
Ezek 44:20 nor let their hair grow l
Ezek 45: 3 twenty-five thousand cubits l
Ezek 45: 5 twenty-five thousand cubits l
Ezek 45: 6 and twenty-five thousand l
Ezek 46:22 courts, forty cubits l and
Dan 8:13 How l will the vision be,
Dan 10: 1 but the appointed time was l
Dan 12: 6 How l shall the fulfillment
Hos 8: 5 How l will it be until they
Hos 13:13 son, for he should not stay l
Hab 1: 2 how l shall I cry, and You
Hab 2: 6 what is not his—how l?
Zech 1:12 how l will You not have mercy
Matt 9:15 l as the bridegroom is with
Matt 11:21 repented l ago in sackcloth
Matt 17:17 how l shall I be with you
Matt 17:17 How l shall I bear with you
Matt 23:14 for a pretense make l prayers
Matt 25:19 After a l time the lord of
Mark 1:35 having risen a l while before
Mark 2:19 As l as they have the
Mark 9:19 how l shall I be with you
Mark 9:19 How l shall I bear with you
Mark 9:21 How l has this been happening
Mark 12:38 to go around in l robes, love
Mark 12:40 for a pretense make l prayers
Mark 16: 5 a young man clothed in a l
Luke 1:21 lingered so l in the temple
Luke 8:27 who had demons for a l time
Luke 9:41 how l shall I be with you and
Luke 18: 7 though He bears l with them
Luke 20: 9 a far country for a l time
Luke 20:46 who desire to walk in l robes
Luke 20:47 for a pretense make l prayers
Luke 23: 8 for a l time to see Him,
John 5: 6 in that condition a l time
John 9: 5 As l as I am in the world, I
John 10:24 How l do You keep us in doubt
John 14: 9 Have I been with you so l
Acts 8:11 his sorceries for a l time
Acts 14: 3 they stayed there a l time
Acts 14:28 So they stayed there a l time
Acts 20:11 and eaten, and talked a l while
Acts 27:14 But not l after, a
Acts 27:21 But after l abstinence from
Acts 28: 6 they had looked for a l time
Rom 1:11 For I l to see you, that I
Rom 7: 1 over a man as l as he lives
Rom 7: 2 her husband as l as he lives
Rom 8:36 sake we are killed all day l
Rom 10:21 All day l I have stretched
1Co 7:39 law as l as her husband lives
1Co 11:14 you that if a man has l hair
1Co 11:15 But if a woman has l hair
1Co 13: 4 Love suffers l and is kind
2Co 9:14 who l for you because of the
Gal 4: 1 as l as he is a child, does
Eph 6: 3 you may live l on the earth
Phil 1: 8 how greatly I l for you all
Heb 4: 7 Today," after such a l time
2Pe 1:13 as l as I am in this tent, to
2Pe 2: 3 for a l time their judgment
Jude 4 who l ago were marked out for
Rev 6:10 How l, O Lord, holy and true,

LONGED (*see* LONG)
2Sa 13:39 King David l to go to Absalom
Ps 119:131 For I l for Your commandments
Is 21: 4 the night for which I l He
Rev 18:14 soul l for has gone from you

LONGED-FOR (*see* LONG)
Phil 4: 1 l brethren, my joy and crown,

LONGER (*see* LONG)
Gen 4:12 it shall no l yield its
Gen 17: 5 No l shall your name be
Gen 32:28 shall no l be called Jacob
Ex 2: 3 when she could no l hide him
Ex 5: 7 You shall no l give the
Ex 9:28 go, and you shall stay no l
Deut 10:16 and be stiff-necked no l
Deut 17:13 and no l act presumptuously
Deut 31: 2 I can no l go out and come in
Josh 5: 1 was no spirit in them any l
Josh 5:12 of Israel no l had manna, but
Josh 23:13 no l drive out these nations
Judg 2:14 so that they could no l stand
Judg 2:21 I also will no l drive out
Judg 10:16 His soul could no l endure
1Sa 1:18 ate, and her face was no l sad
2Sa 19:35 Can I hear any l the voice of
2Sa 20: 5 But he delayed l than the set
2Ki 5:17 for your servant will no l
2Ki 6:33 I wait for the LORD any l
1Ch 23:26 They shall no l carry the
2Ch 35: 3 It shall no l be a burden on
Neh 2:17 we may no l be a reproach
Job 7: 8 are upon me, I shall no l be
Job 7:21 but I will no l be
Job 11: 9 measure is l than the earth
Ps 74: 9 There is no l any prophet
Is 32: 5 will no l be called generous
Is 47: 5 for you shall no l be called
Is 51:22 you shall no l drink it
Is 52: 1 shall no l come to you
Is 54: 9 would no l cover the earth
Is 60:18 Violence shall no l be heard
Is 60:19 The sun shall no l be your
Is 60:20 Your sun shall no l go down
Is 62: 4 You shall no l be termed
Is 62: 8 Surely I will no l give your
Is 65:19 shall no l be heard in her
Jer 9:21 no l to be outside
Jer 9:21 no l on the streets
Jer 23: 7 that they shall no l say, 'As
Jer 44:22 the LORD could no l bear it
Lam 4:15 They shall no l dwell here
Lam 4:16 He no l regards them
Lam 4:22 He will no l send you into
Ezek 13:21 they shall no l be as prey in
Ezek 13:23 no l envision futility nor
Ezek 14:11 Israel may no l stray from Me
Ezek 16:41 and you shall no l hire lovers
Ezek 18: 3 you shall no l use this
Ezek 19: 9 that his voice should no l be
Ezek 21:27 It shall be no l, until He
Ezek 24:27 shall speak and no l be mute
Ezek 28:24 And there shall no l be a
Ezek 29:16 No l shall it be the
Ezek 30:13 there shall no l be princes
Ezek 33:22 opened, and I was no l mute
Ezek 34:10 may no l be food for them
Ezek 34:22 and they shall no l be a prey
Ezek 34:28 they shall no l be a prey for
Ezek 34:29 they shall no l be consumed
Ezek 37:22 they shall no l be two
Ezek 39:28 none of them captive any l
Hos 1: 6 for I will no l have mercy on
Hos 2:16 no l call Me 'My Master,'
Joel 2:19 I will no l make you a
Amos 9:15 no l shall they be pulled up
Nah 1:14 shall be perpetuated no l
Zeph 3:11 you shall no l be haughty In
Zech 11: 6 For I will no l pity the
Zech 13: 2 they shall no l be remembered
Zech 14:11 no l shall there be utter
Zech 14:21 In that day there shall no l
Matt 19: 6 they are no l two but one
Mark 1:45 no l openly enter the city
Mark 2: 2 was no l room to receive them
Mark 7:12 you no l let him do anything
Mark 10: 8 so then they are no l two
Mark 14:25 you, I will no l drink of the
Luke 15:19 I am no l worthy to be called
Luke 15:21 am no l worthy to be called
Luke 16: 2 for you can no l be steward
Luke 22:16 I will no l eat of it until
John 7:33 be with you a little while l
John 11:54 Therefore Jesus no l walked
John 12:35 A little while l the light is
John 13:33 be with you a little while l
John 14:19 A little while l and the world
John 14:30 I will no l talk much with
John 15:15 No l do I call you servants,
John 16:21 child, she no l remembers the
John 16:25 is coming when I will no l
John 17:11 Now I am no l in the world,
Acts 18:20 to stay a l time with them
Acts 25:24 he was not fit to live any l
Rom 6: 2 died to sin live any l in it
Rom 6: 6 should no l be slaves of sin
Rom 6: 9 Death no l has dominion over
Rom 7:17 it is no l I who do it, but
Rom 7:20 it is no l I who do it, but
Rom 11: 6 then it is no l of works
Rom 11: 6 otherwise grace is no l grace
Rom 11: 6 is of works, it is no l grace
Rom 11: 6 otherwise work is no l work
Rom 14:15 you are no l walking in love
Rom 15:23 But now no l having a place
2Co 5:15 live no l for themselves, but
2Co 5:16 yet now we know Him thus no l
Gal 2:20 it is no l I who live, but
Gal 3:18 law, it is no l of promise
Gal 3:25 we are no l under a tutor
Gal 4: 7 are no l a slave but a son
Eph 2:19 you are no l strangers and
Eph 4:14 we should no l be children
Eph 4:17 that you should no l walk as
Eph 4:28 Let him who stole steal no l
1Th 3: 1 when we could no l endure it
1Th 3: 5 when I could no l endure it
1Ti 5:23 No l drink only water, but
Phm 16 no l as a slave but more than
Heb 10:18 there is no l an offering for
Heb 10:26 truth, there no l remains a
1Pe 4: 2 that he no l should live the
Rev 6:11 should rest a little while l
Rev 10: 6 there should be delay no l
Rev 12: 8 for them in heaven any l

LONGING (*see* LONG)
Gen 39: 7 wife cast l eyes on Joseph
Deut 28:32 fail with l for them all day
2Sa 23:15 And David said with l, "Oh,
1Ch 11:17 And David said with l, "Oh,
Ps 107: 9 For He satisfies the l soul
Ps 119:20 My soul breaks with l For
Phil 2:26 since he was l for you all
1Th 2: 8 So, affectionately l for you

LONGS (*see* LONG)
Gen 34: 8 Shechem l for your daughter
Ps 63: 1 My flesh l for You In a dry
Ps 84: 2 My soul l, yes, even faints
Ps 143: 6 My soul l for You like a

LONGSUFFERING
Ex 34: 6 God, merciful and gracious, l
Num 14:18 The LORD is l and abundant in
Ps 86:15 of compassion, and gracious, L
Jer 15:15 Do not take me away in Your l
Rom 2: 4 goodness, forbearance, and l
Rom 9:22 endured with much l the
2Co 6: 6 by purity, by knowledge, by l
Gal 5:22 Spirit is love, joy, peace, l
Eph 4: 2 and gentleness, with l,
Col 1:11 all patience and l with joy
Col 3:12 of mind, meekness, l
1Ti 1:16 Jesus Christ might show all l
2Ti 3:10 of life, purpose, faith, l
2Ti 4: 2 rebuke, exhort, with all l
1Pe 3:20 when once the l of God waited
2Pe 3: 9 but is l toward us, not
2Pe 3:15 account that the l of our

LOOK (*see* LOOKED, LOOKING, LOOKS)
Gen 9:16 I will l on it to remember
Gen 13:14 l from the place where you
Gen 15: 3 L, You have given me no
Gen 15: 5 L now toward heaven, and
Gen 19:17 Do not l behind you nor stay
Gen 22: 7 L, the fire and the wood, but
Gen 25:32 L, I am about to die
Gen 27:11 L, Esau my brother is a hairy
Gen 27:36 away my birthright, and now l
Gen 29: 6 And l, his daughter Rachel is
Gen 29: 7 L, it is still high day
Gen 37: 9 L, I have dreamed another
Gen 37:19 L, this dreamer is coming
Gen 38:13 L, your father-in-law is
Gen 39: 8 L, my master does not know
Gen 39:23 of the prison did not l into
Gen 40: 7 Why do you l so sad today
Gen 42: 1 Why do you l at one another
Gen 44: 8 L, we brought back to you
Gen 47:23 L, here is seed for you, and
Gen 48: 2 L, your son Joseph is coming
Ex 1: 9 L, the people of the children
Ex 3: 4 saw that he turned aside to l
Ex 3: 6 he was afraid to l upon God
Ex 4:14 And l, he is also coming out
Ex 5: 5 L, the people of the land are
Ex 5:21 Let the LORD l on you and
Lev 10:19 L, this day they have offered
Lev 13: 3 The priest shall l at the
Lev 13: 3 the priest shall l at him
Lev 13: 5 the priest shall l at him on
Lev 13: 6 Then the priest shall l at
Lev 13:10 And the priest shall l at him
Lev 13:15 shall l at the raw flesh and
Lev 13:17 And the priest shall l at him
Lev 13:25 then the priest shall l at it
Lev 13:27 the priest shall l at him on
Lev 13:30 priest shall l at the sore
Lev 13:32 priest shall l at the sore
Lev 13:34 priest shall l at the scall
Lev 13:36 the priest shall l at him
Lev 13:39 then the priest shall l
Lev 13:43 Then the priest shall l at it
Lev 13:50 priest shall l at the plague
Lev 13:51 he shall l at the plague on
Lev 13:55 Then the priest shall l at
Lev 14: 3 camp, and the priest shall l
Lev 14:36 into it to l at the plague
Lev 14:36 shall go in to l at the house
Lev 14:37 And he shall l at the plague
Lev 14:39 again on the seventh day and l
Lev 14:44 the priest shall come and l
Lev 26: 9 For I will l on you favorably
Num 15:39 that you may l upon it and
Num 22: 5 L, a people has come from
Num 22:11 L, a people has come out of
Num 22:38 L, I have come to you
Num 23:11 you to curse my enemies, and l
Num 23:24 L, a people rises like a
Num 24:10 you to curse my enemies, and l
Num 31:16 L, these women caused the
Num 32:14 And l! You have risen
Deut 1:21 L, the LORD your God has set
Deut 2:24 L, I have given into your
Deut 9:27 do not l on the stubbornness
Deut 26:15 L down from Your holy
Deut 28:32 people, and your eyes shall l
Josh 9:12 But now l, it is dry and moldy
Judg 3:24 Eglon's servants came to l
Judg 6:37 l, I shall put a fleece of
Judg 7:17 L at me and do likewise
Judg 9:36 L, people are coming down
Judg 13:10 L, the Man has just now
Judg 14:16 L, I have not explained it to
Judg 16:10 L, you have mocked me and told
Judg 19: 9 L, the day is now drawing
Judg 19:24 L, here is my virgin daughter
Judg 20: 7 L! All of you are children
Ruth 1:15 L, your sister-in-law has
1Sa 1:11 if You will indeed l on the
1Sa 8: 5 L, you are old, and your sons
1Sa 9: 3 go and l for the donkeys
1Sa 9: 6 L now, there is in this city
1Sa 9: 7 But l, if we go, what shall
1Sa 9: 8 L, I have here at hand one
1Sa 10: 2 went to l for have been found
1Sa 10:14 said, "To l for the donkeys
1Sa 12: 2 I am old and grayheaded, and l
1Sa 14:11 L, the Hebrews are coming out
1Sa 14:29 L now, how my countenance has
1Sa 14:33 L, the people are sinning
1Sa 16: 7 Do not l at his appearance or
1Sa 16:18 L, I have seen a son of Jesse
1Sa 18:22 David secretly, and say, 'L
1Sa 20:21 If I expressly say to him, 'L
1Sa 20:22 say thus to the young man, 'L
1Sa 21:14 L, you see the man is insane
1Sa 23: 1 L, the Philistines are
1Sa 23: 3 L, we are afraid here in
1Sa 24:10 L, this day your eyes have
1Sa 25:14 L, David sent messengers from
1Sa 28: 9 L, you know what Saul has
1Sa 28:21 L, your maidservant has
2Sa 3:24 L, Abner came to you
2Sa 4:10 someone told me, saying, 'L
2Sa 9: 8 that you should l upon such a

2Sa 13:35 L, the king's sons are coming
2Sa 14:32 L, I sent to you, saying
2Sa 15: 3 L, your case is good and right
2Sa 16:12 LORD will l on my affliction
2Sa 24:22 L, here are oxen for burnt
1Ki 1:18 So now, l! Adonijah has
1Ki 1:25 and l! They are eating
1Ki 1:51 for l, he has taken hold of
1Ki 2:39 L, your slaves are in Gath
1Ki 18:43 Go up now, l toward the sea
1Ki 20:31 L now, we have heard that the
1Ki 22:23 Now therefore, l! The LORD
2Ki 1:14 L, fire has come down from
2Ki 2:16 L now, there are fifty strong
2Ki 3:14 Judah, I would not l at you
2Ki 4: 9 L now, I know that this is a
2Ki 4:13 Say now to her, 'L, you have
2Ki 4:25 L, there is the Shunammite
2Ki 5:20 L, my master has spared
2Ki 6:32 L, when the messenger comes,
2Ki 7: 2 L, if the LORD would make
2Ki 7: 6 L, the king of Israel has
2Ki 7:13 L, they may either become
2Ki 7:19 Now l, if the LORD would make
2Ki 9: 2 l there for Jehu the son of
2Ki 10: 4 L, two kings could not stand
2Ki 18:21 Now l! You are trusting
2Ki 19: 9 L, he has come out to make
2Ki 19:11 L! You have heard what
1Ch 12:17 may the God of our fathers l
1Ch 21:23 L, I also give you the oxen
1Ch 23: 4 thousand were to l after the
2Ch 13:12 Now l, God Himself is with us
2Ch 18:22 Now therefore, l! The LORD
2Ch 24:22 The LORD l on it, and repay
2Ch 28: 9 L, because the LORD God of
Esth 7: 9 L! The gallows, fifty cubits
Job 3: 9 may it l for light, but have
Job 6:19 The caravans of Tema l, the
Job 6:28 be pleased to l at me
Job 7:19 Will You not l away from me
Job 8:17 l for a place in the stones
Job 14: 6 L away from him that he may
Job 21: 5 L at me and be astonished
Job 21:27 L, I know your thoughts, and
Job 23: 8 L, I go forward, but He is
Job 31: 1 why then should I l upon a
Job 33:12 L, in this you are not
Job 35: 5 L to the heavens, and see
Job 36:30 L, He scatters his light upon
Job 37:21 Even now men cannot l at the
Job 40:11 l on everyone who is proud,
Job 40:12 L on everyone who is proud,
Job 40:15 L now at the behemoth, which
Ps 5: 3 it to You, And I will l up
Ps 11: 2 For l! The wicked bend
Ps 17: 2 Let Your eyes l on the things
Ps 22:17 They l and stare at Me
Ps 25:18 L on my affliction and my pain
Ps 35:17 Lord, how long will You l on
Ps 37:10 you will l diligently for his
Ps 40:12 so that I am not able to l up
Ps 59: 3 For l, they lie in wait for
Ps 80:14 L down from heaven and see,
Ps 84: 9 And l upon the face of Your
Ps 85:11 shall l down from heaven
Ps 91: 8 with your eyes shall you l
Ps 101: 5 The one who has a haughty l
Ps 109:25 When they l at me, they shake
Ps 119: 6 When I l into all Your
Ps 119:132 L upon me and be merciful to
Ps 123: 2 l to the hand of their
Ps 123: 2 So our eyes l to the LORD our
Ps 142: 4 L on my right hand and see,
Ps 145:15 The eyes of all l expectantly
Prov 4:25 Let your eyes l straight
Prov 4:25 your eyelids l right before
Prov 6:17 A proud l, a lying tongue,
Prov 21: 4 A haughty l, a proud heart,
Prov 23:31 Do not l on the wine when it
Eccl 1:16 L, I have attained greatness,
Eccl 4: 1 And l! The tears of
Eccl 12: 3 and those that l through the
Song 1: 6 Do not l upon me, because I
Song 4: 8 L from the top of Amana, from
Song 4: 9 heart with one l of your eyes
Song 6:13 that we may l upon you
Is 3: 9 The l on their countenance
Is 8:21 and their God, and l upward
Is 8:22 Then they will l to the earth
Is 17: 7 day a man will l to his Maker
Is 17: 8 He will not l to the altars,
Is 18: 4 I will l from My dwelling
Is 21: 9 And l, here comes a chariot of
Is 22: 4 L away from me, I will weep
Is 22:11 you did not l to its Maker
Is 29: 8 a hungry man dreams, and l
Is 29: 8 a thirsty man dreams, and l
Is 31: 1 but who do not l to the Holy
Is 33:20 L upon Zion, the city of our
Is 36: 6 L! You are trusting
Is 37:11 L! You have heard
Is 40:15 l, He lifts up the isles as a
Is 41:27 first time I said to Zion, 'L
Is 42:18 and l, you blind, that you may
Is 45:22 L to Me, and be saved, all you
Is 49:12 l! Those from the north
Is 49:18 up your eyes, l around and see
Is 50:11 L, all you who kindle a fire,
Is 51: 1 l to the rock from which you
Is 51: 2 L to Abraham your father, and
Is 51: 6 and l on the earth beneath
Is 56:11 they all l to their own way,
Is 59: 9 we l for light, but there is
Is 59:11 we l for justice, but there
Is 63:15 L down from heaven, and see
Is 64: 3 things for which we did not l
Is 64: 9 indeed, please l—we all are
Is 66: 2 But on this one will I l
Is 66:24 l upon the corpses of the men
Jer 8: 8 L, the false pen of the
Jer 18: 6 L, as the clay is in the
Jer 32:24 L, the siege mounds
Jer 38: 5 L, he is in your hand
Jer 39:12 l after him, and do him no
Jer 40: 4 And now l, I free you this day
Jer 40: 4 come, and I will l after you
Jer 46: 5 fled, And did not l back, For
Jer 47: 3 the fathers will not l back
Lam 3:63 L at their sitting down and
Lam 5: 1 l, and behold our reproach
Ezek 12:27 Son of man, l, the house of
Ezek 16:49 L, this was the iniquity of
Ezek 22: 6 L, the princes of Israel
Ezek 25: 8 Because Moab and Seir say, 'L
Ezek 40: 4 l with your eyes and hear with
Dan 3:25 L!" he answered
Dan 8:19 L, I am making known to you
Hos 3: 1 who l to other gods and love
Hos 5: 8 L behind you, O Benjamin
Jon 2: 4 yet I will l again toward
Mic 4:11 and let our eye l upon Zion
Mic 7: 7 I will l to the LORD
Nah 3: 7 come to pass that all who l
Hab 1: 5 L among the nations and watch
Hab 1:13 and cannot l on wickedness
Hab 1:13 Why do You l on those who
Hab 2:15 drunk, that you may l on his
Zech 12:10 then they will l on Me whom
Matt 6:26 L at the birds of the air,
Matt 7: 3 why do you l at the speck in
Matt 7: 4 and l, a plank is in your own
Matt 11: 3 One, or do we l for another
Matt 11:19 and drinking, and they say, 'L
Matt 12: 2 L, Your disciples are doing
Matt 12:47 L, Your mother and Your
Matt 24:23 if anyone says to you, 'L
Matt 24:26 if they say to you, 'L, He is
Matt 24:26 or 'L, He is in the inner
Matt 25:20 l, I have gained five more
Matt 25:22 l, I have gained two more
Matt 25:25 L, there you have what is
Matt 26:65 L, now you have heard His
Mark 2:24 L, why do they do what is not
Mark 3:32 L, Your mother and Your
Mark 8:25 eyes again and made him l up
Mark 11:21 Rabbi, l! The fig tree
Mark 13:21 if anyone says to you, 'L
Mark 13:21 or, 'L, He is there
Mark 15:35 L, He is calling for Elijah
Luke 2:48 L, Your father and I have
Luke 6:41 why do you l at the speck in
Luke 7:19 One, or do we l for another
Luke 7:20 One, or do we l for another
Luke 7:34 and drinking, and you say, 'L
Luke 9:38 l on my son, for he is my
Luke 13: 7 keeper of his vineyard, 'L
Luke 17:23 'L here!' or 'L there!'
Luke 19: 8 L, Lord, I give half of my
Luke 21:28 l up and lift up your heads,
Luke 21:29 L at the fig tree, and all the
Luke 22:38 Lord, l, here are two swords
John 4:35 l at the fields, for they are
John 7:26 But l! He speaks boldly
John 7:52 Search and l, for no prophet
John 12:19 L, the world has gone after
John 19:37 They shall l on Him whom they
John 20:27 finger here, and l at My hands
Acts 2: 7 L, are not all these who
Acts 3: 4 John, Peter said, "L at us
Acts 3:12 Or why l so intently at us,
Acts 4:29 l on their threats, and grant
Acts 5: 9 L, the feet of those who have
Acts 5:25 L, the men whom you put in
Acts 5:28 And l, you have filled
Acts 7:32 Moses trembled and dared not l
Acts 7:56 L! I see the heavens opened
Acts 18:15 own law, l to it yourselves
2Co 3: 7 of Israel could not l
2Co 3:13 of Israel could not l
2Co 4:18 while we do not l at the
2Co 10: 7 Do you l at things according
Phil 2: 4 Let each of you l out not
Jas 3: 4 L also at ships
1Pe 1:12 which angels desire to l into
2Pe 3:13 l for new heavens and a new
2Jn 8 L to yourselves, that we do
Rev 5: 3 the scroll, or to l at it
Rev 5: 4 the scroll, or to l at it

LOOKED (*see* LOOK)
Gen 6:12 So God l upon the earth, and
Gen 8:13 the covering of the ark and l
Gen 18: 2 So he lifted his eyes and l
Gen 18:16 l toward Sodom, and Abraham
Gen 19:26 But his wife l back behind
Gen 19:28 Then he l toward Sodom and
Gen 22:13 Abraham lifted his eyes and l
Gen 24:63 and he lifted his eyes and l
Gen 26: 8 l through a window, and saw,
Gen 29: 2 And he l, and saw a well in the
Gen 29:32 has surely l on my affliction
Gen 33: 1 Jacob lifted his eyes and l
Gen 37:25 they lifted their eyes and l
Gen 40: 6 l at them, and saw that they
Gen 43:33 the men l in astonishment at
Ex 2:11 and l at their burdens
Ex 2:12 So he l this way and that way,
Ex 2:25 God l upon the children of
Ex 3: 2 So he l, and behold, the bush
Ex 4:31 and that He had l on their
Ex 14:24 that the LORD l down upon the
Ex 16:10 that they l toward the
Ex 39:43 Then Moses l over all the
Num 17: 9 and they l, and each man took
Num 21: 9 when he l at the bronze
Num 24:20 Then he l on Amalek, and he
Num 24:21 Then he l on the Kenites, and
Deut 9:16 And I l, and there, you had
Deut 26: 7 l on our affliction and our
Josh 5:13 that he lifted his eyes and l
Josh 8:20 the men of Ai l behind them
Judg 5:28 Sisera l through the window
Judg 9:43 And he l, and there were the
Judg 13:19 while Manoah and his wife l on
Judg 20:40 the Benjamites l behind them
1Sa 6:19 because they had l into the
1Sa 9:16 for I have l upon My people,
1Sa 14:16 Saul in Gibeah of Benjamin l
1Sa 16: 6 that he l at Eliab and said,
1Sa 17:42 when the Philistine l about
1Sa 24: 8 when Saul l behind him, David
2Sa 1: 7 Now when he l behind him, he
2Sa 2:20 Then Abner l behind him and
2Sa 6:16 l through a window and saw
2Sa 13:34 watch lifted his eyes and l
2Sa 18:24 wall, lifted his eyes and l
2Sa 22:42 They l, but there was none to
2Sa 24:20 Now Araunah l, and saw the
1Ki 18:43 So he went up and l, and said
1Ki 19: 6 Then he l, and there by his
2Ki 2:24 l at them, and pronounced a
2Ki 6:30 by on the wall, the people l
2Ki 9:30 head, and l through a window
2Ki 9:32 he l up at the window, and
2Ki 9:32 or three eunuchs l out at him
2Ki 11:14 When she l, there was the
1Ch 21:15 he was destroying, the LORD l
1Ch 21:21 came to Ornan, and Ornan l
2Ch 13:14 And when Judah l around, to
2Ch 20:24 they l toward the multitude

2Ch 23:13 And when she l, there was the
2Ch 26:20 and all the priests l at him
Ezra 8:15 I l among the people and the
Neh 4:14 And I l, and arose and said to
Job 30:26 But when I l for good, evil
Ps 34: 5 They l to Him and were radiant
Ps 63: 2 So I have l for You in the
Ps 69:20 I l for someone to take pity,
Ps 102:19 For He l down from the height
Prov 7: 6 house I l through my lattice
Prov 24:32 I l on it and received
Eccl 2:11 Then I l on all the works
Is 5: 7 He l for justice, but behold,
Is 22: 8 You l in that day to the
Is 41:28 For I l, and there was no man
Is 41:28 I l among them, but there was
Is 63: 5 I l, but there was no one to
Jer 8:15 We l for peace, but no good
Jer 14:19 We l for peace, but there was
Jer 31:26 l around, and my sleep was
Jer 36:16 that they l in fear from one
Ezek 1: 4 Then I l, and behold, a
Ezek 1:15 Now as I l at the living
Ezek 2: 9 Now when I l, there was a
Ezek 8: 2 Then I l, and there was a
Ezek 8: 7 and when I l, there was a hole
Ezek 10: 1 And I l, and there in the
Ezek 10: 9 And when I l, there were four
Ezek 10:10 appearance, all four l alike
Ezek 16: 8 l upon you, indeed your time
Ezek 23:14 she l at men portrayed on the
Ezek 37: 8 Indeed, as I l, the sinews and
Ezek 44: 4 so I l, and behold, the glory
Dan 7: 6 After this I l, and there was
Dan 10: 5 I lifted my eyes and l, and
Dan 12: 5 Then I, Daniel, l
Hab 3: 6 He l and startled the nations
Hag 1: 9 You l for much, but indeed it
Zech 1:18 Then I raised my eyes and l
Zech 2: 1 Then I raised my eyes and l
Zech 5: 9 Then I raised my eyes and l
Zech 6: 1 turned and raised my eyes and l
Matt 19:26 But Jesus l at them and said
Mark 3: 5 So when He had l around at
Mark 3:34 He l around in a circle at
Mark 5:32 He l around to see her who
Mark 6:41 He l up to heaven, blessed and
Mark 8:24 And he l up and said, I see
Mark 8:33 and l at His disciples, He
Mark 9: 8 when they had l around, they
Mark 10:23 Then Jesus l around and said
Mark 11:11 So when He had l around at
Mark 14:67 she l at him and said,
Mark 16: 4 But when they l up, they saw
Luke 1:25 in the days when He l on me
Luke 2:38 of Him to all those who l for
Luke 10:32 at the place, came and l, and
Luke 19: 5 came to the place, He l up
Luke 20:17 And He l at them and said,
Luke 21: 1 Then He l up and saw the rich
Luke 22:56 l intently at him and said,
Luke 22:61 the Lord turned and l at Peter
John 1:42 Now when Jesus l at him, He
John 13:22 disciples l at one another
John 20:11 down and l into the tomb
Acts 1:10 And while they l steadfastly
Acts 13: 9 Spirit, l intently at him
Acts 22:13 that same hour I l up at him
Acts 28: 6 they had l for a long time
Heb 11:26 for he l to the reward
1Jn 1: 1 eyes, which we have l upon
Rev 4: 1 After these things I l, and
Rev 5: 6 And I l, and behold, in the
Rev 5:11 Then I l, and I heard the
Rev 6: 2 And I l, and behold, a white
Rev 6: 5 And I l, and behold, a black
Rev 6: 8 And I l, and behold, a pale
Rev 6:12 I l when He opened the sixth
Rev 7: 9 After these things I l, and
Rev 8:13 And I l, and I heard an angel
Rev 14: 1 Then I l, and behold, a Lamb
Rev 14:14 And I l, and behold, a white
Rev 15: 5 After these things I l, and

LOOKING (*see* LOOK)
Gen 41: 2 the river seven cows, fine l
Gen 41: 4 cows ate up the seven fine l
Gen 41:18 up out of the river, fine l
1Ki 7:25 three l toward the north,
1Ki 7:25 three l toward the west,
1Ki 7:25 three l toward the south, and
1Ki 7:25 and three l toward the east
1Ch 15:29 l through a window, saw King
2Ch 4: 4 three l toward the north,
2Ch 4: 4 three l toward the west,
2Ch 4: 4 three l toward the south, and
2Ch 4: 4 and three l toward the east
Ps 119:37 from l at worthless things
Song 2: 9 he is l through the windows,
Is 38:14 my eyes fail from l upward
Jer 13:16 and while you are l for light
Ezek 23:15 all of them l like captains,
Dan 1:10 l worse than the young men
Dan 4:10 I was l, and behold, A tree in
Dan 8: 2 it so happened while I was l
Zech 4: 2 I am l, and there is a
Matt 14:19 l up to heaven, He blessed and
Matt 24:50 day when he is not l for him
Matt 27:55 were there l on from afar,
Mark 1:37 Everyone is l for You
Mark 7:34 l up to heaven, He sighed, and
Mark 10:21 l at him, loved him, and said
Mark 10:27 But l at them, Jesus said,
Mark 15:40 also women l on from afar
Luke 6:10 l around at them all, He said
Luke 9:16 l up to heaven, He blessed and
Luke 9:62 and l back, is fit for the
Luke 12:46 day when he is not l for him
Luke 23:35 And the people stood l on
John 1:36 l at Jesus as He walked, he
John 20: 5 l in, saw the linen cloths
Acts 6:15 l steadfastly at him, saw his
Acts 23: 1 l earnestly at the council,
Tit 2:13 l for the blessed hope and
Heb 12: 2 l unto Jesus, the author and
Heb 12:15 l diligently lest anyone fall
2Pe 3:12 l for and hastening the coming
2Pe 3:14 l forward to these things, be
Jude 21 l for the mercy of our Lord

LOOKS (*see* LOOK)
Lev 13:12 foot, wherever the priest l
Lev 13:21 But if the priest l at it
Lev 13:26 But if the priest l at it
Lev 13:31 But if the priest l at the
Lev 13:53 But if the priest l, and
Lev 13:56 If the priest l, and indeed
Lev 14:48 l at it, and indeed the plague
Num 21: 8 is bitten, when he l at it
Num 21:20 which l down on the wasteland
1Sa 16: 7 for man l at the outward
1Sa 16: 7 but the LORD l at the heart
2Sa 14:25 as Absalom for his good l
Job 7: 2 who eagerly l for his wages
Job 28:24 For He l to the ends of the
Job 33:27 he l at men and says, 'I have
Job 36:25 man l on it from afar
Ps 14: 2 The LORD l down from heaven
Ps 18:27 But will bring down haughty l
Ps 33:13 The LORD l from heaven
Ps 33:14 l On all the inhabitants of
Ps 53: 2 God l down from heaven upon
Ps 104:32 He l on the earth, and it
Song 6:10 Who is she who l forth as the
Song 7: 4 which l toward Damascus
Is 2:11 The lofty l of man shall be
Is 5:30 if one l to the land, behold,
Is 10:12 and the glory of his haughty l
Lam 3:50 the LORD from heaven l down
Ezek 2: 6 words or dismayed by their l
Ezek 3: 9 nor be dismayed at their l
Ezek 21:21 the images, he l at the liver
Matt 5:28 I say to you that whoever l
Jas 1:25 But he who l into the perfect

LOOM (*see* LOOMING)
Judg 16:13 head into the web of the l"
Judg 16:14 with the batten of the l, and
Judg 16:14 batten and the web from the l
Is 38:12 He cuts me off from the l

LOOMING (*see* LOOM)
2Ch 32:25 wrath was l over him and over

LOOPS
Ex 26: 4 you shall make l of blue yarn
Ex 26: 5 Fifty l you shall make in the
Ex 26: 5 fifty l you shall make on the
Ex 26: 5 that the l may be clasped to
Ex 26:10 You shall make fifty l on the
Ex 26:10 fifty l on the edge of the
Ex 26:11 put the clasps into the l
Ex 36:11 He made l of blue yarn on the
Ex 36:12 Fifty l he made on one
Ex 36:12 fifty l he made on the edge
Ex 36:12 the l held one curtain to
Ex 36:17 he made fifty l on the edge
Ex 36:17 fifty l he made on the edge

LOOSE (*see* LOOSED, LOOSING)
Gen 49:21 Naphtali is a deer let l
Ex 22: 5 and lets l his animal, and it
Ex 28:28 not come l from the ephod
Ex 39:21 not come l from the ephod
Lev 14: 7 bird l in the open field
Lev 14:53 l outside the city in the
Judg 15:14 bonds broke l from his hands
Job 6: 9 me, that He would l his hand
Job 38:31 or l the belt of Orion
Ps 102:20 To l those appointed to death
Is 45: 1 l the armor of kings, to open
Is 52: 2 l yourself from the bonds of
Is 58: 6 to l the bonds of wickedness,
Jer 2:23 breaking l in her ways,
Dan 3:25 I see four men l, walking in
Matt 16:19 whatever you l on earth will
Matt 18:18 whatever you l on earth will
Matt 21: 2 L them and bring them to Me
Mark 1: 7 not worthy to stoop down and l
Mark 11: 2 L it and bring it
Luke 3:16 strap I am not worthy to l
Luke 13:15 l his ox or his donkey from
Luke 19:30 L him and bring him here
John 1:27 strap I am not worthy to l
John 11:44 them, "L him, and let him go
Acts 13:25 feet I am not worthy to l
Rev 5: 2 the scroll and to l its seals
Rev 5: 5 and to l its seven seals

LOOSED (*see* LOOSE)
Job 30:11 Because He has l my bowstring
Job 39: 5 Who l the bonds of the onager
Ps 116:16 You have l my bonds
Eccl 12: 6 before the silver cord is l
Is 5:27 the belt on their loins be l
Is 33:23 your tackle is l, they could
Is 51:14 hastens, that he may be l
Matt 16:19 on earth will be l in heaven
Matt 18:18 on earth will be l in heaven
Mark 7:35 of his tongue was l, and he
Mark 11: 4 on the street, and they l it
Luke 1:64 was opened and his tongue l
Luke 13:12 you are l from your infirmity
Luke 13:16 be l from this bond on the
Acts 2:24 having l the pains of death,
Acts 16:26 and everyone's chains were l
1Co 7:27 Do not seek to be l
1Co 7:27 Are you l from a wife

LOOSENED (*see* LOOSENS)
Dan 5: 6 the joints of his hips were l

LOOSENS (*see* LOOSENED)
Job 12:18 He l the bonds of kings, And

LOOSING (*see* LOOSE)
Mark 11: 5 are you doing, l the colt
Luke 19:31 asks you, 'Why are you l him
Luke 19:33 But as they were l the colt
Luke 19:33 Why are you l the colt
Acts 27:40 meanwhile l the rudder ropes

LOOTER
Judg 5:30 for the neck of the l

LOP
Is 10:33 will l off the bough with

LORD (*see* LORDLY, LORD'S, LORDS, LORDSHIP, THE-LORD-IS-MY-BANNER, THE-LORD-SHALOM, THE-LORD-WILL-PROVIDE)
Gen 2: 4 that the L God made the earth
Gen 2: 5 For the L God had not caused
Gen 2: 7 the L God formed man of the
Gen 2: 8 The L God planted a garden
Gen 2: 9 out of the ground the L God
Gen 2:15 Then the L God took the man
Gen 2:16 the L God commanded the man,
Gen 2:18 the L God said, "It is not
Gen 2:19 Out of the ground the L God
Gen 2:21 the L God caused a deep sleep
Gen 2:22 Then the rib which the L God
Gen 3: 1 which the L God had made
Gen 3: 8 L God walking in the garden
Gen 3: 8 from the presence of the L
Gen 3: 9 Then the L God called to Adam

Gen 3:13 the L God said to the woman,
Gen 3:14 So the L God said to the
Gen 3:21 and his wife the L God made
Gen 3:22 Then the L God said, "Behold
Gen 3:23 therefore the L God sent him
Gen 4: 1 have gotten a man from the L
Gen 4: 3 fruit of the ground to the L
Gen 4: 4 the L respected Abel and his
Gen 4: 6 So the L said to Cain, "Why
Gen 4: 9 Then the L said to Cain
Gen 4:13 And Cain said to the L, "My
Gen 4:15 And the L said to him,
Gen 4:15 the L set a mark on Cain,
Gen 4:16 from the presence of the L
Gen 4:26 to call on the name of the L
Gen 5:29 ground which the L has cursed
Gen 6: 3 And the L said, "My Spirit
Gen 6: 5 Then the L saw that the
Gen 6: 6 the L was sorry that He had
Gen 6: 7 So the L said, "I will
Gen 6: 8 grace in the eyes of the L
Gen 7: 1 Then the L said to Noah
Gen 7: 5 all that the L commanded him
Gen 7:16 and the L shut him in
Gen 8:20 Noah built an altar to the L
Gen 8:21 And the L smelled a soothing
Gen 8:21 Then the L said in His heart,
Gen 9:26 Blessed be the L, the God of
Gen 10: 9 a mighty hunter before the L
Gen 10: 9 mighty hunter before the L
Gen 11: 5 But the L came down to see
Gen 11: 6 And the L said, "Indeed the
Gen 11: 8 So the L scattered them
Gen 11: 9 because there the L confused
Gen 11: 9 from there the L scattered
Gen 12: 1 Now the L had said to Abram
Gen 12: 4 as the L had spoken to him
Gen 12: 7 Then the L appeared to Abram
Gen 12: 7 he built an altar to the L
Gen 12: 8 he built an altar to the L
Gen 12: 8 called on the name of the L
Gen 12:17 But the L plagued Pharaoh and
Gen 13: 4 called on the name of the L
Gen 13:10 (before the L destroyed Sodom
Gen 13:10 like the garden of the L
Gen 13:13 and sinful against the L
Gen 13:14 the L said to Abram, after
Gen 13:18 built an altar there to the L
Gen 14:22 have lifted my hand to the L
Gen 15: 1 things the word of the L came
Gen 15: 2 L GOD, what will You give me,
Gen 15: 4 the word of the L came to him
Gen 15: 6 And he believed in the L, and
Gen 15: 7 I am the L, who brought you
Gen 15: 8 L GOD, how shall I know that
Gen 15:18 On the same day the L made a
Gen 16: 2 the L has restrained me from
Gen 16: 5 The L judge between you and
Gen 16: 7 Now the Angel of the L found
Gen 16: 9 Angel of the L said to her
Gen 16:10 Angel of the L said to her
Gen 16:11 Angel of the L said to her
Gen 16:11 because the L has heard your
Gen 16:13 of the L who spoke to her
Gen 17: 1 the L appeared to Abram and
Gen 18: 1 Then the L appeared to him by
Gen 18: 3 My L, if I have now found
Gen 18:12 pleasure, my l being old also
Gen 18:13 And the L said to Abraham,
Gen 18:14 anything too hard for the L
Gen 18:17 And the L said, "Shall I hide
Gen 18:19 they keep the way of the L
Gen 18:19 that the L may bring to
Gen 18:20 And the L said, "Because the
Gen 18:22 still stood before the L
Gen 18:26 And the L said, "If I
Gen 18:27 upon myself to speak to the L
Gen 18:30 Let not the L be angry, and I
Gen 18:31 upon myself to speak to the L
Gen 18:32 Let not the L be angry, and I
Gen 18:33 So the L went His way as soon
Gen 19:13 before the face of the L, and
Gen 19:13 the L has sent us to destroy
Gen 19:14 for the L will destroy this
Gen 19:16 the L being merciful to him,
Gen 19:24 Then the L rained brimstone
Gen 19:24 from the L out of the heavens
Gen 19:27 he had stood before the L
Gen 20: 4 L, will You slay a righteous
Gen 20:18 for the L had closed up all
Gen 21: 1 the L visited Sarah as He had
Gen 21: 1 the L did for Sarah as He had
Gen 21:33 called on the name of the L
Gen 22:11 But the Angel of the L called
Gen 22:14 In the Mount of The L it
Gen 22:15 Then the Angel of the L
Gen 22:16 I have sworn, says the L,
Gen 23: 6 Hear us, my l
Gen 23:11 No, my l, hear me
Gen 23:15 My l, listen to me
Gen 24: 1 the L had blessed Abraham in
Gen 24: 3 will make you swear by the L
Gen 24: 7 The L God of heaven, who took
Gen 24:12 O L God of my master
Gen 24:18 Drink, my l
Gen 24:21 the L had made his journey
Gen 24:26 his head and worshiped the L
Gen 24:27 Blessed be the L God of my
Gen 24:27 the L led me to the house of
Gen 24:31 Come in, O blessed of the L
Gen 24:35 The L has blessed my master
Gen 24:40 But he said to me, 'The L
Gen 24:42 O L God of my master
Gen 24:44 the L has appointed for my
Gen 24:48 my head and worshiped the L
Gen 24:48 and blessed the L God of my
Gen 24:50 The thing comes from the L
Gen 24:51 wife, as the L has spoken
Gen 24:52 that he worshiped the L,
Gen 24:56 since the L has prospered my
Gen 25:21 with the L for his wife,
Gen 25:21 the L granted his plea, and
Gen 25:22 she went to inquire of the L
Gen 25:23 And the L said to her
Gen 26: 2 Then the L appeared to him and
Gen 26:12 and the L blessed him
Gen 26:22 For now the L has made room
Gen 26:24 the L appeared to him the
Gen 26:25 called on the name of the L
Gen 26:28 seen that the L is with you
Gen 26:29 are now the blessed of the L
Gen 27: 7 of the L before my death
Gen 27:20 Because the L your God
Gen 27:27 field which the L has blessed
Gen 28:13 the L stood above it and said
Gen 28:13 I am the L God of Abraham
Gen 28:16 Surely the L is in this place
Gen 28:21 then the L shall be my God
Gen 29:31 When the L saw that Leah was
Gen 29:32 The L has surely looked on my
Gen 29:33 Because the L has heard that
Gen 29:35 Now I will praise the L
Gen 30:24 The L shall add to me another
Gen 30:27 by experience that the L has
Gen 30:30 the L has blessed you since
Gen 31: 3 Then the L said to Jacob,
Gen 31:35 Let it not displease my l
Gen 31:49 May the L watch between you
Gen 32: 4 Speak thus to my l Esau
Gen 32: 5 and I have sent to tell my l
Gen 32: 9 the L who said to me, 'Return
Gen 32:18 a present sent to my l Esau
Gen 33: 8 favor in the sight of my l
Gen 33:13 My l knows that the children
Gen 33:14 Please let my l go on ahead
Gen 33:14 until I come to my l in Seir
Gen 33:15 favor in the sight of my l
Gen 38: 7 wicked in the sight of the L
Gen 38: 7 and the L killed him
Gen 38:10 which he did displeased the L
Gen 39: 2 The L was with Joseph, and he
Gen 39: 3 saw that the L was with him
Gen 39: 3 that the L made all he did to
Gen 39: 5 had, that the L blessed the
Gen 39: 5 the blessing of the L was on
Gen 39:21 But the L was with Joseph and
Gen 39:23 because the L was with him
Gen 39:23 he did, the L made it prosper
Gen 40: 1 of Egypt offended their l
Gen 42:10 No, my l, but your servants
Gen 42:30 The man who is l of the land
Gen 42:33 the l of the country, said to
Gen 44: 5 one from which my l drinks
Gen 44: 7 Why does my l say these words
Gen 44:16 What shall we say to my l
Gen 44:18 O my l, please let your
Gen 44:19 My l asked his servants,
Gen 44:20 And we said to my l, 'We have
Gen 44:22 And we said to my l, 'The lad
Gen 44:24 we told him the words of my l
Gen 44:33 of the lad as a slave to my l
Gen 45: 8 and l of all his house, and a
Gen 45: 9 has made me l of all Egypt
Gen 47:18 my l that our money is gone
Gen 47:18 my l also has our herds of
Gen 47:18 sight of my l but our bodies
Gen 47:25 favor in the sight of my l
Gen 49:18 for your salvation, O L
Ex 3: 2 the Angel of the L appeared
Ex 3: 4 So when the L saw that he
Ex 3: 7 the L said: "I have surely
Ex 3:15 The L God of your fathers,
Ex 3:16 The L God of your fathers,
Ex 3:18 The L God of the Hebrews has
Ex 3:18 sacrifice to the L our God
Ex 4: 1 The L has not appeared to
Ex 4: 2 So the L said to him, "What
Ex 4: 4 Then the L said to Moses,
Ex 4: 5 the L God of their fathers
Ex 4: 6 Furthermore the L said to him
Ex 4:10 Then Moses said to the L, "O
Ex 4:10 O my L, I am not eloquent,
Ex 4:11 So the L said to him, "Who
Ex 4:11 Have not I, the L
Ex 4:13 O my L, please send by the
Ex 4:14 So the anger of the L was
Ex 4:19 the L said to Moses in Midian
Ex 4:21 And the L said to Moses,
Ex 4:22 to Pharaoh, 'Thus says the L
Ex 4:24 that the L met him and sought
Ex 4:27 And the L said to Aaron,
Ex 4:28 of the L who had sent him
Ex 4:30 the L had spoken to Moses
Ex 4:31 when they heard that the L
Ex 5: 1 Thus says the L God of Israel
Ex 5: 2 Who is the L, that I should
Ex 5: 2 I do not know the L, nor will
Ex 5: 3 and sacrifice to the L our God
Ex 5:17 us go and sacrifice to the L
Ex 5:21 Let the L look on you and
Ex 5:22 So Moses returned to the L
Ex 5:22 L, why have You brought
Ex 6: 1 Then the L said to Moses,
Ex 6: 2 I am the L
Ex 6: 3 Almighty, but by My name, L
Ex 6: 6 I am the L
Ex 6: 7 shall know that I am the L
Ex 6: 8 I am the L
Ex 6:10 the L spoke to Moses, saying,
Ex 6:12 And Moses spoke before the L
Ex 6:13 Then the L spoke to Moses and
Ex 6:26 and Moses to whom the L said
Ex 6:28 on the day when the L spoke
Ex 6:29 that the L spoke to Moses,
Ex 6:29 I am the L
Ex 6:30 But Moses said before the L
Ex 7: 1 So the L said to Moses
Ex 7: 5 shall know that I am the L
Ex 7: 6 just as the L commanded them,
Ex 7: 8 Then the L spoke to Moses and
Ex 7:10 so, just as the L commanded
Ex 7:13 heed them, as the L had said
Ex 7:14 So the L said to Moses
Ex 7:16 The L God of the Hebrews has
Ex 7:17 Thus says the L: "By this
Ex 7:17 shall know that I am the L
Ex 7:19 Then the L spoke to Moses,
Ex 7:20 so, just as the L commanded
Ex 7:22 heed them, as the L had said
Ex 7:25 the L had struck the river
Ex 8: 1 And the L spoke to Moses,
Ex 8: 1 say to him, 'Thus says the L
Ex 8: 5 Then the L spoke to Moses,
Ex 8: 8 Entreat the L that He may
Ex 8: 8 they may sacrifice to the L
Ex 8:10 is no one like the L our God
Ex 8:12 And Moses cried out to the L
Ex 8:13 So the L did according to the
Ex 8:15 heed them, as the L had said
Ex 8:16 So the L said to Moses, "Say
Ex 8:19 them, just as the L had said
Ex 8:20 And the L said to Moses,
Ex 8:20 say to him, 'Thus says the L
Ex 8:22 L in the midst of the land
Ex 8:24 And the L did so
Ex 8:26 Egyptians to the L our God
Ex 8:27 sacrifice to the L our God as
Ex 8:28 you may sacrifice to the L
Ex 8:29 you, and I will entreat the L
Ex 8:29 go to sacrifice to the L

Ex 8:30 Pharaoh and entreated the L
Ex 8:31 the L did according to the
Ex 9: 1 Then the L said to Moses,
Ex 9: 1 Thus says the L God of the
Ex 9: 3 the hand of the L will be on
Ex 9: 4 the L will make a difference
Ex 9: 5 Then the L appointed a set
Ex 9: 5 Tomorrow the L will do this
Ex 9: 6 So the L did this thing on
Ex 9: 8 So the L said to Moses and
Ex 9:12 But the L hardened the heart
Ex 9:12 just as the L had spoken to
Ex 9:13 Then the L said to Moses,
Ex 9:13 Thus says the L God of the
Ex 9:20 the L among the servants of
Ex 9:21 of the L left his servants
Ex 9:22 Then the L said to Moses,
Ex 9:23 the L sent thunder and hail,
Ex 9:23 the L rained hail on the land
Ex 9:27 The L is righteous, and my
Ex 9:28 Entreat the L, that there may
Ex 9:29 spread out my hands to the L
Ex 9:30 will not yet fear the L God
Ex 9:33 spread out his hands to the L
Ex 9:35 as the L had spoken by Moses
Ex 10: 1 Now the L said to Moses, "Go
Ex 10: 2 you may know that I am the L
Ex 10: 3 Thus says the L God of the
Ex 10: 7 may serve the L their God
Ex 10: 8 Go, serve the L your God
Ex 10: 9 we must hold a feast to the L
Ex 10:10 The L had better be with you
Ex 10:11 who are men, and serve the L
Ex 10:12 Then the L said to Moses,
Ex 10:13 the L brought an east wind on
Ex 10:16 sinned against the L your God
Ex 10:17 and entreat the L your God
Ex 10:18 Pharaoh and entreated the L
Ex 10:19 the L turned a very strong
Ex 10:20 But the L hardened Pharaoh's
Ex 10:21 Then the L said to Moses,
Ex 10:24 Go, serve the L
Ex 10:25 sacrifice to the L our God
Ex 10:26 them to serve the L our God
Ex 10:26 the L until we arrive there
Ex 10:27 But the L hardened Pharaoh's
Ex 11: 1 And the L said to Moses,
Ex 11: 3 the L gave the people favor
Ex 11: 4 Thus says the L: 'About
Ex 11: 7 the L does make a difference
Ex 11: 9 But the L said to Moses
Ex 11:10 and the L hardened Pharaoh's
Ex 12: 1 Now the L spoke to Moses and
Ex 12:12 I am the L
Ex 12:14 keep it as a feast to the L
Ex 12:23 For the L will pass through
Ex 12:23 the L will pass over the door
Ex 12:25 which the L will give you
Ex 12:27 Passover sacrifice of the L
Ex 12:28 just as the L had commanded
Ex 12:29 pass at midnight that the L
Ex 12:31 serve the L as you have said
Ex 12:36 the L had given the people
Ex 12:41 L went out from the land of
Ex 12:42 L for bringing them out of
Ex 12:42 This is that night of the L
Ex 12:43 the L said to Moses and Aaron,
Ex 12:48 to keep the Passover to the L
Ex 12:50 as the L commanded Moses and
Ex 12:51 day, that the L brought the
Ex 13: 1 Then the L spoke to Moses,
Ex 13: 3 the L brought you out of this
Ex 13: 5 when the L brings you into
Ex 13: 6 shall be a feast to the L
Ex 13: 8 L did for me when I came up
Ex 13: 9 the L has brought you out of
Ex 13:11 when the L brings you into
Ex 13:12 the L all that open the womb
Ex 13:14 the L brought us out of Egypt
Ex 13:15 that the L killed all the
Ex 13:15 I sacrifice to the L all
Ex 13:16 the L brought us out of Egypt
Ex 13:21 the L went before them by day
Ex 14: 1 Now the L spoke to Moses,
Ex 14: 4 may know that I am the L
Ex 14: 8 the L hardened the heart of
Ex 14:10 of Israel cried out to the L
Ex 14:13 and see the salvation of the L
Ex 14:14 The L will fight for you, and
Ex 14:15 And the L said to Moses,
Ex 14:18 shall know that I am the L
Ex 14:21 the L caused the sea to go
Ex 14:24 that the L looked down upon
Ex 14:25 for the L fights for them
Ex 14:26 Then the L said to Moses,
Ex 14:27 So the L overthrew the
Ex 14:30 So the L saved Israel that
Ex 14:31 which the L had done in Egypt
Ex 14:31 so the people feared the L
Ex 14:31 the L, and believed the L
Ex 15: 1 sang this song to the L, and
Ex 15: 1 I will sing to the L, for He
Ex 15: 2 The L is my strength and song,
Ex 15: 3 The L is a man of war
Ex 15: 3 the L is His name
Ex 15: 6 Your right hand, O L, has
Ex 15: 6 Your right hand, O L, has
Ex 15:11 Who is like You, O L, among
Ex 15:16 Your people pass over, O L
Ex 15:17 in the place, O L, which You
Ex 15:17 dwelling, the sanctuary, O L
Ex 15:18 The L shall reign forever and
Ex 15:19 the L brought back the waters
Ex 15:21 Sing to the L, for He has
Ex 15:25 So he cried out to the L, and
Ex 15:25 and the L showed him a tree
Ex 15:26 the voice of the L your God
Ex 15:26 For I am the L who heals you
Ex 16: 3 of the L in the land of Egypt
Ex 16: 4 Then the L said to Moses,
Ex 16: 6 you shall know that the L has
Ex 16: 7 shall see the glory of the L
Ex 16: 7 your murmurings against the L
Ex 16: 8 L gives you meat to eat in
Ex 16: 8 for the L hears your
Ex 16: 8 against us but against the L
Ex 16: 9 Come near before the L, for
Ex 16:10 the glory of the L appeared
Ex 16:11 the L spoke to Moses, saying,
Ex 16:12 know that I am the L your God
Ex 16:15 the L has given you to eat
Ex 16:16 which the L has commanded
Ex 16:23 This is what the L has said
Ex 16:23 rest, a holy Sabbath to the L
Ex 16:25 today is a Sabbath to the L
Ex 16:28 And the L said to Moses,
Ex 16:29 For the L has given you the
Ex 16:32 which the L has commanded
Ex 16:33 it, and lay it up before the L
Ex 16:34 As the L commanded Moses, so
Ex 17: 1 to the commandment of the L
Ex 17: 2 Why do you tempt the L
Ex 17: 4 So Moses cried out to the L
Ex 17: 5 And the L said to Moses,
Ex 17: 7 and because they tempted the L
Ex 17: 7 Is the L among us or not
Ex 17:14 Then the L said to Moses,
Ex 17:16 Because the L has sworn
Ex 17:16 the L will have war with
Ex 18: 1 that the L had brought Israel
Ex 18: 8 the L had done to Pharaoh
Ex 18: 8 how the L had delivered them
Ex 18: 9 the L had done for Israel
Ex 18:10 Blessed be the L, who has
Ex 18:11 Now I know that the L is
Ex 19: 3 the L called to him from the
Ex 19: 7 which the L commanded him
Ex 19: 8 All that the L has spoken we
Ex 19: 8 words of the people to the L
Ex 19: 9 And the L said to Moses,
Ex 19: 9 words of the people to the L
Ex 19:10 Then the L said to Moses,
Ex 19:11 For on the third day the L
Ex 19:18 because the L descended upon
Ex 19:20 Then the L came down upon
Ex 19:20 the L called Moses to the top
Ex 19:21 And the L said to Moses,
Ex 19:21 through to gaze at the L, and
Ex 19:22 the L sanctify themselves
Ex 19:22 lest the L break out against
Ex 19:23 And Moses said to the L, "The
Ex 19:24 Then the L said to him
Ex 19:24 through to come up to the L
Ex 20: 2 I am the L your God, who
Ex 20: 5 the L your God, am a jealous
Ex 20: 7 of the L your God in vain
Ex 20: 7 for the L will not hold him
Ex 20:10 the Sabbath of the L your God
Ex 20:11 days the L made the heavens
Ex 20:11 Therefore the L blessed the
Ex 20:12 the L your God is giving you
Ex 20:22 Then the L said to Moses,
Ex 22:11 then an oath of the L shall
Ex 22:20 any god, except to the L only
Ex 23:17 shall appear before the L God
Ex 23:19 the house of the L your God
Ex 23:25 shall serve the L your God
Ex 24: 1 Come up to the L, you and
Ex 24: 2 alone shall come near the L
Ex 24: 3 people all the words of the L
Ex 24: 3 the L has said we will do
Ex 24: 4 wrote all the words of the L
Ex 24: 5 offerings of oxen to the L
Ex 24: 7 All that the L has said we
Ex 24: 8 of the covenant which the L
Ex 24:12 Then the L said to Moses,
Ex 24:16 Now the glory of the L rested
Ex 24:17 L was like a consuming fire
Ex 25: 1 Then the L spoke to Moses,
Ex 27:21 until morning before the L
Ex 28:12 L on his two shoulders as a
Ex 28:29 before the L continually
Ex 28:30 when he goes in before the L
Ex 28:30 before the L continually
Ex 28:35 the holy place before the L
Ex 28:36 HOLINESS TO THE L
Ex 28:38 may be accepted before the L
Ex 29:11 kill the bull before the L
Ex 29:18 is a burnt offering to the L
Ex 29:18 made by fire to the L
Ex 29:23 bread that is before the L
Ex 29:24 a wave offering before the L
Ex 29:25 as a sweet aroma before the L
Ex 29:25 made by fire to the L
Ex 29:26 a wave offering before the L
Ex 29:28 their heave offering to the L
Ex 29:41 made by fire to the L
Ex 29:42 of meeting before the L,
Ex 29:46 that I am the L their God
Ex 29:46 I am the L their God
Ex 30: 8 incense before the L
Ex 30:10 It is most holy to the L
Ex 30:11 Then the L spoke to Moses,
Ex 30:12 a ransom for himself to the L
Ex 30:13 shall be an offering to the L
Ex 30:14 give an offering to the L
Ex 30:15 you give an offering to the L
Ex 30:16 of Israel before the L, to
Ex 30:17 Then the L spoke to Moses,
Ex 30:20 made by fire to the L, they
Ex 30:22 Moreover the L spoke to Moses
Ex 30:34 And the L said to Moses
Ex 30:37 be to you holy for the L
Ex 31: 1 Then the L spoke to Moses,
Ex 31:12 the L spoke to Moses, saying,
Ex 31:13 I am the L who sanctifies you
Ex 31:15 of rest, holy to the L
Ex 31:17 days the L made the heavens
Ex 32: 5 Tomorrow is a feast to the L
Ex 32: 7 And the L said to Moses,
Ex 32: 9 And the L said to Moses,
Ex 32:11 pleaded with the L his God
Ex 32:11 L, why does Your wrath burn
Ex 32:14 So the L relented from the
Ex 32:22 the anger of my l become hot
Ex 32:27 Thus says the L God of Israel
Ex 32:29 yourselves today to the L
Ex 32:30 So now I will go up to the L
Ex 32:31 Then Moses returned to the L
Ex 32:33 And the L said to Moses,
Ex 32:35 So the L plagued the people
Ex 33: 1 Then the L said to Moses,
Ex 33: 5 For the L had said to Moses,
Ex 33: 7 everyone who sought the L
Ex 33: 9 and the L talked with Moses
Ex 33:11 So the L spoke to Moses face
Ex 33:12 Then Moses said to the L
Ex 33:17 Then the L said to Moses,
Ex 33:19 the name of the L before you
Ex 33:21 the L said, "Here is a place
Ex 34: 1 the L said to Moses, "Cut two
Ex 34: 4 as the L had commanded him
Ex 34: 5 Then the L descended in the
Ex 34: 5 proclaimed the name of the L
Ex 34: 6 the L passed before him and
Ex 34: 6 The L, the L God, merciful
Ex 34: 9 Your sight, O L, let my L
Ex 34:10 shall see the work of the L
Ex 34:14 no other god, for the L,
Ex 34:23 the L, the L God of Israel

Ex	34:24	go up to appear before the **L**
Ex	34:26	the house of the **L** your God
Ex	34:27	Then the **L** said to Moses,
Ex	34:28	there with the **L** forty days
Ex	34:32	the **L** had spoken with him on
Ex	34:34	the **L** to speak with Him, he
Ex	35: 1	the **L** has commanded you to do
Ex	35: 2	a Sabbath of rest to the **L**
Ex	35: 4	thing which the **L** commanded
Ex	35: 5	you an offering to the **L**
Ex	35: 5	it as an offering to the **L**
Ex	35:10	all that the **L** has commanded
Ex	35:22	an offering of gold to the **L**
Ex	35:29	a freewill offering to the **L**
Ex	35:29	all kinds of work which the **L**
Ex	35:30	See, the **L** has called by name
Ex	36: 1	in whom the **L** has put wisdom
Ex	36: 1	all that the **L** has commanded
Ex	36: 2	heart the **L** had put wisdom
Ex	36: 5	the **L** commanded us to do
Ex	38:22	made all that the **L** had
Ex	39: 1	as the **L** had commanded Moses
Ex	39: 5	as the **L** had commanded Moses
Ex	39: 7	as the **L** had commanded Moses
Ex	39:21	as the **L** had commanded Moses
Ex	39:26	as the **L** had commanded Moses
Ex	39:29	woven as the **L** had commanded
Ex	39:30	HOLINESS TO THE **L**
Ex	39:31	as the **L** had commanded Moses
Ex	39:32	the **L** had commanded Moses
Ex	39:42	the **L** had commanded Moses
Ex	39:43	as the **L** had commanded, just
Ex	40: 1	Then the **L** spoke to Moses,
Ex	40:16	that the **L** had commanded him
Ex	40:19	as the **L** had commanded Moses
Ex	40:21	as the **L** had commanded Moses
Ex	40:23	in order upon it before the **L**
Ex	40:23	as the **L** had commanded Moses
Ex	40:25	he lit the lamps before the **L**
Ex	40:25	as the **L** had commanded Moses
Ex	40:27	as the **L** had commanded Moses
Ex	40:29	as the **L** had commanded Moses
Ex	40:32	as the **L** had commanded Moses
Ex	40:34	the glory of the **L** filled the
Ex	40:35	the glory of the **L** filled the
Ex	40:38	For the cloud of the **L** was
Lev	1: 1	Now the **L** called to Moses, and
Lev	1: 2	brings an offering to the **L**
Lev	1: 3	of meeting before the **L**
Lev	1: 5	kill the bull before the **L**
Lev	1: 9	fire, a sweet aroma to the **L**
Lev	1:11	of the altar before the **L**
Lev	1:13	fire, a sweet aroma to the **L**
Lev	1:14	offering to the **L** is of birds
Lev	1:17	fire, a sweet aroma to the **L**
Lev	2: 1	a grain offering to the **L**
Lev	2: 2	fire, a sweet aroma to the **L**
Lev	2: 3	to the **L** made by fire
Lev	2: 8	made of these things to the **L**
Lev	2: 9	fire, a sweet aroma to the **L**
Lev	2:10	to the **L** made by fire
Lev	2:11	which you bring to the **L**
Lev	2:11	to the **L** made by fire
Lev	2:12	you shall offer them to the **L**
Lev	2:14	of your firstfruits to the **L**
Lev	2:16	made by fire to the **L**
Lev	3: 1	without blemish before the **L**
Lev	3: 3	made by fire to the **L**
Lev	3: 5	fire, a sweet aroma to the **L**
Lev	3: 6	to the **L** is of the flock,
Lev	3: 7	shall offer it before the **L**
Lev	3: 9	made by fire to the **L**, its
Lev	3:11	made by fire to the **L**
Lev	3:12	shall offer it before the **L**
Lev	3:14	made by fire to the **L**
Lev	4: 1	Now the **L** spoke to Moses,
Lev	4: 2	of the commandments of the **L**
Lev	4: 3	**L** for his sin which he has
Lev	4: 4	of meeting before the **L**, lay
Lev	4: 4	and kill the bull before the **L**
Lev	4: 6	seven times before the **L**, in
Lev	4: 7	of sweet incense before the **L**
Lev	4:13	**L** in anything which should
Lev	4:15	head of the bull before the **L**
Lev	4:15	shall be killed before the **L**
Lev	4:17	it seven times before the **L**
Lev	4:18	altar which is before the **L**
Lev	4:22	**L** his God in anything which
Lev	4:24	burnt offering before the **L**
Lev	4:27	of the commandments of the **L**
Lev	4:31	for a sweet aroma to the **L**
Lev	4:35	made by fire to the **L**
Lev	5: 6	**L** for his sin which he has
Lev	5: 7	then he shall bring to the **L**
Lev	5:12	made by fire to the **L**
Lev	5:14	Then the **L** spoke to Moses,
Lev	5:15	to the holy things of the **L**
Lev	5:15	**L** as his trespass offering a
Lev	5:17	by the commandments of the **L**
Lev	5:19	trespassed against the **L**
Lev	6: 1	the **L** spoke to Moses, saying
Lev	6: 2	a trespass against the **L** by
Lev	6: 6	trespass offering to the **L**
Lev	6: 7	for him before the **L**, and he
Lev	6: 8	Then the **L** spoke to Moses,
Lev	6:14	it on the altar before the **L**
Lev	6:15	aroma, as a memorial to the **L**
Lev	6:18	made by fire to the **L**
Lev	6:19	the **L** spoke to Moses, saying,
Lev	6:20	they shall offer to the **L**
Lev	6:21	for a sweet aroma to the **L**
Lev	6:22	is a statute forever to the **L**
Lev	6:24	the **L** spoke to Moses, saying,
Lev	6:25	shall be killed before the **L**
Lev	7: 5	made by fire to the **L**
Lev	7:11	which he shall offer to the **L**
Lev	7:14	as a heave offering to the **L**
Lev	7:20	that belongs to the **L**, while
Lev	7:21	that belongs to the **L**, that
Lev	7:22	the **L** spoke to Moses, saying,
Lev	7:25	made by fire to the **L**, the
Lev	7:28	Then the **L** spoke to Moses,
Lev	7:29	his peace offering to the **L**
Lev	7:29	**L** from the sacrifice of his
Lev	7:30	made by fire to the **L**
Lev	7:30	a wave offering before the **L**
Lev	7:35	made by fire to the **L**, on the
Lev	7:35	minister to the **L** as priests
Lev	7:36	The **L** commanded this to be
Lev	7:38	which the **L** commanded Moses
Lev	7:38	their offerings to the **L** in
Lev	8: 1	the **L** spoke to Moses, saying
Lev	8: 4	did as the **L** commanded him
Lev	8: 5	This is what the **L** commanded
Lev	8: 9	as the **L** had commanded Moses
Lev	8:13	as the **L** had commanded Moses
Lev	8:17	as the **L** had commanded Moses
Lev	8:21	made by fire to the **L**, as the
Lev	8:21	as the **L** had commanded Moses
Lev	8:26	bread that was before the **L**
Lev	8:27	a wave offering before the **L**
Lev	8:28	made by fire to the **L**
Lev	8:29	a wave offering before the **L**
Lev	8:29	as the **L** had commanded Moses
Lev	8:34	so the **L** has commanded to do,
Lev	8:35	and keep the charge of the **L**
Lev	8:36	**L** had commanded by the hand
Lev	9: 2	and offer them before the **L**
Lev	9: 4	to sacrifice before the **L**
Lev	9: 4	for today the **L** will appear
Lev	9: 5	near and stood before the **L**
Lev	9: 6	the **L** commanded you to do
Lev	9: 6	and the glory of the **L** will
Lev	9: 7	for them, as the **L** commanded
Lev	9:10	as the **L** had commanded Moses
Lev	9:21	a wave offering before the **L**
Lev	9:23	Then the glory of the **L**
Lev	9:24	came out from before the **L**
Lev	10: 1	profane fire before the **L**
Lev	10: 2	So fire went out from the **L**
Lev	10: 2	and they died before the **L**
Lev	10: 3	This is what the **L** spoke,
Lev	10: 6	which the **L** has kindled
Lev	10: 7	oil of the **L** is upon you
Lev	10: 8	Then the **L** spoke to Aaron,
Lev	10:11	**L** has spoken to them by the
Lev	10:12	made by fire to the **L**, and eat
Lev	10:13	made by fire to the **L**
Lev	10:15	a wave offering before the **L**
Lev	10:15	as the **L** has commanded
Lev	10:17	for them before the **L**
Lev	10:19	burnt offering before the **L**
Lev	10:19	in the sight of the **L**
Lev	11: 1	the **L** spoke to Moses and Aaron
Lev	11:44	For I am the **L** your God
Lev	11:45	For I am the **L** who brings
Lev	12: 1	Then the **L** spoke to Moses,
Lev	12: 7	shall offer it before the **L**
Lev	13: 1	the **L** spoke to Moses and Aaron
Lev	14: 1	Then the **L** spoke to Moses,
Lev	14:11	and those things, before the **L**
Lev	14:12	a wave offering before the **L**
Lev	14:16	seven times before the **L**
Lev	14:18	for him before the **L**
Lev	14:23	of meeting, before the **L**
Lev	14:24	a wave offering before the **L**
Lev	14:27	hand seven times before the **L**
Lev	14:29	for him before the **L**
Lev	14:31	to be cleansed before the **L**
Lev	14:33	the **L** spoke to Moses and Aaron
Lev	15: 1	the **L** spoke to Moses and Aaron
Lev	15:14	pigeons, and come before the **L**
Lev	15:15	for him before the **L** because
Lev	15:30	for her before the **L** for the
Lev	16: 1	Now the **L** spoke to Moses
Lev	16: 1	profane fire before the **L**
Lev	16: 2	and the **L** said to Moses
Lev	16: 7	the **L** at the door of the
Lev	16: 8	one lot for the **L** and the
Lev	16:10	presented alive before the **L**
Lev	16:12	from the altar before the **L**
Lev	16:13	on the fire before the **L**,
Lev	16:18	altar that is before the **L**
Lev	16:30	all your sins before the **L**
Lev	16:34	he did as the **L** commanded
Lev	17: 1	the **L** spoke to Moses, saying,
Lev	17: 2	which the **L** has commanded
Lev	17: 4	**L** before the tabernacle of
Lev	17: 4	the tabernacle of the **L**,
Lev	17: 5	to the **L** at the door of the
Lev	17: 5	as peace offerings to the **L**
Lev	17: 6	of the **L** at the door of the
Lev	17: 6	for a sweet aroma to the **L**
Lev	17: 9	meeting, to offer it to the **L**
Lev	18: 1	Then the **L** spoke to Moses,
Lev	18: 2	I am the **L** your God
Lev	18: 4	I am the **L** your God
Lev	18: 5	I am the **L**
Lev	18: 6	I am the **L**
Lev	18:21	I am the **L**
Lev	18:30	I am the **L** your God
Lev	19: 1	the **L** spoke to Moses, saying,
Lev	19: 2	for I the **L** your God am holy
Lev	19: 3	I am the **L** your God
Lev	19: 4	I am the **L** your God
Lev	19: 5	of peace offering to the **L**
Lev	19: 8	hallowed offering of the **L**
Lev	19:10	I am the **L** your God
Lev	19:12	I am the **L**
Lev	19:14	I am the **L**
Lev	19:16	I am the **L**
Lev	19:18	I am the **L**
Lev	19:21	trespass offering to the **L**
Lev	19:22	offering before the **L** for his
Lev	19:24	be holy, a praise to the **L**
Lev	19:25	I am the **L** your God
Lev	19:28	I am the **L**
Lev	19:30	I am the **L**
Lev	19:31	I am the **L** your God
Lev	19:32	I am the **L**
Lev	19:34	I am the **L** your God
Lev	19:36	I am the **L** your God, who
Lev	19:37	I am the **L**
Lev	20: 1	Then the **L** spoke to Moses,
Lev	20: 7	holy, for I am the **L** your God
Lev	20: 8	I am the **L** who sanctifies you
Lev	20:24	I am the **L** your God, who
Lev	20:26	to Me, for I the **L** am holy
Lev	21: 1	And the **L** said to Moses,
Lev	21: 6	of the **L** made by fire, and the
Lev	21: 8	be holy to you, for I the **L**
Lev	21:12	I am the **L**
Lev	21:15	for I the **L** sanctify him
Lev	21:16	the **L** spoke to Moses, saying,
Lev	21:21	made by fire to the **L**
Lev	21:23	for I the **L** sanctify them
Lev	22: 1	Then the **L** spoke to Moses,
Lev	22: 2	I am the **L**
Lev	22: 3	of Israel sanctify to the **L**
Lev	22: 3	I am the **L**
Lev	22: 8	I am the **L**
Lev	22: 9	I the **L** sanctify them
Lev	22:15	which they offer to the **L**
Lev	22:16	for I the **L** sanctify them
Lev	22:17	the **L** spoke to Moses, saying,
Lev	22:18	to the **L** as a burnt offering
Lev	22:21	of peace offering to the **L**
Lev	22:22	you shall not offer to the **L**
Lev	22:22	of them on the altar to the **L**
Lev	22:24	**L** what is bruised or crushed

Lev 22:26 the **L** spoke to Moses, saying
Lev 22:27 made by fire to the **L**
Lev 22:29 of thanksgiving to the **L**,
Lev 22:30 I am the **L**
Lev 22:31 I am the **L**
Lev 22:32 I am the **L** who sanctifies you
Lev 22:33 I am the **L**
Lev 23: 1 the **L** spoke to Moses, saying,
Lev 23: 2 The feasts of the **L**, which
Lev 23: 3 the **L** in all your dwellings
Lev 23: 4 These are the feasts of the **L**
Lev 23: 6 of Unleavened Bread to the **L**
Lev 23: 8 fire to the **L** for seven days
Lev 23: 9 the **L** spoke to Moses, saying,
Lev 23:11 wave the sheaf before the **L**
Lev 23:12 as a burnt offering to the **L**
Lev 23:13 made by fire to the **L**, for a
Lev 23:16 a new grain offering to the **L**
Lev 23:17 are the firstfruits to the **L**
Lev 23:18 as a burnt offering to the **L**
Lev 23:18 for a sweet aroma to the **L**
Lev 23:20 a wave offering before the **L**
Lev 23:20 holy to the **L** for the priest
Lev 23:22 I am the **L** your God
Lev 23:23 Then the **L** spoke to Moses,
Lev 23:25 made by fire to the **L**
Lev 23:26 the **L** spoke to Moses, saying
Lev 23:27 made by fire to the **L**
Lev 23:28 for you before the **L** your God
Lev 23:33 Then the **L** spoke to Moses,
Lev 23:34 for seven days to the **L**
Lev 23:36 made by fire to the **L**
Lev 23:36 made by fire to the **L**
Lev 23:37 **L** which you shall proclaim to
Lev 23:37 made by fire to the **L**, a
Lev 23:38 besides the Sabbaths of the **L**
Lev 23:38 which you give to the **L**
Lev 23:39 feast of the **L** for seven days
Lev 23:40 the **L** your God for seven days
Lev 23:41 keep it as a feast to the **L**
Lev 23:43 I am the **L** your God
Lev 23:44 of Israel the feasts of the **L**
Lev 24: 1 Then the **L** spoke to Moses,
Lev 24: 3 before the **L** continually
Lev 24: 4 before the **L** continually
Lev 24: 6 the pure table before the **L**
Lev 24: 7 made by fire to the **L**
Lev 24: 8 before the **L** continually,
Lev 24: 9 of the **L** made by fire, by a
Lev 24:11 the name of the **L**
Lev 24:12 that the mind of the **L** might
Lev 24:13 the **L** spoke to Moses, saying,
Lev 24:16 the **L** shall surely be put to
Lev 24:16 the name of the **L**
Lev 24:22 for I am the **L** your God
Lev 24:23 did as the **L** commanded Moses
Lev 25: 1 the **L** spoke to Moses on Mount
Lev 25: 2 shall keep a sabbath to the **L**
Lev 25: 4 the land, a sabbath to the **L**
Lev 25:17 for I am the **L** your God
Lev 25:38 I am the **L** your God, who
Lev 25:55 I am the **L** your God
Lev 26: 1 for I am the **L** your God
Lev 26: 2 I am the **L**
Lev 26:13 I am the **L** your God, who
Lev 26:44 for I am the **L** their God
Lev 26:45 I am the **L**
Lev 26:46 laws which the **L** made between
Lev 27: 1 Now the **L** spoke to Moses,
Lev 27: 2 vow certain persons to the **L**
Lev 27: 9 bring as an offering to the **L**
Lev 27: 9 gives to the **L** shall be holy
Lev 27:11 offer as a sacrifice to the **L**
Lev 27:14 his house to be holy to the **L**
Lev 27:16 if a man sanctifies to the **L**
Lev 27:21 shall be holy to the **L**, as a
Lev 27:22 if a man sanctifies to the **L**
Lev 27:23 as a holy offering to the **L**
Lev 27:28 to the **L** of all that he has
Lev 27:28 is most holy to the **L**
Lev 27:30 It is holy to the **L**
Lev 27:32 one shall be holy to the **L**
Lev 27:34 the **L** commanded Moses for the
Num 1: 1 Now the **L** spoke to Moses in
Num 1:19 As the **L** commanded Moses, so
Num 1:48 for the **L** had spoken to Moses
Num 1:54 that the **L** commanded Moses
Num 2: 1 the **L** spoke to Moses and Aaron
Num 2:33 just as the **L** commanded Moses
Num 2:34 that the **L** commanded Moses
Num 3: 1 Moses when the **L** spoke with
Num 3: 4 **L** when they offered profane
Num 3: 4 profane fire before the **L** in
Num 3: 5 the **L** spoke to Moses, saying
Num 3:11 Then the **L** spoke to Moses,
Num 3:13 I am the **L**
Num 3:14 Then the **L** spoke to Moses in
Num 3:16 to the word of the **L**, as he
Num 3:39 at the commandment of the **L**
Num 3:40 Then the **L** said to Moses
Num 3:41 I am the **L**
Num 3:42 as the **L** commanded him
Num 3:44 Then the **L** spoke to Moses,
Num 3:45 I am the **L**
Num 3:51 to the word of the **L**, as the
Num 3:51 as the **L** commanded Moses
Num 4: 1 Then the **L** spoke to Moses and
Num 4:17 Then the **L** spoke to Moses and
Num 4:21 Then the **L** spoke to Moses,
Num 4:37 of the **L** by the hand of Moses
Num 4:41 to the commandment of the **L**
Num 4:45 to the word of the **L** by the
Num 4:49 **L** they were numbered by the
Num 4:49 the **L** commanded Moses
Num 5: 1 the **L** spoke to Moses, saying
Num 5: 4 as the **L** spoke to Moses, so
Num 5: 5 Then the **L** spoke to Moses,
Num 5: 6 unfaithfulness against the **L**
Num 5: 8 go to the **L** for the priest
Num 5:11 the **L** spoke to Moses, saying,
Num 5:16 near, and set her before the **L**
Num 5:18 stand the woman before the **L**
Num 5:21 the **L** make you a curse and an
Num 5:21 when the **L** makes your thigh
Num 5:25 the offering before the **L**
Num 5:30 stand the woman before the **L**
Num 6: 1 Then the **L** spoke to Moses,
Num 6: 2 to separate himself to the **L**
Num 6: 5 he separated himself to the **L**
Num 6: 6 **L** he shall not go near a dead
Num 6: 8 he shall be holy to the **L**
Num 6:12 **L** the days of his separation
Num 6:14 present his offering to the **L**
Num 6:16 shall bring them before the **L**
Num 6:17 of peace offering to the **L**
Num 6:20 a wave offering before the **L**
Num 6:21 to the **L** the offering for his
Num 6:22 the **L** spoke to Moses, saying
Num 6:24 The **L** bless you and keep you
Num 6:25 the **L** make His face shine
Num 6:26 the **L** lift up His countenance
Num 7: 3 their offering before the **L**
Num 7: 4 Then the **L** spoke to Moses,
Num 7:11 For the **L** said to Moses
Num 8: 1 the **L** spoke to Moses, saying
Num 8: 3 as the **L** commanded Moses
Num 8: 4 which the **L** had shown Moses
Num 8: 5 Then the **L** spoke to Moses,
Num 8:10 the Levites before the **L**, and
Num 8:11 the Levites before the **L**, as
Num 8:11 may perform the work of the **L**
Num 8:12 as a burnt offering to the **L**
Num 8:13 a wave offering to the **L**
Num 8:20 according to all that the **L**
Num 8:21 a wave offering before the **L**
Num 8:22 as the **L** commanded Moses
Num 8:23 Then the **L** spoke to Moses,
Num 9: 1 Now the **L** spoke to Moses in
Num 9: 5 that the **L** commanded Moses
Num 9: 7 the offering of the **L** at its
Num 9: 8 that I may hear what the **L**
Num 9: 9 Then the **L** spoke to Moses,
Num 9:13 the **L** at its appointed time
Num 9:18 At the command of the **L** the
Num 9:18 of the **L** they would camp
Num 9:19 kept the charge of the **L** and
Num 9:20 to the command of the **L** they
Num 9:20 of the **L** they would journey
Num 9:23 At the command of the **L** they
Num 9:23 of the **L** they journeyed
Num 9:23 they kept the charge of the **L**
Num 9:23 of the **L** by the hand of Moses
Num 10: 1 the **L** spoke to Moses, saying
Num 10: 9 before the **L** your God, and you
Num 10:10 I am the **L** your God
Num 10:13 of the **L** by the hand of Moses
Num 10:29 the place of which the **L** said
Num 10:29 for the **L** has promised good
Num 10:32 good the **L** will do to us, the
Num 10:33 from the mountain of the **L** on
Num 10:33 **L** went before them for the
Num 10:34 the cloud of the **L** was above
Num 10:35 Rise up, O **L**! Let Your
Num 10:36 Return, O **L**, to the many
Num 11: 1 it displeased the **L**
Num 11: 1 for the **L** heard it, and His
Num 11: 1 of the **L** burned among them
Num 11: 2 and when Moses prayed to the **L**
Num 11: 3 the **L** had burned among them
Num 11:10 and the anger of the **L** was
Num 11:11 So Moses said to the **L**, "Why
Num 11:16 So the **L** said to Moses
Num 11:18 wept in the hearing of the **L**
Num 11:18 Therefore the **L** will give
Num 11:20 the **L** who is among you, and
Num 11:23 And the **L** said to Moses,
Num 11:24 the people the words of the **L**
Num 11:25 Then the **L** came down in the
Num 11:28 Moses my **l**, forbid them
Num 11:29 and that the **L** would put His
Num 11:31 a wind went out from the **L**
Num 11:33 the wrath of the **L** was
Num 11:33 the **L** struck the people with
Num 12: 2 Has the **L** indeed spoken only
Num 12: 2 And the **L** heard it
Num 12: 4 Suddenly the **L** said to Moses,
Num 12: 5 Then the **L** came down in the
Num 12: 6 a prophet among you, I, the **L**
Num 12: 8 and he sees the form of the **L**
Num 12: 9 So the anger of the **L** was
Num 12:11 Oh, my **l**! Please do not lay
Num 12:13 So Moses cried out to the **L**
Num 12:14 Then the **L** said to Moses,
Num 13: 1 the **L** spoke to Moses, saying,
Num 13: 3 to the command of the **L**, all
Num 14: 3 Why has the **L** brought us to
Num 14: 8 If the **L** delights in us, then
Num 14: 9 do not rebel against the **L**
Num 14: 9 them, and the **L** is with us
Num 14:10 Now the glory of the **L**
Num 14:11 And the **L** said to Moses
Num 14:13 And Moses said to the **L**
Num 14:14 They have heard that You, **L**
Num 14:14 that You, **L**, are seen face to
Num 14:16 Because the **L** was not able
Num 14:17 the power of my **L** be great
Num 14:18 The **L** is longsuffering and
Num 14:20 the **L** said: "I have pardoned
Num 14:21 with the glory of the **L**
Num 14:26 Then the **L** spoke to Moses and
Num 14:28 them, 'As I live,' says the **L**
Num 14:35 I the **L** have spoken this
Num 14:37 by the plague before the **L**
Num 14:40 which the **L** has promised, for
Num 14:41 the command of the **L**
Num 14:42 for the **L** is not among you
Num 14:43 have turned away from the **L**
Num 14:43 the **L** will not be with you
Num 14:44 ark of the covenant of the **L**
Num 15: 1 the **L** spoke to Moses, saying,
Num 15: 3 an offering by fire to the **L**
Num 15: 3 make a sweet aroma to the **L**
Num 15: 4 to the **L** shall bring a grain
Num 15: 7 as a sweet aroma to the **L**
Num 15: 8 as a peace offering to the **L**
Num 15:10 fire, a sweet aroma to the **L**
Num 15:13 fire, a sweet aroma to the **L**
Num 15:14 fire, a sweet aroma to the **L**
Num 15:15 the stranger be before the **L**
Num 15:17 Again the **L** spoke to Moses,
Num 15:19 up a heave offering to the **L**
Num 15:21 meal you shall give to the **L**
Num 15:22 the **L** has spoken to Moses
Num 15:23 all that the **L** has commanded
Num 15:23 day the **L** gave commandment
Num 15:24 as a sweet aroma to the **L**
Num 15:25 made by fire to the **L**, and
Num 15:25 sin offering before the **L**
Num 15:28 unintentionally before the **L**
Num 15:30 one brings reproach on the **L**
Num 15:31 despised the word of the **L**
Num 15:35 Then the **L** said to Moses,
Num 15:36 as the **L** commanded Moses, all
Num 15:37 Again the **L** spoke to Moses,
Num 15:39 all the commandments of the **L**
Num 15:41 I am the **L** your God, who
Num 15:41 I am the **L** your God
Num 16: 3 them, and the **L** is among them
Num 16: 3 the congregation of the **L**
Num 16: 5 the **L** will show who is His

Num 16: 7 in them before the **L** tomorrow
Num 16: 7 be that the man whom the **L**
Num 16: 9 of the tabernacle of the **L**
Num 16:11 together against the **L**
Num 16:15 very angry, and said to the **L**
Num 16:16 be present before the **L**
Num 16:17 bring his censer before the **L**
Num 16:19 of the **L** appeared to all the
Num 16:20 the **L** spoke to Moses and Aaron
Num 16:23 So the **L** spoke to Moses,
Num 16:28 you shall know that the **L** has
Num 16:29 then the **L** has not sent me
Num 16:30 But if the **L** creates a new
Num 16:30 these men have rejected the **L**
Num 16:35 And a fire came out from the **L**
Num 16:36 Then the **L** spoke to Moses,
Num 16:38 presented them before the **L**
Num 16:40 to offer incense before the **L**
Num 16:40 just as the **L** had said to him
Num 16:41 killed the people of the **L**
Num 16:42 the glory of the **L** appeared
Num 16:44 the **L** spoke to Moses, saying,
Num 16:46 wrath has gone out from the **L**
Num 17: 1 the **L** spoke to Moses, saying
Num 17: 7 the **L** in the tabernacle of
Num 17: 9 the **L** to all the children of
Num 17:10 And the **L** said to Moses,
Num 17:11 just as the **L** had commanded
Num 17:13 tabernacle of the **L** must die
Num 18: 1 Then the **L** said to Aaron
Num 18: 6 a gift to you, given by the **L**
Num 18: 8 And the **L** spoke to Aaron
Num 18:12 which they offer to the **L**
Num 18:13 which they bring to the **L**
Num 18:15 which they bring to the **L**
Num 18:17 for a sweet aroma to the **L**
Num 18:19 of Israel offer to the **L**, I
Num 18:19 forever before the **L** with you
Num 18:20 Then the **L** said to Aaron
Num 18:24 as a heave offering to the **L**
Num 18:25 Then the **L** spoke to Moses,
Num 18:26 heave offering of it to the **L**
Num 18:28 a heave offering to the **L**
Num 18:29 heave offering due to the **L**
Num 19: 1 Now the **L** spoke to Moses and
Num 19: 2 law which the **L** has commanded
Num 19:13 the tabernacle of the **L**
Num 19:20 the sanctuary of the **L**
Num 20: 3 brethren died before the **L**
Num 20: 4 of the **L** into this wilderness
Num 20: 6 of the **L** appeared to them
Num 20: 7 Then the **L** spoke to Moses,
Num 20: 9 the **L** as He commanded him
Num 20:12 Then the **L** spoke to Moses and
Num 20:13 Israel contended with the **L**
Num 20:16 When we cried out to the **L**
Num 20:23 the **L** spoke to Moses and Aaron
Num 20:27 did just as the **L** commanded
Num 21: 2 So Israel made a vow to the **L**
Num 21: 3 the **L** listened to the voice
Num 21: 6 So the **L** sent fiery serpents
Num 21: 7 we have spoken against the **L**
Num 21: 7 pray to the **L** that He take
Num 21: 8 Then the **L** said to Moses,
Num 21:14 the Book of the Wars of the **L**
Num 21:16 where the **L** said to Moses
Num 21:34 Then the **L** said to Moses,
Num 22: 8 to you, as the **L** speaks to me
Num 22:13 for the **L** has refused to give
Num 22:18 the word of the **L** my God, to
Num 22:19 more the **L** will say to me
Num 22:22 the Angel of the **L** took His
Num 22:23 **L** standing in the way with
Num 22:24 Then the Angel of the **L** stood
Num 22:25 donkey saw the Angel of the **L**
Num 22:26 Angel of the **L** went further
Num 22:27 donkey saw the Angel of the **L**
Num 22:28 Then the **L** opened the mouth
Num 22:31 Then the **L** opened Balaam's
Num 22:31 he saw the Angel of the **L**
Num 22:32 Angel of the **L** said to him
Num 22:34 said to the Angel of the **L**
Num 22:35 Angel of the **L** said to Balaam
Num 23: 3 perhaps the **L** will come to
Num 23: 5 Then the **L** put a word in
Num 23: 8 whom the **L** has not denounced
Num 23:12 the **L** has put in my mouth
Num 23:15 while I meet the **L** over there
Num 23:16 Then the **L** met Balaam, and put
Num 23:17 What has the **L** spoken
Num 23:21 The **L** his God is with him, and
Num 23:26 All that the **L** speaks, that
Num 24: 1 pleased the **L** to bless Israel
Num 24: 6 like aloes planted by the **L**
Num 24:11 the **L** has kept you back from
Num 24:13 go beyond the word of the **L**
Num 24:13 but what the **L** says, that I
Num 25: 3 and the anger of the **L** was
Num 25: 4 Then the **L** said to Moses,
Num 25: 4 the offenders before the **L**
Num 25: 4 the fierce anger of the **L** may
Num 25:10 Then the **L** spoke to Moses,
Num 25:16 Then the **L** spoke to Moses,
Num 26: 1 that the **L** spoke to Moses and
Num 26: 4 just as the **L** commanded Moses
Num 26: 9 they contended against the **L**
Num 26:52 Then the **L** spoke to Moses,
Num 26:61 profane fire before the **L**
Num 26:65 For the **L** had said of them,
Num 27: 3 together against the **L**, in
Num 27: 5 their case before the **L**
Num 27: 6 the **L** spoke to Moses, saying
Num 27:11 just as the **L** commanded Moses
Num 27:12 Now the **L** said to Moses
Num 27:15 Then Moses spoke to the **L**
Num 27:16 Let the **L**, the God of the
Num 27:17 the congregation of the **L** may
Num 27:18 And the **L** said to Moses
Num 27:21 shall inquire before the **L**
Num 27:22 did as the **L** commanded him
Num 27:23 just as the **L** commanded by
Num 28: 1 Now the **L** spoke to Moses,
Num 28: 3 you shall offer to the **L**
Num 28: 6 made by fire to the **L**
Num 28: 7 drink to the **L** as an offering
Num 28: 8 fire, a sweet aroma to the **L**
Num 28:11 a burnt offering to the **L**
Num 28:13 made by fire to the **L**
Num 28:15 to the **L** shall be offered
Num 28:16 is the Passover of the **L**
Num 28:19 as a burnt offering to the **L**
Num 28:24 as a sweet aroma to the **L**
Num 28:26 the **L** at your Feast of Weeks
Num 28:27 as a sweet aroma to the **L**
Num 29: 2 as a sweet aroma to the **L**
Num 29: 6 made by fire to the **L**
Num 29: 8 to the **L** as a sweet aroma
Num 29:12 a feast to the **L** seven days
Num 29:13 as a sweet aroma to the **L**
Num 29:36 as a sweet aroma to the **L**
Num 29:39 you shall present to the **L** at
Num 29:40 just as the **L** commanded Moses
Num 30: 1 which the **L** has commanded
Num 30: 2 If a man vows a vow to the **L**
Num 30: 3 a woman vows a vow to the **L**
Num 30: 5 and the **L** will forgive her,
Num 30: 8 and the **L** will forgive her
Num 30:12 and the **L** will forgive her
Num 30:16 which the **L** commanded Moses
Num 31: 1 the **L** spoke to Moses, saying
Num 31: 3 vengeance for the **L** on Midian
Num 31: 7 just as the **L** commanded Moses
Num 31:16 the **L** in the incident of Peor
Num 31:16 the congregation of the **L**
Num 31:21 which the **L** commanded Moses
Num 31:25 the **L** spoke to Moses, saying
Num 31:28 levy a tribute for the **L** on
Num 31:29 as a heave offering to the **L**
Num 31:30 of the tabernacle of the **L**
Num 31:31 did as the **L** commanded Moses
Num 31:41 as the **L** commanded Moses
Num 31:47 of the tabernacle of the **L**
Num 31:47 as the **L** commanded Moses
Num 31:50 brought an offering for the **L**
Num 31:50 for ourselves before the **L**
Num 31:52 that they offered to the **L**
Num 31:54 of Israel before the **L**
Num 32: 4 the **L** defeated before the
Num 32: 7 which the **L** has given them
Num 32: 9 which the **L** had given them
Num 32:12 have wholly followed the **L**
Num 32:13 the sight of the **L** was gone
Num 32:14 anger of the **L** against Israel
Num 32:20 before the **L** for the war,
Num 32:21 over the Jordan before the **L**
Num 32:22 land is subdued before the **L**
Num 32:22 and be blameless before the **L**
Num 32:22 your possession before the **L**
Num 32:23 you have sinned against the **L**
Num 32:25 will do as my **l** commands
Num 32:27 war, before the **L** to battle
Num 32:27 to battle, just as my **l** says
Num 32:29 armed for battle before the **L**
Num 32:31 As the **L** has said to your
Num 32:32 the **L** into the land of Canaan
Num 33: 2 at the command of the **L**
Num 33: 4 whom the **L** had killed among
Num 33: 4 the **L** had executed judgments
Num 33:38 Hor at the command of the **L**
Num 33:50 Now the **L** spoke to Moses in
Num 34: 1 Then the **L** spoke to Moses,
Num 34:13 which the **L** has commanded to
Num 34:16 the **L** spoke to Moses, saying,
Num 34:29 These are the ones the **L**
Num 35: 1 the **L** spoke to Moses in the
Num 35: 9 Then the **L** spoke to Moses,
Num 35:34 for I the **L** dwell among the
Num 36: 2 The **L** commanded my **l** Moses
Num 36: 2 my **l** was commanded by the **L**
Num 36: 5 to the word of the **L**, saying
Num 36: 6 This is what the **L** commands
Num 36:10 Just as the **L** commanded Moses
Num 36:13 the judgments which the **L**
Deut 1: 3 that the **L** had given him as
Deut 1: 6 The **L** our God spoke to us in
Deut 1: 8 the **L** swore to your fathers
Deut 1:10 The **L** your God has
Deut 1:11 May the **L** God of your
Deut 1:19 as the **L** our God had
Deut 1:20 which the **L** our God is giving
Deut 1:21 the **L** your God has set the
Deut 1:21 as the **L** God of your fathers
Deut 1:25 the **L** our God is giving us
Deut 1:26 the command of the **L** your God
Deut 1:27 said, 'Because the **L** hates us
Deut 1:30 The **L** your God, who goes
Deut 1:31 the **L** your God carried you
Deut 1:32 not believe the **L** your God
Deut 1:34 the **L** heard the sound of your
Deut 1:36 he wholly followed the **L**
Deut 1:37 The **L** was also angry with me
Deut 1:41 We have sinned against the **L**
Deut 1:41 fight, just as the **L** our God
Deut 1:42 the **L** said to me, 'Tell them,
Deut 1:43 against the command of the **L**
Deut 1:45 returned and wept before the **L**
Deut 1:45 but the **L** would not listen to
Deut 2: 1 as the **L** spoke to me, and we
Deut 2: 2 the **L** spoke to me, saying
Deut 2: 7 For the **L** your God has
Deut 2: 7 These forty years the **L** your
Deut 2: 9 Then the **L** said to me, 'Do
Deut 2:12 which the **L** gave them
Deut 2:14 just as the **L** had sworn to
Deut 2:15 of the **L** was against them
Deut 2:17 that the **L** spoke to me,
Deut 2:21 But the **L** destroyed them
Deut 2:29 the **L** our God is giving us
Deut 2:30 for the **L** your God hardened
Deut 2:31 the **L** said to me, 'See, I
Deut 2:33 the **L** our God delivered him
Deut 2:36 the **L** our God delivered all
Deut 2:37 or wherever the **L** our God had
Deut 3: 2 the **L** said to me, 'Do not
Deut 3: 3 So the **L** our God also
Deut 3:18 The **L** your God has given you
Deut 3:20 until the **L** has given rest
Deut 3:20 the **L** your God is giving them
Deut 3:21 **L** your God has done to these
Deut 3:21 so will the **L** do to all the
Deut 3:22 for the **L** your God Himself
Deut 3:23 with the **L** at that time,
Deut 3:24 O **L** God, You have begun to
Deut 3:26 But the **L** was angry with me
Deut 3:26 So the **L** said to me
Deut 4: 1 the **L** God of your fathers is
Deut 4: 2 the commandments of the **L**
Deut 4: 3 what the **L** did at Baal Peor
Deut 4: 3 for the **L** your God has
Deut 4: 4 **L** your God are alive today
Deut 4: 5 just as the **L** my God
Deut 4: 7 as the **L** our God is to us,
Deut 4:10 the **L** your God in Horeb, when
Deut 4:10 when the **L** said to me
Deut 4:12 the **L** spoke to you out of the
Deut 4:14 the **L** commanded me at that
Deut 4:15 you saw no form when the **L**
Deut 4:19 which the **L** your God has
Deut 4:20 But the **L** has taken you and
Deut 4:21 Furthermore the **L** was angry

Deut 4:21 the good land which the L
Deut 4:23 forget the covenant of the L
Deut 4:23 L your God has forbidden you
Deut 4:24 For the L your God is a
Deut 4:25 L your God to provoke Him to
Deut 4:27 the L will scatter you among
Deut 4:27 where the L will drive you
Deut 4:29 you will seek the L your God
Deut 4:30 you turn to the L your God
Deut 4:31 (for the L your God is a
Deut 4:34 the L your God did for you in
Deut 4:35 that the L Himself is God
Deut 4:39 that the L Himself is God in
Deut 4:40 L your God is giving you for
Deut 5: 2 The L our God made a covenant
Deut 5: 3 The L did not make this
Deut 5: 4 The L talked with you face to
Deut 5: 5 I stood between the L and you
Deut 5: 5 to you the word of the L
Deut 5: 6 I am the L your God who
Deut 5: 9 the L your God, am a jealous
Deut 5:11 of the L your God in vain
Deut 5:11 for the L will not hold him
Deut 5:12 as the L your God commanded
Deut 5:14 the Sabbath of the L your God
Deut 5:15 that the L your God brought
Deut 5:15 therefore the L your God
Deut 5:16 mother, as the L your God has
Deut 5:16 the L your God is giving you
Deut 5:22 These words the L spoke to
Deut 5:24 Surely the L our God has
Deut 5:25 of the L our God anymore,
Deut 5:27 that the L our God may say
Deut 5:27 the L our God says to you
Deut 5:28 Then the L heard the voice of
Deut 5:28 to me, and the L said to me
Deut 5:32 be careful to do as the L
Deut 5:33 in all the ways which the L
Deut 6: 1 judgments which the L your
Deut 6: 2 you may fear the L your God
Deut 6: 3 the L God of your fathers has
Deut 6: 4 L our God, the L is one
Deut 6: 5 You shall love the L your God
Deut 6:10 when the L your God brings
Deut 6:12 lest you forget the L who
Deut 6:13 You shall fear the L your God
Deut 6:15 (for the L your God is a
Deut 6:15 lest the anger of the L your
Deut 6:16 You shall not tempt the L
Deut 6:17 of the L your God, His
Deut 6:18 and good in the sight of the L
Deut 6:18 the L swore to your fathers
Deut 6:19 you, as the L has spoken
Deut 6:20 the judgments which the L our
Deut 6:21 the L brought us out of Egypt
Deut 6:22 the L showed signs and wonders
Deut 6:24 the L commanded us to observe
Deut 6:24 to fear the L our God, for
Deut 6:25 before the L our God, as He
Deut 7: 1 When the L your God brings
Deut 7: 2 when the L your God delivers
Deut 7: 4 so the anger of the L will be
Deut 7: 6 holy people to the L your God
Deut 7: 6 the L your God has chosen you
Deut 7: 7 The L did not set His love on
Deut 7: 8 but because the L loves you
Deut 7: 8 the L has brought you out
Deut 7: 9 know that the L your God, He
Deut 7:12 that the L your God will keep
Deut 7:15 the L will take away from you
Deut 7:16 all the peoples whom the L
Deut 7:18 remember well what the L your
Deut 7:19 arm, by which the L your God
Deut 7:19 So shall the L your God do to
Deut 7:20 Moreover the L your God will
Deut 7:21 for the L your God, the great
Deut 7:22 the L your God will drive out
Deut 7:23 But the L your God will
Deut 7:25 abomination to the L your God
Deut 8: 1 the L swore to your fathers
Deut 8: 2 L your God led you all the
Deut 8: 3 from the mouth of the L
Deut 8: 5 so the L your God chastens
Deut 8: 6 of the L your God, to walk in
Deut 8: 7 For the L your God is
Deut 8:10 then you shall bless the L
Deut 8:11 that you do not forget the L
Deut 8:14 you forget the L your God who
Deut 8:18 shall remember the L your God
Deut 8:19 means forget the L your God
Deut 8:20 the L destroys before you
Deut 8:20 the voice of the L your God
Deut 9: 3 the L your God is He who goes
Deut 9: 3 as the L has said to you
Deut 9: 4 after the L your God has cast
Deut 9: 4 the L has brought me in to
Deut 9: 4 L is driving them out from
Deut 9: 5 L your God drives them out
Deut 9: 5 the L swore to your fathers
Deut 9: 6 understand that the L your
Deut 9: 7 L your God to wrath in the
Deut 9: 7 been rebellious against the L
Deut 9: 8 you provoked the L to wrath
Deut 9: 8 so that the L was angry
Deut 9: 9 which the L made with you
Deut 9:10 Then the L delivered to me
Deut 9:10 all the words which the L had
Deut 9:11 that the L gave me the two
Deut 9:12 Then the L said to me, 'Arise
Deut 9:13 Furthermore the L spoke to me
Deut 9:16 sinned against the L your God
Deut 9:16 which the L had commanded
Deut 9:18 And I fell down before the L
Deut 9:18 in the sight of the L, to
Deut 9:19 the L was angry with you, to
Deut 9:19 But the L listened to me at
Deut 9:20 the L was very angry with
Deut 9:22 you provoked the L to wrath
Deut 9:23 when the L sent you from
Deut 9:23 commandment of the L your
Deut 9:24 L from the day that I knew
Deut 9:25 myself before the L
Deut 9:25 because the L had said He
Deut 9:26 Therefore I prayed to the L
Deut 9:26 O L God, do not destroy Your
Deut 9:28 Because the L was not able to
Deut 10: 1 At that time the L said to me
Deut 10: 4 which the L had spoken to you
Deut 10: 4 and the L gave them to me
Deut 10: 5 just as the L commanded me
Deut 10: 8 At that time the L separated
Deut 10: 8 ark of the covenant of the L
Deut 10: 8 the L to minister to Him and
Deut 10: 9 the L is his inheritance,
Deut 10: 9 just as the L your God
Deut 10:10 the L also heard me at that
Deut 10:10 the L chose not to destroy
Deut 10:11 Then the L said to me, 'Arise
Deut 10:12 what does the L your God
Deut 10:12 but to fear the L your God
Deut 10:12 to serve the L your God with
Deut 10:13 the commandments of the L
Deut 10:14 belong to the L your God,
Deut 10:15 The L delighted only in your
Deut 10:17 For the L your God is God of
Deut 10:17 L of lords, the great God,
Deut 10:20 You shall fear the L your God
Deut 10:22 now the L your God has made
Deut 11: 1 you shall love the L your God
Deut 11: 2 chastening of the L your God
Deut 11: 4 how the L has destroyed them
Deut 11: 7 act of the L which He did
Deut 11: 9 L swore to give your fathers
Deut 11:12 which the L your God cares
Deut 11:12 the eyes of the L your God
Deut 11:13 today, to love the L your God
Deut 11:17 which the L is giving you
Deut 11:21 L swore to your fathers to
Deut 11:22 to love the L your God, to
Deut 11:23 then the L will drive out all
Deut 11:25 the L your God will put the
Deut 11:27 the commandments of the L
Deut 11:28 of the L your God, but turn
Deut 11:29 be, when the L your God has
Deut 11:31 the L your God is giving you
Deut 12: 1 in the land which the L God
Deut 12: 4 L your God with such things
Deut 12: 5 where the L your God chooses
Deut 12: 7 eat before the L your God
Deut 12: 7 in which the L your God has
Deut 12: 9 the L your God is giving you
Deut 12:10 L your God is giving you to
Deut 12:11 L your God chooses to make
Deut 12:11 which you vow to the L
Deut 12:12 rejoice before the L your God
Deut 12:14 the place which the L chooses
Deut 12:15 to the blessing of the L your
Deut 12:18 must eat them before the L
Deut 12:18 which the L your God chooses
Deut 12:18 L your God in all to which
Deut 12:20 When the L your God enlarges
Deut 12:21 If the place where the L your
Deut 12:21 which the L has given you
Deut 12:25 right in the sight of the L
Deut 12:26 the place which the L chooses
Deut 12:27 the altar of the L your God
Deut 12:27 the altar of the L your God
Deut 12:28 the sight of the L your God
Deut 12:29 When the L your God cuts off
Deut 12:31 the L your God in that way
Deut 12:31 L which He hates they have
Deut 13: 3 for the L your God is testing
Deut 13: 3 the L your God with all your
Deut 13: 4 walk after the L your God
Deut 13: 5 you away from the L your God
Deut 13: 5 L your God commanded you to
Deut 13:10 you away from the L your God
Deut 13:12 which the L your God gives
Deut 13:16 plunder, for the L your God
Deut 13:17 that the L may turn from the
Deut 13:18 the voice of the L your God
Deut 13:18 in the eyes of the L your God
Deut 14: 1 children of the L your God
Deut 14: 2 holy people to the L your God
Deut 14: 2 the L has chosen you to be a
Deut 14:21 holy people to the L your God
Deut 14:23 eat before the L your God
Deut 14:23 to fear the L your God always
Deut 14:24 or if the place where the L
Deut 14:24 you, when the L your God has
Deut 14:25 which the L your God chooses
Deut 14:26 there before the L your God
Deut 14:29 that the L your God may bless
Deut 15: 4 for the L will greatly bless
Deut 15: 4 L your God is giving you to
Deut 15: 5 the voice of the L your God
Deut 15: 6 For the L your God will bless
Deut 15: 7 the L your God is giving you
Deut 15: 9 cry out to the L against you
Deut 15:10 L your God will bless you in
Deut 15:14 From what the L has blessed
Deut 15:15 the L your God redeemed you
Deut 15:18 Then the L your God will
Deut 15:19 sanctify to the L your God
Deut 15:20 shall eat it before the L
Deut 15:20 the place which the L chooses
Deut 15:21 it to the L your God
Deut 16: 1 Passover to the L your God
Deut 16: 1 in the month of Abib the L
Deut 16: 2 Passover to the L your God
Deut 16: 2 in the place where the L
Deut 16: 5 the L your God gives you
Deut 16: 6 L your God chooses to make
Deut 16: 7 which the L your God chooses
Deut 16: 8 assembly to the L your God
Deut 16:10 L your God with the tribute
Deut 16:10 as the L your God blesses you
Deut 16:11 rejoice before the L your God
Deut 16:11 at the place where the L your
Deut 16:15 keep a sacred feast to the L
Deut 16:15 the place which the L chooses
Deut 16:15 because the L your God will
Deut 16:16 shall appear before the L
Deut 16:16 before the L empty-handed
Deut 16:17 to the blessing of the L your
Deut 16:18 which the L your God gives
Deut 16:20 the L your God is giving you
Deut 16:21 yourself to the L your God
Deut 16:22 which the L your God hates
Deut 17: 1 L your God a bull or sheep
Deut 17: 1 abomination to the L your God
Deut 17: 2 the L your God gives you, a
Deut 17: 2 the sight of the L your God
Deut 17: 8 which the L your God chooses
Deut 17:10 place which the L chooses
Deut 17:12 there before the L your God
Deut 17:14 the L your God is giving you
Deut 17:15 whom the L your God chooses
Deut 17:16 for the L has said to you
Deut 17:19 learn to fear the L his God
Deut 18: 1 of the L made by fire, and His
Deut 18: 2 the L is their inheritance,
Deut 18: 5 For the L your God has chosen
Deut 18: 5 minister in the name of the L
Deut 18: 6 the place which the L chooses
Deut 18: 7 serve in the name of the L
Deut 18: 7 who stand there before the L
Deut 18: 9 the L your God is giving you
Deut 18:12 are an abomination to the L
Deut 18:12 L your God drives them out

Deut 18:13 before the **L** your God
Deut 18:14 you, the **L** your God has not
Deut 18:15 The **L** your God will raise up
Deut 18:16 **L** your God in Horeb in the
Deut 18:16 the voice of the **L** my God
Deut 18:17 And the **L** said to me
Deut 18:21 which the **L** has not spoken
Deut 18:22 speaks in the name of the **L**
Deut 18:22 which the **L** has not spoken
Deut 19: 1 When the **L** your God has cut
Deut 19: 1 the **L** your God is giving you
Deut 19: 2 of your land which the **L** your
Deut 19: 3 of your land which the **L** your
Deut 19: 8 Now if the **L** your God
Deut 19: 9 today, to love the **L** your God
Deut 19:10 of your land which the **L** your
Deut 19:14 in the land that the **L** your
Deut 19:17 shall stand before the **L**,
Deut 20: 1 for the **L** your God is with
Deut 20: 4 for the **L** your God is He who
Deut 20:13 when the **L** your God delivers
Deut 20:14 the **L** your God gives you
Deut 20:16 **L** your God gives you as an
Deut 20:17 just as the **L** your God has
Deut 20:18 sin against the **L** your God
Deut 21: 1 **L** your God is giving you to
Deut 21: 5 for the **L** your God has chosen
Deut 21: 5 to bless in the name of the **L**
Deut 21: 8 Provide atonement, O **L**, for
Deut 21: 9 right in the sight of the **L**
Deut 21:10 the **L** your God delivers them
Deut 21:23 **L** your God is giving you as
Deut 22: 5 abomination to the **L** your God
Deut 23: 1 the congregation of the **L**
Deut 23: 2 the congregation of the **L**
Deut 23: 2 the congregation of the **L**
Deut 23: 3 the congregation of the **L**
Deut 23: 3 congregation of the **L** forever
Deut 23: 5 Nevertheless the **L** your God
Deut 23: 5 but the **L** your God turned the
Deut 23: 5 because the **L** your God loves
Deut 23: 8 the congregation of the **L**
Deut 23:14 For the **L** your God walks in
Deut 23:18 the **L** your God for any vowed
Deut 23:18 abomination to the **L** your God
Deut 23:20 that the **L** your God may bless
Deut 23:21 make a vow to the **L** your God
Deut 23:21 for the **L** your God will
Deut 23:23 the **L** your God what you have
Deut 24: 4 an abomination before the **L**
Deut 24: 4 **L** your God is giving you as
Deut 24: 9 Remember what the **L** your God
Deut 24:13 to you before the **L** your God
Deut 24:15 cry out against you to the **L**
Deut 24:18 the **L** your God redeemed you
Deut 24:19 that the **L** your God may bless
Deut 25:15 in the land which the **L** your
Deut 25:16 abomination to the **L** your God
Deut 25:19 when the **L** your God has given
Deut 25:19 in the land which the **L** your
Deut 26: 1 into the land which the **L**
Deut 26: 2 the **L** your God is giving you
Deut 26: 2 **L** your God chooses to make
Deut 26: 3 I declare today to the **L**
Deut 26: 3 the **L** swore to our fathers to
Deut 26: 4 the altar of the **L** your God
Deut 26: 5 and say before the **L** your God
Deut 26: 7 to the **L** God of our fathers
Deut 26: 7 and the **L** heard our voice and
Deut 26: 8 So the **L** brought us out of
Deut 26:10 of the land which you, O **L**
Deut 26:10 set it before the **L** your God
Deut 26:10 worship before the **L** your God
Deut 26:11 **L** your God has given to you
Deut 26:13 say before the **L** your God
Deut 26:14 the voice of the **L** my God
Deut 26:16 This day the **L** your God
Deut 26:17 the **L** to be your God, and that
Deut 26:18 Also today the **L** has
Deut 26:19 holy people to the **L** your God
Deut 27: 2 to the land which the **L** your
Deut 27: 3 the **L** your God is giving you
Deut 27: 3 just as the **L** God of your
Deut 27: 5 an altar to the **L** your God
Deut 27: 6 the altar of the **L** your God
Deut 27: 6 on it to the **L** your God
Deut 27: 7 rejoice before the **L** your God
Deut 27: 9 the people of the **L** your God
Deut 27:10 the voice of the **L** your God
Deut 27:15 an abomination to the **L**, the
Deut 28: 1 the voice of the **L** your God
Deut 28: 1 that the **L** your God will set
Deut 28: 2 the voice of the **L** your God
Deut 28: 7 The **L** will cause your enemies
Deut 28: 8 The **L** will command the
Deut 28: 8 the **L** your God is giving you
Deut 28: 9 The **L** will establish you as a
Deut 28: 9 of the **L** your God and walk in
Deut 28:10 called by the name of the **L**
Deut 28:11 the **L** will grant you plenty
Deut 28:11 **L** swore to your fathers to
Deut 28:12 The **L** will open to you His
Deut 28:13 the **L** will make you the head
Deut 28:13 of the **L** your God, which I
Deut 28:15 the voice of the **L** your God
Deut 28:20 The **L** will send on you
Deut 28:21 The **L** will make the plague
Deut 28:22 The **L** will strike you with
Deut 28:24 The **L** will change the rain of
Deut 28:25 The **L** will cause you to be
Deut 28:27 The **L** will strike you with
Deut 28:28 The **L** will strike you with
Deut 28:35 The **L** will strike you in the
Deut 28:36 The **L** will bring you and the
Deut 28:37 where the **L** will lead you
Deut 28:45 the voice of the **L** your God
Deut 28:47 serve the **L** your God with joy
Deut 28:48 whom the **L** will send against
Deut 28:49 The **L** will bring a nation
Deut 28:52 the **L** your God has given you
Deut 28:53 the **L** your God has given you
Deut 28:58 awesome name, THE **L** YOUR
Deut 28:59 then the **L** will bring upon
Deut 28:61 will the **L** bring upon you
Deut 28:62 the voice of the **L** your God
Deut 28:63 that just as the **L** rejoiced
Deut 28:63 so the **L** will rejoice over
Deut 28:64 Then the **L** will scatter you
Deut 28:65 but there the **L** will give you
Deut 28:68 the **L** will take you back to
Deut 29: 1 the **L** commanded Moses to
Deut 29: 2 You have seen all that the **L**
Deut 29: 4 Yet the **L** has not given you a
Deut 29: 6 know that I am the **L** your God
Deut 29:10 today before the **L** your God
Deut 29:12 covenant with the **L** your God
Deut 29:12 which the **L** your God makes
Deut 29:15 us today before the **L** our God
Deut 29:18 away today from the **L** our God
Deut 29:20 The **L** would not spare him
Deut 29:20 for then the anger of the **L**
Deut 29:20 the **L** would blot out his name
Deut 29:21 the **L** would separate him from
Deut 29:22 which the **L** has laid on it
Deut 29:23 which the **L** overthrew in His
Deut 29:24 Why has the **L** done so to
Deut 29:25 the covenant of the **L** God of
Deut 29:27 Then the anger of the **L** was
Deut 29:28 And the **L** uprooted them from
Deut 29:29 belong to the **L** our God, but
Deut 30: 1 the **L** your God drives you
Deut 30: 2 you return to the **L** your God
Deut 30: 3 that the **L** your God will
Deut 30: 3 all the nations where the **L**
Deut 30: 4 from there the **L** your God
Deut 30: 5 Then the **L** your God will
Deut 30: 6 And the **L** your God will
Deut 30: 6 to love the **L** your God with
Deut 30: 7 Also the **L** your God will put
Deut 30: 8 again obey the voice of the **L**
Deut 30: 9 The **L** your God will make you
Deut 30: 9 For the **L** will again rejoice
Deut 30:10 the voice of the **L** your God
Deut 30:10 if you turn to the **L** your God
Deut 30:16 today to love the **L** your God
Deut 30:16 the **L** your God will bless you
Deut 30:20 you may love the **L** your God
Deut 30:20 the **L** swore to your fathers
Deut 31: 2 Also the **L** has said to me
Deut 31: 3 The **L** your God Himself
Deut 31: 3 you, just as the **L** has said
Deut 31: 4 the **L** will do to them as He
Deut 31: 5 The **L** will give them over to
Deut 31: 6 for the **L** your God, He is the
Deut 31: 7 to the land which the **L** has
Deut 31: 8 And the **L**, He is the one who
Deut 31: 9 ark of the covenant of the **L**
Deut 31:11 comes to appear before the **L**
Deut 31:12 learn to fear the **L** your God
Deut 31:13 learn to fear the **L** your God
Deut 31:14 Then the **L** said to Moses,
Deut 31:15 Now the **L** appeared at the
Deut 31:16 And the **L** said to Moses
Deut 31:25 ark of the covenant of the **L**
Deut 31:26 covenant of the **L** your God
Deut 31:27 been rebellious against the **L**
Deut 31:29 do evil in the sight of the **L**
Deut 32: 3 I proclaim the name of the **L**
Deut 32: 6 Do you thus deal with the **L**
Deut 32:12 so the **L** alone led him, and
Deut 32:19 And when the **L** saw it, He
Deut 32:27 it is not the **L** who has done
Deut 32:30 the **L** had surrendered them
Deut 32:36 For the **L** will judge His
Deut 32:48 Then the **L** spoke to Moses
Deut 33: 2 The **L** came from Sinai, and
Deut 33: 7 Hear, **L**, the voice of Judah,
Deut 33:11 Bless his substance, **L**, and
Deut 33:12 The beloved of the **L** shall
Deut 33:13 Blessed of the **L** is his land
Deut 33:21 the justice of the **L**, and His
Deut 33:23 full of the blessing of the **L**
Deut 33:29 you, a people saved by the **L**
Deut 34: 1 the **L** showed him all the land
Deut 34: 4 Then the **L** said to him
Deut 34: 5 **L** died there in the land of
Deut 34: 5 to the word of the **L**
Deut 34: 9 did as the **L** had commanded
Deut 34:10 whom the **L** knew face to face,
Deut 34:11 wonders which the **L** sent him
Josh 1: 1 of Moses the servant of the **L**
Josh 1: 1 it came to pass that the **L**
Josh 1: 9 for the **L** your God is with
Josh 1:11 **L** your God is giving you to
Josh 1:13 of the **L** commanded you,
Josh 1:13 The **L** your God is giving you
Josh 1:15 until the **L** has given your
Josh 1:15 of the land which the **L** your
Josh 1:17 Only the **L** your God be with
Josh 2: 9 I know that the **L** has given
Josh 2:10 **L** dried up the water of the
Josh 2:11 for the **L** your God, He is God
Josh 2:12 beg you, swear to me by the **L**
Josh 2:14 when the **L** has given us the
Josh 2:24 Truly the **L** has delivered all
Josh 3: 3 covenant of the **L** your God
Josh 3: 5 for tomorrow the **L** will do
Josh 3: 7 And the **L** said to Joshua,
Josh 3: 9 the words of the **L** your God
Josh 3:11 of the **L** of all the earth is
Josh 3:13 who bear the ark of the **L**
Josh 3:13 the **L** of all the earth, shall
Josh 3:17 ark of the covenant of the **L**
Josh 4: 1 that the **L** spoke to Joshua,
Josh 4: 5 **L** your God into the midst of
Josh 4: 7 ark of the covenant of the **L**
Josh 4: 8 as the **L** had spoken to Joshua
Josh 4:10 was finished that the **L** had
Josh 4:11 over, that the ark of the **L**
Josh 4:13 over before the **L** for battle
Josh 4:14 On that day the **L** magnified
Josh 4:15 Then the **L** spoke to Joshua,
Josh 4:18 **L** had come from the midst of
Josh 4:23 for the **L** your God dried up
Josh 4:23 as the **L** your God did to the
Josh 4:24 may know the hand of the **L**
Josh 4:24 fear the **L** your God forever
Josh 5: 1 heard that the **L** had dried up
Josh 5: 2 time the **L** said to Joshua
Josh 5: 6 not obey the voice of the **L**
Josh 5: 6 to whom the **L** swore that He
Josh 5: 6 them the land which the **L** had
Josh 5: 9 Then the **L** said to Joshua,
Josh 5:14 army of the **L** I have now come
Josh 5:14 What does my **L** say to His
Josh 6: 2 And the **L** said to Joshua
Josh 6: 6 horns before the ark of the **L**
Josh 6: 7 before the ark of the **L**
Josh 6: 8 horns before the **L** advanced
Josh 6: 8 of the **L** followed them
Josh 6:11 ark of the **L** circle the city
Josh 6:12 took up the ark of the **L**
Josh 6:13 of the **L** went on continually
Josh 6:13 came after the ark of the **L**
Josh 6:16 for the **L** has given you the
Josh 6:17 by the **L** to destruction, it
Josh 6:19 are consecrated to the **L**
Josh 6:19 into the treasury of the **L**
Josh 6:24 of the house of the **L**
Josh 6:26 man before the **L** who rises up

Josh 6:27 So the L was with Joshua, and
Josh 7: 1 so the anger of the L burned
Josh 7: 6 ark of the L until evening
Josh 7: 7 L God, why have You brought
Josh 7: 8 O L, what shall I say when
Josh 7:10 So the L said to Joshua
Josh 7:13 thus says the L God of Israel
Josh 7:14 L takes shall come according
Josh 7:14 the L takes shall come by
Josh 7:14 the household which the L
Josh 7:15 the covenant of the L, and
Josh 7:19 glory to the L God of Israel
Josh 7:20 against the L God of Israel
Josh 7:23 and laid them out before the L
Josh 7:25 The L will trouble you this
Josh 7:26 So the L turned from the
Josh 8: 1 Then the L said to Joshua
Josh 8: 7 city, for the L your God will
Josh 8: 8 of the L you shall do
Josh 8:18 Then the L said to Joshua,
Josh 8:27 to the word of the L which He
Josh 8:30 built an altar to the L God
Josh 8:31 L had commanded the children
Josh 8:31 it burnt offerings to the L
Josh 8:33 ark of the covenant of the L
Josh 8:33 of the L had commanded before
Josh 9: 9 of the name of the L your God
Josh 9:14 did not ask counsel of the L
Josh 9:18 them by the L God of Israel
Josh 9:19 them by the L God of Israel
Josh 9:24 the L your God commanded His
Josh 9:27 and for the altar of the L
Josh 10: 8 And the L said to Joshua,
Josh 10:10 So the L routed them before
Josh 10:11 that the L cast down large
Josh 10:12 L in the day when the L
Josh 10:14 that the L heeded the voice
Josh 10:14 for the L fought for Israel
Josh 10:19 for the L your God has
Josh 10:25 for thus the L will do to all
Josh 10:30 the L also delivered it and
Josh 10:32 the L delivered Lachish into
Josh 10:40 as the L God of Israel had
Josh 10:42 because the L God of Israel
Josh 11: 6 But the L said to Joshua,
Josh 11: 8 the L delivered them into the
Josh 11: 9 to them as the L had told him
Josh 11:12 of the L had commanded
Josh 11:15 L had commanded Moses
Josh 11:15 the L had commanded Moses
Josh 11:20 For it was of the L to harden
Josh 11:20 as the L had commanded Moses
Josh 11:23 that the L had said to Moses
Josh 12: 6 Moses the servant of the L
Josh 12: 6 of the L had given it as a
Josh 13: 1 the L said to him: "You are
Josh 13: 8 of the L had given them
Josh 13:14 the sacrifices of the L God
Josh 13:33 the L God of Israel was their
Josh 14: 2 as the L had commanded by the
Josh 14: 5 L had commanded Moses,
Josh 14: 6 L said to Moses the man of
Josh 14: 7 Moses the servant of the L
Josh 14: 8 wholly followed the L my God
Josh 14: 9 wholly followed the L my God
Josh 14:10 the L has kept me alive, as
Josh 14:10 ever since the L spoke this
Josh 14:12 which the L spoke in that day
Josh 14:12 be that the L will be with me
Josh 14:12 drive them out as the L said
Josh 14:14 followed the L God of Israel
Josh 15:13 of the L to Joshua, namely,
Josh 17: 4 The L commanded Moses to
Josh 17: 4 to the commandment of the L
Josh 17:14 inasmuch as the L has blessed
Josh 18: 3 the L God of your fathers has
Josh 18: 6 you here before the L our God
Josh 18: 7 of the L is their inheritance
Josh 18: 7 servant of the L gave them
Josh 18: 8 here before the L in Shiloh
Josh 18:10 them in Shiloh before the L
Josh 19:50 to the word of the L they
Josh 19:51 by lot in Shiloh before the L
Josh 20: 1 The L also spoke to Joshua,
Josh 21: 2 The L commanded through
Josh 21: 3 at the commandment of the L
Josh 21: 8 as the L had commanded by the
Josh 21:43 So the L gave to Israel all
Josh 21:44 The L gave them rest all
Josh 21:44 the L delivered all their
Josh 21:45 L had spoken to the house of
Josh 22: 2 of the L commanded you, and
Josh 22: 3 commandment of the L your
Josh 22: 4 now the L your God has given
Josh 22: 4 Moses the servant of the L
Josh 22: 5 of the L commanded you, to
Josh 22: 5 you, to love the L your God
Josh 22: 9 to the word of the L by the
Josh 22:16 whole congregation of the L
Josh 22:16 this day from following the L
Josh 22:16 rebel this day against the L
Josh 22:17 in the congregation of the L
Josh 22:18 this day from following the L
Josh 22:18 you rebel today against the L
Josh 22:19 of the possession of the L
Josh 22:19 do not rebel against the L
Josh 22:19 the altar of the L our God
Josh 22:22 The L God of gods, the L
Josh 22:22 if in treachery against the L
Josh 22:23 to turn from following the L
Josh 22:23 let the L Himself require an
Josh 22:24 do with the L God of Israel
Josh 22:25 For the L has made the Jordan
Josh 22:25 You have no part in the L
Josh 22:25 cease fearing the L
Josh 22:27 L before Him with our burnt
Josh 22:27 You have no part in the L
Josh 22:28 the L which our fathers made
Josh 22:29 we should rebel against the L
Josh 22:29 from following the L this day
Josh 22:29 besides the altar of the L
Josh 22:31 that the L is among us,
Josh 22:31 this treachery against the L
Josh 22:31 out of the hand of the L
Josh 22:34 between us that the L is God
Josh 23: 1 a long time after the L had
Josh 23: 3 L your God has done to all
Josh 23: 3 for the L your God is He who
Josh 23: 5 the L your God will expel
Josh 23: 5 land, as the L your God has
Josh 23: 8 hold fast to the L your God
Josh 23: 9 For the L has driven out from
Josh 23:10 for the L your God is He who
Josh 23:11 that you love the L your God
Josh 23:13 the L your God will no longer
Josh 23:13 the L your God has given you
Josh 23:14 L your God spoke concerning
Josh 23:15 the L your God promised you
Josh 23:15 so the L will bring upon you
Josh 23:15 the L your God has given you
Josh 23:16 covenant of the L your God
Josh 23:16 the L will burn against you
Josh 24: 2 Thus says the L God of Israel
Josh 24: 7 So they cried out to the L
Josh 24:14 Now therefore, fear the L
Josh 24:14 and in Egypt. Serve the L!
Josh 24:15 evil to you to serve the L
Josh 24:15 my house, we will serve the L
Josh 24:16 the L to serve other gods
Josh 24:17 for the L our God is He who
Josh 24:18 the L drove out from before
Josh 24:18 We also will serve the L, for
Josh 24:19 You cannot serve the L, for
Josh 24:20 If you forsake the L and serve
Josh 24:21 No, but we will serve the L
Josh 24:22 chosen the L for yourselves
Josh 24:23 heart to the L God of Israel
Josh 24:24 The L our God we will serve,
Josh 24:26 was by the sanctuary of the L
Josh 24:27 of the L which He spoke to us
Josh 24:29 of Nun, the servant of the L
Josh 24:31 Israel served the L all the
Josh 24:31 the L which He had done for
Judg 1: 1 of Israel asked the L, saying
Judg 1: 2 And the L said, "Judah shall
Judg 1: 4 up, and the L delivered the
Judg 1:19 So the L was with Judah
Judg 1:22 and the L was with them
Judg 2: 1 Then the Angel of the L came
Judg 2: 4 when the Angel of the L spoke
Judg 2: 5 sacrificed there to the L
Judg 2: 7 the L all the days of Joshua
Judg 2: 7 the L which He had done for
Judg 2: 8 of Nun, the servant of the L
Judg 2:10 L nor the work which He had
Judg 2:11 evil in the sight of the L
Judg 2:12 they forsook the L God of
Judg 2:12 they provoked the L to anger
Judg 2:13 They forsook the L and served
Judg 2:14 the anger of the L was hot
Judg 2:15 the hand of the L was against
Judg 2:15 as the L had said, and as the
Judg 2:15 as the L had sworn to them
Judg 2:16 Then the L raised up judges
Judg 2:17 the commandments of the L
Judg 2:18 when the L raised up judges
Judg 2:18 the L was with the judge and
Judg 2:18 for the L was moved to pity
Judg 2:20 Then the anger of the L was
Judg 2:22 will keep the ways of the L
Judg 2:23 Therefore the L left those
Judg 3: 1 the nations which the L left
Judg 3: 4 the commandments of the L
Judg 3: 7 evil in the sight of the L
Judg 3: 7 They forgot the L their God
Judg 3: 8 the L was hot against Israel
Judg 3: 9 of Israel cried out to the L
Judg 3: 9 the L raised up a deliverer
Judg 3:10 Spirit of the L came upon him
Judg 3:10 to war, and the L delivered
Judg 3:12 evil in the sight of the L
Judg 3:12 So the L strengthened Eglon
Judg 3:12 evil in the sight of the L
Judg 3:15 of Israel cried out to the L
Judg 3:15 the L raised up a deliverer
Judg 3:28 for the L has delivered your
Judg 4: 1 evil in the sight of the L
Judg 4: 2 So the L sold them into the
Judg 4: 3 of Israel cried out to the L
Judg 4: 6 Has not the L God of Israel
Judg 4: 9 for the L will sell Sisera
Judg 4:14 is the day in which the L has
Judg 4:14 Has not the L gone out before
Judg 4:15 the L routed Sisera and all
Judg 4:18 Turn aside, my l, turn aside
Judg 5: 2 offer themselves, bless the L
Judg 5: 3 I, even I, will sing to the L
Judg 5: 3 praise to the L God of Israel
Judg 5: 4 L, when You went out from
Judg 5: 5 mountains gushed before the L
Judg 5: 5 before the L God of Israel
Judg 5: 9 Bless the L!
Judg 5:11 the righteous acts of the L
Judg 5:11 then the people of the L
Judg 5:13 the L came down for me
Judg 5:23 said the angel of the L
Judg 5:23 not come to the help of the L
Judg 5:23 of the L against the mighty
Judg 5:31 all Your enemies perish, O L
Judg 6: 1 evil in the sight of the L
Judg 6: 1 So the L delivered them into
Judg 6: 6 of Israel cried out to the L
Judg 6: 7 L because of the Midianites
Judg 6: 8 that the L sent a prophet to
Judg 6: 8 Thus says the L God of Israel
Judg 6:10 I am the L your God
Judg 6:11 Now the Angel of the L came
Judg 6:12 of the L appeared to him, and
Judg 6:12 The L is with you, you mighty
Judg 6:13 O my l, if the L is with
Judg 6:13 Did not the L bring us up
Judg 6:13 But now the L has forsaken
Judg 6:14 Then the L turned to him and
Judg 6:15 O my L, how can I save Israel
Judg 6:16 And the L said to him,
Judg 6:21 Then the Angel of the L put
Judg 6:21 the Angel of the L departed
Judg 6:22 He was the Angel of the L
Judg 6:22 Gideon said, "Alas, O L God
Judg 6:22 Angel of the L face to face
Judg 6:23 Then the L said to him
Judg 6:24 built an altar there to the L
Judg 6:25 night that the L said to him
Judg 6:26 build an altar to the L your
Judg 6:27 did as the L had said to him
Judg 6:34 of the L came upon Gideon
Judg 7: 2 And the L said to Gideon,
Judg 7: 4 And the L said to Gideon,
Judg 7: 5 And the L said to Gideon,
Judg 7: 7 Then the L said to Gideon,
Judg 7: 9 night that the L said to him
Judg 7:15 for the L has delivered the
Judg 7:18 and say, 'The sword of the L
Judg 7:20 The sword of the L and of
Judg 7:22 the L set every man's sword
Judg 8: 7 when the L has delivered
Judg 8:19 As the L lives, if you had
Judg 8:23 the L shall rule over you
Judg 8:34 not remember the L their God

Judg 10: 6 evil in the sight of the L
Judg 10: 6 and they forsook the L and did
Judg 10: 7 So the anger of the L was hot
Judg 10:10 of Israel cried out to the L
Judg 10:11 So the L said to the children
Judg 10:15 of Israel said to the L, We
Judg 10:16 among them and served the L
Judg 11: 9 the L delivers them to me,
Judg 11:10 The L will be a witness
Judg 11:11 words before the L in Mizpah
Judg 11:21 the L God of Israel delivered
Judg 11:23 So now the L God of Israel
Judg 11:24 So whatever the L our God
Judg 11:27 May the L, the Judge, render
Judg 11:29 of the L came upon Jephthah
Judg 11:30 Jephthah made a vow to the L
Judg 11:32 the L delivered them into his
Judg 11:35 I have given my word to the L
Judg 11:36 have given your word to the L
Judg 11:36 because the L has avenged you
Judg 12: 3 the L delivered them into my
Judg 13: 1 evil in the sight of the L
Judg 13: 1 the L delivered them into the
Judg 13: 3 the Angel of the L appeared
Judg 13: 8 Then Manoah prayed to the L
Judg 13: 8 O my L, please let the Man of
Judg 13:13 Angel of the L said to Manoah
Judg 13:15 said to the Angel of the L
Judg 13:16 Angel of the L said to Manoah
Judg 13:16 you must offer it to the L
Judg 13:16 He was the Angel of the L
Judg 13:17 said to the Angel of the L
Judg 13:18 Angel of the L said to him
Judg 13:19 it upon the rock to the L
Judg 13:20 that the Angel of the L
Judg 13:21 When the Angel of the L
Judg 13:21 He was the Angel of the L
Judg 13:23 If the L had desired to kill
Judg 13:24 grew, and the L blessed him
Judg 13:25 the Spirit of the L began to
Judg 14: 4 not know that it was of the L
Judg 14: 6 And the Spirit of the L came
Judg 14:19 the L came upon him mightily
Judg 15:14 the L came mightily upon him
Judg 15:18 so he cried out to the L and
Judg 16:20 the L had departed from him
Judg 16:28 Then Samson called to the L
Judg 16:28 O L God, remember me, I pray
Judg 17: 2 May you be blessed by the L
Judg 17: 3 my hand to the L for my son
Judg 17:13 that the L will be good to me
Judg 18: 6 the L be with you on your way
Judg 19:18 going to the house of the L
Judg 20: 1 man before the L at Mizpah
Judg 20:18 And the L said, "Judah
Judg 20:23 before the L until evening
Judg 20:23 and asked counsel of the L
Judg 20:23 And the L said, "Go up
Judg 20:26 They sat there before the L
Judg 20:26 peace offerings before the L
Judg 20:27 of Israel inquired of the L
Judg 20:28 And the L said,
Judg 20:35 The L defeated Benjamin
Judg 21: 3 O L God of Israel, why has
Judg 21: 5 up with the assembly to the L
Judg 21: 5 come up to the L at Mizpah
Judg 21: 7 L that we will not give them
Judg 21: 8 come up to Mizpah to the L
Judg 21:15 because the L had made a void
Judg 21:19 feast of the L in Shiloh,
Ruth 1: 6 country of Moab that the L
Ruth 1: 8 The L deal kindly with you,
Ruth 1: 9 The L grant that you may find
Ruth 1:13 the L has gone out against me
Ruth 1:17 The L do so to me, and more
Ruth 1:21 the L has brought me home
Ruth 1:21 since the L has testified
Ruth 2: 4 reapers, "The L be with you
Ruth 2: 4 him, "The L bless you
Ruth 2:12 The L repay your work, and a
Ruth 2:12 you by the L God of Israel
Ruth 2:13 favor in your sight, my l
Ruth 2:20 Blessed be he of the L, who
Ruth 3:10 Blessed are you of the L, my
Ruth 3:13 duty for you, as the L lives
Ruth 4:11 The L make the woman who is
Ruth 4:12 the L will give you from this
Ruth 4:13 the L gave her conception, and
Ruth 4:14 Blessed be the L, who has not
1Sa 1: 3 sacrifice to the L of hosts
1Sa 1: 3 the priests of the L, were
1Sa 1: 5 although the L had closed her
1Sa 1: 6 because the L had closed her
1Sa 1: 7 went up to the house of the L
1Sa 1: 9 of the tabernacle of the L
1Sa 1:10 of soul, and prayed to the L
1Sa 1:11 O L of hosts, if You will
1Sa 1:11 L all the days of his life
1Sa 1:12 praying before the L, that
1Sa 1:15 No, my l, I am a woman of
1Sa 1:15 out my soul before the L
1Sa 1:19 and worshiped before the L
1Sa 1:19 wife, and the L remembered her
1Sa 1:20 have asked for him from the L
1Sa 1:21 to the L the yearly sacrifice
1Sa 1:22 he may appear before the L
1Sa 1:23 Only let the L establish His
1Sa 1:24 the house of the L in Shiloh
1Sa 1:26 O my l! As your soul lives
1Sa 1:26 As your soul lives, my l, I
1Sa 1:26 by you here, praying to the L
1Sa 1:27 and the L has granted me my
1Sa 1:28 I also have lent him to the L
1Sa 1:28 he shall be lent to the L
1Sa 1:28 So they worshiped the L there
1Sa 2: 1 My heart rejoices in the L
1Sa 2: 1 my horn is exalted in the L
1Sa 2: 2 There is none holy like the L
1Sa 2: 3 for the L is the God of
1Sa 2: 6 The L kills and makes alive
1Sa 2: 7 The L makes poor and makes
1Sa 2:10 The adversaries of the L
1Sa 2:10 The L will judge the ends of
1Sa 2:11 the L before Eli the priest
1Sa 2:12 they did not know the L
1Sa 2:17 was very great before the L
1Sa 2:17 the offering of the L
1Sa 2:18 ministered before the L, even
1Sa 2:20 The L give you descendants
1Sa 2:20 loan that was lent to the L
1Sa 2:21 the L visited Hannah, so that
1Sa 2:21 Samuel grew before the L
1Sa 2:25 if a man sins against the L
1Sa 2:25 because the L desired to kill
1Sa 2:26 and in favor both with the L
1Sa 2:27 Thus says the L: 'Did I
1Sa 2:30 Therefore the L God of Israel
1Sa 2:30 the L says: 'Far be it from
1Sa 3: 1 to the L before Eli
1Sa 3: 1 the word of the L was rare in
1Sa 3: 3 L where the ark of God was
1Sa 3: 4 that the L called Samuel
1Sa 3: 6 And the L called yet again,
1Sa 3: 7 Samuel did not yet know the L
1Sa 3: 7 of the L yet revealed to him
1Sa 3: 8 the L called Samuel again the
1Sa 3: 8 that the L had called the boy
1Sa 3: 9 that you must say, 'Speak, L
1Sa 3:10 Then the L came and stood and
1Sa 3:11 Then the L said to Samuel
1Sa 3:15 doors of the house of the L
1Sa 3:17 that the L has said to you
1Sa 3:18 It is the L
1Sa 3:19 the L was with him and let
1Sa 3:20 as a prophet of the L
1Sa 3:21 Then the L appeared again in
1Sa 3:21 For the L revealed Himself to
1Sa 3:21 Shiloh by the word of the L
1Sa 4: 3 Why has the L defeated us
1Sa 4: 3 of the L from Shiloh to us
1Sa 4: 4 covenant of the L of hosts
1Sa 4: 5 of the L came into the camp
1Sa 4: 6 that the ark of the L had
1Sa 5: 3 earth before the ark of the L
1Sa 5: 4 before the ark of the L
1Sa 5: 6 But the hand of the L was
1Sa 5: 9 that the hand of the L was
1Sa 6: 1 Now the ark of the L was in
1Sa 6: 2 we do with the ark of the L
1Sa 6: 8 Then take the ark of the L
1Sa 6:11 the ark of the L on the cart
1Sa 6:14 as a burnt offering to the L
1Sa 6:15 took down the ark of the L
1Sa 6:15 the same day to the L
1Sa 6:17 a trespass offering to the L
1Sa 6:18 they set the ark of the L
1Sa 6:19 looked into the ark of the L
1Sa 6:19 L had struck the people with
1Sa 6:20 stand before this holy L God
1Sa 6:21 brought back the ark of the L
1Sa 7: 1 came and took the ark of the L
1Sa 7: 1 son to keep the ark of the L
1Sa 7: 2 Israel lamented after the L
1Sa 7: 3 to the L with all your hearts
1Sa 7: 3 prepare your hearts for the L
1Sa 7: 4 and served the L only
1Sa 7: 5 I will pray to the L for you
1Sa 7: 6 and poured it out before the L
1Sa 7: 6 We have sinned against the L
1Sa 7: 8 out to the L our God for us
1Sa 7: 9 whole burnt offering to the L
1Sa 7: 9 cried out to the L for Israel
1Sa 7: 9 Israel, and the L answered him
1Sa 7:10 But the L thundered with a
1Sa 7:12 Thus far the L has helped us
1Sa 7:13 the hand of the L was against
1Sa 7:17 he built an altar to the L
1Sa 8: 6 So Samuel prayed to the L
1Sa 8: 7 And the L said to Samuel,
1Sa 8:10 told all the words of the L
1Sa 8:18 the L will not hear you in
1Sa 8:21 them in the hearing of the L
1Sa 8:22 So the L said to Samuel
1Sa 9:15 Now the L had told Samuel in
1Sa 9:17 saw Saul, the L said to him,
1Sa 10: 1 Is it not because the L has
1Sa 10: 6 of the L will come upon you
1Sa 10:17 together to the L at Mizpah
1Sa 10:18 Thus says the L God of Israel
1Sa 10:19 before the L by your tribes
1Sa 10:22 inquired of the L further
1Sa 10:22 And the L answered,
1Sa 10:24 see him whom the L has chosen
1Sa 10:25 and laid it up before the L
1Sa 11: 7 the fear of the L fell on the
1Sa 11:13 this day, for today the L has
1Sa 11:15 king before the L in Gilgal
1Sa 11:15 peace offerings before the L
1Sa 12: 3 against me before the L and
1Sa 12: 5 The L is witness against you,
1Sa 12: 6 It is the L who raised up
1Sa 12: 7 the L concerning all the
1Sa 12: 7 of the L which He did to you
1Sa 12: 8 fathers cried out to the L
1Sa 12: 8 then the L sent Moses and
1Sa 12: 9 they forgot the L their God
1Sa 12:10 Then they cried out to the L
1Sa 12:10 we have forsaken the L and
1Sa 12:11 the L sent Jerubbaal, Bedan,
1Sa 12:12 when the L your God was your
1Sa 12:13 the L has set a king over you
1Sa 12:14 If you fear the L and serve
1Sa 12:14 the commandment of the L,
1Sa 12:14 following the L your God
1Sa 12:15 not obey the voice of the L
1Sa 12:15 the commandment of the L,
1Sa 12:15 of the L will be against you
1Sa 12:16 L will do before your eyes
1Sa 12:17 I will call to the L, and He
1Sa 12:17 done in the sight of the L
1Sa 12:18 So Samuel called to the L
1Sa 12:18 the L sent thunder and rain
1Sa 12:18 people greatly feared the L
1Sa 12:19 servants to the L your God
1Sa 12:20 aside from following the L
1Sa 12:20 but serve the L with all your
1Sa 12:22 For the L will not forsake
1Sa 12:22 the L to make you His people
1Sa 12:23 I should sin against the L in
1Sa 12:24 Only fear the L, and serve Him
1Sa 13:12 made supplication to the L
1Sa 13:13 commandment of the L your
1Sa 13:13 For now the L would have
1Sa 13:14 The L has sought for Himself
1Sa 13:14 the L has commanded him to be
1Sa 13:14 kept what the L commanded
1Sa 14: 6 that the L will work for us
1Sa 14: 6 L from saving by many or by
1Sa 14:10 For the L has delivered them
1Sa 14:12 for the L has delivered them
1Sa 14:23 So the L saved Israel that
1Sa 14:33 are sinning against the L by
1Sa 14:34 do not sin against the L by
1Sa 14:35 Saul built an altar to the L
1Sa 14:35 altar that he built to the L
1Sa 14:39 For as the L lives, who saves
1Sa 14:41 said to the L God of Israel
1Sa 14:45 As the L lives, not one hair
1Sa 15: 1 The L sent me to anoint you
1Sa 15: 1 voice of the words of the L

1Sa 15: 2 Thus says the L of hosts
1Sa 15:10 word of the L came to Samuel
1Sa 15:11 cried out to the L all night
1Sa 15:13 Blessed are you of the L
1Sa 15:13 the commandment of the L
1Sa 15:15 sacrifice to the L your God
1Sa 15:16 the L said to me last night
1Sa 15:17 did not the L anoint you king
1Sa 15:18 Now the L sent you on a
1Sa 15:19 not obey the voice of the L
1Sa 15:19 do evil in the sight of the L
1Sa 15:20 obeyed the voice of the L
1Sa 15:20 on which the L sent me, and
1Sa 15:21 to the L your God in Gilgal
1Sa 15:22 Has the L as great delight in
1Sa 15:22 in obeying the voice of the L
1Sa 15:23 rejected the word of the L
1Sa 15:24 the commandment of the L and
1Sa 15:25 me, that I may worship the L
1Sa 15:26 rejected the word of the L
1Sa 15:26 the L has rejected you from
1Sa 15:28 The L has torn the kingdom of
1Sa 15:30 I may worship the L your God
1Sa 15:31 Saul, and Saul worshiped the L
1Sa 15:33 pieces before the L in Gilgal
1Sa 15:35 the L regretted that He had
1Sa 16: 1 Then the L said to Samuel,
1Sa 16: 2 the L said, "Take a heifer
1Sa 16: 2 come to sacrifice to the L
1Sa 16: 4 So Samuel did what the L said
1Sa 16: 5 come to sacrifice to the L
1Sa 16: 7 But the L said to Samuel,
1Sa 16: 7 For the L does not see as
1Sa 16: 7 but the L looks at the heart
1Sa 16: 8 has the L chosen this one
1Sa 16: 9 has the L chosen this one
1Sa 16:10 The L has not chosen these
1Sa 16:12 And the L said, "Arise, anoint
1Sa 16:13 the Spirit of the L came upon
1Sa 16:14 of the L departed from Saul
1Sa 16:14 from the L troubled him
1Sa 16:18 and the L is with him
1Sa 17:37 The L, who delivered me from
1Sa 17:37 Go, and the L be with you
1Sa 17:45 in the name of the L of hosts
1Sa 17:46 This day the L will deliver
1Sa 17:47 shall know that the L does
1Sa 18:12 because the L was with him,
1Sa 18:14 ways, and the L was with him
1Sa 18:28 and knew that the L was with
1Sa 19: 5 the L brought about a great
1Sa 19: 6 As the L lives, he shall not
1Sa 19: 9 L came upon Saul as he sat in
1Sa 20: 3 But truly, as the L lives
1Sa 20: 8 a covenant of the L with you
1Sa 20:12 The L God of Israel is
1Sa 20:13 may the L do so and much more
1Sa 20:13 the L be with you as He has
1Sa 20:14 of the L while I still live
1Sa 20:15 not when the L has cut off
1Sa 20:16 Let the L require it at the
1Sa 20:21 then, as the L lives, there
1Sa 20:22 for the L has sent you away
1Sa 20:23 indeed the L be between you
1Sa 20:42 sworn in the name of the L
1Sa 20:42 May the L be between you and
1Sa 21: 6 been taken from before the L
1Sa 21: 7 day, detained before the L
1Sa 22:10 he inquired of the L for him
1Sa 22:12 Here I am, my l
1Sa 22:17 and kill the priests of the L
1Sa 22:17 strike the priests of the L
1Sa 23: 2 David inquired of the L,
1Sa 23: 2 And the L said to David,
1Sa 23: 4 inquired of the L once again
1Sa 23: 4 the L answered him and said,
1Sa 23:10 O L God of Israel, Your
1Sa 23:11 O L God of Israel, I pray,
1Sa 23:11 And the L said, "He will come
1Sa 23:12 And the L said, "They will
1Sa 23:18 made a covenant before the L
1Sa 23:21 Blessed are you of the L, for
1Sa 24: 4 of which the L said to you
1Sa 24: 6 The L forbid that I should do
1Sa 24: 6 he is the anointed of the L
1Sa 24: 8 Saul, saying, "My l the king
1Sa 24:10 eyes have seen that the L
1Sa 24:10 out my hand against my l, for
1Sa 24:12 Let the L judge between you
1Sa 24:12 let the L avenge me on you
1Sa 24:15 Therefore let the L be judge
1Sa 24:18 for when the L delivered me
1Sa 24:19 Therefore may the L reward
1Sa 24:21 swear now to me by the L that
1Sa 25:24 On me, my l, on me let this
1Sa 25:25 let not my l regard this
1Sa 25:25 men of my l whom you sent
1Sa 25:26 my l, as the L lives and
1Sa 25:26 since the L has held you back
1Sa 25:26 harm for my l be as Nabal
1Sa 25:27 has brought to my l, let it
1Sa 25:27 the young men who follow my l
1Sa 25:28 For the L will certainly make
1Sa 25:28 for my l an enduring house
1Sa 25:28 because my l fights the
1Sa 25:28 fights the battles of the L
1Sa 25:29 but the life of my l shall be
1Sa 25:29 living with the L your God
1Sa 25:30 when the L has done for my
1Sa 25:30 the L has done for my l
1Sa 25:31 nor offense of heart to my l
1Sa 25:31 or that my l has avenged
1Sa 25:31 L has dealt well with my l
1Sa 25:32 be the L God of Israel, who
1Sa 25:34 as the L God of Israel lives,
1Sa 25:38 that the L struck Nabal, and
1Sa 25:39 Blessed be the L, who has
1Sa 25:39 For the L has returned the
1Sa 25:41 feet of the servants of my l
1Sa 26:10 As the L lives
1Sa 26:10 the L shall strike him, or
1Sa 26:11 The L forbid that I should
1Sa 26:12 from the L had fallen on them
1Sa 26:15 not guarded your l the king
1Sa 26:15 in to destroy your l the king
1Sa 26:16 As the L lives, you are
1Sa 26:17 It is my voice, my l, O king
1Sa 26:18 Why does my l thus pursue his
1Sa 26:19 let my l the king hear the
1Sa 26:19 If the L has stirred you up
1Sa 26:19 they be cursed before the L
1Sa 26:19 in the inheritance of the L
1Sa 26:20 before the face of the L
1Sa 26:23 May the L repay every man for
1Sa 26:23 for the L delivered you into
1Sa 26:24 much in the eyes of the L
1Sa 28: 6 when Saul inquired of the L
1Sa 28: 6 the L did not answer him,
1Sa 28:10 And Saul swore to her by the L
1Sa 28:10 As the L lives, no punishment
1Sa 28:16 seeing the L has departed
1Sa 28:17 the L has done for Himself as
1Sa 28:17 For the L has torn the
1Sa 28:18 the L nor execute His fierce
1Sa 28:18 therefore the L has done this
1Sa 28:19 Moreover the L will also
1Sa 28:19 The L will also deliver the
1Sa 29: 6 Surely, as the L lives, you
1Sa 29: 8 the enemies of my l the king
1Sa 30: 6 himself in the L his God
1Sa 30: 8 So David inquired of the L
1Sa 30:23 with what the L has given us
1Sa 30:26 of the enemies of the L"
2Sa 1:10 brought them here to my l
2Sa 1:12 son, for the people of the L
2Sa 2: 1 that David inquired of the L
2Sa 2: 1 And the L said to him,
2Sa 2: 5 You are blessed of the L, for
2Sa 2: 5 shown this kindness to your l
2Sa 2: 6 now may the L show kindness
2Sa 3: 9 as the L has sworn to him
2Sa 3:18 For the L has spoken of David
2Sa 3:21 all Israel to my l the king
2Sa 3:28 the L forever of the blood of
2Sa 3:39 The L shall repay the
2Sa 4: 8 the L has avenged my l the
2Sa 4: 9 As the L lives, who has
2Sa 5: 2 the L said to you, 'You shall
2Sa 5: 3 them at Hebron before the L
2Sa 5:10 the L God of hosts was with
2Sa 5:12 So David knew that the L had
2Sa 5:19 And David inquired of the L
2Sa 5:19 And the L said to David,
2Sa 5:20 The L has broken through my
2Sa 5:23 when David inquired of the L
2Sa 5:24 For then the L will go out
2Sa 5:25 so, as the L commanded him
2Sa 6: 2 the L of Hosts, who dwells
2Sa 6: 5 played music before the L on
2Sa 6: 7 Then the anger of the L was
2Sa 6: 9 was afraid of the L that day
2Sa 6: 9 the ark of the L come to me
2Sa 6:10 not move the ark of the L
2Sa 6:11 The ark of the L remained in
2Sa 6:11 the L blessed Obed-Edom and
2Sa 6:12 The L has blessed the house
2Sa 6:13 of the L had gone six paces
2Sa 6:14 the L with all his might
2Sa 6:15 ark of the L with shouting
2Sa 6:16 as the ark of the L came into
2Sa 6:16 and whirling before the L
2Sa 6:17 they brought the ark of the L
2Sa 6:17 peace offerings before the L
2Sa 6:18 in the name of the L of hosts
2Sa 6:21 It was before the L, who
2Sa 6:21 over the people of the L,
2Sa 6:21 will play music before the L
2Sa 7: 1 the L had given him rest from
2Sa 7: 3 heart, for the L is with you
2Sa 7: 4 word of the L came to Nathan
2Sa 7: 5 David, 'Thus says the L
2Sa 7: 8 Thus says the L of hosts
2Sa 7:11 Also the L tells you that He
2Sa 7:18 went in and sat before the L
2Sa 7:18 Who am I, O L God
2Sa 7:19 thing in Your sight, O L God
2Sa 7:19 the manner of man, O L God
2Sa 7:20 L God, know Your servant
2Sa 7:22 You are great, O L God
2Sa 7:24 and You, L, have become their
2Sa 7:25 O L God, the word which You
2Sa 7:26 The L of hosts is the God
2Sa 7:27 O L of hosts, God of Israel,
2Sa 7:28 O L God, You are God, and
2Sa 7:29 O L God, have spoken it, and
2Sa 8: 6 The L preserved David
2Sa 8:11 dedicated these to the L,
2Sa 8:14 And the L preserved David
2Sa 9:11 According to all that my l
2Sa 10: 3 Ammon said to Hanun their l
2Sa 10:12 may the L do what seems good
2Sa 11: 9 all the servants of his l
2Sa 11:11 my l Joab and the servants of
2Sa 11:11 and the servants of my l are
2Sa 11:13 with the servants of his l
2Sa 11:27 had done displeased the L
2Sa 12: 1 Then the L sent Nathan to
2Sa 12: 5 As the L lives, the man who
2Sa 12: 7 Thus says the L God of Israel
2Sa 12: 9 the commandment of the L, to
2Sa 12:11 Thus says the L: 'Behold, I
2Sa 12:13 I have sinned against the L
2Sa 12:13 The L also has put away your
2Sa 12:14 enemies of the L to blaspheme
2Sa 12:15 the L struck the child that
2Sa 12:20 went into the house of the L
2Sa 12:22 the L will be gracious to me
2Sa 12:24 And the L loved him
2Sa 12:25 Jedidiah, because of the L
2Sa 13:32 Let not my l suppose that
2Sa 13:33 let not my l the king take
2Sa 14: 9 My l, O king, let the
2Sa 14:11 king remember the L your God
2Sa 14:11 As the L lives, not one hair
2Sa 14:12 another word to my l the king
2Sa 14:15 speak of this thing to my l
2Sa 14:17 The word of my l the king
2Sa 14:17 God, so is my l the king in
2Sa 14:17 may the L your God be with
2Sa 14:18 let my l the king speak
2Sa 14:19 my l the king, no one can
2Sa 14:19 that my l the king has spoken
2Sa 14:20 but my l is wise, according
2Sa 14:22 favor in your sight, my l
2Sa 15: 7 vow which I vowed to the L
2Sa 15: 8 If the L indeed brings me
2Sa 15: 8 then I will serve the L
2Sa 15:15 my l the king commands
2Sa 15:21 As the L lives
2Sa 15:21 and as my l the king lives,
2Sa 15:21 place my l the king shall be
2Sa 15:25 favor in the eyes of the L
2Sa 15:31 O L, I pray, turn the counsel
2Sa 16: 4 favor in your sight, my l
2Sa 16: 8 The L has brought upon you
2Sa 16: 8 and the L has delivered the
2Sa 16: 9 dead dog curse my l the king
2Sa 16:10 because the L has said to him
2Sa 16:11 for so the L has ordered him
2Sa 16:12 It may be that the L will

2Sa 16:12 that the L will repay me with
2Sa 16:18 No, but whom the L and this
2Sa 17:14 For the L had purposed to
2Sa 17:14 to the intent that the L
2Sa 18:19 how the L has avenged him of
2Sa 18:28 Blessed be the L your God
2Sa 18:28 hand against my l the king
2Sa 18:31 is good news, my l the king
2Sa 18:31 For the L has avenged you
2Sa 18:32 the enemies of my l the king
2Sa 19: 7 For I swear by the L, if you
2Sa 19:19 Do not let my l impute
2Sa 19:19 did on the day that my l the
2Sa 19:20 go down to meet my l the king
2Sa 19:26 My l, O king, my servant
2Sa 19:27 your servant to my l the king
2Sa 19:27 but my l the king is like the
2Sa 19:28 dead men before my l the king
2Sa 19:30 inasmuch as my l the king has
2Sa 19:35 burden to my l the king
2Sa 19:37 cross over with my l the king
2Sa 20:19 up the inheritance of the L
2Sa 21: 1 and David inquired of the L
2Sa 21: 1 And the L answered, It is
2Sa 21: 3 the inheritance of the L
2Sa 21: 6 the L in Gibeah of Saul, whom
2Sa 21: 6 of Saul, whom the L chose
2Sa 21: 9 them on the hill before the L
2Sa 22: 1 the L the words of this song
2Sa 22: 1 on the day when the L had
2Sa 22: 2 The L is my rock, my fortress
2Sa 22: 4 I will call upon the L, who
2Sa 22: 7 distress I called upon the L
2Sa 22:14 The L thundered from heaven,
2Sa 22:16 at the rebuke of the L, at
2Sa 22:19 but the L was my support
2Sa 22:21 The L rewarded me according
2Sa 22:22 I have kept the ways of the L
2Sa 22:25 the L has recompensed me
2Sa 22:29 For You are my lamp, O L
2Sa 22:29 the L shall enlighten my
2Sa 22:31 the word of the L is proven
2Sa 22:32 For who is God, except the L
2Sa 22:42 even to the L, but He did not
2Sa 22:47 The L lives
2Sa 22:50 will give thanks to You, O L
2Sa 23: 2 Spirit of the L spoke by me
2Sa 23:10 The L brought about a great
2Sa 23:12 the L brought about a great
2Sa 23:16 but poured it out to the L
2Sa 23:17 Far be it from me, O L, that
2Sa 24: 1 Again the anger of the L was
2Sa 24: 3 Now may the L your God add to
2Sa 24: 3 eyes of my l the king see it
2Sa 24: 3 But why does my l the king
2Sa 24:10 So David said to the L, "I
2Sa 24:10 but now, I pray, O L, take
2Sa 24:11 the word of the L came to the
2Sa 24:12 tell David, 'Thus says the L
2Sa 24:14 fall into the hand of the L
2Sa 24:15 So the L sent a plague upon
2Sa 24:16 it, the L relented from the
2Sa 24:16 the angel of the L was by the
2Sa 24:17 Then David spoke to the L
2Sa 24:18 erect an altar to the L on
2Sa 24:19 went up as the L commanded
2Sa 24:21 Why has my l the king come to
2Sa 24:21 to build an altar to the L
2Sa 24:22 Let my l the king take and
2Sa 24:23 May the L your God accept you
2Sa 24:24 the L my God with that which
2Sa 24:25 built there an altar to the L
2Sa 24:25 So the L heeded the prayers
1Ki 1: 2 be sought for our l the king
1Ki 1: 2 that our l the king may be
1Ki 1:11 David our l does not know it
1Ki 1:13 to him, 'Did you not, my l
1Ki 1:17 My l, you swore by the L
1Ki 1:18 my l the king, you do not
1Ki 1:20 And as for you, my l, O king,
1Ki 1:20 of my l the king after him
1Ki 1:21 when my l the king rests with
1Ki 1:24 My l, O king, have you said
1Ki 1:27 been done by my l the king
1Ki 1:27 of my l the king after him
1Ki 1:29 As the L lives, who has
1Ki 1:30 to you by the L God of Israel
1Ki 1:31 Let my l King David live
1Ki 1:33 you the servants of your l
1Ki 1:36 May the L God of my l the
1Ki 1:37 As the L has been with my
1Ki 1:37 has been with my l the king
1Ki 1:37 the throne of my l King David
1Ki 1:43 Our l King David has made
1Ki 1:47 to bless our l King David
1Ki 1:48 be the L God of Israel, who
1Ki 2: 3 the charge of the L your God
1Ki 2: 4 that the L may fulfill His
1Ki 2: 8 and I swore to him by the L
1Ki 2:15 for it was his from the L
1Ki 2:23 King Solomon swore by the L
1Ki 2:24 Now therefore, as the L lives
1Ki 2:26 L GOD before my father David
1Ki 2:27 from being priest to the L
1Ki 2:27 fulfill the word of the L
1Ki 2:28 to the tabernacle of the L
1Ki 2:29 to the tabernacle of the L
1Ki 2:30 to the tabernacle of the L
1Ki 2:32 So the L will return his
1Ki 2:33 be peace forever from the L
1Ki 2:38 As my l the king has said, so
1Ki 2:42 I not make you swear by the L
1Ki 2:43 not kept the oath of the L
1Ki 2:44 therefore the L will return
1Ki 2:45 before the L forever
1Ki 3: 1 house, and the house of the L
1Ki 3: 2 of the L until those days
1Ki 3: 3 And Solomon loved the L,
1Ki 3: 5 At Gibeon the L appeared to
1Ki 3: 7 O L my God, You have made
1Ki 3:10 And the speech pleased the L
1Ki 3:15 ark of the covenant of the L
1Ki 3:17 O my l, this woman and I dwell
1Ki 3:26 O my l, give her the living
1Ki 5: 3 L his God because of the wars
1Ki 5: 3 until the L put his foes
1Ki 5: 4 But now the L my God has
1Ki 5: 5 for the name of the L my God
1Ki 5: 5 as the L spoke to my father
1Ki 5: 7 Blessed be the L this day
1Ki 5:12 So the L gave Solomon wisdom,
1Ki 6: 1 to build the house of the L
1Ki 6: 2 King Solomon built for the L
1Ki 6:11 word of the L came to Solomon
1Ki 6:19 the covenant of the L there
1Ki 6:37 the house of the L was laid
1Ki 7:12 court of the house of the L
1Ki 7:40 Solomon on the house of the L
1Ki 7:45 for the house of the L were
1Ki 7:48 made for the house of the L
1Ki 7:51 house of the L was finished
1Ki 7:51 of the house of the L
1Ki 8: 1 the L from the City of David
1Ki 8: 4 brought up the ark of the L
1Ki 8: 6 of the L to its place, into
1Ki 8: 9 when the L made a covenant
1Ki 8:10 filled the house of the L
1Ki 8:11 for the glory of the L filled
1Ki 8:11 filled the house of the L
1Ki 8:12 The L said He would dwell in
1Ki 8:15 be the L God of Israel, who
1Ki 8:17 name of the L God of Israel
1Ki 8:18 But the L said to my father
1Ki 8:20 So the L has fulfilled His
1Ki 8:20 of Israel, as the L promised
1Ki 8:20 name of the L God of Israel
1Ki 8:21 the L which He made with our
1Ki 8:22 before the altar of the L in
1Ki 8:23 L God of Israel, there is no
1Ki 8:25 L God of Israel, now keep
1Ki 8:28 O L my God, and listen to the
1Ki 8:44 and when they pray to the L
1Ki 8:53 fathers out of Egypt, O L GOD
1Ki 8:54 and supplication to the L,
1Ki 8:54 before the altar of the L
1Ki 8:56 Blessed be the L, who has
1Ki 8:57 May the L our God be with us,
1Ki 8:59 supplication before the L
1Ki 8:59 be near the L our God day
1Ki 8:60 may know that the L is God
1Ki 8:61 be loyal to the L our God
1Ki 8:62 sacrifices before the L
1Ki 8:63 which he offered to the L
1Ki 8:63 dedicated the house of the L
1Ki 8:64 front of the house of the L
1Ki 8:64 L was too small to receive
1Ki 8:65 Egypt, before the L our God
1Ki 8:66 L had done for His servant
1Ki 9: 1 building the house of the L
1Ki 9: 2 that the L appeared to
1Ki 9: 3 the L said to him: "I have
1Ki 9: 8 Why has the L done thus to
1Ki 9: 9 they forsook the L their God
1Ki 9: 9 therefore the L has brought
1Ki 9:10 houses, the house of the L
1Ki 9:15 to build the house of the L
1Ki 9:25 which he had built for the L
1Ki 9:25 altar that was before the L
1Ki 10: 1 concerning the name of the L
1Ki 10: 5 went up to the house of the L
1Ki 10: 9 Blessed be the L your God
1Ki 10: 9 Because the L has loved
1Ki 10:12 wood for the house of the L
1Ki 11: 2 the nations of whom the L had
1Ki 11: 4 not loyal to the L his God
1Ki 11: 6 evil in the sight of the L
1Ki 11: 6 and did not fully follow the L
1Ki 11: 9 So the L became angry with
1Ki 11: 9 from the L God of Israel, who
1Ki 11:10 keep what the L had
1Ki 11:11 Therefore the L said to
1Ki 11:14 Now the L raised up an
1Ki 11:23 who had fled from his l,
1Ki 11:31 pieces, for thus says the L
1Ki 12:15 of affairs was from the L
1Ki 12:15 which the L had spoken by
1Ki 12:24 Thus says the L: "You shall
1Ki 12:24 they obeyed the word of the L
1Ki 12:24 to the word of the L
1Ki 12:27 house of the L at Jerusalem
1Ki 12:27 will turn back to their l
1Ki 13: 1 Bethel by the word of the L
1Ki 13: 2 altar by the word of the L
1Ki 13: 2 Thus says the L: 'Behold,
1Ki 13: 3 sign which the L has spoken
1Ki 13: 5 given by the word of the L
1Ki 13: 6 the favor of the L your God
1Ki 13: 6 man of God entreated the L
1Ki 13: 9 me by the word of the L,
1Ki 13:17 told by the word of the L
1Ki 13:18 to me by the word of the L
1Ki 13:20 that the word of the L came
1Ki 13:21 Thus says the L: 'Because
1Ki 13:21 disobeyed the word of the L
1Ki 13:21 the L your God commanded you
1Ki 13:22 of which the L said to you
1Ki 13:26 to the word of the L
1Ki 13:26 Therefore the L has delivered
1Ki 13:26 to the word of the L which He
1Ki 13:32 out by the word of the L
1Ki 14: 5 Now the L had said to Ahijah,
1Ki 14: 7 Thus says the L God of Israel
1Ki 14:11 for the L has spoken it
1Ki 14:13 something good toward the L
1Ki 14:14 Moreover the L will raise up
1Ki 14:15 For the L will strike Israel,
1Ki 14:15 provoking the L to anger
1Ki 14:18 to the word of the L which He
1Ki 14:21 the city which the L had
1Ki 14:22 evil in the sight of the L
1Ki 14:24 the L had cast out before the
1Ki 14:26 of the house of the L and the
1Ki 14:28 went into the house of the L
1Ki 15: 3 not loyal to the L his God
1Ki 15: 4 for David's sake the L his
1Ki 15: 5 right in the eyes of the L
1Ki 15:11 right in the eyes of the L
1Ki 15:14 loyal to the L all his days
1Ki 15:15 into the house of the L the
1Ki 15:18 of the house of the L and the
1Ki 15:26 evil in the sight of the L
1Ki 15:29 to the word of the L which He
1Ki 15:30 the L God of Israel to anger
1Ki 15:34 evil in the sight of the L
1Ki 16: 1 Then the word of the L came
1Ki 16: 7 also the word of the L came
1Ki 16: 7 L in provoking Him to anger
1Ki 16:12 to the word of the L, which
1Ki 16:13 in provoking the L God of
1Ki 16:19 evil in the sight of the L
1Ki 16:25 did evil in the eyes of the L
1Ki 16:26 provoking the L God of Israel
1Ki 16:30 evil in the sight of the L
1Ki 16:33 did more to provoke the L God
1Ki 16:34 to the word of the L, which
1Ki 17: 1 As the L God of Israel lives,
1Ki 17: 2 the word of the L came to him
1Ki 17: 5 to the word of the L, for he
1Ki 17: 8 the word of the L came to him
1Ki 17:12 As the L your God lives, I do

1Ki 17:14 thus says the L God of Israel
1Ki 17:14 until the day the L sends
1Ki 17:16 to the word of the L which He
1Ki 17:20 Then he cried out to the L
1Ki 17:20 O L my God, have You also
1Ki 17:21 times, and cried out to the L
1Ki 17:21 O L my God, I pray, let this
1Ki 17:22 Then the L heard the voice of
1Ki 17:24 that the word of the L in
1Ki 18: 1 word of the L came to Elijah
1Ki 18: 3 Obadiah feared the L greatly
1Ki 18: 4 the prophets of the L, that
1Ki 18: 7 Is that you, my l Elijah
1Ki 18:10 As the L your God lives,
1Ki 18:12 that the Spirit of the L will
1Ki 18:12 feared the L from my youth
1Ki 18:13 my l what I did when Jezebel
1Ki 18:13 killed the prophets of the L
1Ki 18:15 As the L of hosts lives,
1Ki 18:18 the commandments of the L
1Ki 18:21 If the L is God, follow Him
1Ki 18:22 am left a prophet of the L
1Ki 18:24 call on the name of the L
1Ki 18:30 of the L that was broken down
1Ki 18:31 the word of the L had come
1Ki 18:32 an altar in the name of the L
1Ki 18:36 L God of Abraham, Isaac, and
1Ki 18:37 Hear me, O L, hear me, that
1Ki 18:37 know that You are the L God
1Ki 18:38 Then the fire of the L fell
1Ki 18:39 The L, He is God
1Ki 18:39 The L, He is God
1Ki 18:46 of the L came upon Elijah
1Ki 19: 4 Now, L, take my life, for I
1Ki 19: 7 the angel of the L came back
1Ki 19: 9 the word of the L came to him
1Ki 19:10 for the L God of hosts
1Ki 19:11 on the mountain before the L
1Ki 19:11 the L passed by, and a great
1Ki 19:11 rocks in pieces before the L
1Ki 19:11 but the L was not in the wind
1Ki 19:11 but the L was not in the
1Ki 19:12 but the L was not in the fire
1Ki 19:14 for the L God of hosts
1Ki 19:15 Then the L said to him
1Ki 20: 4 My l, O king, just as you say
1Ki 20: 9 Tell my l the king, 'All that
1Ki 20:13 Thus says the L: 'Have you
1Ki 20:13 shall know that I am the L
1Ki 20:14 Thus says the L: 'By the
1Ki 20:28 Thus says the L: 'Because
1Ki 20:28 The L is God of the hills,
1Ki 20:28 shall know that I am the L
1Ki 20:35 neighbor by the word of the L
1Ki 20:36 not obeyed the voice of the L
1Ki 20:42 Thus says the L: 'Because
1Ki 21: 3 The L forbid that I should
1Ki 21:17 Then the word of the L came
1Ki 21:19 him, saying, 'Thus says the L
1Ki 21:19 him, saying, 'Thus says the L
1Ki 21:20 do evil in the sight of the L
1Ki 21:23 Jezebel the L also spoke,
1Ki 21:25 in the sight of the L,
1Ki 21:26 done, whom the L had cast out
1Ki 21:28 the word of the L came to
1Ki 22: 5 for the word of the L today
1Ki 22: 6 for the L will deliver it
1Ki 22: 7 still a prophet of the L here
1Ki 22: 8 whom we may inquire of the L
1Ki 22:11 Thus says the L: 'With these
1Ki 22:12 for the L will deliver it
1Ki 22:14 As the L lives, whatever the
1Ki 22:14 whatever the L says to me
1Ki 22:15 for the L will deliver it
1Ki 22:16 truth in the name of the L
1Ki 22:17 the L said, 'These have no
1Ki 22:19 hear the word of the L
1Ki 22:19 I saw the L sitting on His
1Ki 22:20 And the L said, 'Who will
1Ki 22:21 forward and stood before the L
1Ki 22:22 The L said to him, 'In what
1Ki 22:23 The L has put a lying spirit
1Ki 22:23 the L has declared disaster
1Ki 22:24 L go from me to speak to you
1Ki 22:28 the L has not spoken by me
1Ki 22:38 to the word of the L which He
1Ki 22:43 right in the eyes of the L
1Ki 22:52 evil in the sight of the L
1Ki 22:53 provoked the L God of Israel
2Ki 1: 3 But the angel of the L said
2Ki 1: 4 therefore, thus says the L
2Ki 1: 6 Thus says the L: 'Is it
2Ki 1:15 angel of the L said to Elijah
2Ki 1:16 Thus says the L: 'Because
2Ki 1:17 to the word of the L which
2Ki 2: 1 when the L was about to take
2Ki 2: 2 for the L has sent me on to
2Ki 2: 2 As the L lives, and as your
2Ki 2: 3 Do you know that the L will
2Ki 2: 4 for the L has sent me on to
2Ki 2: 4 As the L lives, and as your
2Ki 2: 5 Do you know that the L will
2Ki 2: 6 for the L has sent me on to
2Ki 2: 6 As the L lives, and as your
2Ki 2:14 Where is the L God of Elijah
2Ki 2:16 of the L has taken him up
2Ki 2:19 is pleasant, as my l sees
2Ki 2:21 Thus says the L: 'I have
2Ki 2:24 on them in the name of the L
2Ki 3: 2 evil in the sight of the L
2Ki 3:10 For the L has called these
2Ki 3:11 no prophet of the L here,
2Ki 3:11 may inquire of the L by him
2Ki 3:12 The word of the L is with him
2Ki 3:13 for the L has called these
2Ki 3:14 As the L of hosts lives,
2Ki 3:15 hand of the L came upon him
2Ki 3:16 Thus says the L: 'Make this
2Ki 3:17 thus says the L: 'You shall
2Ki 3:18 thing in the sight of the L
2Ki 4: 1 your servant feared the L
2Ki 4:16 my l. Man of God, do not
2Ki 4:27 the L has hidden it from me,
2Ki 4:28 Did I ask a son of my l
2Ki 4:30 As the L lives, and as your
2Ki 4:33 of them, and prayed to the L
2Ki 4:43 thus says the L: 'They shall
2Ki 4:44 to the word of the L
2Ki 5: 1 because by him the L had
2Ki 5:11 on the name of the L his God
2Ki 5:16 As the L lives, before whom I
2Ki 5:17 to other gods, but to the L
2Ki 5:18 may the L pardon your servant
2Ki 5:18 may the L please pardon your
2Ki 5:20 but as the L lives, I will
2Ki 6:12 None, my l, O king
2Ki 6:17 L, I pray, open his eyes that
2Ki 6:17 Then the L opened the eyes
2Ki 6:18 him, Elisha prayed to the L
2Ki 6:20 L, open the eyes of these men
2Ki 6:20 the L opened their eyes, and
2Ki 6:26 Help, my l, O king
2Ki 6:27 If the L does not help you,
2Ki 6:33 this calamity is from the L
2Ki 6:33 I wait for the L any longer
2Ki 7: 1 Hear the word of the L
2Ki 7: 1 Thus says the L: 'Tomorrow
2Ki 7: 2 if the L would make windows
2Ki 7: 6 For the L had caused the army
2Ki 7:16 to the word of the L
2Ki 7:19 if the L would make windows
2Ki 8: 1 for the L has called for a
2Ki 8: 5 My l, O king, this is the
2Ki 8: 8 and inquire of the L by him
2Ki 8:10 However the L has shown me
2Ki 8:12 Why is my l weeping
2Ki 8:13 The L has shown me that you
2Ki 8:18 evil in the sight of the L
2Ki 8:19 Yet the L would not destroy
2Ki 8:27 evil in the sight of the L
2Ki 9: 3 and say, 'Thus says the L
2Ki 9: 6 Thus says the L God of Israel
2Ki 9: 6 king over the people of the L
2Ki 9: 7 of all the servants of the L
2Ki 9:12 me, saying, 'Thus says the L
2Ki 9:25 that the L laid this burden
2Ki 9:26 of his sons,' says the L, 'and
2Ki 9:26 you in this plot,' says the L
2Ki 9:26 to the word of the L
2Ki 9:36 This is the word of the L
2Ki 10:10 of the L which the L spoke
2Ki 10:10 for the L has done what He
2Ki 10:16 me, and see my zeal for the L
2Ki 10:17 to the word of the L which He
2Ki 10:23 of the L are here with you
2Ki 10:30 And the L said to Jehu,
2Ki 10:31 to walk in the law of the L
2Ki 10:32 In those days the L began to
2Ki 11: 3 house of the L for six years
2Ki 11: 4 the house of the L to him
2Ki 11: 4 them in the house of the L
2Ki 11: 7 house of the L for the king
2Ki 11:10 were in the temple of the L
2Ki 11:13 into the temple of the L
2Ki 11:15 killed in the house of the L
2Ki 11:17 made a covenant between the L
2Ki 11:18 over the house of the L
2Ki 11:19 down from the house of the L
2Ki 12: 2 the L all the days in which
2Ki 12: 4 into the house of the L
2Ki 12: 4 bring into the house of the L
2Ki 12: 9 comes into the house of the L
2Ki 12: 9 into the house of the L
2Ki 12:10 found in the house of the L
2Ki 12:11 of the house of the L
2Ki 12:11 worked on the house of the L
2Ki 12:12 damage of the house of the L
2Ki 12:13 of the L basins of silver
2Ki 12:13 into the house of the L
2Ki 12:14 the house of the L with it
2Ki 12:16 into the house of the L
2Ki 12:18 of the house of the L and in
2Ki 13: 2 evil in the sight of the L
2Ki 13: 3 Then the anger of the L was
2Ki 13: 4 Jehoahaz pleaded with the L
2Ki 13: 4 and the L listened to him
2Ki 13: 5 Then the L gave Israel a
2Ki 13:11 evil in the sight of the L
2Ki 13:23 But the L was gracious to
2Ki 14: 3 right in the sight of the L
2Ki 14: 6 in which the L commanded
2Ki 14:14 found in the house of the L
2Ki 14:24 evil in the sight of the L
2Ki 14:25 word of the L God of Israel
2Ki 14:26 For the L saw that the
2Ki 14:27 the L did not say that He
2Ki 15: 3 right in the sight of the L
2Ki 15: 5 Then the L struck the king,
2Ki 15: 9 evil in the sight of the L
2Ki 15:12 the L which He spoke to Jehu
2Ki 15:18 evil in the sight of the L
2Ki 15:24 evil in the sight of the L
2Ki 15:28 evil in the sight of the L
2Ki 15:34 right in the sight of the L
2Ki 15:35 Gate of the house of the L
2Ki 15:37 In those days the L began to
2Ki 16: 2 in the sight of the L his God
2Ki 16: 3 of the nations whom the L had
2Ki 16: 8 found in the house of the L
2Ki 16:14 altar which was before the L
2Ki 16:14 altar and the house of the L
2Ki 16:18 from the house of the L, on
2Ki 17: 2 evil in the sight of the L
2Ki 17: 7 against the L their God, who
2Ki 17: 8 of the nations whom the L had
2Ki 17: 9 secretly did against the L
2Ki 17:11 the L had carried away before
2Ki 17:11 to provoke the L to anger
2Ki 17:12 of which the L had said to
2Ki 17:13 Yet the L testified against
2Ki 17:14 believe in the L their God
2Ki 17:15 concerning whom the L had
2Ki 17:16 of the L their God, made for
2Ki 17:17 do evil in the sight of the L
2Ki 17:18 Therefore the L was very
2Ki 17:19 of the L their God, but
2Ki 17:20 And the L rejected all the
2Ki 17:21 Israel from following the L
2Ki 17:23 until the L removed Israel
2Ki 17:25 that they did not fear the L
2Ki 17:25 therefore the L sent lions
2Ki 17:28 how they should fear the L
2Ki 17:32 So they feared the L, and from
2Ki 17:33 They feared the L, yet served
2Ki 17:34 they do not fear the L, nor
2Ki 17:34 commandment which the L had
2Ki 17:35 with whom the L had made a
2Ki 17:36 but the L, who brought you up
2Ki 17:39 But the L your God you shall
2Ki 17:41 So these nations feared the L
2Ki 18: 3 right in the sight of the L
2Ki 18: 5 in the L God of Israel, so
2Ki 18: 6 For he held fast to the L
2Ki 18: 6 which the L had commanded
2Ki 18: 7 The L was with him
2Ki 18:12 the voice of the L their God
2Ki 18:12 of the L had commanded
2Ki 18:15 found in the house of the L
2Ki 18:16 doors of the temple of the L
2Ki 18:22 We trust in the L our God

2Ki 18:25 the L against this place to
2Ki 18:25 The L said to me, Go up
2Ki 18:30 make you trust in the L,
2Ki 18:30 The L will surely deliver us
2Ki 18:32 The L will deliver us
2Ki 18:35 that the L should deliver
2Ki 19: 1 went into the house of the L
2Ki 19: 4 It may be that the L your
2Ki 19: 4 the L your God has heard
2Ki 19: 6 your master, Thus says the L
2Ki 19:14 went up to the house of the L
2Ki 19:14 and spread it before the L
2Ki 19:15 Hezekiah prayed before the L
2Ki 19:15 O L God of Israel, the One
2Ki 19:16 Incline Your ear, O L, and
2Ki 19:16 open Your eyes, O L, and see
2Ki 19:17 Truly, L, the kings of
2Ki 19:19 O L our God, I pray, save us
2Ki 19:19 know that You are the L God
2Ki 19:20 Thus says the L God of Israel
2Ki 19:21 L has spoken concerning him
2Ki 19:23 you have reproached the L
2Ki 19:31 The zeal of the L of hosts
2Ki 19:32 the L concerning the king of
2Ki 19:33 into this city,' says the L
2Ki 19:35 the angel of the L went out
2Ki 20: 1 Thus says the L: 'Set your
2Ki 20: 2 the wall, and prayed to the L
2Ki 20: 3 Remember now, O L, I pray,
2Ki 20: 4 the word of the L came to him
2Ki 20: 5 My people, 'Thus says the L
2Ki 20: 5 go up to the house of the L
2Ki 20: 8 sign that the L will heal me
2Ki 20: 8 house of the L the third day
2Ki 20: 9 is the sign to you from the L
2Ki 20: 9 that the L will do the thing
2Ki 20:11 prophet cried out to the L
2Ki 20:16 Hear the word of the L
2Ki 20:17 shall be left,' says the L
2Ki 20:19 The word of the L which you
2Ki 21: 2 evil in the sight of the L
2Ki 21: 2 the L had cast out before the
2Ki 21: 4 altars in the house of the L
2Ki 21: 4 of which the L had said
2Ki 21: 5 courts of the house of the L
2Ki 21: 6 evil in the sight of the L
2Ki 21: 7 which the L had said to David
2Ki 21: 9 L had destroyed before the
2Ki 21:10 the L spoke by His servants
2Ki 21:12 thus says the L God of Israel
2Ki 21:16 evil in the sight of the L
2Ki 21:20 evil in the sight of the L
2Ki 21:22 He forsook the L God of his
2Ki 21:22 not walk in the way of the L
2Ki 22: 2 right in the sight of the L
2Ki 22: 3 to the house of the L,
2Ki 22: 4 into the house of the L,
2Ki 22: 5 in the house of the L
2Ki 22: 5 house of the L doing the work
2Ki 22: 8 the Law in the house of the L
2Ki 22: 9 oversee the house of the L
2Ki 22:13 Go, inquire of the L for me
2Ki 22:13 great is the wrath of the L
2Ki 22:15 Thus says the L God of Israel
2Ki 22:16 Thus says the L
2Ki 22:18 sent you to inquire of the L
2Ki 22:18 Thus says the L God of Israel
2Ki 22:19 L when you heard what I spoke
2Ki 22:19 have heard you," says the L
2Ki 23: 2 L with all the men of Judah
2Ki 23: 2 found in the house of the L
2Ki 23: 3 made a covenant before the L
2Ki 23: 3 to follow the L
2Ki 23: 4 out of the temple of the L
2Ki 23: 6 image from the house of the L
2Ki 23: 7 were in the house of the L
2Ki 23: 9 altar of the L in Jerusalem
2Ki 23:11 to the house of the L, by the
2Ki 23:12 courts of the house of the L
2Ki 23:16 to the word of the L which
2Ki 23:19 to provoke the L to anger
2Ki 23:21 Passover to the L your God
2Ki 23:23 before the L in Jerusalem
2Ki 23:24 found in the house of the L
2Ki 23:25 who turned to the L with all
2Ki 23:26 Nevertheless the L did not
2Ki 23:27 And the L said,
2Ki 23:32 evil in the sight of the L
2Ki 23:37 evil in the sight of the L
2Ki 24: 2 And the L sent against him
2Ki 24: 2 to the word of the L which He
2Ki 24: 3 of the L this came upon Judah
2Ki 24: 4 which the L would not pardon
2Ki 24: 9 evil in the sight of the L
2Ki 24:13 of the house of the L and the
2Ki 24:13 made in the temple of the L
2Ki 24:13 as the L had said
2Ki 24:19 evil in the sight of the L
2Ki 24:20 L this happened in Jerusalem
2Ki 25: 9 He burned the house of the L
2Ki 25:13 were in the house of the L
2Ki 25:13 were in the house of the L
2Ki 25:16 made for the house of the L
1Ch 2: 3 wicked in the sight of the L
1Ch 6:15 when the L carried Judah and
1Ch 6:31 of song in the house of the L
1Ch 6:32 house of the L in Jerusalem
1Ch 9:19 entrance to the camp of the L
1Ch 9:20 the L was with him
1Ch 9:23 gates of the house of the L
1Ch 10:13 had committed against the L
1Ch 10:13 not keep the word of the L
1Ch 10:14 he did not inquire of the L
1Ch 11: 2 the L your God said to you
1Ch 11: 3 them at Hebron before the L
1Ch 11: 3 the word of the L by Samuel
1Ch 11: 9 the L of hosts was with him
1Ch 11:10 of the L concerning Israel
1Ch 11:14 the L saved them by a great
1Ch 11:18 but poured it out to the L
1Ch 12:23 to the word of the L
1Ch 13: 2 and if it is of the L our God
1Ch 13: 6 there the ark of God the L
1Ch 13:10 Then the anger of the L was
1Ch 13:14 the L blessed the house of
1Ch 14: 2 David perceived that the L
1Ch 14:10 And the L said to him,
1Ch 14:17 the L brought the fear of him
1Ch 15: 2 for the L has chosen them to
1Ch 15: 3 the ark of the L to its place
1Ch 15:12 L God of Israel to the place
1Ch 15:13 time, the L our God broke out
1Ch 15:14 ark of the L God of Israel
1Ch 15:15 to the word of the L
1Ch 15:25 ark of the covenant of the L
1Ch 15:26 ark of the covenant of the L
1Ch 15:28 of the L with shouting and
1Ch 15:29 L came to the City of David
1Ch 16: 2 people in the name of the L
1Ch 16: 4 before the ark of the L, to
1Ch 16: 4 to praise the L God of Israel
1Ch 16: 7 his brethren, to thank the L
1Ch 16: 8 Oh, give thanks to the L
1Ch 16:10 those rejoice who seek the L
1Ch 16:11 Seek the L and His strength
1Ch 16:14 He is the L our God
1Ch 16:23 Sing to the L, all the earth
1Ch 16:25 For the L is great and greatly
1Ch 16:26 but the L made the heavens
1Ch 16:28 Give to the L, O kindreds of
1Ch 16:28 peoples, give to the L glory
1Ch 16:29 Give to the L the glory due
1Ch 16:29 worship the L in the beauty
1Ch 16:31 the nations, "The L reigns
1Ch 16:33 shall rejoice before the L
1Ch 16:34 Oh, give thanks to the L, for
1Ch 16:36 Blessed be the L God of
1Ch 16:36 and praised the L
1Ch 16:37 L to minister before the ark
1Ch 16:39 the tabernacle of the L at
1Ch 16:40 the L on the altar of burnt
1Ch 16:40 L which He commanded Israel
1Ch 16:41 name, to give thanks to the L
1Ch 17: 1 the L is under tent curtains
1Ch 17: 4 David, 'Thus says the L
1Ch 17: 7 Thus says the L of hosts
1Ch 17:10 I tell you that the L will
1Ch 17:16 went in and sat before the L
1Ch 17:16 Who am I, O L God
1Ch 17:17 a man of high degree, O L God
1Ch 17:19 O L, for Your servant's sake,
1Ch 17:20 O L, there is none like You,
1Ch 17:22 and You, L, have become their
1Ch 17:23 And now, O L, the word which
1Ch 17:24 The L of hosts, the God of
1Ch 17:26 And now, L, You are God, and
1Ch 17:27 for You have blessed it, O L
1Ch 18: 6 Thus the L preserved David
1Ch 18:11 also dedicated these to the L
1Ch 18:13 And the L preserved David
1Ch 19:13 may the L do what is good in
1Ch 21: 3 May the L make His people a
1Ch 21: 3 my l the king, are they not
1Ch 21: 3 Why then does my l require
1Ch 21: 9 the L spoke to Gad, David's
1Ch 21:10 saying, 'Thus says the L
1Ch 21:11 Thus says the L
1Ch 21:12 three days the sword of the L
1Ch 21:12 land, with the angel of the L
1Ch 21:13 fall into the hand of the L
1Ch 21:14 So the L sent a plague upon
1Ch 21:15 the L looked and relented of
1Ch 21:15 the angel of the L stood by
1Ch 21:16 and saw the angel of the L
1Ch 21:17 O L my God, be against me and
1Ch 21:18 Then the angel of the L
1Ch 21:18 erect an altar to the L on
1Ch 21:19 spoken in the name of the L
1Ch 21:22 build an altar on it to the L
1Ch 21:23 let my l the king do what is
1Ch 21:24 take what is yours for the L
1Ch 21:26 built there an altar to the L
1Ch 21:26 offerings, and called on the L
1Ch 21:27 Then the L commanded the
1Ch 21:28 the L had answered him on the
1Ch 21:29 For the tabernacle of the L
1Ch 21:30 sword of the angel of the L
1Ch 22: 1 is the house of the L God
1Ch 22: 5 for the L must be exceedingly
1Ch 22: 6 house for the L God of Israel
1Ch 22: 7 to the name of the L my God
1Ch 22: 8 the word of the L came to me
1Ch 22:11 my son, may the L be with you
1Ch 22:11 the house of the L your God
1Ch 22:12 Only may the L give you
1Ch 22:12 the law of the L your God
1Ch 22:13 L charged Moses concerning
1Ch 22:14 of the L one hundred thousand
1Ch 22:16 working, and the L be with you
1Ch 22:18 Is not the L your God with
1Ch 22:18 land is subdued before the L
1Ch 22:19 soul to seek the L your God
1Ch 22:19 the sanctuary of the L God
1Ch 22:19 ark of the covenant of the L
1Ch 22:19 built for the name of the L
1Ch 23: 4 work of the house of the L
1Ch 23: 5 L with musical instruments
1Ch 23:13 to burn incense before the L
1Ch 23:24 service of the house of the L
1Ch 23:25 The L God of Israel has given
1Ch 23:28 service of the house of the L
1Ch 23:30 to thank and praise the L, and
1Ch 23:31 to the L on the Sabbaths and
1Ch 23:31 them, regularly before the L
1Ch 23:32 work of the house of the L
1Ch 24:19 of the L according to their
1Ch 24:19 as the L God of Israel had
1Ch 25: 3 thanks and to praise the L
1Ch 25: 6 music in the house of the L
1Ch 25: 7 in the songs of the L, all
1Ch 26:12 serve in the house of the L
1Ch 26:22 of the house of the L
1Ch 26:27 maintain the house of the L
1Ch 26:30 for all the business of the L
1Ch 27:23 because the L had said He
1Ch 28: 2 ark of the covenant of the L
1Ch 28: 4 However the L God of Israel
1Ch 28: 5 of all my sons (for the L has
1Ch 28: 5 kingdom of the L over Israel
1Ch 28: 8 the congregation of the L
1Ch 28: 8 of the L your God, that you
1Ch 28: 9 for the L searches all hearts
1Ch 28:10 for the L has chosen you to
1Ch 28:12 courts of the house of the L
1Ch 28:13 service of the house of the L
1Ch 28:13 service in the house of the L
1Ch 28:18 ark of the covenant of the L
1Ch 28:19 the L made me understand in
1Ch 28:20 be dismayed, for the L God
1Ch 28:20 service of the house of the L
1Ch 29: 1 not for man but for the L God
1Ch 29: 5 himself this day to the L
1Ch 29: 8 of the house of the L, into
1Ch 29: 9 offered willingly to the L
1Ch 29:10 L before all the congregation
1Ch 29:10 L God of Israel, our Father,
1Ch 29:11 Yours, O L, is the greatness,
1Ch 29:11 Yours is the kingdom, O L
1Ch 29:16 O L our God, all this
1Ch 29:18 O L God of Abraham, Isaac,

1Ch 29:20 Now bless the L your God
1Ch 29:20 the L God of their fathers
1Ch 29:20 themselves before the L and
1Ch 29:21 they made sacrifices to the L
1Ch 29:21 to the L on the next day
1Ch 29:22 drank before the L with great
1Ch 29:22 before the L to be the leader
1Ch 29:23 L as king instead of David
1Ch 29:25 So the L exalted Solomon
2Ch 1: 1 the L his God was with him and
2Ch 1: 3 Moses the servant of the L
2Ch 1: 5 the tabernacle of the L
2Ch 1: 6 the bronze altar before the L
2Ch 1: 9 O L God, let Your promise to
2Ch 2: 1 temple for the name of the L
2Ch 2: 4 for the name of the L my God
2Ch 2: 4 set feasts of the L our God
2Ch 2:11 Because the L loves His
2Ch 2:12 be the L God of Israel, who
2Ch 2:12 will build a temple for the L
2Ch 2:14 men of my l David your father
2Ch 2:15 wine which my l has spoken of
2Ch 3: 1 the L at Jerusalem on Mount
2Ch 3: 1 where the L had appeared to
2Ch 4:16 for the house of the L
2Ch 5: 1 house of the L was finished
2Ch 5: 2 L up from the City of David
2Ch 5: 7 of the L to its place, into
2Ch 5:10 when the L made a covenant
2Ch 5:13 in praising and thanking the L
2Ch 5:13 of music, and praised the L
2Ch 5:13 the house, the house of the L
2Ch 5:14 for the glory of the L filled
2Ch 6: 1 The L said He would dwell in
2Ch 6: 4 be the L God of Israel, who
2Ch 6: 7 name of the L God of Israel
2Ch 6: 8 But the L said to my father
2Ch 6:10 So the L has fulfilled His
2Ch 6:10 of Israel, as the L promised
2Ch 6:10 name of the L God of Israel
2Ch 6:11 the L which He made with the
2Ch 6:12 before the altar of the L in
2Ch 6:14 L God of Israel, there is no
2Ch 6:16 L God of Israel, now keep
2Ch 6:17 O L God of Israel, let Your
2Ch 6:19 O L my God, and listen to the
2Ch 6:41 O L God, to Your resting
2Ch 6:41 O L God, be clothed with
2Ch 6:42 O L God, do not turn away the
2Ch 7: 1 the glory of the L filled the
2Ch 7: 2 not enter the house of the L
2Ch 7: 2 because the glory of the L
2Ch 7: 3 glory of the L on the temple
2Ch 7: 3 and worshiped and praised the L
2Ch 7: 4 sacrifices before the L
2Ch 7: 6 of the music of the L, which
2Ch 7: 6 had made to praise the L,
2Ch 7: 7 front of the house of the L
2Ch 7:10 that the L had done for David
2Ch 7:11 finished the house of the L
2Ch 7:11 to make in the house of the L
2Ch 7:12 Then the L appeared to
2Ch 7:21 Why has the L done thus to
2Ch 7:22 the L God of their fathers
2Ch 8: 1 had built the house of the L
2Ch 8:11 of the L has come are holy
2Ch 8:12 burnt offerings to the L
2Ch 8:12 on the altar of the L
2Ch 8:16 of the house of the L until
2Ch 8:16 house of the L was completed
2Ch 9: 4 went up to the house of the L
2Ch 9: 8 Blessed be the L your God
2Ch 9: 8 to be king for the L your God
2Ch 9:11 wood for the house of the L
2Ch 10:15 that the L might fulfill His
2Ch 11: 2 But the word of the L came to
2Ch 11: 4 Thus says the L
2Ch 11: 4 obeyed the words of the L
2Ch 11:14 serving as priests to the L
2Ch 11:16 to seek the L God of Israel
2Ch 11:16 to sacrifice to the L God of
2Ch 12: 1 he forsook the law of the L
2Ch 12: 2 transgressed against the L
2Ch 12: 5 Thus says the L
2Ch 12: 6 said, "The L is righteous
2Ch 12: 7 Now when the L saw that they
2Ch 12: 7 the word of the L came to
2Ch 12: 9 of the house of the L and the
2Ch 12:11 entered the house of the L
2Ch 12:12 of the L turned from him, so
2Ch 12:13 the city which the L had
2Ch 12:14 his heart to seek the L
2Ch 13: 5 you not know that the L God
2Ch 13: 6 up and rebelled against his l
2Ch 13: 8 the kingdom of the L, which
2Ch 13: 9 cast out the priests of the L
2Ch 13:10 the L is our God, and we have
2Ch 13:10 the L are the sons of Aaron
2Ch 13:11 burn to the L every morning
2Ch 13:11 the command of the L our God
2Ch 13:12 the L God of your fathers
2Ch 13:14 and they cried out to the L
2Ch 13:18 on the L God of their fathers
2Ch 13:20 the L struck him, and he died
2Ch 14: 2 in the eyes of the L his God
2Ch 14: 4 the L God of their fathers
2Ch 14: 6 because the L had given him
2Ch 14: 7 we have sought the L our God
2Ch 14:11 cried out to the L his God
2Ch 14:11 L, it is nothing for You to
2Ch 14:11 O L our God, for we rest on
2Ch 14:11 O L, You are our God
2Ch 14:12 So the L struck the
2Ch 14:13 they were broken before the L
2Ch 14:14 fear of the L came upon them
2Ch 15: 2 The L is with you while you
2Ch 15: 4 turned to the L God of Israel
2Ch 15: 8 of the L that was before the
2Ch 15: 8 before the vestibule of the L
2Ch 15: 9 the L his God was with him
2Ch 15:11 they offered to the L at that
2Ch 15:12 L God of their fathers with
2Ch 15:13 whoever would not seek the L
2Ch 15:14 the L with a loud voice, with
2Ch 15:15 and the L gave them rest all
2Ch 16: 2 of the house of the L and of
2Ch 16: 7 not relied on the L your God
2Ch 16: 8 because you relied on the L
2Ch 16: 9 For the eyes of the L run to
2Ch 16:12 disease he did not seek the L
2Ch 17: 3 Now the L was with
2Ch 17: 5 Therefore the L established
2Ch 17: 6 delight in the ways of the L
2Ch 17: 9 of the Law of the L with them
2Ch 17:10 the fear of the L fell on all
2Ch 17:16 offered himself to the L, and
2Ch 18: 4 for the word of the L today
2Ch 18: 6 still a prophet of the L here
2Ch 18: 7 whom we may inquire of the L
2Ch 18:10 Thus says the L
2Ch 18:11 for the L will deliver it
2Ch 18:13 As the L lives, whatever my
2Ch 18:15 truth in the name of the L
2Ch 18:16 the L said, 'These have no
2Ch 18:18 hear the word of the L
2Ch 18:18 I saw the L sitting on His
2Ch 18:19 And the L said, 'Who will
2Ch 18:20 forward and stood before the L
2Ch 18:20 The L said to him, 'In what
2Ch 18:21 And the L said, 'You shall
2Ch 18:22 The L has put a lying spirit
2Ch 18:22 the L has declared disaster
2Ch 18:23 L go from me to speak to you
2Ch 18:27 the L has not spoken by me
2Ch 18:31 and the L helped him, and God
2Ch 19: 2 and love those who hate the L
2Ch 19: 2 wrath of the L is upon you
2Ch 19: 4 to the L God of their fathers
2Ch 19: 6 judge for man but for the L
2Ch 19: 7 the fear of the L be upon you
2Ch 19: 7 iniquity with the L our God
2Ch 19: 8 for the judgment of the L
2Ch 19: 9 act in the fear of the L,
2Ch 19:10 they trespass against the L
2Ch 19:11 you in all matters of the L
2Ch 19:11 the L will be with the good
2Ch 20: 3 and set himself to seek the L
2Ch 20: 4 to ask help from the L
2Ch 20: 4 Judah they came to seek the L
2Ch 20: 5 in the house of the L,
2Ch 20: 6 O L God of our fathers, are
2Ch 20:13 children, stood before the L
2Ch 20:14 Then the Spirit of the L came
2Ch 20:15 Thus says the L to you
2Ch 20:17 and see the salvation of the L
2Ch 20:17 them, for the L is with you
2Ch 20:18 Jerusalem bowed before the L
2Ch 20:18 worshiping the L
2Ch 20:19 stood up to praise the L God
2Ch 20:20 Believe in the L your God
2Ch 20:21 who should sing to the L, and
2Ch 20:21 Praise the L, for His mercy
2Ch 20:22 the L set ambushes against
2Ch 20:26 for there they blessed the L
2Ch 20:27 joy, for the L had made them
2Ch 20:28 to the house of the L
2Ch 20:29 the L had fought against the
2Ch 20:32 right in the sight of the L
2Ch 20:37 the L has destroyed your
2Ch 21: 6 evil in the sight of the L
2Ch 21: 7 Yet the L would not destroy
2Ch 21:10 the L God of his fathers
2Ch 21:12 Thus says the L God of your
2Ch 21:14 the L will strike your people
2Ch 21:16 Moreover the L stirred up
2Ch 21:18 this the L struck him in his
2Ch 22: 4 evil in the sight of the L
2Ch 22: 7 whom the L had anointed to
2Ch 22: 9 who sought the L with all his
2Ch 23: 3 as the L has said of the sons
2Ch 23: 5 courts of the house of the L
2Ch 23: 6 of the L except the priests
2Ch 23: 6 shall keep the watch of the L
2Ch 23:12 people in the temple of the L
2Ch 23:14 her in the house of the L
2Ch 23:18 of the house of the L to the
2Ch 23:18 in the house of the L, to
2Ch 23:18 the burnt offerings of the L
2Ch 23:19 gates of the house of the L
2Ch 23:20 down from the house of the L
2Ch 24: 2 L all the days of Jehoiada
2Ch 24: 4 repairing the house of the L
2Ch 24: 6 of Moses the servant of the L
2Ch 24: 7 house of the L to the Baals
2Ch 24: 8 gate of the house of the L
2Ch 24: 9 L the collection that Moses
2Ch 24:12 service of the house of the L
2Ch 24:12 to repair the house of the L
2Ch 24:12 to restore the house of the L
2Ch 24:14 for the house of the L,
2Ch 24:14 in the house of the L
2Ch 24:18 of the L God of their fathers
2Ch 24:19 to bring them back to the L
2Ch 24:20 the commandments of the L
2Ch 24:20 you have forsaken the L, He
2Ch 24:21 court of the house of the L
2Ch 24:22 The L look on it, and repay
2Ch 24:24 but the L delivered a very
2Ch 24:24 the L God of their fathers
2Ch 25: 2 right in the sight of the L
2Ch 25: 4 Moses, where the L commanded
2Ch 25: 7 for the L is not with Israel
2Ch 25: 9 The L is able to give you
2Ch 25:15 Therefore the anger of the L
2Ch 25:27 away from following the L
2Ch 26: 4 right in the sight of the L
2Ch 26: 5 and as long as he sought the L
2Ch 26:16 the L his God by entering the
2Ch 26:16 the L to burn incense on the
2Ch 26:17 were eighty priests of the L
2Ch 26:18 to burn incense to the L
2Ch 26:18 have no honor from the L God
2Ch 26:19 priests in the house of the L
2Ch 26:20 because the L had struck him
2Ch 26:21 off from the house of the L
2Ch 27: 2 right in the sight of the L
2Ch 27: 2 enter the temple of the L)
2Ch 27: 3 Gate of the house of the L
2Ch 27: 6 his ways before the L his God
2Ch 28: 1 right in the sight of the L
2Ch 28: 3 the L had cast out before the
2Ch 28: 5 Therefore the L his God
2Ch 28: 6 the L God of their fathers
2Ch 28: 9 a prophet of the L was there
2Ch 28: 9 because the L God of your
2Ch 28:10 guilty before the L your God
2Ch 28:11 wrath of the L is upon you
2Ch 28:13 already have offended the L
2Ch 28:19 For the L brought Judah low
2Ch 28:19 unfaithful to the L
2Ch 28:21 from the house of the L, from
2Ch 28:22 unfaithful to the L
2Ch 28:24 doors of the house of the L
2Ch 28:25 the L God of his fathers
2Ch 29: 2 right in the sight of the L
2Ch 29: 3 doors of the house of the L
2Ch 29: 5 of the L God of your fathers
2Ch 29: 6 in the eyes of the L our God
2Ch 29: 6 from the habitation of the L
2Ch 29: 8 of the L fell upon Judah and

2Ch 29:10 with the **L** God of Israel,
2Ch 29:11 for the **L** has chosen you to
2Ch 29:15 king, at the words of the **L**
2Ch 29:15 to cleanse the house of the **L**
2Ch 29:16 house of the **L** to cleanse it
2Ch 29:16 **L** to the court of the house
2Ch 29:16 court of the house of the **L**
2Ch 29:17 to the vestibule of the **L**
2Ch 29:17 house of the **L** in eight days
2Ch 29:18 all the house of the **L**, the
2Ch 29:19 before the altar of the **L**
2Ch 29:20 went up to the house of the **L**
2Ch 29:21 them on the altar of the **L**
2Ch 29:25 house of the **L** with cymbals
2Ch 29:25 of the **L** by his prophets
2Ch 29:27 the song of the **L** also began
2Ch 29:30 to sing praise to the **L** with
2Ch 29:31 yourselves to the **L**, come
2Ch 29:31 into the house of the **L**
2Ch 29:32 for a burnt offering to the **L**
2Ch 29:35 of the **L** was set in order
2Ch 30: 1 house of the **L** at Jerusalem
2Ch 30: 1 to the **L** God of Israel
2Ch 30: 5 **L** God of Israel at Jerusalem
2Ch 30: 6 return to the **L** God of
2Ch 30: 7 the **L** God of their fathers
2Ch 30: 8 but yield yourselves to the **L**
2Ch 30: 8 and serve the **L** your God,
2Ch 30: 9 For if you return to the **L**
2Ch 30: 9 for the **L** your God is
2Ch 30:12 leaders, at the word of the **L**
2Ch 30:15 to the house of the **L**
2Ch 30:17 to sanctify them to the **L**
2Ch 30:18 May the good **L** provide
2Ch 30:19 the **L** God of his fathers,
2Ch 30:20 the **L** listened to Hezekiah and
2Ch 30:21 praised the **L** day by day,
2Ch 30:21 day by day, singing to the **L**
2Ch 30:22 the good knowledge of the **L**
2Ch 30:22 to the **L** God of their fathers
2Ch 31: 2 gates of the camp of the **L**
2Ch 31: 3 written in the Law of the **L**
2Ch 31: 4 to the Law of the **L**
2Ch 31: 6 the **L** their God they laid in
2Ch 31: 8 the heaps, they blessed the **L**
2Ch 31:10 into the house of the **L**, we
2Ch 31:10 for the **L** has blessed His
2Ch 31:11 rooms in the house of the **L**
2Ch 31:14 the offerings of the **L** and the
2Ch 31:16 entered the house of the **L**
2Ch 31:20 and true before the **L** his God
2Ch 32: 8 but with us is the **L** our God
2Ch 32:11 The **L** our God will deliver us
2Ch 32:16 even more against the **L** God
2Ch 32:17 to revile the **L** God of Israel
2Ch 32:21 Then the **L** sent an angel who
2Ch 32:22 Thus the **L** saved Hezekiah and
2Ch 32:23 gifts to the **L** at Jerusalem
2Ch 32:24 death, and he prayed to the **L**
2Ch 32:26 so that the wrath of the **L**
2Ch 33: 2 evil in the sight of the **L**
2Ch 33: 2 the **L** had cast out before the
2Ch 33: 4 altars in the house of the **L**
2Ch 33: 4 of which the **L** had said
2Ch 33: 5 courts of the house of the **L**
2Ch 33: 6 evil in the sight of the **L**
2Ch 33: 9 **L** had destroyed before the
2Ch 33:10 the **L** spoke to Manasseh and
2Ch 33:11 Therefore the **L** brought upon
2Ch 33:12 he implored the **L** his God
2Ch 33:13 knew that the **L** was God
2Ch 33:15 idol from the house of the **L**
2Ch 33:15 mount of the house of the **L**
2Ch 33:16 repaired the altar of the **L**
2Ch 33:16 to serve the **L** God of Israel
2Ch 33:17 but only to the **L** their God
2Ch 33:18 name of the **L** God of Israel
2Ch 33:22 evil in the sight of the **L**
2Ch 33:23 humble himself before the **L**
2Ch 34: 2 right in the sight of the **L**
2Ch 34: 8 the house of the **L** his God
2Ch 34:10 of the house of the **L**
2Ch 34:10 worked in the house of the **L**
2Ch 34:14 into the house of the **L**,
2Ch 34:14 Law of the **L** given by Moses
2Ch 34:15 the Law in the house of the **L**
2Ch 34:17 found in the house of the **L**
2Ch 34:21 Go, inquire of the **L** for me
2Ch 34:21 **L** that is poured out on us
2Ch 34:21 not kept the word of the **L**
2Ch 34:23 Thus says the **L** God of Israel
2Ch 34:24 Thus says the **L**
2Ch 34:26 sent you to inquire of the **L**
2Ch 34:26 Thus says the **L** God of Israel
2Ch 34:27 have heard you," says the **L**
2Ch 34:30 went up to the house of the **L**
2Ch 34:30 found in the house of the **L**
2Ch 34:31 made a covenant before the **L**
2Ch 34:31 to follow the **L**
2Ch 34:33 serve the **L** their God
2Ch 34:33 the **L** God of their fathers
2Ch 35: 1 to the **L** in Jerusalem, and
2Ch 35: 2 service of the house of the **L**
2Ch 35: 3 who were holy to the **L**
2Ch 35: 3 Now serve the **L** your God and
2Ch 35: 6 to the word of the **L** by the
2Ch 35:12 lay people, to offer to the **L**
2Ch 35:16 **L** was prepared the same day
2Ch 35:16 on the altar of the **L**,
2Ch 35:26 written in the Law of the **L**
2Ch 36: 5 in the sight of the **L** his God
2Ch 36: 7 the house of the **L** to Babylon
2Ch 36: 9 evil in the sight of the **L**
2Ch 36:10 from the house of the **L**, and
2Ch 36:12 in the sight of the **L** his God
2Ch 36:12 spoke from the mouth of the **L**
2Ch 36:13 to the **L** God of Israel
2Ch 36:14 defiled the house of the **L**
2Ch 36:15 the **L** God of their fathers
2Ch 36:16 until the wrath of the **L**
2Ch 36:18 of the house of the **L**, and the
2Ch 36:21 **L** by the mouth of Jeremiah
2Ch 36:22 that the word of the **L** spoken
2Ch 36:22 the **L** stirred up the spirit
2Ch 36:23 kingdoms of the earth the **L**
2Ch 36:23 May the **L** his God be with him
Ezra 1: 1 that the word of the **L** spoken
Ezra 1: 1 the **L** stirred up the spirit
Ezra 1: 2 kingdoms of the earth the **L**
Ezra 1: 3 build the house of the **L** God
Ezra 1: 5 the **L** which is in Jerusalem
Ezra 1: 7 of the house of the **L**, which
Ezra 2:68 the **L** which is in Jerusalem
Ezra 3: 3 offerings on it to the **L**,
Ezra 3: 5 the **L** that were consecrated
Ezra 3: 5 a freewill offering to the **L**
Ezra 3: 6 burnt offerings to the **L**
Ezra 3: 6 of the temple of the **L** had
Ezra 3: 8 work of the house of the **L**
Ezra 3:10 of the temple of the **L**, the
Ezra 3:10 with cymbals, to praise the **L**
Ezra 3:11 and giving thanks to the **L**
Ezra 3:11 when they praised the **L**,
Ezra 3:11 the house of the **L** was laid
Ezra 4: 1 temple of the **L** God of Israel
Ezra 4: 3 build to the **L** God of Israel
Ezra 6:21 to seek the **L** God of Israel
Ezra 6:22 for the **L** made them joyful,
Ezra 7: 6 which the **L** God of Israel had
Ezra 7: 6 of the **L** his God upon him
Ezra 7:10 to seek the Law of the **L**, and
Ezra 7:11 of the commandments of the **L**
Ezra 7:27 Blessed be the **L** God of our
Ezra 7:27 the **L** which is in Jerusalem
Ezra 7:28 of the **L** my God was upon me
Ezra 8:28 You are holy to the **L**
Ezra 8:28 to the **L** God of your fathers
Ezra 8:29 of the house of the **L**
Ezra 8:35 was a burnt offering to the **L**
Ezra 9: 5 out my hands to the **L** my God
Ezra 9: 8 been shown from the **L** our God
Ezra 9:15 O **L** God of Israel, You are
Ezra 10:11 to the **L** God of your fathers
Neh 1: 5 **L** God of heaven, O great and
Neh 1:11 O **L**, I pray, please let Your
Neh 3: 5 to the work of their **L**
Neh 4:14 Remember the **L**, great and
Neh 5:13 and praised the **L**
Neh 8: 1 which the **L** had commanded
Neh 8: 6 And Ezra blessed the **L**, the
Neh 8: 6 worshiped the **L** with their
Neh 8: 9 day is holy to the **L** your God
Neh 8:10 for this day is holy to our **L**
Neh 8:10 joy of the **L** is your strength
Neh 8:14 which the **L** had commanded by
Neh 9: 3 the Book of the Law of the **L**
Neh 9: 3 and worshiped the **L** their God
Neh 9: 4 loud voice to the **L** their God
Neh 9: 5 bless the **L** your God forever
Neh 9: 6 You alone are the **L**
Neh 9: 7 You are the **L** God, Who chose
Neh 10:29 of the **L** our **L**, and His
Neh 10:34 **L** our God as it is written in
Neh 10:35 year, to the house of the **L**
Job 1: 6 themselves before the **L**, and
Job 1: 7 And the **L** said to Satan,
Job 1: 7 So Satan answered the **L**
Job 1: 8 Then the **L** said to Satan,
Job 1: 9 So Satan answered the **L** and
Job 1:12 So the **L** said to Satan
Job 1:12 from the presence of the **L**
Job 1:21 The **L** gave, and the **L** has
Job 1:21 gave, and the **L** has taken away
Job 1:21 blessed be the name of the **L**
Job 2: 1 themselves before the **L**, and
Job 2: 1 present himself before the **L**
Job 2: 2 And the **L** said to Satan,
Job 2: 2 So Satan answered the **L**
Job 2: 3 Then the **L** said to Satan,
Job 2: 4 So Satan answered the **L** and
Job 2: 6 So the **L** said to Satan
Job 2: 7 from the presence of the **L**
Job 12: 9 hand of the **L** has done this
Job 28:28 Behold, the fear of the **L**
Job 38: 1 Then the **L** answered Job out
Job 40: 1 Moreover the **L** answered Job
Job 40: 3 Then Job answered the **L** and
Job 40: 6 Then the **L** answered Job out
Job 42: 1 Then Job answered the **L** and
Job 42: 7 after the **L** had spoken these
Job 42: 7 that the **L** said to Eliphaz
Job 42: 9 did as the **L** commanded them
Job 42: 9 for the **L** had accepted Job
Job 42:10 the **L** restored Job's losses
Job 42:10 Indeed the **L** gave Job twice
Job 42:11 the **L** had brought upon him
Job 42:12 Now the **L** blessed the latter
Ps 1: 2 is in the law of the **L**, And in
Ps 1: 6 For the **L** knows the way of
Ps 2: 2 together, Against the **L** and
Ps 2: 4 The **L** shall hold them in
Ps 2: 7 The **L** has said to Me, "You
Ps 2:11 Serve the **L** with fear, And
Ps 3: 1 **L**, how they have increased
Ps 3: 3 But You, O **L**, are a shield
Ps 3: 4 cried to the **L** with my voice
Ps 3: 5 awoke, for the **L** sustained me
Ps 3: 7 Arise, O **L**; Save
Ps 3: 8 Salvation belongs to the **L**
Ps 4: 3 But know that the **L** has set
Ps 4: 3 The **L** will hear when I call
Ps 4: 5 And put your trust in the **L**
Ps 4: 6 **L**, lift up the light of
Ps 4: 8 For You alone, O **L**, make me
Ps 5: 1 Give ear to my words, O **L**
Ps 5: 3 hear in the morning, O **L**
Ps 5: 6 The **L** abhors the bloodthirsty
Ps 5: 8 Lead me, O **L**, in Your
Ps 5:12 For You, O **L**, will bless the
Ps 6: 1 O **L**, do not rebuke me in Your
Ps 6: 2 Have mercy on me, O **L**, for I
Ps 6: 2 O **L**, heal me, for my bones
Ps 6: 3 But You, O **L**—how long?
Ps 6: 4 Return, O **L**, deliver me
Ps 6: 8 For the **L** has heard the voice
Ps 6: 9 The **L** has heard my
Ps 6: 9 The **L** will receive my prayer
Ps 7: 1 O **L** my God, in You I put my
Ps 7: 3 O **L** my God, if I have done
Ps 7: 6 Arise, O **L**, in Your anger
Ps 7: 8 The **L** shall judge the peoples
Ps 7: 8 Judge me, O **L**, according to
Ps 7:17 praise the **L** according to His
Ps 7:17 the name of the **L** Most High
Ps 8: 1 O **L**, our **L**, How excellent
Ps 8: 9 O **L**, our **L**, How excellent
Ps 9: 1 I will praise You, O **L**, with
Ps 9: 7 But the **L** shall endure
Ps 9: 9 The **L** also will be a refuge
Ps 9:10 For You, **L**, have not forsaken
Ps 9:11 Sing praises to the **L**, who
Ps 9:13 Have mercy on me, O **L**
Ps 9:16 The **L** is known by the
Ps 9:19 Arise, O **L**, Do not let man
Ps 9:20 Put them in fear, O **L**, That
Ps 10: 1 do You stand afar off, O **L**
Ps 10: 3 the greedy and renounces the **L**
Ps 10:12 Arise, O **L**! O God, lift up
Ps 10:16 The **L** is King forever and ever
Ps 10:17 **L**, You have heard the desire

Ps 11: 1 In the L I put my trust
Ps 11: 4 The L is in His holy temple,
Ps 11: 5 The L tests the righteous,
Ps 11: 7 For the L is righteous, He
Ps 12: 1 Help, L, for the godly man
Ps 12: 3 May the L cut off all
Ps 12: 4 Who is l over us
Ps 12: 5 I will arise," says the L
Ps 12: 6 words of the L are pure words
Ps 12: 7 You shall keep them, O L, You
Ps 13: 1 How long, O L
Ps 13: 3 and hear me, O L my God
Ps 13: 6 I will sing to the L, Because
Ps 14: 2 The L looks down from heaven
Ps 14: 4 And do not call on the L
Ps 14: 6 poor, But the L is his refuge
Ps 14: 7 When the L brings back the
Ps 15: 1 L, who may abide in Your
Ps 15: 4 honors those who fear the L
Ps 16: 2 soul, you have said to the L
Ps 16: 2 You are my L, My goodness is
Ps 16: 5 You, O L, are the portion of
Ps 16: 7 I will bless the L who has
Ps 16: 8 I have set the L always
Ps 17: 1 Hear a just cause, O L,
Ps 17:13 Arise, O L, Confront him,
Ps 17:14 With Your hand from men, O L
Ps 18: 1 I will love You, O L, my
Ps 18: 2 The L is my rock and my
Ps 18: 3 I will call upon the L, who
Ps 18: 6 distress I called upon the L
Ps 18:13 The L also thundered in the
Ps 18:15 uncovered At Your rebuke, O L
Ps 18:18 But the L was my support
Ps 18:20 The L rewarded me according
Ps 18:21 I have kept the ways of the L
Ps 18:24 Therefore the L has
Ps 18:28 The L my God will enlighten
Ps 18:30 The word of the L is proven
Ps 18:31 For who is God, except the L
Ps 18:41 to save them, Even to the L
Ps 18:46 The L lives! Blessed be my
Ps 18:49 will give thanks to You, O L
Ps 19: 7 The law of the L is perfect
Ps 19: 7 testimony of the L is sure
Ps 19: 8 statutes of the L are right
Ps 19: 8 commandment of the L is pure
Ps 19: 9 The fear of the L is clean
Ps 19: 9 judgments of the L are true
Ps 19:14 acceptable in Your sight, O L
Ps 20: 1 May the L answer you in the
Ps 20: 5 May the L fulfill all your
Ps 20: 6 that the L saves His anointed
Ps 20: 7 the name of the L our God
Ps 20: 9 Save, L! May the King
Ps 21: 1 joy in Your strength, O L
Ps 21: 7 For the king trusts in the L
Ps 21: 9 The L shall swallow them up
Ps 21:13 Be exalted, O L, in Your own
Ps 22: 8 He trusted in the L, let Him
Ps 22:19 But You, O L, do not be far
Ps 22:23 You who fear the L, praise
Ps 22:26 seek Him will praise the L
Ps 22:27 remember and turn to the L
Ps 22:30 the L to the next generation
Ps 23: 1 The L is my shepherd
Ps 23: 6 in the house of the L Forever
Ps 24: 3 ascend into the hill of the L
Ps 24: 5 receive blessing from the L
Ps 24: 8 The L strong and mighty, The
Ps 24: 8 The L mighty in battle
Ps 24:10 The L of hosts, He is the
Ps 25: 1 To You, O L, I lift up my
Ps 25: 4 Show me Your ways, O L
Ps 25: 6 Remember, O L, Your tender
Ps 25: 7 For Your goodness' sake, O L
Ps 25: 8 Good and upright is the L
Ps 25:10 the paths of the L are mercy
Ps 25:11 For Your name's sake, O L
Ps 25:12 is the man that fears the L
Ps 25:14 The secret of the L is with
Ps 25:15 My eyes are ever toward the L
Ps 26: 1 Vindicate me, O L, For I have
Ps 26: 1 I have also trusted in the L
Ps 26: 2 Examine me, O L, and prove me
Ps 26: 6 will go about Your altar, O L
Ps 26: 8 L, I have loved the
Ps 26:12 I will bless the L
Ps 27: 1 The L is my light and my
Ps 27: 1 The L is the strength of my
Ps 27: 4 thing I have desired of the L
Ps 27: 4 the L All the days of my life
Ps 27: 4 To behold the beauty of the L
Ps 27: 6 I will sing praises to the L
Ps 27: 7 Hear, O L, when I cry with my
Ps 27: 8 Your face, L, I will seek
Ps 27:10 Then the L will take care of
Ps 27:11 Teach me Your way, O L, And
Ps 27:13 see the goodness of the L In
Ps 27:14 Wait on the L
Ps 27:14 Wait, I say, on the L
Ps 28: 1 You I will cry, O L my Rock
Ps 28: 5 not regard the works of the L
Ps 28: 6 Blessed be the L, Because He
Ps 28: 7 The L is my strength and my
Ps 28: 8 The L is their strength, And
Ps 29: 1 Give unto the L, O you mighty
Ps 29: 1 ones, Give unto the L glory
Ps 29: 2 Give unto the L the glory due
Ps 29: 2 Worship the L in the beauty
Ps 29: 3 The voice of the L is over
Ps 29: 3 The L is over many waters
Ps 29: 4 voice of the L is powerful
Ps 29: 4 The voice of the L is full of
Ps 29: 5 The voice of the L breaks the
Ps 29: 5 the L splinters the cedars of
Ps 29: 7 The voice of the L divides
Ps 29: 8 The voice of the L shakes the
Ps 29: 8 The L shakes the Wilderness
Ps 29: 9 The voice of the L makes the
Ps 29:10 The L sat enthroned at the
Ps 29:10 the L sits as King forever
Ps 29:11 The L will give strength to
Ps 29:11 The L will bless His people
Ps 30: 1 I will extol You, O L, for
Ps 30: 2 O L my God, I cried out to
Ps 30: 3 O L, You have brought my soul
Ps 30: 4 Sing praise to the L, You
Ps 30: 7 L, by Your favor You have
Ps 30: 8 I cried out to You, O L
Ps 30: 8 to the L I made supplication
Ps 30:10 Hear, O L, and have mercy on
Ps 30:10 L, be my helper
Ps 30:12 O L my God, I will give
Ps 31: 1 In You, O L, I put my trust
Ps 31: 5 redeemed me, O L God of truth
Ps 31: 6 But I trust in the L
Ps 31: 9 Have mercy on me, O L, for I
Ps 31:14 for me, I trust in You, O L
Ps 31:17 Do not let me be ashamed, O L
Ps 31:21 Blessed be the L, For He has
Ps 31:23 Oh, love the L, all you His
Ps 31:23 For the L preserves the
Ps 31:24 All you who hope in the L
Ps 32: 2 is the man to whom the L does
Ps 32: 5 my transgressions to the L
Ps 32:10 But he who trusts in the L
Ps 32:11 Be glad in the L and rejoice,
Ps 33: 1 Rejoice in the L, O you
Ps 33: 2 Praise the L with the harp
Ps 33: 4 the word of the L is right
Ps 33: 5 full of the goodness of the L
Ps 33: 6 By the word of the L the
Ps 33: 8 Let all the earth fear the L
Ps 33:10 The L brings the counsel of
Ps 33:11 of the L stands forever, The
Ps 33:12 the nation whose God is the L
Ps 33:13 The L looks from heaven
Ps 33:18 the eye of the L is on those
Ps 33:20 Our soul waits for the L
Ps 33:22 Let Your mercy, O L, be upon
Ps 34: 1 will bless the L at all times
Ps 34: 2 shall make its boast in the L
Ps 34: 3 Oh, magnify the L with me
Ps 34: 4 I sought the L, and He heard
Ps 34: 6 the L heard him, And saved him
Ps 34: 7 The angel of the L encamps
Ps 34: 8 and see that the L is good
Ps 34: 9 Oh, fear the L, you His
Ps 34:10 But those who seek the L
Ps 34:11 teach you the fear of the L
Ps 34:15 The eyes of the L are on the
Ps 34:16 The face of the L is against
Ps 34:17 the L hears, And delivers them
Ps 34:18 The L is near to those who
Ps 34:19 But the L delivers him out of
Ps 34:22 The L redeems the soul of His
Ps 35: 1 Plead my cause, O L, with
Ps 35: 5 the angel of the L chase them
Ps 35: 6 angel of the L pursue them
Ps 35: 9 soul shall be joyful in the L
Ps 35:10 L, who is like You,
Ps 35:17 L, how long will You look on
Ps 35:22 This You have seen, O L
Ps 35:22 O L, do not be far from me
Ps 35:23 To my cause, my God and my L
Ps 35:24 O L my God, according to Your
Ps 35:27 Let the L be magnified, Who
Ps 36: 5 Your mercy, O L, is in the
Ps 36: 6 O L, You preserve man and
Ps 37: 3 Trust in the L, and do good
Ps 37: 4 yourself also in the L, And He
Ps 37: 5 Commit your way to the L,
Ps 37: 7 Rest in the L, and wait
Ps 37: 9 But those who wait on the L
Ps 37:13 The L laughs at him, For He
Ps 37:17 broken, But the L upholds the
Ps 37:18 The L knows the days of the
Ps 37:20 And the enemies of the L, Like
Ps 37:23 good man are ordered by the L
Ps 37:24 For the L upholds him with
Ps 37:28 For the L loves justice, And
Ps 37:33 The L will not leave him in
Ps 37:34 Wait on the L, And keep His
Ps 37:39 the righteous is from the L
Ps 37:40 And the L shall help them and
Ps 38: 1 O l, do not rebuke me in Your
Ps 38: 9 L, all my desire is before
Ps 38:15 For in You, O L, I hope
Ps 38:15 You will hear, O L my God
Ps 38:21 Do not forsake me, O L
Ps 38:22 Make haste to help me, O L
Ps 39: 4 L, make me to know my end,
Ps 39: 7 And now, L, what do I wait for
Ps 39:12 Hear my prayer, O L, And give
Ps 40: 1 I waited patiently for the L
Ps 40: 3 fear, And will trust in the L
Ps 40: 4 man who makes the L his trust
Ps 40: 5 Many, O L my God, are Your
Ps 40: 9 do not restrain my lips, O L
Ps 40:11 tender mercies from me, O L
Ps 40:13 Be pleased, O L, to deliver
Ps 40:13 O L, make haste to help me
Ps 40:16 The L be magnified
Ps 40:17 Yet the L thinks upon me
Ps 41: 1 The L will deliver him in
Ps 41: 2 The L will preserve him and
Ps 41: 3 The L will strengthen him on
Ps 41: 4 L, be merciful to me
Ps 41:10 But You, O L, be merciful to
Ps 41:13 Blessed be the L God of
Ps 42: 8 The L will command His
Ps 44:23 Why do You sleep, O L
Ps 45:11 Because He is your L, worship
Ps 46: 7 The L of hosts is with us
Ps 46: 8 behold the works of the L
Ps 46:11 The L of hosts is with us
Ps 47: 2 For the L Most High is
Ps 47: 5 The L with the sound of a
Ps 48: 1 Great is the L, and greatly to
Ps 48: 8 In the city of the L of hosts
Ps 50: 1 The Mighty One, God the L
Ps 51:15 O L, open my lips, And my
Ps 54: 4 The L is with those who
Ps 54: 6 I will praise Your name, O L
Ps 55: 9 Destroy, O L, and divide their
Ps 55:16 God, And the L shall save me
Ps 55:22 Cast your burden on the L
Ps 56:10 In the L (I will praise His
Ps 57: 9 I will praise You, O L, among
Ps 58: 6 fangs of the young lions, O L
Ps 59: 3 nor for my sin, O L
Ps 59: 5 O L God of hosts, the God of
Ps 59: 8 But You, O L, shall laugh at
Ps 59:11 them down, O L our shield
Ps 62:12 Also to You, O L, belongs
Ps 64:10 shall be glad in the L, and
Ps 66:18 my heart, The L will not hear
Ps 68:11 The L gave the word
Ps 68:16 Yes, the L will dwell in it
Ps 68:17 The L is among them as in
Ps 68:18 That the L God might dwell
Ps 68:19 Blessed be the L, Who daily
Ps 68:20 to GOD the L belong escapes
Ps 68:22 The L said, "I will bring
Ps 68:26 in the congregations, The L
Ps 68:32 Oh, sing praises to the L
Ps 69: 6 O L GOD of hosts, be ashamed
Ps 69:13 me, my prayer is to You, O L
Ps 69:16 Hear me, O L, for Your

Ps 69:31 L better than an ox or bull
Ps 69:33 For the L hears the poor, And
Ps 70: 1 Make haste to help me, O L
Ps 70: 5 O L, do not delay
Ps 71: 1 In You, O L, I put my trust
Ps 71: 5 For You are my hope, O L God
Ps 71:16 in the strength of the L God
Ps 72:18 Blessed be the L God, the God
Ps 73:20 dream when one awakes, So, L
Ps 73:28 put my trust in the L God
Ps 74:18 the enemy has reproached, O L
Ps 75: 8 hand of the L there is a cup
Ps 76:11 Make vows to the L your God
Ps 77: 2 of my trouble I sought the L
Ps 77: 7 Will the L cast off forever
Ps 77:11 remember the works of the L
Ps 78: 4 to come the praises of the L
Ps 78:21 Therefore the L heard this
Ps 78:65 Then the L awoke as one out
Ps 79: 5 How long, L? Will You be
Ps 79:12 they have reproached You, O L
Ps 80: 4 O L God of hosts, How long
Ps 80:19 Restore us, O L God of hosts
Ps 81:10 I am the L your God, Who
Ps 81:15 The haters of the L would
Ps 83:16 they may seek Your name, O L
Ps 83:18 whose name alone is the L
Ps 84: 1 Your tabernacle, O L of hosts
Ps 84: 2 For the courts of the L
Ps 84: 3 O L of hosts, My King and my
Ps 84: 8 O L God of hosts, hear my
Ps 84:11 For the L God is a sun and
Ps 84:11 The L will give grace and
Ps 84:12 O L of hosts, Blessed is the
Ps 85: 1 L, You have been favorable to
Ps 85: 7 Show us Your mercy, O L, And
Ps 85: 8 what God the L will speak
Ps 85:12 the L will give what is good
Ps 86: 1 Bow down Your ear, O L, hear
Ps 86: 3 Be merciful to me, O L, For I
Ps 86: 4 Your servant, For to You, O L
Ps 86: 5 For You, L, are good, and
Ps 86: 6 Give ear, O L, to my prayer
Ps 86: 8 there is none like You, O L
Ps 86: 9 and worship before You, O L
Ps 86:11 Teach me Your way, O L
Ps 86:12 O L my God, with all my heart
Ps 86:15 But You, O L, are a God full
Ps 86:17 be ashamed, Because You, L
Ps 87: 2 The L loves the gates of Zion
Ps 87: 6 The L will record, When He
Ps 88: 1 O L, God of my salvation, I
Ps 88: 9 L, I have called daily upon
Ps 88:13 to You I have cried out, O L
Ps 88:14 L, why do You cast off my
Ps 89: 1 the mercies of the L forever
Ps 89: 5 will praise Your wonders, O L
Ps 89: 6 can be compared to the L
Ps 89: 6 can be likened to the L
Ps 89: 8 O L God of hosts, Who is
Ps 89: 8 Who is mighty like You, O L
Ps 89:15 They walk, O L, in the light
Ps 89:18 our shield belongs to the L
Ps 89:46 How long, L? Will You hide
Ps 89:49 L, where are Your former
Ps 89:50 Remember, L, the reproach of
Ps 89:51 enemies have reproached, O L
Ps 89:52 Blessed be the L forevermore
Ps 90: 1 L, You have been our dwelling
Ps 90:13 Return, O L! How long?
Ps 90:17 of the L our God be upon us
Ps 91: 2 I will say of the L, "He is
Ps 91: 9 Because you have made the L
Ps 92: 1 good to give thanks to the L
Ps 92: 4 For You, L, have made me glad
Ps 92: 5 O L, how great are Your works
Ps 92: 8 But You, L, are on high
Ps 92: 9 For behold, Your enemies, O L
Ps 92:13 the L Shall flourish in the
Ps 92:15 declare that the L is upright
Ps 93: 1 The L reigns, He is clothed
Ps 93: 1 The L is clothed, He has
Ps 93: 3 floods have lifted up, O L
Ps 93: 4 The L on high is mightier
Ps 93: 5 adorns Your house, O L,
Ps 94: 1 O L God, to whom vengeance
Ps 94: 3 L, how long will the wicked,
Ps 94: 5 in pieces Your people, O L
Ps 94: 7 The L does not see, Nor does
Ps 94:11 The L knows the thoughts of
Ps 94:12 man whom You instruct, O L
Ps 94:14 For the L will not cast off
Ps 94:17 Unless the L had been my help
Ps 94:18 foot slips," Your mercy, O L
Ps 94:22 But the L has been my defense
Ps 94:23 The L our God shall cut them
Ps 95: 1 Oh come, let us sing to the L
Ps 95: 3 For the L is the great God,
Ps 95: 6 kneel before the L our Maker
Ps 96: 1 Oh, sing to the L a new song
Ps 96: 1 Sing to the L, all the earth
Ps 96: 2 Sing to the L, bless His name
Ps 96: 4 For the L is great and greatly
Ps 96: 5 But the L made the heavens
Ps 96: 7 Give to the L, O kindreds of
Ps 96: 7 peoples, Give to the L glory
Ps 96: 8 Give to the L the glory due
Ps 96: 9 worship the L in the beauty
Ps 96:10 the nations, "The L reigns
Ps 96:12 will rejoice before the L
Ps 97: 1 The L reigns
Ps 97: 5 wax at the presence of the L
Ps 97: 5 of the L of the whole earth
Ps 97: 8 of Your judgments, O L
Ps 97: 9 For You, L, are most high
Ps 97:10 You who love the L, hate evil
Ps 97:12 Rejoice in the L, you
Ps 98: 1 Oh, sing to the L a new song
Ps 98: 2 The L has made known His
Ps 98: 4 Shout joyfully to the L, all
Ps 98: 5 Sing to the L with the harp,
Ps 98: 6 Shout joyfully before the L
Ps 98: 8 joyful together before the L
Ps 99: 1 The L reigns
Ps 99: 2 The L is great in Zion, And He
Ps 99: 5 Exalt the L our God, And
Ps 99: 6 They called upon the L, and He
Ps 99: 8 answered them, O L our God
Ps 99: 9 Exalt the L our God, And
Ps 99: 9 For the L our God is holy
Ps 100: 1 Make a joyful shout to the L
Ps 100: 2 Serve the L with gladness
Ps 100: 3 Know that the L, He is God
Ps 100: 5 For the L is good
Ps 101: 1 To You, O L, I will sing
Ps 101: 8 from the city of the L
Ps 102: 1 Hear my prayer, O L, And let
Ps 102:12 But You, O L, shall endure
Ps 102:15 shall fear the name of the L
Ps 102:16 For the L shall build up Zion
Ps 102:18 be created may praise the L
Ps 102:19 From heaven the L viewed the
Ps 102:21 the name of the L in Zion
Ps 102:22 the kingdoms, to serve the L
Ps 103: 1 Bless the L, O my soul
Ps 103: 2 Bless the L, O my soul, And
Ps 103: 6 The L executes righteousness
Ps 103: 8 The L is merciful and gracious
Ps 103:13 So the L pities those who
Ps 103:17 But the mercy of the L is
Ps 103:19 The L has established His
Ps 103:20 Bless the L, you His angels,
Ps 103:21 Bless the L, all you His
Ps 103:22 Bless the L, all His works,
Ps 103:22 Bless the L, O my soul
Ps 104: 1 Bless the L, O my soul
Ps 104: 1 O L my God, You are very
Ps 104:16 of the L are full of sap, The
Ps 104:24 O L, how manifold are Your
Ps 104:31 glory of the L endure forever
Ps 104:31 May the L rejoice in His
Ps 104:33 to the L as long as I live
Ps 104:34 I will be glad in the L
Ps 104:35 Bless the L, O my soul
Ps 104:35 Praise the L!
Ps 105: 1 Oh, give thanks to the L
Ps 105: 3 those rejoice who seek the L
Ps 105: 4 Seek the L and His strength
Ps 105: 7 He is the L our God
Ps 105:19 The word of the L tested him
Ps 105:21 He made him l of his house,
Ps 105:45 Praise the L!
Ps 106: 1 Praise the L!
Ps 106: 1 Oh, give thanks to the L, for
Ps 106: 2 the mighty acts of the L
Ps 106: 4 Remember me, O L, with the
Ps 106:16 And Aaron the saint of the L
Ps 106:25 not heed the voice of the L
Ps 106:34 whom the L had commanded
Ps 106:40 the L was kindled against His
Ps 106:47 O L our God, And gather us
Ps 106:48 Blessed be the L God of
Ps 106:48 Praise the L!
Ps 107: 1 Oh, give thanks to the L, for
Ps 107: 2 the redeemed of the L say so
Ps 107: 6 out to the L in their trouble
Ps 107: 8 to the L for His goodness
Ps 107:13 out to the L in their trouble
Ps 107:15 to the L for His goodness
Ps 107:19 out to the L in their trouble
Ps 107:21 to the L for His goodness
Ps 107:24 They see the works of the L
Ps 107:28 out to the L in their trouble
Ps 107:31 to the L for His goodness
Ps 107:43 the lovingkindness of the L
Ps 108: 3 I will praise You, O L, among
Ps 109:14 be remembered before the L
Ps 109:15 be continually before the L
Ps 109:21 But You, O God the L, Deal
Ps 109:26 Help me, O L my God
Ps 109:27 That You, L, have done it
Ps 109:30 praise the L with my mouth
Ps 110: 1 The L said to my L, "Sit
Ps 110: 1 The L said to my L, "Sit
Ps 110: 2 The L shall send the rod of
Ps 110: 4 The L has sworn And will not
Ps 110: 5 The L is at Your right hand
Ps 111: 1 Praise the L!
Ps 111: 1 I will praise the L with my
Ps 111: 2 The works of the L are great
Ps 111: 4 The L is gracious and full of
Ps 111:10 The fear of the L is the
Ps 112: 1 Praise the L!
Ps 112: 1 is the man who fears the L
Ps 112: 7 steadfast, trusting in the L
Ps 113: 1 Praise the L!
Ps 113: 1 Praise, O servants of the L
Ps 113: 1 Praise the name of the L
Ps 113: 2 of the L From this time forth
Ps 113: 4 The L is high above all
Ps 113: 5 Who is like the L our God
Ps 113: 9 Praise the L!
Ps 114: 7 at the presence of the L
Ps 115: 1 Not unto us, O L, not unto us
Ps 115: 9 O Israel, trust in the L
Ps 115:10 of Aaron, trust in the L
Ps 115:11 fear the L, trust in the L
Ps 115:12 The L has been mindful of us
Ps 115:13 bless those who fear the L
Ps 115:14 May the L give you increase
Ps 115:15 May you be blessed by the L
Ps 115:17 The dead do not praise the L
Ps 115:18 the L From this time forth
Ps 115:18 Praise the L!
Ps 116: 1 I love the L, because He has
Ps 116: 4 called upon the name of the L
Ps 116: 4 O L, I implore You, deliver
Ps 116: 5 Gracious is the L, and
Ps 116: 6 The L preserves the simple
Ps 116: 7 my soul, For the L has dealt
Ps 116: 9 I will walk before the L In
Ps 116:12 What shall I render to the L
Ps 116:13 call upon the name of the L
Ps 116:14 I will pay my vows to the L
Ps 116:15 in the sight of the L Is the
Ps 116:16 O L, truly I am Your servant
Ps 116:17 call upon the name of the L
Ps 116:18 I will pay my vows to the L
Ps 116:19 Praise the L!
Ps 117: 1 Oh, praise the L, all you
Ps 117: 2 of the L endures forever
Ps 117: 2 Praise the L!
Ps 118: 1 Oh, give thanks to the L, for
Ps 118: 4 those who fear the L now say
Ps 118: 5 I called on the L in distress
Ps 118: 5 The L answered me and set me
Ps 118: 6 The L is on my side
Ps 118: 7 The L is for me among those
Ps 118: 8 L Than to put confidence in
Ps 118: 9 L Than to put confidence in
Ps 118:10 of the L I will destroy them
Ps 118:11 of the L I will destroy them
Ps 118:12 of the L I will destroy them
Ps 118:13 fall, But the L helped me
Ps 118:14 The L is my strength and song,
Ps 118:15 hand of the L does valiantly
Ps 118:16 hand of the L is exalted
Ps 118:16 hand of the L does valiantly
Ps 118:17 And declare the works of the L
Ps 118:18 The L has chastened me

Ps 118:19 them, And I will praise the L
Ps 118:20 This is the gate of the L
Ps 118:24 the day which the L has made
Ps 118:25 Save now, I pray, O L
Ps 118:25 O L, I pray, send now
Ps 118:26 comes in the name of the L
Ps 118:26 you from the house of the L
Ps 118:27 God is the L, And He has given
Ps 118:29 Oh, give thanks to the L, for
Ps 119: 1 Who walk in the law of the L
Ps 119:12 Blessed are You, O L
Ps 119:31 O L, do not put me to shame
Ps 119:33 Teach me, O L, the way of
Ps 119:41 mercies come also to me, O L
Ps 119:52 Your judgments of old, O L
Ps 119:55 Your name in the night, O L
Ps 119:57 You are my portion, O L
Ps 119:64 The earth, O L, is full of
Ps 119:65 well with Your servant, O L
Ps 119:75 I know, O L, that Your
Ps 119:89 Forever, O L, Your word is
Ps 119:107 Revive me, O L, according to
Ps 119:108 offerings of my mouth, O L
Ps 119:126 is time for You to act, O L
Ps 119:137 Righteous are You, O L, And
Ps 119:145 Hear me, O L!
Ps 119:149 O L, revive me according to
Ps 119:151 You are near, O L, And all
Ps 119:156 are Your tender mercies, O L
Ps 119:159 Revive me, O L, according to
Ps 119:166 L, I hope for Your salvation,
Ps 119:169 my cry come before You, O L
Ps 119:174 long for Your salvation, O L
Ps 120: 1 my distress I cried to the L
Ps 120: 2 Deliver my soul, O L, from
Ps 121: 2 My help comes from the L, Who
Ps 121: 5 The L is your keeper
Ps 121: 5 The L is your shade at your
Ps 121: 7 The L shall preserve you from
Ps 121: 8 The L shall preserve your
Ps 122: 1 us go into the house of the L
Ps 122: 4 go up, The tribes of the L
Ps 122: 4 thanks to the name of the L
Ps 122: 9 L our God I will seek your
Ps 123: 2 eyes look to the L our God
Ps 123: 3 Have mercy on us, O L, have
Ps 124: 1 the L who was on our side
Ps 124: 2 the L who was on our side
Ps 124: 6 Blessed be the L, Who has not
Ps 124: 8 help is in the name of the L
Ps 125: 1 in the L Are like Mount Zion
Ps 125: 2 So the L surrounds His people
Ps 125: 4 Do good, O L, to those who
Ps 125: 5 The L shall lead them away
Ps 126: 1 When the L brought back the
Ps 126: 2 The L has done great things
Ps 126: 3 The L has done great things
Ps 126: 4 Bring back our captivity, O L
Ps 127: 1 Unless the L builds the house
Ps 127: 1 Unless the L guards the city,
Ps 127: 3 are a heritage from the L
Ps 128: 1 is every one who fears the L
Ps 128: 4 be blessed Who fears the L
Ps 128: 5 The L bless you out of Zion,
Ps 129: 4 The L is righteous
Ps 129: 8 blessing of the L be upon you
Ps 129: 8 you in the name of the L
Ps 130: 1 I have cried to You, O L
Ps 130: 2 L, hear my voice
Ps 130: 3 If You, L, should mark
Ps 130: 3 should mark iniquities, O L
Ps 130: 5 I wait for the L, my soul
Ps 130: 6 My soul waits for the L More
Ps 130: 7 O Israel, hope in the L
Ps 130: 7 For with the L there is mercy
Ps 131: 1 L, my heart is not haughty,
Ps 131: 3 hope in the L From this time
Ps 132: 1 L, remember David And all his
Ps 132: 2 How he swore to the L, And
Ps 132: 5 I find a place for the L, A
Ps 132: 8 Arise, O L, to Your resting
Ps 132:11 The L has sworn in truth to
Ps 132:13 For the L has chosen Zion
Ps 133: 3 For there the L commanded the
Ps 134: 1 Behold, bless the L, All you
Ps 134: 1 All you servants of the L
Ps 134: 1 stand in the house of the L
Ps 134: 2 the sanctuary, And bless the L
Ps 134: 3 The L who made heaven and
Ps 135: 1 Praise the L!
Ps 135: 1 Praise the name of the L
Ps 135: 1 Him, O you servants of the L
Ps 135: 2 stand in the house of the L
Ps 135: 3 Praise the L,
Ps 135: 3 for the L is good
Ps 135: 4 For the L has chosen Jacob
Ps 135: 5 I know that the L is great
Ps 135: 5 And our L is above all gods
Ps 135: 6 Whatever the L pleases He
Ps 135:13 Your name, O L, endures
Ps 135:13 forever, Your fame, O L,
Ps 135:14 For the L will judge His
Ps 135:19 Bless the L, O house of
Ps 135:19 Bless the L, O house of Aaron
Ps 135:20 Bless the L, O house of Levi
Ps 135:20 fear the L, bless the L
Ps 135:21 Blessed be the L out of Zion
Ps 135:21 Praise the L!
Ps 136: 1 Oh, give thanks to the L, for
Ps 136: 3 give thanks to the L of lords
Ps 137: 7 Remember, O L, against the
Ps 138: 4 earth shall praise You, O L
Ps 138: 5 sing of the ways of the L
Ps 138: 5 great is the glory of the L
Ps 138: 6 Though the L is on high, Yet
Ps 138: 8 The L will perfect that which
Ps 138: 8 Your mercy, O L, endures
Ps 139: 1 O L, You have searched me and
Ps 139: 4 on my tongue, But behold, O L
Ps 139:21 Do I not hate them, O L, who
Ps 140: 1 Deliver me, O L, from evil
Ps 140: 4 Keep me, O L, from the hands
Ps 140: 6 I said to the L
Ps 140: 6 of my supplications, O L
Ps 140: 7 O GOD the L, the strength of
Ps 140: 8 Do not grant, O L, the
Ps 140:12 I know that the L will
Ps 141: 1 L, I cry out to You
Ps 141: 3 Set a guard, O L, over my
Ps 141: 8 are upon You, O GOD the L
Ps 142: 1 out to the L with my voice
Ps 142: 1 With my voice to the L I make
Ps 142: 5 I cried out to You, O L
Ps 143: 1 Hear my prayer, O L, Give ear
Ps 143: 7 Answer me speedily, O L
Ps 143: 9 Deliver me, O L, from my
Ps 143:11 Revive me, O L, for Your
Ps 144: 1 Blessed be the L my Rock, Who
Ps 144: 3 L, what is man, that You take
Ps 144: 5 Bow down Your heavens, O L
Ps 144:15 the people whose God is the L
Ps 145: 3 Great is the L, and greatly to
Ps 145: 8 The L is gracious and full of
Ps 145: 9 The L is good to all, And His
Ps 145:10 works shall praise You, O L
Ps 145:14 The L upholds all who fall,
Ps 145:17 The L is righteous in all His
Ps 145:18 The L is near to all who call
Ps 145:20 The L preserves all who love
Ps 145:21 speak the praise of the L
Ps 146: 1 Praise the L! Praise the L,
Ps 146: 2 I live I will praise the L
Ps 146: 5 hope is in the L his God,
Ps 146: 7 The L gives freedom to the
Ps 146: 8 The L opens the eyes of the
Ps 146: 8 The L raises those who are
Ps 146: 8 The L loves the righteous
Ps 146: 9 The L watches over the
Ps 146:10 The L shall reign forever
Ps 146:10 Praise the L!
Ps 147: 1 Praise the L!
Ps 147: 2 The L builds up Jerusalem
Ps 147: 5 Great is our L, and mighty in
Ps 147: 6 The L lifts up the humble
Ps 147: 7 Sing to the L with
Ps 147:11 The L takes pleasure in those
Ps 147:12 Praise the L, O Jerusalem
Ps 147:20 Praise the L!
Ps 148: 1 Praise the L! Praise the L
Ps 148: 5 them praise the name of the L
Ps 148: 7 Praise the L from the earth,
Ps 148:13 them praise the name of the L
Ps 148:14 Praise the L!
Ps 149: 1 Praise the L!
Ps 149: 1 Sing to the L a new song, And
Ps 149: 4 For the L takes pleasure in
Ps 149: 9 Praise the L!
Ps 150: 1 Praise the L!
Ps 150: 6 praise the L. Praise the L!
Prov 1: 7 The fear of the L is the
Prov 1:29 not choose the fear of the L
Prov 2: 5 understand the fear of the L
Prov 2: 6 For the L gives wisdom
Prov 3: 5 Trust in the L with all your
Prov 3: 7 fear the L and depart from
Prov 3: 9 Honor the L with your
Prov 3:11 the chastening of the L, nor
Prov 3:12 for whom the L loves He
Prov 3:19 The L by wisdom founded the
Prov 3:26 for the L will be your
Prov 3:32 is an abomination to the L
Prov 3:33 The curse of the L is on the
Prov 5:21 are before the eyes of the L
Prov 6:16 These six things the L hates
Prov 8:13 fear of the L is to hate evil
Prov 8:22 The L possessed me at the
Prov 8:35 and obtains favor from the L
Prov 9:10 The fear of the L is the
Prov 10: 3 The L will not allow the
Prov 10:22 of the L makes one rich, and
Prov 10:27 fear of the L prolongs days
Prov 10:29 The way of the L is strength
Prov 11: 1 is an abomination to the L
Prov 11:20 are an abomination to the L
Prov 12: 2 man obtains favor from the L
Prov 12:22 are an abomination to the L
Prov 14: 2 his uprightness fears the L
Prov 14:26 In the fear of the L there is
Prov 14:27 The fear of the L is a
Prov 15: 3 The eyes of the L are in
Prov 15: 8 is an abomination to the L
Prov 15: 9 is an abomination to the L
Prov 15:11 Destruction are before the L
Prov 15:16 little with the fear of the L
Prov 15:25 The L will destroy the house
Prov 15:26 are an abomination to the L
Prov 15:29 The L is far from the wicked,
Prov 15:33 The fear of the L is the
Prov 16: 1 of the tongue is from the L
Prov 16: 2 but the L weighs the spirits
Prov 16: 3 Commit your works to the L
Prov 16: 4 The L has made all things for
Prov 16: 5 is an abomination to the L
Prov 16: 6 and by the fear of the L one
Prov 16: 7 a man's ways please the L
Prov 16: 9 but the L directs his steps
Prov 16:20 and whoever trusts in the L
Prov 16:33 every decision is from the L
Prov 17: 3 but the L tests the hearts
Prov 17:15 are an abomination to the L
Prov 18:10 The name of the L is a strong
Prov 18:22 and obtains favor from the L
Prov 19: 3 his heart frets against the L
Prov 19:14 a prudent wife is from the L
Prov 19:17 on the poor lends to the L
Prov 19:23 fear of the L leads to life
Prov 20:10 an abomination to the L
Prov 20:12 the L has made both of them
Prov 20:22 wait for the L, and He will
Prov 20:23 are an abomination to the L
Prov 20:24 A man's steps are of the L
Prov 20:27 of a man is the lamp of the L
Prov 21: 1 heart is in the hand of the L
Prov 21: 2 but the L weighs the hearts
Prov 21: 3 to the L than sacrifice
Prov 21:30 or counsel against the L
Prov 21:31 but deliverance is of the L
Prov 22: 2 the L is the maker of them
Prov 22: 4 the fear of the L are riches
Prov 22:12 The eyes of the L preserve
Prov 22:14 of the L will fall there
Prov 22:19 your trust may be in the L
Prov 22:23 for the L will plead their
Prov 23:17 the L continue all day long
Prov 24:18 lest the L see it, and it
Prov 24:21 My son, fear the L and the
Prov 25:22 and the L will reward you
Prov 28: 5 who seek the L understand all
Prov 28:25 in the L will be prospered
Prov 29:13 the L gives light to the eyes
Prov 29:25 trusts in the L shall be safe
Prov 29:26 for man comes from the L
Prov 30: 9 Who is the L
Prov 31:30 but a woman who fears the L
Is 1: 2 For the L has spoken
Is 1: 4 They have forsaken the L,
Is 1: 9 Unless the L of hosts had
Is 1:10 Hear the word of the L, you
Is 1:11 sacrifices to Me?" says the L
Is 1:18 reason together," says the L

Is 1:20 the mouth of the L has spoken
Is 1:24 Therefore the L says, the
Is 1:24 the L of hosts, the Mighty
Is 1:28 the L shall be consumed
Is 2: 3 up to the mountain of the L
Is 2: 3 word of the L from Jerusalem
Is 2: 5 us walk in the light of the L
Is 2:10 from the terror of the L
Is 2:11 the L alone shall be exalted
Is 2:12 For the day of the L of hosts
Is 2:17 the L alone will be exalted
Is 2:19 from the terror of the L
Is 2:21 from the terror of the L
Is 3: 1 behold, the L, the L of hosts
Is 3: 8 doings Are against the L, to
Is 3:13 The L stands up to plead, and
Is 3:14 The L will enter into
Is 3:15 says the L GOD of hosts
Is 3:16 the L says: "Because the
Is 3:17 therefore the L will strike
Is 3:17 and the L will uncover their
Is 3:18 In that day the L will take
Is 4: 2 of the L shall be beautiful
Is 4: 4 When the L has washed away
Is 4: 5 then the L will create above
Is 5: 7 For the vineyard of the L of
Is 5: 9 hearing the L of hosts said
Is 5:12 not regard the work of the L
Is 5:16 But the L of hosts shall be
Is 5:24 the law of the L of hosts
Is 5:25 the L is aroused against His
Is 6: 1 I saw the L sitting on a
Is 6: 3 holy, holy is the L of hosts
Is 6: 5 seen the King, the L of hosts
Is 6: 8 I heard the voice of the L
Is 6:11 Then I said, "L, how long?"
Is 6:12 The L has removed men far
Is 7: 3 Then the L said to Isaiah,
Is 7: 7 thus says the L GOD
Is 7:10 Moreover the L spoke again to
Is 7:11 yourself from the L your God
Is 7:12 ask, nor will I test the L
Is 7:14 Therefore the L Himself will
Is 7:17 The L will bring the king of
Is 7:18 L will whistle for the fly
Is 7:20 In the same day the L will
Is 8: 1 Moreover the L said to me
Is 8: 3 Then the L said to me,
Is 8: 5 The L also spoke to me again,
Is 8: 7 the L brings up over them the
Is 8:11 For the L spoke thus to me
Is 8:13 The L of hosts, Him you shall
Is 8:17 And I will wait on the L, Who
Is 8:18 whom the L has given me
Is 8:18 in Israel From the L of hosts
Is 9: 7 The zeal of the L of hosts
Is 9: 8 The L sent a word against
Is 9:11 Therefore the L shall set up
Is 9:13 do they seek the L of hosts
Is 9:14 Therefore the L will cut off
Is 9:17 Therefore the L will have no
Is 9:19 Through the wrath of the L of
Is 10:12 when the L has performed all
Is 10:16 the L, the L of hosts, will send
Is 10:20 but will depend on the L
Is 10:23 For the L GOD of hosts will
Is 10:24 thus says the L GOD of hosts
Is 10:26 the L of hosts will stir up a
Is 10:33 the L, the L of hosts, will lop
Is 11: 2 The Spirit of the L shall
Is 11: 2 and of the fear of the L
Is 11: 3 is in the fear of the L, and
Is 11: 9 of the knowledge of the L as
Is 11:11 L shall set His hand again
Is 11:15 The L will utterly destroy
Is 12: 1 O L, I will praise You
Is 12: 2 For YAH, the L, is my
Is 12: 4 Praise the L, call upon His
Is 12: 5 Sing to the L, For He has
Is 13: 4 The L of hosts musters the
Is 13: 5 the end of heaven, even the L
Is 13: 6 the day of the L is at hand
Is 13: 9 the day of the L comes,
Is 13:13 the wrath of the L of hosts
Is 14: 1 For the L will have mercy on
Is 14: 2 and maids in the land of the L
Is 14: 3 L gives you rest from your
Is 14: 5 The L has broken the staff of
Is 14:22 them," says the L of hosts
Is 14:22 and posterity," says the L
Is 14:23 says the L of hosts
Is 14:24 The L of hosts has sworn,
Is 14:27 For the L of hosts has
Is 14:32 That the L has founded Zion,
Is 16:13 L has spoken concerning Moab
Is 16:14 But now the L has spoken,
Is 17: 3 Israel," says the L of hosts
Is 17: 6 Says the L God of Israel
Is 18: 4 For so the L said to me, "I
Is 18: 7 will be brought to the L of
Is 18: 7 of the name of the L of hosts
Is 19: 1 the L rides on a swift cloud,
Is 19: 4 says the L, the L of hosts
Is 19:12 the L of hosts has purposed
Is 19:14 The L has mingled a perverse
Is 19:16 of the hand of the L of hosts
Is 19:17 the L of hosts which He has
Is 19:18 and swear by the L of hosts
Is 19:19 will be an altar to the L in
Is 19:19 pillar to the L at its border
Is 19:20 for a witness to the L of
Is 19:20 for they will cry to the L
Is 19:21 Then the L will be known to
Is 19:21 will know the L in that day
Is 19:21 they will make a vow to the L
Is 19:22 the L will strike Egypt, He
Is 19:22 they will return to the L
Is 19:25 whom the L of hosts shall
Is 20: 2 at the same time the L spoke
Is 20: 3 Then the L said, "Just as My
Is 21: 6 For thus has the L said to me
Is 21: 8 Then he cried, "A lion, my L!
Is 21:10 heard from the L of hosts
Is 21:16 For thus the L has said to me
Is 21:17 for the L God of Israel has
Is 22: 5 perplexity by the L GOD of
Is 22:12 And in that day the L GOD of
Is 22:14 my hearing by the L of hosts
Is 22:14 says the L GOD of hosts
Is 22:15 Thus says the L GOD of hosts
Is 22:17 the L will throw you away
Is 22:25 day,' says the L of hosts
Is 22:25 for the L has spoken
Is 23: 9 The L of hosts has purposed
Is 23:11 the L has given a commandment
Is 23:17 that the L will visit Tyre
Is 23:18 will be set apart for the L
Is 23:18 those who dwell before the L
Is 24: 1 the L makes the earth empty
Is 24: 3 for the L has spoken this
Is 24:14 for the majesty of the L they
Is 24:15 the L in the dawning light
Is 24:15 the name of the L God of
Is 24:21 the L will punish on high the
Is 24:23 for the L of hosts will reign
Is 25: 1 O L, You are my God
Is 25: 6 in this mountain the L of
Is 25: 8 and the L GOD will wipe away
Is 25: 8 for the L has spoken
Is 25: 9 This is the L
Is 25:10 the hand of the L will rest
Is 26: 4 Trust in the L forever, for
Is 26: 4 forever, for in YAH, the L
Is 26: 8 way of Your judgments, O L
Is 26:10 behold the majesty of the L
Is 26:11 L, when Your hand is lifted
Is 26:12 L, You will establish peace
Is 26:13 O L our God, other masters
Is 26:15 increased the nation, O L
Is 26:16 L, in trouble they have
Is 26:17 we been in Your sight, O L
Is 26:21 the L comes out of His place
Is 27: 1 In that day the L with His
Is 27: 3 I, the L, keep it, I water it
Is 27:12 day that the L will thresh
Is 27:13 shall worship the L in the
Is 28: 2 the L has a mighty and strong
Is 28: 5 In that day the L of hosts
Is 28:13 the word of the L was to them
Is 28:14 hear the word of the L, you
Is 28:16 Therefore thus says the L GOD
Is 28:21 For the L will rise up as at
Is 28:22 heard from the L GOD of hosts
Is 28:29 comes from the L of hosts
Is 29: 6 the L of hosts with thunder
Is 29:10 For the L has poured out on
Is 29:13 the L said: "Inasmuch as
Is 29:15 their counsel far from the L
Is 29:19 increase their joy in the L
Is 29:22 Therefore thus says the L
Is 30: 1 children," says the L, "Who
Is 30: 9 not hear the law of the L
Is 30:15 For thus says the L GOD, the
Is 30:18 Therefore the L will wait
Is 30:18 For the L is a God of justice
Is 30:20 though the L gives you the
Is 30:26 in the day that the L binds
Is 30:27 name of the L comes from afar
Is 30:29 into the mountain of the L
Is 30:30 The L will cause His glorious
Is 30:31 through the voice of the L
Is 30:32 which the L lays on him, it
Is 30:33 the breath of the L, like a
Is 31: 1 One of Israel, nor seek the L
Is 31: 3 When the L stretches out His
Is 31: 4 For thus the L has spoken to
Is 31: 4 so the L of hosts will come
Is 31: 5 so will the L of hosts defend
Is 31: 9 of the banner," says the L
Is 32: 6 to utter error against the L
Is 33: 2 O L, be gracious to us
Is 33: 5 The L is exalted, for He
Is 33: 6 fear of the L is His treasure
Is 33:10 Now I will rise," says the L
Is 33:21 But there the majestic L will
Is 33:22 (for the L is our Judge, the
Is 33:22 the L is our Lawgiver, the
Is 33:22 Lawgiver, the L is our King
Is 34: 2 the L is against all nations
Is 34: 6 The sword of the L is filled
Is 34: 6 For the L has a sacrifice in
Is 34:16 Search from the book of the L
Is 35: 2 shall see the glory of the L
Is 35:10 of the L shall return, and
Is 36: 7 We trust in the L our God
Is 36:10 the L against this land to
Is 36:10 The L said to me, 'Go up
Is 36:15 make you trust in the L,
Is 36:15 The L will surely deliver us
Is 36:18 The L will deliver us
Is 36:20 that the L should deliver
Is 37: 1 went into the house of the L
Is 37: 4 It may be that the L your
Is 37: 4 the L your God has heard
Is 37: 6 your master, 'Thus says the L
Is 37:14 went up to the house of the L
Is 37:14 and spread it before the L
Is 37:15 Then Hezekiah prayed to the L
Is 37:16 O L of hosts, God of Israel,
Is 37:17 Incline Your ear, O L, and
Is 37:17 open Your eyes, O L, and see
Is 37:18 Truly, L, the kings of
Is 37:20 O L our God, save us from his
Is 37:20 may know that You are the L
Is 37:21 Thus says the L God of Israel
Is 37:22 L has spoken concerning him
Is 37:24 you have reproached the L
Is 37:32 The zeal of the L of hosts
Is 37:33 the L concerning the king of
Is 37:34 into this city,' says the L
Is 37:36 the angel of the L went out
Is 38: 1 Thus says the L: 'Set your
Is 38: 2 the wall, and prayed to the L
Is 38: 3 Remember now, O L, I pray,
Is 38: 4 word of the L came to Isaiah
Is 38: 5 to Hezekiah, 'Thus says the L
Is 38: 7 is the sign to you from the L
Is 38: 7 that the L will do this thing
Is 38:11 YAH, the L in the land of the
Is 38:14 O L, I am oppressed
Is 38:16 O L, by these things men live
Is 38:20 The L was ready to save me
Is 38:20 life, in the house of the L
Is 38:22 go up to the house of the L
Is 39: 5 the word of the L of hosts
Is 39: 6 shall be left,' says the L
Is 39: 8 The word of the L which you
Is 40: 3 Prepare the way of the L
Is 40: 5 the glory of the L shall be
Is 40: 5 the mouth of the L has spoken
Is 40: 7 breath of the L blows upon it
Is 40:10 the L GOD shall come with a
Is 40:13 directed the Spirit of the L
Is 40:27 My way is hidden from the L
Is 40:28 The everlasting God, the L
Is 40:31 But those who wait on the L
Is 41: 4 I, the L, am the first
Is 41:13 the L your God, will hold
Is 41:14 I will help you," says the L
Is 41:16 you shall rejoice in the L

Is 41:17 fail for thirst, I, the L
Is 41:20 hand of the L has done this
Is 41:21 your case," says the L
Is 42: 5 Thus says God the L, Who
Is 42: 6 I, the L, have called You in
Is 42: 8 I am the L, that is My name
Is 42:10 Sing to the L a new song, and
Is 42:12 Let them give glory to the L
Is 42:13 The L shall go forth like a
Is 42:21 The L is well pleased for His
Is 42:24 Was it not the L, He against
Is 43: 1 But now, thus says the L, who
Is 43: 3 For I am the L your God, the
Is 43:10 My witnesses," says the L
Is 43:11 I, even I, am the L, and
Is 43:12 My witnesses," says the L
Is 43:14 Thus says the L, your
Is 43:15 I am the L, your Holy One,
Is 43:16 Thus says the L, who makes a
Is 44: 2 Thus says the L who made you
Is 44: 6 Thus says the L, the King of
Is 44: 6 his Redeemer, the L of hosts
Is 44:23 for the L has done it
Is 44:23 for the L has redeemed Jacob,
Is 44:24 Thus says the L, your
Is 44:24 I am the L, who makes all
Is 45: 1 Thus says the L to His
Is 45: 3 you may know that I, the L
Is 45: 5 I am the L, and there is no
Is 45: 6 I am the L, and there is no
Is 45: 7 I, the L, do all these things
Is 45: 8 I, the L, have created it
Is 45:11 Thus says the L, the Holy One
Is 45:13 reward," says the L of hosts
Is 45:14 Thus says the L: "The labor
Is 45:17 by the L with an everlasting
Is 45:18 For thus says the L, Who
Is 45:18 I am the L, and there is no
Is 45:19 I, the L, speak righteousness
Is 45:21 Have not I, the L
Is 45:24 say, 'Surely in the L I have
Is 45:25 In the L all the descendants
Is 47: 4 the L of hosts is His name,
Is 48: 1 swear by the name of the L
Is 48: 2 the L of hosts is His name
Is 48:14 The L loves him
Is 48:16 And now the L God and His
Is 48:17 Thus says the L, your
Is 48:17 I am the L your God, Who
Is 48:20 say, "The L has redeemed His
Is 48:22 is no peace," says the L
Is 49: 1 The L has called Me from the
Is 49: 4 my just reward is with the L
Is 49: 5 And now the L says, who
Is 49: 5 glorious in the eyes of the L
Is 49: 7 Thus says the L, the Redeemer
Is 49: 7 because of the L who is
Is 49: 8 Thus says the L: "In an
Is 49:13 For the L has comforted His
Is 49:14 The L has forsaken me, and my
Is 49:14 me, and my L has forgotten me
Is 49:18 As I live," says the L
Is 49:22 Thus says the L God
Is 49:23 you will know that I am the L
Is 49:25 thus says the L: "Even the
Is 49:26 shall know that I, the L, am
Is 50: 1 Thus says the L: "Where is
Is 50: 4 The L God has given Me the
Is 50: 5 The L God has opened My ear
Is 50: 7 For the L God will help Me
Is 50: 9 Surely the L God will help Me
Is 50:10 Who among you fears the L
Is 50:10 trust in the name of the L
Is 51: 1 you who seek the L
Is 51: 3 For the L will comfort Zion,
Is 51: 3 like the garden of the L
Is 51: 9 on strength, O arm of the L
Is 51:11 of the L shall return, and
Is 51:13 you forget the L your Maker
Is 51:15 But I am the L your God, who
Is 51:15 the L of hosts is His name
Is 51:17 of the L the cup of His fury
Is 51:20 are full of the fury of the L
Is 51:22 Thus says your L, the L and
Is 52: 3 thus says the L: "You have
Is 52: 4 For thus says the L God
Is 52: 5 have I here," says the L
Is 52: 5 make them wail," says the L
Is 52: 8 when the L brings back Zion
Is 52: 9 For the L has comforted His
Is 52:10 The L has made bare His holy
Is 52:11 who bear the vessels of the L
Is 52:12 for the L will go before you,
Is 53: 1 arm of the L been revealed
Is 53: 6 the L has laid on Him the
Is 53:10 pleased the L to bruise Him
Is 53:10 the pleasure of the L shall
Is 54: 1 married woman," says the L
Is 54: 5 the L of hosts is His name
Is 54: 6 For the L has called you like
Is 54: 8 mercy on you," says the L
Is 54:10 be removed," says the L, who
Is 54:13 shall be taught by the L, and
Is 54:17 of the servants of the L, and
Is 54:17 is from Me," says the L
Is 55: 5 because of the L your God
Is 55: 6 Seek the L while He may be
Is 55: 7 let him return to the L, and
Is 55: 8 ways My ways," says the L
Is 55:13 shall be to the L for a name
Is 56: 1 Thus says the L: "Keep
Is 56: 3 joined himself to the L speak
Is 56: 3 The L has utterly separated
Is 56: 4 For thus says the L
Is 56: 6 who join themselves to the L
Is 56: 6 and to love the name of the L
Is 56: 8 The L God, who gathers the
Is 57:19 him who is near," says the L
Is 58: 5 and an acceptable day to the L
Is 58: 8 the glory of the L shall be
Is 58: 9 call, and the L will answer
Is 58:11 The L will guide you
Is 58:13 holy day of the L honorable
Is 58:14 delight yourself in the L
Is 58:14 The mouth of the L has spoken
Is 59:13 and lying against the L, and
Is 59:15 Then the L saw it, and it
Is 59:19 name of the L from the west
Is 59:19 the Spirit of the L will lift
Is 59:20 in Jacob," says the L
Is 59:21 As for Me," says the L
Is 59:21 descendants," says the L
Is 60: 1 the glory of the L is risen
Is 60: 2 but the L will arise over you
Is 60: 6 proclaim the praises of the L
Is 60: 9 to the name of the L your God
Is 60:14 call you The City of the L
Is 60:16 you shall know that I, the L
Is 60:19 but the L will be to you an
Is 60:20 for the L will be your
Is 60:22 I, the L, will hasten it in
Is 61: 1 of the L God is upon Me,
Is 61: 1 because the L has anointed Me
Is 61: 2 the acceptable year of the L
Is 61: 3 the planting of the L, that
Is 61: 6 be named the Priests of the L
Is 61: 8 For I, the L, love justice
Is 61: 9 whom the L has blessed
Is 61:10 will greatly rejoice in the L
Is 61:11 so the L God will cause
Is 62: 2 the mouth of the L will name
Is 62: 3 of glory in the hand of the L
Is 62: 4 for the L delights in you, and
Is 62: 6 You who make mention of the L
Is 62: 8 The L has sworn by His right
Is 62: 9 shall eat it, and praise the L
Is 62:11 Indeed the L has proclaimed
Is 62:12 People, the Redeemed of the L
Is 63: 7 the lovingkindnesses of the L
Is 63: 7 and the praises of the L
Is 63: 7 that the L has bestowed on us
Is 63:14 the Spirit of the L causes
Is 63:16 You, O L, are our Father
Is 63:17 O L, why have You made us
Is 64: 8 But now, O L, You are our
Is 64: 9 Do not be furious, O L, nor
Is 64:12 because of these things, O L
Is 65: 7 together," says the L, "Who
Is 65: 8 Thus says the L: "As the new
Is 65:11 are those who forsake the L
Is 65:13 Therefore thus says the L God
Is 65:15 for the L God will slay you,
Is 65:23 of the blessed of the L, and
Is 65:25 holy mountain," says the L
Is 66: 1 Thus says the L: "Heaven
Is 66: 2 things exist," says the L
Is 66: 5 Hear the word of the L, you
Is 66: 5 let the L be glorified, that
Is 66: 6 The voice of the L, Who fully
Is 66: 9 cause delivery?" says the L
Is 66:12 For thus says the L
Is 66:14 the hand of the L shall be
Is 66:15 the L will come with fire and
Is 66:16 by His sword the L will judge
Is 66:16 slain of the L shall be many
Is 66:17 together," says the L
Is 66:20 to the L out of all nations
Is 66:20 Jerusalem," says the L, "as
Is 66:20 into the house of the L
Is 66:21 and Levites," says the L
Is 66:22 before Me," says the L, "So
Is 66:23 before Me," says the L
Jer 1: 2 to whom the word of the L
Jer 1: 4 the word of the L came to me
Jer 1: 6 Ah, L God! Behold, I cannot
Jer 1: 7 But the L said to me
Jer 1: 8 to deliver you," says the L
Jer 1: 9 Then the L put forth His hand
Jer 1: 9 my mouth, and the L said to me
Jer 1:11 the word of the L came to me
Jer 1:12 Then the L said to me, "You
Jer 1:13 the word of the L came to me
Jer 1:14 Then the L said to me
Jer 1:15 of the north," says the L
Jer 1:19 I am with you," says the L
Jer 2: 1 the word of the L came to me
Jer 2: 2 saying, 'Thus says the L
Jer 2: 3 Israel was holiness to the L
Jer 2: 3 come upon them," says the L
Jer 2: 4 Hear the word of the L, O
Jer 2: 5 Thus says the L: "What
Jer 2: 6 did they say, 'Where is the L
Jer 2: 8 did not say, 'Where is the L
Jer 2: 9 against you," says the L
Jer 2:12 very desolate," says the L
Jer 2:17 that you have forsaken the L
Jer 2:19 have forsaken the L your God
Jer 2:19 says the L God of hosts
Jer 2:22 before Me," says the L God
Jer 2:29 against Me," says the L
Jer 2:31 see the word of the L
Jer 2:37 for the L has rejected your
Jer 3: 1 return to Me," says the L
Jer 3: 6 The L said also to me in the
Jer 3:10 but in pretense," says the L
Jer 3:11 Then the L said to me
Jer 3:12 Israel,' says the L, 'and I
Jer 3:12 I am merciful,' says the L
Jer 3:13 against the L your God, and
Jer 3:13 obeyed My voice,' says the L
Jer 3:14 children," says the L
Jer 3:16 in those days," says the L
Jer 3:16 ark of the covenant of the L
Jer 3:17 be called The Throne of the L
Jer 3:17 to it, to the name of the L
Jer 3:20 house of Israel," says the L
Jer 3:21 forgotten the L their God
Jer 3:22 for You are the L our God
Jer 3:23 in the L our God is the
Jer 3:25 sinned against the L our God
Jer 3:25 the voice of the L our God
Jer 4: 1 O Israel," says the L
Jer 4: 2 The L lives,' in truth, in
Jer 4: 3 For thus says the L to the
Jer 4: 4 yourselves to the L, and take
Jer 4: 8 L has not turned back from us
Jer 4: 9 in that day," says the L
Jer 4:10 Then I said, "Ah, L God
Jer 4:17 against Me," says the L
Jer 4:26 down at the presence of the L
Jer 4:27 thus says the L: "The whole
Jer 5: 2 they say, 'As the L lives
Jer 5: 3 O L, are not Your eyes on the
Jer 5: 4 do not know the way of the L
Jer 5: 5 have known the way of the L
Jer 5: 9 for these things?" says the L
Jer 5:11 with Me," says the L
Jer 5:12 They have lied about the L
Jer 5:14 thus says the L God of hosts
Jer 5:15 house of Israel," says the L
Jer 5:18 in those days," says the L
Jer 5:19 Why does the L our God do
Jer 5:22 you not fear Me?' says the L
Jer 5:24 Let us now fear the L our God
Jer 5:29 for these things?' says the L
Jer 6: 6 thus has the L of hosts said
Jer 6: 9 Thus says the L of hosts
Jer 6:10 the word of the L is a
Jer 6:11 am full of the fury of the L
Jer 6:12 of the land," says the L

Jer 6:15 be cast down," says the L
Jer 6:16 Thus says the L: "Stand in
Jer 6:21 Therefore thus says the L
Jer 6:22 Thus says the L: "Behold, a
Jer 6:30 because the L has rejected
Jer 7: 1 came to Jeremiah from the L
Jer 7: 2 say, 'Hear the word of the L
Jer 7: 2 these gates to worship the L
Jer 7: 3 Thus says the L of hosts, the
Jer 7: 4 saying, 'The temple of the L
Jer 7: 4 the temple of the L are these
Jer 7:11 I, have seen it," says the L
Jer 7:13 all these works," says the L
Jer 7:19 Me to anger?" says the L
Jer 7:20 Therefore thus says the L GOD
Jer 7:21 Thus says the L of hosts, the
Jer 7:28 the L their God nor receive
Jer 7:29 for the L has rejected and
Jer 7:30 in My sight," says the L
Jer 7:32 days are coming," says the L
Jer 8: 1 At that time," says the L
Jer 8: 3 them," says the L of hosts
Jer 8: 4 say to them, 'Thus says the L
Jer 8: 7 know the judgment of the L
Jer 8: 8 the law of the L is with us'
Jer 8: 9 rejected the word of the L
Jer 8:12 be cast down," says the L
Jer 8:13 consume them," says the L
Jer 8:14 For the L our God has put us
Jer 8:14 we have sinned against the L
Jer 8:17 shall bite you," says the L
Jer 8:19 Is not the L in Zion
Jer 9: 3 do not know Me," says the L
Jer 9: 6 to know Me," says the L
Jer 9: 7 thus says the L of hosts
Jer 9: 9 for these things?" says the L
Jer 9:12 the mouth of the L has spoken
Jer 9:13 the L said, "Because they
Jer 9:15 thus says the L of hosts, the
Jer 9:17 Thus says the L of hosts
Jer 9:20 Yet hear the word of the L
Jer 9:22 Thus says the L: 'Even the
Jer 9:23 Thus says the L: "Let not
Jer 9:24 and knows Me, that I am the L
Jer 9:24 these I delight," says the L
Jer 9:25 days are coming," says the L
Jer 10: 1 which the L speaks to you
Jer 10: 2 Thus says the L: "Do not
Jer 10: 6 O L (You are great, and Your
Jer 10:10 But the L is the true God
Jer 10:16 the L of hosts is His name
Jer 10:18 For thus says the L
Jer 10:21 and have not sought the L
Jer 10:23 O L, I know the way of man is
Jer 10:24 O L, correct me, but with
Jer 11: 1 came to Jeremiah from the L
Jer 11: 3 Thus says the L God of Israel
Jer 11: 5 So be it, L
Jer 11: 6 Then the L said to me
Jer 11: 9 And the L said to me,
Jer 11:11 Therefore thus says the L
Jer 11:16 The L called your name, green
Jer 11:17 For the L of hosts, who
Jer 11:18 Now the L gave me knowledge
Jer 11:20 O L of hosts, you who judge
Jer 11:21 the L concerning the men of
Jer 11:21 prophesy in the name of the L
Jer 11:22 thus says the L of hosts
Jer 12: 1 Righteous are You, O L, when
Jer 12: 3 But You, O L, know me
Jer 12:12 for the sword of the L shall
Jer 12:13 of the fierce anger of the L
Jer 12:14 Thus says the L: "Against all
Jer 12:16 by My name, 'As the L lives
Jer 12:17 that nation," says the L
Jer 13: 1 Thus the L said to me
Jer 13: 2 to the word of the L, and put
Jer 13: 3 the word of the L came to me
Jer 13: 5 as the L commanded me
Jer 13: 6 days that the L said to me
Jer 13: 8 the word of the L came to me
Jer 13: 9 Thus says the L: 'In this
Jer 13:11 to cling to Me,' says the L
Jer 13:12 Thus says the L God of Israel
Jer 13:13 say to them, 'Thus says the L
Jer 13:14 sons together," says the L
Jer 13:15 proud, for the L has spoken
Jer 13:16 Give glory to the L your God
Jer 13:25 from Me," says the L
Jer 14: 1 The word of the L that came
Jer 14: 7 O L, though our iniquities
Jer 14: 9 Yet You, O L, are in our
Jer 14:10 Thus says the L to this
Jer 14:10 Therefore the L does not
Jer 14:11 Then the L said to me, "Do
Jer 14:13 Then I said, "Ah, L GOD
Jer 14:14 And the L said to me,
Jer 14:15 Therefore thus says the L
Jer 14:20 We acknowledge, O L, our
Jer 14:22 Are You not He, O L our God
Jer 15: 1 Then the L said to me
Jer 15: 2 tell them, 'Thus says the L
Jer 15: 3 of destruction," says the L
Jer 15: 6 forsaken Me," says the L
Jer 15: 9 their enemies," says the L
Jer 15:11 The L said: "Surely
Jer 15:15 O L, You know
Jer 15:16 Your name, O L God of hosts
Jer 15:19 Therefore thus says the L
Jer 15:20 and deliver you," says the L
Jer 16: 1 word of the L also came to me
Jer 16: 3 thus says the L concerning
Jer 16: 5 thus says the L: "Do not
Jer 16: 5 this people," says the L
Jer 16: 9 For thus says the L of hosts
Jer 16:10 Why has the L pronounced all
Jer 16:10 against the L our God
Jer 16:11 have forsaken Me,' says the L
Jer 16:14 days are coming," says the L
Jer 16:14 The L lives who brought up
Jer 16:15 The L lives who brought up
Jer 16:16 many fishermen," says the L
Jer 16:19 O L, my strength and my
Jer 16:21 know that My name is the L
Jer 17: 5 Thus says the L: "Cursed is
Jer 17: 5 heart departs from the L
Jer 17: 7 the man who trusts in the L
Jer 17: 7 and whose hope is the L
Jer 17:10 I, the L, search the heart, I
Jer 17:13 O L, the hope of Israel, all
Jer 17:13 they have forsaken the L, the
Jer 17:14 Heal me, O L, and I shall be
Jer 17:15 Where is the word of the L
Jer 17:19 Thus the L said to me
Jer 17:20 them, 'Hear the word of the L
Jer 17:21 Thus says the L: "Take heed
Jer 17:24 heed Me," says the L, "to
Jer 17:26 praise to the house of the L
Jer 18: 1 came to Jeremiah from the L
Jer 18: 5 the word of the L came to me
Jer 18: 6 as this potter?" says the L
Jer 18:11 saying, 'Thus says the L
Jer 18:13 Therefore thus says the L
Jer 18:19 Give heed to me, O L, and
Jer 18:23 Yet, L, You know all their
Jer 19: 1 Thus says the L: "Go and get
Jer 19: 3 say, 'Hear the word of the L
Jer 19: 3 Thus says the L of hosts, the
Jer 19: 6 days are coming," says the L
Jer 19:11 Thus says the L of hosts
Jer 19:12 to this place," says the L
Jer 19:14 where the L had sent him to
Jer 19:15 Thus says the L of hosts, the
Jer 20: 1 in the house of the L, heard
Jer 20: 2 was by the house of the L
Jer 20: 3 The L has not called your
Jer 20: 4 thus says the L: 'Behold, I
Jer 20: 7 O L, You induced me, and I was
Jer 20: 8 L was made to me a reproach
Jer 20:11 But the L is with me as a
Jer 20:12 O L of hosts, You who test
Jer 20:13 Sing to the L! Praise the L!
Jer 20:16 cities which the L overthrew
Jer 21: 1 came to Jeremiah from the L
Jer 21: 2 inquire of the L for us, for
Jer 21: 2 Perhaps the L will deal with
Jer 21: 4 Thus says the L God of Israel
Jer 21: 7 And afterward," says the L
Jer 21: 8 this people, 'Thus says the L
Jer 21:10 and not for good," says the L
Jer 21:11 say, 'Hear the word of the L
Jer 21:12 of David! Thus says the L
Jer 21:13 of the plain," says the L
Jer 21:14 of your doings," says the L
Jer 22: 1 Thus says the L: "Go down
Jer 22: 2 say, 'Hear the word of the L
Jer 22: 3 Thus says the L: "Execute
Jer 22: 5 swear by Myself," says the L
Jer 22: 6 For thus says the L to the
Jer 22: 8 Why has the L done so to
Jer 22: 9 covenant of the L their God
Jer 22:11 For thus says the L
Jer 22:16 this knowing Me?" says the L
Jer 22:18 Therefore thus says the L
Jer 22:24 As I live," says the L
Jer 22:29 earth, hear the word of the L
Jer 22:30 Thus says the L
Jer 23: 1 of My pasture!" says the L
Jer 23: 2 Therefore thus says the L God
Jer 23: 2 of your doings," says the L
Jer 23: 4 they be lacking," says the L
Jer 23: 5 days are coming," says the L
Jer 23: 6 L OUR RIGHTEOUSNESS
Jer 23: 7 days are coming," says the L
Jer 23: 7 As the L lives who brought
Jer 23: 8 As the L lives who brought
Jer 23: 9 overcome, because of the L
Jer 23:11 wickedness," says the L
Jer 23:12 punishment," says the L
Jer 23:15 the L of hosts concerning the
Jer 23:16 Thus says the L of hosts
Jer 23:16 not from the mouth of the L
Jer 23:17 despise Me, 'The L has said,
Jer 23:18 stood in the counsel of the L
Jer 23:19 a whirlwind of the L has gone
Jer 23:20 The anger of the L will not
Jer 23:23 near at hand," says the L
Jer 23:24 not see him?" says the L
Jer 23:24 heaven and earth?" says the L
Jer 23:28 to the wheat?" says the L.
Jer 23:29 says the L, "And like a
Jer 23:30 the prophets," says the L
Jer 23:31 the prophets," says the L
Jer 23:32 false dreams," says the L
Jer 23:32 people at all," says the L
Jer 23:33 What is the oracle of the L
Jer 23:33 forsake you," says the L
Jer 23:34 who say, The oracle of the L
Jer 23:35 What has the L answered
Jer 23:35 and, 'What has the L spoken
Jer 23:36 the oracle of the L you shall
Jer 23:36 God, the L of hosts, our God
Jer 23:37 What has the L answered you
Jer 23:37 and, 'What has the L spoken
Jer 23:38 you say, 'The oracle of the L
Jer 23:38 therefore thus says the L
Jer 23:38 The oracle of the L
Jer 23:38 not say, 'The oracle of the L
Jer 24: 1 The L showed me, and there
Jer 24: 1 before the temple of the L
Jer 24: 3 Then the L said to me, "What
Jer 24: 4 the word of the L came to me
Jer 24: 5 Thus says the L, the God of
Jer 24: 7 to know Me, that I am the L
Jer 24: 8 surely thus says the L
Jer 25: 3 word of the L has come to me
Jer 25: 4 the L has sent to you all His
Jer 25: 5 that the L has given to you
Jer 25: 7 listened to Me," says the L
Jer 25: 8 thus says the L of hosts
Jer 25: 9 of the north,' says the L
Jer 25:12 their iniquity,' says the L
Jer 25:15 For thus says the L God of
Jer 25:17 to whom the L had sent me
Jer 25:27 Thus says the L of hosts
Jer 25:28 Thus says the L of hosts
Jer 25:29 earth," says the L of hosts
Jer 25:30 The L will roar from on high
Jer 25:31 for the L has a controversy
Jer 25:31 to the sword,' says the L
Jer 25:32 Thus says the L of hosts
Jer 25:33 L shall be from one end of
Jer 25:36 For the L has plundered their
Jer 25:37 of the fierce anger of the L
Jer 26: 1 this word came from the L
Jer 26: 2 Thus says the L: 'Stand in
Jer 26: 4 say to them, 'Thus says the L
Jer 26: 7 words in the house of the L
Jer 26: 8 of speaking all that the L
Jer 26: 9 in the name of the L, saying,
Jer 26: 9 in the house of the L
Jer 26:10 house to the house of the L
Jer 26:12 The L sent me to prophesy
Jer 26:13 the voice of the L your God
Jer 26:13 then the L will relent
Jer 26:15 for truly the L has sent me
Jer 26:16 in the name of the L our God
Jer 26:18 Thus says the L of hosts
Jer 26:19 Did he not fear the L and seek
Jer 26:19 the L relented concerning the

Jer 26:20 in the name of the **L**, Urijah
Jer 27: 1 came to Jeremiah from the **L**
Jer 27: 2 Thus says the **L** to me
Jer 27: 4 Thus says the **L** of hosts, the
Jer 27: 8 I will punish,' says the **L**
Jer 27:11 their own land,' says the **L**
Jer 27:13 as the **L** has spoken against
Jer 27:15 not sent them," says the **L**
Jer 27:16 Thus says the **L**: 'Do not
Jer 27:18 word of the **L** is with them
Jer 27:18 to the **L** of hosts, that the
Jer 27:18 left in the house of the **L**
Jer 27:19 For thus says the **L** of hosts
Jer 27:21 yes, thus says the **L** of hosts
Jer 27:21 remain in the house of the **L**
Jer 27:22 I visit them,' says the **L**
Jer 28: 1 the **L** in the presence of the
Jer 28: 2 Thus speaks the **L** of hosts
Jer 28: 4 went to Babylon,' says the **L**
Jer 28: 5 stood in the house of the **L**
Jer 28: 6 Amen! The **L** do so
Jer 28: 6 the **L** perform your words
Jer 28: 9 one whom the **L** has truly sent.
Jer 28:11 Thus says the **L**
Jer 28:12 of the **L** came to Jeremiah
Jer 28:13 saying, 'Thus says the **L**
Jer 28:14 For thus says the **L** of hosts
Jer 28:15 the **L** has not sent you, but
Jer 28:16 Therefore thus says the **L**
Jer 28:16 rebellion against the **L**
Jer 29: 4 Thus says the **L** of hosts, the
Jer 29: 7 and pray to the **L** for it
Jer 29: 8 For thus says the **L** of hosts
Jer 29: 9 not sent them, says the **L**.
Jer 29:10 For thus says the **L**
Jer 29:11 think toward you, says the **L**
Jer 29:14 be found by you, says the **L**
Jer 29:14 I have driven you, says the **L**
Jer 29:15 The **L** has raised up prophets
Jer 29:16 the **L** concerning the king who
Jer 29:17 thus says the **L** of hosts
Jer 29:19 heeded My words, says the **L**
Jer 29:19 would you heed, says the **L**
Jer 29:20 hear the word of the **L**, all
Jer 29:21 Thus says the **L** of hosts, the
Jer 29:22 The **L** make you like Zedekiah
Jer 29:23 and am a witness, says the **L**
Jer 29:25 Thus speaks the **L** of hosts
Jer 29:26 The **L** has made you priest
Jer 29:26 in the house of the **L** over
Jer 29:30 of the **L** came to Jeremiah
Jer 29:31 Thus says the **L** concerning
Jer 29:32 thus says the **L**: "Behold,
Jer 29:32 for My people," says the **L**
Jer 29:32 rebellion against the **L**
Jer 30: 1 came to Jeremiah from the **L**
Jer 30: 2 speaks the **L** God of Israel
Jer 30: 3 days are coming,' says the **L**
Jer 30: 3 Israel and Judah,' says the **L**
Jer 30: 4 are the words that the **L**
Jer 30: 5 For thus says the **L**
Jer 30: 8 day,' says the **L** of hosts
Jer 30: 9 shall serve the **L** their God
Jer 30:10 My servant Jacob,' says the **L**
Jer 30:11 I am with you,' says the **L**
Jer 30:12 says the **L**: 'Your affliction
Jer 30:17 of your wounds,' says the **L**
Jer 30:18 Thus says the **L**: 'Behold,
Jer 30:21 to approach Me?' says the **L**
Jer 30:23 of the **L** goes forth with fury
Jer 30:24 The fierce anger of the **L**
Jer 31: 1 the same time," says the **L**
Jer 31: 2 Thus says the **L**: "The people
Jer 31: 3 The **L** has appeared of old to
Jer 31: 6 up to Zion, to the **L** our God
Jer 31: 7 For thus says the **L**
Jer 31: 7 give praise, and say, 'O **L**
Jer 31:10 Hear the word of the **L**, O
Jer 31:11 For the **L** has redeemed Jacob,
Jer 31:12 to the goodness of the **L**
Jer 31:14 My goodness," says the **L**
Jer 31:15 Thus says the **L**: "A voice
Jer 31:16 Thus says the **L**: "Refrain your
Jer 31:16 be rewarded," says the **L**
Jer 31:17 in your future," says the **L**
Jer 31:18 for You are the **L** my God
Jer 31:20 mercy on him," says the **L**
Jer 31:22 For the **L** has created a new
Jer 31:23 Thus says the **L** of hosts, the
Jer 31:23 The **L** bless you, O
Jer 31:27 days are coming," says the **L**
Jer 31:28 and to plant," says the **L**
Jer 31:31 days are coming," says the **L**
Jer 31:32 husband to them," says the **L**
Jer 31:33 After those days, says the **L**
Jer 31:34 brother, saying, 'Know the **L**
Jer 31:34 of them," says the **L**
Jer 31:35 Thus says the **L**, Who gives
Jer 31:35 and its waves roar (the **L** of
Jer 31:36 from before Me," says the **L**
Jer 31:37 Thus says the **L**: "If heaven
Jer 31:37 they have done," says the **L**
Jer 31:38 days are coming," says the **L**
Jer 31:38 **L** from the Tower of Hananeel
Jer 31:40 east, shall be holy to the **L**
Jer 32: 1 the **L** in the tenth year of
Jer 32: 3 and say, 'Thus says the **L**
Jer 32: 5 I visit him," says the **L**
Jer 32: 6 The word of the **L** came to me
Jer 32: 8 to the word of the **L**, and said
Jer 32: 8 this was the word of the **L**
Jer 32:14 Thus says the **L** of hosts
Jer 32:15 For thus says the **L** of hosts
Jer 32:16 of Neriah, I prayed to the **L**
Jer 32:17 Ah, **L** GOD! Behold
Jer 32:18 whose name is the **L** of hosts
Jer 32:25 You have said to me, O **L** GOD,
Jer 32:26 of the **L** came to Jeremiah
Jer 32:27 Behold, I am the **L**, the God
Jer 32:28 Therefore thus says the **L**
Jer 32:30 of their hands," says the **L**
Jer 32:36 therefore, thus says the **L**
Jer 32:42 For thus says the **L**
Jer 32:44 to return,' says the **L**
Jer 33: 1 Moreover the word of the **L**
Jer 33: 2 Thus says the **L** who made it
Jer 33: 2 it, the **L** who formed it to
Jer 33: 2 it (the **L** is His name)
Jer 33: 4 For thus says the **L**, the God
Jer 33:10 Thus says the **L**: 'Again there
Jer 33:11 Praise the **L** of hosts, for
Jer 33:11 of hosts, for the **L** is good
Jer 33:11 into the house of the **L**
Jer 33:11 as at the first,' says the **L**
Jer 33:12 Thus says the **L** of hosts
Jer 33:13 who counts them,' says the **L**
Jer 33:14 days are coming,' says the **L**
Jer 33:16 **L** OUR RIGHTEOUSNESS
Jer 33:17 For thus says the **L**: 'David
Jer 33:19 the word of the **L** came to
Jer 33:20 Thus says the **L**: 'If you
Jer 33:23 of the **L** came to Jeremiah
Jer 33:24 which the **L** has chosen, He
Jer 33:25 Thus says the **L**
Jer 34: 1 came to Jeremiah from the **L**
Jer 34: 2 Thus says the **L**, the God of
Jer 34: 2 Thus says the **L**: 'Behold,
Jer 34: 4 Yet hear the word of the **L**
Jer 34: 4 Thus says the **L** concerning
Jer 34: 5 saying, "Alas, **l**!"
Jer 34: 5 the word," says the **L**
Jer 34: 8 came to Jeremiah from the **L**
Jer 34:12 **L** came to Jeremiah from the
Jer 34:12 came to Jeremiah from the **L**
Jer 34:13 Thus says the **L**, the God of
Jer 34:17 Therefore thus says the **L**
Jer 34:17 liberty to you,' says the **L**
Jer 34:22 I will command,' says the **L**
Jer 35: 1 **L** in the days of Jehoiakim
Jer 35: 2 them into the house of the **L**
Jer 35: 4 them into the house of the **L**
Jer 35:12 the word of the **L** to Jeremiah
Jer 35:13 Thus says the **L** of hosts, the
Jer 35:13 obey My words?" says the **L**
Jer 35:17 thus says the **L** God of hosts
Jer 35:18 Thus says the **L** of hosts, the
Jer 35:19 thus says the **L** of hosts, the
Jer 36: 1 came to Jeremiah from the **L**
Jer 36: 4 all the words of the **L** which
Jer 36: 5 go into the house of the **L**
Jer 36: 6 the words of the **L**, in the
Jer 36: 7 supplication before the **L**
Jer 36: 7 and the fury that the **L** has
Jer 36: 8 of the **L** in the LORD's house
Jer 36: 9 a fast before the **L** to all
Jer 36:10 in the house of the **L**, in the
Jer 36:11 words of the **L** from the book
Jer 36:26 prophet, but the **L** hid them
Jer 36:27 the word of the **L** came to
Jer 36:29 of Judah, 'Thus says the **L**
Jer 36:30 Therefore thus says the **L**
Jer 37: 2 the **L** which He spoke by the
Jer 37: 3 now to the **L** our God for us
Jer 37: 6 the word of the **L** came to the
Jer 37: 7 Thus says the **L**, the God of
Jer 37: 9 Thus says the **L**: 'Do not
Jer 37:17 Is there any word from the **L**
Jer 37:20 hear now, O my **l** the king
Jer 38: 2 Thus says the **L**: 'He who
Jer 38: 3 Thus says the **L**: 'This city
Jer 38: 9 My **l** the king, these men have
Jer 38:14 of the house of the **L**
Jer 38:16 As the **L** lives, who made our
Jer 38:17 Thus says the **L**, the God of
Jer 38:20 of the **L** which I speak to you
Jer 38:21 word that the **L** has shown me
Jer 39:15 Now the word of the **L** had
Jer 39:16 Thus says the **L** of hosts
Jer 39:17 you in that day," says the **L**
Jer 39:18 trust in Me," says the **L**
Jer 40: 1 the **L** after Nebuzaradan the
Jer 40: 2 The **L** your God has pronounced
Jer 40: 3 Now the **L** has brought it, and
Jer 40: 3 have sinned against the **L**
Jer 41: 5 them to the house of the **L**
Jer 42: 2 pray for us to the **L** your God
Jer 42: 3 that the **L** your God may show
Jer 42: 4 I will pray to the **L** your God
Jer 42: 4 whatever the **L** answers you
Jer 42: 5 Let the **L** be a true and
Jer 42: 5 to everything which the **L**
Jer 42: 6 will obey the voice of the **L**
Jer 42: 6 the voice of the **L** our God
Jer 42: 7 of the **L** came to Jeremiah
Jer 42: 9 Thus says the **L**, the God of
Jer 42:11 be afraid of him,' says the **L**
Jer 42:13 the voice of the **L** your God
Jer 42:15 hear now the word of the **L**
Jer 42:15 Thus says the **L** of hosts, the
Jer 42:18 For thus says the **L** of hosts
Jer 42:19 The **L** has said concerning you
Jer 42:20 you sent me to the **L** your God
Jer 42:20 Pray for us to the **L** our God
Jer 42:20 all that the **L** your God says
Jer 42:21 the voice of the **L** your God
Jer 43: 1 the words of the **L** their God
Jer 43: 1 for which the **L** their God had
Jer 43: 2 The **L** our God has not sent
Jer 43: 4 not obey the voice of the **L**
Jer 43: 7 not obey the voice of the **L**
Jer 43: 8 of the **L** came to Jeremiah in
Jer 43:10 Thus says the **L** of hosts
Jer 44: 2 Thus says the **L** of hosts, the
Jer 44: 7 therefore, thus says the **L**
Jer 44:11 thus says the **L** of hosts, the
Jer 44:16 to us in the name of the **L**
Jer 44:21 did not the **L** remember them,
Jer 44:22 So the **L** could no longer bear
Jer 44:23 you have sinned against the **L**
Jer 44:23 of the **L** or walked in His law
Jer 44:24 Hear the word of the **L**, all
Jer 44:25 Thus says the **L** of hosts, the
Jer 44:26 hear the word of the **L**, all
Jer 44:26 by My great name,' says the **L**
Jer 44:26 saying, "The **L** GOD lives
Jer 44:29 be a sign to you,' says the **L**
Jer 44:30 Thus says the **L**: 'Behold,
Jer 45: 2 Thus says the **L**, the God of
Jer 45: 3 For the **L** has added grief to
Jer 45: 4 say to him, "Thus says the **L**
Jer 45: 5 on all flesh," says the **L**
Jer 46: 1 The word of the **L** which came
Jer 46: 5 was all around," says the **L**
Jer 46:10 the day of the **L** GOD of hosts
Jer 46:10 for the **L** GOD of hosts has a
Jer 46:13 The word that the **L** spoke to
Jer 46:15 because the **L** drove them away
Jer 46:18 whose name is the **L** of hosts
Jer 46:23 down her forest," says the **L**
Jer 46:25 The **L** of hosts, the God of
Jer 46:26 the days of old," says the **L**
Jer 46:28 My servant," says the **L**
Jer 47: 1 The word of the **L** that came
Jer 47: 2 Thus says the **L**: "Behold,
Jer 47: 4 for the **L** shall plunder the
Jer 47: 6 O you sword of the **L**, how
Jer 47: 7 seeing the **L** has given it a
Jer 48: 1 Thus says the **L** of hosts, the
Jer 48: 8 as the **L** has spoken
Jer 48:10 the work of the **L** deceitfully

Jer 48:12 days are coming," says the **L**
Jer 48:15 Whose name is the **L** of hosts
Jer 48:25 arm is broken," says the **L**
Jer 48:26 himself against the **L**
Jer 48:30 know his wrath," says the **L**
Jer 48:35 Moreover," says the **L**, "I
Jer 48:38 is no pleasure," says the **L**
Jer 48:40 thus says the **L**: "Behold,
Jer 48:42 himself against the **L**
Jer 48:43 of Moab," says the **L**
Jer 48:44 punishment," says the **L**
Jer 48:47 the latter days," says the **L**
Jer 49: 1 Thus says the **L**: "Has Israel
Jer 49: 2 days are coming," says the **L**
Jer 49: 2 his inheritance," says the **L**
Jer 49: 5 says the **L** GOD of hosts,
Jer 49: 6 people of Ammon," says the **L**
Jer 49: 7 Thus says the **L** of hosts
Jer 49:12 For thus says the **L**
Jer 49:13 sworn by Myself," says the **L**
Jer 49:14 heard a message from the **L**
Jer 49:16 down from there," says the **L**
Jer 49:18 cities," says the **L**, No
Jer 49:20 hear the counsel of the **L**
Jer 49:26 day," says the **L** of hosts
Jer 49:28 Thus says the **L**: "Arise, go
Jer 49:30 of Hazor!" says the **L**
Jer 49:31 dwells securely," says the **L**
Jer 49:32 all its sides," says the **L**
Jer 49:34 The word of the **L** that came
Jer 49:35 Thus says the **L** of hosts
Jer 49:37 my fierce anger,' says the **L**
Jer 49:38 and the princes,' says the **L**
Jer 49:39 captives of Elam,' says the **L**
Jer 50: 1 The word that the **L** spoke
Jer 50: 4 and in that time," says the **L**
Jer 50: 4 come, and seek the **L** their God
Jer 50: 5 the **L** In a perpetual covenant
Jer 50: 7 have sinned against the **L**
Jer 50: 7 habitation of justice, the **L**
Jer 50:10 be satisfied," says the **L**
Jer 50:13 **L** she shall not be inhabited
Jer 50:14 she has sinned against the **L**
Jer 50:15 it is the vengeance of the **L**
Jer 50:18 thus says the **L** of hosts, the
Jer 50:20 and in that time," says the **L**
Jer 50:21 destroy them," says the **L**
Jer 50:24 have contended against the **L**
Jer 50:25 The **L** has opened His armory,
Jer 50:25 **L** God of hosts in the land of
Jer 50:28 vengeance of the **L** our God
Jer 50:29 has been proud against the **L**
Jer 50:30 off in that day," says the **L**
Jer 50:31 says the **L** GOD of hosts
Jer 50:33 Thus says the **L** of hosts
Jer 50:34 the **L** of hosts is His name
Jer 50:35 the Chaldeans," says the **L**
Jer 50:40 cities," says the **L**, "So no
Jer 50:45 hear the counsel of the **L**
Jer 51: 1 Thus says the **L**: "Behold, I
Jer 51: 5 the **L** of hosts, though their
Jer 51:10 The **L** has revealed our
Jer 51:10 the work of the **L** our God
Jer 51:11 The **L** has raised up the
Jer 51:11 it is the vengeance of the **L**
Jer 51:12 For the **L** has both devised and
Jer 51:14 The **L** of hosts has sworn by
Jer 51:19 The **L** of hosts is His name
Jer 51:24 in your sight," says the **L**
Jer 51:25 all the earth," says the **L**
Jer 51:26 forever," says the **L**
Jer 51:29 for every purpose of the **L**
Jer 51:33 For thus says the **L** of hosts
Jer 51:36 Therefore thus says the **L**
Jer 51:39 and not awake," says the **L**
Jer 51:45 the fierce anger of the **L**
Jer 51:48 from the north," says the **L**
Jer 51:50 Remember the **L** afar off, and
Jer 51:52 days are coming," says the **L**
Jer 51:53 come to her," says the **L**
Jer 51:55 because the **L** is plundering
Jer 51:56 for the **L** is the God of
Jer 51:57 Whose name is the **L** of hosts
Jer 51:58 Thus says the **L** of hosts
Jer 51:62 then you shall say, 'O **L**, You
Jer 52: 2 evil in the sight of the **L**
Jer 52: 3 **L** this happened in Jerusalem
Jer 52:13 He burned the house of the **L**
Jer 52:17 were in the house of the **L**
Jer 52:17 were in the house of the **L**
Jer 52:20 made for the house of the **L**
Lam 1: 5 for the **L** has afflicted her
Lam 1: 9 O **L**, behold my affliction,
Lam 1:11 See, O **L**, and consider, for I
Lam 1:12 which the **L** has inflicted on
Lam 1:14 the **L** delivered me into the
Lam 1:15 The **L** has trampled underfoot
Lam 1:15 The **L** trampled as in a
Lam 1:17 the **L** has commanded
Lam 1:18 The **L** is righteous, for I
Lam 1:20 See, O **L**, that I am in
Lam 2: 1 How the **L** has covered the
Lam 2: 2 The **L** has swallowed up and has
Lam 2: 5 The **L** was like an enemy
Lam 2: 6 the **L** has caused the
Lam 2: 7 The **L** has spurned His altar,
Lam 2: 7 the **L** as on the day of a set
Lam 2: 8 The **L** has purposed to destroy
Lam 2: 9 find no vision from the **L**
Lam 2:17 The **L** has done what He
Lam 2:18 heart cried out to the **L**, "O
Lam 2:19 before the face of the **L**
Lam 2:20 See, O **L**, and consider
Lam 2:20 in the sanctuary of the **L**
Lam 3:18 hope Have perished from the **L**
Lam 3:24 The **L** is my portion," says
Lam 3:25 The **L** is good to those who
Lam 3:26 for the salvation of the **L**
Lam 3:31 For the **L** will not cast off
Lam 3:36 the **L** does not approve
Lam 3:37 when the **L** has not commanded
Lam 3:40 ways, and turn back to the **L**
Lam 3:50 till the **L** from heaven looks
Lam 3:55 I called on Your name, O **L**
Lam 3:58 O **L**, You have pleaded the
Lam 3:59 O **L**, You have seen how I am
Lam 3:61 heard their reproach, O **L**
Lam 3:64 Repay them, O **L**, according to
Lam 3:66 under the heavens of the **L**
Lam 4:11 The **L** has fulfilled His fury,
Lam 4:16 face of the **L** scattered them
Lam 4:20 the anointed of the **L**, was
Lam 5: 1 Remember, O **L**, what has come
Lam 5:19 You, O **L**, remain forever
Lam 5:21 Turn us back to You, O **L**, and
Ezek 1: 3 the word of the **L** came
Ezek 1: 3 the hand of the **L** was upon
Ezek 1:28 of the glory of the **L**
Ezek 2: 4 to them, 'Thus says the **L** GOD
Ezek 3:11 them, 'Thus says the **L** GOD
Ezek 3:12 glory of the **L** from His place
Ezek 3:14 of the **L** was strong upon me
Ezek 3:16 the word of the **L** came to me
Ezek 3:22 of the **L** was upon me there
Ezek 3:23 glory of the **L** stood there
Ezek 3:27 to them, 'Thus says the **L** GOD
Ezek 4:13 Then the **L** said, "So shall
Ezek 4:14 So I said, 'Ah, **L** GOD
Ezek 5: 5 Thus says the **L** GOD
Ezek 5: 7 Therefore thus says the **L** GOD
Ezek 5: 8 therefore thus says the **L** GOD
Ezek 5:11 as I live,' says the **L** GOD
Ezek 5:13 they shall know that I, the **L**
Ezek 5:15 I, the **L**, have spoken
Ezek 5:17 I, the **L**, have spoken
Ezek 6: 1 the word of the **L** came to me
Ezek 6: 3 hear the word of the **L** GOD
Ezek 6: 3 Thus says the **L** GOD to the
Ezek 6: 7 shall know that I am the **L**
Ezek 6:10 shall know that I am the **L**
Ezek 6:11 Thus says the **L** GOD
Ezek 6:13 shall know that I am the **L**
Ezek 6:14 shall know that I am the **L**
Ezek 7: 1 the word of the **L** came to me
Ezek 7: 2 thus says the **L** GOD to the
Ezek 7: 4 shall know that I am the **L**
Ezek 7: 5 Thus says the **L** GOD
Ezek 7: 9 that I am the **L** who strikes
Ezek 7:19 the day of the wrath of the **L**
Ezek 7:27 shall know that I am the **L**
Ezek 8: 1 that the hand of the **L** GOD
Ezek 8:12 The **L** does not see us, the
Ezek 8:12 the **L** has forsaken the land
Ezek 8:16 door of the temple of the **L**
Ezek 8:16 toward the temple of the **L**
Ezek 9: 4 and the **L** said to him,
Ezek 9: 8 out, and said, "Ah, **L** GOD
Ezek 9: 9 The **L** has forsaken the land,
Ezek 9: 9 land, and the **L** does not see
Ezek 10: 4 Then the glory of the **L** went
Ezek 10:18 Then the glory of the **L**
Ezek 11: 5 Spirit of the **L** fell upon me
Ezek 11: 5 Thus says the **L**: "Thus you
Ezek 11: 7 Therefore thus says the **L** GOD
Ezek 11: 8 upon you," says the **L** GOD
Ezek 11:10 shall know that I am the **L**
Ezek 11:12 shall know that I am the **L**
Ezek 11:13 voice, and said, "Ah, **L** GOD
Ezek 11:14 the word of the **L** came to me
Ezek 11:15 Get far away from the **L**
Ezek 11:16 say, 'Thus says the **L** GOD
Ezek 11:17 say, 'Thus says the **L** GOD
Ezek 11:21 own heads," says the **L** GOD
Ezek 11:23 the glory of the **L** went up
Ezek 11:25 the things the **L** had shown me
Ezek 12: 1 the word of the **L** came to me
Ezek 12: 8 the word of the **L** came to me
Ezek 12:10 to them, 'Thus says the **L** GOD
Ezek 12:15 shall know that I am the **L**
Ezek 12:16 shall know that I am the **L**
Ezek 12:17 the word of the **L** came to me
Ezek 12:19 Thus says the **L** GOD to the
Ezek 12:20 shall know that I am the **L**
Ezek 12:21 the word of the **L** came to me
Ezek 12:23 Thus says the **L** GOD
Ezek 12:25 For I am the **L**
Ezek 12:25 perform it," says the **L** GOD
Ezek 12:26 the word of the **L** came to me
Ezek 12:28 to them, "Thus says the **L** GOD
Ezek 12:28 be done," says the **L** GOD
Ezek 13: 1 the word of the **L** came to me
Ezek 13: 2 Hear the word of the **L**
Ezek 13: 3 Thus says the **L** GOD
Ezek 13: 5 in battle on the day of the **L**
Ezek 13: 6 saying, 'Thus says the **L**
Ezek 13: 6 But the **L** has not sent them
Ezek 13: 7 You say, 'The **L** says,' but I
Ezek 13: 8 Therefore thus says the **L** GOD
Ezek 13: 8 against you," says the **L** GOD
Ezek 13: 9 know that I am the **L** GOD
Ezek 13:13 Therefore thus says the **L** GOD
Ezek 13:14 shall know that I am the **L**
Ezek 13:16 no peace,'" says the **L** GOD
Ezek 13:18 and say, 'Thus says the **L** GOD
Ezek 13:20 Therefore thus says the **L** GOD
Ezek 13:21 shall know that I am the **L**
Ezek 13:23 shall know that I am the **L**
Ezek 14: 2 the word of the **L** came to me
Ezek 14: 4 to them, 'Thus says the **L** GOD
Ezek 14: 4 I the **L** will answer him who
Ezek 14: 6 Israel, 'Thus says the **L** GOD
Ezek 14: 7 I the **L** will answer him by
Ezek 14: 8 shall know that I am the **L**
Ezek 14: 9 I the **L** have induced that
Ezek 14:11 their God," says the **L** GOD
Ezek 14:12 The word of the **L** came again
Ezek 14:14 says the **L** GOD
Ezek 14:16 as I live," says the **L** GOD
Ezek 14:18 as I live," says the **L** GOD
Ezek 14:20 as I live," says the **L** GOD
Ezek 14:21 For thus says the **L** GOD
Ezek 14:23 done in it," says the **L** GOD
Ezek 15: 1 the word of the **L** came to me
Ezek 15: 6 Therefore thus says the **L** GOD
Ezek 15: 7 shall know that I am the **L**
Ezek 15: 8 says the **L** GOD
Ezek 16: 1 the word of the **L** came to me
Ezek 16: 3 say, 'Thus says the **L** GOD to
Ezek 16: 8 became Mine," says the **L** GOD
Ezek 16:14 on you," says the **L** GOD
Ezek 16:19 so it was," says the **L** GOD
Ezek 16:23 woe to you!' says the **L** GOD
Ezek 16:30 says the **L** GOD, "seeing
Ezek 16:35 hear the word of the **L**
Ezek 16:36 Thus says the **L** GOD
Ezek 16:43 own head," says the **L** GOD
Ezek 16:48 As I live," says the **L** GOD
Ezek 16:58 abominations," says the **L**
Ezek 16:59 For thus says the **L** GOD
Ezek 16:62 shall know that I am the **L**
Ezek 16:63 have done," says the **L** GOD
Ezek 17: 1 the word of the **L** came to me
Ezek 17: 3 and say, 'Thus says the **L** GOD
Ezek 17: 9 Say, 'Thus says the **L** GOD
Ezek 17:11 the word of the **L** came to me
Ezek 17:16 As I live,' says the **L** GOD
Ezek 17:19 Therefore thus says the **L** GOD
Ezek 17:21 you shall know that I, the **L**
Ezek 17:22 Thus says the **L** GOD
Ezek 17:24 shall know that I, the **L**,

Ezek 17:24 I, the L, have spoken and have
Ezek 18: 1 The word of the L came to me
Ezek 18: 3 As I live," says the L GOD
Ezek 18: 9 surely live!" says the L GOD
Ezek 18:23 says the L GOD, "and not
Ezek 18:25 The way of the L is not fair
Ezek 18:29 The way of the L is not fair
Ezek 18:30 to his ways," says the L GOD
Ezek 18:32 who dies," says the L GOD
Ezek 20: 1 came to inquire of the L, and
Ezek 20: 2 the word of the L came to me
Ezek 20: 3 to them, 'Thus says the L GOD
Ezek 20: 3 As I live," says the L GOD
Ezek 20: 5 to them, 'Thus says the L GOD
Ezek 20: 5 saying, 'I am the L your God
Ezek 20: 7 I am the L your God
Ezek 20:12 am the L who sanctifies them
Ezek 20:19 I am the L your God
Ezek 20:20 know that I am the L your God
Ezek 20:26 might know that I am the L
Ezek 20:27 to them, 'Thus says the L GOD
Ezek 20:30 Israel, 'Thus says the L GOD
Ezek 20:31 As I live," says the L GOD
Ezek 20:33 As I live," says the L GOD
Ezek 20:36 with you," says the L GOD
Ezek 20:38 you will know that I am the L
Ezek 20:39 Israel," thus says the L GOD
Ezek 20:40 of Israel," says the L GOD
Ezek 20:42 shall know that I am the L
Ezek 20:44 shall know that I am the L
Ezek 20:44 of Israel," says the L GOD
Ezek 20:45 the word of the L came to me
Ezek 20:47 Hear the word of the L
Ezek 20:47 Thus says the L GOD
Ezek 20:48 flesh shall see that I, the L
Ezek 20:49 Then I said, "Ah, L GOD
Ezek 21: 1 the word of the L came to me
Ezek 21: 3 of Israel, 'Thus says the L
Ezek 21: 5 flesh may know that I, the L
Ezek 21: 7 to pass,' says the L GOD
Ezek 21: 8 the word of the L came to me
Ezek 21: 9 and say, 'Thus says the L
Ezek 21:13 be no more," says the L GOD
Ezek 21:17 I, the L, have spoken
Ezek 21:18 The word of the L came to me
Ezek 21:24 Therefore thus says the L GOD
Ezek 21:26 thus says the L GOD
Ezek 21:28 and say, 'Thus says the L GOD
Ezek 21:32 for I the L have spoken
Ezek 22: 1 the word of the L came to me
Ezek 22: 3 say, 'Thus says the L GOD
Ezek 22:12 Me," says the L GOD
Ezek 22:14 I, the L, have spoken, and
Ezek 22:16 shall know that I am the L
Ezek 22:17 The word of the L came to me
Ezek 22:19 Therefore thus says the L GOD
Ezek 22:22 you shall know that I, the L
Ezek 22:23 the word of the L came to me
Ezek 22:28 saying, 'Thus says the L GOD
Ezek 22:28 when the L had not spoken
Ezek 22:31 own heads," says the L GOD
Ezek 23: 1 The word of the L came again
Ezek 23:22 Oholibah, thus says the L GOD
Ezek 23:28 For thus says the L GOD
Ezek 23:32 Thus says the L GOD
Ezek 23:34 have spoken,' says the L GOD
Ezek 23:35 Therefore thus says the L GOD
Ezek 23:36 The L also said to me
Ezek 23:46 For thus says the L GOD
Ezek 23:49 know that I am the L GOD
Ezek 24: 1 the word of the L came to me
Ezek 24: 3 to them, 'Thus says the L GOD
Ezek 24: 6 Therefore thus says the L GOD
Ezek 24: 9 Therefore thus says the L GOD
Ezek 24:14 I, the L, have spoken it
Ezek 24:14 judge you," says the L GOD
Ezek 24:15 the word of the L came to me
Ezek 24:20 The word of the L came to me
Ezek 24:21 Thus says the L GOD
Ezek 24:24 know that I am the L GOD
Ezek 24:27 will know that I am the L
Ezek 25: 1 The word of the L came to me
Ezek 25: 3 Hear the word of the L GOD
Ezek 25: 3 Thus says the L GOD
Ezek 25: 5 shall know that I am the L
Ezek 25: 6 For thus says the L GOD
Ezek 25: 7 shall know that I am the L
Ezek 25: 8 Thus says the L GOD
Ezek 25:11 shall know that I am the L
Ezek 25:12 Thus says the L GOD
Ezek 25:13 therefore thus says the L GOD
Ezek 25:14 vengeance," says the L GOD
Ezek 25:15 Thus says the L GOD
Ezek 25:16 therefore thus says the L GOD
Ezek 25:17 shall know that I am the L
Ezek 26: 1 the word of the L came to me
Ezek 26: 3 Therefore thus says the L GOD
Ezek 26: 5 have spoken,' says the L GOD
Ezek 26: 6 shall know that I am the L
Ezek 26: 7 For thus says the L GOD
Ezek 26:14 for I the L have spoken,'
Ezek 26:14 have spoken,' says the L GOD
Ezek 26:15 Thus says the L GOD to Tyre
Ezek 26:19 For thus says the L GOD
Ezek 26:21 found again,' says the L GOD
Ezek 27: 1 The word of the L came again
Ezek 27: 3 thus says the L GOD
Ezek 28: 1 The word of the L came to me
Ezek 28: 2 of Tyre, 'Thus says the L GOD
Ezek 28: 6 Therefore thus says the L GOD
Ezek 28:10 have spoken," says the L GOD
Ezek 28:11 the word of the L came to me
Ezek 28:12 to him, 'Thus says the L GOD
Ezek 28:20 the word of the L came to me
Ezek 28:22 and say, 'Thus says the L GOD
Ezek 28:22 shall know that I am the L
Ezek 28:23 shall know that I am the L
Ezek 28:24 know that I am the L GOD
Ezek 28:25 Thus says the L GOD
Ezek 28:26 that I am the L their God
Ezek 29: 1 the word of the L came to me
Ezek 29: 3 and say, 'Thus says the L GOD
Ezek 29: 6 shall know that I am the L
Ezek 29: 8 Therefore thus says the L GOD
Ezek 29: 9 will know that I am the L
Ezek 29:13 Yet, thus says the L GOD
Ezek 29:16 know that I am the L GOD
Ezek 29:17 the word of the L came to me
Ezek 29:19 Therefore thus says the L GOD
Ezek 29:20 for Me,' says the L GOD
Ezek 29:21 shall know that I am the L
Ezek 30: 1 The word of the L came to me
Ezek 30: 2 and say, 'Thus says the L GOD
Ezek 30: 3 even the day of the L is near
Ezek 30: 6 Thus says the L: "Those who
Ezek 30: 6 the sword," says the L GOD
Ezek 30: 8 will know that I am the L
Ezek 30:10 Thus says the L GOD
Ezek 30:12 I, the L, have spoken
Ezek 30:13 Thus says the L GOD
Ezek 30:19 shall know that I am the L
Ezek 30:20 the word of the L came to me
Ezek 30:22 Therefore thus says the L GOD
Ezek 30:25 shall know that I am the L
Ezek 30:26 shall know that I am the L
Ezek 31: 1 the word of the L came to me
Ezek 31:10 Therefore thus says the L GOD
Ezek 31:15 Thus says the L GOD
Ezek 31:18 multitude,' says the L GOD
Ezek 32: 1 the word of the L came to me
Ezek 32: 3 Thus says the L GOD
Ezek 32: 8 your land,' says the L GOD
Ezek 32:11 For thus says the L GOD
Ezek 32:14 run like oil,' says the L GOD
Ezek 32:15 shall know that I am the L
Ezek 32:16 multitude,' says the L GOD
Ezek 32:17 the word of the L came to me
Ezek 32:31 the sword," says the L GOD
Ezek 32:32 multitude," says the L GOD
Ezek 33: 1 the word of the L came to me
Ezek 33:11 As I live,' says the L GOD
Ezek 33:17 The way of the L is not fair
Ezek 33:20 The way of the L is not fair
Ezek 33:22 Now the hand of the L had
Ezek 33:23 the word of the L came to me
Ezek 33:25 to them, 'Thus says the L GOD
Ezek 33:27 to them, 'Thus says the L GOD
Ezek 33:29 shall know that I am the L
Ezek 33:30 word is that comes from the L
Ezek 34: 1 the word of the L came to me
Ezek 34: 2 Thus says the L GOD to the
Ezek 34: 7 hear the word of the L
Ezek 34: 8 as I live," says the L GOD
Ezek 34: 9 hear the word of the L
Ezek 34:10 Thus says the L GOD
Ezek 34:11 For thus says the L GOD
Ezek 34:15 lie down," says the L GOD
Ezek 34:17 My flock, thus says the L GOD
Ezek 34:20 thus says the L GOD to them
Ezek 34:24 And I, the L, will be their
Ezek 34:24 I, the L, have spoken
Ezek 34:27 shall know that I am the L
Ezek 34:30 the L their God, am with them
Ezek 34:30 My people," says the L GOD
Ezek 34:31 am your God," says the L GOD
Ezek 35: 1 the word of the L came to me
Ezek 35: 3 to it, 'Thus says the L GOD
Ezek 35: 4 shall know that I am the L
Ezek 35: 6 as I live," says the L GOD
Ezek 35: 9 shall know that I am the L
Ezek 35:10 although the L was there
Ezek 35:11 as I live," says the L GOD
Ezek 35:12 shall know that I am the L
Ezek 35:14 Thus says the L GOD
Ezek 35:15 shall know that I am the L
Ezek 36: 1 hear the word of the L
Ezek 36: 2 Thus says the L GOD
Ezek 36: 3 and say, 'Thus says the L GOD
Ezek 36: 4 hear the word of the L GOD
Ezek 36: 4 Thus says the L GOD to the
Ezek 36: 5 therefore thus says the L GOD
Ezek 36: 6 valleys, 'Thus says the L GOD
Ezek 36: 7 Therefore thus says the L GOD
Ezek 36:11 shall know that I am the L
Ezek 36:13 Thus says the L GOD
Ezek 36:14 anymore," says the L GOD
Ezek 36:15 anymore," says the L GOD
Ezek 36:16 the word of the L came to me
Ezek 36:20 These are the people of the L
Ezek 36:22 Israel, 'Thus says the L GOD
Ezek 36:23 I am the L," says the L GOD
Ezek 36:32 I do this," says the L GOD
Ezek 36:33 Thus says the L GOD
Ezek 36:36 you shall know that I, the L
Ezek 36:36 I, the L, have spoken it, and
Ezek 36:37 Thus says the L GOD
Ezek 36:38 shall know that I am the L
Ezek 37: 1 hand of the L came upon me
Ezek 37: 1 me out in the Spirit of the L
Ezek 37: 3 answered, "O L GOD, You
Ezek 37: 4 bones, hear the word of the L
Ezek 37: 5 Thus says the L GOD to these
Ezek 37: 6 shall know that I am the L
Ezek 37: 9 breath, 'Thus says the L GOD
Ezek 37:12 to them, 'Thus says the L GOD
Ezek 37:13 shall know that I am the L
Ezek 37:14 you shall know that I, the L
Ezek 37:14 and performed it," says the L
Ezek 37:15 the word of the L came to me
Ezek 37:19 to them, 'Thus says the L GOD
Ezek 37:21 to them, 'Thus says the L GOD
Ezek 37:28 also will know that I, the L
Ezek 38: 1 the word of the L came to me
Ezek 38: 3 and say, 'Thus says the L GOD
Ezek 38:10 Thus says the L GOD
Ezek 38:14 to Gog, 'Thus says the L GOD
Ezek 38:17 Thus says the L GOD
Ezek 38:18 of Israel," says the L GOD
Ezek 38:21 mountains," says the L GOD
Ezek 38:23 shall know that I am the L
Ezek 39: 1 and say, 'Thus says the L GOD
Ezek 39: 5 have spoken," says the L GOD
Ezek 39: 6 shall know that I am the L
Ezek 39: 7 shall know that I am the L
Ezek 39: 8 be done," says the L GOD
Ezek 39:10 them," says the L GOD
Ezek 39:13 glorified," says the L GOD
Ezek 39:17 of man, thus says the L GOD
Ezek 39:20 men of war," says the L GOD
Ezek 39:22 the L their God from that day
Ezek 39:25 Therefore thus says the L GOD
Ezek 39:28 that I am the L their God
Ezek 39:29 of Israel,' says the L GOD
Ezek 40: 1 the hand of the L was upon me
Ezek 40:46 Levi, who come near the L to
Ezek 41:22 table that is before the L
Ezek 42:13 the L shall eat the most holy
Ezek 43: 4 the glory of the L came into
Ezek 43: 5 the glory of the L filled the
Ezek 43:18 of man, thus says the L GOD
Ezek 43:19 to Me,' says the L GOD
Ezek 43:24 you offer them before the L
Ezek 43:24 as a burnt offering to the L
Ezek 43:27 accept you,' says the L GOD
Ezek 44: 2 And the L said to me,
Ezek 44: 2 because the L God of Israel
Ezek 44: 3 it to eat bread before the L
Ezek 44: 4 the glory of the L filled the
Ezek 44: 4 filled the house of the L
Ezek 44: 5 And the L said to me,

Ezek 44: 5 of the house of the L and all
Ezek 44: 6 Israel, Thus says the L GOD
Ezek 44: 9 Thus says the L GOD
Ezek 44:12 them," says the L GOD
Ezek 44:15 the blood," says the L GOD
Ezek 44:27 inner court," says the L GOD
Ezek 45: 1 apart a district for the L
Ezek 45: 4 near to minister to the L
Ezek 45: 9 Thus says the L GOD
Ezek 45: 9 My people," says the L GOD
Ezek 45:15 for them," says the L GOD
Ezek 45:18 Thus says the L GOD
Ezek 45:23 a burnt offering to the L
Ezek 46: 1 Thus says the L GOD
Ezek 46: 3 before the L on the Sabbaths
Ezek 46: 4 the prince offers to the L on
Ezek 46: 9 L on the appointed feast days
Ezek 46:12 peace offering to the L, the
Ezek 46:13 a burnt offering to the L of
Ezek 46:14 to be made regularly to the L
Ezek 46:16 Thus says the L GOD
Ezek 47:13 Thus says the L GOD
Ezek 47:23 inheritance," says the L GOD
Ezek 48: 9 the L shall be twenty-five
Ezek 48:10 The sanctuary of the L shall
Ezek 48:14 land, for it is holy to the L
Ezek 48:29 portions," says the L GOD
Ezek 48:35 THE L IS THERE
Dan 1: 2 the L gave Jehoiakim king of
Dan 1:10 I fear my l the king, who has
Dan 2:10 therefore no king, l, or
Dan 2:47 the L of kings, and a revealer
Dan 4:19 My l, may the dream concern
Dan 4:24 has come upon my l the king
Dan 5:23 up against the L of heaven
Dan 9: 2 by the word of the L, given
Dan 9: 3 the L God to make request by
Dan 9: 4 And I prayed to the L my God
Dan 9: 4 O L, great and awesome God,
Dan 9: 7 O L, righteousness belongs to
Dan 9: 8 O L, to us belongs shame of
Dan 9: 9 To the L our God belong mercy
Dan 9:10 the voice of the L our God
Dan 9:13 prayer before the L our God
Dan 9:14 Therefore the L has kept the
Dan 9:14 for the L our God is
Dan 9:15 O L our God, who brought Your
Dan 9:16 O L, according to all Your
Dan 9:19 O L, hear! O L, forgive!
Dan 9:19 O L, listen and act
Dan 9:20 the L my God for the holy
Dan 10:16 My l, because of the vision
Dan 10:17 my l talk with you, my l
Dan 10:19 Let my l speak, for you have
Dan 12: 8 My l, what shall be the end
Hos 1: 1 The word of the L that came
Hos 1: 2 When the L began to speak by
Hos 1: 2 by Hosea, the L said to Hosea
Hos 1: 2 by departing from the L
Hos 1: 4 Then the L said to him
Hos 1: 7 save them by the L their God
Hos 2:13 she forgot Me," says the L
Hos 2:16 be, in that day," says the L
Hos 2:20 and you shall know the L
Hos 2:21 I will answer," says the L
Hos 3: 1 Then the L said to me, Go
Hos 3: 1 just like the love of the L
Hos 3: 5 seek the L their God and David
Hos 3: 5 their king, and fear the L
Hos 4: 1 Hear the word of the L, you
Hos 4: 1 for the L brings a charge
Hos 4:10 have ceased obeying the L
Hos 4:15 saying, As the L lives'
Hos 4:16 now the L will let them
Hos 5: 4 and they do not know the L
Hos 5: 6 they shall go to seek the L
Hos 5: 7 treacherously with the L, for
Hos 6: 1 and let us return to the L
Hos 6: 3 pursue the knowledge of the L
Hos 7:10 not return to the L their God
Hos 8: 1 against the house of the L
Hos 8:13 but the L does not accept
Hos 9: 4 offer wine offerings to the L
Hos 9: 4 come into the house of the L
Hos 9: 5 the day of the feast of the L
Hos 9:14 Give them, O L—what will You
Hos 10: 3 Because we did not fear the L
Hos 10:12 for it is time to seek the L
Hos 11:10 They shall walk after the L
Hos 11:11 in their houses," says the L
Hos 12: 2 The L also brings a charge
Hos 12: 5 that is, the L God of hosts
Hos 12: 5 The L is His memorial
Hos 12: 9 But I am the L your God, ever
Hos 12:13 By a prophet the L brought
Hos 12:14 therefore his L will leave on
Hos 13: 4 Yet I am the L your God ever
Hos 13:15 the wind of the L shall come
Hos 14: 1 return to the L your God
Hos 14: 2 with you, and return to the L
Hos 14: 9 the ways of the L are right
Joel 1: 1 The word of the L that came
Joel 1: 9 off from the house of the L
Joel 1: 9 mourn, who minister to the L
Joel 1:14 the house of the L your God
Joel 1:14 your God, and cry out to the L
Joel 1:15 the day of the L is at hand
Joel 1:19 O L, to You I cry out
Joel 2: 1 the day of the L is coming
Joel 2:11 The L gives voice before His
Joel 2:11 For the day of the L is great
Joel 2:12 Now, therefore," says the L
Joel 2:13 return to the L your God, for
Joel 2:14 offering for the L your God
Joel 2:17 who minister to the L, weep
Joel 2:17 Spare Your people, O L, and do
Joel 2:18 Then the L will be zealous
Joel 2:19 The L will answer and say to
Joel 2:21 for the L has done marvelous
Joel 2:23 and rejoice in the L your God
Joel 2:26 the name of the L your God
Joel 2:27 and that I am the L your God
Joel 2:31 and terrible day of the L
Joel 2:32 name of the L shall be saved
Joel 2:32 as the L has said, among the
Joel 2:32 the remnant whom the L calls
Joel 3: 8 for the L has spoken
Joel 3:11 ones to go down there, O L
Joel 3:14 For the day of the L is near
Joel 3:16 The L also will roar from
Joel 3:16 but the L will be a shelter
Joel 3:17 know that I am the L your God
Joel 3:18 flow from the house of the L
Joel 3:21 for the L dwells in Zion
Amos 1: 2 The L roars from Zion, and
Amos 1: 3 Thus says the L: "For three
Amos 1: 5 captive to Kir," says the L
Amos 1: 6 Thus says the L: "For three
Amos 1: 8 perish," says the L GOD
Amos 1: 9 Thus says the L: "For three
Amos 1:11 Thus says the L: "For three
Amos 1:13 Thus says the L: "For three
Amos 1:15 together," says the L
Amos 2: 1 Thus says the L: "For three
Amos 2: 3 with him," says the L
Amos 2: 4 Thus says the L: "For three
Amos 2: 4 despised the law of the L
Amos 2: 6 Thus says the L: "For three
Amos 2:11 of Israel?" says the L
Amos 2:16 in that day," says the L
Amos 3: 1 the L has spoken against you
Amos 3: 6 will not the L have done it
Amos 3: 7 Surely the L GOD does nothing
Amos 3: 8 The L GOD has spoken
Amos 3:10 know to do right,' says the L
Amos 3:11 Therefore thus says the L GOD
Amos 3:12 Thus says the L: "As a
Amos 3:13 of Jacob," says the L GOD
Amos 3:15 have an end," says the L
Amos 4: 2 The L GOD has sworn by His
Amos 4: 3 into Harmon," says the L
Amos 4: 5 Israel!" says the L GOD
Amos 4: 6 returned to Me," says the L
Amos 4: 8 returned to Me," says the L
Amos 4: 9 returned to Me," says the L
Amos 4:10 returned to Me," says the L
Amos 4:11 returned to Me," says the L
Amos 4:13 The L God of hosts is His
Amos 5: 3 For thus says the L GOD
Amos 5: 4 For thus says the L to the
Amos 5: 6 Seek the L and live, lest He
Amos 5: 8 the L is His name
Amos 5:14 so the L God of hosts will be
Amos 5:15 It may be that the L God of
Amos 5:16 the L God of hosts, the L
Amos 5:17 through you," says the L
Amos 5:18 who desire the day of the L
Amos 5:18 is the day of the L to you
Amos 5:20 not the day of the L darkness
Amos 5:27 beyond Damascus," says the L
Amos 6: 8 The L GOD has sworn by
Amos 6: 8 the L God of hosts says
Amos 6:10 not mention the name of the L
Amos 6:11 behold, the L gives a command
Amos 6:14 says the L God of hosts
Amos 7: 1 Thus the L GOD showed me
Amos 7: 2 O L GOD, forgive, I pray
Amos 7: 3 So the L relented concerning
Amos 7: 3 It shall not be," said the L
Amos 7: 4 Thus the L GOD showed me
Amos 7: 4 the L GOD called for conflict
Amos 7: 5 O L GOD, cease, I pray
Amos 7: 6 So the L relented concerning
Amos 7: 6 not be," said the L GOD
Amos 7: 7 the L stood on a wall made
Amos 7: 8 And the L said to me,
Amos 7: 8 Then the L said: "Behold, I
Amos 7:15 Then the L took me as I
Amos 7:15 and the L said to me, "Go,
Amos 7:16 hear the word of the L
Amos 7:17 Therefore thus says the L
Amos 8: 1 Thus the L GOD showed me
Amos 8: 2 Then the L said to me
Amos 8: 3 in that day," says the L GOD
Amos 8: 7 The L has sworn by the pride
Amos 8: 9 in that day," says the L GOD
Amos 8:11 are coming," says the L GOD
Amos 8:11 of hearing the words of the L
Amos 8:12 seeking the word of the L
Amos 9: 1 I saw the L standing by the
Amos 9: 5 The L GOD of hosts, He who
Amos 9: 6 the L is His name
Amos 9: 7 of Israel?" says the L
Amos 9: 8 the eyes of the L GOD are on
Amos 9: 8 house of Jacob," says the L
Amos 9:12 says the L who does this
Amos 9:13 days are coming," says the L
Amos 9:15 them," says the L your God
Obad 1 Thus says the L GOD
Obad 1 heard a report from the L
Obad 4 bring you down," says the L
Obad 8 not in that day," says the L
Obad 15 For the day of the L upon all
Obad 18 Esau," for the L has spoken
Jon 1: 1 Now the word of the L came to
Jon 1: 3 from the presence of the L
Jon 1: 3 from the presence of the L
Jon 1: 4 But the L sent out a great
Jon 1: 9 and I fear the L, the God of
Jon 1:10 from the presence of the L
Jon 1:14 they cried out to the L and
Jon 1:14 We pray, O L, please do not
Jon 1:14 for You, O L, have done as it
Jon 1:16 men feared the L exceedingly
Jon 1:16 offered a sacrifice to the L
Jon 1:17 Now the L had prepared a
Jon 2: 1 the L his God from the fish's
Jon 2: 2 I cried out to the L because
Jon 2: 6 up my life from the pit, O L
Jon 2: 7 within me, I remembered the L
Jon 2: 9 Salvation is of the L
Jon 2:10 So the L spoke to the fish,
Jon 3: 1 Now the word of the L came to
Jon 3: 3 to the word of the L
Jon 4: 2 So he prayed to the L, and
Jon 4: 2 Ah, L, was not this what I
Jon 4: 3 Therefore now, O L, please
Jon 4: 4 Then the L said, "Is it
Jon 4: 6 the L God prepared a plant and
Jon 4:10 But the L said, You have
Mic 1: 1 The word of the L that came
Mic 1: 2 Let the L GOD be a witness
Mic 1: 2 the L from His holy temple
Mic 1: 3 the L is coming out of His
Mic 1:12 L to the gate of Jerusalem
Mic 2: 3 Therefore thus says the L
Mic 2: 5 in the congregation of the L
Mic 2: 7 Spirit of the L restricted
Mic 2:13 with the L at their head
Mic 3: 4 Then they will cry to the L
Mic 3: 5 Thus says the L concerning
Mic 3: 8 power by the Spirit of the L
Mic 3:11 yet they lean on the L, and
Mic 3:11 Is not the L among us
Mic 4: 2 up to the mountain of the L
Mic 4: 2 word of the L from Jerusalem
Mic 4: 4 of the L of hosts has spoken
Mic 4: 5 name of the L our God forever
Mic 4: 6 In that day," says the L
Mic 4: 7 so the L will reign over them

Mic 4:10 there the **L** will redeem you
Mic 4:12 know the thoughts of the **L**
Mic 4:13 their gain to the **L**, and their
Mic 4:13 to the **L** of the whole earth
Mic 5: 4 in the strength of the **L**, in
Mic 5: 4 of the name of the **L** His God
Mic 5: 7 peoples, like dew from the **L**
Mic 5:10 be in that day," says the **L**
Mic 6: 1 Hear now what the **L** says
Mic 6: 2 for the **L** has a complaint
Mic 6: 5 the righteousness of the **L**
Mic 6: 6 shall I come before the **L**
Mic 6: 7 Will the **L** be pleased with
Mic 6: 8 what does the **L** require of
Mic 7: 7 I will look to the **L**
Mic 7: 8 the **L** will be a light to me
Mic 7: 9 bear the indignation of the **L**
Mic 7:10 Where is the **L** your God
Mic 7:17 be afraid of the **L** our God
Nah 1: 2 is jealous, and the **L** avenges
Nah 1: 2 the **L** avenges and is furious
Nah 1: 2 the **L** will take vengeance on
Nah 1: 3 the **L** is slow to anger and
Nah 1: 3 the **L** has His way in the
Nah 1: 7 The **L** is good, a stronghold
Nah 1: 9 do you conspire against the **L**
Nah 1:11 who plots evil against the **L**
Nah 1:12 Thus says the **L**: "Though they
Nah 1:14 The **L** has given a command
Nah 2: 2 For the **L** will restore the
Nah 2:13 you," says the **L** of hosts
Nah 3: 5 you," says the **L** of hosts
Hab 1: 2 O **L**, how long shall I cry, and
Hab 1:12 O **L** my God, my Holy One
Hab 1:12 O **L**, You have appointed them
Hab 2: 2 Then the **L** answered me and
Hab 2:13 is it not of the **L** of hosts
Hab 2:14 of the glory of the **L**, as the
Hab 2:20 But the **L** is in His holy
Hab 3: 2 O **L**, I have heard your speech
Hab 3: 2 O **L**, revive Your work in the
Hab 3: 8 O **L**, were You displeased with
Hab 3:18 Yet I will rejoice in the **L**
Hab 3:19 The **L** God is my strength
Zeph 1: 1 The word of the **L** which came
Zeph 1: 2 of the land," says the **L**
Zeph 1: 3 of the land," says the **L**
Zeph 1: 5 and swear oaths by the **L**, but
Zeph 1: 6 back from following the **L**
Zeph 1: 6 and have not sought the **L**
Zeph 1: 7 in the presence of the **L** GOD
Zeph 1: 7 the day of the **L** is at hand
Zeph 1: 7 for the **L** has prepared a
Zeph 1:10 be on that day," says the **L**
Zeph 1:12 The **L** will not do good, nor
Zeph 1:14 great day of the **L** is near
Zeph 1:14 of the day of the **L** is bitter
Zeph 1:17 have sinned against the **L**
Zeph 2: 3 Seek the **L**, all you meek of
Zeph 2: 5 word of the **L** is against you
Zeph 2: 7 for the **L** their God will
Zeph 2: 9 I live," says the **L** of hosts
Zeph 2:10 the people of the **L** of hosts
Zeph 2:11 The **L** will be awesome to them
Zeph 3: 2 she has not trusted in the **L**
Zeph 3: 5 The **L** is righteous, he is in
Zeph 3: 8 wait for Me," says the **L**
Zeph 3: 9 may call on the name of the **L**
Zeph 3:12 trust in the name of the **L**
Zeph 3:15 The **L** has taken away your
Zeph 3:15 the King of Israel, the **L**
Zeph 3:17 The **L** your God in your midst,
Zeph 3:20 your eyes," says the **L**
Hag 1: 1 the word of the **L** came by
Hag 1: 2 Thus speaks the **L** of hosts
Hag 1: 3 Then the word of the **L** came
Hag 1: 5 thus says the **L** of hosts
Hag 1: 7 Thus says the **L** of hosts
Hag 1: 8 and be glorified," says the **L**
Hag 1: 9 says the **L** of hosts
Hag 1:12 the voice of the **L** their God
Hag 1:12 as the **L** their God had sent
Hag 1:12 feared the presence of the **L**
Hag 1:13 I am with you, says the **L**
Hag 1:14 So the **L** stirred up the
Hag 1:14 the house of the **L** of hosts
Hag 2: 1 the word of the **L** came by
Hag 2: 4 Zerubbabel,' says the **L**
Hag 2: 4 of the land,' says the **L**, and
Hag 2: 4 you,' says the **L** of hosts
Hag 2: 6 For thus says the **L** of hosts
Hag 2: 7 glory,' says the **L** of hosts
Hag 2: 8 is Mine,' says the **L** of hosts
Hag 2: 9 former,' says the **L** of hosts
Hag 2: 9 peace,' says the **L** of hosts
Hag 2:10 the word of the **L** came by
Hag 2:11 Thus says the **L** of hosts
Hag 2:14 nation before Me,' says the **L**
Hag 2:15 stone in the temple of the **L**
Hag 2:17 not turn to Me,' says the **L**
Hag 2:20 the **L** came to Haggai on the
Hag 2:23 day,' says the **L** of hosts
Hag 2:23 son of Shealtiel,' says the **L**
Hag 2:23 you,' says the **L** of hosts
Zech 1: 1 the word of the **L** came to
Zech 1: 2 The **L** has been very angry
Zech 1: 3 Thus says the **L** of hosts
Zech 1: 3 to Me," says the **L** of hosts
Zech 1: 3 to you," says the **L** of hosts
Zech 1: 4 Thus says the **L** of hosts
Zech 1: 4 nor heed Me," says the **L**
Zech 1: 6 Just as the **L** of hosts
Zech 1: 7 the word of the **L** came to
Zech 1: 9 My **l**, what are these
Zech 1:10 the **L** has sent to walk to
Zech 1:11 answered the Angel of the **L**
Zech 1:12 the Angel of the **L** answered
Zech 1:12 O **L** of hosts, how long will
Zech 1:13 the **L** answered the angel who
Zech 1:14 Thus says the **L** of hosts
Zech 1:16 Therefore thus says the **L**
Zech 1:16 in it," says the **L** of hosts
Zech 1:17 Thus says the **L** of hosts
Zech 1:17 the **L** will again comfort Zion
Zech 1:20 Then the **L** showed me four
Zech 2: 5 For I,' says the **L**, 'will be
Zech 2: 6 of the north," says the **L**
Zech 2: 6 winds of heaven," says the **L**
Zech 2: 8 For thus says the **L** of hosts
Zech 2: 9 the **L** of hosts has sent Me
Zech 2:10 in your midst," says the **L**
Zech 2:11 joined to the **L** in that day
Zech 2:11 **L** of hosts has sent Me to you
Zech 2:12 the **L** will take possession of
Zech 2:13 all flesh, before the **L**, for
Zech 3: 1 before the Angel of the **L**
Zech 3: 2 And the **L** said to Satan,
Zech 3: 2 The **L** rebuke you, Satan
Zech 3: 2 The **L** who has chosen
Zech 3: 5 the Angel of the **L** stood by
Zech 3: 6 of the **L** admonished Joshua
Zech 3: 7 Thus says the **L** of hosts
Zech 3: 9 says the **L** of hosts, 'And I
Zech 3:10 day,' says the **L** of hosts
Zech 4: 4 What are these, my **l**
Zech 4: 5 And I said, "No, my **l**."
Zech 4: 6 word of the **L** to Zerubbabel
Zech 4: 6 Spirit,' says the **L** of hosts
Zech 4: 8 the word of the **L** came to me
Zech 4: 9 **L** of hosts has sent Me to you
Zech 4:10 They are the eyes of the **L**
Zech 4:13 And I said, "No, my **l**."
Zech 4:14 the **L** of the whole earth
Zech 5: 4 curse," says the **L** of hosts
Zech 6: 4 What are these, my **l**
Zech 6: 5 before the **L** of all the earth
Zech 6: 9 the word of the **L** came to me
Zech 6:12 Thus says the **L** of hosts
Zech 6:12 build the temple of the **L**
Zech 6:13 build the temple of the **L**
Zech 6:14 the temple of the **L** for Helem
Zech 6:15 and build the temple of the **L**
Zech 6:15 you shall know that the **L** of
Zech 6:15 the voice of the **L** your God
Zech 7: 1 of the **L** came to Zechariah
Zech 7: 2 of God, to pray before the **L**
Zech 7: 3 the house of the **L** of hosts
Zech 7: 4 of the **L** of hosts came to me
Zech 7: 7 the **L** proclaimed through the
Zech 7: 8 of the **L** came to Zechariah
Zech 7: 9 Thus says the **L** of hosts
Zech 7:12 and the words which the **L** of
Zech 7:12 came from the **L** of hosts
Zech 7:13 listen," says the **L** of hosts
Zech 8: 1 word of the **L** of hosts came
Zech 8: 2 Thus says the **L** of hosts
Zech 8: 3 Thus says the **L**: 'I will
Zech 8: 3 Mountain of the **L** of hosts
Zech 8: 4 Thus says the **L** of hosts
Zech 8: 6 Thus says the **L** of hosts
Zech 8: 6 says the **L** of hosts
Zech 8: 7 Thus says the **L** of hosts
Zech 8: 9 Thus says the **L** of hosts
Zech 8: 9 the house of the **L** of hosts
Zech 8:11 days,' says the **L** of hosts
Zech 8:14 For thus says the **L** of hosts
Zech 8:14 wrath,' says the **L** of hosts
Zech 8:17 that I hate,' says the **L**
Zech 8:18 of the **L** of hosts came to me
Zech 8:19 Thus says the **L** of hosts
Zech 8:20 Thus says the **L** of hosts
Zech 8:21 to go and pray before the **L**
Zech 8:21 and seek the **L** of hosts
Zech 8:22 the **L** of hosts in Jerusalem
Zech 8:22 and to pray before the **L**
Zech 8:23 Thus says the **L** of hosts
Zech 9: 1 burden of the word of the **L**
Zech 9: 1 of Israel are on the **L**)
Zech 9: 4 the **L** will cast her out
Zech 9:14 Then the **L** will be seen over
Zech 9:14 The **L** GOD will blow the
Zech 9:15 The **L** of hosts will defend
Zech 9:16 The **L** their God will save
Zech 10: 1 Ask the **L** for rain in the
Zech 10: 1 the **L** will make flashing
Zech 10: 3 For the **L** of hosts will visit
Zech 10: 5 because the **L** is with them
Zech 10: 6 for I am the **L** their God, and
Zech 10: 7 heart shall rejoice in the **L**
Zech 10:12 will strengthen them in the **L**
Zech 10:12 in His name," says the **L**
Zech 11: 4 Thus says the **L** my God
Zech 11: 5 them say, 'Blessed be the **L**
Zech 11: 6 of the land," says the **L**
Zech 11:11 that it was the word of the **L**
Zech 11:13 And the **L** said to me,
Zech 11:13 house of the **L** for the potter
Zech 11:15 And the **L** said to me,
Zech 12: 1 word of the **L** against Israel
Zech 12: 1 Thus says the **L**, who
Zech 12: 4 In that day," says the **L**
Zech 12: 5 my strength in the **L** of hosts
Zech 12: 7 The **L** will save the tents of
Zech 12: 8 In that day the **L** will defend
Zech 12: 8 Angel of the **L** before them
Zech 13: 2 day," says the **L** of hosts
Zech 13: 3 lies in the name of the **L**
Zech 13: 7 says the **L** of hosts
Zech 13: 8 in all the land," says the **L**
Zech 13: 9 will say, 'The **L** is my God
Zech 14: 1 the day of the **L** is coming
Zech 14: 3 Then the **L** will go forth and
Zech 14: 5 Thus the **L** my God will come,
Zech 14: 7 day which is known to the **L**
Zech 14: 9 the **L** shall be King over all
Zech 14: 9 the **L** is one," and His name
Zech 14:12 the plague with which the **L**
Zech 14:13 from the **L** will be among them
Zech 14:16 the **L** of hosts, and to keep
Zech 14:17 the **L** of hosts, on them there
Zech 14:18 the plague with which the **L**
Zech 14:20 HOLINESS TO THE **L**" shall
Zech 14:21 be holiness to the **L** of hosts
Zech 14:21 the house of the **L** of hosts
Mal 1: 1 of the **L** to Israel by Malachi
Mal 1: 2 have loved you," says the **L**
Mal 1: 2 Jacob's brother?" says the **L**
Mal 1: 4 Thus says the **L** of hosts
Mal 1: 4 the **L** will have indignation
Mal 1: 5 The **L** is magnified beyond
Mal 1: 6 Says the **L** of hosts to you
Mal 1: 7 of the **L** is contemptible
Mal 1: 8 says the **L** of hosts
Mal 1: 9 says the **L** of hosts
Mal 1:10 in you," Says the **L** of hosts
Mal 1:11 says the **L** of hosts
Mal 1:12 The table of the **L** is defiled
Mal 1:13 at it," says the **L** of hosts
Mal 1:13 from your hand?" says the **L**
Mal 1:14 to the **L** what is blemished
Mal 1:14 King," says the **L** of hosts
Mal 2: 2 name," says the **L** of hosts
Mal 2: 4 says the **L** of hosts
Mal 2: 7 messenger of the **L** of hosts
Mal 2: 8 Levi," says the **L** of hosts
Mal 2:12 May the **L** cut off from the
Mal 2:12 an offering to the **L** of hosts
Mal 2:13 the altar of the **L** with tears
Mal 2:14 because the **L** has been
Mal 2:16 For the **L** God of Israel says

Mal 2:16 says the L of hosts
Mal 2:17 wearied the L with your words
Mal 2:17 is good in the sight of the L
Mal 3: 1 And the L, whom you seek, will
Mal 3: 1 coming," says the L of hosts
Mal 3: 3 offer to the L an offering in
Mal 3: 4 will be pleasant to the L
Mal 3: 5 Me," says the L of hosts
Mal 3: 6 For I am the L, I do not
Mal 3: 7 to you," says the L of hosts
Mal 3:10 this," says the L of hosts
Mal 3:11 field," says the L of hosts
Mal 3:12 land," says the L of hosts
Mal 3:13 against Me," says the L
Mal 3:14 before the L of hosts
Mal 3:16 the L spoke to one another
Mal 3:16 the L listened and heard them
Mal 3:16 Him for those who fear the L
Mal 3:17 Mine," says the L of hosts
Mal 4: 1 up," says the L of hosts
Mal 4: 3 this," says the L of hosts
Mal 4: 5 and dreadful day of the L
Matt 1:20 an angel of the L appeared to
Matt 1:22 by the L through the prophet
Matt 1:24 angel of the L commanded him
Matt 2:13 an angel of the L appeared to
Matt 2:15 by the L through the prophet
Matt 2:19 an angel of the L appeared in
Matt 3: 3 Prepare the way of the L
Matt 4: 7 not tempt the L your God
Matt 4:10 shall worship the L your God
Matt 5:33 perform your oaths to the L
Matt 7:21 who says to Me, 'L, L,'
Matt 7:22 say to Me in that day, 'L
Matt 7:22 to Me in that day, 'L, L
Matt 8: 2 L, if You are willing, You
Matt 8: 6 L, my servant is lying at
Matt 8: 8 L, I am not worthy that You
Matt 8:21 L, let me first go and bury my
Matt 8:25 L, save us! We are perishing!
Matt 9:28 They said to Him, "Yes, L."
Matt 9:38 Therefore pray the L of the
Matt 11:25 L of heaven and earth, because
Matt 12: 8 Man is L even of the Sabbath
Matt 13:51 They said to Him, "Yes, L."
Matt 14:28 L, if it is You, command me
Matt 14:30 saying, "L, save me!"
Matt 15:22 Have mercy on me, O L, Son of
Matt 15:25 saying, "L, help me!"
Matt 15:27 True, L, yet even the little
Matt 16:22 Far be it from You, L
Matt 17: 4 L, it is good for us to be
Matt 17:15 L, have mercy on my son, for
Matt 18:21 L, how often shall my brother
Matt 20:25 the Gentiles l it over them
Matt 20:30 Have mercy on us, O L, Son of
Matt 20:31 Have mercy on us, O L, Son of
Matt 20:33 L, that our eyes may be
Matt 21: 3 The L has need of them,' and
Matt 21: 9 comes in the name of the L
Matt 22:37 You shall love the L your
Matt 22:43 in the Spirit call Him 'L
Matt 22:44 The L said to my L, "Sit
Matt 22:45 If David then calls Him 'L
Matt 23:39 comes in the name of the L
Matt 24:42 what hour your L is coming
Matt 25:11 came also, saying, 'L, L
Matt 25:19 After a long time the l of
Matt 25:20 other talents, saying, L
Matt 25:21 His l said to him, 'Well done
Matt 25:21 Enter into the joy of your l
Matt 25:22 two talents came and said, L
Matt 25:23 His l said to him, 'Well done
Matt 25:23 Enter into the joy of your l
Matt 25:24 one talent came and said, 'L
Matt 25:26 But his l answered and said to
Matt 25:37 will answer Him, saying, 'L
Matt 25:44 will answer Him, saying, 'L
Matt 26:22 say to Him, "L, is it I?"
Matt 27:10 field, as the L directed me
Matt 28: 2 for an angel of the L
Matt 28: 6 see the place where the L lay
Mark 1: 3 Prepare the way of the L
Mark 2:28 Man is also L of the Sabbath
Mark 5:19 things the L has done for you
Mark 7:28 Yes, L, yet even the little
Mark 9:24 L, I believe; help my
Mark 10:42 the Gentiles l it over them
Mark 11: 3 The L has need of it,' and
Mark 11: 9 comes in the name of the L
Mark 11:10 comes in the name of the L
Mark 12:29 L our God, the L is one
Mark 12:30 you shall love the L your God
Mark 12:36 The L said to my L,
Mark 12:37 David himself calls Him 'L'
Mark 13:20 unless the L had shortened
Mark 16:19 after the L had spoken to
Mark 16:20 the L working with them and
Luke 1: 6 ordinances of the L blameless
Luke 1: 9 went into the temple of the L
Luke 1:11 of the L appeared to him,
Luke 1:15 great in the sight of the L
Luke 1:16 of Israel to the L their God
Luke 1:17 a people prepared for the L
Luke 1:25 Thus the L has dealt with me,
Luke 1:28 one, the L is with you
Luke 1:32 the L God will give Him the
Luke 1:38 the maidservant of the L
Luke 1:43 of my L should come to me
Luke 1:45 were told her from the L
Luke 1:46 My soul magnifies the L,
Luke 1:58 relatives heard how the L had
Luke 1:66 hand of the L was with him
Luke 1:68 is the L God of Israel, for
Luke 1:76 of the L to prepare His ways
Luke 2: 9 an angel of the L stood
Luke 2: 9 and the glory of the L shone
Luke 2:11 a Savior, who is Christ the L
Luke 2:15 which the L has made known to
Luke 2:22 to present Him to the L
Luke 2:23 written in the law of the L
Luke 2:23 be called holy to the L")
Luke 2:24 is said in the law of the L
Luke 2:29 L, now You are letting Your
Luke 2:38 she gave thanks to the L, and
Luke 2:39 according to the law of the L
Luke 3: 4 Prepare the way of the L
Luke 4: 8 shall worship the L your God
Luke 4:12 not tempt the L your God
Luke 4:18 Spirit of the L is upon Me
Luke 4:19 the acceptable year of the L
Luke 5: 8 for I am a sinful man, O L
Luke 5:12 L, if You are willing, You
Luke 5:17 And the power of the L was
Luke 6: 5 Man is also L of the Sabbath
Luke 6:46 why do you call Me 'L, L
Luke 7: 6 L, do not trouble Yourself,
Luke 7:13 When the L saw her, He had
Luke 7:31 the L said, "To what then
Luke 9:54 L, do You want us to command
Luke 9:57 L, I will follow You wherever
Luke 9:59 L, let me first go and bury my
Luke 9:61 L, I will follow You, but let
Luke 10: 1 After these things the L
Luke 10: 2 therefore pray the L of the
Luke 10:17 L, even the demons are
Luke 10:21 L of heaven and earth, that
Luke 10:27 You shall love the L your
Luke 10:40 L, do You not care that my
Luke 11: 1 L, teach us to pray, as John
Luke 11:39 But the L said to him, "Now
Luke 12:41 L, do You speak this parable
Luke 12:42 the L said, "Who then is
Luke 13:15 The L then answered him and
Luke 13:23 L, are there few who are
Luke 13:25 at the door, saying, 'L, L
Luke 13:35 Comes in the name of the L
Luke 17: 5 And the apostles said to the L
Luke 17: 6 So the L said, "If you have
Luke 17:37 said to Him, "Where, L?"
Luke 18: 6 Then the L said, "Hear what
Luke 18:41 L, that I may receive my
Luke 19: 8 stood and said to the L
Luke 19: 8 Look, L, I give half of my
Luke 19:31 Because the L has need of
Luke 19:34 said, "The L has need of him
Luke 19:38 comes in the name of the L
Luke 20:37 when he called the L the God
Luke 20:42 The L said to my L,
Luke 20:44 David therefore calls Him L'
Luke 22:31 the L said, "Simon, Simon!
Luke 22:33 L, I am ready to go with You,
Luke 22:38 L, look, here are two swords
Luke 22:49 L, shall we strike with the
Luke 22:61 the L turned and looked at
Luke 22:61 remembered the word of the L
Luke 23:42 L, remember me when You
Luke 24: 3 find the body of the L Jesus
Luke 24:34 The L is risen indeed, and has
John 1:23 straight the way of the L
John 4: 1 when the L knew that the
John 6:23 after the L had given thanks
John 6:34 L, give us this bread always
John 6:68 L, to whom shall we go
John 8:11 She said, "No one, L."
John 9:36 Who is He, L, that I may
John 9:38 Then he said, "L, I believe!"
John 11: 2 the L with fragrant oil and
John 11: 3 L, behold, he whom You love
John 11:12 L, if he sleeps he will get
John 11:21 L, if You had been here, my
John 11:27 Yes, L, I believe that You
John 11:32 L, if You had been here, my
John 11:34 L, come and see
John 11:39 L, by this time there is a
John 12:13 comes in the name of the L
John 12:38 L, who has believed our
John 12:38 arm of the L been revealed
John 13: 6 L, are You washing my feet
John 13: 9 L, not my feet only, but also
John 13:13 You call me Teacher and L, and
John 13:14 If I then, your L and Teacher,
John 13:25 to Him, "L, who is it?"
John 13:36 L, where are You going
John 13:37 L, why can I not follow You
John 14: 5 L, we do not know where You
John 14: 8 L, show us the Father, and it
John 14:22 L, how is it that You will
John 20: 2 away the L out of the tomb
John 20:13 they have taken away my L
John 20:18 that she had seen the L, and
John 20:20 were glad when they saw the L
John 20:25 We have seen the L
John 20:28 My L and my God
John 21: 7 It is the L
John 21: 7 Peter heard that it was the L
John 21:12 knowing that it was the L
John 21:15 Yes, L; You know that I love
John 21:16 Yes, L; You know that I love
John 21:17 L, You know all things
John 21:20 L, who is the one who betrays
John 21:21 But L, what about this man
Acts 1: 6 L, will You at this time
Acts 1:21 time that the L Jesus went in
Acts 1:24 You, O L, who know the hearts
Acts 2:20 great and notable day of the L
Acts 2:21 name of the L shall be saved
Acts 2:25 I foresaw the L always
Acts 2:34 The L said to my L,
Acts 2:36 whom you crucified, both L
Acts 2:39 as many as the L our God will
Acts 2:47 the L added to the church
Acts 3:19 from the presence of the L
Acts 3:22 The L your God will raise up
Acts 4:24 L, You are God, who made
Acts 4:26 together against the L and
Acts 4:29 Now, L, look on their threats
Acts 4:33 resurrection of the L Jesus
Acts 5: 9 to test the Spirit of the L
Acts 5:14 increasingly added to the L
Acts 5:19 the L opened the prison doors
Acts 7:30 an Angel of the L appeared to
Acts 7:31 voice of the L came to him
Acts 7:33 Then the L said to him
Acts 7:37 The L your God will raise up
Acts 7:49 says the L, or what is the
Acts 7:59 L Jesus, receive my spirit
Acts 7:60 L, do not charge them with
Acts 8:16 in the name of the L Jesus
Acts 8:24 Pray to the L for me, that
Acts 8:25 and preached the word of the L
Acts 8:26 of the L spoke to Philip,
Acts 8:39 the Spirit of the L caught
Acts 9: 1 the disciples of the L, went
Acts 9: 5 Who are You, L
Acts 9: 5 the L said, "I am Jesus,
Acts 9: 6 L, what do You want me to do
Acts 9: 6 And the L said to him,
Acts 9:10 to him the L said in a vision
Acts 9:10 And he said, "Here I am, L."
Acts 9:11 So the L said to him, "Arise
Acts 9:13 L, I have heard from many
Acts 9:15 But the L said to him, "Go,
Acts 9:17 the L Jesus, who appeared to
Acts 9:27 he had seen the L on the road
Acts 9:29 in the name of the L Jesus
Acts 9:31 walking in the fear of the L
Acts 9:35 saw him and turned to the L
Acts 9:42 and many believed on the L
Acts 10: 4 What is it, l

Acts 10:14 But Peter said, "Not so, L!
Acts 10:36 He is L of all
Acts 10:48 baptized in the name of the L
Acts 11: 8 But I said, 'Not so, L
Acts 11:16 remembered the word of the L
Acts 11:17 on the L Jesus Christ, who
Acts 11:20 preaching the L Jesus
Acts 11:21 hand of the L was with them
Acts 11:21 believed and turned to the L
Acts 11:23 should continue with the L
Acts 11:24 people were added to the L
Acts 12: 7 angel of the L stood by him
Acts 12:11 that the L has sent His angel
Acts 12:17 L had brought him out of the
Acts 12:23 an angel of the L struck him
Acts 13: 2 As they ministered to the L
Acts 13:10 the straight ways of the L
Acts 13:11 the hand of the L is upon you
Acts 13:12 at the teaching of the L
Acts 13:47 For so the L has commanded us
Acts 13:48 glorified the word of the L
Acts 13:49 the word of the L was being
Acts 14: 3 speaking boldly in the L
Acts 14:23 L in whom they had believed
Acts 15:11 L Jesus Christ we shall be
Acts 15:17 of mankind may seek the L
Acts 15:17 Says the L who does all these
Acts 15:26 name of our L Jesus Christ
Acts 15:35 preaching the word of the L
Acts 15:36 preached the word of the L
Acts 16:10 concluding that the L had
Acts 16:14 The L opened her heart to
Acts 16:15 me to be faithful to the L
Acts 16:31 Believe on the L Jesus Christ
Acts 16:32 the word of the L to him and
Acts 17:24 it, since He is L of heaven
Acts 17:27 that they should seek the L
Acts 18: 8 believed on the L with all
Acts 18: 9 Now the L spoke to Paul in
Acts 18:25 in the way of the L
Acts 18:25 the things of the L, though
Acts 19: 5 in the name of the L Jesus
Acts 19:10 heard the word of the L Jesus
Acts 19:13 to call the name of the L
Acts 19:17 the name of the L Jesus was
Acts 19:20 word of the L grew mightily
Acts 20:19 serving the L with all
Acts 20:21 toward our L Jesus Christ
Acts 20:24 I received from the L Jesus
Acts 20:35 the words of the L Jesus,
Acts 21:13 for the name of the L Jesus
Acts 21:14 The will of the L be done
Acts 21:20 it, they glorified the L
Acts 22: 8 I answered, 'Who are You, L
Acts 22:10 I said, 'What shall I do, L
Acts 22:10 the L said to me, 'Arise and
Acts 22:16 calling on the name of the L
Acts 22:19 So I said, 'L, they know that
Acts 23:11 night the L stood by him and
Acts 25:26 write to my l concerning him
Acts 26:15 So I said, 'Who are You, L
Acts 28:31 the L Jesus Christ with all
Rom 1: 3 His Son Jesus Christ our L
Rom 1: 7 Father and the L Jesus Christ
Rom 4: 8 the L shall not impute sin
Rom 4:24 up Jesus our L from the dead
Rom 5: 1 through our L Jesus Christ
Rom 5:11 through our L Jesus Christ
Rom 5:21 through Jesus Christ our L
Rom 6:11 to God in Christ Jesus our L
Rom 6:23 life in Christ Jesus our L
Rom 7:25 through Jesus Christ our L
Rom 8:39 is in Christ Jesus our L
Rom 9:28 because the L will make a
Rom 9:29 Unless the L of Sabaoth had
Rom 10: 9 with your mouth the L Jesus
Rom 10:12 for the same L over all is
Rom 10:13 name of the L shall be saved
Rom 10:16 L, who has believed our
Rom 11: 3 L, they have killed Your
Rom 11:34 has known the mind of the L
Rom 12:11 in spirit, serving the L
Rom 12:19 I will repay," says the L
Rom 13:14 But put on the L Jesus Christ
Rom 14: 6 the day, observes it to the L
Rom 14: 6 to the L he does not observe
Rom 14: 6 He who eats, eats to the L
Rom 14: 6 to the L he does not eat, and
Rom 14: 8 if we live, we live to the L
Rom 14: 8 and if we die, we die to the L
Rom 14: 9 might be L of both the dead
Rom 14:11 As I live, says the L, every
Rom 14:14 am convinced by the L Jesus
Rom 15: 6 Father of our L Jesus Christ
Rom 15:11 Praise the L, all you
Rom 15:30 through the L Jesus Christ,
Rom 16: 2 L in a manner worthy of the
Rom 16: 8 Amplias, my beloved in the L
Rom 16:11 of Narcissus who are in the L
Rom 16:12 who have labored in the L
Rom 16:12 who labored much in the L
Rom 16:13 Greet Rufus, chosen in the L
Rom 16:18 not serve our L Jesus Christ
Rom 16:20 The grace of our L Jesus
Rom 16:22 epistle, greet you in the L
Rom 16:24 The grace of our L Jesus
1Co 1: 2 name of Jesus Christ our L
1Co 1: 3 Father and the L Jesus Christ
1Co 1: 7 of our L Jesus Christ,
1Co 1: 8 the day of our L Jesus Christ
1Co 1: 9 His Son, Jesus Christ our L
1Co 1:10 name of our L Jesus Christ
1Co 1:31 let him glory in the L
1Co 2: 8 have crucified the L of glory
1Co 2:16 L that he may instruct Him
1Co 3: 5 as the L gave to each one
1Co 3:20 The L knows the thoughts of
1Co 4: 4 but He who judges me is the L
1Co 4: 5 the time, until the L comes
1Co 4:17 and faithful son in the L, who
1Co 4:19 you shortly, if the L wills
1Co 5: 4 name of our L Jesus Christ
1Co 5: 4 power of our L Jesus Christ
1Co 5: 5 in the day of the L Jesus
1Co 6:11 in the name of the L Jesus
1Co 6:13 immorality but for the L
1Co 6:13 and the L for the body
1Co 6:14 And God both raised up the L
1Co 6:17 the L is one spirit with Him
1Co 7:10 command, yet not I but the L
1Co 7:12 But to the rest I, not the L
1Co 7:17 as the L has called each one,
1Co 7:22 L while a slave is the Lord's
1Co 7:25 no commandment from the L
1Co 7:25 the L in His mercy has made
1Co 7:32 things that belong to the L
1Co 7:32 how he may please the L
1Co 7:34 about the things of the L
1Co 7:35 the L without distraction
1Co 7:39 she wishes, only in the L
1Co 8: 6 one L Jesus Christ, through
1Co 9: 1 I not seen Jesus Christ our L
1Co 9: 1 Are you not my work in the L
1Co 9: 2 of my apostleship in the L
1Co 9: 5 the brothers of the L, and
1Co 9:14 Even so the L has commanded
1Co 10:21 cannot drink the cup of the L
1Co 10:22 we provoke the L to jealousy
1Co 11:11 independent of man, in the L
1Co 11:23 For I received from the L
1Co 11:23 that the L Jesus on the same
1Co 11:27 or drinks this cup of the L
1Co 11:27 of the body and blood of the L
1Co 11:32 we are chastened by the L
1Co 12: 3 L except by the Holy Spirit
1Co 12: 5 of ministries, but the same L
1Co 14:21 not hear Me," says the L
1Co 14:37 are the commandments of the L
1Co 15:31 I have in Christ Jesus our L
1Co 15:47 Man is the L from heaven
1Co 15:57 through our L Jesus Christ
1Co 15:58 in the work of the L, knowing
1Co 15:58 labor is not in vain in the L
1Co 16: 7 with you, if the L permits
1Co 16:10 for he does the work of the L
1Co 16:19 greet you heartily in the L
1Co 16:22 not love the L Jesus Christ
1Co 16:22 be accursed. O L, come!
1Co 16:23 The grace of our L Jesus
2Co 1: 2 Father and the L Jesus Christ
2Co 1: 3 Father of our L Jesus Christ
2Co 1:14 in the day of the L Jesus
2Co 2:12 was opened to me by the L
2Co 3:16 when one turns to the L, the
2Co 3:17 Now the L is the Spirit
2Co 3:17 where the Spirit of the L is
2Co 3:18 a mirror the glory of the L
2Co 3:18 as by the Spirit of the L
2Co 4: 5 but Christ Jesus the L, and
2Co 4:10 body the dying of the L Jesus
2Co 4:14 that He who raised up the L
2Co 5: 6 body we are absent from the L
2Co 5: 8 and to be present with the L
2Co 5:11 the terror of the L, we
2Co 6:17 and be separate, says the L
2Co 6:18 says the L Almighty
2Co 8: 5 gave themselves to the L, and
2Co 8: 9 grace of our L Jesus Christ
2Co 8:19 to the glory of the L Himself
2Co 8:21 only in the sight of the L
2Co 10: 8 which the L gave us for
2Co 10:17 let him glory in the L
2Co 10:18 but whom the L commends
2Co 11:17 speak not according to the L
2Co 11:31 Father of our L Jesus Christ
2Co 12: 1 and revelations of the L
2Co 12: 8 thing I pleaded with the L
2Co 13:10 which the L has given me for
2Co 13:14 grace of the L Jesus Christ
Gal 1: 3 Father and our L Jesus Christ,
Gal 5:10 confidence in you, in the L
Gal 6:14 cross of our L Jesus Christ
Gal 6:17 body the marks of the L Jesus
Gal 6:18 the grace of our L Jesus
Eph 1: 2 Father and the L Jesus Christ
Eph 1: 3 Father of our L Jesus Christ
Eph 1:15 of your faith in the L Jesus
Eph 1:17 the God of our L Jesus Christ
Eph 2:21 into a holy temple in the L
Eph 3:11 in Christ Jesus our L,
Eph 3:14 Father of our L Jesus Christ
Eph 4: 1 the prisoner of the L,
Eph 4: 5 one L, one faith, one baptism
Eph 4:17 and testify in the L, that
Eph 5: 8 now you are light in the L
Eph 5:10 what is acceptable to the L
Eph 5:17 what the will of the L is
Eph 5:19 melody in your heart to the L
Eph 5:20 name of our L Jesus Christ
Eph 5:22 own husbands, as to the L
Eph 5:29 just as the L does the church
Eph 6: 1 obey your parents in the L
Eph 6: 4 and admonition of the L
Eph 6: 7 doing service, as to the L
Eph 6: 8 receive the same from the L
Eph 6:10 brethren, be strong in the L
Eph 6:21 and faithful minister in the L
Eph 6:23 Father and the L Jesus Christ
Eph 6:24 L Jesus Christ in sincerity
Phil 1: 2 Father and the L Jesus Christ
Phil 1:14 most of the brethren in the L
Phil 2:11 that Jesus Christ is L, to
Phil 2:19 But I trust in the L Jesus to
Phil 2:24 But I trust in the L that I
Phil 2:29 in the L with all gladness
Phil 3: 1 my brethren, rejoice in the L
Phil 3: 8 of Christ Jesus my L, for
Phil 3:20 Savior, the L Jesus Christ,
Phil 4: 1 crown, so stand fast in the L
Phil 4: 2 be of the same mind in the L
Phil 4: 4 Rejoice in the L always
Phil 4: 5 The L is at hand
Phil 4:10 But I rejoiced in the L
Phil 4:23 The grace of our L Jesus
Col 1: 2 Father and the L Jesus Christ
Col 1: 3 Father of our L Jesus Christ
Col 1:10 have a walk worthy of the L
Col 2: 6 received Christ Jesus the L
Col 3:16 grace in your hearts to the L
Col 3:17 in the name of the L Jesus
Col 3:18 as is fitting in the L
Col 3:20 is well pleasing to the L
Col 3:23 do it heartily, as to the L
Col 3:24 knowing that from the L you
Col 3:24 for you serve the L Christ
Col 4: 7 and a fellow servant in the L
Col 4:17 you have received in the L
1Th 1: 1 Father and the L Jesus Christ
1Th 1: 1 Father and the L Jesus Christ
1Th 1: 3 patience of hope in our L
1Th 1: 6 followers of us and of the L
1Th 1: 8 of the L has sounded forth
1Th 2:15 who killed both the L Jesus
1Th 2:19 L Jesus Christ at His coming
1Th 3: 8 if you stand fast in the L
1Th 3:11 our L Jesus Christ, direct
1Th 3:12 may the L make you increase
1Th 3:13 L Jesus Christ with all His
1Th 4: 1 exhort in the L Jesus that
1Th 4: 2 gave you through the L Jesus

1Th 4: 6 because the L is the avenger
1Th 4:15 to you by the word of the L
1Th 4:15 until the coming of the L
1Th 4:16 For the L Himself will
1Th 4:17 to meet the L in the air
1Th 4:17 we shall always be with the L
1Th 5: 2 that the day of the L so
1Th 5: 9 through our L Jesus Christ
1Th 5:12 you, and are over you in the L
1Th 5:23 coming of our L Jesus Christ
1Th 5:27 I charge you by the L that
1Th 5:28 The grace of our L Jesus
2Th 1: 1 Father and the L Jesus Christ
2Th 1: 2 Father and the L Jesus Christ
2Th 1: 7 rest with us when the L Jesus
2Th 1: 8 gospel of our L Jesus Christ
2Th 1: 9 from the presence of the L
2Th 1:12 of our L Jesus Christ may be
2Th 1:12 our God and the L Jesus Christ
2Th 2: 1 coming of our L Jesus Christ
2Th 2: 8 whom the L will consume with
2Th 2:13 brethren beloved by the L
2Th 2:14 glory of our L Jesus Christ
2Th 2:16 Now may our L Jesus Christ
2Th 3: 1 of the L may have free course
2Th 3: 3 But the L is faithful, who
2Th 3: 4 in the L concerning you, both
2Th 3: 5 Now may the L direct your
2Th 3: 6 name of our L Jesus Christ
2Th 3:12 exhort through our L Jesus
2Th 3:16 Now may the L of peace
2Th 3:16 The L be with you all
2Th 3:18 The grace of our L Jesus
1Ti 1: 1 the L Jesus Christ, our hope,
1Ti 1: 2 Father and Jesus Christ our L
1Ti 1:12 our L who has enabled me,
1Ti 1:14 And the grace of our L was
1Ti 5:21 the L Jesus Christ and the
1Ti 6: 3 words of our L Jesus Christ
1Ti 6:14 blameless until our L Jesus
1Ti 6:15 King of kings and L of lords,
2Ti 1: 2 Father and Christ Jesus our L
2Ti 1: 8 of the testimony of our L
2Ti 1:16 The L grant mercy to the
2Ti 1:18 The L grant to him that he
2Ti 1:18 mercy from the L in that Day
2Ti 2: 7 I say, and may the L give you
2Ti 2:14 charging them before the L
2Ti 2:19 The L knows those who are His
2Ti 2:22 on the L out of a pure heart
2Ti 2:24 a servant of the L must not
2Ti 3:11 them all the L delivered me
2Ti 4: 1 the L Jesus Christ, who will
2Ti 4: 8 of righteousness, which the L
2Ti 4:14 May the L repay him according
2Ti 4:17 But the L stood with me and
2Ti 4:18 the L will deliver me from
2Ti 4:22 The L Jesus Christ be with
Tit 1: 4 the L Jesus Christ our Savior
Phm 3 Father and the L Jesus Christ
Phm 5 you have toward the L Jesus
Phm 16 both in the flesh and in the L
Phm 20 me have joy from you in the L
Phm 20 refresh my heart in the L
Phm 25 The grace of our L Jesus
Heb 1:10 You, L, in the beginning laid
Heb 2: 3 began to be spoken by the L
Heb 7:14 that our L arose from Judah
Heb 7:21 The L has sworn and will not
Heb 8: 2 which the L erected, and not
Heb 8: 8 days are coming," says the L
Heb 8: 9 them," says the L
Heb 8:10 those days," says the L, "I
Heb 8:11 brother, saying, 'Know the L
Heb 10:16 after those days, says the L
Heb 10:30 I will repay, says the L
Heb 10:30 The L will judge His people
Heb 12: 5 the chastening of the L, nor
Heb 12: 6 For whom the L loves He
Heb 12:14 which no one will see the L
Heb 13: 6 The L is my helper
Heb 13:20 up our L Jesus from the dead
Jas 1: 1 of the L Jesus Christ, To the
Jas 1: 7 receive anything from the L
Jas 1:12 L has promised to those who
Jas 2: 1 faith of our L Jesus Christ
Jas 2: 1 Christ, the L of glory, with
Jas 4:10 in the sight of the L, and He
Jas 4:15 If the L wills, we shall live
Jas 5: 4 the ears of the L of Sabaoth
Jas 5: 7 until the coming of the L
Jas 5: 8 coming of the L is at hand
Jas 5:10 spoke in the name of the L
Jas 5:11 the end intended by the L
Jas 5:11 the L is very compassionate
Jas 5:14 with oil in the name of the L
Jas 5:15 and the L will raise him up
1Pe 1: 3 Father of our L Jesus Christ
1Pe 1:25 word of the L endures forever
1Pe 2: 3 tasted that the L is gracious
1Pe 3: 6 obeyed Abraham, calling him l
1Pe 3:12 For the eyes of the L are on
1Pe 3:12 but the face of the L is
1Pe 3:15 But sanctify the L God in
2Pe 1: 2 of God and of Jesus our L,
2Pe 1: 8 of our L Jesus Christ
2Pe 1:11 everlasting kingdom of our L
2Pe 1:14 just as our L Jesus Christ
2Pe 1:16 coming of our L Jesus Christ
2Pe 2: 1 denying the L who bought them
2Pe 2: 9 then the L knows how to
2Pe 2:11 against them before the L
2Pe 2:20 the knowledge of the L and
2Pe 3: 2 of us the apostles of the L
2Pe 3: 8 that with the L one day is as
2Pe 3: 9 The L is not slack concerning
2Pe 3:10 But the day of the L will
2Pe 3:15 of our L is salvation
2Pe 3:18 grace and knowledge of our L
2Jn 3 from the L Jesus Christ, the
Jude 4 and deny the only L God and
Jude 4 God and our L Jesus Christ
Jude 5 once knew this, that the L
Jude 9 but said, "The L rebuke you
Jude 14 Behold, the L comes with ten
Jude 17 of our L Jesus Christ
Jude 21 for the mercy of our L Jesus
Rev 1: 8 and the End," says the L
Rev 4: 8 L God Almighty, Who was and
Rev 4:11 You are worthy, O L, to
Rev 6:10 How long, O L, holy and true,
Rev 11: 8 also our L was crucified
Rev 11:15 become the kingdoms of our L
Rev 11:17 O L God Almighty, the One
Rev 14:13 who die in the L from now on
Rev 15: 3 Your works, L God Almighty
Rev 15: 4 Who shall not fear You, O L
Rev 16: 5 You are righteous, O L, the
Rev 16: 7 so, L God Almighty, true and
Rev 17:14 them, for He is L of lords
Rev 18: 8 for strong is the L God who
Rev 19: 1 and power to the L our God
Rev 19: 6 For the L God Omnipotent
Rev 19:16 OF KINGS AND L OF LORDS
Rev 21:22 for the L God Almighty and the
Rev 22: 5 sun, for the L God gives them
Rev 22: 6 And the L God of the holy
Rev 22:20 Even so, come, L Jesus
Rev 22:21 The grace of our L Jesus

LORDLY (*see* LORD)

Judg 5:25 brought out cream in a l bowl

LORD'S (*see* LORD)

Gen 40: 7 in the custody of his l house
Gen 44: 8 or gold from your l house
Gen 44: 9 we also will be my l slaves
Gen 44:16 my l slaves, both we and he
Gen 44:18 speak a word in my l hearing
Ex 9:29 know that the earth is the L
Ex 12:11 It is the L Passover
Ex 13: 9 that the L law may be in your
Ex 13:12 the males shall be the L
Ex 32:26 Whoever is on the L side, let
Ex 35:21 they brought the L offering
Ex 35:24 bronze brought the L offering
Lev 3:16 all the fat is the L
Lev 16: 9 goat on which the L lot fell
Lev 23: 5 at twilight is the L Passover
Lev 27:26 should be the L firstling
Lev 27:26 an ox or sheep, it is the L
Lev 27:30 fruit of the tree, is the L
Num 9:10 may still keep the L Passover
Num 9:14 and would keep the L Passover
Num 11:23 Has the L arm been shortened
Num 11:29 that all the L people were
Num 18:28 you shall give the L heave
Num 31:37 the L tribute of the sheep
Num 31:38 of which the L tribute was
Num 31:39 of which the L tribute was
Num 31:40 of which the L tribute was
Num 31:41 L heave offering to Eleazar
Num 32:10 So the L anger was aroused on
Num 32:13 So the L anger was aroused
Deut 11:17 lest the L anger be aroused
Deut 15: 2 it is called the L release
Deut 32: 9 For the L portion is His
Josh 1:15 which Moses the L servant
Josh 5:15 of the L army said to Joshua
Josh 22:19 where the L tabernacle stands
Judg 11:31 Ammon, shall surely be the L
1Sa 2: 8 of the earth are the L, and He
1Sa 2:24 You make the L people
1Sa 14: 3 the L priest in Shiloh, was
1Sa 16: 6 Surely the L anointed is
1Sa 17:47 for the battle is the L, and
1Sa 18:17 me, and fight the L battles
1Sa 22:21 Saul had killed the L priests
1Sa 24: 6 the L anointed, to stretch
1Sa 24:10 for he is the L anointed
1Sa 26: 9 hand against the L anointed
1Sa 26:11 hand against the L anointed
1Sa 26:16 your master, the L anointed
1Sa 26:23 hand against the L anointed
2Sa 1:14 to destroy the L anointed
2Sa 1:16 I have killed the L anointed
2Sa 6: 8 the L outbreak against Uzzah
2Sa 19:21 he cursed the L anointed
2Sa 20: 6 Take your l servants and
2Sa 21: 7 because of the L oath that
1Ki 18:13 hundred men of the L prophets
2Ki 11:17 they should be the L people
2Ki 13:17 arrow of the L deliverance
1Ch 13:11 the L outbreak against Uzza
1Ch 21: 3 they not all my l servants
2Ch 7: 2 LORD had filled the L house
2Ch 23:16 they should be the L people
Ps 11: 4 The L throne is in heaven
Ps 22:28 For the kingdom is the L, And
Ps 24: 1 The earth is the L, and all
Ps 109:20 Let this be the L reward to
Ps 113: 3 The L name is to be praised
Ps 115:16 even the heavens, are the L
Ps 116:19 In the courts of the L house
Ps 118:23 This was the L doing
Ps 137: 4 How shall we sing the L song
Prov 16:11 weight and balance are the L
Prov 19:21 Nevertheless the L counsel
Is 2: 2 that the mountain of the L
Is 34: 8 is the day of the L vengeance
Is 40: 2 the L hand double for all her
Is 42:19 and blind as the L servant
Is 44: 5 One will say, I am the L'
Is 44: 5 write with his hand, The L
Is 59: 1 the L hand is not shortened,
Jer 5:10 for they are not the L
Jer 7: 2 in the gate of the L house
Jer 13:17 because the L flock has been
Jer 19:14 in the court of the L house
Jer 25:17 took the cup from the L hand
Jer 26: 2 in the court of the L house
Jer 26: 2 to worship in the L house
Jer 26:10 the new gate of the L house
Jer 26:19 the LORD and seek the L favor
Jer 27:16 the vessels of the L house
Jer 28: 3 the vessels of the L house
Jer 28: 6 the vessels of the L house
Jer 36: 6 of the people in the L house
Jer 36: 8 of the LORD in the L house
Jer 36:10 the New Gate of the L house
Jer 51: 6 the time of the L vengeance
Jer 51: 7 a golden cup in the L hand
Jer 51:51 sanctuaries of the L house
Lam 2:22 In the day of the L anger
Lam 3:22 Through the L mercies we are
Ezek 8:14 the north gate of the L house
Ezek 8:16 inner court of the L house
Ezek 10: 4 the brightness of the L glory
Ezek 10:19 the east gate of the L house
Ezek 11: 1 the east gate of the L house
Dan 9:17 for the L sake cause Your
Hos 9: 3 shall not dwell in the L land
Obad 21 and the kingdom shall be the L
Mic 4: 1 That the mountain of the L
Mic 6: 2 the L complaint, and you
Mic 6: 9 The L voice cries to the city
Hab 2:16 The cup of the L right hand
Zeph 1: 8 in the day of the L sacrifice
Zeph 1:18 in the day of the L wrath
Zeph 2: 2 before the L fierce anger

Zeph 2: 2 of the **L** anger comes upon you
Zeph 2: 3 in the day of the **L** anger
Hag 1: 2 the time that the **L** house
Hag 1:13 the **L** messenger, spoke the
Hag 1:13 spoke the **L** message to the
Hag 2:18 of the **L** temple was laid
Zech 14:20 The pots in the **L** house shall
Mal 2:11 **L** holy institution which He
Matt 21:42 This was the **L** doing, and it
Matt 25:18 ground, and hid his **l** money
Mark 12:11 This was the **L** doing, and it
Luke 2:26 he had seen the **L** Christ
Rom 14: 8 we live or die, we are the **L**
1Co 7:22 a slave is the **L** freedman
1Co 10:21 cannot partake of the **L** table
1Co 10:26 The earth is the **L**, and all
1Co 10:28 The earth is the **L**, and all
1Co 11:20 it is not to eat the **L** Supper
1Co 11:26 you proclaim the **L** death till
1Co 11:29 not discerning the **L** body
Gal 1:19 except James, the **L** brother
1Pe 2:13 of man for the **L** sake,
Rev 1:10 in the Spirit on the **L** Day

LORDS (*see* LORD)
Gen 19: 2 Here now, my **l**, please turn
Gen 19:18 Please, no, my **l**
Num 21:28 the **l** of the heights of the
Deut 10:17 is God of gods and Lord of **l**
Josh 13: 3 the five **l** of the Philistines
Judg 3: 3 five **l** of the Philistines,
Judg 16: 5 the **l** of the Philistines came
Judg 16: 8 So the **l** of the Philistines
Judg 16:18 and called for the **l** of the
Judg 16:18 So the **l** of the Philistines
Judg 16:23 Now the **l** of the Philistines
Judg 16:27 all the **l** of the Philistines
Judg 16:30 and the temple fell on the **l**
1Sa 5: 8 all the **l** of the Philistines
1Sa 5:11 all the **l** of the Philistines
1Sa 6: 4 of the **l** of the Philistines
1Sa 6: 4 on all of you and on your **l**
1Sa 6:12 the **l** of the Philistines went
1Sa 6:16 So when the five **l** of the
1Sa 6:18 belonging to the five **l**, both
1Sa 7: 7 the **l** of the Philistines went
1Sa 29: 2 And the **l** of the Philistines
1Sa 29: 6 the **l** do not favor you
1Sa 29: 7 the **l** of the Philistines
1Ch 12:19 for the **l** of the Philistines
Ps 136: 3 give thanks to the Lord of **l**
Is 16: 8 the **l** of the nations have
Jer 2:31 do My people say, 'We are **l**
Dan 5: 1 feast for a thousand of his **l**
Dan 5: 2 that the king and his **l**, his
Dan 5: 3 and the king and his **l**, his
Dan 5: 9 and his **l** were astonished
Dan 5:10 words of the king and his **l**
Dan 5:23 before you, and you and your **l**
Dan 6:17 and with the signets of his **l**
1Co 8: 5 are many gods and many **l**),
1Ti 6:15 King of kings and Lord of **l**
1Pe 5: 3 nor as being **l** over those
Rev 17:14 them, for He is Lord of **l**
Rev 19:16 AND LORD OF **L**

LORDSHIP (*see* LORD)
Luke 22:25 Gentiles exercise **l** over them

LO-RUHAMAH
Hos 1: 6 Call her name **L**, for I will
Hos 1: 8 Now when she had weaned **L**

LOSE (*see* LOSES, LOSS, LOST)
Judg 18:25 you **l** your life, with the
Job 31:39 its owners to **l** their lives
Eccl 3: 6 time to gain, and a time to **l**
Matt 10:39 who finds his life will **l** it
Matt 10:42 by no means **l** his reward
Matt 16:25 to save his life will **l** it
Mark 8:35 to save his life will **l** it
Mark 9:41 will by no means **l** his reward
Luke 9:24 to save his life will **l** it
Luke 17:33 to save his life will **l** it
Luke 18: 1 ought to pray and not **l** heart,
John 6:39 given Me I should **l** nothing
John 12:25 who loves his life will **l** it
2Co 4: 1 mercy, we do not **l** heart
2Co 4:16 Therefore we do not **l** heart
Gal 6: 9 reap if we do not **l** heart
Eph 3:13 I ask that you do not **l** heart
2Jn 8 that we do not **l** those things

LOSES (*see* LOSE)
Matt 5:13 but if the salt **l** its flavor
Matt 10:39 he who **l** his life for My sake
Matt 16:25 whoever **l** his life for My
Matt 16:26 world, and **l** his own soul
Mark 8:35 but whoever **l** his life for My
Mark 8:36 world, and **l** his own soul
Mark 9:50 but if the salt **l** its flavor
Luke 9:24 but whoever **l** his life for My
Luke 15: 4 if he **l** one of them, does not
Luke 15: 8 if she **l** one coin, does not
Luke 17:33 and whoever **l** his life will

LOSS (*see* LOSE, LOSSES)
Gen 31:39 I bore the **l** of it
Ex 21:19 pay for the **l** of his time
Esth 7: 4 compensate for the king's **l**
Job 11:20 and their hope—**l** of life!
Is 47: 8 I know the **l** of children'
Is 47: 9 the **l** of children, and
Dan 6: 2 the king would suffer no **l**
Acts 27:10 end with disaster and much **l**
Acts 27:21 incurred this disaster and **l**
Acts 27:22 be no **l** of life among you
1Co 3:15 is burned, he will suffer **l**
2Co 7: 9 suffer **l** from us in nothing
Phil 3: 7 I have counted **l** for Christ
Phil 3: 8 I also count all things **l** for
Phil 3: 8 suffered the **l** of all things

LOSSES (*see* LOSS)
Job 42:10 **l** when he prayed for his

LOST (*see* LOSE)
Ex 22: 9 or for any kind of **l** thing
Lev 6: 3 or if he has found what was **l**
Lev 6: 4 or the **l** thing which he found
Num 6:12 the former days shall be **l**
Deut 22: 3 with any **l** thing of your
Deut 22: 3 brother's, which he has **l**
1Sa 9: 3 Kish, Saul's father, were **l**
1Sa 9:20 that were **l** three days ago
2Sa 4: 1 he **l** heart, and all Israel was
1Ki 20:25 like the army that you have **l**
Ps 27:13 I would have **l** heart, unless
Ps 119:176 gone astray like a **l** sheep
Is 49:20 after you have **l** the others
Is 49:21 since I have **l** my children
Jer 50: 6 My people have been **l** sheep
Ezek 19: 5 waited, that her hope was **l**
Ezek 34: 4 away, nor sought what was **l**
Ezek 34:16 I will seek what was **l** and
Ezek 37:11 bones are dry, our hope is **l**
Matt 10: 6 But go rather to the **l** sheep
Matt 15:24 the **l** sheep of the house of
Matt 18:11 come to save that which was **l**
Luke 9:25 and is himself destroyed or **l**
Luke 14:34 if the salt has **l** its flavor
Luke 15: 4 which is **l** until he finds it
Luke 15: 6 found my sheep which was **l**
Luke 15: 9 found the piece which I **l**
Luke 15:24 he was **l** and is found
Luke 15:32 dead and is alive, and was **l**
Luke 19:10 and to save that which was **l**
Luke 21:18 hair of your head shall be **l**
John 6:12 remain, so that nothing is **l**
John 17:12 none of them is **l** except the
John 18: 9 You gave Me I have **l** none

LOT (*see* LOTS)
Lev 16: 8 one **l** for the LORD and the
Lev 16: 8 the other **l** for the scapegoat
Lev 16: 9 on which the LORD's **l** fell
Lev 16:10 **l** fell to be the scapegoat
Num 26:55 land shall be divided by **l**
Num 26:56 According to the **l** their
Num 33:54 by **l** as an inheritance among
Num 33:54 be whatever falls to him by **l**
Num 34:13 which you shall inherit by **l**
Num 36: 2 **l** to the children of Israel
Num 36: 3 from the **l** of our inheritance
Josh 13: 6 only divide it by **l** to Israel
Josh 14: 2 Their inheritance was by **l**
Josh 15: 1 This then was the **l** of the
Josh 16: 1 The **l** fell to the children of
Josh 17: 1 There was also a **l** for the
Josh 17: 2 there was a **l** for the rest of
Josh 17:14 have you given us but one **l**
Josh 17:17 you shall not have one **l** only
Josh 18:11 Now the **l** of the tribe of the
Josh 18:11 their **l** came out between the
Josh 19: 1 The second **l** came out for
Josh 19:10 The third **l** came out for the
Josh 19:17 The fourth **l** came out to
Josh 19:24 The fifth **l** came out for the
Josh 19:32 The sixth **l** came out to the
Josh 19:40 The seventh **l** came out for
Josh 19:51 as an inheritance by **l** in
Josh 21: 4 Now the **l** came out for the
Josh 21: 4 had thirteen cities by **l** from
Josh 21: 5 by **l** from the families of the
Josh 21: 6 had thirteen cities by **l** from
Josh 21: 8 by **l** to the Levites, as the
Josh 21:10 for the **l** was theirs first
Josh 21:20 had the cities of their **l**
Josh 21:40 were by their **l** twelve cities
Josh 23: 4 I have divided to you by **l**
Judg 20: 9 We will go up against it by **l**
1Sa 14:41 Give a perfect **l**
1Ch 6:54 by **l** to the sons of Aaron
1Ch 6:61 by **l** ten cities from half the
1Ch 6:65 they gave by **l** from the tribe
1Ch 24: 5 Thus they were divided by **l**
1Ch 24: 7 Now the first **l** fell to
1Ch 25: 9 Now the first **l** for Asaph
1Ch 26:14 The **l** for the East Gate fell
1Ch 26:14 his **l** came out for the North
1Ch 26:16 Hosah the **l** came out for the
Esth 3: 7 cast Pur (that is, the **l**)
Esth 9:24 had cast Pur (that is, the **l**)
Ps 16: 5 You maintain my **l**
Prov 1:14 cast in your **l** among us, let
Prov 16:33 The **l** is cast into the lap,
Is 17:14 the **l** of those who rob us
Is 34:17 He has cast the **l** for them
Is 57: 6 they, they, are your **l**
Jer 13:25 This is your **l**, the portion
Ezek 24: 6 on which no **l** has fallen
Ezek 45: 1 land by **l** into inheritance
Ezek 47:22 it by **l** as an inheritance for
Ezek 48:29 which you shall divide by **l**
Jon 1: 7 lots, and the **l** fell on Jonah
Mic 2: 5 **l** in the congregation of the
Luke 1: 9 his **l** fell to burn incense
Acts 1:26 and the **l** fell on Matthias

LOT* (*see* LOT'S)
Gen 11:27 Haran begot **L**
Gen 11:31 son Abram and his grandson **L**
Gen 12: 4 to him, and **L** went with him
Gen 12: 5 **L** his brother's son, and all
Gen 13: 1 and **L** with him, to the South
Gen 13: 5 **L** also, who went with Abram,
Gen 13: 8 So Abram said to **L**, "Please
Gen 13:10 **L** lifted his eyes and saw all
Gen 13:11 Then **L** chose for himself all
Gen 13:11 Jordan, and **L** journeyed east
Gen 13:12 **L** dwelt in the cities of the
Gen 13:14 after **L** had separated from
Gen 14:12 They also took **L**, Abram's
Gen 14:16 brought back his brother **L**
Gen 19: 1 **L** was sitting in the gate of
Gen 19: 1 When **L** saw them, he rose to
Gen 19: 5 And they called to **L** and said
Gen 19: 6 So **L** went out to them through
Gen 19: 9 hard against the man **L**, and
Gen 19:10 pulled **L** into the house with
Gen 19:12 Then the men said to **L**
Gen 19:14 So **L** went out and spoke to his
Gen 19:15 the angels urged **L** to hurry
Gen 19:18 Then **L** said to them, "Please
Gen 19:23 the earth when **L** entered Zoar
Gen 19:29 sent **L** out of the midst of
Gen 19:29 cities in which **L** had dwelt
Gen 19:30 Then **L** went up out of Zoar and
Gen 19:36 of **L** were with child by their
Deut 2: 9 of **L** as a possession
Deut 2:19 of **L** as a possession
Ps 83: 8 have helped the children of **L**
Luke 17:28 it was also in the days of **L**
Luke 17:29 but on the day that **L** went
2Pe 2: 7 and delivered righteous **L**, who

LOTAN (*see* LOTAN'S)
Gen 36:20 **L**, Shobal, Zibeon, Anah,
Gen 36:22 And the sons of **L** were Hori
Gen 36:29 Chief **L**, Chief Shobal, Chief
1Ch 1:38 The sons of Seir were **L**,
1Ch 1:39 And the sons of **L** were Hori

LOTAN'S (*see* LOTAN)
Gen 36:22 **L** sister was Timna
1Ch 1:39 **L** sister was Timna

LOT'S (*see* LOT*)
Gen 13: 7 the herdsmen of L livestock
Luke 17:32 Remember L wife

LOTS (*see* LOT)
Lev 16: 8 cast l for the two goats
Josh 18: 6 that I may cast l for you
Josh 18: 8 that I may cast l for you
Josh 18:10 Then Joshua cast l for them
1Sa 14:42 said, "Cast l between my son
1Ch 24:31 These also cast l just as
1Ch 25: 8 they cast l for their duty,
1Ch 26:13 they cast l for each gate,
1Ch 26:14 Then they cast l for his son
Neh 10:34 We cast l among the priests,
Neh 11: 1 l to bring one out of ten to
Ps 22:18 for My clothing they cast l
Prov 18:18 Casting l causes contentions
Joel 3: 3 have cast l for My people
Obad 11 gates and cast l for Jerusalem
Jon 1: 7 Come, let us cast l, that we
Jon 1: 7 So they cast l, and the lot
Nah 3:10 they cast l for her honorable
Matt 27:35 His garments, casting l, that
Matt 27:35 for My clothing they cast l
Mark 15:24 casting l for them to
Luke 23:34 His garments and cast l
John 19:24 tear it, but cast l for it
John 19:24 for My clothing they cast l
Acts 1:26 And they cast their l, and the

LOTUS
Job 40:21 He lies under the l trees
Job 40:22 The l trees cover him with

LOUD (*see* LOUDER, LOUDLY)
Gen 39:14 and I cried out with a l voice
Ex 19:16 of the trumpet was very l
Deut 5:22 darkness, with a l voice
Deut 27:14 shall speak with a l voice
1Sa 7:10 with a l thunder upon the
1Sa 28:12 she cried out with a l voice
2Sa 15:23 country wept with a l voice
2Sa 19: 4 king cried out with a l voice
1Ki 8:55 of Israel with a l voice,
2Ki 18:28 out with a l voice in Hebrew
2Ch 15:14 the LORD with a l voice, with
2Ch 20:19 God of Israel with voices l
2Ch 30:21 accompanied by l instruments
2Ch 32:18 a l voice in Hebrew to the
Ezra 3:12 wept with a l voice when the
Ezra 3:13 people shouted with a l shout
Ezra 10:12 and said with a l voice, "Yes
Neh 9: 4 cried out with a l voice to
Esth 4: 1 He cried out with a l and
Ps 150: 5 Praise Him with l cymbals
Prov 7:11 She was l and rebellious, her
Prov 27:14 his friend with a l voice
Is 36:13 out with a l voice in Hebrew
Jer 51:55 and silencing her l voice,
Ezek 8:18 cry in My ears with a l voice
Ezek 9: 1 in my hearing with a l voice
Ezek 11:13 face and cried with a l voice
Mic 2:12 they shall make a l noise
Zeph 1:10 a l crashing from the hills
Matt 27:46 cried out with a l voice,
Matt 27:50 out again with a l voice,
Mark 1:26 and cried out with a l voice
Mark 5: 7 he cried out with a l voice
Mark 15:34 cried out with a l voice,
Mark 15:37 cried out with a l voice, and
Luke 1:42 she spoke out with a l voice
Luke 4:33 he cried out with a l voice
Luke 8:28 Him, and with a l voice said,
Luke 17:15 with a l voice glorified God,
Luke 19:37 praise God with a l voice for
Luke 23:23 demanding with l voices that
Luke 23:46 had cried out with a l voice
John 11:43 He cried with a l voice
Acts 7:57 they cried out with a l voice
Acts 7:60 and cried out with a l voice
Acts 8: 7 crying with a l voice, came
Acts 14:10 said with a l voice, "Stand
Acts 16:28 Paul called with a l voice
Acts 23: 9 Then there arose a l outcry
Acts 26:24 Festus said with a l voice
Rev 1:10 I heard behind me a l voice
Rev 5: 2 proclaiming with a l voice
Rev 5:12 saying with a l voice
Rev 6:10 And they cried with a l voice
Rev 7: 2 he cried with a l voice to
Rev 7:10 and crying out with a l voice
Rev 8:13 heaven, saying with a l voice
Rev 10: 3 and cried with a l voice, as
Rev 11:12 they heard a l voice from
Rev 11:15 there were l voices in heaven
Rev 12:10 Then I heard a l voice saying
Rev 14: 2 like the voice of l thunder
Rev 14: 7 saying with a l voice, "Fear
Rev 14: 9 them, saying with a l voice
Rev 14:15 crying with a l voice to Him
Rev 14:18 he cried with a l cry to him
Rev 16: 1 Then I heard a l voice from
Rev 16:17 a l voice came out of the
Rev 18: 2 cried mightily with a l voice
Rev 19: 1 these things I heard a l
Rev 19:17 and he cried with a l voice
Rev 21: 3 I heard a l voice from heaven

LOUDER (*see* LOUD)
Ex 19:19 sounded long and became l and
Ex 19:19 long and became l and l

LOUDLY (*see* LOUD)
1Sa 4: 5 so l that the earth shook
Neh 12:42 The singers sang l with
Mark 5:38 and those who wept and wailed l

LOVE (*see* LOVED, LOVER, LOVE'S, LOVES, LOVESICK, LOVING, LOVINGKINDNESS, UNLOVED)
Gen 22: 2 only son Isaac, whom you l
Gen 27: 4 me savory food, such as I l
Gen 29:20 of the l he had for her
Gen 29:32 my husband will l me
Ex 20: 6 thousands, to those who l Me
Ex 21: 5 I l my master, my wife, and
Lev 19:18 but you shall l your neighbor
Lev 19:34 you shall l him as yourself
Deut 5:10 thousands, to those who l Me
Deut 6: 5 You shall l the LORD your God
Deut 7: 7 His l on you nor choose you
Deut 7: 9 with those who l Him and keep
Deut 7:13 And He will l you and bless you
Deut 10:12 to l Him, to serve the LORD
Deut 10:15 in your fathers, to l them
Deut 10:19 Therefore l the stranger, for
Deut 11: 1 you shall l the LORD your God
Deut 11:13 to l the LORD your God and
Deut 11:22 to l the LORD your God, to
Deut 13: 3 you to know whether you l the
Deut 19: 9 to l the LORD your God and to
Deut 30: 6 to l the LORD your God with
Deut 30:16 today to l the LORD your God
Deut 30:20 that you may l the LORD your
Josh 22: 5 to l the LORD your God, to
Josh 23:11 that you l the LORD your God
Judg 5:31 But let those who l Him be
Judg 14:16 You do not l me
Judg 16:15 I l you,' when your heart is
1Sa 18:22 and all his servants l you
2Sa 1:26 Your l to me was wonderful,
2Sa 1:26 surpassing the l of women
2Sa 13: 4 him, "I l Tamar, my brother
2Sa 13:15 her was greater than the l
2Sa 19: 6 in that you l your enemies and
1Ki 11: 2 Solomon clung to these in l
2Ch 19: 2 l those who hate the LORD
Neh 1: 5 and mercy with those who l You
Job 19:19 those whom I l have turned
Ps 4: 2 long will you l worthlessness
Ps 5:11 Let those also who l Your
Ps 18: 1 I will l You, O LORD, my
Ps 31:23 Oh, l the LORD, all you His
Ps 40:16 Let such as l Your salvation
Ps 45: 7 You l righteousness and hate
Ps 52: 3 You l evil more than good, And
Ps 52: 4 You l all devouring words,
Ps 69:36 those who l His name shall
Ps 70: 4 And let those who l Your
Ps 91:14 he has set his l upon Me,
Ps 97:10 You who l the LORD, hate evil
Ps 109: 4 In return for my l they are
Ps 109: 5 for good, And hatred for my l
Ps 116: 1 I l the LORD, because He has
Ps 119:47 Your commandments, Which I l
Ps 119:48 Your commandments, Which I l
Ps 119:97 Oh, how I l Your law
Ps 119:113 But I l Your law
Ps 119:119 I l Your testimonies
Ps 119:127 I l Your commandments
Ps 119:132 toward those who l Your name
Ps 119:159 how I l Your precepts
Ps 119:163 abhor lying, But I l Your law
Ps 119:165 have those who l Your law
Ps 119:167 And I l them exceedingly
Ps 122: 6 May they prosper who l you
Ps 145:20 LORD preserves all who l Him
Prov 1:22 ones, will you l simplicity
Prov 4: 6 l her, and she will keep you
Prov 5:19 be enraptured with her l
Prov 7:18 our fill of l until morning
Prov 7:18 us delight ourselves with l
Prov 8:17 I l those who l me, and
Prov 8:21 who l me to inherit wealth
Prov 8:36 all those who hate me l death
Prov 9: 8 a wise man, and he will l you
Prov 10:12 strife, but l covers all sins
Prov 15:12 A scoffer does not l one who
Prov 15:17 a dinner of herbs where l is
Prov 16:13 they l him who speaks what is
Prov 17: 9 a transgression seeks l, but
Prov 18:21 those who l it will eat its
Prov 20:13 Do not l sleep, lest you come
Prov 27: 5 than l carefully concealed
Eccl 3: 8 a time to l, and a time to
Eccl 9: 1 People know neither l nor
Eccl 9: 6 Also their l, their hatred,
Eccl 9: 9 with the wife whom you l all
Song 1: 2 for your l is better than
Song 1: 3 therefore the virgins l you
Song 1: 4 your l more than wine
Song 1: 4 Rightly do they l you
Song 1: 7 Tell me, O you whom I l,
Song 1: 9 I have compared you, my l
Song 1:15 Behold, you are fair, my l
Song 2: 2 thorns, so is my l among the
Song 2: 4 and his banner over me was l
Song 2: 7 nor awaken l until it pleases
Song 2:10 Rise up, my l, my fair one,
Song 2:13 rise up, my l, my fair one,
Song 3: 1 my bed I sought the one I l
Song 3: 2 I will seek the one I l
Song 3: 3 Have you seen the one I l
Song 3: 4 when I found the one I l
Song 3: 5 nor awaken l until it pleases
Song 3:10 with l by the daughters of
Song 4: 1 Behold, you are fair, my l
Song 4: 7 You are all fair, my l, and
Song 4:10 How fair is your l, my sister
Song 4:10 better than wine is your l
Song 5: 2 Open for me, my sister, my l
Song 6: 4 O my l, you are as beautiful
Song 7: 6 and how pleasant you are, O l
Song 7:12 There I will give you my l
Song 8: 4 nor awaken l until it pleases
Song 8: 6 for l is as strong as death,
Song 8: 7 Many waters cannot quench l
Song 8: 7 If a man would give for l all
Is 56: 6 to l the name of the LORD, to
Is 61: 8 For I, the LORD, l justice
Is 63: 9 in His l and in His pity He
Is 66:10 with her, all you who l her
Jer 2: 2 the l of your betrothal, when
Jer 2:33 beautify your way to seek l
Jer 5:31 My people l to have it so
Jer 31: 3 you with an everlasting l
Ezek 16: 8 your time was the time of l
Ezek 23:11 in her inordinate l than she
Ezek 23:17 to her, into the bed of l
Ezek 33:31 their mouth they show much l
Dan 9: 4 and mercy with those who l Him
Hos 3: 1 l a woman who is loved by a
Hos 3: 1 just like the l of the LORD
Hos 3: 1 l the raisin cakes of the
Hos 4:18 Her rulers dearly l dishonor
Hos 9:15 I will l them no more
Hos 11: 4 gentle cords, with bands of l
Hos 14: 4 I will l them freely, for My
Amos 4: 5 for this you l, you children
Amos 5:15 Hate evil, l good
Mic 3: 2 You who hate good and l evil
Mic 6: 8 to l mercy, and to walk humbly
Zeph 3:17 He will quiet you in His l
Zech 8:17 and do not l a false oath
Zech 8:19 Therefore l truth and peace
Matt 5:43 You shall l your neighbor and
Matt 5:44 l your enemies, bless those
Matt 5:46 if you l those who l you
Matt 6: 5 For they l to pray standing
Matt 6:24 l the other, or else he will
Matt 19:19 You shall l your neighbor as
Matt 22:37 You shall l the LORD your
Matt 22:39 You shall l your neighbor as

Matt 23: 6 They l the best places at
Matt 24:12 the l of many will grow cold
Mark 12:30 you shall l the LORD your God
Mark 12:31 You shall l your neighbor as
Mark 12:33 to l Him with all the heart,
Mark 12:33 and to l one's neighbor as
Mark 12:38 robes, l greetings in the
Luke 6:27 L your enemies, do good to
Luke 6:32 if you l those who l you
Luke 6:32 sinners l those who l them
Luke 6:35 But l your enemies, do good,
Luke 7:42 which of them will l him more
Luke 10:27 You shall l the LORD your
Luke 11:42 by justice and the l of God
Luke 11:43 For you l the best seats in
Luke 16:13 l the other, or else he will
Luke 20:46 robes, l greetings in the
John 5:42 not have the l of God in you
John 8:42 your Father, you would l Me
John 11: 3 behold, he whom You l is sick
John 13:34 you, that you l one another
John 13:34 that you also l one another
John 13:35 if you have l for one another
John 14:15 If you l Me, keep My
John 14:21 by My Father, and I will l him
John 14:23 and My Father will l him, and
John 14:24 He who does not l Me does not
John 14:31 may know that I l the Father
John 15: 9 abide in My l
John 15:10 you will abide in My l, just
John 15:10 and abide in His l
John 15:12 that you l one another as I
John 15:13 Greater l has no one than
John 15:17 you, that you l one another
John 15:19 the world would l its own
John 17:26 that the l with which You
John 21:15 do you l Me more than these
John 21:15 You know that I l You
John 21:16 son of Jonah, do you l Me
John 21:16 You know that I l You
John 21:17 son of Jonah, do you l Me
John 21:17 Do you l Me
John 21:17 You know that I l You
Rom 5: 5 because the l of God has been
Rom 5: 8 His own l toward us, in that
Rom 8:28 for good to those who l God
Rom 8:35 us from the l of Christ
Rom 8:39 to separate us from the l of
Rom 12: 9 Let l be without hypocrisy
Rom 12:10 one another with brotherly l
Rom 13: 8 except to l one another, for
Rom 13: 9 You shall l your neighbor as
Rom 13:10 L does no harm to a neighbor
Rom 13:10 therefore l is the
Rom 14:15 are no longer walking in l
Rom 15:30 through the l of the Spirit,
1Co 2: 9 prepared for those who l Him
1Co 4:21 to you with a rod, or in l
1Co 8: 1 puffs up, but l edifies
1Co 13: 1 and of angels, but have not l
1Co 13: 2 mountains, but have not l
1Co 13: 3 to be burned, but have not l
1Co 13: 4 L suffers long and is kind
1Co 13: 4 l does not envy
1Co 13: 4 l does not parade itself, is
1Co 13: 8 L never fails
1Co 13:13 And now abide faith, hope, l
1Co 13:13 the greatest of these is l
1Co 14: 1 Pursue l, and desire spiritual
1Co 16:14 that you do be done with l
1Co 16:22 If anyone does not l the Lord
1Co 16:24 My l be with you all in
2Co 2: 4 l which I have so abundantly
2Co 2: 8 you to reaffirm your l to him
2Co 5:14 For the l of Christ
2Co 6: 6 the Holy Spirit, by sincere l
2Co 8: 7 and in your l for us
2Co 8: 8 the sincerity of your l by
2Co 8:24 churches, the proof of your l
2Co 11:11 Because I do not l you
2Co 12:15 the more abundantly I l you
2Co 13:11 and the God of l and peace will
2Co 13:14 and the l of God, and the
Gal 5: 6 but faith working through l
Gal 5:13 but through l serve one
Gal 5:14 You shall l your neighbor as
Gal 5:22 the fruit of the Spirit is l
Eph 1: 4 without blame before Him in l
Eph 1:15 your l for all the saints,
Eph 2: 4 because of His great l with
Eph 3:17 being rooted and grounded in l
Eph 3:19 to know the l of Christ which
Eph 4: 2 bearing with one another in l
Eph 4:15 but, speaking the truth in l
Eph 4:16 the edifying of itself in l
Eph 5: 2 And walk in l, as Christ also
Eph 5:25 l your wives, just as Christ
Eph 5:28 So husbands ought to l their
Eph 5:33 so l his own wife as himself
Eph 6:23 l with faith, from God the
Eph 6:24 l our Lord Jesus Christ in
Phil 1: 9 that your l may abound still
Phil 1:17 but the latter out of l,
Phil 2: 1 Christ, if any comfort of l
Phil 2: 2 having the same l, being of
Col 1: 4 of your l for all the saints
Col 1: 8 to us your l in the Spirit
Col 1:13 kingdom of the Son of His l
Col 2: 2 being knit together in l
Col 3:14 all these things put on l
Col 3:19 l your wives and do not be
1Th 1: 3 work of faith, labor of l
1Th 3: 6 good news of your faith and l
1Th 3:12 abound in l to one another and
1Th 4: 9 l you have no need that I
1Th 4: 9 by God to l one another
1Th 5: 8 the breastplate of faith and l
1Th 5:13 in l for their work's sake
2Th 1: 3 the l of every one of you all
2Th 2:10 receive the l of the truth
2Th 3: 5 your hearts into the l of God
1Ti 1: 5 is l from a pure heart, from
1Ti 1:14 l which are in Christ Jesus
1Ti 2:15 if they continue in faith, l
1Ti 4:12 in word, in conduct, in l
1Ti 6:10 For the l of money is a root
1Ti 6:11 godliness, faith, l,
2Ti 1: 7 of fear, but of power and of l
2Ti 1:13 l which are in Christ Jesus
2Ti 2:22 righteousness, faith, l,
2Ti 3:10 faith, longsuffering, l,
Tit 2: 2 sound in faith, in l, in
Tit 2: 4 women to l their husbands
Tit 2: 4 to l their children,
Tit 3: 4 and the l of God our Savior
Tit 3:15 those who l us in the faith
Phm 5 hearing of your l and faith
Phm 7 joy and consolation in your l
Heb 6:10 labor of l which you have
Heb 10:24 another in order to stir up l
Heb 13: 1 Let brotherly l continue
Jas 1:12 promised to those who l Him
Jas 2: 5 promised to those who l Him
Jas 2: 8 You shall l your neighbor as
1Pe 1: 8 whom having not seen you l
1Pe 1:22 in sincere l of the brethren
1Pe 1:22 l one another fervently with
1Pe 2:17 L the brotherhood
1Pe 3: 8 l as brothers, be
1Pe 3:10 He who would l life and see
1Pe 4: 8 fervent l for one another
1Pe 4: 8 l will cover a multitude of
1Pe 5:14 one another with a kiss of l
2Pe 1: 7 and to brotherly kindness l
1Jn 2: 5 word, truly the l of God is
1Jn 2:15 Do not l the world or the
1Jn 2:15 the l of the Father is not in
1Jn 3: 1 Behold what manner of l the
1Jn 3:10 he who does not l his brother
1Jn 3:11 that we should l one another
1Jn 3:14 because we l the brethren
1Jn 3:14 He who does not l his brother
1Jn 3:16 By this we know l, because He
1Jn 3:17 how does the l of God abide
1Jn 3:18 let us not l in word or in
1Jn 3:23 l one another, as He gave us
1Jn 4: 7 let us l one another, for
1Jn 4: 7 one another, for l is of God
1Jn 4: 8 He who does not l does not
1Jn 4: 8 not know God, for God is l
1Jn 4: 9 In this the l of God was
1Jn 4:10 In this is l, not that we
1Jn 4:11 also ought to l one another
1Jn 4:12 If we l one another, God
1Jn 4:12 His l has been perfected in
1Jn 4:16 believed the l that God has
1Jn 4:16 God is l, and he who abides in
1Jn 4:16 who abides in l abides in God
1Jn 4:17 L has been perfected among us
1Jn 4:18 There is no fear in l
1Jn 4:18 but perfect l casts out fear,
1Jn 4:18 not been made perfect in l
1Jn 4:19 We l Him because He first
1Jn 4:20 I l God," and hates his
1Jn 4:20 for he who does not l his
1Jn 4:20 how can he l God whom he has
1Jn 4:21 God must l his brother also
1Jn 5: 2 that we l the children of God
1Jn 5: 2 of God, when we l God and keep
1Jn 5: 3 For this is the l of God,
2Jn 1 whom I l in truth, and not
2Jn 3 of the Father, in truth and l
2Jn 5 that we l one another
2Jn 6 This is l, that we walk
3Jn 1 Gaius, whom I l in truth
3Jn 6 of your l before the church
Jude 2 and l be multiplied to you
Jude 12 are spots in your l feasts
Jude 21 yourselves in the l of God
Rev 2: 4 you have left your first l
Rev 2:19 I know your works, l, service
Rev 3:19 As many as I l, I rebuke and
Rev 12:11 they did not l their lives to

LOVED (*see* LOVE)

Gen 24:67 became his wife, and he l her
Gen 25:28 Isaac l Esau because he ate
Gen 25:28 his game, but Rebekah l Jacob
Gen 27:14 food, such as his father l
Gen 29:18 Now Jacob l Rachel
Gen 29:30 he also l Rachel more than
Gen 34: 3 he l the young woman and spoke
Gen 37: 3 Now Israel l Joseph more than
Gen 37: 4 l him more than all his
Deut 4:37 because He l your fathers,
Deut 21:15 If a man has two wives, one l
Deut 21:15 him children, both the l and
Deut 21:16 status on the son of the l
Judg 16: 4 it happened that he l a woman
1Sa 1: 5 portion, for he l Hannah,
1Sa 16:21 And he l him greatly, and he
1Sa 18: 1 Jonathan l him as his own
1Sa 18: 3 because he l him as his own
1Sa 18:16 all Israel and Judah l David
1Sa 18:20 Saul's daughter, l David
1Sa 18:28 Saul's daughter, l him
1Sa 20:17 to vow, because he l him
1Sa 20:17 l him as he l his own soul
2Sa 12:24 And the LORD l him
2Sa 13: 1 Amnon the son of David l her
2Sa 13:15 love with which he had l her
1Ki 3: 3 Solomon l the LORD, walking
1Ki 5: 1 for Hiram had always l David
1Ki 10: 9 the LORD has l Israel forever
1Ki 11: 1 But King Solomon l many
2Ch 9: 8 Because your God has l Israel
2Ch 11:21 Now Rehoboam l Maacah the
2Ch 26:10 in Carmel, for he l the soil
Esth 2:17 The king l Esther more than
Ps 26: 8 I have l the habitation of
Ps 38:11 My l ones and my friends stand
Ps 78:68 Judah, Mount Zion which He l
Ps 88:18 L one and friend You have put
Ps 109:17 As he l cursing, so let it
Is 43: 4 been honored, and I have l you
Is 57: 8 you have l their bed, where
Jer 2:25 For I have l aliens, and after
Jer 8: 2 of heaven, which they have l
Jer 14:10 Thus they have l to wander
Jer 31: 3 Yes, I have l you with an
Ezek 16:37 pleasure, all those you l
Hos 3: 1 a woman who is l by a lover
Hos 9: 1 You have l for reward on
Hos 9:10 like the thing they l
Hos 11: 1 I l him, and out of Egypt I
Mal 1: 2 I have l you," says the LORD
Mal 1: 2 In what way have You l us
Mal 1: 2 Yet Jacob I have l
Mark 10:21 him, l him, and said to him,
Luke 7:47 are forgiven, for she l much
John 3:16 For God so l the world that
John 3:19 men l darkness rather than
John 11: 5 Now Jesus l Martha and her
John 11:36 See how He l him
John 12:43 for they l the praise of men
John 13: 1 having l His own who were in
John 13: 1 world, He l them to the end
John 13:23 His disciples, whom Jesus l
John 13:34 as I have l you, that you
John 14:21 Me will be l by My Father
John 14:28 If you l Me, you would

John 15: 9 As the Father l Me, I also
John 15: 9 l Me, I also have l you
John 15:12 one another as I have l you
John 16:27 you, because you have l Me
John 17:23 l them as You have l Me
John 17:24 for You l Me before the
John 17:26 which You l Me may be in them
John 19:26 whom He l standing by, He
John 20: 2 other disciple, whom Jesus l
John 21: 7 whom Jesus l said to Peter
John 21:20 whom Jesus l following, who
Rom 8:37 through Him who l us
Rom 9:13 Jacob I have l, but Esau I
2Co 12:15 I love you, the less I am l
Gal 2:20 in the Son of God, who l me
Eph 2: 4 great love with which He l us
Eph 5: 2 love, as Christ also has l us
Eph 5:25 as Christ also l the church
2Th 2:16 God and Father, who has l us
2Ti 4: 8 all who have l His appearing
2Ti 4:10 having l this present world,
Heb 1: 9 You have l righteousness and
2Pe 2:15 of Beor, who l the wages of
1Jn 4:10 is love, not that we l God
1Jn 4:10 but that He l us
1Jn 4:11 Beloved, if God so l us, we
1Jn 4:19 Him because He first l us
Rev 1: 5 To Him who l us and washed us
Rev 3: 9 and to know that I have l you

LOVELIEST (*see* LOVELY)
1Ki 20: 3 your l wives and children are

LOVELINESS (*see* LOVELY)
Is 40: 6 all its l is like the flower

LOVELY (*see* LOVELIEST, LOVELINESS)
Num 24: 5 How l are your tents, O Jacob
2Sa 13: 1 son of David had a l sister
1Ki 1: 3 So they sought for a l young
1Ki 1: 4 the young woman was very l
Esth 2: 7 The young woman was l and
Ps 84: 1 How l is Your tabernacle, O
Prov 11:22 so is a l woman who lacks
Song 1: 5 I am dark, but l, O daughters
Song 1:10 cheeks are l with ornaments
Song 2:14 and your countenance is l
Song 4: 3 scarlet, and your mouth is l
Song 5:16 yes, he is altogether l
Song 6: 4 l as Jerusalem, awesome as an
Jer 6: 2 the daughter of Zion to a l
Jer 11:16 name, Green Olive Tree, L
Ezek 33:32 very l song of one who has a
Dan 4:12 Its leaves were l, its fruit
Dan 4:21 whose leaves were l and its
Phil 4: 8 pure, whatever things are l

LOVER (*see* LOVE, LOVERS)
Hos 3: 1 a woman who is loved by a l
Tit 1: 8 a l of what is good,

LOVERS (*see* LOVER)
Jer 3: 1 played the harlot with many l
Jer 4:30 your l will despise you
Jer 22:20 for all your l are destroyed
Jer 22:22 and your l shall go into
Jer 30:14 All your l have forgotten you
Lam 1: 2 among all her l she has none
Lam 1:19 I called for my l, but they
Ezek 16:33 your payments to all your l
Ezek 16:36 in your harlotry with your l
Ezek 16:37 I will gather all your l with
Ezek 16:41 and you shall no longer hire l
Ezek 23: 5 and she lusted for her l, the
Ezek 23: 9 her into the hand of her l
Ezek 23:22 stir up your l against you
Hos 2: 5 said, "I will go after my l
Hos 2: 7 She will chase her l, but not
Hos 2:10 in the sight of her l, and no
Hos 2:12 that my l have given me
Hos 2:13 jewelry, And went after her l
Hos 8: 9 Ephraim has hired l
Luke 16:14 who were l of money, also
2Ti 3: 2 men will be l of themselves
2Ti 3: 2 l of money, boasters, proud,
2Ti 3: 4 l of pleasure rather than
2Ti 3: 4 pleasure rather than l of God

LOVE'S (*see* LOVE)
Phm 9 yet for l sake I rather

LOVES (*see* LOVE)
Gen 27: 9 for your father, such as he l
Gen 44:20 children, and his father l him
Deut 7: 8 but because the LORD l you
Deut 10:18 l the stranger, giving him
Deut 15:16 from you,' because he l you
Deut 23: 5 the LORD your God l you
Deut 33: 3 Yes, He l the people
Ruth 4:15 daughter-in-law, who l you
2Ch 2:11 Because the LORD l His people
Ps 11: 5 the one who l violence His
Ps 11: 7 righteous, He l righteousness
Ps 33: 5 He l righteousness and justice
Ps 34:12 l many days, that he may see
Ps 37:28 For the LORD l justice, And
Ps 47: 4 excellence of Jacob whom He l
Ps 87: 2 The LORD l the gates of Zion
Ps 99: 4 strength also l justice
Ps 119:140 Therefore Your servant l it
Ps 146: 8 The LORD l the righteous
Prov 3:12 whom the LORD l He corrects
Prov 12: 1 l instruction l knowledge
Prov 13:24 but he who l him disciplines
Prov 15: 9 but He l him who follows
Prov 17:17 A friend l at all times, and a
Prov 17:19 who l transgression l strife
Prov 19: 8 gets wisdom l his own soul
Prov 21:17 He who l pleasure will be a
Prov 21:17 he who l wine and oil will not
Prov 22:11 He who l purity of heart and
Prov 29: 3 Whoever l wisdom makes his
Eccl 5:10 He who l silver will not be
Eccl 5:10 nor he who l abundance, with
Is 1:23 Everyone l bribes, and follows
Is 48:14 The LORD l him
Hos 10:11 heifer that l to thresh grain
Hos 12: 7 he l to oppress
Mal 2:11 holy institution which He l
Matt 10:37 He who l father or mother
Matt 10:37 he who l son or daughter more
Luke 7: 5 for he l our nation, and has
Luke 7:47 forgiven, the same l little
John 3:35 The Father l the Son, and has
John 5:20 For the Father l the Son, and
John 10:17 Therefore My Father l Me,
John 12:25 He who l his life will lose
John 14:21 keeps them, it is he who l Me
John 14:21 he who l Me will be loved by
John 14:23 If anyone l Me, he will keep
John 16:27 for the Father Himself l you
Rom 13: 8 for he who l another has
1Co 8: 3 But if anyone l God, this one
2Co 9: 7 for God l a cheerful giver
Eph 5:28 who l his wife l himself
Heb 12: 6 whom the LORD l He chastens
1Jn 2:10 He who l his brother abides
1Jn 2:15 If anyone l the world, the
1Jn 4: 7 everyone who l is born of God
1Jn 4:21 that he who l God must love
1Jn 5: 1 who l Him who begot also l
3Jn 9 who l to have the preeminence
Rev 22:15 and idolaters, and whoever l

LOVESICK (*see* LOVE)
Song 2: 5 me with apples, for I am l
Song 5: 8 that you tell him I am l

LOVING (*see* LOVE, LOVINGLY)
Prov 5:19 As a l deer and a graceful doe
Prov 22: 1 l favor rather than silver and
Is 56:10 lying down, l to slumber

LOVINGKINDNESS (*see* LOVE, LOVINGKINDNESSES)
Ps 17: 7 l by Your right hand, O You
Ps 26: 3 For Your l is before my eyes,
Ps 36: 7 How precious is Your l, O God
Ps 36:10 continue Your l to those who
Ps 40:10 I have not concealed Your l
Ps 40:11 Let Your l and Your truth
Ps 42: 8 command His l in the daytime
Ps 48: 9 thought, O God, on Your l
Ps 51: 1 O God, According to Your l
Ps 63: 3 Because Your l is better than
Ps 69:16 O LORD, for Your l is good
Ps 88:11 Shall Your l be declared in
Ps 89:33 Nevertheless My l I will not
Ps 92: 2 declare Your l in the morning
Ps 103: 4 Who crowns you with l and
Ps 107:43 understand the l of the LORD
Ps 119:88 Revive me according to Your l
Ps 119:149 my voice according to Your l
Ps 119:159 O LORD, according to Your l
Ps 138: 2 praise Your name For Your l
Ps 143: 8 to hear Your l in the morning
Ps 144: 2 My l and my fortress, My high
Prov 20:28 by l he upholds his throne
Jer 9:24 I am the LORD, exercising l
Jer 16: 5 says the LORD, "l and mercies
Jer 31: 3 therefore with l I have drawn
Jer 32:18 You show l to thousands, and
Hos 2:19 and justice, in l and mercy
Jon 4: 2 to anger and abundant in l

LOVINGKINDNESSES (*see* LOVINGKINDNESS)
Ps 25: 6 Your tender mercies and Your l
Ps 89:49 Lord, where are Your former l
Is 63: 7 mention the l of the LORD
Is 63: 7 to the multitude of His l

LOVINGLY (*see* LOVING)
Is 38:17 but You have l delivered my

LOW (*see* PREFACE)

LOWER (*see* PREFACE)

LOWEST (*see* PREFACE)

LOWING
1Sa 6:12 l as they went, and did not
1Sa 15:14 the l of the oxen which I

LOWLAND (*see* LOWLANDS)
Deut 1: 7 in the mountains and in the l
Josh 9: 1 in the hills and in the l
Josh 10:40 country and the South and the l
Josh 11: 2 south of Chinneroth, in the l
Josh 11:16 all the land of Goshen, the l
Josh 15:33 In the l
Judg 1: 9 in the South, and in the l
Judg 1:19 out the inhabitants of the l
1Ki 10:27 sycamores which are in the l
2Ch 1:15 sycamores which are in the l
2Ch 9:27 sycamores which are in the l
2Ch 28:18 invaded the cities of the l
Jer 17:26 of Benjamin and from the l
Jer 32:44 in the cities of the l, and
Jer 33:13 in the cities of the l, in
Obad 19 of the Philistine l
Zech 7: 7 South and the L were inhabited

LOWLANDS (*see* LOWLAND)
Josh 11:16 mountains of Israel and its l
Josh 12: 8 mountain country, in the l
1Ch 27:28 trees that were in the l, and
2Ch 26:10 much livestock, both in the l

LOWLIEST (*see* LOWLY)
Ezek 29:15 It shall be the l of kingdoms

LOWLINESS (*see* LOWLY)
Eph 4: 2 with all l and gentleness,
Phil 2: 3 but in l of mind let each

LOWLY (*see* LOWLIEST, LOWLINESS)
Job 5:11 sets on high those who are l
Ps 136:23 remembered us in our l state
Ps 138: 6 on high, Yet He regards the l
Prov 16:19 of a humble spirit with the l
Eccl 10: 6 the rich sit in a l place
Ezek 21:26 Exalt the l, and abase the
Ezek 29:14 they shall be a l kingdom
Zech 9: 9 just and having salvation, l
Matt 11:29 l in heart, and you will find
Matt 21: 5 your King is coming to you, l
Luke 1:48 For He has regarded the l
Luke 1:52 thrones, and exalted the l
2Co 10: 1 in presence am l among you
Phil 3:21 our l body that it may be
Jas 1: 9 Let the l brother glory in

LOYAL (*see* LOYALTY)
2Sa 20: 2 remained l to their king
1Ki 8:61 be l to the LORD our God, to
1Ki 11: 4 his heart was not l to the
1Ki 15: 3 his heart was not l to the
1Ki 15:14 Asa's heart was l to the LORD
2Ki 20: 3 in truth and with a l heart
1Ch 12:29 l to the house of Saul)
1Ch 12:38 came to Hebron with a l heart
1Ch 28: 9 and serve Him with a l heart
1Ch 29: 9 because with a l heart they
1Ch 29:19 a l heart to keep Your
2Ch 15:17 of Asa was l all his days
2Ch 16: 9 those whose heart is l to Him
2Ch 19: 9 faithfully and with a l heart
2Ch 25: 2 LORD, but not with a l heart
Is 38: 3 in truth and with a l heart

Matt 6:24 else he will be l to the one
Luke 16:13 else he will be l to the one

LOYALTY (*see* LOYAL)
2Sa 3: 8 Today I show l to the house
2Sa 16:17 Is this your l to your friend

LUBIM (*see* LEHABIM)
2Ch 12: 3 the L and the Sukkiim and the
2Ch 16: 8 the L not a huge army with
Nah 3: 9 Put and L were your helpers

LUCIFER
Is 14:12 are fallen from heaven, O L

LUCIUS
Acts 13: 1 L of Cyrene, Manaen who had
Rom 16:21 my fellow worker, and L,

LUD (*see* LUDIM, LYDIA)
Gen 10:22 Elam, Asshur, Arphaxad, L
1Ch 1:17 Elam, Asshur, Arphaxad, L
Is 66:19 to Tarshish and Pul and L, who

LUDIM (*see* LUD, LYDIA)
Gen 10:13 Mizraim begot L, Anamim,
1Ch 1:11 Mizraim begot L, Anamim,

LUHITH
Is 15: 5 of L they will go up with
Jer 48: 5 For in the ascent of L they

LUKE
Col 4:14 L the beloved physician and
2Ti 4:11 Only L is with me
Phm 24 Mark, Aristarchus, Demas, L

LUKEWARM
Rev 3:16 So then, because you are l

LULLED
Judg 16:19 Then she l him to sleep on

LUMP
2Ki 20: 7 said, "Take a l of figs
Is 38:21 Let them take a l of figs
Rom 9:21 from the same l to make one
Rom 11:16 is holy, the l is also holy
1Co 5: 6 leaven leavens the whole l
1Co 5: 7 that you may be a new l,
Gal 5: 9 leaven leavens the whole l

LUNGE
Joel 2: 8 And when they l between the

LURK (*see* LURKED, LURKING)
Job 38:40 or l in their lairs to lie in
Prov 1:11 Let us l secretly for the
Prov 1:18 They l secretly for their own

LURKED (*see* LURK)
Job 31: 9 a woman, or if I have l at my

LURKING (*see* LURK)
1Sa 23:23 the l places where he hides
Ps 10: 8 He sits in the l places of
Ps 17:12 as a young lion l in secret
Prov 7:12 square, l at every corner

LUST (*see* LUSTED, LUSTFUL, LUSTS, LUSTY)
Prov 6:25 Do not l after her beauty in
Prov 11: 6 will be taken by their own l
Matt 5:28 to l for her has already
Rom 1:27 in their l for one another
1Co 10: 6 l after evil things as they
Gal 5:16 fulfill the l of the flesh
1Th 4: 5 not in passion of l, like the
Jas 4: 2 You l and do not have
2Pe 1: 4 is in the world through l
2Pe 2:10 flesh in the l of uncleanness
1Jn 2:16 the l of the flesh
1Jn 2:16 the l of the eyes
1Jn 2:17 passing away, and the l of it

LUSTED (*see* LUST)
Ps 106:14 But l exceedingly in the
Ezek 23: 5 she l for her lovers, the
Ezek 23: 7 and with all for whom she l
Ezek 23: 9 the Assyrians, for whom she l
Ezek 23:12 She l for the neighboring
Ezek 23:16 them, she l for them and sent
Ezek 23:20 For she l for her paramours,
1Co 10: 6 evil things as they also l

LUSTFUL (*see* LUST)
Jer 13:27 and your l neighings, the

LUSTS (*see* LUST)
Rom 1:24 in the l of their hearts, to
Rom 6:12 you should obey it in its l
Rom 13:14 the flesh, to fulfill its l
Gal 5:17 For the flesh l against the
Eph 2: 3 in the l of our flesh,
Eph 4:22 according to the deceitful l
1Ti 6: 9 harmful l which drown men in
2Ti 2:22 Flee also youthful l
2Ti 3: 6 sins, led away by various l
Tit 2:12 ungodliness and worldly l, we
Tit 3: 3 deceived, serving various l
1Pe 1:14 yourselves to the former l
1Pe 2:11 abstain from fleshly l which
1Pe 4: 2 in the flesh for the l of men
1Pe 4: 3 walked in licentiousness, l
2Pe 2:18 through the l of the flesh
2Pe 3: 3 according to their own l,
Jude 16 according to their own l
Jude 18 to their own ungodly l

LUSTY (*see* LUST)
Jer 5: 8 like well-fed l stallions

LUTE
Ps 57: 8 Awake, l and harp
Ps 71:22 Also with the l I will praise
Ps 81: 2 The pleasant harp with the l
Ps 92: 3 of ten strings, On the l, And
Ps 108: 2 Awake, l and harp
Ps 150: 3 Praise Him with the l and harp

LUXURIOUSLY (*see* LUXURY)
Rev 18: 7 glorified herself and lived l
Rev 18: 9 lived l with her will weep and

LUXURY (*see* LUXURIOUSLY)
2Sa 1:24 you in scarlet, with l
Prov 19:10 L is not fitting for a fool,
Ezek 27:12 because of your many l goods
Ezek 27:18 because of your many l items
Ezek 27:33 earth with your many l goods
Luke 7:25 and live in l are in kings'
Jas 5: 5 on the earth in pleasure and l
Rev 18: 3 the abundance of her l

LUZ
Gen 28:19 city had been L previously
Gen 35: 6 So Jacob came to L (that is
Gen 48: 3 me at L in the land of Canaan
Josh 16: 2 went out from Bethel to L
Josh 18:13 went over from there toward L
Josh 18:13 to the side of L (which is
Judg 1:23 of the city was formerly L
Judg 1:26 a city, and called its name L

LYCAONIA
Acts 14: 6 Lystra and Derbe, cities of L

LYCAONIAN
Acts 14:11 saying in the L language

LYCIA
Acts 27: 5 we came to Myra, a city of L

LYDDA (*see* LOD)
Acts 9:32 to the saints who dwelt in L
Acts 9:35 So all who dwelt at L and
Acts 9:38 since L was near Joppa, and

LYDIA (*see* LUD, LUDIM, LYDIANS)
Ezek 27:10 Those from Persia, L, and
Ezek 30: 5 Ethiopia, Libya, L, all the
Acts 16:14 woman named L heard us
Acts 16:40 and entered the house of L

LYDIANS (*see* LYDIA)
Jer 46: 9 the L who handle and bend the

LYE
Jer 2:22 you wash yourself with l, and

LYING (*see* LIE)
Gen 29: 2 three flocks of sheep l by it
Gen 34: 7 thing in Israel by l with
Gen 49:14 l down between two burdens
Ex 23: 5 hates you l under its burden
Lev 6: 2 against the LORD by l to his
Num 35:20 or, while l in wait, hurls
Num 35:22 at him without l in wait,
Deut 21: 1 l in the field in the land
Deut 22:22 If a man is found l with a
Deut 33:13 dew, and the deep l beneath
Judg 7:12 East, were l in the valley as
Judg 9:35 with him rose from l in wait
Judg 16: 9 Now there were men l in wait
Judg 16:12 And there were men l in wait
Ruth 3: 8 a woman was l at his feet
1Sa 3: 2 while Eli was l down in his
1Sa 3: 3 Samuel was l down to sleep
2Sa 4: 5 who was l on his bed at noon
2Sa 4: 7 he was l on his bed in his
2Sa 13: 8 and he was l down
1Ki 22:22 be a l spirit in the mouth of
1Ki 22:23 The LORD has put a l spirit
2Ki 4:32 the child, l dead on his bed
2Ch 18:21 be a l spirit in the mouth of
2Ch 18:22 The LORD has put a l spirit
Ps 31:18 Let the l lips be put to
Ps 52: 3 And l rather than speaking
Ps 59:12 cursing and l which they speak
Ps 109: 2 against me with a l tongue
Ps 119:29 Remove from me the way of l
Ps 119:163 I hate and abhor l, But I love
Ps 120: 2 my soul, O LORD, from l lips
Ps 139: 3 my l down, And are acquainted
Prov 6:17 a l tongue, hands that shed
Prov 10:18 hides hatred has l lips, and
Prov 12:19 but a l tongue is but for a
Prov 12:22 L lips are an abomination to
Prov 13: 5 A righteous man hates l, but
Prov 17: 7 much less l lips to a prince
Prov 21: 6 by a l tongue is the fleeting
Prov 26:28 A l tongue hates those who
Is 30: 9 l children, children who will
Is 32: 7 destroy the poor with l words
Is 56:10 l down, loving to slumber
Is 59:13 and l against the LORD, and
Jer 7: 4 Do not trust in these l words
Jer 7: 8 you trust in l words that
Jer 29:23 have spoken l words in My
Lam 3:10 to me like a bear l in wait
Ezek 13:19 by your l to My people who
Ezek 36:34 of l desolate in the sight of
Dan 2: 9 you have agreed to speak l
Hos 4: 2 By swearing and l, killing and
Matt 8: 6 Lord, my servant is l at home
Matt 8:14 mother l sick with a fever
Matt 9: 2 to Him a paralytic l on a bed
Mark 2: 4 on which the paralytic was l
Mark 5:40 entered where the child was l
Mark 7:30 and her daughter l on the bed
Luke 2:12 cloths, l in a manger
Luke 2:16 and the Babe l in a manger
Luke 5:25 took up what he had been l on
Luke 11:54 l in wait for Him, and seeking
Luke 24:12 linen cloths l by themselves
John 5: 6 When Jesus saw him l there
John 11:41 where the dead man was l
John 20: 5 saw the linen cloths l there
John 20: 6 saw the linen cloths l there
John 20: 7 not l with the linen cloths,
Rom 9: 1 truth in Christ, I am not l
2Co 11:31 knows that I am not l
Eph 4:25 Therefore, putting away l
2Th 2: 9 power, signs, and l wonders,
1Ti 2: 7 the truth in Christ and not l

LYRE
Dan 3: 5 of the horn, flute, harp, l
Dan 3: 7 the horn, flute, harp, and l
Dan 3:10 of the horn, flute, harp, l
Dan 3:15 of the horn, flute, harp, l

LYSANIAS
Luke 3: 1 and L tetrarch of Abilene,

LYSIAS
Acts 23:26 Claudius L, to the most
Acts 24: 7 But the commander L came by
Acts 24:22 When L the commander comes

LYSTRA
Acts 14: 6 aware of it and fled to L and
Acts 14: 8 in L a certain man without
Acts 14:21 disciples, they returned to L
Acts 16: 1 Then he came to Derbe and L
Acts 16: 2 by the brethren who were at L
2Ti 3:11 at Antioch, at Iconium, at L

M

MAACAH (*see* MAACATHITE, MAACHAH)
2Sa 3: 3 third, Absalom the son of **M**
2Sa 10: 6 from King **M** one thousand men,
2Sa 10: 8 **M** were by themselves in the
1Ch 3: 2 third, Absalom the son of **M**
1Ch 8:29 whose wife's name was **M**,
1Ch 9:35 whose wife's name was **M**,
2Ch 11:20 After her he took **M** the
2Ch 11:21 Now Rehoboam loved **M** the
2Ch 11:22 Abijah the son of **M** as chief
2Ch 15:16 Also he removed **M**, the mother

MAACATHITE (*see* MAACAH, MAACATHITES)
2Sa 23:34 of Ahasbai, the son of the **M**

MAACATHITES (*see* MAACATHITE)
Deut 3:14 of the Geshurites and the **M**

MAACHAH (*see* BETH MAACHAH, MAACAH, MAACHATHITE)
Gen 22:24 Gaham, Thahash, and **M**
1Ki 2:39 away to Achish the son of **M**
1Ki 15: 2 was **M** the granddaughter of
1Ki 15:10 was **M** the granddaughter of
1Ki 15:13 Also he removed **M** his
1Ch 2:48 **M**, Caleb's concubine, bore
1Ch 7:15 Shuppim, whose name was **M**
1Ch 7:16 (**M** the wife of Machir bore a
1Ch 11:43 Hanan the son of **M**, Joshaphat
1Ch 19: 6 Mesopotamia, from Syrian **M**
1Ch 19: 7 chariots, with the king of **M**
1Ch 27:16 Shephatiah the son of **M**

MAACHATHITE (*see* MAACHAH, MAACHATHITES)
2Ki 25:23 and Jaazaniah the son of a **M**
1Ch 4:19 Garmite and of Eshtemoa the **M**
Jer 40: 8 and Jezaniah the son of a **M**

MAACHATHITES (*see* MAACHATHITE)
Josh 12: 5 of the Geshurites and the **M**
Josh 13:11 border of the Geshurites and **M**
Josh 13:13 out the Geshurites or the **M**
Josh 13:13 and the **M** dwell among the

MAADAI
Ezra 10:34 **M**, Amram, Uel,

MAADIAH (*see* MOADIAH)
Neh 12: 5 Mijamin, **M**, Bilgah,

MAAI
Neh 12:36 Azarel, Milalai, Gilalai, **M**

MAARATH
Josh 15:59 **M**, Beth Anoth, and Eltekon

MAASAI
1Ch 9:12 **M** the son of Adiel, the son

MAASEIAH
1Ch 15:18 Unni, Eliab, Benaiah, **M**,
1Ch 15:20 Jehiel, Unni, Eliab, **M**, and
2Ch 23: 1 Obed, **M** the son of Adaiah, and
2Ch 26:11 **M** the officer, under the hand
2Ch 28: 7 killed **M** the king's son,
2Ch 34: 8 **M** the governor of the city,
Ezra 10:18 **M**, Eliezer, Jarib, and
Ezra 10:21 **M**, Elijah, Shemaiah, Jehiel,
Ezra 10:22 Elioenai, **M**, Ishmael,
Ezra 10:30 Adna, Chelal, Benaiah, **M**,
Neh 3:23 them Azariah the son of **M**
Neh 8: 4 Anaiah, Urijah, Hilkiah, and **M**
Neh 8: 7 Shabbethai, Hodijah, **M**
Neh 10:25 Rehum, Hashabnah, **M**,
Neh 11: 5 **M** the son of Baruch, the son
Neh 11: 7 son of Kolaiah, the son of **M**
Neh 12:41 and the priests, Eliakim, **M**
Neh 12:42 also **M**, Shemaiah, Eleazar,
Jer 21: 1 and Zephaniah the son of **M**
Jer 29:21 and Zedekiah the son of **M**
Jer 29:25 the son of **M** the priest, and
Jer 35: 4 of **M** the son of Shallum, the
Jer 37: 3 and Zephaniah the son of **M**

MAATH
Luke 3:26 the son of **M**, the son of

MAAZ
1Ch 2:27 of Jerahmeel, were **M**, Jamin,

MAAZIAH
1Ch 24:18 the twenty-fourth to **M**
Neh 10: 8 **M**, Bilgai, and Shemaiah

MACEDONIA (*see* MACEDONIAN)
Acts 16: 9 A man of **M** stood and pleaded
Acts 16: 9 Come over to **M** and help us
Acts 16:10 we sought to go to **M**,
Acts 16:12 city of that part of **M**, a
Acts 18: 5 and Timothy had come from **M**
Acts 19:21 when he had passed through **M**
Acts 19:22 So he sent into **M** two of
Acts 20: 1 them, and departed to go to **M**
Acts 20: 3 decided to return through **M**
Rom 15:26 For it pleased those from **M**
1Co 16: 5 **M** (for I am passing through
1Co 16: 5 (for I am passing through **M**)
2Co 1:16 to pass by way of you to **M**
2Co 1:16 to come again from **M** to you
2Co 2:13 of them, I departed for **M**
2Co 7: 5 For indeed, when we came to **M**
2Co 8: 1 bestowed on the churches of **M**
2Co 11: 9 who came from **M** supplied
Phil 4:15 when I departed from **M**, no
1Th 1: 7 became examples to all in **M**
1Th 1: 8 sounded forth, not only in **M**
1Th 4:10 the brethren who are in all **M**
1Ti 1: 3 urged you when I went into **M**

MACEDONIAN (*see* MACEDONIA, MACEDONIANS)
Acts 27: 2 a **M** of Thessalonica, was with

MACEDONIANS (*see* MACEDONIAN)
Acts 19:29 Gaius and Aristarchus, **M**,
2Co 9: 2 which I boast of you to the **M**
2Co 9: 4 lest if some **M** come with me

MACHBANAI
1Ch 12:13 the tenth, and **M** the eleventh

MACHBENAH
1Ch 2:49 Sheva the father of **M** and the

MACHI
Num 13:15 of Gad, Geuel the son of **M**

MACHIR (*see* MACHIRITES)
Gen 50:23 The children of **M**, the son of
Num 26:29 of **M**, the family of the
Num 26:29 and **M** begot Gilead
Num 27: 1 son of Gilead, the son of **M**
Num 32:39 the children of **M** the son of
Num 32:40 to **M** the son of Manasseh, and
Num 36: 1 of Gilead the son of **M**, the
Deut 3:15 And I gave Gilead to **M**
Josh 13:31 of **M** the son of Manasseh, for
Josh 13:31 **M** according to their families
Josh 17: 1 namely for **M** the firstborn of
Josh 17: 3 son of Gilead, the son of **M**
Judg 5:14 from **M** rulers came down, and
2Sa 9: 4 house of **M** the son of Ammiel
2Sa 9: 5 house of **M** the son of Ammiel
2Sa 17:27 **M** the son of Ammiel from Lo
1Ch 2:21 of **M** the father of Gilead
1Ch 2:23 of **M** the father of Gilead
1Ch 7:14 him **M** the father of Gilead
1Ch 7:15 **M** took as his wife the sister
1Ch 7:16 the wife of **M** bore a son, and
1Ch 7:17 of Gilead the son of **M**, the

MACHIRITES (*see* MACHIR)
Num 26:29 Machir, the family of the **M**

MACHNADEBAI
Ezra 10:40 **M**, Shashai, Sharai,

MACHPELAH
Gen 23: 9 me the cave of **M** which he has
Gen 23:17 of Ephron which was in **M**,
Gen 23:19 in the cave of the field of **M**
Gen 25: 9 buried him in the cave of **M**
Gen 49:30 that is in the field of **M**
Gen 50:13 in the cave of the field of **M**

MAD (*see* MADMAN, MADNESS)
Deut 28:34 So you shall be driven **m**
Is 44:25 and drives diviners **m**
Jer 25:16 go **m** because of the sword
John 10:20 He has a demon and is **m**
Acts 26:24 learning is driving you **m**
Acts 26:25 I am not **m**, most noble Festus

MADAI (*see* MEDIA)
Gen 10: 2 were Gomer, Magog, **M**
1Ch 1: 5 were Gomer, Magog, **M**

MADE (*see* MAKE)
Gen 1: 7 Thus God **m** the firmament, and
Gen 1:16 Then God **m** two great lights
Gen 1:16 He **m** the stars also
Gen 1:25 God **m** the beast of the earth
Gen 1:31 saw everything that He had **m**
Gen 2: 3 which God had created and **m**
Gen 2: 4 that the LORD God **m** the earth
Gen 2: 9 God **m** every tree grow that is
Gen 2:22 from man He **m** into a woman
Gen 3: 1 which the LORD God had **m**
Gen 3: 7 and **m** themselves coverings
Gen 3:21 the LORD God **m** tunics of skin
Gen 5: 1 He **m** him in the likeness of
Gen 6: 6 He had **m** man on the earth
Gen 6: 7 I am sorry that I have **m** them
Gen 7: 4 living things that I have **m**
Gen 8: 1 God **m** a wind to pass over the
Gen 8: 6 of the ark which he had **m**
Gen 9: 6 in the image of God He **m** man
Gen 13: 4 which he had **m** there at first
Gen 14: 2 that they **m** war with Bera
Gen 14:23 say, I have **m** Abram rich'
Gen 15:18 LORD **m** a covenant with Abram
Gen 17: 5 for I have **m** you a father of
Gen 19: 3 Then he **m** them a feast, and
Gen 19:33 So they **m** their father drink
Gen 19:35 Then they **m** their father
Gen 21: 6 God has **m** me laugh, so that
Gen 21: 8 Abraham **m** a great feast on
Gen 21:27 the two of them **m** a covenant
Gen 21:32 Thus they **m** a covenant at
Gen 24:11 he **m** his camels kneel down
Gen 24:21 **m** his journey prosperous or
Gen 24:37 Now my master **m** me swear,
Gen 24:46 And she **m** haste and let her
Gen 26:22 the LORD has **m** room for us
Gen 26:30 So he **m** them a feast, and they
Gen 27:14 his mother **m** savory food,
Gen 27:31 He also had **m** savory food
Gen 27:37 Indeed I have **m** him your
Gen 28:20 Then Jacob **m** a vow, saying
Gen 29:22 men of the place and **m** a feast
Gen 30:40 **m** the flocks face toward the
Gen 31:13 and where you **m** a vow to Me
Gen 31:46 **m** a heap, and they ate there
Gen 33:17 **m** booths for his livestock
Gen 37: 3 Also he **m** him a tunic of many
Gen 39: 3 that the LORD **m** all he did to
Gen 39: 4 Then he **m** him overseer of his
Gen 39: 5 **m** him overseer of his house
Gen 39:23 he did, the LORD **m** it prosper
Gen 40:20 that he **m** a feast for all his
Gen 41:51 For God has **m** me forget all
Gen 43:25 Then they **m** the present ready
Gen 43:30 so Joseph **m** haste and sought
Gen 45: 1 Joseph **m** himself known to his
Gen 45: 8 and He has **m** me a father to
Gen 45: 9 God has **m** me lord of all
Gen 46:29 So Joseph **m** ready his chariot
Gen 47:26 Joseph **m** it a law over the
Gen 49:24 **m** strong by the hands of the
Gen 50: 5 My father **m** me swear, saying
Gen 50: 6 father, as he **m** you swear
Ex 1:13 So the Egyptians **m** the
Ex 1:14 they **m** their lives bitter
Ex 1:14 **m** them serve was with rigor
Ex 2:14 Who **m** you a prince and a judge
Ex 4:11 him, Who has **m** man's mouth
Ex 5: 8 of bricks which they **m** before
Ex 5:21 judge, because you have **m** us
Ex 7: 1 See, I have **m** you as God to
Ex 9:20 of Pharaoh **m** his servants
Ex 14: 6 So he **m** ready his chariot and
Ex 14:21 **m** the sea into dry land, and
Ex 15:17 which You have **m** for Your own
Ex 15:25 the waters were **m** sweet
Ex 15:25 There He **m** a statute and an
Ex 16:31 was like wafers **m** with honey
Ex 18:25 **m** them heads over the people
Ex 20:11 days the LORD **m** the heavens
Ex 21:29 it has been **m** known to his
Ex 24: 8 **m** with you according to all
Ex 25:33 Three bowls shall be **m** like
Ex 25:33 three bowls **m** like almond
Ex 25:34 be **m** like almond blossoms
Ex 25:39 It shall be **m** of a talent of

Ex 26:36 linen thread, **m** by a weaver
Ex 27:16 linen thread, **m** by a weaver
Ex 29:18 an offering **m** by fire to the
Ex 29:23 of bread, one cake **m** with oil
Ex 29:25 It is an offering **m** by fire
Ex 29:33 which the atonement was **m**
Ex 29:41 an offering **m** by fire to the
Ex 30:20 **m** by fire to the LORD, they
Ex 31:17 days the LORD **m** the heavens
Ex 31:18 And when He had **m** an end of
Ex 32: 4 tool, and **m** a molded calf
Ex 32: 5 Aaron **m** a proclamation and
Ex 32: 8 They have **m** themselves a
Ex 32:20 the calf which they had **m**
Ex 32:20 and **m** the children of Israel
Ex 32:31 have **m** for themselves a god
Ex 32:35 with the calf which Aaron **m**
Ex 34: 8 So Moses **m** haste and bowed his
Ex 34:27 I have **m** a covenant with you
Ex 36: 8 worked on the tabernacle **m**
Ex 36: 8 of cherubim they **m** them
Ex 36:11 He **m** loops of blue yarn on
Ex 36:12 loops he **m** on one curtain
Ex 36:12 fifty loops he **m** on the edge
Ex 36:13 he **m** fifty clasps of gold, and
Ex 36:14 He **m** curtains of goats' hair
Ex 36:14 he **m** eleven curtains
Ex 36:17 he **m** fifty loops on the edge
Ex 36:17 fifty loops he **m** on the edge
Ex 36:18 He also **m** fifty bronze clasps
Ex 36:19 Then he **m** a covering for the
Ex 36:20 he **m** boards of acacia wood
Ex 36:22 Thus he **m** for all the boards
Ex 36:23 And he **m** boards for the
Ex 36:24 he **m** to go under the twenty
Ex 36:25 side, he **m** twenty boards
Ex 36:27 tabernacle he **m** six boards
Ex 36:28 He also **m** two boards for the
Ex 36:29 Thus he **m** both of them for
Ex 36:31 And he **m** bars of acacia wood
Ex 36:33 he **m** the middle bar to pass
Ex 36:34 **m** their rings of gold to be
Ex 36:35 he **m** a veil woven of blue and
Ex 36:36 He **m** for it four pillars of
Ex 36:37 He also **m** a screen for the
Ex 36:37 linen thread, **m** by a weaver,
Ex 37: 1 Then Bezaleel **m** the ark of
Ex 37: 2 and **m** a molding of gold all
Ex 37: 4 He **m** poles of acacia wood, and
Ex 37: 6 He also **m** the mercy seat of
Ex 37: 7 He **m** two cherubim of beaten
Ex 37: 7 he **m** them of one piece at the
Ex 37: 8 He **m** the cherubim at the two
Ex 37:10 He **m** the table of acacia wood
Ex 37:11 and **m** a molding of gold all
Ex 37:12 Also he **m** a frame of a
Ex 37:12 **m** a molding of gold for the
Ex 37:15 he **m** the poles of acacia wood
Ex 37:16 He **m** of pure gold the
Ex 37:17 He also **m** the lampstand of
Ex 37:17 work he **m** the lampstand
Ex 37:19 There were three bowls **m** like
Ex 37:19 three bowls **m** like almond
Ex 37:20 bowls **m** like almond blossoms
Ex 37:23 he **m** its seven lamps, its
Ex 37:24 a talent of pure gold he **m** it
Ex 37:25 He **m** the incense altar of
Ex 37:26 He also **m** for it a molding of
Ex 37:27 He **m** two rings of gold for it
Ex 37:28 he **m** the poles of acacia wood
Ex 37:29 He also **m** the holy anointing
Ex 38: 1 He **m** the altar of burnt
Ex 38: 2 He **m** its horns on its four
Ex 38: 3 He **m** all the utensils for the
Ex 38: 3 its utensils he **m** of bronze
Ex 38: 4 And he **m** a grate of bronze
Ex 38: 6 he **m** the poles of acacia wood
Ex 38: 7 He **m** the altar hollow with
Ex 38: 8 He **m** the laver of bronze and
Ex 38: 9 Then he **m** the court on the
Ex 38:22 **m** all that the LORD had
Ex 38:28 he **m** hooks for the pillars
Ex 38:28 capitals, and **m** bands for them
Ex 38:30 with it he **m** the sockets for
Ex 39: 1 and scarlet thread they **m**
Ex 39: 1 **m** the holy garments for Aaron
Ex 39: 2 He **m** the ephod of gold and
Ex 39: 4 They **m** shoulder straps for it
Ex 39: 8 And he **m** the breastplate,
Ex 39: 9 They **m** the breastplate square

Ex 39:15 And they **m** chains for the
Ex 39:16 They also **m** two settings of
Ex 39:19 they **m** two rings of gold and
Ex 39:20 They **m** two other gold rings
Ex 39:22 He **m** the robe of the ephod of
Ex 39:24 They **m** on the hem of the robe
Ex 39:25 they **m** bells of pure gold, and
Ex 39:27 They **m** tunics, artistically
Ex 39:30 Then they **m** the plate of the
Lev 1: 9 an offering **m** by fire, a
Lev 1:13 an offering **m** by fire, a
Lev 1:17 an offering **m** by fire, a
Lev 2: 2 altar, an offering **m** by fire
Lev 2: 3 to the LORD **m** by fire
Lev 2: 7 it shall be **m** of fine flour
Lev 2: 8 the grain offering that is **m**
Lev 2: 9 It is an offering **m** by fire
Lev 2:10 to the LORD **m** by fire
Lev 2:11 LORD shall be **m** with leaven
Lev 2:11 to the LORD **m** by fire
Lev 2:16 as an offering **m** by fire to
Lev 3: 3 **m** by fire to the LORD
Lev 3: 5 as an offering **m** by fire
Lev 3: 9 as an offering **m** by fire to
Lev 3:11 an offering **m** by fire to the
Lev 3:14 as an offering **m** by fire to
Lev 3:16 an offering **m** by fire for a
Lev 4:35 **m** by fire to the LORD
Lev 5:12 **m** by fire to the LORD
Lev 6:17 of My offerings **m** by fire
Lev 6:18 **m** by fire to the LORD
Lev 6:21 It shall be **m** in a pan with
Lev 7: 5 **m** by fire to the LORD
Lev 7:25 **m** by fire to the LORD, the
Lev 7:30 **m** by fire to the LORD
Lev 7:35 from the offerings **m** by fire
Lev 8:21 an offering **m** by fire to the
Lev 8:28 **m** by fire to the LORD
Lev 10:12 **m** by fire to the LORD, and eat
Lev 10:13 of the sacrifices **m** by fire
Lev 10:15 offerings of fat **m** by fire
Lev 10:16 Then Moses diligently **m**
Lev 13:48 or in anything **m** of leather
Lev 13:49 or in anything **m** of leather
Lev 13:51 or in anything **m** of leather
Lev 13:53 or in anything **m** of leather
Lev 13:57 or in anything **m** of leather
Lev 13:58 or whatever is **m** of leather
Lev 13:59 or in anything **m** of leather
Lev 14:11 the man who is to be **m** clean
Lev 14:36 house may not be **m** unclean
Lev 16:20 And when he has **m** an end of
Lev 21: 6 of the LORD **m** by fire, and the
Lev 21:21 **m** by fire to the LORD
Lev 22: 4 **m** unclean by a corpse, or a
Lev 22: 5 which he would be **m** unclean
Lev 22:27 **m** by fire to the LORD
Lev 23: 8 **m** by fire to the LORD for
Lev 23:13 an offering **m** by fire to the
Lev 23:18 an offering **m** by fire for a
Lev 23:25 **m** by fire to the LORD
Lev 23:27 offer an offering **m** by fire
Lev 23:36 **m** by fire to the LORD
Lev 23:36 **m** by fire to the LORD
Lev 23:37 **m** by fire to the LORD, a
Lev 23:43 I **m** the children of Israel
Lev 24: 7 an offering **m** by fire to the
Lev 24: 9 of the LORD **m** by fire, by a
Lev 26:13 yoke and **m** you walk upright
Lev 26:46 the LORD **m** between Himself
Num 4:26 and all that is **m** for these
Num 5: 8 may be **m** for the wrong, the
Num 5: 8 which atonement is **m** for him
Num 5:27 When he has **m** her drink the
Num 6: 3 **m** from wine nor vinegar **m**
Num 7: 2 were numbered, **m** an offering
Num 8: 4 Moses, so he **m** the lampstand
Num 8:21 Aaron **m** atonement for them to
Num 11: 8 it in pans, and **m** cakes of it
Num 14:36 **m** all the congregation murmur
Num 15:10 wine as an offering **m** by fire
Num 15:13 an offering **m** by fire, a
Num 15:14 present an offering **m** by fire
Num 15:25 an offering **m** by fire to the
Num 16:38 let them be **m** into hammered
Num 16:47 **m** atonement for the people
Num 18:17 their fat as an offering **m** by
Num 20: 5 why have you **m** us come up out
Num 21: 2 So Israel **m** a vow to the LORD
Num 21: 9 So Moses **m** a bronze serpent,

Num 25:13 **m** atonement for the children
Num 28: 2 My food for My offerings **m** by
Num 28: 3 This is the offering **m** by
Num 28: 6 an offering **m** by fire to the
Num 28: 8 it as an offering **m** by fire
Num 28:13 an offering **m** by fire to the
Num 28:19 shall present an offering **m**
Num 28:24 **m** by fire daily for seven
Num 29: 6 an offering **m** by fire to the
Num 29:13 an offering **m** by fire as a
Num 29:36 an offering **m** by fire as a
Num 30:11 **m** no response to her and did
Num 30:12 **m** them void on the day he
Num 30:12 her husband has **m** them void
Num 30:14 because he **m** no response to
Num 31:20 everything **m** of leather,
Num 31:20 hair, and everything **m** of wood
Num 32:13 and He **m** them wander in the
Num 35:33 can be **m** for the land, for
Deut 1:15 and **m** them heads over you,
Deut 2:30 **m** his heart obstinate, that
Deut 4:23 your God which He **m** with you
Deut 5: 2 The LORD our God **m** a covenant
Deut 9: 9 which the LORD **m** with you
Deut 9:12 they have **m** themselves a
Deut 9:16 had **m** for yourselves a molded
Deut 9:21 sin, the calf which you had **m**
Deut 10: 3 So I **m** an ark of acacia wood,
Deut 10: 5 in the ark which I had **m**
Deut 10:22 now the LORD your God has **m**
Deut 11: 4 how He **m** the waters of the
Deut 18: 1 of the LORD **m** by fire, and His
Deut 26:19 all nations which He has **m**
Deut 29: 1 which He **m** with them in Horeb
Deut 29:25 which He **m** with them when He
Deut 31:16 which I have **m** with them
Deut 32: 6 has He not **m** you and
Deut 32:13 He **m** him ride in the heights
Deut 32:13 He **m** him to draw honey from
Deut 32:15 then he forsook God who **m** him
Josh 2:17 which you have **m** us swear
Josh 2:20 oath which you **m** us swear
Josh 5: 3 So Joshua **m** flint knives for
Josh 8:15 all Israel **m** as if they were
Josh 8:24 to pass when Israel had **m** an
Josh 8:28 Ai and **m** it a heap forever, a
Josh 9:15 So Joshua **m** peace with them,
Josh 9:15 **m** a covenant with them to let
Josh 9:16 after they had **m** a covenant
Josh 9:27 And that day Joshua **m** them
Josh 10: 1 had **m** peace with Israel and
Josh 10: 4 for it has **m** peace with
Josh 10: 5 Gibeon and **m** war against it
Josh 10:20 the children of Israel **m** an
Josh 11:18 Joshua **m** war a long time with
Josh 11:19 There was not a city that **m**
Josh 13:14 of Israel **m** by fire are their
Josh 14: 8 who went up with me **m** the
Josh 19:49 When they had **m** an end of
Josh 19:51 So they **m** an end of dividing
Josh 22:25 For the LORD has **m** the Jordan
Josh 22:28 the LORD which our fathers **m**
Josh 24:25 So Joshua **m** a covenant with
Josh 24:25 **m** for them a statute and an
Judg 3:16 Now Ehud **m** himself a dagger
Judg 6: 2 the children of Israel **m** for
Judg 8:27 Then Gideon **m** it into an
Judg 8:33 and **m** Baal-Berith their god
Judg 9: 6 **m** Abimelech king beside the
Judg 9:18 **m** Abimelech, the son of his
Judg 9:27 and trod them, and **m** merry
Judg 11: 4 of Ammon **m** war against Israel
Judg 11: 5 of Ammon **m** war against Israel
Judg 11:11 and the people **m** him head
Judg 11:30 Jephthah **m** a vow to the LORD,
Judg 17: 4 he **m** it into a carved image
Judg 17: 5 **m** an ephod and household idols
Judg 18:24 taken away my gods which I **m**
Judg 18:27 took the things Micah had **m**
Judg 18:31 carved image which he **m**, all
Judg 21: 5 For they had **m** a great oath
Judg 21:15 because the LORD had **m** a void
1Sa 1:11 Then she **m** a vow and said, "O
1Sa 2:28 children of Israel **m** by fire
1Sa 3:13 his sons **m** themselves vile
1Sa 4:18 when he **m** mention of the ark
1Sa 6:15 **m** sacrifices the same day to
1Sa 8: 1 **m** his sons judges over Israel
1Sa 11:15 there they **m** Saul king before
1Sa 11:15 There they **m** sacrifices of

1Sa 12: 1 me, and have **m** a king over you
1Sa 12: 8 **m** them dwell in this place
1Sa 13:12 I have not **m** supplication to
1Sa 14:14 his armorbearer **m** was about
1Sa 15:33 sword has **m** women childless
1Sa 15:35 had **m** Saul king over Israel
1Sa 16: 8 and **m** him pass before Samuel
1Sa 16: 9 Then Jesse **m** Shammah pass by
1Sa 16:10 Thus Jesse **m** seven of his
1Sa 18: 3 David **m** a covenant, because
1Sa 18:13 and **m** him his captain over a
1Sa 20:16 So Jonathan **m** a covenant with
1Sa 22: 8 to me that my son has **m** a
1Sa 23:18 So the two of them **m** a
1Sa 23:26 So David **m** haste to get away
1Sa 25:18 Then Abigail **m** haste and took
1Sa 27:10 Where have you **m** a raid today
1Sa 27:12 He has **m** his people Israel
1Sa 30:14 We **m** an invasion of the
1Sa 30:21 whom they also had **m** to stay
1Sa 30:25 he **m** it a statute and an
2Sa 2: 9 he **m** him king over Gilead,
2Sa 3:20 David **m** a feast for Abner and
2Sa 4: 4 as she **m** haste to flee, that
2Sa 5: 3 King David **m** a covenant with
2Sa 6: 5 of instruments **m** of fir wood
2Sa 7: 9 have **m** you a great name, like
2Sa 7:24 For You have **m** Your people
2Sa 8:13 David **m** himself a name when
2Sa 10: 6 had **m** themselves repulsive to
2Sa 10:19 they **m** peace with Israel and
2Sa 11:13 and he **m** him drunk
2Sa 12:31 and **m** them cross over to the
2Sa 13: 8 it, **m** cakes in his sight, and
2Sa 13:10 the cakes which she had **m**
2Sa 14:15 the people have **m** me afraid
2Sa 15: 4 that I were **m** judge in the
2Sa 17:25 Absalom **m** Amasa captain of
2Sa 22: 5 of ungodliness **m** me afraid
2Sa 22:12 He **m** darkness canopies around
2Sa 22:36 gentleness has **m** me great
2Sa 23: 5 God, yet He has **m** with me an
1Ki 1:43 King David has **m** Solomon king
1Ki 1:44 they have **m** him ride on the
1Ki 2:24 who has **m** me a house, as He
1Ki 3: 1 Now Solomon **m** a treaty with
1Ki 3: 7 You have **m** Your servant king
1Ki 3:15 and **m** a feast for all his
1Ki 4: 7 each one **m** provision for one
1Ki 5:12 the two of them **m** a treaty
1Ki 6: 4 he **m** for the house windows
1Ki 6: 5 Thus he **m** side chambers all
1Ki 6: 6 for he **m** narrow ledges around
1Ki 6:23 the inner sanctuary he **m** two
1Ki 6:31 he **m** doors of olive wood
1Ki 6:33 **m** doorposts of olive wood
1Ki 7: 6 He also **m** the Hall of Pillars
1Ki 7: 7 Then he **m** a hall for the
1Ki 7: 8 Solomon also **m** a house like
1Ki 7:16 Then he **m** two capitals of
1Ki 7:17 He **m** a lattice network, with
1Ki 7:18 So he **m** the pillars, and two
1Ki 7:23 Then he **m** the Sea of cast
1Ki 7:27 He also **m** ten carts of bronze
1Ki 7:37 manner he **m** the ten carts
1Ki 7:38 Then he **m** ten lavers of
1Ki 7:40 Hiram **m** the lavers and the
1Ki 7:45 **m** for King Solomon for the
1Ki 7:48 had all the furnishings **m** for
1Ki 8: 9 when the LORD **m** a covenant
1Ki 8:21 there I have **m** a place for
1Ki 8:21 which He **m** with our fathers
1Ki 8:38 supplication is **m** by anyone
1Ki 8:59 of mine, with which I have **m**
1Ki 9: 3 that you have **m** before Me
1Ki 9:22 Solomon **m** no forced laborers
1Ki 10: 9 therefore He **m** you king, to
1Ki 10:12 the king **m** steps of the almug
1Ki 10:16 King Solomon **m** two hundred
1Ki 10:17 He also **m** three hundred
1Ki 10:18 Moreover the king **m** a great
1Ki 10:20 been **m** for any other kingdom
1Ki 10:27 The king **m** silver as common
1Ki 10:27 he **m** cedars as abundant as
1Ki 11:28 **m** him the officer over all
1Ki 11:34 because I have **m** him ruler
1Ki 12: 4 Your father **m** our yoke heavy
1Ki 12:10 Your father **m** our yoke heavy
1Ki 12:14 My father **m** your yoke heavy,
1Ki 12:20 **m** him king over all Israel
1Ki 12:28 **m** two calves of gold, and said
1Ki 12:31 He **m** shrines on the high
1Ki 12:31 **m** priests from every class of
1Ki 12:32 to the calves that he had **m**
1Ki 12:32 high places which he had **m**
1Ki 12:33 So he **m** offerings on the
1Ki 12:33 on the altar which he had **m**
1Ki 13:33 but again he **m** priests from
1Ki 14: 7 **m** you ruler over My people
1Ki 14: 9 **m** for yourself other gods and
1Ki 14:15 because they have **m** their
1Ki 14:16 sinned and who **m** Israel sin
1Ki 14:19 of Jeroboam, how he **m** war
1Ki 14:26 shields which Solomon had **m**
1Ki 14:27 Then King Rehoboam **m** bronze
1Ki 15:12 idols that his fathers had **m**
1Ki 15:13 because she had **m** an obscene
1Ki 15:22 Then King Asa **m** a
1Ki 15:26 by which he had **m** Israel sin
1Ki 15:30 by which he had **m** Israel sin
1Ki 15:34 by which he had **m** Israel sin
1Ki 16: 2 **m** you ruler over My people
1Ki 16: 2 have **m** My people Israel sin,
1Ki 16:13 which they had **m** Israel sin
1Ki 16:16 So all Israel **m** Omri, the
1Ki 16:26 by which he had **m** Israel sin
1Ki 16:33 And Ahab **m** a wooden image
1Ki 18:26 the altar which they had **m**
1Ki 18:32 and he **m** a trench around the
1Ki 20: 1 Samaria, and **m** war against it
1Ki 20:34 So he **m** a treaty with him
1Ki 21:22 Me to anger, and **m** Israel sin
1Ki 22:11 the son of Chenaanah had **m**
1Ki 22:44 Also Jehoshaphat **m** peace with
1Ki 22:45 he showed, and how he **m** war
1Ki 22:48 Jehoshaphat **m** merchant ships
1Ki 22:52 Nebat, who had **m** Israel sin
2Ki 3: 2 of Baal that his father had **m**
2Ki 3: 3 Nebat, who had **m** Israel sin
2Ki 6: 6 and he **m** the iron float
2Ki 8:20 and **m** a king over themselves
2Ki 9:21 And his chariot was **m** ready
2Ki 10:25 as soon as he had **m** an end of
2Ki 10:27 **m** it a refuse dump to this
2Ki 10:29 who had **m** Israel sin, that is
2Ki 10:31 who had **m** Israel sin
2Ki 11: 4 he **m** a covenant with them and
2Ki 11:12 they **m** him king and anointed
2Ki 11:17 Then Jehoiada **m** a covenant
2Ki 12:13 However there were not **m** for
2Ki 12:20 **m** a conspiracy, and killed
2Ki 13: 2 Nebat, who had **m** Israel sin
2Ki 13: 6 who had **m** Israel sin, but
2Ki 13: 7 and **m** them like the dust at
2Ki 13:11 Nebat, who had **m** Israel sin
2Ki 14:19 they **m** a conspiracy against
2Ki 14:21 **m** him king instead of his
2Ki 14:24 Nebat, who had **m** Israel sin
2Ki 14:28 his might, how he **m** war, and
2Ki 15: 9 Nebat, who had **m** Israel sin
2Ki 15:18 Nebat, who had **m** Israel sin
2Ki 15:24 Nebat, who had **m** Israel sin
2Ki 15:28 Nebat, who had **m** Israel sin
2Ki 16: 3 indeed he **m** his son pass
2Ki 16:11 So Urijah the priest **m** it
2Ki 16:12 altar and **m** offerings on it
2Ki 17: 8 of Israel, which they had **m**
2Ki 17:15 He had **m** with their fathers
2Ki 17:16 **m** for themselves a molded
2Ki 17:16 **m** a wooden image and
2Ki 17:19 of Israel which they **m**
2Ki 17:21 they **m** Jeroboam the son of
2Ki 17:21 **m** them commit a great sin
2Ki 17:29 which the Samaritans had **m**
2Ki 17:30 of Babylon **m** Succoth Benoth
2Ki 17:30 the men of Cuth **m** Nergal
2Ki 17:30 the men of Hamath **m** Ashima
2Ki 17:31 and the Avites **m** Nibhaz and
2Ki 17:35 the LORD had **m** a covenant
2Ki 17:38 that I have **m** with you, you
2Ki 18: 4 serpent that Moses had **m**
2Ki 19:15 You have **m** heaven and earth
2Ki 19:25 not hear long ago how I **m** it
2Ki 20:20 his might, and how he **m** a pool
2Ki 21: 3 **m** a wooden image, as Ahab
2Ki 21: 6 Also he **m** his son pass
2Ki 21: 7 of Asherah that he had **m**, in
2Ki 21:11 has also **m** Judah sin with his
2Ki 21:16 sin with which he **m** Judah sin
2Ki 21:24 **m** his son Josiah king in his
2Ki 22: 7 **m** with them of the money
2Ki 23: 3 **m** a covenant before the LORD,
2Ki 23: 4 articles that were **m** for Baal
2Ki 23:12 the kings of Judah had **m**, and
2Ki 23:12 **m** in the two courts of the
2Ki 23:15 who **m** Israel sin, had **m**,
2Ki 23:15 who **m** Israel sin, had **m**
2Ki 23:19 had **m** to provoke the LORD to
2Ki 23:30 **m** him king in his father's
2Ki 23:34 Then Pharaoh Necho **m** Eliakim
2Ki 24:13 **m** in the temple of the LORD
2Ki 24:17 king of Babylon **m** Mattaniah
2Ki 25:15 the things **m** of solid gold and
2Ki 25:16 which Solomon had **m** for the
2Ki 25:22 Then he **m** Gedaliah the son of
2Ki 25:23 had **m** Gedaliah governor, they
1Ch 5:10 they **m** war with the Hagrites
1Ch 5:19 They **m** war with the Hagrites,
1Ch 9:30 **m** the ointment of the spices
1Ch 11: 3 David **m** a covenant with them
1Ch 12:18 **m** them captains of the troop
1Ch 14: 9 **m** a raid on the Valley of
1Ch 14:13 again **m** a raid on the valley
1Ch 16: 5 harps, but Asaph **m** music with
1Ch 16:16 which He **m** with Abraham, and
1Ch 16:26 but the LORD **m** the heavens
1Ch 17: 8 have **m** you a name like the
1Ch 17:22 For You have **m** Your people
1Ch 18: 8 Solomon **m** the bronze Sea, the
1Ch 19: 6 had **m** themselves repulsive to
1Ch 19:19 they **m** peace with David and
1Ch 21:29 which Moses had **m** in the
1Ch 22: 5 So David **m** abundant
1Ch 22: 8 blood and have **m** great wars
1Ch 23: 1 he **m** his son Solomon king
1Ch 23: 5 which I **m**," said David
1Ch 26:10 his father **m** him the first),
1Ch 26:32 whom King David **m** officials
1Ch 28: 2 had **m** preparations to build
1Ch 28:19 the LORD **m** me understand in
1Ch 29: 2 for things to be **m** of gold
1Ch 29:19 for which I have **m** provision
1Ch 29:21 they **m** sacrifices to the LORD
1Ch 29:22 they **m** Solomon the son of
2Ch 1: 3 LORD had **m** in the wilderness
2Ch 1: 5 of Uri, the son of Hur, had **m**
2Ch 1: 8 have **m** me king in his place
2Ch 1: 9 for You have **m** me king over a
2Ch 1:11 over whom I have **m** you king
2Ch 1:15 Also the king **m** silver and
2Ch 1:15 he **m** cedars as abundant as
2Ch 2:11 He has **m** you king over them
2Ch 2:12 who **m** heaven and earth, for He
2Ch 2:18 he **m** seventy thousand of them
2Ch 3: 8 And he **m** the Most Holy Place
2Ch 3:10 Holy Place he **m** two cherubim
2Ch 3:14 And he **m** the veil of blue and
2Ch 3:15 Also he **m** in front of the
2Ch 3:16 He **m** wreaths of chainwork, as
2Ch 3:16 he **m** one hundred
2Ch 4: 1 Moreover he **m** a bronze altar
2Ch 4: 2 Then he **m** the Sea of cast
2Ch 4: 6 He also **m** ten lavers, and put
2Ch 4: 7 he **m** ten lampstands of gold
2Ch 4: 8 He also **m** ten tables, and
2Ch 4: 8 he **m** one hundred bowls of
2Ch 4: 9 Furthermore he **m** the court of
2Ch 4:11 Then Huram **m** the pots and the
2Ch 4:14 he also **m** carts and the lavers
2Ch 4:16 **m** of burnished bronze for
2Ch 4:18 had all these articles **m** in
2Ch 4:19 **m** for the house of God
2Ch 5:10 when the LORD **m** a covenant
2Ch 6:11 of the LORD which He **m** with
2Ch 6:13 (for Solomon had **m** a bronze
2Ch 6:29 supplication is **m** by anyone
2Ch 6:40 to the prayer **m** in this place
2Ch 7: 6 had **m** to praise the LORD,
2Ch 7: 7 altar which Solomon had **m** was
2Ch 7:15 to prayer **m** in this place
2Ch 9: 8 therefore He **m** you king over
2Ch 9:11 the king **m** walkways of the
2Ch 9:15 King Solomon **m** two hundred
2Ch 9:16 He also **m** three hundred
2Ch 9:17 Moreover the king **m** a great
2Ch 9:19 been **m** for any other kingdom
2Ch 9:27 The king **m** silver as common
2Ch 9:27 he **m** cedar trees as abundant
2Ch 10: 4 Your father **m** our yoke heavy
2Ch 10:10 Your father **m** our yoke heavy

2Ch 10:14 My father **m** your yoke heavy,
2Ch 11:12 **m** them very strong, having
2Ch 11:15 the calf idols which he had **m**
2Ch 11:17 **m** Rehoboam the son of
2Ch 12: 9 shields which Solomon had **m**
2Ch 12:10 Rehoboam **m** bronze shields
2Ch 13: 8 Jeroboam **m** for you as gods
2Ch 13: 9 **m** for yourselves priests,
2Ch 15:16 because she had **m** an obscene
2Ch 16:14 which he had **m** for himself in
2Ch 16:14 They **m** a very great burning
2Ch 18:10 the son of Chenaanah had **m**
2Ch 20:23 when they had **m** an end of the
2Ch 20:27 joy, for the LORD had **m** them
2Ch 20:36 they **m** the ships in Ezion
2Ch 21: 7 that He had **m** with David, and
2Ch 21: 8 and **m** a king over themselves
2Ch 21:11 Moreover he **m** high places in
2Ch 21:13 and have **m** Judah and the
2Ch 21:19 his people **m** no burning for
2Ch 22: 1 **m** Ahaziah his youngest son
2Ch 23: 1 and **m** a covenant with the
2Ch 23: 3 Then all the congregation **m** a
2Ch 23:11 the Testimony, and **m** him king
2Ch 23:16 Then Jehoiada **m** a covenant
2Ch 24: 8 commandment they **m** a chest
2Ch 24: 9 And they **m** a proclamation
2Ch 24:14 they **m** from it articles for
2Ch 25:16 Have we **m** you the king's
2Ch 25:27 they **m** a conspiracy against
2Ch 26: 1 **m** him king instead of his
2Ch 26: 5 the LORD, God **m** him prosper
2Ch 26: 6 **m** war against the Philistines
2Ch 26:13 that **m** war with mighty power,
2Ch 26:15 he **m** devices in Jerusalem,
2Ch 28: 2 **m** molded images for the Baals
2Ch 28:24 **m** for himself altars in every
2Ch 28:25 single city of Judah he **m**
2Ch 29:24 offering be **m** for all Israel
2Ch 32: 5 and **m** weapons and shields in
2Ch 32:27 he **m** himself treasuries for
2Ch 33: 3 the Baals, and **m** wooden images
2Ch 33: 7 the idol which he had **m**, in
2Ch 33:22 his father Manasseh had **m**
2Ch 33:25 **m** his son Josiah king in his
2Ch 34: 4 **m** dust of them and scattered
2Ch 34:31 **m** a covenant before the LORD,
2Ch 34:32 he **m** all who were present in
2Ch 34:33 **m** all who were present in
2Ch 35:25 They **m** it a custom in Israel
2Ch 36: 1 **m** him king in his father's
2Ch 36: 4 Then the king of Egypt **m** his
2Ch 36:10 and **m** Zedekiah, Jehoiakim's
2Ch 36:13 who had **m** him swear an oath
2Ch 36:22 so that he **m** a proclamation
Ezra 1: 1 so that he **m** a proclamation
Ezra 4:15 that search may be **m** in the
Ezra 4:19 and a search has been **m**, and
Ezra 4:19 city in former times has **m**
Ezra 4:23 by force of arms **m** them cease
Ezra 5:14 whom he had **m** governor
Ezra 5:17 let a search be **m** in the
Ezra 6: 1 and a search was **m** in the
Ezra 6:11 let his house be **m** a refuse
Ezra 6:22 for the LORD **m** them joyful
Ezra 10: 5 **m** the leaders of the priests,
Neh 3: 4 the son of Koz, **m** repairs
Neh 3: 4 son of Meshezabeel, **m** repairs
Neh 3: 4 the son of Baana **m** repairs
Neh 3: 5 them the Tekoites **m** repairs
Neh 3: 8 of the goldsmiths, **m** repairs
Neh 3: 8 of the perfumers, **m** repairs
Neh 3: 9 of Jerusalem, **m** repairs
Neh 3:10 **m** repairs in front of his
Neh 3:10 son of Hashabniah **m** repairs
Neh 3:12 he and his daughters **m** repairs
Neh 3:16 **m** repairs as far as the place
Neh 3:17 the son of Bani, **m** repairs
Neh 3:17 **m** repairs for his district
Neh 3:18 district of Keilah, **m** repairs
Neh 3:22 men of the plain, **m** repairs
Neh 3:23 Hasshub **m** repairs opposite
Neh 3:23 **m** repairs by his house
Neh 3:25 Uzai **m** repairs opposite the
Neh 3:25 the son of Parosh **m** repairs
Neh 3:26 **m** repairs as far as the place
Neh 3:28 Gate the priests **m** repairs
Neh 3:29 **m** repairs in front of his own
Neh 3:29 of the East Gate, **m** repairs
Neh 3:30 the son of Berechiah **m**
Neh 3:31 **m** repairs as far as the house
Neh 3:32 and the merchants **m** repairs
Neh 4: 9 Nevertheless we **m** our prayer
Neh 6:14 who would have **m** me afraid
Neh 8: 4 they had **m** for the purpose
Neh 8:16 **m** themselves booths, each one
Neh 8:17 from the captivity **m** booths
Neh 9: 6 You have **m** heaven, the heaven
Neh 9: 8 **m** a covenant with him to give
Neh 9:10 So You **m** a name for Yourself,
Neh 9:14 You **m** known to them Your
Neh 9:18 Even when they **m** a molded
Neh 10:32 Also we **m** ordinances for
Neh 10:35 we **m** ordinances to bring the
Neh 12:43 for God had **m** them rejoice
Neh 13:25 **m** them swear by God, saying,
Neh 13:26 and God **m** him king over all
Esth 1: 3 he **m** a feast for all his
Esth 1: 5 the king **m** a feast lasting
Esth 1: 9 Queen Vashti also **m** a feast
Esth 2:17 **m** her queen instead of Vashti
Esth 2:18 Then the king **m** a great feast
Esth 2:23 inquiry was **m** into the matter
Esth 5:14 Let a gallows be **m**, fifty
Esth 5:14 so he had the gallows **m**
Esth 7: 9 which Haman **m** for Mordecai,
Esth 9:17 **m** it a day of feasting and
Esth 9:18 **m** it a day of feasting and
Job 1:10 Have You not **m** a hedge around
Job 2:11 For they had **m** an appointment
Job 4:14 which **m** all my bones shake
Job 9: 9 He **m** the Bear, Orion, and the
Job 10: 8 Your hands have **m** me and
Job 10: 9 that You have **m** me like clay
Job 12: 5 it is **m** ready for those whose
Job 15: 7 Or were you **m** before the
Job 15:27 **m** his waist heavy with fat,
Job 16: 7 you have **m** desolate all my
Job 17: 6 But He has **m** me a byword of
Job 23:16 For God **m** my heart weak, and
Job 27: 2 who has **m** my soul bitter,
Job 28:18 shall be **m** of coral or quartz
Job 28:26 When He **m** a law for the rain,
Job 31: 1 I have **m** a covenant with my
Job 31:15 Did not He who **m** me in the
Job 31:24 If I have **m** gold my hope, or
Job 33: 4 The Spirit of God has **m** me
Job 38: 9 when I **m** the clouds its
Job 39: 6 home I have **m** the wilderness
Job 40:15 which I **m** along with you
Job 40:19 only He who **m** him can bring
Job 41:33 him, which is **m** without fear
Ps 7:15 He **m** a pit and dug it out, And
Ps 7:15 into the ditch which he **m**
Ps 8: 5 For You have **m** him a little
Ps 8: 6 You have **m** him to have
Ps 9:15 down in the pit which they **m**
Ps 18: 4 of ungodliness **m** me afraid
Ps 18:11 He **m** darkness His secret
Ps 18:35 gentleness has **m** me great
Ps 18:43 You have **m** me the head of the
Ps 21: 6 For You have **m** him most
Ps 21: 6 You have **m** him exceedingly
Ps 22: 9 You **m** Me trust when I was on
Ps 30: 7 by Your favor You have **m** my
Ps 30: 8 to the LORD I **m** supplication
Ps 33: 6 the LORD the heavens were **m**
Ps 39: 5 Indeed, You have **m** my days as
Ps 45: 8 by which they have **m** You glad
Ps 46: 8 Who has **m** desolations in the
Ps 50: 5 Those who have **m** a covenant
Ps 56:12 Vows **m** to You are binding
Ps 60: 2 You have **m** the earth tremble
Ps 60: 3 You have **m** us drink the wine
Ps 69:11 I also **m** sackcloth my garment
Ps 72:15 will be **m** for Him continually
Ps 74:17 You have **m** summer and winter
Ps 78:13 He **m** the waters stand up like
Ps 78:50 He **m** a path for His anger
Ps 78:52 But He **m** His own people go
Ps 78:55 **m** the tribes of Israel dwell
Ps 78:64 their widows **m** no lamentation
Ps 80: 6 You have **m** us a strife to our
Ps 80:15 You **m** strong for Yourself
Ps 80:17 You **m** strong for Yourself
Ps 86: 9 whom You have **m** Shall come
Ps 88: 8 You have **m** me an abomination
Ps 89: 3 I have **m** a covenant with My
Ps 89:42 You have **m** all his enemies
Ps 89:44 You have **m** his glory cease,
Ps 91: 9 Because you have **m** the LORD
Ps 92: 4 have **m** me glad through Your
Ps 95: 5 The sea is His, for He **m** it
Ps 96: 5 But the LORD **m** the heavens
Ps 98: 2 The LORD has **m** known His
Ps 100: 3 It is He who has **m** us, and not
Ps 103: 7 He **m** known His ways to Moses,
Ps 104:24 In wisdom You have **m** them all
Ps 104:26 You have **m** to play there
Ps 105: 9 which He **m** with Abraham,
Ps 105:21 He **m** him lord of his house,
Ps 105:24 **m** them stronger than their
Ps 105:28 sent darkness, and **m** it dark
Ps 106:19 They **m** a calf in Horeb, And
Ps 106:28 ate sacrifices **m** to the dead
Ps 106:46 He also **m** them to be pitied
Ps 111: 4 He has **m** His wonderful works
Ps 115:15 LORD, Who **m** heaven and earth
Ps 118:24 the day which the LORD has **m**
Ps 119:60 I **m** haste, and did not delay
Ps 119:73 Your hands have **m** me and
Ps 119:87 They almost **m** an end of me on
Ps 121: 2 LORD, Who **m** heaven and earth
Ps 124: 8 LORD, Who **m** heaven and earth
Ps 129: 3 They **m** their furrows long
Ps 134: 3 The LORD who **m** heaven and
Ps 136: 5 who by wisdom **m** the heavens
Ps 136: 7 To Him who **m** great lights,
Ps 136:14 **m** Israel pass through the
Ps 138: 3 **m** me bold with strength in my
Ps 139:14 am fearfully and wonderfully **m**
Ps 139:15 You, When I was **m** in secret
Ps 143: 3 He has **m** me dwell in darkness
Ps 146: 6 Who **m** heaven and earth, The
Ps 148: 6 He has **m** a decree which shall
Prov 8:26 not **m** the earth or the fields
Prov 11:25 generous soul will be **m** rich
Prov 13: 4 the diligent shall be **m** rich
Prov 14:33 the heart of fools is **m** known
Prov 16: 4 The LORD has **m** all things for
Prov 20: 9 I have **m** my heart clean, I am
Prov 20:12 the LORD has **m** both of them
Prov 21:11 the simple is **m** wise
Eccl 1:15 crooked cannot be **m** straight
Eccl 2: 4 I **m** my works great, I built
Eccl 2: 5 I **m** myself gardens and
Eccl 2: 6 I **m** myself waterpools from
Eccl 3:11 He has **m** everything beautiful
Eccl 4:16 over whom he was **m** king
Eccl 7: 3 the heart is **m** better
Eccl 7:13 what He has **m** crooked
Eccl 7:29 that God **m** man upright, but
Eccl 10:19 A feast is **m** for laughter, and
Song 1: 6 they **m** me the keeper of the
Song 3: 9 King **m** himself a palanquin
Song 3:10 He **m** its pillars of silver,
Song 6:12 my soul had **m** me as the
Is 1: 9 have been **m** like Gomorrah
Is 2: 8 their own fingers have **m**
Is 2:20 idols of gold, which they **m**
Is 5: 2 and also **m** a winepress in it
Is 14: 3 in which you were **m** to serve
Is 14:16 man who **m** the earth tremble
Is 14:17 who **m** the world as a
Is 16:10 I have **m** their shouting cease
Is 17: 8 what his fingers have **m**, nor
Is 21: 2 its sighing I have **m** to cease
Is 22:11 You also **m** a reservoir
Is 25: 2 For You have **m** a city a ruin,
Is 26:14 **m** all their memory to perish
Is 27:11 therefore He who **m** them will
Is 28:15 We have **m** a covenant with
Is 28:15 for we have **m** lies our refuge
Is 28:22 lest your bonds be **m** strong
Is 29:16 thing **m** say of him who **m** it
Is 30:33 He has **m** it deep and large
Is 31: 7 hands have **m** for yourselves
Is 34: 6 it is **m** overflowing with
Is 37:16 You have **m** heaven and earth
Is 37:26 not hear long ago how I **m** it
Is 40: 4 and hill shall be **m** low
Is 40: 4 places shall be **m** straight
Is 41: 2 him, and **m** him rule over kings
Is 43: 7 formed him, yes, I have **m** him
Is 44: 2 Thus says the LORD who **m** you
Is 45:12 I have **m** the earth, and
Is 45:18 **m** it, Who has established it,
Is 46: 4 I have **m**, and I will bear
Is 48: 6 I have **m** you hear new things
Is 49: 1 He has **m** mention of My name

Is 49: 2 And He has **m** My mouth like a
Is 49: 2 Me, and **m** Me a polished shaft
Is 51:10 that **m** the depths of the sea
Is 51:12 man who will be **m** like grass
Is 52:10 The LORD has **m** bare His holy
Is 53: 9 they **m** His grave with the
Is 53:12 and **m** intercession for the
Is 57: 8 bed and **m** a covenant with them
Is 57:16 and the souls which I have **m**
Is 59: 8 they have **m** themselves
Is 63: 6 **m** them drunk in My fury, and
Is 63:17 why have You **m** us stray from
Is 66: 2 those things My hand has **m**
Is 66: 8 Shall the earth be **m** to give
Jer 1:18 I have **m** you this day a
Jer 2: 7 **m** My heritage an abomination
Jer 2:15 they **m** his land waste
Jer 2:28 you have **m** for yourselves
Jer 3:16 it, nor shall it be **m** anymore
Jer 5: 3 They have **m** their faces
Jer 10:11 that have not **m** the heavens
Jer 10:12 He has **m** the earth by His
Jer 10:25 **m** his habitation desolate
Jer 11:10 which I **m** with their fathers
Jer 12:10 they have **m** My pleasant
Jer 12:11 They have **m** it desolate
Jer 12:11 the whole land is **m** desolate
Jer 13:22 uncovered, your heels **m** bare
Jer 13:27 Will you still not be **m** clean
Jer 14:22 since You have **m** all these
Jer 17:23 but **m** their neck stiff, that
Jer 18: 4 the vessel that he **m** of clay
Jer 18: 4 so he **m** it again into another
Jer 19: 4 Me and **m** this an alien place,
Jer 19:11 which cannot be **m** whole again
Jer 20: 8 LORD was **m** to me a reproach
Jer 25:17 **m** all the nations drink, to
Jer 26: 8 when Jeremiah had **m** an end of
Jer 27: 5 I have **m** the earth, the man
Jer 28:13 but you have **m** in their place
Jer 29:26 The LORD has **m** you priest
Jer 31:32 to the covenant that I **m** with
Jer 32:17 You have **m** the heavens and the
Jer 32:20 You have **m** Yourself a name,
Jer 33: 2 Thus says the LORD who **m** it
Jer 34: 8 had **m** a covenant with all the
Jer 34:11 **m** the male and female slaves
Jer 34:13 I **m** a covenant with your
Jer 34:15 you **m** a covenant before Me in
Jer 34:18 which they **m** before Me, when
Jer 37: 1 king of Babylon **m** king in the
Jer 37:15 For they had **m** that the
Jer 38:16 who **m** our very souls, I will
Jer 40: 5 the king of Babylon has **m**
Jer 40: 7 the king of Babylon had **m**
Jer 41: 2 had **m** governor over the land
Jer 41: 9 same one Asa the king had **m**
Jer 41:18 had **m** governor in the land
Jer 44:25 our vows that we have **m**, to
Jer 46:10 and **m** drunk with their blood
Jer 46:16 He **m** many fall
Jer 48:30 his lies have **m** nothing right
Jer 49:10 But I have **m** Esau bare
Jer 51: 7 that **m** all the earth drunk
Jer 51:15 He has **m** the earth by His
Jer 51:34 he has **m** me an empty vessel,
Jer 52:20 which King Solomon had **m** for
Lam 1:13 He has **m** me desolate and faint
Lam 1:14 He **m** my strength fail
Lam 2: 7 They have **m** a noise in the
Lam 3: 2 **m** me walk in darkness and not
Lam 3: 7 he has **m** my chain heavy
Lam 3: 9 He has **m** my paths crooked
Lam 3:11 He has **m** me desolate
Lam 3:15 He has **m** me drink wormwood
Lam 3:45 You have **m** us an offscouring
Ezek 3: 8 I have **m** your face strong
Ezek 3: 9 flint, I have **m** your forehead
Ezek 3:17 I have **m** you a watchman for
Ezek 6: 6 **m** desolate, your idols may be
Ezek 6: 6 and **m** to cease, your incense
Ezek 7:14 **m** everyone ready, but no one
Ezek 7:20 but they **m** from it the images
Ezek 7:20 therefore I have **m** it like
Ezek 12: 6 for I have **m** you a sign to
Ezek 13:22 **m** the heart of the righteous
Ezek 13:22 sad, whom I have not **m** sad
Ezek 15: 5 no object could be **m** from it
Ezek 16: 7 I **m** you thrive like a plant
Ezek 16:17 **m** for yourself male images and
Ezek 16:24 **m** a high place for yourself
Ezek 16:25 **m** your beauty to be abhorred
Ezek 16:33 but you **m** your payments to
Ezek 17:13 **m** a covenant with him, and put
Ezek 17:16 king dwells who **m** him king
Ezek 17:24 and **m** the dry tree flourish
Ezek 19: 5 cubs and **m** him a young lion
Ezek 20: 5 **m** Myself known to them in the
Ezek 20: 9 I had **m** Myself known to them
Ezek 20:10 Therefore I **m** them go out of
Ezek 21:15 It is **m** bright
Ezek 21:24 Because you have **m** your
Ezek 22: 4 the idols which you have **m**
Ezek 22: 4 therefore I have **m** you a
Ezek 22: 7 they have **m** light of father
Ezek 22:12 you have **m** profit from your
Ezek 22:13 profit which you have **m**, and
Ezek 22:25 they have **m** many widows in
Ezek 22:26 nor have they **m** known the
Ezek 26:15 when slaughter is **m** in the
Ezek 27: 5 They **m** all your planks of fir
Ezek 27: 6 from Bashan they **m** your oars
Ezek 27:11 they **m** your beauty perfect
Ezek 27:16 the abundance of goods you **m**
Ezek 27:18 the abundance of goods you **m**
Ezek 29: 3 I have **m** it for myself
Ezek 29: 7 and **m** all their loins shake
Ezek 29: 9 River is mine, and I have **m** it
Ezek 29:18 every head was **m** bald, and
Ezek 31: 4 The waters **m** it grow
Ezek 31: 6 the birds of the heavens **m**
Ezek 31: 6 great nations **m** their home
Ezek 31: 9 I **m** it beautiful with a
Ezek 31:16 I **m** the nations shake at the
Ezek 33: 7 I have **m** you a watchman for
Ezek 33:29 when I have **m** the land most
Ezek 36: 3 Because they **m** you desolate
Ezek 39:26 land and no one **m** them afraid
Ezek 40:17 a pavement **m** all around the
Ezek 41:18 it was **m** with cherubim and
Ezek 41:19 thus it was **m** throughout the
Ezek 43:18 altar on the day when it is **m**
Ezek 46:14 to be **m** regularly to the LORD
Ezek 46:23 cooking hearths were **m** under
Dan 2: 5 houses shall be **m** an ash heap
Dan 2:15 Then Arioch **m** the decision
Dan 2:17 and **m** the decision known to
Dan 2:23 have now **m** known to me what
Dan 2:23 for You have **m** known to us
Dan 2:28 and He has **m** known to King
Dan 2:29 **m** known to you what will be
Dan 2:38 has **m** you ruler over them all
Dan 2:45 the great God has **m** known to
Dan 2:48 he **m** him ruler over the whole
Dan 3: 1 the king **m** an image of gold
Dan 3:10 have **m** a decree that everyone
Dan 3:15 the image which I have **m**,
Dan 3:29 houses shall be **m** an ash heap
Dan 4: 5 saw a dream which **m** me afraid
Dan 5: 1 king **m** a great feast for a
Dan 5:11 **m** him chief of the magicians,
Dan 5:21 men, his heart was **m** like the
Dan 5:29 **m** a proclamation concerning
Dan 7: 4 **m** to stand on two feet like a
Dan 7:16 told me and **m** known to me the
Dan 7:22 a judgment was **m** in favor of
Dan 9: 1 who was **m** king over the realm
Dan 9: 4 and **m** confession, and said,
Dan 9:13 yet we have not **m** our prayer
Dan 9:15 **m** Yourself a name, as it is
Dan 10:10 me, which **m** me tremble on my
Dan 11:23 after the league is **m** with
Dan 12:10 **m** white, and refined, but the
Hos 7: 5 king princes have **m** him sick
Hos 8: 4 they **m** princes, and I did not
Hos 8: 4 and gold they **m** idols for
Hos 8: 6 a workman **m** it, and it is not
Hos 8:11 has **m** many altars for sin
Hos 13: 2 have **m** for themselves molded
Joel 1: 7 its branches are **m** white
Amos 4: 7 I **m** it rain on one city, I
Amos 4:10 I **m** the stench of your camps
Amos 5: 8 He **m** the Pleiades and Orion
Amos 5:26 which you **m** for yourselves
Amos 7: 7 on a wall **m** with a plumb line
Jon 1: 9 who **m** the sea and the dry land
Jon 1:16 to the LORD and **m** vows
Jon 4: 5 There he **m** himself a shelter
Jon 4: 6 **m** it come up over Jonah, that
Jon 4:10 nor **m** it grow, which came up
Nah 2: 3 of his mighty men are **m** red
Nah 2:11 cub, and no one **m** them afraid
Hab 2:17 of beasts which **m** them afraid
Hab 3: 9 Your bow was **m** quite ready
Zeph 2: 8 **m** arrogant threats against
Zeph 2:10 **m** arrogant threats against
Zeph 3: 6 I have **m** their streets
Zech 7:12 Yes, they **m** their hearts like
Zech 7:14 for they **m** the pleasant land
Zech 9:13 **m** you like the sword of a
Zech 11:10 I had **m** with all the peoples
Mal 2: 9 also have **m** you contemptible
Matt 9:16 and the tear is **m** worse
Matt 9:21 garment, I shall be **m** well
Matt 9:22 your faith has **m** you well
Matt 9:22 the woman was **m** well from
Matt 14:22 Immediately Jesus **m** His
Matt 14:36 it were **m** perfectly well
Matt 15: 6 Thus you have **m** the
Matt 15:31 speaking, the maimed **m** whole
Matt 18:25 he had, and that payment be **m**
Matt 19: 4 you not read that He who **m**
Matt 19: 4 at the beginning **m** them male
Matt 19:12 who were **m** eunuchs by men
Matt 19:12 **m** themselves eunuchs for the
Matt 20:12 you **m** them equal to us who
Matt 21:13 but you have **m** it a den of
Matt 22: 5 But they **m** light of it and
Matt 24:45 whom his master **m** ruler over
Matt 25:16 and **m** another five talents
Matt 26:31 All of you will be **m** to
Matt 26:33 Even if all are **m** to stumble
Matt 26:33 I will never be **m** to stumble
Matt 27:64 command that the tomb be **m**
Matt 27:66 **m** the tomb secure, sealing
Mark 2:21 old, and the tear is **m** worse
Mark 2:27 The Sabbath was **m** for man
Mark 5:28 clothes, I shall be **m** well
Mark 5:34 your faith has **m** you well
Mark 6:45 Immediately He **m** His
Mark 6:56 as touched Him were **m** well
Mark 8:25 eyes again and **m** him look up
Mark 10: 6 God '**m** them male and female
Mark 10:52 your faith has **m** you well
Mark 11:17 But you have **m** it a 'den of
Mark 14:27 All of you will be **m** to
Mark 14:29 Even if all are **m** to stumble
Mark 14:58 temple that is **m** with hands
Mark 14:58 build another **m** without hands
Luke 1:62 So they **m** signs to his father
Luke 2:15 the Lord has **m** known to us
Luke 2:17 Him, they **m** widely known the
Luke 3: 5 places shall be **m** straight
Luke 3: 5 and the rough ways **m** smooth
Luke 4:38 and they **m** request of Him
Luke 8:48 your faith has **m** you well
Luke 8:50 and she will be **m** well
Luke 9:15 so, and **m** them all sit down
Luke 11:40 Did not He who **m** the outside
Luke 12:14 Man, who **m** Me a judge or an
Luke 13:13 she was **m** straight, and
Luke 17:19 Your faith has **m** you well
Luke 19: 6 So he **m** haste and came down,
Luke 19:46 but you have **m** it a 'den of
Luke 23:19 insurrection **m** in the city
John 1: 3 All things were **m** through Him
John 1: 3 nothing was **m** that was **m**
John 1:10 the world was **m** through Him
John 2: 9 the water that was **m** wine
John 2:15 When He had **m** a whip of cords
John 4: 1 had heard that Jesus **m** and
John 4:46 where He had **m** the water wine
John 5: 4 water, was **m** well of whatever
John 5: 6 Do you want to be **m** well
John 5: 9 the man was **m** well, took up
John 5:11 He who **m** me well said to me
John 5:14 See, you have been **m** well
John 5:15 was Jesus who had **m** him well
John 7:23 I **m** a man completely well on
John 8:33 you say, 'You will be **m** free'
John 9: 6 and **m** clay with the saliva
John 9:11 A Man called Jesus **m** clay
John 9:14 Sabbath when Jesus **m** the clay
John 9:39 those who see may be **m** blind
John 12: 2 There they **m** Him a supper
John 15:15 Father I have **m** known to you
John 16: 1 should not be **m** to stumble
John 17:23 they may be **m** perfect in one
John 18:18 officers who had **m** a fire of
John 19: 7 because He **m** Himself the Son

John 19:23 **m** four parts, to each soldier
Acts 1: 1 The former account I **m**, O
Acts 2:28 You have **m** known to me the
Acts 2:36 that God has **m** this Jesus
Acts 3:12 we had **m** this man walk
Acts 3:16 has **m** this man strong, whom
Acts 3:25 which God **m** with our fathers
Acts 4: 9 what means he has been **m** well
Acts 4:24 who **m** heaven and earth and the
Acts 7:10 he **m** him governor over Egypt
Acts 7:13 was **m** known to his brothers
Acts 7:27 Who **m** you a ruler and a judge
Acts 7:35 Who **m** you a ruler and a judge
Acts 7:41 they **m** a calf in those days,
Acts 7:43 images which you **m** to worship
Acts 7:48 dwell in temples **m** with hands
Acts 7:50 Has My hand not **m** all these
Acts 8: 2 **m** great lamentation over him
Acts 8: 3 he **m** havoc of the church,
Acts 9:39 had **m** while she was with them
Acts 10:10 but while they **m** ready, he
Acts 10:17 sent from Cornelius had **m**
Acts 12:20 having **m** Blastus the king's
Acts 13:32 which was **m** to the fathers
Acts 14: 5 was **m** by both the Gentiles
Acts 14:15 who **m** the heaven, the earth,
Acts 14:21 and **m** many disciples, they
Acts 15: 9 **m** no distinction between us
Acts 16:13 prayer was customarily **m**
Acts 17:24 who **m** the world and everything
Acts 17:24 dwell in temples **m** with hands
Acts 17:26 He has **m** from one blood every
Acts 19:24 who **m** silver shrines of Diana
Acts 19:26 gods which are **m** with hands
Acts 20:28 Spirit has **m** you overseers
Acts 21:26 be **m** for each one of them
Acts 26: 6 **m** by God to our fathers
Acts 26:24 Now as he thus **m** his defense
Acts 27:40 to the wind and **m** for shore
Acts 28: 2 **m** us all welcome, because of
Rom 1:20 by the things that are **m**,
Rom 1:23 God into an image **m** like
Rom 4:14 are heirs, faith is **m** void
Rom 4:14 the promise **m** of no effect,
Rom 4:17 I have **m** you a father of many
Rom 5:19 many were **m** sinners, so also
Rom 5:19 many will be **m** righteous
Rom 8: 2 **m** me free from the law of sin
Rom 9:20 Why have you **m** me like this
Rom 9:29 have been **m** like Gomorrah
Rom 10:10 confession is **m** to salvation
Rom 10:20 I was **m** manifest to those who
Rom 14: 4 Indeed, he will be **m** to stand
Rom 14:21 or is offended or is **m** weak
Rom 15: 8 the promises **m** to the fathers
Rom 15:20 And so I have **m** it my aim to
Rom 16:26 but now has been **m** manifest
Rom 16:26 Scriptures has been **m** known
1Co 1:17 should be **m** of no effect
1Co 1:20 Has not God **m** foolish the
1Co 4: 9 for we have been **m** a
1Co 4:13 We have been **m** as the filth
1Co 7:21 but if you can be **m** free,
1Co 7:25 His mercy has **m** trustworthy
1Co 9:19 I have **m** myself a servant to
1Co 12:13 have all been **m** to drink into
1Co 15:22 Christ all shall be **m** alive
1Co 15:28 things are **m** subject to Him
1Co 15:36 what you sow is not **m** alive
1Co 15:47 was of the earth, **m** of dust
1Co 15:48 are those who are **m** of dust
2Co 2: 2 one who is **m** sorrowful by me
2Co 3: 6 who also **m** us sufficient as
2Co 3:10 For even what was **m** glorious
2Co 5: 1 God, a house not **m** with hands
2Co 5:21 For He **m** Him who knew no sin
2Co 7: 8 For even if I **m** you sorry
2Co 7: 8 the same epistle **m** you sorry
2Co 7: 9 not that you were **m** sorry
2Co 7: 9 For you were **m** sorry in a
2Co 11: 6 **m** manifest among you in all
2Co 11:29 Who is **m** to stumble, and I do
2Co 12: 9 for My strength is **m** perfect
2Co 13: 9 that you may be **m** complete
Gal 3: 3 are you now being **m** perfect
Gal 3:16 his Seed were the promises **m**
Gal 3:19 to whom the promise was **m**
Gal 5: 1 by which Christ has **m** us free
Eph 1: 6 by which He has **m** us accepted
Eph 1: 8 which He **m** to abound toward
Eph 1: 9 having **m** known to us the
Eph 2: 1 And you He **m** alive, who were
Eph 2: 5 **m** us alive together with
Eph 2: 6 and **m** us sit together in the
Eph 2:11 **m** in the flesh by hands
Eph 2:13 **m** near by the blood of Christ
Eph 2:14 who has **m** both one, and has
Eph 3: 3 how that by revelation He **m**
Eph 3: 5 **m** known to the sons of men
Eph 3:10 wisdom of God might be **m**
Eph 5:13 are **m** manifest by the light
Phil 2: 7 but **m** Himself of no
Phil 4: 6 requests be **m** known to God
Col 1:20 having **m** peace through the
Col 2:11 circumcision **m** without hands
Col 2:13 He has **m** alive together with
Col 2:15 He **m** a public spectacle of
1Th 2: 6 when we might have **m** demands
1Ti 1: 9 that the law is not **m** for a
1Ti 1:18 previously **m** concerning you
1Ti 2: 1 of thanks be **m** for all men
Heb 1: 2 whom also He **m** the worlds
Heb 2: 7 You **m** him a little lower than
Heb 2: 9 who was **m** a little lower than
Heb 2:17 had to be **m** like His brethren
Heb 6:13 For when God **m** a promise to
Heb 7: 3 but **m** like the Son of God,
Heb 7:19 for the law **m** nothing perfect
Heb 7:20 not **m** priest without an oath
Heb 8: 9 to the covenant that I **m** with
Heb 8:13 He has **m** the first obsolete
Heb 9: 8 **m** manifest while the first
Heb 9:11 tabernacle not **m** with hands
Heb 9:24 the holy places **m** with hands
Heb 10:13 enemies are **m** His footstool
Heb 10:33 were **m** a spectacle both by
Heb 11: 3 which are seen were not **m** of
Heb 11:22 **m** mention of the departure of
Heb 11:34 out of weakness were **m** strong
Heb 11:40 be **m** perfect apart from us
Heb 12:23 spirits of just men **m** perfect
Heb 12:27 as of things that are **m**,
Jas 2:22 by works faith was **m** perfect
Jas 3: 9 men, who have been **m** in the
1Pe 3:18 but **m** alive by the Spirit
1Pe 3:22 having been **m** subject to Him
2Pe 1:16 we **m** known to you the power
2Pe 1:19 prophetic word **m** more sure
2Pe 2:12 brute beasts **m** to be caught
1Jn 2:19 that they might be **m** manifest
1Jn 4:18 not been **m** perfect in love
1Jn 5:10 believe God has **m** Him a liar
Rev 1: 6 has **m** us kings and priests to
Rev 5:10 have **m** us kings and priests to
Rev 7:14 **m** them white in the blood of
Rev 8:11 because it was **m** bitter
Rev 14: 7 and worship Him who **m** heaven
Rev 14: 8 because she has **m** all nations
Rev 17: 2 of the earth were **m** drunk
Rev 18:19 in one hour she is **m** desolate
Rev 19: 7 His wife has **m** herself ready

MADMAN (*see* MAD, MADMEN)
1Sa 21:15 to play the **m** in my presence
2Ki 9:11 Why did this **m** come to you
Prov 26:18 Like a **m** who throws

MADMANNAH
Josh 15:31 Ziklag, **M**, Sansannah,
1Ch 2:49 bore Shaaph the father of **M**

MADMEN (*see* MADMAN)
1Sa 21:15 Have I need of **m**, that you
Jer 48: 2 also shall be cut down, O **M**

MADMENAH
Is 10:31 **M** has fled, the inhabitants

MADNESS (*see* MAD)
Deut 28:28 LORD will strike you with **m**
1Sa 21:13 feigned **m** in their hands,
Eccl 1:17 to know wisdom and to know **m**
Eccl 2: 2 I said of laughter, "It is **m**"
Eccl 2:12 to consider wisdom and **m** and
Eccl 7:25 even of foolishness and **m**
Eccl 9: 3 **m** is in their hearts while
Eccl 10:13 end of his talk is raving **m**
Zech 12: 4 and its rider with **m**
2Pe 2:16 the **m** of the prophet

MADON
Josh 11: 1 he sent to Jobab king of **M**
Josh 12:19 the king of **M**, one

MAGBISH
Ezra 2:30 the people of **M**, one hundred

MAGDALA (*see* MAGDALENE)
Matt 15:39 and came to the region of **M**

MAGDALENE (*see* MAGDALA)
Matt 27:56 among whom were Mary **M**,
Matt 27:61 And Mary **M** was there, and the
Matt 28: 1 week began to dawn, Mary **M**
Mark 15:40 among whom were Mary **M**
Mark 15:47 And Mary **M** and Mary the
Mark 16: 1 the Sabbath was past, Mary **M**
Mark 16: 9 He appeared first to Mary **M**
Luke 8: 2 Mary called **M**, out of whom
Luke 24:10 It was Mary **M**, Joanna, Mary
John 19:25 the wife of Clopas, and Mary **M**
John 20: 1 Mary **M** came to the tomb early
John 20:18 Mary **M** came and told the

MAGDIEL
Gen 36:43 Chief **M**, and Chief Iram
1Ch 1:54 Chief **M**, and Chief Iram

MAGGOT
Job 25: 6 how much less man, who is a **m**
Is 14:11 the **m** is spread under you, and

MAGIC (*see* MAGICIAN)
Ezek 13:18 sew **m** charms on their sleeves
Ezek 13:20 I am against your **m** charms by
Acts 19:19 **m** brought their books

MAGICIAN (*see* MAGIC, MAGICIANS)
Dan 2:10 asked such things of any **m**

MAGICIANS (*see* MAGICIAN)
Gen 41: 8 called for all the **m** of Egypt
Gen 41:24 So I told this to the **m**, but
Ex 7:11 so the **m** of Egypt, they also
Ex 7:22 Then the **m** of Egypt did so
Ex 8: 7 And the **m** did so with their
Ex 8:18 Now the **m** so worked with
Ex 8:19 Then the **m** said to Pharaoh,
Ex 9:11 the **m** could not stand before
Ex 9:11 for the boils were on the **m**
Dan 1:20 times better than all the **m**
Dan 2: 2 the command to call the **m**
Dan 2:27 men, the astrologers, the **m**
Dan 4: 7 Then the **m**, the astrologers,
Dan 4: 9 Belteshazzar, chief of the **m**
Dan 5:11 made him chief of the **m**,

MAGISTRATE (*see* MAGISTRATES)
Luke 12:58 with your adversary to the **m**

MAGISTRATES (*see* MAGISTRATE)
Ezra 7:25 your God-given wisdom, set **m**
Is 60:17 and your **m** righteousness
Dan 3: 2 treasurers, the judges, the **m**
Dan 3: 3 treasurers, the judges, the **m**
Luke 12:11 you to the synagogues and **m**
Acts 16:20 And they brought them to the **m**
Acts 16:22 the **m** tore off their clothes
Acts 16:35 day, the **m** sent the officers,
Acts 16:36 The **m** have sent to let you go
Acts 16:38 told these words to the **m**

MAGNIFICENCE (*see* MAGNIFICENT)
Job 31:23 because of His **m** I could not
Acts 19:27 her **m** destroyed, whom all

MAGNIFICENT (*see* MAGNIFICENCE, MAGNIFY)
1Ch 22: 5 LORD must be exceedingly **m**

MAGNIFIED (*see* MAGNIFY)
Josh 4:14 On that day the LORD **m** Joshua
2Sa 7:26 So let Your name be **m** forever
1Ch 17:24 Your name may be **m** forever
Ps 35:27 Let the LORD be **m**, Who has
Ps 40:16 The LORD be **m**
Ps 55:12 who has **m** himself against me
Ps 70: 4 Let God be **m**
Ps 138: 2 For You have **m** Your word
Jer 48:26 for he **m** himself against the
Jer 48:42 because he has **m** himself
Lam 1: 9 for the enemy has **m** himself
Mal 1: 5 The LORD is **m** beyond the
Acts 19:17 name of the Lord Jesus was **m**
Phil 1:20 Christ will be **m** in my body

MAINSAIL
Acts 27:40 hoisted the **m** to the wind

MAINSTAY
Is 19:13 who are the **m** of its tribes

MAINTAIN (*see* MAINTAINED, MAINTAINING)
1Ki 8:45 and **m** their cause
1Ki 8:49 and **m** their cause,
1Ki 8:59 that He may **m** the cause of
1Ch 26:27 to **m** the house of the LORD
2Ch 6:35 and **m** their cause
2Ch 6:39 **m** their cause, and forgive
Ps 16: 5 You **m** my lot
Ps 140:12 I know that the LORD will **m**
Tit 3: 8 be careful to **m** good works
Tit 3:14 also learn to **m** good works

MAINTAINED (*see* MAINTAIN)
1Ch 4:33 and they **m** their genealogy
Ps 9: 4 For You have **m** my right and my

MAINTAINING (*see* MAINTAIN)
Acts 24: 9 **m** that these things were so

MAJESTIC (*see* MAJESTY)
Job 37: 4 He thunders with His **m** voice
Job 39:20 His **m** snorting strikes terror
Prov 30:29 things which are **m** in pace
Is 33:21 But there the **m** LORD will be
Is 33:21 sail, nor **m** ships pass by
Ezek 17: 8 fruit, and become a **m** vine
Ezek 17:23 bear fruit, and be a **m** cedar

MAJESTY (*see* MAJESTIC)
Deut 33:29 help and the sword of your **m**
1Ch 16:27 Honor and **m** are before Him
1Ch 29:11 glory, the victory and the **m**
1Ch 29:25 bestowed on him such royal **m**
Esth 1: 4 his excellent **m** for many days
Job 37:22 with God is awesome **m**
Job 40:10 Then adorn yourself with **m**
Ps 21: 5 **m** You have placed upon him
Ps 29: 4 of the LORD is full of **m**
Ps 45: 3 With Your glory and Your **m**
Ps 45: 4 in Your **m** ride prosperously
Ps 93: 1 reigns, He is clothed with **m**
Ps 96: 6 Honor and **m** are before Him
Ps 104: 1 are clothed with honor and **m**
Ps 145: 5 glorious splendor of Your **m**
Ps 145:12 the glorious **m** of His kingdom
Is 2:10 LORD and the glory of His **m**
Is 2:19 LORD and the glory of His **m**
Is 2:21 LORD and the glory of His **m**
Is 24:14 for the **m** of the LORD they
Is 26:10 not behold the **m** of the LORD
Ezek 7:20 his ornaments, he set it in **m**
Dan 4:30 and for the honor of my **m**
Dan 4:36 excellent **m** was added to me
Dan 5:18 your father a kingdom and **m**
Dan 5:19 because of the **m** that He gave
Mic 5: 4 in the **m** of the name of the
Luke 9:43 all amazed at the **m** of God
Heb 1: 3 right hand of the **M** on high
Heb 8: 1 of the **M** in the heavens,
2Pe 1:16 were eyewitnesses of His **m**
Jude 25 alone is wise, be glory and **m**

MAJORITY
Acts 27:12 the **m** advised to set sail
2Co 2: 6 **m** is sufficient for such a
2Co 9: 2 zeal has stirred up the **m**

MAKAZ
1Ki 4: 9 Ben-Deker, in **M**, Shaalbim,

MAKE (*see* MADE, MAKER, MAKES, MAKING, MAN-MADE)
Gen 1:26 Let Us **m** man in Our image,
Gen 2:18 I will **m** him a helper
Gen 3: 6 tree desirable to **m** one wise
Gen 6:14 **M** yourself an ark of
Gen 6:14 **m** rooms in the ark, and cover
Gen 6:15 And this is how you shall **m** it
Gen 6:16 You shall **m** a window for the
Gen 6:16 You shall **m** it with lower,
Gen 9:12 covenant which I **m** between Me
Gen 11: 3 Come, let us **m** bricks and bake
Gen 11: 4 let us **m** a name for ourselves
Gen 12: 2 I will **m** you a great nation
Gen 12: 2 you and **m** your name great
Gen 13:16 I will **m** your descendants as
Gen 17: 2 I will **m** My covenant between
Gen 17: 6 I will **m** you exceedingly
Gen 17: 6 I will **m** nations of you, and
Gen 17:20 will **m** him fruitful, and will
Gen 17:20 I will **m** him a great nation
Gen 18: 6 **m** ready three measures of
Gen 18: 6 knead it and **m** cakes
Gen 19:32 let us **m** our father drink
Gen 19:34 let us **m** him drink wine
Gen 21:13 Yet I will also **m** a nation of
Gen 21:18 for I will **m** him a great
Gen 24: 3 I will **m** you swear by the
Gen 26: 4 I will **m** your descendants
Gen 26:28 let us **m** a covenant with you,
Gen 27: 4 **m** me savory food, such as I
Gen 27: 7 **m** savory food for me, that I
Gen 27: 9 I will **m** savory food from
Gen 28: 3 **m** you fruitful and multiply
Gen 31:44 let us **m** a covenant, you and I
Gen 32:12 **m** your descendants as the
Gen 34: 9 And **m** marriages with us
Gen 35: 1 **m** an altar there to God, who
Gen 35: 3 I will **m** an altar there to
Gen 40:14 **m** mention of me to Pharaoh,
Gen 43:16 an animal and **m** ready
Gen 45: 1 **M** everyone go out from me
Gen 46: 3 for I will **m** of you a great
Gen 47: 6 then **m** them chief herdsmen
Gen 48: 4 I will **m** you fruitful and
Gen 48: 4 I will **m** of you a multitude
Gen 48:20 May God **m** you as Ephraim
Ex 5: 5 you **m** them rest from their
Ex 5: 7 straw to **m** brick as before
Ex 5:16 and they say to us, '**M** brick
Ex 8:23 I will **m** a difference between
Ex 9: 4 the LORD will **m** a difference
Ex 11: 7 **m** a difference between the
Ex 12: 4 **m** your count for the lamb
Ex 16: 8 which you **m** against Him
Ex 18:16 I **m** known the statutes of God
Ex 20: 4 You shall not **m** for yourself
Ex 20:23 You shall not **m** anything to
Ex 20:23 shall not **m** for yourselves
Ex 20:24 of earth you shall **m** for Me
Ex 20:25 if you **m** Me an altar of stone
Ex 21:34 of the pit shall **m** it good
Ex 22: 3 He should **m** full restitution
Ex 22: 5 he shall **m** restitution from
Ex 22: 6 shall surely **m** restitution
Ex 22:11 and he shall not **m** it good
Ex 22:12 he shall **m** restitution to the
Ex 22:13 he shall not **m** good what was
Ex 22:14 it, he shall surely **m** it good
Ex 22:15 it, he shall not **m** it good
Ex 23:13 **m** no mention of the name of
Ex 23:27 will **m** all your enemies turn
Ex 23:32 You shall **m** no covenant with
Ex 23:33 lest they **m** you sin against
Ex 25: 8 let them **m** Me a sanctuary,
Ex 25: 9 just so you shall **m** it
Ex 25:10 they shall **m** an ark of acacia
Ex 25:11 shall **m** on it a molding of
Ex 25:13 you shall **m** poles of acacia
Ex 25:17 You shall **m** a mercy seat of
Ex 25:18 you shall **m** two cherubim of
Ex 25:18 of hammered work you shall **m**
Ex 25:19 **M** one cherub at one end, and
Ex 25:19 you shall **m** the cherubim at
Ex 25:23 You shall also **m** a table of
Ex 25:24 and **m** a molding of gold all
Ex 25:25 You shall **m** for it a frame of
Ex 25:25 you shall **m** a gold molding
Ex 25:26 you shall **m** for it four rings
Ex 25:28 And you shall **m** the poles of
Ex 25:29 You shall **m** its dishes, its
Ex 25:29 You shall **m** them of pure gold
Ex 25:31 You shall also **m** a lampstand
Ex 25:37 You shall **m** seven lamps for
Ex 25:40 see to it that you **m** them
Ex 26: 1 Moreover you shall **m** the
Ex 26: 4 you shall **m** loops of blue
Ex 26: 5 shall **m** in the one curtain
Ex 26: 5 fifty loops you shall **m** on
Ex 26: 6 you shall **m** fifty clasps of
Ex 26: 7 You shall also **m** curtains of
Ex 26: 7 You shall **m** eleven curtains
Ex 26:10 You shall **m** fifty loops on
Ex 26:11 And you shall **m** fifty bronze
Ex 26:14 You shall also **m** a covering
Ex 26:15 the tabernacle you shall **m**
Ex 26:17 Thus you shall **m** for all the
Ex 26:18 you shall **m** the boards for
Ex 26:19 You shall **m** forty sockets of
Ex 26:22 you shall **m** six boards
Ex 26:23 you shall also **m** two boards
Ex 26:26 you shall **m** bars of acacia
Ex 26:29 **m** their rings of gold as
Ex 26:31 You shall **m** a veil woven of
Ex 26:36 You shall **m** a screen for the
Ex 26:37 you shall **m** for the screen
Ex 27: 1 You shall **m** an altar of
Ex 27: 2 You shall **m** its horns on its
Ex 27: 3 Also you shall **m** its pans to
Ex 27: 3 you shall **m** all its utensils
Ex 27: 4 You shall **m** a grate for it, a
Ex 27: 4 **m** four bronze rings at its
Ex 27: 6 you shall **m** poles for the
Ex 27: 8 You shall **m** it hollow with
Ex 27: 8 mountain, so shall they **m** it
Ex 27: 9 You shall also **m** the court of
Ex 28: 2 you shall **m** holy garments for
Ex 28: 3 that they may **m** Aaron's
Ex 28: 4 garments which they shall **m**
Ex 28: 4 So they shall **m** holy garments
Ex 28: 6 they shall **m** the ephod of
Ex 28:13 You shall also **m** settings of
Ex 28:14 you shall **m** two chains of
Ex 28:15 You shall **m** the breastplate
Ex 28:15 of the ephod you shall **m** it
Ex 28:15 linen thread, you shall **m** it
Ex 28:22 You shall **m** chains for the
Ex 28:23 you shall **m** two rings of gold
Ex 28:26 You shall **m** two rings of gold
Ex 28:27 rings of gold you shall **m**
Ex 28:31 You shall **m** the robe of the
Ex 28:33 shall **m** pomegranates of blue
Ex 28:36 You shall also **m** a plate of
Ex 28:39 you shall **m** the turban of
Ex 28:39 you shall **m** the sash of woven
Ex 28:40 sons you shall **m** tunics, and
Ex 28:40 you shall **m** sashes for them
Ex 28:40 you shall **m** hats for them,
Ex 28:42 you shall **m** for them linen
Ex 29: 2 with oil (you shall **m** them of
Ex 29:36 when you **m** atonement for it
Ex 29:37 Seven days you shall **m**
Ex 30: 1 You shall **m** an altar to burn
Ex 30: 1 you shall **m** it of acacia wood
Ex 30: 3 you shall **m** for it a molding
Ex 30: 4 gold rings you shall **m** for it
Ex 30: 5 You shall **m** the poles of
Ex 30:10 Aaron shall **m** atonement upon
Ex 30:10 he shall **m** atonement upon it
Ex 30:15 to **m** atonement for yourselves
Ex 30:16 to **m** atonement for yourselves
Ex 30:18 You shall also **m** a laver of
Ex 30:25 you shall **m** from these a holy
Ex 30:32 nor shall you **m** any other
Ex 30:35 You shall **m** of these an
Ex 30:37 the incense which you shall **m**
Ex 30:37 you shall not **m** any for
Ex 31: 6 that they may **m** all that I
Ex 32: 1 Come, **m** us gods that shall go
Ex 32:10 And I will **m** of you a great
Ex 32:23 me, '**M** us gods that shall go
Ex 32:30 perhaps I can **m** atonement for
Ex 33:19 I will **m** all My goodness pass
Ex 34:10 Behold, I **m** a covenant
Ex 34:12 lest you **m** a covenant with
Ex 34:15 lest you **m** a covenant with
Ex 34:15 **m** sacrifice to their gods, and
Ex 34:16 **m** your sons play the harlot
Ex 34:17 You shall **m** no molded gods
Ex 35:10 and **m** all that the LORD has
Lev 1: 4 behalf to **m** atonement for him
Lev 4:20 shall **m** atonement for them
Lev 4:26 shall **m** atonement for him
Lev 4:31 shall **m** atonement for him
Lev 4:35 So the priest shall **m**
Lev 5: 6 shall **m** atonement for him
Lev 5:10 So the priest shall **m**
Lev 5:13 shall **m** atonement for him
Lev 5:16 he shall **m** restitution for
Lev 5:16 So the priest shall **m**
Lev 5:18 So the priest shall **m**
Lev 6: 7 So the priest shall **m**
Lev 6:30 to **m** atonement in the holy
Lev 8:15 it, to **m** atonement for it
Lev 8:34 to do, to **m** atonement for you
Lev 9: 7 **m** atonement for yourself and
Lev 9: 7 **m** atonement for them, as the
Lev 10:17 to **m** atonement for them
Lev 11:43 You shall not **m** yourselves

Lev 11:43 nor shall you **m** yourselves
Lev 12: 7 LORD, and **m** atonement for her
Lev 12: 8 shall **m** atonement for her
Lev 14:18 So the priest shall **m**
Lev 14:19 **m** atonement for him who is to
Lev 14:20 shall **m** atonement for him
Lev 14:21 to **m** atonement for him,
Lev 14:29 to **m** atonement for him before
Lev 14:31 So the priest shall **m**
Lev 14:53 **m** atonement for the house, and
Lev 15:15 So the priest shall **m**
Lev 15:30 the priest shall **m** atonement
Lev 16: 6 **m** atonement for himself and
Lev 16:10 to **m** atonement upon it, and to
Lev 16:11 **m** atonement for himself and
Lev 16:16 So he shall **m** atonement for
Lev 16:17 meeting when he goes in to **m**
Lev 16:17 that he may **m** atonement for
Lev 16:18 **m** atonement for it, and shall
Lev 16:24 **m** atonement for himself and
Lev 16:27 blood was brought in to **m**
Lev 16:30 shall **m** atonement for you
Lev 16:32 shall **m** atonement, and put on
Lev 16:33 then he shall **m** atonement for
Lev 16:33 he shall **m** atonement for the
Lev 16:33 he shall **m** atonement for the
Lev 16:34 you, to **m** atonement for the
Lev 17:11 to **m** atonement for your souls
Lev 19: 4 nor **m** for yourselves molded
Lev 19:22 The priest shall **m** atonement
Lev 19:28 You shall not **m** any cuttings
Lev 20:25 you shall not **m** yourselves
Lev 21: 5 They shall not **m** any bald
Lev 21: 5 edges of their beards nor **m**
Lev 22:22 nor **m** an offering by fire of
Lev 22:24 nor shall you **m** any offering
Lev 23:28 to **m** atonement for you before
Lev 24: 2 light, to **m** the lamps burn
Lev 24:18 an animal shall **m** it good
Lev 25: 9 shall **m** the trumpet to sound
Lev 26: 1 You shall not **m** idols for
Lev 26: 6 and none will **m** you afraid
Lev 26: 9 **m** you fruitful, multiply you
Lev 26:19 I will **m** your heavens like
Lev 26:22 and **m** you few in number
Num 5: 7 He shall **m** restitution for
Num 5:21 the LORD **m** you a curse and an
Num 5:22 **m** your belly swell and your
Num 5:24 he shall **m** the woman drink
Num 5:26 afterward **m** the woman drink
Num 6: 7 He shall not **m** himself
Num 6:11 **m** atonement for him, because
Num 6:25 the LORD **m** His face shine
Num 8: 7 and so **m** themselves clean
Num 8:12 LORD, to **m** atonement for the
Num 8:19 and to **m** atonement for the
Num 10: 2 **M** two silver trumpets for
Num 10: 2 you shall **m** them of hammered
Num 12: 6 **m** Myself known to him in a
Num 14:12 and I will **m** of you a nation
Num 14:30 swore I would **m** you dwell in
Num 15: 3 you **m** an offering by fire to
Num 15: 3 to **m** a sweet aroma to the
Num 15:25 So the priest shall **m**
Num 15:28 So the priest shall **m**
Num 15:28 LORD, to **m** atonement for him
Num 15:38 Tell them to **m** tassels on the
Num 16:46 and **m** atonement for them
Num 21: 8 **M** a fiery serpent, and set it
Num 23:19 and will He not **m** it good
Num 28:22 to **m** atonement for you
Num 28:30 goats, to **m** atonement for you
Num 29: 5 to **m** atonement for you
Num 30: 8 he shall **m** void her vow which
Num 30:13 or her husband may **m** it void
Num 30:15 But if he does **m** them void
Num 31:50 to **m** atonement for ourselves
Deut 1:11 LORD God of your fathers **m**
Deut 1:13 I will **m** them heads over you
Deut 4:16 **m** for yourselves a carved
Deut 4:23 **m** for yourselves a carved
Deut 4:25 **m** a carved image in the form
Deut 5: 3 The LORD did not **m** this
Deut 5: 8 You shall not **m** for yourself
Deut 7: 2 You shall **m** no covenant with
Deut 7: 3 Nor shall you **m** marriages
Deut 8: 3 that He might **m** you know that
Deut 9:14 and I will **m** of you a nation
Deut 10: 1 **m** yourself an ark of wood
Deut 12:11 chooses to **m** His name abide
Deut 14:23 chooses to **m** His name abide
Deut 16: 6 chooses to **m** His name abide
Deut 16:11 chooses to **m** His name abide
Deut 19:18 shall **m** diligent inquiry, and
Deut 20: 9 that they shall **m** captains of
Deut 20:12 will not **m** peace with you
Deut 20:12 but would **m** war against you,
Deut 22: 8 then you shall **m** a parapet
Deut 22:12 You shall **m** tassels on the
Deut 23:21 When you **m** a vow to the LORD
Deut 26: 2 chooses to **m** His name abide
Deut 28:13 the LORD will **m** you the head
Deut 28:21 The LORD will **m** the plague
Deut 29: 1 **m** with the children of Israel
Deut 29:14 I **m** this covenant and this
Deut 30: 9 The LORD your God will **m** you
Deut 32:26 I will **m** the memory of them
Deut 32:39 I kill and I **m** alive
Deut 32:42 I will **m** My arrows drunk with
Josh 1: 8 For then you will **m** your way
Josh 5: 2 **M** flint knives for yourself,
Josh 6: 5 when they **m** a long blast with
Josh 6:10 You shall not shout or **m** any
Josh 6:18 **m** the camp of Israel a curse,
Josh 7:19 **m** confession to Him, and tell
Josh 9: 6 **m** a covenant with us
Josh 9: 7 so how can we **m** a covenant
Josh 9:11 **m** a covenant with us
Josh 22:25 would **m** our descendants cease
Josh 23: 7 You shall not **m** mention of
Josh 23:12 **m** marriages with them, and go
Josh 24: 9 arose to **m** war against Israel
Judg 2: 2 you shall **m** no covenant with
Judg 8:24 I would like to **m** a request
Judg 9:48 **m** haste and do as I have done
Judg 17: 3 son, to **m** a carved image and a
Judg 20:10 to **m** provisions for the
Judg 20:38 ambush was that they would **m**
Ruth 3: 3 but do not **m** yourself known
Ruth 4:11 The LORD **m** the woman who is
1Sa 1: 4 for Elkanah to **m** an offering
1Sa 1: 6 to **m** her miserable, because
1Sa 2: 8 **m** them inherit the throne of
1Sa 2:19 used to **m** him a little robe
1Sa 2:24 You **m** the LORD's people
1Sa 2:29 to **m** yourselves fat with the
1Sa 6: 5 Therefore you shall **m** images
1Sa 6: 7 **m** a new cart, take two milk
1Sa 8: 5 Now **m** for us a king to judge
1Sa 8:12 some to **m** his weapons of war
1Sa 8:22 their voice, and **m** them a king
1Sa 10: 8 and **m** sacrifices of peace
1Sa 11: 1 **M** a covenant with us, and we
1Sa 11: 2 I will **m** a covenant with you
1Sa 12:22 the LORD to **m** you His people
1Sa 13:19 Hebrews **m** swords or spears
1Sa 18:25 But Saul thought to **m**
1Sa 20:38 **M** haste, hurry, do not delay
1Sa 22: 7 and **m** you all captains of
1Sa 25:28 **m** for my lord an enduring
1Sa 28: 2 Therefore I will **m** you one of
1Sa 28:15 Philistines **m** war against me
1Sa 29: 4 **M** this fellow return, that he
2Sa 3:12 **M** your covenant with me, and
2Sa 3:13 I will **m** a covenant with you
2Sa 3:21 that they may **m** a covenant
2Sa 7:11 that He will **m** you a house
2Sa 7:21 to **m** Your servant know them
2Sa 7:23 to **m** for Himself a name
2Sa 13: 6 **m** a couple of cakes for me in
2Sa 15:14 **M** haste to depart, lest he
2Sa 15:20 Should I **m** you wander up and
2Sa 17: 2 and weak, and **m** him afraid
2Sa 21: 3 with what shall I **m** atonement
2Sa 22:35 He teaches my hands to **m** war
2Sa 23: 5 will He not **m** it increase
1Ki 1:37 **m** his throne greater than the
1Ki 1:47 May God **m** the name of
1Ki 1:47 may He **m** his throne greater
1Ki 2:42 Did I not **m** you swear by the
1Ki 8:33 **m** supplication to You in this
1Ki 8:47 **m** supplication to You in the
1Ki 12: 1 gone to Shechem to **m** him king
1Ki 12:10 but you **m** it lighter on us'
1Ki 16: 3 I will **m** your house like the
1Ki 16:19 had committed to **m** Israel sin
1Ki 16:21 to **m** him king, and half
1Ki 17:13 but **m** me a small cake from it
1Ki 17:13 afterward **m** some for yourself
1Ki 19: 2 if I do not **m** your life as
1Ki 21:22 I will **m** your house like the
1Ki 22:16 How many times shall I **m** you
2Ki 3:16 **M** this valley full of
2Ki 4:10 let us **m** a small upper room
2Ki 5: 7 **m** alive, that this man sends
2Ki 6: 2 let us **m** there a place where
2Ki 7: 2 would **m** windows in heaven
2Ki 7:19 would **m** windows in heaven
2Ki 8: 3 she went to **m** an appeal to
2Ki 9: 2 **m** him rise up from among his
2Ki 9: 9 So I will **m** the house of
2Ki 9:21 So Joram said, "**M** ready
2Ki 10: 5 but we will not **m** anyone king
2Ki 10:19 great sacrifice to **m** to Baal
2Ki 16: 5 came up to Jerusalem to **m** war
2Ki 17:29 to **m** gods of its own, and put
2Ki 18:30 nor let Hezekiah **m** you trust
2Ki 18:31 **M** peace with me by a present
2Ki 19: 9 come out to **m** war with you
2Ki 21: 8 and I will not **m** the feet of
2Ki 23:10 that no man might **m** his son
1Ch 6:49 to **m** atonement for Israel,
1Ch 11:10 to **m** him king, according to
1Ch 12:31 name to come and **m** David king
1Ch 12:38 to **m** David king over all
1Ch 12:38 of one mind to **m** David king
1Ch 16: 8 **m** known His deeds among the
1Ch 17:21 to **m** for Yourself a name by
1Ch 21: 3 May the LORD **m** His people a
1Ch 22: 5 I will now **m** preparation for
1Ch 28: 4 to **m** me king over all Israel
1Ch 29:12 in Your hand it is to **m** great
2Ch 2:14 and to **m** any engraving and to
2Ch 2:18 to **m** the people work
2Ch 5:13 to **m** one sound to be heard in
2Ch 6:24 **m** supplication before You in
2Ch 6:37 **m** supplication to You in the
2Ch 7:11 to **m** in the house of the LORD
2Ch 7:20 will **m** it to be a proverb and
2Ch 8: 9 But Solomon did not **m** the
2Ch 10: 1 gone to Shechem to **m** him king
2Ch 10:10 but you **m** it lighter on us'
2Ch 11:22 for he intended to **m** him king
2Ch 14: 7 and **m** walls around them, and
2Ch 17:10 so that they did not **m** war
2Ch 18:15 How many times shall I **m** you
2Ch 20:36 to **m** ships to go to Tarshish
2Ch 22: 5 of Ahab king of Israel to **m**
2Ch 25: 8 God shall **m** you fall before
2Ch 29:10 to **m** a covenant with the LORD
2Ch 29:24 altar as a sin offering to **m**
2Ch 30: 5 So they resolved to **m** a
2Ch 32: 2 to **m** war against Jerusalem
2Ch 35:21 God commanded me to **m** haste
Ezra 4:21 command to **m** these men cease
Ezra 5: 5 so that they could not **m** them
Ezra 10: 3 let us **m** a covenant with our
Ezra 10:11 **m** confession to the LORD God
Neh 2: 8 he must give me timber to **m**
Neh 6: 9 were trying to **m** us afraid
Neh 8:15 to **m** booths, as it is written
Neh 9:38 we **m** a sure covenant, and
Neh 10:33 to **m** atonement for Israel
Esth 1:20 **m** is proclaimed throughout
Esth 4: 8 king to **m** supplication to him
Esth 9:22 that they should **m** them days
Job 5:18 wounds, but His hands **m** whole
Job 8: 5 **m** your supplication to the
Job 11: 3 talk **m** men hold their peace
Job 11:19 and no one would **m** you afraid
Job 13:11 His excellence **m** you afraid
Job 13:21 the dread of You **m** me afraid
Job 13:23 **M** me know my transgression
Job 13:26 **m** me inherit the iniquities
Job 15:24 and anguish **m** him afraid
Job 17:13 if I **m** my bed in the darkness
Job 20: 2 anxious thoughts **m** me answer
Job 22: 3 you **m** your ways blameless
Job 22:27 You will **m** your prayer to Him
Job 23:13 and who can **m** Him change
Job 24:25 **m** my speech worth nothing
Job 31:15 made me in the womb **m** them
Job 34:29 who then can **m** trouble
Job 39:27 and **m** its nest on high
Job 41: 3 Will he **m** many supplications
Job 41: 4 Will he **m** a covenant with you
Job 41: 6 companions **m** a banquet of him
Job 41:28 The arrow cannot **m** him flee
Ps 4: 8 O LORD, **m** me dwell in safety
Ps 5: 8 **M** Your way straight before my

Ps 6: 6 All night I **m** my bed swim
Ps 11: 2 They **m** ready their arrow on
Ps 18:34 He teaches my hands to **m** war
Ps 21: 9 You shall **m** them as a fiery
Ps 21:12 Therefore You will **m** them
Ps 21:12 You will **m** ready Your arrows
Ps 31:16 **M** Your face shine upon Your
Ps 33: 2 **M** melody to Him with an
Ps 34: 2 My soul shall **m** its boast in
Ps 38:22 **M** haste to help me, O Lord,
Ps 39: 4 **m** me to know my end, And
Ps 39: 8 Do not **m** me the reproach of
Ps 39:11 You **m** his beauty melt away
Ps 40:13 O LORD, **m** haste to help me
Ps 44:10 You **m** us turn back from the
Ps 44:13 You **m** us a reproach to our
Ps 44:14 You **m** us a byword among the
Ps 45:16 Whom You shall **m** princes in
Ps 45:17 I will **m** Your name to be
Ps 46: 4 shall **m** glad the city of God
Ps 51: 6 You will **m** me to know wisdom
Ps 51: 8 **M** me to hear joy and gladness,
Ps 52: 7 did not **m** God his strength
Ps 57: 1 Your wings I will **m** my refuge
Ps 64: 8 So He will **m** them stumble
Ps 65: 8 You **m** the outgoings of the
Ps 65:10 You **m** it soft with showers,
Ps 66: 1 **M** a joyful shout to God, all
Ps 66: 2 **M** His praise glorious
Ps 66: 8 **m** the voice of His praise to
Ps 69:23 And **m** their loins shake
Ps 70: 1 **M** haste, O God, to deliver me
Ps 70: 1 **M** haste to help me, O LORD
Ps 70: 5 **M** haste to me, O God
Ps 71:12 O my God, **m** haste to help me
Ps 71:16 I will **m** mention of Your
Ps 76:11 **M** vows to the LORD your God,
Ps 78: 5 That they should **m** them known
Ps 81: 1 **M** a joyful shout to the God
Ps 83: 2 Your enemies **m** a tumult
Ps 83:11 **M** their nobles like Oreb and
Ps 83:13 **m** them like the whirling dust
Ps 84: 6 of Baca, They **m** it a spring
Ps 85:13 shall **m** His footsteps our
Ps 87: 4 I will **m** mention of Rahab and
Ps 89: 1 With my mouth will I **m** known
Ps 89:27 Also I will **m** him My
Ps 89:29 I will **m** to endure forever
Ps 90:15 **M** us glad according to the
Ps 100: 1 **M** a joyful shout to the LORD,
Ps 104:15 Oil to **m** his face shine, And
Ps 104:17 Where the birds **m** their nests
Ps 104:20 You **m** darkness, and it is
Ps 105: 1 **M** known His deeds among the
Ps 106: 8 That He might **m** His mighty
Ps 110: 1 Till I **m** Your enemies Your
Ps 115: 8 Those who **m** them are like
Ps 119:27 **M** me understand the way of
Ps 119:35 **M** me walk in the path of Your
Ps 119:98 **m** me wiser than my enemies
Ps 119:135 **M** Your face shine upon Your
Ps 132:17 There I will **m** the horn of
Ps 135:18 Those who **m** them are like
Ps 139: 8 If I **m** my bed in hell, behold
Ps 140: 4 to **m** my steps stumble
Ps 141: 1 **M** haste to me
Ps 142: 1 the LORD I **m** my supplication
Ps 145:12 To **m** known to the sons of men
Prov 1:16 they **m** haste to shed blood
Prov 1:23 I will **m** my words known to
Prov 4:16 unless they **m** someone fall
Prov 22:21 That I may **m** you know the
Prov 22:24 **M** no friendship with an angry
Prov 23: 5 certainly **m** themselves wings
Prov 24:27 **m** it fit for yourself in the
Prov 27:11 **m** my heart glad, that I may
Prov 30:26 yet they **m** their homes in the
Eccl 5: 4 When you **m** a vow to God, do
Eccl 7:13 for who can **m** straight what
Song 1: 7 where you **m** it rest at noon
Song 1:11 We will **m** you ornaments of
Song 8:14 **M** haste, my beloved, and be
Is 1:15 though you **m** many prayers
Is 1:16 **m** yourselves clean
Is 3: 7 do not **m** me a ruler of the
Is 5:19 Let Him **m** speed and hasten His
Is 6:10 **M** the heart of this people
Is 7: 1 Jerusalem to **m** war against it
Is 7: 6 let us **m** a gap in its wall
Is 10:23 **m** a determined end in the
Is 11:15 and **m** men cross over dryshod
Is 12: 4 **m** mention that His name is
Is 13:12 I will **m** a mortal more rare
Is 13:20 **m** their sheepfolds there
Is 14:23 I will also **m** it a possession
Is 16: 3 **m** your shadow like the night
Is 17: 2 and no one will **m** them afraid
Is 17:11 you will **m** your plant to grow
Is 17:11 will **m** your seed to flourish
Is 17:12 of many people who **m** a noise
Is 17:12 **m** a rushing like the rushing
Is 19:10 All who **m** wages will be
Is 19:21 will **m** sacrifice and offering
Is 19:21 they will **m** a vow to the LORD
Is 23:16 **m** sweet melody, sing many
Is 25: 6 the LORD of hosts will **m** for
Is 26:13 but by You only we **m** mention
Is 27: 5 that he may **m** peace with Me
Is 27: 5 and he shall **m** peace with Me
Is 28: 9 whom will he **m** to understand
Is 28:17 Also I will **m** justice the
Is 29:16 He did not **m** me"
Is 29:21 who **m** a man an offender by a
Is 32:11 **m** yourselves bare, and gird
Is 33: 1 when you **m** an end of dealing
Is 34:15 arrow snake shall **m** her nest
Is 35: 3 and **m** firm the feeble knees
Is 36:15 nor let Hezekiah **m** you trust
Is 36:16 **M** peace with me by a present
Is 37: 9 come out to **m** war with you
Is 38:12 night You **m** an end of me
Is 38:13 night You **m** an end of me
Is 38:16 will restore me and **m** me live
Is 38:19 the father shall **m** known Your
Is 40: 3 **m** straight in the desert a
Is 41:15 I will **m** you into a new
Is 41:15 and **m** the hills like chaff
Is 41:18 I will **m** the wilderness a
Is 42:15 I will **m** the rivers
Is 42:16 I will **m** darkness light
Is 42:21 the law and **m** it honorable
Is 43:19 I will even **m** a road in the
Is 44: 9 Those who **m** a graven image,
Is 44:19 shall I **m** the rest of it an
Is 45: 2 **m** the crooked places straight
Is 45: 7 I **m** peace and create calamity
Is 45:14 They will **m** supplication to
Is 46: 5 **m** Me equal and compare Me,
Is 48: 1 and **m** mention of the God of
Is 49:11 I will **m** each of My mountains
Is 49:17 Your sons shall **m** haste
Is 50: 2 I **m** the rivers a wilderness
Is 50: 3 I **m** sackcloth their covering
Is 51: 3 He will **m** her wilderness like
Is 51: 4 I will **m** My justice rest as a
Is 52: 5 rule over them **m** them wail
Is 53:10 When You **m** His soul an
Is 54: 3 and **m** the desolate cities
Is 54:12 I will **m** your pinnacles of
Is 55: 3 and I will **m** an everlasting
Is 55:10 **m** it bring forth and bud, that
Is 56: 7 **m** them joyful in My house of
Is 57: 4 whom do you **m** a wide mouth
Is 58: 4 to **m** your voice heard on high
Is 59: 7 they **m** haste to shed innocent
Is 60:13 I will **m** the place of My feet
Is 60:15 you, I will **m** you an eternal
Is 60:17 I will also **m** your officers
Is 61: 8 truth, and will **m** with them an
Is 62: 6 You who **m** mention of the LORD
Is 63:12 the water before them to **m**
Is 63:14 to **m** Yourself a glorious name
Is 64: 2 to **m** Your name known to Your
Is 66:22 will **m** shall remain before Me
Jer 4: 7 place to **m** your land desolate
Jer 4:16 **M** mention to the nations, yes
Jer 4:27 yet I will not **m** a full end
Jer 4:30 vain you will **m** yourself fair
Jer 5:10 but do not **m** a complete end
Jer 5:14 I will **m** My words in your
Jer 5:18 I will not **m** a complete end
Jer 6: 8 lest I **m** you desolate, a land
Jer 6:26 **M** mourning as for an only son
Jer 7:16 nor **m** intercession to Me
Jer 7:18 to **m** cakes for the queen of
Jer 9:11 I will **m** Jerusalem a heap of
Jer 9:11 I will **m** the cities of Judah
Jer 9:18 Let them **m** haste and take up a
Jer 10:22 to **m** the cities of Judah
Jer 15:14 I will **m** you cross over with
Jer 15:20 I will **m** you to this people a
Jer 16: 6 nor **m** themselves bald for
Jer 16:20 Will a man **m** gods for himself
Jer 18: 4 good to the potter to **m**
Jer 18:11 **m** your ways and your doings
Jer 18:16 to **m** their land desolate and a
Jer 19: 7 I will **m** void the counsel of
Jer 19: 8 I will **m** this city desolate
Jer 19:12 and **m** this city like Tophet
Jer 20: 4 I will **m** you a terror to
Jer 20: 9 I will not **m** mention of Him,
Jer 22: 6 will **m** you a wilderness, and
Jer 23:15 **m** them drink the water of
Jer 23:16 They **m** you worthless
Jer 23:27 who try to **m** My people forget
Jer 25: 9 **m** them an astonishment, a
Jer 25:12 and I will **m** it a perpetual
Jer 25:18 to **m** them a desolation, an
Jer 26: 6 then I will **m** this house like
Jer 26: 6 will **m** this city a curse to
Jer 27: 2 **M** for yourselves bonds and
Jer 27: 7 kings shall **m** him serve them
Jer 27:18 let them now **m** intercession
Jer 28:15 but you **m** this people trust
Jer 29:17 will **m** them like rotten figs
Jer 29:22 The LORD **m** you like Zedekiah
Jer 30:10 and no one shall **m** him afraid
Jer 30:11 though I **m** a full end of all
Jer 30:11 yet I will not **m** a complete
Jer 30:16 prey upon you I will **m** a prey
Jer 30:19 voice of those who **m** merry
Jer 31:13 **m** them rejoice rather than
Jer 31:21 Set up signposts, **m** landmarks
Jer 31:31 when I will **m** a new covenant
Jer 31:33 **m** with the house of Israel
Jer 32:40 And I will **m** an everlasting
Jer 34:22 I will **m** the cities of Judah
Jer 37:20 do not **m** me return to the
Jer 38:26 that he would not **m** me return
Jer 44:19 did we **m** cakes for her, to
Jer 46:27 No one shall **m** him afraid
Jer 46:28 For I will **m** a complete end
Jer 46:28 but I will not **m** a complete
Jer 48:26 **M** him drunk, for he magnified
Jer 49:15 I will **m** you small among
Jer 49:16 Though you **m** your nest as
Jer 49:19 but I will suddenly **m** him run
Jer 49:20 surely He shall **m** their
Jer 50: 3 her, which shall **m** her land
Jer 50:44 but I will **m** them suddenly
Jer 50:45 surely He will **m** their
Jer 51:11 **M** the arrows bright
Jer 51:12 **m** the guard strong, set up
Jer 51:25 and **m** you a burnt mountain
Jer 51:29 to **m** the land of Babylon a
Jer 51:36 her sea and **m** her springs dry
Jer 51:39 I will **m** them drunk, that
Jer 51:57 I will **m** drunk her princes and
Lam 4:21 drunk and **m** yourself naked
Ezek 3:26 I will **m** your tongue cling to
Ezek 4: 9 **m** bread of them for yourself
Ezek 5:14 Moreover I will **m** you a waste
Ezek 6:14 **m** the land desolate, yes,
Ezek 7:23 **M** a chain, for the land is
Ezek 8: 6 to **m** Me go far away from My
Ezek 11:13 Will You **m** a complete end of
Ezek 13:18 and **m** veils for the heads of
Ezek 14: 8 **m** him a sign and a proverb, and
Ezek 14:15 **m** it so desolate that no man
Ezek 15: 3 taken from it to **m** any object
Ezek 15: 3 Or can men **m** a peg from it to
Ezek 15: 8 Thus I will **m** the land
Ezek 16:33 Men **m** payment to all harlots,
Ezek 16:41 I will **m** you cease playing
Ezek 20: 4 Then **m** known to them the
Ezek 20:17 I did not **m** an end of them in
Ezek 20:26 that I might **m** them desolate
Ezek 20:31 **m** your sons pass through the
Ezek 20:37 I will **m** you pass under the
Ezek 21:10 Sharpened to **m** a dreadful
Ezek 21:10 Should we then **m** mirth
Ezek 21:19 **M** a sign; put it at the head
Ezek 21:27 I will **m** it overthrown
Ezek 22:30 among them who would **m** a wall
Ezek 23:27 Thus I will **m** you cease your
Ezek 24: 5 **m** it boil well, and let the
Ezek 24: 9 I too will **m** the pyre great
Ezek 24:17 **m** no mourning for the dead
Ezek 25: 4 **m** their dwellings among you
Ezek 25: 5 I will **m** Rabbah a stable for

Ezek 25:13 and **m** it desolate from Teman
Ezek 26: 4 **m** her like the top of a rock
Ezek 26:14 I will **m** you like the top of
Ezek 26:19 When I **m** you a desolate city
Ezek 26:20 I will **m** you dwell in the
Ezek 26:21 I will **m** you a terror, and
Ezek 27: 5 from Lebanon to **m** you a mast
Ezek 27:30 They will **m** their voice heard
Ezek 29:10 I will **m** the land of Egypt
Ezek 29:12 I will **m** the land of Egypt
Ezek 30: 9 to **m** the careless Ethiopians
Ezek 30:10 I will also **m** a multitude of
Ezek 30:12 I will **m** the rivers dry, and
Ezek 30:12 I will **m** the land waste, and
Ezek 30:14 I will **m** Pathros desolate,
Ezek 30:21 to **m** it strong enough to hold
Ezek 30:22 I will **m** the sword fall out
Ezek 32: 7 heavens, and **m** its stars dark
Ezek 32: 8 I will **m** dark over you, and
Ezek 32:10 Yes, I will **m** many peoples
Ezek 32:14 Then I will **m** their waters
Ezek 32:14 **m** their rivers run like oil,'
Ezek 32:15 When I **m** the land of Egypt
Ezek 33: 2 and **m** him their watchman,
Ezek 33:28 For I will **m** the land most
Ezek 34:15 I will **m** them lie down,"
Ezek 34:25 I will **m** a covenant of peace
Ezek 34:26 I will **m** them and the places
Ezek 34:28 and no one shall **m** them afraid
Ezek 35: 3 you, and **m** you most desolate
Ezek 35: 7 Thus I will **m** Mount Seir most
Ezek 35: 9 I will **m** you perpetually
Ezek 35:11 I will **m** Myself known among
Ezek 35:14 rejoice when I **m** you desolate
Ezek 36:11 I will **m** you inhabited as in
Ezek 37:19 **m** them one stick, and they
Ezek 37:22 I will **m** them one nation in
Ezek 37:26 Moreover I will **m** a covenant
Ezek 38:10 and you will **m** an evil plan
Ezek 39: 7 So I will **m** My holy name
Ezek 39: 9 they will **m** fires with them
Ezek 39:10 because they will **m** fires
Ezek 39:14 months they will **m** a search
Ezek 43:11 **m** known to them the design of
Ezek 43:20 it and **m** atonement for it
Ezek 43:26 Seven days they shall **m**
Ezek 44:14 Nevertheless I will **m** them
Ezek 45:15 to **m** atonement for them,"
Ezek 45:17 and the peace offerings to **m**
Ezek 45:20 Thus you shall **m** atonement
Ezek 46:13 You shall daily **m** a burnt
Dan 2: 5 if you do not **m** known the
Dan 2: 9 if you do not **m** known the
Dan 2:25 who will **m** known to the king
Dan 2:26 Are you able to **m** known to me
Dan 2:30 but for our sakes who **m** known
Dan 3:29 Therefore I **m** a decree that
Dan 4: 6 they might **m** known to me the
Dan 4: 7 did not **m** known to me its
Dan 4:18 not able to **m** known to me the
Dan 4:25 they shall **m** you eat grass
Dan 4:32 They shall **m** you eat grass
Dan 5: 8 or **m** known to the king its
Dan 5:15 writing and **m** known to me its
Dan 5:16 writing and **m** known to me its
Dan 5:17 king, and **m** known to him the
Dan 6: 7 and to **m** a firm decree, that
Dan 6:26 I **m** a decree that in every
Dan 8:16 **m** this man understand the
Dan 9: 3 God to **m** request by prayer
Dan 9:24 to **m** an end of sins
Dan 9:24 to **m** reconciliation for
Dan 10:14 Now I have come to **m** you
Dan 11: 6 the North to **m** an agreement
Dan 11:35 **m** them white, until the time
Hos 2: 3 **m** her like a wilderness, and
Hos 2:12 So I will **m** them a forest,
Hos 2:18 In that day I will **m** a
Hos 2:18 to **m** them lie down safely
Hos 5: 9 Israel I **m** known what is sure
Hos 7: 3 They **m** a king glad with their
Hos 10:11 I will **m** Ephraim pull a plow
Hos 11: 8 How can I **m** you like Admah
Hos 12: 1 Also they **m** a covenant with
Hos 12: 9 I will again **m** you dwell in
Joel 2:19 I will no longer **m** you a
Amos 8: 4 **m** the poor of the land fail,
Amos 8: 9 That I will **m** the sun go down
Amos 8:10 I will **m** it like mourning for
Amos 9:14 They shall also **m** gardens
Obad 2 I will **m** you small among the
Mic 1: 6 Therefore I will **m** Samaria a
Mic 1: 8 I will **m** a wailing like the
Mic 1:16 **M** yourself bald and cut off
Mic 2:12 they shall **m** a loud noise
Mic 3: 5 who **m** my people stray
Mic 4: 4 and no one shall **m** them afraid
Mic 4: 7 I will **m** the lame a remnant,
Mic 4:13 for I will **m** your horn iron,
Mic 4:13 I will **m** your hooves bronze
Mic 6:13 Therefore I will also **m** you
Mic 6:15 **m** sweet wine, but not drink
Mic 6:16 that I may **m** you a desolation
Nah 1: 8 **m** an utter end of its place
Nah 1: 9 He will **m** an utter end of it
Nah 2: 5 they **m** haste to her walls, and
Nah 3: 6 **m** you vile, and **m** you a
Nah 3:14 **M** strong the brick kiln
Nah 3:15 **M** yourself many—like the
Nah 3:15 **M** yourself many—like the
Hab 1:14 Why do You **m** men like fish of
Hab 2: 2 **m** it plain on tablets, that
Hab 2:15 even to **m** him drunk, that you
Hab 2:18 trust in it, to **m** mute idols
Hab 3: 2 midst of the years **m** it known
Hab 3:19 he will **m** my feet like deer's
Hab 3:19 He will **m** me walk on my high
Zeph 1:18 for He will **m** speedy riddance
Zeph 2:13 **m** Nineveh a desolation, as
Zeph 3:13 and no one shall **m** them afraid
Hag 2:23 will **m** you as a signet ring
Zech 6:11 **m** an elaborate crown, and set
Zech 9:17 Grain shall **m** the young men
Zech 10: 1 the LORD will **m** flashing
Zech 10: 3 and will **m** them as His royal
Zech 12: 2 I will **m** Jerusalem a cup of
Zech 12: 3 will **m** Jerusalem a very heavy
Zech 12: 6 In that day I will **m** the
Mal 2:15 But did He not **m** them one
Mal 3:17 day that I **m** them My jewels
Matt 1:19 not wanting to **m** her a public
Matt 3: 3 LORD, **m** His paths straight
Matt 4:19 I will **m** you fishers of men
Matt 5:36 because you cannot **m** one hair
Matt 8: 2 willing, You can **m** me clean
Matt 9:24 **M** room, for the girl is not
Matt 12:16 them not to **m** Him known,
Matt 12:33 Either **m** the tree good and its
Matt 12:33 or else **m** the tree bad and its
Matt 17: 4 You wish, let us **m** here three
Matt 22:44 till I **m** Your enemies Your
Matt 23: 5 They **m** their phylacteries
Matt 23:14 for a pretense **m** long prayers
Matt 23:15 you **m** him twice as much a son
Matt 24:47 will **m** him ruler over all his
Matt 25:21 I will **m** you ruler over many
Matt 25:23 I will **m** you ruler over many
Matt 27:65 **m** it as secure as you know
Matt 28:14 appease him and **m** you secure
Matt 28:19 and **m** disciples of all the
Mark 1: 3 LORD, **m** His paths straight
Mark 1:17 I will **m** you become fishers
Mark 1:40 willing, You can **m** me clean
Mark 3:12 they should not **m** Him known
Mark 5:39 Why **m** this commotion and
Mark 6:39 Then He commanded them to **m**
Mark 9: 5 let us **m** three tabernacles
Mark 12:36 till I **m** Your enemies Your
Mark 12:40 for a pretense **m** long prayers
Mark 12:42 two mites, which **m** a quadrans
Mark 14:15 there **m** ready for us
Luke 1:17 to **m** ready a people prepared
Luke 3: 4 LORD, **m** His paths straight
Luke 5:12 willing, You can **m** me clean
Luke 5:14 and **m** an offering for your
Luke 5:33 **m** prayers, and likewise those
Luke 5:34 Can you **m** the friends of the
Luke 9:14 **M** them sit down in groups of
Luke 9:33 let us **m** three tabernacles
Luke 11:39 Now you Pharisees **m** the
Luke 11:40 the outside **m** the inside also
Luke 12:42 whom his master will **m** ruler
Luke 12:44 I say to you that he will **m**
Luke 12:58 **m** every effort along the way
Luke 14:18 one accord began to **m** excuses
Luke 14:31 king, going to **m** war against
Luke 15:19 **M** me like one of your hired
Luke 15:29 that I might **m** merry with my
Luke 15:32 right that we should **m** merry
Luke 16: 9 **m** friends for yourselves by
Luke 19: 5 **m** haste and come down, for
Luke 19:42 things that **m** for your peace
Luke 20:43 till I **m** Your enemies Your
Luke 20:47 for a pretense **m** long prayers
Luke 22:12 furnished upper room; there **m**
John 1:23 **M** straight the way of the
John 2:16 Do not **m** My Father's house a
John 6:10 said, "**M** the people sit down
John 6:15 Him by force to **m** Him king
John 8:32 and the truth shall **m** you free
John 8:53 Whom do You **m** Yourself out
John 10:33 being a Man, **m** Yourself God
John 14:23 to him and **m** Our home with
Acts 2:28 you will **m** me full of joy in
Acts 2:35 till I **m** Your enemies Your
Acts 7:40 **M** us gods to go before us
Acts 7:44 instructing Moses to **m** it
Acts 9:34 Arise and **m** your bed
Acts 19:33 wanted to **m** his defense to
Acts 19:39 have any other inquiry to **m**
Acts 22:18 to me, '**M** haste and get out of
Acts 23:15 going to **m** further inquiries
Acts 24:22 I will **m** a decision on your
Acts 26:16 to **m** you a minister and a
Rom 1: 9 Son, that without ceasing I **m**
Rom 2:17 law, and **m** your boast in God,
Rom 2:23 You who **m** your boast in the
Rom 3: 3 Will their unbelief **m** the
Rom 3:31 Do we then **m** void the law
Rom 9:21 to **m** one vessel for honor
Rom 9:22 to **m** His power known, endured
Rom 9:23 that He might **m** known the
Rom 9:28 because the LORD will **m** a
Rom 13:14 **m** no provision for the flesh,
Rom 14: 4 God is able to **m** him stand
Rom 14:19 the things which **m** for peace
Rom 15:18 to **m** the Gentiles obedient
Rom 15:26 and Achaia to **m** a certain
1Co 6:15 **m** them members of a harlot
1Co 8:13 lest I **m** my brother stumble
1Co 9:15 should **m** my boasting void
1Co 10:13 will also **m** the way of escape
1Co 12: 3 Therefore I **m** known to you
1Co 14: 7 or harp, when they **m** a sound
1Co 14: 7 unless they **m** a distinction
2Co 2: 2 For if I **m** you sorrowful,
2Co 5: 9 Therefore we **m** it our aim
2Co 8: 1 we **m** known to you the grace
2Co 9: 8 God is able to **m** all grace
Gal 1:11 But I **m** known to you,
Gal 2:18 I **m** myself a transgressor
Gal 3:17 that it should **m** the promise
Gal 6:12 As many as desire to **m** a good
Eph 3: 9 to **m** all people see what is
Eph 6:19 to **m** known the mystery of the
Eph 6:21 will **m** all things known to
Col 1:27 To them God willed to **m** known
Col 4: 4 that I may **m** it manifest, as
Col 4: 9 They will **m** known to you all
1Th 3:12 may the Lord **m** you increase
2Th 3: 9 but to **m** ourselves an example
2Ti 3: 6 **m** captives of gullible women
2Ti 3:15 which are able to **m** you wise
Heb 1:13 Till I **m** Your enemies Your
Heb 2:10 to **m** the author of their
Heb 2:17 to **m** propitiation for the
Heb 7:25 to **m** intercession for them
Heb 8: 5 was about to **m** the tabernacle
Heb 8: 5 See that you **m** all things
Heb 8: 8 when I will **m** a new covenant
Heb 8:10 **m** with the house of Israel
Heb 9: 9 **m** him who performed the
Heb 10: 1 **m** those who approach perfect
Heb 10:16 **m** with them after those days
Heb 12:13 **m** straight paths for your
Heb 13:21 **m** you complete in every good
Jas 3:18 in peace by those who **m** peace
Jas 4:13 buy and sell, and **m** a profit"
2Pe 1:10 diligent to **m** your calling
1Jn 1:10 we **m** Him a liar, and His word
Rev 3: 9 Indeed I will **m** those of the
Rev 3: 9 indeed I will **m** them come
Rev 3:12 I will **m** him a pillar in the
Rev 10: 9 it will **m** your stomach bitter
Rev 11: 7 pit will **m** war against them
Rev 11:10 **m** merry, and send gifts to one
Rev 12:17 he went to **m** war with the
Rev 13: 4 Who is able to **m** war with him
Rev 13: 7 him to **m** war with the saints
Rev 13:14 **m** an image to the beast who

Rev 17:14 These will **m** war with the
Rev 17:16 **m** her desolate and naked, eat
Rev 19:19 gathered together to **m** war
Rev 21: 5 Behold, I **m** all things new

MAKER (*see* MAKE, MAKERS)
Ex 35:35 designer and the tapestry **m**
Job 4:17 a man be more pure than his **M**
Job 32:22 else my **M** would soon take me
Job 35:10 one says, "Where is God my **M**
Job 36: 3 ascribe righteousness to my **M**
Ps 95: 6 kneel before the LORD our **M**
Ps 149: 2 Let Israel rejoice in their **M**
Prov 14:31 the poor reproaches his **M**
Prov 17: 5 the poor reproaches his **M**
Prov 22: 2 the LORD is the **m** of them all
Is 17: 7 day a man will look to his **M**
Is 22:11 But you did not look to its **M**
Is 45: 9 to him who strives with his **M**
Is 45:11 Holy One of Israel, and his **M**
Is 51:13 And you forget the LORD your **M**
Is 54: 5 For your **M** is your husband,
Jer 10:16 for He is the **M** of all things
Jer 51:19 for He is the **M** of all things
Hos 8:14 Israel has forgotten his **M**
Hab 2:18 that its **m** should carve it,
Hab 2:18 that the **m** of its mold should
Heb 11:10 whose builder and **m** is God

MAKERS (*see* MAKER)
Is 45:16 together, who are **m** of idols

MAKES (*see* MAKE)
Ex 4:11 Or who **m** the mute, the deaf,
Ex 30:38 Whoever **m** any like it, to
Lev 7: 7 the priest who **m** atonement
Lev 14:11 Then the priest who **m** him
Lev 17:11 that **m** atonement for the soul
Num 5:21 when the LORD **m** your thigh
Num 30: 7 **m** no response to her on the
Num 30:14 But if her husband **m** no
Deut 18:10 who **m** his son or his daughter
Deut 20:20 the city that **m** war with you
Deut 27:15 Cursed is the one who **m** any
Deut 27:18 Cursed is the one who **m** the
Deut 29:12 your God **m** with you today
1Sa 2: 6 The LORD kills and **m** alive
1Sa 2: 7 The LORD **m** poor and **m** rich
2Sa 22:33 power, and He **m** my way
2Sa 22:34 He **m** my feet like the feet of
1Ki 8:29 servant **m** toward this place
Job 12:17 and **m** fools of the judges
Job 12:23 He **m** nations great, and
Job 12:24 **m** them wander in a pathless
Job 12:25 and He **m** them stagger like a
Job 25: 2 He **m** peace in His high places
Job 27:18 a booth which a watchman **m**
Job 34:11 and **m** man to find a reward
Job 35:11 **m** us wiser than the birds of
Job 41:31 He **m** the deep boil like a pot
Job 41:31 he **m** the sea like a pot of
Ps 7:12 bends His bow and **m** it ready
Ps 7:13 He **m** His arrows into fiery
Ps 18:32 strength, And **m** my way perfect
Ps 18:33 He **m** my feet like the feet of
Ps 23: 2 He **m** me to lie down in green
Ps 29: 6 He **m** them also skip like a
Ps 29: 9 LORD **m** the deer give birth
Ps 33:10 He **m** the plans of the peoples
Ps 40: 4 man who **m** the LORD his trust
Ps 46: 9 He **m** wars cease to the end of
Ps 77: 6 my spirit **m** diligent search
Ps 104: 3 Who **m** the clouds His chariot,
Ps 104: 4 Who **m** His angels spirits, His
Ps 104:15 wine that **m** glad the heart of
Ps 107:36 There He **m** the hungry dwell,
Ps 107:41 **m** their families like a flock
Ps 135: 7 He **m** lightning for the rain
Ps 147: 8 Who **m** grass to grow on the
Ps 147:14 He **m** peace in your borders,
Prov 4:19 not know what **m** them stumble
Prov 10: 1 A wise son **m** a glad father,
Prov 10: 4 of the diligent **m** one rich
Prov 10:22 of the LORD **m** one rich, and He
Prov 12:25 but a good word **m** it glad
Prov 13: 7 is one who **m** himself rich
Prov 13: 7 one who **m** himself poor, yet
Prov 13:12 Hope deferred **m** the heart
Prov 15:13 A merry heart **m** a cheerful
Prov 15:20 A wise son **m** a father glad,
Prov 15:30 a good report **m** the bones
Prov 16: 7 he **m** even his enemies to be
Prov 18:16 A man's gift **m** room for him
Prov 19: 4 Wealth **m** many friends, but
Prov 19:11 of a man **m** him slow to anger
Prov 29: 3 wisdom **m** his father rejoice
Prov 31:22 She **m** tapestry for herself
Prov 31:24 She **m** linen garments and sells
Eccl 8: 1 man's wisdom **m** his face shine
Eccl 10:19 for laughter, and wine **m** merry
Eccl 11: 5 works of God who **m** all things
Is 19:17 everyone who **m** mention of it
Is 24: 1 the LORD **m** the earth empty and
Is 24: 1 and **m** it waste, distorts its
Is 27: 9 when he **m** all the stones of
Is 40:23 He **m** the judges of the earth
Is 43:16 who **m** a way in the sea and a
Is 44:13 **m** it like the figure of a man
Is 44:15 indeed he **m** a god and worships
Is 44:15 he **m** it a carved image, and
Is 44:17 rest of it he **m** into a god
Is 44:24 LORD, who **m** all things, Who
Is 44:25 **m** their knowledge foolishness
Is 46: 6 a goldsmith, and he **m** it a god
Is 59:15 from evil **m** himself a prey
Is 62: 7 till He **m** Jerusalem a praise
Jer 4:19 My heart **m** a noise in me
Jer 10:13 He **m** lightning for the rain,
Jer 13:16 death and **m** it dense darkness
Jer 17: 5 **m** flesh his strength, whose
Jer 21: 2 of Babylon **m** war against us
Jer 29:27 **m** himself a prophet to you
Jer 48:28 be like the dove which **m** her
Jer 51:16 He **m** lightnings for the rain
Ezek 22: 3 she **m** idols within herself to
Ezek 46:12 Now when the prince **m** a
Dan 6:13 but **m** his petition three
Dan 9:27 shall be one who **m** desolate
Amos 4:13 **m** the morning darkness, who
Amos 5: 8 and **m** the day dark as night
Nah 1: 4 **m** it dry, and dries up all the
Mal 1:14 **m** a vow, but sacrifices to
Matt 5:45 for He **m** His sun rise on the
Mark 7:37 He **m** both the deaf to hear and
Mark 9:43 And if your hand **m** you sin
Mark 9:45 And if your foot **m** you sin
Mark 9:47 And if your eye **m** you sin,
Luke 5:36 otherwise the new **m** a tear
John 8:36 if the Son **m** you free, you
John 19:12 Whoever **m** himself a king
Rom 8:26 but the Spirit Himself **m**
Rom 8:27 because He **m** intercession for
Rom 8:34 who also **m** intercession for
1Co 4: 7 For who **m** you differ from
1Co 8:13 if food **m** my brother stumble,
1Co 14: 8 trumpet **m** an uncertain sound
2Co 2: 2 then who is he who **m** me glad
Gal 2: 6 it **m** no difference to me
Eph 5:13 for whatever **m** manifest is
Heb 1: 7 Who **m** His angels spirits and
Jas 4: 4 **m** himself an enemy of God
Rev 13:13 so that he even **m** fire come
Rev 19:11 He judges and **m** war

MAKHELOTH
Num 33:25 from Haradah and camped at **M**
Num 33:26 They moved from **M** and

MAKING (*see* MAKE)
Gen 34:30 by **m** me obnoxious among the
Ex 5:14 in **m** brick both yesterday
Ex 36: 3 service of **m** the sanctuary
Deut 20:19 while **m** war against it to
Judg 9:16 sincerity in **m** Abimelech king
Judg 21:22 **m** yourselves guilty of your
2Ki 6: 8 was **m** war against Israel
1Ch 15:28 **m** music with stringed
1Ch 17:19 in **m** known all these great
2Ch 30:22 **m** confession to the LORD God
Ps 19: 7 is sure, **m** wise the simple
Eccl 12:12 Of **m** many books there is no
Is 3:16 **m** a jingling with their feet,
Is 45: 9 who forms it, 'What are you **m**
Jer 18: 3 was, **m** something at the wheel
Jer 20:15 **M** him very glad
Jer 22:23 **m** your nest in the cedars,
Dan 6:11 **m** supplication before his God
Dan 7:21 and the same horn was **m** war
Dan 8:19 I am **m** known to you what
Hos 10: 4 falsely in **m** a covenant
Amos 8: 5 **M** the ephah small and the
Mic 6:13 by **m** you desolate because of
Zech 14: 4 west, **m** a very large valley
Mark 7:13 **m** the word of God of no
John 5:18 **m** Himself equal with God
Acts 7:19 **m** them expose their babies,
Rom 1:10 **m** request if, by some means,
2Co 6:10 as poor, yet **m** many rich
Eph 1:16 you, **m** mention of you in my
Eph 2:15 from the two, thus **m** peace,
Eph 5:19 **m** melody in your heart to the
Phil 1: 4 in every prayer of mine **m**
1Th 1: 2 all, **m** mention of you in our
Phm 4 **m** mention of you always in my
2Pe 2: 6 **m** them an example to those
Jude 22 compassion, **m** a distinction

MAKKEDAH
Josh 10:10 down as far as Azekah and **M**
Josh 10:16 themselves in a cave at **M**
Josh 10:17 found hidden in the cave at **M**
Josh 10:21 to the camp, to Joshua at **M**
Josh 10:28 On that day Joshua took **M**
Josh 10:28 **M** as he had done to the king
Josh 10:29 Then Joshua passed from **M**
Josh 12:16 the king of **M**, one
Josh 15:41 Beth Dagon, Naamah, and **M**

MAKTESH
Zeph 1:11 Wail, you inhabitants of **M**

MALACHI
Mal 1: 1 of the LORD to Israel by **M**

MALADY
2Ch 16:12 and his **m** was very severe

MALCAM
1Ch 8: 9 begot Jobab, Zibia, Mesha, **M**

MALCHIAH (*see* MALCHIJAH, MELCHIAH)
Ezra 10:25 Ramiah, Jeziah, **M**, Mijamin,
Jer 38: 1 Pashhur the son of **M** heard
Jer 38: 6 dungeon of **M** the king's son

MALCHIEL (*see* MALCHIELITES)
Gen 46:17 of Beriah were Heber and **M**
Num 26:45 of **M**, the family of the
1Ch 7:31 of Beriah were Heber and **M**

MALCHIELITES (*see* MALCHIEL)
Num 26:45 Malchiel, the family of the **M**

MALCHIJAH (*see* MALCHIAH)
1Ch 6:40 son of Baaseiah, the son of **M**
1Ch 9:12 son of Pashur, the son of **M**
1Ch 24: 9 the fifth to **M**, the sixth to
Ezra 10:25 Malchiah, Mijamin, Eleazar, **M**
Ezra 10:31 Eliezer, Ishijah, **M**, Shemaiah
Neh 3:11 **M** the son of Harim and Hashub
Neh 3:14 **M** the son of Rechab, leader
Neh 3:31 After him **M**, one of the
Neh 8: 4 left hand Pedaiah, Mishael, **M**
Neh 10: 3 Pashhur, Amariah, **M**,
Neh 11:12 son of Pashhur, the son of **M**
Neh 12:42 Eleazar, Uzzi, Jehohanan, **M**

MALCHIRAM
1Ch 3:18 and **M**, Pedaiah, Shenazzar,

MALCHISHUA (*see* MELCHI)
1Sa 14:49 were Jonathan and Jishui and **M**
1Sa 31: 2 Jonathan, Abinadab, and **M**,
1Ch 8:33 and Saul begot Jonathan, **M**
1Ch 9:39 and Saul begot Jonathan, **M**
1Ch 10: 2 Jonathan, Abinadab, and **M**,

MALCHUS
John 18:10 The servant's name was **M**

MALE (*see* MALES)
Gen 1:27 **m** and female He created them
Gen 5: 2 He created them **m** and female,
Gen 6:19 they shall be **m** and female
Gen 7: 2 of every clean animal, a **m**
Gen 7: 2 animals that are unclean, a **m**
Gen 7: 3 each of birds of the air, **m**
Gen 7: 9 went into the ark to Noah, **m**
Gen 7:16 So those that entered, **m** and
Gen 12:16 **m** donkeys, **m** and female
Gen 12:16 sheep, oxen, **m** donkeys, **m**
Gen 17:10 Every **m** child among you shall
Gen 17:12 every **m** child in your
Gen 17:14 And the uncircumcised **m** child
Gen 17:23 every **m** among the men of
Gen 20:14 took sheep, oxen, and **m** and
Gen 24:35 and herds, silver and gold, **m**
Gen 30:35 **m** goats that were speckled
Gen 30:43 and **m** servants, and camels and
Gen 32: 5 oxen, donkeys, flocks, and **m**

Gen 32:14 goats and twenty **m** goats, two
Gen 34:15 we are, if every **m** of you is
Gen 34:22 if every **m** among us is
Gen 34:24 every **m** was circumcised, all
Ex 1:17 but saved the **m** children
Ex 1:18 saved the **m** children alive
Ex 12: 5 a **m** of the first year
Ex 34:19 every **m** firstling among your
Lev 1: 3 him offer a **m** without blemish
Lev 1:10 bring a **m** without blemish
Lev 3: 1 whether **m** or female, he shall
Lev 3: 6 whether **m** or female, he shall
Lev 4:23 goats, a **m** without blemish
Lev 7: 6 Every **m** among the priests
Lev 12: 2 conceived, and borne a **m** child
Lev 12: 7 who has borne a **m** or a female
Lev 14:10 two **m** lambs without blemish
Lev 14:12 priest shall take one **m** lamb
Lev 14:21 then he shall take one **m** lamb
Lev 18:22 lie with a **m** as with a woman
Lev 20:13 If a man lies with a **m** as he
Lev 22:19 of your own free will a **m**
Lev 23:12 a **m** lamb of the first year,
Lev 23:19 two **m** lambs of the first year
Lev 25:44 And as for your **m** and female
Lev 25:44 you, from them you may buy **m**
Lev 27: 3 if your valuation is of a **m**
Lev 27: 5 a **m** shall be twenty shekels
Lev 27: 6 a **m** shall be five shekels of
Lev 27: 7 old and above, if it is a **m**
Num 1: 2 names, every **m** individually,
Num 1:20 every **m** individually, from
Num 1:22 every **m** individually, from
Num 3:15 every **m** from a month old and
Num 5: 3 You shall put out both **m** and
Num 6:12 bring a **m** lamb in its first
Num 6:14 one **m** lamb in its first year
Num 7:15 one **m** lamb in its first year,
Num 7:17 five **m** goats, and five **m** lambs
Num 7:21 one **m** lamb in its first year,
Num 7:23 five **m** goats, and five **m** lambs
Num 7:27 one **m** lamb in its first year,
Num 7:29 five **m** goats, and five **m** lambs
Num 7:33 one **m** lamb in its first year,
Num 7:35 five **m** goats, and five **m** lambs
Num 7:39 one **m** lamb in its first year,
Num 7:41 five **m** goats, and five **m** lambs
Num 7:45 one **m** lamb in its first year,
Num 7:47 five **m** goats, and five **m** lambs
Num 7:51 one **m** lamb in its first year,
Num 7:53 five **m** goats, and five **m** lambs
Num 7:57 one **m** lamb in its first year,
Num 7:59 five **m** goats, and five **m** lambs
Num 7:63 one **m** lamb in its first year,
Num 7:65 five **m** goats, and five **m** lambs
Num 7:69 one **m** lamb in its first year,
Num 7:71 five **m** goats, and five **m** lambs
Num 7:75 one **m** lamb in its first year,
Num 7:77 five **m** goats, and five **m** lambs
Num 7:81 one **m** lamb in its first year,
Num 7:83 five **m** goats, and five **m** lambs
Num 7:87 the **m** lambs in their first
Num 7:88 the **m** goats sixty, and the
Num 18:10 every **m** shall eat it
Num 26:62 every **m** from a month old and
Num 28: 3 two **m** lambs in their first
Num 31:17 kill every **m** among the little
Deut 4:16 the likeness of **m** or female
Deut 7:14 there shall not be a **m** or
Deut 20:13 you shall strike every **m** in
Deut 28:68 for sale to your enemies as **m**
Josh 17: 2 these were the **m** children of
Judg 21:11 shall utterly destroy every **m**
1Sa 1:11 your maidservant a **m** child
1Sa 25:22 if I leave one **m** of all who
1Ki 11:15 he had killed every **m** in Edom
1Ki 11:16 had cut down every **m** in Edom)
1Ki 14:10 Jeroboam every **m** in Israel
1Ki 16:11 he did not leave him one **m**
1Ki 21:21 from Ahab every **m** in Israel
2Ki 5:26 vineyards, sheep and oxen, **m**
2Ch 17:11 seven hundred **m** goats
2Ch 28:10 and Jerusalem to be your **m**
2Ch 29:21 and seven **m** goats for a sin
2Ch 29:23 Then they brought out the **m**
Ezra 2:65 besides their **m** and female
Ezra 6:17 for all Israel twelve **m** goats
Ezra 8:35 and twelve **m** goats as a sin
Neh 7:67 besides their **m** and female
Esth 7: 4 Had we been sold as **m** and
Job 3: 3 said, 'A **m** child is conceived
Prov 30:31 a **m** goat also, and a king
Eccl 2: 7 I acquired **m** and female
Eccl 2: 8 I acquired **m** and female
Is 66: 7 came, she delivered a **m** child
Jer 20:15 A **m** child has been born to
Jer 34: 9 man should set free his **m**
Jer 34:10 should set free his **m** and
Jer 34:11 their minds and made the **m**
Jer 34:11 them into subjection as **m**
Jer 34:16 one of you brought back his **m**
Jer 34:16 into subjection, to be your **m**
Jer 51:40 like rams with **m** goats
Ezek 16:17 and made for yourself **m** images
Dan 8: 5 suddenly a **m** goat came from
Dan 8: 8 Therefore the **m** goat grew
Dan 8:21 the **m** goat is the kingdom of
Mal 1:14 who has in his flock a **m**, and
Matt 2:16 the **m** children who were in
Matt 19: 4 at the beginning 'made them **m**
Mark 10: 6 creation, God 'made them **m**
Luke 2:23 Every **m** who opens the womb
Gal 3:28 there is neither **m** nor female
Rev 12: 5 she bore a **m** Child who was to
Rev 12:13 who gave birth to the **m** Child

MALES (*see* MALE)
Gen 34:25 the city and killed all the **m**
Ex 12:48 let all his **m** be circumcised,
Ex 13:12 the **m** shall be the LORD's
Ex 13:15 LORD all **m** that open the womb
Ex 23:17 **m** shall appear before the
Lev 6:18 All the **m** among the children
Lev 6:29 All the **m** among the priests
Num 3:22 of all the **m** from a month old
Num 3:28 to the number of all the **m**
Num 3:34 of all the **m** from a month old
Num 3:39 all the **m** from a month old and
Num 3:40 Number all the firstborn **m** of
Num 3:43 And all the firstborn **m**,
Num 31: 7 and they killed all the **m**
Deut 15:19 All the firstborn **m** that come
Deut 16:16 **m** shall appear before the
Josh 5: 4 came out of Egypt who were **m**
1Sa 25:34 no **m** would have been left to
2Ki 9: 8 from Ahab all the **m** in Israel
1Ch 23: 3 the number of individual **m**
2Ch 31:16 Besides those **m** from three
2Ch 31:19 all the **m** among the priests
Ezra 8: 3 were one hundred and fifty **m**
Ezra 8: 4 and with him two hundred **m**
Ezra 8: 5 and with him three hundred **m**
Ezra 8: 6 Jonathan, and with him fifty **m**
Ezra 8: 7 and with him seventy **m**
Ezra 8: 8 Michael, and with him eighty **m**
Ezra 8: 9 two hundred and eighteen **m**
Ezra 8:10 him one hundred and sixty **m**
Ezra 8:11 and with him twenty-eight **m**
Ezra 8:12 with him one hundred and ten **m**
Ezra 8:13 and with them sixty **m**
Ezra 8:14 and with them seventy **m**

MALICE (*see* MALICIOUS)
1Co 5: 8 nor with the leaven of **m**
1Co 14:20 in **m** be babes, but in
Eph 4:31 put away from you, with all **m**
Col 3: 8 anger, wrath, **m**, blasphemy,
Tit 3: 3 and pleasures, living in **m**
1Pe 2: 1 Therefore, laying aside all **m**

MALICIOUS (*see* MALICE, MALICIOUSNESS)
1Ki 2: 8 who cursed me with a **m** curse
3Jn 10 against us with **m** words

MALICIOUSNESS (*see* MALICIOUS)
Rom 1:29 wickedness, covetousness, **m**

MALIGN
Prov 30:10 Do not **m** a servant to his

MALLOTHI
1Ch 25: 4 Joshbekashah, **M**
1Ch 25:26 the nineteenth for **M**, his

MALLOW
Job 30: 4 who pluck **m** by the bushes, and

MALLUCH
1Ch 6:44 the son of Abdi, the son of **M**
Ezra 10:29 Meshullam, **M**, Adaiah, Jashub,
Ezra 10:32 Benjamin, **M**, and Shemariah
Neh 10: 4 Hattush, Shebaniah, **M**,
Neh 10:27 **M**, Harim, and Baanah
Neh 12: 2 Amariah, **M**, Hattush,

MALTA
Acts 28: 1 that the island was called **M**

MAMMON
Matt 6:24 You cannot serve God and **m**
Luke 16: 9 yourselves by unrighteous **m**
Luke 16:11 faithful in the unrighteous **m**
Luke 16:13 You cannot serve God and **m**

MAMRE
Gen 13:18 by the terebinth trees of **M**
Gen 14:13 trees of **M** the Amorite,
Gen 14:24 Aner, Eshcol, and **M**
Gen 18: 1 by the terebinth trees of **M**
Gen 23:17 Machpelah, which was before **M**
Gen 23:19 before **M** (that is, Hebron) in
Gen 25: 9 Machpelah, which is before **M**
Gen 35:27 came to his father Isaac at **M**
Gen 49:30 which is before **M** in the land
Gen 50:13 field of Machpelah, before **M**

MAN (*see* MANKIND, MAN'S, MEN)
Gen 1:26 Let Us make **m** in Our image,
Gen 1:27 So God created **m** in His own
Gen 2: 5 there was no **m** to till the
Gen 2: 7 the LORD God formed **m** of the
Gen 2: 7 and **m** became a living being
Gen 2: 8 there He put the **m** whom He
Gen 2:15 Then the LORD God took the **m**
Gen 2:16 LORD God commanded the **m**
Gen 2:18 good that **m** should be alone
Gen 2:22 from **m** He made into a woman
Gen 2:22 and He brought her to the **m**
Gen 2:23 she was taken out of **M**
Gen 2:24 Therefore a **m** shall leave his
Gen 2:25 they were both naked, the **m**
Gen 3:12 Then the **m** said, "The woman
Gen 3:22 the **m** has become like one of
Gen 3:24 So He drove out the **m**
Gen 4: 1 have gotten a **m** from the LORD
Gen 4:23 killed a **m** for wounding me
Gen 4:23 even a young **m** for hurting me
Gen 5: 1 In the day that God created **m**
Gen 6: 3 not strive with **m** forever
Gen 6: 5 of **m** was great in the earth
Gen 6: 6 He had made **m** on the earth
Gen 6: 7 I will destroy **m** whom I have
Gen 6: 7 the face of the earth, both **m**
Gen 6: 9 Noah was a just **m**, perfect in
Gen 7:21 on the earth, and every **m**
Gen 7:23 both **m** and cattle, creeping
Gen 9: 5 it, and from the hand of **m**
Gen 9: 5 I will require the life of **m**
Gen 9: 6 by **m** his blood shall be shed
Gen 9: 6 in the image of God He made **m**
Gen 13:16 so that if a **m** could number
Gen 16:12 He shall be a wild **m**
Gen 16:12 hand shall be against every **m**
Gen 17:17 a **m** who is one hundred years
Gen 18: 7 calf, gave it to a young **m**
Gen 19: 8 who have not known a **m**
Gen 19: 9 hard against the **m** Lot, and
Gen 19:31 there is no **m** on the earth to
Gen 20: 3 Indeed you are a dead **m**
Gen 24:16 no **m** had known her
Gen 24:21 And the **m**, wondering at her,
Gen 24:22 that the **m** took a golden nose
Gen 24:26 Then the **m** bowed down his
Gen 24:29 ran out to the **m** by the well
Gen 24:30 Thus the **m** spoke to me,"
Gen 24:30 me," that he went to the **m**
Gen 24:32 Then the **m** came to the house
Gen 24:58 Will you go with this **m**
Gen 24:61 the camels and followed the **m**
Gen 24:65 Who is this **m** walking in the
Gen 25: 8 in a good old age, an old **m**
Gen 25:27 hunter, a **m** of the field
Gen 25:27 but Jacob was a mild **m**,
Gen 26:11 He who touches this **m** or his
Gen 26:13 The **m** began to prosper, and
Gen 27:11 Esau my brother is a hairy **m**
Gen 27:11 and I am a smooth-skinned **m**
Gen 29:19 should give her to another **m**
Gen 30:43 Thus the **m** became exceedingly
Gen 31:50 although no **m** is with us
Gen 32:24 a **M** wrestled with him until
Gen 34:19 So the young **m** did not delay
Gen 37:15 Now a certain **m** found him
Gen 37:15 And the **m** asked him, saying,
Gen 37:17 And the **m** said,
Gen 38:25 By the **m** to whom these belong
Gen 39: 2 and he was a successful **m**

Gen 41:12 young Hebrew **m** with us there
Gen 41:12 to each **m** he interpreted
Gen 41:33 select a discerning and wise **m**
Gen 41:38 a **m** in whom is the Spirit of
Gen 41:44 without your consent no **m** may
Gen 42:13 the sons of one **m** in the land
Gen 42:30 The **m** who is lord of the land
Gen 42:33 Then the **m**, the lord of the
Gen 43: 3 The **m** solemnly warned us,
Gen 43: 5 for the **m** said to us, 'You
Gen 43: 6 the **m** whether you had still
Gen 43: 7 The **m** asked us pointedly
Gen 43:11 down a present for the **m**
Gen 43:13 and arise, go back to the **m**
Gen 43:14 give you mercy before the **m**
Gen 43:17 Then the **m** did as Joseph
Gen 43:17 the **m** brought the men into
Gen 43:24 So the **m** brought the men into
Gen 43:27 the old **m** of whom you spoke
Gen 44:11 Then each **m** speedily let down
Gen 44:13 each **m** loaded his donkey and
Gen 44:15 you not know that such a **m** as
Gen 44:17 but the **m** in whose hand the
Gen 44:20 We have a father, an old **m**
Gen 45:22 to all of them, to each **m**
Gen 47:20 for every **m** of the Egyptians
Gen 49: 6 in their anger they slew a **m**
Ex 1: 1 each **m** and his household came
Ex 2: 1 a **m** of the house of Levi went
Ex 2:20 it that you have left the **m**
Ex 2:21 content to live with the **m**
Ex 7:12 For every **m** threw down his
Ex 8:17 earth, and it became lice on **m**
Ex 8:18 So there were lice on **m** and
Ex 9: 9 that break out in sores on **m**
Ex 9:10 that break out in sores on **m**
Ex 9:19 shall come down on every **m**
Ex 9:22 on **m**, on beast, and on every
Ex 9:25 that was in the field, both **m**
Ex 10: 7 shall this **m** be a snare to us
Ex 11: 2 and let every **m** ask from his
Ex 11: 3 Moreover the **m** Moses was very
Ex 11: 7 against **m** or beast, that you
Ex 12: 3 day of this month every **m**
Ex 12:12 in the land of Egypt, both **m**
Ex 13: 2 children of Israel, both of **m**
Ex 13:13 all the firstborn of **m** among
Ex 13:15 both the firstborn of **m** and
Ex 15: 3 The LORD is a **m** of war
Ex 16:16 Let every **m** gather it
Ex 16:16 let every **m** take for those
Ex 16:18 Every **m** had gathered
Ex 16:21 every **m** according to his need
Ex 16:29 Let every **m** remain in his
Ex 16:29 let no **m** go out of his place
Ex 19:13 whether **m** or beast, he shall
Ex 21: 7 if a **m** sells his daughter to
Ex 21:12 He who strikes a **m** so that he
Ex 21:14 But if a **m** acts with
Ex 21:16 He who kidnaps a **m** and sells
Ex 21:20 if a **m** beats his servant or
Ex 21:26 if a **m** strikes the eye of his
Ex 21:28 If an ox gores a **m** or a woman
Ex 21:29 it has killed a **m** or a woman
Ex 21:33 if a **m** opens a pit, or if a
Ex 21:33 or if a **m** digs a pit and does
Ex 22: 1 If a **m** steals an ox or a
Ex 22: 5 If a **m** causes a field or
Ex 22: 7 If a **m** delivers to his
Ex 22:10 If a **m** delivers to his
Ex 22:14 if a **m** borrows anything from
Ex 22:16 if a **m** entices a virgin who
Ex 23: 3 to a poor **m** in his dispute
Ex 24:14 If any **m** has a difficulty,
Ex 30:12 then every **m** shall give a
Ex 32: 1 the **m** who brought us up out
Ex 32:23 the **m** who brought us out of
Ex 32:27 Let every **m** put his sword on
Ex 32:27 let every **m** kill his brother,
Ex 32:27 every **m** his companion, and
Ex 32:27 and every **m** his neighbor
Ex 32:29 for every **m** has opposed his
Ex 33: 8 each **m** stood at his tent door
Ex 33:10 each **m** in his tent door
Ex 33:11 as a **m** speaks to his friend
Ex 33:11 the son of Nun, a young **m**
Ex 33:20 for no **m** shall see Me, and
Ex 34: 3 no **m** shall come up with you,
Ex 34: 3 let no **m** be seen throughout
Ex 34:24 neither will any **m** covet your
Ex 35:22 is, every **m** who offered an
Ex 35:23 And every **m**, with whom was
Ex 36: 6 Let neither **m** nor woman do
Ex 38:26 a bekah for each **m** (that is
Lev 5: 3 with which a **m** may be defiled
Lev 5: 4 whatever it is that a **m** may
Lev 6: 3 a **m** may do in which he sins
Lev 13: 2 When a **m** has on the skin of
Lev 13:29 If a **m** or woman has a sore on
Lev 13:38 If a **m** or a woman has bright
Lev 13:40 As for the **m** whose hair has
Lev 13:44 he is a leprous **m**
Lev 14:11 the **m** who is to be made clean
Lev 15: 2 When any **m** has a discharge
Lev 15:16 If any **m** has an emission of
Lev 15:18 when a woman lies with a **m**
Lev 15:24 if any **m** lies with her at all
Lev 15:33 either **m** or woman, and for him
Lev 16:17 There shall be no **m** in the
Lev 16:21 by the hand of a suitable **m**
Lev 17: 3 Whatever **m** of the house of
Lev 17: 4 shall be imputed to that **m**
Lev 17: 4 that **m** shall be cut off from
Lev 17: 8 Whatever **m** of the house of
Lev 17: 9 that **m** shall be cut off from
Lev 17:10 whatever **m** of the house of
Lev 17:13 whatever **m** of the children of
Lev 18: 5 judgments, which if a **m** does
Lev 19:20 as a concubine to another **m**
Lev 19:32 the presence of an old **m**, and
Lev 20: 3 set My face against that **m**
Lev 20: 4 hide their eyes from the **m**
Lev 20: 5 set My face against that **m**
Lev 20:10 The **m** who commits adultery
Lev 20:11 The **m** who lies with his
Lev 20:12 If a **m** lies with his
Lev 20:13 If a **m** lies with a male as
Lev 20:14 If a **m** marries a woman and
Lev 20:15 If a **m** mates with a beast,
Lev 20:17 If a **m** takes his sister, his
Lev 20:18 If a **m** lies with a woman
Lev 20:20 If a **m** lies with his uncle's
Lev 20:21 If a **m** takes his brother's
Lev 20:27 A **m** or a woman who is a
Lev 21: 4 being a chief **m** among his
Lev 21:17 No **m** of your descendants in
Lev 21:18 For any **m** who has a defect
Lev 21:18 a **m** blind or lame, who has a
Lev 21:19 a **m** who has a broken foot or
Lev 21:20 or a **m** who has a defect in
Lev 21:21 No **m** of the descendants of
Lev 22: 4 Whatever **m** of the
Lev 22: 4 corpse, or a **m** who has had an
Lev 22:14 if a **m** eats the holy offering
Lev 22:18 Whatever **m** of the house of
Lev 24:10 a **m** of Israel fought each
Lev 24:17 Whoever kills any **m** shall
Lev 24:19 If a **m** causes disfigurement
Lev 24:20 caused disfigurement of a **m**
Lev 24:21 but whoever kills a **m** shall
Lev 25:26 Or if the **m** has no one to
Lev 25:27 to the **m** to whom he sold it
Lev 25:29 if a **m** sells a house in a
Lev 25:33 if a **m** purchases a house from
Lev 27: 2 When a **m** consecrates by a
Lev 27: 9 all such that any **m** gives to
Lev 27:14 when a **m** sanctifies his house
Lev 27:16 if a **m** sanctifies to the LORD
Lev 27:20 sold the field to another **m**
Lev 27:22 if a **m** sanctifies to the LORD
Lev 27:26 no **m** shall sanctify
Lev 27:28 a **m** may devote to the LORD of
Lev 27:28 of all that he has, both **m**
Lev 27:31 If a **m** wants at all to
Num 1: 4 shall be a **m** from every tribe
Num 3:13 firstborn in Israel, both **m**
Num 4:32 you shall assign to each **m** by
Num 5: 6 When a **m** or woman commits
Num 5: 8 But if the **m** has no kinsman
Num 5:10 whatever any **m** gives the
Num 5:13 a **m** lies with her carnally,
Num 5:15 then the **m** shall bring his
Num 5:19 If no **m** has lain with you, and
Num 5:20 and some **m** other than your
Num 5:30 of jealousy comes upon a **m**
Num 5:31 Then the **m** shall be free
Num 6: 2 When either a **m** or woman
Num 7: 5 to every **m** according to his
Num 8:17 of Israel are Mine, both **m**
Num 9: 6 by the dead body of a **m**, so
Num 9: 7 by the dead body of a **m**
Num 9:13 But the **m** who is clean and is
Num 9:13 that **m** shall bear his sin
Num 11:27 And a young **m** ran and told
Num 12: 3 (Now the **m** Moses was very
Num 13: 2 fathers you shall send a **m**
Num 14:15 kill these people as one **m**
Num 15:32 they found a **m** gathering
Num 15:35 The **m** must surely be put to
Num 16: 7 it shall be that the **m** whom
Num 16:18 So every **m** took his censer,
Num 16:22 of all flesh, shall one **m** sin
Num 17: 5 be that the rod of the **m** whom
Num 17: 9 and each **m** took his rod
Num 18:15 whether **m** or beast, shall be
Num 18:15 the firstborn of **m** you shall
Num 19: 9 Then a **m** who is clean shall
Num 19:14 law when a **m** dies in a tent
Num 19:16 has died, or a bone of a **m**
Num 19:20 But the **m** who is unclean and
Num 23:19 God is not a **m**, that He
Num 23:19 He should lie, nor a son of **m**
Num 24: 3 the utterance of the **m** whose
Num 24:15 the utterance of the **m** whose
Num 25: 8 he went after the **m** of Israel
Num 25: 8 the **m** of Israel, and the woman
Num 26:64 **m** of those who were numbered
Num 26:65 was not left a **m** of them,
Num 27: 8 If a **m** dies and has no son,
Num 27:16 set a **m** over the congregation
Num 27:18 a **m** in whom is the Spirit, and
Num 30: 2 If a **m** vows a vow to the LORD
Num 30:16 Moses, between a **m**
Num 31:11 and all the booty, both of **m**
Num 31:17 who has known a **m** intimately
Num 31:18 have not known a **m** intimately
Num 31:26 that was taken, both of **m**
Num 31:35 had not known a **m** intimately
Num 31:47 of every fifty, drawn from **m**
Num 31:49 and not a **m** of us is missing
Num 31:50 LORD, what every **m** found of
Num 31:53 spoil, every **m** for himself
Num 32:27 every **m** armed for war, before
Num 32:29 you, every **m** armed for battle
Num 35:23 stone, by which a **m** could die
Deut 1:16 judge righteously between a **m**
Deut 1:23 men, one **m** from each tribe
Deut 1:31 as a **m** carries his son, in
Deut 4:32 God created **m** on the earth
Deut 5:24 day that God speaks with **m**
Deut 8: 3 **m** shall not live by bread
Deut 8: 3 but **m** lives by every word
Deut 8: 5 that as a **m** chastens his son
Deut 11:25 No **m** shall be able to stand
Deut 12: 8 every **m** doing whatever is
Deut 15: 7 you a poor **m** of your brethren
Deut 15:12 If your brother, a Hebrew **m**
Deut 16:17 Every **m** shall give as he is
Deut 17: 2 a **m** or a woman who has been
Deut 17: 5 out to your gates that **m** or
Deut 17: 5 that **m** or woman with stones
Deut 17:12 Now the **m** who acts
Deut 17:12 the judge, that **m** shall die
Deut 19: 5 as when a **m** goes to the woods
Deut 19:15 shall not rise against a **m**
Deut 19:16 **m** to testify against him of
Deut 20: 5 What **m** is there who has
Deut 20: 5 and another **m** dedicate it
Deut 20: 6 And what **m** is there who has
Deut 20: 6 battle and another **m** eat of it
Deut 20: 7 And what **m** is there who is
Deut 20: 7 battle and another **m** marry her
Deut 20: 8 say, 'What **m** is there who is
Deut 21: 2 **m** to the surrounding cities
Deut 21: 3 **m** will take a heifer which
Deut 21: 6 city nearest to the slain **m**
Deut 21:15 If a **m** has two wives, one
Deut 21:18 If a **m** has a stubborn and
Deut 21:22 If a **m** has committed a sin
Deut 22: 5 anything that pertains to a **m**
Deut 22: 5 a **m**, nor shall a **m** put on a
Deut 22:13 If any **m** takes a wife, and
Deut 22:16 my daughter to this **m** as wife
Deut 22:18 that city shall take that **m**
Deut 22:22 If a **m** is found lying with a
Deut 22:22 both the **m** that lay with the
Deut 22:23 a **m** finds her in the city and
Deut 22:24 the **m** because he humbled his
Deut 22:25 But if a **m** finds a betrothed
Deut 22:25 the **m** forces her and lies with

Deut 22:25 then only the **m** who lay with
Deut 22:26 for just as when a **m** rises
Deut 22:28 If a **m** finds a young woman
Deut 22:29 then the **m** who lay with her
Deut 22:30 A **m** shall not take his
Deut 23:10 If there is any **m** among you
Deut 24: 1 When a **m** takes a wife and
Deut 24: 5 When a **m** has taken a new wife
Deut 24: 6 No **m** shall take the lower or
Deut 24: 7 If a **m** is found kidnapping
Deut 24:11 the **m** to whom you lend shall
Deut 24:12 if the **m** is poor, you shall
Deut 25: 2 if the wicked **m** deserves to
Deut 25: 5 the widow of the dead **m** shall
Deut 25: 7 But if the **m** does not want to
Deut 25: 9 **m** who will not build up his
Deut 28:29 as a blind **m** gropes in
Deut 28:30 but another **m** shall lie with
Deut 28:54 The **m** among you who is
Deut 29:18 there may not be among you **m**
Deut 29:20 would burn against that **m**
Deut 32:25 terror within for the young **m**
Deut 32:25 with the **m** of gray hairs
Deut 33: 1 with which Moses the **m** of God
Josh 1: 5 No **m** shall be able to stand
Josh 3:12 one **m** from every tribe
Josh 4: 2 one **m** from every tribe,
Josh 4: 4 one **m** from every tribe
Josh 5:13 a **M** stood opposite him with
Josh 6: 5 every **m** straight before him
Josh 6:20 every **m** straight before him,
Josh 6:21 that was in the city, both **m**
Josh 6:26 Cursed be the **m** before the
Josh 7:14 takes shall come **m** by **m**
Josh 7:14 takes shall come **m** by **m**
Josh 7:17 of the Zarhites **m** by **m**, and
Josh 7:17 of the Zarhites **m** by **m**, and
Josh 7:18 his household **m** by **m**, and
Josh 7:18 his household **m** by **m**, and
Josh 8:17 There was not a **m** left in Ai
Josh 8:31 **m** has wielded any iron tool
Josh 10: 8 not a **m** of them shall stand
Josh 10:14 LORD heeded the voice of a **m**
Josh 11:14 but they struck every **m** with
Josh 14: 6 the **m** of God concerning you
Josh 14:15 greatest **m** among the Anakim
Josh 17: 1 because he was a **m** of war
Josh 21:44 not a **m** of all their enemies
Josh 22:20 that **m** did not perish alone
Josh 23:10 One **m** of you shall chase a
Judg 1:24 when the spies saw a **m** coming
Judg 1:25 but they let the **m** and all his
Judg 1:26 the **m** went to the land of the
Judg 3:15 Benjamite, a left-handed **m**
Judg 3:17 (Now Eglon was a very fat **m**
Judg 3:29 not a **m** escaped
Judg 4:16 not a **m** was left
Judg 4:20 the tent, and if any **m** comes
Judg 4:20 and says, 'Is there any **m** here
Judg 4:22 show you the **m** whom you seek
Judg 5:30 to every **m** a girl or two
Judg 6:12 you, you mighty **m** of valor
Judg 6:16 the Midianites as one **m**
Judg 7: 7 go, every **m** to his place
Judg 7: 8 every **m** to his tent, and
Judg 7:13 there was a **m** telling a dream
Judg 7:14 son of Joash, a **m** of Israel
Judg 7:21 every **m** stood in his place
Judg 8:14 he caught a young **m** of the
Judg 8:21 for as a **m** is, so is his
Judg 8:25 and each **m** threw into it the
Judg 9:54 called quickly to the young **m**
Judg 9:54 So his young **m** thrust him
Judg 9:55 every **m** to his own place
Judg 10: 1 son of Dodo, a **m** of Issachar
Judg 10:18 Who is the **m** who will begin
Judg 11: 1 was a mighty **m** of valor, but
Judg 11:39 She knew no **m**
Judg 13: 2 was a certain **m** from Zorah
Judg 13: 6 A **M** of God came to me, and
Judg 13: 8 please let the **M** of God whom
Judg 13:10 the **M** has just now appeared
Judg 13:11 When he came to the **M**, he
Judg 13:11 Are You the **M** who spoke to
Judg 14:20 who had been his best **m**
Judg 16: 7 weak, and be like any other **m**
Judg 16:11 weak, and be like any other **m**
Judg 16:17 weak, and be like any other **m**
Judg 16:19 her knees, and called for a **m**
Judg 17: 1 Now there was a **m** from the
Judg 17: 5 The **m** Micah had a shrine, and
Judg 17: 7 Now there was a young **m** from
Judg 17: 8 The **m** departed from the city
Judg 17:11 content to dwell with the **m**
Judg 17:11 the young **m** became like one
Judg 17:12 the young **m** became his priest
Judg 18:15 house of the young Levite **m**
Judg 18:19 to the household of one **m**
Judg 19: 6 woman's father said to the **m**
Judg 19: 7 when the **m** stood to depart,
Judg 19: 9 when the **m** stood to depart
Judg 19:10 But the **m** was not willing to
Judg 19:16 Just then an old **m** came in
Judg 19:17 and the old **m** said, "Where
Judg 19:19 for the young **m** who is with
Judg 19:20 And the old **m** said, "Peace be
Judg 19:22 of the house, the old **m**,
Judg 19:22 Bring out the **m** who came to
Judg 19:23 But the **m**, the master of the
Judg 19:23 Seeing this **m** has come into
Judg 19:24 but to this **m** do not do such
Judg 19:25 So the **m** took his concubine
Judg 19:28 So the **m** lifted her onto the
Judg 19:28 the **m** got up and went to his
Judg 20: 1 gathered together as one **m**
Judg 20: 8 all the people arose as one **m**
Judg 20:11 united together as one **m**
Judg 21:11 who has known a **m** intimately
Judg 21:12 had not known a **m** intimately
Judg 21:21 and every **m** catch a wife for
Judg 21:24 time, every **m** to his tribe and
Judg 21:24 every **m** to his inheritance
Ruth 1: 1 a certain **m** of Bethlehem,
Ruth 1: 2 name of the **m** was Elimelech
Ruth 2: 1 a **m** of great wealth, of the
Ruth 2:20 The **m** is a relative of ours,
Ruth 3: 3 the **m** until he has finished
Ruth 3: 8 that the **m** was startled, and
Ruth 3:16 that the **m** had done for her
Ruth 3:18 for the **m** will not rest until
Ruth 4: 7 one **m** took off his sandal and
1Sa 1: 1 **m** of Ramathaim Zophim
1Sa 1: 3 This **m** went up from his city
1Sa 1:21 And the **m** Elkanah and all his
1Sa 2: 9 strength no **m** shall prevail
1Sa 2:13 any **m** offered a sacrifice
1Sa 2:15 say to the **m** who sacrificed,
1Sa 2:16 And if the **m** said to him,
1Sa 2:25 If one **m** sins against another
1Sa 2:25 But if a **m** sins against the
1Sa 2:27 Then a **m** of God came to Eli
1Sa 2:31 not be an old **m** in your house
1Sa 2:32 old **m** in your house forever
1Sa 4:10 and every **m** fled to his tent
1Sa 4:12 Then a **m** of Benjamin ran from
1Sa 4:13 when the **m** came into the city
1Sa 4:14 the **m** came hastily and told
1Sa 4:16 Then the **m** said to Eli, "I
1Sa 4:18 and he died, for the **m** was old
1Sa 8:22 Every **m** go to his city
1Sa 9: 1 There was a **m** of Benjamin
1Sa 9: 1 a mighty **m** of power
1Sa 9: 2 a choice and handsome young **m**
1Sa 9: 6 is in this city a **m** of God
1Sa 9: 6 God, and he is an honorable **m**
1Sa 9: 7 go, what shall we bring the **m**
1Sa 9: 7 to bring to the **m** of God
1Sa 9: 8 give that to the **m** of God
1Sa 9: 9 when a **m** went to inquire of
1Sa 9:10 city where the **m** of God was
1Sa 9:16 a **m** from the land of Benjamin
1Sa 9:17 the **m** of whom I spoke to you
1Sa 10: 6 and be turned into another **m**
1Sa 10:12 Then a **m** from there answered
1Sa 10:22 Has the **m** come here yet
1Sa 10:25 away, every **m** to his house
1Sa 10:27 How can this **m** save us
1Sa 11:13 Not a **m** shall be put to death
1Sa 13: 2 away, every **m** to his tent
1Sa 13:14 a **m** after His own heart, and
1Sa 14: 1 young **m** who bore his armor
1Sa 14: 6 young **m** who bore his armor
1Sa 14:24 Cursed is the **m** who eats any
1Sa 14:28 Cursed is the **m** who eats
1Sa 14:36 let us not leave a **m** of them
1Sa 14:39 But not a **m** among all the
1Sa 14:52 strong **m** or any valiant **m**
1Sa 15: 3 But kill both **m** and woman,
1Sa 15:29 For He is not a **m**, that He
1Sa 16: 7 LORD does not see as **m** sees
1Sa 16: 7 for **m** looks at the outward
1Sa 16:16 you, to seek out a **m** who is a
1Sa 16:17 Provide me now a **m** who can
1Sa 16:18 playing, a mighty **m** of valor
1Sa 16:18 a **m** of war, prudent in speech
1Sa 17: 8 Choose a **m** for yourselves, and
1Sa 17:10 give me a **m**, that we may
1Sa 17:12 the **m** was old, advanced in
1Sa 17:24 Israel, when they saw the **m**
1Sa 17:25 seen this **m** who has come up
1Sa 17:25 it shall be that the **m** who
1Sa 17:26 **m** who kills this Philistine
1Sa 17:27 done for the **m** who kills him
1Sa 17:33 he a **m** of war from his youth
1Sa 17:41 the **m** who bore the shield
1Sa 17:56 whose son this young **m** is
1Sa 17:58 Whose son are you, young **m**
1Sa 18:23 a poor and lightly esteemed **m**
1Sa 20:22 if I say thus to the young **m**
1Sa 21: 7 Now a certain **m** of the
1Sa 21:14 Look, you see the **m** is insane
1Sa 24:19 For if a **m** finds his enemy,
1Sa 25: 2 Now there was a **m** in Maon
1Sa 25: 2 and the **m** was very rich
1Sa 25: 3 The name of the **m** was Nabal
1Sa 25: 3 but the **m** was harsh and evil
1Sa 25:13 Every **m** gird on his sword
1Sa 25:13 So every **m** girded on his
1Sa 25:29 Yet a **m** has risen to pursue
1Sa 26:12 no **m** saw it or knew it or
1Sa 26:15 Are you not a **m**
1Sa 26:23 every **m** for his righteousness
1Sa 27: 3 each **m** with his household, and
1Sa 27: 9 neither **m** nor woman alive
1Sa 27:11 neither **m** nor woman alive
1Sa 28:14 An old **m** is coming up, and he
1Sa 30: 6 every **m** for his sons and his
1Sa 30:13 I am a young **m** from Egypt
1Sa 30:17 Not a **m** of them escaped,
2Sa 1: 2 it happened that a **m** came
2Sa 1: 5 to the young **m** who told him
2Sa 1: 6 the young **m** who told him said
2Sa 1:13 to the young **m** who told him
2Sa 2: 3 every **m** with his household
2Sa 3:34 as a **m** falls before wicked
2Sa 3:38 a great **m** has fallen this day
2Sa 7:19 Is this the manner of **m**, O
2Sa 12: 2 The rich **m** had exceedingly
2Sa 12: 3 But the poor **m** had nothing
2Sa 12: 4 a traveler came to the rich **m**
2Sa 12: 4 **m** who had come to him
2Sa 12: 4 for the **m** who had come to him
2Sa 12: 5 greatly aroused against the **m**
2Sa 12: 5 the **m** who has done this shall
2Sa 12: 7 You are the **m**
2Sa 13: 3 Jonadab was a very crafty **m**
2Sa 13:34 the young **m** who was keeping
2Sa 14:16 of the **m** who would destroy me
2Sa 14:21 back the young **m** Absalom
2Sa 16: 5 there was a **m** from the family
2Sa 16: 7 You bloodthirsty **m**, you rogue
2Sa 16: 8 you are a bloodthirsty **m**
2Sa 17: 3 except the **m** whom you seek
2Sa 17: 8 and your father is a **m** of war
2Sa 17:10 your father is a mighty **m**
2Sa 17:25 of a **m** whose name was Jithra
2Sa 18: 5 sake with the young **m** Absalom
2Sa 18:10 Now a certain **m** saw it and
2Sa 18:11 said to the **m** who told him
2Sa 18:12 But the **m** said to Joab
2Sa 18:12 touch the young **m** Absalom
2Sa 18:24 and looked, and there was a **m**
2Sa 18:26 saw another **m** running, and the
2Sa 18:26 There is another **m**, running
2Sa 18:27 He is a good **m**, and comes with
2Sa 18:29 Is the young **m** Absalom safe
2Sa 18:32 Is the young **m** Absalom safe
2Sa 18:32 harm, be as that young **m** is
2Sa 19:14 just as the heart of one **m**
2Sa 19:22 Shall any **m** be put to death
2Sa 19:32 Barzillai was a very aged **m**
2Sa 19:32 for he was a very rich **m**
2Sa 20: 1 every **m** to his tents, O
2Sa 20: 2 So every **m** of Israel deserted
2Sa 20:12 when the **m** saw that all the
2Sa 20:21 But a **m** from the mountains of
2Sa 20:22 the city, every **m** to his tent
2Sa 21: 4 kill any **m** in Israel for us
2Sa 21: 5 As for the **m** who consumed us
2Sa 21:20 was a **m** of great stature, who

2Sa 22:26 with a blameless **m** You will
2Sa 22:49 me from the violent **m**
2Sa 23: 1 thus says the **m** raised up on
2Sa 23: 7 But the **m** who touches them
2Sa 23:20 of a valiant **m** from Kabzeel
2Sa 23:21 an Egyptian, a spectacular **m**
2Sa 24:14 me fall into the hand of **m**
1Ki 1: 6 also a very good-looking **m**
1Ki 1:42 in, for you are a prominent **m**
1Ki 1:52 he proves himself a worthy **m**
1Ki 2: 2 and prove yourself a **m**
1Ki 2: 4 you shall not lack a **m** on
1Ki 2: 9 for you are a wise **m** and know
1Ki 4:25 each **m** under his vine and his
1Ki 4:27 each **m** in his month, provided
1Ki 4:28 each **m** according to his
1Ki 7:14 and his father was a **m** of Tyre
1Ki 8:25 shall not fail to have a **m**
1Ki 9: 5 a **m** on the throne of Israel
1Ki 10:25 Each **m** brought his present
1Ki 11:28 The **m** Jeroboam was a mighty
1Ki 11:28 was a mighty **m** of valor
1Ki 11:28 the young **m** was industrious
1Ki 12:22 came to Shemaiah the **m** of God
1Ki 12:24 Let every **m** return to his
1Ki 13: 1 a **m** of God went from Judah to
1Ki 13: 4 the saying of the **m** of God
1Ki 13: 5 to the sign which the **m** of
1Ki 13: 6 and said to the **m** of God
1Ki 13: 6 So the **m** of God entreated
1Ki 13: 7 the king said to the **m** of God
1Ki 13: 8 But the **m** of God said to the
1Ki 13:11 him all the works that the **m**
1Ki 13:12 **m** of God went who came from
1Ki 13:14 and went after the **m** of God
1Ki 13:14 Are you the **m** of God who came
1Ki 13:21 he cried out to the **m** of God
1Ki 13:26 It is the **m** of God who was
1Ki 13:29 up the corpse of the **m** of God
1Ki 13:31 where the **m** of God is buried
1Ki 17:18 I to do with you, O **m** of God
1Ki 17:24 know that you are a **m** of God
1Ki 20: 7 see how this **m** seeks trouble,
1Ki 20:20 And each one killed his **m**
1Ki 20:28 Then a **m** of God came and
1Ki 20:35 Now a certain **m** of the sons
1Ki 20:35 the **m** refused to strike him
1Ki 20:37 And he found another **m**, and
1Ki 20:37 So the **m** struck him,
1Ki 20:39 a **m** came over and brought a
1Ki 20:39 over and brought a **m** to me
1Ki 20:39 to me, and said, 'Guard this **m**
1Ki 20:42 a **m** whom I appointed to utter
1Ki 22: 8 There is still one **m**, Micaiah
1Ki 22:34 Now a certain **m** drew a bow at
1Ki 22:36 Every **m** to his city, and every
1Ki 22:36 every **m** to his own country
2Ki 1: 6 A **m** came up to meet us, and
2Ki 1: 7 What kind of **m** was it who
2Ki 1: 8 He was a hairy **m**, and wore a
2Ki 1: 9 **M** of God, the king has said
2Ki 1:10 If I am a **m** of God, then let
2Ki 1:11 **M** of God, thus has the king
2Ki 1:12 If I am a **m** of God, let fire
2Ki 1:13 **M** of God, please let my life
2Ki 3:25 each **m** threw a stone on every
2Ki 4: 7 she came and told the **m** of God
2Ki 4: 9 that this is a holy **m** of God
2Ki 4:16 **M** of God, do not lie to your
2Ki 4:21 on the bed of the **m** of God
2Ki 4:22 I may run to the **m** of God
2Ki 4:25 went to the **m** of God at Mount
2Ki 4:25 when the **m** of God saw her
2Ki 4:27 to the **m** of God at the hill
2Ki 4:27 But the **m** of God said,
2Ki 4:40 O **m** of God, there is death in
2Ki 4:42 Then a **m** came from Baal
2Ki 4:42 brought the **m** of God bread of
2Ki 5: 1 honorable **m** in the eyes of
2Ki 5: 1 was also a mighty **m** of valor
2Ki 5: 7 that this **m** sends a **m** to me
2Ki 5: 8 was, when Elisha the **m** of God
2Ki 5:14 to the saying of the **m** of God
2Ki 5:15 he returned to the **m** of God
2Ki 5:20 of Elisha the **m** of God, said,
2Ki 5:26 the **m** turned back from his
2Ki 6: 2 let every **m** take a beam from
2Ki 6: 6 And the **m** of God said,
2Ki 6: 9 the **m** of God sent to the king
2Ki 6:10 the **m** of God had told him
2Ki 6:15 of the **m** of God arose early
2Ki 6:17 the eyes of the young **m**, and
2Ki 6:19 you to the **m** whom you seek
2Ki 6:32 king sent a **m** ahead of him
2Ki 7: 2 leaned answered the **m** of God
2Ki 7:17 just as the **m** of God had said
2Ki 7:18 **m** of God had spoken to the
2Ki 7:19 had answered the **m** of God
2Ki 8: 2 to the saying of the **m** of God
2Ki 8: 4 the servant of the **m** of God
2Ki 8: 7 The **m** of God has come here
2Ki 8: 8 and go to meet the **m** of God
2Ki 8:11 and the **m** of God wept
2Ki 9: 4 So the young **m**, the servant
2Ki 9:11 You know the **m** and his babble
2Ki 9:13 Then each **m** hastened to take
2Ki 10:21 not a **m** left who did not come
2Ki 11: 8 every **m** with his weapons in
2Ki 11:11 every **m** with his weapons in
2Ki 12: 4 and all the money that a **m**
2Ki 13:19 the **m** of God was angry with
2Ki 13:21 was, as they were burying a **m**
2Ki 13:21 they put the **m** in the tomb of
2Ki 13:21 when the **m** was let down and
2Ki 14:12 and every **m** fled to his tent
2Ki 15:20 from each **m** fifty shekels of
2Ki 18:21 Egypt, on which if a **m** leans
2Ki 22:15 Tell the **m** who sent you to
2Ki 23:10 that no **m** might make his son
2Ki 23:16 which the **m** of God proclaimed
2Ki 23:17 It is the tomb of the **m** of
1Ch 11:22 of a valiant **m** from Kabzeel
1Ch 11:23 a **m** of great height, five
1Ch 12: 4 a mighty **m** among the thirty,
1Ch 12:28 Zadok, a young **m**, a valiant
1Ch 16: 3 to everyone of Israel, both **m**
1Ch 16:21 He permitted no **m** to do them
1Ch 16:43 every **m** to his house
1Ch 17:17 estate of a **m** of high degree
1Ch 20: 6 was a **m** of great stature,
1Ch 21:13 me fall into the hand of **m**
1Ch 22: 9 you, who shall be a **m** of rest
1Ch 23:14 Now the sons of Moses the **m**
1Ch 27:32 was a counselor, a wise **m**
1Ch 28: 3 you have been a **m** of war and
1Ch 29: 1 for **m** but for the LORD God
2Ch 2: 7 a **m** skillful to work in gold
2Ch 2:13 now I have sent a skillful **m**
2Ch 2:14 his father was a **m** of Tyre)
2Ch 6: 5 nor did I choose any **m** to be
2Ch 6:16 shall not fail to have a **m**
2Ch 7:18 have a **m** as ruler in Israel
2Ch 8:14 for so David the **m** of God had
2Ch 9:24 Each **m** brought his present
2Ch 10:16 Every **m** to your tents, O
2Ch 11: 2 came to Shemaiah the **m** of God
2Ch 11: 4 Let every **m** return to his
2Ch 14:11 do not let **m** prevail against
2Ch 15:13 or great, whether **m** or woman
2Ch 17:17 Eliada a mighty **m** of valor
2Ch 18: 7 There is still one **m** by whom
2Ch 18:33 Now a certain **m** drew a bow at
2Ch 19: 6 judge for **m** but for the LORD
2Ch 20:27 every **m** of Judah and Jerusalem
2Ch 23: 7 every **m** with his weapons in
2Ch 23: 8 each **m** took his men who were
2Ch 23:10 every **m** with his weapon in
2Ch 25: 7 But a **m** of God came to him,
2Ch 25: 9 Amaziah said to the **m** of God
2Ch 25: 9 And the **m** of God answered,
2Ch 25:22 and every **m** fled to his tent
2Ch 28: 7 a mighty **m** of Ephraim, killed
2Ch 30:16 the Law of Moses the **m** of God
2Ch 31: 1 every **m** to his possession
2Ch 31: 2 each **m** according to his
2Ch 32:21 down every mighty **m** of valor
2Ch 34:23 Tell the **m** who sent you to
2Ch 36:17 on young **m** or virgin, on the
Ezra 3: 1 as one **m** to Jerusalem
Ezra 3: 2 the Law of Moses the **m** of God
Ezra 8:17 chief **m** at the place Casiphia
Ezra 8:18 us a **m** of understanding, of
Neh 1:11 mercy in the sight of this **m**
Neh 2:10 that a **m** had come to seek the
Neh 4:22 Let each **m** and his servant
Neh 5:13 out each **m** from his house
Neh 6:11 Should such a **m** as I flee
Neh 7: 2 for he was a faithful **m** and
Neh 8: 1 gathered together as one **m** in
Neh 9:29 judgments, 'which if a **m** does
Neh 12:24 command of David the **m** of
Neh 12:36 of David the **m** of God
Esth 1:22 that each **m** should be master
Esth 4:11 provinces know that any **m** or
Esth 6: 6 **m** whom the king delights to
Esth 6: 7 For the **m** whom the king
Esth 6: 9 that he may array the **m** whom
Esth 6: 9 shall it be done to the **m**
Esth 6:11 shall it be done to the **m** the
Esth 9: 4 for this **m** Mordecai became
Job 1: 1 There was a **m** in the land of
Job 1: 1 and that **m** was blameless and
Job 1: 8 a blameless and upright **m**
Job 2: 3 a blameless and upright **m**
Job 2: 4 all that a **m** has he will give
Job 3:23 to a **m** whose way is hidden
Job 4:17 Can a **m** be more pure than his
Job 5: 2 For wrath kills a foolish **m**
Job 5: 7 yet **m** is born to trouble, as
Job 5:17 happy is the **m** whom God
Job 7: 1 hard service for **m** on earth
Job 7: 1 like the days of a hired **m**
Job 7: 2 like a hired **m** who eagerly
Job 7:17 What is **m**, that You should
Job 9: 2 but how can a **m** be righteous
Job 9:32 For He is not a **m**, as I am,
Job 10: 4 Or do You see as **m** sees
Job 10: 5 like the days of a mortal **m**
Job 10: 5 like the days of a mighty **m**
Job 11: 2 should a **m** full of talk be
Job 11:12 empty-headed **m** will be wise
Job 11:12 donkey's colt is born a **m**
Job 12:14 if He imprisons a **m**, there
Job 12:25 them stagger like a drunken **m**
Job 13: 9 you mock Him as one mocks a **m**
Job 13:28 **M** decays like a rotten thing,
Job 14: 1 **M** who is born of woman is of
Job 14: 6 rest, till like a hired **m** he
Job 14:10 But **m** dies and is laid away
Job 14:12 so **m** lies down and does not
Job 14:14 If a **m** dies, shall he live
Job 14:19 so You destroy the hope of **m**
Job 15: 2 Should a wise **m** answer with
Job 15: 7 you the first **m** who was born
Job 15:14 What is **m**, that he could be
Job 15:16 how much less **m**, who is
Job 15:20 the wicked **m** writhes with
Job 16:21 might plead for a **m** with God
Job 16:21 God, as a **m** pleads for his
Job 17:10 not find one wise **m** among you
Job 20: 4 since **m** was placed on earth,
Job 20:29 from God for a wicked **m**, the
Job 21: 4 me, is my complaint against **m**
Job 21:25 Another **m** dies in the
Job 22: 2 Can a **m** be profitable to God,
Job 22: 8 But the mighty **m** possessed
Job 22: 8 the honorable **m** dwelt in it
Job 24:22 up, but no **m** is sure of life
Job 25: 4 How then can **m** be righteous
Job 25: 6 how much less **m**, who is a
Job 25: 6 is a maggot, and a son of **m**
Job 27:13 of a wicked **m** with God, and
Job 27:19 The rich **m** will lie down, but
Job 28: 3 **M** puts an end to darkness, and
Job 28:13 **M** does not know its value,
Job 28:28 to **m** He said, 'Behold, the
Job 29:13 of a perishing **m** came upon me
Job 31:19 or any poor **m** without
Job 32: 8 But there is a spirit in **m**
Job 32:13 God will vanquish him, not **m**
Job 32:21 nor let me flatter any **m**
Job 33:12 for God is greater than **m**
Job 33:14 yet **m** does not perceive it
Job 33:17 order to turn **m** from his deed
Job 33:17 deed, and conceal pride from **m**
Job 33:19 **M** is also chastened with pain
Job 33:23 to show **m** His uprightness,
Job 33:26 to **m** His righteousness
Job 33:29 in fact, three times with a **m**
Job 34: 7 What **m** is like Job, who
Job 34: 9 It profits a **m** nothing that
Job 34:11 For He repays **m** according to
Job 34:11 and makes **m** to find a reward
Job 34:15 and **m** would return to dust
Job 34:21 His eyes are on the ways of **m**
Job 34:23 need not further consider a **m**
Job 34:29 against a nation or a **m** alone
Job 35: 8 affects a **m** such as you, and
Job 35: 8 your righteousness a son of **m**
Job 36:25 **m** looks on it from afar

Job 36:28 down and pour abundantly on **m**
Job 37: 7 He seals the hand of every **m**
Job 37:20 If a **m** were to speak, surely
Job 38: 3 Now prepare yourself like a **m**
Job 38:26 in which there is no **m**
Job 40: 7 Now prepare yourself like a **m**
Ps 1: 1 Blessed is the **m** Who walks
Ps 5: 6 bloodthirsty and deceitful **m**
Ps 8: 4 What is **m** that You are
Ps 8: 4 the son of **m** that You visit
Ps 9:19 O LORD, Do not let **m** prevail
Ps 10:15 of the wicked and the evil **m**
Ps 10:18 That the **m** of the earth may
Ps 12: 1 LORD, for the godly **m** ceases
Ps 18:25 With a blameless **m** You will
Ps 18:48 me from the violent **m**
Ps 19: 5 a strong **m** to run its race
Ps 22: 6 But I am a worm, and no **m**
Ps 25:12 Who is the **m** that fears the
Ps 31:12 I am forgotten like a dead **m**
Ps 31:20 presence From the plots of **m**
Ps 32: 2 Blessed is the **m** to whom the
Ps 33:16 A mighty **m** is not delivered
Ps 34: 6 This poor **m** cried out, and the
Ps 34: 8 Blessed is the **m** who trusts
Ps 34:12 Who is the **m** who desires life
Ps 36: 6 O LORD, You preserve **m** and
Ps 37: 7 Because of the **m** who brings
Ps 37:16 **m** has Is better than the
Ps 37:23 The steps of a good **m** are
Ps 37:37 Mark the blameless **m**, and
Ps 37:37 the future of that **m** is peace
Ps 38:13 But I, like a deaf **m**, do not
Ps 38:14 Thus I am like a **m** who does
Ps 39: 5 Certainly every **m** at his best
Ps 39: 6 Surely every **m** walks about
Ps 39:11 You correct **m** for iniquity
Ps 39:11 Surely every **m** is vapor
Ps 40: 4 Blessed is that **m** who makes
Ps 43: 1 the deceitful and unjust **m**
Ps 49:12 Nevertheless **m**, though in
Ps 49:20 **M** who is in honor, yet does
Ps 52: 1 you boast in evil, O mighty **m**
Ps 52: 7 Here is the **m** who did not
Ps 55:13 a **m** my equal, My companion
Ps 56: 1 for **m** would swallow me up
Ps 56:11 What can **m** do to me
Ps 60:11 For vain is the help of **m**
Ps 62: 3 How long will you attack a **m**
Ps 64: 6 and the heart of **m** are deep
Ps 65: 4 Blessed is the **m** whom You
Ps 71: 4 of the unrighteous and cruel **m**
Ps 74:22 **m** reproaches You daily
Ps 76:10 wrath of **m** shall praise You
Ps 78:65 like a mighty **m** who shouts
Ps 80:17 upon the **m** of Your right hand
Ps 80:17 Upon the son of **m** whom You
Ps 84: 5 Blessed is the **m** whose
Ps 84:12 Blessed is the **m** who trusts
Ps 88: 4 I am like a **m** who has no
Ps 89:48 What **m** can live and not see
Ps 90: 3 You turn **m** to destruction, And
Ps 92: 6 A senseless **m** does not know,
Ps 94:10 He who teaches **m** knowledge
Ps 94:11 LORD knows the thoughts of **m**
Ps 94:12 Blessed is the **m** whom You
Ps 103:15 As for **m**, his days are like
Ps 104:14 for the service of **m**, That he
Ps 104:15 makes glad the heart of **m**
Ps 104:23 **M** goes out to his work And to
Ps 105:17 He sent a **m** before them
Ps 107:27 and stagger like a drunken **m**
Ps 108:12 For vain is the help of **m**
Ps 109: 6 Set a wicked **m** over him, And
Ps 109:16 the poor and needy **m**, That he
Ps 112: 1 Blessed is the **m** who fears
Ps 112: 5 A good **m** deals graciously and
Ps 118: 6 What can **m** do to me
Ps 118: 8 Than to put confidence in **m**
Ps 119: 9 can a young **m** cleanse his way
Ps 119:134 me from the oppression of **m**
Ps 127: 5 Happy is the **m** who has his
Ps 128: 4 thus shall the **m** be blessed
Ps 135: 8 firstborn of Egypt, Both of **m**
Ps 140:11 violent **m** to overthrow him
Ps 144: 3 LORD, what is **m**, that You
Ps 144: 3 Or the son of **m**, that You are
Ps 144: 4 **M** is like a breath
Ps 146: 3 in princes, Nor in a son of **m**
Ps 147:10 pleasure in the legs of a **m**
Prov 1: 4 to the young **m** knowledge
Prov 1: 5 A wise **m** will hear and
Prov 1: 5 a **m** of understanding will
Prov 2:12 evil, from the **m** who speaks
Prov 3: 4 in the sight of God and **m**
Prov 3:13 Happy is the **m** who finds
Prov 3:13 the **m** who gains understanding
Prov 3:30 strive with a **m** without cause
Prov 5:21 For the ways of **m** are before
Prov 5:22 entrap the wicked **m**, and he is
Prov 6:11 and your need like an armed **m**
Prov 6:12 worthless person, a wicked **m**
Prov 6:26 a **m** is reduced to a crust of
Prov 6:27 can a **m** take fire to his
Prov 7: 7 youths, a young **m** devoid of
Prov 8:34 Blessed is the **m** who listens
Prov 9: 7 **m** gets himself a blemish
Prov 9: 8 rebuke a wise **m**, and he will
Prov 9: 9 Give instruction to a wise **m**
Prov 9: 9 teach a just **m**, and he will
Prov 10:23 but a **m** of understanding has
Prov 11: 7 When a wicked **m** dies, his
Prov 11:12 but a **m** of understanding
Prov 11:17 The merciful **m** does good for
Prov 11:18 The wicked **m** does deceptive
Prov 12: 2 A good **m** obtains favor from
Prov 12: 2 but a **m** of wicked devices He
Prov 12: 3 A **m** is not established by
Prov 12: 8 A **m** will be commended
Prov 12:10 A righteous **m** regards the
Prov 12:14 A **m** will be satisifed with
Prov 12:16 but a prudent **m** covers shame
Prov 12:23 A prudent **m** conceals
Prov 12:25 heart of **m** causes depression
Prov 12:27 The slothful **m** does not roast
Prov 13: 2 A **m** shall eat well by the
Prov 13: 5 A righteous **m** hates lying
Prov 13: 5 but a wicked **m** is loathsome
Prov 13:16 Every prudent **m** acts with
Prov 13:22 A good **m** leaves an
Prov 14: 7 the presence of a foolish **m**
Prov 14:12 way which seems right to a **m**
Prov 14:14 ways, but a good **m** will be
Prov 14:15 but the prudent **m** considers
Prov 14:16 A wise **m** fears and departs
Prov 14:17 a **m** of wicked intentions is
Prov 14:20 The poor **m** is hated even by
Prov 15:18 A wrathful **m** stirs up strife,
Prov 15:19 The way of the slothful **m** is
Prov 15:20 but a foolish **m** despises his
Prov 15:21 but a **m** of understanding
Prov 15:23 A **m** has joy by the answer of
Prov 16: 1 of the heart belong to **m**, but
Prov 16: 2 All the ways of a **m** are pure
Prov 16:14 but a wise **m** will appease it
Prov 16:25 a way that seems right to a **m**
Prov 16:27 An ungodly **m** digs up evil, and
Prov 16:28 A perverse **m** sows strife, and
Prov 16:29 A violent **m** entices his
Prov 17:10 **m** than a hundred blows on a
Prov 17:11 An evil **m** seeks only
Prov 17:12 Let a **m** meet a bear robbed of
Prov 17:18 A **m** devoid of understanding
Prov 17:23 A wicked **m** accepts a bribe
Prov 17:27 a **m** of understanding is of a
Prov 18: 1 A **m** who isolates himself
Prov 18:12 the heart of a **m** is haughty
Prov 18:14 The spirit of a **m** will
Prov 18:23 The poor **m** uses entreaties,
Prov 18:24 A **m** who has friends must
Prov 19: 3 of a **m** twists his way, and his
Prov 19: 6 every **m** is a friend to one
Prov 19:11 The discretion of a **m** makes
Prov 19:19 A **m** of great wrath will
Prov 19:22 is desired in a **m** is kindness
Prov 19:22 a poor **m** is better than a
Prov 19:24 A slothful **m** buries his hand
Prov 20: 3 for a **m** to stop striving,
Prov 20: 5 heart of **m** is like deep water
Prov 20: 5 but a **m** of understanding will
Prov 20: 6 but who can find a faithful **m**
Prov 20: 7 The righteous **m** walks in his
Prov 20:17 by deceit is sweet to a **m**
Prov 20:24 how then can a **m** understand
Prov 20:25 It is a snare for a **m** to
Prov 20:27 The spirit of a **m** is the lamp
Prov 21: 2 Every way of a **m** is right in
Prov 21: 8 way of a guilty **m** is perverse
Prov 21:16 A **m** who wanders from the way
Prov 21:17 pleasure will be a poor **m**
Prov 21:20 but a foolish **m** squanders it
Prov 21:22 A wise **m** scales the city of
Prov 21:24 A proud and haughty **m**
Prov 21:28 but the **m** who hears him will
Prov 21:29 A wicked **m** hardens his face,
Prov 22: 3 A prudent **m** foresees evil and
Prov 22:13 The slothful **m** says, "There
Prov 22:24 no friendship with an angry **m**
Prov 22:24 and with a furious **m** do not go
Prov 22:29 Do you see a **m** who excels in
Prov 23: 2 you are a **m** given to appetite
Prov 23:21 will clothe a **m** with rags
Prov 24: 5 A wise **m** is strong, yes, a
Prov 24: 5 a **m** of knowledge increases
Prov 24:12 each **m** according to his deeds
Prov 24:15 not lie in wait, O wicked **m**
Prov 24:16 for a righteous **m** may fall
Prov 24:20 be no prospect for the evil **m**
Prov 24:29 I will render to the **m**
Prov 24:30 and by the vineyard of the **m**
Prov 24:34 and your want like an armed **m**
Prov 25:18 A **m** who bears false witness
Prov 25:19 **m** in time of trouble is like
Prov 25:26 A righteous **m** who falters
Prov 26:12 Do you see a **m** wise in his
Prov 26:13 The slothful **m** says, "There
Prov 26:15 The slothful **m** buries his
Prov 26:19 is the **m** who deceives his
Prov 26:21 **m** to kindle strife
Prov 27: 2 Let another **m** praise you, and
Prov 27: 8 **m** who wanders from his place
Prov 27:12 A prudent **m** foresees evil and
Prov 27:17 iron, so a **m** sharpens the
Prov 27:19 a man's heart reveals the **m**
Prov 27:20 so the eyes of **m** are never
Prov 27:21 a **m** is valued by what others
Prov 28: 2 but by a **m** of understanding
Prov 28: 3 A poor **m** who oppresses the
Prov 28:11 The rich **m** is wise in his own
Prov 28:14 Happy is the **m** who is always
Prov 28:17 A **m** burdened with bloodshed
Prov 28:20 A faithful **m** will abound with
Prov 28:21 of bread a **m** will transgress
Prov 28:22 A **m** with an evil eye hastens
Prov 28:23 He who rebukes a **m** will find
Prov 29: 2 but when a wicked **m** rules
Prov 29: 5 A **m** who flatters his neighbor
Prov 29: 6 an evil **m** is snared, but the
Prov 29: 9 **m** contends with a foolish **m**
Prov 29:11 but a wise **m** holds them back
Prov 29:13 The poor **m** and the oppressor
Prov 29:20 Do you see a **m** hasty in his
Prov 29:22 An angry **m** stirs up strife,
Prov 29:22 and a furious **m** abounds in
Prov 29:25 The fear of **m** brings a snare,
Prov 29:26 but justice for **m** comes from
Prov 29:27 An unjust **m** is an abomination
Prov 30: 1 This **m** declared to Ithiel
Prov 30: 2 I am more stupid than any **m**
Prov 30: 2 have the understanding of a **m**
Prov 30:19 the way of a **m** with a virgin
Eccl 1: 3 What profit has a **m** from all
Eccl 1: 8 **m** cannot express it
Eccl 1:13 has given to the sons of **m**
Eccl 2:12 for what can the **m** do who
Eccl 2:16 and how does a wise **m** die
Eccl 2:18 the **m** who will come after me
Eccl 2:19 he will be a wise **m** or a fool
Eccl 2:21 For there is a **m** whose labor
Eccl 2:21 leave his heritage to a **m** who
Eccl 2:22 For what has **m** for all his
Eccl 2:24 a **m** than that he should eat
Eccl 2:26 joy to a **m** who is good in His
Eccl 3:13 also that every **m** should eat
Eccl 3:19 **m** has no advantage over
Eccl 3:22 a **m** should rejoice in his own
Eccl 4: 4 every skillful work a **m** is
Eccl 5:12 of a laboring **m** is sweet,
Eccl 5:19 As for every **m** to whom God
Eccl 6: 2 A **m** to whom God has given
Eccl 6: 3 If a **m** begets a hundred
Eccl 6: 5 has more rest than that **m**
Eccl 6: 7 labor of **m** is for his mouth
Eccl 6: 8 has the wise **m** than the fool
Eccl 6: 8 What does the poor **m** have
Eccl 6:10 for it is known that he is **m**
Eccl 6:11 vanity, how is **m** the better
Eccl 6:12 what is good for **m** in life
Eccl 6:12 Who can tell a **m** what will
Eccl 7: 5 of the wise than for a **m** to

Eccl 7:14 so that **m** can find nothing
Eccl 7:15 There is a just **m** who
Eccl 7:15 and there is a wicked **m** who
Eccl 7:20 just **m** on earth who does good
Eccl 7:28 one **m** among a thousand I have
Eccl 7:29 that God made **m** upright, but
Eccl 8: 1 Who is like a wise **m**
Eccl 8: 6 misery of **m** increases greatly
Eccl 8: 9 is a time in which one **m**
Eccl 8:15 because a **m** has nothing
Eccl 8:17 that a **m** cannot find out the
Eccl 8:17 For though a **m** labors to
Eccl 8:17 though a wise **m** attempts to
Eccl 9:12 For **m** also does not know his
Eccl 9:15 was found in it a poor wise **m**
Eccl 9:15 remembered that same poor **m**
Eccl 10:14 No **m** knows what is to be
Eccl 11: 8 But if a **m** lives many years
Eccl 11: 9 Rejoice, O young **m**, in your
Eccl 12: 5 For **m** goes to his eternal
Eccl 12:13 this is the whole duty of **m**
Song 3: 8 every **m** has his sword on his
Song 8: 7 If a **m** would give for love
Is 2: 9 and each **m** humbles himself
Is 2:11 looks of **m** shall be humbled
Is 2:17 The loftiness of **m** shall be
Is 2:20 In that day a **m** will cast
Is 2:22 yourselves from such a **m**,
Is 3: 2 the mighty **m** and the **m** of war
Is 3: 3 of fifty and the honorable **m**
Is 3: 6 When a **m** takes hold of his
Is 4: 1 shall take hold of one **m**,
Is 5:15 Each **m** shall be humbled, and
Is 5:23 justice from the righteous **m**
Is 6: 5 Because I am a **m** of unclean
Is 6:11 the houses are without a **m**
Is 7:21 **m** will keep alive a young cow
Is 9:19 no **m** shall spare his brother
Is 9:20 every **m** shall eat the flesh
Is 10:13 inhabitants like a valiant **m**
Is 10:18 as when a sick **m** wastes away
Is 13:12 a **m** more than the golden
Is 13:14 as a sheep that no **m** takes up
Is 13:14 every **m** will turn to his own
Is 14:16 Is this the **m** who made the
Is 16:14 as the years of a hired **m**
Is 17: 7 In that day a **m** will look to
Is 19:14 as a drunken **m** staggers in
Is 21:16 to the year of a hired **m**, all
Is 22:17 away violently, O mighty **m**
Is 28:20 for a **m** to stretch out on
Is 29: 8 be as when a hungry **m** dreams
Is 29: 8 or as when a thirsty **m** dreams
Is 29:21 who make a **m** an offender by a
Is 31: 7 For in that day every **m** shall
Is 31: 8 fall by a sword not of **m**, and
Is 32: 2 A **m** will be as a hiding place
Is 32: 8 But a generous **m** devises
Is 33: 8 waste, the wayfaring **m** ceases
Is 33: 8 the cities, He regards no **m**
Is 36: 6 Egypt, on which if a **m** leans
Is 38:11 I shall observe **m** no more
Is 38:19 The living, the living **m**, he
Is 41:28 I looked, and there was no **m**
Is 42:13 go forth like a mighty **m**
Is 42:13 up His zeal like a **m** of war
Is 44:13 it like the figure of a **m**
Is 44:13 to the beauty of a **m**, that it
Is 44:15 it shall be for a **m** to burn
Is 45:12 the earth, and created **m** on it
Is 46:11 the **m** who executes My counsel
Is 47: 3 I will not arbitrate with a **m**
Is 49: 7 One, to Him whom **m** despises
Is 50: 2 when I came, was there no **m**
Is 51:12 be afraid of a **m** who will die
Is 51:12 of the son of a **m** who will be
Is 52:14 was marred more than any **m**
Is 53: 3 a **m** of sorrows and acquainted
Is 55: 7 unrighteous **m** his thoughts
Is 56: 2 is the **m** who does this, and
Is 56: 2 the son of **m** who lays hold on
Is 57: 1 and no **m** takes it to heart
Is 58: 5 a day for a **m** to afflict his
Is 59:16 He saw that there was no **m**
Is 62: 5 For as a young **m** marries a
Is 65:20 nor an old **m** who has not
Is 66: 3 a bull is as if he slays a **m**
Jer 3: 1 If a **m** divorces his wife, and
Jer 4:25 and indeed there was no **m**
Jer 4:29 not a **m** shall dwell in it
Jer 5: 1 places if you can find a **m**
Jer 7: 5 execute judgment between a **m**
Jer 7:20 on **m** and on beast, on the
Jer 8: 6 No **m** repented of his
Jer 9:12 Who is the wise **m** who may
Jer 9:23 Let not the wise **m** glory in
Jer 9:23 mighty **m** glory in his might
Jer 9:23 nor let the rich **m** glory in
Jer 10:23 way of **m** is not in himself
Jer 10:23 it is not in **m** who walks to
Jer 11: 3 Cursed is the **m** who does not
Jer 13:11 clings to the waist of a **m**
Jer 14: 8 like a wayfaring **m** who turns
Jer 14: 9 You be like a **m** astonished
Jer 15:10 a **m** of strife
Jer 15:10 and a **m** of contention to the
Jer 16:20 Will a **m** make gods for
Jer 17: 5 is the **m** who trusts in **m**
Jer 17: 7 Blessed is the **m** who trusts
Jer 17:10 mind, even to give every **m**
Jer 18:14 Will a **m** leave the snow-water
Jer 20:15 Let the **m** be cursed who
Jer 20:16 let that **m** be like the cities
Jer 21: 6 of this city, both **m** and beast
Jer 22:28 Is this **m** Coniah a despised,
Jer 22:30 Write this **m** down as
Jer 22:30 a **m** who shall not prosper in
Jer 23: 9 I am like a drunken **m**, and
Jer 23: 9 and like a **m** whom wine has
Jer 23:34 I will even punish that **m**
Jer 26:11 This **m** deserves to die
Jer 26:16 This **m** does not deserve to
Jer 26:20 Now there was also a **m** who
Jer 27: 5 I have made the earth, the **m**
Jer 29:26 over every **m** who is demented
Jer 30: 6 whether a **m** is ever in labor
Jer 30: 6 So why do I see every **m** with
Jer 31:22 a woman shall encompass a **m**
Jer 31:27 of Judah with the seed of **m**
Jer 31:30 every **m** who eats the sour
Jer 31:34 every **m** teach his neighbor
Jer 31:34 every **m** his brother, saying
Jer 32:43 desolate, without **m** or beast
Jer 33:10 It is desolate, without **m**
Jer 33:10 that are desolate, without **m**
Jer 33:12 which is desolate, without **m**
Jer 33:17 David shall never lack a **m**
Jer 33:18 lack a **m** to offer burnt
Jer 34: 9 that every **m** should set free
Jer 34: 9 a Hebrew **m** or woman
Jer 34:14 of seven years let every **m**
Jer 34:15 every **m** proclaiming liberty
Jer 35: 4 a **m** of God, which was by the
Jer 35:19 **m** to stand before Me forever
Jer 36:29 destroy this land, and cause **m**
Jer 37:10 every **m** in his tent, and burn
Jer 38: 4 let this **m** be put to death,
Jer 38: 4 For this **m** does not seek the
Jer 44: 7 to cut off from you **m** and
Jer 44:26 named in the mouth of any **m**
Jer 46: 6 away, nor the mighty **m** escape
Jer 46:12 for the mighty **m** has stumbled
Jer 49:18 shall a son of **m** dwell in it
Jer 49:19 who is a chosen **m** that I may
Jer 49:33 nor son of **m** dwell in it
Jer 50: 3 they shall depart, both **m**
Jer 50:40 nor son of **m** dwell in it
Jer 50:42 like a **m** for the battle,
Jer 50:44 who is a chosen **m** that I may
Jer 51:22 also I will break in pieces **m**
Jer 51:22 break in pieces the young **m**
Jer 51:43 which no son of **m** passes
Jer 51:62 neither **m** nor beast, but it
Lam 3: 1 I am the **m** who has seen
Lam 3:27 It is good for a **m** to bear
Lam 3:35 aside the justice due a **m**
Lam 3:36 or subvert a **m** in his cause
Lam 3:39 should a living **m** complain
Lam 3:39 a **m** for the punishment of his
Ezek 1: 5 they had the likeness of a **m**
Ezek 1: 8 They had the hands of a **m**
Ezek 1:10 each had the face of a **m**
Ezek 1:26 of a **m** high above it
Ezek 2: 1 Son of **m**, stand on your feet,
Ezek 2: 3 Son of **m**, I am sending you to
Ezek 2: 6 And you, son of **m**, do not be
Ezek 2: 8 But you, son of **m**, hear what
Ezek 3: 1 Son of **m**, eat what you find
Ezek 3: 3 Son of **m**, feed your belly, and
Ezek 3: 4 Son of **m**, go to the house of
Ezek 3:10 Son of **m**, receive into your
Ezek 3:17 Son of **m**, I have made you a
Ezek 3:18 that same wicked **m** shall die
Ezek 3:20 a righteous **m** turns from his
Ezek 3:21 **m** that the righteous should
Ezek 3:25 And you, O son of **m**, surely
Ezek 4: 1 You also, son of **m**, take a
Ezek 4:16 Son of **m**, surely I will cut
Ezek 5: 1 And you, son of **m**, take a
Ezek 6: 2 Son of **m**, set your face
Ezek 7: 2 And you, son of **m**, thus says
Ezek 8: 5 Son of **m**, lift your eyes now
Ezek 8: 6 Son of **m**, do you see what
Ezek 8: 8 Son of **m**, dig into the wall"
Ezek 8:11 Each **m** had a censer in his
Ezek 8:12 Son of **m**, have you seen what
Ezek 8:12 every **m** in the room of his
Ezek 8:15 you seen this, O son of **m**
Ezek 8:17 you seen this, O son of **m**
Ezek 9: 2 One **m** among them was clothed
Ezek 9: 3 He called to the **m** clothed
Ezek 9:11 the **m** clothed with linen, who
Ezek 10: 2 He spoke to the **m** clothed
Ezek 10: 3 the temple when the **m** went in
Ezek 10: 6 the **m** clothed in linen,
Ezek 10: 7 of the **m** clothed with linen
Ezek 10:14 second face the face of a **m**
Ezek 10:21 of a **m** was under their wings
Ezek 11: 2 Son of **m**, these are the men
Ezek 11: 4 them, prophesy, O son of **m**
Ezek 11:15 Son of **m**, your brethren, your
Ezek 12: 2 Son of **m**, you dwell in the
Ezek 12: 3 Therefore, son of **m**, prepare
Ezek 12: 9 Son of **m**, has not the house
Ezek 12:18 Son of **m**, eat your bread with
Ezek 12:22 Son of **m**, what is this
Ezek 12:27 Son of **m**, look, the house of
Ezek 13: 2 Son of **m**, prophesy against
Ezek 13:17 Likewise, son of **m**, set your
Ezek 14: 3 Son of **m**, these men have set
Ezek 14: 8 set My face against that **m**
Ezek 14:13 Son of **m**, when a land sins
Ezek 14:13 famine on it, and cut off **m**
Ezek 14:15 **m** may pass through because of
Ezek 14:17 the land,' and I cut off **m**
Ezek 14:19 blood, and cut off from it **m**
Ezek 14:21 to cut off **m** and beast from it
Ezek 15: 2 Son of **m**, how is the wood of
Ezek 16: 2 Son of **m**, cause Jerusalem to
Ezek 17: 2 Son of **m**, pose a riddle, and
Ezek 18: 5 But if a **m** is just and does
Ezek 18: 8 true judgment between **m** and **m**
Ezek 18:21 But if a wicked **m** turns from
Ezek 18:24 **m** turns away from his
Ezek 18:24 that the wicked **m** does, shall
Ezek 18:26 When a righteous **m** turns away
Ezek 18:27 when a wicked **m** turns away
Ezek 20: 3 Son of **m**, speak to the elders
Ezek 20: 4 Will you judge them, son of **m**
Ezek 20:11 which, if a **m** does, he
Ezek 20:13 judgments, which, if a **m** does
Ezek 20:21 which, if a **m** does, he
Ezek 20:27 Therefore, son of **m**, speak to
Ezek 20:46 Son of **m**, set your face
Ezek 21: 2 Son of **m**, set your face
Ezek 21: 6 Sigh therefore, son of **m**,
Ezek 21: 9 Son of **m**, prophesy and say
Ezek 21:12 Cry and wail, son of **m**
Ezek 21:14 You therefore, son of **m**,
Ezek 21:19 And son of **m**, appoint for
Ezek 21:28 And you, son of **m**, prophesy
Ezek 22: 2 Now, son of **m**, will you judge
Ezek 22:18 Son of **m**, the house of Israel
Ezek 22:24 Son of **m**, say to her
Ezek 22:30 So I sought for a **m** among
Ezek 23: 2 Son of **m**, there were two
Ezek 23:36 Son of **m**, will you judge
Ezek 24: 2 Son of **m**, write down the name
Ezek 24:16 Son of **m**, behold, I take away
Ezek 24:25 And you, son of **m**
Ezek 25: 2 Son of **m**, set your face
Ezek 25:13 hand against Edom, cut off **m**
Ezek 26: 2 Son of **m**, because Tyre has
Ezek 27: 2 Now, son of **m**, take up a
Ezek 28: 2 Son of **m**, say to the prince
Ezek 28: 2 of the seas,' yet you are a **m**
Ezek 28: 9 But you shall be a **m**, and not
Ezek 28:12 Son of **m**, take up a
Ezek 28:21 Son of **m**, set your face
Ezek 29: 2 Son of **m**, set your face

Ezek 29: 8 you and cut off from you **m**
Ezek 29:11 Neither foot of **m** shall pass
Ezek 29:18 Son of **m**, Nebuchadnezzar king
Ezek 30: 2 Son of **m**, prophesy and say
Ezek 30:21 Son of **m**, I have broken the
Ezek 30:24 of a mortally wounded **m**
Ezek 31: 2 Son of **m**, say to Pharaoh king
Ezek 32: 2 Son of **m**, take up a
Ezek 32:10 every **m** for his own life, in
Ezek 32:13 the foot of **m** shall muddy
Ezek 32:18 Son of **m**, wail over the
Ezek 33: 2 Son of **m**, speak to the
Ezek 33: 2 take a **m** from their territory
Ezek 33: 7 So you, son of **m**
Ezek 33: 8 to the wicked, 'O wicked **m**
Ezek 33: 8 that wicked **m** shall die in
Ezek 33:10 Therefore you, O son of **m**
Ezek 33:12 Therefore you, O son of **m**
Ezek 33:12 of the righteous **m** shall not
Ezek 33:22 the **m** came who had escaped
Ezek 33:24 Son of **m**, they who inhabit
Ezek 33:30 As for you, son of **m**, the
Ezek 34: 2 Son of **m**, prophesy against
Ezek 35: 2 Son of **m**, set your face
Ezek 36: 1 And you, son of **m**, prophesy to
Ezek 36:11 I will multiply upon you **m**
Ezek 36:17 Son of **m**, when the house of
Ezek 37: 3 Son of **m**, can these bones
Ezek 37: 9 breath, prophesy, son of **m**
Ezek 37:11 Son of **m**, these bones are the
Ezek 37:16 As for you, son of **m**, take a
Ezek 38: 2 Son of **m**, set your face
Ezek 38:14 Therefore, son of **m**, prophesy
Ezek 39: 1 And you, son of **m**, prophesy
Ezek 39:17 And as for you, son of **m**, thus
Ezek 40: 3 behold, there was a **m** whose
Ezek 40: 4 And the **m** said to me,
Ezek 40: 4 Son of **m**, look with your eyes
Ezek 41:19 so that the face of a **m** was
Ezek 43: 6 while a **m** stood beside me
Ezek 43: 7 Son of **m**, this is the place
Ezek 43:10 Son of **m**, describe the temple
Ezek 43:18 Son of **m**, thus says the Lord
Ezek 44: 2 and no **m** shall enter by it,
Ezek 44: 5 Son of **m**, mark well, see with
Ezek 47: 3 when the **m** went out to the
Ezek 47: 6 Son of **m**, have you seen this
Dan 2:10 There is not a **m** on earth who
Dan 2:25 I have found a **m** of the
Dan 4:16 be changed from that of a **m**
Dan 5:11 There is a **m** in your kingdom
Dan 6: 7 any god or **m** for thirty days
Dan 6:12 **m** who petitions any god or
Dan 6:12 god or **m** within thirty days
Dan 7: 4 to stand on two feet like a **m**
Dan 7: 8 eyes like the eyes of a **m**
Dan 7:13 behold, One like the Son of **M**
Dan 8:15 having the appearance of a **m**
Dan 8:16 make this **m** understand the
Dan 8:17 Understand, son of **m**, that
Dan 9:21 the **m** Gabriel, whom I had
Dan 10: 5 a certain **m** clothed in linen,
Dan 10:11 **m** greatly beloved, understand
Dan 10:18 likeness of a **m** touched me
Dan 10:19 O **m** greatly beloved, fear not
Dan 12: 6 one said to the **m** clothed in
Dan 12: 7 heard the **m** clothed in linen
Hos 3: 3 nor shall you have a **m**
Hos 4: 4 Now let no **m** contend, or
Hos 6: 9 robbers lie in wait for a **m**
Hos 9: 7 the spiritual **m** is insane
Hos 9:12 bereave them to the last **m**
Hos 11: 9 For I am God, and not **m**, the
Amos 2: 7 a **m** and his father go in to
Amos 4:13 who declares to **m** what his
Amos 5:19 though a **m** fled from a lion
Jon 1: 5 every **m** cried out to his god,
Jon 3: 7 Let neither **m** nor beast, herd
Jon 3: 8 But let **m** and beast be covered
Mic 2: 2 So they oppress a **m** and his
Mic 2: 2 a **m** and his inheritance
Mic 2:11 If a **m** should walk in a false
Mic 5: 7 that tarry for no **m** nor wait
Mic 6: 8 He has shown you, O **m**, what
Mic 7: 2 The faithful **m** has perished
Mic 7: 2 every **m** hunts his brother
Mic 7: 3 the great **m** utters his evil
Nah 2: 1 **M** the fort! Watch the road!
Hab 2: 5 by wine, he is a proud **m**, and
Zeph 1: 3 I will consume **m** and beast
Zeph 1: 3 I will cut off **m** from the
Zech 1: 8 a **m** riding on a red horse, and
Zech 1:10 the **m** who stood among the
Zech 2: 1 a **m** with a measuring line in
Zech 2: 4 Run, speak to this young **m**
Zech 4: 1 as a **m** who is wakened out of
Zech 6:12 the **M** whose name is the
Zech 8:10 for **m** nor any hire for beast
Zech 8:16 speak each **m** the truth to his
Zech 8:23 the sleeve of a Jewish **m**,
Zech 9:13 like the sword of a mighty **m**
Zech 10: 7 shall be like a mighty **m**, and
Zech 12: 1 the spirit of **m** within him
Zech 13: 5 for a **m** taught me to keep
Zech 13: 7 against the **M** who is My
Mal 2:12 of Jacob the **m** who does this
Mal 3: 8 Will a **m** rob God
Mal 3:17 as a **m** spares his own son who
Matt 1:19 her husband, being a just **m**
Matt 4: 4 **M** shall not live by bread
Matt 7: 9 Or what **m** is there among you
Matt 7:24 **m** who built his house on the
Matt 7:26 will be like a foolish **m** who
Matt 8: 9 I also am a **m** under authority
Matt 8:20 but the Son of **M** has nowhere
Matt 9: 3 This **M** blasphemes
Matt 9: 6 of **M** has power on earth to
Matt 9: 9 He saw a **m** named Matthew
Matt 9:32 they brought to Him a **m**,
Matt 10:23 before the Son of **M** comes
Matt 10:35 set a **m** against his father
Matt 10:41 **m** in the name of a righteous
Matt 10:41 **m** shall receive a righteous
Matt 11: 8 A **m** clothed in soft garments
Matt 11:19 The Son of **M** came eating and
Matt 11:19 say, 'Look, a gluttonous **m**
Matt 12: 8 For the Son of **M** is Lord even
Matt 12:10 there was a **m** who had a
Matt 12:11 What **m** is there among you who
Matt 12:12 then is a **m** than a sheep
Matt 12:13 Then He said to the **m**
Matt 12:22 and mute **m** both spoke and saw
Matt 12:29 he first binds the strong **m**
Matt 12:32 a word against the Son of **M**
Matt 12:35 A good **m** out of the good
Matt 12:35 an evil **m** out of the evil
Matt 12:40 the Son of **M** be three days
Matt 12:43 spirit goes out of a **m**, he
Matt 12:45 the last state of that **m** is
Matt 13:24 **m** who sowed good seed in his
Matt 13:31 mustard seed, which a **m** took
Matt 13:37 the good seed is the Son of **M**
Matt 13:41 The Son of **M** will send out
Matt 13:44 in a field, which a **m** found
Matt 13:54 Where did this **M** get this
Matt 13:56 Where then did this **M** get all
Matt 15:11 into the mouth defiles a **m**
Matt 15:11 the mouth, this defiles a **m**
Matt 15:18 the heart, and they defile a **m**
Matt 15:20 the things which defile a **m**
Matt 15:20 hands does not defile a **m**
Matt 16:13 men say that I, the Son of **M**
Matt 16:26 For what is a **m** profited if
Matt 16:26 Or what will a **m** give in
Matt 16:27 For the Son of **M** will come in
Matt 16:28 of **M** coming in His kingdom
Matt 17: 9 of **M** is risen from the dead
Matt 17:12 Likewise the Son of **M** is also
Matt 17:14 a **m** came to Him, kneeling
Matt 17:22 The Son of **M** is about to be
Matt 18: 7 but woe to that **m** by whom the
Matt 18:11 For the Son of **M** has come to
Matt 18:12 If a **m** has a hundred sheep,
Matt 19: 3 Is it lawful for a **m** to
Matt 19: 5 For this reason a **m** shall
Matt 19: 6 together, let not **m** separate
Matt 19:10 case of the **m** with his wife
Matt 19:20 The young **m** said to Him
Matt 19:22 the young **m** heard that saying
Matt 19:23 **m** to enter the kingdom of
Matt 19:24 **m** to enter the kingdom of God
Matt 19:28 when the Son of **M** sits on the
Matt 20:14 last **m** the same as to you
Matt 20:18 the Son of **M** will be betrayed
Matt 20:28 just as the Son of **M** did not
Matt 21:28 A **m** had two sons, and he came
Matt 22:11 he saw a **m** there who did not
Matt 22:24 Moses said that if a **m** dies
Matt 24:27 the coming of the Son of **M** be
Matt 24:30 of **M** will appear in heaven
Matt 24:30 of **M** coming on the clouds of
Matt 24:37 the coming of the Son of **M** be
Matt 24:39 the coming of the Son of **M** be
Matt 24:44 for the Son of **M** is coming at
Matt 25:13 which the Son of **M** is coming
Matt 25:14 **m** traveling to a far country
Matt 25:24 I knew you to be a hard **m**
Matt 25:31 When the Son of **M** comes in
Matt 26: 2 and the Son of **M** will be
Matt 26:18 into the city to a certain **m**
Matt 26:24 The Son of **M** goes as it is
Matt 26:24 but woe to that **m** by whom the
Matt 26:24 whom the Son of **M** is betrayed
Matt 26:24 **m** if he had not been born
Matt 26:45 and the Son of **M** is being
Matt 26:64 you will see the Son of **M**
Matt 26:72 I do not know the **M**
Matt 26:74 I do not know the **M**
Matt 27:19 to do with that just **M**, for I
Matt 27:32 out, they found a **m** of Cyrene
Matt 27:47 This **M** is calling for Elijah
Matt 27:57 came a rich **m** from Arimathea
Matt 27:58 This **m** went to Pilate and
Mark 1:23 Now there was a **m** in their
Mark 2: 7 Why does this **M** speak
Mark 2:10 of **M** has power on earth to
Mark 2:27 The Sabbath was made for **m**
Mark 2:27 and not **m** for the Sabbath
Mark 2:28 Therefore the Son of **M** is
Mark 3: 1 and a **m** was there who had a
Mark 3: 3 Then He said to the **m** who had
Mark 3: 5 hearts, He said to the **m**
Mark 3:27 he first binds the strong **m**
Mark 4:26 kingdom of God is as if a **m**
Mark 5: 2 a **m** with an unclean spirit
Mark 5: 8 Come out of the **m**, unclean
Mark 6: 2 Where did this **M** get these
Mark 6:20 that he was a just and holy **m**
Mark 7:11 If a **m** says to his father or
Mark 7:15 a **m** from outside which can
Mark 7:15 the things that defile a **m**
Mark 7:18 that whatever enters a **m** from
Mark 7:20 What comes out of a **m**,
Mark 7:20 that defiles a **m**
Mark 7:23 from within and defile a **m**
Mark 8:22 they brought a blind **m** to Him
Mark 8:23 took the blind **m** by the hand
Mark 8:31 of **M** must suffer many things
Mark 8:36 For what will it profit a **m**
Mark 8:37 Or what will a **m** give in
Mark 8:38 of him the Son of **M** also will
Mark 9: 9 till the Son of **M** had risen
Mark 9:12 concerning the Son of **M**, that
Mark 9:31 them, "The Son of **M** is being
Mark 10: 2 Is it lawful for a **m** to
Mark 10: 4 Moses permitted a **m** to write
Mark 10: 7 For this reason a **m** shall
Mark 10: 9 together, let not **m** separate
Mark 10:25 **m** to enter the kingdom of God
Mark 10:33 and the Son of **M** will be
Mark 10:45 For even the Son of **M** did not
Mark 10:49 Then they called the blind **m**
Mark 10:51 The blind **m** said to Him
Mark 12: 1 A **m** planted a vineyard and set
Mark 13:26 they will see the Son of **M**
Mark 13:34 It is like a **m** going to a far
Mark 14:13 a **m** will meet you carrying a
Mark 14:21 The Son of **M** indeed goes just
Mark 14:21 but woe to that **m** by whom the
Mark 14:21 whom the Son of **M** is betrayed
Mark 14:21 have been good for that **m** if
Mark 14:41 behold, the Son of **M** is being
Mark 14:51 certain young **m** followed Him
Mark 14:62 you will see the Son of **M**
Mark 14:71 know this **M** of whom you speak
Mark 15:21 they compelled a certain **m**
Mark 15:24 what every **m** should take
Mark 15:39 Truly this **M** was the Son of
Mark 16: 5 they saw a young **m** clothed in
Luke 1:18 For I am an old **m**, and my wife
Luke 1:27 to a **m** whose name was Joseph
Luke 1:34 be, since I do not know a **m**
Luke 2:25 there was a **m** in Jerusalem
Luke 2:25 this **m** was just and devout,
Luke 4: 4 **M** shall not live by bread
Luke 4:33 a **m** who had a spirit of an
Luke 5: 8 from me, for I am a sinful **m**
Luke 5:12 a **m** who was full of leprosy
Luke 5:18 a bed a **m** who was paralyzed
Luke 5:20 **M**, your sins are forgiven you

Luke 5:24 of **M** has power on earth to
Luke 5:24 He said to the **m** who was
Luke 6: 5 The Son of **M** is also Lord of
Luke 6: 6 a **m** was there whose right
Luke 6: 8 said to the **m** who had the
Luke 6:10 at them all, He said to the **m**
Luke 6:45 A good **m** out of the good
Luke 6:45 an evil **m** out of the evil
Luke 6:48 He is like a **m** building a
Luke 6:49 did nothing is like a **m** who
Luke 7: 8 For I also am a **m** placed
Luke 7:12 a dead **m** was being carried
Luke 7:14 Young **m**, I say to you, arise
Luke 7:25 A **m** clothed in soft garments
Luke 7:34 The Son of **M** has come eating
Luke 7:39 This **m**, if He were a prophet,
Luke 8:27 **m** from the city who had
Luke 8:29 spirit to come out of the **m**
Luke 8:33 the demons went out of the **m**
Luke 8:35 found the **m** from whom the
Luke 8:38 Now the **m** from whom the
Luke 8:41 there came a **m** named Jairus
Luke 9:22 The Son of **M** must suffer many
Luke 9:25 what advantage is it to a **m**
Luke 9:26 of him the Son of **M** will be
Luke 9:38 Suddenly a **m** from the
Luke 9:44 for the Son of **M** is about to
Luke 9:56 For the Son of **M** did not come
Luke 9:58 but the Son of **M** has nowhere
Luke 10:30 A certain **m** went down from
Luke 11:21 When a strong **m**, fully armed,
Luke 11:24 spirit goes out of a **m**, he
Luke 11:26 the last state of that **m** is
Luke 11:30 so also the Son of **M** will be
Luke 12: 8 him the Son of **M** also will
Luke 12:10 a word against the Son of **M**
Luke 12:14 **M**, who made Me a judge or an
Luke 12:16 rich **m** yielded plentifully
Luke 12:40 for the Son of **M** is coming at
Luke 13: 6 A certain **m** had a fig tree
Luke 13:19 mustard seed, which a **m** took
Luke 14: 2 there was a certain **m** before
Luke 14: 9 to you, 'Give place to this **m**
Luke 14:16 A certain **m** gave a great
Luke 14:30 This **m** began to build and was
Luke 15: 2 This **m** receives sinners and
Luke 15: 4 What **m** of you, having a
Luke 15:11 A certain **m** had two sons
Luke 16: 1 rich **m** who had a steward, and
Luke 16: 1 this **m** was wasting his goods
Luke 16:19 There was a certain rich **m**
Luke 16:22 The rich **m** also died and was
Luke 17:22 of the days of the Son of **M**
Luke 17:24 Son of **M** will be in His day
Luke 17:26 in the days of the Son of **M**
Luke 17:30 when the Son of **M** is revealed
Luke 18: 2 did not fear God nor regard **m**
Luke 18: 4 do not fear God nor regard **m**
Luke 18: 8 when the Son of **M** comes,
Luke 18:14 this **m** went down to his house
Luke 18:25 eye than for a rich **m** to
Luke 18:31 Son of **M** will be accomplished
Luke 18:35 that a certain blind **m** sat by
Luke 19: 2 there was a **m** named Zacchaeus
Luke 19: 7 with a **m** who is a sinner
Luke 19:10 for the Son of **M** has come to
Luke 19:14 have this **m** to reign over us
Luke 19:15 every **m** had gained by trading
Luke 19:21 because you are an austere **m**
Luke 19:22 knew that I was an austere **m**
Luke 20: 9 A certain **m** planted a
Luke 21:27 of **M** coming in a cloud with
Luke 21:36 to stand before the Son of **M**
Luke 22:10 a **m** will meet you carrying a
Luke 22:22 truly the Son of **M** goes as it
Luke 22:22 but woe to that **m** by whom He
Luke 22:48 the Son of **M** with a kiss
Luke 22:56 This **m** was also with Him
Luke 22:58 Peter said, "**M**, I am not!
Luke 22:60 **M**, I do not know what you are
Luke 22:69 Hereafter the Son of **M** will
Luke 23: 4 I find no fault in this **M**
Luke 23: 6 if the **M** were a Galilean
Luke 23:14 You have brought this **M** to me
Luke 23:14 **M** concerning those things of
Luke 23:18 Away with this **M**, and release
Luke 23:26 they laid hold of a certain **m**
Luke 23:41 but this **M** has done nothing
Luke 23:47 this was a righteous **M**
Luke 23:50 there was a **m** named Joseph, a
Luke 23:50 member, a good and just **m**
Luke 23:52 This **m** went to Pilate and
Luke 24: 7 saying, 'The Son of **M** must be
John 1: 6 There was a **m** sent from God,
John 1: 7 This **m** came for a witness, to
John 1: 9 **m** who comes into the world
John 1:13 flesh, nor of the will of **m**
John 1:30 After me comes a **M** who is
John 1:51 descending upon the Son of **M**
John 2:10 Every **m** at the beginning sets
John 2:25 anyone should testify of **m**
John 2:25 for He knew what was in **m**
John 3: 1 There was a **m** of the
John 3: 2 This **m** came to Jesus by night
John 3: 4 How can a **m** be born when he
John 3:13 the Son of **M** who is in heaven
John 3:14 the Son of **M** be lifted up
John 3:27 A **m** can receive nothing
John 4:29 Come, see a **M** who told me all
John 4:50 So the **m** believed the word
John 5: 5 Now a certain **m** was there who
John 5: 7 The sick **m** answered Him
John 5: 7 I have no **m** to put me into
John 5: 9 the **m** was made well, took up
John 5:12 Who is the **M** who said to you,
John 5:15 The **m** departed and told the
John 5:27 because He is the Son of **M**
John 5:34 not receive testimony from **m**
John 6:27 the Son of **M** will give you
John 6:52 How can this **M** give us His
John 6:53 eat the flesh of the Son of **M**
John 6:62 you should see the Son of **M**
John 7:15 How does this **M** know letters
John 7:22 circumcise a **m** on the Sabbath
John 7:23 If a **m** receives circumcision
John 7:23 a **m** completely well on the
John 7:27 we know where this **M** is from
John 7:31 these which this **M** has done
John 7:46 No **m** ever spoke like this **M**
John 7:51 judge a **m** before it hears him
John 8:28 When you lift up the Son of **M**
John 8:40 Me, a **M** who has told you the
John 9: 1 He saw a **m** who was blind from
John 9: 2 this **m** or his parents, that
John 9: 3 Neither this **m** nor his
John 9: 6 of the blind **m** with the clay
John 9:11 A **M** called Jesus made clay and
John 9:16 This **M** is not from God,
John 9:16 How can a **m** who is a sinner
John 9:17 said to the blind **m** again
John 9:24 called the **m** who was blind
John 9:24 know that this **M** is a sinner
John 9:30 The **m** answered and said to
John 9:33 If this **M** were not from God,
John 10:33 and because You, being a **M**
John 10:41 spoke about this **M** were true
John 11: 1 Now a certain **m** was sick,
John 11:37 Could not this **M**, who opened
John 11:37 have kept this **m** from dying
John 11:41 where the dead **m** was lying
John 11:47 For this **M** works many signs
John 11:50 **m** should die for the people
John 12:23 Son of **M** should be glorified
John 12:34 The Son of **M** must be lifted
John 12:34 Who is this Son of **M**
John 13:31 Now the Son of **M** is glorified
John 18:14 **m** should die for the people
John 18:29 do you bring against this **M**
John 18:40 Not this **M**, but Barabbas
John 19: 5 said to them, "Behold the **M**!"
John 19:12 If you let this **M** go, you are
John 21:21 But Lord, what about this **m**
Acts 1:18 (Now this **m** purchased a field
Acts 2:22 a **M** attested by God to you by
Acts 3: 2 a certain **m** lame from his
Acts 3:11 Now as the lame **m** who was
Acts 3:12 we had made this **m** walk
Acts 3:16 name, has made this **m** strong
Acts 4: 9 deed done to the helpless **m**
Acts 4:10 by Him this **m** stands here
Acts 4:14 seeing the **m** who had been
Acts 4:17 speak to no **m** in this name
Acts 4:22 For the **m** was over forty
Acts 5: 1 But a certain **m** named Ananias
Acts 5:37 After this **m**, Judas of
Acts 6: 5 a **m** full of faith and the Holy
Acts 6:13 This **m** does not cease to
Acts 7:19 This **m** dealt treacherously
Acts 7:56 the Son of **M** standing at the
Acts 7:58 feet of a young **m** named Saul
Acts 8: 9 was a certain **m** called Simon
Acts 8:10 This **m** is the great power of
Acts 8:27 a **m** of Ethiopia, a eunuch of
Acts 8:34 of himself or of some other **m**
Acts 9:12 a **m** named Ananias coming in
Acts 9:13 heard from many about this **m**
Acts 9:33 a certain **m** named Aeneas, who
Acts 10: 1 certain **m** in Caesarea called
Acts 10: 2 a devout **m** and one who feared
Acts 10:22 the centurion, a just **m**, one
Acts 10:26 I myself am also a **m**
Acts 10:28 **m** to keep company with or go
Acts 10:28 call any **m** common or unclean
Acts 10:30 a **m** stood before me in bright
Acts 11:24 For he was a good **m**, full of
Acts 12:22 voice of a god and not of a **m**
Acts 13: 7 Paulus, an intelligent **m**
Acts 13: 7 This **m** called for Barnabas and
Acts 13:21 a **m** of the tribe of Benjamin,
Acts 13:22 a **m** after My own heart, who
Acts 13:38 that through this **M** is
Acts 14: 8 in Lystra a certain **m** without
Acts 14: 9 This **m** heard Paul speaking
Acts 16: 9 A **m** of Macedonia stood and
Acts 17:31 by the **M** whom He has ordained
Acts 18: 7 of a certain **m** named Justus
Acts 18:24 at Alexandria, an eloquent **m**
Acts 18:25 This **m** had been instructed in
Acts 19:16 Then the **m** in whom the evil
Acts 19:24 For a certain **m** named
Acts 19:35 what **m** is there who does not
Acts 20: 9 young **m** named Eutychus, who
Acts 20:12 brought the young **m** in alive
Acts 21: 9 Now this **m** had four virgin
Acts 21:11 bind the **m** who owns this belt
Acts 21:28 This is the **m** who teaches all
Acts 22:12 a devout **m** according to the
Acts 22:25 to scourge a **m** who is a Roman
Acts 22:26 you do, for this **m** is a Roman
Acts 23: 9 We find no evil in this **m**
Acts 23:17 Take this young **m** to the
Acts 23:18 to bring this young **m** to you
Acts 23:22 let the young **m** depart, and
Acts 23:27 This **m** was seized by the Jews
Acts 23:30 Jews lay in wait for the **m**
Acts 24: 5 we have found this **m** a plague
Acts 25: 5 down with me and accuse this **m**
Acts 25:14 There is a certain **m** left a
Acts 25:16 **m** to destruction before the
Acts 25:17 commanded the **m** to be brought
Acts 25:22 like to hear the **m** myself
Acts 25:24 you see this **m** about whom the
Acts 26:31 This **m** is doing nothing
Acts 26:32 This **m** might have been set
Acts 28: 4 No doubt this **m** is a murderer
Rom 1:23 image made like corruptible **m**
Rom 2: 1 you are inexcusable, O **m**,
Rom 2: 3 And do you think this, O **m**
Rom 2: 9 every soul of **m** who does evil
Rom 2:21 that a **m** should not steal
Rom 2:26 **m** keeps the righteous
Rom 3: 4 be true but every **m** a liar
Rom 3: 5 (I speak as a **m**
Rom 3:28 we conclude that a **m** is
Rom 4: 6 of the **m** to whom God imputes
Rom 4: 8 blessed is the **m** to whom the
Rom 5: 7 a righteous **m** will one die
Rom 5: 7 yet perhaps for a good **m**
Rom 5:12 just as through one **m** sin
Rom 5:15 by the grace of the one **M**
Rom 6: 6 that our old **m** was crucified
Rom 7: 1 over a **m** as long as he lives
Rom 7: 3 lives, she marries another **m**
Rom 7: 3 she has married another **m**
Rom 7:22 God according to the inward **m**
Rom 7:24 O wretched **m** that I am
Rom 9:10 also had conceived by one **m**
Rom 9:20 But indeed, O **m**, who are you
Rom 10: 5 The **m** who does those things
Rom 14:20 the **m** who eats with offense
1Co 2: 9 of **m** the things which God has
1Co 2:11 For what **m** knows the things
1Co 2:11 a **m** except the spirit of the
1Co 2:11 of the **m** which is in him
1Co 2:14 But the natural **m** does not
1Co 4: 1 Let a **m** so consider us, as
1Co 5: 1 that a **m** has his father's
1Co 6: 5 is not a wise **m** among you
1Co 6:18 Every sin that a **m** does is
1Co 7: 1 It is good for a **m** not to

1Co 7: 2 let each **m** have his own wife,
1Co 7:26 for a **m** to remain as he is
1Co 7:36 But if any **m** thinks he is
1Co 9: 8 say these things as a mere **m**
1Co 10:13 except such as is common to **m**
1Co 11: 3 the head of every **m** is Christ
1Co 11: 3 the head of woman is **m**, and
1Co 11: 4 Every **m** praying or
1Co 11: 7 For a **m** indeed ought not to
1Co 11: 7 but woman is the glory of **m**
1Co 11: 8 For **m** is not from woman, but
1Co 11: 8 woman, but woman from **m**
1Co 11: 9 Nor was **m** created for the
1Co 11: 9 woman, but woman for the **m**
1Co 11:11 neither is **m** independent of
1Co 11:11 nor woman independent of **m**
1Co 11:12 as the woman was from the **m**
1Co 11:12 even so the **m** also is through
1Co 11:14 you that if a **m** has long hair
1Co 11:28 But let a **m** examine himself,
1Co 13:11 but when I became a **m**, I put
1Co 15:21 For since by **m** came death
1Co 15:21 death, by **M** also came the
1Co 15:45 The first **m** Adam became a
1Co 15:47 The first **m** was of the earth,
1Co 15:47 the second **M** is the Lord from
1Co 15:48 As was the **m** of dust, so also
1Co 15:48 and as is the heavenly **M**, so
1Co 15:49 the image of the **m** of dust
1Co 15:49 the image of the heavenly **M**
2Co 2: 6 is sufficient for such a **m**
2Co 4:16 our outward **m** is perishing
2Co 4:16 yet the inward **m** is being
2Co 12: 2 I know a **m** in Christ who
2Co 12: 3 And I know such a **m**
2Co 12: 4 not lawful for a **m** to utter
Gal 1: 1 (not from men nor through **m**
Gal 1:11 by me is not according to **m**
Gal 1:12 I neither received it from **m**
Gal 2: 6 personal favoritism to no **m**
Gal 2:16 knowing that a **m** is not
Gal 3:12 The **m** who does them shall
Gal 5: 3 **m** who becomes circumcised
Gal 6: 1 if a **m** is overtaken in any
Gal 6: 7 for whatever a **m** sows, that
Eph 2:15 one new **m** from the two, thus
Eph 3:16 His Spirit in the inner **m**
Eph 4:13 Son of God, to a perfect **m**
Eph 4:22 the old **m** which grows corrupt
Eph 4:24 that you put on the new **m**
Eph 5: 5 person, nor covetous **m**, who
Eph 5:31 For this reason a **m** shall
Phil 2: 8 found in appearance as a **m**
Col 1:28 we preach, warning every **m**
Col 1:28 every **m** in all wisdom, that
Col 1:28 **m** perfect in Christ Jesus
Col 3: 9 off the old **m** with his deeds
Col 3:10 have put on the new **m** who is
1Th 4: 8 this does not reject **m**, but
2Th 2: 3 the **m** of sin is revealed, the
1Ti 1:13 persecutor, and an insolent **m**
1Ti 2: 5 and men, the **M** Christ Jesus,
1Ti 2:12 or to have authority over a **m**
1Ti 3: 1 If a **m** desires the position
1Ti 3: 5 (for if a **m** does not know how
1Ti 5: 1 Do not rebuke an older **m**, but
1Ti 5: 9 has been the wife of one **m**
1Ti 5:16 If any believing **m** or woman
1Ti 6:11 O **m** of God, flee these things
1Ti 6:16 whom no **m** has seen or can see
2Ti 3:17 that the **m** of God may be
Tit 1: 6 if a **m** is blameless, the
Tit 3: 4 our Savior toward **m** appeared
Tit 3:10 a divisive **m** after the first
Heb 2: 6 What is **m** that You are
Heb 2: 6 or the son of **m** that You take
Heb 5: 4 And no **m** takes this honor to
Heb 7: 4 consider how great this **m** was
Heb 7:13 tribe, from which no **m** has
Heb 8: 2 the Lord erected, and not **m**
Heb 10:12 But this **M**, after He had
Heb 11:12 Therefore from one **m**, and him
Heb 13: 6 What can **m** do to me
Jas 1: 7 For let not that **m** suppose
Jas 1: 8 he is a double-minded **m**,
Jas 1:11 So the rich **m** also will fade
Jas 1:12 Blessed is the **m** who endures
Jas 1:19 let every **m** be swift to hear,
Jas 1:20 for the wrath of **m** does not
Jas 1:23 he is like a **m** observing his
Jas 1:24 forgets what kind of **m** he was
Jas 2: 2 assembly a **m** with gold rings
Jas 2: 2 in a poor **m** in filthy clothes
Jas 2: 3 place," and say to the poor **m**
Jas 2: 6 have dishonored the poor **m**
Jas 2:20 you want to know, O foolish **m**
Jas 2:24 You see then that a **m** is
Jas 3: 2 in word, he is a perfect **m**
Jas 3: 8 But no **m** can tame the tongue
Jas 5:16 of a righteous **m** avails much
Jas 5:17 Elijah was a **m** with a nature
1Pe 1:24 all the glory of **m** as the
1Pe 2:13 of **m** for the Lord's sake,
2Pe 1:21 never came by the will of **m**
2Pe 2: 8 (for that righteous **m**,
Rev 1:13 One like the Son of **M**,
Rev 4: 7 creature had a face like a **m**
Rev 6:15 every slave and every free **m**
Rev 9: 5 scorpion when it strikes a **m**
Rev 13:18 for it is the number of a **m**
Rev 14:14 sat One like the Son of **M**
Rev 16: 3 became blood as of a dead **m**
Rev 21:17 to the measure of a **m**, that

MANAEN

Acts 13: 1 **M** who had been brought up

MANAGE

1Ti 5:14 **m** the house, give no

MANAHATH

Gen 36:23 Alvan, **M**, Ebal, Shepho, and
1Ch 1:40 sons of Shobal were Alian, **M**
1Ch 8: 6 who forced them to move to **M**

MANAHETHITES

1Ch 2:54 Beth Joab, half of the **M**, and

MANASSEH (*see* MANASSEH'S, MANASSITES)

Gen 41:51 the name of the firstborn **M**
Gen 46:20 the land of Egypt were born **M**
Gen 48: 1 took with him his two sons, **M**
Gen 48: 5 your two sons, Ephraim and **M**
Gen 48:13 **M** with his left hand toward
Gen 48:14 for **M** was the firstborn
Gen 48:20 make you as Ephraim and as **M**
Gen 48:20 thus he set Ephraim before **M**
Gen 50:23 of Machir, the son of **M**, were
Num 1:10 from **M**, Gamaliel the son of
Num 1:34 From the children of **M**, their
Num 1:35 of **M** were thirty-two thousand
Num 2:20 him shall be the tribe of **M**
Num 2:20 **M** shall be Gamaliel the son
Num 7:54 leader of the children of **M**
Num 10:23 of **M** was Gamaliel the son of
Num 13:11 that is, from the tribe of **M**
Num 26:28 to their families, by **M** and
Num 26:29 The sons of **M**
Num 26:34 These are the families of **M**
Num 27: 1 son of Machir, the son of **M**
Num 27: 1 of **M** the son of Joseph
Num 32:33 tribe of **M** the son of Joseph
Num 32:39 the son of **M** went to Gilead
Num 32:40 Gilead to Machir the son of **M**
Num 32:41 Also Jair the son of **M** went
Num 34:14 of **M** has received its
Num 34:23 tribe of the children of **M**
Num 36: 1 son of Machir, the son of **M**
Num 36:12 of **M** the son of Joseph, and
Deut 3:13 I gave to half the tribe of **M**
Deut 3:14 Jair the son of **M** took all
Deut 29: 8 and to half the tribe of **M**
Deut 33:17 they are the thousands of **M**
Deut 34: 2 and the land of Ephraim and **M**
Josh 1:12 the tribe of **M** Joshua spoke
Josh 4:12 half the tribe of **M** crossed
Josh 12: 6 and half the tribe of **M**
Josh 13: 7 tribes and half the tribe of **M**
Josh 13:29 to half the tribe of **M**
Josh 13:29 tribe of the children of **M**
Josh 13:31 of Machir the son of **M**, for
Josh 14: 4 two tribes: **M** and Ephraim
Josh 16: 4 So the children of Joseph, **M**
Josh 16: 9 of the children of **M**, all the
Josh 17: 1 also a lot for the tribe of **M**
Josh 17: 1 for Machir the firstborn of **M**
Josh 17: 2 **M** according to their families
Josh 17: 2 were the male children of **M**
Josh 17: 3 son of Machir, the son of **M**
Josh 17: 5 Ten portions fell to **M**,
Josh 17: 6 of **M** received an inheritance
Josh 17: 7 the territory of **M** was from
Josh 17: 8 **M** had the land of Tappuah,
Josh 17: 8 Tappuah on the border of **M**
Josh 17: 9 are among the cities of **M**
Josh 17: 9 The border of **M** was on the
Josh 17:11 **M** had Beth Shean and its towns
Josh 17:12 Yet the children of **M** could
Josh 17:17 to Ephraim and **M**
Josh 18: 7 and half the tribe of **M** have
Josh 20: 8 Bashan, from the tribe of **M**
Josh 21: 5 and from the half-tribe of **M**
Josh 21: 6 the half-tribe of **M** in Bashan
Josh 21:25 and from the half-tribe of **M**
Josh 21:27 the other half-tribe of **M**
Josh 22: 1 and half the tribe of **M**,
Josh 22: 7 tribe of **M** Moses had given a
Josh 22: 9 half the tribe of **M** returned
Josh 22:10 half the tribe of **M** built an
Josh 22:11 and half the tribe of **M** have
Josh 22:13 and to half the tribe of **M**
Josh 22:15 and to half the tribe of **M**
Josh 22:21 half the tribe of **M** answered
Josh 22:30 and the children of **M** spoke
Josh 22:31 of Gad, and the children of **M**
Judg 1:27 **M** did not drive out the
Judg 6:15 my clan is the weakest in **M**
Judg 6:35 messengers throughout all **M**
Judg 7:23 Naphtali, Asher, and all **M**
Judg 11:29 he passed through Gilead and **M**
Judg 18:30 son of Gershom, the son of **M**
1Ki 4:13 towns of Jair the son of **M**
2Ki 10:33 Gad, Reuben, and **M**
2Ki 20:21 Then **M** his son reigned in his
2Ki 21: 1 **M** was twelve years old when
2Ki 21: 9 **M** seduced them to do more
2Ki 21:11 Because **M** king of Judah has
2Ki 21:16 Moreover **M** shed very much
2Ki 21:17 Now the rest of the acts of **M**
2Ki 21:18 So **M** rested with his fathers,
2Ki 21:20 as his father **M** had done
2Ki 23:12 the altars which **M** had made
2Ki 23:26 which **M** had provoked Him
2Ki 24: 3 because of the sins of **M**,
1Ch 3:13 Hezekiah his son, **M** his son,
1Ch 5:18 and half the tribe of **M** had
1Ch 5:23 of **M** dwelt in the land
1Ch 5:26 of **M** into captivity
1Ch 6:61 from half the tribe of **M**
1Ch 6:62 from the tribe of **M** in Bashan
1Ch 6:70 And from the half-tribe of **M**
1Ch 6:71 of **M** the sons of Gershon were
1Ch 7:14 The descendants of **M**
1Ch 7:17 son of Machir, the son of **M**
1Ch 7:29 children of **M** were Beth Shean
1Ch 9: 3 the children of Ephraim and **M**
1Ch 12:19 some from **M** defected to David
1Ch 12:20 those of **M** who defected to
1Ch 12:20 the thousands who were from **M**
1Ch 12:31 of **M** eighteen thousand, who
1Ch 12:37 and the half-tribe of **M**, from
1Ch 26:32 and the half-tribe of **M**, for
1Ch 27:20 over the half-tribe of **M**,
1Ch 27:21 the half-tribe of **M** in Gilead
2Ch 15: 9 with them from Ephraim, **M**
2Ch 30: 1 wrote letters to Ephraim and **M**
2Ch 30:10 the country of Ephraim and **M**
2Ch 30:11 some from Asher, **M**, and
2Ch 30:18 people, many from Ephraim, **M**
2Ch 31: 1 Benjamin, Ephraim, and **M**
2Ch 32:33 Then **M** his son reigned in his
2Ch 33: 1 **M** was twelve years old when
2Ch 33: 9 So **M** seduced Judah and the
2Ch 33:10 And the LORD spoke to **M** and
2Ch 33:11 who took **M** with hooks, bound
2Ch 33:13 Then **M** knew that the LORD was
2Ch 33:18 Now the rest of the acts of **M**
2Ch 33:20 So **M** rested with his fathers,
2Ch 33:22 as his father **M** had done
2Ch 33:22 which his father **M** had made
2Ch 33:23 as his father **M** had humbled
2Ch 34: 6 so he did in the cities of **M**
2Ch 34: 9 gathered from the hand of **M**
Ezra 10:30 Bezaleel, Binnui, and **M**
Ezra 10:33 Zabad, Eliphelet, Jeremai, **M**
Ps 60: 7 Gilead is Mine, and **M** is Mine
Ps 80: 2 Ephraim, Benjamin, and **M**,
Ps 108: 8 Gilead is Mine; **M** is Mine
Is 9:21 **M** shall devour Ephraim, and
Is 9:21 Ephraim, and Ephraim **M**
Jer 15: 4 because of **M** the son of
Ezek 48: 4 the west, one portion for **M**
Ezek 48: 5 by the border of **M**, from the

Matt 1:10 Hezekiah begot **M**, **M** begot
Rev 7: 6 of the tribe of **M** twelve

MANASSEH'S (*see* MANASSEH)
Gen 48:14 and his left hand on **M** head
Gen 48:17 from Ephraim's head to **M** head
Josh 17: 6 the rest of **M** sons had the
Josh 17:10 Ephraim's, northward it was **M**
Josh 17:10 **M** territory was adjoining

MANASSITES (*see* MANASSEH)
Deut 4:43 and Golan in Bashan for the **M**
Judg 12: 4 Ephraimites and among the **M**

MANDRAKES
Gen 30:14 and found **m** in the field, and
Gen 30:14 give me some of your son's **m**
Gen 30:15 you take away my son's **m** also
Gen 30:15 you tonight for your son's **m**
Gen 30:16 hired you with my son's **m**
Song 7:13 The **m** give off a fragrance,

MANGER
Job 39: 9 Will he bed by your **m**
Luke 2: 7 cloths, and laid Him in a **m**
Luke 2:12 cloths, lying in a **m**
Luke 2:16 and the Babe lying in a **m**

MANIFEST (*see* MANIFESTATION, MANIFESTED, MANIFESTLY)
John 14:21 love him and **m** Myself to him
John 14:22 You will **m** Yourself to us
Rom 1:19 be known of God is **m** in them
Rom 10:20 I was made **m** to those who did
Rom 16:26 but now has been made **m**, and
1Co 3:13 each one's work will become **m**
2Co 11: 6 **m** among you in all things
Eph 5:13 are made **m** by the light, for
Eph 5:13 for whatever makes **m** is light
Col 4: 4 that I may make it **m**, as I
2Th 1: 5 which is **m** evidence of the
1Ti 6:15 which He will **m** in His own
2Ti 3: 9 their folly will be **m** to all
Heb 9: 8 of All was not yet made **m**
1Pe 1:20 but was **m** in these last times
1Jn 2:19 out that they might be made **m**
1Jn 3:10 children of the devil are **m**

MANIFESTATION (*see* MANIFEST)
Luke 1:80 the day of his **m** to Israel
1Co 12: 7 But the **m** of the Spirit is
2Co 4: 2 but by **m** of the truth

MANIFESTED (*see* MANIFEST)
John 2:11 of Galilee, and **m** His glory
John 17: 6 I have **m** Your name to the men
2Co 4:10 also may be **m** in our body
2Co 4:11 may be **m** in our mortal flesh
1Ti 3:16 God was **m** in the flesh,
Tit 1: 3 but has in due time **m** His
1Jn 1: 2 the life was **m**, and we have
1Jn 1: 2 the Father and was **m** to us
1Jn 3: 5 you know that He was **m** to
1Jn 3: 8 purpose the Son of God was **m**
1Jn 4: 9 love of God was **m** toward us
Rev 15: 4 Your judgments have been **m**

MANIFESTLY (*see* MANIFEST)
2Co 3: 3 you are **m** an epistle of

MANIFOLD
Neh 9:19 Yet in Your **m** mercies You did
Ps 104:24 O LORD, how **m** are Your works
Amos 5:12 I know your **m** transgressions
Eph 3:10 to the intent that now the **m**
1Pe 4:10 of the **m** grace of God

MANKIND (*see* MAN)
Gen 5: 2 called them **M** in the day they
Job 12:10 thing, and the breath of all **m**
Is 31: 8 a sword not of **m** shall devour
Acts 15:17 rest of **m** may seek the LORD
Jas 3: 7 tamed and has been tamed by **m**
Rev 9:15 released to kill a third of **m**
Rev 9:18 a third of **m** was killed
Rev 9:20 But the rest of **m**, who were

MAN-MADE (*see* MAKE)
Neh 3:16 tombs of David, to the **m** pool

MANNA
Ex 16:31 of Israel called its name **M**
Ex 16:33 pot and put an omer of **m** in it
Ex 16:35 of Israel ate **m** forty years
Ex 16:35 they ate **m** until they came to
Num 11: 6 except this **m** before our eyes
Num 11: 7 Now the **m** was like coriander
Num 11: 9 the night, the **m** fell on it
Deut 8: 3 fed you with **m** which you did
Deut 8:16 you in the wilderness with **m**
Josh 5:12 Now the **m** ceased on the day
Josh 5:12 of Israel no longer had **m**
Neh 9:20 Your **m** from their mouth, and
Ps 78:24 rained down **m** on them to eat
John 6:31 ate the **m** in the desert
John 6:49 ate the **m** in the wilderness
John 6:58 not as your fathers ate the **m**
Heb 9: 4 the golden pot that had the **m**
Rev 2:17 some of the hidden **m** to eat

MANNER
Gen 31:35 for the **m** of women is with me
Gen 32:19 In this **m** you shall speak to
Gen 39:19 did to me after this **m**,"
Gen 40:13 according to the former **m**
Gen 42:15 In this **m** you shall be tested
Ex 1:14 in all **m** of service in the
Ex 7:11 they also did in like **m** with
Ex 12:16 No **m** of work shall be done on
Ex 23:11 In like **m** you shall do with
Ex 31: 3 and in all **m** of workmanship,
Ex 31: 5 work in all **m** of workmanship
Ex 35:31 and all **m** of workmanship,
Ex 35:33 to work in all **m** of artistic
Ex 35:35 all **m** of work of the engraver
Ex 36: 1 to know how to do all **m** of
Lev 5:10 according to the prescribed **m**
Lev 9:16 according to the prescribed **m**
Lev 23:31 You shall do no **m** of work
Num 15:13 do these things in this **m**
Num 28:24 In this **m** you shall offer
Josh 6:15 seven times in the same **m**
Judg 11:17 in like **m** they sent to the
Judg 18: 7 in the **m** of the Sidonians,
1Sa 17:27 people answered him in this **m**
1Sa 18:24 In this **m** David spoke
1Sa 19:24 before Samuel in like **m**, and
2Sa 7:19 Is this the **m** of man, O Lord
2Sa 14: 3 and speak to him in this **m**
2Sa 15: 6 In this **m** Absalom acted
2Sa 17: 6 has spoken in this **m**
1Ki 7:37 After this **m** he made the ten
1Ki 22:20 So one spoke in this **m**, and
1Ki 22:20 and another spoke in that **m**
2Ki 22:18 in this **m** you shall speak to
1Ch 28:21 you for all **m** of workmanship
2Ch 4:20 **m** in front of the inner
2Ch 18:19 And one spoke in this **m**, and
2Ch 18:19 and another spoke in that **m**
2Ch 30: 5 long time in the prescribed **m**
2Ch 34:26 in this **m** you shall speak to
Neh 6: 4 I answered them in the same **m**
Neh 8:18 according to the prescribed **m**
Esth 1:13 **m** toward all who knew law
Ps 107:18 soul abhorred all **m** of food
Song 7:13 are pleasant fruits, all **m**
Is 10:24 you, in the **m** of Egypt
Is 10:26 lift it up in the **m** of Egypt
Is 51: 6 in it will die in like **m**
Jer 13: 9 In this **m** I will ruin the
Jer 22:21 been your **m** from your youth
Ezek 20:30 in the **m** of your fathers, and
Ezek 23:15 in the **m** of the Babylonians
Ezek 23:45 after the **m** of adulteresses
Ezek 23:45 after the **m** of women who shed
Amos 4:10 a plague after the **m** of Egypt
Nah 1:12 yet in this **m** they will be
Matt 6: 9 In this **m**, therefore, pray
Mark 13: 1 see what **m** of stones and what
Luke 1:29 considered what **m** of greeting
Luke 6:23 for in like **m** their fathers
Luke 7:39 what **m** of woman this is who
Luke 9:55 what **m** of spirit you are of
Luke 11:42 all **m** of herbs, and pass by
Luke 20:31 and in like **m** the seven also
John 2: 6 stone, according to the **m** of
John 5:19 the Son also does in like **m**
Acts 1:11 will so come in like **m** as you
Acts 15:11 saved in the same **m** as they
Acts 20:18 in what **m** I always lived
Acts 23:25 a letter in the following **m**
Acts 26: 4 My **m** of life from my youth,
Rom 7: 8 in me all **m** of evil desire
Rom 16: 2 in a **m** worthy of the saints
1Co 7: 7 gift from God, one in this **m**
1Co 11:25 In the same **m** He also took
1Co 11:27 **m** will be guilty of the body
1Co 11:29 drinks in an unworthy **m** eats
1Co 15:32 If, in the **m** of men, I have
2Co 7: 9 were made sorry in a godly **m**
2Co 7:11 you sorrowed in a godly **m**
Gal 2:14 live in the **m** of Gentiles
Gal 3:15 I speak in the **m** of men
1Th 1: 9 what **m** of entry we had to you
2Th 3:11 among you in a disorderly **m**
1Ti 2: 9 in like **m** also, that the
2Ti 3:10 **m** of life, purpose, faith,
Heb 6: 9 though we speak in this **m**
Heb 10:25 together, as is the **m** of some
1Pe 1:11 what, or what **m** of time, the
1Pe 3: 5 For in this **m**, in former
2Pe 3:11 what **m** of persons ought you
1Jn 3: 1 Behold what **m** of love the
3Jn 6 journey in a **m** worthy of God
Jude 7 them in a similar **m** to these
Rev 11: 5 he must be killed in this **m**

MANOAH
Judg 13: 2 the Danites, whose name was **M**
Judg 13: 8 Then **M** prayed to the LORD, and
Judg 13: 9 listened to the voice of **M**
Judg 13: 9 but **M** her husband was not
Judg 13:11 So **M** arose and followed his
Judg 13:12 And **M** said, "Now let Your
Judg 13:13 Angel of the LORD said to **M**
Judg 13:15 Then **M** said to the Angel of
Judg 13:16 Angel of the LORD said to **M**
Judg 13:16 (For **M** did not know He was
Judg 13:17 Then **M** said to the Angel of
Judg 13:19 So **M** took the young goat with
Judg 13:19 did a wondrous thing while **M**
Judg 13:20 When **M** and his wife saw this,
Judg 13:21 LORD appeared no more to **M**
Judg 13:21 then **M** knew that He was the
Judg 13:22 And **M** said to his wife,
Judg 16:31 in the tomb of his father **M**

MAN'S (*see* MAN)
Gen 8:21 curse the ground for **m** sake
Gen 8:21 of **m** heart is evil from his
Gen 9: 5 From the hand of every **m**
Gen 9: 6 Whoever sheds **m** blood, by man
Gen 16:12 and every **m** hand against him
Gen 20: 3 taken, for she is a **m** wife
Gen 20: 7 therefore, restore the **m** wife
Gen 40: 5 each **m** dream in one night and
Gen 40: 5 each **m** dream with its own
Gen 42:11 We are all one **m** sons
Gen 42:25 to restore every **m** money to
Gen 42:35 that surprisingly each **m**
Gen 43:21 each **m** money was in the mouth
Gen 44: 1 put each **m** money in the mouth
Gen 44:26 for we may not see the **m** face
Ex 4:11 Who has made **m** mouth
Ex 12: 4 according to each **m** need you
Ex 12:44 But every **m** servant who is
Ex 21:35 if one **m** ox hurts another's,
Ex 22: 5 it feeds in another **m** field
Ex 22: 7 is stolen out of the **m** house
Ex 30:32 not be poured on **m** flesh
Lev 20:10 adultery with another **m** wife
Num 5:10 every **m** holy things shall be
Num 5:12 If any **m** wife goes astray and
Num 17: 2 Write each **m** name on his rod
Deut 1:17 be afraid in any **m** presence
Deut 20:19 tree of the field is **m** food
Deut 24: 2 and becomes another **m** wife
Judg 7:16 a trumpet into every **m** hand
Judg 7:22 the LORD set every **m** sword
Judg 19:24 daughter and the **m** concubine
Judg 19:26 down at the door of the **m**
Ruth 2:19 The **m** name with whom I
1Sa 12: 4 anything from any **m** hand
1Sa 13:20 to sharpen each **m** plowshare
1Sa 14:20 and indeed every **m** sword was
1Sa 14:34 every **m** ox and every **m** sheep
1Sa 17:32 Let no **m** heart fail because
1Sa 30:22 except for every **m** wife and
2Sa 12: 4 but he took the poor **m** lamb
2Sa 17:18 came to a **m** house in Bahurim,
1Ki 18:44 a cloud, as small as a **m** hand
2Ki 12: 4 each **m** census money, each
2Ki 12: 4 each **m** assessment money
Esth 1: 8 according to each **m** pleasure
Ps 104:15 which strengthens **m** heart
Prov 10:15 The rich **m** wealth is his
Prov 12:14 the recompense of a **m** hands
Prov 12:27 but diligence is **m** precious

Prov 13: 8 The ransom of a **m** life is his
Prov 16: 7 When a **m** ways please the LORD
Prov 16: 9 A **m** heart plans his way, but
Prov 18: 4 The words of a **m** mouth are
Prov 18:11 The rich **m** wealth is his
Prov 18:16 A **m** gift makes room for him,
Prov 18:20 A **m** stomach shall be
Prov 19:21 are many plans in a **m** heart
Prov 20:24 A **m** steps are of the LORD
Prov 27: 9 the sweetness of a **m** friend
Prov 27:19 so a **m** heart reveals the man
Prov 29:23 A **m** pride will bring him low,
Eccl 2:14 The wise **m** eyes are in his
Eccl 7: 7 destroys a wise **m** reason, and
Eccl 8: 1 A **m** wisdom makes his face
Eccl 8: 5 a wise **m** heart discerns both
Eccl 9:16 the poor **m** wisdom is despised
Eccl 10: 2 A wise **m** heart is at his
Eccl 10:12 a wise **m** mouth are gracious
Is 8: 1 on it with a **m** pen concerning
Is 13: 7 every **m** heart will melt,
Jer 3: 1 him and becomes another **m**
Jer 23:36 For every **m** word will be his
Ezek 10: 8 to have the form of a **m** hand
Ezek 24:17 do not eat **m** bread of sorrow
Ezek 24:22 nor eat **m** bread of sorrow
Ezek 38:21 Every **m** sword will be against
Ezek 39:15 whenever anyone sees a **m** bone
Ezek 40: 5 In the **m** hand was a measuring
Dan 5: 5 fingers of a **m** hand appeared
Dan 7: 4 a **m** heart was given to it
Dan 8:16 I heard a **m** voice between the
Jon 1:14 let us perish for this **m** life
Mic 7: 6 a **m** enemies are the men of
Matt 10:36 a **m** foes will be those of
Matt 10:41 receive a righteous **m** reward
Matt 12:29 one enter a strong **m** house
Mark 3:27 can enter a strong **m** house
Mark 12:19 us that if a **m** brother dies
Luke 6:22 evil, for the Son of **M** sake
Luke 16:12 faithful in what is another **m**
Luke 16:21 fell from the rich **m** table
Luke 20:28 us that if a **m** brother dies
John 18:17 also one of this **M** disciples
Acts 5:28 to bring this **M** blood on us
Acts 11:12 me, and we entered the **m** house
Acts 13:23 From this **m** seed, according
Acts 17:29 shaped by art and **m** devising
Rom 5:15 the one **m** offense many died
Rom 5:17 For if by the one **m** offense
Rom 5:18 as through one **m** offense
Rom 5:18 even so through one **M**
Rom 5:19 For as by one **m** disobedience
Rom 5:19 so also by one **M** obedience
Rom 15:20 build on another **m** foundation
1Co 2:13 not in words which **m** wisdom
1Co 10:29 by another **m** conscience
2Co 4: 2 ourselves to every **m**
2Co 10:16 not to boast in another **m**
Gal 3:15 it is only a **m** covenant, yet
2Pe 2:16 with a **m** voice restrained the

MANSERVANT (*see* MENSERVANTS, SERVANT)
Ex 20:10 nor your daughter, nor your **m**
Ex 20:17 neighbor's wife, nor his **m**
Ex 21:32 ox gores a **m** or a maidservant
Deut 5:14 nor your daughter, nor your **m**
Deut 5:14 your gates, that your **m** and
Deut 5:21 house, his field, his **m**, his
Deut 12:18 son and your daughter, your **m**
Deut 16:11 son and your daughter, your **m**
Deut 16:14 son and your daughter, your **m**
Job 31:13 despised the cause of my **m** or

MANSIONS
John 14: 2 My Father's house are many **m**

MANSLAYER (*see* MANSLAYERS)
Num 35: 6 refuge, to which a **m** may flee
Num 35:11 you, that the **m** who kills any
Num 35:12 that the **m** may not die until
Num 35:24 shall judge between the **m**
Num 35:25 shall deliver the **m** from the
Num 35:26 But if the **m** at any time
Num 35:27 avenger of blood kills the **m**
Num 35:28 of the high priest the **m** may
Deut 4:42 that the **m** might flee there,
Deut 19: 3 that any **m** may flee there
Deut 19: 4 case of the **m** who flees there
Deut 19: 6 anger is hot, pursue the **m**

MANSLAYERS (*see* MANSLAYER)
1Ti 1: 9 murderers of mothers, for **m**

MANTLE (*see* MANTLES)
1Sa 28:14 up, and he is covered with a **m**
1Ki 19:13 he wrapped his face in his **m**
1Ki 19:19 by him and threw his **m** on him
2Ki 2: 8 Now Elijah took his **m**, rolled
2Ki 2:13 He also took up the **m** of
2Ki 2:14 Then he took the **m** of Elijah
Ps 109:29 own disgrace as with a **m**

MANTLES (*see* MANTLE)
Is 3:22 the festal apparel, and the **m**

MANUHOTH
1Ch 2:52 and half of the families of **M**

MANY (*see* PREFACE)

MAOCH
1Sa 27: 2 him to Achish the son of **M**

MAON (*see* MAONITES)
Josh 15:55 **M**, Carmel, Ziph, Juttah,
1Sa 23:24 were in the Wilderness of **M**
1Sa 23:25 stayed in the Wilderness of **M**
1Sa 23:25 David in the Wilderness of **M**
1Sa 25: 2 in **M** whose business was in
1Ch 2:45 And the son of Shammai was **M**
1Ch 2:45 **M** was the father of Beth Zur

MAONITES (*see* MAON)
Judg 10:12 Amalekites and **M** oppressed

MARA
Ruth 1:20 call me **M**, for the Almighty

MARAH
Ex 15:23 Now when they came to **M**, they
Ex 15:23 not drink the waters of **M**
Ex 15:23 the name of it was called **M**
Num 33: 8 of Etham, and camped at **M**
Num 33: 9 They moved from **M** and came

MARALAH
Josh 19:11 went toward the west and to **M**

MARBLE
1Ch 29: 2 and **m** slabs in abundance
Esth 1: 6 on silver rods and **m** pillars
Esth 1: 6 and white and black **m**
Song 5:15 His legs are pillars of **m** set
Rev 18:12 wood, bronze, iron, and **m**

MARCH (*see* MARCHED, MARCHES, MARCHING)
Num 10:28 Thus was the order of **m** of
Josh 6: 3 You shall **m** around the city,
Josh 6: 4 the seventh day you shall **m**
Josh 6: 7 **m** around the city, and let him
Judg 5:21 O my soul, **m** on in strength
Jer 46:22 for they shall **m** with an army

MARCHED (*see* MARCH)
Ex 14:10 the Egyptians **m** after them
Josh 6:14 the second day they **m** around
Josh 6:15 **m** around the city seven times
Josh 6:15 On that day only they **m**
Josh 10: 9 having **m** all night from
Judg 5: 4 when You **m** from the field of
2Ki 3: 9 they **m** on that roundabout
Ps 68: 7 When You **m** through the
Hab 3:12 You **m** through the land in

MARCHES (*see* MARCH)
Joel 2: 7 every one **m** in formation, and
Joel 2: 8 every one **m** in his own column
Hab 1: 6 hasty nation which **m** through

MARCHING (*see* MARCH)
2Sa 5:24 when you hear the sound of **m**
1Ch 14:15 when you hear a sound of **m** in

MARESHAH
Josh 15:44 Keilah, Achzib, and **M**
1Ch 2:42 the sons of **M** the father of
1Ch 4:21 Lecah, Laadah the father of **M**
2Ch 11: 8 Gath, **M**, Ziph,
2Ch 14: 9 chariots, and he came to **M**
2Ch 14:10 the Valley of Zephathah at **M**
2Ch 20:37 of **M** prophesied against
Mic 1:15 to you, O inhabitant of **M**

MARINERS
Ezek 27:27 wares, and merchandise, your **m**
Ezek 27:29 All who handle the oar, the **m**
Jon 1: 5 Then the **m** were afraid

MARK (*see* MARKED, MARKER, MARKS)
Gen 4:15 And the LORD set a **m** on Cain
Num 34: 7 **m** out your border line to
Num 34: 8 **m** out your border to the
Num 34:10 You shall **m** out your eastern
Job 10:14 If I sin, then You **m** me, and
Job 31:35 Here is my **m**
Job 39: 1 Or can you **m** when the deer
Ps 37:37 **M** the blameless man, and
Ps 48:13 **M** well her bulwarks
Ps 56: 6 they **m** my steps, When they
Ps 130: 3 should **m** iniquities, O Lord,
Ezek 9: 4 put a **m** on the foreheads of
Ezek 9: 6 near anyone on whom is the **m**
Ezek 44: 5 **m** well, see with your eyes and
Ezek 44: 5 **M** well who may enter the
Ezek 47:18 On the east side you shall **m**
Rev 13:16 to receive a **m** on their right
Rev 13:17 **m** or the name of the beast
Rev 14: 9 and receives his **m** on his
Rev 14:11 receives the **m** of his name
Rev 15: 2 over his image and over his **m**
Rev 16: 2 who had the **m** of the beast
Rev 19:20 received the **m** of the beast
Rev 20: 4 had not received his **m** on

MARK* (*see* JOHN)
Acts 12:12 of John whose surname was **M**
Acts 12:25 John whose surname was **M**
Acts 15:37 take with them John called **M**
Acts 15:39 And so Barnabas took **M** and
Col 4:10 with **M** the cousin of Barnabas
2Ti 4:11 Get **M** and bring him with you,
Phm 24 as do **M**, Aristarchus, Demas,
1Pe 5:13 and so does **M** my son

MARKED (*see* MARK)
Job 24:16 they **m** for themselves in the
Prov 8:29 when He **m** out the foundations
Jer 2:22 your iniquity is **m** before Me
Jer 23:18 Who has **m** His word and heard
Hab 1:12 O Rock, You have **m** them for
Jude 4 who long ago were **m** out for

MARKER (*see* MARK)
Ezek 39:15 he shall set up a **m** by it

MARKET (*see* MARKETPLACE)
Ezek 27: 9 in you to **m** your merchandise
Ezek 27:15 isles were the **m** of your hand
1Co 10:25 is sold in the meat **m**, asking

MARKETPLACE (*see* MARKET, MARKETPLACES)
Is 23: 3 she is a **m** for the nations
Ezek 27:24 cords, which were in your **m**
Matt 20: 3 others standing idle in the **m**
Mark 7: 4 When they come from the **m**
Luke 7:32 children sitting in the **m**
Acts 16:19 into the **m** to the authorities
Acts 17: 5 of the evil men from the **m**
Acts 17:17 in the **m** daily with those who

MARKETPLACES (*see* MARKETPLACE)
1Ki 20:34 you may set up **m** for yourself
Matt 11:16 children sitting in the **m**
Matt 23: 7 greetings in the **m**, and to be
Mark 6:56 they laid the sick in the **m**
Mark 12:38 love greetings in the **m**,
Luke 11:43 and greetings in the **m**
Luke 20:46 love greetings in the **m**, the

MARKS (*see* MARK)
Lev 19:28 dead, nor tattoo any **m** on you
Job 41:30 spreads pointed **m** in the mire
Is 44:13 rule, he **m** one out with chalk
Is 44:13 he **m** it out with the compass,
Gal 6:17 body the **m** of the Lord Jesus

MAROTH
Mic 1:12 of **M** pined for good, but

MARRED
Lev 21:18 who has a **m** face or any limb
Is 52:14 was **m** more than any man, and
Jer 18: 4 that he made of clay was **m** in

MARRIAGE (*see* MARRIAGES, MARRY)
Ex 21:10 her clothing, and her **m** rights
Judg 12: 9 away thirty daughters in **m**
2Ch 18: 1 by **m** he allied himself with
Ezra 9:14 join in **m** with the people of
Ps 78:63 maidens were not given in **m**
Matt 22: 2 who arranged a **m** for his son
Matt 22:30 marry nor are given in **m**, but

Matt 24:38 marrying and giving in **m**,
Mark 12:25 marry nor are given in **m**, but
Luke 17:27 wives, they were given in **m**
Luke 20:34 age marry and are given in **m**
Luke 20:35 marry nor are given in **m**
1Co 7:38 who gives her in **m** does well
1Co 7:38 not give her in **m** does better
Heb 13: 4 **M** is honorable among all, and
Rev 19: 7 for the **m** of the Lamb has
Rev 19: 9 to the **m** supper of the Lamb

MARRIAGES (*see* MARRIAGE)
Gen 34: 9 And make **m** with us
Deut 7: 3 shall you make **m** with them
Josh 23:12 make **m** with them, and go in to

MARRIED (*see* MARRY)
Gen 19:14 who had **m** his daughters, and
Gen 38: 2 he **m** her and went in to her
Ex 21: 3 if he comes in **m**, then his
Lev 22:12 daughter is **m** to an outsider
Num 12: 1 woman whom he had **m**
Num 12: 1 for he had **m** an Ethiopian
Num 36: 3 Now if they are **m** to any of
Num 36:11 were **m** to the sons of their
Num 36:12 They were **m** into the families
Deut 20: 7 a woman and has not yet **m** her
Deut 22:22 with a woman **m** to a husband
Deut 25: 5 **m** to a stranger outside the
1Ki 3: 1 and **m** Pharaoh's daughter
1Ch 2:21 whom he **m** when he was sixty
2Ch 13:21 **m** fourteen wives, and begot
Neh 6:18 his son Jehohanan had **m** the
Neh 13:23 who had **m** women of Ashdod
Prov 30:23 a hateful woman when she is **m**
Is 54: 1 the children of the **m** woman
Is 62: 4 you, and your land shall be **m**
Jer 3:14 for I am **m** to you
Mal 2:11 he has **m** the daughter of a
Matt 22:25 The first died after he had **m**
Mark 6:17 for he had **m** her
Luke 14:20 said, 'I have **m** a wife, and
Luke 17:27 they **m** wives, they were given
Rom 7: 3 though she has **m** another man
Rom 7: 4 that you may be **m** to another
1Co 7:10 Now to the **m** I command, yet
1Co 7:33 But he who is **m** cares about
1Co 7:34 But she who is **m** cares about
1Co 7:39 to be **m** to whom she wishes

MARRIES (*see* MARRY)
Lev 20:14 If a man **m** a woman and her
Deut 24: 1 **m** her, and it happens that she
Is 62: 5 For as a young man **m** a virgin
Matt 5:32 and whoever **m** a woman who is
Matt 19: 9 **m** another, commits adultery
Matt 19: 9 whoever **m** her who is divorced
Mark 10:11 **m** another commits adultery
Mark 10:12 and **m** another, she commits
Luke 16:18 **m** another commits adultery
Luke 16:18 whoever **m** her who is divorced
Rom 7: 3 she **m** another man, she will
1Co 7:28 and if a virgin **m**, she has not

MARROW
Job 21:24 the **m** of his bones is moist
Ps 63: 5 shall be satisfied as with **m**
Is 25: 6 lees, of fat things full of **m**
Heb 4:12 and spirit, and of joints and **m**

MARRY (*see* MARRIAGE, MARRIED, MARRIES, MARRYING, UNMARRIED)
Gen 38: 8 **m** her, and raise up an heir to
Lev 21:14 these he shall not **m**
Num 36: 3 the tribe into which they **m**
Num 36: 4 the tribe into which they **m**
Num 36: 6 Let them **m** whom they think
Num 36: 6 but they may **m** only within
Deut 20: 7 battle and another man **m** her
Is 62: 5 so shall your sons **m** you
Matt 19:10 wife, it is better not to **m**
Matt 22:24 his brother shall **m** his wife
Matt 22:30 **m** nor are given in marriage
Mark 12:25 they neither **m** nor are given
Luke 20:34 The sons of this age **m** and are
Luke 20:35 neither **m** nor are given in
1Co 7: 9 self-control, let them **m**
1Co 7: 9 For it is better to **m** than to
1Co 7:28 But even if you do **m**, you
1Co 7:36 he does not sin; let them **m**.
1Ti 4: 3 forbidding to **m**, and
1Ti 5:11 Christ, they desire to **m**,
1Ti 5:14 that the younger widows **m**

MARRYING (*see* MARRY)
Neh 13:27 our God by **m** pagan women
Matt 24:38 were eating and drinking, **m**

MARSENA
Esth 1:14 Admatha, Tarshish, Meres, **M**

MARSH (*see* MARSHES)
Job 8:11 papyrus grow up without a **m**
Job 40:21 in a covert of reeds and **m**

MARSHAL
Jer 51:27 Appoint a **m** against her

MARSHES (*see* MARSH)
Is 14:23 and **m** of muddy water
Ezek 47:11 and **m** will not be healed

MARTHA
Luke 10:38 and a certain woman named **M**
Luke 10:40 But **M** was distracted with
Luke 10:41 **M**, **M**, you are worried and
John 11: 1 town of Mary and her sister **M**
John 11: 5 Now Jesus loved **M** and her
John 11:19 had joined the women around **M**
John 11:20 Then **M**, as soon as she heard
John 11:21 Then **M** said to Jesus, "Lord,
John 11:24 **M** said to Him, "I know that
John 11:30 in the place where **M** met Him
John 11:39 **M**, the sister of him who
John 12: 2 **M** served, but Lazarus was one

MARTYR (*see* MARTYRS)
Acts 22:20 of Your **m** Stephen was shed
Rev 2:13 Antipas was My faithful **m**

MARTYRS (*see* MARTYR)
Rev 17: 6 the blood of the **m** of Jesus

MARVEL (*see* MARVELED, MARVELING, MARVELOUS, MARVELS)
Eccl 5: 8 do not **m** at the matter
John 3: 7 Do not **m** that I said to you
John 5:20 than these, that you may **m**
John 5:28 Do not **m** at this
John 7:21 I did one work, and you all **m**
Acts 3:12 Israel, why do you **m** at this
Acts 13:41 Behold, you despisers, **m** and
Gal 1: 6 I **m** that you are turning away
1Jn 3:13 Do not **m**, my brethren, if the
Rev 17: 7 Why did you **m**
Rev 17: 8 who dwell on the earth will **m**

MARVELED (*see* MARVEL)
Ps 48: 5 They saw it, and so they **m**
Matt 8:10 When Jesus heard it, He **m**
Matt 8:27 And the men **m**, saying, "Who
Matt 9: 8 the multitudes saw it, they **m**
Matt 9:33 And the multitudes **m**, saying,
Matt 15:31 So the multitude **m** when they
Matt 21:20 the disciples saw it, they **m**
Matt 22:22 had heard these words, they **m**
Matt 27:14 that the governor **m** greatly
Mark 5:20 had done for him; and all **m**.
Mark 6: 6 And He **m** because of their
Mark 6:51 beyond measure, and **m**
Mark 12:17 And they **m** at Him
Mark 15: 5 nothing, so that Pilate **m**
Mark 15:44 Pilate **m** that He was already
Luke 1:21 **m** that he lingered so long in
Luke 1:63 And they all **m**
Luke 2:18 all those who heard it **m** at
Luke 2:33 His mother **m** at those things
Luke 4:22 **m** at the gracious words which
Luke 7: 9 He **m** at him, and turned around
Luke 8:25 And they were afraid, and **m**
Luke 9:43 But while everyone **m** at all
Luke 11:14 and the multitudes **m**
Luke 11:38 he **m** that He had not first
Luke 20:26 they **m** at His answer and kept
Luke 24:41 did not believe for joy, and **m**
John 4:27 they **m** that He talked with a
John 7:15 And the Jews **m**, saying, "How
Acts 2: 7 they were all amazed and **m**
Acts 4:13 and untrained men, they **m**
Acts 7:31 saw it, he **m** at the sight
Rev 13: 3 And all the world **m** and
Rev 17: 6 her, I **m** with great amazement

MARVELING (*see* MARVEL)
Luke 24:12 **m** to himself at what had

MARVELOUS (*see* MARVEL, MARVELOUSLY)
1Ch 16:12 Remember His **m** works which
Job 5: 9 **m** things without number
Ps 9: 1 will tell of all Your **m** works
Ps 17: 7 Show Your **m** lovingkindness by
Ps 31:21 For He has shown me His **m**
Ps 78:12 **M** things He did in the sight
Ps 98: 1 For He has done **m** things
Ps 105: 5 Remember His **m** works which
Ps 118:23 It is **m** in our eyes
Ps 139:14 **M** are Your works, And that my
Is 29:14 I will again do a **m** work
Is 29:14 people, a **m** work and a wonder
Joel 2:21 the LORD has done **m** things
Mic 7:15 I will show them **m** things
Zech 8: 6 If it is **m** in the eyes of
Zech 8: 6 will it also be **m** in My eyes
Matt 21:42 and it is **m** in our eyes'
Mark 12:11 and it is **m** in our eyes'
John 9:30 Why, this is a **m** thing, that
1Pe 2: 9 of darkness into His **m** light
Rev 15: 1 sign in heaven, great and **m**
Rev 15: 3 **m** are Your works, Lord God

MARVELOUSLY (*see* MARVELOUS)
2Ch 26:15 for he was **m** helped till he
Job 37: 5 God thunders **m** with His voice

MARVELS (*see* MARVEL)
Ex 34:10 all your people I will do **m**

MARY
Matt 1:16 begot Joseph the husband of **M**
Matt 1:18 After His mother **M** was
Matt 1:20 to take to you **M** your wife
Matt 2:11 young Child with **M** His mother
Matt 13:55 Is not His mother called **M**
Matt 27:56 were **M** Magdalene
Matt 27:56 **M** the mother of James and
Matt 27:61 **M** Magdalene was there, and the
Matt 27:61 was there, and the other **M**
Matt 28: 1 **M** Magdalene and the other **M**
Mark 6: 3 the carpenter, the Son of **M**
Mark 15:40 were **M** Magdalene
Mark 15:40 **M** the mother of James the
Mark 15:47 **M** Magdalene and **M** the mother
Mark 16: 1 **M** Magdalene, **M** the mother
Mark 16: 9 appeared first to **M** Magdalene
Luke 1:27 The virgin's name was **M**
Luke 1:30 Do not be afraid, **M**, for you
Luke 1:34 Then **M** said to the angel,
Luke 1:38 Then **M** said, "Behold the
Luke 1:39 Now **M** arose in those days and
Luke 1:41 heard the greeting of **M**, that
Luke 1:46 And **M** said: "My soul
Luke 1:56 **M** remained with her about
Luke 2: 5 to be registered with **M**, his
Luke 2:16 came with haste and found **M**
Luke 2:19 But **M** kept all these things
Luke 2:34 and said to **M** His mother,
Luke 8: 2 **M** called Magdalene, out of
Luke 10:39 And she had a sister called **M**
Luke 10:42 **M** has chosen that good part,
Luke 24:10 It was **M** Magdalene, Joanna,
Luke 24:10 **M** the mother of James, and the
John 11: 1 of Bethany, the town of **M**
John 11: 2 It was that **M** who anointed
John 11:19 women around Martha and **M**
John 11:20 Him, but **M** was sitting in the
John 11:28 secretly called **M** her sister
John 11:31 saw that **M** rose up quickly
John 11:32 when **M** came where Jesus was,
John 11:45 of the Jews who had come to **M**
John 12: 3 Then **M** took a pound of very
John 19:25 **M** the wife of Clopas
John 19:25 and **M** Magdalene
John 20: 1 the first day of the week **M**
John 20:11 But **M** stood outside by the
John 20:16 Jesus said to her, "**M**!"
John 20:18 **M** Magdalene came and told the
Acts 1:14 **M** the mother of Jesus, and
Acts 12:12 he came to the house of **M**
Rom 16: 6 Greet **M**, who labored much for

MASH
Gen 10:23 were Uz, Hul, Gether, and **M**

MASHAL
1Ch 6:74 **M** with its common-lands,

MASONS
2Sa 5:11 trees, and carpenters and **m**
2Ki 12:12 and to **m** and stonecutters, and
2Ki 22: 6 carpenters and builders and **m**
1Ch 14: 1 David, and cedar trees, with **m**
1Ch 22: 2 he appointed **m** to cut hewn
2Ch 24:12 and they hired **m** and carpenters

Ezra 3: 7 They also gave money to the **m**

MASREKAH

Gen 36:36 Samlah of **M** reigned in his
1Ch 1:47 Samlah of **M** reigned in his

MASSA

Gen 25:14 Mishma, Dumah, **M**,
1Ch 1:30 Mishma, Dumah, **M**, Hadad,

MASSACRED

1Ki 18: 4 while Jezebel **m** the prophets

MASSAH (*see* MERIBAH)

Ex 17: 7 the name of the place **M** and
Deut 6:16 God as you tempted Him in **M**
Deut 9:22 Also at Taberah and **M** and
Deut 33: 8 one, whom You tested at **M**

MAST

Prov 23:34 who lies at the top of the **m**
Is 33:23 could not strengthen their **m**
Ezek 27: 5 from Lebanon to make you a **m**

MASTER (*see* MASTER'S, MASTERS)

Gen 24: 9 the thigh of Abraham his **m**
Gen 24:12 O LORD God of my **m** Abraham
Gen 24:12 show kindness to my **m**
Gen 24:14 have shown kindness to my **m**
Gen 24:27 the LORD God of my **m**
Gen 24:27 and His truth toward my **m**
Gen 24:35 LORD has blessed my **m** greatly
Gen 24:36 son to my **m** when she was old
Gen 24:37 Now my **m** made me swear,
Gen 24:39 And I said to my **m**, 'Perhaps
Gen 24:42 O LORD God of my **m** Abraham
Gen 24:48 the LORD God of my **m**
Gen 24:49 kindly and truly with my **m**
Gen 24:54 Send me away to my **m**
Gen 24:56 away so that I may go to my **m**
Gen 24:65 It is my **m**
Gen 27:29 Be **m** over your brethren, and
Gen 27:37 Indeed I have made him your **m**
Gen 39: 2 house of his **m** the Egyptian
Gen 39: 3 his **m** saw that the LORD was
Gen 39: 8 my **m** does not know what is
Gen 39:16 her until his **m** came home
Gen 39:19 when his **m** heard the words
Gen 39:20 Then Joseph's **m** took him and
Ex 21: 4 If his **m** has given him a wife
Ex 21: 5 plainly says, 'I love my **m**
Ex 21: 6 then his **m** shall bring him to
Ex 21: 6 his **m** shall pierce his ear
Ex 21: 8 If she does not please her **m**
Ex 21:32 he shall give to their **m**
Ex 22: 8 then the **m** of the house shall
Deut 23:15 **m** the slave who has escaped
Deut 23:15 has escaped from his **m** to you
Judg 3:25 And there was their **m**, fallen
Judg 19:11 and the servant said to his **m**
Judg 19:12 But his **m** said to him, "We
Judg 19:22 spoke to the **m** of the house
Judg 19:23 the **m** of the house, went out
Judg 19:26 man's house where her **m** was
Judg 19:27 When her **m** arose in the
1Sa 16:16 Let our **m** now command your
1Sa 20:38 arrows and came back to his **m**
1Sa 24: 6 should do this thing to my **m**
1Sa 25:10 away each one from his **m**
1Sa 25:14 the wilderness to greet our **m**
1Sa 25:17 is determined against our **m**
1Sa 26:16 you have not guarded your **m**
1Sa 29: 4 he reconcile himself to his **m**
1Sa 30:13 my **m** left me behind, because
1Sa 30:15 me into the hands of my **m**
2Sa 2: 7 for your **m** Saul is dead, and
1Ki 18: 8 Go, tell your **m**, 'Elijah is
1Ki 18:10 my **m** has not sent someone to
1Ki 18:11 now you say, 'Go, tell your **m**
1Ki 18:14 now you say, 'Go, tell your **m**
1Ki 22:17 LORD said, "These have no **m**
2Ki 2: 3 your **m** from over you today
2Ki 2: 5 your **m** from over you today
2Ki 2:16 them go and search for your **m**
2Ki 5: 1 man in the eyes of his **m**,
2Ki 5: 3 If only my **m** were with the
2Ki 5: 4 Naaman went in and told his **m**
2Ki 5:18 when my **m** goes into the
2Ki 5:20 my **m** has spared Naaman this
2Ki 5:22 My **m** has sent me, saying
2Ki 5:25 went in and stood before his **m**
2Ki 6: 5 Alas, **m**! For it was borrowed
2Ki 6:15 Alas, my **m**! What shall we do?
2Ki 6:22 eat and drink and go to their **m**
2Ki 6:23 away and they went to their **m**
2Ki 8:14 from Elisha, and came to his **m**
2Ki 9: 7 down the house of Ahab your **m**
2Ki 9:11 out to the servants of his **m**
2Ki 9:31 Zimri, murderer of your **m**
2Ki 10: 9 I conspired against my **m** and
2Ki 18:23 to my **m** the king of Assyria
2Ki 18:27 my **m** sent me to your **m**
2Ki 19: 4 whom his **m** the king of
2Ki 19: 6 Thus you shall say to your **m**
1Ch 12:19 He may defect to his **m** Saul
1Ch 15:27 the music **m** with the singers
2Ch 2:13 Huram my **m** craftsman
2Ch 4:16 their articles Huram his **m**
2Ch 18:16 LORD said, 'These have no **m**
Ezra 10: 3 to the counsel of my **m** and of
Esth 1:22 should be **m** in his own house
Job 3:19 servant is free from his **m**
Prov 8:30 beside Him, as a **m** craftsman
Prov 27:18 on his **m** will be honored
Prov 30:10 not malign a servant to his **m**
Is 19: 4 into the hand of a cruel **m**
Is 24: 2 the servant, so with his **m**
Is 36: 8 to my **m** the king of Assyria
Is 36:12 my **m** sent me to your **m**
Is 37: 4 whom his **m** the king of
Is 37: 6 Thus shall you say to your **m**
Jer 22:18 for him, saying, 'Alas, **m**
Lam 1: 5 adversaries have become the **m**
Dan 1: 3 the **m** of his eunuchs, to
Hos 2:16 and no longer call Me 'My **M**
Mal 1: 6 father, and a servant his **m**
Mal 1: 6 And if I am a **M**, where is My
Matt 10:24 nor a servant above his **m**
Matt 10:25 and a servant like his **m**
Matt 10:25 the **m** of the house Beelzebub
Matt 18:25 his **m** commanded that he be
Matt 18:26 down before him, saying, '**M**
Matt 18:27 Then the **m** of that servant
Matt 18:31 told their **m** all that had
Matt 18:32 Then his **m**, after he had
Matt 18:34 his **m** was angry, and delivered
Matt 24:43 that if the **m** of the house
Matt 24:45 whom his **m** made ruler over
Matt 24:46 is that servant whom his **m**
Matt 24:48 My **m** is delaying his coming,
Matt 24:50 the **m** of that servant will
Mark 13:35 the **m** of the house is coming
Mark 14:14 say to the **m** of the house
Luke 5: 5 **M**, we have toiled all night
Luke 8:24 **M**, **M**, we are perishing
Luke 8:45 **M**, the multitudes throng You
Luke 9:33 **M**, it is good for us to be
Luke 9:49 **M**, we saw someone casting out
Luke 12:36 like men who wait for their **m**
Luke 12:37 are those servants whom the **m**
Luke 12:39 that if the **m** of the house
Luke 12:42 whom his **m** will make ruler
Luke 12:43 is that servant whom his **m**
Luke 12:45 My **m** is delaying his coming,
Luke 12:46 the **m** of that servant will
Luke 13:25 When once the **M** of the house
Luke 14:21 these things to his **m**
Luke 14:21 Then the **m** of the house,
Luke 14:22 And the servant said, '**M**, it
Luke 14:23 Then the **m** said to the
Luke 16: 3 For my **m** is taking the
Luke 16: 5 How much do you owe my **m**
Luke 16: 8 So the **m** commended the unjust
Luke 17:13 Jesus, **M**, have mercy on us
Luke 19:16 came the first, saying, '**M**
Luke 19:18 the second came, saying, '**M**
Luke 19:20 And another came, saying, '**M**
Luke 19:25 But they said to him, **M**, he
Luke 22:11 say to the **m** of the house
John 2: 8 take it to the **m** of the feast
John 2: 9 When the **m** of the feast had
John 2: 9 the **m** of the feast called the
John 13:16 is not greater than his **m**
John 15:15 not know what his **m** is doing
John 15:20 is not greater than his **m**
Rom 14: 4 To his own **m** he stands or
1Co 3:10 as a wise **m** builder I have
Gal 4: 1 slave, though he is **m** of all
Eph 6: 9 your own **M** also is in heaven
Col 4: 1 you also have a **M** in heaven
2Ti 2:21 and useful for the **M**, prepared

MASTER'S (*see* MASTER)

Gen 24:10 took ten of his **m** camels and
Gen 24:10 for all his **m** goods were in
Gen 24:27 to the house of my **m** brethren
Gen 24:36 Sarah my **m** wife bore a son to
Gen 24:44 has appointed for my **m** son
Gen 24:48 of my **m** brother for his son
Gen 24:51 let her be your **m** son's wife
Gen 39: 7 **m** wife cast longing eyes on
Gen 39: 8 refused and said to his **m** wife
Ex 21: 4 her children shall be her **m**
1Sa 29:10 in the morning with your **m**
2Sa 9: 9 I have given to your **m** son
2Sa 9:10 that your **m** son may have food
2Sa 9:10 But Mephibosheth your **m** son
2Sa 12: 8 I gave you your **m** house and
2Sa 12: 8 and your **m** wives into your
2Sa 16: 3 And where is your **m** son
2Ki 6:32 of his **m** feet behind him
2Ki 10: 2 since your **m** sons are with
2Ki 10: 3 best qualified of your **m** sons
2Ki 10: 3 and fight for your **m** house
2Ki 10: 6 heads of the men, your **m** sons
2Ki 18:24 of the least of my **m** servants
Is 1: 3 And the donkey its **m** crib
Is 22:18 be the shame of your **m** house
Is 36: 9 of the least of my **m** servants
Luke 12:47 servant who knew his **m** will
Luke 16: 5 one of his **m** debtors to him

MASTERS (*see* MASTER, MASTERS', TASKMASTERS)

Ps 123: 2 look to the hand of their **m**
Prov 25:13 refreshes the soul of his **m**
Is 26:13 other **m** besides You have had
Jer 27: 4 them to say to their **m**
Jer 27: 4 thus you shall say to your **m**
Matt 6:24 No one can serve two **m**
Luke 16:13 No servant can serve two **m**
Acts 16:16 brought her **m** much profit by
Acts 16:19 But when her **m** saw that their
Eph 6: 5 to those who are your **m**
Eph 6: 9 And you, **m**, do the same things
Col 3:22 your **m** according to the flesh
Col 4: 1 **M**, give your servants what is
1Ti 6: 1 own **m** worthy of all honor
1Ti 6: 2 And those who have believing **m**
Tit 2: 9 to be obedient to their own **m**
1Pe 2:18 to your **m** with all fear, not

MASTERS' (*see* MASTERS)

Zeph 1: 9 who fill their **m** houses with
Matt 15:27 which fall from their **m** table

MATCH

Luke 5:36 of the new does not **m** the old

MATE (*see* MATES, MATING)

Lev 18:23 shall you **m** with any beast
Lev 18:23 before a beast to **m** with it
Is 34:15 every one with her **m**
Is 34:16 not one shall lack her **m**

MATERIAL

Ex 35:29 were willing to bring **m** for
Ex 36: 7 for the **m** they had was
Rom 15:27 minister to them in **m** things
1Co 9:11 if we reap your **m** things

MATES (*see* MATE)

Lev 20:15 If a man **m** with a beast, he
Lev 20:16 **m** with it, you shall kill the

MATING (*see* MATE)

Jer 2:24 in her time of **m**, who can

MATRED

Gen 36:39 Mehetabel, the daughter of **M**
1Ch 1:50 Mehetabel the daughter of **M**

MATRI

1Sa 10:21 the family of **M** was chosen

MATRIX

Is 49: 1 from the **m** of My mother He

MATTAN

2Ki 11:18 killed **M** the priest of Baal
2Ch 23:17 killed **M** the priest of Baal
Jer 38: 1 Now Shephatiah the son of **M**

MATTANAH

Num 21:18 the wilderness they went to **M**
Num 21:19 from **M** to Nahaliel, from

MATTANIAH (*see* ZEDEKIAH)
2Ki 24:17 the king of Babylon made **M**
1Ch 9:15 **M** the son of Micah, the son
1Ch 25: 4 Bukkiah, **M**, Uzziel, Shebuel,
1Ch 25:16 the ninth for **M**, his sons and
2Ch 20:14 son of Jeiel, the son of **M**
2Ch 29:13 sons of Asaph, Zechariah and **M**
Ezra 10:26 **M**, Zechariah, Jehiel, Abdi,
Ezra 10:27 Elioenai, Eliashib, **M**,
Ezra 10:30 Chelal, Benaiah, Maaseiah, **M**
Ezra 10:37 **M**, Mattenai, Jaasai,
Neh 11:17 **M** the son of Micha, the son
Neh 11:22 of Hashabiah, the son of **M**
Neh 12: 8 **M** who led the thanksgiving
Neh 12:25 **M**, Bakbukiah, Obadiah,
Neh 12:35 son of Shemaiah, the son of **M**
Neh 13:13 son of Zaccur, the son of **M**

MATTATHAH
Luke 3:31 son of Menan, the son of **M**

MATTATHIAH
Luke 3:25 the son of **M**, the son of Amos
Luke 3:26 son of Maath, the son of **M**

MATTATTAH
Ezra 10:33 Mattenai, **M**, Zabad, Eliphelet

MATTENAI
Ezra 10:33 **M**, Mattattah, Zabad,
Ezra 10:37 Mattaniah, **M**, Jaasai,
Neh 12:19 of Joiarib, **M**

MATTER (*see* PREFACE)

MATTERS (*see* PREFACE)

MATTHAN
Matt 1:15 Eleazar, Eleazar begot **M**,
Matt 1:15 and **M** begot Jacob

MATTHAT
Luke 3:24 the son of **M**, the son of Levi
Luke 3:29 son of Jorim, the son of **M**

MATTHEW (*see* LEVI)
Matt 9: 9 He saw a man named **M** sitting
Matt 10: 3 Thomas and **M** the tax collector
Mark 3:18 Philip, Bartholomew, **M**,
Luke 6:15 **M** and Thomas
Acts 1:13 Bartholomew and **M**

MATTHIAS
Acts 1:23 was surnamed Justus, and **M**
Acts 1:26 lots, and the lot fell on **M**

MATTITHIAH
1Ch 9:31 **M** of the Levites, the
1Ch 15:18 Eliab, Benaiah, Maaseiah, **M**
1Ch 15:21 **M**, Elipheleh, Mikneiah,
1Ch 16: 5 Jeiel, Shemiramoth, Jehiel, **M**
1Ch 25: 3 Shimei, Hashabiah, and **M**, six
1Ch 25:21 the fourteenth for **M**, his
Ezra 10:43 Jeiel, **M**, Zabad, Zebina,
Neh 8: 4 at his right hand, stood **M**

MATTOCK (*see* MATTOCKS)
1Sa 13:20 each man's plowshare, his **m**

MATTOCKS (*see* MATTOCK)
1Sa 13:21 pim for the plowshares, the **m**

MATURE (*see* MATURED, MATURITY)
1Co 2: 6 wisdom among those who are **m**
1Co 14:20 but in understanding be **m**
Phil 3:15 let us, as many as are **m**,

MATURED (*see* MATURE)
Ezek 16: 7 and you grew, **m**, and became

MATURITY (*see* MATURE)
Luke 8:14 life, and bring no fruit to **m**

MAULED
2Ki 2:24 **m** forty-two of the youths

MAY (*see* PREFACE)

MAZZAROTH
Job 38:32 you bring out **M** in its season

ME (*see* PREFACE)

MEADOW (*see* MEADOWS)
Gen 41: 2 and they fed in the **m**
Gen 41:18 and they fed in the **m**

MEADOWS (*see* MEADOW)
Ps 37:20 Like the splendor of the **m**

MEAL (*see* MEALTIME)
Gen 18: 6 three measures of fine **m**
Gen 37:25 And they sat down to eat a **m**
Ex 30: 9 offering, or a **m** offering
Num 5:15 of an ephah of barley **m**
Num 15:20 ground **m** as a heave offering
Num 15:21 **m** you shall give to the LORD
1Ki 4:22 fine flour, sixty kors of **m**
Is 47: 2 the millstones and grind **m**
Ezek 39:17 **m** which I am sacrificing for
Ezek 39:17 A great sacrificial **m** on the
Ezek 39:19 at My sacrificial **m** which I
Ezek 44:30 the first of your ground **m**
Hos 8: 7 it shall never produce **m**
Matt 13:33 of **m** till it was all leavened
Luke 13:21 of **m** till it was all leavened

MEALTIME (*see* MEAL)
Ruth 2:14 Now Boaz said to her at **m**

MEAN (*see* MEANING, MEANS, MEANT)
Gen 33: 8 What do you **m** by all this
Ex 12:26 you, 'What do you **m** by this
Deut 29:24 heat of this great anger **m**
Josh 4: 6 What do these stones **m** to you
1Sa 4: 6 in the camp of the Hebrews **m**
1Sa 4:14 the sound of this tumult **m**
2Sa 16: 2 What do you **m** to do with
Is 3:15 What do you **m** by crushing My
Is 10: 7 Yet he does not **m** so, nor
Ezek 17:12 not know what these things **m**
Ezek 18: 2 What do you **m** when you use
Ezek 37:18 show us what you **m** by these
Jon 1: 6 What do you **m**, sleeper
Luke 8: 9 What does this parable **m**
Acts 2:12 Whatever could this **m**
Acts 17:20 to know what these things **m**
Acts 21:13 What do you **m** by weeping and
Acts 21:39 a citizen of no **m** city
1Co 5:10 Yet I certainly did not **m**
2Co 8:13 For I do not **m** that others
Eph 4: 9 what does it **m** but that He
Phil 1:22 this will **m** fruit from my

MEANING (*see* MEAN)
Gen 21:29 What is the **m** of these seven
Deut 6:20 saying, 'What is the **m** of the
Dan 8:15 vision and was seeking the **m**
Acts 27: 2 **m** to sail along the coasts of
1Co 14:11 know the **m** of the language
Heb 7: 2 and then also king of Salem, **m**

MEANS (*see* MEAN)
Ex 28:28 bind the breastplate by **m** of
Ex 34: 7 by no **m** clearing the guilty,
Ex 39:21 bound the breastplate by **m** of
Lev 7:24 but you shall by no **m** eat it
Num 14:18 but He by no **m** clears the
Num 14:30 you shall by no **m** enter the
Deut 8:19 if you by any **m** forget the
Josh 6:18 by all **m** keep yourselves from
Judg 16: 5 by what **m** we may overpower
1Sa 6: 3 but by all **m** return it to Him
1Sa 20: 2 By no **m**! You shall not die!
2Sa 14:14 but He devises **m**, so that His
1Ki 3:26 child, and by no **m** kill him
1Ki 3:27 child, and by no **m** kill him
1Ki 20:39 if by any **m** he is missing,
Ps 49: 7 by any **m** redeem his brother
Prov 6:26 For by **m** of a harlot a man is
Matt 5:18 or one tittle will by no **m**
Matt 5:20 you will by no **m** enter the
Matt 5:26 you will by no **m** get out of
Matt 9:13 But go and learn what this **m**
Matt 10:42 he shall by no **m** lose his
Matt 12: 7 if you had known what this **m**
Matt 18: 3 you will by no **m** enter the
Matt 24:34 no **m** pass away till all these
Matt 24:35 words will by no **m** pass away
Mark 9:41 you, he will by no **m** lose his
Mark 10:15 child will by no **m** enter it
Mark 13:30 no **m** pass away till all these
Mark 13:31 words will by no **m** pass away
Mark 16:18 it will by no **m** hurt them
Luke 8:36 by what **m** he who had been
Luke 10:19 shall by any **m** hurt you
Luke 18:17 child will by no **m** enter it
Luke 21:32 **m** pass away till all things
Luke 21:33 words will by no **m** pass away
Luke 22:67 you, you will by no **m** believe
Luke 22:68 you will by no **m** answer Me or
John 4:48 you will by no **m** believe
John 6:37 to Me I will by no **m** cast out
John 9:21 but by what **m** he now sees we
John 10: 5 by no **m** follow a stranger
Acts 4: 9 by what **m** he has been made
Acts 13:41 you will by no **m** believe,
Acts 18:21 I must by all **m** keep this
Acts 27:12 if by any **m** they could reach
Rom 1:10 making request if, by some **m**
Rom 11:14 if by any **m** I may provoke to
1Co 9:22 I might by all **m** save some
Gal 2: 2 lest by any **m** I might run
Phil 3:11 if, by any **m**, I may attain to
1Th 3: 5 lest by some **m** the tempter
1Th 4:15 by no **m** precede those who are
2Th 2: 3 no one deceive you by any **m**
1Ti 6: 5 that godliness is a **m** of gain
Heb 9:15 by **m** of death, for the
1Pe 2: 6 will by no **m** be put to shame
Rev 21:27 But there shall by no **m** enter

MEANT (*see* MEAN)
Gen 50:20 you, you **m** evil against me
Gen 50:20 but God **m** it for good, in
Mark 9:10 the rising from the dead **m**
Luke 15:26 and asked what these things **m**
Luke 18:36 by, he asked what it **m**
Acts 10:17 vision which he had seen **m**

MEANTIME (*see* PREFACE)

MEANWHILE (*see* PREFACE)

MEARAH
Josh 13: 4 and **M** that belongs to the

MEASURE (*see* MEASURED, MEASUREMENT, MEASURES, MEASURING)
Num 35: 5 you shall **m** outside the city
Deut 21: 2 they shall **m** the distance
Deut 25:15 weight, a perfect and just **m**
Josh 3: 4 two thousand cubits by **m**
1Ki 7:37 were of the same mold, one **m**
2Ki 25:16 these articles was beyond **m**
1Ch 22: 3 bronze in abundance beyond **m**
1Ch 22:14 and bronze and iron beyond **m**
2Ch 3: 3 according to the former **m**)
Ezra 9: 8 give us a **m** of revival in our
Job 11: 9 Their **m** is longer than the
Job 28:25 and mete out the waters by **m**
Ps 39: 4 And what is the **m** of my days
Ps 60: 6 **m** out the Valley of Succoth
Ps 80: 5 tears to drink in great **m**
Ps 108: 7 **m** out the Valley of Succoth
Is 5:14 and opened its mouth beyond **m**
Is 27: 8 In **m**, by sending it away, you
Is 40:12 the dust of the earth in a **m**
Is 65: 7 therefore I will **m** their
Jer 51:13 the **m** of your covetousness
Jer 52:20 these articles was beyond **m**
Jer 52:21 could **m** its circumference
Ezek 4:11 shall also drink water by **m**
Ezek 4:16 and shall drink water by **m**
Ezek 41:17 inside and outside, by **m**
Ezek 43:10 and let them **m** the pattern
Ezek 45: 3 is the district you shall **m**
Ezek 45:11 bath shall be of the same **m**
Ezek 45:11 their **m** shall be according to
Mic 6:10 and the short **m** that is an
Zech 2: 2 To **m** Jerusalem, to see what
Matt 7: 2 and with the same **m** you use
Matt 23:32 the **m** of your fathers' guilt
Mark 4:24 With the same **m** you use, it
Mark 6:51 amazed in themselves beyond **m**
Mark 7:37 they were astonished beyond **m**
Mark 10:26 they were astonished beyond **m**
Luke 6:38 good **m**, pressed down, shaken
Luke 6:38 with the same **m** that you use
John 3:34 does not give the Spirit by **m**
Rom 12: 3 to each one a **m** of faith
2Co 1: 8 we were burdened beyond **m**
2Co 10:13 will not boast beyond **m**, but
2Co 10:15 boasting of things beyond **m**
2Co 11:23 abundant, in stripes above **m**
2Co 12: 7 **m** by the abundance of the
2Co 12: 7 me, lest I be exalted above **m**
Gal 1:13 the church of God beyond **m**
Eph 4: 7 to the **m** of Christ's gift
Eph 4:13 to the **m** of the stature of
1Th 2:16 fill up the **m** of their sins
Rev 11: 1 and **m** the temple of God, the
Rev 11: 2 the temple, and do not **m** it
Rev 18: 7 In the **m** that she glorified
Rev 18: 7 in the same **m** give her

Rev 21:15 had a gold reed to **m** the city
Rev 21:17 according to the **m** of a man

MEASURED (*see* MEASURE)
Ex 16:18 So when they **m** it by omers
Ruth 3:15 he **m** six ephahs of barley, and
2Sa 8: 2 he **m** them off with a line
2Sa 8: 2 With two lines he **m** off those
1Ki 7:15 a line of twelve cubits **m** the
1Ki 7:23 cubits **m** its circumference
2Ch 4: 2 cubits **m** its circumference
Is 40:12 Who has **m** the waters in the
Is 40:12 hand, **m** heaven with a span and
Jer 31:37 If heaven above can be **m**, and
Jer 33:22 nor the sand of the sea **m**
Ezek 40: 5 he **m** the width of the wall
Ezek 40: 6 and **m** the threshold of the
Ezek 40: 8 He also **m** the vestibule of
Ezek 40: 9 Then he **m** the vestibule of
Ezek 40:11 He **m** the width of the
Ezek 40:13 Then he **m** the gateway from
Ezek 40:14 He **m** the gateposts, sixty
Ezek 40:19 Then he **m** the width from the
Ezek 40:20 he **m** its length and its width
Ezek 40:23 he **m** from gateway to gateway,
Ezek 40:24 and he **m** its gateposts and
Ezek 40:27 he **m** from gateway to gateway
Ezek 40:28 he **m** the southern gateway
Ezek 40:32 he **m** the gateway according to
Ezek 40:35 **m** it according to these same
Ezek 40:47 he **m** the court, one hundred
Ezek 40:48 and **m** the doorposts of the
Ezek 41: 1 **m** the doorposts, six cubits
Ezek 41: 2 he **m** its length, forty cubits
Ezek 41: 3 **m** the doorposts, two cubits
Ezek 41: 4 He **m** the length, twenty
Ezek 41: 5 he **m** the wall of the temple,
Ezek 41:13 So he **m** the temple, one
Ezek 41:15 He **m** the length of the
Ezek 42:15 the east, and **m** it all around
Ezek 42:16 He **m** the east side with the
Ezek 42:17 He **m** the north side, five
Ezek 42:18 He **m** the south side, five
Ezek 42:19 **m** five hundred rods by the
Ezek 42:20 He **m** it on the four sides
Ezek 47: 3 he **m** one thousand cubits, and
Ezek 47: 4 Again he **m** one thousand and
Ezek 47: 4 Again he **m** one thousand and
Ezek 47: 5 Again he **m** one thousand, and
Hos 1:10 which cannot be **m** or numbered
Hab 3: 6 He stood and **m** the earth
Matt 7: 2 use, it will be **m** back to you
Mark 4:24 you use, it will be **m** to you
Luke 6:38 use, it will be **m** back to you
Rev 21:16 he **m** the city with the reed
Rev 21:17 Then he **m** its wall

MEASUREMENT (*see* MEASURE, MEASUREMENTS)
Lev 19:35 in **m** of length, weight, or

MEASUREMENTS (*see* MEASUREMENT)
Ex 26: 2 shall have the same **m**
Ex 26: 8 shall all have the same **m**
Job 38: 5 Who determined its **m**
Ezek 40:21 had the same **m** as the first
Ezek 40:22 had the same **m** as the gateway
Ezek 40:24 according to these same **m**
Ezek 40:28 according to these same **m**
Ezek 40:29 according to these same **m**
Ezek 40:32 according to these same **m**
Ezek 40:33 according to these same **m**
Ezek 40:35 it according to these same **m**
Ezek 43:13 These are the **m** of the altar
Ezek 48:16 These shall be its **m**

MEASURES (*see* MEASURE)
Gen 18: 6 ready three **m** of fine meal
Deut 25:14 in your house differing **m**
1Ch 23:29 mixed and with all kinds of **m**
Prov 20:10 Diverse weights and diverse **m**
Jer 13:25 the portion of your **m** from Me
Matt 13:33 hid in three **m** of meal till
Luke 13:21 hid in three **m** of meal till
Luke 16: 6 he said, A hundred **m** of oil
Luke 16: 7 said, A hundred **m** of wheat

MEASURING (*see* MEASURE)
2Ki 21:13 the **m** line of Samaria and the
Is 28:17 will make justice the **m** line
Is 34:17 it among them with a **m** line
Jer 52:21 a **m** line of twelve cubits
Ezek 40: 3 a **m** rod in his hand, and he
Ezek 40: 5 was a **m** rod six cubits long
Ezek 42:15 finished **m** the inner temple
Ezek 42:16 the east side with the **m** rod
Ezek 42:16 rods by the **m** rod all around
Ezek 42:17 rods by the **m** rod all around
Ezek 42:18 hundred rods by the **m** rod
Ezek 42:19 hundred rods by the **m** rod
Ezek 48:30 **m** four thousand five hundred
Ezek 48:33 **m** four thousand five hundred
Zech 2: 1 a man with a **m** line in his
2Co 10:12 **m** themselves by themselves,
Rev 11: 1 was given a reed like a **m** rod

MEAT
Ex 16: 3 when we sat by the pots of **m**
Ex 16: 8 you **m** to eat in the evening
Ex 16:12 At twilight you shall eat **m**
Ex 22:31 you shall not eat any **m** which
Num 11: 4 Who will give us **m** to eat
Num 11:13 Where am I to get **m** to give
Num 11:13 over me, saying, 'Give us **m**
Num 11:18 tomorrow, and you shall eat **m**
Num 11:18 Who will give us **m** to eat
Num 11:18 the LORD will give you **m**, and
Num 11:21 said, 'I will give them **m**
Num 11:33 But while the **m** was still
Deut 12:15 eat **m** within all your gates,
Deut 12:20 and you say, 'Let me eat **m**
Deut 12:20 because you long to eat **m**
Deut 12:20 you may eat as much **m** as your
Deut 12:23 not eat the life with the **m**
Deut 12:27 your burnt offerings, the **m**
Deut 12:27 God, and you shall eat the **m**
Deut 16: 4 nor shall any of the **m** which
Judg 6:19 The **m** he put in a basket, and
Judg 6:20 Take the **m** and the unleavened
Judg 6:21 in His hand, and touched the **m**
Judg 6:21 of the rock and consumed the **m**
1Sa 2:13 hand while the **m** was boiling
1Sa 2:15 Give **m** for roasting to the
1Sa 2:15 not take boiled **m** from you
1Sa 25:11 my **m** that I have killed for
2Sa 6:19 a loaf of bread, a piece of **m**
1Ki 17: 6 **m** in the morning, and bread and
1Ki 17: 6 and bread and **m** in the evening
1Ch 16: 3 a loaf of bread, a piece of **m**
Job 31:31 not been satisfied with his **m**
Ps 78:20 He provide **m** for His people
Ps 78:27 He also rained **m** on them like
Prov 9: 2 she has slaughtered her **m**
Prov 23:20 with gluttonous eaters of **m**
Is 22:13 and killing sheep, eating **m**
Is 44:16 with this half he eats **m**
Is 44:19 I have roasted **m** and eaten it
Jer 7:21 to your sacrifices and eat **m**
Jer 16: 4 their corpses shall be **m** for
Jer 19: 7 corpses I will give as **m** for
Jer 34:20 dead bodies shall be for **m**
Ezek 11: 3 the caldron, and we are the **m**
Ezek 11: 7 in its midst, they are the **m**
Ezek 11:11 you be the **m** in its midst
Ezek 24: 4 Gather pieces of **m** in it,
Ezek 24:10 cook the **m** well, Mix in the
Ezek 33:25 You eat **m** with blood, you
Dan 10: 3 no **m** or wine came into my
Mic 3: 3 in pieces like **m** for the pot
Hag 2:12 If one carries holy **m** in the
Rom 14:21 eat **m** nor drink wine nor do
1Co 8:13 I will never again eat **m**
1Co 10:25 is sold in the **m** market,

MEBUNNAI (*see* SIBBECHAI)
2Sa 23:27 **M** the Hushathite,

MECHERATHITE
1Ch 11:36 Hepher the **M**, Ahijah the

MECONAH
Neh 11:28 in Ziklag and **M** and its

MEDAD
Num 11:26 and the name of the other **M**
Num 11:27 **M** are prophesying in the camp

MEDAN
Gen 25: 2 bore him Zimran, Jokshan, **M**
1Ch 1:32 were Zimran, Jokshan, **M**,

MEDDLE (*see* MEDDLES, MEDDLING)
Deut 2: 5 Do not **m** with them, for I
Deut 2:19 harass them or **m** with them
2Ki 14:10 for why should you **m** with
2Ch 25:19 why should you **m** with trouble

MEDDLES (*see* MEDDLE)
Prov 26:17 **m** in a quarrel not his own is

MEDDLING (*see* MEDDLE)
2Ch 35:21 Refrain from **m** with God, who

MEDE (*see* MEDES, MEDIA)
Dan 5:31 Darius the **M** received the
Dan 11: 1 first year of Darius the **M**

MEDEBA
Num 21:30 as Nophah, which reaches to **M**
Josh 13: 9 plain of **M** as far as Dibon
Josh 13:16 ravine, and all the plain by **M**
1Ch 19: 7 came and encamped before **M**
Is 15: 2 will wail over Nebo and over **M**

MEDES (*see* MEDE)
2Ki 17: 6 and in the cities of the **M**
2Ki 18:11 and in the cities of the **M**
Esth 1:19 laws of the Persians and the **M**
Is 13:17 stir up the **M** against them
Jer 25:25 and all the kings of the **M**
Jer 51:11 spirit of the kings of the **M**
Jer 51:28 with the kings of the **M**, its
Dan 5:28 divided, and given to the **M**
Dan 6: 8 according to the law of the **M**
Dan 6:12 according to the law of the **M**
Dan 6:15 that it is the law of the **M**
Dan 9: 1 of the lineage of the **M**, who
Acts 2: 9 Parthians and **M** and Elamites,

MEDIA (*see* MADAI, MEDE)
Ezra 6: 2 that is in the province of **M**
Esth 1: 3 the powers of Persia and **M**
Esth 1:14 seven princes of Persia and **M**
Esth 1:18 **M** will say to all the king's
Esth 10: 2 chronicles of the kings of **M**
Is 21: 2 Go up, O Elam! Besiege, O **M**!
Dan 8:20 they are the kings of **M** and

MEDIATE (*see* MEDIATOR)
Gal 3:20 does not **m** for one only, but

MEDIATOR (*see* MEDIATE, MEDIATORS)
Job 9:33 Nor is there any **m** between us
Job 33:23 is a messenger for him, a **m**
Gal 3:19 angels by the hand of a **m**
Gal 3:20 Now a **m** does not mediate for
1Ti 2: 5 one **M** between God and men,
Heb 8: 6 also **M** of a better covenant
Heb 9:15 is the **M** of the new covenant
Heb 12:24 to Jesus the **M** of the new

MEDIATORS (*see* MEDIATOR)
Is 43:27 and your **m** have transgressed

MEDICINE (*see* MEDICINES)
Prov 17:22 merry heart does good, like **m**
Ezek 47:12 food, and their leaves for **m**

MEDICINES (*see* MEDICINE)
Jer 30:13 you have no healing **m**
Jer 46:11 In vain you will use many **m**

MEDITATE (*see* MEDITATES, MEDITATING, MEDITATION)
Gen 24:63 Isaac went out to **m** in the
Josh 1: 8 but you shall **m** in it day
Ps 4: 4 **M** within your heart on your
Ps 63: 6 bed, I **m** on You in the night
Ps 77: 6 I **m** within my heart, And my
Ps 77:12 I will also **m** on all Your
Ps 119:15 I will **m** on Your precepts, And
Ps 119:27 So shall I **m** on Your wondrous
Ps 119:48 I will **m** on Your statutes
Ps 119:78 But I will **m** on Your precepts
Ps 119:148 That I may **m** on Your word
Ps 143: 5 I **m** on all Your works
Ps 145: 5 I will **m** on the glorious
Is 33:18 Your heart will **m** on terror
Mal 3:16 the LORD and who **m** on His
Luke 21:14 it in your hearts not to **m**
Phil 4: 8 **m** on these things
1Ti 4:15 **M** on these things

MEDITATES (*see* MEDITATE)
Ps 1: 2 LORD, And in His law he **m** day
Ps 119:23 servant **m** on Your statutes

MEDITATING (*see* MEDITATE)
1Ki 18:27 either he is **m**, or he is busy

MEDITATION (*see* MEDITATE)
Ps 5: 1 words, O LORD, Consider my **m**
Ps 9:16 of his own hands. **M**
Ps 19:14 mouth and the **m** of my heart Be

Ps 49: 3 the **m** of my heart shall bring
Ps 64: 1 Hear my voice, O God, in my **m**
Ps 104:34 May my **m** be sweet to Him
Ps 119:97 It is my **m** all the day
Ps 119:99 For Your testimonies are my **m**

MEDIUM (*see* MEDIUM'S, MEDIUMS)
Lev 20:27 A man or a woman who is a **m**
Deut 18:11 who conjures spells, or a **m**
1Sa 28: 7 Find me a woman who is a **m**
1Sa 28: 7 a woman who is a **m** at En Dor
1Ch 10:13 he consulted a **m** for guidance

MEDIUM'S (*see* MEDIUM)
Is 29: 4 Your voice shall be like a **m**

MEDIUMS (*see* MEDIUM)
Lev 19:31 Give no regard to **m** and
Lev 20: 6 the person who turns after **m**
1Sa 28: 3 And Saul had put the **m** and the
1Sa 28: 9 how he has cut off the **m**
2Ki 21: 6 and consulted spiritists and **m**
2Ki 23:24 away those who consulted **m**
2Ch 33: 6 and sorcery, and consulted **m**
Is 8:19 Seek those who are **m** and
Is 19: 3 idols and the charmers, the **m**

MEEK (*see* MEEKNESS)
Ps 37:11 But the **m** shall inherit the
Is 11: 4 equity for the **m** of the earth
Zeph 2: 3 all you **m** of the earth, who
Zeph 3:12 will leave in your midst a **m**
Matt 5: 5 Blessed are the **m**, for they

MEEKNESS (*see* MEEK)
2Co 10: 1 am pleading with you by the **m**
Col 3:12 humbleness of mind, **m**,
Jas 1:21 receive with **m** the implanted
Jas 3:13 are done in the **m** of wisdom
1Pe 3:15 hope that is in you, with **m**

MEET (*see* MEETING, MEETS, MET)
Gen 14:17 king of Sodom went out to **m**
Gen 18: 2 from the tent door to **m** them
Gen 19: 1 saw them, he rose to **m** them
Gen 23: 8 and **m** with Ephron the son of
Gen 24:17 And the servant ran to **m** her
Gen 24:65 walking in the field to **m** us
Gen 29:13 son, that he ran to **m** him
Gen 30:16 Leah went out to **m** him and
Gen 32: 6 and he also is coming to **m** you
Gen 33: 4 But Esau ran to **m** him, and
Gen 46:29 Goshen to **m** his father Israel
Ex 4:14 is also coming out to **m** you
Ex 4:27 the wilderness to **m** Moses
Ex 5:20 who stood there to **m** them
Ex 7:15 by the river's bank to **m** him
Ex 18: 7 out to **m** his father-in-law
Ex 19:17 out of the camp to **m** with God
Ex 23: 4 If you **m** your enemy's ox or
Ex 25:22 And there I will **m** with you
Ex 29:42 where I will **m** you to speak
Ex 29:43 And there I will **m** with the
Ex 30: 6 where I will **m** with you
Ex 30:36 where I will **m** with you
Num 3:38 to **m** the needs of the
Num 17: 4 Testimony, where I **m** with you
Num 22:36 he went out to **m** him at the
Num 23: 3 the LORD will come to **m** me
Num 23:15 while I **m** the LORD over there
Num 31:13 went to **m** them outside the
Deut 23: 4 they did not **m** you with bread
Josh 2:16 lest the pursuers **m** you
Josh 9:11 the journey, and go to **m** them
Judg 4:18 And Jael went out to **m** Sisera
Judg 4:22 Jael came out to **m** him, and
Judg 6:35 and they came up to **m** them
Judg 11:31 the doors of my house to **m** me
Judg 11:34 coming out to **m** him with
Judg 19: 3 saw him, he was glad to **m** him
Ruth 2:22 that people do not **m** you in
1Sa 10: 3 to God at Bethel will **m** you
1Sa 10: 5 that you will **m** a group of
1Sa 10:10 a group of prophets to **m** him
1Sa 13:10 and Saul went out to **m** him
1Sa 15:12 in the morning to **m** Saul, it
1Sa 17:48 came and drew near to **m** David
1Sa 17:48 the army to **m** the Philistine
1Sa 18: 6 dancing, to **m** King Saul, with
1Sa 25:32 who sent you this day to **m** me
1Sa 25:34 had hastened and come to **m** me
1Sa 30:21 So they went out to **m** David
1Sa 30:21 to **m** the people who were with
2Sa 6:20 of Saul came out to **m** David
2Sa 10: 5 told David, he sent to **m** them
2Sa 15:32 coming to **m** him with his robe
2Sa 19:15 Gilgal, to go to **m** the king
2Sa 19:16 men of Judah to **m** King David
2Sa 19:20 go down to **m** my lord the king
2Sa 19:24 Saul came down to **m** the king
2Sa 19:25 to Jerusalem to **m** the king
1Ki 2: 8 down to **m** me at the Jordan
1Ki 2:19 And the king rose up to **m** her
1Ki 18:16 So Obadiah went to **m** Ahab
1Ki 18:16 and Ahab went to **m** Elijah
1Ki 21:18 go down to **m** Ahab king of
2Ki 1: 3 go up to **m** the messengers of
2Ki 1: 6 A man came up to **m** us, and
2Ki 1: 7 was it who came up to **m** you
2Ki 2:15 And they came to **m** him, and
2Ki 4:26 Please run now to **m** her, and
2Ki 4:29 If you **m** anyone, do not greet
2Ki 4:31 he went back to **m** him, and
2Ki 5:21 from the chariot to **m** him
2Ki 5:26 from his chariot to **m** you
2Ki 8: 8 go to **m** the man of God, and
2Ki 8: 9 So Hazael went to **m** him and
2Ki 9:17 and send him to **m** them, and let
2Ki 9:18 So the horseman went to **m** him
2Ki 9:21 and they went out to **m** Jehu
2Ki 10:15 of Rechab, coming to **m** him
2Ki 16:10 to **m** Tiglath-Pileser king of
1Ch 12:17 And David went out to **m** them
1Ch 19: 5 and he sent to **m** them, because
2Ch 15: 2 And he went out to **m** Asa, and
2Ch 19: 2 the seer went out to **m** him
Neh 6: 2 let us **m** together in one of
Neh 6:10 Let us **m** together in the
Job 5:14 They **m** with darkness in the
Ps 21: 3 For You **m** him with the
Ps 59:10 God shall come to **m** me
Ps 79: 8 mercies come speedily to **m** us
Prov 7:15 So I came out to **m** you,
Prov 8: 2 the way, where the paths **m**
Prov 17:12 Let a man **m** a bear robbed of
Is 7: 3 Go out now to **m** Ahaz, you and
Is 14: 9 you, to **m** you at your coming
Is 34:14 shall also **m** with the jackals
Is 64: 5 You **m** him who rejoices and
Jer 41: 6 out from Mizpah to **m** them
Jer 51:31 runner will run to **m** another
Jer 51:31 and one messenger to **m** another
Hos 13: 8 I will **m** them like a bear
Amos 4:12 to you, prepare to **m** your God
Zech 2: 3 angel was coming out to **m** him
Matt 8:34 city came out to **m** Jesus
Matt 25: 1 went out to **m** the bridegroom
Matt 25: 6 go out to **m** him
Mark 14:13 a man will **m** you carrying a
Luke 14:31 **m** him who comes against him
Luke 22:10 a man will **m** you carrying a
John 12:13 trees and went out to **m** Him
John 18:20 where the Jews always **m**, and
Acts 21:22 The assembly must certainly **m**
Acts 28:15 they came to **m** us as far as
1Th 4:17 to **m** the Lord in the air
Tit 3:14 to **m** urgent needs, that they

MEETING (*see* MEET, MEETINGS)
Ex 27:21 In the tabernacle of **m**,
Ex 28:43 come into the tabernacle of **m**
Ex 29: 4 door of the tabernacle of **m**
Ex 29:10 before the tabernacle of **m**
Ex 29:11 door of the tabernacle of **m**
Ex 29:30 of **m** to minister in the holy
Ex 29:32 door of the tabernacle of **m**
Ex 29:42 of **m** before the LORD, where I
Ex 29:44 sanctify the tabernacle of **m**
Ex 30:16 of the tabernacle of **m**, that
Ex 30:18 between the tabernacle of **m**
Ex 30:20 go into the tabernacle of **m**
Ex 30:26 anoint the tabernacle of **m**
Ex 30:36 in the tabernacle of **m** where
Ex 31: 7 the tabernacle of **m**, the ark
Ex 33: 7 called it the tabernacle of **m**
Ex 33: 7 out to the tabernacle of **m**
Ex 35:21 work of the tabernacle of **m**
Ex 38: 8 door of the tabernacle of **m**
Ex 38:30 door of the tabernacle of **m**
Ex 39:32 of the tent of **m** was finished
Ex 39:40 tabernacle, for the tent of **m**
Ex 40: 2 tabernacle of the tent of **m**
Ex 40: 6 tabernacle of the tent of **m**
Ex 40: 7 between the tabernacle of **m**
Ex 40:12 door of the tabernacle of **m**
Ex 40:22 table in the tabernacle of **m**
Ex 40:24 in the tabernacle of **m**,
Ex 40:26 of **m** in front of the veil
Ex 40:29 tabernacle of the tent of **m**
Ex 40:30 between the tabernacle of **m**
Ex 40:32 went into the tabernacle of **m**
Ex 40:34 covered the tabernacle of **m**
Ex 40:35 to enter the tabernacle of **m**
Lev 1: 1 him from the tabernacle of **m**
Lev 1: 3 of **m** before the LORD
Lev 1: 5 door of the tabernacle of **m**
Lev 3: 2 door of the tabernacle of **m**
Lev 3: 8 it before the tabernacle of **m**
Lev 3:13 it before the tabernacle of **m**
Lev 4: 4 of **m** before the LORD, lay his
Lev 4: 5 it to the tabernacle of **m**
Lev 4: 7 is in the tabernacle of **m**
Lev 4: 7 door of the tabernacle of **m**
Lev 4:14 it before the tabernacle of **m**
Lev 4:16 blood to the tabernacle of **m**
Lev 4:18 is in the tabernacle of **m**
Lev 4:18 door of the tabernacle of **m**
Lev 6:16 of **m** they shall eat it
Lev 6:26 court of the tabernacle of **m**
Lev 6:30 into the tabernacle of **m**, to
Lev 8: 3 door of the tabernacle of **m**
Lev 8: 4 door of the tabernacle of **m**
Lev 8:31 door of the tabernacle of **m**
Lev 8:33 of **m** for seven days, until
Lev 8:35 of the tabernacle of **m** day
Lev 9: 5 before the tabernacle of **m**
Lev 9:23 went into the tabernacle of **m**
Lev 10: 7 door of the tabernacle of **m**
Lev 10: 9 go into the tabernacle of **m**
Lev 12: 6 door of the tabernacle of **m**
Lev 14:11 door of the tabernacle of **m**
Lev 14:23 door of the tabernacle of **m**
Lev 15:14 door of the tabernacle of **m**
Lev 15:29 door of the tabernacle of **m**
Lev 16: 7 door of the tabernacle of **m**
Lev 16:16 do for the tabernacle of **m**
Lev 16:17 of **m** when he goes in to make
Lev 16:20 Place, the tabernacle of **m**
Lev 16:23 come into the tabernacle of **m**
Lev 16:33 for the tabernacle of **m** and
Lev 17: 4 door of the tabernacle of **m**
Lev 17: 5 door of the tabernacle of **m**
Lev 17: 6 door of the tabernacle of **m**
Lev 17: 9 door of the tabernacle of **m**
Lev 19:21 door of the tabernacle of **m**
Lev 24: 3 in the tabernacle of **m**,
Num 1: 1 Sinai, in the tabernacle of **m**
Num 2: 2 from the tabernacle of **m**
Num 2:17 Then the tabernacle of **m**
Num 3: 7 before the tabernacle of **m**
Num 3: 8 of the tabernacle of **m**, and to
Num 3:25 in the tabernacle of **m**
Num 3:25 door of the tabernacle of **m**
Num 3:38 before the tabernacle of **m**
Num 4: 3 work in the tabernacle of **m**
Num 4: 4 Kohath in the tabernacle of **m**
Num 4:15 of **m** which the sons of Kohath
Num 4:23 work in the tabernacle of **m**
Num 4:25 of **m** with its covering, the
Num 4:25 door of the tabernacle of **m**
Num 4:28 in the tabernacle of **m**
Num 4:30 work of the tabernacle of **m**
Num 4:31 for the tabernacle of **m**
Num 4:33 for the tabernacle of **m**,
Num 4:35 work in the tabernacle of **m**
Num 4:37 serve in the tabernacle of **m**
Num 4:39 work in the tabernacle of **m**
Num 4:41 serve in the tabernacle of **m**
Num 4:43 work in the tabernacle of **m**
Num 4:47 in the tabernacle of **m**
Num 6:10 door of the tabernacle of **m**
Num 6:13 door of the tabernacle of **m**
Num 6:18 door of the tabernacle of **m**
Num 7: 5 work of the tabernacle of **m**
Num 7:89 of **m** to speak with Him, he
Num 8: 9 before the tabernacle of **m**
Num 8:15 service the tabernacle of **m**
Num 8:19 Israel in the tabernacle of **m**
Num 8:22 tabernacle of **m** before Aaron
Num 8:24 work of the tabernacle of **m**
Num 8:26 in the tabernacle of **m**, to
Num 10: 3 door of the tabernacle of **m**
Num 11:16 them to the tabernacle of **m**
Num 12: 4 three, to the tabernacle of **m**

Num 14:10 in the tabernacle of **m** before
Num 16:18 tabernacle of **m** with Moses
Num 16:19 door of the tabernacle of **m**
Num 16:42 toward the tabernacle of **m**
Num 16:43 before the tabernacle of **m**
Num 16:50 door of the tabernacle of **m**
Num 17: 4 of **m** before the Testimony
Num 18: 4 needs of the tabernacle of **m**
Num 18: 6 work of the tabernacle of **m**
Num 18:21 work of the tabernacle of **m**
Num 18:22 come near the tabernacle of **m**
Num 18:23 work of the tabernacle of **m**
Num 18:31 work in the tabernacle of **m**
Num 19: 4 front of the tabernacle of **m**
Num 20: 6 door of the tabernacle of **m**
Num 25: 6 door of the tabernacle of **m**
Num 27: 2 of the tabernacle of **m**,
Num 31:54 of **m** as a memorial for the
Deut 31:14 in the tabernacle of **m**, that
Deut 31:14 in the tabernacle of **m**
Josh 18: 1 up the tabernacle of **m** there
Josh 19:51 door of the tabernacle of **m**
1Sa 2:22 door of the tabernacle of **m**
1Ki 8: 4 the LORD, the tabernacle of **m**
1Ch 6:32 place of the tabernacle of **m**
1Ch 9:21 door of the tabernacle of **m**
1Ch 23:32 needs of the tabernacle of **m**
2Ch 1: 3 of **m** with God was there,
2Ch 1: 6 was at the tabernacle of **m**
2Ch 1:13 before the tabernacle of **m**
2Ch 5: 5 the ark, the tabernacle of **m**
Ps 74: 4 in the midst of Your **m** place
Ps 74: 8 **m** places of God in the land
Is 1:13 iniquity and the sacred **m**

MEETINGS (*see* MEETING)
Ezek 44:24 in all My appointed **m**, and

MEETS (*see* MEET)
Gen 32:17 When Esau my brother **m** you
Num 35:19 when he **m** him, he shall put
Num 35:21 to death when he **m** him
Acts 25:16 before the accused **m** the

MEGIDDO
Josh 12:21 the king of **M**, one
Josh 17:11 and the inhabitants of **M** and
Judg 1:27 or the inhabitants of **M** and
Judg 5:19 Taanach, by the waters of **M**
1Ki 4:12 son of Ahilud, in Taanach, **M**
1Ki 9:15 wall of Jerusalem, Hazor, **M**
2Ki 9:27 Then he fled to **M**, and died
2Ki 23:29 at **M** when he confronted him
2Ki 23:30 his body in a chariot from **M**
1Ch 7:29 Taanach and its towns, **M** and
2Ch 35:22 to fight in the Valley of **M**
Zech 12:11 Rimmon in the plain of **M**

MEHETABEEL (*see* MEHETABEL)
Neh 6:10 son of Delaiah, the son of **M**

MEHETABEL (*see* MEHETABEEL)
Gen 36:39 His wife's name was **M**, the
1Ch 1:50 His wife's name was **M** the

MEHIDA
Ezra 2:52 of Bazluth, the sons of **M**
Neh 7:54 of Bazlith, the children of **M**

MEHIR
1Ch 4:11 the brother of Shuhah begot **M**

MEHOLATHITE (*see* ABEL MEHOLAH)
1Sa 18:19 to Adriel the **M** as a wife
2Sa 21: 8 the son of Barzillai the **M**

MEHUJAEL
Gen 4:18 and Irad begot **M**,
Gen 4:18 and **M** begot Methushael, and

MEHUMAN
Esth 1:10 with wine, he commanded **M**

ME JARKON
Josh 19:46 **M**, and Rakkon, with the region

MELATIAH
Neh 3: 7 next to them **M** the Gibeonite,

MELCHI (*see* MALCHISHUA)
Luke 3:24 the son of Levi, the son of **M**
Luke 3:28 the son of **M**, the son of Addi

MELCHIAH (*see* MALCHIAH)
Jer 21: 1 to him Pashhur the son of **M**

MELCHIZEDEK
Gen 14:18 Then **M** king of Salem brought
Ps 110: 4 According to the order of **M**
Heb 5: 6 according to the order of **M**"
Heb 5:10 according to the order of **M**
Heb 6:20 according to the order of **M**
Heb 7: 1 For this **M**, king of Salem,
Heb 7:10 of his father when **M** met him
Heb 7:11 according to the order of **M**
Heb 7:15 if, in the likeness of **M**,
Heb 7:17 according to the order of **M**
Heb 7:21 to the order of **M**'"),

MELEA
Luke 3:31 the son of **M**, the son of

MELECH (*see* EBED-MELECH, NATHAN-MELECH, REGEM-MELECH)
1Ch 8:35 sons of Micah were Pithon, **M**
1Ch 9:41 sons of Micah were Pithon, **M**

MELICHU
Neh 12:14 of **M**, Jonathan

MELODY
Ps 33: 2 Make **m** to Him with an
Is 23:16 make sweet **m**, sing many songs
Is 51: 3 and the voice of **m**
Amos 5:23 hear the **m** of your stringed
Eph 5:19 making **m** in your heart to the

MELONS
Num 11: 5 Egypt, the cucumbers, the **m**

MELT (*see* MELTED, MELTING, MELTS)
Ex 15:15 of Canaan will **m** away
Josh 14: 8 the heart of the people **m**
2Sa 17:10 of a lion, will **m** completely
Ps 39:11 his beauty **m** away like a moth
Ps 97: 5 The mountains **m** like wax at
Ps 112:10 gnash his teeth and **m** away
Is 13: 7 every man's heart will **m**
Is 19: 1 of Egypt will **m** in its midst
Ezek 21: 7 it comes, every heart will **m**
Ezek 21:15 gates, that the heart may **m**
Ezek 22:20 to blow fire on it, to **m** it
Ezek 22:20 will leave you there and **m** you
Mic 1: 4 mountains will **m** under him
Nah 1: 5 quake before Him, the hills **m**
2Pe 3:10 will **m** with fervent heat
2Pe 3:12 will **m** with fervent heat

MELTED (*see* MELT)
Ex 16:21 when the sun became hot, it **m**
Josh 2:11 these things, our hearts **m**
Josh 5: 1 over, that their heart **m**
Josh 7: 5 the hearts of the people **m**
Ps 22:14 It has **m** within Me
Ps 46: 6 His voice, the earth **m**
Is 34: 3 shall be **m** with their blood
Ezek 22:21 you shall be **m** in its midst
Ezek 22:22 As silver is **m** in the midst
Ezek 22:22 shall you be **m** in its midst
Ezek 24:11 its filthiness may be **m** in it

MELTING (*see* MELT)
1Sa 14:16 was the multitude, **m** away

MELTS (*see* MELT)
Ps 58: 8 snail which **m** away as it goes
Ps 68: 2 As wax **m** before the fire, So
Ps 107:26 Their soul **m** because of
Ps 119:28 My soul **m** from heaviness
Ps 147:18 sends out His word and **m** them
Amos 9: 5 who touches the earth and it **m**
Nah 2:10 The heart **m**, and the knees

MEMBER (*see* MEMBERS)
Lev 25:47 or to a **m** of the stranger's
Mark 15:43 a prominent council **m**, who
Luke 23:50 man named Joseph, a council **m**
1Co 12:14 body is not one **m** but many
1Co 12:19 And if they were all one **m**
1Co 12:26 if one **m** suffers, all the
1Co 12:26 or if one **m** is honored, all
Jas 3: 5 so the tongue is a little **m**

MEMBERS (*see* MEMBER)
Job 17: 7 all my **m** are like shadows
Matt 5:29 you that one of your **m** perish
Matt 5:30 you that one of your **m** perish
Rom 6:13 your **m** as instruments of
Rom 6:13 and your **m** as instruments of
Rom 6:19 **m** as slaves of uncleanness
Rom 6:19 so now present your **m** as
Rom 7: 5 our **m** to bear fruit to death
Rom 7:23 But I see another law in my **m**
Rom 7:23 law of sin which is in my **m**
Rom 12: 4 as we have many **m** in one body
Rom 12: 4 but all the **m** do not have the
Rom 12: 5 individually **m** of one another
1Co 6:15 your bodies are **m** of Christ
1Co 6:15 I then take the **m** of Christ
1Co 6:15 and make them **m** of a harlot
1Co 12:12 the body is one and has many **m**
1Co 12:12 but all the **m** of that one
1Co 12:18 But now God has set the **m**
1Co 12:20 now indeed there are many **m**
1Co 12:22 those **m** of the body which
1Co 12:23 those **m** of the body which we
1Co 12:25 but that the **m** should have
1Co 12:26 all the **m** suffer with it
1Co 12:26 all the **m** rejoice with it
1Co 12:27 of Christ, and **m** individually
Eph 2:19 **m** of the household of God,
Eph 4:25 for we are **m** of one another
Eph 5:30 For we are **m** of His body, of
Col 3: 5 your **m** which are on the earth
Jas 3: 6 **m** that it defiles the whole
Jas 4: 1 pleasure that war in your **m**

MEMORIAL (*see* MEMORY)
Ex 3:15 and this is My **m** to all
Ex 12:14 this day shall be to you a **m**
Ex 13: 9 as a **m** between your eyes,
Ex 17:14 this for a **m** in the book and
Ex 28:12 as **m** stones for the sons of
Ex 28:12 on his two shoulders as a **m**
Ex 28:29 place, as a **m** before the LORD
Ex 30:16 that it may be a **m** for the
Ex 39: 7 a **m** for the sons of Israel
Lev 2: 2 burn it as a **m** on the altar
Lev 2: 9 grain offering a **m** portion
Lev 2:16 shall burn the **m** portion
Lev 5:12 handful of it as a **m** portion
Lev 6:15 aroma, as a **m** to the LORD
Lev 23:24 a **m** of blowing of trumpets, a
Lev 24: 7 may be on the bread for a **m**
Num 5:26 as its **m** portion, burn it on
Num 10:10 they shall be a **m** for you
Num 16:40 to be a **m** to the children of
Num 31:54 **m** for the children of Israel
Josh 4: 7 a **m** to the children of Israel
Neh 2:20 or right or **m** in Jerusalem
Hos 12: 5 The LORD is His **m**
Zech 6:14 crown shall be for a **m** in the
Matt 26:13 also be told as a **m** to her
Mark 14: 9 be spoken of as a **m** to her
Acts 10: 4 come up for a **m** before God

MEMORY (*see* MEMORIAL)
Deut 32:26 I will make the **m** of them to
Esth 9:28 that the **m** of them should not
Job 18:17 The **m** of him perishes from
Ps 9: 6 Even their **m** has perished
Ps 109:15 the **m** of them from the earth
Ps 145: 7 They shall utter the **m** of
Prov 10: 7 The **m** of the righteous is
Eccl 9: 5 reward, for the **m** of them is
Is 26:14 and made all their **m** to perish

MEMPHIS (*see* NOPH)
Hos 9: 6 **M** shall bury them

MEMUCAN
Esth 1:14 Meres, Marsena, and **M**, the
Esth 1:16 **M** answered before the king and
Esth 1:21 according to the word of **M**

MEN (*see* MAN, MEN-PLEASERS, MEN'S)
Gen 4:26 Then **m** began to call on the
Gen 6: 1 when **m** began to multiply on
Gen 6: 2 of God saw the daughters of **m**
Gen 6: 4 came in to the daughters of **m**
Gen 6: 4 the mighty **m** who were of old
Gen 6: 4 who were of old, **m** of renown
Gen 11: 5 which the sons of **m** had built
Gen 12:20 his **m** concerning him
Gen 13:13 But the **m** of Sodom were
Gen 14:24 what the young **m** have eaten
Gen 14:24 of the **m** who went with me
Gen 17:23 the **m** of Abraham's house, and
Gen 17:27 all the **m** of his house, born
Gen 18: 2 three **m** were standing by him
Gen 18:16 Then the **m** rose from there and
Gen 18:22 Then the **m** turned away from
Gen 19: 4 the **m** of the city, the **m** of
Gen 19: 4 the **m** of Sodom, both old and
Gen 19: 5 Where are the **m** who came to

Gen 19: 8 only do nothing to these **m**
Gen 19:10 But the **m** reached out their
Gen 19:11 they struck the **m** who were at
Gen 19:12 Then the **m** said to Lot
Gen 19:16 the **m** took hold of his hand,
Gen 20: 8 and the **m** were very afraid
Gen 22: 3 two of his young **m** with him
Gen 22: 5 Abraham said to his young **m**
Gen 22:19 returned to his young **m**, and
Gen 24:13 the daughters of the **m** of the
Gen 24:32 the feet of the **m** who were
Gen 24:54 the **m** who were with him ate
Gen 24:59 Abraham's servant and his **m**
Gen 26: 7 the **m** of the place asked him
Gen 26: 7 lest the **m** of the place
Gen 29:22 all the **m** of the place and
Gen 32: 6 four hundred **m** are with him
Gen 32:28 struggled with God and with **m**
Gen 33: 1 with him were four hundred **m**
Gen 33:13 if the **m** should drive them
Gen 34: 7 the **m** were grieved and very
Gen 34:20 with the **m** of their city,
Gen 34:21 These **m** are at peace with us
Gen 34:22 **m** consent to dwell with us
Gen 38:21 he asked the **m** of that place
Gen 38:22 the **m** of the place said there
Gen 39:11 none of the **m** of the house
Gen 39:14 called to the **m** of her house
Gen 41: 8 of Egypt and all its wise **m**
Gen 42:11 we are honest **m**
Gen 42:19 If you are honest **m**, let one
Gen 42:31 said to him, "We are honest **m**
Gen 42:33 know that you are honest **m**
Gen 42:34 but that you are honest **m**
Gen 43:15 So the **m** took that present and
Gen 43:16 Take these **m** to my home, and
Gen 43:16 for these **m** will dine with me
Gen 43:17 the **m** into Joseph's house
Gen 43:18 Now the **m** were afraid because
Gen 43:24 the **m** into Joseph's house
Gen 43:33 the **m** looked in astonishment
Gen 44: 3 the **m** were sent away, they and
Gen 44: 4 Get up, follow the **m**
Gen 46:32 And the **m** are shepherds, for
Gen 47: 2 he took five **m** from among his
Gen 47: 6 any competent **m** among them
Ex 2:13 two Hebrew **m** were fighting,
Ex 4:19 for all the **m** are dead who
Ex 5: 9 more work be laid on the **m**
Ex 7:11 also called the wise **m** and the
Ex 10: 7 Let the **m** go, that they may
Ex 10:11 Go now, you who are **m**, and
Ex 12:37 hundred thousand **m** on foot
Ex 15:15 the mighty **m** of Moab,
Ex 17: 9 Choose us some **m** and go out,
Ex 18:21 from all the people able **m**
Ex 18:21 fear God, **m** of truth, hating
Ex 18:25 Moses chose able **m** out of all
Ex 21:18 If **m** contend with each other,
Ex 21:22 If **m** fight, and hurt a woman
Ex 22:31 And you shall be holy **m** to Me
Ex 24: 5 Then he sent young **m** of the
Ex 32:28 about three thousand **m** of the
Ex 34:23 **m** shall appear before the
Ex 35:22 They came, both **m** and women,
Ex 35:29 to the LORD, all the **m** and
Ex 38:26 five hundred and fifty **m**
Lev 7:25 **m** offer an offering made by
Lev 18:27 the **m** of the land have done
Lev 27: 9 if it is a beast such as **m**
Lev 27:29 doomed to destruction among **m**
Num 1: 5 **m** who shall stand with you
Num 1:17 Aaron took these **m** who had
Num 1:44 leaders of Israel, twelve **m**
Num 5: 6 **m** commit in unfaithfulness
Num 9: 6 Now there were certain **m** who
Num 9: 7 And those **m** said to him,
Num 11:16 Gather to Me seventy **m** of the
Num 11:21 hundred thousand **m** on foot
Num 11:24 he gathered the seventy **m** of
Num 11:26 But two **m** had remained in the
Num 11:28 one of his choice **m**,
Num 12: 3 more than all **m** who were on
Num 13: 2 Send **m** to spy out the land of
Num 13: 3 all of them **m** who were heads
Num 13:16 **m** whom Moses sent to spy out
Num 13:24 **m** of Israel cut down there
Num 13:31 But the **m** who had gone up
Num 13:32 in it are **m** of great stature
Num 14:22 because all these **m** who have
Num 14:36 the **m** whom Moses sent to spy
Num 14:37 those very **m** who brought the
Num 14:38 of the **m** who went to spy out
Num 16: 1 sons of Reuben, took **m**
Num 16: 2 the congregation, **m** of renown
Num 16:14 put out the eyes of these **m**
Num 16:26 the tents of these wicked **m**
Num 16:29 **m** die naturally like all **m**
Num 16:29 by the common fate of all **m**
Num 16:30 **m** have rejected the LORD
Num 16:32 all the **m** with Korah, with
Num 16:35 fifty **m** who were offering
Num 16:38 The censers of these **m** who
Num 20:20 out against them with many **m**
Num 22: 9 Who are these **m** with you
Num 22:20 If the **m** come to call you,
Num 22:35 Go with the **m**, but only the
Num 25: 5 Every one of you kill his **m**
Num 26:10 two hundred and fifty **m**
Num 31:21 the priest said to the **m** of
Num 31:28 the **m** of war who went out to
Num 31:32 which the **m** of war had taken,
Num 31:42 from the **m** who fought
Num 31:49 **m** of war who are under our
Num 31:53 (The **m** of war had taken spoil
Num 32:11 Surely none of the **m** who
Num 32:14 place, a brood of sinful **m**
Num 32:21 all your armed **m** cross over
Num 34:17 **m** who shall divide the land
Num 34:19 These are the names of the **m**
Deut 1:13 knowledgeable **m** from among
Deut 1:15 wise and knowledgeable **m**, and
Deut 1:22 Let us send **m** before us
Deut 1:23 so I took twelve of your **m**
Deut 1:35 **m** of this evil generation
Deut 2:14 **m** of war was consumed from
Deut 2:16 when all the **m** of war had
Deut 2:34 and we utterly destroyed the **m**
Deut 3: 6 utterly destroying the **m**
Deut 3:18 All you **m** of valor shall
Deut 4: 3 from among you all the **m** who
Deut 13:13 Certain corrupt **m** have gone
Deut 19:14 which the **m** of old have set,
Deut 19:17 then both **m** in the
Deut 21:21 Then all the **m** of his city
Deut 22:21 the **m** of her city shall stone
Deut 25: 1 there is a dispute between **m**
Deut 25:11 If two **m** fight together, and
Deut 27:14 and say to all the **m** of Israel
Deut 29:10 all the **m** of Israel,
Deut 29:25 Then **m** would say
Deut 31:12 Gather the people together, **m**
Deut 32:26 of them to cease from among **m**
Deut 33: 6 not die, nor let his **m** be few
Josh 1:14 all your mighty **m** of valor
Josh 2: 1 **m** from Acacia Grove to spy
Josh 2: 2 **m** have come here tonight from
Josh 2: 3 Bring out the **m** who have come
Josh 2: 4 Then the woman took the two **m**
Josh 2: 4 the **m** came to me, but I did
Josh 2: 5 was dark, that the **m** went out
Josh 2: 5 Where the **m** went I do not
Josh 2: 7 Then the **m** pursued them by
Josh 2: 9 and said to the **m**
Josh 2:14 So the **m** answered her, "Our
Josh 2:17 Then the **m** said to her
Josh 2:23 So the two **m** returned,
Josh 3:12 **m** from the tribes of Israel
Josh 4: 2 twelve **m** from the people, one
Josh 4: 4 Joshua called the twelve **m**
Josh 4:12 the **m** of Reuben, the **m** of Gad
Josh 5: 4 were males, all the **m** of war
Josh 5: 6 the people who were **m** of war
Josh 6: 2 and the mighty **m** of valor
Josh 6: 3 the city, all you **m** of war
Josh 6: 9 The armed **m** went before the
Josh 6:13 the armed **m** went before them
Josh 6:22 two **m** who had spied out the
Josh 6:23 And the young **m** who had been
Josh 7: 2 Now Joshua sent **m** from
Josh 7: 2 So the **m** went up and spied
Josh 7: 3 two or three thousand **m** go up
Josh 7: 4 **m** went up there from the
Josh 7: 4 they fled before the **m** of Ai
Josh 7: 5 the **m** of Ai struck down about
Josh 7: 5 down about thirty-six **m**, for
Josh 8: 3 thousand mighty **m** of valor
Josh 8:12 he took about five thousand **m**
Josh 8:14 it, that the **m** of the city
Josh 8:20 And when the **m** of Ai looked
Josh 8:21 and struck down the **m** of Ai
Josh 8:25 all who fell that day, both **m**
Josh 9: 6 to him and to the **m** of Israel,
Josh 9: 7 But the **m** of Israel said to
Josh 9:14 Then the **m** of Israel took
Josh 10: 2 Ai, and all its **m** were mighty
Josh 10: 6 And the **m** of Gibeon sent to
Josh 10: 7 and all the mighty **m** of valor
Josh 10:18 set **m** by it to guard them
Josh 10:24 for all the **m** of Israel, and
Josh 10:24 **m** of war who went with him
Josh 18: 4 you three **m** for each tribe
Josh 18: 8 Then the **m** arose to go away
Josh 18: 9 So the **m** went, passed through
Josh 24:11 And the **m** of Jericho fought
Judg 1: 4 ten thousand **m** at Bezek
Judg 1:23 sent **m** to spy out Bethel
Judg 3:29 about ten thousand **m** of Moab
Judg 3:29 of Moab, all stout **m** of valor
Judg 3:31 who killed six hundred **m** of
Judg 4: 6 **m** of the sons of Naphtali
Judg 4:10 thousand **m** under his command
Judg 4:14 ten thousand **m** following him
Judg 6:27 So Gideon took ten **m** from
Judg 6:27 the **m** of the city too much to
Judg 6:28 when the **m** of the city arose
Judg 6:30 Then the **m** of the city said
Judg 7: 6 mouth, was three hundred **m**
Judg 7: 7 By the three hundred **m** who
Judg 7: 8 those three hundred **m**
Judg 7:11 armed **m** who were in the camp
Judg 7:16 **m** into three companies, and he
Judg 7:19 the hundred **m** who were with
Judg 7:23 And the **m** of Israel gathered
Judg 7:24 Then all the **m** of Ephraim
Judg 8: 1 Now the **m** of Ephraim said to
Judg 8: 4 the three hundred **m** who were
Judg 8: 5 he said to the **m** of Succoth
Judg 8: 8 the **m** of Penuel answered him
Judg 8: 8 Penuel answered him as the **m**
Judg 8: 9 also spoke to the **m** of Penuel
Judg 8:10 about fifteen thousand **m**
Judg 8:10 twenty thousand **m** who drew
Judg 8:14 young man of the **m** of Succoth
Judg 8:14 its elders, seventy-seven **m**
Judg 8:15 he came to the **m** of Succoth
Judg 8:15 give bread to your weary **m**
Judg 8:16 he taught the **m** of Succoth
Judg 8:17 and killed the **m** of the city
Judg 8:18 What kind of **m** were they whom
Judg 8:22 Then the **m** of Israel said to
Judg 9: 2 of all the **m** of Shechem
Judg 9: 3 of all the **m** of Shechem
Judg 9: 4 hired worthless and reckless **m**
Judg 9: 6 all the **m** of Shechem gathered
Judg 9: 7 you **m** of Shechem, that God
Judg 9: 9 which they honor God and **m**
Judg 9:13 which cheers both God and **m**
Judg 9:18 king over the **m** of Shechem
Judg 9:20 and devour the **m** of Shechem
Judg 9:20 come from the **m** of Shechem
Judg 9:23 and the **m** of Shechem
Judg 9:23 and the **m** of Shechem dealt
Judg 9:24 and on the **m** of Shechem, who
Judg 9:25 the **m** of Shechem set **m** in
Judg 9:26 the **m** of Shechem put their
Judg 9:28 Serve the **m** of Hamor the
Judg 9:36 mountains as if they were **m**
Judg 9:39 out, leading the **m** of Shechem
Judg 9:46 Now when all the **m** of the
Judg 9:47 the **m** of the tower of Shechem
Judg 9:49 died, about a thousand **m** and
Judg 9:51 in the city, and all the **m**
Judg 9:54 lest **m** say of me, 'A woman
Judg 9:55 when the **m** of Israel saw that
Judg 9:57 And all the evil of the **m** of
Judg 11: 3 worthless **m** banded together
Judg 12: 1 Then the **m** of Ephraim
Judg 12: 4 together all the **m** of Gilead
Judg 12: 4 And the **m** of Gilead defeated
Judg 12: 5 the **m** of Gilead would say
Judg 14:10 for young **m** used to do so
Judg 14:18 So the **m** of the city said to
Judg 14:19 and killed thirty of their **m**
Judg 15:10 And the **m** of Judah said,
Judg 15:11 Then three thousand **m** of
Judg 15:15 killed a thousand **m** with it
Judg 15:16 I have slain a thousand **m**
Judg 16: 9 there were **m** lying in wait
Judg 16:12 there were **m** lying in wait,

Judg 16:27 Now the temple was full of **m**
Judg 16:27 were about three thousand **m**
Judg 18: 2 children of Dan sent five **m**
Judg 18: 2 **m** of valor from Zorah and
Judg 18: 7 So the five **m** departed and
Judg 18:11 six hundred **m** of the family
Judg 18:14 Then the five **m** who had gone
Judg 18:16 The six hundred **m** armed with
Judg 18:17 Then the five **m** who had gone
Judg 18:17 gate with the six hundred **m**
Judg 18:22 the **m** who were in the houses
Judg 18:25 lest angry **m** fall upon you,
Judg 19:16 whereas the **m** of the place
Judg 19:22 **m** of the city, perverted **m**
Judg 19:25 But the **m** would not heed him
Judg 20: 5 the **m** of Gibeah rose against
Judg 20:10 We will take ten **m** out of
Judg 20:11 So all the **m** of Israel were
Judg 20:12 **m** through all the tribe of
Judg 20:13 therefore, deliver up the **m**
Judg 20:13 the perverted **m** who are in
Judg 20:15 thousand **m** who drew the sword
Judg 20:15 seven hundred select **m**
Judg 20:16 select **m** who were left-handed
Judg 20:17 the **m** of Israel numbered four
Judg 20:17 thousand **m** who drew the sword
Judg 20:17 all of these were **m** of war
Judg 20:20 the **m** of Israel went out to
Judg 20:20 and the **m** of Israel put
Judg 20:21 thousand **m** of the Israelites
Judg 20:22 the **m** of Israel, encouraged
Judg 20:29 Then Israel set **m** in ambush
Judg 20:31 about thirty **m** of Israel
Judg 20:33 So all the **m** of Israel rose
Judg 20:33 Then Israel's **m** in ambush
Judg 20:34 ten thousand select **m** from
Judg 20:36 The **m** of Israel had given
Judg 20:36 because they relied on the **m**
Judg 20:37 And the **m** in ambush quickly
Judg 20:37 the **m** in ambush spread out and
Judg 20:38 between the **m** of Israel and
Judg 20:38 the **m** in ambush was that they
Judg 20:39 whereupon the **m** of Israel
Judg 20:39 thirty of the **m** of Israel
Judg 20:41 when the **m** of Israel turned
Judg 20:41 the **m** of Benjamin panicked,
Judg 20:42 their backs before the **m** of
Judg 20:44 thousand **m** of Benjamin fell
Judg 20:44 all these were **m** of valor
Judg 20:46 thousand **m** who drew the sword
Judg 20:46 all these were **m** of valor
Judg 20:47 But six hundred **m** turned and
Judg 20:48 the **m** of Israel turned back
Judg 20:48 from every city, **m** and beasts,
Judg 21: 1 Now the **m** of Israel had sworn
Judg 21:10 of their most valiant **m**, and
Ruth 2: 9 the young **m** not to touch you
Ruth 2: 9 what the young **m** have drawn
Ruth 2:15 Boaz commanded his young **m**
Ruth 2:21 stay close by my young **m**
Ruth 3:10 you did not go after young **m**
Ruth 4: 2 he took ten **m** of the elders
1Sa 2: 4 of the mighty **m** are broken
1Sa 2:17 the sin of the young **m** was
1Sa 2:17 for **m** abhorred the offering
1Sa 2:26 favor both with the LORD and **m**
1Sa 2:33 But any of your **m** whom I do
1Sa 4: 2 **m** of the army in the field
1Sa 4: 9 and conduct yourselves like **m**
1Sa 4: 9 Conduct yourselves like **m**
1Sa 5: 7 when the **m** of Ashdod saw how
1Sa 5: 9 He struck the **m** of the city
1Sa 5:12 the **m** who did not die were
1Sa 6:10 Then the **m** did so
1Sa 6:15 Then the **m** of Beth Shemesh
1Sa 6:19 struck the **m** of Beth Shemesh
1Sa 6:19 seventy **m** of the people, and
1Sa 6:20 the **m** of Beth Shemesh said,
1Sa 7: 1 Then the **m** of Kirjath Jearim
1Sa 7:11 the **m** of Israel went out of
1Sa 8:16 and your finest young **m** and
1Sa 8:22 said to the **m** of Israel
1Sa 10: 2 today, you will find two **m** by
1Sa 10: 3 There three **m** going up to God
1Sa 10:26 and valiant **m** went with him,
1Sa 11: 1 all the **m** of Jabesh said to
1Sa 11: 5 the words of the **m** of Jabesh
1Sa 11: 8 and the **m** of Judah thirty
1Sa 11: 9 say to the **m** of Jabesh Gilead
1Sa 11: 9 it to the **m** of Jabesh, and

1Sa 11:10 Therefore the **m** of Jabesh
1Sa 11:12 Bring the **m**, that we may put
1Sa 11:15 all the **m** of Israel rejoiced
1Sa 13: 2 three thousand **m** of Israel
1Sa 13: 6 When the **m** of Israel saw that
1Sa 13:15 with him, about six hundred **m**
1Sa 14: 2 him were about six hundred **m**
1Sa 14: 8 let us cross over to these **m**
1Sa 14:12 Then the **m** of the garrison
1Sa 14:14 made was about twenty **m**
1Sa 14:22 Likewise all the **m** of Israel
1Sa 14:24 And the **m** of Israel were
1Sa 15: 4 and ten thousand **m** of Judah
1Sa 16:11 Are all the young **m** here
1Sa 17: 2 the **m** of Israel were gathered
1Sa 17:19 all the **m** of Israel were in
1Sa 17:24 all the **m** of Israel, when
1Sa 17:25 So the **m** of Israel said
1Sa 17:26 to the **m** who stood by him
1Sa 17:28 heard when he spoke to the **m**
1Sa 17:52 Now the **m** of Israel and Judah
1Sa 18: 5 set him over the **m** of war
1Sa 18:27 arose and went, he and his **m**
1Sa 18:27 hundred **m** of the Philistines
1Sa 21: 2 directed my young **m** to such
1Sa 21: 4 if the young **m** have at least
1Sa 21: 5 of the young **m** are holy, and
1Sa 22: 2 about four hundred **m** with him
1Sa 22: 6 the **m** who were with him had
1Sa 22:18 **m** who wore a linen ephod
1Sa 22:19 the edge of the sword, both **m**
1Sa 23: 3 And David's **m** said to him,
1Sa 23: 5 and his **m** went to Keilah and
1Sa 23: 8 to besiege David and his **m**
1Sa 23:11 Will the **m** of Keilah deliver
1Sa 23:12 Will the **m** of Keilah deliver
1Sa 23:12 my **m** into the hand of Saul
1Sa 23:13 So David and his **m**, about six
1Sa 23:24 his **m** were in the Wilderness
1Sa 23:25 his **m** went to seek him, they
1Sa 23:26 his **m** on the other side of
1Sa 23:26 his **m** were encircling David
1Sa 23:26 David and his **m** to take them
1Sa 24: 2 chosen **m** from all Israel, and
1Sa 24: 2 his **m** on the Rocks of the
1Sa 24: 3 his **m** were staying in the
1Sa 24: 4 Then the **m** of David said to
1Sa 24: 6 And he said to his **m**, "The
1Sa 24: 9 to the words of **m** who say
1Sa 24:22 David and his **m** went up to the
1Sa 25: 5 David sent ten young **m**
1Sa 25: 5 and David said to the young **m**
1Sa 25: 8 Ask your young **m**, and they
1Sa 25: 8 Therefore let my young **m** find
1Sa 25: 9 So when David's young **m** came
1Sa 25:11 give it to **m** when I do not
1Sa 25:12 So David's young **m** turned on
1Sa 25:13 Then David said to his **m**
1Sa 25:13 hundred **m** went with David
1Sa 25:14 of the young **m** told Abigail
1Sa 25:15 But the **m** were very good to
1Sa 25:20 and there were David and his **m**
1Sa 25:25 did not see the young **m** of my
1Sa 25:27 young **m** who follow my lord
1Sa 26: 2 chosen **m** of Israel with him
1Sa 26:19 if it is the children of **m**
1Sa 26:22 one of the young **m** come over
1Sa 27: 2 over with the six hundred **m**
1Sa 27: 3 Achish at Gath, he and his **m**
1Sa 27: 8 his **m** went up and raided the
1Sa 28: 1 me to battle, you and your **m**
1Sa 28: 8 he went, and two **m** with him
1Sa 29: 2 his **m** passed in review at the
1Sa 29: 4 not with the heads of these **m**
1Sa 29:11 his **m** rose early to depart in
1Sa 30: 1 his **m** came to Ziklag, on the
1Sa 30: 3 his **m** came to the city, and
1Sa 30: 9 the six hundred **m** who were
1Sa 30:10 pursued, he and four hundred **m**
1Sa 30:17 young **m** who rode on camels
1Sa 30:21 came to the two hundred **m** who
1Sa 30:22 worthless **m** of those who went
1Sa 30:31 his **m** were accustomed to rove
1Sa 31: 1 the **m** of Israel fled from
1Sa 31: 4 these uncircumcised **m** come
1Sa 31: 6 all his **m** died together that
1Sa 31: 7 when the **m** of Israel who were
1Sa 31: 7 saw that the **m** of Israel had
1Sa 31:12 all the valiant **m** arose and
2Sa 1:11 so did all the **m** who were

2Sa 1:15 called one of the young **m**
2Sa 2: 3 up the **m** who were with him
2Sa 2: 4 Then the **m** of Judah came, and
2Sa 2: 4 The **m** of Jabesh Gilead were
2Sa 2: 5 to the **m** of Jabesh Gilead
2Sa 2:14 Let the young **m** now arise
2Sa 2:17 the **m** of Israel were beaten
2Sa 2:21 hold on one of the young **m**
2Sa 2:29 his **m** went on all that night
2Sa 2:30 David's servants nineteen **m**
2Sa 2:31 of Benjamin and Abner's **m**
2Sa 2:31 hundred and sixty **m** who died
2Sa 2:32 his **m** went all night, and they
2Sa 3:20 twenty **m** with him came to
2Sa 3:20 and the **m** who were with him
2Sa 3:34 a man falls before wicked **m**
2Sa 3:39 and these **m**, the sons of
2Sa 4: 2 Now Saul's son had two **m** who
2Sa 4:11 when wicked **m** have killed a
2Sa 4:12 David commanded his young **m**
2Sa 5: 6 and his **m** went to Jerusalem
2Sa 5:21 and his **m** carried them away
2Sa 6: 1 all the choice **m** of Israel
2Sa 6:19 both the women and the **m**, to
2Sa 7: 9 great **m** who are on the earth
2Sa 7:14 chasten him with the rod of **m**
2Sa 7:14 the blows of the sons of **m**
2Sa 10: 5 because the **m** were greatly
2Sa 10: 6 King Maacah one thousand **m**
2Sa 10: 6 Ish-Tob twelve thousand **m**
2Sa 10: 7 all the army of the mighty **m**
2Sa 10: 9 of the choice **m** of Israel
2Sa 11:16 he knew there were valiant **m**
2Sa 11:17 Then the **m** of the city came
2Sa 11:23 Surely the **m** prevailed
2Sa 12: 1 There were two **m** in one city
2Sa 13:32 have killed all the young **m**
2Sa 15: 1 fifty **m** to run before him
2Sa 15: 6 the hearts of the **m** of Israel
2Sa 15:11 **m** from Jerusalem who were
2Sa 15:13 The hearts of the **m** of Israel
2Sa 15:18 six hundred **m** who had
2Sa 15:22 the Gittite and all his **m** and
2Sa 16: 2 fruit for the young **m** to eat
2Sa 16: 6 all the mighty **m** were on his
2Sa 16:13 his **m** went along the road,
2Sa 16:15 the **m** of Israel, came to
2Sa 16:18 all the **m** of Israel choose,
2Sa 17: 1 me choose twelve thousand **m**
2Sa 17: 8 you know your father and his **m**
2Sa 17: 8 that they are mighty **m**
2Sa 17:10 are with him are valiant **m**
2Sa 17:12 all the **m** who are with him
2Sa 17:14 all the **m** of Israel said,
2Sa 17:24 all the **m** of Israel with him
2Sa 18: 7 of twenty thousand **m** took
2Sa 18:15 ten young **m** who bore Joab's
2Sa 18:28 the **m** who raised their hand
2Sa 19:14 hearts of all the **m** of Judah
2Sa 19:16 came down with the **m** of Judah
2Sa 19:17 **m** of Benjamin with him, and
2Sa 19:28 house were but dead **m** before
2Sa 19:35 longer the voice of singing **m**
2Sa 19:41 Just then all the **m** of Israel
2Sa 19:41 the **m** of Judah, stolen you
2Sa 19:41 all David's **m** with him across
2Sa 19:42 So all the **m** of Judah
2Sa 19:42 answered the **m** of Israel
2Sa 19:43 the **m** of Israel answered the
2Sa 19:43 answered the **m** of Judah, and
2Sa 19:43 Yet the words of the **m** of
2Sa 19:43 the words of the **m** of Israel
2Sa 20: 2 But the **m** of Judah, from the
2Sa 20: 4 Assemble the **m** of Judah for
2Sa 20: 5 to assemble the **m** of Judah
2Sa 20: 7 So Joab's **m**, with the
2Sa 20: 7 and all the mighty **m**, went
2Sa 20:11 of Joab's **m** stood near Amasa
2Sa 21: 6 let seven **m** of his
2Sa 21:12 from the **m** of Jabesh Gilead
2Sa 21:17 Then the **m** of David swore to
2Sa 23: 3 who rules over **m** must be just
2Sa 23: 8 the mighty **m** whom David had
2Sa 23: 8 eight hundred **m** at one time
2Sa 23: 9 one of the three mighty **m**
2Sa 23: 9 the **m** of Israel had retreated
2Sa 23:13 **m** went down at harvest time
2Sa 23:16 So the three mighty **m** broke
2Sa 23:17 the **m** who went in jeopardy of
2Sa 23:17 done by the three mighty **m**

2Sa 23:18 spear against three hundred **m**
2Sa 23:22 a name among three mighty **m**
2Sa 24: 9 valiant **m** who drew the sword
2Sa 24: 9 and the **m** of Judah were five
2Sa 24: 9 were five hundred thousand **m**
2Sa 24:15 thousand **m** of the people died
1Ki 1: 5 fifty **m** to run before him
1Ki 1: 8 the mighty **m** who belonged to
1Ki 1: 9 and all the **m** of Judah, the
1Ki 1:10 Benaiah, the mighty **m**, or
1Ki 2:32 down two **m** more righteous
1Ki 4:30 of all the **m** of the East and
1Ki 4:31 For he was wiser than all **m**
1Ki 4:34 **m** of all nations, from all
1Ki 5:13 force was thirty thousand **m**
1Ki 8: 2 all the **m** of Israel assembled
1Ki 8:39 hearts of all the sons of **m**)
1Ki 9:22 because they were **m** of war
1Ki 10: 8 Happy are your **m** and happy are
1Ki 11:18 they took **m** with them from
1Ki 11:24 So he gathered **m** to him and
1Ki 12: 8 consulted the young **m** who had
1Ki 12:10 Then the young **m** who had
1Ki 12:14 to the counsel of the young **m**
1Ki 12:21 chosen **m** who were warriors
1Ki 13:25 **m** passed by and saw the corpse
1Ki 18:13 how I hid one hundred **m** of
1Ki 18:22 are four hundred and fifty **m**
1Ki 20:17 **M** are coming out of Samaria
1Ki 20:30 of the **m** who were left
1Ki 20:33 Now the **m** were diligently
1Ki 21:10 and seat two **m**, scoundrels,
1Ki 21:11 So the **m** of his city, the
1Ki 21:13 And two **m**, scoundrels, came in
1Ki 22: 6 about four hundred **m**, and
2Ki 1: 9 of fifty with his fifty **m**
2Ki 1:10 consume you and your fifty **m**
2Ki 1:11 of fifty with his fifty **m**
2Ki 1:12 consume you and your fifty **m**
2Ki 1:13 of fifty with his fifty **m**
2Ki 2: 7 fifty **m** of the sons of the
2Ki 2:16 strong **m** with your servants
2Ki 2:17 Therefore they sent fifty **m**
2Ki 2:19 Then the **m** of the city said
2Ki 3:26 hundred **m** who drew swords
2Ki 4:22 send me one of the young **m**
2Ki 4:40 served it to the **m** to eat
2Ki 4:43 set this before one hundred **m**
2Ki 5:22 just now two young **m** of the
2Ki 5:24 then he let the **m** go, and they
2Ki 6:20 open the eyes of these **m**
2Ki 7: 3 **m** at the entrance of the gate
2Ki 7:13 let several **m** take five of
2Ki 8:12 their young **m** you will kill
2Ki 9:17 I see a company of **m**
2Ki 10: 6 take the heads of the **m**,
2Ki 10: 6 with the great **m** of the city
2Ki 10:11 Jezreel, and all his great **m**
2Ki 10:14 of Beth Eked, forty-two **m**
2Ki 10:24 eighty **m** on the outside, and
2Ki 10:24 If any of the **m** whom I have
2Ki 11: 9 Each of them took his **m** who
2Ki 12:15 the **m** into whose hand they
2Ki 15:25 him were fifty **m** of Gilead
2Ki 16: 6 drove the **m** of Judah from
2Ki 17:30 The **m** of Babylon made Succoth
2Ki 17:30 the **m** of Cuth made Nergal,
2Ki 17:30 the **m** of Hamath made Ashima,
2Ki 18:27 not to the **m** who sit on the
2Ki 20:14 What did these **m** say, and from
2Ki 23: 2 LORD with all the **m** of Judah
2Ki 23:14 places with the bones of **m**
2Ki 23:17 the **m** of the city told him,
2Ki 24:14 and all the mighty **m** of valor
2Ki 24:16 All the valiant **m**, seven
2Ki 25: 4 and all the **m** of war fled at
2Ki 25: 9 all the houses of the great **m**
2Ki 25:19 had charge of the **m** of war
2Ki 25:19 five **m** of the king's close
2Ki 25:19 sixty **m** of the people of the
2Ki 25:23 the armies, they and their **m**
2Ki 25:23 Maachathite, they and their **m**
2Ki 25:24 oath before them and their **m**
2Ki 25:25 royal family, came with ten **m**
1Ch 4:12 These were the **m** of Rechah
1Ch 4:22 the **m** of Chozeba, and Joash
1Ch 4:42 five hundred **m** of the sons of
1Ch 5:18 hundred and sixty valiant **m**
1Ch 5:18 **m** able to bear shield and
1Ch 5:21 hundred thousand of their **m**
1Ch 5:24 mighty **m** of valor, famous **m**
1Ch 6:31 Now these are the **m** whom
1Ch 7: 2 mighty **m** of valor in their
1Ch 7: 3 All five of them were chief **m**
1Ch 7: 5 were mighty **m** of valor,
1Ch 7: 7 thirty-four mighty **m** of valor
1Ch 7: 9 two hundred mighty **m** of valor
1Ch 7:11 **m** of valor fit to go out for
1Ch 7:40 fathers' houses, choice **m**
1Ch 7:40 choice **m**, mighty **m** of valor
1Ch 8:28 by their generations, chief **m**
1Ch 8:40 Ulam were mighty **m** of valor
1Ch 9: 9 All these **m** were heads of a
1Ch 9:13 They were very able **m** for the
1Ch 10: 1 the **m** of Israel fled from
1Ch 10: 4 these uncircumcised **m** come
1Ch 10: 7 when all the **m** of Israel who
1Ch 10:12 all the valiant **m** arose and
1Ch 11:10 the mighty **m** whom David had
1Ch 11:11 the mighty **m** whom David had
1Ch 11:12 was one of the three mighty **m**
1Ch 11:15 **m** went down to the rock to
1Ch 11:19 I drink the blood of these **m**
1Ch 11:19 done by the three mighty **m**
1Ch 11:20 spear against three hundred **m**
1Ch 11:21 honored than the other two **m**
1Ch 11:24 a name among three mighty **m**
1Ch 12: 1 Now these were the **m** who came
1Ch 12: 1 they were among the mighty **m**
1Ch 12: 8 mighty **m** of valor, **m** trained
1Ch 12:21 were all mighty **m** of valor
1Ch 12:25 mighty **m** of valor fit for war
1Ch 12:30 mighty **m** of valor, famous **m**
1Ch 12:33 stouthearted **m** who could keep
1Ch 12:38 All these **m** of war, who could
1Ch 17: 8 great **m** who are on the earth
1Ch 19: 5 and told David about the **m**
1Ch 19: 5 because the **m** were greatly
1Ch 19: 8 all the army of the mighty **m**
1Ch 19:10 of the choice **m** of Israel
1Ch 21: 5 thousand **m** who drew the sword
1Ch 21: 5 seventy thousand **m** who drew
1Ch 21:14 thousand **m** of Israel fell
1Ch 22:15 all types of skillful **m** for
1Ch 26: 6 they were **m** of great ability
1Ch 26: 7 and Semachiah were able **m**
1Ch 26: 8 able **m** with strength for the
1Ch 26: 9 and brethren, eighteen able **m**
1Ch 26:12 among the chief **m**, having
1Ch 26:30 thousand seven hundred able **m**
1Ch 26:31 capable **m** at Jazer of Gilead
1Ch 26:32 thousand seven hundred able **m**
1Ch 28: 1 the officials, the valiant **m**
1Ch 28: 1 and all the mighty **m** of valor
1Ch 29:24 the leaders and the mighty **m**
2Ch 2: 2 thousand **m** to bear burdens
2Ch 2: 7 **m** who are with me in Judah
2Ch 2:14 to him, with your skillful **m**
2Ch 2:14 with the skillful **m** of my
2Ch 5: 3 Therefore all the **m** of Israel
2Ch 6:18 dwell with **m** on the earth
2Ch 6:30 the hearts of the sons of **m**)
2Ch 8: 9 Some were **m** of war, captains
2Ch 9: 7 Happy are your **m** and happy are
2Ch 10: 8 consulted the young **m** who had
2Ch 10:10 Then the young **m** who had
2Ch 10:14 to the counsel of the young **m**
2Ch 11: 1 chosen **m** who were warriors
2Ch 13: 3 hundred thousand choice **m**
2Ch 13: 3 choice **m**, mighty **m** of valor
2Ch 13:15 Then the **m** of Judah gave a
2Ch 13:15 as the **m** of Judah shouted, it
2Ch 13:17 choice **m** of Israel fell slain
2Ch 14: 8 **m** from Judah who carried
2Ch 14: 8 eighty thousand **m** who carried
2Ch 14: 8 these were mighty **m** of valor
2Ch 14: 9 with an army of a million **m**
2Ch 17:13 **m** of war, mighty **m** of valor
2Ch 17:14 thousand mighty **m** of valor
2Ch 17:16 thousand mighty **m** of valor
2Ch 17:17 thousand **m** armed with bow
2Ch 18: 5 together, four hundred **m**, and
2Ch 23: 8 each man took his **m** who were
2Ch 24:24 with a small company of **m**
2Ch 25: 5 hundred thousand choice **m**
2Ch 25: 6 **m** of valor from Israel for
2Ch 26:11 **m** who went out to war by
2Ch 26:12 officers of the mighty **m** of
2Ch 26:15 invented by skillful **m**, to
2Ch 26:17 the LORD, who were valiant **m**
2Ch 28: 6 in one day, all valiant **m**
2Ch 28:14 So the armed **m** left the
2Ch 28:15 Then the **m** who were
2Ch 31:19 city, there were **m** who were
2Ch 34:12 the **m** did the work faithfully
2Ch 34:30 LORD, with all the **m** of Judah
2Ch 35:25 to this day all the singing **m**
2Ch 36:17 who killed their young **m** with
Ezra 1: 4 let the **m** of his place help
Ezra 2: 2 The number of the **m** of the
Ezra 2:22 the **m** of Netophah, fifty-six
Ezra 2:23 the **m** of Anathoth, one
Ezra 2:27 the **m** of Michmas, one hundred
Ezra 2:28 the **m** of Bethel and Ai, two
Ezra 2:65 and they had two hundred **m**
Ezra 3:12 houses, who were old **m**, who
Ezra 4:11 from your servants the **m** of
Ezra 4:21 command to make these **m** cease
Ezra 5: 4 **m** who were constructing this
Ezra 5:10 write the names of the **m** who
Ezra 6: 8 given immediately to these **m**
Ezra 7:28 I gathered chief **m** of Israel
Ezra 8:16 Elnathan, **m** of understanding
Ezra 8:18 sons and brothers, eighteen **m**
Ezra 8:19 and their sons, twenty **m**
Ezra 10: 1 very large congregation of **m**
Ezra 10: 9 So all the **m** of Judah and
Ezra 10:17 questioning all the **m** who had
Neh 1: 2 came with **m** from Judah
Neh 2:12 night, I and a few **m** with me
Neh 3: 2 the **m** of Jericho built
Neh 3: 7 the **m** of Gibeon and Mizpah,
Neh 3:22 the **m** of the plain, made
Neh 4:13 Therefore I positioned **m**
Neh 4:21 half of the **m** held the spears
Neh 4:23 nor the **m** of the guard who
Neh 5: 5 for other **m** have our lands and
Neh 7: 7 The number of the **m** of the
Neh 7:26 the **m** of Bethlehem and
Neh 7:27 the **m** of Anathoth, one
Neh 7:28 the **m** of Beth Azmaveth,
Neh 7:29 the **m** of Kirjath Jearim,
Neh 7:30 the **m** of Ramah and Geba, six
Neh 7:31 the **m** of Michmas, one hundred
Neh 7:32 the **m** of Bethel and Ai, one
Neh 7:33 the **m** of the other Nebo,
Neh 7:67 two hundred and forty-five **m**
Neh 8: 2 before the congregation, of **m**
Neh 8: 3 until midday, before the **m**
Neh 11: 2 the **m** who willingly offered
Neh 11: 6 and sixty-eight valiant **m**
Neh 11:14 mighty **m** of valor, were one
Neh 11:14 the son of one of the great **m**
Neh 13:16 **M** of Tyre dwelt there also,
Esth 1:13 **m** who understood the times
Esth 6:13 happened to him, his wise **m**
Esth 9: 6 and destroyed five hundred **m**
Esth 9:12 **m** in Shushan the citadel, and
Esth 9:15 three hundred **m** at Shushan
Job 1:19 and it fell on the young **m**
Job 4:13 when deep sleep falls on **m**
Job 7:20 I done to You, O watcher of **m**
Job 11: 3 talk make **m** hold their peace
Job 11:11 For He knows deceitful **m**
Job 12:12 Wisdom is with aged **m**, and
Job 15:18 what wise **m** have told, not
Job 17: 6 one in whose face **m** spit
Job 17: 8 Upright **m** are astonished at
Job 22:15 way which wicked **m** have trod
Job 27:23 **M** shall clap their hands at
Job 28: 4 they hang far away from **m**
Job 29: 8 the young **m** saw me and hid,
Job 29:21 **M** listened to me and waited,
Job 30: 1 me, **m** younger than I, whose
Job 30: 5 were driven out from among **m**
Job 30: 8 of fools, yes, sons of vile **m**
Job 31:31 if the **m** of my tent have not
Job 32: 1 So these three **m** ceased
Job 32: 5 in the mouth of these three **m**
Job 32: 9 Great **m** are not always wise,
Job 33:15 when deep sleep falls upon **m**
Job 33:16 Then He opens the ears of **m**
Job 33:27 And he looks at **m** and says, 'I
Job 34: 2 Hear my words, you wise **m**
Job 34: 8 and walks with wicked **m**
Job 34:10 to me, you **m** of understanding
Job 34:24 mighty **m** without inquiry, and
Job 34:26 He strikes them as wicked **m**
Job 34:34 **M** of understanding say to me,
Job 34:34 me, wise **m** who listen to me

Job 34:36 are like those of wicked **m**
Job 35:12 of the pride of evil **m**
Job 36:24 work, of which **m** have sung
Job 37: 7 that all **m** may know His work
Job 37:21 Even now **m** cannot look at the
Job 37:24 Therefore **m** fear Him
Ps 4: 2 How long, O you sons of **m**
Ps 9:20 know themselves to be but **m**
Ps 11: 4 eyelids test the sons of **m**
Ps 12: 1 from among the sons of **m**
Ps 12: 8 exalted among the sons of **m**
Ps 14: 2 heaven upon the children of **m**
Ps 17: 4 Concerning the works of **m**
Ps 17:14 With Your hand from **m**,
Ps 17:14 From **m** of the world who have
Ps 21:10 from among the sons of **m**
Ps 22: 6 A reproach of **m**, and despised
Ps 26: 9 my life with bloodthirsty **m**
Ps 31:19 the presence of the sons of **m**
Ps 33:13 He sees all the sons of **m**
Ps 36: 7 **m** put their trust under the
Ps 45: 2 are fairer than the sons of **m**
Ps 49:10 For he sees that wise **m** die
Ps 49:18 he blesses himself (For **m**
Ps 53: 2 heaven upon the children of **m**
Ps 55:23 deceitful **m** shall not live
Ps 57: 4 sons of **m** Who are set on fire
Ps 58: 1 uprightly, you sons of **m**
Ps 58:11 So that **m** will say, "Surely
Ps 59: 2 save me from bloodthirsty **m**
Ps 62: 9 Surely **m** of low degree are a
Ps 62: 9 **M** of high degree are a lie
Ps 64: 9 All **m** shall fear, And shall
Ps 66: 5 doing toward the sons of **m**
Ps 66:12 You have caused **m** to ride
Ps 68:18 have received gifts among **m**
Ps 72:17 **m** shall be blessed in Him
Ps 73: 5 are not in trouble as other **m**
Ps 73: 5 are they plagued like other **m**
Ps 74: 5 They seem like **m** who lift up
Ps 76: 5 none of the mighty **m** have
Ps 78:25 **M** ate angels' food
Ps 78:31 down the choice **m** of Israel
Ps 78:60 which He had placed among **m**
Ps 78:63 fire consumed their young **m**
Ps 82: 7 But you shall die like **m**, And
Ps 83:18 That **m** may know that You,
Ps 86:14 And a mob of violent **m** have
Ps 89:47 created all the children of **m**
Ps 90: 3 Return, O children of **m**
Ps 107: 8 that **m** would give thanks to
Ps 107: 8 works to the children of **m**
Ps 107:15 that **m** would give thanks to
Ps 107:15 works to the children of **m**
Ps 107:21 that **m** would give thanks to
Ps 107:21 works to the children of **m**
Ps 107:31 that **m** would give thanks to
Ps 107:31 works to the children of **m**
Ps 115:16 given to the children of **m**
Ps 116:11 my haste, "All **m** are liars
Ps 119:136 Because **m** do not keep Your
Ps 124: 2 When **m** rose up against us,
Ps 139:19 therefore, you bloodthirsty **m**
Ps 140: 1 me, O LORD, from evil **m**
Ps 140: 1 Preserve me from violent **m**
Ps 140: 4 Preserve me from violent **m**
Ps 141: 4 With **m** who work iniquity
Ps 145: 6 **M** shall speak of the might of
Ps 145:12 the sons of **m** His mighty acts
Ps 148:12 Both young **m** and maidens
Ps 148:12 Old **m** and children
Prov 7:26 slain by her were strong **m**
Prov 8: 4 To you, O **m**, I call, and my
Prov 8: 4 my voice is to the sons of **m**
Prov 8:31 was with the sons of **m**
Prov 11:16 but ruthless **m** retain riches
Prov 12:12 covet the catch of evil **m**
Prov 13:20 with wise **m** will be wise, but
Prov 15:11 the hearts of the sons of **m**
Prov 17: 6 are the crown of old **m**, and
Prov 18:16 and brings him before great **m**
Prov 20: 6 Most **m** will proclaim each his
Prov 20:29 of young **m** is their strength
Prov 20:29 of old **m** is their gray head
Prov 22:29 not stand before unknown **m**
Prov 23:28 the unfaithful among **m**
Prov 24: 1 Do not be envious of evil **m**
Prov 24: 9 is an abomination to **m**
Prov 25: 1 of Solomon which the **m** of
Prov 25: 6 stand in the place of great **m**
Prov 26:16 **m** who can answer sensibly
Prov 28: 5 Evil **m** do not understand
Prov 28:12 arise, **m** hide themselves
Prov 28:28 arise, **m** hide themselves
Prov 29: 8 but wise **m** turn away wrath
Prov 30:14 and the needy from among **m**
Eccl 2: 3 was good for the sons of **m** to
Eccl 2: 8 the delights of the sons of **m**
Eccl 3:10 sons of **m** are to be occupied
Eccl 3:14 that **m** should fear before Him
Eccl 3:18 the estate of the sons of **m**
Eccl 3:19 of **m** also happens to beasts
Eccl 3:21 the spirit of the sons of **m**
Eccl 6: 1 sun, and it is common among **m**
Eccl 7: 2 for that is the end of all **m**
Eccl 8:11 the heart of the sons of **m** is
Eccl 8:14 are just **m** to whom it happens
Eccl 8:14 there are wicked **m** to whom it
Eccl 9: 3 sons of **m** are full of evil
Eccl 9:11 the wise, nor riches to **m** of
Eccl 9:11 nor favor to **m** of skill
Eccl 9:12 so the sons of **m** are snared
Eccl 9:14 little city with few **m** in it
Eccl 12: 3 and the strong **m** bow down
Song 3: 7 sixty valiant **m** around it
Song 4: 4 all shields of mighty **m**
Is 2:11 the haughtiness of **m** shall be
Is 2:17 the haughtiness of **m** shall be
Is 3:25 Your **m** shall fall by the
Is 5: 3 **m** of Judah, judge, please,
Is 5: 7 and the **m** of Judah are His
Is 5:13 honorable **m** are famished, and
Is 5:22 Woe to **m** mighty at drinking
Is 5:22 woe to **m** valiant for mixing
Is 6:12 LORD has removed **m** far away
Is 7:13 thing for you to weary **m**, but
Is 7:24 and bows **m** will come there,
Is 9: 3 as **m** rejoice when they divide
Is 9:17 have no joy in their young **m**
Is 11:15 make **m** cross over dryshod
Is 13:18 dash the young **m** to pieces
Is 19:12 Where are your wise **m**
Is 21: 9 of **m** with a pair of horsemen
Is 21:17 the mighty **m** of the people of
Is 22: 2 Your slain **m** are not slain
Is 22: 6 the quiver with chariots of **m**
Is 23: 4 neither do I rear young **m**
Is 24: 6 are burned, and few **m** are left
Is 28:14 of the LORD, you scornful **m**
Is 29:11 which **m** deliver to one who is
Is 29:13 by the commandment of **m**,
Is 29:14 of their wise **m** shall perish
Is 29:14 prudent **m** shall be hidden
Is 29:19 and the poor among **m** shall
Is 31: 3 Now the Egyptians are **m**, and
Is 31: 8 and his young **m** shall become
Is 36:12 not to the **m** who sit on the
Is 38:16 LORD, by these things **m** live
Is 39: 3 What did these **m** say, and from
Is 40:30 the young **m** shall utterly
Is 41:14 worm Jacob, you **m** of Israel
Is 43: 4 I will give **m** for you, and
Is 44:11 the workmen, they are mere **m**
Is 44:25 Who turns wise **m** backward
Is 45:14 **m** of stature, shall come over
Is 45:24 To Him **m** shall come, and all
Is 46: 8 this, and show yourselves **m**
Is 51: 7 do not fear the reproach of **m**
Is 52:14 form more than the sons of **m**
Is 53: 3 is despised and rejected by **m**
Is 57: 1 merciful **m** are taken away,
Is 59:10 we are as dead **m** in desolate
Is 60:11 that **m** may bring to you the
Is 61: 6 **m** shall call you the Servants
Is 64: 4 world **m** have not heard nor
Is 66:24 the **m** who have transgressed
Jer 3: 2 have you not lain with **m**
Jer 4: 3 the LORD to the **m** of Judah
Jer 4: 4 you **m** of Judah and inhabitants
Jer 5: 5 I will go to the great **m** and
Jer 5:16 they are all mighty **m**
Jer 5:26 My people are found wicked **m**
Jer 5:26 they set a trap; they catch **m**
Jer 6:11 assembly of young **m** together
Jer 6:23 as **m** of war set in array
Jer 8: 9 The wise **m** are ashamed, they
Jer 9: 2 lodging place for wayfaring **m**
Jer 9: 2 an assembly of treacherous **m**
Jer 9:10 nor can **m** hear the voice of
Jer 9:21 and the young **m**
Jer 9:22 Even the carcasses of **m**
Jer 10: 7 all the wise **m** of the nations
Jer 10: 9 all the work of skillful **m**
Jer 11: 2 and speak to the **m** of Judah
Jer 11: 9 found among the **m** of Judah
Jer 11:21 the LORD concerning the **m** of
Jer 11:22 The young **m** shall die by the
Jer 11:23 on the **m** of Anathoth, even
Jer 15: 8 the mother of the young **m**
Jer 15:10 nor have **m** lent to me for
Jer 16: 6 neither shall **m** lament for
Jer 16: 7 Nor shall **m** break bread in
Jer 16: 7 nor shall **m** give them the cup
Jer 17:25 accompanied by the **m** of Judah
Jer 18:11 speak to the **m** of Judah and
Jer 18:21 Let their **m** be put to death,
Jer 18:21 their young **m** be slain by the
Jer 19:10 of the **m** who go with you,
Jer 26:21 king, with all his mighty **m**
Jer 26:22 the king sent **m** to Egypt
Jer 26:22 other **m** who went with him to
Jer 31:13 in the dance, and the young **m**
Jer 32:19 all the ways of the sons of **m**
Jer 32:20 and in Israel and among other **m**
Jer 32:32 the **m** of Judah, and the
Jer 32:44 **M** will buy fields for money,
Jer 33: 5 of **m** whom I will slay in My
Jer 34:18 I will give the **m** who have
Jer 35:13 Go and tell the **m** of Judah
Jer 36:31 on the **m** of Judah all the
Jer 37:10 only wounded **m** among them
Jer 38: 4 **m** of war who remain in this
Jer 38: 9 these **m** have done evil in all
Jer 38:10 from here thirty **m** with you
Jer 38:11 took the **m** with him and went
Jer 38:16 of these **m** who seek your life
Jer 39: 4 all the **m** of war saw them,
Jer 39:17 the **m** of whom you are afraid
Jer 40: 7 the fields, they and their **m**
Jer 40: 7 and had committed to him **m**
Jer 40: 8 Maachathite, they and their **m**
Jer 40: 9 oath before them and their **m**
Jer 41: 1 came with ten **m** to Gedaliah
Jer 41: 2 the ten **m** who were with him,
Jer 41: 3 found there, the **m** of war
Jer 41: 5 that certain **m** came from
Jer 41: 5 eighty **m** with their beards
Jer 41: 7 he and the **m** who were with him
Jer 41: 8 But ten **m** were found among
Jer 41: 9 of the **m** whom he had slain
Jer 41:12 they took all the **m** and went
Jer 41:15 from Johanan with eight **m**
Jer 41:16 the mighty **m** of war and the
Jer 42:17 **m** who set their faces to go
Jer 43: 2 and all the proud **m** spoke
Jer 43: 6 **m**, women, children, the
Jer 43: 9 the sight of the **m** of Judah
Jer 44:15 Then all the **m** who knew that
Jer 44:20 the **m**, the women, and all the
Jer 44:27 all the **m** of Judah who are in
Jer 46: 9 let the mighty **m** come forth
Jer 46:15 are your valiant **m** swept away
Jer 47: 2 then the **m** shall cry, and all
Jer 48:14 and strong **m** for the war'
Jer 48:15 Her chosen young **m** have gone
Jer 48:31 mourn for the **m** of Kir Heres
Jer 48:36 wail for the **m** of Kir Heres
Jer 49:15 nations, despised among **m**
Jer 49:22 The heart of the mighty **m** of
Jer 49:26 Therefore her young **m** shall
Jer 49:26 all the **m** of war shall be cut
Jer 49:28 devastate the **m** of the East
Jer 50:30 Therefore her young **m** shall
Jer 50:30 all her **m** of war shall be cut
Jer 50:35 her princes and her wise **m**
Jer 50:36 sword is against her mighty **m**
Jer 51: 3 Do not spare her young **m**
Jer 51:14 Surely I will fill you with **m**
Jer 51:30 The mighty **m** of Babylon have
Jer 51:32 the **m** of war are terrified
Jer 51:56 and her mighty **m** are taken
Jer 51:57 drunk her princes and wise **m**
Jer 51:57 her deputies, and her mighty **m**
Jer 52: 7 all the **m** of war fled and went
Jer 52:13 all the houses of the great **m**
Jer 52:25 had charge of the **m** of war
Jer 52:25 seven **m** of the king's close
Jer 52:25 sixty **m** of the people of the
Lam 1:15 all my mighty **m** in my midst
Lam 1:15 me to crush my young **m**

Lam 1:18 my young **m** have gone into
Lam 2:21 my young **m** have fallen by the
Lam 3:33 nor grieve the children of **m**
Lam 5:13 Young **m** ground at the
Lam 5:14 the young **m** from their music
Ezek 6: 4 slain **m** before your idols
Ezek 6:13 when their slain **m** are among
Ezek 8:11 stood before them seventy **m**
Ezek 8:16 were about twenty-five **m** with
Ezek 9: 2 suddenly six **m** came from the
Ezek 9: 4 foreheads of the **m** who sigh
Ezek 9: 6 Utterly slay old and young **m**
Ezek 11: 1 the gate were twenty-five **m**
Ezek 11: 2 these are the **m** who devise
Ezek 12:16 few of their **m** from the sword
Ezek 14: 3 these **m** have set up their
Ezek 14:14 Though these three **m**, Noah,
Ezek 14:16 these three **m** were in it, as
Ezek 14:18 these three **m** were in it, as
Ezek 15: 3 Or can **m** make a peg from it
Ezek 16:33 **M** make payment to all harlots
Ezek 19: 3 catch prey, and he devoured **m**
Ezek 19: 6 he devoured **m**
Ezek 21:14 sword that slays the great **m**
Ezek 21:31 into the hands of brutal **m**
Ezek 22: 9 In you are **m** who slander to
Ezek 22:10 In you **m** uncover their
Ezek 22:20 As **m** gather silver, bronze,
Ezek 23: 6 all of them desirable young **m**
Ezek 23: 7 of them choice **m** of Assyria
Ezek 23:12 all of them desirable young **m**
Ezek 23:14 she looked at **m** portrayed on
Ezek 23:23 all of them desirable young **m**
Ezek 23:23 and **m** of renown, all of them
Ezek 23:40 sent for **m** to come from afar
Ezek 23:42 with **m** of the common sort
Ezek 23:44 as **m** go in to a woman who
Ezek 23:45 But righteous **m** will judge
Ezek 25: 4 to the **m** of the East, and they
Ezek 25:10 To the **m** of the East I will
Ezek 26:10 as **m** enter a city that has
Ezek 26:17 one inhabited by seafaring **m**
Ezek 27: 8 your own wise **m**, O Tyre, were
Ezek 27: 9 its wise **m** were in you to
Ezek 27:10 were in your army as **m** of war
Ezek 27:11 **M** of Arvad with your army
Ezek 27:11 the **m** of Gammad were in your
Ezek 27:15 The **m** of Dedan were your
Ezek 27:27 all your **m** of war who are in
Ezek 30: 5 the **m** of the lands who are
Ezek 30:17 The young **m** of Aven and Pi
Ezek 31:14 among the children of **m** who
Ezek 34:31 you are **m**, and I am your God,
Ezek 36:10 I will multiply **m** upon you
Ezek 36:12 I will cause **m** to walk on you
Ezek 36:13 say to you, 'You devour **m**
Ezek 36:14 you shall devour **m** no more
Ezek 36:37 increase their **m** like a flock
Ezek 36:38 be filled with flocks of **m**
Ezek 38:20 all **m** who are on the face of
Ezek 39:14 apart **m** regularly employed
Ezek 39:20 **m** and with all the **m** of war
Dan 1: 4 young **m** in whom there was no
Dan 1:10 the young **m** who are your age
Dan 1:13 countenances of the young **m**
Dan 1:15 **m** who ate the portion of the
Dan 1:17 As for these four young **m**
Dan 2:12 all the wise **m** of Babylon
Dan 2:13 they began killing the wise **m**
Dan 2:14 to kill the wise **m** of Babylon
Dan 2:18 rest of the wise **m** of Babylon
Dan 2:24 destroy the wise **m** of Babylon
Dan 2:24 destroy the wise **m** of Babylon
Dan 2:27 king has demanded, the wise **m**
Dan 2:38 the children of **m** dwell, or
Dan 2:43 mingle with the seed of **m**
Dan 2:48 all the wise **m** of Babylon
Dan 3:12 these **m**, O king, have not
Dan 3:13 these **m** before the king
Dan 3:20 **m** of valor who were in his
Dan 3:21 Then these **m** were bound in
Dan 3:22 those **m** who took up Shadrach
Dan 3:23 And these three **m**, Shadrach,
Dan 3:24 Did we not cast three **m** bound
Dan 3:25 I see four **m** loose, walking
Dan 3:27 they saw these **m** on whose
Dan 4: 6 wise **m** of Babylon before me
Dan 4:17 rules in the kingdom of **m**
Dan 4:17 sets over it the lowest of **m**
Dan 4:18 since all the wise **m** of my
Dan 4:25 They shall drive you from **m**
Dan 4:25 rules in the kingdom of **m**
Dan 4:32 they shall drive you from **m**
Dan 4:32 rules in the kingdom of **m**
Dan 4:33 he was driven from **m** and ate
Dan 5: 7 to the wise **m** of Babylon
Dan 5: 8 all the king's wise **m** came
Dan 5:15 Now the wise **m**, the
Dan 5:21 was driven from the sons of **m**
Dan 5:21 God rules in the kingdom of **m**
Dan 6: 5 Then these **m** said, "We shall
Dan 6:11 Then these **m** assembled and
Dan 6:15 Then these **m** approached the
Dan 6:24 they brought those **m** who had
Dan 6:26 of my kingdom **m** must tremble
Dan 9: 7 to the **m** of Judah, to the
Dan 10: 7 for the **m** who were with me
Dan 10:16 the sons of **m** touched my lips
Dan 11:14 also certain violent **m** of
Hos 4:14 for the **m** themselves go apart
Hos 6: 7 But like **m** they transgressed
Hos 10:13 multitude of your mighty **m**
Hos 13: 2 Let the **m** who sacrifice kiss
Joel 1:12 away from the sons of **m**
Joel 2: 7 They run like mighty **m**, they
Joel 2: 7 climb the wall like **m** of war
Joel 2:28 your old **m** shall dream dreams
Joel 2:28 your young **m** shall see
Joel 3: 9 Wake up the mighty **m**, let all
Joel 3: 9 let all the **m** of war draw
Amos 2:11 of your young **m** as Nazirites
Amos 2:16 The most courageous **m** of
Amos 4:10 your young **m** I killed with a
Amos 6: 9 that if ten **m** remain in one
Amos 8:13 strong young **m** shall faint
Obad 7 All the **m** in your confederacy
Obad 7 the **m** at peace with you shall
Obad 8 destroy the wise **m** from Edom
Obad 9 Then your mighty **m**, O Teman,
Jon 1:10 Then the **m** were exceedingly
Jon 1:10 For the **m** knew that he fled
Jon 1:13 Nevertheless the **m** rowed hard
Jon 1:16 Then the **m** feared the LORD
Mic 2: 8 by, like **m** returned from war
Mic 2:12 noise because of so many **m**
Mic 5: 5 shepherds and eight princely **m**
Mic 5: 7 nor wait for the sons of **m**
Mic 6:12 For her rich **m** are full of
Mic 7: 2 is no one upright among **m**
Mic 7: 6 are the **m** of his own house
Nah 2: 3 of his mighty **m** are made red
Nah 2: 3 the valiant **m** are in scarlet
Nah 3:10 cast lots for her honorable **m**
Nah 3:10 all her great **m** were bound in
Hab 1:14 Why do You make **m** like fish
Zeph 1:12 punish the **m** who are settled
Zeph 1:14 the mighty **m** shall cry out
Zeph 1:17 I will bring distress upon **m**
Zeph 1:17 they shall walk like blind **m**
Hag 1:11 the ground brings forth, on **m**
Zech 2: 4 because of the multitude of **m**
Zech 7: 2 with Regem-Melech and his **m**
Zech 8: 4 Old **m** and old women shall
Zech 8:10 for I set all **m**, everyone,
Zech 8:23 In those days ten **m** from
Zech 9: 1 place (for the eyes of **m** and
Zech 9:17 shall make the young **m** thrive
Zech 10: 5 They shall be like mighty **m**
Matt 2: 1 wise **m** from the East came to
Matt 2: 7 secretly called the wise **m**
Matt 2:16 he was deceived by the wise **m**
Matt 2:16 determined from the wise **m**
Matt 4:19 I will make you fishers of **m**
Matt 5:13 and trampled under foot by **m**
Matt 5:16 your light so shine before **m**
Matt 5:19 commandments, and teaches **m**
Matt 6: 1 charitable deeds before **m**
Matt 6: 2 they may have glory from **m**
Matt 6: 5 that they may be seen by **m**
Matt 6:14 forgive **m** their trespasses
Matt 6:15 forgive **m** their trespasses
Matt 6:16 may appear to **m** to be fasting
Matt 6:18 not appear to **m** to be fasting
Matt 7:12 you want **m** to do to you, do
Matt 7:16 Do **m** gather grapes from
Matt 8:27 And the **m** marveled, saying,
Matt 8:28 Him two demon-possessed **m**
Matt 8:33 to the demon-possessed **m**
Matt 9: 8 who had given such power to **m**
Matt 9:27 two blind **m** followed Him,
Matt 9:28 the blind **m** came to Him
Matt 10:17 But beware of **m**, for they
Matt 10:32 whoever confesses Me before **m**
Matt 10:33 whoever denies Me before **m**
Matt 12:31 blasphemy will be forgiven **m**
Matt 12:31 Spirit will not be forgiven **m**
Matt 12:36 every idle word **m** may speak
Matt 12:41 The **m** of Nineveh will rise in
Matt 13:17 righteous **m** desired to see
Matt 13:25 but while **m** slept, his enemy
Matt 14:21 were about five thousand **m**
Matt 14:35 And when the **m** of that place
Matt 15: 9 the commandments of **m**
Matt 15:38 who ate were four thousand **m**
Matt 16:13 Who do **m** say that I, the Son
Matt 16:23 of God, but the things of **m**
Matt 17:22 betrayed into the hands of **m**
Matt 19:12 who were made eunuchs by **m**
Matt 19:26 With **m** this is impossible,
Matt 20:12 These last **m** have worked
Matt 20:30 two blind **m** sitting by the
Matt 21:25 From heaven or from **m**
Matt 21:26 But if we say, 'From **m**,' we
Matt 21:41 those wicked **m** miserably, and
Matt 22:16 do not regard the person of **m**
Matt 23: 5 works they do to be seen by **m**
Matt 23: 7 and to be called by **m**, 'Rabbi
Matt 23:13 kingdom of heaven against **m**
Matt 23:28 appear righteous to **m**, but
Matt 23:34 I send you prophets, wise **m**
Matt 24:40 Then two **m** will be in the
Matt 26:62 these **m** testify against You
Matt 28: 4 of him, and became like dead **m**
Mark 1:17 make you become fishers of **m**
Mark 2: 3 who was carried by four **m**
Mark 3:28 be forgiven the sons of **m**
Mark 6:21 and the chief **m** of Galilee
Mark 6:44 were about five thousand **m**
Mark 7: 7 the commandments of **m**
Mark 7: 8 you hold the tradition of **m**
Mark 7:21 within, out of the heart of **m**
Mark 8:24 I see **m** like trees, walking
Mark 8:27 Who do **m** say that I am
Mark 8:33 of God, but the things of **m**
Mark 9:31 delivered into the hands of **m**
Mark 10:27 With **m** it is impossible, but
Mark 11:30 was it from heaven or from **m**
Mark 11:32 But if we say, 'From **m**' "
Mark 12:14 do not regard the person of **m**
Mark 13:13 by all **m** for My name's sake
Mark 14:51 the young **m** laid hold of him,
Mark 14:60 What is it these **m** testify
Luke 1:25 away my reproach among **m**
Luke 2:14 peace, good will toward **m**
Luke 2:52 and in favor with God and **m**
Luke 5:10 From now on you will catch **m**
Luke 5:18 **m** brought on a bed a man who
Luke 6:22 are you when **m** hate you, and
Luke 6:26 when all **m** speak well of you
Luke 6:31 as you want **m** to do to you
Luke 6:44 For **m** do not gather figs from
Luke 7:20 When the **m** had come to Him,
Luke 7:31 the **m** of this generation, and
Luke 9:14 were about five thousand **m**
Luke 9:30 two **m** talked with Him, who
Luke 9:32 the two **m** who stood with Him
Luke 9:44 delivered into the hands of **m**
Luke 11:31 with the **m** of this generation
Luke 11:32 The **m** of Nineveh will rise up
Luke 11:44 the **m** who walk over them are
Luke 11:46 For you load **m** with burdens
Luke 12: 8 whoever confesses Me before **m**
Luke 12: 9 **m** will be denied before the
Luke 12:36 you yourselves be like **m** who
Luke 13: 4 **m** who dwelt in Jerusalem
Luke 13:14 days on which **m** ought to work
Luke 14:24 **m** who were invited shall
Luke 14:35 dunghill, but **m** throw it out
Luke 16:15 justify yourselves before **m**
Luke 16:15 **m** is an abomination in the
Luke 17:12 met Him ten **m** who were lepers
Luke 17:34 will be two **m** in one bed
Luke 17:36 Two **m** will be in the field
Luke 18: 1 that **m** always ought to pray
Luke 18:10 Two **m** went up to the temple
Luke 18:11 that I am not like other **m**
Luke 18:27 with **m** are possible with God
Luke 20: 4 was it from heaven or from **m**
Luke 20: 6 But if we say, 'From **m**,' all
Luke 22:63 Now the **m** who held Jesus

Luke 23:11 Then Herod, with his **m** of war
Luke 23:23 And the voices of these **m** and
Luke 24: 4 two **m** stood by them in
Luke 24: 7 into the hands of sinful **m**
John 1: 4 the life was the light of **m**
John 2:24 them, because He knew all **m**
John 3:19 **m** loved darkness rather than
John 4:28 the city, and said to the **m**
John 5:41 I do not receive honor from **m**
John 6:10 So the **m** sat down, in number
John 6:14 Then those **m**, when they had
John 8:17 testimony of two **m** is true
John 12:43 they loved the praise of **m**
John 17: 6 **m** whom You have given Me out
Acts 1:10 two **m** stood by them in white
Acts 1:11 **M** of Galilee, why do you
Acts 1:16 **M** and brethren, this Scripture
Acts 1:21 of these **m** who have
Acts 2: 5 in Jerusalem Jews, devout **m**
Acts 2:14 **M** of Judea and all who dwell
Acts 2:17 your young **m** shall see
Acts 2:17 your old **m** shall dream dreams
Acts 2:22 **M** of Israel, hear these words
Acts 2:29 **M** and brethren, let me speak
Acts 2:37 **M** and brethren, what shall we
Acts 3:12 **M** of Israel, why do you
Acts 4: 4 the number of the **m** came to
Acts 4:12 under heaven given among **m** by
Acts 4:13 uneducated and untrained **m**
Acts 4:16 What shall we do to these **m**
Acts 5: 4 have not lied to **m** but to God
Acts 5: 6 And the young **m** arose and
Acts 5:10 And the young **m** came in and
Acts 5:14 Lord, multitudes of both **m**
Acts 5:25 the **m** whom you put in prison
Acts 5:29 to obey God rather than **m**
Acts 5:35 **M** of Israel, take heed to
Acts 5:35 to do regarding these **m**
Acts 5:36 A number of **m**, about four
Acts 5:38 you, keep away from these **m**
Acts 5:38 plan or this work is of **m**
Acts 6: 3 seven **m** of good reputation
Acts 6:11 secretly induced **m** to say
Acts 7: 2 **M** and brethren and fathers,
Acts 7:26 to reconcile them, saying, **M**
Acts 8: 2 devout **m** carried Stephen to
Acts 8: 3 house, and dragging off **m** and
Acts 8:12 name of Jesus Christ, both **m**
Acts 9: 2 whether **m** or women, he might
Acts 9: 7 the **m** who journeyed with him
Acts 9:38 there, they sent two **m** to him
Acts 10: 5 Now send **m** to Joppa, and send
Acts 10:17 the **m** who had been sent from
Acts 10:19 three **m** are seeking you
Acts 10:21 **m** who had been sent to him
Acts 11: 3 went in to uncircumcised **m**
Acts 11:11 three **m** stood before the
Acts 11:13 Send **m** to Joppa, and call for
Acts 11:20 of them were **m** from Cyprus
Acts 13:15 **M** and brethren, if you have
Acts 13:16 **M** of Israel, and you who fear
Acts 13:26 **M** and brethren, sons of the
Acts 13:50 and the chief **m** of the city,
Acts 14:11 to us in the likeness of **m**
Acts 14:15 **M**, why are you doing these
Acts 14:15 We also are **m** with the same
Acts 15: 1 And certain **m** came down from
Acts 15: 7 **M** and brethren, you know that
Acts 15:13 **M** and brethren, listen to me
Acts 15:22 to send chosen **m** of their own
Acts 15:22 leading **m** among the brethren
Acts 15:25 to send chosen **m** to you with
Acts 15:26 **m** who have risked their lives
Acts 16:17 These **m** are the servants of
Acts 16:20 These **m**, being Jews,
Acts 16:35 Let those **m** go
Acts 17: 5 evil **m** from the marketplace
Acts 17:12 prominent women as well as **m**
Acts 17:22 **M** of Athens, I perceive that
Acts 17:26 one blood every nation of **m**
Acts 17:30 all **m** everywhere to repent
Acts 17:34 some **m** joined him and believed
Acts 18:13 This fellow persuades **m** to
Acts 19: 7 Now the **m** were about twelve
Acts 19:25 **M**, you know that we have our
Acts 19:35 **M** of Ephesus, what man is
Acts 19:37 these **m** here who are neither
Acts 20: 5 These **m**, going ahead, waited
Acts 20:26 of the blood of all **m**
Acts 20:30 yourselves **m** will rise up
Acts 21:23 We have four **m** who have taken
Acts 21:26 Then Paul took the **m**, and the
Acts 21:28 out, "**M** of Israel, help
Acts 21:28 all **m** everywhere against the
Acts 22: 1 **M**, brethren, and fathers, hear
Acts 22: 4 into prisons both **m** and women,
Acts 22:15 all **m** of what you have seen
Acts 23: 1 **M** and brethren, I have lived
Acts 23: 6 **M** and brethren, I am a
Acts 23:21 **m** who have bound themselves
Acts 24:16 offense toward God and **m**
Acts 25: 2 and the chief **m** of the Jews
Acts 25:11 of which these **m** accuse me
Acts 25:23 the prominent **m** of the city
Acts 25:24 and all the **m** who are here
Acts 27:10 **M**, I perceive that this
Acts 27:21 **M**, you should have listened
Acts 27:25 Therefore take heart, **m**, for
Acts 27:31 Unless these **m** stay in the
Acts 28:17 **M** and brethren, though I have
Rom 1:18 and unrighteousness of **m**, who
Rom 1:27 Likewise also the **m**, leaving
Rom 1:27 **m** with **m** committing what is
Rom 2:16 secrets of **m** by Jesus Christ
Rom 2:29 is not from **m** but from God
Rom 5:12 and thus death spread to all **m**
Rom 5:18 judgment came to all **m**,
Rom 5:18 the free gift came to all **m**
Rom 11: 4 for Myself seven thousand **m**
Rom 12:17 things in the sight of all **m**
Rom 12:18 live peaceably with all **m**
Rom 14:18 to God and approved by **m**
1Co 1:25 of God is wiser than **m**, and
1Co 1:25 of God is stronger than **m**
1Co 2: 5 of **m** but in the power of God
1Co 3: 3 and behaving like mere **m**
1Co 3:21 let no one glory in **m**
1Co 4: 9 last, as **m** condemned to death
1Co 4: 9 world, both to angels and to **m**
1Co 7: 7 For I wish that all **m** were
1Co 7:23 do not become slaves of **m**
1Co 9:19 though I am free from all **m**
1Co 9:22 become all things to all **m**
1Co 10:15 I speak as to wise **m**
1Co 10:33 please all **m** in all things
1Co 13: 1 I speak with the tongues of **m**
1Co 14: 2 not speak to **m** but to God
1Co 14: 3 exhortation and comfort to **m**
1Co 14:21 With **m** of other tongues and
1Co 15:19 we are of all **m** the most
1Co 15:32 If, in the manner of **m**, I
1Co 15:39 is one kind of flesh of **m**
1Co 16:18 therefore acknowledge such **m**
2Co 3: 2 known and read by all **m**
2Co 5:11 of the Lord, we persuade **m**
2Co 8:21 but also in the sight of **m**
2Co 9:13 sharing with them and all **m**
Gal 1: 1 (not from **m** nor through man
Gal 1:10 For do I now persuade **m**, or
Gal 1:10 Or do I seek to please **m**
Gal 1:10 For if I still pleased **m**, I
Gal 2:12 certain **m** came from James
Gal 3:15 I speak in the manner of **m**
Eph 3: 5 made known to the sons of **m**
Eph 4: 8 captive, and gave gifts to **m**
Eph 4:14 by the trickery of **m**, in the
Eph 6: 7 as to the Lord, and not to **m**
Phil 2: 7 coming in the likeness of **m**
Phil 2:29 and hold such **m** in esteem
Phil 4: 5 gentleness be known to all **m**
Col 2: 8 to the tradition of **m**,
Col 2:22 and doctrines of **m**
Col 3:23 as to the Lord and not to **m**
1Th 1: 5 as you know what kind of **m** we
1Th 2: 4 we speak, not as pleasing **m**
1Th 2: 6 Nor did we seek glory from **m**
1Th 2:13 it not as the word of **m**, but
1Th 2:15 God and are contrary to all **m**
2Th 3: 2 unreasonable and wicked **m**
1Ti 2: 1 of thanks be made for all **m**
1Ti 2: 4 who desires all **m** to be saved
1Ti 2: 5 Mediator between God and **m**
1Ti 2: 8 that the **m** pray everywhere
1Ti 4:10 who is the Savior of all **m**
1Ti 5: 1 the younger **m** as brothers
1Ti 5:24 those of some **m** follow later
1Ti 6: 5 of **m** of corrupt minds and
1Ti 6: 9 which drown **m** in destruction
2Ti 2: 2 commit these to faithful **m**
2Ti 3: 2 For **m** will be lovers of
2Ti 3: 8 **m** of corrupt minds,
2Ti 3:13 But evil **m** and impostors will
Tit 1:14 commandments of **m** who turn
Tit 2: 2 that the older **m** be sober
Tit 2: 6 young **m** to be sober-minded
Tit 2:11 has appeared to all **m**,
Tit 3: 2 showing all humility to all **m**
Tit 3: 8 are good and profitable to **m**
Heb 5: 1 among **m** is appointed for **m**
Heb 6:16 For **m** indeed swear by the
Heb 7: 8 Here mortal **m** receive tithes,
Heb 7:28 priests **m** who have weakness
Heb 9:17 is in force after **m** are dead
Heb 9:27 appointed for **m** to die once
Heb 12:14 Pursue peace with all **m**, and
Heb 12:23 of just **m** made perfect,
Jas 3: 9 Father, and with it we curse **m**
1Pe 2: 4 stone, rejected indeed by **m**
1Pe 2:15 the ignorance of foolish **m**
1Pe 4: 2 the flesh for the lusts of **m**
1Pe 4: 6 according to **m** in the flesh
2Pe 1:21 but holy **m** of God spoke as
2Pe 3: 7 and perdition of ungodly **m**
1Jn 2:13 I write to you, young **m**,
1Jn 2:14 have written to you, young **m**
1Jn 5: 9 we receive the witness of **m**
Jude 4 For certain **m** have crept in
Jude 4 this condemnation, ungodly **m**
Jude 14 prophesied about these **m** also
Rev 6:15 the great **m**, the rich **m**
Rev 6:15 the commanders, the mighty **m**
Rev 8:11 many **m** died from the water,
Rev 9: 4 but only those **m** who do not
Rev 9: 6 In those days **m** will seek
Rev 9: 7 were like the faces of **m**
Rev 9:10 was to hurt **m** five months
Rev 11:13 seven thousand **m** were killed
Rev 13:13 the earth in the sight of **m**
Rev 14: 4 were redeemed from among **m**
Rev 16: 2 sore came upon the **m** who had
Rev 16: 8 to him to scorch **m** with fire
Rev 16: 9 **m** were scorched with great
Rev 16:18 since **m** were on the earth
Rev 16:21 hail from heaven fell upon **m**
Rev 16:21 **m** blasphemed God because of
Rev 18:13 and bodies and souls of **m**
Rev 18:23 were the great **m** of the earth
Rev 19:18 the flesh of mighty **m**, the
Rev 21: 3 tabernacle of God is with **m**

MENAHEM
2Ki 15:14 For **M** the son of Gadi went up
2Ki 15:16 **M** attacked Tiphsah, all who
2Ki 15:17 **M** the son of Gadi became king
2Ki 15:19 **M** gave Pul a thousand talents
2Ki 15:20 And **M** exacted the money from
2Ki 15:21 Now the rest of the acts of **M**
2Ki 15:22 So **M** rested with his fathers
2Ki 15:23 Pekahiah the son of **M** became

MENAN
Luke 3:31 son of Melea, the son of **M**

MENDED (*see* MENDING)
Josh 9: 4 old wineskins torn and **m**,

MENDING (*see* MENDED)
Matt 4:21 their father, **m** their nets
Mark 1:19 were in the boat **m** their nets

MENE
Dan 5:25 **M**, **M**, TEKEL, UPHARSIN
Dan 5:26 **M**: God has numbered

MENI
Is 65:11 a drink offering for **M**

MEN-PLEASERS (*see* MEN)
Eph 6: 6 not with eyeservice, as **m**
Col 3:22 not with eyeservice, as **m**

MEN'S (*see* MEN)
Gen 44: 1 Fill the **m** sacks with food,
Deut 4:28 gods, the work of **m** hands
1Ki 13: 2 **m** bones shall be burned on
2Ki 19:18 gods, but the work of **m** hands
2Ki 23:20 and burned **m** bones on them
2Ch 32:19 the work of **m** hands
Ps 115: 4 and gold, The work of **m** hands
Ps 135:15 and gold, The work of **m** hands
Is 37:19 gods, but the work of **m** hands
Jer 48:41 the mighty **m** hearts in Moab
Hab 2: 8 you, because of **m** blood and
Hab 2:17 afraid, because of **m** blood

Matt 23: 4 and lay them on **m** shoulders
Matt 23:27 are full of dead **m** bones and
Luke 9:56 **m** lives but to save them
Luke 21:26 **m** hearts failing them from
Acts 17:25 is He worshiped with **m** hands
2Co 10:15 that is, in other **m** labors
1Ti 5:24 Some **m** sins are clearly

MENSERVANTS (*see* MANSERVANT)
Ex 21: 7 shall not go out as the **m** do
Deut 12:12 and your daughters, your **m**
1Sa 8:16 And he will take your **m** and
Joel 2:29 And also on My **m** and on My
Luke 12:45 and begins to beat the **m**
Acts 2:18 and on My **m** and on My

MENTION (*see* MENTIONED)
Gen 40:14 make **m** of me to Pharaoh, and
Ex 23:13 and make no **m** of the name of
Josh 23: 7 You shall not make **m** of the
1Sa 4:18 when he made **m** of the ark of
Job 28:18 No **m** shall be made of coral
Ps 71:16 I will make **m** of Your
Ps 87: 4 I will make **m** of Rahab and
Is 12: 4 make **m** that His name is
Is 19:17 everyone who makes **m** of it
Is 26:13 only we make **m** of Your name
Is 48: 1 make **m** of the God of Israel,
Is 49: 1 He has made **m** of My name
Is 62: 6 You who make **m** of the LORD
Is 63: 7 I will **m** the lovingkindnesses
Jer 4:16 Make **m** to the nations, yes,
Jer 20: 9 I will not make **m** of Him, nor
Jer 23:36 the LORD you shall **m** no more
Amos 6:10 For we dare not **m** the name of
Rom 1: 9 **m** of you always in my prayers
2Co 9: 4 unprepared, we (not to **m** you
Eph 1:16 making **m** of you in my prayers
1Th 1: 2 all, making **m** of you in our
Phm 4 making **m** of you always in my
Phm 19 not to **m** to you that you owe
Heb 11:22 made **m** of the departure of

MENTIONED (*see* MENTION)
Num 1:17 men who had been **m** by name
Josh 21: 9 which are **m** here by name,
1Ch 4:38 these **m** by name were leaders
2Ch 20:34 which is **m** in the book of the

MEONOTHAI
1Ch 4:14 and **M** who begot Ophrah

MEPHAATH
Josh 13:18 Jahaza, Kedemoth, **M**,
Josh 21:37 and **M** with its common-land
1Ch 6:79 and **M** with its common-lands
Jer 48:21 on Holon and Jahzah and **M**,

MEPHIBOSHETH (*see* MERIB-BAAL)
2Sa 4: 4 So his name was **M**
2Sa 9: 6 Now when **M** the son of
2Sa 9: 6 Then David said, "**M**?"
2Sa 9:10 But **M** your master's son shall
2Sa 9:11 As for **M**," said the king
2Sa 9:12 **M** had a young son whose name
2Sa 9:12 of Ziba were servants of **M**
2Sa 9:13 So **M** dwelt in Jerusalem, for
2Sa 16: 1 was Ziba the servant of **M**
2Sa 16: 4 that belongs to **M** is yours
2Sa 19:24 Now **M** the son of Saul came
2Sa 19:25 Why did you not go with me, **M**
2Sa 19:30 Then **M** said to the king
2Sa 21: 7 spared **M** the son of Jonathan
2Sa 21: 8 So the king took Armoni and **M**

MERAB
1Sa 14:49 the name of the firstborn **M**
1Sa 18:17 Here is my older daughter **M**
1Sa 18:19 happened at the time when **M**

MERAIAH
Neh 12:12 of Seraiah, **M**

MERAIOTH (*see* MEREMOTH)
1Ch 6: 6 and Zerahiah begot **M**
1Ch 6: 7 **M** begot Amariah, and Amariah
1Ch 6:52 **M** his son, Amariah his son,
1Ch 9:11 son of Zadok, the son of **M**
Ezra 7: 3 son of Azariah, the son of **M**
Neh 11:11 son of Zadok, the son of **M**
Neh 12:15 of **M**, Helkai

MERARI (*see* MERARITES)
Gen 46:11 were Gershon, Kohath, and **M**
Ex 6:16 Gershon, Kohath, and **M**
Ex 6:19 The sons of **M** were Mahali
Num 3:17 Gershon, Kohath, and **M**
Num 3:20 And the sons of **M** by their
Num 3:33 From **M** came the family of the
Num 3:33 these were the families of **M**
Num 3:35 of **M** was Zuriel the son of
Num 3:36 duty of the children of **M**
Num 4:29 As for the sons of **M**, you
Num 4:33 the families of the sons of **M**
Num 4:42 sons of **M** who were numbered
Num 4:45 the families of the sons of **M**
Num 7: 8 oxen he gave to the sons of **M**
Num 10:17 and the sons of **M** set out,
Num 26:57 of **M**, the family of the
Josh 21: 7 The children of **M** according
Josh 21:34 families of the children of **M**
Josh 21:40 cities for the children of **M**
1Ch 6: 1 were Gershon, Kohath, and **M**
1Ch 6:16 were Gershon, Kohath, and **M**
1Ch 6:19 The sons of **M** were Mahli and
1Ch 6:29 The sons of **M** were Mahli,
1Ch 6:44 their brethren, the sons of **M**
1Ch 6:47 son of Mushi, the son of **M**
1Ch 6:63 To the sons of **M**, throughout
1Ch 6:77 **M** were given Rimmon with its
1Ch 9:14 Hashabiah, of the sons of **M**
1Ch 15: 6 of the sons of **M**, Asaiah the
1Ch 15:17 their brethren, the sons of **M**
1Ch 23: 6 Gershon, Kohath, and **M**
1Ch 23:21 The sons of **M** were Mahli and
1Ch 24:26 The sons of **M** were Mahli and
1Ch 24:27 The sons of **M** by Jaaziah were
1Ch 26:10 Hosah, of the children of **M**
1Ch 26:19 Korah and among the sons of **M**
2Ch 29:12 of the sons of **M**, Kish the
2Ch 34:12 the Levites, of the sons of **M**
Ezra 8:19 him Jeshaiah of the sons of **M**

MERARITES (*see* MERARI)
Num 26:57 Merari, the family of the **M**

MERATHAIM
Jer 50:21 Go up against the land of **M**

MERCENARIES
Jer 46:21 Also her **m** are in her midst

MERCHANDISE (*see* MERCHANDISERS)
Prov 31:18 perceives that her **m** is good
Is 45:14 **m** of Cush and of the Sabeans,
Ezek 26:12 your riches and pillage your **m**
Ezek 27: 9 were in you to market your **m**
Ezek 27:13 vessels of bronze for your **m**
Ezek 27:17 for your **m** wheat of Minnith
Ezek 27:19 and cane were among your **m**
Ezek 27:25 were carriers of your **m**
Ezek 27:27 Your riches, wares, and **m**,
Ezek 27:33 many luxury goods and your **m**
Ezek 27:34 depths of the waters, your **m**
John 2:16 Father's house a house of **m**
Rev 18:11 no one buys their **m** anymore
Rev 18:12 **m** of gold and silver, precious

MERCHANDISERS (*see* MERCHANDISE)
Ezek 27:27 and pilots, your caulkers and **m**

MERCHANT (*see* MERCHANT'S, MERCHANTS)
1Ki 10:22 For the king had **m** ships at
1Ki 10:22 **m** ships came bringing gold
1Ki 22:48 Jehoshaphat made **m** ships to
2Ch 9:21 three years the **m** ships came
Prov 31:14 She is like the **m** ships, she
Ezek 27: 3 sea, **m** of the peoples on many
Ezek 27:12 Tarshish was your **m** because
Ezek 27:16 Syria was your **m** because of
Ezek 27:18 Damascus was your **m** because
Ezek 27:20 Dedan was your **m** in
Zeph 1:11 for all the **m** people are cut
Matt 13:45 a **m** seeking beautiful pearls

MERCHANT'S (*see* MERCHANT)
Song 3: 6 with all the **m** fragrant

MERCHANTS (*see* MERCHANT)
Gen 23:16 of silver, currency of the **m**
1Ki 10:15 that from the traveling **m**
1Ki 10:28 the king's **m** bought them in
2Ch 1:16 the king's **m** bought them in
2Ch 9:14 besides what the traveling **m**
Neh 3:31 of the Nethinim and of the **m**
Neh 3:32 and the **m** made repairs
Neh 13:20 Now the **m** and sellers of all
Job 41: 6 apportion him among the **m**
Prov 31:24 and supplies sashes for the **m**
Is 23: 2 you **m** of Sidon, whom those
Is 23: 8 whose **m** are princes, whose
Is 47:15 your **m** from your youth
Ezek 17: 4 he set it in a city of **m**
Ezek 27:21 of Kedar were your regular **m**
Ezek 27:22 The **m** of Sheba and Raamah
Ezek 27:22 Sheba and Raamah were your **m**
Ezek 27:23 the **m** of Sheba, Assyria, and
Ezek 27:23 and Chilmad were your **m**
Ezek 27:24 were your **m** in choice items
Ezek 27:36 The **m** among the peoples will
Ezek 38:13 the **m** of Tarshish, and all
Nah 3:16 your **m** more than the stars of
Rev 18: 3 and the **m** of the earth have
Rev 18:11 the **m** of the earth will weep
Rev 18:15 The **m** of these things, who
Rev 18:23 For your **m** were the great men

MERCIES (*see* MERCIES', MERCY)
Gen 32:10 of the least of all the **m**
2Sa 24:14 the LORD, for His **m** are great
1Ch 21:13 for His **m** are very great
2Ch 6:42 remember the **m** of Your
Neh 9:19 Yet in Your manifold **m** You
Neh 9:27 **m** You gave them deliverers
Neh 9:28 them according to Your **m**,
Ps 25: 6 O LORD, Your tender **m** and
Ps 40:11 Your tender **m** from me
Ps 51: 1 multitude of Your tender **m**
Ps 69:16 multitude of Your tender **m**
Ps 77: 9 in anger shut up His tender **m**
Ps 79: 8 Let Your tender **m** come
Ps 89: 1 I will sing of the **m** of the
Ps 103: 4 lovingkindness and tender **m**
Ps 106: 7 the multitude of Your **m**, But
Ps 106:45 to the multitude of His **m**
Ps 119:41 Let Your **m** come also to me, O
Ps 119:77 Let Your tender **m** come to me
Ps 119:156 Great are Your tender **m**, O
Ps 145: 9 His tender **m** are over all His
Prov 12:10 but the tender **m** of the
Is 54: 7 you, but with great **m** I will
Is 55: 3 the sure **m** of David
Is 63: 7 on them according to His **m**
Is 63:15 heart and Your **m** toward me
Jer 16: 5 lovingkindness and **m**
Lam 3:22 Through the LORD's **m** we are
Lam 3:32 to the multitude of His **m**
Dan 2:18 that they might seek **m** from
Dan 9:18 but because of Your great **m**
Acts 13:34 give you the sure **m** of David
Rom 12: 1 brethren, by the **m** of God
2Co 1: 3 Jesus Christ, the Father of **m**
Col 3:12 and beloved, put on tender **m**

MERCIES' (*see* MERCIES, MERCY)
Ps 6: 4 Oh, save me for Your **m** sake
Ps 31:16 Save me for Your **m** sake
Ps 44:26 And redeem us for Your **m** sake

MERCIFUL (*see* MERCY, UNMERCIFUL)
Gen 19:16 the LORD being **m** to him, and
Ex 34: 6 The LORD, the LORD God, **m**
Deut 4:31 the LORD your God is a **m** God)
2Sa 22:26 With the **m** You will show
2Sa 22:26 You will show Yourself **m**
1Ki 20:31 house of Israel are **m** kings
2Ch 30: 9 your God is gracious and **m**
Neh 9:17 to pardon, gracious and **m**,
Neh 9:31 You are God, gracious and **m**
Ps 18:25 With the **m** You will show
Ps 18:25 You will show Yourself **m**
Ps 26:11 Redeem me and be **m** to me
Ps 37:26 He is ever **m**, and lends
Ps 41: 4 I said, "LORD, be **m** to me
Ps 41:10 be **m** to me, and raise me up,
Ps 56: 1 Be **m** to me, O God, for man
Ps 57: 1 Be **m** to me, O God, be
Ps 57: 1 to me, O God, be **m** to me
Ps 59: 5 Do not be **m** to any wicked
Ps 59:10 My **m** God shall come to meet
Ps 67: 1 God be **m** to us and bless us,
Ps 86: 3 Be **m** to me, O Lord, For I cry
Ps 103: 8 The LORD is **m** and gracious,
Ps 116: 5 Yes, our God is **m**
Ps 117: 2 For His **m** kindness is great
Ps 119:58 Be **m** to me according to Your
Ps 119:76 Your **m** kindness be for my
Ps 119:132 be **m** to me, As Your custom is

Prov 11:17 The **m** man does good for his
Is 57: 1 **m** men are taken away, while
Jer 3:12 For I am **m**,' says the LORD
Joel 2:13 God, for He is gracious and **m**
Jon 4: 2 and **m** God, slow to anger and
Matt 5: 7 Blessed are the **m**, for they
Luke 6:36 Therefore be **m**, just as your
Luke 6:36 just as your Father also is **m**
Luke 18:13 God be **m** to me a sinner
Heb 2:17 that He might be a **m** and
Heb 8:12 For I will be **m** to their
Jas 5:11 is very compassionate and **m**

MERCY (*see* MERCIES, MERCIES', MERCIFUL)
Gen 19:19 you have increased your **m**
Gen 24:27 who has not forsaken His **m**
Gen 39:21 with Joseph and showed him **m**
Gen 43:14 give you **m** before the man
Ex 15:13 You in Your **m** have led forth
Ex 20: 6 but showing **m** to thousands,
Ex 25:17 You shall make a **m** seat of
Ex 25:18 at the two ends of the **m** seat
Ex 25:19 of one piece with the **m** seat
Ex 25:20 covering the **m** seat with
Ex 25:20 shall be toward the **m** seat
Ex 25:21 You shall put the **m** seat on
Ex 25:22 you from above the **m** seat
Ex 26:34 You shall put the **m** seat upon
Ex 30: 6 before the **m** seat that is
Ex 31: 7 the **m** seat that is on it, and
Ex 34: 7 keeping **m** for thousands,
Ex 35:12 and its poles, with the **m** seat
Ex 37: 6 He also made the **m** seat of
Ex 37: 7 at the two ends of the **m** seat
Ex 37: 8 of one piece with the **m** seat
Ex 37: 9 covered the **m** seat with their
Ex 37: 9 were toward the **m** seat
Ex 39:35 with its poles, and the **m** seat
Ex 40:20 put the **m** seat on top of the
Lev 16: 2 before the **m** seat which is on
Lev 16: 2 in the cloud above the **m** seat
Lev 16:13 the **m** seat that is on the
Lev 16:14 the **m** seat on the east side
Lev 16:14 before the **m** seat he shall
Lev 16:15 and sprinkle it on the **m** seat
Lev 16:15 seat and before the **m** seat
Num 7:89 to him from above the **m** seat
Num 14:18 and abundant in **m**, forgiving
Num 14:19 to the greatness of Your **m**
Deut 5:10 but showing **m** to thousands,
Deut 7: 2 with them nor show **m** to them
Deut 7: 9 **m** for a thousand generations
Deut 7:12 the **m** which He swore to your
Deut 13:17 of His anger and show you **m**
Josh 11:20 that they might receive no **m**
Judg 1:24 city, and we will show you **m**
2Sa 7:15 But My **m** shall not depart
2Sa 15:20 **M** and truth be with you
2Sa 22:51 shows **m** to His anointed, to
1Ki 3: 6 You have shown great **m** to
1Ki 8:23 **m** with Your servants who walk
1Ki 20:33 sign of **m** would come from him
1Ch 16:34 For His **m** endures forever
1Ch 16:41 because His **m** endures forever
1Ch 17:13 not take My **m** away from him
1Ch 28:11 and the place of the **m** seat
2Ch 1: 8 great **m** to David my father
2Ch 5:13 for His **m** endures forever,"
2Ch 6:14 **m** with Your servants who walk
2Ch 7: 3 for His **m** endures forever
2Ch 7: 6 For His **m** endures forever,"
2Ch 20:21 for His **m** endures forever
Ezra 3:11 For His **m** endures forever
Ezra 7:28 has extended **m** to me before
Ezra 9: 9 but He extended **m** to us in
Neh 1: 5 **m** with those who love You and
Neh 1:11 grant him **m** in the sight of
Neh 9:31 Nevertheless in Your great **m**
Neh 9:32 Who keeps covenant and **m**
Neh 13:22 to the greatness of Your **m**
Job 9:15 I would beg **m** of my Judge
Job 37:13 or for His land, or for **m**
Ps 4: 1 Have **m** on me, and hear my
Ps 5: 7 in the multitude of Your **m**
Ps 6: 2 Have **m** on me, O LORD, for I
Ps 9:13 Have **m** on me, O LORD
Ps 13: 5 But I have trusted in Your **m**
Ps 18:50 shows **m** to His anointed, To
Ps 21: 7 through the **m** of the Most
Ps 23: 6 **m** shall follow me All the
Ps 25: 7 to Your **m** remember me, For
Ps 25:10 the paths of the LORD are **m**
Ps 25:16 me, and have **m** on me, For I am
Ps 27: 7 Have **m** also upon me, and
Ps 30:10 Hear, O LORD, and have **m** on
Ps 31: 7 be glad and rejoice in Your **m**
Ps 31: 9 Have **m** on me, O LORD, for I
Ps 32:10 LORD, **m** shall surround him
Ps 33:18 On those who hope in His **m**
Ps 33:22 Let Your **m**, O LORD, be upon
Ps 36: 5 Your **m**, O LORD, is in the
Ps 37:21 But the righteous shows **m**
Ps 51: 1 Have **m** upon me, O God,
Ps 52: 8 trust in the **m** of God forever
Ps 57: 3 God shall send forth His **m**
Ps 57:10 For Your **m** reaches unto the
Ps 59:16 of Your **m** in the morning
Ps 59:17 my defense, The God of my **m**
Ps 61: 7 Oh, prepare **m** and truth, which
Ps 62:12 to You, O Lord, belongs **m**
Ps 66:20 my prayer, Nor His **m** from me
Ps 69:13 in the multitude of Your **m**
Ps 77: 8 Has His **m** ceased forever
Ps 85: 7 Show us Your **m**, O LORD, And
Ps 85:10 **M** and truth have met together
Ps 86: 5 abundant in **m** to all those
Ps 86:13 For great is Your **m** toward me
Ps 86:15 and abundant in **m** and truth
Ps 86:16 turn to me, and have **m** on me
Ps 89: 2 **M** shall be built up forever
Ps 89:14 **M** and truth go before Your
Ps 89:24 My **m** shall be with him, And in
Ps 89:28 My **m** I will keep for him
Ps 90:14 satisfy us early with Your **m**
Ps 94:18 My foot slips," Your **m**, O
Ps 98: 3 He has remembered His **m** and
Ps 100: 5 His **m** is everlasting, And His
Ps 101: 1 I will sing of **m** and justice
Ps 102:13 will arise and have **m** on Zion
Ps 103: 8 to anger, and abounding in **m**
Ps 103:11 So great is His **m** toward
Ps 103:17 But the **m** of the LORD is from
Ps 106: 1 For His **m** endures forever
Ps 107: 1 For His **m** endures forever
Ps 108: 4 For Your **m** is great above the
Ps 109:12 be none to extend **m** to him
Ps 109:16 he did not remember to show **m**
Ps 109:21 Because Your **m** is good,
Ps 109:26 save me according to Your **m**
Ps 115: 1 give glory, Because of Your **m**
Ps 118: 1 Because His **m** endures forever
Ps 118: 2 say, "His **m** endures forever
Ps 118: 3 say, "His **m** endures forever
Ps 118: 4 say, "His **m** endures forever
Ps 118:29 For His **m** endures forever
Ps 119:64 O LORD, is full of Your **m**
Ps 119:124 servant according to Your **m**
Ps 123: 2 our God, Until He has **m** on us
Ps 123: 3 Have **m** on us, O LORD, have
Ps 123: 3 on us, O LORD, have **m** on us
Ps 130: 7 For with the LORD there is **m**
Ps 136: 1 For His **m** endures forever
Ps 136: 2 For His **m** endures forever
Ps 136: 3 For His **m** endures forever
Ps 136: 4 For His **m** endures forever
Ps 136: 5 For His **m** endures forever
Ps 136: 6 For His **m** endures forever
Ps 136: 7 For His **m** endures forever
Ps 136: 8 For His **m** endures forever
Ps 136: 9 For His **m** endures forever
Ps 136:10 For His **m** endures forever
Ps 136:11 For His **m** endures forever
Ps 136:12 For His **m** endures forever
Ps 136:13 For His **m** endures forever
Ps 136:14 For His **m** endures forever
Ps 136:15 For His **m** endures forever
Ps 136:16 For His **m** endures forever
Ps 136:17 For His **m** endures forever
Ps 136:18 For His **m** endures forever
Ps 136:19 For His **m** endures forever
Ps 136:20 For His **m** endures forever
Ps 136:21 For His **m** endures forever
Ps 136:22 For His **m** endures forever
Ps 136:23 For His **m** endures forever
Ps 136:24 For His **m** endures forever
Ps 136:25 For His **m** endures forever
Ps 136:26 For His **m** endures forever
Ps 138: 8 Your **m**, O LORD, endures
Ps 143:12 In Your **m** cut off my enemies,
Ps 145: 8 Slow to anger and great in **m**
Ps 147:11 In those who hope in His **m**
Prov 3: 3 let not **m** and truth forsake
Prov 14:21 but he who has **m** on the poor
Prov 14:22 but **m** and truth belong to
Prov 14:31 honors Him has **m** on the needy
Prov 16: 6 In **m** and truth atonement is
Prov 20:28 **M** and truth preserve the king,
Prov 21:21 **m** finds life, righteousness
Prov 28:13 and forsakes them will have **m**
Is 9:17 men, nor have **m** on their
Is 14: 1 the LORD will have **m** on Jacob
Is 16: 5 In **m** the throne will be
Is 27:11 them will not have **m** on them
Is 30:18 that He may have **m** on you
Is 47: 6 You showed them no **m**
Is 49:10 for He who has **m** on them will
Is 49:13 will have **m** on His afflicted
Is 54: 8 kindness I will have **m** on you
Is 54:10 the LORD, who has **m** on you
Is 55: 7 and He will have **m** on him
Is 60:10 My favor I have had **m** on you
Jer 6:23 they are cruel and have no **m**
Jer 13:14 not pity nor spare nor have **m**
Jer 21: 7 spare them, or have pity or **m**
Jer 30:18 have **m** on his dwelling places
Jer 31:20 I will surely have **m** on him
Jer 33:11 for His **m** endures forever"
Jer 33:26 and will have **m** on them
Jer 42:12 And I will show you **m**, that
Jer 42:12 that he may have **m** on you
Jer 50:42 are cruel and shall not show **m**
Ezek 39:25 have **m** on the whole house of
Dan 4:27 by showing **m** to the poor
Dan 9: 4 **m** with those who love Him, and
Dan 9: 9 To the Lord our God belong **m**
Hos 1: 6 have **m** on the house of Israel
Hos 1: 7 Yet I will have **m** on the
Hos 2: 1 to your sisters, '**M** is shown
Hos 2: 4 not have **m** on her children
Hos 2:19 in lovingkindness and **m**
Hos 2:23 I will have **m** on her who had
Hos 2:23 on her who had not obtained **m**
Hos 4: 1 There is no truth or **m** or
Hos 6: 6 For I desire **m** and not
Hos 10:12 reap in **m**; break up your
Hos 12: 6 observe **m** and justice, and wait
Hos 14: 3 in You the fatherless finds **m**
Jon 2: 8 idols forsake their own **M**
Mic 6: 8 but to do justly, to love **m**
Mic 7:18 because He delights in **m**
Mic 7:20 **m** to Abraham, which You have
Hab 3: 2 in wrath remember **m**
Zech 1:12 You not have **m** on Jerusalem
Zech 1:16 returning to Jerusalem with **m**
Zech 7: 9 Execute true justice, show **m**
Zech 10: 6 because I have **m** on them
Matt 5: 7 for they shall obtain **m**
Matt 9:13 I desire **m** and not sacrifice
Matt 9:27 Son of David, have **m** on us
Matt 12: 7 what this means, 'I desire **m**
Matt 15:22 Have **m** on me, O Lord, Son of
Matt 17:15 have **m** on my son, for he is
Matt 20:30 Have **m** on us, O Lord, Son of
Matt 20:31 Have **m** on us, O Lord, Son of
Matt 23:23 justice and **m** and faith
Mark 10:47 Son of David, have **m** on me
Mark 10:48 Son of David, have **m** on me
Luke 1:50 His **m** is on those who fear
Luke 1:54 in remembrance of His **m**,
Luke 1:58 Lord had shown great **m** to her
Luke 1:72 to perform the **m** promised to
Luke 1:78 the tender **m** of our God, with
Luke 10:37 He who showed **m** on him
Luke 16:24 have **m** on me, and send Lazarus
Luke 17:13 Jesus, Master, have **m** on us
Luke 18:38 Son of David, have **m** on me
Luke 18:39 Son of David, have **m** on me
Rom 9:15 I will have **m** on whomever I
Rom 9:15 on whomever I will have **m**
Rom 9:16 runs, but of God who shows **m**
Rom 9:18 He has **m** on whom He wills
Rom 9:23 His glory on the vessels of **m**
Rom 11:30 God, yet have now obtained **m**
Rom 11:31 that through the **m** shown you
Rom 11:31 you they also may obtain **m**
Rom 11:32 that He might have **m** on all
Rom 12: 8 he who shows **m**, with
Rom 15: 9 might glorify God for His **m**
1Co 7:25 in His **m** has made trustworthy
2Co 4: 1 as we have received **m**, we do
Gal 6:16 **m** be upon them, and upon the

Eph 2: 4 But God, who is rich in **m**
Phil 2: 1 Spirit, if any affection and **m**
Phil 2:27 but God had **m** on him, and not
1Ti 1: 2 Grace, **m**, and peace from God
1Ti 1:13 but I obtained **m** because I
1Ti 1:16 for this reason I obtained **m**
2Ti 1: 2 Grace, **m**, and peace from God
2Ti 1:16 The Lord grant **m** to the
2Ti 1:18 to him that he may find **m**
Tit 1: 4 Grace, **m**, and peace from God
Tit 3: 5 to His **m** He saved us, through
Heb 4:16 grace, that we may obtain **m**
Heb 9: 5 overshadowing the **m** seat
Heb 10:28 Moses' law dies without **m** on
Jas 2:13 For judgment is without **m** to
Jas 2:13 to the one who has shown no **m**
Jas 2:13 **M** triumphs over judgment
Jas 3:17 willing to yield, full of **m**
1Pe 1: 3 according to His abundant **m**
1Pe 2:10 who had not obtained **m**
1Pe 2:10 but now have obtained **m**
2Jn 3 Grace, **m**, and peace will be
Jude 2 **M**, peace, and love be
Jude 21 looking for the **m** of our Lord

MERE (*see* PREFACE)

MERED (*see* MERED'S)
1Ch 4:17 sons of Ezrah were Jether, **M**
1Ch 4:18 of Pharaoh, whom **M** took

MERED'S (*see* MERED)
1Ch 4:17 **M** wife bore Miriam, Shammai,

MEREMOTH (*see* MERAIOTH)
Ezra 8:33 of our God by the hand of **M**
Ezra 10:36 Vaniah, **M**, Eliashib,
Neh 3: 4 next to them **M** the son of
Neh 3:21 After him **M** the son of Urijah
Neh 10: 5 Harim, **M**, Obadiah,
Neh 12: 3 Shechaniah, Rehum, **M**,

MERES
Esth 1:14 Shethar, Admatha, Tarshish, **M**

MERIBAH (*see* MASSAH, MERIBAH KADESH)
Ex 17: 7 name of the place Massah and **M**
Num 20:13 This was the water of **M**,
Num 20:24 My word at the water of **M**
Num 27:14 (These are the waters of **M**
Deut 32:51 at the waters of **M** Kadesh
Deut 33: 8 contended at the waters of **M**
Ps 81: 7 proved you at the waters of **M**
Ezek 47:19 to the waters of **M** by Kadesh
Ezek 48:28 to the waters of **M** by Kadesh

MERIB-BAAL (*see* MEPHIBOSHETH)
1Ch 8:34 The son of Jonathan was **M**
1Ch 8:34 and **M** begot Micah
1Ch 9:40 The son of Jonathan was **M**
1Ch 9:40 and **M** begot Micah

MERODACH (*see* EVIL-MERODACH)
Jer 50: 2 **M** is broken in pieces

MERODACH-BALADAN (*see* BALADAN, BERODACH-BALADAN)
Is 39: 1 At that time **M** the son of

MEROM
Josh 11: 5 of **M** to fight against Israel
Josh 11: 7 suddenly by the waters of **M**

MERONOTHITE
1Ch 27:30 Jehdeiah the **M** was over the
Neh 3: 7 the Gibeonite, Jadon the **M**

MEROZ
Judg 5:23 Curse **M**,' said the angel of

MERRILY (*see* MERRY)
Esth 5:14 then go **m** with the king to

MERRY (*see* MERRILY, MERRY-HEARTED)
Gen 43:34 they drank and were **m** with him
Judg 9:27 and trod them, and made **m**
Judg 16:25 when their hearts were **m**
Judg 19: 6 night, and let your heart be **m**
Judg 19: 9 that your heart may be **m**
1Sa 25:36 heart was **m** within him, for
2Sa 13:28 Amnon's heart is **m** with wine
Esth 1:10 of the king was **m** with wine
Prov 15:13 A **m** heart makes a cheerful
Prov 15:15 but he who is of a **m** heart
Prov 17:22 A **m** heart does good, like
Eccl 8:15 than to eat, drink, and be **m**
Eccl 9: 7 your wine with a **m** heart
Eccl 10:19 for laughter, and wine makes **m**
Jer 30:19 the voice of those who make **m**
Luke 12:19 eat, drink, and be **m**
Luke 15:23 it, and let us eat and be **m**
Luke 15:24 And they began to be **m**
Luke 15:29 might make **m** with my friends
Luke 15:32 right that we should make **m**
Rev 11:10 rejoice over them, make **m**

MERRY-HEARTED (*see* MERRY)
Is 24: 7 languishes, all the **m** sigh

MESHA
Gen 10:30 **M** as you go toward Sephar
2Ki 3: 4 Now **M** king of Moab was a
1Ch 2:42 brother of Jerahmeel were **M**
1Ch 8: 9 wife he begot Jobab, Zibia, **M**

MESHACH (*see* MISHAEL)
Dan 1: 7 to Mishael, **M**
Dan 2:49 king, and he set Shadrach, **M**
Dan 3:12 Shadrach, **M**, and Abed-Nego
Dan 3:13 command to bring Shadrach, **M**
Dan 3:14 Is it true, Shadrach, **M**, and
Dan 3:16 Shadrach, **M**, and Abed-Nego
Dan 3:19 changed toward Shadrach, **M**
Dan 3:20 his army to bind Shadrach, **M**
Dan 3:22 men who took up Shadrach, **M**
Dan 3:23 these three men, Shadrach, **M**
Dan 3:26 Shadrach, **M**, and Abed-Nego,
Dan 3:26 Then Shadrach, **M**, and
Dan 3:28 be the God of Shadrach, **M**
Dan 3:29 the God of Shadrach, **M**, and
Dan 3:30 the king promoted Shadrach, **M**

MESHECH
Gen 10: 2 Magog, Madai, Javan, Tubal, **M**
1Ch 1: 5 Magog, Madai, Javan, Tubal, **M**
1Ch 1:17 Aram, Uz, Hul, Gether, and **M**
Ps 120: 5 is me, that I sojourn in **M**
Ezek 27:13 Tubal, and **M** were your traders
Ezek 32:26 There are **M** and Tubal and all
Ezek 38: 2 Magog, the prince of Rosh, **M**
Ezek 38: 3 O Gog, the prince of Rosh, **M**
Ezek 39: 1 you, O Gog, prince of Rosh, **M**

MESHELEMIAH (*see* MESHULLAM, SHALLUM, SHELEMIAH)
1Ch 9:21 Zechariah the son of **M** was
1Ch 26: 1 **M** the son of Kore, of the
1Ch 26: 2 the sons of **M** were Zechariah
1Ch 26: 9 And **M** had sons and brethren,

MESHEZABEEL
Neh 3: 4 of Berechiah, the son of **M**
Neh 10:21 **M**, Zadok, Jaddua,
Neh 11:24 Pethahiah the son of **M**, of

MESHILLEMITH (*see* MESHILLEMOTH)
1Ch 9:12 of Meshullam, the son of **M**

MESHILLEMOTH (*see* MESHILLEMITH)
2Ch 28:12 Berechiah the son of **M**,
Neh 11:13 son of Ahzai, the son of **M**

MESHOBAB
1Ch 4:34 **M**, Jamlech, and Joshah the son

MESHULLAM (*see* MESHELEMIAH)
2Ki 22: 3 son of Azaliah, the son of **M**
1Ch 3:19 The sons of Zerubbabel were **M**
1Ch 5:13 Michael, **M**, Sheba, Jorai,
1Ch 8:17 Zebadiah, **M**, Hizki, Heber,
1Ch 9: 7 Sallu the son of **M**, the son
1Ch 9: 8 **M** the son of Shephatiah, the
1Ch 9:11 son of Hilkiah, the son of **M**
1Ch 9:12 son of Jahzerah, the son of **M**
2Ch 34:12 of Merari, and Zechariah and **M**
Ezra 8:16 Nathan, Zechariah, and **M**,
Ezra 10:15 of Tikvah opposed this, and **M**
Ezra 10:29 **M**, Malluch, Adaiah, Jashub,
Neh 3: 4 Next to them **M** the son of
Neh 3: 6 and **M** the son of Besodeiah
Neh 3:30 After him **M** the son of
Neh 6:18 of **M** the son of Berechiah
Neh 8: 4 Hashbadana, Zechariah, and **M**
Neh 10: 7 **M**, Abijah, Mijamin,
Neh 10:20 Magpiash, **M**, Hezir,
Neh 11: 7 Sallu the son of **M**, the son
Neh 11:11 son of Hilkiah, the son of **M**
Neh 12:13 of Ezra, **M**
Neh 12:16 of Ginnethon, **M**
Neh 12:25 Bakbukiah, Obadiah, **M**,
Neh 12:33 and Azariah, Ezra, **M**,

MESHULLEMETH
2Ki 21:19 His mother's name was **M** the

MESOPOTAMIA (*see* ARAM)
Gen 24:10 And he arose and went to **M**, to
Deut 23: 4 son of Beor from Pethor of **M**
Judg 3: 8 Cushan-Rishathaim king of **M**
Judg 3:10 king of **M** into his hand
1Ch 19: 6 chariots and horsemen from **M**
Acts 2: 9 Elamites, those dwelling in **M**
Acts 7: 2 Abraham when he was in **M**,

MESSAGE (*see* MESSENGER)
Ex 4: 8 nor heed the **m** of the first
Ex 4: 8 the **m** of the latter sign
Judg 3:19 I have a secret **m** for you
Judg 3:20 I have a **m** from God for you
1Ki 5: 8 the **m** which you sent me, and I
1Ki 20:12 when Ben-Hadad heard this **m**
2Ki 9: 5 I have a **m** for you, O
Neh 6: 4 sent me this **m** four times
Prov 26: 6 He who sends a **m** by the hand
Is 28: 9 he make to understand the **m**
Jer 49:14 have heard a **m** from the LORD
Dan 10: 1 a **m** was revealed to Daniel
Dan 10: 1 The **m** was true, but the
Dan 10: 1 and he understood the **m**, and
Jon 3: 2 to it the **m** that I tell you
Hag 1:13 the LORD's **m** to the people
Acts 20: 7 them and continued his **m** until
1Co 1:18 For the **m** of the cross is
1Co 1:21 the foolishness of the **m**
2Ti 2:17 And their **m** will spread like
2Ti 4:17 me, so that the **m** might be
1Jn 1: 5 This is the **m** which we have
1Jn 3:11 For this is the **m** that you

MESSENGER (*see* MESSAGE, MESSENGERS)
1Sa 4:17 So the **m** answered and said,
1Sa 23:27 But a **m** came to Saul, saying,
2Sa 11:19 and charged the **m**, saying
2Sa 11:22 So the **m** went, and came and
2Sa 11:23 And the **m** said to David,
2Sa 11:25 Then David said to the **m**
2Sa 15:13 a **m** came to David, saying,
1Ki 19: 2 Jezebel sent a **m** to Elijah
1Ki 22:13 Then the **m** who had gone to
2Ki 5:10 And Elisha sent a **m** to him
2Ki 6:32 but before the **m** came to him
2Ki 6:32 Look, when the **m** comes, shut
2Ki 6:33 with them, there was the **m**
2Ki 9:18 The **m** went to them, but is
2Ki 10: 8 Then a **m** came and told him,
2Ch 18:12 Then the **m** who had gone to
Job 1:14 and a **m** came to Job and said,
Job 33:23 If there is a **m** for him, a
Prov 13:17 A wicked **m** falls into trouble
Prov 17:11 therefore a cruel **m** will be
Prov 25:13 **m** to those who send him, for
Eccl 5: 6 nor say before the **m** of God
Is 42:19 or deaf as My **m** whom I send
Jer 51:31 one **m** to meet another, to
Ezek 23:40 afar, to whom a **m** was sent
Obad 1 a **m** has been sent among the
Hag 1:13 Then Haggai, the LORD's **m**
Mal 2: 7 for he is the **m** of the LORD
Mal 3: 1 Behold, I send My **m**, and he
Mal 3: 1 even the **M** of the covenant,
Matt 11:10 I send My **m** before Your face,
Mark 1: 2 I send My **m** before Your face,
Luke 7:27 I send My **m** before Your face,
2Co 12: 7 a **m** of Satan to buffet me,
Phil 2:25 and fellow soldier, but your **m**

MESSENGERS (*see* MESSENGER)
Gen 32: 3 Then Jacob sent **m** before him
Gen 32: 6 Then the **m** returned to Jacob,
Gen 50:16 So they sent **m** to Joseph,
Num 20:14 Now Moses sent **m** from Kadesh
Num 21:21 Then Israel sent **m** to Sihon
Num 22: 5 Then he sent **m** to Balaam the
Num 24:12 to your **m** whom you sent to me
Deut 2:26 I sent **m** from the Wilderness
Josh 6:17 she hid the **m** that we sent
Josh 6:25 because she hid the **m** whom
Josh 7:22 So Joshua sent **m**, and they ran
Judg 6:35 And he sent **m** throughout all
Judg 6:35 He also sent **m** to Asher,
Judg 7:24 Then Gideon sent **m** throughout
Judg 9:31 And he sent **m** to Abimelech
Judg 11:12 Now Jephthah sent **m** to the
Judg 11:13 answered the **m** of Jephthah

Judg 11:14 So Jephthah again sent **m** to
Judg 11:17 Then Israel sent **m** to the
Judg 11:19 Then Israel sent **m** to Sihon
1Sa 6:21 So they sent **m** to the
1Sa 11: 3 that we may send **m** to all the
1Sa 11: 4 So the **m** came to Gibeah of
1Sa 11: 7 of Israel by the hands of **m**
1Sa 11: 9 they said to the **m** who came
1Sa 11: 9 Then the **m** came and
1Sa 16:19 Saul sent **m** to Jesse, and said
1Sa 19:11 Saul also sent **m** to David's
1Sa 19:14 Saul sent **m** to take David
1Sa 19:15 sent the **m** back to see David
1Sa 19:16 when the **m** had come in, there
1Sa 19:20 Saul sent **m** to take David
1Sa 19:20 God came upon the **m** of Saul
1Sa 19:21 was told, he sent other **m**
1Sa 19:21 Then Saul sent **m** again the
1Sa 25:14 Look, David sent **m** from the
1Sa 25:42 she followed the **m** of David
2Sa 2: 5 So David sent **m** to the men of
2Sa 3:12 Then Abner sent **m** on his
2Sa 3:14 So David sent **m** to Ishbosheth
2Sa 3:26 he sent **m** after Abner, who
2Sa 5:11 king of Tyre sent **m** to David
2Sa 11: 4 Then David sent **m**, and took
2Sa 12:27 And Joab sent **m** to David, and
1Ki 20: 2 Then he sent **m** into the city
1Ki 20: 5 Then the **m** came back and said,
1Ki 20: 9 he said to the **m** of Ben-Hadad
1Ki 20: 9 the **m** departed and brought
2Ki 1: 2 so he sent **m** and said to them,
2Ki 1: 3 go up to meet the **m** of the
2Ki 1: 5 when the **m** returned to him,
2Ki 1:16 Because you have sent **m** to
2Ki 7:15 So the **m** returned and told the
2Ki 14: 8 Then Amaziah sent **m** to
2Ki 16: 7 So Ahaz sent **m** to
2Ki 17: 4 for he had sent **m** to So, king
2Ki 19: 9 he again sent **m** to Hezekiah
2Ki 19:14 letter from the hand of the **m**
2Ki 19:23 By your **m** you have reproached
1Ch 14: 1 king of Tyre sent **m** to David
1Ch 19: 2 So David sent **m** to comfort
1Ch 19:16 by Israel, they sent **m** and
2Ch 35:21 But he sent **m** to him, saying,
2Ch 36:15 warnings to them by His **m**
2Ch 36:16 But they mocked the **m** of God
Neh 6: 3 So I sent **m** to them, saying,
Prov 16:14 As **m** of death is the king's
Is 14:32 answer the **m** of the nation
Is 18: 2 Go, swift **m**, to a nation tall
Is 37: 9 he sent **m** to Hezekiah, saying
Is 37:14 letter from the hand of the **m**
Is 44:26 performs the counsel of His **m**
Is 57: 9 you sent your **m** far off, and
Jer 27: 3 by the hand of the **m** who come
Ezek 23:16 sent **m** to them in Chaldea
Ezek 30: 9 On that day **m** shall go forth
Nah 2:13 the voice of your **m** shall be
Luke 7:24 When the **m** of John had
Luke 9:52 and sent **m** before His face
2Co 8:23 they are **m** of the churches,
Jas 2:25 works when she received the **m**

MESSIAH
Dan 9:25 Jerusalem until **M** the Prince
Dan 9:26 weeks **M** shall be cut off, but
John 1:41 We have found the **M**" (which
John 4:25 I know that **M** is coming"

MET (*see* MEET)
Gen 32: 1 and the angels of God **m** him
Gen 33: 8 by all this company which I **m**
Ex 3:18 of the Hebrews has **m** with us
Ex 4:24 that the LORD **m** him and
Ex 4:27 **m** him on the mountain of God,
Ex 5: 3 of the Hebrews has **m** with us
Ex 5:20 they **m** Moses and Aaron who
Num 23: 4 God **m** Balaam, and he said to
Num 23:16 Then the LORD **m** Balaam, and
Deut 25:18 how he **m** you on the way and
Josh 11: 5 these kings had **m** together
1Sa 9:11 they **m** some young women
1Sa 21: 1 was afraid when he **m** David
1Sa 25:20 toward her, and she **m** them
2Sa 2:13 **m** them by the pool of Gibeon
2Sa 16: 1 who **m** him with a couple of
2Sa 18: 9 Then Absalom **m** the servants
1Ki 11:29 Shilonite **m** him on the way
1Ki 13:24 a lion **m** him on the road and
1Ki 18: 7 way, suddenly Elijah **m** him
2Ki 9:21 and **m** him on the property of
2Ki 10:13 Jehu **m** with the brothers of
2Ki 10:15 he **m** Jehonadab the son of
Neh 13: 2 because they had not **m** the
Ps 85:10 and truth have **m** together
Prov 7:10 And there a woman **m** him, with
Is 21:14 bread they **m** him who fled
Jer 41: 6 it happened as he **m** them that
Amos 5:19 from a lion, and a bear **m** him
Matt 8:28 Gergesenes, there **m** Him two
Matt 28: 9 behold, Jesus **m** them, saying
Mark 5: 2 immediately there **m** Him out
Luke 8:27 there **m** Him a certain man
Luke 9:37 that a great multitude **m** Him
Luke 17:12 there **m** Him ten men who were
John 4:51 down, his servants **m** him and
John 11:20 **m** Him, but Mary was sitting
John 11:30 the place where Martha **m** Him
John 12:18 reason the people also **m** Him
John 18: 2 for Jesus often **m** there with
Acts 10:25 coming in, Cornelius **m** him
Acts 16:13 to the women who **m** there
Acts 16:16 a spirit of divination **m** us
Acts 20:14 when he **m** us at Assos, we
Acts 27:41 a place where two seas **m**,
Heb 7: 1 who **m** Abraham returning from
Heb 7:10 father when Melchizedek **m** him

METAL (*see* METALSMITH)
Job 37:18 strong as a cast **m** mirror

METALSMITH (*see* METAL)
Jer 10: 9 and of the hands of the **m**
Jer 10:14 every **m** is put to shame by
Jer 51:17 every **m** is put to shame by

METE
Job 28:25 **m** out the waters by measure

METHEG AMMAH
2Sa 8: 1 David took **M** from the hand of

METHUSELAH
Gen 5:21 sixty-five years, and begot **M**
Gen 5:22 After he begot **M**, Enoch
Gen 5:25 **M** lived one hundred and
Gen 5:26 **M** lived seven hundred and
Gen 5:27 days of **M** were nine hundred
1Ch 1: 3 Enoch, **M**, Lamech,
Luke 3:37 the son of **M**, the son of

METHUSHAEL
Gen 4:18 and Mehujael begot **M**
Gen 4:18 and **M** begot Lamech

MEUNIM
Ezra 2:50 sons of Asnah, the sons of **M**
Neh 7:52 of Besai, the children of **M**

MEUNITES
1Ch 4:41 the **M** who were found there,
2Ch 26: 7 in Gur Baal, and against the **M**

MEZAHAB
Gen 36:39 of Matred, the daughter of **M**
1Ch 1:50 of Matred, the daughter of **M**

MEZOBAITE
1Ch 11:47 Eliel, Obed, and Jaasiel the **M**

MIBHAR
1Ch 11:38 Nathan, **M** the son of Hagri,

MIBSAM
Gen 25:13 then Kedar, Adbeel, **M**,
1Ch 1:29 then Kedar, Adbeel, **M**,
1Ch 4:25 **M** his son, and Mishma his son

MIBZAR
Gen 36:42 Kenaz, Chief Teman, Chief **M**
1Ch 1:53 Kenaz, Chief Teman, Chief **M**

MICAH (*see* MICAH'S, MICAIAH, MICHA, MICHAH)
Judg 17: 1 of Ephraim, whose name was **M**
Judg 17: 4 they were in the house of **M**
Judg 17: 5 The man **M** had a shrine, and
Judg 17: 8 of Ephraim, to the house of **M**
Judg 17: 9 **M** said to him, "Where do
Judg 17:10 **M** said to him, "Dwell with
Judg 17:12 So **M** consecrated the Levite,
Judg 17:12 and lived in the house of **M**
Judg 17:13 Then **M** said, "Now I know
Judg 18: 2 of Ephraim, to the house of **M**
Judg 18: 3 they were at the house of **M**
Judg 18: 4 Thus and so **M** did for me
Judg 18:13 and came to the house of **M**
Judg 18:15 that is, to the house of **M**
Judg 18:22 good way from the house of **M**
Judg 18:23 turned around and said to **M**
Judg 18:26 when **M** saw that they were too
Judg 18:27 took the things **M** had made
1Ch 5: 5 **M** his son, Reaiah his son,
1Ch 8:34 and Merib-Baal begot **M**
1Ch 8:35 The sons of **M** were Pithon
1Ch 9:15 and Mattaniah the son of **M**
1Ch 9:40 and Merib-Baal begot **M**
1Ch 9:41 The sons of **M** were Pithon
2Ch 34:20 Shaphan, Abdon the son of **M**
Jer 26:18 **M** of Moresheth prophesied in
Mic 1: 1 of the LORD that came to **M** of

MICAH'S (*see* MICAH)
Judg 18:18 When these went into **M** house
Judg 18:22 **M** house gathered together
Judg 18:31 **M** carved image which he made

MICAIAH (*see* MICAH, MICHA, MICHAIAH)
1Ki 22: 8 **M** the son of Imlah, by whom
1Ki 22: 9 Bring **M** the son of Imlah
1Ki 22:13 gone to call **M** spoke to him
1Ki 22:14 **M** said, "As the LORD lives
1Ki 22:15 **M**, shall we go to war against
1Ki 22:19 Then **M** said, "Therefore hear
1Ki 22:24 struck **M** on the cheek, and
1Ki 22:25 **M** said, "Indeed, you shall
1Ki 22:26 Take **M**, and return him to
1Ki 22:28 Then **M** said, "If you ever
2Ch 18: 7 He is **M** the son of Imla
2Ch 18: 8 Bring **M** the son of Imla
2Ch 18:12 gone to call **M** spoke to him
2Ch 18:13 **M** said, "As the LORD lives
2Ch 18:14 **M**, shall we go to war against
2Ch 18:18 Then **M** said, "Therefore hear
2Ch 18:23 struck **M** on the cheek, and
2Ch 18:24 **M** said, "Indeed you shall
2Ch 18:25 Take **M**, and return him to
2Ch 18:27 Then **M** said, "If you ever

MICHA (*see* MICAH, MICAIAH, MICHAIAH)
2Sa 9:12 a young son whose name was **M**
Neh 10:11 **M**, Rehob, Hashabiah,
Neh 11:17 and Mattaniah the son of **M**
Neh 11:22 of Mattaniah, the son of **M**

MICHAEL
Num 13:13 of Asher, Sethur the son of **M**
1Ch 5:13 **M**, Meshullam, Sheba, Jorai,
1Ch 5:14 son of Gilead, the son of **M**
1Ch 6:40 the son of **M**, the son of
1Ch 7: 3 the sons of Izrahiah were **M**
1Ch 8:16 **M**, Ispah, and Joha were the
1Ch 12:20 Adnah, Jozabad, Jediael, **M**
1Ch 27:18 Issachar, Omri the son of **M**
2Ch 21: 2 Zechariah, Azaryahu, **M**, and
Ezra 8: 8 Zebadiah the son of **M**, and
Dan 10:13 and behold, **M**, one of the
Dan 10:21 these, except **M** your prince
Dan 12: 1 At that time **M** shall stand up
Jude 9 Yet **M** the archangel, in
Rev 12: 7 **M** and his angels fought

MICHAH (*see* MICAH, MICHAIAH)
1Ch 23:20 **M** was the first and Jesshiah
1Ch 24:24 Of the sons of Uzziel, **M**
1Ch 24:24 of the sons of **M**, Shamir
1Ch 24:25 The brother of **M**, Isshiah

MICHAIAH (*see* MICAIAH, MICHA, MICHAH)
2Ki 22:12 Shaphan, Achbor the son of **M**
2Ch 13: 2 His mother's name was **M** the
2Ch 17: 7 Zechariah, Nethaneel, and **M**
Neh 12:35 of Mattaniah, the son of **M**
Neh 12:41 Maaseiah, Minjamin, **M**,
Jer 36:11 When **M** the son of Gemariah,
Jer 36:13 Then **M** declared to them all

MICHAL (*see* EGLAH)
1Sa 14:49 and the name of the younger **M**
1Sa 18:20 Now **M**, Saul's daughter, loved
1Sa 18:27 Then Saul gave him **M** his
1Sa 18:28 was with David, and that **M**
1Sa 19:11 And **M**, David's wife, told him,
1Sa 19:12 So **M** let David down through a
1Sa 19:13 **M** took an image and laid it in
1Sa 19:17 Then Saul said to **M**, "Why
1Sa 19:17 And **M** answered Saul, "He said
1Sa 25:44 Saul had given **M** his daughter
2Sa 3:13 face unless you first bring **M**
2Sa 3:14 Give me my wife **M**, whom I

2Sa 6:16 into the City of David, **M**
2Sa 6:20 **M** the daughter of Saul came
2Sa 6:21 So David said to **M**, "It was
2Sa 6:23 Therefore **M** the daughter of
2Sa 21: 8 and the five sons of **M** the
1Ch 15:29 that **M** the daughter of Saul,

MICHMAS (*see* MICHMASH)
Ezra 2:27 the men of **M**, one hundred and
Neh 7:31 the men of **M**, one hundred and

MICHMASH (*see* MICHMAS)
1Sa 13: 2 thousand were with Saul in **M**
1Sa 13: 5 came up and encamped in **M**
1Sa 13:11 gathered together at **M**,
1Sa 13:16 the Philistines encamped in **M**
1Sa 13:23 went out to the pass of **M**
1Sa 14: 5 faced northward opposite **M**
1Sa 14:31 that day from **M** to Aijalon
Neh 11:31 Benjamin from Geba dwelt in **M**
Is 10:28 at **M** he has attended to his

MICHMETHATH
Josh 16: 6 sea on the north side of **M**
Josh 17: 7 Manasseh was from Asher to **M**

MICHRI
1Ch 9: 8 the son of Uzzi, the son of **M**

MIDDAY
1Ki 18:29 when **m** was past, that they
Neh 8: 3 Gate from morning until **m**
Acts 26:13 at **m**, O king, along the road

MIDDIN
Josh 15:61 Beth Arabah, **M**, Secacah,

MIDDLE
Gen 15:10 cut them in two, down the **m**
Ex 26:28 The **m** bar shall pass through
Ex 28:32 for his head in the **m** of it
Ex 36:33 he made the **m** bar to pass
Ex 39:23 opening in the **m** of the robe
Num 2:17 Levites in the **m** of the camps
Num 35: 5 The city shall be in the **m**
Deut 3:16 the **m** of the river as the
Deut 13:16 into the **m** of the street, and
Josh 12: 2 from the **m** of that river,
Judg 7:19 the beginning of the **m** watch
Judg 16:29 **m** pillars which supported the
2Sa 10: 4 off their garments in the **m**
2Sa 20:12 blood in the **m** of the highway
2Sa 23:12 himself in the **m** of the field
1Ki 3:20 arose in the **m** of the night
1Ki 6: 6 the **m** was six cubits wide, and
1Ki 6: 8 The doorway for the **m** story
1Ki 6: 8 up by stairs to the **m** story
1Ki 6: 8 and from the **m** to the third
1Ki 6:27 other in the **m** of the room
1Ki 8:64 **m** of the court that was in
2Ki 20: 4 had gone out into the **m** court
1Ch 19: 4 off their garments in the **m**
2Ch 7: 7 Solomon consecrated the **m** of
Job 34:20 die, in the **m** of the night
Is 16: 3 the night in the **m** of the day
Jer 39: 3 came in and sat in the **M** Gate
Ezek 1:16 a wheel in the **m** of a wheel
Ezek 10:10 a wheel in the **m** of a wheel
Ezek 15: 4 of it, and its **m** is burned
Ezek 41: 7 highest by way of the **m** one
Ezek 42: 5 **m** stories of the building
Ezek 42: 6 **m** levels from the ground up
Dan 9:27 but in the **m** of the week He
Matt 14:24 was now in the **m** of the sea
Mark 6:47 boat was in the **m** of the sea
John 7:14 Now about the **m** of the feast
Acts 1:18 he burst open in the **m** and
Eph 2:14 has broken down the **m** wall of
Rev 22: 2 In the **m** of its street, and on

MIDIAN (*see* MIDIANITE)
Gen 25: 2 Zimran, Jokshan, Medan, **M**
Gen 25: 4 And the sons of **M** were Ephah
Gen 36:35 who attacked **M** in the field
Ex 2:15 and dwelt in the land of **M**
Ex 2:16 Now the priest of **M** had seven
Ex 3: 1 the priest of **M**
Ex 4:19 the LORD said to Moses in **M**
Ex 18: 1 And Jethro, the priest of **M**
Num 22: 4 Moab said to the elders of **M**
Num 22: 7 the elders of **M** departed with
Num 25:15 of a father's house in **M**
Num 25:18 the daughter of a leader of **M**
Num 31: 3 vengeance for the LORD on **M**
Num 31: 8 They killed the kings of **M**
Num 31: 8 and Reba, the five kings of **M**
Num 31: 9 all the women of **M** captive
Josh 13:21 struck with the princes of **M**
Judg 6: 1 the hand of **M** for seven years
Judg 6: 2 and the hand of **M** prevailed
Judg 7: 8 Now the camp of **M** was below
Judg 7:13 tumbled into the camp of **M**
Judg 7:14 his hand God has delivered **M**
Judg 7:15 the camp of **M** into your hand
Judg 7:25 They pursued **M** and brought
Judg 8: 3 your hands the princes of **M**
Judg 8: 5 and Zalmunna, kings of **M**
Judg 8:12 and he took the two kings of **M**
Judg 8:22 us from the hand of **M**
Judg 8:26 which were on the kings of **M**
Judg 8:28 Thus **M** was subdued before the
Judg 9:17 you out of the hand of **M**
1Ki 11:18 Then they arose from **M** and
1Ch 1:32 Zimran, Jokshan, Medan, **M**
1Ch 1:33 The sons of **M** were Ephah,
1Ch 1:46 who attacked **M** in the field
Ps 83: 9 Deal with them as with **M**, As
Is 9: 4 oppressor, as in the day of **M**
Is 10:26 of **M** at the rock of Oreb
Is 60: 6 land, the dromedaries of **M**
Hab 3: 7 of the land of **M** trembled
Acts 7:29 a sojourner in the land of **M**

MIDIANITE (*see* MIDIAN, MIDIANITES)
Gen 37:28 Then **M** traders passed by
Num 10:29 Hobab the son of Reuel the **M**
Num 25: 6 **M** woman in the sight of Moses
Num 25:14 was killed with the **M** woman
Num 25:15 the name of the **M** woman who

MIDIANITES (*see* KENITES, MIDIANITE)
Gen 37:36 Now the **M** had sold him in
Num 25:17 Harass the **M**, and attack them
Num 31: 2 children of Israel on the **M**
Num 31: 3 let them go against the **M** to
Num 31: 7 And they warred against the **M**
Judg 6: 2 Because of the **M**, the
Judg 6: 3 had sown, **M** would come up
Judg 6: 6 impoverished because of the **M**
Judg 6: 7 to the LORD because of the **M**
Judg 6:11 order to hide it from the **M**
Judg 6:13 us into the hands of the **M**
Judg 6:14 Israel from the hand of the **M**
Judg 6:16 shall defeat the **M** as one man
Judg 6:33 Then all the **M** and Amalekites,
Judg 7: 1 so that the camp of the **M** was
Judg 7: 2 give the **M** into their hands
Judg 7: 7 deliver the **M** into your hand
Judg 7:12 Now the **M** and Amalekites, all
Judg 7:23 Manasseh, and pursued the **M**
Judg 7:24 Come down against the **M**, and
Judg 7:25 captured two princes of the **M**
Judg 8: 1 you went to fight with the **M**

MIDNIGHT
Ex 11: 4 About **m** I will go out into
Ex 12:29 it came to pass at **m** that the
Judg 16: 3 And Samson lay low till **m**
Judg 16: 3 then he arose at **m**, took hold
Ruth 3: 8 Now it happened at **m** that the
Ps 119:62 At **m** I will rise to give
Matt 25: 6 And at **m** a cry was heard
Mark 13:35 in the evening, at **m**, at the
Luke 11: 5 a friend, and go to him at **m**
Acts 16:25 But at **m** Paul and Silas were
Acts 20: 7 continued his message until **m**
Acts 27:27 about **m** the sailors sensed

MIDST (*see* PREFACE)

MIDWAY
Ex 27: 5 network may be **m** up the altar
Ex 38: 4 its rim, **m** from the bottom

MIDWIFE (*see* MIDWIVES)
Gen 35:17 that the **m** said to her,
Gen 38:28 the **m** took a scarlet thread
Ex 1:16 of a **m** for the Hebrew women

MIDWIVES (*see* MIDWIFE)
Ex 1:15 Egypt spoke to the Hebrew **m**
Ex 1:17 But the **m** feared God, and did
Ex 1:18 of Egypt called for the **m**
Ex 1:19 And the **m** said to Pharaoh,
Ex 1:19 before the **m** come to them
Ex 1:20 God dealt well with the **m**
Ex 1:21 was, because the **m** feared God

MIGDAL EL
Josh 19:38 Iron, **M**, Horem, Beth Anath,

MIGDAL GAD (*see* GAD)
Josh 15:37 Zenan, Hadashah, **M**,

MIGDOL
Ex 14: 2 before Pi Hahiroth, between **M**
Num 33: 7 and they camped near **M**.
Jer 44: 1 land of Egypt, who dwell at **M**
Jer 46:14 in Egypt, and proclaim in **M**
Ezek 29:10 from **M** to Syene, as far as
Ezek 30: 6 From **M** to Syene those within

MIGHT (*see* PREFACE)

MIGHT* (*see* MIGHTIER, MIGHTILY, MIGHTY)
Gen 49: 3 you are my firstborn, my **m**
Num 14:13 for by Your **m** You brought
Deut 6: 5 your soul, and with all your **m**
Deut 8:17 the **m** of my hand have gained
Judg 6:14 Go in this **m** of yours, and you
2Sa 6:14 the LORD with all his **m**
1Ki 15:23 the acts of Asa, all his **m**
1Ki 16: 5 Baasha, what he did, and his **m**
1Ki 16:27 the **m** that he showed, are
2Ki 10:34 all that he did, and all his **m**
2Ki 13: 8 all that he did, and his **m**
2Ki 13:12 his **m** with which he fought
2Ki 14:15 his **m**, and how he fought with
2Ki 14:28 his **m**, how he made war, and
2Ki 20:20 all his **m**, and how he made a
2Ki 23:25 his soul, and with all his **m**
1Ch 13: 8 before God with all their **m**
1Ch 29: 2 I have prepared with all my **m**
1Ch 29:12 In Your hand is power and **m**
1Ch 29:30 with all his reign and his **m**
2Ch 20: 6 hand is there not power and **m**
Esth 10: 2 acts of his power and his **m**
Ps 145: 6 of the **m** of Your awesome acts
Eccl 9:10 to do, do it with your **m**
Is 11: 2 the Spirit of counsel and **m**
Is 40:26 by the greatness of His **m**
Jer 9:23 the mighty man glory in his **m**
Jer 10: 6 and Your name is great in **m**)
Jer 16:21 to know My hand and My **m**
Jer 49:35 Elam, the foremost of their **m**
Jer 51:30 their **m** has failed, they
Ezek 32:30 which they caused by their **m**
Dan 2:20 ever, for wisdom and **m** are His
Dan 2:23 have given me wisdom and **m**
Amos 2:16 of **m** shall flee naked in that
Mic 3: 8 the LORD, and of justice and **m**
Mic 7:16 and be ashamed of all their **m**
Zech 4: 6 Not by **m** nor by power, but
Eph 1:21 principality and power and **m**
Eph 3:16 to be strengthened with **m**
Eph 6:10 Lord and in the power of His **m**
Col 1:11 strengthened with all **m**,
2Pe 2:11 who are greater in power and **m**
Rev 7:12 and honor and power and **m**, be

MIGHTIER (*see* MIGHT*, MIGHTY)
Gen 26:16 for you are much **m** than we
Ex 1: 9 Israel are more and **m** than we
Num 14:12 nation greater and **m** than they
Deut 4:38 **m** than you, to bring you in,
Deut 7: 1 greater and **m** than you,
Deut 9: 1 **m** than yourself, cities great
Deut 9:14 I will make of you a nation **m**
Deut 11:23 **m** nations than yourselves
Ps 93: 4 The LORD on high is **m** Than
Eccl 6:10 with Him who is **m** than he
Matt 3:11 coming after me is **m** than I
Mark 1: 7 One after me who is **m** than I
Luke 3:16 but One **m** than I is coming,

MIGHTILY (*see* MIGHT*)
Judg 14: 6 of the LORD came **m** upon him
Judg 14:19 of the LORD came upon him **m**
Judg 15:14 of the LORD came **m** upon him
Is 2:19 arises to shake the earth **m**
Is 2:21 arises to shake the earth **m**
Jer 25:30 He will roar **m** against His
Jon 3: 8 sackcloth, and cry **m** to God
Nah 2: 1 Fortify your power **m**
Acts 19:20 the word of the Lord grew **m**
Col 1:29 working which works in me **m**
Rev 18: 2 he cried **m** with a loud voice,

MIGHTY (*see* MIGHT*, MIGHTIER)
Gen 6: 4 Those were the **m** men who were
Gen 10: 8 to be a **m** one on the earth
Gen 10: 9 He was a **m** hunter before the

Gen 10: 9 Like Nimrod the **m** hunter
Gen 18:18 **m** nation, and all the nations
Gen 23: 6 You are a **m** prince among us
Gen 49:24 strong by the hands of the **M**
Ex 1: 7 and grew exceedingly **m**
Ex 1:20 multiplied and grew very **m**
Ex 3:19 go, no, not even by a **m** hand
Ex • 9:28 may be no more **m** thundering
Ex 10: 2 your son's son the **m** things I
Ex 15:10 like lead in the **m** waters
Ex 15:15 the **m** men of Moab, trembling
Ex 32:11 great power and with a **m** hand
Lev 19:15 nor honor the person of the **m**
Num 22: 6 me, for they are too **m** for me
Deut 3:24 greatness and Your **m** hand
Deut 3:24 Your works and Your **m** deeds
Deut 4:34 wonders, by war, by a **m** hand
Deut 4:37 Presence, with His **m** power
Deut 5:15 out from there by a **m** hand
Deut 6:21 us out of Egypt with a **m** hand
Deut 7: 8 brought you out with a **m** hand
Deut 7:19 wonders, the **m** hand and the
Deut 9:26 out of Egypt with a **m** hand
Deut 9:29 brought out by Your **m** power
Deut 10:17 of lords, the great God, **m**
Deut 11: 2 and His **m** hand and His
Deut 26: 5 he became a nation, great, **m**
Deut 26: 8 us out of Egypt with a **m** hand
Deut 34:12 and by all that **m** power and all
Josh 1:14 all your **m** men of valor, and
Josh 4:24 of the LORD, that it is **m**
Josh 6: 2 king, and the **m** men of valor
Josh 8: 3 thousand **m** men of valor and
Josh 10: 2 Ai, and all its men were **m**
Josh 10: 7 and all the **m** men of valor
Judg 5:13 down for me against the **m**
Judg 5:23 of the LORD against the **m**
Judg 6:12 with you, you **m** man of valor
Judg 11: 1 was a **m** man of valor, but he
1Sa 2: 4 bows of the **m** men are broken
1Sa 4: 8 from the hand of these **m** gods
1Sa 6: 6 When He did **m** things among
1Sa 9: 1 a Benjamite, a **m** man of power
1Sa 16:18 a **m** man of valor, a man of
1Sa 19: 8 and struck them with a **m** blow
1Sa 23: 5 struck them with a **m** blow
2Sa 1:19 How the **m** have fallen
2Sa 1:21 of the **m** is cast away there
2Sa 1:22 slain, from the fat of the **m**
2Sa 1:25 How the **m** have fallen in the
2Sa 1:27 How the **m** have fallen, and the
2Sa 10: 7 and all the army of the **m** men
2Sa 16: 6 all the **m** men were on his
2Sa 17: 8 his men, that they are **m** men
2Sa 17:10 that your father is a **m** man
2Sa 20: 7 Pelethites, and all the **m** men
2Sa 23: 8 of the **m** men whom David had
2Sa 23: 9 one of the three **m** men with
2Sa 23:16 So the three **m** men broke
2Sa 23:17 were done by the three **m** men
2Sa 23:22 won a name among three **m** men
1Ki 1: 8 the **m** men who belonged to
1Ki 1:10 prophet, Benaiah, the **m** men
1Ki 11:28 Jeroboam was a **m** man of valor
2Ki 5: 1 He was also a **m** man of valor
2Ki 24:14 all the **m** men of valor, ten
2Ki 24:15 the **m** of the land he carried
1Ch 1:10 to be a **m** one on the earth
1Ch 5:24 They were **m** men of valor,
1Ch 7: 2 were **m** men of valor in their
1Ch 7: 5 Issachar were **m** men of valor
1Ch 7: 7 thirty-four **m** men of valor
1Ch 7: 9 two hundred **m** men of valor
1Ch 7:11 thousand two hundred **m** men of
1Ch 7:40 **m** men of valor, chief leaders
1Ch 8:40 of Ulam were **m** men of valor
1Ch 11:10 of the **m** men whom David had
1Ch 11:11 of the **m** men whom David had
1Ch 11:12 was one of the three **m** men
1Ch 11:19 were done by the three **m** men
1Ch 11:24 won a name among three **m** men
1Ch 11:26 Also the **m** warriors were
1Ch 12: 1 and they were among the **m** men
1Ch 12: 4 a **m** man among the thirty, and
1Ch 12: 8 **m** men of valor, men trained
1Ch 12:21 they were all **m** men of valor
1Ch 12:25 **m** men of valor fit for war,
1Ch 12:30 **m** men of valor, famous men
1Ch 19: 8 and all the army of the **m** men
1Ch 27: 6 who was **m** among the thirty
1Ch 28: 1 and all the **m** men of valor
1Ch 29:24 All the leaders and the **m** men
2Ch 6:32 great name and Your **m** hand
2Ch 13: 3 choice men, **m** men of valor
2Ch 13:21 But Abijah grew **m**, married
2Ch 14: 8 all these were **m** men of valor
2Ch 17:13 war, **m** men of valor, were in
2Ch 17:14 thousand **m** men of valor
2Ch 17:16 thousand **m** men of valor
2Ch 17:17 Eliada a **m** man of valor, and
2Ch 25: 6 **m** men of valor from Israel
2Ch 26:12 of the **m** men of valor was two
2Ch 26:13 that made war with **m** power
2Ch 27: 6 So Jotham became **m**, because
2Ch 28: 7 a **m** man of Ephraim, killed
2Ch 32:21 cut down every **m** man of valor
Ezra 4:20 been **m** kings over Jerusalem
Ezra 7:28 all the king's **m** princes
Neh 3:16 as far as the House of the **M**
Neh 9:11 as a stone into the **m** waters
Neh 9:32 our God, the great, the **m**
Neh 11:14 **m** men of valor, were one
Job 5:15 from the mouth of the **m**, and
Job 9: 4 in heart and **m** in strength
Job 10: 5 like the days of a **m** man,
Job 12:19 and overthrows the **m**
Job 12:21 on princes, and disarms the **m**
Job 21: 7 old, yes, become **m** in power
Job 22: 8 But the **m** man possessed the
Job 24:22 But God draws the **m** away with
Job 34:20 the **m** are taken away without
Job 34:24 pieces **m** men without inquiry
Job 35: 9 because of the arm of the **m**
Job 36: 5 Behold, God is **m**, but
Job 36: 5 He is **m** in strength of
Job 36:19 riches, or all the **m** forces
Job 41:12 his **m** power, or his graceful
Job 41:25 himself up, the **m** are afraid
Ps 24: 8 The LORD strong and **m**,
Ps 24: 8 The LORD **m** in battle
Ps 29: 1 unto the LORD, O you **m** ones
Ps 33:16 A **m** man is not delivered by
Ps 45: 3 O **M** One, With Your glory and
Ps 50: 1 The **M** One, God the LORD, Has
Ps 52: 1 do you boast in evil, O **m** man
Ps 59: 3 The **m** gather against me, Not
Ps 68:33 out His voice, a **m** voice
Ps 69: 4 They are **m** who would destroy
Ps 74:15 You dried up **m** rivers
Ps 76: 5 none of the **m** men have found
Ps 78:65 And like a **m** man who shouts
Ps 80:10 the **m** cedars with its boughs
Ps 82: 1 in the congregation of the **m**
Ps 89: 6 Who among the sons of the **m**
Ps 89: 8 Who is **m** like You, O LORD
Ps 89:10 Your enemies with Your **m** arm
Ps 89:13 You have a **m** arm
Ps 89:19 given help to one who is **m**
Ps 93: 4 Than the **m** waves of the sea
Ps 106: 2 utter the **m** acts of the LORD
Ps 106: 8 might make His **m** power known
Ps 112: 2 will be **m** on earth
Ps 132: 2 vowed to the **M** God of Jacob
Ps 132: 5 place for the **M** God of Jacob
Ps 135:10 many nations And slew **m** kings
Ps 145: 4 And shall declare Your **m** acts
Ps 145:12 to the sons of men His **m** acts
Ps 147: 5 is our Lord, and **m** in power
Ps 150: 1 Praise Him in His **m** firmament
Ps 150: 2 Praise Him for His **m** acts
Prov 16:32 to anger is better than the **m**
Prov 18:18 cease, and keeps the **m** apart
Prov 21:22 man scales the city of the **m**
Prov 23:11 for their Redeemer is **m**
Prov 30:30 which is **m** among beasts and
Song 4: 4 all shields of **m** men
Is 1:24 hosts, the **M** One of Israel,
Is 3: 2 the **m** man and the man of war,
Is 3:25 sword, and your **m** in the war
Is 5:22 Woe to men **m** at drinking wine
Is 8: 7 of the River, strong and **m**
Is 9: 6 **M** God, Everlasting Father,
Is 10:21 of Jacob, to the **M** God
Is 10:34 will fall by the **M** One
Is 11:15 with His **m** wind He will shake
Is 13: 3 called My **m** ones for My anger
Is 17:12 like the rushing of **m** waters
Is 19:20 a **M** One, and He will deliver
Is 21:17 the **m** men of the people of
Is 22:17 O **m** man, and will surely seize
Is 28: 2 Behold, the Lord has a **m** and
Is 28: 2 like a flood of **m** waters
Is 30:29 LORD, to the **M** One of Israel
Is 34: 7 young bulls with the **m** bulls
Is 42:13 shall go forth like a **m** man
Is 43:16 a path through the **m** waters
Is 49:24 the prey be taken from the **m**
Is 49:25 of the **m** shall be taken away
Is 49:26 Redeemer, the **M** One of Jacob
Is 60:16 Redeemer, the **M** One of Jacob
Is 63: 1 in righteousness, **m** to save
Jer 5:15 It is a **m** nation, it is an
Jer 5:16 they are all **m** men
Jer 9:23 let not the **m** man glory in
Jer 14: 9 like a **m** one who cannot save
Jer 14:17 been broken with a **m** stroke
Jer 20:11 the LORD is with me as a **m**
Jer 26:21 the king, with all his **m** men
Jer 32:18 the Great, the **M** God, whose
Jer 32:19 **m** in work, for your eyes are
Jer 33: 3 **m** things, which you do not
Jer 41:16 the **m** men of war and the
Jer 46: 5 Their **m** ones are beaten down
Jer 46: 6 away, nor the **m** man escape
Jer 46: 9 And let the **m** men come forth
Jer 46:12 for the **m** man has stumbled
Jer 46:12 has stumbled against the **m**
Jer 48:14 How can you say, "We are **m**
Jer 48:41 the **m** men's hearts in Moab on
Jer 49:22 The heart of the **m** men of
Jer 50:36 A sword is against her **m** men
Jer 51:30 The **m** men of Babylon have
Jer 51:56 and her **m** men are taken
Jer 51:57 her deputies, and her **m** men
Lam 1:15 all my **m** men in my midst
Ezek 17:13 took away the **m** of the land
Ezek 17:17 will Pharaoh with his **m** army
Ezek 20:33 surely with a **m** hand, with an
Ezek 20:34 are scattered, with a **m** hand
Ezek 31:11 of the **m** one of the nations
Ezek 32:12 the swords of the **m** warriors
Ezek 32:21 The strong among the **m** Shall
Ezek 32:27 the **m** who are fallen of the
Ezek 32:27 of the terror of the **m** in the
Ezek 38:15 a great company and a **m** army
Ezek 39:18 shall eat the flesh of the **m**
Ezek 39:20 horses and riders, with **m** men
Dan 3:20 he commanded certain **m** men of
Dan 4: 3 signs, and how **m** His wonders
Dan 4:30 royal dwelling by my **m** power
Dan 8:24 His power shall be **m**, but not
Dan 8:24 he shall destroy the **m**, and
Dan 9:15 land of Egypt with a **m** hand
Dan 11: 3 Then a **m** king shall arise,
Dan 11:25 with a very great and **m** army
Hos 10:13 the multitude of your **m** men
Joel 2: 7 They run like **m** men, they
Joel 3: 9 Wake up the **m** men, let all
Joel 3:11 Cause Your **m** ones to go down
Amos 2:14 nor shall the **m** deliver
Amos 5:12 transgressions and your **m** sins
Amos 5:24 righteousness like a **m** stream
Obad 9 Then your **m** men, O Teman,
Jon 1: 4 there was a **m** tempest on the
Nah 2: 3 of his **m** men are made red
Zeph 1:14 there the **m** men shall cry out
Zeph 3:17 God in your midst, the **M** One
Zech 9:13 you like the sword of a **m** man
Zech 10: 5 They shall be like **m** men, who
Zech 10: 7 Ephraim shall be like a **m** man
Zech 11: 2 because the **m** trees are
Matt 11:20 of His **m** works had been done
Matt 11:21 For if the **m** works which were
Matt 11:23 for if the **m** works which were
Matt 13:54 this wisdom and these **m** works
Matt 13:58 He did not do many **m** works
Mark 6: 2 to Him, that such **m** works are
Mark 6: 5 He could do no **m** work there
Luke 1:49 For He who is **m** has done
Luke 1:52 down the **m** from their thrones
Luke 10:13 For if the **m** works which were
Luke 19:37 all the **m** works they had seen
Luke 24:19 who was a Prophet **m** in deed
Acts 2: 2 as of a rushing **m** wind, and
Acts 7:22 and was **m** in words and deeds
Acts 18:24 **m** in the Scriptures, came to
Rom 15:19 in **m** signs and wonders, by the
1Co 1:26 to the flesh, not many **m**, not
1Co 1:27 shame the things which are **m**
2Co 10: 4 but **m** in God for pulling down

2Co 12:12 signs and wonders and **m** deeds
2Co 13: 3 weak toward you, but **m** in you
Eph 1:19 to the working of His **m** power
2Th 1: 7 from heaven with His **m** angels
1Pe 5: 6 under the **m** hand of God, that
Rev 6:13 when it is shaken by a **m** wind
Rev 6:15 the commanders, the **m** men
Rev 10: 1 I saw still another **m** angel
Rev 16:18 a great earthquake, such a **m**
Rev 18:10 city Babylon, that **m** city
Rev 18:21 Then a **m** angel took up a
Rev 19: 6 as the sound of **m** thunderings
Rev 19:18 captains, the flesh of **m** men

MIGRON
1Sa 14: 2 tree which is in **M**
Is 10:28 to Aiath, he has passed **M**

MIJAMIN
1Ch 24: 9 to Malchijah, the sixth to **M**
Ezra 10:25 Ramiah, Jeziah, Malchiah, **M**
Neh 10: 7 Meshullam, Abijah, **M**,
Neh 12: 5 **M**, Maadiah, Bilgah,

MIKLOTH
1Ch 8:32 and **M**, who begot Shimeah
1Ch 9:37 Gedor, Ahio, Zechariah, and **M**
1Ch 9:38 And **M** begot Shimeam
1Ch 27: 4 of his division **M** also was

MIKNEIAH
1Ch 15:18 Mattithiah, Elipheleh, **M**
1Ch 15:21 Mattithiah, Elipheleh, **M**,

MILALAI
Neh 12:36 brethren, Shemaiah, Azarel, **M**

MILCAH (*see* MILCAH'S)
Gen 11:29 the name of Nahor's wife, **M**
Gen 11:29 of Haran the father of **M** and
Gen 22:20 Indeed **M** also has borne
Gen 22:23 These eight **M** bore to Nahor,
Gen 24:15 was born to Bethuel, son of **M**
Gen 24:47 son, whom **M** bore to him
Num 26:33 were Mahlah, Noah, Hoglah, **M**
Num 27: 1 Mahlah, Noah, Hoglah, **M**, and
Num 36:11 for Mahlah, Tirzah, Hoglah, **M**
Josh 17: 3 Mahlah, Noah, Hoglah, **M**, and

MILCAH'S (*see* MILCAH)
Gen 24:24 **M** son, whom she bore to Nahor

MILCHAM
Jer 49: 1 Why then does **M** inherit Gad
Jer 49: 3 for **M** shall go into captivity

MILCOM (*see* MOLECH, MOLOCH)
1Ki 11: 5 after **M** the abomination of
1Ki 11:33 **M** the god of the people of
2Ki 23:13 for **M** the abomination of the
Zeph 1: 5 LORD, but who also swear by **M**

MILD
Gen 25:27 but Jacob was a **m** man,

MILDEW
Deut 28:22 with scorching, and with **m**
1Ki 8:37 or pestilence, blight or **m**
2Ch 6:28 pestilence or blight or **m**
Amos 4: 9 blasted you with blight and **m**
Hag 2:17 I struck you with blight and **m**

MILE (*see* MILES)
Matt 5:41 compels you to go one **m**, go

MILES (*see* MILE)
Luke 24:13 about seven **m** from Jerusalem
John 6:19 rowed about three or four **m**
John 11:18 Jerusalem, about two **m** away

MILETUS
Acts 20:15 the next day we came to **M**
Acts 20:17 From **M** he sent to Ephesus and
2Ti 4:20 I have left in **M** sick

MILITARY
1Ch 27: 1 matter of the **m** divisions
2Ch 32: 6 Then he set **m** captains over
2Ch 33:14 Then he put **m** captains in all

MILK
Gen 18: 8 So he took butter and **m** and the
Gen 32:15 thirty **m** camels with their
Gen 49:12 and his teeth whiter than **m**
Ex 3: 8 to a land flowing with **m**
Ex 3:17 to a land flowing with **m**
Ex 13: 5 you, a land flowing with **m**
Ex 23:19 young goat in its mother's **m**
Ex 33: 3 up to a land flowing with **m**
Ex 34:26 young goat in its mother's **m**
Lev 20:24 a land flowing with **m** and
Num 13:27 It truly flows with **m** and
Num 14: 8 a land which flows with **m**
Num 16:13 out of a land flowing with **m**
Num 16:14 us into a land flowing with **m**
Deut 6: 3 a land flowing with **m** and
Deut 11: 9 a land flowing with **m** and
Deut 14:21 young goat in its mother's **m**
Deut 26: 9 a land flowing with **m** and
Deut 26:15 a land flowing with **m** and
Deut 27: 3 you, 'a land flowing with **m**
Deut 31:20 to the land flowing with **m**
Deut 32:14 **m** of the flock, with fat of
Josh 5: 6 a land flowing with **m** and
Judg 4:19 So she opened a jug of **m**
Judg 5:25 asked for water, she gave **m**
1Sa 6: 7 take two **m** cows which have
1Sa 6:10 they took two **m** cows and
Job 10:10 you not pour me out like **m**
Job 21:24 His pails are full of **m**, and
Prov 27:27 enough goats' **m** for your food
Prov 30:33 churning of **m** produces butter
Song 4:11 and **m** are under your tongue
Song 5: 1 have drunk my wine with my **m**
Song 5:12 of waters, washed with **m**, and
Is 7:22 the abundance of **m** they give
Is 28: 9 Those just weaned from **m**
Is 55: 1 **m** without money and without
Is 60:16 dry the **m** of the Gentiles
Is 60:16 shall **m** the breast of kings
Jer 11: 5 them a land flowing with **m**
Jer 32:22 a land flowing with **m** and
Lam 4: 7 than snow and whiter than **m**
Ezek 20: 6 out for them, flowing with **m**
Ezek 20:15 given them, flowing with **m**
Ezek 25: 4 and they shall drink your **m**
Joel 3:18 the hills shall flow with **m**
1Co 3: 2 I fed you with **m** and not with
1Co 9: 7 drink of the **m** of the flock
Heb 5:12 and you have come to need **m**
Heb 5:13 who partakes only of **m** is
1Pe 2: 2 desire the pure **m** of the word

MILL
Matt 24:41 will be grinding at the **m**

MILLET
Ezek 4: 9 barley, beans, lentils, **m**
Ezek 27:17 wheat of Minnith, **m**, honey,

MILLION
1Ch 21: 5 All Israel had one **m** one
1Ch 22:14 one **m** talents of silver, and
2Ch 14: 9 them with an army of a **m** men
Rev 9:16 horsemen was two hundred **m**

MILLO
2Sa 5: 9 built all around from the **M**
1Ki 9:15 LORD, his own house, the **M**
1Ki 9:24 Then he built the **M**
1Ki 11:27 Solomon had built the **M** and
2Ki 12:20 Joash in the house of the **M**
1Ch 11: 8 from the **M** to the surrounding
2Ch 32: 5 the **M** in the City of David

MILLSTONE (*see* MILLSTONES)
Deut 24: 6 or the upper **m** in pledge, for
Judg 9:53 upper **m** on Abimelech's head
2Sa 11:21 of a **m** on him from the wall
Job 41:24 even as hard as the lower **m**
Matt 18: 6 be better for him if a **m** were
Mark 9:42 be better for him if a **m** were
Luke 17: 2 be better for him if a **m** were
Rev 18:21 up a stone like a great **m**
Rev 18:22 the sound of a **m** shall not be

MILLSTONES (*see* MILLSTONE)
Num 11: 8 ground it on **m** or beat it in
Is 47: 2 Take the **m** and grind meal
Jer 25:10 the bride, the sound of the **m**
Lam 5:13 Young men ground at the **m**

MINA
Ezek 45:12 shekels shall be your **m**
Luke 19:16 your **m** has earned ten minas
Luke 19:18 your **m** has earned five minas
Luke 19:20 Master, here is your **m**,
Luke 19:24 by, 'Take the **m** from him, and

MINAS
1Ki 10:17 three **m** of gold went into
Ezra 2:69 five thousand **m** of silver
Neh 7:71 thousand two hundred silver **m**
Neh 7:72 two thousand silver **m**, and
Luke 19:13 delivered to them ten **m**, and
Luke 19:16 your mina has earned ten **m**
Luke 19:18 your mina has earned five **m**
Luke 19:24 give it to him who has ten **m**
Luke 19:25 to him, "Master, he has ten **m**

MINCING
Is 3:16 and **m** as they go, making a

MIND (*see* MINDED, MINDFUL, MINDS, UNMINDFUL)
Gen 26:35 were a grief of **m** to Isaac
Gen 37:11 father kept the matter in **m**
Lev 24:12 that the **m** of the LORD might
Deut 18: 6 with all the desire of his **m**
Deut 30: 1 you call them to **m** among all
1Sa 2:35 is in My heart and in My **m**
1Ch 12:38 of one **m** to make David king
1Ch 22: 7 it was in my **m** to build a
1Ch 28: 9 heart and with a willing **m**
Neh 4: 6 the people had a **m** to work
Job 38:36 Who has put wisdom in the **m**
Ps 26: 2 Try my **m** and my heart
Ps 31:12 like a dead man, out of **m**
Ps 73:21 And I was vexed in my **m**
Is 26: 3 whose **m** is stayed on You,
Is 46: 8 recall to **m**, O you
Is 65:17 be remembered or come to **m**
Jer 3:16 It shall not come to **m**, nor
Jer 11:20 righteously, testing the **m**
Jer 12: 2 mouth but far from their **m**
Jer 15: 1 Me, yet My **m** could not be
Jer 17:10 the heart, I test the **m**, even
Jer 19: 5 nor did it come into My **m**)
Jer 20:12 the righteous, and see the **m**
Jer 32:35 nor did it come into My **m**
Jer 44:21 and did it not come into His **m**
Jer 51:50 let Jerusalem come to your **m**
Lam 3:21 This I recall to my **m**,
Ezek 11: 5 things that come into your **m**
Ezek 20:32 have in your **m** shall never be
Ezek 38:10 thoughts will arise in your **m**
Ezek 40: 4 fix your **m** on everything I
Dan 2:29 to your **m** while on your bed
Dan 9:14 has kept the disaster in **m**
Hab 1:11 Then his **m** changes, and he
Matt 22:37 your soul, and with all your **m**
Mark 3:21 He is out of His **m**
Mark 5:15 and clothed and in his right **m**
Mark 12:30 your soul, with all your **m**
Mark 14:72 Peter called to **m** the word
Luke 8:35 clothed and in his right **m**
Luke 10:27 strength, and with all your **m**
Luke 12:29 drink, nor have an anxious **m**
Rom 1:28 gave them over to a debased **m**
Rom 7:23 against the law of my **m**, and
Rom 7:25 with the **m** I myself serve the
Rom 8: 7 Because the carnal **m** is
Rom 8:27 what the **m** of the Spirit is
Rom 11:34 has known the **m** of the LORD
Rom 12: 2 by the renewing of your **m**
Rom 12:16 Be of the same **m** toward one
Rom 12:16 not set your **m** on high things
Rom 14: 5 fully convinced in his own **m**
Rom 15: 6 that you may with one **m** and
1Co 1:10 joined together in the same **m**
1Co 2:16 Who has known the **m** of the
1Co 2:16 But we have the **m** of Christ
1Co 14:23 that you are out of your **m**
2Co 5:13 or if we are of sound **m**, it
2Co 8:12 if there is first a willing **m**
2Co 8:19 and to show your ready **m**,
2Co 13:11 of good comfort, be of one **m**
Gal 5:10 that you will have no other **m**
Eph 2: 3 of the flesh and of the **m**, and
Eph 4:17 in the futility of their **m**
Eph 4:23 in the spirit of your **m**,
Phil 1:27 with one **m** striving together
Phil 2: 2 being of one accord, of one **m**
Phil 2: 3 but in lowliness of **m** let
Phil 2: 5 Let this **m** be in you which
Phil 3:15 as are mature, have this **m**
Phil 3:16 rule, let us be of the same **m**
Phil 3:19 who set their **m** on earthly
Phil 4: 2 be of the same **m** in the Lord
Col 1:21 in your **m** by wicked works

Acts 4:16 that a notable **m** has been
Acts 4:22 this **m** of healing had been

MIRACLES (*see* MIRACLE)
Judg 6:13 where are all His **m** which our
John 9:16 man who is a sinner do such **m**
Acts 2:22 attested by God to you by **m**
Acts 8: 6 seeing the **m** which he did
Acts 8:13 and was amazed, seeing the **m**
Acts 15:12 and Paul declaring how many **m**
Acts 19:11 **m** by the hands of Paul,
1Co 12:10 to another the working of **m**
1Co 12:28 third teachers, after that **m**
1Co 12:29 Are all workers of **m**
Gal 3: 5 works **m** among you, does He do
Heb 2: 4 and wonders, with various **m**

MIRE (*see* MIRY)
Job 30:19 He has cast me into the **m**
Job 41:30 pointed marks in the **m**
Ps 69: 2 I sink in deep **m**, Where there
Ps 69:14 Deliver me out of the **m**, And
Is 10: 6 like the **m** of the streets
Is 57:20 rest, whose waters cast up **m**
Jer 38: 6 there was no water, but **m**
Jer 38: 6 So Jeremiah sank in the **m**
Jer 38:22 your feet have sunk in the **m**
Mic 7:10 down like **m** in the streets
Zech 9: 3 and gold like the **m** of the
Zech 10: 5 the **m** of the streets in the
2Pe 2:22 to her wallowing in the **m**

MIRIAM
Ex 15:20 Then **M** the prophetess, the
Ex 15:21 And **M** answered them
Num 12: 1 Then **M** and Aaron spoke
Num 12: 4 said to Moses, Aaron, and **M**
Num 12: 5 and called Aaron and **M**
Num 12:10 suddenly **M** became leprous, as
Num 12:10 Then Aaron turned toward **M**
Num 12:15 So **M** was shut out of the camp
Num 12:15 till **M** was brought in again
Num 20: 1 **M** died there and was buried
Num 26:59 and Moses and their sister **M**
Deut 24: 9 to **M** on the way when you came
1Ch 4:17 And Mered's wife bore **M**,
1Ch 6: 3 were Aaron, Moses, and **M**
Mic 6: 4 you Moses, Aaron, and **M**

MIRMAH
1Ch 8:10 Jeuz, Sachiah, and **M**

MIRROR (*see* MIRRORS)
Job 37:18 strong as a cast metal **m**
1Co 13:12 For now we see in a **m**, dimly,
2Co 3:18 beholding as in a **m** the glory
Jas 1:23 his natural face in a **m**

MIRRORS (*see* MIRROR)
Ex 38: 8 from the bronze **m** of the
Is 3:23 and the **m**; the fine linen

MIRTH
Ps 137: 3 plundered us required of us **m**
Prov 14:13 the end of **m** may be grief
Eccl 2: 1 now, I will test you with **m**
Eccl 2: 2 and of **m**, "What does it
Eccl 7: 4 of fools is in the house of **m**
Is 24: 8 The **m** of the tambourine
Is 24:11 the **m** of the land is gone
Jer 7:34 of Jerusalem the voice of **m**
Jer 16: 9 in your days, the voice of **m**
Jer 25:10 take from them the voice of **m**
Ezek 21:10 Should we then make **m**
Hos 2:11 also cause all her **m** to cease

MIRY (*see* MIRE)
Ps 40: 2 pit, Out of the **m** clay, And

MISCARRIAGE (*see* MISCARRIED)
Ex 23:26 No one shall suffer **m** or be
Job 21:10 their cow calves without **m**

MISCARRIED (*see* MISCARRIAGE, MISCARRYING)
Gen 31:38 goats have not **m** their young

MISCARRYING (*see* MISCARRIED)
Hos 9:14 Give them a **m** womb and dry

MISER
Prov 23: 6 Do not eat the bread of a **m**
Is 32: 5 nor the **m** said to be

MISERABLE (*see* MISERABLY, MISERY)
1Sa 1: 6 her severely, to make her **m**
Job 16: 2 **m** comforters are you all
Rev 3:17 know that you are wretched, **m**

MISERABLY (*see* MISERABLE)
Matt 21:41 destroy those wicked men **m**

MISERIES (*see* MISERY)
Jas 5: 1 and howl for your **m** that are

MISERY (*see* MISERABLE, MISERIES)
Judg 10:16 longer endure the **m** of Israel
Job 3:20 given to him who is in **m**, and
Job 10:15 full of disgrace; see my **m**!
Job 11:16 you would forget your **m**, and
Job 20:22 every hand of **m** will come
Prov 31: 7 and remember his **m** no more
Eccl 8: 6 though the **m** of man increases
Jon 4: 6 to deliver him from his **m**
Rom 3:16 and **m** are in their ways

MISFORTUNE
Eccl 4: 8 also is vanity and a grave **m**
Eccl 5:14 those riches perish through **m**
Is 10: 1 decrees, who write **m**, which

MISHAEL (*see* MESHACH, MISHAL)
Ex 6:22 And the sons of Uzziel were **M**
Lev 10: 4 And Moses called **M** and
Neh 8: 4 at his left hand Pedaiah, **M**
Dan 1: 6 were Daniel, Hananiah, **M**, and
Dan 1: 7 to **M**, Meshach
Dan 1:11 set over Daniel, Hananiah, **M**
Dan 1:19 like Daniel, Hananiah, **M**, and
Dan 2:17 decision known to Hananiah, **M**

MISHAL (*see* MISHAEL)
Josh 19:26 Alammelech, Amad, and **M**
Josh 21:30 **M** with its common-land,

MISHAM
1Ch 8:12 sons of Elpaal were Eber, **M**

MISHMA
Gen 25:14 **M**, Dumah, Massa,
1Ch 1:30 **M**, Dumah, Massa, Hadad,
1Ch 4:25 Mibsam his son, and **M** his son
1Ch 4:26 the sons of **M** were Hamuel his

MISHMANNAH
1Ch 12:10 **M** the fourth, Jeremiah the

MISHRAITES
1Ch 2:53 the Shumathites, and the **M**

MISLEADS
Luke 23:14 me, as one who **m** the people

MISPAR
Ezra 2: 2 Mordecai, Bilshan, **M**, Bigvai

MISPERETH
Neh 7: 7 Mordecai, Bilshan, **M**, Bigvai

MISREPHOTH
Josh 11: 8 Greater Sidon, to the Brook **M**
Josh 13: 6 Lebanon as far as the Brook **M**

MISS (*see* MISSED, MISSES, MISSING)
Judg 20:16 at a hair's breadth and not **m**
1Sa 25:15 nor did we **m** anything as long

MISSED (*see* MISS)
1Sa 20:18 and you will be **m**, because
1Sa 25:21 so that nothing was **m** of all

MISSES (*see* MISS)
1Sa 20: 6 If your father **m** me at all

MISSING (*see* MISS)
Num 31:49 and not a man of us is **m**
Judg 21: 3 be one tribe **m** in Israel
1Sa 25: 7 nor was there anything **m** from
2Sa 2:30 there were **m** of David's
1Ki 20:39 if by any means he is **m**, your
2Ki 10:19 Let no one be **m**, for I have a
2Ki 10:19 Whoever is **m** shall not live
Is 40:26 not one is **m**

MISSION
1Sa 15:18 Now the LORD sent you on a **m**
1Sa 15:20 gone on the **m** on which the

MIST
Gen 2: 6 but a **m** went up from the
Job 36:27 distill as rain from the **m**
Acts 13:11 a dark **m** fell on him, and he

MISTAKEN
Matt 22:29 You are **m**, not knowing the
Mark 12:24 Are you not therefore **m**,
Mark 12:27 You are therefore greatly **m**

MISTREAT (*see* MISTREATED, MISTREATS)
Ex 22:21 You shall neither **m** a
Lev 19:33 land, you shall not **m** him

MISTREATED (*see* MISTREAT)
Deut 26: 6 But the Egyptians **m** us,
Ezek 22: 7 they have **m** the fatherless
Ezek 22:29 and **m** the poor and needy
Heb 13: 3 with them, and those who are **m**

MISTREATS (*see* MISTREAT)
Deut 24: 7 **m** him or sells him, then that
Prov 19:26 He who **m** his father and chases

MISTRESS
Gen 16: 4 her **m** became despised in her
Gen 16: 8 the presence of my **m** Sarai
Gen 16: 9 Return to your **m**, and submit
2Ki 5: 3 Then she said to her **m**, "If
Ps 123: 2 a maid to the hand of her **m**
Prov 30:23 who succeeds her **m**
Is 24: 2 with the maid, so with her **m**
Nah 3: 4 the **m** of sorceries, who sells

MISUNDERSTAND
Deut 32:27 their adversaries should **m**

MISUSING
1Co 7:31 use this world as not **m** it

MITE (*see* MITES)
Luke 12:59 you have paid the very last **m**

MITES (*see* MITE)
Mark 12:42 widow came and threw in two **m**
Luke 21: 2 poor widow putting in two **m**

MITHKAH
Num 33:28 from Terah and camped at **M**
Num 33:29 They went from **M** and camped

MITHNITE
1Ch 11:43 of Maachah, Joshaphat the **M**

MITHREDATH
Ezra 1: 8 the hand of **M** the treasurer
Ezra 4: 7 Artaxerxes also, Bishlam, **M**

MITYLENE
Acts 20:14 him on board and came to **M**

MIX (*see* MIXED, MIXING, MIXTURE)
Prov 23:20 Do not **m** with winebibbers, or
Ezek 24:10 **M** in the spices, and let the
Dan 2:43 as iron does not **m** with clay
Rev 18: 6 has mixed, **m** for her double

MIXED (*see* MIX)
Ex 12:38 A **m** multitude went up with
Ex 29: 2 unleavened cakes **m** with oil
Ex 29:40 of an ephah of flour **m** with
Lev 2: 4 of fine flour **m** with oil, or
Lev 2: 5 flour, unleavened, **m** with oil
Lev 6:21 When it is well **m**, you shall
Lev 7:10 grain offering **m** with oil
Lev 7:12 unleavened cakes **m** with oil
Lev 7:12 blended flour **m** with oil
Lev 9: 4 a grain offering **m** with oil
Lev 14:10 flour **m** with oil as a grain
Lev 14:21 flour **m** with oil as a grain
Lev 19:19 sow your field with **m** seed
Lev 19:19 shall a garment of **m** linen
Lev 23:13 of fine flour **m** with oil, an
Num 6:15 of fine flour **m** with oil,
Num 7:13 flour **m** with oil as a grain
Num 7:19 flour **m** with oil as a grain
Num 7:25 flour **m** with oil as a grain
Num 7:31 flour **m** with oil as a grain
Num 7:37 flour **m** with oil as a grain
Num 7:43 flour **m** with oil as a grain
Num 7:49 flour **m** with oil as a grain
Num 7:55 flour **m** with oil as a grain
Num 7:61 flour **m** with oil as a grain
Num 7:67 flour **m** with oil as a grain
Num 7:73 flour **m** with oil as a grain
Num 7:79 flour **m** with oil as a grain
Num 8: 8 of fine flour **m** with oil, and
Num 11: 4 Now the **m** multitude who were
Num 15: 4 of an ephah of fine flour **m**
Num 15: 6 of an ephah of fine flour **m**
Num 15: 9 **m** with half a hin of oil
Num 28: 5 flour as a grain offering **m**

Num 28: 9 **m** with oil, with its drink
Num 28:12 **m** with oil, for each bull
Num 28:12 **m** with oil, for the one ram
Num 28:13 flour, **m** with oil, as a grain
Num 28:20 be of fine flour **m** with oil
Num 28:28 of fine flour **m** with oil
Num 29: 3 be fine flour **m** with oil
Num 29: 9 be of fine flour **m** with oil
Num 29:14 be of fine flour **m** with oil
Deut 22:11 as wool and linen **m** together
1Ch 23:29 in the pan, with what is **m**
Neh 13: 3 the **m** multitude from Israel
Ps 75: 8 It is fully **m**, and He pours it
Prov 9: 2 she has **m** her wine, she has
Prov 9: 5 of the wine which I have **m**
Prov 23:30 who go in search of **m** wine
Is 1:22 dross, your wine **m** with water
Jer 25:20 all the **m** multitude, all the
Jer 25:24 and all the kings of the **m**
Jer 50:37 against all the **m** peoples who
Dan 2:41 the iron **m** with ceramic clay
Dan 2:43 As you saw iron **m** with
Hos 7: 8 Ephraim has **m** himself among
Zech 9: 6 A **m** race shall settle in
Heb 4: 2 not being **m** with faith in
Rev 18: 6 in the cup which she has **m**

MIXING (*see* MIX)
Is 5:22 for **m** intoxicating drink,

MIXTURE (*see* MIX)
2Ch 16:14 prepared in a **m** of ointments
John 19:39 came, bringing a **m** of myrrh

MIZAR
Ps 42: 6 of Hermon, From the Hill **M**

MIZPAH
Gen 31:49 also **M**, because he said
Josh 11: 3 below Hermon in the land of **M**
Josh 11: 8 to the Valley of **M** eastward
Josh 15:38 Dilean, **M**, Joktheel,
Josh 18:26 **M**, Chephirah, Mozah,
Judg 10:17 together and encamped in **M**
Judg 11:11 words before the LORD in **M**
Judg 11:29 and passed through **M** of Gilead
Judg 11:29 from **M** of Gilead he advanced
Judg 11:34 came to his house at **M**, there
Judg 20: 1 one man before the LORD at **M**
Judg 20: 3 of Israel had gone up to **M**
Judg 21: 1 Israel had sworn an oath at **M**
Judg 21: 5 not come up to the LORD at **M**
Judg 21: 8 not come up to **M** to the LORD
1Sa 7: 5 Gather all Israel to **M**, and I
1Sa 7: 6 they gathered together at **M**
1Sa 7: 6 the children of Israel at **M**
1Sa 7: 7 had gathered together at **M**
1Sa 7:11 men of Israel went out of **M**
1Sa 7:12 stone and set it up between **M**
1Sa 7:16 to Bethel, Gilgal, and **M**, and
1Sa 10:17 together to the LORD at **M**
1Sa 22: 3 went from there to **M** of Moab
1Ki 15:22 built Geba of Benjamin, and **M**
2Ki 25:23 they came to Gedaliah at **M**
2Ki 25:25 who were with him at **M**
2Ch 16: 6 with them he built Geba and **M**
Neh 3: 7 the men of Gibeon and **M**,
Neh 3:15 leader of the district of **M**
Neh 3:19 of Jeshua, the leader of **M**
Jer 40: 6 the son of Ahikam, to **M**, and
Jer 40: 8 they came to Gedaliah at **M**
Jer 40:10 me, I will indeed dwell at **M**
Jer 40:12 of Judah, to Gedaliah at **M**
Jer 40:13 fields came to Gedaliah at **M**
Jer 40:15 secretly to Gedaliah in **M**
Jer 41: 1 the son of Ahikam, at **M**
Jer 41: 1 they ate bread together in **M**
Jer 41: 3 that is, with Gedaliah at **M**
Jer 41: 6 went out from **M** to meet them
Jer 41:10 of the people who were in **M**
Jer 41:10 the people who remained in **M**
Jer 41:14 captive from **M** turned around
Jer 41:16 took from **M** all the rest of
Hos 5: 1 you have been a snare to **M**

MIZRAIM (*see* ABEL MIZRAIM, EGYPT)
Gen 10: 6 The sons of Ham were Cush, **M**
Gen 10:13 **M** begot Ludim, Anamim,
1Ch 1: 8 The sons of Ham were Cush, **M**
1Ch 1:11 **M** begot Ludim, Anamim,

MIZZAH
Gen 36:13 Zerah, Shammah, and **M**
Gen 36:17 Chief Shammah, and Chief **M**
1Ch 1:37 Zerah, Shammah, and **M**

MNASON
Acts 21:16 one, **M** of Cyprus, an early

MOAB (*see* MOABITE, MOABITESS, PAHATH-MOAB)
Gen 19:37 a son and called his name **M**
Gen 36:35 Midian in the field of **M**,
Ex 15:15 the mighty men of **M**,
Num 21:11 wilderness which is east of **M**
Num 21:13 the border of **M**, between **M**
Num 21:15 and lies on the border of **M**
Num 21:20 that is in the country of **M**
Num 21:26 against the former king of **M**
Num 21:28 it consumed Ar of **M**, the
Num 21:29 Woe to you, **M**
Num 22: 1 camped in the plains of **M** on
Num 22: 3 **M** was exceedingly afraid of
Num 22: 3 **M** was sick with dread because
Num 22: 4 So **M** said to the elders of
Num 22: 7 So the elders of **M** and the
Num 22: 8 of **M** stayed with Balaam
Num 22:10 the son of Zippor, king of **M**
Num 22:14 And the princes of **M** rose and
Num 22:21 and went with the princes of **M**
Num 22:36 to meet him at the city of **M**
Num 23: 6 he and all the princes of **M**
Num 23: 7 Balak the king of **M** has
Num 23:17 princes of **M** were with him
Num 24:17 and batter the brow of **M**, and
Num 25: 1 harlotry with the women of **M**
Num 26: 3 the plains of **M** by the Jordan
Num 26:63 the plains of **M** by the Jordan
Num 31:12 the plains of **M** by the Jordan
Num 33:44 Abarim, at the border of **M**
Num 33:48 the plains of **M** by the Jordan
Num 33:49 Grove in the plains of **M**
Num 33:50 the plains of **M** by the Jordan
Num 35: 1 **M** by the Jordan across from
Num 36:13 the plains of **M** by the Jordan
Deut 1: 5 the Jordan in the land of **M**
Deut 2: 8 by way of the Wilderness of **M**
Deut 2: 9 said to me, Do not harass **M**
Deut 2:18 over at Ar, the boundary of **M**
Deut 29: 1 of Israel in the land of **M**
Deut 32:49 which is in the land of **M**
Deut 34: 1 the plains of **M** to Mount Nebo
Deut 34: 5 died there in the land of **M**
Deut 34: 6 in a valley in the land of **M**
Deut 34: 8 the plains of **M** thirty days
Josh 13:32 in the plains of **M** on the
Josh 24: 9 the son of Zippor, king of **M**
Judg 3:12 king of **M** against Israel,
Judg 3:14 king of **M** eighteen years
Judg 3:15 tribute to Eglon king of **M**
Judg 3:17 tribute to Eglon king of **M**
Judg 3:28 of the Jordan leading to **M**
Judg 3:29 about ten thousand men of **M**
Judg 3:30 So **M** was subdued that day
Judg 10: 6 gods of Sidon, the gods of **M**
Judg 11:15 not take away the land of **M**
Judg 11:17 they sent to the king of **M**
Judg 11:18 land of Edom and the land of **M**
Judg 11:18 east side of the land of **M**
Judg 11:18 did not enter the border of **M**
Judg 11:18 the Arnon was the border of **M**
Judg 11:25 the son of Zippor, king of **M**
Ruth 1: 1 sojourn in the country of **M**
Ruth 1: 2 they went to the country of **M**
Ruth 1: 4 took wives of the women of **M**
Ruth 1: 6 return from the country of **M**
Ruth 1: 6 **M** that the LORD had visited
Ruth 1:22 from the country of **M**
Ruth 2: 6 Naomi from the country of **M**
Ruth 4: 3 back from the country of **M**
1Sa 12: 9 the hand of the king of **M**
1Sa 14:47 on every side, against **M**,
1Sa 22: 3 from there to Mizpah of **M**
1Sa 22: 3 and he said to the king of **M**
1Sa 22: 4 them before the king of **M**
2Sa 8: 2 Then he defeated **M**
2Sa 8:12 from Syria, from **M**, from the
2Sa 23:20 two lion-like heroes of **M**
1Ki 11: 7 Chemosh the abomination of **M**
2Ki 1: 1 **M** rebelled against Israel
2Ki 3: 4 Now Mesha king of **M** was a
2Ki 3: 5 that the king of **M** rebelled
2Ki 3: 7 The king of **M** has rebelled
2Ki 3: 7 go with me to fight against **M**
2Ki 3:10 them into the hand of **M**
2Ki 3:13 them into the hand of **M**
2Ki 3:23 now therefore, **M**, to the
2Ki 3:26 when the king of **M** saw that
2Ki 13:20 And the raiding bands from **M**
1Ch 1:46 Midian in the field of **M**,
1Ch 4:22 Saraph, who ruled in **M**, and
1Ch 8: 8 children in the country of **M**
1Ch 11:22 two lion-like heroes of **M**
1Ch 18: 2 Then he defeated **M**, and the
1Ch 18:11 from Edom, from **M**, from the
2Ch 20: 1 this that the people of **M**
2Ch 20:10 are the people of Ammon, **M**
2Ch 20:22 the people of Ammon, **M**, and
2Ch 20:23 and **M** stood up against the
Neh 13:23 of Ashdod, Ammon, and **M**
Ps 60: 8 **M** is My washpot
Ps 83: 6 **M** and the Hagarites
Ps 108: 9 **M** is My washpot
Is 11:14 lay their hand on Edom and **M**
Is 15: 1 The burden against **M**
Is 15: 1 night Ar of **M** is laid waste
Is 15: 1 night Kir of **M** is laid waste
Is 15: 2 **M** will wail over Nebo and over
Is 15: 4 soldiers of **M** will cry out
Is 15: 5 My heart will cry out for **M**
Is 15: 8 all around the borders of **M**
Is 15: 9 upon him who escapes from **M**
Is 16: 2 **M** at the fords of the Arnon
Is 16: 4 outcasts dwell with you, O **M**
Is 16: 6 have heard of the pride of **M**
Is 16: 7 **M** shall wail for **M**
Is 16:11 resound like a harp for **M**
Is 16:12 when it is seen that **M** is
Is 16:13 concerning **M** since that time
Is 16:14 man, the glory of **M** will be
Is 25:10 and **M** shall be trampled down
Jer 9:26 the people of Ammon, **M**
Jer 25:21 Edom, **M**, and the people of
Jer 27: 3 king of Edom, the king of **M**
Jer 40:11 all the Jews who were in **M**
Jer 48: 1 Against **M**. Thus says the LORD
Jer 48: 2 No more praise of **M**
Jer 48: 4 **M** is destroyed; her little
Jer 48: 9 Give wings to **M**, that she may
Jer 48:11 **M** has been at ease from his
Jer 48:13 **M** shall be ashamed of Chemosh
Jer 48:15 **M** is plundered and gone up
Jer 48:16 calamity of **M** is near at hand
Jer 48:18 of **M** has come against you
Jer 48:20 **M** is shamed, for he is broken
Jer 48:20 in Arnon, that **M** is plundered
Jer 48:24 the cities of the land of **M**
Jer 48:25 The horn of **M** is cut off, and
Jer 48:26 **M** shall wallow in his vomit,
Jer 48:28 You who dwell in **M**, leave the
Jer 48:29 **M** (he is exceedingly proud)
Jer 48:31 Therefore I will wail for **M**
Jer 48:31 and I will cry out for all **M**
Jer 48:33 field and from the land of **M**
Jer 48:35 cease in **M** the one who offers
Jer 48:36 shall wail like flutes for **M**
Jer 48:38 on all the housetops of **M**
Jer 48:38 for I have broken **M** like a
Jer 48:39 How **M** has turned her back
Jer 48:39 So **M** shall be a derision and a
Jer 48:40 and spread his wings over **M**
Jer 48:41 **M** on that day shall be like
Jer 48:42 **M** shall be destroyed as a
Jer 48:43 upon you, O inhabitant of **M**
Jer 48:44 For upon **M**, upon it I will
Jer 48:45 and shall devour the brow of **M**
Jer 48:46 Woe to you, O **M**
Jer 48:47 of **M** in the latter days,"
Jer 48:47 Thus far is the judgment of **M**
Ezek 25: 8 Because **M** and Seir say, 'Look
Ezek 25: 9 the territory of **M** of cities
Ezek 25:11 will execute judgments upon **M**
Dan 11:41 Edom, **M**, and the prominent
Amos 2: 1 For three transgressions of **M**
Amos 2: 2 But I will send a fire upon **M**
Amos 2: 2 **M** shall die with tumult, with
Mic 6: 5 Balak king of **M** counseled
Zeph 2: 8 have heard the reproach of **M**
Zeph 2: 9 Surely **M** shall be like Sodom,

MOABITE (*see* MOAB, MOABITES)
Deut 23: 3 An Ammonite or **M** shall not
Ruth 2: 6 It is the young **M** woman who
1Ch 11:46 sons of Elnaam, Ithmah the **M**
Neh 13: 1 **M** should ever come into the

MOABITES (*see* MOABITE)
Gen 19:37 father of the **M** to this day
Num 22: 4 king of the **M** at that time
Deut 2:11 but the **M** call them Emim
Deut 2:29 the **M** who dwell in Ar did for
Judg 3:28 enemies the **M** into your hand
2Sa 8: 2 So the **M** became David's
1Ki 11: 1 women of the **M**, Ammonites,
1Ki 11:33 Chemosh the god of the **M**
2Ki 3:18 deliver the **M** into your hand
2Ki 3:21 when all the **M** heard that the
2Ki 3:22 the **M** saw the water on the
2Ki 3:24 rose up and attacked the **M**
2Ki 3:24 their land, killing the **M**
2Ki 23:13 the abomination of the **M**, and
2Ki 24: 2 bands of Syrians, bands of **M**
1Ch 18: 2 the **M** became David's servants
Ezra 9: 1 the Ammonites, the **M**, the

MOABITESS (*see* MOAB)
Ruth 1:22 returned, and Ruth the **M** her
Ruth 2: 2 So Ruth the **M** said to Naomi,
Ruth 2:21 Then Ruth the **M** said, "He
Ruth 4: 5 also buy it from Ruth the **M**
Ruth 4:10 Moreover, Ruth the **M**, the
2Ch 24:26 the son of Shimrith the **M**

MOADIAH (*see* MAADIAH)
Neh 12:17 of **M**, Piltai

MOAN
Ps 55: 2 my complaint, and **m** noisily,
Is 59:11 bears, and **m** sadly like doves

MOB
Ps 86:14 And a **m** of violent men have
Acts 17: 5 marketplace, and gathering a **m**
Acts 21:35 of the violence of the **m**

MOCK (*see* MOCKED, MOCKER, MOCKERY, MOCKING, MOCKS)
Gen 39:14 in to us a Hebrew to **m** us
Gen 39:17 to us came in to me to **m** me
Job 11: 3 And when you **m**, should no one
Job 13: 9 Or can you **m** Him as one mocks
Job 30: 1 But now they **m** at me, men
Prov 1:26 I will **m** when your terror
Prov 14: 9 Fools **m** at sin, but among the
Ezek 22: 5 you will **m** you as infamous
Matt 20:19 Him to the Gentiles to **m** and
Mark 10:34 and they will **m** Him, and
Luke 14:29 all who see it begin to **m** him

MOCKED (*see* MOCK)
Judg 16:10 Look, you have **m** me and told
Judg 16:13 Until now you have **m** me and
Judg 16:15 You have **m** me these three
1Ki 18:27 at noon, that Elijah **m** them
2Ki 2:23 and **m** him, and said to him,
2Ch 30:10 them to scorn and **m** them
2Ch 36:16 But they **m** the messengers of
Neh 4: 1 very indignant, and **m** the Jews
Job 12: 4 I am one **m** by his friends,
Job 29:24 If I **m** at them, they did not
Lam 1: 7 saw her and **m** at her downfall
Matt 27:29 before Him and **m** Him, saying,
Matt 27:31 Then when they had **m** Him,
Mark 15:20 And when they had **m** Him, they
Mark 15:31 together with the scribes, **m**
Luke 18:32 to the Gentiles and will be **m**
Luke 22:63 the men who held Jesus **m** Him
Luke 23:11 and **m** Him, arrayed Him in a
Luke 23:36 And the soldiers also **m** Him
Acts 17:32 of the dead, some **m**, while
Gal 6: 7 not be deceived, God is not **m**

MOCKER (*see* MOCK, MOCKERS)
Prov 20: 1 Wine is a **m**, intoxicating

MOCKERS (*see* MOCKER)
Job 17: 2 Are not **m** with me
Ps 35:16 With ungodly **m** at feasts They
Is 28:22 Now therefore, do not be **m**
Jer 15:17 sit in the assembly of the **m**
Jude 18 you that there would be **m** in

MOCKERY (*see* MOCK)
Ezek 22: 4 and a **m** to all countries
Ezek 36: 4 **m** to the rest of the nations

MOCKING (*see* MOCK, MOCKINGS)
Job 21: 3 after I have spoken, keep **m**
Jer 20:10 For I heard many **m**
Matt 27:41 also **m** with the scribes and
Acts 2:13 Others **m** said, "They are

MOCKINGS (*see* MOCKING)
Heb 11:36 Still others had trial of **m**

MOCKS (*see* MOCK)
Job 13: 9 you mock Him as one **m** a man
Job 39:22 He **m** at fear, and is not
Prov 17: 5 He who **m** the poor reproaches
Prov 30:17 The eye that **m** his father
Jer 20: 7 everyone **m** me

MODERATION (*see* MODEST)
1Ti 2: 9 apparel, with propriety and **m**

MODEST (*see* MODERATION, MODESTY)
1Ti 2: 9 adorn themselves in **m** apparel

MODESTY (*see* MODEST)
1Co 12:23 parts have greater **m**,

MOIST (*see* MOISTEN)
Job 21:24 the marrow of his bones is **m**

MOISTEN (*see* MOIST, MOISTURE)
Ezek 46:14 of oil to **m** the fine flour

MOISTURE (*see* MOISTEN)
Job 37:11 Also with **m** He saturates the
Luke 8: 6 away because it lacked **m**

MOLADAH
Josh 15:26 Amam, Shema, **M**,
Josh 19: 2 Beersheba (Sheba), **M**,
1Ch 4:28 They dwelt at Beersheba, **M**
Neh 11:26 in Jeshua, **M**, Beth Pelet,

MOLD (*see* MOLDED, MOLDING, MOLDS)
1Ki 7:37 of them were of the same **m**
Hab 2:18 of its **m** should trust in it

MOLDED (*see* MOLD)
Ex 32: 4 tool, and made a **m** calf
Ex 32: 8 have made themselves a **m** calf
Ex 34:17 You shall make no **m** gods for
Lev 19: 4 make for yourselves **m** gods
Num 33:52 destroy all their **m** images
Deut 9:12 made themselves a **m** image
Deut 9:16 made for yourselves a **m** calf
Deut 27:15 makes any carved or **m** image
Judg 17: 3 a carved image and a **m** image
Judg 17: 4 a carved image and a **m** image
Judg 18:14 a carved image, and a **m** image
Judg 18:17 idols, and the **m** image
Judg 18:18 the **m** image, the priest said
1Ki 14: 9 **m** images to provoke Me to
2Ki 17:16 made for themselves a **m** image
2Ch 28: 2 made **m** images for the Baals
2Ch 34: 3 images, and the **m** images
2Ch 34: 4 and the **m** images he broke in
Neh 9:18 made a **m** calf for themselves
Ps 106:19 And worshiped the **m** image
Is 30:22 of your **m** images of gold
Is 41:29 their **m** images are wind and
Is 42:17 who say to the **m** images
Is 48: 5 my **m** image have commanded
Jer 10:14 for his **m** image is falsehood,
Jer 51:17 for his **m** image is falsehood,
Hos 13: 2 made for themselves **m** images
Nah 1:14 carved image and the **m** image
Hab 2:18 the **m** image, a teacher of

MOLDING (*see* MOLD)
Ex 25:11 on it a **m** of gold all around
Ex 25:24 make a **m** of gold all around
Ex 25:25 you shall make a gold **m** for
Ex 30: 3 for it a **m** of gold all around
Ex 30: 4 under the **m** on both its sides
Ex 37: 2 made a **m** of gold all around
Ex 37:11 made a **m** of gold all around
Ex 37:12 and made a **m** of gold for the
Ex 37:26 it a **m** of gold all around it
Ex 37:27 of gold for it under its **m**

MOLDS (*see* MOLD)
1Ki 7:46 king had them cast in clay **m**
2Ch 4:17 king had them cast in clay **m**
Is 40:19 The workman **m** a graven

MOLDY
Josh 9: 5 their provision was dry and **m**
Josh 9:12 But now look, it is dry and **m**

MOLE (*see* MOLES)
Lev 11:29 the **m**, the mouse, and the

MOLECH (*see* MILCOM, MOLOCH)
Lev 18:21 pass through the fire to **M**
Lev 20: 2 any of his descendants to **M**
Lev 20: 3 some of his descendants to **M**
Lev 20: 4 some of his descendants to **M**
Lev 20: 5 him to commit harlotry with **M**
1Ki 11: 7 for **M** the abomination of the
2Ki 23:10 pass through the fire to **M**
Jer 32:35 to pass through the fire to **M**

MOLES (*see* MOLE)
Is 2:20 himself to worship, to the **m**

MOLID
1Ch 2:29 and she bore him Ahban and **M**

MOLOCH (*see* MILCOM, MOLECH)
Acts 7:43 took up the tabernacle of **M**

MOMENT
Ex 33: 5 up into your midst in one **m**
Num 16:21 I may consume them in a **m**
Num 16:45 I may consume them in a **m**
2Sa 3:22 At that **m** the servants of
Job 7:18 morning, and test him every **m**
Job 20: 5 the hypocrite is but for a **m**
Job 21:13 in a **m** go down to the grave
Job 34:20 In a **m** they die, in the
Ps 30: 5 For His anger is but for a **m**
Ps 73:19 to desolation, as in a **m**
Prov 12:19 a lying tongue is but for a **m**
Is 26:20 as it were, for a little **m**
Is 27: 3 keep it, I water it every **m**
Is 47: 9 shall come to you in a **m**, in
Is 54: 7 For a mere **m** I have forsaken
Is 54: 8 hid My face from you for a **m**
Jer 4:20 and my curtains in a **m**
Lam 4: 6 which was overthrown in a **m**
Ezek 26:16 the ground, tremble every **m**
Ezek 32:10 and they shall tremble every **m**
Luke 4: 5 of the world in a **m** of time
Acts 11:11 At that very **m**, three men
1Co 15:52 in a **m**, in the twinkling of
2Co 4:17 which is but for a **m**, is

MONEY (*see* MONEYBELTS, MONEYCHANGERS, MONEYLENDER)
Gen 17:12 **m** from any stranger who is
Gen 17:13 your **m** must be circumcised
Gen 17:23 who were bought with his **m**
Gen 17:27 bought with **m** from a stranger
Gen 23:13 will give you **m** for the field
Gen 31:15 completely consumed our **m**
Gen 33:19 for one hundred pieces of **m**
Gen 42:25 every man's **m** to his sack
Gen 42:27 the encampment, he saw his **m**
Gen 42:28 My **m** has been restored, and
Gen 42:35 bundle of **m** was in his sack
Gen 42:35 father saw the bundles of **m**
Gen 43:12 Take double **m** in your hand,
Gen 43:12 **m** that was returned in the
Gen 43:15 took double **m** in their hand
Gen 43:18 It is because of the **m**, which
Gen 43:21 each man's **m** was in the mouth
Gen 43:21 sack, our **m** in full weight
Gen 43:22 **m** in our hands to buy food
Gen 43:22 who put our **m** in our sacks
Gen 43:23 I had your **m**
Gen 44: 1 put each man's **m** in the mouth
Gen 44: 2 the youngest, and his grain **m**
Gen 44: 8 **m** which we found in the mouth
Gen 47:14 **m** that was found in the land
Gen 47:14 Joseph brought the **m** into
Gen 47:15 So when the **m** failed in the
Gen 47:15 For the **m** has failed
Gen 47:16 livestock, if the **m** is gone
Gen 47:18 my lord that our **m** is gone
Ex 12:44 servant who is bought for **m**
Ex 21:11 go out free, without paying **m**
Ex 21:30 is imposed on him a sum of **m**
Ex 21:34 he shall give **m** to their
Ex 21:35 ox and divide the **m** from it
Ex 22: 7 **m** or articles to keep, and it
Ex 22:17 he shall pay **m** according to
Ex 22:25 If you lend **m** to any of My
Ex 30:16 shall take the atonement **m** of
Lev 22:11 buys a person with his **m**, he

Lev 25:37 not lend him your **m** for usury
Lev 25:51 **m** with which he was bought
Lev 27:15 the **m** of your valuation to it
Lev 27:18 shall reckon to him the **m** due
Lev 27:19 the **m** of your valuation to it
Num 3:48 And you shall give the **m**, with
Num 3:49 **m** from those who were over
Num 3:50 of Israel he took the **m**, one
Num 3:51 their redemption **m** to Aaron
Deut 2: 6 buy food from them with **m**
Deut 2: 6 buy water from them with **m**
Deut 2:28 You shall sell me food for **m**
Deut 2:28 eat, and give me water for **m**
Deut 14:25 you shall exchange it for **m**
Deut 14:25 take the **m** in your hand, and
Deut 14:26 you shall spend that **m** for
Deut 21:14 shall not sell her for **m**
Deut 23:19 interest on **m** or food or
Judg 16:18 brought the **m** in their hand
1Ki 21: 2 will give you its worth in **m**
1Ki 21: 6 Give me your vineyard for **m**
1Ki 21:15 he refused to give you for **m**
2Ki 5:26 Is it time to receive **m** and to
2Ki 12: 4 All the **m** of the dedicated
2Ki 12: 4 each man's census **m**, each
2Ki 12: 4 each man's assessment **m**
2Ki 12: 4 all the **m** that a man purposes
2Ki 12: 7 do not take any more **m** from
2Ki 12: 8 any more **m** from the people
2Ki 12: 9 **m** that was brought into the
2Ki 12:10 there was much **m** in the chest
2Ki 12:10 counted the **m** that was found
2Ki 12:11 Then they gave the **m**, which
2Ki 12:13 from the **m** that was brought
2Ki 12:15 the **m** to be paid to workmen
2Ki 12:16 The **m** from the trespass
2Ki 12:16 the **m** from the sin offerings
2Ki 15:20 exacted the **m** from Israel
2Ki 17: 3 vassal, and paid him tribute **m**
2Ki 22: 4 that he may count the **m** which
2Ki 22: 7 made with them of the **m**
2Ki 22: 9 servants have gathered the **m**
2Ki 23:35 to give **m** according to the
2Ch 24: 5 gather from all Israel **m** to
2Ch 24:11 saw that there was much **m**
2Ch 24:11 and gathered **m** in abundance
2Ch 24:14 rest of the **m** before the king
2Ch 34: 9 they delivered the **m** that was
2Ch 34:14 **m** that was brought into the
2Ch 34:17 they have gathered the **m** that
Ezra 3: 7 also gave **m** to the masons
Ezra 7:17 to buy with this **m** bulls,
Neh 5: 4 We have borrowed **m** for the
Neh 5:10 servants, am lending them **m**
Neh 5:11 the hundredth part of the **m**
Esth 3:11 The **m** and the people are given
Esth 4: 7 the sum of **m** that Haman had
Job 31:39 eaten its fruit without **m**
Ps 15: 5 not put out his **m** at usury
Prov 7:20 has taken a bag of **m** with him
Eccl 7:12 a defense as **m** is a defense
Eccl 10:19 but **m** answers every thing
Is 43:24 Me no sweet cane with **m**, nor
Is 52: 3 shall be redeemed without **m**
Is 55: 1 and you who have no **m**, come,
Is 55: 1 buy wine and milk without **m**
Is 55: 2 Why do you spend **m** for what
Jer 32: 9 and weighed out to him the **m**
Jer 32:10 weighed the **m** in the balances
Jer 32:25 Buy the field for **m**, and take
Jer 32:44 Men will buy fields for **m**
Mic 3:11 and her prophets divine for **m**
Zeph 1:11 who handle **m** are cut off
Matt 17:27 you will find a piece of **m**
Matt 22:19 Show Me the tax **m**
Matt 25:18 ground, and hid his lord's **m**
Matt 25:27 my **m** with the bankers, and at
Matt 28:12 sum of **m** to the soldiers,
Matt 28:15 So they took the **m** and did as
Mark 6: 8 no copper in their **m** belts
Mark 12:41 put **m** into the treasury
Mark 14:11 and promised to give him **m**
Luke 9: 3 nor bag nor bread nor **m**
Luke 10: 4 Carry neither **m** bag, sack,
Luke 12:33 provide yourselves **m** bags
Luke 16:14 who were lovers of **m**, also
Luke 19:15 to whom he had given the **m**
Luke 19:23 you not put my **m** in the bank
Luke 22: 5 glad, and agreed to give him **m**
Luke 22:35 When I sent you without **m** bag
Luke 22:36 But now, he who has a **m** bag
John 2:15 and poured out the changers' **m**
John 12: 6 was a thief, and had the **m** box
John 13:29 because Judas had the **m** box
Acts 4:37 sold it, and brought the **m**
Acts 7:16 of **m** from the sons of Hamor
Acts 8:18 was given, he offered them **m**
Acts 8:20 Your **m** perish with you,
Acts 8:20 God could be purchased with **m**
Acts 24:26 he also hoped that **m** would be
1Ti 3: 3 not violent, not greedy for **m**
1Ti 3: 8 much wine, not greedy for **m**
1Ti 6:10 For the love of **m** is a root
2Ti 3: 2 of themselves, lovers of **m**
Tit 1: 7 not violent, not greedy for **m**

MONEYBELTS (*see* MONEY)
Matt 10: 9 silver nor copper in your **m**

MONEYCHANGERS (*see* MONEY)
Matt 21:12 the tables of the **m** and the
Mark 11:15 the tables of the **m** and the
John 2:14 and the **m** doing business

MONEYLENDER (*see* MONEY)
Ex 22:25 shall not be like a **m** to him

MONITOR
Lev 11:30 gecko, the **m** lizard, the sand

MONKEYS
1Ki 10:22 silver, ivory, apes, and **m**
2Ch 9:21 silver, ivory, apes, and **m**

MONSTER (*see* MONSTROUS)
Jer 51:34 has swallowed me up like a **m**
Ezek 29: 3 O great **m** who lies in the
Ezek 32: 2 you are like a **m** in the seas

MONSTROUS (*see* MONSTER)
Joel 2:20 because he has done **m** things

MONTH (*see* MONTHLY, MONTHS)
Gen 7:11 Noah's life, in the second **m**
Gen 7:11 the seventeenth day of the **m**
Gen 8: 4 ark rested in the seventh **m**
Gen 8: 4 the seventeenth day of the **m**
Gen 8: 5 continually until the tenth **m**
Gen 8: 5 In the tenth **m**, on the first
Gen 8: 5 on the first day of the **m**
Gen 8:13 and first year, in the first **m**
Gen 8:13 the first day of the **m**
Gen 8:14 And in the second **m**, on the
Gen 8:14 twenty-seventh day of the **m**
Gen 29:14 And he stayed with him for a **m**
Ex 12: 2 This **m** shall be your
Ex 12: 2 first **m** of the year to you
Ex 12: 3 **m** every man shall take for
Ex 12: 6 fourteenth day of the same **m**
Ex 12:18 In the first **m**, on the
Ex 12:18 day of the **m** at evening, you
Ex 12:18 day of the **m** at evening
Ex 13: 4 are going out, in the **m** Abib
Ex 13: 5 keep this service in this **m**
Ex 16: 1 **m** after they departed from
Ex 19: 1 In the third **m** after the
Ex 23:15 appointed in the **m** of Abib
Ex 34:18 time of the **m** of Abib
Ex 34:18 for in the **m** of Abib you came
Ex 40: 2 first **m** you shall set up the
Ex 40:17 first **m** of the second year
Ex 40:17 on the first day of the **m**
Lev 16:29 In the seventh **m**, on the
Lev 16:29 on the tenth day of the **m**
Lev 23: 5 **m** at twilight is the LORD's
Lev 23: 6 fifteenth day of the same **m**
Lev 23:24 In the seventh **m**, on the
Lev 23:24 on the first day of the **m**
Lev 23:27 seventh **m** shall be the Day of
Lev 23:32 ninth day of the **m** at evening
Lev 23:34 day of this seventh **m** shall
Lev 23:39 day of the seventh **m**, when
Lev 23:41 celebrate it in the seventh **m**
Lev 25: 9 tenth day of the seventh **m**
Lev 27: 6 if from a **m** old up to five
Num 1: 1 the first day of the second **m**
Num 1:18 the first day of the second **m**
Num 3:15 every male from a **m** old and
Num 3:22 of all the males from a **m** old
Num 3:28 all the males, from a **m** old
Num 3:34 of all the males from a **m** old
Num 3:39 all the males from a **m** old
Num 3:40 of Israel from a **m** old and
Num 3:43 number of names from a **m** old
Num 9: 1 in the first **m** of the second
Num 9: 3 the fourteenth day of this **m**
Num 9: 5 fourteenth day of the first **m**
Num 9:11 day of the second **m**, at
Num 9:22 Whether it was two days, a **m**
Num 10:11 twentieth day of the second **m**
Num 11:20 but for a whole **m**, until it
Num 11:21 they may eat for a whole **m**
Num 18:16 shall redeem when one **m** old
Num 20: 1 of Zin in the first **m**, and the
Num 26:62 every male from a **m** old and
Num 28:14 **m** throughout the months of
Num 28:16 **m** is the Passover of the LORD
Num 28:17 day of this **m** is the feast
Num 29: 1 And in the seventh **m**, on the
Num 29: 1 on the first day of the **m**
Num 29: 7 **m** you shall have a holy
Num 29:12 day of the seventh **m** you
Num 33: 3 from Rameses in the first **m**
Num 33: 3 fifteenth day of the first **m**
Num 33:38 the first day of the fifth **m**
Deut 1: 3 year, in the eleventh **m**, on
Deut 1: 3 on the first day of the **m**
Deut 16: 1 Observe the **m** of Abib, and
Deut 16: 1 for in the **m** of Abib the LORD
Deut 21:13 father and her mother a full **m**
Josh 4:19 the tenth day of the first **m**
Josh 5:10 **m** at twilight on the plains
1Sa 20:27 day, the second day of the **m**
1Sa 20:34 food the second day of the **m**
1Ki 4: 7 for one **m** of the year
1Ki 4:27 governors, each man in his **m**
1Ki 5:14 ten thousand a **m** in shifts
1Ki 5:14 they were one **m** in Lebanon
1Ki 6: 1 over Israel, in the **m** of Ziv
1Ki 6: 1 of Ziv, which is the second **m**
1Ki 6:37 was laid, in the **m** of Ziv
1Ki 6:38 year, in the **m** of Bul, which
1Ki 6:38 of Bul, which is the eighth **m**
1Ki 8: 2 the feast in the **m** of Ethanim
1Ki 8: 2 which is the seventh **m**
1Ki 12:32 fifteenth day of the eighth **m**
1Ki 12:33 fifteenth day of the eighth **m**
1Ki 12:33 in the **m** which he had devised
2Ki 15:13 reigned a full **m** in Samaria
2Ki 25: 1 of his reign, in the tenth **m**
2Ki 25: 1 on the tenth day of the **m**
2Ki 25: 3 **m** the famine had become so
2Ki 25: 8 Now in the fifth **m**, on the
2Ki 25: 8 **m** (which was the nineteenth
2Ki 25:25 **m** that Ishmael the son of
2Ki 25:27 of Judah, in the twelfth **m**
2Ki 25:27 twenty-seventh day of the **m**
1Ch 12:15 the Jordan in the first **m**
1Ch 27: 1 in and went out **m** by **m**
1Ch 27: 2 division for the first **m** was
1Ch 27: 3 of the army for the first **m**
1Ch 27: 4 second **m** was Dodai an Ahohite
1Ch 27: 5 for the third **m** was Benaiah
1Ch 27: 7 captain for the fourth **m** was
1Ch 27: 8 **m** was Shamhuth the Izrahite
1Ch 27: 9 **m** was Ira the son of Ikkesh
1Ch 27:10 **m** was Helez the Pelonite, of
1Ch 27:11 eighth **m** was Sibbechai the
1Ch 27:12 **m** was Abiezer the Anathothite
1Ch 27:13 the tenth **m** was Maharai the
1Ch 27:14 captain for the eleventh **m**
1Ch 27:15 captain for the twelfth **m** was
2Ch 3: 2 second day of the second **m** in
2Ch 5: 3 which was in the seventh **m**
2Ch 7:10 day of the seventh **m** he sent
2Ch 15:10 at Jerusalem in the third **m**
2Ch 29: 3 of his reign, in the first **m**
2Ch 29:17 the first day of the first **m**
2Ch 29:17 on the eighth day of the **m**
2Ch 29:17 of the first **m** they finished
2Ch 30: 2 the Passover in the second **m**
2Ch 30:13 Bread in the second **m**
2Ch 30:15 day of the second **m**
2Ch 31: 7 In the third **m** they began
2Ch 31: 7 finished in the seventh **m**
2Ch 35: 1 fourteenth day of the first **m**
Ezra 3: 1 when the seventh **m** had come
Ezra 3: 6 first day of the seventh **m**
Ezra 3: 8 Now in the second **m** of the
Ezra 6:15 third day of the **m** of Adar
Ezra 6:19 fourteenth day of the first **m**
Ezra 7: 8 to Jerusalem in the fifth **m**
Ezra 7: 9 **m** he began his journey from
Ezra 7: 9 fifth **m** he came to Jerusalem

Ezra 8:31 twelfth day of the first **m**
Ezra 10: 9 It was the ninth **m**, on the
Ezra 10: 9 on the twentieth day of the **m**
Ezra 10:16 tenth **m** to examine the matter
Ezra 10:17 **m** they finished questioning
Neh 1: 1 to pass in the **m** of Chislev
Neh 2: 1 to pass in the **m** of Nisan
Neh 6:15 day of the **m** of Elul, in
Neh 7:73 When the seventh **m** came, the
Neh 8: 2 first day of the seventh **m**
Neh 8:14 the feast of the seventh **m**
Neh 9: 1 twenty-fourth day of this **m**
Esth 2:16 royal palace, in the tenth **m**
Esth 2:16 which is the **m** of Tebeth
Esth 3: 7 In the first **m**, which is the
Esth 3: 7 which is the **m** of Nisan, in
Esth 3: 7 to determine the day and the **m**
Esth 3: 7 it fell on the twelfth **m**,
Esth 3: 7 which is the **m** of Adar
Esth 3:12 thirteenth day of the first **m**
Esth 3:13 thirteenth day of the twelfth **m**,
Esth 3:13 which is the **m** of Adar
Esth 8: 9 at that time, in the third **m**
Esth 8: 9 which is the **m** of Sivan, on
Esth 8:12 day of the twelfth **m**,
Esth 8:12 which is the **m** of Adar
Esth 9: 1 Now in the twelfth **m**, that is
Esth 9: 1 is, the **m** of Adar, on the
Esth 9:15 day of the **m** of Adar and
Esth 9:17 day of the **m** of Adar
Esth 9:17 day of the **m** they rested and
Esth 9:18 day of the **m** they rested, and
Esth 9:19 of the **m** of Adar as a day of
Esth 9:21 days of the **m** of Adar,
Esth 9:22 as the **m** which was turned
Jer 1: 3 captive in the fifth **m**
Jer 2:24 in her **m** they will find her
Jer 28: 1 fourth year and in the fifth **m**
Jer 28:17 same year in the seventh **m**
Jer 36: 9 king of Judah, in the ninth **m**
Jer 36:22 winter house in the ninth **m**
Jer 39: 1 king of Judah, in the tenth **m**
Jer 39: 2 of Zedekiah, in the fourth **m**
Jer 39: 2 on the ninth day of the **m**
Jer 41: 1 **m** that Ishmael the son of
Jer 52: 4 of his reign, in the tenth **m**
Jer 52: 4 on the tenth day of the **m**
Jer 52: 6 By the fourth **m**, on the ninth
Jer 52: 6 on the ninth day of the **m**
Jer 52:12 Now in the fifth **m**, on the
Jer 52:12 on the tenth day of the **m**
Jer 52:31 of Judah, in the twelfth **m**
Jer 52:31 the twenty-fifth day of the **m**
Ezek 1: 1 year, in the fourth **m**, on the
Ezek 1: 1 on the fifth day of the **m**
Ezek 1: 2 On the fifth day of the **m**
Ezek 8: 1 sixth year, in the sixth **m**
Ezek 8: 1 on the fifth day of the **m**
Ezek 20: 1 seventh year, in the fifth **m**
Ezek 20: 1 on the tenth day of the **m**
Ezek 24: 1 ninth year, in the tenth **m**
Ezek 24: 1 on the tenth day of the **m**
Ezek 26: 1 on the first day of the **m**
Ezek 29: 1 tenth year, in the tenth **m**
Ezek 29: 1 on the twelfth day of the **m**
Ezek 29:17 year, in the first **m**, on the
Ezek 29:17 on the first day of the **m**
Ezek 30:20 eleventh year, in the first **m**
Ezek 30:20 on the seventh day of the **m**
Ezek 31: 1 eleventh year, in the third **m**
Ezek 31: 1 on the first day of the **m**
Ezek 32: 1 year, in the twelfth **m**, on
Ezek 32: 1 on the first day of the **m**
Ezek 32:17 on the fifteenth day of the **m**
Ezek 33:21 our captivity, in the tenth **m**
Ezek 33:21 on the fifth day of the **m**
Ezek 40: 1 on the tenth day of the **m**
Ezek 45:18 In the first **m**, on the first
Ezek 45:18 on the first day of the **m**
Ezek 45:20 on the seventh day of the **m**
Ezek 45:21 In the first **m**, on the
Ezek 45:21 the fourteenth day of the **m**
Ezek 45:25 In the seventh **m**, on the
Ezek 45:25 on the fifteenth day of the **m**
Ezek 47:12 They will bear fruit every **m**
Dan 10: 4 day of the first **m**, as I was
Joel 2:23 latter rain in the first **m**
Hag 1: 1 King Darius, in the sixth **m**
Hag 1: 1 on the first day of the **m**
Hag 1:15 day of the sixth **m**, in the
Hag 2: 1 In the seventh **m**, on the
Hag 2: 1 the twenty-first day of the **m**
Hag 2:10 day of the ninth **m**, in the
Hag 2:18 day of the ninth **m**, from the
Hag 2:20 twenty-fourth day of the **m**
Zech 1: 1 In the eighth **m** of the second
Zech 1: 7 day of the eleventh **m**
Zech 1: 7 which is the **m** Shebat
Zech 7: 1 the fourth day of the ninth **m**
Zech 7: 3 Should I weep in the fifth **m**
Zech 8:19 The fast of the fourth **m**
Zech 11: 8 the three shepherds in one **m**
Luke 1:26 Now in the sixth **m** the angel
Luke 1:36 this is now the sixth **m** for
Rev 9:15 for the hour and day and **m** and
Rev 22: 2 yielding its fruit every **m**

MONTHLY (*see* MONTH)
Is 47:13 the **m** prognosticators stand

MONTHS (*see* MONTH, MONTHS')
Gen 38:24 to pass, about three **m** after
Ex 2: 2 child, she hid him three **m**
Ex 12: 2 shall be your beginning of **m**
Num 10:10 and at the beginning of your **m**
Num 28:11 **m** you shall present a burnt
Num 28:14 throughout the **m** of the year
Deut 33:14 the precious produce of the **m**
Judg 11:37 let me alone for two **m**, that
Judg 11:38 And he sent her away for two **m**
Judg 11:39 **m** that she returned to her
Judg 19: 2 and was there four whole **m**
Judg 20:47 the rock of Rimmon for four **m**
1Sa 6: 1 of the Philistines seven **m**
1Sa 27: 7 was one full year and four **m**
2Sa 2:11 was seven years and six **m**
2Sa 5: 5 Judah seven years and six **m**
2Sa 6:11 Obed-Edom the Gittite three **m**
2Sa 24: 8 at the end of nine **m** and
2Sa 24:13 three **m** before your enemies
1Ki 5:14 in Lebanon and two **m** at home
1Ki 11:16 (because for six **m** Joab
2Ki 15: 8 over Israel in Samaria six **m**
2Ki 23:31 reigned three **m** in Jerusalem
2Ki 24: 8 reigned in Jerusalem three **m**
1Ch 3: 4 reigned seven years and six **m**
1Ch 13:14 in his house three **m**
1Ch 21:12 or three **m** to be defeated by
1Ch 27: 1 all the **m** of the year, each
2Ch 36: 2 reigned three **m** in Jerusalem
2Ch 36: 9 reigned in Jerusalem three **m**
Esth 2:12 six **m** with oil of myrrh, and
Esth 2:12 and six **m** with perfumes and
Job 3: 6 come into the number of the **m**
Job 7: 3 been allotted **m** of futility
Job 14: 5 number of his **m** is with You
Job 21:21 of his **m** is cut in half
Job 29: 2 Oh, that I were as in **m** past
Job 39: 2 the **m** that they fulfill
Ezek 39:12 For seven **m** the house of
Ezek 39:14 At the end of seven **m** they
Dan 4:29 **m** he was walking about the
Amos 4: 7 still three **m** to the harvest
Zech 7: 5 and seventh **m** during those
Luke 1:24 and she hid herself five **m**
Luke 1:56 with her about three **m**, and
Luke 4:25 shut up three years and six **m**
John 4:35 say, 'There are still four **m**
Acts 7:20 father's house for three **m**
Acts 18:11 there a year and six **m**,
Acts 19: 8 and spoke boldly for three **m**
Acts 20: 3 and stayed three **m**
Acts 28:11 After three **m** we sailed in an
Gal 4:10 You observe days and **m** and
Heb 11:23 hidden three **m** by his parents
Jas 5:17 land for three years and six **m**
Rev 9: 5 to torment them for five **m**
Rev 9:10 power was to hurt men five **m**
Rev 11: 2 under foot for forty-two **m**
Rev 13: 5 to continue for forty-two **m**

MONTHS' (*see* MONTHS)
Esth 2:12 twelve **m** preparation,

MONUMENT (*see* MONUMENTS)
1Sa 15:12 he set up a **m** for himself
2Sa 18:18 day it is called Absalom's **M**

MONUMENTS (*see* MONUMENT)
Matt 23:29 adorn the **m** of the righteous,

MOON (*see* MOONS)
Gen 37: 9 And this time, the sun, the **m**
Num 29: 6 grain offering for the New **M**
Deut 4:19 when you see the sun, the **m**
Deut 17: 3 either the sun or **m** or any of
Josh 10:12 and **M**, in the Valley of
Josh 10:13 and the **m** stopped, till the
1Sa 20: 5 Indeed tomorrow is the New **M**
1Sa 20:18 Tomorrow is the New **M**
1Sa 20:24 And when the New **M** had come
2Ki 4:23 the New **M** nor the Sabbath
2Ki 23: 5 to Baal, to the sun, to the **m**
Job 25: 5 If even the **m** does not shine,
Job 31:26 or the **m** moving in brightness
Ps 8: 3 work of Your fingers, The **m**
Ps 72: 5 and **m** endure, Throughout all
Ps 72: 7 peace, Until the **m** is no more
Ps 81: 3 at the time of the New **M**, At
Ps 81: 3 the New **M**, At the full **m**
Ps 89:37 forever like the **m**, Even like
Ps 104:19 appointed the **m** for seasons
Ps 121: 6 by day, Nor the **m** by night
Ps 136: 9 The **m** and stars to rule by
Ps 148: 3 Praise Him, sun and **m**
Eccl 12: 2 the sun and the light, the **m**
Song 6:10 as the morning, fair as the **m**
Is 13:10 and the **m** will not cause its
Is 24:23 Then the **m** will be disgraced
Is 30:26 Moreover the light of the **m**
Is 60:19 shall the **m** give light to you
Is 60:20 nor shall your **m** withdraw
Is 66:23 from one New **M** to another
Jer 8: 2 them before the sun and the **m**
Jer 31:35 and the ordinances of the **m**
Ezek 32: 7 and the **m** shall not give her
Ezek 46: 1 the New **M** it shall be opened
Ezek 46: 6 On the day of the New **M** it
Hos 5: 7 Now a New **M** shall devour them
Joel 2:10 **m** grow dark, and the stars
Joel 2:31 the **m** into blood, before the
Joel 3:15 and **m** will grow dark, and the
Amos 8: 5 When will the New **M** be past
Hab 3:11 sun and **m** stood still in their
Matt 24:29 the **m** will not give its light
Mark 13:24 the **m** will not give its light
Luke 21:25 be signs in the sun, in the **m**
Acts 2:20 the **m** into blood, before the
1Co 15:41 sun, another glory of the **m**
Col 2:16 or a new **m** or sabbaths,
Rev 6:12 and the **m** became like blood
Rev 8:12 was struck, a third of the **m**
Rev 12: 1 with the **m** under her feet, and
Rev 21:23 or of the **m** to shine in it

MOONS (*see* MOON)
1Ch 23:31 the Sabbaths and on the New **M**
2Ch 2: 4 on the Sabbaths, on the New **M**
2Ch 8:13 for the Sabbaths, the New **M**
2Ch 31: 3 for the Sabbaths and the New **M**
Ezra 3: 5 offering, and those for New **M**
Neh 10:33 of the Sabbaths, the New **M**
Is 1:13 The New **M**, the Sabbaths, and
Is 1:14 Your New **M** and your
Ezek 45:17 at the feasts, the New **M**
Ezek 46: 3 on the Sabbaths and the New **M**
Hos 2:11 her feast days, her New **M**

MOORINGS
Jon 2: 6 to the **m** of the mountains

MORAL
2Ch 28:19 encouraged **m** decline in Judah

MORDECAI (*see* MORDECAI'S)
Ezra 2: 2 Seraiah, Reelaiah, **M**,
Neh 7: 7 Raamiah, Nahamani, **M**
Esth 2: 5 name was **M** the son of Jair
Esth 2: 7 **M** had brought up Hadassah,
Esth 2: 7 died, **M** took her as his own
Esth 2:10 for **M** had charged her not to
Esth 2:11 every day **M** paced in front of
Esth 2:15 of Abihail the uncle of **M**
Esth 2:19 **M** sat within the king's gate
Esth 2:20 just as **M** had charged her,
Esth 2:20 obeyed the command of **M** as
Esth 2:21 while **M** sat within the king's
Esth 2:22 the matter became known to **M**
Esth 3: 2 But **M** would not bow or pay
Esth 3: 3 the king's gate said to **M**
Esth 3: 4 for **M** had told them that he
Esth 3: 5 When Haman saw that **M** did
Esth 3: 6 to lay hands on **M** alone, for

Esth 3: 6 told him of the people of **M**
Esth 3: 6 the people of **M**
Esth 4: 1 When **M** learned all that had
Esth 4: 4 she sent garments to clothe **M**
Esth 4: 5 him a command concerning **M**
Esth 4: 6 So Hathach went out to **M** in
Esth 4: 7 And **M** told him all that had
Esth 4: 9 and told Esther the words of **M**
Esth 4:10 and gave him a command for **M**
Esth 4:12 So they told **M** Esther's words
Esth 4:13 Then **M** told them to answer
Esth 4:15 to return this answer to **M**
Esth 4:17 Then **M** went his way and did
Esth 5: 9 saw **M** in the king's gate, and
Esth 5: 9 with indignation against **M**
Esth 5:13 so long as I see **M** the Jew
Esth 5:14 king that **M** be hanged on it
Esth 6: 2 that **M** had told of Bigthana
Esth 6: 3 been bestowed on **M** for this
Esth 6: 4 **M** on the gallows that he had
Esth 6:10 do so for **M** the Jew who sits
Esth 6:11 robe and the horse, arrayed **M**
Esth 6:12 Afterward **M** went back to the
Esth 6:13 If **M**, before whom you have
Esth 7: 9 high, which Haman made for **M**
Esth 7:10 that he had prepared for **M**
Esth 8: 1 **M** came before the king, for
Esth 8: 2 from Haman, and gave it to **M**
Esth 8: 2 Esther appointed **M** over the
Esth 8: 7 to Queen Esther and **M** the Jew,
Esth 8: 9 to all that **M** commanded, to
Esth 8:15 Now **M** went out from the
Esth 9: 3 the fear of **M** fell upon them
Esth 9: 4 For **M** was great in the king's
Esth 9: 4 for this man **M** became
Esth 9:20 **M** wrote these things and sent
Esth 9:23 as **M** had written to them,
Esth 9:29 with **M** the Jew, wrote with
Esth 9:30 **M** sent letters to all the
Esth 9:31 as **M** the Jew and Queen Esther
Esth 10: 2 account of the greatness of **M**
Esth 10: 3 For **M** the Jew was second to

MORDECAI'S (*see* MORDECAI)
Esth 2:22 informed the king in **M** name
Esth 3: 4 to see whether **M** words would

MORE (*see* PREFACE)

MOREH
Gen 12: 6 as the terebinth tree of **M**
Deut 11:30 the terebinth trees of **M**
Judg 7: 1 the hill of **M** in the valley

MOREOVER (*see* PREFACE)

MORESHETH
Jer 26:18 Micah of **M** prophesied in the
Mic 1: 1 of **M** in the days of Jotham

MORESHETH GATH (*see* GATH)
Mic 1:14 you shall give presents to **M**

MORIAH
Gen 22: 2 love, and go to the land of **M**
2Ch 3: 1 LORD at Jerusalem on Mount **M**

MORNING (*see* MORNINGS)
Gen 1: 5 and the **m** were the first day
Gen 1: 8 the **m** were the second day
Gen 1:13 and the **m** were the third day
Gen 1:19 the **m** were the fourth day
Gen 1:23 and the **m** were the fifth day
Gen 1:31 and the **m** were the sixth day
Gen 19:15 When the **m** dawned, the angels
Gen 19:27 **m** to the place where he had
Gen 20: 8 Abimelech rose early in the **m**
Gen 21:14 Abraham rose early in the **m**
Gen 22: 3 Abraham rose early in the **m**
Gen 24:54 Then they arose in the **m**, and
Gen 26:31 they arose early in the **m**
Gen 28:18 Jacob rose early in the **m**
Gen 29:25 So it came to pass in the **m**
Gen 31:55 And early in the **m** Laban arose
Gen 40: 6 came in to them in the **m** and
Gen 41: 8 in the **m** that his spirit was
Gen 44: 3 As soon as the **m** dawned, the
Gen 49:27 in the **m** he shall devour the
Ex 7:15 Go to Pharaoh in the **m**, when
Ex 8:20 Rise early in the **m** and stand
Ex 9:13 Rise early in the **m** and stand
Ex 10:13 And when it was **m**, the east
Ex 12:10 let none of it remain until **m**
Ex 12:10 **m** you shall burn with fire
Ex 12:22 the door of his house until **m**
Ex 14:24 came to pass, in the **m** watch
Ex 14:27 and when the **m** appeared, the
Ex 16: 7 in the **m** you shall see the
Ex 16: 8 in the **m** bread to the full
Ex 16:12 in the **m** you shall be filled
Ex 16:13 and in the **m** the dew lay all
Ex 16:19 no one leave any of it till **m**
Ex 16:20 them left part of it until **m**
Ex 16:21 So they gathered it every **m**
Ex 16:23 remains, to be kept until **m**
Ex 16:24 So they laid it up till **m**
Ex 18:13 Moses from **m** until evening
Ex 18:14 you from **m** until evening
Ex 19:16 on the third day, in the **m**
Ex 23:18 My sacrifice remain until **m**
Ex 24: 4 And he rose early in the **m**
Ex 27:21 until **m** before the LORD
Ex 29:34 bread, remains until the **m**
Ex 29:39 lamb you shall offer in the **m**
Ex 29:41 drink offering, as in the **m**
Ex 30: 7 on it sweet incense every **m**
Ex 34: 2 So be ready in the **m**, and come
Ex 34: 2 up in the **m** to Mount Sinai
Ex 34: 4 Moses rose early in the **m**
Ex 34:25 the Passover be left until **m**
Ex 36: 3 freewill offerings every **m**
Lev 6: 9 the altar all night until **m**
Lev 6:12 shall burn wood on it every **m**
Lev 6:20 offering, half of it in the **m**
Lev 7:15 not leave any of it until **m**
Lev 9:17 the burnt sacrifice of the **m**
Lev 19:13 with you all night until **m**
Lev 22:30 leave none of it until **m**
Lev 24: 3 of it from evening until **m**
Num 9:12 leave none of it until **m**, nor
Num 9:15 from evening until **m** it was
Num 9:21 only from evening until **m**
Num 9:21 cloud was taken up in the **m**
Num 14:40 And they rose early in the **m**
Num 16: 5 Tomorrow **m** the LORD will show
Num 22:13 So Balaam rose in the **m** and
Num 22:21 So Balaam rose in the **m**,
Num 28: 4 lamb you shall offer in the **m**
Num 28: 8 as the **m** grain offering and
Num 28:23 the burnt offering of the **m**
Deut 16: 4 remain overnight until **m**
Deut 16: 7 in the **m** you shall turn and go
Deut 28:67 In the **m** you shall say, 'Oh,
Deut 28:67 say, 'Oh, that it were **m**
Josh 3: 1 Joshua rose early in the **m**
Josh 6:12 And Joshua rose early in the **m**
Josh 7:14 In the **m** therefore you shall
Josh 7:16 So Joshua rose early in the **m**
Josh 8:10 Joshua rose up early in the **m**
Judg 6:28 the city arose early in the **m**
Judg 6:31 for him be put to death by **m**
Judg 6:38 When he rose early the next **m**
Judg 9:33 as the sun is up in the **m**
Judg 16: 2 In the **m**, when it is daylight
Judg 19: 5 they arose early in the **m**
Judg 19: 8 **m** on the fifth day to depart
Judg 19:25 abused her all night until **m**
Judg 19:27 her master arose in the **m**
Judg 20:19 of Israel rose in the **m** and
Judg 21: 4 So it was, on the next **m**,
Ruth 2: 7 continued from **m** until now
Ruth 3:13 in the **m** it shall be that if
Ruth 3:13 Lie down until **m**
Ruth 3:14 she lay at his feet until **m**
1Sa 1:19 Then they rose early in the **m**
1Sa 3:15 So Samuel lay down until **m**
1Sa 5: 3 Ashdod arose early in the **m**
1Sa 5: 4 they arose early the next **m**
1Sa 11:11 of the camp in the **m** watch
1Sa 14:36 them until the **m** light
1Sa 15:12 early in the **m** to meet Saul
1Sa 17:16 himself forty days, **m** and
1Sa 17:20 So David rose early in the **m**
1Sa 19: 2 be on your guard until **m**, and
1Sa 19:11 him and to kill him in the **m**
1Sa 20:35 And so it was, in the **m**, that
1Sa 25:22 who belong to him by **m** light
1Sa 25:34 surely by **m** light no males
1Sa 25:36 little or much, until **m** light
1Sa 25:37 So it was, in the **m**, when the
1Sa 29:10 rise early in the **m** with your
1Sa 29:10 as you are up early in the **m**
1Sa 29:11 rose early to depart in the **m**
2Sa 2:27 surely then by **m** all the
2Sa 11:14 Then in the **m** it was so that
2Sa 17:22 By **m** light not one of them
2Sa 23: 4 of the **m** when the sun rises
2Sa 23: 4 a **m** without clouds, Like the
2Sa 24:11 Now when David arose in the **m**
2Sa 24:15 the **m** till the appointed time
1Ki 3:21 rose in the **m** to nurse my son
1Ki 3:21 I had examined him in the **m**
1Ki 17: 6 him bread and meat in the **m**
1Ki 18:26 of Baal from **m** even till noon
2Ki 3:20 Now it happened in the **m**,
2Ki 3:22 they rose up early in the **m**
2Ki 7: 9 If we wait until **m** light,
2Ki 10: 8 entrance of the gate until **m**
2Ki 10: 9 So it was, in the **m**, that he
2Ki 16:15 burn the **m** burnt offering
2Ki 19:35 people arose early in the **m**
1Ch 9:27 charge of opening it every **m**
1Ch 16:40 of burnt offering regularly **m**
1Ch 23:30 to stand every **m** to thank
2Ch 2: 4 for the burnt offerings **m**
2Ch 13:11 they burn to the LORD every **m**
2Ch 20:20 And they rose early in the **m**
2Ch 31: 3 for the **m** and evening burnt
Ezra 3: 3 on it to the LORD, both the **m**
Neh 8: 3 Gate from **m** until midday,
Esth 2:14 in the **m** she returned to the
Esth 5:14 in the **m** suggest to the king
Job 1: 5 he would rise early in the **m**
Job 3: 9 the stars of its **m** be dark
Job 4:20 in pieces from **m** till evening
Job 7:18 You should visit him every **m**
Job 11:17 dark, you would be like the **m**
Job 24:17 For the **m** is the same to them
Job 38: 7 when the **m** stars sang
Job 38:12 the **m** since your days began
Job 41:18 are like the eyelids of the **m**
Ps 5: 3 voice You shall hear in the **m**
Ps 5: 3 In the **m** I will direct it to
Ps 30: 5 night, But joy comes in the **m**
Ps 49:14 dominion over them in the **m**
Ps 55:17 Evening and **m** and at noon I
Ps 59:16 aloud of Your mercy in the **m**
Ps 65: 8 make the outgoings of the **m**
Ps 73:14 And chastened every **m**
Ps 88:13 And in the **m** my prayer comes
Ps 90: 5 In the **m** they are like grass
Ps 90: 6 In the **m** it flourishes and
Ps 92: 2 Your lovingkindness in the **m**
Ps 110: 3 from the womb of the **m**, You
Ps 119:147 before the dawning of the **m**
Ps 130: 6 those who watch for the **m**
Ps 130: 6 those who watch for the **m**
Ps 139: 9 If I take the wings of the **m**
Ps 143: 8 Your lovingkindness in the **m**
Prov 7:18 take our fill of love until **m**
Prov 27:14 voice, rising early in the **m**
Eccl 10:16 your princes feast in the **m**
Eccl 11: 6 In the **m** sow your seed, and in
Song 6:10 she who looks forth as the **m**
Is 5:11 those who rise early in the **m**
Is 14:12 O Lucifer, son of the **m**
Is 17:11 in the **m** you will make your
Is 17:14 and before the **m**, he is no
Is 21:12 The **m** comes, and also the
Is 28:19 for **m** by **m** it will pass
Is 33: 2 Be their arm every **m**, our
Is 37:36 people arose early in the **m**
Is 38:13 I have considered until **m**
Is 50: 4 He awakens Me **m** by **m**
Is 58: 8 shall break forth like the **m**
Jer 20:16 Let him hear the cry in the **m**
Jer 21:12 Execute judgment in the **m**
Lam 3:23 They are new every **m**
Ezek 12: 8 in the **m** the word of the LORD
Ezek 24:18 spoke to the people in the **m**
Ezek 24:18 the next **m** I did as I was
Ezek 33:22 when he came to me in the **m**
Ezek 46:13 you shall prepare it every **m**
Ezek 46:14 offering with it every **m**, a
Ezek 46:15 burnt offering every **m**
Dan 6:19 arose very early in the **m**
Hos 6: 3 forth is established as the **m**
Hos 6: 4 is like a **m** cloud, and like
Hos 7: 6 in the **m** it burns like a
Hos 10:15 In a **m** the king of Israel
Hos 13: 3 shall be like the **m** cloud
Joel 2: 2 like the **m** clouds spread over
Amos 4: 4 bring your sacrifices every **m**
Amos 4:13 is, and makes the **m** darkness

Amos 5: 8 the shadow of death into **m**
Jon 4: 7 But as **m** dawned the next day
Mic 2: 1 At **m** light they practice it,
Zeph 3: 3 that leave not a bone till **m**
Zeph 3: 5 Every **m** He brings His justice
Matt 16: 3 and in the **m**, 'It will be foul
Matt 20: 1 **m** to hire laborers for his
Matt 21:18 Now in the **m**, as He returned
Matt 27: 1 When **m** came, all the chief
Mark 1:35 Now in the **m**, having risen a
Mark 11:20 Now in the **m**, as they passed
Mark 13:35 of the rooster, or in the **m**
Mark 15: 1 Immediately, in the **m**, the
Mark 16: 2 Very early in the **m**, on the
Luke 21:38 Then early in the **m** all the
Luke 24: 1 the week, very early in the **m**
John 8: 2 But early in the **m** He came
John 18:28 Praetorium, and it was early **m**
John 21: 4 But when the **m** had now come
Acts 5:21 the temple early in the **m**
Acts 28:23 Prophets, from **m** till evening
2Pe 1:19 and the **m** star rises in your
Rev 2:28 and I will give him the **m** star
Rev 22:16 David, the Bright and **M** Star

MORNINGS (*see* MORNING)
Dan 8:26 and **m** which was told is true

MORSEL (*see* MORSELS)
Gen 18: 5 And I will bring a **m** of bread
Judg 19: 5 your heart with a **m** of bread
1Sa 2:36 and a **m** of bread, and say,
1Ki 17:11 Please bring me a **m** of bread
Job 31:17 or eaten my **m** by myself, so
Prov 17: 1 is a dry **m** with quietness
Prov 23: 8 The **m** you have eaten, you
Heb 12:16 who for one **m** of food sold

MORSELS (*see* MORSEL)
Ps 147:17 He casts out His hail like **m**

MORTAL (*see* MORTALITY, MORTALLY, MORTALS)
Job 4:17 Can a **m** be more righteous
Job 10: 5 days like the days of a **m** man
Is 13:12 I will make a **m** more rare
Rom 6:12 let sin reign in your **m** body
Rom 8:11 **m** bodies through His Spirit
1Co 15:53 and this **m** must put on
1Co 15:54 this **m** has put on immortality
2Co 4:11 be manifested in our **m** flesh
Heb 7: 8 Here **m** men receive tithes,

MORTALITY (*see* MORTAL)
2Co 5: 4 that **m** may be swallowed up by

MORTALLY (*see* MORTAL)
Deut 19:11 against him and strikes him **m**
Ezek 30:24 groanings of a **m** wounded man
Rev 13: 3 as if it had been **m** wounded

MORTALS (*see* MORTAL)
Ps 26: 4 not sat with idolatrous **m**

MORTAR
Gen 11: 3 and they had asphalt for **m**
Ex 1:14 in **m**, in brick, and in all
Lev 14:42 and he shall take other **m**
Num 11: 8 or beat it in the **m**, cooked
Prov 27:22 you grind a fool in a **m** with
Is 41:25 against princes as though **m**
Ezek 13:10 plaster it with untempered **m**
Ezek 13:11 plaster it with untempered **m**
Ezek 13:12 Where is the **m** with which
Ezek 13:14 plastered with untempered **m**
Ezek 13:15 it with untempered **m**
Ezek 22:28 them with untempered **m**,
Nah 3:14 into the clay and tread the **m**

MORTGAGED
Neh 5: 3 We have **m** our lands and

MOSAIC
Esth 1: 6 silver on a **m** pavement of

MOSERAH (*see* MOSEROTH)
Deut 10: 6 the wells of Bene Jaakan to **M**

MOSEROTH (*see* MOSERAH)
Num 33:30 Hashmonah and camped at **M**
Num 33:31 They departed from **M** and

MOSES (*see* MOSES')
Ex 2:10 So she called his name **M**,
Ex 2:11 when **M** was grown, that he
Ex 2:14 So **M** feared and said,
Ex 2:15 matter, he sought to kill **M**
Ex 2:15 But **M** fled from the face of
Ex 2:17 but **M** stood up and helped them
Ex 2:21 Then **M** was content to live
Ex 2:21 Zipporah his daughter to **M**
Ex 3: 1 Now **M** kept the flock of
Ex 3: 3 Then **M** said, "I will now
Ex 3: 4 the bush and said, "**M**, **M**!"
Ex 3: 6 **M** hid his face, for he was
Ex 3:11 But **M** said to God, "Who am I
Ex 3:13 Then **M** said to God, "Indeed,
Ex 3:14 And God said to **M**, "I AM
Ex 3:15 Moreover God said to **M**
Ex 4: 1 Then **M** answered and said
Ex 4: 3 and **M** fled from it
Ex 4: 4 Then the LORD said to **M**
Ex 4:10 Then **M** said to the LORD, "O
Ex 4:14 LORD was kindled against **M**
Ex 4:18 So **M** went and returned to
Ex 4:18 And Jethro said to **M**, "Go
Ex 4:19 the LORD said to **M** in Midian
Ex 4:20 Then **M** took his wife and his
Ex 4:20 **M** took the rod of God in his
Ex 4:21 And the LORD said to **M**, "When
Ex 4:27 into the wilderness to meet **M**
Ex 4:28 So **M** told Aaron all the words
Ex 4:29 Then **M** and Aaron went and
Ex 4:30 the LORD had spoken to **M**
Ex 5: 1 Afterward **M** and Aaron went in
Ex 5: 4 **M** and Aaron, why do you take
Ex 5:20 out from Pharaoh, they met **M**
Ex 5:22 So **M** returned to the LORD and
Ex 6: 1 Then the LORD said to **M**
Ex 6: 2 And God spoke to **M** and said to
Ex 6: 9 So **M** spoke thus to the
Ex 6: 9 but they would not heed **M**
Ex 6:10 And the LORD spoke to **M**,
Ex 6:12 And **M** spoke before the LORD,
Ex 6:13 Then the LORD spoke to **M** and
Ex 6:20 and she bore him Aaron and **M**
Ex 6:26 and **M** to whom the LORD said,
Ex 6:27 These are the same **M** and
Ex 6:28 to **M** in the land of Egypt
Ex 6:29 that the LORD spoke to **M**,
Ex 6:30 But **M** said before the LORD,
Ex 7: 1 So the LORD said to **M**
Ex 7: 6 Then **M** and Aaron did so
Ex 7: 7 **M** was eighty years old and
Ex 7: 8 Then the LORD spoke to **M** and
Ex 7:10 So **M** and Aaron went in to
Ex 7:14 So the LORD said to **M**
Ex 7:19 Then the LORD spoke to **M**
Ex 7:20 And **M** and Aaron did so, just as
Ex 8: 1 And the LORD spoke to **M**, "Go
Ex 8: 5 Then the LORD spoke to **M**
Ex 8: 8 Then Pharaoh called for **M**
Ex 8: 9 And **M** said to Pharaoh,
Ex 8:12 Then **M** and Aaron went out
Ex 8:12 And **M** cried out to the LORD
Ex 8:13 according to the word of **M**
Ex 8:16 So the LORD said to **M**, "Say
Ex 8:20 And the LORD said to **M**, "Rise
Ex 8:25 Then Pharaoh called for **M**
Ex 8:26 And **M** said, "It is not right
Ex 8:29 Then **M** said, "Indeed I am
Ex 8:30 So **M** went out from Pharaoh
Ex 8:31 according to the word of **M**
Ex 9: 1 Then the LORD said to **M**, "Go
Ex 9: 8 So the LORD said to **M** and
Ex 9: 8 let **M** scatter it toward the
Ex 9:10 and **M** scattered them toward
Ex 9:11 before **M** because of the boils
Ex 9:12 as the LORD had spoken to **M**
Ex 9:13 Then the LORD said to **M**
Ex 9:22 Then the LORD said to **M**
Ex 9:23 And **M** stretched out his rod
Ex 9:27 Pharaoh sent and called for **M**
Ex 9:29 And **M** said to him, "As soon
Ex 9:33 So **M** went out of the city
Ex 9:35 as the LORD had spoken by **M**
Ex 10: 1 Now the LORD said to **M**, "Go
Ex 10: 3 So **M** and Aaron came in to
Ex 10: 8 So **M** and Aaron were brought
Ex 10: 9 And **M** said, "We will go
Ex 10:12 Then the LORD said to **M**
Ex 10:13 So **M** stretched out his rod
Ex 10:16 Then Pharaoh called for **M**
Ex 10:21 Then the LORD said to **M**
Ex 10:22 So **M** stretched out his hand
Ex 10:24 Then Pharaoh called to **M** and
Ex 10:25 But **M** said, "You must also
Ex 10:29 And **M** said, "You have spoken
Ex 11: 1 And the LORD said to **M**, "I
Ex 11: 3 Moreover the man **M** was very
Ex 11: 4 Then **M** said, "Thus says the
Ex 11: 9 the LORD said to **M**, "Pharaoh
Ex 11:10 So **M** and Aaron did all these
Ex 12: 1 Now the LORD spoke to **M** and
Ex 12:21 Then **M** called for all the
Ex 12:28 as the LORD had commanded **M**
Ex 12:31 Then he called for **M** and Aaron
Ex 12:35 according to the word of **M**
Ex 12:43 And the LORD said to **M** and
Ex 12:50 as the LORD commanded **M** and
Ex 13: 1 Then the LORD spoke to **M**,
Ex 13: 3 And **M** said to the people
Ex 13:19 **M** took the bones of Joseph
Ex 14: 1 Now the LORD spoke to **M**,
Ex 14:11 Then they said to **M**
Ex 14:13 And **M** said to the people,
Ex 14:15 And the LORD said to **M**, "Why
Ex 14:21 Then **M** stretched out his hand
Ex 14:26 Then the LORD said to **M**
Ex 14:27 **M** stretched out his hand over
Ex 14:31 the LORD and His servant **M**
Ex 15: 1 Then **M** and the children of
Ex 15:22 So **M** brought Israel from the
Ex 15:24 the people murmured against **M**
Ex 16: 2 of Israel murmured against **M**
Ex 16: 4 Then the LORD said to **M**
Ex 16: 6 Then **M** and Aaron said to all
Ex 16: 8 Also **M** said, "This shall be
Ex 16: 9 Then **M** spoke to Aaron, "Say
Ex 16:11 And the LORD spoke to **M**,
Ex 16:15 And **M** said to them,
Ex 16:19 And **M** said, "Let no one leave
Ex 16:20 they did not heed **M**
Ex 16:20 And **M** was angry with them
Ex 16:22 congregation came and told **M**
Ex 16:24 till morning, as **M** commanded
Ex 16:25 Then **M** said, "Eat that today
Ex 16:28 And the LORD said to **M**, "How
Ex 16:32 Then **M** said, "This is the
Ex 16:33 And **M** said to Aaron,
Ex 16:34 As the LORD commanded **M**, so
Ex 17: 2 the people contended with **M**
Ex 17: 2 And **M** said to them,
Ex 17: 3 the people murmured against **M**
Ex 17: 4 So **M** cried out to the LORD,
Ex 17: 5 And the LORD said to **M**, "Go
Ex 17: 6 **M** did so in the sight of the
Ex 17: 9 And **M** said to Joshua,
Ex 17:10 Joshua did as **M** said to him
Ex 17:10 And **M**, Aaron, and Hur went
Ex 17:11 when **M** held up his hand, that
Ex 17:14 Then the LORD said to **M**
Ex 17:15 **M** built an altar and called
Ex 18: 1 all that God had done for **M**
Ex 18: 5 sons and his wife to **M** in the
Ex 18: 6 Now he had said to **M**, "I,
Ex 18: 7 So **M** went out to meet his
Ex 18: 8 **M** told his father-in-law all
Ex 18:13 day, that **M** sat to judge the
Ex 18:13 the people stood before **M**
Ex 18:15 **M** said to his father-in-law,
Ex 18:24 So **M** heeded the voice of his
Ex 18:25 **M** chose able men out of all
Ex 18:26 hard cases they brought to **M**
Ex 18:27 Then **M** let his father-in-law
Ex 19: 3 **M** went up to God, and the LORD
Ex 19: 7 So **M** came and called for the
Ex 19: 8 So **M** brought back the words
Ex 19: 9 And the LORD said to **M**
Ex 19: 9 So **M** told the words of the
Ex 19:10 Then the LORD said to **M**, "Go
Ex 19:14 Then **M** went down from the
Ex 19:17 **M** brought the people out of
Ex 19:19 **M** spoke, and God answered
Ex 19:20 the LORD called **M** to the top
Ex 19:20 of the mountain, and **M** went up
Ex 19:21 And the LORD said to **M**, "Go
Ex 19:23 And **M** said to the LORD,
Ex 19:25 So **M** went down to the people
Ex 20:19 Then they said to **M**, "You
Ex 20:20 And **M** said to the people,
Ex 20:21 but **M** drew near the thick
Ex 20:22 Then the LORD said to **M**
Ex 24: 1 Now He said to **M**, "Come up
Ex 24: 2 **M** alone shall come near the
Ex 24: 3 So **M** came and told the people
Ex 24: 4 **M** wrote all the words of the

Ex 24: 6 **M** took half the blood and put
Ex 24: 8 **M** took the blood, sprinkled
Ex 24: 9 Then **M** went up, also Aaron,
Ex 24:12 Then the LORD said to **M**
Ex 24:13 So **M** arose with his assistant
Ex 24:13 **M** went up to the mountain of
Ex 24:15 Then **M** went up into the
Ex 24:16 to **M** out of the midst of the
Ex 24:18 So **M** went into the midst of
Ex 24:18 **M** was on the mountain forty
Ex 25: 1 Then the LORD spoke to **M**,
Ex 30:11 Then the LORD spoke to **M**,
Ex 30:17 Then the LORD spoke to **M**,
Ex 30:22 Moreover the LORD spoke to **M**
Ex 30:34 And the LORD said to **M**
Ex 31: 1 Then the LORD spoke to **M**,
Ex 31:12 And the LORD spoke to **M**,
Ex 31:18 He gave **M** two tablets of the
Ex 32: 1 **M** delayed coming down from
Ex 32: 1 for as for this **M**, the man
Ex 32: 7 And the LORD said to **M**, "Go,
Ex 32: 9 And the LORD said to **M**, "I
Ex 32:11 Then **M** pleaded with the LORD
Ex 32:15 **M** turned and went down from
Ex 32:17 as they shouted, he said to **M**
Ex 32:21 And **M** said to Aaron,
Ex 32:23 as for this **M**, the man who
Ex 32:25 Now when **M** saw that the
Ex 32:26 then **M** stood in the entrance
Ex 32:28 according to the word of **M**
Ex 32:29 Then **M** said, "Consecrate
Ex 32:30 day that **M** said to the people
Ex 32:31 Then **M** returned to the LORD
Ex 32:33 And the LORD said to **M**
Ex 33: 1 Then the LORD said to **M**
Ex 33: 5 For the LORD had said to **M**
Ex 33: 7 **M** took his tent and pitched it
Ex 33: 8 whenever **M** went out to the
Ex 33: 8 watched **M** until he had gone
Ex 33: 9 when **M** entered the tabernacle
Ex 33: 9 and the LORD talked with **M**
Ex 33:11 LORD spoke to **M** face to face
Ex 33:12 Then **M** said to the LORD
Ex 33:17 Then the LORD said to **M**, "I
Ex 34: 1 And the LORD said to **M**, "Cut
Ex 34: 4 Then **M** rose early in the
Ex 34: 8 So **M** made haste and bowed his
Ex 34:27 Then the LORD said to **M**
Ex 34:29 when **M** came down from
Ex 34:29 that **M** did not know that the
Ex 34:30 the children of Israel saw **M**
Ex 34:31 Then **M** called to them, and
Ex 34:31 and **M** talked with them
Ex 34:33 when **M** had finished speaking
Ex 34:34 But whenever **M** went in before
Ex 34:35 of Israel saw the face of **M**
Ex 34:35 then **M** would put the veil on
Ex 35: 1 Then **M** gathered all the
Ex 35: 4 And **M** spoke to all the
Ex 35:20 from the presence of **M**
Ex 35:29 the LORD, by the hand of **M**
Ex 35:30 **M** said to the children of
Ex 36: 2 Then **M** called Bezaleel and
Ex 36: 3 they received from **M** all the
Ex 36: 5 and they spoke to **M**, saying
Ex 36: 6 So **M** gave a commandment, and
Ex 38:21 to the commandment of **M**, for
Ex 38:22 the LORD had commanded **M**
Ex 39: 1 as the LORD had commanded **M**
Ex 39: 5 as the LORD had commanded **M**
Ex 39: 7 as the LORD had commanded **M**
Ex 39:21 as the LORD had commanded **M**
Ex 39:26 as the LORD had commanded **M**
Ex 39:29 as the LORD had commanded **M**
Ex 39:31 as the LORD had commanded **M**
Ex 39:32 the LORD had commanded **M**
Ex 39:33 brought the tabernacle to **M**
Ex 39:42 the LORD had commanded **M**
Ex 39:43 Then **M** looked over all the
Ex 39:43 And **M** blessed them
Ex 40: 1 Then the LORD spoke to **M**,
Ex 40:16 Thus **M** did; according to all
Ex 40:18 So **M** raised up the tabernacle
Ex 40:19 as the LORD had commanded **M**
Ex 40:21 as the LORD had commanded **M**
Ex 40:23 as the LORD had commanded **M**
Ex 40:25 as the LORD had commanded **M**
Ex 40:27 as the LORD had commanded **M**
Ex 40:29 as the LORD had commanded **M**
Ex 40:31 and **M**, Aaron, and his sons
Ex 40:32 as the LORD had commanded **M**
Ex 40:33 So **M** finished the work
Ex 40:35 **M** was not able to enter the
Lev 1: 1 Now the LORD called to **M**, and
Lev 4: 1 Now the LORD spoke to **M**,
Lev 5:14 Then the LORD spoke to **M**,
Lev 6: 1 And the LORD spoke to **M**,
Lev 6: 8 Then the LORD spoke to **M**,
Lev 6:19 And the LORD spoke to **M**,
Lev 6:24 And the LORD spoke to **M**,
Lev 7:22 And the LORD spoke to **M**,
Lev 7:28 Then the LORD spoke to **M**,
Lev 7:35 on the day when **M** presented
Lev 7:38 commanded **M** on Mount Sinai
Lev 8: 1 And the LORD spoke to **M**,
Lev 8: 4 So **M** did as the LORD
Lev 8: 5 **M** said to the congregation,
Lev 8: 6 Then **M** brought Aaron and his
Lev 8: 9 as the LORD had commanded **M**
Lev 8:10 Then **M** took the anointing oil
Lev 8:13 Then **M** brought Aaron's sons
Lev 8:13 as the LORD had commanded **M**
Lev 8:15 and **M** killed it
Lev 8:16 **M** burned them on the altar
Lev 8:17 as the LORD had commanded **M**
Lev 8:19 and **M** killed it
Lev 8:20 **M** burned the head, the pieces
Lev 8:21 **M** burned the whole ram on the
Lev 8:21 as the LORD had commanded **M**
Lev 8:23 and **M** killed it
Lev 8:24 **M** put some of the blood on
Lev 8:24 **M** sprinkled the blood all
Lev 8:28 Then **M** took them from their
Lev 8:29 **M** took the breast and waved it
Lev 8:29 as the LORD had commanded **M**
Lev 8:30 Then **M** took some of the
Lev 8:31 **M** said to Aaron and his sons,
Lev 8:36 commanded by the hand of **M**
Lev 9: 1 day that **M** called Aaron and
Lev 9: 5 what **M** commanded before the
Lev 9: 6 Then **M** said, "This is the
Lev 9: 7 And **M** said to Aaron,
Lev 9:10 as the LORD had commanded **M**
Lev 9:21 the LORD, as **M** had commanded
Lev 9:23 And **M** and Aaron went into the
Lev 10: 3 Then **M** said to Aaron, "This
Lev 10: 4 **M** called Mishael and Elzaphan,
Lev 10: 5 of the camp, as **M** had said
Lev 10: 6 And **M** said to Aaron, and to
Lev 10: 7 according to the word of **M**
Lev 10:11 to them by the hand of **M**
Lev 10:12 Then **M** spoke to Aaron, and to
Lev 10:16 Then **M** diligently made
Lev 10:19 And Aaron said to **M**, "Look,
Lev 10:20 So when **M** heard that, he was
Lev 11: 1 And the LORD spoke to **M** and
Lev 12: 1 Then the LORD spoke to **M**,
Lev 13: 1 And the LORD spoke to **M** and
Lev 14: 1 Then the LORD spoke to **M**,
Lev 14:33 And the LORD spoke to **M** and
Lev 15: 1 And the LORD spoke to **M** and
Lev 16: 1 Now the LORD spoke to **M** after
Lev 16: 2 and the LORD said to **M**
Lev 16:34 did as the LORD commanded **M**
Lev 17: 1 And the LORD spoke to **M**,
Lev 18: 1 Then the LORD spoke to **M**,
Lev 19: 1 And the LORD spoke to **M**,
Lev 20: 1 Then the LORD spoke to **M**,
Lev 21: 1 And the LORD said to **M**
Lev 21:16 And the LORD spoke to **M**,
Lev 21:24 **M** told it to Aaron and his
Lev 22: 1 Then the LORD spoke to **M**,
Lev 22:17 And the LORD spoke to **M**,
Lev 22:26 And the LORD spoke to **M**,
Lev 23: 1 And the LORD spoke to **M**,
Lev 23: 9 And the LORD spoke to **M**,
Lev 23:23 Then the LORD spoke to **M**,
Lev 23:26 And the LORD spoke to **M**,
Lev 23:33 Then the LORD spoke to **M**,
Lev 23:44 So **M** declared to the children
Lev 24: 1 Then the LORD spoke to **M**,
Lev 24:11 and so they brought him to **M**
Lev 24:13 And the LORD spoke to **M**,
Lev 24:23 Then **M** spoke to the children
Lev 24:23 did as the LORD commanded **M**
Lev 25: 1 spoke to **M** on Mount Sinai
Lev 27: 1 Now the LORD spoke to **M**,
Lev 27:34 which the LORD commanded **M**
Num 1: 1 Now the LORD spoke to **M** in
Num 1:17 Then **M** and Aaron took these
Num 1:19 As the LORD commanded **M**, so
Num 1:44 who were numbered, whom **M**
Num 1:48 for the LORD had spoken to **M**
Num 1:54 all that the LORD commanded **M**
Num 2: 1 And the LORD spoke to **M** and
Num 2:33 just as the LORD commanded **M**
Num 2:34 all that the LORD commanded **M**
Num 3: 1 **M** when the LORD spoke with
Num 3: 1 spoke with **M** on Mount Sinai
Num 3: 5 And the LORD spoke to **M**,
Num 3:11 Then the LORD spoke to **M**,
Num 3:14 Then the LORD spoke to **M** in
Num 3:16 So **M** numbered them according
Num 3:38 tabernacle of meeting, were **M**
Num 3:39 of the Levites, whom **M** and
Num 3:40 Then the LORD said to **M**
Num 3:42 So **M** numbered all the
Num 3:44 Then the LORD spoke to **M**,
Num 3:49 So **M** took the redemption
Num 3:51 **M** gave their redemption money
Num 3:51 as the LORD commanded **M**
Num 4: 1 Then the LORD spoke to **M** and
Num 4:17 Then the LORD spoke to **M** and
Num 4:21 Then the LORD spoke to **M**,
Num 4:34 And **M**, Aaron, and the leaders
Num 4:37 tabernacle of meeting, whom **M**
Num 4:37 of the LORD by the hand of **M**
Num 4:41 tabernacle of meeting, whom **M**
Num 4:45 of the sons of Merari, whom **M**
Num 4:45 of the LORD by the hand of **M**
Num 4:46 of the Levites, whom **M**, Aaron
Num 4:49 numbered by the hand of **M**
Num 4:49 him, as the LORD commanded **M**
Num 5: 1 And the LORD spoke to **M**,
Num 5: 4 as the LORD spoke to **M**, so
Num 5: 5 Then the LORD spoke to **M**,
Num 5:11 And the LORD spoke to **M**,
Num 6: 1 Then the LORD spoke to **M**,
Num 6:22 And the LORD spoke to **M**,
Num 7: 1 when **M** had finished setting
Num 7: 4 Then the LORD spoke to **M**,
Num 7: 6 So **M** took the carts and the
Num 7:11 For the LORD said to **M**
Num 7:89 Now when **M** went into the
Num 8: 1 And the LORD spoke to **M**,
Num 8: 3 as the LORD commanded **M**
Num 8: 4 which the LORD had shown **M**
Num 8: 5 Then the LORD spoke to **M**,
Num 8:20 Thus **M** and Aaron and all the
Num 8:20 **M** concerning the Levites, so
Num 8:22 as the LORD commanded **M**
Num 8:23 Then the LORD spoke to **M**,
Num 9: 1 Now the LORD spoke to **M** in
Num 9: 4 So **M** told the children of
Num 9: 5 all that the LORD commanded **M**
Num 9: 6 and they came before **M** and
Num 9: 8 And **M** said to them,
Num 9: 9 Then the LORD spoke to **M**,
Num 9:23 of the LORD by the hand of **M**
Num 10: 1 And the LORD spoke to **M**,
Num 10:13 of the LORD by the hand of **M**
Num 10:29 Now **M** said to Hobab the son
Num 10:31 So **M** said, "Please do not
Num 10:35 the ark set out, that **M** said
Num 11: 2 the people cried out to **M**
Num 11: 2 when **M** prayed to the LORD,
Num 11:10 Now **M** heard the people
Num 11:10 **M** also was displeased
Num 11:11 So **M** said to the LORD, "Why
Num 11:16 So the LORD said to **M**
Num 11:21 And **M** said, "The people whom
Num 11:23 And the LORD said to **M**, "Has
Num 11:24 So **M** went out and told the
Num 11:27 a young man ran and told **M**
Num 11:28 **M** my lord, forbid them
Num 11:29 Then **M** said to him, "Are you
Num 11:30 **M** returned to the camp, both
Num 12: 1 Aaron spoke against **M** because
Num 12: 2 indeed spoken only through **M**
Num 12: 3 (Now the man **M** was very
Num 12: 4 Suddenly the LORD said to **M**
Num 12: 7 Not so with My servant **M**
Num 12: 8 to speak against My servant **M**
Num 12:11 So Aaron said to **M**, "Oh, my
Num 12:13 So **M** cried out to the LORD,
Num 12:14 Then the LORD said to **M**, "If
Num 13: 1 And the LORD spoke to **M**,
Num 13: 3 So **M** sent them from the
Num 13:16 **M** sent to spy out the land
Num 13:16 **M** called Hoshea the son of

Num 13:17 So **M** sent them to spy out the
Num 13:26 departed and came back to **M**
Num 13:30 quieted the people before **M**
Num 14: 2 of Israel murmured against **M**
Num 14: 5 Then **M** and Aaron fell on their
Num 14:11 And the LORD said to **M**
Num 14:13 And **M** said to the LORD
Num 14:26 Then the LORD spoke to **M** and
Num 14:36 the men whom **M** sent to spy
Num 14:39 Then **M** told these words to
Num 14:41 Then **M** said, "Now why do you
Num 14:44 nor **M** departed from the camp
Num 15: 1 And the LORD spoke to **M**,
Num 15:17 Again the LORD spoke to **M**
Num 15:22 the LORD has spoken to **M**
Num 15:23 you by the hand of **M**, from
Num 15:33 sticks brought him to **M** and
Num 15:35 Then the LORD said to **M**
Num 15:36 So, as the LORD commanded **M**
Num 15:37 Again the LORD spoke to **M**
Num 16: 2 they rose up before **M** with
Num 16: 3 gathered together against **M**
Num 16: 4 So when **M** heard it, he fell
Num 16: 8 Then **M** said to Korah, "Hear
Num 16:12 And **M** sent to call Dathan and
Num 16:15 Then **M** was very angry, and
Num 16:16 And **M** said to Korah,
Num 16:18 tabernacle of meeting with **M**
Num 16:20 And the LORD spoke to **M** and
Num 16:23 So the LORD spoke to **M**,
Num 16:25 Then **M** rose and went to
Num 16:28 Then **M** said: "By this you
Num 16:36 Then the LORD spoke to **M**,
Num 16:40 had said to him through **M**
Num 16:41 of Israel murmured against **M**
Num 16:42 had gathered against **M** and
Num 16:43 Then **M** and Aaron came before
Num 16:44 And the LORD spoke to **M**,
Num 16:46 So **M** said to Aaron, "Take a
Num 16:47 Aaron took it as **M** commanded
Num 16:50 to **M** at the door of the
Num 17: 1 And the LORD spoke to **M**,
Num 17: 6 So **M** spoke to the children of
Num 17: 7 **M** placed the rods before the
Num 17: 8 pass on the next day that **M**
Num 17: 9 Then **M** brought out all the
Num 17:10 And the LORD said to **M**
Num 17:11 Thus did **M**; just as the LORD
Num 17:12 children of Israel spoke to **M**
Num 18:25 Then the LORD spoke to **M**,
Num 19: 1 Now the LORD spoke to **M** and
Num 20: 2 gathered together against **M**
Num 20: 3 the people contended with **M**
Num 20: 6 So **M** and Aaron went from the
Num 20: 7 Then the LORD spoke to **M**,
Num 20: 9 So **M** took the rod from before
Num 20:10 And **M** and Aaron gathered the
Num 20:11 Then **M** lifted his hand and
Num 20:12 Then the LORD spoke to **M** and
Num 20:14 Now **M** sent messengers from
Num 20:23 And the LORD spoke to **M** and
Num 20:27 So **M** did just as the LORD
Num 20:28 **M** stripped Aaron of his
Num 20:28 Then **M** and Eleazar came down
Num 21: 5 against God and against **M**
Num 21: 7 the people came to **M**, and said
Num 21: 7 So **M** prayed for the people
Num 21: 8 Then the LORD said to **M**
Num 21: 9 So **M** made a bronze serpent,
Num 21:16 well where the LORD said to **M**
Num 21:32 Then **M** sent to spy out Jazer
Num 21:34 Then the LORD said to **M**, "Do
Num 25: 4 Then the LORD said to **M**
Num 25: 5 So **M** said to the judges of
Num 25: 6 woman in the sight of **M** and in
Num 25:10 Then the LORD spoke to **M**,
Num 25:16 Then the LORD spoke to **M**,
Num 26: 1 that the LORD spoke to **M**
Num 26: 3 So **M** and Eleazar the priest
Num 26: 4 just as the LORD commanded **M**
Num 26: 9 who contended against **M** and
Num 26:52 Then the LORD spoke to **M**,
Num 26:59 Amram she bore Aaron and **M**
Num 26:63 those who were numbered by **M**
Num 26:64 those who were numbered by **M**
Num 27: 2 And they stood before **M**,
Num 27: 5 So **M** brought their case
Num 27: 6 And the LORD spoke to **M**,
Num 27:11 just as the LORD commanded **M**
Num 27:12 Now the LORD said to **M**
Num 27:15 Then **M** spoke to the LORD,
Num 27:18 And the LORD said to **M**
Num 27:22 So **M** did as the LORD
Num 27:23 commanded by the hand of **M**
Num 28: 1 Now the LORD spoke to **M**,
Num 29:40 So **M** told the children of
Num 29:40 just as the LORD commanded **M**
Num 30: 1 Then **M** spoke to the heads of
Num 30:16 which the LORD commanded **M**
Num 31: 1 And the LORD spoke to **M**,
Num 31: 3 So **M** spoke to the people,
Num 31: 6 Then **M** sent them to the war,
Num 31: 7 just as the LORD commanded **M**
Num 31:12 the booty, and the spoil to **M**
Num 31:13 And **M**, Eleazar the priest, and
Num 31:14 But **M** was angry with the
Num 31:15 And **M** said to them
Num 31:21 which the LORD commanded **M**
Num 31:25 And the LORD spoke to **M**,
Num 31:31 So **M** and Eleazar the priest
Num 31:31 did as the LORD commanded **M**
Num 31:41 So **M** gave the tribute which
Num 31:41 as the LORD commanded **M**
Num 31:42 which **M** separated from the
Num 31:47 **M** took one of every fifty
Num 31:47 as the LORD commanded **M**
Num 31:48 of hundreds, came near to **M**
Num 31:49 and they said to **M**, "Your
Num 31:51 So **M** and Eleazar the priest
Num 31:54 And **M** and Eleazar the priest
Num 32: 2 of Reuben came and spoke to **M**
Num 32: 6 **M** said to the children of Gad
Num 32:20 Then **M** said to them
Num 32:25 children of Reuben spoke to **M**
Num 32:28 So **M** gave command concerning
Num 32:29 And **M** said to them
Num 32:33 So **M** gave to the children of
Num 32:40 So **M** gave Gilead to Machir
Num 33: 1 armies under the hand of **M**
Num 33: 2 Now **M** wrote down the starting
Num 33:50 Now the LORD spoke to **M** in
Num 34: 1 Then the LORD spoke to **M**,
Num 34:13 **M** commanded the children
Num 34:16 And the LORD spoke to **M**,
Num 35: 1 the LORD spoke to **M** in the
Num 35: 9 Then the LORD spoke to **M**,
Num 36: 1 came near and spoke before **M**
Num 36: 2 lord **M** to give the land as an
Num 36: 5 **M** commanded the children
Num 36:10 Just as the LORD commanded **M**
Num 36:13 of **M** in the plains of Moab by
Deut 1: 1 These are the words which **M**
Deut 1: 3 that **M** spoke to the children
Deut 1: 5 **M** began to explain this law,
Deut 4:41 Then **M** set apart three cities
Deut 4:44 this is the law which **M** set
Deut 4:45 the judgments which **M** spoke
Deut 4:46 who dwelt at Heshbon, whom **M**
Deut 5: 1 **M** called all Israel, and said
Deut 27: 1 Then **M**, with the elders of
Deut 27: 9 Then **M** and the priests, the
Deut 27:11 **M** commanded the people on
Deut 29: 1 which the LORD commanded **M**
Deut 29: 2 Now **M** called all Israel and
Deut 31: 1 Then **M** went and spoke these
Deut 31: 7 Then **M** called Joshua and said
Deut 31: 9 So **M** wrote this law and
Deut 31:10 **M** commanded them, saying
Deut 31:14 Then the LORD said to **M**
Deut 31:14 So **M** and Joshua went and
Deut 31:16 And the LORD said to **M**
Deut 31:22 Therefore **M** wrote this song
Deut 31:24 when **M** had completed writing
Deut 31:25 that **M** commanded the Levites,
Deut 31:30 Then **M** spoke in the hearing
Deut 32:44 So **M** came with Joshua the son
Deut 32:45 **M** finished speaking all these
Deut 32:48 spoke to **M** that very same day
Deut 33: 1 **M** the man of God blessed the
Deut 33: 4 **M** commanded a law for us, a
Deut 34: 1 Then **M** went up from the
Deut 34: 5 So **M** the servant of the LORD
Deut 34: 7 **M** was one hundred and twenty
Deut 34: 8 for **M** in the plains of Moab
Deut 34: 8 and mourning for **M** ended
Deut 34: 9 for **M** had laid his hands on
Deut 34: 9 as the LORD had commanded **M**
Deut 34:10 in Israel a prophet like **M**
Deut 34:12 **M** performed in the sight of
Josh 1: 1 After the death of **M** the
Josh 1: 2 **M** My servant is dead
Josh 1: 3 given you, as I said to **M**
Josh 1: 5 as I was with **M**, so I will be
Josh 1: 7 to all the law which **M** My
Josh 1:13 **M** the servant of the LORD
Josh 1:14 **M** gave you on this side of
Josh 1:15 which **M** the LORD's servant
Josh 1:17 as we heeded **M** in all things
Josh 1:17 be with you, as He was with **M**
Josh 3: 7 know that, as I was with **M**
Josh 4:10 that **M** had commanded Joshua
Josh 4:12 as **M** had spoken to them
Josh 4:14 him, as they had feared **M**
Josh 8:31 as **M** the servant of the LORD
Josh 8:31 in the Book of the Law of **M**
Josh 8:32 stones a copy of the law of **M**
Josh 8:33 as **M** the servant of the LORD
Josh 8:35 **M** had commanded which
Josh 9:24 **M** to give you all the land
Josh 11:12 as **M** the servant of the LORD
Josh 11:15 had commanded **M** his servant
Josh 11:15 so **M** commanded Joshua, and
Josh 11:15 the LORD had commanded **M**
Josh 11:20 as the LORD had commanded **M**
Josh 11:23 that the LORD had said to **M**
Josh 12: 6 These **M** the servant of the
Josh 12: 6 **M** the servant of the LORD had
Josh 13: 8 which **M** had given them,
Josh 13: 8 as **M** the servant of the LORD
Josh 13:12 for **M** had defeated and cast
Josh 13:15 **M** had given to the tribe of
Josh 13:21 whom **M** had struck with the
Josh 13:24 **M** also had given an
Josh 13:29 **M** also gave an inheritance to
Josh 13:32 which **M** had distributed as an
Josh 13:33 **M** had given no inheritance
Josh 14: 2 commanded by the hand of **M**
Josh 14: 3 For **M** had given the
Josh 14: 5 As the LORD had commanded **M**
Josh 14: 6 **M** the man of God concerning
Josh 14: 7 **M** the servant of the LORD
Josh 14: 9 So **M** swore on that day,
Josh 14:10 to **M** while Israel wandered in
Josh 14:11 was on the day that **M** sent me
Josh 17: 4 The LORD commanded **M** to give
Josh 18: 7 which **M** the servant of the
Josh 20: 2 I spoke to you through **M**,
Josh 21: 2 **M** to give us cities to dwell
Josh 21: 8 commanded by the hand of **M**
Josh 22: 2 You have kept all that **M** the
Josh 22: 4 which **M** the servant of the
Josh 22: 5 the law which **M** the servant
Josh 22: 7 **M** had given a possession in
Josh 22: 9 of the LORD by the hand of **M**
Josh 23: 6 in the Book of the Law of **M**
Josh 24: 5 Also I sent **M** and Aaron, and I
Judg 1:20 to Caleb, as **M** had said
Judg 3: 4 fathers by the hand of **M**
Judg 4:11 Hobab the father-in-law of **M**
1Sa 12: 6 is the LORD who raised up **M**
1Sa 12: 8 LORD, then the LORD sent **M**
1Ki 2: 3 it is written in the Law of **M**
1Ki 8: 9 which **M** put there at Horeb
1Ki 8:53 by the hand of Your servant **M**
1Ki 8:56 through His servant **M**
2Ki 14: 6 in the Book of the Law of **M**
2Ki 18: 4 serpent that **M** had made
2Ki 18: 6 the LORD had commanded **M**
2Ki 18:12 all that **M** the servant of the
2Ki 21: 8 My servant **M** commanded them
2Ki 23:25 according to all the Law of **M**
1Ch 6: 3 of Amram were Aaron, **M**, and
1Ch 6:49 according to all that **M** the
1Ch 15:15 as **M** had commanded according
1Ch 21:29 which **M** had made in the
1Ch 22:13 charged **M** concerning Israel
1Ch 23:13 sons of Amram: Aaron and **M**
1Ch 23:14 Now the sons of **M** the man of
1Ch 23:15 The sons of **M** were Gershon
1Ch 26:24 son of Gershom, the son of **M**
2Ch 1: 3 which **M** the servant of the
2Ch 5:10 which **M** put there at Horeb
2Ch 8:13 to the commandment of **M**, for
2Ch 23:18 it is written in the Law of **M**
2Ch 24: 6 to the commandment of **M** the
2Ch 24: 9 that **M** the servant of God had
2Ch 25: 4 in the Law in the Book of **M**
2Ch 30:16 the Law of **M** the man of God
2Ch 33: 8 ordinances by the hand of **M**
2Ch 34:14 Law of the LORD given by **M**

2Ch 35: 6 of the LORD by the hand of **M**
2Ch 35:12 is written in the Book of **M**
Ezra 3: 2 the Law of **M** the man of God
Ezra 6:18 is written in the Book of **M**
Ezra 7: 6 scribe in the Law of **M**, which
Neh 1: 7 commanded Your servant **M**
Neh 1: 8 commanded Your servant **M**
Neh 8: 1 the Book of the Law of **M**,
Neh 8:14 the LORD had commanded by **M**
Neh 9:14 by the hand of **M** Your servant
Neh 10:29 given by **M** the servant of God
Neh 13: 1 of **M** in the hearing of the
Ps 77:20 like a flock By the hand of **M**
Ps 99: 6 **M** and Aaron were among His
Ps 103: 7 He made known His ways to **M**
Ps 105:26 He sent **M** His servant, And
Ps 106:16 they envied **M** in the camp
Ps 106:23 Had not **M** His chosen one
Ps 106:32 ill with **M** on account of them
Is 63:11 remembered the days of old, **M**
Is 63:12 them by the right hand of **M**
Jer 15: 1 Though **M** and Samuel stood
Dan 9:11 of **M** the servant of God have
Dan 9:13 it is written in the Law of **M**
Mic 6: 4 and I sent before you **M**, Aaron
Mal 4: 4 Remember the Law of **M**, My
Matt 8: 4 the gift that **M** commanded
Matt 17: 3 And behold, **M** and Elijah
Matt 17: 4 one for You, one for **M**, and
Matt 19: 7 Why then did **M** command to
Matt 19: 8 **M**, because of the hardness of
Matt 22:24 **M** said that if a man dies,
Mark 1:44 things which **M** commanded, as
Mark 7:10 For **M** said, 'Honor your
Mark 9: 4 appeared to them with **M**, and
Mark 9: 5 one for You, one for **M**, and
Mark 10: 3 What did **M** command you
Mark 10: 4 **M** permitted a man to write a
Mark 12:19 **M** wrote to us that if a man's
Mark 12:26 you not read in the book of **M**
Luke 2:22 the law of **M** were completed
Luke 5:14 to them, just as **M** commanded
Luke 9:30 talked with Him, who were **M**
Luke 9:33 one for You, one for **M**, and
Luke 16:29 said to him, 'They have **M**
Luke 16:31 him, 'If they do not hear **M**
Luke 20:28 **M** wrote to us that if a man's
Luke 20:37 Now even **M** showed in the
Luke 24:27 And beginning at **M** and all the
Luke 24:44 were written in the Law of **M**
John 1:17 the law was given through **M**
John 1:45 Him of whom **M** in the law, and
John 3:14 as **M** lifted up the serpent in
John 5:45 **M**, in whom you trust
John 5:46 For if you believed **M**, you
John 6:32 **M** did not give you the bread
John 7:19 Did not **M** give you the law,
John 7:22 **M** therefore gave you
John 7:22 (not that it is from **M**, but
John 7:23 so that the law of **M** should
John 8: 5 Now **M**, in the law, commanded
John 9:29 We know that God spoke to **M**
Acts 3:22 For **M** truly said to the
Acts 6:11 blasphemous words against **M**
Acts 6:14 which **M** delivered to us
Acts 7:20 At this time **M** was born, and
Acts 7:22 And **M** was learned in all the
Acts 7:29 **M** fled and became a sojourner
Acts 7:31 When **M** saw it, he marveled at
Acts 7:32 **M** trembled and dared not look
Acts 7:35 This **M** whom they rejected,
Acts 7:37 This is that **M** who said to
Acts 7:40 as for this **M** who brought us
Acts 7:44 instructing **M** to make it
Acts 13:39 be justified by the law of **M**
Acts 15: 1 according to the custom of **M**
Acts 15: 5 them to keep the law of **M**
Acts 15:21 For **M** has had throughout many
Acts 21:21 the Gentiles to forsake **M**
Acts 26:22 prophets and **M** said would
Acts 28:23 Jesus from both the Law of **M**
Rom 5:14 death reigned from Adam to **M**
Rom 9:15 For He says to **M**, "I will
Rom 10: 5 For **M** writes about the
Rom 10:19 **M** says: "I will provoke
1Co 9: 9 it is written in the law of **M**
1Co 10: 2 baptized into **M** in the cloud
2Co 3: 7 steadily at the face of **M**
2Co 3:13 unlike **M**, who put a veil over
2Co 3:15 when **M** is read, a veil lies
2Ti 3: 8 Jannes and Jambres resisted **M**
Heb 3: 2 as **M** also was faithful in all
Heb 3: 3 worthy of more glory than **M**
Heb 3: 5 **M** indeed was faithful in all
Heb 3:16 came out of Egypt, led by **M**
Heb 7:14 Judah, of which tribe **M** spoke
Heb 8: 5 as **M** was divinely instructed
Heb 9:19 For when **M** had spoken every
Heb 10:28 Anyone who has rejected **M**'
Heb 11:23 By faith **M**, when he was born,
Heb 11:24 By faith **M**, when he became of
Heb 12:21 was the sight that **M** said
Jude 9 disputed about the body of **M**
Rev 15: 3 And they sing the song of **M**

MOSES' (*see* MOSES)
Ex 4:25 her son and cast it at **M** feet
Ex 17:12 But **M** hands became heavy
Ex 18: 1 **M** father-in-law, heard of all
Ex 18: 2 Jethro, **M** father-in-law, took
Ex 18: 2 **M** wife, after he had sent her
Ex 18: 5 **M** father-in-law, came with
Ex 18:12 **M** father-in-law, took a burnt
Ex 18:12 **M** father-in-law before God
Ex 18:14 So when **M** father-in-law saw
Ex 18:17 So **M** father-in-law said to
Ex 32:19 So **M** anger became hot, and he
Ex 34:29 of the Testimony were in **M**
Ex 34:35 that the skin of **M** face shone
Lev 8:29 It was **M** part of the ram of
Num 10:29 Midianite, **M** father-in-law,
Num 11:28 Nun, **M** assistant, one of his
Josh 1: 1 the son of Nun, **M** assistant,
Judg 1:16 **M** father-in-law, went up from
Matt 23: 2 the Pharisees sit in **M** seat
John 9:28 but we are **M** disciples

MOST (*see* PREFACE)

MOTH (*see* MOTH-EATEN)
Job 4:19 who are crushed before a **m**
Job 27:18 He builds his house like a **m**
Ps 39:11 his beauty melt away like a **m**
Is 50: 9 the **m** will eat them up
Is 51: 8 For the **m** will eat them up
Hos 5:12 I will be to Ephraim like a **m**
Matt 6:19 treasures on earth, where **m**
Matt 6:20 where neither **m** nor rust
Luke 12:33 approaches nor **m** destroys

MOTH-EATEN (*see* MOTH)
Job 13:28 like a garment that is **m**
Jas 5: 2 and your garments are **m**

MOTHER (*see* GRANDMOTHER, MOTHER-IN-LAW, MOTHER'S, MOTHERS)
Gen 2:24 shall leave his father and **m**
Gen 3:20 she was the **m** of all living
Gen 17:16 she shall be a **m** of nations
Gen 20:12 but not the daughter of my **m**
Gen 21:21 his **m** took a wife for him
Gen 24:53 to her brother and to her **m**
Gen 24:55 her brother and her **m** said,
Gen 24:60 may you become the **m** of
Gen 24:67 her into his **m** Sarah's tent
Gen 27:11 Jacob said to Rebekah his **m**
Gen 27:13 But his **m** said to him, "Let
Gen 27:14 them and brought them to his **m**
Gen 27:14 his **m** made savory food, such
Gen 28: 5 the **m** of Jacob and Esau
Gen 28: 7 obeyed his father and his **m**
Gen 30:14 and brought them to his **m** Leah
Gen 32:11 me and the **m** with the children
Gen 37:10 Shall your **m** and I and your
Ex 2: 8 went and called the child's **m**
Ex 20:12 Honor your father and your **m**
Ex 21:15 his **m** shall surely be put to
Ex 21:17 his **m** shall surely be put to
Ex 22:30 be with its **m** seven days
Lev 18: 7 your **m** you shall not uncover
Lev 18: 7 She is your **m**
Lev 18: 9 or the daughter of your **m**
Lev 18:13 she is near of kin to your **m**
Lev 19: 3 one of you shall revere his **m**
Lev 20: 9 his **m** shall surely be put to
Lev 20: 9 cursed his father or his **m**
Lev 20:14 man marries a woman and her **m**
Lev 21: 2 his **m**, his father, his son,
Lev 21:11 for his father or his **m**
Lev 22:27 be seven days with its **m**
Num 6: 7 even for his father or his **m**
Deut 5:16 Honor your father and your **m**
Deut 13: 6 brother, the son of your **m**
Deut 21:13 father and her **m** a full month
Deut 21:18 father or the voice of his **m**
Deut 21:19 his **m** shall take hold of him
Deut 22: 6 with the **m** sitting on the
Deut 22: 6 not take the **m** with the young
Deut 22: 7 you shall surely let the **m** go
Deut 22:15 **m** of the young woman shall
Deut 27:16 father or his **m** with contempt
Deut 27:22 or the daughter of his **m**
Deut 33: 9 who says of his father and **m**
Josh 2:13 and spare my father, my **m**, my
Josh 2:18 you bring your father, your **m**
Josh 6:23 out Rahab, her father, her **m**
Judg 5: 7 arose, arose a **m** in Israel
Judg 5:28 The **m** of Sisera looked
Judg 8:19 my brothers, the sons of my **m**
Judg 14: 2 up and told his father and **m**
Judg 14: 3 his father and **m** said to him,
Judg 14: 4 **m** did not know that it was of
Judg 14: 5 Timnah with his father and **m**
Judg 14: 6 or his **m** what he had done
Judg 14: 9 he came to his father and **m**
Judg 14:16 it to my father or my **m**
Judg 17: 2 And he said to his **m**, "The
Judg 17: 2 And his **m** said, "May you be
Judg 17: 3 shekels of silver to his **m**
Judg 17: 3 his **m** said, "I had wholly
Judg 17: 4 returned the silver to his **m**
Judg 17: 4 Then his **m** took two hundred
Ruth 2:11 left your father and your **m**
1Sa 2:19 Moreover his **m** used to make
1Sa 15:33 so shall your **m** be childless
1Sa 22: 3 **m** come here with you, till I
2Sa 17:25 sister of Zeruiah, Joab's **m**
2Sa 19:37 the grave of my father and **m**
2Sa 20:19 a city and a **m** in Israel
1Ki 1: 6 His **m** had borne him after
1Ki 1:11 to Bathsheba the **m** of Solomon
1Ki 2:13 to Bathsheba the **m** of Solomon
1Ki 2:19 a throne set for the king's **m**
1Ki 2:20 Ask it, my **m**, for I will not
1Ki 2:22 answered and said to his **m**
1Ki 3:27 she is his **m**
1Ki 15:13 from being queen **m**, because
1Ki 17:23 house, and gave him to his **m**
1Ki 19:20 let me kiss my father and my **m**
1Ki 22:52 father and in the way of his **m**
2Ki 3: 2 but not like his father and **m**
2Ki 3:13 and the prophets of your **m**
2Ki 4:19 Carry him to his **m**
2Ki 4:20 him and brought him to his **m**
2Ki 4:30 And the **m** of the child said,
2Ki 9:22 harlotries of your **m** Jezebel
2Ki 10:13 and the sons of the queen **m**
2Ki 11: 1 When Athaliah the **m** of
2Ki 24:12 king of Judah, his **m**, his
2Ki 24:15 The king's **m**, the king's
1Ch 2:26 she was the **m** of Onam
1Ch 4: 9 his **m** called his name Jabez,
2Ch 15:16 the **m** of Asa the king, from
2Ch 15:16 the king, from being queen **m**
2Ch 22: 3 for his **m** counseled him to do
2Ch 22:10 Now when Athaliah the **m** of
Esth 2: 7 she had neither father nor **m**
Esth 2: 7 **m** died, Mordecai took her as
Job 17:14 and to the worm, 'You are my **m**
Ps 27:10 my **m** forsake me, Then the
Ps 35:14 as one who mourns for his **m**
Ps 51: 5 And in sin my **m** conceived me
Ps 109:14 sin of his **m** be blotted out
Ps 113: 9 Like a joyful **m** of children
Ps 131: 2 a weaned child with his **m**
Prov 1: 8 not forsake the law of your **m**
Prov 4: 3 only one in the sight of my **m**
Prov 6:20 not forsake the law of your **m**
Prov 10: 1 son is the grief of his **m**
Prov 15:20 a foolish man despises his **m**
Prov 19:26 chases away his **m** is a son
Prov 20:20 curses his father or his **m**
Prov 23:22 your **m** when she is old
Prov 23:25 your **m** be glad, and let her
Prov 28:24 robs his father or his **m**, and
Prov 29:15 himself brings shame to his **m**
Prov 30:11 and does not bless its **m**
Prov 30:17 and scorns obedience to his **m**
Prov 31: 1 which his **m** taught him
Song 3: 4 him to the house of my **m**, and
Song 3:11 the crown with which his **m**
Song 6: 9 one, the only one of her **m**
Song 8: 2 you into the house of my **m**

Song 8: 5 There your **m** brought you
Is 8: 4 to cry 'My father' and 'My **m**
Is 49: 1 from the matrix of My **m** He
Is 50: 1 your **m** has been put away
Is 66:13 As one whom his **m** comforts
Jer 13:18 to the king and to the queen **m**
Jer 15: 8 against the **m** of the young
Jer 15:10 Woe is me, my **m**, that you
Jer 16: 7 for their father or their **m**
Jer 20:14 blessed in which my **m** bore me
Jer 20:17 that my **m** might have been my
Jer 22:26 your **m** who bore you, into
Jer 29: 2 the king, the queen **m**, the
Jer 50:12 your **m** shall be deeply
Ezek 16: 3 Amorite and your **m** a Hittite
Ezek 16:44 Like **m**, like daughter
Ezek 16:45 your **m** was a Hittite and your
Ezek 19: 2 What is your **m**
Ezek 19:10 Your **m** was like a vine in
Ezek 22: 7 made light of father and **m**
Ezek 23: 2 women, the daughters of one **m**
Ezek 44:25 Only for father or **m**, for son
Hos 2: 2 Bring charges against your **m**
Hos 2: 5 For their **m** has played the
Hos 4: 5 and I will destroy your **m**
Hos 10:14 a **m** dashed in pieces upon her
Mic 7: 6 daughter rises against her **m**
Zech 13: 3 **m** who begot him will say to
Zech 13: 3 **m** who begot him shall thrust
Matt 1:18 After His **m** Mary was
Matt 2:11 young Child with Mary His **m**
Matt 2:13 take the young Child and His **m**
Matt 2:14 His **m** by night and departed
Matt 2:20 take the young Child and His **m**
Matt 2:21 took the young Child and His **m**
Matt 8:14 He saw his wife's **m** lying
Matt 10:35 a daughter against her **m**
Matt 10:37 He who loves father or **m** more
Matt 12:46 the multitudes, behold, His **m**
Matt 12:47 Look, Your **m** and Your
Matt 12:48 Who is My **m** and who are My
Matt 12:49 Here are My **m** and My brothers
Matt 12:50 is My brother and sister and **m**
Matt 13:55 Is not His **m** called Mary
Matt 14: 8 having been prompted by her **m**
Matt 14:11 and she brought it to her **m**
Matt 15: 4 Honor your father and your **m**'
Matt 15: 4 He who curses father or **m**
Matt 15: 5 says to his father or **m**
Matt 15: 6 from honoring his father or **m**
Matt 19: 5 shall leave his father and **m**
Matt 19:19 Honor your father and your **m**
Matt 19:29 or **m** or wife or children or
Matt 20:20 Then the **m** of Zebedee's sons
Matt 27:56 Mary the **m** of James and Joses
Matt 27:56 and the **m** of Zebedee's sons
Mark 1:30 But Simon's wife's **m** lay sick
Mark 3:31 and His **m** came, and standing
Mark 3:32 Look, Your **m** and Your
Mark 3:33 Who is My **m**, or My brothers
Mark 3:34 Here are My **m** and My brothers
Mark 3:35 My brother and My sister and **m**
Mark 5:40 the **m** of the child, and those
Mark 6:24 she went out and said to her **m**
Mark 6:28 and the girl gave it to her **m**
Mark 7:10 Honor your father and your **m**'
Mark 7:10 He who curses father or **m**
Mark 7:11 a man says to his father or **m**
Mark 7:12 for his father or his **m**,
Mark 10: 7 shall leave his father and **m**
Mark 10:19 Honor your father and your **m**
Mark 10:29 or **m** or wife or children or
Mark 15:40 Mary the **m** of James the Less
Mark 15:47 Mary the **m** of Joses observed
Mark 16: 1 Mary the **m** of James, and
Luke 1:43 that the **m** of my Lord should
Luke 1:60 And his **m** answered and said,
Luke 2:33 and His **m** marveled at those
Luke 2:34 them, and said to Mary His **m**
Luke 2:43 and His **m** did not know it
Luke 2:48 and His **m** said to Him,
Luke 2:51 but His **m** kept all these
Luke 4:38 But Simon's wife's **m** was sick
Luke 7:12 out, the only son of his **m**
Luke 7:15 And He presented him to his **m**
Luke 8:19 Then His **m** and brothers came
Luke 8:20 Your **m** and Your brothers are
Luke 8:21 My **m** and My brothers are these
Luke 8:51 the father and **m** of the girl
Luke 12:53 father, **m** against daughter and
Luke 12:53 and daughter against **m**,
Luke 14:26 does not hate his father and **m**
Luke 18:20 Honor your father and your **m**
Luke 24:10 Joanna, Mary the **m** of James
John 2: 1 and the **m** of Jesus was there
John 2: 3 the **m** of Jesus said to Him,
John 2: 5 His **m** said to the servants,
John 2:12 down to Capernaum, He, His **m**
John 6:42 whose father and **m** we know
John 19:25 by the cross of Jesus His **m**
John 19:26 Jesus therefore saw His **m**
John 19:26 standing by, He said to His **m**
John 19:27 Behold your **m**
Acts 1:14 women and Mary the **m** of Jesus
Acts 12:12 the **m** of John whose surname
Rom 16:13 chosen in the Lord, and his **m**
Gal 4:26 which is the **m** of us all
Eph 5:31 shall leave his father and **m**
Eph 6: 2 Honor your father and **m**,"
1Th 2: 7 just as a nursing **m** cherishes
2Ti 1: 5 and your **m** Eunice, and I am
Heb 7: 3 without father, without **m**
Rev 17: 5 THE **M** OF HARLOTS AND

MOTHER-IN-LAW (*see* MOTHER)
Deut 27:23 the one who lies with his **m**
Ruth 1:14 and Orpah kissed her **m**, but
Ruth 2:11 **m** since the death of your
Ruth 2:18 and her **m** saw what she had
Ruth 2:19 And her **m** said to her,
Ruth 2:19 So she told her **m** with whom
Ruth 2:23 and she dwelt with her **m**
Ruth 3: 1 Then Naomi her **m** said to her
Ruth 3: 6 all that her **m** instructed her
Ruth 3:16 So when she came to her **m**
Ruth 3:17 not go empty-handed to your **m**
Mic 7: 6 daughter-in-law against her **m**
Matt 10:35 daughter-in-law against her **m**
Luke 12:53 **m** against her daughter-in-law
Luke 12:53 daughter-in-law against her **m**

MOTHER'S (*see* MOTHER)
Gen 24:28 told those of her **m** house
Gen 24:67 comforted after his **m** death
Gen 27:29 let your **m** sons bow down to
Gen 28: 2 of Bethuel your **m** father
Gen 28: 2 of Laban your **m** brother
Gen 29:10 of Laban his **m** brother, and
Gen 29:10 sheep of Laban his **m** brother
Gen 29:10 flock of Laban his **m** brother
Gen 43:29 brother Benjamin, his **m** son
Gen 44:20 is left of his **m** children
Ex 23:19 a young goat in its **m** milk
Ex 34:26 a young goat in its **m** milk
Lev 18:13 nakedness of your **m** sister
Lev 20:17 daughter or his **m** daughter
Lev 20:19 the nakedness of your **m**
Lev 24:11 (His **m** name was Shelomith the
Num 12:12 he comes out of his **m** womb
Deut 14:21 a young goat in its **m** milk
Judg 9: 1 to his **m** brothers, and spoke
Judg 9: 1 of the house of his **m** father
Judg 9: 3 And his **m** brothers spoke all
Judg 16:17 to God from my **m** womb
Ruth 1: 8 return each to her **m** house
1Sa 20:30 the shame of your **m** nakedness
1Ki 11:26 whose **m** name was Zeruah, a
1Ki 14:21 His **m** name was Naamah, an
1Ki 14:31 His **m** name was Naamah, an
1Ki 15: 2 His **m** name was Maachah the
1Ki 22:42 His **m** name was Azubah the
2Ki 8:26 His **m** name was Athaliah the
2Ki 12: 1 His **m** name was Zibiah of
2Ki 14: 2 His **m** name was Jehoaddan of
2Ki 15: 2 His **m** name was Jecholiah of
2Ki 15:33 His **m** name was Jerusha the
2Ki 18: 2 His **m** name was Abi the
2Ki 21: 1 His **m** name was Hephzibah
2Ki 21:19 His **m** name was Meshullemeth
2Ki 22: 1 His **m** name was Jedidah the
2Ki 23:31 His **m** name was Hamutal the
2Ki 23:36 His **m** name was Zebudah the
2Ki 24: 8 His **m** name was Nehushta the
2Ki 24:18 His **m** name was Hamutal the
2Ch 12:13 His **m** name was Naamah, an
2Ch 13: 2 His **m** name was Michaiah the
2Ch 20:31 His **m** name was Azubah the
2Ch 22: 2 His **m** name was Athaliah the
2Ch 24: 1 His **m** name was Zibiah of
2Ch 25: 1 His **m** name was Jehoaddan of
2Ch 26: 3 His **m** name was Jecholiah of
2Ch 27: 1 His **m** name was Jerushah the
2Ch 29: 1 His **m** name was Abijah the
Job 1:21 Naked I came from my **m** womb
Job 3:10 up the doors of my **m** womb
Job 31:18 from my **m** womb I guided the
Ps 22: 9 when I was on My **m** breasts
Ps 22:10 From My **m** womb You have
Ps 50:20 You slander your own **m** son
Ps 69: 8 And an alien to my **m** children
Ps 71: 6 who took me out of my **m** womb
Ps 139:13 have covered me in my **m** womb
Eccl 5:15 As he came from his **m** womb
Song 1: 6 My **m** sons were angry with me
Song 8: 1 who nursed at my **m** breasts
Is 50: 1 certificate of your **m** divorce
Jer 52: 1 His **m** name was Hamutal the
Ezek 16:45 You are your **m** daughter,
Matt 19:12 born thus from their **m** womb
Luke 1:15 Spirit, even from his **m** womb
John 3: 4 a second time into his **m** womb
John 19:25 His **m** sister, Mary the wife
Acts 3: 2 from his **m** womb was carried
Acts 14: 8 a cripple from his **m** womb
Gal 1:15 separated me from my **m** womb

MOTHERS (*see* MOTHER, MOTHERS')
Is 49:23 their queens your nursing **m**
Jer 16: 3 their **m** who bore them and
Lam 2:12 They say to their **m**, "Where
Lam 5: 3 waifs, our **m** are like widows
Mark 10:30 and brothers and sisters and **m**
1Ti 1: 9 of fathers and murderers of **m**
1Ti 5: 2 the older women as **m**, the

MOTHERS' (*see* MOTHERS)
Lam 2:12 poured out in their **m** bosom

MOTIONED (*see* MOTIONING)
John 13:24 Simon Peter therefore **m** to
Acts 19:33 Alexander **m** with his hand, and
Acts 21:40 **m** with his hand to the people

MOTIONING (*see* MOTIONED)
Acts 12:17 But **m** to them with his hand
Acts 13:16 up, and **m** with his hand said,

MOUND (*see* MOUNDS)
2Sa 20:15 up a siege **m** against the city
2Ki 19:32 build a siege **m** against it
Is 29: 3 siege against you with a **m**
Is 37:33 build a siege **m** against it
Jer 6: 6 build a **m** against Jerusalem
Jer 30:18 shall be built upon its own **m**
Jer 49: 2 It shall be a desolate **m**, and
Ezek 4: 2 it, and heap up a **m** against it
Ezek 17:17 when they heap up a siege **m**
Ezek 21:22 gates, to heap up a siege **m**
Ezek 26: 8 heap up a siege **m** against you
Dan 11:15 shall come and build a siege **m**

MOUNDS (*see* MOUND)
Josh 11:13 cities that stood on their **m**
Jer 32:24 Look, the siege **m**
Jer 33: 4 fortify against the siege **m**
Hab 1:10 for they heap up **m** of earth

MOUNT (*see* MOUNTAIN, MOUNTED, MOUNTINGS, MOUNTS)
Gen 22:14 In the **M** of The LORD it shall
Gen 36: 8 So Esau dwelt in **M** Seir
Gen 36: 9 of the Edomites in **M** Seir
Ex 19:11 LORD will come down upon **M**
Ex 19:18 Now **M** Sinai was completely in
Ex 19:20 LORD came down upon **M** Sinai
Ex 19:23 cannot come up to **M** Sinai
Ex 24:16 of the LORD rested on **M** Sinai
Ex 31:18 speaking with him on **M** Sinai
Ex 33: 6 of their ornaments by **M** Horeb
Ex 34: 2 up in the morning to **M** Sinai
Ex 34: 4 morning and went up **M** Sinai
Ex 34:29 Moses came down from **M** Sinai
Ex 34:32 spoken with him on **M** Sinai
Lev 7:38 commanded Moses on **M** Sinai
Lev 25: 1 spoke to Moses on **M** Sinai
Lev 26:46 on **M** Sinai by the hand of
Lev 27:34 children of Israel on **M** Sinai
Num 3: 1 spoke with Moses on **M** Sinai
Num 20:22 Kadesh and came to **M** Hor
Num 20:23 Aaron in **M** Hor by the border
Num 20:25 and bring them up to **M** Hor
Num 20:27 they went up to **M** Hor in the
Num 21: 4 Then they journeyed from **M**
Num 27:12 Go up into this **M** Abarim, and
Num 28: 6 which was ordained at **M** Sinai

Num 33:23 and camped at **M** Shepher
Num 33:24 They moved from **M** Shepher
Num 33:37 Kadesh and camped at **M** Hor
Num 33:38 **M** Hor at the command of the
Num 33:39 old when he died on **M** Hor
Num 33:41 So they departed from **M** Hor
Num 34: 7 out your border line to **M** Hor
Num 34: 8 from **M** Hor you shall mark
Deut 1: 2 from Horeb by way of **M** Seir
Deut 2: 1 we skirted **M** Seir for many
Deut 2: 5 given **M** Seir to Esau as a
Deut 3: 8 the River Arnon to **M** Hermon
Deut 4:48 even to **M** Sion (that is,
Deut 11:29 put the blessing on **M** Gerizim
Deut 11:29 and the curse on **M** Ebal
Deut 27: 4 that on **M** Ebal you shall set
Deut 27:12 These shall stand on **M**
Deut 27:13 stand on **M** Ebal to curse
Deut 32:49 **M** Nebo, which is in the land
Deut 32:50 your brother died on **M** Hor
Deut 33: 2 He shone forth from **M** Paran
Deut 34: 1 the plains of Moab to **M** Nebo
Josh 8:30 LORD God of Israel in **M** Ebal
Josh 8:33 were in front of **M** Gerizim
Josh 8:33 of them in front of **M** Ebal
Josh 11:17 from **M** Halak and the ascent to
Josh 11:17 of Lebanon below **M** Hermon
Josh 12: 1 the River Arnon to **M** Hermon
Josh 12: 5 and reigned over **M** Hermon,
Josh 12: 7 of Lebanon as far as **M** Halak
Josh 13: 5 Baal Gad below **M** Hermon
Josh 13:11 all **M** Hermon, and all Bashan
Josh 15: 9 to the cities of **M** Ephron
Josh 15:10 from Baalah to **M** Seir, passed
Josh 15:10 **M** Jearim on the north (which
Josh 15:11 passed along to **M** Baalah
Josh 19:26 it reached to **M** Carmel
Josh 24:30 on the north side of **M** Gaash
Judg 1:35 to dwell in **M** Heres, in
Judg 2: 9 on the north side of **M** Gaash
Judg 3: 3 who dwelt in **M** Lebanon, from
Judg 3: 3 from **M** Baal Hermon to the
Judg 4: 6 and deploy troops at **M** Tabor
Judg 4:12 had gone up to **M** Tabor
Judg 4:14 So Barak went down from **M**
Judg 7: 3 depart at once from **M** Gilead
Judg 9: 7 and stood on top of **M** Gerizim
Judg 9:48 went up to **M** Zalmon
1Sa 31: 1 and fell slain on **M** Gilboa
1Sa 31: 8 three sons fallen on **M** Gilboa
2Sa 1: 6 by chance to be on **M** Gilboa
2Sa 15:30 the ascent of the **M** of Olives
1Ki 18:19 all Israel to me on **M** Carmel
1Ki 18:20 prophets together on **M** Carmel
2Ki 2:25 went from there to **M** Carmel
2Ki 4:25 to the man of God at **M** Carmel
2Ki 19:31 those who escape from **M** Zion
2Ki 23:13 south of the **M** of Corruption
1Ch 4:42 of Simeon, went to **M** Seir
1Ch 5:23 is, to Senir, or **M** Hermon
1Ch 10: 1 and fell slain on **M** Gilboa
1Ch 10: 8 his sons fallen on **M** Gilboa
2Ch 3: 1 LORD at Jerusalem on **M** Moriah
2Ch 13: 4 Abijah stood on **M** Zemaraim
2Ch 20:10 of Ammon, Moab, and **M** Seir
2Ch 20:22 **M** Seir, who had come against
2Ch 20:23 of **M** Seir to utterly kill
2Ch 33:15 **m** of the house of the LORD
Neh 9:13 You came down also on **M** Sinai
Job 39:27 Does the eagle **m** up at your
Ps 48: 2 Is **M** Zion on the sides of the
Ps 48:11 Let **M** Zion rejoice, Let the
Ps 74: 2 This **M** Zion where You have
Ps 78:68 Judah, **M** Zion which He loved
Ps 107:26 They **m** up to the heavens,
Ps 125: 1 in the LORD Are like **M** Zion
Song 4: 1 going down from **M** Gilead
Song 7: 5 head crowns you like **M** Carmel
Is 4: 5 dwelling place of **M** Zion, and
Is 8:18 hosts, Who dwells in **M** Zion
Is 9:18 they shall **m** up like rising
Is 10:12 all His work on **M** Zion and on
Is 10:32 the **m** of the daughter of Zion
Is 14:13 I will also sit on the **m** of
Is 16: 1 to the **m** of the daughter of
Is 18: 7 the LORD of hosts, to **M** Zion
Is 24:23 of hosts will reign on **M** Zion
Is 27:13 in the holy **m** at Jerusalem
Is 28:21 will rise up as at **M** Perazim
Is 29: 8 be, who fight against **M** Zion
Is 31: 4 come down to fight for **M** Zion
Is 37:32 those who escape from **M** Zion
Is 40:31 they shall **m** up with wings
Jer 4:15 affliction from **M** Ephraim
Jer 31: 6 will cry on **M** Ephraim, 'Arise
Jer 46: 4 horses, and **m** up, you horsemen
Jer 50:19 be satisfied on **M** Ephraim
Jer 51:53 were to **m** up to heaven, and
Lam 5:18 because of **M** Zion which is
Ezek 10:16 wings to **m** up from the earth
Ezek 35: 2 set your face against **M** Seir
Ezek 35: 3 O **M** Seir, I am against you
Ezek 35: 7 Thus I will make **M** Seir most
Ezek 35:15 O **M** Seir, as well as all of
Joel 2:32 For in **M** Zion and in Jerusalem
Amos 6: 1 Zion, and trust in **M** Samaria
Obad 17 But on **M** Zion there shall be
Obad 21 Then saviors shall come to **M**
Mic 4: 7 them in **M** Zion From now on
Hab 3: 3 the Holy One from **M** Paran
Zech 14: 4 will stand on the **M** of Olives
Zech 14: 4 And the **M** of Olives shall be
Matt 21: 1 at the **M** of Olives, then
Matt 24: 3 as He sat on the **M** of Olives
Matt 26:30 went out to the **M** of Olives
Mark 11: 1 at the **M** of Olives, He sent
Mark 13: 3 Now as He sat on the **M** of
Mark 14:26 went out to the **M** of Olives
Luke 19:37 descent of the **M** of Olives
Luke 22:39 He went to the **M** of Olives
John 8: 1 Jesus went to the **M** of Olives
Acts 1:12 from the **M** called Olivet,
Acts 7:30 in the wilderness of **M** Sinai
Acts 7:38 who spoke to him on **M** Sinai
Gal 4:24 the one from **M** Sinai which
Gal 4:25 Hagar is **M** Sinai in Arabia
Heb 12:22 But you have come to **M** Zion
Rev 14: 1 a Lamb standing on **M** Zion

MOUNTAIN (*see* MOUNT, MOUNTAINS, MOUNTAINTOP)
Gen 10:30 Sephar, the **m** of the east
Gen 12: 8 there to the **m** east of Bethel
Gen 14: 6 Horites in their **m** of Seir
Gen 31:54 offered a sacrifice on the **m**
Gen 31:54 and stayed all night on the **m**
Ex 3: 1 came to Horeb, the **m** of God
Ex 3:12 you shall serve God on this **m**
Ex 4:27 and met him on the **m** of God
Ex 15:17 plant them in the **m** of Your
Ex 18: 5 was encamped at the **m** of God
Ex 19: 2 camped there before the **m**
Ex 19: 3 LORD called to him from the **m**
Ex 19:12 up to the **m** or touch its base
Ex 19:12 Whoever touches the **m** shall
Ex 19:13 they shall come near the **m**
Ex 19:14 down from the **m** to the people
Ex 19:16 and a thick cloud on the **m**
Ex 19:17 stood at the foot of the **m**
Ex 19:18 the whole **m** quaked greatly
Ex 19:20 Sinai, on the top of the **m**
Ex 19:20 Moses to the top of the **m**
Ex 19:23 Set bounds around the **m**
Ex 20:18 the trumpet, and the **m** smoking
Ex 24: 4 an altar at the foot of the **m**
Ex 24:12 Come up to Me on the **m** and be
Ex 24:13 Moses went up to the **m** of God
Ex 24:15 Then Moses went up into the **m**
Ex 24:15 and a cloud covered the **m**
Ex 24:17 fire on the top of the **m** in
Ex 24:18 cloud and went up into the **m**
Ex 24:18 Moses was on the **m** forty days
Ex 25:40 which was shown you on the **m**
Ex 26:30 which you were shown on the **m**
Ex 27: 8 as it was shown you on the **m**
Ex 32: 1 coming down from the **m**, the
Ex 32:15 and went down from the **m**, and
Ex 32:19 them at the foot of the **m**
Ex 34: 2 Me there on the top of the **m**
Ex 34: 3 be seen throughout all the **m**
Ex 34: 3 nor herds feed before that **m**
Ex 34:29 when he came down from the **m**)
Num 10:33 So they departed from the **m**
Num 14:40 went up to the top of the **m**
Num 14:45 who dwelt in that **m** came down
Num 20:28 there on the top of the **m**
Num 20:28 Eleazar came down from the **m**
Deut 1: 6 dwelt long enough at this **m**
Deut 1:41 ready to go up into the **m**
Deut 1:43 went up into the **m**
Deut 1:44 that **m** came out against you
Deut 2: 3 skirted this **m** long enough
Deut 4:11 and stood at the foot of the **m**
Deut 4:11 the **m** burned with fire to the
Deut 5: 4 you face to face on the **m**
Deut 5: 5 and you did not go up the **m**
Deut 5:22 in the **m** from the midst of
Deut 5:23 while the **m** was burning with
Deut 9: 9 When I went up into the **m** to
Deut 9: 9 I stayed on the **m** forty days
Deut 9:10 had spoken to you on the **m**
Deut 9:15 and came down from the **m**, and
Deut 9:15 and the **m** burned with fire
Deut 9:21 that descended from the **m**
Deut 10: 1 and come up to Me on the **m**
Deut 10: 3 the first, and went up the **m**
Deut 10: 4 had spoken to you in the **m**
Deut 10: 5 and came down from the **m**, and
Deut 10:10 I stayed in the **m** forty days
Deut 14: 5 the **m** goat, the antelope, and
Deut 14: 5 the antelope, and the **m** sheep
Deut 32:49 Go up this **m** of the Abarim,
Deut 32:50 die on the **m** which you ascend
Deut 33:19 call the peoples to the **m**
Josh 2:16 Get to the **m**, lest the
Josh 2:22 departed and went to the **m**
Josh 2:23 descended from the **m**, and
Josh 10:40 the **m** country and the South and
Josh 11:16 the **m** country, all the South,
Josh 12: 8 in the **m** country, in the
Josh 13:19 Shahar on the **m** of the valley
Josh 14:12 give me this **m** of which the
Josh 15: 8 went up to the top of the **m**
Josh 15:48 And in the **m** country
Josh 17:16 The **m** country is not enough
Josh 17:18 but the **m** country shall be
Josh 18:16 **m** that lies before the Valley
1Sa 17: 3 stood on a **m** on one side, and
1Sa 17: 3 on a **m** on the other side,
1Sa 23:26 went on one side of the **m**
1Sa 23:26 on the other side of the **m**
2Sa 15:32 had come to the top of the **m**
2Sa 16: 1 little past the top of the **m**
1Ki 19: 8 as far as Horeb, the **m** of God
1Ki 19:11 stand on the **m** before the
2Ki 2:16 cast him upon some **m** or into
2Ki 6:17 the **m** was full of horses and
2Ki 23:16 that were there on the **m**
2Ch 2:18 hewers of stone in the **m**, and
Neh 8:15 Go out to the **m**, and bring
Job 14:18 But as a **m** falls and crumbles
Job 39: 1 the wild **m** goats bear young
Ps 11: 1 Flee as a bird to your **m**"
Ps 30: 7 have made my **m** stand strong
Ps 48: 1 of our God, In His holy **m**
Ps 68:15 A **m** of God is the **m** of Bashan
Ps 68:15 A **m** of many peaks is the
Ps 68:15 many peaks is the **m** of Bashan
Ps 68:16 This is the **m** which God
Ps 78:54 This **m** which His right hand
Song 4: 6 go my way to the **m** of myrrh
Is 2: 2 **m** of the LORD's house shall
Is 2: 3 us go up to the **m** of the LORD
Is 11: 9 nor destroy in all My holy **m**
Is 13: 2 up a banner on the high **m**
Is 18: 6 for the **m** birds of prey and
Is 22: 5 walls and of crying to the **m**
Is 25: 6 in this **m** the LORD of hosts
Is 25: 7 He will destroy on this **m** the
Is 25:10 For on this **m** the hand of the
Is 30:17 left as a pole on top of a **m**
Is 30:25 There will be on every high **m**
Is 30:29 come into the **m** of the LORD
Is 40: 4 shall be exalted, and every **m**
Is 40: 9 get up into the high **m**
Is 56: 7 I will bring to My holy **m**
Is 57: 7 high **m** you have set your bed
Is 57:13 and shall inherit My holy **m**
Is 65:11 LORD, who forget My holy **m**
Is 65:25 nor destroy in all My holy **m**
Is 66:20 to My holy **m** Jerusalem,"
Jer 3: 6 has gone up on every high **m**
Jer 16:16 shall hunt them from every **m**
Jer 17: 3 O My **m** in the field, I will
Jer 26:18 the **m** of the temple like the
Jer 31:23 of justice, and **m** of holiness
Jer 50: 6 They have gone from **m** to hill
Jer 51:25 against you, O destroying **m**
Jer 51:25 rocks, and make you a burnt **m**
Ezek 11:23 of the city and stood on the **m**
Ezek 17:22 it on a high and prominent **m**

Ezek 17:23 On the **m** height of Israel I
Ezek 20:40 For on My holy **m**, on the
Ezek 20:40 on the **m** height of Israel,"
Ezek 28:14 you were on the holy **m** of God
Ezek 28:16 thing out of the **m** of God
Ezek 40: 2 and set me on a very high **m**
Dan 2:35 the image became a great **m**
Dan 2:45 out of the **m** without hands
Dan 9:16 city Jerusalem, Your holy **m**
Dan 9:20 God for the holy **m** of my God
Dan 11:45 seas and the glorious holy **m**
Joel 2: 1 sound an alarm in My holy **m**
Joel 3:17 dwelling in Zion My holy **m**
Amos 4: 1 who are on the **m** of Samaria
Obad 16 For as you drank on my holy **m**
Mic 3:12 the **m** of the temple like the
Mic 4: 1 **m** of the LORD's house shall
Mic 4: 2 us go up to the **m** of the LORD
Mic 7:12 sea to sea, and **m** to **m**
Zeph 3:11 be haughty In My holy **m**
Zech 4: 7 Who are you, O great **m**
Zech 8: 3 the **M** of the LORD of hosts,
Zech 8: 3 the LORD of hosts, the Holy **M**
Zech 14: 4 half of the **m** shall move
Zech 14: 5 flee through My **m** valley, for
Zech 14: 5 for the **m** valley shall reach
Matt 4: 8 up on an exceedingly high **m**
Matt 5: 1 multitudes, He went up on a **m**
Matt 8: 1 He had come down from the **m**
Matt 14:23 He went up on a **m** by Himself
Matt 15:29 Galilee, and went up on the **m**
Matt 17: 1 up on a high **m** by themselves
Matt 17: 9 as they came down from the **m**
Matt 17:20 seed, you will say to this **m**
Matt 21:21 but also if you say to this **m**
Matt 28:16 to the **m** which Jesus had
Mark 3:13 And He went up on the **m** and
Mark 6:46 He departed to the **m** to pray
Mark 9: 2 a high **m** apart by themselves
Mark 9: 9 as they came down from the **m**
Mark 11:23 you, whoever says to this **m**
Luke 3: 5 shall be filled and every **m**
Luke 4: 5 taking Him up on a high **m**
Luke 6:12 He went out to the **m** to pray
Luke 8:32 was feeding there on the **m**
Luke 9:28 and went up on the **m** to pray
Luke 9:37 they had come down from the **m**
Luke 19:29 at the **m** called Olivet, that
Luke 21:37 stayed on the **m** called Olivet
John 4:20 fathers worshiped on this **m**
John 4:21 you will neither on this **m**
John 6: 3 And Jesus went up on a **m**, and
John 6:15 again to a **m** by Himself alone
Heb 8: 5 pattern shown you on the **m**
Heb 12:18 to the **m** that may be touched
Heb 12:20 much as a beast touches the **m**
2Pe 1:18 were with Him on the holy **m**
Rev 6:14 it is rolled up, and every **m**
Rev 8: 8 great **m** burning with fire was
Rev 21:10 Spirit to a great and high **m**

MOUNTAINS (*see* MOUNTAIN)
Gen 7:20 upward, and the **m** were covered
Gen 8: 4 the month, on the **m** of Ararat
Gen 8: 5 the tops of the **m** were seen
Gen 14:10 the remainder fled to the **m**
Gen 19:17 Escape to the **m**, lest you be
Gen 19:19 but I cannot escape to the **m**
Gen 19:30 out of Zoar and dwelt in the **m**
Gen 22: 2 offering on one of the **m** of
Gen 31:21 headed toward the **m** of Gilead
Gen 31:23 him in the **m** of Gilead
Gen 31:25 had pitched his tent in the **m**
Gen 31:25 pitched in the **m** of Gilead
Ex 32:12 them, to kill them in the **m**
Num 13:17 the South, and go up to the **m**
Num 13:29 the Amorites dwell in the **m**
Num 23: 7 Aram, from the **m** of the east
Num 33:47 and camped in the **m** of Abarim
Num 33:48 departed from the **m** of Abarim
Deut 1: 7 go to the **m** of the Amorites,
Deut 1: 7 places in the plain, in the **m**
Deut 1:19 way to the **m** of the Amorites
Deut 1:20 come to the **m** of the Amorites
Deut 1:24 and went up into the **m**, and
Deut 2:37 or to the cities of the **m**
Deut 3:12 half the **m** of Gilead and its
Deut 3:25 the Jordan, those pleasant **m**
Deut 12: 2 their gods, on the high **m**
Deut 32:22 fire the foundations of the **m**
Deut 33:15 best things of the ancient **m**

Josh 10: 6 the **m** have gathered together
Josh 11: 2 were from the north, in the **m**
Josh 11: 3 the Jebusite in the **m**, and
Josh 11:16 the **m** of Israel and its
Josh 11:21 cut off the Anakim from the **m**
Josh 11:21 Anab, from all the **m** of Judah
Josh 11:21 and from all the **m** of Israel
Josh 13: 6 **m** from Lebanon as far as the
Josh 16: 1 through the **m** to Bethel,
Josh 17:15 since the **m** of Ephraim are
Josh 18:12 up through the **m** westward
Josh 19:50 Serah in the **m** of Ephraim
Josh 20: 7 in the **m** of Naphtali, Shechem
Josh 20: 7 Shechem in the **m** of Ephraim
Josh 20: 7 is Hebron) in the **m** of Judah
Josh 21:11 in the **m** of Judah, with the
Josh 21:21 the **m** of Ephraim (a city of
Josh 24: 4 gave the **m** of Seir to possess
Josh 24:30 which is in the **m** of Ephraim
Josh 24:33 to him in the **m** of Ephraim
Judg 1: 9 Canaanites who dwelt in the **m**
Judg 1:19 out the inhabitants of the **m**
Judg 1:34 children of Dan into the **m**
Judg 2: 9 in the **m** of Ephraim, on the
Judg 3:27 trumpet in the **m** of Ephraim
Judg 3:27 went down with him from the **m**
Judg 4: 5 and Bethel in the **m** of Ephraim
Judg 5: 5 the **m** gushed before the LORD,
Judg 6: 2 which are in the **m**
Judg 7:24 all the **m** of Ephraim, saying,
Judg 9:25 him on the tops of the **m**, and
Judg 9:36 down from the tops of the **m**
Judg 9:36 of the **m** as if they were men
Judg 10: 1 in Shamir in the **m** of Ephraim
Judg 11:37 I may go and wander on the **m**
Judg 11:38 her virginity on the **m**
Judg 12:15 in the **m** of the Amalekites
Judg 17: 1 a man from the **m** of Ephraim
Judg 17: 8 he came to the **m** of Ephraim
Judg 18: 2 they went to the **m** of Ephraim
Judg 18:13 there to the **m** of Ephraim
Judg 19: 1 in the remote **m** of Ephraim
Judg 19:16 was from the **m** of Ephraim
Judg 19:18 the remote **m** of Ephraim
1Sa 1: 1 of the **m** of Ephraim, and his
1Sa 9: 4 through the **m** of Ephraim and
1Sa 13: 2 and in the **m** of Bethel, and a
1Sa 14:22 hidden in the **m** of Ephraim
1Sa 23:14 and remained in the **m** in the
1Sa 26:20 hunts a partridge in the **m**
2Sa 1:21 O **m** of Gilboa, let there be
2Sa 20:21 a man from the **m** of Ephraim
1Ki 4: 8 Ben-Hur, in the **m** of Ephraim
1Ki 5:15 who quarried stone in the **m**
1Ki 12:25 Shechem in the **m** of Ephraim
1Ki 19:11 strong wind tore into the **m**
1Ki 22:17 all Israel scattered on the **m**
2Ki 5:22 to me from the **m** of Ephraim
2Ki 19:23 up to the height of the **m**
1Ch 6:67 in the **m** of Ephraim, also
1Ch 12: 8 as swift as gazelles on the **m**
2Ch 2: 2 to quarry stone in the **m**, and
2Ch 13: 4 which is in the **m** of Ephraim
2Ch 15: 8 had taken in the **m** of Ephraim
2Ch 18:16 all Israel scattered on the **m**
2Ch 19: 4 Beersheba to the **m** of Ephraim
2Ch 21:11 high places in the **m** of Judah
2Ch 26:10 and vinedressers in the **m** and
2Ch 27: 4 cities in the **m** of Judah, and
Job 9: 5 He removes the **m**, and they do
Job 24: 8 wet with the showers of the **m**
Job 28: 9 overturns the **m** at the roots
Job 39: 8 range of the **m** is his pasture
Job 40:20 Surely the **m** yield food for
Ps 36: 6 is like the great **m**
Ps 46: 2 though the **m** be carried into
Ps 46: 3 Though the **m** shake with its
Ps 50:11 I know all the birds of the **m**
Ps 65: 6 the **m** by His strength, Being
Ps 68:16 envy, you **m** of many peaks
Ps 72: 3 The **m** will bring peace to the
Ps 72:16 earth, On the top of the **m**
Ps 76: 4 excellent Than the **m** of prey
Ps 83:14 the flame sets the **m** on fire
Ps 87: 1 foundation is in the holy **m**
Ps 90: 2 Before the **m** were brought
Ps 97: 5 The **m** melt like wax at the
Ps 104: 6 The waters stood above the **m**
Ps 104: 8 They went up over the **m**
Ps 114: 4 The **m** skipped like rams, The

Ps 114: 6 O **m**, that you skipped like
Ps 125: 2 As the **m** surround Jerusalem,
Ps 133: 3 Descending upon the **m** of Zion
Ps 144: 5 Touch the **m**, and they shall
Ps 147: 8 makes grass to grow on the **m**
Ps 148: 9 **M** and all hills
Prov 8:25 Before the **m** were settled,
Prov 27:25 of the **m** are gathered in,
Song 2: 8 he comes leaping upon the **m**
Song 2:17 stag upon the **m** of Bether
Song 4: 8 from the **m** of the leopards
Song 8:14 young stag on the **m** of spices
Is 2: 2 on the top of the **m**, and shall
Is 2:14 upon all the high **m**, and upon
Is 13: 4 noise of a multitude in the **m**
Is 14:25 on My **m** tread him under foot
Is 17:13 of the **m** before the wind,
Is 18: 3 he lifts up a banner on the **m**
Is 34: 3 the **m** shall be melted with
Is 37:24 up to the height of the **m**
Is 40:12 Weighed the **m** in scales and
Is 41:15 you shall thresh the **m** and
Is 42:11 shout from the top of the **m**
Is 42:15 I will lay waste the **m** and
Is 44:23 forth into singing, you **m**
Is 49:11 will make each of My **m** a road
Is 49:13 And break out in singing, O **m**
Is 52: 7 How beautiful upon the **m** are
Is 54:10 For the **m** shall depart and the
Is 55:12 the **m** and the hills shall
Is 64: 1 That the **m** might shake at
Is 64: 3 the **m** shook at Your presence
Is 65: 7 have burned incense on the **m**
Is 65: 9 and from Judah an heir of My **m**
Jer 3:23 and from the multitude of **m**
Jer 4:24 I beheld the **m**, and indeed
Jer 9:10 weeping and wailing for the **m**
Jer 13:16 feet stumble on the dark **m**
Jer 17:26 from the lowland, from the **m**
Jer 31: 5 vines on the **m** of Samaria
Jer 32:44 Judah, in the cities of the **m**
Jer 33:13 In the cities of the **m**, in
Jer 46:18 as Tabor is among the **m** and as
Jer 50: 6 turned them away on the **m**
Lam 4:19 They pursued us on the **m** and
Ezek 6: 2 face toward the **m** of Israel
Ezek 6: 3 O **m** of Israel, hear the word
Ezek 6: 3 says the Lord GOD to the **m**
Ezek 7: 7 and not of rejoicing in the **m**
Ezek 7:16 be on the **m** like doves of the
Ezek 18: 6 if he has not eaten on the **m**
Ezek 18:11 but has eaten on the **m** or
Ezek 18:15 Who has not eaten on the **m**
Ezek 19: 9 be heard on the **m** of Israel
Ezek 22: 9 are those who eat on the **m**
Ezek 31:12 branches have fallen on the **m**
Ezek 32: 5 will lay your flesh on the **m**
Ezek 32: 6 of your blood, even to the **m**
Ezek 33:28 the **m** of Israel shall be so
Ezek 34: 6 wandered through all the **m**
Ezek 34:13 feed them on the **m** of Israel
Ezek 34:14 be on the high **m** of Israel
Ezek 34:14 pasture on the **m** of Israel
Ezek 35: 8 fill its **m** with the slain
Ezek 35:12 against the **m** of Israel,
Ezek 36: 1 prophesy to the **m** of Israel
Ezek 36: 1 O **m** of Israel, hear the word
Ezek 36: 4 O **m** of Israel, hear the word
Ezek 36: 4 says the Lord GOD to the **m**
Ezek 36: 6 of Israel, and say to the **m**
Ezek 36: 8 you, O **m** of Israel, you shall
Ezek 37:22 the land, on the **m** of Israel
Ezek 38: 8 people on the **m** of Israel
Ezek 38:20 The **m** shall be thrown down,
Ezek 38:21 Gog throughout all My **m**,"
Ezek 39: 2 you against the **m** of Israel
Ezek 39: 4 fall upon the **m** of Israel
Ezek 39:17 meal on the **m** of Israel, that
Hos 10: 8 they shall say to the **m**
Joel 2: 2 clouds spread over the **m**
Joel 3:18 **m** shall drip with new wine
Amos 3: 9 Assemble on the **m** of Samaria
Amos 4:13 For behold, He who forms **m**
Amos 9:13 the **m** shall drip with sweet
Obad 8 from the **m** of Esau
Obad 9 **m** of Esau may be cut off by
Obad 19 shall possess the **m** of Esau
Obad 21 Zion to judge the **m** of Esau
Jon 2: 6 down to the moorings of the **m**
Mic 1: 4 The **m** will melt under him, and

Mic 4: 1 on the top of the **m**, and shall
Mic 6: 1 plead your case before the **m**
Mic 6: 2 Hear, O you **m**, the LORD's
Nah 1: 5 The **m** quake before Him, the
Nah 1:15 on the **m** the feet of him who
Nah 3:18 people are scattered on the **m**
Hab 3: 6 everlasting **m** were scattered
Hab 3:10 The **m** saw You and trembled
Hag 1: 8 Go up to the **m** and bring wood
Hag 1:11 drought on the land and the **m**
Zech 6: 1 coming from between two **m**
Zech 6: 1 **m** were **m** of bronze
Mal 1: 3 hated, and laid waste his **m**
Matt 18:12 go to the **m** to seek the one
Matt 24:16 are in Judea flee to the **m**
Mark 5: 5 night and day, he was in the **m**
Mark 5:11 was feeding there near the **m**
Mark 13:14 are in Judea flee to the **m**
Luke 21:21 those in Judea flee to the **m**
Luke 23:30 will begin 'to say to the **m**
1Co 13: 2 so that I could remove **m**
Heb 11:38 They wandered in deserts and **m**
Rev 6:15 and in the rocks of the **m**,
Rev 6:16 and said to the **m** and rocks
Rev 16:20 away, and the **m** were not found
Rev 17: 9 **m** on which the woman sits

MOUNTAINTOP (*see* MOUNTAIN, MOUNTAINTOPS)
Num 14:44 presumed to go up to the **m**
Ezek 43:12 the **m** shall be most holy

MOUNTAINTOPS (*see* MOUNTAINTOP)
Ezek 6:13 every high hill, on all the **m**
Hos 4:13 offer sacrifices on the **m**
Joel 2: 5 chariots over **m** they leap

MOUNTED (*see* MOUNT)
1Ki 12:18 **m** his chariot in haste to
2Ch 10:18 **m** his chariot in haste to
Ezek 10:19 **m** up from the earth in my

MOUNTINGS (*see* MOUNT)
Ex 39:13 settings of gold in their **m**

MOUNTS (*see* MOUNT)
Job 20: 6 **m** up to the heavens, and his
Acts 23:24 provide **m** to set Paul on, and

MOURN (*see* MOURNED, MOURNER, MOURNFUL, MOURNING, MOURNS)
Gen 23: 2 Abraham came to **m** for Sarah
Deut 21:13 **m** her father and her mother a
1Sa 16: 1 How long will you **m** for Saul
2Sa 3:31 sackcloth, and **m** for Abner
1Ki 13:29 prophet came to the city to **m**
1Ki 14:13 And all Israel shall **m** for him
Neh 8: 9 do not **m** nor weep
Job 2:11 **m** with him, and to comfort him
Job 5:11 those who **m** are lifted to
Job 14:22 and his soul will **m** over it
Prov 5:11 and you **m** at last, when your
Eccl 3: 4 a time to **m**, and a time to
Is 3:26 Her gates shall lament and **m**
Is 16: 7 of Kir Hareseth you shall **m**
Is 19: 8 The fishermen also will **m**
Is 32:12 People shall **m** upon their
Is 61: 2 to comfort all who **m**,
Is 61: 3 console those who **m** in Zion
Is 66:10 her, all you who **m** for her
Jer 4:28 For this shall the earth **m**
Jer 12: 4 How long will the land **m**, and
Jer 14: 2 they **m** for the land, and the
Jer 48:31 I will **m** for the men of Kir
Lam 1: 4 The roads to Zion **m** because
Ezek 7:12 rejoice, nor the seller **m**
Ezek 7:27 The king will **m**, the prince
Ezek 24:16 you shall neither **m** nor weep
Ezek 24:23 you shall neither **m** nor weep
Ezek 24:23 and **m** with one another
Ezek 31:15 I caused Lebanon to **m** for it
Hos 4: 3 Therefore the land will **m**
Hos 10: 5 For its people **m** for it, and
Joel 1: 9 the priests **m**, who minister
Amos 1: 2 pastures of the shepherds **m**
Amos 8: 8 everyone **m** who dwells in it
Amos 9: 5 and all who dwell there **m**
Zech 12:10 they will **m** for Him as one
Zech 12:12 And the land shall **m**, every
Matt 5: 4 Blessed are those who **m**, for
Matt 9:15 **m** as long as the bridegroom
Matt 24:30 tribes of the earth will **m**
Luke 6:25 laugh now, For you shall **m**
2Co 12:21 I shall **m** for many who have
Jas 4: 9 Lament and **m** and weep
Rev 1: 7 earth will **m** because of Him
Rev 18:11 **m** over her, for no one buys

MOURNED (*see* MOURN)
Gen 37:34 and **m** for his son many days
Gen 50: 3 and the Egyptians **m** for him
Gen 50:10 they **m** there with a great and
Ex 33: 4 these grave tidings, they **m**
Num 14:39 and the people **m** greatly
Num 20:29 **m** for Aaron thirty days
1Sa 15:35 Samuel **m** for Saul, and the
2Sa 1:12 And they **m** and wept and fasted
2Sa 11:26 dead, she **m** for her husband
2Sa 13:37 David **m** for his son every day
1Ki 13:30 and they **m** over him, saying,
1Ki 14:18 and all Israel **m** for him,
1Ch 7:22 their father **m** many days, and
2Ch 35:24 and Jerusalem **m** for Josiah
Ezra 10: 6 for he **m** because of the guilt
Neh 1: 4 and wept, and **m** for many days
Is 38:14 I **m** like a dove
Zech 7: 5 **m** in the fifth and seventh
Matt 11:17 we **m** to you, And you did not
Mark 16:10 had been with Him, as they **m**
Luke 7:32 we **m** to you, and you did not
Luke 8:52 Now all wept and **m** for her
Luke 23:27 Him, and women who also **m**
1Co 5: 2 up, and have not rather **m**,

MOURNER (*see* MOURN, MOURNERS)
2Sa 14: 2 Please pretend to be a **m**, and

MOURNERS (*see* MOURNER)
Job 29:25 army, as one who comforts **m**
Eccl 12: 5 the **m** go about the streets
Is 57:18 comforts to him and to his **m**
Hos 9: 4 be like bread of **m** to them
Mal 3:14 and that we have walked as **m**

MOURNFUL (*see* MOURN)
Zeph 1:10 The sound of a **m** cry from the

MOURNING (*see* MOURN)
Gen 27:41 The days of **m** for my father
Gen 37:35 into the grave to my son in **m**
Gen 50: 4 the days of his **m** were past
Gen 50:10 days of **m** for his father
Gen 50:11 saw the **m** at the threshing
Gen 50:11 a grievous **m** of the Egyptians
Deut 26:14 not eaten any of it when in **m**
Deut 34: 8 weeping and **m** for Moses ended
2Sa 11:27 And when her **m** was over,
2Sa 14: 2 mourner, and put on **m** apparel
2Sa 14: 2 **m** a long time for the dead
2Sa 19: 1 is weeping and **m** for Absalom
2Sa 19: 2 into **m** for all the people
1Ki 21:27 in sackcloth, and went about **m**
Esth 4: 3 was great **m** among the Jews
Esth 6:12 hastened to his house, **m** and
Esth 9:22 them, and from **m** to a holiday
Job 30:28 I go about **m**, but not in the
Job 30:31 My harp is turned to **m**, and my
Ps 30:11 for me my **m** into dancing
Ps 38: 6 I go **m** all the day long
Ps 42: 9 Why do I go **m** because of the
Ps 43: 2 Why do I go **m** because of the
Eccl 7: 2 to go to the house of **m** than
Eccl 7: 4 the wise is in the house of **m**
Is 22:12 called for weeping and for **m**
Is 60:20 days of your **m** shall be ended
Is 61: 3 ashes, the oil of joy for **m**
Jer 6:26 Make **m** as for an only son,
Jer 8:21 I am hurt. I am **m**
Jer 9:17 and call for the **m** women, that
Jer 16: 5 Do not enter the house of **m**
Jer 16: 7 men break bread in **m** for them
Jer 31:13 I will turn their **m** to joy
Lam 2: 5 and has increased **m** and
Lam 5:15 our dance has turned into **m**
Ezek 2:10 on it were lamentations and **m**
Ezek 7:16 of the valleys, all of them **m**
Ezek 24:17 make no **m** for the dead
Ezek 31:15 went down to hell, I caused **m**
Dan 10: 2 was **m** three full weeks
Joel 2:12 with weeping, and with **m**
Amos 5:16 shall call the farmer to **m**
Amos 8:10 will turn your feasts into **m**
Amos 8:10 it like **m** for an only son
Mic 1: 8 And a **m** like the ostriches,
Zech 12:11 be a great **m** in Jerusalem
Zech 12:11 like the **m** at Hadad Rimmon in
Matt 2:18 weeping, and great **m**, Rachel
2Co 7: 7 your earnest desire, your **m**
Jas 4: 9 your laughter be turned to **m**
Rev 18: 8 death and **m** and famine

MOURNS (*see* MOURN)
Ps 35:14 as one who **m** for his mother
Is 24: 4 The earth **m** and fades away,
Is 33: 9 The earth **m** and languishes,
Jer 12:11 desolate, it **m** to Me
Jer 14: 2 Judah **m**, and her gates
Jer 23:10 because of a curse the land **m**
Joel 1:10 field is wasted, the land **m**
Mic 1:11 Beth Ezel **m**
Zech 12:10 Him as one **m** for his only son

MOUSE
Lev 11:29 the mole, the **m**, and the large
Is 66:17 and the abomination and the **m**

MOUTH (*see* MOUTHS)
Gen 4:11 which has opened its **m** to
Gen 8:11 olive leaf was in her **m**
Gen 29: 2 stone was on the well's **m**
Gen 29: 3 the stone from the well's **m**
Gen 29: 3 in its place on the well's **m**
Gen 29: 8 the stone from the well's **m**
Gen 29:10 the stone from the well's **m**
Gen 42:27 it was, in the **m** of his sack
Gen 43:12 in the **m** of your sacks
Gen 43:21 was in the **m** of his sack, our
Gen 44: 1 money in the **m** of his sack
Gen 44: 2 in the **m** of the sack of the
Gen 44: 8 found in the **m** of our sacks
Gen 45:12 it is my **m** that speaks to you
Ex 4:11 Who has made man's **m**
Ex 4:12 go, and I will be with your **m**
Ex 4:15 him and put the words in his **m**
Ex 4:15 be with your **m** and with his **m**
Ex 4:16 shall be as a **m** for you, and
Ex 13: 9 LORD's law may be in your **m**
Ex 23:13 let it be heard from your **m**
Num 16:30 and the earth opens its **m**
Num 16:32 and the earth opened its **m**
Num 22:28 opened the **m** of the donkey
Num 22:38 word that God puts in my **m**
Num 23: 5 LORD put a word in Balaam's **m**
Num 23:12 what the LORD has put in my **m**
Num 23:16 and put a word in his **m**, and
Num 26:10 and the earth opened its **m**
Num 30: 2 that proceeds out of his **m**
Num 32:24 has proceeded out of your **m**
Deut 8: 3 from the **m** of the LORD
Deut 11: 6 how the earth opened its **m**
Deut 18:18 and will put My words in His **m**
Deut 19:15 by the **m** of two or three
Deut 23:23 you have promised with your **m**
Deut 30:14 is very near you, in your **m**
Deut 32: 1 O earth, the words of my **m**
Josh 1: 8 shall not depart from your **m**
Josh 6:10 word proceed out of your **m**
Josh 10:18 against the **m** of the cave
Josh 10:22 Open the **m** of the cave, and
Josh 10:27 stones against the cave's **m**
Josh 15: 5 as far as the **m** of the Jordan
Josh 15: 5 sea at the **m** of the Jordan
Judg 7: 6 putting their hand to their **m**
Judg 9:38 Where indeed is your **m** now
Judg 11:36 what has gone out of your **m**
Judg 18:19 put your hand over your **m**
1Sa 1:12 LORD, that Eli watched her **m**
1Sa 2: 3 no arrogance come from your **m**
1Sa 14:26 no one put his hand to his **m**
1Sa 14:27 and put his hand to his **m**
1Sa 17:35 delivered the lamb from its **m**
2Sa 1:16 for your own **m** has testified
2Sa 14: 3 Joab put the words in her **m**
2Sa 14:19 in the **m** of your maidservant
2Sa 17:19 a covering over the well's **m**
2Sa 18:25 alone, there is news in his **m**
2Sa 22: 9 and devouring fire from His **m**
1Ki 8:15 with His **m** to my father David
1Ki 8:24 have both spoken with Your **m**
1Ki 17:24 LORD in your **m** is the truth
1Ki 19:18 every **m** that has not kissed
1Ki 22:22 in the **m** of all his prophets
1Ki 22:23 **m** of all these prophets of
2Ki 4:34 and put his **m** on his **m**
1Ch 16:12 and the judgments of His **m**
2Ch 6: 4 with His **m** to my father David
2Ch 6:15 have both spoken with Your **m**
2Ch 18:21 in the **m** of all his prophets

2Ch 18:22 put a lying spirit in the **m**
2Ch 35:22 of Necho from the **m** of God
2Ch 36:12 spoke from the **m** of the LORD
2Ch 36:21 the LORD by the **m** of Jeremiah
2Ch 36:22 by the **m** of Jeremiah might be
Ezra 1: 1 by the **m** of Jeremiah might be
Neh 9:20 Your manna from their **m**, and
Esth 7: 8 As the word left the king's **m**
Job 3: 1 After this Job opened his **m**
Job 5:15 from the **m** of the mighty, and
Job 5:16 and injustice shuts her **m**
Job 7:11 I will not restrain my **m**
Job 8: 2 the words of your **m** be like a
Job 8:21 yet fill your **m** with laughing
Job 9:20 my own **m** would condemn me
Job 12:11 words and the **m** taste its food
Job 15: 5 your iniquity teaches your **m**
Job 15: 6 Your own **m** condemns you, and
Job 15:13 such words go out of your **m**
Job 15:30 of His **m** he will go away
Job 16: 5 strengthen you with my **m**, and
Job 16:10 They gape at me with their **m**
Job 19:16 I beg him with my **m**
Job 20:12 Though evil is sweet in his **m**
Job 20:13 but still keeps it in his **m**
Job 21: 5 put your hand over your **m**
Job 22:22 instruction from His **m**, and
Job 23: 4 and fill my **m** with arguments
Job 23:12 treasured the words of His **m**
Job 29: 9 and put their hand on their **m**
Job 29:10 stuck to the roof of their **m**
Job 29:23 they opened their **m** wide as
Job 31:27 and my **m** has kissed my hand
Job 31:30 I have not allowed my **m** to
Job 32: 5 in the **m** of these three men
Job 33: 2 Now, I open my **m**
Job 33: 2 my tongue speaks in my **m**
Job 35:16 Job opens his **m** in vain
Job 37: 2 that comes from His **m**
Job 40: 4 I lay my hand over my **m**
Job 40:23 the Jordan gushes into his **m**
Job 41:19 Out of his **m** go burning
Job 41:21 and a flame goes out of his **m**
Ps 5: 9 is no faithfulness in their **m**
Ps 8: 2 Out of the **m** of babes and
Ps 10: 7 His **m** is full of cursing and
Ps 17: 3 my **m** shall not transgress
Ps 18: 8 And devouring fire from His **m**
Ps 19:14 Let the words of my **m** and the
Ps 22:21 Save Me from the lion's **m**
Ps 33: 6 them by the breath of His **m**
Ps 34: 1 shall continually be in my **m**
Ps 35:21 their **m** wide against me, And
Ps 36: 3 words of his **m** are wickedness
Ps 37:30 The **m** of the righteous speaks
Ps 38:13 mute who does not open his **m**
Ps 38:14 in whose **m** is no response
Ps 39: 1 restrain my **m** with a muzzle
Ps 39: 9 was mute, I did not open my **m**
Ps 40: 3 He has put a new song in my **m**
Ps 49: 3 My **m** shall speak wisdom, And
Ps 50:16 Or take My covenant in your **m**
Ps 50:19 You give your **m** to evil, And
Ps 51:15 my **m** shall show forth Your
Ps 54: 2 Give ear to the words of my **m**
Ps 55:21 The words of his **m** were
Ps 58: 6 Break their teeth in their **m**
Ps 59: 7 they belch out with their **m**
Ps 59:12 For the sin of their **m** and the
Ps 62: 4 They bless with their **m**, But
Ps 63: 5 my **m** shall praise You with
Ps 63:11 But the **m** of those who speak
Ps 66:14 my **m** has spoken when I was in
Ps 66:17 I cried to Him with my **m**, And
Ps 69:15 not the pit shut its **m** on me
Ps 71: 8 Let my **m** be filled with Your
Ps 71:15 My **m** shall tell of Your
Ps 73: 9 They set their **m** against the
Ps 78: 1 ears to the words of my **m**
Ps 78: 2 I will open my **m** in a parable
Ps 78:36 flattered Him with their **m**
Ps 81:10 Open your **m** wide, and I will
Ps 89: 1 With my **m** will I make known
Ps 103: 5 your **m** with good things, So
Ps 105: 5 and the judgments of His **m**
Ps 107:42 And all iniquity stops its **m**
Ps 109: 2 For the **m** of the wicked and
Ps 109: 2 the **m** of the deceitful Have
Ps 109:30 praise the LORD with my **m**
Ps 119:13 All the judgments of Your **m**
Ps 119:43 of truth utterly out of my **m**
Ps 119:72 The law of Your **m** is better
Ps 119:88 keep the testimony of Your **m**
Ps 119:103 sweeter than honey to my **m**
Ps 119:108 freewill offerings of my **m**
Ps 119:131 I opened my **m** and panted, For
Ps 126: 2 Then our **m** was filled with
Ps 137: 6 cling to the roof of my **m**
Ps 138: 4 they hear the words of Your **m**
Ps 141: 3 a guard, O LORD, over my **m**
Ps 141: 7 at the **m** of the grave, As
Ps 144: 8 Whose **m** speaks vain words,
Ps 144:11 Whose **m** speaks vain words,
Ps 145:21 My **m** shall speak the praise
Ps 149: 6 praises of God be in their **m**
Prov 2: 6 from His **m** come knowledge
Prov 4: 5 away from the words of my **m**
Prov 4:24 away from you a deceitful **m**
Prov 5: 3 her **m** is smoother than oil
Prov 5: 7 depart from the words of my **m**
Prov 6: 2 by the words of your own **m**
Prov 6: 2 taken by the words of your **m**
Prov 6:12 man, walks with a perverse **m**
Prov 7:24 to the words of my **m**
Prov 8: 7 for my **m** will speak truth
Prov 8: 8 All the words of my **m** are
Prov 8:13 way and the perverse **m** I hate
Prov 10: 6 covers the **m** of the wicked
Prov 10:11 The **m** of the righteous is a
Prov 10:11 covers the **m** of the wicked
Prov 10:14 but the **m** of the foolish is
Prov 10:31 The **m** of the righteous brings
Prov 10:32 but the **m** of the wicked what
Prov 11: 9 his **m** destroys his neighbor
Prov 11:11 by the **m** of the wicked
Prov 12: 6 but the **m** of the upright
Prov 12:14 good by the fruit of his **m**
Prov 13: 2 well by the fruit of his **m**
Prov 13: 3 He who guards his **m** preserves
Prov 14: 3 In the **m** of a fool is a rod
Prov 15: 2 but the **m** of fools pours
Prov 15:14 but the **m** of fools feeds on
Prov 15:23 joy by the answer of his **m**
Prov 15:28 but the **m** of the wicked pours
Prov 16:10 his **m** must not transgress in
Prov 16:23 of the wise teaches his **m**
Prov 16:26 his hungry **m** drives him on
Prov 18: 4 of a man's **m** are deep waters
Prov 18: 6 and his **m** calls for blows
Prov 18: 7 A fool's **m** is his destruction
Prov 18:20 from the fruit of his **m**, and
Prov 19:24 as bring it to his **m** again
Prov 19:28 the **m** of the wicked devours
Prov 20:17 but afterward his **m** will be
Prov 21:23 Whoever guards his **m** and
Prov 22:14 The **m** of an immoral woman is
Prov 24: 7 not open his **m** in the gate
Prov 26: 7 a proverb in the **m** of fools
Prov 26: 9 a proverb in the **m** of fools
Prov 26:15 him to bring it back to his **m**
Prov 26:28 and a flattering **m** works ruin
Prov 27: 2 praise you, and not your own **m**
Prov 30:20 she eats and wipes her **m**, and
Prov 30:32 evil, put your hand on your **m**
Prov 31: 8 Open your **m** for the
Prov 31: 9 Open your **m**, judge
Prov 31:26 She opens her **m** with wisdom
Eccl 5: 2 Do not be rash with your **m**
Eccl 5: 6 Do not let your **m** cause your
Eccl 6: 7 the labor of man is for his **m**
Eccl 10:12 a wise man's **m** are gracious
Eccl 10:13 the words of his **m** begin with
Song 1: 2 me with the kisses of his **m**
Song 4: 3 scarlet, and your **m** is lovely
Song 5:16 His **m** is most sweet, yes, he
Song 7: 9 the roof of your **m** like the
Is 1:20 for the **m** of the LORD has
Is 5:14 opened its **m** beyond measure
Is 6: 7 And he touched my **m** with it
Is 9:12 devour Israel with an open **m**
Is 9:17 and every **m** speaks folly
Is 10:14 nor opened his **m** with even a
Is 11: 4 earth with the rod of His **m**
Is 19: 7 by the **m** of the River, and
Is 34:16 For My **m** has commanded it,
Is 40: 5 for the **m** of the LORD has
Is 45:23 out of My **m** in righteousness
Is 48: 3 they went forth from My **m**
Is 49: 2 He has made My **m** like a sharp
Is 51:16 I have put My words in your **m**
Is 53: 7 yet He opened not His **m**
Is 53: 7 so He opened not his **m**
Is 53: 9 nor was any deceit in His **m**
Is 55:11 be that goes forth from My **m**
Is 57: 4 whom do you make a wide **m**
Is 58:14 The **m** of the LORD has spoken
Is 59:21 which I have put in your **m**
Is 59:21 shall not depart from your **m**
Is 59:21 nor from the **m** of your
Is 59:21 nor from the **m** of your
Is 62: 2 which the **m** of the LORD will
Jer 1: 9 His hand and touched my **m**,
Jer 1: 9 I have put My words in your **m**
Jer 5:14 make My words in your **m** fire
Jer 7:28 has been cut off from their **m**
Jer 9: 8 to his neighbor with his **m**
Jer 9:12 who is he to whom the **m** of
Jer 9:20 ear receive the word of His **m**
Jer 12: 2 You are near in their **m** but
Jer 15:19 vile, you shall be as My **m**
Jer 23:16 not from the **m** of the LORD
Jer 36:18 his **m** all these words to me
Jer 44:17 has gone out of our own **m**
Jer 44:26 no more be named in the **m** of
Jer 48:28 in the sides of the cave's **m**
Jer 51:44 his **m** what he has swallowed
Lam 2:16 opened their **m** against you
Lam 3:29 Let him put his **m** in the dust
Lam 3:38 Is it not from the **m** of the
Lam 4: 4 the roof of its **m** for thirst
Ezek 2: 8 open your **m** and eat what I
Ezek 3: 2 So I opened my **m**, and He
Ezek 3: 3 it was in my **m** like honey in
Ezek 3:17 hear a word from My **m**, and
Ezek 3:26 cling to the roof of your **m**
Ezek 3:27 with you, I will open your **m**
Ezek 4:14 flesh ever come into my **m**
Ezek 16:56 was not a byword in your **m** in
Ezek 16:63 never open your **m** anymore
Ezek 24:27 on that day your **m** will be
Ezek 29:21 I will open your **m** to speak
Ezek 33: 7 shall hear a word from My **m**
Ezek 33:22 And He had opened my **m**
Ezek 33:22 my **m** was opened, and I was no
Ezek 33:31 for with their **m** they show
Ezek 35:13 Thus with your **m** you have
Dan 3:26 went near the **m** of the
Dan 4:31 was still in the king's **m**
Dan 6:17 and laid on the **m** of the den
Dan 7: 5 in its **m** between its teeth
Dan 7: 8 a **m** speaking pompous words
Dan 7:20 a **m** which spoke pompous
Dan 10: 3 meat or wine came into my **m**
Dan 10:16 then I opened my **m** and spoke,
Hos 2:17 her **m** the names of the Baals
Hos 6: 5 them by the words of My **m**
Hos 8: 1 Set the trumpet to your **m**
Joel 1: 5 has been cut off from your **m**
Amos 3:12 the **m** of a lion two legs or a
Mic 4: 4 for the **m** of the LORD of
Mic 6:12 is deceitful in their **m**
Mic 7: 5 Guard the doors of your **m**
Mic 7:16 put their hand over their **m**
Nah 3:12 fall into the **m** of the eater
Zeph 3:13 tongue be found in their **m**
Zech 5: 8 the lead cover over its **m**
Zech 8: 9 by the **m** of the prophets, who
Zech 9: 7 away the blood from his **m**
Mal 2: 6 The law of truth was in his **m**
Mal 2: 7 seek the law from his **m**
Matt 4: 4 proceeds from the **m** of God
Matt 5: 2 Then He opened His **m** and
Matt 12:34 of the heart the **m** speaks
Matt 13:35 I will open My **m** in parables
Matt 15: 8 draw near to Me with their **m**
Matt 15:11 goes into the **m** defiles a man
Matt 15:11 but what comes out of the **m**
Matt 15:17 the **m** goes into the stomach
Matt 15:18 of the **m** come from the heart
Matt 17:27 when you have opened its **m**
Matt 18:16 that 'by the **m** of two or
Matt 21:16 read, 'Out of the **m** of babes
Mark 9:18 he foams at the **m**, gnashes
Mark 9:20 and wallowed, foaming at the **m**
Luke 1:64 Immediately his **m** was opened
Luke 1:70 as He spoke by the **m** of His
Luke 4:22 which proceeded out of His **m**
Luke 6:45 of the heart his **m** speaks
Luke 9:39 him so that he foams at the **m**
Luke 19:22 your own **m** I will judge you

Luke 21:15 for I will give you a **m** and
Luke 22:71 it ourselves from His own **m**
John 19:29 on hyssop, and put it to His **m**
Acts 1:16 **m** of David concerning Judas
Acts 3:18 by the **m** of all His prophets
Acts 3:21 **m** of all His holy prophets
Acts 4:25 who by the **m** of Your servant
Acts 8:32 so He opened not His **m**
Acts 8:35 Then Philip opened his **m**, and
Acts 10:34 Then Peter opened his **m** and
Acts 11: 8 has at any time entered my **m**
Acts 15: 7 that by my **m** the Gentiles
Acts 15:27 the same things by word of **m**
Acts 18:14 Paul was about to open his **m**
Acts 22:14 and hear the voice of His **m**
Acts 23: 2 by him to strike him on the **m**
Rom 3:14 Whose **m** is full of cursing and
Rom 3:19 that every **m** may be stopped,
Rom 10: 8 is near you, even in your **m**
Rom 10: 9 with your **m** the Lord Jesus
Rom 10:10 with the **m** confession is made
Rom 15: 6 and one **m** glorify the God and
2Co 13: 1 By the **m** of two or three
Eph 4:29 proceed out of your **m**, but
Eph 6:19 that I may open my **m** boldly
Col 3: 8 filthy language out of your **m**
2Th 2: 8 with the breath of His **m** and
2Ti 4:17 out of the **m** of the lion
Jas 3:10 Out of the same **m** proceed
1Pe 2:22 was guile found in His **m**"
Jude 16 they **m** great swelling words,
Rev 1:16 out of His **m** went a sharp
Rev 2:16 them with the sword of My **m**
Rev 3:16 I will spew you out of My **m**
Rev 9:19 For their power is in their **m**
Rev 10: 9 as sweet as honey in your **m**
Rev 10:10 was as sweet as honey in my **m**
Rev 11: 5 fire proceeds from their **m**
Rev 12:15 his **m** like a flood after the
Rev 12:16 and the earth opened its **m**
Rev 12:16 had spewed out of his **m**
Rev 13: 2 his **m** like the **m** of a
Rev 13: 2 **m** like the **m** of a lion
Rev 13: 5 he was given a **m** speaking
Rev 13: 6 Then he opened his **m** in
Rev 14: 5 in their **m** was found no guile
Rev 16:13 out of the **m** of the dragon
Rev 16:13 out of the **m** of the beast, and
Rev 16:13 out of the **m** of the false
Rev 19:15 Now out of His **m** goes a sharp
Rev 19:21 which proceeded from the **m** of

MOUTHS (*see* MOUTH)
Deut 31:19 put it in their **m**, that this
Deut 31:21 in the **m** of their descendants
Ps 17:10 With their **m** they speak
Ps 22:13 They gape at Me with their **m**
Ps 78:30 food was still in their **m**
Ps 115: 5 They have **m**, but they do not
Ps 135:16 They have **m**, but they do not
Ps 135:17 there any breath in their **m**
Is 29:13 draw near to Me with their **m**
Is 52:15 shall shut their **m** at Him
Jer 44:25 wives have spoken with your **m**
Lam 3:46 opened their **m** against us
Ezek 34:10 deliver My flock from their **m**
Dan 6:22 angel and shut the lions' **m**
Mic 3: 5 Who puts nothing into their **m**
Zech 14:12 shall dissolve in their **m**
Tit 1:11 whose **m** must be stopped, who
Heb 11:33 stopped the **m** of lions,
Jas 3: 3 **m** that they may obey us, and
Rev 9:17 and out of their **m** came fire
Rev 9:18 which came out of their **m**

MOVE (*see* MOVED, MOVEMENT, MOVES, MOVING)
Ex 11: 7 shall a dog **m** its tongue,
Lev 11:10 all that **m** in the water or
Num 2:17 **m** out with the camp of the
Num 2:17 camp, so they shall **m** out
Num 14:25 **m** out into the wilderness by
Deut 32:21 I will **m** them to anger by a
Judg 13:25 to **m** upon him at Mahaneh Dan
Judg 14: 4 to **m** against the Philistines
2Sa 6:10 So David would not **m** the ark
2Sa 7:10 of their own and **m** no more
2Ki 23:18 let no one **m** his bones
1Ch 8: 6 forced them to **m** to Manahath
1Ch 8: 7 and Gera who forced them to **m**
1Ch 13:13 David would not **m** the ark
1Ch 17: 9 of their own and **m** no more
Is 13:13 the earth will **m** out of her
Is 46: 7 from its place it shall not **m**
Jer 46: 7 whose waters **m** like the
Jer 46: 8 its waters **m** like the rivers
Jer 50: 3 They shall **m**, they shall
Jer 50: 8 **M** from the midst of Babylon,
Zech 14: 4 shall **m** toward the north and
Matt 17:20 **M** from here to there,' and it
Matt 17:20 here to there,' and it will **m**
Matt 23: 4 not **m** them with one of their
Acts 17:28 for in Him we live and **m** and
Acts 20:24 But none of these things **m** me

MOVED (*see* MOVE)
Gen 7:18 and the ark **m** about on the
Gen 7:21 died that **m** on the earth
Gen 12: 8 And he **m** from there to the
Gen 13:18 Then Abram **m** his tent, and
Gen 26:22 And he **m** from there and dug
Gen 47:21 he **m** them into the cities,
Ex 7:23 was his heart **m** by this
Ex 14:19 before the camp of Israel, **m**
Num 11:35 the people **m** to Hazeroth, and
Num 12:16 the people **m** from Hazeroth
Num 21:10 the children of Israel **m** on
Num 21:12 From there they **m** and camped
Num 21:13 From there they **m** and camped
Num 22: 1 Then the children of Israel **m**
Num 33: 5 of Israel **m** from Rameses and
Num 33: 7 They **m** from Etham and turned
Num 33: 9 They **m** from Marah and came to
Num 33:10 They **m** from Elim and camped
Num 33:11 They **m** from the Red Sea and
Num 33:14 They **m** from Alush and camped
Num 33:16 They **m** from the Wilderness of
Num 33:21 They **m** from Libnah and
Num 33:24 They **m** from Mount Shepher
Num 33:25 They **m** from Haradah and
Num 33:26 They **m** from Makheloth and
Num 33:28 They **m** from Terah and camped
Num 33:32 They **m** from Bene Jaakan and
Num 33:34 They **m** from Jotbathah and
Num 33:36 They **m** from Ezion Geber and
Num 33:37 They **m** from Kadesh and
Num 33:46 They **m** from Dibon Gad and
Num 33:47 They **m** from Almon Diblathaim
Deut 32:21 they have **m** Me to anger by
Josh 10:21 No one **m** his tongue against
Judg 2:18 for the LORD was **m** to pity by
1Sa 1:13 only her lips **m**, but her
2Sa 7: 6 but have **m** about in a tent and
2Sa 18:33 Then the king was deeply **m**
2Sa 20:12 he **m** Amasa from the highway
2Sa 22: 8 the foundations of heaven **m**
2Sa 24: 1 He **m** David against them to
2Ki 23:30 Then his servants **m** his body
1Ch 16:30 it shall not be **m**
1Ch 17: 6 Wherever I have **m** about with
1Ch 21: 1 and **m** David to number Israel
2Ch 18:31 God **m** them to turn away from
Ezra 1: 5 those whose spirits God had **m**
Esth 2: 9 he **m** her and her maidservants
Job 14:18 as a rock is **m** from its place
Job 41:23 firm on him and cannot be **m**
Ps 10: 6 I shall not be **m**
Ps 13: 4 me rejoice when I am **m**
Ps 15: 5 these things shall never be **m**
Ps 16: 8 right hand I shall not be **m**
Ps 21: 7 Most High he shall not be **m**
Ps 30: 6 I shall never be **m**
Ps 46: 5 of her, she shall not be **m**
Ps 46: 6 raged, the kingdoms were **m**
Ps 55:22 permit the righteous to be **m**
Ps 62: 2 I shall not be greatly **m**
Ps 62: 6 I shall not be **m**
Ps 66: 9 not allow our feet to be **m**
Ps 68: 8 Sinai itself was **m** at the
Ps 78:58 **m** Him to jealousy with their
Ps 93: 1 so that it cannot be **m**
Ps 96:10 It shall not be **m**
Ps 99: 1 Let the earth be **m**
Ps 104: 5 it should not be **m** forever
Ps 121: 3 not allow your foot to be **m**
Ps 125: 1 Zion, Which cannot be **m**
Prov 12: 3 of the righteous cannot be **m**
Is 7: 2 heart of his people were **m** as
Is 7: 2 the woods are **m** with the wind
Is 10:14 was no one who **m** his wing
Is 30:20 be **m** into a corner anymore
Jer 4: 1 then you shall not be **m**
Jer 4:24 and all the hills **m** back and
Lam 3:17 You have **m** my soul far from
Dan 8: 7 he was **m** with rage against
Dan 11:11 South shall be **m** with rage
Dan 11:28 his heart shall be **m** against
Matt 9:36 He was **m** with compassion for
Matt 14:14 He was **m** with compassion for
Matt 18:27 servant was **m** with compassion
Matt 20:24 they were **m** with indignation
Matt 21:10 Jerusalem, all the city was **m**
Mark 1:41 **m** with compassion, put out
Mark 6:34 was **m** with compassion for
Acts 7: 4 He **m** him to this land in
Col 1:23 are not **m** away from the hope
Heb 11: 7 **m** with godly fear, prepared
2Pe 1:21 were **m** by the Holy Spirit
Rev 6:14 island was **m** out of its place

MOVEMENT (*see* MOVE)
Num 10: 2 directing the **m** of the camps

MOVES (*see* MOVE)
Gen 1:21 and every living thing that **m**
Gen 1:28 thing that **m** on the earth
Gen 9: 2 on all that **m** on the earth,
Lev 11:46 creature that **m** in the waters
Deut 27:17 Cursed is the one who **m** his
Job 9:11 If He **m** past, I do not
Job 40:17 He **m** his tail like a cedar
Ps 69:34 and everything that **m** in them
Ezek 47: 9 every living thing that **m**

MOVING (*see* MOVE)
Gen 9: 3 Every **m** thing that lives
Job 31:26 or the moon **m** in brightness,
Song 7: 9 **m** gently the lips of sleepers
John 5: 3 for the **m** of the water

MOWED (*see* MOWINGS, MOWN)
Jas 5: 4 laborers who **m** your fields

MOWINGS (*see* MOWED)
Amos 7: 1 late crop after the king's **m**

MOWN (*see* MOWED)
Ps 72: 6 like rain upon the **m** grass

MOZA
1Ch 2:46 concubine, bore Haran, **M**, and
1Ch 8:36 and Zimri begot **M**
1Ch 8:37 **M** begot Binea, Raphah his son
1Ch 9:42 and Zimri begot **M**
1Ch 9:43 **M** begot Binea, Rephaiah his

MOZAH
Josh 18:26 Mizpah, Chephirah, **M**,

MUCH (*see* PREFACE)

MUDDY
Is 14:23 and marshes of **m** water
Ezek 32:13 of man shall **m** them no more
Ezek 32:13 the hooves of beasts **m** them

MULBERRY
2Sa 5:23 them in front of the **m** trees
2Sa 5:24 in the tops of the **m** trees
1Ch 14:14 them in front of the **m** trees
1Ch 14:15 in the tops of the **m** trees
Luke 17: 6 you can say to this **m** tree

MULE (*see* MULE-LOADS, MULES)
2Sa 13:29 and each one got on his **m**
2Sa 18: 9 Absalom rode on a **m**
2Sa 18: 9 The **m** went under the thick
2Sa 18: 9 the **m** which was under him
1Ki 1:33 my son ride on my own **m**, and
1Ki 1:38 ride on King David's **m**, and
1Ki 1:44 made him ride on the king's **m**
Ps 32: 9 like the horse or like the **m**
Zech 14:15 plague on the horse and the **m**

MULE-LOADS (*see* MULE)
2Ki 5:17 be given two **m** of earth

MULES (*see* MULE)
1Ki 10:25 armor, spices, horses, and **m**
1Ki 18: 5 **m** alive, so that we will not
1Ch 12:40 on donkeys and camels, on **m**
2Ch 9:24 armor, spices, horses, and **m**
Ezra 2:66 their **m** two hundred and
Neh 7:68 their **m** two hundred and
Is 66:20 chariots and in litters, on **m**
Ezek 27:14 with horses, steeds, and **m**

MULTICOLORED
Ezek 16:16 adorned **m** high places for
Ezek 27:24 in chests of **m** apparel, in

MULTIPLIED (*see* MULTIPLY)
Gen 47:27 and grew and **m** exceedingly
Ex 1: 7 and increased abundantly, **m**
Ex 1:12 them, the more they **m** and grew
Ex 1:20 the midwives, and the people **m**
Ex 11: 9 may be **m** in the land of Egypt
Deut 1:10 The LORD your God has **m** you
Deut 8:13 silver and your gold are **m**
Deut 8:13 and all that you have is **m**
Deut 11:21 of your children may be **m** in
Josh 24: 3 **m** his descendants and gave him
Judg 16:24 and the one who **m** our dead
1Ch 5: 9 had **m** in the land of Gilead
Neh 9:23 You also **m** their children as
Job 27:14 If his children are **m**, it is
Job 35: 6 if your transgressions are **m**
Ps 16: 4 Their sorrows shall be **m** who
Ps 38:19 who hate me wrongfully have **m**
Prov 9:11 For by me your days will be **m**
Prov 29:16 When the wicked are **m**,
Is 9: 3 You have **m** the nation and
Is 59:12 are **m** before You, and our sins
Jer 3:16 come to pass, when you are **m**
Ezek 5: 7 Because you have **m**
Ezek 11: 6 You have **m** your slain in this
Ezek 16:25 and **m** your acts of harlotry
Ezek 16:29 Moreover you **m** your acts of
Ezek 16:51 but you have **m** your
Ezek 23:19 Yet she **m** her harlotry in
Ezek 31: 5 its boughs were **m**, and its
Ezek 35:13 Me and **m** your words against
Dan 4: 1 Peace be **m** to you
Dan 6:25 Peace be **m** to you
Hos 2: 8 oil, and **m** her silver and gold
Hos 8:14 Judah also has **m** fortified
Hos 12:10 prophets, and have **m** visions
Nah 3:16 You have **m** your merchants
Acts 6: 7 **m** greatly in Jerusalem, and a
Acts 7:17 the people grew and **m** in Egypt
Acts 9:31 the Holy Spirit, they were **m**
Acts 12:24 But the word of God grew and **m**
1Pe 1: 2 Grace to you and peace be **m**
2Pe 1: 2 and peace be **m** to you in the
Jude 2 peace, and love be **m** to you

MULTIPLIES (*see* MULTIPLY)
Job 9:17 **m** my wounds without cause
Job 34:37 and **m** his words against God
Job 35:16 he **m** words without knowledge
Eccl 10:14 A fool also **m** words

MULTIPLY (*see* MULTIPLIED, MULTIPLIES, MULTIPLYING)
Gen 1:22 Be fruitful and **m**, and fill the
Gen 1:22 and let birds **m** on the earth
Gen 1:28 Be fruitful and **m**
Gen 3:16 I will greatly **m** your sorrow
Gen 6: 1 when men began to **m** on the
Gen 8:17 be fruitful and **m** on the earth
Gen 9: 1 Be fruitful and **m**, and fill the
Gen 9: 7 as for you, be fruitful and **m**
Gen 9: 7 in the earth and **m** in it
Gen 16:10 I will **m** your descendants
Gen 17: 2 and will **m** you exceedingly
Gen 17:20 and will **m** him exceedingly
Gen 22:17 in multiplying I will **m** your
Gen 26: 4 **m** as the stars of heaven
Gen 26:24 **m** your descendants for My
Gen 28: 3 **m** you, that you may be an
Gen 35:11 Be fruitful and **m**
Gen 48: 4 **m** you, and I will make of you
Ex 1:10 wisely with them, lest they **m**
Ex 7: 3 **m** My signs and My wonders in
Ex 32:13 I will **m** your descendants as
Lev 26: 9 **m** you and confirm My covenant
Deut 6: 3 that you may **m** greatly as the
Deut 7:13 you and bless you and **m** you
Deut 8: 1 that you may live and **m**, and
Deut 8:13 your herds and your flocks **m**
Deut 13:17 **m** you, just as He swore to
Deut 17:16 But he shall not **m** horses for
Deut 17:16 return to Egypt to **m** horses
Deut 17:17 Neither shall he **m** wives for
Deut 17:17 nor shall he greatly **m** silver
Deut 28:63 and **m** you, so the LORD will
Deut 30: 5 **m** you more than your fathers
Deut 30:16 that you may live and **m**
1Ch 4:27 did any of their families **m**
1Ch 27:23 **m** Israel like the stars of
Job 29:18 and **m** my days as the sand
Ps 107:38 them, and they **m** greatly
Jer 30:19 I will **m** them, and they shall
Jer 33:22 so will I **m** the descendants
Ezek 36:10 I will **m** men upon you, all
Ezek 36:11 I will **m** upon you man and
Ezek 36:29 **m** it, and bring no famine upon
Ezek 36:30 I will **m** the fruit of your
Ezek 37:26 and **m** them, and I will set My
Amos 4: 4 at Gilgal **m** transgression
2Co 9:10 **m** the seed you have sown and
Heb 6:14 and multiplying I will **m** you

MULTIPLYING (*see* MULTIPLY)
Gen 22:17 in **m** I will multiply your
Acts 6: 1 number of the disciples was **m**
Heb 6:14 you, and **m** I will multiply you

MULTITUDE (*see* MULTITUDES)
Gen 16:10 shall not be counted for **m**
Gen 32:12 cannot be numbered for **m**
Gen 48: 4 make of you a **m** of people
Gen 48:16 let them grow into a **m** in the
Gen 48:19 shall become a **m** of nations
Ex 12:38 A mixed **m** went up with them
Lev 25:16 According to the **m** of years
Num 11: 4 Now the mixed **m** who were
Num 32: 1 a very great **m** of livestock
Deut 1:10 as the stars of heaven in **m**
Deut 10:22 as the stars of heaven in **m**
Deut 28:62 as the stars of heaven in **m**
Josh 11: 4 that is on the seashore in **m**
Judg 4: 7 his **m** at the River Kishon
Judg 7:12 the sand by the seashore in **m**
1Sa 13: 5 which is on the seashore in **m**
1Sa 14:16 looked, and there was the **m**
2Sa 6:19 among the whole **m** of Israel
2Sa 17:11 sand that is by the sea for **m**
1Ki 4:20 as the sand by the sea in **m**
1Ki 8: 5 be counted or numbered for **m**
1Ki 20:13 you seen all this great **m**
1Ki 20:28 this great **m** into your hand
2Ki 7:13 **m** of Israel that are left in
2Ki 7:13 may become like all the **m** of
2Ki 19:23 By the **m** of my chariots I
2Ki 25:11 with the rest of the **m**
2Ch 1: 9 the dust of the earth in **m**
2Ch 5: 6 be counted or numbered for **m**
2Ch 13: 8 and you are a great **m**, and with
2Ch 14:11 name we go against this **m**
2Ch 20: 2 A great **m** is coming against
2Ch 20:12 **m** that is coming against us
2Ch 20:15 because of this great **m**, for
2Ch 20:24 they looked toward the **m**
2Ch 28: 5 a great **m** of them as captives
2Ch 30:18 For a **m** of the people, many
2Ch 32: 7 all the **m** that is with him
Neh 13: 3 all the mixed **m** from Israel
Esth 5:11 the **m** of his children, all
Esth 10: 3 by the **m** of his brethren,
Job 11: 2 Should not the **m** of words be
Job 31:34 because I feared the great **m**
Job 32: 7 and **m** of years should teach
Job 35: 9 Because of the **m** of
Ps 5: 7 house in the **m** of Your mercy
Ps 5:10 Cast them out in the **m** of
Ps 33:16 is saved by the **m** of an army
Ps 42: 4 For I used to go with the **m**
Ps 42: 4 With a **m** that kept a pilgrim
Ps 49: 6 And boast in the **m** of their
Ps 51: 1 According to the **m** of Your
Ps 69:13 in the **m** of Your mercy, Hear
Ps 69:16 the **m** of Your tender mercies
Ps 94:19 In the **m** of my anxieties
Ps 97: 1 Let the **m** of isles be glad
Ps 106: 7 the **m** of Your mercies, But
Ps 106:45 to the **m** of His mercies
Ps 109:30 I will praise Him among the **m**
Prov 10:19 In the **m** of words sin is not
Prov 11:14 but in the **m** of counselors
Prov 14:28 In a **m** of people is a king's
Prov 15:22 but in the **m** of counselors
Prov 20:15 a **m** of rubies, but the lips
Prov 24: 6 in a **m** of counselors there is
Eccl 5: 7 For in the **m** of dreams and
Is 1:11 To what purpose is the **m** of
Is 5:13 their **m** dried up with thirst
Is 5:14 their glory and their **m** and
Is 13: 4 The noise of a **m** in the
Is 16:14 with all that great **m**, and the
Is 17:12 Woe to the **m** of many people
Is 29: 5 Moreover the **m** of your foes
Is 29: 5 the **m** of the terrible ones
Is 29: 7 The **m** of all the nations who
Is 29: 8 so the **m** of all the nations
Is 31: 4 a **m** of shepherds is summoned
Is 37:24 By the **m** of my chariots I
Is 47: 9 of the **m** of your sorceries
Is 47:12 the **m** of your sorceries, in
Is 47:13 in the **m** of your counsels
Is 60: 6 The **m** of camels shall cover
Is 63: 7 according to the **m** of His
Jer 3:23 and from the **m** of mountains
Jer 10:13 there is a **m** of waters in the
Jer 12: 6 have called a **m** after you
Jer 25:20 all the mixed **m**, all the
Jer 25:24 **m** who dwell in the desert
Jer 30:14 for the **m** of your iniquities,
Jer 30:15 Because of the **m** of your
Jer 44:15 women who stood by, a great **m**
Jer 49:32 the **m** of their cattle for
Jer 51:16 there is a **m** of waters in the
Jer 51:42 with the **m** of its waves
Lam 1: 5 her because of the **m** of her
Lam 3:32 to the **m** of His mercies
Ezek 7:11 shall remain, none of their **m**
Ezek 7:12 for wrath is on their whole **m**
Ezek 7:13 vision concerns the whole **m**
Ezek 7:14 My wrath is on all their **m**
Ezek 14: 4 to the **m** of his idols,
Ezek 23:42 of a carefree **m** was with her
Ezek 28:18 by the **m** of your iniquities
Ezek 30:10 I will also make a **m** of Egypt
Ezek 30:15 I will cut off the **m** of No
Ezek 31: 2 king of Egypt and to his **m**
Ezek 31: 9 with a **m** of branches, so that
Ezek 31:18 This is Pharaoh and all his **m**
Ezek 32:12 I will cause your **m** to fall
Ezek 32:12 all its **m** shall be destroyed
Ezek 32:16 for Egypt, and for all her **m**
Ezek 32:18 man, wail over the **m** of Egypt
Ezek 32:24 There is Elam and all her **m**
Ezek 32:25 of the slain, with all her **m**
Ezek 32:31 be comforted over all his **m**
Ezek 32:32 sword, Pharaoh and all his **m**
Ezek 39:11 will bury Gog and all his **m**
Ezek 47: 9 be a very great **m** of fish
Dan 10: 6 words like the voice of a **m**
Dan 11:10 assemble a **m** of great forces
Dan 11:11 who shall muster a great **m**
Dan 11:11 but the **m** shall be given into
Dan 11:12 When he has taken away the **m**
Dan 11:13 muster a **m** greater than the
Hos 10: 1 According to the **m** of his
Hos 10:13 in the **m** of your mighty men
Nah 3: 3 There is a **m** of slain, a
Nah 3: 4 because of the **m** of
Zech 2: 4 because of the **m** of men and
Matt 13: 2 and the whole **m** stood on the
Matt 13:34 spoke to the **m** in parables
Matt 13:36 Then Jesus sent the **m** away
Matt 14: 5 him to death, he feared the **m**
Matt 14:14 went out He saw a great **m**
Matt 15:10 Then He called the **m** and said
Matt 15:31 So the **m** marveled when they
Matt 15:32 I have compassion on the **m**
Matt 15:33 to fill such a great **m**
Matt 15:35 He commanded the **m** to sit
Matt 15:36 the disciples gave to the **m**
Matt 15:39 And He sent away the **m**, got
Matt 17:14 when they had come to the **m**
Matt 20:29 a great **m** followed Him
Matt 20:31 Then the **m** warned them that
Matt 21: 8 a very great **m** spread their
Matt 21:26 From men,' we fear the **m**
Matt 26:47 with a great **m** with swords
Matt 27:15 to releasing to the **m** one
Matt 27:24 washed his hands before the **m**
Mark 2:13 all the **m** came to Him, and He
Mark 3: 7 And a great **m** from Galilee
Mark 3: 8 from Tyre and Sidon, a great **m**
Mark 3: 9 for Him because of the **m**,
Mark 3:20 the **m** came together again, so
Mark 3:32 a **m** was sitting around Him
Mark 4: 1 a great **m** was gathered to Him
Mark 4: 1 the whole **m** was on the land
Mark 4:36 Now when they had left the **m**
Mark 5:21 a great **m** gathered to Him
Mark 5:24 a great **m** followed Him and
Mark 5:31 You see the **m** thronging You,

Mark 6:34 He came out, saw a great **m**
Mark 6:45 while He sent the **m** away
Mark 7:14 had called all the **m** to Him
Mark 7:33 He took him aside from the **m**
Mark 8: 1 the **m** being very great and
Mark 8: 2 I have compassion on the **m**
Mark 8: 6 He commanded the **m** to sit
Mark 8: 6 and they set them before the **m**
Mark 9:14 He saw a great **m** around them
Mark 9:17 Then one from the **m** answered
Mark 10:46 His disciples and a great **m**
Mark 12:12 hold of Him, but feared the **m**
Mark 14:43 with a great **m** with swords
Mark 15: 8 Then the **m**, crying aloud,
Luke 1:10 the whole **m** of the people was
Luke 2:13 a **m** of the heavenly host
Luke 5: 1 as the **m** pressed about Him to
Luke 6:17 a great **m** of people from all
Luke 6:19 the whole **m** sought to touch
Luke 8: 4 when a great **m** had gathered
Luke 8:37 Then the whole **m** of the
Luke 8:40 that the **m** welcomed Him, for
Luke 9:12 Send the **m** away, that they
Luke 9:16 disciples to set before the **m**
Luke 9:37 that a great **m** met Him
Luke 9:38 a man from the **m** cried out
Luke 12: 1 when an innumerable **m** of
Luke 13:17 all the **m** rejoiced for all
Luke 18:36 hearing a **m** passing by, he
Luke 19:37 the whole **m** of the disciples
Luke 22: 6 them in the absence of the **m**
Luke 22:47 still speaking, behold, a **m**
Luke 23: 1 the whole **m** of them arose
Luke 23:27 And a great **m** of the people
John 5: 3 lay a great **m** of sick people
John 5:13 a **m** being in that place
John 6: 2 Then a great **m** followed Him
John 6: 5 and seeing a great **m** coming
John 12:12 The next day a great **m** that
John 21: 6 in because of the **m** of fish
Acts 2: 6 the **m** came together, and were
Acts 4:32 Now the **m** of those who
Acts 5:16 Also a **m** gathered from the
Acts 6: 2 the **m** of the disciples and
Acts 6: 5 saying pleased the whole **m**
Acts 14: 1 a great **m** both of the Jews
Acts 14: 4 But the **m** of the city was
Acts 14:14 clothes and ran in among the **m**
Acts 15:12 Then all the **m** kept silent
Acts 15:30 had gathered the **m** together
Acts 16:22 Then the **m** rose up together
Acts 17: 4 and a great **m** of the devout
Acts 19: 9 evil of the Way before the **m**
Acts 19:33 drew Alexander out of the **m**
Acts 21:34 some among the **m** cried one
Acts 21:36 For the **m** of the people
Acts 24:18 neither with a **m** nor with
Heb 11:12 as the stars of the sky in **m**
Jas 5:20 death and cover a **m** of sins
1Pe 4: 8 love will cover a **m** of sins
Rev 7: 9 a great **m** which no one could
Rev 19: 1 voice of a great **m** in heaven
Rev 19: 6 were, the voice of a great **m**

MULTITUDES (*see* MULTITUDE)
Ezek 32:20 drawing her and all her **m**
Ezek 32:26 and Tubal and all their **m**, with
Joel 3:14 **M**, **m** in the valley of decision
Matt 4:25 And great **m** followed Him
Matt 5: 1 And seeing the **m**, He went up
Matt 8: 1 great **m** followed Him
Matt 8:18 Jesus saw great **m** about Him
Matt 9: 8 Now when the **m** saw it, they
Matt 9:33 And the **m** marveled, saying,
Matt 9:36 But when He saw the **m**, He was
Matt 11: 7 say to the **m** concerning John
Matt 12:15 great **m** followed Him, and He
Matt 12:23 all the **m** were amazed and said
Matt 12:46 He was still talking to the **m**
Matt 13: 2 And great **m** were gathered
Matt 14:13 But when the **m** heard it, they
Matt 14:15 Send the **m** away, that they
Matt 14:19 Then He commanded the **m** to
Matt 14:19 the disciples gave to the **m**
Matt 14:22 while He sent the **m** away
Matt 14:23 when He had sent the **m** away
Matt 15:30 Then great **m** came to Him,
Matt 19: 2 great **m** followed Him, and He
Matt 21: 9 Then the **m** who went before
Matt 21:11 So the **m** said, This is
Matt 21:46 on Him, they feared the **m**
Matt 22:33 when the **m** heard this, they
Matt 23: 1 Then Jesus spoke to the **m**
Matt 26:55 that hour Jesus said to the **m**
Matt 27:20 elders persuaded the **m** that
Mark 6:33 But the **m** saw them departing,
Luke 3: 7 to the **m** that came out to be
Luke 5: 3 taught the **m** from the boat
Luke 5:15 great **m** came together to hear
Luke 7:24 to the **m** concerning John
Luke 8:42 He went, the **m** thronged Him
Luke 8:45 the **m** throng You and press You
Luke 9:11 But when the **m** knew it, they
Luke 11:14 and the **m** marveled
Luke 12:54 Then He also said to the **m**
Luke 14:25 And great **m** went with Him
Acts 5:14 **m** of both men and women,
Acts 8: 6 the **m** with one accord heeded
Acts 13:45 But when the Jews saw the **m**
Acts 14:13 to sacrifice with the **m**
Acts 14:18 **m** from sacrificing to them
Acts 14:19 and having persuaded the **m**
Rev 17:15 harlot sits, are peoples, **m**

MUPPIM
Gen 46:21 Gera, Naaman, Ehi, Rosh, **M**

MURDER (*see* MURDERED, MURDERER, MURDERS)
Ex 20:13 You shall not **m**
Deut 5:17 You shall not **m**
Ps 94: 6 stranger, And **m** the fatherless
Jer 7: 9 Will you steal, **m**, commit
Jer 40:14 the son of Nethaniah to **m** you
Jer 40:15 Why should he **m** you, so that
Hos 6: 9 **m** on the way to Shechem
Matt 5:21 of old, You shall not **m**,' and
Matt 19:18 You shall not **m**,' 'You shall
Mark 10:19 commit adultery,' 'Do not **m**
Mark 15: 7 they had committed **m** in the
Luke 18:20 commit adultery,' 'Do not **m**
Luke 23:19 made in the city, and for **m**
Luke 23:25 **m** had been thrown into prison
Acts 9: 1 **m** against the disciples of
Rom 1:29 full of envy, **m**, strife,
Rom 13: 9 You shall not **m**," "You
Jas 2:11 Do not **m**
Jas 2:11 commit adultery, but you do **m**
Jas 4: 2 You **m** and covet and cannot
1Jn 3:12 And why did he **m** him

MURDERED (*see* MURDER)
Judg 20: 4 of the woman who was **m**,
1Ki 21:19 Have you **m** and also taken
2Ki 11: 2 king's sons who were being **m**
2Ki 14: 5 who had **m** his father the king
2Ch 22:11 king's sons who were being **m**
2Ch 25: 3 who had **m** his father the king
Jer 41:16 of Nethaniah after he had **m**
Jer 41:18 the son of Nethaniah had **m**
Matt 23:31 of those who **m** the prophets
Matt 23:35 whom you **m** between the
Acts 5:30 you **m** by hanging on a tree
Jas 5: 6 you have **m** the just
1Jn 3:12 wicked one and **m** his brother

MURDERER (*see* MURDER, MURDERERS)
Num 35:16 so that he dies, he is a **m**
Num 35:16 the **m** shall surely be put to
Num 35:17 and he does die, he is a **m**
Num 35:17 the **m** shall surely be put to
Num 35:18 and he does die, he is a **m**
Num 35:18 the **m** shall surely be put to
Num 35:19 shall put the **m** to death
Num 35:21 put to death, for he is a **m**
Num 35:21 of blood shall put the **m** to
Num 35:30 the **m** shall be put to death
Num 35:31 of a **m** who is guilty of death
2Ki 6:32 a **m** has sent someone to take
2Ki 9:31 Zimri, **m** of your master
Job 24:14 The **m** rises with the light
Hos 9:13 out his children to the **m**
John 8:44 He was a **m** from the beginning
Acts 3:14 asked for a **m** to be granted
Acts 28: 4 No doubt this man is a **m**,
1Pe 4:15 let none of you suffer as a **m**
1Jn 3:15 hates his brother is a **m**, and
1Jn 3:15 and you know that no **m** has

MURDERERS (*see* MURDERER)
2Ki 14: 6 of the **m** he did not execute
Is 1:21 lodged in it, but now **m**
Jer 4:31 my soul is weary because of **m**
Matt 22: 7 his armies, destroyed those **m**
Acts 7:52 become the betrayers and **m**
1Ti 1: 9 **m** of fathers and **m** of mothers
Rev 21: 8 unbelieving, abominable, **m**
Rev 22:15 and sexually immoral and **m** and

MURDERS (*see* MURDER)
Ps 10: 8 places he **m** the innocent
Matt 5:21 whoever **m** will be in danger
Matt 15:19 proceed evil thoughts, **m**,
Mark 7:21 adulteries, fornications, **m**
Gal 5:21 envy, **m**, drunkenness,
Rev 9:21 did not repent of their **m** or

MURKY
Prov 25:26 the wicked is like a **m** spring

MURMUR (*see* MURMURED, MURMURERS, MURMURING)
Ex 16: 7 are we, that you **m** against us
Num 14:27 congregation who **m** against Me
Num 14:27 of Israel **m** against Me
Num 14:36 **m** against him by bringing a
Num 16:11 Aaron that you **m** against him
Num 17: 5 which they **m** against you
John 6:43 Do not **m** among yourselves
1Co 10:10 nor **m**, as some of them also

MURMURED (*see* MURMUR)
Ex 15:24 the people **m** against Moses,
Ex 16: 2 of Israel **m** against Moses
Ex 17: 3 the people **m** against Moses,
Num 14: 2 of Israel **m** against Moses
Num 14:29 **m** against Me shall fall in
Num 16:41 of Israel **m** against Moses
Deut 1:27 you **m** in your tents, and said,
Josh 9:18 **m** against the rulers
Ps 106:25 But **m** in their tents, And did
Is 29:24 and those who **m** will learn
Matt 20:11 they **m** against the landowner,
Luke 5:30 the Pharisees **m** against His
Luke 15: 2 And the Pharisees and scribes **m**
Luke 19: 7 when they saw it, they all **m**
John 6:41 The Jews then **m** against Him
John 6:61 His disciples **m** about this
1Co 10:10 as some of them also **m**, and

MURMURERS (*see* MURMUR)
Jude 16 These are **m**, complainers,

MURMURING (*see* MURMUR, MURMURINGS)
John 7:12 there was much **m** among the
John 7:32 Pharisees heard the crowd **m**
Acts 6: 1 there arose a **m** against the
Phil 2:14 Do all things without **m** and

MURMURINGS (*see* MURMURING)
Ex 16: 7 hears your **m** against the LORD
Ex 16: 8 for the LORD hears your **m**
Ex 16: 8 Your **m** are not against us but
Ex 16: 9 LORD, for He has heard your **m**
Ex 16:12 I have heard the **m** of the
Num 14:27 I have heard the **m** which the
Num 17: 5 I will rid Myself of the **m** of
Num 17:10 may put their **m** away from Me

MUSCLE (*see* MUSCLES)
Gen 32:32 do not eat the **m** that shrank
Gen 32:32 hip in the **m** that shrank

MUSCLES (*see* MUSCLE)
Job 40:16 his power is in his stomach **m**

MUSE (*see* MUSING)
Ps 143: 5 I **m** on the work of Your hands

MUSHI (*see* MUSHITES)
Ex 6:19 of Merari were Mahali and **M**
Num 3:20 Mahli and **M**
1Ch 6:19 of Merari were Mahli and **M**
1Ch 6:47 son of Mahli, the son of **M**
1Ch 23:21 of Merari were Mahli and **M**
1Ch 23:23 The sons of **M** were Mahli,
1Ch 24:26 of Merari were Mahli and **M**
1Ch 24:30 Also the sons of **M** were Mahli

MUSHITES (*see* MUSHI)
Num 3:33 and the family of the **M**
Num 26:58 Mahlites, the family of the **M**

MUSIC (*see* MUSICAL, MUSICIAN)
1Sa 18:10 David played **m** with his hand
1Sa 19: 9 was playing **m** with his hand
2Sa 6: 5 **m** before the LORD on all
2Sa 6:21 I will play **m** before the LORD
1Ch 6:32 **m** before the dwelling place
1Ch 13: 8 all Israel played **m** before
1Ch 15:16 by instruments of **m**, stringed

1Ch 15:22 instructor in charge of the **m**
1Ch 15:27 Chenaniah the **m** master with
1Ch 15:28 making **m** with stringed
1Ch 15:29 David whirling and playing **m**
1Ch 16: 5 but Asaph made **m** with cymbals
1Ch 25: 6 of their father for the **m** in
2Ch 5:13 cymbals and instruments of **m**
2Ch 7: 6 of the **m** of the LORD, which
2Ch 23:13 singers with instruments of **m**
2Ch 34:12 with instruments of **m**,
Eccl 12: 4 of **m** are brought low
Lam 5:14 and the young men from their **m**
Dan 3: 5 symphony with all kinds of **m**
Dan 3: 7 symphony with all kinds of **m**
Dan 3:10 symphony with all kinds of **m**
Dan 3:15 symphony with all kinds of **m**
Luke 15:25 near to the house, he heard **m**

MUSICAL (*see* MUSIC)
1Sa 18: 6 joy, and with **m** instruments
1Ch 16:42 and the **m** instruments of God
1Ch 23: 5 the LORD with **m** instruments
Neh 12:36 with the **m** instruments of
Eccl 2: 8 **m** instruments of all kinds
Amos 6: 5 and invent for yourselves **m**

MUSICIAN (*see* MUSIC, MUSICIANS)
2Ki 3:15 But now bring me a **m**
2Ki 3:15 happened, when the **m** played
Hab 3:19 To the Chief **M**

MUSICIANS (*see* MUSICIAN)
Dan 6:18 no **m** were brought before him
Rev 18:22 The sound of harpists, **m**,

MUSING (*see* MUSE)
Ps 39: 3 While I was **m**, the fire

MUST
Gen 17:13 your money **m** be circumcised
Gen 24: 5 **M** I take your son back to the
Gen 29:26 It **m** not be done so in our
Gen 30:16 You **m** come in to me, for I
Gen 43:11 If it **m** be so, then do this
Gen 47:29 drew near that Israel **m** die
Ex 6:11 that he **m** let the children of
Ex 7: 2 that he **m** send the children
Ex 10: 9 for we **m** hold a feast to the
Ex 10:25 You **m** also give us sacrifices
Ex 10:26 For we **m** take some of them to
Ex 10:26 we **m** serve the LORD until we
Ex 12:16 but that which everyone **m** eat
Ex 18:20 the way in which they **m** walk
Ex 18:20 walk and the work they **m** do
Ex 29:37 touches the altar **m** be holy
Ex 30:29 touches them **m** be holy
Lev 6:18 who touches them **m** be holy
Lev 6:27 touches its flesh **m** be holy
Lev 7:17 day **m** be burned with fire
Lev 10: 3 Me I **m** be regarded as holy
Lev 10: 3 the people I **m** be glorified
Lev 11:32 is done, it **m** be put in water
Lev 22:21 sheep, it **m** be perfect to be
Lev 23: 6 seven days you **m** eat
Lev 27:13 then he **m** add one-fifth to
Lev 27:19 then he **m** add one-fifth of
Num 4:31 this is what they **m** carry as
Num 4:32 by name the items he **m** carry
Num 5: 8 **m** go to the LORD for the
Num 6:21 so he **m** do according to the
Num 8:25 **m** cease performing this work
Num 9:14 he **m** do so according to the
Num 15:35 The man **m** surely be put to
Num 17:13 tabernacle of the LORD **m** die
Num 20:10 **M** we bring water for you out
Num 22:38 in my mouth, that I **m** speak
Num 23:12 **M** I not take heed to speak
Num 23:23 It now **m** be said of Jacob and
Num 23:26 the LORD speaks, that I **m** do'
Num 24:13 LORD says, that I **m** speak'
Deut 3:22 You **m** not fear them, for the
Deut 4:22 But I **m** die in this land, I
Deut 4:22 I **m** not cross over the Jordan
Deut 8: 1 you **m** be careful to observe
Deut 12:18 But you **m** eat them before the
Deut 21:16 sons, that he **m** not bestow
Deut 22: 3 you **m** not hide yourself
Deut 24: 4 husband who divorced her **m**
Deut 31: 7 for you **m** go with this people
Deut 31:14 days approach when you **m** die
Josh 3: 4 the way by which you **m** go
Josh 22:18 but that you **m** turn away
Judg 13:16 you **m** offer it to the LORD
Judg 14: 3 all my people, that you **m** go
Judg 21:17 There **m** be an inheritance for
Ruth 4: 5 you **m** also buy it from Ruth
1Sa 2:16 but you **m** give it to me now
1Sa 3: 9 He calls you, that you **m** say
1Sa 5: 7 Israel **m** not remain with us
1Sa 9:13 comes, because he **m** bless the
1Sa 14:43 So now I **m** die
2Sa 23: 3 who rules over men **m** be just
2Sa 23: 7 them **m** be armed with iron
1Ki 18:27 is sleeping and **m** be awakened
2Ki 13:17 for you **m** strike the Syrians
1Ch 17:11 when you **m** go to be with your
1Ch 22: 5 **m** be exceedingly magnificent
Ezra 10: 7 that they **m** gather at
Ezra 10:12 As you have said, so we **m** do
Neh 2: 7 that they **m** permit me to pass
Neh 2: 8 that he **m** give me timber to
Neh 13:19 charged that they **m** not be
Job 32:20 I **m** open my lips and answer
Job 34:33 You **m** choose, and not I
Job 35:14 Him, and you **m** wait for Him
Job 38:11 here your proud waves **m** stop
Ps 32: 9 Which **m** be harnessed with bit
Ps 69: 4 nothing, I still **m** restore it
Prov 6:31 found, he **m** restore sevenfold
Prov 16:10 his mouth **m** not transgress in
Prov 18:24 friends **m** himself be friendly
Eccl 2:18 because I **m** leave it to the
Eccl 2:21 yet he **m** leave his heritage
Eccl 10:10 then he **m** use more strength
Is 28:10 For precept **m** be upon precept
Is 28:28 Bread flour **m** be ground
Jer 10: 5 they **m** be carried, because
Jer 10:19 an infirmity, and I **m** bear it
Jer 15:19 but you **m** not return to them
Ezek 34:18 that you **m** tread down with
Ezek 34:18 that you **m** foul the residue
Ezek 44:27 he **m** offer his sin offering
Ezek 47: 5 water in which one **m** swim
Dan 6:26 of my kingdom men **m** tremble
Dan 10:20 now I **m** return to fight with
Matt 16:21 that He **m** go to Jerusalem
Matt 17:10 say that Elijah **m** come first
Matt 18: 7 For offenses **m** come, but woe
Matt 24: 6 these things **m** come to pass
Matt 26:54 that it **m** happen thus
Mark 2:22 But new wine **m** be put into
Mark 8:31 of Man **m** suffer many things
Mark 9:11 say that Elijah **m** come first
Mark 9:12 that He **m** suffer many things
Mark 13: 7 for such things **m** happen, but
Mark 13:10 And the gospel **m** first be
Mark 14:49 the Scriptures **m** be fulfilled
Luke 2:49 that I **m** be about My Father's
Luke 4:43 I **m** preach the kingdom of God
Luke 5:38 But new wine **m** be put into
Luke 9:22 The Son of Man **m** suffer many
Luke 13:33 I **m** journey today, tomorrow,
Luke 14:18 ground, and I **m** go and see it
Luke 17:25 But first He **m** suffer many
Luke 19: 5 for today I **m** stay at your
Luke 21: 9 for these things **m** come to
Luke 22: 7 when the Passover **m** be killed
Luke 22:37 that this which is written **m**
Luke 24: 7 saying, 'The Son of Man **m** be
Luke 24:44 you, that all things **m** be
John 3: 7 to you, 'You **m** be born again
John 3:14 even so **m** the Son of Man be
John 3:30 He **m** increase
John 3:30 but I **m** decrease
John 4:24 Him **m** worship in spirit and
John 9: 4 I **m** work the works of Him who
John 10:16 them also I **m** bring, and they
John 12:34 Son of Man **m** be lifted up'
John 20: 9 that He **m** rise again from the
Acts 1:22 us, one of these **m** become a
Acts 3:21 whom heaven **m** receive until
Acts 4:12 men by which we **m** be saved
Acts 9: 6 will be told what you **m** do
Acts 9:16 **m** suffer for My name's sake
Acts 10: 6 will tell you what you **m** do
Acts 10:15 you **m** not call common
Acts 11: 9 you **m** not call common
Acts 14:22 saying, "We **m** through many
Acts 15:24 You **m** be circumcised and keep
Acts 16:30 Sirs, what **m** I do to be saved
Acts 18:21 I **m** by all means keep this
Acts 19:21 been there, I **m** also see Rome
Acts 20:35 that you **m** support the weak
Acts 21:22 The assembly **m** certainly meet
Acts 23:11 so you **m** also bear witness at
Acts 26: 9 I myself thought I **m** do many
Acts 27:24 you **m** be brought before
Acts 27:26 we **m** run aground on a certain
Rom 13: 5 Therefore you **m** be subject
1Co 7:36 of her youth, and thus it **m** be
1Co 11:19 For there **m** also be factions
1Co 15:25 For He **m** reign till He has
1Co 15:53 **m** put on incorruption, and
1Co 15:53 and this mortal **m** put on
1Co 16: 1 of Galatia, so you **m** do also
2Co 5:10 For we **m** all appear before
2Co 8:11 but now you also **m** complete
2Co 11:30 If I **m** boast, I will boast in
Col 3: 8 But now you **m** also put off
Col 3:13 forgave you, so you also **m** do
1Ti 3: 2 A bishop then **m** be blameless
1Ti 3: 7 Moreover he **m** have a good
1Ti 3: 8 deacons **m** be reverent, not
1Ti 3:11 their wives **m** be reverent
2Ti 2: 3 You therefore **m** endure
2Ti 2: 6 The hard-working farmer **m** be
2Ti 2:24 a servant of the Lord **m** not
2Ti 4:15 You also **m** beware of him, for
Tit 1: 7 For a bishop **m** be blameless
Tit 1:11 whose mouths **m** be stopped
Heb 2: 1 Therefore we **m** give the more
Heb 4: 6 remains that some **m** enter it
Heb 4:13 Him to whom we **m** give account
Heb 9:16 there **m** also of necessity be
Heb 11: 6 to God **m** believe that He is
Heb 13:17 as those who **m** give account
2Pe 1:14 shortly I **m** put off my tent
1Jn 4:21 God **m** love his brother also
Rev 1: 1 things which **m** shortly take
Rev 4: 1 which **m** take place after this
Rev 10:11 You **m** prophesy again about
Rev 11: 5 he **m** be killed in this manner
Rev 13:10 **m** be killed with the sword
Rev 17:10 he **m** continue a short time
Rev 20: 3 he **m** be released for a little
Rev 22: 6 which **m** shortly take place

MUSTACHE
Lev 13:45 and he shall cover his **m**, and
2Sa 19:24 his feet, nor trimmed his **m**

MUSTARD
Matt 13:31 of heaven is like a **m** seed
Matt 17:20 if you have faith as a **m** seed
Mark 4:31 It is like a **m** seed which
Luke 13:19 It is like a **m** seed, which a
Luke 17: 6 If you have faith as a **m** seed

MUSTER (*see* MUSTERED)
1Ki 20:25 you shall **m** an army like the
Dan 11:11 who shall **m** a great multitude
Dan 11:13 **m** a multitude greater than

MUSTERED (*see* MUSTER)
Josh 8:10 **m** the people, and went up, he
1Ki 20:15 Then he **m** the young leaders
1Ki 20:15 and after them he **m** all the
1Ki 20:26 that Ben-Hadad **m** the Syrians
1Ki 20:27 the children of Israel were **m**
2Ki 3: 6 at that time and **m** all Israel
2Ki 25:19 who **m** the people of the land
Jer 52:25 who **m** the people of the land
Dan 11:31 And forces shall be **m** by him

MUSTERS
Is 13: 4 The LORD of hosts **m** the army

MUTE
Ex 4:11 Or who makes the **m**, the deaf,
Ps 38:13 I am like a **m** who does not
Ps 39: 2 I was **m** with silence, I held
Ps 39: 9 I was **m**, I did not open my
Ezek 3:26 mouth, so that you shall be **m**
Ezek 24:27 shall speak and no longer be **m**
Ezek 33:22 opened, and I was no longer **m**
Hab 2:18 trust in it, to make **m** idols
Matt 9:32 they brought to Him a man, **m**
Matt 9:33 was cast out, the **m** spoke
Matt 12:22 demon-possessed, blind and **m**
Matt 12:22 and **m** man both spoke and saw
Matt 15:30 those who were lame, blind, **m**
Matt 15:31 when they saw the **m** speaking
Mark 7:37 to hear and the **m** to speak
Mark 9:17 my son, who has a **m** spirit
Luke 1:20 But behold, you will be **m**
Luke 11:14 out a demon, and it was **m**

Luke 11:14 gone out, that the **m** spoke

MUTILATION
Deut 23: 1 or **m** shall not enter the
Phil 3: 2 evil workers, beware of the **m**

MUTTER (*see* MUTTERED)
Ps 115: 7 Nor do they **m** through their
Is 8:19 and wizards, who whisper and **m**

MUTTERED (*see* MUTTER)
Is 59: 3 your tongue has **m** perversity

MUTUAL
Ps 35:26 brought to **m** confusion Who
Ps 40:14 brought to **m** confusion Who
Rom 1:12 by the **m** faith both of you

MUZZLE
Deut 25: 4 You shall not **m** an ox while
Ps 39: 1 restrain my mouth with a **m**
1Co 9: 9 You shall not **m** an ox while
1Ti 5:18 You shall not **m** an ox while

MY (*see* PREFACE)

MYRA
Acts 27: 5 and Pamphylia, we came to **M**

MYRIADS
Acts 21:20 how many **m** of Jews there are

MYRRH
Gen 37:25 bearing spices, balm, and **m**
Gen 43:11 a little honey, spices and **m**
Ex 30:23 hundred shekels of liquid **m**
Esth 2:12 six months with oil of **m**, and
Ps 45: 8 garments are scented with **m**
Prov 7:17 I have perfumed my bed with **m**
Song 1:13 A bundle of **m** is my beloved
Song 3: 6 of smoke, perfumed with **m**
Song 4: 6 my way to the mountain of **m**
Song 4:14 all trees of frankincense, **m**
Song 5: 1 gathered my **m** with my spice
Song 5: 5 and my hands dripped with **m**
Song 5: 5 My fingers with liquid **m**
Song 5:13 are lilies, dripping liquid **m**
Matt 2:11 gold, frankincense, and **m**
Mark 15:23 wine mingled with **m** to drink
John 19:39 came, bringing a mixture of **m**

MYRTLE
Neh 8:15 **m** branches, palm branches, and
Is 41:19 and the acacia tree, the **m**
Is 55:13 shall come up the **m** tree
Zech 1: 8 it stood among the **m** trees in
Zech 1:10 among the **m** trees answered
Zech 1:11 who stood among the **m** trees

MYSELF (*see* PREFACE)

MYSIA
Acts 16: 7 After they had come to **M**,
Acts 16: 8 So passing by **M**, they came

MYSTERIES (*see* MYSTERY)
Matt 13:11 **m** of the kingdom of heaven
Luke 8:10 the **m** of the kingdom of God
1Co 4: 1 and stewards of the **m** of God
1Co 13: 2 prophecy, and understand all **m**
1Co 14: 2 in the spirit he speaks **m**

MYSTERIOUS (*see* MYSTERY)
Deut 30:11 it is not too **m** for you, nor

MYSTERY (*see* MYSTERIES, MYSTERIOUS)
Mark 4:11 the **m** of the kingdom of God
Rom 11:25 should be ignorant of this **m**
Rom 16:25 to the revelation of the **m**
1Co 2: 7 the wisdom of God in a **m**, the
1Co 15:51 Behold, I tell you a **m**
Eph 1: 9 known to us the **m** of His will
Eph 3: 3 He made known to me the **m** (as
Eph 3: 4 knowledge in the **m** of Christ)
Eph 3: 9 is the fellowship of the **m**
Eph 5:32 This is a great **m**, but I
Eph 6:19 known the **m** of the gospel
Col 1:26 the **m** which has been hidden
Col 1:27 of this **m** among the Gentiles
Col 2: 2 the knowledge of the **m** of God
Col 4: 3 to speak the **m** of Christ
2Th 2: 7 For the **m** of lawlessness is
1Ti 3: 9 holding the **m** of the faith
1Ti 3:16 great is the **m** of godliness
Rev 1:20 The **m** of the seven stars
Rev 10: 7 sound, the **m** of God would be
Rev 17: 5 **M**, BABYLON THE GREAT,
Rev 17: 7 tell you the **m** of the woman

N

NAAM
1Ch 4:15 were Iru, Elah, and **N**

NAAMAH (*see* NAAMATHITE)
Gen 4:22 sister of Tubal-Cain was **N**
Josh 15:41 Gederoth, Beth Dagon, **N**, and
1Ki 14:21 His mother's name was **N**, an
1Ki 14:31 His mother's name was **N**, an
2Ch 12:13 His mother's name was **N**, an

NAAMAN (*see* NAAMAN'S, NAAMITES)
Gen 46:21 Becher, Ashbel, Gera, **N**, Ehi
Num 26:40 sons of Bela were Ard and **N**
Num 26:40 of **N**, the family of the
2Ki 5: 1 Now **N**, commander of the army
2Ki 5: 4 **N** went in and told his master,
2Ki 5: 6 that I have sent **N** my servant
2Ki 5: 9 Then **N** went with his horses
2Ki 5:11 But **N** became furious, and went
2Ki 5:17 So **N** said, "Then, if not,
2Ki 5:20 has spared **N** this Syrian,
2Ki 5:21 So Gehazi pursued **N**
2Ki 5:21 When **N** saw him running after
2Ki 5:23 So **N** said, "Please, take two
2Ki 5:27 of **N** shall cling to you and
1Ch 8: 4 Abishua, **N**, Ahoah,
1Ch 8: 7 **N**, Ahijah, and Gera who forced
Luke 4:27 cleansed except **N** the Syrian

NAAMAN'S (*see* NAAMAN)
2Ki 5: 2 She waited on **N** wife

NAAMATHITE (*see* NAAMAH)
Job 2:11 the Shuhite, and Zophar the **N**
Job 11: 1 Then Zophar the **N** answered
Job 20: 1 Then Zophar the **N** answered
Job 42: 9 Shuhite and Zophar the **N** went

NAAMITES (*see* NAAMAN)
Num 26:40 Naaman, the family of the **N**

NAARAH (*see* NAARAN)
Josh 16: 7 from Janohah to Ataroth and **N**
1Ch 4: 5 had two wives, Helah and **N**
1Ch 4: 6 **N** bore him Ahuzzam, Hepher,
1Ch 4: 6 These were the sons of **N**

NAARAI
1Ch 11:37 **N** the son of Ezbai,

NAARAN (*see* NAARAH)
1Ch 7:28 to the east **N**, to the west

NABAJOTH
1Ch 1:29 firstborn of Ishmael was **N**

NABAL (*see* NABAL'S)
1Sa 25: 3 The name of the man was **N**
1Sa 25: 4 that **N** was shearing his sheep
1Sa 25: 5 Go up to Carmel, go to **N**, and
1Sa 25: 9 they spoke to **N** according to
1Sa 25:10 Then **N** answered David's
1Sa 25:19 did not tell her husband **N**
1Sa 25:25 lord regard this scoundrel **N**
1Sa 25:25 **N** is his name, and folly is
1Sa 25:26 seek harm for my lord be as **N**
1Sa 25:34 would have been left to **N**
1Sa 25:36 Then Abigail went to **N**, and
1Sa 25:37 when the wine had gone from **N**
1Sa 25:38 days, that the LORD struck **N**
1Sa 25:39 David heard that **N** was dead
1Sa 25:39 reproach from the hand of **N**
1Sa 25:39 of **N** on his own head
1Sa 30: 5 the widow of **N** the Carmelite
2Sa 2: 2 the widow of **N** the Carmelite
2Sa 3: 3 the widow of **N** the Carmelite

NABAL'S (*see* NABAL)
1Sa 25:14 told Abigail, **N** wife, saying,
1Sa 25:36 **N** heart was merry within him,
1Sa 27: 3 the Carmelitess, **N** widow

NABOTH
1Ki 21: 1 that **N** the Jezreelite had a
1Ki 21: 2 So Ahab spoke to **N**, saying
1Ki 21: 3 And **N** said to Ahab,
1Ki 21: 4 **N** the Jezreelite had spoken
1Ki 21: 6 I spoke to **N** the Jezreelite
1Ki 21: 7 vineyard of **N** the Jezreelite
1Ki 21: 8 dwelling in the city with **N**
1Ki 21: 9 seat **N** with high honor among
1Ki 21:12 and seated **N** with high honor
1Ki 21:13 against him, against **N**, in
1Ki 21:13 **N** has blasphemed God and the
1Ki 21:14 **N** has been stoned and is dead
1Ki 21:15 heard that **N** had been stoned
1Ki 21:15 vineyard of **N** the Jezreelite
1Ki 21:15 for **N** is not alive, but dead
1Ki 21:16 Ahab heard that **N** was dead
1Ki 21:16 vineyard of **N** the Jezreelite
1Ki 21:18 he is, in the vineyard of **N**
1Ki 21:19 dogs licked the blood of **N**
2Ki 9:21 property of **N** the Jezreelite
2Ki 9:25 the field of **N** the Jezreelite
2Ki 9:26 saw yesterday the blood of **N**

NACHON'S (*see* CHIDON'S)
2Sa 6: 6 they came to **N** threshingfloor

NADAB
Ex 6:23 and she bore him **N**, Abihu,
Ex 24: 1 to the LORD, you and Aaron, **N**
Ex 24: 9 Moses went up, also Aaron, **N**
Ex 28: 1 **N**, Abihu, Eleazar, and Ithamar
Lev 10: 1 Then **N** and Abihu, the sons of
Num 3: 2 **N**, the firstborn, and Abihu,
Num 3: 4 **N** and Abihu had died before
Num 26:60 were born **N** and Abihu
Num 26:61 And **N** and Abihu died when
1Ki 14:20 Then **N** his son reigned in his
1Ki 15:25 Now **N** the son of Jeroboam
1Ki 15:27 to the Philistines, while **N**
1Ki 15:31 Now the rest of the acts of **N**
1Ch 2:28 The sons of Shammai were **N**
1Ch 2:30 The sons of **N** were Seled and
1Ch 6: 3 And the sons of Aaron were **N**
1Ch 8:30 then Zur, Kish, Baal, **N**,
1Ch 9:36 then Zur, Kish, Baal, Ner, **N**
1Ch 24: 1 The sons of Aaron were **N**,
1Ch 24: 2 And **N** and Abihu died before

NAGGAI
Luke 3:25 the son of Esli, the son of **N**

NAHALAL (*see* NAHALLAL, NAHALOL)
Josh 21:35 and **N** with its common-land

NAHALIEL
Num 21:19 from Mattanah to **N**
Num 21:19 from **N** to Bamoth

NAHALLAL (*see* NAHALAL)
Josh 19:15 Included were Kattath, **N**,

NAHALOL (*see* NAHALAL)
Judg 1:30 or the inhabitants of **N**

NAHAM (*see* ISHBAH)
1Ch 4:19 wife, the sister of **N**, were

NAHAMANI
Neh 7: 7 Azariah, Raamiah, **N**

NAHARAI
2Sa 23:37 **N** the Beerothite (armorbearer
1Ch 11:39 **N** the Berothite (the

NAHASH (*see* IR-NAHASH)
1Sa 11: 1 Then **N** the Ammonite came up
1Sa 11: 1 the men of Jabesh said to **N**
1Sa 11: 2 **N** the Ammonite answered
1Sa 12:12 when you saw that **N** king of
2Sa 10: 2 to Hanun the son of **N**, as his
2Sa 17:25 to Abigail the daughter of **N**
2Sa 17:27 that Shobi the son of **N** from
1Ch 19: 1 **N** the king of the people of
1Ch 19: 2 to Hanun the son of **N**,

NAHATH (*see* TOHU)
Gen 36:13 **N**, Zerah, Shammah, and
Gen 36:17 Chief **N**, Chief Zerah, Chief
1Ch 1:37 The sons of Reuel were **N**,
1Ch 6:26 Zophai his son, **N** his son,
2Ch 31:13 Jehiel, Azaziah, **N**, Asahel,

NAHBI
Num 13:14 Naphtali, **N** the son of Vophsi

NAHOR (*see* NAHOR'S)
Gen 11:22 thirty years, and begot **N**
Gen 11:23 After he begot **N**, Serug lived
Gen 11:24 **N** lived twenty-nine years, and
Gen 11:25 Terah, **N** lived one hundred and
Gen 11:26 years, and begot Abram, **N**, and
Gen 11:27 Terah begot Abram, **N**, and
Gen 11:29 Then Abram and **N** took wives
Gen 22:20 children to your brother **N**

Gen 22:23 These eight Milcah bore to **N**
Gen 24:10 Mesopotamia, to the city of **N**
Gen 24:15 son of Milcah, the wife of **N**
Gen 24:24 son, whom she bore to **N**
Gen 29: 5 you know Laban the son of **N**
Gen 31:53 God of Abraham, the God of **N**
Josh 24: 2 of Abraham and the father of **N**
1Ch 1:26 Serug, **N**, Terah,
Luke 3:34 son of Terah, the son of **N**

NAHOR'S (*see* NAHOR)
Gen 11:29 Sarai, and the name of **N** wife
Gen 24:47 **N** son, whom Milcah bore to

NAHSHON
Ex 6:23 of Amminadab, sister of **N**
Num 1: 7 Judah, **N** the son of Amminadab
Num 2: 3 **N** the son of Amminadab shall
Num 7:12 was **N** the son of Amminadab
Num 7:17 of **N** the son of Amminadab
Num 10:14 over their army was **N** the son
Ruth 4:20 Amminadab begot **N**
Ruth 4:20 and **N** begot Salmon
1Ch 2:10 and Amminadab begot **N**,
1Ch 2:11 **N** begot Salma, and Salma begot
Matt 1: 4 Amminadab begot **N**
Matt 1: 4 and **N** begot Salmon
Luke 3:32 son of Salmon, the son of **N**

NAHUM
Nah 1: 1 the vision of **N** the Elkoshite
Luke 3:25 the son of Amos, the son of **N**

NAILED (*see* NAILS)
Col 2:14 way, having **n** it to the cross

NAILS (*see* NAILED)
Deut 21:12 shave her head and trim her **n**
1Ch 22: 3 **n** of the doors of the gates
2Ch 3: 9 The weight of the **n** was fifty
Eccl 12:11 are like well-driven **n**, given
Jer 10: 4 they fasten it with **n** and
Dan 4:33 and his **n** like birds' claws
Dan 7:19 and its **n** of bronze, which
John 20:25 His hands the print of the **n**
John 20:25 into the print of the **n**, and

NAIN
Luke 7:11 He went into a city called **N**

NAIOTH
1Sa 19:18 Samuel went and stayed in **N**
1Sa 19:19 note, David is at **N** in Ramah
1Sa 19:22 Indeed they are at **N** in Ramah
1Sa 19:23 he went there to **N** in Ramah
1Sa 19:23 until he came to **N** in Ramah
1Sa 20: 1 David fled from **N** in Ramah

NAKED (*see* NAKEDNESS)
Gen 2:25 And they were both **n**, the man
Gen 3: 7 and they knew that they were **n**
Gen 3:10 I was afraid because I was **n**
Gen 3:11 Who told you that you were **n**
1Sa 19:24 lay down **n** all that day and
2Ch 28:15 all who were **n** among them
Job 1:21 **N** I came from my mother's
Job 1:21 and **n** shall I return there
Job 22: 6 and stripped the **n** of their
Job 24: 7 They spend the night **n**,
Job 24:10 They cause the poor to go **n**
Job 26: 6 Sheol is **n** before Him, and
Eccl 5:15 **n** shall he return, to go as
Is 20: 2 And he did so, walking **n**
Is 20: 3 servant Isaiah has walked **n**
Is 20: 4 as captives, young and old, **n**
Is 58: 7 when you see the **n**, that you
Lam 4:21 drunk and make yourself **n**
Ezek 16: 7 hair grew, but you were **n**
Ezek 16:22 your youth, when you were **n**
Ezek 16:39 jewelry, and leave you **n** and
Ezek 18: 7 covered the **n** with clothing
Ezek 18:16 covered the **n** with clothing
Ezek 23:29 worked for, and leave you **n**
Hos 2: 3 Lest I strip her **n** and expose
Amos 2:16 shall flee **n** in that day,"
Mic 1: 8 howl, I will go stripped and **n**
Mic 1:11 Pass by in **n** shame, you
Matt 25:36 I was **n** and you clothed Me
Matt 25:38 stranger and take You in, or **n**
Matt 25:43 and you did not take Me in, **n**
Matt 25:44 or **n** or sick or in prison
Mark 14:51 thrown around his **n** body
Mark 14:52 cloth and fled from them **n**
Acts 19:16 they fled out of that house **n**
2Co 5: 3 we shall not be found **n**
Heb 4:13 sight, but all things are **n**
Jas 2:15 If a brother or sister is **n**
Rev 3:17 miserable, poor, blind, and **n**
Rev 16:15 his garments, lest he walk **n**
Rev 17:16 make her desolate and **n**, eat

NAKEDNESS (*see* NAKED)
Gen 9:22 saw the **n** of his father, and
Gen 9:23 covered the **n** of their father
Gen 9:23 did not see their father's **n**
Gen 42: 9 come to see the **n** of the land
Gen 42:12 come to see the **n** of the land
Ex 20:26 altar, that your **n** may not be
Ex 28:42 trousers to cover their **n**
Lev 18: 6 kin to him, to uncover his **n**
Lev 18: 7 The **n** of your father or the
Lev 18: 7 of your father or the **n** of
Lev 18: 7 you shall not uncover her **n**
Lev 18: 8 The **n** of your father's wife
Lev 18: 8 it is your father's **n**
Lev 18: 9 The **n** of your sister, the
Lev 18: 9 their **n** you shall not uncover
Lev 18:10 The **n** of your son's daughter
Lev 18:10 their **n** you shall not uncover
Lev 18:10 for theirs is your own **n**
Lev 18:11 The **n** of your father's
Lev 18:11 you shall not uncover her **n**
Lev 18:12 the **n** of your father's sister
Lev 18:13 the **n** of your mother's sister
Lev 18:14 **n** of your father's brother
Lev 18:15 the **n** of your daughter-in-law
Lev 18:15 you shall not uncover her **n**
Lev 18:16 the **n** of your brother's wife
Lev 18:16 it is your brother's **n**
Lev 18:17 not uncover the **n** of a woman
Lev 18:17 daughter, to uncover her **n**
Lev 18:18 to uncover her **n** while the
Lev 18:19 a woman to uncover her **n** as
Lev 20:11 has uncovered his father's **n**
Lev 20:17 daughter, and sees her **n**
Lev 20:17 and she sees his **n**
Lev 20:17 has uncovered his sister's **n**
Lev 20:18 sickness and uncovers her **n**
Lev 20:19 You shall not uncover the **n**
Lev 20:20 has uncovered his uncle's **n**
Lev 20:21 has uncovered his brother's **n**
Deut 28:48 in hunger, in thirst, in **n**
1Sa 20:30 the shame of your mother's **n**
Is 47: 3 Your **n** shall be uncovered,
Lam 1: 8 because they have seen her **n**
Ezek 16: 8 over you and covered your **n**
Ezek 16:36 and your **n** uncovered in your
Ezek 16:37 will uncover your **n** to them
Ezek 16:37 that they may see all your **n**
Ezek 22:10 men uncover their fathers' **n**
Ezek 23:10 They uncovered her **n**, took
Ezek 23:18 harlotry and uncovered her **n**
Ezek 23:29 The **n** of your harlotry shall
Hos 2: 9 linen, given to cover her **n**
Nah 3: 5 will show the nations your **n**
Hab 2:15 that you may look on his **n**
Rom 8:35 persecution, or famine, or **n**
2Co 11:27 fastings often, in cold and **n**
Rev 3:18 of your **n** may not be revealed

NAME (*see* NAMED, NAME'S, NAMES)
Gen 2:11 The **n** of the first is Pishon
Gen 2:13 The **n** of the second river is
Gen 2:14 The **n** of the third river is
Gen 2:19 creature, that was its **n**
Gen 3:20 Adam called his wife's **n** Eve
Gen 4:17 and called the **n** of the city
Gen 4:17 city after the **n** of his son
Gen 4:19 the **n** of one was Adah, and the
Gen 4:19 and the **n** of the second was
Gen 4:21 His brother's **n** was Jubal
Gen 4:26 to call on the **n** of the LORD
Gen 5:29 And he called his **n** Noah,
Gen 10:25 the **n** of one was Peleg, for
Gen 10:25 and his brother's **n** was Joktan
Gen 11: 4 let us make a **n** for ourselves
Gen 11: 9 Therefore its **n** is called
Gen 11:29 the **n** of Abram's wife was
Gen 11:29 the **n** of Nahor's wife, Milcah
Gen 12: 2 you and make your **n** great
Gen 12: 8 called on the **n** of the LORD
Gen 13: 4 called on the **n** of the LORD
Gen 16: 1 maidservant whose **n** was Hagar
Gen 16:11 You shall call his **n** Ishmael
Gen 16:13 Then she called the **n** of the
Gen 17: 5 shall your **n** be called Abram
Gen 17: 5 but your **n** shall be Abraham
Gen 17:15 shall not call her **n** Sarai
Gen 17:15 but Sarah shall be her **n**
Gen 17:19 and you shall call his **n** Isaac
Gen 19:22 Therefore the **n** of the city
Gen 19:37 a son and called his **n** Moab
Gen 19:38 son and called his **n** Ben-Ammi
Gen 21: 3 Abraham called the **n** of his
Gen 21:33 called on the **n** of the LORD
Gen 22:14 called the **n** of the place
Gen 22:24 whose **n** was Reumah, also bore
Gen 24:29 a brother whose **n** was Laban
Gen 25: 1 a wife, and her **n** was Keturah
Gen 25:25 so they called his **n** Esau
Gen 25:26 so his **n** was called Jacob
Gen 25:30 his **n** was called Edom
Gen 26:20 called the **n** of the well Esek
Gen 26:21 So he called its **n** Sitnah
Gen 26:22 So he called its **n** Rehoboth
Gen 26:25 called on the **n** of the LORD
Gen 26:33 Therefore the **n** of the city
Gen 28:19 he called the **n** of that place
Gen 28:19 but the **n** of that city had
Gen 29:16 the **n** of the elder was Leah,
Gen 29:16 and the **n** of the younger was
Gen 29:32 and she called his **n** Reuben
Gen 29:33 And she called his **n** Simeon
Gen 29:34 his **n** was called Levi
Gen 29:35 she called his **n** Judah
Gen 30: 6 she called his **n** Dan
Gen 30: 8 So she called his **n** Naphtali
Gen 30:11 So she called his **n** Gad
Gen 30:13 So she called his **n** Asher
Gen 30:18 So she called his **n** Issachar
Gen 30:20 So she called his **n** Zebulun
Gen 30:21 and called her **n** Dinah
Gen 30:24 So she called his **n** Joseph
Gen 30:28 **N** me your wages, and I will
Gen 31:48 Therefore its **n** was called
Gen 32: 2 he called the **n** of that place
Gen 32:27 What is your **n**
Gen 32:28 Your **n** shall no longer be
Gen 32:29 Tell me Your **n**, I pray
Gen 32:29 is it that you ask about My **n**
Gen 32:30 Jacob called the **n** of the
Gen 33:17 Therefore the **n** of the place
Gen 35: 8 So the **n** of it was called
Gen 35:10 to him, Your **n** is Jacob
Gen 35:10 your **n** shall not be called
Gen 35:10 but Israel shall be your **n**
Gen 35:10 So He called his **n** Israel
Gen 35:15 Jacob called the **n** of the
Gen 35:18 that she called his **n** Ben-Oni
Gen 36:32 and the **n** of his city was
Gen 36:35 the **n** of his city was Avith
Gen 36:39 the **n** of his city was Pau
Gen 36:39 His wife's **n** was Mehetabel,
Gen 38: 1 Adullamite whose **n** was Hirah
Gen 38: 2 Canaanite whose **n** was Shua
Gen 38: 3 a son, and he called his **n** Er
Gen 38: 4 son, and she called his **n** Onan
Gen 38: 5 a son, and called his **n** Shelah
Gen 38: 6 firstborn, and her **n** was Tamar
Gen 38:29 Therefore his **n** was called
Gen 38:30 And his **n** was called Zerah
Gen 41:45 Joseph's **n** Zaphnath-Paaneah
Gen 41:51 Joseph called the **n** of the
Gen 41:52 the **n** of the second he called
Gen 48: 6 will be called by the **n** of
Gen 48:16 let my **n** be named upon them,
Gen 48:16 the **n** of my fathers Abraham
Gen 50:11 Therefore its **n** was called
Ex 1:15 of whom the **n** of one was
Ex 1:15 and the **n** of the other Puah
Ex 2:10 So she called his **n** Moses
Ex 2:22 and he called his **n** Gershom
Ex 3:13 say to me, 'What is His **n**
Ex 3:15 This is My **n** forever, and this
Ex 5:23 to Pharaoh to speak in Your **n**
Ex 6: 3 as God Almighty, but by My **n**
Ex 9:16 that My **n** may be declared in
Ex 15: 3 the LORD is His **n**
Ex 15:23 Therefore the **n** of it was
Ex 16:31 of Israel called its **n** Manna
Ex 17: 7 So he called the **n** of the
Ex 17:15 an altar and called its **n**,
Ex 18: 3 of whom the **n** of one was
Ex 18: 4 and the **n** of the other was
Ex 20: 7 You shall not take the **n** of

Ex 20: 7 who takes His **n** in vain
Ex 20:24 My **n** I will come to you, and I
Ex 23:13 of the **n** of other gods, nor
Ex 23:21 for My **n** is in Him
Ex 28:21 each one with its own **n**
Ex 31: 2 I have called by **n** Bezaleel
Ex 33:12 have said, I know you by **n**
Ex 33:17 My sight, and I know you by **n**
Ex 33:19 I will proclaim the **n** of the
Ex 34: 5 proclaimed the **n** of the LORD
Ex 34:14 whose **n** is Jealous, is a
Ex 35:30 See, the LORD has called by **n**
Ex 39:14 each one with its own **n**
Lev 18:21 you profane the **n** of your God
Lev 19:12 not swear by My **n** falsely
Lev 19:12 you profane the **n** of your God
Lev 20: 3 and profane My holy **n**
Lev 21: 6 profane the **n** of their God
Lev 22: 2 **n** in those things which they
Lev 22:32 shall not profane My holy **n**
Lev 24:11 blasphemed the **n** of the LORD
Lev 24:11 (His mother's **n** was Shelomith
Lev 24:16 whoever blasphemes the **n** of
Lev 24:16 blasphemes the **n** of the LORD
Num 1:17 who had been mentioned by **n**
Num 4:32 by **n** the items he must carry
Num 6:27 So they shall put My **n** on the
Num 11: 3 So he called the **n** of the
Num 11:26 the **n** of one was Eldad, and
Num 11:26 and the **n** of the other Medad
Num 11:34 So he called the **n** of that
Num 17: 2 Write each man's **n** on his rod
Num 17: 3 Aaron's **n** on the rod of Levi
Num 21: 3 So the **n** of that place was
Num 25:14 Now the **n** of the Israelite
Num 25:15 the **n** of the Midianite woman
Num 26:46 And the **n** of the daughter of
Num 26:59 The **n** of Amram's wife was
Num 27: 4 Why should the **n** of our
Num 32:42 it Nobah, after his own **n**
Deut 3:14 called Bashan after his own **n**
Deut 5:11 the **n** of the LORD your God in
Deut 5:11 who takes His **n** in vain
Deut 6:13 and shall take oaths in His **n**
Deut 7:24 their **n** from under heaven
Deut 9:14 blot out their **n** from under
Deut 10: 8 to Him and to bless in His **n**
Deut 10:20 fast, and take oaths in His **n**
Deut 12: 5 tribes, to put His **n** for His
Deut 12:11 chooses to make His **n** abide
Deut 12:21 put His **n** is too far from you
Deut 14:23 chooses to make His **n** abide
Deut 14:24 put His **n** is too far from you
Deut 16: 2 the LORD chooses to put His **n**
Deut 16: 6 chooses to make His **n** abide
Deut 16:11 chooses to make His **n** abide
Deut 18: 5 minister in the **n** of the LORD
Deut 18: 7 then he may serve in the **n** of
Deut 18:19 which He speaks in My **n**, I
Deut 18:20 to speak a word in My **n**,
Deut 18:20 speaks in the **n** of other gods
Deut 18:22 speaks in the **n** of the LORD
Deut 21: 5 to bless in the **n** of the LORD
Deut 22:14 and brings a bad **n** on her
Deut 22:19 he has brought a bad **n** on a
Deut 25: 6 to the **n** of his dead brother
Deut 25: 6 that his **n** may not be blotted
Deut 25: 7 refuses to raise up a **n** to
Deut 25:10 And his **n** shall be called in
Deut 26: 2 chooses to make His **n** abide
Deut 26:19 He has made, in praise, in **n**
Deut 28:10 called by the **n** of the LORD
Deut 28:58 this glorious and awesome **n**
Deut 29:20 out his **n** from under heaven
Deut 32: 3 I proclaim the **n** of the LORD
Josh 5: 9 Therefore the **n** of the
Josh 7: 9 cut off our **n** from the earth
Josh 7: 9 will You do for Your great **n**
Josh 7:26 Therefore the **n** of that place
Josh 9: 9 because of the **n** of the LORD
Josh 14:15 the **n** of Hebron formerly was
Josh 15:15 of Debir (formerly the **n** of
Josh 19:47 Dan, after the **n** of Dan their
Josh 21: 9 which are mentioned here by **n**
Josh 23: 7 of the **n** of their gods, nor
Judg 1:10 (Now the **n** of Hebron was
Judg 1:11 (The **n** of Debir was formerly
Judg 1:17 So the **n** of the city was
Judg 1:23 (The **n** of the city was
Judg 1:26 a city, and called its **n** Luz
Judg 1:26 which is its **n** to this day
Judg 2: 5 the **n** of that place Bochim
Judg 8:31 whose **n** he called Abimelech
Judg 13: 2 Danites, whose **n** was Manoah
Judg 13: 6 and He did not tell me His **n**
Judg 13:17 What is Your **n**, that when
Judg 13:18 Why do you ask My **n**, seeing
Judg 13:24 a son and called his **n** Samson
Judg 15:19 he called its **n** En Hakkore
Judg 16: 4 of Sorek, whose **n** was Delilah
Judg 17: 1 of Ephraim, whose **n** was Micah
Judg 18:29 called the **n** of the city Dan
Judg 18:29 Dan, after the **n** of Dan their
Judg 18:29 the **n** of the city formerly
Ruth 1: 2 The **n** of the man was
Ruth 1: 2 the **n** of his wife was Naomi,
Ruth 1: 4 the **n** of the one was Orpah,
Ruth 1: 4 and the **n** of the other Ruth
Ruth 2: 1 his **n** was Boaz
Ruth 2:19 The man's **n** with whom I
Ruth 4: 5 to raise up the **n** of the dead
Ruth 4:10 to raise up the **n** of the dead
Ruth 4:10 that the **n** of the dead may
Ruth 4:14 may his **n** be famous in Israel
Ruth 4:17 neighbor women gave him a **n**
Ruth 4:17 And they called his **n** Obed
1Sa 1: 1 his **n** was Elkanah the son of
1Sa 1: 2 the **n** of one was Hannah, and
1Sa 1: 2 the **n** of the other Peninnah
1Sa 1:20 a son, and called his **n** Samuel
1Sa 7:12 and called its **n** Ebenezer
1Sa 8: 2 The **n** of his firstborn was
1Sa 8: 2 the **n** of his second, Abijah
1Sa 9: 1 **n** was Kish the son of Abiel
1Sa 9: 2 he had a son whose **n** was Saul
1Sa 14: 4 the **n** of one was Bozez, and
1Sa 14: 4 and the **n** of the other Seneh
1Sa 14:49 the **n** of the firstborn Merab,
1Sa 14:49 the **n** of the younger Michal
1Sa 14:50 The **n** of Saul's wife was
1Sa 14:50 the **n** of the commander of his
1Sa 16: 3 for Me the one I **n** to you
1Sa 17:12 whose **n** was Jesse, and who had
1Sa 17:23 of Gath, Goliath by **n**, coming
1Sa 17:45 in the **n** of the LORD of hosts
1Sa 18:30 so that his **n** became highly
1Sa 20:42 sworn in the **n** of the LORD
1Sa 21: 7 his **n** was Doeg, an Edomite,
1Sa 24:21 my **n** from my father's house
1Sa 25: 3 The **n** of the man was Nabal,
1Sa 25: 3 the **n** of his wife Abigail
1Sa 25: 5 Nabal, and greet him in my **n**
1Sa 25: 9 these words in the **n** of David
1Sa 25:25 For as his **n** is, so is he
1Sa 25:25 Nabal is his **n**, and folly is
1Sa 28: 8 me the one I shall **n** to you
2Sa 3: 7 whose **n** was Rizpah, the
2Sa 4: 2 The **n** of one was Baanah and
2Sa 4: 2 the **n** of the other Rechab,
2Sa 4: 4 So his **n** was Mephibosheth
2Sa 5:20 Therefore he called the **n**
2Sa 6: 2 whose **n** is called by the **N**
2Sa 6: 8 he called the **n** of the place
2Sa 6:18 in the **n** of the LORD of hosts
2Sa 7: 9 and have made you a great **n**
2Sa 7: 9 like the **n** of the great men
2Sa 7:13 shall build a house for My **n**
2Sa 7:23 to make for Himself a **n**
2Sa 7:26 So let Your **n** be magnified
2Sa 8:13 David made himself a **n** when
2Sa 9: 2 of Saul whose **n** was Ziba
2Sa 9:12 a young son whose **n** was Micha
2Sa 12:24 and he called his **n** Solomon
2Sa 12:25 so he called his **n** Jedidiah
2Sa 12:28 and it be called after my **n**
2Sa 13: 1 sister, whose **n** was Tamar
2Sa 13: 3 **n** was Jonadab the son of
2Sa 14: 7 **n** nor remnant on the earth
2Sa 14:27 daughter whose **n** was Tamar
2Sa 16: 5 whose **n** was Shimei the son of
2Sa 17:25 of a man whose **n** was Jithra
2Sa 18:18 to keep my **n** in remembrance
2Sa 18:18 the pillar after his own **n**
2Sa 20: 1 whose **n** was Sheba the son of
2Sa 20:21 Sheba the son of Bichri by **n**
2Sa 22:50 and sing praises to Your **n**
2Sa 23:18 won a **n** among these three
2Sa 23:22 won a **n** among three mighty
1Ki 1:47 May God make the **n** of
1Ki 1:47 of Solomon better than your **n**
1Ki 3: 2 the **n** of the LORD until those
1Ki 5: 3 not build a house for the **n**
1Ki 5: 5 for the **n** of the LORD my God
1Ki 5: 5 build the house for My **n**
1Ki 7:21 right and called its **n** Jachin
1Ki 7:21 the left and called its **n** Boaz
1Ki 8:16 that My **n** might be there
1Ki 8:17 to build a house for the **n** of
1Ki 8:18 to build a house for My **n**
1Ki 8:19 build the house for My **n**
1Ki 8:20 **n** of the LORD God of Israel
1Ki 8:29 My **n** shall be there,' that
1Ki 8:33 back to You and confess Your **n**
1Ki 8:35 this place and confess Your **n**
1Ki 8:42 will hear of Your great **n**
1Ki 8:43 of the earth may know Your **n**
1Ki 8:43 built is called by Your **n**
1Ki 8:44 which I have built for Your **n**
1Ki 8:48 which I have built for Your **n**
1Ki 9: 3 to put My **n** there forever
1Ki 9: 7 I have sanctified for My **n** I
1Ki 10: 1 concerning the **n** of the LORD
1Ki 11:26 whose mother's **n** was Zeruah
1Ki 11:36 for Myself, to put My **n** there
1Ki 13: 2 Behold, a child, Josiah by **n**
1Ki 14:21 of Israel, to put His **n** there
1Ki 14:21 His mother's **n** was Naamah
1Ki 14:31 His mother's **n** was Naamah
1Ki 15: 2 His mother's **n** was Maachah
1Ki 15:10 **n** was Maachah the
1Ki 16:24 and called the **n** of the city
1Ki 16:24 after the **n** of Shemer, owner
1Ki 18:24 call on the **n** of your gods
1Ki 18:24 call on the **n** of the LORD
1Ki 18:25 and call on the **n** of your god
1Ki 18:26 called on the **n** of Baal from
1Ki 18:31 Israel shall be your **n**
1Ki 18:32 an altar in the **n** of the LORD
1Ki 21: 8 she wrote letters in Ahab's **n**
1Ki 22:16 truth in the **n** of the LORD
1Ki 22:42 His mother's **n** was Azubah the
2Ki 2:24 on them in the **n** of the LORD
2Ki 5:11 call on the **n** of the LORD his
2Ki 8:26 His mother's **n** was Athaliah
2Ki 12: 1 His mother's **n** was Zibiah of
2Ki 14: 2 His mother's **n** was Jehoaddan
2Ki 14: 7 called its **n** Joktheel to this
2Ki 14:27 that He would blot out the **n**
2Ki 15: 2 His mother's **n** was Jecholiah
2Ki 15:33 His mother's **n** was Jerusha
2Ki 18: 2 His mother's **n** was Abi the
2Ki 21: 1 His mother's **n** was Hephzibah
2Ki 21: 4 In Jerusalem I will put My **n**
2Ki 21: 7 I will put My **n** forever
2Ki 21:19 His mother's **n** was
2Ki 22: 1 His mother's **n** was Jedidah
2Ki 23:27 I said, 'My **n** shall be there
2Ki 23:31 His mother's **n** was Hamutal
2Ki 23:34 changed his **n** to Jehoiakim
2Ki 23:36 His mother's **n** was Zebudah
2Ki 24: 8 His mother's **n** was Nehushta
2Ki 24:17 and changed his **n** to Zedekiah
2Ki 24:18 His mother's **n** was Hamutal
1Ch 1:19 the **n** of one was Peleg, for
1Ch 1:19 and his brother's **n** was Joktan
1Ch 1:43 and the **n** of his city was
1Ch 1:46 The **n** of his city was Avith
1Ch 1:50 the **n** of his city was Pai
1Ch 1:50 His wife's **n** was Mehetabel
1Ch 2:26 wife, whose **n** was Atarah
1Ch 2:29 the **n** of the wife of Abishur
1Ch 2:34 servant whose **n** was Jarha
1Ch 4: 3 the **n** of their sister was
1Ch 4: 9 his mother called his **n** Jabez
1Ch 4:38 these mentioned by **n** were
1Ch 4:41 These recorded by **n** came in
1Ch 7:15 Shuppim, whose **n** was Maachah
1Ch 7:15 The **n** of Gilead's grandson
1Ch 7:16 and she called his **n** Peresh
1Ch 7:16 The **n** of his brother was
1Ch 7:23 and he called his **n** Beriah
1Ch 8:29 whose wife's **n** was Maacah
1Ch 9:35 whose wife's **n** was Maacah
1Ch 11:20 won a **n** among these three
1Ch 11:24 won a **n** among three mighty
1Ch 12:31 were designated by **n** to come
1Ch 13: 6 where His **n** is proclaimed
1Ch 14:11 **n** of that place Baal Perazim
1Ch 16: 2 people in the **n** of the LORD
1Ch 16: 8 Call upon His **n**

1Ch 16:10 Glory in His holy **n**
1Ch 16:29 the LORD the glory due His **n**
1Ch 16:35 to give thanks to Your holy **n**
1Ch 16:41 who were designated by **n**
1Ch 17: 8 made you a **n** like the **n** of
1Ch 17:21 for Yourself a **n** by great
1Ch 17:24 that Your **n** may be magnified
1Ch 21:19 spoken in the **n** of the LORD
1Ch 22: 7 to the **n** of the LORD my God
1Ch 22: 8 not build a house for My **n**
1Ch 22: 9 His **n** shall be Solomon, for I
1Ch 22:10 shall build a house for My **n**
1Ch 22:19 built for the **n** of the LORD
1Ch 23:13 the blessing in His **n** forever
1Ch 28: 3 not build a house for My **n**
1Ch 29:13 You and praise Your glorious **n**
1Ch 29:16 Your holy **n** is from Your hand
2Ch 2: 1 temple for the **n** of the LORD
2Ch 2: 4 for the **n** of the LORD my God
2Ch 3:17 he called the **n** of the one on
2Ch 3:17 the **n** of the one on the left
2Ch 6: 5 that My **n** might be there, nor
2Ch 6: 6 that My **n** may be there
2Ch 6: 7 **n** of the LORD God of Israel
2Ch 6: 8 to build a temple for My **n**
2Ch 6: 9 build the temple for My **n**
2Ch 6:10 built the temple for the **n** of
2Ch 6:20 You said You would put Your **n**
2Ch 6:24 and return and confess Your **n**
2Ch 6:26 this place and confess Your **n**
2Ch 6:32 for the sake of Your great **n**
2Ch 6:33 of the earth may know Your **n**
2Ch 6:33 built is called by Your **n**
2Ch 6:34 which I have built for Your **n**
2Ch 6:38 which I have built for Your **n**
2Ch 7:14 My **n** will humble themselves
2Ch 7:16 house, that My **n** may be there
2Ch 7:20 I have sanctified for My **n** I
2Ch 12:13 of Israel, to put His **n** there
2Ch 12:13 His mother's **n** was Naamah
2Ch 13: 2 His mother's **n** was Michaiah
2Ch 14:11 in Your **n** we go against this
2Ch 18:15 truth in the **n** of the LORD
2Ch 20: 8 a sanctuary in it for Your **n**
2Ch 20: 9 for Your **n** is in this temple)
2Ch 20:26 therefore the **n** of that place
2Ch 20:31 His mother's **n** was Azubah the
2Ch 22: 2 His mother's **n** was Athaliah
2Ch 24: 1 His mother's **n** was Zibiah of
2Ch 25: 1 His mother's **n** was Jehoaddan
2Ch 26: 3 His mother's **n** was Jecholiah
2Ch 27: 1 His mother's **n** was Jerushah
2Ch 28: 9 was there, whose **n** was Oded
2Ch 28:15 were designated by **n** rose up
2Ch 29: 1 His mother's **n** was Abijah the
2Ch 31:19 **n** to distribute portions to
2Ch 33: 4 shall My **n** be forever
2Ch 33: 7 I will put My **n** forever
2Ch 33:18 who spoke to him in the **n** of
2Ch 36: 4 changed his **n** to Jehoiakim
Ezra 2:61 and was called by their **n**
Ezra 5: 1 in the **n** of the God of Israel
Ezra 6:12 **n** to dwell there destroy any
Ezra 8:20 of them were designated by **n**
Ezra 10:16 households, each of them by **n**
Neh 1: 9 chosen as a dwelling for My **n**
Neh 1:11 who desire to fear Your **n**
Neh 7:63 and was called by their **n**
Neh 9: 5 Blessed be Your glorious **n**
Neh 9: 7 and gave him the **n** Abraham
Neh 9:10 So You made a **n** for Yourself
Esth 2: 5 **n** was Mordecai the son of
Esth 2:14 in her and called for her by **n**
Esth 2:22 the king in Mordecai's **n**
Esth 3:12 In the **n** of King Ahasuerus it
Esth 8: 8 you please, in the king's **n**
Esth 8: 8 is written in the king's **n**
Esth 8:10 he wrote in the **n** of King
Esth 9:26 days Purim, after the **n** Pur
Job 1: 1 land of Uz, whose **n** was Job
Job 1:21 blessed be the **n** of the LORD
Job 18:17 and he has no **n** among the
Job 42:14 he called the **n** of the first
Job 42:14 the **n** of the second Keziah,
Job 42:14 Keziah, and the **n** of the third
Ps 5:11 love Your **n** Be joyful in You
Ps 7:17 the **n** of the LORD Most High
Ps 8: 1 is Your **n** in all the earth
Ps 8: 9 is Your **n** in all the earth
Ps 9: 2 I will sing praise to Your **n**
Ps 9: 5 blotted out their **n** forever
Ps 9:10 those who know Your **n** will
Ps 18:49 And sing praises to Your **n**
Ps 20: 1 May the **n** of the God of Jacob
Ps 20: 5 in the **n** of our God we will
Ps 20: 7 the **n** of the LORD our God
Ps 22:22 declare Your **n** to My brethren
Ps 29: 2 LORD the glory due to His **n**
Ps 30: 4 the remembrance of His holy **n**
Ps 33:21 we have trusted in His holy **n**
Ps 34: 3 let us exalt His **n** together
Ps 41: 5 will he die, and his **n** perish
Ps 44: 5 Through Your **n** we will
Ps 44: 8 And praise Your **n** forever
Ps 44:20 forgotten the **n** of our God
Ps 45:17 I will make Your **n** to be
Ps 48:10 According to Your **n**, O God,
Ps 52: 9 saints I will wait on Your **n**
Ps 54: 1 Save me, O God, by Your **n**
Ps 54: 6 I will praise Your **n**, O LORD,
Ps 61: 5 of those who fear Your **n**
Ps 61: 8 sing praise to Your **n** forever
Ps 63: 4 lift up my hands in Your **n**
Ps 66: 2 Sing out the honor of His **n**
Ps 66: 4 shall sing praises to Your **n**
Ps 68: 4 to God, sing praises to His **n**
Ps 68: 4 on the clouds, By His **n** YAH
Ps 69:30 I will praise the **n** of God
Ps 69:36 love His **n** shall dwell in it
Ps 72:17 His **n** shall endure forever
Ps 72:17 His **n** shall continue as long
Ps 72:19 be His glorious **n** forever
Ps 74: 7 place of Your **n** to the ground
Ps 74:10 blaspheme Your **n** forever
Ps 74:18 people has blasphemed Your **n**
Ps 74:21 poor and needy praise Your **n**
Ps 75: 1 declare that Your **n** is near
Ps 76: 1 His **n** is great in Israel
Ps 79: 6 that do not call on Your **n**
Ps 79: 9 For the glory of Your **n**
Ps 80:18 and we will call upon Your **n**
Ps 83: 4 That the **n** of Israel may be
Ps 83:16 That they may seek Your **n**
Ps 83:18 whose **n** alone is the LORD,
Ps 86: 9 Lord, And shall glorify Your **n**
Ps 86:11 Unite my heart to fear Your **n**
Ps 86:12 glorify Your **n** forevermore
Ps 89:12 and Hermon rejoice in Your **n**
Ps 89:16 In Your **n** they rejoice all
Ps 89:24 in My **n** his horn shall be
Ps 91:14 because he has known My **n**
Ps 92: 1 And to sing praises to Your **n**
Ps 96: 2 Sing to the LORD, bless His **n**
Ps 96: 8 the LORD the glory due His **n**
Ps 97:12 the remembrance of His holy **n**
Ps 99: 3 Your great and awesome **n**
Ps 99: 6 those who called upon His **n**
Ps 100: 4 to Him, and bless His **n**
Ps 102:12 of Your **n** to all generations
Ps 102:15 shall fear the **n** of the LORD
Ps 102:21 To declare the **n** of the LORD
Ps 103: 1 within me, bless His holy **n**
Ps 105: 1 Call upon His **n**
Ps 105: 3 Glory in His holy **n**
Ps 106:47 To give thanks to Your holy **n**
Ps 109:13 let their **n** be blotted out
Ps 111: 9 Holy and awesome is His **n**
Ps 113: 1 Praise the **n** of the LORD
Ps 113: 2 Blessed be the **n** of the LORD
Ps 113: 3 The LORD's **n** is to be praised
Ps 115: 1 us, But to Your **n** give glory
Ps 116: 4 called upon the **n** of the LORD
Ps 116:13 call upon the **n** of the LORD
Ps 116:17 call upon the **n** of the LORD
Ps 118:10 But in the **n** of the LORD I
Ps 118:11 But in the **n** of the LORD I
Ps 118:12 For in the **n** of the LORD I
Ps 118:26 comes in the **n** of the LORD
Ps 119:55 remember Your **n** in the night
Ps 119:132 toward those who love Your **n**
Ps 122: 4 thanks to the **n** of the LORD
Ps 124: 8 help is in the **n** of the LORD
Ps 129: 8 you in the **n** of the LORD
Ps 135: 1 Praise the **n** of the LORD
Ps 135: 3 Sing praises to His **n**, for it
Ps 135:13 Your **n**, O LORD, endures
Ps 138: 2 And praise Your **n** For Your
Ps 138: 2 Your word above all Your **n**
Ps 139:20 enemies take Your **n** in vain
Ps 140:13 shall give thanks to Your **n**
Ps 142: 7 That I may praise Your **n**
Ps 145: 1 I will bless Your **n** forever
Ps 145: 2 I will praise Your **n** forever
Ps 145:21 bless His holy **n** Forever and
Ps 147: 4 He calls them all by **n**
Ps 148: 5 them praise the **n** of the LORD
Ps 148:13 them praise the **n** of the LORD
Ps 148:13 For His **n** alone is exalted
Ps 149: 3 praise His **n** with the dance
Prov 10: 7 but the **n** of the wicked will
Prov 18:10 The **n** of the LORD is a strong
Prov 21:24 Scoffer" is his **n**
Prov 22: 1 A good **n** is to be chosen
Prov 30: 4 What is His **n**
Prov 30: 4 and what is His Son's **n**
Prov 30: 9 and profane the **n** of my God
Eccl 6: 4 and its **n** is covered with
Eccl 7: 1 A good **n** is better than
Song 1: 3 your **n** is ointment poured
Is 4: 1 let us be called by your **n**
Is 7:14 and shall call His **n** Immanuel
Is 8: 3 LORD said to me, Call his **n**
Is 9: 6 And His **n** will be called
Is 12: 4 the LORD, call upon His **n**
Is 12: 4 mention that His **n** is exalted
Is 14:22 And cut off from Babylon the **n**
Is 18: 7 to the place of the **n** of the
Is 24:15 the **n** of the LORD God of
Is 25: 1 You, I will praise Your **n**
Is 26: 8 of our soul is for Your **n**
Is 26:13 we make mention of Your **n**
Is 29:23 midst, they will hallow My **n**
Is 30:27 the **n** of the LORD comes from
Is 40:26 He calls them all by **n**, by
Is 41:25 the sun he shall call on My **n**
Is 42: 8 I am the LORD, that is My **n**
Is 43: 1 I have called you by your **n**
Is 43: 7 who is called by My **n**, whom I
Is 44: 5 himself by the **n** of Jacob
Is 44: 5 and **n** himself by the **n** of
Is 45: 3 LORD, Who call you by your **n**
Is 45: 4 even called you by your **n**
Is 47: 4 the LORD of hosts is His **n**
Is 48: 1 are called by the **n** of Israel
Is 48: 1 swear by the **n** of the LORD
Is 48: 2 the LORD of hosts is His **n**
Is 48:11 how should My **n** be profaned
Is 48:19 his **n** would not have been cut
Is 49: 1 He has made mention of My **n**
Is 50:10 trust in the **n** of the LORD
Is 51:15 the LORD of hosts is His **n**
Is 52: 5 And My **n** is blasphemed
Is 52: 6 My people shall know My **n**
Is 54: 5 the LORD of hosts is His **n**
Is 55:13 shall be to the LORD for a **n**
Is 56: 5 a **n** better than that of sons
Is 56: 5 give them an everlasting **n**
Is 56: 6 and to love the **n** of the LORD
Is 57:15 eternity, whose **n** is Holy
Is 59:19 So shall they fear the **n** of
Is 60: 9 to the **n** of the LORD your God
Is 62: 2 shall be called by a new **n**
Is 62: 2 the mouth of the LORD will **n**
Is 63:12 for Himself an everlasting **n**
Is 63:14 to make Yourself a glorious **n**
Is 63:16 from Everlasting is Your **n**
Is 63:19 were never called by Your **n**
Is 64: 2 to make Your **n** known to Your
Is 64: 7 is no one who calls on Your **n**
Is 65: 1 that was not called by My **n**
Is 65:15 You shall leave your **n** as a
Is 65:15 His servants by another **n**
Is 66:22 descendants and your **n** remain
Jer 3:17 it, to the **n** of the LORD, to
Jer 7:10 house which is called by My **n**
Jer 7:11 which is called by My **n**,
Jer 7:12 where I set My **n** at the first
Jer 7:14 house which is called by My **n**
Jer 7:30 house which is called by My **n**
Jer 10: 6 Your **n** is great in might),
Jer 10:16 the LORD of hosts is His **n**
Jer 10:25 who do not call on Your **n**
Jer 11:16 The LORD called your **n**, green
Jer 11:19 that his **n** may be remembered
Jer 11:21 prophesy in the **n** of the LORD
Jer 12:16 My people, to swear by My **n**
Jer 14: 9 and we are called by Your **n**
Jer 14:14 prophesy lies in My **n**
Jer 14:15 prophets who prophesy in My **n**
Jer 15:16 for I am called by Your **n**

Jer 16:21 know that My **n** is the LORD
Jer 20: 3 has not called your **n** Pashhur
Jer 20: 9 nor speak anymore in His **n**
Jer 23: 6 now this is His **n** by which He
Jer 23:25 who prophesy lies in My **n**
Jer 23:27 My **n** by their dreams which
Jer 23:27 fathers forgot My **n** for Baal
Jer 25:29 city which is called by My **n**
Jer 26: 9 in the **n** of the LORD, saying,
Jer 26:16 in the **n** of the LORD our God
Jer 26:20 in the **n** of the LORD, Urijah
Jer 27:15 they prophesy a lie in My **n**
Jer 29: 9 falsely to you in My **n**
Jer 29:21 prophesy a lie to you in My **n**
Jer 29:23 spoken lying words in My **n**
Jer 29:25 **n** to all the people who are
Jer 31:35 (the LORD of hosts is His **n**)
Jer 32:18 whose **n** is the LORD of hosts
Jer 32:20 and You have made Yourself a **n**
Jer 32:34 house which is called by My **n**
Jer 33: 2 it (the LORD is His **n**)
Jer 33: 9 it shall be to Me a **n** of joy
Jer 33:16 this is the **n** by which she
Jer 34:15 house which is called by My **n**
Jer 34:16 around and profaned My **n**, and
Jer 37:13 whose **n** was Irijah the son of
Jer 44:16 to us in the **n** of the LORD
Jer 44:26 I have sworn by My great **n**
Jer 44:26 that My **n** shall no more be
Jer 46:18 whose **n** is the LORD of hosts,
Jer 48:15 Whose **n** is the LORD of hosts
Jer 48:17 and all you who know his **n**
Jer 50:34 the LORD of hosts is His **n**
Jer 51:19 The LORD of hosts is His **n**
Jer 51:57 Whose **n** is the LORD of hosts
Jer 52: 1 His mother's **n** was Hamutal
Lam 3:55 I called on Your **n**, O LORD,
Ezek 20:29 So its **n** is called Bamah to
Ezek 20:39 but profane My holy **n** no more
Ezek 24: 2 write down the **n** of the day
Ezek 36:20 went, they profaned My holy **n**
Ezek 36:21 I had concern for My holy **n**
Ezek 36:23 And I will sanctify My great **n**
Ezek 39: 7 So I will make My holy **n**
Ezek 39: 7 profane My holy **n** anymore
Ezek 39:16 The **n** of the city will also
Ezek 39:25 will be jealous for My holy **n**
Ezek 43: 7 of Israel defile My holy **n**
Ezek 43: 8 they defiled My holy **n** by the
Ezek 48:35 the **n** of the city from that
Dan 1: 7 Daniel the **n** Belteshazzar
Dan 2:20 be the **n** of God forever and
Dan 2:26 whose **n** was Belteshazzar,
Dan 4: 8 me (his **n** is Belteshazzar
Dan 4: 8 according to the **n** of my god
Dan 4:19 whose **n** was Belteshazzar, was
Dan 9: 6 spoke in Your **n** to our kings
Dan 9:15 hand, and made Yourself a **n**
Dan 9:18 which is called by Your **n**
Dan 9:19 people are called by Your **n**
Dan 10: 1 to Daniel, whose **n** was called
Hos 1: 4 Call his **n** Jezreel, for in a
Hos 1: 6 Call her **n** Lo-Ruhamah, for I
Hos 1: 9 Call his **n** Lo-Ammi, for you
Hos 2:17 remembered by their **n** no more
Joel 2:26 praise the **n** of the LORD your
Joel 2:32 that whoever calls on the **n**
Amos 2: 7 girl, to defile My holy **n**
Amos 4:13 LORD God of hosts is His **n**
Amos 5: 8 the LORD is His **n**
Amos 5:27 whose **n** is the God of hosts
Amos 6:10 not mention the **n** of the LORD
Amos 9: 6 the LORD is His **n**
Amos 9:12 who are called by My **n**,"
Mic 4: 5 walk each in the **n** of his god
Mic 4: 5 but we will walk in the **n** of
Mic 5: 4 of the **n** of the LORD His God
Mic 6: 9 wisdom shall see Your **n**
Nah 1:14 Your **n** shall be perpetuated
Zeph 3: 9 may call on the **n** of the LORD
Zeph 3:12 trust in the **n** of the LORD
Zech 5: 4 who swears falsely by My **n**
Zech 6:12 the Man whose **n** is the
Zech 10:12 walk up and down in His **n**,"
Zech 13: 3 lies in the **n** of the LORD
Zech 13: 9 They will call on My **n**, and I
Zech 14: 9 LORD is one," and His **n** one
Mal 1: 6 you priests who despise My **n**
Mal 1: 6 way have we despised Your **n**
Mal 1:11 my **n** shall be great among the
Mal 1:11 shall be offered to My **n**, and
Mal 1:11 For My **n** shall be great among
Mal 1:14 My **n** is to be feared among
Mal 2: 2 heart, to give glory to My **n**
Mal 2: 5 and was reverent before My **n**
Mal 3:16 LORD and who meditate on His **n**
Mal 4: 2 But to you who fear My **n** the
Matt 1:21 and you shall call His **n** JESUS
Matt 1:23 shall call His **n** Immanuel
Matt 1:25 And he called His **n** JESUS
Matt 6: 9 in heaven, hallowed be Your **n**
Matt 7:22 we not prophesied in Your **n**
Matt 7:22 cast out demons in Your **n**
Matt 7:22 done many wonders in Your **n**
Matt 10:41 receives a prophet in the **n**
Matt 10:41 a righteous man in the **n** of a
Matt 10:42 water in the **n** of a disciple
Matt 12:21 in His **n** Gentiles will trust
Matt 18: 5 like this in My **n** receives Me
Matt 18:20 are gathered together in My **n**
Matt 21: 9 comes in the **n** of the LORD
Matt 23:39 comes in the **n** of the LORD
Matt 24: 5 For many will come in My **n**
Matt 27:32 a man of Cyrene, Simon by **n**
Matt 28:19 them in the **n** of the Father
Mark 3:16 to whom He gave the **n** Peter
Mark 3:17 whom He gave the **n** Boanerges
Mark 5: 9 What is your **n**
Mark 5: 9 saying, My **n** is Legion
Mark 5:22 synagogue came, Jairus by **n**
Mark 6:14 of Him, for His **n** had become
Mark 9:37 children in My **n** receives Me
Mark 9:38 casting out demons in Your **n**
Mark 9:39 My **n** can soon afterward speak
Mark 9:41 cup of water to drink in My **n**
Mark 11: 9 comes in the **n** of the LORD
Mark 11:10 comes in the **n** of the Lord
Mark 13: 6 For many will come in My **n**
Mark 16:17 In My **n** they will cast out
Luke 1: 5 Aaron, and her **n** was Elizabeth
Luke 1:13 and you shall call his **n** John
Luke 1:27 to a man whose **n** was Joseph
Luke 1:27 The virgin's **n** was Mary
Luke 1:31 and shall call His **n** JESUS
Luke 1:49 for me, and holy is His **n**
Luke 1:59 him by the **n** of his father
Luke 1:61 who is called by this **n**
Luke 1:63 saying, "His **n** is John
Luke 2:21 His **n** was called JESUS, the
Luke 2:21 the **n** given by the angel
Luke 2:25 Jerusalem whose **n** was Simeon
Luke 6:22 and cast out your **n** as evil
Luke 8:30 What is your **n**
Luke 9:48 child in My **n** receives Me
Luke 9:49 casting out demons in Your **n**
Luke 10:17 are subject to us in Your **n**
Luke 11: 2 in heaven, hallowed be Your **n**
Luke 13:35 Comes in the **n** of the LORD
Luke 19:38 comes in the **n** of the LORD
Luke 21: 8 For many, will come in My **n**
Luke 24:18 Then the one whose **n** was
Luke 24:47 in His **n** to all nations,
John 1: 6 from God, whose **n** was John
John 1:12 to those who believe in His **n**
John 2:23 many believed in His **n** when
John 3:18 he has not believed in the **n**
John 5:43 I have come in My Father's **n**
John 5:43 if another comes in his own **n**
John 10: 3 he calls his own sheep by **n**
John 10:25 that I do in My Father's **n**
John 12:13 comes in the **n** of the LORD
John 12:28 Father, glorify Your **n**
John 14:13 And whatever you ask in My **n**
John 14:14 If you ask anything in My **n**
John 14:26 the Father will send in My **n**
John 15:16 in My **n** He may give you
John 16:23 in My **n** He will give you
John 16:24 have asked nothing in My **n**
John 16:26 that day you will ask in My **n**
John 17: 6 I have manifested Your **n** to
John 17:11 keep through Your **n** those
John 17:12 world, I kept them in Your **n**
John 17:26 have declared to them Your **n**
John 18:10 The servant's **n** was Malchus
John 20:31 you may have life in His **n**
Acts 2:21 that whoever calls on the **n**
Acts 2:38 the **n** of Jesus Christ for the
Acts 3: 6 In the **n** of Jesus Christ of
Acts 3:16 His **n**, through faith in His **n**
Acts 4: 7 by what **n** have you done this
Acts 4:10 that by the **n** of Jesus Christ
Acts 4:12 for there is no other **n** under
Acts 4:17 speak to no man in this **n**
Acts 4:18 nor teach in the **n** of Jesus
Acts 4:30 may be done through the **n** of
Acts 5:28 you not to teach in this **n**
Acts 5:40 not speak in the **n** of Jesus
Acts 5:41 to suffer shame for His **n**
Acts 8:12 the **n** of Jesus Christ, both
Acts 8:16 in the **n** of the Lord Jesus
Acts 9:14 bind all who call on Your **n**
Acts 9:15 to bear My **n** before Gentiles
Acts 9:21 called on this **n** in Jerusalem
Acts 9:27 at Damascus in the **n** of Jesus
Acts 9:29 in the **n** of the Lord Jesus
Acts 10:43 witness that, through His **n**
Acts 10:48 baptized in the **n** of the Lord
Acts 13: 6 a Jew whose **n** was Bar-Jesus,
Acts 13: 8 **n** is translated) withstood
Acts 15:14 of them a people for His **n**
Acts 15:17 who are called by My **n**, Says
Acts 15:26 **n** of our Lord Jesus Christ
Acts 16:18 I command you in the **n** of
Acts 19: 5 in the **n** of the Lord Jesus
Acts 19:13 the **n** of the Lord Jesus over
Acts 19:17 the **n** of the Lord Jesus was
Acts 21:13 for the **n** of the Lord Jesus
Acts 22:16 calling on the **n** of the Lord
Acts 26: 9 to the **n** of Jesus of Nazareth
Acts 28: 7 whose **n** was Publius, who
Rom 1: 5 among all nations for His **n**
Rom 2:24 The **n** of God is blasphemed
Rom 9:17 that My **n** might be declared
Rom 10:13 whoever calls upon the **n** of
Rom 15: 9 Gentiles, and sing to Your **n**
1Co 1: 2 **n** of Jesus Christ our Lord
1Co 1:10 by the **n** of our Lord Jesus
1Co 1:13 you baptized in the **n** of Paul
1Co 1:15 I had baptized in my own **n**
1Co 5: 4 In the **n** of our Lord Jesus
1Co 6:11 in the **n** of the Lord Jesus
Eph 1:21 every **n** that is named, not
Eph 5:20 **n** of our Lord Jesus Christ
Phil 2: 9 the **n** which is above every **n**
Phil 2:10 that at the **n** of Jesus every
Col 3:17 do all in the **n** of the Lord
2Th 1:12 that the **n** of our Lord Jesus
2Th 3: 6 in the **n** of our Lord Jesus
1Ti 6: 1 honor, so that the **n** of God
2Ti 2:19 the **n** of Christ depart from
Heb 1: 4 a more excellent **n** than they
Heb 2:12 declare Your **n** to My brethren
Heb 6:10 you have shown toward His **n**
Heb 13:15 lips, giving thanks to His **n**
Jas 2: 7 **n** by which you are called
Jas 5:10 spoke in the **n** of the Lord
Jas 5:14 with oil in the **n** of the Lord
1Pe 4:14 for the **n** of Christ, blessed
1Jn 3:23 the **n** of His Son Jesus Christ
1Jn 5:13 in the **n** of the Son of God
1Jn 5:13 in the **n** of the Son of God
3Jn 14 Greet the friends by **n**
Rev 2:13 And you hold fast to My **n**, and
Rev 2:17 on the stone a new **n** written
Rev 3: 1 that you have a **n** that you
Rev 3: 5 his **n** from the Book of Life
Rev 3: 5 his **n** before My Father and
Rev 3: 8 word, and have not denied My **n**
Rev 3:12 write on him the **n** of My God
Rev 3:12 the **n** of the city of My God,
Rev 3:12 I will write on him My new **n**
Rev 6: 8 the **n** of him who sat on it
Rev 8:11 the **n** of the star is Wormwood
Rev 9:11 whose **n** in Hebrew is Abaddon,
Rev 9:11 Greek he has the **n** Apollyon
Rev 11:18 and those who fear Your **n**
Rev 13: 1 on his heads a blasphemous **n**
Rev 13: 6 God, to blaspheme His **n**, His
Rev 13:17 mark or the **n** of the beast
Rev 13:17 beast, or the number of his **n**
Rev 14: 1 having His Father's **n** written
Rev 14:11 receives the mark of his **n**
Rev 15: 2 and over the number of his **n**
Rev 15: 4 O Lord, and glorify Your **n**
Rev 16: 9 they blasphemed the **n** of God
Rev 17: 5 her forehead a **n** was written
Rev 19:12 He had a **n** written that no
Rev 19:13 His **n** is called The Word of
Rev 19:16 and on His thigh a **n** written
Rev 22: 4 and His **n** shall be on their

Ezek 48: 4 by the border of **N**, from the
Ezek 48:34 for Asher, and one gate for **N**
Matt 4:13 the regions of Zebulun and **N**
Matt 4:15 of Zebulun and the land of **N**
Rev 7: 6 of the tribe of **N** twelve

NAPHTUHIM
Gen 10:13 Ludim, Anamim, Lehabim, **N**
1Ch 1:11 Ludim, Anamim, Lehabim, **N**

NARCISSUS
Rom 16:11 of **N** who are in the Lord

NARRATIVE
Luke 1: 1 a **n** of those things which are

NARROW
Num 22:24 of the LORD stood in a **n** path
Num 22:26 and stood in a **n** place where
1Ki 6: 6 for he made **n** ledges around
Prov 23:27 and a seductress is a **n** well
Is 28:20 the covering so **n** that he
Matt 7:13 Enter by the **n** gate
Matt 7:14 Because **n** is the gate and
Luke 13:24 to enter through the **n** gate

NATHAN (*see* NATHAN-MELECH)
2Sa 5:14 Shammua, Shobab, **N**,
2Sa 7: 2 king said to **N** the prophet
2Sa 7: 3 Then **N** said to the king, "Go
2Sa 7: 4 word of the LORD came to **N**
2Sa 7:17 vision, so **N** spoke to David
2Sa 12: 1 Then the LORD sent **N** to David
2Sa 12: 5 the man, and he said to **N**
2Sa 12: 7 Then **N** said to David, "You
2Sa 12:13 Then David said to **N**, "I
2Sa 12:13 And **N** said to David,
2Sa 12:15 Then **N** departed to his house
2Sa 12:25 by the hand of **N** the prophet
2Sa 23:36 Igal the son of **N** of Zobah
1Ki 1: 8 **N** the prophet, Shimei, Rei,
1Ki 1:10 did not invite **N** the prophet
1Ki 1:11 So **N** spoke to Bathsheba the
1Ki 1:22 **N** the prophet also came in
1Ki 1:23 Here is **N** the prophet
1Ki 1:24 And **N** said, "My lord, O king
1Ki 1:32 **N** the prophet, and Benaiah the
1Ki 1:34 **N** the prophet anoint him king
1Ki 1:38 **N** the prophet, Benaiah the
1Ki 1:44 **N** the prophet, Benaiah the
1Ki 1:45 **N** the prophet have anointed
1Ki 4: 5 Azariah the son of **N**, over
1Ki 4: 5 Zabud the son of **N**, a priest
1Ch 2:36 Attai begot **N**
1Ch 2:36 and **N** begot Zabad
1Ch 3: 5 Shimea, Shobab, **N**, and
1Ch 11:38 Joel the brother of **N**, Mibhar
1Ch 14: 4 Shammua, Shobab, **N**,
1Ch 17: 1 David said to **N** the prophet
1Ch 17: 2 Then **N** said to David, "Do
1Ch 17: 3 the word of God came to **N**
1Ch 17:15 so did **N** speak to David
1Ch 29:29 in the book of **N** the prophet
2Ch 9:29 in the book of **N** the prophet
2Ch 29:25 seer, and of **N** the prophet
Ezra 8:16 Elnathan, Jarib, Elnathan, **N**
Ezra 10:39 Shelemiah, **N**, Adaiah,
Zech 12:12 of the house of **N** by itself
Luke 3:31 of Mattathah, the son of **N**

NATHANAEL (*see* BARTHOLOMEW)
John 1:45 Philip found **N** and said to him
John 1:46 And **N** said to him,
John 1:47 Jesus saw **N** coming toward Him
John 1:48 **N** said to Him, "How do You
John 1:49 **N** answered and said to Him
John 21: 2 **N** of Cana in Galilee, the

NATHAN-MELECH (*see* MELECH, NATHAN)
2Ki 23:11 the LORD, by the chamber of **N**

NATION (*see* NATION'S, NATIONS)
Gen 12: 2 I will make you a great **n**
Gen 15:14 also the **n** whom they serve I
Gen 17:20 and I will make him a great **n**
Gen 18:18 become a great and mighty **n**
Gen 20: 4 You slay a righteous **n** also
Gen 21:13 Yet I will also make a **n** of
Gen 21:18 for I will make him a great **n**
Gen 35:11 a **n** and a company of nations
Gen 46: 3 make of you a great **n** there
Ex 9:24 of Egypt since it became a **n**
Ex 19: 6 of priests and a holy **n**
Ex 32:10 I will make of you a great **n**
Ex 33:13 that this **n** is Your people
Ex 34:10 all the earth, nor in any **n**
Lev 18:26 own **n** or any stranger who
Lev 20:23 the **n** which I am casting out
Num 14:12 will make of you a **n** greater
Deut 4: 6 Surely this great **n** is a wise
Deut 4: 7 For what great **n** is there
Deut 4: 8 what great **n** is there that
Deut 4:34 take for Himself a **n** from the
Deut 4:34 from the midst of another **n**
Deut 9:14 will make of you a **n** mightier
Deut 26: 5 and there he became a **n**, great
Deut 28:33 A **n** whom you have not known
Deut 28:36 **n** which neither you nor your
Deut 28:49 a **n** against you from afar
Deut 28:49 a **n** whose language you will
Deut 28:50 a **n** of fierce countenance,
Deut 32:21 by those who are not a **n**
Deut 32:21 them to anger by a foolish **n**
Deut 32:28 For they are a **n** void of
Judg 2:20 He said, "Because this **n** has
2Sa 7:23 the one **n** on the earth whom
1Ki 18:10 there is no **n** or kingdom
1Ki 18:10 or **n** that they could not find
2Ki 17:29 However every **n** continued to
2Ki 17:29 every **n** in the cities where
1Ch 16:20 went from one **n** to another
1Ch 17:21 the one **n** on the earth whom
2Ch 15: 6 So **n** was destroyed by **n**,
2Ch 32:15 for no god of any **n** or
Job 34:29 is against a **n** or a man alone
Ps 33:12 Blessed is the **n** whose God is
Ps 43: 1 my cause against an ungodly **n**
Ps 83: 4 cut them off from being a **n**
Ps 105:13 went from one **n** to another
Ps 106: 5 in the gladness of Your **n**
Ps 147:20 has not dealt thus with any **n**
Prov 14:34 Righteousness exalts a **n**, but
Is 1: 4 Alas, sinful **n**, a people
Is 2: 4 **N** shall not lift up sword
Is 2: 4 not lift up sword against **n**
Is 9: 3 You have multiplied the **n**
Is 10: 6 send him against an ungodly **n**
Is 14:32 the messengers of the **n**
Is 18: 2 swift messengers, to a **n** tall
Is 18: 2 a **n** powerful and treading down
Is 18: 7 a **n** powerful and treading down
Is 26: 2 that the righteous **n** which
Is 26:15 You have increased the **n**, O
Is 26:15 you have increased the **n**
Is 49: 7 to Him whom the **n** abhors
Is 51: 4 and give ear to Me, O My **n**
Is 55: 5 call a **n** you do not know, and
Is 58: 2 as a **n** that did righteousness
Is 60:12 For the **n** and kingdom which
Is 60:22 and a small one a strong **n**
Is 65: 1 to a **n** that was not called
Is 66: 8 Or shall a **n** be born at once
Jer 2:11 Has a **n** changed its gods,
Jer 5: 9 Myself on such a **n** as this
Jer 5:15 I will bring a **n** against you
Jer 5:15 mighty **n**, it is an ancient **n**
Jer 5:15 a **n** whose language you do not
Jer 5:29 Myself on such a **n** as this
Jer 6:22 a great **n** will be raised from
Jer 7:28 This is a **n** that does not
Jer 9: 9 Myself on such a **n** as this
Jer 12:17 pluck up and destroy that **n**
Jer 18: 7 I speak concerning a **n** and
Jer 18: 8 if that **n** against whom I have
Jer 18: 9 I speak concerning a **n** and
Jer 25:12 the king of Babylon and that **n**
Jer 25:32 go forth from **n** to **n**
Jer 27: 8 And it shall be, that the **n**
Jer 27: 8 that **n** I will punish,' says
Jer 27:13 the **n** that will not serve the
Jer 31:36 being a **n** before Me forever
Jer 33:24 no more be a **n** before them
Jer 48: 2 and let us cut her off as a **n**
Jer 49:31 **n** that dwells securely,"
Jer 50: 3 a **n** comes up against her,
Jer 50:41 from the north, and a great **n**
Jer 51:20 I will break the **n** in pieces
Lam 4:17 a **n** that could not save us
Ezek 2: 3 to a rebellious **n** that has
Ezek 36:13 and bereave your **n** of children
Ezek 36:14 nor bereave your **n** anymore
Ezek 36:15 your **n** to stumble anymore
Ezek 37:22 make them one **n** in the land
Dan 3:29 a decree that any people, **n**
Dan 8:22 shall arise out of that **n**
Dan 12: 1 never was since there was a **n**
Joel 1: 6 For a **n** has come up against
Amos 6: 1 persons in the chief **n**, to
Amos 6:14 will raise up a **n** against you
Mic 4: 3 **N** shall not lift up sword
Mic 4: 3 not lift up sword against **n**
Mic 4: 7 and the outcast a strong **n**
Hab 1: 6 hasty **n** which marches through
Zeph 2: 1 together, O undesirable **n**
Zeph 2: 5 the **n** of the Cherethites
Zeph 2:14 midst, every beast of the **n**
Hag 2:14 and so is this **n** before Me
Mal 3: 9 robbed Me, even this whole **n**
Matt 21:43 and given to a **n** bearing the
Matt 24: 7 **n** will rise against **n**
Mark 13: 8 **n** will rise against **n**
Luke 7: 5 for he loves our **n**, and has
Luke 21:10 **N** will rise against **n**,
Luke 23: 2 this fellow perverting the **n**
John 11:48 take away both our place and **n**
John 11:50 the whole **n** should perish
John 11:51 Jesus would die for the **n**
John 11:52 and not for that **n** only, but
John 18:35 Your own **n** and the chief
Acts 2: 5 from every **n** under heaven
Acts 7: 7 the **n** to whom they will be in
Acts 10:22 among all the **n** of the Jews
Acts 10:28 or go to one of another **n**
Acts 10:35 But in every **n** whoever fears
Acts 17:26 made from one blood every **n**
Acts 24: 2 to this **n** by your foresight
Acts 24:10 many years a judge of this **n**
Acts 24:17 alms and offerings to my **n**
Acts 26: 4 among my own **n** at Jerusalem
Acts 28:19 of which to accuse my **n**
Rom 10:19 by those who are not a **n**, I
Rom 10:19 will anger you by a foolish **n**
Gal 1:14 my contemporaries in my own **n**
1Pe 2: 9 a royal priesthood, a holy **n**
Rev 5: 9 and tongue and people and **n**,
Rev 13: 7 every tribe, tongue, and **n**
Rev 14: 6 to every **n**, tribe, tongue, and

NATION'S (*see* NATION)
Num 21:18 sank, dug by the **n** nobles

NATIONS (*see* NATION)
Gen 10: 5 their families, into their **n**
Gen 10:20 in their lands and in their **n**
Gen 10:31 lands, according to their **n**
Gen 10:32 their generations, in their **n**
Gen 10:32 from these the **n** were divided
Gen 14: 1 of Elam, and Tidal king of **n**
Gen 14: 9 king of Elam, Tidal king of **n**
Gen 17: 4 shall be a father of many **n**
Gen 17: 5 made you a father of many **n**
Gen 17: 6 and I will make **n** of you, and
Gen 17:16 and she shall be a mother of **n**
Gen 18:18 all the **n** of the earth shall
Gen 22:18 In your seed all the **n** of the
Gen 25:16 princes according to their **n**
Gen 25:23 Two **n** are in your womb, two
Gen 26: 4 in your seed all the **n** of the
Gen 27:29 you, and **n** bow down to you
Gen 35:11 a company of **n** shall proceed
Gen 48:19 shall become a multitude of **n**
Ex 34:24 cast out the **n** before you
Lev 18:24 all these the **n** are defiled
Lev 18:28 the **n** that were before you
Lev 25:44 from the **n** that are around
Lev 26:33 will scatter you among the **n**
Lev 26:38 You shall perish among the **n**
Lev 26:45 Egypt in the sight of the **n**
Num 14:15 then the **n** which have heard
Num 23: 9 reckoning itself among the **n**
Num 24: 8 he shall consume the **n**, his
Num 24:20 Amalek was first among the **n**
Deut 2:25 fear of you upon the **n** under
Deut 4:27 few in number among the **n**
Deut 4:38 out from before you **n** greater
Deut 7: 1 cast out many **n** before you
Deut 7: 1 seven **n** greater and mightier
Deut 7:17 These **n** are greater than I
Deut 7:22 God will drive out those **n**
Deut 8:20 As the **n** which the LORD
Deut 9: 1 go in to dispossess **n** greater
Deut 9: 4 **n** that the LORD is driving
Deut 9: 5 **n** that the LORD your God
Deut 11:23 all these **n** from before you
Deut 11:23 mightier **n** than yourselves

Deut 12: 2 all the places where the **n**
Deut 12:29 off from before you the **n**
Deut 12:30 How did these **n** serve their
Deut 15: 6 you shall lend to many **n**, but
Deut 15: 6 you shall reign over many **n**
Deut 17:14 all the **n** that are around me
Deut 18: 9 the abominations of those **n**
Deut 18:14 For these **n** which you will
Deut 19: 1 **n** whose land the LORD your
Deut 20:15 not of the cities of these **n**
Deut 26:19 above all **n** which He has made
Deut 28: 1 high above all **n** of the earth
Deut 28:12 You shall lend to many **n**, but
Deut 28:37 a byword among all **n** where
Deut 28:65 among those **n** you shall find
Deut 29:16 the **n** which you passed by
Deut 29:18 and serve the gods of these **n**
Deut 29:24 All **n** would say, 'Why has the
Deut 30: 1 the **n** where the LORD your God
Deut 30: 3 you again from all the **n**
Deut 31: 3 these **n** from before you, and
Deut 32: 8 their inheritance to the **n**
Josh 23: 3 to all these **n** because of you
Josh 23: 4 by lot these **n** that remain
Josh 23: 4 with all the **n** that I have
Josh 23: 7 and lest you go among these **n**
Josh 23: 9 before you great and strong **n**
Josh 23:12 to the remnant of these **n**
Josh 23:13 out these **n** from before you
Judg 2:21 **n** which Joshua left when he
Judg 2:23 the LORD left those **n**,
Judg 3: 1 Now these are the **n** which the
1Sa 8: 5 to judge us like all the **n**
1Sa 8:20 we also may be like all the **n**
1Sa 27: 8 For those **n** were the
2Sa 7:23 from Egypt, from the **n** and
2Sa 8:11 the **n** which he had subdued
2Sa 22:44 kept me as the head of the **n**
1Ki 4:31 was in all the surrounding **n**
1Ki 4:34 And men of all **n**, from all the
1Ki 11: 2 from the **n** of whom the LORD
1Ki 14:24 **n** which the LORD had cast out
2Ki 16: 3 **n** whom the LORD had cast out
2Ki 17: 8 in the statutes of the **n** whom
2Ki 17:11 as the **n** had done whom the
2Ki 17:15 went after the **n** who were all
2Ki 17:26 The **n** whom you have removed
2Ki 17:33 to the rituals of the **n** from
2Ki 17:41 So these **n** feared the LORD,
2Ki 18:33 **n** at all delivered its land
2Ki 19:12 Have the gods of the **n**
2Ki 19:17 Assyria have laid waste the **n**
2Ki 21: 2 **n** whom the LORD had cast out
2Ki 21: 9 to do more evil than the **n**
1Ch 14:17 the fear of him upon all **n**
1Ch 16:24 Declare His glory among the **n**
1Ch 16:31 and let them say among the **n**
1Ch 17:21 by driving out **n** from before
1Ch 18:11 had brought from all these **n**
2Ch 7:20 and a byword among all **n**
2Ch 12: 8 of the kingdoms of the **n**
2Ch 20: 6 all the kingdoms of the **n**
2Ch 28: 3 **n** whom the LORD had cast out
2Ch 32:13 Were the gods of the **n** of
2Ch 32:14 **n** that my fathers utterly
2Ch 32:17 As the gods of the **n** of other
2Ch 32:23 the sight of all **n** thereafter
2Ch 33: 2 **n** whom the LORD had cast out
2Ch 33: 9 to do more evil than the **n**
2Ch 36:14 all the abominations of the **n**
Ezra 4:10 rest of the **n** whom the great
Ezra 6:21 from the filth of the **n** of
Neh 1: 8 will scatter you among the **n**
Neh 5: 8 who were sold to the **n**
Neh 5: 9 of the reproach of the **n**, our
Neh 5:17 to us from the **n** around us
Neh 6: 6 It is reported among the **n**
Neh 6:16 all the **n** around us saw these
Neh 9:22 You gave them kingdoms and **n**
Neh 13:26 Yet among many **n** there was no
Job 12:23 He makes **n** great, and destroys
Job 12:23 He enlarges **n**, and guides them
Ps 2: 1 Why do the **n** rage, And the
Ps 2: 8 I will give You The **n** for
Ps 9: 5 You have rebuked the **n**, You
Ps 9:15 The **n** have sunk down in the
Ps 9:17 all the **n** that forget God
Ps 9:19 Let the **n** be judged in Your
Ps 9:20 O LORD, That the **n** may know
Ps 10:16 The **n** have perished out of

Ps 18:43 made me the head of the **n**
Ps 22:27 all the families of the **n**
Ps 22:28 And He rules over the **n**
Ps 33:10 counsel of the **n** to nothing
Ps 44: 2 out the **n** with Your hand, But
Ps 44:11 have scattered us among the **n**
Ps 44:14 make us a byword among the **n**
Ps 46: 6 The **n** raged, the kingdoms
Ps 46:10 I will be exalted among the **n**
Ps 47: 3 us, And the **n** under our feet
Ps 47: 8 God reigns over the **n**
Ps 57: 9 will sing to You among the **n**
Ps 59: 5 Awake to punish all the **n**
Ps 59: 8 have all the **n** in derision
Ps 66: 7 His eyes observe the **n**
Ps 67: 2 Your salvation among all **n**
Ps 67: 4 Oh, let the **n** be glad and sing
Ps 67: 4 And govern the **n** on earth
Ps 72:11 All **n** shall serve Him
Ps 72:17 All **n** shall call Him blessed
Ps 78:55 drove out the **n** before them
Ps 79: 1 the **n** have come into Your
Ps 79: 6 on the **n** that do not know You
Ps 79:10 Why should the **n** say, "Where
Ps 79:10 there be known among the **n** in
Ps 80: 8 You have cast out the **n**, and
Ps 82: 8 For You shall inherit all **n**
Ps 86: 9 All **n** whom You have made
Ps 94:10 He who instructs the **n**, shall
Ps 96: 3 Declare His glory among the **n**
Ps 96:10 Say among the **n**, "The LORD
Ps 98: 2 shown in the sight of the **n**
Ps 102:15 So the **n** shall fear the name
Ps 105:44 inherited the labor of the **n**
Ps 106:27 their descendants among the **n**
Ps 108: 3 praises to You among the **n**
Ps 110: 6 He shall judge among the **n**
Ps 111: 6 them the heritage of the **n**
Ps 113: 4 The LORD is high above all **n**
Ps 118:10 All **n** surrounded me, But in
Ps 126: 2 Then they said among the **n**
Ps 135:10 He defeated many **n** And slew
Ps 135:15 The idols of the **n** are silver
Ps 149: 7 To execute vengeance on the **n**
Prov 24:24 **n** will abhor him
Is 2: 2 and all **n** shall flow to it
Is 2: 4 He shall judge between the **n**
Is 5:26 a banner to the **n** from afar
Is 10: 7 and cut off not a few **n**
Is 11:12 set up a banner for the **n**
Is 13: 4 of **n** gathered together
Is 14: 6 he who ruled the **n** in anger
Is 14: 9 all the kings of the **n**
Is 14:12 you who weakened the **n**
Is 14:18 All the kings of the **n**, all
Is 14:26 stretched out over all the **n**
Is 16: 8 the lords of the **n** have
Is 17:12 to the rushing of **n** that make
Is 17:13 The **n** will rush like the
Is 23: 3 is a marketplace for the **n**
Is 25: 3 the terrible **n** will fear You
Is 25: 7 that is spread over all **n**
Is 29: 7 the **n** who fight against Ariel
Is 29: 8 of all the **n** shall be, who
Is 30:28 to sift the **n** with the sieve
Is 33: 3 up, the **n** shall be scattered
Is 34: 1 Come near, you **n**, to hear
Is 34: 2 of the LORD is against all **n**
Is 36:18 any one of the gods of the **n**
Is 37:12 Have the gods of the **n**
Is 37:18 have laid waste all the **n**
Is 40:15 the **n** are as a drop in a
Is 40:17 All **n** before Him are as
Is 41: 2 Who gave the **n** before him
Is 43: 9 Let all the **n** be gathered
Is 45: 1 to subdue **n** before him and
Is 45:20 who have escaped from the **n**
Is 49:22 My hand in an oath to the **n**
Is 52:10 arm in the eyes of all the **n**
Is 52:15 So shall He sprinkle many **n**
Is 54: 3 will inherit the **n**, and make
Is 55: 5 **n** who do not know you shall
Is 56: 7 a house of prayer for all **n**
Is 60:12 and those **n** shall be utterly
Is 61:11 spring forth before all the **n**
Is 64: 2 that the **n** may tremble at
Is 66:18 be that I will gather all **n**
Is 66:19 escape I will send to the **n**
Is 66:20 to the LORD out of all **n**, on
Jer 1: 5 you a prophet to the **n**

Jer 1:10 this day set you over the **n**
Jer 3:17 all the **n** shall be gathered
Jer 3:19 heritage of the hosts of **n**
Jer 4: 2 the **n** shall bless themselves
Jer 4: 7 destroyer of **n** is on his way
Jer 4:16 Make mention to the **n**, yes,
Jer 6:18 Therefore hear, you **n**, and
Jer 9:26 For all these **n** are
Jer 10: 7 not fear You, O King of the **n**
Jer 10: 7 all the wise men of the **n**
Jer 10:10 the **n** will not be able to
Jer 14:22 of the **n** that can cause rain
Jer 22: 8 many **n** will pass by this city
Jer 25: 9 and against these **n** all around
Jer 25:11 these **n** shall serve the king
Jer 25:13 concerning all the **n**
Jer 25:14 (For many **n** and great kings
Jer 25:15 My hand, and cause all the **n**
Jer 25:17 hand, and made all the **n** drink
Jer 25:31 has a controversy with the **n**
Jer 26: 6 to all the **n** of the earth
Jer 27: 7 So all **n** shall serve him and
Jer 27: 7 and then many **n** and great kings
Jer 27:11 But the **n** that bring their
Jer 28:11 from the neck of all **n** within
Jer 28:14 on the neck of all these **n**
Jer 29:14 gather you from all the **n**
Jer 29:18 **n** where I have driven them
Jer 30:11 I make a full end of all **n**
Jer 31: 7 among the chief of the **n**
Jer 31:10 the word of the LORD, O **n**
Jer 33: 9 before all **n** of the earth
Jer 36: 2 Judah, and against all the **n**
Jer 43: 5 from all **n** where they had
Jer 44: 8 among all the **n** of the earth
Jer 46: 1 the prophet against the **n**
Jer 46:12 The **n** have heard of your
Jer 46:28 a complete end of all the **n**
Jer 49:14 has been sent to the **n**
Jer 49:15 I will make you small among **n**
Jer 49:36 there shall be no **n** where the
Jer 50: 2 Declare among the **n**, Proclaim
Jer 50: 9 An assembly of great **n** from
Jer 50:12 the least of the **n** shall be a
Jer 50:23 a desolation among the **n**
Jer 50:46 the cry is heard among the **n**
Jer 51: 7 The **n** drank her wine
Jer 51: 7 therefore the **n** are deranged
Jer 51:27 blow the trumpet among the **n**
Jer 51:27 Prepare the **n** against her
Jer 51:28 Prepare against her the **n**
Jer 51:41 become desolate among the **n**
Jer 51:44 the **n** shall not stream to him
Jer 51:58 will labor in vain, and the **n**
Lam 1: 1 Who was great among the **n**
Lam 1: 3 she dwells among the **n**, she
Lam 1:10 the **n** enter her sanctuary
Lam 2: 9 her princes are among the **n**
Lam 4:15 those among the **n** said
Lam 4:20 we shall live among the **n**
Ezek 5: 5 set her in the midst of the **n**
Ezek 5: 6 wickedness more than the **n**
Ezek 5: 7 the **n** that are all around you
Ezek 5: 7 the **n** that are all around you
Ezek 5: 8 midst in the sight of the **n**
Ezek 5:14 a reproach among the **n** that
Ezek 5:15 an astonishment to the **n** that
Ezek 6: 8 escape the sword among the **n**
Ezek 6: 9 the **n** where they are carried
Ezek 12:15 I scatter them among the **n**
Ezek 16:14 the **n** because of your beauty
Ezek 19: 4 The **n** also heard of him
Ezek 19: 8 Then the **n** set against him
Ezek 22: 4 made you a reproach to the **n**
Ezek 22:15 will scatter you among the **n**
Ezek 22:16 in the sight of the **n**
Ezek 25: 7 give you as plunder to the **n**
Ezek 25: 8 of Judah is like all the **n**
Ezek 25:10 not be remembered among the **n**
Ezek 26: 3 will cause many **n** to come up
Ezek 26: 5 become plunder for the **n**
Ezek 28: 7 the most terrible of the **n**
Ezek 29:12 the Egyptians among the **n**
Ezek 29:15 exalt itself above the **n**, for
Ezek 29:15 not rule over the **n** anymore
Ezek 30:11 the most terrible of the **n**
Ezek 30:23 the Egyptians among the **n**
Ezek 30:26 the Egyptians among the **n**
Ezek 31: 6 all great **n** made their home
Ezek 31:11 of the mighty one of the **n**

Ezek 31:12 the most terrible of the **n**
Ezek 31:16 I made the **n** shake at the
Ezek 31:17 in its shadows among the **n**
Ezek 32: 2 like a young lion among the **n**
Ezek 32: 9 your destruction among the **n**
Ezek 32:12 the most terrible of the **n**
Ezek 32:16 of the **n** shall lament her
Ezek 32:18 the daughters of the famous **n**
Ezek 34:28 no longer be a prey for the **n**
Ezek 35:10 you have said, 'These two **n**
Ezek 36: 3 of the rest of the **n**, and you
Ezek 36: 4 the rest of the **n** all around
Ezek 36: 5 against the rest of the **n**
Ezek 36: 6 have borne the shame of the **n**
Ezek 36: 7 **n** that are around you shall
Ezek 36:15 the taunts of the **n** anymore
Ezek 36:19 I scattered them among the **n**
Ezek 36:20 When they came to the **n**,
Ezek 36:21 the **n** wherever they went
Ezek 36:22 among the **n** wherever you went
Ezek 36:23 has been profaned among the **n**
Ezek 36:23 the **n** shall know that I am
Ezek 36:24 take you from among the **n**
Ezek 36:30 of famine among the **n**
Ezek 36:36 Then the **n** which are left all
Ezek 37:21 of Israel from among the **n**
Ezek 37:22 they shall no longer be two **n**
Ezek 37:28 The **n** also will know that I,
Ezek 38: 8 were brought out of the **n**
Ezek 38:12 a people gathered from the **n**
Ezek 38:16 so that the **n** may know Me
Ezek 38:23 known in the eyes of many **n**
Ezek 39: 7 Then the **n** shall know that I
Ezek 39:21 will set My glory among the **n**
Ezek 39:21 all the **n** shall see My
Ezek 39:27 them in the sight of many **n**
Ezek 39:28 into captivity among the **n**
Dan 3: 4 it is commanded, O peoples, **n**
Dan 3: 7 of music, all the people, **n**
Dan 4: 1 the king, To all peoples, **n**
Dan 5:19 He gave him, all peoples, **n**
Dan 6:25 To all peoples, **n**, and
Dan 7:14 kingdom, that all peoples, **n**
Hos 8:10 they have hired among the **n**
Hos 9:17 be wanderers among the **n**
Joel 2:17 that the **n** should rule over
Joel 2:19 you a reproach among the **n**
Joel 3: 2 I will also gather all **n**, and
Joel 3: 2 have scattered among the **n**
Joel 3: 9 Proclaim this among the **n**
Joel 3:11 Assemble and come, all you **n**
Joel 3:12 Let the **n** be wakened, and come
Joel 3:12 judge all the surrounding **n**
Amos 9: 9 house of Israel among all **n**
Obad 1 has been sent among the **n**
Obad 2 make you small among the **n**
Obad 15 LORD upon all the **n** is near
Obad 16 so shall all the **n** drink
Mic 4: 2 Many **n** shall come and say,
Mic 4: 3 and rebuke strong **n** afar off
Mic 4:11 Now also many **n** have gathered
Mic 5:15 fury on the **n** that have not
Mic 7:16 The **n** shall see and be ashamed
Nah 3: 4 who sells **n** through her
Nah 3: 5 show the **n** your nakedness
Hab 1: 5 Look among the **n** and watch
Hab 1:17 to slay **n** without pity
Hab 2: 5 he gathers to himself all **n**
Hab 2: 8 you have plundered many **n**
Hab 2:13 **n** weary themselves in vain
Hab 3: 6 He looked and startled the **n**
Hab 3:12 you trampled the **n** in anger
Zeph 2:11 all the shores of the **n**
Zeph 3: 6 I have cut off **n**, their
Zeph 3: 8 is to gather the **n** to My
Hag 2: 7 and I will shake all **n**, and
Hag 2: 7 come to the Desire of All **N**
Zech 1:15 angry with the **n** at ease
Zech 1:21 **n** that lifted up their horn
Zech 2: 8 to the **n** which plunder you
Zech 2:11 Many **n** shall be joined to the
Zech 7:14 **n** which they had not known
Zech 8:13 you were a curse among the **n**
Zech 8:22 strong **n** shall come to seek
Zech 8:23 from every language of the **n**
Zech 9:10 He shall speak peace to the **n**
Zech 12: 3 though all **n** of the earth are
Zech 12: 9 seek to destroy all the **n**
Zech 14: 2 For I will gather all the **n**
Zech 14: 3 and fight against those **n**, as
Zech 14:14 of all the surrounding **n**
Zech 14:16 all the **n** which came against
Zech 14:18 **n** who do not come up to keep
Zech 14:19 the punishment of all the **n**
Mal 1:11 shall be great among the **n**
Mal 1:14 is to be feared among the **n**
Mal 3:12 all **n** will call you blessed,
Matt 24: 9 by all **n** for My name's sake
Matt 24:14 as a witness to all the **n**
Matt 25:32 All the **n** will be gathered
Matt 28:19 make disciples of all the **n**
Mark 11:17 a house of prayer for all **n**'
Mark 13:10 be preached to all the **n**
Luke 12:30 the **n** of the world seek after
Luke 21:24 led away captive into all **n**
Luke 21:25 and on the earth distress of **n**
Luke 24:47 preached in His name to all **n**
Acts 4:25 Why did the **n** rage, and the
Acts 13:19 seven **n** in the land of Canaan
Acts 14:16 generations allowed all **n** to
Rom 1: 5 among all **n** for His name,
Rom 4:17 made you a father of many **n**
Rom 4:18 became the father of many **n**
Rom 16:26 has been made known to all **n**
Gal 3: 8 would justify the **n** by faith
Gal 3: 8 In you all the **n** shall be
Rev 2:26 I will give power over the **n**
Rev 7: 9 no one could number, of all **n**
Rev 10:11 again about many peoples, **n**
Rev 11: 9 **n** will see their dead bodies
Rev 11:18 The **n** were angry, and Your
Rev 12: 5 rule all **n** with a rod of iron
Rev 14: 8 **n** drink of the wine of the
Rev 15: 4 For all **n** shall come and
Rev 16:19 and the cities of the **n** fell
Rev 17:15 are peoples, multitudes, **n**
Rev 18: 3 For all the **n** have drunk of
Rev 18:23 all the **n** were deceived
Rev 19:15 it He should strike the **n**
Rev 20: 3 **n** no more till the thousand
Rev 20: 8 the **n** which are in the four
Rev 21:24 the **n** of those who are saved
Rev 21:26 and the honor of the **n** into it
Rev 22: 2 were for the healing of the **n**

NATIVE (*see* NATIVE-BORN, NATIVES)
Gen 11:28 father Terah in his **n** land
Ex 12:19 a stranger or a **n** of the land
Ex 12:48 shall be as a **n** of the land
Lev 16:29 all, whether a **n** of your own
Lev 17:15 whether he is a **n** of your own
Lev 23:42 All who are **n** Israelites
Num 9:14 stranger and the **n** of the land
Ps 37:35 himself like a **n** green tree
Jer 22:10 more, nor see his **n** country

NATIVE-BORN (*see* NATIVE)
Ex 12:49 One law shall be for the **n**
Num 15:13 All who are **n** shall do these
Num 15:29 both for him who is **n** among
Num 15:30 whether he is **n** or a stranger
Ezek 47:22 as **n** among the children of

NATIVES (*see* NATIVE)
Acts 28: 2 And the **n** showed us unusual
Acts 28: 4 So when the **n** saw the

NATIVITY
Jer 46:16 to the land of our **n** from the
Ezek 16: 3 your **n** are from the land of
Ezek 16: 4 As for your **n**, on the day you
Ezek 21:30 in the land of your **n**
Ezek 23:15 Chaldea, the land of their **n**

NATURAL (*see* NATURALLY, NATURE)
Deut 34: 7 dim nor his **n** vigor abated
Rom 1:26 the **n** use for what is against
Rom 1:27 men, leaving the **n** use of the
Rom 11:21 did not spare the **n** branches
Rom 11:24 these, who are the **n** branches
1Co 2:14 But the **n** man does not
1Co 15:44 It is sown a **n** body, it is
1Co 15:44 There is a **n** body, and there
1Co 15:46 is not first, but the **n**, and
Jas 1:23 his **n** face in a mirror
2Pe 2:12 like **n** brute beasts made to

NATURALLY (*see* NATURAL)
Lev 7:24 fat of a beast that dies **n**
Lev 17:15 person who eats what died **n**
Lev 22: 8 Whatever dies **n** or is torn
Num 16:29 these men die **n** like all men
Ezek 44:31 that died **n** or was torn by
Jude 10 and whatever they know **n**, like

NATURE (*see* NATURAL)
Acts 14:15 men with the same **n** as you
Acts 17:29 to think that the Divine **N** is
Rom 1:26 use for what is against **n**
Rom 2:14 by **n** do the things contained
Rom 11:24 olive tree which is wild by **n**
Rom 11:24 to **n** into a good olive tree
1Co 11:14 Does not even **n** itself teach
Gal 2:15 We who are Jews by **n**, and not
Gal 4: 8 those which by **n** are not gods
Eph 2: 3 were by **n** children of wrath,
Jas 3: 6 sets on fire the course of **n**
Jas 5:17 was a man with a **n** like ours
2Pe 1: 4 be partakers of the divine **n**

NAUGHT
Ps 44:12 You sell Your people for **n**
Is 29:21 the just for a thing of **n**

NAVEL
Song 7: 2 Your **n** is a rounded goblet
Ezek 16: 4 born your **n** cord was not cut

NAZARENE (*see* NAZARENES, NAZARETH)
Matt 2:23 He shall be called a **N**

NAZARENES (*see* NAZARENE)
Acts 24: 5 of the sect of the **N**

NAZARETH (*see* NAZARENE)
Matt 2:23 and dwelt in a city called **N**
Matt 4:13 And leaving **N**, He came and
Matt 21:11 the prophet from **N** of Galilee
Matt 26:71 also was with Jesus of **N**
Mark 1: 9 Jesus came from **N** of Galilee
Mark 1:24 we to do with You, Jesus of **N**
Mark 10:47 heard that it was Jesus of **N**
Mark 14:67 You also were with Jesus of **N**
Mark 16: 6 You seek Jesus of **N**, who was
Luke 1:26 to a city of Galilee named **N**
Luke 2: 4 Galilee, out of the city of **N**
Luke 2:39 Galilee, to their own city, **N**
Luke 2:51 down with them and came to **N**
Luke 4:16 So He came to **N**, where He had
Luke 4:34 we to do with You, Jesus of **N**
Luke 18:37 Jesus of **N** was passing by
Luke 24:19 things concerning Jesus of **N**
John 1:45 Jesus of **N**, the son of Joseph
John 1:46 anything good come out of **N**
John 18: 5 answered Him, "Jesus of **N**."
John 18: 7 And they said, "Jesus of **N**."
John 19:19 Jesus of **N**, The King of the
Acts 2:22 Jesus of **N**, a Man attested by
Acts 3: 6 the name of Jesus Christ of **N**
Acts 4:10 the name of Jesus Christ of **N**
Acts 6:14 of **N** will destroy this place
Acts 10:38 of **N** with the Holy Spirit
Acts 22: 8 said to me, 'I am Jesus of **N**
Acts 26: 9 to the name of Jesus of **N**

NAZIRITE (*see* NAZIRITES)
Num 6: 2 to take the vow of a **N**, to
Num 6:13 Now this is the law of the **N**
Num 6:18 Then the **N** shall shave his
Num 6:19 the **N** after he has shaved his
Num 6:20 that the **N** may drink wine
Num 6:21 This is the law of the **N** who
Judg 13: 5 be a **N** to God from the womb
Judg 13: 7 for the child shall be a **N** to
Judg 16:17 for I have been a **N** to God

NAZIRITES (*see* NAZIRITE)
Lam 4: 7 Her **N** were brighter than snow
Amos 2:11 some of your young men as **N**
Amos 2:12 you gave the **N** wine to drink

NEAH
Josh 19:13 to Rimmon, which borders on **N**

NEAPOLIS
Acts 16:11 and the next day came to **N**

NEAR (*see* PREFACE)

NEARBY (*see* PREFACE)

NEARER (*see* PREFACE)

NEAREST (*see* PREFACE)

NEARIAH
1Ch 3:22 were Hattush, Igal, Bariah, **N**
1Ch 3:23 The sons of **N** were Elioenai,
1Ch 4:42 as their captains Pelatiah, **N**

NEARLY (*see* PREFACE)

NEBAI
Neh 10:19 Hariph, Anathoth, **N**,

NEBAIOTH (*see* NEBAJOTH)
Is 60: 7 the rams of **N** shall minister

NEBAJOTH (*see* NEBAIOTH)
Gen 25:13 The firstborn of Ishmael, **N**
Gen 28: 9 son, the sister of **N**, to be
Gen 36: 3 daughter, sister of **N**

NEBALLAT
Neh 11:34 in Hadid, Zeboim, **N**

NEBAT
1Ki 11:26 Jeroboam the son of **N**, an
1Ki 12: 2 when Jeroboam the son of **N**
1Ki 12:15 to Jeroboam the son of **N**
1Ki 15: 1 of King Jeroboam the son of **N**
1Ki 16: 3 of Jeroboam the son of **N**
1Ki 16:26 ways of Jeroboam the son of **N**
1Ki 16:31 sins of Jeroboam the son of **N**
1Ki 21:22 of Jeroboam the son of **N**, and
1Ki 22:52 way of Jeroboam the son of **N**
2Ki 3: 3 sins of Jeroboam the son of **N**
2Ki 9: 9 of Jeroboam the son of **N**, and
2Ki 10:29 sins of Jeroboam the son of **N**
2Ki 13: 2 sins of Jeroboam the son of **N**
2Ki 13:11 sins of Jeroboam the son of **N**
2Ki 14:24 sins of Jeroboam the son of **N**
2Ki 15: 9 sins of Jeroboam the son of **N**
2Ki 15:18 sins of Jeroboam the son of **N**
2Ki 15:24 sins of Jeroboam the son of **N**
2Ki 15:28 sins of Jeroboam the son of **N**
2Ki 17:21 Jeroboam the son of **N** king
2Ki 23:15 which Jeroboam the son of **N**
2Ch 9:29 Jeroboam the son of **N**
2Ch 10: 2 when Jeroboam the son of **N**
2Ch 10:15 to Jeroboam the son of **N**
2Ch 13: 6 Yet Jeroboam the son of **N**

NEBO (*see* PISGAH)
Num 32: 3 Heshbon, Elealeh, Shebam, **N**
Num 32:38 **N** and Baal Meon (their names
Num 33:47 mountains of Abarim, before **N**
Deut 32:49 of the Abarim, Mount **N**, which
Deut 34: 1 the plains of Moab to Mount **N**
1Ch 5: 8 dwelt in Aroer, as far as **N**
Ezra 2:29 the people of **N**, fifty-two
Ezra 10:43 of the sons of **N**
Neh 7:33 the men of the other **N**,
Is 15: 2 Moab will wail over **N** and over
Is 46: 1 Bel bows down, **N** stoops
Jer 48: 1 Woe to **N**! For it is plundered
Jer 48:22 on Dibon and **N** and Beth

NEBUCHADNEZZAR (*see* NEBUCHADNEZZAR'S)
2Ki 24: 1 In his days **N** king of Babylon
2Ki 24:10 of **N** king of Babylon came up
2Ki 24:11 And **N** king of Babylon came
2Ki 25: 1 that **N** king of Babylon and all
2Ki 25: 8 of King **N** king of Babylon)
2Ki 25:22 whom **N** king of Babylon had
1Ch 6:15 captivity by the hand of **N**
2Ch 36: 6 **N** king of Babylon came up
2Ch 36: 7 **N** also carried off some of
2Ch 36:10 the year King **N** summoned him
2Ch 36:13 also rebelled against King **N**
Ezra 1: 7 LORD, which **N** had taken from
Ezra 2: 1 whom **N** the king of Babylon
Ezra 5:12 the hand of **N** king of Babylon
Ezra 5:14 which **N** had taken from the
Ezra 6: 5 which **N** took from the temple
Neh 7: 6 whom **N** the king of Babylon
Esth 2: 6 whom **N** the king of Babylon
Jer 21: 2 for **N** king of Babylon makes
Jer 21: 7 the hand of **N** king of Babylon
Jer 22:25 the hand of **N** king of Babylon
Jer 24: 1 after **N** king of Babylon had
Jer 25: 1 year of **N** king of Babylon)
Jer 25: 9 **N** the king of Babylon, My
Jer 27: 6 hand of **N** the king of Babylon
Jer 27: 8 serve **N** the king of Babylon
Jer 27:20 which **N** king of Babylon did
Jer 28: 3 that **N** king of Babylon took
Jer 28:11 of **N** king of Babylon from the
Jer 28:14 may serve **N** king of Babylon
Jer 29: 1 all the people whom **N** had
Jer 29: 3 to **N** king of Babylon, saying,
Jer 29:21 the hand of **N** king of Babylon
Jer 32: 1 was the eighteenth year of **N**
Jer 32:28 the hand of **N** king of Babylon
Jer 34: 1 when **N** king of Babylon and all
Jer 35:11 when **N** king of Babylon came
Jer 37: 1 whom **N** king of Babylon made
Jer 39: 1 **N** king of Babylon and all his
Jer 39: 5 him up to **N** king of Babylon
Jer 39:11 Now **N** king of Babylon gave
Jer 43:10 bring **N** the king of Babylon,
Jer 44:30 the hand of **N** king of Babylon
Jer 46: 2 and which **N** king of Babylon
Jer 46:13 how **N** king of Babylon would
Jer 46:26 the hand of **N** king of Babylon
Jer 49:28 which **N** king of Babylon shall
Jer 49:30 For **N** king of Babylon has
Jer 50:17 now at last this **N** king of
Jer 51:34 **N** the king of Babylon has
Jer 52: 4 that **N** king of Babylon and all
Jer 52:12 of King **N** king of Babylon)
Jer 52:28 whom **N** carried away captive
Jer 52:29 of **N** he carried away captive
Jer 52:30 in the twenty-third year of **N**
Ezek 26: 7 the north **N** king of Babylon
Ezek 29:18 **N** king of Babylon caused his
Ezek 29:19 of Egypt to **N** king of Babylon
Ezek 30:10 the hand of **N** king of Babylon
Dan 1: 1 **N** king of Babylon came to
Dan 1:18 brought them in before **N**
Dan 2: 1 reign, **N** had dreams
Dan 2:28 He has made known to King **N**
Dan 2:46 Then King **N** fell on his face,
Dan 3: 1 **N** the king made an image of
Dan 3: 2 King **N** sent word to gather
Dan 3: 2 image which King **N** had set up
Dan 3: 3 image that King **N** had set up
Dan 3: 3 the image that **N** had set up
Dan 3: 5 image that King **N** has set up
Dan 3: 7 image which King **N** had set up
Dan 3: 9 They spoke and said to King **N**
Dan 3:13 Then **N**, in rage and fury, gave
Dan 3:14 **N** spoke, saying to them, "Is
Dan 3:16 O **N**, we have no need to
Dan 3:19 Then **N** was full of fury, and
Dan 3:24 Then King **N** was astonished
Dan 3:26 Then **N** went near the mouth of
Dan 3:28 **N** spoke, saying, "Blessed be
Dan 4: 1 **N** the king, To all peoples,
Dan 4: 4 I, **N**, was at rest in my house
Dan 4:18 This dream I, King **N**, have
Dan 4:28 All this came upon King **N**
Dan 4:31 King **N**, to you it is spoken
Dan 4:33 was fulfilled concerning **N**
Dan 4:34 at the end of the time I, **N**
Dan 4:37 Now I, **N**, praise and extol and
Dan 5: 2 vessels which his father **N**
Dan 5:11 and King **N** your father
Dan 5:18 gave **N** your father a kingdom

NEBUCHADNEZZAR'S (*see* NEBUCHADNEZZAR)
Dan 2: 1 in the second year of **N** reign

NEBUSHASBAN
Jer 39:13 captain of the guard sent **N**

NEBUZARADAN
2Ki 25: 8 **N** the captain of the guard, a
2Ki 25:11 Then **N** the captain of the
2Ki 25:20 So **N**, captain of the guard,
Jer 39: 9 Then **N** the captain of the
Jer 39:10 But **N** the captain of the
Jer 39:11 concerning Jeremiah to **N** the
Jer 39:13 So **N** the captain of the guard
Jer 40: 1 from the LORD after **N** the
Jer 40: 5 not yet gone back, **N** said,
Jer 41:10 whom **N** the captain of the
Jer 43: 6 and every person whom **N** the
Jer 52:12 **N**, the captain of the guard
Jer 52:15 Then **N** the captain of the
Jer 52:16 But **N** the captain of the
Jer 52:26 **N** the captain of the guard
Jer 52:30 **N** the captain of the guard

NECESSARY
Job 23:12 His mouth more than my **n** food
Luke 23:17 (for it was **n** for him to
Luke 24:46 thus it was **n** for the Christ
Acts 13:46 It was **n** that the word of God
Acts 15: 5 It is **n** to circumcise them,
Acts 15:28 burden than these **n** things
Acts 28:10 such things as were **n**
1Co 12:22 which seem to be weaker are **n**
2Co 9: 5 Therefore I thought it **n** to
Eph 4:29 is good for **n** edification
Phil 2:25 Yet I considered it **n** to send
Heb 8: 3 Therefore it is **n** that this
Heb 9:23 Therefore it was **n** that the
Jude 3 I found it **n** to write to you

NECESSITIES (*see* NECESSITY)
Acts 20:34 hands have provided for my **n**
Phil 4:16 aid once and again for my **n**

NECESSITY (*see* NECESSITIES)
1Co 7:37 in his heart, having no **n**
1Co 9:16 of, for **n** is laid upon me
2Co 9: 7 heart, not grudgingly or of **n**
Heb 7:12 of **n** there is also a change
Heb 9:16 there must also of **n** be the

NECHO (*see* PHARAOH)
2Ki 23:29 In his days Pharaoh **N** king of
2Ki 23:29 And Pharaoh **N** killed him at
2Ki 23:33 Now Pharaoh **N** put him in
2Ki 23:34 Then Pharaoh **N** made Eliakim
2Ki 23:35 to give it to Pharaoh **N**
2Ch 35:20 **N** king of Egypt came up to
2Ch 35:22 of **N** from the mouth of God
2Ch 36: 4 **N** took Jehoahaz his brother
Jer 46: 2 the army of Pharaoh **N**, king

NECK (*see* NECKS)
Gen 27:16 on the smooth part of his **n**
Gen 27:40 break his yoke from your **n**
Gen 33: 4 him, and fell on his **n** and
Gen 41:42 put a gold chain around his **n**
Gen 45:14 on his brother Benjamin's **n**
Gen 45:14 and Benjamin wept on his **n**
Gen 46:29 to him, and fell on his **n** and
Gen 46:29 wept on his **n** a good while
Gen 49: 8 be on the **n** of your enemies
Ex 13:13 then you shall break its **n**
Ex 34:20 then you shall break his **n**
Lev 5: 8 wring off its head from its **n**
Deut 21: 4 **n** there in the valley
Deut 21: 6 **n** was broken in the valley
Deut 28:48 **n** until He has destroyed you
Deut 31:27 rebellion and your stiff **n**
Judg 5:30 for the **n** of the looter
1Sa 4:18 his **n** was broken and he died,
2Ch 36:13 but he stiffened his **n** and
Job 16:12 He also has taken me by my **n**
Job 39:19 clothed his **n** with thunder
Job 41:22 Strength dwells in his **n**, and
Ps 69: 1 waters have come up to my **n**
Ps 75: 5 Do not speak with a stiff **n**
Prov 1: 9 head, and chains about your **n**
Prov 3: 3 bind them around your **n**,
Prov 3:22 your soul and grace to your **n**
Prov 6:21 tie them around your **n**
Prov 29: 1 reproved, and hardens his **n**
Song 1:10 your **n** with chains of gold
Song 4: 4 Your **n** is like the tower of
Song 7: 4 Your **n** is like an ivory tower
Is 8: 8 he will reach up to the **n**
Is 10:27 and his yoke from your **n**, and
Is 30:28 which reaches up to the **n**
Is 48: 4 your **n** was an iron sinew, and
Is 52: 2 from the bonds of your **n**, O
Is 66: 3 as if he breaks a dog's **n**
Jer 7:26 ear, but stiffened their **n**
Jer 17:23 ear, but made their **n** stiff
Jer 27: 2 yokes, and put them on your **n**
Jer 27: 8 and which will not put its **n**
Jer 28:10 off the prophet Jeremiah's **n**
Jer 28:11 king of Babylon from the **n** of
Jer 28:12 the **n** of the prophet Jeremiah
Jer 28:14 on the **n** of all these nations
Jer 30: 8 break his yoke from your **n**
Lam 1:14 hands, and thrust upon my **n**
Ezek 16:11 wrists, and a chain on your **n**
Dan 5: 7 a chain of gold around his **n**
Dan 5:16 a chain of gold around your **n**
Dan 5:29 a chain of gold around his **n**
Hos 10:11 but I harnessed her fair **n**
Hos 11: 4 take the yoke from their **n**
Hab 3:13 bare from foundation to **n**
Matt 18: 6 were hung around his **n**, and he
Mark 9:42 were hung around his **n**, and he
Luke 15:20 and ran and fell on his **n** and
Luke 17: 2 were hung around his **n**, and he
Acts 15:10 the **n** of the disciples which
Acts 20:37 freely, and fell on Paul's **n**

NECKLACE (*see* NECKLACES)
Ps 73: 6 pride serves as their **n**
Song 4: 9 eyes, with one link of your **n**

NECKLACES (*see* NECKLACE)
Ex 35:22 and nose rings, rings and **n**
Num 31:50 signet rings and earrings and **n**

NECKS (*see* NECK)
Josh 10:24 feet on the **n** of these kings
Josh 10:24 and put their feet on their **n**
Judg 8:21 that were on their camels' **n**
Judg 8:26 were around their camels' **n**
2Sa 22:41 given me the **n** of my enemies
2Ki 17:14 hear, but stiffened their **n**
2Ki 17:14 like the **n** of their fathers,
Neh 9:16 proudly, hardened their **n**
Neh 9:17 But they hardened their **n**
Neh 9:29 shoulders, stiffened their **n**
Ps 18:40 given me the **n** of my enemies
Is 3:16 and walk with outstretched **n**
Jer 19:15 they have stiffened their **n**
Jer 27:11 nations that bring their **n**
Jer 27:12 Bring your **n** under the yoke
Ezek 21:29 you on the **n** of the wicked
Mic 2: 3 you cannot remove your **n**
Rom 16: 4 their own **n** for my life, to

NEDABIAH
1Ch 3:18 Jecamiah, Hoshama, and **N**

NEED (*see* NEEDED, NEEDFUL, NEEDS, NEEDY)
Gen 33:15 he said, "What **n** is there
Ex 12: 4 according to each man's **n** you
Ex 16:16 it according to each one's **n**
Ex 16:18 according to each one's **n**
Ex 16:21 every man according to his **n**
Lev 13:36 the priest **n** not seek for
Deut 15: 8 lend him sufficient for his **n**
Deut 28:48 and in **n** of all things
1Sa 21:15 Have I **n** of madmen, that you
2Ki 22: 7 However there **n** be no
2Ch 2:16 Lebanon, as much as you **n**
2Ch 20:17 You will not **n** to fight in
Ezra 6: 9 And whatever they **n**
Job 34:23 For He **n** not further consider
Prov 6:11 and your **n** like an armed man
Prov 25:16 Eat only as much as you **n**
Is 64: 5 and we **n** to be saved
Ezek 36:30 so that you **n** never again
Dan 3:16 we have no **n** to answer you in
Matt 3:14 I have **n** to be baptized by
Matt 6: 8 have **n** of before you ask Him
Matt 6:32 that you **n** all these things
Matt 9:12 well have no **n** of a physician
Matt 14:16 They do not **n** to go away
Matt 21: 3 say, 'The Lord has **n** of them
Matt 26:65 What further **n** do we have of
Mark 2:17 well have no **n** of a physician
Mark 2:25 David did when he was in **n**
Mark 11: 3 say, 'The Lord has **n** of it
Mark 14:63 What further **n** do we have of
Luke 5:31 are well do not **n** a physician
Luke 9:11 those who had **n** of healing
Luke 12:30 knows that you **n** these things
Luke 15: 7 persons who **n** no repentance
Luke 19:31 Because the Lord has **n** of him
Luke 19:34 The Lord has **n** of him
Luke 22:71 further testimony do we **n**
John 2:25 had no **n** that anyone should
John 13:29 things we **n** for the feast
John 16:30 have no **n** that anyone should
Acts 2:45 among all, as anyone had **n**
Acts 4:35 to each as anyone had **n**
Rom 16: 2 business she has **n** of you
1Co 5:10 since then you would **n** to go
1Co 12:21 I have no **n** of you"
1Co 12:21 I have no **n** of you
1Co 12:24 presentable parts have no **n**
2Co 3: 1 Or do we **n**, as some others,
2Co 11: 9 was present with you, and in **n**
Eph 4:28 to give him who has **n**
Phil 2:25 one who ministered to my **n**
Phil 4:11 that I speak in regard to **n**
Phil 4:12 both to abound and to suffer **n**
Phil 4:19 God shall supply all your **n**
1Th 1: 8 we do not **n** to say anything
1Th 4: 9 **n** that I should write to you
1Th 5: 1 you have no **n** that I should
2Ti 2:15 who does not **n** to be ashamed
Heb 4:16 grace to help in time of **n**
Heb 5:12 you **n** someone to teach you
Heb 5:12 and you have come to **n** milk
Heb 7:11 what further **n** was there that
Heb 7:27 who does not **n** daily, as
Heb 10:36 For you have **n** of endurance
1Pe 1: 6 for a little while, if **n** be
1Jn 2:27 and you do not **n** that anyone
1Jn 3:17 and sees his brother in **n**
Rev 3:17 and have **n** of nothing'
Rev 21:23 the city had no **n** of the sun
Rev 22: 5 They **n** no lamp nor light of

NEEDED (*see* NEED)
Ezra 7:20 whatever more may be **n** for
Ezek 17: 9 or many people will be **n** to
Luke 10:42 But one thing is **n**, and Mary
John 4: 4 But He **n** to go through
Acts 17:25 as though He **n** anything,
Jas 2:16 which are **n** for the body,

NEEDFUL (*see* NEED)
Phil 1:24 the flesh is more **n** for you

NEEDLE (*see* NEEDLE'S)
Matt 19:24 of a **n** than for a rich man to
Mark 10:25 of a **n** than for a rich man to

NEEDLE'S (*see* NEEDLE)
Luke 18:25 **n** eye than for a rich man to

NEEDS (*see* NEED)
Num 3: 7 his **n** and the **n** of the whole
Num 3: 8 to the **n** of the children of
Num 3:38 to meet the **n** of the children
Num 8:26 of meeting, to attend to **n**
Num 18: 3 They shall attend to your **n**
Num 18: 3 all the **n** of the tabernacle
Num 18: 4 you and attend to the **n** of the
Deut 15: 8 for his need, whatever he **n**
Judg 3:24 to his **n** in the cool chamber
Judg 19:20 However, let all your **n** be my
1Sa 24: 3 went in to attend to his **n**
1Ch 23:32 to the **n** of the tabernacle of
1Ch 23:32 the **n** of the holy place, and
1Ch 23:32 the **n** of the sons of Aaron
Luke 11: 8 and give him as many as he **n**
John 13:10 He who is bathed **n** only to
Rom 12:13 to the **n** of the saints, given
2Co 6: 4 in tribulations, in **n**, in
2Co 9:12 supplies the **n** of the saints
2Co 12:10 in reproaches, in **n**, in
Tit 3:14 good works, to meet urgent **n**

NEEDY (*see* NEED)
Deut 15:11 to your poor and your **n**, in
Deut 24:14 servant who is poor and **n**,
Job 5:15 He saves the **n** from the sword
Job 24: 4 They push the **n** off the road
Job 24:14 he kills the poor and **n**
Ps 9:18 For the **n** shall not always be
Ps 12: 5 for the sighing of the **n**
Ps 35:10 the **n** from him who plunders
Ps 37:14 To cast down the poor and **n**
Ps 40:17 But I am poor and **n**
Ps 70: 5 But I am poor and **n**
Ps 72: 4 save the children of the **n**
Ps 72:12 deliver the **n** when he cries
Ps 72:13 He will spare the poor and **n**
Ps 72:13 will save the souls of the **n**
Ps 74:21 poor and **n** praise Your name
Ps 82: 3 justice to the afflicted and **n**
Ps 82: 4 Deliver the poor and **n**
Ps 86: 1 For I am poor and **n**
Ps 109:16 **n** man, That he might even
Ps 109:22 For I am poor and **n**, And my
Ps 113: 7 lifts the **n** out of the ash
Prov 14:31 honors Him has mercy on the **n**
Prov 30:14 and the **n** from among men
Prov 31: 9 the cause of the poor and **n**
Prov 31:20 out her hands to the **n**
Is 10: 2 to rob the **n** of justice, and
Is 14:30 the **n** will lie down in safety
Is 25: 4 to the **n** in his distress, a
Is 26: 6 poor and the steps of the **n**
Is 32: 7 words, even when the **n** speaks
Is 41:17 **n** seek water, and there is
Jer 5:28 the right of the **n** they do
Jer 22:16 the cause of the poor and **n**
Ezek 16:49 the hand of the poor and **n**
Ezek 18:12 has oppressed the poor and **n**
Ezek 22:29 and mistreated the poor and **n**
Amos 4: 1 the poor, who crush the **n**
Amos 8: 4 you who swallow up the **n**
Amos 8: 6 the **n** for a pair of sandals

NEGLECT (*see* NEGLECTED)
Josh 18: 3 How long will you **n** to go
Neh 10:39 we will not **n** the house of
Col 2:23 **n** of the body, but are of no
1Ti 4:14 Do not **n** the gift that is in
Heb 2: 3 if we **n** so great a salvation

NEGLECTED (*see* NEGLECT)
Matt 23:23 have **n** the weightier matters
Acts 6: 1 **n** in the daily distribution

NEGLIGENT
2Ch 29:11 My sons, do not be **n** now, for
2Pe 1:12 be **n** to remind you always of

NEHELAMITE
Jer 29:24 also speak to Shemaiah the **N**
Jer 29:31 concerning Shemaiah the **N**
Jer 29:32 I will punish Shemaiah the **N**

NEHEMIAH
Ezra 2: 2 Zerubbabel were Jeshua, **N**
Neh 1: 1 The words of **N** the son of
Neh 3:16 After him **N** the son of Azbuk,
Neh 7: 7 Zerubbabel were Jeshua, **N**
Neh 8: 9 And **N**, who was the governor,
Neh 10: 1 **N** the governor, the son of
Neh 12:26 in the days of **N** the governor
Neh 12:47 in the days of **N** all Israel

NEHUM (*see* REHUM)
Neh 7: 7 Bilshan, Mispereth, Bigvai, **N**

NEHUSHTA
2Ki 24: 8 His mother's name was **N** the

NEHUSHTAN
2Ki 18: 4 incense to it, and called it **N**

NEIEL
Josh 19:27 beyond Beth Emek and **N**,

NEIGHBOR (*see* NEIGHBORING, NEIGHBOR'S, NEIGHBORS)
Ex 3:22 woman shall ask of her **n**,
Ex 11: 2 let every man ask from his **n**
Ex 11: 2 and every woman from her **n**
Ex 12: 4 his **n** next to his house take
Ex 20:16 false witness against your **n**
Ex 21:14 premeditation against his **n**
Ex 22: 7 If a man delivers to his **n**
Ex 22: 9 shall pay double to his **n**
Ex 22:10 delivers to his **n** a donkey
Ex 22:14 borrows anything from his **n**
Ex 32:27 companion, and every man his **n**
Lev 6: 2 the LORD by lying to his **n**
Lev 6: 2 if he has extorted from his **n**
Lev 19:13 You shall not defraud your **n**
Lev 19:15 you shall judge your **n**
Lev 19:16 against the life of your **n**
Lev 19:17 shall surely rebuke your **n**
Lev 19:18 shall love your **n** as yourself
Lev 24:19 causes disfigurement of his **n**
Lev 25:14 you sell anything to your **n**
Lev 25:15 you shall buy from your **n**
Deut 4:42 flee there, who kills his **n**
Deut 5:20 false witness against your **n**
Deut 15: 2 to his **n** shall release it
Deut 15: 2 it of his **n** or his brother
Deut 19: 4 kills his **n** unintentionally
Deut 19: 5 with his **n** to cut timber, and
Deut 19: 5 strikes his **n** so that he dies
Deut 19:11 But if anyone hates his **n**
Deut 22:26 a man rises against his **n**
Deut 27:24 who attacks his **n** secretly
Josh 20: 5 struck his **n** unintentionally
Ruth 4:17 Also the **n** women gave him a
1Sa 14:20 man's sword was against his **n**
1Sa 15:28 has given it to a **n** of yours
1Sa 28:17 hand and given it to your **n**
2Sa 12:11 eyes and give them to your **n**
1Ki 8:31 anyone sins against his **n**
1Ki 20:35 his **n** by the word of the LORD
2Ch 6:22 If anyone sins against his **n**
Job 16:21 as a man pleads for his **n**
Ps 12: 2 idly everyone with his **n**
Ps 15: 3 Nor does evil to his **n**, Nor
Ps 101: 5 secretly slanders his **n**, Him
Prov 3:28 Do not say to your **n**, "Go,
Prov 3:29 devise evil against your **n**
Prov 11: 9 with his mouth destroys his **n**
Prov 11:12 of wisdom despises his **n**, but
Prov 14:20 is hated even by his own **n**
Prov 14:21 He who despises his **n** sins
Prov 16:29 A violent man entices his **n**

Prov 18:17 right, until his **n** comes and
Prov 21:10 his **n** finds no favor in his
Prov 24:28 against your **n** without cause
Prov 25: 8 when your **n** has put you to
Prov 25: 9 your case with your **n** himself
Prov 25:18 against his **n** is like a club
Prov 26:19 is the man who deceives his **n**
Prov 27:10 For better is a **n** nearby than
Prov 29: 5 A man who flatters his **n**
Eccl 4: 4 work a man is envied by his **n**
Is 3: 5 another and every one by his **n**
Is 19: 2 and everyone against his **n**
Is 41: 6 Everyone helped his **n**, and
Jer 6:21 The **n** and his friend shall
Jer 7: 5 between a man and his **n**,
Jer 9: 4 Everyone take heed to his **n**
Jer 9: 4 and every **n** will walk with
Jer 9: 5 Everyone will deceive his **n**
Jer 9: 8 to his **n** with his mouth, but
Jer 9:20 everyone her **n** a lamentation
Jer 22: 8 and everyone will say to his **n**
Jer 23:27 which everyone tells his **n**
Jer 23:30 My words every one from his **n**
Jer 23:35 one of you shall say to his **n**
Jer 31:34 shall every man teach his **n**
Jer 34:15 proclaiming liberty to his **n**
Jer 34:17 brother and every one to his **n**
Hab 2:15 him who gives drink to his **n**
Zech 3:10 invite his **n** under his vine
Zech 8:10 men, everyone, against his **n**
Zech 8:16 each man the truth to his **n**
Zech 8:17 in your heart against your **n**
Zech 14:13 will seize the hand of his **n**
Matt 5:43 said, 'You shall love your **n**
Matt 19:19 shall love your **n** as yourself
Matt 22:39 shall love your **n** as yourself
Mark 12:31 shall love your **n** as yourself
Mark 12:33 and to love one's **n** as oneself
Luke 10:27 mind,' and 'your **n** as yourself
Luke 10:29 And who is my **n**
Luke 10:36 three do you think was **n** to
Acts 7:27 But he who did his **n** wrong
Rom 13: 9 shall love your **n** as yourself
Rom 13:10 Love does no harm to a **n**
Rom 15: 2 us please his **n** for his good
Gal 5:14 shall love your **n** as yourself
Eph 4:25 one speak truth with his **n**
Heb 8:11 of them shall teach his **n**
Jas 2: 8 shall love your **n** as yourself

NEIGHBORING (*see* NEIGHBOR)
Deut 1: 7 to all the **n** places in the
Jer 49:18 their **n** cities," says the
Jer 50:40 their **n** cities," says the
Ezek 23: 5 her lovers, the **n** Assyrians,
Ezek 23:12 lusted for the **n** Assyrians

NEIGHBOR'S (*see* NEIGHBOR)
Ex 20:17 shall not covet your **n** house
Ex 20:17 shall not covet your **n** wife
Ex 20:17 nor anything that is your **n**
Ex 22: 8 put his hand into his **n** goods
Ex 22:11 put his hand into his **n** goods
Ex 22:26 your **n** garment as a pledge
Lev 18:20 lie carnally with your **n** wife
Lev 20:10 adultery with his **n** wife, the
Lev 25:14 or buy from your **n** hand, you
Deut 5:21 shall not covet your **n** wife
Deut 5:21 shall not desire your **n** house
Deut 5:21 or anything that is your **n**
Deut 19:14 not remove your **n** landmark
Deut 22:24 because he humbled his **n** wife
Deut 23:24 you come into your **n** vineyard
Deut 23:25 into your **n** standing grain
Deut 23:25 on your **n** standing grain
Deut 27:17 one who moves his **n** landmark
Job 31: 9 if I have lurked at my **n** door
Prov 6:29 he who goes in to his **n** wife
Prov 25:17 set foot in your **n** house,
Jer 5: 8 one neighed after his **n** wife
Jer 22:13 who uses his **n** service
Ezek 18: 6 nor defiled his **n** wife, nor
Ezek 18:11 or defiled his **n** wife
Ezek 18:15 Nor defiled his **n** wife
Ezek 22:11 abomination with his **n** wife
Zech 11: 6 give everyone into his **n** hand
Zech 14:13 his hand against his **n** hand

NEIGHBORS (*see* NEIGHBOR, NEIGHBORS')
Josh 9:16 their **n** who dwelt near them
2Ki 4: 3 everywhere, from all your **n**
Ps 28: 3 Who speak peace to their **n**
Ps 31:11 But especially among my **n**
Ps 44:13 make us a reproach to our **n**
Ps 79: 4 become a reproach to our **n**
Ps 79:12 return to our **n** sevenfold
Ps 80: 6 made us a strife to our **n**
Ps 89:41 He is a reproach to his **n**
Jer 12:14 Against all My evil **n** who
Jer 49:10 his brethren and his **n**, and he
Ezek 16:26 your very fleshly **n**, and
Ezek 22:12 from your **n** by extortion, and
Luke 1:58 When her **n** and relatives heard
Luke 14:12 relatives, nor your rich **n**
Luke 15: 6 together his friends and **n**
Luke 15: 9 **n** together, saying, 'Rejoice
John 9: 8 Therefore the **n** and those who

NEIGHBORS' (*see* NEIGHBORS)
Jer 29:23 adultery with their **n** wives

NEIGHED (*see* NEIGHING)
Jer 5: 8 every one **n** after his

NEIGHING (*see* NEIGHED, NEIGHINGS)
Jer 8:16 of the **n** of His strong ones

NEIGHINGS (*see* NEIGHING)
Jer 13:27 adulteries and your lustful **n**

NEITHER (*see* PREFACE)

NEKODA
Ezra 2:48 sons of Rezin, the sons of **N**
Ezra 2:60 of Tobiah, and the sons of **N**
Neh 7:50 of Rezin, the children of **N**
Neh 7:62 of Tobiah, the children of **N**

NEMUEL (*see* JEMUEL, NEMUELITES)
Num 26: 9 The sons of Eliab were **N**,
Num 26:12 of **N**, the family of the
1Ch 4:24 The sons of Simeon were **N**

NEMUELITES (*see* NEMUEL)
Num 26:12 Nemuel, the family of the **N**

NEPHEG
Ex 6:21 sons of Izhar were Korah, **N**
2Sa 5:15 Ibhar, Elishua, **N**, Japhia,
1Ch 3: 7 Nogah, **N**, Japhia,
1Ch 14: 6 Nogah, **N**, Japhia,

NEPHISHESIM (*see* NEPHUSIM)
Neh 7:52 of Meunim, the children of **N**

NEPHTOAH
Josh 15: 9 fountain of the water of **N**
Josh 18:15 the spring of the waters of **N**

NEPHUSIM (*see* NEPHISHESIM)
Ezra 2:50 sons of Meunim, the sons of **N**

NER
1Sa 14:50 army was Abner the son of **N**
1Sa 14:51 **N** the father of Abner was the
1Sa 26: 5 lay, and Abner the son of **N**
1Sa 26:14 and to Abner the son of **N**,
2Sa 2: 8 But Abner the son of **N**,
2Sa 2:12 Now Abner the son of **N**, and
2Sa 3:23 the son of **N** came to the king
2Sa 3:25 son of **N** came to deceive you
2Sa 3:28 blood of Abner the son of **N**
2Sa 3:37 to kill Abner the son of **N**
1Ki 2: 5 Israel, to Abner the son of **N**
1Ki 2:32 Abner the son of **N**, the
1Ch 8:33 **N** begot Kish, Kish begot Saul
1Ch 9:36 then Zur, Kish, Baal, **N**,
1Ch 9:39 **N** begot Kish, Kish begot Saul
1Ch 26:28 of Kish, Abner the son of **N**

NEREUS
Rom 16:15 Greet Philologus and Julia, **N**

NERGAL (*see* NERGAL-SAREZER, NERGAL-SHAREZER)
2Ki 17:30 the men of Cuth made **N**, the

NERGAL-SAREZER (*see* NERGAL)
Jer 39: 3 Sarsechim, Rabsaris, **N**,

NERGAL-SHAREZER (*see* NERGAL)
Jer 39: 3 **N**, Samgar-Nebo, Sarsechim,
Jer 39:13 sent Nebushasban, Rabsaris, **N**

NERI
Luke 3:27 of Shealtiel, the son of **N**

NERIAH
Jer 32:12 deed to Baruch the son of **N**
Jer 32:16 deed to Baruch the son of **N**
Jer 36: 4 called Baruch the son of **N**
Jer 36: 8 And Baruch the son of **N** did
Jer 36:14 So Baruch the son of **N** took
Jer 36:32 the scribe, the son of **N**, who
Jer 43: 3 But Baruch the son of **N** has
Jer 43: 6 and Baruch the son of **N**
Jer 45: 1 spoke to Baruch the son of **N**
Jer 51:59 Seraiah the son of **N**, the son

NEST (*see* NESTED, NESTS)
Num 24:21 your **n** is set in the rock
Deut 22: 6 If a bird's **n** happens to be
Deut 32:11 As an eagle stirs up its **n**
Job 29:18 I said, 'I shall die in my **n**
Job 39:27 and make its **n** on high
Ps 84: 3 the swallow a **n** for herself
Prov 27: 8 **n** is a man who wanders from
Is 10:14 a **n** the riches of the people
Is 16: 2 bird thrown out of the **n**
Is 34:15 arrow snake shall make her **n**
Jer 22:23 making your **n** in the cedars,
Jer 48:28 the dove which makes her **n** in
Jer 49:16 your **n** as high as the eagle
Obad 4 set your **n** among the stars
Hab 2: 9 that he may set his **n** on high
Matt 13:32 air come and **n** in its branches
Mark 4:32 the air may **n** under its shade

NESTED (*see* NEST)
Luke 13:19 of the air **n** in its branches

NESTLED
Job 30: 7 under the nettles they **n**

NESTS (*see* NEST)
Ps 104:17 Where the birds make their **n**
Ezek 31: 6 made their **n** in its boughs
Matt 8:20 and birds of the air have **n**
Luke 9:58 and birds of the air have **n**

NET (*see* NETS)
Job 18: 8 cast into a **n** by his own feet
Job 18: 9 The **n** takes him by the heel,
Job 19: 6 has surrounded me with His **n**
Ps 9:15 In the **n** which they hid,
Ps 10: 9 when he draws him into his **n**
Ps 25:15 pluck my feet out of the **n**
Ps 31: 4 Pull me out of the **n** which
Ps 35: 7 their **n** for me in a pit,
Ps 35: 8 let his **n** that he has hidden
Ps 57: 6 prepared a **n** for my steps
Ps 66:11 You brought us into the **n**
Ps 140: 5 spread a **n** by the wayside
Prov 1:17 in vain the **n** is spread in
Prov 29: 5 spreads a **n** for his feet
Eccl 9:12 Like fish taken in a cruel **n**
Is 51:20 like an antelope in a **n**
Lam 1:13 He has spread a **n** for my feet
Ezek 12:13 also spread My **n** over him
Ezek 17:20 I will spread My **n** over him
Ezek 19: 8 and spread their **n** over him
Ezek 32: 3 **n** over you with a company of
Ezek 32: 3 they will draw you up in My **n**
Hos 5: 1 Mizpah and a **n** spread on Tabor
Hos 7:12 I will spread My **n** on them
Mic 7: 2 hunts his brother with a **n**
Hab 1:15 they catch them in their **n**
Hab 1:16 they sacrifice to their **n**
Hab 1:17 they therefore empty their **n**
Matt 4:18 casting a **n** into the sea
Mark 1:16 casting a **n** into the sea
Luke 5: 5 word I will let down the **n**
Luke 5: 6 fish, and their **n** was breaking
John 21: 6 Cast the **n** on the right side
John 21: 8 dragging the **n** with fish
John 21:11 up and dragged the **n** to land
John 21:11 so many, the **n** was not broken

NETAIM
1Ch 4:23 and those who dwell at **N** and

NETHANEAL
Neh 12:21 and of Jedaiah, **N**
Neh 12:36 Milalai, Gilalai, Maai, **N**

NETHANEEL
Num 1: 8 Issachar, **N** the son of Zuar
Num 2: 5 **N** the son of Zuar shall be
Num 7:18 second day **N** the son of Zuar
Num 7:23 offering of **N** the son of Zuar
Num 10:15 was **N** the son of Zuar
1Ch 15:24 Shebaniah, Joshaphat, **N**,
1Ch 24: 6 scribe, Shemaiah the son of **N**
2Ch 17: 7 Obadiah, Zechariah, **N**, and
2Ch 35: 9 his brothers Shemaiah and **N**
Ezra 10:22 Maaseiah, Ishmael, **N**,

NETHANEL
1Ch 2:14 **N** the fourth, Raddai the
1Ch 26: 4 the fourth, **N** the fifth,

NETHANIAH
2Ki 25:23 Ishmael the son of **N**, Johanan
2Ki 25:25 that Ishmael the son of **N**
1Ch 25: 2 Zaccur, Joseph, **N**, and
1Ch 25:12 the fifth for **N**, his sons and
2Ch 17: 8 Shemaiah, **N**, Zebadiah, Asahel
Jer 36:14 sent Jehudi the son of **N**, the
Jer 40: 8 Ishmael the son of **N**, Johanan
Jer 40:14 the son of **N** to murder you
Jer 40:15 kill Ishmael the son of **N**
Jer 41: 1 that Ishmael the son of **N**
Jer 41: 2 Then Ishmael the son of **N**
Jer 41: 6 Now Ishmael the son of **N** went
Jer 41: 7 the son of **N** killed them and
Jer 41: 9 Ishmael the son of **N** filled
Jer 41:10 Ishmael the son of **N** carried
Jer 41:11 Ishmael the son of **N** had done
Jer 41:12 with Ishmael the son of **N**
Jer 41:15 But Ishmael the son of **N**
Jer 41:16 of **N** after he had murdered
Jer 41:18 **N** had murdered Gedaliah the

NETHINIM
1Ch 9: 2 priests, Levites, and the **N**
Ezra 2:43 The **N**: the sons of
Ezra 2:58 All the **N** and the children of
Ezra 2:70 the gatekeepers, and the **N**
Ezra 7: 7 the **N** came up to Jerusalem in
Ezra 7:24 singers, gatekeepers, **N**, or
Ezra 8:17 his brethren the **N** at the
Ezra 8:20 also of the **N**, whom David and
Ezra 8:20 two hundred and twenty **N**
Neh 3:26 Moreover the **N** who dwelt in
Neh 3:31 as far as the house of the **N**
Neh 7:46 The **N**: the children of
Neh 7:60 All the **N**, and the children of
Neh 7:73 some of the people, the **N**
Neh 10:28 the singers, the **N**, and all
Neh 11: 3 priests, Levites, **N**, and
Neh 11:21 But the **N** dwelt in Ophel
Neh 11:21 and Gishpa were over the **N**

NETOPHAH (*see* NETOPHATHITE)
Ezra 2:22 the men of **N**, fifty-six
Neh 7:26 the men of Bethlehem and **N**

NETOPHATHITE (*see* NETOPHAH, NETOPHATHITES)
2Sa 23:28 the Ahohite, Maharai the **N**
2Sa 23:29 the son of Baanah (the **N**)
2Ki 25:23 the son of Tanhumeth the **N**
1Ch 11:30 Maharai the **N**, Heled the son
1Ch 11:30 Heled the son of Baanah the **N**
1Ch 27:13 tenth month was Maharai the **N**
1Ch 27:15 month was Heldai the **N**, of
Jer 40: 8 the sons of Ephai the **N**, and

NETOPHATHITES (*see* NETOPHATHITE)
1Ch 2:54 Salma were Bethlehem, the **N**
1Ch 9:16 in the villages of the **N**
Neh 12:28 from the villages of the **N**

NETS (*see* NET)
Ps 141:10 wicked fall into their own **n**
Eccl 7:26 whose heart is snares and **n**
Is 19: 8 who spread **n** on the waters
Ezek 19: 9 they brought him in **n**, that
Ezek 26: 5 **n** in the midst of the sea
Ezek 26:14 be a place for spreading **n**
Ezek 47:10 places for spreading their **n**
Matt 4:20 they immediately left their **n**
Matt 4:21 their father, mending their **n**
Mark 1:18 immediately they left their **n**
Mark 1:19 in the boat mending their **n**
Luke 5: 2 them and were washing their **n**
Luke 5: 4 let down your **n** for a catch

NETTLES
Job 30: 7 under the **n** they nestled
Prov 24:31 surface was covered with **n**
Is 34:13 come up in its palaces, **n**
Hos 9: 6 **N** shall possess their

NETWORK (*see* NETWORKS)
Ex 27: 4 a grate for it, a **n** of bronze
Ex 27: 4 on the **n** you shall make four
Ex 27: 5 that the **n** may be midway up
Ex 38: 4 of bronze a **n** for the altar
1Ki 7:17 He made a lattice **n**, with
1Ki 7:18 the **n** all around to cover the
1Ki 7:20 which was next to the **n**
1Ki 7:42 of pomegranates for each **n**
2Ki 25:17 was three cubits, and the **n**
2Ki 25:17 pillar was the same, with a **n**
2Ch 4:13 of pomegranates for each **n**
Jer 52:22 was five cubits, with a **n**
Jer 52:23 all around on the **n**, were

NETWORKS (*see* NETWORK)
1Ki 7:41 the two **n** covering the two
1Ki 7:42 pomegranates for the two **n**
2Ch 4:12 the two **n** covering the two
2Ch 4:13 pomegranates for the two **n**

NEVER (*see* PREFACE)

NEVERMORE (*see* PREFACE)

NEVERTHELESS (*see* PREFACE)

NEW (*see* NEWBORN, NEWLY, NEWNESS, NEWS)
Ex 1: 8 arose a **n** king over Egypt
Lev 23:16 then you shall offer a **n**
Lev 26:10 out the old because of the **n**
Num 16:30 if the LORD creates a **n** thing
Num 18:12 all the best of the **n** wine
Num 28:26 when you bring a **n** grain
Num 29: 6 grain offering for the **N** Moon
Deut 7:13 your grain and your **n** wine
Deut 11:14 in your grain, your **n** wine
Deut 12:17 or your **n** wine or your oil
Deut 14:23 of your grain and your **n** wine
Deut 18: 4 of your grain and your **n** wine
Deut 20: 5 there who has built a **n** house
Deut 22: 8 When you build a **n** house,
Deut 24: 5 When a man has taken a **n** wife
Deut 28:51 you grain or **n** wine or oil
Deut 32:17 to **n** gods, **n** arrivals that
Deut 33:28 in a land of grain and **n** wine
Josh 9:13 which we filled were **n**, and
Judg 5: 8 They chose **n** gods
Judg 9:13 Should I cease my **n** wine
Judg 15:13 bound him with two **n** ropes
Judg 16:11 **n** ropes that have never been
Judg 16:12 Delilah took **n** ropes and bound
1Sa 6: 7 Now therefore, make a **n** cart
1Sa 20: 5 Indeed tomorrow is the **N** Moon
1Sa 20:18 Tomorrow is the **N** Moon
1Sa 20:24 when the **N** Moon had come, the
2Sa 6: 3 the ark of God on a **n** cart
2Sa 6: 3 of Abinadab, drove the **n** cart
2Sa 21:16 who was bearing a **n** sword
1Ki 11:29 himself with a **n** garment, and
1Ki 11:30 the **n** garment that was on him
2Ki 2:20 Bring me a **n** bowl, and put
2Ki 4:23 It is neither the **N** Moon nor
2Ki 16:14 from between the **n** altar and
2Ki 16:14 the north side of the **n** altar
2Ki 16:15 On the great **n** altar burn the
2Ki 18:32 **n** wine, a land of bread and
1Ch 13: 7 on a **n** cart from the house of
1Ch 23:31 Sabbaths and on the **N** Moons
2Ch 2: 4 the Sabbaths, on the **N** Moons
2Ch 8:13 the **N** Moons, and the three
2Ch 20: 5 the LORD, before the **n** court
2Ch 31: 3 the **N** Moons and the set feasts
Ezra 3: 5 and those for **N** Moons and for
Ezra 6: 4 stones and one row of **n** timber
Neh 5:11 the **n** wine and the oil, that
Neh 10:33 the **N** Moons, and the set
Neh 10:37 the **n** wine and oil, to the
Neh 10:39 of the grain, of the **n** wine
Neh 13: 5 the **n** wine and oil, which were
Neh 13:12 the **n** wine and the oil to the
Job 32:19 to burst like **n** wineskins
Ps 33: 3 Sing to Him a **n** song
Ps 40: 3 He has put a **n** song in my
Ps 81: 3 at the time of the **N** Moon
Ps 96: 1 Oh, sing to the LORD a **n** song
Ps 98: 1 Oh, sing to the LORD a **n** song
Ps 144: 9 I will sing a **n** song to You
Ps 149: 1 Sing to the LORD a **n** song
Prov 3:10 will overflow with **n** wine
Eccl 1: 9 is nothing **n** under the sun
Eccl 1:10 See, this is **n**"
Song 7:13 fruits, all manner, **n** and old,
Is 1:13 The **N** Moons, the Sabbaths,
Is 1:14 Your **N** Moons and your
Is 24: 7 The **n** wine fails, the vine
Is 36:17 **n** wine, a land of bread and
Is 41:15 I will make you into a **n**
Is 42: 9 pass, and **n** things I declare
Is 42:10 Sing to the LORD a **n** song
Is 43:19 Behold, I will do a **n** thing
Is 48: 6 I have made you hear **n** things
Is 62: 2 shall be called by a **n** name
Is 62: 8 shall not drink your **n** wine
Is 65: 8 As the **n** wine is found in the
Is 65:17 **n** heavens and a **n** earth
Is 66:22 For as the **n** heavens and the
Is 66:22 the **n** earth which I will make
Is 66:23 from one **N** Moon to another
Jer 26:10 **n** gate of the LORD's house
Jer 31:12 **n** wine and oil, for the young
Jer 31:22 a **n** thing in the earth
Jer 31:31 when I will make a **n** covenant
Jer 36:10 **N** Gate of the LORD's house
Lam 3:23 They are **n** every morning
Ezek 11:19 I will put a **n** spirit within
Ezek 18:31 a **n** heart and a **n** spirit
Ezek 36:26 I will give you a **n** heart
Ezek 36:26 put a **n** spirit within you
Ezek 45:17 the **N** Moons, the Sabbaths, and
Ezek 46: 1 on the day of the **N** Moon it
Ezek 46: 3 the Sabbaths and the **N** Moons
Ezek 46: 6 On the day of the **N** Moon it
Hos 2: 8 **n** wine, and oil, and multiplied
Hos 2: 9 My **n** wine in its season, and
Hos 2:11 her **N** Moons, her Sabbaths
Hos 2:22 With grain, with **n** wine, and
Hos 4:11 and **n** wine enslave the heart
Hos 5: 7 Now a **N** Moon shall devour
Hos 7:14 **n** wine, They rebel against Me
Hos 9: 2 the **n** wine shall fail in her
Joel 1: 5 wine, because of the **n** wine
Joel 1:10 the **n** wine is dried up, the
Joel 2:19 **n** wine and oil, and you will be
Joel 2:24 shall overflow with **n** wine
Joel 3:18 shall drip with **n** wine, the
Amos 8: 5 When will the **N** Moon be past
Hag 1:11 the **n** wine and the oil, on
Zech 9:17 and **n** wine the young women
Matt 9:17 Nor do people put **n** wine into
Matt 9:17 But they put **n** wine into **n**
Matt 9:17 put **n** wine into **n** wineskins
Matt 13:52 out of his treasure things **n**
Matt 26:28 is My blood of the **n** covenant
Matt 26:29 it **n** with you in My Father's
Matt 27:60 laid it in his **n** tomb which
Mark 1:27 What **n** doctrine is this
Mark 2:21 or else the **n** piece pulls
Mark 2:22 no one puts **n** wine into old
Mark 2:22 or else the **n** wine bursts the
Mark 2:22 But **n** wine must be put into
Mark 2:22 must be put into **n** wineskins
Mark 14:24 is My blood of the **n** covenant
Mark 14:25 it **n** in the kingdom of God
Mark 16:17 will speak with **n** tongues
Luke 5:36 a **n** garment on an old one
Luke 5:36 otherwise the **n** makes a tear
Luke 5:36 the **n** does not match the old
Luke 5:37 no one puts **n** wine into old
Luke 5:37 or else the **n** wine will burst
Luke 5:38 But **n** wine must be put into
Luke 5:38 must be put into **n** wineskins
Luke 5:39 wine, immediately desires **n**
Luke 22:20 This cup is the **n** covenant in
John 13:34 A **n** commandment I give to you
John 19:41 in the garden a **n** tomb in
Acts 2:13 They are full of **n** wine
Acts 17:19 May we know what this **n**
Acts 17:21 tell or to hear some **n** thing
1Co 5: 7 that you may be a **n** lump
1Co 11:25 This cup is the **n** covenant in
2Co 3: 6 ministers of the **n** covenant
2Co 5:17 in Christ, he is a **n** creation
2Co 5:17 all things have become **n**
Gal 6:15 anything, but a **n** creation
Eph 2:15 one **n** man from the two, thus
Eph 4:24 that you put on the **n** man
Col 2:16 or a **n** moon or sabbaths,
Col 3:10 have put on the **n** man who is
Heb 8: 8 when I will make a **n** covenant
Heb 8:13 A **n** covenant," He has made
Heb 9:15 Mediator of the **n** covenant
Heb 10:20 by a **n** and living way which He
Heb 12:24 Mediator of the **n** covenant
2Pe 3:13 promise, look for **n** heavens
2Pe 3:13 heavens and a **n** earth in which
1Jn 2: 7 I write no **n** commandment to
1Jn 2: 8 a **n** commandment I write to
2Jn 5 wrote a **n** commandment to you

Rev 2:17 on the stone a **n** name written
Rev 3:12 the **N** Jerusalem, which comes
Rev 3:12 I will write on him My **n** name
Rev 5: 9 And they sang a **n** song, saying
Rev 14: 3 a **n** song before the throne
Rev 21: 1 I saw a **n** heaven and a **n** earth
Rev 21: 2 **N** Jerusalem, coming down out
Rev 21: 5 Behold, I make all things **n**

NEWBORN (*see* NEW)
1Pe 2: 2 as **n** babes, desire the pure

NEWLY (*see* NEW)
2Ki 4:42 and **n** ripened grain in his

NEWNESS (*see* NEW)
Rom 6: 4 also should walk in **n** of life
Rom 7: 6 serve in the **n** of the Spirit

NEWS (*see* NEW)
1Sa 4:19 when she heard the **n** that the
1Sa 11: 4 told the **n** in the hearing of
1Sa 11: 6 Saul when he heard this **n**
1Sa 17:18 fare, and bring back **n** of them
1Sa 27:11 alive, to bring **n** to Gath
2Sa 4: 4 old when the **n** about Saul
2Sa 4:10 to have brought good **n**, I
2Sa 4:10 give him a reward for his **n**
2Sa 13:30 that **n** came to David, saying,
2Sa 18:19 take the **n** to the king, how
2Sa 18:20 shall not take the **n** this day
2Sa 18:20 shall take the **n** another day
2Sa 18:20 But today you shall take no **n**
2Sa 18:22 since you have no **n** ready
2Sa 18:25 there is **n** in his mouth
2Sa 18:26 He also brings **n**
2Sa 18:27 man, and comes with good **n**
2Sa 18:31 There is good **n**, my lord the
1Ki 2:28 Then **n** came to Joab, for Joab
1Ki 14: 6 been sent to you with bad **n**
2Ki 7: 9 This day is a day of good **n**
1Ch 10: 9 the **n** in the temple of their
1Ch 16:23 proclaim the good **n** of His
Ps 40: 9 **n** of righteousness In the
Ps 96: 2 Proclaim the good **n** of His
Prov 25:25 soul, so is good **n** from a far
Is 52: 7 feet of him who brings good **n**
Jer 20:15 who brought **n** to my father
Jer 37: 5 Jerusalem heard **n** of them
Jer 49:23 for they have heard bad **n**
Ezek 21: 7 answer, 'Because of the **n**
Dan 11:44 But **n** from the east and the
Nah 3:19 All who hear **n** of you will
Matt 9:31 they spread the **n** about Him
Luke 4:14 **n** of Him went out through all
Acts 11:22 Then **n** of these things came
Acts 21:31 **n** came to the commander of
Col 4: 7 tell you all the **n** about me
1Th 3: 6 us good **n** of your faith and

NEXT (*see* PREFACE)

NEZIAH
Ezra 2:54 the sons of **N**, and the sons of
Neh 7:56 the children of **N**, and the

NEZIB
Josh 15:43 Jiphtah, Ashnah, **N**,

NIBHAZ
2Ki 17:31 and the Avites made **N** and

NIBSHAN
Josh 15:62 **N**, the City of Salt, and En

NICANOR
Acts 6: 5 and Philip, Prochorus, **N**,

NICODEMUS
John 3: 1 man of the Pharisees named **N**
John 3: 4 **N** said to Him, "How can a
John 3: 9 **N** answered and said to Him
John 7:50 **N** (he who came to Jesus by
John 19:39 And **N**, who at first came to

NICOLAITANS
Rev 2: 6 you hate the deeds of the **N**
Rev 2:15 hold the doctrine of the **N**

NICOLAS
Acts 6: 5 Timon, Parmenas, and **N**, a

NICOPOLIS
Tit 3:12 diligent to come to me at **N**

NIGER (*see* SIMEON, SIMON)
Acts 13: 1 Simeon who was called **N**,

NIGHT (*see* NIGHTS)
Gen 1: 5 and the darkness He called **N**
Gen 1:14 to divide the day from the **n**
Gen 1:16 lesser light to rule the **n**
Gen 1:18 over the day and over the **n**
Gen 8:22 and day and **n** shall not cease
Gen 14:15 his forces against them by **n**
Gen 19: 2 house and spend the **n**, and wash
Gen 19: 2 the **n** in the open square
Gen 19:33 father drink wine that **n**
Gen 19:34 I lay with my father last **n**
Gen 19:35 father drink wine that **n** also
Gen 20: 3 to Abimelech in a dream by **n**
Gen 24:54 ate and drank and stayed all **n**
Gen 26:24 appeared to him the same **n**
Gen 28:11 place and stayed there all **n**
Gen 30:16 And he lay with her that **n**
Gen 31:24 the Syrian in a dream by **n**
Gen 31:29 father spoke to me last **n**
Gen 31:39 stolen by day or stolen by **n**
Gen 31:40 me, and the frost by **n**, and my
Gen 31:42 hands, and rebuked you last **n**
Gen 31:54 stayed all **n** on the mountain
Gen 32:13 he lodged there that same **n**
Gen 32:21 lodged that **n** in the camp
Gen 32:22 And he arose that **n** and took
Gen 40: 5 each man's dream in one **n**
Gen 41:11 each dreamed a dream in one **n**
Gen 46: 2 in the visions of the **n**, and
Gen 49:27 and at **n** he shall divide the
Ex 10:13 all that day and all that **n**
Ex 12: 8 shall eat the flesh on that **n**
Ex 12:12 the land of Egypt on that **n**
Ex 12:30 So Pharaoh rose in the **n**, he,
Ex 12:31 for Moses and Aaron by **n**, and
Ex 12:42 It is a **n** of solemn
Ex 12:42 This is that **n** of the LORD
Ex 13:21 by **n** in a pillar of fire to
Ex 13:21 so as to go by day and **n**
Ex 13:22 by **n** from before the people
Ex 14:20 gave light by **n** to the other
Ex 14:20 near the other all that **n**
Ex 14:21 a strong east wind all that **n**
Ex 40:38 day, and fire was over it by **n**
Lev 6: 9 the altar all **n** until morning
Lev 6:20 morning and half of it at **n**
Lev 8:35 **n** for seven days, and keep the
Lev 19:13 with you all **n** until morning
Num 9:16 the appearance of fire by **n**
Num 9:21 whether by day or by **n**,
Num 11: 9 dew fell on the camp in the **n**
Num 11:32 up all that day, all that **n**
Num 14: 1 and the people wept that **n**
Num 14:14 and in a pillar of fire by **n**
Num 22:20 And God came to Balaam at **n**
Deut 1:33 should go, in the fire by **n**
Deut 16: 1 brought you out of Egypt by **n**
Deut 23:10 by some occurrence in the **n**
Deut 28:66 you shall fear day and **n**, and
Josh 1: 8 shall meditate in it day and **n**
Josh 8: 3 valor and sent them away by **n**
Josh 8: 9 that **n** among the people
Josh 8:13 Joshua went that **n** into the
Josh 10: 9 marched all **n** from Gilgal
Judg 6:25 it came to pass the same **n**
Judg 6:27 do it by day, he did it by **n**
Judg 6:40 And God did so that **n**
Judg 7: 9 it happened on the same **n**
Judg 9:32 Now therefore, get up by **n**
Judg 9:34 who were with him rose by **n**
Judg 16: 2 all **n** at the gate of the city
Judg 16: 2 They were quiet all **n**, saying
Judg 19: 6 be content to stay all **n**, and
Judg 19: 9 please spend the **n**
Judg 19:10 not willing to spend that **n**
Judg 19:13 spend the **n** in Gibeah or in
Judg 19:15 into his house to spend the **n**
Judg 19:20 the **n** in the open square
Judg 19:25 her all **n** until morning
Judg 20: 4 to Benjamin, to spend the **n**
Judg 20: 5 the house at **n** because of me
Ruth 3:13 Stay this **n**, and in the
1Sa 14:34 his ox with him that **n**, and
1Sa 14:36 after the Philistines by **n**
1Sa 15:11 cried out to the LORD all **n**
1Sa 15:16 the LORD said to me last **n**
1Sa 19:10 David fled and escaped that **n**
1Sa 19:24 all that day and all that **n**
1Sa 25:16 were a wall to us both by **n**
1Sa 26: 7 came to the people by **n**
1Sa 28: 8 they came to the woman by **n**
1Sa 28:20 no food all day or all **n**
1Sa 28:25 they rose and went away that **n**
1Sa 31:12 men arose and traveled all **n**
2Sa 2:29 all that **n** through the plain
2Sa 2:32 And Joab and his men went all **n**
2Sa 4: 7 were all **n** escaping through
2Sa 7: 4 But it happened that **n** that
2Sa 12:16 in and lay all **n** on the ground
2Sa 17:16 Do not spend this **n** in the
2Sa 19: 7 one will stay with you this **n**
2Sa 21:10 the beasts of the field by **n**
1Ki 3: 5 to Solomon in a dream by **n**
1Ki 3:19 woman's son died in the **n**
1Ki 3:20 arose in the middle of the **n**
1Ki 8:29 be open toward this temple **n**
1Ki 8:59 the LORD our God day and **n**
1Ki 19: 9 spent the **n** in that place
2Ki 6:14 army there, and they came by **n**
2Ki 7:12 Then the king arose in the **n**
2Ki 8:21 And he rose by **n** and attacked
2Ki 19:35 came to pass on a certain **n**
2Ki 25: 4 **n** by way of the gate between
1Ch 9:33 in that work day and **n**
1Ch 17: 3 But it happened that **n** that
2Ch 1: 7 On that **n** God appeared to
2Ch 6:20 toward this temple day and **n**
2Ch 7:12 LORD appeared to Solomon by **n**
2Ch 21: 9 And he rose by **n** and attacked
2Ch 35:14 offerings and fat until **n**
Neh 1: 6 pray before You now, day and **n**
Neh 2:12 Then I arose in the **n**, I and a
Neh 2:13 I went out by **n** through the
Neh 2:15 up in the **n** by the valley
Neh 4: 9 a watch against them day and **n**
Neh 4:22 stay at **n** in Jerusalem, that
Neh 4:22 they may be our guard by **n**
Neh 6:10 at **n** they will come to kill
Neh 9:12 by **n** with a pillar of fire,
Neh 9:19 nor the pillar of fire by **n**
Neh 13:21 spend the **n** around the wall
Esth 4:16 for three days, **n** or day
Esth 6: 1 That **n** the king could not
Job 3: 3 the **n** in which it was said
Job 3: 6 As for that **n**, may darkness
Job 3: 7 Oh, may that **n** be barren
Job 4:13 from the visions of the **n**
Job 5:14 grope at noontime as in the **n**
Job 7: 4 I arise, and the **n** be ended
Job 17:12 They change the **n** into day
Job 20: 8 away like a vision of the **n**
Job 24: 7 They spend the **n** naked,
Job 24:14 in the **n** he is like a thief
Job 27:20 steals him away in the **n**
Job 29:19 dew lies all **n** on my branch
Job 30:17 bones are pierced in me at **n**
Job 33:15 a dream, in a vision of the **n**
Job 34:20 die, in the middle of the **n**
Job 34:25 He overthrows them in the **n**
Job 35:10 Who gives songs in the **n**
Job 36:20 Do not desire the **n**, when
Ps 1: 2 His law he meditates day and **n**
Ps 6: 6 All **n** I make my bed swim
Ps 16: 7 instructs me in the **n** seasons
Ps 17: 3 You have visited me in the **n**
Ps 19: 2 And **n** unto **n** reveals
Ps 22: 2 And in the **n** season, and am not
Ps 30: 5 Weeping may endure for a **n**
Ps 32: 4 **n** Your hand was heavy upon me
Ps 42: 3 have been my food day and **n**
Ps 42: 8 in the **n** His song shall be
Ps 55:10 **n** they go around it on its
Ps 63: 6 on You in the **n** watches
Ps 74:16 is Yours, the **n** also is Yours
Ps 77: 2 out in the **n** without ceasing
Ps 77: 6 remembrance my song in the **n**
Ps 78:14 all the **n** with a light of
Ps 88: 1 cried out day and **n** before You
Ps 90: 4 And like a watch in the **n**
Ps 91: 5 be afraid of the terror by **n**
Ps 92: 2 And Your faithfulness every **n**
Ps 104:20 You make darkness, and it is **n**
Ps 105:39 fire to give light in the **n**
Ps 119:55 I remember Your name in the **n**
Ps 119:148 awake through the **n** watches
Ps 121: 6 you by day, Nor the moon by **n**
Ps 134: 1 Who by **n** stand in the house
Ps 136: 9 moon and stars to rule by **n**

Ps 139:11 Even the **n** shall be light
Ps 139:12 But the **n** shines as the day
Prov 7: 9 in the black and dark **n**
Prov 31:15 also rises while it is yet **n**
Prov 31:18 her lamp does not go out by **n**
Eccl 2:23 even in the **n** his heart takes
Eccl 8:16 one sees no sleep day or **n**
Song 1:13 that lies all **n** between my
Song 3: 1 By **n** on my bed I sought the
Song 3: 8 because of fear in the **n**
Song 5: 2 locks with the drops of the **n**
Is 4: 5 of a flaming fire by **n**
Is 5:11 who continue until **n**, till
Is 15: 1 Because in the **n** Ar of Moab
Is 15: 1 because in the **n** Kir of Moab
Is 16: 3 **n** in the middle of the day
Is 21: 4 the **n** for which I longed He
Is 21: 8 I have sat at my post every **n**
Is 21:11 Watchman, what of the **n**
Is 21:11 Watchman, what of the **n**
Is 21:12 morning comes, and also the **n**
Is 26: 9 I have desired You in the **n**
Is 27: 3 lest any hurt it, I keep it **n**
Is 28:19 pass over, and by day and by **n**
Is 29: 7 be as a dream of a **n** vision
Is 30:29 the **n** when a holy festival is
Is 34:10 not be quenched **n** or day
Is 34:14 also the **n** creature shall
Is 38:12 from day until **n** You make an
Is 38:13 from day until **n** You make an
Is 60:11 shall not be shut day or **n**
Is 62: 6 hold their peace day or **n**
Is 65: 4 and spend the **n** in the tombs
Jer 6: 5 Arise, and let us go by **n**, and
Jer 9: 1 day and **n** for the slain of the
Jer 14: 8 turns aside to tarry for a **n**
Jer 14:17 Let my eyes flow with tears **n**
Jer 16:13 serve other gods day and **n**
Jer 31:35 and the stars for a light by **n**
Jer 33:20 day and My covenant with the **n**
Jer 33:20 be day and **n** in their season,
Jer 33:25 covenant is not with day and **n**
Jer 36:30 the day and the frost of the **n**
Jer 39: 4 and went out of the city by **n**
Jer 49: 9 If thieves by **n**, would they
Jer 52: 7 went out of the city at **n** by
Lam 1: 2 She weeps bitterly in the **n**
Lam 2:18 down like a river day and **n**
Lam 2:19 Arise, cry out in the **n**, at
Dan 2:19 to Daniel in a **n** vision
Dan 5:30 That very **n** Belshazzar, king
Dan 6:18 palace and spent the **n** fasting
Dan 7: 2 I saw in my vision by **n**, and
Dan 7: 7 this I saw in the **n** visions
Dan 7:13 was watching in the **n** visions
Hos 4: 5 stumble with you in the **n**
Hos 7: 6 their baker sleeps all **n**
Joel 1:13 lie all **n** in sackcloth, you
Amos 5: 8 and makes the day dark as **n**
Obad 5 come to you, if robbers by **n**
Jon 4:10 in a **n** and perished in a **n**
Mic 3: 6 shall have **n** without vision
Zech 1: 8 I saw by **n**, and behold, a man
Zech 14: 7 neither day nor **n**
Matt 2:14 Child and His mother by **n** and
Matt 14:25 of the **n** Jesus went to them
Matt 26:31 stumble because of Me this **n**
Matt 26:34 I say to you that this **n**
Matt 27:64 lest His disciples come by **n**
Matt 28:13 His disciples came at **n**
Mark 4:27 and should sleep by **n** and rise
Mark 5: 5 And always, **n** and day, he was
Mark 6:48 of the **n** He came to them,
Mark 14:27 stumble because of Me this **n**
Mark 14:30 you that today, even this **n**
Luke 2: 8 watch over their flock by **n**
Luke 2:37 with fastings and prayers **n**
Luke 5: 5 Master, we have toiled all **n**
Luke 6:12 continued all **n** in prayer to
Luke 12:20 This **n** your soul will be
Luke 17:34 in that **n** there will be two
Luke 18: 7 **n** to Him, though He bears
Luke 21:37 but at **n** He went out and
John 3: 2 This man came to Jesus by **n**
John 7:50 (he who came to Jesus by **n**
John 9: 4 the **n** is coming when no one
John 11:10 But if one walks in the **n**
John 13:30 And it was **n**
John 19:39 at first came to Jesus by **n**
John 21: 3 that **n** they caught nothing
Acts 5:19 But at **n** an angel of the Lord
Acts 9:24 watched the gates day and **n**
Acts 9:25 the disciples took him by **n**
Acts 12: 6 that **n** Peter was sleeping,
Acts 16: 9 appeared to Paul in the **n**
Acts 16:33 them the same hour of the **n**
Acts 17:10 and Silas away by **n** to Berea
Acts 18: 9 to Paul in the **n** by a vision
Acts 20:31 not cease to warn everyone **n**
Acts 23:11 But the following **n** the Lord
Acts 23:23 at the third hour of the **n**
Acts 23:31 him by **n** to Antipatris
Acts 26: 7 earnestly serving God **n** and
Acts 27:23 For there stood by me this **n**
Acts 27:27 the fourteenth **n** had come
Rom 13:12 The **n** is far spent, the day
1Co 11:23 **n** in which He was betrayed
2Co 11:25 a **n** and a day I have been in
1Th 2: 9 for laboring **n** and day, that
1Th 3:10 **n** and day praying exceedingly
1Th 5: 2 so comes as a thief in the **n**
1Th 5: 5 not of the **n** nor of darkness
1Th 5: 7 those who sleep, sleep at **n**
1Th 5: 7 who get drunk are drunk at **n**
2Th 3: 8 worked with labor and toil **n**
1Ti 5: 5 in supplications and prayers **n**
2Ti 1: 3 remember you in my prayers **n**
2Pe 3:10 will come as a thief in the **n**
Rev 4: 8 And they do not rest day or **n**
Rev 7:15 Him day and **n** in His temple
Rev 8:12 not shine, and likewise the **n**
Rev 12:10 them before our God day and **n**
Rev 14:11 and they have no rest day or **n**
Rev 20:10 day and **n** forever and ever
Rev 21:25 (there shall be no **n** there)
Rev 22: 5 And there shall be no **n** there

NIGHTS (*see* NIGHT)
Gen 7: 4 earth forty days and forty **n**
Gen 7:12 earth forty days and forty **n**
Ex 24:18 forty days and forty **n**
Ex 34:28 LORD forty days and forty **n**
Deut 9: 9 forty days and forty **n**
Deut 9:11 end of forty days and forty **n**
Deut 9:18 first, forty days and forty **n**
Deut 9:25 forty **n** I kept prostrating
Deut 10:10 forty days and forty **n**
1Sa 30:12 for three days and three **n**
1Ki 19: 8 forty **n** as far as Horeb, the
Job 2:13 ground seven days and seven **n**
Job 7: 3 and wearisome **n** have been
Jon 1:17 fish three days and three **n**
Matt 4: 2 fasted forty days and forty **n**
Matt 12:40 three **n** in the belly of the
Matt 12:40 three **n** in the heart of the

NIMRAH (*see* BETH NIMRAH)
Num 32: 3 Ataroth, Dibon, Jazer, **N**,

NIMRIM
Is 15: 6 waters of **N** will be desolate
Jer 48:34 for the waters of **N** also

NIMROD
Gen 10: 8 Cush begot **N**
Gen 10: 9 Like **N** the mighty hunter
1Ch 1:10 Cush begot **N**
Mic 5: 6 and the land of **N** at its

NIMSHI
1Ki 19:16 son of **N** as king over Israel
2Ki 9: 2 of Jehoshaphat, the son of **N**
2Ki 9:14 of Jehoshaphat, the son of **N**
2Ki 9:20 driving of Jehu the son of **N**
2Ch 22: 7 against Jehu the son of **N**

NINE (*see* NINTH)
Gen 5: 5 Adam lived were **n** hundred
Gen 5: 8 days of Seth were **n** hundred
Gen 5:11 days of Enosh were **n** hundred
Gen 5:14 days of Cainan were **n** hundred
Gen 5:20 days of Jared were **n** hundred
Gen 5:27 of Methuselah were **n** hundred
Gen 9:29 days of Noah were **n** hundred
Gen 11:19 **n** years, and begot sons and
Num 29:26 the fifth day present **n** bulls
Num 34:13 to give to the **n** tribes and to
Deut 3:11 **N** cubits is its length and
Josh 13: 7 inheritance to the **n** tribes
Josh 14: 2 of Moses, for the **n** tribes
Josh 15:44 **n** cities with their villages
Josh 15:54 **n** cities with their villages
Josh 21:16 **n** cities from those two
Judg 4: 3 for Jabin had **n** hundred
Judg 4:13 **n** hundred chariots of iron,
2Sa 24: 8 at the end of **n** months and
2Ki 17: 1 and he reigned **n** years
1Ch 3: 8 **n** in all
1Ch 9: 9 **n** hundred and fifty-six
Ezra 2: 8 **n** hundred and forty-five
Ezra 2:36 **n** hundred and seventy-three
Neh 7:38 three thousand **n** hundred
Neh 7:39 **n** hundred and seventy-three
Neh 11: 8 **n** hundred and twenty-eight
Luke 17:17 But where are the **n**

NINETEEN (*see* NINETEENTH)
Gen 11:25 **n** years, and begot sons and
Josh 19:38 **n** cities with their villages
2Sa 2:30 of David's servants **n** men

NINETEENTH (*see* NINETEEN)
2Ki 25: 8 **n** year of King Nebuchadnezzar
1Ch 24:16 the **n** to Pethahiah, the
1Ch 25:26 the **n** for Mallothi, his sons
Jer 52:12 **n** year of King Nebuchadnezzar

NINE-TENTHS
Neh 11: 1 and **n** were to dwell in other

NINETY
Gen 5: 9 Enosh lived **n** years, and begot
Gen 17:17 who is **n** years old, bear a
1Ch 9: 6 six hundred and **n**
Ezek 4: 5 days, three hundred and **n** days
Ezek 4: 9 and **n** days, you shall eat it
Ezek 41:12 and its length **n** cubits
Dan 12:11 two hundred and **n** days

NINETY-EIGHT
1Sa 4:15 Eli was **n** years old, and his
Ezra 2:16 people of Ater of Hezekiah, **n**
Neh 7:21 of Ater of Hezekiah, **n**

NINETY-FIVE
Gen 5:17 were eight hundred and **n** years
Gen 5:30 **n** years, and begot sons and
Ezra 2:20 the people of Gibbar, **n**
Neh 7:25 the children of Gibeon, **n**

NINETY-NINE
Gen 17: 1 When Abram was **n** years old
Gen 17:24 Abraham was **n** years old when
Matt 18:12 does he not leave the **n** and
Matt 18:13 the **n** that did not go astray
Luke 15: 4 leave the **n** in the wilderness
Luke 15: 7 who repents than over **n** just

NINETY-SIX
Ezra 8:35 **n** rams, seventy-seven lambs,
Jer 52:23 There were **n** pomegranates on

NINETY-TWO
Ezra 2:58 were three hundred and **n**
Neh 7:60 were three hundred and **n**

NINEVEH (*see* NINEVITES)
Gen 10:11 he went to Assyria and built **N**
Gen 10:12 and Resen between **N** and Calah
2Ki 19:36 home, and remained at **N**
Is 37:37 home, and remained at **N**
Jon 1: 2 Arise, go to **N**, that great
Jon 3: 2 Arise, go to **N**, that great
Jon 3: 3 So Jonah arose and went to **N**
Jon 3: 3 Now **N** was an exceedingly
Jon 3: 4 and **N** shall be overthrown
Jon 3: 5 the people of **N** believed God
Jon 3: 6 word came to the king of **N**
Jon 3: 7 published throughout **N** by the
Jon 4:11 And should I not pity **N**, that
Nah 1: 1 The burden against **N**
Nah 2: 8 Though **N** of old was like a
Nah 3: 7 you, and say, **N** is laid waste
Zeph 2:13 make **N** a desolation, as dry
Matt 12:41 The men of **N** will rise in the
Luke 11:32 The men of **N** will rise up in

NINEVITES (*see* NINEVEH)
Luke 11:30 Jonah became a sign to the **N**

NINTH (*see* NINE)
Lev 23:32 on the **n** day of the month at
Lev 25:22 old produce until the **n** year
Num 7:60 On the **n** day Abidan the son
2Ki 17: 6 In the **n** year of Hoshea, the
2Ki 18:10 the **n** year of Hoshea king of
2Ki 25: 1 in the **n** year of his reign
2Ki 25: 3 By the **n** day of the fourth
1Ch 12:12 the eighth, Elzabad the **n**

1Ch 24:11 the n to Jeshua, the tenth to
1Ch 25:16 the n for Mattaniah, his sons
1Ch 27:12 The n captain for the n
Ezra 10: 9 It was the n month, on the
Jer 36: 9 king of Judah, in the n month
Jer 36:22 winter house in the n month
Jer 39: 1 In the n year of Zedekiah
Jer 39: 2 on the n day of the month,
Jer 52: 4 in the n year of his reign
Jer 52: 6 on the n day of the month,
Ezek 24: 1 Again, in the n year, in the
Hag 2:10 day of the n month, in the
Hag 2:18 day of the n month, from the
Zech 7: 1 the fourth day of the n month
Matt 20: 5 the n hour, and did likewise
Matt 27:45 the n hour there was darkness
Matt 27:46 about the n hour Jesus cried
Mark 15:33 whole land until the n hour
Mark 15:34 at the n hour Jesus cried out
Luke 23:44 the earth until the n hour
Acts 3: 1 hour of prayer, the n hour
Acts 10: 3 About the n hour of the day
Acts 10:30 at the n hour I prayed in my
Rev 21:20 beryl, the n topaz, the tenth

NISAN (*see* ABIB)
Neh 2: 1 to pass in the month of N
Esth 3: 7 which is the month of N, in

NISROCH
2Ki 19:37 in the temple of N his god
Is 37:38 in the house of N his god

NO (*see* PREFACE)

NO*
Jer 46:25 bring punishment on Amon of N
Ezek 30:14 and execute judgments in N
Ezek 30:15 cut off the multitude of N
Ezek 30:16 n shall be split open, and
Nah 3: 8 Are you better than N Amon

NOADIAH
Ezra 8:33 and N the son of Binnui,
Neh 6:14 works, and the prophetess N

NOAH (*see* NOAH'S)
Gen 5:29 And he called his name N,
Gen 5:30 After he begot N, Lamech
Gen 5:32 N was five hundred years old,
Gen 5:32 N begot Shem, Ham, and
Gen 6: 8 But N found grace in the eyes
Gen 6: 9 This is the genealogy of N
Gen 6: 9 N was a just man, perfect in
Gen 6: 9 N walked with God
Gen 6:10 And N begot three sons
Gen 6:13 And God said to N, "The end
Gen 6:22 Thus N did; according to all
Gen 7: 1 Then the LORD said to N
Gen 7: 5 N did according to all that
Gen 7: 6 N was six hundred years old
Gen 7: 7 So N, with his sons, his wife
Gen 7: 9 they went into the ark to N
Gen 7: 9 as God had commanded N
Gen 7:13 On the very same day N and
Gen 7:15 they went into the ark to N
Gen 7:23 Only N and those who were with
Gen 8: 1 Then God remembered N, and
Gen 8: 6 that N opened the window of
Gen 8:11 N knew that the waters had
Gen 8:13 N removed the covering of the
Gen 8:15 Then God spoke to N, saying,
Gen 8:18 So N went out, and his sons and
Gen 8:20 Then N built an altar to the
Gen 9: 1 So God blessed N and his sons,
Gen 9: 8 Then God spoke to N and to his
Gen 9:17 And God said to N, "This is
Gen 9:18 Now the sons of N who went
Gen 9:19 three were the sons of N, and
Gen 9:20 N began to be a farmer, and he
Gen 9:24 So N awoke from his wine, and
Gen 9:28 N lived after the flood three
Gen 9:29 days of N were nine hundred
Gen 10: 1 genealogy of the sons of N
Gen 10:32 the families of the sons of N
Num 26:33 of Zelophehad were Mahlah, N
Num 27: 1 Mahlah, N, Hoglah, Milcah,
Num 36:11 Tirzah, Hoglah, Milcah, and N
Josh 17: 3 Mahlah, N, Hoglah, Milcah,
1Ch 1: 4 N, Shem, Ham, and Japheth
Is 54: 9 is like the waters of N to Me
Is 54: 9 sworn that the waters of N
Ezek 14:14 Though these three men, N
Ezek 14:20 even though N, Daniel, and Job
Matt 24:37 But as the days of N were
Matt 24:38 day that N entered the ark
Luke 3:36 the son of Shem, the son of N
Luke 17:26 And as it was in the days of N
Luke 17:27 day that N entered the ark
Heb 11: 7 By faith N, being divinely
1Pe 3:20 God waited in the days of N
2Pe 2: 5 ancient world, but saved N

NOAH'S (*see* NOAH)
Gen 7:11 six hundredth year of N life
Gen 7:13 N sons, Shem, Ham, and
Gen 7:13 N wife and the three wives of

NOB
1Sa 21: 1 Now David came to N, to
1Sa 22: 9 the son of Jesse going to N
1Sa 22:11 the priests who were in N
1Sa 22:19 Also N, the city of the
Neh 11:32 in Anathoth, N, Ananiah
Is 10:32 he will remain at N that day

NOBAH (*see* KENATH, NOPHAH)
Num 32:42 Then N went and took Kenath
Num 32:42 villages, and he called it N
Judg 8:11 in tents on the east of N

NOBILITY (*see* NOBLE)
Prov 19: 6 entreat the favor of the n

NOBLE (*see* NOBILITY, NOBLEMAN, NOBLES)
Ezra 4:10 n Osnapper took captive and
Esth 1:18 day the n ladies of Persia
Esth 6: 9 of the king's most n princes
Song 6:12 the chariots of my n people
Jer 2:21 I had planted you a n vine
Luke 8:15 heard the word with a n and
Acts 24: 3 most n Felix, with all
Acts 26:25 most n Festus, but speak the
1Co 1:26 not many mighty, not many n
Phil 4: 8 true, whatever things are n
Jas 2: 7 that n name by which you are

NOBLEMAN (*see* NOBLE)
Luke 19:12 A certain n went into a far
John 4:46 there was a certain n whose
John 4:49 The n said to Him, "Sir,

NOBLES (*see* NOBLE)
Ex 24:11 But on the n of the children
Num 21:18 sank, dug by the nation's n
Judg 5:13 the people against the n
1Ki 21: 8 the n who were dwelling in
1Ki 21:11 n who were inhabitants of his
2Ch 23:20 captains of hundreds, the n
Neh 2:16 the Jews, the priests, the n
Neh 3: 5 but their n did not put their
Neh 4:14 and arose and said to the n
Neh 4:19 Then I said to the n, the
Neh 5: 7 thought, I rebuked the n and
Neh 6:17 n of Judah sent many letters
Neh 7: 5 into my heart to gather the n
Neh 10:29 with their brethren, their n
Neh 13:17 contended with the n of Judah
Esth 1: 3 of Persia and Media, the n
Job 29:10 the voice of n was hushed
Job 34:18 You are worthless,' and to n
Ps 83:11 Make their n like Oreb and
Ps 149: 8 their n with fetters of iron
Prov 8:16 By me princes rule, and n, all
Eccl 10:17 your king is the son of n
Is 13: 2 may enter the gates of the n
Is 34:12 call its n to the kingdom
Jer 14: 3 Their n have sent their lads
Jer 27:20 and all the n of Judah and
Jer 30:21 Their n shall be from among
Jer 39: 6 killed all the n of Judah
Dan 1: 3 descendants and some of the n
Dan 4:36 and n resorted to me, I was
Jon 3: 7 decree of the king and his n
Nah 3:18 your n rest in the dust
Mark 6:21 gave a feast for his n, the

NOD (*see* NODDED)
Gen 4:16 land of N on the east of Eden

NODAB
1Ch 5:19 Jetur, Naphish, and N

NODDED (*see* NOD)
Acts 24:10 had n to him to speak,

NOGAH
1Ch 3: 7 N, Nepheg, Japhia,
1Ch 14: 6 N, Nepheg, Japhia,

NOHAH
1Ch 8: 2 N the fourth, and Rapha the

NOISE (*see* NOISES, NOISILY, NOISY)
Ex 32:17 the n of the people as they
Ex 32:17 There is a n of war in the
Josh 6:10 or make any n with your voice
Judg 5:11 Far from the n of the archers
1Sa 4: 6 heard the n of the shout,
1Sa 4:14 Eli heard the n of the outcry
1Sa 14:19 that the n which was in the
1Ki 1:45 This is the n that you have
2Ki 7: 6 to hear the n of chariots
2Ki 7: 6 chariots and the n of horses
2Ki 7: 6 the n of a great army
2Ki 11:13 heard the n of the escorts
2Ch 23:12 the n of the people running
Ezra 3:13 could not discern the n of
Ezra 3:13 the n of the weeping of the
Ps 42: 7 at the n of Your waterfalls
Ps 65: 7 who still the n of the seas
Ps 65: 7 The n of their waves, And the
Ps 93: 4 Than the n of many waters
Is 13: 4 The n of a multitude in the
Is 13: 4 A tumultuous n of the
Is 17:12 a n like the roar of the seas
Is 22: 2 you who are full of n, a
Is 24: 8 the n of the jubilant ends,
Is 24:18 that he who flees from the n
Is 25: 5 will reduce the n of aliens
Is 29: 6 and earthquake and great n,
Is 31: 4 nor be disturbed by their n)
Is 33: 3 At the n of the tumult the
Is 66: 6 The sound of n from the city
Jer 4:19 My heart makes a n in me
Jer 4:29 from the n of the horsemen
Jer 10:22 the n of the report has come,
Jer 11:16 With the n of a great tumult
Jer 25:31 A n will come to the ends of
Jer 46:17 king of Egypt, is but a n
Jer 46:22 Her n shall go like a serpent
Jer 47: 3 At the n of the stamping
Jer 49:21 shakes at the n of their fall
Jer 49:21 at the cry its n is heard at
Jer 50:46 At the n of the taking of
Jer 51:55 and the n of their voice is
Lam 2: 7 They have made a n in the
Ezek 1:24 I heard the n of their wings,
Ezek 1:24 like the n of many waters,
Ezek 1:24 tumult like the n of an army
Ezek 3:13 I also heard the n of the
Ezek 3:13 the n of the wheels beside
Ezek 3:13 them, and a great thunderous n
Ezek 19: 7 by the n of his roaring
Ezek 26:10 at the n of the horsemen, the
Ezek 37: 7 I prophesied, there was a n
Joel 2: 5 With a n like chariots over
Joel 2: 5 like the n of a flaming fire
Amos 5:23 from Me the n of your songs
Mic 2:12 loud n because of so many men
Nah 3: 2 The n of a whip
Nah 3: 2 the n of rattling wheels
Zeph 1:14 The n of the day of the LORD
2Pe 3:10 will pass away with a great n

NOISES (*see* NOISE)
Rev 8: 5 And there were n, thunderings,
Rev 11:19 And there were lightnings, n
Rev 16:18 And there were n and

NOISILY (*see* NOISE)
Ps 55: 2 in my complaint, and moan n

NOISY (*see* NOISE)
1Ki 1:41 the city in such a n uproar
Is 9: 5 sandal from the n battle, and
Matt 9:23 and the n crowd wailing,

NONE (*see* PREFACE)

NONEXISTENT
Is 41:12 be as nothing, as a n thing

NONSENSE
Job 27:12 do you behave with complete n
Ezek 13: 8 Because you have spoken n

NOON (*see* NOONDAY, NOONTIME)
Gen 43:16 men will dine with me at n
Gen 43:25 for Joseph's coming at n, for
2Sa 4: 5 who was lying on his bed at n

1Ki 18:26 Baal from morning even till **n**
1Ki 18:27 And so it was, at **n**, that
1Ki 20:16 So they went out at **n**
2Ki 4:20 he sat on her knees till **n**
Ps 55:17 and at **n** I will pray, and cry
Song 1: 7 where you make it rest at **n**
Jer 6: 4 arise, and let us go up at **n**
Jer 20:16 morning and the shouting at **n**
Amos 8: 9 make the sun go down at **n**
Acts 22: 6 came near Damascus at about **n**

NOONDAY (*see* NOON)
Deut 28:29 And you shall grope at **n**, as a
Job 11:17 life would be brighter than **n**
Ps 37: 6 And your justice as the **n**
Ps 91: 6 that lays waste at **n**
Is 58:10 darkness shall be as the **n**
Is 59:10 we stumble at **n** as at
Jer 15: 8 young men, a plunderer at **n**
Zeph 2: 4 shall drive out Ashdod at **n**

NOONTIME (*see* NOON)
Job 5:14 grope at **n** as in the night

NOOSE
Job 18:10 A **n** is hidden for him on the

NOPH (*see* MEMPHIS)
Is 19:13 the princes of **N** are deceived
Jer 2:16 Also the people of **N** and
Jer 44: 1 at Migdol, at Tahpanhes, at **N**
Jer 46:14 Proclaim in **N** and in Tahpanhes
Jer 46:19 For **N** shall be waste and be
Ezek 30:13 the images to cease from **N**
Ezek 30:16 **N** shall be in distress daily

NOPHAH (*see* NOBAH)
Num 21:30 we laid waste as far as **N**

NOR (*see* PREFACE)

NORTH (*see* NORTHERN, NORTHWARD)
Gen 14:15 Hobah, which is **n** of Damascus
Gen 28:14 west and the east, to the **n**
Ex 26:20 the **n** side, there shall be
Ex 26:35 put the table on the **n** side
Ex 27:11 of the **n** side there shall be
Ex 36:25 the **n** side, he made twenty
Ex 38:11 On the **n** side the hangings
Ex 40:22 meeting, on the **n** side of the
Lev 1:11 **n** side of the altar before
Num 2:25 the **n** side according to their
Num 3:35 the **n** side of the tabernacle
Num 35: 5 on the **n** side two thousand
Deut 3:27 eyes toward the west, the **n**
Josh 8:11 and camped on the **n** side of Ai
Josh 8:13 that was on the **n** of the city
Josh 11: 2 the kings who were from the **n**
Josh 15: 6 and passed **n** of Beth Arabah
Josh 15:10 on the **n** (which is Chesalon)
Josh 16: 6 on the **n** side of Michmethath
Josh 17: 9 on the **n** side of the brook
Josh 17:10 was adjoining Asher on the **n**
Josh 18: 5 in their territory on the **n**
Josh 18:12 Their border on the **n** side
Josh 18:12 the side of Jericho on the **n**
Josh 18:16 of the Rephaim on the **n**,
Josh 18:17 And it went around from the **n**
Josh 18:18 toward the **n** side of Arabah
Josh 18:19 to the **n** side of Beth Hoglah
Josh 18:19 at the **n** bay at the Salt Sea
Josh 19:14 it on the **n** side of Hannathon
Josh 24:30 on the **n** side of Mount Gaash
Judg 2: 9 on the **n** side of Mount Gaash
Judg 7: 1 the Midianites was on the **n**
Judg 21:19 which is **n** of Bethel, on the
1Ki 7:25 three looking toward the **n**
2Ki 16:14 put it on the **n** side of the
1Ch 9:24 the east, west, **n**, and south
1Ch 26:14 lot came out for the **N** Gate
1Ch 26:17 on the **n** four each day, on
2Ch 4: 4 three looking toward the **n**
Job 26: 7 out the **n** over empty space
Job 37: 9 the scattering winds of the **n**
Job 37:22 He comes from the **n** as golden
Ps 48: 2 Zion on the sides of the **n**
Ps 89:12 The **n** and the south, You have
Ps 107: 3 and from the west, From the **n**
Prov 25:23 The **n** wind brings forth rain,
Eccl 1: 6 and turns around to the **n**
Eccl 11: 3 falls to the south or the **n**
Song 4:16 O **n** wind, and come, O south
Is 14:13 the farthest sides of the **n**
Is 14:31 smoke will come from the **n**
Is 41:25 have raised up one from the **n**
Is 43: 6 I will say to the **n**, 'Give
Is 49:12 Those from the **n** and the west,
Jer 1:13 it is facing away from the **n**
Jer 1:14 Out of the **n** calamity shall
Jer 1:15 of the kingdoms of the **n**,"
Jer 3:12 these words toward the **n**, and
Jer 3:18 out of the land of the **n** to
Jer 4: 6 bring disaster from the **n**
Jer 6: 1 disaster appears out of the **n**
Jer 6:22 comes from the **n** country, and
Jer 10:22 out of the **n** country, to make
Jer 13:20 see those who come from the **n**
Jer 16:15 Israel from the land of the **n**
Jer 23: 8 of Israel from the **n** country
Jer 25: 9 all the families of the **n**
Jer 25:26 all the kings of the **n**, far
Jer 31: 8 bring them from the **n** country
Jer 46: 6 stumble and fall toward the **n**
Jer 46:10 in the **n** country by the River
Jer 46:20 comes, it comes from the **n**
Jer 46:24 hand of the people of the **n**
Jer 47: 2 waters rise out of the **n**
Jer 50: 3 For out of the **n** a nation
Jer 50: 9 nations from the **n** country
Jer 50:41 people shall come from the **n**
Jer 51:48 shall come to her from the **n**
Ezek 1: 4 was coming out of the **n**, a
Ezek 8: 3 to the door of the **n** gate of
Ezek 8: 5 your eyes now toward the **n**
Ezek 8: 5 I lifted my eyes toward the **n**
Ezek 8: 5 **n** of the altar gate, was this
Ezek 8:14 me to the door of the **n** gate
Ezek 9: 2 the upper gate, which faces **n**
Ezek 16:46 her daughters to the **n** of you
Ezek 20:47 the **n** shall be scorched by it
Ezek 21: 4 all flesh from south to **n**
Ezek 26: 7 the **n** Nebuchadnezzar king of
Ezek 32:30 are the princes of the **n**, all
Ezek 38: 6 of Togarmah from the far **n**
Ezek 38:15 your place out of the far **n**
Ezek 39: 2 you up from the far **n**, and
Ezek 40:19 toward the east and the **n**
Ezek 40:20 was also a gateway facing **n**
Ezek 40:35 brought me to the **n** gateway
Ezek 40:44 the other facing **n** at the
Ezek 40:46 The chamber which faces **n** is
Ezek 41:11 one door toward the **n** and
Ezek 42: 1 by the way toward the **n**
Ezek 42: 1 the building toward the **n**
Ezek 42: 2 fifty cubits), was the **n** door
Ezek 42: 4 and their doors faced **n**
Ezek 42:11 which were toward the **n**
Ezek 42:13 The **n** chambers and the south
Ezek 42:17 He measured the **n** side, five
Ezek 44: 4 **n** gate to the front of the
Ezek 46: 9 enters by way of the **n** gate
Ezek 46: 9 go out by way of the **n** gate
Ezek 46:19 which face toward the **n**
Ezek 47: 2 me out by way of the **n** gate
Ezek 47:15 border of the land on the **n**
Ezek 47:17 and as for the **n**, northward,
Ezek 47:17 This is the **n** side
Ezek 48:10 on the **n** twenty-five thousand
Ezek 48:16 the **n** side four thousand five
Ezek 48:17 to the **n** two hundred and fifty
Ezek 48:30 On the **n** side, measuring four
Dan 11: 6 of the **N** to make an agreement
Dan 11: 7 fortress of the king of the **N**
Dan 11: 8 years than the king of the **N**
Dan 11: 9 Then the king of the **N** shall
Dan 11:11 him, with the king of the **N**
Dan 11:13 the king of the **N** will return
Dan 11:15 the king of the **N** shall come
Dan 11:40 the king of the **N** shall come
Dan 11:44 and the **n** shall trouble him
Amos 8:12 sea to sea, and from **n** to east
Zeph 2:13 out His hand against the **n**
Zech 2: 6 Flee from the land of the **n**
Zech 6: 6 is going to the **n** country
Zech 6: 8 those who go toward the **n**
Zech 6: 8 to My Spirit in the **n** country
Zech 14: 4 shall move toward the **n** and
Luke 13:29 east and the west, from the **n**
Rev 21:13 east, three gates on the **n**

NORTHERN (*see* NORTH)
Num 34: 7 this shall be your **n** border
Num 34: 9 This shall be your **n** border
Josh 15: 5 the border on the **n** quarter
Jer 15:12 the **n** iron and the bronze
Ezek 40:23 was opposite the **n** gateway
Ezek 40:40 the entrance of the **n** gateway
Ezek 40:44 at the side of the **n** gateway
Ezek 48: 1 From the **n** border along the
Joel 2:20 far from you the **n** army, and

NORTHWARD (*see* NORTH)
Gen 13:14 **n**, southward, eastward, and
Deut 2: 3 turn **n**
Josh 13: 3 Ekron **n** (which is counted as
Josh 15: 7 it turned **n** toward Gilgal,
Josh 15: 8 of the Valley of Rephaim **n**
Josh 15:11 out to the side of Ekron **n**
Josh 17:10 **n** it was Manasseh's, and the
Josh 19:27 then **n** beyond Beth Emek and
1Sa 14: 5 one faced **n** opposite Michmash
Ezek 47:17 and as for the north, **n**, it is
Ezek 48: 1 the border of Damascus **n**
Ezek 48:31 of Israel), the three gates **n**
Dan 8: 4 the ram pushing westward, **n**

NORTHWEST
Acts 27:12 toward the southwest and **n**

NOSE (*see* NOSES)
Gen 24:22 that the man took a golden **n**
Gen 24:30 pass, when he saw the **n** ring
Gen 24:47 So I put the **n** ring on her
Gen 24:47 I put the **n** ring on her **n**
Ex 35:22 **n** rings, rings and necklaces,
2Ki 19:28 I will put My hook in your **n**
Job 40:24 pierces his **n** with a snare
Job 41: 2 you put a reed through his **n**
Prov 30:33 wringing the **n** produces blood
Song 7: 4 Your **n** is like the tower of
Is 3:21 and the rings; the **n** jewels,
Is 37:29 I will put My hook in your **n**
Ezek 8:17 put the branch to their **n**
Ezek 16:12 And I put a jewel in your **n**
Ezek 23:25 they shall remove your **n** and

NOSES (*see* NOSE)
Ps 115: 6 **N** they have, but they do not

NOSTRILS
Gen 2: 7 and breathed into his **n** the
Gen 7:22 All in whose **n** was the breath
Ex 15: 8 with the blast of Your **n** the
Num 11:20 until it comes out of your **n**
2Sa 22: 9 Smoke went up from His **n**, and
2Sa 22:16 blast of the breath of His **n**
Job 27: 3 and the breath of God in my **n**
Job 41:20 Smoke goes out of his **n**, as
Ps 18: 8 Smoke went up from His **n**, And
Ps 18:15 blast of the breath of Your **n**
Is 2:22 man, whose breath is in his **n**
Is 65: 5 These are smoke in My **n**, a
Lam 4:20 The breath of our **n**, the
Amos 4:10 camps come up into your **n**

NOT (*see* PREFACE)

NOTABLE (*see* NOTE)
2Ki 4: 8 where there was a **n** woman
Dan 8: 5 the goat had a **n** horn between
Dan 8: 8 in place of it four **n** ones
Amos 6: 1 **n** persons in the chief nation
Acts 2:20 great and **n** day of the LORD
Acts 4:16 that a **n** miracle has been

NOTE (*see* NOTABLE, NOTED, NOTICE)
Num 32:23 you do not do so, then take **n**
Judg 9:31 saying, "Take **n**! Gaal the
1Sa 12:13 And take **n**, the LORD has set a
1Sa 19:19 Take **n**, David is at Naioth in
1Sa 24: 1 saying, "Take **n**! David is
2Sa 3:36 all the people took **n** of it
2Sa 13:24 Kindly **n**, your servant has
1Ki 20:22 take **n**, and see what you
2Ch 16:11 **N** that the acts of Asa, first
Job 23: 6 But He would take **n** of me
Is 30: 8 **n** it on a scroll, that it may
Rom 16: 7 who are of **n** among the
Rom 16:17 **n** those who cause divisions
Phil 3:17 **n** those who so walk, as you
2Th 3:14 **n** that person and do not keep

NOTED (*see* NOTE)
Dan 10:21 **n** in the Scripture of Truth
Luke 14: 7 when He **n** how they chose the

NOTHING (*see* PREFACE)

NOTICE (*see* NOTE, UNNOTICED)
Ruth 2:10 that you should take **n** of me
Ruth 2:19 be the one who took **n** of you
Ruth 3: 4 that you shall **n** the place
2Sa 20:10 But Amasa did not **n** the sword
1Ki 20: 7 **N**, please, and see how this
2Ki 2:19 Please **n**, the situation of
2Ch 19:11 And take **n**: Amariah the
Job 35:15 nor taken much **n** of folly
Is 58: 3 our souls, and You take no **n**
Acts 18:17 took no **n** of these things

NOTORIOUS
Matt 27:16 they had then a **n** prisoner

NOTWITHSTANDING
Ex 16:20 **N** they did not heed Moses
Ex 21:21 **N**, if he remains alive a day
Ezek 20:21 **N**, the children rebelled

NOURISHED (*see* NOURISHES)
2Sa 12: 3 lamb which he had bought and **n**
Is 1: 2 I have **n** and brought up
Ezek 19: 2 young lions she **n** her cubs
Col 2:19 from whom all the body, **n**
1Ti 4: 6 **n** in the words of faith and of
Rev 12:14 where she is **n** for a time

NOURISHER (*see* NOURISHES)
Ruth 4:15 life and a **n** of your old age

NOURISHES (*see* NOURISHED, NOURISHER, NOURISHMENT)
Is 44:14 a pine, and the rain **n** it
Eph 5:29 hated his own flesh, but **n**

NOURISHMENT (*see* NOURISHES)
Prov 27:27 the **n** of your maidservants
Acts 27:34 I urge you to take **n**, for

NOVICE
1Ti 3: 6 not a **n**, lest being puffed up

NOW (*see* PREFACE)

NOWADAYS
1Sa 25:10 **n** who break away each one

NOWHERE (*see* PREFACE)

NUMBER (*see* NUMBERED, NUMBERING, NUMBERS, NUMEROUS)
Gen 13:16 could **n** the dust of the earth
Gen 15: 5 if you are able to **n** them
Gen 26:14 and a great **n** of servants
Gen 34:30 and since I am few in **n**, they
Gen 41:49 for it was without **n**
Gen 47:12 according to the **n** in their
Ex 12: 4 to the **n** of the persons
Ex 16:16 according to the **n** of persons
Ex 23:26 fulfill the **n** of your days
Ex 30:12 of Israel for their **n**, then
Ex 30:12 to the LORD, when you **n** them
Ex 30:12 among them when you **n** them
Lev 25:15 According to the **n** of years
Lev 25:15 according to the **n** of years
Lev 25:16 according to the fewer **n** of
Lev 25:16 to you according to the **n** of
Lev 25:50 according to the **n** of years
Lev 26:22 and make you few in **n**
Num 1: 2 according to the **n** of names
Num 1: 3 Aaron shall **n** them by their
Num 1:18 according to the **n** of names
Num 1:20 according to the **n** of names
Num 1:22 according to the **n** of names
Num 1:24 according to the **n** of names
Num 1:26 according to the **n** of names
Num 1:28 according to the **n** of names
Num 1:30 according to the **n** of names
Num 1:32 according to the **n** of names
Num 1:34 according to the **n** of names
Num 1:36 according to the **n** of names
Num 1:38 according to the **n** of names
Num 1:40 according to the **n** of names
Num 1:42 according to the **n** of names
Num 1:49 tribe of Levi you shall not **n**
Num 3:15 **N** the children of Levi by
Num 3:15 you shall **n** every male from a
Num 3:22 according to the **n** of all the
Num 3:28 to the **n** of all the males
Num 3:34 according to the **n** of all the
Num 3:40 **N** all the firstborn males of
Num 3:40 take the **n** of their names
Num 3:43 according to the **n** of names
Num 3:46 than the **n** of the Levites
Num 3:48 excess **n** of them is redeemed
Num 4:23 years old, you shall **n** them
Num 4:29 you shall **n** them by their
Num 4:30 years old, you shall **n** them
Num 14:29 according to your entire **n**
Num 14:34 According to the **n** of the
Num 15:12 to the **n** that you prepare
Num 15:12 everyone according to their **n**
Num 23:10 or **n** one-fourth of Israel
Num 26:53 according to the **n** of names
Num 29:18 and for the lambs, by their **n**
Num 29:21 and for the lambs, by their **n**
Num 29:24 and for the lambs, by their **n**
Num 29:27 and for the lambs, by their **n**
Num 29:30 and for the lambs, by their **n**
Num 29:33 and for the lambs, by their **n**
Num 29:37 and for the lambs, by their **n**
Num 31:36 was in **n** three hundred and
Deut 4:27 you will be left few in **n**
Deut 7: 7 in **n** than any other people
Deut 25: 2 with a certain **n** of blows
Deut 26: 5 and sojourned there, few in **n**
Deut 28:62 You shall be left few in **n**
Deut 32: 8 peoples according to the **n** of
Josh 4: 5 according to the **n** of the
Josh 4: 8 according to the **n** of the
Judg 6: 5 their camels were without **n**
Judg 7: 6 the **n** of those who lapped,
Judg 7:12 their camels were without **n**
Judg 21:23 their **n** from those who danced
1Sa 6: 4 according to the **n** of the
1Sa 6:18 according to the **n** of all the
2Sa 2:15 they arose and went over by **n**
2Sa 15:12 continually increased in **n**
2Sa 21:20 each foot, twenty-four in **n**
2Sa 24: 1 say, "Go, **n** Israel and Judah
2Sa 24: 2 may know the **n** of the people
2Sa 24: 9 Joab gave the sum of the **n** of
1Ki 18:31 according to the **n** of the
1Ch 7: 2 their **n** in the days of David
1Ch 7:40 their **n** was twenty-six
1Ch 11:11 this is the **n** of the mighty
1Ch 16:19 When you were but few in **n**
1Ch 21: 1 and moved David to **n** Israel
1Ch 21: 2 **n** Israel from Beersheba to
1Ch 21: 2 bring the **n** of them to me
1Ch 21: 5 the **n** of the people to David
1Ch 23: 3 the **n** of individual males was
1Ch 23:24 by the **n** of their names, who
1Ch 23:31 feasts, by **n** according to the
1Ch 25: 1 And the **n** of the workmen
1Ch 25: 7 So the **n** of them, with their
1Ch 27: 1 Israel, according to their **n**
1Ch 27:23 **n** of those twenty years old
1Ch 27:24 nor was the **n** recorded in the
2Ch 12: 3 people without **n** who came
2Ch 26:11 according to the **n** on their
2Ch 26:12 The total **n** of chief officers
2Ch 29:32 the **n** of the burnt offerings
2Ch 30: 3 **n** of priests had not
2Ch 30:24 and a great **n** of priests
2Ch 35: 7 to the **n** of thirty thousand,
Ezra 1: 9 This is the **n** of them
Ezra 2: 2 The **n** of the men of the
Ezra 3: 4 burnt offerings in the **n**
Ezra 6:17 according to the **n** of the
Ezra 8:34 with the **n** and weight of
Neh 7: 7 The **n** of the men of the
Esth 9:11 On that day the **n** of those
Job 1: 5 to the **n** of them all
Job 3: 6 come into the **n** of the months
Job 5: 9 marvelous things without **n**
Job 9:10 out, yes, wonders without **n**
Job 14: 5 the **n** of his months is with
Job 14:16 For now You **n** my steps, but
Job 15:20 the **n** of years is hidden from
Job 21:21 when the **n** of his months is
Job 25: 3 Is there any **n** to His armies
Job 31:37 to Him the **n** of my steps
Job 36:26 nor can the **n** of His years be
Job 38:21 or because the **n** of your days
Job 38:37 who can **n** the clouds by
Job 39: 2 Can you **n** the months that
Ps 56: 8 You **n** my wanderings
Ps 90:12 So teach us to **n** our days
Ps 105:12 When they were but few in **n**
Ps 105:34 came, Young locusts without **n**
Ps 139:18 be more in **n** than the sand
Ps 147: 4 He counts the **n** of the stars
Song 6: 8 and virgins without **n**
Is 10:19 forest will be so few in **n**
Is 21:17 remainder of the **n** of archers
Is 40:26 brings out their host by **n**
Is 65:12 Therefore I will **n** you for
Jer 2:28 for according to the **n** of
Jer 2:32 forgotten Me days without **n**
Jer 11:13 For according to the **n** of
Jer 11:13 according to the **n** of the
Jer 44:28 Yet a small **n** who escape the
Ezek 4: 4 According to the **n** of the
Ezek 4: 5 to the **n** of the days, three
Ezek 4: 9 During the **n** of days that you
Ezek 5: 3 also take a small **n** of them
Dan 9: 2 **n** of the years specified by
Dan 11:23 with a small **n** of people
Hos 1:10 Yet the **n** of the children of
Joel 1: 6 My land, strong, and without **n**
Nah 3: 3 slain, a great **n** of bodies,
Luke 5: 6 they caught a great **n** of fish
Luke 5:29 a great **n** of tax collectors
John 6:10 in **n** about five thousand
Acts 1:15 the **n** of names was about a
Acts 4: 4 the **n** of the men came to be
Acts 5:36 A **n** of men, about four
Acts 6: 1 when the **n** of the disciples
Acts 6: 7 and the **n** of the disciples
Acts 11:21 a great **n** believed and turned
Acts 16: 5 and increased in **n** daily
Rom 9:27 Though the **n** of the children
1Ti 5: 9 years old be taken into the **n**
Rev 5:11 and the **n** of them was ten
Rev 6:11 until both the **n** of their
Rev 7: 4 I heard the **n** of those who
Rev 7: 9 which no one could **n**, of all
Rev 9:16 Now the **n** of the army of the
Rev 9:16 and I heard the **n** of them
Rev 13:17 beast, or the **n** of his name
Rev 13:18 calculate the **n** of the beast
Rev 13:18 for it is the **n** of a man
Rev 13:18 His **n** is 666
Rev 15: 2 and over the **n** of his name,
Rev 20: 8 whose **n** is as the sand of the

NUMBERED (*see* NUMBER)
Gen 13:16 descendants also could be **n**
Gen 32:12 cannot be **n** for multitude
Ex 30:13 those who are **n** shall give
Ex 30:14 among those who are **n**, from
Ex 38:25 silver from those who were **n**
Num 1:19 Moses, so he **n** them in the
Num 1:21 those who were **n** of the tribe
Num 1:22 house, of those who were **n**
Num 1:23 those who were **n** of the tribe
Num 1:25 those who were **n** of the tribe
Num 1:27 those who were **n** of the tribe
Num 1:29 those who were **n** of the tribe
Num 1:31 those who were **n** of the tribe
Num 1:33 those who were **n** of the tribe
Num 1:35 those who were **n** of the tribe
Num 1:37 those who were **n** of the tribe
Num 1:39 those who were **n** of the tribe
Num 1:41 those who were **n** of the tribe
Num 1:43 those who were **n** of the tribe
Num 1:44 These are the ones who were **n**
Num 1:44 whom Moses and Aaron **n**, with
Num 1:45 So all who were **n** of the
Num 1:46 all who were **n** were six
Num 1:47 not **n** among them by their
Num 2: 4 And his army was **n** at
Num 2: 6 his army was **n** at fifty-four
Num 2: 8 his army was **n** at fifty-seven
Num 2: 9 All who were **n** according to
Num 2:11 his army was **n** at forty-six
Num 2:13 his army was **n** at fifty-nine
Num 2:15 his army was **n** at forty-five
Num 2:16 All who were **n** according to
Num 2:19 And his army was **n** at forty
Num 2:21 his army was **n** at thirty-two
Num 2:23 his army was **n** at thirty-five
Num 2:24 All who were **n** according to
Num 2:26 his army was **n** at sixty-two
Num 2:28 his army was **n** at forty-one
Num 2:30 his army was **n** at fifty-three
Num 2:31 All who were **n** of the forces
Num 2:32 **n** of the children of Israel
Num 2:32 All who were **n** according to
Num 2:33 not **n** among the children of
Num 3:16 So Moses **n** them according to
Num 3:22 Those who were **n**, according
Num 3:22 of those who were **n** there
Num 3:34 And those who were **n**,
Num 3:39 All who were **n** of the Levites

Num 3:39 Aaron **n** at the commandment of
Num 3:42 So Moses **n** all the firstborn
Num 3:43 of those who were **n** of them
Num 4:34 **n** the sons of the Kohathites
Num 4:36 those who were **n** by their
Num 4:37 were **n** of the families of the
Num 4:37 and Aaron **n** according to the
Num 4:38 those who were **n** of the sons
Num 4:40 those who were **n** by their
Num 4:41 **n** of the families of the sons
Num 4:41 and Aaron **n** according to the
Num 4:42 the sons of Merari who were **n**
Num 4:44 those who were **n** by their
Num 4:45 **n** of the families of the sons
Num 4:45 Aaron **n** according to the word
Num 4:46 All who were **n** of the Levites
Num 4:46 and the leaders of Israel **n**
Num 4:48 those who were **n** were eight
Num 4:49 were **n** by the hand of Moses
Num 4:49 thus were they **n** by him, as
Num 7: 2 and over those who were **n**,
Num 14:29 all of you who were **n**,
Num 26: 7 those who were **n** of them were
Num 26:18 to those who were **n** of them
Num 26:22 to those who were **n** of them
Num 26:25 to those who were **n** of them
Num 26:27 to those who were **n** of them
Num 26:34 those who were **n** of them were
Num 26:37 to those who were **n** of them
Num 26:41 those who were **n** of them were
Num 26:43 to those who were **n** of them
Num 26:47 to those who were **n** of them
Num 26:50 those who were **n** of them were
Num 26:51 These are those who were **n** of
Num 26:54 to those who were **n** of them
Num 26:57 these are those who were **n** of
Num 26:62 Now those who were **n** of them
Num 26:62 for they were not **n** among the
Num 26:63 are those who were **n** by Moses
Num 26:63 who **n** the children of Israel
Num 26:64 of those who were **n** by Moses
Num 26:64 **n** the children of Israel in
Judg 20:15 the children of Benjamin **n**
Judg 20:15 who **n** seven hundred select
Judg 20:17 the men of Israel **n** four
1Sa 11: 8 When he **n** them in Bezek, the
1Sa 13:15 Saul **n** the people who were
1Sa 15: 4 **n** them in Telaim, two hundred
2Sa 18: 1 David **n** the people who were
2Sa 24:10 him after he had **n** the people
1Ki 3: 8 numerous to be **n** or counted
1Ki 8: 5 be counted or **n** for multitude
1Ch 21:17 commanded the people to be **n**
1Ch 23: 3 Now the Levites were **n** from
1Ch 23:27 were **n** from twenty years old
2Ch 2:17 Then Solomon **n** all the aliens
2Ch 2:17 David his father had **n** them
2Ch 5: 6 be counted or **n** for multitude
2Ch 25: 5 he **n** them from twenty years
Ps 40: 5 They are more than can be **n**
Eccl 1:15 what is lacking cannot be **n**
Is 22:10 You **n** the houses of Jerusalem
Is 53:12 death, and He was **n** with the
Jer 33:22 host of heaven cannot be **n**
Dan 5:26 God has **n** your kingdom, and
Hos 1:10 which cannot be measured or **n**
Matt 10:30 hairs of your head are all **n**
Mark 15:28 says, "And He was **n** with the
Luke 12: 7 hairs of your head are all **n**
Luke 22: 3 who was **n** among the twelve
Luke 22:37 And He was **n** with the
Acts 1:17 for he was **n** with us and
Acts 1:26 And he was **n** with the eleven

NUMBERING (*see* NUMBER)
Ex 38:26 the **n** from twenty years old

NUMBERS (*see* NUMBER)
1Ch 5:23 Their **n** increased from Bashan
1Ch 12:23 Now these were the **n** of the
2Ch 15: 9 **n** from Israel when they saw
2Ch 17:14 These are their **n**, according

NUMEROUS (*see* NUMBER)
Ex 23:29 field become too **n** for you
Num 22:15 again sent princes, more **n**
Deut 1:11 times more **n** than you are
Deut 2:10 past, a people as great and **n**
Deut 2:21 a people as great and **n** and
Deut 7:22 field become too **n** for you
Deut 20: 1 and people more **n** than you
Judg 6: 5 coming in as **n** as locusts
Judg 7:12 in the valley as **n** as locusts
1Ki 3: 8 too **n** to be numbered or
1Ki 4:20 Israel were as **n** as the sand
Jer 46:23 and more **n** than grasshoppers

NUN
Ex 33:11 servant Joshua the son of **N**
Num 11:28 So Joshua the son of **N**,
Num 13: 8 Ephraim, Hoshea the son of **N**
Num 13:16 called Hoshea the son of **N**
Num 14: 6 And Joshua the son of **N** and
Num 14:30 and Joshua the son of **N**, you
Num 14:38 But Joshua the son of **N** and
Num 26:65 and Joshua the son of **N**
Num 27:18 Joshua the son of **N** with you
Num 32:12 and Joshua the son of **N**, for
Num 32:28 to Joshua the son of **N**, and
Num 34:17 priest and Joshua the son of **N**
Deut 1:38 but Joshua the son of **N**, who
Deut 31:23 Joshua the son of **N**, and said,
Deut 32:44 came with Joshua the son of **N**
Deut 34: 9 Now Joshua the son of **N** was
Josh 1: 1 spoke to Joshua the son of **N**
Josh 2: 1 of **N** sent out two men from
Josh 2:23 came to Joshua the son of **N**
Josh 6: 6 son of **N** called the priests
Josh 14: 1 priest, Joshua the son of **N**
Josh 17: 4 before Joshua the son of **N**
Josh 19:49 them to Joshua the son of **N**
Josh 19:51 priest, Joshua the son of **N**
Josh 21: 1 to Joshua the son of **N**, and
Josh 24:29 that Joshua the son of **N**, the
Judg 2: 8 Now Joshua the son of **N**, the
1Ki 16:34 through Joshua the son of **N**
1Ch 7:27 **N** his son, and Joshua his son
Neh 8:17 days of Joshua the son of **N**

NURSE (*see* NURSED, NURSING)
Gen 21: 7 that Sarah would **n** children
Gen 24:59 Rebekah their sister and her **n**
Gen 35: 8 Now Deborah, Rebekah's **n**,
Ex 2: 7 call a **n** for you from the
Ex 2: 7 that she may **n** the child for
Ex 2: 9 **n** him for me, and I will give
Ruth 4:16 bosom, and became a **n** to him
2Sa 4: 4 his **n** took him up and fled
1Ki 3:21 in the morning to **n** my son
2Ki 11: 2 his **n** in the bedroom, from
2Ch 22:11 put him and his **n** in a bedroom
Job 3:12 the breasts, that I should **n**
Lam 4: 3 breasts to **n** their young

NURSED (*see* NURSE)
Ex 2: 9 woman took the child and **n** him
1Sa 1:23 and **n** her son until she had
Song 8: 1 who **n** at my mother's breasts
Is 60: 4 shall be **n** at your side
Luke 11:27 and the breasts which **n** You
Luke 23:29 and the breasts which never **n**

NURSING (*see* NURSE)
Gen 33:13 herds which are **n** are with me
Num 11:12 a guardian carries a **n** child
Deut 32:25 the **n** child with the man of
1Sa 15: 3 **n** child, ox and sheep, camel
1Sa 22:19 **n** infants, oxen and donkeys and
Is 11: 8 The **n** child shall play by the
Is 49:15 a woman forget her **n** child
Is 49:23 their queens your **n** mothers
Joel 2:16 the children and **n** babes
Matt 21:16 **n** infants You have perfected
Matt 24:19 to those with **n** babies in
Mark 13:17 to those with **n** babies in
Luke 21:23 to those who are **n** babies in
1Th 2: 7 just as a **n** mother cherishes

NUTS
Gen 43:11 spices and myrrh, pistachio **n**
Song 6:11 **n** to see the verdure of the

NYMPHAS
Col 4:15 who are in Laodicea, and **N**

O

O (*see* PREFACE)

OAK (*see* OAKS)
Josh 24:26 **o** that was by the sanctuary
1Ki 13:14 found him sitting under an **o**
Is 6:13 a terebinth tree or as an **o**
Is 44:14 and takes the cypress and the **o**
Ezek 6:13 tree, and under every thick **o**

OAKS (*see* OAK)
Is 2:13 and upon all the **o** of Bashan
Ezek 27: 6 Of **o** from Bashan they made
Hos 4:13 incense on the hills, under **o**
Amos 2: 9 and he was as strong as the **o**
Zech 11: 2 O **o** of Bashan, for the thick

OAR (*see* OARS, OARSMEN)
Ezek 27:29 All who handle the **o**, the

OARS (*see* OAR)
Is 33:21 no galley with **o** will sail
Ezek 27: 6 from Bashan they made your **o**

OARSMEN (*see* OAR)
Ezek 27: 8 of Sidon and Arvad were your **o**
Ezek 27: 9 their **o** were in you to market
Ezek 27:26 Your **o** brought you into many

OATH (*see* OATHS)
Gen 21:31 two of them swore an **o** there
Gen 24: 8 will be released from this **o**
Gen 24:41 **o** when you arrive among my
Gen 24:41 will be released from my **o**
Gen 26: 3 I will perform the **o** which I
Gen 26:28 there now be an **o** between us
Gen 26:31 swore an **o** with one another
Gen 50:25 Then Joseph took an **o** from
Ex 13:19 of Israel under solemn **o**,
Ex 22:11 then an **o** of the LORD shall
Lev 5: 1 hearing the utterance of an **o**
Lev 5: 4 a man may pronounce by an **o**
Num 5:19 priest shall put her under **o**
Num 5:21 under the **o** of the curse, and
Num 5:21 an **o** among your people, when
Num 30: 2 LORD, or swears an **o** to bind
Num 30:10 by an agreement with an **o**
Num 30:13 every binding **o** to afflict
Num 32:10 on that day, and He swore an **o**
Deut 1:34 and was angry, and took an **o**
Deut 7: 8 the **o** which He swore to your
Deut 29:12 LORD your God, and into His **o**
Deut 29:14 make this covenant and this **o**
Josh 2:17 **o** of yours which you have
Josh 2:20 **o** which you made us swear
Josh 9:20 the **o** which we swore to them
Judg 21: 1 had sworn an **o** at Mizpah,
Judg 21: 5 **o** concerning anyone who had
Judg 21:18 of Israel have sworn an **o**
Judg 21:22 yourselves guilty of your **o**
1Sa 14:24 had placed the people under **o**
1Sa 14:26 for the people feared the **o**
1Sa 14:27 charge the people with the **o**
1Sa 14:28 charged the people with an **o**
1Sa 20: 3 Then David took an **o** again
2Sa 3:35 still day, David took an **o**
2Sa 21: 7 **o** that was between them,
1Ki 1:29 And the king took an **o** and said
1Ki 2:43 not kept the **o** of the LORD
1Ki 8:31 and is forced to take an **o**
1Ki 8:31 takes an **o** before Your altar
1Ki 18:10 here,' he took an **o** from the
2Ki 11: 4 took an **o** from them in the
2Ki 25:24 took an **o** before them and
1Ch 16:16 Abraham, and His **o** to Isaac,
2Ch 6:22 and is forced to take an **o**
2Ch 6:22 takes an **o** before Your altar
2Ch 15:14 Then they took an **o** before
2Ch 15:15 all Judah rejoiced at the **o**
2Ch 36:13 made him swear an **o** by God
Ezra 10: 5 swear an **o** that they would do
Ezra 10: 5 So they swore an **o**
Neh 5:12 required an **o** from them that
Neh 10:29 an **o** to walk in God's Law,
Ps 102: 8 me swear an **o** against me
Ps 105: 9 Abraham, And His **o** to Isaac,
Ps 106:26 His hand in an **o** against them
Eccl 8: 2 for the sake of your **o** to God
Eccl 9: 2 an **o** as he who fears an **o**
Is 45:23 every tongue shall take an **o**
Is 49:22 hand in an **o** to the nations
Jer 11: 5 that I may establish the **o**
Jer 40: 9 took an **o** before them and
Jer 42:18 And you shall be an **o**, an
Jer 44:12 and they shall be an **o** and an
Ezek 16: 8 Yes, I swore an **o** to you and

Ezek 16:59 done, who despised the **o** by
Ezek 17:13 with him, and put him under **o**
Ezek 17:16 whose **o** he despised and whose
Ezek 17:18 Since he despised the **o** by
Ezek 17:19 surely My **o** which he despised
Ezek 20: 5 lifted My hand in an **o** to the
Ezek 20: 5 My hand in an **o** to them,
Ezek 20: 6 My hand in an **o** to them, to
Ezek 20:15 **o** to them in the wilderness
Ezek 20:23 **o** to those in the wilderness
Ezek 20:28 My hand in an **o** to give them
Ezek 20:42 I lifted My hand in an **o** to
Ezek 36: 7 an **o** that surely the nations
Ezek 44:12 My hand in an **o** against them
Ezek 47:14 **o** to give it to your fathers
Dan 9:11 the **o** written in the Law of
Hos 4:15 to Beth Aven, nor swear an **o**
Zech 8:17 and do not love a false **o**
Matt 14: 7 he promised with an **o** to give
Matt 26:72 But again he denied with an **o**
Luke 1:73 the **o** which He swore to our
Acts 2:30 that God had sworn with an **o**
Acts 23:12 bound themselves under an **o**
Acts 23:14 ourselves under a great **o**
Acts 23:21 **o** that they will neither eat
Heb 6:16 an **o** for confirmation is for
Heb 6:17 counsel, confirmed it by an **o**
Heb 7:20 not made priest without an **o**
Heb 7:21 become priests without an **o**
Heb 7:21 but He with an **o** by Him who
Heb 7:28 but the word of the **o**, which
Jas 5:12 by earth or with any other **o**

OATHS (*see* OATH)
Deut 6:13 and shall take **o** in His name
Deut 10:20 fast, and take **o** in His name
Ezek 21:23 who have sworn **o** with them
Hab 3: 9 **o** were sworn over Your arrows
Zeph 1: 5 swear **o** by the LORD, but who
Matt 5:33 perform your **o** to the Lord
Matt 14: 9 because of the **o** and because
Mark 6:26 yet, because of the **o** and

OBADIAH
1Ki 18: 3 And Ahab had called **O**, who
1Ki 18: 3 (Now **O** feared the LORD
1Ki 18: 4 that **O** had taken one hundred
1Ki 18: 5 And Ahab had said to **O**, "Go
1Ki 18: 6 **O** went another way by himself
1Ki 18: 7 Now as **O** was on his way,
1Ki 18:16 So **O** went to meet Ahab, and
1Ch 3:21 sons of Arnan, the sons of **O**
1Ch 7: 3 of Izrahiah were Michael, **O**
1Ch 8:38 Bocheru, Ishmael, Sheariah, **O**
1Ch 9:16 **O** the son of Shemaiah, the
1Ch 9:44 Bocheru, Ishmael, Sheariah, **O**
1Ch 12: 9 **O** the second, Eliab the third
1Ch 27:19 Ishmaiah the son of **O**
2Ch 17: 7 sent his leaders, Ben-Hail, **O**
2Ch 34:12 **O** the Levites, of the sons of
Ezra 8: 9 **O** the son of Jehiel, and with
Neh 10: 5 Harim, Meremoth, **O**,
Neh 12:25 Mattaniah, Bakbukiah, **O**,
Obad 1 The vision of **O**

OBAL
Gen 10:28 **O**, Abimael, Sheba,

OBED (*see* OBED-EDOM)
Ruth 4:17 And they called his name **O**
Ruth 4:21 begot Boaz, and Boaz begot **O**
Ruth 4:22 **O** begot Jesse, and Jesse begot
1Ch 2:12 Boaz begot **O**
1Ch 2:12 and **O** begot Jesse
1Ch 2:37 Ephlal, and Ephlal begot **O**
1Ch 2:38 **O** begot Jehu, and Jehu begot
1Ch 11:47 Eliel, **O**, and Jaasiel the
1Ch 26: 7 were Othni, Rephael, **O**, and
2Ch 23: 1 Azariah the son of **O**,
Matt 1: 5 Rahab, Boaz begot **O** by Ruth
Matt 1: 5 **O** begot Jesse
Luke 3:32 son of Jesse, the son of **O**

OBED-EDOM (*see* EDOM, OBED)
2Sa 6:10 the house of **O** the Gittite
2Sa 6:11 of **O** the Gittite three months
2Sa 6:11 And the LORD blessed **O** and all
2Sa 6:12 has blessed the house of **O**
2Sa 6:12 of God from the house of **O** to
1Ch 13:13 the house of **O** the Gittite
1Ch 13:14 **O** in his house three months
1Ch 13:14 LORD blessed the house of **O**
1Ch 15:18 Elipheleh, Mikneiah, **O**, and
1Ch 15:21 Elipheleh, Mikneiah, **O**,
1Ch 15:24 and **O** and Jehiah, doorkeepers
1Ch 15:25 from the house of **O** with joy
1Ch 16: 5 Eliab, Benaiah, and **O**
1Ch 16:38 and **O** with his sixty-eight
1Ch 16:38 including **O** the son of
1Ch 26: 4 Moreover the sons of **O** were
1Ch 26: 8 these were of the sons of **O**
1Ch 26: 8 sixty-two of **O**
1Ch 26:15 to **O** the South Gate, and to
2Ch 25:24 in the house of God with **O**

OBEDIENCE (*see* OBEDIENT)
Gen 49:10 shall be the **o** of the people
Prov 30:17 scorns **o** to his mother, the
Rom 1: 5 and apostleship for **o** to the
Rom 5:19 so also by one Man's **o** many
Rom 6:16 or of **o** to righteousness
Rom 16:19 For your **o** has become known
Rom 16:26 God, for **o** to the faith
2Co 7:15 he remembers the **o** of you all
2Co 9:13 they glorify God for the **o** of
2Co 10: 5 captivity to the **o** of Christ
2Co 10: 6 when your **o** is fulfilled
Phm 21 Having confidence in your **o**
Heb 5: 8 Son, yet He learned **o** by the
1Pe 1: 2 of the Spirit, for **o** and

OBEDIENT (*see* OBEDIENCE, OBEY)
Ex 24: 7 has said we will do, and be **o**
Num 27:20 children of Israel may be **o**
Deut 8:20 be **o** to the voice of the LORD
Prov 25:12 a wise reprover to an **o** ear
Is 1:19 If you are willing and **o**, you
Is 42:24 nor were they **o** to His law
Acts 6: 7 priests were **o** to the faith
Rom 15:18 deed, to make the Gentiles **o**
2Co 2: 9 you are **o** in all things
Eph 6: 5 be **o** to those who are your
Phil 2: 8 and became **o** to the point of
Tit 2: 5 **o** to their own husbands, that
Tit 2: 9 to be **o** to their own masters
1Pe 1:14 as **o** children, not conforming

OBEY (*see* OBEDIENT, OBEYED, OBEYING, OBEYS)
Gen 27: 8 **o** my voice according to what
Gen 27:13 only **o** my voice, and go, get
Gen 27:43 therefore, my son, **o** my voice
Ex 5: 2 that I should **o** His voice to
Ex 19: 5 if you will indeed **o** My voice
Ex 23:21 Beware of Him and **o** His voice
Ex 23:22 But if you indeed **o** His voice
Lev 26:14 But if you do not **o** Me, and
Lev 26:18 all this, if you do not **o** Me
Lev 26:21 and are not willing to **o** Me
Lev 26:27 all this, if you do not **o** Me
Deut 4:30 LORD your God and **o** His voice
Deut 9:23 believe Him nor **o** His voice
Deut 11:13 **o** My commandments which I
Deut 11:27 if you **o** the commandments of
Deut 11:28 curse, if you do not **o** the
Deut 12:28 **o** all these words which I
Deut 13: 4 **o** His voice, and you shall
Deut 15: 5 only if you carefully **o** the
Deut 21:18 **o** the voice of his father or
Deut 21:20 he will not **o** our voice
Deut 26:17 and that you will **o** His voice
Deut 27:10 Therefore you shall **o** the
Deut 28: 1 if you diligently **o** the voice
Deut 28: 2 because you **o** the voice of
Deut 28:15 if you do not **o** the voice of
Deut 28:45 because you did not **o** the
Deut 28:62 because you would not **o** the
Deut 30: 2 **o** His voice, according to all
Deut 30: 8 you will again **o** the voice of
Deut 30:10 if you **o** the voice of the
Deut 30:20 God, that you may **o** His voice
Josh 5: 6 because they did not **o** the
Josh 24:24 serve, and His voice we will **o**
Judg 3: 4 **o** the commandments of the
1Sa 8:19 to **o** the voice of Samuel
1Sa 12:14 **o** His voice, and do not rebel
1Sa 12:15 if you do not **o** the voice of
1Sa 15:19 Why then did you not **o** the
1Sa 15:22 to **o** is better than sacrifice
1Sa 28:18 Because you did not **o** the
2Sa 22:45 soon as they hear, they **o** me
2Ki 10: 6 me, and if you will **o** my voice
2Ki 17:40 However they did not **o**, but
2Ki 18:12 because they did not **o** the
Neh 9:17 They refused to **o**, and they
Esth 1:15 did not **o** the command of King
Job 36:11 If they **o** and serve Him, they
Job 36:12 But if they do not **o**, they
Ps 18:44 as they hear of me they **o** me
Is 11:14 people of Ammon shall **o** them
Jer 7:23 **O** My voice, and I will be
Jer 7:24 Yet they did not **o** or incline
Jer 7:26 Yet they did not **o** Me or
Jer 7:27 them, but they will not **o** you
Jer 7:28 is a nation that does not **o**
Jer 11: 3 is the man who does not **o** the
Jer 11: 4 **O** My voice, and do according
Jer 11: 7 saying, "**O** My voice
Jer 11: 8 Yet they did not **o** or
Jer 12:17 But if they do not **o**, I will
Jer 17:23 But they did not **o** nor
Jer 18:10 that it does not **o** My voice
Jer 22:21 that you did not **o** My voice
Jer 26:13 **o** the voice of the LORD your
Jer 34:14 **o** Me nor incline their ear
Jer 35:13 instruction to **o** My words
Jer 35:14 **o** their father's commandment
Jer 35:14 and speaking, you did not **o** Me
Jer 38:20 **o** the voice of the LORD which
Jer 42: 6 we will **o** the voice of the
Jer 42: 6 **o** the voice of the LORD our
Jer 43: 4 not **o** the voice of the LORD
Jer 43: 7 for they did not **o** the voice
Ezek 20: 8 against Me and would not **o** Me
Ezek 20:39 if you will not **o** me
Dan 7:27 shall serve and **o** Him
Dan 9:11 so as not to **o** Your voice
Hos 9:17 because they did not **o** Him
Zech 6:15 to pass if you diligently **o**
Matt 8:27 the winds and the sea **o** Him
Mark 1:27 spirits, and they **o** Him
Mark 4:41 the wind and the sea **o** Him
Luke 8:25 winds and water, and they **o** Him
Luke 17: 6 the sea,' and it would **o** you
Acts 5:29 We ought to **o** God rather than
Acts 5:32 has given to those who **o** Him
Acts 7:39 whom our fathers would not **o**
Rom 2: 8 do not **o** the truth
Rom 2: 8 but **o** unrighteousness
Rom 6:12 you should **o** it in its lusts
Rom 6:16 yourselves slaves to **o**, you
Rom 6:16 that one's slaves whom you **o**
Gal 3: 1 you should not **o** the truth
Eph 6: 1 **o** your parents in the Lord,
Col 3:20 **o** your parents in all things,
Col 3:22 **o** in all things your masters
2Th 1: 8 on those who do not **o** the
2Th 3:14 if anyone does not **o** our word
Tit 3: 1 rulers and authorities, to **o**
Heb 3:18 but to those who did not **o**
Heb 5: 9 salvation to all who **o** Him
Heb 13:17 **O** those who rule over you, and
Jas 3: 3 mouths that they may **o** us
1Pe 3: 1 if some do not **o** the word
1Pe 4:17 do not **o** the gospel of God

OBEYED (*see* OBEY)
Gen 22:18 because you have **o** My voice
Gen 26: 5 because Abraham **o** My voice
Gen 28: 7 that Jacob had **o** his father
Deut 26:14 I have **o** the voice of the
Josh 22: 2 have **o** my voice in all that I
Judg 2: 2 But you have not **o** My voice
Judg 6:10 But you have not **o** My voice
1Sa 15:20 But I have **o** the voice of the
1Sa 15:24 the people and **o** their voice
1Sa 28:21 maidservant has **o** your voice
1Ki 12:24 Therefore they **o** the
1Ki 20:36 Because you have not **o** the
2Ki 22:13 our fathers have not **o** the
1Ch 29:23 and all Israel **o** him
2Ch 11: 4 Therefore they **o** the
Esth 2:20 for Esther **o** the command of
Prov 5:13 I have not **o** the voice of my
Jer 3:13 and you have not **o** My voice
Jer 3:25 have not **o** the voice of the
Jer 9:13 them, and have not **o** My voice
Jer 32:23 it, but they have not **o** Your
Jer 34:10 in bondage anymore, they **o**
Jer 34:17 You have not **o** Me in
Jer 35: 8 Thus we have **o** the voice of
Jer 35:10 dwelt in tents, and have **o**
Jer 35:15 inclined your ear, nor **o** Me
Jer 35:16 but this people has not **o** Me
Jer 35:18 Because you have **o** the
Jer 40: 3 not **o** His voice, therefore

Jer 42:21 but you have not **o** the voice
Jer 44:23 have not **o** the voice of the
Dan 9:10 We have not **o** the voice of
Dan 9:14 we have not **o** His voice
Zeph 3: 2 She has not **o** His voice, she
Hag 1:12 **o** the voice of the LORD their
Zech 7: 7 Should you not have **o** the
Acts 5:36 all who **o** him were scattered
Acts 5:37 all who **o** him were dispersed
Rom 6:17 yet you **o** from the heart that
Rom 10:16 have not all **o** the gospel
Phil 2:12 beloved, as you have always **o**
Heb 11: 8 By faith Abraham **o** when he
1Pe 3: 6 as Sarah **o** Abraham, calling

OBEYING (*see* OBEY)
Judg 2:17 in **o** the commandments of the
1Sa 15:22 as in **o** the voice of the LORD
Hos 4:10 they have ceased **o** the LORD
Gal 5: 7 hindered you from **o** the truth
1Pe 1:22 in **o** the truth through the

OBEYS (*see* OBEY)
Is 50:10 Who **o** the voice of His

OBIL
1Ch 27:30 **O** the Ishmaelite was over the

OBJECT (*see* OBJECTION, OBJECTS)
Ezek 15: 3 taken from it to make any **o**
Ezek 15: 5 no **o** could be made from it
Acts 10:11 an **o** like a great sheet bound
Acts 10:16 And the **o** was taken up into
Acts 11: 5 an **o** descending like a great
Acts 24:19 you to **o** if they had anything
Acts 25:11 of death, I do not **o** to dying
Rev 18:12 every kind of **o** of ivory
Rev 18:12 every kind of **o** of most

OBJECTION (*see* OBJECT)
Acts 10:29 Therefore I came without **o** as

OBJECTS (*see* OBJECT)
Acts 17:23 the **o** of your worship, I even

OBLIGATION (*see* OBLIGED)
2Co 9: 5 and not as a grudging **o**

OBLIGED (*see* OBLIGATION)
Matt 23:16 temple, he is **o** to perform it
Matt 23:18 on it, he is **o** to perform it

OBNOXIOUS
Gen 34:30 me **o** among the inhabitants of

OBOTH
Num 21:10 moved on and camped in **O**
Num 21:11 And they journeyed from **O** and
Num 33:43 from Punon and camped at **O**
Num 33:44 They departed from **O** and

OBSCENE
1Ki 15:13 made an **o** image of Asherah
1Ki 15:13 And Asa cut down her **o** image
2Ch 15:16 made an **o** image of Asherah
2Ch 15:16 and Asa cut down her **o** image

OBSCURE (*see* OBSCURITY)
Is 33:19 people, a people of **o** speech

OBSCURITY (*see* OBSCURE)
Is 29:18 the blind shall see out of **o**

OBSERVANCE (*see* OBSERVE)
Ex 12:42 It is a night of solemn **o** to
Ex 12:42 LORD, a solemn **o** for all the

OBSERVATION (*see* OBSERVE)
Luke 17:20 of God does not come with **o**

OBSERVE (*see* OBSERVANCE, OBSERVATION, OBSERVED, OBSERVER, OBSERVES, OBSERVING)
Gen 16:14 **o**, it is between Kadesh and
Ex 12:17 So you shall **o** the Feast of
Ex 12:17 Therefore you shall **o** this
Ex 12:24 you shall **o** this thing as an
Ex 31:16 to **o** the Sabbath throughout
Ex 34:11 **O** what I command you this day
Ex 34:22 And you shall **o** the Feast of
Lev 18: 4 You shall **o** My judgments and
Lev 19:37 you shall **o** all My statutes
Lev 25:18 So you shall **o** My statutes
Lev 26:14 Me, and do not **o** all these
Num 15:22 and do not **o** all these
Num 22:41 **o** the extent of the people
Deut 4: 1 which I teach you to **o**, that
Deut 4: 6 be careful to **o** them
Deut 4:14 that you might **o** them in the
Deut 5: 1 them and be careful to **o** them
Deut 5:12 **O** the Sabbath day, to keep
Deut 5:31 that they may **o** them in the
Deut 6: 1 that you may **o** them in the
Deut 6: 3 Israel, and be careful to **o** it
Deut 6:24 us to **o** all these statutes
Deut 6:25 if we are careful to **o** all
Deut 7:11 command you today, to **o** them
Deut 8: 1 you must be careful to **o**,
Deut 11:32 careful to **o** all the statutes
Deut 12: 1 you shall be careful to **o** in
Deut 12:28 **O** and obey all these words
Deut 12:32 you, be careful to **o** it
Deut 15: 5 God, to **o** with care all these
Deut 16: 1 **O** the month of Abib, and keep
Deut 16:12 careful to **o** these statutes
Deut 16:13 You shall **o** the Feast of
Deut 17:19 be careful to **o** all the words
Deut 24: 8 that you diligently **o** and do
Deut 26:16 you to **o** these statutes and
Deut 26:16 you shall be careful to **o**
Deut 27:10 **o** His commandments and His
Deut 28: 1 God, to **o** carefully all His
Deut 28:13 and are careful to **o** them
Deut 28:15 God, to **o** carefully all His
Deut 28:58 If you do not carefully **o** all
Deut 31:12 carefully **o** all the words of
Deut 32:46 children to be careful to **o**
Josh 1: 7 that you may **o** to do
Josh 1: 8 night, that you may **o** to do
Judg 13:14 I commanded her let her **o**
1Sa 19: 3 Then what I **o**, I will tell
2Ki 17:37 shall be careful to **o** forever
1Ch 28: 7 to **o** My commandments and My
2Ch 14: 4 and to **o** the law and the
Ezra 7:26 Whoever will not **o** the law of
Neh 1: 5 You and **o** Your
Neh 10:29 the servant of God, and to **o**
Job 39:29 its eyes **o** from afar
Ps 10:14 seen it, for You **o** trouble
Ps 37:37 man, and **o** the upright
Ps 66: 7 His eyes **o** the nations
Ps 105:45 they might **o** His statutes
Ps 107:43 is wise will **o** these things
Ps 119:34 I shall **o** it with my whole
Ps 119:117 And I shall **o** Your statutes
Prov 23:26 and let your eyes **o** my ways
Is 38:11 I shall **o** man no more among
Is 42:20 many things, but you do not **o**
Jer 8: 7 the swallow **o** the time of
Ezek 20:18 nor **o** their judgments, nor
Ezek 20:21 not careful to **o** My judgments
Ezek 37:24 **o** My statutes, and do them
Ezek 45:21 you shall **o** the Passover, a
Hos 12: 6 **o** mercy and justice, and wait
Hos 13: 7 by the road I will **o** them
Matt 23: 3 they tell you to **o**, that **o**
Matt 28:20 teaching them to **o** all things
Acts 7:31 and as he drew near to **o**, the
Acts 16:21 being Romans, to receive or **o**
Acts 21:25 they should **o** no such thing
Rom 14: 6 and he who does not **o** the day
Rom 14: 6 to the Lord he does not **o** it
1Co 10:18 **O** Israel after the flesh
2Co 7:11 For **o** this very thing, that
Gal 4:10 You **o** days and months and
1Ti 5:21 you **o** these things without
1Pe 2:12 your good works which they **o**
1Pe 3: 2 when they **o** your chaste

OBSERVED (*see* OBSERVE)
Gen 50:10 He **o** seven days of mourning
Num 23:21 He has not **o** iniquity in
Deut 33: 9 for they have **o** Your word
2Ch 7: 9 for they **o** the dedication of
Esth 9:28 fail to be **o** among the Jews
Job 31:26 If I have **o** the sun when it
Hos 14: 8 I have heard and **o** him
Mark 10:20 these I have **o** from my youth
Mark 15:47 of Joses **o** where He was laid
Luke 23:55 they **o** the tomb and how His
Acts 10: 4 And when he **o** him, he was
Acts 11: 6 When I **o** it intently and
Acts 27:39 but they **o** a bay with a beach

OBSERVER (*see* OBSERVE)
Is 28: 4 the summer, which an **o** sees

OBSERVES (*see* OBSERVE)
Eccl 11: 4 He who **o** the wind will not
Rom 14: 6 He who **o** the day, **o** it to
Jas 1:24 for he **o** himself, goes away,

OBSERVING (*see* OBSERVE)
Acts 14: 9 **o** him intently and seeing that
Jas 1:23 doer, he is like a man **o** his

OBSESSED
1Ti 6: 4 but is **o** with disputes and

OBSOLETE
Heb 8:13 He has made the first **o**
Heb 8:13 Now what is becoming **o** and

OBSTINATE
Deut 2:30 spirit and made his heart **o**
Is 48: 4 I knew that you were **o**, and

OBSTRUCT
Ezek 39:11 it will **o** travelers, because

OBTAIN (*see* OBTAINED, OBTAINING, OBTAINS)
Gen 16: 2 I shall **o** children by her
Is 35:10 They shall **o** joy and gladness,
Is 51:11 They shall **o** joy and gladness,
Matt 5: 7 for they shall **o** mercy
Rom 11:31 you they also may **o** mercy
1Co 9:24 such a way that you may **o** it
1Co 9:25 Now they do it to **o** a
1Th 5: 9 but to **o** salvation through
1Ti 3:13 **o** for themselves a good
2Ti 2:10 that they also may **o** the
Heb 4:16 of grace, that we may **o** mercy
Heb 11:35 that they might **o** a better
Jas 4: 2 murder and covet and cannot **o**

OBTAINED (*see* OBTAIN)
Lev 6: 4 which he has deceitfully **o**
Neh 13: 6 days I **o** leave from the king
Esth 2: 9 him, and she **o** his favor
Esth 2:15 Esther **o** favor in the sight
Esth 2:17 she **o** grace and favor in his
Hos 2:23 on her who had not **o** mercy
Acts 1:17 **o** a part in this ministry
Acts 22:28 sum I **o** this citizenship
Acts 26:22 having **o** help from God, to
Acts 27:13 that they had **o** their purpose
Rom 11: 7 has not **o** what it seeks
Rom 11: 7 but the elect have **o** it, and
Rom 11:30 yet have now **o** mercy through
Eph 1:11 also we have **o** an inheritance
1Ti 1:13 but I **o** mercy because I did
1Ti 1:16 for this reason I **o** mercy
Heb 1: 4 as He has by inheritance **o** a
Heb 6:15 endured, he **o** the promise
Heb 8: 6 But now He has **o** a more
Heb 9:12 having **o** eternal redemption
Heb 11: 2 the elders **o** a good testimony
Heb 11: 4 through which he **o** witness
Heb 11:33 **o** promises, stopped the
Heb 11:39 having **o** a good testimony
1Pe 2:10 who had not **o** mercy
1Pe 2:10 but now have **o** mercy
2Pe 1: 1 To those who have **o** like

OBTAINING (*see* OBTAIN)
2Th 2:14 for the **o** of the glory of our

OBTAINS (*see* OBTAIN)
Prov 8:35 and **o** favor from the LORD
Prov 12: 2 A good man **o** favor from the
Prov 18:22 and **o** favor from the LORD

OBVIOUSLY
Gen 26: 9 Quite **o** she is your wife

OCCASION (*see* OCCASIONALLY, OCCASIONS)
Gen 43:18 he may seek an **o** against us
Judg 14: 4 an **o** to move against the
1Sa 10: 7 that you do as the **o** demands
2Sa 12:14 deed you have given great **o**
2Ch 22: 7 **o** for Ahaziah's downfall
Ezra 7:20 you may have **o** to provide
Neh 6:13 have **o** for an evil report
Luke 21:13 for you as an **o** for testimony
Rom 7:11 taking **o** by the commandment,

OCCASIONALLY (*see* OCCASION)
1Sa 17:15 But David **o** went and returned

OCCASIONS (*see* OCCASION)
Job 33:10 Yet He finds **o** against me

OCCUPATION
Gen 46:32 for their **o** has been to feed
Gen 46:33 you and says, What is your **o**
Gen 46:34 Your servants' **o** has been
Gen 47: 3 What is your **o**?
Jon 1: 8 What is your **o**?
Acts 18: 3 for by **o** they were tentmakers

Acts 19:25 with the workers of similar **o**

OCCUPIED (*see* OCCUPY)
Josh 22:11 on the side **o** by the children
Eccl 3:10 the sons of men are to be **o**
Acts 26:12 While thus **o**, as I journeyed
Heb 13: 9 who have been **o** with them

OCCUPIES (*see* OCCUPY)
1Co 14:16 how will he who **o** the place

OCCUPY (*see* OCCUPIED, OCCUPIES)
Neh 2: 8 for the house that I will **o**

OCCUR (*see* OCCURRED, OCCURRENCE, OCCURS)
Eccl 8: 7 can tell him when it will **o**
Zech 14: 8 summer and winter it shall **o**

OCCURRED (*see* OCCUR)
Judg 20:12 that has **o** among you
Esth 9: 1 them, the opposite **o**, in that
Acts 2: 6 And when this sound **o**, the
Gal 2: 4 But this **o** because of false
Rev 16:18 **o** since men were on the earth

OCCURRENCE (*see* OCCUR)
Deut 23:10 by some **o** in the night, then
1Ki 5: 4 neither adversary nor evil **o**

OCCURS (*see* OCCUR)
Eccl 8:14 is a vanity which **o** on earth
Eccl 9: 2 Everything **o** alike to all

OCRAN
Num 1:13 Asher, Pagiel the son of **O**
Num 2:27 shall be Pagiel the son of **O**
Num 7:72 day Pagiel the son of **O**,
Num 7:77 of Pagiel the son of **O**
Num 10:26 Asher was Pagiel the son of **O**

ODED
2Ch 15: 1 upon Azariah the son of **O**
2Ch 15: 8 the prophecy of **O** the prophet
2Ch 28: 9 was there, whose name was **O**

ODOR
Eccl 10: 1 cause it to give off a foul **o**
Joel 2:20 his foul **o** will rise, because

OF (*see* PREFACE)

OFF (*see* PREFACE)

OFFAL
Ex 29:14 bull, with its skin and its **o**
Lev 4:11 and legs, its entrails and **o**
Lev 8:17 its hide, its flesh, and its **o**
Lev 16:27 their flesh, and their **o**
Num 19: 5 and its **o** shall be burned

OFFEND (*see* OFFENDED, OFFENDER, OFFENSE, OFFENSIVE)
Job 34:31 I will **o** no more
Jer 2: 3 All that devour him will **o**
Hos 4:15 the harlot, let not Judah **o**
Matt 13:41 His kingdom all things that **o**
Matt 17:27 Nevertheless, lest we **o** them
Luke 17: 2 than that he should **o** one of
John 6:61 Does this **o** you?

OFFENDED (*see* OFFEND)
Gen 20: 9 How have I **o** you, that you
Gen 40: 1 king of Egypt **o** their lord
2Ch 28:13 we already have **o** the LORD
Prov 18:19 A brother **o** is harder to win
Jer 50: 7 said, 'We have not **o**, because
Ezek 25:12 has greatly **o** by avenging
Hos 13: 1 but when he **o** in Baal, he
Matt 11: 6 he who is not **o** because of Me
Matt 13:57 So they were **o** at Him
Matt 15:12 that the Pharisees were **o**
Matt 24:10 And then many will be **o**, will
Mark 6: 3 And they were **o** at Him
Luke 7:23 he who is not **o** because of Me
Acts 25: 8 have I **o** in anything at all
Rom 14:21 or is **o** or is made weak

OFFENDER (*see* OFFEND, OFFENDERS)
Is 29:21 who make a man an **o** by a word
Acts 25:11 For if I am an **o**, or have

OFFENDERS (*see* OFFENDER)
Num 25: 4 hang the **o** before the LORD,
1Ki 1:21 Solomon will be counted as **o**

OFFENSE (*see* OFFEND, OFFENSES)
1Sa 25:31 nor **o** of heart to my lord,
Is 8:14 and a rock of **o** to both the
Jer 37:18 What **o** have I committed
Hos 5:15 till they acknowledge their **o**
Hab 1:11 he commits **o**, imputing this
Matt 16:23 You are an **o** to Me, for you
Matt 18: 7 that man by whom the **o** comes
Acts 24:16 without **o** toward God and men
Rom 5:15 free gift is not like the **o**
Rom 5:15 by the one man's **o** many died
Rom 5:16 which came from one **o**
Rom 5:17 For if by the one man's **o**
Rom 5:18 as through one man's **o**
Rom 5:20 that the **o** might abound
Rom 9:33 stumbling stone and rock of **o**
Rom 14:20 for the man who eats with **o**
1Co 10:32 Give no **o**, either to the Jews
2Co 6: 3 We give no **o** in anything,
Gal 5:11 Then the **o** of the cross has
Phil 1:10 without **o** till the day of
1Pe 2: 8 of stumbling and a rock of **o**

OFFENSES (*see* OFFENSE)
2Ch 19:10 whether of bloodshed or **o**
Eccl 10: 4 conciliation pacifies great **o**
Matt 18: 7 Woe to the world because of **o**
Matt 18: 7 For **o** must come, but woe to
Luke 17: 1 that no **o** should come, but
Rom 4:25 delivered up because of our **o**
Rom 5:16 **o** resulted in justification
Rom 16:17 who cause divisions and **o**,

OFFENSIVE (*see* OFFEND)
Job 19:17 My breath is **o** to my wife

OFFER (*see* OFFERED, OFFERING, OFFERS)
Gen 22: 2 and **o** him there as a burnt
Ex 22:29 to **o** the first of your ripe
Ex 23:18 You shall not **o** the blood of
Ex 29:36 you shall **o** a bull every day
Ex 29:38 what you shall **o** on the altar
Ex 29:39 you shall **o** in the morning
Ex 29:39 lamb you shall **o** at twilight
Ex 29:41 lamb you shall **o** at twilight
Ex 29:41 you shall **o** with it the grain
Ex 30: 9 You shall not **o** strange
Ex 34:25 You shall not **o** the blood of
Lev 1: 3 let him **o** a male without
Lev 1: 3 he shall **o** it of his own free
Lev 2:12 you shall **o** them to the LORD,
Lev 2:13 offerings you shall **o** salt
Lev 2:14 If you **o** a grain offering of
Lev 2:14 you shall **o** for the grain
Lev 3: 1 he shall **o** it without blemish
Lev 3: 3 Then he shall **o** from the
Lev 3: 6 he shall **o** it without blemish
Lev 3: 7 then he shall **o** it before the
Lev 3: 9 Then he shall **o** from the
Lev 3:12 then he shall **o** it before the
Lev 3:14 Then he shall **o** from it his
Lev 4: 3 then let him **o** to the LORD
Lev 4:14 then the assembly shall **o** a
Lev 5: 8 who shall **o** that which is for
Lev 5:10 he shall **o** the second as a
Lev 6:14 The sons of Aaron shall **o** it
Lev 6:20 they shall **o** to the LORD,
Lev 6:21 **o** for a sweet aroma to the
Lev 6:22 in his place, shall **o** it
Lev 7: 3 he shall **o** from it all its
Lev 7:11 which he shall **o** to the LORD
Lev 7:12 thanksgiving, then he shall **o**
Lev 7:13 **o** leavened bread with the
Lev 7:14 from it he shall **o** one cake
Lev 7:25 of the beast of which men **o**
Lev 7:38 the children of Israel to **o**
Lev 9: 2 and **o** them before the LORD
Lev 9: 7 **o** your sin offering and your
Lev 9: 7 **O** the offering of the people,
Lev 10:15 fire, to **o** as a wave offering
Lev 12: 7 Then he shall **o** it before
Lev 14:12 **o** it as a trespass offering,
Lev 14:19 shall **o** the sin offering, and
Lev 14:20 the priest shall **o** the burnt
Lev 14:30 And he shall **o** one of the
Lev 15:15 Then the priest shall **o** them
Lev 15:30 Then the priest shall **o** the
Lev 16: 6 Aaron shall **o** the bull as a
Lev 16: 9 and **o** it as a sin offering
Lev 16:24 **o** his burnt offering and the
Lev 17: 4 to **o** an offering to the LORD
Lev 17: 5 they **o** in the open field,
Lev 17: 5 **o** them as peace offerings to
Lev 17: 7 They shall no more **o** their
Lev 17: 9 to **o** it to the LORD, that man
Lev 19: 5 if you **o** a sacrifice of peace
Lev 19: 5 you shall **o** it of your own
Lev 19: 6 eaten the same day you **o** it
Lev 21: 6 for they **o** the offerings of
Lev 21:17 may approach to **o** the bread
Lev 21:21 shall come near to **o** the
Lev 21:21 to **o** the bread of his God
Lev 22:15 which they **o** to the LORD,
Lev 22:18 which they **o** to the LORD as a
Lev 22:19 you shall **o** of your own free
Lev 22:20 has a defect, you shall not **o**
Lev 22:22 you shall not **o** to the LORD
Lev 22:23 may **o** as a freewill offering
Lev 22:24 You shall not **o** to the LORD
Lev 22:25 **o** any of these as the bread
Lev 22:29 when you **o** a sacrifice of
Lev 22:29 **o** it of your own free will
Lev 23: 8 But you shall **o** an offering
Lev 23:12 you shall **o** on that day, when
Lev 23:16 then you shall **o** a new grain
Lev 23:18 you shall **o** with the bread
Lev 23:25 you shall **o** an offering made
Lev 23:27 **o** an offering made by fire to
Lev 23:36 For seven days you shall **o**
Lev 23:36 you shall **o** an offering made
Lev 23:37 to **o** an offering made by fire
Lev 27:11 beast which they do not **o** as
Num 6:11 the priest shall **o** one as a
Num 6:16 **o** his sin offering and his
Num 6:17 and he shall **o** the ram as a
Num 6:17 also **o** its grain offering
Num 7:11 They shall **o** their offering,
Num 8:11 Aaron shall **o** the Levites
Num 8:12 and you shall **o** one as a sin
Num 8:13 then **o** them as though a wave
Num 8:15 and **o** them, as though a wave
Num 15: 7 **o** one-third of a hin of wine
Num 15:19 that you shall **o** up a heave
Num 15:20 You shall **o** up a cake of the
Num 15:20 floor, so shall you **o** it up
Num 15:24 whole congregation shall **o**
Num 16:40 should come near to **o** incense
Num 18:12 which they **o** to the LORD, I
Num 18:19 of Israel **o** to the LORD, I
Num 18:24 which they **o** up as a heave
Num 18:26 then you shall **o** up a heave
Num 18:28 Thus you shall also **o** a
Num 18:29 **o** up every heave offering due
Num 28: 2 you shall be careful to **o** to
Num 28: 3 which you shall **o** to the LORD
Num 28: 4 you shall **o** in the morning
Num 28: 4 you shall **o** in the evening
Num 28: 8 you shall **o** in the evening
Num 28: 8 you shall **o** it as an offering
Num 28:20 ephah you shall **o** for a bull
Num 28:21 you shall **o** one-tenth of an
Num 28:23 You shall **o** these besides
Num 28:24 **o** the food of the offering
Num 29: 2 You shall **o** a burnt offering
Deut 12:13 not **o** your burnt offerings in
Deut 12:14 there you shall **o** your burnt
Deut 12:27 And you shall **o** your burnt
Deut 18: 3 from those who **o** a sacrifice
Deut 20:10 proclaim an **o** of peace to it
Deut 20:11 they accept your **o** of peace
Deut 27: 6 **o** burnt offerings on it to
Deut 27: 7 You shall **o** peace offerings,
Deut 33:19 there they shall **o** sacrifices
Josh 22:23 LORD, or if to **o** on it burnt
Josh 22:23 or if to **o** peace offerings on
Judg 5: 2 people willingly **o** themselves
Judg 6:26 **o** a burnt sacrifice with the
Judg 11:31 I will **o** it up as a burnt
Judg 13:16 But if you **o** a burnt offering
Judg 13:16 you must **o** it to the LORD
Judg 16:23 gathered together to **o** a
1Sa 1:21 to **o** to the LORD the yearly
1Sa 2:19 to **o** the yearly sacrifice
1Sa 2:28 to **o** upon My altar, to burn
1Sa 10: 8 to you to **o** burnt offerings
2Sa 24:12 I **o** you three things
2Sa 24:22 **o** up whatever seems good to
2Sa 24:24 nor will I **o** burnt offerings
1Ki 12:27 If these people go up to **o**
2Ki 5:17 **o** either burnt offering or
2Ki 10:24 they went in to **o** sacrifices
2Ki 17:36 to Him you shall **o** sacrifice

1Ch 16:40 to **o** burnt offerings to the
1Ch 21:10 I **o** you three things
1Ch 21:24 nor **o** burnt offerings with
1Ch 29:14 to **o** so willingly as this
1Ch 29:17 here to **o** willingly to You
2Ch 23:18 to **o** the burnt offerings of
2Ch 29:21 to **o** them on the altar of the
2Ch 29:27 **o** the burnt offering on the
2Ch 35:12 to **o** to the LORD, as it is
2Ch 35:16 to **o** burnt offerings on the
Ezra 3: 2 to **o** burnt offerings on it,
Ezra 3: 6 **o** burnt offerings to the LORD
Ezra 6:10 that they may **o** sacrifices of
Ezra 7:17 **o** them on the altar of the
Neh 4: 2 Will they **o** sacrifices
Job 1: 5 **o** burnt offerings according
Job 6:22 **O** a bribe for me from your
Job 42: 8 **o** up for yourselves a burnt
Ps 4: 5 **O** the sacrifices of
Ps 16: 4 of blood I will not **o**, Nor
Ps 27: 6 Therefore I will **o** sacrifices
Ps 50:14 **O** to God thanksgiving, And pay
Ps 51:19 Then they shall **o** bulls on
Ps 66:15 I will **o** You burnt sacrifices
Ps 66:15 I will **o** bulls with goats
Ps 72:10 of Sheba and Seba Will **o** gifts
Ps 116:17 I will **o** to You the sacrifice
Is 57: 7 you went up to **o** sacrifice
Jer 11:12 gods to whom they **o** incense
Jer 14:12 when they **o** burnt offering and
Jer 33:18 lack a man to **o** burnt
Ezek 20:31 For when you **o** your gifts
Ezek 43:22 **o** a kid of the goats without
Ezek 43:23 it, you shall **o** a young bull
Ezek 43:24 When you **o** them before the
Ezek 43:24 and they will **o** them up as a
Ezek 43:27 shall **o** your burnt offerings
Ezek 44:15 before Me to **o** to Me the fat
Ezek 44:27 he must **o** his sin offering in
Ezek 45:13 offering which you shall **o**
Hos 4:13 They **o** sacrifices on the
Hos 4:14 **o** sacrifices with a ritual
Hos 9: 4 They shall not **o** wine
Hos 14: 2 for we will **o** the sacrifices
Amos 4: 5 **O** a sacrifice of thanksgiving
Amos 5:22 Though you **o** Me burnt
Amos 5:25 Did you **o** Me sacrifices and
Hag 2:14 what they **o** there is unclean
Mal 1: 7 You **o** defiled food on My
Mal 1: 8 when you **o** the blind as a
Mal 1: 8 And when you **o** the lame and
Mal 1: 8 **O** it then to your governor
Mal 3: 3 that they may **o** to the LORD
Matt 5:24 and then come and **o** your gift
Matt 8: 4 and **o** the gift that Moses
Mark 1:44 **o** for your cleansing those
Luke 2:24 to **o** a sacrifice according to
Luke 6:29 one cheek, **o** the other also
Luke 11:12 egg, will he **o** him a scorpion
Acts 7:42 Did you **o** Me slaughtered
Heb 5: 1 God, that he may **o** both gifts
Heb 5: 3 for himself, to **o** for sins
Heb 7:27 to **o** up sacrifices, first for
Heb 8: 3 is appointed to **o** both gifts
Heb 8: 3 One also have something to **o**
Heb 8: 4 **o** the gifts according to the
Heb 9:25 He should **o** Himself often
Heb 10: 1 which they **o** continually year
Heb 13:15 by Him let us continually **o**
1Pe 2: 5 to **o** up spiritual sacrifices
Rev 8: 3 that he should **o** it with the

OFFERED (*see* OFFER)
Gen 8:20 and **o** burnt offerings on the
Gen 22:13 **o** it up for a burnt offering
Gen 31:54 Then Jacob **o** a sacrifice on
Gen 46: 1 **o** sacrifices to the God of
Ex 24: 5 who **o** burnt offerings and
Ex 32: 6 **o** burnt offerings, and brought
Ex 35:22 every man who **o** an offering
Ex 35:24 Everyone who **o** an offering of
Ex 40:29 **o** upon it the burnt offering
Lev 7: 8 burnt offering which he has **o**
Lev 7:15 be eaten the same day it is **o**
Lev 9:15 **o** it for sin, like the first
Lev 9:16 and **o** it according to the
Lev 10: 1 **o** profane fire before the
Lev 10:19 have **o** their sin offering
Lev 16: 1 when they **o** profane fire
Num 3: 4 **o** profane fire before the
Num 7:10 Now the leaders **o** the
Num 7:10 so the leaders **o** their
Num 7:12 the one who **o** his offering on
Num 7:19 he **o** one silver platter, the
Num 15: 9 then shall be **o** with the
Num 22:40 Then Balak **o** oxen and sheep,
Num 23: 2 and Balak and Balaam **o** a bull
Num 23: 4 I have **o** on each altar a bull
Num 23:14 **o** a bull and a ram on each
Num 23:30 **o** a bull and a ram on every
Num 26:61 and Abihu died when they **o**
Num 28:15 to the LORD shall be **o**,
Num 28:24 it shall be **o** besides the
Num 31:52 that they **o** to the LORD, from
Deut 28:68 there you shall be **o** for sale
Josh 8:31 they **o** on it burnt offerings
Judg 5: 9 the rulers of Israel who **o**
Judg 6:28 the second bull was being **o**
Judg 13:19 **o** it upon the rock to the
Judg 20:26 they **o** burnt offerings and
Judg 21: 4 **o** burnt offerings and peace
1Sa 2:13 when any man **o** a sacrifice
1Sa 6:14 cart and **o** the cows as a burnt
1Sa 6:15 Shemesh **o** burnt offerings
1Sa 7: 9 lamb and **o** it as a whole burnt
1Sa 13: 9 And he **o** the burnt offering
1Sa 13:12 and **o** a burnt offering
2Sa 6:17 Then David **o** burnt offerings
2Sa 15:12 Giloh, while he **o** sacrifices
2Sa 24:25 **o** burnt offerings and peace
1Ki 3: 4 Solomon **o** a thousand burnt
1Ki 3:15 **o** up burnt offerings
1Ki 3:15 **o** peace offerings, and made a
1Ki 8:62 king and all Israel with him **o**
1Ki 8:63 And Solomon **o** a sacrifice of
1Ki 8:63 which he **o** to the LORD,
1Ki 8:64 for there he **o** burnt
1Ki 9:25 Solomon **o** burnt offerings
1Ki 12:32 **o** sacrifices on the altar
1Ki 12:33 **o** sacrifices on the altar and
1Ki 22:43 for the people **o** sacrifices
2Ki 3:20 when the grain offering was **o**
2Ki 3:27 **o** him as a burnt offering
1Ch 6:49 his sons **o** sacrifices on the
1Ch 15:26 that they **o** seven bulls and
1Ch 16: 1 Then they **o** burnt offerings
1Ch 21:26 **o** burnt offerings and peace
1Ch 29: 6 the king's work, **o** willingly
1Ch 29: 9 for they had **o** willingly
1Ch 29: 9 had **o** willingly to the LORD
1Ch 29:17 willingly **o** all these things
1Ch 29:21 **o** burnt offerings to the LORD
2Ch 1: 6 **o** a thousand burnt offerings
2Ch 4: 6 such things as they **o** for the
2Ch 7: 4 all the people **o** sacrifices
2Ch 7: 5 King Solomon **o** a sacrifice of
2Ch 7: 6 whenever David **o** praise by
2Ch 7: 7 for there he **o** burnt
2Ch 8:12 Then Solomon **o** burnt
2Ch 15:11 they **o** to the LORD at that
2Ch 17:16 who willingly **o** himself to
2Ch 24:14 they **o** burnt offerings in the
2Ch 29: 7 have not burned incense or **o**
Ezra 1: 6 all that was willingly **o**
Ezra 2:68 **o** freely for the house of God
Ezra 3: 3 they **o** burnt offerings on it
Ezra 3: 4 **o** the daily burnt offerings
Ezra 3: 5 afterward they **o** the regular
Ezra 3: 5 of everyone who willingly **o** a
Ezra 6: 3 place where they **o** sacrifices
Ezra 6:17 And they **o** sacrifices at the
Ezra 7:15 freely **o** to the God of Israel
Ezra 7:16 are to be freely **o** for the
Ezra 8:25 who were present, had **o**
Ezra 8:35 **o** burnt offerings to the God
Neh 11: 2 **o** themselves to dwell at
Neh 12:43 day they **o** great sacrifices
Is 57: 6 you have **o** a grain offering
Jer 32:29 they have **o** incense to Baal
Ezek 6:13 wherever they **o** sweet incense
Ezek 16:21 **o** them up to them by causing
Ezek 16:25 You **o** yourself to everyone
Ezek 20:28 there they **o** their sacrifices
Ezek 36:38 Like a flock **o** as holy
Ezek 44: 7 and when you **o** My food, the
Jon 1:16 **o** a sacrifice to the LORD and
Mal 1:11 incense shall be **o** to My name
Mark 15:36 **o** it to Him to drink, saying,
Acts 7:41 **o** sacrifices to the idol, and
Acts 8:18 was given, he **o** them money,
Acts 12: 5 was **o** to God for him by the
Acts 15:29 from things **o** to idols, from
Acts 21:25 from things **o** to idols, from
1Co 8: 1 concerning things **o** to idols
1Co 8: 4 eating of things **o** to idols
1Co 8: 7 it as a thing **o** to an idol
1Co 8:10 eat those things **o** to idols
1Co 10:19 or what is **o** to idols is
1Co 10:28 This was **o** to idols," do not
Heb 5: 7 when He had **o** up prayers
Heb 7:27 for all when He **o** up Himself
Heb 9: 7 which he **o** for himself and for
Heb 9: 9 sacrifices are **o** which cannot
Heb 9:14 through the eternal Spirit **o**
Heb 9:28 so Christ was **o** once to bear
Heb 10: 2 they not have ceased to be **o**
Heb 10: 8 in them" (which are **o**
Heb 10:12 after He had **o** one sacrifice
Heb 11: 4 By faith Abel **o** to God a more
Heb 11:17 **o** up Isaac, and he who had
Heb 11:17 **o** up his only begotten son
Jas 2:21 **o** Isaac his son on the altar

OFFERING (*see* OFFER, OFFERINGS)
Gen 4: 3 pass that Cain brought an **o**
Gen 4: 4 LORD respected Abel and his **o**
Gen 4: 5 did not respect Cain and his **o**
Gen 22: 2 **o** on one of the mountains of
Gen 22: 3 the wood for the burnt **o**, and
Gen 22: 6 took the wood of the burnt **o**
Gen 22: 7 is the lamb for a burnt **o**
Gen 22: 8 the lamb for a burnt **o**
Gen 22:13 a burnt **o** instead of his son
Gen 35:14 and he poured a drink **o** on it
Ex 18:12 father-in-law, took a burnt **o**
Ex 25: 2 that they bring Me an **o**
Ex 25: 2 his heart you shall take My **o**
Ex 25: 3 this is the **o** which you shall
Ex 29:14 It is a sin **o**
Ex 29:18 It is a burnt **o** to the LORD
Ex 29:18 an **o** made by fire to the LORD
Ex 29:24 as a wave **o** before the LORD
Ex 29:25 on the altar as a burnt **o**
Ex 29:25 It is an **o** made by fire to
Ex 29:26 as a wave **o** before the LORD
Ex 29:27 of the wave **o** which is waved
Ex 29:27 the heave **o** which is raised
Ex 29:28 For it is a heave **o**
Ex 29:28 it shall be a heave **o** from
Ex 29:28 is, their heave **o** to the LORD
Ex 29:36 day as a sin **o** for atonement
Ex 29:40 of a hin of wine as a drink **o**
Ex 29:41 grain **o** and the drink **o**
Ex 29:41 an **o** made by fire to the LORD
Ex 29:42 shall be a continual burnt **o**
Ex 30: 9 a burnt **o**, or a meal **o**
Ex 30: 9 you pour a drink **o** on it
Ex 30:10 of the sin **o** of atonement
Ex 30:13 shall be an **o** to the LORD
Ex 30:14 shall give an **o** to the LORD
Ex 30:15 you give an **o** to the LORD
Ex 30:20 to burn an **o** made by fire to
Ex 30:28 the altar of burnt **o** with all
Ex 31: 9 the altar of burnt **o** with all
Ex 35: 5 among you an **o** to the LORD
Ex 35: 5 bring it as an **o** to the LORD
Ex 35:16 the altar of burnt **o** with
Ex 35:21 LORD's **o** for the work of the
Ex 35:22 an **o** of gold to the LORD
Ex 35:24 Everyone who offered an **o** of
Ex 35:24 bronze brought the LORD's **o**
Ex 35:29 a freewill **o** to the LORD, all
Ex 36: 3 the **o** which the children of
Ex 36: 6 for the **o** of the sanctuary
Ex 38: 1 of burnt **o** of acacia wood
Ex 38:24 that is, the gold of the **o**
Ex 38:29 The **o** of bronze was seventy
Ex 40: 6 **o** before the door of the
Ex 40:10 the altar of the burnt **o** and
Ex 40:29 **o** before the door of the
Ex 40:29 burnt **o** and the grain **o**
Lev 1: 2 you brings an **o** to the LORD
Lev 1: 2 bring your **o** of the livestock
Lev 1: 3 If his **o** is a burnt
Lev 1: 4 on the head of the burnt **o**
Lev 1: 6 And he shall skin the burnt **o**
Lev 1: 9 an **o** made by fire, a sweet
Lev 1:10 if his **o** is of the flocks
Lev 1:13 an **o** made by fire, a sweet
Lev 1:14 his **o** to the LORD is of birds
Lev 1:14 his **o** of turtledoves or young
Lev 1:17 an **o** made by fire, a sweet

Lev 2: 1 offers a grain **o** to the LORD
Lev 2: 1 his **o** shall be of fine flour
Lev 2: 2 an **o** made by fire, a sweet
Lev 2: 3 the grain **o** shall be Aaron's
Lev 2: 3 It is a most holy **o** of the
Lev 2: 4 bring as an **o** a grain **o**
Lev 2: 5 if your **o** is a grain **o** baked
Lev 2: 6 it is a grain **o**
Lev 2: 7 if your **o** is a grain **o** baked
Lev 2: 8 grain **o** that is made of these
Lev 2: 9 grain **o** a memorial portion
Lev 2: 9 It is an **o** made by fire, a
Lev 2:10 the grain **o** shall be Aaron's
Lev 2:10 It is a most holy **o** of the
Lev 2:11 No grain **o** which you bring
Lev 2:11 **o** to the LORD made by fire
Lev 2:12 As for the **o** of the
Lev 2:13 every **o** of your grain **o** you
Lev 2:13 be lacking from your grain **o**
Lev 2:14 If you offer a grain **o** of
Lev 2:14 **o** of your firstfruits green
Lev 2:15 It is a grain **o**
Lev 2:16 as an **o** made by fire to the
Lev 3: 1 **o** is a sacrifice of peace **o**
Lev 3: 2 his hand on the head of his **o**
Lev 3: 3 the sacrifice of the peace **o**
Lev 3: 3 an **o** made by fire to the LORD
Lev 3: 5 as an **o** made by fire, a sweet
Lev 3: 6 **o** as a sacrifice of peace **o**
Lev 3: 7 If he offers a lamb as his **o**
Lev 3: 8 his hand on the head of his **o**
Lev 3: 9 the sacrifice of the peace **o**
Lev 3: 9 as an **o** made by fire to the
Lev 3:11 an **o** made by fire to the LORD
Lev 3:12 if his **o** is a goat, then he
Lev 3:14 he shall offer from it his **o**
Lev 3:14 as an **o** made by fire to the
Lev 3:16 an **o** made by fire for a sweet
Lev 4: 3 without blemish as a sin **o**
Lev 4: 7 of the altar of the burnt **o**
Lev 4: 8 fat of the bull as the sin **o**
Lev 4:10 the sacrifice of the peace **o**
Lev 4:10 on the altar of the burnt **o**
Lev 4:18 base of the altar of burnt **o**
Lev 4:20 did with the bull as a sin **o**
Lev 4:21 It is a sin **o** for the
Lev 4:23 as his **o** a kid of the goats
Lev 4:24 the burnt **o** before the LORD
Lev 4:24 It is a sin **o**
Lev 4:25 of the sin **o** with his finger
Lev 4:25 horns of the altar of burnt **o**
Lev 4:25 base of the altar of burnt **o**
Lev 4:26 of the sacrifice of peace **o**
Lev 4:28 as his **o** a kid of the goats
Lev 4:29 hand on the head of the sin **o**
Lev 4:29 kill the sin **o**
Lev 4:29 in the place of the burnt **o**
Lev 4:30 horns of the altar of burnt **o**
Lev 4:31 from the sacrifice of peace **o**
Lev 4:32 he brings a lamb as his sin **o**
Lev 4:33 hand on the head of the sin **o**
Lev 4:33 slay it as a sin **o** at the
Lev 4:33 where they kill the burnt **o**
Lev 4:34 of the sin **o** with his finger
Lev 4:34 horns of the altar of burnt **o**
Lev 4:35 the sacrifice of the peace **o**
Lev 5: 6 **o** to the LORD for his sin
Lev 5: 6 a kid of the goats as a sin **o**
Lev 5: 7 as a sin **o**
Lev 5: 7 and the other as a burnt **o**
Lev 5: 8 which is for the sin **o** first
Lev 5: 9 of the blood of the sin **o** on
Lev 5: 9 It is a sin **o**
Lev 5:10 **o** according to the prescribed
Lev 5:11 **o** one-tenth of an ephah of
Lev 5:11 fine flour as a sin **o**
Lev 5:11 on it, for it is a sin **o**
Lev 5:12 It is a sin **o**
Lev 5:13 be the priest's as a grain **o**
Lev 5:15 **o** a ram without blemish from
Lev 5:15 sanctuary, as a trespass **o**
Lev 5:16 the ram of the trespass **o**
Lev 5:18 valuation, as a trespass **o**
Lev 5:19 It is a trespass **o**
Lev 6: 5 on the day of his trespass **o**
Lev 6: 6 his trespass **o** to the LORD
Lev 6: 6 valuation, as a trespass **o**
Lev 6: 9 is the law of the burnt **o**
Lev 6: 9 The burnt **o** shall be on the
Lev 6:10 up the ashes of the burnt **o**
Lev 6:12 lay the burnt **o** in order on
Lev 6:14 is the law of the grain **o**
Lev 6:15 the fine flour of the grain **o**
Lev 6:15 which is on the grain **o**, and
Lev 6:17 the sin **o** and the trespass **o**
Lev 6:20 This is the **o** of Aaron and his
Lev 6:20 fine flour as a daily grain **o**
Lev 6:21 baked pieces of the grain **o**
Lev 6:23 For every grain **o** for the
Lev 6:25 This is the law of the sin **o**
Lev 6:25 where the burnt **o** is killed
Lev 6:25 the sin **o** shall be killed
Lev 6:30 But no sin **o** from which any
Lev 7: 1 trespass **o** (it is most holy)
Lev 7: 2 where they killed the burnt **o**
Lev 7: 2 shall kill the trespass **o**
Lev 7: 5 them on the altar as an **o**
Lev 7: 5 It is a trespass **o**
Lev 7: 7 trespass **o** is like the sin **o**
Lev 7: 8 who offers anyone's burnt **o**
Lev 7: 8 burnt **o** which he has offered
Lev 7: 9 Also every grain **o** that is
Lev 7:10 Every grain **o** mixed with oil
Lev 7:13 as his **o** he shall offer
Lev 7:13 thanksgiving of his peace **o**
Lev 7:14 offer one cake from each **o**
Lev 7:14 as a heave **o** to the LORD
Lev 7:14 the blood of the peace **o**
Lev 7:15 **o** for thanksgiving shall be
Lev 7:16 **o** is a vow or a voluntary **o**
Lev 7:18 **o** is eaten at all on the
Lev 7:20 **o** that belongs to the LORD
Lev 7:21 **o** that belongs to the LORD
Lev 7:25 an **o** made by fire to the LORD
Lev 7:29 the sacrifice of his peace **o**
Lev 7:29 his **o** to the LORD from the
Lev 7:29 the sacrifice of his peace **o**
Lev 7:30 as a wave **o** before the LORD
Lev 7:32 to the priest as a heave **o**
Lev 7:33 the blood of the peace **o**, and
Lev 7:34 For the breast of the wave **o**
Lev 7:34 heave **o** I have taken from the
Lev 7:37 is the law of the burnt **o**
Lev 7:37 the grain **o**, the sin **o**
Lev 7:37 the trespass **o**
Lev 7:37 the sacrifice of the peace **o**
Lev 8: 2 oil, a bull as the sin **o**, two
Lev 8:14 the bull for the sin **o**
Lev 8:14 of the bull for the sin **o**
Lev 8:18 the ram as the burnt **o**
Lev 8:21 an **o** made by fire to the LORD
Lev 8:27 as a wave **o** before the LORD
Lev 8:28 on the altar, on the burnt **o**
Lev 8:28 That was an **o** made by fire to
Lev 8:29 as a wave **o** before the LORD
Lev 9: 2 a young bull as a sin **o** and a
Lev 9: 2 and a ram as a burnt **o**,
Lev 9: 3 a kid of the goats as a sin **o**
Lev 9: 3 without blemish, as a burnt **o**
Lev 9: 4 and a grain **o** mixed with oil
Lev 9: 7 your sin **o** and your burnt **o**
Lev 9: 7 Offer the **o** of the people, and
Lev 9: 8 killed the calf of the sin **o**
Lev 9:10 sin **o** he burned on the altar
Lev 9:12 And he killed the burnt **o**
Lev 9:13 presented the burnt **o** to him
Lev 9:14 with the burnt **o** on the altar
Lev 9:15 he brought the people's **o**
Lev 9:15 was the sin **o** for the people
Lev 9:16 And he brought the burnt **o**
Lev 9:17 Then he brought the grain **o**
Lev 9:21 as a wave **o** before the LORD
Lev 9:22 down from **o** the sin **o**
Lev 9:22 the burnt **o**, and peace offerings
Lev 9:24 LORD and consumed the burnt **o**
Lev 10:12 Take the grain **o** that remains
Lev 10:14 The breast of the wave **o** and
Lev 10:14 the thigh of the heave **o** you
Lev 10:15 The thigh of the heave **o** and
Lev 10:15 the breast of the wave **o** they
Lev 10:15 as a wave **o** before the LORD
Lev 10:16 about the goat of the sin **o**
Lev 10:17 the sin **o** in a holy place
Lev 10:19 they have offered their sin **o**
Lev 10:19 their burnt **o** before the LORD
Lev 10:19 I had eaten the sin **o** today
Lev 12: 6 the first year as a burnt **o**
Lev 12: 6 or a turtledove as a sin **o**
Lev 12: 8 one as a burnt **o**
Lev 12: 8 and the other as a sin **o**
Lev 14:10 mixed with oil as a grain **o**
Lev 14:12 and offer it as a trespass **o**
Lev 14:12 as a wave **o** before the LORD
Lev 14:13 the sin **o** and the burnt **o**
Lev 14:13 for as the sin **o** is the
Lev 14:13 so is the trespass **o**
Lev 14:14 the blood of the trespass **o**
Lev 14:17 the blood of the trespass **o**
Lev 14:19 priest shall offer the sin **o**
Lev 14:19 he shall kill the burnt **o**
Lev 14:20 shall offer the burnt **o** and
Lev 14:20 and the grain **o** on the altar
Lev 14:21 as a trespass **o** to be waved
Lev 14:21 mixed with oil as a grain **o**
Lev 14:22 one shall be a sin **o** and the
Lev 14:22 and the other a burnt **o**
Lev 14:24 the lamb of the trespass **o**
Lev 14:24 as a wave **o** before the LORD
Lev 14:25 the lamb of the trespass **o**
Lev 14:25 the blood of the trespass **o**
Lev 14:28 the blood of the trespass **o**
Lev 14:31 to afford, the one as a sin **o**
Lev 14:31 a burnt **o**, with the grain **o**
Lev 15:15 them, the one as a sin **o** and
Lev 15:15 and the other as a burnt **o**
Lev 15:30 offer the one as a sin **o** and
Lev 15:30 and the other as a burnt **o**
Lev 16: 3 of a young bull as a sin **o**
Lev 16: 3 and of a ram as a burnt **o**
Lev 16: 5 kids of the goats as a sin **o**
Lev 16: 5 and one ram as a burnt **o**
Lev 16: 6 offer the bull as a sin **o**
Lev 16: 9 fell, and offer it as a sin **o**
Lev 16:11 bring the bull of the sin **o**
Lev 16:11 sin **o** which is for himself
Lev 16:15 kill the goat of the sin **o**
Lev 16:24 come out and offer his burnt **o**
Lev 16:24 the burnt **o** of the people, and
Lev 16:25 The fat of the sin **o** he shall
Lev 16:27 The bull for the sin **o** and the
Lev 16:27 and the goat for the sin **o**
Lev 17: 4 to offer an **o** to the LORD
Lev 17: 8 offers a burnt **o** or sacrifice
Lev 19: 5 of peace **o** to the LORD, you
Lev 19: 8 the hallowed **o** of the LORD
Lev 19:21 his trespass **o** to the LORD
Lev 19:21 a ram as a trespass **o**
Lev 19:22 the ram of the trespass **o**
Lev 22:10 outsider shall eat the holy **o**
Lev 22:14 the holy **o** unintentionally
Lev 22:14 a holy **o** to the priest, and
Lev 22:18 to the LORD as a burnt **o**
Lev 22:21 of peace **o** to the LORD, to
Lev 22:21 vow, or a freewill **o** from the
Lev 22:22 nor make an **o** by fire of them
Lev 22:23 you may offer as a freewill **o**
Lev 22:24 any **o** of them in your land
Lev 22:27 an **o** made by fire to the LORD
Lev 23: 8 But you shall offer an **o**
Lev 23:12 as a burnt **o** to the LORD
Lev 23:13 Its grain **o** shall be
Lev 23:13 an **o** made by fire to the LORD
Lev 23:13 its drink **o** shall be of wine,
Lev 23:14 have brought an **o** to your God
Lev 23:15 the sheaf of the wave **o**
Lev 23:16 a new grain **o** to the LORD
Lev 23:18 be as a burnt **o** to the LORD
Lev 23:18 the LORD, with their grain **o**
Lev 23:18 an **o** made by fire for a sweet
Lev 23:19 kid of the goats as a sin **o**
Lev 23:19 as a sacrifice of peace **o**
Lev 23:20 as a wave **o** before the LORD
Lev 23:25 you shall offer an **o** made by
Lev 23:27 offer an **o** made by fire to
Lev 23:36 days you shall offer an **o**
Lev 23:36 you shall offer an **o** made by
Lev 23:37 to offer an **o** made by fire to
Lev 23:37 a burnt **o** and a grain **o**
Lev 24: 7 an **o** made by fire to the LORD
Lev 27: 9 may bring as an **o** to the LORD
Lev 27:23 day as a holy **o** to the LORD
Lev 27:28 **o** that a man may devote to
Lev 27:28 every devoted **o** is most holy
Num 4:16 incense, the daily grain **o**
Num 5: 9 Every **o** of all the holy
Num 5:15 bring the **o** required for her
Num 5:15 it is a grain **o** of jealousy
Num 5:15 an **o** for remembering, for
Num 5:18 put the **o** for remembering in
Num 5:18 is the grain **o** of jealousy

Num 5:25 grain **o** of jealousy from the
Num 5:25 shall wave the **o** before the
Num 5:26 shall take a handful of the **o**
Num 6: 2 an **o** to take the vow of a
Num 6:11 shall offer one as a sin **o**
Num 6:11 and the other as a burnt **o**
Num 6:12 first year as a trespass **o**
Num 6:14 present his **o** to the LORD
Num 6:14 without blemish as a burnt **o**
Num 6:14 without blemish as a sin **o**
Num 6:14 without blemish as a peace **o**
Num 6:15 and their grain **o** with their
Num 6:16 his sin **o** and his burnt **o**
Num 6:17 of peace **o** to the LORD, with
Num 6:17 grain **o** and its drink **o**
Num 6:18 the sacrifice of the peace **o**
Num 6:20 as a wave **o** before the LORD
Num 6:20 with the breast of the wave **o**
Num 6:20 and the thigh of the heave **o**
Num 6:21 LORD the **o** for his separation
Num 7: 2 who were numbered, made an **o**
Num 7: 3 their **o** before the LORD, six
Num 7:10 offered the dedication **o** for
Num 7:10 their **o** before the altar
Num 7:11 They shall offer their **o**, one
Num 7:12 his **o** on the first day was
Num 7:13 His **o** was one silver platter,
Num 7:13 mixed with oil as a grain **o**
Num 7:15 its first year, as a burnt **o**
Num 7:16 kid of the goats as a sin **o**
Num 7:17 This was the **o** of Nahshon the
Num 7:18 of Issachar, presented an **o**
Num 7:19 For his **o** he offered one
Num 7:19 mixed with oil as a grain **o**
Num 7:21 its first year, as a burnt **o**
Num 7:22 kid of the goats as a sin **o**
Num 7:23 This was the **o** of Nethaneel
Num 7:24 of Zebulun, presented an **o**
Num 7:25 His **o** was one silver platter,
Num 7:25 mixed with oil as a grain **o**
Num 7:27 its first year, as a burnt **o**
Num 7:28 kid of the goats as a sin **o**
Num 7:29 This was the **o** of Eliab the
Num 7:30 of Reuben, presented an **o**
Num 7:31 His **o** was one silver platter,
Num 7:31 mixed with oil as a grain **o**
Num 7:33 its first year, as a burnt **o**
Num 7:34 kid of the goats as a sin **o**
Num 7:35 This was the **o** of Elizur the
Num 7:36 of Simeon, presented an **o**
Num 7:37 His **o** was one silver platter,
Num 7:37 mixed with oil as a grain **o**
Num 7:39 its first year, as a burnt **o**
Num 7:40 kid of the goats as a sin **o**
Num 7:41 This was the **o** of Shelumiel
Num 7:42 of Gad, presented an **o**
Num 7:43 His **o** was one silver platter,
Num 7:43 mixed with oil as a grain **o**
Num 7:45 its first year, as a burnt **o**
Num 7:46 kid of the goats as a sin **o**
Num 7:47 This was the **o** of Eliasaph
Num 7:48 of Ephraim, presented an **o**
Num 7:49 His **o** was one silver platter,
Num 7:49 mixed with oil as a grain **o**
Num 7:51 its first year, as a burnt **o**
Num 7:52 kid of the goats as a sin **o**
Num 7:53 This was the **o** of Elishama
Num 7:54 of Manasseh, presented an **o**
Num 7:55 His **o** was one silver platter,
Num 7:55 mixed with oil as a grain **o**
Num 7:57 its first year, as a burnt **o**
Num 7:58 kid of the goats as a sin **o**
Num 7:59 This was the **o** of Gamaliel
Num 7:60 of Benjamin, presented an **o**
Num 7:61 His **o** was one silver platter,
Num 7:61 mixed with oil as a grain **o**
Num 7:63 its first year, as a burnt **o**
Num 7:64 kid of the goats as a sin **o**
Num 7:65 This was the **o** of Abidan the
Num 7:66 of Dan, presented an **o**
Num 7:67 His **o** was one silver platter,
Num 7:67 mixed with oil as a grain **o**
Num 7:69 its first year, as a burnt **o**
Num 7:70 kid of the goats as a sin **o**
Num 7:71 This was the **o** of Ahiezer the
Num 7:72 of Asher, presented an **o**
Num 7:73 His **o** was one silver platter,
Num 7:73 mixed with oil as a grain **o**
Num 7:75 its first year, as a burnt **o**
Num 7:76 kid of the goats as a sin **o**
Num 7:77 This was the **o** of Pagiel the
Num 7:78 of Naphtali, presented an **o**
Num 7:79 His **o** was one silver platter,
Num 7:79 mixed with oil as a grain **o**
Num 7:81 its first year, as a burnt **o**
Num 7:82 kid of the goats as a sin **o**
Num 7:83 This was the **o** of Ahira the
Num 7:84 **o** for the altar from the
Num 7:87 **o** were twelve young bulls
Num 7:87 twelve, with their grain **o**
Num 7:87 the goats as a sin **o** twelve
Num 7:88 This was the dedication **o** for
Num 8: 8 **o** of fine flour mixed with
Num 8: 8 another young bull as a sin **o**
Num 8:11 as though a wave **o** from the
Num 8:12 shall offer one as a sin **o**
Num 8:12 as a burnt **o** to the LORD, to
Num 8:13 though a wave **o** to the LORD
Num 8:15 them, as though a wave **o**
Num 8:21 a wave **o** before the LORD, and
Num 9: 7 the **o** of the LORD at its
Num 9:13 the **o** of the LORD at its
Num 15: 3 you make an **o** by fire to the
Num 15: 3 a burnt **o** or a sacrifice, to
Num 15: 3 a vow or as a freewill **o** or
Num 15: 4 presents his **o** to the LORD
Num 15: 4 shall bring a grain **o** of
Num 15: 5 **o** you shall prepare with the
Num 15: 5 the burnt **o** or the sacrifice
Num 15: 6 shall prepare as a grain **o**
Num 15: 7 as a drink **o** you shall offer
Num 15: 8 a young bull as a burnt **o**
Num 15: 8 or as a peace **o** to the LORD
Num 15: 9 **o** of three-tenths of an ephah
Num 15:10 shall bring as the drink **o**
Num 15:10 of wine as an **o** made by fire
Num 15:13 presenting an **o** made by fire
Num 15:14 present an **o** made by fire
Num 15:19 up a heave **o** to the LORD
Num 15:20 your ground meal as a heave **o**
Num 15:20 as a heave **o** of the threshing
Num 15:21 give to the LORD a heave **o**
Num 15:24 one young bull as a burnt **o**
Num 15:24 grain **o** and its drink **o**
Num 15:24 kid of the goats as a sin **o**
Num 15:25 they shall bring their **o**, an
Num 15:25 an **o** made by fire to the LORD
Num 15:25 their sin **o** before the LORD,
Num 15:27 in its first year as a sin **o**
Num 16:15 Do not respect their **o**
Num 16:35 fifty men who were **o** incense
Num 18: 9 every **o** of theirs, every
Num 18: 9 every grain **o** and every sin **o**
Num 18: 9 every trespass **o** which they
Num 18:11 the heave **o** of their gift,
Num 18:17 burn their fat as an **o** made
Num 18:24 up as a heave **o** to the LORD
Num 18:26 a heave **o** of it to the LORD
Num 18:27 And your heave **o** shall be
Num 18:28 shall also offer a heave **o** to
Num 18:28 **o** from it to Aaron the priest
Num 18:29 every heave **o** due to the LORD
Num 23: 3 Stand by your burnt **o**, and I
Num 23: 6 was, standing by his burnt **o**
Num 23:15 Stand here by your burnt **o**
Num 23:17 was, standing by his burnt **o**
Num 28: 2 Israel, and say to them, 'My **o**
Num 28: 3 This is the **o** made by fire
Num 28: 3 by day, as a regular burnt **o**
Num 28: 5 of fine flour as a grain **o**
Num 28: 6 It is a regular burnt **o**
Num 28: 6 an **o** made by fire to the LORD
Num 28: 7 And its drink **o** shall be
Num 28: 7 the drink to the LORD as an **o**
Num 28: 8 grain **o** and its drink **o**
Num 28: 8 offer it as an **o** made by fire
Num 28: 9 of fine flour as a grain **o**
Num 28: 9 with oil, with its drink **o**
Num 28:10 the burnt **o** for every Sabbath
Num 28:10 **o** with its drink **o**
Num 28:11 present a burnt **o** to the LORD
Num 28:12 of fine flour as a grain **o**
Num 28:13 as a grain **o** for each lamb,
Num 28:13 as a burnt **o** of sweet aroma,
Num 28:13 an **o** made by fire to the LORD
Num 28:14 Their drink **o** shall be half
Num 28:14 this is the burnt **o** for each
Num 28:15 a sin **o** to the LORD shall be
Num 28:15 burnt **o** and its drink **o**
Num 28:19 you shall present an **o** made
Num 28:19 fire as a burnt **o** to the LORD
Num 28:20 Their grain **o** shall be of
Num 28:22 also one goat as a sin **o**
Num 28:23 the burnt **o** of the morning
Num 28:23 is for a regular burnt **o**
Num 28:24 the **o** made by fire daily for
Num 28:24 burnt **o** and its drink **o**
Num 28:26 **o** to the LORD at your Feast
Num 28:27 **o** as a sweet aroma to the
Num 28:28 with their grain **o** of fine
Num 28:31 **o** with its grain **o**
Num 29: 2 **o** as a sweet aroma to the
Num 29: 3 Their grain **o** shall be fine
Num 29: 5 kid of the goats as a sin **o**
Num 29: 6 besides the burnt **o** with its
Num 29: 6 its grain **o** for the New Moon
Num 29: 6 burnt **o** with its grain **o**
Num 29: 6 an **o** made by fire to the LORD
Num 29: 8 **o** to the LORD as a sweet
Num 29: 9 Their grain **o** shall be of
Num 29:11 kid of the goats as a sin **o**
Num 29:11 the sin **o** for atonement, the
Num 29:11 burnt **o** with its grain **o**
Num 29:13 You shall present a burnt **o**
Num 29:13 an **o** made by fire as a sweet
Num 29:14 Their grain **o** shall be of
Num 29:16 kid of the goats as a sin **o**
Num 29:16 besides the regular burnt **o**
Num 29:16 grain **o**, and its drink **o**
Num 29:18 and their grain **o** and their
Num 29:19 kid of the goats as a sin **o**
Num 29:19 **o** with its grain **o**
Num 29:21 and their grain **o** and their
Num 29:22 also one goat as a sin **o**
Num 29:22 besides the regular burnt **o**
Num 29:22 grain **o**, and its drink **o**
Num 29:24 and their grain **o** and their
Num 29:25 kid of the goats as a sin **o**
Num 29:25 besides the regular burnt **o**
Num 29:25 grain **o**, and its drink **o**
Num 29:27 and their grain **o** and their
Num 29:28 also one goat as a sin **o**
Num 29:28 besides the regular burnt **o**
Num 29:28 grain **o**, and its drink **o**
Num 29:30 and their grain **o** and their
Num 29:31 also one goat as a sin **o**
Num 29:31 besides the regular burnt **o**
Num 29:31 grain **o**, and its drink **o**
Num 29:33 and their grain **o** and their
Num 29:34 also one goat as a sin **o**
Num 29:34 besides the regular burnt **o**
Num 29:34 grain **o**, and its drink **o**
Num 29:36 You shall present a burnt **o**
Num 29:36 an **o** made by fire as a sweet
Num 29:37 and their grain **o** and their
Num 29:38 also one goat as a sin **o**
Num 29:38 besides the regular burnt **o**
Num 29:38 grain **o**, and its drink **o**
Num 31:29 as a heave **o** to the LORD
Num 31:41 heave **o** to Eleazar the priest
Num 31:50 brought an **o** for the LORD
Num 31:52 all the gold of the **o** that
Deut 12:17 of the heave **o** of your hand
Deut 16:10 a freewill **o** from your hand
Deut 23:18 LORD your God for any vowed **o**
Deut 32:38 the wine of their drink **o**
Josh 22:26 not for burnt **o** nor for
Judg 6:18 come to You and bring out my **o**
Judg 11:31 will offer it up as a burnt **o**
Judg 13:16 But if you offer a burnt **o**
Judg 13:19 young goat with the grain **o**
Judg 13:23 not have accepted a burnt **o**
Judg 13:23 a grain **o** from our hands, nor
1Sa 1: 4 came for Elkanah to make an **o**
1Sa 2:17 abhorred the **o** of the LORD
1Sa 2:29 My **o** which I have commanded
1Sa 3:14 for by sacrifice or **o** forever
1Sa 6: 3 it to Him with a trespass **o**
1Sa 6: 4 What is the trespass **o** which
1Sa 6: 8 to Him as a trespass **o** in a
1Sa 6:14 cows as a burnt **o** to the LORD
1Sa 6:17 as a trespass **o** to the LORD
1Sa 7: 9 a whole burnt **o** to the LORD
1Sa 7:10 Samuel was **o** up the burnt **o**
1Sa 13: 9 Bring a burnt **o** and peace
1Sa 13: 9 And he offered the burnt **o**
1Sa 13:10 finished **o** the burnt **o**
1Sa 13:12 and offered a burnt **o**
1Sa 26:19 me, let Him accept an **o**
2Sa 6:18 finished **o** burnt offerings

1Ki 18:29 until the time of the o of
1Ki 18:36 at the time of the o of the
2Ki 3:20 when the grain o was offered
2Ki 3:27 as a burnt o upon the wall
2Ki 5:17 longer offer either burnt o
2Ki 10:25 end of o the burnt o
2Ki 16:13 burnt o and his grain o
2Ki 16:13 and he poured his drink o and
2Ki 16:15 burn the morning burnt o
2Ki 16:15 the evening grain o
2Ki 16:15 sacrifice, and his grain o
2Ki 16:15 with the burnt o of all the
2Ki 16:15 of the land, their grain o
2Ki 16:15 all the blood of the burnt o
1Ch 6:49 on the altar of burnt o and on
1Ch 16: 2 o the burnt offerings and the
1Ch 16:29 bring an o, and come before
1Ch 16:40 of burnt o regularly morning
1Ch 21:23 and the wheat for the grain o
1Ch 21:26 fire on the altar of burnt o
1Ch 21:29 and the altar of the burnt o
1Ch 22: 1 altar of burnt o for Israel
1Ch 23:29 fine flour for the grain o
1Ch 23:31 presentation of a burnt o to
2Ch 4: 6 o they would wash in them
2Ch 7: 1 and consumed the burnt o and
2Ch 8:13 rate, o according to the
2Ch 24:14 articles for serving and o
2Ch 29:21 for a sin o for the kingdom
2Ch 29:23 for the sin o before the king
2Ch 29:24 o to make an atonement for
2Ch 29:24 commanded that the burnt o
2Ch 29:24 the sin o be made for all
2Ch 29:27 the burnt o on the altar
2Ch 29:27 And when the burnt o began
2Ch 29:28 the burnt o was finished
2Ch 29:29 And when they had finished o
2Ch 29:32 for a burnt o to the LORD
2Ch 29:35 offerings for every burnt o
2Ch 30:22 o peace offerings and making
2Ch 35:14 Aaron, were busy in o burnt
Ezra 3: 5 offered the regular burnt o
Ezra 3: 5 a freewill o to the LORD
Ezra 6:17 as a sin o for all Israel
Ezra 7:16 the freewill o of the people
Ezra 8:25 the o for the house of our
Ezra 8:28 o to the LORD God of your
Ezra 8:35 twelve male goats as a sin o
Ezra 8:35 was a burnt o to the LORD
Ezra 10:19 the flock as their trespass o
Neh 10:33 for the regular grain o, for
Neh 10:33 burnt o of the Sabbaths, the
Neh 10:34 for bringing the wood o into
Neh 10:39 bring the o of the grain, of
Neh 13: 9 of God, with the grain o and
Neh 13:31 and to bringing the wood o
Job 42: 8 up for yourselves a burnt o
Ps 40: 6 and o You did not desire
Ps 40: 6 Burnt o and sin o You
Ps 51:16 You do not delight in burnt o
Ps 51:19 burnt o and whole burnt o
Ps 96: 8 Bring an o, and come into His
Is 19:21 and will make sacrifice and o
Is 40:16 sufficient for a burnt o
Is 53:10 make His soul an o for sin
Is 57: 6 you have poured a drink o
Is 57: 6 you have offered a grain o
Is 61: 8 I hate robbery for burnt o
Is 65:11 furnish a drink o for Meni
Is 66: 3 he who offers a grain o, as
Is 66:20 an o to the LORD out of all
Is 66:20 o in a clean vessel into the
Jer 11:17 to anger in o incense to Baal
Jer 14:12 burnt o and grain o
Ezek 40:38 where they washed the burnt o
Ezek 40:39 on which to slay the burnt o
Ezek 40:39 sin o, and the trespass o
Ezek 40:42 of hewn stone for the burnt o
Ezek 40:42 they slaughtered the burnt o
Ezek 42:13 the grain o, the sin o
Ezek 42:13 and the trespass o
Ezek 43:19 for a sin o to the priests
Ezek 43:21 take the bull of the sin o
Ezek 43:22 without blemish for a sin o
Ezek 43:24 up as a burnt o to the LORD
Ezek 43:25 prepare a goat for a sin o
Ezek 44:11 they shall slay the burnt o
Ezek 44:27 his sin o in the inner court
Ezek 44:29 They shall eat the grain o
Ezek 44:29 sin o, and the trespass o
Ezek 45:13 This is the o which you shall
Ezek 45:16 o for the prince in Israel
Ezek 45:17 He shall prepare the sin o
Ezek 45:17 grain o, the burnt o
Ezek 45:19 of the blood of the sin o
Ezek 45:22 the land a bull for a sin o
Ezek 45:23 prepare a burnt o to the LORD
Ezek 45:23 the goats daily for a sin o
Ezek 45:24 he shall prepare a grain o of
Ezek 45:25 days, according to the sin o
Ezek 45:25 burnt o, the grain o
Ezek 46: 2 shall prepare his burnt o
Ezek 46: 4 The burnt o that the prince
Ezek 46: 5 and the grain o shall be one
Ezek 46: 5 the grain o for the lambs, as
Ezek 46: 7 o of an ephah for a bull, an
Ezek 46:11 feast days the grain o shall
Ezek 46:12 makes a voluntary burnt o or
Ezek 46:12 voluntary peace o to the LORD
Ezek 46:12 he shall prepare his burnt o
Ezek 46:13 o to the LORD of a lamb of
Ezek 46:14 grain o with it every morning
Ezek 46:14 This grain o is a perpetual
Ezek 46:15 prepare the lamb, the grain o
Ezek 46:15 regular burnt o every morning
Ezek 46:20 trespass o and the sin o
Ezek 46:20 they shall bake the grain o
Dan 2:46 that they should present an o
Dan 9:21 the time of the evening o
Dan 9:27 an end to sacrifice and o
Joel 1: 9 The grain o and the drink
Joel 1: 9 the drink o have been cut off
Joel 1:13 for the grain o and the drink
Joel 1:13 the drink o are withheld from
Joel 2:14 a grain o and a drink o
Zeph 3:10 ones, shall bring My o
Mal 1:10 I accept an o from your hands
Mal 1:11 to My name, and a pure o
Mal 1:13 thus you bring an o
Mal 2:12 who brings an o to the LORD
Mal 2:13 does not regard the o anymore
Mal 3: 3 LORD an o in righteousness
Mal 3: 4 Then the o of Judah and
Luke 5:14 make an o for your cleansing,
Luke 23:36 coming and o Him sour wine,
Acts 21:26 at which time an o should be
Rom 15:16 that the o of the Gentiles
Eph 5: 2 and given Himself for us, an o
Phil 2:17 as a drink o on the sacrifice
2Ti 4: 6 being poured out as a drink o
Heb 10: 5 o You did not desire, but a
Heb 10: 8 Sacrifice and o, burnt
Heb 10:10 o of the body of Jesus Christ
Heb 10:11 and o repeatedly the same
Heb 10:14 For by one o He has perfected
Heb 10:18 is no longer an o for sin

OFFERINGS (*see* OFFERING)
Gen 8:20 offered burnt o on the altar
Ex 10:25 give us sacrifices and burnt o
Ex 20:24 burnt o and your peace o
Ex 24: 5 Israel, who offered burnt o
Ex 24: 5 sacrificed peace o of oxen to
Ex 29:28 sacrifices of their peace o
Ex 29:34 flesh of the consecration o
Ex 32: 6 and brought peace o
Ex 36: 3 him freewill o every morning
Lev 2: 3 o to the LORD made by fire
Lev 2:10 o to the LORD made by fire
Lev 2:13 With all your o you shall
Lev 4:35 according to the o made by
Lev 5:12 o made by fire to the LORD
Lev 6:12 on it the fat of the peace o
Lev 6:17 portion of My o made by fire
Lev 6:18 o made by fire to the LORD
Lev 7:11 of the sacrifice of peace o
Lev 7:30 o made by fire to the LORD
Lev 7:32 sacrifices of your peace o
Lev 7:34 sacrifices of their peace o
Lev 7:35 from the o made by fire to
Lev 7:38 their o to the LORD in the
Lev 8:28 o for a sweet aroma
Lev 8:31 the basket of consecration o
Lev 9: 4 a bull and a ram as peace o
Lev 9:18 ram as sacrifices of peace o
Lev 9:22 burnt offering, and peace o
Lev 10:12 that remains of the o made by
Lev 10:14 the sacrifices of peace o of
Lev 10:15 the o of fat made by fire
Lev 17: 5 them as peace o to the LORD
Lev 21: 6 for they offer the o of the
Lev 21:21 come near to offer the o made
Lev 22: 4 the holy o until he is clean
Lev 22: 6 and shall not eat the holy o
Lev 22: 7 he may eat the holy o,
Lev 22:12 she may not eat of the holy o
Lev 22:15 o of the children of Israel
Lev 22:16 when they eat their holy o
Lev 22:18 or for any of his freewill o
Lev 23:18 offering and their drink o •
Lev 23:37 a sacrifice and drink o,
Lev 23:38 besides all your freewill o
Lev 24: 9 o of the LORD made by fire
Num 6:15 offering with their drink o
Num 7:17 for the sacrifice of peace o
Num 7:23 as the sacrifice of peace o
Num 7:29 for the sacrifice of peace o
Num 7:35 as the sacrifice of peace o
Num 7:41 as the sacrifice of peace o
Num 7:47 as the sacrifice of peace o
Num 7:53 as the sacrifice of peace o
Num 7:59 as the sacrifice of peace o
Num 7:65 as the sacrifice of peace o
Num 7:71 as the sacrifice of peace o
Num 7:77 as the sacrifice of peace o
Num 7:83 as the sacrifice of peace o
Num 7:88 o were twenty-four bulls, the
Num 10:10 trumpets over your burnt o
Num 10:10 sacrifices of your peace o
Num 18: 8 you charge of My heave o, all
Num 18:11 with all the wave o of the
Num 18:19 All the heave o of the holy
Num 28: 2 My food for My o made by fire
Num 28:31 them with their drink o,
Num 29: 6 offering, and their drink o
Num 29:11 offering, and their drink o
Num 29:18 their drink o for the bulls,
Num 29:19 offering, and their drink o
Num 29:21 their drink o for the bulls,
Num 29:24 their drink o for the bulls,
Num 29:27 their drink o for the bulls,
Num 29:30 their drink o for the bulls,
Num 29:33 their drink o for the bulls,
Num 29:37 their drink o for the bull,
Num 29:39 vowed o and your freewill o
Num 29:39 burnt o and your grain o
Num 29:39 drink o and your peace o
Deut 12: 6 you shall take your burnt o
Deut 12: 6 the heave o of your hand,
Deut 12: 6 your vowed o, your freewill o
Deut 12:11 your burnt o, your sacrifices
Deut 12:11 the heave o of your hand, and
Deut 12:11 all your choice o which you
Deut 12:13 o in every place that you see
Deut 12:14 you shall offer your burnt o
Deut 12:17 any of your o which you vow
Deut 12:17 you vow, of your freewill o
Deut 12:26 you have, and your vowed o
Deut 12:27 you shall offer your burnt o
Deut 18: 1 they shall eat the o of the
Deut 27: 6 offer burnt o on it to the
Deut 27: 7 You shall offer peace o, and
Josh 8:31 on it burnt o to the LORD
Josh 8:31 LORD, and sacrificed peace o
Josh 22:23 it burnt o or grain o
Josh 22:23 or if to offer peace o on it
Josh 22:27 before Him with our burnt o
Josh 22:27 and with our peace o
Josh 22:28 burnt o nor for sacrifices
Josh 22:29 for burnt o, for grain o
Judg 20:26 and they offered burnt o and
Judg 20:26 and peace o before the LORD
Judg 21: 4 offered burnt o and peace o
1Sa 2:28 of your father all the o of
1Sa 2:29 all the o of Israel My people
1Sa 6:15 Beth Shemesh offered burnt o
1Sa 10: 8 down to you to offer burnt o
1Sa 10: 8 and make sacrifices of peace o
1Sa 11:15 of peace o before the LORD
1Sa 13: 9 and peace o here to me
1Sa 15:22 as great delight in burnt o
2Sa 1:21 upon you, nor fields of o
2Sa 6:17 Then David offered burnt o
2Sa 6:17 and peace o before the LORD
2Sa 6:18 offering burnt o and peace o
2Sa 24:24 nor will I offer burnt o to
2Sa 24:25 offered burnt o and peace o
1Ki 3: 4 burnt o on that altar
1Ki 3:15 burnt o, offered peace o
1Ki 8:63 a sacrifice of peace o, which
1Ki 8:64 burnt o, grain o, and

1Ki 8:64 and the fat of the peace o
1Ki 8:64 the burnt o, the grain o
1Ki 8:64 and the fat of the peace o
1Ki 9:25 year Solomon offered burnt o
1Ki 9:25 peace o on the altar which he
1Ki 12:33 So he made o on the altar
2Ki 10:24 offer sacrifices and burnt o
2Ki 12:16 The money from the trespass o
2Ki 12:16 the money from the sin o was
2Ki 16:12 the altar and made o on it
2Ki 16:13 of his peace o on the altar
2Ki 16:15 offering, and their drink o
1Ch 16: 1 Then they offered burnt o
1Ch 16: 1 and peace o before God
1Ch 16: 2 the burnt o and the peace o
1Ch 16:40 to offer burnt o to the LORD
1Ch 21:23 give you the oxen for burnt o
1Ch 21:24 nor offer burnt o with that
1Ch 21:26 offered burnt o and peace o
1Ch 29:21 offered burnt o to the LORD
1Ch 29:21 lambs, with their drink o
2Ch 1: 6 a thousand burnt o on it
2Ch 2: 4 for the burnt o morning and
2Ch 7: 7 for there he offered burnt o
2Ch 7: 7 and the fat of the peace o
2Ch 7: 7 the burnt o, the grain o
2Ch 8:12 Then Solomon offered burnt o
2Ch 23:18 offer the burnt o of the LORD
2Ch 24:14 they offered burnt o in the
2Ch 29: 7 o in the holy place to the
2Ch 29:18 the altar of burnt o with all
2Ch 29:31 thank o into the house of the
2Ch 29:31 in sacrifices and thank o, and
2Ch 29:31 willing heart brought burnt o
2Ch 29:32 o which the congregation
2Ch 29:34 not skin all the burnt o
2Ch 29:35 Also the burnt o were in
2Ch 29:35 with the fat of the peace o
2Ch 29:35 with the drink o for every
2Ch 30:15 brought the burnt o to the
2Ch 30:22 seven days, offering peace o
2Ch 31: 2 for burnt o and peace o
2Ch 31: 3 possessions for the burnt o
2Ch 31: 3 morning and evening burnt o
2Ch 31: 3 the burnt o for the Sabbaths
2Ch 31:10 people began to bring the o
2Ch 31:12 faithfully brought in the o
2Ch 31:14 over the freewill o to God
2Ch 31:14 distribute the o of the LORD
2Ch 33:16 peace o and thank o on it
2Ch 35: 6 So slaughter the Passover o
2Ch 35: 7 all for Passover o for all
2Ch 35: 8 o two thousand six hundred
2Ch 35: 9 o five thousand from the
2Ch 35:11 slaughtered the Passover o
2Ch 35:12 o that they might give them
2Ch 35:13 they roasted the Passover o
2Ch 35:13 but the other holy o they
2Ch 35:14 were busy in offering burnt o
2Ch 35:16 to offer burnt o on the altar
Ezra 1: 4 besides the freewill o for
Ezra 3: 2 to offer burnt o on it, as
Ezra 3: 3 burnt o on it to the LORD
Ezra 3: 3 morning and evening burnt o
Ezra 3: 4 offered the daily burnt o in
Ezra 3: 6 to offer burnt o to the LORD
Ezra 6: 9 lambs for the burnt o of the
Ezra 7:17 grain o and their drink o
Ezra 8:35 offered burnt o to the God of
Neh 10:33 things, for the sin o to make
Neh 10:37 of our dough, our o, the
Neh 12:44 of the storehouse for the o
Neh 13: 5 they had stored the grain o
Neh 13: 5 and the o for the priests
Job 1: 5 offer burnt o according to
Ps 16: 4 Their drink o of blood I will
Ps 20: 3 May He remember all your o
Ps 50: 8 sacrifices Or your burnt o
Ps 66:13 into Your house with burnt o
Ps 119:108 the freewill o of my mouth
Prov 7:14 I have peace o with me
Is 1:11 had enough of burnt o of rams
Is 43:23 Me the sheep for your burnt o
Is 43:23 you to serve with grain o
Is 56: 7 Their burnt o and their
Jer 6:20 Your burnt o are not
Jer 7:18 out drink o to other gods
Jer 7:21 Add your burnt o to your
Jer 7:22 burnt o or sacrifices
Jer 17:26 the South, bringing burnt o
Jer 17:26 and sacrifices, grain o and
Jer 19: 5 with fire for burnt o to Baal
Jer 19:13 out drink o to other gods
Jer 32:29 out drink o to other gods
Jer 33:18 to offer burnt o before Me
Jer 33:18 before Me, to kindle grain o
Jer 41: 5 having cut themselves, with o
Jer 44:17 and pour out drink o to her
Jer 44:18 and pouring out drink o to her
Jer 44:19 and poured out drink o to her
Jer 44:19 and pour out drink o to her
Jer 44:25 and pour out drink o to her
Ezek 20:28 and provoked Me with their o
Ezek 20:28 and poured out their drink o
Ezek 20:40 there I will require your o
Ezek 42:13 shall eat the most holy o
Ezek 42:13 shall lay the most holy o
Ezek 43:18 for sacrificing burnt o on it
Ezek 43:27 shall offer your burnt o and
Ezek 43:27 your peace o on the altar
Ezek 45:15 These shall be for grain o
Ezek 45:15 burnt o, and peace o
Ezek 45:17 prince's part to give burnt o
Ezek 45:17 grain o, and drink o
Ezek 45:17 the peace o to make atonement
Ezek 46: 2 burnt offering and his peace o
Ezek 46:12 his peace o as he did on the
Hos 6: 6 of God more than burnt o
Hos 8:13 of My o they sacrifice flesh
Hos 9: 4 not offer wine o to the LORD
Amos 4: 5 and announce the freewill o
Amos 5:22 burnt o and your grain o
Amos 5:22 regard your fattened peace o
Amos 5:25 o in the wilderness forty
Mic 6: 6 come before Him with burnt o
Mal 3: 8 In tithes and o
Mark 12:33 than all the whole burnt o
Luke 21: 4 have put in o for God, but
Acts 24:17 bring alms and o to my nation,
1Co 9:13 partake of the o of the altar
Heb 10: 6 In burnt o and sacrifices for
Heb 10: 8 and offering, burnt o, and
Heb 10: 8 o for sin You did not desire,

OFFERS (*see* OFFER)
Lev 2: 1 When anyone o a grain
Lev 3: 1 if he o it of the herd,
Lev 3: 7 If he o a lamb as his
Lev 6:26 The priest who o it for sin
Lev 7: 8 the priest who o anyone's
Lev 7: 9 be the priest's who o it
Lev 7:12 If he o it for a
Lev 7:16 day that he o his sacrifice
Lev 7:18 whoever o it shall be an
Lev 7:29 He who o the sacrifice of
Lev 7:33 who o the blood of the peace
Lev 17: 8 who o a burnt offering or
Lev 21: 8 for he o the bread of your
Lev 22:18 who o his sacrifice for any
Lev 22:21 And whoever o a sacrifice of
Ps 50:23 Whoever o praise glorifies Me
Is 66: 3 he who o a grain offering, as
Is 66: 3 as if he o swine's blood
Jer 48:35 who o sacrifices in the high
Ezek 46: 4 offering that the prince o to
John 16: 2 think that he o God service

OFFICE (*see* OFFICER)
Gen 41:13 He restored me to my o, and he
1Ch 6:32 and they served in their o
1Ch 9:22 them to their trusted o
1Ch 9:26 For in this trusted o were
1Ch 9:31 had the trusted o over the
Ps 109: 8 And let another take his o
Is 22:19 will drive you out of your o
Matt 9: 9 Matthew sitting at the tax o
Mark 2:14 Alphaeus sitting at the tax o
Luke 5:27 Levi, sitting at the tax o
Acts 1:20 and, 'Let another take his o

OFFICER (*see* OFFICE, OFFICERS)
Gen 37:36 an o of Pharaoh and captain of
Gen 39: 1 an o of Pharaoh, captain of
Judg 9:28 and is not Zebul his o
1Ki 11:28 made him the o over all the
1Ki 22: 9 king of Israel called an o
2Ki 7: 2 So an o on whose hand the
2Ki 7:17 o on whose hand he leaned to
2Ki 7:19 Then that o had answered the
2Ki 8: 6 appointed a certain o for her
2Ki 15:25 an o of his, conspired
2Ki 23:11 the o who was in the court
2Ki 25:19 took out of the city an o who
1Ch 9:11 the o over the house of God
1Ch 9:20 the o over them in time past
1Ch 27:16 the o over the Reubenites was
2Ch 24:11 and the high priest's o came
2Ch 26:11 the scribe and Maaseiah the o
2Ch 28: 7 Azrikam the o over the house,
Jer 52:25 took out of the city an o who
Matt 5:25 judge hand you over to the o
Luke 12:58 judge deliver you to the o
Luke 12:58 the o throw you into prison

OFFICERS (*see* OFFICER)
Gen 40: 2 was angry with his two o, the
Gen 40: 7 So he asked Pharaoh's o who
Gen 41:34 him appoint o over the land
Ex 5: 6 of the people and their o,
Ex 5:10 their o went out and spoke to
Ex 5:14 Also the o of the children of
Ex 5:15 Then the o of the children of
Ex 5:19 And the o of the children of
Num 11:16 of the people and o over them
Num 31:14 angry with the o of the army
Num 31:48 Then the o who were over
Deut 1:15 of tens, and o for your tribes
Deut 16:18 o in all your gates, which
Deut 20: 5 Then the o shall speak to the
Deut 20: 8 Then the o shall speak
Deut 20: 9 be, when the o have finished
Deut 29:10 and your elders and your o, all
Deut 31:28 of your tribes, and your o
Josh 1:10 commanded the o of the people
Josh 3: 2 that the o went through the
Josh 8:33 with their elders and o and
Josh 23: 2 their judges, and for their o
Josh 24: 1 their judges, and for their o
1Sa 8:15 vintage, and give it to his o
1Ki 4: 5 the son of Nathan, over the o
1Ki 9:22 his o, his captains,
2Ki 10:25 the o threw them out, and went
2Ki 11:15 the o of the army, and said to
2Ki 11:18 the priest appointed o over
2Ki 24:12 his o went out to the king of
2Ki 24:15 the king's wives, his o, and
1Ch 23: 4 the LORD, six thousand were o
1Ch 27: 1 and hundreds and their o,
1Ch 28: 1 the o of the tribes and the
1Ch 29: 6 with the o over the king's
2Ch 8: 9 men of war, captains of his o
2Ch 18: 8 of Israel called one of his o
2Ch 21: 9 Jehoram went out with his o
2Ch 26:12 The total number of chief o
2Ch 34:13 the Levites were scribes, o
Esth 1: 8 all the o of his household
Esth 2: 3 let the king appoint o in all
Is 60:17 I will also make your o peace
Jer 29:26 so that there should be o in
Jer 39:13 the king of Babylon's chief o
Jer 41: 1 of the o of the king, came
Mark 6:21 for his nobles, the high o
Mark 14:65 the o struck Him with the
John 7:32 priests sent o to take Him
John 7:45 Then the o came to the chief
John 7:46 The o answered, "No man ever
John 18: 3 o from the chief priests and
John 18:12 the o of the Jews arrested
John 18:18 and o who had made a fire of
John 18:22 one of the o who stood by
John 19: 6 o saw Him, they cried out,
Acts 5:22 But when the o came and did
Acts 5:26 the captain went with the o
Acts 16:35 the magistrates sent the o
Acts 16:38 the o told these words to the

OFFICIAL (*see* OFFICIALS)
2Ch 24:11 was brought to the king's o
Neh 2:10 the Ammonite o heard of it
Neh 2:19 Tobiah the Ammonite o, and
Eccl 5: 8 high o watches over high o

OFFICIALS (*see* OFFICIAL)
1Ki 4: 2 And these were his o
1Ki 9:23 the o who were over Solomon's
1Ch 24: 5 for there were o of the
1Ch 24: 5 o of the house of God, from
1Ch 26:29 sons performed duties as o
1Ch 26:32 made o over the Reubenites
1Ch 27:31 All these were the o over
1Ch 28: 1 and of his sons, with the o
2Ch 8:10 of the o of King Solomon
2Ch 19:11 Levites will be o before you
Neh 2:16 the o did not know where I

Neh 2:16 priests, the nobles, the **o**
Esth 1: 3 he made a feast for all his **o**
Esth 1:11 beauty to the people and the **o**
Esth 1:18 will say to all the king's **o**
Esth 2:18 of Esther, for all his **o** and
Esth 3:12 to the **o** of all people, to
Esth 5:11 had advanced him above the **o**
Esth 9: 3 all the **o** of the provinces,
Eccl 5: 8 and higher **o** are over them
Dan 3: 2 all the **o** of the provinces,
Dan 3: 3 all the **o** of the provinces
Acts 19:31 Then some of the **o** of Asia

OFFICIATED
Heb 7:13 no man has **o** at the altar

OFFSCOURING
Lam 3:45 You have made us an **o** and
1Co 4:13 the **o** of all things until now

OFFSPRING
Gen 15: 3 Look, You have given me no **o**
Gen 21:23 falsely with me, with my **o**
Gen 48: 6 Your **o** whom you beget after
Gen 48:11 God has also shown me your **o**
Deut 7:13 the **o** of your flock, in the
Deut 28: 4 and the **o** of your flocks
Deut 28:18 and the **o** of your flocks
Deut 28:51 or the **o** of your flocks,
Judg 8:30 sons who were his own **o**, for
Ruth 4:12 because of the **o** which the
2Ch 32:21 some of his own **o** struck him
Job 5:25 your **o** like the grass of the
Job 21: 8 their **o** before their eyes
Job 27:14 his **o** shall not be satisfied
Job 39: 3 young, they deliver their **o**
Ps 21:10 Their **o** You shall destroy
Ps 22:23 fear Him, all you **o** of Israel
Is 14:22 the name and remnant, and **o**
Is 14:29 its **o** will be a fiery flying
Is 22:24 of his father's house, the **o**
Is 44: 3 and My blessing on your **o**
Is 48:19 the **o** of your body like the
Is 57: 3 you **o** of the adulterer and the
Is 57: 4 **o** of falsehood,
Is 61: 9 and their **o** among the people
Is 65:23 LORD, and their **o** with them
Jer 46:27 your **o** from the land of their
Lam 2:20 Should the women eat their **o**
Ezek 17:13 And he took the king's **o**,
Mal 2:15 He seeks godly **o**
Matt 22:24 raise up **o** for his brother
Matt 22:25 had married, and having no **o**
Mark 12:19 raise up **o** for his brother
Mark 12:20 and dying, he left no **o**
Mark 12:21 nor did he leave any **o**
Mark 12:22 seven had her and left no **o**
Luke 20:28 raise up **o** for his brother
Acts 17:28 said, 'For we are also His **o**
Acts 17:29 since we are the **o** of God
Rev 12:17 war with the rest of her **o**
Rev 22:16 the **O** of David, the Bright and

OFTEN (*see* PREFACE)

OG
Num 21:33 So **O** king of Bashan went out
Num 32:33 kingdom of **O** king of Bashan
Deut 1: 4 **O** king of Bashan, who dwelt
Deut 3: 1 **O** king of Bashan came out
Deut 3: 3 our hands **O** king of Bashan
Deut 3: 4 the kingdom of **O** in Bashan
Deut 3:10 of the kingdom of **O** in Bashan
Deut 3:11 For only **O** king of Bashan
Deut 3:13 all Bashan, the kingdom of **O**
Deut 4:47 the land of **O** king of Bashan,
Deut 29: 7 **O** king of Bashan came out
Deut 31: 4 them as He did to Sihon and **O**
Josh 2:10 of the Jordan, Sihon and **O**
Josh 9:10 **O** king of Bashan, who was at
Josh 12: 4 **O** king of Bashan and his
Josh 13:12 the kingdom of **O** in Bashan
Josh 13:30 kingdom of **O** king of Bashan
Josh 13:31 of the kingdom of **O** in Bashan
1Ki 4:19 and of **O** king of Bashan
Neh 9:22 the land of **O** king of Bashan
Ps 135:11 **O** king of Bashan, And all the
Ps 136:20 **O** king of Bashan, For His

OH (*see* PREFACE)

OHAD
Gen 46:10 Simeon were Jemuel, Jamin, **O**
Ex 6:15 Simeon were Jemuel, Jamin, **O**

OHEL
1Ch 3:20 and Hashubah, **O**, Berechiah,

OHOLAH
Ezek 23: 4 **O** the elder and Oholibah her
Ezek 23: 4 for their names, Samaria is **O**
Ezek 23: 5 **O** played the harlot even
Ezek 23:36 Son of man, will you judge **O**
Ezek 23:44 thus they went in to **O** and

OHOLIBAH
Ezek 23: 4 the elder and **O** her sister
Ezek 23: 4 is Oholah, and Jerusalem is **O**
Ezek 23:11 her sister **O** saw this, she
Ezek 23:22 Therefore, **O**, thus says the
Ezek 23:36 will you judge Oholah and **O**
Ezek 23:44 they went in to Oholah and **O**

OIL (*see* OILS)
Gen 28:18 and poured **o** on top of it
Gen 35:14 on it, and he poured **o** on it
Ex 25: 6 **o** for the light, and spices
Ex 25: 6 and spices for the anointing **o**
Ex 27:20 that they bring you pure **o** of
Ex 29: 2 unleavened cakes mixed with **o**
Ex 29: 2 wafers anointed with **o** (you
Ex 29: 7 shall take the anointing **o**
Ex 29:21 and some of the anointing **o**
Ex 29:23 bread, one cake made with **o**
Ex 29:40 of a hin of pressed **o**, and
Ex 30:24 and a hin of olive **o**
Ex 30:25 from these a holy anointing **o**
Ex 30:25 shall be a holy anointing **o**
Ex 30:31 **o** to Me throughout your
Ex 31:11 and the anointing **o** and sweet
Ex 35: 8 **o** for the light, and spices
Ex 35: 8 and spices for the anointing **o**
Ex 35:14 lamps, and the **o** for the light
Ex 35:15 its poles, the anointing **o**
Ex 35:28 and **o** for the light, for the
Ex 35:28 light, for the anointing **o**
Ex 37:29 made the holy anointing **o**
Ex 39:37 utensils, and the **o** for light
Ex 39:38 gold altar, the anointing **o**
Ex 40: 9 shall take the anointing **o**
Lev 2: 1 And he shall pour **o** on it, and
Lev 2: 2 **o** with all the frankincense
Lev 2: 4 of fine flour mixed with **o**
Lev 2: 4 wafers anointed with **o**
Lev 2: 5 unleavened, mixed with **o**
Lev 2: 6 it in pieces and pour **o** on it
Lev 2: 7 be made of fine flour with **o**
Lev 2:15 And you shall put **o** on it
Lev 2:16 beaten grain and part of its **o**
Lev 5:11 He shall put no **o** on it, nor
Lev 6:15 grain offering, with its **o**
Lev 6:21 shall be made in a pan with **o**
Lev 7:10 grain offering mixed with **o**
Lev 7:12 unleavened cakes mixed with **o**
Lev 7:12 wafers anointed with **o**, or
Lev 7:12 blended flour mixed with **o**
Lev 8: 2 the garments, the anointing **o**
Lev 8:10 Moses took the anointing **o**
Lev 8:12 anointing **o** on Aaron's head
Lev 8:26 cake of bread anointed with **o**
Lev 8:30 took some of the anointing **o**
Lev 9: 4 a grain offering mixed with **o**
Lev 10: 7 for the anointing **o** of the
Lev 14:10 with **o** as a grain offering
Lev 14:10 offering, and one log of **o**
Lev 14:12 offering, and the log of **o**
Lev 14:15 take some of the log of **o**
Lev 14:16 **o** that is in his left hand
Lev 14:16 shall sprinkle some of the **o**
Lev 14:17 the rest of the **o** in his hand
Lev 14:18 The rest of the **o** that is in
Lev 14:21 with **o** as a grain offering
Lev 14:21 a grain offering, a log of **o**
Lev 14:24 offering and the log of **o**, and
Lev 14:26 shall pour some of the **o** into
Lev 14:27 **o** that is in his left hand
Lev 14:28 shall put some of the **o** that
Lev 14:29 The rest of the **o** that is in
Lev 21:10 the anointing **o** was poured
Lev 21:12 of the anointing **o** of his God
Lev 23:13 of fine flour mixed with **o**
Lev 24: 2 **o** of pressed olives for the
Num 4: 9 trays, and all its **o** vessels
Num 4:16 priest is the **o** for the light
Num 4:16 offering, the anointing **o**
Num 5:15 he shall pour no **o** on it and
Num 6:15 of fine flour mixed with **o**
Num 6:15 wafers anointed with **o**, and
Num 7:13 with **o** as a grain offering
Num 7:19 with **o** as a grain offering
Num 7:25 with **o** as a grain offering
Num 7:31 with **o** as a grain offering
Num 7:37 with **o** as a grain offering
Num 7:43 with **o** as a grain offering
Num 7:49 with **o** as a grain offering
Num 7:55 with **o** as a grain offering
Num 7:61 with **o** as a grain offering
Num 7:67 with **o** as a grain offering
Num 7:73 with **o** as a grain offering
Num 7:79 with **o** as a grain offering
Num 8: 8 of fine flour mixed with **o**
Num 11: 8 of pastry prepared with **o**
Num 15: 4 with one-fourth of a hin of **o**
Num 15: 6 with one-third of a hin of **o**
Num 15: 9 mixed with half a hin of **o**
Num 18:12 All the best of the **o**, all
Num 28: 5 of a hin of pressed **o**
Num 28: 9 grain offering, mixed with **o**
Num 28:12 grain offering, mixed with **o**
Num 28:12 grain offering, mixed with **o**
Num 28:13 of fine flour, mixed with **o**
Num 28:20 be of fine flour mixed with **o**
Num 28:28 of fine flour mixed with **o**
Num 29: 3 be fine flour mixed with **o**
Num 29: 9 be of fine flour mixed with **o**
Num 29:14 be of fine flour mixed with **o**
Num 35:25 was anointed with the holy **o**
Deut 7:13 and your new wine and your **o**
Deut 8: 8 a land of olive **o** and honey
Deut 11:14 your new wine, and your **o**
Deut 12:17 or your new wine or your **o**
Deut 14:23 and your new wine and your **o**
Deut 18: 4 and your new wine and your **o**
Deut 28:40 anoint yourself with the **o**
Deut 28:51 you grain or new wine or **o**
Deut 32:13 and **o** from the flinty rock
Deut 33:24 and let him dip his foot in **o**
Judg 9: 9 Should I cease giving my **o**
1Sa 10: 1 Then Samuel took a flask of **o**
1Sa 16: 1 Fill your horn with **o**, and go
1Sa 16:13 Samuel took the horn of **o**
2Sa 1:21 of Saul, not anointed with **o**
2Sa 14: 2 do not anoint yourself with **o**
1Ki 1:39 horn of **o** from the tabernacle
1Ki 5:11 and twenty kors of pressed **o**
1Ki 17:12 a bin, and a little **o** in a jar
1Ki 17:14 shall the jar of **o** run dry
1Ki 17:16 nor did the jar of **o** run dry
2Ki 4: 2 in the house but a jar of **o**
2Ki 4: 6 So the **o** ceased
2Ki 4: 7 Go, sell the **o** and pay your
2Ki 9: 1 this flask of **o** in your hand
2Ki 9: 3 Then take the flask of **o**, and
2Ki 9: 6 he poured the **o** on his head
1Ch 9:29 flour and the wine and the **o**
1Ch 12:40 cakes of raisins, wine and **o**
1Ch 27:28 Joash was over the store of **o**
2Ch 2:10 and twenty thousand baths of **o**
2Ch 2:15 the wheat, the barley, the **o**
2Ch 11:11 in them, and stores of food, **o**
2Ch 31: 5 of grain and wine, **o** and honey,
2Ch 32:28 harvest of grain, wine, and **o**
Ezra 3: 7 **o** to the people of Sidon and
Ezra 6: 9 wheat, salt, wine, and **o**,
Ezra 7:22 wine, one hundred baths of **o**
Neh 5:11 grain, the new wine and the **o**
Neh 8:15 branches, branches of **o** trees
Neh 10:37 of trees, the new wine and **o**
Neh 10:39 of the new wine and the **o**
Neh 13: 5 of grain, the new wine and **o**
Neh 13:12 and the **o** to the storehouse
Esth 2:12 six months with **o** of myrrh
Job 24:11 They press out **o** within their
Job 29: 6 poured out rivers of **o** for me
Ps 23: 5 You anoint my head with **o**
Ps 45: 7 has anointed You With the **o**
Ps 55:21 His words were softer than **o**
Ps 89:20 With My holy **o** I have
Ps 92:10 been anointed with fresh **o**
Ps 104:15 **O** to make his face shine, And
Ps 109:18 And like **o** into his bones
Ps 133: 2 the precious **o** upon the head
Ps 141: 5 It shall be as excellent **o**

Prov 5: 3 her mouth is smoother than **o**
Prov 21:17 wine and **o** will not be rich
Prov 21:20 **o** in the dwelling of the wise
Prov 27:16 grasps **o** with his right hand
Eccl 9: 8 and let your head lack no **o**
Is 10:27 because of the anointing **o**
Is 41:19 the myrtle and the **o** tree
Is 61: 3 the **o** of joy for mourning,
Jer 31:12 for wheat and new wine and **o**
Jer 40:10 wine and summer fruit and **o**
Jer 41: 8 treasures of wheat, barley, **o**
Ezek 16: 9 and I anointed you with **o**
Ezek 16:13 of fine flour, honey, and **o**
Ezek 16:18 covered them, and you set My **o**
Ezek 16:19 the pastry of fine flour, **o**
Ezek 23:41 had set My incense and My **o**
Ezek 27:17 of Minnith, millet, honey, **o**
Ezek 32:14 make their rivers run like **o**
Ezek 45:14 concerning **o**, the bath of **o**
Ezek 45:24 a hin of **o** for each ephah
Ezek 45:25 the grain offering, and the **o**
Ezek 46: 5 a hin of **o** with every ephah
Ezek 46: 7 a hin of **o** with every ephah
Ezek 46:11 a hin of **o** with every ephah
Ezek 46:14 and a third of a hin of **o** to
Ezek 46:15 the grain offering, and the **o**
Hos 2: 5 my wool and my linen, my **o**
Hos 2: 8 her grain, new wine, and **o**
Hos 2:22 with new wine, and with **o**
Hos 12: 1 and **o** is carried to Egypt
Joel 1:10 wine is dried up, the **o** fails
Joel 2:19 you grain and new wine and **o**
Joel 2:24 overflow with new wine and **o**
Mic 6: 7 or ten thousand rivers of **o**
Mic 6:15 not anoint yourselves with **o**
Hag 1:11 and the new wine and the **o**, on
Hag 2:12 bread or stew, wine or **o**, or
Zech 4:12 which the golden **o** drains
Matt 25: 3 lamps and took no **o** with them,
Matt 25: 4 but the wise took **o** in their
Matt 25: 8 wise, 'Give us some of your **o**
Matt 26: 7 of very costly fragrant **o**
Matt 26: 9 For this fragrant **o** might
Matt 26:12 this fragrant **o** on My body
Mark 6:13 anointed with **o** many who were
Mark 14: 3 of very costly **o** of spikenard
Mark 14: 4 was this fragrant **o** wasted
Luke 7:37 alabaster flask of fragrant **o**
Luke 7:38 them with the fragrant **o**
Luke 7:46 did not anoint My head with **o**
Luke 7:46 My feet with fragrant **o**
Luke 10:34 his wounds, pouring on **o** and
Luke 16: 6 A hundred measures of **o**
John 11: 2 the Lord with fragrant **o** and
John 12: 3 of very costly **o** of spikenard
John 12: 3 with the fragrance of the **o**
John 12: 5 Why was this fragrant **o** not
Heb 1: 9 has anointed You with the **o**
Jas 5:14 anointing him with **o** in the
Rev 6: 6 and do not harm the **o** and the
Rev 18:13 and incense, fragrant **o** and
Rev 18:13 and frankincense, wine and **o**

OILS (*see* OIL)
Luke 23:56 prepared spices and fragrant **o**

OINTMENT (*see* OINTMENTS)
Ex 30:25 an **o** compounded according to
2Ki 20:13 the spices and precious **o**
1Ch 9:30 made the **o** of the spices
Job 41:31 makes the sea like a pot of **o**
Prov 27: 9 **O** and perfume delight the
Eccl 7: 1 is better than precious **o**
Eccl 10: 1 putrefy the perfumer's **o**, and
Song 1: 3 your name is **o** poured forth
Is 1: 6 bound up, or soothed with **o**
Is 39: 2 the spices and precious **o**
Is 57: 9 You went to the king with **o**

OINTMENTS (*see* OINTMENT)
2Ch 16:14 prepared in a mixture of **o**
Song 1: 3 the fragrance of your good **o**
Amos 6: 6 yourselves with the best **o**

OLD (*see* ELDEST, OLDER, OLDEST, OLDNESS)
Gen 5:32 Noah was five hundred years **o**
Gen 6: 4 the mighty men who were of **o**
Gen 7: 6 **o** when the flood of waters
Gen 11:10 Shem was one hundred years **o**
Gen 12: 4 was seventy-five years **o** when
Gen 15:15 be buried at a good **o** age
Gen 16:16 **o** when Hagar bore Ishmael to
Gen 17: 1 Abram was ninety-nine years **o**
Gen 17:12 days **o** among you shall be
Gen 17:17 who is one hundred years **o**
Gen 17:17 Sarah, who is ninety years **o**
Gen 17:24 was ninety-nine years **o** when
Gen 17:25 **o** when he was circumcised in
Gen 18:11 Now Abraham and Sarah were **o**
Gen 18:12 After I have grown **o**, shall I
Gen 18:12 my lord being **o** also
Gen 18:13 bear a child, since I am **o**
Gen 19: 4 the men of Sodom, both **o**
Gen 19:31 Our father is **o**, and there is
Gen 21: 2 Abraham a son in his **o** age
Gen 21: 4 when he was eight days **o**, as
Gen 21: 5 was one hundred years **o** when
Gen 21: 7 borne him a son in his **o** age
Gen 24: 1 Now Abraham was **o**,
Gen 24:36 to my master when she was **o**
Gen 25: 8 last and died in a good **o** age
Gen 25: 8 an **o** man and full of years, and
Gen 25:20 Isaac was forty years **o** when
Gen 25:26 years **o** when she bore them
Gen 26:34 When Esau was forty years **o**
Gen 27: 1 to pass, when Isaac was **o**
Gen 27: 2 Behold now, I am **o**
Gen 35:29 to his people, being **o** and
Gen 37: 2 being seventeen years **o**, was
Gen 37: 3 he was the son of his **o** age
Gen 41:46 years **o** when he stood before
Gen 43:27 the **o** man of whom you spoke
Gen 44:20 an **o** man, and a child of his
Gen 44:20 man, and a child of his **o** age
Gen 47: 8 to Jacob, "How **o** are you
Gen 50:26 one hundred and ten years **o**
Ex 7: 7 And Moses was eighty years **o**
Ex 7: 7 Aaron eighty-three years **o**
Ex 10: 9 go with our young and our **o**
Ex 30:14 numbered, from twenty years **o**
Ex 38:26 numbering from twenty years **o**
Lev 13:11 it is an **o** leprosy on the
Lev 19:32 the presence of an **o** man, and
Lev 25:22 eat **o** produce until the ninth
Lev 25:22 shall eat of the **o** harvest
Lev 26:10 You shall eat the **o** harvest
Lev 26:10 clear out the **o** because of
Lev 27: 3 years **o** up to sixty years **o**
Lev 27: 5 if from five years **o**
Lev 27: 5 up to twenty years **o**,
Lev 27: 6 and if from a month **o**
Lev 27: 6 up to five years **o**
Lev 27: 7 and if from sixty years **o**
Num 1: 3 from twenty years **o** and above
Num 1:18 of names, from twenty years **o**
Num 1:20 from twenty years **o** and above
Num 1:22 from twenty years **o** and above
Num 1:24 of names, from twenty years **o**
Num 1:26 of names, from twenty years **o**
Num 1:28 of names, from twenty years **o**
Num 1:30 of names, from twenty years **o**
Num 1:32 of names, from twenty years **o**
Num 1:34 of names, from twenty years **o**
Num 1:36 of names, from twenty years **o**
Num 1:38 of names, from twenty years **o**
Num 1:40 of names, from twenty years **o**
Num 1:42 of names, from twenty years **o**
Num 1:45 houses, from twenty years **o**
Num 3:15 every male from a month **o**
Num 3:22 all the males from a month **o**
Num 3:28 all the males, from a month **o**
Num 3:34 all the males from a month **o**
Num 3:39 all the males from a month **o**
Num 3:40 of Israel from a month **o** and
Num 3:43 of names from a month **o** and
Num 4: 3 from thirty years **o** and above,
Num 4: 3 above, even to fifty years **o**
Num 4:23 From thirty years **o** and above,
Num 4:23 above, even to fifty years **o**
Num 4:30 From thirty years **o** and above,
Num 4:30 above, even to fifty years **o**
Num 4:35 from thirty years **o** and above,
Num 4:35 above, even to fifty years **o**
Num 4:39 from thirty years **o** and above,
Num 4:39 above, even to fifty years **o**
Num 4:43 from thirty years **o** and above,
Num 4:43 above, even to fifty years **o**
Num 4:47 from thirty years **o** and above,
Num 4:47 above, even to fifty years **o**
Num 8:24 From twenty-five years **o** and
Num 14:29 number, from twenty years **o**
Num 18:16 shall redeem when one month **o**
Num 26: 2 of Israel from twenty years **o**
Num 26: 4 people from twenty years **o**
Num 26:62 every male from a month **o**
Num 32:11 Egypt, from twenty years **o**
Num 33:39 twenty-three years **o** when he
Deut 4:25 have grown **o** in the land, act
Deut 19:14 which the men of **o** have set
Deut 31: 2 and twenty years **o** today
Deut 32: 7 Remember the days of **o**,
Deut 34: 7 twenty years **o** when he died
Josh 6:21 and woman, young and **o**
Josh 9: 4 they took **o** sacks on their
Josh 9: 4 **o** wineskins torn and mended,
Josh 9: 5 **o** and patched sandals on their
Josh 9: 5 and **o** garments on themselves
Josh 9:13 our sandals have become **o**
Josh 13: 1 Now Joshua was **o**, advanced in
Josh 13: 1 You are **o**, advanced in years,
Josh 14: 7 I was forty years **o** when
Josh 14:10 this day, eighty-five years **o**
Josh 23: 1 about, that Joshua was **o**,
Josh 23: 2 I am **o**, advanced in age
Josh 24: 2 side of the River in **o** times
Josh 24:29 one hundred and ten years **o**
Judg 2: 8 one hundred and ten years **o**
Judg 6:25 second bull of seven years **o**
Judg 8:32 of Joash died at a good **o** age
Judg 19:16 Just then an **o** man came in
Judg 19:17 and the **o** man said,
Judg 19:20 And the **o** man said,
Judg 19:22 of the house, the **o** man,
Ruth 1:12 for I am too **o** to have a
Ruth 4:15 and a nourisher of your **o** age
1Sa 2:22 Now Eli was very **o**
1Sa 2:31 not be an **o** man in your house
1Sa 2:32 there shall not be an **o** man
1Sa 4:15 Eli was ninety-eight years **o**
1Sa 4:18 and he died, for the man was **o**
1Sa 8: 1 was **o** that he made his sons
1Sa 8: 5 Look, you are **o**, and your sons
1Sa 12: 2 and I am **o** and grayheaded, and
1Sa 17:12 And the man was **o**, advanced in
1Sa 27: 8 of the land from of **o**, as you
1Sa 28:14 An **o** man is coming up, and he
2Sa 2:10 was forty years **o** when he
2Sa 4: 4 He was five years **o** when the
2Sa 5: 4 **o** when he began to reign, and
2Sa 19:32 very aged man, eighty years **o**
2Sa 19:35 I am today eighty years **o**
1Ki 1: 1 Now King David was **o**,
1Ki 1:15 (Now the king was very **o**, and
1Ki 11: 4 it was so, when Solomon was **o**
1Ki 13:11 Now an **o** prophet dwelt in
1Ki 13:25 where the **o** prophet dwelt
1Ki 13:29 So the **o** prophet came to the
1Ki 14:21 years **o** when he became king
1Ki 15:23 But in the time of his **o** age
1Ki 22:42 years **o** when he became king
2Ki 4:14 no son, and her husband is **o**
2Ki 8:17 years **o** when he became king
2Ki 8:26 years **o** when he became king
2Ki 11:21 years **o** when he became king
2Ki 14: 2 years **o** when he became king
2Ki 14:21 who was sixteen years **o**, and
2Ki 15: 2 years **o** when he became king
2Ki 15:33 years **o** when he became king
2Ki 16: 2 years **o** when he became king
2Ki 18: 2 years **o** when he became king
2Ki 21: 1 years **o** when he became king
2Ki 21:19 years **o** when he became king
2Ki 22: 1 years **o** when he became king
2Ki 23:31 years **o** when he became king
2Ki 23:36 years **o** when he became king
2Ki 24: 8 was eighteen years **o** when he
2Ki 24:18 years **o** when he became king
1Ch 2:21 when he was sixty years **o**
1Ch 23: 1 So when David was **o** and full
1Ch 23:27 numbered from twenty years **o**
1Ch 27:23 of those twenty years **o** and
1Ch 29:28 So he died in a good **o** age
2Ch 12:13 years **o** when he became king
2Ch 20:31 years **o** when he became king
2Ch 21: 5 years **o** when he became king
2Ch 21:20 years **o** when he became king
2Ch 22: 2 years **o** when he became king
2Ch 24: 1 years **o** when he became king
2Ch 24:15 But Jehoiada grew **o** and was
2Ch 24:15 thirty years **o** when he died
2Ch 25: 1 years **o** when he became king
2Ch 25: 5 them from twenty years **o** and

2Ch 26: 1 who was sixteen years **o**, and
2Ch 26: 3 years **o** when he became king
2Ch 27: 1 years **o** when he became king
2Ch 27: 8 years **o** when he became king
2Ch 28: 1 years **o** when he became king
2Ch 29: 1 he was twenty-five years **o**
2Ch 31:16 males from three years **o** and
2Ch 31:17 Levites from twenty years **o**
2Ch 33: 1 years **o** when he became king
2Ch 33:21 years **o** when he became king
2Ch 34: 1 years **o** when he became king
2Ch 36: 2 years **o** when he became king
2Ch 36: 5 years **o** when he became king
2Ch 36: 9 years **o** when he became king
2Ch 36:11 years **o** when he became king
Ezra 3: 8 Levites from twenty years **o**
Ezra 3:12 houses, who were **o** men, who
Neh 3: 6 Besodeiah repaired the **O** Gate
Neh 12:39 of Ephraim, above the **O** Gate
Neh 12:46 Asaph of **o** there were chiefs
Esth 3:13 all the Jews, both young and **o**
Job 4:11 The **o** lion perishes for lack
Job 14: 8 root may grow **o** in the earth
Job 20: 4 Do you not know this of **o**
Job 21: 7 the wicked live and become **o**
Job 22:15 Will you keep to the **o** way
Job 32: 6 in years, and you are very **o**
Job 42:17 So Job died, **o** and full of
Ps 6: 7 It grows **o** because of all my
Ps 25: 6 For they have been from of **o**
Ps 32: 3 my bones grew **o** Through my
Ps 37:25 have been young, and now am **o**
Ps 44: 1 in their days, In days of **o**
Ps 55:19 Even He who abides from of **o**
Ps 68:33 of heavens, which were of **o**
Ps 71: 9 me off in the time of **o** age
Ps 71:18 Now also when I am **o** and
Ps 74: 2 which You have purchased of **o**
Ps 74:12 For God is my King from of **o**
Ps 77: 5 have considered the days of **o**
Ps 77:11 remember Your wonders of **o**
Ps 78: 2 will utter dark sayings of **o**
Ps 92:14 still bear fruit in **o** age
Ps 93: 2 is established from of **o**
Ps 102:25 Of **o** You laid the foundation
Ps 102:26 will grow **o** like a garment
Ps 119:52 Your judgments of **o**, O LORD,
Ps 119:152 I have known of **o** that You
Ps 143: 5 I remember the days of **o**
Ps 148:12 **O** men and children
Prov 8:22 way, before His works of **o**
Prov 17: 6 are the crown of **o** men, and
Prov 20:29 and the splendor of **o** men is
Prov 22: 6 and when he is **o** he will not
Prov 23:22 your mother when she is **o**
Eccl 4:13 poor and wise youth than an **o**
Song 7:13 fruits, all manner, new and **o**
Is 20: 4 as captives, young and **o**,
Is 22:11 for the water of the **o** pool
Is 25: 1 of **o** are faithfulness and
Is 30:33 Tophet was established of **o**
Is 43:18 nor consider the things of **o**
Is 46: 4 even to your **o** age, I am He,
Is 46: 9 the former things of **o**, for I
Is 50: 9 all grow **o** like a garment
Is 51: 6 will grow **o** like a garment
Is 51: 9 days, in the generations of **o**
Is 57:11 of **o** that you do not fear Me
Is 58:12 build the **o** waste places
Is 61: 4 shall rebuild the **o** ruins
Is 63: 9 them all the days of **o**
Is 63:11 he remembered the days of **o**
Is 63:19 have become like those of **o**
Is 65:20 nor an **o** man who has not
Is 65:20 shall die one hundred years **o**
Is 65:20 years **o** shall be accursed
Jer 2:20 For of **o** I have broken your
Jer 6:16 see, and ask for the **o** paths
Jer 28: 8 before you of **o** prophesied
Jer 31: 3 LORD has appeared of **o** to me
Jer 31:13 and the young men and the **o**
Jer 38:11 and took from there **o** clothes
Jer 38:11 **o** rags, and let them down by
Jer 38:12 Please put these **o** clothes
Jer 46:26 inhabited as in the days of **o**
Jer 51:22 you I will break in pieces **o**
Jer 52: 1 years **o** when he became king
Lam 1: 7 that she had in the days of **o**
Lam 2:17 He commanded in days of **o**
Lam 2:21 **o** lie on the ground in the
Lam 5:21 renew our days as of **o**,
Ezek 9: 6 Utterly slay **o** and young men,
Ezek 23:43 who had grown **o** in adulteries
Ezek 25:15 because of the **o** hatred,"
Ezek 26:20 the Pit, to the people of **o**
Dan 5:31 being about sixty-two years **o**
Joel 2:28 your **o** men shall dream dreams
Amos 9:11 it as in the days of **o**
Mic 5: 2 forth have been from of **o**
Mic 6: 6 with calves a year **o**
Mic 7:14 and Gilead, as in days of **o**
Mic 7:20 to our fathers from days of **o**
Nah 2: 8 Though Nineveh of **o** was like
Zech 8: 4 **O** men and **o** women shall
Mal 3: 4 the LORD, as in the days of **o**
Matt 2:16 districts, from two years **o**
Matt 5:21 it was said to those of **o**
Matt 5:27 it was said to those of **o**
Matt 5:33 it was said to those of **o**
Matt 9:16 cloth on an **o** garment
Matt 9:17 put new wine into **o** wineskins
Matt 13:52 his treasure things new and **o**
Mark 2:21 cloth on an **o** garment
Mark 2:21 piece pulls away from the **o**
Mark 2:22 new wine into **o** wineskins
Luke 1:18 For I am an **o** man, and my wife
Luke 1:36 conceived a son in her **o** age
Luke 2:42 And when He was twelve years **o**
Luke 5:36 a new garment on an **o** one
Luke 5:36 the new does not match the **o**
Luke 5:37 new wine into **o** wineskins
Luke 5:39 no one, having drunk **o** wine
Luke 5:39 for he says, 'The **o** is better
Luke 9: 8 **o** prophets had risen again
Luke 9:19 **o** prophets has risen again
Luke 12:33 bags which do not grow **o**, a
John 3: 4 a man be born when he is **o**
John 8:57 You are not yet fifty years **o**
John 21:18 but when you are **o**, you will
Acts 2:17 your **o** men shall dream dreams
Acts 4:22 **o** on whom this miracle of
Acts 7:23 But when he was forty years **o**
Rom 4:19 was about a hundred years **o**)
Rom 6: 6 that our **o** man was crucified
1Co 5: 7 purge out the **o** leaven, that
1Co 5: 8 the feast, not with **o** leaven
2Co 3:14 reading of the **O** Testament
2Co 5:17 **o** things have passed away
Eph 4:22 the **o** man which grows corrupt
Col 3: 9 off the **o** man with his deeds
1Ti 4: 7 **o** wives' fables, and exercise
1Ti 5: 9 **o** be taken into the number
Heb 1:11 all grow **o** like a garment
Heb 8:13 growing **o** is ready to vanish
2Pe 1: 9 he was purged from his **o** sins
2Pe 3: 5 of God the heavens were of **o**
1Jn 2: 7 but an **o** commandment which
1Jn 2: 7 The **o** commandment is the word
Rev 12: 9 cast out, that serpent of **o**
Rev 20: 2 the dragon, that serpent of **o**

OLDER (*see* OLD)
Gen 25:23 the **o** shall serve the younger
Gen 27: 1 that he called Esau his **o** son
Gen 27:42 the words of Esau her **o** son
1Sa 18:17 Here is my **o** daughter Merab
1Ki 2:22 for he is my **o** brother
2Ki 3:21 bear arms and **o** were gathered
2Ch 22: 1 had killed all the **o** sons
Job 15:10 us, much **o** than your father
Job 32: 4 they were years **o** than he
Ezek 16:61 when you receive your **o** and
Luke 15:25 Now his **o** son was in the
Rom 9:12 The **o** shall serve the younger
1Ti 5: 1 Do not rebuke an **o** man, but
1Ti 5: 2 the **o** women as mothers, the
Tit 2: 2 that the **o** men be sober,
Tit 2: 3 the **o** women likewise, that

OLDEST (*see* OLD)
Gen 24: 2 to the **o** servant of his house
Gen 44:12 and he began with the **o** and
Num 1:20 of Reuben, Israel's **o** son
1Sa 17:13 The three **o** sons of Jesse had
1Sa 17:14 the three **o** followed Saul
1Sa 17:28 Now Eliab his **o** brother heard
Job 1:13 in their **o** brother's house
Job 1:18 in their **o** brother's house
John 8: 9 with the **o** even to the last

OLDNESS (*see* OLD)
Rom 7: 6 not in the **o** of the letter

OLIVE (*see* OLIVES)
Gen 8:11 a freshly plucked **o** leaf was
Ex 23:11 your vineyard and your **o** grove
Ex 30:24 sanctuary, and a hin of **o** oil
Deut 6:11 **o** trees which you did not
Deut 8: 8 pomegranates, a land of **o** oil
Deut 24:20 When you beat your **o** trees
Deut 28:40 You shall have **o** trees
Josh 24:13 **o** groves which you did not
Judg 9: 8 And they said to the **o** tree
Judg 9: 9 But the **o** tree said to them
Judg 15: 5 as the vineyards and **o** groves
1Sa 8:14 your **o** groves, and give them
1Ki 6:23 made two cherubim of **o** wood
1Ki 6:31 he made doors of **o** wood
1Ki 6:32 The two doors were of **o** wood
1Ki 6:33 also made doorposts of **o** wood
2Ki 5:26 **o** groves and vineyards, sheep
2Ki 18:32 vineyards, a land of **o** groves
1Ch 27:28 Gederite was over the **o** trees
Neh 5:11 their **o** groves, and their
Neh 8:15 bring **o** branches, branches of
Neh 9:25 **o** groves, and fruit trees in
Job 15:33 his blossom like an **o** tree
Ps 52: 8 But I am like a green **o** tree
Ps 128: 3 Your children like **o** plants
Is 17: 6 like the shaking of an **o** tree
Is 24:13 like the shaking of an **o** tree
Jer 11:16 your name, green **O** Tree,
Hos 14: 6 shall be like an **o** tree, and
Amos 4: 9 and your **o** trees, The locust
Hab 3:17 the labor of the **o** may fail
Hag 2:19 the **o** tree have not yielded
Zech 4: 3 Two **o** trees are by it, one at
Zech 4:11 What are these two **o** trees
Zech 4:12 What are these two **o** branches
Rom 11:17 and you, being a wild **o** tree
Rom 11:17 root and fatness of the **o** tree
Rom 11:24 the **o** tree which is wild by
Rom 11:24 to nature into a good **o** tree
Rom 11:24 grafted into their own **o** tree
Rev 11: 4 These are the two **o** trees

OLIVES (*see* OLIVE)
Ex 27:20 of pressed **o** for the light
Lev 24: 2 of pressed **o** for the light
Deut 28:40 for your **o** shall drop off
2Sa 15:30 the ascent of the Mount of **O**
Is 17: 6 two or three **o** at the top of
Mic 6:15 you shall tread the **o**, but
Zech 14: 4 will stand on the Mount of **O**
Zech 14: 4 the Mount of **O** shall be split
Matt 21: 1 Bethphage, at the Mount of **O**
Matt 24: 3 as He sat on the Mount of **O**
Matt 26:30 went out to the Mount of **O**
Mark 11: 1 and Bethany, at the Mount of **O**
Mark 13: 3 of **O** opposite the temple,
Mark 14:26 went out to the Mount of **O**
Luke 19:37 the descent of the Mount of **O**
Luke 22:39 He went to the Mount of **O**
John 8: 1 Jesus went to the Mount of **O**
Jas 3:12 fig tree, my brethren, bear **o**

OLIVET
Luke 19:29 at the mountain called **O**
Luke 21:37 on the mountain called **O**
Acts 1:12 from the Mount called **O**,

OLYMPAS
Rom 16:15 Nereus and his sister, and **O**

OMAR
Gen 36:11 sons of Eliphaz were Teman, **O**
Gen 36:15 were Chief Teman, Chief **O**
1Ch 1:36 sons of Eliphaz were Teman, **O**

OMEGA
Rev 1: 8 I am the Alpha and the **O**, the
Rev 1:11 I am the Alpha and the **O**, the
Rev 21: 6 I am the Alpha and the **O**, the
Rev 22:13 I am the Alpha and the **O**, the

OMENS
Deut 18:10 or one who interprets **o**, or

OMER (*see* OMERS)
Ex 16:16 need, one **o** for each person,
Ex 16:32 Fill an **o** with it, to be
Ex 16:33 put an **o** of manna in it, and
Ex 16:36 Now an **o** is one-tenth of an

OMERS (*see* OMER)
Ex 16:18 So when they measured it by **o**
Ex 16:22 bread, two **o** for each one

OMNIPOTENT
Rev 19: 6 For the Lord God **O** reigns

OMRI
1Ki 16:16 So all Israel made **O**, the
1Ki 16:17 Then **O** and all Israel with him
1Ki 16:21 him king, and half followed **O**
1Ki 16:22 **O** prevailed over the people
1Ki 16:22 So Tibni died and **O** reigned
1Ki 16:23 **O** became king over Israel, and
1Ki 16:25 **O** did evil in the eyes of the
1Ki 16:27 of the acts of **O** which he did
1Ki 16:28 So **O** rested with his fathers
1Ki 16:29 Ahab the son of **O** became king
1Ki 16:29 Ahab the son of **O** reigned
1Ki 16:30 Now Ahab the son of **O** did
2Ki 8:26 the granddaughter of **O**, king
1Ch 7: 8 Joash, Eliezer, Elioenai, **O**
1Ch 9: 4 son of Ammihud, the son of **O**
1Ch 27:18 **O** the son of Michael
2Ch 22: 2 the granddaughter of **O**
Mic 6:16 the statutes of **O** are kept

ON (*see* PREFACE)

ON*
Gen 41:45 of Poti-Pherah priest of **O**
Gen 41:50 of Poti-Pherah priest of **O**
Gen 46:20 of Poti-Pherah priest of **O**
Num 16: 1 **O** the son of Peleth, sons of

ONAGER
Job 39: 5 Who loosed the bonds of the **o**

ONAM
Gen 36:23 Manahath, Ebal, Shepho, and **O**
1Ch 1:40 Manahath, Ebal, Shephi, and **O**
1Ch 2:26 she was the mother of **O**
1Ch 2:28 The sons of **O** were Shammai

ONAN
Gen 38: 4 son, and she called his name **O**
Gen 38: 8 And Judah said to **O**, "Go in
Gen 38: 9 But **O** knew that the heir
Gen 46:12 The sons of Judah were Er, **O**
Gen 46:12 **O** died in the land of Canaan)
Num 26:19 sons of Judah were Er and **O**
Num 26:19 **O** died in the land of Canaan
1Ch 2: 3 The sons of Judah were Er, **O**

ONCE (*see* ONE)
Gen 18:32 and I will speak but **o** more
Ex 10:17 forgive my sin only this **o**
Ex 30:10 **o** a year with the blood of
Ex 30:10 **o** a year he shall make
Lev 16:34 for all their sins, **o** a year
Num 13:30 Let us go up at **o** and take
Num 22: 6 Therefore please come at **o**
Num 32:15 He will **o** again leave them in
Deut 7:22 unable to destroy them at **o**
Josh 6: 3 go all around the city **o**
Josh 6:11 the city, going around it **o**
Josh 6:14 marched around the city **o**
Judg 6:39 and let me speak just **o** more
Judg 6:39 just **o** more with the fleece
Judg 7: 3 depart at **o** from Mount Gilead
Judg 9: 8 The trees **o** went forth to
Judg 16:18 Come up **o** more, for he has
Judg 16:28 me, I pray, just this **o**, O
1Sa 23: 4 inquired of the LORD **o** again
1Sa 26: 8 him at **o** with the spear,
2Sa 5:22 Philistines went up **o** again
1Ki 10:22 **O** every three years the
2Ki 6:10 there, not just **o** or twice
1Ch 14:13 Then the Philistines **o** again
2Ch 2: 7 Therefore send me at **o** a man
2Ch 9:21 **O** every three years the
Neh 5:18 **o** every ten days an abundance
Neh 13:20 outside Jerusalem **o** or twice
Job 33:21 out which **o** were not seen
Job 40: 5 **O** I have spoken, but I will
Ps 62:11 God has spoken **o**, Twice I
Ps 74: 6 its carved work, all at **o**
Ps 76: 7 presence When **o** You are angry
Ps 89:35 **O** I have sworn by My holiness
Prov 12:16 A fool's wrath is known at **o**
Prov 28:18 in his ways will fall at **o**
Is 42:14 I will pant and gasp at **o**
Is 66: 8 shall a nation be born at **o**
Jer 16:21 I will this **o** cause them to
Ezek 32:15 of all that **o** filled it, when
Hag 2: 6 **O** more (it is a little while)
Zech 10: 8 increase as they **o** increased
Matt 9: 3 at **o** some of the scribes said
Mark 1:30 they told Him about her at **o**
Mark 1:43 him and sent him away at **o**
Mark 5:13 And at **o** Jesus gave them
Mark 6:25 me at **o** the head of John the
Luke 13:25 When **o** the Master of the
Luke 17: 7 in from the field, 'Come at **o**
Luke 23:18 And they all cried out at **o**
Acts 9:18 and he received his sight at **o**
Rom 6:10 He died to sin **o** for all
Rom 7: 9 I was alive **o** without the law
Rom 11:30 For as you were **o** disobedient
1Co 15: 6 five hundred brethren at **o**
2Co 11:25 **o** I was stoned
Gal 1:23 which he **o** tried to destroy
Eph 2: 2 in which you **o** walked
Eph 2: 3 among whom also we all **o**
Eph 2:11 you, **o** Gentiles in the flesh
Eph 2:13 **o** were far off have been made
Eph 5: 8 For you were **o** darkness, but
Phil 2:23 I hope to send him at **o**, as
Phil 4:16 Thessalonica you sent aid **o**
Col 1:21 you, who **o** were alienated and
Col 3: 7 in which you also **o** walked
Tit 3: 3 ourselves were also **o** foolish
Phm 11 who **o** was unprofitable to you
Heb 6: 4 those who were **o** enlightened
Heb 7:27 for this He did **o** for all
Heb 9: 7 priest went alone **o** a year
Heb 9:12 the Most Holy Place **o** for all
Heb 9:26 **o** at the end of the ages, He
Heb 9:27 is appointed for men to die **o**
Heb 9:28 so Christ was offered **o** to
Heb 10: 2 **o** purged, would have had no
Heb 10:10 of Jesus Christ **o** for all
Heb 12:26 Yet **o** more I shake not only
Heb 12:27 Yet **o** more," indicates the
1Pe 2:10 who **o** were not a people but
1Pe 3:18 also suffered **o** for sins, the
1Pe 3:20 when **o** the longsuffering of
Jude 3 for the faith which was **o** for
Jude 5 you, though you **o** knew this

ONE (*see* ONCE)
Gen 1: 9 together into **o** place, and let
Gen 2:11 it is the **o** which encompasses
Gen 2:13 it is the **o** which encompasses
Gen 2:14 it is the **o** which goes toward
Gen 2:21 He took **o** of his ribs, and
Gen 2:24 and they shall become **o** flesh
Gen 3: 6 tree desirable to make **o** wise
Gen 3:22 man has become like **o** of Us
Gen 4:19 the name of **o** was Adah, and
Gen 5: 3 And Adam lived **o** hundred and
Gen 5: 6 Seth lived **o** hundred and five
Gen 5:18 Jared lived **o** hundred and
Gen 5:25 Methuselah lived **o** hundred
Gen 5:28 Lamech lived **o** hundred and
Gen 5:29 This **o** will comfort us
Gen 6: 3 his days shall be **o** hundred
Gen 7:24 on the earth **o** hundred and
Gen 10: 8 to be a mighty **o** on the earth
Gen 10:25 the name of **o** was Peleg, for
Gen 11: 1 had **o** language and **o** speech
Gen 11: 3 Then they said to **o** another
Gen 11: 6 Indeed the people are **o** and
Gen 11: 6 and they all have **o** language
Gen 11: 7 understand **o** another's speech
Gen 11:10 Shem was **o** hundred years old,
Gen 11:25 Terah, Nahor lived **o** hundred
Gen 14:13 Then **o** who had escaped came
Gen 15: 3 indeed **o** born in my house is
Gen 15: 4 This **o** shall not be your heir
Gen 15: 4 but **o** who will come from your
Gen 17:17 who is **o** hundred years old
Gen 19: 9 This **o** came in to sojourn, and
Gen 19:20 flee to, and it is a little **o**
Gen 19:20 there (is it not a little **o**
Gen 21: 5 Now Abraham was **o** hundred
Gen 21:15 the boy under **o** of the shrubs
Gen 22: 2 as a burnt offering on **o** of
Gen 23: 1 Sarah lived **o** hundred and
Gen 24:14 let her be the **o** whom You
Gen 25: 7 **o** hundred and seventy-five
Gen 25:17 **o** hundred and thirty-seven
Gen 25:23 **o** people shall be stronger
Gen 26:10 **O** of the people might soon
Gen 26:21 quarreled over that **o** also
Gen 26:26 **o** of his friends, and Phichol
Gen 26:31 swore an oath with **o** another
Gen 27:33 Where is the **o** who hunted
Gen 27:38 Have you only **o** blessing, my
Gen 27:45 also of you both in **o** day
Gen 28:11 he took **o** of the stones of
Gen 29:27 we will give you this **o** also
Gen 30:33 every **o** that is not speckled
Gen 30:35 every **o** that had some white
Gen 31:49 we are absent **o** from another
Gen 32: 8 Esau comes to the **o** company
Gen 32:17 And he commanded the first **o**
Gen 33:13 should drive them hard **o** day
Gen 33:19 for **o** hundred pieces of money
Gen 34:14 to **o** who is uncircumcised
Gen 34:16 and we will become **o** people
Gen 34:22 dwell with us, to be **o** people
Gen 35:28 days of Isaac were **o** hundred
Gen 37:19 Then they said to **o** another
Gen 38:28 that the **o** put out his hand
Gen 38:28 This **o** came out first
Gen 39: 9 There is no **o** greater in this
Gen 40: 5 each man's dream in **o** night
Gen 41: 5 of grain came up on **o** stalk
Gen 41: 8 but there was no **o** who could
Gen 41:11 dreamed a dream in **o** night
Gen 41:15 and there is no **o** who can
Gen 41:21 no **o** would have known that
Gen 41:22 heads came up on **o** stalk,
Gen 41:24 but there was no **o** who could
Gen 41:25 The dreams of Pharaoh are **o**
Gen 41:26 the dreams are **o**
Gen 41:38 Can we find such a **o** as this
Gen 41:39 there is no **o** as discerning
Gen 42: 1 Why do you look at **o** another
Gen 42:11 We are all **o** man's sons
Gen 42:13 the sons of **o** man in the land
Gen 42:13 father today, and **o** is no more
Gen 42:16 Send **o** of you, and let him
Gen 42:19 let **o** of your brothers be
Gen 42:21 Then they said to **o** another
Gen 42:27 But as **o** of them opened his
Gen 42:28 afraid, saying to **o** another
Gen 42:32 **o** is no more, and the youngest
Gen 42:33 Leave **o** of your brothers here
Gen 43:33 in astonishment at **o** another
Gen 44: 5 Is not this the **o** from which
Gen 44:28 the **o** went out from me, and I
Gen 44:29 you take this **o** also from me
Gen 45: 1 So no **o** stood with him
Gen 47: 9 my pilgrimage are **o** hundred
Gen 47:21 from **o** end of the borders of
Gen 47:28 of Jacob's life was **o** hundred
Gen 48:18 for this **o** is the firstborn
Gen 48:22 I have given to you **o** portion
Gen 49:16 as **o** of the tribes of Israel
Gen 49:28 he blessed each **o** according
Gen 50:22 And Joseph lived **o** hundred
Gen 50:26 being **o** hundred and ten years
Ex 1:15 the name of **o** was Shiphrah
Ex 2: 6 This is **o** of the Hebrews'
Ex 2:11 a Hebrew, **o** of his brethren
Ex 2:12 that way, and when he saw no **o**
Ex 2:13 he said to the **o** who did the
Ex 6:16 life of Levi were **o** hundred
Ex 6:18 life of Kohath were **o** hundred
Ex 6:20 life of Amram were **o** hundred
Ex 6:25 took for himself **o** of the
Ex 8:10 is no **o** like the LORD our God
Ex 8:31 Not **o** remained
Ex 9: 6 of Israel, not **o** died
Ex 9: 7 not even **o** of the livestock
Ex 10: 5 so that no **o** will be able to
Ex 10:19 There remained not **o** locust
Ex 10:23 They did not see **o** another
Ex 11: 1 I will bring yet **o** more
Ex 12:30 where there was not **o** dead
Ex 12:46 In **o** house it shall be eaten
Ex 12:46 you break **o** of its bones
Ex 12:49 **O** law shall be for the
Ex 14: 7 captains over every **o** of them
Ex 14:20 a cloud and darkness to the **o**
Ex 14:20 so that the **o** did not come
Ex 14:28 Not so much as **o** of them
Ex 16:15 it, they said to **o** another
Ex 16:16 need, **o** omer for each person,
Ex 16:19 Let no **o** leave any of it till
Ex 16:22 bread, two omers for each **o**
Ex 17:12 his hands, **o** on **o** side, and
Ex 18: 3 of whom the name of **o** was

Ex 18:16 to me, and I judge between **o**
Ex 21:18 **o** strikes the other with a
Ex 21:35 if **o** man's ox hurts another's
Ex 22:10 driven away, no **o** seeing it,
Ex 23: 5 If you see the donkey of **o**
Ex 23:26 No **o** shall suffer miscarriage
Ex 23:29 out from before you in **o** year
Ex 24: 3 people answered with **o** voice
Ex 25:12 two rings shall be on **o** side
Ex 25:19 Make **o** cherub at **o** end, and
Ex 25:19 at the two ends of it of **o**
Ex 25:20 and they shall face **o** another
Ex 25:31 flowers shall be of **o** piece
Ex 25:32 the lampstand out of **o** side
Ex 25:33 almond blossoms on **o** branch
Ex 25:36 branches shall be of **o** piece
Ex 25:36 all of it shall be **o** hammered
Ex 26: 2 every **o** of the curtains shall
Ex 26: 3 shall be coupled to **o** another
Ex 26: 3 shall be coupled to **o** another
Ex 26: 4 on the selvedge of **o** set, and
Ex 26: 5 shall make in the **o** curtain
Ex 26: 5 may be clasped to **o** another
Ex 26: 6 that it may be **o** tabernacle
Ex 26:10 that is outermost in **o** set
Ex 26:11 together, that it may be **o**
Ex 26:13 And a cubit on **o** side and a
Ex 26:17 for binding **o** to another
Ex 26:19 two sockets under **o** board for
Ex 26:21 two sockets under **o** board
Ex 26:24 together at the top by **o** ring
Ex 26:25 two sockets under **o** board
Ex 26:26 on **o** side of the tabernacle
Ex 27: 2 shall be of **o** piece with it
Ex 27: 9 **o** hundred cubits long for **o**
Ex 27:11 **o** hundred cubits long, with
Ex 27:14 The hangings on **o** side of the
Ex 27:18 shall be **o** hundred cubits
Ex 28:10 six of their names on **o** stone
Ex 28:21 each **o** with its own name
Ex 29: 1 Take **o** young bull and two rams
Ex 29: 3 shall put them in **o** basket
Ex 29:15 You shall also take **o** ram
Ex 29:23 **o** loaf of bread, **o** cake
Ex 29:23 and **o** wafer from the basket
Ex 29:39 **O** lamb you shall offer in the
Ex 29:40 With the **o** lamb shall be
Ex 30: 2 shall be of **o** piece with it
Ex 32:15 on the **o** side and on the other
Ex 33: 4 no **o** put on his ornaments
Ex 33: 5 into your midst in **o** moment
Ex 34:15 **o** of them invites you and you
Ex 36:10 five curtains to **o** another
Ex 36:10 he coupled to **o** another
Ex 36:11 on the selvedge of **o** set
Ex 36:12 loops he made on **o** curtain
Ex 36:12 the loops held **o** curtain to
Ex 36:13 to **o** another with the clasps
Ex 36:13 that it might be **o** tabernacle
Ex 36:17 that is outermost in **o** set
Ex 36:18 together, that it might be **o**
Ex 36:22 for binding **o** to another
Ex 36:24 two sockets under **o** board for
Ex 36:26 two sockets under **o** board
Ex 36:29 together at the top by **o** ring
Ex 36:31 on **o** side of the tabernacle
Ex 36:33 from **o** end to the other
Ex 37: 3 two rings on **o** side, and two
Ex 37: 7 he made them of **o** piece at
Ex 37: 8 **o** cherub at **o** end on this
Ex 37: 8 **o** piece with the mercy seat
Ex 37: 9 They faced **o** another
Ex 37:18 the lampstand out of **o** side
Ex 37:19 almond blossoms on **o** branch
Ex 37:22 branches were of **o** piece
Ex 37:22 all of it was **o** hammered
Ex 37:25 horns were of **o** piece with it
Ex 38: 2 horns were of **o** piece with it
Ex 38: 9 linen, **o** hundred cubits long
Ex 38:11 were **o** hundred cubits long
Ex 38:14 The hangings of **o** side of the
Ex 38:25 was **o** hundred talents and
Ex 38:25 **o** thousand seven hundred and
Ex 38:27 **o** hundred sockets from the
Ex 38:27 **o** talent for each socket
Ex 38:28 Then from the **o** thousand
Ex 39:14 each **o** with its own name
Lev 1: 2 When any **o** of you brings an
Lev 2: 2 **o** of whom shall take from it
Lev 5: 7 **o** as a sin offering and the
Lev 6: 3 in any **o** of these things that
Lev 6: 7 shall be forgiven for any **o**
Lev 7: 7 there is **o** law for them both
Lev 7:10 to **o** as much as the other
Lev 7:14 from it he shall offer **o** cake
Lev 8:26 he took **o** unleavened cake
Lev 8:26 **o** wafer, and put them on the
Lev 9:15 it for sin, like the first **o**
Lev 12: 8 **o** as a burnt offering and the
Lev 13: 2 to **o** of his sons the priests
Lev 13: 4 priest shall isolate the **o**
Lev 13:12 of the **o** who has the sore
Lev 13:23 bright spot stays in **o** place
Lev 13:28 bright spot stays in **o** place
Lev 13:31 the **o** who has the sore of the
Lev 13:33 priest shall isolate the **o**
Lev 14: 5 **o** of the birds be killed in
Lev 14:10 **o** ewe lamb of the first year
Lev 14:10 offering, and **o** log of oil
Lev 14:12 priest shall take **o** male lamb
Lev 14:21 then he shall take **o** male
Lev 14:22 **o** shall be a sin offering and
Lev 14:30 And he shall offer **o** of the
Lev 14:31 the **o** as a sin offering and
Lev 14:32 This is the law for **o** who had
Lev 14:50 Then he shall kill **o** of the
Lev 15:15 the **o** as a sin offering and
Lev 15:30 offer the **o** as a sin offering
Lev 15:32 law for **o** who has a discharge
Lev 15:33 for **o** who has a discharge,
Lev 16: 5 **o** ram as a burnt offering
Lev 16: 8 **o** lot for the LORD and the
Lev 17:12 No **o** among you shall eat
Lev 19: 3 Every **o** of you shall revere
Lev 19:11 falsely, nor lie to **o** another
Lev 19:34 be to you as **o** born among you
Lev 22:10 **o** who sojourns with the
Lev 22:11 **o** who is born in his house
Lev 23:18 **o** young bull, and two rams
Lev 23:19 **o** kid of the goats as a sin
Lev 24:22 for **o** from your own country
Lev 25:14 shall not oppress **o** another
Lev 25:17 shall not oppress **o** another
Lev 25:25 If **o** of your brethren
Lev 25:26 the man has no **o** to redeem it
Lev 25:35 if **o** of your brethren becomes
Lev 25:39 if **o** of your brethren who
Lev 25:46 over **o** another with rigor
Lev 25:47 **o** of your brethren who dwells
Lev 25:48 **O** of his brothers may redeem
Lev 26:17 flee when no **o** pursues you
Lev 26:26 bake your bread in **o** oven
Lev 26:36 shall fall when no **o** pursues
Lev 26:37 shall stumble over **o** another
Lev 26:37 a sword, when no **o** pursues
Lev 27:10 the **o** exchanged for it shall
Lev 27:24 to the **o** who owned the land
Lev 27:32 the tenth **o** shall be holy to
Lev 27:33 the **o** exchanged for it shall
Num 1: 4 tribe, each **o** the head of his
Num 1:18 and above, each **o** individually
Num 1:44 men, each **o** representing his
Num 2: 9 **o** hundred and eighty-six
Num 2:16 **o** hundred and fifty-one
Num 2:24 **o** hundred and eight thousand
Num 2:24 and eight thousand **o** hundred
Num 2:31 Dan, **o** hundred and fifty-seven
Num 2:34 camp, each **o** by his family,
Num 3:47 for each **o** individually
Num 3:50 **o** thousand three hundred and
Num 5: 7 it to the **o** he has wronged
Num 6:11 offer **o** as a sin offering
Num 6:14 **o** male lamb in its first year
Num 6:14 **o** ewe lamb in its first year
Num 6:14 **o** ram without blemish as a
Num 6:19 **o** unleavened cake from the
Num 6:19 **o** unleavened wafer, and put
Num 7: 3 leaders, and for each **o** an ox
Num 7:11 **o** leader each day, for the
Num 7:12 And the **o** who offered his
Num 7:13 offering was **o** silver platter
Num 7:13 weight of which was **o** hundred
Num 7:13 and **o** silver bowl of seventy
Num 7:14 **o** gold pan of ten shekels,
Num 7:15 **o** young bull, **o** ram
Num 7:15 **o** male lamb in its first year
Num 7:16 **o** kid of the goats as a sin
Num 7:19 he offered **o** silver platter
Num 7:19 weight of which was **o** hundred
Num 7:19 and **o** silver bowl of seventy
Num 7:20 **o** gold pan of ten shekels,
Num 7:21 **o** young bull, **o** ram,
Num 7:21 **o** ram, and **o** male lamb in
Num 7:21 **o** male lamb in its first year
Num 7:22 **o** kid of the goats as a sin
Num 7:25 offering was **o** silver platter
Num 7:25 weight of which was **o** hundred
Num 7:25 and **o** silver bowl of seventy
Num 7:26 **o** gold pan of ten shekels,
Num 7:27 **o** young bull, **o** ram,
Num 7:27 **o** male lamb in its first year
Num 7:28 **o** kid of the goats as a sin
Num 7:31 offering was **o** silver platter
Num 7:31 weight of which was **o** hundred
Num 7:31 and **o** silver bowl of seventy
Num 7:32 **o** gold pan of ten shekels,
Num 7:33 **o** young bull, **o** ram,
Num 7:33 **o** male lamb in its first year
Num 7:34 **o** kid of the goats as a sin
Num 7:37 offering was **o** silver platter
Num 7:37 weight of which was **o** hundred
Num 7:37 and **o** silver bowl of seventy
Num 7:38 **o** gold pan of ten shekels,
Num 7:39 **o** young bull, **o** ram,
Num 7:39 **o** male lamb in its first year
Num 7:40 **o** kid of the goats as a sin
Num 7:43 offering was **o** silver platter
Num 7:43 weight of which was **o** hundred
Num 7:43 and **o** silver bowl of seventy
Num 7:44 **o** gold pan of ten shekels,
Num 7:45 **o** young bull, **o** ram,
Num 7:45 **o** male lamb in its first year
Num 7:46 **o** kid of the goats as a sin
Num 7:49 offering was **o** silver platter
Num 7:49 weight of which was **o** hundred
Num 7:49 and **o** silver bowl of seventy
Num 7:50 **o** gold pan of ten shekels,
Num 7:51 **o** young bull, **o** ram,
Num 7:51 **o** male lamb in its first year
Num 7:52 **o** kid of the goats as a sin
Num 7:55 offering was **o** silver platter
Num 7:55 weight of which was **o** hundred
Num 7:55 and **o** silver bowl of seventy
Num 7:56 **o** gold pan of ten shekels,
Num 7:57 **o** young bull, **o** ram,
Num 7:57 **o** male lamb in its first year
Num 7:58 **o** kid of the goats as a sin
Num 7:61 offering was **o** silver platter
Num 7:61 weight of which was **o** hundred
Num 7:61 and **o** silver bowl of seventy
Num 7:62 **o** gold pan of ten shekels,
Num 7:63 **o** young bull, **o** ram,
Num 7:63 **o** male lamb in its first year
Num 7:64 **o** kid of the goats as a sin
Num 7:67 offering was **o** silver platter
Num 7:67 weight of which was **o** hundred
Num 7:67 and **o** silver bowl of seventy
Num 7:68 **o** gold pan of ten shekels,
Num 7:69 **o** young bull, **o** ram,
Num 7:69 **o** male lamb in its first year
Num 7:70 **o** kid of the goats as a sin
Num 7:73 offering was **o** silver platter
Num 7:73 weight of which was **o** hundred
Num 7:73 and **o** silver bowl of seventy
Num 7:74 **o** gold pan of ten shekels,
Num 7:75 **o** young bull, **o** ram,
Num 7:75 **o** male lamb in its first year
Num 7:76 **o** kid of the goats as a sin
Num 7:79 offering was **o** silver platter
Num 7:79 weight of which was **o** hundred
Num 7:79 and **o** silver bowl of seventy
Num 7:80 **o** gold pan of ten shekels,
Num 7:81 **o** young bull, **o** ram, and **o**
Num 7:81 **o** male lamb in its first year
Num 7:82 **o** kid of the goats as a sin
Num 7:85 platter weighed **o** hundred
Num 7:86 of the pans weighed **o** hundred
Num 7:89 Him, he heard the voice of **O**
Num 8:12 you shall offer **o** as a sin
Num 8:24 above **o** may enter to perform
Num 9:12 nor break **o** of its bones
Num 9:14 you shall have **o** ordinance
Num 10: 4 But if they blow only **o**, then
Num 11:19 You shall eat, not **o** day
Num 11:26 the name of **o** was Eldad, and
Num 11:28 **o** of his choice men, answered
Num 12:12 do not let her be as **o** dead
Num 13: 2 every **o** a leader among them
Num 13:23 with **o** cluster of grapes
Num 14: 4 So they said to **o** another

Num 14:15 kill these people as **o** man
Num 14:34 shall bear your guilt **o** year
Num 15:15 **O** ordinance shall be for you
Num 15:16 **O** law and **o** custom shall be
Num 15:24 offer **o** young bull as a burnt
Num 15:24 **o** kid of the goats as a sin
Num 15:29 You shall have **o** law for him
Num 15:30 that **o** brings reproach on the
Num 16: 3 every **o** of them, and the LORD
Num 16: 5 that **o** whom He chooses He
Num 16: 7 chooses shall be the holy **o**
Num 16:15 not taken **o** donkey from them
Num 16:15 nor have I hurt **o** of them
Num 16:22 shall **o** man sin, and You be
Num 17: 3 For there shall be **o** rod for
Num 18:16 shall redeem when **o** month old
Num 19: 8 the **o** who burns it shall wash
Num 19:10 the **o** who gathers the ashes
Num 19:16 in the open field touches **o**
Num 19:18 or on the **o** who touched a
Num 24:19 Out of Jacob **O** shall have
Num 25: 5 Every **o** of you kill his men
Num 25: 6 **o** of the children of Israel
Num 26:51 **o** thousand seven hundred and
Num 28: 4 The **o** lamb you shall offer
Num 28:11 **o** ram, and seven lambs in
Num 28:12 mixed with oil, for the **o** ram
Num 28:15 Also **o** kid of the goats as a
Num 28:19 **o** ram, and seven lambs in
Num 28:22 also **o** goat as a sin
Num 28:27 **o** ram, and seven lambs in
Num 28:28 two-tenths for the **o** ram
Num 28:30 also **o** kid of the goats, to
Num 29: 2 **o** young bull, **o** ram, and
Num 29: 5 also **o** kid of the goats as a
Num 29: 8 **o** young bull, **o** ram, and
Num 29: 9 two-tenths for the **o** ram
Num 29:11 also **o** kid of the goats as a
Num 29:16 also **o** kid of the goats as a
Num 29:19 also **o** kid of the goats as a
Num 29:22 also **o** goat as a sin
Num 29:25 also **o** kid of the goats as a
Num 29:28 also **o** goat as a sin
Num 29:31 also **o** goat as a sin
Num 29:34 also **o** goat as a sin
Num 29:36 **o** bull, **o** ram, seven lambs
Num 29:38 also **o** goat as a sin
Num 31: 5 the divisions of Israel **o**
Num 31: 6 **o** thousand from each tribe
Num 31:28 **o** of every five hundred of
Num 31:30 shall take **o** of every fifty
Num 31:47 Moses took **o** of every fifty
Num 32:18 to our homes until every **o** of
Num 33:39 Aaron was **o** hundred and
Num 34:18 you shall take **o** leader of
Num 35:17 by which **o** could die, and he
Num 35:18 by which **o** could die, and he
Num 35:21 the **o** who struck him shall
Num 35:30 but **o** witness is not
Num 36: 7 for every **o** of the children
Num 36: 8 of **o** of the family of her
Num 36: 9 hands from **o** tribe to another
Deut 1:23 men, **o** man from each tribe
Deut 1:35 Surely not **o** of these men of
Deut 2: 5 no, not so much as **o** footstep
Deut 2:36 there was not **o** city too
Deut 4: 4 alive today, every **o** of you
Deut 4:32 ask from **o** end of heaven to
Deut 4:42 that by fleeing to **o** of these
Deut 6: 4 LORD our God, the LORD is **o**
Deut 7:24 no **o** shall be able to stand
Deut 12:14 in **o** of your tribes, there
Deut 13: 7 from **o** end of the earth to
Deut 13:12 someone in **o** of your cities
Deut 17: 6 on the testimony of **o** witness
Deut 17: 8 between **o** judgment or another
Deut 17: 8 or between **o** punishment or
Deut 17:15 **o** from among your brethren
Deut 17:18 from the **o** before the priests
Deut 18:10 or **o** who practices witchcraft
Deut 18:10 or **o** who interprets omens, or
Deut 18:11 or **o** who conjures spells, or
Deut 18:11 or **o** who calls up the dead
Deut 19: 5 flee to **o** of these cities
Deut 19:11 he flees to **o** of these cities
Deut 19:15 **O** witness shall not rise
Deut 21:15 **o** loved and the other unloved,
Deut 22:19 they shall fine him **o** hundred
Deut 22:27 there was no **o** to save her
Deut 23: 2 **O** of illegitimate birth shall
Deut 23:16 within **o** of your gates, where
Deut 23:17 or a perverted **o** of the sons
Deut 24: 5 shall be free at home **o** year
Deut 24:14 whether **o** of your brethren or
Deut 24:14 or **o** of the aliens who is in
Deut 25: 5 **o** of them dies and has no son,
Deut 25:11 the wife of **o** draws near to
Deut 25:11 hand of the **o** attacking him
Deut 26: 3 you shall go to the **o** who is
Deut 27:15 Cursed is the **o** who makes
Deut 27:16 Cursed is the **o** who treats
Deut 27:17 Cursed is the **o** who moves
Deut 27:18 Cursed is the **o** who makes
Deut 27:19 Cursed is the **o** who perverts
Deut 27:20 Cursed is the **o** who lies
Deut 27:21 Cursed is the **o** who lies
Deut 27:22 Cursed is the **o** who lies
Deut 27:23 Cursed is the **o** who lies
Deut 27:24 Cursed is the **o** who attacks
Deut 27:25 Cursed is the **o** who takes a
Deut 27:26 Cursed is the **o** who does not
Deut 28: 7 come out against you **o** way
Deut 28:25 go out **o** way against them
Deut 28:26 no **o** shall frighten them away
Deut 28:29 and no **o** shall save you
Deut 28:31 have no **o** to rescue them
Deut 28:64 from **o** end of the earth to
Deut 28:68 slaves, but no **o** will buy you
Deut 29:11 from the **o** who cuts your wood
Deut 29:11 to the **o** who draws your water
Deut 31: 2 I am **o** hundred and twenty
Deut 31: 6 He is the **O** who goes with you
Deut 31: 8 He is the **o** who goes before
Deut 32:30 How could **o** chase a thousand,
Deut 32:36 and there is no **o** remaining
Deut 33: 8 Your Urim be with Your holy **o**
Deut 33:26 There is no **o** like the God of
Deut 34: 6 but no **o** knows his grave to
Deut 34: 7 Moses was **o** hundred and
Josh 3:12 **o** man from every tribe
Josh 4: 2 **o** man from every tribe,
Josh 4: 4 **o** man from every tribe
Josh 4: 5 each **o** of you take up a stone
Josh 9: 2 and Israel with **o** accord
Josh 10: 2 like **o** of the royal cities,
Josh 10:21 No **o** moved his tongue against
Josh 10:42 land Joshua took at **o** time
Josh 12: 9 the king of Jericho, **o**
Josh 12: 9 Ai, which is beside Bethel, **o**
Josh 12:10 the king of Jerusalem, **o**
Josh 12:10 the king of Hebron, **o**
Josh 12:11 the king of Jarmuth, **o**
Josh 12:11 the king of Lachish, **o**
Josh 12:12 the king of Eglon, **o**
Josh 12:12 the king of Gezer, **o**
Josh 12:13 the king of Debir, **o**
Josh 12:13 the king of Geder, **o**
Josh 12:14 the king of Hormah, **o**
Josh 12:14 the king of Arad, **o**
Josh 12:15 the king of Libnah, **o**
Josh 12:15 the king of Adullam, **o**
Josh 12:16 the king of Makkedah, **o**
Josh 12:16 the king of Bethel, **o**
Josh 12:17 the king of Tappuah, **o**
Josh 12:17 the king of Hepher, **o**
Josh 12:18 the king of Aphek, **o**
Josh 12:18 the king of Lasharon, **o**
Josh 12:19 the king of Madon, **o**
Josh 12:19 the king of Hazor, **o**
Josh 12:20 the king of Shimron Meron, **o**
Josh 12:20 the king of Achshaph, **o**
Josh 12:21 the king of Taanach, **o**
Josh 12:21 the king of Megiddo, **o**
Josh 12:22 the king of Kedesh, **o**
Josh 12:22 king of Jokneam in Carmel, **o**
Josh 12:23 Dor in the heights of Dor, **o**
Josh 12:23 of the people of Gilgal, **o**
Josh 12:24 the king of Tirzah, **o**
Josh 17:14 have you given us but **o** lot
Josh 17:14 **o** portion to inherit, since
Josh 17:17 you shall not have **o** lot only
Josh 20: 4 he flees to **o** of those cities
Josh 20: 4 into the city as **o** of them
Josh 20: 6 until the death of the **o** who
Josh 21:10 **o** of the families of the
Josh 21:42 Every **o** of these cities had
Josh 22:14 **o** ruler each from the chief
Josh 22:14 each **o** was the head of the
Josh 23: 9 no **o** has been able to stand
Josh 23:10 **O** man of you shall chase a
Josh 23:14 in all your souls that not **o**
Josh 23:14 not **o** word of them has failed
Josh 24:29 being **o** hundred and ten years
Josh 24:32 **o** hundred pieces of silver
Judg 2: 8 died when he was **o** hundred
Judg 6:16 the Midianites as **o** man
Judg 6:29 So they said to **o** another
Judg 6:31 Let the **o** who would plead for
Judg 7: 4 This **o** shall go with you,'
Judg 7: 4 This **o** shall not go with you
Judg 8:10 for **o** hundred and twenty
Judg 8:18 each **o** resembled the son of a
Judg 8:26 that he requested was **o**
Judg 9: 2 you, or that **o** reign over you
Judg 9: 5 sons of Jerubbaal, on **o** stone
Judg 9:18 his seventy sons on **o** stone
Judg 10:18 of Gilead, said to **o** another
Judg 12: 7 was buried in **o** of the cities
Judg 13:10 me, the **O** who came to me the
Judg 14: 6 as **o** would have torn apart a
Judg 16: 5 every **o** of us will give you
Judg 16:24 the **o** who multiplied our dead
Judg 16:28 that I may with **o** blow take
Judg 16:29 **o** on his right and the other
Judg 17: 5 he consecrated **o** of his sons
Judg 17:11 like **o** of his sons to him
Judg 18:19 to the household of **o** man
Judg 19:13 near to **o** of these places
Judg 19:15 for no **o** would take them into
Judg 19:18 But there is no **o** who will
Judg 20: 1 gathered together as **o** man
Judg 20: 8 all the people arose as **o** man
Judg 20:11 united together as **o** man
Judg 20:16 every **o** could sling a stone
Judg 20:31 in the highways (**o** of which
Judg 20:35 thousand **o** hundred Benjamites
Judg 21: 3 be **o** tribe missing in Israel
Judg 21: 6 **O** tribe is cut off from
Judg 21: 8 What **o** is there from the
Judg 21: 8 no **o** had come to the camp
Judg 21: 9 not **o** of the inhabitants of
Judg 21:18 Cursed be the **o** who gives a
Ruth 1: 4 the name of the **o** was Orpah
Ruth 2:13 like **o** of your maidservants
Ruth 2:19 Blessed be the **o** who took
Ruth 2:20 ours, **o** of our near kinsmen
Ruth 3:14 and she arose before **o** could
Ruth 4: 4 for there is no **o** but you to
Ruth 4: 7 **o** man took off his sandal and
1Sa 1: 2 the name of **o** was Hannah, and
1Sa 1:24 **o** ephah of flour, and a skin
1Sa 2:25 If **o** man sins against another
1Sa 2:34 in **o** day they shall die, both
1Sa 2:36 put me in **o** of the priestly
1Sa 6:17 **o** for Ashdod, **o** for Gaza,
1Sa 6:17 **o** for Ashkelon, **o** for Gath,
1Sa 6:17 **o** for Ekron
1Sa 9: 3 take **o** of the servants with
1Sa 9: 8 I have here at hand **o** fourth
1Sa 9:17 This **o** shall reign over My
1Sa 10: 3 **o** carrying three young goats,
1Sa 10:11 the people said to **o** another
1Sa 10:24 that there is no **o** like him
1Sa 11: 3 if there is no **o** to save us
1Sa 11: 7 they came out with **o** consent
1Sa 13: 1 Saul reigned **o** year
1Sa 13:17 **O** company turned to the road
1Sa 14: 1 Now it happened **o** day that
1Sa 14: 4 was a sharp rock on **o** side
1Sa 14: 4 And the name of **o** was Bozez
1Sa 14: 5 The front of **o** faced
1Sa 14:26 but no **o** put his hand to his
1Sa 14:28 Then **o** of the people said,
1Sa 14:34 So every **o** of the people
1Sa 14:40 You be on **o** side, and my son
1Sa 14:45 not **o** hair of his head shall
1Sa 16: 3 for Me the **o** I name to you
1Sa 16: 8 has the LORD chosen this **o**
1Sa 16: 9 has the LORD chosen this **o**
1Sa 16:12 for this is the **o**
1Sa 16:18 Then **o** of the servants
1Sa 17: 3 stood on a mountain on **o** side
1Sa 17:36 will be like **o** of them,
1Sa 18:25 **o** hundred foreskins of the
1Sa 20:15 **o** of the enemies of David
1Sa 20:41 And they kissed **o** another
1Sa 21: 1 alone, and no **o** is with you
1Sa 21: 9 no other except that **o** here
1Sa 21:11 of him to **o** another in dances
1Sa 22: 7 give every **o** of you fields

1Sa 22: 8 there is no **o** who reveals to
1Sa 22: 8 there is not **o** of you who is
1Sa 22:20 Now **o** of the sons of
1Sa 23:26 Then Saul went on **o** side of
1Sa 25:10 away each **o** from his master
1Sa 25:14 Now **o** of the young men told
1Sa 25:17 that **o** cannot speak to him
1Sa 25:18 **o** hundred clusters of raisins
1Sa 25:22 if I leave **o** male of all who
1Sa 26:15 For **o** of the people came in
1Sa 26:20 as when **o** hunts a partridge
1Sa 26:22 Let **o** of the young men come
1Sa 27: 7 Philistines was **o** full year
1Sa 28: 2 you **o** of my chief guardians
1Sa 28: 8 me the **o** I shall name to you
1Sa 29: 5 sang to **o** another in dances
2Sa 1:15 called **o** of the young men
2Sa 2:13 **o** on **o** side of the pool and
2Sa 2:13 **o** on **o** side of the pool and
2Sa 2:16 each **o** grasped his opponent
2Sa 2:21 lay hold on **o** of the young
2Sa 3:13 But **o** thing I require of you
2Sa 3:29 to be in the house of Joab **o**
2Sa 4: 2 The name of **o** was Baanah and
2Sa 4:10 the **o** who thought I would
2Sa 5: 2 you were the **o** who led Israel
2Sa 6:20 as **o** of the base fellows
2Sa 7:23 the **o** nation on the earth
2Sa 8: 2 with **o** full line those to be
2Sa 8: 4 from him **o** thousand chariots
2Sa 8: 4 them for **o** hundred chariots
2Sa 9:11 like **o** of the king's sons
2Sa 10: 6 King Maacah **o** thousand men
2Sa 11: 2 Then it happened **o** evening
2Sa 11:25 devours **o** as well as another
2Sa 12: 1 There were two men in **o** city
2Sa 12: 1 **o** rich and the other poor
2Sa 12: 3 except **o** little ewe lamb
2Sa 12: 4 his own herd to prepare **o** for
2Sa 13:13 you would be like **o** of the
2Sa 13:29 each **o** got on his mule and
2Sa 13:30 and not **o** of them is left
2Sa 14: 6 there was no **o** to part them
2Sa 14: 6 but the **o** struck the other and
2Sa 14:11 not **o** hair of your son shall
2Sa 14:13 this thing as **o** who is guilty
2Sa 14:13 his banished **o** home again
2Sa 14:19 no **o** can turn to the right
2Sa 14:25 **o** who was praised as much as
2Sa 14:27 **o** daughter whose name was
2Sa 16: 1 **o** hundred clusters of raisins
2Sa 16: 1 **o** hundred summer fruits, and a
2Sa 16:23 was as if **o** had inquired at
2Sa 17:12 not be left so much as **o**
2Sa 17:13 until there is not **o** small
2Sa 17:22 By morning light not **o** of
2Sa 18: 2 Then David sent out **o** third
2Sa 18: 2 **o** third under the hand of
2Sa 18: 2 **o** third under the hand of
2Sa 19: 7 not **o** will stay with you this
2Sa 19:14 just as the heart of **o** man
2Sa 20:11 Meanwhile **o** of Joab's men
2Sa 21:16 who was **o** of the sons of the
2Sa 21:18 who was **o** of the sons of the
2Sa 23: 8 eight hundred men at **o** time
2Sa 23: 9 **o** of the three mighty men
2Sa 23:24 of Joab was **o** of the thirty
2Sa 24:12 choose **o** of them for yourself
1Ki 1:48 who has given **o** to sit on my
1Ki 1:49 arose, and each **o** went his way
1Ki 1:52 not **o** hair of him shall fall
1Ki 2:16 Now I ask **o** petition of you
1Ki 2:20 I desire **o** small petition of
1Ki 3:17 **o** woman said, "O my lord,
1Ki 3:18 there was no **o** with us in the
1Ki 3:22 But the living **o** is my son
1Ki 3:22 and the dead **o** is your son
1Ki 3:22 But the dead **o** is your son
1Ki 3:22 and the living **o** is my son
1Ki 3:23 The **o** says, 'This is my son,
1Ki 3:23 and your son is the dead **o**'
1Ki 3:23 But your son is the dead **o**
1Ki 3:23 and my son is the living **o**
1Ki 3:25 in two, and give half to **o**
1Ki 4: 7 each **o** made provision
1Ki 4: 7 for **o** month of the year
1Ki 4:22 **o** day was thirty kors of fine
1Ki 4:23 **o** hundred sheep, besides deer
1Ki 4:32 and his songs were **o** thousand
1Ki 5:14 they were **o** month in Lebanon
1Ki 6:24 **O** wing of the cherub was five
1Ki 6:24 of **o** wing to the tip of the
1Ki 6:26 The height of **o** cherub was
1Ki 6:27 of the **o** touched **o** wall
1Ki 6:34 comprised **o** folding door, and
1Ki 7: 2 length was **o** hundred cubits
1Ki 7:15 each **o** eighteen cubits high,
1Ki 7:16 The height of **o** capital was
1Ki 7:17 seven chains for **o** capital
1Ki 7:23 ten cubits from **o** brim to the
1Ki 7:31 top was **o** cubit in diameter
1Ki 7:31 shaped like a pedestal, **o**
1Ki 7:32 The height of a wheel was **o**
1Ki 7:37 mold, **o** measure, and **o** shape
1Ki 7:44 **o** Sea, and twelve oxen under
1Ki 8:38 when each **o** knows the plague
1Ki 8:46 is no **o** who does not sin)
1Ki 8:56 failed **o** word of all His good
1Ki 8:63 **o** hundred and twenty thousand
1Ki 9:14 Hiram sent the king **o** hundred
1Ki 10:10 she gave the king **o** hundred
1Ki 10:20 **o** on each side of the six
1Ki 10:21 not **o** was of silver, for this
1Ki 10:26 he had **o** thousand four
1Ki 10:29 silver, and a horse **o** hundred
1Ki 11:13 but I will give **o** tribe to
1Ki 11:32 (but he shall have **o** tribe
1Ki 11:36 his son I will give **o** tribe
1Ki 12:21 **o** hundred and eighty thousand
1Ki 12:29 And he set up **o** in Bethel, and
1Ki 12:30 before the **o** as far as Dan
1Ki 13:33 he became **o** of the priests of
1Ki 14:10 as **o** takes away refuse until
1Ki 14:13 him, for he is the only **o** of
1Ki 16:11 he did not leave him **o** male
1Ki 18: 4 had taken **o** hundred prophets
1Ki 18: 6 Ahab went **o** way by himself,
1Ki 18:13 how I hid **o** hundred men of
1Ki 18:23 let them choose **o** bull for
1Ki 18:25 Choose **o** bull for yourselves
1Ki 18:26 no voice; no **o** answered.
1Ki 18:29 no voice; no **o** answered,
1Ki 18:29 no **o** paid attention
1Ki 18:40 Do not let **o** of them escape
1Ki 19: 2 your life as the life of **o** of
1Ki 20:11 Let not the **o** who puts on
1Ki 20:11 like the **o** who takes it off
1Ki 20:20 And each **o** killed his man
1Ki 20:29 **o** hundred thousand foot
1Ki 20:29 of the Syrians in **o** day
1Ki 20:41 him as **o** of the prophets
1Ki 21:25 But there was no **o** like Ahab
1Ki 22: 8 There is still **o** man, Micaiah
1Ki 22:13 **o** accord encourage the king
1Ki 22:13 be like the word of **o** of them
1Ki 22:20 So **o** spoke in this manner,
1Ki 22:31 Fight with no **o** small or
2Ki 3: 4 **o** hundred thousand lambs and
2Ki 3: 4 and the wool of **o** hundred
2Ki 3:11 **o** of the servants of the king
2Ki 3:23 and have killed **o** another
2Ki 4: 8 Now it happened **o** day that
2Ki 4:11 it happened **o** day that he
2Ki 4:18 Now it happened **o** day that he
2Ki 4:22 Please send me **o** of the young
2Ki 4:22 **o** of the donkeys, that I may
2Ki 4:39 So **o** went out into the field
2Ki 4:43 set this before **o** hundred men
2Ki 6: 3 Then **o** said, "Please consent
2Ki 6: 5 But as **o** was cutting down a
2Ki 6:12 And **o** of his servants said,
2Ki 7: 3 and they said to **o** another
2Ki 7: 5 their surprise no **o** was there
2Ki 7: 6 so they said to **o** another
2Ki 7: 8 camp, they went into **o** tent
2Ki 7: 9 Then they said to **o** another
2Ki 7:10 surprisingly no **o** was there
2Ki 7:13 **o** of his servants answered and
2Ki 8:26 king, and he reigned **o** year in
2Ki 9: 1 Elisha the prophet called **o**
2Ki 9: 5 For which **o** of us
2Ki 9:11 his master, and **o** said to him,
2Ki 9:15 let no **o** leave or escape from
2Ki 10:19 Let no **o** be missing, for I
2Ki 10:21 full from **o** end to the other
2Ki 10:22 he said to the **o** in charge of
2Ki 10:25 let no **o** come out
2Ki 12: 9 on the right side as **o** comes
2Ki 14: 8 let us face **o** another in
2Ki 14:11 **o** another at Beth Shemesh
2Ki 17:27 Send there **o** of the priests
2Ki 17:28 Then **o** of the priests whom
2Ki 18:24 How then will you repel **o**
2Ki 18:31 every **o** of you eat from his
2Ki 18:31 every **o** from his own fig tree
2Ki 18:31 and every **o** of you drink the
2Ki 19:15 the **O** who dwells between the
2Ki 19:22 Against the Holy **O** of Israel
2Ki 19:35 of the Assyrians **o** hundred
2Ki 21:13 Jerusalem as **o** wipes a dish
2Ki 21:16 from **o** end to another,
2Ki 23:18 let no **o** move his bones
2Ki 23:33 on the land a tribute of **o**
2Ki 23:35 from every **o** according to his
2Ki 24:16 **o** thousand, all who were
2Ki 25:16 **o** Sea, and the carts, which
2Ki 25:17 The height of **o** pillar was
1Ch 1:10 to be a mighty **o** on the earth
1Ch 1:19 the name of **o** was Peleg, for
1Ch 5:21 also **o** hundred thousand of
1Ch 6:57 **o** of the cities of refuge
1Ch 6:67 And they gave them **o** of the
1Ch 8:40 **o** hundred and fifty in all
1Ch 9:13 **o** thousand seven hundred and
1Ch 11: 2 you were the **o** who led Israel
1Ch 11:11 killed by him at **o** time
1Ch 11:12 who was **o** of the three mighty
1Ch 12:25 war, seven thousand **o** hundred
1Ch 12:34 of Naphtali **o** thousand
1Ch 12:37 **o** hundred and twenty thousand
1Ch 12:38 of **o** mind to make David king
1Ch 15: 2 No **o** may carry the ark of God
1Ch 15: 5 **o** hundred and twenty of his
1Ch 15: 7 **o** hundred and thirty of his
1Ch 15:10 **o** hundred and twelve of his
1Ch 16:20 went from **o** nation to another
1Ch 16:20 from **o** kingdom to another
1Ch 17: 5 from **o** tabernacle to another
1Ch 17:21 the **o** nation on the earth
1Ch 18: 4 from him **o** thousand chariots
1Ch 18: 4 them for **o** hundred chariots
1Ch 20: 4 who was **o** of the sons of the
1Ch 21: 5 **o** million **o** hundred thousand
1Ch 21:10 choose **o** of them for yourself
1Ch 21:17 I am the **o** who has sinned and
1Ch 22:14 for the house of the LORD **o**
1Ch 22:14 **o** million talents of silver,
1Ch 23:11 assigned as **o** father's house
1Ch 24: 5 **o** group as another, for there
1Ch 24: 6 **o** of the Levites, wrote them
1Ch 24: 6 **o** father's house taken for
1Ch 24: 6 for Eleazar and **o** for Ithamar
1Ch 26:30 **o** thousand seven hundred able
1Ch 27:18 Elihu, **o** of David's brothers
1Ch 29: 7 **o** hundred thousand talents of
2Ch 1:14 he had **o** thousand four
2Ch 1:17 and a horse for **o** hundred
2Ch 2:17 were found to be **o** hundred
2Ch 3: 4 and the height was **o** hundred
2Ch 3:11 **o** wing of the **o** cherub was
2Ch 3:12 **o** wing of the other cherub
2Ch 3:16 and he made **o** hundred
2Ch 3:17 **o** on the right hand and the
2Ch 3:17 **o** on the right hand Jachin
2Ch 3:17 the name of the **o** on the left
2Ch 4: 2 ten cubits from **o** brim to the
2Ch 4: 8 he made **o** hundred bowls of
2Ch 4:15 **o** Sea and twelve oxen under it
2Ch 5:12 harps, and with them **o** hundred
2Ch 5:13 and singers were as **o**, to make
2Ch 5:13 to make **o** sound to be heard
2Ch 6:29 when each **o** knows his own
2Ch 6:36 is no **o** who does not sin)
2Ch 7: 5 **o** hundred and twenty thousand
2Ch 9: 9 she gave the king **o** hundred
2Ch 9:19 **o** on each side of the six
2Ch 9:20 Not **o** was of silver, for this
2Ch 11: 1 Judah and Benjamin **o** hundred
2Ch 15: 5 peace to the **o** who went out
2Ch 15: 5 nor to the **o** who came in, but
2Ch 17:18 and with him **o** hundred and
2Ch 18: 7 There is still **o** man by whom
2Ch 18: 8 called **o** of his officers and
2Ch 18:12 **o** accord encourage the king
2Ch 18:12 be like the word of **o** of them
2Ch 18:19 **o** spoke in this manner, and
2Ch 18:30 Fight with no **o** small or
2Ch 20: 6 so that no **o** is able to
2Ch 20:23 helped to destroy **o** another
2Ch 20:24 No **o** had escaped

2Ch 22: 2 king, and he reigned o year in
2Ch 22: 9 no o to assume power over the
2Ch 23: 6 But let no o come into the
2Ch 23:19 so that no o who was in any
2Ch 24:15 he was o hundred and thirty
2Ch 25: 6 He also hired o hundred
2Ch 25: 6 of valor from Israel for o
2Ch 25:17 let us face o another in
2Ch 25:21 o another at Beth Shemesh
2Ch 26:11 o of the king's captains
2Ch 27: 5 o hundred talents of silver
2Ch 28: 6 of Remaliah killed o hundred
2Ch 28: 6 thousand in Judah in o day
2Ch 29:32 bulls, o hundred rams, and two
2Ch 32:12 shall worship before o altar
2Ch 35:24 was buried in o of the tombs
2Ch 36: 3 on the land a tribute of o
Ezra 1: 9 o thousand silver platters,
Ezra 1:10 o thousand other articles
Ezra 2: 3 two thousand o hundred and
Ezra 2: 7 o thousand two hundred and
Ezra 2:12 o thousand two hundred and
Ezra 2:18 of Jorah, o hundred and twelve
Ezra 2:21 o hundred and twenty-three
Ezra 2:23 o hundred and twenty-eight
Ezra 2:27 o hundred and twenty-two
Ezra 2:30 o hundred and fifty-six
Ezra 2:31 o thousand two hundred and
Ezra 2:37 o thousand and fifty-two
Ezra 2:38 o thousand two hundred and
Ezra 2:39 o thousand and seventeen
Ezra 2:41 o hundred and twenty-eight
Ezra 2:42 o hundred and thirty-nine in
Ezra 2:69 o hundred priestly garments
Ezra 3: 1 as o man to Jerusalem
Ezra 3: 9 arose as o to oversee those
Ezra 5:14 given to o named Sheshbazzar
Ezra 6: 4 stones and o row of new timber
Ezra 6:17 o hundred bulls, two hundred
Ezra 7:22 up to o hundred talents of
Ezra 7:22 o hundred kors of wheat,
Ezra 7:22 o hundred baths of wine,
Ezra 7:22 o hundred baths of oil, and
Ezra 8: 3 with him were o hundred and
Ezra 8:10 and with him o hundred and
Ezra 8:12 and with him o hundred and ten
Ezra 8:26 weighing o hundred talents
Ezra 8:26 o hundred talents of gold,
Ezra 9:11 o end to another with their
Ezra 9:15 though no o can stand before
Ezra 10: 2 o of the sons of Elam, spoke
Ezra 10:13 the work of o or two days
Neh 1: 2 that Hanani o of my brethren
Neh 2:12 I told no o what my God had
Neh 2:12 except the o on which I rode
Neh 3: 8 o of the goldsmiths, made
Neh 3: 8 o of the perfumers, made
Neh 3:31 o of the goldsmiths, made
Neh 4:17 with o hand they worked at
Neh 4:18 Every o of the builders had
Neh 4:18 the o who sounded the trumpet
Neh 4:19 from o another on the wall
Neh 5:17 were at my table o hundred
Neh 5:18 for me daily was o ox and six
Neh 6: 2 in o of the villages in the
Neh 7: 3 o at his watch station and
Neh 7: 8 two thousand o hundred and
Neh 7:12 o thousand two hundred and
Neh 7:24 Hariph, o hundred and twelve
Neh 7:26 o hundred and eighty-eight
Neh 7:27 o hundred and twenty-eight
Neh 7:31 o hundred and twenty-two
Neh 7:32 o hundred and twenty-three
Neh 7:34 o thousand two hundred and
Neh 7:40 o thousand and fifty-two
Neh 7:41 o thousand two hundred and
Neh 7:42 o thousand and seventeen
Neh 7:44 o hundred and forty-eight
Neh 7:45 o hundred and thirty-eight
Neh 7:70 gave to the treasury o
Neh 8: 1 o man in the open square that
Neh 8:16 each o on the roof of his
Neh 11: 1 o out of ten to dwell in
Neh 11:14 of valor, were o hundred and
Neh 11:14 the son of o of the great men
Neh 11:19 were o hundred and seventy-two
Neh 12:31 o of which went to the right
Neh 13:24 to the language of o or the
Neh 13:28 o of the sons of Joiada, the
Esth 1: 1 Ethiopia, over o hundred and
Esth 1: 4 o hundred and eighty days in
Esth 3:13 in o day, on the thirteenth
Esth 4: 2 for no o might enter the
Esth 4: 5 o of the king's eunuchs whom
Esth 4:11 been called, he has but o law
Esth 4:11 except the o to whom the king
Esth 5:12 Queen Esther invited no o but
Esth 6: 1 So o was commanded to bring
Esth 6: 9 of o of the king's most noble
Esth 7: 9 o of the eunuchs, said to the
Esth 8: 8 signet ring no o can revoke
Esth 8: 9 o hundred and twenty-seven
Esth 8:12 on o day in all the provinces
Esth 9: 2 no o could withstand them,
Esth 9:19 sending presents to o another
Esth 9:22 sending presents to o another
Esth 9:30 the Jews, to the o hundred and
Job 1: 1 o who feared God and shunned
Job 1: 8 o who fears God and shuns evil
Job 2: 3 o who fears God and shuns evil
Job 2:10 You speak as o of the foolish
Job 2:11 him, each o came from his own
Job 2:12 and each o tore his robe and
Job 2:13 no o spoke a word to him, for
Job 4: 2 If o attempts a word with you
Job 4:20 forever, with no o regarding
Job 5: 2 man, and envy slays a simple o
Job 6:10 the words of the Holy O
Job 6:26 the speeches of a desperate o
Job 9: 3 If o wished to contend with
Job 9: 3 Him o time out of a thousand
Job 9:22 It is all o thing
Job 10: 7 there is no o who can deliver
Job 11: 3 mock, should no o rebuke you
Job 11:19 no o would make you afraid
Job 12: 4 I am o mocked by his friends,
Job 12: 5 thought of o who is at ease
Job 13: 9 you mock Him as o mocks a man
Job 14: 3 open Your eyes on such a o
Job 14: 4 out of an unclean? No o!
Job 15:28 in houses which no o inhabits
Job 16:21 that o might plead for a man
Job 17: 6 I have become o in whose face
Job 17:10 not find o wise man among you
Job 19:11 counts me as o of His enemies
Job 21:23 O dies in his full strength,
Job 22:30 deliver o who is not innocent
Job 24:18 so that no o would turn into
Job 26: 3 counseled o who has no wisdom
Job 29:25 as o who comforts mourners
Job 31:15 Did not the same O fashion us
Job 31:35 Oh, that I had o to hear me
Job 32:12 surely not o of you convinced
Job 33:14 For God may speak in o way
Job 33:23 o among a thousand, to show
Job 34:17 Should o who hates justice
Job 35:10 But no o says, 'Where is God
Job 36: 4 o who is perfect in knowledge
Job 36: 5 is mighty, but despises no o
Job 36:18 He take you away with o blow
Job 38:26 on a land where there is no o
Job 40: 2 Shall the o who contends with
Job 40:24 or o pierces his nose with a
Job 41: 9 shall o not be overwhelmed at
Job 41:10 No o is so fierce that he
Job 41:16 O is so near another that no
Job 41:17 They are joined o to another
Job 41:32 o would think the deep had
Job 42:11 Each o gave him a piece of
Job 42:12 o thousand yoke of oxen, and
Job 42:12 o thousand female donkeys
Job 42:16 this Job lived o hundred and
Ps 3: 3 the O who lifts up my head
Ps 11: 5 the o who loves violence His
Ps 14: 3 none who does good, No, not o
Ps 16:10 Your Holy O to see corruption
Ps 19: 6 is from o end of heaven, And
Ps 25: 3 let no o who waits on You be
Ps 27: 4 O thing I have desired of the
Ps 34:20 Not o of them is broken
Ps 35:14 as o who mourns for his
Ps 45: 3 upon Your thigh, O Mighty O
Ps 49:16 be afraid when o becomes rich
Ps 50: 1 The Mighty O, God the LORD,
Ps 53: 3 Every o of them has turned
Ps 53: 3 none who does good, No, not o
Ps 55:12 Nor is it o who hates me who
Ps 57: 3 He reproaches the o who would
Ps 62:12 each o according to his work
Ps 68:21 The hairy scalp of the o who
Ps 69:25 Let no o dwell in their tents
Ps 71:22 the harp, O Holy O of Israel
Ps 73:20 As a dream when o awakes, So,
Ps 75: 7 He puts down o, And exalts
Ps 78:41 limited the Holy O of Israel
Ps 78:65 Lord awoke as o out of sleep
Ps 79: 3 there was no o to bury them
Ps 82: 7 fall like o of the princes
Ps 83: 5 together with o consent
Ps 84: 7 Every o of them appears
Ps 87: 4 This o was born there
Ps 87: 5 This o and that o were born
Ps 87: 6 This o was born there
Ps 88:18 Loved o and friend You have
Ps 89:10 in pieces, as o who is slain
Ps 89:18 king to the Holy O of Israel
Ps 89:19 in a vision to Your holy o
Ps 89:19 given help to o who is mighty
Ps 89:19 I have exalted o chosen from
Ps 101: 5 The o who has a haughty look
Ps 105:13 went from o nation to another
Ps 105:13 From o kingdom to another
Ps 105:14 He permitted no o to do them
Ps 106:11 There was not o of them left
Ps 106:23 o stood before Him in the
Ps 119:160 every o of Your righteous
Ps 119:162 As o who finds great treasure
Ps 120: 6 long With o who hates peace
Ps 128: 1 Blessed is every o who fears
Ps 137: 3 Sing us o of the songs of
Ps 141: 7 of the grave, As when o plows
Ps 142: 4 and see, For there is no o who
Ps 142: 4 No o cares for my soul
Ps 143: 2 no o living is righteous
Ps 144: 2 the O in whom I take refuge,
Ps 144:10 The O who gives salvation to
Ps 145: 4 O generation shall praise
Prov 1:14 us, let us all have o purse"
Prov 1:24 out my hand and no o regarded,
Prov 4: 3 the only o in the sight of my
Prov 5: 9 and your years to the cruel o
Prov 6:19 and o who sows discord among
Prov 6:28 Can o walk on hot coals, and
Prov 8:11 all the things o may desire
Prov 9:10 the Holy O is understanding
Prov 10: 4 of the diligent makes o rich
Prov 10:22 of the LORD makes o rich, and
Prov 11:15 but o who hates being surety
Prov 11:24 There is o who scatters, yet
Prov 11:24 there is o who withholds more
Prov 12: 9 Better is the o who is
Prov 12:18 There is o who speaks like
Prov 13: 7 There is o who makes himself
Prov 13: 7 o who makes himself poor, yet
Prov 13:14 life, to turn o away from the
Prov 15:12 not love o who reproves him
Prov 16: 6 the LORD o departs from evil
Prov 18:17 The first o to plead his
Prov 19: 1 o who is perverse in his lips
Prov 19: 6 a friend to o who gives gifts
Prov 19:15 casts o into a deep sleep
Prov 19:25 reprove o who has
Prov 20:16 of o who is surety for a
Prov 20:19 do not associate with o who
Prov 22:26 Do not be o of those who
Prov 22:26 o of those who is surety for
Prov 23:34 you will be like o who lies
Prov 23:34 or like o who lies at the top
Prov 25:20 Like o who takes away a
Prov 25:20 is o who sings songs to a
Prov 26: 8 Like o who binds a stone in a
Prov 26:17 o who takes a dog by the ears
Prov 28: 1 wicked flee when no o pursues
Prov 28: 6 than o perverse in his ways
Prov 28: 8 O who increases his
Prov 28: 9 O who turns away his ear from
Prov 28:17 let no o help him
Prov 30: 3 have knowledge of the Holy O
Eccl 1: 4 O generation passes away, and
Eccl 3:11 except that no o can find out
Eccl 3:19 o thing befalls them
Eccl 3:19 as o dies, so dies the other
Eccl 3:19 they all have o breath
Eccl 3:20 All go to o place
Eccl 4: 8 There is o alone, without
Eccl 4: 9 Two are better than o,
Eccl 4:10 o will lift up his companion
Eccl 4:10 for he has no o to help him
Eccl 4:11 but how can o be warm alone
Eccl 4:12 Though o may be overpowered

Eccl 5:18 good and fitting for o to eat
Eccl 6: 6 Do not all go to o place
Eccl 6:10 Whatever o is, he has been
Eccl 7:14 the o as well as the other
Eccl 7:27 Adding o thing to the other
Eccl 7:28 o man among a thousand I have
Eccl 8: 8 No o has power over the
Eccl 8: 8 no o has power in the day of
Eccl 8: 9 There is a time in which o
Eccl 8:16 even though o sees no sleep
Eccl 9: 2 O event happens to the
Eccl 9: 3 that o thing happens to all
Eccl 9:15 Yet no o remembered that same
Eccl 9:18 but o sinner destroys much
Eccl 10: 1 to o respected for wisdom
Eccl 10:10 o does not sharpen the edge,
Eccl 12: 4 when o rises up at the sound
Eccl 12:11 nails, given by o Shepherd
Song 1: 7 For why should I be as o who
Song 2:10 Rise up, my love, my fair o
Song 2:13 rise up, my love, my fair o
Song 3: 1 my bed I sought the o I love
Song 3: 2 I will seek the o I love
Song 3: 3 Have you seen the o I love
Song 3: 4 when I found the o I love
Song 4: 2 every o of which bears twins,
Song 4: 9 with o look of your eyes,
Song 4: 9 with o link of your necklace
Song 5: 2 love, my dove, my perfect o
Song 6: 6 every o bears twins, and none
Song 6: 9 My dove, my perfect o, is the
Song 6: 9 my perfect o, is the only o
Song 6: 9 of the o who bore her
Song 8:10 his eyes as o who found peace
Is 1: 4 to anger the Holy O of Israel
Is 1:24 hosts, the Mighty O of Israel
Is 1:31 and no o shall quench them
Is 3: 5 every o by another and every
Is 3: 5 and every o by his neighbor
Is 4: 1 shall take hold of o man,
Is 5:10 vineyard shall yield o bath
Is 5:10 of seed shall yield o ephah
Is 5:19 Holy O of Israel draw near
Is 5:24 word of the Holy O of Israel
Is 5:27 No o will be weary or stumble
Is 5:27 No o will slumber or sleep
Is 5:29 safely, and no o will deliver
Is 5:30 And if o looks to the land,
Is 6: 2 each o had six wings
Is 6: 3 o cried to another and said
Is 6: 6 Then o of the seraphim flew
Is 9:14 branch and bulrush in o day
Is 10:14 as o gathers eggs that are
Is 10:14 there was no o who moved his
Is 10:17 and his Holy O for a flame
Is 10:17 thorns and his briers in o day
Is 10:20 the Holy O of Israel, in
Is 10:34 will fall by the Mighty O
Is 12: 6 for great is the Holy O of
Is 13: 8 will be amazed at o another
Is 14: 6 is persecuted and no o hinders
Is 14:31 no o will be alone in his
Is 14:32 What will o then answer the
Is 16: 5 O will sit on it in truth, in
Is 17: 2 no o will make them afraid
Is 17: 7 for the Holy O of Israel
Is 19:18 o will be called the City of
Is 19:20 them a Savior and a Mighty O
Is 19:24 will be o of three with Egypt
Is 22:22 open, and no o shall shut
Is 22:22 shut, and no o shall open
Is 23:15 to the days of o king
Is 27:12 you will be gathered o by o
Is 28: 2 Lord has a mighty and strong o
Is 29:11 deliver to o who is literate
Is 29:12 to o who is illiterate,
Is 29:19 In the Holy O of Israel
Is 29:20 For the terrible o is brought
Is 29:20 the scornful o is consumed
Is 29:23 and hallow the Holy O of Jacob
Is 30:11 cause the Holy O of Israel to
Is 30:12 says the Holy O of Israel
Is 30:15 GOD, the Holy O of Israel
Is 30:17 O thousand shall flee at the
Is 30:17 shall flee at the threat of o
Is 30:29 as when o goes with a flute
Is 30:29 to the Mighty O of Israel
Is 31: 1 look to the Holy O of Israel
Is 33:20 not o of its stakes will ever
Is 34:10 no o shall pass through it
Is 34:15 every o with her mate
Is 34:16 not o of these shall fail
Is 34:16 not o shall lack her mate
Is 36: 9 How then will you repel o
Is 36:16 every o of you eat from his
Is 36:16 every o from his own fig tree
Is 36:16 and every o of you drink the
Is 36:18 Has any o of the gods of
Is 37:16 the O who dwells between the
Is 37:23 Against the Holy O of Israel
Is 37:36 of the Assyrians o hundred
Is 40: 3 The voice of o crying in the
Is 40:25 I be equal?" says the Holy O
Is 40:26 not o is missing
Is 41: 2 Who raised up o from the east
Is 41:14 the Holy O of Israel
Is 41:16 glory in the Holy O of Israel
Is 41:20 and the Holy O of Israel has
Is 41:25 raised up o from the north
Is 41:26 there is no o who shows,
Is 41:26 there is no o who declares
Is 41:26 surely there is no o who
Is 41:27 o who brings good tidings
Is 42: 1 My Elect O in whom My soul
Is 42:22 for prey, and no o delivers
Is 42:22 for plunder, and no o says,
Is 43: 3 the Holy O of Israel, your
Is 43:13 there is no o who can deliver
Is 43:14 the Holy O of Israel
Is 43:15 I am the LORD, your Holy O
Is 44: 5 O will say, I am the LORD's'
Is 44: 8 I know not o
Is 44:12 tongs works o in the coals
Is 44:13 he marks o out with chalk
Is 44:19 no o considers in his heart,
Is 45:11 the Holy O of Israel, and his
Is 46: 7 Though o cries out to it, yet
Is 47: 4 name, the Holy O of Israel
Is 47: 8 there is no o else besides me
Is 47: 9 to you in a moment, in o day
Is 47:10 you have said, No o sees me'
Is 47:10 there is no o else besides me
Is 47:15 wander each o to his quarter
Is 47:15 no o shall save you
Is 48:17 the Holy O of Israel
Is 49: 7 of Israel, their Holy O, to
Is 49: 7 the Holy O of Israel
Is 49:26 the Mighty O of Jacob
Is 51:10 Are you not the O who dried
Is 51:18 There is no o to guide her
Is 53: 6 we have turned, every o, to
Is 54: 5 is the Holy O of Israel
Is 54:11 O you afflicted o, tossed
Is 55: 5 God, and the Holy O of Israel
Is 56:11 every o for his own gain,
Is 56:12 Come," o says, "I will
Is 57: 1 while no o considers that the
Is 57: 2 beds, each o walking in his
Is 57:14 And o shall say, Heap it up
Is 57:15 Lofty O Who inhabits eternity
Is 59: 4 No o calls for justice, nor
Is 60: 9 and to the Holy O of Israel
Is 60:14 Zion of the Holy O of Israel
Is 60:15 so that no o went through you
Is 60:16 the Mighty O of Jacob
Is 60:22 A little o shall become a
Is 60:22 a small o a strong nation
Is 63: 1 this O who is glorious in His
Is 63: 2 and Your garments like o who
Is 63: 3 the peoples no o was with Me
Is 63: 5 but there was no o to help
Is 63: 5 that there was no o to uphold
Is 64: 4 Who acts for the o who waits
Is 64: 7 there is no o who calls on
Is 65: 8 o says, 'Do not destroy it,
Is 65:20 shall die o hundred years old
Is 65:20 old, but the sinner being o
Is 66: 2 But on this o will I look
Is 66: 4 no o answered, when I spoke
Is 66: 8 made to give birth in o day
Is 66:13 As o whom his mother comforts
Is 66:23 from o New Moon to another
Is 66:23 from o Sabbath to another,
Jer 1:15 each o set his throne at the
Jer 2: 6 a land that no o crossed and
Jer 2: 6 crossed and where no o dwelt
Jer 3:14 o from a city and two from a
Jer 4: 4 so that no o can quench it
Jer 5: 8 every o neighed after his
Jer 5:26 in wait as o who sets snares
Jer 6: 3 Each o shall pasture in his
Jer 7:33 no o will frighten them away
Jer 8: 4 Will o turn away and not
Jer 9: 8 o speaks peaceably to his
Jer 9:10 so that no o can pass through
Jer 9:12 so that no o can pass through
Jer 9:22 and no o shall gather them
Jer 10: 3 for o cuts a tree from the
Jer 10:20 There is no o to pitch my
Jer 12:11 because no o takes it to
Jer 12:12 from o end of the land to the
Jer 13:14 dash them o against another
Jer 13:19 up, and no o shall open them
Jer 14: 9 like a mighty o who cannot
Jer 14:16 will have no o to bury them
Jer 15:10 every o of them curses me
Jer 16:12 each o walks according to the
Jer 16:12 so that no o listens to Me
Jer 18:11 Return now every o from his
Jer 18:12 and we will every o do the
Jer 19:11 as o breaks a potter's vessel
Jer 20:11 me as a mighty, awesome o
Jer 21:12 so that no o can quench it
Jer 23:14 so that no o turns back from
Jer 23:30 every o from his neighbor
Jer 23:35 Thus every o of you shall say
Jer 23:35 every o to his brother, What
Jer 24: 2 O basket had very good figs,
Jer 25:26 far and near, o with another
Jer 25:33 o end of the earth even to
Jer 28: 9 as o whom the LORD has truly
Jer 30:10 no o shall make him afraid
Jer 30:13 There is no o to plead your
Jer 30:14 the chastisement of a cruel o
Jer 30:16 every o of them, shall go
Jer 30:17 no o seeks her
Jer 31: 8 the o who labors with child,
Jer 31:11 hand of o stronger than he
Jer 31:30 But every o shall die for his
Jer 32:39 then I will give them o heart
Jer 32:39 o way, that they may fear Me
Jer 34: 9 that no o should keep a
Jer 34:10 that no o should keep them in
Jer 34:16 every o of you brought back
Jer 34:17 every o to his brother and
Jer 34:17 and every o to his neighbor
Jer 35: 2 into o of the chambers, and
Jer 36:16 in fear from o to another
Jer 36:19 let no o know where you are
Jer 36:30 He shall have no o to sit on
Jer 38: 7 o of the eunuchs, who was in
Jer 38:24 Let no o know of these words,
Jer 40:15 and no o will know it
Jer 41: 4 when as yet no o knew it
Jer 41: 9 was the same o Asa the king
Jer 44: 2 and no o dwells in them,
Jer 46:16 yes, o fell upon another
Jer 46:27 No o shall make him afraid
Jer 48: 8 No o shall escape
Jer 48:33 no o will tread with joyous
Jer 48:35 o who offers sacrifices in
Jer 48:40 o shall fly like an eagle, and
Jer 49: 5 no o will gather those who
Jer 49:12 And are you the o who will
Jer 49:18 No o shall abide there, nor
Jer 49:33 no o shall reside there, nor
Jer 50: 3 and no o shall dwell therein
Jer 50:29 against the Holy O of Israel
Jer 50:32 and no o will raise him up
Jer 50:40 So no o shall reside there,
Jer 51: 5 against the Holy O of Israel
Jer 51: 6 and every o save his life
Jer 51:31 O runner will run to meet
Jer 51:31 o messenger to meet another,
Jer 51:43 a land where no o dwells
Jer 51:46 (a rumor will come o year
Jer 51:56 Every o of their bows is
Jer 52:20 o Sea, the twelve bronze
Jer 52:21 the height of o pillar was
Jer 52:22 the height of o capital was
Jer 52:23 the network, were o hundred
Lam 1: 4 no o comes to the set feasts
Lam 1: 7 with no o to help her, the
Lam 1:17 there is no o to comfort her
Lam 1:21 sigh, with no o to comfort me
Lam 3:26 It is good that o should hope
Lam 3:30 to the o who strikes him, and
Lam 4: 4 but no o breaks it for them
Lam 4:14 so that no o would touch
Ezek 1: 6 Each o had four faces, and

Ezek 1: 6 and each **o** had four wings
Ezek 1: 9 Their wings touched **o** another
Ezek 1: 9 but each **o** went straight
Ezek 1:11 of each **o** touched **o** another
Ezek 1:12 each **o** went straight forward
Ezek 1:17 any **o** of four directions
Ezek 1:23 straight, **o** toward another
Ezek 1:23 Each **o** had two which covered
Ezek 1:23 had two which covered **o** side
Ezek 1:23 each **o** had two which covered
Ezek 1:28 I heard a voice of **O** speaking
Ezek 3:13 that touched **o** another, and
Ezek 4: 8 **o** side to another till you
Ezek 4: 9 put them into **o** vessel, and
Ezek 4:17 and be dismayed with **o** another
Ezek 7:13 no **o** will strengthen himself
Ezek 7:14 but no **o** goes to battle
Ezek 9: 2 **O** man among them was clothed
Ezek 10: 9 **o** wheel by **o** cherub and
Ezek 10: 9 **o** wheel by **o** cherub and
Ezek 10:14 Each **o** had four faces
Ezek 10:17 when **o** was lifted up, the
Ezek 10:21 Each **o** had four faces and each
Ezek 10:21 each **o** four wings, and the
Ezek 11:19 Then I will give them **o** heart
Ezek 13:10 **o** builds a boundary wall, and
Ezek 14:10 of the **o** who inquired,
Ezek 15: 7 They will go out from **o** fire
Ezek 16:34 because no **o** solicited you to
Ezek 17:22 I will take also **o** of the
Ezek 17:22 of its young twigs a tender **o**
Ezek 18: 7 has robbed no **o** by violence
Ezek 18:30 every **o** according to his ways
Ezek 18:32 in the death of **o** who dies
Ezek 19: 3 She brought up **o** of her cubs
Ezek 20:39 Go, serve every **o** of you his
Ezek 22: 6 each **o** has used his power to
Ezek 22:11 **O** commits abomination with
Ezek 22:30 but I found no **o**
Ezek 23: 2 the daughters of **o** mother
Ezek 23:32 cup, the deep and wide **o**
Ezek 24:16 of your eyes with **o** stroke
Ezek 24:23 and mourn with **o** another
Ezek 24:26 on that day **o** who escapes
Ezek 26:17 O **o** inhabited by seafaring
Ezek 30:22 his arms, both the strong **o**
Ezek 30:22 **o** and the **o** that was broken
Ezek 31:11 the mighty **o** of the nations
Ezek 33:20 I will judge every **o** of you
Ezek 33:21 that **o** who had escaped from
Ezek 33:24 saying, 'Abraham was only **o**
Ezek 33:26 you defile **o** another's wives
Ezek 33:27 and the **o** who is in the open
Ezek 33:28 that no **o** will pass through
Ezek 33:30 and they speak to **o** another
Ezek 33:32 of **o** who has a pleasant voice
Ezek 34: 6 no **o** was seeking or searching
Ezek 34:23 I will establish **o** shepherd
Ezek 34:28 no **o** shall make them afraid
Ezek 35: 7 off from it the **o** who leaves
Ezek 35: 7 leaves and the **o** who returns
Ezek 37:17 Then join them **o** to another
Ezek 37:17 for yourself into **o** stick
Ezek 37:17 will become **o** in your hand
Ezek 37:19 Judah, and make them **o** stick
Ezek 37:19 and they will be **o** in My hand
Ezek 37:22 I will make them **o** nation in
Ezek 37:22 **o** king shall be king over
Ezek 37:24 shall all have **o** shepherd
Ezek 39: 7 LORD, the Holy **O** in Israel
Ezek 39:26 land and no **o** made them afraid
Ezek 40: 5 of the wall structure, **o** rod
Ezek 40: 5 and the height, **o** rod
Ezek 40: 6 gateway, which was **o** rod wide
Ezek 40: 6 threshold was **o** rod wide
Ezek 40: 7 **o** rod long and **o** rod wide
Ezek 40: 7 of the inside gate was **o** rod
Ezek 40: 8 of the inside gate, **o** rod
Ezek 40:10 three gate chambers on **o** side
Ezek 40:12 **o** cubit on this side
Ezek 40:12 and **o** cubit on that side
Ezek 40:13 gateway from the roof of **o**
Ezek 40:19 **o** hundred cubits toward the
Ezek 40:23 to gateway, **o** hundred cubits
Ezek 40:26 **o** on this side and **o** on that
Ezek 40:27 the south, **o** hundred cubits
Ezek 40:40 as **o** goes up to the entrance
Ezek 40:42 **o** cubit and a half long
Ezek 40:42 **o** cubit and a half wide, and
Ezek 40:42 a half wide, and **o** cubit high
Ezek 40:44 **o** facing south at the side of
Ezek 40:47 **o** hundred cubits long
Ezek 40:47 and **o** hundred cubits wide,
Ezek 40:49 **o** on this side and another on
Ezek 41: 1 six cubits wide on **o** side
Ezek 41: 6 **o** above the other, thirty
Ezek 41: 7 As **o** went up from story to
Ezek 41: 7 as **o** went up from the lowest
Ezek 41: 7 by way of the middle **o**
Ezek 41:11 **o** door toward the north and
Ezek 41:13 temple, **o** hundred cubits long
Ezek 41:13 and its walls was **o** hundred
Ezek 41:14 was **o** hundred cubits
Ezek 41:15 its galleries on the **o** side
Ezek 41:15 **o** hundred cubits, as well as
Ezek 41:19 toward a palm tree on **o** side
Ezek 41:21 the appearance of the **o** was
Ezek 41:24 two panels for **o** door and two
Ezek 41:26 and palm trees on **o** side and on
Ezek 42: 2 which was **o** hundred cubits
Ezek 42: 4 at a distance of **o** cubit
Ezek 42: 8 temple was **o** hundred cubits
Ezek 42: 9 as **o** goes into them from the
Ezek 42:12 as **o** enters them, there was a
Ezek 43:13 cubits (the cubit is **o** cubit
Ezek 43:13 the base **o** cubit high
Ezek 43:13 **o** cubit wide, with a rim all
Ezek 43:13 all around its edge of **o** span
Ezek 43:14 width of the ledge, **o** cubit
Ezek 43:14 width of the ledge, **o** cubit
Ezek 43:17 its base, **o** cubit all around
Ezek 45: 7 have a portion on **o** side and
Ezek 45: 7 with **o** of the tribal portions
Ezek 45:15 **o** lamb shall be given from a
Ezek 45:24 of **o** ephah for each bull and
Ezek 45:24 bull and **o** ephah for each ram,
Ezek 46: 5 shall be **o** ephah for a ram
Ezek 46:17 to **o** of his servants, it
Ezek 47: 3 he measured **o** thousand cubits
Ezek 47: 4 Again he measured **o** thousand
Ezek 47: 4 Again he measured **o** thousand
Ezek 47: 5 Again he measured **o** thousand
Ezek 47: 5 water in which **o** must swim
Ezek 47: 7 very many trees on **o** side
Ezek 47:14 it equally with **o** another
Ezek 47:15 Hethlon, as **o** goes to Zedad,
Ezek 47:20 **o** comes to a point opposite
Ezek 48: 1 there shall be **o** portion for
Ezek 48: 2 the west, **o** portion for Asher
Ezek 48: 3 west, **o** portion for Naphtali
Ezek 48: 4 west, **o** portion for Manasseh
Ezek 48: 5 west, **o** portion for Ephraim
Ezek 48: 6 west, **o** portion for Reuben
Ezek 48: 7 the west, **o** portion for Judah
Ezek 48: 8 as **o** of the other portions
Ezek 48:21 on **o** side and on the other of
Ezek 48:23 Benjamin shall have **o** portion
Ezek 48:24 Simeon shall have **o** portion
Ezek 48:25 Issachar shall have **o** portion
Ezek 48:26 Zebulun shall have **o** portion
Ezek 48:27 Gad shall have **o** portion
Ezek 48:31 **o** gate for Reuben
Ezek 48:31 **o** gate for Judah
Ezek 48:31 and **o** gate for Levi
Ezek 48:32 **o** gate for Joseph
Ezek 48:32 **o** gate for Benjamin
Ezek 48:32 and **o** gate for Dan
Ezek 48:33 **o** gate for Simeon
Ezek 48:33 **o** gate for Issachar
Ezek 48:33 and **o** gate for Zebulun
Ezek 48:34 **o** gate for Gad
Ezek 48:34 **o** gate for Asher
Ezek 48:34 and **o** gate for Naphtali
Dan 2: 9 there is only **o** decree for
Dan 2:43 will not adhere to **o** another
Dan 4:13 there was a watcher, a holy **o**
Dan 4:23 king saw a watcher, a holy **o**
Dan 4:35 no **o** can restrain His hand or
Dan 5:13 **o** of the captives from Judah
Dan 6: 1 over the kingdom **o** hundred
Dan 6: 2 of whom Daniel was **o**, that
Dan 6:13 who is **o** of the captives from
Dan 6:26 is the **o** which shall not be
Dan 7: 5 It was raised up on **o** side
Dan 7: 8 was another horn, a little **o**
Dan 7:13 **O** like the Son of Man, coming
Dan 7:14 His kingdom the **o** which shall
Dan 7:16 I came near to **o** of those who
Dan 8: 1 after the **o** that appeared to
Dan 8: 3 but **o** was higher than the
Dan 8: 3 the higher **o** came up last
Dan 8: 7 there was no **o** that could
Dan 8: 9 And out of **o** of them came a
Dan 8:13 I heard a holy **o** speaking
Dan 8:13 another holy **o** said to that
Dan 8:13 certain **o** who was speaking
Dan 8:15 there stood before me **o**
Dan 8:27 but no **o** understood it
Dan 9:27 covenant with many for **o** week
Dan 9:27 shall be **o** who makes desolate
Dan 10:13 **o** of the chief princes, came
Dan 10:16 **o** having the likeness of the
Dan 10:18 the **o** having the likeness of
Dan 10:21 (No **o** upholds me against
Dan 11: 5 as well as **o** of his princes
Dan 11: 7 **o** shall arise in his place
Dan 11:10 **o** shall certainly come and
Dan 11:16 no **o** shall stand against him
Dan 11:20 **o** who imposes taxes on the
Dan 11:45 end, and no **o** will help him
Dan 12: 1 every **o** who is found written
Dan 12: 5 **o** on this riverbank and the
Dan 12: 6 **o** said to the man clothed in
Dan 12:11 there shall be **o** thousand two
Dan 12:12 comes to the **o** thousand three
Hos 1:11 appoint for themselves **o** head
Hos 2:10 no **o** shall deliver her from
Hos 3: 2 shekels of silver, and **o** and
Hos 5:14 away, and no **o** shall rescue
Hos 11: 9 man, the Holy **O** in your midst
Hos 11:12 the Holy **O** who is faithful
Joel 2: 7 every **o** marches in formation,
Joel 2: 8 They do not push **o** another
Joel 2: 8 every **o** marches in his own
Joel 2:11 for strong is the **O** who
Amos 1: 5 the **o** who holds the scepter
Amos 1: 8 the **o** who holds the scepter
Amos 4: 3 each **o** straight ahead of her,
Amos 4: 7 I made it rain on **o** city, I
Amos 4: 7 **O** part was rained upon, and
Amos 5: 2 there is no **o** to raise her up
Amos 5: 6 with no **o** to quench it in
Amos 5:10 They hate the **o** who rebukes
Amos 5:10 they abhor the **o** who speaks
Amos 6: 9 if ten men remain in **o** house
Amos 6:10 with **o** who will burn the
Amos 6:10 he will say to **o** inside the
Amos 6:12 Does **o** plow there with oxen
Obad 7 No **o** is aware of it
Obad 11 even you were as **o** of them
Jon 1: 7 And they said to **o** another
Jon 3: 8 let every **o** turn from his
Jon 4: 2 **O** who relents from doing harm
Jon 4:11 which are more than **o** hundred
Mic 2: 4 In that day **o** shall take up a
Mic 2: 5 **o** to determine boundaries by
Mic 2:13 The **o** who breaks open will
Mic 4: 4 no **o** shall make them afraid
Mic 5: 2 the **O** to be ruler in Israel
Mic 5: 5 And this **O** shall be peace
Mic 7: 2 there is no **o** upright among
Nah 1:11 From you comes forth **o** who
Nah 1:15 For the wicked **o** shall no
Nah 2: 4 they jostle **o** another in the
Nah 2: 8 but no **o** turns back
Nah 2:11 cub, and no **o** made them afraid
Nah 3:18 and no **o** gathers them
Hab 1:12 O LORD my God, my Holy **O**
Hab 1:13 **o** more rightous than he
Hab 3: 3 the Holy **O** from Mount Paran
Zeph 2:11 each **o** from his place, indeed
Zeph 3: 6 there is no **o**, no inhabitant
Zeph 3: 9 to serve Him with **o** accord
Zeph 3:13 no **o** shall make them afraid
Zeph 3:17 in your midst, the Mighty **O**
Hag 1: 6 yourselves, but no **o** is warm
Hag 1: 9 while every **o** of you runs to
Hag 2:12 If **o** carries holy meat in the
Hag 2:13 If **o** who is unclean because
Hag 2:16 when **o** came to a heap of
Hag 2:16 when **o** came to the wine vat
Hag 2:22 every **o** by the sword of his
Zech 1:21 so that no **o** could lift up
Zech 3: 9 of that land in **o** day
Zech 4: 3 **o** at the right of the bowl and
Zech 4:11 trees, **o** at the right of the
Zech 5: 4 the house of the **o** who swears
Zech 6: 6 The **o** with the black horses
Zech 7:14 so that no **o** passed through
Zech 8: 4 each **o** with his staff in his

Zech 8:21 the inhabitants of **o** city
Zech 11: 7 the **o** I called Beauty, and the
Zech 11: 8 three shepherds in **o** month
Zech 12: 8 the **o** who is feeble among
Zech 12:10 as **o** mourns for his only son
Zech 12:10 grieve for Him as **o** grieves
Zech 13: 8 but **o** third shall be left in
Zech 13: 9 I will bring the **o** third
Zech 13: 9 each **o** will say, The LORD is
Zech 14: 7 It shall be **o** day which is
Zech 14: 9 LORD is **o**," and His name **o**
Mal 2: 3 **o** will take you away with it
Mal 2: 5 **o** of life and peace, and I gave
Mal 2:10 Have we not all **o** Father
Mal 2:10 Has not **o** God created us
Mal 2:10 **o** another by profaning the
Mal 2:15 But did He not make them **o**
Mal 2:15 of the Spirit? And why **o**?*
Mal 3:16 the LORD spoke to **o** another
Mal 3:18 between **o** who serves God and
Mal 3:18 and **o** who does not serve Him
Matt 3: 3 The voice of **o** crying in the
Matt 5:18 **o** jot or **o** tittle will by
Matt 5:19 **o** of the least of these
Matt 5:29 that **o** of your members perish
Matt 5:30 that **o** of your members perish
Matt 5:36 make **o** hair white or black
Matt 5:37 than these is from the evil **o**
Matt 5:41 compels you to go **o** mile, go
Matt 6:13 deliver us from the evil **o**
Matt 6:24 No **o** can serve two masters
Matt 6:24 for either he will hate the **o**
Matt 6:24 he will be loyal to the **o**
Matt 6:27 add **o** cubit to his stature
Matt 6:29 not arrayed like **o** of these
Matt 7:29 them as **o** having authority
Matt 8: 4 See that you tell no **o**
Matt 8: 9 And I say to this **o**, 'Go,' and
Matt 8:28 so that no **o** could pass that
Matt 9:16 No **o** puts a piece of unshrunk
Matt 9:30 See that no **o** knows it
Matt 10:29 not **o** of them falls to the
Matt 10:42 And whoever gives **o** of these
Matt 11: 3 Are You the Coming **O**, or do
Matt 11:11 risen **o** greater than John the
Matt 11:27 no **o** knows the Son except the
Matt 12: 6 is **O** greater than the temple
Matt 12:11 among you who has **o** sheep
Matt 12:22 Then **o** was brought to Him who
Matt 12:29 Or else how can **o** enter a
Matt 12:47 Then **o** said to Him, "Look,
Matt 12:48 said to the **o** who told Him,
Matt 13:19 it, then the wicked **o** comes
Matt 13:38 are the sons of the wicked **o**
Matt 13:46 when he had found **o** pearl of
Matt 16:14 Jeremiah or **o** of the prophets
Matt 16:20 no **o** that He was Jesus the
Matt 17: 4 **o** for You, **o** for Moses, and
Matt 17: 4 and **o** for Elijah
Matt 17: 8 they saw no **o** but Jesus only
Matt 17: 9 Tell the vision to no **o** until
Matt 18: 5 whoever receives **o** little
Matt 18: 6 But whoever causes **o** of these
Matt 18: 9 to enter into life with **o** eye
Matt 18:10 **o** of these little ones, for I
Matt 18:12 **o** of them goes astray, does
Matt 18:12 seek the **o** that is straying
Matt 18:14 who is in heaven that **o** of
Matt 18:16 take with you **o** or two more
Matt 18:24 **o** was brought to him who owed
Matt 18:28 out and found **o** of his fellow
Matt 19: 5 the two shall become **o** flesh'
Matt 19: 6 are no longer two but **o** flesh
Matt 19:16 **o** came and said to Him,
Matt 19:17 No **o** is good but **O**, that is
Matt 20: 7 him, 'Because no **o** hired us
Matt 20:12 men have worked only **o** hour
Matt 20:13 But he answered **o** of them
Matt 20:21 **o** on Your right hand and the
Matt 21:24 I also will ask you **o** thing
Matt 21:35 servants, beat **o**, killed **o**
Matt 22: 5 **o** to his own farm, another to
Matt 22:35 Then **o** of them, a lawyer,
Matt 22:46 no **o** was able to answer Him a
Matt 23: 4 them with **o** of their fingers
Matt 23: 8 for **O** is your Teacher, the
Matt 23: 9 for **O** is your Father, He who
Matt 23:10 for **O** is your Teacher, the
Matt 23:15 and sea to win **o** proselyte
Matt 23:37 the **o** who kills the prophets
Matt 24: 2 not **o** stone shall be left
Matt 24: 4 heed that no **o** deceives you
Matt 24:10 will betray **o** another, and
Matt 24:10 and will hate **o** another
Matt 24:31 from **o** end of heaven to the
Matt 24:36 that day and hour no **o** knows
Matt 24:40 **o** will be taken and the other
Matt 24:41 **o** will be taken and the other
Matt 25:15 to **o** he gave five talents, to
Matt 25:15 another two, and to another **o**
Matt 25:18 he who had received **o** went
Matt 25:24 received the **o** talent came
Matt 25:32 separate them **o** from another
Matt 25:40 to **o** of the least of these My
Matt 25:45 it to **o** of the least of these
Matt 26:14 Then **o** of the twelve, called
Matt 26:21 you, **o** of you will betray Me
Matt 26:40 you not watch with Me **o** hour
Matt 26:47 **o** of the twelve, with a great
Matt 26:48 Whomever I kiss, He is the **O**
Matt 26:51 **o** of those who were with
Matt 26:68 Who is the **o** who struck You
Matt 26:73 Surely you also are **o** of them
Matt 27:14 answered him not **o** word
Matt 27:15 **o** prisoner whom they wished
Matt 27:38 **o** on the right and another on
Matt 27:48 Immediately **o** of them ran
Mark 1: 3 The voice of **o** crying in the
Mark 1: 7 There comes **O** after me who is
Mark 1:22 them as **o** having authority
Mark 1:24 the Holy **O** of God
Mark 2:21 No **o** sews a piece of unshrunk
Mark 2:22 no **o** puts new wine into old
Mark 3:27 No **o** can enter a strong man's
Mark 4:41 and said to **o** another, "Who
Mark 5: 3 no **o** could bind him, not even
Mark 5:15 and saw the **o** who had been
Mark 5:22 **o** of the rulers of the
Mark 5:37 He permitted no **o** to follow
Mark 5:43 that no **o** should know it, and
Mark 6:15 or like **o** of the prophets
Mark 7:24 wanted no **o** to know it, but
Mark 7:32 brought to Him **o** who was deaf
Mark 7:36 that they should tell no **o**
Mark 8: 4 How can **o** satisfy these
Mark 8:14 **o** loaf with them in the boat
Mark 8:28 and others, **o** of the prophets
Mark 8:30 should tell no **o** about Him
Mark 9: 5 **o** for You, **o** for Moses,
Mark 9: 5 and **o** for Elijah
Mark 9: 8 around, they saw no **o** anymore
Mark 9: 9 no **o** the things they had seen
Mark 9:17 Then **o** from the multitude
Mark 9:26 And he became as **o** dead, so
Mark 9:37 Whoever receives **o** of these
Mark 9:39 for no **o** who works a miracle
Mark 9:42 whoever causes **o** of these
Mark 9:47 the kingdom of God with **o** eye
Mark 9:50 and have peace with **o** another
Mark 10: 8 the two shall become **o** flesh'
Mark 10: 8 no longer two, but **o** flesh
Mark 10:17 **o** came running, knelt before
Mark 10:18 No **o** is good but **O**, that is
Mark 10:21 to him, "**O** thing you lack
Mark 10:29 there is no **o** who has left
Mark 10:37 **o** on Your right hand and the
Mark 11: 2 tied, on which no **o** has sat
Mark 11:14 Let no **o** eat fruit from you
Mark 11:29 will also ask you **o** question
Mark 12: 6 Therefore still having **o** son
Mark 12:14 are true, and care about no **o**
Mark 12:28 Then **o** of the scribes came,
Mark 12:29 LORD our God, the LORD is **o**
Mark 12:32 the truth, for there is **o** God
Mark 12:34 And after that no **o** dared
Mark 12:42 Then **o** poor widow came and
Mark 13: 1 **o** of His disciples said to
Mark 13: 2 Not **o** stone shall be left
Mark 13: 5 heed that no **o** deceives you
Mark 13:32 that day and hour no **o** knows
Mark 14:10 **o** of the twelve, went to the
Mark 14:18 **o** of you who eats with Me
Mark 14:19 and to say to Him **o** by **o**
Mark 14:20 It is **o** of the twelve, who
Mark 14:37 Could you not watch **o** hour
Mark 14:43 **o** of the twelve, with a great
Mark 14:44 Whomever I kiss, He is the **O**
Mark 14:47 **o** of those who stood by drew
Mark 14:66 **o** of the servant girls of the
Mark 14:69 This is **o** of them
Mark 14:70 Surely you are **o** of them
Mark 15: 6 releasing **o** prisoner to them
Mark 15: 7 there was **o** named Barabbas,
Mark 15:27 **o** on His right and the other
Luke 1:28 Rejoice, highly favored **o**
Luke 1:35 that Holy **O** who is to be born
Luke 1:61 There is no **o** among your
Luke 2:15 shepherds said to **o** another
Luke 2:36 Now there was **o**, Anna, a
Luke 3: 4 The voice of **o** crying in the
Luke 3:16 but **O** mightier than I is
Luke 4:34 the Holy **O** of God
Luke 4:40 His hands on every **o** of them
Luke 5: 3 He got into **o** of the boats
Luke 5:14 He charged him to tell no **o**
Luke 5:36 No **o** puts a piece from a new
Luke 5:36 a new garment on an old **o**
Luke 5:37 no **o** puts new wine into old
Luke 5:39 And no **o**, having drunk old
Luke 6: 9 I will ask you **o** thing
Luke 6:11 discussed with **o** another what
Luke 6:29 strikes you on the **o** cheek
Luke 7: 4 saying that the **o** for whom He
Luke 7: 8 And I say to **o**, 'Go,' and he
Luke 7:19 Are You the Coming **O**, or do
Luke 7:20 saying, 'Are You the Coming **O**
Luke 7:32 and calling to **o** another,
Luke 7:36 Then **o** of the Pharisees asked
Luke 7:41 **O** owed five hundred denarii,
Luke 7:43 I suppose the **o** whom he
Luke 8:16 No **o**, when he has lit a lamp,
Luke 8:25 marveled, saying to **o** another
Luke 8:51 He permitted no **o** to go in
Luke 8:56 tell no **o** what had happened
Luke 9: 8 by others that **o** of the old
Luke 9:19 others say that **o** of the old
Luke 9:21 them to tell this to no **o**
Luke 9:33 **o** for You, **o** for Moses,
Luke 9:33 and **o** for Elijah
Luke 9:36 told no **o** in those days any
Luke 9:62 No **o**, having put his hand to
Luke 10: 4 greet no **o** along the road
Luke 10:22 no **o** knows who the Son is but
Luke 10:22 the **o** to whom the Son wills
Luke 10:42 But **o** thing is needed, and
Luke 11: 1 that **o** of His disciples said
Luke 11: 4 deliver us from the evil **o**
Luke 11:33 No **o**, when he has lit a lamp,
Luke 11:45 Then **o** of the lawyers
Luke 11:46 with **o** of your fingers
Luke 12: 1 that they trampled **o** another
Luke 12: 6 not **o** of them is forgotten
Luke 12:13 Then **o** from the crowd said to
Luke 12:25 add **o** cubit to his stature
Luke 12:27 not arrayed like **o** of these
Luke 12:52 in **o** house will be divided
Luke 13:10 Now He was teaching in **o** of
Luke 13:15 Does not each **o** of you on the
Luke 13:23 Then **o** said to Him, "Lord,
Luke 13:34 the **o** who kills the prophets
Luke 14: 1 of **o** of the rulers of the
Luke 14: 8 lest **o** more honorable than
Luke 14:15 Now when **o** of those who sat
Luke 14:18 But they all with **o** accord
Luke 15: 4 sheep, if he loses **o** of them
Luke 15: 4 go after the **o** which is lost
Luke 15: 7 **o** sinner who repents than
Luke 15: 8 coins, if she loses **o** coin
Luke 15:10 God over **o** sinner who repents
Luke 15:16 and no **o** gave him anything
Luke 15:19 Make me like **o** of your hired
Luke 15:26 So he called **o** of the
Luke 16: 5 So he called every **o** of his
Luke 16:13 for either he will hate the **o**
Luke 16:13 he will be loyal to the **o**
Luke 16:17 **o** tittle of the law to fail
Luke 16:30 but if **o** goes to them from
Luke 16:31 though **o** rise from the dead
Luke 17: 2 offend **o** of these little ones
Luke 17:15 Now **o** of them, when he saw
Luke 17:22 **o** of the days of the Son of
Luke 17:24 that flashes out of **o** part
Luke 17:31 likewise the **o** who is in the
Luke 17:34 will be two men in **o** bed
Luke 17:34 the **o** will be taken and the
Luke 17:35 the **o** will be taken and the
Luke 17:36 the **o** will be taken and the
Luke 18:10 **o** a Pharisee and the other a
Luke 18:19 No **o** is good but **O**, that is
Luke 18:22 You still lack **o** thing

Luke 18:29 there is no **o** who has left
Luke 19:30 on which no **o** has ever sat
Luke 19:44 in you **o** stone upon another
Luke 20: 1 happened on **o** of those days
Luke 20: 3 I will also ask you **o** thing
Luke 21: 6 **o** stone shall be left upon
Luke 22:27 among you as the **O** who serves
Luke 22:29 My Father bestowed **o** upon Me
Luke 22:36 him sell his garment and buy **o**
Luke 22:47 **o** of the twelve, went before
Luke 22:50 **o** of them struck the servant
Luke 23:14 as **o** who misleads the people
Luke 23:17 for him to release **o** to them
Luke 23:25 to them the **o** they requested
Luke 23:33 **o** on the right hand and the
Luke 23:39 Then **o** of the criminals who
Luke 23:53 where no **o** had ever lain
Luke 24:17 with **o** another as you walk
Luke 24:18 Then the **o** whose name was
Luke 24:32 And they said to **o** another
John 1:18 No **o** has seen God at any time
John 1:23 I am The voice of **o** crying
John 1:26 but there stands **O** among you
John 1:40 **O** of the two who heard John
John 3: 2 for no **o** can do these signs
John 3: 3 unless **o** is born again, he
John 3: 5 unless **o** is born of water and
John 3:13 No **o** has ascended to heaven
John 3:32 no **o** receives His testimony
John 4:18 the **o** whom you now have is
John 4:20 where **o** ought to worship
John 4:27 yet no **o** said, "What do You
John 4:33 disciples said to **o** another
John 4:37 **O** sows and another reaps
John 5:13 But the **o** who was healed did
John 5:22 For the Father judges no **o**
John 5:44 receive honor from **o** another
John 5:45 there is **o** who accuses you
John 6: 7 that every **o** of them may have
John 6: 8 **O** of His disciples, Andrew,
John 6:22 except that **o** which His
John 6:37 the **o** who comes to Me I will
John 6:44 No **o** can come to Me unless
John 6:50 that **o** may eat of it and not
John 6:65 no **o** can come to Me unless it
John 6:70 and **o** of you is a devil
John 6:71 Him, being **o** of the twelve
John 7: 4 For no **o** does anything in
John 7:13 no **o** spoke openly of Him for
John 7:18 of the **O** who sent Him is true
John 7:21 I did **o** work, and you all
John 7:27 no **o** knows where He is from
John 7:30 but no **o** laid a hand on Him,
John 7:44 but no **o** laid hands on Him
John 7:50 being **o** of them) said to them
John 8: 9 conscience, went out **o** by **o**
John 8:10 saw no **o** but the woman, He
John 8:10 Has no **o** condemned you
John 8:11 She said, "No **o**, Lord."
John 8:15 I judge no **o**
John 8:18 I am **O** who bears witness of
John 8:20 no **o** laid hands on Him, for
John 8:41 we have **o** Father
John 8:50 there is **O** who seeks and
John 9: 4 is coming when no **o** can work
John 9:25 **O** thing I know
John 9:32 eyes of **o** who was born blind
John 10:12 **o** who does not own the sheep,
John 10:16 and there will be **o** flock and
John 10:16 be **o** flock and **o** shepherd
John 10:18 No **o** takes it from Me, but I
John 10:21 words of **o** who has a demon
John 10:29 no **o** is able to snatch them
John 10:30 I and My Father are **o**
John 11:10 But if **o** walks in the night,
John 11:49 **o** of them, Caiaphas, being
John 11:50 that **o** man should die for the
John 11:52 in **o** the children of God who
John 12: 2 but Lazarus was **o** of those
John 12: 4 Then **o** of His disciples,
John 13:14 to wash **o** another's feet
John 13:21 you, **o** of you will betray Me
John 13:22 disciples looked at **o** another
John 13:23 bosom **o** of His disciples,
John 13:28 But no **o** at the table knew
John 13:34 you, that you love **o** another
John 13:34 that you also love **o** another
John 13:35 you have love for **o** another
John 14: 6 No **o** comes to the Father
John 15:12 that you love **o** another as I
John 15:13 love has no **o** than this, than
John 15:17 you, that you love **o** another
John 15:24 the works which no **o** else did
John 16:22 your joy no **o** will take from
John 17:11 that they may be **o** as We are
John 17:15 keep them from the evil **o**
John 17:21 that they all may be **o**, as
John 17:21 that they also may be **o** in Us
John 17:22 may be **o** just as We are **o**
John 17:23 they may be made perfect in **o**
John 18:14 that **o** man should die for the
John 18:17 You are not also **o** of this
John 18:22 **o** of the officers who stood
John 18:25 not also **o** of His disciples
John 18:26 **O** of the servants of the high
John 19:11 Therefore the **o** who delivered
John 19:18 **o** on either side, and Jesus in
John 19:23 woven from the top in **o** piece
John 19:34 But **o** of the soldiers pierced
John 19:36 Not **o** of His bones shall be
John 19:41 which no **o** had yet been laid
John 20:12 **o** at the head and the other at
John 20:24 **o** of the twelve, was not with
John 21:11 **o** hundred and fifty-three
John 21:20 who is the **o** who betrays You
John 21:25 if they were written **o** by **o**
Acts 1:14 with **o** accord in prayer and
Acts 1:20 and let no **o** live in it'
Acts 1:22 us, **o** of these must become a
Acts 2: 1 with **o** accord in **o** place
Acts 2: 3 and **o** sat upon each of them
Acts 2: 7 marveled, saying to **o** another
Acts 2:12 saying to **o** another
Acts 2:27 Your Holy **O** to see corruption
Acts 2:38 and let every **o** of you be
Acts 2:46 with **o** accord in the temple
Acts 3:14 But you denied the Holy **O**
Acts 3:26 in turning away every **o** of
Acts 4:24 voice to God with **o** accord
Acts 4:32 were of **o** heart and **o** soul
Acts 5:12 they were all with **o** accord
Acts 5:23 them, we found no **o** inside
Acts 5:25 Then **o** came and told them,
Acts 5:34 Then **o** in the council stood
Acts 7:24 seeing **o** of them suffer wrong
Acts 7:26 why do you wrong **o** another
Acts 7:35 is the **o** God sent to be a
Acts 7:38 the **o** who received the living
Acts 7:52 the coming of the Just **O**, of
Acts 7:57 and ran at him with **o** accord
Acts 8: 6 the multitudes with **o** accord
Acts 9: 7 a voice but seeing no **o**
Acts 9: 8 eyes were opened he saw no **o**
Acts 9:11 for **o** called Saul of Tarsus
Acts 10: 2 **o** who feared God with all his
Acts 10:22 **o** who fears God and has a good
Acts 10:28 or go to **o** of another nation
Acts 11:19 to no **o** but the Jews only
Acts 11:28 Then **o** of them, named Agabus,
Acts 12:10 out and went down **o** street
Acts 12:20 came to him with **o** accord
Acts 13:25 there comes **O** after me, the
Acts 13:35 Your Holy **O** to see corruption
Acts 13:41 though **o** were to declare it
Acts 15:25 being assembled with **o** accord
Acts 15:38 not take with them the **o** who
Acts 15:39 they parted from **o** another
Acts 17:23 the **O** whom you worship
Acts 17:26 And He has made from **o** blood
Acts 17:27 is not far from each **o** of us
Acts 18: 7 **o** who worshiped God, whose
Acts 18:10 no **o** will attack you to hurt
Acts 18:12 the Jews with **o** accord rose
Acts 19:29 the theater with **o** accord
Acts 19:32 Some therefore cried **o** thing
Acts 19:34 all with **o** voice cried out
Acts 19:38 charges against **o** another
Acts 21: 6 taken our leave of **o** another
Acts 21: 7 and stayed with them **o** day
Acts 21: 8 who was **o** of the seven, and
Acts 21:16 us and brought with them **o**
Acts 21:26 be made for each **o** of them
Acts 21:34 the multitude cried **o** thing
Acts 22:12 Then **o**, Ananias, a devout man
Acts 22:14 His will, and see the Just **O**
Acts 23: 6 that **o** part were Sadducees
Acts 23:17 Then Paul called **o** of the
Acts 23:22 Tell no **o** that you have
Acts 24:21 unless it is for this **o**
Acts 25:11 no **o** can deliver me to them
Acts 25:19 their own religion and about **o**
Acts 27: 1 prisoners to **o** named Julius
Acts 28: 4 hand, they said to **o** another
Acts 28:13 after **o** day the south wind
Acts 28:25 after Paul had said **o** word
Acts 28:31 no **o** forbidding him
Rom 1:27 in their lust for **o** another
Rom 2: 6 who "will render to each **o**
Rom 2:28 not a Jew who is **o** outwardly
Rom 2:29 he is a Jew who is **o** inwardly
Rom 3:10 is none righteous, no, not **o**
Rom 3:12 none who does good, no, not **o**
Rom 3:26 the justifier of the **o** who
Rom 3:30 since there is **o** God who will
Rom 5: 7 a righteous man will **o** die
Rom 5:12 just as through **o** man sin
Rom 5:15 For if by the **o** man's offense
Rom 5:15 by the grace of the **o** Man
Rom 5:16 came through the **o** who sinned
Rom 5:16 from **o** offense resulted in
Rom 5:17 For if by the **o** man's offense
Rom 5:17 death reigned through the **o**
Rom 5:17 reign in life through the **O**
Rom 5:18 as through **o** man's offense
Rom 5:18 even so through **o** Man's
Rom 5:19 For as by **o** man's
Rom 5:19 so also by **o** Man's obedience
Rom 7:21 the **o** who wills to do good
Rom 8:24 for why does **o** still hope for
Rom 9:10 also had conceived by **o** man
Rom 9:21 to make **o** vessel for honor
Rom 10:10 For with the heart **o** believes
Rom 12: 3 to each **o** a measure of faith
Rom 12: 4 have many members in **o** body
Rom 12: 5 are **o** body in Christ, and
Rom 12: 5 members of **o** another
Rom 12:10 Be kindly affectionate to **o**
Rom 12:10 preference to **o** another
Rom 12:16 same mind toward **o** another
Rom 12:17 Repay no **o** evil for evil
Rom 13: 8 Owe no **o** anything except to
Rom 13: 8 except to love **o** another, for
Rom 14: 1 Receive **o** who is weak in the
Rom 14: 2 For **o** believes he may eat all
Rom 14: 5 **O** person esteems **o** day
Rom 14: 7 and no **o** dies to himself
Rom 14:13 not judge **o** another anymore
Rom 14:15 the **o** for whom Christ died
Rom 14:19 by which **o** may edify another
Rom 15: 5 like-minded toward **o** another
Rom 15: 6 that you may with **o** mind and
Rom 15: 6 **o** mouth glorify the God and
Rom 15: 7 Therefore receive **o** another
Rom 15:14 also to admonish **o** another
Rom 16:16 Greet **o** another with a holy
1Co 2:11 Even so no **o** knows the things
1Co 2:15 is rightly judged by no **o**
1Co 3: 4 For when **o** says, "I am of
1Co 3: 5 as the Lord gave to each **o**
1Co 3: 8 plants and he who waters are **o**
1Co 3: 8 each **o** will receive his own
1Co 3:10 But let each **o** take heed how
1Co 3:18 Let no **o** deceive himself
1Co 3:21 let no **o** glory in men
1Co 4: 2 that **o** be found faithful
1Co 4: 6 behalf of **o** against the other
1Co 5: 5 deliver such a **o** to Satan for
1Co 6: 5 man among you, not even **o**
1Co 6: 7 go to law against **o** another
1Co 6:16 a harlot is **o** body with her
1Co 6:16 shall become **o** flesh
1Co 6:17 the Lord is **o** spirit with Him
1Co 7: 5 Do not deprive **o** another
1Co 7: 7 But each **o** has his own gift
1Co 7: 7 **o** in this manner and another
1Co 7:17 God has distributed to each **o**
1Co 7:17 as the Lord has called each **o**
1Co 7:20 Let each **o** remain in the same
1Co 7:24 let each **o** remain with God in
1Co 7:25 yet I give judgment as **o** whom
1Co 8: 3 God, this **o** is known by Him
1Co 8: 4 there is no other God but **o**
1Co 8: 6 for us there is only **o** God
1Co 8: 6 **o** Lord Jesus Christ, through
1Co 9:24 run, but **o** receives the prize
1Co 9:26 not as **o** who beats the air
1Co 10: 8 did, and in **o** day twenty-three
1Co 10:17 many, are **o** bread and **o** body
1Co 10:17 all partake of that **o** bread
1Co 10:24 Let no **o** seek his own, but

1Co 10:24 own, but each **o** the other's
1Co 10:28 sake of the **o** who told you
1Co 11: 5 her head, for that is **o** and
1Co 11:20 you come together in **o** place
1Co 11:21 each **o** takes his own supper
1Co 11:21 **o** is hungry and another is
1Co 11:33 to eat, wait for **o** another
1Co 12: 3 **o** speaking by the Spirit of
1Co 12: 3 no **o** can say that Jesus is
1Co 12: 7 each **o** for the profit of all
1Co 12: 8 for to **o** is given the word of
1Co 12:11 But **o** and the same Spirit
1Co 12:11 distributing to each **o**
1Co 12:12 For as the body is **o** and has
1Co 12:12 the members of that **o** body
1Co 12:12 are **o** body, so also is Christ
1Co 12:13 For by **o** Spirit we were all
1Co 12:13 were all baptized into **o** body
1Co 12:13 made to drink into **o** Spirit
1Co 12:14 body is not **o** member but many
1Co 12:18 each **o** of them, in the body
1Co 12:19 And if they were all **o** member
1Co 12:20 are many members, yet **o** body
1Co 12:25 the same care for **o** another
1Co 12:26 if **o** member suffers, all the
1Co 12:26 or if **o** member is honored,
1Co 14: 2 God, for no **o** understands him
1Co 14:23 comes together in **o** place
1Co 14:27 in turn, and let **o** interpret
1Co 14:31 you can all prophesy **o** by **o**
1Co 15: 8 as by **o** born out of due time
1Co 15:23 But each **o** in his own order
1Co 15:36 Foolish **o**, what you sow is
1Co 15:39 but there is **o** kind of flesh
1Co 15:40 glory of the celestial is **o**
1Co 15:41 There is **o** glory of the sun,
1Co 15:41 for **o** star differs from
1Co 16: 2 day of the week let each **o** of
1Co 16:11 let no **o** despise him
1Co 16:20 Greet **o** another with a holy
2Co 2: 2 who makes me glad but the **o**
2Co 2: 7 him, lest perhaps such a **o** be
2Co 2:10 I have forgiven that **o** for
2Co 2:16 To the **o** we are the aroma of
2Co 3:16 when **o** turns to the Lord, the
2Co 5:10 that each **o** may receive the
2Co 5:14 that if **O** died for all, then
2Co 5:16 we regard no **o** according to
2Co 7: 2 We have wronged no **o**
2Co 7: 2 we have corrupted no **o**
2Co 7: 2 we have defrauded no **o**
2Co 8:12 according to what **o** has, and
2Co 9: 7 So let each **o** give as he
2Co 11: 2 betrothed you to **o** husband
2Co 11: 9 need, I was a burden to no **o**
2Co 11:10 no **o** shall stop me from this
2Co 11:16 let no **o** think me a fool
2Co 11:20 if **o** brings you into bondage
2Co 11:20 if **o** devours you
2Co 11:20 if **o** takes from you
2Co 11:20 if **o** exalts himself
2Co 11:20 if **o** strikes you on the face
2Co 11:24 forty stripes minus **o**
2Co 12: 2 such a **o** was caught up to the
2Co 12: 5 Of such a **o** I will boast
2Co 13:11 of good comfort, be of **o** mind
2Co 13:12 Greet **o** another with a holy
Gal 3:11 But that no **o** is justified by
Gal 3:15 no **o** annuls or adds to it
Gal 3:16 as of many, but as of **o**
Gal 3:20 for **o** only, but God is **o**
Gal 3:28 you are all **o** in Christ Jesus
Gal 4:22 the **o** by a bondwoman, the
Gal 4:24 the **o** from Mount Sinai which
Gal 5:13 through love serve **o** another
Gal 5:14 law is fulfilled in **o** word
Gal 5:15 devour **o** another, beware lest
Gal 5:15 you be consumed by **o** another
Gal 5:17 are contrary to **o** another
Gal 5:26 provoking **o** another, envying
Gal 5:26 another, envying **o** another
Gal 6: 1 spiritual restore such a **o** in
Gal 6: 2 Bear **o** another's burdens, and
Gal 6: 4 But let each **o** examine his
Gal 6: 5 For each **o** shall bear his own
Gal 6:17 now on let no **o** trouble me
Eph 1:10 in **o** all things in Christ
Eph 2:14 peace, who has made both **o**
Eph 2:15 **o** new man from the two, thus
Eph 2:16 them both to God in **o** body
Eph 2:18 by **o** Spirit to the Father
Eph 4: 2 bearing with **o** another in
Eph 4: 4 There is **o** body and **o** Spirit
Eph 4: 4 in **o** hope of your calling
Eph 4: 5 **o** Lord, **o** faith, **o** baptism
Eph 4: 6 **o** God and Father of all, who
Eph 4: 7 But to each **o** of us grace was
Eph 4:10 who descended is also the **O**
Eph 4:25 each **o** speak truth with his
Eph 4:25 we are members of **o** another
Eph 4:32 And be kind to **o** another,
Eph 4:32 forgiving **o** another, just as
Eph 5: 6 Let no **o** deceive you with
Eph 5:19 speaking to **o** another in
Eph 5:21 submitting to **o** another in
Eph 5:29 For no **o** ever hated his own
Eph 5:31 the two shall become **o** flesh
Eph 5:33 Nevertheless let each **o** of
Eph 6:16 fiery darts of the wicked **o**
Phil 1:27 you stand fast in **o** spirit
Phil 1:27 with **o** mind striving together
Phil 2: 2 of **o** accord, of **o** mind
Phil 2:20 For I have no **o** like-minded
Phil 2:25 the **o** who ministered to my
Phil 3:13 but **o** thing I do, forgetting
Col 2:16 Therefore let no **o** judge you
Col 2:18 Let no **o** defraud you of your
Col 3: 9 Do not lie to **o** another,
Col 3:13 bearing with **o** another, and
Col 3:13 and forgiving **o** another, if
Col 3:15 you were called in **o** body
Col 3:16 and admonishing **o** another in
Col 4: 6 you ought to answer each **o**
Col 4: 9 brother, who is **o** of you
Col 4:12 Epaphras, who is **o** of you
1Th 2:11 and charged every **o** of you
1Th 3: 3 that no **o** should be shaken by
1Th 3:12 abound in love to **o** another
1Th 4: 6 that no **o** should take
1Th 4: 9 by God to love **o** another
1Th 4:18 Therefore comfort **o** another
1Th 5:11 edify **o** another, just as you
1Th 5:15 See that no **o** renders evil
2Th 1: 3 the love of every **o** of you
2Th 2: 3 Let no **o** deceive you by any
2Th 2: 8 lawless **o** will be revealed
2Th 2: 9 The coming of the lawless **o**
2Th 3: 3 and guard you from the evil **o**
1Ti 1: 8 is good if **o** uses it lawfully
1Ti 2: 5 there is **o** God and **o** Mediator
1Ti 3: 2 the husband of **o** wife,
1Ti 3: 4 **o** who rules his own house
1Ti 3:12 be the husbands of **o** wife
1Ti 4:12 Let no **o** despise your youth,
1Ti 5: 9 has been the wife of **o** man
2Ti 2: 4 No **o** engaged in warfare
2Ti 4:16 defense no **o** stood with me
Tit 1: 6 the husband of **o** wife,
Tit 1:12 **O** of them, a prophet of their
Tit 2: 8 that **o** who is an opponent may
Tit 2:15 Let no **o** despise you
Tit 3: 2 to speak evil of no **o**, to be
Tit 3: 3 hateful and hating **o** another
Phm 9 being such a **o** as Paul, the
Heb 2: 6 But **o** testified in a certain
Heb 2:11 being sanctified are all of **o**
Heb 3: 3 For this **O** has been counted
Heb 3:13 but exhort **o** another daily,
Heb 6:11 we desire that each **o** of you
Heb 6:13 could swear by no **o** greater
Heb 7:18 For on the **o** hand there is an
Heb 8: 3 this **O** also have something to
Heb 10:12 Man, after He had offered **o**
Heb 10:14 For by **o** offering He has
Heb 10:24 let us consider **o** another in
Heb 10:25 some, but exhorting **o** another
Heb 11:12 Therefore from **o** man, and him
Heb 12:14 without which no **o** will see
Heb 12:16 who for **o** morsel of food sold
Heb 13:14 but we seek the **o** to come
Jas 1:13 Let no **o** say when he is
Jas 1:14 But each **o** is tempted when he
Jas 1:25 this **o** will be blessed in
Jas 2: 3 **o** wearing the fine clothes
Jas 2:10 and yet stumble in **o** point
Jas 2:13 the **o** who has shown no mercy
Jas 2:16 and **o** of you says to them,
Jas 2:19 believe that there is **o** God
Jas 4:11 not speak evil of **o** another
Jas 4:12 There is **o** Lawgiver, who is
Jas 5: 9 not grumble against **o** another
Jas 5:16 your trespasses to **o** another
Jas 5:16 and pray for **o** another, that
1Pe 1:22 love **o** another fervently with
1Pe 2:19 toward God **o** endures grief
1Pe 3: 8 all of you be of **o** mind,
1Pe 3: 8 compassion for **o** another
1Pe 4: 8 fervent love for **o** another
1Pe 4: 9 Be hospitable to **o** another
1Pe 4:10 As each **o** has received a gift
1Pe 4:10 minister it to **o** another
1Pe 4:18 Now "If the righteous **o** is
1Pe 5: 5 be submissive to **o** another
1Pe 5:14 Greet **o** another with a kiss
2Pe 2: 5 **o** of eight people, a preacher
2Pe 3: 8 do not forget this **o** thing
2Pe 3: 8 that with the Lord **o** day is
2Pe 3: 8 and a thousand years as **o** day
1Jn 1: 7 fellowship with **o** another
1Jn 2:13 have overcome the wicked **o**
1Jn 2:14 have overcome the wicked **o**
1Jn 2:20 an anointing from the Holy **O**
1Jn 3: 7 let no **o** deceive you
1Jn 3:11 that we should love **o** another
1Jn 3:12 Cain who was of the wicked **o**
1Jn 3:23 love **o** another, as He gave us
1Jn 4: 7 let us love **o** another, for
1Jn 4:11 also ought to love **o** another
1Jn 4:12 No **o** has seen God at any time
1Jn 4:12 If we love **o** another, God
1Jn 5: 7 and these three are **o**
1Jn 5: 8 and these three agree as **o**
1Jn 5:18 the wicked **o** does not touch
1Jn 5:19 the sway of the wicked **o**
2Jn 5 that we love **o** another
Rev 1:13 **O** like the Son of Man,
Rev 2:17 no **o** knows except him who
Rev 2:23 I will give to each **o** of you
Rev 3: 7 no **o** shuts, and shuts and no
Rev 3: 7 and shuts and no **o** opens"
Rev 3: 8 door, and no **o** can shut it
Rev 3:11 that no **o** may take your crown
Rev 4: 2 and **O** sat on the throne
Rev 5: 3 And no **o** in heaven or on the
Rev 5: 4 because no **o** was found worthy
Rev 5: 5 But **o** of the elders said to
Rev 6: 1 Lamb opened **o** of the seals
Rev 6: 1 I heard **o** of the four living
Rev 6: 4 it was granted to the **o** who
Rev 6: 4 people should kill **o** another
Rev 7: 4 **O** hundred and forty-four
Rev 7: 9 which no **o** could number, of
Rev 7:13 Then **o** of the elders answered
Rev 9:12 **O** woe is past
Rev 11: 3 they will prophesy **o** thousand
Rev 11:10 and send gifts to **o** another
Rev 11:17 the **O** who is and who was and
Rev 12: 6 there **o** thousand two hundred
Rev 13: 3 I saw **o** of his heads as if it
Rev 13:17 that no **o** may buy or sell
Rev 13:17 **o** who has the mark or the
Rev 14: 1 Zion, and with Him **o** hundred
Rev 14: 3 no **o** could learn that song
Rev 14:14 on the cloud sat **O** like the
Rev 14:20 for **o** thousand six hundred
Rev 15: 7 Then **o** of the four living
Rev 15: 8 no **o** was able to enter the
Rev 16: 5 the **O** who is and who was and
Rev 17: 1 Then **o** of the seven angels
Rev 17:10 **o** is, and the other has not
Rev 17:12 for **o** hour as kings with the
Rev 17:13 These are of **o** mind, and they
Rev 17:17 His purpose, to be of **o** mind
Rev 18: 8 plagues will come in **o** day
Rev 18:10 For in **o** hour your judgment
Rev 18:11 over her, for no **o** buys their
Rev 18:17 For in **o** hour such great
Rev 18:19 For in **o** hour she is made
Rev 19:12 that no **o** knew except Himself
Rev 20:13 each **o** according to his works
Rev 21: 9 Then **o** of the seven angels
Rev 21:17 **o** hundred and forty-four
Rev 21:21 gate was of **o** pearl
Rev 22:12 to give to every **o** according

ONE-FIFTH

Gen 41:34 to collect **o** of the produce
Gen 47:24 you shall give **o** to Pharaoh
Gen 47:26 that Pharaoh should have **o**
Lev 5:16 thing, and shall add **o** to it
Lev 6: 5 add **o** more to it, and give it

Lev 22:14 to the priest, and add **o** to it
Lev 27:13 then he must add **o** to your
Lev 27:15 then he shall add **o** of the
Lev 27:19 then he must add **o** of the
Lev 27:27 and shall add **o** to it
Lev 27:31 tithes, he shall add **o** to it
Num 5: 7 in full value plus **o** of it
1Ki 6:31 doorposts were **o** of the wall

ONE-FOURTH
Ex 29:40 **o** of a hin of pressed oil
Ex 29:40 **o** of a hin of wine as a drink
Lev 23:13 shall be of wine, **o** of a hin
Num 15: 4 mixed with **o** of a hin of oil
Num 15: 5 **o** of a hin of wine as a drink
Num 23:10 Jacob, or number **o** of Israel
Num 28: 5 **o** of a hin of pressed oil
Num 28: 7 be **o** of a hin for each lamb
Num 28:14 ram, and **o** of a hin for a lamb
1Ki 6:33 of olive wood, **o** of the wall
2Ki 6:25 **o** of a kab of dove droppings
Neh 9: 3 their God for **o** of the day

ONE-HALF
Hos 3: 2 and one and **o** homers of barley

ONE'S (*see* PREFACE)

ONES (*see* PREFACE)

ONESELF (*see* PREFACE)

ONESIMUS
Col 4: 9 with **O**, a faithful and beloved
Phm 10 I appeal to you for my son **O**

ONESIPHORUS
2Ti 1:16 mercy to the household of **O**
2Ti 4:19 Aquila, and the household of **O**

ONE-SIXTH
Ezek 4:11 water by measure, **o** of a hin
Ezek 45:13 you shall give **o** of an ephah
Ezek 45:13 **o** of an ephah from a homer of

ONE-TENTH
Ex 16:36 Now an omer is **o** of an ephah
Ex 29:40 **o** of an ephah of flour mixed
Lev 5:11 bring for his offering **o** of
Lev 6:20 **o** of an ephah of fine flour
Lev 14:21 **o** of an ephah of fine flour
Num 5:15 **o** of an ephah of barley meal
Num 15: 4 **o** of an ephah of fine flour
Num 28: 5 **o** of an ephah of fine flour
Num 28:13 **o** of an ephah of fine flour,
Num 28:21 you shall offer **o** of an
Num 28:29 **o** for each of the seven lambs
Num 29: 4 **o** for each of the seven lambs
Num 29:10 **o** for each of the seven lambs
Num 29:15 **o** for each of the fourteen
Ezek 45:11 bath contains **o** of a homer
Ezek 45:11 and the ephah **o** of a homer
Ezek 45:14 is **o** of a bath from a kor

ONE-THIRD
Num 15: 6 mixed with **o** of a hin of oil
Num 15: 7 offering you shall offer **o** of
Num 28:14 **o** of a hin for a ram, and
2Ki 11: 5 **O** of you who come on duty on
2Ki 11: 6 **o** shall be at the gate of Sur
2Ki 11: 6 and **o** at the gate behind the
2Ch 23: 4 **O** of you entering on the
2Ch 23: 5 **o** shall be at the king's
2Ch 23: 5 and **o** at the Gate of the
Neh 10:32 **o** of a shekel for the service
Ezek 5: 2 **o** in the midst of the city
Ezek 5: 2 then you shall take **o** and
Ezek 5: 2 **o** you shall scatter in the
Ezek 5:12 **O** of you shall die of the
Ezek 5:12 **o** shall fall by the sword all

ONIONS
Num 11: 5 the melons, the leeks, the **o**

ONLY (*see* PREFACE)

ONO
1Ch 8:12 and Shemed, who built **O** and
Ezra 2:33 people of Lod, Hadid, and **O**
Neh 6: 2 villages in the plain of **O**
Neh 7:37 children of Lod, Hadid, and **O**
Neh 11:35 in Lod, **O**, and the Valley of

ONTO (*see* PREFACE)

ONWARD
Ex 40:36 went **o** in all their journeys
Num 15:23 **o** throughout your generations
Is 18: 2 from their beginning **o**, a
Is 18: 7 from their beginning **o**, a

ONYCHA
Ex 30:34 sweet spices, stacte and **o**

ONYX
Gen 2:12 and the **o** stone are there
Ex 25: 7 **o** stones, and stones to be set
Ex 28: 9 you shall take two **o** stones
Ex 28:20 the fourth row, a beryl, an **o**
Ex 35: 9 **o** stones, and stones to be
Ex 35:27 The rulers brought **o** stones
Ex 39: 6 And they set **o** stones,
Ex 39:13 the fourth row, a beryl, an **o**
1Ch 29: 2 **o** stones, stones to be set,
Job 28:16 in precious **o** or sapphire
Ezek 28:13 topaz, and diamond, beryl, **o**

OPEN (*see* OPENED, OPENING, OPENLY, OPENS)
Gen 19: 2 the night in the **o** square
Gen 38:14 sat in an **o** place which was
Ex 13:12 the LORD all that **o** the womb
Ex 13:15 all males that **o** the womb
Ex 34:19 All that **o** the womb are Mine,
Lev 14: 7 bird loose in the **o** field
Lev 14:53 the city in the **o** field, and
Lev 17: 5 they offer in the **o** field
Num 8:16 instead of all who **o** the womb
Num 19:15 every **o** vessel, which has no
Num 19:16 Whoever in the **o** field
Deut 15: 8 but you shall **o** your hand
Deut 15:11 You shall **o** your hand wide
Deut 20:11 **o** to you, then all the people
Deut 28:12 The LORD will **o** to you His
Josh 8:17 So they left the city **o** and
Josh 10:22 **O** the mouth of the cave, and
Judg 19:15 in the **o** square of the city
Judg 19:17 in the **o** square of the city
Judg 19:20 the night in the **o** square
2Sa 11:11 are encamped in the **o** fields
1Ki 6:18 ornamental buds and **o** flowers
1Ki 6:29 palm trees, and **o** flowers
1Ki 6:32 **o** flowers, and overlaid them
1Ki 6:35 and **o** flowers on them, and
1Ki 8:29 that Your eyes may be **o**
1Ki 8:52 that Your eyes may be **o** to
2Ki 6:17 **o** his eyes that he may see
2Ki 6:20 **o** the eyes of these men, that
2Ki 8:12 rip **o** their women with child
2Ki 9: 3 Then **o** the door and flee,
2Ki 13:17 said, "**O** the east window"
2Ki 15:16 they did not **o** it to him,
2Ki 15:16 were with child he ripped **o**
2Ki 19:16 **o** Your eyes, O LORD, and see
2Ch 6:20 that Your eyes may be **o**
2Ch 6:40 I pray, let Your eyes be **o**
2Ch 7:15 Now My eyes will be **o** and My
2Ch 32: 6 the **o** square of the city gate
Ezra 10: 9 all the people sat in the **o**
Neh 1: 6 be attentive and Your eyes **o**
Neh 6: 5 with an **o** letter in his hand
Neh 8: 1 together as one man in the **o**
Neh 8: 3 **o** square that was in front of
Neh 8:16 in the **o** square of the Water
Neh 8:16 in the **o** square of the Gate
Job 11: 5 and **o** His lips against you,
Job 14: 3 do You **o** Your eyes on such a
Job 28: 4 He breaks **o** a shaft away from
Job 29: 7 took my seat in the **o** square
Job 32:20 I must **o** my lips and answer
Job 33: 2 Now, I **o** my mouth
Job 34:26 men in the **o** sight of others
Job 41:14 Who can **o** the doors of his
Ps 5: 9 Their throat is an **o** tomb
Ps 34:15 His ears are **o** to their cry
Ps 38:13 mute who does not **o** his mouth
Ps 39: 9 mute, I did not **o** my mouth
Ps 51:15 **o** my lips, And my mouth shall
Ps 74:15 You broke **o** the fountain and
Ps 77: 4 You hold my eyelids **o**
Ps 78: 2 I will **o** my mouth in a
Ps 81:10 **O** your mouth wide, and I will
Ps 104:28 You **o** Your hand, they are
Ps 118:19 **O** to me the gates of
Ps 119:18 **O** my eyes, that I may see
Ps 145:16 You **o** Your hand And satisfy
Prov 1:20 her voice in the **o** squares
Prov 7:12 at times in the **o** square
Prov 13:16 but a fool lays **o** his folly
Prov 20:13 **o** your eyes, and you will be
Prov 24: 7 he does not **o** his mouth in
Prov 27: 5 **O** rebuke is better than love
Prov 31: 8 **O** your mouth for the
Prov 31: 9 **O** your mouth, judge
Song 5: 2 **O** for me, my sister, my love,
Song 5: 5 I arose to **o** for my beloved,
Song 7:12 the grape blossoms are **o**, and
Is 9:12 devour Israel with an **o** mouth
Is 14:17 who did not **o** the house of
Is 22:22 so he shall **o**, and no one
Is 22:22 shall shut, and no one shall **o**
Is 24:18 windows from on high are **o**
Is 24:19 broken, the earth is split **o**
Is 26: 2 **O** the gates, that the
Is 37:17 **o** Your eyes, O LORD, and see
Is 41:18 I will **o** rivers in desolate
Is 42: 7 To **o** blind eyes, to bring out
Is 45: 1 to **o** before him the double
Is 45: 8 let the earth **o**, let them
Is 60:11 gates shall be **o** continually
Jer 5: 1 seek in her **o** places if you
Jer 5:16 quiver is like an **o** tomb
Jer 9:22 fall as refuse on the **o** field
Jer 13:19 up, and no one shall **o** them
Jer 32:11 custom, and that which was **o**
Jer 32:14 and this deed which is **o**, and
Jer 32:19 for your eyes are **o** to all
Jer 50:26 **o** her storehouses; cast her
Ezek 2: 8 **o** your mouth and eat what I
Ezek 3:27 I will **o** your mouth, and you
Ezek 16: 5 thrown out into the **o** field
Ezek 16:63 never **o** your mouth anymore
Ezek 29: 5 you shall fall on the **o** field
Ezek 29:21 I will **o** your mouth to speak
Ezek 30:16 pain, no shall be split **o**
Ezek 32: 4 cast you out on the **o** fields
Ezek 33:27 the one who is in the **o** field
Ezek 36: 5 to plunder its **o** country
Ezek 37: 2 very many in the **o** valley
Ezek 37:12 I will **o** your graves and cause
Ezek 39: 5 You shall fall on the **o** field
Ezek 45: 2 around it for an **o** space
Dan 6:10 windows **o** toward Jerusalem
Dan 9:18 **o** Your eyes and see our
Hos 4:16 like a lamb in **o** country
Hos 13: 8 I will tear **o** their rib cage,
Hos 13:16 women with child ripped **o**
Joel 1:19 has devoured the **o** pastures
Joel 1:20 has devoured the **o** pastures
Joel 2:22 for the **o** pastures are
Amos 1:13 because they ripped **o** the
Mic 2:13 The one who breaks **o** will
Nah 3:13 are wide **o** for your enemies
Zech 11: 1 **O** your doors, O Lebanon, that
Zech 12: 4 I will **o** My eyes on the house
Mal 3:10 If I will not **o** for you the
Matt 13:35 I will **o** My mouth in parables
Matt 25:11 saying, 'Lord, Lord, **o** to us
Luke 7:14 came and touched the **o** coffin
Luke 12:36 and knocks they may **o** to him
Luke 13:25 **o** for us,' and He will answer
John 1:51 you shall see heaven **o**, and
John 9:26 How did He **o** your eyes
John 10:21 Can a demon **o** the eyes of the
Acts 1:18 he burst **o** in the middle and
Acts 12:14 she did not **o** the gate, but
Acts 16:27 and seeing the prison doors **o**
Acts 18:14 Paul was about to **o** his mouth
Acts 19:38 anyone, the courts are **o** and
Acts 26:18 to **o** their eyes and to turn
Rom 3:13 Their throat is an **o** tomb
2Co 6:11 to you, our heart is wide **o**
2Co 6:13 to children), you also be **o**
2Co 7: 2 **O** your hearts to us
Eph 6:19 that I may **o** my mouth boldly
Col 4: 3 that God would **o** to us a door
Heb 4:13 **o** to the eyes of Him to whom
Heb 6: 6 God, and put Him to an **o** shame
1Pe 3:12 and his ears are **o** to their
Rev 3: 8 have set before you an **o** door
Rev 4: 1 a door standing **o** in heaven
Rev 5: 2 Who is worthy to **o** the scroll
Rev 5: 3 was able to **o** the scroll, or
Rev 5: 4 no one was found worthy to **o**
Rev 5: 5 has prevailed to **o** the scroll
Rev 5: 9 the scroll, and to **o** its seals
Rev 10: 2 a little book **o** in his hand
Rev 10: 8 is **o** in the hand of the angel

OPENED (*see* OPEN)
Gen 3: 5 eat of it your eyes will be **o**
Gen 3: 7 eyes of both of them were **o**
Gen 4:11 which has **o** its mouth to
Gen 7:11 the windows of heaven were **o**
Gen 8: 6 that Noah **o** the window of the
Gen 21:19 God **o** her eyes, and she saw a
Gen 29:31 was unloved, He **o** her womb
Gen 30:22 listened to her and **o** her womb
Gen 41:56 Joseph **o** all the storehouses
Gen 42:27 But as one of them **o** his sack
Gen 43:21 that we **o** our sacks, and there
Gen 44:11 ground, and each **o** his sack
Ex 2: 6 And when she had **o** it, she saw
Num 16:32 and the earth **o** its mouth and
Num 22:28 Then the LORD **o** the mouth of
Num 22:31 Then the LORD **o** Balaam's eyes
Num 24: 3 of the man whose eyes are **o**
Num 24: 4 falls down, with eyes **o** wide
Num 24:15 of the man whose eyes are **o**
Num 24:16 falls down, with eyes **o** wide
Num 26:10 and the earth **o** its mouth and
Deut 11: 6 how the earth **o** its mouth
Judg 3:25 still he had not **o** the doors
Judg 3:25 they took the key and **o** them
Judg 4:19 So she **o** a jug of milk,
Judg 19:27 **o** the doors of the house and
1Sa 3:15 **o** the doors of the house of
2Ki 4:35 and the child **o** his eyes
2Ki 6:17 Then the LORD **o** the eyes of
2Ki 6:20 the LORD **o** their eyes, and
2Ki 9:10 And he **o** the door and fled
2Ki 13:17 and he **o** it
2Ch 29: 3 he **o** the doors of the house
Neh 7: 3 be **o** until the sun is hot
Neh 8: 5 Ezra **o** the book in the sight
Neh 8: 5 and when he **o** it, all the
Neh 13:19 that they must not be **o** till
Job 3: 1 After this Job **o** his mouth
Job 29:23 they **o** their mouth wide as
Job 31:32 for I have **o** my doors to the
Ps 35:21 They also **o** their mouth wide
Ps 40: 6 My ears You have **o**
Ps 78:23 And **o** the doors of heaven,
Ps 105:41 He **o** the rock, and water
Ps 106:17 The earth **o** up and swallowed
Ps 109: 2 deceitful Have **o** against me
Ps 119:131 I **o** my mouth and panted, For I
Song 5: 6 I **o** for my beloved, but my
Is 5:14 **o** its mouth beyond measure
Is 10:14 nor **o** his mouth with even a
Is 35: 5 eyes of the blind shall be **o**
Is 48: 8 long ago your ear was not **o**
Is 50: 5 The Lord GOD has **o** My ear
Is 53: 7 yet He **o** not His mouth
Is 53: 7 silent, so He **o** not his mouth
Jer 50:25 The LORD has **o** His armory
Lam 2:16 All your enemies have **o** their
Lam 3:46 All our enemies have **o** their
Ezek 1: 1 that the heavens were **o** and I
Ezek 3: 2 So I **o** my mouth, and He caused
Ezek 24:27 be **o** to him who has escaped
Ezek 33:22 And He had **o** my mouth
Ezek 33:22 the morning, my mouth was **o**
Ezek 37:13 when I have **o** your graves
Ezek 41:11 chambers **o** on the terrace
Ezek 44: 2 it shall not be **o**, and no man
Ezek 46: 1 on the Sabbath it shall be **o**
Ezek 46: 1 of the New Moon it shall be **o**
Ezek 46:12 east shall then be **o** for him
Dan 7:10 seated, and the books were **o**
Dan 10:16 then I **o** my mouth and spoke,
Nah 2: 6 The gates of the rivers are **o**
Zech 13: 1 be **o** for the house of David
Matt 2:11 And when they had **o** their
Matt 3:16 the heavens were **o** to Him
Matt 5: 2 Then He **o** His mouth and taught
Matt 7: 7 knock, and it will be **o** to you
Matt 7: 8 him who knocks it will be **o**
Matt 9:30 And their eyes were **o**
Matt 17:27 And when you have **o** its mouth
Matt 20:33 Lord, that our eyes may be **o**
Matt 27:52 and the graves were **o**
Mark 7:34 Ephphatha," that is, "Be **o**."
Mark 7:35 Immediately his ears were **o**
Luke 1:64 Immediately his mouth was **o**
Luke 3:21 He prayed, the heaven was **o**
Luke 4:17 And when He had **o** the book
Luke 11: 9 knock, and it will be **o** to you
Luke 11:10 him who knocks it will be **o**
Luke 24:31 Then their eyes were **o** and
Luke 24:32 while He **o** the Scriptures to
Luke 24:45 He **o** their understanding,
John 9:10 How were your eyes **o**
John 9:14 made the clay and **o** his eyes
John 9:17 Him because He **o** your eyes
John 9:21 or who **o** his eyes we do not
John 9:30 from, and yet He has **o** my eyes
John 9:32 **o** the eyes of one who was
John 11:37 who **o** the eyes of the blind,
Acts 5:19 the Lord **o** the prison doors
Acts 5:23 but when we **o** them, we found
Acts 7:56 I see the heavens **o** and the
Acts 8:32 so He **o** not His mouth
Acts 8:35 Then Philip **o** his mouth, and
Acts 9: 8 his eyes were **o** he saw no one
Acts 9:40 she **o** her eyes, and when she
Acts 10:11 and saw heaven **o** and an object
Acts 10:34 Then Peter **o** his mouth and
Acts 12:10 which **o** to them of its own
Acts 12:16 and when they **o** the door and
Acts 14:27 that He had **o** the door of
Acts 16:14 The Lord **o** her heart to heed
Acts 16:26 all the doors were **o** and
1Co 16: 9 and effective door has **o** to me
2Co 2:12 a door was **o** to me by the
Rev 6: 1 the Lamb **o** one of the seals
Rev 6: 3 When He **o** the second seal, I
Rev 6: 5 When He **o** the third seal, I
Rev 6: 7 When He **o** the fourth seal, I
Rev 6: 9 When He **o** the fifth seal, I
Rev 6:12 when He **o** the sixth seal, and
Rev 8: 1 When He **o** the seventh seal,
Rev 9: 2 he **o** the bottomless pit, and
Rev 11:19 temple of God was **o** in heaven
Rev 12:16 and the earth **o** its mouth
Rev 13: 6 Then he **o** his mouth in
Rev 15: 5 the testimony in heaven was **o**
Rev 19:11 Then I saw heaven **o**, and
Rev 20:12 before God, and books were **o**
Rev 20:12 And another book was **o**, which

OPENING (*see* OPEN, OPENINGS)
Ex 28:32 There shall be an **o** for his
Ex 28:32 binding all around its **o**,
Ex 28:32 like the **o** in a coat of mail,
Ex 39:23 there was an **o** in the middle
Ex 39:23 like the **o** in a coat of mail,
Ex 39:23 binding all around the **o**, so
1Ki 7:31 Its **o** inside the crown at the
1Ki 7:31 the **o** was round, shaped like
1Ki 7:31 also on the **o** were engravings
1Ch 9:27 charge of **o** it every morning
Prov 8: 6 from the **o** of my lips will
Is 42:20 **o** the ears, but he does not
Is 61: 1 the **o** of the prison to those
Acts 27:12 a harbor of Crete **o** toward
Jas 3:11 and bitter from the same **o**

OPENINGS (*see* OPENING)
Neh 4:13 parts of the wall, at the **o**
Prov 1:21 at the **o** of the gates in the

OPENLY (*see* OPEN)
Gen 38:21 who was **o** by the roadside
Ps 98: 2 His righteousness He has **o**
Matt 6: 4 will Himself reward you **o**
Matt 6: 6 in secret will reward you **o**
Matt 6:18 in secret will reward you **o**
Mark 1:45 no longer **o** enter the city
Mark 8:32 He spoke this word **o**
John 7: 4 himself seeks to be known **o**
John 7:10 went up to the feast, not **o**
John 7:13 no one spoke **o** of Him for
John 11:54 walked **o** among the Jews, but
John 18:20 him, "I spoke **o** to the world
Acts 10:40 third day, and showed Him **o**
Acts 16:37 They have beaten us **o**,
2Co 6:11 We have spoken **o** to you, our

OPENS (*see* OPEN)
Ex 13: 2 whatever **o** the womb among the
Ex 21:33 And if a man **o** a pit, or if a
Num 3:12 of every firstborn who **o** the
Num 16:30 and the earth **o** its mouth
Num 18:15 first **o** the womb of all flesh
Job 27:19 he **o** his eyes, and he is no
Job 33:16 Then He **o** the ears of men, and
Job 35:16 Therefore Job **o** his mouth in
Job 36:10 He also **o** their ear to
Job 36:15 **o** their ears in oppression
Ps 146: 8 The LORD **o** the eyes of the
Prov 13: 3 but he who **o** wide his lips
Prov 31:26 She **o** her mouth with wisdom,
Luke 2:23 Every male who **o** the womb
John 10: 3 To him the doorkeeper **o**, and
Rev 3: 7 the key of David, He who **o**
Rev 3: 7 shuts, and shuts and no one **o**"
Rev 3:20 **o** the door, I will come in to

OPERATION
Ps 28: 5 Nor the **o** of His hands, He
Is 5:12 consider the **o** of His hands

OPHEL
2Ch 27: 3 extensively on the wall of **O**
2Ch 33:14 and it enclosed **O**, and he
Neh 3:26 the Nethinim who dwelt in **O**
Neh 3:27 and as far as the wall of **O**
Neh 11:21 But the Nethinim dwelt in **O**

OPHIR
Gen 10:29 **O**, Havilah, and Jobab
1Ki 9:28 And they went to **O**, and
1Ki 10:11 which brought gold from **O**
1Ki 10:11 and precious stones from **O**
1Ki 22:48 ships to go to **O** for gold
1Ch 1:23 **O**, Havilah, and Jobab
1Ch 29: 4 of gold, of the gold of **O**
2Ch 8:18 the servants of Solomon to **O**
2Ch 9:10 who brought gold from **O**,
Job 22:24 and the gold of **O** among the
Job 28:16 be valued in the gold of **O**
Ps 45: 9 the queen in gold from **O**
Is 13:12 than the golden wedge of **O**

OPHNI
Josh 18:24 Chephar Haammoni, **O**, and

OPHRAH (*see* APHRAH)
Josh 18:23 Avim, Parah, **O**,
Judg 6:11 terebinth tree which was in **O**
Judg 6:24 still in **O** of the Abiezrites
Judg 8:27 and set it up in his city, **O**
Judg 8:32 in **O** of the Abiezrites
Judg 9: 5 to his father's house at **O**
1Sa 13:17 to the road that leads to **O**
1Ch 4:14 and Meonothai who begot **O**

OPINION (*see* OPINIONS)
Job 32: 6 dared not declare my **o** to you
Job 32:10 me, I also will declare my **o**
Job 32:17 part, I too will declare my **o**
Rom 11:25 should be wise in your own **o**
Rom 12:16 Do not be wise in your own **o**

OPINIONS (*see* OPINION)
1Ki 18:21 will you falter between two **o**

OPPONENT (*see* OPPONENT'S)
2Sa 2:16 one grasped his **o** by the head
Tit 2: 8 who is an **o** may be ashamed

OPPONENT'S (*see* OPPONENT)
2Sa 2:16 his sword in his **o** side

OPPORTUNE (*see* OPPORTUNITY)
Mark 6:21 Then an **o** day came when Herod
Luke 4:13 from Him until an **o** time

OPPORTUNITY (*see* OPPORTUNE)
Judg 9:33 then do to them as you find **o**
Matt 26:16 he sought **o** to betray Him
Luke 22: 6 sought **o** to betray Him to
Acts 25:16 has **o** to answer for himself
Rom 7: 8 taking **o** by the commandment,
2Co 5:12 but give you **o** to glory on
2Co 11:12 that I may cut off the **o** from
2Co 11:12 from those who desire an **o** to
Gal 5:13 liberty as an **o** for the flesh
Gal 6:10 Therefore, as we have **o**, let
Phil 4:10 did care, but you lacked **o**
1Ti 5:14 give no **o** to the adversary to
Heb 11:15 would have had **o** to return

OPPOSE (*see* OPPOSED, OPPOSES)
Job 30:21 of Your hand You **o** me
Dan 8:12 to **o** the daily sacrifices
Zech 3: 1 at his right hand to **o** him

OPPOSED (*see* OPPOSE)
Ex 32:29 for every man has **o** his son
Ezra 10:15 the son of Tikvah **o** this, and
Acts 13:45 they **o** the things spoken by
Acts 18: 6 But when they **o** him and

OPPOSES (*see* OPPOSE)
2Th 2: 4 who **o** and exalts himself above

OPPOSITE (*see* OPPOSITION)
Gen 15:10 placed each piece **o** the other
Gen 21:16 So she sat **o** him, and lifted
Ex 14: 2 and the sea, **o** Baal Zephon
Deut 1: 1 in the plain **o** Suph, between
Deut 3:29 in the valley **o** Beth Peor
Deut 4:46 in the valley **o** Beth Peor
Deut 11:30 dwell in the plain **o** Gilgal
Deut 34: 6 the land of Moab, **o** Beth Peor
Josh 3:16 people crossed over **o** Jericho
Josh 5:13 a Man stood **o** him with His
Judg 19:10 to a place **o** Jebus (that is
1Sa 14: 5 faced northward **o** Michmash
1Sa 14: 5 the other southward **o** Gibeah
1Sa 26: 1 Hachilah, which is **o** Jeshimon
1Sa 26: 3 Hachilah, which is **o** Jeshimon
2Sa 16:13 went along the hillside **o** him
1Ki 7: 4 window was **o** window in three
1Ki 7: 5 window was **o** window in three
1Ki 20:29 they encamped **o** each other
1Ch 26:16 watchman **o** watchman
2Ch 7: 6 sounded trumpets **o** them,
Neh 3:23 made repairs **o** their house
Neh 3:25 made repairs **o** the buttress
Neh 12:38 choir went the **o** way, and I
Esth 9: 1 the **o** occurred, in that the
Ezek 16:34 You are the **o** of other women
Ezek 16:34 you, therefore you are the **o**
Ezek 40:23 was **o** the northern gateway
Ezek 41:16 **o** the threshold were paneled
Ezek 42: 1 **o** the separating courtyard
Ezek 42: 1 and which was **o** the building
Ezek 42: 3 **O** the inner court of twenty
Ezek 42: 3 **o** the pavement of the outer
Ezek 42:10 **o** the separating courtyard and
Ezek 42:10 courtyard and **o** the building
Ezek 42:13 which are **o** the separating
Ezek 46: 9 go out through the **o** gate
Ezek 47:20 one comes to a point **o** Hamath
Ezek 48:13 **O** the border of the priests,
Dan 5: 5 wrote **o** the lampstand on the
Matt 21: 2 Go into the village **o** you
Matt 27:61 Mary, sitting **o** the tomb
Mark 11: 2 Go into the village **o** you
Mark 12:41 Now Jesus sat **o** the treasury
Mark 13: 3 Mount of Olives **o** the temple
Mark 15:39 centurion, who stood **o** Him
Luke 8:26 Gadarenes, which is **o** Galilee
Luke 19:30 Go into the village **o** you
Acts 20:15 and the next day came **o** Chios

OPPOSITION (*see* OPPOSITE)
2Ti 2:25 correcting those who are in **o**

OPPRESS (*see* OPPRESSED, OPPRESSES, OPPRESSING, OPPRESSION, OPPRESSOR)
Ex 3: 9 which the Egyptians **o** them
Ex 22:21 mistreat a stranger nor **o** him
Ex 23: 9 you shall not **o** a stranger
Lev 25:14 you shall not **o** one another
Lev 25:17 you shall not **o** one another
Deut 23:16 you shall not **o** him
Deut 24:14 You shall not **o** a hired
2Sa 7:10 of wickedness **o** them anymore
1Ch 17: 9 of wickedness **o** them anymore
Job 10: 3 good to You that You should **o**
Job 37:23 He does not **o**
Ps 10:18 of the earth may **o** no more
Ps 17: 9 From the wicked who **o** me,
Ps 119:122 Do not let the proud **o** me
Prov 22:22 nor **o** the afflicted at the
Is 49:26 I will feed those who **o** you
Jer 7: 6 if you do not **o** the stranger
Jer 30:20 I will punish all who **o** them
Ezek 22:29 wrongfully **o** the stranger
Ezek 45: 8 shall no more **o** My people
Hos 12: 7 he loves to **o**
Amos 4: 1 who **o** the poor, who crush the
Mic 2: 2 So they **o** a man and his house,
Hab 2: 7 they not awaken who **o** you
Zech 7:10 Do not **o** the widow or the
Acts 7: 6 **o** them four hundred years
Jas 2: 6 Do not the rich **o** you and drag

OPPRESSED (*see* OPPRESS)
Deut 28:29 you shall be only **o** and
Deut 28:33 labor, and you shall be only **o**
Judg 2:18 because of those who **o** them
Judg 4: 3 **o** the children of Israel
Judg 6: 9 of the hand of all who **o** you
Judg 10: 8 **o** the children of Israel for
Judg 10:12 Amalekites and Maonites **o** you
1Sa 10:18 and from those who **o** you
1Sa 12: 3 Whom have I **o**, or from whose
1Sa 12: 4 have not defrauded us or **o** us
2Ki 13: 4 the king of Syria **o** them
2Ki 13:22 Hazael king of Syria **o** Israel
2Ch 16:10 Asa **o** some of the people at
Neh 9:27 of their enemies, who **o** them
Job 20:19 For he has **o** and forsaken the
Job 36: 6 but gives justice to the **o**
Ps 9: 9 will be a refuge for the **o**
Ps 10:18 to the fatherless and the **o**
Ps 74:21 not let the **o** return ashamed
Ps 76: 9 all the **o** of the earth
Ps 103: 6 And justice for all who are **o**
Ps 106:42 Their enemies also **o** them
Ps 146: 7 executes justice for the **o**
Eccl 4: 1 The tears of the **o**, but they
Is 3: 5 The people will be **o**, every
Is 9: 1 afterward more heavily **o** her
Is 23:12 O you **o** virgin daughter of
Is 38:14 O LORD, I am **o**
Is 52: 4 then the Assyrian **o** them
Is 53: 7 He was **o** and He was afflicted,
Is 58: 6 burdens, to let the **o** go free
Jer 50:33 The children of Israel were **o**
Ezek 18: 7 if he has not **o** anyone, but
Ezek 18:12 if he has **o** the poor and needy
Ezek 18:16 has not **o** anyone, nor
Ezek 18:18 father, because he cruelly **o**
Ezek 22: 7 they have **o** the stranger
Hos 5:11 Ephraim is **o** and broken in
Amos 3: 9 midst, and the **o** within her
Luke 4:18 at liberty those who are **o**
Acts 7:19 **o** our forefathers, making
Acts 7:24 and avenged him who was **o**, and
Acts 10:38 all who were **o** by the devil
2Pe 2: 7 who was **o** with the filthy

OPPRESSES (*see* OPPRESS)
Num 10: 9 against the enemy who **o** you
Ps 56: 1 Fighting all day he **o** me
Prov 14:31 He who **o** the poor reproaches
Prov 22:16 He who **o** the poor to increase
Prov 28: 3 A poor man who **o** the poor is

OPPRESSING (*see* OPPRESS)
Jer 46:16 our nativity from the **o** sword
Jer 50:16 For fear of the **o** sword
Zeph 3: 1 and polluted, to the **o** city

OPPRESSION (*see* OPPRESS, OPPRESSIONS)
Ex 3: 7 I have surely seen the **o** of
Ex 3: 9 I have also seen the **o** with
Deut 26: 7 and our labor and our **o**
2Ki 13: 4 for He saw the **o** of Israel
Job 36:15 and opens their ears in **o**
Ps 10: 7 of cursing and deceit and **o**
Ps 12: 5 For the **o** of the poor, for
Ps 42: 9 because of the **o** of the enemy
Ps 43: 2 because of the **o** of the enemy
Ps 44:24 our affliction and our **o**
Ps 55: 3 of the **o** of the wicked
Ps 62:10 Do not trust in **o**, Nor vainly
Ps 72:14 will redeem their life from **o**
Ps 73: 8 speak wickedly concerning **o**
Ps 107:39 and brought low Through **o**,
Ps 119:134 Redeem me from the **o** of man
Eccl 4: 1 considered all the **o** that is
Eccl 5: 8 If you see the **o** of the poor
Eccl 7: 7 Surely **o** destroys a wise
Is 5: 7 for justice, but behold, **o**
Is 30:12 this word, and trust in **o** and
Is 54:14 you shall be far from **o**, for
Is 59:13 from our God, speaking **o** and
Jer 6: 6 She is full of **o** in her midst
Jer 22:17 blood, and practicing **o** and
Acts 7:34 the **o** of my people who are in

OPPRESSIONS (*see* OPPRESSION)
Job 35: 9 multitude of **o** they cry out
Is 33:15 he who despises the gain of **o**
Ezek 22:29 of the land have used **o**,

OPPRESSOR (*see* OPPRESS, OPPRESSORS)
Job 3:18 not hear the voice of the **o**
Job 15:20 of years is hidden from the **o**
Ps 72: 4 And will break in pieces the **o**
Prov 3:31 Do not envy the **o**, and choose
Prov 28:16 understanding is a great **o**
Prov 29:13 the **o** have this in common
Is 1:17 seek justice, reprove the **o**
Is 9: 4 shoulder, the rod of his **o**
Is 14: 4 How the **o** has ceased, the
Is 51:13 because of the fury of the **o**
Is 51:13 And where is the fury of the **o**
Jer 21:12 out of the hand of the **o**,
Jer 22: 3 out of the hand of the **o**
Jer 25:38 of the fierceness of the **O**
Zech 9: 8 No more shall an **o** pass

OPPRESSORS (*see* OPPRESSOR)
Job 6:23 Redeem me from the hand of **o**'
Job 27:13 God, and the heritage of **o**
Ps 54: 3 **o** have sought after my life
Ps 119:121 Do not leave me to my **o**
Eccl 4: 1 of their **o** there was power
Is 3:12 people, children are their **o**
Is 14: 2 were, and rule over their **o**
Is 16: 4 the **o** are consumed out of the
Is 19:20 to the LORD because of the **o**

OR (*see* PREFACE)

ORACLE (*see* ORACLES)
Num 23: 7 And he took up his **o** and said
Num 23:18 Then he took up his **o** and said
Num 24: 3 Then he took up his **o** and said
Num 24:15 Then he took up his **o** and said
Num 24:20 Amalek, and he took up his **o**
Num 24:21 Kenites, and he took up his **o**
Num 24:23 Then he took up his **o** and said
2Sa 16:23 had inquired at the **o** of God
Ps 36: 1 An **o** within my heart
Jer 23:33 What is the **o** of the LORD
Jer 23:33 then say to them, 'What **o**
Jer 23:34 who say, 'The **o** of the LORD
Jer 23:36 the **o** of the LORD you shall
Jer 23:36 man's word will be his **o**, for
Jer 23:38 you say, 'The **o** of the LORD
Jer 23:38 word, "The **o** of the LORD
Jer 23:38 not say, 'The **o** of the LORD

ORACLES (*see* ORACLE)
2Ch 24:27 the many **o** about him, and the
Acts 7:38 the living **o** to give to us
Rom 3: 2 were committed the **o** of God
Heb 5:12 principles of the **o** of God
1Pe 4:11 let him speak as the **o** of God

ORATION (*see* ORATOR)
Acts 12:21 throne and gave an **o** to them

ORATOR (*see* ORATION)
Acts 24: 1 a certain **o** named Tertullus

ORCHARD (*see* ORCHARDS)
Song 4:13 Your plants are an **o** of

ORCHARDS (*see* ORCHARD)
Eccl 2: 5 I made myself gardens and **o**

ORDAIN (*see* ORDAINED)
1Co 7:17 so I **o** in all the churches

ORDAINED (*see* ORDAIN)
Num 28: 6 burnt offering which was **o** at
1Ki 12:32 Jeroboam **o** a feast on the
1Ki 12:33 he **o** a feast for the children
2Ki 23: 5 **o** to burn incense on the high
Ps 8: 2 infants You have **o** strength
Ps 8: 3 the stars, which You have **o**
Jer 1: 5 and I **o** you a prophet to the
Acts 10:42 that it is He who was **o** by
Acts 17:31 by the Man whom He has **o**
1Co 2: 7 God **o** before the ages for our

ORDER (*see* ORDERED, ORDERLY, ORDERS, WELL-ORDERED)
Gen 18:19 in **o** that he may command his
Gen 22: 9 there and placed the wood in **o**
Gen 50:20 in **o** to bring it about as it
Ex 8:22 in **o** that you may know that I
Ex 39:37 lamps (the lamps set in **o**)
Ex 40: 4 that are to be set in **o** on it
Ex 40:23 he set the bread in **o** upon it
Lev 1: 7 lay the wood in **o** on the fire
Lev 1: 8 the fat in **o** on the wood that
Lev 1:12 priest shall lay them in **o** on
Lev 6:12 the burnt offering in **o** on it
Lev 24: 8 Sabbath he shall set it in **o**
Num 10:28 Thus was the **o** of march of
Deut 13: 5 because he has spoken in **o** to
Deut 17:10 to all that they **o** you
Josh 2: 6 she had laid in **o** on the roof
Judg 6:11 in **o** to hide it from the
Judg 14:15 us in **o** to take what is ours

1Sa 21: 6 in **o** to put hot bread in its
2Sa 17:23 he put his household in **o**
1Ki 18:33 And he put the wood in **o**, cut
1Ki 20:14 Who will set the battle in **o**
2Ki 20: 1 Set your house in **o**, for you
2Ki 23: 4 the priests of the second **o**
1Ch 6:32 office according to their **o**
1Ch 15:13 Him about the proper **o**
1Ch 25: 2 to the **o** of the king
2Ch 8:14 according to the **o** of David
2Ch 13: 3 in **o** with an army of valiant
2Ch 13:11 in **o** on the pure table, and
2Ch 29:35 of the LORD was set in **o**
2Ch 32:31 in **o** to test him, that He
Ezra 6:21 in **o** to seek the LORD God of
Neh 8:13 in **o** to understand the words
Esth 1:11 in **o** to show her beauty to
Job 10:22 of death, without any **o**,
Job 33: 5 set your words in **o** before me
Job 33:17 In **o** to turn man from his
Ps 40: 5 be recounted to You in **o**
Ps 50:21 set them in **o** before your
Ps 110: 4 to the **o** of Melchizedek
Eccl 12: 9 out and set in **o** many proverbs
Is 9: 7 and over His kingdom, to **o** it
Is 38: 1 Set your house in **o**, for you
Is 44: 7 it and set it in **o** for Me,
Jer 46: 3 **O** the buckler and shield, and
Ezek 36: 5 in **o** to plunder its open
Ezek 39:12 in **o** to cleanse the land
Ezek 39:14 ground, in **o** to cleanse it
Dan 4:17 in **o** that the living may know
Matt 12:44 it empty, swept, and put in **o**
Luke 1: 1 taken in hand to set in **o** a
Luke 1: 8 God in the **o** of his division
Luke 11:25 he finds it swept and put in **o**
Luke 20:20 in **o** to deliver Him to the
Acts 11: 4 them in **o** from the beginning
Acts 18:23 of Galatia and Phrygia in **o**
1Co 11:34 I will set in **o** when I come
1Co 14:40 be done decently and in **o**
1Co 15:23 But each one in his own **o**
Col 2: 5 rejoicing to see your good **o**
Tit 1: 5 that you should set in **o** the
Heb 5: 6 to the **o** of Melchizedek"
Heb 5:10 to the **o** of Melchizedek,"
Heb 6:20 to the **o** of Melchizedek
Heb 7:11 to the **o** of Melchizedek, and
Heb 7:11 according to the **o** of Aaron
Heb 7:17 to the **o** of Melchizedek
Heb 7:21 to the **o** of Melchizedek' ")
Heb 10:24 another in **o** to stir up love

ORDERED (*see* ORDER)
Gen 43:17 Then the man did as Joseph **o**
1Sa 21: 2 The king has **o** me on some
2Sa 16:11 for so the LORD has **o** him
2Sa 23: 5 **o** in all things and secure
Esth 1: 8 for so the king had **o** all the
Ps 37:23 a good man are **o** by the LORD
Ezek 21:16 wherever your edge is **o**
Acts 22:24 the commander **o** him to be

ORDERLY (*see* ORDER)
Ex 13:18 of Israel went up in **o** ranks
Luke 1: 3 to write to you an **o** account
Acts 21:24 that you yourself also walk **o**

ORDERS (*see* ORDER)
2Sa 14: 8 I will give **o** concerning you
2Sa 18: 5 captains **o** concerning Absalom
Ezra 8:36 **o** to the king's satraps and
Ps 50:23 And to him who **o** his conduct
Acts 20:13 for so he had given **o**,
1Co 16: 1 as I have given **o** to the

ORDINANCE (*see* ORDINANCES)
Ex 12:14 a feast by an everlasting **o**
Ex 12:17 as an everlasting **o**
Ex 12:24 this thing as an **o** for you
Ex 12:43 This is the **o** of the Passover
Ex 13:10 shall therefore keep this **o**
Ex 15:25 a statute and an **o** for them
Lev 18:30 Therefore you shall keep My **o**
Lev 22: 9 shall therefore keep My **o**
Num 9:14 you shall have one **o**, both
Num 10: 8 an **o** forever throughout your
Num 15:15 One **o** shall be for you of
Num 15:15 an **o** forever throughout your
Num 15:24 offering, according to the **o**
Num 18: 8 and your sons, as an **o** forever
Num 18:11 with you, as an **o** forever
Num 18:19 with you as an **o** forever
Num 19: 2 This is the **o** of the law
Num 29: 6 according to their **o**, as a
Num 29:18 number, according to the **o**
Num 29:21 number, according to the **o**
Num 29:24 number, according to the **o**
Num 29:27 number, according to the **o**
Num 29:30 number, according to the **o**
Num 29:33 number, according to the **o**
Num 29:37 number, according to the **o**
Num 31:21 This is the **o** of the law
Josh 24:25 a statute and an **o** in Shechem
1Sa 30:25 an **o** for Israel to this day
1Ch 23:31 to the **o** governing them,
1Ch 24:19 **o** by the hand of Aaron their
2Ch 2: 4 This is an **o** forever to
2Ch 35:13 with fire according to the **o**
Ezra 3: 4 required by **o** for each day
Ezra 3:10 according to the **o** of David
Ps 99: 7 and the **o** that He gave them
Is 24: 5 the laws, changed the **o**,
Is 58: 2 forsake the **o** of their God
Ezek 45:14 The **o** concerning oil, the
Ezek 46:14 offering is a perpetual **o**
Mal 3:14 is it that we have kept His **o**
Rom 13: 2 resists the **o** of God, and
1Pe 2:13 **o** of man for the Lord's sake

ORDINANCES (*see* ORDINANCE)
Lev 18: 3 nor shall you walk in their **o**
Lev 18: 4 My judgments and keep My **o**
Num 9:12 According to all the **o** of the
2Ki 17:34 their statutes or their **o**
2Ki 17:37 And the statutes, the **o**, the
2Ch 19:10 against statutes or **o**, you
2Ch 33: 8 the **o** by the hand of Moses
Ezra 7:10 teach statutes and **o** in Israel
Neh 1: 7 nor the **o** which You
Neh 9:13 heaven, and gave them just **o**
Neh 10:29 the LORD our Lord, and His **o**
Neh 10:32 Also we made **o** for ourselves,
Neh 10:35 And we made **o** to bring the
Job 38:33 you know the **o** of the heavens
Ps 119:43 For I have hoped in Your **o**
Ps 119:91 this day according to Your **o**
Is 58: 2 ask of Me the **o** of justice
Jer 31:35 and the **o** of the moon and the
Jer 31:36 If those **o** depart from before
Jer 33:25 not appointed the **o** of heaven
Ezek 43:11 entire design and all its **o**
Ezek 43:11 its whole design and all its **o**
Ezek 43:18 These are the **o** for the
Ezek 44: 5 **o** of the house of the LORD
Mal 3: 7 you have gone away from My **o**
Luke 1: 6 and **o** of the Lord blameless
Eph 2:15 commandments contained in **o**
Heb 9: 1 had **o** of divine service and
Heb 9:10 fleshly **o** imposed until the

ORDINARY
Jer 31: 5 plant and eat them as **o** food

ORE
Job 28: 2 and copper is smelted from **o**
Job 28: 3 recess for **o** in the darkness

OREB
Judg 7:25 princes of the Midianites, **O**
Judg 7:25 killed **O** at the rock of **O**
Judg 7:25 and brought the heads of **O**
Judg 8: 3 the princes of Midian, **O** and
Ps 83:11 Make their nobles like **O** and
Is 10:26 of Midian at the rock of **O**

OREN
1Ch 2:25 the firstborn, and Bunah, **O**

ORIGIN
Ezek 29:14 to the land of their **o**, and

ORIGINAL (*see* ORIGINALLY)
2Ch 24:13 of God to its **o** condition

ORIGINALLY (*see* ORIGINAL)
1Co 14:36 word of God come **o** from you

ORION
Job 9: 9 He made the Bear, **O**, and the
Job 38:31 or loose the belt of **O**
Amos 5: 8 He made the Pleiades and **O**

ORNAMENT (*see* ORNAMENTAL, ORNAMENTS)
Prov 4: 9 on your head an **o** of grace
Prov 25:12 an **o** of fine gold is a wise
Is 30:22 the **o** of your molded images
Is 49:18 with them all as an **o**, and
1Pe 3: 4 incorruptible **o** of a gentle

ORNAMENTAL (*see* ORNAMENT)
Ex 25:31 its **o** knobs, and flowers shall
Ex 25:33 on one branch, with an **o** knob
Ex 25:33 other branch, with an **o** knob
Ex 25:34 each with its **o** knob and
Ex 37:17 its **o** knobs, and its flowers
Ex 37:19 on one branch, with an **o** knob
Ex 37:19 other branch, with an **o** knob
Ex 37:20 each with its **o** knob and
1Ki 6:18 was cedar, carved with **o** buds
1Ki 7:24 below its brim were **o** buds
1Ki 7:24 The **o** buds were cast in two

ORNAMENTS (*see* ORNAMENT)
Ex 33: 4 and no one put on his **o**
Ex 33: 5 therefore, take off your **o**
Ex 33: 6 of their **o** by Mount Horeb
Num 31:50 every man found of **o** of gold
Num 31:51 them, all the fashioned **o**
Judg 8:21 took the crescent **o** that were
Judg 8:26 gold, besides the crescent **o**
2Sa 1:24 who put **o** of gold on your
Prov 1: 9 be graceful **o** on your head
Song 1:10 Your cheeks are lovely with **o**
Song 1:11 We will make you **o** of gold
Is 3:20 the headdresses, the leg **o**
Is 61:10 decks himself with **o**, and as a
Jer 2:32 Can a virgin forget her **o**
Jer 4:30 adorn yourself with **o** of gold
Ezek 7:20 As for the beauty of his **o**
Ezek 16:11 I adorned you with **o**, put
Ezek 23:40 and adorned yourself with **o**

ORNAN (*see* ARAUNAH)
1Ch 21:15 floor of **O** the Jebusite
1Ch 21:18 floor of **O** the Jebusite
1Ch 21:20 Now **O** turned and saw the angel
1Ch 21:20 but **O** continued threshing
1Ch 21:21 Then David came to **O**, and
1Ch 21:21 and **O** looked and saw David
1Ch 21:22 Then David said to **O**, "Grant
1Ch 21:23 And **O** said to David,
1Ch 21:24 Then King David said to **O**
1Ch 21:25 So David gave **O** six hundred
1Ch 21:28 floor of **O** the Jebusite, he
2Ch 3: 1 floor of **O** the Jebusite

ORPAH
Ruth 1: 4 the name of the one was **O**
Ruth 1:14 **O** kissed her mother-in-law,

ORPHANS
Lam 5: 3 We have become **o** and waifs,
John 14:18 I will not leave you **o**
Jas 1:27 to visit **o** and widows in their

OSNAPPER
Ezra 4:10 and noble **O** took captive and

OSTRICH (*see* OSTRICHES)
Lev 11:16 the **o**, the short-eared owl,
Deut 14:15 the **o**, the short-eared owl,
Job 39:13 wings of the **o** wave proudly

OSTRICHES (*see* OSTRICH)
Job 30:29 jackals, and a companion of **o**
Is 13:21 **o** will dwell there, And wild
Is 34:13 of jackals, a courtyard for **o**
Is 43:20 Me, the jackals and the **o**,
Jer 50:39 and the **o** shall dwell in it
Lam 4: 3 like **o** in the wilderness
Mic 1: 8 And a mourning like the **o**,

OTHER (*see* PREFACE)

OTHER'S (*see* PREFACE)

OTHERS (*see* PREFACE)

OTHERWISE (*see* PREFACE)

OTHNI
1Ch 26: 7 The sons of Shemaiah were **O**

OTHNIEL
Josh 15:17 So **O** the son of Kenaz, the
Judg 1:13 **O** the son of Kenaz, Caleb's
Judg 3: 9 **O** the son of Kenaz, Caleb's
Judg 3:11 Then **O** the son of Kenaz died
1Ch 4:13 The sons of Kenaz were **O** and
1Ch 4:13 The sons of **O** were Hathath,
1Ch 27:15 Heldai the Netophathite, of **O**

OUGHT (*see* PREFACE)

OUR (*see* PREFACE)

OURS (*see* PREFACE)

OURSELVES (*see* PREFACE)

OUT (*see* PREFACE)

OUTBREAK
Deut 24: 8 Take heed in an o of leprosy
2Sa 6: 8 of the LORD's o against Uzzah
1Ch 13:11 of the LORD's o against Uzza

OUTBURSTS
2Co 12:20 o of wrath, selfish ambitions
Gal 5:20 o of wrath, selfish ambitions

OUTCAST (*see* OUTCASTS)
Jer 30:17 they called you an o saying
Mic 4: 6 the lame, I will gather the o
Mic 4: 7 and the o a strong nation

OUTCASTS (*see* OUTCAST)
Ps 147: 2 together the o of Israel
Is 11:12 will assemble the o of Israel
Is 16: 3 hide the o, do not betray him
Is 16: 4 Let My o dwell with you, O
Is 27:13 they who are o in the land of
Is 56: 8 who gathers the o of Israel
Jer 49:36 the o of Elam will not go

OUTCOME
Acts 5:24 wondered what the o would be
Heb 13: 7 considering the o of their

OUTCRY
Gen 18:20 Because the o against Sodom
Gen 18:21 o against it that has come to
Gen 19:13 because the o against them
1Sa 4:14 Eli heard the noise of the o
Neh 5: 1 was a great o of the people
Neh 5: 6 angry when I heard their o
Ps 144:14 there be no o in our streets
Acts 23: 9 Then there arose a loud o

OUTER
Ex 26: 4 you shall do on the o edge of
Ex 36:11 likewise he did on the o edge
Num 23:13 see only the o part of them
1Ki 6:29 o sanctuaries, with carved
1Ki 6:30 the inner and o sanctuaries
2Ki 16:18 and he removed the king's o
Esth 6: 4 o court of the king's palace
Job 41:13 Who can remove his o coat
Is 3:22 the o garments, the purses,
Ezek 10: 5 was heard even in the o court
Ezek 40:17 brought me into the o court
Ezek 40:20 On the o court was also a
Ezek 40:31 archways faced the o court
Ezek 40:34 archways faced the o court
Ezek 40:37 gateposts faced the o court
Ezek 40:40 At the o side of the
Ezek 41: 9 The thickness of the o wall
Ezek 42: 1 me out into the o court, by
Ezek 42: 3 the pavement of the o court
Ezek 42: 7 chambers, toward the o court
Ezek 42: 8 the o court was fifty cubits
Ezek 42: 9 into them from the o court
Ezek 42:14 holy chamber into the o court
Ezek 44: 1 He brought me back to the o
Ezek 44:19 they go out to the o court
Ezek 44:19 to the o court to the people,
Ezek 46:20 the o court to sanctify the
Ezek 46:21 me out into the o court and
Ezek 47: 2 on the outside to the o
Matt 8:12 be cast out into o darkness
Matt 22:13 and cast him into o darkness
Matt 25:30 servant into the o darkness
John 21: 7 he put on his o garment (for

OUTERMOST
Ex 26:10 curtain that is o in one set
Ex 36:17 curtain that is o in one set

OUTGOINGS
Ps 65: 8 You make the o of the morning

OUTLET
2Ch 32:30 the water o of Upper Gihon

OUTLIVED
Josh 24:31 of the elders who o Joshua
Judg 2: 7 of the elders who o Joshua

OUTPOST
Judg 7:11 Purah his servant to the o of
Judg 7:19 to the o of the camp at the

OUTRAGE
Judg 19:23 house, do not commit this o
Judg 20: 6 lewdness and o in Israel

OUTRAN
2Sa 18:23 the plain, and o the Cushite
John 20: 4 and the other disciple o Peter

OUTSIDE (*see* PREFACE)

OUTSIDER
Ex 12:43 No o shall eat it
Ex 30:33 puts any of it on an o, shall
Lev 22:10 No o shall eat the holy
Lev 22:12 daughter is married to an o
Lev 22:13 but no o shall eat it
Num 1:51 The o who comes near shall be
Num 3:10 but the o who comes near
Num 3:38 but the o who came near was
Num 16:40 children of Israel that no o
Num 18: 4 but an o shall not come near
Num 18: 7 but the o who comes near

OUTSKIRTS
Num 11: 1 some in the o of the camp
1Sa 9:27 down to the o of the city
1Sa 14: 2 in the o of Gibeah under a
2Sa 15:17 him, and stopped at the o
2Ki 7: 5 to the o of the Syrian camp
2Ki 7: 8 came to the o of the camp

OUTSTRETCHED
Ex 6: 6 will redeem you with an o arm
Deut 4:34 an o arm, and by great terrors
Deut 5:15 a mighty hand and by an o arm
Deut 7:19 the mighty hand and the o arm
Deut 9:29 power and by Your o arm
Deut 11: 2 His mighty hand and His o arm
Deut 26: 8 mighty hand and with an o arm
1Ki 8:42 strong hand and Your o arm)
2Ki 17:36 an o arm, Him you shall fear,
2Ch 6:32 mighty hand and Your o arm
Ps 136:12 strong hand, and with an o arm
Is 3:16 haughty, and walk with o necks
Jer 21: 5 against you with an o hand
Jer 27: 5 power and by My o arm
Jer 32:17 by Your great power and o arm
Jer 32:21 and an o arm, and with great
Ezek 20:33 a mighty hand, with an o arm
Ezek 20:34 a mighty hand, with an o arm

OUTWARD (*see* OUTWARDLY)
Num 35: 4 city o a thousand cubits all
1Sa 16: 7 man looks at the o appearance
Rom 2:28 which is o in the flesh
2Co 4:16 Even though our o man is
2Co 10: 7 according to the o appearance
1Pe 3: 3 o adorning of arranging the

OUTWARDLY (*see* OUTWARD)
Matt 23:27 indeed appear beautiful o
Matt 23:28 Even so you also o appear
Rom 2:28 he is not a Jew who is one o

OUTWIT
Ps 89:22 The enemy shall not o him

OVEN (*see* OVENS)
Gen 15:17 behold, there was a smoking o
Lev 2: 4 grain offering baked in the o
Lev 7: 9 that is baked in the o and all
Lev 11:35 it is an o or cooking stove
Lev 26:26 bake your bread in one o, and
Ps 21: 9 o in the time of Your anger
Lam 5:10 Our skin is hot as an o,
Hos 7: 4 like an o heated by a baker
Hos 7: 6 prepare their heart like an o
Hos 7: 7 They are all hot, like an o
Mal 4: 1 is coming, burning like an o
Matt 6:30 tomorrow is thrown into the o
Luke 12:28 tomorrow is thrown into the o

OVENS (*see* OVEN)
Ex 8: 3 on your people, into your o
Neh 3:11 as well as the Tower of the O
Neh 12:38 O as far as the Broad Wall

OVER (*see* PREFACE)

OVERALL (*see* PREFACE)

OVERBOARD
Acts 27:19 tackle o with our own hands
Acts 27:43 swim should jump o first and

OVERCAME (*see* OVERCOME)
Rev 3:21 Me on My throne, as I also o
Rev 12:11 they o him by the blood of

OVERCOME (*see* OVERCAME, OVERCOMES, OVERCOMING)
Num 13:30 for we are well able to o it
1Sa 7:10 they were o before Israel
2Ki 16: 5 Ahaz but could not o him
Song 6: 5 from me, for they have o me
Is 28: 1 to those who are o with wine
Jer 23: 9 and like a man whom wine has o
Mark 5:42 And they were o with great
John 16:33 cheer, I have o the world
Acts 20: 9 He was o by sleep
Rom 3: 4 may o when You are judged
Rom 12:21 Do not be o by evil, but
Rom 12:21 by evil, but o evil with good
2Pe 2:19 for by whom a person is o
2Pe 2:20 again entangled in them and o
1Jn 2:13 you have o the wicked one
1Jn 2:14 you have o the wicked one
1Jn 4: 4 children, and have o them,
1Jn 5: 4 victory that has o the world
Rev 11: 7 them, o them, and kill them
Rev 13: 7 with the saints and to o them
Rev 17:14 Lamb, and the Lamb will o them

OVERCOMES (*see* OVERCOME)
Luke 11:22 o him, he takes from him all
1Jn 5: 4 is born of God o the world
1Jn 5: 5 Who is he who o the world
Rev 2: 7 To him who o I will give to
Rev 2:11 He who o shall not be hurt by
Rev 2:17 To him who o I will give some
Rev 2:26 And he who o, and keeps My
Rev 3: 5 He who o shall be clothed in
Rev 3:12 He who o, I will make him a
Rev 3:21 To him who o I will grant to
Rev 21: 7 He who o shall inherit all

OVERCOMING (*see* OVERCOME)
Job 41: 9 any hope of o him is vain

OVERFLOW (*see* OVERFLOWED, OVERFLOWING, OVERFLOWS)
Deut 11: 4 o them as they pursued you
Ps 69: 2 waters, Where the floods o me
Ps 69:15 Let not the floodwater o me
Prov 3:10 vats will o with new wine
Is 8: 8 pass through Judah, he will o
Is 10:22 shall o with righteousness
Is 23:10 O through your land like the
Is 28:17 the waters will o the hiding
Is 43: 2 rivers, they shall not o you
Jer 47: 2 They shall o the land and all
Lam 3:48 My eyes o with rivers of
Joel 2:24 vats shall o with new wine
Joel 3:13 winepress is full, the vats o
Jas 1:21 o of wickedness, and receive

OVERFLOWED (*see* OVERFLOW)
1Ch 12:15 when it had o all its banks
Ps 78:20 gushed out, And the streams o

OVERFLOWING (*see* OVERFLOW)
Job 38:25 a channel for the o water
Ps 45: 1 My heart is o with a good
Is 28: 2 a flood of mighty waters o
Is 28:15 When the o scourge passes
Is 28:18 when the o scourge passes
Is 30:28 breath is like an o stream
Is 34: 6 it is made o with fatness, and
Jer 47: 2 north, and shall be an o flood
Nah 1: 8 But with an o flood He will
Hab 3:10 the o of the water passed by

OVERFLOWS (*see* OVERFLOW)
Josh 3:15 o all its banks during the
Lam 1:16 my eye, my eye o with water

OVERGROWN
Prov 24:31 it was, all o with thorns

OVERLAID (*see* OVERLAY)
Ex 26:32 of acacia wood o with gold
Ex 36:34 He o the boards with gold,
Ex 36:34 bars, and o the bars with gold
Ex 36:36 o them with gold, with their
Ex 36:38 he o their capitals and their
Ex 37: 2 He o it with pure gold inside

Ex 37: 4 wood, and **o** them with gold
Ex 37:11 he **o** it with pure gold, and
Ex 37:15 table, and **o** them with gold
Ex 37:26 And he **o** it with pure gold
Ex 37:28 wood, and **o** them with gold
Ex 38: 2 And he **o** it with bronze
Ex 38: 6 wood, and **o** them with bronze
Ex 38:28 **o** their capitals, and made
1Ki 6:20 He **o** it with pure gold, and
1Ki 6:20 gold, and **o** the altar of cedar
1Ki 6:21 So Solomon **o** the inside of
1Ki 6:21 and he **o** it with gold
1Ki 6:22 whole temple he **o** with gold
1Ki 6:22 also he **o** with gold the
1Ki 6:28 Also he **o** the cherubim with
1Ki 6:30 of the temple he **o** with gold
1Ki 6:32 flowers, and **o** them with gold
1Ki 6:35 and **o** them with gold applied
1Ki 10:18 ivory, and **o** it with pure gold
2Ki 18:16 Hezekiah king of Judah had **o**
2Ch 3: 4 He **o** the inside with pure
2Ch 3: 5 which he **o** with fine gold
2Ch 3: 7 He also **o** the house
2Ch 3: 8 He **o** it with six hundred
2Ch 3: 9 he **o** the upper area with gold
2Ch 3:10 carving, and **o** them with gold
2Ch 4: 9 he **o** these doors with bronze
2Ch 9:17 ivory, and **o** it with pure gold
Hab 2:19 it is **o** with gold and silver,
Heb 9: 4 **o** on all sides with gold, in

OVERLAY (*see* OVERLAID)
Ex 25:11 you shall **o** it with pure gold
Ex 25:11 inside and out you shall **o** it
Ex 25:13 wood, and **o** them with gold
Ex 25:24 you shall **o** it with pure gold
Ex 25:28 **o** them with gold, that the
Ex 26:29 You shall **o** the boards with
Ex 26:29 bars, and **o** the bars with gold
Ex 26:37 wood, and **o** them with gold
Ex 27: 2 you shall **o** it with bronze
Ex 27: 6 wood, and **o** them with bronze
Ex 30: 3 And you shall **o** its top, its
Ex 30: 5 wood, and **o** them with gold
Ex 38:17 the **o** of their capitals was
Ex 38:19 the **o** of their capitals and
1Ch 29: 4 to **o** the walls of the houses

OVERLOOK (*see* OVERLOOKED, OVERLOOKING, OVERLOOKS)
Prov 19:11 glory to **o** a transgression

OVERLOOKED (*see* OVERLOOK)
Acts 17:30 times of ignorance God **o**, but

OVERLOOKING (*see* OVERLOOK)
2Ch 20:24 to a place **o** the wilderness

OVERLOOKS (*see* OVERLOOK)
Num 23:28 of Peor, that **o** the wasteland
1Sa 13:18 **o** the Valley of Zeboim toward

OVERLY
Eccl 7:16 Do not be **o** righteous, nor be
Eccl 7:16 righteous, nor be **o** wise
Eccl 7:17 Do not be **o** wicked, nor be

OVERNIGHT
Deut 16: 4 remain **o** until morning
Deut 21:23 not remain **o** on the tree, but
Deut 24:12 shall not keep his pledge **o**

OVERPOWER (*see* OVERPOWERED)
Num 22:11 I shall be able to **o** them
Judg 16: 5 and by what means we may **o**
Esth 9: 1 the Jews had hoped to **o** them
Job 15:24 they **o** him, like a king ready

OVERPOWERED (*see* OVERPOWER)
Esth 9: 1 **o** those who hated them
Eccl 4:12 one may be **o** by another, two
Lam 1:13 into my bones, and it **o** them
Dan 6:24 and the lions **o** them, and broke
Acts 19:16 **o** them, and prevailed against

OVERRULE (*see* OVERRULED, OVERRULES)
Num 30:11 to her and did not **o** her, then

OVERRULED (*see* OVERRULE)
Num 30: 5 her, because her father **o** her

OVERRULES (*see* OVERRULE)
Num 30: 5 But if her father **o** her on
Num 30: 8 But if her husband **o** her on

OVERRUN
Zeph 2: 9 **o** with weeds and saltpits, and

OVERSEE (*see* OVERSEER, OVERSIGHT)
2Ki 22: 9 who **o** the house of the LORD
2Ch 2: 2 six hundred to **o** them
Ezra 3: 8 above to **o** the work of the
Ezra 3: 9 arose as one to **o** those

OVERSEER (*see* OVERSEE)
Gen 39: 4 he made him **o** of his house
Gen 39: 5 had made him **o** of his house
1Ch 26:24 was **o** of the treasuries
Neh 11: 9 the son of Zichri was their **o**
Neh 11:14 Their **o** was Zabdiel the son
Neh 11:22 Also the **o** of the Levites at
Prov 6: 7 no captain, **o** or ruler,
1Pe 2:25 Shepherd and **O** of your souls

OVERSEERS (*see* OVERSEERS)
2Ki 22: 5 who are the **o** in the house of
2Ch 2:18 **o** to make the people work
2Ch 31:13 Benaiah were **o** under the hand
2Ch 34:12 Their **o** were Jahath and
2Ch 34:13 were **o** of all who did work in
2Ch 34:17 it into the hand of the **o**
Acts 20:28 Holy Spirit has made you **o**
1Pe 5: 2 is among you, serving as **o**

OVERSHADOW (*see* OVERSHADOWED, OVERSHADOWING)
Luke 1:35 of the Highest will **o** you

OVERSHADOWED (*see* OVERSHADOW)
1Ki 8: 7 and the cherubim **o** the ark
1Ch 28:18 **o** the ark of the covenant of
2Ch 5: 8 and the cherubim **o** the ark
Matt 17: 5 behold, a bright cloud **o** them
Mark 9: 7 And a cloud came and **o** them
Luke 9:34 this, a cloud came and **o** them

OVERSHADOWING (*see* OVERSHADOW)
Heb 9: 5 of glory **o** the mercy seat

OVERSIGHT (*see* OVERSEE)
Gen 43:12 perhaps it was an **o**
Num 3: 4 as priests under the **o** of
Num 3:32 with **o** of those who kept
Num 4:16 the **o** of all the tabernacle,
2Ki 12:11 who had the **o** of the house of
1Ch 26:30 had the **o** of Israel on the
2Ch 23:18 **o** of the house of the LORD to
2Ch 34:10 **o** of the house of the LORD
Neh 11:16 had the **o** of the business

OVERSPREAD (*see* OVERSPREADS)
Job 15:29 his possessions **o** the earth

OVERSPREADS (*see* OVERSPREAD)
Is 40:19 the goldsmith **o** it with gold

OVERTAKE (*see* OVERTAKEN, OVERTAKING, OVERTOOK)
Gen 19:19 lest some evil **o** me and I die
Gen 44: 4 and when you **o** them, say to
Ex 15: 9 I will pursue, I will **o**
Deut 19: 6 **o** him, because the way is
Deut 28: 2 **o** you, because you obey the
Deut 28:15 will come upon you and **o** you
Deut 28:45 and **o** you, until you are
Josh 2: 5 quickly, for you may **o** them
1Sa 30: 8 Shall I **o** them
1Sa 30: 8 for you shall surely **o** them
2Sa 15:14 lest he **o** us suddenly and
Job 27:20 Terrors **o** him like a flood
Ps 7: 5 the enemy pursue me and **o** me
Prov 12:21 trouble will **o** the righteous
Is 59: 9 nor does righteousness **o** us
Jer 42:16 which you feared shall **o** you
Lam 1: 3 **o** her in dire straits
Hos 2: 7 her lovers, but not **o** them
Hos 10: 9 of iniquity did not **o** them
Amos 9:10 not **o** us nor confront us
Amos 9:13 plowman shall **o** the reaper
Zech 1: 6 did they not **o** your fathers
John 12:35 light, lest darkness **o** you
Acts 8:29 Go near and **o** this chariot
1Th 5: 4 Day should **o** you as a thief

OVERTAKEN (*see* OVERTAKE)
Ps 18:37 pursued my enemies and **o** them
Ps 40:12 My iniquities have **o** me, so
Ps 119:143 Trouble and anguish have **o** me
1Co 10:13 No temptation has **o** you
Gal 6: 1 if a man is **o** in any trespass

OVERTAKING (*see* OVERTAKE)
1Ch 21:12 sword of your enemies **o** you

OVERTHREW (*see* OVERTHROW)
Gen 19:25 So He **o** those cities, all the
Gen 19:29 when He **o** the cities in which
Ex 14:27 So the LORD **o** the Egyptians
Deut 29:23 which the LORD **o** in His anger
1Ch 20: 1 Joab defeated Rabbah and **o** it
Ps 136:15 But **o** Pharaoh and his army in
Is 13:19 will be as when God **o** Sodom
Jer 20:16 the cities which the LORD **o**
Jer 50:40 As God **o** Sodom and Gomorrah
Amos 4:11 I **o** some of you, as God
Amos 4:11 some of you, as God **o** Sodom

OVERTHROW (*see* OVERTHREW, OVERTHROWING, OVERTHROWN, OVERTHROWS)
Gen 19:21 in that I will not **o** this
Gen 19:29 Lot out of the midst of the **o**
Ex 23:24 but you shall utterly **o** them
Deut 29:23 there, like the **o** of Sodom
2Sa 10: 3 to spy it out, and to **o** it
2Sa 11:25 against the city, and **o** it
1Ch 19: 3 come to you to search and to **o**
2Ch 25: 8 God has power to help and to **o**
Ps 106:26 To **o** them in the wilderness,
Ps 106:27 To **o** their descendants among
Ps 140:11 hunt the violent man to **o** him
Prov 18: 5 or to **o** the righteous in
Jer 49:18 As in the **o** of Sodom and
Hag 2:22 I will **o** the throne of
Hag 2:22 I will **o** the chariots and
Acts 5:39 it is of God, you cannot **o** it
2Ti 2:18 and they **o** the faith of some

OVERTHROWING (*see* OVERTHROW)
Prov 21:12 **o** the wicked for their

OVERTHROWN (*see* OVERTHROW)
Ex 15: 7 **o** those who rose against You
2Sa 17: 9 of them are **o** at the first
2Sa 18: 7 **o** there before the servants
2Ch 14:13 So the Ethiopians were **o**, and
Ps 141: 6 Their judges are **o** by the
Prov 11:11 but it is **o** by the mouth of
Prov 12: 7 The wicked are **o** and are no
Prov 14:11 house of the wicked will be **o**
Is 1: 7 desolate, as **o** by strangers
Jer 18:23 but let them be **o** before You
Lam 4: 6 which was **o** in a moment, with
Ezek 21:27 **O**, **o**, I will make it **o**
Dan 11:41 and many countries shall be **o**
Jon 3: 4 days, and Nineveh shall be **o**

OVERTHROWS (*see* OVERTHROW)
Job 12:19 plundered, and **o** the mighty
Job 34:25 He **o** them in the night, and
Prov 13: 6 but wickedness **o** the sinner
Prov 22:12 but He **o** the words of the
Prov 29: 4 he who receives bribes **o** it

OVERTOOK (*see* OVERTAKE)
Gen 31:23 he **o** him in the mountains of
Gen 31:25 So Laban **o** Jacob
Gen 44: 6 So he **o** them, and he spoke to
Ex 14: 9 **o** them camping by the sea
Judg 18:22 and **o** the children of Dan
Judg 20:42 but the battle **o** them, and
2Ki 25: 5 they **o** him in the plains of
Jer 39: 5 **o** Zedekiah in the plains of
Jer 52: 8 they **o** Zedekiah in the plains

OVERTURNED (*see* OVERTURNS)
Judg 7:13 it so that it fell and **o**, and
Lam 1:20 my heart is **o** within me, for
Matt 21:12 and **o** the tables of the
Mark 11:15 and **o** the tables of the
John 2:15 money and **o** the tables

OVERTURNS (*see* OVERTURNED)
Job 9: 5 when He **o** them in His anger
Job 28: 9 he **o** the mountains at the

OVERWHELM (*see* OVERWHELMED)
Job 6:27 you **o** the fatherless, and you
Job 12:15 them out, they **o** the earth
Dan 11:10 one shall certainly come and **o**
Dan 11:40 **o** them, and pass through

OVERWHELMED (*see* OVERWHELM)
Job 41: 9 shall one not be **o** at the
Ps 55: 5 upon me, And horror has **o** me
Ps 61: 2 to You, When my heart is **o**

Ps 77: 3 and my spirit was **o**
Ps 78:53 But the sea **o** their enemies
Ps 124: 4 the waters would have **o** us
Ps 142: 3 my spirit was **o** within me
Ps 143: 4 my spirit is **o** within me
Dan 10:16 vision my sorrows have **o** me

OVERWORK
Prov 23: 4 Do not **o** to be rich

OWE (*see* OWED, OWES)
Matt 18:28 saying, Pay me what you **o**
Luke 16: 5 How much do you **o** my master
Luke 16: 7 And how much do you **o**
Rom 13: 8 **O** no one anything except to
Phm 19 you **o** me even your own self

OWED (*see* OWE)
Deut 15: 3 what is **o** by your brother
Matt 18:24 **o** him ten thousand talents
Matt 18:28 who **o** him a hundred denarii
Luke 7:41 One **o** five hundred denarii,

OWES (*see* OWE)
Phm 18 wronged you or **o** you anything

OWL (*see* OWLS)
Lev 11:16 ostrich, the short-eared **o**
Lev 11:17 the little **o**, the fisher **o**
Lev 11:17 and the screech **o**
Lev 11:18 the white **o**, the jackdaw, and
Deut 14:15 ostrich, the short-eared **o**
Deut 14:16 the little **o**, the screech **o**
Deut 14:16 the white **o**
Deut 14:17 carrion vulture, the fisher **o**
Ps 102: 6 I am like an **o** of the desert
Is 34:11 shall possess it, also the **o**

OWLS (*see* OWL)
Is 13:21 houses will be full of **o**

OWN (*see* OWNED, OWNER, OWNS)
Gen 1:27 created man in His **o** image
Gen 5: 3 begot a son in his **o** likeness
Gen 10: 5 according to his **o** language
Gen 14:14 who were born in his **o** house
Gen 15: 4 **o** body shall be your heir
Gen 30:25 that I may go to my **o** place
Gen 30:30 I also provide for my **o** house
Gen 30:40 but he put his **o** flocks by
Gen 40: 5 with its **o** interpretation
Gen 41:11 interpretation of his **o** dream
Gen 41:12 according to his **o** dream
Gen 47:24 Four-fifths shall be your **o**
Gen 49:28 according to his **o** blessing
Ex 5:16 the fault is in your **o** people
Ex 15:17 have made for Your **o** dwelling
Ex 18:27 he went his way to his **o** land
Ex 21:36 the dead beast shall be his **o**
Ex 22: 5 from the best of his **o** field
Ex 22: 5 and the best of his **o** vineyard
Ex 28:21 each one with its **o** name
Ex 32:13 whom You swore by Your **o** self
Ex 39:14 each one with its **o** name
Lev 1: 3 **o** free will at the door of
Lev 7:30 His **o** hands shall bring the
Lev 14:15 the palm of his **o** left hand
Lev 14:26 the palm of his **o** left hand
Lev 16:29 whether a native of your **o**
Lev 17:15 your **o** country or a stranger
Lev 18:10 theirs is your **o** nakedness
Lev 18:26 either any of your **o** nation
Lev 19: 5 offer it of your **o** free will
Lev 21:14 of his **o** people as wife
Lev 22:19 **o** free will a male without
Lev 22:29 offer it of your **o** free will
Lev 24:22 for one from your **o** country
Lev 25: 5 What grows of its **o** accord
Lev 25:11 what grows of its **o** accord
Lev 25:41 shall return to his **o** family
Num 1:52 tents, everyone by his **o** camp
Num 1:52 everyone by his **o** standard
Num 2: 2 shall camp by his **o** standard
Num 10:30 I will depart to my **o** land
Num 13:33 grasshoppers in our **o** sight
Num 15:39 to which your **o** heart and
Num 15:39 your **o** eyes are inclined,
Num 16:28 not done them of my **o** will
Num 16:38 sinned against their **o** souls
Num 24:13 good or bad of my **o** will
Num 27: 3 but he died in his **o** sin
Num 32:42 it Nobah, after his **o** name
Num 36: 9 shall keep its **o** inheritance
Deut 3:14 Bashan after his **o** name,
Deut 12: 8 is right in his **o** eyes
Deut 13: 6 friend who is as your **o** soul
Deut 22: 2 bring it to your **o** house, and
Deut 24:13 he may sleep in his **o** garment
Deut 24:16 be put to death for his **o** sin
Deut 28:53 eat the fruit of your **o** body
Deut 33: 9 Or know his **o** children
Josh 2:18 household to your **o** home
Josh 2:19 blood shall be on his **o** head
Josh 7:11 put it among their **o** stuff
Josh 20: 6 return and come to his **o** city
Josh 20: 6 his **o** house, to the city from
Josh 24:28 each to his **o** inheritance
Judg 2: 6 **o** inheritance to possess the
Judg 2:19 their **o** doings nor from their
Judg 7: 2 My **o** hand has saved me
Judg 8:29 went and dwelt in his **o** house
Judg 8:30 sons who were his **o** offspring
Judg 9: 2 that I am your **o** flesh and
Judg 9:49 likewise cut down his **o** bough
Judg 9:55 every man to his **o** place
Judg 9:57 God returned on their **o** heads
Judg 17: 6 what was right in his **o** eyes
Judg 21:25 what was right in his **o** eyes
Ruth 4: 6 lest I ruin my **o** inheritance
1Sa 2:20 they would go to their **o** home
1Sa 5:11 let it go back to its **o** place
1Sa 6: 9 the road to its **o** territory
1Sa 8:11 them for his **o** chariots and to
1Sa 13:14 a man after His **o** heart, and
1Sa 14:46 went to their **o** place
1Sa 15:17 were little in your **o** eyes
1Sa 18: 1 loved him as his **o** soul
1Sa 18: 3 he loved him as his **o** soul
1Sa 20:17 him as he loved his **o** soul
1Sa 20:30 son of Jesse to your **o** shame
1Sa 23:18 Jonathan went to his **o** house
1Sa 25:26 yourself with your **o** hand
1Sa 25:33 myself with my **o** hand
1Sa 25:39 of Nabal on his **o** head
1Sa 28: 3 him in Ramah, in his **o** city
2Sa 1:11 took hold of his **o** clothes
2Sa 1:16 Your blood is on your **o** head
2Sa 1:16 head, for your **o** mouth has
2Sa 4:11 in his **o** house on his bed
2Sa 6:22 will be humble in my **o** sight
2Sa 7:10 dwell in a place of their **o**
2Sa 7:21 and according to Your **o** heart
2Sa 7:24 Your very **o** people forever
2Sa 12: 3 It ate of his **o** food and drank
2Sa 12: 3 food and drank from his **o** cup
2Sa 12: 4 to take from his **o** flock and
2Sa 12: 4 from his **o** herd to prepare
2Sa 12:11 against you from your **o** house
2Sa 12:20 Then he went to his **o** house
2Sa 14:24 Let him return to his **o** house
2Sa 14:24 returned to his **o** house, but
2Sa 15:19 an exile from your **o** place
2Sa 16: 8 you are caught in your **o** evil
2Sa 16:11 from my **o** body seeks my life
2Sa 18:13 falsely against my **o** life
2Sa 18:18 the pillar after his **o** name
2Sa 19:28 those who eat at your **o** table
2Sa 19:30 back in peace to his **o** house
2Sa 19:37 that I may die in my **o** city
2Sa 19:39 and he returned to his **o** place
2Sa 23:21 killed him with his **o** spear
1Ki 1:12 that you may save your **o** life
1Ki 1:33 my son ride on my **o** mule, and
1Ki 2:23 this word against his **o** life
1Ki 2:26 to Anathoth, to your **o** fields
1Ki 2:34 he was buried in his **o** house
1Ki 2:37 blood shall be on your **o** head
1Ki 2:44 wickedness on your **o** head
1Ki 3: 1 finished building his **o** house
1Ki 7: 1 years to build his **o** house
1Ki 8:38 the plague of his **o** heart
1Ki 9:15 his **o** house, the Millo, the
1Ki 10: 6 in my **o** land about your words
1Ki 10: 7 came and saw it with my **o** eyes
1Ki 10:13 and went to her **o** country, she
1Ki 11:19 wife the sister of his **o** wife
1Ki 11:21 that I may go to my **o** country
1Ki 11:22 seek to go to your **o** country
1Ki 12:16 Now, see to your **o** house, O
1Ki 12:33 he had devised in his **o** heart
1Ki 13:30 laid the corpse in his **o** tomb
1Ki 14:12 therefore, go to your **o** house
1Ki 17:19 and laid him on his **o** bed
1Ki 22:36 and every man to his **o** country
2Ki 2:12 he took hold of his **o** clothes
2Ki 3:27 and returned to their **o** land
2Ki 4:13 I dwell among my **o** people
2Ki 12:18 his **o** sacred things, and all
2Ki 14: 6 be put to death for his **o** sin
2Ki 17:23 from their **o** land to Assyria
2Ki 17:29 to make gods of its **o**, and put
2Ki 17:33 LORD, yet served their **o** gods
2Ki 18:27 drink their **o** waste with you
2Ki 18:31 of you eat from his **o** vine
2Ki 18:31 every one from his **o** fig tree
2Ki 18:31 the waters of his **o** cistern
2Ki 18:32 to a land like your **o** land
2Ki 19: 7 rumor and return to his **o** land
2Ki 19: 7 by the sword in his **o** land
2Ki 19:34 to save it for My **o** sake
2Ki 20: 6 this city for My **o** sake, and
2Ki 21:18 in the garden of his **o** house
2Ki 21:23 the king in his **o** house
2Ki 23:30 and buried him in his **o** tomb
2Ki 25:21 away captive from its **o** land
1Ch 11:23 killed him with his **o** spear
1Ch 17: 9 dwell in a place of their **o**
1Ch 17:19 and according to Your **o** heart
1Ch 17:22 Your very **o** people forever
1Ch 29: 3 my **o** special treasure of gold
1Ch 29:14 of Your **o** we have given You
1Ch 29:16 Your hand, and is all Your **o**
2Ch 6: 9 come forth from your **o** loins
2Ch 6:23 his way on his **o** head, and
2Ch 6:29 each one knows his **o** burden
2Ch 6:29 his **o** grief, and spreads out
2Ch 7:11 of the LORD and in his **o** house
2Ch 8: 1 of the LORD and his **o** house,
2Ch 9: 5 in my **o** land about your words
2Ch 9: 6 I came and saw with my **o** eyes
2Ch 9:12 and went to her **o** country, she
2Ch 10:16 Now see to your **o** house, O
2Ch 16:14 They buried him in his **o** tomb
2Ch 24:25 his **o** servants conspired
2Ch 25: 4 shall die for his **o** sin
2Ch 25:15 their **o** people from your hand
2Ch 31: 1 returned to their **o** cities
2Ch 32:21 shamefaced to his **o** land
2Ch 32:21 god, some of his **o** offspring
2Ch 33:20 buried him in his **o** house
2Ch 33:24 and killed him in his **o** house
Ezra 2: 1 Judah, everyone to his **o** city
Neh 3:28 each in front of his **o** house
Neh 3:29 in front of his **o** house
Neh 4: 4 reproach on their **o** heads
Neh 6: 8 invent them in your **o** heart
Neh 6:16 disheartened in their **o** eyes
Neh 7: 3 in front of his **o** house
Neh 7: 6 Judah, everyone to his **o** city
Neh 11: 3 **o** possession in their cities
Neh 11:20 everyone in his **o** inheritance
Esth 1:22 each province in its **o** script
Esth 1:22 people in their **o** language
Esth 1:22 be master in his **o** house, and
Esth 1:22 the language of his **o** people
Esth 2: 7 took her as his **o** daughter
Esth 8: 9 province in its **o** script, to
Esth 8: 9 people in their **o** language
Esth 8: 9 to the Jews in their **o** script
Esth 9:25 should return on his **o** head
Job 2:11 one came from his **o** place
Job 4:21 Does not their **o** excellence
Job 5:13 wise in their **o** craftiness
Job 9:20 my **o** mouth would condemn me
Job 9:31 my **o** clothes will abhor me
Job 13:15 defend my **o** ways before Him
Job 15: 6 Your **o** mouth condemns you,
Job 15: 6 your **o** lips testify against
Job 18: 7 his **o** counsel casts him down
Job 18: 8 cast into a net by his **o** feet
Job 19:17 to the children of my **o** body
Job 20: 7 forever like his **o** refuse
Job 32: 1 was righteous in his **o** eyes
Job 40:14 **o** right hand can save you
Ps 5:10 them fall by their **o** counsels
Ps 7:16 shall return upon his **o** head
Ps 7:16 come down on his **o** crown
Ps 9:15 hid, their **o** foot is caught
Ps 9:16 in the work of his **o** hands
Ps 12: 4 Our lips are our **o**
Ps 15: 4 He who swears to his **o** hurt
Ps 21:13 O LORD, in Your **o** strength
Ps 33:12 chosen as His **o** inheritance
Ps 35:13 would return to my **o** heart

Ps 36: 2 himself in his **o** eyes, When
Ps 37:15 shall enter their **o** heart
Ps 41: 9 Even my **o** familiar friend in
Ps 44: 3 of the land by their **o** sword
Ps 44: 3 Nor did their **o** arm save them
Ps 45:10 Forget your **o** people also
Ps 49:11 lands after their **o** names
Ps 50:20 slander your **o** mother's son
Ps 64: 8 stumble over their **o** tongue
Ps 67: 6 God, our **o** God, shall bless
Ps 74:22 O God, plead Your **o** cause
Ps 78:29 He gave them their **o** desire
Ps 78:52 But He made His **o** people go
Ps 81:12 to their **o** stubborn heart
Ps 81:12 To walk in their **o** counsels
Ps 94:23 on them their **o** iniquity, And
Ps 94:23 off in their **o** wickedness
Ps 106:39 were defiled by their **o** works
Ps 106:39 the harlot by their **o** deeds
Ps 106:40 He abhorred His **o** inheritance
Ps 109:29 **o** disgrace as with a mantle
Ps 141:10 wicked fall into their **o** nets
Prov 1:18 lie in wait for their **o** blood
Prov 1:18 secretly for their **o** lives
Prov 1:31 eat the fruit of their **o** way
Prov 1:31 the full with their **o** fancies
Prov 3: 5 not on your **o** understanding
Prov 3: 7 Do not be wise in your **o** eyes
Prov 5:15 water from your **o** cistern
Prov 5:15 water from your **o** well
Prov 5:17 Let them be only your **o**, and
Prov 5:22 His **o** iniquities entrap the
Prov 6: 2 by the words of your **o** mouth
Prov 6:32 does so destroys his **o** soul
Prov 8:36 against me wrongs his **o** soul
Prov 11: 5 will fall by his **o** wickedness
Prov 11: 6 will be taken by their **o** lust
Prov 11:17 man does good for his **o** soul
Prov 11:17 is cruel troubles his **o** flesh
Prov 11:19 pursues it to his **o** death
Prov 11:29 He who troubles his **o** house
Prov 12:15 a fool is right in his **o** eyes
Prov 14:10 heart knows its **o** bitterness
Prov 14:14 be filled with his **o** ways
Prov 14:20 hated even by his **o** neighbor
Prov 15:27 for gain troubles his **o** house
Prov 15:32 despises his **o** soul, but he
Prov 16: 2 a man are pure in his **o** eyes
Prov 18: 1 himself seeks his **o** desire
Prov 18: 2 but in expressing his **o** heart
Prov 18:11 a high wall in his **o** esteem
Prov 19: 8 gets wisdom loves his **o** soul
Prov 20: 2 anger sins against his **o** life
Prov 20: 6 proclaim each his **o** goodness
Prov 20:24 a man understand his **o** way
Prov 21: 2 a man is right in his **o** eyes
Prov 23: 4 of your **o** understanding,
Prov 24: 6 you will wage your **o** war, and
Prov 25:27 so to seek one's **o** glory is
Prov 25:28 has no rule over his **o** spirit
Prov 26: 5 lest he be wise in his **o** eyes
Prov 26: 6 of a fool cuts off his **o** feet
Prov 26:11 a dog returns to his **o** vomit
Prov 26:12 see a man wise in his **o** eyes
Prov 26:16 sluggard is wiser in his **o**
Prov 26:17 in a quarrel not his **o** is
Prov 27: 2 you, and not your **o** mouth
Prov 27: 2 stranger, and not your **o** lips
Prov 27:10 Do not forsake your **o** friend
Prov 28:10 will fall into his **o** pit
Prov 28:11 man is wise in his **o** eyes
Prov 28:26 in his **o** heart is a fool, but
Prov 29:24 with a thief hates his **o** life
Prov 30:12 that is pure in its **o** eyes
Prov 31:31 let her **o** works praise her in
Eccl 3:22 should rejoice in his **o** works
Eccl 4: 5 hands and consumes his **o** flesh
Eccl 7:22 your **o** heart has known that
Eccl 8: 9 over another to his **o** hurt
Song 1: 6 but my **o** vineyard I have not
Song 8:12 My **o** vineyard is before me
Is 2: 8 the work of their **o** hands
Is 2: 8 that which their **o** fingers
Is 4: 1 We will eat our **o** food and
Is 4: 1 food and wear our **o** apparel
Is 5:21 who are wise in their **o** eyes
Is 5:21 and prudent in their **o** sight
Is 9:20 eat the flesh of his **o** arm
Is 13:14 man will turn to his **o** people
Is 13:14 will flee to his **o** land
Is 14: 1 settle them in their **o** land
Is 14:18 everyone in his **o** house
Is 31: 7 which your **o** hands have made
Is 36:12 drink their **o** waste with you
Is 36:16 of you eat from his **o** vine
Is 36:16 every one from his **o** fig tree
Is 36:16 the waters of his **o** cistern
Is 36:17 to a land like your **o** land
Is 37: 7 rumor and return to his **o** land
Is 37: 7 by the sword in his **o** land
Is 37:35 to save it for My **o** sake
Is 38:17 Indeed it was for my **o** peace
Is 43:25 transgressions for My **o** sake
Is 44: 9 they are their **o** witnesses
Is 48:11 My **o** sake, for My **o** sake
Is 49:26 you with their **o** flesh, and
Is 49:26 **o** blood as with sweet wine
Is 53: 6 every one, to his **o** way
Is 56:11 they all look to their **o** way
Is 56:11 every one for his **o** gain
Is 56:11 from his **o** territory
Is 58: 7 yourself from your **o** flesh
Is 58:13 Him, not doing your **o** ways
Is 58:13 nor finding your **o** pleasure
Is 58:13 nor speaking your **o** words
Is 59:16 therefore His **o** arm brought
Is 59:16 and His **o** righteousness, it
Is 63: 5 therefore My **o** arm brought
Is 63: 5 My **o** fury, it sustained Me
Is 65: 2 according to their **o** thoughts
Is 66: 3 they have chosen their **o** ways
Jer 1:16 the works of their **o** hands
Jer 2:19 Your **o** wickedness will
Jer 5:31 priests rule by their **o** power
Jer 6: 3 shall pasture in his **o** place
Jer 7:19 to the shame of their **o** faces
Jer 8: 6 turned to his **o** course, as
Jer 9:14 imagination of their **o** heart
Jer 10:23 walks to direct his **o** steps
Jer 16:12 of his **o** evil heart, so that
Jer 18:12 walk according to our **o** plans
Jer 23: 8 shall dwell in their **o** land
Jer 23:16 a vision of their **o** heart
Jer 23:17 imagination of his **o** heart
Jer 23:26 the deceit of their **o** heart
Jer 24: 5 this place for their **o** good
Jer 25: 7 of your hands to your **o** hurt
Jer 25:14 to the works of their **o** hands
Jer 27:11 them remain in their **o** land
Jer 30:18 be built upon its **o** mound
Jer 30:18 according to its **o** plan
Jer 31:17 come back to their **o** border
Jer 31:30 shall die for his **o** iniquity
Jer 37: 7 to Egypt, to their **o** land
Jer 42:12 you to return to your **o** land
Jer 44: 9 your **o** wickedness, and the
Jer 44:17 has gone out of our **o** mouth
Jer 46:16 us go back to our **o** people
Jer 50:16 shall turn to his **o** people
Jer 50:16 shall flee to his **o** land
Jer 51: 9 go everyone to his **o** country
Jer 52:27 away captive from its **o** land
Lam 4:10 have cooked their **o** children
Ezek 9:10 their deeds on their **o** head
Ezek 11:21 their deeds on their **o** heads
Ezek 13: 2 prophesy out of their **o** heart
Ezek 13: 3 who follow their **o** spirit
Ezek 13:17 prophesy out of their **o** heart
Ezek 16: 6 struggling in your **o** blood
Ezek 16:15 you trusted in your **o** beauty
Ezek 16:43 your deeds on your **o** head
Ezek 16:52 bear your **o** shame also,
Ezek 16:52 also, and bear your **o** shame
Ezek 16:54 you may bear your **o** shame
Ezek 17:19 will recompense on his **o** head
Ezek 20:43 **o** sight because of all the
Ezek 22: 3 sheds blood in her **o** midst
Ezek 22:31 their deeds on their **o** heads
Ezek 23:34 and tear at your **o** breasts
Ezek 27: 8 your **o** wise men, O Tyre, were
Ezek 28:25 **o** land which I gave to My
Ezek 29: 3 has said, 'My River is my **o**
Ezek 32:10 every man for his **o** life
Ezek 33: 4 blood shall be on his **o** head
Ezek 33:13 trusts in his **o** righteousness
Ezek 33:20 you according to his **o** ways
Ezek 33:31 hearts pursue their **o** gain
Ezek 34:13 bring them to their **o** land
Ezek 36: 7 you shall bear their **o** shame
Ezek 36:17 Israel dwelt in their **o** land
Ezek 36:17 defiled it by their **o** ways
Ezek 36:24 and bring you into your **o** land
Ezek 36:31 yourselves in your **o** sight
Ezek 36:32 and confounded for your **o** ways
Ezek 37:14 will place you in your **o** land
Ezek 37:21 bring them into their **o** land
Ezek 39:26 dwelt safely in their **o** land
Ezek 39:28 them back to their **o** land
Ezek 46:18 his sons from his **o** property
Dan 3:28 any god except their **o** God
Dan 6:17 it with his **o** signet ring
Dan 8:24 but not by his **o** power
Dan 9:19 Do not delay for Your **o** sake
Dan 11: 9 shall return to his **o** land
Dan 11:16 do according to his **o** will
Dan 11:19 the fortress of his **o** land
Dan 11:28 and return to his **o** land
Dan 11:36 do according to his **o** will
Hos 7: 2 now their **o** deeds have
Hos 10: 6 be ashamed of his **o** counsel
Hos 10:13 you trusted in your **o** way
Hos 11: 6 because of their **o** counsels
Joel 2: 8 one marches in his **o** column
Joel 3: 4 retaliation upon your **o** head
Joel 3: 7 retaliation upon your **o** head
Amos 6:13 ourselves by our **o** strength
Amos 7:11 captive from their **o** land
Amos 7:17 away captive from his **o** land
Obad 15 shall return upon your **o** head
Jon 2: 8 idols forsake their **o** Mercy
Mic 7: 6 are the men of his **o** house
Hab 3:14 his **o** arrows the head of his
Hag 1: 9 of you runs to his **o** house
Zech 12: 6 again in her **o** place
Mal 3:17 his **o** son who serves him
Matt 2:12 their **o** country another way
Matt 6:34 will worry about its **o** things
Matt 6:34 for the day is its **o** trouble
Matt 7: 3 the plank in your **o** eye
Matt 7: 4 a plank is in your **o** eye
Matt 7: 5 the plank from your **o** eye
Matt 8:22 the dead bury their **o** dead
Matt 9: 1 over, and came to His **o** city
Matt 10:36 be those of his **o** household
Matt 13:54 He had come to His **o** country
Matt 13:57 **o** country and in his **o** house
Matt 16:26 world, and loses his **o** soul
Matt 17:25 from their **o** sons or from
Matt 20:15 what I wish with my **o** things
Matt 22: 5 their ways, one to his **o** farm
Matt 25:14 who called his **o** servants
Matt 25:15 according to his **o** ability
Matt 25:27 back my **o** with interest
Matt 27:31 put His **o** clothes on Him, and
Mark 3:21 But when His **o** people heard
Mark 6: 1 and came to His **o** country, and
Mark 6: 4 honor except in his **o** country
Mark 6: 4 among his **o** relatives,
Mark 6: 4 and in his **o** house
Mark 8: 3 away hungry to their **o** houses
Mark 8:36 world, and loses his **o** soul
Mark 15:20 put His **o** clothes on Him, and
Luke 1:20 be fulfilled in their **o** time
Luke 1:23 he departed to his **o** house
Luke 2: 3 everyone to his **o** city
Luke 2:35 through your **o** soul also)
Luke 2:39 to Galilee, to their **o** city
Luke 4:24 is accepted in his **o** country
Luke 5:25 and departed to his **o** house
Luke 5:29 a great feast in his **o** house
Luke 6:41 the plank in your **o** eye
Luke 6:42 plank that is in your **o** eye
Luke 6:42 the plank from your **o** eye
Luke 6:44 tree is known by its **o** fruit
Luke 8:39 Return to your **o** house, and
Luke 9:26 when He comes in His **o** glory
Luke 9:60 the dead bury their **o** dead
Luke 10:34 and he set him on his **o** animal
Luke 11:21 armed, guards his **o** palace
Luke 14:26 his **o** life also, he cannot be
Luke 16:12 will give you what is your **o**
Luke 18: 7 His **o** elect who cry out day
Luke 19:22 Out of your **o** mouth I will
Luke 19:35 they threw their **o** garments
Luke 22:71 it ourselves from His **o** mouth
John 1:11 He came to His **o**
John 1:11 His **o** did not receive Him
John 1:41 found his **o** brother Simon
John 4:41 because of His **o** word
John 4:44 has no honor in his **o** country

Ex 22: 1 restore five **o** for an ox and
Ex 22:30 you shall do with your **o** and
Ex 24: 5 offerings of **o** to the LORD
Num 7: 3 six covered carts and twelve **o**
Num 7: 6 Moses took the carts and the **o**
Num 7: 7 four **o** he gave to the sons of
Num 7: 8 eight **o** he gave to the sons
Num 7:17 two **o**, five rams, five male
Num 7:23 two **o**, five rams, five male
Num 7:29 two **o**, five rams, five male
Num 7:35 two **o**, five rams, five male
Num 7:41 two **o**, five rams, five male
Num 7:47 two **o**, five rams, five male
Num 7:53 two **o**, five rams, five male
Num 7:59 two **o**, five rams, five male
Num 7:65 two **o**, five rams, five male
Num 7:71 two **o**, five rams, five male
Num 7:77 two **o**, five rams, five male
Num 7:83 two **o**, five rams, five male
Num 7:87 All the **o** for the burnt
Num 7:88 all the **o** for the sacrifice
Num 22:40 Then Balak offered **o** and sheep
Deut 14:26 for **o** or sheep, for wine or
Josh 7:24 sons, his daughters, his **o**
1Sa 11: 7 So he took a yoke of **o** and cut
1Sa 11: 7 so it shall be done to his **o**
1Sa 14:32 the spoil, and took sheep, **o**
1Sa 15: 9 the best of the sheep, the **o**
1Sa 15:14 lowing of the **o** which I hear
1Sa 15:15 best of the sheep and the **o**
1Sa 15:21 of the plunder, sheep and **o**
1Sa 22:19 and nursing infants, **o** and
1Sa 27: 9 took away the sheep, the **o**
2Sa 6: 6 of it, for the **o** stumbled
2Sa 6:13 paces, that he sacrificed **o**
2Sa 24:22 Look, here are **o** for burnt
2Sa 24:22 the yokes of the **o** for wood
2Sa 24:24 the **o** for fifty shekels of
1Ki 1: 9 sacrificed sheep and **o** and
1Ki 1:19 He has sacrificed **o** and
1Ki 1:25 today, and has sacrificed **o**
1Ki 4:23 ten fatted **o**, twenty **o**
1Ki 7:25 It stood on twelve **o**
1Ki 7:29 the frames were lions, **o**, and
1Ki 7:29 **o** were wreaths of plaited
1Ki 7:44 and twelve **o** under the Sea
1Ki 8: 5 **o** that could not be counted
1Ki 19:19 twelve yoke of **o** before him
1Ki 19:20 And he left the **o** and ran after
1Ki 19:21 from him, and took a yoke of **o**
2Ki 5:26 and vineyards, sheep and **o**,
2Ki 16:17 bronze **o** that were under it
1Ch 12:40 and camels, on mules and **o**
1Ch 12:40 of raisins, wine and oil and **o**
1Ch 13: 9 the ark, for the **o** stumbled
1Ch 21:23 you the **o** for burnt offerings
2Ch 4: 3 it was the likeness of **o**
2Ch 4: 3 The **o** were cast in two rows,
2Ch 4: 4 It stood on twelve **o**
2Ch 4:15 one Sea and twelve **o** under it
2Ch 5: 6 **o** that could not be counted
2Ch 18: 2 **o** in abundance for him and the
2Ch 31: 6 Judah, brought the tithe of **o**
Job 1:14 The **o** were plowing and the
Job 42:12 one thousand yoke of **o**, and
Ps 8: 7 All sheep and **o**
Ps 22:21 from the horns of the wild **o**
Ps 144:14 That our **o** may be well-laden
Prov 14: 4 Where no **o** are, the trough is
Is 7:25 it will become a range for **o**
Is 22:13 joy and gladness, slaying **o**
Is 30:24 Likewise the **o** and the young
Is 34: 7 The wild **o** shall come down
Jer 51:23 the farmer and his yoke of **o**
Dan 4:25 make you eat grass like **o**
Dan 4:32 make you eat grass like **o**
Dan 4:33 from men and ate grass like **o**
Dan 5:21 fed him with grass like **o**
Amos 6:12 Does one plow there with **o**
Matt 22: 4 my **o** and fatted cattle are
Luke 14:19 I have bought five yoke of **o**
John 2:14 the temple those who sold **o**
John 2:15 with the sheep and the **o**, and
Acts 14:13 of their city, brought **o** and
1Co 9: 9 Is it **o** God is concerned

OXEN'S (*see* OXEN)
1Ki 19:21 flesh, using the **o** equipment

OZEM
1Ch 2:15 **O** the sixth, and David the
1Ch 2:25 firstborn, and Bunah, Oren, **O**

OZNI (*see* OZNITES)
Num 26:16 of **O**, the family of the

OZNITES (*see* OZNI)
Num 26:16 of Ozni, the family of the **O**

P

PAARAI
2Sa 23:35 the Carmelite, **P** the Arbite,

PACE (*see* PACED, PACES)
Gen 33:14 I will lead on slowly at a **p**
2Ki 4:24 do not slacken the **p** for me
Prov 30:29 which are majestic in **p**, yes,

PACED (*see* PACE)
Esth 2:11 every day Mordecai **p** in front
Ps 35:14 I **p** about as though he were

PACES (*see* PACE)
2Sa 6:13 of the LORD had gone six **p**

PACIFIES
Prov 21:14 A gift in secret **p** anger, and
Eccl 10: 4 conciliation **p** great offenses

PACKED
Acts 21:15 And after those days we **p** and

PADAN (*see* PADAN ARAM)
Gen 48: 7 as for me, when I came from **P**

PADAN ARAM (*see* PADAN)
Gen 25:20 of Bethuel the Syrian of **P**
Gen 28: 2 Arise, go to **P**, to the house
Gen 28: 5 Jacob away, and he went to **P**
Gen 28: 6 sent him away to **P** to take
Gen 28: 7 his mother and had gone to **P**
Gen 31:18 which he had gained in **P**, to
Gen 33:18 Canaan, when he came from **P**
Gen 35: 9 again, when he came from **P**
Gen 35:26 who were born to him in **P**
Gen 46:15 whom she bore to Jacob in **P**

PADON
Ezra 2:44 sons of Siaha, the sons of **P**
Neh 7:47 of Sia, the children of **P**

PAGAN (*see* PAGANS)
Ezra 10: 2 have taken **p** wives from the
Ezra 10:10 and have taken **p** wives, adding
Ezra 10:11 the land, and from the **p** wives
Ezra 10:14 **p** wives come at appointed
Ezra 10:17 the men who had taken **p** wives
Ezra 10:18 **p** wives the following were
Ezra 10:44 All these had taken **p** wives
Neh 13:26 Nevertheless **p** women caused
Neh 13:27 our God by marrying **p** women
Neh 13:30 cleansed them of everything **p**
Hos 5: 7 they have begotten **p** children
Zeph 1: 4 priests with the **p** priests

PAGANS (*see* PAGAN)
Hos 3: 1 the raisin cakes of the **p**

PAGIEL
Num 1:13 Asher, **P** the son of Ocran
Num 2:27 shall be **P** the son of Ocran
Num 7:72 day **P** the son of Ocran,
Num 7:77 of **P** the son of Ocran
Num 10:26 Asher was **P** the son of Ocran

PAHATH-MOAB (*see* MOAB)
Ezra 2: 6 the people of **P**, of the
Ezra 8: 4 of the sons of **P**, Elihoenai
Ezra 10:30 of the sons of **P**
Neh 3:11 Hashub the son of **P** repaired
Neh 7:11 the children of **P**, of the
Neh 10:14 Parosh, **P**, Elam, Zattu, Bani,

PAI (*see* PAU)
1Ch 1:50 and the name of his city was **P**

PAID (*see* PAY)
1Ki 18:29 answered, no one **p** attention
2Ki 3: 4 he regularly **p** the king of
2Ki 12:11 and they **p** it out to the
2Ki 12:12 for all that was **p** out to
2Ki 12:15 the money to be **p** to workmen
2Ki 17: 3 and **p** him tribute money
2Ki 21: 9 But they **p** no attention, and
2Ch 27: 5 The people of Ammon **p** him
Ezra 4:20 and custom were **p** to them
Ezra 6: 4 Let the expenses be **p** from
Ezra 6: 8 Let the cost be **p** at the
Esth 3: 2 **p** homage to Haman, for so the
Job 32:12 I **p** close attention to you
Prov 7:14 today I have **p** my vows
Ezek 16:58 You have **p** for your lewdness
Ezek 27:19 and Javan **p** for your wares,
Dan 3:12 have not **p** due regard to you
Jon 1: 3 so he **p** the fare, and went
Matt 5:26 you have **p** the last penny
Luke 12:59 you have **p** the very last mite
Heb 7: 9 **p** tithes through Abraham, so
Heb 12: 9 us, and we **p** them respect

PAILS
Job 21:24 His **p** are full of milk, and

PAIN (*see* PAINED, PAINFUL, PAINS)
Gen 3:16 in **p** you shall bring forth
Gen 34:25 day, when they were in **p**,
1Ch 4: 9 Because I bore him in **p**
1Ch 4:10 evil, that I may not cause **p**
2Ch 21:19 so he died in severe **p**
Job 14:22 flesh will be in **p** over it
Job 15:20 writhes with **p** all his days
Job 33:19 chastened with **p** on his bed
Job 33:19 with strong **p** in many of his
Ps 25:18 Look on my affliction and my **p**
Ps 48: 6 took hold of them there, And **p**
Is 13: 8 they will be in **p** as a woman
Is 21: 3 my loins are filled with **p**
Is 26:17 As a woman with child is in **p**
Is 26:18 with child, we have been in **p**
Is 66: 7 before her **p** came, she
Jer 6:24 us, **p** as of a woman in labor
Jer 12:13 to **p** but do not profit
Jer 15:18 Why is my **p** perpetual and my
Jer 22:23 you, like the **p** of a woman in
Jer 51: 8 Take balm for her **p**
Ezek 30:16 Sin shall have great **p**, no
Joel 2: 6 them the people writhe in **p**
Mic 4:10 Be in **p**, and labor to bring
Nah 2:10 much **p** is in every side, and
Rev 12: 2 labor and in **p** to give birth
Rev 16:10 tongues because of the **p**
Rev 21: 4 and there shall be no more **p**

PAINED (*see* PAIN)
Ps 55: 4 heart is severely **p** within me
Jer 4:19 I am **p** in my very heart

PAINFUL (*see* PAIN)
Job 2: 7 struck Job with **p** boils from
Ps 73:16 this, It was too **p** for me
Ezek 28:24 or a **p** thorn for the house of

PAINS (*see* PAIN)
1Sa 4:19 for her labor **p** came upon her
Job 30:17 my gnawing **p** take no rest
Ps 116: 3 The **p** of death encompassed me
Acts 2:24 having loosed the **p** of death
1Th 5: 3 as labor **p** upon a pregnant
Rev 16:11 of heaven because of their **p**

PAINT (*see* PAINTED, PAINTING)
2Ki 9:30 and she put **p** on her eyes and
Jer 4:30 you enlarge your eyes with **p**

PAINTED (*see* PAINT)
Ezek 23:40 them, **p** your eyes, and adorned

PAINTING (*see* PAINT)
Jer 22:14 cedar and **p** it with vermilion

PAIR
Judg 15: 4 torch between each **p** of tails
Is 21: 7 chariot with a **p** of horsemen
Is 21: 9 of men with a **p** of horsemen
Amos 2: 6 the poor for a **p** of sandals
Amos 8: 6 the needy for a **p** of sandals
Luke 2:24 A **p** of turtledoves or two
Rev 6: 5 had a **p** of scales in his hand

PALACE (*see* PALACES)
1Ki 21: 1 next to the **p** of Ahab king of
2Ki 20:18 the **p** of the king of Babylon
Ezra 4:14 we receive support from the **p**
Ezra 6: 2 in the **p** that is in the
Esth 1: 5 of the garden of the king's **p**
Esth 1: 9 **p** which belonged to King
Esth 2: 8 was taken to the king's **p**

Esth 2: 9 for her from the king's **p**
Esth 2:13 quarters to the king's **p**
Esth 2:16 Ahasuerus, into his royal **p**
Esth 4:13 will escape in the king's **p**
Esth 5: 1 inner court of the king's **p**
Esth 6: 4 **p** to suggest that the king
Esth 7: 7 and went into the **p** garden
Esth 7: 8 **p** garden to the place of the
Esth 9: 4 was great in the king's **p**
Ps 45:13 is all glorious within the **p**
Ps 45:15 They shall enter the King's **p**
Ps 144:12 Sculptured in **p** style
Is 25: 2 a **p** of foreigners to be a
Is 39: 7 the **p** of the king of Babylon
Jer 30:18 the **p** shall remain according
Dan 1: 4 to serve in the king's **p**, and
Dan 4: 4 house, and flourishing in my **p**
Dan 4:29 about the royal **p** of Babylon
Dan 5: 5 of the wall of the king's **p**
Dan 6:18 Now the king went to his **p**
Dan 11:45 of his **p** between the seas
Nah 2: 6 opened, and the **p** is dissolved
Matt 26: 3 at the **p** of the high priest
Luke 11:21 fully armed, guards his own **p**
Phil 1:13 evident to the whole **p** guard

PALACES (*see* PALACE)
2Ch 36:19 burned all its **p** with fire
Ps 45: 8 and cassia, Out of the ivory **p**
Ps 48: 3 God is in her **p**
Ps 48:13 Consider her **p**
Ps 122: 7 Prosperity within your **p**
Prov 30:28 hands, and it is in kings' **p**
Is 13:22 jackals in their pleasant **p**
Is 23:13 towers, they raised up its **p**
Is 32:14 Because the **p** will be
Is 34:13 thorns shall come up in its **p**
Jer 6: 5 and let us destroy her **p**
Jer 9:21 windows, has entered our **p**
Jer 17:27 devour the **p** of Jerusalem
Jer 49:27 consume the **p** of Ben-Hadad
Lam 2: 5 He has swallowed up all her **p**
Lam 2: 7 given up the walls of her **p**
Hos 8:14 and it shall devour his **p**
Amos 1: 4 devour the **p** of Ben-Hadad
Amos 1: 7 which shall devour its **p**
Amos 1:10 which shall devour its **p**
Amos 1:12 shall devour the **p** of Bozrah
Amos 1:14 and it shall devour its **p**
Amos 2: 2 shall devour the **p** of Kerioth
Amos 2: 5 devour the **p** of Jerusalem
Amos 3: 9 Proclaim in the **p** at Ashdod
Amos 3: 9 in the **p** in the land of Egypt
Amos 3:10 and robbery in their **p**
Amos 3:11 your **p** shall be plundered
Amos 6: 8 pride of Jacob, and hate his **p**
Mic 5: 5 and when he treads in our **p**

PALAL
Neh 3:25 **P** the son of Uzai made

PALANQUIN
Song 3: 9 the King made himself a **p**

PALATE
Job 34: 3 words as the **p** tastes food

PALE
Is 29:22 nor shall his face now grow **p**
Jer 30: 6 labor, and all faces turned **p**
Rev 6: 8 looked, and behold, a **p** horse

PALESTINA (*see* PHILISTIA)
Ex 15:14 hold of the inhabitants of **P**

PALLU (*see* PALLUITES)
Gen 46: 9 sons of Reuben were Hanoch, **P**
Ex 6:14 of Israel, were Hanoch, **P**
Num 26: 5 of **P**, the family of the
Num 26: 8 And the son of **P** was Eliab
1Ch 5: 3 of Israel were Hanoch, **P**,

PALLUITES (*see* PALLU)
Num 26: 5 of Pallu, the family of the **P**

PALM (*see* PALMS)
Ex 15:27 of water and seventy **p** trees
Lev 14:15 pour it into the **p** of his own
Lev 14:26 the **p** of his own left hand
Lev 23:40 trees, branches of **p** trees
Num 33: 9 of water and seventy **p** trees
Deut 34: 3 Jericho, the city of **p** trees
Judg 4: 5 the **p** tree of Deborah between
1Ki 6:29 **p** trees, and open flowers
1Ki 6:32 **p** trees, and open flowers, and
1Ki 6:32 cherubim and on the **p** trees
1Ki 6:35 **p** trees, and open flowers on
1Ki 7:36 **p** trees, wherever there was a
2Ch 3: 5 gold, and he carved **p** trees
2Ch 28:15 Jericho, the city of **p** trees
Neh 8:15 **p** branches, and branches of
Ps 92:12 shall flourish like a **p** tree
Song 7: 7 of yours is like a **p** tree
Song 7: 8 I will go up to the **p** tree
Is 9:14 **p** branch and bulrush in one
Is 19:15 **p** branch or bulrush, may do
Jer 10: 5 are upright, like a **p** tree
Ezek 40:16 on each gatepost were **p** trees
Ezek 40:22 archways, and also its **p** trees
Ezek 40:26 and it had **p** trees on its
Ezek 40:31 **p** trees were on its gateposts
Ezek 40:34 **p** trees were on its gateposts
Ezek 40:37 **p** trees were on its gateposts
Ezek 41:18 **p** trees, a **p** tree between
Ezek 41:19 toward a **p** tree on one side
Ezek 41:19 a **p** tree on the other side
Ezek 41:20 and **p** trees were carved
Ezek 41:25 **p** trees were carved on the
Ezek 41:26 **p** trees on one side and on the
Joel 1:12 the **p** tree also, and the apple
John 12:13 took branches of **p** trees and
John 18:22 Jesus with the **p** of his hand
Rev 7: 9 with **p** branches in their

PALMS (*see* PALM)
Judg 1:16 went up from the city of **p**
Judg 3:13 possession of the city of **p**
1Sa 5: 4 both the **p** of its hands were
2Ki 9:35 feet and the **p** of her hands
Is 49:16 you on the **p** of My hands
Dan 10:10 knees and on the **p** of my hands
Matt 26:67 Him with the **p** of their hands
Mark 14:65 Him with the **p** of their hands

PALTI
Num 13: 9 Benjamin, **P** the son of Raphu
1Sa 25:44 to **P** the son of Laish, who

PALTIEL
Num 34:26 Issachar, **P** the son of Azzan
2Sa 3:15 from **P** the son of Laish

PALTITE (*see* PELONITE)
2Sa 23:26 Helez the **P**, Ira the son of

PAMPERS
Prov 29:21 He who **p** his servant from

PAMPHYLIA
Acts 2:10 Phrygia and **P**, Egypt and the
Acts 13:13 they came to Perga in **P**
Acts 14:24 Pisidia, they came to **P**
Acts 15:38 had departed from them in **P**
Acts 27: 5 sea which is off Cilicia and **P**

PAN (*see* PANS)
Lev 2: 5 a grain offering baked in a **p**
Lev 2: 7 offering baked in a covered **p**
Lev 6:21 shall be made in a **p** with oil
Lev 7: 9 in the covered **p**, or in a **p**
Num 7:14 one gold **p** of ten shekels,
Num 7:20 one gold **p** of ten shekels,
Num 7:26 one gold **p** of ten shekels,
Num 7:32 one gold **p** of ten shekels,
Num 7:38 one gold **p** of ten shekels,
Num 7:44 one gold **p** of ten shekels,
Num 7:50 one gold **p** of ten shekels,
Num 7:56 one gold **p** of ten shekels,
Num 7:62 one gold **p** of ten shekels,
Num 7:68 one gold **p** of ten shekels,
Num 7:74 one gold **p** of ten shekels,
Num 7:80 one gold **p** of ten shekels,
1Sa 2:14 he would thrust it into the **p**
2Sa 13: 9 And she took the **p** and placed
1Ch 23:29 and what is baked in the **p**

PANELED (*see* PANELING, PANELS)
1Ki 6: 9 he **p** the temple with beams and
1Ki 6:15 he **p** them on the inside with
1Ki 7: 3 it was **p** with cedar above the
1Ki 7: 7 and it was **p** with cedar from
2Ch 3: 5 The larger room he **p** with
Ezek 41:16 **p** with wood from the ground
Hag 1: 4 to dwell in your **p** houses

PANELING (*see* PANELED)
Jer 22:14 **p** it with cedar and painting

PANELS (*see* PANELED)
1Ki 6:34 two **p** comprised one folding
1Ki 6:34 two **p** comprised the other
1Ki 7:28 They had **p**, and the **p**
1Ki 7:28 the **p** were between frames
1Ki 7:29 on the **p** that were between
1Ki 7:31 but the **p** were square, not
1Ki 7:32 Under the **p** were the four
1Ki 7:35 and its **p** were of the same
1Ki 7:36 on its **p** he engraved cherubim
2Ki 16:17 cut off the **p** of the carts
Ezek 41:24 two **p** apiece, two folding **p**
Ezek 41:24 two **p** for one door
Ezek 41:24 and two **p** for the other door

PANGS
Ps 18: 4 The **p** of death encompassed me
Ps 73: 4 there are no **p** in their death
Ps 116: 3 the **p** of Sheol laid hold of
Is 13: 8 **P** and sorrows will take hold
Is 21: 3 **p** have taken hold of me
Is 21: 3 me, like the **p** of a woman in
Is 26:17 in her **p**, when she draws
Jer 13:21 Will not **p** seize you, like a
Jer 22:23 you be when **p** come upon you
Jer 48:41 heart of a woman in birth **p**
Jer 49:22 heart of a woman in birth **p**
Jer 50:43 **p** as of a woman in childbirth
Mic 4: 9 For **p** have seized you like a
Mic 4:10 Zion, like a woman in birth **p**
Rom 8:22 labors with birth **p** together

PANIC (*see* PANICKED)
Zech 14:13 in that day that a great **p**

PANICKED (*see* PANIC)
Judg 20:41 back, the men of Benjamin **p**

PANS (*see* PAN)
Ex 25:29 shall make its dishes, its **p**
Ex 27: 3 its **p** to receive its ashes
Ex 38: 3 the **p**, the shovels, the
Num 4: 7 put on it the dishes, the **p**
Num 7:84 bowls, and twelve gold **p**
Num 7:86 The twelve gold **p** full of
Num 7:86 of the **p** weighed one hundred
Num 11: 8 in the mortar, cooked it in **p**
1Ch 9:31 that were baked in the **p**
2Ch 35:13 in pots, in caldrons, and in **p**

PANT (*see* PANTED, PANTS)
Is 42:14 a woman in labor, I will **p**
Amos 2: 7 They **p** after the dust of the

PANTED (*see* PANT)
Ps 119:131 I opened my mouth and **p**, For I

PANTS (*see* PANT)
Ps 38:10 My heart **p**, my strength fails
Ps 42: 1 As the deer **p** for the water
Ps 42: 1 So **p** my soul for You, O God

PAPER
2Jn 12 did not wish to do so with **p**

PAPHOS
Acts 13: 6 gone through the island to **P**
Acts 13:13 and his party set sail from **P**

PAPYRUS
Job 8:11 Can the **p** grow up without a
Is 19: 7 The **p** reeds by the River, by

PARABLE (*see* PARABLES)
Ps 78: 2 I will open my mouth in a **p**
Ezek 17: 2 speak a **p** to the house of
Ezek 24: 3 utter a **p** to the rebellious
Matt 13:18 hear the **p** of the sower
Matt 13:24 Another **p** He put forth to
Matt 13:31 Another **p** He put forth to
Matt 13:33 Another **p** He spoke to them
Matt 13:34 without a **p** He did not speak
Matt 13:36 Explain to us the **p** of the
Matt 15:15 Explain this **p** to us
Matt 21:33 Hear another **p**
Matt 24:32 Now learn this **p** from the fig
Mark 4:10 twelve asked Him about the **p**
Mark 4:13 Do you not understand this **p**
Mark 4:30 Or with what **p** shall we
Mark 4:34 But without a **p** He did not
Mark 7:17 asked Him concerning the **p**
Mark 12:12 had spoken the **p** against them
Mark 13:28 Now learn this **p** from the fig
Luke 5:36 Then He spoke a **p** to them
Luke 6:39 And He spoke a **p** to them
Luke 8: 4 every city, He spoke by a **p**

Luke 8: 9 What does this **p** mean
Luke 8:11 Now the **p** is this
Luke 12:16 Then He spoke a **p** to them
Luke 12:41 You speak this **p** only to us
Luke 13: 6 He also spoke this **p**
Luke 14: 7 So He told a **p** to those who
Luke 15: 3 So He spoke this **p** to them
Luke 18: 1 Then He spoke a **p** to them
Luke 18: 9 Also He spoke this **p** to some
Luke 19:11 things, He spoke another **p**
Luke 20: 9 to tell the people this **p**
Luke 20:19 spoken this **p** against them
Luke 21:29 And He spoke to them a **p**

PARABLES (*see* PARABLE)
Ezek 20:49 of me, 'Does he not speak **p**
Matt 13: 3 many things to them in **p**,
Matt 13:10 Why do You speak to them in **p**
Matt 13:13 I speak to them in **p**, because
Matt 13:34 spoke to the multitude in **p**
Matt 13:35 I will open My mouth in **p**
Matt 13:53 Jesus had finished these **p**
Matt 21:45 and Pharisees heard His **p**,
Matt 22: 1 and spoke to them again by **p**
Mark 3:23 to Him and said to them in **p**
Mark 4: 2 taught them many things by **p**
Mark 4:11 outside, all things come in **p**
Mark 4:13 will you understand all the **p**
Mark 4:33 with many such **p** He spoke the
Mark 12: 1 began to speak to them in **p**
Luke 8:10 to the rest it is given in **p**

PARADE
Esth 6: 9 Then **p** him on horseback
Job 18:14 they **p** him before the king of
1Co 13: 4 love does not **p** itself, is

PARADISE
Luke 23:43 you will be with Me in **P**
2Co 12: 4 how he was caught up into **P**
Rev 2: 7 in the midst of the **P** of God

PARAH
Josh 18:23 Avim, **P**, Ophrah,

PARALLEL
Ezek 42: 7 outside ran **p** to the chambers

PARALYTIC (*see* PARALYTICS, PARALYZED)
Matt 9: 2 to Him a **p** lying on a bed
Matt 9: 2 their faith, said to the **p**
Matt 9: 6 then He said to the **p**
Mark 2: 3 bringing a **p** who was carried
Mark 2: 4 bed on which the **p** was lying
Mark 2: 5 their faith, He said to the **p**
Mark 2: 9 is easier, to say to the **p**
Mark 2:10 He said to the **p**,

PARALYTICS (*see* PARALYTIC)
Matt 4:24 epileptics, and **p**

PARALYZED (*see* PARALYTIC)
Matt 8: 6 my servant is lying at home **p**
Luke 5:18 on a bed a man who was **p**
Luke 5:24 He said to the man who was **p**
John 5: 3 sick people, blind, lame, **p**
Acts 8: 7 and many who were **p** and lame
Acts 9:33 eight years and was **p**

PARAMOURS
Ezek 23:20 For she lusted for her **p**,

PARAN (*see* EL PARAN)
Gen 21:21 dwelt in the Wilderness of **P**
Num 10:12 down in the Wilderness of **P**
Num 12:16 camped in the Wilderness of **P**
Num 13: 3 **P** according to the command of
Num 13:26 Israel in the Wilderness of **P**
Deut 1: 1 opposite Suph, between **P**,
Deut 33: 2 He shone forth from Mount **P**
1Sa 25: 1 down to the Wilderness of **P**
1Ki 11:18 from Midian and came to **P**
1Ki 11:18 took men with them from **P**
Hab 3: 3 the Holy One from Mount **P**

PARAPET
Deut 22: 8 shall make a **p** for your roof

PARBAR
1Ch 26:18 As for the **P** on the west,
1Ch 26:18 the highway and two at the **P**

PARCEL
Gen 33:19 And he bought the **p** of land

PARCHED
Lev 23:14 **p** grain nor fresh grain until
Josh 5:11 **p** grain on the very same day
Ruth 2:14 and he passed **p** grain to her
2Sa 17:28 **p** grain and beans, lentils and
2Sa 17:28 and beans, lentils and **p** seeds,
Job 14:11 the sea, and a river becomes **p**
Is 35: 7 The **p** ground shall become a
Jer 14: 4 Because the ground is **p**, for
Jer 17: 6 but shall inhabit the **p**

PARCHMENTS
2Ti 4:13 the books, especially the **p**

PARDON (*see* PARDONED, PARDONING)
Ex 23:21 Him, for He will not **p** your
Ex 34: 9 **p** our iniquity and our sin, and
Num 14:19 **P** the iniquity of this people
1Sa 15:25 therefore, please **p** my sin
2Ki 5:18 may the LORD **p** your servant
2Ki 5:18 may the LORD please **p** your
2Ki 24: 4 which the LORD would not **p**
Neh 9:17 But You are God, ready to **p**
Job 7:21 do You not **p** my transgression
Ps 25:11 **P** my iniquity, for it is
Is 55: 7 God, for He will abundantly **p**
Jer 5: 1 the truth, and I will **p** her
Jer 5: 7 How shall I **p** you for this
Jer 33: 8 I will **p** all their iniquities
Jer 50:20 for I will **p** those whom I

PARDONED (*see* PARDON)
Num 14:20 I have **p**, according to your
Is 40: 2 ended, that her iniquity is **p**
Lam 3:42 You have not **p**

PARDONING (*see* PARDON)
Mic 7:18 **p** iniquity and passing over

PARENTS
Matt 10:21 will rise up against **p** and
Mark 13:12 will rise up against **p** and
Luke 2:27 when the **p** brought in the
Luke 2:41 His **p** went to Jerusalem every
Luke 8:56 her **p** were astonished, but He
Luke 18:29 or **p** or brothers or wife or
Luke 21:16 will be betrayed even by **p**
John 9: 2 who sinned, this man or his **p**
John 9: 3 this man nor his **p** sinned
John 9:18 until they called the **p** of
John 9:20 His **p** answered them and said,
John 9:22 His **p** said these things
John 9:23 Therefore his **p** said, "He is
Rom 1:30 evil things, disobedient to **p**
2Co 12:14 ought not to lay up for the **p**
2Co 12:14 but the **p** for the children
Eph 6: 1 obey your **p** in the Lord, for
Col 3:20 obey your **p** in all things,
1Ti 5: 4 at home and to repay their **p**
2Ti 3: 2 blasphemers, disobedient to **p**
Heb 11:23 hidden three months by his **p**

PARMASHTA
Esth 9: 9 **P**, Arisai, Aridai, and

PARMENAS
Acts 6: 5 Prochorus, Nicanor, Timon, **P**

PARNACH
Num 34:25 Elizaphan the son of **P**

PAROSH
Ezra 2: 3 the people of **P**, two thousand
Ezra 8: 3 Shecaniah, of the sons of **P**
Ezra 10:25 of the sons of **P**
Neh 3:25 the son of **P** made repairs
Neh 7: 8 the children of **P**, two
Neh 10:14 **P**, Pahath-Moab, Elam, Zattu,

PARSHANDATHA
Esth 9: 7 Also **P**, Dalphon, Aspatha,

PART (*see* PARTED, PARTING, PARTLY, PARTS)
Gen 27:16 on the smooth **p** of his neck
Gen 31:37 what **p** of your household
Ex 16:20 left **p** of it until morning
Lev 2:16 **p** of its beaten grain
Lev 2:16 and **p** of its oil,
Lev 7:33 the right thigh for his **p**
Lev 8:29 It was Moses' **p** of the ram of
Lev 11:25 whoever carries **p** of the
Lev 11:35 everything on which a **p** of
Lev 11:37 if a **p** of any such carcass
Lev 11:38 if a **p** of any such carcass
Lev 27:16 LORD some **p** of a field of his
Num 18:29 the sanctified **p** of them
Num 23:13 see only the outer **p** of them
Num 31:27 those who took **p** in the war
Deut 14:27 gates, for he has no **p** nor
Deut 18: 1 of Levi, shall have no **p** nor
Deut 33:21 the first **p** for himself,
Josh 14: 4 they gave no **p** to the Levites
Josh 18: 7 Levites have no **p** among you
Josh 22:25 You have no **p** in the LORD
Josh 22:27 You have no **p** in the LORD
Ruth 2: 3 **p** of the field belonging to
1Sa 9:24 up the thigh with its upper **p**
1Sa 23:20 our **p** shall be to deliver him
1Sa 27: 1 me anymore in any **p** of Israel
1Sa 30:24 But as his **p** is who goes down
1Sa 30:24 so shall his **p** be who stays
2Sa 4: 2 also was **p** of Benjamin,
2Sa 14: 6 and there was no one to **p** them
2Sa 20: 1 We have no **p** in David, nor do
1Ki 7:34 its supports were **p** of the
2Ki 18:23 your **p** to put riders on them
1Ch 12:29 (until then the greatest **p** of
2Ch 28:21 For Ahaz took **p** of the
2Ch 29:16 **p** of the house of the LORD to
Neh 1: 9 the farthest **p** of the heavens
Neh 5:11 the hundredth **p** of the money
Job 32:17 I also will answer my **p**, I
Ps 5: 9 Their inward **p** is destruction
Ps 51: 6 in the hidden **p** You will make
Is 7:18 **p** of the rivers of Egypt, and
Is 36: 8 your **p** to put riders on them
Ezek 26:20 in the lowest **p** of the earth
Ezek 45:17 **p** to give burnt offerings
Ezek 48:14 this best **p** of the land, for
Dan 5: 5 the king saw the **p** of the
Amos 4: 7 One **p** was rained upon, and
Amos 4: 7 did not rain the **p** withered
Mark 13:27 from the farthest **p** of earth
Mark 13:27 to the farthest **p** of heaven
Luke 10:42 Mary has chosen that good **p**
Luke 11:36 of light, having no **p** dark
Luke 11:39 but your inward **p** is full of
Luke 17:24 that flashes out of one **p**
Luke 17:24 to the other **p** under heaven
John 13: 8 you, you have no **p** with Me
John 19:23 parts, to each soldier a **p**
Acts 1:17 obtained a **p** in this ministry
Acts 1:25 to take **p** in this ministry and
Acts 5: 2 And he kept back **p** of the
Acts 5: 2 of it, and brought a certain **p**
Acts 5: 3 keep back **p** of the price of
Acts 8:21 You have neither **p** nor
Acts 14: 4 **p** sided with the Jews, and
Acts 14: 4 Jews, and **p** with the apostles
Acts 16:12 city of that **p** of Macedonia
Acts 23: 6 that one **p** were Sadducees
Rom 11:25 that hardening in **p** has
1Co 11:18 you, and in **p** I believe it
1Co 12:24 to that **p** which lacks it,
1Co 13: 9 know in **p** and we prophesy in **p**
1Co 13:10 is in **p** will be done away
1Co 13:12 Now I know in **p**, but then I
1Co 15: 6 of whom the greater **p** remain
1Co 16:17 on your **p** they supplied
2Co 1:14 you have understood us in **p**)
2Co 6:15 Or what **p** has a believer with
Eph 4:16 which every **p** does its share
Heb 7: 2 Abraham gave a tenth **p** of all
Heb 9: 2 the first **p**, in which was the
Heb 9: 3 the **p** of the tabernacle which
Heb 9: 6 the first **p** of the tabernacle
Heb 9: 7 But into the second **p** the
1Pe 4:14 On their **p** He is blasphemed,
1Pe 4:14 but on your **p** He is glorified
Rev 20: 6 holy is he who has **p** in the
Rev 21: 8 **p** in the lake which burns
Rev 22:19 his **p** from the Book of Life

PARTAKE (*see* PARTAKEN, PARTAKER, PARTAKES)
Deut 33:19 for they shall **p** of the
1Co 9:13 who serve at the altar **p** of
1Co 10:17 for we all **p** of that one
1Co 10:21 you cannot **p** of the Lord's
1Co 10:30 But if I **p** with thanks, why
2Co 1: 7 so also you will **p** of the
2Ti 2: 6 be first to **p** of the crops
1Pe 4:13 you **p** of Christ's sufferings

PARTAKEN (*see* PARTAKE)
Heb 2:14 the children have **p** of flesh

PARTAKER (*see* PARTAKE, PARTAKERS)
Ps 50:18 have been a **p** with adulterers
Rom 11:17 them became a **p** of the root
1Co 9:10 hope should be **p** of his hope
1Co 9:23 that I may be **p** of it with
1Pe 5: 1 also a **p** of the glory that

PARTAKERS (*see* PARTAKER)
Matt 23:30 we would not have been **p** with
Rom 15:27 **p** of their spiritual things
1Co 9:12 If others are **p** of this right
1Co 10:18 the sacrifices **p** of the altar
2Co 1: 7 you are **p** of the sufferings
Eph 3: 6 **p** of His promise in Christ
Eph 5: 7 do not be **p** with them
Phil 1: 7 you all are **p** with me of
Col 1:12 **p** of the inheritance of the
Heb 3: 1 **p** of the heavenly calling,
Heb 3:14 For we have become **p** of
Heb 6: 4 have become **p** of the Holy
Heb 12: 8 of which all have become **p**
Heb 12:10 that we may be **p** of His
2Pe 1: 4 may be **p** of the divine nature

PARTAKES (*see* PARTAKE)
Heb 5:13 For everyone who **p** only of

PARTED (*see* PART)
Gen 2:10 garden, and from there it **p**
Job 41:17 stick together and cannot be **p**
Luke 24:51 them, that He was **p** from them
Acts 15:39 that they **p** from one another

PARTHIANS
Acts 2: 9 **P** and Medes and Elamites,

PARTIAL (*see* PARTIALITY)
Lev 19:15 shall not be **p** to the poor
Job 34:19 Yet He is not **p** to princes

PARTIALITY (*see* PARTIAL)
Ex 23: 3 You shall not show **p** to a
Deut 1:17 shall not show **p** in judgment
Deut 10:17 who shows no **p** nor takes a
Deut 16:19 you shall not show **p**, nor
2Ch 19: 7 with the LORD our God, no **p**
Job 13: 8 Will you show **p** for Him
Job 13:10 you if you secretly show **p**
Job 32:21 not, I pray, show **p** to anyone
Job 37:24 He shows no **p** to any who are
Ps 82: 2 And show **p** to the wicked
Prov 18: 5 good to show **p** to the wicked
Prov 24:23 good to show **p** in judgment
Prov 28:21 To show **p** is not good,
Mal 2: 9 but have shown **p** in the law
Acts 10:34 perceive that God shows no **p**
Rom 2:11 For there is no **p** with God
Eph 6: 9 and there is no **p** with Him
Col 3:25 he has done, and there is no **p**
1Ti 5:21 doing nothing with **p**
Jas 2: 1 the Lord of glory, with **p**
Jas 2: 4 not shown **p** among yourselves
Jas 2: 9 but if you show **p**, you commit
Jas 3:17 and good fruits, without **p**
1Pe 1:17 Father, who without **p** judges

PARTICULAR
Zech 11: 7 in **p** the poor of the flock
Eph 5:33 let each one of you in **p** so

PARTIES (*see* PARTY)
Ex 22: 9 the cause of both **p** shall
1Pe 4: 3 revelries, drinking **p**, and

PARTING (*see* PART)
Ezek 21:21 stands at the **p** of the road
Mark 1:10 water, He saw the heavens **p**
Luke 9:33 as they were **p** from Him,

PARTITION (*see* PARTITIONED)
Ex 40: 3 **p** off the ark with the veil

PARTITIONED (*see* PARTITION)
Ex 40:21 and **p** off the ark of the

PARTLY (*see* PART)
Dan 2:33 **p** of iron and **p** of clay
Dan 2:41 **p** of potter's clay and **p**
Dan 2:41 **p** of iron, the kingdom shall
Dan 2:42 of the feet were **p** of iron
Dan 2:42 **p** of clay, so the kingdom
Dan 2:42 the kingdom shall be **p** strong
Dan 2:42 be **p** strong and **p** fragile
Heb 10:33 **p** while you were made a
Heb 10:33 **p** while you became companions

PARTNER (*see* PARTNERS)
Prov 29:24 Whoever is a **p** with a thief
2Co 8:23 about Titus, he is my **p** and
Phm 17 If then you count me as a **p**

PARTNERS (*see* PARTNER)
Luke 5: 7 **p** in the other boat to come
Luke 5:10 who were **p** with Simon

PARTRIDGE
1Sa 26:20 hunts a **p** in the mountains
Jer 17:11 As a **p** that broods but does

PARTS (*see* PART)
Lev 1: 8 Aaron's sons, shall lay the **p**
Num 31:27 divide the plunder into two **p**
Deut 14: 6 the hoof split into two **p**
Deut 19: 3 and divide into three **p** the
Deut 30: 4 the farthest **p** under heaven
Josh 18: 5 shall divide it into seven **p**
Josh 18: 6 survey the land in seven **p**
Josh 18: 9 a book in seven **p** by cities
Ruth 1:17 if anything but death **p** you
1Ki 7:25 their back **p** pointed inward
1Ki 16:21 were divided into two **p**
2Ki 10:32 began to cut off **p** of Israel
2Ch 4: 4 their back **p** pointed inward
Neh 4:13 the lower **p** of the wall, at
Ps 51: 6 desire truth in the inward **p**
Ps 63: 9 into the lower **p** of the earth
Ps 65: 8 **p** are afraid of Your signs
Ps 139: 9 in the uttermost **p** of the sea
Ps 139:13 You have formed my inward **p**
Ps 139:15 in the lowest **p** of the earth
Is 3:17 will uncover their secret **p**
Is 44:23 you lower **p** of the earth
Jer 6:22 the farthest **p** of the earth
Jer 25:32 the farthest **p** of the earth
Jer 34:18 and passed between the **p** of it
Jer 34:19 between the **p** of the calf
Ezek 32:24 to the lower **p** of the earth
Jon 1: 5 into the lowest **p** of the ship
John 19:23 His garments and made four **p**
Acts 2:10 and the **p** of Libya adjoining
Acts 9:32 through all **p** of the country
Rom 15:23 having a place in these **p**
1Co 12:23 and our unpresentable **p** have
1Co 12:24 presentable **p** have no need
Eph 4: 9 into the lower **p** of the earth
Rev 16:19 city was divided into three **p**

PARTY (*see* PARTIES)
Neh 4:22 night and a working **p** by day
Ezek 39:14 with the help of a search **p**
Ezek 39:15 The search **p** will pass
Acts 13:13 his **p** set sail from Paphos,
Acts 23: 9 of the Pharisees' **p** arose

PARUAH
1Ki 4:17 Jehoshaphat the son of **P**, in

PARVAIM
2Ch 3: 6 and the gold was gold from **P**

PARZITES
Num 26:20 of Perez, the family of the **P**

PASACH
1Ch 7:33 The sons of Japhlet were **P**

PASDAMMIM (*see* EPHES DAMMIM)
1Ch 11:13 He was with David at **P**

PASEAH
1Ch 4:12 Eshton begot Beth-Rapha, **P**
Ezra 2:49 sons of Uzza, the sons of **P**
Neh 3: 6 Jehoiada the son of **P** and
Neh 7:51 of Uzza, the children of **P**

PASHHUR
Ezra 2:38 the sons of **P**, one thousand
Ezra 10:22 of the sons of **P**
Neh 7:41 the children of **P**, one
Neh 10: 3 **P**, Amariah, Malchijah,
Neh 11:12 of Zechariah, the son of **P**
Jer 20: 1 Now **P** the son of Immer, the
Jer 20: 2 Then **P** struck Jeremiah the
Jer 20: 3 on the next day that **P**
Jer 20: 3 has not called your name **P**
Jer 20: 6 And you, **P**, and all who dwell
Jer 21: 1 to him **P** the son of Melchiah
Jer 38: 1 Mattan, Gedaliah the son of **P**
Jer 38: 1 **P** the son of Malchiah heard

PASHUR
1Ch 9:12 son of Jeroham, the son of **P**

PASS (*see* PASSED, PASSES, PASSING)
Gen 4: 3 to **p** that Cain brought an
Gen 4: 8 and it came to **p**, when they
Gen 6: 1 Now it came to **p**, when men
Gen 7:10 it came to **p** after seven days
Gen 8: 1 a wind to **p** over the earth
Gen 8: 6 So it came to **p**, at the end
Gen 8:13 And it came to **p** in the six
Gen 11: 2 And it came to **p**, as they
Gen 12:11 And it came to **p**, when he was
Gen 14: 1 it came to **p** in the days of
Gen 15:17 And it came to **p**, when the sun
Gen 18: 3 do not **p** on by Your servant
Gen 18: 5 After that you may **p** by,
Gen 19:17 So it came to **p**, when they
Gen 19:29 And it came to **p**, when God
Gen 20:13 And it came to **p**, when God
Gen 21:22 it came to **p** at that time
Gen 22: 1 Now it came to **p** after these
Gen 22:20 Now it came to **p** after these
Gen 24:30 So it came to **p**, when he saw
Gen 24:43 it shall come to **p** that when
Gen 24:52 And it came to **p**, when
Gen 25:11 And it came to **p**, after the
Gen 26: 8 Now it came to **p**, when he had
Gen 26:32 It came to **p** the same day
Gen 27: 1 Now it came to **p**, when Isaac
Gen 27:40 and it shall come to **p**, when
Gen 29:10 And it came to **p**, when Jacob
Gen 29:13 Then it came to **p**, when Laban
Gen 29:23 it came to **p** in the evening
Gen 29:25 So it came to **p** in the
Gen 30:25 And it came to **p**, when Rachel
Gen 30:32 Let me **p** through all your
Gen 30:41 And it came to **p**, whenever the
Gen 31:52 that I will not **p** beyond this
Gen 31:52 you will not **p** beyond this
Gen 32:16 **P** over before me, and put some
Gen 34:25 Now it came to **p** on the third
Gen 35:17 Now it came to **p**, when she
Gen 37:23 So it came to **p**, when Joseph
Gen 38: 1 It came to **p** at that time
Gen 38: 9 and it came to **p**, when he went
Gen 38:24 And it came to **p**, about three
Gen 38:27 Now it came to **p**, at the time
Gen 39: 7 Now it came to **p** after these
Gen 40: 1 It came to **p** after these
Gen 40:20 Now it came to **p** on the third
Gen 41: 1 Then it came to **p**, at the end
Gen 41: 8 Now it came to **p** in the
Gen 41:13 And it came to **p** just as he
Gen 41:32 will shortly bring it to **p**
Gen 43: 2 And it came to **p**, when they
Gen 47:24 it shall come to **p** in the
Gen 48: 1 Now it came to **p** after these
Ex 2:11 it came to **p** in those days
Ex 4:24 And it came to **p** on the way
Ex 6:28 And it came to **p**, on the day
Ex 12:12 For I will **p** through the
Ex 12:13 the blood, I will **p** over you
Ex 12:23 For the LORD will **p** through
Ex 12:23 the LORD will **p** over the door
Ex 12:25 It will come to **p** when you
Ex 12:29 it came to **p** at midnight that
Ex 12:41 it came to **p** at the end of
Ex 12:41 it came to **p** that all the
Ex 12:51 So it came to **p**, on that very
Ex 13:15 And it came to **p**, when
Ex 13:17 Then it came to **p**, when
Ex 14:24 Now it came to **p**, in the
Ex 15:16 till Your people **p** over, O
Ex 15:16 till the people **p** over whom
Ex 16:10 Now it came to **p**, as Aaron
Ex 19:16 Then it came to **p** on the
Ex 26:28 The middle bar shall **p**
Ex 32:30 it came to **p** on the next day
Ex 33: 7 it came to **p** that everyone
Ex 33: 9 And it came to **p**, when Moses
Ex 33:19 all My goodness **p** before you
Ex 33:22 you with My hand while I **p** by
Ex 36:33 he made the middle bar to **p**
Ex 40:17 it came to **p** in the first
Lev 9: 1 It came to **p** on the eighth
Lev 18:21 **p** through the fire to Molech
Num 7: 1 Now it came to **p**, when Moses
Num 10:11 Now it came to **p** on the
Num 16:31 Then it came to **p**, as he
Num 17: 8 Now it came to **p** on the next

Num 20:17 Please let us **p** through your
Num 20:17 We will not **p** through fields
Num 20:18 You shall not **p** through my
Num 20:19 let me only **p** through on foot
Num 20:20 You shall not **p** through
Num 21:22 Let me **p** through your land
Num 21:23 to **p** through his territory
Num 26: 1 And it came to **p**, after the
Num 27: 7 of their father to **p** to them
Num 27: 8 to **p** to his daughter
Deut 1: 3 Now it came to **p** in the
Deut 2: 4 You are about to **p** through
Deut 2:27 Let me **p** through your land
Deut 2:28 only let me **p** through on foot
Deut 2:30 would not let us **p** through
Deut 3:21 kingdoms through which you **p**
Deut 7:12 Then it shall come to **p**,
Deut 9:11 And it came to **p**, at the end
Deut 13: 2 he spoke to you comes to **p**
Deut 18:10 daughter **p** through the fire
Deut 18:22 does not happen or come to **p**
Deut 28: 1 Now it shall come to **p**, if
Deut 28:15 But it shall come to **p**, if
Deut 30: 1 Now it shall come to **p**, when
Josh 1: 1 it came to **p** that the LORD
Josh 1:11 **P** through the camp and
Josh 1:14 But you shall **p** before your
Josh 3:13 And it shall come to **p**, as
Josh 4: 1 And it came to **p**, when all the
Josh 4:11 Then it came to **p**, when all
Josh 4:18 And it came to **p**, when the
Josh 5:13 And it came to **p**, when Joshua
Josh 6: 5 Then it shall come to **p**, when
Josh 6:15 But it came to **p** on the
Josh 8:24 it came to **p** when Israel had
Josh 9: 1 it came to **p** when all the
Josh 10: 1 Now it came to **p** when
Josh 11: 1 And it came to **p**, when Jabin
Josh 21:45 All came to **p**
Josh 23: 1 Now it came to **p**, a long time
Josh 23:14 All have come to **p** for you
Josh 23:15 Therefore it shall come to **p**
Josh 24:29 Now it came to **p** after these
Judg 1: 1 death of Joshua it came to **p**
Judg 1:28 And it came to **p**, when Israel
Judg 2:19 And it came to **p**, when the
Judg 6: 7 And it came to **p**, when the
Judg 6:25 Now it came to **p** the same
Judg 11: 4 Now it came to **p** after a time
Judg 11:17 Please let me **p** through your
Judg 11:19 Please let us **p** through your
Judg 11:20 to **p** through his territory
Judg 11:35 And it came to **p**, when he saw
Judg 13:12 Now let Your words come to **p**
Judg 13:17 come to **p** we may honor You
Judg 14:15 So it came to **p** on the
Judg 16:16 And it came to **p**, when she
Judg 19: 1 it came to **p** in those days,
Judg 19: 5 Then it came to **p** on the
Judg 21: 3 has this come to **p** in Israel
Ruth 1: 1 Now it came to **p**, in the days
1Sa 1:20 So it came to **p** in the
1Sa 2:36 And it shall come to **p** that
1Sa 3: 2 it came to **p** at that time,
1Sa 8: 1 Now it came to **p** when Samuel
1Sa 9: 6 he says surely comes to **p**
1Sa 10: 9 signs came to **p** that day
1Sa 13:23 went out to the **p** of Michmash
1Sa 16: 8 and made him **p** before Samuel
1Sa 16: 9 Then Jesse made Shammah **p** by
1Sa 16:10 of his sons **p** before Samuel
1Sa 25:30 And it shall come to **p**, when
1Sa 31: 8 So it came to **p** the next day
2Sa 1: 1 Now it came to **p** after the
2Sa 7: 1 Now it came to **p** when the
2Sa 8: 1 After this it came to **p** that
2Sa 11: 1 Now it came to **p** in the
2Sa 12:18 came to **p** that the child died
2Sa 13:23 And it came to **p**, after two
2Sa 13:30 And it came to **p**, while they
2Sa 15: 7 And it came to **p** after forty
2Sa 17:21 Now it came to **p**, after they
1Ki 6: 1 And it came to **p** in the four
1Ki 8:10 And it came to **p**, when the
1Ki 9: 1 And it came to **p**, when Solomon
1Ki 12:20 Now it came to **p** when all
1Ki 13: 4 So it came to **p** when King
1Ki 13:32 will surely come to **p**
1Ki 16:11 Then it came to **p**, when he
1Ki 16:31 And it came to **p**, as though it

1Ki 18: 1 Now it came to **p** after many
1Ki 18:12 And it shall come to **p**, as
1Ki 18:36 And it came to **p**, at the time
1Ki 18:44 Then it came to **p** the seventh
1Ki 21: 1 And it came to **p** after these
1Ki 21:15 And it came to **p**, when Jezebel
1Ki 22: 2 Then it came to **p**, in the
2Ki 2: 1 And it came to **p**, when the
2Ki 4: 6 Now it came to **p**, when the
2Ki 6: 9 that you do not **p** this place
2Ki 8: 3 It came to **p**, at the end of
2Ki 16: 3 his son **p** through the fire
2Ki 17:17 daughters to **p** through the
2Ki 18: 1 Now it came to **p** in the third
2Ki 18: 9 Now it came to **p** in the
2Ki 19:25 Now I have brought it to **p**
2Ki 19:35 it came to **p** on a certain
2Ki 19:37 Now it came to **p**, as he was
2Ki 21: 6 his son **p** through the fire
2Ki 22: 3 Now it came to **p**, in the
2Ki 23:10 his son or his daughter **p**
2Ki 25: 1 Now it came to **p** in the ninth
2Ki 25:27 Now it came to **p** in the
1Ch 17: 1 Now it came to **p**, when David
1Ch 18: 1 After this it came to **p** that
2Ch 5:11 it came to **p** when the priests
2Ch 5:13 indeed it came to **p**, when the
2Ch 8: 1 It came to **p** at the end of
2Ch 12: 1 Now it came to **p**, when
2Ch 33: 6 to **p** through the fire in the
Neh 1: 1 It came to **p** in the month of
Neh 2: 1 it came to **p** in the month of
Neh 2: 7 to **p** through till I come to
Neh 2:14 animal that was under me to **p**
Esth 1: 1 Now it came to **p** in the days
Job 6:15 of the brooks that **p** away
Job 9:26 They **p** by like swift ships,
Job 14: 5 limits, so that he cannot **p**
Job 19: 8 up my way, so that I cannot **p**
Job 34:20 people are shaken and **p** away
Ps 8: 8 **p** through the paths of the
Ps 37: 5 And He shall bring it to **p**
Ps 37: 7 brings wicked schemes to **p**
Ps 78:13 and caused them to **p** through
Ps 80:12 So that all who **p** by the way
Ps 84: 6 As they **p** through the Valley
Ps 89:41 All who **p** by the way plunder
Ps 104: 9 that they may not **p** over,
Ps 105:19 time that his word came to **p**
Ps 129: 8 let those who **p** by them say
Ps 136:14 made Israel **p** through the
Ps 148: 6 decree which shall not **p** away
Prov 4:15 turn away from it and **p** on
Prov 9:15 to call to those who **p** by
Prov 22: 3 himself, but the simple **p** on
Prov 27:12 the simple **p** on and are
Is 2: 2 Now it shall come to **p** in the
Is 4: 3 it shall come to **p** that he
Is 7: 1 Now it came to **p** in the days
Is 7: 7 stand, nor shall it come to **p**
Is 7:18 it shall come to **p** in that
Is 8: 8 He will **p** through Judah, he
Is 8: 8 **p** over, he will reach up to
Is 8:21 they will **p** through it hard
Is 10:12 Therefore it shall come to **p**
Is 10:20 it shall come to **p** in that
Is 10:27 It shall come to **p** in that
Is 11:11 It shall come to **p** in that
Is 14: 3 It shall come to **p** in the day
Is 14:24 so it shall come to **p**, and as
Is 16:12 And it shall come to **p**, when
Is 17: 4 to **p** that the glory of Jacob
Is 21: 1 in the South **p** through, so it
Is 22: 7 It shall come to **p** that your
Is 23:15 Now it shall come to **p** in
Is 24:21 It shall come to **p** in that
Is 27:12 it shall come to **p** in that
Is 28:19 by morning it will **p** over
Is 28:21 work, and bring to **p** His act
Is 33:21 sail, nor majestic ships **p** by
Is 34:10 no one shall **p** through it
Is 35: 8 unclean shall not **p** over it
Is 36: 1 Now it came to **p** in the
Is 37:26 Now I have brought it to **p**
Is 37:38 Now it came to **p**, as he was
Is 42: 9 former things have come to **p**
Is 43: 2 When you **p** through the waters
Is 46:11 I will also bring it to **p**
Is 47: 2 thigh, **p** through the rivers
Is 48: 3 I did them, and they came to **p**

Is 48: 5 before it came to **p** I
Is 65:24 It shall come to **p** that
Is 66:23 it shall come to **p** that from
Jer 2:10 For **p** beyond the coasts of
Jer 3: 9 So it came to **p**, through her
Jer 3:16 Then it shall come to **p**, when
Jer 4: 9 shall come to **p** in that day
Jer 5:22 that it cannot **p** beyond it
Jer 5:22 yet they cannot **p** over it
Jer 8:13 them shall **p** away from them
Jer 9:10 no one can **p** through them
Jer 9:12 so that no one can **p** through
Jer 13: 6 it came to **p** after many days
Jer 22: 8 nations will **p** by this city
Jer 25:12 Then it will come to **p**, when
Jer 28: 9 of the prophet comes to **p**
Jer 30: 8 shall come to **p** in that day
Jer 31:28 And it shall come to **p**, that
Jer 32:35 their daughters to **p** through
Jer 33:13 the flocks shall again **p**
Jer 35:11 But it came to **p**, when
Jer 36: 1 Now it came to **p** in the
Jer 36: 9 Now it came to **p** in the fifth
Jer 41: 1 Now it came to **p** in the
Jer 49:39 come to **p** in the latter days
Jer 52: 4 Now it came to **p** in the ninth
Jer 52:31 Now it came to **p** in the
Lam 1:12 to you, all you who **p** by
Lam 2:15 All who **p** by clap their hands
Lam 3:37 who speaks and it comes to **p**
Lam 3:44 prayer should not **p** through
Lam 4:21 cup shall also **p** over to you
Ezek 1: 1 Now it came to **p** in the
Ezek 3:16 Now it came to **p** at the end
Ezek 5: 1 **p** it over your head and your
Ezek 5:14 in the sight of all who **p** by
Ezek 5:17 and blood shall **p** through you
Ezek 8: 1 it came to **p** in the sixth
Ezek 12:25 which I speak will come to **p**
Ezek 14:15 beasts to **p** through the land
Ezek 14:15 may **p** through because of the
Ezek 16:21 them to **p** through the fire
Ezek 20: 1 It came to **p** in the seventh
Ezek 20:26 to **p** through the fire, that I
Ezek 20:31 make your sons **p** through the
Ezek 20:37 will make you **p** under the rod
Ezek 21: 7 and shall be brought to **p**,'
Ezek 24:14 it shall come to **p**, and I will
Ezek 26: 1 it came to **p** in the eleventh
Ezek 29:11 Neither foot of man shall **p**
Ezek 29:11 foot of beast **p** through it
Ezek 29:17 And it came to **p** in the
Ezek 30:20 it came to **p** in the eleventh
Ezek 31: 1 Now it came to **p** in the
Ezek 32: 1 it came to **p** in the twelfth
Ezek 32:17 It came to **p** also in the
Ezek 33:21 it came to **p** in the twelfth
Ezek 33:28 that no one will **p** through
Ezek 33:33 And when this comes to **p**
Ezek 36:34 in the sight of all who **p** by
Ezek 37: 2 me to **p** by them all around
Ezek 38:10 that day it shall come to **p**
Ezek 38:18 it will come to **p** at the same
Ezek 39:11 It will come to **p** in that day
Ezek 39:11 who **p** by east of the sea
Ezek 39:14 to **p** through the land and bury
Ezek 39:15 party will **p** through the land
Ezek 46:21 caused me to **p** by the four
Dan 2:29 would come to **p** after this
Dan 2:45 will come to **p** after this
Dan 4:16 and let seven times **p** over him
Dan 4:23 till seven times **p** over him'
Dan 4:25 seven times shall **p** over you
Dan 4:32 seven times shall **p** over you
Dan 7:14 which shall not **p** away, and
Dan 11:10 and overwhelm and **p** through
Dan 11:40 overwhelm them, and **p** through
Hos 1: 5 It shall come to **p** in that
Hos 1:10 it shall come to **p** in the
Hos 2:21 It shall come to **p** in that
Joel 2:28 it shall come to **p** afterward
Joel 2:32 And it shall come to **p** that
Joel 3:17 ever **p** through her again
Joel 3:18 it will come to **p** in that day
Amos 5: 5 nor **p** over to Beersheba
Amos 5:17 for I will **p** through you,"
Amos 6: 9 Then it shall come to **p**, that
Amos 7: 8 I will not **p** by them anymore
Amos 8: 2 I will not **p** by them anymore
Amos 8: 9 shall come to **p** in that day

Mic 1:11 **P** by in naked shame, you
Mic 2: 8 who trust you, as they **p** by
Mic 2:13 **p** through the gate, and go out
Mic 2:13 their king will **p** before them
Mic 4: 1 Now it shall come to **p** in the
Nah 1:15 shall no more **p** through you
Nah 3: 7 It shall come to **p** that all
Zeph 1:12 it shall come to **p** at that
Zech 6:15 this shall come to **p** if you
Zech 7: 1 **p** that the word of the LORD
Zech 8:13 it shall come to **p** that just
Zech 9: 8 an oppressor **p** through them
Zech 10:11 He shall **p** through the sea
Zech 13: 3 It shall come to **p** that if
Zech 13: 8 come to **p** in all the land
Zech 14: 6 It shall come to **p** in that
Zech 14:13 It shall come to **p** in that
Zech 14:16 And it shall come to **p** that
Matt 5:18 till heaven and earth **p** away
Matt 5:18 **p** from the law till all is
Matt 8:28 that no one could **p** that way
Matt 11: 1 Now it came to **p**, when Jesus
Matt 13:53 Now it came to **p**, when Jesus
Matt 19: 1 Now it came to **p**, when Jesus
Matt 24: 6 these things must come to **p**
Matt 24:34 **p** away till all these things
Matt 24:35 Heaven and earth will **p** away
Matt 24:35 words will by no means **p** away
Matt 26: 1 Now it came to **p**, when Jesus
Matt 26:39 let this cup **p** from Me
Matt 26:42 if this cup cannot **p** away
Mark 1: 9 It came to **p** in those days
Mark 11:23 things he says will come to **p**
Mark 13:30 **p** away till all these things
Mark 13:31 Heaven and earth will **p** away
Mark 13:31 words will by no means **p** away
Mark 14:35 the hour might **p** from Him
Luke 2: 1 it came to **p** in those days
Luke 2:15 this thing that has come to **p**
Luke 3:21 it came to **p** that Jesus also
Luke 6:12 Now it came to **p** in those
Luke 8: 1 Now it came to **p**, afterward,
Luke 9:28 And it came to **p**, about eight
Luke 9:51 Now it came to **p**, when the
Luke 11: 1 And it came to **p**, as He was
Luke 11:42 **p** by justice and the love of
Luke 16:17 earth to **p** away than for one
Luke 16:26 to **p** from here to you cannot
Luke 16:26 can those from there **p** to us
Luke 19: 4 He was going to **p** that way
Luke 19:29 And it came to **p**, when He came
Luke 21: 9 things must come to **p** first
Luke 21:32 **p** away till all things are
Luke 21:33 Heaven and earth will **p** away
Luke 21:33 words will by no means **p** away
Luke 21:36 things that will come to **p**
Luke 24:30 Now it came to **p**, as He sat
Luke 24:51 Now it came to **p**, while He
John 13:19 that when it does come to **p**
John 14:29 that when it does come to **p**
Acts 2:17 come to **p** in the last days
Acts 2:21 And it shall come to **p** that
Acts 3:23 it shall come to **p** that every
Acts 4: 5 And it came to **p**, on the next
Acts 9:32 Now it came to **p**, as Peter
Acts 21: 1 Now it came to **p**, that when
Acts 28:17 it came to **p** after three days
Rom 9:26 it shall come to **p** in the
1Co 15:54 then shall be brought to **p**
1Co 16: 5 I will come to you when I **p**
2Co 1:16 to **p** by way of you to
Jas 1:10 of the field he will **p** away
2Pe 3:10 **p** away with a great noise

PASSAGE (*see* PASSAGES)
Num 20:21 **p** through his territory
Mark 12:26 Moses, in the burning bush **p**
Luke 20:37 **p** that the dead are raised

PASSAGES (*see* PASSAGE)
Jer 51:32 The **p** are blocked, the reeds

PASSED (*see* PASS)
Gen 12: 6 Abram **p** through the land to
Gen 15:17 that **p** between those pieces
Gen 18:11 and Sarah had **p** the age of
Gen 37:28 Then Midianite traders **p** by
Ex 7:25 seven days **p** after the LORD
Ex 12:27 who **p** over the houses of the
Ex 34: 6 And the LORD **p** before him and
Num 14: 7 The land we **p** through to spy
Num 20:17 have **p** through your territory
Num 21:22 Highway until we have **p**
Num 33: 8 **p** through the midst of the
Deut 2: 8 when we **p** beyond our brethren
Deut 2: 8 **p** by way of the Wilderness of
Deut 29:16 the nations which you **p** by
Josh 3: 4 have not **p** this way before
Josh 10:29 Then Joshua **p** from Makkedah,
Josh 10:31 Then Joshua **p** from Libnah
Josh 10:34 Lachish Joshua **p** to Eglon
Josh 15: 3 **p** along to Zin, ascended on
Josh 15: 3 **p** along to Hezron, went up to
Josh 15: 4 From there it **p** toward Azmon
Josh 15: 6 and **p** north of Beth Arabah
Josh 15:10 **p** along to the side of Mount
Josh 15:10 Shemesh, and **p** on to Timnah
Josh 15:11 **p** along to Mount Baalah, and
Josh 16: 2 **p** along to the border of the
Josh 16: 6 and **p** by it on the east of
Josh 18: 9 **p** through the land, and wrote
Josh 18:18 Then it **p** along toward the
Josh 18:19 the border **p** along to the
Josh 19:13 from there it **p** along on the
Josh 24:17 the people through whom we **p**
Judg 3:26 **p** beyond the stone images and
Judg 9:25 they robbed all who **p** by them
Judg 11:29 and he **p** through Gilead and
Judg 11:29 **p** through Mizpah of Gilead
Judg 18:13 And they **p** from there to the
Judg 19:14 And they **p** by and went their
Ruth 2:14 he **p** parched grain to her
1Sa 9: 4 So he **p** through the mountains
1Sa 9: 4 Then they **p** through the land
1Sa 9: 4 Then he **p** through the land of
1Sa 15:12 **p** by, and gone down to Gilgal
1Sa 29: 2 **p** in review by hundreds and by
1Sa 29: 2 his men **p** in review at the
2Sa 15:18 all his servants **p** before him
2Sa 15:18 from Gath, **p** before the king
1Ki 13:25 And there, men **p** by and saw the
1Ki 19:11 And behold, the LORD **p** by
1Ki 19:19 Then Elijah **p** by him and threw
1Ki 20:39 Now as the king **p** by, he
1Ki 22: 1 Now three years **p** without war
2Ki 4: 8 it was, as often as he **p** by
2Ki 6:30 as he **p** by on the wall, the
2Ki 14: 9 that was in Lebanon **p** by and
2Ch 25:18 that was in Lebanon **p** by and
2Ch 30:10 So the runners **p** from city to
Job 4:15 Then a spirit **p** before my
Job 11:16 it as waters that have **p** away
Job 15:19 and no alien **p** among them
Job 28: 8 has the fierce lion **p** over it
Job 30:15 prosperity has **p** like a cloud
Job 37:21 skies, when the wind has **p**
Ps 18:12 clouds **p** with hailstones and
Ps 37:36 Yet he **p** away, and behold, he
Ps 48: 4 assembled, They **p** by together
Ps 57: 1 these calamities have **p** by
Ps 90: 9 have **p** away in Your wrath
Song 3: 4 Scarcely had I **p** by them,
Is 10:28 to Aiath, he has **p** Migron
Is 40:27 claim is **p** over by my God"
Is 41: 3 **p** safely by the way that he
Jer 11:15 the holy flesh has **p** from you
Jer 34:18 **p** between the parts of it
Jer 34:19 **p** between the parts of the
Jer 46:17 He has **p** by the appointed
Ezek 16: 6 And when I **p** by you and saw
Ezek 16: 8 When I **p** by you again and
Ezek 16:25 yourself to everyone who **p** by
Jon 2: 3 and Your waves **p** over me
Nah 3:19 your wickedness **p** continually
Hab 3:10 overflowing of the water **p** by
Zech 7:14 so that no one **p** through or
Matt 9: 9 Then as Jesus **p** on from there
Matt 27:39 those who **p** by blasphemed Him
Mark 2:14 And as He **p** by, He saw Levi
Mark 6:48 sea, and would have **p** them by
Mark 9:30 **p** through Galilee, and He did
Mark 11:20 in the morning, as they **p** by
Mark 15:29 those who **p** by blasphemed Him
Luke 10:31 he **p** by on the other side
Luke 10:32 and **p** by on the other side
Luke 17:11 He **p** through the midst of
Luke 19: 1 entered and **p** through Jericho
Luke 22:59 after about an hour had **p**
John 5:24 but has **p** from death into
John 8:59 the midst of them, and so **p** by
John 9: 1 Now as Jesus **p** by, He saw a
Acts 7:30 And when forty years had **p**
Acts 14:24 And after they had **p** through
Acts 15: 3 they **p** through Phoenicia and
Acts 17: 1 Now when they had **p** through
Acts 19: 1 having **p** through the upper
Acts 19:21 Spirit, when he had **p** through
Acts 21: 3 we **p** it on the left, sailed
Rom 3:25 had **p** over the sins that were
1Co 10: 1 cloud, all **p** through the sea,
2Co 5:17 old things have **p** away
Heb 4:14 who has **p** through the heavens
Heb 11:29 By faith they **p** through the
1Jn 3:14 we have **p** from death to life
Rev 21: 1 and the first earth had **p** away
Rev 21: 4 the former things have **p** away

PASSES (*see* PASS)
Ex 33:22 shall be, while My glory **p** by
Lev 27:32 of whatever **p** under the rod,
1Sa 14: 4 Now between the **p**, by which
1Ki 9: 8 yet everyone who **p** by it will
2Ki 4: 9 of God, who **p** by us regularly
2Ch 7:21 everyone who **p** by it will be
Job 11:10 If He **p** by, imprisons, and
Job 14:20 against him, and he **p** on
Ps 78:39 flesh, A breath that **p** away
Ps 103:16 For the wind **p** over it, and it
Prov 10:25 When the whirlwind **p** by, the
Prov 26:17 He who **p** by and meddles in a
Eccl 1: 4 One generation **p** away, and
Eccl 6:12 life which he **p** like a shadow
Is 28:15 overflowing scourge **p** through
Is 28:18 overflowing scourge **p** through
Is 29: 5 shall be as chaff that **p** away
Is 30:32 the staff of punishment **p**
Jer 13:24 them like stubble that **p** away
Jer 18:16 everyone who **p** by it will be
Jer 19: 8 everyone who **p** by it will be
Jer 51:43 through which no son of man **p**
Hos 13: 3 the early dew that **p** away
Mic 5: 8 if he **p** through, both treads
Nah 1:12 be cut down when he **p** through
Zeph 2: 2 before the day **p** like chaff
Zeph 2:15 Everyone who **p** by her shall
Zech 9: 8 army, because of him who **p** by
Eph 3:19 of Christ which **p** knowledge

PASSING (*see* PASS)
Judg 19:18 We are **p** from Bethlehem in
2Ki 6:26 Israel was **p** by on the wall
Ps 144: 4 His days are like a **p** shadow
Prov 7: 8 **p** along the street near her
Is 31: 5 **p** over, He will preserve it
Ezek 16:15 **p** by who would have it
Ezek 23:37 **p** them through the fire, to
Mic 7:18 **p** over the transgression of
Zeph 3: 6 desolate, With none **p** by
Matt 20:30 heard that Jesus was **p** by
Mark 15:21 and **p** by, to bear His cross
Luke 4:30 Then **p** through the midst of
Luke 18:36 And hearing a multitude **p** by
Luke 18:37 Jesus of Nazareth was **p** by
Acts 5:15 **p** by might fall on some of
Acts 8:40 **p** through, he preached in all
Acts 16: 8 So **p** by Mysia, they came down
Acts 17:23 for as I was **p** through and
Acts 27: 8 **P** it with difficulty, we came
1Co 7:31 form of this world is **p** away
1Co 16: 5 for I am **p** through Macedonia)
2Co 3: 7 which glory was **p** away,
2Co 3:11 For if what is **p** away was
2Co 3:13 at the end of what was **p** away
Heb 11:25 enjoy the **p** pleasures of sin
1Jn 2: 8 the darkness is **p** away, and
1Jn 2:17 And the world is **p** away, and

PASSION (*see* PASSIONS)
1Co 7: 9 to marry than to burn with **p**
Col 3: 5 fornication, uncleanness, **p**
1Th 4: 5 not in **p** of lust, like the

PASSIONS (*see* PASSION)
Rom 1:26 God gave them up to vile **p**
Rom 7: 5 the **p** of sins which were
Gal 5:24 the flesh with its **p** and

PASSOVER
Ex 12:11 It is the LORD'S **P**
Ex 12:21 families, and kill the **P** lamb
Ex 12:27 It is the **P** sacrifice of the
Ex 12:43 is the ordinance of the **P**
Ex 12:48 to keep the **P** to the LORD
Ex 34:25 of the Feast of the **P** be left
Lev 23: 5 at twilight is the LORD'S **P**

Num 9: 2 the **P** at its appointed time
Num 9: 4 that they should keep the **P**
Num 9: 5 And they kept the **P** on the
Num 9: 6 not keep the **P** on that day
Num 9:10 may still keep the LORD's **P**
Num 9:12 of the **P** they shall keep it
Num 9:13 and ceases to keep the **P**,
Num 9:14 and would keep the LORD's **P**
Num 9:14 to the rite of the **P** and
Num 28:16 month is the **P** of the LORD
Num 33: 3 on the day after the **P** the
Deut 16: 1 keep the **P** to the LORD your
Deut 16: 2 the **P** to the LORD your God
Deut 16: 5 **P** within any of your gates
Deut 16: 6 sacrifice the **P** at twilight
Josh 5:10 kept the **P** on the fourteenth
Josh 5:11 land on the day after the **P**
2Ki 23:21 Keep the **P** to the LORD your
2Ki 23:22 Surely such a **P** had never
2Ki 23:23 year of King Josiah this **P**
2Ch 30: 1 to keep the **P** to the LORD God
2Ch 30: 2 the **P** in the second month
2Ch 30: 5 should come to keep the **P** to
2Ch 30:15 Then they slaughtered the **P**
2Ch 30:17 of the slaughter of the **P**
2Ch 30:18 yet they ate the **P** contrary
2Ch 35: 1 Now Josiah kept a **P** to the
2Ch 35: 1 they slaughtered the **P** lambs
2Ch 35: 6 So slaughter the **P** offerings
2Ch 35: 7 all for **P** offerings for all
2Ch 35: 8 **P** offerings two thousand six
2Ch 35: 9 for **P** offerings five thousand
2Ch 35:11 slaughtered the **P** offerings
2Ch 35:13 the **P** offerings with fire
2Ch 35:16 the same day, to keep the **P**
2Ch 35:17 kept the **P** at that time, and
2Ch 35:18 There had been no **P** kept in
2Ch 35:18 kept such a **P** as Josiah kept
2Ch 35:19 of Josiah this **P** was kept
Ezra 6:19 **P** on the fourteenth day of
Ezra 6:20 the **P** lambs for all the
Ezek 45:21 you shall observe the **P**, a
Matt 26: 2 that after two days is the **P**
Matt 26:17 prepare for You to eat the **P**
Matt 26:18 I will keep the **P** at your
Matt 26:19 and they prepared the **P**
Mark 14: 1 After two days it was the **P**
Mark 14:12 when they killed the **P** lamb
Mark 14:12 that You may eat the **P**
Mark 14:14 eat the **P** with My disciples
Mark 14:16 and they prepared the **P**
Luke 2:41 year at the Feast of the **P**
Luke 22: 1 drew near, which is called **P**
Luke 22: 7 when the **P** must be killed
Luke 22: 8 Go and prepare the **P** for us
Luke 22:11 eat the **P** with My disciples
Luke 22:13 them, and they prepared the **P**
Luke 22:15 **P** with you before I suffer
John 2:13 Now the **P** of the Jews was at
John 2:23 He was in Jerusalem at the **P**
John 6: 4 Now the **P**, a feast of the
John 11:55 the **P** of the Jews was near,
John 11:55 up to Jerusalem before the **P**
John 12: 1 Then, six days before the **P**
John 13: 1 Now before the feast of the **P**
John 18:28 but that they might eat the **P**
John 18:39 someone to you at the **P**
John 19:14 the Preparation Day of the **P**
Acts 12: 4 him before the people after **P**
1Co 5: 7 For indeed Christ, our **P**, was
Heb 11:28 By faith he kept the **P** and the

PAST

Gen 50: 4 days of his mourning were **p**
Ex 21:29 with its horn in times **p**, and
Ex 21:36 ox tended to thrust in time **p**
Deut 2:10 had dwelt there in times **p**
Deut 4:32 the days that are **p**, which
Deut 4:42 having hated him in time **p**
Deut 19: 4 having hated him in time **p**
Deut 19: 6 hated the victim in time **p**
1Sa 15:32 the bitterness of death is **p**
1Sa 19: 7 in his presence as in times **p**
2Sa 3:17 In time **p** you were seeking
2Sa 5: 2 Also, in time **p**, when Saul
2Sa 16: 1 **p** the top of the mountain
1Ki 18:29 it was so, when midday was **p**
1Ch 9:20 officer over them in time **p**
1Ch 11: 2 Also, in time **p**, even when
Neh 12:38 going **p** the Tower of the
Job 9:10 great things **p** finding out
Job 9:11 If He moves **p**, I do not
Job 14:13 me until Your wrath is **p**,
Job 17:11 My days are **p**, my purposes
Job 29: 2 that I were as in months **p**
Ps 90: 4 like yesterday when it is **p**
Eccl 3:15 an account of what is **p**
Song 2:11 For lo, the winter is **p**, the
Is 26:20 until the indignation is **p**
Jer 8:20 The harvest is **p**, the summer
Amos 8: 5 When will the New Moon be **p**
Mark 16: 1 Now when the Sabbath was **p**
Acts 9:23 Now after many days were **p**
Acts 12:10 When they were **p** the first
Acts 20:16 had decided to sail **p** Ephesus
Rom 11:33 and His ways **p** finding out
1Co 7:36 if she is **p** the flower of her
Gal 5:21 as I also told you in time **p**
Eph 4:19 being **p** feeling, have given
2Ti 2:18 the resurrection is already **p**
Heb 1: 1 ways spoke in time **p** to the
Heb 11:11 child when she was **p** the age
1Pe 4: 3 **p** lifetime in doing the will
Rev 9:12 One woe is **p**
Rev 11:14 The second woe is **p**

PASTORS

Eph 4:11 some evangelists, and some **p**

PASTRY

Num 11: 8 taste of **p** prepared with oil
Ezek 16:13 You ate **p** of fine flour,
Ezek 16:19 the **p** of fine flour, oil, and

PASTURE (*see* PASTURED, PASTURES)

Gen 47: 4 have no **p** for their flocks
1Ch 4:39 to seek **p** for their flocks
1Ch 4:40 And they found rich, good **p**
1Ch 4:41 because there was **p** for their
Job 39: 8 of the mountains is his **p**
Ps 74: 1 against the sheep of Your **p**
Ps 79:13 people and sheep of Your **p**
Ps 95: 7 And we are the people of His **p**
Ps 100: 3 people and the sheep of His **p**
Is 5:17 lambs shall feed in their **p**
Is 32:14 wild donkeys, a **p** of flocks
Jer 6: 3 Each one shall **p** in his own
Jer 23: 1 and scatter the sheep of My **p**
Jer 25:36 LORD has plundered their **p**
Lam 1: 6 like deer that find no **p**,
Ezek 34:14 I will feed them in good **p**
Ezek 34:14 fold and feed in rich **p** on the
Ezek 34:18 to have eaten up the good **p**
Ezek 34:18 feet the residue of your **p**
Ezek 34:31 My flock, the flock of My **p**
Hos 13: 6 When they had **p**, they were
Joel 1:18 because they have no **p**
Mic 2:12 flock in the midst of their **p**
John 10: 9 will go in and out and find **p**

PASTURED (*see* PASTURE)

Gen 36:24 in the wilderness as he **p** the

PASTURES (*see* PASTURE)

1Ki 4:23 oxen, twenty oxen from the **p**
Ps 23: 2 me to lie down in green **p**
Ps 65:12 They drop on the **p** of the
Ps 65:13 The **p** are clothed with flocks
Ps 83:12 The **p** of God for a possession
Is 7:19 and on all thorns and in all **p**
Is 30:23 cattle will feed in large **p**
Is 49: 9 and their **p** shall be on all
Ezek 45:15 from the rich **p** of Israel
Joel 1:19 fire has devoured the open **p**
Joel 1:20 fire has devoured the open **p**
Joel 2:22 for the open **p** are springing
Amos 1: 2 the **p** of the shepherds mourn,
Zeph 2: 6 The seacoast shall be **p**, with

PATARA

Acts 21: 1 to Rhodes, and from there to **P**

PATCH (*see* PATCHED, PATCHES)

Matt 9:16 for the **p** pulls away from the

PATCHED (*see* PATCH)

Josh 9: 5 **p** sandals on their feet, and

PATCHES (*see* PATCH)

Job 18:13 It devours **p** of his skin

PATH (*see* PATHLESS, PATHS, PATHWAY)

Gen 49:17 by the way, a viper by the **p**
Num 22:24 **p** between the vineyards, with
2Sa 22:37 You enlarged my **p** under me
Job 28: 7 That **p** no bird knows, nor has
Job 28:26 and a **p** for the thunderbolt,
Job 30:13 They break up my **p**, they
Job 38:25 or a **p** for the thunderbolt,
Ps 1: 1 stands in the **p** of sinners
Ps 16:11 will show me the **p** of life
Ps 18:36 You enlarged my **p** under me
Ps 27:11 And lead me in a smooth **p**
Ps 77:19 Your **p** in the great waters,
Ps 78:50 He made a **p** for His anger
Ps 119:35 Make me walk in the **p** of Your
Ps 119:105 to my feet And a light to my **p**
Ps 139: 3 You comprehend my **p** and my
Ps 142: 3 within me, Then You knew my **p**
Prov 1:15 keep your foot from their **p**
Prov 2: 9 equity and every good **p**
Prov 4:14 not enter the **p** of the wicked
Prov 4:18 But the **p** of the just is like
Prov 4:26 Ponder the **p** of your feet, and
Prov 5: 6 Lest you ponder her **p** of life
Prov 7: 8 he took the **p** to her house
Is 26: 7 You weigh the **p** of the just
Is 30:11 way, turn aside from the **p**
Is 40:14 Him in the **p** of justice
Is 43:16 a **p** through the mighty waters

PATHLESS (*see* PATH)

Job 12:24 them wander in a **p** wilderness

PATHROS (*see* PATHRUSIM)

Is 11:11 from Assyria and Egypt, from **P**
Jer 44: 1 Noph, and in the country of **P**
Jer 44:15 in the land of Egypt, in **P**
Ezek 29:14 to return to the land of **P**
Ezek 30:14 I will make **P** desolate, set

PATHRUSIM (*see* PATHROS)

Gen 10:14 **P**, and Casluhim (from whom
1Ch 1:12 **P**, Casluhim (from whom came

PATHS (*see* PATH)

Job 6:18 The **p** of their way turn aside
Job 8:13 So are the **p** of all who
Job 13:27 and watch closely all my **p**
Job 19: 8 He has set darkness in my **p**
Job 24:13 its ways nor abide in its **p**
Job 33:11 stocks, He watches all my **p**
Job 38:20 may know the **p** to its home
Ps 8: 8 through the **p** of the seas
Ps 17: 4 from the **p** of the destroyer
Ps 17: 5 Uphold my steps in Your **p**
Ps 23: 3 He leads me in the **p** of
Ps 25: 4 Teach me Your **p**
Ps 25:10 All the **p** of the LORD are
Ps 65:11 Your **p** drip with abundance
Prov 2: 8 He guards the **p** of justice
Prov 2:13 from those who leave the **p** of
Prov 2:15 and who are devious in their **p**
Prov 2:18 death, and her **p** to the dead
Prov 2:19 do they regain the **p** of life
Prov 2:20 goodness, and keep to the **p** of
Prov 3: 6 and He shall direct your **p**
Prov 3:17 and all her **p** are peace
Prov 4:11 I have led you in right **p**
Prov 5:21 LORD, and He ponders all his **p**
Prov 7:25 ways, do not stray into her **p**
Prov 8: 2 the way, where the **p** meet
Prov 8:20 the midst of the **p** of justice
Is 2: 3 and we shall walk in His **p**
Is 3:12 and destroy the way of your **p**
Is 42:16 them in **p** they have not known
Is 59: 7 and destruction are in their **p**
Is 59: 8 made themselves crooked **p**
Jer 6:16 and see, and ask for the old **p**
Jer 18:15 ways, from the ancient **p**, to
Lam 3: 9 He has made my **p** crooked
Hos 2: 6 so that she cannot find her **p**
Mic 4: 2 and we shall walk in His **p**
Matt 3: 3 the LORD, make His **p** straight
Mark 1: 3 the LORD, make His **p** straight
Luke 3: 4 the LORD, make His **p** straight
Heb 12:13 make straight **p** for your feet

PATHWAY (*see* PATH, PATHWAYS)

Ps 85:13 make His footsteps our **p**
Prov 12:28 in its **p** there is no death

PATHWAYS (*see* PATHWAY)

Jer 18:15 ancient paths, to walk in **p**

PATIENCE (*see* PATIENT)

Neh 9:30 years You had **p** with them
Matt 18:26 have **p** with me, and I will pay
Matt 18:29 Have **p** with me, and I will
Luke 8:15 keep it and bear fruit with **p**

Luke 21:19 In your **p** possess your souls
Rom 15: 4 that we through the **p** and
Rom 15: 5 Now may the God of **p** and
2Co 6: 4 in much **p**, in tribulations,
Col 1:11 His glorious power, for all **p**
1Th 1: 3 **p** of hope in our Lord Jesus
2Th 1: 4 churches of God for your **p**
2Th 3: 5 God and into the **p** of Christ
1Ti 6:11 godliness, faith, love, **p**
Tit 2: 2 sound in faith, in love, in **p**
Heb 6:12 and **p** inherit the promises
Jas 1: 3 of your faith produces **p**
Jas 1: 4 But let **p** have its perfect
Jas 5:10 an example of suffering and **p**
Rev 1: 9 **p** of Jesus Christ, was on the
Rev 2: 2 works, your labor, your **p**
Rev 2: 3 you have persevered and have **p**
Rev 2:19 service, faith, and your **p**
Rev 13:10 Here is the **p** and the faith of
Rev 14:12 Here is the **p** of the saints

PATIENT (*see* PATIENCE, PATIENTLY)
Eccl 7: 8 the **p** in spirit is better
Rom 2: 7 life to those who by **p**
Rom 12:12 **p** in tribulation, continuing
1Th 5:14 the weak, be **p** with all
2Ti 2:24 to all, able to teach, **p**,
Jas 5: 7 Therefore be **p**, brethren,
Jas 5: 8 You also be **p**

PATIENTLY (*see* PATIENT)
Ps 37: 7 the LORD, and wait **p** for Him
Ps 40: 1 I waited **p** for the LORD
Acts 26: 3 I beg you to hear me **p**
Heb 6:15 And so, after he had **p** endured
Jas 5: 7 waiting **p** for it until it
1Pe 2:20 your faults, you take it **p**
1Pe 2:20 for it, if you take it **p**,

PATMOS
Rev 1: 9 called **P** for the word of God

PATRIARCH (*see* PATRIARCHS)
Acts 2:29 freely to you of the **p** David
Heb 7: 4 to whom even the **p** Abraham

PATRIARCHS (*see* PATRIARCH)
Acts 7: 8 and Jacob begot the twelve **p**
Acts 7: 9 And the **p**, becoming envious,

PATROBAS
Rom 16:14 Phlegon, Hermas, **P**, Hermes,

PATROL
1Ki 20:17 And Ben-Hadad sent out a **p**

PATTERN
Ex 25: 9 the **p** of the tabernacle and
Ex 25: 9 the **p** of all its furnishings,
Ex 25:40 **p** which was shown you on the
Ex 26:30 **p** which you were shown on the
Num 8: 4 According to the **p** which the
2Ki 16:10 design of the altar and its **p**
Ezek 43:10 and let them measure the **p**
Acts 7:44 to the **p** that he had seen
Phil 3:17 walk, as you have us for a **p**
1Ti 1:16 as a **p** to those who are going
2Ti 1:13 Hold fast the **p** of sound
Tit 2: 7 to be a **p** of good works
Heb 8: 5 **p** shown you on the mountain

PAU (*see* PAI)
Gen 36:39 and the name of his city was **P**

PAUL (*see* PAUL'S, SAUL)
Acts 13: 9 Saul, who also is called **P**
Acts 13:13 Now when **P** and his party set
Acts 13:16 Then **P** stood up, and motioning
Acts 13:43 devout proselytes followed **P**
Acts 13:45 the things spoken by **P**
Acts 13:46 Then **P** and Barnabas grew bold
Acts 13:50 up persecution against **P** and
Acts 14: 9 This man heard **P** speaking
Acts 14: 9 **P**, observing him intently and
Acts 14:11 people saw what **P** had done
Acts 14:12 they called Zeus, and **P**,
Acts 14:14 **P** heard this, they tore their
Acts 14:19 the multitudes, they stoned **P**
Acts 15: 2 when **P** and Barnabas
Acts 15: 2 them, they determined that **P**
Acts 15:12 **P** declaring how many miracles
Acts 15:22 own company to Antioch with **P**
Acts 15:25 our beloved Barnabas and **P**
Acts 15:35 **P** and Barnabas also remained
Acts 15:36 some days **P** said to Barnabas
Acts 15:38 But **P** insisted that they
Acts 15:40 but **P** chose Silas and departed
Acts 16: 3 **P** wanted to have him go on
Acts 16: 9 appeared to **P** in the night
Acts 16:14 heed the things spoken by **P**
Acts 16:17 This girl followed **P** and us,
Acts 16:18 But **P**, greatly annoyed,
Acts 16:19 was gone, they seized **P** and
Acts 16:25 But at midnight **P** and Silas
Acts 16:28 But **P** called with a loud
Acts 16:29 fell down trembling before **P**
Acts 16:36 reported these words to **P**
Acts 16:37 But **P** said to them, "They
Acts 17: 2 Then **P**, as his custom was,
Acts 17: 4 the leading women, joined **P**
Acts 17:10 brethren immediately sent **P**
Acts 17:13 was preached by **P** at Berea
Acts 17:14 the brethren sent **P** away, to
Acts 17:15 **P** brought him to Athens
Acts 17:16 Now while **P** waited for them
Acts 17:22 Then **P** stood in the midst of
Acts 17:33 So **P** departed from among them
Acts 18: 1 After these things **P** departed
Acts 18: 5 **P** was constrained by the
Acts 18: 9 Now the Lord spoke to **P** in
Acts 18:12 one accord rose up against **P**
Acts 18:14 when **P** was about to open his
Acts 18:18 So **P** still remained a good
Acts 19: 1 was at Corinth, that **P**,
Acts 19: 4 Then **P** said, "John indeed
Acts 19: 6 when **P** had laid hands on them
Acts 19:11 miracles by the hands of **P**
Acts 19:13 by the Jesus whom **P** preaches
Acts 19:15 Jesus I know, and **P** I know
Acts 19:21 **P** purposed in the Spirit,
Acts 19:26 Asia, this **P** has persuaded and
Acts 19:30 when **P** wanted to go in to the
Acts 20: 1 **P** called the disciples to him
Acts 20: 7 together to break bread, **P**
Acts 20: 9 as **P** continued speaking, he
Acts 20:10 But **P** went down, fell on him,
Acts 20:13 intending to take **P** on board
Acts 20:16 For **P** had decided to sail
Acts 21: 4 They told **P** through the
Acts 21:13 Then **P** answered, "What do
Acts 21:18 On the following day **P** went
Acts 21:26 Then **P** took the men, and the
Acts 21:29 whom they supposed that **P** had
Acts 21:30 people ran together, seized **P**
Acts 21:32 they stopped beating **P**
Acts 21:37 as **P** was about to be led into
Acts 21:39 But **P** said, "I am a Jew from
Acts 21:40 **P** stood on the stairs and
Acts 22:25 **P** said to the centurion who
Acts 22:28 And **P** said, "But I was born
Acts 22:30 to appear, and brought **P** down
Acts 23: 1 Then **P**, looking earnestly at
Acts 23: 3 Then **P** said to him, "God
Acts 23: 5 Then **P** said, "I did not know
Acts 23: 6 But when **P** perceived that one
Acts 23:10 fearing lest **P** might be
Acts 23:11 Be of good cheer, **P**
Acts 23:12 drink till they had killed **P**
Acts 23:14 until we have killed **P**
Acts 23:16 the barracks and told **P**
Acts 23:17 Then **P** called one of the
Acts 23:18 **P** the prisoner called me to
Acts 23:20 bring **P** down to the council
Acts 23:24 and provide mounts to set **P** on
Acts 23:31 they were commanded, took **P**
Acts 23:33 they also presented **P** to him
Acts 24: 1 to the governor against **P**
Acts 24:10 Then **P**, after the governor
Acts 24:23 the centurion to keep **P** and to
Acts 24:24 who was Jewish, he sent for **P**
Acts 24:26 money would be given him by **P**
Acts 24:27 Jews a favor, left **P** bound
Acts 25: 2 Jews informed him against **P**
Acts 25: 4 But Festus answered that **P**
Acts 25: 6 he commanded **P** to be brought
Acts 25: 7 serious complaints against **P**
Acts 25: 9 the Jews a favor, answered **P**
Acts 25:10 Then **P** said, "I stand at
Acts 25:19 whom **P** affirmed to be alive
Acts 25:21 But when **P** appealed to be
Acts 25:23 command **P** was brought in
Acts 26: 1 Then Agrippa said to **P**, "You
Acts 26: 1 So **P** stretched out his hand
Acts 26:24 **P**, you are beside yourself
Acts 26:28 Then Agrippa said to **P**, "You
Acts 26:29 And **P** said, "I would to God
Acts 27: 1 to Italy, they delivered **P**
Acts 27: 3 And Julius treated **P** kindly
Acts 27: 9 already over, **P** advised them,
Acts 27:11 by the things spoken by **P**
Acts 27:21 then **P** stood in the midst of
Acts 27:24 saying, "Do not be afraid, **P**
Acts 27:31 **P** said to the centurion and
Acts 27:33 **P** implored them all to take
Acts 27:43 centurion, wanting to save **P**
Acts 28: 3 But when **P** had gathered a
Acts 28: 8 **P** went in to him and prayed,
Acts 28:15 When **P** saw them, he thanked
Acts 28:16 but **P** was permitted to dwell
Acts 28:17 **P** called the leaders of the
Acts 28:25 after **P** had said one word
Acts 28:30 Then **P** dwelt two whole years
Rom 1: 1 **P**, a servant of Jesus Christ,
1Co 1: 1 **P**, called to be an apostle of
1Co 1:12 I am of **P**," or "I am of
1Co 1:13 Was **P** crucified for you
1Co 1:13 you baptized in the name of **P**
1Co 3: 4 I am of **P**," and another, "I
1Co 3: 5 Who then is **P**, and who is
1Co 3:22 whether **P** or Apollos or
1Co 16:21 salutation with my own hand—**P**
2Co 1: 1 **P**, an apostle of Jesus Christ
2Co 10: 1 Now I, **P**, myself am pleading
Gal 1: 1 **P**, an apostle (not from men
Gal 5: 2 Indeed I, **P**, say to you that
Eph 1: 1 **P**, an apostle of Jesus Christ
Eph 3: 1 For this reason I, **P**, the
Phil 1: 1 **P** and Timothy, servants of
Col 1: 1 **P**, an apostle of Jesus Christ
Col 1:23 under heaven, of which I, **P**
Col 4:18 salutation by my own hand—**P**
1Th 1: 1 **P**, Silvanus, and Timothy, To
1Th 2:18 even I, **P**, time and again
2Th 1: 1 **P**, Silvanus, and Timothy, To
2Th 3:17 of **P** with my own hand, which
1Ti 1: 1 **P**, an apostle of Jesus Christ
2Ti 1: 1 **P**, an apostle of Jesus Christ
Tit 1: 1 **P**, a servant of God and an
Phm 1 **P**, a prisoner of Christ Jesus
Phm 9 being such a one as **P**, the
Phm 19 I, **P**, am writing with my own
2Pe 3:15 as also our beloved brother **P**

PAUL'S (*see* PAUL)
Acts 19:29 **P** travel companions
Acts 20:37 freely, and fell on **P** neck
Acts 21: 8 were **P** companions departed
Acts 21:11 come to us, he took **P** belt
Acts 23:16 when **P** sister's son heard of
Acts 25:14 Festus laid **P** case before the

PAULUS
Acts 13: 7 with the proconsul, Sergius **P**

PAUSE (*see* PAUSED)
Is 29: 9 **P** and wonder! Blind

PAUSED (*see* PAUSE)
Ezek 10: 4 **p** over the threshold of the

PAVED (*see* PAVEMENT)
Ex 24:10 a **p** work of sapphire stone
Song 3:10 its interior **p** with love by

PAVEMENT (*see* PAVED)
2Ki 16:17 and put it on a **p** of stones
2Ch 7: 3 faces to the ground on the **p**
Esth 1: 6 on a mosaic **p** of alabaster
Ezek 40:17 a **p** made all around the court
Ezek 40:17 thirty chambers faced the **p**
Ezek 40:18 The **p** was by the side of the
Ezek 40:18 this was the lower **p**
Ezek 42: 3 opposite the **p** of the outer
John 19:13 a place that is called The **P**

PAVILION
2Ki 16:18 **p** which they had built in the
Ps 27: 5 He shall hide me in His **p**
Ps 31:20 keep them secretly in a **p**
Jer 43:10 spread his royal **p** over them

PAW (*see* PAWS)
1Sa 17:37 me from the **p** of the lion
1Sa 17:37 from the **p** of the bear, He

PAWS (*see* PAW)
Lev 11:27 And whatever goes on its **p**
Job 39:21 He **p** in the valley, and

PAY (*see* PAID, PAYING, PAYMENT, PAYS)
Ex 21: 2 go out free and **p** nothing
Ex 21:19 He shall only **p** for the loss
Ex 21:22 and he shall **p** as the judges
Ex 21:30 then he shall **p** to redeem his
Ex 21:36 he shall surely **p** ox for ox
Ex 22: 7 is found, he shall **p** double
Ex 22: 9 **p** double to his neighbor
Ex 22:16 her, he shall surely **p** the
Ex 22:17 he shall **p** money according to
Lev 27: 8 too poor to **p** your valuation
Num 20:19 water, then I will **p** for it
Deut 23:21 you shall not delay to **p** it
2Sa 15: 7 **p** the vow which I vowed to
1Ki 5: 6 I will **p** you wages for your
1Ki 20:39 or else you shall **p** a talent
2Ki 4: 7 sell the oil and **p** your debt
2Ki 18:14 you impose on me I will **p**
Ezra 4:13 they will not **p** tax, tribute
Ezra 7:20 **p** for it from the king's
Esth 3: 2 would not bow or **p** homage
Esth 3: 5 did not bow or **p** him homage
Esth 3: 9 I will **p** ten thousand talents
Esth 4: 7 **p** into the king's treasuries
Job 22:27 you, and you will **p** your vows
Job 41:11 Me, that I should **p** him
Ps 22:25 I will **p** My vows before those
Ps 50:14 **p** your vows to the Most High
Ps 66:13 I will **p** You my vows,
Ps 76:11 the LORD your God, and **p** them
Ps 116:14 I will **p** my vows to the LORD
Ps 116:18 I will **p** my vows to the LORD
Prov 5: 1 son, **p** attention to my wisdom
Prov 7:24 **p** attention to the words of
Prov 19:17 He will **p** back what he has
Prov 22:27 have nothing with which to **p**
Eccl 5: 4 to God, do not delay to **p** it
Eccl 5: 4 **P** what you have vowed
Eccl 5: 5 to vow than to vow and not **p**
Is 23:17 She will return to her **p**, and
Is 23:18 her **p** will be set apart for
Lam 5: 4 We **p** for the water we drink,
Ezek 23:49 and you shall **p** for your
Jon 2: 9 I will **p** what I have vowed
Mic 1: 7 all her **p** as a harlot shall
Mic 1: 7 it from the **p** of a harlot
Mic 1: 7 return to the **p** of a harlot
Mic 3:11 her priests teach for **p**, and
Matt 17:24 Teacher not **p** the temple tax
Matt 18:25 But as he was not able to **p**
Matt 18:26 with me, and I will **p** you all
Matt 18:28 saying, '**P** me what you owe
Matt 18:29 with me, and I will **p** you all
Matt 18:30 till he should **p** the debt
Matt 18:34 **p** all that was due to him
Matt 22:17 lawful to **p** taxes to Caesar
Matt 23:23 For you **p** tithe of mint and
Mark 12:14 lawful to **p** taxes to Caesar
Mark 12:15 Shall we **p**, or shall we not **p**
Luke 20:22 to **p** taxes to Caesar or not
Luke 23: 2 and forbidding to **p** taxes to
Acts 21:24 **p** their expenses so that they
Rom 13: 6 of this you also **p** taxes, for
Jas 2: 3 you **p** attention to the one

PAYING (*see* PAY)
Ex 21:11 go out free, without **p** money

PAYMENT (*see* PAY, PAYMENTS)
Ezek 16:31 harlot, because you scorned **p**
Ezek 16:33 Men make **p** to all harlots,
Ezek 16:34 In that you gave **p** but no
Ezek 16:34 but no **p** was given you,
Ezek 27:15 you ivory tusks and ebony as **p**
Matt 18:25 he had, and that **p** be made

PAYMENTS (*see* PAYMENT)
Ezek 16:33 but you made your **p** to all

PAYS (*see* PAY)
Prov 29:12 If a ruler **p** attention to

PEACE (*see* PEACEABLE, PEACEFUL, PEACEMAKERS, PEACETIME)
Gen 15:15 shall go to your fathers in **p**
Gen 26:29 and have sent you away in **p**
Gen 26:31 they departed from him in **p**
Gen 28:21 to my father's house in **p**
Gen 34: 5 held his **p** until they came
Gen 34:21 These men are at **p** with us
Gen 41:16 give Pharaoh an answer of **p**
Gen 43:23 **P** be with you, do not be
Gen 44:17 go up in **p** to your father
Ex 4:18 said to Moses, Go in **p**."
Ex 14:14 you, and you shall hold your **p**
Ex 18:23 also go to their place in **p**
Ex 20:24 your **p** offerings, your sheep
Ex 24: 5 sacrificed **p** offerings of
Ex 29:28 of their **p** offerings, that is
Ex 32: 6 and brought **p** offerings
Lev 3: 1 is a sacrifice of **p** offering
Lev 3: 3 **p** offering an offering made
Lev 3: 6 **p** offering to the LORD is of
Lev 3: 9 sacrifice of the **p** offering
Lev 4:10 sacrifice of the **p** offering
Lev 4:26 the sacrifice of **p** offering
Lev 4:31 the sacrifice of **p** offering
Lev 4:35 sacrifice of the **p** offering
Lev 6:12 it the fat of the **p** offerings
Lev 7:11 of **p** offerings which he shall
Lev 7:13 of his **p** offering
Lev 7:14 the blood of the **p** offering
Lev 7:15 of the sacrifice of his **p**
Lev 7:18 of the sacrifice of his **p**
Lev 7:20 of the sacrifice of the **p**
Lev 7:21 of the sacrifice of the **p**
Lev 7:29 **p** offering to the LORD shall
Lev 7:29 sacrifice of his **p** offering
Lev 7:32 of your **p** offerings
Lev 7:33 the blood of the **p** offering
Lev 7:34 of their **p** offerings, and I
Lev 7:37 sacrifice of the **p** offering
Lev 9: 4 and a ram as **p** offerings, to
Lev 9:18 as sacrifices of **p** offerings
Lev 9:22 offering, and **p** offerings
Lev 10: 3 So Aaron held his **p**
Lev 10:14 from the sacrifices of **p**
Lev 17: 5 offer them as **p** offerings to
Lev 19: 5 of **p** offering to the LORD
Lev 22:21 of **p** offering to the LORD
Lev 23:19 as a sacrifice of **p** offering
Lev 26: 6 I will give **p** in the land
Num 6:14 blemish as a **p** offering,
Num 6:17 of **p** offering to the LORD
Num 6:18 sacrifice of the **p** offering
Num 6:26 upon you, and give you **p**
Num 7:17 the sacrifice of **p** offerings
Num 7:23 the sacrifice of **p** offerings
Num 7:29 the sacrifice of **p** offerings
Num 7:35 the sacrifice of **p** offerings
Num 7:41 the sacrifice of **p** offerings
Num 7:47 the sacrifice of **p** offerings
Num 7:53 the sacrifice of **p** offerings
Num 7:59 the sacrifice of **p** offerings
Num 7:65 the sacrifice of **p** offerings
Num 7:71 the sacrifice of **p** offerings
Num 7:77 the sacrifice of **p** offerings
Num 7:83 the sacrifice of **p** offerings
Num 7:88 oxen for the sacrifice of **p**
Num 10:10 of your **p** offerings
Num 15: 8 or as a **p** offering to the
Num 25:12 give to him My covenant of **p**
Num 29:39 offerings and your **p** offerings
Num 30: 4 and her father holds his **p**
Deut 2:26 of Heshbon, with words of **p**
Deut 20:10 proclaim an offer of **p** to it
Deut 20:11 they accept your offer of **p**
Deut 20:12 city will not make **p** with you
Deut 23: 6 **p** nor their prosperity all
Deut 27: 7 You shall offer **p** offerings
Deut 29:19 saying, 'I shall have **p**,
Josh 8:31 and sacrificed **p** offerings
Josh 9:15 So Joshua made **p** with them
Josh 10: 1 Gibeon had made **p** with Israel
Josh 10: 4 for it has made **p** with Joshua
Josh 10:21 to Joshua at Makkedah, in **p**
Josh 11:19 was not a city that made **p**
Josh 22:23 or if to offer **p** offerings on
Josh 22:27 and with our **p** offerings
Judg 4:17 for there was **p** between Jabin
Judg 6:23 said to him, "**P** be with you
Judg 8: 9 When I come back in **p**, I will
Judg 11:31 when I return in **p** from the
Judg 18: 6 Go in **p**. May the presence
Judg 19:20 old man said, "**P** be with you
Judg 20:26 **p** offerings before the LORD
Judg 21: 4 offerings and **p** offerings
Judg 21:13 and announced **p** to them
1Sa 1:17 Go in **p**, and the God of Israel
1Sa 7:14 there was **p** between Israel
1Sa 10: 8 sacrifices of **p** offerings
1Sa 10:27 But he held his **p**
1Sa 11:15 they made sacrifices of **p**
1Sa 13: 9 and **p** offerings here to me
1Sa 20:42 Go in **p**, since we have both
1Sa 25: 6 **P** be to you, **p** to your house
1Sa 25: 6 and **p** to all that you have
1Sa 25:35 Go up in **p** to your house
1Sa 29: 7 return now, and go in **p**, that
2Sa 3:21 Abner away, and he went in **p**
2Sa 3:22 him away, and he had gone in **p**
2Sa 3:23 him away, and he has gone in **p**
2Sa 6:17 **p** offerings before the LORD
2Sa 6:18 **p** offerings, he blessed the
2Sa 10:19 they made **p** with Israel and
2Sa 13:20 But now hold your **p**, my
2Sa 15: 9 king said to him, "Go in **p**."
2Sa 15:27 Return to the city in **p**, and
2Sa 17: 3 all the people will be at **p**
2Sa 19:24 the day he came back in **p**
2Sa 19:30 back in **p** to his own house
2Sa 24:25 offerings and **p** offerings
1Ki 2: 6 go down to the grave in **p**
1Ki 2:33 there shall be **p** forever from
1Ki 3:15 offered **p** offerings, and made
1Ki 4:24 he had **p** on every side all
1Ki 5:12 there was **p** between Hiram and
1Ki 8:63 a sacrifice of **p** offerings
1Ki 8:64 and the fat of the **p** offerings
1Ki 8:64 and the fat of the **p** offerings
1Ki 9:25 and **p** offerings on the altar
1Ki 20:18 If they have come out for **p**
1Ki 22:17 each return to his house in **p**
1Ki 22:27 affliction, until I come in **p**
1Ki 22:28 If you ever return in **p**, the
1Ki 22:44 Also Jehoshaphat made **p** with
2Ki 5:19 he said to him, "Go in **p**."
2Ki 9:17 and let him say, 'Is it **p**
2Ki 9:18 says the king: 'Is it **p**?'
2Ki 9:18 What have you to do with **p**
2Ki 9:19 says the king: 'Is it **p**?'
2Ki 9:19 What have you to do with **p**
2Ki 9:22 Is it **p**, Jehu
2Ki 9:22 What **p**, as long as the
2Ki 9:31 Is it **p**, Zimri, murderer of
2Ki 16:13 his **p** offerings on the altar
2Ki 18:31 Make **p** with me by a present
2Ki 18:36 But the people held their **p**
2Ki 20:19 Will there not be **p** and truth
2Ki 22:20 gathered to your grave in **p**
1Ch 12:18 **P**, **p** to you,
1Ch 12:18 and **p** to your helpers
1Ch 16: 1 and **p** offerings before God
1Ch 16: 2 the **p** offerings, he blessed
1Ch 19:19 they made **p** with David and
1Ch 21:26 **p** offerings, and called on the
1Ch 22: 9 be Solomon, for I will give **p**
2Ch 7: 7 and the fat of the **p** offerings
2Ch 15: 5 no **p** to the one who went out
2Ch 18:16 each return to his house in **p**
2Ch 18:26 until I return in **p**
2Ch 18:27 If you ever return in **p**, the
2Ch 29:35 the fat of the **p** offerings
2Ch 30:22 days, offering **p** offerings and
2Ch 31: 2 **p** offerings, to serve, to
2Ch 33:16 LORD, sacrificed **p** offerings
2Ch 34:28 gathered to your grave in **p**
Ezra 4:17 **P**, and so forth
Ezra 5: 7 To Darius the king: All **p**.
Ezra 7:12 Perfect **p**, and so forth
Ezra 9:12 seek their **p** or prosperity
Esth 9:30 of Ahasuerus, with words of **p**
Esth 10: 3 speaking **p** to all his kindred
Job 5:23 field shall be at **p** with you
Job 5:24 know that your tent is in **p**
Job 11: 3 talk make men hold their **p**
Job 13:13 Hold your **p** with me, and let
Job 22:21 yourself with Him, and be at **p**
Job 25: 2 He makes **p** in His high places
Job 33:31 hold your **p**, and I will speak
Job 33:33 hold your **p**, and I will teach
Ps 4: 8 I will both lie down in **p**
Ps 7: 4 to him who was at **p** with me
Ps 28: 3 Who speak **p** to their
Ps 29:11 will bless His people with **p**
Ps 34:14 Seek **p**, and pursue it
Ps 35:20 For they do not speak **p**, But
Ps 37:11 in the abundance of **p**
Ps 37:37 the future of that man is **p**
Ps 39: 2 I held my **p** even from good
Ps 55:18 **p** from the battle which was
Ps 55:20 those who were at **p** with him
Ps 72: 3 will bring **p** to the people

Ps 72: 7 flourish, And abundance of p
Ps 83: 1 Do not hold Your p, And do not
Ps 85: 8 He will speak p To His people
Ps 85:10 and p have kissed each other
Ps 119:165 Great p have those who love
Ps 120: 6 too long With one who hates p
Ps 120: 7 I am for p; But when I speak
Ps 122: 6 Pray for the p of Jerusalem
Ps 122: 7 P be within your walls,
Ps 122: 8 now say, "P be within you
Ps 125: 5 P be upon Israel
Ps 128: 6 P be upon Israel
Ps 147:14 He makes p in your borders,
Prov 3: 2 and p they will add to you
Prov 3:17 and all her paths are p
Prov 7:14 I have p offerings with me
Prov 11:12 of understanding holds his p
Prov 12:20 but counselors of p have joy
Prov 16: 7 enemies to be at p with him
Prov 17:28 wise when he holds his p
Prov 29: 9 or laughs, there is no p
Eccl 3: 8 a time of war, and a time of p
Song 8:10 his eyes as one who found p
Is 9: 6 Father, Prince of P
Is 9: 7 p there will be no end, upon
Is 26: 3 will keep him in perfect p
Is 26:12 You will establish p for us
Is 27: 5 that he may make p with Me
Is 27: 5 and he shall make p with Me
Is 32:17 of righteousness will be p
Is 33: 7 the ambassadors of p shall
Is 36:16 Make p with me by a present
Is 36:21 But they held their p and
Is 38:17 Indeed it was for my own p
Is 39: 8 At least there will be p and
Is 42:14 I have held My p a long time
Is 45: 7 and create darkness, I make p
Is 48:18 Then your p would have been
Is 48:22 There is no p," says the
Is 52: 7 good news, who proclaims p
Is 53: 5 for our p was upon Him, and by
Is 54:10 My covenant of p be removed
Is 54:13 be the p of your children
Is 55:12 joy, and be led out with p
Is 57: 2 He shall enter into p
Is 57:11 not because I have held My p
Is 57:19 p, p to him who is far
Is 57:21 There is no p," says my God,
Is 59: 8 The way of p they have not
Is 59: 8 that way shall not know p
Is 60:17 also make your officers p
Is 62: 1 sake I will not hold My p
Is 62: 6 hold their p day or night
Is 64:12 Will You hold Your p, and
Is 66:12 I will extend p to her like a
Jer 4:10 saying, 'You shall have p
Jer 4:19 I cannot hold my p, because
Jer 6:14 slightly, saying, 'P, p
Jer 6:14 When there is no p
Jer 8:11 slightly, saying, 'P, p
Jer 8:11 When there is no p
Jer 8:15 We looked for p, but no good
Jer 12: 5 And if in the land of p, in
Jer 12:12 no flesh shall have p
Jer 14:13 you assured p in this place
Jer 14:19 We looked for p, but there
Jer 16: 5 away My p from this people
Jer 23:17 You shall have p" '
Jer 28: 9 prophet who prophesies of p
Jer 29: 7 seek the p of the city where
Jer 29: 7 in its p you will have p
Jer 29:11 says the LORD, thoughts of p
Jer 30: 5 of fear, and not of p
Jer 33: 6 to them the abundance of p
Jer 34: 5 But you shall die in p
Jer 43:12 shall go out from there in p
Lam 3:17 have moved my soul far from p
Ezek 7:25 they will seek p, but there
Ezek 13:10 seduced My people, saying, 'P
Ezek 13:10 when there is no p
Ezek 13:16 who see visions of p for her
Ezek 13:16 when there is no p
Ezek 34:25 a covenant of p with them
Ezek 37:26 a covenant of p with them
Ezek 43:27 your p offerings on the altar
Ezek 45:15 and p offerings, to make
Ezek 45:17 and the p offerings to make
Ezek 46: 2 offering and his p offerings
Ezek 46:12 p offering to the LORD, the
Ezek 46:12 his p offerings as he did on
Dan 4: 1 P be multiplied to you
Dan 6:25 P be multiplied to you
Dan 10:19 P be to you; be strong,
Amos 5:22 your fattened p offerings
Obad 7 the men at p with you shall
Mic 3: 5 P" while they chew with
Mic 5: 5 And this One shall be p
Nah 1:15 good tidings, who proclaims p
Hag 2: 9 in this place I will give p
Zech 6:13 the counsel of p shall be
Zech 8:10 there was no p from the enemy
Zech 8:16 for truth, justice, and p
Zech 8:19 Therefore love truth and p
Zech 9:10 shall speak p to the nations
Mal 2: 5 with him, one of life and p
Mal 2: 6 He walked with Me in p and
Matt 10:13 let your p come upon it
Matt 10:13 let your p return to you
Matt 10:34 I came to bring p on earth
Matt 10:34 come to bring p but a sword
Mark 4:39 to the sea, "P, be still!"
Mark 5:34 Go in p, and be healed of your
Mark 9:50 and have p with one another
Luke 1:79 our feet into the way of p
Luke 2:14 the highest, and on earth p
Luke 2:29 Your servant depart in p,
Luke 7:50 faith has saved you. Go in p
Luke 8:48 has made you well. Go in p
Luke 10: 5 first say, 'P to this house
Luke 10: 6 And if a son of p is there
Luke 10: 6 your p will rest on it
Luke 11:21 palace, his goods are in p
Luke 12:51 I came to give p on earth
Luke 14:32 and asks conditions of p
Luke 19:38 P in heaven and glory in the
Luke 19:42 things that make for your p
Luke 24:36 and said to them, "P to you
John 14:27 P I leave with you, My p
John 14:27 with you, My p I give to you
John 16:33 that in Me you may have p
John 20:19 said to them, "P be with you
John 20:21 to them again, "P to you
John 20:26 midst, and said, "P to you
Acts 9:31 Galilee, and Samaria had p
Acts 10:36 preaching p through Jesus
Acts 12:20 friend, they asked for p,
Acts 16:36 therefore depart, and go in p
Acts 24: 2 through you we enjoy great p
Rom 1: 7 p from God our Father and the
Rom 2:10 p to everyone who works what
Rom 3:17 the way of p they have not
Rom 5: 1 we have p with God through
Rom 8: 6 minded is life and p
Rom 10:15 who preach the gospel of p
Rom 14:17 drink, but righteousness and p
Rom 14:19 the things which make for p
Rom 15:13 p in believing, that you may
Rom 15:33 Now the God of p be with you
Rom 16:20 the God of p will crush Satan
1Co 1: 3 p from God our Father and the
1Co 7:15 But God has called us to p
1Co 14:33 author of confusion but of p
1Co 16:11 send him on his journey in p
2Co 1: 2 p from God our Father and the
2Co 13:11 be of one mind, live in p
2Co 13:11 of love and p will be with you
Gal 1: 3 p from God the Father and our
Gal 5:22 of the Spirit is love, joy, p
Gal 6:16 according to this rule, p
Eph 1: 2 p from God our Father and the
Eph 2:14 For He Himself is our p, who
Eph 2:15 from the two, thus making p
Eph 2:17 preached p to you who were
Eph 4: 3 the Spirit in the bond of p
Eph 6:15 of the gospel of p
Eph 6:23 P to the brethren, and love
Phil 1: 2 p from God our Father and the
Phil 4: 7 the p of God, which surpasses
Phil 4: 9 the God of p will be with you
Col 1: 2 p from God our Father and the
Col 1:20 having made p through the
Col 3:15 let the p of God rule in your
1Th 1: 1 p from God our Father and the
1Th 5: 3 they say, "P and safety!"
1Th 5:13 Be at p among yourselves
1Th 5:23 Now may the God of p Himself
2Th 1: 2 p from God our Father and the
2Th 3:16 Now may the Lord of p Himself
2Th 3:16 you p always in every way
1Ti 1: 2 and p from God our Father and
2Ti 1: 2 and p from God the Father and
2Ti 2:22 p with those who call on the
Tit 1: 4 p from God the Father and the
Phm 3 p from God our Father and the
Heb 7: 2 Salem, meaning "king of p,"
Heb 11:31 had received the spies with p
Heb 12:14 Pursue p with all men, and
Heb 13:20 Now may the God of p who
Jas 2:16 Depart in p, be warmed and
Jas 3:18 in p by those who make p
1Pe 1: 2 to you and p be multiplied
1Pe 3:11 let him seek p and pursue it
1Pe 5:14 P to you all who are in
2Pe 1: 2 p be multiplied to you in the
2Pe 3:14 to be found by Him in p,
2Jn 3 p will be with you from God
3Jn 14 P to you. Our friends greet
Jude 2 Mercy, p, and love be
Rev 1: 4 p from Him who is and who was
Rev 6: 4 it to take p from the earth

PEACEABLE (*see* PEACE, PEACEABLY)
2Sa 20:19 I am among the p and faithful
1Ti 2: 2 p life in all godliness and
Tit 3: 2 speak evil of no one, to be p
Heb 12:11 afterward it yields the p
Jas 3:17 above is first pure, then p

PEACEABLY (*see* PEACEABLE)
Gen 37: 4 and could not speak p to him
Judg 11:13 restore those lands p
1Sa 16: 4 Do you come p
1Sa 16: 5 P; I have come to sacrifice
1Ki 2:13 come p?" And he said, "P."
1Ch 12:17 have come p to me to help me
Jer 9: 8 one speaks p to his neighbor
Dan 11:21 but he shall come in p, and
Dan 11:24 He shall enter p, even into
Rom 12:18 on you, live p with all men

PEACEFUL (*see* PEACE)
1Ch 4:40 land was broad, quiet, and p
Is 32:18 will dwell in a p habitation
Jer 25:37 the p habitations are cut
Ezek 38:11 I will go to a p people, who

PEACEMAKERS (*see* PEACE)
Matt 5: 9 Blessed are the p, for they

PEACETIME (*see* PEACE)
1Ki 2: 5 he shed the blood of war in p

PEAKS
Ps 68:15 A mountain of many p is the
Ps 68:16 envy, you mountains of many p

PEARL (*see* PEARLS)
Matt 13:46 found one p of great price
Rev 21:21 individual gate was of one p

PEARLS (*see* PEARL)
Matt 7: 6 nor cast your p before swine
Matt 13:45 merchant seeking beautiful p
1Ti 2: 9 gold or p or costly clothing
Rev 17: 4 gold and precious stones and p
Rev 18:12 silver, precious stones and p
Rev 18:16 gold and precious stones and p
Rev 21:21 twelve gates were twelve p

PEDAHEL
Num 34:28 P the son of Ammihud

PEDAHZUR
Num 1:10 Gamaliel the son of P
Num 2:20 be Gamaliel the son of P
Num 7:54 day Gamaliel the son of P
Num 7:59 of Gamaliel the son of P
Num 10:23 was Gamaliel the son of P

PEDAIAH
2Ki 23:36 the daughter of P of Rumah
1Ch 3:18 and Malchiram, P, Shenazzar,
1Ch 3:19 The sons of P were Zerubbabel
1Ch 27:20 Manasseh, Joel the son of P
Neh 3:25 After him P the son of Parosh
Neh 8: 4 and at his left hand P,
Neh 11: 7 the son of Joed, the son of P
Neh 13:13 scribe, and of the Levites, P

PEDDLING
2Co 2:17 as so many, p the word of God

PEDESTAL
1Ki 7:29 on the frames was a p on top
1Ki 7:31 was round, shaped like a p

PEELED
Gen 30:37 **p** white strips in them, and
Gen 30:38 And the rods which he had **p**

PEEP
Is 10:14 his mouth with even a **p**

PEG (*see* PEGS)
Judg 4:21 Heber's wife, took a tent **p**
Judg 4:21 drove the **p** into his temple,
Judg 4:22 dead with the **p** in his temple
Judg 5:26 her hand to the tent **p**, her
Ezra 9: 8 to give us a **p** in His holy
Is 22:23 him as a **p** in a secure place
Is 22:25 the **p** that is fastened in
Ezek 15: 3 Or can men make a **p** from it
Zech 10: 4 from him the tent **p**, from

PEGS (*see* PEG)
Ex 27:19 all its service, all its **p**
Ex 27:19 all the **p** of the court, shall
Ex 35:18 the **p** of the tabernacle, the
Ex 35:18 the **p** of the court, and their
Ex 38:20 All the **p** of the tabernacle,
Ex 38:31 all the **p** for the tabernacle,
Ex 38:31 all the **p** for the court all
Ex 39:40 gate, its cords, and its **p**
Num 3:37 with their sockets, their **p**
Num 4:32 court with their sockets, **p**
Is 41: 7 then he fastened it with **p**

PEKAH
2Ki 15:25 Then **P** the son of Remaliah,
2Ki 15:27 **P** the son of Remaliah became
2Ki 15:29 the days of **P** king of Israel
2Ki 15:30 against **P** the son of Remaliah
2Ki 15:31 Now the rest of the acts of **P**
2Ki 15:32 year of **P** the son of Remaliah
2Ki 15:37 **P** the son of Remaliah against
2Ki 16: 1 year of **P** the son of Remaliah
2Ki 16: 5 **P** the son of Remaliah, king
2Ch 28: 6 For **P** the son of Remaliah
Is 7: 1 **P** the son of Remaliah, king

PEKAHIAH
2Ki 15:22 Then **P** his son reigned in his
2Ki 15:23 **P** the son of Menahem became
2Ki 15:26 Now the rest of the acts of **P**

PEKOD
Jer 50:21 against the inhabitants of **P**
Ezek 23:23 all the Chaldeans, **P**, Shoa,

PELAIAH
1Ch 3:24 were Hodaviah, Eliashib, **P**
Neh 8: 7 Azariah, Jozabad, Hanan, **P**
Neh 10:10 Shebaniah, Hodijah, Kelita, **P**

PELALIAH
Neh 11:12 son of Jeroham, the son of **P**

PELATIAH
1Ch 3:21 The sons of Hananiah were **P**
1Ch 4:42 having as their captains **P**
Neh 10:22 **P**, Hanan, Anaiah,
Ezek 11: 1 **P** the son of Benaiah, princes
Ezek 11:13 that **P** the son of Benaiah

PELEG
Gen 10:25 the name of one was **P**, for in
Gen 11:16 thirty-four years, and begot **P**
Gen 11:17 After he begot **P**, Eber lived
Gen 11:18 **P** lived thirty years, and
Gen 11:19 **P** lived two hundred and nine
1Ch 1:19 the name of one was **P**, for in
1Ch 1:25 Eber, **P**, Reu,
Luke 3:35 the son of Reu, the son of **P**

PELET (*see* BETH PELET)
1Ch 2:47 Regem, Jotham, Geshan, **P**
1Ch 12: 3 and **P** the sons of Azmaveth

PELETH (*see* PELETHITES)
Num 16: 1 of Eliab, and On the son of **P**
1Ch 2:33 The sons of Jonathan were **P**

PELETHITES (*see* PELETH)
2Sa 8:18 both the Cherethites and the **P**
2Sa 15:18 the Cherethites, all the **P**
2Sa 20: 7 with the Cherethites, the **P**
2Sa 20:23 over the Cherethites and the **P**
1Ki 1:38 and the **P** went down and had
1Ki 1:44 the Cherethites, and the **P**
1Ch 18:17 over the Cherethites and the **P**

PELICAN
Ps 102: 6 I am like a **p** of the
Is 34:11 But the **p** and the porcupine
Zeph 2:14 both the **p** and the bittern

PELONITE (*see* PALTITE)
1Ch 11:27 the Harorite, Helez the **P**
1Ch 11:36 Mecherathite, Ahijah the **P**
1Ch 27:10 seventh month was Helez the **P**

PEN
Job 19:24 on a rock with an iron **p** and
Ps 45: 1 My tongue is the **p** of a ready
Is 8: 1 it with a man's **p** concerning
Jer 8: 8 the false **p** of the scribe
Jer 17: 1 is written with a **p** of iron
3Jn 13 wish to write to you with **p**

PENALTY
Num 35:30 a person for the death **p**
Ezek 23:35 bear the **p** of your lewdness
Rom 1:27 **p** of their error which was

PENDANTS
Judg 8:26 the crescent ornaments, **p**
Is 3:19 the **p**, the bracelets, and the

PENETRATED
Jer 39: 2 of the month, the city was **p**

PENIEL (*see* PENUEL)
Gen 32:30 the name of the place **P**

PENINNAH
1Sa 1: 2 and the name of the other **P**
1Sa 1: 2 **P** had children, but Hannah
1Sa 1: 4 give portions to **P** his wife

PENITENTS
Is 1:27 and her **p** with righteousness

PENNY
Matt 5:26 till you have paid the last **p**

PENTECOST
Acts 2: 1 the Day of **P** had fully come
Acts 20:16 if possible, on the Day of **P**
1Co 16: 8 will tarry in Ephesus until **P**

PENUEL (*see* PENIEL)
Gen 32:31 over **P** the sun rose on him
Judg 8: 8 he went up from there to **P**
Judg 8: 8 the men of **P** answered him as
Judg 8: 9 he also spoke to the men of **P**
Judg 8:17 he tore down the tower of **P**
1Ki 12:25 out from there and built **P**
1Ch 4: 4 **P** was the father of Gedor, and
1Ch 8:25 **P** were the sons of Shashak

PEOPLE (*see* PEOPLE'S, PEOPLES)
Gen 11: 6 Indeed the **p** are one and they
Gen 12: 5 the **p** whom they had acquired
Gen 14:16 as well as the women and the **p**
Gen 17:14 shall be cut off from his **p**
Gen 19: 4 all the **p** from every quarter,
Gen 19:38 of the **p** of Ammon to this day
Gen 23: 7 himself to the **p** of the land
Gen 23:11 presence of the sons of my **p**
Gen 23:12 down before the **p** of the land
Gen 23:13 hearing of the **p** of the land
Gen 25: 8 and was gathered to his **p**
Gen 25:17 and was gathered to his **p**
Gen 25:23 one **p** shall be stronger than
Gen 26:10 One of the **p** might soon have
Gen 26:11 Abimelech charged all his **p**
Gen 29: 1 the land of the **p** of the east
Gen 32: 7 he divided the **p** that were
Gen 33:15 some of the **p** who are with me
Gen 34:16 you, and we will become one **p**
Gen 34:22 to dwell with us, to be one **p**
Gen 35: 6 all the **p** who were with him
Gen 35:29 and was gathered to his **p**
Gen 41:40 and all my **p** shall be ruled
Gen 41:55 the **p** cried to Pharaoh for
Gen 42: 6 sold to all the **p** of the land
Gen 47:21 And as for the **p**, he moved
Gen 47:23 Then Joseph said to the **p**
Gen 48: 4 make of you a multitude of **p**
Gen 48:19 He also shall become a **p**, and
Gen 49:10 be the obedience of the **p**
Gen 49:16 Dan shall judge his **p** as one
Gen 49:29 I am to be gathered to my **p**
Gen 49:33 and was gathered to his **p**
Gen 50:20 day, to save many **p** alive
Ex 1: 9 And he said to his **p**, "Look,
Ex 1: 9 the **p** of the children of
Ex 1:20 the **p** multiplied and grew very
Ex 1:22 Pharaoh commanded all his **p**
Ex 3: 7 of My **p** who are in Egypt, and
Ex 3:10 that you may bring My **p**, the
Ex 3:12 brought the **p** out of Egypt
Ex 3:21 I will give this **p** favor in
Ex 4:16 be your spokesman to the **p**
Ex 4:21 that he will not let the **p** go
Ex 4:30 signs in the sight of the **p**
Ex 4:31 So the **p** believed
Ex 5: 1 Let My **p** go, that they may
Ex 5: 4 take the **p** from their work
Ex 5: 5 the **p** of the land are many
Ex 5: 6 the taskmasters of the **p** and
Ex 5: 7 the **p** straw to make brick as
Ex 5:10 And the taskmasters of the **p**
Ex 5:10 went out and spoke to the **p**
Ex 5:12 So the **p** were scattered
Ex 5:16 the fault is in your own **p**
Ex 5:22 You brought trouble on this **p**
Ex 5:23 he has done evil to this **p**
Ex 5:23 You delivered Your **p** at all
Ex 6: 7 I will take you as My **p**, and
Ex 7: 4 and bring My armies and My **p**
Ex 7:14 he refuses to let the **p** go
Ex 7:16 Let My **p** go, that they may
Ex 8: 1 Let My **p** go, that they may
Ex 8: 3 of your servants, on your **p**
Ex 8: 4 come up on you, on your **p**
Ex 8: 8 frogs from me and from my **p**
Ex 8: 8 and I will let the **p** go, that
Ex 8: 9 your servants, and for your **p**
Ex 8:11 your servants, and from your **p**
Ex 8:20 Let My **p** go, that they may
Ex 8:21 if you will not let My **p** go
Ex 8:21 and your servants, on your **p**
Ex 8:22 Goshen, in which My **p** dwell
Ex 8:23 between My **p** and your **p**
Ex 8:29 his servants, and from his **p**
Ex 8:29 anymore in not letting the **p**
Ex 8:31 his servants, and from his **p**
Ex 8:32 neither would he let the **p** go
Ex 9: 1 Let My **p** go, that they may
Ex 9: 7 and he did not let the **p** go
Ex 9:13 Let My **p** go, that they may
Ex 9:14 on your servants and on your **p**
Ex 9:15 your **p** with pestilence, then
Ex 9:17 My **p** in that you will not let
Ex 9:27 LORD is righteous, and my **p**
Ex 10: 3 Let My **p** go, that they may
Ex 10: 4 if you refuse to let My **p** go
Ex 11: 2 now in the hearing of the **p**
Ex 11: 3 the LORD gave the **p** favor in
Ex 11: 3 and in the sight of the **p**
Ex 11: 8 and all the **p** who follow you
Ex 12:27 So the **p** bowed their heads
Ex 12:31 and go out from among my **p**
Ex 12:33 And the Egyptians urged the **p**
Ex 12:34 So the **p** took their dough
Ex 12:36 And the LORD had given the **p**
Ex 13: 3 And Moses said to the **p**
Ex 13:17 when Pharaoh had let the **p** go
Ex 13:17 Lest perhaps the **p** change
Ex 13:18 So God led the **p** around by
Ex 13:22 by night from before the **p**
Ex 14: 5 of Egypt that the **p** had fled
Ex 14: 5 was turned against the **p**
Ex 14: 6 and took his **p** with him
Ex 14:13 And Moses said to the **p**, "Do
Ex 14:31 so the **p** feared the LORD, and
Ex 15:13 the **p** whom You have redeemed
Ex 15:14 The **p** will hear and be afraid
Ex 15:16 stone, till Your **p** pass over
Ex 15:16 till the **p** pass over whom You
Ex 15:24 the **p** murmured against Moses,
Ex 16: 4 the **p** shall go out and gather
Ex 16:27 happened that some of the **p**
Ex 16:30 So the **p** rested on the
Ex 17: 1 no water for the **p** to drink
Ex 17: 2 Therefore the **p** contended
Ex 17: 3 And the **p** thirsted there for
Ex 17: 3 the **p** murmured against Moses,
Ex 17: 4 What shall I do with this **p**
Ex 17: 5 Go on before the **p**, and take
Ex 17: 6 of it, that the **p** may drink
Ex 17:13 his **p** with the edge of the
Ex 18: 1 for Moses and for Israel His **p**
Ex 18:10 who has delivered the **p** from
Ex 18:13 that Moses sat to judge the **p**
Ex 18:13 the **p** stood before Moses from

Ex 18:14 saw all that he did for the **p**
Ex 18:14 that you are doing for the **p**
Ex 18:14 all the **p** stand before you
Ex 18:15 Because the **p** come to me to
Ex 18:18 these **p** who are with you will
Ex 18:19 Stand before God for the **p**
Ex 18:21 from all the **p** able men, such
Ex 18:22 them judge the **p** at all times
Ex 18:23 all this **p** will also go to
Ex 18:25 and made them heads over the **p**
Ex 18:26 judged the **p** at all times
Ex 19: 5 treasure to Me above all **p**
Ex 19: 7 for the elders of the **p**, and
Ex 19: 8 Then all the **p** answered
Ex 19: 8 words of the **p** to the LORD
Ex 19: 9 that the **p** may hear when I
Ex 19: 9 words of the **p** to the LORD
Ex 19:10 Go to the **p** and sanctify them
Ex 19:11 in the sight of all the **p**
Ex 19:12 bounds for the **p** all around
Ex 19:14 from the mountain to the **p**
Ex 19:14 and sanctified the **p**
Ex 19:15 And he said to the **p**, "Be
Ex 19:16 so that all the **p** who were in
Ex 19:17 Moses brought the **p** out of
Ex 19:21 Go down and warn the **p**, lest
Ex 19:23 The **p** cannot come up to Mount
Ex 19:24 the **p** break through to come
Ex 19:25 So Moses went down to the **p**
Ex 20:18 Now all the **p** witnessed the
Ex 20:18 and when the **p** saw it, they
Ex 20:20 And Moses said to the **p**, "Do
Ex 20:21 So the **p** stood afar off, but
Ex 21: 8 to sell her to a foreign **p**
Ex 22:25 My **p** who are poor among you
Ex 22:28 nor curse a ruler of your **p**
Ex 23:11 the poor of your **p** may eat
Ex 23:27 all the **p** to whom you come
Ex 24: 2 nor shall the **p** go up with
Ex 24: 3 told the **p** all the words of
Ex 24: 3 all the **p** answered with one
Ex 24: 7 read in the hearing of the **p**
Ex 24: 8 blood, sprinkled it on the **p**
Ex 30:33 shall be cut off from his **p**
Ex 30:38 shall be cut off from his **p**
Ex 31:14 be cut off from among his **p**
Ex 32: 1 Now when the **p** saw that Moses
Ex 32: 1 the **p** gathered together to
Ex 32: 3 So all the **p** broke off the
Ex 32: 6 and the **p** sat down to eat and
Ex 32: 7 For your **p** whom you brought
Ex 32: 9 I have seen this **p**, and
Ex 32: 9 indeed it is a stiff-necked **p**
Ex 32:11 **p** whom You have brought out
Ex 32:12 from this harm to Your **p**
Ex 32:14 He said He would do to His **p**
Ex 32:17 of the **p** as they shouted, he
Ex 32:21 What did this **p** do to you
Ex 32:22 You know the **p**, that they are
Ex 32:25 the **p** were unrestrained (for
Ex 32:28 men of the **p** fell that day
Ex 32:30 day that Moses said to the **p**
Ex 32:31 these **p** have sinned a great
Ex 32:34 lead the **p** to the place of
Ex 32:35 So the LORD plagued the **p**
Ex 33: 1 the **p** whom you have brought
Ex 33: 3 for you are a stiff-necked **p**
Ex 33: 4 when the **p** heard these grave
Ex 33: 5 You are a stiff-necked **p**
Ex 33: 8 that all the **p** rose, and each
Ex 33:10 All the **p** saw the pillar of
Ex 33:10 door, and all the **p** rose and
Ex 33:12 say to me, 'Bring up this **p**
Ex 33:13 that this nation is Your **p**
Ex 33:16 will it be known that Your **p**
Ex 33:16 we shall be separate, Your **p**
Ex 33:16 from all the **p** who are upon
Ex 34: 9 we are a stiff-necked **p**
Ex 34:10 Before all your **p** I will do
Ex 34:10 all the **p** among whom you are
Ex 36: 5 The **p** bring much more than
Ex 36: 6 the **p** were restrained from
Lev 4: 3 sins, bringing guilt on the **p**
Lev 4:27 **p** sins unintentionally by
Lev 7:20 shall be cut off from his **p**
Lev 7:21 shall be cut off from his **p**
Lev 7:25 shall be cut off from his **p**
Lev 7:27 shall be cut off from his **p**
Lev 9: 7 for yourself and for the **p**
Lev 9: 7 Offer the offering of the **p**
Lev 9:15 the sin offering for the **p**
Lev 9:18 which were for the **p**
Lev 9:22 lifted his hand toward the **p**
Lev 9:23 and came out and blessed the **p**
Lev 9:23 LORD appeared to all the **p**
Lev 9:24 When all the **p** saw it, they
Lev 10: 3 before all the **p** I must be
Lev 10: 6 and wrath come upon all the **p**
Lev 16:15 offering, which is for the **p**
Lev 16:24 the burnt offering of the **p**
Lev 16:24 for himself and for the **p**
Lev 16:33 and for all the **p** of the
Lev 17: 4 be cut off from among his **p**
Lev 17: 9 be cut off from among his **p**
Lev 17:10 cut him off from among his **p**
Lev 18:29 be cut off from among their **p**
Lev 19: 8 shall be cut off from his **p**
Lev 19:16 as a talebearer among your **p**
Lev 19:18 the children of your **p**, but
Lev 20: 2 The **p** of the land shall stone
Lev 20: 3 will cut him off from his **p**
Lev 20: 4 if the **p** of the land should
Lev 20: 5 I will cut him off from his **p**
Lev 20: 6 and cut him off from his **p**
Lev 20:17 off in the sight of their **p**
Lev 20:18 shall be cut off from their **p**
Lev 21: 1 for the dead among his **p**,
Lev 21: 4 being a chief man among his **p**
Lev 21:14 a virgin of his own **p** as wife
Lev 21:15 his posterity among his **p**
Lev 23:29 shall be cut off from his **p**
Lev 23:30 will destroy from among his **p**
Lev 26:12 God, and you shall be My **p**
Num 5:21 curse and an oath among your **p**
Num 5:27 become a curse among her **p**
Num 9:13 be cut off from among his **p**
Num 11: 1 Now when the **p** complained
Num 11: 2 Then the **p** cried out to Moses
Num 11: 8 The **p** went about and gathered
Num 11:10 Now Moses heard the **p** weeping
Num 11:11 burden of all these **p** on me
Num 11:12 Did I conceive all these **p**
Num 11:13 meat to give to all these **p**
Num 11:14 to bear all these **p** alone
Num 11:16 to be the elders of the **p**
Num 11:17 the burden of the **p** with you
Num 11:18 Then you shall say to the **p**
Num 11:21 The **p** whom I am among are six
Num 11:24 told the **p** the words of the
Num 11:24 men of the elders of the **p**
Num 11:29 the LORD's **p** were prophets
Num 11:32 the **p** stayed up all that day,
Num 11:33 was aroused against the **p**
Num 11:33 the LORD struck the **p** with a
Num 11:34 there they buried the **p** who
Num 11:35 the **p** moved to Hazeroth, and
Num 12:15 the **p** did not journey on till
Num 12:16 afterward the **p** moved from
Num 13:18 whether the **p** who dwell in it
Num 13:28 Nevertheless the **p** who dwell
Num 13:30 quieted the **p** before Moses
Num 13:31 able to go up against the **p**
Num 13:32 all the **p** whom we saw in it
Num 14: 1 and the **p** wept that night
Num 14: 9 nor fear the **p** of the land
Num 14:11 long will these **p** reject Me
Num 14:13 these **p** up from among them
Num 14:14 You, LORD, are among these **p**
Num 14:15 You kill these **p** as one man
Num 14:16 **p** to the land which He swore
Num 14:19 Pardon the iniquity of this **p**
Num 14:19 as You have forgiven this **p**
Num 14:39 and the **p** mourned greatly
Num 15:26 because all the **p** did it
Num 15:30 be cut off from among his **p**
Num 16:41 have killed the **p** of the LORD
Num 16:47 plague had begun among the **p**
Num 16:47 and made atonement for the **p**
Num 20: 1 and the **p** stayed in Kadesh
Num 20: 3 the **p** contended with Moses and
Num 20:24 shall be gathered to his **p**
Num 20:26 shall be gathered to his **p**
Num 21: 2 deliver this **p** into my hand
Num 21: 4 the soul of the **p** became very
Num 21: 5 the **p** spoke against God and
Num 21: 6 fiery serpents among the **p**
Num 21: 6 and they bit the **p**
Num 21: 6 many of the **p** of Israel died
Num 21: 7 Therefore the **p** came to Moses
Num 21: 7 So Moses prayed for the **p**
Num 21:16 Gather the **p** together, and I
Num 21:23 gathered all his **p** together
Num 21:24 as far as the **p** of Ammon
Num 21:24 for the border of the **p** of
Num 21:29 have perished, O **p** of Chemosh
Num 21:33 against them, he and all his **p**
Num 21:34 your hand, with all his **p**
Num 21:35 him, his sons, and all his **p**
Num 22: 3 the **p** because they were many
Num 22: 5 the land of the sons of his **p**
Num 22: 5 Look, a **p** has come from Egypt
Num 22: 6 at once, curse this **p** for me
Num 22:11 a **p** has come out of Egypt, and
Num 22:12 you shall not curse the **p**
Num 22:17 come, curse this **p** for me
Num 22:41 observe the extent of the **p**
Num 23: 9 A **p** dwelling alone, not
Num 23:24 a **p** rises like a lioness, And
Num 24:14 indeed, I am going to my **p**
Num 24:14 **p** will do to your **p** in
Num 25: 1 and the **p** began to commit
Num 25: 2 They invited the **p** to the
Num 25: 2 of their gods, and the **p** ate
Num 25: 4 Take all the leaders of the **p**
Num 25:15 he was head of the **p** of a
Num 26: 4 Take a census of the **p** from
Num 27:13 shall be gathered to your **p**
Num 31: 2 shall be gathered to your **p**
Num 31: 3 So Moses spoke to the **p**,
Num 32:15 you will destroy all these **p**
Num 33:14 no water for the **p** to drink
Deut 1:28 The **p** are greater and taller
Deut 2: 4 And command the **p**, saying
Deut 2:10 a **p** as great and numerous and
Deut 2:16 perished from among the **p**
Deut 2:19 you come near the **p** of Ammon
Deut 2:19 **p** of Ammon as a possession
Deut 2:21 a **p** as great and numerous and
Deut 2:32 all his **p** came out against us
Deut 2:33 him, his sons, and all his **p**
Deut 2:37 the land of the **p** of Ammon
Deut 3: 1 against us, he and all his **p**
Deut 3: 2 delivered him and all his **p**
Deut 3: 3 of Bashan, with all his **p**
Deut 3:11 in Rabbah of the **p** of Ammon
Deut 3:16 the border of the **p** of Ammon
Deut 3:28 shall go over before this **p**
Deut 4: 6 is a wise and understanding **p**
Deut 4:10 to me, 'Gather the **p** to Me
Deut 4:20 out of Egypt, to be His **p**
Deut 4:33 Did any **p** ever hear the voice
Deut 5:28 **p** which they have spoken to
Deut 7: 6 For you are a holy **p** to the
Deut 7: 6 you to be a **p** for Himself
Deut 7: 7 in number than any other **p**
Deut 9: 2 a **p** great and tall, the
Deut 9: 6 for you are a stiff-necked **p**
Deut 9:12 for your **p** whom you brought
Deut 9:13 saying, 'I have seen this **p**
Deut 9:13 they are a stiff-necked **p**
Deut 9:26 GOD, do not destroy Your **p**
Deut 9:27 on the stubbornness of this **p**
Deut 9:29 Yet they are Your **p** and Your
Deut 10:11 your journey before the **p**
Deut 13: 7 of the gods of the **p** which
Deut 13: 9 the hand of all the **p**
Deut 14: 2 For you are a holy **p** to the
Deut 14: 2 you to be a **p** for Himself
Deut 14:21 for you are a holy **p** to the
Deut 16:18 the **p** with just judgment
Deut 17: 7 the hands of all the **p**
Deut 17:13 all the **p** shall hear and fear,
Deut 17:16 nor cause the **p** to return to
Deut 18: 3 the priest's due from the **p**
Deut 20: 1 **p** more numerous than you, do
Deut 20: 2 approach and speak to the **p**
Deut 20: 5 officers shall speak to the **p**
Deut 20: 8 shall speak further to the **p**
Deut 20: 9 finished speaking to the **p**
Deut 20: 9 of the armies to lead the **p**
Deut 20:11 then all the **p** who are found
Deut 21: 8 O LORD, for Your **p** Israel
Deut 21: 8 the charge of Your **p** Israel
Deut 26:15 and bless Your **p** Israel and
Deut 26:18 you to be His special **p**, just
Deut 26:19 a holy **p** to the LORD your God
Deut 27: 1 of Israel, commanded the **p**
Deut 27: 9 the **p** of the LORD your God
Deut 27:11 the **p** on the same day, saying
Deut 27:12 Mount Gerizim to bless the **p**

Deut 27:15 all the **p** shall answer and say
Deut 27:16 all the **p** shall say, 'Amen
Deut 27:17 all the **p** shall say, 'Amen
Deut 27:18 all the **p** shall say, 'Amen
Deut 27:19 all the **p** shall say, 'Amen
Deut 27:20 all the **p** shall say, 'Amen
Deut 27:21 all the **p** shall say, 'Amen
Deut 27:22 all the **p** shall say, 'Amen
Deut 27:23 all the **p** shall say, 'Amen
Deut 27:24 all the **p** shall say, 'Amen
Deut 27:25 all the **p** shall say, 'Amen
Deut 27:26 all the **p** shall say, 'Amen
Deut 28: 9 you as a holy **p** to Himself
Deut 28:32 shall be given to another **p**
Deut 29:13 you today as a **p** for Himself
Deut 31: 7 for you must go with this **p**
Deut 31:12 Gather the **p** together, men and
Deut 31:16 this **p** will rise and play the
Deut 32: 6 LORD, O foolish and unwise **p**
Deut 32: 9 the LORD's portion is His **p**
Deut 32:36 For the LORD will judge His **p**
Deut 32:43 O Gentiles, with His **p**
Deut 32:43 for His land and His **p**
Deut 32:44 song in the hearing of the **p**
Deut 32:50 and be gathered to your **p**
Deut 32:50 Hor and was gathered to his **p**
Deut 33: 3 Yes, He loves the **p**
Deut 33: 5 of the **p** were gathered, all
Deut 33: 7 Judah, and bring him to his **p**
Deut 33:21 came with the heads of the **p**
Deut 33:29 a **p** saved by the LORD, the
Josh 1: 2 Jordan, you and all this **p**
Josh 1: 6 for to this **p** you shall
Josh 1:10 the officers of the **p**, saying
Josh 1:11 the camp and command the **p**
Josh 3: 3 and they commanded the **p**,
Josh 3: 5 And Joshua said to the **p**
Josh 3: 6 and cross over before the **p**
Josh 3: 6 covenant and went before the **p**
Josh 3:14 when the **p** set out from their
Josh 3:14 of the covenant before the **p**
Josh 3:16 the **p** crossed over opposite
Josh 3:17 until all the **p** had crossed
Josh 4: 1 when all the **p** had completely
Josh 4: 2 twelve men from the **p**, one
Josh 4:10 Joshua to speak to the **p**,
Josh 4:10 the **p** hastened and crossed
Josh 4:11 when all the **p** had completely
Josh 4:11 over in the presence of the **p**
Josh 4:19 Now the **p** came up from the
Josh 5: 4 All the **p** who came out of
Josh 5: 5 For all the **p** who came out
Josh 5: 5 but all the **p** who were born
Josh 5: 6 till all the **p** who were men
Josh 5: 8 circumcising all the **p**, that
Josh 6: 5 that all the **p** shall shout
Josh 6: 5 the **p** shall go up every man
Josh 6: 7 And he said to the **p**
Josh 6: 8 Joshua had spoken to the **p**
Josh 6:10 Joshua had commanded the **p**
Josh 6:16 that Joshua said to the **p**
Josh 6:20 So the **p** shouted when the
Josh 6:20 it happened when the **p** heard
Josh 6:20 the **p** shouted with a great
Josh 6:20 Then the **p** went up into the
Josh 7: 3 Do not let all the **p** go up
Josh 7: 3 Do not weary all the **p** there
Josh 7: 3 for the **p** of Ai are few
Josh 7: 4 men went up there from the **p**
Josh 7: 5 the hearts of the **p** melted
Josh 7: 7 this **p** over the Jordan at all
Josh 7:13 Get up, sanctify the **p**, and
Josh 8: 1 take all the **p** of war with
Josh 8: 1 hand the king of Ai, his **p**
Josh 8: 3 arose, and all the **p** of war
Josh 8: 5 all the **p** who are with me
Josh 8: 9 lodged that night among the **p**
Josh 8:10 the morning and mustered the **p**
Josh 8:10 of Israel, before the **p** to Ai
Josh 8:11 all the **p** of war who were
Josh 8:13 And when they had set the **p**
Josh 8:14 to battle, he and all his **p**
Josh 8:16 So all the **p** who were in Ai
Josh 8:20 the **p** who had fled to the
Josh 8:25 all the **p** of Ai
Josh 8:33 should bless the **p** of Israel
Josh 10: 7 all the **p** of war with him, and
Josh 10:13 till the **p** had revenge upon
Josh 10:21 all the **p** returned to the
Josh 10:28 all the **p** who were in it
Josh 10:30 all the **p** who were in it with
Josh 10:32 all the **p** who were in it with
Josh 10:33 and Joshua struck him and his **p**
Josh 10:35 all the **p** who were in it he
Josh 10:37 and all the **p** who were in it
Josh 10:37 and all the **p** who were in it
Josh 10:39 all the **p** who were in it
Josh 11: 4 as many **p** as the sand that is
Josh 11: 7 all the **p** of war with him
Josh 11:11 they struck all the **p** who
Josh 12:23 the king of the **p** of Gilgal
Josh 14: 8 made the heart of the **p** melt
Josh 17:14 since we are a great **p**,
Josh 17:15 If you are a great **p**, then go
Josh 17:17 You are a great **p** and have
Josh 19: 9 the inheritance of that **p**
Josh 24: 2 And Joshua said to all the **p**
Josh 24:16 So the **p** answered and said
*Josh 24:17 among all the **p** through whom
Josh 24:18 out from before us all the **p**
Josh 24:19 But Joshua said to the **p**
Josh 24:21 And the **p** said to Joshua,
Josh 24:22 So Joshua said to the **p**
Josh 24:24 And the **p** said to Joshua,
Josh 24:25 covenant with the **p** that day
Josh 24:27 And Joshua said to all the **p**
Josh 24:28 So Joshua let the **p** depart
Judg 1:16 went and dwelt among the **p**
Judg 2: 4 that the **p** lifted up their
Judg 2: 6 Joshua had dismissed the **p**
Judg 2: 7 So the **p** served the LORD all
Judg 2:12 **p** who were all around them
Judg 3:13 to himself the **p** of Ammon
Judg 3:18 he sent away the **p** who had
Judg 4:13 all the **p** who were with him,
Judg 5: 2 when the **p** willingly offer
Judg 5: 9 willingly with the **p**
Judg 5:11 then the **p** of the LORD shall
Judg 5:13 the **p** against the nobles
Judg 5:18 Zebulun is a **p** who
Judg 6: 3 the **p** of the East would come
Judg 6:33 the **p** of the East, gathered
Judg 7: 1 all the **p** who were with him
Judg 7: 2 The **p** who are with you are
Judg 7: 3 in the hearing of the **p**,
Judg 7: 3 thousand of the **p** returned
Judg 7: 4 The **p** are still too many
Judg 7: 5 the **p** down to the water
Judg 7: 6 but all the rest of the **p** got
Judg 7: 7 Let all the other **p** go, every
Judg 7: 8 So the **p** took provisions and
Judg 7:12 all the **p** of the East, were
Judg 8: 5 bread to the **p** who follow me
Judg 8:10 the army of the **p** of the East
Judg 9:29 If only this **p** were under my
Judg 9:32 the **p** who are with you, and
Judg 9:33 the **p** who are with him come
Judg 9:34 all the **p** who were with him
Judg 9:35 the **p** who were with him rose
Judg 9:36 And when Gaal saw the **p**, he
Judg 9:36 **p** are coming down from the
Judg 9:37 **p** are coming down from the
Judg 9:38 these the **p** whom you despised
Judg 9:42 the **p** went out into the field
Judg 9:43 So he took his **p**, divided
Judg 9:43 looked, and there were the **p**
Judg 9:45 killed the **p** who were in it
Judg 9:48 all the **p** who were with him
Judg 9:48 to the **p** who were with him
Judg 9:49 So each of the **p** likewise cut
Judg 9:49 so that all the **p** of the
Judg 9:51 all the **p** of the city
Judg 10: 6 the gods of the **p** of Ammon
Judg 10: 7 the hands of the **p** of Ammon
Judg 10: 9 Moreover the **p** of Ammon
Judg 10:11 and from the **p** of Ammon and
Judg 10:17 Then the **p** of Ammon gathered
Judg 10:18 And the **p**, the leaders of
Judg 10:18 fight against the **p** of Ammon
Judg 11: 4 **p** of Ammon made war against
Judg 11: 5 when the **p** of Ammon made war
Judg 11: 6 fight against the **p** of Ammon
Judg 11: 8 fight against the **p** of Ammon
Judg 11: 9 fight against the **p** of Ammon
Judg 11:11 and the **p** made him head and
Judg 11:12 to the king of the **p** of Ammon
Judg 11:13 the king of the **p** of Ammon
Judg 11:14 to the king of the **p** of Ammon
Judg 11:15 the land of the **p** of Ammon
Judg 11:20 gathered all his **p** together
Judg 11:21 all his **p** into the hand of
Judg 11:23 from before His **p** Israel
Judg 11:27 of Israel and the **p** of Ammon
Judg 11:28 the king of the **p** of Ammon
Judg 11:29 toward the **p** of Ammon
Judg 11:30 the **p** of Ammon into my hands
Judg 11:31 in peace from the **p** of Ammon
Judg 11:32 advanced toward the **p** of
Judg 11:33 Thus the **p** of Ammon were
Judg 11:36 your enemies, the **p** of Ammon
Judg 12: 1 fight against the **p** of Ammon
Judg 12: 2 My **p** and I were in a great
Judg 12: 2 struggle with the **p** of Ammon
Judg 12: 3 over against the **p** of Ammon
Judg 14: 3 brethren, or among all my **p**
Judg 14:16 a riddle to the sons of my **p**
Judg 14:17 riddle to the sons of her **p**
Judg 16:24 When the **p** saw him, they
Judg 16:30 and all the **p** who were in it
Judg 18: 7 They saw the **p** who were there
Judg 18:10 you will come to a secure **p**
Judg 18:20 and took his place among the **p**
Judg 18:27 to a **p** who were quiet and
Judg 20: 2 And the leaders of all the **p**
Judg 20: 2 the assembly of the **p** of God
Judg 20: 8 Then all the **p** arose as one
Judg 20:10 to make provisions for the **p**
Judg 20:16 Among all this **p** there were
Judg 20:22 And the **p**, that is, the men of
Judg 20:26 of Israel, that is, all the **p**
Judg 20:31 went out against the **p**, and
Judg 20:31 down and kill some of the **p**
Judg 21: 2 Then the **p** came to the house
Judg 21: 4 that the **p** rose early and
Judg 21: 9 For when the **p** were counted
Judg 21:15 the **p** grieved for Benjamin,
Ruth 1: 6 His **p** in giving them bread
Ruth 1:10 return with you to your **p**
Ruth 1:15 has gone back to her **p** and to
Ruth 1:16 your **p** shall be my **p**, and
Ruth 1:16 your **p** shall be my **p**
Ruth 2:11 have come to a **p** whom you did
Ruth 2:22 that **p** do not meet you in any
Ruth 3:11 for all the **p** of my town know
Ruth 4: 4 and the elders of my **p**
Ruth 4: 9 to the elders and to all the **p**
Ruth 4:11 all the **p** who were at the
1Sa 2:13 the **p** was that when any man
1Sa 2:23 evil dealings from all the **p**
1Sa 2:24 make the LORD's **p** transgress
1Sa 2:29 the offerings of Israel My **p**
1Sa 4: 3 when the **p** had come into the
1Sa 4: 4 So the **p** sent to Shiloh, that
1Sa 4:17 a great slaughter among the **p**
1Sa 5: 3 when the **p** of Ashdod arose
1Sa 5: 6 was heavy on the **p** of Ashdod
1Sa 5:10 to us, to kill us and our **p**
1Sa 5:11 it does not kill us and our **p**
1Sa 6: 6 did they not let the **p** go
1Sa 6:13 Now the **p** of Beth Shemesh
1Sa 6:19 and seventy men of the **p**, and
1Sa 6:19 the **p** lamented because the
1Sa 6:19 the **p** with a great slaughter
1Sa 8: 7 Heed the voice of the **p** in
1Sa 8:10 **p** who asked him for a king
1Sa 8:19 Nevertheless the **p** refused to
1Sa 8:21 heard all the words of the **p**
1Sa 9: 2 was taller than any of the **p**
1Sa 9:12 the **p** today on the high place
1Sa 9:13 For the **p** will not eat until
1Sa 9:16 commander over My **p** Israel
1Sa 9:16 that he may save My **p** from
1Sa 9:16 for I have looked upon My **p**
1Sa 9:17 one shall reign over My **p**
1Sa 9:24 since I said I invited the **p**
1Sa 10:11 that the **p** said to one
1Sa 10:17 Then Samuel called the **p**
1Sa 10:23 and when he stood among the **p**
1Sa 10:23 **p** from his shoulders upward
1Sa 10:24 And Samuel said to all the **p**
1Sa 10:24 one like him among all the **p**
1Sa 10:24 So all the **p** shouted and
1Sa 10:25 the **p** the behavior of royalty
1Sa 10:25 And Samuel sent all the **p** away
1Sa 11: 4 news in the hearing of the **p**
1Sa 11: 4 all the **p** lifted up their
1Sa 11: 5 What troubles the **p**, that
1Sa 11: 7 of the LORD fell on the **p**
1Sa 11:11 that Saul put the **p** in three
1Sa 11:12 Then the **p** said to Samuel,

1Sa 11:14 Then Samuel said to the **p**
1Sa 11:15 So all the **p** went to Gilgal,
1Sa 12: 6 And Samuel said to the **p**, "It
1Sa 12:18 all the **p** greatly feared the
1Sa 12:19 all the **p** said to Samuel,
1Sa 12:20 Then Samuel said to the **p**
1Sa 12:22 LORD will not forsake His **p**
1Sa 12:22 the LORD to make you His **p**
1Sa 13: 2 rest of the **p** he sent away
1Sa 13: 4 the **p** were called together to
1Sa 13: 5 **p** as the sand which is on the
1Sa 13: 6 (for the **p** were distressed)
1Sa 13: 6 then the **p** hid in caves, in
1Sa 13: 7 and all the **p** followed him
1Sa 13: 8 the **p** were scattered from him
1Sa 13:11 When I saw that the **p** were
1Sa 13:14 to be commander over His **p**
1Sa 13:15 Saul numbered the **p** who were
1Sa 13:16 the **p** who were present with
1Sa 13:22 of the **p** who were with Saul
1Sa 14: 2 The **p** who were with him were
1Sa 14: 3 But the **p** did not know that
1Sa 14:15 the field, and among all the **p**
1Sa 14:17 to the **p** who were with him
1Sa 14:20 all the **p** who were with him
1Sa 14:24 had placed the **p** under oath
1Sa 14:24 So none of the **p** tasted food
1Sa 14:25 Now all the **p** of the land
1Sa 14:26 when the **p** had come into the
1Sa 14:26 for the **p** feared the oath
1Sa 14:27 charge the **p** with the oath
1Sa 14:28 Then one of the **p** said
1Sa 14:28 charged the **p** with an oath
1Sa 14:28 And the **p** were faint
1Sa 14:30 How much better if the **p** had
1Sa 14:31 So the **p** were very faint
1Sa 14:32 the **p** rushed on the spoil, and
1Sa 14:32 the **p** ate them with the blood
1Sa 14:33 the **p** are sinning against the
1Sa 14:34 yourselves among the **p**, and
1Sa 14:34 So every one of the **p**
1Sa 14:38 here, all you chiefs of the **p**
1Sa 14:39 among all the **p** answered him
1Sa 14:40 And the **p** said to Saul,
1Sa 14:41 were taken, but the **p** escaped
1Sa 14:45 But the **p** said to Saul
1Sa 14:45 So the **p** rescued Jonathan,
1Sa 14:47 Moab, against the **p** of Ammon
1Sa 15: 1 to anoint you king over His **p**
1Sa 15: 4 Saul gathered the **p** together
1Sa 15: 8 utterly destroyed all the **p**
1Sa 15: 9 the **p** spared Agag and the best
1Sa 15:15 for the **p** spared the best of
1Sa 15:21 But the **p** took of the plunder
1Sa 15:24 words, because I feared the **p**
1Sa 15:30 before the elders of my **p**
1Sa 17:27 the **p** answered him in this
1Sa 17:30 these **p** answered him as the
1Sa 18: 5 in the sight of all the **p**
1Sa 18:13 out and came in before the **p**
1Sa 23: 8 all the **p** together for war
1Sa 26: 5 camp, with the **p** encamped all
1Sa 26: 7 came to the **p** by night
1Sa 26: 7 and the **p** lay all around him
1Sa 26:14 And David called out to the **p**
1Sa 26:15 For one of the **p** came in to
1Sa 27:12 He has made his **p** Israel
1Sa 30: 4 and the **p** who were with him
1Sa 30: 6 for the **p** spoke of stoning
1Sa 30: 6 soul of all the **p** was grieved
1Sa 30:21 to meet the **p** who were with
1Sa 30:21 when David came near the **p**
1Sa 31: 9 of their idols and among the **p**
2Sa 1: 4 The **p** have fled from the
2Sa 1: 4 many of the **p** are fallen
2Sa 1:12 for the **p** of the LORD and for
2Sa 2:26 the **p** to return from pursuing
2Sa 2:27 all the **p** would have given up
2Sa 2:28 all the **p** stood still and did
2Sa 2:30 gathered all the **p** together
2Sa 3:18 I will save My **p** Israel from
2Sa 3:31 to all the **p** who were with
2Sa 3:32 of Abner, and all the **p** wept
2Sa 3:34 Then all the **p** wept over
2Sa 3:35 And when all the **p** came to
2Sa 3:36 Now all the **p** took note of it
2Sa 3:36 king did pleased all the **p**
2Sa 3:37 For all the **p** and all Israel
2Sa 5: 2 shall shepherd My **p** Israel
2Sa 5:12 for His **p** Israel's sake

2Sa 6: 2 went with all the **p** who were
2Sa 6:18 he blessed the **p** in the name
2Sa 6:19 distributed among all the **p**
2Sa 6:19 So all the **p** departed,
2Sa 6:21 ruler over the **p** of the LORD
2Sa 7: 7 to shepherd My **p** Israel,
2Sa 7: 8 sheep, to be ruler over My **p**
2Sa 7:10 a place for My **p** Israel, and
2Sa 7:11 judges to be over My **p** Israel
2Sa 7:23 And who is like Your **p**, like
2Sa 7:23 to redeem for Himself as a **p**
2Sa 7:23 before Your **p** whom You
2Sa 7:24 For You have made Your **p**
2Sa 7:24 Your very own **p** forever
2Sa 8:12 Moab, from the **p** of Ammon
2Sa 8:15 and justice to all his **p**
2Sa 10: 1 king of the **p** of Ammon died
2Sa 10: 2 the land of the **p** of Ammon
2Sa 10: 3 the **p** of Ammon said to Hanun
2Sa 10: 6 So when the **p** of Ammon saw
2Sa 10: 6 the **p** of Ammon sent and hired
2Sa 10: 8 Then the **p** of Ammon came out
2Sa 10:10 And the rest of the **p** he put
2Sa 10:10 array against the **p** of Ammon
2Sa 10:11 But if the **p** of Ammon are too
2Sa 10:12 and let us be strong for our **p**
2Sa 10:13 the **p** who were with him drew
2Sa 10:14 when the **p** of Ammon saw that
2Sa 10:14 returned from the **p** of Ammon
2Sa 10:19 help the **p** of Ammon anymore
2Sa 11: 1 they destroyed the **p** of Ammon
2Sa 11: 7 how the **p** were doing, and how
2Sa 11:17 some of the **p** of the servants
2Sa 12: 9 the sword of the **p** of Ammon
2Sa 12:26 Rabbah of the **p** of Ammon, and
2Sa 12:28 the rest of the **p** together
2Sa 12:29 gathered all the **p** together
2Sa 12:31 out the **p** who were in it, and
2Sa 12:31 the cities of the **p** of Ammon
2Sa 12:31 and all the **p** returned to
2Sa 13:34 many **p** were coming from the
2Sa 14:13 a thing against the **p** of God
2Sa 14:15 the **p** have made me afraid
2Sa 15:12 for the **p** with Absalom
2Sa 15:17 out with all the **p** after him
2Sa 15:23 and all the **p** crossed over
2Sa 15:23 all the **p** crossed over toward
2Sa 15:24 went up until all the **p** had
2Sa 15:30 all the **p** who were with him
2Sa 16: 6 And all the **p** and all the
2Sa 16:14 all the **p** who were with him
2Sa 16:15 Absalom and all the **p**, the men
2Sa 16:18 but whom the LORD and this **p**
2Sa 17: 2 all the **p** who are with him
2Sa 17: 3 bring back all the **p** to you
2Sa 17: 3 then all the **p** will be at
2Sa 17: 8 and will not camp with the **p**
2Sa 17: 9 the **p** who follow Absalom
2Sa 17:16 all the **p** who are with him be
2Sa 17:22 all the **p** who were with him
2Sa 17:27 from Rabbah of the **p** of
2Sa 17:29 the **p** who were with him to
2Sa 17:29 The **p** are hungry and weary and
2Sa 18: 1 the **p** who were with him, and
2Sa 18: 2 the **p** under the hand of Joab
2Sa 18: 2 And the king said to the **p**
2Sa 18: 3 But the **p** answered, "You
2Sa 18: 4 and all the **p** went out by
2Sa 18: 5 all the **p** heard when the king
2Sa 18: 6 So the **p** went out into the
2Sa 18: 7 The **p** of Israel were
2Sa 18: 8 **p** that day than the sword
2Sa 18:16 the **p** returned from pursuing
2Sa 18:16 For Joab held back the **p**
2Sa 19: 2 into mourning for all the **p**
2Sa 19: 2 For the **p** heard it said that
2Sa 19: 3 the **p** stole back into the
2Sa 19: 3 as **p** who are ashamed steal
2Sa 19: 8 And they told all the **p**,
2Sa 19: 8 So all the **p** came before
2Sa 19: 9 Now all the **p** were in a
2Sa 19:39 Then all the **p** went over the
2Sa 19:40 all the **p** of Judah escorted
2Sa 19:40 and also half the **p** of Israel
2Sa 20:12 that all the **p** stood still
2Sa 20:13 all the **p** went on after Joab
2Sa 20:15 all the **p** who were with Joab
2Sa 20:22 her wisdom went to all the **p**
2Sa 22:28 You will save the humble **p**
2Sa 22:44 me from the strivings of my **p**

2Sa 22:44 A **p** whom I have not known
2Sa 22:48 who subdues the **p** under me
2Sa 23:10 the **p** returned after him only
2Sa 23:11 Then the **p** fled from the
2Sa 24: 2 to Beersheba, and count the **p**
2Sa 24: 2 may know the number of the **p**
2Sa 24: 3 the **p** a hundredfold more than
2Sa 24: 4 king to count the **p** of Israel
2Sa 24: 9 number of the **p** to the king
2Sa 24:10 after he had numbered the **p**
2Sa 24:15 thousand men of the **p** died
2Sa 24:16 who was destroying the **p**
2Sa 24:17 angel who was striking the **p**
2Sa 24:21 may be withdrawn from the **p**
1Ki 1:39 the horn, and all the **p** said
1Ki 1:40 all the **p** went up after him
1Ki 1:40 the **p** played the flutes and
1Ki 3: 2 Meanwhile the **p** sacrificed at
1Ki 3: 8 Your **p** whom You have chosen
1Ki 3: 8 a great **p**, too numerous
1Ki 3: 9 heart to judge Your **p**, that I
1Ki 3: 9 judge this great **p** of Yours
1Ki 5: 7 a wise son over this great **p**
1Ki 5:16 who supervised the **p** who
1Ki 6:13 will not forsake My **p** Israel
1Ki 8:16 My **p** Israel out of Egypt, I
1Ki 8:16 David to be over My **p** Israel
1Ki 8:30 servant and of Your **p** Israel
1Ki 8:33 When Your **p** Israel are
1Ki 8:34 the sin of Your **p** Israel, and
1Ki 8:36 Your **p** Israel, that You may
1Ki 8:36 to Your **p** as an inheritance
1Ki 8:38 or by all Your **p** Israel,
1Ki 8:41 who is not of Your **p** Israel
1Ki 8:43 fear You, as do Your **p** Israel
1Ki 8:44 When Your **p** go out to battle
1Ki 8:50 and forgive Your **p** who have
1Ki 8:51 (for they are Your **p** and Your
1Ki 8:52 supplication of Your **p** Israel
1Ki 8:56 given rest to His **p** Israel
1Ki 8:59 and the cause of His **p** Israel
1Ki 8:66 eighth day he sent the **p** away
1Ki 8:66 David, and for Israel His **p**
1Ki 9:20 All the **p** who were left of
1Ki 9:23 over the **p** who did the work
1Ki 11: 7 abomination of the **p** of Ammon
1Ki 11:33 the god of the **p** of Ammon
1Ki 12: 5 And the **p** departed
1Ki 12: 6 advise me to answer these **p**
1Ki 12: 7 be a servant to these **p** today
1Ki 12: 9 this **p** who have spoken to me
1Ki 12:10 this **p** who have spoken to you
1Ki 12:12 all the **p** came to Rehoboam
1Ki 12:13 king answered the **p** roughly
1Ki 12:15 king did not listen to the **p**
1Ki 12:16 the **p** answered the king,
1Ki 12:23 and to the rest of the **p**,
1Ki 12:27 If these **p** go up to offer
1Ki 12:27 then the heart of this **p** will
1Ki 12:28 of gold, and said to the **p**
1Ki 12:30 for the **p** went to worship
1Ki 12:31 priests from every class of **p**
1Ki 13:33 of **p** for the high places
1Ki 14: 2 I would be king over this **p**
1Ki 14: 7 exalted you from among the **p**
1Ki 14: 7 you ruler over My **p** Israel
1Ki 16: 2 you ruler over My **p** Israel
1Ki 16: 2 and have made My **p** Israel sin
1Ki 16:15 the **p** were encamped against
1Ki 16:16 Now the **p** who were encamped
1Ki 16:21 Then the **p** of Israel were
1Ki 16:21 half of the **p** followed Tibni
1Ki 16:22 But the **p** who followed Omri
1Ki 16:22 prevailed over the **p** who
1Ki 18:21 And Elijah came to all the **p**
1Ki 18:21 But the **p** answered him not
1Ki 18:22 Then Elijah said to the **p**
1Ki 18:24 So all the **p** answered and
1Ki 18:30 Then Elijah said to all the **p**
1Ki 18:30 So all the **p** came near to
1Ki 18:37 that this **p** may know that You
1Ki 18:39 Now when all the **p** saw it
1Ki 19:21 and gave it to the **p**, and they
1Ki 20: 8 and all the **p** said to him,
1Ki 20:10 each of the **p** who follow me
1Ki 20:15 them he mustered all the **p**
1Ki 20:42 and your **p** for his **p**
1Ki 21: 9 with high honor among the **p**
1Ki 21:12 with high honor among the **p**
1Ki 21:13 in the presence of the **p**

1Ki 22: 4 are, my **p** as your **p**, my
1Ki 22: 4 you are, my **p** as your **p**
1Ki 22:28 Take heed, all you **p**
1Ki 22:43 for the **p** offered sacrifices
2Ki 3: 7 are, my **p** as your **p**, my
2Ki 3: 7 you are, my **p** as your **p**
2Ki 4:13 I dwell among my own **p**
2Ki 4:41 Serve it to the **p**, that they
2Ki 4:42 Give it to the **p**, that they
2Ki 4:43 Give it to the **p**, that they
2Ki 6:18 Strike this **p**, I pray, with
2Ki 6:30 wall, the **p** looked, and there
2Ki 7:16 Then the **p** went out and
2Ki 7:17 But the **p** trampled him in the
2Ki 7:20 for the **p** trampled him in the
2Ki 8:21 but his **p** fled to their tents
2Ki 9: 6 king over the **p** of the LORD
2Ki 10: 9 stood, and said to all the **p**
2Ki 10:18 gathered all the **p** together
2Ki 11:13 noise of the escorts and the **p**
2Ki 11:13 she came to the **p**
2Ki 11:14 All the **p** of the land were
2Ki 11:17 the LORD, the king, and the **p**
2Ki 11:17 they should be the LORD's **p**
2Ki 11:17 between the king and the **p**
2Ki 11:18 all the **p** of the land went to
2Ki 11:19 and all the **p** of the land
2Ki 11:20 So all the **p** of the land
2Ki 12: 3 the **p** still sacrificed and
2Ki 12: 8 any more money from the **p**
2Ki 14: 4 the **p** still sacrificed and
2Ki 14:21 And all the **p** of Judah took
2Ki 15: 4 the **p** still sacrificed and
2Ki 15: 5 judging the **p** of the land
2Ki 15:10 killed him in front of the **p**
2Ki 15:35 the **p** still sacrificed and
2Ki 16: 9 carried its **p** captive to Kir,
2Ki 16:15 of all the **p** of the land,
2Ki 17:24 brought **p** from Babylon,
2Ki 18:26 of the **p** who are on the wall
2Ki 18:36 But the **p** held their peace and
2Ki 19:12 the **p** of Eden who were in
2Ki 19:35 when **p** arose early in the
2Ki 20: 5 Hezekiah the leader of My **p**
2Ki 21:24 But the **p** of the land
2Ki 21:24 Then the **p** of the land made
2Ki 22: 4 have gathered from the **p**
2Ki 22:13 of the LORD for me, for the **p**
2Ki 23: 2 and the prophets and all the **p**
2Ki 23: 3 all the **p** took their stand
2Ki 23: 6 on the graves of the common **p**
2Ki 23:13 abomination of the **p** of Ammon
2Ki 23:21 the king commanded all the **p**
2Ki 23:30 And the **p** of the land took
2Ki 23:35 gold from the **p** of the land
2Ki 24: 2 and bands of the **p** of Ammon
2Ki 24:14 the poorest **p** of the land
2Ki 25: 3 no food for the **p** of the land
2Ki 25:11 captive the rest of the **p** who
2Ki 25:19 mustered the **p** of the land
2Ki 25:19 sixty men of the **p** of the
2Ki 25:22 governor over the **p** who
2Ki 25:26 And all the **p**, small and great,
1Ch 10: 9 of their idols and among the **p**
1Ch 11: 2 shall shepherd My **p** Israel
1Ch 11: 2 and be ruler over My **p** Israel
1Ch 11:13 And the **p** fled from the
1Ch 13: 4 in the eyes of all the **p**
1Ch 14: 2 because of His **p** Israel
1Ch 16: 2 he blessed the **p** in the name
1Ch 16:20 from one kingdom to another **p**
1Ch 16:36 And all the **p** said, "Amen
1Ch 16:43 Then all the **p** departed,
1Ch 17: 6 I commanded to shepherd My **p**
1Ch 17: 7 be ruler over My **p** Israel
1Ch 17: 9 a place for My **p** Israel, and
1Ch 17:10 judges to be over My **p** Israel
1Ch 17:21 And who is like Your **p** Israel
1Ch 17:21 to redeem for Himself as a **p**
1Ch 17:21 Your **p** whom You redeemed
1Ch 17:22 For You have made Your **p**
1Ch 17:22 Your very own **p** forever
1Ch 18:11 Moab, from the **p** of Ammon
1Ch 18:14 and justice to all his **p**
1Ch 19: 1 king of the **p** of Ammon died
1Ch 19: 2 the **p** of Ammon to comfort him
1Ch 19: 3 the princes of the **p** of Ammon
1Ch 19: 6 When the **p** of Ammon saw that
1Ch 19: 6 and the **p** of Ammon sent a
1Ch 19: 7 the king of Maachah and his **p**
1Ch 19: 7 Also the **p** of Ammon gathered
1Ch 19: 9 Then the **p** of Ammon came out
1Ch 19:11 And the rest of the **p** he put
1Ch 19:11 array against the **p** of Ammon
1Ch 19:12 but if the **p** of Ammon are too
1Ch 19:13 and let us be strong for our **p**
1Ch 19:14 the **p** who were with him drew
1Ch 19:15 When the **p** of Ammon saw that
1Ch 19:19 help the **p** of Ammon anymore
1Ch 20: 1 the country of the **p** of Ammon
1Ch 20: 3 out the **p** who were in it, and
1Ch 20: 3 the cities of the **p** of Ammon
1Ch 20: 3 and all the **p** returned to
1Ch 21: 2 and to the leaders of the **p**
1Ch 21: 3 May the LORD make His **p** a
1Ch 21: 5 the number of the **p** to David
1Ch 21:17 the **p** to be numbered
1Ch 21:17 but not against Your **p** that
1Ch 21:22 may be withdrawn from the **p**
1Ch 22:18 the LORD and before His **p**
1Ch 23:25 has given rest to His **p**, that
1Ch 28: 2 Hear me, my brethren and my **p**
1Ch 28:21 all the **p** will be completely
1Ch 29: 9 Then the **p** rejoiced, for they
1Ch 29:14 But who am I, and who are my **p**
1Ch 29:17 with joy I have seen Your **p**
1Ch 29:18 of the heart of Your **p**, and
2Ch 1: 9 have made me king over a **p**
2Ch 1:10 out and come in before this **p**
2Ch 1:10 judge this great **p** of Yours
2Ch 1:11 that you may judge My **p** over
2Ch 2:11 Because the LORD loves His **p**
2Ch 2:18 overseers to make the **p** work
2Ch 6: 5 My **p** out of the land of Egypt
2Ch 6: 5 be a ruler over My **p** Israel
2Ch 6: 6 David to be over My **p** Israel
2Ch 6:21 servant and of Your **p** Israel
2Ch 6:24 Or if Your **p** Israel are
2Ch 6:25 the sin of Your **p** Israel, and
2Ch 6:27 Your **p** Israel, that You may
2Ch 6:27 to Your **p** as an inheritance
2Ch 6:29 or by all Your **p** Israel,
2Ch 6:32 who is not of Your **p** Israel
2Ch 6:33 that all **p** of the earth may
2Ch 6:33 fear You, as do Your **p** Israel
2Ch 6:34 When Your **p** go out to battle
2Ch 6:39 and forgive Your **p** who have
2Ch 7: 4 all the **p** offered sacrifices
2Ch 7: 5 all the **p** dedicated the house
2Ch 7:10 the **p** away to their tents
2Ch 7:10 Solomon, and for His **p** Israel
2Ch 7:13 or send pestilence among My **p**
2Ch 7:14 if My **p** who are called by My
2Ch 8: 7 All the **p** who were left of
2Ch 8:10 fifty, who ruled over the **p**
2Ch 10: 5 And the **p** departed
2Ch 10: 6 advise me to answer these **p**
2Ch 10: 7 If you are kind to these **p**
2Ch 10: 9 this **p** who have spoken to me
2Ch 10:10 the **p** who have spoken to you
2Ch 10:12 all the **p** came to Rehoboam on
2Ch 10:15 king did not listen to the **p**
2Ch 10:16 the **p** answered the king,
2Ch 12: 3 **p** without number who came
2Ch 13:17 and his **p** struck them with a
2Ch 14:13 and the **p** who were with him
2Ch 16:10 some of the **p** at that time
2Ch 17: 9 of Judah and taught the **p**
2Ch 18: 2 the **p** who were with him, and
2Ch 18: 3 are, and my **p** as your **p**
2Ch 18:27 Take heed, all you **p**
2Ch 19: 4 the **p** from Beersheba to the
2Ch 20: 1 **p** of Moab with the **p** of Ammon
2Ch 20: 7 land before Your **p** Israel
2Ch 20:10 now, here are the **p** of Ammon
2Ch 20:21 he had consulted with the **p**
2Ch 20:22 against the **p** of Ammon, Moab,
2Ch 20:23 For the **p** of Ammon and Moab
2Ch 20:25 his **p** came to take away their
2Ch 20:33 for as yet the **p** had not
2Ch 21:14 **p** with a serious affliction
2Ch 21:19 his **p** made no burning for him
2Ch 23: 5 All the **p** shall be in the
2Ch 23: 6 but all the **p** shall keep the
2Ch 23:10 Then he set all the **p**, every
2Ch 23:12 the noise of the **p** running
2Ch 23:12 she came to the **p** in the
2Ch 23:13 were all the **p** of the land
2Ch 23:16 between himself, the **p**, and
2Ch 23:16 they should be the LORD's **p**
2Ch 23:17 all the **p** went to the temple
2Ch 23:20 the governors of the **p**, and
2Ch 23:20 all the **p** of the land, and
2Ch 23:21 So all the **p** of the land
2Ch 24:10 all the **p** rejoiced, brought
2Ch 24:20 priest, who stood above the **p**
2Ch 24:23 the **p** from among the **p**
2Ch 25:11 himself, and leading his **p**
2Ch 25:11 ten thousand of the **p** of Seir
2Ch 25:14 the gods of the **p** of Seir
2Ch 25:15 you sought the gods of the **p**
2Ch 25:15 their own **p** from your hand
2Ch 26: 1 Now all the **p** of Judah took
2Ch 26:21 judging the **p** of the land
2Ch 27: 2 But still the **p** acted
2Ch 27: 5 the **p** of Ammon gave him in
2Ch 27: 5 The **p** of Ammon paid him this
2Ch 29:36 all the **p** rejoiced
2Ch 29:36 that God had prepared the **p**
2Ch 30: 3 nor had the **p** gathered
2Ch 30:13 Now many **p**, a very great
2Ch 30:18 For a multitude of the **p**,
2Ch 30:20 to Hezekiah and healed the **p**
2Ch 30:27 arose and blessed the **p**, and
2Ch 31: 4 **p** who dwelt in Jerusalem to
2Ch 31: 8 the LORD and His **p** Israel
2Ch 31:10 Since the **p** began to bring
2Ch 31:10 the LORD has blessed His **p**
2Ch 32: 4 Thus many **p** gathered together
2Ch 32: 6 military captains over the **p**
2Ch 32: 8 the **p** were strengthened by
2Ch 32:14 deliver his **p** from my hand
2Ch 32:15 was able to deliver his **p**
2Ch 32:17 their **p** from my hand, so the
2Ch 32:17 deliver His **p** from my hand
2Ch 32:18 **p** of Jerusalem who were on
2Ch 32:19 gods of the **p** of the earth
2Ch 33:10 spoke to Manasseh and his **p**
2Ch 33:17 Nevertheless the **p** still
2Ch 33:25 But the **p** of the land
2Ch 33:25 Then the **p** of the land made
2Ch 34:30 and the Levites, and all the **p**
2Ch 35: 3 LORD your God and His **p** Israel
2Ch 35: 5 of your brethren the lay **p**
2Ch 35: 7 Josiah gave the lay **p** lambs
2Ch 35: 8 gave willingly to the **p**, to
2Ch 35:12 fathers' houses of the lay **p**
2Ch 35:13 quickly among all the lay **p**
2Ch 36: 1 Then the **p** of the land took
2Ch 36:14 the **p** transgressed more and
2Ch 36:15 He had compassion on His **p**
2Ch 36:16 the LORD arose against His **p**
2Ch 36:23 there among you of all His **p**
Ezra 1: 3 there among you of all His **p**
Ezra 2: 1 Now these are the **p** of the
Ezra 2: 2 of the men of the **p** of Israel
Ezra 2: 3 the **p** of Parosh, two thousand
Ezra 2: 4 the **p** of Shephatiah, three
Ezra 2: 5 the **p** of Arah, seven hundred
Ezra 2: 6 the **p** of Pahath-Moab, of the
Ezra 2: 6 of the **p** of Jeshua and Joab,
Ezra 2: 7 the **p** of Elam, one thousand
Ezra 2: 8 the **p** of Zattu, nine hundred
Ezra 2: 9 the **p** of Zaccai, seven
Ezra 2:10 the **p** of Bani, six hundred and
Ezra 2:11 the **p** of Bebai, six hundred
Ezra 2:12 the **p** of Azgad, one thousand
Ezra 2:13 the **p** of Adonikam, six
Ezra 2:14 the **p** of Bigvai, two thousand
Ezra 2:15 the **p** of Adin, four hundred
Ezra 2:16 the **p** of Ater of Hezekiah,
Ezra 2:17 the **p** of Bezai, three hundred
Ezra 2:18 the **p** of Jorah, one hundred
Ezra 2:19 the **p** of Hashum, two hundred
Ezra 2:20 the **p** of Gibbar, ninety-five
Ezra 2:21 the **p** of Bethlehem, one
Ezra 2:24 the **p** of Azmaveth, forty-two
Ezra 2:25 the **p** of Kirjath Arim,
Ezra 2:26 the **p** of Ramah and Geba, six
Ezra 2:29 the **p** of Nebo, fifty-two
Ezra 2:30 the **p** of Magbish, one hundred
Ezra 2:31 the **p** of the other Elam, one
Ezra 2:32 the **p** of Harim, three hundred
Ezra 2:33 the **p** of Lod, Hadid, and Ono,
Ezra 2:34 the **p** of Jericho, three
Ezra 2:35 the **p** of Senaah, three
Ezra 2:70 and the Levites, some of the **p**
Ezra 3: 1 the **p** gathered together as
Ezra 3: 3 of the **p** of those countries
Ezra 3: 7 and oil to the **p** of Sidon

Ezra 3:11 Then all the **p** shouted with
Ezra 3:13 so that the **p** could not
Ezra 3:13 noise of the weeping of the **p**
Ezra 3:13 for the **p** shouted with a loud
Ezra 4: 4 Then the **p** of the land tried
Ezra 4: 4 to discourage the **p** of Judah
Ezra 4: 9 the **p** of Persia and Erech and
Ezra 5:12 carried the **p** away to Babylon
Ezra 6:12 there destroy any king or **p**
Ezra 7:13 all those of the **p** of Israel
Ezra 7:16 freewill offering of the **p**
Ezra 7:25 the **p** who are in the region
Ezra 8:15 And I looked among the **p** and
Ezra 8:36 So they gave support to the **p**
Ezra 9: 1 The **p** of Israel and the
Ezra 9:14 the **p** of these abominations
Ezra 10: 1 for the **p** wept very bitterly
Ezra 10: 9 all the **p** sat in the open
Ezra 10:13 But there are many **p**
Neh 1:10 are Your servants and Your **p**
Neh 4: 6 for the **p** had a mind to work
Neh 4:13 and I set the **p** according to
Neh 4:14 and to the rest of the **p**
Neh 4:19 rulers, and the rest of the **p**
Neh 4:22 time I also said to the **p**
Neh 5: 1 was a great outcry of the **p**
Neh 5:13 Then the **p** did according to
Neh 5:15 me laid burdens on the **p**, and
Neh 5:15 servants bore rule over the **p**
Neh 5:18 bondage was heavy on this **p**
Neh 5:19 that I have done for this **p**
Neh 7: 4 but the **p** in it were few, and
Neh 7: 5 nobles, the rulers, and the **p**
Neh 7: 6 These are the **p** of the
Neh 7: 7 of the men of the **p** of Israel
Neh 7:72 **p** gave was twenty thousand
Neh 7:73 the singers, some of the **p**
Neh 8: 1 Now all the **p** gathered
Neh 8: 3 the ears of all the **p** were
Neh 8: 5 in the sight of all the **p**
Neh 8: 5 was standing above all the **p**
Neh 8: 5 opened it, all the **p** stood up
Neh 8: 6 Then all the **p** answered
Neh 8: 7 helped the **p** to understand
Neh 8: 7 the **p** stood in their place
Neh 8: 9 the **p** said to all the **p**
Neh 8: 9 For all the **p** wept, when
Neh 8:11 the Levites quieted all the **p**
Neh 8:12 all the **p** went their way to
Neh 8:13 fathers' houses of all the **p**
Neh 8:16 Then the **p** went out and
Neh 9:10 against all the **p** of his land
Neh 9:24 So the **p** went in and possessed
Neh 9:24 the **p** of the land, that they
Neh 9:32 our fathers and on all Your **p**
Neh 10:14 The leaders of the **p**
Neh 10:28 rest of the **p** (the priests
Neh 10:34 the Levites, and the **p**, for
Neh 11: 1 of the **p** dwelt at Jerusalem
Neh 11: 1 the rest of the **p** cast lots
Neh 11: 2 the **p** blessed all the men who
Neh 11:24 all matters concerning the **p**
Neh 12:30 themselves, and purified the **p**
Neh 12:38 half of the **p** on the wall
Neh 13: 1 Moses in the hearing of the **p**
Neh 13:15 **p** treading wine presses on
Neh 13:24 of one or the other **p**
Esth 1: 5 seven days for all the **p** who
Esth 1:11 to show her beauty to the **p**
Esth 1:16 all the **p** who are in all the
Esth 1:22 and to every **p** in their own
Esth 1:22 in the language of his own **p**
Esth 2:10 not revealed her **p** or kindred
Esth 2:20 revealed her kindred and her **p**
Esth 3: 6 told him of the **p** of Mordecai
Esth 3: 6 the **p** of Mordecai
Esth 3: 8 is a certain **p** scattered and
Esth 3: 8 dispersed among the **p** in all
Esth 3:11 the **p** are given to you, to do
Esth 3:12 to the officials of all **p**
Esth 3:12 to every **p** in their language
Esth 3:14 being published for all **p**
Esth 4: 8 and plead before him for her **p**
Esth 4:11 the **p** of the king's provinces
Esth 7: 3 and my **p** at my request
Esth 7: 4 For we have been sold, my **p**
Esth 8: 6 evil that will come to my **p**
Esth 8: 9 to every **p** in their own
Esth 8:11 all the forces of any **p** or
Esth 8:13 and published to all **p**, so
Esth 8:17 Then many of the **p** of the
Esth 9: 2 fear of them fell upon all **p**
Esth 10: 3 seeking the good of his **p**
Job 12: 2 No doubt you are the **p**, and
Job 12:24 chiefs of the **p** of the earth
Job 17: 6 has made me a byword of the **p**
Job 18:19 son nor posterity among his **p**
Job 28: 4 open a shaft away from **p**
Job 34:20 the **p** are shaken and pass away
Job 34:30 reign, lest the **p** be ensnared
Job 36:20 when **p** are cut off in their
Ps 2: 1 And the **p** plot a vain thing
Ps 3: 6 of **p** Who have set themselves
Ps 3: 8 Your blessing is upon Your **p**
Ps 9:11 Declare His deeds among the **p**
Ps 14: 4 Who eat up my **p** as they eat
Ps 14: 7 back the captivity of His **p**
Ps 18:27 You will save the humble **p**
Ps 18:43 from the strivings of the **p**
Ps 18:43 A **p** I have not known shall
Ps 22: 6 of men, and despised of the **p**
Ps 22:31 to a **p** who will be born, That
Ps 28: 9 Save Your **p**, And bless Your
Ps 29:11 will give strength to His **p**
Ps 29:11 will bless His **p** with peace
Ps 33:12 the **p** whom He has chosen as
Ps 35:18 will praise You among many **p**
Ps 44:12 You sell Your **p** for naught
Ps 45:10 Forget your own **p** also, and
Ps 45:12 The rich among the **p** will
Ps 45:17 Therefore the **p** shall praise
Ps 47: 9 The princes of the **p** have
Ps 47: 9 The **p** of the God of Abraham
Ps 50: 4 that He may judge His **p**
Ps 50: 7 Hear, O My **p**, and I will speak
Ps 53: 4 Who eat up my **p** as they eat
Ps 53: 6 back the captivity of His **p**
Ps 59:11 slay them, lest my **p** forget
Ps 60: 3 have shown Your **p** hard things
Ps 62: 8 in Him at all times, you **p**
Ps 67: 4 shall judge the **p** righteously
Ps 68: 7 You went out before Your **p**
Ps 68:35 strength and power to His **p**
Ps 72: 2 Your **p** with righteousness
Ps 72: 3 will bring peace to the **p**
Ps 72: 4 justice to the poor of the **p**
Ps 73:10 Therefore his **p** return here
Ps 74:14 gave him as food to the **p**
Ps 74:18 LORD, And that a foolish **p** has
Ps 77:15 Your arm redeemed Your **p**
Ps 77:20 You led Your **p** like a flock
Ps 78: 1 Give ear, O my **p**, to my law
Ps 78:20 Can He provide meat for His **p**
Ps 78:52 His own **p** go forth like sheep
Ps 78:62 He also gave His **p** over to
Ps 78:71 him, To shepherd Jacob His **p**
Ps 79:13 So we, Your **p** and sheep of
Ps 80: 4 Against the prayer of Your **p**
Ps 81: 8 Hear, O My **p**, and I will
Ps 81:11 But My **p** would not heed My
Ps 81:13 that My **p** would listen to Me,
Ps 83: 3 crafty counsel against Your **p**
Ps 85: 2 the iniquity of Your **p**
Ps 85: 6 That Your **p** may rejoice in
Ps 85: 8 He will speak peace To His **p**
Ps 89:15 Blessed are the **p** who know
Ps 89:19 exalted one chosen from the **p**
Ps 94: 5 They break in pieces Your **p**
Ps 94: 8 you senseless among the **p**
Ps 94:14 LORD will not cast off His **p**
Ps 95: 7 we are the **p** of His pasture,
Ps 95:10 It is a **p** who go astray in
Ps 100: 3 We are His **p** and the sheep of
Ps 102:18 That a **p** yet to be created
Ps 105:13 From one kingdom to another **p**
Ps 105:20 of the **p** let him go free
Ps 105:24 And He increased His **p** greatly
Ps 105:25 their heart to hate His **p**
Ps 105:40 The **p** asked, and He brought
Ps 105:43 He brought out His **p** with joy
Ps 106: 4 favor You have toward Your **p**
Ps 106:40 was kindled against His **p**
Ps 106:48 And let all the **p** say, "Amen
Ps 107:32 in the congregation of the **p**
Ps 110: 3 Your **p** shall be volunteers In
Ps 111: 6 His **p** the power of His works
Ps 111: 9 has sent redemption to His **p**
Ps 113: 8 With the princes of His **p**
Ps 114: 1 from a **p** of strange language
Ps 116:14 in the presence of all His **p**
Ps 116:18 in the presence of all His **p**
Ps 125: 2 His **p** From this time forth
Ps 135:12 A heritage to Israel His **p**
Ps 135:14 For the LORD will judge His **p**
Ps 136:16 To Him who led His **p** through
Ps 144: 2 Who subdues my **p** under me
Ps 144:15 Happy are the **p** who are in
Ps 144:15 Happy are the **p** whose God is
Ps 148:14 has exalted the horn of His **p**
Ps 148:14 of Israel, A **p** near to Him
Ps 149: 4 LORD takes pleasure in His **p**
Prov 6:30 **P** do not despise a thief if
Prov 10:14 Wise **p** store up knowledge,
Prov 11:14 is no counsel, the **p** fall
Prov 11:26 The **p** will curse him who
Prov 14:28 of **p** is a king's honor, but
Prov 14:28 but in the lack of **p** is the
Prov 14:34 sin is a reproach to any **p**
Prov 24:24 him the **p** will curse
Prov 28:15 is a wicked ruler over poor **p**
Prov 29: 2 in authority, the **p** rejoice
Prov 29: 2 wicked man rules, the **p** groan
Prov 29:18 the **p** cast off restraint
Prov 30:25 the ants are a **p** not strong
Eccl 4:16 **p** over whom he was made king
Eccl 7:21 to heart everything **p** say
Eccl 9: 1 **P** know neither love nor
Eccl 12: 9 still taught the **p** knowledge
Song 6:12 as the chariots of my noble **p**
Is 1: 3 know, My **p** do not consider
Is 1: 4 a **p** laden with iniquity, a
Is 1:10 of our God, you **p** of Gomorrah
Is 2: 3 Many **p** shall come and say,
Is 2: 4 and shall rebuke many **p**
Is 2: 6 For You have forsaken Your **p**
Is 2: 9 **P** bow down, and each man
Is 3: 5 The **p** will be oppressed,
Is 3: 7 not make me a ruler of the **p**
Is 3:12 As for My **p**, children are
Is 3:12 O My **p**! Those who lead you
Is 3:13 and stands to judge the **p**
Is 3:14 with the elders of His **p** and
Is 3:15 do you mean by crushing My **p**
Is 5:13 Therefore my **p** have gone into
Is 5:15 **P** shall be brought down, Each
Is 5:25 LORD is aroused against His **p**
Is 6: 5 midst of a **p** of unclean lips
Is 6: 9 Go, and tell this **p**
Is 6:10 Make the heart of this **p** dull
Is 7: 2 the heart of his **p** were moved
Is 7: 8 so that it will not be a **p**
Is 7:17 of Assyria upon you and your **p**
Is 8: 6 Inasmuch as these **p** refused
Is 8:11 not walk in the way of this **p**
Is 8:12 that this **p** call a conspiracy
Is 8:19 should not a **p** seek their God
Is 9: 2 The **p** who walked in darkness
Is 9: 9 All the **p** will know
Is 9:13 For the **p** do not turn to Him
Is 9:16 of this **p** cause them to err
Is 9:19 the **p** shall be as fuel for
Is 10: 2 right from the poor of My **p**
Is 10: 6 against the **p** of My wrath I
Is 10:13 the boundaries of the **p**, and
Is 10:14 a nest the riches of the **p**
Is 10:22 For though your **p**, O Israel,
Is 10:24 O My **p**, who dwell in Zion, do
Is 11:10 stand as a banner to the **p**
Is 11:11 remnant of His **p** who are left
Is 11:14 plunder the **p** of the east
Is 11:14 the **p** of Ammon shall obey
Is 11:16 His **p** who will be left from
Is 13: 4 like that of many **p**
Is 13:14 man will turn to his own **p**
Is 14: 2 Then **p** will take them and
Is 14: 6 He who struck the **p** in wrath
Is 14:20 your land and slain your **p**
Is 14:32 the poor of His **p** shall take
Is 17:12 to the multitude of many **p**
Is 18: 2 to a **p** terrible from their
Is 18: 7 LORD of hosts from a **p** tall
Is 18: 7 from a **p** terrible from their
Is 19:25 Blessed is Egypt My **p**, and
Is 21:17 mighty men of the **p** of Kedar
Is 22: 4 of the daughter of my **p**
Is 23:13 this **p** which was not
Is 24: 2 as with the **p**, so with the
Is 24: 4 the haughty **p** of the earth
Is 24:13 midst of the land among the **p**
Is 25: 3 the strong **p** will glorify You

Is 25: 6 **p** a feast of choice pieces
Is 25: 7 the covering cast over all **p**
Is 25: 8 the rebuke of His **p** He will
Is 26:11 ashamed for their envy of **p**
Is 26:20 Come, my **p**, enter your
Is 27:11 For it is a **p** of no
Is 28: 5 to the remnant of His **p**,
Is 28:11 He will speak to this **p**,
Is 28:14 who rule this **p** who are in
Is 29:13 Inasmuch as these **p** draw near
Is 29:14 a marvelous work among this **p**
Is 30: 5 **p** who could not benefit them
Is 30: 6 to a **p** who shall not benefit
Is 30: 9 that this is a rebellious **p**
Is 30:19 For the **p** shall dwell in Zion
Is 30:26 binds up the bruise of His **p**
Is 30:28 a bridle in the jaws of the **p**
Is 32:12 **P** shall mourn upon their
Is 32:13 On the land of my **p** will come
Is 32:18 My **p** will dwell in a peaceful
Is 33: 3 the tumult the **p** shall flee
Is 33:12 And the **p** shall be like the
Is 33:19 You will not see a fierce **p**
Is 33:19 a **p** of obscure speech, beyond
Is 33:24 the **p** who dwell in it will be
Is 34: 1 and heed, you **p**
Is 34: 5 on the **p** of My curse, for
Is 36:11 of the **p** who are on the wall
Is 37:12 the **p** of Eden who were in
Is 37:36 when **p** arose early in the
Is 40: 1 Comfort, yes, comfort My **p**
Is 40: 7 surely the **p** are grass
Is 41: 1 and let the **p** renew their
Is 42: 5 gives breath to the **p** on it
Is 42: 6 You as a covenant to the **p**
Is 42:22 But this is a **p** robbed and
Is 43: 4 for you, and **p** for your life
Is 43: 8 out the blind **p** who have eyes
Is 43: 9 and let the **p** be assembled
Is 43:20 desert, to give drink to My **p**
Is 43:21 This **p** I have formed for
Is 44: 7 I appointed the ancient **p**
Is 47: 6 I was angry with My **p**
Is 49: 8 You as a covenant to the **p**
Is 49:13 the LORD has comforted His **p**
Is 51: 4 Listen to Me, My **p**
Is 51: 7 you **p** in whose heart is My
Is 51:16 and say to Zion, 'You are My **p**
Is 51:22 Who pleads the cause of His **p**
Is 52: 4 My **p** went down at first into
Is 52: 5 That My **p** are taken away for
Is 52: 6 Therefore My **p** shall know My
Is 52: 9 the LORD has comforted His **p**
Is 53: 8 of My **p** He was stricken
Is 55: 4 him as a witness to the **p**
Is 55: 4 leader and commander for the **p**
Is 56: 3 separated me from His **p**"
Is 57:14 block out of the way of My **p**
Is 58: 1 tell My **p** their transgression
Is 60: 2 earth, and deep darkness the **p**
Is 60:21 Also your **p** shall all be
Is 61: 9 their offspring among the **p**
Is 62:10 Prepare the way for the **p**
Is 62:12 shall call them The Holy **P**
Is 63: 8 Surely they are My **p**,
Is 63:11 days of old, Moses and his **p**
Is 63:14 to rest, so You lead Your **p**
Is 63:18 Your holy **p** have possessed it
Is 64: 9 we all are Your **p**
Is 65: 2 day long to a rebellious **p**
Is 65: 3 a **p** who provoke Me to anger
Is 65:10 for My **p** who have sought Me
Is 65:18 a rejoicing, and her **p** a joy
Is 65:19 in Jerusalem, and joy in My **p**
Is 65:22 so shall be the days of My **p**
Jer 1:18 and against the **p** of the land
Jer 2:11 But My **p** have changed their
Jer 2:13 For My **p** have committed two
Jer 2:16 Also the **p** of Noph and
Jer 2:31 Why do My **p** say, "We are
Jer 2:32 Yet My **p** have forgotten Me
Jer 4:10 have greatly deceived this **p**
Jer 4:11 it will be said to this **p**
Jer 4:11 toward the daughter of My **p**
Jer 4:22 For My **p** are foolish, they
Jer 5:14 mouth fire, and this **p** wood
Jer 5:21 Hear this now, O foolish **p**
Jer 5:23 But this **p** has a defiant and
Jer 5:26 For among My **p** are found
Jer 5:31 and My **p** love to have it so

Jer 6:14 the hurt of My **p** slightly
Jer 6:19 bring calamity on this **p**,
Jer 6:21 blocks before this **p**, And the
Jer 6:22 a **p** comes from the north
Jer 6:26 O daughter of my **p**, clothe
Jer 6:27 and a fortress among My **p**,
Jer 6:30 **P** will call them rejected
Jer 7:12 the wickedness of My **p** Israel
Jer 7:16 do not pray for this **p**, nor
Jer 7:23 God, and you shall be My **p**
Jer 7:33 The corpses of this **p** will be
Jer 8: 5 then has this **p** slidden back
Jer 8: 7 But My **p** do not know the
Jer 8:11 the daughter of My **p** slightly
Jer 8:19 of my **p** from a far country
Jer 8:21 daughter of my **p** I am hurt
Jer 8:22 of the daughter of my **p**
Jer 9: 1 slain of the daughter of my **p**
Jer 9: 2 that I might leave my **p**, and
Jer 9: 7 with the daughter of My **p**
Jer 9:15 I will feed them, this **p**
Jer 9:26 the **p** of Ammon, Moab, and all
Jer 11: 4 so shall you be My **p**, and I
Jer 11:14 do not pray for this **p**, or
Jer 12:14 caused My **p** Israel to inherit
Jer 12:16 learn the ways of My **p**, to
Jer 12:16 taught My **p** to swear by Baal
Jer 12:16 in the midst of My **p**
Jer 13:10 This evil **p**, who refuse to
Jer 13:11 that they may become My **p**
Jer 14:10 Thus says the LORD to this **p**
Jer 14:11 Do not pray for this **p**, for
Jer 14:16 the **p** to whom they prophesy
Jer 14:17 my **p** has been broken with a
Jer 15: 1 be favorable toward this **p**
Jer 15: 7 I will destroy My **p**, since
Jer 15:20 **p** a fortified bronze wall
Jer 16: 5 away My peace from this **p**
Jer 16:10 show this **p** all these words
Jer 17:19 gate of the children of the **p**
Jer 18:15 Because My **p** have forgotten
Jer 19: 1 some of the elders of the **p**
Jer 19:11 Even so I will break this **p**
Jer 19:14 house and said to all the **p**
Jer 21: 7 Judah, his servants and the **p**
Jer 21: 8 Now you shall say to this **p**
Jer 22: 2 your **p** who enter these gates
Jer 22: 4 accompanied by servants and **p**
Jer 23: 2 the shepherds who feed My **p**
Jer 23:13 caused My **p** Israel to err
Jer 23:22 had caused My **p** to hear My
Jer 23:27 who try to make My **p** forget
Jer 23:32 cause My **p** to err by their
Jer 23:32 not profit this **p** at all,"
Jer 23:33 So when these **p** or the
Jer 23:34 the **p** who say, 'The oracle of
Jer 24: 7 and they shall be My **p**, and I
Jer 25: 1 concerning all the **p** of Judah
Jer 25: 2 spoke to all the **p** of Judah
Jer 25:19 his princes, and all his **p**
Jer 25:21 Edom, Moab, and the **p** of
Jer 26: 7 and all the **p** heard Jeremiah
Jer 26: 8 him to speak to all the **p**
Jer 26: 8 all the **p** seized him, saying,
Jer 26: 9 And all the **p** were gathered
Jer 26:11 to the princes and all the **p**
Jer 26:12 all the princes and all the **p**
Jer 26:16 all the **p** said to the priests
Jer 26:17 to all the assembly of the **p**
Jer 26:18 spoke to all the **p** of Judah
Jer 26:23 the graves of the common **p**
Jer 26:24 of the **p** to put him to death
Jer 27:12 and serve him and his **p**, and
Jer 27:13 will you die, you and your **p**
Jer 27:16 the priests and to all this **p**
Jer 28: 1 the priests and of all the **p**
Jer 28: 5 **p** who stood in the house of
Jer 28: 7 in the hearing of all the **p**
Jer 28:11 in the presence of all the **p**
Jer 28:15 make this **p** trust in a lie
Jer 29: 1 all the **p** whom Nebuchadnezzar
Jer 29:16 concerning all the **p** who
Jer 29:25 the **p** who are at Jerusalem
Jer 29:32 anyone to dwell among this **p**
Jer 29:32 good that I will do for My **p**
Jer 30: 3 from captivity My **p** Israel
Jer 30:22 You shall be My **p**, and I will
Jer 31: 1 Israel, and they shall be My **p**
Jer 31: 2 The **p** who survived the sword
Jer 31: 7 and say, 'O LORD, save Your **p**

Jer 31:14 My **p** shall be satisfied with
Jer 31:33 God, and they shall be My **p**
Jer 32:21 You have brought Your **p**
Jer 32:38 They shall be My **p**, and I
Jer 32:42 this great calamity on this **p**
Jer 33:24 what these **p** have spoken,
Jer 33:24 Thus they have despised My **p**
Jer 34: 1 his dominion, and all the **p**
Jer 34: 8 a covenant with all the **p** who
Jer 34:10 all the princes and all the **p**
Jer 34:19 all the **p** of the land who
Jer 35:16 but this **p** has not obeyed Me
Jer 36: 6 in the hearing of the **p** in
Jer 36: 7 has pronounced against this **p**
Jer 36: 9 to all the **p** in Jerusalem
Jer 36: 9 to all the **p** who came from
Jer 36:10 in the hearing of all the **p**
Jer 36:13 book in the hearing of the **p**
Jer 36:14 read in the hearing of the **p**
Jer 37: 2 **p** of the land gave heed to
Jer 37: 4 coming and going among the **p**
Jer 37:12 property there among the **p**
Jer 37:18 servants, or against this **p**
Jer 38: 1 had spoken to all the **p**,
Jer 38: 4 and the hands of all the **p**
Jer 38: 4 seek the welfare of this **p**
Jer 39: 8 the houses of the **p** with fire
Jer 39: 9 **p** who remained in the city
Jer 39: 9 rest of the **p** who remained
Jer 39:10 the land of Judah the poor **p**
Jer 39:14 So he dwelt among the **p**
Jer 40: 3 Because you **p** have sinned
Jer 40: 5 and dwell with him among the **p**
Jer 40: 6 dwelt with him among the **p**
Jer 41:10 of the **p** who were in Mizpah
Jer 41:10 all the **p** who remained in
Jer 41:13 when all the **p** who were with
Jer 41:14 Then all the **p** whom Ishmael
Jer 41:16 **p** whom he had recovered from
Jer 42: 1 son of Hoshaiah, and all the **p**
Jer 42: 8 all the **p** from the least even
Jer 43: 1 **p** all the words of the LORD
Jer 43: 4 all the **p** would not obey the
Jer 44:15 all the **p** who dwelt in the
Jer 44:20 Jeremiah spoke to all the **p**
Jer 44:20 all the **p** who had given him
Jer 44:21 the **p** of the land, did not
Jer 44:24 Jeremiah said to all the **p**
Jer 46:16 Let us go back to our own **p**
Jer 46:24 hand of the **p** of the north
Jer 48:42 shall be destroyed as a **p**
Jer 48:46 The **p** of Chemosh perish
Jer 49: 1 his **p** dwell in its cities
Jer 49: 6 captives of the **p** of Ammon
Jer 50: 6 My **p** have been lost sheep
Jer 50:16 shall turn to his own **p**, and
Jer 50:41 a **p** shall come from the north
Jer 51:45 My **p**, go out of the midst of
Jer 51:58 the **p** will labor in vain, and
Jer 52: 6 no food for the **p** of the land
Jer 52:15 captive some of the poor **p**
Jer 52:15 **p**, the rest of the **p** who
Jer 52:25 mustered the **p** of the land
Jer 52:25 sixty men of the **p** of the
Jer 52:28 These are the **p** whom
Lam 1: 1 the city that was full of **p**
Lam 1: 7 When her **p** fell into the hand
Lam 1:11 All her **p** sigh, they seek
Lam 2:11 of the daughter of my **p**,
Lam 3:14 the ridicule of all my **p**, and
Lam 3:48 of the daughter of my **p**
Lam 4: 3 of my **p** has become cruel,
Lam 4: 6 of my **p** is greater than the
Lam 4:10 of the daughter of my **p**
Lam 4:16 The **p** do not respect the
Ezek 3: 5 to a **p** of unfamiliar speech
Ezek 3: 6 not to many **p** of unfamiliar
Ezek 3:11 to the children of your **p**
Ezek 7:27 of the common **p** will tremble
Ezek 11: 1 of Benaiah, princes of the **p**
Ezek 11:20 and they shall be My **p**, and I
Ezek 12:19 say to the **p** of the land
Ezek 12:22 you **p** have about the land of
Ezek 13: 9 be in the assembly of My **p**
Ezek 13:10 they have seduced My **p**,
Ezek 13:17 the daughters of your **p**, who
Ezek 13:18 of **p** of every height to hunt
Ezek 13:18 you hunt the souls of My **p**
Ezek 13:19 My **p** for handfuls of barley
Ezek 13:19 killing **p** who should not die,

Ezek 13:19 keeping **p** alive who should
Ezek 13:19 to My **p** who listen to lies
Ezek 13:21 deliver My **p** out of your hand
Ezek 13:23 deliver My **p** out of your hand
Ezek 14: 8 off from the midst of My **p**
Ezek 14: 9 him from among My **p** Israel
Ezek 14:11 but that they may be My **p**
Ezek 17: 9 no great power or many **p** will
Ezek 17:15 give him horses and many **p**
Ezek 18:18 what is not good among his **p**
Ezek 21:12 for it will be against My **p**
Ezek 21:12 sword will be against My **p**
Ezek 22:25 they have devoured **p**
Ezek 22:27 to shed blood, to destroy **p**
Ezek 22:29 The **p** of the land have used
Ezek 23:24 war-horses, With a horde of **p**
Ezek 24:18 spoke to the **p** in the morning
Ezek 24:19 And the **p** said to me,
Ezek 25:14 by the hand of My **p** Israel
Ezek 26: 7 and an army with many **p**
Ezek 26:11 will slay your **p** by the sword
Ezek 26:20 into the Pit, to the **p** of old
Ezek 27:33 by sea, you satisfied many **p**
Ezek 30: 5 Lydia, all the mingled **p**
Ezek 30:11 and his **p** with him, the most
Ezek 32: 3 you with a company of many **p**
Ezek 33: 2 to the children of your **p**
Ezek 33: 2 the **p** of the land take a man
Ezek 33: 3 the trumpet and warns the **p**
Ezek 33: 6 the **p** are not warned, and the
Ezek 33:12 say to the children of your **p**
Ezek 33:17 the children of your **p** say
Ezek 33:30 the children of your **p** are
Ezek 33:31 So they come to you as **p** do
Ezek 33:31 they sit before you as My **p**
Ezek 34:30 the house of Israel, are My **p**
Ezek 36: 3 and slandered by the **p**"
Ezek 36: 8 your fruit to My **p** Israel
Ezek 36:12 to walk on you, My **p** Israel
Ezek 36:20 These are the **p** of the LORD
Ezek 36:28 you shall be My **p**, and I will
Ezek 37:12 Behold, O My **p**, I will open
Ezek 37:13 opened your graves, O My **p**
Ezek 37:18 of your **p** speak to you,
Ezek 37:23 Then they shall be My **p**, and I
Ezek 37:27 God, and they shall be My **p**
Ezek 38: 6 many **p** are with you
Ezek 38: 8 gathered from many **p** on the
Ezek 38:11 I will go to a peaceful **p**
Ezek 38:12 against a **p** gathered from the
Ezek 38:14 when My **p** Israel dwell safely
Ezek 38:16 My **p** Israel like a cloud, to
Ezek 39: 7 in the midst of My **p** Israel
Ezek 39:13 Indeed all the **p** of the land
Ezek 42:14 that which is for the **p**
Ezek 44:11 and the sacrifice for the **p**
Ezek 44:19 to the outer court to the **p**
Ezek 44:19 they shall not sanctify the **p**
Ezek 44:23 they shall teach My **p** the
Ezek 45: 8 shall no more oppress My **p**
Ezek 45: 9 and stop dispossessing My **p**
Ezek 45:16 All the **p** of the land shall
Ezek 45:22 for all the **p** of the land a
Ezek 46: 3 Likewise the **p** of the land
Ezek 46: 9 But when the **p** of the land
Ezek 46:18 so that none of My **p** may be
Ezek 46:20 outer court to sanctify the **p**
Ezek 46:24 boil the sacrifices of the **p**
Dan 2:44 shall not be left to other **p**
Dan 3: 7 when all the **p** heard the
Dan 3: 7 all kinds of music, all the **p**
Dan 3:29 I make a decree that any **p**
Dan 7:27 shall be given to the **p**, the
Dan 8:24 mighty, and also the holy **p**
Dan 9: 6 and all the **p** of the land
Dan 9:15 who brought Your **p** out of the
Dan 9:16 Your **p** have become a reproach
Dan 9:19 Your **p** are called by Your
Dan 9:20 sin and the sin of my **p** Israel
Dan 9:24 are determined for your **p**
Dan 9:26 the **p** of the prince who is to
Dan 10:14 to your **p** in the latter days
Dan 11:14 **p** shall exalt themselves in
Dan 11:23 with a small number of **p**
Dan 11:32 but the **p** who know their God
Dan 11:33 those of the **p** who understand
Dan 11:41 and the prominent **p** of Ammon
Dan 12: 1 watch over the sons of your **p**
Dan 12: 1 at that time your **p** shall be
Dan 12: 7 holy **p** has been completely

Hos 1: 9 Lo-Ammi, for you are not My **p**
Hos 1:10 to them, 'You are not My **p**
Hos 2: 1 Say to your brethren, 'My **p**
Hos 2:23 to those who were not My **p**
Hos 2:23 You are My **p**!'
Hos 4: 4 for your **p** are like those who
Hos 4: 6 My **p** are destroyed for lack
Hos 4: 8 They eat up the sin of My **p**
Hos 4: 9 like **p**, like priest
Hos 4:12 My **p** ask counsel from their
Hos 4:14 Therefore **p** who do not
Hos 6:11 I return the captives of My **p**
Hos 10: 5 For its **p** mourn for it, and
Hos 10:14 shall arise among your **p**, and
Hos 11: 7 My **p** are bent on backsliding
Joel 2: 2 a **p** come, great and strong,
Joel 2: 5 like a strong **p** set in battle
Joel 2: 6 them the **p** writhe in pain
Joel 2:16 gather the **p**, sanctify the
Joel 2:17 Spare Your **p**, O LORD, and do
Joel 2:18 for His land, and pity His **p**
Joel 2:19 will answer and say to His **p**
Joel 2:26 My **p** shall never be put to
Joel 2:27 My **p** shall never be put to
Joel 3: 2 them there on account of My **p**
Joel 3: 3 They have cast lots for My **p**
Joel 3: 6 Also the **p** of Judah and the
Joel 3: 6 the **p** of Jerusalem You have
Joel 3: 8 the hand of the **p** of Judah
Joel 3: 8 the Sabeans, to a **p** far off
Joel 3:16 will be a shelter for His **p**
Joel 3:19 against the **p** of Judah, for
Amos 1: 5 the **p** of Syria shall go
Amos 1:13 of the **p** of Ammon, and for
Amos 3: 6 will not the **p** be afraid
Amos 7: 8 in the midst of My **p** Israel
Amos 7:15 Go, prophesy to My **p** Israel
Amos 8: 2 end has come upon my **p** Israel
Amos 9: 7 like the **p** of Ethiopia to Me
Amos 9:10 All the sinners of My **p** shall
Amos 9:14 the captives of My **p** Israel
Obad 13 of My **p** in the day of their
Jon 1: 8 And of what **p** are you
Jon 3: 5 So the **p** of Nineveh believed
Mic 1: 9 has come to the gate of My **p**
Mic 2: 4 changed the heritage of my **p**
Mic 2: 8 Lately My **p** have risen up as
Mic 2: 9 The women of My **p** you cast
Mic 2:11 be the prattler of this **p**
Mic 3: 2 who strip the skin from My **p**
Mic 3: 3 also eat the flesh of My **p**
Mic 3: 5 prophets who make my **p** stray
Mic 4: 5 For all **p** walk each in the
Mic 6: 2 has a complaint against His **p**
Mic 6: 3 O My **p**, what have I done to
Mic 6: 5 O My **p**, remember now what
Mic 6:16 bear the reproach of My **p**
Mic 7:14 Shepherd Your **p** with Your
Nah 3:13 your **p** in your midst are
Nah 3:18 Your **p** are scattered on the
Hab 2: 8 of the **p** shall plunder you
Hab 3:13 for the salvation of Your **p**
Hab 3:16 When he comes up to the **p**
Zeph 1:11 the merchant **p** are cut down
Zeph 2: 8 revilings of the **p** of Ammon
Zeph 2: 8 they have reproached My **p**
Zeph 2: 9 the **p** of Ammon like Gomorrah
Zeph 2: 9 the residue of My **p** shall
Zeph 2: 9 the remnant of My **p** shall
Zeph 2:10 threats against the **p** of the
Zeph 2:11 **p** shall worship Him, each one
Zeph 3: 4 are insolent, treacherous **p**
Zeph 3:12 your midst a meek and humble **p**
Hag 1: 2 This **p** says, "The time has
Hag 1:12 with all the remnant of the **p**
Hag 1:12 the **p** feared the presence of
Hag 1:13 the LORD's message to the **p**
Hag 1:14 of all the remnant of the **p**
Hag 2: 2 and to the remnant of the **p**
Hag 2: 4 all you **p** of the land,' says
Hag 2:14 So is this **p**, and so is this
Zech 2:11 and they shall become My **p**
Zech 7: 2 when the **p** sent Sherezer,
Zech 7: 5 Say to all the **p** of the land
Zech 8: 6 of this **p** in these days, will
Zech 8: 7 I will save My **p** from the
Zech 8: 8 They shall be My **p** and I will
Zech 8:11 this **p** as in the former days
Zech 8:12 cause the remnant of this **p**
Zech 9:16 day, as the flock of His **p**

Zech 10: 2 Therefore the **p** wend their
Zech 13: 9 I will say, 'This is My **p**'
Zech 14: 2 but the remnant of the **p**
Zech 14:11 The **p** shall dwell in it
Zech 14:12 all the **p** who fought against
Mal 1: 4 the **p** against whom the LORD
Mal 2: 7 **p** should seek the law from
Mal 2: 9 and base before all the **p**,
Matt 1:21 save His **p** from their sins
Matt 2: 4 and scribes of the **p** together
Matt 2: 6 who will shepherd My **p** Israel
Matt 4:16 the **p** who sat in darkness saw
Matt 4:23 kinds of disease among the **p**
Matt 4:24 **p** who were afflicted with
Matt 7:28 that the **p** were astonished at
Matt 9:17 Nor do **p** put new wine into
Matt 9:35 and every disease among the **p**
Matt 13:15 of this **p** has grown dull
Matt 15: 8 These **p** draw near to Me with
Matt 21:23 and the elders of the **p**
Matt 26: 3 the elders of the **p** assembled
Matt 26: 5 be an uproar among the **p**
Matt 26:47 priests and elders of the **p**
Matt 27: 1 elders of the **p** took counsel
Matt 27:25 all the **p** answered and said,
Matt 27:64 Him away, and say to the **p**
Mark 3:21 His own **p** heard about this
Mark 6: 5 His hands on a few sick **p**
Mark 6:12 preached that **p** should repent
Mark 6:54 the **p** recognized Him,
Mark 7: 6 This **p** honors Me with their
Mark 8: 4 **p** with bread here in the
Mark 8:34 He had called the **p** to Him
Mark 9:15 all the **p** were greatly amazed
Mark 9:25 the **p** came running together
Mark 10: 1 the **p** gathered to Him again,
Mark 11:18 Him, because all the **p** were
Mark 11:32 they feared the **p**, for all
Mark 12:37 the common **p** heard Him gladly
Mark 12:41 saw how the **p** put money into
Mark 14: 2 there be an uproar of the **p**
Luke 1:10 **p** was praying outside at the
Luke 1:17 to make ready a **p** prepared
Luke 1:21 the **p** waited for Zacharias,
Luke 1:68 has visited and redeemed His **p**
Luke 1:77 of salvation to His **p** by the
Luke 2:10 joy which will be to all **p**
Luke 2:32 and the glory of Your **p** Israel
Luke 3:10 So the **p** asked him, saying,
Luke 3:15 Now as the **p** were in
Luke 3:18 he preached to the **p**
Luke 3:21 when all the **p** were baptized
Luke 6:17 multitude of **p** from all Judea
Luke 7: 1 in the hearing of the **p**, He
Luke 7:16 God has visited His **p**
Luke 7:21 many **p** of their infirmities
Luke 7:29 And when all the **p** heard Him
Luke 8:47 **p** the reason she had touched
Luke 9:13 and buy food for all these **p**
Luke 12: 1 of **p** had gathered together
Luke 12:41 only to us, or to all **p**
Luke 18:43 And all the **p**, when they saw
Luke 19:47 the leaders of the **p** sought
Luke 19:48 for all the **p** were very
Luke 20: 1 He taught the **p** in the temple
Luke 20: 6 all the **p** will stone us, for
Luke 20: 9 to tell the **p** this parable
Luke 20:19 on Him, but they feared the **p**
Luke 20:26 in the presence of the **p**
Luke 20:45 in the hearing of all the **p**
Luke 21:23 the land and wrath upon this **p**
Luke 21:38 in the morning all the **p** came
Luke 22: 2 Him, for they feared the **p**
Luke 22:66 was day, the elders of the **p**
Luke 23: 5 He stirs up the **p**, teaching
Luke 23:13 priests, the rulers, and the **p**
Luke 23:14 me, as one who misleads the **p**
Luke 23:27 of the **p** followed Him, and
Luke 23:35 And the **p** stood looking on
Luke 24:19 word before God and all the **p**
John 4:48 Unless you **p** see signs and
John 5: 3 a great multitude of sick **p**
John 6:10 Make the **p** sit down
John 6:22 when the **p** who were standing
John 6:24 when the **p** therefore saw that
John 7:12 among the **p** concerning Him
John 7:12 contrary, He deceives the **p**
John 7:20 The **p** answered and said, "You
John 7:31 many of the **p** believed in Him
John 7:43 among the **p** because of Him

John 8: 2 and all the **p** came to Him
John 11:42 but because of the **p** who are
John 11:50 one man should die for the **p**
John 12:17 Therefore the **p**, who were
John 12:18 reason the **p** also met Him
John 12:29 Therefore the **p** who stood by
John 12:34 The **p** answered Him, "We have
John 18:14 one man should die for the **p**
Acts 2:47 having favor with all the **p**
Acts 3: 9 all the **p** saw him walking and
Acts 3:11 all the **p** ran together to
Acts 3:12 saw it, he responded to the **p**
Acts 3:23 destroyed from among the **p**
Acts 4: 1 Now as they spoke to the **p**
Acts 4: 2 that they taught the **p** and
Acts 4: 8 Rulers of the **p** and elders of
Acts 4:10 and to all the **p** of Israel
Acts 4:17 no further among the **p**, let
Acts 4:21 them, because of the **p**, since
Acts 4:25 and the **p** plot vain things
Acts 4:27 and the **p** of Israel, were
Acts 5:12 wonders were done among the **p**
Acts 5:13 them, but the **p** esteemed them
Acts 5:16 to Jerusalem, bringing sick **p**
Acts 5:20 speak to the **p** all the words
Acts 5:25 the temple and teaching the **p**
Acts 5:26 for they feared the **p**, lest
Acts 5:34 held in respect by all the **p**
Acts 5:37 and drew away many **p** after him
Acts 6: 8 wonders and signs among the **p**
Acts 6:12 And they stirred up the **p**, the
Acts 7:14 to him, seventy-five **p**
Acts 7:17 the **p** grew and multiplied in
Acts 7:19 treacherously with our **p**, and
Acts 7:34 of my **p** who are in Egypt
Acts 8: 9 astonished the **p** of Samaria
Acts 10: 2 gave alms generously to the **p**
Acts 10:41 not to all the **p**, but to
Acts 10:42 us to preach to the **p**, and to
Acts 11:24 a great many **p** were added to
Acts 11:26 and taught a great many **p**
Acts 12: 4 before the **p** after Passover
Acts 12:11 expectation of the Jewish **p**
Acts 12:20 very angry with the **p** of Tyre
Acts 12:22 And the **p** kept shouting,
Acts 13:15 word of exhortation for the **p**
Acts 13:17 The God of this **p** Israel
Acts 13:17 exalted the **p** when they dwelt
Acts 13:24 to all the **p** of Israel
Acts 13:31 are His witnesses to the **p**
Acts 14:11 Now when the **p** saw what Paul
Acts 15:14 out of them a **p** for His name
Acts 17: 5 to bring them out to the **p**
Acts 18:10 I have many **p** in this city
Acts 19: 4 saying to the **p** that they
Acts 19:26 and turned away many **p**, saying
Acts 19:30 Paul wanted to go in to the **p**
Acts 19:33 to make his defense to the **p**
Acts 21:28 men everywhere against the **p**
Acts 21:30 the **p** ran together, seized
Acts 21:36 of the **p** followed after,
Acts 21:39 permit me to speak to the **p**
Acts 21:40 with his hand to the **p**
Acts 23: 5 evil of the ruler of your **p**
Acts 26:17 deliver you from the Jewish **p**
Acts 26:23 light to the Jewish **p** and to
Acts 28:17 our **p** or the customs of our
Acts 28:26 saying, 'Go to this **p** and say
Acts 28:27 of this **p** has grown dull
Rom 9:25 My **p**, who were not My **p**
Rom 9:26 to them, 'You are not My **p**
Rom 10:21 a disobedient and contrary **p**
Rom 11: 1 then, has God cast away His **p**
Rom 11: 2 away His **p** whom He foreknew
Rom 15:10 O Gentiles, with His **p**
1Co 3: 1 spiritual **p** but as to carnal
1Co 5: 9 with sexually immoral **p**
1Co 5:10 immoral **p** of this world, or
1Co 10: 7 The **p** sat down to eat and
1Co 14:21 lips I will speak to this **p**
2Co 6:16 God, and they shall be My **p**
Eph 3: 9 to make all **p** see what is the
2Ti 3: 5 And from such **p** turn away
Tit 2:14 for Himself His own special **p**
Tit 3:14 And let our **p** also learn to
Heb 2:17 for the sins of the **p**
Heb 4: 9 a rest for the **p** of God
Heb 5: 3 he is required as for the **p**
Heb 7: 5 the **p** according to the law
Heb 7:11 it the **p** received the law)
Heb 8:10 God, and they shall be My **p**
Heb 9:19 the **p** according to the law
Heb 9:19 the book itself and all the **p**
Heb 10:30 The LORD will judge His **p**
Heb 11:25 **p** of God than to enjoy the
Heb 13:12 the **p** with His own blood,
1Pe 2: 9 nation, His own special **p**
1Pe 2:10 who once were not a **p**
1Pe 2:10 but are now the **p** of God, who
1Pe 2:17 Honor all **p**
1Pe 5: 5 Likewise you younger **p**,
2Pe 2: 1 false prophets among the **p**
2Pe 2: 5 saved Noah, one of eight **p**
Jude 5 having saved the **p** out of the
Jude 16 words, flattering **p** to gain
Rev 5: 9 of every tribe and tongue and **p**
Rev 6: 4 and that **p** should kill one
Rev 14: 6 nation, tribe, tongue, and **p**
Rev 18: 4 Come out of her, my **p**, lest
Rev 19:18 them, and the flesh of all **p**
Rev 21: 3 them, and they shall be His **p**

PEOPLE'S (*see* PEOPLE)
Lev 9:15 he brought the **p** offering
Esth 3: 8 different from all other **p**
Ezek 46:18 the **p** inheritance by evicting
1Ti 5:22 nor share in other **p** sins
Heb 7:27 own sins and then for the **p**
Heb 9: 7 for the **p** sins committed in
1Pe 4:15 a busybody in other **p** matters

PEOPLES (*see* PEOPLE)
Gen 10: 5 **p** of the Gentiles were
Gen 17:16 kings of **p** shall be from her
Gen 25:23 two **p** shall be separated from
Gen 27:29 Let **p** serve you, and nations
Gen 28: 3 you may be an assembly of **p**
Lev 20:24 has separated you from the **p**
Lev 20:26 have separated you from the **p**
Deut 4: 6 in the sight of the **p** who
Deut 4:19 God has given to all the **p**
Deut 4:27 will scatter you among the **p**
Deut 6:14 the gods of the **p** who are all
Deut 7: 6 treasure above all the **p** on
Deut 7: 7 you were the least of all **p**
Deut 7:14 shall be blessed above all **p**
Deut 7:16 the **p** whom the LORD your God
Deut 7:19 the **p** of whom you are afraid
Deut 10:15 after them, you above all **p**
Deut 14: 2 treasure above all the **p** who
Deut 20:16 **p** which the LORD your God
Deut 28:10 Then all **p** of the earth shall
Deut 28:64 will scatter you among all **p**
Deut 32: 8 set the boundaries of the **p**
Deut 33:17 **p** to the ends of the earth
Deut 33:19 call the **p** to the mountain
Josh 4:24 that all the **p** of the earth
Judg 5:14 you, Benjamin, with your **p**
1Ki 8:43 that all **p** of the earth may
1Ki 8:53 the **p** of the earth to be Your
1Ki 8:60 that all the **p** of the earth
1Ki 9: 7 and a byword among all **p**
1Ch 5:25 the gods of the **p** of the land
1Ch 16: 8 known His deeds among the **p**
1Ch 16:24 His wonders among all **p**
1Ch 16:26 the gods of the **p** are idols
1Ch 16:28 the LORD, O kindreds of the **p**
2Ch 13: 9 like the **p** of other lands, so
2Ch 32:13 to all the **p** of other lands
Ezra 9: 1 from the **p** of the lands, with
Ezra 9: 2 with the **p** of those lands
Ezra 9:11 of the **p** of the lands, with
Ezra 10: 2 wives from the **p** of the land
Ezra 10:11 from the **p** of the land, and
Neh 9:30 hand of the **p** of the lands
Neh 10:28 themselves from the **p** of the
Neh 10:30 as wives to the **p** of the land
Neh 10:31 that if the **p** of the land
Job 36:31 For by these He judges the **p**
Ps 7: 7 of the **p** shall surround You
Ps 7: 8 The LORD shall judge the **p**
Ps 9: 8 for the **p** in uprightness
Ps 18:47 me, And subdues the **p** under
Ps 33:10 plans of the **p** of no effect
Ps 44: 2 How You afflicted the **p**, and
Ps 44:14 of the head among the **p**
Ps 45: 5 The **p** fall under You
Ps 47: 1 clap your hands, all you **p**
Ps 47: 3 He will subdue the **p** under us
Ps 49: 1 Hear this, all you **p**
Ps 56: 7 In anger cast down the **p**, O
Ps 57: 9 You, O Lord, among the **p**
Ps 65: 7 waves, And the tumult of the **p**
Ps 66: 8 Oh, bless our God, you **p**
Ps 67: 3 Let the **p** praise You, O God
Ps 67: 3 Let all the **p** praise You
Ps 67: 5 Let the **p** praise You, O God
Ps 67: 5 Let all the **p** praise You
Ps 68:30 with the calves of the **p**,
Ps 68:30 Scatter the **p** who delight in
Ps 77:14 Your strength among the **p**
Ps 87: 6 When He registers the **p**
Ps 89:50 reproach of all the many **p**
Ps 96: 3 His wonders among all **p**
Ps 96: 5 the gods of the **p** are idols
Ps 96: 7 the LORD, O kindreds of the **p**
Ps 96:10 shall judge the **p** righteously
Ps 96:13 And the **p** with His truth
Ps 97: 6 And all the **p** see His glory
Ps 98: 9 world, And the **p** with equity
Ps 99: 1 Let the **p** tremble
Ps 99: 2 And He is high above all the **p**
Ps 102:22 When the **p** are gathered
Ps 105: 1 known His deeds among the **p**
Ps 106:34 They did not destroy the **p**
Ps 108: 3 You, O LORD, among the **p**,
Ps 117: 1 Laud Him, all you **p**
Ps 148:11 Kings of the earth and all **p**
Ps 149: 7 And punishments on the **p**
Is 8: 9 Be shattered, O you **p**, and be
Is 12: 4 declare His deeds among the **p**
Is 49: 1 and take heed, you **p** from afar
Is 49:22 set up My standard for the **p**
Is 51: 4 rest as a light of the **p**
Is 51: 5 and My arms will judge the **p**
Is 62:10 lift up a banner for the **p**
Is 63: 3 from the **p** no one was with Me
Is 63: 6 down the **p** in My anger, made
Jer 10: 3 customs of the **p** are futile
Jer 50:37 mixed **p** who are in her midst
Lam 1:18 Hear now, all **p**, and behold my
Lam 3:45 refuse in the midst of the **p**
Ezek 11:17 I will gather you from the **p**
Ezek 20:34 will bring you out from the **p**
Ezek 20:35 into the wilderness of the **p**
Ezek 20:41 I bring you out from the **p**
Ezek 25: 7 I will cut you off from the **p**
Ezek 26: 2 who was the gateway of the **p**
Ezek 27: 3 merchant of the **p** on many
Ezek 27:36 among the **p** will hiss at you
Ezek 28:19 the **p** are astonished at you
Ezek 28:25 the **p** among whom they are
Ezek 29:13 the **p** among whom they were
Ezek 31:12 all the **p** of the earth have
Ezek 32: 9 trouble the hearts of many **p**
Ezek 32:10 I will make many **p** astonished
Ezek 34:13 bring them out from the **p**
Ezek 36:15 the reproach of the **p** anymore
Ezek 38: 9 troops and many **p** with you
Ezek 38:15 many **p** with you, all of them
Ezek 38:22 on the many **p** who are with
Ezek 39: 4 and the **p** who are with you
Ezek 39:27 brought them back from the **p**
Dan 3: 4 To you it is commanded, O **p**
Dan 4: 1 the king, To all **p**, nations
Dan 5:19 that He gave him, all **p**,
Dan 6:25 To all **p**, nations, and
Dan 7:14 and a kingdom, that all **p**,
Hos 7: 8 has mixed himself among the **p**
Hos 9: 1 Israel, with joy like other **p**
Hos 10:10 **P** shall be gathered against
Joel 2:17 should they say among the **p**
Mic 1: 2 Hear, all you **p**
Mic 4: 1 and **p** shall flow to it
Mic 4: 3 He shall judge between many **p**
Mic 4:13 shall beat in pieces many **p**
Mic 5: 7 be in the midst of many **p**
Mic 5: 8 in the midst of many **p**, like
Hab 2: 5 and heaps up for himself all **p**
Hab 2:10 house, cutting off many **p**
Hab 2:13 the **p** labor to feed the fire
Zeph 3: 9 to the **p** a pure language,
Zeph 3:20 among all the **p** of the earth
Zech 8:20 **P** shall yet come,
Zech 8:22 Yes, many **p** and strong nations
Zech 10: 9 I will sow them among the **p**
Zech 11:10 I had made with all the **p**
Zech 12: 2 to all the surrounding **p**,
Zech 12: 3 a very heavy stone for all **p**
Zech 12: 4 horse of the **p** with blindness
Zech 12: 6 **p** on the right hand and on the

Luke 2:31 before the face of all **p**,
John 12:32 will draw all **p** to Myself
Rom 15:11 laud Him, all you **p**
Rev 7: 9 of all nations, tribes, **p**
Rev 10:11 prophesy again about many **p**
Rev 11: 9 Then those from the **p**, tribes
Rev 17:15 where the harlot sits, are **p**

PEOR
Num 23:28 took Balaam to the top of **P**
Num 25: 3 was joined to Baal of **P**, and
Num 25: 5 who were joined to Baal of **P**
Num 25:18 you in the matter of **P** and in
Num 25:18 of the plague because of **P**
Num 31:16 the LORD in the incident of **P**
Deut 4: 3 what the LORD did at Baal **P**
Deut 4: 3 men who followed Baal of **P**
Josh 22:17 of **P** not enough for us, from
Ps 106:28 themselves also to Baal of **P**
Hos 9:10 But they went to Baal **P**, and

PER (*see* PREFACE)

PERAZIM (*see* BAAL PERAZIM)
Is 28:21 will rise up as at Mount **P**

PERCEIVE (*see* PERCEIVED, PERCEIVES, PERCEIVING, PERCEPTION, PERCEPTIVE)
Deut 29: 4 not given you a heart to **p**
Josh 22:31 This day we **p** that the LORD
1Sa 12:17 and rain, that you may **p** and
2Sa 19: 6 for today I **p** that if Absalom
Job 9:11 He moves past, I do not **p** Him
Job 14:21 low, and he does not **p** it
Job 23: 8 backward, but I cannot **p** Him
Job 33:14 yet man does not **p** it
Prov 1: 2 to **p** the words of
Prov 14: 7 when you do not **p** in him the
Is 6: 9 keep on seeing, but do not **p**
Matt 13:14 seeing you will see and not **p**
Mark 4:12 seeing they may see and not **p**
Mark 7:18 Do you not **p** that whatever
Mark 8:17 you not yet **p** nor understand
Luke 6:41 but do not **p** the plank in
Luke 9:45 so that they did not **p** it
John 4:19 I **p** that You are a prophet
Acts 10:34 In truth I **p** that God shows
Acts 17:22 I **p** that in all things you
Acts 27:10 I **p** that this voyage will end
Acts 28:26 seeing you will see, and not **p**
2Co 7: 8 For I **p** that the same epistle

PERCEIVED (*see* PERCEIVE)
Judg 6:22 Now Gideon **p** that He was the
1Sa 3: 8 Then Eli **p** that the LORD
1Sa 28:14 Saul **p** that it was Samuel, and
2Sa 12:19 David **p** that the child was
2Sa 14: 1 **p** that the king's heart was
1Ch 14: 2 David **p** that the LORD had
Neh 6:12 Then I **p** that God had not
Neh 6:16 for they **p** that this work was
Prov 7: 7 I **p** among the youths, a young
Eccl 1:17 I **p** that this also is
Eccl 2:14 Yet I myself **p** that the same
Eccl 3:22 So I **p** that there is nothing
Is 64: 4 not heard nor **p** by the ear
Jer 23:18 counsel of the LORD, and has **p**
Matt 16: 8 But when Jesus **p** it, He said
Matt 21:45 they **p** that He was speaking
Matt 22:18 But Jesus **p** their wickedness,
Mark 2: 8 when Jesus **p** in His spirit
Luke 1:22 they **p** that he had seen a
Luke 5:22 when Jesus **p** their thoughts
Luke 8:46 for I **p** power going out from
Luke 20:23 But He **p** their craftiness, and
John 6:15 Therefore when Jesus **p** that
Acts 4:13 **p** that they were uneducated
Acts 23: 6 But when Paul **p** that one part
Gal 2: 9 **p** the grace that had been

PERCEIVES (*see* PERCEIVE)
Prov 31:18 She **p** that her merchandise is

PERCEIVING (*see* PERCEIVE)
Mark 12:28 **p** that He had answered them
Luke 9:47 **p** the thought of their heart,

PERCEPTION (*see* PERCEIVE)
Is 33:19 of obscure speech, beyond **p**

PERCEPTIVE (*see* PERCEIVE)
Prov 17:28 his lips, he is considered **p**

PERDITION
John 17:12 is lost except the son of **p**
Phil 1:28 which is to them a proof of **p**
2Th 2: 3 sin is revealed, the son of **p**
1Ti 6: 9 drown men in destruction and **p**
Heb 10:39 of those who draw back to **p**
2Pe 3: 7 judgment and **p** of ungodly men
Rev 17: 8 the bottomless pit and go to **p**
Rev 17:11 the seven, and is going to **p**

PERES (*see* UPHARSIN)
Dan 5:28 **P**: Your kingdom has been

PERESH
1Ch 7:16 son, and she called his name **P**

PEREZ (*see* PEREZ UZZAH)
Gen 38:29 his name was called **P**
Gen 46:12 were Er, Onan, Shelah, **P**, and
Gen 46:12 The sons of **P** were Hezron
Num 26:20 of **P**, the family of the
Num 26:21 And the sons of **P** were
Ruth 4:12 house be like the house of **P**
Ruth 4:18 this is the genealogy of **P**
Ruth 4:18 **P** begot Hezron
1Ch 2: 4 daughter-in-law, bore him **P**
1Ch 2: 5 The sons of **P** were Hezron
1Ch 4: 1 The sons of Judah were **P**,
1Ch 9: 4 Bani, of the descendants of **P**
1Ch 13:11 is called **P** Uzza to this day
1Ch 27: 3 he was of the children of **P**
Neh 11: 4 of the children of **P**
Neh 11: 6 All the sons of **P** who dwelt
Matt 1: 3 Judah begot **P** and Zerah by
Matt 1: 3 **P** begot Hezron, and Hezron
Luke 3:33 son of Hezron, the son of **P**

PEREZ UZZAH (*see* PEREZ)
2Sa 6: 8 of the place **P** to this day

PERFECT (*see* PERFECTED, PERFECTING, PERFECTION, PERFECTLY)
Gen 6: 9 man, **p** in his generations
Lev 22:21 it must be **p** to be accepted
Deut 25:15 You shall have a **p** and just
Deut 25:15 a **p** and just weight, a **p**
Deut 32: 4 He is the Rock, His work is **p**
1Sa 14:41 Give a **p** lot
2Sa 22:31 As for God, His way is **p**
2Sa 22:33 power, and He makes my way **p**
Ezra 7:12 **P** peace, and so forth
Job 36: 4 one who is **p** in knowledge is
Job 37:16 of Him who is **p** in knowledge
Ps 18:30 As for God, His way is **p**
Ps 18:32 strength, And makes my way **p**
Ps 19: 7 The law of the LORD is **p**,
Ps 101: 2 will behave wisely in a **p** way
Ps 101: 2 my house with a **p** heart
Ps 101: 6 He who walks in a **p** way, He
Ps 138: 8 The LORD will **p** that which
Ps 139:22 I hate them with **p** hatred
Prov 4:18 ever brighter unto the **p** day
Song 5: 2 my love, my dove, my **p** one
Song 6: 9 my **p** one, is the only one,
Is 18: 5 harvest, when the bud is **p**
Is 26: 3 You will keep him in **p** peace
Is 42:19 Who is blind as he who is **p**
Ezek 16:14 for it was **p** through My
Ezek 27: 3 have said, 'I am **p** in beauty
Ezek 27:11 they made your beauty **p**
Ezek 28:12 full of wisdom and **p** in beauty
Ezek 28:15 You were **p** in your ways from
Matt 5:48 Therefore you shall be **p**,
Matt 5:48 as your Father in heaven is **p**
Matt 19:21 If you want to be **p**, go, sell
Luke 1: 3 having had **p** understanding of
John 17:23 they may be made **p** in one
Acts 3:16 Him has given him this **p**
Rom 12: 2 acceptable and **p** will of God
1Co 13:10 when that which is **p** has come
2Co 12: 9 is made **p** in weakness
Gal 3: 3 now being made **p** by the flesh
Eph 4:13 of the Son of God, to a **p** man
Col 1:28 every man **p** in Christ Jesus
Col 4:12 prayers, that you may stand **p**
1Th 3:10 **p** what is lacking in your
Heb 2:10 **p** through sufferings
Heb 7:19 for the law made nothing **p**
Heb 9: 9 who performed the service **p**
Heb 9:11 more **p** tabernacle not made
Heb 10: 1 make those who approach **p**
Heb 11:40 not be made **p** apart from us
Heb 12:23 spirits of just men made **p**
Jas 1: 4 let patience have its **p** work
Jas 1: 4 that you may be **p** and
Jas 1:17 every **p** gift is from above,
Jas 1:25 into the **p** law of liberty
Jas 2:22 and by works faith was made **p**
Jas 3: 2 in word, he is a **p** man, able
1Pe 5:10 you have suffered a while, **p**
1Jn 4:18 but **p** love casts out fear,
1Jn 4:18 has not been made **p** in love
Rev 3: 2 found your works **p** before God

PERFECTED (*see* PERFECT)
Ps 64: 6 We have **p** a shrewd scheme
Ezek 27: 4 builders have **p** your beauty
Matt 21:16 infants You have **p** praise'
Luke 13:32 and the third day I shall be **p**
Phil 3:12 attained, or am already **p**
Heb 5: 9 And having been **p**, He became
Heb 7:28 Son who has been **p** forever
Heb 10:14 For by one offering He has **p**
1Jn 2: 5 the love of God is **p** in him
1Jn 4:12 and His love has been **p** in us
1Jn 4:17 Love has been **p** among us in

PERFECTING (*see* PERFECT)
2Co 7: 1 **p** holiness in the fear of God

PERFECTION (*see* PERFECT)
Ps 50: 2 the **p** of beauty, God will
Ps 119:96 the consummation of all **p**
Lam 2:15 is called 'the **p** of beauty
Ezek 28:12 You were the seal of **p**, full
Col 3:14 love, which is the bond of **p**
Heb 6: 1 of Christ, let us go on to **p**
Heb 7:11 if **p** were through the

PERFECTLY (*see* PERFECT)
1Ki 7:35 half a cubit, it was **p** round
Jer 23:20 days you will understand it **p**
Matt 14:36 touched it were made **p** well
Luke 6:40 but everyone who is **p** trained
1Co 1:10 you, but that you be **p** joined
1Th 5: 2 For you yourselves know **p**

PERFORM (*see* PERFORMED, PERFORMING, PERFORMS)
Gen 26: 3 I will **p** the oath which I
Ex 18:18 not able to **p** it by yourself
Lev 19:37 all My judgments, and **p** them
Lev 20: 8 keep My statutes, and **p** them
Lev 20:22 **p** them, that the land where I
Lev 22:31 My commandments, and **p**
Lev 25:18 keep My judgments, and **p** them
Lev 26: 3 My commandments, and **p**
Lev 26:15 so that you do not **p** all My
Num 4:23 who enter to **p** the service
Num 8:11 that they may **p** the work of
Num 8:24 and above one may enter to **p**
Num 18:21 for the work which they **p**
Num 18:23 But the Levites shall **p** the
Deut 4:13 which He commanded you to **p**
Deut 23:23 your lips you shall keep and **p**
Deut 25: 5 **p** the duty of a husband's
Deut 25: 7 he will not **p** the duty of my
Josh 22:27 that we may **p** the service of
Judg 16:25 Samson, that he may **p** for us
Judg 21:21 come out to **p** their dances
Ruth 3:13 **p** the duty of a near kinsman
Ruth 3:13 want to **p** the duty for you
Ruth 3:13 then I will **p** the duty for
1Sa 3:12 In that day I will **p** against
2Sa 14:15 will **p** the request of his
1Ki 6:12 then I will **p** My word with
2Ki 23: 3 soul, to **p** the words of this
2Ki 23:24 that he might **p** the words of
2Ch 34:31 soul, to **p** the words of the
Neh 5:13 who does not **p** this promise
Ps 21:11 which they are not able to **p**
Ps 61: 8 That I may daily **p** my vows
Ps 119:112 to **p** Your statutes Forever
Eccl 9: 9 which you **p** under the sun
Is 9: 7 the LORD of hosts will **p** this
Is 19:21 a vow to the LORD and **p** it
Is 44:28 he shall **p** all My pleasure,
Jer 1:12 for I am ready to **p** My word
Jer 28: 6 the LORD **p** your words which
Jer 29:10 **p** My good word toward you,
Jer 33:14 that I will **p** that good
Jer 44:25 We will surely **p** our vows
Jer 44:25 your vows and **p** your vows
Ezek 12:25 **p** it," says the Lord GOD
Ezek 43:11 all its ordinances, and **p** them

Nah 1:15 appointed feasts, **p** your vows
Matt 5:33 but shall **p** your oaths to the
Matt 23:16 temple, he is obliged to **p** it
Matt 23:18 on it, he is obliged to **p** it
Luke 1:72 to **p** the mercy promised to
Luke 13:32 **p** cures today and tomorrow,
John 6:30 What sign will You **p** then
Rom 4:21 He was also able to **p**
Rom 7:18 but how to **p** what is good I

PERFORMED (*see* PERFORM)
Num 14:11 which I have **p** among them
Deut 34:12 great terror which Moses **p** in
Judg 16:25 the prison, and he **p** for them
Judg 16:27 who watched while Samson **p**
1Sa 15:11 has not **p** My commandments
1Sa 15:13 I have **p** the commandment of
2Sa 21:14 So they **p** all that the king
1Ch 26:29 and his sons **p** duties as
Neh 9: 8 You have **p** Your words, for
Ps 65: 1 And to You the vow shall be **p**
Ps 105:27 They **p** His signs among them,
Is 10:12 when the LORD has **p** all His
Is 41: 4 Who has **p** and done it, calling
Jer 23:20 **p** the thoughts of His heart
Jer 30:24 until He has **p** the intents of
Jer 34:18 who have not **p** the words of
Jer 35:14 not to drink wine, are **p**
Jer 35:16 the son of Rechab have **p** the
Jer 39:16 they shall be **p** in that day
Jer 51:29 shall be **p** against Babylon
Ezek 37:14 it and **p** it," says the LORD
Mark 6: 2 works are **p** by His hands
Luke 2:39 So when they had **p** all things
John 6: 2 **p** on those who were diseased
John 10:41 John **p** no sign, but all the
Acts 4:22 miracle of healing had been **p**
Rom 15:28 Therefore, when I have **p** this
Heb 9: 9 who **p** the service perfect in

PERFORMING (*see* PERFORM)
Num 8:25 they must cease **p** this work
Heb 9: 6 tabernacle, **p** the services
Rev 16:14 **p** signs, which go out to the

PERFORMS (*see* PERFORM)
Job 23:14 For He **p** what is appointed
Ps 57: 2 To God who **p** all things for
Is 44:26 and **p** the counsel of His
Rev 13:13 He **p** great signs, so that he

PERFUME (*see* PERFUMED, PERFUMER, PERFUMES)
Prov 27: 9 **p** delight the heart, and the
Is 3:20 the **p** boxes, the charms,

PERFUMED (*see* PERFUME)
Prov 7:17 I have **p** my bed with myrrh,
Song 3: 6 **p** with myrrh and frankincense,

PERFUMER (*see* PERFUME, PERFUMER'S, PERFUMERS)
Ex 30:25 according to the art of the **p**
Ex 30:35 according to the art of the **p**
Ex 37:29 to the work of the **p**

PERFUMER'S (*see* PERFUMER)
Eccl 10: 1 flies putrefy the **p** ointment

PERFUMERS (*see* PERFUMER)
1Sa 8:13 take your daughters to be **p**
Neh 3: 8 to him Hananiah, one of the **p**

PERFUMES (*see* PERFUME)
Esth 2:12 myrrh, and six months with **p**
Song 4:10 of your **p** than all spices
Is 57: 9 ointment, and increased your **p**

PERGA
Acts 13:13 they came to **P** in Pamphylia
Acts 13:14 But when they departed from **P**
Acts 14:25 had preached the word in **P**

PERGAMOS
Rev 1:11 to Ephesus, to Smyrna, to **P**
Rev 2:12 of the church in **P** write

PERHAPS (*see* PREFACE)

PERIDA (*see* PERUDA)
Neh 7:57 Sophereth, the children of **P**

PERIL (*see* PERILOUS, PERILS)
Rom 8:35 or famine, or nakedness, or **p**

PERILOUS (*see* PERIL)
Ps 91: 3 And from the **p** pestilence
2Ti 3: 1 last days **p** times will come

PERILS (*see* PERIL)
2Co 11:26 in **p** of waters,
2Co 11:26 in **p** of robbers,
2Co 11:26 in **p** of my own countrymen,
2Co 11:26 in **p** of the Gentiles,
2Co 11:26 in **p** in the city,
2Co 11:26 in **p** in the wilderness,
2Co 11:26 in **p** in the sea,
2Co 11:26 in **p** among false brethren

PERIOD
1Ki 2:11 The **p** that David reigned over
1Ki 11:42 the **p** that Solomon reigned in
1Ki 14:20 The **p** that Jeroboam reigned
2Ki 10:36 the **p** that Jehu reigned over
1Ch 29:27 the **p** that he reigned over

PERISH (*see* PERISHABLE, PERISHED, PERISHES, PERISHING)
Gen 41:36 may not **p** during the famine
Ex 19:21 the LORD, and many of them **p**
Lev 26:38 You shall **p** among the nations
Num 17:12 we die, we **p**, we all **p**
Deut 4:26 **p** from the land which you
Deut 8:19 day that you shall surely **p**
Deut 8:20 before you, so you shall **p**
Deut 11:17 you **p** quickly from the good
Deut 26: 5 was a Syrian, about to **p**, and
Deut 28:20 and until you **p** quickly,
Deut 28:22 shall pursue you until you **p**
Deut 30:18 today that you shall surely **p**
Josh 22:20 that man did not **p** alone in
Josh 23:13 until you **p** from this good
Josh 23:16 you shall **p** quickly from the
Judg 5:31 Thus let all Your enemies **p**
1Sa 26:10 shall go out to battle and **p**
1Sa 27: 1 Now I shall **p** someday by the
2Ki 9: 8 whole house of Ahab shall **p**
Esth 4:14 and your father's house will **p**
Esth 4:16 and if I **p**, I **p**
Esth 9:28 not **p** among their descendants
Job 3: 3 May the day **p** on which I was
Job 3:11 Why did I not **p** when I came
Job 4: 9 By the blast of God they **p**
Job 4:20 they **p** forever, with no one
Job 6:18 aside, they go nowhere and **p**
Job 8:13 hope of the hypocrite shall **p**
Job 13:19 If now I hold my tongue, I **p**
Job 20: 7 Yet he will **p** forever like
Job 31:19 anyone **p** for lack of clothing
Job 34:15 All flesh would **p** together
Job 36:12 they shall **p** by the sword, and
Ps 1: 6 way of the ungodly shall **p**
Ps 2:12 you **p** in the way, When His
Ps 9: 3 fall and **p** at Your presence
Ps 9:18 the poor shall not **p** forever
Ps 37:20 But the wicked shall **p**
Ps 41: 5 will he die, and his name **p**
Ps 49:10 and the senseless person **p**
Ps 49:12 He is like the beasts that **p**
Ps 49:20 Is like the beasts that **p**
Ps 68: 2 So let the wicked **p** at the
Ps 73:27 who are far from You shall **p**
Ps 80:16 They **p** at the rebuke of Your
Ps 83:17 let them be put to shame and **p**
Ps 92: 9 behold, Your enemies shall **p**
Ps 102:26 They will **p**, but You will
Ps 112:10 desire of the wicked shall **p**
Ps 146: 4 In that very day his plans **p**
Prov 10:28 of the wicked will **p**
Prov 11: 7 dies, his expectation will **p**
Prov 11:10 and when the wicked **p**, there
Prov 19: 9 and he who speaks lies shall **p**
Prov 21:28 A false witness shall **p**, but
Prov 28:28 but when they **p**, the
Eccl 5:14 But those riches **p** through
Is 26:14 and made all their memory to **p**
Is 27:13 who are about to **p** in the
Is 29:14 of their wise men shall **p**
Is 31: 3 they all will **p** together
Is 41:11 who strive with you shall **p**
Is 60:12 will not serve you shall **p**
Jer 4: 9 the heart of the king shall **p**
Jer 6:21 and his friend shall **p**
Jer 9:12 Why does the land **p** and burn
Jer 10:11 earth shall **p** from the earth
Jer 10:15 their punishment they shall **p**
Jer 18:18 shall not **p** from the priest
Jer 27:10 drive you out, and you will **p**
Jer 27:15 you out, and that you may **p**
Jer 40:15 and the remnant in Judah **p**
Jer 48: 8 The valley also shall **p**, and
Jer 48:46 The people of Chemosh **p**
Jer 51:18 their punishment they shall **p**
Ezek 7:26 law will **p** from the priest
Ezek 25: 7 you to **p** from the countries
Dan 2:18 his companions might not **p**
Amos 1: 8 of the Philistines shall **p**
Amos 2:14 flight shall **p** from the swift
Amos 3:15 the houses of ivory shall **p**
Jon 1: 6 us, so that we may not **p**
Jon 1:14 let us **p** for this man's life
Jon 3: 9 anger, so that we may not **p**
Zech 9: 5 The king shall **p** from Gaza
Zech 11: 9 die, and what is perishing **p**
Matt 5:29 that one of your members **p**
Matt 5:30 that one of your members **p**
Matt 18:14 of these little ones should **p**
Matt 26:52 the sword will **p** by the sword
Luke 13: 3 you will all likewise **p**
Luke 13: 5 you will all likewise **p**
Luke 13:33 should **p** outside of Jerusalem
Luke 15:17 to spare, and I **p** with hunger
John 3:15 not **p** but have eternal life
John 3:16 **p** but have everlasting life
John 10:28 life, and they shall never **p**
John 11:50 the whole nation should **p**
Acts 8:20 Your money **p** with you,
Acts 13:41 you despisers, marvel and **p**
Rom 2:12 law will also **p** without law
1Co 8:11 shall the weak brother **p**, for
Col 2:22 things which **p** with the using
2Th 2:10 deception among those who **p**
Heb 1:11 They will **p**, but You remain
Heb 11:31 not **p** with those who did not
2Pe 2:12 will utterly **p** in their own
2Pe 3: 9 **p** but that all should come to

PERISHABLE (*see* PERISH)
1Co 9:25 do it to obtain a **p** crown

PERISHED (*see* PERISH)
Num 16:33 and they **p** from among the
Num 21:29 You have **p**, O people of
Num 21:30 Heshbon has **p** as far as Dibon
Deut 2:16 **p** from among the people,
2Sa 1:27 and the weapons of war **p**
Job 4: 7 who ever **p** being innocent
Job 10:18 Oh, that I had **p** and no eye
Job 30: 2 Their vigor has **p**
Ps 9: 6 Even their memory has **p**
Ps 10:16 have **p** out of His land
Ps 83:10 Who **p** at Endor, Who became
Ps 119:92 then have **p** in my affliction
Eccl 9: 6 and their envy have now **p**
Jer 7:28 Truth has **p** and has been cut
Jer 48:36 they have acquired have **p**
Jer 49: 7 has counsel **p** from the
Lam 3:18 my hope Have **p** from the LORD
Ezek 26:17 How you have **p**, O one
Joel 1:11 harvest of the field has **p**
Jon 4:10 up in a night and **p** in a night
Mic 4: 9 Has your counselor **p**
Mic 7: 2 man has **p** from the earth, and
Matt 8:32 the sea, and **p** in the water
Luke 11:51 who **p** between the altar and
Acts 5:37 He also **p**, and all who obeyed
1Co 15:18 asleep in Christ have **p**
2Pe 3: 6 the world that then existed **p**
Jude 11 **p** in the rebellion of Korah

PERISHES (*see* PERISH)
Num 24:20 But shall be last until he **p**
Num 24:24 so shall Amalek, until he **p**
Job 4:11 The old lion **p** for lack of
Job 18:17 of him **p** from the earth, and
Prov 11: 7 and the hope of the unjust **p**
Eccl 7:15 who **p** in his righteousness
Is 57: 1 The righteous **p**, and no man
John 6:27 labor for the food which **p**
Jas 1:11 and its beautiful appearance **p**
1Pe 1: 7 precious than gold that **p**

PERISHING (*see* PERISH)
Job 29:13 of a **p** man came upon me, and I
Job 33:18 his life from **p** by the sword
Prov 31: 6 strong drink to him who is **p**
Zech 11: 9 die, and what is **p** perish
Matt 8:25 Lord, save us! We are **p**!"
Mark 4:38 do You not care that we are **p**

Luke 8:24 Master, Master, we are **p**
1Co 1:18 to those who are **p**, but to us
2Co 2:15 and among those who are **p**
2Co 4: 3 is veiled to those who are **p**
2Co 4:16 though our outward man is **p**

PERIZZITE (*see* PERIZZITES)
Ex 33: 2 and the Hittite and the **P** and
Ex 34:11 and the Hittite and the **P** and
Deut 20:17 and the Canaanite and the **P**
Josh 9: 1 Amorite, the Canaanite, the **P**
Josh 11: 3 Amorite, the Hittite, the **P**

PERIZZITES (*see* PERIZZITE)
Gen 13: 7 the **P** then dwelt in the land
Gen 15:20 the Hittites, the **P**, and the
Gen 34:30 among the Canaanites and the **P**
Ex 3: 8 and the Amorites and the **P** and
Ex 3:17 and the Amorites and the **P** and
Ex 23:23 and the Hittites and the **P** and
Deut 7: 1 and the Canaanites and the **P**
Josh 3:10 and the Hivites and the **P** and
Josh 12: 8 the Canaanites, the **P**, the
Josh 17:15 there in the land of the **P**
Josh 24:11 also the Amorites, the **P**, the
Judg 1: 4 and the **P** into their hand
Judg 1: 5 the Canaanites and the **P**
Judg 3: 5 Hittites, the Amorites, the **P**
1Ki 9:20 of the Amorites, Hittites, **P**
2Ch 8: 7 of the Hittites, Amorites, **P**
Ezra 9: 1 the Hittites, the **P**, the
Neh 9: 8 Hittites, the Amorites, the **P**

PERJURER (*see* PERJURERS)
Zech 5: 3 Every **p** shall be expelled,'

PERJURERS (*see* PERJURER)
Mal 3: 5 against adulterers, against **p**
1Ti 1:10 kidnappers, for liars, for **p**

PERMANENT (*see* PERMANENTLY)
Lev 25:46 they shall be your **p** slaves

PERMANENTLY (*see* PERMANENT)
Lev 25:23 The land shall not be sold **p**
Lev 25:30 belong **p** to him who bought it

PERMISSION (*see* PERMIT)
Num 22:13 to give me **p** to go with you
1Sa 20: 6 David earnestly asked **p** of
1Sa 20:28 David earnestly asked **p** of me
Ezra 3: 7 according to the **p** which they
Jer 44:19 her without our husbands' **p**
Mark 5:13 And at once Jesus gave them **p**
John 19:38 and Pilate gave him **p**
Acts 21:40 So when he had given him **p**

PERMIT (*see* PERMISSION, PERMITS, PERMITTED, PERMITTING)
Ex 22:18 You shall not **p** a sorceress
Judg 15: 1 would not **p** him to go in
2Sa 14:11 do not **p** the avenger of blood
Neh 2: 7 that they must **p** me to pass
Ps 55:22 He shall never **p** the
Eccl 5:12 rich will not **p** him to sleep
Matt 3:15 **P** it to be so now, for thus
Matt 8:31 **p** us to go away into the herd
Mark 5:19 However, Jesus did not **p** him
Luke 8:32 He would **p** them to enter them
Luke 22:51 and said, "**P** even this
Acts 16: 7 but the Spirit did not **p** them
Acts 21:39 **p** me to speak to the people
1Ti 2:12 I do not **p** a woman to teach

PERMITS (*see* PERMIT)
1Co 16: 7 while with you, if the Lord **p**
Heb 6: 3 And this we will do if God **p**

PERMITTED (*see* PERMIT)
Deut 22:29 he shall not be **p** to divorce
1Ch 16:21 He **p** no man to do them wrong
Esth 8:11 By these letters the king **p**
Ps 105:14 He **p** no one to do them wrong
Matt 19: 8 **p** you to divorce your wives,
Mark 5:37 He **p** no one to follow Him
Mark 10: 4 Moses **p** a man to write a
Luke 8:32 And He **p** them
Luke 8:51 He **p** no one to go in except
Acts 26: 1 You are **p** to speak for
Acts 28:16 but Paul was **p** to dwell by
1Co 14:34 for they are not **p** to speak

PERMITTING (*see* PERMIT)
Acts 27: 7 the wind not **p** us to proceed,

PERPETUAL (*see* PERPETUALLY, PERPETUATED)
Gen 9:12 with you, for **p** generations
Ex 29: 9 be theirs for a **p** statute
Ex 30: 8 a **p** incense before the LORD
Ex 31:16 generations as a **p** covenant
Lev 3:17 This shall be a **p** statute
Lev 6:13 A **p** fire shall burn on the
Lev 24: 9 made by fire, by a **p** statute
Lev 25:34 for it is their **p** possession
Num 19:21 It shall be a **p** statute for
Ps 74: 3 feet to the **p** desolations
Ps 78:66 He put them to a **p** reproach
Jer 5:22 by a **p** decree, that it cannot
Jer 8: 5 Jerusalem, in a **p** backsliding
Jer 15:18 Why is my pain **p** and my wound
Jer 18:16 land desolate and a **p** hissing
Jer 23:40 a **p** shame, which shall not be
Jer 25: 9 a hissing, and **p** desolations
Jer 25:12 I will make it a **p** desolation
Jer 49:13 its cities shall be **p** wastes
Jer 50: 5 a **p** covenant That will not be
Jer 51:39 rejoice, and sleep a **p** sleep
Jer 51:57 and they shall sleep a **p** sleep
Ezek 46:14 offering is a **p** ordinance
Hab 3: 6 scattered, the **p** hills bowed
Zeph 2: 9 saltpits, and a **p** desolation

PERPETUALLY (*see* PERPETUAL)
1Ki 9: 3 and My heart will be there **p**
2Ch 7:16 and My heart will be there **p**
Ezek 35: 9 I will make you **p** desolate
Amos 1:11 his anger tore **p**, and he kept

PERPETUATED (*see* PERPETUAL)
Nah 1:14 name shall be **p** no longer

PERPLEXED (*see* PERPLEXITY)
Esth 3:15 but the city of Shushan was **p**
Luke 9: 7 and he was **p**, because it was
Luke 24: 4 were greatly **p** about this
John 13:22 **p** about whom He spoke
Acts 2:12 So they were all amazed and **p**
2Co 4: 8 we are **p**, but not in despair

PERPLEXITY (*see* PERPLEXED)
Is 22: 5 **p** by the Lord GOD of hosts in
Mic 7: 4 now shall be their **p**
Luke 21:25 distress of nations, with **p**

PERSECUTE (*see* PERSECUTED, PERSECUTES, PERSECUTING, PERSECUTION, PERSECUTOR)
Job 19:22 Why do you **p** me as God does,
Job 19:28 say, 'How shall we **p** him
Ps 7: 1 me from all those who **p** me
Ps 31:15 And from those who **p** me
Ps 69:26 For they **p** him whom You have
Ps 119:84 judgment on those who **p** me
Ps 119:86 They **p** me wrongfully
Ps 119:161 Princes **p** me without a cause,
Jer 17:18 Let them be ashamed who **p** me
Dan 7:25 shall **p** the saints of the
Matt 5:11 **p** you, and say all kinds of
Matt 5:44 spitefully use you and **p** you,
Matt 10:23 But when they **p** you in this
Matt 23:34 and **p** from city to city,
Luke 11:49 of them they will kill and **p**
Luke 21:12 **p** you, delivering you up to
John 15:20 Me, they will also **p** you
Acts 7:52 did your fathers not **p**
Rom 12:14 Bless those who **p** you

PERSECUTED (*see* PERSECUTE)
Deut 30: 7 those who hate you, who **p** you
Ps 109:16 But **p** the poor and needy man,
Ps 143: 3 For the enemy has **p** my soul
Is 14: 6 the nations in anger, is **p**
Matt 5:10 are **p** for righteousness' sake
Matt 5:12 for so they **p** the prophets
John 5:16 this reason the Jews **p** Jesus
John 15:20 If they **p** Me, they will also
Acts 22: 4 I **p** this Way to the death,
Acts 26:11 I **p** them even to foreign
1Co 4:12 being **p**, we endure it
1Co 15: 9 because I **p** the church of God
2Co 4: 9 **p**, but not forsaken
Gal 1:13 how I **p** the church of God
Gal 1:23 He who formerly **p** us now
Gal 4:29 **p** him who was born according
1Th 2:15 own prophets, and have **p** us
Rev 12:13 he **p** the woman who gave birth

PERSECUTES (*see* PERSECUTE)
Ps 10: 2 in his pride **p** the poor

PERSECUTING (*see* PERSECUTE)
Acts 9: 4 Saul, Saul, why are you **p** Me
Acts 9: 5 I am Jesus, whom you are **p**
Acts 22: 7 Saul, Saul, why are you **p** Me
Acts 22: 8 of Nazareth, whom you are **p**
Acts 26:14 Saul, Saul, why are you **p** Me
Acts 26:15 I am Jesus, whom you are **p**
Phil 3: 6 concerning zeal, **p** the church

PERSECUTION (*see* PERSECUTE, PERSECUTIONS)
Matt 13:21 For when tribulation or **p**
Mark 4:17 when tribulation or **p** arises
Acts 8: 1 At that time a great **p** arose
Acts 11:19 the **p** that arose over Stephen
Acts 13:50 raised up **p** against Paul and
Rom 8:35 or distress, or **p**, or famine
Gal 5:11 why do I still suffer **p**
Gal 6:12 **p** for the cross of Christ
2Ti 3:12 in Christ Jesus will suffer **p**

PERSECUTIONS (*see* PERSECUTION)
Mark 10:30 and children and lands, with **p**
2Co 12:10 in reproaches, in needs, in **p**
2Th 1: 4 and faith in all your **p** and
2Ti 3:11 **p**, afflictions, which
2Ti 3:11 what **p** I endured

PERSECUTOR (*see* PERSECUTE, PERSECUTORS)
1Ti 1:13 formerly a blasphemer, a **p**

PERSECUTORS (*see* PERSECUTOR)
Neh 9:11 their **p** You threw into the
Ps 119:157 Many are my **p** and my enemies,
Ps 142: 6 Deliver me from my **p**, For
Jer 15:15 take vengeance for me on my **p**
Jer 20:11 Therefore my **p** will stumble
Lam 1: 3 all her **p** overtake her in

PERSEVERANCE (*see* PERSEVERE)
Rom 5: 3 that tribulation produces **p**
Rom 5: 4 and **p**, character
Rom 8:25 we eagerly wait for it with **p**
2Co 12:12 among you with all **p**, in
Eph 6:18 to this end with all **p** and
2Ti 3:10 faith, longsuffering, love, **p**
Jas 5:11 have heard of the **p** of Job
2Pe 1: 6 to self-control **p**,
2Pe 1: 6 to **p** godliness,

PERSEVERE (*see* PERSEVERANCE, PERSEVERED)
Rev 3:10 you have kept My command to **p**

PERSEVERED (*see* PERSEVERE)
Rev 2: 3 and you have **p** and have

PERSIA (*see* ELAM, PERSIAN)
2Ch 36:20 the reign of the kingdom of **P**
2Ch 36:22 first year of Cyrus king of **P**
2Ch 36:22 the spirit of Cyrus king of **P**
2Ch 36:23 Thus says Cyrus king of **P**
Ezra 1: 1 first year of Cyrus king of **P**
Ezra 1: 1 the spirit of Cyrus king of **P**
Ezra 1: 2 Thus says Cyrus king of **P**
Ezra 1: 8 Cyrus king of **P** brought them
Ezra 3: 7 they had from Cyrus king of **P**
Ezra 4: 3 king of **P** has commanded us
Ezra 4: 5 the days of Cyrus king of **P**
Ezra 4: 5 the reign of Darius king of **P**
Ezra 4: 7 wrote to Artaxerxes king of **P**
Ezra 4: 9 Tarpelites, the people of **P**
Ezra 4:24 the reign of Darius king of **P**
Ezra 6:14 and Artaxerxes king of **P**
Ezra 7: 1 reign of Artaxerxes king of **P**
Ezra 9: 9 the sight of the kings of **P**
Esth 1: 3 the powers of **P** and Media, the
Esth 1:14 the seven princes of **P** and
Esth 1:18 day the noble ladies of **P**
Esth 10: 2 of the kings of Media and **P**
Ezek 27:10 Those from **P**, Lydia, and Libya
Ezek 38: 5 **P**, Ethiopia, and Libya are
Dan 8:20 are the kings of Media and **P**
Dan 10: 1 **P** a message was revealed to
Dan 10:13 of **P** withstood me twenty-one
Dan 10:13 there with the kings of **P**
Dan 10:20 to fight with the prince of **P**
Dan 11: 2 more kings will arise in **P**

PERSIAN (*see* ELAMITES, PERSIA, PERSIANS)
Neh 12:22 the reign of Darius the **P**
Dan 6:28 in the reign of Cyrus the **P**

PERSIANS (*see* PERSIAN)
Ezra 5: 6 the **P** who were in the region
Ezra 6: 6 your companions the **P** who are
Esth 1:19 recorded in the laws of the **P**
Dan 5:28 and given to the Medes and **P**
Dan 6: 8 to the law of the Medes and **P**
Dan 6:12 to the law of the Medes and **P**
Dan 6:15 **P** that no decree or statute

PERSIS
Rom 16:12 Greet the beloved **P**, who

PERSISTED (*see* PERSISTENCE)
2Ki 3: 3 Nevertheless he **p** in the sins
Ezek 15: 8 they have **p** in unfaithfulness

PERSISTENCE (*see* PERSISTED, PERSISTENT)
Luke 11: 8 because of his **p** he will rise

PERSISTENT (*see* PERSISTENCE)
Ezek 14:13 Me by **p** unfaithfulness, I

PERSON (*see* PERSONAL, PERSONS)
Gen 17:14 that **p** shall be cut off from
Ex 12:15 that **p** shall be cut off from
Ex 12:19 that same **p** shall be cut off
Ex 12:48 uncircumcised **p** shall eat it
Ex 16:16 need, one omer for each **p**
Ex 31:14 that **p** shall be cut off from
Lev 4: 2 If a **p** sins unintentionally
Lev 5: 1 If a **p** sins in hearing the
Lev 5: 2 Or if a **p** touches any
Lev 5: 4 Or if a **p** swears, speaking
Lev 5:15 If a **p** commits a trespass, and
Lev 5:17 If a **p** sins, and commits any
Lev 6: 2 If a **p** sins and commits a
Lev 7:18 the **p** who eats of it shall
Lev 7:20 But the **p** who eats the flesh
Lev 7:20 that **p** shall be cut off from
Lev 7:21 Moreover the **p** who touches
Lev 7:21 that **p** shall be cut off from
Lev 7:25 the **p** who eats it shall be
Lev 7:27 that **p** shall be cut off from
Lev 13: 9 the leprous sore is on a **p**
Lev 17:10 against that **p** who eats blood
Lev 17:15 every **p** who eats what died
Lev 19: 8 that **p** shall be cut off from
Lev 19:15 nor honor the **p** of the mighty
Lev 20: 6 the **p** who turns after mediums
Lev 20: 6 set My face against that **p**
Lev 22: 3 that **p** shall be cut off from
Lev 22: 5 or any **p** by whom he would
Lev 22: 6 the **p** who has touched any
Lev 22:11 buys a **p** with his money, he
Lev 23:29 For any **p** who is not
Lev 23:30 any **p** who does any work on
Lev 23:30 that **p** I will destroy from
Lev 27:29 No **p** under the ban, who may
Num 5: 6 LORD, and that **p** is guilty,
Num 9:13 that same **p** shall be cut off
Num 15:27 if a **p** sins unintentionally,
Num 15:28 make atonement for the **p** who
Num 15:30 But the **p** who does anything
Num 15:31 that **p** shall be completely
Num 19:13 That **p** shall be cut off from
Num 19:17 for an unclean **p** they shall
Num 19:18 A clean **p** shall take hyssop
Num 19:19 The clean **p** shall sprinkle
Num 19:20 that **p** shall be cut off from
Num 19:22 Whatever the unclean **p**
Num 19:22 the **p** who touches it shall be
Num 31:19 whoever has killed any **p**, and
Num 35:11 **p** accidentally may flee there
Num 35:15 that anyone who kills a **p**
Num 35:30 Whoever kills a **p**, the
Num 35:30 testimony against a **p** for the
Deut 15:22 the clean **p** alike may eat it,
Deut 17: 7 the evil **p** from among you
Deut 17:12 away the evil **p** from Israel
Deut 19:19 the evil **p** from among you
Deut 21:21 the evil **p** from among you
Deut 22:21 the evil **p** from among you
Deut 22:22 away the evil **p** from Israel
Deut 22:24 the evil **p** from among you
Deut 24: 7 the evil **p** from among you
Deut 24:16 a **p** shall be put to death for
Deut 27:25 a bribe to slay an innocent **p**
Josh 20: 3 kills any **p** accidentally or
Josh 20: 9 any **p** accidentally might flee
1Sa 9: 2 was not a more handsome **p**
1Sa 16:18 in speech, and a handsome **p**
1Sa 25:35 voice and respected your **p**
2Sa 4:11 **p** in his own house on his bed
2Sa 17:11 and that you go to battle in **p**
1Ki 14: 6 you pretend to be another **p**
2Ki 14: 6 but a **p** shall be put to death
2Ch 25: 4 but a **p** shall die for his own
Job 1:12 do not lay a hand on his **p**
Job 22:29 He will save the humble **p**
Ps 15: 4 eyes a vile **p** is despised
Ps 31:23 And fully repays the proud **p**
Ps 49:10 and the senseless **p** perish
Ps 109:20 who speak evil against my **p**
Prov 3:32 for the perverse **p** is an
Prov 6:12 A worthless **p**, a wicked man,
Prov 16:26 The **p** who labors, labors for
Prov 19:15 an idle **p** will suffer hunger
Is 32: 5 The foolish **p** will no longer
Is 32: 6 for the foolish **p** will speak
Jer 43: 6 every **p** whom Nebuzaradan the
Ezek 33: 6 takes any **p** from among them,
Ezek 44:25 by coming near a dead **p**
Dan 11:21 place shall arise a vile **p**
Matt 5:39 you not to resist an evil **p**
Matt 22:16 do not regard the **p** of men
Matt 27:24 of the blood of this just **P**
Mark 12:14 do not regard the **p** of men
Rom 14: 5 One **p** esteems one day above
1Co 5:11 not even to eat with such a **p**
1Co 5:13 from yourselves that wicked **p**
1Co 14:24 or an uninformed **p** comes in
2Co 10:11 Let such a **p** consider this,
Eph 5: 5 that no fornicator, unclean **p**
2Th 3:14 in this epistle, note that **p**
1Ti 1: 9 is not made for a righteous **p**
Tit 3:11 that such a **p** is warped and
Heb 1: 3 and the express image of His **p**
Heb 12:16 or profane **p** like Esau, who
1Pe 3: 4 be the hidden **p** of the heart
2Pe 2:19 for by whom a **p** is overcome

PERSONAL (*see* PERSON, PERSONALLY)
Luke 20:21 You do not show **p** favoritism
Gal 2: 6 God shows **p** favoritism to no

PERSONALLY (*see* PERSONAL)
Gen 24:57 the young woman and ask her **p**

PERSONS (*see* PERSON)
Gen 14:21 Give me the **p**, and take the
Gen 36: 6 all the **p** of his household,
Gen 46:15 All the **p**, his sons and his
Gen 46:18 she bore to Jacob: sixteen **p**
Gen 46:22 fourteen **p** in all
Gen 46:25 to Jacob: seven **p** in all.
Gen 46:26 All the **p** who went with Jacob
Gen 46:26 were sixty-six **p** in all
Gen 46:27 to him in Egypt were two **p**
Gen 46:27 All the **p** of the house of
Ex 1: 5 of Jacob were seventy **p** (for
Ex 12: 4 to the number of the **p**
Ex 16:16 according to the number of **p**
Lev 18:29 the **p** who commit them shall
Lev 27: 2 a vow certain **p** to the LORD
Num 19:18 on the **p** who were there, or
Num 31:28 every five hundred of the **p**
Num 31:30 every fifty, drawn from the **p**
Num 31:35 thirty-two thousand **p** in all
Num 31:40 The **p** were sixteen thousand,
Num 31:40 tribute was thirty-two **p**
Num 31:46 and sixteen thousand **p**
Deut 10:22 down to Egypt with seventy **p**
1Sa 9:22 there were about thirty **p**
1Sa 22:22 the **p** of your father's house
1Ki 14:24 also perverted **p** in the land
1Ki 15:12 the perverted **p** from the land
1Ki 22:46 the rest of the perverted **p**
2Ki 10: 6 the king's sons, seventy **p**
2Ki 10: 7 sons and slaughtered seventy **p**
2Ki 23: 7 booths of the perverted **p**
Job 36:14 ends among the perverted **p**
Jer 52:29 eight hundred and thirty-two **p**
Jer 52:30 seven hundred and forty-five **p**
Jer 52:30 All the **p** were four thousand
Ezek 10:22 their appearance and their **p**
Ezek 17:17 a wall to cut off many **p**
Amos 6: 1 notable **p** in the chief nation
Jon 4:11 twenty thousand **p** who cannot
Luke 15: 7 just **p** who need no repentance
Acts 27:37 and seventy-six **p** on the ship
2Co 1:11 **p** on our behalf for the gift
2Pe 3:11 what manner of **p** ought you to
Jude 19 These are sensual **p**, who

PERSUADE (*see* PERSUADED, PERSUADES, PERSUADING, PERSUASION, PERSUASIVE)
2Sa 3:35 **p** David to eat food while it
1Ki 22:20 Who will **p** Ahab to go up,
1Ki 22:21 LORD, and said, 'I will **p** him
1Ki 22:22 And He said, 'You shall **p** him
2Ki 18:32 to Hezekiah, lest he **p** you
2Ch 18:19 Who will **p** Ahab king of
2Ch 18:20 LORD, and said, 'I will **p** him
2Ch 18:21 LORD said, 'You shall **p** him
2Ch 32:11 Does not Hezekiah **p** you to
2Ch 32:15 you or **p** you like this, and do
Is 36:18 Beware lest Hezekiah **p** you
Acts 26:28 You almost **p** me to become a
2Co 5:11 terror of the Lord, we **p** men
Gal 1:10 For do I now **p** men, or God

PERSUADED (*see* PERSUADE)
Josh 15:18 that she **p** him to ask her
2Ch 18: 2 **p** him to go up with him to
Prov 25:15 long forbearance a ruler is **p**
Jer 20: 7 You induced me, and I was **p**
Matt 27:20 elders **p** the multitudes that
Luke 16:31 neither will they be **p** though
Luke 20: 6 for they are **p** that John was
Acts 13:43 **p** them to continue in the
Acts 14:19 having **p** the multitudes, they
Acts 17: 4 And some of them were **p**
Acts 17: 5 But the Jews who were not **p**
Acts 18: 4 and **p** both Jews and Greeks
Acts 19:26 all Asia, this Paul has **p**
Acts 21:14 So when he would not be **p**
Acts 27:11 was more **p** by the helmsman
Acts 28:24 some were **p** by the things
Rom 8:38 For I am **p** that neither death
2Ti 1: 5 and I am **p** is in you also
2Ti 1:12 am **p** that He is able to keep

PERSUADES (*see* PERSUADE)
Acts 18:13 This fellow **p** men to worship

PERSUADING (*see* PERSUADE)
Acts 19: 8 **p** concerning the things of
Acts 28:23 **p** them concerning Jesus from

PERSUASION (*see* PERSUADE)
Gal 5: 8 This **p** does not come from Him

PERSUASIVE (*see* PERSUADE)
1Co 2: 4 with **p** words of human wisdom
Col 2: 4 deceive you with **p** words

PERTAIN (*see* PERTAINING, PERTAINS)
Rom 9: 4 to whom **p** the adoption, the
Rom 15:17 in the things which **p** to God
1Co 6: 3 things that **p** to this life
2Pe 1: 3 us all things that **p** to life

PERTAINING (*see* PERTAIN)
1Ch 26:32 for every matter **p** to God
Acts 1: 3 **p** to the kingdom of God
1Co 6: 4 things **p** to this life, do you
Heb 2:17 Priest in things **p** to God
Heb 5: 1 for men in things **p** to God

PERTAINS (*see* PERTAIN)
Num 8:24 This is what **p** to the Levites
Deut 22: 5 wear anything that **p** to a man
Neh 2: 8 citadel which **p** to the temple

PERTURBED
Prov 30:21 three things the earth is **p**

PERUDA (*see* PERIDA)
Ezra 2:55 of Sophereth, the sons of **P**

PERVERSE (*see* PERVERSENESS, PERVERSION, PERVERSITY, PERVERT)
Num 22:32 your way is **p** before Me
Deut 32: 5 a **p** and crooked generation
Deut 32:20 for they are a **p** generation
1Sa 20:30 You son of a **p**, rebellious
Job 9:20 it would prove me **p**
Ps 101: 4 A **p** heart shall depart from
Prov 2:12 the man who speaks **p** things
Prov 3:32 for the **p** person is an
Prov 4:24 and put **p** lips far from you
Prov 6:12 man, walks with a **p** mouth
Prov 8: 8 crooked or **p** is in them
Prov 8:13 way and the **p** mouth I hate
Prov 10:31 but the **p** tongue will be cut
Prov 10:32 mouth of the wicked what is **p**
Prov 11:20 Those who are of a **p** heart

Prov 12: 8 but he who is of a **p** heart
Prov 14: 2 but he who is **p** in his ways
Prov 16:28 A **p** man sows strife, and a
Prov 16:30 his eye to devise **p** things
Prov 17:20 he who has a **p** tongue falls
Prov 19: 1 than one who is **p** in his lips
Prov 21: 8 The way of a guilty man is **p**
Prov 22: 5 are in the way of the **p**
Prov 23:33 heart will utter **p** things
Prov 28: 6 than one **p** in his ways,
Prov 28:18 but he who is **p** in his ways
Is 19:14 a **p** spirit in her midst
Hab 1: 4 therefore **p** judgment proceeds
Matt 17:17 **p** generation, how long shall
Luke 9:41 **p** generation, how long shall
Acts 2:40 saved from this **p** generation
Acts 20:30 rise up, speaking **p** things
Phil 2:15 **p** generation, among whom you

PERVERSENESS (*see* PERVERSE)
Prov 15: 4 but **p** in it breaks the spirit

PERVERSION (*see* PERVERSE,)
Lev 18:23 to mate with it. It is **p**.
Lev 20:12 They have committed **p**
Eccl 5: 8 and the violent **p** of justice

PERVERSITY (*see* PERVERSE)
Prov 2:14 in the **p** of the wicked
Prov 6:14 **p** is in his heart, he devises
Prov 11: 3 but the **p** of the unfaithful
Is 30:12 and trust in oppression and **p**
Is 59: 3 your tongue has muttered **p**
Ezek 9: 9 and the city full of **p**

PERVERT (*see* PERVERSE, PERVERTED, PERVERTING, PERVERTS)
Ex 23: 2 aside after many to **p** justice
Ex 23: 6 You shall not **p** the judgment
Deut 16:19 You shall not **p** justice
Deut 24:17 You shall not **p** justice due
Job 8: 3 does the Almighty **p** justice
Job 34:12 will the Almighty **p** justice
Prov 17:23 back to **p** the ways of justice
Prov 31: 5 and **p** the justice of all the
Amos 2: 7 and **p** the way of the humble
Mic 3: 9 justice and **p** all equity,
Gal 1: 7 and want to **p** the gospel of

PERVERTED (*see* PERVERT)
Deut 23:17 or a **p** one of the sons of
Judg 19:22 **p** men, surrounded the house
Judg 20:13 the **p** men who are in Gibeah,
1Sa 8: 3 took bribes, and **p** justice
1Ki 14:24 there were also **p** persons in
1Ki 15:12 he banished the **p** persons
1Ki 22:46 And the rest of the **p** persons
2Ki 23: 7 **p** persons that were in the
Job 33:27 **p** what was right, and it did
Job 36:14 life ends among the **p** persons
Jer 3:21 for they have **p** their way
Jer 23:36 for you have **p** the words of

PERVERTING (*see* PERVERT)
Luke 23: 2 this fellow **p** the nation, and
Acts 13:10 will you not cease **p** the

PERVERTS (*see* PERVERT)
Ex 23: 8 **p** the words of the righteous
Deut 27:19 one who **p** the justice due the
Prov 10: 9 but he who **p** his ways will

PESTERED
Judg 16:16 when she **p** him daily with her

PESTILENCE (*see* PESTILENCES)
Ex 5: 3 us with **p** or with the sword
Ex 9: 3 There will be a very severe **p**
Ex 9:15 you and your people with **p**
Lev 26:25 I will send **p** among you
Num 14:12 I will strike them with the **p**
Deut 32:24 with hunger, devoured by **p**
1Ki 8:37 is famine in the land, or **p**
2Ch 6:28 land, **p** or blight or mildew,
2Ch 7:13 or send **p** among My people,
2Ch 20: 9 as the sword, judgment, **p**
Ps 91: 3 fowler And from the perilous **p**
Ps 91: 6 Nor of the **p** that walks in
Jer 14:12 by the famine, and by the **p**
Jer 21: 6 they shall die of a great **p**
Jer 21: 7 left in this city from the **p**
Jer 21: 9 the sword, by famine, and by **p**
Jer 24:10 the **p** among them, till they
Jer 27: 8 sword, the famine, and the **p**
Jer 27:13 by the famine, and by the **p**
Jer 28: 8 of war and disaster and **p**
Jer 29:17 sword, the famine, and the **p**
Jer 29:18 sword, with famine, and with **p**
Jer 32:24 of the sword and famine and **p**
Jer 32:36 by the famine, and by the **p**'
Jer 34:17 to the sword, to **p**, and to
Jer 38: 2 the sword, by famine, and by **p**
Jer 42:17 the sword, by famine, and by **p**
Jer 42:22 by **p** in the place where you
Jer 44:13 the sword, by famine, and by **p**
Ezek 5:12 of you shall die of the **p**
Ezek 5:17 **P** and blood shall pass through
Ezek 6:11 the sword, by famine, and by **p**
Ezek 6:12 is far off shall die by the **p**
Ezek 7:15 sword is outside, and the **p**
Ezek 7:15 famine and **p** will devour him
Ezek 12:16 sword, from famine, and from **p**
Ezek 14:19 if I send a **p** into that land
Ezek 14:21 famine and wild beasts and **p**
Ezek 28:23 For I will send **p** upon her
Ezek 33:27 and caves shall die of the **p**
Ezek 38:22 bring him to judgment with **p**
Hab 3: 5 Before Him went **p**, and fever

PESTILENCES (*see* PESTILENCE)
Matt 24: 7 And there will be famines, **p**
Luke 21:11 places, and famines and **p**

PESTLE
Prov 27:22 a **p** along with crushed grain

PETER (*see* CEPHAS, PETER'S, SIMON)
Matt 4:18 two brothers, Simon called **P**
Matt 10: 2 first, Simon, who is called **P**
Matt 14:28 And **P** answered Him and said,
Matt 14:29 when **P** had come down out of
Matt 15:15 Then **P** answered and said to
Matt 16:16 Simon **P** answered and said,
Matt 16:18 say to you that you are **P**
Matt 16:22 Then **P** took Him aside and
Matt 16:23 But He turned and said to **P**
Matt 17: 1 after six days Jesus took **P**
Matt 17: 4 Then **P** answered and said to
Matt 17:24 the temple tax came to **P** and
Matt 17:26 **P** said to Him, "From
Matt 18:21 Then **P** came to Him and said,
Matt 19:27 Then **P** answered and said to
Matt 26:33 **P** answered and said to Him
Matt 26:35 **P** said to Him, "Even if I
Matt 26:37 And He took with Him **P** and
Matt 26:40 them asleep, and said to **P**
Matt 26:58 But **P** followed Him at a
Matt 26:69 Now **P** sat outside in the
Matt 26:73 by came to him and said to **P**
Matt 26:75 And **P** remembered the word of
Mark 3:16 to whom He gave the name **P**
Mark 5:37 no one to follow Him except **P**
Mark 8:29 **P** answered and said to Him,
Mark 8:32 **P** took Him aside and began to
Mark 8:33 His disciples, He rebuked **P**
Mark 9: 2 after six days Jesus took **P**
Mark 9: 5 Then **P** answered and said to
Mark 10:28 Then **P** began to say to Him,
Mark 11:21 And **P**, remembering, said to
Mark 13: 3 Olives opposite the temple, **P**
Mark 14:29 But **P** said to Him, "Even if
Mark 14:33 took **P**, James, and John
Mark 14:37 them sleeping, and said to **P**
Mark 14:54 But **P** followed Him at a
Mark 14:66 Now as **P** was below in the
Mark 14:67 And when she saw **P** warming
Mark 14:70 who stood by said to **P** again
Mark 14:72 **P** called to mind the word
Mark 16: 7 tell His disciples—and **P**
Luke 5: 8 When Simon **P** saw it, he fell
Luke 6:14 Simon, whom He also named **P**
Luke 8:45 When all denied it, **P** and
Luke 8:51 no one to go in except **P**,
Luke 9:20 **P** answered and said,
Luke 9:28 these sayings, that He took **P**
Luke 9:32 But **P** and those with him were
Luke 9:33 Him, that **P** said to Jesus,
Luke 12:41 Then **P** said to Him, "Lord,
Luke 18:28 Then **P** said, "See, we have
Luke 22: 8 And He sent **P** and John, saying,
Luke 22:34 I tell you, **P**, the rooster
Luke 22:54 And **P** followed at a distance
Luke 22:55 together, **P** sat among them
Luke 22:58 But **P** said, "Man, I am not
Luke 22:60 But **P** said, "Man, I do not
Luke 22:61 Lord turned and looked at **P**
Luke 22:61 **P** remembered the word of the
Luke 22:62 Then **P** went out and wept
Luke 24:12 But **P** arose and ran to the
John 1:44 the city of Andrew and **P**
John 6:68 Then Simon **P** answered Him,
John 13: 6 Then He came to Simon **P**
John 13: 6 And **P** said to Him,
John 13: 8 **P** said to Him, "You shall
John 13: 9 Simon **P** said to Him, "Lord,
John 13:24 Simon **P** therefore motioned to
John 13:36 Simon **P** said to Him, "Lord,
John 13:37 **P** said to Him, "Lord, why
John 18:10 Then Simon **P**, having a sword,
John 18:11 Then Jesus said to **P**, "Put
John 18:15 Simon **P** followed Jesus, and so
John 18:16 But **P** stood at the door
John 18:16 the door, and brought **P** in
John 18:17 who kept the door said to **P**
John 18:18 **P** stood with them and warmed
John 18:25 Now Simon **P** stood and warmed
John 18:26 of him whose ear **P** cut off
John 18:27 **P** then denied again
John 20: 2 she ran and came to Simon **P**
John 20: 3 **P** therefore went out, and the
John 20: 4 the other disciple outran **P**
John 20: 6 Then Simon **P** came, following
John 21: 2 Simon **P**, Thomas called
John 21: 3 Simon **P** said to them, "I am
John 21: 7 whom Jesus loved said to **P**
John 21: 7 Now when Simon **P** heard that
John 21:11 Simon **P** went up and dragged
John 21:15 Jesus said to Simon **P**
John 21:17 **P** was grieved because He
John 21:20 Then **P**, turning around, saw
John 21:21 **P**, seeing him, said to Jesus,
Acts 1:13 **P**, James, John, and Andrew
Acts 1:15 in those days **P** stood up in
Acts 2:14 But **P**, standing up with the
Acts 2:37 to the heart, and said to **P**
Acts 2:38 Then **P** said to them, "Repent
Acts 3: 1 Now **P** and John went up
Acts 3: 3 who, seeing **P** and John about
Acts 3: 4 on him, with John, **P** said,
Acts 3: 6 Then **P** said, "Silver and gold
Acts 3:11 who was healed held on to **P**
Acts 3:12 So when **P** saw it, he
Acts 4: 8 Then **P**, filled with the Holy
Acts 4:13 they saw the boldness of **P**
Acts 4:19 But **P** and John answered and
Acts 5: 3 But **P** said, "Ananias, why
Acts 5: 8 And **P** answered her,
Acts 5: 9 Then **P** said to her, "How is
Acts 5:15 of **P** passing by might fall on
Acts 5:29 Then **P** and the other apostles
Acts 8:14 the word of God, they sent **P**
Acts 8:20 But **P** said to him, "Your
Acts 9:32 as **P** went through all parts
Acts 9:34 And **P** said to him,
Acts 9:38 had heard that **P** was there
Acts 9:39 Then **P** arose and went with
Acts 9:40 But **P** put them all out, and
Acts 9:40 and when she saw **P** she sat up
Acts 10: 5 for Simon whose surname is **P**
Acts 10: 9 **P** went up on the housetop to
Acts 10:13 Rise, **P**; kill and eat."
Acts 10:14 But **P** said, "Not so, Lord
Acts 10:17 Now while **P** wondered within
Acts 10:18 Simon, whose surname was **P**
Acts 10:19 While **P** thought about the
Acts 10:21 Then **P** went down to the men
Acts 10:23 On the next day **P** went away
Acts 10:25 As **P** was coming in, Cornelius
Acts 10:26 But **P** lifted him up, saying,
Acts 10:32 here, whose surname is **P**
Acts 10:34 Then **P** opened his mouth and
Acts 10:44 While **P** was still speaking
Acts 10:45 as many as came with **P**,
Acts 10:46 Then **P** answered,
Acts 11: 2 when **P** came up to Jerusalem,
Acts 11: 4 But **P** explained it to them in
Acts 11: 7 voice saying to me, 'Rise, **P**
Acts 11:13 for Simon whose surname is **P**
Acts 12: 3 further to seize **P** also
Acts 12: 5 **P** was therefore kept in
Acts 12: 6 that night **P** was sleeping,
Acts 12: 7 he struck **P** on the side and
Acts 12:11 when **P** had come to himself,
Acts 12:13 as **P** knocked at the door of
Acts 12:14 announced that **P** stood before
Acts 12:16 Now **P** continued knocking
Acts 12:18 about what had become of **P**

Acts 15: 7 **P** rose up and said to them
Gal 1:18 went up to Jerusalem to see **P**
Gal 2: 7 for the circumcised was to **P**
Gal 2: 8 who worked effectively in **P**
Gal 2:11 But when **P** had come to
Gal 2:14 I said to **P** before them all,
1Pe 1: 1 **P**, an apostle of Jesus Christ
2Pe 1: 1 Simon **P**, a servant and apostle

PETER'S (*see* PETER)
Matt 8:14 Jesus had come into **P** house
John 1:40 was Andrew, Simon **P** brother
John 6: 8 Simon **P** brother, said to Him,
Acts 12:14 When she recognized **P** voice

PETHAHIAH
1Ch 24:16 the nineteenth to **P**, the
Ezra 10:23 (the same is Kelita), **P**,
Neh 9: 5 Hodijah, Shebaniah, and **P**
Neh 11:24 **P** the son of Meshezabeel, of

PETHOR
Num 22: 5 Balaam the son of Beor at **P**
Deut 23: 4 of Beor from **P** of Mesopotamia

PETHUEL
Joel 1: 1 came to Joel the son of **P**

PETITION (*see* PETITIONED, PETITIONS)
1Sa 1:17 God of Israel grant your **p**
1Sa 1:27 me my **p** which I asked of Him
1Ki 2:16 Now I ask one **p** of you
1Ki 2:20 I desire one small **p** of you
Esth 5: 6 What is your **p**
Esth 5: 7 My **p** and request is this
Esth 5: 8 the king to grant my **p** and
Esth 7: 2 What is your **p**, Queen Esther
Esth 7: 3 my life be given me at my **p**
Esth 9:12 Now what is your **p**
Jer 37:20 let my **p** be accepted before
Jer 42: 2 let our **p** be acceptable to
Jer 42: 9 to present your **p** before Him
Dan 6:13 but makes his **p** three times a

PETITIONED (*see* PETITION)
Dan 2:49 Also Daniel **p** the king, and he
Acts 25: 2 and they **p** him,
Acts 25:24 assembly of the Jews **p** me

PETITIONS (*see* PETITION)
Ps 20: 5 the LORD fulfill all your **p**
Dan 6: 7 that whoever **p** any god or man
Dan 6:12 who **p** any god or man within
1Jn 5:15 we know that we have the **p**

PEULTHAI
1Ch 26: 5 the seventh, **P** the eighth

PHANUEL
Luke 2:36 prophetess, the daughter of **P**

PHARAOH (*see* HOPHRA, NECHO, PHARAOH'S)
Gen 12:15 The princes of **P** also saw her
Gen 12:15 and commended her to **P**
Gen 12:17 But the LORD plagued **P** and his
Gen 12:18 And **P** called Abram and said,
Gen 12:20 So **P** commanded his men
Gen 37:36 to Potiphar, an officer of **P**
Gen 39: 1 And Potiphar, an officer of **P**
Gen 40: 2 And **P** was angry with his two
Gen 40:13 Now within three days **P** will
Gen 40:14 make mention of me to **P**, and
Gen 40:17 kinds of baked goods for **P**
Gen 40:19 Within three days **P** will lift
Gen 41: 1 years, that **P** had a dream
Gen 41: 4 So **P** awoke
Gen 41: 7 So **P** awoke, and indeed, it was
Gen 41: 8 **P** told them his dreams, but
Gen 41: 8 could interpret them for **P**
Gen 41: 9 the chief butler spoke to **P**
Gen 41:10 When **P** was angry with his
Gen 41:14 Then **P** sent and called Joseph,
Gen 41:14 his clothing, and came to **P**
Gen 41:15 And **P** said to Joseph,
Gen 41:16 So Joseph answered **P**, saying,
Gen 41:16 God will give **P** an answer of
Gen 41:17 Then **P** said to Joseph
Gen 41:25 Then Joseph said to **P**
Gen 41:25 The dreams of **P** are one
Gen 41:25 God has shown **P** what He is
Gen 41:28 which I have spoken to **P**
Gen 41:28 God has shown **P** what He is
Gen 41:32 the dream was repeated to **P**
Gen 41:33 let **P** select a discerning and
Gen 41:34 Let **P** do this, and let him
Gen 41:35 under the authority of **P**, and
Gen 41:37 was good in the eyes of **P**
Gen 41:38 And **P** said to his servants,
Gen 41:39 Then **P** said to Joseph
Gen 41:41 And **P** said to Joseph,
Gen 41:42 Then **P** took his signet ring
Gen 41:44 **P** also said to Joseph
Gen 41:44 I am **P**, and without your
Gen 41:45 And **P** called Joseph's name
Gen 41:46 stood before **P** king of Egypt
Gen 41:46 out from the presence of **P**
Gen 41:55 people cried to **P** for bread
Gen 41:55 Then **P** said to all the
Gen 42:15 By the life of **P**, you shall
Gen 42:16 or else, by the life of **P**
Gen 44:18 for you are even like **P**
Gen 45: 2 and the house of **P** heard it
Gen 45: 8 He has made me a father to **P**
Gen 45:16 So it pleased **P** and his
Gen 45:17 And **P** said to Joseph,
Gen 45:21 according to the command of **P**
Gen 46: 5 in the carts which **P** had sent
Gen 46:31 I will go up and tell **P**, and
Gen 46:33 when **P** calls you and says
Gen 47: 1 Then Joseph went and told **P**
Gen 47: 2 and presented them to **P**
Gen 47: 3 Then **P** said to his brothers,
Gen 47: 3 And they said to **P**, "Your
Gen 47: 4 And they said to **P**, "We have
Gen 47: 5 Then **P** spoke to Joseph,
Gen 47: 7 Jacob and set him before **P**
Gen 47: 7 and Jacob blessed **P**
Gen 47: 8 **P** said to Jacob, "How old
Gen 47: 9 And Jacob said to **P**, "The
Gen 47:10 So Jacob blessed **P**
Gen 47:10 and went out from before **P**
Gen 47:11 Rameses, as **P** had commanded
Gen 47:19 land will be servants of **P**
Gen 47:20 all the land of Egypt for **P**
Gen 47:22 rations allotted to them by **P**
Gen 47:22 rations which **P** gave them
Gen 47:23 and your land this day for **P**
Gen 47:24 you shall give one-fifth to **P**
Gen 47:26 that **P** should have one-fifth,
Gen 50: 4 to the household of **P** saying
Gen 50: 4 speak in the hearing of **P**
Gen 50: 6 And **P** said, "Go up and bury
Gen 50: 7 went up all the servants of **P**
Ex 1:11 built for **P** supply cities
Ex 1:19 And the midwives said to **P**
Ex 1:22 So **P** commanded all his people
Ex 2: 5 Then the daughter of **P** came
Ex 2:15 When **P** heard of this matter,
Ex 2:15 Moses fled from the face of **P**
Ex 3:10 I will send you to **P** that you
Ex 3:11 am I that I should go to **P**
Ex 4:21 **P** which I have put in your
Ex 4:22 Then you shall say to **P**
Ex 5: 1 and Aaron went in and told **P**
Ex 5: 2 **P** said, "Who is the LORD,
Ex 5: 5 And **P** said, "Look, the people
Ex 5: 6 So the same day **P** commanded
Ex 5:10 Thus says **P**: "I will
Ex 5:15 Israel came and cried out to **P**
Ex 5:20 Then, as they came out from **P**
Ex 5:21 abhorrent in the sight of **P**
Ex 5:23 For since I came to **P** to
Ex 6: 1 shall see what I will do to **P**
Ex 6:11 speak to **P** king of Egypt,
Ex 6:12 How then shall **P** heed me, for
Ex 6:13 for **P** king of Egypt, to bring
Ex 6:27 who spoke to **P** king of Egypt
Ex 6:29 Speak to **P** king of Egypt all
Ex 6:30 lips, and how shall **P** heed me
Ex 7: 1 I have made you as God to **P**
Ex 7: 2 your brother shall speak to **P**
Ex 7: 4 But **P** will not heed you, so
Ex 7: 7 old when they spoke to **P**
Ex 7: 9 When **P** speaks to you, saying,
Ex 7: 9 your rod and cast it before **P**
Ex 7:10 Moses and Aaron went in to **P**
Ex 7:10 cast down his rod before **P**
Ex 7:11 But **P** also called the wise
Ex 7:15 Go to **P** in the morning, when
Ex 7:20 the river, in the sight of **P**
Ex 7:23 **P** turned and went into his
Ex 8: 1 Go to **P** and say to him, "Thus
Ex 8: 8 Then **P** called for Moses and
Ex 8: 9 And Moses said to **P**, "Accept
Ex 8:12 and Aaron went out from **P**
Ex 8:12 He had brought against **P**
Ex 8:15 But when **P** saw that there was
Ex 8:19 Then the magicians said to **P**
Ex 8:20 stand before **P** as he comes
Ex 8:24 came into the house of **P**,
Ex 8:25 Then **P** called for Moses and
Ex 8:28 **P** said, "I will let you go,
Ex 8:29 may depart tomorrow from **P**
Ex 8:29 But let **P** not deal
Ex 8:30 So Moses went out from **P** and
Ex 8:31 the swarms of flies from **P**
Ex 8:32 But **P** hardened his heart at
Ex 9: 1 Go in to **P** and tell him, 'Thus
Ex 9: 7 Then **P** sent, and indeed, not
Ex 9: 7 the heart of **P** became hard
Ex 9: 8 the heavens in the sight of **P**
Ex 9:10 the furnace and stood before **P**
Ex 9:12 LORD hardened the heart of **P**
Ex 9:13 the morning and stand before **P**
Ex 9:20 of **P** made his servants and his
Ex 9:27 **P** sent and called for Moses and
Ex 9:33 went out of the city from **P**
Ex 9:34 when **P** saw that the rain, the
Ex 9:35 So the heart of **P** was hard
Ex 10: 1 Go in to **P**; for I have
Ex 10: 3 Moses and Aaron came in to **P**
Ex 10: 6 he turned and went out from **P**
Ex 10: 8 Aaron were brought again to **P**
Ex 10:16 Then **P** called for Moses and
Ex 10:18 So he went out from **P** and
Ex 10:24 Then **P** called to Moses and
Ex 10:28 Then **P** said to him, "Get
Ex 11: 1 yet one more plague on **P** and
Ex 11: 5 from the firstborn of **P** who
Ex 11: 8 out from **P** in great anger
Ex 11: 9 **P** will not heed you, so that
Ex 11:10 all these wonders before **P**
Ex 12:29 from the firstborn of **P** who
Ex 12:30 So **P** rose in the night, he,
Ex 13:15 when **P** was stubborn about
Ex 13:17 when **P** had let the people go,
Ex 14: 3 For **P** will say of the
Ex 14: 4 and I will gain honor over **P**
Ex 14: 5 had fled, and the heart of **P**
Ex 14: 8 the heart of **P** king of Egypt
Ex 14: 9 the horses and chariots of **P**
Ex 14:10 And when **P** drew near, the
Ex 14:17 So I will gain honor over **P**
Ex 14:18 honor for Myself over **P**, his
Ex 14:28 all the army of **P** that came
Ex 15:19 For the horses of **P** went with
Ex 18: 4 me from the sword of **P**")
Ex 18: 8 that the LORD had done to **P**
Ex 18:10 and out of the hand of **P**, and
Deut 6:21 We were slaves of **P** in Egypt
Deut 6:22 and severe, against Egypt, **P**
Deut 7: 8 the hand of **P** king of Egypt
Deut 7:18 the LORD your God did to **P**
Deut 11: 3 to **P** king of Egypt, and to all
Deut 29: 2 in the land of Egypt, to **P**
Deut 34:11 the land of Egypt, before **P**
1Sa 6: 6 and **P** hardened their hearts
1Ki 3: 1 a treaty with **P** king of Egypt
1Ki 9:16 (**P** king of Egypt had gone up
1Ki 11: 1 as well as the daughter of **P**
1Ki 11:19 to **P** king of Egypt, who gave
1Ki 11:19 great favor in the sight of **P**
1Ki 11:20 household among the sons of **P**
1Ki 11:21 was dead, Hadad said to **P**
1Ki 11:22 Then **P** said to him, "But
2Ki 17: 7 the hand of **P** king of Egypt
2Ki 18:21 So is **P** king of Egypt to all
2Ki 23:29 In his days **P** Necho king of
2Ki 23:29 **P** Necho killed him at Megiddo
2Ki 23:33 Now **P** Necho put him in prison
2Ki 23:34 Then **P** Necho made Eliakim the
2Ki 23:34 **P** took Jehoahaz and went to
2Ki 23:35 gave the silver and gold to **P**
2Ki 23:35 to the commandment of **P**
2Ki 23:35 to give it to **P** Necho
1Ch 4:18 of Bithiah the daughter of **P**
2Ch 8:11 brought the daughter of **P** up
Neh 9:10 signs and wonders against **P**
Ps 135: 9 midst of you, O Egypt, Upon **P**
Ps 136:15 But overthrew **P** and his army
Is 19:11 How do you say to **P**, "I am
Is 30: 2 in the strength of **P**, and to
Is 30: 3 of **P** shall be your shame, and
Is 36: 6 So is **P** king of Egypt to all
Jer 25:19 **P** king of Egypt, his servants

Jer 44:30 I will give **P** Hophra king of
Jer 46: 2 the army of **P** Necho, king of
Jer 46:17 They cried there, '**P**, king of
Jer 46:25 on Amon of No, and **P** and
Jer 46:25 **P** and those who trust in him
Jer 47: 1 before **P** attacked Gaza
Ezek 17:17 Nor will **P** with his mighty
Ezek 29: 2 face against **P** king of Egypt
Ezek 29: 3 O **P** king of Egypt, O great
Ezek 30:21 the arm of **P** king of Egypt
Ezek 30:22 I am against **P** king of Egypt
Ezek 30:25 the arms of **P** shall fall down
Ezek 31: 2 say to **P** king of Egypt and to
Ezek 31:18 This is **P** and all his
Ezek 32: 2 for **P** king of Egypt, and say
Ezek 32:31 **P** will see them and be
Ezek 32:31 over all his multitude, **P**
Ezek 32:32 those slain by the sword, **P**
Acts 7:10 wisdom in the presence of **P**
Acts 7:13 family became known to the **P**
Rom 9:17 For the Scripture says to **P**

PHARAOH'S (*see* PHARAOH)
Gen 12:15 woman was taken to **P** house
Gen 40: 7 So he asked **P** officers who
Gen 40:11 Then **P** cup was in my hand
Gen 40:11 and pressed them into **P** cup
Gen 40:11 and placed the cup in **P** hand
Gen 40:13 you will put **P** cup in his
Gen 40:20 day, which was **P** birthday
Gen 40:21 he placed the cup in **P** hand
Gen 45:16 of it was heard in **P** house
Gen 47:14 the money into **P** house
Gen 47:20 So the land became **P**
Gen 47:25 and we will be **P** servants
Gen 47:26 only, which did not become **P**
Ex 2: 7 his sister said to **P** daughter
Ex 2: 8 And **P** daughter said to her,
Ex 2: 9 Then **P** daughter said to her,
Ex 2:10 she brought him to **P** daughter
Ex 5:14 whom **P** taskmasters had set
Ex 7: 3 And I will harden **P** heart, and
Ex 7:13 **P** heart grew hard, and he did
Ex 7:14 **P** heart is hard
Ex 7:22 **P** heart grew hard, and he did
Ex 8:19 But **P** heart grew hard, and
Ex 10: 7 Then **P** servants said to him,
Ex 10:11 driven out from **P** presence
Ex 10:20 But the LORD hardened **P** heart
Ex 10:27 But the LORD hardened **P** heart
Ex 11: 3 in the sight of **P** servants
Ex 11:10 and the LORD hardened **P** heart
Ex 14: 4 Then I will harden **P** heart
Ex 14:23 all **P** horses, his chariots,
Ex 15: 4 **P** chariots and his army He has
1Sa 2:27 they were in Egypt in **P** house
1Ki 3: 1 Egypt, and married **P** daughter
1Ki 7: 8 like this hall for **P** daughter
1Ki 9:24 But **P** daughter came up from
1Ki 11:20 Tahpenes weaned in **P** house
1Ki 11:20 Genubath was in **P** household
Song 1: 9 to my filly among **P** chariots
Is 19:11 **P** wise counselors give
Jer 37: 5 Then **P** army came up from
Jer 37: 7 **P** army which has come up to
Jer 37:11 Jerusalem for fear of **P** army
Jer 43: 9 to **P** house in Tahpanhes
Ezek 30:24 but I will break **P** arms, and
Acts 7:21 **P** daughter took him away and
Heb 11:24 called the son of **P** daughter

PHARISEE (*see* PHARISEE'S, PHARISEES)
Matt 23:26 Blind **P**, first cleanse the
Luke 7:39 Now when the **P** who had
Luke 11:37 a certain **P** asked Him to dine
Luke 11:38 And when the **P** saw it, he
Luke 18:10 the temple to pray, one a **P**
Luke 18:11 The **P** stood and prayed thus
Acts 5:34 a **P** named Gamaliel, a teacher
Acts 23: 6 I am a **P**, the son of a **P**;
Acts 26: 5 of our religion I lived a **P**
Phil 3: 5 concerning the law, a **P**

PHARISEE'S (*see* PHARISEE)
Luke 7:36 And He went to the **P** house
Luke 7:37 at the table in the **P** house

PHARISEES (*see* PHARISEE)
Matt 3: 7 But when he saw many of the **P**
Matt 5:20 of the scribes and **P**, you will
Matt 9:11 And when the **P** saw it, they
Matt 9:14 the **P** fast often, but Your
Matt 9:34 But the **P** said, "He casts
Matt 12: 2 But when the **P** saw it, they
Matt 12:14 Then the **P** went out and took
Matt 12:24 But when the **P** heard it they
Matt 12:38 and **P** answered, saying,
Matt 15: 1 **P** who were from Jerusalem
Matt 15:12 Do You know that the **P** were
Matt 16: 1 Then the **P** and Sadducees
Matt 16: 6 beware of the leaven of the **P**
Matt 16:11 beware of the leaven of the **P**
Matt 16:12 but of the doctrine of the **P**
Matt 19: 3 The **P** also came to Him,
Matt 21:45 **P** heard His parables, they
Matt 22:15 Then the **P** went and plotted
Matt 22:34 But when the **P** heard that He
Matt 22:41 While the **P** were gathered
Matt 23: 2 and the **P** sit in Moses' seat
Matt 23:13 But woe to you, scribes and **P**
Matt 23:14 Woe to you, scribes and **P**,
Matt 23:15 Woe to you, scribes and **P**,
Matt 23:23 Woe to you, scribes and **P**,
Matt 23:25 Woe to you, scribes and **P**,
Matt 23:27 Woe to you, scribes and **P**,
Matt 23:29 Woe to you, scribes and **P**,
Matt 27:62 **P** gathered together to Pilate
Mark 2:16 **P** saw Him eating with the tax
Mark 2:18 John and of the **P** were fasting
Mark 2:18 of John and of the **P** fast, but
Mark 2:24 And the **P** said to Him,
Mark 3: 6 Then the **P** went out and
Mark 7: 1 Then the **P** and some of the
Mark 7: 3 For the **P** and all the Jews do
Mark 7: 5 Then the **P** and scribes asked
Mark 8:11 the **P** came out and began to
Mark 8:15 beware of the leaven of the **P**
Mark 10: 2 The **P** came and asked Him, "Is
Mark 12:13 sent to Him some of the **P**
Luke 5:17 teaching, that there were **P**
Luke 5:21 the **P** began to reason, saying
Luke 5:30 the **P** murmured against His
Luke 5:33 and likewise those of the **P**
Luke 6: 2 some of the **P** said to them,
Luke 6: 7 and **P** watched Him closely,
Luke 7:30 But the **P** and lawyers rejected
Luke 7:36 Then one of the **P** asked Him
Luke 11:39 Now you **P** make the outside of
Luke 11:42 But woe to you **P**
Luke 11:43 Woe to you **P**! For you love
Luke 11:44 Woe to you, scribes and **P**,
Luke 11:53 the **P** began to assail Him
Luke 12: 1 Beware of the leaven of the **P**
Luke 13:31 On that very day some **P** came
Luke 14: 1 **P** to eat bread on the Sabbath
Luke 14: 3 spoke to the lawyers and **P**
Luke 15: 2 And the **P** and scribes
Luke 16:14 Now the **P**, who were lovers of
Luke 17:20 the **P** when the kingdom of God
Luke 19:39 some of the **P** called to Him
John 1:24 who were sent were from the **P**
John 3: 1 man of the **P** named Nicodemus
John 4: 1 **P** had heard that Jesus made
John 7:32 The **P** heard the crowd
John 7:32 concerning Him, and the **P** and
John 7:45 to the chief priests and **P**
John 7:47 Then the **P** answered them,
John 7:48 or the **P** believed in Him
John 8: 3 and **P** brought to Him a woman
John 8:13 The **P** therefore said to Him,
John 9:13 formerly was blind to the **P**
John 9:15 Then the **P** also asked him
John 9:16 Therefore some of the **P** said
John 9:40 Then some of the **P** who were
John 11:46 of them went away to the **P**
John 11:47 the **P** gathered a council and
John 11:57 the **P** had given a command,
John 12:19 The **P** therefore said among
John 12:42 but because of the **P** they did
John 18: 3 from the chief priests and **P**
Acts 15: 5 of the **P** who believed rose up
Acts 23: 6 were Sadducees and the other **P**
Acts 23: 7 arose between the **P** and the
Acts 23: 8 but the **P** confess both

PHARISEES'
Acts 23: 9 who were of the **P** party arose

PHARPAR
2Ki 5:12 Are not the Abanah and the **P**

PHICHOL
Gen 21:22 that time that Abimelech and **P**
Gen 21:32 So Abimelech rose with **P**, the
Gen 26:26 **P** the commander of his army

PHILADELPHIA
Rev 1:11 to Thyatira, to Sardis, to **P**
Rev 3: 7 of the church in **P** write

PHILEMON
Phm 1 To **P** our beloved friend and

PHILETUS
2Ti 2:17 and **P** are of this sort,

PHILIP (*see* PHILIP'S)
Matt 10: 3 **P** and Bartholomew
Mark 3:18 Andrew, **P**, Bartholomew,
Luke 3: 1 his brother **P** tetrarch of
Luke 6:14 **P** and Bartholomew
John 1:43 go to Galilee, and He found **P**
John 1:44 Now **P** was from Bethsaida, the
John 1:45 **P** found Nathanael and said to
John 1:46 **P** said to him, "Come and
John 1:48 Before **P** called you, when you
John 6: 5 toward Him, He said to **P**
John 6: 7 **P** answered Him, "Two hundred
John 12:21 Then they came to **P**, who was
John 12:22 **P** came and told Andrew, and in
John 12:22 turn Andrew and **P** told Jesus
John 14: 8 **P** said to Him, "Lord, show
John 14: 9 yet you have not known Me, **P**
Acts 1:13 **P** and Thomas
Acts 6: 5 and the Holy Spirit, and **P**,
Acts 8: 5 Then **P** went down to the city
Acts 8: 6 heeded the things spoken by **P**
Acts 8:12 But when they believed **P** as
Acts 8:13 baptized he continued with **P**
Acts 8:26 angel of the Lord spoke to **P**
Acts 8:29 Then the Spirit said to **P**
Acts 8:30 So **P** ran to him, and heard him
Acts 8:31 he asked **P** to come up and sit
Acts 8:34 So the eunuch answered **P** and
Acts 8:35 Then **P** opened his mouth, and
Acts 8:37 Then **P** said, "If you believe
Acts 8:38 And both **P** and the eunuch went
Acts 8:39 of the Lord caught **P** away
Acts 8:40 But **P** was found at Azotus
Acts 21: 8 the house of **P** the evangelist

PHILIPPI (*see* PHILIPPIANS)
Acts 16:12 and from there to **P**, which is
Acts 20: 6 away from **P** after the Days of
Phil 1: 1 in Christ Jesus who are in **P**
1Th 2: 2 were spitefully treated at **P**

PHILIPPIANS (*see* PHILIPPI)
Phil 4:15 Now you **P** know also that in

PHILIP'S (*see* PHILIP)
Matt 14: 3 Herodias, his brother **P** wife
Mark 6:17 Herodias, his brother **P** wife
Luke 3:19 Herodias, his brother **P** wife

PHILISTIA (*see* PALESTINA, PHILISTINE)
Ps 60: 8 **P**, shout in triumph because
Ps 83: 7 **P** with the inhabitants of
Ps 87: 4 Behold, O **P** and Tyre, with
Ps 108: 9 Over **P** I will triumph
Is 14:29 Do not rejoice, all you of **P**
Is 14:31 All you of **P** are dissolved
Joel 3: 4 Sidon, and all the coasts of **P**

PHILISTINE (*see* PHILISTIA, PHILISTINES)
1Sa 10: 5 God where the **P** garrison is
1Sa 17: 8 Am I not a **P**, and you the
1Sa 17:10 And the **P** said,
1Sa 17:11 heard these words of the **P**
1Sa 17:16 the **P** drew near and presented
1Sa 17:23 the **P** of Gath, Goliath by
1Sa 17:26 for the man who kills this **P**
1Sa 17:26 who is this uncircumcised **P**
1Sa 17:32 will go and fight with this **P**
1Sa 17:33 this **P** to fight with him
1Sa 17:36 this uncircumcised **P** will be
1Sa 17:37 me from the hand of this **P**
1Sa 17:40 And he drew near to the **P**
1Sa 17:41 So the **P** came, and began
1Sa 17:42 when the **P** looked about and
1Sa 17:43 So the **P** said to David, "Am
1Sa 17:43 the **P** cursed David by his
1Sa 17:44 And the **P** said to David,
1Sa 17:45 Then David said to the **P**
1Sa 17:48 it was so, when the **P** arose
1Sa 17:48 toward the army to meet the **P**

1Sa 17:49 struck the **P** in his forehead,
1Sa 17:50 over the **P** with a sling and a
1Sa 17:50 stone, and struck the **P**
1Sa 17:51 David ran and stood over the **P**
1Sa 17:54 David took the head of the **P**
1Sa 17:55 David going out against the **P**
1Sa 17:57 from the slaughter of the **P**
1Sa 17:57 the head of the **P** in his hand
1Sa 18: 6 from the slaughter of the **P**
1Sa 19: 5 in his hands and killed the **P**
1Sa 21: 9 The sword of Goliath the **P**
1Sa 22:10 the sword of Goliath the **P**
2Sa 21:17 to his aid, and struck the **P**
Obad 19 inhabitants of the **P** lowland

PHILISTINES (*see* PHILISTINE)
Gen 10:14 (from whom came the **P** and
Gen 21:32 returned to the land of the **P**
Gen 21:34 the land of the **P** many days
Gen 26: 1 to Abimelech king of the **P**
Gen 26: 8 the **P** looked through a window
Gen 26:14 So the **P** envied him
Gen 26:15 Now the **P** had stopped up all
Gen 26:18 for the **P** had stopped them up
Ex 13:17 by way of the land of the **P**
Ex 23:31 Red Sea to the Sea of the **P**
Josh 13: 2 all the territory of the **P**
Josh 13: 3 the five lords of the **P**
Judg 3: 3 namely, five lords of the **P**
Judg 3:31 men of the **P** with an ox goad
Judg 10: 6 Ammon, and the gods of the **P**
Judg 10: 7 them into the hands of the **P**
Judg 10:11 of Ammon and from the **P**
Judg 13: 1 hand of the **P** for forty years
Judg 13: 5 out of the hand of the **P**
Judg 14: 1 of the daughters of the **P**
Judg 14: 2 of the daughters of the **P**
Judg 14: 3 wife from the uncircumcised **P**
Judg 14: 4 to move against the **P**
Judg 14: 4 For at that time the **P** had
Judg 15: 3 the **P** if I harm them
Judg 15: 5 the standing grain of the **P**
Judg 15: 6 Then the **P** said, "Who has
Judg 15: 6 So the **P** came up and burned
Judg 15: 9 Now the **P** went up, encamped
Judg 15:11 know that the **P** rule over us
Judg 15:12 you into the hand of the **P**
Judg 15:14 the **P** came shouting against
Judg 15:20 years in the days of the **P**
Judg 16: 5 lords of the **P** came up to her
Judg 16: 8 So the lords of the **P** brought
Judg 16: 9 The **P** are upon you, Samson
Judg 16:12 The **P** are upon you, Samson
Judg 16:14 The **P** are upon you, Samson
Judg 16:18 called for the lords of the **P**
Judg 16:18 lords of the **P** came up to her
Judg 16:20 The **P** are upon you, Samson
Judg 16:21 Then the **P** took him and put
Judg 16:23 Now the lords of the **P**
Judg 16:27 the lords of the **P** were there
Judg 16:28 on the **P** for my two eyes
Judg 16:30 Let me die with the **P**
1Sa 4: 1 out to battle against the **P**
1Sa 4: 1 and the **P** encamped in Aphek
1Sa 4: 2 Then the **P** put themselves in
1Sa 4: 2 Israel was defeated by the **P**
1Sa 4: 3 us today before the **P**
1Sa 4: 6 Now when the **P** heard the
1Sa 4: 7 So the **P** were afraid, for
1Sa 4: 9 yourselves like men, you **P**
1Sa 4:10 So the **P** fought, and Israel
1Sa 4:17 Israel has fled before the **P**
1Sa 5: 1 Then the **P** took the ark of
1Sa 5: 2 When the **P** took the ark of
1Sa 5: 8 all the lords of the **P**, and
1Sa 5:11 all the lords of the **P**, and
1Sa 6: 1 country of the **P** seven months
1Sa 6: 2 the **P** called for the priests
1Sa 6: 4 number of the lords of the **P**
1Sa 6:12 the lords of the **P** went after
1Sa 6:16 lords of the **P** had seen it
1Sa 6:17 the **P** returned as a trespass
1Sa 6:18 of all the cities of the **P**
1Sa 6:21 The **P** have brought back the
1Sa 7: 3 you from the hand of the **P**
1Sa 7: 7 Now when the **P** heard that the
1Sa 7: 7 the lords of the **P** went up
1Sa 7: 7 it, they were afraid of the **P**
1Sa 7: 8 us from the hand of the **P**
1Sa 7:10 the **P** drew near to battle
1Sa 7:10 thunder upon the **P** that day
1Sa 7:11 of Mizpah and pursued the **P**
1Sa 7:13 So the **P** were subdued, and
1Sa 7:13 the **P** all the days of Samuel
1Sa 7:14 Then the cities which the **P**
1Sa 7:14 from the hands of the **P**
1Sa 9:16 people from the hand of the **P**
1Sa 12: 9 Hazor, into the hand of the **P**
1Sa 13: 3 of the **P** that was in Geba
1Sa 13: 3 and the **P** heard of it
1Sa 13: 4 attacked a garrison of the **P**
1Sa 13: 4 an abomination to the **P**
1Sa 13: 5 Then the **P** gathered together
1Sa 13:11 that the **P** gathered together
1Sa 13:12 The **P** will now come down on
1Sa 13:16 But the **P** encamped in
1Sa 13:17 of the **P** in three companies
1Sa 13:19 of Israel, for the **P** said
1Sa 13:20 would go down to the **P** to
1Sa 13:23 the garrison of the **P** went
1Sa 14: 1 let us go over to the **P**'
1Sa 14: 4 to go over to the **P**' garrison
1Sa 14:11 to the garrison of the **P**
1Sa 14:11 And the **P** said,
1Sa 14:19 the **P** continued to increase
1Sa 14:21 with the **P** before that time
1Sa 14:22 they heard that the **P** fled
1Sa 14:30 greater slaughter among the **P**
1Sa 14:31 they had driven back the **P**
1Sa 14:36 go down after the **P** by night
1Sa 14:37 Shall I go down after the **P**
1Sa 14:46 returned from pursuing the **P**
1Sa 14:46 the **P** went to their own place
1Sa 14:47 of Zobah, and against the **P**
1Sa 14:52 the **P** all the days of Saul
1Sa 17: 1 Now the **P** gathered their
1Sa 17: 2 in battle array against the **P**
1Sa 17: 3 The **P** stood on a mountain on
1Sa 17: 4 out from the camp of the **P**
1Sa 17:19 of Elah, fighting with the **P**
1Sa 17:21 the **P** had drawn up in battle
1Sa 17:23 up from the armies of the **P**
1Sa 17:46 of the camp of the **P** to the
1Sa 17:51 when the **P** saw that their
1Sa 17:52 pursued the **P** as far as the
1Sa 17:52 the wounded of the **P** fell
1Sa 17:53 returned from chasing the **P**
1Sa 18:17 hand of the **P** be against him
1Sa 18:21 of the **P** may be against him
1Sa 18:25 hundred foreskins of the **P**
1Sa 18:25 fall by the hand of the **P**
1Sa 18:27 two hundred men of the **P**
1Sa 18:30 of the **P** went out to war
1Sa 19: 8 went out and fought with the **P**
1Sa 23: 1 the **P** are fighting against
1Sa 23: 2 Shall I go and attack these **P**
1Sa 23: 2 Go and attack the **P**, and save
1Sa 23: 3 against the armies of the **P**
1Sa 23: 4 deliver the **P** into your hand
1Sa 23: 5 Keilah and fought with the **P**
1Sa 23:27 for the **P** have invaded the
1Sa 23:28 David, and went against the **P**
1Sa 24: 1 returned from following the **P**
1Sa 27: 1 escape to the land of the **P**
1Sa 27: 7 of the **P** was one full year
1Sa 27:11 dwelt in the country of the **P**
1Sa 28: 1 the **P** gathered their armies
1Sa 28: 4 Then the **P** gathered together,
1Sa 28: 5 Saul saw the army of the **P**
1Sa 28:15 for the **P** make war against me
1Sa 28:19 you into the hand of the **P**
1Sa 28:19 Israel into the hand of the **P**
1Sa 29: 1 Then the **P** gathered together
1Sa 29: 2 the lords of the **P** passed in
1Sa 29: 3 the princes of the **P** said
1Sa 29: 3 said to the princes of the **P**
1Sa 29: 4 of the **P** were angry with him
1Sa 29: 4 princes of the **P** said to him
1Sa 29: 7 displease the lords of the **P**
1Sa 29: 9 princes of the **P** have said
1Sa 29:11 return to the land of the **P**
1Sa 29:11 And the **P** went up to Jezreel
1Sa 30:16 taken from the land of the **P**
1Sa 31: 1 So the **P** fought against
1Sa 31: 1 Israel fled from before the **P**
1Sa 31: 2 Then the **P** followed hard
1Sa 31: 2 And the **P** killed Jonathan,
1Sa 31: 7 the **P** came and dwelt in them
1Sa 31: 8 when the **P** came to strip the
1Sa 31: 9 throughout the land of the **P**
1Sa 31:11 what the **P** had done to Saul
2Sa 1:20 daughters of the **P** rejoice
2Sa 3:14 a hundred foreskins of the **P**
2Sa 3:18 Israel from the hand of the **P**
2Sa 5:17 Now when the **P** heard that
2Sa 5:17 all the **P** went up to search
2Sa 5:18 The **P** also went and deployed
2Sa 5:19 Shall I go up against the **P**
2Sa 5:19 deliver the **P** into your hand
2Sa 5:22 Then the **P** went up once again
2Sa 5:24 to strike the camp of the **P**
2Sa 5:25 he drove back the **P** from Geba
2Sa 8: 1 that David attacked the **P**
2Sa 8: 1 Ammah from the hand of the **P**
2Sa 8:12 people of Ammon, from the **P**
2Sa 19: 9 us from the hand of the **P**
2Sa 21:12 where the **P** had hung them up,
2Sa 21:12 after the **P** had struck down
2Sa 21:15 When the **P** were at war again
2Sa 21:15 down and fought against the **P**
2Sa 21:18 a battle with the **P** at Gob
2Sa 21:19 a battle in Gob with the **P**
2Sa 23: 9 David when they defied the **P**
2Sa 23:10 attacked the **P** until his hand
2Sa 23:11 The **P** had gathered together
2Sa 23:11 the people fled from the **P**
2Sa 23:12 defended it, and killed the **P**
2Sa 23:13 the troop of **P** encamped in
2Sa 23:14 the garrison of the **P** was
2Sa 23:16 through the camp of the **P**
1Ki 4:21 River to the land of the **P**
1Ki 15:27 which belonged to the **P**,
1Ki 16:15 which belonged to the **P**
2Ki 8: 2 the land of the **P** seven years
2Ki 8: 3 from the land of the **P**
2Ki 18: 8 He subdued the **P**, as far as
1Ch 1:12 (from whom came the **P** and the
1Ch 10: 1 Now the **P** fought against
1Ch 10: 1 Israel fled from before the **P**
1Ch 10: 2 Then the **P** followed hard
1Ch 10: 2 And the **P** killed Jonathan,
1Ch 10: 7 then the **P** came and dwelt in
1Ch 10: 8 when the **P** came to strip the
1Ch 10: 9 throughout the land of the **P**
1Ch 10:11 that the **P** had done to Saul
1Ch 11:13 Now there the **P** were gathered
1Ch 11:13 And the people fled from the **P**
1Ch 11:14 defended it, and killed the **P**
1Ch 11:15 the army of the **P** encamped in
1Ch 11:16 the garrison of the **P** was
1Ch 11:18 through the camp of the **P**
1Ch 12:19 the **P** to battle against Saul
1Ch 12:19 for the lords of the **P** sent
1Ch 14: 8 Now when the **P** heard that
1Ch 14: 8 all the **P** went up to search
1Ch 14: 9 Then the **P** went and made a
1Ch 14:10 Shall I go up against the **P**
1Ch 14:13 Then the **P** once again made a
1Ch 14:15 to strike the camp of the **P**
1Ch 14:16 drove back the army of the **P**
1Ch 18: 1 that David attacked the **P**
1Ch 18: 1 towns from the hand of the **P**
1Ch 18:11 people of Ammon, from the **P**
1Ch 20: 4 broke out at Gezer with the **P**
1Ch 20: 5 there was war with the **P**, and
2Ch 9:26 River to the land of the **P**
2Ch 17:11 Also some of the **P** brought
2Ch 21:16 Jehoram the spirit of the **P**
2Ch 26: 6 out and made war against the **P**
2Ch 26: 6 Ashdod and among the **P**
2Ch 26: 7 God helped him against the **P**
2Ch 28:18 The **P** also had invaded the
Is 2: 6 are soothsayers like the **P**
Is 9:12 before and the **P** behind
Is 11:14 of the **P** toward the west
Jer 25:20 of the land of the **P** (namely
Jer 47: 1 the prophet against the **P**
Jer 47: 4 comes to plunder all the **P**
Jer 47: 4 the LORD shall plunder the **P**
Ezek 16:27 you, the daughters of the **P**
Ezek 16:57 and of the daughters of the **P**
Ezek 25:15 Because the **P** dealt
Ezek 25:16 out My hand against the **P**
Amos 1: 8 remnant of the **P** shall perish
Amos 6: 2 Then go down to Gath of the **P**
Amos 9: 7 the **P** from Caphtor, and the
Zeph 2: 5 you, O Canaan, land of the **P**
Zech 9: 6 cut off the pride of the **P**

PHILOLOGUS
Rom 16:15 Greet **P** and Julia, Nereus and

PHILOSOPHERS (*see* PHILOSOPHY)
Acts 17:18 and Stoic **p** encountered him

PHILOSOPHY (*see* PHILOSOPHERS)
Col 2: 8 anyone cheat you through **p**

PHINEHAS
Ex 6:25 and she bore him **P**
Num 25: 7 Now when **P** the son of Eleazar
Num 25:11 **P** the son of Eleazar, the son
Num 31: 6 with **P** the son of Eleazar the
Josh 22:13 sent **P** the son of Eleazar the
Josh 22:30 And when **P** the priest and the
Josh 22:31 Then **P** the son of Eleazar the
Josh 22:32 And **P** the son of Eleazar the
Josh 24:33 that belonged to **P** his son
Judg 20:28 **P** the son of Eleazar, the son
1Sa 1: 3 two sons of Eli, Hophni and **P**
1Sa 2:34 your two sons, on Hophni and **P**
1Sa 4: 4 two sons of Eli, Hophni and **P**
1Sa 4:11 two sons of Eli, Hophni and **P**
1Sa 4:17 your two sons, Hophni and **P**
1Sa 4:19 **P'** wife, was with child, due
1Sa 14: 3 brother, the son of **P**, the
1Ch 6: 4 Eleazar begot **P**, and **P**
1Ch 6: 4 **P**, and **P** begot Abishua
1Ch 6:50 **P** his son, Abishua his son,
1Ch 9:20 **P** the son of Eleazar had been
Ezra 7: 5 son of Abishua, the son of **P**
Ezra 8: 2 of the sons of **P**, Gershom
Ezra 8:33 him was Eleazar the son of **P**
Ps 106:30 Then **P** stood up and intervened

PHLEGON
Rom 16:14 Greet Asyncritus, **P**, Hermas,

PHOEBE
Rom 16: 1 I commend to you **P** our sister

PHOENICIA
Acts 11:19 Stephen traveled as far as **P**
Acts 15: 3 church, they passed through **P**
Acts 21: 2 a ship sailing over to **P**, we

PHOENIX
Acts 27:12 any means they could reach **P**

PHRYGIA
Acts 2:10 **P** and Pamphylia, Egypt and the
Acts 16: 6 when they had gone through **P**
Acts 18:23 **P** in order, strengthening all

PHYGELLUS
2Ti 1:15 from me, among whom are **P**

PHYLACTERIES
Matt 23: 5 They make their **p** broad and

PHYSICAL (*see* PHYSICALLY)
Gal 4:13 of **p** infirmity I preached the

PHYSICALLY (*see* PHYSICAL)
Rom 2:27 will not the **p** uncircumcised,

PHYSICIAN (*see* PHYSICIANS)
Jer 8:22 Gilead, is there no **p** there
Matt 9:12 are well have no need of a **p**
Mark 2:17 are well have no need of a **p**
Luke 4:23 say this proverb to Me, '**P**
Luke 5:31 who are well do not need a **p**
Col 4:14 Luke the beloved **p** and Demas

PHYSICIANS (*see* PHYSICIAN)
Gen 50: 2 the **p** to embalm his father
Gen 50: 2 So the **p** embalmed Israel
2Ch 16:12 not seek the LORD, but the **p**
Job 13: 4 lies, you are all worthless **p**
Mark 5:26 many things from many **p**
Luke 8:43 spent all her livelihood on **p**

PI BESETH
Ezek 30:17 **P** shall fall by the sword, and

PICK (*see* PICKED, PICKS)
Ex 12:21 **P** out and take lambs for
Num 16:37 to **p** up the censers out of
Josh 18: 4 **P** out from among you three
2Ki 4:36 him, he said, "**P** up your son
2Ki 6: 7 said, "**P** it up for yourself
2Ki 9:25 **P** him up, and throw him into
Prov 30:17 of the valley will **p** it out
Jon 1:12 **P** me up and throw me into the

PICKED (*see* PICK)
2Ki 4:37 then she **p** up her son and went
Ezek 29: 5 shall not be **p** up or gathered
Jon 1:15 So they **p** up Jonah and threw

PICKS (*see* PICK)
2Sa 12:31 to work with saws and iron **p**
1Ch 20: 3 work with saws, with iron **p**
Amos 6:10 **p** up the bodies to take them

PICTURE
Mark 4:30 what parable shall we **p** it

PIECE (*see* PIECES)
Gen 15:10 placed each **p** opposite the
Ex 25:19 of one **p** with the mercy seat
Ex 25:31 and flowers shall be of one **p**
Ex 25:36 branches shall be of one **p**
Ex 25:36 one hammered **p** of pure gold
Ex 27: 2 shall be of one **p** with it
Ex 30: 2 shall be of one **p** with it
Ex 37: 7 he made them of one **p** at the
Ex 37: 8 of one **p** with the mercy seat
Ex 37:17 flowers were of the same **p**
Ex 37:22 their branches were of one **p**
Ex 37:22 one hammered **p** of pure gold
Ex 37:25 horns were of one **p** with it
Ex 38: 2 horns were of one **p** with it
Ruth 2:14 dip your **p** of bread in the
Ruth 4: 3 sold the **p** of land which
1Sa 2:36 down to him for a **p** of silver
1Sa 2:36 that I may eat a **p** of bread
1Sa 28:22 and let me set a **p** of bread
1Sa 30:12 they gave him a **p** of a cake
2Sa 6:19 a **p** of meat, and a cake of
2Sa 11:21 it not a woman who cast a **p**
2Sa 23:11 a **p** of ground full of lentils
2Ki 3:19 ruin every good **p** of land
2Ki 3:25 stone on every good **p** of land
1Ch 11:13 there was a **p** of ground full
1Ch 16: 3 a **p** of meat, and a cake of
Job 42:11 one gave him a **p** of silver
Prov 28:21 because for a **p** of bread a
Song 4: 3 are like a **p** of pomegranate
Song 6: 7 Like a **p** of pomegranate are
Jer 37:21 should give him daily a **p** of
Ezek 24: 4 of meat in it, every good **p**
Ezek 24: 6 Bring it out **p** by **p**, on
Amos 3:12 two legs or a **p** of an ear
Matt 9:16 No one puts a **p** of unshrunk
Matt 17:27 you will find a **p** of money
Mark 2:21 No one sews a **p** of unshrunk
Mark 2:21 or else the new **p** pulls away
Luke 5:36 No one puts a **p** from a new
Luke 5:36 also the **p** that was taken out
Luke 14:18 I have bought a **p** of ground
Luke 15: 9 have found the **p** which I lost
Luke 24:42 Him a **p** of a broiled fish
John 13:26 he to whom I shall give a **p**
John 13:27 Now after the **p** of bread,
John 13:30 received the **p** of bread, he
John 19:23 woven from the top in one **p**

PIECES (*see* PIECE)
Gen 15:17 that passed between those **p**
Gen 20:16 a thousand **p** of silver
Gen 33:19 for one hundred **p** of money
Gen 37:33 doubt Joseph is torn to **p**
Gen 44:28 Surely he is torn to **p**"
Gen 45:22 three hundred **p** of silver
Ex 15: 6 has dashed the enemy in **p**
Ex 22:13 it is torn to **p** by an animal
Ex 29:17 you shall cut the ram in **p**
Ex 29:17 legs, and put them with its **p**
Lev 1: 6 offering and cut it into its **p**
Lev 1:12 And he shall cut it into its **p**
Lev 2: 6 You shall break it in **p** and
Lev 6:21 And the baked **p** of the grain
Lev 8:20 And he cut the ram into **p**
Lev 8:20 Moses burned the head, the **p**
Lev 9:13 offering to him, with its **p**
Deut 32:26 I will dash them in **p**, I will
Josh 24:32 for one hundred **p** of silver
Judg 5:30 two **p** of dyed embroidery for
Judg 16: 5 eleven hundred **p** of silver
Judg 19:29 dismembered her into twelve **p**
Judg 20: 6 of my concubine, cut her in **p**
1Sa 2:10 the LORD shall be broken in **p**
1Sa 11: 7 yoke of oxen and cut them in **p**
1Sa 15:33 And Samuel hacked Agag in **p**
1Ki 11:30 him, and tore it into twelve **p**
1Ki 11:31 Take for yourself ten **p**, for
1Ki 18:23 for themselves, cut it in **p**
1Ki 18:33 in order, cut the bull in **p**
1Ki 19:11 rocks in **p** before the LORD
2Ki 2:12 and tore them into two **p**
2Ki 11:18 broke in **p** its altars and
2Ki 18: 4 broke in **p** the bronze serpent
2Ki 23:14 And he broke in **p** the sacred
2Ki 24:13 he cut in **p** all the articles
2Ki 25:13 the Chaldeans broke in **p**
2Ch 23:17 They broke in **p** its altars
2Ch 25:12 they all were dashed in **p**
2Ch 28:24 cut in **p** the articles of the
2Ch 31: 1 broke the sacred pillars in **p**
2Ch 34: 4 molded images he broke in **p**
Job 4:20 They are broken in **p** from
Job 16:12 by my neck, and shaken me to **p**
Job 19: 2 and break me in **p** with words
Job 34:24 He breaks in **p** mighty men
Ps 2: 3 Let us break Their bonds in **p**
Ps 2: 9 in **p** like a potter's vessel
Ps 7: 2 like a lion, Rending me in **p**
Ps 50:22 God, Lest I tear you in **p**
Ps 58: 7 his arrows be as if cut in **p**
Ps 68:30 himself with **p** of silver
Ps 72: 4 will break in **p** the oppressor
Ps 74:14 the heads of Leviathan in **p**
Ps 89:10 You have broken Rahab in **p**
Ps 94: 5 They break in **p** Your people
Ps 107:14 And broke their chains in **p**
Ps 129: 4 He has cut in **p** the cords of
Song 8:11 fruit a thousand **p** of silver
Is 8: 9 peoples, and be broken in **p**
Is 8: 9 but be broken in **p**
Is 8: 9 but be broken in **p**
Is 13:16 dashed to **p** before their eyes
Is 13:18 will dash the young men to **p**
Is 25: 6 people a feast of choice **p**
Is 30:14 vessel, which is broken in **p**
Is 45: 2 I will break in **p** the gates
Jer 5: 6 from there shall be torn in **p**
Jer 23:29 that breaks the rock in **p**
Jer 50: 2 Merodach is broken in **p**
Jer 50: 2 her images are broken in **p**
Jer 51:20 I will break the nation in **p**
Jer 51:21 I will break in **p** the horse
Jer 51:21 I will break in **p** the chariot
Jer 51:22 also I will break in **p** man
Jer 51:22 you I will break in **p** old
Jer 51:22 will break in **p** the young man
Jer 51:23 will break in **p** the shepherd
Jer 51:23 I will break in **p** the farmer
Jer 51:23 I will break in **p** governors
Jer 52:17 the Chaldeans broke in **p**
Lam 3:11 aside my ways and torn me in **p**
Ezek 13:19 and for **p** of bread, killing
Ezek 24: 4 Gather **p** of meat in it, every
Dan 2: 5 you shall be cut in **p**, and
Dan 2:34 and clay, and broke them in **p**
Dan 2:40 inasmuch as iron breaks in **p**
Dan 2:40 that kingdom will break in **p**
Dan 2:44 it shall break in **p** and
Dan 2:45 that it broke in **p** the iron
Dan 3:29 Abed-Nego shall be cut in **p**
Dan 6:24 in **p** before they ever came to
Dan 7: 7 was devouring, breaking in **p**
Dan 7:19 which devoured, broke in **p**
Dan 7:23 trample it and break it in **p**
Hos 8: 6 Samaria shall be broken to **p**
Hos 10:14 dashed in **p** upon her children
Hos 13:16 infants shall be dashed in **p**
Amos 6:11 and the little house into **p**
Mic 1: 7 images shall be beaten to **p**
Mic 3: 3 chop them in **p** like meat for
Mic 4:13 shall beat in **p** many peoples
Mic 5: 8 treads down and tears in **p**
Nah 2:12 The lion tore in **p** enough for
Nah 3:10 also were dashed to **p** at the
Zech 11:12 my wages thirty **p** of silver
Zech 11:13 I took the thirty **p** of silver
Zech 11:16 fat and tear their hooves in **p**
Zech 12: 3 away will surely be cut in **p**
Matt 7: 6 and turn and tear you in **p**
Matt 26:15 out to him thirty **p** of silver
Matt 27: 3 **p** of silver to the chief
Matt 27: 5 Then he threw down the **p** of
Matt 27: 6 priests took the silver **p**
Matt 27: 9 took the thirty **p** of silver
Mark 5: 4 and the shackles broken in **p**
Acts 19:19 fifty thousand **p** of silver
Acts 23:10 might be pulled to **p** by them

Acts 27:44 some on broken **p** of the ship
Rev 2:27 vessels shall be broken to **p**'

PIERCE (*see* PIERCED, PIERCES, PIERCING)
Ex 21: 6 his master shall **p** his ear
Num 24: 8 and **p** them with his arrows
2Ki 18:21 will go into his hand and **p** it
Job 20:24 bronze bow will **p** him through
Job 41: 2 or **p** his jaw with a hook
Ps 38: 2 For Your arrows **p** me deeply
Is 36: 6 will go into his hand and **p** it
Lam 3:13 of His quiver to **p** my loins
Luke 2:35 a sword will **p** through your

PIERCED (*see* PIERCE)
Judg 5:26 she **p** his head, she split and
Job 26:13 His hand **p** the fleeing
Job 30:17 My bones are **p** in me at night
Ps 22:16 They **p** My hands and My feet
Zech 12:10 look on Me whom they have **p**
John 19:34 **p** His side with a spear, and
John 19:37 shall look on Him whom they **p**
1Ti 6:10 **p** themselves through with
Rev 1: 7 Him, and they also who **p** Him

PIERCES (*see* PIERCE)
Job 16:13 He **p** my heart and does not
Job 40:24 or one **p** his nose with a

PIERCING (*see* PIERCE, PIERCINGS)
Heb 4:12 **p** even to the division of

PIERCINGS (*see* PIERCING)
Prov 12:18 speaks like the **p** of a sword

PIETY
1Ti 5: 4 first learn to show **p** at home

PIGEON (*see* PIGEONS)
Gen 15: 9 a turtledove, and a young **p**
Lev 12: 6 a young **p** or a turtledove as

PIGEONS (*see* PIGEON)
Lev 1:14 of turtledoves or young **p**
Lev 5: 7 turtledoves or two young **p**
Lev 5:11 turtledoves or two young **p**
Lev 12: 8 turtledoves or two young **p**
Lev 14:22 turtledoves or two young **p**
Lev 14:30 of the turtledoves or young **p**
Lev 15:14 turtledoves or two young **p**
Lev 15:29 turtledoves or two young **p**
Num 6:10 or two young **p** to the priest
Luke 2:24 of turtledoves or two young **p**

PI HAHIROTH (*see* HAHIROTH)
Ex 14: 2 they turn and camp before **P**
Ex 14: 9 camping by the sea beside **P**
Num 33: 7 Etham and turned back to **P**

PILATE (*see* PONTIUS)
Matt 27: 2 Him to Pontius **P** the governor
Matt 27:13 Then **P** said to Him, "Do You
Matt 27:17 together, **P** said to them,
Matt 27:22 **P** said to them, "What then
Matt 27:24 When **P** saw that he could not
Matt 27:58 This man went to **P** and asked
Matt 27:58 Then **P** commanded the body to
Matt 27:62 gathered together to **P**,
Matt 27:65 **P** said to them, "You have a
Mark 15: 1 away, and delivered Him to **P**
Mark 15: 2 Then **P** asked Him, "Are You
Mark 15: 4 Then **P** asked Him again,
Mark 15: 5 nothing, so that **P** marveled
Mark 15: 9 But **P** answered them, saying,
Mark 15:12 **P** answered and said to them
Mark 15:14 Then **P** said to them, "Why,
Mark 15:15 So **P**, wanting to gratify the
Mark 15:43 taking courage, went in to **P**
Mark 15:44 **P** marveled that He was
Luke 3: 1 Pontius **P** being governor of
Luke 13: 1 **P** had mingled with their
Luke 23: 1 of them arose and led Him to **P**
Luke 23: 3 So **P** asked Him, saying, "Are
Luke 23: 4 Then **P** said to the chief
Luke 23: 6 When **P** heard of Galilee, he
Luke 23:11 robe, and sent Him back to **P**
Luke 23:12 That very day **P** and Herod
Luke 23:13 Then **P**, when he had called
Luke 23:20 **P**, therefore, wishing to
Luke 23:24 So **P** gave sentence that it
Luke 23:52 This man went to **P** and asked
John 18:29 **P** then went out to them and
John 18:31 Then **P** said to them, "You
John 18:33 Then **P** entered the Praetorium
John 18:35 **P** answered, "Am I a Jew
John 18:37 **P** therefore said to Him
John 18:38 **P** said to Him, "What is
John 19: 1 So then **P** took Jesus and
John 19: 4 **P** then went out again, and
John 19: 5 And **P** said to them,
John 19: 6 **P** said to them,
John 19: 8 when **P** heard that saying, he
John 19:10 Then **P** said to Him, "Are You
John 19:12 From then on **P** sought to
John 19:13 When **P** therefore heard that
John 19:15 **P** said to them,
John 19:19 Now **P** wrote a title and put it
John 19:21 priests of the Jews said to **P**
John 19:22 **P** answered, "What I have
John 19:31 the Jews asked **P** that their
John 19:38 asked **P** that he might take
John 19:38 and **P** gave him permission
Acts 3:13 denied in the presence of **P**
Acts 4:27 both Herod and Pontius **P**,
Acts 13:28 they asked **P** that He should
1Ti 6:13 confession before Pontius **P**

PILDASH
Gen 22:22 Chesed, Hazo, **P**, Jidlaph, and

PILE (*see* PILES)
Job 27:17 he may **p** it up, but the just
Ezek 24: 5 also **p** fuel bones under it,

PILES (*see* PILE)
Job 27:16 and **p** up clothing like clay

PILFERING
Tit 2:10 not **p**, but showing all good

PILGRIM (*see* PILGRIMAGE, PILGRIMS)
Ps 42: 4 multitude that kept a **p** feast

PILGRIMAGE (*see* PILGRIM)
Gen 47: 9 years of my **p** are one hundred
Gen 47: 9 in the days of their **p**
Ex 6: 4 Canaan, the land of their **p**
Ps 84: 5 You, Whose heart is set on **p**
Ps 119:54 my songs In the house of my **p**

PILGRIMS (*see* PILGRIM)
1Ch 29:15 **p** before You, as were all our
Heb 11:13 strangers and **p** on the earth
1Pe 1: 1 To the **p** of the Dispersion in
1Pe 2:11 I beg you as sojourners and **p**

PILHA
Neh 10:24 Hallohesh, **P**, Shobek,

PILLAGE (*see* PILLAGED)
Ezek 26:12 riches and **p** your merchandise
Ezek 29:19 her spoil, and remove her **p**
Ezek 39:10 **p** those who pillaged them,"

PILLAGED (*see* PILLAGE)
Ezek 39:10 and pillage those who **p** them

PILLAR (*see* PILLARS)
Gen 19:26 and she became a **p** of salt
Gen 28:18 at his head, set it up as a **p**
Gen 28:22 as a **p** shall be God's house
Gen 31:13 where you anointed the **p**
Gen 31:45 a stone and set it up as a **p**
Gen 31:51 this heap and here is this **p**
Gen 31:52 this **p** is a witness, that I
Gen 31:52 and this **p** to me, for harm
Gen 35:14 So Jacob set up a **p** in the
Gen 35:14 talked with him, a **p** of stone
Gen 35:20 Jacob set a **p** on her grave,
Gen 35:20 which is the **p** of Rachel's
Ex 13:21 before them by day in a **p** of
Ex 13:21 by night in a **p** of fire to
Ex 13:22 the **p** of cloud by day or the
Ex 13:22 the **p** of fire by night from
Ex 14:19 and the **p** of cloud went from
Ex 14:24 through the **p** of fire and
Ex 33: 9 that the **p** of cloud descended
Ex 33:10 All the people saw the **p** of
Lev 26: 1 **p** shall you rear up for
Num 12: 5 came down in the **p** of cloud
Num 14:14 them in a **p** of cloud by day
Num 14:14 and in a **p** of fire by night
Deut 16:22 shall not set up a sacred **p**
Deut 31:15 tabernacle in a **p** of cloud
Deut 31:15 the **p** of cloud stood above
Judg 9: 6 at the **p** that was in Shechem
2Sa 18:18 set up a **p** for himself, which
2Sa 18:18 He called the **p** after his
1Ki 7:21 he set up the **p** on the right
1Ki 7:21 he set up the **p** on the left
2Ki 3: 2 for he put away the sacred **p**
2Ki 10:27 down the sacred **p** of Baal
2Ki 11:14 standing by a **p** according to
2Ki 23: 3 Then the king stood by a **p**
2Ki 25:17 The height of one **p** was
2Ki 25:17 The second **p** was the same,
2Ch 23:13 by his **p** at the entrance
Neh 9:12 them by day with a cloudy **p**
Neh 9:12 and by night with a **p** of fire
Neh 9:19 The **p** of the cloud did not
Neh 9:19 nor the **p** of fire by night,
Ps 99: 7 spoke to them in the cloudy **p**
Is 19:19 a **p** to the LORD at its border
Jer 1:18 a fortified city and an iron **p**
Jer 52:21 the height of one **p** was
Jer 52:22 The second **p**, with
Hos 3: 4 without sacrifice or sacred **p**
1Ti 3:15 of the living God, the **p** and
Rev 3:12 I will make him a **p** in the

PILLARS (*see* PILLAR)
Ex 23:24 break down their sacred **p**
Ex 24: 4 twelve **p** according to the
Ex 26:32 **p** of acacia wood overlaid
Ex 26:37 screen five **p** of acacia wood
Ex 27:10 And its twenty **p** and their
Ex 27:10 The hooks of the **p** and their
Ex 27:11 long, with its twenty **p** and
Ex 27:11 bronze, and the hooks of the **p**
Ex 27:12 cubits, with their ten **p** and
Ex 27:14 cubits, with their three **p**
Ex 27:15 cubits, with their three **p**
Ex 27:16 It shall have four **p** and four
Ex 27:17 All the **p** around the court
Ex 34:13 altars, break their sacred **p**
Ex 35:11 its boards, its bars, its **p**
Ex 35:17 hangings of the court, its **p**
Ex 36:36 for it four **p** of acacia wood
Ex 36:38 its five **p** with their hooks
Ex 38:10 There were twenty **p** for them
Ex 38:10 The hooks of the **p** and their
Ex 38:11 cubits long, with twenty **p**
Ex 38:11 The hooks of the **p** and their
Ex 38:12 of fifty cubits, with ten **p**
Ex 38:12 The hooks of the **p** and their
Ex 38:14 long, with their three **p** and
Ex 38:15 cubits, with their three **p**
Ex 38:17 for the **p** were of bronze
Ex 38:17 the hooks of the **p**
Ex 38:17 all the **p** of the court had
Ex 38:19 there were four **p** with their
Ex 38:28 he made hooks for the **p**,
Ex 39:33 its boards, its bars, its **p**
Ex 39:40 hangings of the court, its **p**
Ex 40:18 its bars, and raised up its **p**
Num 3:36 tabernacle, its bars, its **p**
Num 3:37 the **p** of the court all around
Num 4:31 tabernacle, its bars, its **p**
Num 4:32 the **p** around the court with
Deut 7: 5 and break down their sacred **p**
Deut 12: 3 altars, break their sacred **p**
Judg 16:25 stationed him between the **p**
Judg 16:26 Let me feel the **p** which
Judg 16:29 **p** which supported the temple
1Sa 2: 8 For the **p** of the earth are
1Ki 7: 2 with four rows of cedar **p**
1Ki 7: 2 and cedar beams on the **p**
1Ki 7: 3 that were on forty-five **p**
1Ki 7: 6 He also made the Hall of **P**
1Ki 7: 6 of them was a portico with **p**
1Ki 7:15 And he cast two **p** of bronze
1Ki 7:16 to set on the tops of the **p**
1Ki 7:17 which were on top of the **p**
1Ki 7:18 So he made the **p**, and two rows
1Ki 7:19 the **p** in the hall were in the
1Ki 7:20 The capitals on the two **p**
1Ki 7:21 Then he set up the **p** by the
1Ki 7:22 The tops of the **p** were in the
1Ki 7:22 work of the **p** was finished
1Ki 7:41 the two **p**, the two
1Ki 7:41 that were on top of the two **p**
1Ki 7:41 which were on top of the **p**
1Ki 7:42 that were on top of the **p**)
1Ki 14:23 high places, sacred **p**, and
2Ki 10:26 they brought the sacred **p** out
2Ki 17:10 up for themselves sacred **p**
2Ki 18: 4 places and broke the sacred **p**
2Ki 18:16 from the **p** which Hezekiah
2Ki 23:14 broke in pieces the sacred **p**
2Ki 25:13 The bronze **p** that were in the
2Ki 25:16 The two **p**, one Sea, and the
1Ch 18: 8 made the bronze Sea, the **p**

2Ch 3:15 two **p** thirty-five cubits high
2Ch 3:16 and put them on top of the **p**
2Ch 3:17 up the **p** before the temple
2Ch 4:12 the two **p** and the bowl-shaped
2Ch 4:12 that were on top of the two **p**
2Ch 4:12 which were on top of the **p**
2Ch 4:13 capitals that were on the **p**)
2Ch 14: 3 and broke down the sacred **p**
2Ch 31: 1 broke the sacred **p** in pieces
Esth 1: 6 on silver rods and marble **p**
Job 9: 6 its place, and its **p** tremble
Job 26:11 The **p** of heaven tremble, and
Ps 75: 3 I set up its **p** firmly
Ps 144:12 our daughters may be as **p**
Prov 9: 1 she has hewn out her seven **p**
Song 3: 6 wilderness like **p** of smoke
Song 3:10 He made its **p** of silver, its
Song 5:15 His legs are **p** of marble set
Jer 27:19 of hosts concerning the **p**
Jer 43:13 **p** of Beth Shemesh that are in
Jer 52:17 The bronze **p** that were in the
Jer 52:20 The two **p**, one Sea, the
Jer 52:21 Now concerning the **p**
Ezek 26:11 your strong **p** will fall to
Ezek 40:49 there were **p** by the doorposts
Ezek 42: 6 **p** like the **p** of the courts
Hos 10: 1 have embellished his sacred **p**
Hos 10: 2 he will ruin their sacred **p**
Joel 2:30 blood and fire and **p** of smoke
Mic 5:13 your sacred **p** from your midst
Zeph 2:14 on the capitals of her **p**
Gal 2: 9 and John, who seemed to be **p**
Rev 10: 1 and his feet like **p** of fire

PILLOW
Mark 4:38 in the stern, asleep on a **p**

PILOT (*see* PILOTS)
Jas 3: 4 rudder wherever the **p** desires

PILOTS (*see* PILOT)
Ezek 27: 8 they became your **p**
Ezek 27:27 your mariners and **p**, your
Ezek 27:28 sound of the cry of your **p**
Ezek 27:29 all the **p** of the sea will

PILTAI
Neh 12:17 of Moadiah, **P**

PIM
1Sa 13:21 was a **p** for the plowshares

PIN (*see* PINS)
1Sa 18:11 I will **p** David to the wall
1Sa 19:10 Then Saul sought to **p** David

PINE (*see* PINED)
Is 41:19 the cypress tree and the **p**
Is 44:14 he plants a **p**, and the rain
Is 60:13 to you, the cypress, the **p**
Lam 4: 9 for these **p** away, stricken
Ezek 24:23 but you shall **p** away in your
Ezek 33:10 we **p** away in them, how can we

PINED (*see* PINE)
Mic 1:12 of Maroth **p** for good, but

PINIONS
Job 39:13 **p** like the kindly stork's
Ezek 17: 3 with large wings and long **p**

PINNACLE (*see* PINNACLES)
Matt 4: 5 Him on the **p** of the temple
Luke 4: 9 Him on the **p** of the temple

PINNACLES (*see* PINNACLE)
Is 54:12 I will make your **p** of rubies

PINON
Gen 36:41 Chief Elah, Chief **P**,
1Ch 1:52 Chief Elah, Chief **P**,

PINS (*see* PIN)
1Ki 7:33 their axle **p**, their rims,

PIPED (*see* PIPES, PIPINGS)
1Co 14: 7 be known what is **p** or played

PIPES (*see* PIPED)
Ezek 28:13 **p** was prepared for you on the
Zech 4: 2 seven **p** to the seven lamps
Zech 4:12 **p** from which the golden oil

PIPINGS (*see* PIPED)
Judg 5:16 to hear the **p** for the flocks

PIRAM
Josh 10: 3 **P** king of Jarmuth, Japhia

PIRATHON (*see* PIRATHONITE)
Judg 12:15 was buried in **P** in the land

PIRATHONITE (*see* PIRATHON)
Judg 12:13 of Hillel the **P** judged Israel
Judg 12:15 the son of Hillel the **P** died
2Sa 23:30 Benaiah a **P**, Hiddai from the
1Ch 11:31 of Benjamin, Benaiah the **P**
1Ch 27:14 month was Benaiah the **P**, of

PISGAH (*see* NEBO)
Num 21:20 to the top of **P** which looks
Num 23:14 of Zophim, to the top of **P**
Deut 3:17 Sea), below the slopes of **P**
Deut 3:27 Go up to the top of **P**, and
Deut 4:49 Arabah, below the slopes of **P**
Deut 34: 1 Mount Nebo, to the top of **P**
Josh 12: 3 below the slopes of **P**
Josh 13:20 Beth Peor, the slopes of **P**

PISHON
Gen 2:11 The name of the first is **P**

PISIDIA
Acts 13:14 they came to Antioch in **P**
Acts 14:24 they had passed through **P**

PISPAH
1Ch 7:38 of Jether were Jephunneh, **P**

PISTACHIO
Gen 43:11 and myrrh, **p** nuts and almonds

PIT (*see* PITS)
Gen 37:20 him and cast him into some **p**
Gen 37:22 but cast him into this **p**
Gen 37:24 took him and cast him into a **p**
Gen 37:24 And the **p** was empty
Gen 37:28 up and lifted him out of the **p**
Gen 37:29 Then Reuben returned to the **p**
Gen 37:29 Joseph was not in the **p**
Ex 21:33 And if a man opens a **p**,
Ex 21:33 or if a man digs a **p**
Ex 21:34 the owner of the **p** shall make
Num 16:30 they go down alive into the **p**
Num 16:33 went down alive into the **p**
2Sa 17: 9 by now he is hidden in some **p**
2Sa 18:17 into a large **p** in the woods
2Sa 23:20 midst of a **p** on a snowy day
1Ch 11:22 midst of a **p** on a snowy day
Job 9:31 You will plunge me into the **p**
Job 33:18 back his soul from the **P**, and
Job 33:22 his soul draws near the **P**
Job 33:24 him from going down to the **P**
Job 33:28 soul from going down to the **P**
Job 33:30 back his soul from the **P**,
Ps 7:15 He made a **p** and dug it out, And
Ps 9:15 down in the **p** which they made
Ps 28: 1 those who go down to the **p**
Ps 30: 3 I should not go down to the **p**
Ps 30: 9 When I go down to the **p**
Ps 35: 7 their net for me in a **p**,
Ps 40: 2 me up out of a horrible **p**
Ps 49: 9 eternally, And not see the **P**
Ps 55:23 down to the **p** of destruction
Ps 57: 6 They have dug a **p** before me
Ps 69:15 let not the **p** shut its mouth
Ps 88: 4 those who go down to the **p**
Ps 88: 6 have laid me in the lowest **p**
Ps 94:13 Until the **p** is dug for the
Ps 143: 7 those who go down into the **p**
Prov 1:12 those who go down to the **P**
Prov 22:14 an immoral woman is a deep **p**
Prov 23:27 For a harlot is a deep **p**, and
Prov 26:27 Whoever digs a **p** will fall
Prov 28:10 will fall into his own **p**
Prov 28:17 bloodshed will flee into a **p**
Eccl 10: 8 He who digs a **p** will fall
Is 14:15 to the lowest depths of the **P**
Is 14:19 down to the stones of the **p**
Is 24:17 Fear and the **p** and the snare
Is 24:18 fear shall fall into the **p**
Is 24:18 the **p** shall be caught in the
Is 24:22 are gathered in the **p**, and
Is 38:17 soul from the **p** of corruption
Is 38:18 those who go down to the **p**
Is 51: 1 to the hole of the **p** from
Is 51:14 he should not die in the **p**
Jer 18:20 they have dug a **p** for my life
Jer 18:22 they have dug a **p** to take me
Jer 41: 7 them into the midst of a **p**
Jer 41: 9 Now the **p** into which Ishmael
Jer 48:43 Fear and the **p** and the snare
Jer 48:44 fear shall fall into the **p**
Jer 48:44 the **p** shall be caught in the
Lam 3:53 silenced my life in the **p**
Lam 3:55 O LORD, from the lowest **p**
Ezek 19: 4 he was trapped in their **p**
Ezek 19: 8 he was trapped in their **p**
Ezek 26:20 those who descend into the **P**
Ezek 26:20 those who go down to the **P**
Ezek 28: 8 throw you down into the **P**
Ezek 31:14 of men who go down to the **P**
Ezek 31:16 those who descend into the **P**
Ezek 32:18 those who go down to the **P**
Ezek 32:23 set in the recesses of the **P**
Ezek 32:24 those who go down to the **P**
Ezek 32:25 those who go down to the **P**
Ezek 32:29 those who go down to the **P**
Ezek 32:30 those who go down to the **P**
Jon 2: 6 brought up my life from the **p**
Zech 9:11 free from the waterless **p**
Matt 12:11 falls into a **p** on the Sabbath
Luke 14: 5 ox that has fallen into a **p**
Rev 9: 1 the key to the bottomless **p**
Rev 9: 2 And he opened the bottomless **p**
Rev 9: 2 smoke arose out of the **p** like
Rev 9: 2 because of the smoke of the **p**
Rev 9:11 the angel of the bottomless **p**
Rev 11: 7 out of the bottomless **p** will
Rev 17: 8 out of the bottomless **p** and go
Rev 20: 1 the key to the bottomless **p**
Rev 20: 3 him into the bottomless **p**

PITCH (*see* PITCHED)
Gen 6:14 it inside and outside with **p**
Ex 2: 3 daubed it with asphalt and **p**
Num 1:52 of Israel shall **p** their tents
Num 9:17 of Israel would **p** their tents
Deut 1:33 place for you to **p** your tents
Is 13:20 the Arabian **p** tents there
Is 34: 9 shall be turned into **p**, and
Is 34: 9 land shall become burning **p**
Jer 6: 3 They shall **p** their tents
Jer 10:20 no one to **p** my tent anymore

PITCHED (*see* PITCH)
Gen 12: 8 he **p** his tent with Bethel on
Gen 13:12 **p** his tent even as far as
Gen 26:17 **p** his tent in the Valley of
Gen 26:25 LORD, and he **p** his tent there
Gen 31:25 Now Jacob had **p** his tent in
Gen 31:25 Laban with his brethren **p** in
Gen 33:18 he **p** his tent before the city
Gen 33:19 land, where he had **p** his tent
Gen 35:21 **p** his tent beyond the tower
Ex 33: 7 **p** it outside the camp, far
Judg 4:11 **p** his tent near the terebinth
2Sa 16:22 So they **p** a tent for Absalom
1Ch 15: 1 of God, and **p** a tent for it
2Ch 1: 4 for he had **p** a tent for it at

PITCHER (*see* PITCHERS)
Gen 24:14 down your **p** that I may drink
Gen 24:15 with her **p** on her shoulder
Gen 24:16 to the well, filled her **p**
Gen 24:17 a little water from your **p**
Gen 24:18 let her **p** down to her hand,
Gen 24:20 emptied her **p** into the trough
Gen 24:43 water from your **p** to drink
Gen 24:45 with her **p** on her shoulder
Gen 24:46 and let her **p** down from her
Eccl 12: 6 or the **p** shattered at the
Mark 14:13 you carrying a **p** of water
Luke 22:10 you carrying a **p** of water

PITCHERS (*see* PITCHER)
Ex 25:29 its dishes, its pans, its **p**
Ex 37:16 bowls, and its **p** for pouring
Num 4: 7 bowls, and the **p** for pouring
Judg 7:16 man's hand, with empty **p**, and
Judg 7:16 and torches inside the **p**
Judg 7:19 and broke the **p** that were in
Judg 7:20 the trumpets and broke the **p**
1Ch 28:17 the **p** of pure gold, and the
Is 22:24 from the cups to all the **p**
Mark 7: 4 like the washing of cups, **p**
Mark 7: 8 the washing of **p** and cups, and

PITHOM
Ex 1:11 for Pharaoh supply cities, **P**

PITHON
1Ch 8:35 The sons of Micah were **P**,
1Ch 9:41 The sons of Micah were **P**,

PITIABLE (*see* PITY)
1Co 15:19 we are of all men the most **p**

PITIED (*see* PITY)
Ps 106:46 He also made them to be **p** By
Lam 2: 2 has not **p** all the habitations
Lam 2:17 has thrown down and has not **p**
Lam 2:21 you have slaughtered and not **p**
Lam 3:43 You have slain and not **p**
Ezek 16: 5 No eye **p** you, to do any of

PITIES (*see* PITY)
Ps 103:13 As a father **p** his children,
Ps 103:13 So the LORD **p** those who fear

PITS (*see* PIT)
Gen 14:10 Siddim was full of asphalt **p**
1Sa 13: 6 in rocks, in holes, and in **p**
Ps 119:85 The proud have dug **p** for me
Ps 140:10 into the fire, Into deep **p**
Jer 2: 6 a land of deserts and **p**,
Lam 4:20 LORD, was caught in their **p**

PITY (*see* PITIABLE, PITIED, PITIES)
Deut 7:16 eye shall have no **p** on them
Deut 13: 8 him, nor shall your eye **p** him
Deut 19:13 Your eye shall not **p** him, but
Deut 19:21 Your eye shall not **p**
Deut 25:12 your eye shall not **p** her
Judg 2:18 **p** by their groaning because
2Sa 12: 6 thing and because he had no **p**
Job 16:13 my heart and does not **p**
Job 19:21 Have **p** on me, have **p** on me
Job 19:21 on me, have **p** on me, O you my
Ps 69:20 looked for someone to take **p**
Prov 19:17 He who has **p** on the poor
Prov 28: 8 for him who will **p** the poor
Is 13:18 they will have no **p** on the
Is 63: 9 in His **p** He redeemed them
Jer 13:14 I will not **p** nor spare nor
Jer 15: 5 For who will have **p** on you
Jer 21: 7 them, or have **p** or mercy
Ezek 5:11 spare, nor will I have any **p**
Ezek 7: 4 spare you, nor will I have **p**
Ezek 7: 9 not spare, nor will I have **p**
Ezek 8:18 not spare nor will I have **p**
Ezek 9: 5 eye spare, nor have any **p**
Ezek 9:10 spare, nor will I have **p**, but
Hos 13:14 **P** is hidden from My eyes
Joel 2:18 for His land, and **p** His people
Amos 1:11 the sword, and cast off all **p**
Jon 4:10 You have had **p** on the plant
Jon 4:11 And should I not **p** Nineveh
Hab 1:17 to slay nations without **p**
Zech 11: 5 their shepherds do not **p** them
Zech 11: 6 For I will no longer **p** the
Matt 18:33 just as I had **p** on you

PLACE (*see* PREFACE)

PLACED (*see* PREFACE)

PLACENTA
Deut 28:57 her **p** which comes out from

PLACES (*see* PREFACE)

PLAGUE (*see* PLAGUED, PLAGUES)
Ex 11: 1 yet one more **p** on Pharaoh
Ex 12:13 the **p** shall not be on you to
Ex 30:12 that there may be no **p** among
Lev 13:47 garment has a leprous **p** in it
Lev 13:49 and if the **p** is greenish or
Lev 13:49 of leather, it is a leprous **p**
Lev 13:50 priest shall look at the **p**
Lev 13:50 which has the **p** seven days
Lev 13:51 at the **p** on the seventh day
Lev 13:51 If the **p** has spread in the
Lev 13:51 the **p** is an active leprosy
Lev 13:52 garment in which is the **p**
Lev 13:53 indeed the **p** has not spread
Lev 13:54 the thing in which is the **p**
Lev 13:55 **p** after it has been washed
Lev 13:55 and indeed if the **p** has not
Lev 13:55 though the **p** has not spread,
Lev 13:56 indeed the **p** has faded after
Lev 13:57 leather, it is a spreading **p**
Lev 13:57 fire that in which is the **p**
Lev 13:58 if the **p** has disappeared from
Lev 13:59 **p** in a garment of wool or
Lev 14:34 and I put the leprous **p** in a
Lev 14:35 there is some **p** in the house
Lev 14:36 goes into it to look at the **p**
Lev 14:37 And he shall look at the **p**
Lev 14:37 indeed if the **p** is on the
Lev 14:39 indeed if the **p** has spread on
Lev 14:40 the stones in which is the **p**
Lev 14:43 if the **p** comes back and breaks
Lev 14:44 indeed if the **p** has spread in
Lev 14:48 indeed the **p** has not spread
Lev 14:48 because the **p** is healed
Num 8:19 that there be no **p** among the
Num 11:33 people with a very great **p**
Num 14:37 died by the **p** before the LORD
Num 16:46 The **p** has begun
Num 16:47 already the **p** had begun among
Num 16:48 so the **p** was stopped
Num 16:49 the **p** were fourteen thousand
Num 16:50 for the **p** had stopped
Num 25: 8 So the **p** was stopped among
Num 25: 9 those who died in the **p** were
Num 25:18 day of the **p** because of Peor
Num 26: 1 it came to pass, after the **p**
Num 31:16 and there was a **p** among the
Deut 28:21 The LORD will make the **p**
Deut 28:61 every sickness and every **p**
Josh 22:17 although there was a **p** in the
1Sa 6: 4 For the same **p** was on all of
2Sa 24:13 be three days' **p** in your land
2Sa 24:15 So the LORD sent a **p** upon
2Sa 24:21 that the **p** may be withdrawn
2Sa 24:25 and the **p** was withdrawn from
1Ki 8:37 whatever **p** or whatever
1Ki 8:38 knows the **p** of his own heart
1Ch 21:12 the **p** in the land, with the
1Ch 21:14 the LORD sent a **p** upon Israel
1Ch 21:22 that the **p** may be withdrawn
2Ch 6:28 whatever **p** or whatever
Ps 38:11 friends stand aloof from my **p**
Ps 39:10 Remove Your **p** from me
Ps 78:50 gave their life over to the **p**
Ps 89:23 face, And **p** those who hate him
Ps 91:10 Nor shall any **p** come near
Ps 106:29 the **p** broke out among them
Ps 106:30 And so the **p** was stopped
Amos 4:10 I sent among you a **p** after
Zech 14:12 And this shall be the **p** with
Zech 14:15 shall be the **p** on the horse
Zech 14:15 So shall this **p** be
Zech 14:18 they shall receive the **p** with
Acts 24: 5 we have found this man a **p**
Rev 16:21 because of the **p** of the hail
Rev 16:21 since that **p** was exceedingly

PLAGUED (*see* PLAGUE)
Gen 12:17 But the LORD **p** Pharaoh and his
Ex 32:35 So the LORD **p** the people
Josh 24: 5 I **p** Egypt, according to what
1Ch 21:17 people that they should be **p**
Ps 73: 5 Nor are they **p** like other men
Ps 73:14 all day long I have been **p**

PLAGUES (*see* PLAGUE)
Gen 12:17 with great **p** because of Sarai
Ex 9:14 all My **p** to your very heart
Lev 26:21 on you seven times more **p**
Deut 28:59 descendants extraordinary **p**
Deut 28:59 great and prolonged **p**
Deut 29:22 they see the **p** of that land
1Sa 4: 8 all the **p** in the wilderness
Jer 19: 8 and hiss because of all its **p**
Jer 49:17 and will hiss at all its **p**
Jer 50:13 and hiss at all her **p**
Hos 13:14 O Death, I will be your **p**
Rev 9:18 By these three **p** a third of
Rev 9:20 were not killed by these **p**
Rev 11: 6 strike the earth with all **p**
Rev 15: 1 having the seven last **p**, for
Rev 15: 6 angels having the seven **p**
Rev 15: 8 **p** of the seven angels were
Rev 16: 9 who has power over these **p**
Rev 18: 4 and lest you receive of her **p**
Rev 18: 8 Therefore her **p** will come in
Rev 21: 9 the seven last **p** came to me
Rev 22:18 God will add to him the **p**

PLAIN (*see* PLAINLY, PLAINS)
Gen 11: 2 that they found a **p** in the
Gen 13:10 and saw all the **p** of Jordan
Gen 13:11 himself all the **p** of Jordan
Gen 13:12 dwelt in the cities of the **p**
Gen 19:17 nor stay anywhere in the **p**
Gen 19:25 those cities, all the **p**, all
Gen 19:28 toward all the land of the **p**
Gen 19:29 destroyed the cities of the **p**
Deut 1: 1 in the **p** opposite Suph,
Deut 1: 7 neighboring places in the **p**
Deut 2: 8 away from the road of the **p**
Deut 3:10 all the cities of the **p**, all
Deut 3:17 the **p** also, with the Jordan
Deut 4:49 all the **p** on the east side of
Deut 11:30 in the **p** opposite Gilgal,
Deut 34: 3 and the **p** of the Valley of
Josh 8:14 appointed place before the **p**
Josh 11: 2 in the **p** south of Chinneroth,
Josh 11:16 the lowland, and the Jordan **p**
Josh 12: 1 and all the eastern Jordan **p**
Josh 12: 3 the eastern Jordan **p** from the
Josh 12: 8 the lowlands, in the Jordan **p**
Josh 13: 9 all the **p** of Medeba as far as
Josh 13:16 and all the **p** by Medeba
Josh 13:17 its cities that are in the **p**
Josh 13:21 all the cities of the **p** and
Josh 20: 8 in the wilderness on the **p**
Judg 20:33 position in the **p** of Geba
1Sa 23:24 in the **p** on the south of
2Sa 2:29 all that night through the **p**
2Sa 4: 7 night escaping through the **p**
2Sa 18:23 Ahimaaz ran by way of the **p**
1Ki 7:46 In the **p** of Jordan the king
1Ki 20:23 fight against them in the **p**
1Ki 20:25 fight against them in the **p**
2Ki 25: 4 the king went by way of the **p**
2Ch 4:17 In the **p** of Jordan the king
Neh 3:22 the priests, the men of the **p**
Neh 6: 2 the villages in the **p** of Ono
Prov 8: 9 They are all **p** to him who
Jer 21:13 the valley, and rock of the **p**
Jer 39: 4 he went out by way of the **p**
Jer 48: 8 the **p** shall be destroyed, as
Jer 48:21 has come on the **p** country
Jer 52: 7 And they went by way of the **p**
Ezek 3:22 Arise, go out into the **p**, and
Ezek 3:23 arose and went out into the **p**
Ezek 8: 4 vision that I saw in the **p**
Dan 3: 1 He set it up in the **p** of Dura
Hab 2: 2 make it **p** on tablets, that he
Zech 4: 7 you shall become a **p**
Zech 12:11 Rimmon in the **p** of Megiddo
Zech 14:10 a **p** from Geba to Rimmon south

PLAINLY (*see* PLAIN)
Ex 21: 5 But if the servant **p** says
Num 12: 8 with him face to face, even **p**
Deut 27: 8 you shall write very **p** on the
1Sa 10:16 He told us **p** that the donkeys
Is 32: 4 will be ready to speak **p**
Jer 2:34 but **p** on all these things
Mark 7:35 was loosed, and he spoke **p**
John 10:24 You are the Christ, tell us **p**
John 11:14 Then Jesus said to them **p**
John 16:25 tell you **p** about the Father
John 16:29 See, now You are speaking **p**
Heb 11:14 **p** that they seek a homeland

PLAINS (*see* PLAIN)
Num 22: 1 camped in the **p** of Moab on
Num 26: 3 the **p** of Moab by the Jordan
Num 26:63 the **p** of Moab by the Jordan
Num 31:12 to the camp in the **p** of Moab
Num 33:48 camped in the **p** of Moab by
Num 33:49 Acacia Grove in the **p** of Moab
Num 33:50 the **p** of Moab by the Jordan
Num 35: 1 the **p** of Moab by the Jordan
Num 36:13 the **p** of Moab by the Jordan
Deut 34: 1 the **p** of Moab to Mount Nebo
Deut 34: 8 in the **p** of Moab thirty days
Josh 4:13 battle, to the **p** of Jericho
Josh 5:10 twilight on the **p** of Jericho
Josh 13:32 as an inheritance in the **p** of
2Sa 15:28 I will wait in the **p** of the
2Sa 17:16 in the **p** of the wilderness
2Ki 25: 5 him in the **p** of Jericho
2Ch 26:10 in the lowlands and in the **p**
Jer 39: 5 Zedekiah in the **p** of Jericho
Jer 52: 8 Zedekiah in the **p** of Jericho

PLAITED
1Ki 7:29 oxen were wreaths of **p** work

PLAN (*see* PLANNED, PLANNING, PLANS)
Deut 1:23 And the **p** pleased me well
2Ch 2:14 to accomplish any **p** which may
Neh 6: 6 you and the Jews **p** to rebel
Ps 38:12 **p** deception all the day long

Ps 140: 2 Who **p** evil things in their
Jer 18:11 and devising a **p** against you
Jer 30:18 remain according to its own **p**
Jer 49:30 has conceived a **p** against you
Jer 51:11 For His **p** is against Babylon
Ezek 38:10 and you will make an evil **p**
Ezek 42:11 entrances were according to **p**
Zech 7:10 Let none of you **p** evil in his
Acts 5:38 for if this **p** or this work is
Acts 27:42 Now the soldiers' **p** was to
2Co 1:17 Or the things I **p**
2Co 1:17 do I **p** according to the flesh

PLANE
Is 44:13 he fashions it with a **p**, he

PLANK (*see* PLANKS)
Matt 7: 3 the **p** in your own eye
Matt 7: 4 look, a **p** is in your own eye
Matt 7: 5 First remove the **p** from your
Luke 6:41 the **p** in your own eye
Luke 6:42 the **p** that is in your own eye
Luke 6:42 First remove the **p** from your

PLANKS (*see* PLANK)
1Ki 6:15 the temple with **p** of cypress
Ezek 27: 5 They made all your **p** of fir
Ezek 27: 6 **p** with ivory from the coasts

PLANNED (*see* PLAN)
Acts 27:39 onto which they **p** to run the
Rom 1:13 that I often **p** to come to you

PLANNING (*see* PLAN)
2Co 1:17 Therefore, when I was **p** this

PLANS (*see* PLAN)
1Ki 6:38 and according to all its **p**
1Ch 28:11 the **p** for the vestibule, its
1Ch 28:12 the **p** for all that he had by
1Ch 28:19 me, all the works of these **p**
Job 5:12 cannot carry out their **p**
Ps 33:10 He makes the **p** of the peoples
Ps 33:11 The **p** of His heart to all
Ps 146: 4 In that very day his **p** perish
Prov 6:18 a heart that devises wicked **p**
Prov 15:22 **p** go awry, but in the
Prov 16: 9 A man's heart **p** his way, but
Prov 19:21 There are many **p** in a man's
Prov 21: 5 The **p** of the diligent lead
Is 30: 1 not of Me, and who devise **p**
Is 32: 7 he devises wicked **p** to
Jer 18:12 walk according to our own **p**
Jer 18:18 and let us devise **p** against
Dan 11:24 he shall devise his **p** against
Dan 11:25 shall devise **p** against him

PLANT (*see* PLANTED, PLANTERS, PLANTING, PLANTS)
Gen 2: 5 before any **p** of the field was
Ex 15:17 **p** them in the mountain of
Deut 6:11 trees which you did not **p**
Deut 16:21 You shall not **p** for yourself
Deut 28:30 you shall **p** a vineyard, but
Deut 28:39 You shall **p** vineyards and tend
Josh 24:13 groves which you did not **p**
2Sa 7:10 people Israel, and will **p** them
2Ki 19:29 **p** vineyards and eat the fruit
1Ch 17: 9 people Israel, and will **p** them
Job 8:12 it withers before any other **p**
Job 14: 9 bring forth branches like a **p**
Ps 107:37 **p** vineyards, That they may
Eccl 3: 2 a time to **p**, and a time to
Is 5: 7 of Judah are His pleasant **p**
Is 17:10 you will **p** pleasant plants
Is 17:11 you will make your **p** to grow
Is 28:25 **p** the wheat in rows, the
Is 37:30 **p** vineyards, and eat the fruit
Is 41:19 I will **p** in the wilderness
Is 51:16 that I may **p** the heavens, lay
Is 53: 2 up before Him as a tender **p**
Is 65:21 they shall **p** vineyards and eat
Is 65:22 they shall not **p** and another
Jer 1:10 throw down, to build and to **p**
Jer 2:21 degenerate **p** of an alien vine
Jer 18: 9 kingdom, to build and to **p** it
Jer 24: 6 them down, and I will **p** them
Jer 29: 5 **p** gardens and eat their fruit
Jer 29:28 **p** gardens and eat their fruit
Jer 31: 5 You shall yet **p** vines on the
Jer 31: 5 the planters shall **p** and eat
Jer 31:28 over them to build and to **p**
Jer 32:41 I will assuredly **p** them in
Jer 35: 7 **p** a vineyard, nor have any of
Jer 42:10 you down, and I will **p** you
Ezek 16: 7 thrive like a **p** in the field
Ezek 17:22 and will **p** it on a high and
Ezek 17:23 height of Israel I will **p** it
Ezek 28:26 build houses, and **p** vineyards
Dan 11:45 he shall **p** the tents of his
Amos 9:14 they shall **p** vineyards and
Amos 9:15 I will **p** them in their land,
Jon 4: 6 And the LORD God prepared a **p**
Jon 4: 6 was very grateful for the **p**
Jon 4: 7 the **p** that it withered
Jon 4: 9 you to be angry about the **p**
Jon 4:10 the **p** for which you have not
Zeph 1:13 they shall **p** vineyards, but
Matt 15:13 Every **p** which My heavenly

PLANTED (*see* PLANT)
Gen 2: 8 The LORD God **p** a garden
Gen 9:20 a farmer, and he **p** a vineyard
Gen 21:33 Then Abraham **p** a tamarisk
Lev 19:23 have **p** all kinds of trees for
Num 24: 6 like aloes **p** by the LORD,
Deut 20: 6 is there who has **p** a vineyard
Ps 1: 3 tree **P** by the rivers of water
Ps 44: 2 Your hand, But them You **p**
Ps 80: 8 cast out the nations, and **p** it
Ps 80:15 which Your right hand has **p**
Ps 92:13 Those who are **p** in the house
Ps 94: 9 He who **p** the ear, shall He
Ps 104:16 cedars of Lebanon which He **p**
Eccl 2: 4 houses, and **p** myself vineyards
Eccl 2: 5 I **p** all kinds of fruit trees
Eccl 3: 2 and a time to pluck what is **p**
Is 5: 2 **p** it with the choicest vine
Is 40:24 Scarcely shall they be **p**,
Jer 2:21 Yet I had **p** you a noble vine,
Jer 11:17 the LORD of hosts, who **p** you
Jer 12: 2 You have **p** them, yes, they
Jer 17: 8 like a tree **p** by the waters
Jer 45: 4 what I have **p** I will pluck up
Ezek 17: 5 and **p** it in a fertile field
Ezek 17: 7 terrace where it had been **p**
Ezek 17: 8 It was **p** in good soil by many
Ezek 17:10 Behold, it is **p**, will it
Ezek 19:10 **P** by the waters, fruitful and
Ezek 19:13 And now she is **p** in the
Ezek 31: 4 the place where it was **p**, and
Ezek 36:36 places and **p** what was desolate
Hos 9:13 **p** in a pleasant place, so
Amos 5:11 you have **p** pleasant vineyards
Matt 15:13 has not **p** will be uprooted
Matt 21:33 landowner who **p** a vineyard
Mark 12: 1 A man **p** a vineyard and set a
Luke 13: 6 a fig tree **p** in his vineyard
Luke 17: 6 be **p** in the sea,' and it would
Luke 17:28 bought, they sold, they **p**
Luke 20: 9 A certain man **p** a vineyard
1Co 3: 6 I **p**, Apollos watered, but God

PLANTERS (*see* PLANT)
Jer 31: 5 the **p** shall plant and eat them

PLANTING (*see* PLANT)
Lev 11:37 **p** seed which is to be sown
Is 60:21 forever, the branch of My **p**
Is 61: 3 the **p** of the LORD, that He
Mic 1: 6 places for **p** a vineyard

PLANTS (*see* PLANT)
Ex 10:15 on the trees or on the **p** of
Ps 128: 3 olive **p** All around your table
Ps 144:12 as **p** grown up in their youth
Prov 31:16 her profits she **p** a vineyard
Song 4:13 Your **p** are an orchard of
Is 16: 8 have broken down its choice **p**
Is 17:10 you will plant pleasant **p**
Is 44:14 he **p** a pine, and the rain
Jer 48:32 Your **p** have gone over the sea
1Co 3: 7 neither he who **p** is anything
1Co 3: 8 Now he who **p** and he who
1Co 9: 7 Who **p** a vineyard and does not

PLASTER (*see* PLASTERED)
Lev 14:42 other mortar and **p** the house
Lev 14:45 all the **p** of the house, and he
Ezek 13:10 they **p** it with untempered
Ezek 13:11 say to those who **p** it with
Dan 5: 5 the lampstand on the **p** of the

PLASTERED (*see* PLASTER)
Lev 14:43 the house, and after it is **p**
Lev 14:48 house after the house was **p**
Ezek 13:12 mortar with which you **p** it
Ezek 13:14 have **p** with untempered mortar
Ezek 13:15 on those who have **p** it with
Ezek 13:15 no more, nor those who **p** it
Ezek 22:28 Her prophets **p** them with

PLATE (*see* PLATES)
Ex 28:36 also make a **p** of pure gold
Ex 39:30 Then they made the **p** of the
Lev 8: 9 front, he put the golden **p**
Ezek 4: 3 take for yourself an iron **p**

PLATEAU
Deut 4:43 on the **p** for the Reubenites

PLATES (*see* PLATE)
Num 16:38 them be made into hammered **p**
1Ki 7:36 On the **p** of its flanges and on
Jer 10: 9 Silver is beaten into **p**

PLATFORM
2Ch 6:13 a bronze **p** five cubits long
Neh 8: 4 Ezra the scribe stood on a **p**

PLATITUDES
Job 13:12 Your **p** are proverbs of ashes,

PLATTER (*see* PLATTERS)
Num 7:13 His offering was one silver **p**
Num 7:19 he offered one silver **p**, the
Num 7:25 His offering was one silver **p**
Num 7:31 His offering was one silver **p**
Num 7:37 His offering was one silver **p**
Num 7:43 His offering was one silver **p**
Num 7:49 His offering was one silver **p**
Num 7:55 His offering was one silver **p**
Num 7:61 His offering was one silver **p**
Num 7:67 His offering was one silver **p**
Num 7:73 His offering was one silver **p**
Num 7:79 His offering was one silver **p**
Num 7:85 Each silver **p** weighed one
Matt 14: 8 Baptist's head here on a **p**
Matt 14:11 his head was brought on a **p**
Mark 6:25 of John the Baptist on a **p**
Mark 6:28 brought his head on a **p**, and

PLATTERS (*see* PLATTER)
Num 7:84 twelve silver **p**, twelve
Ezra 1: 9 gold **p**, one thousand silver **p**

PLAY (*see* PLAYED, PLAYING, PLAYS)
Gen 4:21 of all those who **p** the harp
Ex 32: 6 eat and drink, and rose up to **p**
Ex 34:15 they **p** the harlot with their
Ex 34:16 his daughters **p** the harlot
Ex 34:16 make your sons **p** the harlot
Deut 22:21 to **p** the harlot in her
Deut 31:16 **p** the harlot with the gods of
1Sa 16:16 it shall be that he will **p** it
1Sa 16:17 me now a man who can **p** well
1Sa 16:23 a harp and **p** it with his hand
1Sa 21:15 **p** the madman in my presence
2Sa 6:21 Therefore I will **p** music
2Ch 21:13 to **p** the harlot like the
Job 40:20 beasts of the field **p** there
Job 41: 5 Will you **p** with him as with a
Ps 33: 3 **P** skillfully with a shout of
Ps 104:26 You have made to **p** there
Is 11: 8 shall **p** by the cobra's hole
Ezek 6: 9 by their eyes which **p** the
Ezek 33:32 can **p** well on an instrument
Hos 3: 3 you shall not **p** the harlot
Hos 4:15 **p** the harlot, let not Judah
1Co 10: 7 eat and drink, and rose up to **p**

PLAYED (*see* PLAY)
Gen 38:24 has **p** the harlot
Lev 17: 7 whom they have **p** the harlot
Judg 2:17 but they **p** the harlot with
Judg 8:27 all Israel **p** the harlot with
Judg 8:33 children of Israel again **p**
Judg 19: 2 But his concubine **p** the
1Sa 18:10 So David **p** music with his
1Sa 26:21 Indeed I have **p** the fool and
2Sa 6: 5 all the house of Israel **p**
1Ki 1:40 and the people **p** the flutes
2Ki 3:15 happened, when the musician **p**
1Ch 5:25 **p** the harlot after the gods
1Ch 13: 8 all Israel **p** music before God
Ps 106:39 **p** the harlot by their own
Jer 3: 1 But you have **p** the harlot
Jer 3: 6 tree, and there **p** the harlot
Jer 3: 8 but went and **p** the harlot also
Ezek 16:15 **p** the harlot because of your
Ezek 16:16 and **p** the harlot on them
Ezek 16:17 and **p** the harlot with them

Ezek 16:28 You also **p** the harlot with
Ezek 16:28 indeed you **p** the harlot with
Ezek 23: 5 Oholah **p** the harlot even
Ezek 23:19 when she had **p** the harlot in
Hos 2: 5 their mother has **p** the harlot
Hos 4:12 and they have **p** the harlot
Hos 9: 1 for you have **p** the harlot
Matt 11:17 We **p** the flute for you, And
Luke 7:32 We **p** the flute for you, and
1Co 14: 7 be known what is piped or **p**
Gal 2:13 also **p** the hypocrite with him

PLAYER (*see* PLAYERS)
1Sa 16:16 is a skillful **p** on the harp

PLAYERS (*see* PLAYER)
Ps 68:25 the **p** on instruments followed
Ps 87: 7 the **p** on instruments say,
Matt 9:23 house, and saw the flute **p**

PLAYING (*see* PLAY)
Lev 21: 9 herself by **p** the harlot, she
1Sa 16:18 who is skillful in **p**, a
1Sa 19: 9 David was **p** music with his
1Ch 15:29 David whirling and **p** music
Ps 68:25 were the maidens **p** timbrels
Jer 2:20 you lay down, **p** the harlot
Ezek 16:41 make you cease **p** the harlot
Zech 8: 5 and girls **p** in its streets
Rev 14: 2 of harpists **p** their harps

PLAYS (*see* PLAY)
Ezek 23:44 to a woman who **p** the harlot

PLEA (*see* PLEAD)
Gen 25:21 and the LORD granted his **p**

PLEAD (*see* PLEA, PLEADED, PLEADING, PLEADS)
Judg 6:31 Would you **p** for Baal
Judg 6:31 Let the one who would **p** for
Judg 6:31 a god, let him **p** for himself,
Judg 6:32 Let Baal **p** against him,
1Sa 24:15 **p** my case, and deliver me out
Esth 4: 8 **p** before him for her people
Job 16:21 that one might **p** for a man
Job 19: 5 **p** my disgrace against me,
Ps 35: 1 **P** my cause, O LORD, with
Ps 43: 1 **p** my cause against an ungodly
Ps 74:22 O God, **p** Your own cause
Ps 119:154 **P** my cause and redeem me
Prov 6: 3 **p** with your friend
Prov 18:17 The first one to **p** his cause
Prov 22:23 the LORD will **p** their cause
Prov 23:11 he will **p** their cause against
Prov 31: 9 **p** the cause of the poor and
Is 1:17 fatherless, **p** for the widow
Is 3:13 The LORD stands up to **p**, and
Is 59: 4 nor does any **p** for truth
Jer 2:29 Why will you **p** with Me
Jer 2:35 I will **p** My case against you,
Jer 5:28 they do not **p** the cause, the
Jer 12: 1 O LORD, when I **p** with You
Jer 25:31 He will **p** His case with all
Jer 30:13 is no one to **p** your cause
Jer 50:34 will thoroughly **p** their case
Jer 51:36 I will **p** your case and take
Ezek 20:35 there I will **p** My case with
Ezek 20:36 so I will **p** My case with you,
Mic 6: 1 Arise, **p** your case before the
Mark 5:17 Then they began to **p** with Him
1Co 1:10 Now I **p** with you, brethren,
2Co 6: 1 together with Him also **p** with
2Jn 5 now I **p** with you, lady, not

PLEADED (*see* PLEAD)
Gen 25:21 Now Isaac **p** with the LORD for
Gen 42:21 of his soul when he **p** with us
Ex 32:11 Then Moses **p** with the LORD
Deut 3:23 Then I **p** with the LORD at
1Sa 25:39 who has **p** the cause of my
2Sa 12:16 David therefore **p** with God
2Ki 1:13 **p** with him, and said to him
2Ki 13: 4 So Jehoahaz **p** with the LORD,
Jer 20:12 for I have **p** my cause before
Lam 3:58 You have **p** the case for my
Ezek 20:36 Just as I **p** My case with your
Luke 15:28 father came out and **p** with him
Acts 16: 9 stood and **p** with him, saying,
Acts 16:39 **p** with them and brought them
Acts 21:12 those from that place **p** with
2Co 12: 8 Concerning this thing I **p**

PLEADING (*see* PLEAD, PLEADINGS)
Esth 7: 7 **p** for his life, for he saw
Matt 8: 5 came to Him, **p** with Him,
Luke 7: 3 **p** with Him to come and heal
Acts 19:31 sent to him **p** that he would
2Co 5:20 though God were **p** through us
2Co 10: 1 myself am **p** with you by the

PLEADINGS (*see* PLEADING)
Job 13: 6 and heed the **p** of my lips

PLEADS (*see* PLEAD)
Job 16:21 as a man **p** for his neighbor
Is 51:22 Who **p** the cause of His people
Mic 7: 9 Him, until He **p** my case and
Rom 11: 2 how he **p** with God against

PLEASANT (*see* PLEASANTNESS)
Gen 2: 9 grow that is **p** to the sight
Gen 3: 6 that it was **p** to the eyes
Gen 49:15 good, and that the land was **p**
Deut 3:25 those **p** mountains, and
2Sa 1:23 **p** in their lives, and in their
2Sa 1:26 you have been very **p** to me
1Ki 20: 6 whatever is **p** in your eyes
2Ki 2:19 situation of this city is **p**
Ps 16: 6 have fallen to me in **p** places
Ps 81: 2 The **p** harp with the lute
Ps 106:24 Then they despised the **p** land
Ps 133: 1 how **p** it is For brethren to
Ps 135: 3 to His name, for it is **p**
Ps 147: 1 For it is **p**, and praise is
Prov 2:10 knowledge is **p** to your soul
Prov 9:17 and bread eaten in secret is **p**
Prov 15:26 the words of the pure are **p**
Prov 16:24 **P** words are like a honeycomb,
Prov 22:18 for it is a **p** thing if you
Prov 23: 8 up, and waste your **p** words
Prov 24: 4 with all precious and **p** riches
Eccl 11: 7 and it is **p** for the eyes to
Song 1:16 handsome, my beloved! Yes, **p**!
Song 4:13 of pomegranates with **p** fruits
Song 4:16 garden and eat its **p** fruits
Song 7: 6 how **p** you are, O love, with
Song 7:13 and at our gates are **p** fruits
Is 5: 7 men of Judah are His **p** plant
Is 13:22 and jackals in their **p** palaces
Is 17:10 you will plant **p** plants and
Is 32:12 breasts for the **p** fields, for
Is 64:11 all our **p** things are laid
Jer 3:19 children and give you a **p** land
Jer 12:10 they have made My **p** portion a
Jer 23:10 The **p** places of the
Jer 31:20 Is he a **p** child
Lam 1: 7 **p** things that she had in the
Lam 1:10 hand over all her **p** things
Ezek 26:12 and destroy your **p** houses
Ezek 33:32 song of one who has a **p** voice
Dan 10: 3 I ate no **p** food, no meat or
Dan 11:38 precious stones and **p** things
Hos 9:13 Tyre, planted in a **p** place
Amos 5:11 you have planted **p** vineyards
Mic 2: 9 cast out from their **p** houses
Zech 7:14 they made the **p** land desolate
Mal 3: 4 will be **p** to the LORD, as in

PLEASANTNESS (*see* PLEASANT)
Prov 3:17 Her ways are ways of **p**, and

PLEASE (*see* PLEASED, PLEASES, PLEASING)
Gen 12:13 **P** say you are my sister, that
Gen 13: 8 **P** let there be no strife
Gen 13: 9 **P** separate from me
Gen 16: 2 **P**, go in to my maid
Gen 16: 6 do to her as you **p**
Gen 18: 4 **P** let a little water be
Gen 19: 2 **p** turn in to your servant's
Gen 19: 7 **P**, my brethren, do not do so
Gen 19: 8 **p**, let me bring them out to
Gen 19:18 **P**, no, my lords
Gen 19:20 **p** let me escape there (is it
Gen 23:13 you will give it, **p** hear me
Gen 24: 2 **P**, put your hand under my
Gen 24:12 **p** give me success this day,
Gen 24:14 **P** let down your pitcher that
Gen 24:17 **P** let me drink a little water
Gen 24:23 Tell me, **p**, is there room in
Gen 24:43 **P** give me a little water from
Gen 24:45 said to her, '**P** let me drink
Gen 25:30 **P** feed me with that same red
Gen 27: 3 **p** take your weapons, your
Gen 27:19 **p** arise, sit and eat of my
Gen 27:21 **P** come near, that I may feel
Gen 28: 8 did not **p** his father Isaac
Gen 30:14 **P** give me some of your son's
Gen 30:27 **P** stay, if I have found favor
Gen 33:10 No, **p**, if I have now found
Gen 33:11 **P**, take my blessing that is
Gen 33:14 **P** let my lord go on ahead
Gen 34: 8 **P** give her to him as a wife
Gen 37: 6 **P** hear this dream which I
Gen 37:14 **P** go and see if it is well
Gen 37:16 **P** tell me where they are
Gen 38:16 **P** let me come in to you"
Gen 38:25 **P** determine whose these are
Gen 40: 8 Tell them to me, **p**
Gen 40:14 you, and **p** show kindness to me
Gen 44:18 **p** let your servant speak a
Gen 44:33 **p** let your servant remain
Gen 45: 4 brothers, "**P** come near to me
Gen 47: 4 **p** let your servants dwell in
Gen 47:29 **p** put your hand under my
Gen 47:29 **P** do not bury me in Egypt,
Gen 48: 9 **P** bring them to me, and I will
Gen 50: 4 **p** speak in the hearing of
Gen 50: 5 **p** let me go up and bury my
Gen 50:17 **p** forgive the trespass of
Gen 50:17 Now, **p**, forgive the
Ex 3:18 and now, **p**, let us go three
Ex 4:13 Lord, **p** send by the hand of
Ex 4:18 **P** let me go and return to my
Ex 5: 3 **P**, let us go three days'
Ex 10:17 **p** forgive my sin only this
Ex 21: 8 If she does not **p** her master
Ex 33:18 **P**, show me Your glory
Num 10:31 **P** do not leave, inasmuch as
Num 11:15 this, **p** kill me here and now
Num 12:11 **P** do not lay this sin on us,
Num 12:12 **P** do not let her be as one
Num 12:13 **P** heal her, O God, I pray
Num 20:17 **P** let us pass through your
Num 22: 6 Therefore **p** come at once,
Num 22:16 **P** let nothing hinder you
Num 22:17 Therefore **p** come, curse this
Num 22:19 Now therefore, **p**, you also
Num 23:13 **P** come with me to another
Num 23:27 **P** come, I will take you to
Num 23:27 perhaps it will **p** God that
Judg 1:24 **P** show us the entrance to the
Judg 4:19 **P** give me a little water to
Judg 8: 5 **P** give loaves of bread to the
Judg 9: 2 **P** speak in the hearing of all
Judg 11:17 **P** let me pass through your
Judg 11:19 **P** let us pass through your
Judg 13: 4 **p** be careful not to drink
Judg 13: 8 **p** let the Man of God whom You
Judg 13:15 **P** let us detain You, and we
Judg 15: 2 **P**, take her instead
Judg 16: 6 **P** tell me where your great
Judg 16:10 **p** tell me what you may be
Judg 18: 5 **P** inquire of God, that we may
Judg 19: 6 **P** be content to stay all
Judg 19: 8 said, "**P** refresh your heart
Judg 19: 9 **p** spend the night
Judg 19:11 Come, **p**, and let us turn aside
Judg 19:24 and do with them as you **p**
Ruth 2: 2 **P** let me go to the field, and
Ruth 2: 7 **P** let me glean and gather
1Sa 2:36 **P**, put me in one of the
1Sa 3:17 **P** do not hide it from me
1Sa 9: 3 **P**, take one of the servants
1Sa 9:18 **P** tell me, where is the
1Sa 10:15 Tell me, **p**, what Samuel said
1Sa 15:25 **p** pardon my sin, and return
1Sa 15:30 yet honor me now, **p**, before
1Sa 16:22 **P** let David stand before me,
1Sa 19: 2 Therefore **p** be on your guard
1Sa 20:29 **P** let me go, for our family
1Sa 20:29 **p** let me get away and see my
1Sa 22: 3 **P** let my father and mother
1Sa 23:22 **P** go and find out for sure, and
1Sa 25: 8 **P** give whatever comes to your
1Sa 25:24 **p** let your maidservant speak
1Sa 25:25 **P**, let not my lord regard
1Sa 25:28 **P** forgive the trespass of
1Sa 26: 8 Now therefore, **p**, let me
1Sa 26:11 But **p**, take now the spear and
1Sa 26:19 Now therefore, **p**, let my lord
1Sa 28: 8 **P** conduct a seance for me, and
1Sa 28:22 Now therefore, **p**, heed also
1Sa 30: 7 **P** bring the ephod here to me
2Sa 1: 4 the matter go? **P** tell me.
2Sa 1: 9 **P** stand over me and kill me,
2Sa 7:29 let it **p** You to bless the

2Sa 13: 5 **P** let my sister Tamar come
2Sa 13: 6 **P** let Tamar my sister come and
2Sa 13:13 **p** speak to the king
2Sa 13:24 **p**, let the king and his
2Sa 13:26 **p** let my brother Amnon go
2Sa 14: 2 **P** pretend to be a mourner, and
2Sa 14:11 **P** let the king remember the
2Sa 14:12 **P**, let your maidservant speak
2Sa 14:18 **P** do not hide from me
2Sa 14:18 **P**, let my lord the king speak
2Sa 15: 7 **P**, let me go to Hebron and pay
2Sa 16: 9 **P**, let me go over and take off
2Sa 18:22 **p** let me also run after the
2Sa 19:37 **P** let your servant turn back
2Sa 20:16 **P** say to Joab, 'Come nearby,
2Sa 24:14 **P** let us fall into the hand
1Ki 1:12 Come, **p**, let me now give you
1Ki 2:17 **P** speak to King Solomon, for
1Ki 9:12 him, but they did not **p** him
1Ki 13: 6 **P** entreat the favor of the
1Ki 14: 2 **P** arise, and disguise yourself
1Ki 17:10 **P** bring me a little water in
1Ki 17:11 **P** bring me a morsel of bread
1Ki 19:20 **P** let me kiss my father and my
1Ki 20: 7 Notice, **p**, and see how this
1Ki 20:31 **P**, let us put sackcloth
1Ki 20:32 says, '**P** let me live
1Ki 20:35 Strike me, **p**." And the man
1Ki 20:37 and said, "Strike me, **p**."
1Ki 22: 5 **P** inquire for the word of the
1Ki 22:13 **P**, let your word be like the
2Ki 1:13 **p** let my life and the life of
2Ki 2: 2 Stay here, **p**, for the LORD
2Ki 2: 4 Elisha, stay here, **p**, for the
2Ki 2: 6 Stay here, **p**, for the LORD
2Ki 2: 9 **P** let a double portion of
2Ki 2:16 **P** let them go and search for
2Ki 2:19 **P** notice, the situation of
2Ki 4:10 **P**, let us make a small upper
2Ki 4:22 **P** send me one of the young
2Ki 4:26 **P** run now to meet her, and say
2Ki 5: 7 Therefore **p** consider, and see
2Ki 5: 8 **P** let him come to me, and he
2Ki 5:15 **p** take a gift from your
2Ki 5:17 **p** let your servant be given
2Ki 5:18 may the LORD **p** pardon your
2Ki 5:22 **P** give them a talent of
2Ki 5:23 **P**, take two talents
2Ki 6: 2 **P**, let us go to the Jordan,
2Ki 6: 3 **P** consent to go with your
2Ki 7:13 **P**, let several men take five
2Ki 8: 4 Tell me, **p**, all the great
2Ki 18:26 **P** speak to your servants in
1Ch 21:13 **P** let me fall into the hand
2Ch 10: 7 **p** them, and speak good words
2Ch 18: 4 **P** inquire for the word of the
2Ch 18:12 Therefore **p** let your word be
Ezra 10:14 **P**, let the leaders of our
Neh 1: 6 **p** let Your ear be attentive
Neh 1:11 **p** let Your ear be attentive
Neh 5:10 **P**, let us stop this usury
Esth 8: 8 decree for the Jews, as you **p**
Job 6: 9 That it would **p** God to crush
Job 8: 8 For inquire, **p**, of the former
Job 17:10 But **p**, come back again, all
Job 22:22 Receive, **p**, instruction from
Job 33: 1 But **p**, Job, hear my speech,
Job 42: 4 Listen, **p**, and let me speak
Ps 69:31 This also shall **p** the LORD
Prov 16: 7 When a man's ways **p** the LORD
Is 5: 3 and men of Judah, judge, **p**
Is 5: 5 **p** let Me tell you what I will
Is 29:11 saying, "Read this, **p**"
Is 29:12 saying, "Read this, **p**"
Is 36:11 **P** speak to your servants in
Is 51:21 Therefore **p** hear this, you
Is 55:11 it shall accomplish what I **p**
Is 64: 9 indeed, **p** look—we all are
Jer 21: 2 **P** inquire of the LORD for us,
Jer 32: 8 **P** buy my field that is in
Jer 37:20 Therefore **p** hear now, O my
Jer 37:20 **P**, let my petition be
Jer 38: 4 **P**, let this man be put to
Jer 38:12 **P** put these old clothes and
Jer 38:20 **P**, obey the voice of the LORD
Jer 40:15 Let me go, **p**, and I will kill
Jer 42: 2 **P**, let our petition be
Ezek 33:30 **P** come and hear what the word
Dan 1:12 **P** test your servants for ten
Jon 1: 8 they said to him, "**P** tell us
Jon 1:14 **p** do not let us perish for
Jon 4: 3 **p** take my life from me, for
John 8:29 do those things that **p** Him
Rom 8: 8 are in the flesh cannot **p** God
Rom 15: 1 weak, and not to **p** ourselves
Rom 15: 2 Let each of us **p** his neighbor
Rom 15: 3 even Christ did not **p** Himself
1Co 7:32 how he may **p** the Lord
1Co 7:33 how he may **p** his wife
1Co 7:34 how she may **p** her husband
1Co 10:33 just as I also **p** all men in
Gal 1:10 Or do I seek to **p** men
1Th 2:15 and they do not **p** God and are
1Th 4: 1 you ought to walk and to **p** God
2Ti 2: 4 life, that he may **p** him who
Heb 11: 6 it is impossible to **p** Him

PLEASED (*see* PLEASE)
Gen 33:10 of God, and you were **p** with me
Gen 34:18 And their words **p** Hamor and
Gen 45:16 So it **p** Pharaoh and his
Num 24: 1 it **p** the LORD to bless Israel
Deut 1:23 And the plan **p** me well
Josh 22:30 of Manasseh spoke, it **p** them
Josh 22:33 So the thing **p** the children
Judg 14: 7 and she **p** Samson well
1Sa 12:22 because it has **p** the LORD to
1Sa 18:20 told Saul, and the thing **p** him
1Sa 18:26 it **p** David well to become the
2Sa 3:36 it **p** them, since whatever the
2Sa 3:36 the king did **p** all the people
2Sa 17: 4 And the saying **p** Absalom and
2Sa 19: 6 then it would have **p** you well
1Ki 3:10 And the speech **p** the LORD,
1Ch 17:27 Now You have been **p** to bless
1Ch 28: 4 He was **p** with me to make me
2Ch 30: 4 And the matter **p** the king and
Neh 2: 6 So it **p** the king to send me
Esth 1:21 And the reply **p** the king and
Esth 2: 4 This thing **p** the king, and
Esth 2: 9 Now the young woman **p** him
Esth 5:14 And the thing **p** Haman
Esth 9: 5 did what they **p** with those
Job 6:28 therefore, be **p** to look at me
Ps 40:13 Be **p**, O LORD, to deliver me
Ps 41:11 that You are well **p** with me
Ps 51:19 Then You shall be **p** with the
Is 2: 6 they are **p** with the children
Is 39: 2 And Hezekiah was **p** with them
Is 42:21 The LORD is well **p** for His
Is 53:10 Yet it **p** the LORD to bruise
Dan 6: 1 It **p** Darius to set over the
Jon 1:14 O LORD, have done as it **p** You
Mic 6: 7 Will the LORD be **p** with
Mal 1: 8 Would he be **p** with you
Matt 3:17 Son, in whom I am well **p**
Matt 12:18 in whom My soul is well **p**
Matt 14: 6 danced before them and **p**
Matt 17: 5 Son, in whom I am well **p**
Mark 1:11 Son, in whom I am well **p**
Mark 6:22 **p** Herod and those who sat with
Luke 3:22 in You I am well **p**
Acts 6: 5 And the saying **p** the whole
Acts 12: 3 he saw that it **p** the Jews
Acts 15:22 Then it **p** the apostles and
Rom 15:26 For it **p** those from Macedonia
Rom 15:27 It **p** them indeed, and they are
1Co 1:21 God, it **p** God through the
1Co 10: 5 of them God was not well **p**
1Co 12:18 in the body just as He **p**
2Co 5: 8 well **p** rather to be absent
Gal 1:10 For if I still **p** men, I would
Gal 1:15 But when it **p** God, who
Col 1:19 For it **p** the Father that in
1Th 2: 8 we were well **p** to impart to
Heb 11: 5 this testimony, that he **p** God
Heb 13:16 such sacrifices God is well **p**
2Pe 1:17 Son, in whom I am well **p**

PLEASES (*see* PLEASE)
Gen 20:15 dwell where it **p** you
Judg 14: 3 her for me, for she **p** me well
1Sa 20:13 But if it **p** my father to do
1Ki 21: 6 or else, if it **p** you, I will
Neh 2: 5 If it **p** the king, and if your
Neh 2: 7 If it **p** the king, let letters
Esth 1:19 If it **p** the king, let a royal
Esth 2: 4 let the young woman who **p** the
Esth 3: 9 If it **p** the king, let a
Esth 5: 4 If it **p** the king, let the
Esth 5: 8 if it **p** the king to grant my
Esth 7: 3 if it **p** the king, let my life
Esth 8: 5 If it **p** the king, and if I
Esth 9:13 If it **p** the king, let it be
Ps 115: 3 He does whatever He **p**
Ps 135: 6 Whatever the LORD **p** He does
Eccl 7:26 He who **p** God shall escape
Eccl 8: 3 for he does whatever **p** him
Song 2: 7 up nor awaken love until it **p**
Song 3: 5 up nor awaken love until it **p**
Song 8: 4 up nor awaken love until it **p**
Is 56: 4 Sabbaths, and choose what **p** Me
1Co 15:38 God gives it a body as He **p**

PLEASING (*see* PLEASE)
Esth 8: 5 I am **p** in his eyes, let it be
Jer 42: 6 Whether it is **p** or
Lam 2: 4 all who were **p** to His eye
Hos 9: 4 their sacrifices be **p** to Him
Acts 7:20 born, and was well **p** to God
2Co 5: 9 absent, to be well **p** to Him
Phil 4:18 sacrifice, well **p** to God
Col 1:10 of the Lord, fully **p** Him,
Col 3:20 this is well **p** to the Lord
1Th 2: 4 so we speak, not as **p** men
Tit 2: 9 to be well **p** in all things,
Heb 13:21 what is well **p** in His sight
1Jn 3:22 that are **p** in His sight

PLEASURE (*see* PLEASURES)
Gen 18:12 grown old, shall I have **p**
Deut 23:24 your fill of grapes at your **p**
1Ch 29:17 and have **p** in uprightness
Ezra 5:17 his **p** concerning this matter
Neh 9:37 and our cattle at their **p**
Esth 1: 8 do according to each man's **p**
Job 21:25 never having eaten with **p**
Job 22: 3 Is it any **p** to the Almighty
Ps 5: 4 God who takes **p** in wickedness
Ps 35:27 Who has **p** in the prosperity
Ps 51:18 good in Your good **p** to Zion
Ps 102:14 servants take **p** in her stones
Ps 103:21 of His, who do His **p**
Ps 105:22 To bind his princes at his **p**
Ps 111: 2 by all who have **p** in them
Ps 147:10 He takes no **p** in the legs of
Ps 147:11 The LORD takes **p** in those who
Ps 149: 4 LORD takes **p** in His people
Prov 21:17 He who loves **p** will be a poor
Eccl 2: 1 therefore enjoy **p**"
Eccl 2:10 withhold my heart from any **p**
Eccl 5: 4 for He has no **p** in fools
Eccl 12: 1 I have no **p** in them"
Is 44:28 and he shall perform all My **p**
Is 46:10 stand, and I will do all My **p**
Is 48:14 he shall do His **p** on Babylon
Is 53:10 and the **p** of the LORD shall
Is 58: 3 day of your fast you find **p**
Is 58:13 doing your **p** on My holy day
Is 58:13 ways, nor finding your own **p**
Jer 22:28 he a vessel in which is no **p**
Jer 34:16 set at liberty, at their **p**
Jer 48:38 a vessel in which is no **p**
Ezek 16:37 lovers with whom you took **p**
Ezek 18:23 Do I have any **p** at all that
Ezek 18:32 For I have no **p** in the death
Ezek 33:11 I have no **p** in the death of
Hos 8: 8 vessel in which there is no **p**
Hag 1: 8 that I may take **p** in it and
Mal 1:10 I have no **p** in you," Says
Luke 12:32 **p** to give you the kingdom
2Co 12:10 I take **p** in infirmities, in
Eph 1: 5 to the good **p** of His will
Eph 1: 9 good **p** which He purposed in
Phil 2:13 will and to do for His good **p**
2Th 1:11 the good **p** of His goodness
2Th 2:12 but had **p** in unrighteousness
1Ti 5: 6 But she who lives in **p** is
2Ti 3: 4 lovers of **p** rather than
Heb 10: 6 for sin you had no **p**
Heb 10: 8 nor had **p** in them" (which
Heb 10:38 back, my soul has no **p** in him
Jas 4: 1 **p** that war in your members
Jas 5: 5 have lived on the earth in **p**
2Pe 2:13 as those who count it **p** to

PLEASURES (*see* PLEASURE)
Job 36:11 and their years in **p**
Ps 16:11 right hand are **p** forevermore
Ps 36: 8 from the river of Your **p**
Is 47: 8 now, you who are given to **p**
Luke 8:14 **p** of life, and bring no fruit
Tit 3: 3 serving various lusts and **p**

Heb 11:25 to enjoy the passing **p** of sin
Jas 4: 3 you may spend it on your **p**

PLEDGE (*see* PLEDGED, PLEDGES)
Gen 38:17 give me a **p** till you send it
Gen 38:18 What **p** shall I give you
Gen 38:20 to receive his **p** from the
Ex 22:26 neighbor's garment as a **p**
Lev 6: 2 for safekeeping, or about a **p**
Deut 24: 6 or the upper millstone in **p**
Deut 24: 6 he takes one's living in **p**
Deut 24:10 into his house to get his **p**
Deut 24:11 shall bring the **p** out to you
Deut 24:12 not keep his **p** overnight
Deut 24:13 in any case return the **p** to
Deut 24:17 take a widow's garment as a **p**
2Ki 18:23 give a **p** to my master the
Job 17: 3 Now put down a **p** for me with
Job 24: 3 take the widow's ox as a **p**
Job 24: 9 and take a **p** from the poor
Prov 6: 1 hands in **p** for a stranger
Prov 17:18 shakes hands in a **p**, and
Prov 20:16 hold it as a **p** when it is for
Prov 22:26 those who shakes hands in a **p**
Prov 27:13 and hold it in **p** when he is
Is 36: 8 give a **p** to my master the
Ezek 18: 7 restored to the debtor his **p**
Ezek 18:12 violence, not restored the **p**
Ezek 18:16 anyone, nor withheld a **p**, nor
Ezek 33:15 if the wicked restores the **p**
Amos 2: 8 altar on clothes taken in **p**

PLEDGED (*see* PLEDGE)
Neh 6:18 many in Judah were **p** to him
Jer 30:21 for who is this who **p** his

PLEDGES (*see* PLEDGE)
Job 22: 6 For you have taken **p** from
Hab 2: 6 loads himself with many **p**'

PLEIADES
Job 9: 9 the Bear, Orion, and the **P**
Job 38:31 you bind the cluster of the **P**
Amos 5: 8 He made the **P** and Orion

PLENTEOUS (*see* PLENTY)
Is 30:23 it will be fat and **p**
Hab 1:16 is sumptuous and their food **p**

PLENTIFUL (*see* PLENTIFULLY, PLENTY)
Gen 41:34 of Egypt in the seven **p** years
Gen 41:47 Now in the seven **p** years the
Ps 68: 9 You, O God, sent a **p** rain
Is 16:10 away, and joy from the **p** field
Jer 48:33 are taken from the **p** field
Matt 9:37 The harvest truly is **p**, but

PLENTIFULLY (*see* PLENTIFUL)
Luke 12:16 a certain rich man yielded **p**

PLENTY (*see* PLENTEOUS, PLENTIFUL)
Gen 27:28 earth, and **p** of grain and wine
Gen 41:29 **p** will come throughout all
Gen 41:30 all the **p** will be forgotten
Gen 41:31 So the **p** will not be known in
Gen 41:53 Then the seven years of **p**
Lev 11:36 in which there is **p** of water
Deut 28:11 will grant you **p** of goods
2Ch 31:10 enough to eat and have **p** left
Prov 3:10 barns will be filled with **p**
Prov 21: 5 the diligent lead surely to **p**
Prov 28:19 his land will have **p** of bread
Jer 44:17 For then we had **p** of food
Joel 2:26 You shall eat in **p** and be

PLIGHT
Job 9:23 at the **p** of the innocent
Job 30:16 is poured out because of my **p**

PLOT (*see* PLOTS, PLOTTED, PLOTTING)
Josh 24:32 in the **p** of ground which
2Ki 9:26 and I will repay you in this **p**
2Ki 9:26 throw him on the **p** of ground
2Ki 9:36 On the **p** of ground at
2Ki 9:37 in the **p** at Jezreel, so that
Esth 8: 3 evil **p** of Haman the Agagite
Esth 9:25 **p** which Haman had devised
Ps 2: 1 the people **p** a vain thing
Ps 21:11 They devised a **p** which they
Ps 35: 4 to confusion Who **p** my hurt
Ezek 45: 2 a square **p** for the sanctuary
John 4: 5 near the **p** of ground that
Acts 4:25 and the people **p** vain things
Acts 9:24 But their **p** became known to

PLOTS (*see* PLOT)
Ps 10: 2 the **p** which they have devised
Ps 31:20 presence From the **p** of man
Ps 37:12 The wicked **p** against the just
Prov 24: 8 He who **p** to do evil will be
Nah 1:11 who **p** evil against the LORD

PLOTTED (*see* PLOT)
1Sa 23: 9 that Saul **p** evil against him
2Sa 21: 5 **p** against us, that we should
Esth 9:24 had **p** against the Jews to
Matt 22:15 **p** how they might entangle Him
Matt 26: 4 **p** to take Jesus by trickery
Mark 3: 6 out and immediately **p** with the
John 11:53 on they **p** to put Him to death
Acts 9:23 past, the Jews **p** to kill him
Acts 20: 3 when the Jews **p** against him

PLOTTING (*see* PLOT)
Acts 20:19 to me by the **p** of the Jews

PLOW (*see* PLOWED, PLOWERS, PLOWING, PLOWMAN, PLOWS, PLOWSHARE)
Deut 22:10 You shall not **p** with an ox
1Sa 8:12 will set some to **p** his ground
Job 4: 8 seen, those who **p** iniquity
Job 39:10 Or will he **p** the valleys
Prov 20: 4 will not **p** because of winter
Hos 10:11 I will make Ephraim pull a **p**
Hos 10:11 Judah shall **p**
Amos 6:12 Does one **p** there with oxen
Luke 9:62 having put his hand to the **p**
1Co 9:10 he who plows should **p** in hope

PLOWED (*see* PLOW)
Deut 21: 4 which is neither **p** nor sown
Judg 14:18 you had not **p** with my heifer
Ps 129: 3 The plowers **p** on my back
Jer 26:18 Zion shall be **p** like a field
Hos 10:13 You have **p** wickedness
Mic 3:12 Zion shall be **p** like a field

PLOWERS (*see* PLOW)
Ps 129: 3 The **p** plowed on my back

PLOWING (*see* PLOW)
Gen 45: 6 be neither **p** nor harvesting
Ex 34:21 in **p** time and in harvest you
1Ki 19:19 who was **p** with twelve yoke of
Job 1:14 The oxen were **p** and the
Prov 21: 4 the **p** of the wicked are sin
Is 28:24 plowman keep **p** all day to sow
Luke 17: 7 a servant **p** or tending sheep

PLOWMAN (*see* PLOW, PLOWMEN)
Is 28:24 Does the **p** keep plowing all
Amos 9:13 When the **p** shall overtake the

PLOWMEN (*see* PLOWMAN)
Is 61: 5 the foreigner shall be your **p**
Jer 14: 4 the land, the **p** were ashamed

PLOWS (*see* PLOW)
Ps 141: 7 of the grave, As when one **p**
1Co 9:10 that he who **p** should plow in

PLOWSHARE (*see* PLOW, PLOWSHARES)
1Sa 13:20 to sharpen each man's **p**, his

PLOWSHARES (*see* PLOWSHARE)
1Sa 13:21 was a pim for the **p**, the
Is 2: 4 beat their swords into **p**, and
Joel 3:10 Beat your **p** into swords and
Mic 4: 3 beat their swords into **p**, and

PLUCK (*see* PLUCKED)
Deut 23:25 you may **p** the heads with your
Job 30: 4 who **p** mallow by the bushes,
Ps 25:15 For He shall **p** my feet out of
Ps 52: 5 **p** you out of your dwelling
Ps 80:12 pass by the way **p** her fruit
Eccl 3: 2 a time to **p** what is planted
Jer 12:14 I will **p** them out of their
Jer 12:14 **p** out the house of Judah from
Jer 12:17 not obey, I will utterly **p** up
Jer 18: 7 concerning a kingdom, to **p** up
Jer 22:24 hand, yet I would **p** you off
Jer 24: 6 plant them and not **p** them up
Jer 31:28 watched over them to **p** up
Jer 42:10 plant you and not **p** you up
Jer 45: 4 I have planted I will **p** up
Ezek 17: 9 to **p** it up by its roots
Mic 5:14 I will **p** your wooden images
Matt 5:29 **p** it out and cast it from you
Matt 12: 1 began to **p** heads of grain and
Matt 18: 9 **p** it out and cast it from you
Mark 2:23 began to **p** the heads of grain
Mark 9:47 eye makes you sin, **p** it out

PLUCKED (*see* PLUCK)
Gen 8:11 a freshly **p** olive leaf was in
Deut 28:63 you shall be **p** from off the
Ezra 9: 3 **p** out some of the hair of my
Job 29:17 **p** the victim from his teeth
Is 50: 6 to those who **p** out the beard
Jer 12:15 be, after I have **p** them out
Jer 31:40 It shall not be **p** up or
Ezek 19:12 But she was **p** up in fury, she
Dan 7: 4 till its wings were **p** off
Dan 7: 8 horns were **p** out by the roots
Amos 4:11 firebrand **p** from the burning
Zech 3: 2 not a brand **p** from the fire
Luke 6: 1 His disciples **p** the heads of
Gal 4:15 you would have **p** out your own

PLUMB
Amos 7: 7 on a wall made with a **p** line
Amos 7: 7 with a **p** line in His hand
Amos 7: 8 And I said, "A **p** line
Amos 7: 8 I am setting a **p** line in the
Zech 4:10 see the **p** line in the hand of

PLUMMET
2Ki 21:13 the **p** of the house of Ahab
Is 28:17 line, and righteousness the **p**

PLUMP
Gen 41: 5 grain came up on one stalk, **p**
Gen 41: 7 heads devoured the seven **p**

PLUNDER (*see* PLUNDERED, PLUNDERER, PLUNDERING, PLUNDERS)
Ex 3:22 So you shall **p** the Egyptians
Num 31:26 Count up the **p** that was taken
Num 31:27 divide the **p** into two parts,
Num 31:32 booty remaining from the **p**
Deut 2:35 livestock as **p** for ourselves
Deut 13:16 its **p** into the middle of the
Deut 13:16 fire the city and all its **p**
Deut 20:14 you shall **p** for yourself
Deut 20:14 **p** which the LORD your God
Judg 5:30 **p** of dyed garments,
Judg 5:30 **p** of garments embroidered and
Judg 8:24 me the earrings from his **p**
Judg 8:25 it the earrings from his **p**
1Sa 14:36 and **p** them until the morning
1Sa 15:21 But the people took of the **p**
2Sa 23:10 returned after him only to **p**
2Ki 21:14 of **p** to all their enemies
Ezra 9: 7 the sword, to captivity, to **p**
Neh 4: 4 give them as **p** to a land of
Esth 3:13 and to **p** their possessions
Esth 8:11 and to **p** their possessions,
Esth 9:10 did not lay a hand on the **p**
Esth 9:15 did not lay a hand on the **p**
Esth 9:16 did not lay a hand on the **p**
Ps 89:41 All who pass by the way **p** him
Ps 109:11 And let strangers **p** his labor
Prov 22:23 **p** the soul of those who **p**
Prov 24:15 do not **p** his resting place
Is 3:14 the **p** of the poor is in your
Is 11:14 together they shall **p** the
Is 17:14 the portion of those who **p** us
Is 33: 1 Woe to you who **p**, though you
Is 33: 4 Your **p** shall be gathered like
Is 33:23 prey of great **p** is divided
Is 42:22 for **p**, and no one says
Is 42:24 Who gave Jacob for **p**, and
Jer 15:13 will give as **p** without price
Jer 17: 3 I will give as **p** your wealth
Jer 20: 5 enemies, who will **p** them,
Jer 20: 8 I shouted, "Violence and **p**!"
Jer 30:16 **p** you shall become **p**
Jer 47: 4 to **p** all the Philistines, to
Jer 47: 4 LORD shall **p** the Philistines
Jer 49:32 of their cattle for **p**
Jer 50:10 And Chaldea shall become **p**
Jer 50:10 all who **p** her shall be
Ezek 7:21 I will give it as **p** into the
Ezek 23:46 give them up to trouble and **p**
Ezek 25: 7 give you as **p** to the nations
Ezek 26: 5 become **p** for the nations
Ezek 26:12 They will **p** your riches and
Ezek 32:12 They shall **p** the pomp of
Ezek 36: 4 been forsaken, which became **p**
Ezek 36: 5 minds, in order to **p** its open
Ezek 38:12 to take **p** and to take booty,
Ezek 38:13 you, 'Have you come to take **p**
Ezek 38:13 and goods, to take great **p**

Ezek 39:10 and they will **p** those who
Dan 11:24 disperse among them the **p**
Hos 13:15 He shall **p** the treasury of
Hab 2: 8 of the people shall **p** you
Hab 2:17 the **p** of beasts which made
Zeph 2: 9 of My people shall **p** them
Zeph 3: 8 Until the day I rise up for **p**
Zech 2: 8 to the nations which **p** you
Matt 12:29 **p** his goods, unless he first
Matt 12:29 And then he will **p** his house
Mark 3:27 **p** his goods, unless he first
Mark 3:27 and then he will **p** his house

PLUNDERED (*see* PLUNDER)
Gen 34:27 **p** the city, because their
Gen 34:29 they **p** even all that was in
Ex 12:36 Thus they **p** the Egyptians
Deut 28:29 and **p** continually, and no one
Judg 2:16 the hand of those who **p** them
1Sa 14:48 the hands of those who **p** them
1Sa 17:53 and they **p** their tents
2Ki 7:16 **p** the tents of the Syrians
2Ch 14:14 they **p** all the cities, for
Job 12:17 He leads counselors away **p**
Job 12:19 He leads princes away **p**, and
Ps 7: 4 Or have **p** my enemy without
Ps 76: 5 The stouthearted were **p**
Ps 137: 3 those who **p** us required of us
Is 13:16 their houses will be **p** and
Is 24: 3 entirely emptied and utterly **p**
Is 33: 1 though you have not been **p**
Is 33: 1 plundering, you will be **p**
Is 42:22 this is a people robbed and **p**
Jer 2:14 Why is he **p**
Jer 4:13 woe to us, for we are **p**
Jer 4:20 for the whole land is **p**
Jer 4:20 Suddenly my tents are **p**, and
Jer 4:30 And when you are **p**, What will
Jer 9:19 How we are **p**! We are greatly
Jer 10:20 My tent is **p**, and all my cords
Jer 21:12 deliver him who is **p** out of
Jer 22: 3 deliver the **p** out of the hand
Jer 25:36 the LORD has **p** their pasture
Jer 48: 1 For it is **p**, Kirjathaim is
Jer 48:15 Moab is **p** and gone up from her
Jer 48:20 it in Arnon, that Moab is **p**
Jer 49: 3 Wail, O Heshbon, for Ai is **p**
Jer 49:10 His descendants are **p**, his
Ezek 39:10 will plunder those who **p** them
Hos 10:14 be **p** as Shalman **p** Beth Arbel
Amos 3:11 and your palaces shall be **p**
Hab 2: 8 you have **p** many nations, all

PLUNDERER (*see* PLUNDER, PLUNDERERS)
Is 21: 2 and the **p** plunders
Jer 6:26 for the **p** will suddenly come
Jer 15: 8 the young men, a **p** at noonday
Jer 48: 8 And the **p** shall come against
Jer 48:18 for the **p** of Moab has come
Jer 48:32 The **p** has fallen on your
Jer 51:56 because the **p** comes against

PLUNDERERS (*see* PLUNDERER)
Judg 2:14 hands of **p** who despoiled them
2Ki 17:20 them into the hand of **p**,
Jer 12:12 The **p** have come on all the
Jer 51:48 for the **p** shall come to her
Jer 51:53 yet from Me **p** would come to

PLUNDERING (*see* PLUNDER)
Is 22: 4 the **p** of the daughter of my
Is 33: 1 When you cease **p**, you will be
Jer 6: 7 and **p** are heard in her
Jer 48: 3 **P** and great destruction
Jer 51:55 because the LORD is **p** Babylon
Ezek 45: 9 Remove violence and **p**, execute
Dan 11:33 and flame, by captivity and **p**
Hab 1: 3 For **p** and violence are before
Heb 10:34 accepted the **p** of your goods

PLUNDERS (*see* PLUNDER)
Ps 35:10 the needy from him who **p** him
Is 21: 2 and the plunderer **p**
Nah 3:16 The locust **p** and flies away

PLUNGE (*see* PLUNGED)
Job 9:31 yet You will **p** me into the

PLUNGED (*see* PLUNGE)
John 21: 7 it), and **p** into the sea

PLUS
Num 5: 7 full value **p** one-fifth of it

POCHERETH
Ezra 2:57 the sons of **P** of Zebaim, and
Neh 7:59 the children of **P** of Zebaim

POCKET
1Sa 25:29 out, as from the **p** of a sling

PODS
Luke 15:16 with the **p** that the swine ate

POETS
Acts 17:28 some of your own **p** have said

POINT (*see* POINTED, POINTING, POINTS)
Gen 46:28 to **p** out before him the way
Judg 5:18 their lives to the **p** of death
Job 20:25 the glittering **p** comes out of
Jer 17: 1 with the **p** of a diamond it is
Ezek 21:15 I have set the **p** of the sword
Ezek 47:20 comes to a **p** opposite Hamath
Mark 5:23 lies at the **p** of death
John 4:27 at this **p** His disciples came,
John 4:47 for he was at the **p** of death
Phil 2: 8 obedient to the **p** of death
2Ti 2: 9 even to the **p** of chains
Heb 8: 1 Now this is the main **p** of the
Jas 2:10 law, and yet stumble in one **p**

POINTED (*see* POINT, POINTEDLY)
1Ki 7:25 all their back parts **p** inward
2Ch 4: 4 all their back parts **p** inward
Job 41:30 he spreads **p** marks in the

POINTEDLY (*see* POINTED)
Gen 43: 7 asked us **p** about ourselves

POINTING (*see* POINT)
Is 58: 9 the **p** of the finger, and

POINTS (*see* POINT)
Num 33: 2 wrote down the starting **p** of
Num 33: 2 according to their starting **p**
1Sa 13:21 to set the **p** of the goads
Prov 6:13 feet, he **p** with his fingers
Rom 15:15 more boldly to you on some **p**
Heb 4:15 but was in all **p** tempted as

POISON (*see* POISONED)
Deut 32:24 with the **p** of serpents of the
Deut 32:33 wine is the **p** of serpents
Job 6: 4 my spirit drinks in their **p**
Job 20:16 He will suck the **p** of cobras
Ps 58: 4 Their **p** is like the **p** of
Ps 140: 3 The **p** of asps is under their
Rom 3:13 The **p** of asps is under their
Jas 3: 8 unruly evil, full of deadly **p**

POISONED (*see* POISON)
Acts 8:23 that you are **p** by bitterness
Acts 14: 2 **p** their minds against the

POLE (*see* POLES)
Num 13:23 it between two of them on a **p**
Num 21: 8 serpent, and set it on a **p**
Num 21: 9 serpent, and put it on a **p**
Is 30:17 as a **p** on top of a mountain

POLES (*see* POLE)
Ex 25:13 shall make **p** of acacia wood
Ex 25:14 You shall put the **p** into the
Ex 25:15 The **p** shall be in the rings
Ex 25:27 for the **p** to bear the table
Ex 25:28 make the **p** of acacia wood
Ex 27: 6 shall make **p** for the altar
Ex 27: 6 **p** of acacia wood, and overlay
Ex 27: 7 The **p** shall be put in the
Ex 27: 7 the **p** shall be on the two
Ex 30: 4 the **p** with which to bear it
Ex 30: 5 make the **p** of acacia wood
Ex 35:12 the ark and its **p**, with the
Ex 35:13 the table and its **p**, all its
Ex 35:15 the incense altar, its **p**
Ex 35:16 its bronze grating, its **p**
Ex 37: 4 He made **p** of acacia wood, and
Ex 37: 5 he put the **p** into the rings
Ex 37:14 for the **p** to bear the table
Ex 37:15 he made the **p** of acacia wood
Ex 37:27 as holders for the **p** with
Ex 37:28 he made the **p** of acacia wood,
Ex 38: 5 grating, as holders for the **p**
Ex 38: 6 he made the **p** of acacia wood,
Ex 38: 7 Then he put the **p** into the
Ex 39:35 of the Testimony with its **p**
Ex 39:39 its grate of bronze, its **p**
Ex 40:20 inserted the **p** through the
Num 4: 6 and they shall insert its **p**
Num 4: 8 and they shall insert its **p**
Num 4:11 and they shall insert its **p**
Num 4:14 badger skins, and insert its **p**
1Ki 8: 7 overshadowed the ark and its **p**
1Ki 8: 8 the **p** extended so that the
1Ki 8: 8 ends of the **p** could be seen
1Ch 15:15 on their shoulders, by its **p**
2Ch 5: 8 overshadowed the ark and its **p**
2Ch 5: 9 the **p** extended so that the
2Ch 5: 9 ends of the **p** of the ark

POLISH (*see* POLISHED)
Jer 46: 4 **p** the spears, put on the

POLISHED (*see* POLISH)
Ezra 8:27 two vessels of fine **p** bronze
Is 49: 2 Me, and made Me a **p** shaft
Ezek 21: 9 sword is sharpened and also **p**
Ezek 21:10 **p** to flash like lightning
Ezek 21:11 And He has given it to be **p**
Ezek 21:11 it is **p** to be given into the
Ezek 21:28 drawn, **p** for slaughter, for

POLLUTE (*see* POLLUTED, POLLUTIONS)
Num 35:33 So you shall not **p** the land
Jer 7:30 is called by My name, to **p** it

POLLUTED (*see* POLLUTE)
Ps 106:38 And the land was **p** with blood
Prov 25:26 a murky spring and a **p** well
Jer 2:23 How can you say, 'I am not **p**
Jer 3: 1 not that land be greatly **p**
Jer 3: 2 you have **p** the land with your
Zeph 3: 1 to her who is rebellious and **p**
Zeph 3: 4 priests have **p** the sanctuary
Acts 15:20 from things **p** by idols, from

POLLUTIONS (*see* POLLUTE)
2Pe 2:20 **p** of the world through the

POMEGRANATE (*see* POMEGRANATES)
Ex 28:34 a golden bell and a **p**, a
Ex 28:34 a golden bell and a **p**, upon
Ex 39:26 a bell and a **p**, a bell and a
Ex 39:26 a **p**, a bell and a **p**
1Sa 14: 2 a **p** tree which is in Migron
Song 4: 3 veil are like a piece of **p**
Song 6: 7 Like a piece of **p** are your
Song 8: 2 wine, of the juice of my **p**
Joel 1:12 the **p** tree, the palm tree
Hag 2:19 the vine, the fig tree, the **p**

POMEGRANATES (*see* POMEGRANATE)
Ex 28:33 hem you shall make **p** of blue
Ex 39:24 the hem of the robe **p** of blue
Ex 39:25 put the bells between the **p**
Ex 39:25 robe all around between the **p**
Num 13:23 also brought some of the **p**
Num 20: 5 grain or figs or vines or **p**
Deut 8: 8 of vines and fig trees and **p**
1Ki 7:18 and two rows of **p** above the
1Ki 7:20 two pillars also had **p** above
1Ki 7:20 such **p** in rows on each of the
1Ki 7:42 four hundred **p** for the two
1Ki 7:42 rows of **p** for each network
2Ki 25:17 **p** all around the capital were
2Ch 3:16 and he made one hundred **p**, and
2Ch 4:13 four hundred **p** for the two
2Ch 4:13 rows of **p** for each network
Song 4:13 of **p** with pleasant fruits
Song 6:11 budded and the **p** had bloomed
Song 7:12 open, and the **p** are in bloom
Jer 52:22 **p** all around the capital, all
Jer 52:22 pillar, with **p** was the same
Jer 52:23 ninety-six **p** on the sides
Jer 52:23 all the **p**, all around on the

POMP (*see* POMPOUS)
Is 5:14 and their multitude and their **p**
Is 14:11 Your **p** is brought down to
Ezek 7:24 I will cause the **p** of the
Ezek 32:12 shall plunder the **p** of Egypt
Acts 25:23 Bernice had come with great **p**

POMPOUS (*see* POMP)
Dan 7: 8 and a mouth speaking **p** words
Dan 7:11 **p** words which the horn was
Dan 7:20 a mouth which spoke **p** words
Dan 7:25 He shall speak **p** words

PONDER (*see* PONDERED, PONDERS)
Prov 4:26 **P** the path of your feet, and
Prov 5: 6 Lest you **p** her path of life

PONDERED (*see* PONDER)
Eccl 12: 9 yes, he **p** and sought out and
Luke 2:19 things and **p** them in her heart

PONDERS (*see* PONDER)
Prov 5:21 LORD, and He **p** all his paths

PONDS
Ex 7:19 their rivers, over their **p**
Ex 8: 5 the rivers, and over the **p**

PONTIUS (*see* PILATE)
Matt 27: 2 delivered Him to **P** Pilate the
Luke 3: 1 **P** Pilate being governor of
Acts 4:27 **P** Pilate, with the Gentiles
1Ti 6:13 confession before **P** Pilate

PONTUS
Acts 2: 9 Judea and Cappadocia, **P** and
Acts 18: 2 Jew named Aquila, born in **P**
1Pe 1: 1 of the Dispersion in **P**,

POOL (*see* POOLS, WATERPOOLS)
2Sa 2:13 met them by the **p** of Gibeon
2Sa 2:13 one on one side of the **p**
2Sa 2:13 on the other side of the **p**
2Sa 4:12 them by the **p** in Hebron
1Ki 22:38 the chariot at a **p** in Samaria
2Ki 18:17 the aqueduct from the upper **p**
2Ki 20:20 his might, and how he made a **p**
Neh 2:14 Gate and to the King's **P**, but
Neh 3:15 the **P** of Shelah by the King's
Neh 3:16 of David, to the man-made **p**
Ps 114: 8 the rock into a **p** of water
Is 7: 3 the aqueduct from the upper **p**
Is 22: 9 the waters of the lower **p**
Is 22:11 for the water of the old **p**
Is 35: 7 ground shall become a **p**, and
Is 36: 2 the aqueduct from the upper **p**
Is 41:18 the wilderness a **p** of water
Jer 41:12 the great **p** that is in Gibeon
Nah 2: 8 of old was like a **p** of water
John 5: 2 by the Sheep Gate a **p**, which
John 5: 4 at a certain time into the **p**
John 5: 7 **p** when the water is stirred
John 9: 7 wash in the **p** of Siloam"
John 9:11 to me, 'Go to the **p** of Siloam

POOLS (*see* POOL)
Ex 7:19 and over all their **p** of water
Ps 84: 6 rain also covers it with **p**
Ps 107:35 a wilderness into **p** of water
Song 7: 4 your eyes like the **p** in
Is 42:15 and I will dry up the **p**

POOR (*see* POOREST, POORLY)
Gen 41:19 cows came up after them, **p**
Ex 22:25 My people who are **p** among you
Ex 23: 3 to a **p** man in his dispute
Ex 23: 6 of your **p** in his dispute
Ex 23:11 that the **p** of your people may
Ex 30:15 the **p** shall not give less
Lev 14:21 But if he is **p** and cannot
Lev 19:10 shall leave them for the **p**
Lev 19:15 shall not be partial to the **p**
Lev 23:22 shall leave them for the **p**
Lev 25:25 of your brethren becomes **p**
Lev 25:35 of your brethren becomes **p**
Lev 25:39 who dwells by you becomes **p**
Lev 25:47 who dwells by him becomes **p**
Lev 27: 8 But if he is too **p** to pay
Num 13:20 whether the land is rich or **p**
Deut 15: 4 there may be no **p** among you
Deut 15: 7 you a **p** man of your brethren
Deut 15: 7 your hand from your **p** brother
Deut 15: 9 evil against your **p** brother
Deut 15:11 For the **p** will never cease
Deut 15:11 to your brother, to your **p**
Deut 24:12 And if the man is **p**, you shall
Deut 24:14 a hired servant who is **p** and
Deut 24:15 go down on it, for he is **p**
Ruth 3:10 young men, whether **p** or rich
1Sa 2: 7 The LORD makes **p** and makes
1Sa 2: 8 He raises the **p** from the dust
1Sa 18:23 son-in-law, seeing I am a **p**
2Sa 12: 1 city, one rich and the other **p**
2Sa 12: 3 But the **p** man had nothing,
2Sa 12: 4 but he took the **p** man's lamb
2Ki 25:12 the guard left some of the **p**
Esth 9:22 one another and gifts to the **p**
Job 5:16 So the **p** have hope, and
Job 20:10 will seek the favor of the **p**
Job 20:19 oppressed and forsaken the **p**
Job 24: 4 so that the **p** of the land are
Job 24: 9 and take a pledge from the **p**
Job 24:10 They cause the **p** to go naked
Job 24:14 he kills the **p** and needy
Job 29:12 delivered the **p** who cried out
Job 29:16 I was a father to the **p**, and I
Job 30:25 not my soul grieved for the **p**
Job 31:16 kept the **p** from their desire
Job 31:19 or any **p** man without covering
Job 34:19 the rich more than the **p**
Job 34:28 cry of the **p** to come to Him
Job 36:15 He delivers the **p** in their
Ps 9:18 The expectation of the **p**
Ps 10: 2 in his pride persecutes the **p**
Ps 10: 9 lies in wait to catch the **p**
Ps 10: 9 He catches the **p** when he
Ps 12: 5 For the oppression of the **p**
Ps 14: 6 shame the counsel of the **p**
Ps 22:26 The **p** shall eat and be
Ps 34: 6 This **p** man cried out, and the
Ps 35:10 Delivering the **p** from him who
Ps 35:10 strong for him, Yes, the **p**
Ps 37:14 their bow, To cast down the **p**
Ps 40:17 But I am **p** and needy
Ps 41: 1 is he who considers the **p**
Ps 49: 2 and high, Rich and **p** together
Ps 68:10 from Your goodness for the **p**
Ps 69:29 But I am **p** and sorrowful
Ps 69:33 For the LORD hears the **p**, And
Ps 70: 5 But I am **p** and needy
Ps 72: 2 And Your **p** with justice
Ps 72: 4 to the **p** of the people
Ps 72:12 The **p** also, and him who has no
Ps 72:13 He will spare the **p** and needy,
Ps 74:19 the life of Your **p** forever
Ps 74:21 Let the **p** and needy praise
Ps 82: 3 Defend the **p** and fatherless
Ps 82: 4 Deliver the **p** and needy
Ps 86: 1 For I am **p** and needy
Ps 107:41 Yet He sets the **p** on high
Ps 109:16 mercy, But persecuted the **p**
Ps 109:22 For I am **p** and needy, And my
Ps 109:31 at the right hand of the **p**
Ps 112: 9 abroad, He has given to the **p**
Ps 113: 7 He raises the **p** out of the
Ps 132:15 will satisfy her **p** with bread
Ps 140:12 And justice for the **p**
Prov 10: 4 with a slack hand becomes **p**
Prov 10:15 of the **p** is their poverty
Prov 13: 7 and one who makes himself **p**
Prov 13: 8 but the **p** does not hear
Prov 13:23 in the fallow ground of the **p**
Prov 14:20 The **p** man is hated even by
Prov 14:21 but he who has mercy on the **p**
Prov 14:31 the **p** reproaches his Maker
Prov 17: 5 He who mocks the **p** reproaches
Prov 18:23 The **p** man uses entreaties,
Prov 19: 1 Better is the **p** who walks in
Prov 19: 4 but the **p** is separated from
Prov 19: 7 brothers of the **p** hate him
Prov 19:17 on the **p** lends to the LORD
Prov 19:22 a **p** man is better than a liar
Prov 21:13 the **p** will also cry himself
Prov 21:17 pleasure will be a **p** man
Prov 22: 2 the **p** have this in common,
Prov 22: 7 The rich rules over the **p**
Prov 22: 9 gives of his bread to the **p**
Prov 22:16 He who oppresses the **p** to
Prov 22:22 not rob the **p** because he is **p**
Prov 28: 3 A **p** man who oppresses the
Prov 28: 3 the **p** is like a driving rain
Prov 28: 6 Better is the **p** who walks in
Prov 28: 8 for him who will pity the **p**
Prov 28:11 own eyes, but the **p** who has
Prov 28:15 a wicked ruler over **p** people
Prov 28:27 gives to the **p** will not lack
Prov 29: 7 considers the cause of the **p**
Prov 29:13 The **p** man and the oppressor
Prov 29:14 who judges the **p** with truth
Prov 30: 9 Or lest I be **p** and steal, and
Prov 30:14 to devour the **p** from off the
Prov 31: 9 and plead the cause of the **p**
Prov 31:20 She extends her hand to the **p**
Eccl 4:13 Better is a **p** and wise youth
Eccl 4:14 he was born **p** in his kingdom
Eccl 5: 8 see the oppression of the **p**
Eccl 6: 8 What does the **p** man have, who
Eccl 9:15 was found in it a **p** wise man
Eccl 9:15 remembered that same **p** man
Eccl 9:16 Nevertheless the **p** man's
Is 3:14 of the **p** is in your houses
Is 3:15 grinding the faces of the **p**
Is 10: 2 right from the **p** of My people
Is 10:30 far as Laish—O **p** Anathoth!
Is 11: 4 He shall judge the **p**, and
Is 14:30 firstborn of the **p** will feed
Is 14:32 the **p** of His people shall
Is 25: 4 have been a strength to the **p**
Is 26: 6 the feet of the **p** and the
Is 29:19 the **p** among men shall rejoice
Is 32: 7 the **p** with lying words, even
Is 41:17 When the **p** and needy seek
Is 58: 7 house the **p** who are cast out
Is 61: 1 preach good tidings to the **p**
Is 66: 2 on him who is **p** and of a
Jer 2:34 the lives of the **p** innocents
Jer 5: 4 Surely these are **p**
Jer 20:13 delivered the life of the **p**
Jer 22:16 He judged the cause of the **p**
Jer 39:10 land of Judah the **p** people
Jer 52:15 captive some of the **p** people
Jer 52:16 the guard left some of the **p**
Ezek 16:49 strengthen the hand of the **p**
Ezek 18:12 if he has oppressed the **p**
Ezek 18:17 withdrawn his hand from the **p**
Ezek 22:29 robbery, and mistreated the **p**
Dan 4:27 by showing mercy to the **p**
Amos 2: 6 the **p** for a pair of sandals
Amos 2: 7 which is on the head of the **p**
Amos 4: 1 of Samaria, who oppress the **p**
Amos 5:11 because you tread down the **p**
Amos 5:12 you divert the **p** from justice
Amos 8: 4 make the **p** of the land fail,
Amos 8: 6 we may buy the **p** for silver
Hab 3:14 feasting on the **p** in secret
Zech 7:10 the alien or the **p**
Zech 11: 7 particular the **p** of the flock
Zech 11:11 Thus the **p** of the flock, who
Matt 5: 3 Blessed are the **p** in spirit
Matt 11: 5 up and the **p** have the gospel
Matt 19:21 you have and give to the **p**
Matt 26: 9 for much and given to the **p**
Matt 26:11 have the **p** with you always
Mark 10:21 you have and give to the **p**
Mark 12:42 Then one **p** widow came and
Mark 12:43 I say to you that this **p**
Mark 14: 5 denarii and given to the **p**
Mark 14: 7 have the **p** with you always
Luke 4:18 to preach the gospel to the **p**
Luke 6:20 Blessed are you **p**, for yours
Luke 7:22 raised, the **p** have the gospel
Luke 14:13 give a feast, invite the **p**
Luke 14:21 city, and bring in here the **p**
Luke 18:22 have and distribute to the **p**
Luke 19: 8 half of my goods to the **p**
Luke 21: 2 He saw also a certain **p** widow
Luke 21: 3 I say to you that this **p**
John 12: 5 denarii and given to the **p**
John 12: 6 not that he cared for the **p**
John 12: 8 For the **p** you have with you
John 13:29 give something to the **p**
Rom 15:26 contribution for the **p** among
1Co 13: 3 all my goods to feed the **p**
2Co 6:10 as **p**, yet making many rich
2Co 8: 9 for your sakes He became **p**
2Co 9: 9 abroad, He has given to the **p**
Gal 2:10 that we should remember the **p**
Jas 2: 2 in a **p** man in filthy clothes
Jas 2: 3 place," and say to the **p** man
Jas 2: 5 Has God not chosen the **p** of
Jas 2: 6 you have dishonored the **p** man
Rev 3:17 are wretched, miserable, **p**
Rev 13:16 small and great, rich and **p**

POOREST (*see* POOR)
2Ki 24:14 the **p** people of the land
Jer 40: 7 the **p** of the land who had not

POORLY (*see* POOR)
1Co 4:11 we are **p** clothed, and beaten,

POPLAR (*see* POPLARS)
Gen 30:37 for himself rods of green **p**

POPLARS (*see* POPLAR)
Hos 4:13 on the hills, under oaks, **p**

POPULATED (*see* POPULOUS)
Gen 9:19 these the whole earth was **p**

POPULOUS (*see* POPULATED)
Deut 26: 5 a nation, great, mighty, and **p**

PORATHA
Esth 9: 8 **P**, Adalia, Aridatha,

PORCH (*see* PORCHES)
Judg 3:23 Ehud went out through the **p**
Ezek 8:16 of the LORD, between the **p**
Joel 2:17 the LORD, weep between the **p**
Mark 14:68 And he went out on the **p**
John 10:23 in the temple, in Solomon's **p**
Acts 3:11 **p** which is called Solomon's
Acts 5:12 one accord in Solomon's **P**

PORCHES (*see* PORCH)
Ezek 41:15 temple and the **p** of the court,
John 5: 2 Bethesda, having five **p**

PORCIUS (*see* FESTUS)
Acts 24:27 But after two years **P** Festus

PORCUPINE
Is 14:23 it a possession for the **p**
Is 34:11 the **p** shall possess it, also

PORTICO
1Ki 7: 6 of them was a **p** with pillars

PORTION (*see* PORTIONS)
Gen 14:24 the **p** of the men who went
Gen 14:24 let them take their **p**
Gen 31:14 Is there still any **p** or
Gen 48:22 you one **p** above your brothers
Ex 29:26 and it shall be your **p**
Lev 2: 9 grain offering a memorial **p**
Lev 2:16 shall burn the memorial **p**
Lev 5:12 handful of it as a memorial **p**
Lev 6:17 **p** of My offerings made by
Lev 7:35 the consecrated **p** for Aaron
Num 5:26 offering, as its memorial **p**
Num 18: 8 have given them as a **p** to you
Num 18:20 you have any **p** among them
Num 18:20 I am your **p** and your
Num 31:36 the **p** for those who had gone
Deut 10: 9 Therefore Levi has no **p** nor
Deut 12:12 gates, since he has no **p** nor
Deut 14:29 because he has no **p** nor
Deut 18: 1 LORD made by fire, and His **p**
Deut 21:17 a double **p** of all that he has
Deut 32: 9 the LORD's **p** is His people
Deut 33:21 **p** was reserved there
Josh 15:13 son of Jephunneh he gave a **p**
Josh 17:14 one **p** to inherit, since we
Josh 19: 9 **p** of the children of Judah
Josh 19: 9 for the **p** of the children of
1Sa 1: 5 he would give a double **p**, for
1Sa 9:23 Bring the **p** which I gave you,
1Ki 12:16 What **p** have we in David
2Ki 2: 9 Please let a double **p** of your
2Ki 25:30 a **p** for each day, all the
2Ch 10:16 What **p** have we in David
2Ch 31: 3 The king also appointed a **p**
2Ch 31:16 **p** for the work of his service
Neh 11:23 them that a certain **p** should
Neh 12:47 gatekeepers, a **p** for each day
Job 20:29 This is the **p** from God for a
Job 24:18 their **p** should be cursed in
Job 27:13 This is the **p** of a wicked man
Ps 11: 6 shall be the **p** of their cup
Ps 16: 5 are the **p** of my inheritance
Ps 17:14 who have their **p** in this life
Ps 63:10 They shall be a **p** for jackals
Ps 68:23 their **p** from your enemies
Ps 73:26 of my heart and my **p** forever
Ps 119:57 You are my **p**, O LORD
Ps 142: 5 My **p** in the land of the
Prov 31:15 and a **p** for her maidservants
Eccl 9: 9 for that is your **p** in life
Is 17:14 This is the **p** of those who
Is 53:12 divide Him a **p** with the great
Is 57: 6 of the stream is your **p**
Is 61: 7 they shall rejoice in their **p**
Jer 10:16 The **P** of Jacob is not like
Jer 12:10 have trodden My **p** under foot
Jer 12:10 **p** a desolate wilderness
Jer 13:25 the **p** of your measures from
Jer 51:19 The **P** of Jacob is not like
Jer 52:34 a **p** for each day until the
Lam 3:24 The LORD is my **p**," says my
Ezek 45: 1 LORD, a holy **p** of the land
Ezek 45: 4 shall be a holy **p** of the land
Ezek 45: 6 to the district of the holy **p**
Ezek 45: 7 shall have a **p** on one side
Ezek 48: 1 there shall be one **p** for Dan
Ezek 48: 2 to the west, one **p** for Asher
Ezek 48: 3 the west, one **p** for Naphtali
Ezek 48: 4 the west, one **p** for Manasseh
Ezek 48: 5 the west, one **p** for Ephraim
Ezek 48: 6 to the west, one **p** for Reuben
Ezek 48: 7 to the west, one **p** for Judah
Ezek 48:18 the district of the holy **p**
Ezek 48:18 to the district of the holy **p**
Ezek 48:23 Benjamin shall have one **p**
Ezek 48:24 west, Simeon shall have one **p**
Ezek 48:25 Issachar shall have one **p**
Ezek 48:26 Zebulun shall have one **p**
Ezek 48:27 west, Gad shall have one **p**
Dan 1: 8 **p** of the king's delicacies
Dan 1:13 **p** of the king's delicacies
Dan 1:15 **p** of the king's delicacies
Dan 1:16 away their **p** of delicacies
Dan 11:26 those who eat of the **p** of his
Matt 24:51 appoint him his **p** with the
Luke 12:42 to give them their **p** of food
Luke 12:46 appoint him his **p** with the
Luke 15:12 give me the **p** of goods that
Acts 8:21 part nor **p** in this matter

PORTIONS (*see* PORTION)
Deut 18: 8 shall have equal **p** to eat
Josh 17: 5 Ten **p** fell to Manasseh,
1Sa 1: 4 he would give **p** to Peninnah
2Ch 31:19 by name to distribute **p** to
2Ch 35:14 prepared **p** for themselves
2Ch 35:14 prepared **p** for themselves
2Ch 35:15 Levites prepared **p** for them
Neh 8:10 and send **p** to those for whom
Neh 8:12 to eat and drink, to send **p**
Neh 12:44 **p** specified by the Law for
Neh 12:47 gave the **p** for the singers
Neh 13:10 the **p** for the Levites had not
Ezek 45: 7 side with one of the tribal **p**
Ezek 47:13 Joseph shall have two **p**
Ezek 48: 8 same as one of the other **p**
Ezek 48:21 adjacent to the tribal **p**
Ezek 48:29 Israel, and these are their **p**

PORTRAY (*see* PORTRAYED)
Ezek 4: 1 **p** on it a city, Jerusalem

PORTRAYED (*see* PORTRAY)
Ezek 8:10 **p** all around on the walls
Ezek 23:14 looked at men **p** on the wall
Ezek 23:14 of Chaldeans **p** in vermilion
Gal 3: 1 **p** among you as crucified

POSE (*see* POSED)
Judg 14:12 Let me **p** a riddle to you
Judg 14:13 **P** your riddle, that we may
Ezek 17: 2 man, **p** a riddle, and speak a

POSED (*see* POSE)
Judg 14:16 You have **p** a riddle to the

POSITION (*see* POSITIONED, POSITIONS)
Judg 20:33 their **p** in the plain of Geba
1Ki 8:20 I have filled the **p** of my
1Ki 20:24 the kings, each from his **p**
2Ch 6:10 I have filled the **p** of my
2Ch 20:17 **P** yourselves, stand still and
2Ch 35:15 did not have to leave their **p**
Esth 1:19 **p** to another who is better
Ps 62: 4 cast him down from his high **p**
Is 22:19 from your **p** he will pull you
1Ti 3: 1 man desires the **p** of a bishop

POSITIONED (*see* POSITION)
Neh 4:13 Therefore I **p** men behind the

POSITIONS (*see* POSITION)
1Sa 2:36 me in one of the priestly **p**

POSSESS (*see* POSSESSED, POSSESSES, POSSESSING, POSSESSION, POSSESSOR)
Gen 22:17 your descendants shall **p** the
Gen 24:60 may your descendants **p** the
Gen 47: 1 herds and all that they **p**,
Lev 20:24 and I will give it to you to **p**
Num 27:11 his family, and he shall **p** it
Num 33:53 have given you the land to **p**
Num 36: 8 may **p** the inheritance of his
Deut 1: 8 **p** the land which the LORD
Deut 1:21 **p** it, as the LORD God of your
Deut 1:39 give it, and they shall **p** it
Deut 2:24 Begin to **p** it, and engage him
Deut 2:31 Begin to **p** it, that you may
Deut 3:18 has given you this land to **p**
Deut 3:20 they also **p** the land which
Deut 4: 1 **p** the land which the LORD God
Deut 4: 5 in the land which you go to **p**
Deut 4:14 which you cross over to **p**
Deut 4:22 over and **p** that good land
Deut 4:26 cross over the Jordan to **p**
Deut 5:31 which I am giving them to **p**
Deut 5:33 in the land which you shall **p**
Deut 6: 1 you are crossing over to **p**
Deut 6:18 **p** the good land of which the
Deut 7: 1 the land which you go to **p**
Deut 8: 1 **p** the land of which the LORD
Deut 9: 4 brought me in to **p** this land'
Deut 9: 5 you go in to **p** their land
Deut 9: 6 land to **p** because of your
Deut 9:23 **p** the land which I have given
Deut 10:11 **p** the land which I swore to
Deut 11: 8 go in and **p** the land
Deut 11: 8 which you cross over to **p**
Deut 11:10 to **p** is not like the land of
Deut 11:11 over to **p** is a land of hills
Deut 11:29 the land which you go to **p**
Deut 11:31 go in to **p** the land which the
Deut 11:31 giving you, and you will **p** it
Deut 12: 1 fathers is giving you to **p**
Deut 15: 4 you to **p** as an inheritance
Deut 17:14 **p** it and dwell in it, and say
Deut 19: 2 your God is giving you to **p**
Deut 19:14 your God is giving you to **p**
Deut 21: 1 your God is giving you to **p**
Deut 23:20 which you are entering to **p**
Deut 25:19 you to **p** as an inheritance
Deut 26: 1 an inheritance, and you **p** it
Deut 28:21 land which you are going to **p**
Deut 28:63 the land which you go to **p**
Deut 30: 5 possessed, and you shall **p** it
Deut 30:16 in the land which you go to **p**
Deut 30:18 over the Jordan to go in and **p**
Deut 31:13 you cross the Jordan to **p**
Deut 32:47 cross over the Jordan to **p**
Deut 33:23 LORD, **p** the west and the south
Josh 1:11 to go in to **p** the land which
Josh 1:11 your God is giving you to **p**
Josh 18: 3 **p** the land which the LORD God
Josh 23: 5 So you shall **p** their land
Josh 24: 4 the mountains of Seir to **p**
Josh 24: 8 that you might **p** their land
Judg 2: 6 own inheritance to **p** the land
Judg 11:23 should you then **p** it
Judg 11:24 Will you not **p** whatever
Judg 11:24 your god gives you to **p**
Judg 11:24 of before us, we will **p**
Judg 18: 9 you may enter to **p** the land
1Ch 28: 8 that you may **p** this good land
Ezra 9:11 to **p** is an unclean land, with
Neh 9:15 told them to go in to **p** the
Neh 9:23 their fathers to go in and **p**
Ps 69:35 they may dwell there and **p** it
Is 14: 2 will **p** them for servants and
Is 14:21 **p** the land, and fill the face
Is 34:11 and the porcupine shall **p** it
Is 34:17 they shall **p** it forever
Is 57:13 trust in Me shall **p** the land
Is 61: 7 land they shall **p** double
Jer 30: 3 fathers, and they shall **p** it
Ezek 7:24 and they will **p** their houses
Ezek 33:25 Should you then **p** the land
Ezek 33:26 Should you then **p** the land
Ezek 35:10 be mine, and we will **p** them
Dan 7:18 **p** the kingdom forever, even
Dan 7:22 the saints to **p** the kingdom
Hos 9: 6 Nettles shall **p** their
Amos 2:10 to **p** the land of the Amorite
Amos 9:12 that they may **p** the remnant
Obad 17 shall **p** their possessions
Obad 19 of the South shall **p** the
Obad 19 They shall **p** the fields of
Obad 19 Benjamin shall **p** Gilead
Obad 20 children of Israel shall **p**
Obad 20 **p** the cities of the South
Hab 1: 6 to **p** dwelling places that are
Zeph 2: 9 of My people shall **p** them
Zech 8:12 people to **p** all these things
Luke 18:12 I give tithes of all that I **p**
Luke 21:19 In your patience **p** your souls
1Co 7:30 buy as though they did not **p**
1Th 4: 4 how to **p** his own vessel in

POSSESSED (*see* POSSESS)
Deut 3:12 which we **p** at that time, from
Deut 30: 5 the land which your fathers **p**
Josh 12: 1 and whose land they **p** on the
Josh 13: 1 very much land yet to be **p**
Josh 22: 9 which they **p** according to the
Neh 9:24 people went in and **p** the land
Neh 9:25 **p** houses full of all goods,
Job 22: 8 But the mighty man **p** the land
Prov 8:22 The LORD **p** me at the
Is 63:18 have **p** it but a little while
Jer 32:15 shall be **p** again in this land
Acts 4:32 the things he **p** was his own
Acts 7:45 the land **p** by the Gentiles
Acts 8: 7 came out of many who were **p**
Acts 16:16 that a certain slave girl **p**

POSSESSES (*see* POSSESS)
Num 36: 8 And every daughter who **p** an
Luke 12:15 abundance of the things he **p**

POSSESSING (*see* POSSESS)
Dan 1: 4 **p** knowledge and quick to
2Co 6:10 nothing, and yet **p** all things

POSSESSION (*see* POSSESS, POSSESSIONS)
Gen 17: 8 Canaan, as an everlasting **p**
Gen 23:18 to Abraham as a **p** in the
Gen 36:43 in the land of their **p**
Gen 47:11 gave them a **p** in the land of
Gen 48: 4 after you as an everlasting **p**
Gen 49:30 as a **p** for a burial place
Lev 14:34 which I give you as a **p**, and
Lev 14:34 a house in the land of your **p**
Lev 25:10 of you shall return to his **p**
Lev 25:13 of you shall return to his **p**
Lev 25:24 in all the land of your **p** you
Lev 25:25 and has sold some of his **p**
Lev 25:27 that he may return to his **p**
Lev 25:28 and he shall return to his **p**
Lev 25:32 in the cities of their **p**, the
Lev 25:33 **p** shall be released in the
Lev 25:33 their **p** among the children of
Lev 25:34 for it is their perpetual **p**
Lev 25:41 to the **p** of his fathers
Lev 25:46 you, to inherit them as a **p**
Lev 27:16 some part of a field of his **p**
Lev 27:21 shall be the **p** of the priest
Lev 27:22 is not the field of his **p**
Lev 27:24 one who owned the land as a **p**
Lev 27:28 beast, or the field of his **p**
Num 13:30 us go up at once and take **p**
Num 21:24 took **p** of his land from the
Num 21:35 and they took **p** of his land
Num 24:18 And Edom shall be a **p**
Num 24:18 his enemies, shall be a **p**
Num 27: 4 Therefore give us a **p** among
Num 27: 7 shall surely give them a **p** of
Num 32: 5 given to your servants as a **p**
Num 32:22 be your **p** before the LORD
Num 32:29 the land of Gilead as a **p**
Num 32:32 but the **p** of our inheritance
Num 35: 2 the inheritance of their **p**
Num 35: 8 **p** of the children of Israel
Num 35:28 return to the land of his **p**
Deut 2: 5 Mount Seir to Esau as a **p**
Deut 2: 9 you any of their land as a **p**
Deut 2: 9 the descendants of Lot as a **p**
Deut 2:12 **p** which the LORD gave them
Deut 2:19 of the people of Ammon as a **p**
Deut 2:19 the descendants of Lot as a **p**
Deut 3:20 his **p** which I have given you
Deut 4:47 they took **p** of his land and
Deut 11: 6 substance that was in their **p**
Deut 32:49 the children of Israel as a **p**
Josh 1:15 they also have taken **p** of the
Josh 1:15 return to the land of your **p**
Josh 12: 6 it as a **p** to the Reubenites
Josh 12: 7 as a **p** according to their
Josh 19:47 took **p** of it, and dwelt in it
Josh 21:12 the son of Jephunneh as his **p**
Josh 21:41 **p** of the children of Israel
Josh 21:43 fathers, and they took **p** of it
Josh 22: 4 and to the land of your **p**,
Josh 22: 7 Moses had given a **p** in Bashan
Josh 22: 7 a **p** among their brethren on
Josh 22: 9 to the land of their **p**,
Josh 22:19 the land of your **p** is unclean
Josh 22:19 the land of the **p** of the LORD
Josh 22:19 stands, and take **p** among us
Judg 3:13 took **p** of the city of palms
Judg 11:21 Thus Israel gained **p** of all
Judg 11:22 They took **p** of all the
Judg 11:24 our God takes **p** of before us
1Ki 21:15 take **p** of the vineyard of
1Ki 21:16 went down to take **p** of the
1Ki 21:18 has gone down to take **p** of it
1Ki 21:19 you murdered and also taken **p**
2Ki 17:24 they took **p** of Samaria and
2Ch 20:11 to throw us out of Your **p**
2Ch 31: 1 cities, every man to his **p**
Neh 9:22 So they took **p** of the land of
Neh 11: 3 in his own **p** in their cities
Ps 2: 8 ends of the earth for Your **p**
Ps 44: 3 For they did not gain **p** of
Ps 83:12 The pastures of God for a **p**
Prov 12:27 diligence is man's precious **p**
Is 14:23 make it a **p** for the porcupine
Jer 32:23 took **p** of it, but they have
Jer 49: 2 take **p** of his inheritance
Ezek 11:15 has been given to us as a **p**
Ezek 25: 4 as a **p** to the men of the East
Ezek 25:10 East I will give it as a **p**
Ezek 33:24 has been given to us as a **p**
Ezek 36: 2 heights have become our **p**
Ezek 36: 3 so that you became the **p** of
Ezek 36: 5 My land to themselves as a **p**
Ezek 36:12 they shall take **p** of you, and
Ezek 44:28 give them no **p** in Israel
Ezek 44:28 for I am their **p**
Ezek 45: 5 have twenty chambers as a **p**
Ezek 45: 8 land shall be his **p** in Israel
Ezek 46:16 it is their **p** by inheritance
Ezek 48:22 from the **p** of the Levites
Ezek 48:22 the **p** of the city which are
Zech 2:12 the LORD will take **p** of Judah
Acts 5: 1 Sapphira his wife, sold a **p**
Acts 7: 5 to give it to him for a **p**
Eph 1:14 redemption of the purchased **p**
Heb 10:34 an enduring **p** for yourselves

POSSESSIONS (*see* POSSESSION)
Gen 12: 5 all their **p** that they had
Gen 13: 6 for their **p** were so great
Gen 15:14 shall come out with great **p**
Gen 26:14 for he had **p** of flocks and
Gen 26:14 **p** of herds and a great number
Gen 31:18 all his **p** which he had gained
Gen 34:10 acquire **p** for yourselves in
Gen 36: 7 For their **p** were too great
Gen 47:27 and they had **p** there and grew
Num 32:30 they shall have **p** among you
Deut 21:16 bequeaths his **p** to his sons
1Ch 7:28 Now their **p** and habitations
1Ch 9: 2 who dwelt in their **p** in their
1Ch 28: 1 **p** of the king and of his sons,
2Ch 11:14 their common-lands and their **p**
2Ch 21:14 your wives, and all your **p**
2Ch 21:17 carried away all the **p** that
2Ch 31: 3 his **p** for the burnt offerings
2Ch 32:29 and **p** of flocks and herds in
2Ch 35: 7 these were from the king's **p**
2Ch 36:19 destroyed all its precious **p**
Ezra 8:21 our little ones and all our **p**
Esth 3:13 Adar, and to plunder their **p**
Esth 8:11 women, and to plunder their **p**
Job 1:10 his **p** have increased in the
Job 15:29 nor will his **p** overspread the
Ps 104:24 The earth is full of Your **p**
Ps 105:21 house, And ruler of all his **p**
Prov 1:13 find all kinds of precious **p**
Prov 3: 9 Honor the LORD with your **p**
Prov 28: 8 who increases his **p** by usury
Eccl 2: 7 Yes, I had greater **p** of herds
Joel 3: 5 into your temples My prized **p**
Obad 17 Jacob shall possess their **p**
Matt 19:22 sorrowful, for he had great **p**
Mark 10:22 grieved, for he had great **p**
Luke 15:13 and there wasted his **p** with
Acts 2:45 and sold their **p** and goods, and

POSSESSOR (*see* POSSESS, POSSESSORS)
Gen 14:19 High, **P** of heaven and earth
Gen 14:22 the **P** of heaven and earth,
Prov 17: 8 stone in the eyes of its **p**

POSSESSORS (*see* POSSESSOR)
Acts 4:34 for all who were **p** of lands

POSSIBLE
Matt 19:26 but with God all things are **p**
Matt 24:24 so as to deceive, if **p**, even
Matt 26:39 O My Father, if it is **p**, let
Mark 9:23 all things are **p** to him who
Mark 10:27 for with God all things are **p**
Mark 13:22 and wonders to deceive, if **p**
Mark 14:35 and prayed that if it were **p**
Mark 14:36 all things are **p** for You
Luke 18:27 with men are **p** with God
Acts 2:24 because it was not **p** that He
Acts 20:16 to be at Jerusalem, if **p**, on
Acts 27:39 planned to run the ship if **p**
Rom 12:18 If it is **p**, as much as
Gal 4:15 I bear you witness that, if **p**
Heb 10: 4 For it is not **p** that the

POSSIBLY (*see* PREFACE)

POST (*see* POSTED, POSTS)
1Ki 20:12 drinking at the command **p**
1Ki 20:16 drunk at the command **p**
Eccl 10: 4 you, do not leave your **p**
Is 21: 8 have sat at my **p** every night

POSTED (*see* POST)
Judg 7:19 just as they had **p** the watch
Neh 13:19 Then I **p** some of my servants

POSTERITY
Gen 21:23 my offspring, or with my **p**
Gen 45: 7 a **p** for you in the earth, and
Lev 21:15 his **p** among his people, for I
Num 9:10 **p** is unclean because of a
1Ki 16: 3 take away the **p** of Baasha
1Ki 16: 3 the **p** of his house, and I will
1Ki 21:21 I will take away your **p**, and
Job 18:19 son nor **p** among his people
Ps 22:30 A **p** shall serve Him
Ps 49:13 of their **p** who approve their
Ps 109:13 Let his **p** be cut off, And in
Prov 11:21 but the **p** of the righteous
Is 14:22 remnant, and offspring and **p**
Is 61: 9 that they are the **p** whom the
Jer 7:15 the whole **p** of Ephraim
Dan 11: 4 but not among his **p** nor
Amos 4: 2 and your **p** with fishhooks

POSTPONED
Ezek 12:25 it will no more be **p**
Ezek 12:28 My words will be **p** any more

POSTS (*see* POST)
Prov 8:34 waiting at the **p** of my doors
Is 6: 4 the **p** of the door were shaken
Is 57: 8 their **p** you have set up your
Acts 12:10 first and the second guard **p**

POT (*see* POTS, POTSHERD, WASHPOT, WATERPOT)
Ex 16:33 Take a **p** and put an omer of
Lev 6:28 if it is boiled in a bronze **p**
Judg 6:19 and he put the broth in a **p**
1Sa 2:14 or kettle, or caldron, or **p**
2Ki 4:38 Put on the large **p**, and boil
2Ki 4:39 them into the **p** of stew,
2Ki 4:40 God, there is death in the **p**
2Ki 4:41 And he put it into the **p**
2Ki 4:41 was nothing harmful in the **p**
Job 41:20 nostrils, as from a boiling **p**
Job 41:31 makes the deep boil like a **p**
Job 41:31 the sea like a **p** of ointment
Prov 17: 3 The refining **p** is for silver
Prov 27:21 The refining **p** is for silver
Eccl 7: 6 crackling of thorns under a **p**
Jer 1:13 I see a boiling **p**, and it is
Ezek 24: 3 Put on a **p**, set it on, and
Ezek 24: 6 to the **p** whose scum is in it,
Ezek 24:11 Then set the **p** empty on the
Mic 3: 3 in pieces like meat for the **p**
Zech 14:21 every **p** in Jerusalem and Judah
Heb 9: 4 golden **p** that had the manna

POTENTATE
1Ti 6:15 who is the blessed and only **P**

POTIPHAR
Gen 37:36 had sold him in Egypt to **P**
Gen 39: 1 And **P**, an officer of Pharaoh,

POTI-PHERAH
Gen 41:45 daughter of **P** priest of On
Gen 41:50 daughter of **P** priest of On
Gen 46:20 daughter of **P** priest of On

POTS (*see* POT)
Ex 16: 3 when we sat by the **p** of meat
1Ki 7:45 the **p**, the shovels, and the
2Ki 25:14 They also took away the **p**
2Ch 4:11 Then Huram made the **p** and the
2Ch 4:16 also the **p**, the shovels, the

Num 14:17 let the **p** of my LORD be great
Num 22:38 have I any **p** at all to say
Deut 4:37 Presence, with His mighty **p**
Deut 8:17 you say in your heart, 'My **p**
Deut 8:18 who gives you **p** to get wealth
Deut 9:29 brought out by Your mighty **p**
Deut 32:36 He sees that their **p** is gone
Deut 34:12 and by all that mighty **p** and
Josh 8:20 So they had no **p** to flee this
Josh 17:17 great people and have great **p**
1Sa 9: 1 Benjamite, a mighty man of **p**
1Sa 30: 4 they had no more **p** to weep
2Sa 22:33 God is my strength and **p**, and
2Ki 17:36 land of Egypt with great **p**
2Ki 19:26 inhabitants had little **p**
1Ch 18: 3 his **p** by the River Euphrates
1Ch 29:11 LORD, is the greatness, the **p**
1Ch 29:12 In Your hand is **p** and might
2Ch 14:11 or with those who have no **p**
2Ch 20: 6 in Your hand is there not **p**
2Ch 20:12 For we have no **p** against this
2Ch 22: 9 to assume **p** over the kingdom
2Ch 25: 8 for God has **p** to help and to
2Ch 26:13 that made war with mighty **p**
Ezra 8:22 good who seek Him, but His **p**
Neh 1:10 have redeemed by Your great **p**
Neh 5: 5 not in our **p** to redeem them
Esth 10: 2 Now all the acts of his **p**
Job 1:12 all that he has is in your **p**
Job 5:20 war from the **p** of the sword
Job 21: 7 old, yes, become mighty in **p**
Job 23: 6 with me in His great **p**
Job 24:22 the mighty away with His **p**
Job 26: 2 helped him who is without **p**
Job 26:12 stirs up the sea with His **p**
Job 26:14 of His **p** who can understand
Job 27:22 flees desperately from its **p**
Job 36:22 God is exalted by His **p**
Job 37:23 He is excellent in **p**, in
Job 40:16 and his **p** is in his stomach
Job 41:12 his limbs, his mighty **p**, or
Ps 21:13 We will sing and praise Your **p**
Ps 22:20 life from the **p** of the dog
Ps 37:35 seen the wicked in great **p**
Ps 49:15 soul from the **p** of the grave
Ps 59:11 Scatter them by Your **p**, And
Ps 59:16 But I will sing of Your **p**
Ps 62:11 That **p** belongs to God
Ps 63: 2 the sanctuary, To see Your **p**
Ps 65: 6 Being clothed with **p**
Ps 66: 3 the greatness of Your **p** Your
Ps 66: 7 He rules by His **p** forever
Ps 68:35 strength and **p** to His people
Ps 71:18 Your **p** to everyone who is to
Ps 78:26 by His **p** He brought in the
Ps 78:42 They did not remember His **p**
Ps 79:11 Your **p** Preserve those who are
Ps 89:48 life from the **p** of the grave
Ps 90:11 Who knows the **p** of Your anger
Ps 106: 8 might make His mighty **p** known
Ps 110: 3 In the day of Your **p**
Ps 111: 6 His people the **p** of His works
Ps 145:11 kingdom, And talk of Your **p**
Ps 147: 5 is our Lord, and mighty in **p**
Prov 3:27 when it is in the **p** of your
Prov 18:21 are in the **p** of the tongue
Eccl 4: 1 their oppressors there was **p**
Eccl 5:19 given him **p** to eat of it, to
Eccl 6: 2 not give him **p** to eat of it
Eccl 8: 4 word of a king is, there is **p**
Eccl 8: 8 No one has **p** over the spirit
Eccl 8: 8 no one has **p** in the day of
Is 37:27 inhabitants had little **p**
Is 40:26 and the strength of His **p**
Is 40:29 He gives **p** to the weak, and to
Is 43:17 the **p** (they shall lie down
Is 47:14 from the **p** of the flame
Is 50: 2 Or have I no **p** to deliver
Jer 5:31 priests rule by their own **p**
Jer 10:12 has made the earth by His **p**
Jer 27: 5 on the ground, by My great **p**
Jer 32:17 and the earth by Your great **p**
Jer 51:15 has made the earth by His **p**
Ezek 17: 9 no great **p** or many people
Ezek 22: 6 his **p** to shed blood in you
Ezek 30: 6 of her **p** shall come down
Ezek 35: 5 children of Israel by the **p**
Dan 2:37 has given you a kingdom, **p**
Dan 3:27 bodies the fire had no **p**
Dan 4:30 royal dwelling by my mighty **p**
Dan 6:27 from the **p** of the lions
Dan 8: 6 and ran at him with furious **p**
Dan 8: 7 There was no **p** in the ram to
Dan 8:22 nation, but not with its **p**
Dan 8:24 His **p** shall be mighty, but
Dan 8:24 mighty, but not by his own **p**
Dan 11: 5 and he shall gain **p** over him
Dan 11: 6 retain the **p** of her authority
Dan 11:16 with destruction in his **p**
Dan 11:25 He shall stir up his **p** and his
Dan 11:43 He shall have **p** over the
Dan 12: 7 when the **p** of the holy people
Hos 13:14 them from the **p** of the grave
Amos 2:14 shall not strengthen his **p**
Mic 2: 1 it is in the **p** of their hand
Mic 3: 8 But truly I am full of **p** by
Nah 1: 3 slow to anger and great in **p**
Nah 2: 1 Fortify your **p** mightily
Hab 1:11 imputing this **p** to his god
Hab 2: 9 from the **p** of disaster
Hab 3: 4 and there His **p** was hidden
Zech 4: 6 Not by might nor by **p**, but
Zech 9: 4 will destroy her **p** in the sea
Matt 6:13 Yours is the kingdom and the **p**
Matt 9: 6 that the Son of Man has **p** on
Matt 9: 8 who had given such **p** to men
Matt 10: 1 He gave them **p** over unclean
Matt 22:29 Scriptures nor the **p** of God
Matt 24:30 the clouds of heaven with **p**
Matt 26:64 at the right hand of the **P**
Mark 2:10 that the Son of Man has **p** on
Mark 3:15 to have **p** to heal sicknesses
Mark 5:30 that **p** had gone out of Him
Mark 6: 7 and gave them **p** over unclean
Mark 9: 1 kingdom of God present with **p**
Mark 12:24 Scriptures nor the **p** of God
Mark 13:26 in the clouds with great **p**
Mark 14:62 at the right hand of the **P**
Luke 1:17 **p** of Elijah, 'to turn the
Luke 1:35 the **p** of the Highest will
Luke 4:14 **p** of the Spirit to Galilee
Luke 4:36 **p** He commands the unclean
Luke 5:17 the **p** of the Lord was present
Luke 5:24 that the Son of Man has **p** on
Luke 6:19 for **p** went out from Him and
Luke 8:46 for I perceived **p** going out
Luke 9: 1 together and gave them **p** and
Luke 10:19 over all the **p** of the enemy
Luke 12: 5 has **p** to cast into hell
Luke 20:20 order to deliver Him to the **p**
Luke 21:27 Man coming in a cloud with **p**
Luke 22:53 hour, and the **p** of darkness
Luke 22:69 right hand of the **p** of God
Luke 24:49 endued with **p** from on high
John 10:18 I have **p** to lay it down, and I
John 10:18 I have **p** to take it again
John 19:10 that I have **p** to crucify You
John 19:10 and **p** to release You
John 19:11 You could have no **p** at all
Acts 1: 8 But you shall receive **p** when
Acts 3:12 as though by our own **p** or
Acts 4: 7 By what **p** or by what name
Acts 4:33 with great **p** the apostles
Acts 6: 8 Stephen, full of faith and **p**
Acts 8:10 man is the great **p** of God
Acts 8:19 Give me this **p** also, that
Acts 10:38 the Holy Spirit and with **p**
Acts 26:18 from the **p** of Satan to God,
Rom 1: 4 to be the Son of God with **p**
Rom 1:16 for it is the **p** of God to
Rom 1:20 are made, even His eternal **p**
Rom 9:17 that I might show My **p** in you
Rom 9:21 potter have **p** over the clay
Rom 9:22 wrath and to make His **p** known
Rom 15:13 by the **p** of the Holy Spirit
Rom 15:19 by the **p** of the Spirit of God
1Co 1:18 saved it is the **p** of God
1Co 1:24 Greeks, Christ the **p** of God
1Co 2: 4 of the Spirit and of **p**,
1Co 2: 5 of men but in the **p** of God
1Co 4:19 who are puffed up, but the **p**
1Co 4:20 God is not in word but in **p**
1Co 5: 4 with the **p** of our Lord Jesus
1Co 6:12 be brought under the **p** of any
1Co 6:14 also raise us up by His **p**
1Co 7:37 but has **p** over his own will,
1Co 15:24 rule and all authority and **p**
1Co 15:43 weakness, it is raised in **p**
2Co 4: 7 of the **p** may be of God and not
2Co 6: 7 of truth, by the **p** of God
2Co 12: 9 that the **p** of Christ may rest
2Co 13: 4 yet He lives by the **p** of God
2Co 13: 4 by the **p** of God toward you
Eph 1:19 His **p** toward us who believe
Eph 1:19 the working of His mighty **p**
Eph 1:21 above all principality and **p**
Eph 2: 2 prince of the **p** of the air
Eph 3: 7 effective working of His **p**
Eph 3:20 to the **p** that works in us
Eph 6:10 Lord and in the **p** of His might
Phil 3:10 the **p** of His resurrection, and
Col 1:11 according to His glorious **p**
Col 1:13 us from the **p** of darkness
Col 2:10 head of all principality and **p**
1Th 1: 5 in word only, but also in **p**
2Th 1: 9 and from the glory of His **p**
2Th 1:11 and the work of faith with **p**
2Th 2: 9 working of Satan, with all **p**
1Ti 6:16 be honor and everlasting **p**
2Ti 1: 7 us a spirit of fear, but of **p**
2Ti 1: 8 according to the **p** of God
2Ti 3: 5 godliness but denying its **p**
Heb 1: 3 things by the word of His **p**
Heb 2:14 him who had the **p** of death
Heb 7:16 to the **p** of an endless life
Heb 9:17 since it has no **p** at all
1Pe 1: 5 who are kept by the **p** of God
2Pe 1: 3 as His divine **p** has given to
2Pe 1:16 we made known to you the **p**
2Pe 2:11 angels, who are greater in **p**
Jude 25 and majesty, dominion and **p**
Rev 2:26 will give **p** over the nations
Rev 4:11 receive glory and honor and **p**
Rev 5:12 who was slain to receive **p**
Rev 5:13 **p** be to Him who sits on the
Rev 6: 8 **p** was given to them over a
Rev 7:12 thanksgiving and honor and **p**
Rev 9: 3 And to them was given **p**, as
Rev 9: 3 scorpions of the earth have **p**
Rev 9:10 their **p** was to hurt men five
Rev 9:19 For their **p** is in their mouth
Rev 11: 3 And I will give **p** to my two
Rev 11: 6 These have **p** to shut heaven,
Rev 11: 6 they have **p** over waters to
Rev 11:17 You have taken Your great **p**
Rev 12:10 the **p** of His Christ have come
Rev 13: 2 And the dragon gave him his **p**
Rev 13:15 He was granted **p** to give
Rev 14:18 who had **p** over fire, and he
Rev 15: 8 glory of God and from His **p**
Rev 16: 8 **p** was given to him to scorch
Rev 16: 9 who has **p** over these plagues
Rev 17:13 and they will give their **p**
Rev 19: 1 and **p** to the Lord our God
Rev 20: 6 the second death has no **p**

POWERFUL (*see* POWER)
2Ch 17:12 became increasingly **p**, and he
Ps 29: 4 The voice of the LORD is **p**
Is 18: 2 beginning onward, a nation **p**
Is 18: 7 beginning onward, a nation **p**
2Co 10:10 are weighty and **p**, but his
Heb 4:12 word of God is living and **p**

POWERLESS (*see* POWER)
Hab 1: 4 Therefore the law is **p**, and

POWERS (*see* POWER)
Esth 1: 3 the **p** of Persia and Media, the
Matt 14: 2 therefore these **p** are at work
Matt 24:29 the **p** of the heavens will be
Mark 6:14 therefore these **p** are at work
Mark 13:25 and the **p** in heaven will be
Luke 21:26 for the **p** of heaven will be
Rom 8:38 nor principalities nor **p**, nor
Eph 3:10 **p** in the heavenly places,
Eph 6:12 principalities, against **p**
Col 1:16 or principalities or **p**
Col 2:15 disarmed principalities and **p**
Heb 6: 5 the **p** of the age to come,
1Pe 3:22 **p** having been made subject to

PRACTICE (*see* PRACTICED, PRACTICES, PRACTICING)
Gen 44:15 I can certainly **p** divination
Lev 19:26 nor shall you **p** divination or
Ps 141: 4 To **p** wicked works With men
Is 32: 6 to **p** ungodliness, to utter
Ezek 13:23 futility nor **p** divination
Ezek 23:48 taught not to **p** your lewdness
Mic 2: 1 At morning light they **p** it
Matt 7:23 Me, you who **p** lawlessness

Matt 13:41 and those who **p** lawlessness,
Rom 1:32 that those who **p** such things
Rom 1:32 approve of those who **p** them
Rom 2: 1 who judge **p** the same things
Rom 2: 2 those who **p** such things
Rom 7:15 I will to do, that I do not **p**
Rom 7:19 I will not to do, that I **p**
Gal 5:21 that those who **p** such things
1Jn 1: 6 we lie and do not **p** the truth
1Jn 3:10 Whoever does not **p**

PRACTICED (*see* PRACTICE)
2Ki 17:17 **p** witchcraft and soothsaying,
2Ki 21: 6 the fire, **p** soothsaying, used
2Ch 33: 6 he **p** soothsaying, used
Acts 8: 9 who previously **p** sorcery in
Acts 19:19 many of those who had **p** magic
Rom 3:13 tongues they have **p** deceit"
2Co 12:21 which they have **p**

PRACTICES (*see* PRACTICE)
Gen 44: 5 which he indeed **p** divination
Deut 18:10 fire, or one who **p** witchcraft
Rom 13: 4 wrath on him who **p** evil
2Pe 2:14 a heart trained in covetous **p**
1Jn 2:29 **p** righteousness is born of
1Jn 3: 7 He who **p** righteousness is
Rev 22:15 and whoever loves and **p** a lie

PRACTICING (*see* PRACTICE)
2Ki 17:34 continue **p** the former rituals
Jer 22:17 and **p** oppression and violence
John 3:20 For everyone **p** evil hates the
Rom 2: 3 who judge those **p** such things

PRAETORIUM
Matt 27:27 took Jesus into the **P** and
Mark 15:16 away into the hall called **P**
John 18:28 Jesus from Caiaphas to the **P**
John 18:28 did not go into the **P**, lest
John 18:33 Pilate entered the **P** again
John 19: 9 and went again into the **P**, and
Acts 23:35 him to be kept in Herod's **P**

PRAISE (*see* PRAISED, PRAISES, PRAISEWORTHY, PRAISING)
Gen 29:35 Now I will **p** the LORD
Gen 49: 8 he whom your brothers shall **p**
Ex 15: 2 He is my God, and I will **p** Him
Lev 19:24 be holy, a **p** to the LORD
Deut 10:21 He is your **p**, and He is your
Deut 26:19 which He has made, in **p**, in
Judg 5: 3 I will sing **p** to the LORD God
1Ch 16: 4 to **p** the LORD God of Israel
1Ch 16:35 name, to triumph in Your **p**
1Ch 23: 5 said David, "for giving **p**."
1Ch 23:30 **p** the LORD, and likewise at
1Ch 25: 3 give thanks and to **p** the LORD
1Ch 29:13 You and **p** Your glorious name
2Ch 7: 6 David had made to **p** the LORD
2Ch 7: 6 offered **p** by their ministry
2Ch 8:14 for their duties (to **p** and
2Ch 20:19 the Korahites stood up to **p**
2Ch 20:21 who should **p** the beauty of
2Ch 20:21 **P** the LORD, for His mercy
2Ch 20:22 they began to sing and to **p**
2Ch 23:13 music, and those who led in **p**
2Ch 29:30 the Levites to sing **p** to the
2Ch 31: 2 to **p** in the gates of the camp
Ezra 3:10 to **p** the LORD, according to
Neh 9: 5 above all blessing and **p**
Neh 12:24 across from them, to **p** and
Neh 12:46 of the singers, and songs of **p**
Ps 7:17 I will **p** the LORD according
Ps 7:17 will sing **p** to the name of
Ps 9: 1 I will **p** You, O LORD, with my
Ps 9: 2 I will sing **p** to Your name, O
Ps 9:14 Your **p** In the gates of the
Ps 21:13 We will sing and **p** Your power
Ps 22:22 the congregation I will **p** You
Ps 22:23 You who fear the LORD, **p** Him
Ps 22:25 My **p** shall be of You in the
Ps 22:26 who seek Him will **p** the LORD
Ps 28: 7 And with my song I will **p** Him
Ps 30: 4 Sing **p** to the LORD, You
Ps 30: 9 Will the dust **p** You
Ps 30:12 my glory may sing **p** to You
Ps 33: 1 For **p** from the upright is
Ps 33: 2 **P** the LORD with the harp
Ps 34: 1 His **p** shall continually be in
Ps 35:18 I will **p** You among many
Ps 35:28 of Your **p** all the day long
Ps 40: 3 song in my mouth—**P** to our God
Ps 42: 4 With the voice of joy and **p**
Ps 42: 5 for I shall yet **p** Him For the
Ps 42:11 For I shall yet **p** Him, The
Ps 43: 4 And on the harp I will **p** You
Ps 43: 5 For I shall yet **p** Him, The
Ps 44: 8 long, And **p** Your name forever
Ps 45:17 people shall **p** You forever
Ps 48:10 So is Your **p** to the ends of
Ps 49:18 himself (For men will **p** you
Ps 50:23 Whoever offers **p** glorifies Me
Ps 51:15 mouth shall show forth Your **p**
Ps 52: 9 I will **p** You forever, Because
Ps 54: 6 I will **p** Your name, O LORD,
Ps 56: 4 In God (I will **p** His word)
Ps 56:10 In God (I will **p** His word)
Ps 56:10 the LORD (I will **p** His word)
Ps 57: 7 I will sing and give **p**
Ps 57: 9 I will **p** You, O Lord, among
Ps 61: 8 So I will sing **p** to Your name
Ps 63: 3 life, My lips shall **p** You
Ps 63: 5 my mouth shall **p** You with
Ps 65: 1 **P** is awaiting You, O God, in
Ps 66: 2 Make His **p** glorious
Ps 66: 8 voice of His **p** to be heard
Ps 67: 3 Let the peoples **p** You, O God
Ps 67: 3 Let all the peoples **p** You
Ps 67: 5 Let the peoples **p** You, O God
Ps 67: 5 Let all the peoples **p** You
Ps 69:30 I will **p** the name of God with
Ps 69:34 Let heaven and earth **p** Him
Ps 71: 6 My **p** shall be continually of
Ps 71: 8 mouth be filled with Your **p**
Ps 71:14 will **p** You yet more and more
Ps 71:22 with the lute I will **p** you
Ps 74:21 the poor and needy **p** Your
Ps 76:10 the wrath of man shall **p** You
Ps 79:13 Your **p** to all generations
Ps 86:12 I will **p** You, O Lord my God,
Ps 88:10 Shall the dead arise and **p** You
Ps 89: 5 heavens will **p** Your wonders
Ps 99: 3 Let them **p** Your great and
Ps 100: 4 And into His courts with **p**
Ps 102:18 to be created may **p** the LORD
Ps 102:21 Zion, And His **p** in Jerusalem,
Ps 104:33 I will sing **p** to my God while
Ps 104:35 O my soul! **P** the LORD!
Ps 105:45 keep His laws. **P** the LORD!
Ps 106: 1 **P** the LORD! Oh, give thanks
Ps 106: 2 Or can declare all His **p**
Ps 106:12 They sang His **p**
Ps 106:47 name, And to triumph in Your **p**
Ps 106:48 say, "Amen!" **P** the LORD!
Ps 107:32 **p** Him in the assembly of the
Ps 108: 1 I will sing and give **p**, even
Ps 108: 3 I will **p** You, O LORD, among
Ps 109: 1 keep silent, O God of my **p**
Ps 109:30 I will greatly **p** the LORD
Ps 109:30 Yes, I will **p** Him among the
Ps 111: 1 **P** the LORD! I will **p**
Ps 111: 1 I will **p** the LORD with my
Ps 111:10 His **p** endures forever
Ps 112: 1 **P** the LORD! Blessed is
Ps 113: 1 **P** the LORD! **P**, O
Ps 113: 1 **P**, O servants of the LORD,
Ps 113: 1 **P** the name of the LORD
Ps 113: 9 of children. **P** the LORD!
Ps 115:17 The dead do not **p** the LORD
Ps 115:18 forevermore. **P** the LORD!
Ps 116:19 O Jerusalem. **P** the LORD!
Ps 117: 1 **p** the LORD, all you Gentiles
Ps 117: 2 endures forever. **P** the LORD!
Ps 118:19 them, And I will **p** the LORD
Ps 118:21 I will **p** You, For You have
Ps 118:28 are my God, and I will **p** You
Ps 119: 7 I will **p** You with uprightness
Ps 119:164 Seven times a day I **p** You
Ps 119:171 My lips shall utter **p**, For
Ps 119:175 soul live, and it shall **p** You
Ps 135: 1 **P** the LORD! **P** the name
Ps 135: 1 **P** the name of the LORD
Ps 135: 1 **P** Him, O you servants of the
Ps 135: 3 **P** the LORD, for the LORD is
Ps 135:21 in Jerusalem! **P** the LORD!
Ps 138: 1 I will **p** You with my whole
Ps 138: 2 And **p** Your name For Your
Ps 138: 4 of the earth shall **p** You, O
Ps 139:14 I will **p** You, for I am
Ps 142: 7 That I may **p** Your name
Ps 145: 2 I will **p** Your name forever and
Ps 145: 4 One generation shall **p** Your
Ps 145:10 All Your works shall **p** You
Ps 145:21 shall speak the **p** of the LORD
Ps 146: 1 **P** the LORD! **P** the LORD,
Ps 146: 2 I live I will **p** the LORD
Ps 146:10 all generations. **P** the LORD!
Ps 147: 1 **P** the LORD! For it is good
Ps 147: 1 pleasant, and **p** is beautiful
Ps 147:12 **P** the LORD, O Jerusalem
Ps 147:12 **P** your God, O Zion
Ps 147:20 known them. **P** the LORD!
Ps 148: 1 **P** the LORD! **P** the LORD
Ps 148: 1 **P** the LORD from the heavens
Ps 148: 1 **P** Him in the heights
Ps 148: 2 **P** Him, all His angels
Ps 148: 2 **P** Him, all His hosts
Ps 148: 3 **P** Him, sun and moon
Ps 148: 3 **P** Him, all you stars of light
Ps 148: 4 **P** Him, you heavens of heavens
Ps 148: 5 Let them **p** the name of the
Ps 148: 7 **P** the LORD from the earth,
Ps 148:13 Let them **p** the name of the
Ps 148:14 The **p** of all His saints
Ps 148:14 near to Him. **P** the LORD!
Ps 149: 1 **P** the LORD! Sing to the LORD
Ps 149: 1 His **p** in the congregation of
Ps 149: 3 Let them **p** His name with the
Ps 149: 9 all His saints. **P** the LORD!
Ps 150: 1 **P** the LORD! **P** God
Ps 150: 1 **P** God in His sanctuary
Ps 150: 1 **P** Him in His mighty firmament
Ps 150: 2 **P** Him for His mighty acts
Ps 150: 2 **P** Him according to His
Ps 150: 3 **P** Him with the sound of the
Ps 150: 3 **P** Him with the lute and harp
Ps 150: 4 **P** Him with the timbrel and
Ps 150: 4 **P** Him with stringed
Ps 150: 5 **P** Him with loud cymbals
Ps 150: 5 **P** Him with high sounding
Ps 150: 6 **p** the LORD. **P** the LORD!
Prov 27: 2 Let another man **p** you, and not
Prov 28: 4 forsake the law **p** the wicked
Prov 31:31 own works **p** her in the gates
Is 12: 1 O LORD, I will **p** You
Is 12: 4 **P** the LORD, call upon His
Is 25: 1 I will **p** Your name, for You
Is 38:18 thank You, death cannot **p** You
Is 38:19 living man, he shall **p** You
Is 42: 8 nor My **p** to graven images
Is 42:10 His **p** from the ends of the
Is 42:12 LORD, and declare His **p** in the
Is 43:21 they shall declare My **p**
Is 48: 9 for My **p** I will restrain it
Is 60:18 Salvation, and your gates **P**
Is 61: 3 the garment of **p** for the
Is 61:11 **p** to spring forth before all
Is 62: 7 Jerusalem a **p** in the earth
Is 62: 9 shall eat it, and **p** the LORD
Jer 13:11 My people, for renown, for **p**
Jer 17:14 be saved, for You are my **p**
Jer 17:26 bringing sacrifices of **p** to
Jer 20:13 Sing to the LORD! **P** the LORD!
Jer 31: 7 proclaim, give **p**, and say, 'O
Jer 33: 9 be to Me a name of joy, a **p**
Jer 33:11 **P** the LORD of hosts, for the
Jer 33:11 **p** into the house of the LORD
Jer 48: 2 No more **p** of Moab
Jer 49:25 is the city of **p** not deserted
Jer 51:41 how the **p** of the whole earth
Dan 2:23 **p** You, O God of my fathers
Dan 4:37 Now I, Nebuchadnezzar, **p** and
Joel 2:26 **p** the name of the LORD your
Hab 3: 3 the earth was full of His **p**
Zeph 3:19 I will appoint them for **p**
Zeph 3:20 **p** among all the peoples of
Matt 21:16 infants You have perfected **p**'
Luke 10:21 I **p** You, Father, Lord of
Luke 18:43 they saw it, gave **p** to God
Luke 19:37 **p** God with a loud voice for
John 12:43 for they loved the **p** of men
John 12:43 more than the **p** of God
Rom 2:29 whose **p** is not from men but
Rom 13: 3 you will have **p** from the same
Rom 15:11 **P** the LORD, all you Gentiles
1Co 4: 5 then each one's **p** will come
1Co 11: 2 Now I **p** you, brethren, that
1Co 11:17 instructions I do not **p** you
1Co 11:22 Shall I **p** you in this
1Co 11:22 I do not **p** you

2Co 8:18 with him the brother whose **p**
Eph 1: 6 to the **p** of the glory of His
Eph 1:12 be to the **p** of His glory
Eph 1:14 to the **p** of His glory
Phil 1:11 to the glory and **p** of God
Heb 2:12 I will sing **p** to You
Heb 13:15 the sacrifice of **p** to God
1Pe 1: 7 by fire, may be found to **p**
1Pe 2:14 for the **p** of those who do
Rev 19: 5 **P** our God, all you His

PRAISED (*see* PRAISE)
Judg 16:24 saw him, they **p** their god
2Sa 14:25 there was no one who was **p** as
2Sa 22: 4 LORD, who is worthy to be **p**
1Ch 16:25 is great and greatly to be **p**
1Ch 16:36 and **p** the LORD
1Ch 23: 5 four thousand **p** the LORD with
2Ch 5:13 music, and **p** the LORD, saying
2Ch 7: 3 and **p** the LORD, saying
2Ch 30:21 the priests **p** the LORD day by
Ezra 3:11 shout, when they **p** the LORD
Neh 5:13 and **p** the LORD
Ps 18: 3 LORD, who is worthy to be **p**
Ps 48: 1 greatly to be **p** In the city
Ps 72:15 And daily He shall be **p**
Ps 96: 4 is great and greatly to be **p**
Ps 113: 3 The LORD's name is to be **p**
Ps 145: 3 the LORD, and greatly to be **p**
Prov 31:30 the LORD, she shall be **p**
Eccl 4: 2 Therefore I **p** the dead who
Song 6: 9 the concubines, and they **p** her
Is 64:11 where our fathers **p** You, is
Dan 4:34 I blessed the Most High and **p**
Dan 5: 4 **p** the gods of gold and silver,
Dan 5:23 you have **p** the gods of silver

PRAISES (*see* PRAISE)
Ex 15:11 in holiness, fearful in **p**
2Sa 22:50 and sing **p** to Your name
2Ch 29:30 So they sang **p** with gladness,
Ps 9:11 Sing **p** to the LORD, who
Ps 18:49 And sing **p** to Your name
Ps 22: 3 Who inhabit the **p** of Israel
Ps 27: 6 I will sing **p** to the LORD
Ps 47: 6 Sing **p** to God, sing **p**
Ps 47: 6 Sing **p** to our King, sing **p**
Ps 47: 7 Sing **p** with understanding
Ps 56:12 I will render **p** to You,
Ps 59:17 O my Strength, I will sing **p**
Ps 66: 4 worship You And sing **p** to You
Ps 66: 4 shall sing **p** to Your name
Ps 68: 4 to God, sing **p** to His name
Ps 68:32 sing **p** to the Lord, Selah
Ps 75: 9 I will sing **p** to the God of
Ps 78: 4 to come the **p** of the LORD
Ps 92: 1 to sing **p** to Your name, O
Ps 98: 4 in song, rejoice, and sing **p**
Ps 101: 1 To You, O LORD, I will sing **p**
Ps 108: 3 I will sing **p** to You among
Ps 135: 3 Sing **p** to His name, for it is
Ps 138: 1 the gods I will sing **p** to You
Ps 144: 9 strings I will sing **p** to You
Ps 146: 2 I will sing **p** to my God while
Ps 147: 1 is good to sing **p** to our God
Ps 147: 7 Sing **p** on the harp to our God
Ps 149: 3 Let them sing **p** to Him with
Ps 149: 6 Let the high **p** of God be in
Prov 31:28 her husband also, and he **p** her
Is 60: 6 proclaim the **p** of the LORD
Is 63: 7 the **p** of the LORD, according
1Pe 2: 9 **p** of Him who called you out

PRAISEWORTHY (*see* PRAISE)
Phil 4: 8 and if there is anything **p**

PRAISING (*see* PRAISE)
2Ch 5:13 one sound to be heard in **p**
2Ch 23:12 **p** the king, she came to the
Ezra 3:11 And they sang responsively, **p**
Ps 84: 4 They will still be **p** You
Luke 1:64 loosed, and he spoke, **p** God
Luke 2:13 of the heavenly host **p** God
Luke 2:20 **p** God for all the things that
Luke 24:53 continually in the temple **p**
Acts 2:47 **p** God and having favor with
Acts 3: 8 walking, leaping, and **p** God
Acts 3: 9 saw him walking and **p** God

PRATING
Prov 10: 8 but a **p** fool will fall
Prov 10:10 but a **p** fool will fall
3Jn 10 **p** against us with malicious

PRATTLE (*see* PRATTLER)
Mic 2: 6 Do not **p**," you say to those

PRATTLER (*see* PRATTLE)
Mic 2:11 would be the **p** of this people

PRAY (*see* PRAYED, PRAYER, PRAYING, PRAYS)
Gen 20: 7 prophet, and he will **p** for you
Gen 32:11 Deliver me, I **p**, from the
Gen 32:29 Tell me Your name, I **p**
Ex 32:32 but if not, I **p**, blot me out
Ex 33:13 Now therefore, I **p**, if I have
Ex 34: 9 O Lord, let my Lord, I **p**
Num 12:13 Please heal her, O God, I **p**
Num 14:17 And now, I **p**, let the power of
Num 14:19 iniquity of this people, I **p**
Num 21: 7 **p** to the LORD that He take
Deut 3:25 I **p**, let me cross over and
Judg 6:18 Do not depart from here, I **p**
Judg 6:39 Let me test, I **p**, just once
Judg 10:15 deliver us this day, we **p**
Judg 16:28 O Lord GOD, remember me, I **p**
Judg 16:28 Strengthen me, I **p**, just this
1Sa 7: 5 I will **p** to the LORD for you
1Sa 12:19 **P** for your servants to the
1Sa 12:23 LORD in ceasing to **p** for you
1Sa 23:11 O LORD God of Israel, I **p**
2Sa 7:27 heart to **p** this prayer to You
2Sa 15:31 O LORD, I **p**, turn the counsel
2Sa 24:10 but now, I **p**, O LORD, take
2Sa 24:17 Let Your hand, I **p**, be
1Ki 8:26 And now I **p**, O God of Israel,
1Ki 8:30 When they **p** toward this place
1Ki 8:33 and confess Your name, and **p**
1Ki 8:35 when they **p** toward this place
1Ki 8:44 and when they **p** to the LORD
1Ki 8:48 **p** to You toward their land
1Ki 13: 6 **p** for me, that my hand may be
1Ki 17:21 O LORD my God, I **p**, let this
2Ki 6:17 LORD, I **p**, open his eyes that
2Ki 6:18 Strike this people, I **p**, with
2Ki 19:19 O LORD our God, I **p**, save us
2Ki 20: 3 Remember now, O LORD, I **p**
1Ch 17:25 in his heart to **p** before You
1Ch 21: 8 but now, I **p**, take away the
1Ch 21:17 Let Your hand, I **p**, O LORD my
2Ch 6:21 when they **p** toward this place
2Ch 6:24 and confess Your name, and **p**
2Ch 6:26 when they **p** toward this place
2Ch 6:32 they come and **p** in this temple
2Ch 6:34 when they **p** to You toward
2Ch 6:38 **p** toward their land which You
2Ch 6:40 Now, my God, I **p**, let Your
2Ch 7:14 will humble themselves, and **p**
Ezra 6:10 **p** for the life of the king and
Neh 1: 5 I **p**, LORD God of heaven, O
Neh 1: 6 which I **p** before You now, day
Neh 1: 8 Remember, I **p**, the word that
Neh 1:11 O Lord, I **p**, please let Your
Neh 1:11 servant prosper this day, I **p**
Job 10: 9 Remember, I **p**, that You have
Job 21:15 do we have if we **p** to Him
Job 32:21 Let me not, I **p**, show
Job 33:26 He shall **p** to God, and He will
Job 42: 8 servant Job shall **p** for you
Ps 5: 2 my God, For to You I will **p**
Ps 32: 6 **p** to You In a time when You
Ps 55:17 morning and at noon I will **p**
Ps 118:25 Save now, I **p**, O LORD
Ps 118:25 I **p**, send now prosperity.
Ps 119:76 Let, I **p**, Your merciful
Ps 119:108 Accept, I **p**, the freewill
Ps 122: 6 **P** for the peace of Jerusalem
Is 16:12 come to his sanctuary to **p**
Is 38: 3 Remember now, O LORD, I **p**
Is 45:20 **p** to a god that cannot save
Jer 7:16 do not **p** for this people, nor
Jer 11:14 do not **p** for this people, or
Jer 14:11 Do not **p** for this people, for
Jer 29: 7 and **p** to the LORD for it
Jer 29:12 **p** to Me, and I will listen to
Jer 37: 3 **P** now to the LORD our God for
Jer 42: 2 **p** for us to the LORD your God
Jer 42: 4 I will **p** to the LORD your God
Jer 42:20 **P** for us to the LORD our God
Dan 9:16 all Your righteousness, I **p**
Amos 7: 2 O Lord GOD, forgive, I **p**
Amos 7: 5 O Lord GOD, cease, I **p**
Jon 1:14 We **p**, O LORD, please do not
Zech 7: 2 of God, to **p** before the LORD,
Zech 8:21 **p** before the LORD, and seek
Zech 8:22 and to **p** before the LORD
Matt 5:44 **p** for those who spitefully
Matt 6: 5 And when you **p**, you shall not
Matt 6: 5 For they love to **p** standing
Matt 6: 6 But you, when you **p**, go into
Matt 6: 6 **p** to your Father who is in
Matt 6: 7 But when you **p**, do not use
Matt 6: 9 In this manner, therefore, **p**
Matt 9:38 Therefore **p** the Lord of the
Matt 14:23 on a mountain by Himself to **p**
Matt 19:13 put His hands on them and **p**
Matt 24:20 **p** that your flight may not be
Matt 26:36 while I go and **p** over there
Matt 26:41 Watch and **p**, lest you enter
Matt 26:53 I cannot now **p** to My Father
Mark 6:46 departed to the mountain to **p**
Mark 11:24 things you ask when you **p**
Mark 13:18 **p** that your flight may not be
Mark 13:33 Take heed, watch and **p**
Mark 14:32 Sit here while I **p**
Mark 14:38 Watch and **p**, lest you enter
Luke 6:12 went out to the mountain to **p**
Luke 6:28 **p** for those who spitefully
Luke 9:28 went up on the mountain to **p**
Luke 10: 2 therefore **p** the Lord of the
Luke 11: 1 Lord, teach us to **p**, as John
Luke 11: 2 When you **p**, say
Luke 18: 1 that men always ought to **p**
Luke 18:10 went up to the temple to **p**
Luke 21:36 and **p** always that you may be
Luke 22:40 **P** that you may not enter into
Luke 22:46 Rise and **p**, lest you enter
John 14:16 I will **p** the Father, and He
John 16:26 I shall **p** the Father for you
John 17: 9 I **p** for them. I do not **p**
John 17: 9 I do not **p** for the world but
John 17:15 I do not **p** that You should
John 17:20 I do not **p** for these alone,
Acts 8:22 **p** God if perhaps the thought
Acts 8:24 **P** to the Lord for me, that
Acts 10: 9 went up on the housetop to **p**
Rom 8:26 we should **p** for as we ought
1Co 11:13 to **p** to God with her head
1Co 14:13 **p** that he may interpret
1Co 14:14 For if I **p** in a tongue, my
1Co 14:15 I will **p** with the spirit, and
1Co 14:15 and I will also **p** with the
2Co 13: 7 Now I **p** to God that you do no
2Co 13: 9 And this also we **p**, that you
Phil 1: 9 And this I **p**, that your love
Col 1: 9 it, do not cease to **p** for you
1Th 5:17 **p** without ceasing,
1Th 5:25 Brethren, **p** for us
2Th 1:11 Therefore we also **p** always
2Th 3: 1 **p** for us, that the word of
1Ti 2: 8 that the men **p** everywhere
Heb 13:18 **P** for us; for we are
Jas 5:13 you suffering? Let him **p**.
Jas 5:14 and let them **p** over him,
Jas 5:16 **p** for one another, that you
1Jn 5:16 that he should **p** about that
3Jn 2 I **p** that you may prosper in

PRAYED (*see* PRAY)
Gen 20:17 So Abraham **p** to God
Num 11: 2 when Moses **p** to the LORD, the
Num 21: 7 So Moses **p** for the people
Deut 9:20 so I **p** for Aaron also at the
Deut 9:26 Therefore I **p** to the LORD
Judg 13: 8 Then Manoah **p** to the LORD
1Sa 1:10 and **p** to the LORD and wept in
1Sa 1:27 For this child I **p**, and the
1Sa 2: 1 And Hannah **p** and said
1Sa 8: 6 So Samuel **p** to the LORD
1Ki 19: 4 he **p** that he might die, and
2Ki 4:33 two of them, and **p** to the LORD
2Ki 6:17 And Elisha **p**, and said, "LORD,
2Ki 6:18 Elisha **p** to the LORD, and said
2Ki 19:15 Then Hezekiah **p** before the
2Ki 19:20 That which you have **p** to Me
2Ki 20: 2 and **p** to the LORD, saying,
2Ch 30:18 But Hezekiah **p** for them,
2Ch 32:20 Isaiah, the son of Amoz, **p**
2Ch 32:24 death, and he **p** to the LORD
2Ch 33:13 **p** to Him; and He received
Neh 2: 4 So I **p** to the God of heaven
Job 42:10 when he **p** for his friends
Is 37:15 Then Hezekiah **p** to the LORD
Is 37:21 Because you have **p** to Me
Is 38: 2 the wall, and **p** to the LORD,
Jer 32:16 I **p** to the LORD, saying

Dan 6:10 three times that day, and **p**
Dan 9: 4 I **p** to the LORD my God, and
Jon 2: 1 Then Jonah **p** to the LORD his
Jon 4: 2 So he **p** to the LORD, and said,
Matt 26:39 and fell on His face, and **p**
Matt 26:42 away again a second time and **p**
Matt 26:44 **p** the third time, saying the
Mark 1:35 and there He **p**
Mark 14:35 **p** that if it were possible,
Mark 14:39 Again He went away and **p**, and
Luke 3:21 and while He **p**, the heaven was
Luke 5:16 into the wilderness and **p**
Luke 9:29 And as He **p**, the appearance of
Luke 18:11 **p** thus with himself, 'God, I
Luke 22:32 But I have **p** for you, that
Luke 22:41 throw, and He knelt down and **p**
Luke 22:44 in agony, He **p** more earnestly
Acts 1:24 And they **p** and said, "You, O
Acts 4:31 And when they had **p**, the place
Acts 6: 6 and when they had **p**, they laid
Acts 8:15 **p** for them that they might
Acts 9:40 all out, and knelt down and **p**
Acts 10: 2 people, and **p** to God always
Acts 10:30 ninth hour I **p** in my house
Acts 13: 3 Then, having fasted and **p**, and
Acts 14:23 and **p** with fasting, they
Acts 20:36 knelt down and **p** with them all
Acts 21: 5 knelt down on the shore and **p**
Acts 27:29 stern, and **p** for day to come
Acts 28: 8 Paul went in to him and **p**, and
Jas 5:17 he **p** earnestly that it would
Jas 5:18 he **p** again, and the heaven

PRAYER (*see* PRAY, PRAYERS)
2Sa 7:27 heart to pray this **p** to You
2Sa 21:14 God heeded the **p** for the land
1Ki 8:28 Yet regard the **p** of Your
1Ki 8:28 the **p** which Your servant is
1Ki 8:29 that You may hear the **p**
1Ki 8:38 whatever **p**, whatever
1Ki 8:45 then hear in heaven their **p**
1Ki 8:49 Your dwelling place their **p**
1Ki 8:54 finished praying all this **p**
1Ki 9: 3 I have heard your **p** and your
2Ki 19: 4 Therefore lift up your **p** for
2Ki 20: 5 I have heard your **p**, I have
1Ch 5:20 He heeded their **p**, because
2Ch 6:19 Yet regard the **p** of Your
2Ch 6:19 to the **p** which Your servant
2Ch 6:20 that You may hear the **p** which
2Ch 6:29 whatever **p**, whatever
2Ch 6:35 then hear from heaven their **p**
2Ch 6:39 Your dwelling place their **p**
2Ch 6:40 to the **p** made in this place
2Ch 7:12 I have heard your **p**, and have
2Ch 7:15 to **p** made in this place
2Ch 30:27 their **p** came up to His holy
2Ch 33:18 his **p** to his God, and the
2Ch 33:19 Also his **p** and how God
Ezra 8:23 this, and He answered our **p**
Neh 1: 6 that You may hear the **p** of
Neh 1:11 to the **p** of Your servant, and
Neh 1:11 to the **p** of Your servants who
Neh 4: 9 we made our **p** to our God, and
Neh 11:17 began the thanksgiving with **p**
Job 15: 4 and restrain **p** before God
Job 16:17 in my hands, and my **p** is pure
Job 22:27 You will make your **p** to Him
Ps 4: 1 mercy on me, and hear my **p**
Ps 6: 9 The LORD will receive my **p**
Ps 17: 1 Give ear to my **p** that is not
Ps 35:13 my **p** would return to my own
Ps 39:12 Hear my **p**, O LORD, And give
Ps 42: 8 A **p** to the God of my life
Ps 54: 2 Hear my **p**, O God
Ps 55: 1 Give ear to my **p**, O God, And
Ps 61: 1 Attend to my **p**
Ps 65: 2 O You who hear **p**, To You all
Ps 66:19 attended to the voice of my **p**
Ps 66:20 Who has not turned away my **p**
Ps 69:13 my **p** is to You, O LORD, in
Ps 72:15 **P** also will be made for Him
Ps 80: 4 Against the **p** of Your people
Ps 84: 8 LORD God of hosts, hear my **p**
Ps 86: 6 Give ear, O LORD, to my **p**
Ps 88: 2 Let my **p** come before You
Ps 88:13 morning my **p** comes before You
Ps 102: 1 Hear my **p**, O LORD, And let my
Ps 102:17 regard the **p** of the destitute
Ps 102:17 And shall not despise their **p**
Ps 109: 4 But I give myself to **p**
Ps 109: 7 And let his **p** become sin
Ps 141: 2 Let my **p** be set before You as
Ps 141: 5 For still my **p** is against the
Ps 143: 1 Hear my **p**, O LORD, Give ear
Prov 15: 8 but the **p** of the upright is
Prov 15:29 hears the **p** of the righteous
Prov 28: 9 law, even his **p** shall be an
Is 26:16 they poured out a **p** when Your
Is 37: 4 Therefore lift up your **p** for
Is 38: 5 I have heard your **p**, I have
Is 56: 7 them joyful in My house of **p**
Is 56: 7 a house of **p** for all nations
Jer 7:16 lift up a cry or **p** for them
Jer 11:14 lift up a cry or **p** for them
Lam 3: 8 and shout, He shuts out my **p**
Lam 3:44 cloud, that **p** should not pass
Dan 9: 3 Lord God to make request by **p**
Dan 9:13 our **p** before the LORD our God
Dan 9:17 hear the **p** of Your servant,
Dan 9:21 while I was speaking in **p**
Jon 2: 7 my **p** went up to You, into
Hab 3: 1 A **p** of Habakkuk the prophet,
Matt 17:21 does not go out except by **p**
Matt 21:13 shall be called a house of **p**
Matt 21:22 things, whatever you ask in **p**
Mark 9:29 can come out by nothing but **p**
Mark 11:17 a house of **p** for all nations'
Luke 1:13 for your **p** is heard
Luke 6:12 all night in **p** to God
Luke 19:46 My house is a house of **p**
Luke 22:45 When He rose up from **p**, and
Acts 1:14 with one accord in **p** and
Acts 3: 1 the temple at the hour of **p**
Acts 6: 4 ourselves continually to **p**
Acts 10:31 your **p** has been heard, and
Acts 12: 5 but constant **p** was offered to
Acts 16:13 where **p** was customarily made
Acts 16:16 it happened, as we went to **p**
Rom 10: 1 **p** to God for Israel is that
Rom 12:12 continuing steadfastly in **p**
1Co 7: 5 yourselves to fasting and **p**
2Co 1:11 helping together in **p** for us
2Co 9:14 and by their **p** for you, who
Eph 6:18 praying always with all **p**
Phil 1: 4 always in every **p** of mine
Phil 1:19 my salvation through your **p**
Phil 4: 6 but in everything by **p** and
Col 4: 2 Continue earnestly in **p**,
1Ti 4: 5 by the word of God and **p**
Jas 5:15 the **p** of faith will save the
Jas 5:16 fervent **p** of a righteous man

PRAYERS (*see* PRAYER)
2Sa 24:25 heeded the **p** for the land
Ps 72:20 The **p** of David the son of
Is 1:15 even though you make many **p**
Matt 23:14 and for a pretense make long **p**
Mark 12:40 and for a pretense make long **p**
Luke 2:37 fastings and **p** night and day
Luke 5:33 of John fast often and make **p**
Luke 20:47 and for a pretense make long **p**
Acts 2:42 breaking of bread, and in **p**
Acts 10: 4 Your **p** and your alms have come
Rom 1: 9 mention of you always in my **p**
Rom 15:30 me in your **p** to God for me
Eph 1:16 making mention of you in my **p**
Col 4:12 fervently for you in **p**, that
1Th 1: 2 mention of you in our **p**,
1Ti 2: 1 of all that supplications, **p**
1Ti 5: 5 and **p** night and day
2Ti 1: 3 I remember you in my **p** night
Phm 4 mention of you always in my **p**
Phm 22 **p** I shall be granted to you
Heb 5: 7 when He had offered up **p**
1Pe 3: 7 life, that your **p** may not be
1Pe 3:12 his ears are open to their **p**
1Pe 4: 7 serious and watchful in your **p**
Rev 5: 8 which are the **p** of the saints
Rev 8: 3 **p** of all the saints upon the
Rev 8: 4 with the **p** of the saints,

PRAYING (*see* PRAY)
1Sa 1:12 continued **p** before the LORD
1Sa 1:26 by you here, **p** to the LORD
1Ki 8:28 servant is **p** before You today
1Ki 8:54 finished **p** all this prayer
2Ch 6:19 Your servant is **p** before You
2Ch 7: 1 when Solomon had finished **p**
Ezra 10: 1 Now while Ezra was **p**, and
Neh 1: 4 **p** before the God of heaven
Dan 6:11 assembled and found Daniel **p**
Dan 9:20 Now while I was speaking, **p**
Mark 11:25 And whenever you stand **p**, if
Luke 1:10 was **p** outside at the hour of
Luke 9:18 happened, as He was alone **p**
Luke 11: 1 as He was **p** in a certain
Acts 9:11 Tarsus, for behold, he is **p**
Acts 11: 5 I was in the city of Joppa **p**
Acts 12:12 many were gathered together **p**
Acts 16:25 midnight Paul and Silas were **p**
Acts 22:17 was **p** in the temple, that I
1Co 11: 4 Every man **p** or prophesying,
Eph 6:18 **p** always with all prayer and
Col 1: 3 Christ, **p** always for you,
Col 4: 3 meanwhile **p** also for us, that
1Th 3:10 day **p** exceedingly that we may
Jude 20 faith, **p** in the Holy Spirit,

PRAYS (*see* PRAY)
1Ki 8:42 and **p** toward this temple,
2Ch 6:20 servant **p** toward this place
Is 44:17 worships it, **p** to it and says,
1Co 11: 5 But every woman who **p** or
1Co 14:14 pray in a tongue, my spirit **p**

PREACH (*see* PREACHED, PREACHER, PREACHES, PREACHING)
Is 61: 1 to **p** good tidings to the poor
Ezek 20:46 **p** against the south and
Ezek 21: 2 **p** against the holy places, and
Jon 3: 2 **p** to it the message that I
Matt 4:17 that time Jesus began to **p**
Matt 10: 7 And as you go, **p**, saying, 'The
Matt 10:27 the ear, **p** on the housetops
Matt 11: 1 teach and to **p** in their cities
Mark 1:38 that I may **p** there also,
Mark 3:14 He might send them out to **p**
Mark 16:15 and **p** the gospel to every
Luke 4:18 He has anointed Me to **p** the
Luke 4:18 to **p** deliverance to the
Luke 4:19 to **p** the acceptable year of
Luke 4:43 I must **p** the kingdom of God
Luke 9: 2 He sent them to **p** the kingdom
Luke 9:60 go and **p** the kingdom of God
Acts 10:42 us to **p** to the people, and to
Acts 14:15 **p** to you that you should turn
Acts 15:21 those who **p** him in every city
Acts 16: 6 Spirit to **p** the word in Asia
Acts 16:10 us to **p** the gospel to them
Acts 17: 3 This Jesus whom I **p** to you is
Rom 1:15 I am ready to **p** the gospel to
Rom 2:21 You who **p** that a man should
Rom 10: 8 the word of faith which we **p**)
Rom 10:15 how shall they **p** unless they
Rom 10:15 who **p** the gospel of peace
Rom 15:20 it my aim to **p** the gospel
1Co 1:17 but to **p** the gospel, not with
1Co 1:23 but we **p** Christ crucified, to
1Co 9:14 commanded that those who **p**
1Co 9:16 For if I **p** the gospel, I have
1Co 9:16 me if I do not **p** the gospel
1Co 9:18 That when I **p** the gospel, I
1Co 15:11 it was I or they, so we **p**
2Co 2:12 to Troas to **p** Christ's gospel
2Co 4: 5 For we do not **p** ourselves
2Co 10:16 to **p** the gospel in the
Gal 1: 8 **p** any other gospel to you
Gal 1:16 that I might **p** Him among the
Gal 2: 2 which I **p** among the Gentiles
Gal 5:11 if I still **p** circumcision,
Eph 3: 8 that I should **p** among the
Phil 1:15 Some indeed **p** Christ even
Phil 1:16 The former **p** Christ from
Col 1:28 Him we **p**, warning every man
2Ti 4: 2 **P** the word! Be ready
Rev 14: 6 **p** to those who dwell on the

PREACHED (*see* PREACH)
Zech 1: 4 to whom the former prophets **p**
Matt 11: 5 have the gospel **p** to them
Matt 24:14 be **p** in all the world as a
Matt 26:13 is **p** in the whole world, what
Mark 1: 7 And he **p**, saying, "There
Mark 2: 2 And He **p** the word to them
Mark 6:12 **p** that people should repent
Mark 13:10 first be **p** to all the nations
Mark 14: 9 wherever this gospel is **p**
Mark 16:20 out and **p** everywhere, the Lord
Luke 3:18 he **p** to the people
Luke 7:22 have the gospel **p** to them
Luke 16:16 the kingdom of God has been **p**
Luke 20: 1 **p** the gospel, that the chief
Luke 24:47 **p** in His name to all nations

Acts 3:20 who was **p** to you before,
Acts 4: 2 **p** in Jesus the resurrection
Acts 8: 5 Samaria and **p** Christ to them
Acts 8:12 **p** the things concerning the
Acts 8:25 **p** the word of the Lord, they
Acts 8:35 Scripture, **p** Jesus to him
Acts 8:40 he **p** in all the cities till
Acts 9:20 Immediately he **p** the Christ
Acts 9:27 and how he had **p** boldly at
Acts 10:37 the baptism which John **p**
Acts 13: 5 they **p** the word of God in the
Acts 13:24 after John had first **p**,
Acts 13:38 that through this Man is **p** to
Acts 13:42 be **p** to them the next Sabbath
Acts 14:21 when they had **p** the gospel to
Acts 14:25 they had **p** the word in Perga
Acts 15:36 have **p** the word of the Lord
Acts 17:13 of God was **p** by Paul at Berea
Acts 17:18 because he **p** to them Jesus
Rom 15:19 fully **p** the gospel of Christ
1Co 1:21 **p** to save those who believe
1Co 9:27 lest, when I have **p** to others
1Co 15: 1 the gospel which I **p** to you
1Co 15: 2 that word which I **p** to you
1Co 15:12 Now if Christ is **p** that He
2Co 1:19 who was **p** among you by us
2Co 11: 4 Jesus whom we have not **p**, or
2Co 11: 7 because I **p** the gospel of God
Gal 1: 8 than what we have **p** to you
Gal 1:11 **p** by me is not according to
Gal 3: 8 **p** the gospel to Abraham
Gal 4:13 of physical infirmity I **p** the
Eph 2:17 **p** peace to you who were afar
Phil 1:18 or in truth, Christ is **p**
Col 1:23 which was **p** to every creature
1Th 2: 9 we **p** to you the gospel of God
1Ti 3:16 angels, **p** among the Gentiles,
2Ti 4:17 might be **p** fully through me
Heb 4: 2 **p** to us as well as to them
Heb 4: 6 **p** did not enter because of
1Pe 1:12 **p** the gospel to you by the
1Pe 1:25 by the gospel was **p** to you
1Pe 3:19 **p** to the spirits in prison,
1Pe 4: 6 **p** also to those who are dead

PREACHER (*see* PREACH)
Eccl 1: 1 The words of the **P**, the son
Eccl 1: 2 of vanities," says the **P**
Eccl 1:12 I, the **P**, was king over
Eccl 7:27 I have found," says the **P**
Eccl 12: 8 of vanities," says the **P**
Eccl 12: 9 because the **P** was wise, he
Eccl 12:10 The **P** sought to find
Rom 10:14 shall they hear without a **p**
1Ti 2: 7 for which I was appointed a **p**
2Ti 1:11 to which I was appointed a **p**
2Pe 2: 5 people, a **p** of righteousness,

PREACHES (*see* PREACH)
Acts 19:13 you by the Jesus whom Paul **p**
2Co 11: 4 For if he who comes **p** another
Gal 1: 9 if anyone **p** any other gospel
Gal 1:23 now **p** the faith which he once

PREACHING (*see* PREACH)
Matt 3: 1 **p** in the wilderness of Judea
Matt 4:23 **p** the gospel of the kingdom,
Matt 9:35 **p** the gospel of the kingdom,
Matt 12:41 repented at the **p** of Jonah
Mark 1: 4 **p** a baptism of repentance for
Mark 1:14 **p** the gospel of the kingdom
Mark 1:39 He was **p** in their synagogues
Luke 3: 3 **p** a baptism of repentance for
Luke 4:44 He was **p** in the synagogues of
Luke 8: 1 every city and village, **p** and
Luke 9: 6 **p** the gospel and healing
Luke 11:32 repented at the **p** of Jonah
Acts 5:42 and **p** Jesus as the Christ
Acts 8: 4 went everywhere **p** the word
Acts 8:25 **p** the gospel in many villages
Acts 10:36 **p** peace through Jesus Christ
Acts 11:19 **p** the word to no one but the
Acts 11:20 Hellenists, **p** the Lord Jesus
Acts 14: 7 they were **p** the gospel there
Acts 15:35 **p** the word of the Lord, with
Acts 20:25 gone **p** the kingdom of God
Acts 28:31 **p** the kingdom of God and
Rom 16:25 and the **p** of Jesus Christ,
1Co 2: 4 my **p** were not with persuasive
1Co 15:14 not risen, then our **p** is vain
Tit 1: 3 manifested His word through **p**

PREAPPOINTED
Acts 17:26 has determined their **p** times

PRECEDE (*see* PRECEDED, PRECEDING)
1Th 4:15 means **p** those who are asleep

PRECEDED (*see* PRECEDE)
Job 41:11 Who has **p** Me, that I should

PRECEDING (*see* PRECEDE)
1Ti 5:24 **p** them to judgment, but those

PRECEPT (*see* PRECEPTS)
Is 28:10 For **p** must be upon **p**
Is 28:10 **p** upon **p**, line upon
Is 28:13 **P** upon **p**, **p** upon **p**
Hos 5:11 willingly walked by human **p**
Mark 10: 5 heart he wrote you this **p**
Heb 9:19 **p** to all the people according

PRECEPTS (*see* PRECEPT)
Neh 9:14 and commanded them **p**
Ps 111: 7 All His **p** are sure
Ps 119: 4 us To keep Your **p** diligently
Ps 119:15 I will meditate on Your **p**
Ps 119:27 understand the way of Your **p**
Ps 119:40 Behold, I long for Your **p**
Ps 119:45 at liberty, For I seek Your **p**
Ps 119:56 mine, Because I kept Your **p**
Ps 119:63 And of those who keep Your **p**
Ps 119:69 Your **p** with my whole heart
Ps 119:78 But I will meditate on Your **p**
Ps 119:87 But I did not forsake Your **p**
Ps 119:93 I will never forget Your **p**
Ps 119:94 For I have sought Your **p**
Ps 119:100 Because I keep Your **p**
Ps 119:104 Through Your **p** I get
Ps 119:110 have not strayed from Your **p**
Ps 119:128 Therefore all Your **p**
Ps 119:134 man, That I may keep Your **p**
Ps 119:141 Yet I do not forget Your **p**
Ps 119:159 Consider how I love Your **p**
Ps 119:168 I keep Your **p** and Your
Ps 119:173 For I have chosen Your **p**
Jer 35:18 father, and kept all his **p**
Dan 9: 5 even by departing from Your **p**

PRECIOUS
Gen 24:53 He also gave **p** things to her
Deut 33:13 with the **p** things of heaven,
Deut 33:14 with the **p** fruits of the sun,
Deut 33:14 with the **p** produce of the
Deut 33:15 with the **p** things of the
Deut 33:16 with the **p** things of the
1Sa 26:21 because my life was **p** in your
2Sa 12:30 talent of gold, with **p** stones
1Ki 10: 2 very much gold, and **p** stones
1Ki 10:10 great abundance, and **p** stones
1Ki 10:11 wood and **p** stones from Ophir
2Ki 1:13 of yours be **p** in your sight
2Ki 1:14 life now be **p** in your sight
2Ki 20:13 **p** ointment, and all his armory
1Ch 20: 2 there were **p** stones in it
1Ch 29: 2 colors, all kinds of **p** stones
1Ch 29: 8 whoever had **p** stones gave
2Ch 3: 6 with **p** stones for beauty, and
2Ch 9: 1 in abundance, and **p** stones
2Ch 9: 9 great abundance, and **p** stones
2Ch 9:10 algum wood and **p** stones
2Ch 20:25 and **p** jewelry, which they
2Ch 21: 3 and **p** things, with fortified
2Ch 32:27 for **p** stones, for spices, for
2Ch 36:19 all its **p** possessions
Ezra 1: 6 with **p** things, besides all
Ezra 8:27 polished bronze, **p** as gold
Job 22:25 be your gold and your **p** silver
Job 28:10 and his eye sees every **p** thing
Job 28:16 Ophir, in **p** onyx or sapphire
Ps 22:20 My **p** life from the power of
Ps 35:17 My **p** life from the lions
Ps 36: 7 How **p** is Your lovingkindness,
Ps 72:14 **p** shall be their blood in His
Ps 116:15 **P** in the sight of the LORD Is
Ps 133: 2 It is like the **p** oil upon the
Ps 139:17 How **p** also are Your thoughts
Prov 1:13 all kinds of **p** possessions
Prov 3:15 She is more **p** than rubies
Prov 6:26 will prey upon his **p** life
Prov 12:27 is man's **p** possession
Prov 17: 8 A present is a **p** stone in the
Prov 20:15 of knowledge are a **p** jewel
Prov 24: 4 rooms are filled with all **p**
Eccl 7: 1 is better than **p** ointment
Is 28:16 a **p** cornerstone, a sure
Is 39: 2 **p** ointment, and all his armory
Is 43: 4 Since you were **p** in My sight
Is 44: 9 and their **p** things shall not
Is 54:12 and all your walls of **p** stones
Jer 15:19 take out the **p** from the vile
Jer 20: 5 produce, and all its **p** things
Jer 25:34 shall fall like a **p** vessel
Lam 4: 2 The **p** sons of Zion, valuable
Ezek 22:25 taken treasure and **p** things
Ezek 27:22 spices, all kinds of **p** stones
Ezek 28:13 every **p** stone was your
Dan 11: 8 their **p** articles of silver and
Dan 11:38 with **p** stones and pleasant
Dan 11:43 and over all the **p** things of
Mic 1:16 because of your **p** children
1Co 3:12 **p** stones, wood, hay, straw,
Jas 5: 7 for the **p** fruit of the earth
1Pe 1: 7 being much more **p** than gold
1Pe 1:19 but with the **p** blood of
1Pe 2: 4 men, but chosen by God and **p**
1Pe 2: 6 a chief cornerstone, elect, **p**
1Pe 2: 7 to you who believe, He is **p**
1Pe 3: 4 which is very **p** in the sight
2Pe 1: 1 like **p** faith with us by the
2Pe 1: 4 and **p** promises, that through
Rev 17: 4 **p** stones and pearls, having in
Rev 18:12 **p** stones and pearls, fine
Rev 18:12 kind of object of most **p** wood
Rev 18:16 gold and **p** stones and pearls
Rev 21:11 light was like a most **p** stone
Rev 21:19 with all kinds of **p** stones

PREDESTINED
Rom 8:29 He also **p** to be conformed to
Rom 8:30 Moreover whom He **p**, these He
Eph 1: 5 having **p** us to adoption as
Eph 1:11 being **p** according to the

PREEMINENCE
Col 1:18 all things He may have the **p**
3Jn 9 to have the **p** among them,

PREFERENCE (*see* PREFERRED)
Deut 21:16 son of the loved wife in **p** to
Rom 12:10 honor giving **p** to one another

PREFERRED (*see* PREFERENCE)
John 1:15 comes after me is **p** before me
John 1:27 is **p** before me, whose sandal
John 1:30 a Man who is **p** before me, for

PREGNANCY (*see* PREGNANT)
Hos 9:11 no birth, no **p**, and no

PREGNANT (*see* PREGNANCY)
Matt 24:19 But woe to those who are **p**
Mark 13:17 But woe to those who are **p**
Luke 21:23 But woe to those who are **p**
1Th 5: 3 as labor pains upon a **p** woman

PREJUDICE
1Ti 5:21 these things without **p**, doing

PREMATURELY
Ex 21:22 so that she gives birth **p**

PREMEDITATE (*see* PREMEDITATION)
Mark 13:11 or **p** what you will speak

PREMEDITATION (*see* PREMEDITATE)
Ex 21:14 with **p** against his neighbor

PREPARATION (*see* PREPARATIONS, PREPARE)
1Ch 22: 5 I will now make **p** for it
Esth 2:12 completed twelve months' **p**
Esth 2:12 days of their **p** apportioned
Nah 2: 3 torches in the day of his **p**
Matt 27:62 which followed the Day of **P**
Mark 15:42 because it was the **P** Day
Luke 23:54 That day was the **P**, and the
John 19:14 Now it was the **P** Day of the
John 19:31 because it was the **P** Day
John 19:42 because of the Jews' **P** Day
Eph 6:15 the **p** of the gospel of peace

PREPARATIONS (*see* PREPARATION)
1Ch 22: 5 abundant **p** before his death
1Ch 28: 2 and had made **p** to build it
Esth 2: 3 let beauty **p** be given them
Esth 2: 9 readily gave beauty **p** to her
Esth 2:12 and **p** for beautifying women
Prov 16: 1 The **p** of the heart belong to

PREPARE (*see* PREPARATION, PREPARED, PREPARES, PREPARING, UNPREPARED)
Gen 18: 7 man, and he hastened to **p** it
Ex 16: 5 shall **p** what they bring in
Num 15: 5 **p** with the burnt offering or
Num 15: 6 shall **p** as a grain offering
Num 15: 8 when you **p** a young bull as a
Num 15:12 to the number that you **p**, so
Num 23: 1 **p** for me here seven bulls and
Num 23:29 **p** for me here seven bulls and
Deut 19: 3 You shall **p** roads for
Josh 1:11 **P** provisions for yourselves,
Josh 22:26 said, 'Let us now **p** to build
Judg 13:15 we will **p** a young goat for
1Sa 7: 3 **p** your hearts for the LORD,
2Sa 12: 4 from his own herd to **p** one
2Sa 13: 5 **p** the food in my sight, that
2Sa 13: 7 house, and **p** food for him
1Ki 17:12 **p** it for myself and my son,
1Ki 18:23 I will **p** the other bull, and
1Ki 18:25 **p** it first, for you are many
1Ki 18:44 **P** your chariot, and go down
1Ch 22:14 **p** for the house of the LORD
2Ch 2: 9 to **p** timber for me in
2Ch 12:14 because he did not **p** his
2Ch 31:11 **p** rooms in the house of the
2Ch 35: 4 **P** yourselves according to
2Ch 35: 6 **p** them for your brethren,
Esth 5: 8 which I will **p** for them, and
Job 11:13 If you would **p** your heart
Job 37:19 for we can **p** nothing because
Job 38: 3 Now **p** yourself like a man
Job 40: 7 Now **p** yourself like a man
Ps 10:17 You will **p** their heart
Ps 23: 5 You **p** a table before me in
Ps 59: 4 **p** themselves through no fault
Ps 61: 7 **p** mercy and truth, which may
Ps 78:19 Can God **p** a table in the
Ps 132:17 I will **p** a lamp for My
Prov 24:27 **P** your outside work, make it
Prov 30:25 yet they **p** their food in the
Is 14:21 **P** slaughter for his children
Is 21: 5 **P** the table, set a watchman
Is 40: 3 **P** the way of the LORD
Is 40:20 a skillful workman to **p** a
Is 57:14 **P** the way, take the stumbling
Is 62:10 **P** the way for the people
Is 65:11 who **p** a table for Gad, and who
Jer 1:17 Therefore **p** yourself and arise
Jer 6: 4 **P** war against her
Jer 12: 3 and **p** them for the day of
Jer 22: 7 I will **p** destroyers against
Jer 46:14 **p** yourselves, for the sword
Jer 46:19 Egypt, **p** yourself to go into
Jer 51:12 the watchmen, **p** the ambushes
Jer 51:27 **P** the nations against her,
Jer 51:28 **P** against her the nations,
Jer 51:39 I will **p** their feasts
Ezek 4:15 you shall **p** your bread over
Ezek 12: 3 of man, **p** your belongings for
Ezek 35: 6 I will **p** you for blood, and
Ezek 38: 7 **P** yourself and be ready, you
Ezek 43:25 for seven days you shall **p** a
Ezek 43:25 shall also **p** a young bull
Ezek 45:17 He shall **p** the sin offering,
Ezek 45:22 prince shall **p** for himself
Ezek 45:23 **p** a burnt offering to the
Ezek 45:24 he shall **p** a grain offering
Ezek 46: 2 The priests shall **p** his burnt
Ezek 46: 7 He shall **p** a grain offering
Ezek 46:12 he shall **p** his burnt offering
Ezek 46:13 you shall **p** it every morning
Ezek 46:14 you shall **p** a grain offering
Ezek 46:15 Thus they shall **p** the lamb
Hos 7: 6 They **p** their heart like an
Joel 3: 9 **P** for war! Wake up the mighty
Amos 4:12 **p** to meet your God, O Israel
Mic 3: 5 But who **p** war against him Who
Mal 3: 1 he will **p** the way before Me
Matt 3: 3 **P** the way of the LORD, make
Matt 11:10 who will **p** Your way before
Matt 26:17 Where do You want us to **p** for
Mark 1: 2 who will **p** Your way before
Mark 1: 3 **P** the way of the LORD, make
Mark 14:12 do You want us to go and **p**
Luke 1:76 of the Lord to **p** His ways
Luke 3: 4 **P** the way of the LORD, make
Luke 7:27 who will **p** Your way before
Luke 9:52 the Samaritans, to **p** for Him
Luke 12:47 and did not **p** himself or do
Luke 17: 8 **P** something for my supper,
Luke 22: 8 **p** the Passover for us, that
Luke 22: 9 Where do You want us to **p**
John 14: 2 I go to **p** a place for you
John 14: 3 **p** a place for you, I will
Acts 23:23 **P** two hundred soldiers,
1Co 14: 8 who will **p** himself for battle
2Co 9: 5 and **p** your bountiful gift
Phm 22 also **p** a guest room for me,

PREPARED (*see* PREPARE)
Gen 18: 8 and the calf which he had **p**
Gen 24:31 For I have **p** the house, and a
Gen 27:17 and the bread, which she had **p**
Ex 12:16 that only may be **p** by you
Ex 12:39 nor had they **p** provisions for
Ex 23:20 into the place which I have **p**
Lev 7: 9 all that is **p** in the covered
Num 10:21 would be **p** for their arrival
Num 11: 8 taste of pastry **p** with oil
Num 23: 4 I have **p** the seven altars, and
Josh 4:13 About forty thousand **p** for
Judg 6:19 **p** a young goat, and unleavened
2Sa 12: 4 **p** it for the man who had come
1Ki 1: 5 he **p** for himself chariots and
1Ki 5:18 they **p** timber and stones to
1Ki 6:19 And he **p** the inner sanctuary
1Ki 18:26 was given them, and they **p** it
2Ki 6:23 Then he **p** a great feast for
1Ch 12:39 their brethren had **p** for them
1Ch 15: 1 he **p** a place for the ark of
1Ch 15: 3 place, which he had **p** for it
1Ch 15:12 to the place I have **p** for it
1Ch 22: 3 David **p** iron in abundance for
1Ch 22:14 I have **p** timber and stone also
1Ch 29: 2 I have **p** with all my might
1Ch 29: 3 I have **p** for the holy house
1Ch 29:16 **p** to build You a house for
2Ch 1: 4 the place David had **p** for it
2Ch 3: 1 **p** on the threshing floor of
2Ch 16:14 various ingredients **p** in a
2Ch 17:18 and eighty thousand **p** for war
2Ch 19: 3 have **p** your heart to seek God
2Ch 26:11 roll as **p** by Jeiel the scribe
2Ch 26:14 Then Uzziah **p** for them, for
2Ch 27: 6 because he **p** his ways before
2Ch 29:19 his transgression we have **p**
2Ch 29:36 that God had **p** the people
2Ch 31:11 of the LORD, and they **p** them
2Ch 35:10 So the service was **p**, and the
2Ch 35:14 Then afterward they **p**
2Ch 35:14 therefore the Levites **p**
2Ch 35:15 Levites **p** portions for them
2Ch 35:16 the LORD was **p** the same day
2Ch 35:20 when Josiah had **p** the temple
Ezra 7:10 For Ezra had **p** his heart to
Neh 5:18 Now that which was **p** for me
Neh 5:18 also fowl were **p** for me, and
Neh 8:10 those for whom nothing is **p**
Neh 13: 5 he had **p** for him a large room
Esth 2:13 Thus **p**, each young woman went
Esth 5: 4 banquet that I have **p** for him
Esth 5: 5 the banquet that Esther had **p**
Esth 5:12 to the banquet that she **p**
Esth 6: 4 gallows that he had **p** for him
Esth 6:14 banquet which Esther had **p**
Esth 7:10 that he had **p** for Mordecai
Job 13:18 I have **p** my case, I know that
Job 28:27 He **p** it, indeed, He searched
Ps 9: 7 He has **p** His throne for
Ps 31:19 Which You have **p** for those
Ps 57: 6 They have **p** a net for my
Ps 65: 9 grain, For so You have **p** it
Ps 74:16 You have **p** the light and the
Ps 80: 9 You **p** room for it, And caused
Prov 8:27 When He **p** the heavens, I was
Prov 19:29 Judgments are **p** for scoffers
Prov 21:31 The horse is **p** for the day of
Is 30:33 yes, for the king it is **p**
Is 51:13 when he has **p** to destroy
Ezek 23:41 with a table **p** before it
Ezek 28:13 pipes was **p** for you on the
Hos 2: 8 which they **p** for Baal
Jon 1:17 Now the LORD had **p** a great
Jon 4: 6 And the LORD God **p** a plant
Jon 4: 7 the next day God **p** a worm
Jon 4: 8 that God **p** a vehement east
Nah 2: 5 walls, and the defense is **p**
Zeph 1: 7 the LORD has **p** a sacrifice
Matt 20:23 for whom it is **p** by My Father
Matt 22: 4 See, I have **p** my dinner
Matt 25:34 inherit the kingdom **p** for you
Matt 25:41 fire **p** for the devil and his
Matt 26:19 and they **p** the Passover
Mark 10:40 is for those for whom it is **p**
Mark 14:15 upper room, furnished and **p**
Mark 14:16 and they **p** the Passover
Luke 1:17 ready a people **p** for the Lord
Luke 2:31 which You have **p** before the
Luke 22:13 them, and they **p** the Passover
Luke 23:56 **p** spices and fragrant oils
Luke 24: 1 the spices which they had **p**
Rom 9:22 of wrath **p** for destruction
Rom 9:23 which He had **p** beforehand for
1Co 2: 9 has **p** for those who love Him
2Co 5: 5 Now He who has **p** us for this
Eph 2:10 which God **p** beforehand that
2Ti 2:21 Master, **p** for every good work
Heb 9: 2 For a tabernacle was **p**
Heb 9: 6 these things had been thus **p**
Heb 10: 5 but a body You have **p** for Me
Heb 11: 7 **p** an ark for the saving of
Heb 11:16 for He has **p** a city for them
1Pe 3:20 while the ark was being **p**
Rev 8: 6 **p** themselves to sound
Rev 9: 7 was like horses **p** for battle
Rev 9:15 who had been **p** for the hour
Rev 12: 6 she has a place **p** by God,
Rev 16:12 from the east might be **p**
Rev 21: 2 **p** as a bride adorned for her

PREPARES (*see* PREPARE)
Num 4: 5 When the camp **p** to journey
2Ch 30:19 who **p** his heart to seek God,
Job 15:35 their womb **p** deceit
Ps 7:13 He also **p** for Himself
Ps 147: 8 Who **p** rain for the earth, Who

PREPARING (*see* PREPARE)
1Ch 9:32 were in charge of **p** the
Neh 13: 7 in **p** a room for him in the

PRESBYTERY
1Ti 4:14 on of the hands of the **p**

PRESCRIBE (*see* PRESCRIBED)
Prov 30: 8 me with the food You **p** for me

PRESCRIBED (*see* PRESCRIBE)
Lev 5:10 according to the **p** manner
Lev 9:16 it according to the **p** manner
2Ch 4:20 to burn in the **p** manner in
2Ch 30: 5 a long time in the **p** manner
Ezra 7:22 oil, and salt without **p** limit
Neh 8:18 according to the **p** manner
Esth 9:27 and according to the **p** time
Esth 9:31 Queen Esther had **p** for them
Is 10: 1 misfortune, which they have **p**

PRESENCE (*see* PRESENT)
Gen 3: 8 hid themselves from the **p** of
Gen 4:16 out from the **p** of the LORD
Gen 16: 6 with her, she fled from her **p**
Gen 16: 8 the **p** of my mistress Sarai
Gen 16:12 in the **p** of all his brethren
Gen 23:10 in the **p** of the sons of Heth
Gen 23:11 I give it to you in the **p** of
Gen 23:18 in the **p** of the sons of Heth
Gen 25:18 he died in the **p** of all his
Gen 27: 7 bless you in the **p** of the
Gen 27:30 the **p** of Isaac his father
Gen 31:32 In the **p** of our brethren,
Gen 36: 6 the **p** of his brother Jacob
Gen 41:46 out from the **p** of Pharaoh
Gen 45: 3 they were dismayed in his **p**
Gen 47:15 why should we die in your **p**
Ex 10:11 driven out from Pharaoh's **p**
Ex 33:14 My **P** will go with you, and I
Ex 33:15 If Your **P** does not go with us
Ex 35:20 departed from the **p** of Moses
Lev 19:32 honor the **p** of an old man, and
Lev 22: 3 shall be cut off from My **p**
Num 20: 6 Aaron went from the **p** of the
Deut 1:17 not be afraid in any man's **p**
Deut 4:37 you out of Egypt with His **P**
Deut 25: 2 down and be beaten in his **p**
Deut 25: 9 to him in the **p** of the elders
Josh 4:11 over in the **p** of the people
Josh 8:32 in the **p** of the children of
Judg 4:23 **p** of the children of Israel
Judg 18: 6 May the **p** of the LORD be with
Ruth 4: 4 in the **p** of the inhabitants
1Sa 18:11 But David escaped his **p** twice
1Sa 18:13 Saul removed him from his **p**

1Sa 19: 7 he was in his **p** as in times
1Sa 19:10 he slipped away from Saul's **p**
1Sa 21:15 to play the madman in my **p**
2Sa 3:26 Joab had gone from David's **p**
2Sa 16:19 not serve in the **p** of his son
2Sa 16:19 served in your father's **p**
2Sa 16:19 so will I be in your **p**
2Sa 24: 4 **p** of the king to count the
1Ki 1:28 So she came into the king's **p**
1Ki 8:22 altar of the LORD in the **p** of
1Ki 10:24 the **p** of Solomon to hear his
1Ki 12: 2 from the **p** of King Solomon
1Ki 21:13 in the **p** of the people,
2Ki 3:14 the **p** of Jehoshaphat king of
2Ki 5:27 went out from his **p** leprous
2Ki 13:23 them or cast them from His **p**
2Ki 24:20 cast them out from His **p**
1Ch 24:31 in the **p** of King David, Zadok
2Ch 6:12 altar of the LORD in the **p** of
2Ch 9:23 the **p** of Solomon to hear his
2Ch 10: 2 the **p** of Solomon the king)
2Ch 20: 9 in Your **p** (for Your name is
2Ch 34: 4 altars of the Baals in his **p**
Neh 2: 1 been sad in his **p** before
Esth 1:10 in the **p** of King Ahasuerus
Esth 1:14 had access to the king's **p**
Esth 2:23 in the **p** of the king
Esth 8:15 the **p** of the king in royal
Job 1:12 out from the **p** of the LORD
Job 2: 7 out from the **p** of the LORD
Job 23:15 I am terrified at His **p**
Job 23:17 off from the **p** of darkness
Ps 9: 3 fall and perish at Your **p**
Ps 16:11 In Your **p** is fullness of joy
Ps 17: 2 vindication come from Your **p**
Ps 21: 6 exceedingly glad with Your **p**
Ps 23: 5 me in the **p** of my enemies
Ps 31:19 In the **p** of the sons of men
Ps 31:20 Your **p** From the plots of man
Ps 51:11 not cast me away from Your **p**
Ps 52: 9 in the **p** of Your saints I
Ps 68: 2 wicked perish at the **p** of God
Ps 68: 8 dropped rain at the **p** of God
Ps 68: 8 was moved at the **p** of God
Ps 76: 7 who may stand in Your **p** When
Ps 95: 2 His **p** with thanksgiving
Ps 97: 5 like wax at the **p** of the LORD
Ps 97: 5 At the **p** of the Lord of the
Ps 100: 2 before His **p** with singing
Ps 101: 7 shall not continue in my **p**
Ps 114: 7 at the **p** of the Lord,
Ps 114: 7 At the **p** of the God of Jacob,
Ps 116:14 in the **p** of all His people
Ps 116:18 in the **p** of all His people
Ps 139: 7 where can I flee from Your **p**
Ps 140:13 upright shall dwell in Your **p**
Prov 14: 7 Go from the **p** of a foolish
Prov 25: 6 yourself in the **p** of the king
Prov 25: 7 lower in the **p** of the prince
Eccl 8: 3 not be hasty to go from his **p**
Is 1: 7 devour your land in your **p**
Is 19: 1 of Egypt will totter at His **p**
Is 63: 9 the Angel of His **P** saved them
Is 64: 1 might shake at Your **p**
Is 64: 2 nations may tremble at Your **p**
Is 64: 3 the mountains shook at Your **p**
Jer 4:26 down at the **p** of the LORD
Jer 5:22 Will you not tremble at My **p**
Jer 23:39 and will cast you out of My **p**
Jer 28: 1 LORD in the **p** of the priests
Jer 28: 5 in the **p** of the priests and in
Jer 28: 5 in the **p** of all the people
Jer 28:11 in the **p** of all the people
Jer 32:12 in the **p** of Hanameel my
Jer 32:12 in the **p** of the witnesses who
Jer 52: 3 cast them out from His **p**
Ezek 38:20 the earth shall shake at My **p**
Dan 2:27 answered in the **p** of the king
Dan 5: 1 wine in the **p** of the thousand
Jon 1: 3 from the **p** of the LORD
Jon 1: 3 from the **p** of the LORD
Jon 1:10 fled from the **p** of the LORD
Nah 1: 5 and the earth heaves at His **p**
Zeph 1: 7 in the **p** of the Lord GOD
Hag 1:12 feared the **p** of the LORD
Mark 2:12 went out in the **p** of them all
Luke 1:19 who stands in the **p** of God
Luke 8:47 the **p** of all the people the
Luke 13:26 We ate and drank in Your **p**
Luke 14:10 the **p** of those who sit at the
Luke 15:10 there is joy in the **p** of the
Luke 20:26 words in the **p** of the people
Luke 23:14 having examined Him in your **p**
Luke 24:43 He took it and ate in their **p**
John 20:30 in the **p** of His disciples
Acts 2:28 make me full of joy in Your **p**
Acts 3:13 and denied in the **p** of Pilate
Acts 3:16 soundness in the **p** of you all
Acts 3:19 come from the **p** of the Lord
Acts 5:41 from the **p** of the council
Acts 7:10 and wisdom in the **p** of Pharaoh
Acts 27:35 to God in the **p** of them all
Rom 4:17 the **p** of Him whom he believed
1Co 1:29 flesh should glory in His **p**
2Co 2:10 your sakes in the **p** of Christ
2Co 10: 1 who in **p** am lowly among you,
2Co 10:10 but his bodily **p** is weak
Phil 2:12 obeyed, not as in my **p** only
1Th 2:17 you for a short time in **p**
1Th 2:19 Is it not even you in the **p**
2Th 1: 9 from the **p** of the Lord and
1Ti 5:20 rebuke in the **p** of all, that
1Ti 6:12 in the **p** of many witnesses
Heb 6:19 enters the **P** behind the veil
Heb 9:24 appear in the **p** of God for us
Jude 24 you faultless before the **p** of
Rev 12:14 from the **p** of the serpent
Rev 13:12 of the first beast in his **p**
Rev 14:10 brimstone in the **p** of the
Rev 14:10 and in the **p** of the Lamb
Rev 19:20 who worked signs in his **p**

PRESENT (*see* PRESENCE, PRESENTABLE, PRESENTATION, PRESENTED, PRESENTING, PRESENTS, UNPRESENTABLE)
Gen 32:13 as a **p** for Esau his brother
Gen 32:18 It is a **p** sent to my lord
Gen 32:20 the **p** that goes before me
Gen 32:21 So the **p** went on over before
Gen 33:10 receive my **p** from my hand
Gen 43:11 and carry down a **p** for the man
Gen 43:15 So the men took that **p** and
Gen 43:25 Then they made the **p** ready
Gen 43:26 they brought him the **p** which
Ex 34: 2 **p** yourself to Me there on the
Lev 14:11 **p** the man who is to be made
Lev 16: 7 **p** them before the LORD at the
Lev 27: 8 then he shall **p** himself
Lev 27:11 then he shall **p** the beast
Num 3: 6 and **p** them before Aaron the
Num 6:14 he shall **p** his offering to
Num 15:14 would **p** an offering made by
Num 16:16 company be **p** before the LORD
Num 28:11 **p** a burnt offering to the
Num 28:19 you shall **p** an offering made
Num 28:27 You shall **p** a burnt offering
Num 28:31 You shall **p** them with their
Num 29: 8 You shall **p** a burnt offering
Num 29:13 You shall **p** a burnt offering
Num 29:17 day **p** twelve young bulls, two
Num 29:20 the third day **p** eleven bulls
Num 29:23 On the fourth day **p** ten bulls
Num 29:26 On the fifth day **p** nine bulls
Num 29:29 the sixth day **p** eight bulls
Num 29:32 the seventh day **p** seven bulls
Num 29:36 You shall **p** a burnt offering
Num 29:39 shall **p** to the LORD at your
Deut 31:14 and **p** yourselves in the
1Sa 9: 7 there is no **p** to bring to the
1Sa 10:19 **p** yourselves before the LORD
1Sa 13:15 people who were **p** with him
1Sa 13:16 the people who were **p** with
1Sa 25:27 And now this **p** which your
1Sa 30:26 Here is a **p** for you from the
2Sa 20: 4 days, and be **p** here yourself
1Ki 10:25 Each man brought his **p**
1Ki 15:19 I have sent you a **p** of silver
1Ki 18: 1 **p** yourself to Ahab, and I will
1Ki 18: 2 went to **p** himself to Ahab
1Ki 18:15 I will surely **p** myself to him
2Ki 8: 8 Take a **p** in your hand, and go
2Ki 8: 9 took a **p** with him, of every
2Ki 16: 8 sent it as a **p** to the king of
2Ki 18:31 Make peace with me by a **p**
2Ki 20:12 a **p** to Hezekiah, for he heard
1Ch 29:17 who are **p** here to offer
2Ch 5:11 all the priests who were **p**
2Ch 9:24 Each man brought his **p**
2Ch 29:29 all who were **p** with him bowed
2Ch 30:21 **p** at Jerusalem kept the Feast
2Ch 31: 1 all Israel who were **p** went
2Ch 34:32 all who were **p** in Jerusalem
2Ch 34:33 made all who were **p** in Israel
2Ch 35: 7 offerings for all who were **p**
2Ch 35:17 **p** kept the Passover at that
2Ch 35:18 Judah and Israel who were **p**
Ezra 8:25 and all Israel who were **p**
Esth 1: 5 were **p** in Shushan the citadel
Esth 4:16 the Jews who are **p** in Shushan
Job 1: 6 the sons of God came to **p**
Job 2: 1 the sons of God came to **p**
Job 2: 1 to **p** himself before the LORD
Job 23: 4 I would **p** my case before Him,
Ps 46: 1 A very **p** help in trouble
Prov 17: 8 A **p** is a precious stone in
Is 18: 7 In that time a **p** will be
Is 36:16 Make peace with me by a **p**
Is 39: 1 a **p** to Hezekiah, for he heard
Is 41:21 **P** your case," says the LORD
Jer 36: 7 It may be that they will **p**
Jer 42: 9 to whom you sent me to **p** your
Lam 4: 3 Even the jackals **p** their
Dan 2:46 they should **p** an offering
Dan 9:18 for we do not **p** our
Hos 10: 6 Assyria as a **p** for King Jareb
Mark 9: 1 kingdom of God **p** with power
Luke 2:22 to **p** Him to the Lord
Luke 5:17 the Lord was **p** to heal them
Luke 13: 1 There were **p** at that season
Luke 18:30 times more in this **p** time
John 14:25 to you while being **p** with you
Acts 10:33 we are all **p** before God, to
Acts 21:18 and all the elders were **p**
Acts 25:24 men who are here **p** with us
Rom 3:26 to demonstrate at the **p** time
Rom 6:13 And do not **p** your members as
Rom 6:13 but **p** yourselves to God as
Rom 6:16 **p** yourselves slaves to obey
Rom 6:19 so now **p** your members as
Rom 7:18 for to will is **p** with me, but
Rom 7:21 a law, that evil is **p** with me
Rom 8:18 **p** time are not worthy to be
Rom 8:38 nor things **p** nor things to
Rom 11: 5 at this **p** time there is a
Rom 12: 1 God, that you **p** your bodies a
1Co 3:22 or things **p** or things to come
1Co 4:11 Even to the **p** hour we both
1Co 5: 3 in body but **p** in spirit, have
1Co 5: 3 judged, as though I were **p**
1Co 7:26 because of the **p** distress
1Co 9:18 I may **p** the gospel of Christ
1Co 15: 6 greater part remain to the **p**
2Co 4:14 Jesus, and will **p** us with you
2Co 5: 8 body and to be **p** with the Lord
2Co 5: 9 whether **p** or absent, to be
2Co 10: 2 I beg you that when I am **p** I
2Co 10:11 also be in deed when we are **p**
2Co 11: 2 that I may **p** you as a chaste
2Co 11: 9 And when I was **p** with you, and
2Co 13: 2 if I were **p** the second time
2Co 13:10 lest being **p** I should use
Gal 1: 4 us from this **p** evil age,
Gal 4:18 not only when I am **p** with you
Gal 4:20 like to be **p** with you now
Eph 5:27 that He might **p** it to Himself
Col 1:22 to **p** you holy, and blameless,
Col 1:28 that we may **p** every man
1Ti 6:17 this **p** age not to be haughty
2Ti 2:15 Be diligent to **p** yourself
2Ti 4:10 me, having loved this **p** world
Tit 2:12 and godly in the **p** age,
Heb 9: 9 It was symbolic for the **p**
Heb 12:11 seems to be joyful for the **p**
2Pe 1:12 established in the **p** truth
Jude 24 to **p** you faultless before the

PRESENTABLE (*see* PRESENT)
1Co 12:24 but our **p** parts have no need

PRESENTATION (*see* PRESENT)
1Ch 23:31 and at every **p** of a burnt

PRESENTED (*see* PRESENT)
Gen 46:29 he **p** himself to him, and fell
Gen 47: 2 brothers and **p** them to Pharaoh
Lev 2: 8 when it is **p** to the priest,
Lev 7:35 on the day when Moses **p** them
Lev 9:12 Aaron's sons **p** to him the
Lev 9:13 Then they **p** the burnt
Lev 9:18 Aaron's sons **p** to him the
Lev 16:10 be **p** alive before the LORD
Num 7: 3 and they **p** them before the
Num 7:18 of Issachar, **p** an offering

Num 7:24 of Zebulun, **p** an offering
Num 7:30 of Reuben, **p** an offering
Num 7:36 of Simeon, **p** an offering
Num 7:42 of Gad, **p** an offering
Num 7:48 of Ephraim, **p** an offering
Num 7:54 of Manasseh, **p** an offering
Num 7:60 of Benjamin, **p** an offering
Num 7:66 of Dan, **p** an offering
Num 7:72 of Asher, **p** an offering
Num 7:78 of Naphtali, **p** an offering
Num 8:21 then Aaron **p** them, as though
Num 16:38 Because they **p** them before
Num 16:39 who were burned up had **p**, and
Num 25: 6 **p** to his brethren a Midianite
Deut 31:14 went and **p** themselves in the
Josh 24: 1 they **p** themselves before God
Judg 6:19 the terebinth tree and **p** them
Judg 20: 2 **p** themselves in the assembly
1Sa 17:16 **p** himself forty days, morning
2Ch 24: 7 had also **p** all the dedicated
2Ch 29:24 they **p** their blood on the
Ezra 10:19 they **p** a ram of the flock as
Jer 38:26 I **p** my request before the
Matt 2:11 they **p** gifts to Him
Luke 7:15 And He **p** him to his mother
Acts 1: 3 to whom He also **p** Himself
Acts 9:41 and widows, he **p** her alive
Acts 23:33 they also **p** Paul to him
Rom 6:19 For just as you **p** your

PRESENTING (*see* PRESENT)
Num 9: 7 Why are we kept from **p** the
Num 15:13 in **p** an offering made by fire
Judg 3:18 he had finished **p** the tribute
Dan 9:20 **p** my supplication before the

PRESENTS (*see* PRESENT)
Num 15: 4 then he who **p** his offering
1Sa 10:27 him, and brought him no **p**
2Ch 17: 5 Judah gave **p** to Jehoshaphat
2Ch 17:11 brought Jehoshaphat **p** and
2Ch 32:23 **p** to Hezekiah king of Judah,
Esth 9:19 for sending **p** to one another
Esth 9:22 of sending **p** to one another
Ps 68:29 Kings will bring **p** to You
Ps 72:10 and of the isles Will bring **p**
Ps 76:11 **p** to Him who ought to be
Mic 1:14 give **p** to Moresheth Gath

PRESERVE (*see* PRESERVED, PRESERVES)
Gen 19:32 that we may **p** the lineage of
Gen 19:34 that we may **p** the lineage of
Gen 45: 5 sent me before you to **p** life
Gen 45: 7 God sent me before you to **p** a
Deut 6:24 that He might **p** us alive
Neh 9: 6 is in them, and You **p** them all
Job 36: 6 He does not **p** the life of the
Ps 12: 7 You shall **p** them from this
Ps 16: 1 **P** me, O God, for in You I put
Ps 25:21 integrity and uprightness **p** me
Ps 32: 7 You shall **p** me from trouble
Ps 36: 6 O LORD, You **p** man and beast
Ps 40:11 Your truth continually **p** me
Ps 41: 2 The LORD will **p** him and keep
Ps 61: 7 and truth, which may **p** him
Ps 64: 1 **P** my life from fear of the
Ps 79:11 **P** those who are appointed to
Ps 86: 2 **P** my life, for I am holy
Ps 121: 7 The LORD shall **p** you from all
Ps 121: 7 He shall **p** your soul
Ps 121: 8 LORD shall **p** your going out
Ps 140: 1 **P** me from violent men,
Ps 140: 4 **P** me from violent men, Who
Prov 2:11 discretion will **p** you
Prov 4: 6 her, and she will **p** you
Prov 5: 2 that you may **p** discretion
Prov 14: 3 lips of the wise will **p** them
Prov 20:28 and truth **p** the king, and by
Prov 22:12 eyes of the LORD **p** knowledge
Is 31: 5 passing over, He will **p** it
Is 49: 8 I will **p** You and give You as a
Jer 49:11 children, I will **p** them alive
Jer 50:20 I will pardon those whom I **p**
Luke 17:33 loses his life will **p** it
2Ti 4:18 **p** me for His heavenly kingdom

PRESERVED (*see* PRESERVE)
Gen 32:30 face to face, and my life is **p**
Josh 24:17 **p** us in all the way that we
1Sa 30:23 has given us, who has **p** us
2Sa 8: 6 The LORD **p** David wherever he
2Sa 8:14 the LORD **p** David wherever he
1Ch 18: 6 Thus the LORD **p** David
1Ch 18:13 the LORD **p** David wherever he
Job 10:12 and Your care has **p** my spirit
Ps 37:28 They are **p** forever, But the
Is 49: 6 restore the **p** ones of Israel
Hos 12:13 and by a prophet he was **p**
Matt 9:17 new wineskins, and both are **p**
Luke 5:38 new wineskins, and both are **p**
1Th 5:23 body be **p** blameless at the
Jude 1 Father, and **p** in Jesus Christ

PRESERVES (*see* PRESERVE)
Ps 31:23 For the LORD **p** the faithful
Ps 97:10 He **p** the souls of His saints
Ps 116: 6 The LORD **p** the simple
Ps 145:20 The LORD **p** all who love Him,
Prov 2: 8 and **p** the way of His saints
Prov 13: 3 guards his mouth **p** his life
Prov 16:17 who keeps his way **p** his soul
Ezek 18:27 and right, he **p** himself alive

PRESS (*see* PRESSED, PRESSES, PRESSING)
Job 24:11 They **p** out oil within their
Hag 2:16 out fifty baths from the **p**
Luke 8:45 and **p** You, and You say, 'Who
Phil 3:12 but I **p** on, that I may lay
Phil 3:14 I **p** toward the goal for the

PRESSED (*see* PRESS)
Gen 19: 9 So they **p** hard against the
Gen 40:11 **p** them into Pharaoh's cup, and
Ex 27:20 oil of **p** olives for the light
Ex 29:40 one-fourth of a hin of **p** oil
Lev 24: 2 oil of **p** olives for the light
Num 28: 5 one-fourth of a hin of **p** oil
Judg 14:17 because she **p** him so much
Judg 16:16 **p** him, so that his soul was
1Ki 5:11 and twenty kors of **p** oil
Esth 8:14 **p** on by the king's command
Is 8:21 will pass through it hard **p**
Ezek 23: 3 virgin bosom was there **p**
Ezek 23: 8 **p** her virgin bosom, and poured
Ezek 23:21 when the Egyptians **p** your
Mark 3:10 **p** about Him to touch Him
Luke 5: 1 as the multitude **p** about Him
Luke 6:38 **p** down, shaken together, and
2Co 4: 8 We are hard **p** on every side,
Phil 1:23 For I am hard **p** between the

PRESSES (*see* PRESS)
Neh 13:15 wine **p** on the Sabbath, and
Ps 38: 2 And Your hand **p** me down
Is 16:10 tread out wine in their **p**

PRESSING (*see* PRESS)
Hab 2:15 **p** him to your bottle, even to
Luke 16:16 and everyone is **p** into it

PRESUME (*see* PRESUMED, PRESUMES, PRESUMPTUOUS)
Esth 7: 5 who would dare **p** in his heart

PRESUMED (*see* PRESUME)
Num 14:44 But they **p** to go up to the

PRESUMES (*see* PRESUME)
Deut 18:20 But the prophet who **p** to

PRESUMPTUOUS (*see* PRESUME, PRESUMPTUOUSLY)
Ps 19:13 Your servant also from **p** sins
2Pe 2:10 They are **p**, self-willed

PRESUMPTUOUSLY (*see* PRESUMPTUOUS)
Num 15:30 person who does anything **p**
Deut 1:43 **p** went up into the mountain
Deut 17:12 Now the man who acts **p** and
Deut 17:13 and fear, and no longer act **p**
Deut 18:22 the prophet has spoken it **p**

PRETEND (*see* PRETENDED)
2Sa 13: 5 on your bed and **p** to be ill
2Sa 14: 2 Please **p** to be a mourner, and
1Ki 14: 5 that she will **p** to be another
1Ki 14: 6 Why do you **p** to be another
Ps 81:15 would **p** submission to Him

PRETENDED (*see* PRETEND)
Josh 9: 4 went and **p** to be ambassadors
2Sa 13: 6 Amnon lay down and **p** to be ill
Luke 20:20 and sent spies who **p** to be

PRETENSE
Jer 3:10 her whole heart, but in **p**
Matt 23:14 for a **p** make long prayers
Mark 12:40 for a **p** make long prayers
Luke 20:47 for a **p** make long prayers
Acts 27:30 sea, under **p** of putting out
Phil 1:18 whether in **p** or in truth,

PRETTY
Jer 46:20 Egypt is like a very **p** heifer

PREVAIL (*see* PREVAILED, PREVAILING)
Gen 32:25 that He did not **p** against him
1Sa 2: 9 by strength no man shall **p**
1Sa 17: 9 But if I **p** against him and
1Sa 26:25 great things and also still **p**
1Ki 22:22 shall persuade him, and also **p**
2Ch 14:11 do not let man **p** against You
2Ch 18:21 shall persuade him and also **p**
Esth 6:13 you will not **p** against him
Job 14:20 You **p** forever against him, and
Ps 9:19 O LORD, Do not let man **p**
Ps 12: 4 With our tongue we will **p**
Ps 65: 3 Iniquities **p** against me
Is 7: 1 but could not **p** against it
Is 16:12 but he will not **p**
Is 42:13 He shall **p** against His
Is 47:12 to profit, perhaps you will **p**
Jer 1:19 they shall not **p** against you
Jer 5:22 to and fro, yet they cannot **p**
Jer 15:20 they shall not **p** against you
Jer 20:10 Then we will **p** against him
Jer 20:11 will stumble, and will not **p**
Dan 11: 7 North, and deal with them and **p**
Dan 11:12 thousands, but he will not **p**
Obad 7 deceive you and **p** against you
Matt 16:18 Hades shall not **p** against it
Matt 27:24 that he could not **p** at all
Rev 12: 8 but they did not **p**, nor was a

PREVAILED (*see* PREVAIL)
Gen 7:18 The waters **p** and greatly
Gen 7:19 the waters **p** exceedingly on
Gen 7:20 The waters **p** fifteen cubits
Gen 7:24 the waters **p** on the earth one
Gen 30: 8 my sister, and indeed I have **p**
Gen 32:28 God and with men, and have **p**
Ex 17:11 up his hand, that Israel **p**
Ex 17:11 let down his hand, Amalek **p**
Judg 3:10 and his hand **p** over
Judg 6: 2 of Midian **p** against Israel
1Sa 17:50 So David **p** over the
2Sa 11:23 Surely the men **p** against us
2Sa 24: 4 king's word **p** against Joab
1Ki 16:22 Omri **p** over the people who
1Ch 5: 2 yet Judah **p** over his brothers
1Ch 21: 4 king's word **p** against Joab
2Ch 13:18 and the children of Judah **p**
Ps 13: 4 say, "I have **p** against him"
Ps 129: 2 they have not **p** against me
Jer 20: 7 stronger than I, and have **p**
Jer 38:22 set upon you and **p** against you
Lam 1:16 desolate because the enemy **p**
Hos 12: 4 struggled with the Angel and **p**
Luke 23:23 men and of the chief priests **p**
Acts 19:16 **p** against them, so that they
Acts 19:20 the Lord grew mightily and **p**
Rev 5: 5 has **p** to open the scroll and

PREVAILING (*see* PREVAIL)
Dan 7:21 saints, and **p** against them,

PREVENT (*see* PREVENTED)
Matt 3:14 And John tried to **p** Him,

PREVENTED (*see* PREVENT)
Heb 7:23 because they were **p** by death

PREVIOUSLY
Gen 28:19 of that city had been Luz **p**
Ex 10:14 **p** there had been no such
2Sa 7:10 oppress them anymore, as **p**
2Sa 15:34 been your father's servant **p**
1Ch 17: 9 oppress them anymore, as **p**
Neh 13: 5 where **p** they had stored the
Jon 4: 2 I fled **p** to Tarshish
John 9: 8 those who **p** had seen that he
Acts 8: 9 who **p** practiced sorcery in
Acts 21:29 (For they had **p** seen
Rom 3: 9 For we have **p** charged both
Rom 3:25 sins that were **p** committed
2Co 9: 5 which you had **p** promised
1Ti 1:18 **p** made concerning you, that
Heb 10: 8 **P** saying, "Sacrifice and

PREY (*see* PREYS)
Gen 49: 9 from the **p**, my son, you have
Gen 49:27 morning he shall devour the **p**
Num 23:24 down until it devours the **p**

Job 4:11 lion perishes for lack of **p**
Job 9:26 an eagle swooping on its **p**
Job 38:39 you hunt the **p** for the lion
Job 39:29 From there it spies out the **p**
Ps 17:12 that is eager to tear his **p**
Ps 76: 4 Than the mountains of **p**
Ps 104:21 lions roar after their **p**, And
Ps 124: 6 given us as **p** to their teeth
Prov 6:26 an adulteress will **p** upon his
Is 5:29 roar and lay hold of the **p**
Is 10: 2 that widows may be their **p**
Is 10: 6 the spoil, to take the **p**, and
Is 18: 6 for the mountain birds of **p**
Is 18: 6 the birds of **p** will summer on
Is 31: 4 his **p** (when a multitude of
Is 33:23 Then the **p** of great plunder
Is 33:23 the lame take the **p**
Is 42:22 they are for **p**, and no one
Is 46:11 a bird of **p** from the east
Is 49:24 Shall the **p** be taken from the
Is 49:25 and the **p** of the terrible be
Is 59:15 from evil makes himself a **p**
Jer 30:16 who **p** upon you I will make a **p**
Ezek 13:21 longer be as **p** in your hand
Ezek 19: 3 he learned to catch **p**, and he
Ezek 19: 6 he learned to catch **p**
Ezek 22:25 a roaring lion tearing the **p**
Ezek 22:27 are like wolves tearing the **p**
Ezek 34: 8 because My flock became a **p**
Ezek 34:22 they shall no longer be a **p**
Ezek 34:28 longer be a **p** for the nations
Ezek 39: 4 to birds of **p** of every sort
Amos 3: 4 the forest, when he has no **p**
Nah 2:12 filled his caves with **p**, and
Nah 2:13 cut off your **p** from the earth

PREYS (*see* PREY)
Job 24:21 For he **p** on the barren who do

PRICE (*see* PRICED)
Gen 23: 9 give it to me at the full **p**
Lev 25:16 you shall increase its **p**, and
Lev 25:16 you shall diminish its **p**
Lev 25:50 The **p** of his release shall be
Lev 25:51 **p** of his redemption from the
Lev 25:52 him the **p** of his redemption
Deut 23:18 **p** of a dog to the house of
2Sa 24:24 buy it from you for a **p**
1Ki 10:28 in Keveh at the current **p**
1Ch 21:22 grant it to me at the full **p**
1Ch 21:24 surely buy it for the full **p**
2Ch 1:16 in Keveh at the current **p**
Job 28:15 silver be weighed for its **p**
Job 28:18 for the **p** of wisdom is above
Ps 44:12 are not enriched by their **p**
Prov 17:16 fool the purchase **p** of wisdom
Prov 27:26 and the goats the **p** of a field
Is 45:13 not for **p** nor reward," says
Is 55: 1 without money and without **p**
Jer 15:13 give as plunder without **p**
Lam 5: 4 and our wood comes at a **p**
Zech 11:13 that princely **p** they set on
Matt 13:46 found one pearl of great **p**
Matt 27: 6 they are the **p** of blood
Acts 5: 3 keep back part of the **p** of
1Co 6:20 For you were bought at a **p**
1Co 7:23 You were bought at a **p**

PRICED (*see* PRICE)
Matt 27: 9 the value of Him who was **p**
Matt 27: 9 of the children of Israel **p**

PRICKING
Ezek 28:24 a **p** brier or a painful thorn

PRIDE (*see* PROUD)
Lev 26:19 break the **p** of your power
1Sa 17:28 I know your **p** and the
2Ch 32:26 for the **p** of his heart, he and
Job 33:17 deed, and conceal **p** from man,
Job 35:12 because of the **p** of evil men
Job 41:15 His rows of scales are his **p**
Job 41:34 over all the children of **p**
Ps 10: 2 The wicked in his **p**
Ps 36:11 the foot of **p** come against me
Ps 59:12 them even be taken in their **p**
Ps 73: 6 Therefore **p** serves as their
Prov 8:13 **p** and arrogance and the evil
Prov 11: 2 When **p** comes, then comes
Prov 13:10 By **p** comes only contention,
Prov 14: 3 mouth of a fool is a rod of **p**
Prov 16:18 **P** goes before destruction, and
Prov 21:24 he acts with arrogant **p**
Prov 29:23 A man's **p** will bring him low,
Is 9: 9 who say in **p** and arrogance of
Is 13:19 beauty of the Chaldeans' **p**
Is 16: 6 have heard of the **p** of Moab
Is 16: 6 of his haughtiness and his **p**
Is 23: 9 dishonor the **p** of all glory
Is 25:11 He will bring down their **p**
Is 28: 1 Woe to the crown of **p**, to the
Is 28: 3 The crown of **p**, the drunkards
Jer 13: 9 I will ruin the **p** of Judah
Jer 13: 9 and the great **p** of Jerusalem
Jer 13:17 weep in secret for your **p**
Jer 48:29 We have heard the **p** of Moab
Jer 48:29 loftiness and arrogance and **p**
Jer 49:16 the **p** of your heart, O you
Ezek 7:10 has blossomed, **p** has budded
Ezek 16:49 She and her daughter had **p**
Ezek 16:56 mouth in the days of your **p**
Ezek 30: 6 the **p** of her power shall come
Dan 4:37 those who walk in **p** He is
Dan 5:20 his spirit was hardened in **p**
Hos 5: 5 The **p** of Israel testifies to
Hos 7:10 the **p** of Israel testifies to
Amos 6: 8 I abhor the **p** of Jacob, and
Amos 8: 7 has sworn by the **p** of Jacob
Obad 3 The **p** of your heart has
Zeph 2:10 they shall have for their **p**
Zeph 3:11 those who rejoice in your **p**
Zech 9: 6 off the **p** of the Philistines
Zech 10:11 Then the **p** of Assyria shall
Zech 11: 3 For the **p** of the Jordan is in
Mark 7:22 an evil eye, blasphemy, **p**
1Ti 3: 6 with **p** he fall into the same
1Jn 2:16 of the eyes, and the **p** of life

PRIEST (*see* PRIESTHOOD, PRIESTLY, PRIEST'S, PRIESTS)
Gen 14:18 he was the **p** of God Most High
Gen 41:45 of Poti-Pherah **p** of On
Gen 41:50 of Poti-Pherah **p** of On, bore
Gen 46:20 of Poti-Pherah **p** of On, bore
Ex 2:16 Now the **p** of Midian had seven
Ex 3: 1 the **p** of Midian
Ex 18: 1 the **p** of Midian, Moses'
Ex 28: 1 he may minister to Me as **p**
Ex 28: 3 he may minister to Me as **p**
Ex 28: 4 he may minister to Me as **p**
Ex 29:30 That son who becomes **p** in his
Ex 31:10 holy garments for Aaron the **p**
Ex 35:19 holy garments for Aaron the **p**
Ex 38:21 Ithamar, son of Aaron the **p**
Ex 39:41 holy garments for Aaron the **p**
Ex 40:13 he may minister to Me as **p**
Lev 1: 7 The sons of Aaron the **p**
Lev 1: 9 the **p** shall burn all on the
Lev 1:12 the **p** shall lay them in order
Lev 1:13 the **p** shall bring it all and
Lev 1:15 The **p** shall bring it to the
Lev 1:17 the **p** shall burn it on the
Lev 2: 2 And the **p** shall burn it as a
Lev 2: 8 when it is presented to the **p**
Lev 2: 9 Then the **p** shall take from
Lev 2:16 Then the **p** shall burn the
Lev 3:11 the **p** shall burn them on the
Lev 3:16 the **p** shall burn them on the
Lev 4: 3 if the anointed **p** sins,
Lev 4: 5 Then the anointed **p** shall
Lev 4: 6 The **p** shall dip his finger
Lev 4: 7 the **p** shall put some of the
Lev 4:10 the **p** shall burn them on the
Lev 4:16 The anointed **p** shall bring
Lev 4:17 Then the **p** shall dip his
Lev 4:20 So the **p** shall make atonement
Lev 4:25 The **p** shall take some of the
Lev 4:26 So the **p** shall make atonement
Lev 4:30 Then the **p** shall take some
Lev 4:31 the **p** shall burn it on the
Lev 4:31 So the **p** shall make atonement
Lev 4:34 The **p** shall take some of the
Lev 4:35 Then the **p** shall burn it on
Lev 4:35 So the **p** shall make atonement
Lev 5: 6 So the **p** shall make atonement
Lev 5: 8 he shall bring them to the **p**
Lev 5:10 So the **p** shall make atonement
Lev 5:12 he shall bring it to the **p**
Lev 5:12 the **p** shall take his handful
Lev 5:13 The **p** shall make atonement
Lev 5:16 to it and give it to the **p**
Lev 5:16 So the **p** shall make atonement
Lev 5:18 he shall bring to the **p** a ram
Lev 5:18 So the **p** shall make atonement
Lev 6: 6 a trespass offering, to the **p**
Lev 6: 7 So the **p** shall make atonement
Lev 6:10 the **p** shall put on his linen
Lev 6:12 the **p** shall burn wood on it
Lev 6:22 The **p** from among his sons,
Lev 6:23 the **p** shall be wholly burned
Lev 6:26 The **p** who offers it for sin
Lev 7: 5 the **p** shall burn them on the
Lev 7: 7 the **p** who makes atonement
Lev 7: 8 the **p** who offers anyone's
Lev 7: 8 that **p** shall have for himself
Lev 7:14 It shall belong to the **p** who
Lev 7:31 the **p** shall burn the fat on
Lev 7:32 **p** as a heave offering from
Lev 7:34 given them to Aaron the **p**
Lev 12: 6 she shall bring to the **p** a
Lev 12: 8 So the **p** shall make atonement
Lev 13: 2 be brought to Aaron the **p** or
Lev 13: 3 The **p** shall look at the sore
Lev 13: 3 Then the **p** shall look at him,
Lev 13: 4 then the **p** shall isolate the
Lev 13: 5 the **p** shall look at him on
Lev 13: 5 then the **p** shall isolate him
Lev 13: 6 Then the **p** shall look at him
Lev 13: 6 then the **p** shall pronounce
Lev 13: 7 by the **p** for his cleansing
Lev 13: 7 shall be seen by the **p** again
Lev 13: 8 if the **p** sees that the scab
Lev 13: 8 then the **p** shall pronounce
Lev 13: 9 he shall be brought to the **p**
Lev 13:10 And the **p** shall look at him
Lev 13:11 The **p** shall pronounce him
Lev 13:12 foot, wherever the **p** looks
Lev 13:13 then the **p** shall consider
Lev 13:15 the **p** shall look at the raw
Lev 13:16 again, he shall come to the **p**
Lev 13:17 And the **p** shall look at him
Lev 13:17 then the **p** shall pronounce
Lev 13:19 it shall be shown to the **p**
Lev 13:20 and if, when the **p** sees it
Lev 13:20 the **p** shall pronounce him
Lev 13:21 But if the **p** looks at it, and
Lev 13:21 then the **p** shall isolate him
Lev 13:22 then the **p** shall pronounce
Lev 13:23 the **p** shall pronounce him
Lev 13:25 then the **p** shall look at it
Lev 13:25 Therefore the **p** shall
Lev 13:26 But if the **p** looks at it, and
Lev 13:26 then the **p** shall isolate him
Lev 13:27 the **p** shall look at him on
Lev 13:27 then the **p** shall pronounce
Lev 13:28 The **p** shall pronounce him
Lev 13:30 then the **p** shall look at the
Lev 13:30 then the **p** shall pronounce
Lev 13:31 But if the **p** looks at the
Lev 13:31 then the **p** shall isolate the
Lev 13:32 the **p** shall look at the sore
Lev 13:33 the **p** shall isolate the one
Lev 13:34 On the seventh day the **p**
Lev 13:34 then the **p** shall pronounce
Lev 13:36 then the **p** shall look at him
Lev 13:36 skin, the **p** need not seek for
Lev 13:37 the **p** shall pronounce him
Lev 13:39 then the **p** shall look
Lev 13:43 Then the **p** shall look at it
Lev 13:44 The **p** shall surely pronounce
Lev 13:49 and shall be shown to the **p**
Lev 13:50 The **p** shall look at the
Lev 13:53 But if the **p** looks, and indeed
Lev 13:54 then the **p** shall command that
Lev 13:55 Then the **p** shall look at the
Lev 13:56 If the **p** looks, and indeed the
Lev 14: 2 He shall be brought to the **p**
Lev 14: 3 the **p** shall go out of the
Lev 14: 3 and the **p** shall look
Lev 14: 4 then the **p** shall command to
Lev 14: 5 the **p** shall command that one
Lev 14:11 Then the **p** who makes him
Lev 14:12 the **p** shall take one male
Lev 14:14 The **p** shall take some of the
Lev 14:14 the **p** shall put it on the tip
Lev 14:15 the **p** shall take some of the
Lev 14:16 Then the **p** shall dip his
Lev 14:17 the **p** shall put some on the
Lev 14:18 So the **p** shall make atonement
Lev 14:19 Then the **p** shall offer the
Lev 14:20 the **p** shall offer the burnt
Lev 14:20 So the **p** shall make atonement
Lev 14:23 **p** on the eighth day for his
Lev 14:24 the **p** shall take the lamb of

Lev 14:24 the p shall wave them as a
Lev 14:25 the p shall take some of the
Lev 14:26 the p shall pour some of the
Lev 14:27 Then the p shall sprinkle
Lev 14:28 the p shall put some of the
Lev 14:31 So the p shall make atonement
Lev 14:35 house comes and tells the p
Lev 14:36 then the p shall command that
Lev 14:36 before the p goes into it to
Lev 14:36 afterward the p shall go in
Lev 14:38 then the p shall go out of
Lev 14:39 the p shall come again on the
Lev 14:40 then the p shall command that
Lev 14:44 then the p shall come and look
Lev 14:48 But if the p comes in and
Lev 14:48 then the p shall pronounce
Lev 15:14 and give them to the p
Lev 15:15 Then the p shall offer them,
Lev 15:15 So the p shall make atonement
Lev 15:29 and bring them to the p, to
Lev 15:30 Then the p shall offer the
Lev 15:30 the p shall make atonement
Lev 16:30 For on that day the p shall
Lev 16:32 And the p, who is anointed and
Lev 16:32 as p in his father's place
Lev 17: 5 of meeting, to the p, and
Lev 17: 6 And the p shall sprinkle the
Lev 19:22 The p shall make atonement
Lev 21: 7 for the p is holy to his God
Lev 21: 9 The daughter of any p, if
Lev 21:10 the high p among his brethren
Lev 21:21 descendants of Aaron the p
Lev 22:10 one who sojourns with the p
Lev 22:11 But if the p buys a person
Lev 22:14 a holy offering to the p, and
Lev 23:10 of your harvest to the p
Lev 23:11 Sabbath the p shall wave it
Lev 23:20 The p shall wave them with
Lev 23:20 be holy to the LORD for the p
Lev 27: 8 present himself before the p
Lev 27: 8 the p shall set a value for
Lev 27: 8 vowed, the p shall value him
Lev 27:11 the beast before the p
Lev 27:12 the p shall set a value for
Lev 27:12 as you, the p, value it, so
Lev 27:14 then the p shall set a value
Lev 27:14 as the p values it, so it
Lev 27:18 then the p shall reckon to
Lev 27:21 be the possession of the p
Lev 27:23 then the p shall reckon to
Num 3: 6 them before Aaron the p, that
Num 3:32 the son of Aaron the p was to
Num 4:16 the son of Aaron the p is the
Num 4:28 the son of Aaron the p
Num 4:33 the son of Aaron the p
Num 5: 8 must go to the LORD for the p
Num 5: 9 which they bring to the p
Num 5:10 man gives the p shall be his
Num 5:15 shall bring his wife to the p
Num 5:16 the p shall bring her near,
Num 5:17 The p shall take holy water
Num 5:18 Then the p shall stand the
Num 5:18 the p shall have in his hand
Num 5:19 the p shall put her under
Num 5:21 then the p shall put the
Num 5:23 Then the p shall write these
Num 5:25 Then the p shall take the
Num 5:26 the p shall take a handful of
Num 5:30 the p shall execute all this
Num 6:10 or two young pigeons to the p
Num 6:11 the p shall offer one as a
Num 6:16 Then the p shall bring them
Num 6:17 the p shall also offer its
Num 6:19 the p shall take the boiled
Num 6:20 the p shall wave them as a
Num 6:20 they are holy for the p,
Num 7: 8 the son of Aaron the p
Num 15:25 So the p shall make
Num 15:28 So the p shall make
Num 16:37 the son of Aaron the p, to
Num 16:39 So Eleazar the p took the
Num 18:28 from it to Aaron the p
Num 19: 3 give it to Eleazar the p,
Num 19: 4 Eleazar the p shall take some
Num 19: 6 the p shall take cedar wood
Num 19: 7 Then the p shall wash his
Num 19: 7 the p shall be unclean until
Num 25: 7 the son of Aaron the p, saw
Num 25:11 the son of Aaron the p, has
Num 26: 1 the son of Aaron the p,

Num 26: 3 Eleazar the p spoke with them
Num 26:63 by Moses and Eleazar the p
Num 26:64 and Aaron the p when they
Num 27: 2 Moses, before Eleazar the p
Num 27:19 set him before Eleazar the p
Num 27:21 stand before Eleazar the p
Num 27:22 set him before Eleazar the p
Num 31: 6 the son of Eleazar the p,
Num 31:12 to Moses, to Eleazar the p
Num 31:13 And Moses, Eleazar the p, and
Num 31:21 Then Eleazar the p said to
Num 31:26 beast, you and Eleazar the p
Num 31:29 give it to Eleazar the p as a
Num 31:31 Eleazar the p did as the LORD
Num 31:41 offering to Eleazar the p
Num 31:51 Eleazar the p received the
Num 31:54 Eleazar the p received the
Num 32: 2 to Moses, to Eleazar the p
Num 32:28 them to Eleazar the p, to
Num 33:38 Then Aaron the p went up to
Num 34:17 Eleazar the p and Joshua the
Num 35:25 p who was anointed with the
Num 35:28 until the death of the high p
Num 35:28 p the manslayer may return to
Num 35:32 before the death of the p
Deut 10: 6 ministered as p in his stead
Deut 17:12 and will not heed the p who
Deut 18: 3 give to the p the shoulder
Deut 20: 2 that the p shall approach and
Deut 26: 3 one who is p in those days
Deut 26: 4 Then the p shall take the
Josh 14: 1 Canaan, which Eleazar the p
Josh 17: 4 near before Eleazar the p
Josh 19:51 which Eleazar the p, Joshua
Josh 20: 6 who is high p in those days
Josh 21: 1 came near to Eleazar the p
Josh 21: 4 the children of Aaron the p
Josh 21:13 p they gave Hebron with its
Josh 22:13 the son of Eleazar the p to
Josh 22:30 when Phinehas the p and the
Josh 22:31 the son of Eleazar the p said
Josh 22:32 the son of Eleazar the p, and
Judg 17: 5 of his sons, who became his p
Judg 17:10 a p to me, and I will give you
Judg 17:12 and the young man became his p
Judg 17:13 since I have a Levite as p
Judg 18: 4 me, and I have become his p
Judg 18: 6 And the p said to them,
Judg 18:17 The p stood at the entrance
Judg 18:18 image, the p said to them,
Judg 18:19 be a father and a p to us
Judg 18:19 it better for you to be a p
Judg 18:19 or that you be a p to a tribe
Judg 18:24 gods which I made, and the p
Judg 18:27 the p who had belonged to him
1Sa 1: 9 Now Eli the p was sitting on
1Sa 2:11 to the LORD before Eli the p
1Sa 2:14 the p would take for himself
1Sa 2:15 meat for roasting to the p
1Sa 2:28 tribes of Israel to be My p
1Sa 2:35 up for Myself a faithful p
1Sa 14: 3 Eli, the LORD's p in Shiloh
1Sa 14:19 while Saul talked to the p
1Sa 14:19 so Saul said to the p
1Sa 14:36 Then the p said, "Let us
1Sa 21: 1 to Nob, to Ahimelech the p
1Sa 21: 2 David said to Ahimelech the p
1Sa 21: 4 the p answered David and said,
1Sa 21: 5 Then David answered the p
1Sa 21: 6 So the p gave him holy bread
1Sa 21: 9 So the p said, "The sword of
1Sa 22:11 sent to call Ahimelech the p
1Sa 23: 9 he said to Abiathar the p
1Sa 30: 7 David said to Abiathar the p
2Sa 15:27 king also said to Zadok the p
1Ki 1: 7 and with Abiathar the p, and
1Ki 1: 8 But Zadok the p, Benaiah the
1Ki 1:19 of the king, Abiathar the p
1Ki 1:25 the army, and Abiathar the p
1Ki 1:26 your servant, nor Zadok the p
1Ki 1:32 Call to me Zadok the p,
1Ki 1:34 There let Zadok the p and
1Ki 1:38 So Zadok the p, Nathan the
1Ki 1:39 Then Zadok the p took a horn
1Ki 1:42 the son of Abiathar the p
1Ki 1:44 has sent with him Zadok the p
1Ki 1:45 So Zadok the p and Nathan the
1Ki 2:22 him, and for Abiathar the p
1Ki 2:26 Abiathar the p the king said
1Ki 2:27 from being p to the LORD,

1Ki 2:35 the king put Zadok the p in
1Ki 4: 2 the son of Zadok, the p
1Ki 4: 5 Zabud the son of Nathan, a p
2Ki 11: 9 that Jehoiada the p commanded
2Ki 11: 9 and came to Jehoiada the p
2Ki 11:10 the p gave the captains of
2Ki 11:15 Then Jehoiada the p
2Ki 11:15 For the p had said, "Do
2Ki 11:18 killed Mattan the p of Baal
2Ki 11:18 the p appointed officers over
2Ki 12: 2 Jehoiada the p instructed him
2Ki 12: 7 Jehoash called Jehoiada the p
2Ki 12: 9 Jehoiada the p took a chest
2Ki 12:10 scribe and the high p came up
2Ki 16:10 the p the design of the altar
2Ki 16:11 Then Urijah the p built an
2Ki 16:11 So Urijah the p made it
2Ki 16:15 Ahaz commanded Urijah the p
2Ki 16:16 Thus did Urijah the p,
2Ki 22: 4 Go up to Hilkiah the high p
2Ki 22: 8 Then Hilkiah the high p said
2Ki 22:10 Hilkiah the p has given me a
2Ki 22:12 king commanded Hilkiah the p
2Ki 22:14 So Hilkiah the p, Ahikam,
2Ki 23: 4 commanded Hilkiah the high p
2Ki 23:24 p found in the house of the
2Ki 25:18 took Seraiah the chief p,
2Ki 25:18 Zephaniah the second p, and
1Ch 6:10 p in the temple that Solomon
1Ch 16:39 and Zadok the p and his
1Ch 24: 6 the leaders, Zadok the p
1Ch 27: 5 the son of Jehoiada the p
1Ch 29:22 the leader, and Zadok to be p
2Ch 13: 9 and seven rams may be a p of
2Ch 15: 3 God, without a teaching p
2Ch 19:11 Amariah the chief p is over
2Ch 22:11 the wife of Jehoiada the p
2Ch 23: 8 that Jehoiada the p commanded
2Ch 23: 8 for Jehoiada the p had not
2Ch 23: 9 Jehoiada the p gave to the
2Ch 23:14 Then Jehoiada the p brought
2Ch 23:14 For the p said, 'Do not
2Ch 23:17 killed Mattan the p of Baal
2Ch 24: 2 the days of Jehoiada the p
2Ch 24: 6 called Jehoiada the chief p
2Ch 24:20 the son of Jehoiada the p
2Ch 24:25 of the sons of Jehoiada the p
2Ch 26:17 So Azariah the p went in
2Ch 26:20 And Azariah the chief p and all
2Ch 31:10 And Azariah the chief p, from
2Ch 34: 9 came to Hilkiah the high p
2Ch 34:14 Hilkiah the p found the Book
2Ch 34:18 Hilkiah the p has given me a
Ezra 2:63 p could consult with the Urim
Ezra 7: 5 the son of Aaron the chief p
Ezra 7:11 Artaxerxes gave Ezra the p
Ezra 7:12 king of kings, To Ezra the p
Ezra 7:21 that whatever Ezra the p
Ezra 8:33 the son of Uriah the p, and
Ezra 10:10 Then Ezra the p stood up and
Ezra 10:16 And Ezra the p, with certain
Neh 3: 1 Then Eliashib the high p rose
Neh 3:20 house of Eliashib the high p
Neh 7:65 p could consult with the Urim
Neh 8: 2 So Ezra the p brought the Law
Neh 8: 9 was the governor, Ezra the p
Neh 10:38 And the p, the descendant of
Neh 12:26 governor, and of Ezra the p
Neh 13: 4 before this, Eliashib the p
Neh 13:13 storehouse Shelemiah the p
Neh 13:28 son of Eliashib the high p
Ps 110: 4 You are a p forever According
Is 8: 2 to record, Uriah the p and
Is 24: 2 the people, so with the p
Is 28: 7 the p and the prophet have
Jer 6:13 the prophet even to the p
Jer 8:10 the p Everyone deals falsely
Jer 14:18 p go about in a land they do
Jer 18:18 shall not perish from the p
Jer 20: 1 the p who was also chief
Jer 21: 1 the son of Maaseiah, the p
Jer 23:11 both prophet and p are profane
Jer 23:33 the prophet or the p ask you
Jer 23:34 as for the prophet and the p
Jer 29:25 the son of Maaseiah the p
Jer 29:26 The LORD has made you p
Jer 29:26 instead of Jehoiada the p
Jer 29:29 Now Zephaniah the p read this
Jer 37: 3 the son of Maaseiah, the p
Jer 52:24 took Seraiah the chief p,

Jer 52:24 Zephaniah the second **p**, and
Lam 2: 6 has spurned the king and the **p**
Lam 2:20 Should the **p** and prophet be
Ezek 1: 3 expressly to Ezekiel the **p**
Ezek 7:26 law will perish from the **p**
Ezek 44:13 Me to minister to Me as **p**
Ezek 44:21 No **p** shall drink wine when he
Ezek 44:30 **p** the first of your ground
Ezek 45:19 The **p** shall take some of the
Hos 4: 4 those who contend with the **p**
Hos 4: 6 you from being **p** for Me
Hos 4: 9 like people, like **p**
Amos 7:10 Then Amaziah the **p** of Bethel
Hag 1: 1 son of Jehozadak, the high **p**
Hag 1:12 son of Jehozadak, the high **p**
Hag 1:14 son of Jehozadak, the high **p**
Hag 2: 2 son of Jehozadak, the high **p**
Hag 2: 4 son of Jehozadak, the high **p**
Zech 3: 1 **p** standing before the Angel
Zech 3: 8 Hear, O Joshua, the high **p**
Zech 6:11 son of Jehozadak, the high **p**
Zech 6:13 He shall be a **p** on His throne
Mal 2: 7 For the lips of a **p** should
Matt 8: 4 way, show yourself to the **p**
Matt 26: 3 at the palace of the high **p**
Matt 26:51 the servant of the high **p**
Matt 26:57 away to Caiaphas the high **p**
Matt 26:62 And the high **p** arose and said
Matt 26:63 And the high **p** answered and
Matt 26:65 Then the high **p** tore his
Mark 1:44 way, show yourself to the **p**
Mark 2:26 days of Abiathar the high **p**
Mark 14:47 the servant of the high **p**
Mark 14:53 led Jesus away to the high **p**
Mark 14:54 the courtyard of the high **p**
Mark 14:60 the high **p** stood up in the
Mark 14:61 Again the high **p** asked Him
Mark 14:63 Then the high **p** tore his
Mark 14:66 girls of the high **p** came
Luke 1: 5 a certain **p** named Zacharias,
Luke 1: 8 while he was serving as **p**
Luke 5:14 go and show yourself to the **p**
Luke 10:31 certain **p** came down that road
Luke 22:50 the servant of the high **p**
John 11:49 being high **p** that year, said
John 11:51 but being high **p** that year he
John 18:13 who was high **p** that year
John 18:15 was known to the high **p**, and
John 18:15 the courtyard of the high **p**
John 18:16 who was known to the high **p**
John 18:19 The high **p** then asked Jesus
John 18:22 answer the high **p** like that
John 18:24 bound to Caiaphas the high p
John 18:26 of the servants of the high **p**
Acts 4: 6 as well as Annas the high **p**
Acts 4: 6 of the family of the high **p**
Acts 5:17 Then the high **p** rose up, and
Acts 5:21 But the high **p** and those with
Acts 5:24 Now when the high **p**, the
Acts 5:27 And the high **p** asked them,
Acts 7: 1 Then the high **p** said, "Are
Acts 9: 1 the Lord, went to the high **p**
Acts 14:13 Then the **p** of Zeus, whose
Acts 19:14 of Sceva, a Jewish chief **p**
Acts 22: 5 the high **p** bears me witness
Acts 23: 2 the high **p** Ananias commanded
Acts 23: 4 Do you revile God's high **p**
Acts 23: 5 that he was the high **p**
Acts 24: 1 **p** came down with the elders
Acts 25: 2 Then the high **p** and the chief
Heb 2:17 faithful High **P** in things
Heb 3: 1 High **P** of our confession,
Heb 4:14 that we have a great High **P**
Heb 4:15 For we do not have a High **P**
Heb 5: 1 For every **p** taken from among
Heb 5: 5 Himself to become High **P**, but
Heb 5: 6 You are a **p** forever according
Heb 5:10 called by God as High **P**
Heb 6:20 having become High **P** forever
Heb 7: 1 **p** of the Most High God, who
Heb 7: 3 God, remains a **p** continually
Heb 7:11 **p** should rise according to
Heb 7:15 there arises another **p**
Heb 7:17 You are a **p** forever according
Heb 7:20 not made **p** without an oath
Heb 7:21 relent, 'You are a **p** forever
Heb 7:26 For such a High **P** was fitting
Heb 8: 1 We have such a High **P**, who is
Heb 8: 3 For every high **p** is appointed
Heb 8: 4 on earth, He would not be a **p**
Heb 9: 7 high **p** went alone once a year
Heb 9:11 But Christ came as High **P** of
Heb 9:25 as the high **p** enters the Most
Heb 10:11 every **p** stands ministering
Heb 10:21 and having a High **P** over the
Heb 13:11 by the high **p** for sin, are

PRIESTHOOD (*see* PRIEST)
Ex 29: 9 The **p** shall be theirs for a
Ex 40:15 **p** throughout their
Num 3:10 they shall attend to their **p**
Num 16:10 And are you seeking the **p** also
Num 18: 1 associated with your **p**
Num 18: 7 you shall attend to your **p**
Num 18: 7 I give your **p** to you as a
Num 25:13 covenant of an everlasting **p**
Josh 18: 7 you, for the **p** of the LORD is
Ezra 2:62 from the **p** as defiled
Neh 7:64 from the **p** as defiled
Neh 13:29 they have defiled the **p** and
Neh 13:29 and the covenant of the **p** and
Luke 1: 9 to the custom of the **p**, his
Heb 7: 5 of Levi, who receive the **p**
Heb 7:11 **p** (for under it the people
Heb 7:12 For the **p** being changed, of
Heb 7:14 spoke nothing concerning **p**
Heb 7:24 has an unchangeable **p**
1Pe 2: 5 a spiritual house, a holy **p**
1Pe 2: 9 chosen generation, a royal **p**

PRIESTLY (*see* PRIEST)
1Sa 2:36 me in one of the **p** positions
Ezra 2:69 and one hundred **p** garments
Neh 7:70 hundred and thirty **p** garments
Neh 7:72 and sixty-seven **p** garments

PRIEST'S (*see* PRIEST)
Lev 5:13 be the **p** as a grain offering
Lev 7: 9 shall be the **p** who offers it
Lev 14:13 as the sin offering is the **p**
Lev 14:18 **p** hand he shall put on the
Lev 14:29 **p** hand he shall put on the
Lev 22:12 If the **p** daughter is married
Lev 22:13 But if the **p** daughter is a
Deut 18: 3 this shall be the **p** due from
Judg 18:20 So the **p** heart was glad
1Sa 2:13 the **p** servant would come with
1Sa 2:15 the **p** servant would come and
2Ch 24:11 the high **p** officer came and
Ezek 44:30 sacrifices, shall be the **p**
Matt 26:58 to the high **p** courtyard
Luke 22:54 Him into the high **p** house
John 18:10 and struck the high **p** servant

PRIESTS (*see* PRIEST, PRIESTS')
Gen 47:22 land of the **p** he did not buy
Gen 47:22 for the **p** had rations
Gen 47:26 for the land of the **p** only
Ex 19: 6 shall be to Me a kingdom of **p**
Ex 19:22 Also let the **p** who come near
Ex 19:24 But do not let the **p** and the
Ex 28:41 they may minister to Me as **p**
Ex 29: 1 for ministering to Me as **p**
Ex 29:44 sons to minister to Me as **p**
Ex 30:30 they may minister to Me as **p**
Ex 31:10 of his sons, to minister as **p**
Ex 35:19 of his sons, to minister as **p**
Ex 39:41 garments, to minister as **p**
Ex 40:15 they may minister to Me as **p**
Lev 1: 5 and the **p**, Aaron's sons, shall
Lev 1: 8 Then the **p**, Aaron's sons,
Lev 1:11 and the **p**, Aaron's sons, shall
Lev 2: 2 it to Aaron's sons, the **p**
Lev 3: 2 and Aaron's sons, the **p**, shall
Lev 6:29 males among the **p** may eat it
Lev 7: 6 male among the **p** may eat it
Lev 7:35 to minister to the LORD as **p**
Lev 13: 2 or to one of his sons the **p**
Lev 16:33 make atonement for the **p** and
Lev 21: 1 Speak to the **p**, the sons of
Num 3: 3 sons of Aaron, the anointed **p**
Num 3: 3 consecrated to minister as **p**
Num 3: 4 Ithamar ministered as **p** under
Num 10: 8 The sons of Aaron, the **p**,
Deut 17: 9 and you shall come to the **p**
Deut 17:18 from the one before the **p**
Deut 18: 1 The **p**, the Levites, indeed
Deut 19:17 before the LORD, before the **p**
Deut 21: 5 Then the **p**, the sons of Levi,
Deut 24: 8 according to all that the **p**
Deut 27: 9 Then Moses and the **p**, the
Deut 31: 9 law and delivered it to the **p**
Josh 3: 3 the LORD your God, and the **p**
Josh 3: 6 Then Joshua spoke to the **p**
Josh 3: 8 You shall command the **p** who
Josh 3:13 the **p** who bear the ark of the
Josh 3:14 with the **p** bearing the ark of
Josh 3:15 the feet of the **p** who bore
Josh 3:17 Then the **p** who bore the ark
Josh 4: 9 the **p** who bore the ark of the
Josh 4:10 So the **p** who bore the ark
Josh 4:11 the **p** crossed over in the
Josh 4:16 Command the **p** who bear the
Josh 4:17 therefore commanded the **p**
Josh 4:18 when the **p** who bore the ark
Josh 6: 4 And seven **p** shall bear seven
Josh 6: 4 the **p** shall blow the trumpets
Josh 6: 6 the son of Nun called the **p**
Josh 6: 6 and let seven **p** bear seven
Josh 6: 8 that the seven **p** bearing the
Josh 6: 9 the **p** who blew the trumpets
Josh 6: 9 while the **p** continued blowing
Josh 6:12 the **p** took up the ark of the
Josh 6:13 Then seven **p** bearing seven
Josh 6:13 while the **p** continued blowing
Josh 6:16 when the **p** blew the trumpets,
Josh 6:20 when the **p** blew the trumpets
Josh 8:33 side of the ark before the **p**
Josh 21:19 the children of Aaron, the **p**
Judg 18:30 his sons were **p** to the tribe
1Sa 1: 3 the **p** of the LORD, were there
1Sa 5: 5 Therefore neither the **p** of
1Sa 6: 2 Philistines called for the **p**
1Sa 22:11 house, the **p** who were in Nob
1Sa 22:17 and kill the **p** of the LORD,
1Sa 22:17 to strike the **p** of the LORD
1Sa 22:18 You turn and kill the **p**
1Sa 22:18 turned and struck the **p**, and
1Sa 22:19 Also Nob, the city of the **p**
1Sa 22:21 Saul had killed the LORD's **p**
2Sa 8:17 son of Abiathar were the **p**
2Sa 15:35 Abiathar the **p** with you there
2Sa 15:35 to Zadok and Abiathar the **p**
2Sa 17:15 to Zadok and Abiathar the **p**
2Sa 19:11 to Zadok and Abiathar the **p**
2Sa 20:25 Zadok and Abiathar were the **p**
1Ki 4: 4 Zadok and Abiathar, the **p**
1Ki 8: 3 and the **p** took up the ark
1Ki 8: 4 The **p** and the Levites brought
1Ki 8: 6 Then the **p** brought in the ark
1Ki 8:10 when the **p** came out of the
1Ki 8:11 so that the **p** could not
1Ki 12:31 made **p** from every class of
1Ki 12:32 at Bethel he installed the **p**
1Ki 13: 2 you he shall sacrifice the **p**
1Ki 13:33 way, but again he made **p** from
1Ki 13:33 of the **p** of the high places
2Ki 10:11 close acquaintances and his **p**
2Ki 10:19 his servants, and all his **p**
2Ki 12: 4 And Jehoash said to the **p**
2Ki 12: 5 let the **p** take it themselves,
2Ki 12: 6 that the **p** had not repaired
2Ki 12: 7 the priest and the other **p**
2Ki 12: 8 the **p** agreed that they would
2Ki 12: 9 the **p** who kept the door put
2Ki 12:16 It belonged to the **p**
2Ki 17:27 Send there one of the **p** whom
2Ki 17:28 Then one of the **p** whom they
2Ki 17:32 **p** of the high places, who
2Ki 19: 2 and the elders of the **p**,
2Ki 23: 2 the **p** and the prophets and all
2Ki 23: 4 the **p** of the second order, and
2Ki 23: 5 he removed the idolatrous **p**
2Ki 23: 8 he brought all the **p** from the
2Ki 23: 8 the **p** had burned incense,
2Ki 23: 9 Nevertheless the **p** of the
2Ki 23:20 He executed all the **p** of the
2Ki 25:14 with which the **p** ministered
1Ch 9: 2 cities were Israelites, **p**
1Ch 9:10 Of the **p**: Jedaiah, Jehoiarib
1Ch 9:30 some of the sons of the **p**
1Ch 13: 2 Israel, and with them to the **p**
1Ch 15:11 for Zadok and Abiathar the **p**
1Ch 15:14 So the **p** and the Levites
1Ch 15:24 Benaiah, and Eliezer, the **p**
1Ch 16: 6 Jahaziel the **p** regularly blew
1Ch 16:39 priest and his brethren the **p**
1Ch 18:16 son of Abiathar were the **p**
1Ch 23: 2 leaders of Israel, with the **p**
1Ch 24: 2 and Ithamar ministered as **p**
1Ch 24: 6 the fathers' houses of the **p**
1Ch 24:31 the fathers' houses of the **p**

Acts 26:10 authority from the chief **p**
Acts 26:12 commission from the chief **p**
Heb 7:21 have become **p** without an oath
Heb 7:23 And there were many **p**,
Heb 7:27 need daily, as those high **p**
Heb 7:28 high **p** men who have weakness
Heb 8: 4 since there are **p** who offer
Heb 9: 6 the **p** always went into the
Rev 1: 6 **p** to His God and Father, to
Rev 5:10 made us kings and **p** to our God
Rev 20: 6 but they shall be **p** of God

PRIESTS' (*see* PRIESTS)
Josh 4: 3 where the **p** feet stood firm
Josh 4:18 and the soles of the **p** feet
1Sa 2:13 the **p** custom with the people
Neh 12:35 certain of the **p** sons with

PRIME
Job 29: 4 as I was in the days of my **p**
Is 38:10 In the **p** of my life I shall

PRIMEVAL
Prov 8:26 or the **p** dust of the world

PRINCE (*see* PRINCELY, PRINCE'S, PRINCES)
Gen 23: 6 You are a mighty **p** among us
Gen 34: 2 **p** of the country, saw her, he
Ex 2:14 Who made you a **p** and a judge
Num 16:13 keep acting like a **p** over us
2Sa 3:38 Do you not know that a **p** and a
Ezra 1: 8 to Sheshbazzar the **p** of Judah
Job 21:28 Where is the house of the **p**
Job 31:37 like a **p** I would approach Him
Prov 14:28 people is the downfall of a **p**
Prov 17: 7 much less lying lips to a **p**
Prov 25: 7 in the presence of the **p**,
Is 9: 6 Father, **P** of Peace
Ezek 7:27 the **p** will be clothed with
Ezek 12:10 concerns the **p** in Jerusalem
Ezek 12:12 the **p** who is among them shall
Ezek 21:25 wicked **p** of Israel, whose day
Ezek 28: 2 of man, say to the **p** of Tyre
Ezek 34:24 servant David a **p** among them
Ezek 37:25 shall be their **p** forever
Ezek 38: 2 the **p** of Rosh, Meshech, and
Ezek 38: 3 the **p** of Rosh, Meshech, and
Ezek 39: 1 **p** of Rosh, Meshech, and Tubal
Ezek 44: 3 **p**, because he is the **p**
Ezek 45: 7 The **p** shall have a portion on
Ezek 45:16 offering for the **p** in Israel
Ezek 45:22 And on that day the **p** shall
Ezek 46: 2 The **p** shall enter by way of
Ezek 46: 4 **p** offers to the LORD on the
Ezek 46: 8 When the **p** enters, he shall
Ezek 46:10 The **p** shall then be in their
Ezek 46:12 Now when the **p** makes a
Ezek 46:16 If the **p** gives a gift of some
Ezek 46:17 it shall return to the **p**
Ezek 46:18 Moreover the **p** shall not take
Ezek 48:21 rest shall belong to the **p**
Ezek 48:21 it shall belong to the **p**
Ezek 48:22 of what belongs to the **p**, the
Ezek 48:22 shall belong to the **p**
Dan 8:11 as high as the **P** of the host
Dan 8:25 rise against the **P** of princes
Dan 9:25 Jerusalem until Messiah the **P**
Dan 9:26 the people of the **p** who is to
Dan 10:13 But the **p** of the kingdom of
Dan 10:20 to fight with the **p** of Persia
Dan 10:20 indeed the **p** of Greece will
Dan 10:21 these, except Michael your **p**
Dan 11:22 also the **p** of the covenant
Dan 12: 1 the great **p** who stands watch
Hos 3: 4 many days without king or **p**
Mic 7: 3 the **p** asks for gifts, the
Acts 3:15 and killed the **P** of life, whom
Acts 5:31 to His right hand to be **P**
Eph 2: 2 according to the **p** of the

PRINCELY (*see* PRINCE)
Mic 5: 5 shepherds and eight **p** men
Zech 11:13 that **p** price they set on me

PRINCE'S (*see* PRINCE)
Song 7: 1 feet in sandals, O **p** daughter
Ezek 45:17 be the **p** part to give burnt

PRINCES (*see* PRINCE)
Gen 12:15 The **p** of Pharaoh also saw her
Gen 17:20 He shall beget twelve **p**, and I
Gen 25:16 twelve **p** according to their
Num 22: 8 So the **p** of Moab stayed
Num 22:13 and said to the **p** of Balak
Num 22:14 the **p** of Moab rose and went to
Num 22:15 Then Balak again sent **p**, more
Num 22:21 and went with the **p** of Moab
Num 22:35 went with the **p** of Balak
Num 22:40 to the **p** who were with him
Num 23: 6 he and all the **p** of Moab
Num 23:17 the **p** of Moab were with him
Josh 13:21 struck with the **p** of Midian
Josh 13:21 who were **p** of Sihon dwelling
Judg 5: 3 Hear, O kings! Give ear, O **p**
Judg 5:15 the **p** of Issachar were with
Judg 7:25 two **p** of the Midianites, Oreb
Judg 8: 3 your hands the **p** of Midian
1Sa 2: 8 ash heap, To set them among **p**
1Sa 18:30 Then the **p** of the Philistines
1Sa 29: 3 Then the **p** of the Philistines
1Sa 29: 3 to the **p** of the Philistines
1Sa 29: 4 But the **p** of the Philistines
1Sa 29: 4 so the **p** of the Philistines
1Sa 29: 9 nevertheless the **p** of the
2Sa 10: 3 Then the **p** of the people of
2Sa 19: 6 regard neither **p** nor servants
2Ki 24:12 mother, his servants, his **p**
1Ch 19: 3 the **p** of the people of Ammon
2Ch 21: 4 others of the **p** of Israel
2Ch 22: 8 Ahab, and found the **p** of Judah
2Ch 32:31 of the **p** of Babylon, whom
Ezra 7:28 all the king's mighty **p**
Ezra 8:25 and his counselors and his **p**
Neh 9:32 upon us, our kings and our **p**
Neh 9:34 Neither our kings nor our **p**
Esth 1: 3 the **p** of the provinces being
Esth 1:14 the seven **p** of Persia and
Esth 1:16 before the king and the **p**
Esth 1:16 the king, but also all the **p**
Esth 1:21 pleased the king and the **p**
Esth 3: 1 all the **p** who were with him
Esth 6: 9 of the king's most noble **p**
Esth 8: 9 the **p** of the provinces from
Job 3:15 or with **p** who had gold, who
Job 12:19 He leads **p** away plundered, and
Job 12:21 He pours contempt on **p**, and
Job 29: 9 the **p** refrained from talking,
Job 34:19 Yet He is not partial to **p**
Ps 45:16 shall make **p** in all the earth
Ps 47: 9 The **p** of the people have
Ps 68:27 The **p** of Judah and their
Ps 68:27 The **p** of Zebulun
Ps 68:27 and the **p** of Naphtali
Ps 76:12 shall cut off the spirit of **p**
Ps 82: 7 And fall like one of the **p**
Ps 83:11 all their **p** like Zebah and
Ps 105:22 To bind his **p** at his pleasure
Ps 107:40 He pours contempt on **p**, And
Ps 113: 8 That He may seat him with **p**
Ps 113: 8 With the **p** of His people
Ps 118: 9 Than to put confidence in **p**
Ps 119:23 **P** also sit and speak against
Ps 119:161 **P** persecute me without a
Ps 146: 3 Do not put your trust in **p**
Ps 148:11 **P** and all judges of the earth
Prov 8:16 By me **p** rule, and nobles, all
Prov 17:26 nor to strike **p** for their
Prov 19:10 for a servant to rule over **p**
Prov 28: 2 of a land, many are its **p**
Prov 31: 4 nor for **p** intoxicating drink
Eccl 10: 7 while **p** walk on the ground
Eccl 10:16 your **p** feast in the morning
Eccl 10:17 your **p** feast at the proper
Is 1:23 Your **p** are rebellious, and
Is 3: 4 give children to be their **p**
Is 3:14 elders of His people and His **p**
Is 10: 8 are not my **p** altogether
Is 19:11 Surely the **p** of Zoan are
Is 19:13 The **p** of Zoan have become
Is 19:13 the **p** of Noph are deceived
Is 21: 5 Arise, you **p**, anoint the
Is 23: 8 city, whose merchants are **p**
Is 30: 4 For his **p** were at Zoan, and
Is 31: 9 his **p** shall be afraid of the
Is 32: 1 and **p** will rule with justice
Is 34:12 all its **p** shall be nothing
Is 40:23 He brings the **p** to nothing
Is 41:25 against **p** as though mortar
Is 43:28 the **p** of the sanctuary
Is 49: 7 **p** also shall worship, because
Jer 1:18 kings of Judah, against its **p**
Jer 2:26 and their kings and their **p**
Jer 4: 9 perish, and the heart of the **p**
Jer 8: 1 Judah, and the bones of its **p**
Jer 17:25 **p** sitting on the throne of
Jer 17:25 and on horses, they and their **p**
Jer 24: 1 and the **p** of Judah with the
Jer 24: 8 the king of Judah, his **p**, the
Jer 25:18 of Judah, its kings and its **p**
Jer 25:19 of Egypt, his servants, his **p**
Jer 26:10 When the **p** of Judah heard
Jer 26:11 the prophets spoke to the **p**
Jer 26:12 Jeremiah spoke to all the **p**
Jer 26:16 So the **p** and all the people
Jer 26:21 his mighty men and all the **p**
Jer 29: 2 the **p** of Judah and Jerusalem,
Jer 32:32 they, their kings, their **p**
Jer 34:10 Now when all the **p** and all the
Jer 34:19 the **p** of Judah
Jer 34:19 the **p** of Jerusalem, the
Jer 34:21 his **p** into the hand of their
Jer 35: 4 was by the chamber of the **p**
Jer 36:12 there all the **p** were sitting
Jer 36:12 son of Hananiah, and all the **p**
Jer 36:14 Therefore all the **p** sent
Jer 36:19 Then the **p** said to Baruch,
Jer 36:21 **p** who stood beside the king
Jer 37:14 and brought him to the **p**
Jer 37:15 Therefore the **p** were angry
Jer 38: 4 Therefore the **p** said to the
Jer 38:17 to the king of Babylon's **p**
Jer 38:18 to the king of Babylon's **p**
Jer 38:22 to the king of Babylon's **p**
Jer 38:25 But if the **p** hear that I have
Jer 38:27 Then all the **p** came to
Jer 39: 3 Then all the **p** of the king of
Jer 39: 3 with the rest of the **p** of the
Jer 44:17 fathers, our kings and our **p**
Jer 44:21 fathers, your kings and your **p**
Jer 48: 7 his priests and his **p** together
Jer 49: 3 his priests and his **p** together
Jer 49:38 from there the king and the **p**
Jer 50:35 of Babylon, and against her **p**
Jer 51:57 And I will make drunk her **p**
Jer 52:10 he killed all the **p** of Judah
Lam 1: 6 Her **p** have become like deer
Lam 2: 2 profaned the kingdom and its **p**
Lam 2: 9 her **p** are among the nations
Lam 5:12 **P** were hung up by their hands
Ezek 11: 1 of Benaiah, **p** of the people
Ezek 17:12 and took its king and **p**, and led
Ezek 19: 1 for the **p** of Israel,
Ezek 21:12 against all the **p** of Israel
Ezek 22: 6 Look, the **p** of Israel
Ezek 22:27 Her **p** in her midst are like
Ezek 26:16 Then all the **p** of the sea
Ezek 27:21 all the **p** of Kedar were your
Ezek 30:13 be **p** from the land of Egypt
Ezek 32:29 Edom, her kings and all her **p**
Ezek 32:30 There are the **p** of the north
Ezek 39:18 blood of the **p** of the earth
Ezek 45: 8 My **p** shall no more oppress My
Ezek 45: 9 Enough, O **p** of Israel
Dan 8:25 rise against the Prince of **p**
Dan 9: 6 name to our kings and our **p**
Dan 9: 8 of face, to our kings, our **p**
Dan 10:13 Michael, one of the chief **p**
Dan 11: 5 as well as one of his **p**
Dan 11: 8 to Egypt, with their **p** and
Hos 5:10 The **p** of Judah are like those
Hos 7: 3 and **p** with their lies
Hos 7: 5 our king **p** have made him sick
Hos 7:16 their **p** shall fall by the
Hos 8: 4 they made **p**, and I did not
Hos 8:10 the burden of the king of **p**
Hos 9:15 All their **p** are rebellious
Hos 13:10 said, 'Give me a king and **p**'
Amos 1:15 his **p** together," says the
Amos 2: 3 and slay all its **p** with him
Hab 1:10 and **p** are scorned by them
Zeph 1: 8 that I will punish the **p**
Zeph 3: 3 Her **p** in her midst are

PRINCESS (*see* PRINCESSES)
Lam 1: 1 The **p** among the provinces has

PRINCESSES (*see* PRINCESS)
1Ki 11: 3 he had seven hundred wives, **p**

PRINCIPAL (*see* PRINCIPALITY)
Gen 10:12 and Calah (that is the **p** city)
2Ki 25:19 the **p** scribe of the army who
Prov 4: 7 Wisdom is the **p** thing
Jer 52:25 the **p** scribe of the army who

PRINCIPALITIES (*see* PRINCIPALITY)
Rom 8:38 nor angels nor **p** nor powers
Eph 3:10 known by the church to the **p**
Eph 6:12 flesh and blood, but against **p**
Col 1:16 or dominions or **p** or powers
Col 2:15 Having disarmed **p** and powers,

PRINCIPALITY (*see* PRINCIPAL, PRINCIPALITIES)
Eph 1:21 far above all **p** and power and
Col 2:10 Him, who is the head of all **p**

PRINCIPLES
Col 2: 8 to the basic **p** of the world
Col 2:20 from the basic **p** of the world
Heb 5:12 first **p** of the oracles of God
Heb 6: 1 of the elementary **p** of Christ

PRINT
John 20:25 His hands the **p** of the nails
John 20:25 into the **p** of the nails, and

PRISCA (*see* PRISCILLA)
2Ti 4:19 Greet **P** and Aquila, and the

PRISCILLA (*see* PRISCA)
Acts 18: 2 wife **P** (because Claudius had
Acts 18:18 and sailed for Syria, and **P**
Acts 18:26 **P** heard him, they took him
Rom 16: 3 Greet **P** and Aquila, my fellow
1Co 16:19 **P** greet you heartily in the

PRISON (*see* PRISONER, PRISONS)
Gen 39:20 him and put him into the **p**
Gen 39:20 And he was there in the **p**
Gen 39:21 sight of the keeper of the **p**
Gen 39:22 the keeper of the **p** committed
Gen 39:22 prisoners who were in the **p**
Gen 39:23 The keeper of the **p** did not
Gen 40: 3 of the guard, in the **p**, the
Gen 40: 5 who were confined in the **p**
Gen 42:16 and you shall be kept in **p**
Gen 42:17 all together in **p** three days
Gen 42:19 be confined to your **p** house
Judg 16:21 he became a grinder in the **p**
Judg 16:25 called for Samson from the **p**
1Ki 22:27 Put this fellow in **p**, and feed
2Ki 17: 4 him up, and bound him in **p**
2Ki 23:33 in **p** at Riblah in the land of
2Ki 25:27 king of Judah from **p**
2Ki 25:29 changed from his **p** garments
2Ch 16:10 the seer, and put him in **p**
2Ch 18:26 Put this fellow in **p**, and feed
Neh 3:25 was by the court of the **p**
Neh 12:39 stopped by the Gate of the **P**
Ps 142: 7 Bring my soul out of **p**, That
Eccl 4:14 he comes out of **p** to be king
Is 24:22 and will be shut up in the **p**
Is 42: 7 out prisoners from the **p**,
Is 42: 7 in darkness from the **p** house
Is 42:22 they are hidden in **p** houses
Is 53: 8 He was taken from **p** and from
Is 61: 1 the opening of the **p** to those
Jer 29:26 that you should put him in **p**
Jer 32: 2 shut up in the court of the **p**
Jer 32: 8 **p** according to the word of
Jer 32:12 who sat in the court of the **p**
Jer 33: 1 shut up in the court of the **p**
Jer 37: 4 they had not yet put him in **p**
Jer 37:15 put him in **p** in the house of
Jer 37:15 For they had made that the **p**
Jer 37:18 that you have put me in **p**
Jer 37:21 to the court of the **p**, and
Jer 37:21 in the court of the **p**
Jer 38: 6 was in the court of the **p**
Jer 38:13 in the court of the **p**
Jer 38:28 of the **p** until the day that
Jer 39:14 from the court of the **p**, and
Jer 39:15 shut up in the court of the **p**
Jer 52:11 put him in **p** till the day of
Jer 52:31 Judah and brought him out of **p**
Jer 52:33 changed from his **p** garments
Matt 4:12 that John had been put in **p**
Matt 5:25 and you are thrown into **p**
Matt 11: 2 And when John had heard in **p**
Matt 14: 3 put him in **p** for the sake of
Matt 14:10 and had John beheaded in **p**
Matt 18:30 and threw him into **p** till he
Matt 25:36 I was in **p** and you came to Me
Matt 25:39 did we see You sick, or in **p**
Matt 25:43 not clothe Me, sick and in **p**
Matt 25:44 or naked or sick or in **p**, and
Mark 1:14 Now after John was put in **p**
Mark 6:17 bound him in **p** for the sake
Mark 6:27 he went and beheaded him in **p**
Luke 3:20 that he shut John up in **p**
Luke 12:58 the officer throw you into **p**
Luke 22:33 to go with You, both to **p**
Luke 23:19 who had been thrown into **p**
Luke 23:25 murder had been thrown into **p**
John 3:24 not yet been thrown into **p**
Acts 5:18 and put them in the common **p**
Acts 5:19 the Lord opened the **p** doors
Acts 5:21 sent to the **p** to have them
Acts 5:22 and did not find them in the **p**
Acts 5:23 we found the **p** shut securely
Acts 5:25 the men whom you put in **p** are
Acts 8: 3 women, committing them to **p**
Acts 12: 4 him, he put him in **p**, and
Acts 12: 5 Peter was therefore kept in **p**
Acts 12: 6 the door were keeping the **p**
Acts 12: 7 and a light shone in the **p**
Acts 12:17 had brought him out of the **p**
Acts 16:23 them, they threw them into **p**
Acts 16:24 he put them into the inner **p**
Acts 16:26 of the **p** were shaken
Acts 16:27 And the keeper of the **p**,
Acts 16:27 and seeing the **p** doors open
Acts 16:36 So the keeper of the **p**
Acts 16:37 and have thrown us into **p**
Acts 16:40 So they went out of the **p**
Acts 26:10 of the saints I shut up in **p**
1Pe 3:19 preached to the spirits in **p**
Rev 2:10 to throw some of you into **p**
Rev 18: 2 a **p** for every foul spirit, and
Rev 20: 7 will be released from his **p**

PRISONER (*see* PRISON, PRISONERS)
2Ki 24:12 year of his reign, took him **p**
Ps 79:11 of the **p** come before You
Ps 102:20 To hear the groaning of the **p**
Matt 27:15 one **p** whom they wished
Matt 27:16 a notorious **p** called Barabbas
Mark 15: 6 to releasing one **p** to them
Acts 23:18 Paul the **p** called me to him
Acts 25:14 certain man left a **p** by Felix
Acts 25:27 me unreasonable to send a **p**
Acts 28:17 a **p** from Jerusalem into the
Eph 3: 1 the **p** of Jesus Christ for you
Eph 4: 1 the **p** of the Lord, beseech
Col 4:10 my fellow **p** greets you, with
2Ti 1: 8 of our Lord, nor of me His **p**
Phm 1 Paul, a **p** of Christ Jesus, and
Phm 9 now also a **p** of Jesus Christ
Phm 23 my fellow **p** in Christ Jesus,

PRISONERS (*see* PRISONER)
Gen 39:20 the king's **p** were confined
Gen 39:22 the **p** who were in the prison
Num 21: 1 Israel and took some of them **p**
Job 3:18 There the **p** rest together
Ps 69:33 And does not despise His **p**
Ps 146: 7 LORD gives freedom to the **p**
Is 10: 4 shall bow down among the **p**
Is 14:17 not open the house of his **p**
Is 20: 4 lead away the Egyptians as **p**
Is 24:22 as **p** are gathered in the pit,
Is 42: 7 eyes, to bring out **p** from the
Is 49: 9 that You may say to the **p**
Lam 3:34 feet all the **p** of the earth
Zech 9:11 I will set your **p** free from
Zech 9:12 the stronghold, you **p** of hope
Acts 16:25 the **p** were listening to them
Acts 16:27 supposing the **p** had fled
Acts 27: 1 some other **p** to one named
Acts 27:42 plan was to kill the **p**, lest
Acts 28:16 **p** to the captain of the guard
Rom 16: 7 my kinsmen and my fellow **p**
Heb 13: 3 Remember the **p** as if chained

PRISONS (*see* PRISON)
Luke 21:12 you up to the synagogues and **p**
Acts 22: 4 and delivering into **p** both men
2Co 11:23 in **p** more frequently, in

PRIVATE (*see* PRIVATELY)
Judg 3:20 in his cool **p** chamber)
Ezek 21:14 that enters their **p** chambers
2Pe 1:20 is of any **p** interpretation

PRIVATELY (*see* PRIVATE)
2Sa 3:27 the gate to speak with him **p**
Matt 17:19 the disciples came to Jesus **p**
Matt 24: 3 the disciples came to Him **p**
Mark 9:28 His disciples asked Him **p**
Mark 13: 3 John, and Andrew asked Him **p**
Luke 9:10 went aside **p** into a deserted
Luke 10:23 to His disciples and said **p**
Acts 23:19 went aside and asked him **p**
Gal 2: 2 but **p** to those who were of

PRIZE (*see* PRIZED)
Jer 21: 9 life shall be as a **p** to him
Jer 38: 2 life shall be as a **p** to him
Jer 39:18 life shall be as a **p** to you
Jer 45: 5 to you as a **p** in all places
Hos 13:15 treasury of every desirable **p**
Nah 2: 9 wealth of every desirable **p**
1Co 9:24 run, but one receives the **p**
1Co 9:25 who competes for the **p** is
Phil 3:14 toward the goal for the **p** of

PRIZED (*see* PRIZE)
Joel 3: 5 your temples My **p** possessions

PROBABLY
Judg 3:24 He is **p** attending to his
Luke 20:13 **P** they will respect him when

PROBLEMS
Deut 1:12 How can I alone bear your **p**

PROCEED (*see* PROCEEDED, PROCEEDING, PROCEEDS)
Gen 35:11 of nations shall **p** from you
Num 34: 9 the border shall **p** to Ziphron
Josh 6: 7 **P**, and march around the city,
Josh 6:10 any word **p** out of your mouth
Job 40: 5 but I will **p** no further
Is 22:15 **p** to this steward, to Shebna,
Is 51: 4 for law will **p** from Me, and I
Jer 9: 3 For they **p** from evil to evil,
Jer 30:19 of them shall **p** thanksgiving
Lam 3:38 High that woe and well-being **p**
Hab 1: 7 and their dignity **p** from
Matt 15:18 But those things which **p** out
Matt 15:19 of the heart **p** evil thoughts
Mark 7:21 **p** evil thoughts, adulteries,
Acts 27: 7 wind not permitting us to **p**
Eph 4:29 **p** out of your mouth, but what
Jas 3:10 of the same mouth **p** blessing

PROCEEDED (*see* PROCEED)
Num 30:12 then whatever **p** from her lips
Num 32:24 do what has **p** out of your
Job 36: 1 Elihu also **p** and said
Luke 4:22 which **p** out of His mouth
John 8:42 would love Me, for I **p** forth
Acts 12: 3 he **p** further to seize Peter
Rev 4: 5 from the throne **p** lightnings
Rev 19:21 **p** from the mouth of Him who

PROCEEDING (*see* PROCEED, PROCEEDINGS)
Eccl 10: 5 as an error **p** from the ruler
Rev 22: 1 **p** from the throne of God and

PROCEEDINGS (*see* PROCEEDING)
Acts 24:22 the Way, he adjourned the **p**

PROCEEDS (*see* PROCEED)
Num 30: 2 all that **p** out of his mouth
Deut 8: 3 lives by every word that **p**
1Sa 24:13 Wickedness **p** from the wicked
2Ki 8: 6 all the **p** of the field from
Job 20:18 from the **p** of his business he
Prov 3:14 for her **p** are better than the
Hab 1: 4 therefore perverse judgment **p**
Matt 4: 4 that **p** from the mouth of God
John 15:26 truth who **p** from the Father
Acts 4:34 brought the **p** of the things
Acts 5: 2 And he kept back part of the **p**
Rev 11: 5 fire **p** from their mouth and

PROCESS
Gen 4: 3 in the **p** of time it came to
Gen 38:12 Now in the **p** of time the
Ex 2:23 Now it happened in the **p** of
1Sa 1:20 in the **p** of time that Hannah

PROCESSION
Ps 68:24 They have seen Your **p**, O God,
Ps 68:24 The **p** of my God, my King,
Is 60:11 Gentiles, and their kings in **p**

PROCHORUS
Acts 6: 5 the Holy Spirit, and Philip, **P**

PROCLAIM (*see* PROCLAIMED, PROCLAIMER, PROCLAIMING, PROCLAIMS, PROCLAMATION)
Ex 33:19 I will **p** the name of the LORD
Lev 23: 2 which you shall **p** to be holy
Lev 23: 4 which you shall **p** at their
Lev 23:21 you shall **p** on the same day

Lev 23:37 **p** to be holy convocations
Lev 25:10 **p** liberty throughout all the
Deut 20:10 then **p** an offer of peace to
Deut 32: 3 For I **p** the name of the LORD
Judg 7: 3 **p** in the hearing of the
1Sa 31: 9 to **p** it in the temple of
2Sa 1:20 **p** it not in the streets of
1Ki 21: 9 **P** a fast, and seat Naboth with
2Ki 10:20 **P** a solemn assembly for Baal
1Ch 10: 9 **p** the news in the temple of
1Ch 16:23 **p** the good news of His
Neh 6: 7 also appointed prophets to **p**
Neh 8:15 **p** in all their cities and in
Esth 6: 9 city square, and **p** before him
Ps 26: 7 That I may **p** with the voice
Ps 96: 2 **P** the good news of His
Prov 20: 6 Most men will **p** each his own
Is 44: 7 And who can **p** as I do
Is 48:20 **p** this, utter it even to the
Is 60: 6 they shall **p** the praises of
Is 61: 1 to **p** liberty to the captives,
Is 61: 2 to **p** the acceptable year of
Jer 3:12 and **p** these words toward the
Jer 4: 5 and **p** in Jerusalem, and say
Jer 4:16 **p** against Jerusalem, that
Jer 5:20 and **p** it in Judah, saying,
Jer 7: 2 **p** there this word, and say
Jer 11: 6 **P** all these words in the
Jer 19: 2 **p** there the words that I will
Jer 31: 7 **p**, give praise, and say, 'O
Jer 34: 8 to **p** liberty to them
Jer 34:17 I **p** liberty to you,' says the
Jer 46:14 in Egypt, and **p** in Migdol
Jer 46:14 **P** in Noph and in Tahpanhes
Jer 50: 2 Declare among the nations, **P**
Jer 50: 2 **p**, and do not conceal it
Joel 3: 9 **P** this among the nations
Amos 3: 9 **P** in the palaces at Ashdod,
Amos 4: 5 thanksgiving with leaven, **p**
Zech 1:14 **P**, saying, 'Thus says the
Zech 1:17 Again **p**, saying, 'Thus says
Mark 1:45 began to **p** it freely, and to
Mark 5:20 began to **p** in Decapolis all
Acts 16:17 God, who **p** to us the way of
Acts 17:23 knowing, Him I **p** to you
Acts 26:23 would **p** light to the Jewish
1Co 11:26 you **p** the Lord's death till
1Pe 2: 9 that you may **p** the praises of

PROCLAIMED (*see* PROCLAIM)
Ex 34: 5 and **p** the name of the LORD
Ex 34: 6 LORD passed before him and **p**
Ex 36: 6 to be **p** throughout the camp
Deut 26:17 Today you have **p** the LORD to
Deut 26:18 has **p** you to be His special
1Ki 21:12 They **p** a fast, and seated
2Ki 10:20 So they **p** it
2Ki 23:16 man of God **p**, who **p** these
2Ki 23:17 **p** these things which you have
1Ch 13: 6 cherubim, where His name is **p**
2Ch 20: 3 **p** a fast throughout all Judah
Ezra 8:21 Then I **p** a fast there at the
Esth 1:20 which he will make is **p**
Esth 2:18 and he **p** a holiday in the
Esth 3:15 the decree was **p** in Shushan
Esth 6:11 city square, and **p** before him,
Ps 40: 9 I have **p** the good news of
Ps 68:11 the company of those who **p** it
Is 43:12 declared and saved, I have **p**
Is 48: 5 it came to pass I **p** it to you
Is 62:11 Indeed the LORD has **p** to the
Jer 36: 9 that they **p** a fast before the
Jer 36:18 He **p** with his mouth all these
Jon 3: 5 **p** a fast, and put on sackcloth
Jon 3: 7 And he caused it to be **p** and
Zech 7: 7 the words which the LORD **p**
Zech 7:13 happened, that just as He **p**
Mark 7:36 the more widely they **p** it
Luke 8:39 **p** throughout the whole city
Luke 12: 3 will be **p** on the housetops
Acts 10:37 which was **p** throughout all
Acts 20:20 but **p** it to you, and taught

PROCLAIMER (*see* PROCLAIM)
Acts 17:18 to be a **p** of foreign gods

PROCLAIMING (*see* PROCLAIM)
Jer 34:15 every man **p** liberty to his
Jer 34:17 not obeyed Me in **p** liberty
Rev 5: 2 angel **p** with a loud voice

PROCLAIMS (*see* PROCLAIM)
Prov 12:23 heart of fools **p** foolishness
Is 52: 7 who **p** peace, who brings glad
Is 52: 7 who **p** salvation, who says to
Jer 4:15 and **p** affliction from Mount
Nah 1:15 good tidings, who **p** peace

PROCLAMATION (*see* PROCLAIM)
Ex 32: 5 And Aaron made a **p** and said
1Ki 15:22 made a **p** throughout all Judah
2Ch 24: 9 And they made a **p** throughout
2Ch 30: 5 a **p** throughout all Israel
2Ch 36:22 Persia, so that he made a **p**
Ezra 1: 1 Persia, so that he made a **p**
Ezra 10: 7 they issued a **p** throughout
Dan 5:29 made a **p** concerning him that

PROCONSUL (*see* PROCONSULS)
Acts 13: 7 who was with the **p**, Sergius
Acts 13: 8 the **p** away from the faith
Acts 13:12 Then the **p** believed, when he
Acts 18:12 when Gallio was **p** of Achaia

PROCONSULS (*see* PROCONSUL)
Acts 19:38 are open and there are **p**

PROCURED
Jer 4:18 and your doings have **p** these

PRODIGAL
Luke 15:13 his possessions with **p** living

PRODUCE (*see* PRODUCED, PRODUCES, PRODUCING)
Gen 41:34 **p** of the land of Egypt in the
Ex 22:29 the first of your ripe **p** and
Ex 23:10 your land and gather in its **p**
Lev 25: 6 the sabbath **p** of the land
Lev 25: 7 all its **p** shall be for food
Lev 25:12 eat its **p** from the field
Lev 25:20 not sow nor gather in our **p**
Lev 25:21 it will bring forth **p** enough
Lev 25:22 eat old **p** until the ninth
Lev 25:22 until its **p** comes in, you
Lev 26: 4 the land shall yield its **p**
Lev 26:20 land shall not yield its **p**
Num 18:30 to the Levites as the **p** of
Num 18:30 as the **p** of the winepress
Deut 11:17 rain, and the land yield no **p**
Deut 14:28 tithe of your **p** of that year
Deut 16:15 will bless you in all your **p**
Deut 26: 2 of all the **p** of the ground
Deut 28: 4 the **p** of your ground and the
Deut 28:11 in the **p** of your ground, in
Deut 28:18 and the **p** of your land, the
Deut 28:33 the **p** of your labor, and you
Deut 28:42 trees and the **p** of your land
Deut 28:51 the **p** of your land, until you
Deut 30: 9 in the **p** of your land for
Deut 32:13 might eat the **p** of the fields
Deut 33:14 the precious **p** of the months
Josh 5:11 they ate of the **p** of the land
Josh 5:12 had eaten the **p** of the land
Judg 6: 4 destroy the **p** of the earth as
1Ch 27:27 **p** of the vineyards for the
2Ch 31: 5 of all the **p** of the field
Neh 10:31 forego the seventh year's **p**
Ps 144:13 Supplying all kinds of **p**
Prov 18:20 from the **p** of his lips he
Jer 20: 5 of this city, all its **p**, and
Ezek 48:18 its **p** shall be food for the
Hos 8: 7 it shall never **p** meal
Hos 8: 7 If it should **p**, aliens would
Jas 1:20 **p** the righteousness of God

PRODUCED (*see* PRODUCE)
Num 6: 4 that is **p** by the grapevine
Num 17: 8 had **p** blossoms and yielded
Matt 13:26 **p** a crop, then the tares also
Mark 4: 8 sprang up, increased and **p**
Rom 7: 8 **p** in me all manner of evil
2Co 7:11 What diligence it **p** in you
Jas 5:18 and the earth **p** its fruit

PRODUCES (*see* PRODUCE)
Deut 14:22 that the field **p** year by year
Prov 30:33 the churning of milk **p** butter
Prov 30:33 as wringing the nose **p** blood
Prov 30:33 the forcing of wrath **p** strife
Matt 13:23 who indeed bears fruit and **p**
John 12:24 if it dies, it **p** much grain
Rom 5: 3 tribulation **p** perseverance
2Co 7:10 For godly sorrow **p** repentance
2Co 7:10 sorrow of the world **p** death

Jas 1: 3 of your faith **p** patience

PRODUCING (*see* PRODUCE)
Rom 7:13 was **p** death in me through

PROFANE (*see* PROFANED, PROFANENESS, PROFANES, PROFANING)
Lev 10: 1 offered **p** fire before the
Lev 16: 1 when they offered **p** fire
Lev 18:21 nor shall you **p** the name of
Lev 19:12 nor shall you **p** the name of
Lev 20: 3 sanctuary and **p** My holy name
Lev 21: 4 his people, to **p** himself
Lev 21: 6 not **p** the name of their God,
Lev 21:12 nor **p** the sanctuary of his
Lev 21:15 Nor shall he **p** his posterity
Lev 21:23 lest he **p** My sanctuaries
Lev 22: 2 that they do not **p** My holy
Lev 22: 9 and die thereby, if they **p** it
Lev 22:15 They shall not **p** the holy
Lev 22:32 You shall not **p** My holy name
Num 3: 4 the LORD when they offered **p**
Num 18:32 But you shall not **p** the holy
Num 26:61 **p** fire before the LORD
Neh 13:17 by which you **p** the Sabbath
Prov 30: 9 and **p** the name of my God
Is 43:28 Therefore I will **p** the
Jer 23:11 both prophet and priest are **p**
Ezek 13:19 will you **p** Me among My people
Ezek 20:39 but **p** My holy name no more
Ezek 21:25 Now to you, O **p**, wicked
Ezek 23:39 into My sanctuary to **p** it
Ezek 24:21 I will **p** My sanctuary, your
Ezek 28:16 a **p** thing out of the mountain
Ezek 39: 7 I will not let them **p** My holy
Mal 1:12 But you **p** it, in that you say
Matt 12: 5 in the temple **p** the Sabbath
Acts 24: 6 He even tried to **p** the temple
1Ti 1: 9 sinners, for the unholy and **p**
1Ti 4: 7 But reject **p** and old wives'
1Ti 6:20 to your trust, avoiding the **p**
2Ti 2:16 But shun **p** and vain babblings,
Heb 12:16 or **p** person like Esau, who

PROFANED (*see* PROFANE)
Ex 20:25 tool on it, you have **p** it
Lev 19: 8 because he has **p** the hallowed
Ps 89:39 You have **p** his crown by
Is 47: 6 I have **p** My inheritance, and
Is 48:11 for how should My name be **p**
Jer 34:16 **p** My name, and every one of
Lam 2: 2 He has **p** the kingdom and its
Ezek 14:11 nor be **p** anymore with all
Ezek 20: 9 sake, that it should not be **p**
Ezek 20:14 not be **p** before the Gentiles
Ezek 20:16 statutes, but **p** My Sabbaths
Ezek 20:21 but they **p** My Sabbaths
Ezek 20:22 not be **p** in the sight of the
Ezek 20:24 **p** My Sabbaths, and their eyes
Ezek 22: 8 holy things and **p** My Sabbaths
Ezek 22:26 My law and **p** My holy things
Ezek 22:26 so that I am **p** among them
Ezek 23:38 the same day and **p** My Sabbaths
Ezek 25: 3 My sanctuary when it was **p**
Ezek 36:20 went, they **p** My holy name
Ezek 36:21 the house of Israel had **p**
Ezek 36:22 which you have **p** among the
Ezek 36:23 which has been **p** among the
Ezek 36:23 you have **p** in their midst
Mal 2:11 for Judah has **p** the LORD's

PROFANENESS (*see* PROFANE)
Jer 23:15 **p** has gone out into all the

PROFANES (*see* PROFANE)
Ex 31:14 Everyone who **p** it shall
Lev 21: 9 if she **p** herself by playing
Lev 21: 9 the harlot, she **p** her father

PROFANING (*see* PROFANE)
Neh 13:18 on Israel by **p** the Sabbath
Mal 2:10 with one another by **p** the

PROFESS (*see* PROFESSING)
Tit 1:16 They **p** to know God, but in

PROFESSING (*see* PROFESS)
Rom 1:22 **P** to be wise, they became
1Ti 2:10 proper for women **p** godliness
1Ti 6:21 by **p** it, some have strayed

PROFIT (*see* PROFITABLE, PROFITED, PROFITS)
Gen 25:32 so what **p** shall this
Gen 37:26 What **p** is there if we kill
Lev 25:37 nor lend him your food at a **p**

1Sa 12:21 which cannot **p** or deliver
Job 21:15 what **p** do we have if we pray
Job 30: 2 what **p** is the strength of
Job 33:27 was right, and it did not **p** me
Job 35: 3 What **p** shall I have, more
Ps 30: 9 What **p** is there in my blood,
Prov 10: 2 of wickedness **p** nothing, but
Prov 11: 4 Riches do not **p** in the day of
Prov 14:23 In all labor there is **p**, but
Eccl 1: 3 What **p** has a man from all his
Eccl 2:11 there was no **p** under the sun
Eccl 3: 9 What **p** has the worker from
Eccl 5: 9 Moreover the **p** of the land is
Eccl 5:11 So what **p** have the owners
Eccl 5:16 what **p** has he who has labored
Is 44: 9 precious things shall not **p**
Is 47:12 perhaps you will be able to **p**
Is 48:17 God, Who teaches you to **p**
Is 57:12 for they will not **p** you
Jer 2: 8 after things that do not **p**
Jer 2:11 Glory for what does not **p**
Jer 7: 8 in lying words that cannot **p**
Jer 12:13 to pain but do not **p**
Jer 23:32 not **p** this people at all,"
Ezek 22:12 you have made **p** from your
Ezek 22:13 **p** which you have made, and at
Hab 2:18 What **p** is the image, that its
Mal 3:14 what **p** is it that we have
Matt 15: 5 Whatever **p** you might have
Mark 7:11 Whatever **p** you might have
Mark 8:36 For what will it **p** a man if
Acts 16:16 much **p** by fortune-telling
Acts 16:19 that their hope of **p** was gone
Acts 19:24 no small **p** to the craftsmen
Rom 3: 1 the Jew, or what is the **p** of
1Co 7:35 And this I say for your own **p**
1Co 10:33 my own **p**, but the **p** of many
1Co 12: 7 to each one for the **p** of all
1Co 14: 6 what shall I **p** you unless I
Gal 5: 2 Christ will **p** you nothing
2Ti 2:14 to strive about words to no **p**
Heb 4: 2 they heard did not **p** them
Heb 12:10 to them, but He for our **p**
Jas 2:14 What does it **p**, my brethren,
Jas 2:16 for the body, what does it **p**
Jas 4:13 buy and sell, and make a **p**"
Jude 11 in the error of Balaam for **p**

PROFITABLE (*see* PROFIT, UNPROFITABLE)
Job 22: 2 Can a man be **p** to God, though
Job 22: 2 is wise may be **p** to himself
Eccl 7:11 **p** to those who see the sun
Jer 13: 7 It was **p** for nothing
Jer 13:10 sash which is **p** for nothing
Matt 5:29 for it is more **p** for you that
Matt 5:30 for it is more **p** for you that
Rom 2:25 indeed **p** if you keep the law
2Co 12: 1 not **p** for me to boast
1Ti 4: 8 godliness is **p** for all things
2Ti 3:16 and is **p** for doctrine, for
Tit 3: 8 things are good and **p** to men
Phm 11 to you, but now is **p** to you

PROFITED (*see* PROFIT)
Matt 16:26 For what is a man **p** if he
Heb 13: 9 not **p** those who have been

PROFITS (*see* PROFIT)
Job 34: 9 It **p** a man nothing that he
Prov 3:14 better than the **p** of silver
Prov 31:16 from her **p** she plants a
Is 44:10 image that **p** him nothing
John 6:63 the flesh **p** nothing
1Co 13: 3 not love, it **p** me nothing
1Ti 4: 8 bodily exercise **p** a little

PROFOUND
Ps 131: 1 Nor with things too **p** for me

PROGNOSTICATORS
Is 47:13 and the monthly **p** stand up

PROGRESS
Phil 1:25 with you all for your **p** and
1Ti 4:15 that your **p** may be evident to
2Ti 3: 9 but they will **p** no further

PROJECTING (*see* PROJECTS)
Neh 3:26 the east, and on the **p** tower
Neh 3:27 next to the great **p** tower

PROJECTS (*see* PROJECTING)
Neh 3:25 on the tower which **p** from the

PROLONG (*see* PROLONGED, PROLONGS)
Deut 4:26 you will not **p** your days in
Deut 4:40 that you may **p** your days in
Deut 5:33 that you may **p** your days in
Deut 11: 9 that you may **p** your days in
Deut 17:20 that he may **p** his days in his
Deut 22: 7 and that you may **p** your days
Deut 30:18 you shall not **p** your days in
Deut 32:47 by this word you shall **p** your
Job 6:11 end, that I should **p** my life
Ps 61: 6 You will **p** the king's life,
Ps 85: 5 Will You **p** Your anger to all
Prov 28:16 covetousness will **p** his days
Eccl 8:13 nor will he **p** his days, which
Is 53:10 His seed, He shall **p** His days

PROLONGED (*see* PROLONG)
Deut 6: 2 and that your days may be **p**
Deut 28:59 great and **p** plagues
Deut 28:59 and serious and **p** sicknesses
Prov 28: 2 and knowledge right will be **p**
Eccl 8:12 times, and his days are **p**, yet
Is 13:22 and her days will not be **p**
Ezek 12:22 which says, 'The days are **p**
Dan 7:12 lives were **p** for a season

PROLONGS (*see* PROLONG)
Prov 10:27 The fear of the LORD **p** days
Eccl 7:15 there is a wicked man who **p**

PROMINENT
1Ki 1:42 Come in, for you are a **p** man
2Ki 25:28 gave him a more **p** seat than
Esth 9: 4 became increasingly **p**
Jer 52:32 gave him a more **p** seat than
Ezek 17:22 it on a high and **p** mountain
Dan 11:41 and the **p** people of Ammon
Mark 15:43 a **p** council member, who was
Acts 13:50 **p** women and the chief men of
Acts 17:12 **p** women as well as men
Acts 25:23 the **p** men of the city, at

PROMISE (*see* PROMISED, PROMISES)
1Ki 8:56 one word of all His good **p**
2Ch 1: 9 let Your **p** to David my father
Ezra 10:19 they gave their **p** that they
Neh 5:12 would do according to this **p**
Neh 5:13 who does not perform this **p**
Neh 5:13 did according to this **p**
Ps 77: 8 Has His **p** failed forevermore
Ps 105:42 For He remembered His holy **p**
Luke 24:49 I send the **P** of My Father
Acts 1: 4 wait for the **P** of the Father
Acts 2:33 the **p** of the Holy Spirit, He
Acts 2:39 For the **p** is to you and to
Acts 7:17 the **p** drew near which God had
Acts 13:23 seed, according to the **p**, God
Acts 13:32 that **p** which was made to the
Acts 23:21 waiting for the **p** from you
Acts 26: 6 **p** made by God to our fathers
Acts 26: 7 To this **p** our twelve tribes,
Rom 4:13 For the **p** that he would be
Rom 4:14 and the **p** made of no effect,
Rom 4:16 so that the **p** might be sure
Rom 4:20 the **p** of God through unbelief
Rom 9: 8 the **p** are counted as the seed
Rom 9: 9 For this is the word of **p**
Gal 3:14 that we might receive the **p**
Gal 3:17 make the **p** of no effect
Gal 3:18 the law, it is no longer of **p**
Gal 3:18 God gave it to Abraham by **p**
Gal 3:19 come to whom the **p** was made
Gal 3:22 that the **p** by faith in Jesus
Gal 3:29 and heirs according to the **p**
Gal 4:23 he of the freewoman through **p**
Gal 4:28 Isaac was, are children of **p**
Eph 1:13 with the Holy Spirit of **p**
Eph 2:12 from the covenants of **p**,
Eph 3: 6 partakers of His **p** in Christ
Eph 6: 2 the first commandment with **p**
1Ti 4: 8 having **p** of the life that now
2Ti 1: 1 according to the **p** of life
Heb 4: 1 since a **p** remains of entering
Heb 6:13 when God made a **p** to Abraham
Heb 6:15 endured, he obtained the **p**
Heb 6:17 of **p** the immutability of His
Heb 9:15 **p** of the eternal inheritance
Heb 10:36 of God, you may receive the **p**
Heb 11: 9 of **p** as in a foreign country
Heb 11: 9 heirs with him of the same **p**
Heb 11:39 faith, did not receive the **p**
2Pe 2:19 While they **p** them liberty,
2Pe 3: 4 Where is the **p** of His coming
2Pe 3: 9 is not slack concerning His **p**
2Pe 3:13 we, according to His **p**, look
1Jn 2:25 this is the **p** that He has

PROMISED (*see* PROMISE)
Ex 12:25 will give you, just as He **p**
Num 10:29 for the LORD has **p** good
Num 14:40 place which the LORD has **p**
Deut 1:11 and bless you as He has **p** you
Deut 6: 3 God of your fathers has **p** you
Deut 9:28 to the land which He **p** them
Deut 10: 9 as the LORD your God **p** him
Deut 12:20 your border as He has **p** you
Deut 15: 6 bless you just as He **p** you
Deut 19: 8 He **p** to give to your fathers
Deut 23:23 you have **p** with your mouth
Deut 26:18 people, just as He has **p** you
Deut 27: 3 God of your fathers has **p** you
Josh 9:21 as the rulers had **p** them
Josh 22: 4 your brethren, as He **p** them
Josh 23: 5 the LORD your God has **p** you
Josh 23:10 for you, as He has **p** you
Josh 23:15 which the LORD your God **p** you
2Sa 7:28 You have **p** this goodness to
1Ki 2:24 has made me a house, as He **p**
1Ki 5:12 wisdom, as He had **p** him
1Ki 8:20 of Israel, as the LORD **p**
1Ki 8:24 You **p** Your servant David my
1Ki 8:25 now keep what You **p** Your
1Ki 8:56 according to all that He **p**
1Ki 8:56 which He **p** through His
1Ki 9: 5 as I **p** David your father,
2Ki 8:19 as He **p** him to give a lamp to
1Ch 17:26 have **p** this goodness to Your
2Ch 6:10 of Israel, as the LORD **p**
2Ch 6:15 You **p** Your servant David my
2Ch 6:16 now keep what You **p** Your
2Ch 21: 7 since He had **p** to give a lamp
Esth 4: 7 had **p** to pay into the king's
Jer 32:42 the good that I have **p** them
Jer 33:14 have **p** to the house of Israel
Matt 14: 7 Therefore he **p** with an oath
Mark 14:11 glad, and **p** to give him money
Luke 1:72 the mercy **p** to our fathers
Luke 22: 6 Then he **p** and sought
Acts 7: 5 He **p** to give it to him for a
Rom 1: 2 which He **p** before through His
Rom 4:21 convinced that what He had **p**
2Co 9: 5 which you had previously **p**
Tit 1: 2 lie, **p** before time began,
Heb 10:23 for He who **p** is faithful
Heb 11:11 judged Him faithful who had **p**
Heb 12:26 but now He has **p**, saying
Jas 1:12 has **p** to those who love Him
Jas 2: 5 He **p** to those who love Him
1Jn 2:25 the promise that He has **p** us

PROMISES (*see* PROMISE)
Rom 9: 4 the service of God, and the **p**
Rom 15: 8 to confirm the **p** made to the
2Co 1:20 For all the **p** of God in Him
2Co 7: 1 Therefore, having these **p**
Gal 3:16 and his Seed were the **p** made
Gal 3:21 law then against the **p** of God
Heb 6:12 and patience inherit the **p**
Heb 7: 6 and blessed him who had the **p**
Heb 8: 6 was established on better **p**
Heb 11:13 not having received the **p**
Heb 11:17 the **p** offered up his only
Heb 11:33 righteousness, obtained **p**
2Pe 1: 4 great and precious **p**, that

PROMOTE (*see* PROMOTED, PROMOTES)
Job 30:13 my path, they **p** my calamity
Prov 4: 8 Exalt her, and she will **p** you

PROMOTED (*see* PROMOTE)
Esth 3: 1 things King Ahasuerus **p** Haman
Esth 5:11 in which the king had **p** him
Dan 2:48 Then the king **p** Daniel and
Dan 3:30 Then the king **p** Shadrach,

PROMOTES (*see* PROMOTE)
Prov 12:18 tongue of the wise **p** health

PROMPTED
Matt 14: 8 having been **p** by her mother,

PROMPTLY
Prov 13:24 loves him disciplines him **p**

PRONOUNCE (*see* PRONOUNCED)
Lev 5: 4 that a man may **p** by an oath
Lev 13: 3 look at him, and **p** him unclean
Lev 13: 6 the priest shall **p** him clean
Lev 13: 8 priest shall **p** him unclean
Lev 13:11 priest shall **p** him unclean
Lev 13:13 he shall **p** him clean who has
Lev 13:15 flesh and **p** him to be unclean
Lev 13:17 then the priest shall **p** him
Lev 13:20 priest shall **p** him unclean
Lev 13:22 priest shall **p** him unclean
Lev 13:23 the priest shall **p** him clean
Lev 13:25 priest shall **p** him unclean
Lev 13:27 priest shall **p** him unclean
Lev 13:28 The priest shall **p** him clean
Lev 13:30 priest shall **p** him unclean
Lev 13:34 the priest shall **p** him clean
Lev 13:37 the priest shall **p** him clean
Lev 13:44 shall surely **p** him unclean
Lev 13:59 **p** it clean or to **p** it unclean
Lev 14: 7 shall **p** him clean, and shall
Lev 14:48 shall **p** the house clean,
Deut 17: 9 they shall **p** upon you the
Deut 17:10 they **p** upon you in that place
Deut 17:11 which they **p** upon you
Judg 12: 6 for he could not **p** it right
Ps 5:10 **P** them guilty, O God

PRONOUNCED (*see* PRONOUNCE)
2Ki 2:24 **p** a curse on them in the name
2Ki 25: 6 and they **p** judgment on him
Neh 6:12 but that he **p** this prophecy
Jer 11:17 has **p** doom against you for
Jer 16:10 Why has the LORD **p** all this
Jer 19:15 doom that I have **p** against it
Jer 25:13 which I have **p** against it
Jer 26:13 that He has **p** against you
Jer 26:19 which He had **p** against them
Jer 34: 5 For I have **p** the word,"
Jer 35:17 that I have **p** against them
Jer 36: 7 has **p** against this people
Jer 36:31 that I have **p** against them
Jer 39: 5 where he **p** judgment on him
Jer 40: 2 The LORD your God has **p** this
Jer 52: 9 and he **p** judgment on him
Ezek 20:26 I **p** them unclean because of

PROOF (*see* PROOFS)
2Co 8:24 the **p** of your love and of our
2Co 9:13 while, through the **p** of this
2Co 13: 3 since you seek a **p** of Christ
Phil 1:28 is to them a **p** of perdition

PROOFS (*see* PROOF)
Acts 1: 3 by many infallible **p**, being

PROPER (*see* PROPERLY)
Judg 6:26 rock in the **p** arrangement
1Ki 4:28 and straw to the **p** place, for
1Ch 15:13 consult Him about the **p** order
Ezra 4:14 it was not **p** for us to see
Ps 75: 2 When I choose the **p** time, I
Eccl 10:17 princes feast at the **p** time
Jer 26:14 me as seems good and **p** to you
Jer 27: 5 it to whom it seemed **p** to Me
1Co 7:35 on you, but for what is **p**
1Co 11:13 Is it **p** for a woman to pray
1Ti 2:10 but, which is **p** for women
Tit 2: 1 are **p** for sound doctrine
Jude 6 did not keep their **p** domain

PROPERLY (*see* PROPER)
Rom 13:13 Let us walk **p**, as in the day,
1Th 4:12 that you may walk **p** toward

PROPERTY
Gen 23: 4 Give me **p** for a burial place
Gen 23: 9 as **p** for a burial place among
Gen 23:20 Heth as **p** for a burial place
Gen 34:23 not their livestock, their **p**
Gen 50:13 as **p** for a burial place
Ex 21:21 for he is his **p**
Lev 25:45 and they shall become your **p**
Josh 14: 4 their livestock and their **p**
2Ki 9:21 met him on the **p** of Naboth
1Ch 27:31 officials over King David's **p**
2Ch 17:13 He had much **p** in the cities
2Ch 32:29 God had given him very much **p**
Ezra 10: 8 and elders, all his **p** would be
Neh 5:13 from his house, and from his **p**
Jer 37:12 his **p** there among the people
Ezek 45: 6 **p** of the city an area five
Ezek 45: 7 holy district and the city's **p**
Ezek 45: 7 holy district and the city's **p**
Ezek 46:18 by evicting them from their **p**
Ezek 46:18 for his sons from his own **p**
Ezek 46:18 may be scattered from his **p**
Ezek 48:20 with the **p** of the city
Ezek 48:21 district and of the city's **p**

PROPHECIES (*see* PROPHECY)
Lam 2:14 envisioned for you false **p**
1Co 13: 8 But whether there are **p**, they
1Th 5:20 Do not despise **p**
1Ti 1:18 according to the **p** previously

PROPHECY (*see* PROPHECIES, PROPHESY, PROPHETIC)
2Ch 9:29 in the **p** of Ahijah the
2Ch 15: 8 the **p** of Oded the prophet, he
Neh 6:12 **p** against me because Tobiah
Dan 9:24 to seal up vision and **p**, and
Matt 13:14 in them the **p** of Isaiah is
Rom 12: 6 if **p**, let us prophesy in
1Co 12:10 of miracles, to another **p**
1Co 13: 2 though I have the gift of **p**
1Ti 4:14 **p** with the laying on of the
2Pe 1:20 that no **p** of Scripture is of
2Pe 1:21 for **p** never came by the will
Rev 1: 3 who hear the words of this **p**
Rev 11: 6 falls in the days of their **p**
Rev 19:10 of Jesus is the spirit of **p**
Rev 22: 7 words of the **p** of this book
Rev 22:10 words of the **p** of this book
Rev 22:18 words of the **p** of this book
Rev 22:19 words of the book of this **p**

PROPHESIED (*see* PROPHESY)
Num 11:25 rested upon them, that they **p**
Num 11:26 yet they **p** in the camp
1Sa 10:10 upon him, and he **p** among them
1Sa 10:11 indeed **p** among the prophets
1Sa 18:10 and he **p** inside the house
1Sa 19:20 of Saul, and they also **p**
1Sa 19:21 and they **p** likewise
1Sa 19:21 third time, and they **p** also
1Sa 19:23 **p** until he came to Naioth in
1Sa 19:24 and **p** before Samuel in like
1Ki 18:29 that they **p** until the time of
1Ki 22:10 the prophets **p** before them
1Ki 22:12 And all the prophets **p** so,
1Ch 25: 2 who **p** according to the order
1Ch 25: 3 who **p** with a harp to give
2Ch 18: 9 the prophets **p** before them
2Ch 18:11 And all the prophets **p** so,
2Ch 20:37 **p** against Jehoshaphat, saying
Ezra 5: 1 **p** to the Jews who were in
Jer 2: 8 the prophets **p** by Baal, and
Jer 20: 1 that Jeremiah **p** these things
Jer 20: 6 to whom you have **p** lies
Jer 23:13 they **p** by Baal and caused My
Jer 23:21 spoken to them, yet they **p**
Jer 25:13 book, which Jeremiah has **p**
Jer 26: 9 Why have you **p** in the name of
Jer 26:11 For he has **p** against this
Jer 26:18 Micah of Moresheth **p** in the
Jer 26:20 who **p** in the name of the LORD
Jer 26:20 who **p** against this city and
Jer 28: 6 your words which you have **p**
Jer 28: 8 before you of old **p** against
Jer 29:31 Because Shemaiah has **p** to you
Jer 37:19 your prophets who **p** to you
Ezek 37: 7 So I **p** as I was commanded
Ezek 37: 7 and as I **p**, there was a noise,
Ezek 37:10 So I **p** as He commanded me,
Ezek 38:17 who **p** for years in those days
Matt 7:22 have we not **p** in Your name,
Matt 11:13 and the law **p** until John
Luke 1:67 with the Holy Spirit, and **p**
John 11:51 he **p** that Jesus would die for
Acts 19: 6 they spoke with tongues and **p**
Acts 21: 9 four virgin daughters who **p**
1Co 14: 5 but even more that you **p**
1Pe 1:10 who **p** of the grace that would
Jude 14 Adam, **p** about these men also,

PROPHESIES (*see* PROPHESY)
2Ch 18: 7 him, because he never **p** good
Jer 28: 9 the prophet who **p** of peace
Ezek 12:27 now, and he **p** of times far off
Zech 13: 3 pass that if anyone still **p**
Zech 13: 3 thrust him through when he **p**
Zech 13: 4 of his vision when he **p**
1Co 11: 5 or **p** with her head uncovered
1Co 14: 3 But he who **p** speaks
1Co 14: 4 but he who **p** edifies the
1Co 14: 5 for he who **p** is greater than

PROPHESY (*see* PROPHECY, PROPHESIED, PROPHESIES, PROPHESYING, PROPHET, PROPHETESS)
1Sa 10: 6 you will **p** with them and be
1Ki 22: 8 does not **p** good concerning me
1Ki 22:18 not **p** good concerning me, but
1Ch 25: 1 who should **p** with harps,
2Ch 18:17 not **p** good concerning me, but
Is 30:10 Do not **p** to us right things
Is 30:10 us smooth things, **p** deceits
Jer 5:31 the prophets **p** falsely, and
Jer 11:21 Do not **p** in the name of the
Jer 14:14 The prophets **p** lies in My
Jer 14:14 they **p** to you a false vision,
Jer 14:15 the prophets who **p** in My name
Jer 14:16 the people to whom they **p**
Jer 19:14 the LORD had sent him to **p**
Jer 23:16 of the prophets who **p** to you
Jer 23:25 said who **p** lies in My name
Jer 23:26 of the prophets who **p** lies
Jer 23:32 those who **p** false dreams,"
Jer 25:30 Therefore **p** against them all
Jer 26:12 me to **p** against this house
Jer 27:10 For they **p** a lie to you, to
Jer 27:14 for they **p** a lie to you
Jer 27:15 yet they **p** a lie in My name,
Jer 27:15 and the prophets who **p** to you
Jer 27:16 of your prophets who **p** to you
Jer 27:16 for they **p** a lie to you
Jer 29: 9 For they **p** falsely to you in
Jer 29:21 who **p** a lie to you in My name
Jer 32: 3 Why do you **p** and say, 'Thus
Ezek 4: 7 and you shall **p** against it
Ezek 6: 2 of Israel, and **p** against them,
Ezek 11: 4 **p** against them, **p**, O
Ezek 13: 2 **p** against the prophets of
Ezek 13: 2 the prophets of Israel who **p**
Ezek 13: 2 say to those who **p** out of
Ezek 13:16 who **p** concerning Jerusalem
Ezek 13:17 who **p** out of their own heart
Ezek 13:17 **p** against them,
Ezek 20:46 **p** against the forest land,
Ezek 21: 2 **p** against the land of Israel
Ezek 21: 9 Son of man, **p** and say, 'Thus
Ezek 21:14 You therefore, son of man, **p**
Ezek 21:28 And you, son of man, **p** and say,
Ezek 25: 2 Ammonites, and **p** against them
Ezek 28:21 Sidon, and **p** against her,
Ezek 29: 2 **p** against him, and against all
Ezek 30: 2 Son of man, **p** and say, 'Thus
Ezek 34: 2 **p** against the shepherds of
Ezek 34: 2 the shepherds of Israel, **p**
Ezek 35: 2 Mount Seir and **p** against it,
Ezek 36: 1 **p** to the mountains of Israel,
Ezek 36: 3 therefore **p**, and say, 'Thus
Ezek 36: 6 Therefore **p** concerning the
Ezek 37: 4 **P** to these bones, and say to
Ezek 37: 9 **P** to the breath, **p**,
Ezek 37:12 Therefore **p** and say to them
Ezek 38: 2 and Tubal, and **p** against him,
Ezek 38:14 Therefore, son of man, **p** and
Ezek 39: 1 **p** against Gog, and say, 'Thus
Joel 2:28 and your daughters shall **p**
Amos 2:12 prophets saying, 'Do not **p**
Amos 3: 8 Who can but **p**
Amos 7:12 There eat bread, and there **p**
Amos 7:13 But never again **p** at Bethel
Amos 7:15 Go, **p** to My people Israel
Amos 7:16 Do not **p** against Israel, and
Mic 2: 6 you say to those who **p**
Mic 2: 6 So they shall not **p** to you
Mic 2:11 I will **p** to you of wine and
Matt 15: 7 Well did Isaiah **p** about you
Matt 26:68 saying, "**P** to us, Christ
Mark 7: 6 Well did Isaiah **p** of you
Mark 14:65 and to say to Him, "**P**!"
Luke 22:64 **P**! Who is it that struck You?
Acts 2:17 and your daughters shall **p**
Acts 2:18 and they shall **p**
Rom 12: 6 let us **p** in proportion to our
1Co 13: 9 know in part and we **p** in part
1Co 14: 1 but especially that you may **p**
1Co 14:24 But if all **p**, and an
1Co 14:31 For you can all **p** one by one
1Co 14:39 desire earnestly to **p**, and do
Rev 10:11 You must **p** again about many

Rev 11: 3 they will **p** one thousand two

PROPHESYING (*see* PROPHESY)
Num 11:27 and Medad are **p** in the camp
1Sa 10: 5 and they will be **p**
1Sa 10:13 And when he had finished **p**
1Sa 19:20 saw the group of prophets **p**
Ezra 6:14 the **p** of Haggai the prophet
Ezek 11:13 it happened, while I was **p**
1Co 11: 4 Every man praying or **p**,
1Co 14: 6 by knowledge, by **p**, or by
1Co 14:22 but **p** is not for unbelievers

PROPHET (*see* PROPHESY, PROPHET'S, PROPHETS)
Gen 20: 7 for he is a **p**, and he will
Ex 7: 1 your brother shall be your **p**
Num 12: 6 If there is a **p** among you
Deut 13: 1 a **p** or a dreamer of dreams
Deut 13: 3 **p** or that dreamer of dreams
Deut 13: 5 But that **p** or that dreamer of
Deut 18:15 a **P** like me from your midst
Deut 18:18 a **P** like you from among their
Deut 18:20 But the **p** who presumes to
Deut 18:20 other gods, that **p** shall die
Deut 18:22 when a **p** speaks in the name
Deut 18:22 the **p** has spoken it
Deut 34:10 in Israel a **p** like Moses,
Judg 6: 8 that the LORD sent a **p** to the
1Sa 3:20 as a **p** of the LORD
1Sa 9: 9 **p** was formerly called a seer
1Sa 22: 5 Then the **p** Gad said to David,
2Sa 7: 2 the king said to Nathan the **p**
2Sa 12:25 by the hand of Nathan the **p**
2Sa 24:11 of the LORD came to the **p** Gad
1Ki 1: 8 son of Jehoiada, Nathan the **p**
1Ki 1:10 did not invite Nathan the **p**
1Ki 1:22 Nathan the **p** also came in
1Ki 1:23 Here is Nathan the **p**
1Ki 1:32 the priest, Nathan the **p**, and
1Ki 1:34 Nathan the **p** anoint him king
1Ki 1:38 the priest, Nathan the **p**,
1Ki 1:44 the priest, Nathan the **p**,
1Ki 1:45 Nathan the **p** have anointed
1Ki 11:29 that the **p** Ahijah the
1Ki 13:11 Now an old **p** dwelt in Bethel,
1Ki 13:18 I too am a **p** as you are, and
1Ki 13:20 of the LORD came to the **p** who
1Ki 13:23 the **p** whom he had brought
1Ki 13:25 city where the old **p** dwelt
1Ki 13:26 So when the **p** who had brought
1Ki 13:29 the **p** took up the corpse of
1Ki 13:29 So the old **p** came to the city
1Ki 14: 2 Indeed, Ahijah the **p** is there
1Ki 14:18 His servant Ahijah the **p**
1Ki 16: 7 the **p** Jehu the son of Hanani
1Ki 16:12 against Baasha by Jehu the **p**
1Ki 18:22 alone am left a **p** of the LORD
1Ki 18:36 that Elijah the **p** came near
1Ki 19:16 anoint as **p** in your place
1Ki 20:13 Suddenly a **p** approached Ahab
1Ki 20:22 the **p** came to the king of
1Ki 20:38 Then the **p** departed and waited
1Ki 22: 7 still a **p** of the LORD here
2Ki 3:11 Is there no **p** of the LORD
2Ki 5: 3 with the **p** who is in Samaria
2Ki 5: 8 that there is a **p** in Israel
2Ki 5:13 if the **p** had told you to do
2Ki 6:12 the **p** who is in Israel, tells
2Ki 9: 1 Elisha the **p** called one of
2Ki 9: 4 man, the servant of the **p**
2Ki 14:25 the **p** who was from Gath
2Ki 19: 2 sackcloth, to Isaiah the **p**
2Ki 20: 1 And Isaiah the **p**, the son of
2Ki 20:11 So Isaiah the **p** cried out to
2Ki 20:14 Then Isaiah the **p** went to
2Ki 23:18 the **p** who came from Samaria
1Ch 17: 1 David said to Nathan the **p**
1Ch 29:29 in the book of Nathan the **p**
2Ch 9:29 in the book of Nathan the **p**
2Ch 12: 5 the **p** came to Rehoboam and
2Ch 12:15 in the book of Shemaiah the **p**
2Ch 13:22 in the annals of the **p** Iddo
2Ch 15: 8 and the prophecy of Oded the **p**
2Ch 18: 6 still a **p** of the LORD here
2Ch 21:12 came to him from Elijah the **p**
2Ch 25:15 He sent him a **p** who said to
2Ch 25:16 Then the **p** ceased, and said,
2Ch 26:22 the **p** Isaiah the son of Amoz
2Ch 28: 9 But a **p** of the LORD was there
2Ch 29:25 seer, and of Nathan the **p**
2Ch 32:20 the **p** Isaiah, the son of Amoz
2Ch 32:32 in the vision of Isaiah the **p**
2Ch 35:18 the days of Samuel the **p**
2Ch 36:12 himself before Jeremiah the **p**
Ezra 5: 1 Then the **p** Haggai and
Ezra 6:14 prophesying of Haggai the **p**
Ps 74: 9 There is no longer any **p**
Is 3: 2 of war, the judge and the **p**
Is 9:15 the **p** who teaches lies, he is
Is 28: 7 and the **p** have erred through
Is 37: 2 sackcloth, to Isaiah the **p**
Is 38: 1 And Isaiah the **p**, the son of
Is 39: 3 Then Isaiah the **p** went to
Jer 1: 5 you a **p** to the nations
Jer 6:13 from the **p** even to the priest
Jer 8:10 From the **p** even to the priest
Jer 14:18 Yes, both **p** and priest go
Jer 18:18 wise, nor the word from the **p**
Jer 20: 2 Pashhur struck Jeremiah the **p**
Jer 23:11 For both **p** and priest are
Jer 23:28 The **p** who has a dream, let
Jer 23:33 the **p** or the priest ask you
Jer 23:34 And as for the **p** and the priest
Jer 23:37 Thus you shall say to the **p**
Jer 25: 2 which Jeremiah the **p** spoke to
Jer 28: 1 the son of Azur the **p**, who
Jer 28: 5 Then the **p** Jeremiah spoke to
Jer 28: 5 Jeremiah spoke to the **p**
Jer 28: 6 and the **p** Jeremiah said,
Jer 28: 9 As for the **p** who prophesies
Jer 28: 9 word of the **p** comes to pass
Jer 28: 9 the **p** will be known as one
Jer 28:10 Then Hananiah the **p** took the
Jer 28:10 off the **p** Jeremiah's neck
Jer 28:11 the **p** Jeremiah went his way
Jer 28:12 after Hananiah the **p** had
Jer 28:12 the neck of the **p** Jeremiah
Jer 28:15 Then the **p** Jeremiah said to
Jer 28:15 said to Hananiah the **p**
Jer 28:17 So Hananiah the **p** died the
Jer 29: 1 letter that Jeremiah the **p**
Jer 29:26 and considers himself a **p**,
Jer 29:27 who makes himself a **p** to you
Jer 29:29 the hearing of Jeremiah the **p**
Jer 32: 2 Jeremiah the **p** was shut up in
Jer 34: 6 Then Jeremiah the **p** spoke all
Jer 36: 8 Jeremiah the **p** commanded him
Jer 36:26 the scribe and Jeremiah the **p**
Jer 37: 2 He spoke by the **p** Jeremiah
Jer 37: 3 to the **p** Jeremiah, saying,
Jer 37: 6 LORD came to the **p** Jeremiah
Jer 37:13 and he seized Jeremiah the **p**
Jer 38: 9 have done to Jeremiah the **p**
Jer 38:10 lift Jeremiah the **p** out of
Jer 38:14 had Jeremiah the **p** brought to
Jer 42: 2 and said to Jeremiah the **p**
Jer 42: 4 Jeremiah the **p** said to them
Jer 43: 6 of Shaphan, and Jeremiah the **p**
Jer 45: 1 **p** spoke to Baruch the son of
Jer 46: 1 the **p** against the nations
Jer 46:13 LORD spoke to Jeremiah the **p**
Jer 47: 1 the **p** against the Philistines
Jer 49:34 Jeremiah the **p** against Elam
Jer 50: 1 Chaldeans by Jeremiah the **p**
Jer 51:59 **p** commanded Seraiah the son
Lam 2:20 **p** be slain in the sanctuary
Ezek 2: 5 that a **p** has been among them
Ezek 7:26 will seek a vision from a **p**
Ezek 14: 4 and then comes to the **p**, I
Ezek 14: 7 then comes to a **p** to inquire
Ezek 14: 9 if the **p** is induced to speak
Ezek 14: 9 the LORD have induced that **p**
Ezek 14:10 the punishment of the **p** shall
Ezek 33:33 that a **p** has been among them
Dan 9: 2 given through Jeremiah the **p**
Hos 4: 5 the **p** also shall stumble with
Hos 9: 7 The **p** is a fool, the
Hos 9: 8 but the **p** is a fowler's snare
Hos 12:13 By a **p** the LORD brought
Hos 12:13 and by a **p** he was preserved
Amos 7:14 I was no **p**, nor was I a son
Amos 7:14 nor was I a son of a **p**, but
Hab 1: 1 which the **p** Habakkuk saw
Hab 3: 1 A prayer of Habakkuk the **p**
Hag 1: 1 **p** to Zerubbabel the son of
Hag 1: 3 the LORD came by Haggai the **p**
Hag 1:12 and the words of Haggai the **p**
Hag 2: 1 the LORD came by Haggai the **p**
Hag 2:10 the LORD came by Haggai the **p**
Zech 1: 1 the son of Iddo the **p**,
Zech 1: 7 the son of Iddo the **p**
Zech 13: 4 **p** will be ashamed of his
Zech 13: 5 But he will say, 'I am no **p**
Mal 4: 5 **p** before the coming of the
Matt 1:22 by the Lord through the **p**
Matt 2: 5 thus it is written by the **p**
Matt 2:15 by the Lord through the **p**
Matt 2:17 was spoken by Jeremiah the **p**
Matt 3: 3 was spoken of by the **p** Isaiah
Matt 4:14 was spoken by Isaiah the **p**
Matt 8:17 was spoken by Isaiah the **p**
Matt 10:41 He who receives a **p** in the
Matt 10:41 a **p** shall receive a prophet's
Matt 11: 9 did you go out to see? A **p**?
Matt 11: 9 say to you, and more than a **p**
Matt 12:17 was spoken by Isaiah the **p**
Matt 12:39 the sign of the **p** Jonah
Matt 13:35 which was spoken by the **p**
Matt 13:57 A **p** is not without honor
Matt 14: 5 they counted him as a **p**
Matt 16: 4 the sign of the **p** Jonah
Matt 21: 4 which was spoken by the **p**
Matt 21:11 Jesus, the **p** from Nazareth of
Matt 21:26 for all count John as a **p**
Matt 21:46 because they took Him for a **p**
Matt 24:15 spoken of by Daniel the **p**
Matt 27: 9 was spoken by Jeremiah the **p**
Matt 27:35 which was spoken by the **p**
Mark 6: 4 A **p** is not without honor
Mark 6:15 It is the **P**, or like one of
Mark 11:32 John to have been a **p** indeed
Mark 13:14 spoken of by Daniel the **p**
Luke 1:76 called the **p** of the Highest
Luke 3: 4 of the words of Isaiah the **p**
Luke 4:17 the book of the **p** Isaiah
Luke 4:24 no **p** is accepted in his own
Luke 4:27 in the time of Elisha the **p**
Luke 7:16 A great **p** has risen up among
Luke 7:26 did you go out to see? A **p**?
Luke 7:26 say to you, and more than a **p**
Luke 7:28 **p** than John the Baptist
Luke 7:39 This man, if He were a **p**,
Luke 11:29 the sign of Jonah the **p**
Luke 13:33 for it cannot be that a **p**
Luke 20: 6 persuaded that John was a **p**
Luke 24:19 who was a **P** mighty in deed and
John 1:21 Are you the **P**
John 1:23 LORD," ' as the **p** Isaiah said
John 1:25 Christ, nor Elijah, nor the **P**
John 4:19 I perceive that You are a **p**
John 4:44 a **p** has no honor in his own
John 6:14 This is truly the **P** who is to
John 7:40 Truly this is the **P**
John 7:52 for no **p** has arisen out of
John 9:17 He said, "He is a **p**."
John 12:38 the **p** might be fulfilled,
Acts 2:16 what was spoken by the **p** Joel
Acts 2:30 Therefore, being a **p**, and
Acts 3:22 **P** like me from your brethren
Acts 3:23 **P** shall be utterly destroyed
Acts 7:37 **P** like me from your brethren
Acts 7:48 with hands, as the **p** says
Acts 8:28 he was reading Isaiah the **p**
Acts 8:30 him reading the **p** Isaiah, and
Acts 8:34 of whom does the **p** say this
Acts 13: 6 a certain sorcerer, a false **p**
Acts 13:20 years, until Samuel the **p**
Acts 21:10 a certain **p** named Agabus came
Acts 28:25 Isaiah the **p** to our fathers
1Co 14:37 to be a **p** or spiritual, let
Tit 1:12 them, a **p** of their own, said,
2Pe 2:16 the madness of the **p**
Rev 16:13 of the mouth of the false **p**
Rev 19:20 and with him the false **p** who
Rev 20:10 the beast and the false **p** are

PROPHETESS (*see* PROPHESY)
Ex 15:20 Then Miriam the **p**, the sister
Judg 4: 4 Now Deborah, a **p**, the wife of
2Ki 22:14 Asaiah went to Huldah the **p**
2Ch 34:22 went to Huldah the **p**, the
Neh 6:14 the **p** Noadiah and the rest of
Is 8: 3 Then I went to the **p**, and she
Luke 2:36 Now there was one, Anna, a **p**
Rev 2:20 who calls herself a **p**, to

PROPHETIC (*see* PROPHECY)
Rom 16:26 by the **p** Scriptures has been
2Pe 1:19 We also have the **p** word made

PROPHET'S (*see* PROPHET)
Matt 10:41 shall receive a **p** reward

PROPHETS (*see* PROPHET)
Num 11:29 all the LORD's people were **p**
1Sa 10: 5 you will meet a group of **p**
1Sa 10:10 was a group of **p** to meet him
1Sa 10:11 indeed prophesied among the **p**
1Sa 10:11 Is Saul also among the **p**
1Sa 10:12 Is Saul also among the **p**
1Sa 19:20 the group of **p** prophesying
1Sa 19:24 Is Saul also among the **p**
1Sa 28: 6 dreams or by Urim or by the **p**
1Sa 28:15 neither by **p** nor by dreams
1Ki 18: 4 massacred the **p** of the LORD
1Ki 18: 4 had taken one hundred **p** and
1Ki 18:13 killed the **p** of the LORD, how
1Ki 18:13 hundred men of the LORD's **p**
1Ki 18:19 fifty **p** of Baal, and the four
1Ki 18:19 the four hundred **p** of Asherah
1Ki 18:20 gathered the **p** together on
1Ki 18:22 but Baal's **p** are four hundred
1Ki 18:25 Elijah said to the **p** of Baal
1Ki 18:40 Seize the **p** of Baal
1Ki 19: 1 all the **p** with the sword
1Ki 19:10 killed Your **p** with the sword
1Ki 19:14 killed Your **p** with the sword
1Ki 20:35 man of the sons of the **p** said
1Ki 20:41 him as one of the **p**
1Ki 22: 6 gathered the **p** together,
1Ki 22:10 all the **p** prophesied before
1Ki 22:12 And all the **p** prophesied so,
1Ki 22:13 the words of the **p** with one
1Ki 22:22 in the mouth of all his **p**
1Ki 22:23 mouth of all these **p** of yours
2Ki 2: 3 the sons of the **p** who were at
2Ki 2: 5 the sons of the **p** who were at
2Ki 2: 7 men of the sons of the **p** went
2Ki 2:15 Now when the sons of the **p**
2Ki 3:13 Go to the **p** of your father and
2Ki 3:13 and the **p** of your mother
2Ki 4: 1 of the **p** cried out to Elisha
2Ki 4:38 Now the sons of the **p** were
2Ki 4:38 stew for the sons of the **p**
2Ki 5:22 men of the sons of the **p** have
2Ki 6: 1 sons of the **p** said to Elisha
2Ki 9: 1 one of the sons of the **p**, and
2Ki 9: 7 blood of My servants the **p**
2Ki 10:19 call to me all the **p** of Baal
2Ki 17:13 Judah, by all of His **p**,
2Ki 17:13 to you by My servants the **p**
2Ki 17:23 by all His servants the **p**
2Ki 21:10 spoke by His servants the **p**
2Ki 23: 2 the priests and the **p** and all
2Ki 24: 2 spoken by His servants the **p**
1Ch 16:22 ones, and do My **p** no harm
2Ch 18: 5 gathered the **p** together, four
2Ch 18: 9 all the **p** prophesied before
2Ch 18:11 And all the **p** prophesied so,
2Ch 18:12 the words of the **p** with one
2Ch 18:21 in the mouth of all his **p**
2Ch 18:22 the mouth of these **p** of yours
2Ch 20:20 believe His **p**, and you shall
2Ch 24:19 Yet He sent **p** to them, to
2Ch 29:25 of the LORD by his **p**
2Ch 36:16 words, and scoffed at His **p**
Ezra 5: 1 Zechariah the son of Iddo, **p**
Ezra 5: 2 the **p** of God were with them,
Ezra 9:11 by Your servants the **p**,
Neh 6: 7 you have also appointed **p** to
Neh 6:14 the rest of the **p** who would
Neh 9:26 their backs and killed Your **p**
Neh 9:30 them by Your Spirit in Your **p**
Neh 9:32 princes, our priests and our **p**
Ps 105:15 ones, And do My **p** no harm
Is 29:10 your eyes, namely, the **p**
Is 30:10 Do not see," and to the **p**
Jer 2: 8 the **p** prophesied by Baal, and
Jer 2:26 and their priests and their **p**
Jer 2:30 your **p** like a destroying lion
Jer 4: 9 and the **p** shall wonder
Jer 5:13 the **p** become wind, for the
Jer 5:31 the **p** prophesy falsely, and
Jer 7:25 to you all My servants the **p**
Jer 8: 1 and the bones of the **p**, and
Jer 13:13 throne, the priests, the **p**
Jer 14:13 the **p** say to them, 'You shall
Jer 14:14 The **p** prophesy lies in My
Jer 14:15 the **p** who prophesy in My name
Jer 14:15 and famine those **p** shall be
Jer 23: 9 me is broken because of the **p**
Jer 23:13 folly in the **p** of Samaria
Jer 23:14 thing in the **p** of Jerusalem
Jer 23:15 of hosts concerning the **p**
Jer 23:15 for from the **p** of Jerusalem
Jer 23:16 of the **p** who prophesy to you
Jer 23:21 I have not sent these **p**, yet
Jer 23:25 I have heard what the **p** have
Jer 23:26 of the **p** who prophesy lies
Jer 23:26 Indeed they are **p** of the
Jer 23:30 behold, I am against the **p**
Jer 23:31 Behold, I am against the **p**
Jer 25: 4 to you all His servants the **p**
Jer 26: 5 the **p** whom I sent to you,
Jer 26: 7 So the priests and the **p** and
Jer 26: 8 that the priests and the **p**
Jer 26:11 the **p** spoke to the princes and
Jer 26:16 said to the priests and the **p**
Jer 27: 9 do not listen to your **p**, your
Jer 27:14 of the **p** who speak to you
Jer 27:15 the **p** who prophesy to you
Jer 27:16 of your **p** who prophesy to you
Jer 27:18 But if they are **p**, and if the
Jer 28: 8 The **p** who have been before me
Jer 29: 1 to the priests, the **p**, and all
Jer 29: 8 Do not let your **p** and your
Jer 29:15 up **p** for us in Babylon"
Jer 29:19 to them by My servants the **p**
Jer 32:32 their priests, their **p**, the
Jer 35:15 to you all My servants the **p**
Jer 37:19 Where now are your **p** who
Jer 44: 4 to you all My servants the **p**
Lam 2: 9 her **p** find no vision from the
Lam 2:14 Your **p** have seen for you
Lam 4:13 Because of the sins of her **p**
Ezek 13: 2 prophesy against the **p** of
Ezek 13: 3 Woe to the foolish **p**, who
Ezek 13: 4 your **p** are like foxes in the
Ezek 13: 9 the **p** who envision futility
Ezek 13:16 the **p** of Israel who prophesy
Ezek 22:25 The conspiracy of her **p** in
Ezek 22:28 Her **p** plastered them with
Ezek 38:17 My servants the **p** of Israel
Dan 9: 6 we heeded Your servants the **p**
Dan 9:10 us by His servants the **p**
Hos 6: 5 I have hewn them by the **p**
Hos 12:10 I have also spoken by the **p**
Hos 12:10 through the witness of the **p**
Amos 2:11 up some of your sons as **p**
Amos 2:12 and commanded the **p** saying
Amos 3: 7 secret to His servants the **p**
Mic 3: 5 the LORD concerning the **p** who
Mic 3: 6 sun shall go down on the **p**
Mic 3:11 and her **p** divine for money
Zeph 3: 4 Her **p** are insolent,
Zech 1: 4 to whom the former **p** preached
Zech 1: 5 And the **p**, do they live
Zech 1: 6 I commanded My servants the **p**
Zech 7: 3 the LORD of hosts, and the **p**
Zech 7: 7 the former **p** when Jerusalem
Zech 7:12 Spirit through the former **p**
Zech 8: 9 words by the mouth of the **p**
Zech 13: 2 I will also cause the **p** and
Matt 2:23 which was spoken by the **p**
Matt 5:12 the **p** who were before you
Matt 5:17 to destroy the Law or the **P**
Matt 7:12 for this is the Law and the **P**
Matt 7:15 Beware of false **p**, who come
Matt 11:13 For all the **p** and the law
Matt 13:17 I say to you that many **p**
Matt 16:14 Jeremiah or one of the **p**
Matt 22:40 hang all the Law and the **P**
Matt 23:29 you build the tombs of the **p**
Matt 23:30 them in the blood of the **p**
Matt 23:31 of those who murdered the **p**
Matt 23:34 indeed, I send you **p**, wise
Matt 23:37 the one who kills the **p** and
Matt 24:11 many false **p** will rise up
Matt 24:24 false **p** will arise and show
Matt 26:56 of the **p** might be fulfilled
Mark 1: 2 As it is written in the **P**
Mark 6:15 Prophet, or like one of the **p**
Mark 8:28 and others, one of the **p**
Mark 13:22 false **p** will rise and show
Luke 1:70 by the mouth of His holy **p**
Luke 6:23 their fathers did to the **p**
Luke 6:26 their fathers to the false **p**
Luke 9: 8 of the old **p** had risen again
Luke 9:19 of the old **p** has risen again
Luke 10:24 for I tell you that many **p**
Luke 11:47 you build the tombs of the **p**
Luke 11:49 said, 'I will send them **p**
Luke 11:50 the **p** which was shed from the
Luke 13:28 all the **p** in the kingdom of
Luke 13:34 the one who kills the **p** and
Luke 16:16 law and the **p** were until John
Luke 16:29 They have Moses and the **p**
Luke 16:31 do not hear Moses and the **p**
Luke 18:31 that are written by the **p**
Luke 24:25 in all that the **p** have spoken
Luke 24:27 at Moses and all the **P**, He
Luke 24:44 in the Law of Moses and the **P**
John 1:45 in the law, and also the **p**
John 6:45 It is written in the **p**, 'And
John 8:52 Abraham is dead, and the **p**
John 8:53 And the **p** are dead
Acts 3:18 by the mouth of all His **p**
Acts 3:21 holy **p** since the world began
Acts 3:24 Yes, and all the **p**, from
Acts 3:25 You are sons of the **p**, and of
Acts 7:42 written in the book of the **P**
Acts 7:52 Which of the **p** did your
Acts 10:43 To Him all the **p** witness that
Acts 11:27 in these days **p** came from
Acts 13: 1 Antioch there were certain **p**
Acts 13:15 reading of the Law and the **P**
Acts 13:27 of the **P** which are read every
Acts 13:40 spoken in the **p** come upon you
Acts 15:15 this the words of the **p** agree
Acts 15:32 themselves being **p** also,
Acts 24:14 in the Law and in the **P**
Acts 26:22 things than those which the **p**
Acts 26:27 Agrippa, do you believe the **p**
Acts 28:23 the Law of Moses and the **P**
Rom 1: 2 His **p** in the Holy Scriptures
Rom 3:21 witnessed by the Law and the **P**
Rom 11: 3 LORD, they have killed Your **p**
1Co 12:28 first apostles, second **p**,
1Co 12:29 Are all apostles? Are all **p**?
1Co 14:29 Let two or three **p** speak, and
1Co 14:32 of the **p** are subject to the **p**
Eph 2:20 of the apostles and **p**, Jesus
Eph 3: 5 to His holy apostles and **p**
Eph 4:11 some to be apostles, some **p**
1Th 2:15 the Lord Jesus and their own **p**
Heb 1: 1 past to the fathers by the **p**
Heb 11:32 of David and Samuel and the **p**
Jas 5:10 My brethren, take the **p**, who
1Pe 1:10 salvation the **p** have inquired
2Pe 2: 1 also false **p** among the people
2Pe 3: 2 spoken before by the holy **p**
1Jn 4: 1 because many false **p** have
Rev 10: 7 to His servants the **p**
Rev 11:10 because these two **p** tormented
Rev 11:18 reward Your servants the **p**
Rev 16: 6 shed the blood of saints and **p**
Rev 18:20 and you holy apostles and **p**
Rev 18:24 her was found the blood of **p**
Rev 22: 6 the Lord God of the holy **p**
Rev 22: 9 and of your brethren the **p**

PROPITIATION
Rom 3:25 forth to be a **p** by His blood
Heb 2:17 to make **p** for the sins of the
1Jn 2: 2 Himself is the **p** for our sins
1Jn 4:10 Son to be the **p** for our sins

PROPORTION (*see* PROPORTIONS)
Num 35: 8 in **p** to the inheritance that
Rom 12: 6 us prophesy in **p** to our faith

PROPORTIONS (*see* PROPORTION)
Job 41:12 power, or his graceful **p**

PROPOSE (*see* PROPOSED)
Gen 11: 6 now nothing that they **p** to do
1Ki 5: 5 I **p** to build a house for the
2Ch 28:10 And now you **p** to force the

PROPOSED (*see* PROPOSE)
1Sa 25:39 **p** to Abigail, to take her as
Jer 49:20 His purposes that He has **p**
Jer 50:45 has **p** against the land of the
Acts 1:23 And they **p** two

PROPPED
1Ki 22:35 and the king was **p** up in his
2Ch 18:34 the king of Israel **p** himself

PROPRIETY
1Ti 2: 9 in modest apparel, with **p**

PROSECUTOR
Job 31:35 that my **P** had written a book

PROSELYTE (*see* PROSELYTES)
Matt 23:15 land and sea to win one **p**, and
Acts 6: 5 and Nicolas, a **p** from Antioch,

PROSELYTES (*see* PROSELYTE)
Acts 2:10 from Rome, both Jews and **p**
Acts 13:43 devout **p** followed Paul and

PROSPECT
Prov 24:14 have found it, there is a **p**
Prov 24:20 will be no **p** for the evil man

PROSPER (*see* PROSPERED, PROSPERING, PROSPERITY, PROSPEROUS, PROSPERS)
Gen 24:40 angel with you and **p** your way
Gen 24:42 if You will now **p** the way in
Gen 26:13 The man began to **p**, and
Gen 39: 3 all he did to **p** in his hand
Gen 39:23 he did, the LORD made it **p**
Deut 28:29 you shall not **p** in your ways
Deut 29: 9 that you may **p** in all that
Deut 30: 5 He will **p** you and multiply you
Josh 1: 7 that you may **p** wherever you
Ruth 4:11 may you **p** in Ephrathah and be
1Ki 2: 3 that you may **p** in all that
1Ki 22:12 Go up to Ramoth Gilead and **p**
1Ki 22:15 Go and **p**, for the LORD will
1Ch 22:11 and may you **p**, and build the
1Ch 22:13 Then you will **p**, if you take
2Ch 13:12 fathers, for you shall not **p**
2Ch 18:11 Go up to Ramoth Gilead and **p**
2Ch 18:14 Go and **p**, and they shall be
2Ch 20:20 His prophets, and you shall **p**
2Ch 24:20 LORD, so that you cannot **p**
2Ch 26: 5 the LORD, God made him **p**
Neh 1:11 let Your servant **p** this day
Neh 2:20 of heaven Himself will **p** us
Job 8: 6 **p** your rightful habitation
Job 12: 6 The tents of robbers **p**, and
Ps 1: 3 And whatever he does shall **p**
Ps 122: 6 May they **p** who love you
Prov 28:13 covers his sins will not **p**
Eccl 11: 6 you do not know which will **p**
Is 48:15 him, and his way will **p**
Is 53:10 the LORD shall **p** in His hand
Is 54:17 formed against you shall **p**
Is 55:11 it shall **p** in the thing for
Jer 2:37 and you will not **p** by them
Jer 5:28 yet they **p**, and the right of
Jer 10:21 therefore they shall not **p**
Jer 12: 1 does the way of the wicked **p**
Jer 20:11 ashamed, for they will not **p**
Jer 22:30 who shall not **p** in his days
Jer 22:30 of his descendants shall **p**
Jer 23: 5 a King shall reign and **p**, and
Lam 1: 5 the master, her enemies **p**
Ezek 17:15 Will he **p**? Will he who does
Dan 8:24 destroy fearfully, and shall **p**
Dan 8:25 deceit to **p** under his hand
Dan 11:27 but it shall not **p**, for the
Dan 11:36 shall **p** till the wrath has
1Co 16: 2 aside, storing up as he may **p**
3Jn 2 that you may **p** in all things

PROSPERED (*see* PROSPER)
Gen 24:56 since the LORD has **p** my way
2Sa 11: 7 were doing, and how the war **p**
2Ki 18: 7 he **p** wherever he went
1Ch 29:23 of David his father, and **p**
2Ch 14: 7 So they built and **p**
2Ch 31:21 all his heart. So he **p**
2Ch 32:30 Hezekiah **p** in all his works
Ezra 6:14 built, and they **p** through the
Job 9: 4 himself against Him and **p**
Prov 28:25 trusts in the LORD will be **p**
Dan 6:28 So this Daniel **p** in the reign
Dan 8:12 He did all this and **p**

PROSPERING (*see* PROSPER)
Gen 26:13 continued **p** until he became
Ps 10: 5 His ways are always **p**

PROSPERITY (*see* PROSPER)
Deut 23: 6 their **p** all your days forever
1Sa 25: 6 say to him who lives in **p**
1Ki 10: 7 **p** exceed the fame of which I
Ezra 9:12 never seek their peace or **p**
Job 15:21 in **p** the destroyer comes upon
Job 21:16 Indeed their **p** is not in
Job 30:15 my **p** has passed like a cloud
Job 36:11 shall spend their days in **p**
Ps 25:13 He himself shall dwell in **p**
Ps 30: 6 Now in my **p** I said, "I shall
Ps 35:27 in the **p** of His servant
Ps 68: 6 those who are bound into **p**
Ps 73: 3 I saw the **p** of the wicked
Ps 118:25 O LORD, I pray, send now **p**
Ps 122: 7 walls, **P** within your palaces
Eccl 7:14 In the day of **p** be joyful
Jer 22:21 I spoke to you in your **p**, but
Jer 33: 9 all the **p** that I provide for
Lam 3:17 I have forgotten **p**
Dan 4:27 be a lengthening of your **p**
Dan 8:25 shall destroy many in their **p**
Zech 1:17 again spread out through **p**
Acts 19:25 we have our **p** by this trade
Acts 24: 2 **p** is being brought to this

PROSPEROUS (*see* PROSPER, PROSPEROUSLY)
Gen 24:21 had made his journey **p** or not
Gen 26:13 until he became very **p**
Gen 30:43 the man became exceedingly **p**
Josh 1: 8 then you will make your way **p**
Judg 18: 5 on which we go will be **p**
Ps 22:29 All the **p** of the earth Shall
Zech 7: 7 around it were inhabited and **p**
Zech 8:12 For the seed shall be **p**, the

PROSPEROUSLY (*see* PROSPEROUS)
Ps 45: 4 ride **p** because of truth,

PROSPERS (*see* PROSPER)
Deut 15:16 house, since he **p** with you
Ezra 5: 8 and **p** in their hands
Ps 37: 7 of him who **p** in his way,
Prov 17: 8 wherever he turns, he **p**
3Jn 2 health, just as your soul **p**

PROSTITUTE
Lev 19:29 Do not **p** your daughter, to
Lev 20: 5 all who **p** themselves with him
Lev 20: 6 to **p** himself with them, I

PROSTRATE (*see* PROSTRATED, PROSTRATING)
Job 9:13 the proud lie **p** beneath Him
Is 46: 6 they **p** themselves, yes, they
Is 60:14 **p** at the soles of your feet
Dan 2:46 **p** before Daniel, and

PROSTRATED (*see* PROSTRATE)
Gen 43:28 heads down and **p** themselves
Deut 9:25 Thus I **p** myself before the
2Sa 1: 2 to the ground and **p** himself
2Sa 9: 6 fell on his face and **p** himself
2Sa 14: 4 ground and **p** herself, and said,
1Ch 29:20 **p** themselves before the LORD

PROSTRATING (*see* PROSTRATE)
Deut 9:25 forty nights I kept **p** myself

PROTECT (*see* PROTECTED, PROTECTION)
Esth 8:11 together and **p** their lives

PROTECTED (*see* PROTECT)
1Sa 25:21 Surely in vain I have **p** all
Esth 9:16 **p** their lives, had rest from
Mark 6:20 just and holy man, and he **p** him

PROTECTION (*see* PROTECT)
Num 14: 9 their **p** has departed from
2Sa 21: 2 of Israel had sworn **p** to them
Is 22: 8 He removed the **p** of Judah

PROTEST (*see* PROTESTED)
Is 3: 7 in that day he will **p**, saying

PROTESTED (*see* PROTEST)
Acts 23: 9 Pharisees' party arose and **p**

PROUD (*see* PRIDE, PROUDLY)
Job 9:13 the allies of the **p** lie
Job 28: 8 The **p** lions have not trodden
Job 38:11 here your **p** waves must stop
Job 40:11 look on everyone who is **p**
Job 40:12 Look on everyone who is **p**
Ps 10: 4 The wicked in his **p**
Ps 12: 3 tongue that speaks **p** things
Ps 31:23 And fully repays the **p** person
Ps 40: 4 And does not respect the **p**
Ps 86:14 the **p** have risen against me,
Ps 94: 2 Render punishment to the **p**
Ps 101: 5 a **p** heart, Him I will not
Ps 119:21 You rebuke the **p**
Ps 119:51 The **p** have me in great
Ps 119:69 The **p** have forged a lie
Ps 119:78 Let the **p** be ashamed, For
Ps 119:85 The **p** have dug pits for me,
Ps 119:122 Do not let the **p** oppress me
Ps 123: 4 With the contempt of the **p**
Ps 138: 6 But the **p** He knows from afar
Ps 140: 5 The **p** have hidden a snare for
Prov 6:17 A **p** look, a lying tongue,
Prov 15:25 destroy the house of the **p**
Prov 16: 5 Everyone who is **p** in heart is
Prov 16:19 divide the spoil with the **p**
Prov 21: 4 a **p** heart, and the plowing of
Prov 21:24 A **p** and haughty man
Prov 28:25 He who is of a **p** heart stirs
Eccl 7: 8 better than the **p** in spirit
Is 2:12 shall come upon everything **p**
Is 13:11 halt the arrogance of the **p**
Is 16: 6 he is very **p**
Jer 13:15 Do not be **p**, for the LORD has
Jer 43: 2 all the **p** men spoke, saying
Jer 48:29 of Moab (he is exceedingly **p**)
Jer 50:29 has been **p** against the LORD
Jer 50:31 am against you, O you most **p**
Jer 50:32 The most **p** shall stumble and
Hab 2: 4 Behold the **p**, his soul is not
Hab 2: 5 by wine, he is a **p** man, and he
Mal 3:15 So now we call the **p** blessed
Mal 4: 1 like an oven, and all the **p**
Luke 1:51 he has scattered the **p** in the
Rom 1:30 haters of God, violent, **p**
1Ti 6: 4 he is **p**, knowing nothing, but
2Ti 3: 2 lovers of money, boasters, **p**
Jas 4: 6 God resists the **p**, but gives
1Pe 5: 5 God resists the **p**, but gives

PROUDLY (*see* PROUD)
Ex 18:11 thing in which they behaved **p**
1Sa 2: 3 Talk no more so very **p**
Neh 9:10 they acted **p** against them
Neh 9:16 they and our fathers acted **p**
Neh 9:29 Yet they acted **p**, and did not
Job 39:13 wings of the ostrich wave **p**
Ps 17:10 their mouths they speak **p**
Ps 31:18 Which speak insolent things **p**
Obad 12 **p** in the day of distress

PROVE (*see* PROVED, PROVEN, PROVES, PROVING)
1Ki 2: 2 and **p** yourself a man
Job 6:25 But what does your arguing **p**
Job 9:20 it would **p** me perverse
Job 24:25 who will **p** me a liar, and make
Ps 26: 2 Examine me, O LORD, and **p** me
Mal 3:10 **p** Me now in this," says the
Acts 24:13 Nor can they **p** the things of
Acts 25: 7 Paul, which they could not **p**
Rom 12: 2 that you may **p** what is that
2Co 13: 5 in the faith. **P** yourselves.

PROVED (*see* PROVE)
Ps 66:10 For You, O God, have **p** us
Ps 81: 7 I **p** you at the waters of
Ps 95: 9 They **p** Me, though they saw My
Eccl 7:23 All this I have **p** by wisdom
2Co 7:11 In all things you **p**
2Co 8:22 **p** diligent in many things
Col 4:11 they have **p** to be a comfort
1Ti 3:10 But let these also first be **p**
Heb 2: 2 through angels **p** steadfast
Heb 3: 9 **p** Me, and saw My works forty
Jas 1:12 for when he has been **p**, he

PROVEN (*see* PROVE)
2Sa 22:31 the word of the LORD is **p**
Ps 18:30 The word of the LORD is **p**
Phil 2:22 But you know his **p** character

PROVERB (*see* PROVERBS)
Deut 28:37 become an astonishment, a **p**
1Sa 10:12 Therefore it became a **p**
1Sa 24:13 As the **p** of the ancients says
1Ki 9: 7 Israel will be a **p** and a
2Ch 7:20 and will make it to be a **p**
Ps 49: 4 I will incline my ear to a **p**
Prov 1: 6 to understand a **p** and an
Prov 26: 7 is a **p** in the mouth of fools
Prov 26: 9 is a **p** in the mouth of fools
Is 14: 4 that you will take up this **p**
Ezek 12:22 man, what is this **p** that you
Ezek 12:23 I will lay this **p** to rest
Ezek 12:23 more use it as a **p** in Israel
Ezek 14: 8 man and make him a sign and a **p**
Ezek 16:44 will use this **p** against you
Ezek 18: 2 this **p** concerning the land of
Ezek 18: 3 longer use this **p** in Israel
Mic 2: 4 shall take up a **p** against you
Hab 2: 6 these take up a **p** against him

Luke 4:23 will surely say this **p** to Me
2Pe 2:22 them according to the true **p**

PROVERBS (*see* PROVERB)
Num 21:27 those who speak in **p** say
1Ki 4:32 He spoke three thousand **p**
Job 13:12 platitudes are **p** of ashes
Prov 1: 1 The **p** of Solomon the son of
Prov 10: 1 The **P** of Solomon
Prov 25: 1 These also are **p** of Solomon
Eccl 12: 9 out and set in order many **p**
Ezek 16:44 **p** will use this proverb

PROVES (*see* PROVE)
1Ki 1:52 If he **p** himself a worthy man,

PROVIDE (*see* PROVIDED, PROVIDES, PROVIDING, PROVISION)
Gen 22: 8 God will **p** for Himself the
Gen 30:30 I also **p** for my own house
Gen 45:11 There I will **p** for you, lest
Gen 50:21 I will **p** for you and your
Ex 21:19 and shall **p** for him to be
Num 6:21 else his hand is able to **p**
Num 11:22 them, to **p** enough for them
Num 11:22 them, to **p** enough for them
Deut 21: 8 **P** atonement, O LORD, for
Deut 32:43 He will **p** atonement for His
1Sa 16:17 **P** me now a man who can play
2Sa 19:33 I will **p** for you while you
1Ki 17: 9 a widow there to **p** for you
2Ch 30:18 May the good LORD **p**
Ezra 7:20 you may have occasion to **p**
Ps 65: 3 You will **p** atonement for them
Ps 65: 9 You **p** their grain, For so You
Ps 78:20 Can He **p** meat for His people
Ps 79: 9 **p** atonement for our sins, For
Prov 27:26 lambs will **p** your clothing
Jer 18:23 **P** no atonement for their
Jer 33: 9 prosperity that I **p** for it
Ezek 16:63 when I **p** you an atonement for
Ezek 46:18 he shall **p** an inheritance for
Matt 10: 9 **P** neither gold nor silver nor
Matt 26:53 He will **p** Me with more than
Luke 12:33 **p** yourselves money bags which
Acts 23:24 **p** mounts to set Paul on, and
Acts 24:23 friends to **p** for or visit him
1Ti 5: 8 anyone does not **p** for his own

PROVIDED (*see* PROVIDE)
Gen 22:14 of The LORD it shall be **p**
Gen 24:32 and **p** straw and feed for the
Gen 47:12 Then Joseph **p** his father, his
Ex 1:21 that He **p** households for them
Deut 21: 8 atonement shall be **p** on their
Deut 33:21 He **p** the first part for
1Sa 16: 1 For I have **p** Myself a king
2Sa 15: 1 **p** himself with chariots and
2Sa 19:32 And he had **p** the king with
1Ki 4: 7 who **p** food for the king and
1Ki 4:27 **p** food for King Solomon and
2Ch 2: 7 whom David my father **p**
2Ch 32:29 Moreover he **p** cities for
Esth 2: 9 **p** for her from the king's
Ps 68:10 **p** from Your goodness for the
Prov 16: 6 atonement is **p** for iniquity
Luke 8: 3 many others who **p** for Him
Luke 12:20 things be which you have **p**
Acts 20:34 have **p** for my necessities
Acts 28:10 they **p** such things as were
Heb 11:40 God having **p** something better

PROVIDES (*see* PROVIDE)
Job 12: 6 in what God **p** by His hand
Job 38:41 Who **p** food for the raven,
Prov 6: 8 **p** her supplies in the summer,
Prov 31:15 **p** food for her household, and

PROVIDING (*see* PROVIDE)
2Co 8:21 **p** honorable things, not only

PROVINCE (*see* PROVINCES)
Ezra 2: 1 the **p** who came back from the
Ezra 5: 8 we went into the **p** of Judea
Ezra 6: 2 that is in the **p** of Media
Ezra 7:16 find in all the **p** of Babylon
Neh 1: 3 from the captivity in the **p**
Neh 7: 6 the **p** who came back from the
Neh 11: 3 the **p** who dwelt in Jerusalem
Esth 1:22 to each **p** in its own script,
Esth 3:12 who were over each **p**, to the
Esth 3:12 to every **p** according to its
Esth 3:14 be issued as law in every **p**
Esth 4: 3 in every **p** where the king's
Esth 8: 9 to every **p** in its own script,
Esth 8:11 or **p** that would assault them
Esth 8:13 issued as a decree in every **p**
Esth 8:17 And in every **p** and city,
Esth 9:28 every family, every **p**, and
Eccl 5: 8 and righteousness in a **p**, do
Dan 2:48 over the whole **p** of Babylon
Dan 2:49 affairs of the **p** of Babylon
Dan 3: 1 of Dura, in the **p** of Babylon
Dan 3:12 affairs of the **p** of Babylon
Dan 3:30 Abed-Nego in the **p** of Babylon
Dan 8: 2 which is in the **p** of Elam
Dan 11:24 the richest places of the **p**
Acts 23:34 he asked what **p** he was from
Acts 25: 1 when Festus had come to the **p**

PROVINCES (*see* PROVINCE)
1Ki 20:14 By the young leaders of the **p**
1Ki 20:15 the young leaders of the **p**
1Ki 20:17 of the **p** went out first
1Ki 20:19 **p** went out of the city with
Ezra 4:15 city, harmful to kings and **p**
Ezra 4:20 all the **p** beyond the River
Esth 1: 1 hundred and twenty-seven **p**)
Esth 1: 3 of the **p** being before him
Esth 1:16 all the **p** of King Ahasuerus
Esth 1:22 letters to all the king's **p**
Esth 2: 3 in all the **p** of his kingdom
Esth 2:18 proclaimed a holiday in the **p**
Esth 3: 8 in all the **p** of your kingdom
Esth 3:13 into all the king's **p**, to
Esth 4:11 the people of the king's **p**
Esth 8: 5 who are in all the king's **p**
Esth 8: 9 the princes of the **p** from
Esth 8: 9 and twenty-seven **p** in all, to
Esth 8:12 all the **p** of King Ahasuerus
Esth 9: 2 **p** of King Ahasuerus to lay
Esth 9: 3 And all the officials of the **p**
Esth 9: 4 spread throughout all the **p**
Esth 9:12 in the rest of the king's **p**
Esth 9:16 king's **p** gathered together
Esth 9:20 all the **p** of King Ahasuerus
Esth 9:30 twenty-seven **p** of the kingdom
Eccl 2: 8 of kings and of the **p**
Lam 1: 1 the **p** has become a slave
Ezek 19: 8 him from the **p** on every side
Dan 3: 2 and all the officials of the **p**
Dan 3: 3 all the officials of the **p**

PROVING (*see* PROVE)
Acts 9:22 **p** that this Jesus is the
Eph 5:10 **p** what is acceptable to the

PROVISION (*see* PROVIDE, PROVISIONS)
Josh 9: 5 the bread of their **p** was dry
Josh 9:12 **p** from our houses on the day
1Ki 4: 7 each one made **p** for one month
1Ki 4:22 Now Solomon's **p** for one day
1Ch 29:19 for which I have made **p**
Ps 105:16 destroyed all the **p** of bread
Ps 132:15 I will abundantly bless her **p**
Dan 1: 5 **p** of the king's delicacies
Rom 13:14 make no **p** for the flesh, to

PROVISIONS (*see* PROVISION)
Gen 14:11 and Gomorrah, and all their **p**
Gen 42:25 and to give them **p** for the
Gen 45:21 and he gave them **p** for the
Ex 12:39 prepared **p** for themselves
Josh 1:11 Prepare **p** for yourselves,
Josh 9:11 Take **p** with you for the
Josh 9:14 Israel took some of their **p**
Judg 7: 8 So the people took **p** and their
Judg 20:10 to make **p** for the people,
1Sa 22:10 the LORD for him, gave him **p**
1Ki 20:27 were mustered and given **p**, and
2Ki 25:30 And as for his **p**, there was a
1Ch 12:40 **p** of flour and cakes of figs
2Ch 11:23 he gave them **p** in abundance
Neh 5:14 brothers ate the governor's **p**
Neh 5:18 not demand the governor's **p**
Neh 13:15 on which they were selling **p**
Jer 52:34 And as for his **p**, there was a
Luke 9:12 and country, and lodge and get **p**

PROVOCATION (*see* PROVOCATIONS, PROVOKE)
Deut 32:19 because of the **p** of His sons
1Ki 15:30 because of his **p** with which
1Ki 21:22 because of the **p** with which
Job 17: 2 not my eye dwell on their **p**
Jer 32:31 been to Me a **p** of My anger

PROVOCATIONS (*see* PROVOCATION)
2Ki 23:26 because of all the **p** with
Neh 9:18 of Egypt,' and worked great **p**
Neh 9:26 and they worked great **p**

PROVOKE (*see* PROVOCATION, PROVOKED, PROVOKES, PROVOKING)
Ex 23:21 do not **p** Him, for He will not
Deut 4:25 your God to **p** Him to anger
Deut 9:18 the LORD, to **p** Him to anger
Deut 31:20 and they will **p** Me and break My
Deut 31:29 to **p** Him to anger through the
Deut 32:21 But I will **p** them to jealousy
1Ki 14: 9 images to **p** Me to anger, and
1Ki 16: 2 to **p** Me to anger with their
1Ki 16:33 Ahab did more to **p** the LORD
2Ki 17:11 things to **p** the LORD to anger
2Ki 17:17 the LORD, to **p** Him to anger
2Ki 21: 6 the LORD, to **p** Him to anger
2Ki 22:17 that they might **p** Me to anger
2Ki 23:19 made to **p** the LORD to anger
2Ch 33: 6 the LORD, to **p** Him to anger
2Ch 34:25 that they might **p** Me to anger
Job 12: 6 those who **p** God are secure
Is 3: 8 to **p** the eyes of His glory
Is 65: 3 a people who **p** Me to anger
Jer 7:18 that they may **p** Me to anger
Jer 7:19 Do they **p** Me to anger
Jer 7:19 Do they not **p** themselves, to
Jer 11:17 to **p** Me to anger in offering
Jer 25: 6 do not **p** Me to anger with the
Jer 25: 7 that you might **p** Me to anger
Jer 32:29 other gods, to **p** Me to anger
Jer 32:32 have done to **p** Me to anger
Jer 44: 3 committed to **p** Me to anger
Jer 44: 8 in that you **p** Me to wrath
Ezek 8:17 returned to **p** Me to anger
Ezek 16:26 of harlotry to **p** Me to anger
Rom 10:19 I will **p** you to jealousy by
Rom 11:11 fall, to **p** them to jealousy,
Rom 11:14 if by any means I may **p** to
1Co 10:22 Or do we **p** the Lord to
Eph 6: 4 do not **p** your children to
Col 3:21 do not **p** your children, lest

PROVOKED (*see* PROVOKE)
Deut 9: 7 do not forget how you **p** the
Deut 9: 8 Horeb you **p** the LORD to wrath
Deut 9:22 you **p** the LORD to wrath
Deut 32:16 They **p** Him to jealousy with
Deut 32:16 they **p** Him to anger
Deut 32:21 They have **p** Me to jealousy by
Judg 2:12 and they **p** the LORD to anger
1Sa 1: 6 her rival also **p** her severely
1Sa 1: 7 of the LORD, that she **p** her
1Ki 14:22 they **p** Him to jealousy with
1Ki 15:30 with which he had **p** the LORD
1Ki 21:22 which you have **p** Me to anger
1Ki 22:53 **p** the LORD God of Israel to
2Ki 21:15 have **p** Me to anger since the
2Ki 23:26 with which Manasseh had **p** Him
2Ch 28:25 **p** to anger the LORD God of
Ezra 5:12 But because our fathers **p** the
Neh 4: 5 for they have **p** You to anger
Ps 78:40 How often they **p** Him in the
Ps 78:56 **p** the Most High God, And did
Ps 78:58 For they **p** Him to anger with
Ps 106:29 Thus they **p** Him to anger with
Is 1: 4 they have **p** to anger the Holy
Jer 8:19 Why have they **p** Me to anger
Jer 32:30 **p** Me only to anger with the
Ezek 20:28 **p** Me with their offerings
Hos 12:14 Ephraim **p** Him to anger most
Zech 8:14 your fathers **p** Me to wrath
Acts 17:16 his spirit was **p** within him
1Co 13: 5 not seek its own, is not **p**

PROVOKES (*see* PROVOKE)
Job 16: 3 Or what **p** you that you answer
Prov 20: 2 whoever **p** him to anger sins
Ezek 8: 3 was, which **p** to jealousy

PROVOKING (*see* PROVOKE)
1Ki 14:15 images, **p** the LORD to anger
1Ki 16: 7 **p** Him to anger with the work
1Ki 16:13 in **p** the LORD God of Israel
1Ki 16:26 **p** the LORD God of Israel to
Gal 5:26 **p** one another, envying one

PROW
Acts 27:30 out anchors from the **p**,
Acts 27:41 the **p** stuck fast and remained

PROWL (*see* PROWLER)
Ps 12: 8 The wicked **p** on every side,

PROWLER (*see* PROWL)
Prov 24:34 poverty will come like a **p**

PRUDENCE (*see* PRUDENT)
2Ch 2:12 a wise son, endowed with **p**
Job 11: 6 For they would double your **p**
Job 12:16 With Him are strength and **p**
Prov 1: 4 to give **p** to the simple, to
Prov 8: 5 you simple ones, understand **p**
Prov 8:12 I, wisdom, dwell with **p**, and
Eph 1: 8 toward us in all wisdom and **p**

PRUDENT (*see* PRUDENCE, PRUDENTLY)
1Sa 16:18 **p** in speech, and a handsome
Prov 12:16 but a **p** man covers shame
Prov 12:23 A **p** man conceals knowledge,
Prov 13:16 Every **p** man acts with
Prov 14: 8 The wisdom of the **p** is to
Prov 14:15 but the **p** man considers well
Prov 14:18 but the **p** are crowned with
Prov 15: 5 he who receives reproof is **p**
Prov 16:21 in heart will be called **p**
Prov 18:15 The heart of the **p** acquires
Prov 19:14 but a **p** wife is from the LORD
Prov 22: 3 A **p** man foresees evil and
Prov 27:12 A **p** man foresees evil and
Is 5:21 eyes, and **p** in their own sight
Is 10:13 and by my wisdom, for I am **p**
Is 29:14 their **p** men shall be hidden
Jer 49: 7 counsel perished from the **p**
Hos 14: 9 Who is **p**? Let him know them.
Amos 5:13 Therefore the **p** keep silent
Matt 11:25 things from the wise and **p**
Luke 10:21 things from the wise and **p**
1Co 1:19 the understanding of the **p**

PRUDENTLY (*see* PRUDENT)
Eccl 5: 1 Walk **p** when you go to the
Is 52:13 My Servant shall deal **p**, He

PRUNE (*see* PRUNED, PRUNES, PRUNING, PRUNINGHOOKS)
Lev 25: 3 you shall **p** your vineyard
Lev 25: 4 field nor **p** your vineyard

PRUNED (*see* PRUNE)
Is 5: 6 it shall not be **p** or dug, but

PRUNES (*see* PRUNE)
John 15: 2 branch that bears fruit He **p**

PRUNING (*see* PRUNE)
Is 2: 4 and their spears into **p** hooks
Is 18: 5 off the sprigs with **p** hooks
Mic 4: 3 and their spears into **p** hooks

PRUNINGHOOKS (*see* PRUNE)
Joel 3:10 swords and your **p** into spears

PSALM (*see* PSALMIST, PSALMS, PSALTERY)
1Ch 16: 7 this **p** into the hand of Asaph
Ps 98: 5 the harp and the sound of a **p**
Acts 13:33 also written in the second **P**
Acts 13:35 He also says in another **P**
1Co 14:26 together, each of you has a **p**

PSALMIST (*see* PSALM)
2Sa 23: 1 and the sweet **p** of Israel

PSALMS (*see* PSALM)
1Ch 16: 9 Sing to Him, sing **p** to Him
Neh 12: 8 who led the thanksgiving **p**
Ps 95: 2 shout joyfully to Him with **p**
Ps 105: 2 Sing to Him, sing **p** to Him
Luke 20:42 himself said in the Book of **P**
Luke 24:44 and the **P** concerning Me
Acts 1:20 is written in the book of **P**
Eph 5:19 speaking to one another in **p**
Col 3:16 admonishing one another in **p**
Jas 5:13 Let him sing **p**

PSALTERY (*see* PSALM)
Dan 3: 5 horn, flute, harp, lyre, and **p**
Dan 3:10 horn, flute, harp, lyre, and **p**
Dan 3:15 horn, flute, harp, lyre, and **p**

PTOLEMAIS
Acts 21: 7 from Tyre, we came to **P**,

PUAH
Ex 1:15 and the name of the other **P**
Num 26:23 of **P**, the family of the
Judg 10: 1 save Israel Tola the son of **P**
1Ch 7: 1 sons of Issachar were Tola, **P**

PUBLIC (*see* PUBLICLY)
Matt 1:19 to make her a **p** example, was
Col 2:15 He made a **p** spectacle of them

PUBLICLY (*see* PUBLIC)
Acts 18:28 vigorously refuted the Jews **p**
Acts 20:20 it to you, and taught you **p**

PUBLISHED
Esth 3:14 being **p** for all people, that
Esth 8:13 **p** to all people, so that the
Jon 3: 7 **p** throughout Nineveh by the

PUBLIUS
Acts 28: 7 the island, whose name was **P**
Acts 28: 8 of **P** lay sick of a fever and

PUDENS
2Ti 4:21 greets you, as well as **P**,

PUFFED (*see* PUFFS)
1Co 4: 6 that none of you may be **p** up
1Co 4:18 Now some are **p** up, as though
1Co 4:19 word of those who are **p** up
1Co 5: 2 And you are **p** up, and have not
1Co 13: 4 parade itself, is not **p** up
Col 2:18 vainly **p** up by his fleshly
1Ti 3: 6 lest being **p** up with pride he

PUFFS (*see* PUFFED)
1Co 8: 1 Knowledge **p** up, but love

PUL
2Ki 15:19 **P** king of Assyria came
2Ki 15:19 Menahem gave **P** a thousand
1Ch 5:26 spirit of **P** king of Assyria
Is 66:19 to Tarshish and **P** and Lud, who

PULL (*see* PULLED, PULLING, PULLS)
2Sa 17:13 we will **p** it into the river,
1Ki 13: 4 not **p** it back to himself
Ps 31: 4 **P** me out of the net which
Is 22:19 position he will **p** you down
Jer 1:10 to **p** down, to destroy and to
Jer 12: 3 **P** them out like sheep for the
Jer 18: 7 to **p** down, and to destroy it,
Jer 24: 6 not **p** them down, and I will
Jer 42:10 not **p** you down, and I will
Ezek 17: 9 will he not **p** up its roots,
Hos 10:11 I will make Ephraim **p** a plow
Mic 2: 8 you **p** off the robe with the
Luke 12:18 I will **p** down my barns and
Luke 14: 5 will not immediately **p** him

PULLED (*see* PULL)
Gen 19:10 **p** Lot into the house with
Gen 37:28 so the brothers **p** Joseph up
Deut 21: 3 which has not **p** with a yoke
Judg 16: 3 **p** them up, bar and all, put
Judg 16:14 **p** out the batten and the web
Ezra 6:11 a timber be **p** from his house
Neh 13:25 **p** out their hair, and made
Jer 33: 4 which have been **p** down to
Jer 38:13 So they **p** Jeremiah up with
Amos 9:15 be **p** up from the land I have
Mark 5: 4 had been **p** apart by him, and
Luke 17: 6 Be **p** up by the roots and be
Acts 23:10 might be **p** to pieces by them
Jude 12 twice dead, **p** up by the roots

PULLING (*see* PULL)
2Co 10: 4 in God for **p** down strongholds
Jude 23 fear, **p** them out of the fire,

PULLS (*see* PULL)
Prov 14: 1 but the foolish **p** it down
Matt 9:16 for the patch **p** away from the
Mark 2:21 new piece **p** away from the old

PULVERIZED
2Ki 23:12 **p** there, and threw their dust

PUNISH (*see* PUNISHED, PUNISHES, PUNISHING, PUNISHMENT, UNPUNISHED)
Lev 26:18 then I will **p** you seven times
Lev 26:24 I will **p** you yet seven times
Deut 22:18 shall take that man and **p** him
1Sa 15: 2 I will **p** what Amalek did to
Ps 59: 5 Awake to **p** all the nations
Prov 17:26 to **p** the righteous is not
Is 10:12 I will **p** the fruit of the
Is 13:11 I will **p** the world for its
Is 24:21 **p** on high the host of exalted
Is 26:21 to **p** the inhabitants of the
Is 27: 1 will **p** Leviathan the fleeing
Jer 5: 9 Shall I not **p** them for these
Jer 5:29 Shall I not **p** them for these
Jer 6:15 at the time I **p** them, they
Jer 9: 9 Shall I not **p** them for these
Jer 9:25 that I will **p** all those who
Jer 11:22 Behold, I will **p** them
Jer 14:10 iniquity now, and **p** their sins
Jer 21:14 But I will **p** you according to
Jer 23:34 I will even **p** that man and
Jer 25:12 that I will **p** the king of
Jer 27: 8 Babylon, that nation I will **p**
Jer 29:32 Behold, I will **p** Shemaiah the
Jer 30:20 I will **p** all who oppress them
Jer 36:31 I will **p** him, his family, and
Jer 44:13 For I will **p** those who dwell
Jer 44:29 that I will **p** you in this
Jer 49: 8 the time that I will **p** him
Jer 50:18 I will **p** the king of Babylon
Jer 50:31 the time that I will **p** you
Jer 51:44 I will **p** Bel in Babylon, and I
Lam 4:22 He will **p** your iniquity, O
Hos 2:13 I will **p** her for the days of
Hos 4: 9 So I will **p** them for their
Hos 4:14 I will not **p** your daughters
Hos 8:13 iniquity and **p** their sins
Hos 9: 9 He will **p** their sins
Hos 12: 2 will **p** Jacob according to his
Amos 3: 2 therefore I will **p** you for
Amos 3:14 the day I **p** Israel for their
Zeph 1: 8 that I will **p** the princes
Zeph 1: 9 In the same day I will **p** all
Zeph 1:12 **p** the men who are settled in
Zech 8:14 to **p** you when your fathers
Zech 10: 3 and I will **p** the goatherds
2Co 10: 6 and being ready to **p** all

PUNISHED (*see* PUNISH)
Ex 21:20 hand, he shall surely be **p**
Ex 21:21 day or two, he shall not be **p**
Ex 21:22 follows, he shall surely be **p**
Ezra 9:13 since You our God have **p** us
Job 35:15 He has not **p** in His anger
Ps 103:10 Nor **p** us according to our
Prov 21:11 When the scoffer is **p**, the
Prov 22: 3 the simple pass on and are **p**
Prov 27:12 the simple pass on and are **p**
Is 24:22 many days they will be **p**
Is 26:14 Therefore You have **p** and
Is 29: 6 You will be **p** by the LORD of
Jer 6: 6 This is the city to be **p**
Jer 44:13 Egypt, as I have **p** Jerusalem
Jer 50:18 land, as I have **p** the king of
Zeph 3: 7 everything for which I **p** her
Acts 22: 5 there to Jerusalem to be **p**
Acts 26:11 And I **p** them often in every
2Th 1: 9 These shall be **p** with

PUNISHES (*see* PUNISH)
Job 31:14 When He **p**, how shall I answer
Jer 13:21 will you say when He **p** you

PUNISHING (*see* PUNISH)
Acts 4:21 go, finding no way of **p** them

PUNISHMENT (*see* PUNISH, PUNISHMENTS)
Gen 4:13 My **p** is greater than I can
Gen 19:15 consumed in the **p** of the city
Ex 32:34 in the day when I visit for **p**
Ex 32:34 I will visit **p** upon them for
Lev 18:25 therefore I visit the **p** of
Deut 17: 8 or between one **p** or another
1Sa 28:10 no **p** shall come upon you for
2Ki 7: 9 some **p** will come upon us
Job 19:29 brings the **p** of the sword
Ps 94: 2 Render **p** to the proud
Prov 19:19 of great wrath will suffer **p**
Is 10: 3 will you do in the day of **p**
Is 30:32 where the staff of **p** passes
Jer 8:12 in the time of their **p** they
Jer 10:15 of their **p** they shall perish
Jer 11:23 even the year of their **p**
Jer 23:12 on them, the year of their **p**
Jer 46:21 them, the time of their **p**
Jer 46:25 I will bring **p** on Amon of No,
Jer 48:44 bring the year of their **p**
Jer 50:27 has come, the time of their **p**
Jer 51:18 of their **p** they shall perish
Lam 3:39 a man for the **p** of his sins
Lam 4: 6 The **p** of the iniquity of the
Lam 4: 6 the **p** of the sin of Sodom
Lam 4:22 The **p** of your iniquity is
Ezek 14:10 the **p** of the prophet shall be
Ezek 14:10 the **p** of the one who inquired
Hos 9: 7 The days of **p** have come

Joel 1:18 flocks of sheep suffer your **p**
Amos 1: 3 I will not turn away its **p**
Amos 1: 6 I will not turn away its **p**
Amos 1: 9 I will not turn away its **p**
Amos 1:11 I will not turn away its **p**
Amos 1:13 I will not turn away its **p**
Amos 2: 1 I will not turn away its **p**
Amos 2: 4 I will not turn away its **p**
Amos 2: 6 I will not turn away its **p**
Mic 7: 4 your watchman and your **p**
Zech 14:19 This shall be the **p** of Egypt
Zech 14:19 the **p** of all the nations that
Matt 25:46 go away into everlasting **p**
2Co 2: 6 This **p** which was inflicted by
Heb 10:29 Of how much worse **p**, do you
1Pe 2:14 by him for the **p** of evildoers
2Pe 2: 9 **p** for the day of judgment

PUNISHMENTS (*see* PUNISHMENT)
Ps 149: 7 nations, And **p** on the peoples

PUNITES
Num 26:23 of Puah, the family of the **P**

PUNON
Num 33:42 Zalmonah and camped at **P**
Num 33:43 They departed from **P** and

PUR
Esth 3: 7 they cast **P** (that is, the
Esth 9:24 them, and had cast **P** (that is
Esth 9:26 days Purim, after the name **P**

PURAH
Judg 7:10 the camp with **P** your servant
Judg 7:11 Then he went down with **P**

PURCHASE (*see* PURCHASED, PURCHASES)
Prov 17:16 a fool the **p** price of wisdom
Jer 32:11 So I took the **p** deed, both
Jer 32:12 I gave the **p** deed to Baruch
Jer 32:12 who signed the **p** deed, before
Jer 32:14 both this **p** deed which is
Jer 32:16 when I had delivered the **p**

PURCHASED (*see* PURCHASE)
Gen 25:10 **p** from the sons of Heth
Gen 49:32 were **p** from the sons of Heth
Ex 15:16 pass over whom You have **p**
Job 28:15 It cannot be **p** for gold, nor
Ps 74: 2 which You have **p** of old, The
Acts 1:18 (Now this man **p** a field with
Acts 8:20 of God could be **p** with money
Acts 20:28 which He **p** with His own blood
Eph 1:14 of the **p** possession, to the

PURCHASES (*see* PURCHASE)
Lev 25:33 if a man **p** a house from the

PURE (*see* PURER, PUREST, PURIFY, PURITY)
Ex 25:11 shall overlay it with **p** gold
Ex 25:17 make a mercy seat of **p** gold
Ex 25:24 shall overlay it with **p** gold
Ex 25:29 You shall make them of **p** gold
Ex 25:31 make a lampstand of **p** gold
Ex 25:36 one hammered piece of **p** gold
Ex 25:38 trays shall be of **p** gold
Ex 25:39 be made of a talent of **p** gold
Ex 27:20 **p** oil of pressed olives for
Ex 28:14 of **p** gold like braided cords
Ex 28:22 like braided cords of **p** gold
Ex 28:36 also make a plate of **p** gold
Ex 30: 3 and its horns with **p** gold
Ex 30:34 **p** frankincense with these
Ex 30:35 of the perfumer, salted, **p**
Ex 31: 8 the **p** lampstand with all its
Ex 37: 2 it with **p** gold inside and
Ex 37: 6 made the mercy seat of **p** gold
Ex 37:11 And he overlaid it with **p** gold
Ex 37:16 He made of **p** gold the
Ex 37:17 made the lampstand of **p** gold
Ex 37:22 one hammered piece of **p** gold
Ex 37:23 and its trays of **p** gold
Ex 37:24 Of a talent of **p** gold he made
Ex 37:26 And he overlaid it with **p** gold
Ex 37:29 the **p** incense of sweet spices
Ex 39:15 like braided cords of **p** gold
Ex 39:25 And they made bells of **p** gold
Ex 39:30 of the holy crown of **p** gold
Ex 39:37 the **p** lampstand with its
Lev 24: 2 that they bring to you **p** oil
Lev 24: 4 **p** gold lampstand before the
Lev 24: 6 on the **p** table before the
Lev 24: 7 you shall put **p** frankincense
2Sa 22:27 **p** You will show Yourself **p**
1Ki 6:20 He overlaid it with **p** gold
1Ki 6:21 of the temple with **p** gold
1Ki 7:49 the lampstands of **p** gold,
1Ki 7:50 and the censers of **p** gold
1Ki 10:18 and overlaid it with **p** gold
1Ki 10:21 of Lebanon were of **p** gold
1Ch 28:17 also **p** gold for the forks,
1Ch 28:17 the pitchers of **p** gold, and
2Ch 3: 4 the inside with **p** gold
2Ch 4:20 with their lamps of **p** gold
2Ch 4:22 and the censers of **p** gold
2Ch 9:17 and overlaid it with **p** gold
2Ch 9:20 of Lebanon were of **p** gold
2Ch 13:11 in order on the **p** table, and
Job 4:17 man be more **p** than his Maker
Job 8: 6 if you were **p** and upright,
Job 11: 4 have said, My doctrine is **p**
Job 15:14 is man, that he could be **p**
Job 15:15 are not **p** in His sight,
Job 16:17 my hands, and my prayer is **p**
Job 25: 4 Or how can he be **p** who is
Job 25: 5 stars are not **p** in His sight
Job 28:19 can it be valued in **p** gold
Job 33: 3 my lips utter **p** knowledge
Job 33: 9 I am **p**, without
Ps 12: 6 words of the LORD are **p** words
Ps 18:26 **p** You will show Yourself **p**
Ps 19: 8 commandment of the LORD is **p**
Ps 21: 3 crown of **p** gold upon his head
Ps 24: 4 a **p** heart, Who has not lifted
Ps 73: 1 To such as are **p** in heart
Ps 119:140 Your word is very **p**
Prov 15:26 words of the **p** are pleasant
Prov 16: 2 a man are **p** in his own eyes
Prov 20: 9 clean, I am **p** from my sin"
Prov 20:11 by whether what he does is **p**
Prov 21: 8 but as for the **p**, his work is
Prov 30: 5 Every word of God is **p**
Prov 30:12 that is **p** in its own eyes
Dan 7: 9 of His head was like **p** wool
Mic 6:11 Shall I count **p** those with
Zeph 3: 9 to the peoples a **p** language
Mal 1:11 to My name, and a **p** offering
Matt 5: 8 Blessed are the **p** in heart
Rom 14:20 All things indeed are **p**, but
Phil 4: 8 just, whatever things are **p**
1Ti 1: 5 is love from a **p** heart, from
1Ti 3: 9 the faith with a **p** conscience
1Ti 5:22 keep yourself **p**
2Ti 1: 3 I serve with a **p** conscience
2Ti 2:22 on the Lord out of a **p** heart
Tit 1:15 To the **p** all things are **p**,
Tit 1:15 and unbelieving nothing is **p**
Heb 10:22 bodies washed with **p** water
Jas 1:27 **P** and undefiled religion
Jas 3:17 that is from above is first **p**
1Pe 1:22 fervently with a **p** heart,
1Pe 2: 2 desire the **p** milk of the word
2Pe 3: 1 of which I stir up your **p**
1Jn 3: 3 himself, just as He is **p**
Rev 15: 6 clothed in **p** bright linen, and
Rev 21:18 and the city was **p** gold, like
Rev 21:21 street of the city was **p** gold
Rev 22: 1 he showed me a **p** river of

PURER (*see* PURE)
Hab 1:13 You are of **p** eyes than to

PUREST (*see* PURE)
2Ch 4:21 of gold, of **p** gold

PURGE (*see* PURGED)
2Ch 34: 3 year he began to **p** Judah and
Ps 51: 7 **P** me with hyssop, and I shall
Is 1:25 thoroughly **p** away your dross,
Ezek 20:38 I will **p** the rebels from
Dan 11:35 **p** them, and make them white,
Mal 3: 3 **p** them as gold and silver,
Matt 3:12 and He will thoroughly **p** His
Luke 3:17 and He will thoroughly **p** His
1Co 5: 7 Therefore **p** out the old
Heb 9:14 **p** your conscience from dead

PURGED (*see* PURGE)
2Ch 34: 8 reign, when he had **p** the land
Is 4: 4 **p** the blood of Jerusalem from
Is 6: 7 is taken away, and your sin **p**
Ezek 24:13 **p** you, and you were not **p**
Ezek 24:13 you will not be **p** of your
Heb 1: 3 He had by Himself **p** our sins
Heb 9:22 all things are **p** with blood
Heb 10: 2 For the worshipers, once **p**
2Pe 1: 9 he was **p** from his old sins

PURIFICATION (*see* PURIFY)
Lev 12: 4 of her **p** thirty-three days
Lev 12: 4 days of her **p** are fulfilled
Lev 12: 5 blood of her **p** sixty-six days
Lev 12: 6 days of her **p** are fulfilled
Num 8: 7 Sprinkle water of **p** on them
Num 19: 9 of Israel for the water of **p**
Num 19:13 because the water of **p** was
Num 19:17 heifer burnt for **p** from sin
Num 19:20 The water of **p** has not been
Num 19:21 of **p** shall wash his clothes
Num 19:21 of **p** shall be unclean until
Num 31:23 purified with the water of **p**
2Ch 30:19 to the **p** of the sanctuary
Neh 12:45 God and the charge of the **p**
Luke 2:22 her **p** according to the law of
John 2: 6 the manner of **p** of the Jews
John 3:25 disciples and the Jews about **p**
Acts 21:26 expiration of the days of **p**

PURIFIED (*see* PURIFY)
Lev 8:15 his finger, and **p** the altar
Num 8:21 And the Levites **p** themselves
Num 31:23 it shall be **p** with the water
Ezra 6:20 the Levites had **p** themselves
Neh 12:30 and Levites **p** themselves, and
Neh 12:30 **p** the people, the gates, and
Ps 12: 6 of earth, **P** seven times
Dan 12:10 Many shall be **p**, made white,
Acts 21:24 be **p** with them, and pay their
Acts 21:26 day, having been **p** with them
Acts 24:18 Asia found me **p** in the temple
Heb 9:23 should be **p** with these, but
1Pe 1:22 Since you have **p** your souls

PURIFIER (*see* PURIFY)
Mal 3: 3 as a refiner and a **p** of silver

PURIFIES (*see* PURIFY)
1Jn 3: 3 this hope in Him **p** himself

PURIFY (*see* PURE, PURIFICATION, PURIFIED, PURIFIER, PURIFIES, PURIFYING)
Gen 35: 2 **p** yourselves, and change your
Num 19:12 He shall **p** himself with the
Num 19:12 But if he does not **p** himself
Num 19:13 died, and does not **p** himself
Num 19:19 day he shall **p** himself, wash
Num 19:20 unclean and does not **p** himself
Num 31:19 **p** yourselves and your captives
Num 31:20 **P** every garment, everything
Is 66:17 **p** themselves, to go to the
Ezek 43:26 **p** it, and so consecrate it
Mal 3: 3 He will **p** the sons of Levi,
John 11:55 the Passover, to **p** themselves
Tit 2:14 **p** for Himself His own special
Jas 4: 8 and **p** your hearts, you

PURIFYING (*see* PURIFY)
Num 19: 9 it is for **p** from sin
1Ch 23:28 in the **p** of all holy things
Mark 7:19 eliminated, thus **p** all foods
Acts 15: 9 them, **p** their hearts by faith
Heb 9:13 for the **p** of the flesh,

PURIM
Esth 9:26 So they called these days **P**
Esth 9:28 that these days of **P** should
Esth 9:29 this second letter about **P**
Esth 9:31 of **P** at their appointed time
Esth 9:32 confirmed these matters of **P**

PURITY (*see* PURE)
Job 22:30 by the **p** of your hands
Prov 22:11 He who loves **p** of heart and
2Co 6: 6 by **p**, by knowledge, by
1Ti 4:12 in spirit, in faith, in **p**
1Ti 5: 2 as sisters, with all **p**

PURPLE
Ex 25: 4 blue and **p** and scarlet yarn,
Ex 26: 1 linen thread, and blue and **p**
Ex 26:31 a veil woven of blue and **p**
Ex 26:36 woven of blue and **p** and
Ex 27:16 long, woven of blue and **p** and
Ex 28: 5 take the gold and blue and **p**
Ex 28: 6 ephod of gold and blue and **p**
Ex 28: 8 woven of gold and blue and **p**
Ex 28:15 of gold and blue and **p** and
Ex 28:33 pomegranates of blue and **p**
Ex 35: 6 blue and **p** and scarlet yarn,
Ex 35:23 with whom was found blue and **p**
Ex 35:25 they had spun, of blue and **p**

Ex 35:35 tapestry maker, in blue and **p**
Ex 36: 8 linen thread, and blue and **p**
Ex 36:35 a veil woven of blue and **p**
Ex 36:37 door, woven of blue and **p** and
Ex 38:18 court was woven of blue and **p**
Ex 38:23 a weaver in blue and **p** and
Ex 39: 1 Of the blue and **p** and scarlet
Ex 39: 2 ephod of gold and blue and **p**
Ex 39: 3 work it in with the blue and **p**
Ex 39: 5 woven of gold and blue and **p**
Ex 39: 8 ephod, of gold and blue and **p**
Ex 39:24 pomegranates of blue and **p**
Ex 39:29 of fine linen and blue and **p**
Num 4:13 and spread a **p** cloth over it
Judg 8:26 **p** robes which were on the
2Ch 2: 7 in bronze and iron, in **p** and
2Ch 2:14 and iron, stone and wood, **p**
2Ch 3:14 he made the veil of blue and **p**
Esth 1: 6 **p** on silver rods and marble
Esth 8:15 a garment of fine linen and **p**
Prov 31:22 clothing is fine linen and **p**
Song 3:10 of gold, its seat of **p**, its
Song 7: 5 hair of your head is like **p**
Jer 10: 9 blue and **p** are their clothing
Ezek 23: 6 who were clothed in **p**,
Ezek 27: 7 **p** from the coasts of Elishah
Ezek 27:16 for your wares emeralds, **p**
Ezek 27:24 in **p** clothes, in embroidered
Dan 5: 7 shall be clothed with **p** and
Dan 5:16 you shall be clothed with **p**
Dan 5:29 and they clothed Daniel with **p**
Mark 15:17 And they clothed Him with **p**
Mark 15:20 Him, they took the **p** off Him
Luke 16:19 rich man who was clothed in **p**
John 19: 2 and they put on Him a **p** robe
John 19: 5 crown of thorns and the **p** robe
Acts 16:14 She was a seller of **p** from
Rev 17: 4 The woman was arrayed in **p**
Rev 18:12 and pearls, fine linen and **p**
Rev 18:16 was clothed in fine linen, **p**

PURPOSE (*see* PURPOSED, PURPOSES)
Ex 9:16 But indeed for this **p** I have
2Ch 32: 2 that his **p** was to make war
Ezra 4: 5 them to frustrate their **p** all
Neh 8: 4 which they had made for the **p**
Job 42: 2 that no **p** of Yours can be
Ps 20: 4 desire, And fulfill all your **p**
Prov 20:18 Every **p** is established by
Eccl 3: 1 time for every **p** under heaven
Eccl 3:17 be a time there for every **p**
Is 1:11 To what **p** is the multitude of
Is 14:26 This is the **p** that is
Is 30: 7 shall help in vain and to no **p**
Jer 6:20 For what **p** to Me comes
Jer 26: 3 the calamity which I **p** to
Jer 36: 3 which I **p** to bring upon them
Jer 51:29 for every **p** of the LORD shall
Dan 6:17 that the **p** concerning Daniel
Matt 26: 8 To what **p** is this waste
Mark 1:38 because for this **p** I have
Luke 4:43 for this **p** I have been sent
John 12:27 But for this **p** I came to this
Acts 4:28 Your **p** determined before to
Acts 9:21 and has come here for that **p**
Acts 11:23 them all that with **p** of heart
Acts 26:16 appeared to you for this **p**
Acts 27:13 they had obtained their **p**
Acts 27:43 Paul, kept them from their **p**
Rom 8:28 the called according to His **p**
Rom 9:11 that the **p** of God according
Rom 9:17 Even for this same **p** I have
Gal 3:19 What **p** then does the law
Eph 1:11 according to the **p** of Him who
Eph 3:11 **p** which He accomplished in
Eph 6:22 sent to you for this very **p**
Col 4: 8 him to you for this very **p**
1Ti 1: 5 Now the **p** of the commandment
2Ti 1: 9 but according to His own **p**
2Ti 3:10 doctrine, manner of life, **p**
Phm 15 for a while for this **p**, that
1Jn 3: 8 For this **p** the Son of God was
Rev 17:17 their hearts to fulfill His **p**

PURPOSED (*see* PURPOSE)
2Sa 17:14 For the LORD had **p** to
Ps 17: 3 I have **p** that my mouth shall
Ps 140: 4 Who have **p** to make my steps
Is 14:24 come to pass, and as I have **p**
Is 14:26 is **p** against the whole earth
Is 14:27 For the LORD of hosts has **p**
Is 19:12 of hosts has **p** against Egypt
Is 23: 9 The LORD of hosts has **p** it
Is 46:11 I have **p** it
Jer 4:28 I have **p** and will not relent,
Lam 2: 8 The LORD has **p** to destroy the
Lam 2:17 The LORD has done what He **p**
Dan 1: 8 But Daniel **p** in his heart
Acts 19:21 Paul **p** in the Spirit, when he
Eph 1: 9 which He **p** in Himself,

PURPOSELY
Ruth 2:16 the bundles fall **p** for her

PURPOSES (*see* PURPOSE)
2Ki 12: 4 all the money that a man **p** in
Job 17:11 my **p** are broken off, even the
Jer 49:20 His **p** that He has proposed
Jer 50:45 His **p** that He has proposed
2Co 9: 7 one give as he **p** in his heart

PURSE (*see* PURSES)
Prov 1:14 us, let us all have one **p**"

PURSES (*see* PURSE)
Prov 16:30 he **p** his lips and brings about
Is 3:22 the outer garments, the **p**

PURSUE (*see* PURSUED, PURSUER, PURSUES, PURSUING, PURSUIT)
Gen 35: 5 they did not **p** the sons of
Ex 14: 4 heart, so that he will **p** them
Ex 15: 9 The enemy said, 'I will **p**
Deut 19: 6 **p** the manslayer and overtake
Deut 28:22 they shall **p** you until you
Deut 28:45 shall come upon you and **p** and
Josh 2: 5 **p** them quickly, for you may
Josh 8:16 called together to **p** them
Josh 10:19 but **p** your enemies, and attack
1Sa 24:14 Whom do you **p**?
1Sa 25:29 Yet a man has risen to **p** you
1Sa 26:18 my lord thus **p** his servant
1Sa 30: 8 Shall I **p** this troop
1Sa 30: 8 **P**, for you shall surely
2Sa 2:28 did not **p** Israel anymore, nor
2Sa 17: 1 will arise and **p** David tonight
2Sa 20: 6 and **p** him, lest he find for
2Sa 20: 7 to **p** Sheba the son of Bichri
2Sa 20:13 went on after Joab to **p** Sheba
2Sa 24:13 enemies, while they **p** you
Job 13:25 And will You **p** dry stubble
Job 30:15 they **p** my honor as the wind,
Ps 7: 5 Let the enemy **p** me and
Ps 34:14 Seek peace, and **p** it
Ps 35: 3 spear, And stop those who **p** me
Ps 35: 6 the angel of the LORD **p** them
Ps 71:11 **P** and take him, for there is
Ps 83:15 So **p** them with Your tempest,
Prov 19: 7 He may **p** them with words, yet
Is 30:16 who **p** you shall be swift
Jer 29:18 I will **p** them with the sword,
Jer 48: 2 The sword shall **p** you
Lam 3:66 In Your anger, **p** and destroy
Lam 5: 5 They **p** at our heels
Ezek 33:31 their hearts **p** their own gain
Ezek 35: 6 blood, and blood shall **p** you
Ezek 35: 6 therefore blood shall **p** you
Hos 6: 3 let us **p** the knowledge of the
Hos 8: 3 the enemy will **p** him
Nah 1: 8 darkness will **p** His enemies
Rom 9:30 who did not **p** righteousness,
Rom 14:19 Therefore let us **p** the things
1Co 14: 1 **P** love, and desire spiritual
1Th 5:15 but always **p** what is good
1Ti 6:11 **p** righteousness, godliness,
2Ti 2:22 but **p** righteousness, faith,
Heb 12:14 **P** peace with all men, and
1Pe 3:11 let him seek peace and **p** it

PURSUED (*see* PURSUE)
Gen 14:15 **p** them as far as Hobah, which
Gen 31:23 **p** him for seven days' journey
Gen 31:36 that you have so hotly **p** me
Ex 14: 8 he **p** the children of Israel
Ex 14: 9 So the Egyptians **p** them, all
Ex 14:23 And the Egyptians **p** and went
Deut 11: 4 overflow them as they **p** you
Josh 2: 7 Then the men **p** them by the
Josh 2: 7 those who **p** them had gone out
Josh 8:16 they **p** Joshua and were drawn
Josh 8:17 the city open and **p** Israel
Josh 8:24 wilderness where they **p** them
Josh 24: 6 the Egyptians **p** your fathers
Judg 1: 6 fled, and they **p** him and caught
Judg 4:16 But Barak **p** the chariots and
Judg 4:22 And then, as Barak **p** Sisera
Judg 7:23 Manasseh, and **p** the Midianites
Judg 7:25 They **p** Midian and brought the
Judg 8:12 and Zalmunna fled, he **p** them
Judg 20:45 Then they **p** them relentlessly
1Sa 7:11 **p** the Philistines, and drove
1Sa 17:52 **p** the Philistines as far as
1Sa 23:25 he **p** David in the Wilderness
1Sa 30:10 But David **p**, he and four
2Sa 2:19 So Asahel **p** Abner, and in
2Sa 2:24 Joab and Abishai also **p** Abner
2Sa 20:10 Abishai his brother **p** Sheba
2Sa 22:38 I have **p** my enemies and
1Ki 20:20 fled, and Israel **p** them
2Ki 5:21 So Gehazi **p** Naaman
2Ki 9:27 So Jehu **p** him, and said
2Ki 25: 5 of the Chaldeans **p** the king
2Ch 13:19 Abijah **p** Jeroboam and took
2Ch 14:13 were with him **p** them to Gerar
Ps 18:37 I have **p** my enemies and
Is 41: 3 Who **p** them, and passed safely
Jer 39: 5 But the Chaldean army **p** them
Jer 52: 8 of the Chaldeans **p** the king
Lam 3:43 Yourself with anger and **p** us
Lam 4:19 They **p** us on the mountains and
Amos 1:11 because he **p** his brother with

PURSUER (*see* PURSUE, PURSUERS)
Lam 1: 6 without strength before the **p**

PURSUERS (*see* PURSUER)
Josh 2:16 mountain, lest the **p** meet you
Josh 2:16 until the **p** have returned
Josh 2:22 days until the **p** returned
Josh 2:22 The **p** sought them all along
Josh 8:20 turned back on the **p**
Lam 4:19 Our **p** were swifter than the

PURSUES (*see* PURSUE)
Lev 26:17 shall flee when no one **p** you
Lev 26:36 they shall fall when no one **p**
Lev 26:37 before a sword, when no one **p**
Josh 20: 5 if the avenger of blood **p** him
Prov 11:19 so he who **p** evil **p** it
Prov 13:21 Evil **p** sinners, but to the
Prov 28: 1 The wicked flee when no one **p**
Hos 12: 1 the wind, and **p** the east wind

PURSUING (*see* PURSUE)
Judg 8: 5 I am **p** Zebah and Zalmunna,
1Sa 14:46 from **p** the Philistines, and
1Sa 23:28 Saul returned from **p** David
2Sa 2:26 return from **p** their brethren
2Sa 2:27 given up **p** their brethren
2Sa 2:30 So Joab returned from **p** Abner
2Sa 18:16 people returned from **p** Israel
1Ki 22:33 they turned back from **p** him
2Ch 18:32 they turned back from **p** him
Rom 9:31 **p** the law of righteousness,

PURSUIT (*see* PURSUE, PURSUITS)
Gen 14:14 and went in **p** as far as Dan
Judg 8: 4 exhausted but still in **p**

PURSUITS (*see* PURSUIT)
Jas 1:11 also will fade away in his **p**

PUSH (*see* PUSHED, PUSHES, PUSHING)
Deut 33:17 **p** the peoples to the ends of
2Ki 4:27 came near to **p** her away
Job 24: 4 They **p** the needy off the road
Job 30:12 they **p** away my feet, and they
Ps 44: 5 we will **p** down our enemies
Joel 2: 8 They do not **p** one another

PUSHED (*see* PUSH)
Num 22:25 she **p** herself against the
Judg 16:30 he **p** with all his might, and
Ps 118:13 You **p** me violently, that I
Ezek 34:21 Because you have **p** with side
Acts 7:27 his neighbor wrong **p** him away

PUSHES (*see* PUSH)
Num 35:20 If he **p** him out of hatred or
Num 35:22 But if he **p** him suddenly

PUSHING (*see* PUSH)
Dan 8: 4 I saw the ram **p** westward,

PUT (*see* PREFACE)

PUT*
Gen 10: 6 of Ham were Cush, Mizraim, **P**
1Ch 1: 8 of Ham were Cush, Mizraim, **P**
Nah 3: 9 **P** and Lubim were your helpers

PUTEOLI
Acts 28:13 and the next day we came to **P**

PUTHITES
1Ch 2:53 were the Ithrites, the **P**, the

PUTIEL
Ex 6:25 of the daughters of **P** as wife

PUTREFY (*see* PUTREFYING)
Eccl 10: 1 Dead flies **p** the perfumer's

PUTREFYING (*see* PUTREFY)
Is 1: 6 wounds and bruises and **p** sores

PUTS (*see* PREFACE)

PUTTING (*see* PREFACE)

PUVAH
Gen 46:13 sons of Issachar were Tola, **P**

PYRE
Is 30:33 its **p** is fire with much wood
Ezek 24: 9 I too will make the **p** great

QUADRANS
Mark 12:42 in two mites, which make a **q**

QUAIL (*see* QUAILS)
Num 11:31 it brought **q** from the sea and
Num 11:32 and gathered the **q** (he who
Ps 105:40 people asked, and He brought **q**

QUAILS (*see* QUAIL)
Ex 16:13 So it was that **q** came up at

QUAKE (*see* QUAKED, QUAKES, QUAKING)
Nah 1: 5 The mountains **q** before Him

QUAKED (*see* QUAKE)
Ex 19:18 the whole mountain **q** greatly
1Sa 14:15 and the earth **q**, so that it
Ps 18: 7 of the hills also **q** and were
Matt 27:51 and the earth **q**, and the rocks

QUAKES (*see* QUAKE)
Joel 2:10 The earth **q** before them, the

QUAKING (*see* QUAKE)
Ezek 12:18 of man, eat your bread with **q**

QUALIFIED
2Ki 10: 3 choose the best **q** of your
Col 1:12 to the Father who has **q** us to

QUALITY
Ex 30:23 take for yourself **q** spices
Jer 2:21 vine, a seed of highest **q**

QUANTITIES (*see* QUANTITY)
1Ki 10:11 brought great **q** of almug wood

QUANTITY (*see* QUANTITIES)
Is 22:24 issue, all vessels of small **q**

QUARREL (*see* QUARRELED, QUARRELSOME)
Gen 26:22 and they did not **q** over it
2Ki 5: 7 see how he seeks a **q** with me
Prov 17:14 contention before a **q** starts
Prov 20: 3 since any fool can start a **q**
Prov 26:17 meddles in a **q** not his own is
Matt 12:19 He will not **q** nor cry out
2Ti 2:24 not **q** but be gentle to all

QUARRELED (*see* QUARREL)
Gen 26:20 Gerar **q** with Isaac's herdsmen
Gen 26:20 Esek, because they **q** with him
Gen 26:21 they **q** over that one also
John 6:52 therefore **q** among themselves

QUARRELSOME (*see* QUARREL)
1Ti 3: 3 for money, but gentle, not **q**

QUARRIED (*see* QUARRY)
1Ki 5:15 eighty thousand who **q** stone
1Ki 5:18 and the Gebalites **q** them

QUARRIES (*see* QUARRY)
Eccl 10: 9 He who **q** stones may be hurt

QUARRY (*see* QUARRIED, QUARRIES)
1Ki 5:17 them to **q** large stones,
1Ki 6: 7 with stone finished at the **q**
2Ch 2: 2 eighty thousand to **q** stone in

QUART (*see* QUARTS)
Rev 6: 6 A **q** of wheat for a denarius,

QUARTER (*see* QUARTERS)
Gen 19: 4 all the people from every **q**
Josh 15: 5 the border on the northern **q**
2Ki 22:14 in Jerusalem in the Second **Q**
2Ch 34:22 in Jerusalem in the Second **Q**
Is 47:15 wander each one to his **q**
Zeph 1:10 a wailing from the Second **Q**
Mark 1:45 they came to Him from every **q**

QUARTERMASTER
Jer 51:59 And Seraiah was the **q**

QUARTERS (*see* QUARTER)
Ex 13: 7 seen among you in all your **q**
Esth 2: 3 citadel, into the women's **q**
Esth 2:11 of the court of the women's **q**
Esth 2:13 **q** to the king's palace
Jer 49:36 from the four **q** of heaven

QUARTS (*see* QUART)
Rev 6: 6 and three **q** of barley for a

QUARTUS
Rom 16:23 of the city, greets you, and **Q**

QUARTZ
Job 28:18 shall be made of coral or **q**

QUEEN (*see* QUEEN'S, QUEENS)
1Ki 10: 1 Now when the **q** of Sheba heard
1Ki 10: 4 when the **q** of Sheba had seen
1Ki 10:10 the **q** of Sheba gave to King
1Ki 10:13 King Solomon gave the **q** of
1Ki 11:19 is, the sister of **Q** Tahpenes
1Ki 15:13 from being **q** mother, because
2Ki 10:13 and the sons of the **q** mother
2Ch 9: 1 Now when the **q** of Sheba heard
2Ch 9: 3 when the **q** of Sheba had seen
2Ch 9: 9 the **q** of Sheba gave to King
2Ch 9:12 **q** of Sheba all she desired
2Ch 15:16 the king, from being **q** mother
Neh 2: 6 **q** also sitting beside him)
Esth 1: 9 **Q** Vashti also made a feast
Esth 1:11 to bring **Q** Vashti before the
Esth 1:12 But **Q** Vashti refused to come
Esth 1:15 What shall we do to **Q** Vashti
Esth 1:16 **Q** Vashti has not only wronged
Esth 1:17 **Q** Vashti to be brought in
Esth 1:18 of the behavior of the **q**
Esth 2: 4 king be **q** instead of Vashti
Esth 2:17 made her **q** instead of Vashti
Esth 2:22 Mordecai, who told **Q** Esther
Esth 4: 4 the **q** was deeply distressed
Esth 5: 2 when the king saw **Q** Esther
Esth 5: 3 What do you wish, **Q** Esther
Esth 5:12 **Q** Esther invited no one but
Esth 7: 1 went to dine with **Q** Esther
Esth 7: 2 is your petition, **Q** Esther
Esth 7: 3 Then **Q** Esther answered and
Esth 7: 5 answered and said to **Q** Esther
Esth 7: 6 before the king and **q**
Esth 7: 7 Haman stood before **Q** Esther
Esth 7: 8 the **q** while I am in the house
Esth 8: 1 day King Ahasuerus gave **Q**
Esth 8: 7 Ahasuerus said to **Q** Esther
Esth 9:12 And the king said to **Q** Esther
Esth 9:29 Then **Q** Esther, the daughter
Esth 9:31 **Q** Esther had prescribed for
Ps 45: 9 the **q** in gold from Ophir
Jer 7:18 cakes for the **q** of heaven
Jer 13:18 the king and to the **q** mother
Jer 29: 2 the **q** mother, the eunuchs,
Jer 44:17 incense to the **q** of heaven
Jer 44:18 incense to the **q** of heaven
Jer 44:19 incense to the **q** of heaven
Jer 44:25 incense to the **q** of heaven
Dan 5:10 The **q**, because of the words
Dan 5:10 And the **q** spoke, saying,
Matt 12:42 The **q** of the South will rise
Luke 11:31 The **q** of the South will rise
Acts 8:27 the **q** of the Ethiopians, who
Rev 18: 7 in her heart, 'I sit as **q**

QUEEN'S (*see* QUEEN)
Esth 1:17 For the **q** behavior will

QUEENS (*see* QUEEN)
Song 6: 8 There are sixty **q** and eighty
Song 6: 9 and called her blessed, the **q**
Is 49:23 their **q** your nursing mothers

QUENCH (*see* QUENCHED, UNQUENCHABLE)
2Sa 21:17 lest you **q** the lamp of Israel
Ps 104:11 wild donkeys **q** their thirst
Song 8: 7 Many waters cannot **q** love
Is 1:31 and no one shall **q** them
Is 42: 3 and smoking flax He will not **q**
Jer 4: 4 burn so that no one can **q** it
Jer 21:12 burn so that no one can **q** it
Amos 5: 6 with no one to **q** it in Bethel
Matt 12:20 and smoking flax He will not **q**
Eph 6:16 which you will be able to **q**
1Th 5:19 Do not **q** the Spirit

QUENCHED (*see* QUENCH)
Num 11: 2 to the LORD, the fire was **q**
2Ki 22:17 this place and shall not be **q**
2Ch 34:25 on this place, and not be **q**
Ps 118:12 They were **q** like a fire of
Is 34:10 shall not be **q** night or day
Is 43:17 they are **q** like a wick)
Is 66:24 die, and their fire is not **q**
Jer 7:20 And it will burn and not be **q**
Jer 17:27 and it shall not be **q**
Ezek 20:47 blazing flame shall not be **q**
Ezek 20:48 it shall not be **q**
Mark 9:43 fire that shall never be **q**
Mark 9:44 not die and the fire is not **q**
Mark 9:45 fire that shall never be **q**
Mark 9:46 not die and the fire is not **q**
Mark 9:48 not die and the fire is not **q**
Heb 11:34 **q** the violence of fire,

QUESTION (*see* QUESTIONED, QUESTIONING, QUESTIONS)
Job 38: 3 I will **q** you, and you shall
Job 40: 7 I will **q** you, and you shall
Job 42: 4 You said, 'I will **q** you, and
Matt 22:35 them, a lawyer, asked Him a **q**
Matt 22:46 did anyone dare **q** Him anymore
Mark 11:29 I will also ask you one **q**
Mark 12:34 after that no one dared **q** Him
Luke 20:40 they dared not **q** Him anymore
Luke 22:23 began to **q** among themselves
John 16:30 need that anyone should **q** You
Acts 15: 2 and elders, about this **q**
Acts 18:15 But if it is a **q** of words
Acts 19:40 in **q** for today's uproar,
1Co 10:27 asking no **q** for conscience'

QUESTIONED (*see* QUESTION)
2Ch 31: 9 Then Hezekiah **q** the priests
Mark 1:27 amazed, so that they **q** among
Luke 23: 9 Then he **q** Him with many words

QUESTIONING (*see* QUESTION)
Ezra 10:17 **q** all the men who had taken
Mark 9:10 **q** what the rising from the

QUESTIONS (*see* QUESTION)
1Ki 10: 1 came to test him with hard **q**
1Ki 10: 3 So Solomon answered all her **q**
2Ch 9: 1 to test Solomon with hard **q**
2Ch 9: 2 So Solomon answered all her **q**
Luke 2:46 to them and asking them **q**
Acts 23:29 concerning **q** of their law
Acts 25:19 but had some **q** against him
Acts 25:20 I was uncertain of such **q**
Acts 26: 3 **q** which have to do with the
1Co 10:25 asking no **q** for conscience'

QUICK (*see* QUICKLY, QUICK-TEMPERED)
Dan 1: 4 and **q** to understand, who had

QUICKLY (*see* QUICK)
Gen 18: 6 **Q**, make ready three measures
Gen 27:20 that you have found it so **q**
Ex 32: 8 **q** out of the way which I
Num 16:46 take it **q** to the congregation
Deut 9: 3 them out and destroy them **q**
Deut 9:12 go down **q** from here, for your
Deut 9:12 they have **q** turned aside from
Deut 9:16 You had turned aside **q** from
Deut 11:17 you perish **q** from the good
Deut 28:20 and until you perish **q**,
Josh 2: 5 pursue them **q**, for you may
Josh 8:19 arose **q** out of their place
Josh 10: 6 come up to us **q**, save us and
Josh 23:16 you shall perish **q** from the
Judg 2:17 They turned **q** from the way in
Judg 9:54 Then he called **q** to the young
Judg 20:37 the men in ambush **q** rushed
1Sa 20:19 stayed three days, go down **q**
2Sa 5:24 then you shall advance **q**
2Sa 17:16 Now therefore, send **q** and tell

R

Gen 48: 7 **R** died beside me in the land
Ruth 4:11 coming to your house like **R**
Jer 31:15 **R** weeping for her children,
Matt 2:18 **R** weeping for her children,

RACHEL'S (*see* RACHEL)
Gen 30: 7 **R** maid Bilhah conceived again
Gen 31:33 Leah's tent and entered **R** tent
Gen 35:20 pillar of **R** grave to this day
Gen 35:25 **R** maidservant, were Dan and
1Sa 10: 2 by **R** tomb in the territory of

RADDAI
1Ch 2:14 the fourth, **R** the fifth,

RADIANT
Ps 34: 5 They looked to Him and were **r**
Is 60: 5 you shall see and become **r**

RADIATING
Ezek 1: 4 **r** out of its midst like the

RAFTERS
Song 1:17 are cedar, and our **r** of fir

RAFTS
1Ki 5: 9 I will float them in **r** by sea
2Ch 2:16 to you in **r** by sea to Joppa

RAGE (*see* RAGED, RAGES, RAGING)
2Ki 5:12 he turned and went away in a **r**
2Ki 19:27 in, and your **r** against Me
2Ki 19:28 Because your **r** against Me
2Ch 28: 9 a **r** that reaches up to heaven
Job 39:24 distance with fierceness and **r**
Job 40:11 Disperse the **r** of your wrath
Job 40:23 Indeed the river may **r**, Yet
Ps 2: 1 Why do the nations **r**, And the
Ps 7: 6 of the **r** of my enemies, And
Is 37:28 in, and your **r** against Me
Is 37:29 Because your **r** against Me
Jer 46: 9 Come up, O horses, and **r**, O
Dan 3:13 Then Nebuchadnezzar, in **r**
Dan 8: 7 was moved with **r** against him
Dan 11:11 South shall be moved with **r**
Dan 11:30 return in **r** against the holy
Nah 2: 4 The chariots **r** in the streets
Luke 6:11 But they were filled with **r**
Acts 4:25 Why did the nations **r**, and

RAGED (*see* RAGE)
Ps 46: 6 The nations **r**, the kingdoms

RAGES (*see* RAGE)
Prov 14:16 from evil, but a fool **r** and is
Prov 18: 1 he **r** against all wise
Prov 29: 9 whether the fool **r** or laughs

RAGING (*see* RAGE)
Ps 22:13 Me with their mouths, As a **r**
Ps 89: 9 You rule the **r** of the sea
Ezek 1: 4 a great cloud with **r** fire
Jon 1:15 and the sea ceased from its **r**
Luke 8:24 wind and the **r** of the water
Jude 13 **r** waves of the sea, foaming

RAGS
Prov 23:21 will clothe a man with **r**
Is 64: 6 are like filthy **r**
Jer 38:11 there old clothes and old **r**
Jer 38:12 **r** under your armpits, under

RAHAB
Josh 2: 1 the house of a harlot named **R**
Josh 2: 3 the king of Jericho sent to **R**
Josh 6:17 Only **R** the harlot shall live,
Josh 6:23 went in and brought out **R**, her
Josh 6:25 And Joshua spared **R** the harlot
Ps 87: 4 I will make mention of **R** and
Ps 89:10 You have broken **R** in pieces
Is 51: 9 not the arm that cut **R** apart
Matt 1: 5 Salmon begot Boaz by **R**, Boaz
Heb 11:31 By faith the harlot **R** did not
Jas 2:25 was not **R** the harlot also

RAHAB-HEM-SHEBETH
Is 30: 7 Therefore I have called her **R**

RAHAM
1Ch 2:44 Shema begot **R** the father of

RAID (*see* RAIDED, RAIDERS, RAIDING, RAIDS)
1Sa 27:10 Where have you made a **r** today
2Sa 3:22 David and Joab came from a **r**
1Ch 14: 9 made a **r** on the Valley of
1Ch 14:13 again made a **r** on the valley

RAIDED (*see* RAID)
1Sa 27: 8 up and **r** the Geshurites, the
2Ch 25:13 they **r** the cities of Judah
Job 1:15 when the Sabeans **r** them and
Job 1:17 **r** the camels and took them

RAIDERS (*see* RAID)
1Sa 13:17 Then **r** came out of the camp
1Sa 14:15 and the **r** also trembled
1Ki 11:24 captain over a band of **r**,
2Ki 6:23 So the bands of Syrian **r** came
2Ki 13:21 they spied a band of **r**
1Ch 12:21 David against the bands of **r**
2Ch 22: 1 for the **r** who came with the

RAIDING (*see* RAID)
Judg 11: 3 and went out **r** with him
2Ki 13:20 the **r** bands from Moab invaded
2Ki 24: 2 him **r** bands of Chaldeans,

RAIDS (*see* RAID)
2Ki 5: 2 the Syrians had gone out on **r**

RAIN (*see* RAINDROPS, RAINED, RAINS, RAINY)
Gen 2: 5 caused it to **r** on the earth
Gen 7: 4 to **r** on the earth forty days
Gen 7:12 the **r** was on the earth forty
Gen 8: 2 and the **r** from heaven was
Ex 9:18 very heavy hail to **r** down
Ex 9:33 the **r** was not poured on the
Ex 9:34 when Pharaoh saw that the **r**
Ex 16: 4 I will **r** bread from heaven
Lev 26: 4 will give you **r** in its season
Deut 11:11 water from the **r** of heaven
Deut 11:14 then I will give you the **r**
Deut 11:14 early **r** and the latter **r**
Deut 11:17 heavens so that there be no **r**
Deut 28:12 to give the **r** to your land in
Deut 28:24 the **r** of your land to powder
Deut 32: 2 Let my teaching drop as the **r**
1Sa 12:17 and He will send thunder and **r**
1Sa 12:18 sent thunder and **r** that day
2Sa 1:21 nor let there be **r** upon you
2Sa 23: 4 by clear shining after **r**
1Ki 8:35 there is no **r** because they
1Ki 8:36 give **r** on Your land which You
1Ki 17: 1 not be dew nor **r** these years
1Ki 17: 7 had been no **r** in the land
1Ki 17:14 the LORD sends **r** on the earth
1Ki 18: 1 I will send **r** on the earth
1Ki 18:41 the sound of abundance of **r**
1Ki 18:44 down before the **r** stops you
1Ki 18:45 wind, and there was a heavy **r**
2Ki 3:17 see wind, nor shall you see **r**
2Ch 6:26 there is no **r** because they
2Ch 6:27 send **r** on Your land which You
2Ch 7:13 up heaven and there is no **r**
Ezra 10: 9 matter and because of heavy **r**
Ezra 10:13 it is the season for heavy **r**
Job 5:10 He gives **r** on the earth, and
Job 20:23 will **r** it on him while he is
Job 28:26 When He made a law for the **r**
Job 29:23 waited for me as for the **r**
Job 29:23 wide as for the spring **r**
Job 36:27 distill as **r** from the mist
Job 37: 6 likewise to the gentle **r** and
Job 37: 6 the heavy **r** of His strength
Job 38:26 to cause it to **r** on a land
Job 38:28 Has the **r** a father
Ps 11: 6 the wicked He will **r** coals
Ps 68: 8 **r** at the presence of God
Ps 68: 9 O God, sent a plentiful **r**
Ps 72: 6 like **r** upon the mown grass
Ps 84: 6 The **r** also covers it with
Ps 105:32 He gave them hail for **r**, And
Ps 135: 7 He makes lightning for the **r**
Ps 147: 8 Who prepares **r** for the earth,
Prov 16:15 like a cloud of the latter **r**
Prov 25:14 like clouds and wind without **r**
Prov 25:23 The north wind brings forth **r**
Prov 26: 1 **r** in harvest, so honor is not
Prov 28: 3 **r** which leaves no food
Eccl 11: 3 If the clouds are full of **r**
Eccl 12: 2 do not return after the **r**
Song 2:11 past, the **r** is over and gone
Is 4: 6 for a shelter from storm and **r**
Is 5: 6 that they **r** no **r** on it
Is 30:23 Then He will give the **r** for
Is 44:14 a pine, and the **r** nourishes it
Is 45: 8 **R** down, you heavens, from
Is 55:10 For as the **r** comes down, and
Jer 3: 3 and there has been no latter **r**
Jer 5:24 the LORD our God, Who gives **r**
Jer 10:13 He makes lightning for the **r**
Jer 14: 4 there was no **r** in the land
Jer 14:22 the nations that can cause **r**
Jer 51:16 He makes lightnings for the **r**
Ezek 13:11 There will be flooding **r**, and
Ezek 13:13 be a flooding **r** in My anger
Ezek 38:22 I will **r** down on him, on his
Ezek 38:22 who are with him, flooding **r**
Hos 6: 3 He will come to us like the **r**
Hos 6: 3 and former **r** to the earth
Joel 2:23 you the former **r** faithfully
Joel 2:23 He will cause the **r** to come
Joel 2:23 former **r**, and the latter **r**
Amos 4: 7 I also withheld **r** from you
Amos 4: 7 I made it **r** on one city, I
Amos 4: 7 I withheld **r** from another
Amos 4: 7 where it did not **r** the part
Zech 10: 1 Ask the LORD for **r**
Zech 10: 1 in the time of the latter **r**
Zech 10: 1 will give them showers of **r**
Zech 14:17 on them there will be no **r**
Zech 14:18 in, they shall have no **r**
Matt 5:45 sends **r** on the just and on the
Matt 7:25 the **r** descended, the floods
Matt 7:27 the **r** descended, the floods
Acts 14:17 gave us **r** from heaven and
Acts 28: 2 because of the **r** that was
Heb 6: 7 **r** that often comes upon it
Jas 5: 7 the early and latter **r**
Jas 5:17 would not **r**; and it did not **r**
Jas 5:18 again, and the heaven gave **r**
Rev 11: 6 so that no **r** falls in the

RAINBOW
Gen 9:13 I set My **r** in the cloud, and
Gen 9:14 that the **r** shall be seen in
Gen 9:16 The **r** shall be in the cloud,
Ezek 1:28 Like the appearance of a **r** in
Rev 4: 3 and there was a **r** around the
Rev 10: 1 a **r** was on his head, his face

RAINDROPS (*see* RAIN)
Deut 32: 2 as **r** on the tender herb, and

RAINED (*see* RAIN)
Gen 19:24 Then the LORD **r** brimstone
Ex 9:23 the LORD **r** hail on the land
Ps 78:24 Had **r** down manna on them to
Ps 78:27 He also **r** meat on them like
Ezek 22:24 or **r** on in the day of
Amos 4: 7 One part was **r** upon, and where
Luke 17:29 went out of Sodom it **r** fire

RAINS (*see* RAIN)
2Sa 21:10 of harvest until the late **r**
Hos 10:12 and **r** righteousness on you
Amos 5: 9 He **r** ruin upon the strong, so

RAINY (*see* RAIN)
Prov 27:15 dripping on a very **r** day and a
Ezek 1:28 rainbow in a cloud on a **r** day

RAISE (*see* RAISED, RAISES, RAISING, UPRAISED)
Gen 38: 8 **r** up an heir to your brother
Ex 26:30 you shall **r** up the tabernacle
Deut 18:15 The LORD your God will **r** up
Deut 18:18 I will **r** up for them a
Deut 25: 7 brother refuses to **r** up a
Josh 8:29 **r** over it a great heap of
Ruth 4: 5 to **r** up the name of the dead
Ruth 4:10 to **r** up the name of the dead
1Sa 2:35 Then I will **r** up for Myself
2Sa 12:11 I will **r** up adversity against
2Sa 12:17 to **r** him up from the ground
2Sa 18:12 I would not **r** my hand against
1Ki 14:14 Moreover the LORD will **r** up
Job 30:12 they **r** against me their ways
Ps 41:10 **r** me up, That I may repay
Ps 81: 2 **R** a song and strike the
Is 13: 2 **r** your voice to them
Is 15: 5 **r** up a cry of destruction
Is 29: 3 I will **r** siegeworks against
Is 42: 2 nor **r** His voice, nor cause
Is 44:26 I will **r** up her waste places
Is 49: 6 to **r** up the tribes of Jacob
Is 58:12 you shall **r** up the
Is 61: 4 they shall **r** up the former
Jer 4:16 **r** their voice against the
Jer 23: 5 That I will **r** to David a
Jer 30: 9 whom I will **r** up for them
Jer 50: 9 For behold, I will **r** and cause

Jer 50:32 fall, and no one will **r** him up
Jer 51: 1 I will **r** up against Babylon,
Ezek 24: 8 That it may **r** up fury and take
Ezek 26: 8 and **r** a defense against you
Ezek 34:29 I will **r** up for them a garden
Hos 6: 2 the third day He will **r** us up
Joel 3: 7 I will **r** them out of the
Amos 5: 2 there is no one to **r** her up
Amos 6:14 I will **r** up a nation against
Amos 9:11 On that day I will **r** up The
Amos 9:11 I will **r** up its ruins, and
Mic 5: 5 then we will **r** against him
Zech 11:16 For indeed I will **r** up a
Zech 14:13 and **r** his hand against his
Matt 3: 9 to you that God is able to **r**
Matt 10: 8 **r** the dead, cast out demons
Matt 22:24 and **r** up offspring for his
Mark 12:19 and **r** up offspring for his
Luke 3: 8 to you that God is able to **r**
Luke 13:11 could in no way **r** herself up
Luke 18:13 much as **r** his eyes to heaven
Luke 20:28 and **r** up offspring for his
John 2:19 in three days I will **r** it up
John 2:20 will You **r** it up in three
John 6:39 but should **r** it up at the
John 6:40 I will **r** him up at the last
John 6:44 I will **r** him up at the last
John 6:54 I will **r** him up at the last
Acts 2:30 He would **r** up the Christ to
Acts 3:22 The LORD your God will **r** up
Acts 7:37 The LORD your God will **r** up
1Co 6:14 and will also **r** us up by His
1Co 15:15 Christ, whom He did not **r** up
2Co 4:14 will also **r** us up with Jesus
Heb 11:19 that God was able to **r** him up
Jas 5:15 and the Lord will **r** him up

RAISED (*see* RAISE)
Ex 9:16 this purpose I have **r** you up
Ex 29:27 the heave offering which is **r**
Ex 40:17 that the tabernacle was **r** up
Ex 40:18 So Moses **r** up the tabernacle,
Ex 40:18 its bars, and **r** up its pillars
Ex 40:33 he **r** up the court all around
Num 9:15 that the tabernacle was **r** up
Num 24: 2 Balaam **r** his eyes, and saw
Josh 5: 7 whom He **r** up in their place
Josh 7:26 Then they **r** over him a great
Judg 2:16 Then the LORD **r** up judges who
Judg 2:18 when the LORD **r** up judges for
Judg 3: 9 the LORD **r** up a deliverer for
Judg 3:15 the LORD **r** up a deliverer for
Judg 19:17 when he **r** his eyes, he saw
1Sa 12: 6 It is the LORD who **r** up Moses
2Sa 18:28 delivered up the men who **r**
2Sa 20:21 has **r** his hand against the
2Sa 23: 1 says the man **r** up on high
1Ki 5:13 Then King Solomon **r** up a
1Ki 9:15 force which King Solomon **r**
1Ki 9:21 these Solomon **r** forced labor
1Ki 11:14 Now the LORD **r** up an
1Ki 11:23 God **r** up another adversary
2Ki 19:22 whom have you **r** your voice
2Ki 21: 3 he **r** up altars for Baal, and
2Ch 8: 8 these Solomon **r** forced labor
2Ch 32: 5 **r** it up to the towers, and
2Ch 33: 3 he **r** up altars for the Baals,
2Ch 33:14 and he **r** it to a very great
Job 2:12 when they **r** their eyes from
Job 31:21 if I have **r** my hand against
Is 14: 9 it has **r** up from their
Is 23:13 they **r** up its palaces, and
Is 37:23 whom have you **r** your voice
Is 41: 2 Who **r** up one from the east
Is 41:25 I have **r** up one from the
Is 45:13 I have **r** him up in
Jer 6:22 a great nation will be **r** from
Jer 25:32 **r** up from the farthest parts
Jer 29:15 The LORD has **r** up prophets
Jer 50:41 many kings shall be **r** up from
Jer 51:11 The LORD has **r** up the spirit
Dan 7: 5 It was **r** up on one side, and
Amos 2:11 I **r** up some of your sons as
Zech 1:18 Then I **r** my eyes and looked,
Zech 2: 1 Then I **r** my eyes and looked,
Zech 5: 1 **r** my eyes, and saw there a
Zech 5: 9 Then I **r** my eyes and looked,
Zech 6: 1 and **r** my eyes and looked, and
Zech 9:13 and **r** up your sons, O Zion,
Zech 14:10 Jerusalem shall be **r** up and
Mal 3:15 who do wickedness are **r** up
Matt 11: 5 the dead are **r** up and the poor
Matt 16:21 and be **r** again the third day
Matt 17:23 the third day He will be **r** up
Matt 26:32 But after I have been **r**, I
Matt 27:52 who had fallen asleep were **r**
Mark 6:16 he has been **r** from the dead
Mark 14:28 But after I have been **r**, I
Luke 1:69 has **r** up a horn of salvation
Luke 7:22 the deaf hear, the dead are **r**
Luke 9:22 killed, and be **r** the third day
Luke 11:27 from the crowd **r** her voice
Luke 20:37 passage that the dead are **r**
John 8: 7 He **r** Himself up and said to
John 8:10 When Jesus had **r** Himself up
John 12: 1 whom He had **r** from the dead
John 12: 9 whom He had **r** from the dead
John 12:17 **r** him from the dead, bore
John 21:14 after He was **r** from the dead
Acts 2:14 **r** his voice and said to them,
Acts 2:24 whom God **r** up, having loosed
Acts 2:32 This Jesus God has **r** up, of
Acts 3:15 whom God **r** from the dead, of
Acts 3:26 having **r** up His Servant Jesus
Acts 4:10 whom God **r** from the dead, by
Acts 4:24 they **r** their voice to God
Acts 5:30 The God of our fathers **r** up
Acts 10:40 Him God **r** up on the third day
Acts 12: 7 the side and **r** him up, saying,
Acts 13:22 He **r** up for them David as
Acts 13:23 God **r** up for Israel a Savior
Acts 13:30 But God **r** Him from the dead
Acts 13:33 in that He has **r** up Jesus
Acts 13:34 that He **r** Him from the dead,
Acts 13:37 but He whom God **r** up saw no
Acts 13:50 **r** up persecution against Paul
Acts 14:11 they **r** their voices, saying
Acts 21:38 time ago **r** an insurrection
Acts 22:22 then they **r** their voices and
Rom 4:24 us who believe in Him who **r**
Rom 4:25 and was **r** because of our
Rom 6: 4 that just as Christ was **r**
Rom 6: 9 having been **r** from the dead,
Rom 7: 4 Him who was **r** from the dead
Rom 8:11 if the Spirit of Him who **r**
Rom 8:11 He who **r** Christ from the dead
Rom 9:17 same purpose I have **r** you up
Rom 10: 9 God has **r** Him from the dead
1Co 6:14 God both **r** up the Lord and
1Co 15:12 He has been **r** from the dead
1Co 15:15 of God that He **r** up Christ
1Co 15:35 How are the dead **r** up
1Co 15:42 it is **r** in incorruption
1Co 15:43 in dishonor, it is **r** in glory
1Co 15:43 in weakness, it is **r** in power
1Co 15:44 it is **r** a spiritual body
1Co 15:52 dead will be **r** incorruptible
2Co 4:14 knowing that He who **r** up the
Gal 1: 1 who **r** Him from the dead),
Eph 1:20 when He **r** Him from the dead
Eph 2: 6 **r** us up together, and made us
Col 2:12 in which you also were **r** with
Col 2:12 God, who **r** Him from the dead
Col 3: 1 then you were **r** with Christ
1Th 1:10 whom He **r** from the dead, even
2Ti 2: 8 was **r** from the dead according
Heb 11:35 their dead **r** to life again
1Pe 1:21 who **r** Him from the dead and

RAISES (*see* RAISE)
1Sa 2: 8 He **r** the poor from the dust
Job 41:25 When he **r** himself up, the
Ps 107:25 and **r** the stormy wind, Which
Ps 113: 7 He **r** the poor out of the dust
Ps 145:14 **r** up all those who are bowed
Ps 146: 8 The LORD **r** those who are
Prov 1:20 she **r** her voice in the open
Dan 2:21 removes kings and **r** up kings
John 5:21 For as the Father **r** the dead
Acts 26: 8 by you that God **r** the dead
2Co 1: 9 but in God who **r** the dead

RAISIN (*see* RAISINS)
Hos 3: 1 and love the **r** cakes of the

RAISING (*see* RAISE)
1Ch 15:16 cymbals, by **r** the voice with
Hab 1: 6 For indeed I am **r** up the
Acts 17:31 to all by **r** Him from the dead

RAISINS (*see* RAISIN)
Num 6: 3 nor eat fresh grapes or **r**
1Sa 25:18 one hundred clusters of **r**
1Sa 30:12 of figs and two clusters of **r**
2Sa 6:19 piece of meat, and a cake of **r**
2Sa 16: 1 one hundred clusters of **r**
1Ch 12:40 cakes of figs and cakes of **r**
1Ch 16: 3 piece of meat, and a cake of **r**
Song 2: 5 Sustain me with cakes of **r**

RAKEM
1Ch 7:16 and his sons were Ulam and **R**

RAKKATH
Josh 19:35 are Ziddim, Zer, Hammath, **R**

RAKKON
Josh 19:46 Me Jarkon, and **R**, with the

RALLY
Neh 4:20 of the trumpet, **r** to us there

RAM (*see* RAM'S, RAMS)
Gen 15: 9 goat, a three-year-old **r**, a
Gen 22:13 and there behind him was a **r**
Gen 22:13 So Abraham went and took the **r**
Ex 29:15 You shall also take one **r**
Ex 29:15 hands on the head of the **r**
Ex 29:16 and you shall kill the **r**, and
Ex 29:17 you shall cut the **r** in pieces
Ex 29:18 burn the whole **r** on the altar
Ex 29:19 shall also take the other **r**
Ex 29:19 hands on the head of the **r**
Ex 29:20 Then you shall kill the **r**
Ex 29:22 shall take the fat of the **r**
Ex 29:22 it is a **r** of consecration)
Ex 29:26 take the breast of the **r** of
Ex 29:27 And from the **r** of the
Ex 29:31 you shall take the **r** of the
Ex 29:32 shall eat the flesh of the **r**
Lev 5:15 a **r** without blemish from the
Lev 5:16 **r** of the trespass offering
Lev 5:18 a **r** without blemish from the
Lev 6: 6 a **r** without blemish from the
Lev 8:18 Then he brought the **r** as the
Lev 8:18 hands on the head of the **r**
Lev 8:20 And he cut the **r** into pieces
Lev 8:21 the whole **r** on the altar
Lev 8:22 And he brought the second **r**
Lev 8:22 the **r** of consecration
Lev 8:22 hands on the head of the **r**
Lev 8:29 part of the **r** of consecration
Lev 9: 2 and a **r** as a burnt offering,
Lev 9: 4 a **r** as peace offerings, to
Lev 9:18 the **r** as sacrifices of peace
Lev 9:19 fat from the bull and the **r**
Lev 16: 3 of a **r** as a burnt offering
Lev 16: 5 one **r** as a burnt offering
Lev 19:21 a **r** as a trespass offering
Lev 19:22 **r** of the trespass offering
Num 5: 8 in addition to the **r** of the
Num 6:14 one **r** without blemish as a
Num 6:17 he shall offer the **r** as a
Num 6:19 the boiled shoulder of the **r**
Num 7:15 one young bull, one **r**, and one
Num 7:21 one young bull, one **r**, and one
Num 7:27 one young bull, one **r**, and one
Num 7:33 one young bull, one **r**, and one
Num 7:39 one young bull, one **r**, and one
Num 7:45 one young bull, one **r**, and one
Num 7:51 one young bull, one **r**, and one
Num 7:57 one young bull, one **r**, and one
Num 7:63 one young bull, one **r**, and one
Num 7:69 one young bull, one **r**, and one
Num 7:75 one young bull, one **r**, and one
Num 7:81 one young bull, one **r**, and one
Num 15: 6 Or for a **r** you shall prepare
Num 15:11 each young bull, for each **r**
Num 23: 2 a bull and a **r** on each altar
Num 23: 4 on each altar a bull and a **r**
Num 23:14 a bull and a **r** on each altar
Num 23:30 a bull and a **r** on every altar
Num 28:11 two young bulls, one **r**, and
Num 28:12 mixed with oil, for the one **r**
Num 28:14 one-third of a hin for a **r**
Num 28:19 two young bulls, one **r**, and
Num 28:20 a bull, and two-tenths for a **r**
Num 28:27 two young bulls, one **r**, and
Num 28:28 two-tenths for the one **r**
Num 29: 2 one young bull, one **r**, and
Num 29: 3 bull, two-tenths for the **r**
Num 29: 8 one young bull, one **r**, and
Num 29: 9 two-tenths for the one **r**

Num 29:36 one bull, one **r**, seven lambs
Num 29:37 for the bull, for the **r**, and
Ezra 10:19 they presented a **r** of the
Ezek 43:23 a **r** from the flock without
Ezek 43:25 and a **r** from the flock, both
Ezek 45:24 bull and one ephah for each **r**
Ezek 46: 4 and a **r** without blemish
Ezek 46: 5 shall be one ephah for a **r**
Ezek 46: 6 blemish, six lambs, and a **r**
Ezek 46: 7 for a bull, an ephah for a **r**
Ezek 46:11 for a bull, an ephah for a **r**
Dan 8: 3 was a **r** which had two horns,
Dan 8: 4 I saw the **r** pushing westward,
Dan 8: 6 to the **r** that had two horns
Dan 8: 7 I saw him confronting the **r**
Dan 8: 7 against him, attacked the **r**
Dan 8: 7 in the **r** to withstand him
Dan 8: 7 deliver the **r** from his hand
Dan 8:20 The **r** which you saw, having

RAM*
Ruth 4:19 Hezron begot **R**,
Ruth 4:19 and **R** begot Amminadab
1Ch 2: 9 born to him were Jerahmeel, **R**
1Ch 2:10 **R** begot Amminadab, and
1Ch 2:25 firstborn of Hezron, were **R**
1Ch 2:27 The sons of **R**, the firstborn
Job 32: 2 Buzite, of the family of **R**
Matt 1: 3 Hezron, and Hezron begot **R**
Matt 1: 4 **R** begot Amminadab,
Luke 3:33 of Amminadab, the son of **R**

RAMAH (*see* RAMATH, RAMOTH)
Josh 18:25 Gibeon, **R**, Beeroth,
Josh 19: 8 Baalath Beer, **R** of the South
Josh 19:29 And the border turned to **R**
Josh 19:36 Adamah, **R**, Hazor,
Judg 4: 5 tree of Deborah between **R**
Judg 19:13 the night in Gibeah or in **R**
1Sa 1:19 and came to their house at **R**
1Sa 2:11 went to his house at **R**
1Sa 7:17 But he always returned to **R**
1Sa 8: 4 and came to Samuel at **R**,
1Sa 15:34 Then Samuel went to **R**, and
1Sa 16:13 So Samuel arose and went to **R**
1Sa 19:18 and went to Samuel at **R**, and
1Sa 19:19 note, David is at Naioth in **R**
1Sa 19:22 Then he also went to **R**, and
1Sa 19:22 they are at Naioth in **R**
1Sa 19:23 he went there to Naioth in **R**
1Sa 19:23 until he came to Naioth in **R**
1Sa 20: 1 David fled from Naioth in **R**
1Sa 22: 6 under a tamarisk tree in **R**
1Sa 25: 1 buried him at his home in **R**
1Sa 28: 3 for him and buried him in **R**
1Ki 15:17 up against Judah, and built **R**
1Ki 15:21 that he stopped building **R**
1Ki 15:22 the stones and timber of **R**
2Ki 8:29 had inflicted on him at **R**
2Ch 16: 1 up against Judah and built **R**
2Ch 16: 5 that he stopped building **R**
2Ch 16: 6 the stones and timber of **R**
2Ch 22: 6 which he had received at **R**
Ezra 2:26 the people of **R** and Geba, six
Neh 7:30 the men of **R** and Geba, six
Neh 11:33 in Hazor, **R**, Gittaim
Is 10:29 **R** is afraid, Gibeah of Saul
Jer 31:15 A voice was heard in **R**,
Jer 40: 1 guard had let him go from **R**
Hos 5: 8 in Gibeah, the trumpet in **R**
Matt 2:18 A voice was heard in **R**,

RAMATH (*see* RAMAH, RAMATHAIM ZOPHIM, RAMATHITE, RAMATH MIZPAH)
Judg 15:17 and called that place **R** Lehi

RAMATHAIM ZOPHIM (*see* RAMATH, ZOPHIM)
1Sa 1: 1 there was a certain man of **R**

RAMATHITE (*see* RAMATH)
1Ch 27:27 Shimei the **R** was over the

RAMATH MIZPAH (*see* RAMATH)
Josh 13:26 and from Heshbon to **R** and

RAMESES (*see* RAAMSES)
Gen 47:11 of the land, in the land of **R**
Ex 12:37 journeyed from **R** to Succoth
Num 33: 3 from **R** in the first month
Num 33: 5 of Israel moved from **R** and

RAMIAH
Ezra 10:25 **R**, Jeziah, Malchiah, Mijamin,

RAMOTH (*see* JARMUTH, RAMAH, REMETH)
Deut 4:43 **R** in Gilead for the Gadites,
Josh 20: 8 **R** in Gilead, from the tribe
Josh 21:38 of Gad, **R** in Gilead with its
1Sa 30:27 who were in **R** of the South
1Ki 4:13 Ben-Geber, in **R** Gilead
1Ki 22: 3 Do you know that **R** in Gilead
1Ki 22: 4 with me to fight at **R** Gilead
1Ki 22: 6 go against **R** Gilead to fight
1Ki 22:12 Go up to **R** Gilead and prosper,
1Ki 22:15 we go to war against **R** Gilead
1Ki 22:20 that he may fall at **R** Gilead
1Ki 22:29 of Judah went up to **R** Gilead
2Ki 8:28 king of Syria at **R** Gilead
2Ki 9: 1 your hand, and go to **R** Gilead
2Ki 9: 4 the prophet, went to **R** Gilead
2Ki 9:14 had been defending **R** Gilead
1Ch 6:73 **R** with its common-lands, and
1Ch 6:80 **R** in Gilead with its
2Ch 18: 2 to go up with him to **R** Gilead
2Ch 18: 3 go with me against **R** Gilead
2Ch 18: 5 we go to war against **R** Gilead
2Ch 18:11 Go up to **R** Gilead and prosper,
2Ch 18:14 we go to war against **R** Gilead
2Ch 18:19 that he may fall at **R** Gilead
2Ch 18:28 of Judah went up to **R** Gilead
2Ch 22: 5 king of Syria at **R** Gilead
Ezra 10:29 Adaiah, Jashub, Sheal, and **R**

RAMPART
2Sa 20:15 city, and it stood by the **r**
Lam 2: 8 therefore He has caused the **r**
Nah 3: 8 whose **r** was like the sea,
Hab 2: 1 watch and set myself on the **r**

RAM'S (*see* RAM)
Josh 6: 5 a long blast with the **r** horn
Hos 5: 8 Blow the **r** horn in Gibeah,

RAMS (*see* RAM, RAMS')
Gen 31:10 the **r** which leaped upon the
Gen 31:12 all the **r** which leap on the
Gen 31:38 not eaten the **r** of your flock
Gen 32:14 two hundred ewes and twenty **r**
Ex 29: 1 and two **r** without blemish,
Ex 29: 3 with the bull and the two **r**
Ex 35:23 goats' hair, red skins of **r**
Lev 8: 2 as the sin offering, two **r**
Lev 23:18 one young bull, and two **r**
Num 7:17 two oxen, five **r**, five male
Num 7:23 two oxen, five **r**, five male
Num 7:29 two oxen, five **r**, five male
Num 7:35 two oxen, five **r**, five male
Num 7:41 two oxen, five **r**, five male
Num 7:47 two oxen, five **r**, five male
Num 7:53 two oxen, five **r**, five male
Num 7:59 two oxen, five **r**, five male
Num 7:65 two oxen, five **r**, five male
Num 7:71 two oxen, five **r**, five male
Num 7:77 two oxen, five **r**, five male
Num 7:83 two oxen, five **r**, five male
Num 7:87 the **r** twelve, the male lambs
Num 7:88 the **r** sixty, the male goats
Num 23: 1 here seven bulls and seven **r**
Num 23:29 here seven bulls and seven **r**
Num 29:13 thirteen young bulls, two **r**
Num 29:14 for each of the two **r**,
Num 29:17 twelve young bulls, two **r**
Num 29:18 for the bulls, for the **r**, and
Num 29:20 present eleven bulls, two **r**
Num 29:21 for the bulls, for the **r**, and
Num 29:23 day present ten bulls, two **r**
Num 29:24 for the bulls, for the **r**, and
Num 29:26 day present nine bulls, two **r**
Num 29:27 for the bulls, for the **r**, and
Num 29:29 present eight bulls, two **r**
Num 29:30 for the bulls, for the **r**, and
Num 29:32 present seven bulls, two **r**
Num 29:33 for the bulls, for the **r**, and
Deut 32:14 **r** of the breed of Bashan, and
1Sa 15:22 and to heed than the fat of **r**
2Ki 3: 4 of one hundred thousand **r**
1Ch 15:26 seven bulls and seven **r**
1Ch 29:21 thousand bulls, a thousand **r**
2Ch 13: 9 seven **r** may be a priest of
2Ch 17:11 thousand seven hundred **r** and
2Ch 29:21 brought seven bulls, seven **r**
2Ch 29:22 Likewise they killed the **r**
2Ch 29:32 seventy bulls, one hundred **r**
Ezra 6: 9 young bulls, **r**, and lambs for
Ezra 6:17 hundred bulls, two hundred **r**
Ezra 7:17 buy with this money bulls, **r**
Ezra 8:35 for all Israel, ninety-six **r**
Job 42: 8 seven bulls and seven **r**, go to
Ps 66:15 With the sweet aroma of **r**
Ps 114: 4 The mountains skipped like **r**
Ps 114: 6 that you skipped like **r**
Is 1:11 of burnt offerings of **r** and
Is 34: 6 the fat of the kidneys of **r**
Is 60: 7 you, the **r** of Nebaioth shall
Jer 50: 8 and be like the **r** before the
Jer 51:40 like **r** with male goats
Ezek 4: 2 place battering **r** against it
Ezek 21:22 to set up battering **r**, to
Ezek 21:22 to set battering **r** against
Ezek 26: 9 **r** against your walls, and with
Ezek 27:21 traded with you in lambs, **r**
Ezek 34:17 sheep and sheep, between **r**
Ezek 39:18 princes of the earth, of **r**
Ezek 45:23 and seven **r** without blemish,
Mic 6: 7 **r** or ten thousand rivers of

RAMS' (*see* RAMS)
Ex 25: 5 **r** skins dyed red, badger
Ex 26:14 also make a covering of **r**
Ex 35: 7 **r** skins dyed red, badger
Ex 36:19 the tent of **r** skins dyed red
Ex 39:34 covering of **r** skins dyed red
Josh 6: 4 of **r** horns before the ark
Josh 6: 6 bear seven trumpets of **r**
Josh 6: 8 of **r** horns before the LORD
Josh 6:13 bearing seven trumpets of **r**
2Ch 15:14 and trumpets and **r** horns

RAN (*see* RUN)
Gen 18: 2 he **r** from the tent door to
Gen 18: 7 Abraham **r** to the herd, took a
Gen 24:17 And the servant **r** to meet her
Gen 24:20 **r** back to the well to draw
Gen 24:28 So the young woman **r** and told
Gen 24:29 Laban **r** out to the man by the
Gen 29:12 So she **r** and told her father
Gen 29:13 that he **r** to meet him, and
Gen 33: 4 But Esau **r** to meet him, and
Gen 39:12 hand, and fled and **r** outside
Num 11:27 And a young man **r** and told
Num 16:47 and **r** into the midst of the
Josh 7:22 and they **r** to the tent
Josh 8:19 they **r** as soon as he had
Judg 7:21 and the whole army **r** and cried
Judg 9:21 And Jotham **r** away and fled
Judg 13:10 Then the woman **r** in haste
1Sa 3: 5 So he **r** to Eli and said
1Sa 4:12 Then a man of Benjamin **r** from
1Sa 10:23 So they **r** and brought him from
1Sa 17:22 **r** to the army, and came and
1Sa 17:48 **r** toward the army to meet the
1Sa 17:51 Therefore David **r** and stood
1Sa 20:36 As the lad **r**, he shot an
2Sa 18:21 bowed himself to Joab and **r**
2Sa 18:23 Then Ahimaaz **r** by way of
1Ki 2:39 **r** away to Achish the son of
1Ki 18:35 So the water **r** all around the
1Ki 18:46 and **r** ahead of Ahab to the
1Ki 19: 3 **r** for his life, and went to
1Ki 19:20 and **r** after Elijah, and said,
1Ki 22:35 The blood **r** out from the
2Ch 32: 4 the brook that **r** through the
Ps 105:41 It **r** in the dry places like a
Jer 23:21 these prophets, yet they **r**
Ezek 1:14 the living creatures **r** back
Ezek 42: 7 **r** parallel to the chambers
Dan 8: 6 **r** at him with furious power
Matt 8:32 the whole herd of swine **r**
Matt 27:48 Immediately one of them **r**
Matt 28: 8 **r** to bring His disciples word
Mark 5: 6 he saw Jesus from afar, he **r**
Mark 5:13 the herd **r** violently down the
Mark 6:33 **r** there on foot from all the
Mark 6:55 **r** through that whole
Mark 15:36 Then someone **r** and filled a
Luke 8:33 the herd **r** violently down the
Luke 15:20 him and had compassion, and **r**
Luke 19: 4 So he **r** ahead and climbed up
Luke 24:12 Peter arose and **r** to the tomb
John 2: 3 when they **r** out of wine, the
John 20: 2 Then she **r** and came to Simon
John 20: 4 So they both **r** together, and
Acts 3:11 all the people **r** together to

Acts 7:57 and **r** at him with one accord
Acts 8:30 So Philip **r** to him, and heard
Acts 12:14 not open the gate, but **r** in
Acts 14:14 **r** in among the multitude,
Acts 16:11 we **r** a straight course to
Acts 16:29 **r** in, and fell down trembling
Acts 21:30 and the people **r** together,
Acts 21:32 centurions, and **r** down to them
Acts 27:41 met, they **r** the ship aground
Gal 5: 7 You **r** well

RANDOM
1Ki 22:34 a certain man drew a bow at **r**
2Ch 18:33 a certain man drew a bow at **r**

RANGE
2Ki 11: 8 and whoever comes within **r**
Job 39: 8 The **r** of the mountains is his
Is 7:25 it will become a **r** for oxen

RANK (*see* RANKED, RANKS)
1Ch 15:18 brethren of the second **r**

RANKED (*see* RANK)
Esth 1:14 who **r** highest in the kingdom)

RANKS (*see* RANK)
Ex 13:18 **r** out of the land of Egypt
Deut 25:18 way and attacked your rear **r**
Josh 10:19 and attack their rear **r**
1Ch 12:33 men who could keep **r**
1Ch 12:38 men of war, who could keep **r**
Prov 30:27 yet they all advance in **r**
Joel 2: 7 and they do not break **r**
Mark 6:40 So they sat down in **r**, in

RANSOM (*see* RANSOMED)
Ex 30:12 a **r** for himself to the LORD
Num 35:31 **r** for the life of a murderer
Num 35:32 you shall take no **r** for him
Job 33:24 I have found a **r**'
Job 36:18 for a large **r** would not help
Ps 49: 7 Nor give to God a **r** for him
Prov 13: 8 The **r** of a man's life is his
Prov 21:18 be a **r** for the righteous, and
Is 43: 3 I gave Egypt for your **r**,
Hos 13:14 I will **r** them from the power
Matt 20:28 to give His life a **r** for many
Mark 10:45 to give His life a **r** for many
1Ti 2: 6 who gave Himself a **r** for all

RANSOMED (*see* RANSOM)
Is 35:10 And the **r** of the LORD shall
Is 51:11 So the **r** of the LORD shall
Jer 31:11 **r** him from the hand of one

RAPHA (*see* BETH-RAPHA)
1Ch 8: 2 the fourth, and **R** the fifth

RAPHAH
1Ch 8:37 **R** his son, Eleasah his son,

RAPHU
Num 13: 9 Benjamin, Palti the son of **R**

RAPIDLY
2Sa 18:25 And he came **r** and drew near

RARE
1Sa 3: 1 the LORD was **r** in those days
Is 13:12 mortal more **r** than fine gold

RASH (*see* RASHLY)
Num 30: 6 bound by her vows or by a **r**
Job 6: 3 my words have been **r**
Eccl 5: 2 Do not be **r** with your mouth,
Is 32: 4 Also the heart of the **r** will

RASHLY (*see* RASH)
Ps 106:33 that he spoke **r** with his lips
Prov 20:25 to devote **r** something as holy
Acts 19:36 to be quiet and do nothing **r**

RATE
1Ki 10:25 at a set **r** year by year
2Ch 8:13 according to the daily **r**,
2Ch 9:24 at a set **r** year by year

RATHER (*see* PREFACE)

RATION (*see* RATIONS)
2Ki 25:30 there was a regular **r** given
Jer 52:34 there was a regular **r** given

RATIONS (*see* RATION)
Gen 47:22 for the priests had **r**
Gen 47:22 and they ate their **r** which
Jer 40: 5 of the guard gave him **r** and a

RATS
1Sa 6: 4 tumors and five golden **r**,
1Sa 6: 5 images of your **r** that ravage
1Sa 6:11 and the chest with the gold **r**
1Sa 6:18 and the gold **r**, according to

RATTLES (*see* RATTLING)
Job 39:23 The quiver **r** against him, the

RATTLING (*see* RATTLES)
Ezek 37: 7 was a noise, and suddenly a **r**
Nah 3: 2 whip and the noise of **r** wheels

RAVAGE (*see* RAVAGED)
1Sa 6: 5 of your rats that **r** the land

RAVAGED (*see* RAVAGE)
1Sa 5: 6 He **r** them and struck them with
1Ch 20: 1 **r** the country of the people

RAVEN (*see* RAVENS)
Gen 8: 7 Then he sent out a **r**, which
Lev 11:15 every **r** after its kind,
Deut 14:14 every **r** after its kind
Job 38:41 Who provides food for the **r**
Song 5:11 are wavy, and black as a **r**
Is 34:11 and the **r** shall dwell in it

RAVENOUS
Gen 49:27 Benjamin is a **r** wolf
Is 35: 9 nor shall any **r** beast go up
Matt 7:15 inwardly they are **r** wolves

RAVENS (*see* RAVEN)
1Ki 17: 4 the **r** to feed you there
1Ki 17: 6 The **r** brought him bread and
Ps 147: 9 And to the young **r** that cry
Prov 30:17 the **r** of the valley will pick
Luke 12:24 Consider the **r**, for they

RAVINE (*see* RAVINES)
Deut 2:36 the city that is in the **r**
Josh 13: 9 that is in the midst of the **r**
Josh 13:16 that is in the midst of the **r**
2Sa 24: 5 in the midst of the **r** of Gad

RAVINES (*see* RAVINE)
Ezek 6: 3 to the hills, to the **r**, and
Ezek 35: 8 in all your **r** those who are

RAVING
Eccl 10:13 end of his talk is **r** madness

RAVISHED
Judg 20: 5 me, but instead they **r** my
Song 4: 9 You have **r** my heart, my
Song 4: 9 you have **r** my heart with one
Is 13:16 be plundered and their wives **r**
Lam 5:11 They **r** the women in Zion, the
Zech 14: 2 houses rifled, and the women **r**

RAW
Ex 12: 9 Do not eat it **r**, nor boiled
Lev 13:10 there is a spot of **r** flesh in
Lev 13:14 But when **r** flesh appears on
Lev 13:15 shall look at the **r** flesh
Lev 13:15 for the **r** flesh is unclean
Lev 13:16 Or if the **r** flesh changes and
Lev 13:24 and the **r** flesh of the burn
1Sa 2:15 boiled meat from you, but **r**
Ezek 29:18 and every shoulder rubbed **r**

RAYS
Hab 3: 4 He had **r** flashing from His

RAZE
Ps 137: 7 **R** it, **r** it, To its very

RAZOR
Num 6: 5 no **r** shall come upon his head
Judg 13: 5 no **r** shall come upon his head
Judg 16:17 No **r** has ever come upon my
1Sa 1:11 no **r** shall come upon his head
Ps 52: 2 destruction, Like a sharp **r**
Is 7:20 will shave with a hired **r**
Ezek 5: 1 take it as a barber's **r**, and

REACH (*see* PREFACE)

REACHED (*see* PREFACE)

REACHES (*see* PREFACE)

REACHING (*see* PREFACE)

READ (*see* READER, READING, READS)
Ex 24: 7 and **r** in the hearing of the
Deut 17:19 he shall **r** it all the days of
Deut 31:11 you shall **r** this law before
Josh 8:34 afterward he **r** all the words
Josh 8:35 which Joshua did not **r** before
2Ki 5: 7 king of Israel **r** the letter
2Ki 19:14 of the messengers, and **r** it
2Ki 22: 8 book to Shaphan, and he **r** it
2Ki 22:10 Shaphan **r** it before the king
2Ki 22:16 which the king of Judah has **r**
2Ki 23: 2 he **r** in their hearing all the
2Ch 34:18 Shaphan **r** it before the king
2Ch 34:24 **r** before the king of Judah
2Ch 34:30 he **r** in their hearing all the
Ezra 4:18 has been clearly **r** before me
Ezra 4:23 letter was **r** before Rehum
Neh 8: 3 Then he **r** from it in the open
Neh 8: 8 So they **r** distinctly from the
Neh 8:18 he **r** from the Book of the Law
Neh 9: 3 **r** from the Book of the Law of
Neh 13: 1 On that day they **r** from the
Esth 6: 1 they were **r** before the king
Is 29:11 saying, "**R** this, please"
Is 29:12 saying, "**R** this, please"
Is 34:16 the book of the LORD, and **r**
Is 37:14 of the messengers, and **r** it
Jer 29:29 Now Zephaniah the priest **r**
Jer 36: 6 **r** from the scroll which you
Jer 36: 6 you shall also **r** them in the
Jer 36:10 Then Baruch **r** from the book
Jer 36:13 he had heard when Baruch **r**
Jer 36:14 have **r** in the hearing of the
Jer 36:15 now, and **r** it in our hearing
Jer 36:15 So Baruch **r** it in their
Jer 36:21 Jehudi **r** it in the hearing of
Jer 36:23 when Jehudi had **r** three or
Jer 51:61 see it, and **r** all these words,
Dan 5: 8 they could not **r** the writing
Dan 5:15 they should **r** this writing
Dan 5:16 Now if you can **r** the writing
Dan 5:17 yet I will **r** the writing to
Matt 12: 3 Have you not **r** what David did
Matt 12: 5 Or have you not **r** in the law
Matt 19: 4 Have you not **r** that He who
Matt 21:16 Have you never **r**, Out of the
Matt 21:42 Did you never **r** in the
Matt 22:31 dead, have you not **r** what was
Mark 2:25 Have you never **r** what David
Mark 12:10 Have you not **r** this Scripture
Mark 12:26 have you not **r** in the book of
Luke 4:16 Sabbath day, and stood up to **r**
Luke 6: 3 Have you not even **r** this,
John 19:20 many of the Jews **r** this title
Acts 8:32 Scripture which he **r** was this
Acts 13:27 which are **r** every Sabbath
Acts 15:21 being **r** in the synagogues
Acts 15:31 When they had **r** it, they
Acts 23:34 And when the governor had **r** it
2Co 1:13 than what you **r** or understand
2Co 3: 2 hearts, known and **r** by all men
2Co 3:15 to this day, when Moses is **r**
Eph 3: 4 by which, when you **r**, you may
Col 4:16 this epistle is **r** among you
Col 4:16 see that it is **r** also in the
Col 4:16 and that you likewise **r** the
1Th 5:27 be **r** to all the holy brethren
Rev 5: 4 **r** the scroll, or to look at

READER (*see* READ)
Mark 13:14 not" (let the **r** understand)

READILY (*see* READY)
Esth 2: 9 so he **r** gave beauty
Heb 12: 9 Shall we not much more **r** be

READINESS (*see* READY)
Acts 17:11 received the word with all **r**
2Co 8:11 as there was a **r** to desire it

READING (*see* READ)
Neh 8: 8 them to understand the **r**
Jer 36: 8 **r** from the book the words of
Jer 51:63 you have finished **r** this book
Luke 10:26 What is your **r** of it
Acts 8:28 he was **r** Isaiah the prophet
Acts 8:30 and heard him **r** the prophet
Acts 8:30 you understand what you are **r**
Acts 13:15 after the **r** of the Law and the
2Co 3:14 in the **r** of the Old Testament
1Ti 4:13 I come, give attention to **r**

READS (*see* READ)
Dan 5: 7 Whoever **r** this writing, and
Hab 2: 2 that he may run who **r** it
Matt 24:15 the holy place" (whoever **r**
Rev 1: 3 Blessed is he who **r** and those

READY (*see* READILY, READINESS)
Gen 18: 6 make **r** three measures of fine
Gen 43:16 slaughter an animal and make **r**
Gen 43:25 Then they made the present **r**
Gen 46:29 So Joseph made **r** his chariot
Ex 14: 6 So he made **r** his chariot and
Ex 17: 4 They are almost **r** to stone me
Ex 19:11 let them be **r** for the third
Ex 19:15 Be **r** for the third day
Ex 34: 2 So be **r** in the morning, and
Num 32:17 **r** to go before the children
Deut 1:41 you were **r** to go up into the
Josh 8: 4 the city, but all of you be **r**
2Sa 15:15 **r** to do whatever my lord the
2Sa 18:22 son, since you have no news **r**
1Ki 20:12 Get **r**
1Ki 20:12 they got **r** to attack the city
2Ki 4:29 Get yourself **r**, and take my
2Ki 9: 1 Get yourself **r**, take this
2Ki 9:21 So Joram said, "Make **r**."
2Ki 9:21 And his chariot was made **r**
1Ch 7: 4 troops of the army **r** for war
Neh 9:17 God, **r** to pardon, gracious and
Esth 3:14 they should be **r** for that day
Esth 8:13 be **r** on that day to avenge
Job 3: 8 those who are **r** to arouse
Job 12: 5 it is made **r** for those whose
Job 15:23 of darkness is **r** at his hand
Job 15:24 him, like a king **r** for battle
Job 17: 1 the grave is **r** for me
Job 18:12 destruction is **r** at his side
Job 32:19 it is **r** to burst like new
Ps 7:12 bends His bow and makes it **r**
Ps 11: 2 They make **r** their arrow on
Ps 21:12 You will make **r** Your arrows
Ps 38:17 For I am **r** to fall, And my
Ps 45: 1 is the pen of a **r** writer
Ps 86: 5 **r** to forgive, And abundant in
Ps 88:15 **r** to die from my youth up
Is 30:13 you like a breach **r** to fall
Is 32: 4 will be **r** to speak plainly
Is 38:20 The LORD was **r** to save me
Is 41: 7 It is **r** for the soldering"
Jer 1:12 for I am **r** to perform My word
Ezek 7:14 trumpet and made everyone **r**
Ezek 21:16 Swords at the **r**
Ezek 38: 7 Prepare yourself and be **r**, you
Dan 3:15 Now if you are **r** at the time
Hab 3: 9 Your bow was made quite **r**
Zech 5:11 when it is **r**, the basket will
Matt 22: 4 killed, and all things are **r**
Matt 22: 8 servants, "The wedding is **r**
Matt 24:44 Therefore you also be **r**, for
Matt 25:10 those who were **r** went in with
Mark 3: 9 kept **r** for Him because of the
Mark 14:15 there make **r** for us
Mark 14:38 The spirit truly is **r**, but
Luke 1:17 to make **r** a people prepared
Luke 7: 2 to him, was sick and **r** to die
Luke 12:40 Therefore you also be **r**, for
Luke 14:17 for all things are now **r**
Luke 22:12 there make **r**
Luke 22:33 I am **r** to go with You, both
John 7: 6 but your time is always **r**
Acts 10:10 but while they made **r**, he
Acts 20: 7 **r** to depart the next day,
Acts 21:13 For I am **r** not only to be
Acts 23:15 but we are **r** to kill him
Acts 23:21 and now they are **r**, waiting
Rom 1:15 I am **r** to preach the gospel
2Co 8:19 and to show your **r** mind,
2Co 9: 2 that Achaia was **r** a year ago
2Co 9: 3 that, as I said, you may be **r**
2Co 9: 5 that it may be **r** as a matter
2Co 10: 6 and being **r** to punish all
2Co 12:14 time I am **r** to come to you
1Ti 6:18 **r** to give, willing to share,
2Ti 4: 2 Be **r** in season and out of
Tit 3: 1 to be **r** for every good work,
Heb 8:13 old is **r** to vanish away
1Pe 1: 5 **r** to be revealed in the last
1Pe 3:15 always be **r** to give a defense
1Pe 4: 5 who is **r** to judge the living
Rev 3: 2 remain, that are **r** to die
Rev 12: 4 woman who was **r** to give birth
Rev 19: 7 His wife has made herself **r**

REAFFIRM
2Co 2: 8 you to **r** your love to him

REAIAH (*see* HAROEH)
1Ch 4: 2 **R** the son of Shobal begot
1Ch 5: 5 son, **R** his son, Baal his son,
Ezra 2:47 sons of Gahar, the sons of **R**
Neh 7:50 the children of **R**, the

REAL (*see* REALLY)
Acts 12: 9 was done by the angel was **r**

REALIZE (*see* REALIZED, REALIZES)
2Sa 3:25 Surely you **r** that Abner the

REALIZED (*see* REALIZE)
Neh 13:10 I also **r** that the portions
Acts 4:13 they **r** that they had been

REALIZES (*see* REALIZE)
Lev 5: 3 when he **r** it, then he shall
Lev 5: 4 when he **r** it, then he shall

REALLY (*see* REAL)
Gen 27:21 whether you are **r** my son Esau
Gen 27:24 said, "Are you **r** my son Esau
Gen 31:16 from our father are **r** ours
Judg 15: 2 said, "I **r** thought that you
1Sa 2:16 They should **r** burn the fat
2Sa 10: 3 Do you think that David **r**
2Ki 8:10 shown me that he will **r** die
1Ch 19: 3 Do you think that David **r**
Zech 7: 5 years, did you **r** fast for Me
Luke 18: 8 will He **r** find faith on the
1Ti 5: 3 Honor widows who are **r** widows
1Ti 5: 5 Now she who is **r** a widow, and
1Ti 5:16 those who are **r** widows
Jas 2: 8 If you **r** fulfill the royal

REALM
2Ch 20:30 Then the **r** of Jehoshaphat was
Ezra 7:13 priests and Levites in my **r**
Ezra 7:23 against the **r** of the king
Dan 1:20 who were in all his **r**
Dan 6: 3 setting him over the whole **r**
Dan 9: 1 over the **r** of the Chaldeans
Dan 11: 2 all against the **r** of Greece

REAP (*see* REAPED, REAPER, REAPING, REAPS)
Lev 19: 9 When you **r** the harvest of
Lev 19: 9 you shall not wholly **r** the
Lev 23:10 **r** its harvest, then you shall
Lev 23:22 When you **r** the harvest of
Lev 23:22 you shall not wholly **r** the
Lev 23:22 of your field when you **r**, nor
Lev 25: 5 your harvest you shall not **r**
Lev 25:11 nor **r** what grows of its own
Deut 24:19 When you **r** your harvest in
Ruth 2: 9 be on the field which they **r**
1Sa 8:12 **r** his harvest, and some to
2Ki 19:29 in the third year sow and **r**
Job 4: 8 and sow trouble **r** the same
Ps 126: 5 sow in tears Shall **r** in joy
Prov 22: 8 sows iniquity will **r** sorrow
Eccl 11: 4 regards the clouds will not **r**
Is 37:30 in the third year sow and **r**
Hos 8: 7 the wind, and **r** the whirlwind
Hos 10:12 **r** in mercy
Mic 6:15 You shall sow, but not **r**
Matt 6:26 nor **r** nor gather into barns
Matt 25:26 you knew that I **r** where I
Luke 12:24 for they neither sow nor **r**
Luke 19:21 and **r** what you did not sow
John 4:38 I sent you to **r** that for
1Co 9:11 if we **r** your material things
2Co 9: 6 will also **r** sparingly, and he
2Co 9: 6 will also **r** bountifully
Gal 6: 7 man sows, that he will also **r**
Gal 6: 8 of the flesh **r** corruption
Gal 6: 8 the Spirit **r** everlasting life
Gal 6: 9 **r** if we do not lose heart
Rev 14:15 Thrust in Your sickle and **r**
Rev 14:15 time has come for You to **r**

REAPED (*see* REAP)
Gen 26:12 land, and **r** in the same year a
Jer 12:13 have sown wheat but **r** thorns
Hos 10:13 you have **r** iniquity
Rev 14:16 the earth, and the earth was **r**

REAPER (*see* REAP, REAPERS)
Ps 129: 7 With which the **r** does not
Amos 9:13 plowman shall overtake the **r**

REAPERS (*see* REAPER)
Ruth 2: 3 in the field after the **r**
Ruth 2: 4 Bethlehem, and said to the **r**
Ruth 2: 5 who was in charge of the **r**
Ruth 2: 6 in charge of the **r** answered
Ruth 2: 7 gather after the **r** among the
Ruth 2:14 So she sat beside the **r**
2Ki 4:18 out to his father, to the **r**
Matt 13:30 harvest I will say to the **r**
Matt 13:39 age, and the **r** are the angels
Jas 5: 4 and the cries of the **r** have

REAPING (*see* REAP)
1Sa 6:13 **r** their wheat harvest in the
Matt 25:24 **r** where you have not sown, and
Luke 19:22 and **r** what I did not sow

REAPS (*see* REAP)
Is 17: 5 and **r** the heads with his arm
John 4:36 he who **r** receives wages, and
John 4:36 he who **r** may rejoice together
John 4:37 One sows and another **r**

REAR (*see* REARED, REARING)
Lev 26: 1 shall you **r** up for yourselves
Num 10:25 which formed the **r** guard of
Deut 25:18 way and attacked your **r** ranks
Deut 25:18 all the stragglers at your **r**
Josh 6: 9 the **r** guard came after the
Josh 6:13 But the **r** guard came after
Josh 8:13 its **r** guard on the west of
Josh 10:19 and attack their **r** ranks
1Sa 29: 2 review at the **r** with Achish
1Ki 6:16 room at the **r** of the temple
2Ch 13:14 line was at both front and **r**
Is 23: 4 neither do I **r** young men, nor
Is 52:12 Israel will be your **r** guard
Is 58: 8 LORD shall be your **r** guard

REARED (*see* REAR)
2Ki 10: 1 and to those who **r** Ahab's sons
2Ki 10: 5 also, and those who **r** the sons
Job 31:18 my youth I **r** him as a father

REARING (*see* REAR)
2Ki 10: 6 of the city, who were **r** them

REASON (*see* REASONABLE, REASONED, REASONING, REASONS)
Gen 19: 8 since this is the **r** they have
Num 6:11 sinned by **r** of the dead body
Deut 4: 7 for whatever **r** we may call
Josh 5: 4 And this is the **r** why Joshua
Josh 22:24 done it for fear, for a **r**
1Sa 12: 7 that I may **r** with you before
1Ki 9:15 this is the **r** for the labor
1Ki 14: 4 were glazed by **r** of his age
2Ch 21:15 come out by **r** of the sickness
Neh 6:13 For this **r** he was hired, that
Job 9:14 choose my words to **r** with Him
Job 13: 3 and I desire to **r** with God
Job 15: 3 Should he **r** with unprofitable
Job 22: 6 from your brother for no **r**
Job 23: 7 the upright could **r** with Him
Ps 90:10 if by **r** of strength they are
Eccl 7: 7 destroys a wise man's **r**, and a
Eccl 7:25 the **r** of things, to know the
Eccl 7:27 the other to find out the **r**
Is 1:18 let us **r** together," says the
Dan 2:12 For this **r** the king was angry
Dan 4:36 same time my **r** returned to me
Mal 2:14 For what **r**
Matt 5:32 **r** except sexual immorality
Matt 16: 8 why do you **r** among yourselves
Matt 19: 3 his wife for just any **r**
Matt 19: 5 For this **r** a man shall leave
Mark 2: 8 Why do you **r** about these
Mark 8:17 Why do you **r** because you have
Mark 10: 7 For this **r** a man shall leave
Luke 5:21 and the Pharisees began to **r**
Luke 8:47 the **r** she had touched Him
Luke 23:22 I have found no **r** for death
John 5:16 For this **r** the Jews
John 12:18 For this **r** the people also
John 13:28 what **r** He said this to him
Acts 10:21 For what **r** have you come
Acts 10:29 for what **r** have you sent for
Acts 18:14 there would be **r** why I should
Acts 19:40 there being no **r** which we may
Acts 23:28 know the **r** they accused him
Acts 26:25 speak the words of truth and **r**
Acts 28:20 For this **r** therefore I have
Rom 1:26 For this **r** God gave them up
Rom 15: 9 For this **r** I will confess to
Rom 15:17 Therefore I have **r** to glory
Rom 15:22 For this **r** I also have been
1Co 4:17 For this **r** I have sent

1Co 11:10 For this **r** the woman ought to
1Co 11:30 For this **r** many are weak and
Eph 3: 1 For this **r** I, Paul, the
Eph 3:14 For this **r** I bow my knees to
Eph 5:31 For this **r** a man shall leave
Phil 2:18 For the same **r** you also be
Col 1: 9 For this **r** we also, since the
1Th 2:13 For this **r** we also thank God
1Th 3: 5 For this **r**, when I could no
2Th 2:11 for this **r** God will send them
1Ti 1:16 for this **r** I obtained mercy,
2Ti 1:12 For this **r** I also suffer
Tit 1: 5 For this **r** I left you in
Heb 2:11 for which **r** He is not ashamed
Heb 5:14 those who by **r** of use have
Heb 9:15 for this **r** He is the Mediator
1Pe 3:15 to everyone who asks you a **r**
1Pe 4: 6 For this **r** the gospel was
2Pe 1: 5 But also for this very **r**,

REASONABLE (*see* REASON, UNREASONABLE)
Rom 12: 1 God, which is your **r** service

REASONED (*see* REASON)
Matt 16: 7 And they **r** among themselves,
Matt 21:25 And they **r** among themselves,
Mark 2: 8 they **r** thus within themselves
Mark 8:16 So they **r** among themselves,
Mark 11:31 And they **r** among themselves,
Luke 3:15 all **r** in their hearts about
Luke 20: 5 And they **r** among themselves,
Luke 20:14 him, they **r** among themselves,
Luke 24:15 while they conversed and **r**
Acts 17: 2 Sabbaths **r** with them from the
Acts 17:17 Therefore he **r** in the
Acts 18: 4 he **r** in the synagogue every
Acts 18:19 synagogue and **r** with the Jews
Acts 24:25 Now as he **r** about

REASONING (*see* REASON, REASONINGS)
Job 13: 6 Now hear my **r**, and heed the
Mark 2: 6 there and **r** in their hearts,
Mark 12:28 having heard them **r** together
Luke 5:22 Why are you **r** in your hearts
Acts 19: 8 boldly for three months, **r**
Acts 19: 9 **r** daily in the school of

REASONINGS (*see* REASONING)
Job 32:11 words, I listened to your **r**

REASONS (*see* REASON)
Is 41:21 Bring forth your strong **r**
Acts 26:21 For these **r** the Jews seized

REBA
Num 31: 8 Evi, Rekem, Zur, Hur, and **R**
Josh 13:21 Evi, Rekem, Zur, Hur, and **R**

REBECCA (*see* REBEKAH)
Rom 9:10 but when **R** also had conceived

REBEKAH (*see* REBECCA, REBEKAH'S)
Gen 22:23 And Bethuel begot **R**
Gen 24:15 speaking, that behold, **R**, who
Gen 24:29 Now **R** had a brother whose
Gen 24:30 the words of his sister **R**
Gen 24:45 in my heart, there was **R**,
Gen 24:51 Here is **R** before you
Gen 24:53 clothing, and gave them to **R**
Gen 24:58 Then they called **R** and said to
Gen 24:59 they sent away **R** their sister
Gen 24:60 And they blessed **R** and said to
Gen 24:61 Then **R** and her maids arose,
Gen 24:61 So the servant took **R** and
Gen 24:64 Then **R** lifted her eyes, and
Gen 24:67 and he took **R** and she became
Gen 25:20 old when he took **R** as wife
Gen 25:21 plea, and **R** his wife conceived
Gen 25:28 his game, but **R** loved Jacob
Gen 26: 7 place should kill me for **R**
Gen 26: 8 endearment to **R** his wife
Gen 26:35 a grief of mind to Isaac and **R**
Gen 27: 5 Now **R** was listening when
Gen 27: 6 So **R** spoke to Jacob her son,
Gen 27:11 And Jacob said to **R** his mother
Gen 27:15 Then **R** took the choice
Gen 27:42 her older son were told to **R**
Gen 27:46 And **R** said to Isaac,
Gen 28: 5 the Syrian, the brother of **R**
Gen 49:31 **R** his wife, and there I buried

REBEKAH'S (*see* REBEKAH)
Gen 29:12 relative and that he was **R** son
Gen 35: 8 **R** nurse, died, and she was

REBEL (*see* REBELLED, REBELLING, REBELLION, REBELLIOUS, REBELS)
Num 14: 9 Only do not **r** against the
Josh 22:16 that you might **r** this day
Josh 22:18 if you **r** today against the
Josh 22:19 but do not **r** against the LORD
Josh 22:19 nor **r** against us, by building
Josh 22:29 we should **r** against the LORD
1Sa 12:14 and do not **r** against the
1Sa 12:15 but **r** against the commandment
2Sa 20: 1 happened to be there a **r**,
1Ki 11:27 him to **r** against the king
2Ki 18:20 trust, that you **r** against me
Neh 2:19 Will you **r** against the king
Neh 6: 6 you and the Jews plan to **r**
Job 24:13 those who **r** against the light
Ps 105:28 they did not **r** against His
Is 1:20 but if you refuse and **r**, you
Is 36: 5 trust, that you **r** against me
Hos 7:14 new wine, They **r** against Me

REBELLED (*see* REBEL)
Gen 14: 4 in the thirteenth year they **r**
Num 20:24 because you **r** against My word
Num 27:14 you **r** against My command to
Deut 1:26 but **r** against the command of
Deut 1:43 but **r** against the command of
Deut 9:23 you,' then you **r** against the
1Ki 11:26 also **r** against the king
2Ki 1: 1 Moab **r** against Israel after
2Ki 3: 5 died, that the king of Moab **r**
2Ki 3: 7 king of Moab has **r** against me
2Ki 18: 7 And he **r** against the king of
2Ki 24: 1 he turned and **r** against him
2Ki 24:20 Then Zedekiah **r** against the
2Ch 13: 6 rose up and **r** against his lord
2Ch 36:13 And he also **r** against King
Neh 9:26 **r** against You, cast Your law
Ps 5:10 For they have **r** against You
Ps 106: 7 mercies, But **r** by the sea
Ps 106:33 Because they **r** against His
Ps 106:43 But they **r** against Him by
Ps 107:11 Because they **r** against the
Is 1: 2 and they have **r** against Me
Is 63:10 But they **r** and grieved His
Jer 52: 3 Then Zedekiah **r** against the
Lam 1:18 for I **r** against His
Lam 3:42 We have transgressed and **r**
Ezek 2: 3 nation that has **r** against Me
Ezek 5: 6 She has **r** against My
Ezek 17:15 But he **r** against him by
Ezek 20: 8 But they **r** against Me and
Ezek 20:13 of Israel **r** against Me in the
Ezek 20:21 the children **r** against Me
Dan 9: 5 we have done wickedly and **r**
Dan 9: 9 though we have **r** against Him
Hos 8: 1 covenant and **r** against My law
Hos 13:16 for she has **r** against her God
Heb 3:16 For who, having heard, **r**

REBELLING (*see* REBEL)
Ps 78:17 By **r** against the Most High in

REBELLION (*see* REBEL)
Deut 31:27 for I know your **r** and your
Josh 22:22 if it is in **r**, or if in
1Sa 15:23 For **r** is as the sin of
1Sa 24:11 neither evil nor **r** in my hand
2Sa 23: 6 But the sons of **r** shall all
1Ki 12:19 So Israel has been in **r**
2Ch 10:19 So Israel has been in **r**
Ezra 4:19 against kings, and that **r** and
Neh 9:17 in their **r** they appointed a
Job 34:37 For he adds **r** to his sin
Ps 95: 8 your hearts, as in the **r**, And
Prov 17:11 An evil man seeks only **r**
Jer 28:16 taught **r** against the LORD
Jer 29:32 has taught **r** against the LORD
Hos 4:18 Their drink is **r**, they commit
Heb 3: 8 your hearts as in the **r**, in
Heb 3:15 your hearts as in the **r**
Jude 11 and perished in the **r** of Korah

REBELLIOUS (*see* REBEL)
Deut 9: 7 you have been **r** against the
Deut 9:24 You have been **r** against the
Deut 21:18 **r** son who will not obey the
Deut 21:20 son of ours is stubborn and **r**
Deut 31:27 you have been **r** against the
1Sa 20:30 son of a perverse, **r** woman
Ezra 4:12 and are building the **r** and
Ezra 4:15 that this city is a **r** city
Ps 66: 7 Do not let the **r** exalt
Ps 68: 6 But the **r** dwell in a dry land
Ps 68:18 among men, Even among the **r**
Ps 78: 8 **r** generation, A generation
Prov 7:11 She was loud and **r**, her feet
Is 1:23 Your princes are **r**, and
Is 30: 1 Woe to the **r** children," says
Is 30: 9 that this is a **r** people,
Is 50: 5 and I was not **r**, nor did I
Is 65: 2 all day long to a **r** people
Jer 4:17 she has been **r** against Me
Jer 5:23 has a defiant and **r** heart
Lam 1:20 me, for I have been very **r**
Ezek 2: 3 to a **r** nation that has
Ezek 2: 5 for they are a **r** house
Ezek 2: 6 though they are a **r** house
Ezek 2: 7 they refuse, for they are **r**
Ezek 2: 8 Do not be **r** like that **r** house
Ezek 3: 9 though they are a **r** house
Ezek 3:26 them, for they are a **r** house
Ezek 3:27 for they are a **r** house
Ezek 12: 2 in the midst of a **r** house
Ezek 12: 2 for they are a **r** house
Ezek 12: 3 though they are a **r** house
Ezek 12: 9 the **r** house, said to you
Ezek 12:25 O **r** house, I will say the
Ezek 17:12 Say now to the **r** house
Ezek 24: 3 a parable to the **r** house, and
Ezek 44: 6 Now say to the **r**, to the
Hos 9:15 All their princes are **r**
Zeph 3: 1 Woe to her who is **r** and

REBELS (*see* REBEL)
Num 17:10 kept as a sign against the **r**
Num 20:10 Hear now, you **r**
Josh 1:18 Whoever **r** against your
1Sa 10:27 But some **r** said, "How can
Jer 6:28 They are all stubborn **r**,
Ezek 20:38 purge the **r** from among you

REBUILD (*see* REBUILDING, REBUILT)
Ezra 9: 9 to **r** its ruins, and to give us
Neh 2: 5 tombs, that I may **r** it
Is 9:10 down, but we will **r** with hewn
Is 61: 4 they shall **r** the old ruins,
Jer 33: 7 will **r** those places as at the
Amos 9:11 **r** it as in the days of old
Acts 15:16 and will **r** the tabernacle of
Acts 15:16 I will **r** its ruins, and I will

REBUILDING (*see* REBUILD)
Ezra 5:11 we are **r** the temple that was
Neh 4: 1 heard that we were **r** the wall
Neh 6: 6 you are **r** the wall, that you

REBUILT (*see* REBUILD)
Judg 18:28 So they **r** the city and dwelt
Judg 21:23 they **r** the cities and dwelt in
2Ki 21: 3 For he **r** the high places
2Ch 33: 3 For he **r** the high places
Ezra 4:16 king that if this city is **r**
Ezra 5:15 God be **r** on its former site
Ezra 6: 3 Let the house be **r**, the place
Neh 6: 1 heard that I had **r** the wall
Neh 7: 4 few, and the houses were not **r**
Job 12:14 a thing down, it cannot be **r**
Is 25: 2 it will never be **r**
Jer 31: 4 build you, and you shall be **r**
Ezek 26:14 nets, and you shall never be **r**
Ezek 36:10 be inhabited and the ruins **r**
Ezek 36:33 and the ruins shall be **r**
Ezek 36:36 have **r** the ruined places and

REBUKE (*see* REBUKED, REBUKES, REBUKING)
Lev 19:17 shall surely **r** your neighbor
Deut 28:20 **r** in all that you set your
Ruth 2:16 may glean, and do not **r** her
2Sa 22:16 at the **r** of the LORD, at the
2Ki 19: 3 day is a day of trouble, and **r**
Job 11: 3 you mock, should no one **r** you
Ps 6: 1 do not **r** me in Your anger,
Ps 18:15 were uncovered At Your **r**, O
Ps 38: 1 do not **r** me in Your wrath,
Ps 68:30 **R** the beasts of the reeds,
Ps 76: 6 At Your **r**, O God of Jacob,
Ps 80:16 They perish at the **r** of Your
Ps 104: 7 At Your **r** they fled
Ps 119:21 You **r** the proud
Prov 9: 8 **r** a wise man, and he will love
Prov 13: 1 scoffer does not listen to **r**

Prov 13: 8 but the poor does not hear **r**
Prov 24:25 But those who **r** the wicked
Prov 27: 5 Open **r** is better than love
Eccl 7: 5 It is better to hear the **r** of
Is 2: 4 and shall **r** many people
Is 17:13 but God will **r** them and they
Is 25: 8 the **r** of His people He will
Is 37: 3 day is a day of trouble and **r**
Is 50: 2 Indeed with My **r** I dry up the
Is 51:20 the LORD, the **r** of your God
Is 54: 9 be angry with you, nor **r** you
Is 66:15 His **r** with flames of fire
Jer 15:15 Your sake I have suffered **r**
Hos 5: 2 though I **r** them all
Hos 5: 9 be desolate in the day of **r**
Mic 4: 3 **r** strong nations afar off
Zech 3: 2 The LORD **r** you, Satan
Zech 3: 2 has chosen Jerusalem **r** you
Mal 2: 3 I will **r** your descendants and
Mal 3:11 I will **r** the devourer for
Matt 16:22 Him aside and began to **r** Him
Mark 8:32 Him aside and began to **r** Him
Luke 17: 3 sins against you, **r** him
Luke 19:39 Teacher, **r** Your disciples
1Ti 5: 1 Do not **r** an older man, but
1Ti 5:20 Those who are sinning **r** in
2Ti 4: 2 Convince, **r**, exhort, with all
Tit 1:13 Therefore **r** them sharply,
Tit 2:15 and **r** with all authority
Jude 9 The Lord **r** you
Rev 3:19 As many as I love, I **r** and

REBUKED (*see* REBUKE)
Gen 31:36 **r** Laban, and Jacob answered
Gen 31:42 my hands, and **r** you last night
Gen 37:10 and his father **r** him and said
1Ki 1: 6 his father had not **r** him at
Neh 5: 7 I **r** the nobles and rulers, and
Ps 9: 5 You have **r** the nations, You
Ps 106: 9 He **r** the Red Sea also, and it
Matt 8:26 and **r** the winds and the sea
Matt 17:18 Jesus **r** the demon, and he came
Matt 19:13 but the disciples **r** them
Mark 1:25 But Jesus **r** him, saying, Be
Mark 4:39 **r** the wind, and said to the
Mark 8:33 He **r** Peter, saying,
Mark 9:25 He **r** the unclean spirit,
Mark 10:13 but the disciples **r** those who
Mark 16:14 and He **r** their unbelief and
Luke 3:19 being **r** by him concerning
Luke 4:35 But Jesus **r** him, saying, "Be
Luke 4:39 **r** the fever, and it left her
Luke 8:24 **r** the wind and the raging of
Luke 9:42 Then Jesus **r** the unclean
Luke 9:55 He turned and **r** them, and said,
Luke 18:15 disciples saw it, they **r** them
Luke 23:40 answering, **r** him, saying,
Heb 12: 5 when you are **r** by Him
2Pe 2:16 but he was **r** for his iniquity

REBUKES (*see* REBUKE)
Job 40: 2 He who **r** God, let him answer
Ps 39:11 When with **r** You correct man
Prov 9: 7 he who **r** a wicked man gets
Prov 28:23 He who **r** a man will find more
Ezek 5:15 and in fury and in furious **r**
Ezek 25:17 on them with furious **r**
Amos 5:10 the one who **r** in the gate
Nah 1: 4 He **r** the sea and makes it dry,

REBUKING (*see* REBUKE)
Luke 4:41 **r** them, did not allow them to

RECALL
Is 46: 8 **r** to mind, O you
Lam 3:21 This I **r** to my mind,
Heb 10:32 But **r** the former days in

RECAPTURED
2Ki 13:25 **r** from the hand of Ben-Hadad
2Ki 13:25 him and **r** the cities of Israel
2Ki 14:28 how he **r** for Israel, from

RECEDED
Gen 8: 3 the waters **r** continually from
Rev 6:14 Then the sky **r** as a scroll

RECEIVE (*see* RECEIVED, RECEIVES, RECEIVING, WELL-RECEIVED)
Gen 4:11 has opened its mouth to **r**
Gen 33:10 then **r** my present from my
Gen 38:20 to **r** his pledge from the
Ex 27: 3 make its pans to **r** its ashes
Ex 29:25 You shall **r** them back from
Num 18:28 all your tithes which you **r**
Deut 9: 9 to **r** the tablets of stone
Josh 11:20 and that they might **r** no mercy
1Sa 10: 4 which you shall **r** from their
2Sa 18:12 Though I were to **r** a thousand
1Ki 8:64 to **r** the burnt offerings, the
2Ki 5:16 I stand, I will **r** nothing
2Ki 5:26 Is it time to **r** money and to
2Ki 5:26 to **r** clothing, olive groves
2Ki 12: 8 **r** any more money from the
2Ch 7: 7 able to **r** the burnt offerings
Ezra 4:14 Now because we **r** support from
Neh 10:37 **r** the tithes in all our
Neh 10:38 when the Levites **r** tithes
Job 3:12 Why did the knees **r** me
Job 22:22 **R**, please, instruction from
Job 35: 7 what does He **r** from your hand
Ps 6: 9 The LORD will **r** my prayer
Ps 24: 5 He shall **r** blessing from the
Ps 49:15 the grave, For He shall **r** me
Ps 73:24 And afterward **r** me to glory
Prov 1: 3 to **r** the instruction of
Prov 2: 1 My son, if you **r** my words, and
Prov 4:10 **r** my sayings, and the years of
Prov 8:10 **R** my instruction, and not
Prov 10: 8 wise in heart will **r** commands
Prov 19:20 **r** instruction, that you may
Is 57: 6 Should I **r** comfort in these
Jer 5: 3 have refused to **r** correction
Jer 7:28 their God nor **r** correction
Jer 9:20 let your ear **r** the word of
Jer 17:23 not hear nor **r** instruction
Jer 32:33 not listened to **r** instruction
Jer 35:13 Will you not **r** instruction to
Ezek 3:10 man, **r** into your heart all My
Ezek 16:61 when you **r** your older and your
Dan 2: 6 you shall **r** from me gifts,
Dan 7:18 Most High shall **r** the kingdom
Hos 10: 6 Ephraim shall **r** shame, and
Hos 14: 2 **r** us graciously, for we will
Zeph 3: 7 Me, you will **r** instruction'
Zech 6:10 **R** the gift from the captives
Zech 14:18 they shall **r** the plague with
Mal 2:13 nor **r** it with good will from
Mal 3:10 not be room enough to **r** it
Matt 10:14 whoever will not **r** you nor
Matt 10:41 shall **r** a prophet's reward
Matt 10:41 **r** a righteous man's reward
Matt 11: 5 The blind **r** their sight and
Matt 11:14 And if you are willing to **r** it
Matt 19:29 shall **r** a hundredfold, and
Matt 20: 7 whatever is right you will **r**
Matt 20:10 that they would **r** more
Matt 21:22 prayer, believing, you will **r**
Matt 21:34 that they might **r** its fruit
Matt 23:14 Therefore you will **r** greater
Mark 2: 2 was no longer room to **r** them
Mark 4:16 word, immediately **r** it with
Mark 6:11 will not **r** you nor hear you
Mark 10:15 you, whoever does not **r** the
Mark 10:30 who shall not **r** a hundredfold
Mark 10:51 that I may **r** my sight
Mark 11:24 pray, believe that you **r** them
Mark 12: 2 that he might **r** some of the
Mark 12:40 These will **r** greater
Luke 6:34 from whom you hope to **r** back
Luke 6:34 to sinners to **r** as much back
Luke 8:13 hear, **r** the word with joy
Luke 9: 5 And whoever will not **r** you
Luke 9:53 But they did not **r** Him,
Luke 10: 8 city you enter, and they **r** you
Luke 10:10 enter, and they do not **r** you
Luke 16: 4 they may **r** me into their
Luke 16: 9 you fail, they may **r** you into
Luke 18:17 you, whoever does not **r** the
Luke 18:30 who shall not **r** many times
Luke 18:41 Lord, that I may **r** my sight
Luke 18:42 said to him, "**R** your sight
Luke 19:12 to **r** for himself a kingdom
Luke 20:47 These will **r** greater
Luke 23:41 for we **r** the due reward of
John 1:11 own, and His own did not **r** Him
John 3:11 and you do not **r** Our witness
John 3:27 A man can **r** nothing unless it
John 5:34 Yet I do not **r** testimony from
John 5:41 I do not **r** honor from men
John 5:43 name, and you do not **r** Me
John 5:43 his own name, him you will **r**
John 5:44 who **r** honor from one another,
John 7:39 believing in Him would **r**
John 12:48 Me, and does not **r** My words
John 14: 3 come again and **r** you to Myself
John 14:17 whom the world cannot **r**,
John 16:24 Ask, and you will **r**, that your
John 20:22 to them, "**R** the Holy Spirit
Acts 1: 8 But you shall **r** power when
Acts 2:38 you shall **r** the gift of the
Acts 3: 5 expecting to **r** something from
Acts 3:21 whom heaven must **r** until the
Acts 7:59 Lord Jesus, **r** my spirit
Acts 8:15 they might **r** the Holy Spirit
Acts 8:19 hands may **r** the Holy Spirit
Acts 9:12 so that he might **r** his sight
Acts 9:17 me that you may **r** your sight
Acts 10:43 Him will **r** remission of sins
Acts 16:21 being Romans, to **r** or observe
Acts 18:27 the disciples to **r** him
Acts 19: 2 Did you **r** the Holy Spirit
Acts 20:35 blessed to give than to **r**
Acts 22:13 Brother Saul, **r** your sight
Acts 22:18 for they will not **r** your
Acts 26:18 that they may **r** forgiveness
Acts 27: 3 go to his friends and **r** care
Rom 5:17 who **r** abundance of grace and
Rom 8:15 For you did not **r** the spirit
Rom 14: 1 **R** one who is weak in the
Rom 15: 7 Therefore **r** one another, just
Rom 16: 2 that you may **r** her in the
1Co 2:14 the natural man does not **r**
1Co 3: 2 now you were not able to **r** it
1Co 3: 8 and each one will **r** his own
1Co 3:14 endures, he will **r** a reward
1Co 4: 7 you have that you did not **r**
1Co 4: 7 Now if you did indeed **r** it
1Co 14: 5 the church may **r** edification
2Co 5:10 that each one may **r** the
2Co 6: 1 to **r** the grace of God in vain
2Co 6:17 is unclean, and I will **r** you
2Co 8: 4 that we would **r** the gift and
2Co 11: 4 or if you **r** a different
2Co 11:16 at least **r** me as a fool, that
Gal 3: 2 Did you **r** the Spirit by the
Gal 3:14 that we might **r** the promise
Gal 4: 5 that we might **r** the adoption
Eph 6: 8 he will **r** the same from the
Phil 2:29 **R** him therefore in the Lord
Col 3:24 you will **r** the reward of the
2Th 2:10 because they did not **r** the
1Ti 5:19 Do not **r** an accusation
Phm 12 You therefore **r** him, that is,
Phm 15 that you might **r** him forever
Phm 17 **r** him as you would me
Heb 7: 5 who **r** the priesthood, have a
Heb 7: 5 have a commandment to **r**
Heb 7: 8 Here mortal men **r** tithes, but
Heb 9:15 those who are called may **r**
Heb 10:36 of God, you may **r** the promise
Heb 11: 8 afterward **r** as an inheritance
Heb 11:39 faith, did not **r** the promise,
Jas 1: 7 will **r** anything from the Lord
Jas 1:12 he will **r** the crown of life
Jas 1:21 **r** with meekness the implanted
Jas 3: 1 shall **r** a stricter judgment
Jas 4: 3 You ask and do not **r**, because
1Pe 5: 4 you will **r** the crown of glory
2Pe 2:13 and will **r** the wages of
1Jn 3:22 whatever we ask we **r** from Him
1Jn 5: 9 If we **r** the witness of men,
2Jn 8 that we may **r** a full reward
2Jn 10 do not **r** him into your house
3Jn 8 We therefore ought to **r** such
3Jn 9 among them, does not **r** us
3Jn 10 does not **r** the brethren, and
Rev 4:11 to **r** glory and honor and power
Rev 5:12 Lamb who was slain to **r** power
Rev 13:16 to **r** a mark on their right
Rev 17:12 but they **r** authority for one
Rev 18: 4 lest you **r** of her plagues

RECEIVED (*see* RECEIVE)
Ex 32: 4 he **r** the gold from their hand
Ex 36: 3 they **r** from Moses all the
Num 12:14 after that she may be **r** again
Num 23:20 I have **r** a command to bless
Num 31:51 priest **r** the gold from them
Num 31:54 Eleazar the priest **r** the gold
Num 32:18 Israel has **r** his inheritance
Num 34:14 have **r** their inheritance
Num 34:14 has **r** its inheritance
Num 34:15 the half-tribe have **r** their
Josh 13: 8 and the Gadites **r** their

Josh 17: 6 r an inheritance among his
Josh 18: 2 not yet r their inheritance
Josh 18: 7 r their inheritance beyond
1Sa 12: 3 I r any bribe with which to
1Sa 25:35 So David r from her hand what
2Ki 19:14 Hezekiah r the letter from
1Ch 12:18 So David r them, and made
2Ch 22: 6 which he had r at Ramah, when
2Ch 29:22 and the priests r the blood
2Ch 30:16 they r from the hand of the
2Ch 33:13 He r his entreaty, heard his
2Ch 33:19 how God r his entreaty, and
Ezra 8:30 and the Levites r the silver
Job 4:12 and my ear r a whisper of it
Job 15:18 anything r from their fathers
Job 27:13 r from the Almighty
Ps 68:18 You have r gifts among men,
Prov 24:32 looked on it and r instruction
Is 37:14 Hezekiah r the letter from
Is 40: 2 for she has r from the LORD's
Jer 2:30 they r no correction
Ezek 18:17 not r usury or increase, but
Ezek 29:18 his army r wages from Tyre
Dan 5:31 Darius the Mede r the kingdom
Zeph 3: 2 she has not r correction
Matt 10: 8 Freely you have r, freely
Matt 13:19 This is he who r seed by the
Matt 13:20 But he who r the seed on
Matt 13:22 Now he who r seed among the
Matt 13:23 But he who r seed on the good
Matt 15: 5 profit you might have r from
Matt 17:24 those who r the temple tax
Matt 20: 9 hour, they each r a denarius
Matt 20:10 and they likewise r each a
Matt 20:11 And when they had r it, they
Matt 20:34 their eyes r sight, and they
Matt 25:16 Then he who had r the five
Matt 25:17 likewise he who had r two
Matt 25:18 But he who had r one went
Matt 25:20 So he who had r five talents
Matt 25:22 He also who had r two talents
Matt 25:24 Then he who had r the one
Matt 25:27 r back my own with interest
Mark 7: 4 things which they have r and
Mark 7:11 profit you might have r from
Mark 10:52 And immediately he r his sight
Mark 16:19 He was r up into heaven, and
Luke 6:24 are rich, For you have r your
Luke 9:11 He r them and spoke to them
Luke 9:51 had come for Him to be r up
Luke 15:27 and because he has r him safe
Luke 16:25 you r your good things, and
Luke 18:43 And immediately he r his sight
Luke 19: 6 came down, and r Him joyfully
Luke 19:15 having r the kingdom, he then
John 1:12 But as many as r Him, to them
John 1:16 of His fullness we have all r
John 3:33 He who has r His testimony
John 4:45 Galilee, the Galileans r Him
John 6:21 willingly r Him into the boat
John 9:11 went and washed, and I r sight
John 9:15 again how he had r his sight
John 9:18 and r his sight, until they
John 9:18 of him who had r his sight
John 10:18 I have r from My Father
John 13:30 Having r the piece of bread,
John 17: 8 and they have r them, and have
John 18: 3 having r a detachment of
John 19:30 Jesus had r the sour wine
Acts 1: 9 a cloud r Him out of their
Acts 2:33 having r from the Father the
Acts 2:41 Then those who gladly r his
Acts 3: 7 and ankle bones r strength
Acts 7:38 the one who r the living
Acts 7:45 having r it in turn, also
Acts 7:53 who have r the law by the
Acts 8:14 Samaria had r the word of God
Acts 8:17 and they r the Holy Spirit
Acts 9:18 and he r his sight at once
Acts 9:19 And when he had r food, he was
Acts 10:47 not be baptized who have r
Acts 11: 1 had also r the word of God
Acts 15: 4 they were r by the church and
Acts 16:24 Having r such a charge, he
Acts 17:11 in that they r the word with
Acts 20:24 which I r from the Lord Jesus
Acts 21:17 the brethren r us gladly
Acts 22: 5 from whom I also r letters to
Acts 26:10 having r authority from the
Acts 28: 7 name was Publius, who r us
Acts 28:21 We neither r letters from
Acts 28:30 and r all who came to him,
Rom 1: 5 through whom we have r grace
Rom 4:11 he r the sign of circumcision
Rom 5:11 have now r the reconciliation
Rom 8:15 fear, but you r the Spirit of
Rom 14: 3 for God has r him
Rom 15: 7 just as Christ also r us
1Co 2:12 Now we have r, not the spirit
1Co 4: 7 glory as if you had not r it
1Co 11:23 For I r from the Lord that
1Co 15: 1 to you, which also you r and
1Co 15: 3 of all that which I also r
2Co 4: 1 ministry, as we have r mercy
2Co 7:15 fear and trembling you r him
2Co 11: 4 spirit which you have not r
2Co 11:24 I r forty stripes minus one
Gal 1: 9 to you than what you have r
Gal 1:12 For I neither r it from man
Gal 4:14 but you r me as an angel of
Phil 4: 9 things which you learned and r
Phil 4:18 having r from Epaphroditus
Col 2: 6 r Christ Jesus the Lord, so
Col 4:10 about whom you r instructions
Col 4:17 which you have r in the Lord
1Th 1: 6 having r the word in much
1Th 2:13 because when you r the word
1Th 4: 1 just as you r from us how you
2Th 3: 6 tradition which he r from us
1Ti 3:16 in the world, r up in glory
1Ti 4: 3 which God created to be r
1Ti 4: 4 if it is r with thanksgiving
Heb 2: 2 disobedience r a just reward,
Heb 7: 6 them r tithes from Abraham
Heb 7:11 it the people r the law),
Heb 10:26 r the knowledge of the truth
Heb 11:11 r strength to conceive seed
Heb 11:13 not having r the promises,
Heb 11:17 he who had r the promises
Heb 11:19 from which he also r him in a
Heb 11:31 when she had r the spies with
Heb 11:35 Women r their dead raised to
Jas 2:25 when she r the messengers
1Pe 1:18 r by tradition from your
1Pe 4:10 As each one has r a gift,
2Pe 1:17 For He r from God the Father
1Jn 2:27 have r from Him abides in you
2Jn 4 as we r commandment from the
Rev 2:27 I also have r from My Father
Rev 3: 3 therefore how you have r and
Rev 17:12 who have r no kingdom as yet
Rev 19:20 who r the mark of the beast
Rev 20: 4 had not r his mark on their

RECEIVES (*see* RECEIVE)
Lev 13:24 Or if the body r a burn on
Deut 33: 3 everyone r Your words
Prov 15: 5 but he who r reproof is
Prov 21:11 is instructed, he r knowledge
Prov 29: 4 justice, but he who r bribes
Matt 7: 8 For everyone who asks r, and
Matt 10:40 He who r you r Me, and
Matt 10:40 he who r Me r Him who
Matt 10:41 He who r a prophet in the
Matt 10:41 he who r a righteous man in
Matt 13:20 and immediately r it with joy
Matt 18: 5 whoever r one little child
Matt 18: 5 like this in My name r Me
Mark 9:37 Whoever r one of these little
Mark 9:37 children in My name r Me
Mark 9:37 whoever r Me, r not Me
Luke 9:48 Whoever r this little child
Luke 9:48 in My name r Me
Luke 9:48 whoever r Me r Him who sent
Luke 11:10 For everyone who asks r, and
Luke 15: 2 This man r sinners and eats
John 3:32 and no one r His testimony
John 4:36 And he who reaps r wages, and
John 7:23 If a man r circumcision on
John 13:20 who r whomever I send r Me
John 13:20 who r Me r Him who sent Me
1Co 9:24 all run, but one r the prize
Heb 6: 7 r blessing from God
Heb 7: 8 tithes, but there he r them
Heb 7: 9 who r tithes, paid tithes
Heb 12: 6 scourges every son whom He r
Jas 5: 7 for it until it r the early
Rev 2:17 one knows except him who r it
Rev 14: 9 r his mark on his forehead or
Rev 14:11 whoever r the mark of his

RECEIVING (*see* RECEIVE)
2Ki 5:20 while not r from his hands
Acts 17:15 and r a command for Silas and
Rom 1:27 r in themselves the penalty
Phil 4:15 giving and r but you only
Heb 12:28 since we are r a kingdom
1Pe 1: 9 r the end of your faith

RECENTLY
Jer 34:15 Then you r turned and did
Acts 18: 2 who had r come from Italy

RECEPTACLES
Zech 4:12 r of the two gold pipes from

RECESS (*see* RECESSES)
Job 28: 3 searches every r for ore in

RECESSES (*see* RECESS)
1Sa 24: 3 staying in the r of the cave
Ezek 32:23 are set in the r of the Pit

RECHAB (*see* RECHABITES)
2Sa 4: 2 and the name of the other R
2Sa 4: 5 of Rimmon the Beerothite, R
2Sa 4: 6 Then R and Baanah his brother
2Sa 4: 9 Then David answered R and
2Ki 10:15 he met Jehonadab the son of R
2Ki 10:23 Jehonadab the son of R went
1Ch 2:55 the father of the house of R
Neh 3:14 Malchijah the son of R,
Jer 35: 6 for Jonadab the son of R
Jer 35: 8 voice of Jonadab the son of R
Jer 35:14 words of Jonadab the son of R
Jer 35:16 son of R have performed the
Jer 35:19 Jonadab the son of R shall

RECHABITES (*see* RECHAB)
Jer 35: 2 Go to the house of the R,
Jer 35: 3 and the whole house of the R
Jer 35: 5 of the R bowls full of wine
Jer 35:18 said to the house of the R

RECHAH
1Ch 4:12 These were the men of R

RECITE (*see* RECITED)
Ps 45: 1 I r my composition concerning

RECITED (*see* RECITE)
Num 1:18 and they r their ancestry by

RECKLESS (*see* RECKLESSNESS)
Judg 9: 4 hired worthless and r men

RECKLESSNESS (*see* RECKLESS)
Jer 23:32 by their lies and by their r

RECKON (*see* RECKONED, RECKONING)
Lev 25:50 Thus he shall r with him who
Lev 25:52 then he shall r with him
Lev 27:18 shall r to him the money due
Lev 27:23 then the priest shall r to
Rom 6:11 also, r yourselves to be dead

RECKONED (*see* RECKON)
Num 18:27 heave offering shall be r to
1Ch 23:14 were r to the tribe of Levi

RECKONING (*see* RECKON)
Gen 9: 5 lifeblood I will demand a r
Num 23: 9 alone, not r itself among the

RECLINE
Amos 6: 7 those who r at banquets shall

RECOGNIZE (*see* RECOGNIZED, RECOGNIZES, UNRECOGNIZED)
Gen 27:23 And he did not r him, because
Gen 42: 8 but they did not r him
Ruth 3:14 before one could r another
1Ki 14: 2 that they may not r you as
Job 2:12 from afar, and did not r him
Acts 27:39 day, they did not r the land
1Th 5:12 to r those who labor among

RECOGNIZED (*see* RECOGNIZE)
Gen 37:33 And he r it and said, It is
Gen 42: 7 r them, but he acted as a
Gen 42: 8 So Joseph r his brothers, but
Judg 18: 3 they r the voice of the young
1Ki 18: 7 he r him, and fell on his face
1Ki 20:41 the king of Israel r him as
Matt 14:35 the men of that place r Him
Mark 6:54 immediately the people r Him
Acts 12:14 When she r Peter's voice,
1Co 11:19 approved may be r among you

Lev 27:27 or if it is not **r**, then it
Lev 27:28 shall be sold or **r**
Lev 27:29 among men, shall be **r**, but
Lev 27:33 it shall not be **r**
Num 3:48 excess number of them is **r**
Num 3:49 who were **r** by the Levites
Num 18:16 those **r** of the devoted things
Deut 7: 8 and **r** you from the house of
Deut 9:26 have **r** through Your greatness
Deut 13: 5 and **r** you from the house of
Deut 15:15 and the LORD your God **r** you
Deut 21: 8 Israel, whom You have **r**, and
Deut 24:18 your God **r** you from there
2Sa 4: 9 who has **r** my life from all
2Sa 7:23 You **r** for Yourself from Egypt
1Ki 1:29 who has **r** my life from every
1Ch 17:21 people whom You **r** from Egypt
Neh 1:10 whom You have **r** by Your great
Neh 5: 8 to our ability we have **r** our
Ps 31: 5 You have **r** me, O LORD God of
Ps 55:18 He has **r** my soul in peace
Ps 71:23 And my soul, which You have **r**
Ps 74: 2 inheritance, which You have **r**
Ps 77:15 with Your arm **r** Your people
Ps 78:42 The day when He **r** them from
Ps 106:10 **r** them from the hand of the
Ps 107: 2 Let the **r** of the LORD say so,
Ps 107: 2 Whom He has **r** from the hand
Is 1:27 Zion shall be **r** with justice
Is 29:22 who **r** Abraham, concerning the
Is 35: 9 But the **r** shall walk there,
Is 43: 1 Fear not, for I have **r** you
Is 44:22 to Me, for I have **r** you
Is 44:23 for the LORD has **r** Jacob, and
Is 48:20 The LORD has **r** His servant
Is 51:10 road for the **r** to cross over
Is 52: 3 you shall be **r** without money
Is 52: 9 people, He has **r** Jerusalem
Is 62:12 People, the **R** of the LORD
Is 63: 4 and the year of My **r** has come
Is 63: 9 love and in His pity He **r** them
Jer 31:11 For the LORD has **r** Jacob, and
Lam 3:58 You have **r** my life
Hos 7:13 Though I **r** them, yet they
Mic 6: 4 I **r** you from the house of
Luke 1:68 has visited and **r** His people,
Gal 3:13 Christ has **r** us from the
1Pe 1:18 not **r** with corruptible things
Rev 5: 9 and have **r** us to God by Your
Rev 14: 3 who were **r** from the earth
Rev 14: 4 These were **r** from among men,

REDEEMER (*see* REDEEM)
Job 19:25 For I know that my **R** lives
Ps 19:14 O LORD, my strength and my **r**
Ps 78:35 And the Most High God their **r**
Prov 23:11 for their **R** is mighty
Is 41:14 says the LORD and your **R**
Is 43:14 Thus says the LORD, your **R**
Is 44: 6 the King of Israel, and his **R**
Is 44:24 Thus says the LORD, your **R**
Is 47: 4 As for our **R**, the LORD of
Is 48:17 Thus says the LORD, your **R**
Is 49: 7 the **R** of Israel, their Holy
Is 49:26 am your Savior, and your **R**
Is 54: 5 your **R** is the Holy One of
Is 54: 8 you," says the LORD, your **R**
Is 59:20 The **R** will come to Zion, and
Is 60:16 am your Savior and your **R**
Is 63:16 our **R** from Everlasting is
Jer 50:34 Their **R** is strong

REDEEMING (*see* REDEEM)
Ruth 4: 7 times in Israel concerning **r**
Eph 5:16 **r** the time, because the days
Col 4: 5 who are outside, **r** the time

REDEEMS (*see* REDEEM)
Ps 34:22 The LORD **r** the soul of His
Ps 103: 4 Who **r** your life from

REDEMPTION (*see* REDEEM)
Lev 25:24 you shall grant **r** of the land
Lev 25:51 repay the price of his **r** from
Lev 25:52 repay him the price of his **r**
Num 3:46 for the **r** of the two hundred
Num 3:49 So Moses took the **r** money
Num 3:51 gave their **r** money to Aaron
Ruth 4: 6 my right of **r** for yourself
Ps 49: 8 For the **r** of their souls is
Ps 111: 9 He has sent **r** to His people
Ps 130: 7 And with Him is abundant **r**
Jer 32: 7 for the right of **r** is yours
Jer 32: 8 is yours, and the **r** yours
Luke 2:38 who looked for **r** in Jerusalem
Luke 21:28 because your **r** draws near
Rom 3:24 the **r** that is in Christ Jesus
Rom 8:23 adoption, the **r** of our body
1Co 1:30 and sanctification and **r**
Eph 1: 7 In Him we have **r** through His
Eph 1:14 our inheritance until the **r**
Eph 4:30 were sealed for the day of **r**
Col 1:14 in whom we have **r** through His
Heb 9:12 having obtained eternal **r**
Heb 9:15 of death, for the **r** of the

REDNESS (*see* RED)
Prov 23:29 Who has **r** of eyes

REDUCE (*see* REDUCED)
Is 25: 5 You will **r** the noise of
Zeph 2:11 for He will **r** to nothing all

REDUCED (*see* REDUCE)
Prov 6:26 man is **r** to a crust of bread

REED (*see* REEDS)
1Ki 14:15 as a **r** is shaken in the water
2Ki 18:21 in the staff of this broken **r**
Job 41: 2 Can you put a **r** through his
Is 18: 2 in vessels of **r** on the waters
Is 36: 6 in the staff of this broken **r**
Is 42: 3 A bruised **r** He will not break
Ezek 29: 6 of **r** to the house of Israel
Matt 11: 7 A **r** shaken by the wind
Matt 12:20 A bruised **r** He will not break
Matt 27:29 and a **r** in His right hand
Matt 27:30 spat on Him, and took the **r**
Matt 27:48 sour wine and put it on a **r**
Mark 15:19 Him on the head with a **r** and
Mark 15:36 of sour wine, put it on a **r**
Luke 7:24 A **r** shaken by the wind
Rev 11: 1 Then I was given a **r** like a
Rev 21:15 a gold **r** to measure the city
Rev 21:16 measured the city with the **r**

REEDS (*see* REED)
Ex 2: 3 and laid it in the **r** by the
Ex 2: 5 she saw the ark among the **r**
Job 8:11 Can the **r** flourish without
Job 40:21 lotus trees, in a covert of **r**
Ps 68:30 Rebuke the beasts of the **r**
Is 19: 6 the **r** and rushes will wither
Is 19: 7 The papyrus **r** by the River,
Is 35: 7 there shall be grass with **r**
Jer 51:32 the **r** they have burned with

REEL
Ps 107:27 They **r** to and fro, and stagger
Is 24:20 The earth shall **r** to and fro

REELAIAH
Ezra 2: 2 Jeshua, Nehemiah, Seraiah, **R**

REFERS
Dan 8:17 that the vision **r** to the time
Dan 8:26 for it **r** to many days in the
Dan 10:14 for the vision **r** to many days

REFINE (*see* REFINED, REFINER, REFINES, REFINING, WELL-REFINED)
Jer 9: 7 Behold, I will **r** them and try
Dan 11:35 to **r** them, purge them, and
Zech 13: 9 will **r** them as silver is

REFINED (*see* REFINE)
Deut 28:54 very **r** will be hostile toward
1Ch 28:18 and **r** gold by weight for the
1Ch 29: 4 thousand talents of **r** silver
Job 28: 1 and a place where gold is **r**
Ps 66:10 **r** us as silver is **r**
Is 48:10 Behold, I have **r** you, but not
Dan 12:10 be purified, made white, and **r**
Zech 13: 9 refine them as silver is **r**
Rev 1:15 as if **r** in a furnace, and His
Rev 3:18 from Me gold **r** in the fire

REFINER (*see* REFINE, REFINER'S)
Mal 3: 3 He will sit as a **r** and a

REFINER'S (*see* REFINER)
Mal 3: 2 For He is like a **r** fire And

REFINES (*see* REFINE)
Jer 6:29 the smelter **r** in vain, for

REFINING (*see* REFINE)
Prov 17: 3 The **r** pot is for silver and
Prov 27:21 The **r** pot is for silver and

REFORMATION (*see* REFORMED)
Heb 9:10 imposed until the time of **r**

REFORMED (*see* REFORMATION)
Lev 26:23 things you are not **r** by Me

REFRAIN (*see* REFRAINED)
Ex 23: 5 you would **r** from helping it,
1Ki 22: 6 Gilead to fight, or shall I **r**
1Ki 22:15 Ramoth Gilead, or shall we **r**
2Ch 18: 5 Ramoth Gilead, or shall I **r**
2Ch 18:14 Ramoth Gilead, or shall I **r**
2Ch 35:21 **R** from meddling with God, who
Eccl 3: 5 a time to **r** from embracing
Jer 31:16 **R** your voice from weeping, and
Zech 11:12 and if not, **r**
1Co 9: 6 no right to **r** from working
1Pe 3:10 let him **r** his tongue from

REFRAINED (*see* REFRAIN)
Job 29: 9 the princes **r** from talking,

REFRESH (*see* REFRESHED, REFRESHES, REFRESHING)
Gen 18: 5 that you may **r** your hearts
Judg 19: 5 **R** your heart with a morsel of
Judg 19: 8 said, "Please **r** your heart
1Ki 13: 7 **r** yourself, and I will give
Song 2: 5 **r** me with apples, for I am
Phm 20 **r** my heart in the Lord

REFRESHED (*see* REFRESH)
Ex 23:12 and the stranger may be **r**
Ex 31:17 day He rested and was **r**
1Sa 16:23 Then Saul would become **r** and
2Sa 16:14 so they **r** themselves there
Rom 15:32 may be **r** together with you
1Co 16:18 For they **r** my spirit and yours
2Co 7:13 spirit has been **r** by you all
2Ti 1:16 for he often **r** me, and was
Phm 7 the saints have been **r** by you

REFRESHES (*see* REFRESH)
Prov 25:13 him, for he **r** the soul of his

REFRESHING (*see* REFRESH)
Is 28:12 This is the **r**"
Acts 3:19 so that times of **r** may come

REFUGE (*see* REFUGEE)
Num 35: 6 shall appoint six cities of **r**
Num 35:11 to be cities of **r** for you
Num 35:12 of **r** for you from the avenger
Num 35:13 shall have six cities of **r**
Num 35:14 which will be cities of **r**
Num 35:15 six cities shall be for **r** for
Num 35:25 city of **r** where he had fled
Num 35:26 the city of **r** where he fled
Num 35:27 the limits of his city of **r**
Num 35:28 remained in his city of **r**
Num 35:32 who has fled to his city of **r**
Deut 32:37 rock in which they sought **r**
Deut 32:38 and help you, and be your **r**
Deut 33:27 The eternal God is your **r**
Josh 20: 2 for yourselves cities of **r**
Josh 20: 3 they shall be your **r** from the
Josh 21:13 (a city of **r** for the slayer)
Josh 21:21 (a city of **r** for the slayer)
Josh 21:27 (a city of **r** for the slayer)
Josh 21:32 (a city of **r** for the slayer)
Josh 21:38 (a city of **r** for the slayer)
Ruth 2:12 wings you have come for **r**
2Sa 22: 3 my stronghold and my **r**
1Ch 6:57 gave one of the cities of **r**
1Ch 6:67 them one of the cities of **r**
Ps 9: 9 will be a **r** for the oppressed
Ps 9: 9 A **r** in times of trouble
Ps 14: 6 poor, But the LORD is his **r**
Ps 28: 8 the saving **r** of His anointed
Ps 31: 2 Be my rock of **r**, A fortress
Ps 46: 1 God is our **r** and strength, A
Ps 46: 7 The God of Jacob is our **r**
Ps 46:11 The God of Jacob is our **r**
Ps 48: 3 He is known as her **r**
Ps 57: 1 Your wings I will make my **r**
Ps 59:16 **r** in the day of my trouble
Ps 62: 7 rock of my strength, And my **r**
Ps 62: 8 God is a **r** for us
Ps 71: 7 many, But You are my strong **r**
Ps 91: 2 He is my **r** and my fortress
Ps 91: 4 His wings you shall take **r**

Ps 91: 9 made the LORD, who is my **r**
Ps 94:22 And my God the rock of my **r**
Ps 104:18 The cliffs are a **r** for the
Ps 141: 8 In You I take **r**
Ps 142: 4 **R** has failed me
Ps 142: 5 You are my **r**, My portion in
Ps 144: 2 and the One in whom I take **r**
Prov 14:26 will have a place of **r**
Prov 14:32 has a **r** in his death
Is 4: 6 the heat, for a place of **r**
Is 10:31 inhabitants of Gebim seek **r**
Is 14:32 His people shall take **r** in it
Is 25: 4 a **r** from the storm, a shade
Is 28:15 for we have made lies our **r**
Is 28:17 will sweep away the **r** of lies
Jer 4: 6 Take **r**! Do not delay!
Jer 16:19 my **r** in the day of affliction
Nah 3:11 will seek **r** from the enemy
Heb 6:18 who have fled for **r** to lay

REFUGEE (*see* REFUGE)
Lam 2:22 there was no **r** or survivor

REFUSE (*see* REFUSED, REFUSES, REFUSING)
Ex 4:23 But if you **r** to let him go,
Ex 8: 2 But if you **r** to let them go,
Ex 9: 2 For if you **r** to let them go,
Ex 10: 3 How long will you **r** to
Ex 10: 4 if you **r** to let My people go,
Ex 16:28 How long do you **r** to keep My
Deut 23:13 it and turn and cover your **r**
Deut 28:56 will **r** to the husband of her
1Ki 2:17 for he will not **r** you, that
1Ki 2:20 do not **r** me
1Ki 2:20 mother, for I will not **r** you
1Ki 14:10 as one takes away **r** until it
2Ki 9:37 of Jezebel shall be as **r** on
2Ki 10:27 made it a **r** dump to this day
Ezra 6:11 made a **r** heap because of this
Neh 2:13 the **R** Gate, and viewed the
Neh 3:13 the wall as far as the **R** Gate
Neh 3:14 Haccerem, repaired the **R** Gate
Neh 12:31 on the wall toward the **R** Gate
Job 20: 7 perish forever like his own **r**
Ps 83:10 Who became as **r** on the earth
Ps 141: 5 Let my head not **r** it
Prov 21: 7 because they **r** to do justice
Prov 21:25 him, for his hands **r** to labor
Is 1:20 but if you **r** and rebel, you
Is 5:25 Their carcasses were as **r** in
Is 7:15 He may know to **r** the evil
Is 7:16 shall know to **r** the evil and
Is 25:10 trampled down for the **r** heap
Jer 3: 3 you **r** to be ashamed
Jer 8: 2 they shall be like **r** on the
Jer 8: 5 to deceit, they **r** to return
Jer 9: 6 deceit they **r** to know Me,"
Jer 9:22 fall as **r** on the open field
Jer 13:10 who **r** to hear My words, who
Jer 16: 4 but they shall be like **r** on
Jer 25:28 if they **r** to take the cup
Jer 25:33 shall become **r** on the ground
Jer 38:21 But if you **r** to surrender,
Lam 3:45 **r** in the midst of the peoples
Ezek 2: 5 they hear or whether they **r**
Ezek 2: 7 they hear or whether they **r**
Ezek 3:11 they hear, or whether they **r**
Ezek 3:27 and he who refuses, let him **r**
Ezek 7:19 and their gold will be like **r**
Ezek 7:20 I have made it like **r** to them
Zeph 1:17 dust, and their flesh like **r**
Mal 2: 3 spread **r** on your faces,
Mal 2: 3 the **r** of your solemn feasts
Mark 6:26 him, he did not want to **r** her
1Ti 5:11 But **r** the younger widows
Heb 12:25 you do not **r** Him who speaks

REFUSED (*see* REFUSE)
Gen 37:35 but he **r** to be comforted, and
Gen 39: 8 But he **r** and said to his
Gen 48:19 But his father **r** and said, "I
Num 20:21 Thus Edom **r** to give Israel
Num 22:13 for the LORD has **r** to give me
1Sa 8:19 Nevertheless the people **r** to
1Sa 16: 7 stature, because I have **r** him
1Sa 28:23 But he **r** and said, I will
2Sa 2:23 However, he **r** to turn aside
2Sa 12: 4 who **r** to take from his own
2Sa 13: 9 before him, but he **r** to eat
1Ki 20:35 And the man **r** to strike him
1Ki 21:15 which he **r** to give you for
2Ki 5:16 him to take it, but he **r**
Neh 9:17 They **r** to obey, and they were
Esth 1:12 But Queen Vashti **r** to come at
Ps 77: 2 My soul **r** to be comforted
Ps 78:10 They **r** to walk in His law,
Prov 1:24 I have called and you **r**, I
Is 8: 6 Inasmuch as these people **r**
Is 54: 6 youthful wife when you were **r**
Jer 5: 3 but they have **r** to receive
Jer 5: 3 they have **r** to return
Jer 11:10 who **r** to hear My words, and
Jer 50:33 they have **r** to let them go
Ezek 5: 6 for they have **r** My judgments
Hos 11: 5 because they **r** to repent
Zech 7:11 But they **r** to heed, shrugged
1Ti 4: 4 nothing is to be **r** if it is
Heb 11:24 **r** to be called the son of
Heb 12:25 who **r** Him who spoke on earth

REFUSES (*see* REFUSE)
Ex 7:14 he **r** to let the people go
Ex 22:17 utterly **r** to give her to him
Num 22:14 Balaam **r** to come with us
Deut 25: 7 My husband's brother **r** to
Job 6: 7 My soul **r** to touch them
Prov 10:17 but he who **r** reproof goes
Jer 15:18 which **r** to be healed
Ezek 3:27 and he who **r**, let him refuse
Matt 18:17 if he **r** to hear them, tell it
Matt 18:17 But if he **r** even to hear the

REFUSING (*see* REFUSE)
Is 33:15 **r** bribes, who stops his ears
Jer 31:15 **r** to be comforted for her
Zech 7:12 **r** to hear the law and the
Matt 2:18 **r** to be comforted, because

REFUTED
Acts 18:28 **r** the Jews publicly, showing

REGAIN
Ps 39:13 me, that I may **r** strength
Prov 2:19 nor do they **r** the paths of

REGARD (*see* REGARDED, REGARDING, REGARDS)
Gen 41:40 only in **r** to the throne will
Ex 5: 9 and let them not **r** false words
Ex 9:21 But he who did not **r** the word
Lev 5:15 sins unintentionally in **r** to
Lev 5:16 done in **r** to the holy thing
Lev 11:11 flesh, but you shall **r** their
Lev 11:13 And these you shall **r** as an
Lev 15: 3 in **r** to his discharge
Lev 19:31 Give no **r** to mediums and
Num 4:19 but do this in **r** to them,
1Sa 4:20 not answer, nor did she **r** it
1Sa 25:25 let not my lord **r** this
2Sa 19: 6 you **r** neither princes nor
1Ki 8:28 Yet **r** the prayer of Your
2Ki 3:14 surely were it not that I **r**
2Ch 6:19 Yet **r** the prayer of Your
Ezra 7:14 with **r** to the Law of your God
Job 13:24 face, and **r** me as Your enemy
Job 30:20 I stand up, and You **r** me
Job 34:19 nor does He **r** the rich more
Job 35:13 nor will the Almighty **r** it
Ps 28: 5 Because they do not **r** the
Ps 31: 6 hated those who **r** vain idols
Ps 66:18 If I **r** iniquity in my heart,
Ps 102:17 He shall **r** the prayer of the
Is 5:12 but they do not **r** the work of
Is 13:17 them, who will not **r** silver
Ezek 44:28 in **r** to their inheritance,
Dan 3:12 have not paid due **r** to you
Dan 6:13 does not show due **r** for you
Dan 11:30 show **r** for those who forsake
Dan 11:37 He shall **r** neither the God of
Dan 11:37 of women, nor **r** any god
Amos 5:22 Nor will I **r** your fattened
Jon 2: 8 Those who **r** worthless idols
Mal 2:13 so He does not **r** the offering
Matt 22:16 for You do not **r** the person
Mark 12:14 for You do not **r** the person
Luke 18: 2 did not fear God nor **r** man
Luke 18: 4 I do not fear God nor **r** man
Rom 6:20 free in **r** to righteousness
Rom 12:17 Have **r** for good things in the
2Co 5:16 we **r** no one according to the
Phil 4:11 Not that I speak in **r** to need
Heb 9: 9 in **r** to the conscience
1Pe 4: 4 In **r** to these, they think it

REGARDED (*see* REGARD)
Lev 10: 3 near Me I must be **r** as holy
Deut 2:11 They were also **r** as giants
Deut 2:20 (That was also **r** as a land of
2Ki 13:23 and **r** them, because of His
1Ch 17:17 have **r** me according to the
Job 18: 3 **r** as stupid in your sight
Job 41:29 Darts are **r** as straw
Ps 106:44 Nevertheless He **r** their
Ps 119:126 For they have **r** Your law as
Prov 1:24 out my hand and no one **r**,
Lam 4: 2 how they are **r** as clay pots
Luke 1:48 For He has **r** the lowly state
2Co 11:12 to be **r** just as we are in the

REGARDING (*see* REGARD)
Lev 5:18 make atonement for him **r** his
Lev 25:46 But **r** your brethren, the
Num 8:26 to the Levites **r** their duties
Josh 7: 1 **r** the accursed things, for
Judg 15: 3 **r** the Philistines if I harm
2Ch 32:31 **r** the ambassadors of the
Job 4:20 perish forever, with no one **r**
Ps 119:80 be blameless **r** Your statutes
Is 5: 1 of my Beloved **r** His vineyard
Luke 14: 6 not answer Him **r** these things
Acts 5:35 you intend to do **r** these men
Phil 2:30 not **r** his life, to supply
Col 2:16 or **r** a festival or a new moon

REGARDS (*see* REGARD)
Job 41:27 He **r** iron as straw, and bronze
Ps 138: 6 on high, Yet He **r** the lowly
Prov 12:10 A righteous man **r** the life of
Prov 13:18 but he who **r** reproof will be
Eccl 11: 4 he who **r** the clouds will not
Is 33: 8 the cities, He **r** no man
Lam 4:16 He no longer **r** them

REGEM (*see* REGEM-MELECH)
1Ch 2:47 And the sons of Jahdai were **R**

REGEM-MELECH (*see* MELECH, REGEM)
Zech 7: 2 people sent Sherezer, with **R**

REGENERATION
Matt 19:28 I say to you, that in the **r**
Tit 3: 5 us, through the washing of **r**

REGIMENT
Acts 10: 1 what was called the Italian **R**
Acts 27: 1 a centurion of the Augustan **R**

REGION (*see* REGIONS)
Num 32: 1 that indeed the **r** was a place
Deut 3: 4 all the **r** of Argob, the
Deut 3:13 (All the **r** of Argob, with all
Deut 3:14 took all the **r** of Argob, as
Josh 19:29 at the sea by the **r** of Achzib
Josh 19:46 Rakkon, with the **r** near Joppa
Josh 22:10 when they came to the **r** of
Josh 22:11 in the **r** of the Jordan, on
1Ki 4:13 the **r** of Argob in Bashan
1Ki 4:24 **r** on this side of the River
Ezra 4:10 the rest of the **r** beyond the
Ezra 4:11 men of the **r** beyond the River
Ezra 4:16 over the **r** beyond the River
Ezra 4:17 in the **r** beyond the River
Ezra 5: 3 of the **r** beyond the River
Ezra 5: 6 of the **r** beyond the River
Ezra 5: 6 in the **r** beyond the River
Ezra 6: 6 governor of the **r** beyond the
Ezra 6: 8 on the **r** beyond the River
Ezra 6:13 governor of the **r** beyond the
Ezra 7:21 are in the **r** beyond the River
Ezra 7:25 are in the **r** beyond the River
Ezra 8:36 in the **r** beyond the River
Neh 2: 7 of the **r** beyond the River
Neh 2: 9 in the **r** beyond the River
Neh 3: 7 of the **r** beyond the River
Ezek 47: 8 flows toward the eastern **r**
Matt 2:22 aside into the **r** of Galilee
Matt 3: 5 all the **r** around the Jordan
Matt 4:16 upon those who sat in the **r**
Matt 8:34 Him to depart from their **r**
Matt 14:35 into all that surrounding **r**
Matt 15:21 and departed to the **r** of Tyre
Matt 15:22 of Canaan came from that **r**
Matt 15:39 and came to the **r** of Magdala
Matt 16:13 the **r** of Caesarea Philippi
Matt 19: 1 came to the **r** of Judea beyond
Mark 1:28 all the **r** around Galilee
Mark 5:17 Him to depart from their **r**
Mark 6:55 that whole surrounding **r**, and

Mark 7:24 and went to the **r** of Tyre and
Mark 7:31 departing from the **r** of Tyre
Mark 7:31 through the midst of the **r** of
Mark 8:10 came to the **r** of Dalmanutha
Mark 10: 1 came to the **r** of Judea by the
Luke 3: 1 and the **r** of Trachonitis, and
Luke 3: 3 all the **r** around the Jordan
Luke 4:14 through all the surrounding **r**
Luke 4:26 in the **r** of Sidon, to a woman
Luke 4:37 place in the surrounding **r**
Luke 7:17 and all the surrounding **r**
Luke 8:37 of the surrounding **r** of the
Acts 13:49 spread throughout all the **r**
Acts 13:50 and expelled them from their **r**
Acts 14: 6 and to the surrounding **r**
Acts 16: 3 the Jews who were in that **r**
Acts 16: 6 the **r** of Galatia, they were
Acts 18:23 over all the **r** of Galatia
Acts 20: 2 when he had gone over that **r**
Acts 26:20 throughout all the **r** of Judea
Acts 28: 7 Now in that **r** there was an

REGIONS (*see* REGION)
Josh 17:11 three hilly **r**
1Ki 4:11 in all the **r** of Dor
Is 41: 9 and called from its farthest **r**
Matt 4:13 sea, in the **r** of Zebulun and
Acts 8: 1 throughout the **r** of Judea
Acts 19: 1 passed through the upper **r**
2Co 10:16 gospel in the **r** beyond you
2Co 11:10 boasting in the **r** of Achaia
Gal 1:21 I went into the **r** of Syria

REGISTER (*see* REGISTERED, REGISTERS)
Neh 7: 5 I found a **r** of the genealogy

REGISTERED (*see* REGISTER)
1Ch 5: 7 of their generations was **r**
1Ch 5:17 All these were **r** by
Ezra 2:62 those who were **r** by genealogy
Ezra 8: 3 **r** with him were one hundred
Neh 7: 5 they might be **r** by genealogy
Neh 7:64 those who were **r** by genealogy
Luke 2: 1 all the world should be **r**
Luke 2: 3 So all went to be **r**, everyone
Luke 2: 5 to be **r** with Mary, his
Heb 12:23 firstborn who are **r** in heaven

REGISTERS (*see* REGISTER)
Ps 87: 6 record, When He **r** the peoples

REGRET (*see* REGRETTED)
1Sa 15:11 I greatly **r** that I have set
2Co 7: 8 with my letter, I do not **r** it
2Co 7: 8 though I did **r** it

REGRETTED (*see* REGRET)
1Sa 15:35 the LORD **r** that He had made
Matt 21:29 not,' but afterward he **r** it
2Co 7:10 to salvation, not to be **r**

REGULAR (*see* REGULARLY)
Num 28: 3 by day, as a **r** burnt offering
Num 28: 6 It is a **r** burnt offering
Num 28:10 besides the **r** burnt offering
Num 28:15 besides the **r** burnt offering
Num 28:23 is for a **r** burnt offering
Num 28:24 besides the **r** burnt offering
Num 28:31 besides the **r** burnt offering
Num 29: 6 the **r** burnt offering with its
Num 29:11 the **r** burnt offering with its
Num 29:16 besides the **r** burnt offering,
Num 29:19 besides the **r** burnt offering
Num 29:22 besides the **r** burnt offering,
Num 29:25 besides the **r** burnt offering,
Num 29:28 besides the **r** burnt offering,
Num 29:31 besides the **r** burnt offering,
Num 29:34 besides the **r** burnt offering,
Num 29:38 besides the **r** burnt offering,
2Ki 25:30 there was a **r** ration given
Ezra 3: 5 offered the **r** burnt offering
Neh 10:33 for the **r** grain offering,
Neh 10:33 for the **r** burnt offering of
Jer 52:34 there was a **r** ration given
Ezek 27:21 Kedar were your **r** merchants
Ezek 46:15 as a **r** burnt offering every

REGULARLY (*see* REGULAR)
2Ki 3: 4 he **r** paid the king of Israel
2Ki 4: 9 of God, who passes by us **r**
2Ki 25:29 he ate bread **r** before the
1Ch 16: 6 Jahaziel the priests **r** blew
1Ch 16:37 to minister before the ark **r**
1Ch 16:40 of burnt offering **r** morning
1Ch 23:31 them, **r** before the LORD
Job 1: 5 Thus Job did **r**
Jer 52:33 he ate bread **r** before the
Ezek 39:14 will set apart men **r** employed
Ezek 46:14 to be made **r** to the LORD

REGULATIONS
Esth 2:12 to the **r** for the women, for
Col 2:20 you subject yourselves to **r**

REHABIAH
1Ch 23:17 of Eliezer, **R** was the first
1Ch 23:17 the sons of **R** were very many
1Ch 24:21 Concerning **R**, of the sons of **R**
1Ch 26:25 by Eliezer were **R** his son

REHOB (*see* BETH REHOB)
Num 13:21 Wilderness of Zin as far as **R**
Josh 19:28 including Ebron, **R**, Hammon,
Josh 19:30 Aphek, and **R** were included
Josh 21:31 and **R** with its common-land
Judg 1:31 Achzib, Helbah, Aphik, or **R**
2Sa 8: 3 Hadadezer the son of **R**, king
2Sa 8:12 of Hadadezer the son of **R**
2Sa 10: 8 And the Syrians of Zoba, **R**
1Ch 6:75 and **R** with its common-lands
Neh 10:11 Micha, **R**, Hashabiah,

REHOBOAM
1Ki 11:43 And **R** his son reigned in his
1Ki 12: 1 Now **R** went to Shechem, for
1Ki 12: 3 of Israel came and spoke to **R**
1Ki 12: 6 Then King **R** consulted the
1Ki 12:12 came to **R** the third day, as
1Ki 12:17 But **R** reigned over the
1Ki 12:18 Then King **R** sent Adoram, who
1Ki 12:18 Therefore King **R** mounted his
1Ki 12:21 when **R** came to Jerusalem, he
1Ki 12:21 to **R** the son of Solomon
1Ki 12:23 Speak to **R** the son of Solomon
1Ki 12:27 **R** king of Judah, and they will
1Ki 12:27 go back to **R** king of Judah
1Ki 14:21 **R** the son of Solomon reigned
1Ki 14:21 **R** was forty-one years old
1Ki 14:25 in the fifth year of King **R**
1Ki 14:27 Then King **R** made bronze
1Ki 14:29 Now the rest of the acts of **R**
1Ki 14:30 And there was war between **R**
1Ki 14:31 So **R** rested with his fathers,
1Ki 15: 6 And there was war between **R**
1Ch 3:10 Solomon's son was **R**
2Ch 9:31 And **R** his son reigned in his
2Ch 10: 1 **R** went to Shechem, for all
2Ch 10: 3 all Israel came and spoke to **R**
2Ch 10: 6 Then King **R** consulted the
2Ch 10:12 came to **R** on the third day
2Ch 10:13 King **R** rejected the counsel
2Ch 10:17 But **R** reigned over the
2Ch 10:18 Then King **R** sent Hadoram,
2Ch 10:18 Therefore King **R** mounted his
2Ch 11: 1 Now when **R** came to Jerusalem,
2Ch 11: 1 restore the kingdom to **R**
2Ch 11: 3 Speak to **R** the son of Solomon
2Ch 11: 5 So **R** dwelt in Jerusalem, and
2Ch 11:17 made **R** the son of Solomon
2Ch 11:18 Then **R** took for himself as
2Ch 11:21 Now **R** loved Maacah the
2Ch 11:22 **R** appointed Abijah the son of
2Ch 12: 1 when **R** had established the
2Ch 12: 2 in the fifth year of King **R**
2Ch 12: 5 the prophet came to **R** and the
2Ch 12:10 King **R** made bronze shields
2Ch 12:13 So King **R** strengthened
2Ch 12:13 Now **R** was forty-one years old
2Ch 12:15 The acts of **R**, first and last,
2Ch 12:15 And there were wars between **R**
2Ch 12:16 So **R** rested with his fathers,
2Ch 13: 7 against **R** the son of Solomon
2Ch 13: 7 Solomon, when **R** was young
Matt 1: 7 Solomon begot **R**,
Matt 1: 7 **R** begot Abijah

REHOBOTH
Gen 26:22 So he called its name **R**,

REHOBOTH-BY-THE-RIVER
Gen 36:37 Saul of **R** reigned in his
1Ch 1:48 Saul of **R** reigned in his

REHOBOTH IR
Gen 10:11 Assyria and built Nineveh, **R**

REHUM (*see* NEHUM)
Ezra 2: 2 Bilshan, Mispar, Bigvai, **R**
Ezra 4: 8 **R** the commander and Shimshai
Ezra 4: 9 From **R** the commander,
Ezra 4:17 To **R** the commander, to
Ezra 4:23 letter was read before **R**
Neh 3:17 under **R** the son of Bani, made
Neh 10:25 **R**, Hashabnah, Maaseiah,
Neh 12: 3 Shechaniah, **R**, Meremoth,

REI
1Ki 1: 8 Nathan the prophet, Shimei, **R**

REIGN (*see* REIGNED, REIGNING, REIGNS)
Gen 37: 8 Shall you indeed **r** over us
Ex 15:18 The LORD shall **r** forever and
Lev 26:17 who hate you shall **r** over you
Deut 15: 6 you shall **r** over many nations
Deut 15: 6 but they shall not **r** over you
Judg 9: 2 sons of Jerubbaal **r** over you
Judg 9: 2 or that one **r** over you
Judg 9: 8 to the olive tree, '**R** over us
Judg 9:10 tree, 'You come and **r** over us
Judg 9:12 vine, 'You come and **r** over us
Judg 9:14 You come and **r** over us
1Sa 8: 7 that I should not **r** over them
1Sa 8: 9 the king who will **r** over them
1Sa 8:11 the king who will **r** over you
1Sa 9:17 one shall **r** over My people
1Sa 11:12 said, 'Shall Saul **r** over us
1Sa 12:12 but a king shall **r** over us
2Sa 2:10 he began to **r** over Israel
2Sa 3:21 that you may **r** over all that
2Sa 5: 4 years old when he began to **r**
1Ki 1:13 son Solomon shall **r** after me
1Ki 1:17 your son shall **r** after me
1Ki 1:24 Adonijah shall **r** after me
1Ki 2:15 on me, that I should **r**
1Ki 6: 1 of Solomon's **r** over Israel
1Ki 11:37 you shall **r** over all your
1Ki 16:11 to pass, when he began to **r**
2Ki 8:16 began to **r** as king of Judah
2Ki 8:25 king of Judah, began to **r**
2Ki 15:32 king of Judah, began to **r**
2Ki 16: 1 king of Judah, began to **r**
2Ki 18: 1 king of Judah, began to **r**
2Ki 23:33 he might not **r** in Jerusalem
2Ki 24:12 in the eighth year of his **r**
2Ki 25: 1 in the ninth year of his **r**
2Ki 25:27 the year that he began to **r**
1Ch 4:31 cities until the **r** of David
1Ch 26:31 **r** of David they were sought
1Ch 29:12 from You, and You **r** over all
1Ch 29:30 with all his **r** and his might,
2Ch 3: 2 in the fourth year of his **r**
2Ch 15:10 year of the **r** of Asa
2Ch 15:19 year of the **r** of Asa
2Ch 16: 1 year of the **r** of Asa, Baasha
2Ch 16:12 thirty-ninth year of his **r**
2Ch 16:13 the forty-first year of his **r**
2Ch 17: 7 of his **r** he sent his leaders
2Ch 23: 3 the king's son shall **r**, as
2Ch 29: 3 In the first year of his **r**
2Ch 29:19 his **r** had cast aside in his
2Ch 34: 3 in the eighth year of his **r**
2Ch 34: 8 the eighteenth year of his **r**
2Ch 35:19 the eighteenth year of the **r**
2Ch 36:20 his sons until the **r** of the
Ezra 4: 5 even until the **r** of Darius
Ezra 4: 6 Now in the **r** of Ahasuerus, in
Ezra 4: 6 in the beginning of his **r**
Ezra 4:24 the second year of the **r** of
Ezra 6:15 year of the **r** of King Darius
Ezra 7: 1 in the **r** of Artaxerxes king
Ezra 8: 1 in the **r** of King Artaxerxes
Neh 12:22 During the **r** of Darius the
Esth 1: 3 in the third year of his **r** he
Esth 2:16 in the seventh year of his **r**
Job 34:30 the hypocrite should not **r**
Ps 146:10 The LORD shall **r** forever
Prov 8:15 By me kings **r**, and rulers
Is 24:23 of hosts will **r** on Mount Zion
Is 32: 1 Behold, a king will **r** in
Jer 1: 2 the thirteenth year of his **r**
Jer 22:15 Shall you **r** because you
Jer 23: 5 a King shall **r** and prosper, and
Jer 26: 1 the **r** of Jehoiakim the son of
Jer 27: 1 the **r** of Jehoiakim the son of
Jer 28: 1 at the beginning of the **r** of
Jer 33:21 have a son to **r** on his throne
Jer 49:34 in the beginning of the **r** of

Jer 51:59 in the fourth year of his **r**
Jer 52: 4 in the ninth year of his **r**
Jer 52:31 in the first year of his **r**
Dan 1: 1 In the third year of the **r** of
Dan 2: 1 year of Nebuchadnezzar's **r**
Dan 6:28 prospered in the **r** of Darius
Dan 6:28 in the **r** of Cyrus the Persian
Dan 8: 1 In the third year of the **r** of
Dan 9: 2 in the first year of his **r** I
Mic 4: 7 so the LORD will **r** over them
Luke 1:33 He will **r** over the house of
Luke 3: 1 of the **r** of Tiberius Caesar
Luke 19:14 have this man to **r** over us
Luke 19:27 not want me to **r** over them
Rom 5:17 **r** in life through the One
Rom 5:21 even so grace might **r** through
Rom 6:12 let sin **r** in your mortal body
Rom 15:12 rise to **r** over the Gentiles
1Co 4: 8 indeed I could wish you did **r**
1Co 4: 8 that we also might **r** with you
1Co 15:25 For He must **r** till He has put
2Ti 2:12 we shall also **r** with Him
Rev 5:10 and we shall **r** on the earth
Rev 11:15 Christ, and He shall **r** forever
Rev 20: 6 shall **r** with Him a thousand
Rev 22: 5 And they shall **r** forever and

REIGNED (*see* REIGN)
Gen 36:31 these were the kings who **r** in
Gen 36:31 of Edom before any king **r**
Gen 36:32 the son of Beor **r** in Edom
Gen 36:33 of Bozrah **r** in his place
Gen 36:34 the Temanites **r** in his place
Gen 36:35 field of Moab, **r** in his place
Gen 36:36 of Masrekah **r** in his place
Gen 36:37 **r** in his place
Gen 36:38 son of Achbor **r** in his place
Gen 36:39 died, Hadar **r** in his place
Josh 12: 5 **r** over Mount Hermon, over
Josh 13:10 who **r** in Heshbon, as far as
Josh 13:12 who **r** in Ashtaroth and Edrei,
Josh 13:21 who **r** in Heshbon, whom Moses
Judg 4: 2 of Canaan, who **r** in Hazor
Judg 9:22 After Abimelech had **r** over
1Sa 13: 1 Saul **r** one year
1Sa 13: 1 when he had **r** two years over
2Sa 2:10 Israel, and he **r** two years
2Sa 5: 4 to reign, and he **r** forty years
2Sa 5: 5 In Hebron he **r** over Judah
2Sa 5: 5 months, and in Jerusalem he **r**
2Sa 8:15 So David **r** over all Israel
2Sa 10: 1 Hanun his son **r** in his place
2Sa 16: 8 in whose place you have **r**
1Ki 2:11 The period that David **r** over
1Ki 2:11 seven years he **r** in Hebron
1Ki 2:11 and in Jerusalem he **r**
1Ki 4:21 So Solomon **r** over all
1Ki 11:24 dwelt there, and **r** in Damascus
1Ki 11:25 Israel, and **r** over Syria
1Ki 11:42 **r** in Jerusalem over all
1Ki 11:43 his son **r** in his place
1Ki 12:17 But Rehoboam **r** over the
1Ki 14:19 how he made war and how he **r**
1Ki 14:20 **r** was twenty-two years
1Ki 14:20 Nadab his son **r** in his place
1Ki 14:21 the son of Solomon **r** in Judah
1Ki 14:21 He **r** seventeen years in
1Ki 14:31 Abijam his son **r** in his place
1Ki 15: 2 He **r** three years in Jerusalem
1Ki 15: 8 Asa his son **r** in his place
1Ki 15:10 And he **r** forty-one years in
1Ki 15:24 his son **r** in his place
1Ki 15:25 he **r** over Israel two years
1Ki 15:28 of Judah, and **r** in his place
1Ki 15:33 and **r** twenty-four years
1Ki 16: 6 Elah his son **r** in his place
1Ki 16: 8 and **r** two years in Tirzah
1Ki 16:10 of Judah, and **r** in his place
1Ki 16:15 Zimri had **r** in Tirzah seven
1Ki 16:22 So Tibni died and Omri **r**
1Ki 16:23 Israel, and **r** twelve years
1Ki 16:23 Six years he **r** in Tirzah
1Ki 16:28 Ahab his son **r** in his place
1Ki 16:29 Ahab the son of Omri **r** over
1Ki 22:40 his son **r** in his place
1Ki 22:42 he **r** twenty-five years in
1Ki 22:50 his son **r** in his place
1Ki 22:51 and **r** two years over Israel
2Ki 3: 1 of Judah, and **r** twelve years
2Ki 3:27 who would have **r** in his place
2Ki 8:15 and Hazael **r** in his place
2Ki 8:17 he **r** eight years in Jerusalem
2Ki 8:24 his son **r** in his place
2Ki 8:26 he **r** one year in Jerusalem
2Ki 10:35 his son **r** in his place
2Ki 10:36 the period that Jehu **r** over
2Ki 11: 3 Athaliah **r** over the land
2Ki 12: 1 he **r** forty years in Jerusalem
2Ki 12:21 his son **r** in his place
2Ki 13: 1 Samaria, and **r** seventeen years
2Ki 13: 9 Joash his son **r** in his place
2Ki 13:10 Samaria, and **r** sixteen years
2Ki 13:24 his son **r** in his place
2Ki 14: 2 he **r** twenty-nine years in
2Ki 14:16 his son **r** in his place
2Ki 14:23 Samaria, and **r** forty-one years
2Ki 14:29 his son **r** in his place
2Ki 15: 2 and he **r** fifty-two years in
2Ki 15: 7 Jotham his son **r** in his place
2Ki 15: 8 the son of Jeroboam **r** over
2Ki 15:10 and he **r** in his place
2Ki 15:13 he **r** a full month in Samaria
2Ki 15:14 and he **r** in his place
2Ki 15:17 and **r** ten years in Samaria
2Ki 15:22 his son **r** in his place
2Ki 15:23 in Samaria, and **r** two years
2Ki 15:25 killed him and **r** in his place
2Ki 15:27 in Samaria, and **r** twenty years
2Ki 15:30 so he **r** in his place in the
2Ki 15:33 and he **r** sixteen years in
2Ki 15:38 Ahaz his son **r** in his place
2Ki 16: 2 and he **r** sixteen years in
2Ki 16:20 his son **r** in his place
2Ki 17: 1 Samaria, and he **r** nine years
2Ki 18: 2 he **r** twenty-nine years in
2Ki 19:37 his son **r** in his place
2Ki 20:21 his son **r** in his place
2Ki 21: 1 and he **r** fifty-five years in
2Ki 21:18 his son Amon **r** in his place
2Ki 21:19 he **r** two years in Jerusalem
2Ki 21:26 Josiah his son **r** in his place
2Ki 22: 1 and he **r** thirty-one years in
2Ki 23:31 king, and he **r** three months in
2Ki 23:36 king, and he **r** eleven years in
2Ki 24: 6 his son **r** in his place
2Ki 24: 8 and he **r** in Jerusalem three
2Ki 24:18 king, and he **r** eleven years in
1Ch 1:43 these were the kings who **r** in
1Ch 1:43 of Edom before any king **r**
1Ch 1:44 of Bozrah **r** in his place
1Ch 1:45 the Temanites **r** in his place
1Ch 1:46 field of Moab, **r** in his place
1Ch 1:47 of Masrekah **r** in his place
1Ch 1:48 **r** in his place
1Ch 1:49 son of Achbor **r** in his place
1Ch 1:50 died, Hadad **r** in his place
1Ch 3: 4 There he **r** seven years and six
1Ch 3: 4 months, and in Jerusalem he **r**
1Ch 18:14 So David **r** over all Israel,
1Ch 19: 1 and his son **r** in his place
1Ch 29:26 of Jesse **r** over all Israel
1Ch 29:27 the period that he **r** over
1Ch 29:27 seven years he **r** in Hebron
1Ch 29:27 years he **r** in Jerusalem
1Ch 29:28 his son **r** in his place
2Ch 1:13 of meeting, and **r** over Israel
2Ch 9:26 So he **r** over all the kings
2Ch 9:30 Solomon **r** in Jerusalem over
2Ch 9:31 his son **r** in his place
2Ch 10:17 But Rehoboam **r** over the
2Ch 12:13 himself in Jerusalem and **r**
2Ch 12:13 and he **r** seventeen years in
2Ch 12:16 Abijah his son **r** in his place
2Ch 13: 2 He **r** three years in Jerusalem
2Ch 14: 1 Asa his son **r** in his place
2Ch 17: 1 his son **r** in his place, and
2Ch 20:31 he **r** twenty-five years in
2Ch 21: 1 his son **r** in his place
2Ch 21: 5 he **r** eight years in Jerusalem
2Ch 21:20 He **r** in Jerusalem eight years
2Ch 22: 1 of Jehoram, king of Judah, **r**
2Ch 22: 2 he **r** one year in Jerusalem
2Ch 22:12 Athaliah **r** over the land
2Ch 24: 1 he **r** forty years in Jerusalem
2Ch 24:27 his son **r** in his place
2Ch 25: 1 he **r** twenty-nine years in
2Ch 26: 3 and he **r** fifty-two years in
2Ch 26:23 Jotham his son **r** in his place
2Ch 27: 1 and he **r** sixteen years in
2Ch 27: 8 and he **r** sixteen years in
2Ch 27: 9 Ahaz his son **r** in his place
2Ch 28: 1 and he **r** sixteen years in
2Ch 28:27 his son **r** in his place
2Ch 29: 1 he **r** twenty-nine years in
2Ch 32:33 his son **r** in his place
2Ch 33: 1 and he **r** fifty-five years in
2Ch 33:20 his son Amon **r** in his place
2Ch 33:21 he **r** two years in Jerusalem
2Ch 34: 1 and he **r** thirty-one years in
2Ch 36: 2 king, and he **r** three months in
2Ch 36: 5 king, and he **r** eleven years in
2Ch 36: 8 his son **r** in his place
2Ch 36: 9 and he **r** in Jerusalem three
2Ch 36:11 king, and he **r** eleven years in
Esth 1: 1 who **r** from India to Ethiopia
Is 37:38 his son **r** in his place
Jer 22:11 who **r** instead of Josiah his
Jer 37: 1 **r** instead of Coniah the son
Jer 52: 1 king, and he **r** eleven years in
Rom 5:14 death **r** from Adam to Moses
Rom 5:17 death **r** through the one, much
Rom 5:21 so that as sin **r** in death
1Co 4: 8 You have **r** as kings without
Rev 11:17 taken Your great power and **r**
Rev 20: 4 **r** with Christ for a thousand

REIGNING (*see* REIGN)
1Sa 16: 1 him from **r** over Israel
Matt 2:22 **r** over Judea instead of his

REIGNS (*see* REIGN)
1Sa 12:14 the king who **r** over you will
2Sa 15:10 say, 'Absalom **r** in Hebron
1Ch 16:31 The LORD **r**
Ps 47: 8 God **r** over the nations
Ps 93: 1 The LORD **r**, He is clothed
Ps 96:10 The LORD **r**
Ps 97: 1 The LORD **r**
Ps 99: 1 The LORD **r**
Prov 30:22 for a servant when he **r**, a
Is 52: 7 Your God **r**
Rev 17:18 is that great city which **r**
Rev 19: 6 For the Lord God Omnipotent **r**

REINFORCED
2Ch 24:13 original condition and **r** it

REJECT (*see* REJECTED, REJECTION, REJECTS)
Num 14:11 long will these people **r** Me
Ps 119:118 You **r** all those who stray
Hos 4: 6 I also will **r** you from being
Mark 7: 9 All too well you **r** the
Acts 13:46 but since you **r** it, and judge
Gal 4:14 you did not despise or **r**, but
1Th 4: 8 rejects this does not **r** man
1Ti 4: 7 But **r** profane and old wives'
Tit 3:10 **R** a divisive man after the
Jude 8 **r** authority, and speak evil of

REJECTED (*see* REJECT)
Num 14:23 any of those who **r** Me see it
Num 16:30 these men have **r** the LORD
1Sa 8: 7 for they have not **r** you
1Sa 8: 7 but they have **r** Me, that
1Sa 10:19 But you have today **r** your God
1Sa 15:23 Because you have **r** the word
1Sa 15:23 He also has **r** you from being
1Sa 15:26 for you have **r** the word of
1Sa 15:26 the LORD has **r** you from being
1Sa 16: 1 seeing I have **r** him from
1Ki 12: 8 But he **r** the counsel which
1Ki 12:13 and **r** the counsel which the
2Ki 17:15 they **r** His statutes and His
2Ki 17:20 And the LORD **r** all the
2Ch 10: 8 But he **r** the counsel which
2Ch 10:13 King Rehoboam **r** the counsel
2Ch 11:14 and his sons had **r** them from
Ps 78:67 Moreover He **r** the tent of
Ps 118:22 **r** Has become the chief
Is 5:24 because they have **r** the law
Is 53: 3 **r** by men, a man of sorrows and
Jer 2:37 for the LORD has **r** your
Jer 6:19 words, nor My law, but **r** it
Jer 6:30 will call them **r** silver,
Jer 6:30 because the LORD has **r** them
Jer 7:29 for the LORD has **r** and
Jer 8: 9 they have **r** the word of the
Jer 14:19 Have You utterly **r** Judah
Lam 5:22 unless You have utterly **r** us
Hos 4: 6 Because you have **r** knowledge
Hos 8: 5 Your calf is **r**, O Samaria
Matt 21:42 stone which the builders **r**
Mark 8:31 be **r** by the elders and chief
Mark 12:10 stone which the builders **r**

Luke 7:30 lawyers **r** the counsel of God
Luke 9:22 be **r** by the elders and chief
Luke 17:25 and be **r** by this generation
Luke 20:17 stone which the builders **r**
Acts 4:11 which was **r** by you builders
Acts 7:35 This Moses whom they **r**,
Acts 7:39 fathers would not obey, but **r**
1Ti 1:19 which some having **r**,
Heb 6: 8 thorns and briars, it is **r**
Heb 10:28 Anyone who has **r** Moses' law
Heb 12:17 the blessing, he was **r**, for
1Pe 2: 4 **r** indeed by men, but chosen
1Pe 2: 7 stone which the builders **r**

REJECTION (*see* REJECT)
Num 14:34 years, and you shall know My **r**

REJECTS (*see* REJECT)
Luke 10:16 he who **r** you **r** Me, and
Luke 10:16 who **r** Me **r** Him who sent Me
John 12:48 He who **r** Me, and does not
1Th 4: 8 Therefore he who **r** this does

REJOICE (*see* REJOICED, REJOICES, REJOICING)
Lev 23:40 you shall **r** before the LORD
Deut 12: 7 you shall **r** in all to which
Deut 12:12 you shall **r** before the LORD
Deut 12:18 you shall **r** before the LORD
Deut 14:26 LORD your God, and you shall **r**
Deut 16:11 You shall **r** before the LORD
Deut 16:14 you shall **r** in your feast,
Deut 16:15 hands, so that you surely **r**
Deut 26:11 So you shall **r** in every good
Deut 27: 7 **r** before the LORD your God
Deut 28:63 so the LORD will **r** over you
Deut 30: 9 **r** over you for good as He
Deut 32:43 **R**, O Gentiles, with His
Deut 33:18 **R**, Zebulun, in your going out
Judg 9:19 then **r** in Abimelech, and let
Judg 9:19 and let him also **r** in you
Judg 16:23 to Dagon their god, and to **r**
1Sa 2: 1 because I **r** in Your salvation
2Sa 1:20 of the Philistines **r**, lest
1Ch 16:10 of those **r** who seek the LORD
1Ch 16:31 Let the heavens **r**, and let the
1Ch 16:32 let the field **r**, and all that
1Ch 16:33 woods shall **r** before the LORD
2Ch 6:41 let Your saints **r** in goodness
2Ch 20:27 them **r** over their enemies
Neh 8:12 and **r** greatly, because they
Neh 12:43 made them **r** with great joy
Job 3:22 who **r** exceedingly, and are
Job 21:12 **r** to the sound of the flute
Ps 2:11 fear, And **r** with trembling
Ps 5:11 But let all those **r** who put
Ps 9: 2 I will be glad and **r** in You
Ps 9:14 I will **r** in Your salvation
Ps 13: 4 trouble me **r** when I am moved
Ps 13: 5 My heart shall **r** in Your
Ps 14: 7 of His people, Let Jacob **r**
Ps 20: 5 We will **r** in your salvation,
Ps 21: 1 how greatly shall he **r**
Ps 30: 1 not let my foes **r** over me
Ps 31: 7 **r** in Your mercy, For You have
Ps 32:11 Be glad in the LORD and **r**, you
Ps 33: 1 **R** in the LORD, O you
Ps 33:21 For our heart shall **r** in Him
Ps 35: 9 It shall **r** in His salvation
Ps 35:19 Let them not **r** over me who
Ps 35:24 And let them not **r** over me
Ps 35:26 confusion Who **r** at my hurt
Ps 38:16 Hear me, lest they **r** over me
Ps 40:16 Let all those who seek You **r**
Ps 48:11 Let Mount Zion **r**, Let the
Ps 51: 8 which You have broken may **r**
Ps 53: 6 of His people, Let Jacob **r**
Ps 58:10 The righteous shall **r** when he
Ps 60: 6 I will **r**
Ps 63: 7 shadow of Your wings I will **r**
Ps 63:11 But the king shall **r** in God
Ps 65: 8 of the morning and evening **r**
Ps 65:12 little hills **r** on every side
Ps 66: 6 There we will **r** in Him
Ps 68: 3 Let them **r** before God
Ps 68: 3 Yes, let them **r** exceedingly
Ps 68: 4 name YAH, And **r** before Him
Ps 70: 4 Let all those who seek You **r**
Ps 71:23 greatly **r** when I sing to You
Ps 85: 6 That Your people may **r** in You
Ps 86: 4 **R** the soul of Your servant,
Ps 89:12 and Hermon **r** in Your name
Ps 89:16 Your name they **r** all day long
Ps 89:42 have made all his enemies **r**
Ps 90:14 Your mercy, That we may **r**
Ps 96:11 Let the heavens **r**, and let the
Ps 96:12 woods will **r** before the LORD
Ps 97: 1 Let the earth **r**
Ps 97: 8 And the daughters of Judah **r**
Ps 97:12 **R** in the LORD, you righteous,
Ps 98: 4 Break forth in song, **r**, and
Ps 104:31 May the LORD **r** in His works
Ps 105: 3 of those **r** who seek the LORD
Ps 106: 5 That I may **r** in the gladness
Ps 107:42 The righteous see it and **r**
Ps 108: 7 I will **r**
Ps 109:28 But let Your servant **r**
Ps 118:24 We will **r** and be glad in it
Ps 119:162 I **r** at Your word As one who
Ps 149: 2 Let Israel **r** in their Maker
Prov 2:14 who **r** in doing evil, and
Prov 5:18 **r** with the wife of your youth
Prov 23:15 is wise, my heart will **r**
Prov 23:16 my inmost being will **r** when
Prov 23:24 the righteous will greatly **r**
Prov 23:25 and let her who bore you **r**
Prov 24:17 Do not **r** when your enemy
Prov 28:12 When the righteous **r**, there
Prov 29: 2 in authority, the people **r**
Prov 29: 3 wisdom makes his father **r**
Prov 31:25 she shall **r** in time to come
Eccl 3:12 better for them than to **r**
Eccl 3:22 man should **r** in his own works
Eccl 4:16 afterward will not **r** in him
Eccl 5:19 heritage and **r** in his labor
Eccl 11: 9 **R**, O young man, in your youth
Song 1: 4 We will be glad and **r** in you
Is 8: 6 **r** in Rezin and in Remaliah's
Is 9: 3 they **r** before You According
Is 9: 3 as men **r** when they divide the
Is 13: 3 those who **r** in My exaltation
Is 14: 8 the cypress trees **r** over you
Is 14:29 Do not **r**, all you of
Is 23:12 You will **r** no more, O you
Is 25: 9 be glad and **r** in His salvation
Is 29:19 the poor among men shall **r** In
Is 35: 1 them, and the desert shall **r**
Is 35: 2 shall blossom abundantly and **r**
Is 41:16 you shall **r** in the LORD, and
Is 43:14 who **r** in their ships
Is 61: 7 they shall **r** in their portion
Is 61:10 I will greatly **r** in the LORD
Is 62: 5 so shall your God **r** over you
Is 65:13 behold, My servants shall **r**
Is 65:18 **r** forever in what I create
Is 65:19 I will **r** in Jerusalem, and joy
Is 66:10 **R** with Jerusalem, and be glad
Is 66:10 **r** for joy with her, all you
Is 66:14 see this, your heart shall **r**
Jer 11:15 When you do evil, then you **r**
Jer 15:17 of the mockers, nor did I **r**
Jer 31: 4 in the dances of those who **r**
Jer 31:13 the virgin **r** in the dance
Jer 31:13 and make them **r** rather than
Jer 32:41 I will **r** over them to do them
Jer 51:39 them drunk, that they may **r**
Lam 2:17 your enemy to **r** over you
Lam 4:21 **R** and be glad, O daughter of
Ezek 7:12 Let not the buyer **r**, nor the
Ezek 35:14 The whole earth will **r** when I
Hos 9: 1 Do not **r**, O Israel, with joy
Joel 2:21 be glad and **r**, for the LORD
Joel 2:23 and **r** in the LORD your God
Amos 6:13 you who **r** over Lo Debar, who
Mic 7: 8 Do not **r** over me, my enemy
Hab 1:15 Therefore they **r** and are glad
Hab 3:18 Yet I will **r** in the LORD, I
Zeph 3:11 those who **r** in your pride
Zeph 3:14 and **r** with all your heart, O
Zeph 3:17 He will **r** over you with
Zeph 3:17 love, He will **r** over you with
Zech 2:10 Sing and **r**, O daughter of Zion
Zech 4:10 for these seven **r** to see the
Zech 9: 9 **R** greatly, O daughter of Zion
Zech 10: 7 heart shall **r** as if with wine
Zech 10: 7 heart shall **r** in the LORD
Matt 5:12 **R** and be exceedingly glad, for
Matt 28: 9 Jesus met them, saying, "**R**!"
Luke 1:14 and many will **r** at his birth
Luke 1:28 **R**, highly favored one, the
Luke 6:23 **R** in that day and leap for joy
Luke 10:20 Nevertheless do not **r** in this
Luke 10:20 but rather **r** because your
Luke 15: 6 **R** with me, for I have found
Luke 15: 9 **R** with me, for I have found
Luke 19:37 of the disciples began to **r**
John 4:36 he who reaps may **r** together
John 5:35 for a time to **r** in his light
John 14:28 you would **r** because I said
John 16:20 lament, but the world will **r**
John 16:22 again and your heart will **r**
Rom 5: 2 **r** in hope of the glory of God
Rom 5:11 but we also **r** in God through
Rom 12:15 **R** with those who **r**, and
Rom 15:10 **R**, O Gentiles, with His
1Co 7:30 **r** as though they did not **r**
1Co 12:26 all the members **r** with it
1Co 13: 6 does not **r** in iniquity, but
2Co 7: 9 Now I **r**, not that you were
2Co 7:16 Therefore I **r** that I have
Gal 4:27 **R**, O barren, you who do not
Phil 1:18 and in this I **r**, yes, and will
Phil 1:18 I **r**, yes, and will **r**
Phil 2:16 so that I may **r** in the day of
Phil 2:17 I am glad and **r** with you all
Phil 2:18 you also be glad and **r** with me
Phil 2:28 you see him again you may **r**
Phil 3: 1 my brethren, **r** in the Lord
Phil 3: 3 **r** in Christ Jesus, and have no
Phil 4: 4 **R** in the Lord always
Phil 4: 4 Again I will say, **r**
Col 1:24 I now **r** in my sufferings for
1Th 3: 9 we **r** for your sake before our
1Th 5:16 **R** always,
1Pe 1: 6 In this you greatly **r**, though
1Pe 1: 8 you **r** with joy inexpressible
1Pe 4:13 but **r** to the extent that you
Rev 11:10 on the earth will **r** over them
Rev 12:12 Therefore **r**, O heavens, and
Rev 18:20 **R** over her, O heaven, and you
Rev 19: 7 Let us be glad and **r** and give

REJOICED (*see* REJOICE)
Ex 18: 9 Then Jethro **r** for all the
Deut 28:63 that just as the LORD **r** over
Deut 30: 9 as He **r** over your fathers
1Sa 6:13 saw the ark, and **r** to see it
1Sa 11:15 the men of Israel **r** greatly
1Sa 19: 5 You saw it and **r**
1Ki 1:40 **r** with great joy, so that the
1Ki 5: 7 of Solomon, that he **r** greatly
2Ki 11:20 all the people of the land **r**
1Ch 29: 9 Then the people **r**, for they
1Ch 29: 9 and King David also **r** greatly
2Ch 15:15 all Judah **r** at the oath, for
2Ch 23:21 all the people of the land **r**
2Ch 24:10 leaders and all the people **r**
2Ch 29:36 all the people **r** that God had
2Ch 30:25 whole congregation of Judah **r**
Neh 12:43 great sacrifices, and **r**, for
Neh 12:43 women and the children also **r**
Neh 12:44 for Judah **r** over the priests
Esth 8:15 and the city of Shushan **r** and
Job 31:25 If I have **r** because my wealth
Job 31:29 If I have **r** at the
Ps 35:15 But in my adversity they **r**
Ps 119:14 I have **r** in the way of Your
Eccl 2:10 for my heart **r** in all my
Jer 50:11 you were glad, because you **r**
Ezek 25: 6 and **r** in heart with all your
Ezek 35:15 As you **r** because the
Obad 12 nor should you have **r** over
Matt 2:10 they **r** with exceedingly great
Luke 1:47 my spirit has **r** in God my
Luke 1:58 mercy to her, they **r** with her
Luke 10:21 hour Jesus **r** in the Spirit
Luke 13:17 all the multitude **r** for all
John 8:56 Abraham **r** to see My day, and
Acts 2:26 therefore my heart **r**, and my
Acts 7:41 **r** in the works of their own
Acts 15:31 they **r** over its encouragement
Acts 16:34 and he **r**, having believed in
2Co 7: 7 for me, so that I **r** even more
2Co 7:13 we **r** exceedingly more for the
Phil 4:10 But I **r** in the Lord greatly
2Jn 4 I **r** greatly that I have found
3Jn 3 For I **r** greatly when brethren

REJOICES (*see* REJOICE)
1Sa 2: 1 My heart **r** in the LORD
Job 39:21 valley, and **r** in his strength
Ps 16: 9 heart is glad, and my glory **r**
Ps 19: 5 **r** like a strong man to run
Ps 28: 7 Therefore my heart greatly **r**

Prov 11:10 the righteous, the city **r**
Prov 13: 9 The light of the righteous **r**
Prov 15:30 light of the eyes **r** the heart
Prov 29: 6 but the righteous sings and **r**
Eccl 11: 8 **r** in them all, yet let him
Is 62: 5 bridegroom **r** over the bride
Is 64: 5 You meet him who **r** and does
Matt 18:13 he **r** more over that sheep
John 3:29 him, **r** greatly because of the
1Co 13: 6 iniquity, but **r** in the truth

REJOICING (*see* REJOICE)
1Ki 1:45 have gone up from there **r**
1Ki 4:20 eating and drinking and **r**
2Ki 11:14 the people of the land were **r**
2Ch 23:13 all the people of the land, **r**
2Ch 23:18 in the Law of Moses, with **r**
Job 8:21 laughing, and your lips with **r**
Ps 19: 8 LORD are right, **r** the heart
Ps 45:15 and **r** they shall be brought
Ps 107:22 And declare His works with **r**
Ps 118:15 The voice of **r** and salvation
Ps 119:111 they are the **r** of my heart
Ps 126: 6 doubtless come again with **r**
Prov 8:30 delight, **r** always before Him,
Prov 8:31 **r** in His inhabited world, and
Is 65:18 I create Jerusalem as a **r**
Jer 15:16 me the joy and **r** of my heart
Ezek 7: 7 not of **r** in the mountains
Hab 3:14 their **r** was like feasting on
Zeph 2:15 This is the **r** city that dwelt
Luke 15: 5 lays it on his shoulders, **r**
Acts 5:41 **r** that they were counted
Acts 8:39 and he went on his way **r**
Rom 12:12 **r** in hope, patient in
2Co 6:10 as sorrowful, yet always **r**
Gal 6: 4 will have **r** in himself alone
Phil 1:26 that your **r** for me may be
Col 2: 5 **r** to see your good order and
1Th 2:19 hope, or joy, or crown of **r**
Heb 3: 6 the **r** of the hope firm to the

REKEM
Num 31: 8 Evi, **R**, Zur, Hur, and Reba,
Josh 13:21 Evi, **R**, Zur, Hur, and Reba,
Josh 18:27 **R**, Irpeel, Taralah,
1Ch 2:43 were Korah, Tappuah, **R**
1Ch 2:44 Jorkoam, and **R** begot Shammai

RELATED (*see* RELATING, RELATIVE)
Num 18: 1 iniquity **r** to the sanctuary
Esth 8: 1 had told how he was **r** to her

RELATING (*see* RELATED)
Num 3:26 to all the work **r** to them
Num 3:31 and all the work **r** to them
Num 3:36 all the work **r** to them,
Num 4: 4 **r** to the most holy things

RELATIVE (*see* RELATED, RELATIVES)
Gen 29:12 that he was her father's **r**
Gen 29:15 Because you are my **r**, should
Ruth 2:20 The man is a **r** of ours, one
2Sa 19:42 the king is a close **r** of ours
Luke 1:36 Elizabeth your **r** has also
John 18:26 a **r** of him whose ear Peter

RELATIVES (*see* RELATIVE)
Lev 21: 2 except for his **r** who are
Josh 6:23 So they brought out all her **r**
1Ch 8:32 their **r** in Jerusalem, with
1Ch 9:38 their **r** in Jerusalem, with
Job 19:14 my **r** have failed, and my close
Ezek 11:15 of man, your brethren, your **r**
Mark 6: 4 own country, among his own **r**
Luke 1:58 and **r** heard how the Lord had
Luke 1:61 **r** who is called by this name
Luke 2:44 and sought Him among their **r**
Luke 14:12 your brothers, your **r**, nor
Luke 21:16 by parents and brothers, **r**
Acts 7: 3 your country and from your **r**
Acts 7:14 Jacob and all his **r** to him
Acts 10:24 and had called together his **r**

RELEASE (*see* RELEASED, RELEASING)
Gen 43:14 man, that he may **r** your other
Lev 16:22 he shall **r** the goat in the
Lev 25:50 The price of his **r** shall be
Deut 15: 1 you shall grant a **r** of debts
Deut 15: 2 And this is the form of the **r**
Deut 15: 2 to his neighbor shall **r** it
Deut 15: 2 it is called the LORD's **r**
Deut 15: 3 but your hand shall **r** what is
Deut 15: 9 seventh year, the year of **r**
Deut 31:10 time in the year of **r**, at the
Job 12:14 a man, there can be no **r**
Matt 27:17 do you want me to **r** to you
Matt 27:21 do you want me to **r** to you
Mark 15: 9 Do you want me to **r** to you
Mark 15:11 rather **r** Barabbas to them
Luke 23:16 chastise Him and **r** Him"
Luke 23:17 **r** one to them at the feast)
Luke 23:18 Man, and **r** to us Barabbas"
Luke 23:20 therefore, wishing to **r** Jesus
John 18:39 **r** someone to you at the
John 18:39 **r** to you the King of the Jews
John 19:10 You, and power to **r** You
John 19:12 on Pilate sought to **r** Him
Acts 24:26 by Paul, that he might **r** him
Heb 2:15 **r** those who through fear of
Rev 9:14 **R** the four angels who are

RELEASED (*see* RELEASE)
Gen 24: 8 you will be **r** from this oath
Gen 24:41 you will be **r** from my oath
Lev 16:26 And he who **r** the goat as the
Lev 25:28 in the Jubilee it shall be **r**
Lev 25:30 shall not be **r** in the Jubilee
Lev 25:31 and they shall be **r** in the
Lev 25:33 be **r** in the Year of Jubilee
Lev 25:54 then he shall be **r** in the
Lev 27:21 when it is **r** in the Jubilee,
2Ki 25:27 **r** Jehoiachin king of Judah
Ps 105:20 and **r** him, The ruler of the
Matt 15: 6 is **r** from honoring his
Matt 18:27 **r** him, and forgave him the
Matt 27:26 Then he **r** Barabbas to them
Mark 15:15 the crowd, **r** Barabbas to them
Luke 23:25 he **r** to them the one they
Acts 22:30 he **r** him from his bonds, and
Rom 7: 2 she is **r** from the law of her
Rev 9:15 were **r** to kill a third of
Rev 20: 3 must be **r** for a little while
Rev 20: 7 Satan will be **r** from his

RELEASING (*see* RELEASE)
Prov 17:14 of strife is like **r** water
Matt 27:15 to **r** to the multitude one
Mark 15: 6 to **r** one prisoner to them

RELENT (*see* RELENTED, RELENTING, RELENTLESSLY, RELENTS)
Ex 32:12 and **r** from this harm to Your
1Sa 15:29 of Israel will not lie nor **r**
1Sa 15:29 not a man, that He should **r**
Ps 110: 4 LORD has sworn And will not **r**
Jer 4:28 I have purposed and will not **r**
Jer 18: 8 I will **r** of the disaster that
Jer 18:10 then I will **r** concerning the
Jer 20:16 LORD overthrew, and did not **r**
Jer 26: 3 that I may **r** concerning the
Jer 26:13 then the LORD will **r**
Jer 42:10 For I **r** concerning the
Ezek 24:14 will I spare, nor will I **r**
Joel 2:14 knows if He will turn and **r**
Jon 3: 9 tell if God will turn and **r**
Zech 8:14 of hosts, And I would not **r**
Matt 21:32 it, you did not afterward **r**
Heb 7:21 LORD has sworn and will not **r**

RELENTED (*see* RELENT)
Ex 32:14 So the LORD **r** from the harm
2Sa 24:16 it, the LORD **r** from the
1Ch 21:15 **r** of the disaster, and said to
Ps 106:45 **r** according to the multitude
Jer 26:19 the Lord **r** concerning the
Amos 7: 3 So the LORD **r** concerning this
Amos 7: 6 So the LORD **r** concerning this
Jon 3:10 God **r** from the disaster that

RELENTING (*see* RELENT)
Jer 15: 6 I am weary of **r**

RELENTLESSLY (*see* RELENT)
Judg 20:45 pursued them **r** up to Gidom

RELENTS (*see* RELENT)
Joel 2:13 and He **r** from doing harm
Jon 4: 2 One who **r** from doing harm

RELIED (*see* RELY)
Judg 20:36 because they **r** on the men in
2Ch 13:18 because they **r** on the LORD
2Ch 16: 7 Because you have **r** on the
2Ch 16: 7 have not **r** on the LORD your
2Ch 16: 8 because you **r** on the LORD

RELIEF (*see* RELIEVE)
Ex 8:15 Pharaoh saw that there was **r**
Esth 4:14 silent at this time, **r** and
Job 32:20 will speak, that I may find **r**
Lam 2:18 give yourself no **r**
Acts 11:29 determined to send **r** to the

RELIEVE (*see* RELIEF, RELIEVED, RELIEVES)
Job 16: 5 of my lips would **r** your grief
1Ti 5:16 has widows, let them **r** them
1Ti 5:16 that it may **r** those who are

RELIEVED (*see* RELIEVE)
Job 16: 6 I speak, my grief is not **r**
Ps 4: 1 You have **r** me when I was in
1Ti 5:10 if she has **r** the afflicted,

RELIEVES (*see* RELIEVE)
Ps 146: 9 He **r** the fatherless and widow

RELIGION (*see* RELIGIOUS)
Acts 25:19 against him about their own **r**
Acts 26: 5 of our **r** I lived a Pharisee
Col 2:23 of wisdom in self-imposed **r**
Jas 1:26 this one's **r** is useless
Jas 1:27 undefiled **r** before God and the

RELIGIOUS (*see* RELIGION)
Acts 17:22 in all things you are very **r**
Jas 1:26 among you thinks he is **r**, and

RELY (*see* RELIED, UNRELIABLE)
Job 24:23 security, and they **r** on it
Is 30:12 and perversity, and **r** on them,
Is 31: 1 **r** on horses, who trust in
Is 50:10 of the LORD and **r** upon his God
Ezek 33:26 You **r** on your sword, you

REMAIN (*see* REMAINDER, REMAINED, REMAINING, REMAINS, REMNANT)
Gen 38:11 **R** a widow in your father's
Gen 44:33 **r** instead of the lad as a
Ex 8: 9 that they may **r** in the river
Ex 8:11 They shall **r** in the river
Ex 12:10 none of it **r** until morning
Ex 16:29 Let every man **r** in his place
Ex 23:18 My sacrifice **r** until morning
Lev 19:13 **r** with you all night until
Lev 25:28 **r** in the hand of him who
Lev 25:52 if there **r** but a few years
Lev 27:18 **r** till the Year of Jubilee
Num 9:20 LORD they would **r** encamped
Num 9:22 of Israel would **r** encamped
Num 31:19 **r** outside the camp seven days
Num 32:32 of our inheritance shall **r**
Num 33:55 **r** shall be irritants in your
Num 35:25 he shall **r** there until the
Deut 13:17 things shall **r** in your hand
Deut 16: 4 **r** overnight until morning
Deut 19:20 those who **r** shall hear and
Deut 20:16 nothing that breathes **r** alive
Deut 21:13 **r** in your house, and mourn her
Deut 21:23 his body shall not **r**
Deut 22: 2 it shall **r** with you until
Josh 1:14 your livestock shall **r** in the
Josh 2:11 neither did there **r** any more
Josh 8:22 let none of them **r** or escape
Josh 10:27 which **r** until this very day
Josh 10:28 He let none **r**
Josh 10:30 He let none **r** in it, but did
Josh 18: 5 Judah shall **r** in their
Josh 18: 5 **r** in their territory on the
Josh 23: 4 by lot these nations that **r**
Josh 23: 7 these who **r** among you
Josh 23:12 these that **r** among you
Judg 5:17 and why did Dan **r** on ships
Judg 21: 7 do for wives for those who **r**
Judg 21:16 do for wives for those who **r**
1Sa 1:22 the LORD and **r** there forever
1Sa 5: 7 of Israel must not **r** with us
1Sa 20:19 and **r** by the stone Ezel
2Sa 15:19 Return and **r** with the king
2Sa 16:18 will be, and with him I will **r**
2Ki 7: 9 of good news, and we **r** silent
2Ch 32:10 that you **r** under siege in
Esth 3: 8 for the king to let them **r**
Esth 4:14 For if you **r** completely
Job 16: 6 and though I **r** silent, how am
Job 37: 8 dens, and **r** in their lairs
Ps 49:12 though in honor, does not **r**
Ps 55: 7 off, And **r** in the wilderness
Prov 2:21 and the blameless will **r** in it
Eccl 8:15 for this will **r** with him in
Is 10:32 As yet he will **r** at Nob that

Is 32:16 and righteousness r in the
Is 44:13 that it may r in the house
Is 66:22 I will make shall r before Me
Is 66:22 descendants and your name r
Jer 3: 5 Will He r angry forever
Jer 3:12 I will not r angry forever
Jer 8: 3 who r of this evil family
Jer 8: 3 who r in all the places where
Jer 17:25 and this city shall r forever
Jer 24: 8 Jerusalem who r in this land
Jer 27:11 I will let them r in their
Jer 27:19 vessels that r in this city
Jer 27:21 r in the house of the LORD
Jer 30:18 the palace shall r according
Jer 38: 4 men of war who r in this city
Jer 40: 4 with me to Babylon, r here
Jer 42:17 And none of them shall r or
Jer 43: 4 to r in the land of Judah
Jer 44: 7 of Judah, leaving none to r
Jer 51:62 so that none shall r in it
Lam 5:19 You, O LORD, r forever
Ezek 5:10 and all of you who r I will
Ezek 7:11 none of them shall r, none of
Ezek 17:21 and those who r shall be
Ezek 21:26 nothing shall r the same
Ezek 22:14 or can your hands r strong
Ezek 31:13 On its ruin will r all the
Ezek 48:15 cubits in width that r, along
Amos 6: 9 if ten men r in one house
Obad 18 no survivor shall r of the
Zech 5: 4 It shall r in the midst of
Zech 12:14 all the families that r,
Luke 10: 7 r in the same house, eating
John 6:12 up the fragments that r, so
John 15:11 you, that My joy may r in you
John 15:16 and that your fruit should r
John 19:31 that the bodies should not r
John 21:22 I will that he r till I come
John 21:23 I will that he r till I come
Acts 15:34 good to Silas to r there
1Co 7: 8 them if they r even as I am
1Co 7:11 let her r unmarried or be
1Co 7:20 Let each one r in the same
1Co 7:24 let each one r with God in
1Co 7:26 good for a man to r as he is
1Co 15: 6 greater part r to the present
1Co 16: 6 But it may be that I will r
Phil 1:24 Nevertheless to r in the
Phil 1:25 this, I know that I shall r
1Th 4:15 r until the coming of the
1Th 4:17 r shall be caught up together
1Ti 1: 3 r in Ephesus that you may
Heb 1:11 They will perish, but You r
Heb 12:27 which cannot be shaken may r
Rev 3: 2 strengthen the things which r

REMAINDER (*see* REMAIN)
Gen 14:10 the r fled to the mountains
Ex 29:34 shall burn the r with fire
Lev 6:16 the r of it Aaron and his sons
Lev 7:16 the r of it also may be eaten
Lev 7:17 the r of the flesh of the
Esth 9:16 The r of the Jews in the
Ps 76:10 With the r of wrath You shall
Is 21:17 and the r of the number of
Is 38:10 deprived of the r of my years
Jer 27:19 and concerning the r of the
Jer 29: 1 the r of the elders who were

REMAINED (*see* REMAIN)
Gen 7:23 with him in the ark r alive
Gen 24:21 her, r silent so as to know
Gen 49:24 But his bow r in strength
Ex 8:31 Not one r
Ex 10:15 So there r nothing green on
Ex 10:19 There r not one locust in all
Ex 14:28 Not so much as one of them r
Num 9:18 tabernacle they r encamped
Num 9:21 when the cloud r only from
Num 9:22 cloud r above the tabernacle
Num 9:23 of the LORD they r encamped
Num 11:26 But two men had r in the camp
Num 14:38 the son of Jephunneh r alive
Num 25: 1 Then Israel r in Acacia Grove
Num 35:28 because he should have r in
Num 36:12 their inheritance r in the
Deut 1:46 So you r in Kadesh many days,
Deut 3:11 r of the remnant of the
Josh 11:22 they r only in Gaza, in Gath,
Josh 13:12 who r of the remnant of the
Josh 18: 2 But there r among the
Judg 7: 3 returned, and ten thousand r
Judg 11:17 So Israel r in Kadesh
Judg 21: 2 and r there before God till
Ruth 1: 2 country of Moab and r there
1Sa 7: 2 So it was that the ark r in
1Sa 13:16 them r in Gibeah of Benjamin
1Sa 23:14 r in the mountains in the
2Sa 6:11 The ark of the LORD r in the
2Sa 11: 1 But David r at Jerusalem
2Sa 11:12 So Uriah r in Jerusalem
2Sa 13:20 So Tamar r desolate in her
2Sa 15:29 And they r there
2Sa 20: 2 r loyal to their king
1Ki 11:16 Joab r there with all Israel
1Ki 15:21 Ramah, and r in Tirzah
1Ki 22:46 who r in the days of his
2Ki 10:11 So Jehu killed all who r of
2Ki 10:17 he killed all who r to Ahab
2Ki 13: 6 images also r in Samaria
2Ki 19:36 home, and r at Nineveh
2Ki 24:14 None r except the poorest
2Ki 25:11 the people who r in the city
2Ki 25:22 over the people who r in the
1Ch 12:29 greatest part of them had r
1Ch 13:14 The ark of God r with the
Eccl 2: 9 Also my wisdom r with me
Is 37:37 home, and r at Nineveh
Jer 34: 7 r of the cities of Judah
Jer 37:10 and there r only wounded men
Jer 37:16 Jeremiah had r there many
Jer 37:21 Thus Jeremiah r in the court
Jer 38:13 Jeremiah r in the court of
Jer 38:28 Now Jeremiah r in the court
Jer 39: 9 the people who r in the city
Jer 39: 9 the rest of the people who r
Jer 41:10 the people who r in Mizpah
Jer 48:11 Therefore his taste r in him
Jer 51:30 they have r in their
Jer 52:15 the people who r in the city
Ezek 3:15 r there astonished among them
Dan 10: 8 and no strength r in me
Obad 14 who r in the day of distress
Matt 11:23 it would have r until this
Matt 14:20 full of the fragments that r
Luke 1:22 to them and r speechless
Luke 1:56 Mary r with her about three
John 1:32 like a dove, and He r upon Him
John 1:39 r with Him that day (now it
John 3:22 and there He r with them and
John 7: 9 to them, He r in Galilee
John 11:54 there r with His disciples
Acts 5: 4 While it r, was it not your
Acts 15:35 and Barnabas also r in Antioch
Acts 17:14 both Silas and Timothy r there
Acts 18:18 So Paul still r a good while
Acts 25: 6 when he had r among them
Acts 27:41 r immovable, but the stern
Gal 1:18 and r with him fifteen days

REMAINING (*see* REMAIN)
Ex 28:10 the r six names on the other
Lev 4: 7 he shall pour the r blood of
Lev 4:18 he shall pour the r blood at
Lev 4:30 pour its r blood at the base
Lev 4:34 pour its r blood at the base
Lev 25:51 there are still many years r
Num 31:32 the booty r from the plunder,
Deut 2:34 we left none r
Deut 3: 3 until he had no survivors r
Deut 32:36 is gone, and there is no one r
Josh 10:33 until he left him none r
Josh 10:37 he left none r, according to
Josh 10:39 He left none r
Josh 10:40 he left none r, but utterly
Josh 11: 8 they left none of them r
2Sa 21: 5 r in any of the territories
2Ki 7:13 men take five of the r horses
2Ki 10:11 until he left him none r
Job 18:19 nor any r in his dwellings
Ezek 39:14 those bodies r on the ground
Ezek 41: 9 so also the r terrace by the
John 1:33 and r on Him, this is He who
Rev 8:13 because of the r blasts of

REMAINS (*see* REMAIN)
Gen 8:22 While the earth r, seedtime
Ex 10: 5 which r to you from the hail,
Ex 12:10 what r of it until morning
Ex 16:23 up for yourselves all that r
Ex 21:21 if he r alive a day or two,
Ex 26:12 The remnant that r of the
Ex 26:12 tent, the half curtain that r
Ex 26:13 of what r of the length of
Ex 29:34 r until the morning, then you
Lev 8:32 What r of the flesh and of the
Lev 10:12 the grain offering that r of
Lev 11:37 is to be sown, it r clean
Lev 16:16 r among them in the midst of
Lev 19: 6 if any r until the third day,
Num 24:19 and destroy the r of the city
Josh 8:29 of stones that r to this day
Josh 13: 1 there r very much land yet to
Josh 13: 2 This is the land that yet r
1Sa 6:18 which stone r to this day in
1Sa 16:11 There r yet the youngest, and
2Sa 1: 9 me, but my life still r in me
2Ki 2:22 So the water r healed to this
2Ki 6:31 son of Shaphat r on him today
Ezra 1: 4 whoever r in any place where
Job 19: 4 erred, my error r with me
Job 21:34 falsehood r in your answers
Ps 68:12 she who r at home divides the
Is 4: 3 he who r in Jerusalem will be
Is 6:13 whose stump r when it is cut
Jer 21: 9 He who r in this city shall
Jer 38: 2 He who r in this city shall
Jer 47: 4 and Sidon every helper who r
Ezek 6:12 by the sword, and he who r
Dan 10:17 me, no strength r in me now
Hag 2: 5 so My Spirit r among you
Zech 9: 7 But he who r, even he shall
John 9:41 Therefore your sin r
John 12:24 ground and dies, it r alone
John 12:34 law that the Christ r forever
1Co 7:40 is happier if she r as she is
2Co 3:11 what r is much more glorious
2Co 3:14 this day the same veil r
2Co 9: 9 His righteousness r forever
2Ti 2:13 are faithless, He r faithful
Heb 4: 1 since a promise r of entering
Heb 4: 6 Since therefore it r that
Heb 4: 9 There r therefore a rest for
Heb 7: 3 God, r a priest continually
Heb 10:26 there no longer r a sacrifice
1Jn 3: 9 sin, for His seed r in him

REMALIAH (*see* REMALIAH'S)
2Ki 15:25 Then Pekah the son of R, an
2Ki 15:27 Pekah the son of R became
2Ki 15:30 against Pekah the son of R
2Ki 15:32 year of Pekah the son of R
2Ki 15:37 the son of R against Judah
2Ki 16: 1 year of Pekah the son of R
2Ki 16: 5 Syria and Pekah the son of R
2Ch 28: 6 son of R killed one hundred
Is 7: 1 Syria and Pekah the son of R
Is 7: 4 and Syria, and the son of R
Is 7: 5 the son of R have taken evil

REMALIAH'S (*see* REMALIAH)
Is 7: 9 the head of Samaria is R son
Is 8: 6 rejoice in Rezin and in R son

REMEDY
2Ch 36:16 people, till there was no r
Prov 6:15 he shall be broken without r
Prov 29: 1 destroyed, and that without r

REMEMBER (*see* REMEMBERED, REMEMBERING, REMEMBERS, REMEMBRANCE)
Gen 9:15 I will r My covenant which is
Gen 9:16 I will look on it to r the
Gen 40:14 But r me when it is well with
Gen 40:23 chief butler did not r Joseph
Gen 41: 9 I r my faults this day
Ex 13: 3 R this day in which you went
Ex 20: 8 R the Sabbath day, to keep it
Ex 32:13 R Abraham, Isaac, and Israel,
Lev 26:42 then I will r My covenant
Lev 26:42 with Abraham I will r
Lev 26:42 I will r the land
Lev 26:45 will r the covenant of their
Num 11: 5 We r the fish which we ate
Num 15:39 r all the commandments of the
Num 15:40 and that you may r and do all
Deut 5:15 r that you were a slave in
Deut 7:18 but you shall r well what the
Deut 8: 2 you shall r that the LORD
Deut 8:18 you shall r the LORD your God
Deut 9: 7 R and do not forget how you
Deut 9:27 R Your servants, Abraham,
Deut 15:15 You shall r that you were a
Deut 16: 3 that you may r the day in

Deut 16:12 you shall **r** that you were a
Deut 24: 9 **R** what the LORD your God did
Deut 24:18 But you shall **r** that you were
Deut 24:22 you shall **r** that you were a
Deut 25:17 **R** what Amalek did to you on
Deut 32: 7 **R** the days of old, consider
Josh 1:13 **R** the word which Moses the
Judg 8:34 did not **r** the LORD their God
Judg 9: 2 **R** that I am your own flesh
Judg 16:28 O Lord GOD, **r** me, I pray
1Sa 1:11 and **r** me, and not forget your
1Sa 25:31 lord, then **r** your maidservant
2Sa 14:11 the king **r** the LORD your God
2Sa 19:19 or **r** what wrong your servant
2Ki 9:25 for **r**, when you and I were
2Ki 20: 3 **R** now, O LORD, I pray, how I
1Ch 16:12 **R** His marvelous works which
1Ch 16:15 **R** His covenant always, the
2Ch 6:42 **r** the mercies of Your servant
2Ch 24:22 **r** the kindness which Jehoiada
Neh 1: 8 **R**, I pray, the word that You
Neh 4:14 **R** the Lord, great and awesome,
Neh 5:19 **R** me, my God, for good,
Neh 6:14 God, **r** Tobiah and Sanballat,
Neh 13:14 **R** me, O my God, concerning
Neh 13:22 **R** me, O my God, concerning
Neh 13:29 **R** them, O my God, because
Neh 13:31 **R** me, O my God, for good
Job 4: 7 **R** now, who ever perished
Job 7: 7 **r** that my life is a breath
Job 10: 9 **R**, I pray, that You have made
Job 11:16 and **r** it as waters that have
Job 14:13 me a set time, and **r** me
Job 21: 6 Even when I **r** I am terrified,
Job 36:24 **R** to magnify His work, of
Job 41: 8 **r** the battle
Ps 20: 3 May He **r** all your offerings,
Ps 20: 7 But we will **r** the name of the
Ps 22:27 the ends of the world Shall **r**
Ps 25: 6 **R**, O LORD, Your tender
Ps 25: 7 Do not **r** the sins of my youth
Ps 25: 7 According to Your mercy **r** me
Ps 42: 4 When I **r** these things, I pour
Ps 42: 6 Therefore I will **r** You from
Ps 63: 6 When I **r** You on my bed, I
Ps 74: 2 **R** Your congregation, which
Ps 74:18 **R** this, that the enemy has
Ps 74:22 **R** how the foolish man
Ps 77:10 But I will **r** the years of the
Ps 77:11 I will **r** the works of the
Ps 77:11 Surely I will **r** Your wonders
Ps 78:42 They did not **r** His power
Ps 79: 8 do not **r** former iniquities
Ps 88: 5 the grave, Whom You **r** no more
Ps 89:47 **R** how short my time is
Ps 89:50 **R**, Lord, the reproach of Your
Ps 103:18 And to those who **r** His
Ps 105: 5 **R** His marvelous works which
Ps 106: 4 **R** me, O LORD, with the favor
Ps 106: 7 They did not **r** the multitude
Ps 109:16 he did not **r** to show mercy
Ps 119:49 **R** the word to Your servant,
Ps 119:55 I **r** Your name in the night, O
Ps 132: 1 Lord, **r** David And all his
Ps 137: 6 If I do not **r** you, Let my
Ps 137: 7 **R**, O LORD, against the sons
Ps 143: 5 I **r** the days of old
Prov 31: 7 and **r** his misery no more
Eccl 11: 8 yet let him **r** the days of
Eccl 12: 1 **R** now your Creator in the
Eccl 12: 6 **R** your Creator before the
Song 1: 4 We will **r** your love more than
Is 38: 3 **R** now, O LORD, I pray, how I
Is 43:18 Do not **r** the former things,
Is 43:25 and I will not **r** your sins
Is 44:21 **R** these, O Jacob, And Israel,
Is 46: 8 **R** this, and show yourselves
Is 46: 9 **R** the former things of old,
Is 47: 7 nor **r** the latter end of them
Is 54: 4 will not **r** the reproach of
Is 64: 9 LORD, nor **r** iniquity forever
Jer 2: 2 I **r** you, the kindness of your
Jer 3:16 to mind, nor shall they **r** it
Jer 14:10 He will **r** their iniquity now,
Jer 14:21 **R**, do not break Your covenant
Jer 15:15 **r** me and visit me, and take
Jer 17: 2 their children **r** their altars
Jer 18:20 **R** that I stood before You to
Jer 31:20 him, I earnestly **r** him still
Jer 31:34 and their sin I will **r** no more
Jer 44:21 land, did not the LORD **r** them
Jer 51:50 **R** the LORD afar off, and let
Lam 2: 1 did not **r** His footstool in
Lam 3:19 **R** my affliction and roaming,
Lam 5: 1 **R**, O LORD, what has come upon
Ezek 6: 9 of you who escape will **r** Me
Ezek 16:22 not **r** the days of your youth
Ezek 16:43 Because you did not **r** the
Ezek 16:60 Nevertheless I will **r** My
Ezek 16:61 Then you will **r** your ways
Ezek 16:63 that you may **r** and be ashamed,
Ezek 20:43 there you shall **r** your ways
Ezek 23:27 to them, nor **r** Egypt anymore
Ezek 36:31 Then you will **r** your evil
Hos 7: 2 that I **r** all their wickedness
Hos 8:13 Now He will **r** their iniquity
Hos 9: 9 He will **r** their iniquity
Amos 1: 9 did not **r** the covenant of
Mic 6: 5 **r** now what Balak king of Moab
Hab 3: 2 in wrath **r** mercy
Zech 10: 9 and they shall **r** Me in far
Mal 4: 4 **R** the Law of Moses, My
Matt 5:23 there **r** that your brother has
Matt 16: 9 or **r** the five loaves of the
Matt 27:63 Sir, we **r**, while He was still
Mark 8:18 And do you not **r**
Luke 1:72 and to **r** His holy covenant,
Luke 16:25 **r** that in your lifetime you
Luke 17:32 **R** Lot's wife
Luke 23:42 **r** me when You come into Your
Luke 24: 6 **R** how He spoke to you when He
John 15:20 **R** the word that I said to you
John 16: 4 you may **r** that I told you of
Acts 20:31 **r** that for three years I did
Acts 20:35 **r** the words of the Lord Jesus
Rom 11:18 **r** that you do not support the
1Co 11: 2 that you **r** me in all things
Gal 2:10 that we should **r** the poor
Eph 2:11 Therefore **r** that you, once
Col 4:18 **R** my chains
1Th 2: 9 For you **r**, brethren, our
2Th 2: 5 Do you not **r** that when I was
2Ti 1: 3 as without ceasing I **r** you in
2Ti 2: 8 **R** that Jesus Christ, of the
Heb 8:12 deeds I will **r** no more
Heb 10:17 deeds I will **r** no more
Heb 13: 3 **R** the prisoners as if chained
Heb 13: 7 **R** those who rule over you,
Jude 17 **r** the words which were spoken
Rev 2: 5 **R** therefore from where you
Rev 3: 3 **R** therefore how you have

REMEMBERED (*see* REMEMBER)
Gen 8: 1 Then God **r** Noah, and every
Gen 19:29 the plain, that God **r** Abraham
Gen 30:22 Then God **r** Rachel, and God
Gen 42: 9 Then Joseph **r** the dreams
Ex 2:24 and God **r** His covenant with
Ex 6: 5 and I have **r** My covenant
Num 10: 9 you will be **r** before the LORD
1Sa 1:19 his wife, and the LORD **r** her
Esth 2: 1 he **r** Vashti, what she had
Esth 9:28 that these days should be **r**
Job 24:20 he should be **r** no more, and
Ps 45:17 to be **r** in all generations
Ps 77: 3 I **r** God, and was troubled
Ps 78:35 Then they **r** that God was
Ps 78:39 For He **r** that they were but
Ps 83: 4 of Israel may be **r** no more
Ps 98: 3 He has **r** His mercy and His
Ps 105: 8 He has **r** His covenant forever
Ps 105:42 For He **r** His holy promise, And
Ps 106:45 their sake He **r** His covenant
Ps 109:14 fathers be **r** before the LORD
Ps 111: 4 His wonderful works to be **r**
Ps 119:52 I **r** Your judgments of old, O
Ps 136:23 Who **r** us in our lowly state,
Ps 137: 1 yea, we wept When we **r** Zion
Eccl 9:15 Yet no one **r** that same poor
Is 23:16 many songs, that you may be **r**
Is 57:11 you have lied and not **r** Me
Is 63:11 Then he **r** the days of old,
Is 65:17 not be **r** or come to mind
Jer 11:19 his name may be **r** no more
Ezek 3:20 he has done shall not be **r**
Ezek 18:22 shall be **r** against him
Ezek 18:24 he has done shall not be **r**
Ezek 21:24 made your iniquity to be **r**
Ezek 21:32 You shall not be **r**, for I the
Ezek 25:10 not be **r** among the nations
Ezek 33:13 righteous works shall be **r**
Ezek 33:16 shall be **r** against him
Hos 2:17 they shall be **r** by their name
Jon 2: 7 within me, I **r** the LORD
Zech 13: 2 and they shall no longer be **r**
Matt 26:75 Peter **r** the word of Jesus who
Luke 22:61 Peter **r** the word of the Lord,
Luke 24: 8 And they **r** His words
John 2:17 Then His disciples **r** that it
John 2:22 His disciples **r** that He had
John 12:16 then they **r** that these things
Acts 10:31 your alms are **r** in the sight
Acts 11:16 Then I **r** the word of the Lord
Rev 16:19 Babylon was **r** before God, to
Rev 18: 5 and God has **r** her iniquities

REMEMBERING (*see* REMEMBER)
Num 5:15 jealousy, an offering for **r**
Num 5:18 offering for **r** in her hands
Mark 11:21 And Peter, **r**, said to Him
1Th 1: 3 **r** without ceasing your work

REMEMBERS (*see* REMEMBER)
Ps 9:12 He avenges blood, He **r** them
Ps 103:14 He **r** that we are dust
Ps 103:16 And its place **r** it no more
Is 64: 5 who **r** You in Your ways
Lam 1: 7 Jerusalem **r** all her pleasant
Lam 3:20 My soul still **r** and sinks
Nah 2: 5 He **r** his worthies
John 16:21 she no longer **r** the anguish
2Co 7:15 he **r** the obedience of you all

REMEMBRANCE (*see* REMEMBER)
Ex 17:14 **r** of Amalek from under heaven
Num 5:15 for bringing iniquity to **r**
Deut 25:19 that you will blot out the **r**
2Sa 18:18 no son to keep my name in **r**
1Ki 17:18 to me to bring my sin to **r**
Ps 6: 5 in death there is no **r** of You
Ps 30: 4 at the **r** of His holy name
Ps 34:16 To cut off the **r** of them from
Ps 77: 6 I call to **r** my song in the
Ps 97:12 at the **r** of His holy name
Ps 102:12 the **r** of Your name to all
Ps 112: 6 will be in everlasting **r**
Eccl 1:11 There is no **r** of former
Eccl 1:11 nor will there be any **r** of
Eccl 2:16 For there is no more **r** of the
Is 26: 8 Your name and for the **r** of You
Is 43:26 Put Me in **r**
Is 57: 8 posts you have set up your **r**
Ezek 21:23 bring their iniquity to **r**
Ezek 21:24 because you have come to **r**
Ezek 23:19 to **r** the days of her youth
Ezek 23:21 Thus you called to **r** the
Mal 3:16 so a book of **r** was written
Luke 1:54 Israel, in **r** of His mercy,
Luke 22:19 do this in **r** of Me
John 14:26 bring to your **r** all things
1Co 11:24 do this in **r** of Me
1Co 11:25 as you drink it, in **r** of Me
Phil 1: 3 my God upon every **r** of you
1Th 3: 6 you always have good **r** of us
2Ti 1: 5 when I call to **r** the genuine

REMETH (*see* JARMUTH, RAMOTH)
Josh 19:21 **R**, En Gannim, En Haddah, and

REMIND (*see* REMINDER, REMINDING)
Ezek 29:16 but will **r** them of their
1Co 4:17 who will **r** you of my ways in
2Ti 1: 6 Therefore I **r** you to stir up
2Ti 2:14 **R** them of these things,
Tit 3: 1 **R** them to be subject to
2Pe 1:12 **r** you always of these things
Jude 5 But I want to **r** you, though

REMINDER (*see* REMIND)
Heb 10: 3 is a **r** of sins every year
2Pe 1:15 that you always have a **r** of
2Pe 3: 1 your pure minds by way of **r**)

REMINDING (*see* REMIND)
Rom 15:15 as **r** you, because of the
2Pe 1:13 tent, to stir you up by **r** you

REMISSION
Matt 26:28 for many for the **r** of sins
Mark 1: 4 repentance for the **r** of sins
Luke 1:77 people by the **r** of their sins
Luke 3: 3 repentance for the **r** of sins
Luke 24:47 **r** of sins should be preached
Acts 2:38 Christ for the **r** of sins
Acts 10:43 in Him will receive **r** of sins

Heb 9:22 of blood there is no **r**
Heb 10:18 Now where there is **r** of these

REMNANT (*see* REMAIN)
Ex 26:12 The **r** that remains of the
Deut 3:11 of the **r** of the giants
Josh 12: 4 was of the **r** of the giants
Josh 13:12 of the **r** of the giants
Josh 23:12 and cling to the **r** of these
2Sa 14: 7 name nor **r** on the earth
2Sa 21: 2 but of the **r** of the Amorites
1Ki 14:10 I will take away the **r** of the
2Ki 19: 4 prayer for the **r** that is left
2Ki 19:30 the **r** who have escaped of the
2Ki 19:31 out of Jerusalem shall go a **r**
2Ki 21:14 the **r** of My inheritance and
2Ch 30: 6 the **r** of you who have escaped
2Ch 34: 9 from all the **r** of Israel
Ezra 9: 8 to leave us a **r** to escape
Ezra 9:14 would be no **r** or survivor
Ezra 9:15 for we are left as a **r**, as
Job 22:20 and the fire consumes their **r**
Is 1: 9 had left to us a very small **r**
Is 10:20 that day that the **r** of Israel
Is 10:21 The **r** will return, the
Is 10:21 the **r** of Jacob, to the Mighty
Is 10:22 yet a **r** of them will return
Is 11:11 **r** of His people who are left
Is 11:16 **r** of His people who will be
Is 14:22 from Babylon the name and **r**
Is 14:30 and it will slay your **r**
Is 15: 9 Moab, and on the **r** of the land
Is 16:14 the **r** will be very small and
Is 17: 3 Damascus, and the **r** of Syria
Is 28: 5 beauty to the **r** of His people
Is 37: 4 prayer for the **r** that is left
Is 37:31 the **r** who have escaped of the
Is 37:32 out of Jerusalem shall go a **r**
Is 46: 3 all the **r** of the house of
Jer 6: 9 as a vine the **r** of Israel
Jer 11:23 there shall be no **r** of them
Jer 15: 9 the **r** of them I will deliver
Jer 15:11 it will be well with your **r**
Jer 23: 3 But I will gather the **r** of My
Jer 25:20 Ekron, and the **r** of Ashdod)
Jer 31: 7 Your people, the **r** of Israel
Jer 39: 9 **r** of the people who remained
Jer 40:11 Babylon had left a **r** of Judah
Jer 40:15 and the **r** in Judah perish
Jer 42: 2 for all this **r** (since we are
Jer 42:15 of the LORD, O **r** of Judah
Jer 42:19 O **r** of Judah, 'Do not go to
Jer 43: 5 **r** of Judah who had returned
Jer 44:12 I will take the **r** of Judah
Jer 44:14 so that none of the **r** of
Jer 44:28 all the **r** of Judah, who have
Jer 47: 4 the **r** of the country of
Jer 47: 5 with the **r** of their valley
Ezek 6: 8 Yet I will leave a **r**, so that
Ezek 9: 8 **r** of Israel in pouring out
Ezek 11:13 end of the **r** of Israel
Ezek 14:22 a **r** who will be brought out
Ezek 23:25 and your **r** shall fall by the
Ezek 23:25 your **r** shall be devoured by
Ezek 25:16 destroy the **r** of the seacoast
Joel 2:32 among the **r** whom the LORD
Amos 1: 8 and the **r** of the Philistines
Amos 5:15 gracious to the **r** of Joseph
Amos 9:12 may possess the **r** of Edom
Mic 2:12 surely gather the **r** of Israel
Mic 4: 7 I will make the lame a **r**, and
Mic 5: 3 then the **r** of His brethren
Mic 5: 7 Then the **r** of Jacob shall be
Mic 5: 8 the **r** of Jacob shall be among
Mic 7:18 of the **r** of His heritage
Hab 2: 8 all the **r** of the people shall
Zeph 2: 7 the **r** of the house of Judah
Zeph 2: 9 and the **r** of My people shall
Zeph 3:13 The **r** of Israel shall do no
Hag 1:12 with all the **r** of the people,
Hag 1:14 of all the **r** of the people
Hag 2: 2 and to the **r** of the people,
Zech 8: 6 in the eyes of the **r** of this
Zech 8:11 **r** of this people as in the
Zech 8:12 I will cause the **r** of this
Zech 14: 2 but the **r** of the people shall
Mal 2:15 one, having a **r** of the Spirit
Rom 9:27 the sea, the **r** will be saved
Rom 11: 5 present time there is a **r**

REMORSEFUL
Matt 27: 3 He had been condemned, was **r**

REMOTE
Judg 19: 1 in the **r** mountains of Ephraim
Judg 19:18 in Judah toward the **r**

REMOVAL (*see* REMOVE)
Heb 12:27 indicates the **r** of those
1Pe 3:21 namely baptism (not the **r** of

REMOVE (*see* REMOVAL, REMOVED, REMOVES)
Gen 48:17 of his father's hand to **r** it
Ex 12:15 **r** leaven from your houses
Lev 1:16 he shall **r** its crop with its
Lev 3: 4 above the kidneys, he shall **r**
Lev 3: 9 shall **r** close to the backbone
Lev 3:10 above the kidneys, he shall **r**
Lev 3:15 above the kidneys, he shall **r**
Lev 4: 9 above the kidneys, he shall **r**
Lev 4:31 He shall **r** all its fat, as
Lev 4:35 He shall **r** all its fat, as
Lev 7: 4 above the kidneys, he shall **r**
Deut 19:14 You shall not **r** your
Deut 25: 9 **r** his sandal from his foot,
Judg 9:29 Then I would **r** Abimelech
Judg 20:13 and **r** the evil from Israel
2Sa 4:11 hand and **r** you from the earth
2Ki 23:27 I will also **r** Judah from My
2Ki 24: 3 to **r** them from His sight
2Ch 33: 8 I will not again **r** the foot
Job 22:23 you will **r** iniquity far from
Job 24: 2 Some **r** landmarks
Job 41:13 Who can **r** his outer coat
Ps 39:10 **R** Your plague from me
Ps 39:13 **R** Your gaze from me, that I
Ps 119:22 **R** from me reproach and
Ps 119:29 **R** from me the way of lying,
Prov 4:27 **r** your foot from evil
Prov 5: 8 **R** your way far from her, and
Prov 22:28 Do not **r** the ancient landmark
Prov 23:10 Do not **r** the ancient landmark
Prov 30: 8 **r** falsehood and lies far from
Eccl 7:18 also not **r** your hand from the
Eccl 11:10 Therefore **r** sorrow from your
Is 7:20 and will also **r** the beard
Is 20: 2 **r** the sackcloth from your
Is 47: 2 **R** your veil, take off the
Jer 27:10 to **r** you far from your land
Jer 32:31 so I will **r** it from before My
Ezek 21:26 **R** the turban, and take off
Ezek 22:15 **r** your filthiness completely
Ezek 23:25 they shall **r** your nose and
Ezek 29:19 her spoil, and **r** her pillage
Ezek 45: 9 **R** violence and plundering,
Hos 5:10 like those who **r** a landmark
Joel 2:20 But I will **r** far from you the
Joel 3: 6 that you may **r** them far from
Mic 2: 3 which you cannot **r** your necks
Zech 3: 9 I will **r** the iniquity of that
Matt 7: 4 Let me **r** the speck out of
Matt 7: 5 First **r** the plank from your
Matt 7: 5 to **r** the speck out of your
Luke 6:42 let me **r** the speck that is in
Luke 6:42 First **r** the plank from your
Luke 6:42 you will see clearly to **r** the
Luke 22:42 Your will, **r** this cup from Me
1Co 13: 2 so that I could **r** mountains
Rev 2: 5 **r** your lampstand from its

REMOVED (*see* REMOVE)
Gen 8:13 Noah **r** the covering of the
Gen 30:35 So he **r** that day the male
Ex 8:31 He **r** the swarms of flies from
Lev 4:31 its fat, as fat is **r** from the
Lev 4:35 **r** from the sacrifice of the
Num 27: 4 be **r** from among his family
Deut 25:10 of him who had his sandal **r**
Deut 26:13 I have **r** the holy tithe from
Deut 26:14 nor have I **r** any of it for
1Sa 6: 3 His hand is not **r** from you
1Sa 18:13 Therefore Saul **r** him from his
2Sa 7:15 whom I **r** from before you
2Sa 20:13 When he was **r** from the
1Ki 2:27 So Solomon **r** Abiathar from
1Ki 15:12 and **r** all the idols that his
1Ki 15:13 Also he **r** Maachah his
1Ki 15:14 the high places were not **r**
2Ki 15: 4 the high places were not **r**
2Ki 15:35 the high places were not **r**
2Ki 16:17 and **r** the lavers from them
2Ki 16:18 Also he **r** the Sabbath
2Ki 16:18 and he **r** the king's outer
2Ki 17:18 and **r** them from His sight
2Ki 17:23 until the LORD **r** Israel out
2Ki 17:26 The nations whom you have **r**
2Ki 18: 4 He **r** the high places and broke
2Ki 23: 5 Then he **r** the idolatrous
2Ki 23:11 Then he **r** the horses that the
2Ki 23:27 My sight, as I have **r** Israel
2Ch 14: 3 for he **r** the altars of the
2Ch 14: 5 He also **r** the high places and
2Ch 15: 8 **r** the abominable idols from
2Ch 15:16 Also he **r** Maacah, the mother
2Ch 15:17 places were not **r** from Israel
2Ch 17: 6 moreover he **r** the high places
2Ch 19: 3 in that you have **r** the wooden
2Ch 34:33 Thus Josiah **r** all the
2Ch 35:12 Then they **r** the burnt
Job 18: 4 the rock be **r** from its place
Job 19:13 He has **r** my brothers far from
Ps 46: 2 fear, Though the earth be **r**
Ps 81: 6 I **r** his shoulder from the
Ps 103:12 the west, So far has He **r** our
Prov 10:30 The righteous will never be **r**
Prov 27:25 When the hay is **r**, and the
Is 6:12 The LORD has **r** men far away
Is 10:13 also I have **r** the boundaries
Is 14:25 his yoke shall be **r** from them
Is 14:25 and his burden **r** from their
Is 22: 8 He **r** the protection of Judah
Is 22:25 in the secure place will be **r**
Is 29:13 but have **r** their hearts far
Is 33:20 of its stakes will ever be **r**
Is 54:10 depart and the hills be **r**, but
Is 54:10 My covenant of peace be **r**
Dan 11:18 and with the reproach **r**, he
Amos 6: 7 at banquets shall be **r**
Mic 2: 4 how He has **r** it from me
Zech 3: 4 I have **r** your iniquity from
Matt 21:21 say to this mountain, 'Be **r**
Mark 11:23 says to this mountain, 'Be **r**
John 21: 7 garment (for he had **r** it)
Acts 13:22 And when He had **r** him, He

REMOVES (*see* REMOVE)
Job 9: 5 He **r** the mountains, and they
Is 27: 8 He **r** it by His rough wind in
Dan 2:21 He **r** kings and raises up kings

REMOVING
Gen 30:32 **r** from there all the speckled

REMPHAN (*see* CHIUN)
Acts 7:43 and the star of your god **R**

REND (*see* RENDING)
Is 64: 1 that You would **r** the heavens
Joel 2:13 So **r** your heart, and not your

RENDER (*see* RENDERED, RENDERS)
Num 18: 9 offering which they **r** to Me
Deut 32:41 I will **r** vengeance to My
Deut 32:43 and **r** vengeance to His
Judg 11:27 **r** judgment this day between
Ps 28: 4 **R** to them what they deserve
Ps 38:20 also who **r** evil for good,
Ps 56:12 I will **r** praises to You,
Ps 62:12 For You **r** to each one
Ps 94: 2 **R** punishment to the proud
Ps 116:12 What shall I **r** to the LORD
Prov 24:12 will He not **r** to each man
Prov 24:29 I will **r** to the man according
Is 66:15 to **r** His anger with fury, and
Matt 21:41 **r** to him the fruits in their
Matt 22:21 **R** therefore to Caesar the
Mark 12:17 **R** to Caesar the things that
Luke 20:25 **R** therefore to Caesar the
Rom 2: 6 will **r** to each one according
Rom 13: 7 **R** therefore to all their due
1Co 7: 3 Let the husband **r** to his wife
1Th 3: 9 can we **r** to God for you, for
Rev 18: 6 **R** to her just as she rendered

RENDERED (*see* RENDER)
1Ki 3:28 judgment which the king had **r**
Prov 12:14 man's hands will be **r** to him
Rev 18: 6 to her just as she **r** to you

RENDERS (*see* RENDER)
1Th 5:15 See that no one **r** evil for

RENDING (*see* REND)
Ps 7: 2 **R** me in pieces, while there

RENEW (*see* RENEWED, RENEWING)
1Sa 11:14 Gilgal and **r** the kingdom there
Job 10:17 You **r** Your witnesses against
Ps 51:10 **r** a steadfast spirit within
Ps 104:30 You **r** the face of the earth
Is 40:31 LORD shall **r** their strength
Is 41: 1 the people **r** their strength
Lam 5:21 **r** our days as of old,
Heb 6: 6 to **r** them again to repentance

RENEWED (*see* RENEW)
Job 29:20 me, and my bow is **r** in my hand
Ps 103: 5 youth is **r** like the eagle's
2Co 4:16 man is being **r** day by day
Eph 4:23 be **r** in the spirit of your
Col 3:10 **r** in knowledge according to

RENEWING (*see* RENEW)
Rom 12: 2 by the **r** of your mind, that
Tit 3: 5 and **r** of the Holy Spirit,

RENOUNCE (*see* RENOUNCED, RENOUNCES)
Ps 10:13 Why do the wicked **r** God

RENOUNCED (*see* RENOUNCE)
Ps 89:39 You have **r** the covenant of
2Co 4: 2 But we have **r** the hidden

RENOUNCES (*see* RENOUNCE)
Ps 10: 3 the greedy and **r** the LORD

RENOWN (*see* RENOWNED)
Gen 6: 4 men who were of old, men of **r**
Num 16: 2 of the congregation, men of **r**
Jer 13:11 may become My people, for **r**
Ezek 23:23 rulers, captains and men of **r**
Ezek 34:29 up for them a garden of **r**
Ezek 39:13 they will gain **r** for it on

RENOWNED (*see* RENOWN)
Job 18:17 and he has no name among the **r**
Ezek 26:17 O **r** city, who was strong at

RENTED
Acts 28:30 years in his own **r** house, and

REPAID (*see* REPAY)
Gen 44: 4 Why have you **r** evil for good
Judg 1: 7 I have done, so God has **r** me
Judg 9:56 Thus God **r** the wickedness of
1Sa 25:21 he has **r** me evil for good
Ps 7: 4 If I have **r** evil to him who
Prov 13:21 righteous, good shall be **r**
Jer 18:20 Shall evil be **r** for good
Luke 14:12 invite you back, and you be **r**
Luke 14:14 for you shall be **r** at the
Rom 11:35 Him and it shall be **r** to him
Col 3:25 he who does wrong will be **r**

REPAIR (*see* REPAIRED, REPAIRER, REPAIRING, REPAIRS)
2Ki 12: 5 let them **r** the damages of the
2Ki 12: 8 nor **r** the damages of the
2Ki 12:12 to **r** the damage of the house
2Ki 12:12 was paid out to **r** the temple
2Ki 22: 5 to **r** the damages of the house
2Ki 22: 6 and hewn stone to **r** the house
2Ch 24: 5 from all Israel money to **r**
2Ch 24:12 carpenters to **r** the house of
2Ch 34: 8 to **r** the house of the LORD
2Ch 34:10 the house of the LORD, to **r**
Ezra 9: 9 to **r** the house of our God, to
Is 61: 4 and they shall **r** the ruined
Amos 9:11 fallen down, and **r** its damages

REPAIRED (*see* REPAIR)
Num 21:27 let the city of Sihon be **r**
1Ki 11:27 **r** the damages to the City of
1Ki 18:30 he **r** the altar of the LORD
2Ki 12: 6 that the priests had not **r**
2Ki 12: 7 Why have you not **r** the
2Ki 12:14 they **r** the house of the LORD
1Ch 11: 8 Joab **r** the rest of the city
2Ch 29: 3 house of the LORD and **r** them
2Ch 32: 5 also he **r** the Millo in the
2Ch 33:16 He also **r** the altar of the
Neh 3: 6 of Besodeiah **r** the Old Gate
Neh 3: 7 **r** the residence of the
Neh 3:11 Pahath-Moab **r** another section
Neh 3:13 of Zanoah **r** the Valley Gate
Neh 3:13 **r** a thousand cubits of the
Neh 3:14 Haccerem, **r** the Refuse Gate
Neh 3:15 Mizpah, **r** the Fountain Gate
Neh 3:15 **r** the wall of the Pool of
Neh 3:19 **r** another section in front of
Neh 3:20 **r** the other section, from the
Neh 3:21 **r** another section, from the
Neh 3:24 of Henadad **r** another section
Neh 3:27 Tekoites **r** another section
Neh 3:30 of Zalaph, **r** another section

REPAIRER (*see* REPAIR)
Is 58:12 be called the **R** of the Breach

REPAIRING (*see* REPAIR)
2Ki 12: 7 but deliver it for **r** the
2Ch 24: 4 on **r** the house of the LORD
2Ch 24:27 the **r** of the house of God,
Ezra 4:12 walls and **r** the foundations

REPAIRS (*see* REPAIR)
Neh 3: 4 the son of Koz, made **r**
Neh 3: 4 son of Meshezabeel, made **r**
Neh 3: 4 Zadok the son of Baana made **r**
Neh 3: 5 to them the Tekoites made **r**
Neh 3: 8 one of the goldsmiths, made **r**
Neh 3: 8 one of the perfumers, made **r**
Neh 3: 9 district of Jerusalem, made **r**
Neh 3:10 made **r** in front of his house
Neh 3:10 the son of Hashabniah made **r**
Neh 3:12 he and his daughters made **r**
Neh 3:16 made **r** as far as the place in
Neh 3:17 Rehum the son of Bani, made **r**
Neh 3:17 made **r** for his district
Neh 3:18 district of Keilah, made **r**
Neh 3:22 the men of the plain, made **r**
Neh 3:23 Hasshub made **r** opposite their
Neh 3:23 Ananiah, made **r** by his house
Neh 3:25 made **r** opposite the buttress
Neh 3:25 the son of Parosh made **r**
Neh 3:26 made **r** as far as the place in
Neh 3:28 Horse Gate the priests made **r**
Neh 3:29 **r** in front of his own house
Neh 3:29 of the East Gate, made **r**
Neh 3:30 **r** in front of his dwelling
Neh 3:31 made **r** as far as the house of
Neh 3:32 and the merchants made **r**

REPAY (*see* REPAID, REPAYS)
Gen 50:15 may actually **r** us for all the
Lev 25:51 according to them he shall **r**
Lev 25:52 shall **r** him the price of his
Deut 7:10 He will **r** him to his face
Deut 32:41 and **r** those who hate Me
Judg 20:10 they may **r** all the vileness
Ruth 2:12 The LORD **r** your work, and a
1Sa 26:23 May the LORD **r** every man for
2Sa 2: 6 I also will **r** you this
2Sa 3:39 The LORD shall **r** the evildoer
2Sa 16:12 that the LORD will **r** me with
2Sa 19:36 why should the king **r** me with
2Ki 9:26 I will **r** you in this plot,'
2Ch 24:22 The LORD look on it, and **r**
2Ch 32:25 But Hezekiah did not **r**
Job 34:33 Should He **r** it according to
Ps 10:14 grief, To **r** it by Your hand
Ps 37:21 wicked borrows and does not **r**
Ps 41:10 me up, That I may **r** them
Ps 54: 5 He will **r** my enemies for
Is 59:18 deeds, accordingly He will **r**
Is 59:18 coastlands He will fully **r**
Is 65: 6 not keep silence, but will **r**
Is 65: 6 even **r** into their bosom
Jer 16:18 first I will **r** double for
Jer 25:14 I will **r** them according to
Jer 32:18 **r** the iniquity of the fathers
Jer 50:29 **R** her according to her work
Jer 51:24 I will **r** Babylon and all the
Jer 51:56 recompense, He will surely **r**
Lam 3:64 **R** them, O LORD, according to
Ezek 7: 3 I will **r** you for all your
Ezek 7: 4 but I will **r** your ways, and
Ezek 7: 8 I will **r** you for all your
Ezek 7: 9 I will **r** you according to
Ezek 23:49 They shall **r** you for your
Luke 7:42 had nothing with which to **r**
Luke 10:35 I come again, I will **r** you
Luke 14:14 because they cannot **r** you
Rom 12:17 **R** no one evil for evil
Rom 12:19 Vengeance is Mine, I will **r**
2Th 1: 6 **r** with tribulation those who
1Ti 5: 4 at home and to **r** their parents
2Ti 4:14 May the Lord **r** him according
Phm 19 I will **r**
Heb 10:30 I will **r**, says the Lord
Rev 18: 6 **r** her double according to her

REPAYS (*see* REPAY)
Deut 7:10 He **r** those who hate Him to
Job 21:31 who **r** him for what he has
Job 34:11 For He **r** man according to his
Ps 31:23 And fully **r** the proud person
Ps 137: 8 Happy shall he be who **r** you
Is 66: 6 LORD, Who fully **r** His enemies

REPEATED (*see* REPEATEDLY, REPEATS, REPETITIONS)
Gen 41:32 the dream was **r** to Pharaoh
1Sa 8:21 he **r** them in the hearing of

REPEATEDLY (*see* REPEATED)
Heb 10:11 daily and offering **r** the same

REPEATS (*see* REPEATED)
Prov 17: 9 love, but he who **r** a matter
Prov 26:11 vomit, so a fool **r** his folly

REPEL
2Sa 5: 6 blind and the lame will **r** you
2Ki 18:24 How then will you **r** one
Is 36: 9 How then will you **r** one

REPENT (*see* REPENTANCE, REPENTED, REPENTS)
Num 23:19 son of man, that He should **r**
1Ki 8:47 were carried captive, and **r**
2Ch 6:37 were carried captive, and **r**
Job 42: 6 myself, and **r** in dust and ashes
Jer 25: 5 **R** now everyone of his evil
Ezek 14: 6 **R**, turn away from your idols,
Ezek 18:30 **R**, and turn from all your
Hos 11: 5 because they refused to **r**
Matt 3: 2 **R**, for the kingdom of heaven
Matt 4:17 **R**, for the kingdom of heaven
Matt 11:20 done, because they did not **r**
Mark 1:15 **R**, and believe in the gospel
Mark 6:12 preached that people should **r**
Luke 13: 3 but unless you **r** you will all
Luke 13: 5 but unless you **r** you will all
Luke 16:30 from the dead, they will **r**
Luke 17: 4 returns to you, saying, 'I **r**
Acts 2:38 **R**, and let every one of you be
Acts 3:19 **R** therefore and be converted,
Acts 8:22 **R** therefore of this your
Acts 17:30 all men everywhere to **r**,
Acts 26:20 Gentiles, that they should **r**
Rev 2: 5 **r** and do the first works, or
Rev 2: 5 from its place—unless you **r**
Rev 2:16 **R**, or else I will come to
Rev 2:21 I gave her time to **r** of her
Rev 2:21 immorality, and she did not **r**
Rev 2:22 unless they **r** of their deeds
Rev 3: 3 hold fast and **r**
Rev 3:19 Therefore be zealous and **r**
Rev 9:20 did not **r** of the works of
Rev 9:21 and they did not **r** of their
Rev 16: 9 and they did not **r** and give Him
Rev 16:11 and did not **r** of their deeds

REPENTANCE (*see* REPENT)
Matt 3: 8 bear fruits worthy of **r**,
Matt 3:11 baptize you with water unto **r**
Matt 9:13 righteous, but sinners, to **r**
Mark 1: 4 preaching a baptism of **r** for
Mark 2:17 righteous, but sinners, to **r**
Luke 3: 3 preaching a baptism of **r** for
Luke 3: 8 bear fruits worthy of **r**, and
Luke 5:32 righteous, but sinners, to **r**
Luke 15: 7 just persons who need no **r**
Luke 24:47 and that **r** and remission of
Acts 5:31 to give **r** to Israel and
Acts 11:18 to the Gentiles **r** to life
Acts 13:24 the baptism of **r** to all the
Acts 19: 4 baptized with a baptism of **r**
Acts 20:21 **r** toward God and faith toward
Acts 26:20 God, and do works befitting **r**
Rom 2: 4 of God leads you to **r**
2Co 7: 9 but that your sorrow led to **r**
2Co 7:10 produces **r** to salvation, not
2Ti 2:25 God perhaps will grant them **r**
Heb 6: 1 of **r** from dead works and of
Heb 6: 6 to renew them again to **r**
Heb 12:17 for he found no place for **r**
2Pe 3: 9 but that all should come to **r**

REPENTED (*see* REPENT)
Jer 8: 6 No man **r** of his wickedness,
Jer 31:19 Surely, after my turning, I **r**
Matt 11:21 they would have **r** long ago in
Matt 12:41 it, because they **r** at the
Luke 10:13 they would have **r** a great

Luke 11:32 for they **r** at the preaching
2Co 12:21 have not **r** of the uncleanness

REPENTS (*see* REPENT)
Luke 15: 7 **r** than over ninety-nine just
Luke 15:10 of God over one sinner who **r**
Luke 17: 3 and if he **r**, forgive him

REPETITIONS (*see* REPEATED)
Matt 6: 7 do not use vain **r** as the

REPHAEL
1Ch 26: 7 of Shemaiah were Othni, **R**

REPHAH (*see* REPHAIAH)
1Ch 7:25 **R** was his son, as well as

REPHAIAH (*see* REPHAH, RHESA)
1Ch 3:21 and Jeshaiah, the sons of **R**
1Ch 4:42 captains Pelatiah, Neariah, **R**
1Ch 7: 2 The sons of Tola were Uzzi, **R**
1Ch 9:43 **R** his son, Eleasah his son,
Neh 3: 9 next to them **R** the son of Hur

REPHAIM
Gen 14: 5 attacked the **R** in Ashteroth
Gen 15:20 the Perizzites, and the **R**
Josh 15: 8 of the Valley of **R** northward
Josh 18:16 Valley of the **R** on the north
2Sa 5:18 themselves in the Valley of **R**
2Sa 5:22 themselves in the Valley of **R**
2Sa 23:13 encamped in the Valley of **R**
1Ch 11:15 encamped in the Valley of **R**
1Ch 14: 9 a raid on the Valley of **R**
Is 17: 5 of grain in the Valley of **R**

REPHIDIM
Ex 17: 1 of the LORD, and camped in **R**
Ex 17: 8 and fought with Israel in **R**
Ex 19: 2 For they had departed from **R**
Num 33:14 from Alush and camped at **R**
Num 33:15 They departed from **R** and

REPLACE
Is 9:10 down, but we will **r** them with

REPLENISHED
Jer 31:25 I have **r** every sorrowful soul

REPLICA
Josh 22:28 Here is the **r** of the altar

REPLIED (*see* PREFACE)

REPLIES (*see* PREFACE)

REPLY (*see* PREFACE)

REPORT (*see* REPORTED)
Gen 29:13 when Laban heard the **r** about
Gen 37: 2 Joseph brought a bad **r** of
Gen 45:16 Now the **r** of it was heard in
Ex 23: 1 shall not circulate a false **r**
Num 13:32 children of Israel a bad **r** of
Num 14:36 bringing a bad **r** of the land
Num 14:37 the evil **r** about the land
Deut 2:25 who shall hear the **r** of you
Judg 18: 8 What is your **r**
1Sa 2:24 is not a good **r** that I hear
1Sa 20:13 evil, then I will **r** it to you
1Ki 10: 6 It was a true **r** which I heard
2Ch 9: 5 It was a true **r** which I heard
Ezra 5: 5 till a **r** could go to Darius
Neh 6:13 have occasion for an evil **r**
Esth 1:17 in their eyes, when they **r**
Job 28:22 We have heard a **r** about it
Prov 15:30 and a good **r** makes the bones
Is 23: 5 When the **r** comes to Egypt,
Is 23: 5 be in agony at the **r** of Tyre
Is 28:19 just to understand the **r**
Is 53: 1 Who has believed our **r**
Jer 6:24 We have heard the **r** of it
Jer 10:22 the noise of the **r** has come
Jer 20:10 **R**," they say, "and we will
Jer 20:10 and we will **r** it
Jer 50:43 has heard the **r** about them
Obad 1 have heard a **r** from the LORD
Matt 9:26 the **r** of this went out into
Matt 14: 1 heard the **r** about Jesus
Luke 4:37 the **r** about Him went out into
Luke 5:15 Then the **r** went around
Luke 7:17 And this **r** about Him went
John 11:57 where He was, he should **r** it
John 12:38 Lord, who has believed our **r**
Acts 15:27 who will also **r** the same
Rom 10:16 Lord, who has believed our **r**
1Co 14:25 **r** that God is truly among you
2Co 6: 8 by evil **r** and good **r**
Phil 4: 8 whatever things are of good **r**

REPORTED (*see* REPORT)
Judg 4:12 they **r** to Sisera that Barak
Ruth 2:11 It has been fully **r** to me
1Sa 11: 9 **r** it to the men of Jabesh, and
1Sa 17:31 heard, they **r** them to Saul
1Ki 18:13 Was it not **r** to my lord what
2Ki 9:18 And the watchman **r**, saying,
2Ki 9:20 And the watchman **r**, saying
Neh 6: 6 It is **r** among the nations, and
Neh 6: 7 matters will be **r** to the king
Neh 6:19 Also they **r** his good deeds
Neh 6:19 me, and **r** my words to him
Ezek 9:11 at his side, **r** back and said,
Matt 28:11 **r** to the chief priests all
Matt 28:15 this saying is commonly **r**
Luke 7:18 Then the disciples of John **r**
Luke 14:21 **r** these things to his master
Acts 4:23 **r** all that the chief priests
Acts 5:22 prison, they returned and **r**
Acts 14:27 they **r** all that God had done
Acts 15: 4 they **r** all things that God
Acts 16:36 prison **r** these words to Paul
Acts 28:21 of the brethren who came **r** or
Rom 3: 8 as we are slanderously **r** and
1Co 5: 1 It is actually **r** that there
1Ti 5:10 well **r** for good works
1Pe 1:12 **r** to you through those who

REPRESENTATIVES (*see* REPRESENTING)
Num 16: 2 **r** of the congregation, men of
Num 26: 9 **r** of the congregation, who
Ezra 4: 9 **r** of the Dinaites, the

REPRESENTING (*see* REPRESENTATIVES)
Num 1:44 each one **r** his father's house

REPRIMANDED
Judg 8: 1 And they **r** him sharply

REPRISAL
Obad 15 your **r** shall return upon your

REPROACH (*see* REPROACHED, REPROACHES, REPROACHFULLY)
Gen 30:23 God has taken away my **r**
Gen 34:14 for that would be a **r** to us
Num 15:30 that one brings **r** on the LORD
Josh 5: 9 away the **r** of Egypt from you
Ruth 2:15 the sheaves, and do not **r** her
1Sa 11: 2 and bring **r** on all Israel
1Sa 17:26 takes away the **r** from Israel
1Sa 25:39 my **r** from the hand of Nabal
2Ki 19: 4 has sent to **r** the living God
2Ki 19:16 has sent to **r** the living God
Neh 1: 3 there in great distress and **r**
Neh 2:17 that we may no longer be a **r**
Neh 4: 4 turn their **r** on their own
Neh 5: 9 of the **r** of the nations, our
Neh 6:13 report, that they might **r** me
Job 27: 6 my heart shall not **r** me as
Ps 15: 3 up a **r** against his friend
Ps 22: 6 A **r** of men, and despised of
Ps 31:11 I am a **r** among all my enemies
Ps 39: 8 make me the **r** of the foolish
Ps 42:10 of my bones, My enemies **r** me
Ps 44:13 You make us a **r** to our
Ps 69: 7 for Your sake I have borne **r**
Ps 69: 9 who **r** You have fallen on me
Ps 69:10 fasting, That became my **r**
Ps 69:19 You know my **r**, my shame, and
Ps 69:20 **R** has broken my heart, And I
Ps 71:13 Let them be covered with **r**
Ps 74:10 how long will the adversary **r**
Ps 78:66 He put them to a perpetual **r**
Ps 79: 4 become a **r** to our neighbors
Ps 79:12 Their **r** with which they have
Ps 89:41 He is a **r** to his neighbors
Ps 89:50 Lord, the **r** of Your servants
Ps 89:50 the **r** of all the many peoples
Ps 102: 8 My enemies **r** me all day long,
Ps 109:25 also have become a **r** to them
Ps 119:22 Remove from me **r** and
Ps 119:39 Turn away my **r** which I dread,
Prov 6:33 his **r** will not be wiped away
Prov 14:34 but sin is a **r** to any people
Prov 18: 3 and with dishonor comes **r**
Prov 19:26 who causes shame and brings **r**
Prov 22:10 yes, strife and **r** will cease
Is 4: 1 your name, to take away our **r**
Is 30: 5 but a shame and also a **r**
Is 37: 4 has sent to **r** the living God
Is 37:17 has sent to **r** the living God
Is 51: 7 do not fear the **r** of men, nor
Is 54: 4 will not remember the **r** of
Jer 3:25 our shame, and our **r** covers us
Jer 6:10 of the LORD is a **r** to them
Jer 20: 8 the LORD was made to me a **r**
Jer 23:40 an everlasting **r** upon you
Jer 24: 9 for their harm, to be a **r**
Jer 29:18 a **r** among all the nations
Jer 31:19 I bore the **r** of my youth
Jer 42:18 astonishment, a curse, and a **r**
Jer 44: 8 a **r** among all the nations of
Jer 44:12 and a curse and a **r**
Jer 49:13 become a desolation, a **r**, a
Jer 51:51 because we have heard **r**
Lam 3:30 strikes him, and be full of **r**
Lam 3:61 You have heard their **r**, O
Lam 5: 1 look, and behold our **r**
Ezek 5:14 a **r** among the nations that
Ezek 5:15 So it shall be a **r**, a taunt,
Ezek 16:57 **r** of the daughters of Syria
Ezek 21:28 and concerning their **r**,' and
Ezek 22: 4 made you a **r** to the nations
Ezek 36:15 nor bear the **r** of the peoples
Ezek 36:30 need never again bear the **r**
Dan 9:16 a **r** to all who are around us
Dan 11:18 the **r** against them to an end
Dan 11:18 and with the **r** removed, he
Hos 12:14 and return his **r** upon him
Joel 2:17 not give Your heritage to **r**
Joel 2:19 you a **r** among the nations
Mic 6:16 shall bear the **r** of My people
Zeph 2: 8 I have heard the **r** of Moab
Zeph 3:18 to whom its **r** is a burden
Luke 1:25 to take away my **r** among men
Luke 11:45 these things You **r** us also
1Ti 3: 7 outside, lest he fall into **r**
1Ti 4:10 end we both labor and suffer **r**
Heb 11:26 esteeming the **r** of Christ
Heb 13:13 the camp, bearing His **r**
Jas 1: 5 to all liberally and without **r**

REPROACHED (*see* REPROACH)
2Ki 19:22 Whom have you **r** and
2Ki 19:23 you have **r** the Lord, and said
Job 19: 3 These ten times you have **r** me
Ps 74:18 this, that the enemy has **r**
Ps 79:12 with which they have **r** You
Ps 89:51 which Your enemies have **r**
Ps 89:51 With which they have **r** the
Is 37:23 Whom have you **r** and
Is 37:24 servants you have **r** the Lord
Zeph 2: 8 which they have **r** My people
Zeph 2:10 pride, because they have **r**
Rom 15: 3 of those who **r** You fell on Me
1Pe 4:14 If you are **r** for the name of

REPROACHES (*see* REPROACH)
Job 20: 3 heard the reproof that **r** me
Ps 44:16 of the voice of him who **r**
Ps 55:12 it is not an enemy who **r** me
Ps 57: 3 He **r** the one who would
Ps 69: 9 the **r** of those who reproach
Ps 74:22 the foolish man **r** You daily
Ps 119:42 an answer for him who **r** me
Prov 14:31 the poor **r** his Maker, but he
Prov 17: 5 mocks the poor **r** his Maker
Prov 27:11 I may answer him who **r** me
Is 43:28 to the curse, and Israel to **r**
Rom 15: 3 The **r** of those who reproached
2Co 12:10 pleasure in infirmities, in **r**
Heb 10:33 made a spectacle both by **r**

REPROACHFULLY (*see* REPROACH)
Job 16:10 they strike me **r** on the cheek
1Ti 5:14 to the adversary to speak **r**

REPROOF (*see* REPROOFS, REPROVE)
Job 20: 3 I have heard the **r** that
Job 26:11 and are astonished at His **r**
Prov 1:23 Turn at my **r**; Surely I will
Prov 1:25 and would have none of my **r**
Prov 1:30 counsel and despised all my **r**
Prov 5:12 And my heart despised **r**
Prov 10:17 he who refuses **r** goes astray
Prov 12: 1 but he who hates **r** is stupid
Prov 13:18 who regards **r** will be honored
Prov 15: 5 he who receives **r** is prudent
Prov 15:10 and he who hates **r** will die
Prov 15:31 The ear that hears the **r** of
Prov 15:32 soul, but he who heeds **r** gets

RESORTED (*see* RESORT)
Dan 4:36 counselors and nobles **r** to me

RESOUND (*see* RESOUNDING)
Is 16:11 shall **r** like a harp for Moab

RESOUNDING (*see* RESOUND)
1Ch 15:16 raising the voice with **r** joy

RESOURCES
John 8:44 lie, he speaks from his own **r**

RESPECT (*see* RESPECTED, RESPECTS)
Gen 4: 5 but He did not **r** Cain and his
Num 16:15 Do not **r** their offering
Deut 28:50 which does not **r** the elderly
Ezra 9: 1 with **r** to the abominations of
Ps 40: 4 does not **r** the proud, nor
Ps 74:20 Have **r** to the covenant
Is 17: 7 his eyes will have **r** for the
Is 17: 8 he will not **r** what his
Is 22:11 nor did you have **r** for Him
Lam 4:16 The people do not **r** the
Matt 21:37 saying, 'They will **r** my son
Mark 12: 6 saying, 'They will **r** my son
Luke 20:13 Probably they will **r** him when
Acts 5:34 held in **r** by all the people
2Co 3:10 had no glory in this **r**,
2Co 9: 3 should be in vain in this **r**
Heb 12: 9 us, and we paid them **r**

RESPECTED (*see* RESPECT)
Gen 4: 4 And the LORD **r** Abel and his
1Sa 25:35 your voice and **r** your person
Eccl 10: 1 folly to one **r** for wisdom
Lam 5:12 hands, and elders were not **r**

RESPECTS (*see* RESPECT)
Eph 5:33 see that she **r** her husband

RESPOND (*see* RESPONDED, RESPONSE)
Job 13:22 me speak, then You **r** to me
Prov 29:19 he understands, he will not **r**

RESPONDED (*see* RESPOND)
Acts 3:12 saw it, he **r** to the people

RESPONSE (*see* RESPOND, RESPONSIVELY)
Num 30: 7 makes no **r** to her on the day
Num 30:11 heard it, and made no **r** to her
Num 30:14 **r** whatever to her from day to
Num 30:14 because he made no **r** to her
Ps 38:14 And in whose mouth is no **r**
Mark 11:14 In **r** Jesus said to it, "Let
Rom 11: 4 does the divine **r** say to him

RESPONSIBILITY
Judg 19:20 let all your needs be my **r**
1Ch 9:27 of God because they had the **r**
Ezra 10: 4 for this matter is your **r**
Is 22:21 commit your **r** into his hand

RESPONSIVELY (*see* RESPONSE)
Ezra 3:11 And they sang **r**, praising and

REST (*see* RESTED, RESTING, RESTLESS, RESTS)
Gen 18: 4 **r** yourselves under the tree
Gen 30:36 Jacob fed the **r** of Laban's
Gen 49:15 he saw that **r** was good, and
Ex 5: 5 you make them **r** from their
Ex 16:23 Tomorrow is a Sabbath **r**, a
Ex 23:11 year you shall let it **r** and
Ex 23:12 the seventh day you shall **r**
Ex 23:12 your ox and your donkey may **r**
Ex 31:15 seventh is the Sabbath of **r**
Ex 33:14 you, and I will give you **r**
Ex 34:21 the seventh day you shall **r**
Ex 34:21 and in harvest you shall **r**
Ex 35: 2 a Sabbath of **r** to the LORD
Lev 2: 3 The **r** of the grain offering
Lev 5: 9 the **r** of the blood shall be
Lev 5:13 The **r** shall be the priest's
Lev 14:17 of the **r** of the oil in his
Lev 14:18 The **r** of the oil that is in
Lev 14:29 The **r** of the oil that is in
Lev 16:31 a sabbath of solemn **r** for you
Lev 23: 3 day is a Sabbath of solemn **r**
Lev 23:32 to you a sabbath of solemn **r**
Lev 25: 4 of solemn **r** for the land, a
Lev 25: 5 is a year of **r** for the land
Lev 26:34 then the land shall **r** and
Lev 26:35 it lies desolate it shall **r**
Lev 26:35 for the time it did not **r** on
Num 18:30 then the **r** shall be accounted
Num 31: 8 **r** of those who were killed
Deut 3:13 The **r** of Gilead, and all
Deut 3:20 until the LORD has given **r**
Deut 5:14 may **r** as well as you
Deut 12: 9 you have not come to the **r**
Deut 12:10 when He gives you **r** from all
Deut 25:19 you **r** from your enemies all
Deut 28:54 toward the **r** of his children
Deut 28:65 nations you shall find no **r**
Deut 31:16 you will **r** with your fathers
Josh 1:13 LORD your God is giving you **r**
Josh 1:15 has given your brethren **r**
Josh 3:13 shall **r** in the waters of the
Josh 13:27 the **r** of the kingdom of Sihon
Josh 14:15 Then the land had **r** from war
Josh 17: 2 there was a lot for the **r** of
Josh 17: 6 the **r** of Manasseh's sons had
Josh 21: 5 The **r** of the children of
Josh 21:20 the **r** of the children of
Josh 21:26 the **r** of the families of the
Josh 21:34 the **r** of the Levites, from
Josh 21:40 the **r** of the families of the
Josh 21:44 LORD gave them **r** all around
Josh 22: 4 has given **r** to your brethren
Josh 23: 1 **r** to Israel from all their
Judg 3:11 land had **r** for forty years
Judg 3:30 the land had **r** for eighty
Judg 5:31 land had **r** for forty years
Judg 7: 6 but all the **r** of the people
Judg 7: 8 sent away all the **r** of Israel
Ruth 1: 9 grant that you may find **r**
Ruth 3:18 for the man will not **r** until
1Sa 13: 2 The **r** of the people he sent
1Sa 15:15 and the **r** we have utterly
2Sa 3:29 Let it **r** on the head of Joab
2Sa 7: 1 the LORD had given him **r** from
2Sa 7:11 have caused you to **r** from all
2Sa 7:12 you **r** with your fathers, I
2Sa 10:10 the **r** of the people he put
2Sa 12:28 gather the **r** of the people
2Sa 21:10 to **r** on them by day nor the
1Ki 5: 4 has given me **r** on every side
1Ki 8:56 who has given **r** to His people
1Ki 11:41 Now the **r** of the acts of
1Ki 12:23 and to the **r** of the people,
1Ki 14:19 Now the **r** of the acts of
1Ki 14:29 Now the **r** of the acts of
1Ki 15: 7 Now the **r** of the acts of
1Ki 15:23 The **r** of all the acts of Asa,
1Ki 15:31 Now the **r** of the acts of
1Ki 16: 5 Now the **r** of the acts of
1Ki 16:14 Now the **r** of the acts of Elah
1Ki 16:20 Now the **r** of the acts of
1Ki 16:27 Now the **r** of the acts of Omri
1Ki 20:30 But the **r** fled to Aphek, into
1Ki 22:39 Now the **r** of the acts of Ahab
1Ki 22:45 Now the **r** of the acts of
1Ki 22:46 And the **r** of the perverted
2Ki 1:18 Now the **r** of the acts of
2Ki 4: 7 and your sons live on the **r**
2Ki 8:23 Now the **r** of the acts of
2Ki 10:34 Now the **r** of the acts of Jehu
2Ki 12:19 Now the **r** of the acts of
2Ki 13: 8 Now the **r** of the acts of
2Ki 13:12 Now the **r** of the acts of
2Ki 14:15 Now the **r** of the acts of
2Ki 14:18 Now the **r** of the acts of
2Ki 14:28 Now the **r** of the acts of
2Ki 15: 6 Now the **r** of the acts of
2Ki 15:11 Now the **r** of the acts of
2Ki 15:15 Now the **r** of the acts of
2Ki 15:21 Now the **r** of the acts of
2Ki 15:26 Now the **r** of the acts of
2Ki 15:31 Now the **r** of the acts of
2Ki 15:36 Now the **r** of the acts of
2Ki 16:19 Now the **r** of the acts of Ahaz
2Ki 20:20 Now the **r** of the acts of
2Ki 21:17 Now the **r** of the acts of
2Ki 21:25 Now the **r** of the acts of Amon
2Ki 23:28 Now the **r** of the acts of
2Ki 24: 5 Now the **r** of the acts of
2Ki 25:11 carried away captive the **r** of
2Ki 25:11 with the **r** of the multitude
1Ch 4:43 they defeated the **r** of the
1Ch 6:31 LORD, after the ark came to **r**
1Ch 6:61 To the **r** of the family of the
1Ch 6:70 for the **r** of the family of
1Ch 6:77 the tribe of Zebulun the **r** of
1Ch 11: 8 repaired the **r** of the city
1Ch 12:38 all the **r** of Israel were of
1Ch 16:41 the **r** who were chosen, who
1Ch 19:11 the **r** of the people he put
1Ch 22: 9 you, who shall be a man of **r**
1Ch 22: 9 I will give him **r** from all
1Ch 22:18 not given you **r** on every side
1Ch 23:25 has given **r** to His people
1Ch 24:20 Now the **r** of the sons of Levi
1Ch 28: 2 heart to build a house of **r**
2Ch 9:29 Now the **r** of the acts of
2Ch 13:22 Now the **r** of the acts of
2Ch 14: 6 in Judah, for the land had **r**
2Ch 14: 6 the LORD had given him **r**
2Ch 14: 7 has given us **r** on every side
2Ch 14:11 LORD our God, for we **r** on You
2Ch 15:15 LORD gave them **r** all around
2Ch 20:30 his God gave him **r** all around
2Ch 20:34 Now the **r** of the acts of
2Ch 24:14 they brought the **r** of the
2Ch 25:26 Now the **r** of the acts of
2Ch 26:22 Now the **r** of the acts of
2Ch 27: 7 Now the **r** of the acts of
2Ch 28:26 Now the **r** of his acts and all
2Ch 32:32 Now the **r** of the acts of
2Ch 33:18 Now the **r** of the acts of
2Ch 35:26 Now the **r** of the acts of
2Ch 36: 8 Now the **r** of the acts of
Ezra 3: 8 the **r** of their brethren the
Ezra 4: 3 the **r** of the heads of the
Ezra 4: 7 the **r** of their companions
Ezra 4: 9 the **r** of their companions
Ezra 4:10 the **r** of the nations whom the
Ezra 4:10 the **r** of the region beyond
Ezra 4:17 to the **r** of their companions
Ezra 4:17 to the **r** in the region beyond
Ezra 6:16 the **r** of the descendants of
Ezra 7:18 do with the **r** of the silver
Neh 4:14 and to the **r** of the people,
Neh 4:19 and the **r** of the people,
Neh 6: 1 the **r** of our enemies heard
Neh 6:14 the **r** of the prophets who
Neh 7:72 And that which the **r** of the
Neh 9:28 But after they had **r**, they
Neh 10:28 Now the **r** of the people (the
Neh 11: 1 the **r** of the people cast lots
Neh 11:20 And the **r** of Israel, of the
Esth 9:12 the **r** of the king's provinces
Esth 9:16 had **r** from their enemies, and
Esth 9:22 Jews had **r** from their enemies
Job 3:13 then I would have been at **r**
Job 3:17 and there the weary are at **r**
Job 3:18 the prisoners **r** together
Job 3:26 I have no **r**, for trouble
Job 11:18 you, and take your **r** in safety
Job 14: 6 away from him that he may **r**
Job 17:16 Shall we have **r** together in
Job 30:17 and my gnawing pains take no **r**
Job 30:27 is in turmoil and cannot **r**
Ps 16: 9 My flesh also will **r** in hope
Ps 17:14 And leave the **r** of their
Ps 37: 7 **R** in the LORD, and wait
Ps 55: 6 I would fly away and be at **r**
Ps 94:13 That You may give him **r** from
Ps 95:11 They shall not enter My **r**
Ps 116: 7 Return to your **r**, O my soul,
Ps 125: 3 of wickedness shall not **r** On
Prov 21:16 way of understanding will **r**
Prov 24:33 folding of the hands to **r**
Prov 29:17 son, and he will give you **r**
Eccl 2:23 night his heart takes no **r**
Eccl 6: 5 this has more **r** than that man
Song 1: 7 where you make it **r** at noon
Is 7:19 all of them will **r** in the
Is 10:19 Then the **r** of the trees of
Is 11: 2 of the LORD shall **r** upon Him
Is 14: 3 gives you **r** from your sorrow
Is 14: 7 The whole earth is at **r** and
Is 18: 4 I will take My **r**, and I will
Is 23:12 there also you will have no **r**
Is 25:10 the hand of the LORD will **r**
Is 28:12 This is the **r** with which you
Is 28:12 you may cause the weary to **r**
Is 30:15 and **r** you shall be saved
Is 34:14 night creature shall **r** there
Is 34:14 find for herself a place of **r**
Is 44:17 the **r** of it he makes into a
Is 44:19 shall I make the **r** of it an
Is 51: 4 I will make My justice **r** as a
Is 57: 2 they shall **r** in their beds,
Is 57:20 sea, when it cannot **r**, whose
Is 62: 1 Jerusalem's sake I will not **r**
Is 62: 7 and give Him no **r** till He
Is 63:14 of the LORD causes him to **r**

Is 66: 1 And where is the place of My **r**
Jer 6:16 will find **r** for your souls
Jer 30:10 Jacob shall return, have **r**
Jer 31: 2 when I went to give him **r**
Jer 39: 3 with the **r** of the princes of
Jer 39: 9 with the **r** of the people who
Jer 41:10 away captive all the **r** of the
Jer 41:16 took from Mizpah all the **r** of
Jer 45: 3 in my sighing, and I find no **r**
Jer 46:27 Jacob shall return, have **r**
Jer 47: 6 up into your scabbard, **r** and
Jer 50:34 He may give **r** to the land
Jer 52:15 the **r** of the people who
Jer 52:15 and the **r** of the craftsmen
Lam 1: 3 the nations, she finds no **r**
Lam 2:18 give your eyes no **r**
Lam 5: 5 we labor and have no **r**
Ezek 5:13 cause My fury to **r** upon them
Ezek 12:23 I will lay this proverb to **r**
Ezek 16:42 So I will lay to **r** My fury
Ezek 21:17 and I will cause My fury to **r**
Ezek 24:13 caused My fury to **r** upon you
Ezek 36: 3 of the **r** of the nations, and
Ezek 36: 4 and mockery to the **r** of the
Ezek 36: 5 against the **r** of the nations
Ezek 44:30 a blessing to **r** on your house
Ezek 45: 8 but they shall give the **r** of
Ezek 48:18 The **r** of the length,
Ezek 48:21 The **r** shall belong to the
Ezek 48:23 As for the **r** of the tribes,
Dan 2:18 might not perish with the **r**
Dan 4: 4 was at **r** in my house, and
Dan 7:12 As for the **r** of the beasts,
Dan 12:13 for you shall **r**, and will
Amos 5: 7 to **r** in the earth
Mic 2:10 for this is not your **r**
Nah 3:18 your nobles **r** in the dust
Hab 3:16 that I might **r** in the day of
Zech 6: 8 north country have given **r** to
Matt 11:28 laden, and I will give you **r**
Matt 11:29 and you will find **r** for your
Matt 12:43 through dry places, seeking **r**
Matt 22: 6 the **r** seized his servants,
Matt 27:49 The **r** said, "Let Him alone
Mark 6:31 a deserted place and **r** a while
Mark 16:13 they went and told it to the **r**
Luke 8:10 but to the **r** it is given in
Luke 10: 6 your peace will **r** on it
Luke 11:24 through dry places, seeking **r**
Luke 12:26 why are you anxious for the **r**
Luke 24: 9 to the eleven and to all the **r**
John 11:13 about taking **r** in sleep
Acts 2:26 my flesh will also **r** in hope
Acts 2:37 and the **r** of the apostles,
Acts 5:13 none of the **r** dared join them
Acts 7:49 or what is the place of My **r**
Acts 15:17 so that the **r** of mankind may
Acts 17: 9 security from Jason and the **r**
Acts 27:44 and the **r**, some on boards and
Acts 28: 9 the **r** of those on the island
Rom 2:17 **r** on the law, and make your
Rom 11: 7 it, and the **r** were hardened
1Co 7:12 But to the **r** I, not the Lord,
1Co 11:34 the **r** I will set in order
2Co 2:13 I had no **r** in my spirit,
2Co 7: 5 Macedonia, our flesh had no **r**
2Co 12: 9 power of Christ may **r** upon me
2Co 13: 2 before, and to all the **r**, that
Gal 2:13 the **r** of the Jews also played
Eph 4:17 as the **r** of the Gentiles walk
Phil 1:13 palace guard, and to all the **r**
Phil 4: 3 the **r** of my fellow workers,
2Th 1: 7 give you who are troubled **r**
1Ti 5:20 all, that the **r** also may fear
Heb 3:11 They shall not enter My **r**
Heb 3:18 they would not enter His **r**
Heb 4: 1 remains of entering His **r**
Heb 4: 3 have believed do enter that **r**
Heb 4: 3 they shall not enter My **r**
Heb 4: 5 They shall not enter My **r**
Heb 4: 8 if Joshua had given them **r**
Heb 4: 9 a **r** for the people of God
Heb 4:10 His **r** has himself also ceased
Heb 4:11 be diligent to enter that **r**
1Pe 1:13 **r** your hope fully upon the
1Pe 4: 2 **r** of his time in the flesh
2Pe 3:16 also the **r** of the Scriptures
Rev 2:24 to the **r** in Thyatira, as many
Rev 4: 8 they do not **r** day or night,
Rev 6:11 **r** a little while longer,
Rev 9:20 But the **r** of mankind, who
Rev 11:13 the **r** were afraid and gave
Rev 12:17 with the **r** of her offspring
Rev 14:11 they have no **r** day or night
Rev 14:13 that they may **r** from their
Rev 19:21 the **r** were killed with the
Rev 20: 5 But the **r** of the dead did not

RESTED (*see* REST)
Gen 2: 2 He **r** on the seventh day from
Gen 2: 3 because in it He **r** from all
Gen 8: 4 Then the ark **r** in the seventh
Ex 10:14 **r** on all the territory of
Ex 16:30 So the people **r** on the
Ex 20:11 in them, and **r** the seventh day
Ex 24:16 of the LORD **r** on Mount Sinai
Ex 31:17 and on the seventh day He **r**
Ex 40:35 because the cloud **r** above it
Num 10:36 And when it **r**, he said
Num 11:25 when the Spirit **r** upon them
Num 11:26 And the Spirit **r** upon them
Josh 11:23 Then the land **r** from war
Ruth 2: 7 though she **r** a little in the
1Ki 2:10 So David **r** with his fathers,
1Ki 11:21 that David **r** with his fathers,
1Ki 11:43 Then Solomon **r** with his
1Ki 14:20 So he **r** with his fathers
1Ki 14:31 So Rehoboam **r** with his
1Ki 15: 8 So Abijam **r** with his fathers,
1Ki 15:24 So Asa **r** with his fathers, and
1Ki 16: 6 So Baasha **r** with his fathers
1Ki 16:28 So Omri **r** with his fathers and
1Ki 22:40 So Ahab **r** with his fathers
1Ki 22:50 And Jehoshaphat **r** with his
2Ki 8:24 So Joram **r** with his fathers,
2Ki 10:35 So Jehu **r** with his fathers,
2Ki 13: 9 So Jehoahaz **r** with his
2Ki 13:13 So Joash **r** with his fathers
2Ki 14:16 So Jehoash **r** with his fathers
2Ki 14:22 after the king **r** with his
2Ki 14:29 So Jeroboam **r** with his
2Ki 15: 7 So Azariah **r** with his fathers
2Ki 15:22 So Menahem **r** with his fathers
2Ki 15:38 So Jotham **r** with his fathers,
2Ki 16:20 So Ahaz **r** with his fathers,
2Ki 20:21 So Hezekiah **r** with his
2Ki 21:18 So Manasseh **r** with his
2Ki 24: 6 So Jehoiakim **r** with his
2Ch 9:31 Then Solomon **r** with his
2Ch 12:16 So Rehoboam **r** with his
2Ch 14: 1 So Abijah **r** with his fathers,
2Ch 16:13 So Asa **r** with his fathers
2Ch 21: 1 And Jehoshaphat **r** with his
2Ch 26: 2 after the king **r** with his
2Ch 26:23 So Uzziah **r** with his fathers,
2Ch 27: 9 So Jotham **r** with his fathers,
2Ch 28:27 So Ahaz **r** with his fathers,
2Ch 32:33 So Hezekiah **r** with his
2Ch 33:20 So Manasseh **r** with his
Esth 9:17 day of the month they **r** and
Esth 9:18 day of the month they **r**, and
Ezek 41: 6 they **r** on ledges which were
Luke 23:56 And they **r** on the Sabbath
Heb 4: 4 God **r** on the seventh day from

RESTING (*see* REST)
Gen 8: 9 But the dove found no **r** place
Num 10:33 search out a **r** place for them
Deut 28:65 of your foot have a **r** place
2Ch 6:41 O LORD God, to Your **r** place
Job 16:18 and let my cry have no **r** place
Ps 132: 8 O LORD, to Your **r** place, You
Ps 132:14 This is My **r** place forever
Prov 24:15 do not plunder his **r** place
Is 11:10 His **r** place shall be glorious
Is 32:18 and in quiet **r** places,
Jer 50: 6 have forgotten their **r** place
Ezek 25: 5 Ammon a **r** place for flocks
Zech 1:11 all the earth is **r** quietly
Zech 9: 1 Damascus its **r** place (for the
Matt 26:45 Are you still sleeping and **r**
Mark 14:41 Are you still sleeping and **r**

RESTITUTION
Ex 22: 3 He should make full **r**
Ex 22: 5 he shall make **r** from the best
Ex 22: 6 the fire shall surely make **r**
Ex 22:12 he shall make **r** to the owner
Lev 5:16 he shall make **r** for the harm
Num 5: 7 He shall make **r** for his
Num 5: 8 **r** may be made for the wrong
Num 5: 8 the **r** for the wrong must go

RESTLESS (*see* REST)
Gen 27:40 to pass, when you become **r**
Ps 55: 2 I am **r** in my complaint, and
Joel 1:18 The herds of cattle are **r**

RESTORATION (*see* RESTORE)
Acts 3:21 the times of **r** of all things

RESTORE (*see* RESTORATION, RESTORED, RESTORER, RESTORES)
Gen 20: 7 therefore, **r** the man's wife
Gen 20: 7 But if you do not **r** her, know
Gen 40:13 **r** you to your place, and you
Gen 42:25 to **r** every man's money to his
Ex 22: 1 he shall **r** five oxen for an
Ex 22: 4 or sheep, he shall **r** double
Lev 6: 4 that he shall **r** what he has
Lev 6: 5 He shall **r** its full value,
Lev 22:14 then he shall **r** a holy
Lev 24:21 kills an animal shall **r** it
Lev 25:27 **r** the balance to the man to
Deut 22: 2 then you shall **r** it to him
Judg 11:13 **r** those lands peaceably
1Sa 12: 3 I will **r** it to you
2Sa 9: 7 will **r** to you all the land of
2Sa 12: 6 he shall **r** fourfold for the
2Sa 16: 3 the house of Israel will **r**
1Ki 12:21 that he might **r** the kingdom
1Ki 20:34 from your father I will **r**
2Ki 8: 6 **R** all that was hers, and all
2Ch 11: 1 that he might **r** the kingdom
2Ch 24:12 bronze to **r** the house of the
2Ch 34:10 to repair and **r** the house
Neh 5:11 **R** now to them, even this day,
Neh 5:12 We will **r** it, and will require
Job 20:10 his hands will **r** his wealth
Job 20:18 He will **r** that for which he
Ps 51:12 **R** to me the joy of Your
Ps 60: 1 Oh, **r** us again
Ps 69: 4 nothing, I still must **r** it
Ps 80: 3 **R** us, O God; Cause Your face
Ps 80: 7 **R** us, O God of hosts
Ps 80:19 **R** us, O LORD God of hosts
Ps 85: 4 **R** us, O God of our salvation,
Prov 6:31 is found, he must **r** sevenfold
Is 1:26 I will **r** your judges as at
Is 38:16 so You will **r** me and make me
Is 42:22 and no one says, "**R**!"
Is 49: 6 to **r** the preserved ones of
Is 49: 8 to **r** the earth, to cause them
Is 57:18 **r** comforts to him and to his
Jer 27:22 up and **r** them to this place
Jer 30:17 For I will **r** health to you and
Jer 31:18 **r** me, and I will return, for
Lam 1:11 valuables for food to **r** life
Lam 1:16 who should **r** my life, is far
Lam 1:19 sought food to **r** their life
Dan 9:25 forth of the command to **r**
Joel 2:25 So I will **r** to you the years
Nah 2: 2 For the LORD will **r** the
Zeph 3: 9 For then I will **r** to the
Zech 9:12 that I will **r** double to you
Matt 17:11 first and will **r** all things
Luke 19: 8 accusation, I **r** fourfold
Acts 1: 6 time **r** the kingdom to Israel
Gal 6: 1 you who are spiritual **r** such

RESTORED (*see* RESTORE)
Gen 20:14 he **r** Sarah his wife to him
Gen 40:21 Then he **r** the chief butler to
Gen 41:13 He **r** me to my office, and he
Gen 42:28 My money has been **r**, and there
Ex 4: 7 it was **r** like his other flesh
Lev 25:28 able to have it **r** to himself
Deut 28:31 you, and shall not be **r** to you
1Sa 7:14 from Israel were **r** to Israel
1Ki 13: 6 that my hand may be **r** to me
1Ki 13: 6 the king's hand was **r** to him
2Ki 5:10 your flesh shall be **r** to you
2Ki 5:14 and his flesh was **r** like the
2Ki 8: 1 whose son he had **r** to life
2Ki 8: 5 how he had **r** the dead to life
2Ki 8: 5 whose son he had **r** to life
2Ki 8: 5 her son whom Elisha **r** to life
2Ki 14:22 **r** it to Judah, after the king
2Ki 14:25 He **r** the territory of Israel
2Ch 15: 8 he **r** the altar of the LORD
2Ch 24:13 they **r** the house of God to
2Ch 26: 2 **r** it to Judah, after the king
Ezra 6: 5 and brought to Babylon, be **r**
Neh 4: 7 of Jerusalem were being **r**
Job 42:10 the LORD **r** Job's losses when

Lam 5:21 You, O LORD, and we will be **r**
Ezek 18: 7 but has **r** to the debtor his
Ezek 18:12 not **r** the pledge, lifted his
Dan 4:36 I was **r** to my kingdom, and
Matt 12:13 and it was **r** as whole as the
Mark 3: 5 his hand was **r** as whole as
Mark 8:25 And he was **r** and saw everyone
Luke 6:10 his hand was **r** as whole as
Heb 13:19 that I may be **r** to you the

RESTORER (*see* RESTORE)
Ruth 4:15 may he be to you a **r** of life
Is 58:12 the **R** of Streets to Dwell In

RESTORES (*see* RESTORE)
Job 33:26 with joy, for He **r** to man His
Ps 23: 3 He **r** my soul
Ezek 33:15 if the wicked **r** the pledge
Mark 9:12 come first, and **r** all things

RESTRAIN (*see* RESTRAINED, RESTRAINING, RESTRAINS, RESTRAINT, UNRESTRAINED)
Gen 45: 1 Then Joseph could not **r**
Ruth 1:13 Would you **r** yourselves from
1Sa 3:13 vile, and he did not **r** them
2Sa 24:16 now **r** Your hand
1Ch 21:15 now **r** your hand
Job 7:11 I will not **r** my mouth
Job 15: 4 fear, and **r** prayer before God
Job 37: 4 He does not **r** them when His
Ps 39: 1 I will **r** my mouth with a
Ps 40: 9 Indeed, I do not **r** my lips
Is 48: 9 praise I will **r** it from you
Is 64:12 Will You **r** Yourself because
Dan 4:35 no one can **r** His hand or say
Acts 14:18 **r** the multitudes from

RESTRAINED (*see* RESTRAIN)
Gen 8: 2 and the rain from heaven was **r**
Gen 16: 2 now, the LORD has **r** me from
Gen 43:31 and he **r** himself, and said,
Ex 32:25 (for Aaron had not **r** them
Ex 36: 6 people were **r** from bringing
1Sa 24: 7 So David **r** his servants with
Esth 5:10 Nevertheless Haman **r** himself
Ps 119:101 I have **r** my feet from every
Is 42:14 I have been still and **r** Myself
Is 63:15 toward me? Are they **r**?
Jer 14:10 they have not **r** their feet
Ezek 31:15 I **r** its rivers, and the great
Luke 24:16 But their eyes were **r**, so
2Pe 2:16 **r** the madness of the prophet

RESTRAINING (*see* RESTRAIN)
2Th 2: 6 And now you know what is **r**

RESTRAINS (*see* RESTRAIN)
1Sa 14: 6 For nothing **r** the LORD from
Prov 10:19 but he who **r** his lips is wise
Prov 27:16 whoever **r** her **r** the wind,
2Th 2: 7 only He who now **r** will do so

RESTRAINT (*see* RESTRAIN)
Job 30:11 have cast off **r** before me
Job 36:16 place where there is no **r**
Prov 29:18 the people cast off **r**
Hos 4: 2 adultery, they break all **r**

RESTRICTED
Mic 2: 7 Is the Spirit of the LORD **r**
2Co 6:12 You are not **r** by us, but you
2Co 6:12 but you are **r** by your own

RESTS (*see* REST)
1Ki 1:21 the king **r** with his fathers
2Ki 2:15 spirit of Elijah **r** on Elisha
Prov 14:33 Wisdom **r** quietly in the heart
Eccl 7: 9 for anger **r** in the bosom of
1Pe 4:14 of glory and of God **r** upon you

RESULT (*see* RESULTED, RESULTING)
Ezra 4:16 the **r** will be that you will
1Co 14:15 What is the **r** then

RESULTED (*see* RESULT)
Rom 5:16 one offense **r** in condemnation
Rom 5:16 offenses **r** in justification

RESULTING (*see* RESULT)
Rom 5:18 **r** in condemnation, even so
Rom 5:18 **r** in justification of life

RESURRECTION
Matt 22:23 who say there is no **r**, came
Matt 22:28 Therefore, in the **r**, whose
Matt 22:30 For in the **r** they neither
Matt 22:31 concerning the **r** of the dead
Matt 27:53 out of the graves after His **r**
Mark 12:18 who say there is no **r**, came
Mark 12:23 Therefore, in the **r**, when
Luke 14:14 repaid at the **r** of the just
Luke 20:27 who deny that there is a **r**
Luke 20:33 Therefore, in the **r**, whose
Luke 20:35 the **r** from the dead, neither
Luke 20:36 of God, being sons of the **r**
John 5:29 to the **r** of life, and those
John 5:29 to the **r** of condemnation
John 11:24 in the **r** at the last day
John 11:25 I am the **r** and the life
Acts 1:22 a witness with us of His **r**
Acts 2:31 the **r** of the Christ, that His
Acts 4: 2 in Jesus the **r** from the dead
Acts 4:33 to the **r** of the Lord Jesus
Acts 17:18 to them Jesus and the **r**
Acts 17:32 heard of the **r** of the dead
Acts 23: 6 and **r** of the dead I am being
Acts 23: 8 say that there is no **r**
Acts 24:15 there will be a **r** of the dead
Acts 24:21 Concerning the **r** of the dead
Rom 1: 4 by the **r** from the dead,
Rom 6: 5 be in the likeness of His **r**
1Co 15:12 there is no **r** of the dead
1Co 15:13 if there is no **r** of the dead
1Co 15:21 also came the **r** of the dead
1Co 15:42 So also is the **r** of the dead
Phil 3:10 Him and the power of His **r**
Phil 3:11 attain to the **r** from the dead
2Ti 2:18 that the **r** is already past
Heb 6: 2 of **r** of the dead, and of
Heb 11:35 they might obtain a better **r**
1Pe 1: 3 **r** of Jesus Christ from the
1Pe 3:21 through the **r** of Jesus Christ
Rev 20: 5 This is the first **r**
Rev 20: 6 who has part in the first **r**

RETAIN (*see* RETAINED, RETAINS)
Prov 3:18 and happy are all who **r** her
Prov 4: 4 Let your heart **r** my words
Prov 11:16 but ruthless men **r** riches
Prov 29:23 humble in spirit will **r** honor
Eccl 8: 8 the spirit to **r** the spirit
Dan 11: 6 but she shall not **r** the power
Mic 7:18 He does not **r** His anger
John 20:23 if you **r** the sins of any,
Rom 1:28 to **r** God in their knowledge

RETAINED (*see* RETAIN)
Judg 7: 8 **r** those three hundred men
Dan 10: 8 in me, and I **r** no strength
Dan 10:16 me, and I have **r** no strength
John 20:23 the sins of any, they are **r**

RETAINS (*see* RETAIN)
Prov 11:16 A gracious woman **r** honor, but

RETALIATE (*see* RETALIATION)
Joel 3: 4 Will you **r** against Me
Joel 3: 4 But if you **r** against Me,

RETALIATION (*see* RETALIATE)
Joel 3: 4 your **r** upon your own head
Joel 3: 7 will return your **r** upon your

RETINUE
1Ki 10: 2 Jerusalem with a very great **r**
2Ch 9: 1 having a very great **r**,

RETREAT (*see* RETREATED)
2Sa 11:15 **r** from him, that he may be

RETREATED (*see* RETREAT)
2Sa 23: 9 and the men of Israel had **r**

RETRIBUTION
2Ch 6:23 bringing **r** on the wicked by

RETURN (*see* RETURNED, RETURNING, RETURNS)
Gen 3:19 till you **r** to the ground, for
Gen 3:19 are, and to dust you shall **r**
Gen 8:12 which did not **r** again to him
Gen 14:17 after his **r** from the defeat
Gen 15:16 generation they shall **r** here
Gen 16: 9 **R** to your mistress, and submit
Gen 18:10 I will certainly **r** to you
Gen 18:14 time I will **r** to you,
Gen 31: 3 **R** to the land of your fathers
Gen 31:13 **r** to the land of your kindred
Gen 32: 9 **R** to your country and to your
Ex 4:18 **r** to my brethren who are in
Ex 4:19 in Midian, "Go, **r** to Egypt
Ex 13:17 they see war, and **r** to Egypt
Ex 22:26 you shall **r** it to him before
Ex 33:11 he would **r** to the camp, but
Lev 25:10 you shall **r** to his possession
Lev 25:10 of you shall **r** to his family
Lev 25:13 you shall **r** to his possession
Lev 25:27 sold it, that he may **r** to his
Lev 25:28 he shall **r** to his possession
Lev 25:41 shall **r** to his own family
Lev 25:41 he shall **r** to the possession
Lev 27:24 **r** to him from whom it was
Num 10:36 **R**, O LORD, to the many
Num 14: 3 better for us to **r** to Egypt
Num 14: 4 select a leader and **r** to Egypt
Num 18:21 in **r** for the work which they
Num 23: 5 **R** to Balak, and thus you shall
Num 32:18 We will not **r** to our homes
Num 32:22 then afterward you may **r**
Num 35:25 the congregation shall **r** him
Num 35:28 may **r** to the land of his
Num 35:32 that he may **r** to dwell in the
Deut 3:20 Then each of you may **r** to his
Deut 5:30 to them, "**R** to your tents
Deut 17:16 nor cause the people to **r** to
Deut 17:16 shall not **r** that way again
Deut 20: 5 **r** to his house, lest he die
Deut 20: 6 **r** to his house, lest he die
Deut 20: 7 **r** to his house, lest he die
Deut 20: 8 and **r** to his house, lest the
Deut 24:13 You shall in any case **r** the
Deut 30: 2 you **r** to the LORD your God and
Josh 1:15 Then you shall **r** to the land
Josh 20: 6 Then the slayer may **r** and come
Josh 22: 4 now therefore, **r** and go to
Josh 22: 8 **R** with much riches to your
Judg 11:31 when I **r** in peace from the
Judg 17: 3 therefore, I will **r** it to you
Ruth 1: 6 that she might **r** from the
Ruth 1: 7 way to **r** to the land of Judah
Ruth 1: 8 **r** each to her mother's house
Ruth 1:10 Surely we will **r** with you to
Ruth 1:15 **r** after your sister-in-law
1Sa 6: 3 but by all means **r** it to Him
1Sa 6: 4 which we shall **r** to Him
1Sa 7: 3 If you **r** to the LORD with all
1Sa 9: 5 Come, let us **r**, lest my
1Sa 15:25 **r** with me, that I may worship
1Sa 15:26 I will not **r** with you, for
1Sa 15:30 **r** with me, that I may worship
1Sa 26:21 **R**, my son David
1Sa 29: 4 Make this fellow **r**, that he
1Sa 29: 7 Therefore **r** now, and go in
1Sa 29:11 to **r** to the land of the
2Sa 1:22 sword of Saul did not **r** empty
2Sa 2:26 to **r** from pursuing their
2Sa 3:16 Abner said to him, "Go, **r**!"
2Sa 10: 5 beards have grown, and then **r**
2Sa 12:23 him, but he shall not **r** to me
2Sa 14:24 Let him **r** to his own house,
2Sa 15:19 **R** and remain with the king
2Sa 15:20 **R**, and take your brethren back
2Sa 15:27 **R** to the city in peace, and
2Sa 15:34 But if you **r** to the city, and
2Sa 17: 3 When all **r** except the man
2Sa 19:14 **R**, you and all your servants
1Ki 2:32 So the LORD will **r** his blood
1Ki 2:33 **r** upon the head of Joab and
1Ki 2:44 therefore the LORD will **r**
1Ki 8:48 when they **r** to You with all
1Ki 12:24 Let every man **r** to his house
1Ki 12:26 Now the kingdom may **r** to the
1Ki 13: 9 nor **r** by the same way you
1Ki 13:10 did not **r** by the way he came
1Ki 13:16 I cannot **r** with you nor go in
1Ki 13:17 nor **r** by going the way you
1Ki 19:15 Go, **r** on your way to the
1Ki 22:17 Let each **r** to his house in
1Ki 22:26 **r** him to Amon the governor of
1Ki 22:28 If you ever **r** in peace, the
2Ki 1: 6 **r** to the king who sent you,
2Ki 19: 7 a rumor and **r** to his own land
2Ki 19:33 came, by the same shall he **r**
2Ki 20: 5 **R** and tell Hezekiah the leader
1Ch 19: 5 beards have grown, and then **r**
2Ch 6:24 have sinned against You, and **r**
2Ch 6:38 when they **r** to You with all
2Ch 11: 4 Let every man **r** to his house
2Ch 18:16 Let each **r** to his house in
2Ch 18:25 **r** him to Amon the governor of
2Ch 18:26 affliction until I **r** in peace
2Ch 18:27 If you ever **r** in peace, the

2Ch 28:11 **r** the captives, whom you have
2Ch 30: 6 **r** to the LORD God of Abraham,
2Ch 30: 6 then He will **r** to the remnant
2Ch 30: 9 For if you **r** to the LORD,
2Ch 30: 9 face from you if you **r** to Him
Neh 1: 9 but if you **r** to Me, and keep
Neh 2: 6 And when will you **r**
Neh 7: 5 had come up in the first **r**
Neh 9:17 leader to **r** to their bondage
Esth 4:15 to **r** this answer to Mordecai
Esth 9:25 Jews should **r** on his own head
Job 1:21 and naked shall I **r** there
Job 7:10 He shall never **r** to his house
Job 10:21 from which I shall not **r**, to
Job 15:22 that he will **r** from darkness
Job 16:22 I shall go the way of no **r**
Job 22:23 If you **r** to the Almighty, you
Job 33:25 He shall **r** to the days of his
Job 34:15 and man would **r** to dust
Job 39: 4 depart and do not **r** to them
Ps 6: 4 **R**, O LORD, deliver me
Ps 7: 7 sakes, therefore, **r** on high
Ps 7:16 shall **r** upon his own head
Ps 35:13 would **r** to my own heart
Ps 59: 6 At evening they **r**, They growl
Ps 59:14 And at evening they **r**, They
Ps 73:10 Therefore his people **r** here
Ps 74:21 let the oppressed **r** ashamed
Ps 79:12 **r** to our neighbors sevenfold
Ps 80:14 **R**, we beseech You, O God of
Ps 90: 3 **R**, O children of men
Ps 90:13 **R**, O LORD! How long?
Ps 94:15 will **r** to righteousness, And
Ps 104: 9 That they may not **r** to cover
Ps 104:29 they die and **r** to their dust
Ps 109: 4 In **r** for my love they are my
Ps 116: 7 **R** to your rest, O my soul,
Prov 2:19 none who go to her **r**, nor do
Eccl 1: 7 come, there they **r** again
Eccl 3:20 the dust, and all **r** to dust
Eccl 5:15 womb, naked shall he **r**, to go
Eccl 12: 2 do not **r** after the rain
Eccl 12: 7 Then the dust will **r** to the
Eccl 12: 7 the spirit will **r** to God who
Song 6:13 **R**, **r**, O Shulamite
Song 6:13 **r**, **r**, that we may look
Is 6:10 with their heart, and **r** and be
Is 6:13 will be in it, and will **r** and
Is 10:21 The remnant will **r**, the
Is 10:22 yet a remnant of them will **r**
Is 19:22 they will **r** to the LORD, and
Is 21:12 **R**! Come back!
Is 23:17 She will **r** to her pay, and
Is 31: 6 **R** to Him against whom the
Is 35:10 ransomed of the LORD shall **r**
Is 37: 7 a rumor and **r** to his own land
Is 37:34 came, by the same shall he **r**
Is 44:22 **R** to Me, for I have redeemed
Is 45:23 righteousness, and shall not **r**
Is 51:11 ransomed of the LORD shall **r**
Is 55: 7 let him **r** to the LORD, and He
Is 55:10 heaven, and do not **r** there
Is 55:11 it shall not **r** to Me void
Is 63:17 **R** for Your servants' sake,
Jer 3: 1 man's, may he **r** to her again
Jer 3: 1 yet **r** to Me," says the LORD
Jer 3: 7 all these things, '**R** to Me
Jer 3: 7 But she did not **r**
Jer 3:12 **R**, backsliding Israel,' says
Jer 3:14 **R**, O backsliding children,"
Jer 3:22 **R**, you backsliding children,
Jer 4: 1 If you will **r**, O Israel,"
Jer 4: 1 says the LORD, "**R** to Me
Jer 5: 3 they have refused to **r**
Jer 8: 4 Will one turn away and not **r**
Jer 8: 5 to deceit, they refuse to **r**
Jer 12:15 them out, that I will **r** and
Jer 15: 7 they do not **r** from their ways
Jer 15:19 If you **r**, then I will bring
Jer 15:19 Let them **r** to you
Jer 15:19 but you must not **r** to them
Jer 18:11 **R** now every one from his evil
Jer 22:10 away, for he shall **r** no more
Jer 22:11 He shall not **r** here anymore
Jer 22:27 to which they desire to **r**
Jer 22:27 there they shall not **r**
Jer 24: 7 for they shall **r** to Me with
Jer 29:10 cause you to **r** to this place
Jer 30: 3 I will cause them to **r** to the
Jer 30:10 Jacob shall **r**, have rest and
Jer 30:24 not **r** until He has done it
Jer 31: 8 a great throng shall **r** there
Jer 31:18 restore me, and I will **r**, for
Jer 32:44 cause their captives to **r**
Jer 33: 7 the captives of Israel to **r**
Jer 33:11 the land to **r** as at the first
Jer 33:26 cause their captives to **r**
Jer 34:11 the male and female slaves **r**
Jer 34:22 cause them to **r** to this city
Jer 37: 7 to help you will **r** to Egypt
Jer 37:20 do not make me **r** to the house
Jer 38:26 that he would not make me **r**
Jer 42:12 cause you to **r** to your own
Jer 44:14 lest they **r** to the land of
Jer 44:14 to which they desire to **r**
Jer 44:14 For none shall **r** except those
Jer 44:28 **r** from the land of Egypt to
Jer 46:27 Jacob shall **r**, have rest and
Jer 50: 9 none shall **r** in vain
Ezek 7:13 not **r** to what has been sold
Ezek 16:55 **r** to their former state, and
Ezek 16:55 and her daughters **r** to their
Ezek 16:55 your daughters will **r** to your
Ezek 21: 5 it shall not **r** anymore
Ezek 21:30 **R** it to its sheath
Ezek 29:14 cause them to **r** to the land
Ezek 46: 9 He shall not **r** by way of the
Ezek 46:17 it shall **r** to the prince
Dan 10:20 now I must **r** to fight with
Dan 11: 9 but shall **r** to his own land
Dan 11:10 then he shall **r** to his
Dan 11:13 the king of the North will **r**
Dan 11:28 damage and **r** to his own land
Dan 11:29 the appointed time he shall **r**
Dan 11:30 **r** in rage against the holy
Dan 11:30 So he shall **r** and show regard
Hos 2: 7 **r** to my first husband, for
Hos 2: 9 Therefore I will **r** and take
Hos 3: 5 children of Israel shall **r**
Hos 5:15 I will **r** again to My place
Hos 6: 1 Come, and let us **r** to the LORD
Hos 6:11 when I **r** the captives of My
Hos 7:10 but they do not **r** to the LORD
Hos 7:16 They **r**, but not to the Most
Hos 8:13 They shall **r** to Egypt
Hos 9: 3 but Ephraim shall **r** to Egypt
Hos 11: 5 He shall not **r** to the land of
Hos 12: 6 by the help of your God, **r**
Hos 12:14 and **r** his reproach upon him
Hos 14: 1 **r** to the LORD your God, for
Hos 14: 2 with you, and **r** to the LORD
Hos 14: 7 under his shadow shall **r**
Joel 2:13 **r** to the LORD your God, for
Joel 3: 4 and speedily I will **r** your
Joel 3: 7 will **r** your retaliation upon
Obad 15 shall **r** upon your own head
Mic 1: 7 they shall **r** to the pay of a
Mic 2: 6 they shall not **r** insult for
Mic 5: 3 of His brethren shall **r** to
Zeph 2: 7 for them, and **r** their captives
Zeph 3:20 when I **r** your captives before
Zech 1: 3 **R** to Me," says the LORD of
Zech 1: 3 and I will **r** to you," says
Zech 8: 3 I will **r** to Zion, and dwell
Zech 9:12 **R** to the stronghold, you
Zech 10: 9 children, and they shall **r**
Mal 1: 4 impoverished, but we will **r**
Mal 3: 7 **R** to Me, and I will **r** to
Mal 3: 7 said, In what way shall we **r**
Matt 2:12 they should not **r** to Herod
Matt 10:13 let your peace **r** to you
Matt 12:44 I will **r** to my house from
Luke 6:35 lend, hoping for nothing in **r**
Luke 8:39 **R** to your own house, and tell
Luke 10: 6 if not, it will **r** to you
Luke 11:24 I will **r** to my house from
Luke 12:36 when he will **r** from the
Luke 19:12 for himself a kingdom and to **r**
Acts 13:34 no more to **r** to corruption,
Acts 15:16 After this I will **r** and will
Acts 18:21 but I will **r** again to you,
Acts 20: 3 he decided to **r** through
2Co 6:13 Now in **r** for the same (I
Heb 11:15 have had opportunity to **r**
1Pe 2:23 reviled, did not revile in **r**

RETURNED (*see* RETURN)
Gen 8: 9 she **r** into the ark to him,
Gen 18:33 and Abraham **r** to his place
Gen 21:32 they **r** to the land of the
Gen 22:19 So Abraham **r** to his young men
Gen 31:55 departed and **r** to his place
Gen 32: 6 the messengers **r** to Jacob
Gen 33:16 So Esau **r** that day on his way
Gen 37:29 Then Reuben **r** to the pit, and
Gen 37:30 he **r** to his brothers and said,
Gen 38:22 And he **r** to Judah and said,
Gen 42:24 Then he **r** to them again, and
Gen 43:10 would have **r** this second time
Gen 43:12 hand the money that was **r** in
Gen 43:18 which was **r** in our sacks the
Gen 44:13 his donkey and **r** to the city
Gen 50:14 Joseph **r** to Egypt, he and his
Ex 4:18 **r** to Jethro his father-in-law
Ex 4:20 he **r** to the land of Egypt
Ex 5:22 So Moses **r** to the LORD and
Ex 14:27 the sea **r** to its full depth,
Ex 14:28 Then the waters **r** and covered
Ex 32:31 Then Moses **r** to the LORD and
Ex 34:31 of the congregation **r** to him
Lev 22:13 has **r** to her father's house
Num 11:30 Moses **r** to the camp, both he
Num 13:25 they **r** from spying out the
Num 14:36 to spy out the land, who **r**
Num 16:50 So Aaron **r** to Moses at the
Num 23: 6 So he **r** to him, and there he
Num 24:25 and departed and **r** to his place
Deut 1:45 Then you **r** and wept before the
Josh 2:16 until the pursuers have **r**
Josh 2:22 days until the pursuers **r**
Josh 2:23 So the two men **r**, descended
Josh 4:18 the Jordan **r** to their place
Josh 6:14 city once and **r** to the camp
Josh 7: 3 they **r** to Joshua and said to
Josh 8:24 all the Israelites **r** to Ai
Josh 10:15 Then Joshua **r**, and all Israel
Josh 10:21 all the people **r** to the camp
Josh 10:38 Then Joshua **r**, and all Israel
Josh 10:43 Then Joshua **r**, and all Israel
Josh 22: 9 half the tribe of Manasseh **r**
Josh 22:32 **r** from the children of Reuben
Judg 7: 3 thousand of the people **r**, and
Judg 7:15 He **r** to the camp of Israel,
Judg 8:13 son of Joash **r** from battle
Judg 9:57 God **r** on their own heads, and
Judg 11:39 that she **r** to her father, and
Judg 14: 8 when he **r** to get her, he
Judg 15:19 and his spirit **r**, and he
Judg 17: 3 So when he had **r** the eleven
Judg 17: 4 Thus he **r** the silver to his
Judg 21:23 **r** to their inheritance, and
Ruth 1:22 So Naomi **r**, and Ruth the
Ruth 1:22 who **r** from the country of
1Sa 1:19 before the LORD, and **r** and came
1Sa 6:16 they **r** to Ekron the same day
1Sa 6:17 which the Philistines **r** as a
1Sa 7:17 But he always **r** to Ramah, for
1Sa 14:46 Then Saul **r** from pursuing the
1Sa 17:15 and **r** from Saul to feed his
1Sa 17:53 of Israel **r** from chasing the
1Sa 17:57 as David **r** from the slaughter
1Sa 23:28 Therefore Saul **r** from
1Sa 24: 1 when Saul had **r** from
1Sa 25:39 For the LORD has **r** the
1Sa 26:25 way, and Saul **r** to his place
1Sa 27: 9 camels, and the apparel, and **r**
2Sa 1: 1 when David had **r** from the
2Sa 2:30 So Joab **r** from pursuing Abner
2Sa 3:16 Go, return!" And he **r**.
2Sa 3:27 when Abner had **r** to Hebron
2Sa 6:20 Then David **r** to bless his
2Sa 8:13 he **r** from killing eighteen
2Sa 10:14 So Joab **r** from the people of
2Sa 11: 4 and she **r** to her house
2Sa 12:31 all the people **r** to Jerusalem
2Sa 14:24 So Absalom **r** to his own
2Sa 17:20 them, they **r** to Jerusalem
2Sa 18:16 the people **r** from pursuing
2Sa 19:15 Then the king **r** and came to
2Sa 19:39 him, and he **r** to his own place
2Sa 20:22 So Joab **r** to the king at
2Sa 23:10 the people **r** after him only
2Ki 1: 5 when the messengers **r** to him
2Ki 2:25 and from there he **r** to Samaria
2Ki 3:27 him and **r** to their own land
2Ki 4:35 He **r** and walked back and forth
2Ki 4:38 Elisha **r** to Gilgal, and there
2Ki 5:15 Then he **r** to the man of God,
2Ki 7:15 So the messengers **r** and told
2Ki 8: 3 that the woman **r** from the
2Ki 9:15 But King Joram had **r** to

2Ki 14:14 and hostages, and **r** to Samaria
2Ki 19: 8 So the Rabshakeh **r** and found
2Ki 19:36 away, **r** home, and remained at
2Ki 23:20 and he **r** to Jerusalem
1Ch 16:43 David **r** to bless his house
1Ch 20: 3 all the people **r** to Jerusalem
1Ch 21:27 he **r** his sword to its sheath
2Ch 10: 2 that Jeroboam **r** from Egypt
2Ch 14:15 abundance, and **r** to Jerusalem
2Ch 19: 1 the king of Judah **r** safely to
2Ch 19: 8 when they **r** to Jerusalem
2Ch 20:27 Then they **r**, every man of
2Ch 22: 6 Then he **r** to Jezreel to
2Ch 24:11 took it and **r** it to its place
2Ch 25:10 they **r** home in great anger
2Ch 25:24 and hostages, and **r** to Samaria
2Ch 28:15 Then they **r** to Samaria
2Ch 31: 1 Israel **r** to their own cities
2Ch 32:21 So he **r** shamefaced to his own
2Ch 34: 7 of Israel, he **r** to Jerusalem
Ezra 2: 1 who **r** to Jerusalem and Judah,
Ezra 5: 5 was **r** concerning this matter
Ezra 5:11 thus they **r** us an answer,
Ezra 6:21 had **r** from the captivity ate
Neh 2:15 by the Valley Gate, and so **r**
Neh 4:15 that all of us **r** to the wall
Neh 7: 6 who **r** to Jerusalem and Judah,
Neh 8:17 of those who had **r** from the
Neh 9:28 yet when they **r** and cried out
Neh 13: 6 Babylon I had **r** to the king
Esth 2:14 in the morning she **r** to the
Esth 4: 9 So Hathach **r** and told Esther
Esth 7: 8 When the king **r** from the
Ps 78:34 And they **r** and sought
Eccl 4: 1 Then I **r** and considered all
Eccl 4: 7 Then I **r**, and I saw vanity
Eccl 9:11 I **r** and saw under the sun that
Is 37: 8 So the Rabshakeh **r**, and found
Is 37:37 away, **r** home, and remained at
Is 38: 8 So the sun **r** ten degrees on
Jer 14: 3 They **r** with their vessels
Jer 40:12 then all the Jews **r** out of
Jer 43: 5 had **r** to dwell in the land of
Ezek 8:17 then they have **r** to provoke
Ezek 47: 6 **r** me to the bank of the river
Ezek 47: 7 When I **r**, there, along the
Dan 4:34 and my understanding **r** to me
Dan 4:36 same time my reason **r** to me
Dan 4:36 my honor and splendor **r** to me
Amos 4: 6 yet you have not **r** to Me,"
Amos 4: 8 yet you have not **r** to Me,"
Amos 4: 9 yet you have not **r** to Me,"
Amos 4:10 yet you have not **r** to Me,"
Amos 4:11 yet you have not **r** to Me,"
Mic 2: 8 pass by, like men **r** from war
Zech 1: 6 So they **r** and said
Zech 7:14 no one passed through or **r**
Matt 21:18 as He **r** to the city, He was
Mark 14:40 And when He **r**, He found them
Luke 1:56 months, and **r** to her house
Luke 2:20 Then the shepherds **r**,
Luke 2:39 they **r** to Galilee, to their
Luke 2:43 finished the days, as they **r**
Luke 2:45 they **r** to Jerusalem, seeking
Luke 4: 1 **r** from the Jordan and was led
Luke 4:14 Then Jesus **r** in the power of
Luke 8:37 And He got into the boat and **r**
Luke 8:40 So it was, when Jesus **r**, that
Luke 8:55 Then her spirit **r**, and she
Luke 9:10 the apostles, when they had **r**
Luke 10:17 Then the seventy **r** with joy
Luke 17:15 he saw that he was healed, **r**
Luke 17:18 there not any found who **r** to
Luke 19:15 And so it was that when he **r**
Luke 22:32 and when you have **r** to Me,
Luke 23:48 done, beat their breasts and **r**
Luke 23:56 Then they **r** and prepared
Luke 24: 9 Then they **r** from the tomb and
Luke 24:33 **r** to Jerusalem, and found the
Luke 24:52 **r** to Jerusalem with great joy
Acts 1:12 Then they **r** to Jerusalem from
Acts 5:22 them in the prison, they **r**
Acts 8:25 Lord, they **r** to Jerusalem,
Acts 12:25 Saul **r** from Jerusalem when
Acts 13:13 from them, **r** to Jerusalem
Acts 14:21 they **r** to Lystra, Iconium, and
Acts 21: 6 the ship, and they **r** home
Acts 22:17 when I **r** to Jerusalem and was
Acts 23:32 him, and **r** to the barracks
Gal 1:17 and **r** again to Damascus
1Pe 2:25 astray, but have now **r** to the

RETURNING (*see* RETURN)
1Sa 6: 8 are **r** to Him as a trespass
1Sa 18: 6 when David was **r** from the
Is 30:15 In **r** and rest you shall be
Dan 11:28 While **r** to his land with
Zech 1:16 I am **r** to Jerusalem with
Luke 7:10 **r** to the house, found the
Acts 8:28 was **r**. And sitting in his
Heb 7: 1 who met Abraham **r** from the
1Pe 3: 9 not **r** evil for evil or

RETURNS (*see* RETURN)
Ps 146: 4 departs, he **r** to his earth
Prov 26:11 As a dog **r** to his own vomit,
Ezek 35: 7 who leaves and the one who **r**
Zech 9: 8 who passes by and him who **r**
Luke 17: 4 seven times in a day **r** to you
2Pe 2:22 A dog **r** to his own vomit,"

REU
Gen 11:18 thirty years, and begot **R**
Gen 11:19 After he begot **R**, Peleg lived
Gen 11:20 **R** lived thirty-two years, and
Gen 11:21 **R** lived two hundred and seven
1Ch 1:25 Eber, Peleg, **R**,
Luke 3:35 son of Serug, the son of **R**

REUBEN (*see* REUBENITE)
Gen 29:32 son, and she called his name **R**
Gen 30:14 Now **R** went in the days of
Gen 35:22 in that land, that **R** went
Gen 35:23 the sons of Leah were **R**,
Gen 37:21 But **R** heard it, and he
Gen 37:22 And **R** said to them,
Gen 37:29 Then **R** returned to the pit,
Gen 42:22 And **R** answered them, saying,
Gen 42:37 Then **R** spoke to his father,
Gen 46: 8 **R** was Jacob's firstborn
Gen 46: 9 The sons of **R** were Hanoch
Gen 48: 5 as **R** and Simeon, they shall be
Gen 49: 3 **R**, you are my firstborn, my
Ex 1: 2 **R**, Simeon, Levi, and Judah
Ex 6:14 The sons of **R**, the firstborn
Ex 6:14 These are the families of **R**
Num 1: 5 from **R**, Elizur the son of
Num 1:20 Now the children of **R**,
Num 1:21 of **R** were forty-six thousand
Num 2:10 **R** according to their armies
Num 2:10 leader of the children of **R**
Num 2:16 armies of the forces with **R**
Num 7:30 leader of the children of **R**
Num 10:18 **R** set out according to their
Num 13: 4 from the tribe of **R**, Shammua
Num 16: 1 the son of Peleth, sons of **R**
Num 26: 5 **R** was the firstborn of Israel
Num 26: 5 The children of **R** were
Num 32: 1 Now the children of **R** and the
Num 32: 2 Gad and the children of **R** came
Num 32: 6 Gad and to the children of **R**
Num 32:25 children of **R** spoke to Moses
Num 32:29 the children of **R** cross over
Num 32:31 and the children of **R** answered
Num 32:33 of Gad, to the children of **R**
Num 32:37 children of **R** built Heshbon
Num 34:14 tribe of the children of **R**
Deut 11: 6 sons of Eliab, the son of **R**
Deut 27:13 **R**, Gad, Asher, Zebulun, Dan,
Deut 33: 6 Let **R** live, and not die, nor
Josh 4:12 And the men of **R**, the men of
Josh 13:15 tribe of the children of **R** an
Josh 13:23 border of the children of **R**
Josh 13:23 of the children of **R**
Josh 15: 6 stone of Bohan the son of **R**
Josh 18: 7 And Gad, **R**, and half the tribe
Josh 18:17 stone of Bohan the son of **R**
Josh 20: 8 plain, from the tribe of **R**
Josh 21: 7 cities from the tribe of **R**
Josh 21:36 and from the tribe of **R**, Bezer
Josh 22: 9 So the children of **R**, the
Josh 22:10 of Canaan, the children of **R**
Josh 22:11 Behold, the children of **R**
Josh 22:13 priest to the children of **R**
Josh 22:15 came to the children of **R**
Josh 22:21 Then the children of **R**, the
Josh 22:25 you and us, you children of **R**
Josh 22:30 words that the children of **R**
Josh 22:31 said to the children of **R**
Josh 22:32 from the children of **R** and the
Josh 22:33 land where the children of **R**
Josh 22:34 And the children of **R** and the
Judg 5:15 among the divisions of **R**
Judg 5:16 The divisions of **R** have great
2Ki 10:33 Gad, **R**, and Manasseh
1Ch 2: 1 **R**, Simeon, Levi, Judah,
1Ch 5: 1 Now the sons of **R** the
1Ch 5: 3 the sons of **R** the firstborn
1Ch 5:18 The sons of **R**, the Gadites,
1Ch 6:63 cities from the tribe of **R**
1Ch 6:78 given from the tribe of **R**
Ezek 48: 6 the west, one portion for **R**
Ezek 48: 7 by the border of **R**, from the
Ezek 48:31 one gate for **R**, one gate for
Rev 7: 5 of the tribe of **R** twelve

REUBENITE (*see* REUBEN, REUBENITES)
1Ch 11:42 Adina the son of Shiza the **R**

REUBENITES (*see* REUBENITE)
Num 26: 7 are the families of the **R**
Deut 3:12 its cities, I gave to the **R**
Deut 3:16 And to the **R** and the Gadites I
Deut 4:43 on the plateau for the **R**,
Deut 29: 8 it as an inheritance to the **R**
Josh 1:12 And to the **R**, the Gadites, and
Josh 12: 6 it as a possession to the **R**
Josh 13: 8 the other half tribe the **R**
Josh 22: 1 Then Joshua called the **R**, the
1Ch 5: 6 He was leader of the **R**
1Ch 5:26 He carried the **R**, the Gadites
1Ch 11:42 Reubenite (a chief of the **R**)
1Ch 12:37 of the **R** and the Gadites and
1Ch 26:32 made officials over the **R**
1Ch 27:16 the officer over the **R** was

REUEL (*see* DEUEL, JETHRO)
Gen 36: 4 to Esau, and Basemath bore **R**
Gen 36:10 **R** the son of Basemath the
Gen 36:13 These were the sons of **R**
Gen 36:17 These were the sons of **R**,
Gen 36:17 of **R** in the land of Edom
Ex 2:18 they came to **R** their father
Num 2:14 be Eliasaph the son of **R**
Num 10:29 the son of **R** the Midianite
1Ch 1:35 sons of Esau were Eliphaz, **R**
1Ch 1:37 The sons of **R** were Nahath
1Ch 9: 8 of Shephatiah, the son of **R**

REUMAH
Gen 22:24 concubine, whose name was **R**

REVEAL (*see* REVEALED, REVEALER, REVEALING, REVEALS, REVELATION)
1Sa 2:27 Did I not clearly **r** Myself
1Sa 28:15 that you may **r** to me what I
Esth 2:10 had charged her not to **r** it
Job 20:27 heavens will **r** his iniquity
Jer 33: 6 **r** to them the abundance of
Dan 2:47 since you could **r** this secret
Matt 11:27 whom the Son wills to **r** Him
Luke 10:22 whom the Son wills to **r** Him
Acts 26:16 which I will yet **r** to you
1Co 4: 5 **r** the counsels of the hearts
Gal 1:16 to **r** His Son in me, that I
Phil 3:15 God will **r** even this to you

REVEALED (*see* REVEAL)
Deut 29:29 which are **r** belong to us and
1Sa 3: 7 word of the LORD yet **r** to him
1Sa 3:21 For the LORD **r** Himself to
2Sa 7:27 have **r** this to Your servant,
Esth 2:10 Esther had not **r** her people
Esth 2:20 had not yet **r** her kindred
Job 38:17 gates of death been **r** to you
Prov 26:26 will be **r** before the whole
Is 22:14 Then it was **r** in my hearing
Is 23: 1 of Cyprus it is **r** to them
Is 40: 5 glory of the LORD shall be **r**
Is 53: 1 the arm of the LORD been **r**
Is 56: 1 and My righteousness to be **r**
Jer 11:20 for to You I have **r** my cause
Jer 51:10 The LORD has **r** our
Ezek 23:18 She **r** her harlotry and
Dan 2:19 Then the secret was **r** to
Dan 2:30 this secret has not been **r** to
Dan 10: 1 a message was **r** to Daniel
Matt 10:26 covered that will not be **r**
Matt 11:25 and have **r** them to babes
Matt 16:17 blood has not **r** this to you
Mark 4:22 hidden which will not be **r**
Luke 2:26 it had been **r** to him by the
Luke 2:35 of many hearts may be **r**
Luke 8:17 is secret that will not be **r**
Luke 10:21 and prudent and **r** them to babes

Luke 12: 2 covered that will not be **r**
Luke 17:30 day when the Son of Man is **r**
John 1:31 that He should be **r** to Israel
John 9: 3 of God should be **r** in him
John 12:38 the arm of the LORD been **r**
Acts 23:22 you have **r** these things to me
Rom 1:17 God is **r** from faith to faith
Rom 1:18 is **r** from heaven against all
Rom 3:21 God apart from the law is **r**
Rom 8:18 glory which shall be **r** in us
1Co 2:10 But God has **r** them to us
1Co 3:13 because it will be **r** by fire
1Co 14:25 secrets of his heart are **r**
1Co 14:30 But if anything is **r** to
Gal 3:23 which would afterward be **r**
Eph 3: 5 as it has now been **r** by the
Col 1:26 now has been **r** to His saints
2Th 1: 7 us when the Lord Jesus is **r**
2Th 2: 3 first, and the man of sin is **r**
2Th 2: 6 that he may be **r** in his own
2Th 2: 8 the lawless one will be **r**
2Ti 1:10 but has now been **r** by the
1Pe 1: 5 to be **r** in the last time
1Pe 1:12 To them it was **r** that, not to
1Pe 4:13 that when His glory is **r**
1Pe 5: 1 of the glory that will be **r**
1Jn 3: 2 yet been **r** what we shall be
1Jn 3: 2 but we know that when He is **r**
Rev 3:18 your nakedness may not be **r**

REVEALER (*see* REVEAL)
Dan 2:47 a **r** of secrets, since you

REVEALING (*see* REVEAL)
Rom 8:19 for the **r** of the sons of God

REVEALS (*see* REVEAL)
1Sa 22: 8 there is no one who **r** to me
1Sa 22: 8 me or **r** to me that my son has
Ps 19: 2 night unto night **r** knowledge
Prov 11:13 A talebearer **r** secrets, but
Prov 20:19 as a talebearer **r** secrets
Prov 27:19 As in water face **r** face, so a
Prov 27:19 so a man's heart **r** the man
Prov 29:24 tell the truth, but **r** nothing
Dan 2:22 He **r** deep and secret things
Dan 2:28 a God in heaven who **r** secrets
Dan 2:29 He who **r** secrets has made
Amos 3: 7 unless He **r** His secret to His

REVELATION (*see* REVEAL, REVELATIONS)
1Sa 3: 1 there was no widespread **r**
Prov 29:18 Where there is no **r**, the
Luke 2:32 to bring **r** to the Gentiles
Rom 2: 5 **r** of the righteous judgment
Rom 16:25 according to the **r** of the
1Co 1: 7 eagerly waiting for the **r** of
1Co 14: 6 I speak to you either by **r**
1Co 14:26 has a tongue, has a **r**, has
Gal 1:12 through the **r** of Jesus Christ
Gal 2: 2 And I went up by **r**, and
Eph 1:17 **r** in the knowledge of Him,
Eph 3: 3 how that by **r** He made known
1Pe 1: 7 and glory at the **r** of Jesus
1Pe 1:13 you at the **r** of Jesus Christ
Rev 1: 1 The **R** of Jesus Christ, which

REVELATIONS (*see* REVELATION)
2Co 12: 1 to visions and **r** of the Lord
2Co 12: 7 by the abundance of the **r**

REVELRIES (*see* REVELRY)
Gal 5:21 envy, murders, drunkenness, **r**
1Pe 4: 3 lusts, drunkenness, **r**,

REVELRY (*see* REVELRIES)
Rom 13:13 as in the day, not in **r** and

REVENGE
Josh 10:13 had **r** upon their enemies
Judg 15: 7 I will surely take **r** on you
Jer 20:10 and we will take our **r** on him

REVENUE (*see* REVENUES)
2Sa 20:24 Adoram was in charge of **r**
1Ki 12:18 who was in charge of the **r**
2Ch 10:18 who was in charge of **r**
Prov 8:19 and my **r** than choice silver
Prov 15: 6 but in the **r** of the wicked is
Is 23: 3 of the River, is her **r**

REVENUES (*see* REVENUE)
Prov 16: 8 than vast **r** without justice

REVERE (*see* REVERENCE, REVERENT)
Lev 19: 3 one of you shall **r** his mother

REVERENCE (*see* REVERE)
Lev 19:30 and **r** My sanctuary
Lev 26: 2 and **r** My sanctuary
Job 4: 6 Is not your **r** your confidence
Ps 89: 7 to be held in **r** by all those
Mal 1: 6 I am a Master, where is My **r**
1Ti 2: 2 life in all godliness and **r**
1Ti 3: 4 in submission with all **r**
Tit 2: 7 doctrine showing integrity, **r**
Heb 12:28 serve God acceptably with **r**

REVERENT (*see* REVERE)
Prov 28:14 is the man who is always **r**
Mal 2: 5 Me and was **r** before My name
1Ti 3: 8 Likewise deacons must be **r**
1Ti 3:11 their wives must be **r**, not
Tit 2: 2 the older men be sober, **r**
Tit 2: 3 that they be **r** in behavior

REVERSE
Num 23:20 has blessed, and I cannot **r** it
Is 43:13 I work, and who will **r** it

REVERTED
Judg 2:19 judge was dead, that they **r**

REVIEW
1Sa 29: 2 passed in **r** by hundreds and by
1Sa 29: 2 his men passed in **r** at the

REVILE (*see* REVILED, REVILER, REVILERS, REVILES, REVILING)
Ex 22:28 You shall not **r** God, nor
2Ch 32:17 to **r** the LORD God of Israel
Matt 5:11 Blessed are you when they **r**
Luke 6:22 **r** you, and cast out your name
Acts 23: 4 Do you **r** God's high priest
1Pe 2:23 reviled, did not **r** in return
1Pe 3:16 those who **r** your good conduct

REVILED (*see* REVILE)
1Sa 25:14 and he **r** them
Matt 27:44 Him **r** Him with the same thing
Mark 15:32 were crucified with Him **r** Him
John 9:28 Then they **r** him and said
1Co 4:12 Being **r**, we bless
1Pe 2:23 who, when He was **r**, did not

REVILER (*see* REVILE)
1Co 5:11 or an idolater, or a **r**, or a

REVILERS (*see* REVILE)
1Co 6:10 nor drunkards, nor **r**, nor

REVILES (*see* REVILE)
Ps 44:16 of him who reproaches and **r**

REVILING (*see* REVILE, REVILINGS)
1Ti 6: 4 which come envy, strife, **r**
1Pe 3: 9 for evil or **r** for **r**
2Pe 2:11 do not bring a **r** accusation
Jude 9 against him a **r** accusation

REVILINGS (*see* REVILING)
Is 51: 7 men, nor be afraid of their **r**
Zeph 2: 8 the **r** of the people of Ammon,

REVIVAL (*see* REVIVE)
Ezra 9: 8 a measure of **r** in our bondage

REVIVE (*see* REVIVAL, REVIVED)
Ezra 9: 9 the kings of Persia, to **r** us
Neh 4: 2 Will they **r** the stones from
Ps 71:20 Shall **r** me again, And bring me
Ps 80:18 **R** us, and we will call upon
Ps 85: 6 Will You not **r** us again, That
Ps 119:25 **R** me according to Your word
Ps 119:37 things, And **r** me in Your way
Ps 119:40 **R** me in Your righteousness
Ps 119:88 **R** me according to Your
Ps 119:107 **R** me, O LORD, according to
Ps 119:149 LORD, **r** me according to Your
Ps 119:154 **R** me according to Your word
Ps 119:156 **R** me according to Your
Ps 119:159 **R** me, O LORD, according to
Ps 138: 7 of trouble, You will **r** me
Ps 143:11 **R** me, O LORD, for Your name's
Is 57:15 to **r** the spirit of the humble
Is 57:15 and to **r** the heart of the
Hos 6: 2 After two days He will **r** us
Hab 3: 2 **r** Your work in the midst of

REVIVED (*see* REVIVE)
Gen 45:27 of Jacob their father **r**
Judg 15:19 his spirit returned, and he **r**
1Ki 17:22 came back to him, and he **r**
2Ki 13:21 the bones of Elisha, he **r**
Hos 14: 7 they shall be **r** like grain
Rom 7: 9 the commandment came, sin **r**

REVOKE
Esth 8: 5 let it be written to **r** the
Esth 8: 8 signet ring no one can **r**

REVOLT (*see* REVOLTED, REVOLTERS)
2Ki 8:22 Thus Edom has been in **r**
2Ch 21:10 **r** against Judah's authority
Is 1: 5 You will **r** more and more
Is 59:13 God, speaking oppression and **r**

REVOLTED (*see* REVOLT)
2Ki 8:20 In his days Edom **r** against
2Ki 8:22 And Libnah **r** at that time
2Ch 21: 8 In his days the Edomites **r**
2Ch 21:10 Libnah **r** against his rule
Is 31: 6 of Israel have deeply **r**
Jer 5:23 they have **r** and departed

REVOLTERS (*see* REVOLT)
Hos 5: 2 The **r** are deeply involved in

REWARD (*see* REWARDED, REWARDER, REWARDING, REWARDS)
Gen 15: 1 your exceedingly great **r**
Num 18:31 for it is your **r** for your
Ruth 2:12 a full **r** be given you by the
1Sa 24:19 Therefore may the LORD **r** you
2Sa 4:10 give him a **r** for his news
2Sa 19:36 king repay me with such a **r**
1Ki 13: 7 and I will give you a **r**
Job 15:31 for futility will be his **r**
Job 34:11 and makes man to find a **r**
Ps 19:11 keeping them there is great **r**
Ps 35:12 They **r** me evil for good, To
Ps 58:11 is a **r** for the righteous
Ps 91: 8 And see the **r** of the wicked
Ps 109:20 the LORD's **r** to my accusers
Ps 127: 3 fruit of the womb is His **r**
Prov 11:18 will be a sure **r**
Prov 25:22 head, and the LORD will **r** you
Eccl 2:10 this was my **r** from all my
Eccl 4: 9 have a good **r** for their labor
Eccl 9: 5 and they have no more **r**, for
Is 3:11 for the **r** of his hands shall
Is 40:10 His **r** is with Him, and His
Is 45:13 go free, not for price nor **r**
Is 49: 4 my just **r** is with the LORD
Is 62:11 His **r** is with Him, and His
Hos 4: 9 and **r** them for their deeds
Hos 9: 1 You have loved for **r** on every
Matt 5:12 for great is your **r** in heaven
Matt 5:46 who love you, what **r** have you
Matt 6: 1 Otherwise you have no **r** from
Matt 6: 2 say to you, they have their **r**
Matt 6: 4 will Himself **r** you openly
Matt 6: 5 say to you, they have their **r**
Matt 6: 6 in secret will **r** you openly
Matt 6:16 say to you, they have their **r**
Matt 6:18 in secret will **r** you openly
Matt 10:41 shall receive a prophet's **r**
Matt 10:41 receive a righteous man's **r**
Matt 10:42 shall by no means lose his **r**
Matt 16:27 then He will **r** each according
Mark 9:41 will by no means lose his **r**
Luke 6:23 for indeed your **r** is great in
Luke 6:35 your **r** will be great, and you
Luke 23:41 the due **r** of our deeds
1Co 3: 8 one will receive his own **r**
1Co 3:14 endures, he will receive a **r**
1Co 9:17 do this willingly, I have a **r**
1Co 9:18 What is my **r** then
Col 2:18 no one defraud you of your **r**
Col 3:24 the **r** of the inheritance
Heb 2: 2 received a just **r**,
Heb 10:35 confidence, which has great **r**
Heb 11:26 for he looked to the **r**
2Jn 8 that we may receive a full **r**
Rev 11:18 and that You should **r** Your
Rev 22:12 My **r** is with Me, to give to

REWARDED (*see* REWARD)
1Sa 24:17 for you have **r** me with good
1Sa 24:17 I have **r** you with evil
2Sa 22:21 The LORD **r** me according to my
2Ch 15: 7 for your work shall be **r**

Ps 63: 8 Your **r** hand upholds me
Ps 73:23 You hold me by my **r** hand
Ps 74:11 Your hand, even Your **r** hand
Ps 77:10 the **r** hand of the Most High
Ps 78:54 which His **r** hand had acquired
Ps 80:15 which Your **r** hand has planted
Ps 80:17 upon the man of Your **r** hand
Ps 89:13 hand, and high is Your **r** hand
Ps 89:25 his **r** hand over the rivers
Ps 89:42 You have exalted the **r** hand
Ps 91: 7 ten thousand at your **r** hand
Ps 98: 1 His **r** hand and His holy arm
Ps 107: 7 led them forth by the **r** way
Ps 108: 6 Save with Your **r** hand, and
Ps 109: 6 accuser stand at his **r** hand
Ps 109:31 at the **r** hand of the poor
Ps 110: 1 Sit at My **r** hand, Till I make
Ps 110: 5 The Lord is at Your **r** hand
Ps 118:15 The **r** hand of the LORD does
Ps 118:16 The **r** hand of the LORD is
Ps 118:16 The **r** hand of the LORD does
Ps 119:75 that Your judgments are **r**
Ps 119:128 all things I consider to be **r**
Ps 121: 5 is your shade at your **r** hand
Ps 137: 5 Let my **r** hand forget her
Ps 138: 7 And Your **r** hand will save me
Ps 139:10 Your **r** hand shall hold me
Ps 142: 4 Look on my **r** hand and see, For
Ps 144: 8 whose **r** hand is a **r** hand
Ps 144:11 whose **r** hand is a **r** hand
Prov 3:16 of days is in her **r** hand, in
Prov 4:11 I have led you in **r** paths
Prov 4:25 eyelids look **r** before you
Prov 4:27 not turn to the **r** or the left
Prov 8: 6 of my lips will come **r** things
Prov 8: 9 **r** to those who find knowledge
Prov 11:24 who withholds more than is **r**
Prov 12: 5 of the righteous are **r**, but
Prov 12:15 a fool is **r** in his own eyes
Prov 14:12 a way which seems **r** to a man
Prov 16:13 love him who speaks what is **r**
Prov 16:25 a way that seems **r** to a man
Prov 18:17 to plead his cause seems **r**
Prov 20:11 what he does is pure and **r**
Prov 21: 2 of a man is **r** in his own eyes
Prov 21: 8 for the pure, his work is **r**
Prov 23:16 when your lips speak **r** things
Prov 24:26 He who gives a **r** answer
Prov 27:16 and grasps oil with his **r** hand
Prov 28: 2 knowledge **r** will be prolonged
Eccl 10: 2 man's heart is at his **r** hand
Song 2: 6 and his **r** hand embraces me
Song 8: 3 and his **r** hand embraces me
Is 9:20 he shall snatch on the **r** hand
Is 10: 2 to take what is **r** from the
Is 28:26 instructs him in **r** judgment
Is 30:10 not prophesy to us **r** things
Is 30:21 **r** hand or whenever you turn
Is 41:10 you with My righteous **r** hand
Is 41:13 God, will hold your **r** hand
Is 44:20 there not a lie in my **r** hand
Is 45: 1 whose **r** hand I have held
Is 45:19 I declare things that are **r**
Is 48:13 My **r** hand has stretched out
Is 54: 3 For you shall expand to the **r**
Is 62: 8 LORD has sworn by His **r** hand
Is 63:12 them by the **r** hand of Moses
Jer 5:28 the **r** of the needy they do
Jer 17:11 who gets riches, but not by **r**
Jer 17:16 it was **r** there before You
Jer 22:24 were the signet on My **r** hand
Jer 23:10 evil, and their might is not **r**
Jer 32: 7 for the **r** of redemption is
Jer 32: 8 for the **r** of inheritance is
Jer 34:15 and did what was **r** in My sight
Jer 48:30 But it is not **r**
Jer 48:30 his lies have made nothing **r**
Lam 2: 3 He has drawn back His **r** hand
Lam 2: 4 with His **r** hand, like an
Ezek 1:10 face of a lion on the **r** side
Ezek 4: 6 lie again on your **r** side
Ezek 18: 5 and does what is lawful and **r**
Ezek 18:19 has done what is lawful and **r**
Ezek 18:21 and does what is lawful and **r**
Ezek 18:27 and does what is lawful and **r**
Ezek 21:16 Thrust **r**! Set your blade!
Ezek 21:22 In his **r** hand is the
Ezek 21:27 until He comes whose **r** it is
Ezek 33:14 and does what is lawful and **r**
Ezek 33:16 has done what is lawful and **r**
Ezek 33:19 and does what is lawful and **r**
Ezek 39: 3 to fall out of your **r** hand
Ezek 47: 1 the **r** side of the temple,
Ezek 47: 2 running out on the **r** side
Dan 12: 7 when he held up his **r** hand
Hos 14: 9 the ways of the LORD are **r**
Amos 3:10 For they do not know to do **r**
Jon 4: 4 Is it **r** for you to be angry
Jon 4: 9 Is it **r** for you to be angry
Jon 4: 9 It is **r** for me to be angry,
Jon 4:11 discern between their **r** hand
Hab 2:16 The cup of the LORD's **r** hand
Zech 3: 1 at his **r** hand to oppose him
Zech 4: 3 one at the **r** of the bowl and
Zech 4:11 one at the **r** of the lampstand
Zech 11:17 his arm and against his **r** eye
Zech 11:17 his **r** eye shall be totally
Zech 12: 6 peoples on the **r** hand and on
Matt 5:29 if your **r** eye causes you to
Matt 5:30 if your **r** hand causes you to
Matt 5:39 slaps you on your **r** cheek
Matt 6: 3 what your **r** hand is doing
Matt 20: 4 whatever is **r** I will give you
Matt 20: 7 and whatever is **r** you will
Matt 20:21 may sit, one on Your **r** hand
Matt 20:23 but to sit on My **r** hand and on
Matt 22:44 Sit at My **r** hand, till I make
Matt 25:33 set the sheep on His **r** hand
Matt 25:34 say to those on His **r** hand
Matt 26:64 at the **r** hand of the Power
Matt 27:29 head, and a reed in His **r** hand
Matt 27:38 with Him, one on the **r** and
Mark 5:15 and clothed and in his **r** mind
Mark 10:37 may sit, one on Your **r** hand
Mark 10:40 but to sit on My **r** hand and on
Mark 12:36 Sit at My **r** hand, till I make
Mark 14:54 **r** into the courtyard of the
Mark 14:62 at the **r** hand of the Power
Mark 15:27 two robbers, one on His **r**
Mark 16: 5 robe sitting on the **r** side
Mark 16:19 sat down at the **r** hand of God
Luke 1:11 standing on the **r** side of the
Luke 6: 6 whose **r** hand was withered
Luke 8:35 clothed and in his **r** mind
Luke 12:57 do you not judge what is **r**
Luke 15:32 It was **r** that we should make
Luke 20:42 sit at My **r** hand,
Luke 22:50 priest and cut off his **r** ear
Luke 22:69 **r** hand of the power of God
Luke 23:33 criminals, one on the **r** hand
John 1:12 Him, to them He gave the **r** to
John 18:10 servant, and cut off his **r** ear
John 21: 6 net on the **r** side of the boat
Acts 2:25 face, for He is at my **r** hand
Acts 2:33 exalted to the **r** hand of God
Acts 2:34 Sit at My **r** hand,
Acts 3: 7 And he took him by the **r** hand
Acts 4:19 Whether it is **r** in the sight
Acts 5:31 to His **r** hand to be Prince
Acts 7:55 standing at the **r** hand of God
Acts 7:56 standing at the **r** hand of God
Acts 8:21 is not **r** in the sight of God
Rom 8:34 is even at the **r** hand of God
1Co 9: 4 Do we have no **r** to eat and
1Co 9: 5 Do we have no **r** to take along
1Co 9: 6 I who have no **r** to refrain
1Co 9:12 partakers of this **r** over you
1Co 9:12 we have not used this **r**, but
2Co 6: 7 righteousness on the **r** hand
Gal 2: 9 me and Barnabas the **r** hand of
Eph 1:20 seated Him at His **r** hand in
Eph 6: 1 in the Lord, for this is **r**
Phil 1: 7 just as it is **r** for me to
Col 3: 1 sitting at the **r** hand of God
Heb 1: 3 sat down at the **r** hand of the
Heb 1:13 Sit at My **r** hand, Till I make
Heb 8: 1 who is seated at the **r** hand
Heb 10:12 sat down at the **r** hand of God
Heb 12: 2 has sat down at the **r** hand of
Heb 13:10 tabernacle have no **r** to eat
1Pe 3:22 and is at the **r** hand of God,
2Pe 1:13 Yes, I think it is **r**, as long
2Pe 2:15 They have forsaken the **r** way
Rev 1:16 He had in His **r** hand seven
Rev 1:17 But He laid His **r** hand on me
Rev 1:20 which you saw in My **r** hand
Rev 2: 1 the seven stars in His **r** hand
Rev 5: 1 I saw in the **r** hand of Him
Rev 5: 7 **r** hand of Him who sat on the
Rev 10: 2 he set his **r** foot on the sea
Rev 13:16 **r** hand or on their foreheads
Rev 22:14 the **r** to the tree of life

RIGHTEOUS (*see* RIGHTEOUSLY, RIGHTEOUSNESS, UNRIGHTEOUS)

Gen 7: 1 you are **r** before Me in this
Gen 18:23 destroy the **r** with the wicked
Gen 18:24 were fifty **r** within the city
Gen 18:24 the fifty **r** that were in it
Gen 18:25 to slay the **r** with the wicked
Gen 18:25 so that the **r** should be as
Gen 18:26 Sodom fifty **r** within the city
Gen 18:28 five less than the fifty **r**
Gen 20: 4 will You slay a **r** nation also
Gen 38:26 She has been more **r** than I
Ex 9:27 The LORD is **r**, and my people
Ex 23: 7 do not kill the innocent and **r**
Ex 23: 8 perverts the words of the **r**
Num 23:10 Let me die the death of the **r**
Deut 4: 8 **r** judgments as are in all
Deut 16:19 and twists the words of the **r**
Deut 25: 1 them, and they justify the **r**
Deut 32: 4 **r** and upright is He
Judg 5:11 the **r** acts of the LORD, the
Judg 5:11 the **r** acts for His villagers
1Sa 12: 7 **r** acts of the LORD which He
1Sa 24:17 You are more **r** than I
2Sa 4:11 wicked men have killed a **r**
1Ki 2:32 he struck down two men more **r**
1Ki 8:32 justifying the **r** by giving
2Ki 10: 9 You are **r**
2Ch 6:23 justifying the **r** by giving
2Ch 12: 6 The LORD is **r**
Ezra 9:15 LORD God of Israel, You are **r**
Neh 9: 8 Your words, for You are **r**
Job 4:17 a mortal be more **r** than God
Job 9: 2 how can a man be **r** before God
Job 9:15 For though I were **r**, I could
Job 9:20 Though I were **r**, my own mouth
Job 10:15 even if I am **r**, I cannot lift
Job 15:14 a woman, that he could be **r**
Job 17: 9 Yet the **r** will hold to his
Job 22: 3 the Almighty that you are **r**
Job 22:19 The **r** see it and are glad, and
Job 25: 4 then can man be **r** before God
Job 32: 1 because he was **r** in his own
Job 33:12 Look, in this you are not **r**
Job 34: 5 For Job has said, I am **r**
Job 35: 7 If you are **r**, what do you
Job 36: 7 withdraw His eyes from the **r**
Ps 1: 5 in the congregation of the **r**
Ps 1: 6 LORD knows the way of the **r**
Ps 5:12 You, O LORD, will bless the **r**
Ps 7: 9 For the **r** God tests the
Ps 11: 3 destroyed, What can the **r** do
Ps 11: 5 The LORD tests the **r**, But the
Ps 11: 7 For the LORD is **r**, He loves
Ps 14: 5 with the generation of the **r**
Ps 19: 9 LORD are true and **r** altogether
Ps 31:18 contemptuously against the **r**
Ps 32:11 in the LORD and rejoice, you **r**
Ps 33: 1 Rejoice in the LORD, O you **r**
Ps 34:15 eyes of the LORD are on the **r**
Ps 34:17 The **r** cry out, and the LORD
Ps 34:19 are the afflictions of the **r**
Ps 34:21 hate the **r** shall be condemned
Ps 35:27 be glad, Who favor my **r** cause
Ps 37:16 A little that a **r** man has Is
Ps 37:17 But the LORD upholds the **r**
Ps 37:21 But the **r** shows mercy and
Ps 37:25 have not seen the **r** forsaken
Ps 37:29 The **r** shall inherit the land,
Ps 37:30 mouth of the **r** speaks wisdom
Ps 37:32 The wicked watches the **r**, And
Ps 37:39 of the **r** is from the LORD
Ps 52: 6 The **r** also shall see and fear,
Ps 55:22 permit the **r** to be moved
Ps 58:10 The **r** shall rejoice when he
Ps 58:11 there is a reward for the **r**
Ps 64:10 The **r** shall be glad in the
Ps 68: 3 But let the **r** be glad
Ps 69:28 And not be written with the **r**
Ps 72: 7 His days the **r** shall flourish
Ps 75:10 of the **r** shall be exalted
Ps 92:12 The **r** shall flourish like a
Ps 94:21 against the life of the **r**
Ps 97:11 Light is sown for the **r**, And
Ps 97:12 Rejoice in the LORD, you **r**
Ps 107:42 The **r** see it and rejoice, And
Ps 112: 4 and full of compassion, and **r**
Ps 112: 6 The **r** will be in everlasting

Ps 116: 5 Gracious is the LORD, and **r**
Ps 118:15 Is in the tents of the **r**
Ps 118:20 which the **r** shall enter
Ps 119: 7 When I learn Your **r** judgments
Ps 119:62 Because of Your **r** judgments
Ps 119:106 I will keep Your **r** judgments
Ps 119:123 Your salvation And Your **r**
Ps 119:137 **R** are You, O LORD, And
Ps 119:138 You have commanded, Are **r**
Ps 119:160 every one of Your **r** judgments
Ps 119:164 Because of Your **r** judgments
Ps 125: 3 On the land allotted to the **r**
Ps 125: 3 Lest the **r** reach out their
Ps 129: 4 The LORD is **r**
Ps 140:13 Surely the **r** shall give
Ps 141: 5 Let the **r** strike me
Ps 142: 7 The **r** shall surround me, For
Ps 143: 2 Your sight no one living is **r**
Ps 145:17 The LORD is **r** in all His ways
Ps 146: 8 The LORD loves the **r**
Prov 10: 3 allow the **r** soul to famish
Prov 10: 6 are on the head of the **r**, but
Prov 10: 7 memory of the **r** is blessed
Prov 10:11 The mouth of the **r** is a well
Prov 10:16 labor of the **r** leads to life
Prov 10:20 of the **r** is choice silver
Prov 10:21 The lips of the **r** feed many
Prov 10:24 of the **r** will be granted
Prov 10:25 but the **r** has an everlasting
Prov 10:28 The hope of the **r** will be
Prov 10:30 The **r** will never be removed,
Prov 10:31 The mouth of the **r** brings
Prov 10:32 The lips of the **r** know what
Prov 11: 8 The **r** is delivered from
Prov 11: 9 the **r** will be delivered
Prov 11:10 When it goes well with the **r**
Prov 11:21 of the **r** will be delivered
Prov 11:23 desire of the **r** is only good
Prov 11:28 but the **r** will flourish like
Prov 11:30 The fruit of the **r** is a tree
Prov 11:31 If the **r** will be recompensed
Prov 12: 3 root of the **r** cannot be moved
Prov 12: 5 thoughts of the **r** are right
Prov 12: 7 the house of the **r** will stand
Prov 12:10 A **r** man regards the life of
Prov 12:12 root of the **r** yields fruit
Prov 12:13 but the **r** will come through
Prov 12:21 trouble will overtake the **r**
Prov 12:26 The **r** should choose his
Prov 13: 5 A **r** man hates lying, but a
Prov 13: 9 The light of the **r** rejoices
Prov 13:21 pursues sinners, but to the **r**
Prov 13:22 sinner is stored up for the **r**
Prov 13:25 The **r** eats to the satisfying
Prov 14:19 wicked at the gates of the **r**
Prov 14:32 but the **r** has a refuge in his
Prov 15: 6 In the house of the **r** there
Prov 15:28 The heart of the **r** studies
Prov 15:29 He hears the prayer of the **r**
Prov 16:13 **R** lips are the delight of
Prov 17:26 to punish the **r** is not good
Prov 18: 5 overthrow the **r** in judgment
Prov 18:10 the **r** run to it and are safe
Prov 20: 7 The **r** man walks in his
Prov 21:12 The **r** God wisely considers
Prov 21:18 shall be a ransom for the **r**
Prov 21:26 all day long, but the **r** gives
Prov 23:24 The father of the **r** will
Prov 24:15 against the dwelling of the **r**
Prov 24:16 for a **r** man may fall seven
Prov 24:24 You are **r**," him the people
Prov 25:26 A **r** man who falters before
Prov 28: 1 but the **r** are bold as a lion
Prov 28:12 When the **r** rejoice, there is
Prov 28:28 they perish, the **r** increase
Prov 29: 2 When the **r** are in authority,
Prov 29: 6 is snared, but the **r** sings
Prov 29: 7 The **r** considers the cause of
Prov 29:16 but the **r** will see their fall
Prov 29:27 is an abomination to the **r**
Eccl 3:17 God shall judge the **r** and the
Eccl 7:16 Do not be overly **r**, nor be
Eccl 8:14 to the work of the **r**
Eccl 9: 1 that the **r** and the wise and
Eccl 9: 2 One event happens to the **r**
Is 3:10 Say to the **r** that it shall be
Is 5:23 away justice from the **r** man
Is 24:16 Glory to the **r**
Is 26: 2 that the **r** nation which keeps
Is 41:10 you with My **r** right hand
Is 41:26 that we may say, 'He is **r**'
Is 49:24 of the **r** be delivered
Is 53:11 by His knowledge My **r** Servant
Is 57: 1 The **r** perishes, and no man
Is 57: 1 the **r** is taken away from evil
Is 60:21 your people shall all be **r**
Jer 3:11 more **r** than treacherous Judah
Jer 12: 1 **R** are You, O LORD, when I
Jer 20:12 of hosts, You who test the **r**
Lam 1:18 The LORD is **r**, for I rebelled
Ezek 3:20 when a **r** man turns from his
Ezek 3:21 if you warn the **r** man
Ezek 3:21 that the **r** should not sin
Ezek 13:22 made the heart of the **r** sad
Ezek 16:52 they are more **r** than you
Ezek 18:20 the **r** shall be upon himself
Ezek 18:24 But when a **r** man turns away
Ezek 18:26 When a **r** man turns away from
Ezek 21: 3 its sheath and cut off both **r**
Ezek 21: 4 Because I will cut off both **r**
Ezek 23:45 But **r** men will judge them
Ezek 33:12 **r** man shall not deliver him
Ezek 33:12 nor shall the **r** be able to
Ezek 33:13 When I say to the **r** that he
Ezek 33:13 none of his **r** works shall be
Ezek 33:18 When the **r** turns from his
Dan 4:27 off your sins by being **r**, and
Dan 9:14 for the LORD our God is **r** in
Dan 9:18 You because of our **r** deeds
Hos 14: 9 the **r** walk in them, but
Amos 2: 6 they sell the **r** for silver
Hab 1: 4 For the wicked surround the **r**
Hab 1:13 devours one more **r** than he
Zeph 3: 5 The LORD is **r**, he is in her
Mal 3:18 again discern between the **r**
Matt 9:13 I did not come to call the **r**
Matt 10:41 he who receives a **r** man
Matt 10:41 in the name of a **r** man shall
Matt 10:41 receive a **r** man's reward
Matt 13:17 **r** men desired to see what you
Matt 13:43 Then the **r** will shine forth
Matt 23:28 outwardly appear **r** to men
Matt 23:29 adorn the monuments of the **r**
Matt 23:35 the **r** blood shed on the earth
Matt 23:35 from the blood of **r** Abel to
Matt 25:37 Then the **r** will answer Him,
Matt 25:46 but the **r** into eternal life
Mark 2:17 I did not come to call the **r**
Luke 1: 6 they were both **r** before God
Luke 5:32 I have not come to call the **r**
Luke 18: 9 themselves that they were **r**
Luke 20:20 spies who pretended to be **r**
Luke 23:47 Certainly this was a **r** Man
John 5:30 and My judgment is **r**, because
John 7:24 but judge with **r** judgment
John 17:25 O **r** Father! The world has
Rom 1:32 knowing the **r** judgment of God
Rom 2: 5 of the **r** judgment of God,
Rom 2:26 the **r** requirements of the law
Rom 3:10 There is none **r**, no, not one
Rom 5: 7 for a **r** man will one die
Rom 5:18 **r** act the free gift came to
Rom 5:19 obedience many will be made **r**
Rom 8: 4 that the **r** requirement of the
2Th 1: 5 of the **r** judgment of God,
2Th 1: 6 since it is a **r** thing with
1Ti 1: 9 is not made for a **r** person
2Ti 4: 8 the **r** Judge, will give to me
Heb 11: 4 witness that he was **r**, God
Jas 5:16 prayer of a **r** man avails much
1Pe 3:12 eyes of the LORD are on the **r**
1Pe 4:18 If the **r** one is scarcely
2Pe 2: 7 and delivered **r** Lot, who was
2Pe 2: 8 (for that **r** man, dwelling
2Pe 2: 8 tormented his **r** soul from day
1Jn 2: 1 Father, Jesus Christ the **r**
1Jn 2:29 If you know that He is **r**, you
1Jn 3: 7 is **r**, just as He is **r**
1Jn 3:12 were evil and his brother's **r**
Rev 16: 5 You are **r**, O Lord, the One
Rev 16: 7 true and **r** are Your judgments
Rev 19: 2 **r** are His judgments, because
Rev 19: 8 is the **r** acts of the saints
Rev 22:11 who is **r**, let him be **r** still

RIGHTEOUSLY (*see* RIGHTEOUS)
Deut 1:16 judge **r** between a man and his
Ps 67: 4 You shall judge the people **r**
Ps 96:10 He shall judge the peoples **r**
Prov 31: 9 Open your mouth, judge **r**, and
Is 33:15 He who walks **r** and speaks
Jer 11:20 of hosts, you who judge **r**
Tit 2:12 we should live soberly, **r**
1Pe 2:23 Himself to Him who judges **r**

RIGHTEOUSNESS (*see* RIGHTEOUS, RIGHTEOUSNESS', RIGHTEOUSNESSES)
Gen 15: 6 He accounted it to him for **r**
Gen 18:19 the way of the LORD, to do **r**
Gen 30:33 So my **r** will answer for me in
Lev 19:15 But in **r** you shall judge your
Deut 6:25 Then it will be **r** for us
Deut 9: 4 Because of my **r** the LORD has
Deut 9: 5 It is not because of your **r**
Deut 9: 6 to possess because of your **r**
Deut 24:13 it shall be **r** to you before
Deut 33:19 shall offer sacrifices of **r**
1Sa 26:23 repay every man for his **r**
2Sa 22:21 rewarded me according to my **r**
2Sa 22:25 me according to my **r**,
1Ki 3: 6 before You in truth, in **r**
1Ki 8:32 giving him according to his **r**
1Ki 10: 9 you king, to do justice and **r**
2Ch 6:23 giving him according to his **r**
2Ch 9: 8 over them, to do justice and **r**
Job 6:29 turn again, my **r** still stands
Job 27: 6 My **r** I hold fast, and will not
Job 29:14 I put on **r**, and it clothed me
Job 33:26 for He restores to man His **r**
Job 35: 2 My **r** is more than God's'
Job 35: 8 you, and your **r** a son of man
Job 36: 3 I will ascribe **r** to my Maker
Ps 4: 1 me when I call, O God of my **r**
Ps 4: 5 Offer the sacrifices of **r**
Ps 5: 8 LORD, in Your **r** because of my
Ps 7: 8 me, O LORD, according to my **r**
Ps 7:17 the LORD according to His **r**
Ps 9: 4 on the throne judging in **r**
Ps 9: 8 He shall judge the world in **r**
Ps 11: 7 LORD is righteous, He loves **r**
Ps 15: 2 walks uprightly, And works **r**
Ps 17:15 me, I will see Your face in **r**
Ps 18:20 rewarded me according to my **r**
Ps 18:24 me according to my **r**,
Ps 22:31 declare His **r** to a people who
Ps 23: 3 of **r** For His name's sake
Ps 24: 5 And **r** from the God of his
Ps 31: 1 Deliver me in Your **r**
Ps 33: 5 He loves **r** and justice
Ps 35:24 my God, according to Your **r**
Ps 35:28 tongue shall speak of Your **r**
Ps 36: 6 Your **r** is like the great
Ps 36:10 And Your **r** to the upright in
Ps 37: 6 forth your **r** as the light
Ps 40: 9 **r** In the great congregation
Ps 40:10 hidden Your **r** within my heart
Ps 45: 4 of truth, humility, and **r**
Ps 45: 6 A scepter of **r** is the scepter
Ps 45: 7 You love **r** and hate wickedness
Ps 48:10 Your right hand is full of **r**
Ps 50: 6 Let the heavens declare His **r**
Ps 51:14 shall sing aloud of Your **r**
Ps 51:19 with the sacrifices of **r**,
Ps 52: 3 lying rather than speaking **r**
Ps 58: 1 Do you indeed speak **r**, you
Ps 65: 5 deeds in **r** You will answer us
Ps 69:27 let them not come into Your **r**
Ps 71: 2 Deliver me in Your **r**, and
Ps 71:15 My mouth shall tell of Your **r**
Ps 71:16 I will make mention of Your **r**
Ps 71:19 Also Your **r**, O God, is very
Ps 71:24 of Your **r** all the day long
Ps 72: 1 And Your **r** to the king's Son
Ps 72: 2 will judge Your people with **r**
Ps 72: 3 And the little hills, by **r**
Ps 85:10 **R** and peace have kissed each
Ps 85:11 **r** shall look down from heaven
Ps 85:13 **R** will go before Him, And
Ps 88:12 And Your **r** in the land of
Ps 89:14 **R** and justice are the
Ps 89:16 in Your **r** they are exalted
Ps 94:15 But judgment will return to **r**
Ps 96:13 shall judge the world with **r**
Ps 97: 2 **R** and justice are the
Ps 97: 6 The heavens declare His **r**
Ps 98: 2 His **r** He has openly shown in
Ps 98: 9 With **r** He shall judge the
Ps 99: 4 justice and **r** in Jacob
Ps 103: 6 The LORD executes **r** And
Ps 103:17 His **r** to children's children,
Ps 106: 3 he who does **r** at all times
Ps 106:31 him for **r** To all generations

Ps 111: 3 And His **r** endures forever
Ps 112: 3 And his **r** endures forever
Ps 112: 9 His **r** endures forever
Ps 118:19 Open to me the gates of **r**
Ps 119:40 Revive me in Your **r**
Ps 119:121 I have done justice and **r**
Ps 119:142 Your **r** is an everlasting **r**
Ps 119:144 The **r** of Your testimonies is
Ps 119:172 all Your commandments are **r**
Ps 132: 9 priests be clothed with **r**
Ps 143: 1 answer me, And in Your **r**
Ps 145: 7 And shall sing of Your **r**
Prov 2: 9 Then you will understand **r**
Prov 2:20 and keep to the paths of **r**
Prov 8: 8 words of my mouth are with **r**
Prov 8:18 with me, enduring riches and **r**
Prov 8:20 I traverse the way of **r**, in
Prov 10: 2 but **r** delivers from death
Prov 11: 4 but **r** delivers from death
Prov 11: 5 The **r** of the blameless will
Prov 11: 6 The **r** of the upright will
Prov 11:18 but to him who sows **r** will be
Prov 11:19 As **r** leads to life, so he who
Prov 12:17 who speaks truth declares **r**
Prov 12:28 In the way of **r** is life, and
Prov 13: 6 **R** keeps him whose way is
Prov 14:34 **R** exalts a nation, but sin is
Prov 15: 9 He loves him who follows **r**
Prov 16: 8 Better is a little with **r**
Prov 16:12 a throne is established by **r**
Prov 16:31 it is found in the way of **r**
Prov 21: 3 To do **r** and justice is more
Prov 21:21 He who follows **r** and mercy
Prov 21:21 finds life, **r** and honor
Prov 25: 5 will be established in **r**
Eccl 3:16 and in the place of **r**,
Eccl 5: 8 and **r** in a province, do not
Eccl 7:15 man who perishes in his **r**
Is 1:21 **r** lodged in it, but now
Is 1:26 shall be called the city of **r**
Is 1:27 and her penitents with **r**
Is 5: 7 for **r**, but behold, weeping
Is 5:16 holy shall be hallowed in **r**
Is 10:22 decreed shall overflow with **r**
Is 11: 4 but with **r** He shall judge the
Is 11: 5 **R** shall be the belt of His
Is 16: 5 justice and hastening **r**
Is 26: 9 of the world will learn **r**
Is 26:10 yet he will not learn **r**
Is 28:17 line, and **r** the plummet
Is 32: 1 a king will reign in **r**, and
Is 32:16 and **r** remain in the fruitful
Is 32:17 The work of **r** will be peace,
Is 32:17 the effect of **r**, quietness
Is 33: 5 filled Zion with justice and **r**
Is 41: 2 Who in **r** called him to His
Is 42: 6 LORD, have called You in **r**
Is 42:21 well pleased for His **r**' sake
Is 45: 8 and let the skies pour down **r**
Is 45: 8 and let **r** spring up together
Is 45:13 I have raised him up in **r**
Is 45:19 I, the LORD, speak **r**, I
Is 45:23 has gone out of My mouth in **r**
Is 45:24 Surely in the LORD I have **r**
Is 46:12 who are far from **r**
Is 46:13 I bring My **r** near, it shall
Is 48: 1 but not in truth or in **r**
Is 48:18 your **r** like the waves of the
Is 51: 1 to Me, you who follow after **r**
Is 51: 5 My **r** is near, My salvation
Is 51: 6 My **r** will not be abolished
Is 51: 7 Listen to Me, you who know **r**
Is 51: 8 but My **r** will be forever, and
Is 54:14 In **r** you shall be established
Is 54:17 their **r** is from Me," says
Is 56: 1 Keep justice, and do **r**, for My
Is 56: 1 come, and My **r** to be revealed
Is 57:12 I will declare your **r** and your
Is 58: 2 ways, as a nation that did **r**
Is 58: 8 your **r** shall go before you
Is 59: 9 us, nor does **r** overtake us
Is 59:14 back, and **r** stands afar off
Is 59:16 and His own **r**, it sustained
Is 59:17 For He put on **r** as a
Is 60:17 peace, and your magistrates **r**
Is 61: 3 they may be called trees of **r**
Is 61:10 covered me with the robe of **r**
Is 61:11 so the Lord GOD will cause **r**
Is 62: 1 until her **r** goes forth as
Is 62: 2 The Gentiles shall see your **r**
Is 63: 1 I who speak in **r**, mighty to
Is 64: 5 him who rejoices and does **r**
Jer 4: 2 truth, in judgment, and in **r**
Jer 9:24 judgment, and **r** in the earth
Jer 22: 3 Execute judgment and **r**, and
Jer 22:15 and drink, and do justice and **r**
Jer 23: 5 raise to David a Branch of **r**
Jer 23: 5 judgment and **r** in the earth
Jer 23: 6 THE LORD OUR **R**
Jer 33:15 up to David a Branch of **r**
Jer 33:15 judgment and **r** in the earth
Jer 33:16 THE LORD OUR **R**
Jer 51:10 The LORD has revealed our **r**
Ezek 3:20 man turns from his **r** and
Ezek 3:20 his **r** which he has done shall
Ezek 14:14 only themselves by their **r**
Ezek 14:20 only themselves by their **r**
Ezek 18:20 The **r** of the righteous shall
Ezek 18:22 because of the **r** which he has
Ezek 18:24 man turns away from his **r**
Ezek 18:24 All the **r** which he has done
Ezek 18:26 man turns away from his **r**
Ezek 33:12 The **r** of the righteous man
Ezek 33:12 his **r** in the day that he sins
Ezek 33:13 but he trusts in his own **r**
Ezek 33:18 righteous turns from his **r**
Ezek 45: 9 execute justice and **r**, and
Dan 9: 7 **r** belongs to You, but to us
Dan 9:16 Lord, according to all Your **r**
Dan 9:24 to bring in everlasting **r**
Dan 12: 3 to **r** like the stars forever
Hos 2:19 I will betroth you to Me in **r**
Hos 10:12 Sow for yourselves **r**
Hos 10:12 He comes and rains **r** on you
Amos 5: 7 lay **r** to rest in the earth
Amos 5:24 and **r** like a mighty stream
Amos 6:12 the fruit of **r** into wormwood,
Mic 6: 5 may know the **r** of the LORD
Mic 7: 9 light, and I will see His **r**
Zeph 2: 3 Seek **r**, seek humility
Zech 8: 8 be their God, in truth and **r**
Mal 3: 3 to the LORD an offering in **r**
Mal 4: 2 **R** shall arise with healing in
Matt 3:15 for us to fulfill all **r**
Matt 5: 6 who hunger and thirst for **r**
Matt 5:20 unless your **r** exceeds the **r**
Matt 6:33 the kingdom of God and His **r**
Matt 21:32 came to you in the way of **r**
Luke 1:75 **r** before Him all the days of
John 16: 8 the world of sin, and of **r**
John 16:10 of **r**, because I go to My
Acts 10:35 works **r** is accepted by Him
Acts 13:10 the devil, you enemy of all **r**
Acts 17:31 in **r** by the Man whom He has
Acts 24:25 Now as he reasoned about **r**
Rom 1:17 For in it the **r** of God is
Rom 3: 5 demonstrates the **r** of God
Rom 3:21 But now the **r** of God apart
Rom 3:22 even the **r** of God which is
Rom 3:25 faith, to demonstrate His **r**
Rom 3:26 at the present time His **r**
Rom 4: 3 it was accounted to him for **r**
Rom 4: 5 his faith is accounted for **r**
Rom 4: 6 imputes **r** apart from works
Rom 4: 9 accounted to Abraham for **r**
Rom 4:11 a seal of the **r** of the faith
Rom 4:11 that **r** might be imputed to
Rom 4:13 but through the **r** of faith
Rom 4:22 it was accounted to him for **r**
Rom 5:17 of the gift of **r** will reign
Rom 5:21 **r** to eternal life through
Rom 6:13 as instruments of **r** to God
Rom 6:16 death, or of obedience to **r**
Rom 6:18 sin, you became slaves of **r**
Rom 6:19 as slaves of **r** for holiness
Rom 6:20 you were free in regard to **r**
Rom 8:10 Spirit is life because of **r**
Rom 9:28 the work and cut it short in **r**
Rom 9:30 who did not pursue **r**
Rom 9:30 have attained to **r**
Rom 9:30 even the **r** of faith
Rom 9:31 Israel, pursuing the law of **r**
Rom 9:31 not attained to the law of **r**
Rom 10: 3 being ignorant of God's **r**
Rom 10: 3 to establish their own **r**,
Rom 10: 3 not submitted to the **r** of God
Rom 10: 4 **r** to everyone who believes
Rom 10: 5 the **r** which is of the law
Rom 10: 6 But the **r** of faith speaks in
Rom 10:10 the heart one believes to **r**
Rom 14:17 is not food and drink, but **r**
1Co 1:30 and **r** and sanctification and
1Co 15:34 Awake to **r**, and do not sin
2Co 3: 9 the ministry of **r** exceeds
2Co 5:21 become the **r** of God in Him
2Co 6: 7 God, by the armor of **r** on the
2Co 6:14 has **r** with lawlessness
2Co 9: 9 His **r** remains forever
2Co 9:10 increase the fruits of your **r**
2Co 11:15 into ministers of **r**, whose
Gal 2:21 for if **r** comes through the
Gal 3: 6 it was accounted to him for **r**
Gal 3:21 truly **r** would have been by
Gal 5: 5 for the hope of **r** by faith
Eph 4:24 according to God, in **r** and
Eph 5: 9 Spirit is in all goodness, **r**
Eph 6:14 put on the breastplate of **r**
Phil 1:11 **r** which are by Jesus Christ
Phil 3: 6 concerning the **r** which is in
Phil 3: 9 in Him, not having my own **r**
Phil 3: 9 the **r** which is from God by
1Ti 6:11 flee these things and pursue **r**
2Ti 2:22 but pursue **r**, faith, love,
2Ti 3:16 for instruction in **r**,
2Ti 4: 8 laid up for me the crown of **r**
Tit 3: 5 not by works of **r** which we
Heb 1: 8 a scepter of **r** is the scepter
Heb 1: 9 You have loved **r** and hated
Heb 5:13 is unskilled in the word of **r**
Heb 7: 2 king of **r**," and then also
Heb 11: 7 became heir of the **r** which is
Heb 11:33 subdued kingdoms, worked **r**
Heb 12:11 of **r** to those who have been
Jas 1:20 does not produce the **r** of God
Jas 2:23 it was accounted to him for **r**
Jas 3:18 Now the fruit of **r** is sown in
1Pe 2:24 to sins, might live for **r**
2Pe 1: 1 with us by the **r** of our God
2Pe 2: 5 eight people, a preacher of **r**
2Pe 2:21 to have known the way of **r**
2Pe 3:13 a new earth in which **r** dwells
1Jn 2:29 practices **r** is born of Him
1Jn 3: 7 who practices **r** is righteous
1Jn 3:10 not practice **r** is not of God
Rev 19:11 in **r** He judges and makes war

RIGHTEOUSNESS' (*see* RIGHTEOUSNESS)
Ps 143:11 For Your **r** sake bring my soul
Matt 5:10 who are persecuted for **r** sake
1Pe 3:14 you should suffer for **r** sake

RIGHTEOUSNESSES (*see* RIGHTEOUSNESS)
Is 64: 6 all our **r** are like filthy

RIGHTFUL (*see* RIGHT)
Job 8: 6 and prosper your **r** habitation
Jer 10: 7 For this is Your **r** due, for

RIGHTLY (*see* RIGHT)
Gen 27:36 Is he not **r** named Jacob
Prov 15: 2 of the wise uses knowledge **r**
Song 1: 4 **R** do they love
Jer 46:28 I will **r** correct you, for I
Luke 7:43 You have **r** judged
Luke 10:28 You have answered **r**
Luke 20:21 know that You say and teach **r**
Luke 22:70 them, "You **r** say that I am
John 8:48 Do we not say **r** that You are
John 18:37 You say **r** that I am a king
Acts 28:25 The Holy Spirit spoke **r**
1Co 2:15 himself is **r** judged by no one
2Ti 2:15 **r** dividing the word of truth

RIGHTS
Ex 21:10 clothing, and her marriage **r**

RIGID
Mark 9:18 his teeth, and becomes **r**

RIGOR
Ex 1:13 of Israel serve with **r**
Ex 1:14 made them serve was with **r**
Lev 25:43 not rule over him with **r**, but
Lev 25:46 rule over one another with **r**
Lev 25:53 with **r** over him in your sight

RIM (*see* RIMS)
Ex 27: 5 the **r** of the altar beneath
Ex 38: 4 for the altar, under its **r**
Ezek 43:13 with a **r** all around its edge
Ezek 43:17 with a **r** of half a cubit
Ezek 43:20 ledge, and on the **r** around it

RIMMON (*see* RIMMON PEREZ)
Josh 15:32 Lebaoth, Shilhim, Ain, and **R**
Josh 19: 7 Ain, **R**, Ether, and Ashan
Josh 19:13 Eth Kazin, and extended to **R**
Judg 20:45 wilderness to the rock of **R**
Judg 20:47 wilderness to the rock of **R**
Judg 20:47 the rock of **R** for four months
Judg 21:13 who were at the rock of **R**
2Sa 4: 2 the sons of **R** the Beerothite,
2Sa 4: 5 the sons of **R** the Beerothite
2Sa 4: 9 the sons of **R** the Beerothite,
2Ki 5:18 temple of **R** to worship there
2Ki 5:18 I bow down in the temple of **R**
2Ki 5:18 I bow down in the temple of **R**
1Ch 4:32 villages were Etam, Ain, **R**
1Ch 6:77 of Merari were given **R** with
Zech 14:10 Geba to **R** south of Jerusalem

RIMMON PEREZ (*see* RIMMON)
Num 33:19 from Rithmah and camped at **R**
Num 33:20 They departed from **R** and

RIMS (*see* RIM)
1Ki 7:33 their axle pins, their **r**,
Ezek 1:18 As for their **r**, they were so
Ezek 1:18 their **r** were full of eyes,

RING (*see* RINGS)
Gen 24:22 nose **r** weighing half a shekel
Gen 24:30 pass, when he saw the nose **r**
Gen 24:47 I put the nose **r** on her nose
Gen 41:42 his signet **r** off his hand
Ex 26:24 together at the top by one **r**
Ex 36:29 together at the top by one **r**
Esth 3:10 his signet **r** from his hand
Esth 3:12 with the king's signet **r**
Esth 8: 2 king took off his signet **r**
Esth 8: 8 it with the king's signet **r**
Esth 8: 8 signet **r** no one can revoke
Esth 8:10 it with the king's signet **r**
Job 42:11 of silver and each a **r** of gold
Prov 11:22 As a **r** of gold in a swine's
Dan 6:17 it with his own signet **r** and
Hag 2:23 will make you as a signet **r**
Luke 15:22 and put a **r** on his hand and

RINGLEADER
Acts 24: 5 and a **r** of the sect of the

RINGS (*see* RING)
Ex 25:12 cast four **r** of gold for it
Ex 25:12 two **r** shall be on one side,
Ex 25:12 and two **r** on the other side
Ex 25:14 put the poles into the **r** on
Ex 25:15 shall be in the **r** of the ark
Ex 25:26 make for it four **r** of gold
Ex 25:26 put the **r** on the four corners
Ex 25:27 The **r** shall be close to the
Ex 26:29 gold, make their **r** of gold as
Ex 27: 4 bronze **r** at its four corners
Ex 27: 7 poles shall be put in the **r**
Ex 28:23 you shall make two **r** of gold
Ex 28:23 put the two **r** on the two ends
Ex 28:24 **r** which are on the ends of
Ex 28:26 You shall make two **r** of gold
Ex 28:27 two other **r** of gold you shall
Ex 28:28 **r** to the **r** of the ephod
Ex 30: 4 Two gold **r** you shall make for
Ex 35:22 earrings and nose **r**, **r**
Ex 36:34 made their **r** of gold to be
Ex 36:38 their **r** with gold, but their
Ex 37: 3 he cast for it four **r** of gold
Ex 37: 3 two **r** on one side, and two
Ex 37: 3 two **r** on the other side of it
Ex 37: 5 the **r** at the sides of the ark
Ex 37:13 he cast for it four **r** of gold
Ex 37:13 put the **r** on the four corners
Ex 37:14 The **r** were close to the frame
Ex 37:27 He made two **r** of gold for it
Ex 38: 5 He cast four **r** for the four
Ex 38: 7 **r** on the sides of the altar
Ex 39:16 of gold and two gold **r**, and put
Ex 39:16 put the two **r** on the two ends
Ex 39:17 the two **r** on the ends of the
Ex 39:19 And they made two **r** of gold
Ex 39:20 They made two other gold **r**
Ex 39:21 **r** to the **r** of the ephod
Ex 40:20 through the **r** of the ark, and
Num 31:50 and bracelets and signet **r** and
Is 3:21 and the **r**; the nose jewels
Jas 2: 2 assembly a man with gold **r**

RINNAH
1Ch 4:20 sons of Shimon were Amnon, **R**

RINSED
Lev 6:28 be both scoured and **r** in water
Lev 15:11 has not **r** his hands in water,
Lev 15:12 of wood shall be **r** in water

RIP (*see* RIPPED)
2Ki 8:12 **r** open their women with child

RIPE (*see* RIPENS, UNRIPE)
Gen 40:10 brought forth **r** grapes
Ex 22:29 the first of your **r** produce
Num 13:20 season of the first **r** grapes
Num 17: 8 blossoms and yielded **r** almonds
Num 18:13 Whatever first **r** fruit is in
Jer 24: 2 the figs that are first **r**
Joel 3:13 sickle, for the harvest is **r**
Rev 14:15 the harvest of the earth is **r**
Rev 14:18 for her grapes are fully **r**

RIPENED (*see* RIPENS)
2Ki 4:42 newly **r** grain in his knapsack
Nah 3:12 are fig trees with **r** figs

RIPENING (*see* RIPENS)
Is 18: 5 sour grape is **r** in the flower

RIPENS (*see* RIPE, RIPENED, RIPENING)
Job 5:26 of grain **r** in its season
Mark 4:29 But when the grain **r**,

RIPHATH
Gen 10: 3 of Gomer were Ashkenaz, **R**

RIPPED (*see* RIP)
2Ki 15:16 who were with child he **r** open
Hos 13:16 their women with child **r** open
Amos 1:13 because they **r** open the women

RISE (*see* RISEN, RISES, RISING, ROSE)
Gen 19: 2 then you may **r** early and go on
Gen 31:35 that I cannot **r** before you
Ex 8:20 **R** early in the morning and
Ex 9:13 **R** early in the morning and
Ex 10:23 nor did anyone **r** from his
Ex 12:31 **R** and go out from among my
Lev 19:32 You shall **r** before the gray
Num 10:35 **R** up, O LORD
Num 22:20 the men come to call you, **r**
Num 23:18 **R** up, Balak, and hear
Num 24:17 Scepter shall **r** out of Israel
Deut 2:13 Now **r** and cross over the
Deut 2:24 **R**, take your journey, and
Deut 6: 7 lie down, and when you **r** up
Deut 11:19 lie down, and when you **r** up
Deut 19:15 One witness shall not **r**
Deut 28: 7 **r** against you to be defeated
Deut 28:43 is among you shall **r** higher
Deut 29:22 children who **r** up after you
Deut 31:16 and this people will **r** and play
Deut 32:38 Let them **r** and help you, and be
Deut 33:11 of those who **r** against him
Deut 33:11 him, that they **r** not again
Josh 8: 7 Then you shall **r** from the
Josh 18: 4 they shall **r** and go through
Judg 8:20 **R**, kill them!
Judg 8:21 **R** yourself, and kill us
Judg 9:33 that you shall **r** early and
Judg 20:38 of smoke **r** up from the city
Judg 20:40 **r** from the city in a column
1Sa 22:13 that he should **r** against me
1Sa 24: 7 allow them to **r** against Saul
1Sa 29:10 **r** early in the morning with
2Sa 15: 2 Now Absalom would **r** early
2Sa 18:32 all who **r** against you to do
2Sa 22:39 so that they could not **r**
2Sa 22:49 above those who **r** against me
2Ki 9: 2 make him **r** up from among his
2Ki 16: 7 Israel, who **r** up against me
Neh 2:18 Let us **r** up and build
Job 1: 5 and he would **r** early in the
Job 9: 7 the sun, and it does not **r**
Job 14:12 man lies down and does not **r**
Job 20:27 earth will **r** up against him
Job 25: 3 whom does His light not **r**
Ps 3: 1 are they who **r** up against me
Ps 17: 7 those who **r** up against them
Ps 18:38 that they were not able to **r**
Ps 18:48 above those who **r** against me
Ps 27: 3 war should **r** against me, In
Ps 35:11 Fierce witnesses **r** up
Ps 36:12 down and are not able to **r**
Ps 41: 8 down, he will **r** up no more
Ps 44: 5 those who **r** up against us
Ps 59: 1 those who **r** up against me
Ps 74:23 The tumult of those who **r** up
Ps 89: 9 When its waves **r**, You still
Ps 92:11 wicked Who **r** up against me
Ps 94: 2 **R** up, O Judge of the earth
Ps 94:16 Who will **r** up for me against
Ps 119:62 At midnight I will **r** to give
Ps 119:147 I **r** before the dawning of the
Ps 127: 2 is vain for you to **r** up early
Ps 139:21 those who **r** up against You
Ps 140:10 that they **r** not up again
Prov 6: 9 When will you **r** from your
Prov 24:16 **r** again, but the wicked shall
Prov 24:22 calamity will **r** suddenly, and
Prov 31:28 Her children **r** up and call her
Song 2:10 **R** up, my love, my fair one,
Song 2:13 **r** up, my love, my fair one,
Song 3: 2 I will **r** now," I said, "And
Is 5:11 Woe to those who **r** early in
Is 14:21 their fathers, lest they **r** up
Is 14:22 For I will **r** up against them,
Is 24:20 it will fall, and not **r** again
Is 26:14 are deceased, they will not **r**
Is 28:21 For the LORD will **r** up as at
Is 32: 9 **R** up, you women who are at
Is 33:10 Now I will **r**," says the LORD
Is 34: 3 shall **r** from their corpses
Is 43:17 together, they shall not **r**
Jer 8: 4 Will they fall and not **r**
Jer 25:27 **r** no more, because of the
Jer 37:10 among them, they would **r** up
Jer 47: 2 waters **r** out of the north, and
Jer 49:14 her, and **r** up to battle
Jer 51:64 not **r** from the catastrophe
Dan 7:24 And another shall **r** after them
Dan 8:25 he shall even **r** against the
Dan 11:14 in those times many shall **r**
Joel 2:20 up, and his foul odor will **r**
Amos 5: 2 she will **r** no more
Amos 7: 9 I will **r** with the sword
Amos 8:14 shall fall and never **r** again
Obad 1 let us **r** up against her for
Nah 1: 9 will not **r** up a second time
Hab 2: 7 your creditors **r** up suddenly
Zeph 3: 8 the day I **r** up for plunder
Matt 5:45 makes His sun **r** on the evil
Matt 10:21 children will **r** up against
Matt 12:41 The men of Nineveh will **r** in
Matt 12:42 **r** up in the judgment with
Matt 20:19 the third day He will **r** again
Matt 24: 7 nation will **r** against nation
Matt 24:11 many false prophets will **r** up
Matt 26:46 **R**, let us be going
Matt 27:63 After three days I will **r**
Mark 4:27 **r** by day, and the seed should
Mark 8:31 and after three days **r** again
Mark 9:31 He will **r** the third day
Mark 10:34 the third day He will **r** again
Mark 10:49 **R**, He is calling you
Mark 12:23 the resurrection, when they **r**
Mark 12:25 For when they **r** from the dead
Mark 12:26 the dead, that they **r**, have
Mark 13: 8 nation will **r** against nation
Mark 13:12 children will **r** up against
Mark 13:22 and false prophets will **r** and
Mark 14:42 **R** up, let us go
Luke 5:23 or to say, '**R** up and walk'
Luke 11: 7 I cannot **r** and give to you'
Luke 11: 8 to you, though he will not **r**
Luke 11: 8 of his persistence he will **r**
Luke 11:31 **r** up in the judgment with the
Luke 11:32 **r** up in the judgment with
Luke 16:31 though one **r** from the dead
Luke 18:33 the third day He will **r** again
Luke 21:10 Nation will **r** against nation,
Luke 22:46 **R** and pray, lest you enter
Luke 24: 7 and the third day **r** again
Luke 24:46 to **r** from the dead the third
John 5: 8 **R**, take up your bed and walk
John 11:23 Your brother will **r** again
John 11:24 I know that he will **r** again
John 20: 9 that He must **r** again from the
Acts 3: 6 of Nazareth, **r** up and walk
Acts 10:13 **R**, Peter; kill and eat.
Acts 11: 7 a voice saying to me, '**R**,
Acts 17: 3 **r** again from the dead, and
Acts 20:30 yourselves men will **r** up,
Acts 26:16 But **r** and stand on your feet
Acts 26:23 the first to **r** from the dead

Rom 15:12 He who shall **r** to reign over
1Co 15:15 if in fact the dead do not **r**
1Co 15:16 For if the dead do not **r**,
1Co 15:29 if the dead do not **r** at all
1Co 15:32 If the dead do not **r**, "Let
1Th 4:16 dead in Christ will **r** first
Heb 7:11 **r** according to the order of
Rev 11: 1 **R** and measure the temple of

RISEN (*see* RISE)
Gen 19:23 The sun had **r** upon the earth
Ex 22: 3 If the sun has **r** on him,
Num 32:14 You have **r** in your father's
Judg 9:18 but you have **r** up against my
1Sa 25:29 Yet a man has **r** to pursue you
2Sa 14: 7 now the whole family has **r** up
Ezra 9: 6 have **r** higher than our heads
Ps 20: 8 But we have **r** and stand
Ps 27:12 witnesses have **r** against me
Ps 54: 3 have **r** up against me, And
Ps 86:14 the proud have **r** against me
Is 60: 1 of the LORD is **r** upon you
Ezek 7:11 Violence has **r** up into a rod
Mic 2: 8 people have **r** up as an enemy
Matt 11:11 **r** one greater than John the
Matt 14: 2 he is **r** from the dead, and
Matt 17: 9 Son of Man is **r** from the dead
Matt 27:64 He has **r** from the dead
Matt 28: 6 for He is **r**, as He said
Matt 28: 7 that He is **r** from the dead
Mark 1:35 having **r** a long while before
Mark 3:26 if Satan has **r** up against
Mark 6:14 Baptist is **r** from the dead
Mark 9: 9 of Man had **r** from the dead
Mark 16: 2 the tomb when the sun had **r**
Mark 16: 6 He is **r**! He is not here.
Mark 16:14 had seen Him after He had **r**
Luke 7:16 prophet has **r** up among us"
Luke 9: 7 that John had **r** from the dead
Luke 9: 8 the old prophets had **r** again
Luke 9:19 the old prophets has **r** again
Luke 13:25 Master of the house has **r** up
Luke 24: 6 He is not here, but is **r**
Luke 24:34 The Lord is **r** indeed, and has
John 2:22 when He had **r** from the dead,
Rom 8:34 and furthermore is also **r**
1Co 15:13 dead, then Christ is not **r**
1Co 15:14 And if Christ is not **r**, then
1Co 15:16 rise, then Christ is not **r**
1Co 15:17 And if Christ is not **r**, your
1Co 15:20 now Christ is **r** from the dead
Jas 1:11 For no sooner has the sun **r**

RISES (*see* RISE)
Ex 21:19 if he **r** again and walks about
Num 23:24 a people **r** like a lioness, And
Deut 19:11 **r** against him and strikes him
Deut 19:16 If a false witness **r** against
Deut 22:26 a man **r** against his neighbor
Josh 6:26 man before the LORD who **r** up
2Sa 11:20 that the king's wrath **r**, and
2Sa 23: 4 of the morning when the sun **r**
Job 16: 8 my leanness **r** up against me
Job 24:14 The murderer **r** with the light
Job 24:22 He **r** up, but no man is sure
Job 27: 7 he who **r** up against me like
Job 31:14 then shall I do when God **r** up
Prov 31:15 She also **r** while it is yet
Eccl 1: 5 The sun also **r**, and the sun
Eccl 10: 4 of the ruler **r** against you
Eccl 12: 4 when one **r** up at the sound of
Is 54:17 every tongue which **r** against
Jer 46: 8 Egypt **r** up like a flood, and
Mic 7: 6 daughter **r** against her mother
Nah 3:17 when the sun **r** they flee away
2Pe 1:19 morning star **r** in your hearts
Rev 19: 3 her smoke **r** up forever and

RISING (*see* RISE)
Num 2: 3 side, toward the **r** of the sun
Deut 4:41 toward the **r** of the sun,
Deut 4:47 toward the **r** of the sun,
Josh 12: 1 toward the **r** of the sun, from
1Ki 18:44 man's hand, **r** out of the sea
2Ch 36:15 **r** up early and sending them,
Job 36:33 also, concerning the **r** storm
Ps 19: 6 Its **r** is from one end of
Ps 50: 1 the **r** of the sun to its going
Ps 113: 3 From the **r** of the sun to its
Ps 139: 2 my sitting down and my **r** up
Prov 27:14 **r** early in the morning, it
Is 9:18 shall mount up like **r** smoke
Is 41:25 from the **r** of the sun he
Is 45: 6 **r** of the sun to its setting
Is 59:19 glory from the **r** of the sun
Is 60: 3 to the brightness of your **r**
Jer 7:13 **r** up early and speaking, but
Jer 7:25 daily **r** up early and sending
Jer 11: 7 **r** early and exhorting, saying,
Jer 25: 3 **r** early and speaking, but you
Jer 25: 4 **r** early and sending them, but
Jer 26: 5 both **r** up early and sending
Jer 29:19 **r** up early and sending them
Jer 32:33 **r** up early and teaching them,
Jer 35:14 **r** early and speaking, you did
Jer 35:15 **r** up early and sending them,
Jer 44: 4 **r** early and sending them,
Lam 3:63 sitting down and their **r** up
Mal 1:11 For from the **r** of the sun
Matt 27:24 rather that a tumult was **r**
Mark 9:10 the **r** from the dead meant
Luke 2:34 **r** of many in Israel, and for a
Luke 12:54 see a cloud **r** out of the west
Rev 13: 1 I saw a beast **r** up out of the

RISK (*see* RISKED)
1Ch 11:19 For at the **r** of their lives
Lam 5: 9 bread at the **r** of our lives

RISKED (*see* RISK)
Judg 9:17 **r** his life, and delivered you
Acts 15:26 men who have **r** their lives
Rom 16: 4 who **r** their own necks for my

RISSAH
Num 33:21 from Libnah and camped at **R**
Num 33:22 They journeyed from **R** and

RITE (*see* RITES)
Num 9:14 to the **r** of the Passover and

RITES (*see* RITE)
Num 9: 3 According to all its **r** and

RITHMAH
Num 33:18 from Hazeroth and camped at **R**
Num 33:19 They departed from **R** and

RITUAL (*see* RITUALLY, RITUALS)
Deut 23:17 There shall be no **r** harlot of
2Ki 23: 7 Then he tore down the **r**
Ezek 20:26 because of their **r** gifts, in
Hos 4:14 sacrifices with a **r** harlot

RITUALLY (*see* RITUAL)
Ezra 6:20 all of them were **r** clean

RITUALS (*see* RITUAL)
2Ki 17:26 the **r** of the God of the land
2Ki 17:26 they do not know the **r** of the
2Ki 17:27 the **r** of the God of the land
2Ki 17:33 according to the **r** of the
2Ki 17:34 practicing the former **r**
2Ki 17:40 they followed their former **r**

RIVAL (*see* RIVALRY)
Lev 18:18 a woman as a **r** to her sister
1Sa 1: 6 And her **r** also provoked her

RIVALRY (*see* RIVAL)
Luke 22:24 there was also **r** among them

RIVER (*see* RIVERBANK, RIVERBEDS, RIVERHEADS, RIVER'S, RIVERS, RIVERSIDE)
Gen 2:10 Now a **r** went out of Eden to
Gen 2:13 name of the second **r** is Gihon
Gen 2:14 of the third **r** is Hiddekel
Gen 2:14 The fourth **r** is the Euphrates
Gen 15:18 from the **r** of Egypt to the
Gen 15:18 great **r**, the **R** Euphrates
Gen 31:21 He arose and crossed the **r**
Gen 41: 1 and behold, he stood by the **r**
Gen 41: 2 up out of the **r** seven cows
Gen 41: 3 up after them out of the **r**
Gen 41: 3 cows on the bank of the **r**
Gen 41:17 I stood on the bank of the **r**
Gen 41:18 cows came up out of the **r**
Ex 1:22 you shall cast into the **r**
Ex 2: 5 down to wash herself at the **r**
Ex 4: 9 shall take water from the **r**
Ex 4: 9 which you take from the **r**
Ex 7:17 **r** with the rod that is in my
Ex 7:18 that are in the **r** shall die
Ex 7:18 the **r** shall stink, and the
Ex 7:18 to drink the water of the **r**
Ex 7:20 the waters that were in the **r**
Ex 7:20 in the **r** were turned to blood
Ex 7:21 fish that were in the **r** died
Ex 7:21 the **r** stank, and the Egyptians
Ex 7:21 not drink the water of the **r**
Ex 7:24 the **r** for water to drink,
Ex 7:24 not drink the water of the **r**
Ex 7:25 the LORD had struck the **r**
Ex 8: 3 So the **r** shall bring forth
Ex 8: 9 they may remain in the **r** only
Ex 8:11 shall remain in the **r** only
Ex 17: 5 with which you struck the **r**
Ex 23:31 and from the desert to the **R**
Num 22: 5 which is near the **R** in the
Deut 1: 7 great **r**, the **R** Euphrates
Deut 2:24 and cross over the **R** Arnon
Deut 2:36 is on the bank of the **R** Arnon
Deut 2:37 anywhere along the **R** Jabbok
Deut 3: 8 from the **R** Arnon to Mount
Deut 3:12 which is by the **R** Arnon, and
Deut 3:16 Gilead as far as the **R** Arnon
Deut 3:16 middle of the **r** as the border
Deut 3:16 as far as the **R** Jabbok, the
Deut 4:48 is on the bank of the **R** Arnon
Deut 11:24 and Lebanon, from the **r**, the
Deut 11:24 the **R** Euphrates, even to the
Josh 1: 4 Lebanon as far as the great **r**
Josh 1: 4 the **R** Euphrates, all the land
Josh 12: 1 from the **R** Arnon to Mount
Josh 12: 2 is on the bank of the **R** Arnon
Josh 12: 2 from the middle of that **r**
Josh 12: 2 even as far as the **R** Jabbok
Josh 13: 9 is on the bank of the **R** Arnon
Josh 13:16 is on the bank of the **R** Arnon
Josh 24: 2 side of the **R** in old times
Josh 24: 3 from the other side of the **R**
Josh 24:14 on the other side of the **R**
Josh 24:15 on the other side of the **R**
Judg 4: 7 his multitude at the **R** Kishon
Judg 4:13 Hagoyim to the **R** Kishon
2Sa 8: 3 territory at the **R** Euphrates
2Sa 10:16 Syrians who were beyond the **R**
2Sa 17:13 and we will pull it into the **r**
1Ki 4:21 from the **R** to the land of the
1Ki 4:24 **R** from Tiphsah even to Gaza
1Ki 4:24 kings on this side of the **R**
1Ki 14:15 scatter them beyond the **R**
2Ki 10:33 which is by the **R** Arnon,
2Ki 17: 6 the **R** of Gozan, and in the
2Ki 18:11 the **R** of Gozan, and in the
2Ki 23:29 Assyria, to the **R** Euphrates
2Ki 24: 7 of Egypt to the **R** Euphrates
1Ch 5: 9 this side of the **R** Euphrates
1Ch 5:26 the **r** of Gozan to this day
1Ch 18: 3 his power by the **R** Euphrates
1Ch 19:16 Syrians who were beyond the **R**
2Ch 9:26 from the **R** to the land of the
Ezra 4:10 of the region beyond the **R**
Ezra 4:11 of the region beyond the **R**
Ezra 4:16 over the region beyond the **R**
Ezra 4:17 in the region beyond the **R**
Ezra 4:20 the provinces beyond the **R**
Ezra 5: 3 of the region beyond the **R**
Ezra 5: 6 of the region beyond the **R**
Ezra 5: 6 in the region beyond the **R**
Ezra 6: 6 of the region beyond the **R**
Ezra 6: 6 Persians who are beyond the **R**
Ezra 6: 8 on the region beyond the **R**
Ezra 6:13 of the region beyond the **R**
Ezra 7:21 in the region beyond the **R**
Ezra 7:25 in the region beyond the **R**
Ezra 8:15 by the **r** that flows to Ahava
Ezra 8:21 fast there at the **r** of Ahava
Ezra 8:31 Then we departed from the **r**
Ezra 8:36 in the region beyond the **R**
Neh 2: 7 of the region beyond the **R**
Neh 2: 9 in the region beyond the **R**
Neh 3: 7 of the region beyond the **R**
Job 14:11 a **r** becomes parched and dries
Job 40:23 Indeed the **r** may rage, Yet he
Ps 36: 8 from the **r** of Your pleasures
Ps 46: 4 There is a **r** whose streams
Ps 65: 9 The **r** of God is full of water
Ps 66: 6 went through the **r** on foot
Ps 72: 8 from the **R** to the ends of the
Ps 80:11 Sea, And her branches to the **R**
Ps 105:41 in the dry places like a **r**
Is 7:20 with those from beyond the **R**
Is 8: 7 over them the waters of the **R**
Is 11:15 shake His fist over the **R**
Is 19: 5 the **r** will be wasted and dried
Is 19: 7 The papyrus reeds by the **R**
Is 19: 7 **R**, by the mouth of the **R**

Is 19: 7 and everything sown by the **R**
Is 19: 8 who cast hooks into the **R**
Is 23: 3 Shihor, the harvest of the **R**
Is 23:10 through your land like the **R**
Is 27:12 the **R** to the Brook of Egypt
Is 48:18 would have been like a **r**, and
Is 66:12 extend peace to her like a **r**
Jer 2:18 to drink the waters of the **R**
Jer 17: 8 out its roots by the **r**, and
Jer 46: 2 which was by the **R** Euphrates
Jer 46: 6 the north, by the **R** Euphrates
Jer 46:10 country by the **R** Euphrates
Lam 2:18 tears run down like a **r** day
Ezek 1: 1 the captives by the **R** Chebar
Ezek 1: 3 the Chaldeans by the **R** Chebar
Ezek 3:15 who dwelt by the **R** Chebar
Ezek 3:23 which I saw by the **R** Chebar
Ezek 10:15 I saw by the **R** Chebar
Ezek 10:20 God of Israel by the **R** Chebar
Ezek 10:22 I had seen by the **R** Chebar
Ezek 29: 3 who has said, 'My **R** is my own
Ezek 29: 9 The **R** is mine, and I have
Ezek 43: 3 which I saw by the **R** Chebar
Ezek 47: 5 it was a **r** that I could not
Ezek 47: 5 a **r** that could not be crossed
Ezek 47: 6 me to the bank of the **r**
Ezek 47: 7 along the bank of the **r**,
Ezek 47: 9 will live wherever the **r** goes
Ezek 47:12 Along the bank of the **r**, on
Dan 8: 2 that I was by the **R** Ulai
Dan 8: 3 there, standing beside the **r**
Dan 8: 6 seen standing beside the **r**
Dan 10: 4 by the side of the great **r**
Dan 12: 6 was above the waters of the **r**
Dan 12: 7 was above the waters of the **r**
Amos 8: 8 of it shall swell like the **R**
Amos 8: 8 subside like the **R** of Egypt
Amos 9: 5 of it shall swell like the **R**
Amos 9: 5 subside like the **R** of Egypt
Mic 7:12 from the fortress to the **R**
Nah 3: 8 that was situated by the **R**
Zech 9:10 from the **R** to the ends of the
Zech 10:11 depths of the **R** shall dry up
Mark 1: 5 by him in the Jordan **R**,
Rev 9:14 at the great **r** Euphrates
Rev 16:12 bowl on the great **r** Euphrates
Rev 22: 1 me a pure **r** of water of life
Rev 22: 2 and on either side of the **r**

RIVERBANK (*see* RIVER)
Dan 12: 5 two others, one on this **r**
Dan 12: 5 and the other on that **r**

RIVERBEDS (*see* RIVER)
Ezek 32: 6 the **r** will be full of you

RIVERHEADS (*see* RIVER)
Gen 2:10 it parted and became four **r**

RIVER'S (*see* RIVER)
Ex 2: 3 it in the reeds by the **r** bank
Ex 2: 5 walked along the **r** side
Ex 7:15 by the **r** bank to meet him

RIVERS (*see* RIVER)
Ex 7:19 their streams, over their **r**
Ex 8: 5 over the streams, over the **r**
Lev 11: 9 in the seas or in the **r**
Lev 11:10 the **r** that do not have fins
Deut 10: 7 a land of **r** of water
2Ki 5:12 the **r** of Damascus, better
Job 20:17 the **r** flowing with honey and
Job 29: 6 poured out **r** of oil for me
Ps 1: 3 Planted by the **r** of water
Ps 74:15 You dried up mighty **r**
Ps 78:16 waters to run down like **r**
Ps 78:44 Turned their **r** into blood
Ps 89:25 And his right hand over the **r**
Ps 98: 8 Let the **r** clap their hands
Ps 107:33 He turns **r** into a wilderness,
Ps 119:136 **R** of water run down from my
Ps 137: 1 By the **r** of Babylon, There we
Prov 21: 1 the LORD, like the **r** of water
Eccl 1: 7 All the **r** run into the sea,
Eccl 1: 7 place from which the **r** come
Song 5:12 like doves by the **r** of waters
Is 7:18 part of the **r** of Egypt, and
Is 18: 1 is beyond the **r** of Ethiopia
Is 18: 2 down, whose land the **r** divide
Is 18: 7 down, whose land the **r** divide
Is 19: 6 The **r** will turn foul, and the
Is 30:25 and on every high hill **r** and
Is 32: 2 as **r** of water in a dry place,
Is 33:21 be for us a place of broad **r**
Is 41:18 I will open **r** in desolate
Is 42:15 I will make the **r** coastlands
Is 43: 2 and through the **r**, they shall
Is 43:19 wilderness and **r** in the desert
Is 43:20 and **r** in the desert, to give
Is 44:27 and I will dry up your **r**'
Is 47: 2 the thigh, pass through the **r**
Is 50: 2 I make the **r** a wilderness
Jer 31: 9 to walk by the **r** of waters
Jer 46: 7 whose waters move like the **r**
Jer 46: 8 and its waters move like the **r**
Lam 3:48 with **r** of water for the
Ezek 29: 3 lies in the midst of his **r**
Ezek 29: 4 cause the fish of your **r** to
Ezek 29: 4 up out of the midst of your **r**
Ezek 29: 4 all the fish in your **r** will
Ezek 29: 5 you and all the fish of your **r**
Ezek 29:10 against you and against your **r**
Ezek 30:12 I will make the **r** dry, and
Ezek 31: 4 with their **r** running around
Ezek 31:12 by all the **r** of the land
Ezek 31:15 I restrained its **r**, and the
Ezek 32: 2 bursting forth in your **r**
Ezek 32: 2 your feet, and fouling their **r**
Ezek 32:14 make their **r** run like oil,'
Ezek 36: 4 mountains, the hills, the **r**
Ezek 36: 6 mountains, the hills, the **r**
Ezek 47: 9 that moves, wherever the **r** go
Mic 6: 7 rams or ten thousand **r** of oil
Nah 1: 4 it dry, and dries up all the **r**
Nah 2: 6 The gates of the **r** are opened
Hab 3: 8 You displeased with the **r**
Hab 3: 8 was Your anger against the **r**
Hab 3: 9 You divided the earth with **r**
Zeph 3:10 From beyond the **r** of Ethiopia
John 7:38 will flow **r** of living water
Rev 8:10 it fell on a third of the **r**
Rev 16: 4 poured out his bowl on the **r**

RIVERSIDE (*see* RIVER)
Num 24: 6 out, like gardens by the **r**
Acts 16:13 went out of the city to the **r**

RIVULETS
Ezek 31: 4 sent out **r** to all the trees

RIZIA
1Ch 7:39 Ulla were Arah, Haniel, and **R**

RIZPAH
2Sa 3: 7 a concubine, whose name was **R**
2Sa 21: 8 the two sons of **R** the
2Sa 21:10 Now **R** the daughter of Aiah
2Sa 21:11 David was told what **R** the

ROAD (*see* ROADS, ROADSIDE)
Num 21: 1 coming on the **r** to Atharim
Num 22:23 to turn her back onto the **r**
Deut 2: 8 away from the **r** of the plain
Deut 2:27 I will keep strictly to the **r**
Deut 3: 1 and went up the **r** to Bashan
Deut 22: 4 his ox fall down along the **r**
Deut 23: 4 water on the **r** when you came
Deut 27:18 the blind to wander off the **r**
Josh 2: 7 them by the **r** to the Jordan
Josh 10:10 chased them along the **r** that
Josh 12: 3 the **r** to Beth Jeshimoth, and
Judg 5:10 and who walk along the **r**
Judg 8:11 Then Gideon went up by the **r**
1Sa 6: 9 if it goes up the **r** to its
1Sa 6:12 for the **r** to Beth Shemesh
1Sa 13:17 to the **r** that leads to Ophrah
1Sa 13:18 turned to the **r** to Beth Horon
1Sa 13:18 to the **r** of the border that
1Sa 17:52 fell along the **r** to Shaaraim
1Sa 24: 3 to the sheepfolds by the **r**
1Sa 26: 3 opposite Jeshimon, by the **r**
2Sa 2:24 **r** to the Wilderness of Gibeon
2Sa 13:34 **r** on the hillside behind him
2Sa 16:13 and his men went along the **r**
1Ki 13:24 gone, a lion met him on the **r**
1Ki 13:24 corpse was thrown on the **r**
1Ki 13:25 the corpse thrown on the **r**
1Ki 13:28 his corpse thrown on the **r**
1Ki 20:38 waited for the king by the **r**
2Ki 2:23 and as he was going up the **r**
2Ki 7:15 indeed all the **r** was full of
2Ki 9:27 fled by the **r** to Beth Haggan
Ezra 8:22 us against the enemy on the **r**
Ezra 8:31 and from ambush along the **r**
Neh 9:12 **r** which they should travel
Neh 9:19 by day, to lead them on the **r**
Job 18:10 and a trap for him in the **r**
Job 19:12 build up their **r** against me
Job 21:29 asked those who travel the **r**
Job 24: 4 They push the needy off the **r**
Prov 26:13 There is a lion in the **r**
Is 35: 8 shall be there, and a **r**, and it
Is 35: 8 Whoever walks the **r**, although
Is 43:19 make a **r** in the wilderness
Is 49:11 make each of My mountains a **r**
Is 51:10 the depths of the sea a **r** for
Jer 2:18 now why take the **r** to Egypt
Jer 2:18 Or why take the **r** to Assyria
Jer 3: 2 By the **r** you have sat for
Ezek 16:25 places at the head of every **r**
Ezek 16:31 shrine at the head of every **r**
Ezek 21:19 the head of the **r** to the city
Ezek 21:20 Appoint a **r** for the sword to
Ezek 21:21 at the parting of the **r**, at
Ezek 47:15 by the **r** to Hethlon, as one
Ezek 48: 1 northern border along the **r**
Hos 13: 7 by the **r** I will observe them
Nah 2: 1 Man the fort! Watch the **r**!
Matt 20:17 disciples aside on the **r** and
Matt 20:30 blind men sitting by the **r**
Matt 21: 8 their garments on the **r**
Matt 21: 8 trees and spread them on the **r**
Matt 21:19 And seeing a fig tree by the **r**
Mark 8:27 and on the **r** He asked His
Mark 9:33 among yourselves on the **r**
Mark 9:34 silent, for on the **r** they had
Mark 10:17 as He was going out on the **r**
Mark 10:32 Now they were on the **r**, going
Mark 10:46 Timaeus, sat by the **r** begging
Mark 10:52 and followed Jesus on the **r**
Mark 11: 8 their garments on the **r**, and
Mark 11: 8 trees and spread them on the **r**
Luke 9:57 as they journeyed on the **r**
Luke 10: 4 and greet no one along the **r**
Luke 10:31 priest came down that **r**
Luke 18:35 man sat by the **r** begging
Luke 19:36 spread their clothes on the **r**
Luke 24:32 He talked with us on the **r**
Luke 24:35 that had happened on the **r**
Acts 8:26 the **r** which goes down from
Acts 8:36 Now as they went down the **r**
Acts 9:17 to you on the **r** as you came
Acts 9:27 he had seen the Lord on the **r**
Acts 25: 3 along the **r** to kill him
Acts 26:13 along the **r** I saw a light

ROADS (*see* ROAD)
Deut 19: 3 shall prepare **r** for yourself
Is 49: 9 They shall feed along the **r**
Lam 1: 4 The **r** to Zion mourn because
Ezek 21:21 at the fork of the two **r**
Nah 2: 4 one another in the broad **r**

ROADSIDE (*see* ROAD)
Gen 38:21 who was openly by the **r**

ROAM (*see* ROAMING)
Prov 6:22 When you **r**, they will lead
Is 7:25 and a place for sheep to **r**

ROAMING (*see* ROAM)
Lam 1: 7 days of her affliction and **r**
Lam 3:19 Remember my affliction and **r**

ROAR (*see* ROARED, ROARING, ROARS)
1Ch 16:32 Let the sea **r**, and all its
Ps 46: 3 Though its waters **r** and be
Ps 74: 4 Your enemies **r** in the midst
Ps 96:11 Let the sea **r**, and all its
Ps 98: 7 Let the sea **r**, and all its
Ps 104:21 The young lions **r** after their
Is 5:29 they will **r** like young lions
Is 5:29 yes, they will **r** and lay hold
Is 5:30 will **r** against them like the
Is 17:12 noise like the **r** of the seas
Jer 5:22 though they **r**, yet they
Jer 25:30 The LORD will **r** from on high
Jer 25:30 He will **r** mightily against
Jer 31:35 and its waves **r** (the LORD of
Jer 50:42 voice shall **r** like the sea
Jer 51:38 They shall **r** together like
Jer 51:55 though her waves **r** like great
Hos 11:10 He will **r** like a lion
Joel 3:16 LORD also will **r** from Zion
Amos 3: 4 Will a lion **r** in the forest,
Zech 9:15 drink and **r** as if with wine

ROARED (*see* ROAR)
Is 51:15 divided the sea whose waves **r**
Jer 2:15 The young lions **r** at him, and
Amos 3: 8 A lion has **r**

ROARING (*see* ROAR)
Judg 14: 5 young lion came **r** against him
Job 4:10 The **r** of the lion, the voice
Ps 22:13 mouths, As a raging and **r** lion
Prov 19:12 wrath is like the **r** of a lion
Prov 20: 2 king is like the **r** of a lion
Prov 28:15 Like a **r** lion and a charging
Is 5:29 Their **r** will be like a lion,
Is 5:30 them like the **r** of the sea
Ezek 19: 7 by the noise of his **r**
Ezek 22:25 a **r** lion tearing the prey
Zeph 3: 3 in her midst are **r** lions
Zech 11: 3 There is the sound of **r** lions
Luke 21:25 the sea and the waves **r**
1Pe 5: 8 walks about like a **r** lion

ROARS (*see* ROAR)
Job 37: 4 After it a voice **r**
Is 31: 4 As a lion **r**, and a young lion
Jer 6:23 their voice **r** like the sea
Hos 11:10 When He **r**, then His sons
Amos 1: 2 The LORD **r** from Zion, and
Rev 10: 3 loud voice, as when a lion **r**

ROAST (*see* ROASTED, ROASTING, ROASTS)
Deut 16: 7 And you shall **r** and eat it in
Prov 12:27 not **r** what he took in hunting
Is 44:16 he roasts a **r**, and is

ROASTED (*see* ROAST)
Ex 12: 8 **r** in fire, with unleavened
Ex 12: 9 all with water, but **r** in fire
Lev 2:14 heads of grain **r** on the fire
1Sa 25:18 five seahs of **r** grain, one
2Ch 35:13 Also they **r** the Passover
Is 44:19 I have **r** meat and eaten it
Jer 29:22 of Babylon **r** in the fire"

ROASTING (*see* ROAST)
1Sa 2:15 Give meat for **r** to the priest

ROASTS (*see* ROAST)
Is 44:16 he **r** a roast, and is satisfied

ROB (*see* ROBBED, ROBBER, ROBBERY, ROBBING, ROBS)
Lev 19:13 your neighbor, nor **r** him
Lev 26:22 which shall **r** you of your
Prov 22:22 Do not **r** the poor because he
Is 10: 2 to **r** the needy of justice, and
Is 10: 2 prey, and that they may **r** the
Is 17:14 and the lot of those who **r** us
Mal 3: 8 Will a man **r** God
Rom 2:22 abhor idols, do you **r** temples

ROBBED (*see* ROB)
Judg 9:25 they **r** all who passed by them
2Sa 17: 8 like a bear **r** of her cubs in
Prov 17:12 man meet a bear **r** of her cubs
Is 10:13 and have **r** their treasuries
Is 42:22 But this is a people **r** and
Jer 50:37 treasures, and they will be **r**
Ezek 18: 7 has **r** no one by violence, but
Ezek 18:12 **r** by violence, not restored
Ezek 18:16 nor **r** by violence, but has
Ezek 18:18 **r** his brother by violence, and
Mal 3: 8 Yet you have **r** Me
Mal 3: 8 In what way have we **r** You
Mal 3: 9 a curse, for you have **r** Me
2Co 11: 8 I **r** other churches, taking

ROBBER (*see* ROB, ROBBERS)
Prov 6:11 poverty come on you like a **r**
Ezek 18:10 is a **r** or a shedder of blood
Matt 26:55 you come out, as against a **r**
Mark 14:48 you come out, as against a **r**
Luke 22:52 you come out, as against a **r**
John 10: 1 the same is a thief and a **r**
John 18:40 Now Barabbas was a **r**

ROBBERS (*see* ROBBER)
Job 12: 6 The tents of **r** prosper, and
Is 42:24 plunder, and Israel to the **r**
Ezek 7:22 for **r** shall enter it and
Hos 6: 9 As bands of **r** lie in wait for
Hos 7: 1 A band of **r** takes spoil
Obad 5 come to you, if **r** by night
Matt 27:38 Then two **r** were crucified
Matt 27:44 Even the **r** who were crucified
Mark 15:27 Him they also crucified two **r**
John 10: 8 before Me are thieves and **r**
Acts 19:37 men here who are neither **r** of
2Co 11:26 of waters, in perils of **r**

ROBBERY (*see* ROB)
Lev 6: 2 about a pledge, or about a **r**
Ps 62:10 Nor vainly hope in **r**
Is 61: 8 I hate **r** for burnt offering
Ezek 22:29 used oppressions, committed **r**
Amos 3:10 and **r** in their palaces
Nah 3: 1 It is all full of lies and **r**
Phil 2: 6 did not consider it **r** to be

ROBBING (*see* ROB)
1Sa 23: 1 and they are **r** the threshing

ROBE (*see* ROBES)
Ex 28: 4 a breastplate, an ephod, a **r**
Ex 28:31 You shall make the **r** of the
Ex 28:34 the hem of the **r** all around
Ex 29: 5 the **r** of the ephod, the ephod
Ex 39:22 He made the **r** of the ephod of
Ex 39:23 in the middle of the **r**, like
Ex 39:24 of the **r** pomegranates of blue
Ex 39:25 on the hem of the **r** all
Ex 39:26 hem of the **r** to minister in
Lev 8: 7 sash, clothed him with the **r**
1Sa 2:19 used to make him a little **r**
1Sa 15:27 Saul seized the edge of his **r**
1Sa 18: 4 off the **r** that was on him
1Sa 24: 4 cut off a corner of Saul's **r**
1Sa 24: 5 because he had cut Saul's **r**
1Sa 24:11 corner of your **r** in my hand
1Sa 24:11 cut off the corner of your **r**
2Sa 13:18 she had on a **r** of many colors
2Sa 13:19 tore her **r** of many colors
2Sa 15:32 to meet him with his **r** torn
1Ch 15:27 with a **r** of fine linen, as
Ezra 9: 3 I tore my garment and my **r**
Ezra 9: 5 torn my garment and my **r**, I
Esth 6: 8 let a royal **r** be brought
Esth 6: 9 Then let this **r** and horse be
Esth 6:10 Hasten, take the **r** and the
Esth 6:11 So Haman took the **r** and the
Job 1:20 Then Job arose and tore his **r**
Job 2:12 and each one tore his **r** and
Job 29:14 my justice was like a **r** and a
Song 5: 3 I have taken off my **r**
Is 3:24 instead of a rich **r**, a
Is 6: 1 the train of His **r** filled the
Is 22:21 I will clothe him with your **r**
Is 61:10 with the **r** of righteousness
Jon 3: 6 throne and laid aside his **r**
Mic 2: 8 you pull off the **r** with the
Zech 13: 4 they will not wear a **r** of
Matt 27:28 Him and put a scarlet **r** on Him
Matt 27:31 Him, they took the **r** off Him
Mark 16: 5 **r** sitting on the right side
Luke 9:29 and His **r** became white and
Luke 15:22 Bring out the best **r** and put
Luke 23:11 arrayed Him in a gorgeous **r**
John 19: 2 and they put on Him a purple **r**
John 19: 5 of thorns and the purple **r**
Rev 6:11 a white **r** was given to each
Rev 19:13 with a **r** dipped in blood, and
Rev 19:16 And He has on His **r** and on His

ROBES (*see* ROBE)
Judg 8:26 purple **r** which were on the
1Ki 22:10 Judah, having put on their **r**
1Ki 22:30 but you put on your **r**
2Ch 18: 9 of Judah, clothed in their **r**
2Ch 18:29 but you put on your **r**
Esth 5: 1 Esther put on her royal **r**
Ps 45:14 the King in **r** of many colors
Is 3:23 linen, the turbans, and the **r**
Is 63: 3 and I have stained all My **r**
Ezek 26:16 thrones, lay aside their **r**
Zech 3: 4 I will clothe you with rich **r**
Mark 12:38 desire to go around in long **r**
Luke 20:46 who desire to walk in long **r**
Rev 4: 4 sitting, clothed in white **r**
Rev 7: 9 Lamb, clothed with white **r**
Rev 7:13 are these arrayed in white **r**
Rev 7:14 and washed their **r** and made

ROBS (*see* ROB)
Prov 28:24 Whoever **r** his father or his

ROCK (*see* ROCKS)
Ex 17: 6 you there on the **r** in Horeb
Ex 17: 6 and you shall strike the **r**
Ex 33:21 and you shall stand on the **r**
Ex 33:22 put you in the cleft of the **r**
Lev 11: 5 the **r** hyrax, because it
Num 20: 8 Speak to the **r** before their
Num 20: 8 water for them out of the **r**
Num 20:10 together before the **r**
Num 20:10 water for you out of this **r**
Num 20:11 struck the **r** twice with his
Num 24:21 and your nest is set in the **r**
Deut 8:15 for you out of the **r** of flint
Deut 14: 7 the hare, and the **r** hyrax
Deut 32: 4 He is the **R**, His work is
Deut 32:13 him to draw honey from the **r**
Deut 32:13 and oil from the flinty **r**
Deut 32:15 the **R** of his salvation
Deut 32:18 Of the **R** who begot you, you
Deut 32:30 unless their **R** had sold them,
Deut 32:31 their **r** is not like our **R**
Deut 32:37 the **r** in which they sought
Judg 6:20 bread and lay them on this **r**
Judg 6:21 and fire rose out of the **r**
Judg 6:26 your God on top of this **r** in
Judg 7:25 killed Oreb at the **r** of Oreb
Judg 13:19 it upon the **r** to the LORD
Judg 15: 8 in the cleft of the **r** of Etam
Judg 15:11 to the cleft of the **r** of Etam
Judg 15:13 and brought him up from the **r**
Judg 20:45 wilderness to the **r** of Rimmon
Judg 20:47 wilderness to the **r** of Rimmon
Judg 20:47 and they stayed at the **r** of
Judg 21:13 who were at the **r** of Rimmon
1Sa 2: 2 is there any **r** like our God
1Sa 14: 4 was a sharp **r** on one side
1Sa 14: 4 a sharp **r** on the other side
1Sa 23:25 he went down to the **r**, and
1Sa 23:28 that place the **R** of Escaping
2Sa 21:10 it for herself on the **r**, from
2Sa 22: 2 The LORD is my **r**, my fortress
2Sa 22:32 And who is a **r**, except our God
2Sa 22:47 Blessed be my **R**
2Sa 22:47 the **R** of my salvation
2Sa 23: 3 the **R** of Israel spoke to me
1Ch 11:15 went down to the **r** to David
2Ch 25:12 them to the top of the **r**, and
2Ch 25:12 down from the top of the **r**
Neh 9:15 out of the **r** for their thirst
Job 8:17 roots wrap around the **r** heap
Job 14:18 and as a **r** is moved from its
Job 18: 4 Or shall the **r** be removed
Job 19:24 on a **r** with an iron pen and
Job 24: 8 huddle around the **r** for want
Job 29: 6 the **r** poured out rivers of
Job 39:28 It dwells on the **r**, and
Job 39:28 resides on the crag of the **r**
Ps 18: 2 The LORD is my **r** and my
Ps 18:31 And who is a **r**, except our God
Ps 18:46 Blessed be my **R**
Ps 27: 5 He shall set me high upon a **r**
Ps 28: 1 You I will cry, O LORD my **R**
Ps 31: 2 Be my **r** of refuge, A fortress
Ps 31: 3 For You are my **r** and my
Ps 40: 2 clay, And set my feet upon a **r**
Ps 42: 9 I will say to God my **R**, "Why
Ps 61: 2 Lead me to the **r** that is
Ps 62: 2 He only is my **r** and my
Ps 62: 6 He only is my **r** and my
Ps 62: 7 The **r** of my strength, And my
Ps 71: 3 to save me, For You are my **r**
Ps 78:16 brought streams out of the **r**
Ps 78:20 Behold, He struck the **r**, So
Ps 78:35 that God was their **r**, And the
Ps 81:16 with honey from the **r** I would
Ps 89:26 God, and the **r** of my salvation
Ps 92:15 He is my **r**, and there is no
Ps 94:22 my God the **r** of my refuge
Ps 95: 1 to the **R** of our salvation
Ps 104:18 a refuge for the **r** badgers
Ps 105:41 He opened the **r**, and water
Ps 114: 8 Who turned the **r** into a pool
Ps 137: 9 little ones against the **r**
Ps 144: 1 Blessed be the LORD my **R**, Who
Prov 30:19 the way of a serpent on a **r**
Prov 30:26 the **r** badgers are a feeble
Song 2:14 dove, in the clefts of the **r**
Is 2:10 Enter into the **r**, and hide in
Is 8:14 a **r** of offense to both the
Is 10:26 of Midian at the **r** of Oreb
Is 17:10 of the **R** of your stronghold
Is 22:16 a tomb for himself in a **r**
Is 32: 2 of a great **r** in a weary land
Is 44: 8 Indeed there is no other **R**

Is 48:21 to flow from the **r** for them
Is 48:21 He also split the **r**, and the
Is 51: 1 look to the **r** from which you
Jer 5: 3 their faces harder than **r**
Jer 13: 4 it there in a hole in the **r**
Jer 18:14 comes from the **r** of the field
Jer 21:13 **r** of the plain," says the
Jer 23:29 that breaks the **r** in pieces
Jer 48:28 the cities and dwell in the **r**
Jer 49:16 dwell in the clefts of the **r**
Ezek 24: 7 she set it on top of a **r**
Ezek 24: 8 set her blood on top of a **r**
Ezek 26: 4 make her like the top of a **r**
Ezek 26:14 make you like the top of a **r**
Obad 3 dwell in the clefts of the **r**
Hab 1:12 O **R**, You have marked them for
Matt 7:24 who built his house on the **r**
Matt 7:25 for it was founded on the **r**
Matt 16:18 on this **r** I will build My
Matt 27:60 he had hewn out of the **r**
Mark 15:46 had been hewn out of the **r**
Luke 6:48 laid the foundation on the **r**
Luke 6:48 for it was founded on the **r**
Luke 8: 6 Some fell on **r**
Luke 8:13 ones on the **r** are those who
Luke 23:53 that was hewn out of the **r**
Rom 9:33 and **r** of offense, and whoever
1Co 10: 4 **R** that followed them,
1Co 10: 4 and that **R** was Christ
1Pe 2: 8 stumbling and a **r** of offense

ROCKS (*see* ROCK)
Num 23: 9 the top of the **r** I see him
1Sa 13: 6 in caves, in thickets, in **r**
1Sa 24: 2 his men on the **R** of the Wild
1Ki 19:11 broke the **r** in pieces before
Job 28:10 He cuts out channels in the **r**
Job 30: 6 caves of the earth and the **r**
Ps 78:15 He split the **r** in the
Is 2:19 go into the holes of the **r**
Is 2:21 go into the clefts of the **r**
Is 2:21 the crags of the rugged **r**
Is 7:19 and in the clefts of the **r**
Is 33:16 will be the fortress of **r**
Is 57: 5 under the clefts of the **r**
Jer 4:29 thickets and climb up on the **r**
Jer 16:16 and out of the holes of the **r**
Jer 51:25 you, roll you down from the **r**
Amos 6:12 Do horses run on **r**
Nah 1: 6 the **r** are thrown down by Him
Matt 27:51 quaked, and the **r** were split,
Acts 27:29 should run aground on the **r**
Rev 6:15 in the **r** of the mountains,
Rev 6:16 and said to the mountains and **r**

ROD (*see* RODS)
Ex 4: 2 And he said, "A **r**."
Ex 4: 4 it became a **r** in his hand),
Ex 4:17 take this **r** in your hand,
Ex 4:20 Moses took the **r** of God in
Ex 7: 9 say to Aaron, 'Take your **r**
Ex 7:10 down his **r** before Pharaoh
Ex 7:12 every man threw down his **r**
Ex 7:12 But Aaron's **r** swallowed up
Ex 7:15 the **r** which was turned to a
Ex 7:17 with the **r** that is in my hand
Ex 7:19 Say to Aaron, 'Take your **r**
Ex 7:20 So he lifted up the **r** and
Ex 8: 5 with your **r** over the streams
Ex 8:16 to Aaron, 'Stretch out your **r**
Ex 8:17 out his hand with his **r** and
Ex 9:23 out his **r** toward heaven
Ex 10:13 his **r** over the land of Egypt
Ex 14:16 But lift up your **r**, and
Ex 17: 5 **r** with which you struck the
Ex 17: 9 with the **r** of God in my hand
Ex 21:20 or his maidservant with a **r**
Lev 27:32 whatever passes under the **r**
Num 17: 2 get from them a **r** from each
Num 17: 2 each man's name on his **r**
Num 17: 3 Aaron's name on the **r** of Levi
Num 17: 3 be one **r** for the head of each
Num 17: 5 it shall be that the **r** of the
Num 17: 6 leaders gave him a **r** apiece
Num 17: 6 and the **r** of Aaron was among
Num 17: 8 the **r** of Aaron, of the house
Num 17: 9 and each man took his **r**
Num 17:10 Bring Aaron's **r** back before
Num 20: 8 Take the **r**; you and your
Num 20: 9 So Moses took the **r** from
Num 20:11 the rock twice with his **r**
1Sa 14:27 out the end of the **r** that was
1Sa 14:43 of the **r** that was in my hand
2Sa 7:14 chasten him with the **r** of men
Job 9:34 Him take His **r** away from me
Job 21: 9 neither is the **r** of God upon
Ps 2: 9 break them with a **r** of iron
Ps 23: 4 Your **r** and Your staff, they
Ps 89:32 transgression with the **r**, And
Ps 110: 2 the **r** of Your strength out of
Prov 10:13 but a **r** is for the back of
Prov 13:24 spares his **r** hates his son
Prov 14: 3 of a fool is a **r** of pride
Prov 22: 8 the **r** of his anger will fail
Prov 22:15 but the **r** of correction will
Prov 23:13 for if you beat him with a **r**
Prov 23:14 You shall beat him with a **r**
Prov 26: 3 and a **r** for the fool's back
Prov 29:15 The **r** and reproof give wisdom,
Is 9: 4 the **r** of his oppressor, as in
Is 10: 5 the **r** of My anger and the
Is 10:15 As if a **r** could wield itself
Is 10:24 He shall strike you with a **r**
Is 10:26 as His **r** was on the sea, so
Is 11: 1 a **R** from the stem of Jesse
Is 11: 4 earth with the **r** of His mouth
Is 14:29 because the **r** that struck you
Is 28:27 stick, and the cummin with a **r**
Is 30:31 down, who struck with a **r**
Jer 48:17 is broken, the beautiful **r**
Lam 3: 1 by the **r** of His wrath
Ezek 7:10 the **r** has blossomed, pride
Ezek 7:11 up into a **r** of wickedness
Ezek 19:14 out from a **r** of her branches
Ezek 20:37 make you pass under the **r**
Ezek 40: 3 and a measuring **r** in his hand
Ezek 40: 5 a measuring **r** six cubits long
Ezek 40: 5 of the wall structure, one **r**
Ezek 40: 5 and the height, one **r**
Ezek 40: 6 gateway, which was one **r** wide
Ezek 40: 6 threshold was one **r** wide
Ezek 40: 7 one **r** long and one **r** wide
Ezek 40: 7 of the inside gate was one **r**
Ezek 40: 8 of the inside gate, one **r**
Ezek 41: 8 the side chambers, a full **r**
Ezek 42:16 side with the measuring **r**
Ezek 42:16 by the measuring **r** all around
Ezek 42:17 by the measuring **r** all around
Ezek 42:18 rods by the measuring **r**
Ezek 42:19 rods by the measuring **r**
Mic 5: 1 Israel with a **r** on the cheek
Mic 6: 9 Hear the **R**! Who has appointed
1Co 4:21 Shall I come to you with a **r**
Heb 9: 4 Aaron's **r** that budded, and the
Rev 2:27 rule them with a **r** of iron
Rev 11: 1 a reed like a measuring **r**
Rev 12: 5 all nations with a **r** of iron
Rev 19:15 rule them with a **r** of iron

RODANIM (*see* DODANIM)
1Ch 1: 7 Tarshishah, Kittim, and **R**

RODE (*see* RIDE)
Gen 24:61 and they **r** on the camels and
Judg 10: 4 sons who **r** on thirty donkeys
Judg 12:14 who **r** on seventy young
1Sa 25:20 as she **r** on the donkey, that
1Sa 25:42 **r** on a donkey, attended by
1Sa 30:17 young men who **r** on camels
2Sa 18: 9 Absalom **r** on a mule
2Sa 22:11 He **r** upon a cherub, and flew
1Ki 13:13 and he **r** on it,
1Ki 18:45 So Ahab **r** away and went to
2Ki 9:16 So Jehu **r** in a chariot and
Neh 2:12 except the one on which I **r**
Esth 8:14 Then the couriers who **r** on
Ps 18:10 He **r** upon a cherub, and flew
Hab 3: 8 that You **r** on Your horses,

RODS (*see* ROD)
Gen 30:37 for himself **r** of green poplar
Gen 30:37 the white which was in the **r**
Gen 30:38 the **r** which he had peeled, he
Gen 30:39 flocks conceived before the **r**
Gen 30:41 that Jacob placed the **r**
Gen 30:41 might conceive among the **r**
Ex 7:12 rod swallowed up their **r**
Num 17: 2 fathers' houses—twelve **r**
Num 17: 6 fathers' houses, twelve **r**
Num 17: 6 of Aaron was among their **r**
Num 17: 7 Moses placed the **r** before the
Num 17: 9 Moses brought out all the **r**
Esth 1: 6 linen and purple on silver **r**
Song 5:14 His hands are **r** of gold set
Ezek 42:16 rod, five hundred **r** by the
Ezek 42:17 side, five hundred **r** by the
Ezek 42:18 side, five hundred **r** by the
Ezek 42:19 **r** by the measuring rod
Ezek 45: 2 hundred by five hundred **r**
Acts 16:22 them to be beaten with **r**
2Co 11:25 times I was beaten with **r**

ROE
Deut 14: 5 the **r** deer, the wild goat,

ROEBUCKS
1Ki 4:23 besides deer, gazelles, **r**

ROGELIM
2Sa 17:27 the Gileadite from **R**,
2Sa 19:31 Gileadite came down from **R**

ROGUE (*see* ROGUES)
2Sa 16: 7 You bloodthirsty man, you **r**

ROGUES (*see* ROGUE)
2Ch 13: 7 Then worthless **r** gathered to

ROHGAH
1Ch 7:34 sons of Shemer were Ahi, **R**

ROLL (*see* ROLLED, ROLLING, ROLLS)
Gen 29: 3 they would **r** the stone from
Josh 10:18 **R** large stones against the
1Sa 14:17 Now call the **r** and see who has
1Sa 14:17 And when they had called the **r**
1Sa 14:33 **r** a large stone to me this
2Ch 26:11 to the number on their **r** as
Job 30:14 ruinous storm they **r** along
Prov 26:27 will have it **r** back on him
Jer 6:26 and **r** about in ashes
Jer 25:34 **R** about in the ashes, you
Jer 51:25 **r** you down from the rocks, and
Ezek 27:30 they will **r** about in ashes
Mic 1:10 **r** yourself in the dust
Mark 16: 3 Who will **r** away the stone

ROLLED (*see* ROLL)
Gen 29: 8 they have **r** the stone from
Gen 29:10 **r** the stone from the well's
Josh 5: 9 This day I have **r** away the
2Ki 2: 8 **r** it up, and struck the water
Is 9: 5 and garments **r** in blood, will
Is 28:27 a cartwheel **r** over the cummin
Is 34: 4 shall be **r** up like a scroll
Matt 27:60 he **r** a large stone against
Matt 28: 2 **r** back the stone from the
Mark 15:46 **r** a stone against the door of
Mark 16: 4 the stone had been **r** away
Luke 24: 2 stone **r** away from the tomb
Rev 6:14 as a scroll when it is **r** up

ROLLING (*see* ROLL)
Is 17:13 like a **r** thing before the

ROLLS (*see* ROLL)
Prov 26:27 he who **r** a stone will have it

ROMAMTI-EZER (*see* EZER)
1Ch 25: 4 Hanani, Eliathah, Giddalti, **R**
1Ch 25:31 the twenty-fourth for **R**, his

ROMAN (*see* ROMANS, ROME)
Acts 22:25 to scourge a man who is a **R**
Acts 22:26 you do, for this man is a **R**
Acts 22:27 Tell me, are you a **R**
Acts 22:29 he found out that he was a **R**
Acts 23:27 learned that he was a **R**

ROMANS (*see* ROMAN)
John 11:48 the **R** will come and take away
Acts 16:21 not lawful for us, being **R**
Acts 16:37 us openly, uncondemned **R**, and
Acts 16:38 they heard that they were **R**
Acts 25:16 the **R** to deliver any man to
Acts 28:17 into the hands of the **R**,

ROME (*see* ROMAN)
Acts 2:10 Cyrene, visitors from **R**, both
Acts 18: 2 the Jews to depart from **R**)
Acts 19:21 been there, I must also see **R**
Acts 23:11 must also bear witness at **R**
Acts 28:14 And so we went toward **R**
Acts 28:16 Now when we came to **R**, the
Rom 1: 7 To all who are in **R**, beloved
Rom 1:15 to you who are in **R** also
2Ti 1:17 but when he arrived in **R**, he

ROOF (*see* ROOFS)
Gen 19: 8 come under the shadow of my **r**
Deut 22: 8 make a parapet for your **r**
Josh 2: 6 had brought them up to the **r**
Josh 2: 6 had laid in order on the **r**
Josh 2: 8 she came up to them on the **r**
Judg 16:27 women on the **r** who watched
2Sa 11: 2 walked on the **r** of the king's
2Sa 11: 2 from the **r** he saw a woman
2Sa 18:24 up to the **r** over the gate
2Ki 23:12 The altars that were on the **r**
Neh 8:16 one on the **r** of his house
Job 29:10 stuck to the **r** of their mouth
Ps 137: 6 cling to the **r** of my mouth
Song 7: 9 the **r** of your mouth like the
Lam 4: 4 the **r** of its mouth for thirst
Ezek 3:26 cling to the **r** of your mouth
Ezek 40:13 the gateway from the **r** of one
Ezek 40:13 chamber to the **r** of the other
Matt 8: 8 You should come under my **r**
Mark 2: 4 uncovered the **r** where He was
Luke 7: 6 You should enter under my **r**

ROOFS (*see* ROOF)
Jer 19:13 of all the houses on whose **r**
Jer 32:29 with the houses on whose **r**

ROOM (*see* ROOMS)
Gen 24:23 is there **r** in your father's
Gen 24:25 and feed enough, and **r** to lodge
Gen 26:22 the LORD has made **r** for us
Judg 3:23 of the upper **r** behind him
Judg 3:24 of the upper **r** were locked
Judg 3:25 the doors of the upper **r**
Judg 15: 1 go in to my wife, into her **r**
Judg 16: 9 staying with her in the **r**
Judg 16:12 in wait, staying in the **r**
1Ki 6:16 **r** at the rear of the temple
1Ki 6:27 cherubim inside the inner **r**
1Ki 6:27 other in the middle of the **r**
1Ki 7:50 inner **r** (the Most Holy Place)
1Ki 17:19 upper **r** where he was staying
1Ki 17:23 the upper **r** into the house
2Ki 1: 2 of his upper **r** in Samaria
2Ki 4:10 a small upper **r** on the wall
2Ki 4:11 he turned in to the upper **r**
2Ki 9: 2 and take him to an inner **r**
2Ki 10:25 went into the inner **r** of the
2Ch 3: 5 The larger **r** he paneled with
2Ch 3:11 touching the wall of the **r**
2Ch 3:12 touching the wall of the **r**
Neh 2:14 but there was no **r** for the
Neh 3:31 as the upper **r** at the corner
Neh 3:32 the upper **r** at the corner
Neh 13: 5 prepared for him a large **r**
Neh 13: 7 in preparing a **r** for him in
Neh 13: 8 goods of Tobiah out of the **r**
Ps 80: 9 You prepared **r** for it, And
Prov 18:16 A man's gift makes **r** for him
Jer 7:32 in Tophet until there is no **r**
Ezek 8:12 man in the **r** of his idols
Ezek 41:17 the door, even to the inner **r**
Dan 6:10 And in his upper **r**, with his
Joel 2:16 the bride from her dressing **r**
Zech 10:10 until no more **r** is found for
Mal 3:10 not be **r** enough to receive it
Matt 6: 6 when you pray, go into your **r**
Matt 9:24 Make **r**, for the girl is not
Mark 2: 2 no longer **r** to receive them
Mark 14:14 Where is the guest **r** in which
Mark 14:15 will show you a large upper **r**
Luke 2: 7 was no **r** for them in the inn
Luke 12:17 since I have no **r** to store my
Luke 14:22 and still there is **r**
Luke 22:11 Where is the guest **r** in which
Luke 22:12 a large, furnished upper **r**
Acts 1:13 **r** where they were staying
Acts 9:37 they laid her in an upper **r**
Acts 9:39 brought him to the upper **r**
Acts 20: 8 many lamps in the upper **r**
Phm 22 also prepare a guest **r** for me

ROOMS (*see* ROOM)
Gen 6:14 make **r** in the ark, and cover
2Ch 31:11 **r** in the house of the LORD
Neh 10:38 to the **r** of the storehouse
Neh 12:44 were appointed over the **r** of
Neh 13: 9 them to cleanse the **r**
Prov 24: 4 by knowledge the **r** are filled
Matt 24:26 Look, He is in the inner **r**
Luke 12: 3 **r** will be proclaimed on the

ROOSTER
Matt 26:34 night, before the **r** crows
Matt 26:74 And immediately a **r** crowed
Matt 26:75 Before the **r** crows, you will
Mark 13:35 at the crowing of the **r**, or
Mark 14:30 before the **r** crows twice, you
Mark 14:68 on the porch, and a **r** crowed
Mark 14:72 And a second time the **r** crowed
Mark 14:72 Before the **r** crows twice, you
Luke 22:34 the **r** will not crow this day
Luke 22:60 still speaking, the **r** crowed
Luke 22:61 Before the **r** crows, you will
John 13:38 the **r** shall not crow till you
John 18:27 and immediately a **r** crowed

ROOSTS
Is 60: 8 and like doves to their **r**

ROOT (*see* ROOTED, ROOTS)
Deut 29:18 you a **r** bearing bitterness or
2Ki 19:30 shall again take **r** downward
Job 5: 3 seen the foolish taking **r**
Job 14: 8 Though its **r** may grow old in
Job 19:28 Since the **r** of the matter is
Job 29:19 My **r** is spread out to the
Job 31:12 would **r** out all my increase
Ps 80: 9 And caused it to take deep **r**
Prov 12: 3 but the **r** of the righteous
Prov 12:12 but the **r** of the righteous
Is 5:24 chaff, so their **r** will be as
Is 11:10 there shall be a **R** of Jesse
Is 27: 6 cause to take **r** in Jacob
Is 37:31 shall again take **r** downward
Is 40:24 stock take **r** in the earth
Is 53: 2 and as a **r** out of dry ground
Jer 1:10 to **r** out and to pull down, to
Jer 12: 2 them, yes, they have taken **r**
Hos 9:16 stricken, their **r** is dried up
Mal 4: 1 them neither **r** nor branch
Matt 3:10 is laid to the **r** of the trees
Matt 13: 6 had no **r** they withered away
Matt 13:21 yet he has no **r** in himself
Mark 4: 6 it had no **r** it withered away
Mark 4:17 they have no **r** in themselves,
Luke 3: 9 is laid to the **r** of the trees
Luke 8:13 and these have no **r**, who
Rom 11:16 if the **r** is holy, so are the
Rom 11:17 became a partaker of the **r**
Rom 11:18 that you do not support the **r**
Rom 11:18 but the **r** supports you
Rom 15:12 There shall be a **r** of Jesse
1Ti 6:10 is a **r** of all kinds of evil
Heb 12:15 lest any **r** of bitterness
Rev 5: 5 the **R** of David, has prevailed
Rev 22:16 I am the **R** and the Offspring

ROOTED (*see* ROOT)
Job 31: 8 yes, let my harvest be **r** out
Eph 3:17 that you, being **r** and grounded
Col 2: 7 **r** and built up in Him and

ROOTS (*see* ROOT)
Judg 5:14 those whose **r** were in Amalek
Job 8:17 His **r** wrap around the rock
Job 18:16 His **r** are dried out below, and
Job 28: 9 the mountains at the **r**
Job 30: 4 broom tree **r** for their food
Is 11: 1 shall grow out of his **r**
Is 14:29 **r** will come forth a viper
Is 14:30 will kill your **r** with famine
Jer 17: 8 out its **r** by the river, and
Ezek 17: 6 him, but its **r** were under it
Ezek 17: 7 vine bent its **r** toward him
Ezek 17: 9 will he not pull up its **r**
Ezek 17: 9 to pluck it up by its **r**
Ezek 31: 7 because its **r** reached to
Dan 4:15 **r** in the earth, bound with a
Dan 4:23 **r** in the earth, bound with a
Dan 4:26 **r** of the tree, your kingdom
Dan 7: 8 were plucked out by the **r**
Dan 11: 7 her **r** one shall arise in his
Hos 14: 5 lengthen his **r** like Lebanon
Amos 2: 9 fruit above and his **r** beneath
Mark 11:20 fig tree dried up from the **r**
Luke 17: 6 tree, 'Be pulled up by the **r**
Jude 12 dead, pulled up by the **r**

ROPE (*see* ROPES)
Josh 2:15 by a **r** through the window
Is 3:24 instead of a sash, a **r**
Is 5:18 and sin as if with a cart **r**

ROPES (*see* ROPE)
Judg 15:13 they bound him with two new **r**
Judg 15:14 the **r** that were on his arms
Judg 16:11 **r** that have never been used
Judg 16:12 Therefore Delilah took new **r**
2Sa 17:13 shall bring **r** to that city
1Ki 20:31 **r** around our heads, and go out
1Ki 20:32 put **r** around their heads, and
Job 39:10 wild ox in the furrow with **r**
Jer 38: 6 they let Jeremiah down with **r**
Jer 38:11 let them down by **r** into the
Jer 38:12 your armpits, under the **r**
Jer 38:13 pulled Jeremiah up with **r**
Ezek 3:25 surely they will put **r** on you
Acts 27:32 cut away the **r** of the skiff
Acts 27:40 loosing the rudder **r**

ROSE (*see* RISE)
Gen 4: 8 that Cain **r** against Abel his
Gen 7:17 it **r** high above the earth
Gen 18:16 Then the men **r** from there
Gen 19: 1 he **r** to meet them, and he
Gen 20: 8 So Abimelech **r** early in the
Gen 21:14 So Abraham **r** early in the
Gen 21:32 So Abimelech **r** with Phichol
Gen 22: 3 So Abraham **r** early in the
Gen 22:19 to his young men, and they **r**
Gen 28:18 Then Jacob **r** early in the
Gen 31:17 Then Jacob **r** and set his sons
Gen 32:31 over Penuel the sun **r** on him
Ex 12:30 So Pharaoh **r** in the night, he
Ex 15: 7 those who **r** against You
Ex 24: 4 he **r** early in the morning, and
Ex 32: 6 Then they **r** early on the next
Ex 32: 6 eat and drink, and **r** up to play
Ex 33: 8 that all the people **r**, and
Ex 33:10 door, and all the people **r**
Ex 34: 4 Then Moses **r** early in the
Num 14:40 they **r** early in the morning
Num 16: 2 they **r** up before Moses with
Num 16:25 Then Moses **r** and went to
Num 22:13 So Balaam **r** in the morning and
Num 22:14 And the princes of Moab **r** and
Num 22:21 So Balaam **r** in the morning,
Num 24:25 Then Balaam **r** and departed
Num 25: 7 saw it, he **r** from among the
Josh 3: 1 Then Joshua **r** early in the
Josh 3:16 **r** in a heap very far away at
Josh 6:12 Joshua **r** early in the morning
Josh 6:15 seventh day that they **r** early
Josh 7:16 So Joshua **r** early in the
Josh 8:10 Then Joshua **r** up early in the
Josh 8:14 **r** early and went out against
Judg 6:21 fire **r** out of the rock and
Judg 6:38 When he **r** early the next
Judg 7: 1 who were with him **r** early
Judg 9:34 who were with him **r** by night
Judg 9:35 with him **r** from lying in wait
Judg 9:43 he **r** against them and attacked
Judg 19:10 so he **r** and departed, and came
Judg 20: 5 men of Gibeah **r** against me
Judg 20:19 of Israel **r** in the morning
Judg 20:33 of Israel **r** from their place
Judg 21: 4 that the people **r** early and
Ruth 2:15 when she **r** up to glean, Boaz
1Sa 1:19 Then they **r** early in the
1Sa 15:12 So when Samuel **r** early in the
1Sa 17:20 So David **r** early in the
1Sa 25:42 So Abigail **r** in haste and rode
1Sa 28:25 Then they **r** and went away that
1Sa 29:11 his men **r** early to depart in
2Sa 18:31 all those who **r** against you
2Sa 22:40 me those who **r** against me
1Ki 2:19 the king **r** up to meet her and
1Ki 3:21 when I **r** in the morning to
2Ki 3:22 Then they **r** up early in the
2Ki 3:24 camp of Israel, Israel **r** up
2Ki 7: 5 they **r** at twilight to go to
2Ki 8:21 he **r** by night and attacked the
1Ch 28: 2 Then King David **r** to his feet
2Ch 13: 6 **r** up and rebelled against his
2Ch 20:20 they **r** early in the morning
2Ch 21: 9 he **r** by night and attacked the
2Ch 28:15 were designated by name **r** up
2Ch 29:20 Then King Hezekiah **r** early
Ezra 5: 2 the son of Jozadak **r** up and
Ezra 10: 6 Then Ezra **r** up from before
Neh 3: 1 **r** up with his brethren the
Ps 18:39 me those who **r** up against me
Ps 124: 2 When men **r** up against us,
Song 2: 1 I am the **r** of Sharon, and the

Is 35: 1 rejoice and blossom as the **r**
Jer 26:17 the elders of the land **r** up
Dan 3:24 and he **r** in haste and spoke,
Zeph 3: 7 But they **r** early and corrupted
Mark 10:50 aside his garment, he **r** and
Mark 14:57 And some **r** up and bore false
Mark 16: 9 Now when He **r** early on the
Luke 4:29 **r** up and thrust Him out of the
Luke 5:25 he **r** up before them, took up
Luke 5:28 all, **r** up, and followed Him
Luke 22:45 When He **r** up from prayer, and
Luke 24:33 So they **r** up that very hour
John 11:31 saw that Mary **r** up quickly
John 13: 4 **r** from supper and laid aside
Acts 5:17 Then the high priest **r** up
Acts 5:36 some time ago Theudas **r** up
Acts 5:37 Judas of Galilee **r** up in the
Acts 14:20 gathered around him, he **r** up
Acts 15: 5 Pharisees who believed **r** up
Acts 15: 7 been much dispute, Peter **r** up
Acts 16:22 Then the multitude **r** up
Acts 18:12 one accord **r** up against Paul
Rom 14: 9 to this end Christ died and **r**
1Co 10: 7 eat and drink, and **r** up to play
1Co 15: 4 that He **r** again the third day
2Co 5:15 who died for them and **r** again
1Th 4:14 **r** again, even so God will

ROSH
Gen 46:21 Ashbel, Gera, Naaman, Ehi, **R**
Ezek 38: 2 of Magog, the prince of **R**
Ezek 38: 3 you, O Gog, the prince of **R**
Ezek 39: 1 you, O Gog, prince of **R**,

ROT (*see* ROTTEN)
Num 5:21 the LORD makes your thigh **r**
Num 5:22 belly swell and your thigh **r**
Num 5:27 will swell, her thigh will **r**
Prov 10: 7 the name of the wicked will **r**
Is 40:20 a tree that will not **r**

ROTTEN (*see* ROT, ROTTENNESS)
Job 13:28 Man decays like a **r** thing
Job 41:27 as straw, and bronze as **r** wood
Jer 29:17 will make them like **r** figs

ROTTENNESS (*see* ROTTEN)
Prov 12: 4 shame is like **r** in his bones
Prov 14:30 but envy is **r** to the bones
Is 5:24 so their root will be as **r**
Hos 5:12 to the house of Judah like **r**
Hab 3:16 **r** entered my bones

ROUGH (*see* ROUGHLY)
Is 27: 8 He removes it by His **r** wind
Is 40: 4 and the **r** places smooth
Luke 3: 5 and the **r** ways made smooth

ROUGHLY (*see* ROUGH)
Gen 42: 7 to them and spoke **r** to them
Gen 42:30 of the land spoke **r** to us
1Sa 20:10 if your father answers you **r**
1Ki 12:13 king answered the people **r**
2Ch 10:13 Then the king answered them **r**
Prov 18:23 but the rich answers **r**

ROUND (*see* ROUNDED)
Ex 16:14 was a small **r** substance, as
Deut 12:10 from all your enemies **r** about
Josh 23: 1 all their enemies **r** about
1Ki 7:23 it was completely **r**
1Ki 7:31 and the opening was **r**, shaped
1Ki 7:31 the panels were square, not **r**
1Ki 7:35 a cubit, it was perfectly **r**
1Ki 10:19 the throne was **r** at the back
2Ch 4: 2 it was completely **r**
Ps 97: 3 burns up His enemies **r** about
Acts 28:13 From there we circled **r** and
Rom 15:19 **r** about to Illyricum I have

ROUNDABOUT
2Ki 3: 9 on that **r** route seven days

ROUNDED (*see* ROUND)
Song 7: 2 Your navel is a **r** goblet

ROUSE (*see* ROUSED)
Gen 49: 9 and as a lion, who shall **r** him
Num 24: 9 and as a lion, who will **r** him

ROUSED (*see* ROUSE)
Job 14:12 nor be **r** from their sleep

ROUTE
2Ki 3: 9 that roundabout **r** seven days

ROUTED
Josh 10:10 So the LORD **r** them before
Judg 4:15 And the LORD **r** Sisera and all
Judg 8:12 and **r** the whole army

ROVE (*see* ROVED)
1Sa 30:31 his men were accustomed to **r**

ROVED (*see* ROVE)
Ezek 19: 6 He **r** among the lions, and

ROW (*see* ROWED, ROWING, ROWS)
Ex 28:17 The first **r** shall be a
Ex 28:17 this shall be the first **r**
Ex 28:18 the second **r** shall be a
Ex 28:19 the third **r**, a jacinth, an
Ex 28:20 and the fourth **r**, a beryl, an
Ex 39:10 a **r** with a sardius, a topaz,
Ex 39:10 and an emerald was the first **r**
Ex 39:11 the second **r**, a turquoise, a
Ex 39:12 the third **r**, a jacinth, an
Ex 39:13 the fourth **r**, a beryl, an
Lev 24: 6 them in two rows, six in a **r**
Lev 24: 7 pure frankincense on each **r**
1Ki 6:36 stone and a **r** of cedar beams
1Ki 7: 3 pillars, fifteen to a **r**
1Ki 7:12 stones and a **r** of cedar beams
Ezra 6: 4 stones and one **r** of new timber
Ezek 46:23 There was a **r** of building

ROWED (*see* ROW)
Jon 1:13 Nevertheless the men **r** hard
John 6:19 So when they had **r** about

ROWING (*see* ROW)
Mark 6:48 He saw them straining at **r**

ROWS (*see* ROW)
Ex 28:17 in it, four **r** of stones
Ex 39:10 set in it four **r** of stones
Lev 24: 6 You shall set them in two **r**
1Ki 6:36 with three **r** of hewn stone
1Ki 7: 2 with four **r** of cedar pillars,
1Ki 7: 4 beveled frames in three **r**
1Ki 7:12 with three **r** of hewn stones
1Ki 7:18 two **r** of pomegranates above
1Ki 7:20 such pomegranates in **r** on
1Ki 7:24 in two **r** when it was cast
1Ki 7:42 **r** of pomegranates for each
2Ch 4: 3 The oxen were cast in two **r**
2Ch 4:13 **r** of pomegranates for each
Ezra 6: 4 with three **r** of heavy stones
Job 41:15 His **r** of scales are his pride
Is 28:25 cummin, plant the wheat in **r**
Ezek 46:23 the **r** of stones all around

ROYAL (*see* ROYALTY)
Gen 49:20 and he shall yield **r** dainties
Josh 10: 2 like one of the **r** cities
1Sa 27: 5 dwell in the **r** city with you
2Sa 12:26 of Ammon, and took the **r** city
1Ki 10:13 her according to the **r** bounty
2Ki 11: 1 and destroyed all the **r** heirs
2Ki 15: 5 son was over the **r** house,
2Ki 25:25 of Elishama, of the **r** family
1Ch 29:25 and bestowed on him such **r**
2Ch 2: 1 and a **r** house for himself
2Ch 2:12 LORD and a **r** house for himself
2Ch 22:10 destroyed all the **r** heirs of
Esth 1: 7 with **r** wine in abundance,
Esth 1: 9 **r** palace which belonged to
Esth 1:11 the king, wearing her **r** crown
Esth 1:19 let a **r** decree go out from
Esth 1:19 and let the king give her **r**
Esth 2:16 Ahasuerus, into his **r** palace
Esth 2:17 so he set the **r** crown upon
Esth 5: 1 Esther put on her **r** robes
Esth 5: 1 **r** throne in the **r** house
Esth 6: 8 let a **r** robe be brought which
Esth 6: 8 which has a **r** crest placed on
Esth 8:10 riding on **r** horses bred from
Esth 8:14 who rode on **r** horses went out
Esth 8:15 the king in **r** apparel of blue
Ps 45:13 The **r** daughter is all
Is 62: 3 a **r** diadem in the hand of
Jer 41: 1 of Elishama, of the **r** family
Jer 43:10 his **r** pavilion over them
Dan 4:29 about the **r** palace of Babylon
Dan 4:30 that I have built for a **r**
Dan 6: 7 to establish a **r** statute and
Amos 7:13 and it is the **r** residence
Zech 10: 3 as His **r** horse in the battle
Acts 12:21 Herod, arrayed in **r** apparel
Jas 2: 8 the **r** law according to the
1Pe 2: 9 a **r** priesthood, a holy nation

ROYALTY (*see* ROYAL)
1Sa 10:25 the people the behavior of **r**
Ezek 16:13 beautiful, and succeeded to **r**
Dan 11:21 will not give the honor of **r**

RUBBED (*see* RUBBING)
Ezek 16: 4 you were not **r** with salt nor
Ezek 29:18 bald, and every shoulder **r** raw

RUBBING (*see* RUBBED)
Luke 6: 1 them, **r** them in their hands

RUBBISH
2Ch 29: 5 carry out the **r** from the holy
Neh 4: 2 stones from the heaps of **r**
Neh 4:10 there is so much **r** that we
Phil 3: 8 things, and count them as **r**

RUBIES
Job 28:18 price of wisdom is above **r**
Prov 3:15 She is more precious than **r**
Prov 8:11 for wisdom is better than **r**
Prov 20:15 is gold and a multitude of **r**
Prov 31:10 For her worth is far above **r**
Is 54:12 will make your pinnacles of **r**
Lam 4: 7 more ruddy in body than **r**
Ezek 27:16 fine linen, corals, and **r**

RUDDER
Acts 27:40 meanwhile loosing the **r** ropes
Jas 3: 4 **r** wherever the pilot desires

RUDDY
1Sa 16:12 Now he was **r**, with bright
1Sa 17:42 for he was but a youth, **r**
Song 5:10 My beloved is white and **r**,
Lam 4: 7 they were more **r** in body than

RUDELY
1Co 13: 5 does not behave **r**, does not

RUE
Luke 11:42 For you tithe mint and **r** and

RUFUS
Mark 15:21 the father of Alexander and **R**
Rom 16:13 Greet **R**, chosen in the Lord,

RUGGED
Is 2:21 into the crags of the **r** rocks

RUIN (*see* RUINED, RUINOUS, RUINS)
Ruth 4: 6 lest I **r** my own inheritance
2Ki 3:19 **r** every good piece of land
2Ch 28:23 But they were the **r** of him
Ps 89:40 brought his strongholds to **r**
Prov 5:14 I was on the verge of total **r**
Prov 19:13 son is the **r** of his father
Prov 24:22 who knows the **r** those two can
Prov 26:28 and a flattering mouth works **r**
Is 23:13 palaces, and brought it to **r**
Is 25: 2 a **r**, a fortified city a **r**
Jer 13: 9 I will **r** the pride of Judah
Lam 2:13 For your **r** is spread wide as
Ezek 18:30 iniquity will not be your **r**
Ezek 27:27 the seas on the day of your **r**
Ezek 31:13 On its **r** will remain all the
Hos 10: 2 he will **r** their sacred
Amos 5: 9 He rains **r** upon the strong,
Luke 6:49 the **r** of that house was great
2Ti 2:14 to the **r** of the hearers

RUINED (*see* RUIN)
Prov 25:10 and your reputation be **r**
Is 24:16 I am **r**, **r**! Woe to me!
Is 60:12 nations shall be utterly **r**
Is 61: 4 shall repair the **r** cities
Jer 13: 7 and there was the sash, **r**
Ezek 36:35 **r** cities are now fortified and
Ezek 36:36 have rebuilt the **r** places
Ezek 36:38 so shall the **r** cities be
Joel 1: 7 My vine, and **r** My fig tree
Joel 1:10 for the grain is **r**, the new
Nah 2: 2 out and **r** their vine branches
Zech 11: 2 the mighty trees are **r**
Matt 9:17 and the wineskins are **r**
Mark 2:22 and the wineskins are **r**
Luke 5:37 and the wineskins will be **r**

RUINOUS (*see* RUIN)
Job 30:14 under the **r** storm they roll
Is 17: 1 city, and it will be a **r** heap

RUINS (*see* RUIN)
2Ki 19:25 cities into heaps of **r**
Ezra 9: 9 of our God, to rebuild its **r**
Job 3:14 who built **r** for themselves,
Job 15:28 are destined to become **r**
Job 30:24 His hand against a heap of **r**
Is 3: 6 let these **r** be under your
Is 17:11 heap of **r** in the day of grief
Is 37:26 cities into heaps of **r**
Is 61: 4 they shall rebuild the old **r**
Jer 9:11 make Jerusalem a heap of **r**
Jer 26:18 shall become heaps of **r**, and
Jer 50:26 cast her up as heaps of **r**
Ezek 33:24 they who inhabit those **r** in
Ezek 33:27 the **r** shall fall by the sword
Ezek 36:10 be inhabited and the **r** rebuilt
Ezek 36:33 and the **r** shall be rebuilt
Amos 9:11 I will raise up its **r**, and
Mic 1: 6 a heap of **r** in the field,
Mic 3:12 shall become heaps of **r**, and
Hag 1: 4 and this temple to lie in **r**
Hag 1: 9 of My house that is in **r**,
Zech 11: 3 for their glory is in **r**
Zech 11: 3 pride of the Jordan is in **r**
Acts 15:16 I will rebuild its **r**, and I

RULE (*see* RULED, RULER, RULES, RULING)
Gen 1:16 greater light to **r** the day
Gen 1:16 lesser light to **r** the night
Gen 1:18 to **r** over the day and over the
Gen 3:16 and he shall **r** over you
Gen 4: 7 you, but you should **r** over it
Lev 25:43 You shall not **r** over him
Lev 25:46 you shall not **r** over one
Lev 25:53 he shall not **r** with rigor
Judg 8:22 **R** over us, both you and your
Judg 8:23 I will not **r** over you
Judg 8:23 nor shall my son **r** over you
Judg 8:23 the LORD shall **r** over you
Judg 13:12 will be the boy's **r** of life
Judg 15:11 the Philistines **r** over us
2Ch 20: 6 do You not **r** over all the
2Ch 21:10 Libnah revolted against his **r**
Neh 5:15 bore **r** over the people, but I
Ps 89: 9 You **r** the raging of the sea
Ps 110: 2 **R** in the midst of Your
Ps 136: 8 The sun to **r** by day, For His
Ps 136: 9 moon and stars to **r** by night
Prov 8:16 By me princes **r**, and nobles,
Prov 12:24 hand of the diligent will **r**
Prov 17: 2 A wise servant will **r** over a
Prov 19:10 a servant to **r** over princes
Prov 25:28 Whoever has no **r** over his own
Eccl 2:19 Yet he will **r** over all my
Is 3: 4 and babes shall **r** over them
Is 3:12 and women **r** over them
Is 14: 2 and **r** over their oppressors
Is 19: 4 fierce king will **r** over them
Is 28:14 who **r** this people who are in
Is 32: 1 princes will **r** with justice
Is 40:10 and His arm shall **r** for Him
Is 41: 2 him, and made him **r** over kings
Is 44:13 craftsman stretches out his **r**
Is 52: 5 Those who **r** over them make
Jer 5:31 the priests **r** by their own
Jer 13:18 for your **r** shall collapse,
Lam 5: 8 Servants **r** over us
Ezek 20:33 poured out, I will **r** over you
Ezek 29:15 **r** over the nations anymore
Dan 2:39 which shall **r** over all the
Dan 11: 3 arise, who shall **r** with great
Dan 11:39 cause them to **r** over many
Joel 2:17 nations should **r** over them
Zech 6:13 shall sit and **r** on His throne
1Co 15:24 when He puts an end to all **r**
Gal 6:16 as walk according to this **r**
Phil 3:16 let us walk by the same **r**
Col 3:15 peace of God **r** in your hearts
1Ti 3: 5 know how to **r** his own house
1Ti 5:17 Let the elders who **r** well be
Heb 13: 7 Remember those who **r** over
Heb 13:17 Obey those who **r** over you
Heb 13:24 all those who **r** over you, and
Rev 2:27 He shall **r** them with a rod
Rev 12: 5 a male Child who was to **r** all
Rev 19:15 He Himself will **r** them with a

RULED (*see* RULE)
Gen 24: 2 who **r** over all that he had,
Gen 41:40 be **r** according to your word
Josh 12: 2 **r** half of Gilead, from Aroer,
Ruth 1: 1 in the days when the judges **r**
1Ki 9:23 who **r** over the people who did
1Ch 4:22 Saraph, who **r** in Moab, and
2Ch 8:10 fifty, who **r** over the people
Ezra 4:20 who have **r** over all the
Ps 106:41 who hated them **r** over them
Is 14: 6 he who **r** the nations in anger
Is 63:19 of old, over whom You never **r**
Ezek 34: 4 and cruelty you have **r** them
Dan 11: 4 his dominion with which he **r**

RULER (*see* RULE, RULER'S, RULERS)
Gen 45: 8 a **r** throughout all the land
Ex 22:28 nor curse a **r** of your people
Lev 4:22 When a **r** has sinned, and done
Josh 22:14 one **r** each from the chief
Judg 9:30 the **r** of the city, heard the
1Sa 25:30 appointed you **r** over Israel
2Sa 5: 2 Israel, and be **r** over Israel
2Sa 6:21 to appoint me **r** over the
2Sa 7: 8 to be **r** over My people, over
1Ki 1:35 him to be **r** over Israel and
1Ki 11:34 because I have made him **r** all
1Ki 14: 7 made you **r** over My people
1Ki 16: 2 made you **r** over My people
1Ch 5: 2 and from him came a **r**,
1Ch 11: 2 be **r** over My people Israel
1Ch 17: 7 that you should be **r** over My
1Ch 28: 4 has chosen Judah to be the **r**
2Ch 6: 5 be a **r** over My people Israel
2Ch 7:18 to have a man as **r** in Israel
2Ch 19:11 the **r** of the house of Judah,
2Ch 31:12 the Levite was **r** over them
2Ch 31:13 Azariah the **r** of the house of
Ps 105:20 The **r** of the people let him
Ps 105:21 **r** of all his possessions,
Prov 6: 7 no captain, overseer or **r**
Prov 23: 1 you sit down to eat with a **r**
Prov 25:15 forbearance a **r** is persuaded
Prov 28:15 a wicked **r** over poor people
Prov 28:16 A **r** who lacks understanding
Prov 29:12 If a **r** pays attention to lies
Eccl 9:17 the shout of a **r** of fools
Eccl 10: 4 of the **r** rises against you
Eccl 10: 5 error proceeding from the **r**
Is 3: 6 you be our **r**, and let these
Is 3: 7 not make me a **r** of the people
Is 16: 1 the lamb to the **r** of the land
Jer 51:46 in the land, **r** against **r**)
Dan 2:10 or **r** has ever asked such
Dan 2:38 has made you **r** over them all
Dan 2:48 he made him **r** over the whole
Dan 5: 7 be the third **r** in the kingdom
Dan 5:16 be the third **r** in the kingdom
Dan 5:29 be the third **r** in the kingdom
Dan 11:18 But a **r** shall bring the
Mic 5: 2 Me the One to be **r** in Israel
Hab 1:14 that have no **r** over them
Zech 10: 4 from him every **r** together
Matt 2: 6 **R** who will shepherd My people
Matt 9:18 a **r** came and worshiped Him,
Matt 9:34 demons by the **r** of the demons
Matt 12:24 the **r** of the demons
Matt 24:45 made **r** over his household
Matt 24:47 make him **r** over all his goods
Matt 25:21 I will make you **r** over many
Matt 25:23 I will make you **r** over many
Mark 3:22 By the **r** of the demons He
Mark 5:35 some came from the **r** of the
Mark 5:36 He said to the **r** of the
Mark 5:38 of the **r** of the synagogue
Luke 8:41 he was a **r** of the synagogue
Luke 8:49 someone came from the **r** of
Luke 11:15 the **r** of the demons
Luke 12:42 make **r** over his household
Luke 12:44 him **r** over all that he has
Luke 13:14 But the **r** of the synagogue
Luke 18:18 Now a certain **r** asked Him
John 3: 1 Nicodemus, a **r** of the Jews
John 12:31 now the **r** of this world will
John 14:30 for the **r** of this world is
John 16:11 because the **r** of this world
Acts 7:27 saying, 'Who made you a **r**
Acts 7:35 saying, 'Who made you a **r**
Acts 7:35 is the one God sent to be a **r**
Acts 18: 8 the **r** of the synagogue,
Acts 18:17 the **r** of the synagogue, and
Acts 23: 5 evil of the **r** of your people
Rev 1: 5 the **r** over the kings of the

RULER'S (*see* RULER)
Prov 29:26 Many seek the **r** favor, but
Matt 9:23 Jesus came into the **r** house

RULERS (*see* RULER)
Ex 16:22 all the **r** of the congregation
Ex 18:21 them to be **r** of thousands
Ex 18:21 **r** of hundreds, **r** of fifties
Ex 18:21 and **r** of tens
Ex 18:25 **r** of thousands, **r** of hundreds
Ex 18:25 **r** of fifties, and **r** of tens
Ex 34:31 all the **r** of the congregation
Ex 35:27 The **r** brought onyx stones, and
Josh 9:15 the **r** of the congregation
Josh 9:18 them, because the **r** of the
Josh 9:18 murmured against the **r**
Josh 9:19 Then all the **r** said to all
Josh 9:21 And the **r** said to them,
Josh 9:21 as the **r** had promised them
Josh 17: 4 son of Nun, and before the **r**
Josh 22:14 and with him ten **r**, one ruler
Josh 22:30 the **r** of the congregation,
Josh 22:32 Eleazar the priest, and the **r**
Judg 5: 9 My heart is with the **r** of
Judg 5:14 from Machir **r** came down, and
Judg 18: 7 There were no **r** in the land
2Ki 10: 1 to the **r** of Jezreel, to the
2Ch 29:20 gathered the **r** of the city
2Ch 35: 8 **r** of the house of God, gave
Ezra 9: 2 **r** has been foremost in this
Neh 4:19 I said to the nobles, the **r**
Neh 5: 7 I rebuked the nobles and **r**
Neh 5:17 hundred and fifty Jews and **r**
Neh 7: 5 to gather the nobles, the **r**
Neh 12:40 and the half of the **r** with me
Neh 13:11 So I contended with the **r**
Ps 2: 2 the **r** take counsel together,
Prov 8:15 reign, and **r** decree justice
Eccl 7:19 more than ten **r** of the city
Is 1:10 of the LORD, you **r** of Sodom
Is 14: 5 wicked, the scepter of the **r**
Is 22: 3 All your **r** have fled together
Is 49: 7 abhors, to the Servant of **r**
Jer 2: 8 the **r** also transgressed
Jer 12:10 Many **r** have destroyed My
Jer 22:22 wind shall eat up all your **r**
Jer 33:26 be **r** over the descendants of
Jer 51:23 in pieces governors and **r**
Jer 51:28 its governors and all its **r**
Ezek 19:11 branches for scepters of **r**
Ezek 23: 6 in purple, captains and **r**, all
Ezek 23:12 Assyrians, Captains and **r**,
Ezek 23:23 young men, governors and **r**
Hos 4:18 Her **r** dearly love dishonor
Mic 3: 1 you **r** of the house of Israel
Mic 3: 9 **r** of the house of Israel, who
Matt 2: 6 least among the **r** of Judah
Matt 20:25 You know that the **r** of the
Mark 5:22 one of the **r** of the synagogue
Mark 10:42 those who are considered **r**
Mark 13: 9 you will be brought before **r**
Luke 14: 1 the **r** of the Pharisees to eat
Luke 21:12 kings and **r** for My name's sake
Luke 23:13 the chief priests, the **r**, and
Luke 23:35 But even the **r** with them
Luke 24:20 our **r** delivered Him to be
John 7:26 Do the **r** know indeed that
John 7:48 Have any of the **r** or the
John 12:42 the **r** many believed in Him
Acts 3:17 ignorance, as did also your **r**
Acts 4: 5 on the next day, that their **r**
Acts 4: 8 **R** of the people and elders of
Acts 4:26 the **r** were gathered together
Acts 13:15 the **r** of the synagogue sent
Acts 13:27 in Jerusalem, and their **r**,
Acts 14: 5 and Jews, with their **r**, to
Acts 17: 6 brethren to the **r** of the city
Acts 17: 8 the **r** of the city when they
Rom 13: 3 For **r** are not a terror to
1Co 2: 6 nor of the **r** of this age, who
1Co 2: 8 of the **r** of this age knew
Eph 6:12 against the **r** of the darkness
Tit 3: 1 them to be subject to **r** and

RULES (*see* RULE)
2Sa 23: 3 He who **r** over men must be
Ps 22:28 And He **r** over the nations
Ps 59:13 let them know that God **r** in
Ps 66: 7 He **r** by His power forever

Ps 103:19 And His kingdom **r** over all
Prov 16:32 he who **r** his spirit than he
Prov 22: 7 The rich **r** over the poor, and
Prov 29: 2 but when a wicked man **r**, the
Eccl 8: 9 man **r** over another to his own
Dan 4:17 High **r** in the kingdom of men
Dan 4:25 High **r** in the kingdom of men
Dan 4:26 come to know that Heaven **r**
Dan 4:32 High **r** in the kingdom of men
Dan 5:21 God **r** in the kingdom of men
1Ti 3: 4 one who **r** his own house well,
2Ti 2: 5 competes according to the **r**

RULING (*see* RULE)
2Sa 23: 4 **r** in the fear of God
Jer 22:30 David, and **r** anymore in Judah
Ezek 19:14 a scepter for **r**
1Ti 3:12 **r** their children and their own

RUMAH (*see* ARUMAH)
2Ki 23:36 the daughter of Pedaiah of **R**

RUMBLING
Job 37: 2 the **r** that comes from His
Jer 47: 3 at the **r** of his wheels, the

RUMOR (*see* RUMORS)
2Ki 19: 7 him, and he shall hear a **r**
Is 37: 7 him, and he shall hear a **r**
Jer 51:46 you fear for the **r** that will
Jer 51:46 land (a **r** will come one year
Jer 51:46 in another year a **r** will come
Ezek 7:26 and **r** will be upon **r**

RUMORS (*see* RUMOR)
Neh 6: 6 according to these **r**, you
Matt 24: 6 hear of wars and **r** of wars
Mark 13: 7 **r** of wars, do not be troubled

RUN (*see* RAN, RUNNER, RUNNING, RUNS)
Gen 49:22 his branches **r** over the wall
1Sa 8:11 and some will **r** before his
1Sa 17:17 **r** to your brothers at the
1Sa 20: 6 he might **r** over to Bethlehem
1Sa 20:36 Now **r**, find the arrows which
2Sa 15: 1 and fifty men to **r** before him
2Sa 18:19 Let me **r** now and take the news
2Sa 18:22 me also **r** after the Cushite
2Sa 18:22 Why will you **r**, my son, since
2Sa 18:23 he said, "let me **r**."
2Sa 18:23 So he said to him, "**R**."
2Sa 22:30 You I can **r** against a troop
1Ki 1: 5 and fifty men to **r** before him
1Ki 17:14 shall the jar of oil **r** dry
1Ki 17:16 nor did the jar of oil **r** dry
2Ki 4:22 that I may **r** to the man of
2Ki 4:26 Please **r** now to meet her, and
2Ki 5:20 I will **r** after him and take
2Ch 16: 9 For the eyes of the LORD **r** to
Job 1: 5 feasting had **r** their course
Ps 18:29 You I can **r** against a troop
Ps 19: 5 a strong man to **r** its race
Ps 58: 7 as waters which **r** continually
Ps 59: 4 They **r** and prepare themselves
Ps 78:16 waters to **r** down like rivers
Ps 119:32 I will **r** in the way of Your
Ps 119:136 Rivers of water **r** down from
Prov 1:16 for their feet **r** to evil, and
Prov 4:12 be hindered, and when you **r**
Prov 18:10 the righteous **r** to it and are
Eccl 1: 7 All the rivers **r** into the sea
Song 1: 4 We will **r** after you
Is 33: 4 locusts, He shall **r** upon them
Is 40:31 like eagles, they shall **r**
Is 55: 5 not know you shall **r** to you
Is 59: 7 Their feet **r** to evil, and they
Jer 5: 1 **R** to and fro through the
Jer 9:18 our eyes may **r** with tears
Jer 12: 5 If you have **r** with the
Jer 13:17 **r** down with tears, because
Jer 49: 3 and **r** to and fro by the walls
Jer 49:19 make him **r** away from her
Jer 50:44 them suddenly **r** away from her
Jer 51:31 runner will **r** to meet another
Lam 2:18 let tears **r** down like a river
Ezek 24:16 nor shall your tears **r** down
Ezek 32:14 make their rivers **r** like oil
Dan 12: 4 many shall **r** to and fro, and
Joel 2: 4 like swift steeds, so they **r**
Joel 2: 7 They **r** like mighty men, they
Joel 2: 9 They **r** to and fro in the city,
Joel 2: 9 they **r** on the wall;
Amos 5:24 let justice **r** down like water
Amos 6:12 Do horses **r** on rocks
Amos 8:12 they shall **r** to and fro,
Nah 2: 4 they **r** like lightning
Hab 2: 2 that he may **r** who reads it
Zech 2: 4 **R**, speak to this young man,
Acts 27:17 fearing lest they should **r**
Acts 27:26 we must **r** aground on a
Acts 27:29 should **r** aground on the rocks
Acts 27:39 to **r** the ship if possible
1Co 9:24 those who **r** in a race all **r**
1Co 9:24 **R** in such a way that you may
1Co 9:26 Therefore I **r** thus
Gal 2: 2 means I might **r**, or had **r**
Phil 2:16 of Christ that I have not **r**
Heb 12: 1 let us **r** with endurance the
1Pe 4: 4 it strange that you do not **r**
Jude 11 have **r** greedily in the error

RUNNER (*see* RUN, RUNNERS)
Job 9:25 my days are swifter than a **r**
Jer 51:31 One **r** will run to meet

RUNNERS (*see* RUNNER)
2Ch 30: 6 Then the **r** went throughout
2Ch 30:10 So the **r** passed from city to

RUNNING (*see* RUN)
Gen 26:19 found a well of **r** water there
Lev 14: 5 earthen vessel over **r** water
Lev 14: 6 was killed over the **r** water
Lev 14:50 earthen vessel over **r** water
Lev 14:51 slain bird and in the **r** water
Lev 14:52 the **r** water and the living
Lev 15:13 and bathe his body in **r** water
Num 19:17 **r** water shall be put on them
2Sa 18:24 and there was a man, **r** alone
2Sa 18:26 watchman saw another man **r**
2Sa 18:26 There is another man, **r** alone
2Sa 18:27 I think the **r** of the first is
2Sa 18:27 like the **r** of Ahimaaz
2Ki 5:21 Naaman saw him **r** after him
2Ch 23:12 the noise of the people **r**
Job 15:26 **r** stubbornly against Him with
Ps 133: 2 **R** down on the beard, The
Ps 133: 2 **R** down on the edge of his
Prov 5:15 **r** water from your own well
Prov 6:18 that are swift in **r** to evil
Is 33: 4 as the **r** to and fro of locusts
Ezek 31: 4 with their rivers **r** around
Ezek 47: 2 **r** out on the right side
Mark 9:15 and **r** to Him, greeted Him
Mark 9:25 the people came **r** together
Mark 10:17 out on the road, one came **r**
Luke 6:38 **r** over will be put into your
Acts 21: 1 **r** a straight course we came
Acts 27:16 **r** under the shelter of an
Rev 9: 9 many horses **r** into battle

RUNS (*see* RUN)
Lev 15: 3 whether his body **r** with his
Lev 15:25 or if it **r** beyond her usual
Job 16:14 He **r** at me like a warrior
Ps 23: 5 My cup **r** over
Ps 147:15 His word **r** very swiftly
Hag 1: 9 one of you **r** to his own house
Rom 9:16 who wills, nor of him who **r**

RURAL
Deut 3: 5 besides a great many **r** towns

RUSH (*see* RUSHED, RUSHES, RUSHING)
Judg 9:33 rise early and **r** upon the city
Is 17:13 The nations will **r** like the

RUSHED (*see* RUSH)
Judg 9:44 that was with him **r** forward
Judg 9:44 the other two companies **r**
Judg 20:37 ambush quickly **r** upon Gibeah
1Sa 14:32 the people **r** on the spoil, and
Acts 19:29 **r** into the theater with one

RUSHES (*see* RUSH)
Job 41:20 a boiling pot and burning **r**
Is 19: 6 the reeds and **r** will wither
Is 35: 7 be grass with reeds and **r**
Jer 8: 6 as the horse **r** into the

RUSHING (*see* RUSH)
Is 17:12 the **r** of nations that make a **r**
Is 17:12 like the **r** of mighty waters
Is 17:13 like the **r** of many waters
Jer 47: 3 at the **r** of his chariots, at
Acts 2: 2 as of a **r** mighty wind, and it

RUST
Matt 6:19 **r** destroy and where thieves
Matt 6:20 neither moth nor **r** destroys

RUTH
Ruth 1: 4 and the name of the other **R**
Ruth 1:14 but **R** clung to her
Ruth 1:16 But **R** said: "Entreat me not
Ruth 1:22 and **R** the Moabitess her
Ruth 2: 2 So **R** the Moabitess said to
Ruth 2: 8 Then Boaz said to **R**, "You
Ruth 2:21 Then **R** the Moabitess said,
Ruth 2:22 And Naomi said to **R** her
Ruth 3: 9 I am **R**, your maidservant
Ruth 4: 5 buy it from **R** the Moabitess
Ruth 4:10 **R** the Moabitess, the wife of
Ruth 4:13 So Boaz took **R** and she became
Matt 1: 5 Rahab, Boaz begot Obed by **R**

RUTHLESS
Prov 11:16 but **r** men retain riches

S

SABACHTHANI
Matt 27:46 Eli, Eli, lama **s**
Mark 15:34 Eloi, Eloi, lama **s**

SABAOTH
Rom 9:29 LORD of **S** had left us a seed
Jas 5: 4 the ears of the Lord of **S**

SABBATH (*see* SABBATH-REST, SABBATHS)
Ex 16:23 **S** rest, a holy **S** to the LORD
Ex 16:25 for today is a **S** to the LORD
Ex 16:26 seventh day, which is the **S**
Ex 16:29 the LORD has given you the **S**
Ex 20: 8 Remember the **S** day, to keep
Ex 20:10 is the **S** of the LORD your God
Ex 20:11 the LORD blessed the **S** day
Ex 31:14 You shall keep the **S**,
Ex 31:15 the seventh is the **S** of rest
Ex 31:15 does any work on the **S** day
Ex 31:16 of Israel shall keep the **S**
Ex 31:16 to observe the **S** throughout
Ex 35: 2 you, a **S** of rest to the LORD
Ex 35: 3 your habitations on the **S** day
Lev 16:31 It is a **s** of solemn rest for
Lev 23: 3 day is a **S** of solemn rest
Lev 23: 3 it is the **S** of the LORD in
Lev 23:11 on the day after the **S** the
Lev 23:15 from the day after the **S**,
Lev 23:16 the day after the seventh **S**
Lev 23:32 be to you a **s** of solemn rest
Lev 23:32 you shall celebrate your **s**
Lev 24: 8 Every **S** he shall set it in
Lev 25: 2 shall keep a **s** to the LORD
Lev 25: 4 year there shall be a **s** of
Lev 25: 4 for the land, a **s** to the LORD
Lev 25: 6 the **s** produce of the land
Num 15:32 gathering sticks on the **S** day
Num 28: 9 on the **S** day two lambs in
Num 28:10 burnt offering for every **S**
Deut 5:12 Observe the **S** day, to keep
Deut 5:14 is the **S** of the LORD your God
Deut 5:15 you to keep the **S** day
2Ki 4:23 the New Moon nor the **S**
2Ki 11: 5 **S** shall be keeping watch over
2Ki 11: 7 you who go off duty on the **S**
2Ki 11: 9 were to be on duty on the **S**
2Ki 11: 9 were going off duty on the **S**
2Ki 16:18 Also he removed the **S**
1Ch 9:32 the showbread for every **S**
2Ch 23: 4 of you entering on the **S**, of
2Ch 23: 8 were to be on duty on the **S**
2Ch 23: 8 were going off duty on the **S**
2Ch 36:21 she lay desolate she kept **S**
Neh 9:14 known to them Your holy **S**
Neh 10:31 grain to sell on the **S** day
Neh 10:31 not buy it from them on the **S**
Neh 13:15 wine presses on the **S**, and
Neh 13:15 into Jerusalem on the **S** day
Neh 13:16 sold them on the **S** to the
Neh 13:17 which you profane the **S** day
Neh 13:18 on Israel by profaning the **S**
Neh 13:19 began to be dark before the **S**
Neh 13:19 be opened till after the **S**
Neh 13:19 be brought in on the **S** day

Neh 13:21 on they came no more on the **S**
Neh 13:22 gates, to sanctify the **S** day
Is 56: 2 who keeps from defiling the **S**
Is 56: 6 who keeps from defiling the **S**
Is 58:13 away your foot from the **S**
Is 58:13 call the **S** a delight, the
Is 66:23 from one **S** to another, all
Jer 17:21 bear no burden on the **S** day
Jer 17:22 of your houses on the **S** day
Jer 17:22 work, but hallow the **S** day
Jer 17:24 of this city on the **S** day
Jer 17:24 but hallow the **S** day
Jer 17:27 heed Me to hallow the **S** day
Jer 17:27 of Jerusalem on the **S** day
Ezek 46: 1 but on the **S** it shall be
Ezek 46: 4 the **S** day shall be six lambs
Ezek 46:12 as he did on the **S** day
Amos 8: 5 And the **S**, that we may trade
Matt 12: 1 the grainfields on the **S**
Matt 12: 2 is not lawful to do on the **S**
Matt 12: 5 on the **S** the priests
Matt 12: 5 in the temple profane the **S**
Matt 12: 8 of Man is Lord even of the **S**
Matt 12:10 Is it lawful to heal on the **S**
Matt 12:11 it falls into a pit on the **S**
Matt 12:12 is lawful to do good on the **S**
Matt 24:20 not be in winter or on the **S**
Matt 28: 1 Now after the **S**, as the first
Mark 1:21 and immediately on the **S** He
Mark 2:23 the grainfields on the **S**
Mark 2:24 what is not lawful on the **S**
Mark 2:27 The **S** was made for man,
Mark 2:27 and not man for the **S**
Mark 2:28 of Man is also Lord of the **S**
Mark 3: 2 He would heal him on the **S**
Mark 3: 4 Is it lawful on the **S** to do
Mark 6: 2 And when the **S** had come, He
Mark 15:42 that is, the day before the **S**
Mark 16: 1 Now when the **S** was past, Mary
Luke 4:16 the synagogue on the **S** day
Luke 6: 1 **S** after the first that He
Luke 6: 2 is not lawful to do on the **S**
Luke 6: 5 of Man is also Lord of the **S**
Luke 6: 6 Now it happened on another **S**
Luke 6: 7 He would heal on the **S**, that
Luke 6: 9 Is it lawful on the **S** to do
Luke 13:10 of the synagogues on the **S**
Luke 13:14 Jesus had healed on the **S**
Luke 13:14 on them, and not on the **S** day
Luke 13:15 **S** loose his ox or his donkey
Luke 13:16 from this bond on the **S**
Luke 14: 1 to eat bread on the **S**, that
Luke 14: 3 Is it lawful to heal on the **S**
Luke 14: 5 pull him out on the **S** day
Luke 23:54 and the **S** drew near
Luke 23:56 on the **S** according to the
John 5: 9 And that day was the **S**
John 5:10 It is the **S**; it is not lawful
John 5:16 done these things on the **S**
John 5:18 He not only broke the **S**, but
John 7:22 you circumcise a man on the **S**
John 7:23 circumcision on the **S**, so
John 7:23 man completely well on the **S**
John 9:14 Now it was a **S** when Jesus
John 9:16 He does not keep the **S**
John 19:31 the **S** (for that **S** was a
Acts 1:12 Jerusalem, a **S** day's journey
Acts 13:14 the synagogue on the **S** day
Acts 13:27 which are read every **S**, have
Acts 13:42 preached to them the next **S**
Acts 13:44 the next **S** almost the whole
Acts 15:21 in the synagogues every **S**
Acts 16:13 on the **S** day we went out of
Acts 18: 4 in the synagogue every **S**, and

SABBATH-REST (*see* SABBATH)
Lev 23:24 the month, you shall have a **s**
Lev 23:39 first day there shall be a **s**
Lev 23:39 and on the eighth day a **s**

SABBATHS (*see* SABBATH)
Ex 31:13 Surely My **S** you shall keep,
Lev 19: 3 and his father, and keep My **S**
Lev 19:30 You shall keep My **S** and
Lev 23:15 seven **S** shall be completed
Lev 23:38 besides the **S** of the LORD
Lev 25: 8 seven **s** of years for yourself
Lev 25: 8 the time of the seven **s** of
Lev 26: 2 You shall keep My **S** and
Lev 26:34 the land shall enjoy its **s** as
Lev 26:34 shall rest and enjoy its **s**
Lev 26:35 your **s** when you dwelt in it
Lev 26:43 will enjoy its **s** while it
1Ch 23:31 offering to the LORD on the **S**
2Ch 2: 4 morning and evening, on the **S**
2Ch 8:13 of Moses, for the **S**, the New
2Ch 31: 3 the burnt offerings for the **S**
2Ch 36:21 the land had enjoyed her **S**
Neh 10:33 burnt offering of the **S**, the
Is 1:13 The New Moons, the **S**, and the
Is 56: 4 To the eunuchs who keep My **S**
Lam 2: 6 **S** to be forgotten in Zion
Ezek 20:12 I also gave them My **S**, to be
Ezek 20:13 and they greatly defiled My **S**
Ezek 20:16 statutes, but profaned My **S**
Ezek 20:20 hallow My **S**, and they will be
Ezek 20:21 but they profaned My **S**
Ezek 20:24 My statutes, profaned My **S**
Ezek 22: 8 holy things and profaned My **S**
Ezek 22:26 hidden their eyes from My **S**
Ezek 23:38 the same day and profaned My **S**
Ezek 44:24 and they shall hallow My **S**
Ezek 45:17 feasts, the New Moons, the **S**
Ezek 46: 3 before the LORD on the **S** and
Hos 2:11 days, her New Moons, her **S**
Luke 4:31 and was teaching them on the **S**
Acts 17: 2 for three **S** reasoned with
Col 2:16 a festival or a new moon or **s**

SABEANS
Job 1:15 when the **S** raided them and
Is 45:14 of Cush and of the **S**, men of
Ezek 23:42 and **S** were brought from the
Joel 3: 8 they will sell them to the **S**

SABTA (*see* SABTAH)
1Ch 1: 9 of Cush were Seba, Havilah, **S**

SABTAH (*see* SABTA)
Gen 10: 7 of Cush were Seba, Havilah, **S**

SABTECHA (*see* SABTECHAH)
1Ch 1: 9 Havilah, Sabta, Raama, and **S**

SABTECHAH (*see* SABTECHA)
Gen 10: 7 Sabtah, Raamah, and **S**

SACAR (*see* SHARAR)
1Ch 11:35 the son of **S** the Hararite
1Ch 26: 4 **S** the fourth, Nethanel the

SACHIAH
1Ch 8:10 Jeuz, **S**, and Mirmah

SACK (*see* SACKS)
Gen 42:25 every man's money to his **s**
Gen 42:27 as one of them opened his **s**
Gen 42:27 it was, in the mouth of his **s**
Gen 42:28 and there it is, in my **s**
Gen 42:35 bundle of money was in his **s**
Gen 43:21 was in the mouth of his **s**
Gen 44: 1 money in the mouth of his **s**
Gen 44: 2 of the **s** of the youngest, and
Gen 44:11 let down his **s** to the ground
Gen 44:11 and each opened his **s**
Gen 44:12 cup was found in Benjamin's **s**
Lev 11:32 wood or clothing or skin or **s**
Luke 10: 4 Carry neither money bag, **s**
Luke 22:35 sent you without money bag, **s**
Luke 22:36 him take it, and likewise a **s**

SACKCLOTH
Gen 37:34 put **s** on his waist, and
2Sa 3:31 gird yourselves with **s**, and
2Sa 21:10 the daughter of Aiah took **s**
1Ki 20:31 let us put **s** around our
1Ki 20:32 So they wore **s** around their
1Ki 21:27 put **s** on his body
1Ki 21:27 and fasted and lay in **s**
2Ki 6:30 he had **s** on his body
2Ki 19: 1 covered himself with **s**, and
2Ki 19: 2 the priests, covered with **s**
1Ch 21:16 and the elders, clothed in **s**
Neh 9: 1 assembled with fasting, in **s**
Esth 4: 1 tore his clothes and put on **s**
Esth 4: 2 king's gate clothed with **s**
Esth 4: 3 and many lay in **s** and ashes
Esth 4: 4 take his **s** away from him, but
Job 16:15 I have sewn **s** over my skin,
Ps 30:11 You have put off my **s** and
Ps 35:13 were sick, My clothing was **s**
Ps 69:11 I also made **s** my garment
Is 3:24 a rich robe, a girding of **s**
Is 15: 3 will clothe themselves with **s**
Is 20: 2 remove the **s** from your body,
Is 22:12 and for girding with **s**
Is 32:11 and gird **s** on your waists
Is 37: 1 covered himself with **s**, and
Is 37: 2 the priests, covered with **s**
Is 50: 3 and I make **s** their covering
Is 58: 5 a bulrush, and to spread out **s**
Jer 4: 8 this, clothe yourself with **s**
Jer 6:26 clothe yourself with **s**, and
Jer 48:37 be cuts, and on the loins **s**
Jer 49: 3 gird yourselves with **s**
Lam 2:10 and gird themselves with **s**
Ezek 7:18 will also be girded with **s**
Ezek 27:31 you, gird themselves with **s**
Dan 9: 3 with fasting, **s**, and ashes
Joel 1: 8 with **s** for the husband of her
Joel 1:13 come, lie all night in **s**, you
Amos 8:10 I will bring **s** on every waist
Jon 3: 5 a fast, and put on **s**, from the
Jon 3: 6 robe, covered himself with **s**
Jon 3: 8 and beast be covered with **s**
Matt 11:21 have repented long ago in **s**
Luke 10:13 great while ago, sitting in **s**
Rev 6:12 sun became black as **s** of hair
Rev 11: 3 and sixty days, clothed in **s**

SACKS (*see* SACK)
Gen 42:25 to fill their **s** with grain
Gen 42:35 as they emptied their **s**, that
Gen 43:12 in the mouth of your **s**
Gen 43:18 in our **s** the first time, that
Gen 43:21 that we opened our **s**, and
Gen 43:22 who put our money in our **s**
Gen 43:23 given you treasure in your **s**
Gen 44: 1 Fill the men's **s** with food
Gen 44: 8 found in the mouth of our **s**
Josh 9: 4 And they took old **s** on their

SACRED
Ex 23:24 break down their **s** pillars
Ex 34:13 altars, break their **s** pillars
Lev 23:36 It is a **s** assembly, and you
Lev 26: 1 a carved image nor a **s** pillar
Num 29:35 you shall have a **s** assembly
Deut 7: 5 and break down their **s** pillars
Deut 12: 3 altars, break their **s** pillars
Deut 16: 8 day there shall be a **s**
Deut 16:15 **s** feast to the LORD your God
Deut 16:22 shall not set up a **s** pillar
1Ki 14:23 **s** pillars, and wooden images
2Ki 3: 2 for he put away the **s** pillar
2Ki 10:26 they brought the **s** pillars
2Ki 10:27 down the **s** pillar of Baal
2Ki 12:18 the **s** things that his fathers
2Ki 12:18 and his own **s** things, and all
2Ki 17:10 up for themselves **s** pillars
2Ki 18: 4 places and broke the **s** pillars
2Ki 23:14 broke in pieces the **s** pillars
2Ch 7: 9 day they held a **s** assembly
2Ch 14: 3 and broke down the **s** pillars
2Ch 31: 1 broke the **s** pillars in pieces
Neh 8:18 day there was a **s** assembly
Is 1:13 iniquity and the **s** meeting
Jer 43:13 the **s** pillars of Beth Shemesh
Hos 3: 4 without sacrifice or **s** pillar
Hos 10: 1 embellished his **s** pillars
Hos 10: 2 he will ruin their **s** pillars
Joel 1:14 a fast, call a **s** assembly
Joel 2:15 a fast, call a **s** assembly
Amos 5:21 not savor your **s** assemblies
Mic 5:13 and your **s** pillars from your

SACRIFICE (*see* SACRIFICED, SACRIFICES, SACRIFICIAL, SACRIFICING)
Gen 31:54 offered a **s** on the mountain
Ex 3:18 that we may **s** to the LORD our
Ex 5: 3 **s** to the LORD our God, lest
Ex 5: 8 Let us go and **s** to our God
Ex 5:17 Let us go and **s** to the LORD
Ex 8: 8 that they may **s** to the LORD
Ex 8:25 **s** to your God in the land
Ex 8:26 If we **s** the abomination of
Ex 8:27 **s** to the LORD our God as He
Ex 8:28 that you may **s** to the LORD
Ex 8:29 people go to **s** to the LORD
Ex 10:25 that we may **s** to the LORD our
Ex 12:27 is the Passover **s** of the LORD
Ex 13:15 Therefore I **s** to the LORD all
Ex 20:24 you shall **s** on it your burnt
Ex 23:18 of My **s** with leavened bread
Ex 23:18 of My **s** remain until morning
Ex 34:15 make **s** to their gods, and one
Ex 34:15 you and you eat of his **s**,
Ex 34:25 the blood of My **s** with leaven

Ex 34:25 nor shall the s of the Feast
Lev 1: 3 is a burnt s of the herd, let
Lev 1: 9 all on the altar as a burnt s
Lev 1:10 as a burnt s, he shall bring
Lev 1:13 it is a burnt s, an offering
Lev 1:14 And if the burnt s of his
Lev 1:17 It is a burnt s, an offering
Lev 3: 1 is a s of peace offering, if
Lev 3: 3 he shall offer from the s of
Lev 3: 5 on the altar upon the burnt s
Lev 3: 6 If his offering as a s of
Lev 3: 9 the s of the peace offering
Lev 4:10 the s of the peace offering
Lev 4:26 of the s of peace offering
Lev 4:31 from the s of peace offering
Lev 4:35 the s of the peace offering
Lev 7:11 This is the law of the s of
Lev 7:12 with the s of thanksgiving,
Lev 7:13 the s of thanksgiving of his
Lev 7:15 The flesh of the s of his
Lev 7:16 But if the s of his offering
Lev 7:16 same day that he offers his s
Lev 7:17 of the flesh of the s on the
Lev 7:18 s of his peace offering is
Lev 7:20 who eats the flesh of the s
Lev 7:21 who eats the flesh of the s
Lev 7:29 He who offers the s of his
Lev 7:29 to the LORD from the s of his
Lev 7:37 the s of the peace offering,
Lev 8:21 It was a burnt s for a sweet
Lev 9: 4 to s before the LORD, and a
Lev 9:17 the burnt s of the morning
Lev 17: 8 offers a burnt offering or s
Lev 19: 5 if you offer a s of peace
Lev 22:18 who offers his s for any of
Lev 22:21 whoever offers a s of peace
Lev 22:29 And when you offer a s of
Lev 23:19 Then you shall s one kid of
Lev 23:19 year as a s of peace offering
Lev 23:37 and a grain offering, a s and
Lev 27:11 not offer as a s to the LORD
Num 6:17 a s of peace offering to the
Num 6:18 the s of the peace offering
Num 7:17 for the s of peace offerings
Num 7:23 as the s of peace offerings
Num 7:29 for the s of peace offerings
Num 7:35 as the s of peace offerings
Num 7:41 as the s of peace offerings
Num 7:47 as the s of peace offerings
Num 7:53 as the s of peace offerings
Num 7:59 as the s of peace offerings
Num 7:65 as the s of peace offerings
Num 7:71 as the s of peace offerings
Num 7:77 as the s of peace offerings
Num 7:83 as the s of peace offerings
Num 7:88 all the oxen for the s of
Num 15: 3 LORD, a burnt offering or a s
Num 15: 5 the burnt offering or the s
Num 15: 8 or as a s to fulfill a vow,
Deut 15:21 you shall not s it to the
Deut 16: 2 Therefore you shall s the
Deut 16: 4 s the first day at twilight
Deut 16: 5 You may not s the Passover
Deut 16: 6 abide, there you shall s the
Deut 17: 1 You shall not s to the LORD
Deut 18: 3 from those who offer a s
Deut 33:10 a whole burnt s on Your altar
Josh 22:26 for burnt offering nor for s
Judg 6:26 offer a burnt s with the wood
Judg 16:23 a great s to Dagon their god
1Sa 1: 3 s to the LORD of hosts in
1Sa 1:21 to the LORD the yearly s and
1Sa 2:13 that when any man offered a s
1Sa 2:19 husband to offer the yearly s
1Sa 2:29 Why do you kick at My s and
1Sa 3:14 for by s or offering forever
1Sa 9:12 because there is a s of the
1Sa 9:13 because he must bless the s
1Sa 15:15 to s to the LORD your God
1Sa 15:21 to s to the LORD your God in
1Sa 15:22 to obey is better than s
1Sa 16: 2 I have come to s to the LORD
1Sa 16: 3 Then invite Jesse to the s
1Sa 16: 5 I have come to s to the LORD
1Sa 16: 5 and come with me to the s
1Sa 16: 5 and invited them to the s
1Sa 20: 6 for there is a yearly s there
1Sa 20:29 family has a s in the city
2Sa 24:22 here are oxen for burnt s
1Ki 3: 4 went to Gibeon to s there
1Ki 8:63 Solomon offered a s of peace
1Ki 13: 2 on you he shall s the priests
1Ki 18:29 the offering of the evening s
1Ki 18:33 and pour it on the burnt s
1Ki 18:36 the offering of the evening s
1Ki 18:38 fell and consumed the burnt s
2Ki 5:17 offering or s to other gods
2Ki 10:19 a great s to make to Baal
2Ki 16:15 offering, the king's burnt s
2Ki 16:15 and all the blood of the s
2Ki 17:35 nor serve them nor s to them
2Ki 17:36 and to Him you shall offer s
2Ch 2: 6 except to burn s before Him
2Ch 7: 5 a s of twenty-two thousand
2Ch 7:12 for Myself as a house of s
2Ch 11:16 came to Jerusalem to s to the
2Ch 28:23 I will s to them that they
Ezra 9: 4 until the evening s
Ezra 9: 5 At the evening s I arose from
Ps 20: 3 And accept your burnt s
Ps 40: 6 S and offering You did not
Ps 50: 5 made a covenant with Me by s
Ps 51:16 For You do not desire s, or
Ps 54: 6 I will freely s to You
Ps 107:22 Let them s the sacrifices of
Ps 116:17 to You the s of thanksgiving
Ps 118:27 Bind the s with cords to the
Ps 141: 2 of my hands as the evening s
Prov 15: 8 The s of the wicked is an
Prov 21: 3 acceptable to the LORD than s
Prov 21:27 The s of the wicked is an
Eccl 5: 1 than to give the s of fools
Eccl 9: 2 and him who does not s
Is 19:21 in that day, and will make s
Is 34: 6 the LORD has a s in Bozrah
Is 57: 7 there you went up to offer s
Is 65: 3 who s in gardens, and burn
Jer 33:11 s of praise into the house of
Jer 33:18 and to s continually
Jer 46:10 s in the north country by the
Ezek 40:42 the burnt offering and the s
Ezek 44:11 the s for the people, and they
Ezek 44:30 every s of any kind from all
Dan 9:27 He shall bring an end to s
Dan 12:11 the daily s is taken away
Hos 3: 4 without s or sacred pillar,
Hos 6: 6 For I desire mercy and not s
Hos 8:13 of My offerings they s flesh
Hos 12:11 though they s bulls in Gilgal
Hos 13: 2 the men who s kiss the calves
Amos 4: 5 Offer a s of thanksgiving
Jon 1:16 offered a s to the LORD and
Jon 2: 9 But I will s to You with the
Hab 1:16 Therefore they s to their net
Zeph 1: 7 for the LORD has prepared a s
Zeph 1: 8 in the day of the LORD's s
Mal 1: 8 you offer the blind as a s
Matt 9:13 I desire mercy and not s
Matt 12: 7 I desire mercy and not s
Mark 9:49 every s will be seasoned with
Luke 2:24 to offer a s according to
Acts 14:13 intending to s with the
Rom 12: 1 your bodies a living s, holy,
1Co 10:20 s they s to demons
Eph 5: 2 offering and a s to God for a
Phil 2:17 as a drink offering on the s
Phil 4:18 aroma, an acceptable s, well
Heb 9:26 away sin by the s of Himself
Heb 10: 5 S and offering You did not
Heb 10: 8 S and offering, burnt
Heb 10:12 one s for sins forever, sat
Heb 10:26 longer remains a s for sins
Heb 11: 4 a more excellent s than Cain
Heb 13:15 offer the s of praise to God

SACRIFICED (*see* SACRIFICE)
Ex 24: 5 s peace offerings of oxen to
Ex 32: 8 s to it, and said, 'This is
Deut 32:17 They s to demons, not to God,
Josh 8:31 LORD, and s peace offerings
Judg 2: 5 and they s there to the LORD
1Sa 2:15 come and say to the man who s
2Sa 6:13 six paces, that he s oxen
1Ki 1: 9 And Adonijah s sheep and oxen
1Ki 1:19 He has s oxen and fattened
1Ki 1:25 has s oxen and fattened cattle
1Ki 3: 2 people s at the high places
1Ki 3: 3 David, except that he s and
1Ki 11: 8 incense and s to their gods
2Ki 12: 3 the people still s and burned
2Ki 14: 4 away, and the people still s
2Ki 15: 4 the people still s and burned
2Ki 15:35 the people still s and burned
2Ki 16: 4 And he s and burned incense on
2Ki 17:32 who s for them in the shrines
1Ch 21:28 the Jebusite, he s there
2Ch 28: 4 And he s and burned incense on
2Ch 28:23 For he s to the gods of
2Ch 33:16 s peace offerings and thank
2Ch 33:17 the people still s on the
2Ch 33:22 for Amon s to all the carved
2Ch 34: 4 of those who had s to them
Ezra 4: 2 we have s to Him since the
Ps 106:37 They even s their sons And
Ps 106:38 Whom they s to the idols of
Ezek 16:20 these you s to them to be
Ezek 23:37 even s their sons whom they
Hos 11: 2 them, They s to the Baals, and
1Co 5: 7 our Passover, was s for us
Rev 2:14 to eat things s to idols
Rev 2:20 and to eat things s to idols

SACRIFICES (*see* SACRIFICE)
Gen 46: 1 offered s to the God of his
Ex 10:25 You must also give us s and
Ex 18:12 a burnt offering and s to God
Ex 22:20 He who s to any god, except
Ex 29:28 s of their peace offerings
Lev 7:32 the s of your peace offerings
Lev 7:34 from the s of their peace
Lev 9:18 bull and the ram as s of peace
Lev 10:13 of the s made by fire to the
Lev 10:14 which are given from the s of
Lev 17: 5 s which they offer in the
Lev 17: 7 more offer their s to demons
Num 10:10 and over the s of your peace
Num 25: 2 people to the s of their gods
Deut 12: 6 your burnt offerings, your s
Deut 12:11 your burnt offerings, your s
Deut 12:27 the blood of your s shall be
Deut 32:38 Who ate the fat of their s
Deut 33:19 offer s of righteousness
Josh 13:14 the s of the LORD God of
Josh 22:27 burnt offerings, with our s
Josh 22:28 for burnt offerings nor for s
Josh 22:29 for grain offerings, or for s
1Sa 6:15 made s the same day to the
1Sa 10: 8 make s of peace offerings
1Sa 11:15 There they made s of peace
1Sa 15:22 in burnt offerings and s, as
2Sa 15:12 Giloh, while he offered s
1Ki 8:62 him offered s before the LORD
1Ki 12:27 s in the house of the LORD at
1Ki 12:32 and offered s on the altar
1Ki 12:33 offered s on the altar and
1Ki 22:43 for the people offered s
2Ki 10:24 So they went in to offer s
1Ch 6:49 his sons offered s on the
1Ch 29:21 they made s to the LORD and
1Ch 29:21 s in abundance for all Israel
2Ch 7: 1 the burnt offering and the s
2Ch 7: 4 offered s before the LORD
2Ch 13:11 and every evening burnt s and
2Ch 29:31 LORD, come near, and bring s
2Ch 29:31 the congregation brought in s
Ezra 6: 3 place where they offered s
Ezra 6:10 that they may offer s of
Ezra 6:17 And they offered s at the
Neh 4: 2 Will they offer s
Neh 12:43 that day they offered great s
Ps 4: 5 Offer the s of righteousness,
Ps 27: 6 Therefore I will offer s of
Ps 50: 8 s Or your burnt offerings
Ps 51:17 The s of God are a broken
Ps 51:19 with the s of righteousness
Ps 66:15 You burnt s of fat animals
Ps 106:28 And ate s made to the dead
Ps 107:22 the s of thanksgiving, And
Eccl 9: 2 to him who s and him who does
Is 1:11 the multitude of your s to Me
Is 1:13 Bring no more futile s
Is 43:23 you honored Me with your s
Is 43:24 Me with the fat of your s
Is 56: 7 their s will be accepted on
Is 66: 3 he who s a lamb, as if he
Jer 6:20 nor your s sweet to Me
Jer 7:21 burnt offerings to your s
Jer 7:22 burnt offerings or s
Jer 17:26 bringing burnt offerings and s
Jer 17:26 bringing s of praise to the
Jer 48:35 offers s in the high places
Ezek 20:28 there they offered their s

Ezek 20:40 and the firstfruits of your s
Ezek 36:38 a flock offered as holy s
Ezek 40:41 which they slaughtered the s
Ezek 40:43 the flesh of the s was on the
Ezek 44:30 of any kind from all your s
Ezek 46:24 boil the s of the people
Dan 8:11 the daily s were taken away
Dan 8:12 horn to oppose the daily s
Dan 8:13 be, concerning the daily s
Dan 11:31 shall take away the daily s
Hos 4:13 They offer s on the
Hos 4:14 offer s with a ritual harlot
Hos 4:19 be ashamed because of their s
Hos 8:13 For the s of My offerings
Hos 9: 4 nor shall their s be pleasing
Hos 14: 2 will offer the s of our lips
Amos 4: 4 bring your s every morning,
Amos 5:25 Did you offer Me s and
Zech 14:21 Everyone who s shall come
Mal 1:14 but s to the Lord what is
Mark 12:33 whole burnt offerings and s
Luke 13: 1 had mingled with their s
Acts 7:41 offered s to the idol, and
Acts 7:42 s during forty years in the
1Co 10:18 the s partakers of the altar
Heb 5: 1 both gifts and s for sins
Heb 7:27 high priests, to offer up s
Heb 8: 3 to offer both gifts and s
Heb 9: 9 s are offered which cannot
Heb 9:23 with better s than these
Heb 10: 1 can never with these same s
Heb 10: 3 But in those s there is a
Heb 10: 6 s for sin you had no pleasure
Heb 10:11 repeatedly the same s, which
Heb 13:16 for with such s God is well
1Pe 2: 5 to offer up spiritual s

SACRIFICIAL (*see* SACRIFICE)
Ezek 39:17 from all sides to My s meal
Ezek 39:17 you, A great s meal on the
Ezek 39:19 at My s meal which I am

SACRIFICING (*see* SACRIFICE)
Ex 8:26 do so, for we would be s the
1Ki 8: 5 s sheep and oxen that could
1Ki 12:32 s to the calves that he had
2Ch 5: 6 were s sheep and oxen that
Ezek 39:17 meal which I am s for you
Ezek 39:19 meal which I am s for you
Ezek 43:18 for s burnt offerings on it,
Acts 14:18 the multitudes from s to them

SAD (*see* SADLY)
Gen 40: 6 them, and saw that they were s
Gen 40: 7 Why do you look so s today
1Sa 1:18 and her face was no longer s
Neh 2: 1 Now I had never been s in his
Neh 2: 2 Why is your face s, since you
Neh 2: 3 Why should my face not be s
Job 9:27 I will put off my s face
Eccl 7: 3 for by a s countenance the
Ezek 13:22 the heart of the righteous s
Ezek 13:22 whom I have not made s
Matt 6:16 with a s countenance
Mark 10:22 But he was s at this word, and
Luke 24:17 another as you walk and are s

SADDLE (*see* SADDLECLOTHS, SADDLED)
Gen 31:34 put them in the camel's s
Lev 15: 9 Any s on which he who has
2Sa 19:26 I will s a donkey for myself
1Ki 13:13 sons, "S the donkey for me
1Ki 13:27 saying, "S the donkey for me

SADDLECLOTHS (*see* SADDLE)
Ezek 27:20 your merchant in s for riding

SADDLED (*see* SADDLE)
Gen 22: 3 s his donkey, and took two of
Num 22:21 s his donkey, and went with
Judg 19:10 him were the two s donkeys
2Sa 16: 1 with a couple of s donkeys
2Sa 17:23 he s his donkey, and arose and
1Ki 2:40 s his donkey, and went to
1Ki 13:13 So they s the donkey for
1Ki 13:23 that he s the donkey for him,
1Ki 13:27 And they s it
2Ki 4:24 Then she s a donkey, and said

SADDUCEES
Matt 3: 7 S coming to his baptism, he
Matt 16: 1 S came, and testing Him asked
Matt 16: 6 of the Pharisees and the S
Matt 16:11 leaven of the Pharisees and S
Matt 16:12 of the Pharisees and S
Matt 22:23 The same day the S, who say
Matt 22:34 that He had silenced the S
Mark 12:18 Then some S, who say there is
Luke 20:27 Then some of the S, who deny
Acts 4: 1 and the S came upon them,
Acts 5:17 (which is the sect of the S)
Acts 23: 6 that one part were S and the
Acts 23: 7 the Pharisees and the S
Acts 23: 8 For the S say that there is

SADLY (*see* SAD)
Is 59:11 bears, and moan s like doves

SAFE (*see* SAFEKEEPING, SAFELY, SAFETY)
1Sa 20: 7 well,' your servant will be s
1Sa 22:23 but with me you shall be s
2Sa 18:29 Is the young man Absalom s
2Sa 18:32 Is the young man Absalom s
Job 21: 9 Their houses are s from fear
Ps 119:117 Hold me up, and I shall be s
Prov 18:10 righteous run to it and are s
Prov 29:25 trusts in the LORD shall be s
Ezek 34:27 They shall be s in their land
Nah 1:12 Though they are s, and
Luke 15:27 because he has received him s
Phil 3: 1 tedious, but for you it is s

SAFEKEEPING (*see* SAFE)
Lev 6: 2 was delivered to him for s
Lev 6: 4 was delivered to him for s

SAFELY (*see* SAFE)
Gen 33:18 Then Jacob came s to the city
Lev 26: 5 full, and dwell in your land s
Judg 18: 7 were there, how they dwelt s
1Sa 24:19 will he let him get away s
1Ki 4:25 And Judah and Israel dwelt s
2Ch 19: 1 s to his house in Jerusalem
Ps 78:53 And He led them on s, so that
Ps 141:10 own nets, While I escape s
Prov 1:33 listens to me will dwell s
Prov 3:23 you will walk s in your way
Prov 31:11 of her husband s trusts her
Is 5:29 they will carry it away s
Is 41: 3 passed s by the way that he
Jer 23: 6 saved, and Israel will dwell s
Jer 32:37 I will cause them to dwell s
Jer 33:16 and Jerusalem will dwell s
Ezek 28:26 And they will dwell s there
Ezek 34:25 and they will dwell s in the
Ezek 34:28 but they shall dwell s, and no
Ezek 38: 8 and now all of them dwell s
Ezek 38:11 peaceful people, who dwell s
Ezek 38:14 when My people Israel dwell s
Ezek 39:26 when they dwelt s in their
Hos 2:18 to make them lie down s
Zech 14:11 shall be s inhabited
Mark 14:44 take Him and lead Him away s
Acts 23:24 and bring him s to Felix the
Acts 27:44 they all escaped s to land

SAFETY (*see* SAFE, SAFETY'S)
Lev 25:18 will dwell in the land in s
Lev 25:19 fill, and dwell there in s
Deut 12:10 about, so that you dwell in s
Deut 33:12 LORD shall dwell in s by Him
Deut 33:28 Then Israel shall dwell in s
1Sa 12:11 and you dwelt in s
1Sa 20:13 away, that you may go in s
1Sa 20:21 lives, there is s for you
Job 5: 4 His sons are far from s, they
Job 5:11 who mourn are lifted to s
Job 11:18 you, and take your rest in s
Ps 4: 8 O LORD, make me dwell in s
Ps 12: 5 in the s for which he yearns
Ps 33:17 A horse is a vain hope for s
Prov 11:14 of counselors there is s
Prov 24: 6 of counselors there is s
Is 14:30 the needy will lie down in s
1Th 5: 3 when they say, Peace and s!"

SAFETY'S (*see* SAFETY)
Prov 3:29 he dwells by you for s sake

SAFFRON
Song 4:14 spikenard and s, calamus and

SAID (*see* PREFACE)

SAIL (*see* SAILED, SAILING)
Ps 104:26 There the ships s about
Is 33:21 no galley with oars will s
Is 33:23 they could not spread the s
Ezek 27: 7 what you spread for your s
Acts 13:13 his party set s from Paphos
Acts 20: 3 as he was about to s to Syria
Acts 20:16 had decided to s past Ephesus
Acts 21: 1 departed from them and set s
Acts 21: 2 we went aboard and set s
Acts 27: 1 that we should s to Italy
Acts 27: 2 meaning to s along the coasts
Acts 27:12 to set s from there also, if
Acts 27:17 Syrtis Sands, they struck s
Acts 27:24 you all those who s with you

SAILED (*see* SAIL)
1Ki 22:48 but they never s, for the
Luke 8:23 But as they s He fell asleep
Luke 8:26 Then they s to the country of
Acts 13: 4 from there they s to Cyprus
Acts 14:26 From there they s to Antioch
Acts 15:39 took Mark and s to Cyprus
Acts 18:18 s for Syria, and Priscilla and
Acts 18:21 And he s from Ephesus
Acts 20: 6 But we s away from Philippi
Acts 20:13 s to Assos, there intending
Acts 20:15 We s from there, and the next
Acts 21: 3 s to Syria, and landed at Tyre
Acts 27: 4 we s under the shelter of
Acts 27: 5 when we had s over the sea
Acts 27: 7 when we had s slowly many
Acts 27: 7 we s under the shelter of
Acts 27:13 to sea, they s close by Crete
Acts 27:21 and not have s from Crete and
Acts 28:11 After three months we s in an

SAILING (*see* SAIL)
Acts 16:11 s from Troas, we ran a
Acts 21: 2 And finding a ship s over to
Acts 27: 6 Alexandrian ship s to Italy
Acts 27: 9 s was now dangerous because

SAILORS
Acts 27:27 about midnight the s sensed
Acts 27:30 And as the s were seeking to
Rev 18:17 all who travel by ship, s

SAINT (*see* SAINTS)
Ps 106:16 And Aaron the s of the LORD,
Phil 4:21 Greet every s in Christ Jesus

SAINTS (*see* SAINT, SAINTS')
Deut 33: 2 came with ten thousands of s
Deut 33: 3 all His s are in Your hand
1Sa 2: 9 will guard the feet of His s
2Ch 6:41 and let Your s rejoice in
Job 15:15 If God puts no trust in His s
Ps 16: 3 to the s who are on the earth
Ps 30: 4 You s of His, And give thanks
Ps 31:23 love the LORD, all you His s
Ps 34: 9 Oh, fear the LORD, you His s
Ps 37:28 And does not forsake His s
Ps 50: 5 Gather My s together to Me,
Ps 52: 9 in the presence of Your s I
Ps 79: 2 The flesh of Your s to the
Ps 85: 8 To His people and to His s
Ps 89: 5 in the congregation of the s
Ps 89: 7 in the assembly of the s, And
Ps 97:10 preserves the souls of His s
Ps 116:15 LORD Is the death of His s
Ps 132: 9 And let Your s shout for joy
Ps 132:16 her s shall shout aloud for
Ps 145:10 And Your s shall bless You
Ps 148:14 The praise of all His s
Ps 149: 1 in the congregation of s
Ps 149: 5 Let the s be joyful in glory
Ps 149: 9 This honor have all His s
Prov 2: 8 and preserves the way of His s
Dan 7:18 But the s of the Most High
Dan 7:21 was making war against the s
Dan 7:22 of the s of the Most High
Dan 7:22 the time came for the s to
Dan 7:25 the s of the Most High, and
Dan 7:25 Then the s shall be given
Dan 7:27 the s of the Most High
Zech 14: 5 come, and all the s with You
Matt 27:52 many bodies of the s who had
Acts 9:13 done to Your s in Jerusalem
Acts 9:32 to the s who dwelt in Lydda
Acts 9:41 and when he had called the s
Acts 26:10 many of the s I shut up in
Rom 1: 7 of God, called to be s
Rom 8:27 s according to the will of
Rom 12:13 to the needs of the s, given
Rom 15:25 to minister to the s
Rom 15:26 the s who are in Jerusalem
Rom 15:31 may be acceptable to the s

Rom 16: 2 in a manner worthy of the s
Rom 16:15 all the s who are with them
1Co 1: 2 Christ Jesus, called to be s
1Co 6: 1 and not before the s
1Co 6: 2 the s will judge the world
1Co 14:33 in all the churches of the s
1Co 16: 1 the collection for the s, as
1Co 16:15 to the ministry of the s
2Co 1: 1 with all the s who are in all
2Co 8: 4 of the ministering to the s
2Co 9: 1 the ministering to the s, it
2Co 9:12 supplies the needs of the s
2Co 13:13 All the s greet you
Eph 1: 1 To the s who are in Ephesus,
Eph 1:15 and your love for all the s
Eph 1:18 of His inheritance in the s
Eph 2:19 fellow citizens with the s
Eph 3: 8 than the least of all the s
Eph 3:18 all the s what is the width
Eph 4:12 s for the work of ministry
Eph 5: 3 you, as is fitting for s
Eph 6:18 and supplication for all the s
Phil 1: 1 To all the s in Christ Jesus
Phil 4:22 All the s greet you, but
Col 1: 2 To the s and faithful brethren
Col 1: 4 and of your love for all the s
Col 1:12 of the s in the light
Col 1:26 has been revealed to His s
1Th 3:13 Jesus Christ with all His s
2Th 1:10 Day, to be glorified in His s
Phm 5 Jesus and toward all the s
Phm 7 because the hearts of the s
Heb 6:10 you have ministered to the s
Heb 13:24 rule over you, and all the s
Jude 3 for all delivered to the s
Jude 14 with ten thousands of His s
Rev 5: 8 are the prayers of the s
Rev 8: 3 s upon the golden altar which
Rev 8: 4 with the prayers of the s
Rev 11:18 the prophets and the s, and
Rev 13: 7 to him to make war with the s
Rev 13:10 and the faith of the s
Rev 14:12 Here is the patience of the s
Rev 15: 3 Your ways, O King of the s
Rev 16: 6 they have shed the blood of s
Rev 17: 6 drunk with the blood of the s
Rev 18:24 the blood of prophets and s
Rev 19: 8 the righteous acts of the s
Rev 20: 9 surrounded the camp of the s

SAINTS' (*see* SAINTS)
1Ti 5:10 if she has washed the s feet

SAKE (*see* SAKES)
Gen 3:17 is the ground for your s
Gen 8:21 curse the ground for man's s
Gen 12:13 be well with me for your s
Gen 12:16 treated Abram well for her s
Gen 18:29 not do it for the s of forty
Gen 18:31 it for the s of twenty
Gen 18:32 destroy it for the s of ten
Gen 26:24 for My servant Abraham's s
Gen 30:27 has blessed me for your s
Gen 39: 5 house for Joseph's s
Ex 18: 8 the Egyptians for Israel's s
Ex 21:26 go free for the s of his eye
Ex 21:27 free for the s of his tooth
Lev 26:45 But for their s I will
Num 11:29 Are you zealous for my s
1Sa 12:22 for His great name's s,
1Sa 23:10 to destroy the city for my s
2Sa 5:12 for His people Israel's s
2Sa 7:21 For Your word's s, and
2Sa 9: 1 him kindness for Jonathan's s
2Sa 9: 7 for Jonathan your father's s
2Sa 18: 5 Deal gently for my s with the
1Ki 8:41 far country for Your name's s
1Ki 11:12 for the s of your father
1Ki 11:13 for the s of my servant David
1Ki 11:13 for the s of Jerusalem which
1Ki 11:32 for the s of My servant David
1Ki 11:32 for the s of Jerusalem, the
1Ki 11:34 for the s of My servant David
1Ki 15: 4 Nevertheless for David's s
2Ki 8:19 for the s of his servant
2Ki 19:34 city, to save it for My own s
2Ki 19:34 and for My servant David's s
2Ki 20: 6 defend this city for My own s
2Ki 20: 6 for the s of My servant David
1Ch 17:19 O LORD, for Your servant's s
2Ch 6:32 for the s of Your great name
Ps 6: 4 save me for Your mercies' s
Ps 23: 3 For His name's s
Ps 25: 7 me, For Your goodness' s, O
Ps 25:11 For Your name's s, O LORD,
Ps 31: 3 Therefore, for Your name's s
Ps 31:16 Save me for Your mercies' s
Ps 44:22 Yet for Your s we are killed
Ps 44:26 redeem us for Your mercies' s
Ps 69: 7 Because for Your s I have
Ps 79: 9 our sins, For Your name's s
Ps 106: 8 saved them for His name's s
Ps 106:45 for their s He remembered His
Ps 109:21 with me for Your name's s
Ps 122: 8 For the s of my brethren and
Ps 132:10 For Your servant David's s
Ps 143:11 me, O LORD, for Your name's s
Ps 143:11 s bring my soul out of
Prov 3:29 dwells by you for safety's s
Eccl 8: 2 for the s of your oath to God
Is 37:35 city, to save it for My own s
Is 37:35 and for My servant David's s
Is 42:21 for His righteousness' s
Is 43:14 For your s I will send to
Is 43:25 transgressions for My own s
Is 45: 4 For Jacob My servant's s, and
Is 48: 9 For My name's s I will defer
Is 48:11 For My own s, for My own s
Is 54:15 you shall fall for your s
Is 62: 1 For Zion's s I will not hold
Is 62: 1 Jerusalem's s I will not rest
Is 63:17 Return for Your servants' s
Is 65: 8 will I do for My servants' s
Is 66: 5 cast you out for My name's s
Jer 14: 7 us, do it for Your name's s
Jer 14:21 abhor us, for Your name's s
Jer 15:15 Know that for Your s I have
Ezek 20: 9 But I acted for My name's s
Ezek 20:14 But I acted for My name's s
Ezek 20:22 hand and acted for My name's s
Ezek 20:44 with you for My name's s, not
Ezek 28:17 for the s of your splendor
Ezek 36:22 I do not do this for your s
Ezek 36:22 but for My holy name's s
Ezek 36:32 Not for your s do I do this
Dan 9:17 for the Lord's s cause Your
Dan 9:19 Do not delay for Your own s
Matt 5:10 for righteousness' s, for
Matt 5:11 against you falsely for My s
Matt 10:18 governors and kings for My s
Matt 10:22 hated by all for My name's s
Matt 10:39 life for My s will find it
Matt 14: 3 prison for the s of Herodias
Matt 16:25 life for My s will find it
Matt 19:12 for the kingdom of heaven's s
Matt 19:29 or lands, for My name's s
Matt 24: 9 all nations for My name's s
Matt 24:22 elect's s those days will be
Mark 4:17 arises for the word's s,
Mark 6:17 prison for the s of Herodias
Mark 8:35 loses his life for My s and
Mark 10:29 children or lands, for My s
Mark 13: 9 rulers and kings for My s, for
Mark 13:13 by all men for My name's s
Mark 13:20 but for the elect's s, whom
Luke 6:22 evil, for the Son of Man's s
Luke 9:24 life for My s will save it
Luke 18:29 for the s of the kingdom of
Luke 21:12 and rulers for My name's s
Luke 21:17 hated by all for My name's s
John 12: 9 came, not for Jesus' s only
John 12:30 because of Me, but for your s
John 13:37 lay down my life for Your s
John 13:38 lay down your life for My s
John 14:11 the s of the works themselves
John 15:21 do to you for My name's s
Acts 9:16 must suffer for My name's s
Acts 26: 7 For this hope's s, King
Rom 4:23 s alone that it was imputed
Rom 8:36 For Your s we are killed all
Rom 11:28 they are enemies for your s
Rom 11:28 for the s of the fathers
Rom 13: 5 but also for conscience' s
Rom 14:20 work of God for the s of food
1Co 4:10 We are fools for Christ's s
1Co 9:23 this I do for the gospel's s
1Co 10:25 questions for conscience' s
1Co 10:27 no question for conscience' s
1Co 10:28 the s of the one who told you
1Co 10:28 you, and for conscience' s
2Co 4: 5 your servants for Jesus' s
2Co 4:11 to death for Jesus' s, that
2Co 7:12 the s of him who had done the
2Co 7:12 nor for the s of him who
2Co 12:10 in distresses, for Christ's s
Phil 1:29 but also to suffer for His s
Col 1:24 for the s of His body, which
1Th 1: 5 we were among you for your s
1Th 3: 9 for your s before our God
1Th 5:13 in love for their work's s
1Ti 5:23 wine for your stomach's s
2Ti 2:10 things for the s of the elect
Tit 1:11 for the s of dishonest gain
Phm 9 yet for love's s I rather
1Pe 2:13 of man for the Lord's s,
1Pe 3:14 suffer for righteousness' s
1Jn 2:12 forgiven you for His name's s
3Jn 7 went forth for His name's s
Rev 2: 3 have labored for My name's s

SAKES (*see* SAKE)
Gen 18:26 all the place for their s
Deut 1:37 also angry with me for your s
Deut 4:21 was angry with me for your s
Judg 21:22 Be kind to them for our s
Ruth 1:13 me very much for your s that
1Ch 16:21 He reproved kings for their s
Ps 7: 7 For their s, therefore,
Ps 105:14 He reproved kings for their s
Dan 2:30 but for our s who make known
Mal 3:11 the devourer for your s, so
John 11:15 I am glad for your s that I
John 17:19 for their s I sanctify Myself
1Co 4: 6 myself and Apollos for your s
1Co 9:10 say it altogether for our s
1Co 9:10 For our s, no doubt, this is
2Co 2:10 s in the presence of Christ
2Co 4:15 For all things are for your s
2Co 8: 9 yet for your s He became poor

SALAH
Gen 10:24 Arphaxad begot **S**
Gen 10:24 and **S** begot Eber
Gen 11:12 thirty-five years, and begot **S**
Gen 11:13 After he begot **S**, Arphaxad
Gen 11:14 **S** lived thirty years, and
Gen 11:15 **S** lived four hundred and three

SALAMIS
Acts 13: 5 And when they arrived in **S**

SALCAH
Deut 3:10 and all Bashan, as far as **S**
Josh 12: 5 over Mount Hermon, over **S**
Josh 13:11 and all Bashan as far as **S**
1Ch 5:11 land of Bashan as far as **S**

SALE
Lev 25:27 count the years since its s
Deut 18: 8 from the s of his inheritance
Deut 28:68 for s to your enemies as male

SALEM (*see* JERUSALEM)
Gen 14:18 king of **S** brought out bread
Ps 76: 2 In **S** also is His tabernacle,
Heb 7: 1 this Melchizedek, king of **S**
Heb 7: 2 and then also king of **S**

SALIM
John 3:23 was baptizing in Aenon near **S**

SALIVA
1Sa 21:13 let his s fall down on his
Job 7:19 me alone till I swallow my s
John 9: 6 and made clay with the s

SALLAI
Neh 11: 8 and after him Gabbai and **S**,
Neh 12:20 of **S**, Kallai

SALLU
1Ch 9: 7 **S** the son of Meshullam, the
Neh 11: 7 **S** the son of Meshullam, the
Neh 12: 7 **S**, Amok, Hilkiah, and Jedaiah

SALMA
1Ch 2:11 Nahshon begot **S**
1Ch 2:11 and **S** begot Boaz
1Ch 2:51 **S** the father of Bethlehem, and
1Ch 2:54 The sons of **S** were Bethlehem,

SALMAI
Neh 7:48 of Hagaba, the children of **S**

SALMON (*see* ILAI)
Ruth 4:20 Nahshon, and Nahshon begot **S**
Ruth 4:21 **S** begot Boaz, and Boaz begot
Matt 1: 4 Nahshon, and Nahshon begot **S**

Matt 1: 5 S begot Boaz by Rahab, Boaz
Luke 3:32 the son of Boaz, the son of S

SALMONE
Acts 27: 7 the shelter of Crete off S

SALOME
Mark 15:40 the Less and of Joses, and S
Mark 16: 1 S bought spices, that they

SALT (*see* SALTED, SALTPITS)
Gen 14: 3 Siddim (that is, the S Sea)
Gen 19:26 and she became a pillar of s
Lev 2:13 you shall season with s
Lev 2:13 you shall not allow the s of
Lev 2:13 offerings you shall offer s
Num 18:19 it is a covenant of s forever
Num 34: 3 to the end of the S Sea
Num 34:12 and it shall end at the S Sea
Deut 3:17 Sea of the Arabah (the S Sea)
Deut 29:23 whole land is brimstone, s
Josh 3:16 Sea of the Arabah, the S Sea
Josh 12: 3 Sea of the Arabah (the S Sea)
Josh 15: 2 at the shore of the S Sea
Josh 15: 5 The east border was the S Sea
Josh 15:62 Nibshan, the City of S, and En
Josh 18:19 at the north bay at the S Sea
Judg 9:45 the city and sowed it with s
2Sa 8:13 Syrians in the Valley of S
2Ki 2:20 me a new bowl, and put s in it
2Ki 2:21 water, and cast in the s there
2Ki 14: 7 Edomites in the Valley of S
1Ch 18:12 Edomites in the Valley of S
2Ch 13: 5 his sons, by a covenant of s
2Ch 25:11 he went to the Valley of S
Ezra 6: 9 the God of heaven, wheat, s
Ezra 7:22 s without prescribed limit
Job 6: 6 food be eaten without s
Jer 17: 6 in a s land which is not
Ezek 16: 4 s nor swathed in swaddling
Ezek 43:24 priests shall throw s on them
Ezek 47:11 they will be given over to s
Matt 5:13 You are the s of the earth
Matt 5:13 but if the s loses its flavor
Mark 9:49 will be seasoned with s
Mark 9:50 S is good, but if the s loses
Mark 9:50 Have s in yourselves, and have
Luke 14:34 S is good; but if the s has
Col 4: 6 with grace, seasoned with s
Jas 3:12 spring can yield both s water

SALTED (*see* SALT)
Ex 30:35 to the art of the perfumer, s

SALTPITS (*see* SALT)
Zeph 2: 9 overrun with weeds and s, and a

SALU
Num 25:14 woman, was Zimri the son of S

SALUTATION (*see* SALUTE)
1Co 16:21 The s with my own hand
Col 4:18 This s by my own hand
2Th 3:17 The s of Paul with my own

SALUTE (*see* SALUTATION)
Mark 15:18 and began to s Him, "Hail,

SALVATION (*see* SAVE)
Gen 49:18 I have waited for your s, O
Ex 14:13 see the s of the LORD, which
Ex 15: 2 song, and He has become my s
Deut 32:15 esteemed the Rock of his s
1Sa 2: 1 because I rejoice in Your s
1Sa 11:13 has accomplished s in Israel
1Sa 14:45 this great s in Israel
1Sa 19: 5 a great s for all Israel
2Sa 22: 3 my shield and the horn of my s
2Sa 22:36 given me the shield of Your s
2Sa 22:47 be exalted, the Rock of my s
2Sa 22:51 is the tower of s to His king
2Sa 23: 5 For this is all my s and all
1Ch 16:23 news of His s from day to day
1Ch 16:35 Save us, O God of our s
2Ch 6:41 O LORD God, be clothed with s
2Ch 20:17 see the s of the LORD, who is
Job 13:16 He also shall be my s, for a
Ps 3: 8 S belongs to the LORD
Ps 9:14 I will rejoice in Your s
Ps 13: 5 heart shall rejoice in Your s
Ps 14: 7 that the s of Israel would
Ps 18: 2 My shield and the horn of my s
Ps 18:35 given me the shield of Your s
Ps 18:46 the God of my s be exalted
Ps 20: 5 We will rejoice in your s
Ps 21: 1 in Your s how greatly shall
Ps 21: 5 His glory is great in Your s
Ps 24: 5 from the God of his s
Ps 25: 5 For You are the God of my s
Ps 27: 1 The LORD is my light and my s
Ps 27: 9 nor forsake me, O God of my s
Ps 35: 3 to my soul, "I am your s."
Ps 35: 9 It shall rejoice in His s
Ps 37:39 But the s of the righteous is
Ps 38:22 to help me, O Lord, my s
Ps 40:10 Your faithfulness and Your s
Ps 40:16 love Your s say continually
Ps 50:23 I will show the s of God
Ps 51:12 to me the joy of Your s, And
Ps 51:14 O God, The God of my s, And
Ps 53: 6 that the s of Israel would
Ps 62: 1 From Him comes my s
Ps 62: 2 He only is my rock and my s
Ps 62: 6 He only is my rock and my s
Ps 62: 7 In God is my s and my glory
Ps 65: 5 answer us, O God of our s
Ps 67: 2 Your s among all nations
Ps 68:19 benefits, The God of our s
Ps 68:20 Our God is the God of s
Ps 69:13 me in the truth of Your s
Ps 69:29 Let Your s, O God, set me up
Ps 70: 4 love Your s say continually
Ps 71:15 Your s all the day, For I do
Ps 74:12 Working s in the midst of the
Ps 78:22 And did not trust in His s
Ps 79: 9 Help us, O God of our s, For
Ps 85: 4 Restore us, O God of our s
Ps 85: 7 O LORD, And grant us Your s
Ps 85: 9 Surely His s is near to those
Ps 88: 1 O LORD, God of my s, I have
Ps 89:26 My God, and the rock of my s
Ps 91:16 satisfy him, And show him My s
Ps 95: 1 joyfully to the Rock of our s
Ps 96: 2 news of His s from day to day
Ps 98: 2 The LORD has made known His s
Ps 98: 3 have seen the s of our God
Ps 106: 4 Oh, visit me with Your s,
Ps 116:13 I will take up the cup of s
Ps 118:14 song, And He has become my s
Ps 118:15 and s Is in the tents of the
Ps 118:21 me, And have become my s
Ps 119:41 Your s according to Your word
Ps 119:81 My soul faints for Your s
Ps 119:123 eyes fail from seeking Your s
Ps 119:155 S is far from the wicked, For
Ps 119:166 LORD, I hope for Your s, And I
Ps 119:174 I long for Your s, O LORD, And
Ps 132:16 clothe her priests with s
Ps 140: 7 Lord, the strength of my s
Ps 144:10 The One who gives s to kings
Ps 149: 4 beautify the humble with s
Is 12: 2 Behold, God is my s, I will
Is 12: 2 He also has become my s
Is 12: 3 water from the wells of s
Is 17:10 forgotten the God of your s
Is 25: 9 be glad and rejoice in His s
Is 26: 1 God will appoint s for walls
Is 33: 2 our s also in the time of
Is 33: 6 times, and the strength of s
Is 45: 8 open, let them bring forth s
Is 45:17 LORD with an everlasting s
Is 46:13 My s shall not linger
Is 46:13 And I will place s in Zion
Is 49: 6 that You should be My s to
Is 49: 8 in the day of s I have helped
Is 51: 5 My s has gone forth, and My
Is 51: 6 but My s will be forever, and
Is 51: 8 and My s from generation to
Is 52: 7 good things, who proclaims s
Is 52:10 shall see the s of our God
Is 56: 1 for My s is about to come, and
Is 59:11 for s, but it is far from us
Is 59:16 His own arm brought s for Him
Is 59:17 and a helmet of s on His head
Is 60:18 you shall call your walls S
Is 61:10 me with the garments of s
Is 62: 1 her s as a lamp that burns
Is 62:11 Surely your s is coming
Is 63: 5 My own arm brought s for Me
Jer 3:23 in vain is s hoped for from
Jer 3:23 our God is the s of Israel
Lam 3:26 quietly for the s of the LORD
Jon 2: 9 S is of the LORD
Mic 7: 7 will wait for the God of my s
Hab 3: 8 horses, your chariots of s
Hab 3:13 for the s of Your people
Hab 3:13 for s with Your Anointed
Hab 3:18 I will joy in the God of my s
Zech 9: 9 He is just and having s, lowly
Luke 1:69 has raised up a horn of s for
Luke 1:77 of s to His people by the
Luke 2:30 for my eyes have seen Your s
Luke 3: 6 flesh shall see the s of God
Luke 19: 9 Today s has come to this
John 4:22 worship, for s is of the Jews
Acts 4:12 Nor is there s in any other
Acts 13:26 word of this s has been sent
Acts 13:47 that you should be for s to
Acts 16:17 proclaim to us the way of s
Acts 28:28 s of God has been sent to the
Rom 1:16 s for everyone who believes
Rom 10:10 mouth confession is made to s
Rom 11:11 s has come to the Gentiles
Rom 13:11 for now our s is nearer than
2Co 1: 6 is for your consolation and s
2Co 1: 6 is for your consolation and s
2Co 6: 2 in the day of s I have helped
2Co 6: 2 behold, now is the day of s
2Co 7:10 produces repentance to s, not
Eph 1:13 truth, the gospel of your s
Eph 6:17 And take the helmet of s, and
Phil 1:19 for my s through your prayer
Phil 1:28 of perdition, but to you of s
Phil 2:12 work out your own s with fear
1Th 5: 8 and as a helmet the hope of s
1Th 5: 9 but to obtain s through our
2Th 2:13 s through sanctification by
2Ti 2:10 s which is in Christ Jesus
2Ti 3:15 s through faith which is in
Tit 2:11 s has appeared to all men
Heb 1:14 for those who will inherit s
Heb 2: 3 if we neglect so great a s
Heb 2:10 s perfect through sufferings
Heb 5: 9 eternal s to all who obey Him
Heb 6: 9 yes, things that accompany s
Heb 9:28 time, apart from sin, for s
1Pe 1: 5 of God through faith for s
1Pe 1: 9 the s of your souls
1Pe 1:10 Of this s the prophets have
2Pe 3:15 of our Lord is s
Jude 3 you concerning our common s
Rev 7:10 S belongs to our God who sits
Rev 12:10 Now s, and strength, and the
Rev 19: 1 S and glory and honor and

SALVE
Rev 3:18 anoint your eyes with eye s

SAMARIA (*see* SAMARITAN)
1Ki 13:32 which are in the cities of S
1Ki 16:24 he bought the hill of S from
1Ki 16:24 of the city which he built, S
1Ki 16:28 fathers and was buried in S
1Ki 16:29 Israel in S twenty-two years
1Ki 16:32 Baal, which he had built in S
1Ki 18: 2 was a severe famine in S
1Ki 20: 1 And he went up and besieged S
1Ki 20:10 S for a handful for each of
1Ki 20:17 Men are coming out of S
1Ki 20:34 as my father did in S
1Ki 20:43 and displeased, and came to S
1Ki 21: 1 the palace of Ahab king of S
1Ki 21:18 of Israel, who lives in S
1Ki 22:10 the entrance of the gate of S
1Ki 22:37 died, and was brought to S
1Ki 22:37 And they buried the king in S
1Ki 22:38 the chariot at a pool in S
1Ki 22:51 S in the seventeenth year of
2Ki 1: 2 of his upper room in S, and
2Ki 1: 3 messengers of the king of S
2Ki 2:25 from there he returned to S
2Ki 3: 1 S in the eighteenth year of
2Ki 3: 6 went out of S at that time
2Ki 5: 3 with the prophet who is in S
2Ki 6:19 But he led them to S
2Ki 6:20 was, when they had come to S
2Ki 6:20 and there they were, inside S
2Ki 6:24 and went up and besieged S
2Ki 6:25 there was a great famine in S
2Ki 7: 1 a shekel, at the gate of S
2Ki 7:18 this time in the gate of S
2Ki 10: 1 Ahab had seventy sons in S
2Ki 10: 1 letters and sent them to S
2Ki 10:12 and departed and went to S
2Ki 10:17 And when he came to S, he
2Ki 10:17 all who remained to Ahab in S

2Ki 10:35 and they buried him in **S**
2Ki 10:36 in **S** was twenty-eight years
2Ki 13: 1 became king over Israel in **S**
2Ki 13: 6 images also remained in **S**
2Ki 13: 9 and they buried him in **S**
2Ki 13:10 became king over Israel in **S**
2Ki 13:13 Joash was buried in **S** with
2Ki 14:14 and hostages, and returned to **S**
2Ki 14:16 and was buried in **S** with the
2Ki 14:23 of Israel, became king in **S**
2Ki 15: 8 over Israel in **S** six months
2Ki 15:13 he reigned a full month in **S**
2Ki 15:14 up from Tirzah, came to **S**
2Ki 15:14 the son of Jabesh in **S** and
2Ki 15:17 and reigned ten years in **S**
2Ki 15:23 became king over Israel in **S**
2Ki 15:25 him and killed him in **S**, in
2Ki 15:27 became king over Israel in **S**
2Ki 17: 1 became king of Israel in **S**
2Ki 17: 5 all the land, and went up to **S**
2Ki 17: 6 the king of Assyria took **S**
2Ki 17:24 them in the cities of **S**
2Ki 17:24 and they took possession of **S**
2Ki 17:26 placed in the cities of **S** do
2Ki 17:28 had carried away from **S** came
2Ki 18: 9 of Assyria came up against **S**
2Ki 18:10 king of Israel, **S** was taken
2Ki 18:34 they delivered **S** from my hand
2Ki 21:13 the measuring line of **S** and
2Ki 23:18 the prophet who came from **S**
2Ki 23:19 that were in the cities of **S**
2Ch 18: 2 went down to visit Ahab in **S**
2Ch 18: 9 the entrance of the gate of **S**
2Ch 22: 9 him (he was hiding in **S**), and
2Ch 25:13 of Judah from **S** to Beth Horon
2Ch 25:24 and hostages, and returned to **S**
2Ch 28: 8 and brought the spoil to **S**
2Ch 28: 9 the army that came to **S**, and
2Ch 28:15 Then they returned to **S**
Ezra 4:10 and settled in the cities of **S**
Ezra 4:17 companions who dwell in **S**
Neh 4: 2 his brethren and the army of **S**
Is 7: 9 The head of Ephraim is **S**, and
Is 7: 9 the head of **S** is Remaliah's
Is 8: 4 the spoil of **S** will be taken
Is 9: 9 and the inhabitant of **S**
Is 10: 9 Is not **S** like Damascus
Is 10:10 those of Jerusalem and **S**,
Is 10:11 as I have done to **S** and her
Is 36:19 they delivered **S** from my hand
Jer 23:13 folly in the prophets of **S**
Jer 31: 5 vines on the mountains of **S**
Jer 41: 5 from Shiloh, and from **S**,
Ezek 16:46 Your elder sister is **S**, who
Ezek 16:51 **S** did not commit half of your
Ezek 16:53 and the captives of **S** and her
Ezek 16:55 to their former state, and **S**
Ezek 23: 4 **S** is Oholah, and Jerusalem is
Ezek 23:33 The cup of your sister **S**
Hos 7: 1 and the wickedness of **S**
Hos 8: 5 Your calf is rejected, O **S**
Hos 8: 6 But the calf of **S** shall be
Hos 10: 5 The inhabitants of **S** fear
Hos 10: 7 As for **S**, her king is cut off
Hos 13:16 **S** is held guilty, for she has
Amos 3: 9 on the mountains of **S**
Amos 3:12 be taken out who dwell in **S**
Amos 4: 1 who are on the mountain of **S**
Amos 6: 1 in Zion, and trust in Mount **S**
Amos 8:14 who swear by the sin of **S**
Obad 19 of Ephraim and the fields of **S**
Mic 1: 1 which he saw concerning **S**
Mic 1: 5 Is it not **S**
Mic 1: 6 Therefore I will make **S** a
Luke 17:11 passed through the midst of **S**
John 4: 4 But He needed to go through **S**
John 4: 5 of **S** which is called Sychar
John 4: 7 A woman of **S** came to draw
John 4: 9 the woman of **S** said to Him
Acts 1: 8 and in all Judea and **S**, and to
Acts 8: 1 the regions of Judea and **S**
Acts 8: 5 went down to the city of **S**
Acts 8: 9 and astonished the people of **S**
Acts 8:14 at Jerusalem heard that **S** had
Acts 9:31 **S** had peace and were edified
Acts 15: 3 passed through Phoenicia and **S**

SAMARITAN (*see* SAMARIA, SAMARITANS)
Luke 10:33 But a certain **S**, as he
Luke 17:16 And he was a **S**
John 4: 9 a drink from me, a **S** woman
John 8:48 say rightly that You are a **S**

SAMARITANS (*see* SAMARITAN)
2Ki 17:29 places which the **S** had made
Matt 10: 5 do not enter a city of the **S**
Luke 9:52 entered a village of the **S**
John 4: 9 Jews have no dealings with **S**
John 4:39 many of the **S** of that city
John 4:40 So when the **S** had come to Him
Acts 8:25 in many villages of the **S**

SAME (*see* PREFACE)

SAMGAR-NEBO
Jer 39: 3 Nergal-Sharezer, **S**, Sarsechim

SAMLAH
Gen 36:36 **S** of Masrekah reigned in his
Gen 36:37 And when **S** died, Saul of
1Ch 1:47 **S** of Masrekah reigned in his
1Ch 1:48 And when **S** died, Saul of

SAMOS
Acts 20:15 following day we arrived at **S**

SAMOTHRACE
Acts 16:11 we ran a straight course to **S**

SAMSON (*see* SAMSON'S)
Judg 13:24 a son and called his name **S**
Judg 14: 1 Now **S** went down to Timnah,
Judg 14: 3 And **S** said to his father,
Judg 14: 5 So **S** went down to Timnah with
Judg 14: 7 and she pleased **S** well
Judg 14:10 **S** gave a feast there, for
Judg 14:12 Then **S** said to them, "Let me
Judg 15: 1 it happened that **S** visited
Judg 15: 3 **S** said to them, "This time
Judg 15: 4 Then **S** went and caught three
Judg 15: 6 **S**, the son-in-law of the
Judg 15: 7 **S** said to them, "Since you
Judg 15:10 We have come up to arrest **S**
Judg 15:11 rock of Etam, and said to **S**
Judg 15:12 Then **S** said to them,
Judg 15:16 **S** said: "With the jawbone
Judg 16: 1 Then **S** went to Gaza and saw a
Judg 16: 2 were told, "**S** has come here
Judg 16: 3 And **S** lay low till midnight
Judg 16: 6 So Delilah said to **S**
Judg 16: 7 **S** said to her, "If they bind
Judg 16: 9 Philistines are upon you, **S**
Judg 16:10 Then Delilah said to **S**
Judg 16:12 Philistines are upon you, **S**
Judg 16:13 Then Delilah said to **S**
Judg 16:14 Philistines are upon you, **S**
Judg 16:20 Philistines are upon you, **S**
Judg 16:23 into our hands **S** our enemy
Judg 16:25 Call for **S**, that he may
Judg 16:25 called for **S** from the prison
Judg 16:26 Then **S** said to the lad who
Judg 16:27 who watched while **S** performed
Judg 16:28 Then **S** called to the LORD,
Judg 16:29 **S** took hold of the two middle
Judg 16:30 Then **S** said, "Let me die
Heb 11:32 tell of Gideon and Barak and **S**

SAMSON'S (*see* SAMSON)
Judg 14:15 day that they said to **S** wife
Judg 14:16 Then **S** wife wept on him, and
Judg 14:20 And **S** wife was given to his

SAMUEL (*see* SHEMUEL)
1Sa 1:20 a son, and called his name **S**
1Sa 2:18 But **S** ministered before the
1Sa 2:21 Meanwhile the child **S** grew
1Sa 2:26 the child **S** grew in stature,
1Sa 3: 1 Then the boy **S** ministered to
1Sa 3: 3 while **S** was lying down to
1Sa 3: 4 that the LORD called **S**
1Sa 3: 6 **S**!" So **S** arose and went
1Sa 3: 7 (Now **S** did not yet know the
1Sa 3: 8 the LORD called **S** again the
1Sa 3: 9 Therefore Eli said to **S**, "Go
1Sa 3: 9 So **S** went and lay down in
1Sa 3:10 **S**! **S**!" And **S** answered, Speak
1Sa 3:11 Then the LORD said to **S**
1Sa 3:15 So **S** lay down until morning,
1Sa 3:15 **S** was afraid to tell Eli the
1Sa 3:16 Then Eli called **S** and said
1Sa 3:16 and said, "**S**, my son!"
1Sa 3:18 Then **S** told him everything,
1Sa 3:19 So **S** grew, and the LORD was
1Sa 3:20 **S** had been established as a
1Sa 3:21 to **S** in Shiloh by the word of
1Sa 4: 1 the word of **S** came to all
1Sa 7: 3 Then **S** spoke to all the house
1Sa 7: 5 And **S** said, "Gather all
1Sa 7: 6 And **S** judged the children of
1Sa 7: 8 children of Israel said to **S**
1Sa 7: 9 **S** took a suckling lamb and
1Sa 7: 9 Then **S** cried out to the LORD
1Sa 7:10 Now as **S** was offering up the
1Sa 7:12 Then **S** took a stone and set it
1Sa 7:13 Philistines all the days of **S**
1Sa 7:15 So **S** judged Israel all the
1Sa 8: 1 **S** was old that he made his
1Sa 8: 4 and came to **S** at Ramah,
1Sa 8: 6 displeased **S** when they said
1Sa 8: 6 So **S** prayed to the LORD
1Sa 8: 7 And the LORD said to **S**, "Heed
1Sa 8:10 So **S** told all the words of
1Sa 8:19 to obey the voice of **S**
1Sa 8:21 **S** heard all the words of the
1Sa 8:22 So the LORD said to **S**, "Heed
1Sa 8:22 **S** said to the men of Israel,
1Sa 9:14 into the city, there was **S**
1Sa 9:15 Now the LORD had told **S** in
1Sa 9:17 when **S** saw Saul, the LORD
1Sa 9:18 drew near to **S** in the gate
1Sa 9:19 And **S** answered Saul and said,
1Sa 9:22 Then **S** took Saul and his
1Sa 9:23 And **S** said to the cook,
1Sa 9:24 And **S** said, "Here it is
1Sa 9:24 So Saul ate with **S** that day
1Sa 9:25 **S** spoke with Saul on the top
1Sa 9:26 **S** called to Saul on the top
1Sa 9:26 of them went outside, he and **S**
1Sa 9:27 of the city, **S** said to Saul,
1Sa 10: 1 Then **S** took a flask of oil and
1Sa 10: 9 turned his back to go from **S**
1Sa 10:14 to be found, we went to **S**
1Sa 10:15 please, what **S** said to you
1Sa 10:16 not tell him what **S** had said
1Sa 10:17 Then **S** called the people
1Sa 10:20 when **S** had caused all the
1Sa 10:24 **S** said to all the people,
1Sa 10:25 Then **S** explained to the
1Sa 10:25 **S** sent all the people away,
1Sa 11: 7 **S** to battle, so it shall be
1Sa 11:12 Then the people said to **S**
1Sa 11:14 Then **S** said to the people,
1Sa 12: 1 Now **S** said to all Israel
1Sa 12: 6 And **S** said to the people,
1Sa 12:11 Bedan, Jephthah, and **S**, and
1Sa 12:18 So **S** called to the LORD, and
1Sa 12:18 greatly feared the LORD and **S**
1Sa 12:19 And all the people said to **S**
1Sa 12:20 Then **S** said to the people,
1Sa 13: 8 to the time set by **S**
1Sa 13: 8 But **S** did not come to Gilgal
1Sa 13:10 burnt offering, that **S** came
1Sa 13:11 And **S** said, "What have you
1Sa 13:13 And **S** said to Saul,
1Sa 13:15 Then **S** arose and went up from
1Sa 15: 1 **S** also said to Saul, "The
1Sa 15:10 word of the LORD came to **S**
1Sa 15:11 And it grieved **S**, and he
1Sa 15:12 So when **S** rose early in the
1Sa 15:12 to meet Saul, it was told **S**
1Sa 15:13 Then **S** went to Saul, and Saul
1Sa 15:14 But **S** said, "What then is
1Sa 15:16 Then **S** said to Saul, Be
1Sa 15:17 So **S** said, "When you were
1Sa 15:20 And Saul said to **S**, "But I
1Sa 15:22 Then **S** said: "Has the LORD
1Sa 15:24 Then Saul said to **S**, "I have
1Sa 15:26 But **S** said to Saul, "I will
1Sa 15:27 as **S** turned around to go away
1Sa 15:28 So **S** said to him, "The LORD
1Sa 15:31 So **S** turned back after Saul,
1Sa 15:32 Then **S** said, "Bring Agag
1Sa 15:33 But **S** said, "As your sword
1Sa 15:33 And **S** hacked Agag in pieces
1Sa 15:34 Then **S** went to Ramah, and Saul
1Sa 15:35 **S** went no more to see Saul
1Sa 15:35 Nevertheless **S** mourned for
1Sa 16: 1 Then the LORD said to **S**
1Sa 16: 2 And **S** said, "How can I go?
1Sa 16: 4 So **S** did what the LORD said,
1Sa 16: 7 But the LORD said to **S**, "Do
1Sa 16: 8 and made him pass before **S**
1Sa 16:10 of his sons pass before **S**
1Sa 16:10 And **S** said to Jesse,
1Sa 16:11 And **S** said to Jesse,
1Sa 16:11 And **S** said to Jesse,

1Sa 16:13 Then **S** took the horn of oil
1Sa 16:13 So **S** arose and went to Ramah
1Sa 19:18 went to **S** at Ramah, and told
1Sa 19:18 **S** went and stayed in Naioth
1Sa 19:20 **S** standing as leader over
1Sa 19:22 Where are **S** and David
1Sa 19:24 before **S** in like manner, and
1Sa 25: 1 **S** died; and the Israelites
1Sa 28: 3 Now **S** had died, and all Israel
1Sa 28:11 Bring up **S** for me
1Sa 28:12 When the woman saw **S**, she
1Sa 28:14 Saul perceived that it was **S**
1Sa 28:15 Now **S** said to Saul, "Why
1Sa 28:16 Then **S** said: "Why then do
1Sa 28:20 because of the words of **S**
1Ch 6:28 The sons of **S** were Joel the
1Ch 6:33 the son of Joel, the son of **S**
1Ch 9:22 **S** the seer had appointed them
1Ch 11: 3 to the word of the LORD by **S**
1Ch 26:28 And all that **S** the seer, Saul
1Ch 29:29 in the book of **S** the seer
2Ch 35:18 the days of **S** the prophet
Ps 99: 6 **S** was among those who called
Jer 15: 1 **S** stood before Me, yet My
Acts 3:24 and all the prophets, from **S**
Acts 13:20 years, until **S** the prophet
Heb 11:32 Jephthah, also of David and **S**

SANBALLAT
Neh 2:10 When **S** the Horonite and
Neh 2:19 But when **S** the Horonite,
Neh 4: 1 when **S** heard that we were
Neh 4: 7 Now it happened, when **S**,
Neh 6: 1 Now it happened when **S**,
Neh 6: 2 that **S** and Geshem sent to me,
Neh 6: 5 Then **S** sent his servant to me
Neh 6:12 Tobiah and **S** had hired him
Neh 6:14 God, remember Tobiah and **S**
Neh 13:28 son-in-law of **S** the Horonite

SANCTIFICATION (*see* SANCTIFY)
1Co 1:30 and righteousness and **s** and
1Th 4: 3 is the will of God, your **s**
1Th 4: 4 possess his own vessel in **s**
2Th 2:13 through **s** by the Spirit and
1Pe 1: 2 in **s** of the Spirit, for

SANCTIFIED (*see* SANCTIFY)
Gen 2: 3 **s** it, because in it He rested
Ex 19:14 **s** the people, and they washed
Ex 29:43 shall be **s** by My glory
Lev 8:10 all that was in it, and **s** them
Lev 8:15 **s** it, to make atonement for
Lev 8:30 he **s** Aaron, his garments, his
Lev 27:15 If he who **s** it wants to
Num 3:13 Egypt, I **s** to Myself all the
Num 7: 1 **s** it and all its furnishings,
Num 7: 1 so he anointed them and **s** them
Num 8:17 of Egypt I **s** them to Myself
Num 18:29 of them, the **s** part of them
1Sa 16: 5 Then he **s** Jesse and his sons
1Sa 21: 5 even though it was **s** in the
1Ki 9: 3 I have **s** this house which you
1Ki 9: 7 this house which I have **s** for
1Ch 15:14 the Levites **s** themselves to
2Ch 5:11 were present had **s** themselves
2Ch 7:16 **s** this house, that My name
2Ch 7:20 this house which I have **s** for
2Ch 29:15 **s** themselves, and went
2Ch 29:17 Then they **s** the house of the
2Ch 29:19 we have prepared and **s**
2Ch 29:34 priests had **s** themselves, for
2Ch 30: 3 priests had not **s** themselves
2Ch 30: 8 which He has **s** forever, and
2Ch 30:15 **s** themselves, and brought the
2Ch 30:17 who had not **s** themselves
2Ch 30:24 of priests **s** themselves
2Ch 31:18 they **s** themselves in holiness
Is 13: 3 I have commanded My **s** ones
Jer 1: 5 before you were born I **s** you
Ezek 48:11 the sons of Zadok, who are **s**
John 10:36 say of Him whom the Father **s**
John 17:19 also may be **s** by the truth
Acts 20:32 among all those who are **s**
Acts 26:18 who are **s** by faith in Me
Rom 15:16 **s** by the Holy Spirit
1Co 1: 2 who are **s** in Christ Jesus
1Co 6:11 were washed, but you were **s**
1Co 7:14 husband is **s** by the wife, and
1Co 7:14 wife is **s** by the husband
1Ti 4: 5 for it is **s** by the word of
2Ti 2:21 will be a vessel for honor, **s**
Heb 2:11 are being **s** are all of one
Heb 10:10 By that will we have been **s**
Heb 10:14 forever those who are being **s**
Heb 10:29 which he was **s** a common thing
Jude 1 **s** by God the Father, and

SANCTIFIES (*see* SANCTIFY)
Ex 31:13 that I am the LORD who **s** you
Lev 20: 8 I am the LORD who **s** you
Lev 22:32 I am the LORD who **s** you,
Lev 27:14 when a man **s** his house to be
Lev 27:16 if a man **s** to the LORD some
Lev 27:17 If he **s** his field from the
Lev 27:18 But if he **s** his field after
Lev 27:19 if he who **s** the field ever
Lev 27:22 And if a man **s** to the LORD a
Ezek 20:12 that I am the LORD who **s** them
Matt 23:17 or the temple that **s** the gold
Matt 23:19 or the altar that **s** the gift
Heb 2:11 For both He who **s** and those
Heb 9:13 **s** for the purifying of the

SANCTIFY (*see* SANCTIFICATION, SANCTIFIED, SANCTIFIES, SANCTIFYING)
Ex 13: 2 **S** to Me all the firstborn,
Ex 19:10 **s** them today and tomorrow, and
Ex 19:22 near the LORD **s** themselves
Ex 19:23 around the mountain and **s** it
Ex 28: 3 to **s** him, that he may
Ex 28:41 and **s** them, that they may
Ex 29:27 **s** the breast of the wave
Ex 29:33 to consecrate and to **s** them
Ex 29:36 you shall anoint it to **s** it
Ex 29:37 for the altar and **s** it
Ex 29:44 So I will **s** the tabernacle of
Ex 29:44 I will also **s** both Aaron and
Ex 30:29 You shall **s** them, that they
Ex 30:30 and **s** them, that they may
Ex 40:10 its utensils, and **s** the altar
Ex 40:11 laver and its base, and **s** it
Ex 40:13 **s** him, that he may minister
Lev 8:11 laver and its base, to **s** them
Lev 8:12 and anointed him, to **s** him
Lev 11:44 shall therefore **s** yourselves
Lev 16:19 **s** it from the uncleanness of
Lev 20: 7 **S** yourselves therefore, and
Lev 21: 8 Therefore you shall **s** him
Lev 21: 8 for I the LORD, who **s** you
Lev 21:15 people, for I the LORD **s** him
Lev 21:23 for I the LORD **s** them
Lev 22: 2 things which they **s** to Me
Lev 22: 3 of Israel **s** to the LORD,
Lev 22: 9 I the LORD **s** them
Lev 22:16 for I the LORD **s** them
Lev 27:26 firstling, no man shall **s**
Num 6:11 he shall **s** his head that same
Num 11:18 **S** yourselves for tomorrow,
Deut 15:19 shall **s** to the LORD your God
Josh 3: 5 **S** yourselves, for tomorrow
Josh 7:13 up, **s** the people, and say
Josh 7:13 **S** yourselves for tomorrow,
1Sa 16: 5 **S** yourselves, and come with me
1Ch 15:12 **s** yourselves, you and your
1Ch 23:13 that he should **s** the most
2Ch 29: 5 **s** yourselves, **s** the house
2Ch 29:17 Now they began to **s** on the
2Ch 30:17 clean, to **s** them to the LORD
2Ch 35: 6 **s** yourselves, and prepare them
Neh 13:22 gates, to **s** the Sabbath day
Job 1: 5 and **s** them, and he would rise
Is 66:17 Those who **s** themselves and
Ezek 36:23 I will **s** My great name, which
Ezek 37:28 **s** Israel, when My sanctuary
Ezek 38:23 **s** Myself, and I will be known
Ezek 44:19 they shall not **s** the people
Ezek 46:20 outer court to **s** the people
Joel 2:16 **s** the congregation, assemble
John 17:17 **S** them by Your truth
John 17:19 And for their sakes I **s** Myself
Eph 5:26 that He might **s** and cleanse it
1Th 5:23 Himself **s** you completely
Heb 13:12 that He might **s** the people
1Pe 3:15 But **s** the Lord God in your

SANCTIFYING (*see* SANCTIFY)
2Ch 29:34 were more diligent in **s**

SANCTUARIES (*see* SANCTUARY)
Lev 21:23 defect, lest he profane My **s**
Lev 26:31 bring your **s** to desolation,
1Ki 6:29 both the inner and outer **s**
1Ki 6:30 both the inner and outer **s**
Jer 51:51 have come into the **s** of the
Ezek 28:18 You defiled your **s** by the
Amos 7: 9 the **s** of Israel shall be laid

SANCTUARY (*see* SANCTUARIES)
Ex 15:17 for Your own dwelling, the **s**
Ex 25: 8 And let them make Me a **s**, that
Ex 30:13 to the shekel of the **s** (a
Ex 30:24 to the shekel of the **s**, and a
Ex 36: 1 work for the service of the **s**
Ex 36: 3 the service of making the **s**
Ex 36: 4 all the work of the **s** came
Ex 36: 6 for the offering of the **s**
Ex 38:24 to the shekel of the **s**
Ex 38:25 to the shekel of the **s**
Ex 38:26 to the shekel of the **s**), for
Ex 38:27 cast the sockets of the **s**
Lev 4: 6 in front of the veil of the **s**
Lev 5:15 to the shekel of the **s**, as a
Lev 10: 4 before the **s** out of the camp
Lev 12: 4 nor come into the **s** until the
Lev 16:33 make atonement for the Holy **S**
Lev 19:30 Sabbaths and reverence My **s**
Lev 20: 3 to Molech, to defile My **s**
Lev 21:12 nor shall he go out of the **s**
Lev 21:12 nor profane the **s** of his God
Lev 26: 2 Sabbaths and reverence My **s**
Lev 27: 3 to the shekel of the **s**
Lev 27:25 to the shekel of the **s**
Num 3:28 keeping charge of the **s**
Num 3:31 the utensils of the **s** with
Num 3:32 who kept charge of the **s**
Num 3:38 sons, keeping charge of the **s**
Num 3:47 of the shekel of the **s**, the
Num 3:50 to the shekel of the **s**
Num 4:12 which they minister in the **s**
Num 4:15 have finished covering the **s**
Num 4:15 all the furnishings of the **s**
Num 4:16 all that is in it, with the **s**
Num 7:13 to the shekel of the **s**, both
Num 7:19 to the shekel of the **s**, both
Num 7:25 to the shekel of the **s**, both
Num 7:31 to the shekel of the **s**, both
Num 7:37 to the shekel of the **s**, both
Num 7:43 to the shekel of the **s**, both
Num 7:49 to the shekel of the **s**, both
Num 7:55 to the shekel of the **s**, both
Num 7:61 to the shekel of the **s**, both
Num 7:67 to the shekel of the **s**, both
Num 7:73 to the shekel of the **s**, both
Num 7:79 to the shekel of the **s**, both
Num 7:85 to the shekel of the **s**
Num 7:86 to the shekel of the **s**
Num 8:19 of Israel come near the **s**
Num 18: 1 the iniquity related to the **s**
Num 18: 3 near the articles of the **s**
Num 18: 5 attend to the duties of the **s**
Num 18:16 to the shekel of the **s**, which
Num 19:20 has defiled the **s** of the LORD
Josh 24:26 that was by the **s** of the LORD
1Ki 6: 3 the **s** of the house was twenty
1Ki 6: 5 both the **s** and the inner **s**
1Ki 6:16 it inside as the inner **s**, as
1Ki 6:17 **s** was forty cubits long
1Ki 6:19 the inner **s** inside the temple
1Ki 6:20 The inner **s** was twenty cubits
1Ki 6:21 the front of the inner **s**
1Ki 6:22 altar that was by the inner **s**
1Ki 6:23 Inside the inner **s** he made
1Ki 6:31 the entrance of the inner **s**
1Ki 6:33 So for the door of the **s** he
1Ki 7:49 left in front of the inner **s**
1Ki 8: 6 the inner **s** of the temple
1Ki 8: 8 in front of the inner **s**
1Ch 9:29 all the implements of the **s**
1Ch 22:19 build the **s** of the LORD God,
1Ch 24: 5 there were officials of the **s**
1Ch 28:10 to build a house for the **s**
2Ch 3: 4 the **s** was twenty cubits long
2Ch 3:16 chainwork, as in the inner **s**
2Ch 4:20 in front of the inner **s**,
2Ch 4:22 As for the entry of the **s**
2Ch 5: 7 the inner **s** of the temple
2Ch 5: 9 in front of the inner **s**
2Ch 20: 8 have built You a **s** in it for
2Ch 26:18 Get out of the **s**, for you
2Ch 29:21 for the kingdom, for the **s**
2Ch 30: 8 and enter His **s**, which He has
2Ch 30:19 to the purification of the **s**
2Ch 36:17 sword in the house of their **s**
Neh 10:39 the articles of the **s** are

Ps 20: 2 He send you help from the s
Ps 28: 2 my hands toward Your holy s
Ps 63: 2 have looked for You in the s
Ps 68:24 my God, my King, into the s
Ps 73:17 I went into the s of God
Ps 74: 3 damaged everything in the s
Ps 74: 7 They have set fire to Your s
Ps 77:13 Your way, O God, is in the s
Ps 78:69 And He built His s like the
Ps 96: 6 and beauty are in His s
Ps 102:19 down from the height of His s
Ps 114: 2 Judah became His s, And Israel
Ps 134: 2 Lift up your hands in the s
Ps 150: 1 Praise God in His s
Is 8:14 He will be as a s, but a
Is 16:12 he will come to his s to pray
Is 43:28 profane the princes of the s
Is 60:13 to beautify the place of My s
Is 63:18 have trodden down Your s
Jer 17:12 is the place of our s
Lam 1:10 seen the nations enter her s
Lam 2: 7 altar, He has abandoned His s
Lam 2:20 be slain in the s of the Lord
Lam 4: 1 The stones of the s are
Ezek 5:11 My s with all your detestable
Ezek 8: 6 make Me go far away from My s
Ezek 9: 6 and begin at My s
Ezek 11:16 yet I shall be a little s for
Ezek 23:38 defiled My s on the same day
Ezek 23:39 came into My s to profane it
Ezek 24:21 Behold, I will profane My s
Ezek 25: 3 against My s when it was
Ezek 37:26 and I will set My s in their
Ezek 37:28 when My s is in their midst
Ezek 41: 1 Then he brought me into the s
Ezek 41: 4 twenty cubits, beyond the s
Ezek 41:20 door, and on the wall of the s
Ezek 41:21 and so also the front of the s
Ezek 41:23 temple and the s had two doors
Ezek 43:21 of the temple, outside the s
Ezek 44: 1 to the outer gate of the s
Ezek 44: 5 and all who go out from the s
Ezek 44: 7 to be in My s to defile it
Ezek 44: 8 keep charge of My s for you
Ezek 44: 9 in flesh, shall enter My s
Ezek 44:11 shall be ministers in My s
Ezek 44:15 who kept charge of My s when
Ezek 44:16 They shall enter My s, and
Ezek 44:27 to the s to minister in the s
Ezek 45: 2 be a square plot for the s
Ezek 45: 3 in it shall be the s, the
Ezek 45: 4 the ministers of the s, who
Ezek 45: 4 and a holy place for the s
Ezek 45:18 blemish and cleanse the s
Ezek 47:12 their water flows from the s
Ezek 48: 8 with the s in the center
Ezek 48:10 The s of the LORD shall be in
Ezek 48:21 the s of the temple shall be
Dan 8:11 place of His s was cast down
Dan 8:13 the giving of both the s
Dan 8:14 then the s shall be cleansed
Dan 9:17 Your face to shine on Your s
Dan 9:26 destroy the city and the s
Dan 11:31 shall defile the s fortress
Amos 7:13 for it is the king's s, and
Zeph 3: 4 priests have polluted the s
Heb 8: 2 a Minister of the s and of the
Heb 9: 1 service and the earthly s
Heb 9: 2 which is called the s
Heb 13:11 blood is brought into the s

SAND (*see* SANDS)
Gen 22:17 and as the s which is on the
Gen 32:12 as the s of the sea, which
Gen 41:49 as the s of the sea, until he
Ex 2:12 Egyptian and hid him in the s
Lev 11:30 the s reptile, the s lizard
Deut 33:19 of treasures hidden in the s
Josh 11: 4 as many people as the s that
Judg 7:12 as the s by the seashore in
1Sa 13: 5 people as the s which is on
2Sa 17:11 like the s that is by the sea
1Ki 4:20 the s by the sea in multitude
1Ki 4:29 like the s on the seashore
Job 6: 3 heavier than the s of the sea
Job 29:18 and multiply my days as the s
Ps 78:27 fowl like the s of the seas
Ps 139:18 be more in number than the s
Prov 27: 3 s is weighty, but a fool's
Is 10:22 be as the s of the sea, yet a
Is 48:19 would have been like the s
Is 48:19 body like the grains of s
Jer 5:22 Who have placed the s as the
Jer 15: 8 more than the s of the seas
Jer 33:22 nor the s of the sea measured
Hos 1:10 shall be as the s of the sea
Hab 1: 9 They gather captives like s
Matt 7:26 who built his house on the s
Rom 9:27 Israel be as the s of the sea
Heb 11:12 innumerable as the s which is
Rev 13: 1 I stood on the s of the sea
Rev 20: 8 number is as the s of the sea

SANDAL (*see* SANDALS)
Gen 14:23 from a thread to a s strap
Deut 25: 9 remove his s from his foot,
Deut 25:10 of him who had his s removed
Josh 5:15 Take your s off your foot,
Ruth 4: 7 one man took off his s and
Ruth 4: 8 So he took off his s
Is 9: 5 For every warrior's s from
Mark 1: 7 whose s strap I am not worthy
Luke 3:16 whose s strap I am not worthy
John 1:27 whose s strap I am not worthy

SANDALS (*see* SANDAL)
Ex 3: 5 Take your s off your feet,
Ex 12:11 your s on your feet, and your
Deut 29: 5 your s have not worn out on
Deut 33:25 Your s shall be iron and
Josh 9: 5 patched s on their feet, and
Josh 9:13 our s have become old because
1Ki 2: 5 on his s that were on his
2Ch 28:15 dressed them and gave them s
Song 7: 1 beautiful are your feet in s
Is 5:27 strap of their s be broken
Is 20: 2 take your s off your feet
Ezek 16:10 gave you s of badger skin
Ezek 24:17 and put your s on your feet
Ezek 24:23 heads and your s on your feet
Amos 2: 6 and the poor for a pair of s
Amos 8: 6 and the needy for a pair of s
Matt 3:11 whose s I am not worthy to
Matt 10:10 nor two tunics, nor s, nor
Mark 6: 9 but to wear s, and not to put
Luke 10: 4 money bag, sack, nor s
Luke 15:22 on his hand and s on his feet
Luke 22:35 without money bag, sack, and s
Acts 7:33 Take your s off your feet,
Acts 12: 8 yourself and tie on your s"
Acts 13:25 the s of whose feet I am not

SANDS (*see* SAND)
Acts 27:17 run aground on the Syrtis S

SANG (*see* SING)
Ex 15: 1 s this song to the LORD, and
Num 21:17 Then Israel s this song
Judg 5: 1 son of Abinoam s on that day
1Sa 18: 7 So the women s as they danced
1Sa 29: 5 of whom they s to one another
2Sa 3:33 And the king s a lament over
2Ch 29:28 worshiped, the singers s, and
2Ch 29:30 So they s praises with
Ezra 3:11 they s responsively, praising
Neh 12:42 The singers s loudly with
Job 38: 7 the morning stars s together
Ps 106:12 They s His praise
Rev 5: 9 they s a new song, saying
Rev 14: 3 they s as it were a new song

SANK (*see* SINK)
Ex 15: 5 they s to the bottom like a
Ex 15:10 they s like lead in the
Num 21:18 the well the leaders s, dug
Judg 5:27 At her feet he s, he fell, he
Judg 5:27 at her feet he s, he fell
Judg 5:27 where he s, there he fell
1Sa 17:49 the stone s into his forehead
2Ki 9:24 and he s down in his chariot
Jer 38: 6 So Jeremiah s in the mire

SANSANNAH (*see* KIRJATH SANNAH)
Josh 15:31 Ziklag, Madmannah, S,

SAP
Ps 104:16 of the LORD are full of s
Amos 3:11 he shall s your strength from

SAPH (*see* SIPPAI)
2Sa 21:18 the Hushathite killed S, who

SAPPHIRA
Acts 5: 1 with S his wife, sold a

SAPPHIRE (*see* SAPPHIRES)
Ex 24:10 were a paved work of s stone
Ex 28:18 row shall be a turquoise, a s
Ex 39:11 second row, a turquoise, a s
Job 28:16 Ophir, in precious onyx or s
Lam 4: 7 like s in their appearance
Ezek 1:26 in appearance like a s stone
Ezek 10: 1 something like a s stone,
Ezek 28:13 beryl, onyx, and jasper, s
Rev 21:19 was jasper, the second s, the

SAPPHIRES (*see* SAPPHIRE)
Job 28: 6 stones are the source of s
Song 5:14 is carved ivory inlaid with s
Is 54:11 lay your foundations with s

SARAH (*see* ISCAH, SARAH'S, SARAI, SERAH)
Gen 17:15 but S shall be her name
Gen 17:17 And shall S, who is ninety
Gen 17:19 S your wife shall bear you a
Gen 17:21 whom S shall bear to you at
Gen 18: 6 hastened into the tent to S
Gen 18: 9 him, "Where is S your wife
Gen 18:10 S your wife shall have a son
Gen 18:10 S was listening in the tent
Gen 18:11 S were old, well-advanced in
Gen 18:11 and S had passed the age of
Gen 18:12 Therefore S laughed within
Gen 18:13 Why did S laugh, saying
Gen 18:14 life, and S shall have a son
Gen 18:15 But S denied it, saying, "I
Gen 20: 2 Abraham said of S his wife
Gen 20: 2 king of Gerar sent and took S
Gen 20:14 he restored S his wife to him
Gen 20:16 Then to S he said, "Behold,
Gen 20:18 of Abimelech because of S
Gen 21: 1 LORD visited S as He had said
Gen 21: 1 did for S as He had spoken
Gen 21: 2 For S conceived and bore
Gen 21: 3 whom S bore to him
Gen 21: 6 And S said, "God has made me
Gen 21: 7 that S would nurse children
Gen 21: 9 S saw the son of Hagar the
Gen 21:12 Whatever S has said to you,
Gen 23: 1 S lived one hundred and
Gen 23: 1 the years of the life of S
Gen 23: 2 So S died in Kirjath Arba
Gen 23: 2 Abraham came to mourn for S
Gen 23:19 Abraham buried S his wife in
Gen 24:36 S my master's wife bore a son
Gen 25:10 was buried, and S his wife
Gen 49:31 S his wife, there they buried
Is 51: 2 father, and to S who bore you
Rom 9: 9 come and S shall have a son
Heb 11:11 By faith S herself also
1Pe 3: 6 as S obeyed Abraham, calling

SARAH'S (*see* SARAH)
Gen 24:67 her into his mother S tent
Gen 25:12 S maidservant, bore to
Rom 4:19 and the deadness of S womb

SARAI (*see* SARAH, SARAI'S)
Gen 11:29 name of Abram's wife was S
Gen 11:30 But S was barren
Gen 11:31 and his daughter-in-law S
Gen 12: 5 Then Abram took S his wife
Gen 12:11 that he said to S his wife
Gen 12:17 great plagues because of S
Gen 16: 1 Now S, Abram's wife, had
Gen 16: 2 So S said to Abram, "See now
Gen 16: 2 Abram heeded the voice of S
Gen 16: 3 Then S, Abram's wife, took
Gen 16: 5 Then S said to Abram, "My
Gen 16: 6 So Abram said to S, "Indeed
Gen 16: 6 when S dealt harshly with her
Gen 16: 8 the presence of my mistress S
Gen 17:15 As for S your wife
Gen 17:15 you shall not call her name S

SARAI'S (*see* SARAI)
Gen 16: 8 S maid, where have you come

SARAPH
1Ch 4:22 S, who ruled in Moab, and

SARDIS
Rev 1:11 Pergamos, to Thyatira, to S
Rev 3: 1 of the church in S write
Rev 3: 4 have a few names even in S

SARDITES
Num 26:26 of Sered, the family of the **S**

SARDIUS
Ex 28:17 The first row shall be a **s**
Ex 39:10 a row with a **s**, a topaz, and
Ezek 28:13 the **s**, topaz, and diamond,
Rev 4: 3 and a **s** stone in appearance
Rev 21:20 fifth sardonyx, the sixth **s**

SARDONYX
Rev 21:20 the fifth **s**, the sixth

SARGON
Is 20: 1 when **S** the king of Assyria

SARID
Josh 19:10 inheritance was as far as **S**
Josh 19:12 Then from **S** it went eastward

SARSECHIM
Jer 39: 3 Samgar-Nebo, **S**, Rabsaris,

SASH (*see* SASHES)
Ex 28: 4 woven tunic, a turban, and a **s**
Ex 28:39 make the **s** of woven work
Ex 39:29 a **s** of fine linen and blue and
Lev 8: 7 on him, girded him with the **s**
Lev 16: 4 be girded with a linen **s**, and
Is 3:24 instead of a **s**, a rope
Jer 13: 1 Go and get yourself a linen **s**
Jer 13: 2 So I got a **s** according to the
Jer 13: 4 Take the **s** that you acquired,
Jer 13: 6 take from there the **s** which I
Jer 13: 7 I took the **s** from the place
Jer 13: 7 and there was the **s**, ruined
Jer 13:10 **s** which is profitable for
Jer 13:11 For as the **s** clings to the

SASHES (*see* SASH)
Ex 28:40 and you shall make **s** for them
Ex 29: 9 And you shall gird them with **s**
Lev 8:13 on them, girded them with **s**
Prov 31:24 supplies **s** for the merchants

SAT (*see* SIT)
Gen 21:16 **s** down across from him at a
Gen 21:16 So she **s** opposite him, and
Gen 31:34 camel's saddle, and **s** on them
Gen 37:25 they **s** down to eat a meal
Gen 38:14 **s** in an open place which was
Gen 43:33 And they **s** before him, the
Gen 48: 2 himself and **s** up on the bed
Ex 2:15 and he **s** down by a well
Ex 12:29 who **s** on his throne to the
Ex 16: 3 when we **s** by the pots of meat
Ex 17:12 it under him, and he **s** on it
Ex 18:13 that Moses **s** to judge the
Ex 32: 6 the people **s** down to eat and
Lev 15: 6 **s** shall wash his clothes and
Lev 15:22 **s** on shall wash his clothes
Judg 6:11 **s** under the terebinth tree
Judg 19: 6 So they **s** down, and the two of
Judg 19:15 he **s** down in the open square
Judg 20:26 They **s** there before the LORD
Ruth 2:14 So she **s** beside the reapers
Ruth 4: 1 to the gate and **s** down there
Ruth 4: 1 So he came aside and **s** down
Ruth 4: 2 So they **s** down
1Sa 19: 9 LORD came upon Saul as he **s**
1Sa 20:24 the king **s** down to eat the
1Sa 20:25 Now the king **s** on his seat
1Sa 20:25 Abner **s** by Saul's side, but
1Sa 28:23 the ground and **s** on the bed
2Sa 2:13 So they **s** down, one on one
2Sa 7:18 went in and **s** before the LORD
2Sa 19: 8 king arose and **s** in the gate
1Ki 2:12 Then Solomon **s** on the throne
1Ki 2:19 **s** down on his throne and had a
1Ki 2:19 so she **s** at his right hand
1Ki 13:20 as they **s** at the table, that
1Ki 19: 4 **s** down under a broom tree
1Ki 21:13 came in and **s** before him
1Ki 22:10 **s** each on his throne, at a
2Ki 4:20 he **s** on her knees till noon,
2Ki 11:19 he **s** on the throne of the
2Ki 13:13 Then Jeroboam **s** on his throne
1Ch 17:16 went in and **s** before the LORD
1Ch 29:23 Then Solomon **s** on the throne
2Ch 18: 9 robes, **s** each on his throne
2Ch 18: 9 they **s** at a threshing floor
Ezra 9: 3 beard, and **s** down astonished
Ezra 9: 4 and I **s** astonished until the
Ezra 10: 9 all the people **s** in the open
Ezra 10:16 they **s** down on the first day
Neh 1: 4 these words, that I **s** down
Neh 8:17 booths and **s** under the booths
Esth 1: 2 **s** on the throne of his
Esth 2:19 Mordecai **s** within the king's
Esth 2:21 while Mordecai **s** within the
Esth 3:15 Haman **s** down to drink, but
Esth 5: 1 while the king **s** on his royal
Job 2: 8 **s** in the midst of the ashes
Job 2:13 So they **s** down with him on
Job 29:25 way for them, and **s** as chief
Ps 9: 4 You **s** on the throne judging
Ps 26: 4 I have not **s** with idolatrous
Ps 29:10 The LORD **s** enthroned at the
Ps 107:10 Those who **s** in darkness and in
Ps 137: 1 of Babylon, There we **s** down
Song 2: 3 I **s** down in his shade with
Is 21: 8 I have **s** at my post every
Jer 3: 2 By the road you have **s** for
Jer 15:17 I **s** alone because of Your
Jer 26:10 **s** down in the entry of the
Jer 32:12 before all the Jews who **s** in
Jer 39: 3 in and **s** in the Middle Gate
Ezek 3:15 and I **s** where they **s**, and
Ezek 8: 1 as I **s** in my house with the
Ezek 14: 1 came to me and **s** before me
Ezek 20: 1 of the LORD, and **s** before me
Ezek 23:41 You **s** on a stately couch,
Dan 2:49 but Daniel **s** in the gate of
Jon 3: 6 with sackcloth and **s** in ashes
Jon 4: 5 **s** on the east side of the
Jon 4: 5 **s** under it in the shade, till
Matt 4:16 the people who **s** in darkness
Matt 4:16 those who **s** in the region
Matt 9:10 as Jesus **s** at the table in
Matt 9:10 and **s** down with Him and His
Matt 13: 1 of the house and **s** by the sea
Matt 13: 2 that He got into a boat and **s**
Matt 13:48 and they **s** down and gathered
Matt 14: 9 because of those who **s** with
Matt 15:29 the mountain and **s** down there
Matt 24: 3 Now as He **s** on the Mount of
Matt 26: 7 His head as He **s** at the table
Matt 26:20 He **s** down with the twelve
Matt 26:55 I **s** daily with you, teaching
Matt 26:58 **s** with the servants to see
Matt 26:69 Now Peter **s** outside in the
Matt 28: 2 from the door, and **s** on it
Mark 2:15 sinners also **s** together with
Mark 3:34 at those who **s** about Him, and
Mark 4: 1 a boat and **s** in it on the sea
Mark 6:22 Herod and those who **s** with him
Mark 6:26 of those who **s** with him, he
Mark 6:40 So they **s** down in ranks, in
Mark 9:35 He **s** down, called the twelve,
Mark 10:46 **s** by the road begging
Mark 11: 2 tied, on which no one has **s**
Mark 11: 7 garments on it, and He **s** on it
Mark 12:41 Now Jesus **s** opposite the
Mark 13: 3 Now as He **s** on the Mount of
Mark 14: 3 as He **s** at the table, a woman
Mark 14:18 Now as they **s** and ate, Jesus
Mark 14:54 he **s** with the servants and
Mark 16:14 eleven as they **s** at the table
Mark 16:19 **s** down at the right hand of
Luke 4:20 to the attendant and **s** down
Luke 5: 3 And He **s** down and taught the
Luke 5:29 others who **s** down with them
Luke 7:15 And he who was dead **s** up and
Luke 7:36 house, and **s** down to eat
Luke 7:37 Jesus **s** at the table in the
Luke 7:49 those who **s** at the table with
Luke 10:39 who also **s** at Jesus' feet and
Luke 11:37 He went in and **s** down to eat
Luke 14:15 Now when one of those who **s**
Luke 18:35 man **s** by the road begging
Luke 19:30 on which no one has ever **s**
Luke 22:14 He **s** down, and the twelve
Luke 22:55 **s** down together, Peter **s** among
Luke 22:56 him as he **s** by the fire,
Luke 24:30 as He **s** at the table with
John 4: 6 journey, **s** thus by the well
John 6: 3 there He **s** with His disciples
John 6:10 So the men **s** down, in number
John 8: 2 and He **s** down and taught them
John 9: 8 Is not this he who **s** and
John 12: 2 was one of those who **s** at the
John 12:14 found a young donkey, **s** on it
John 13:12 **s** down again, He said to them
John 19:13 **s** down in the judgment seat
Acts 2: 3 and one **s** upon each of them
Acts 3:10 he who **s** begging alms at the
Acts 6:15 all who **s** in the council,
Acts 9:40 when she saw Peter she **s** up
Acts 12:21 **s** on his throne and gave an
Acts 13:14 on the Sabbath day and **s** down
Acts 16:13 we **s** down and spoke to the
Acts 20: 9 in a window **s** a certain young
Acts 25:17 the next day I **s** on the
Acts 26:30 and those who **s** with them
1Co 10: 7 The people **s** down to eat and
Heb 1: 3 **s** down at the right hand of
Heb 10:12 **s** down at the right hand of
Heb 12: 2 has **s** down at the right hand
Rev 3:21 **s** down with My Father on His
Rev 4: 2 and One **s** on the throne
Rev 4: 3 He who **s** there was like a
Rev 5: 1 who **s** on the throne a scroll
Rev 5: 7 of Him who **s** on the throne
Rev 6: 2 And he who **s** on it had a bow
Rev 6: 4 **s** on it to take peace from
Rev 6: 5 he who **s** on it had a pair of
Rev 6: 8 of him who **s** on it was Death
Rev 9:17 those who **s** on them had
Rev 11:16 the twenty-four elders who **s**
Rev 14:14 on the cloud **s** One like the
Rev 14:15 to Him who **s** on the cloud
Rev 14:16 So He who **s** on the cloud
Rev 19: 4 God who **s** on the throne,
Rev 19:11 He who **s** on him was called
Rev 19:19 Him who **s** on the horse and
Rev 19:21 of Him who **s** on the horse
Rev 20: 4 they **s** on them, and judgment
Rev 20:11 throne and Him who **s** on it
Rev 21: 5 Then He who **s** on the throne

SATAN (*see* SATAN'S)
1Ch 21: 1 Now **S** stood up against Israel
Job 1: 6 and **S** also came among them
Job 1: 7 And the LORD said to **S**, "From
Job 1: 7 So **S** answered the LORD and
Job 1: 8 Then the LORD said to **S**
Job 1: 9 So **S** answered the LORD and
Job 1:12 So the LORD said to **S**
Job 1:12 Then **S** went out from the
Job 2: 1 **S** came also among them to
Job 2: 2 And the LORD said to **S**, "From
Job 2: 2 So **S** answered the LORD and
Job 2: 3 Then the LORD said to **S**
Job 2: 4 So **S** answered the LORD and
Job 2: 6 So the LORD said to **S**
Job 2: 7 Then **S** went out from the
Zech 3: 1 **S** standing at his right hand
Zech 3: 2 And the LORD said to **S**
Zech 3: 2 The LORD rebuke you, **S**
Matt 4:10 Away with you, **S**
Matt 12:26 if **S** casts out **S**, he is
Matt 16:23 Get behind Me, **S**
Mark 1:13 forty days, tempted by **S**, and
Mark 3:23 How can **S** cast out **S**
Mark 3:26 if **S** has risen up against
Mark 4:15 **S** comes immediately and takes
Luke 4: 8 Get behind Me, **S**
Luke 10:18 I saw **S** fall like lightning
Luke 11:18 If **S** also is divided against
Luke 13:16 of Abraham, whom **S** has bound
Luke 22: 3 Then **S** entered Judas,
Luke 22:31 **S** has asked for you, that he
John 13:27 piece of bread, **S** entered him
Acts 5: 3 why has **S** filled your heart
Acts 26:18 and from the power of **S** to God
Rom 16:20 **S** under your feet shortly
1Co 5: 5 deliver such a one to **S** for
1Co 7: 5 **S** does not tempt you because
2Co 2:11 lest **S** should take advantage
2Co 11:14 For **S** himself transforms
2Co 12: 7 a messenger of **S** to buffet me
1Th 2:18 but **S** hindered us
2Th 2: 9 according to the working of **S**
1Ti 1:20 whom I delivered to **S** that
1Ti 5:15 already turned aside after **S**
Rev 2: 9 not, but are a synagogue of **S**
Rev 2:13 among you, where **S** dwells
Rev 2:24 not known the depths of **S**
Rev 3: 9 those of the synagogue of **S**
Rev 12: 9 of old, called the Devil and **S**
Rev 20: 2 of old, who is the Devil and **S**
Rev 20: 7 **S** will be released from his

SATAN'S (*see* SATAN)
Rev 2:13 you dwell, where **S** throne is

SATIATE (*see* SATIATED)
Jer 31:14 I will **s** the soul of the

SATIATED (*see* SATIATE)
Jer 31:25 For I have **s** the weary soul,
Jer 46:10 It shall be **s** and made drunk

SATISFACTION (*see* SATISFY)
Prov 19:23 he who has it will abide in **s**

SATISFIED (*see* SATISFY)
Ex 15: 9 my desire shall be **s** on them
Lev 26:26 and you shall eat and not be **s**
Deut 14:29 may come and eat and be **s**,
Deut 33:23 **s** with favor, and full of the
Ruth 2:14 and she ate and was **s**, and kept
Ruth 2:18 back after she had been **s**
Job 19:22 and are not **s** with my flesh
Job 27:14 shall not be **s** with bread
Job 31:31 has not been **s** with his meat
Ps 17:14 They are **s** with children, And
Ps 17:15 I shall be **s** when I awake in
Ps 22:26 The poor shall eat and be **s**
Ps 36: 8 They are abundantly **s** with
Ps 37:19 of famine they shall be **s**
Ps 59:15 And howl if they are not **s**
Ps 63: 5 shall be **s** as with marrow
Ps 65: 4 We shall be **s** with the
Ps 81:16 the rock I would have **s** you
Ps 104:13 The earth is **s** with the fruit
Ps 105:40 And **s** them with the bread of
Prov 12:11 his land will be **s** with bread
Prov 12:14 A man will be **s** with good by
Prov 14:14 good man will be **s** from above
Prov 18:20 A man's stomach shall be **s**
Prov 20:13 and you will be **s** with bread
Prov 27: 7 A **s** soul loathes the
Prov 27:20 the eyes of man are never **s**
Prov 30:15 three things that are never **s**
Prov 30:16 that is not **s** with water, and
Eccl 1: 8 The eye is not **s** with seeing
Eccl 4: 8 nor is his eye **s** with riches
Eccl 5:10 will not be **s** with silver
Eccl 6: 3 soul is not **s** with goodness
Eccl 6: 7 and yet the soul is not **s**
Is 9:20 on the left hand and not be **s**
Is 43:24 nor have you **s** Me with the
Is 44:16 he roasts a roast, and is **s**
Is 53:11 travail of His soul, and be **s**
Is 66:11 be **s** with the consolation of
Jer 31:14 shall be **s** with My goodness
Jer 50:10 who plunder her shall be **s**
Jer 50:19 shall be **s** on Mount Ephraim
Lam 5: 6 Assyrians, to be **s** with bread
Ezek 16:28 with them and still were not **s**
Ezek 16:29 and even then you were not **s**
Ezek 27:33 out by sea, you **s** many people
Joel 2:19 oil, and you will be **s** by them
Joel 2:26 shall eat in plenty and be **s**
Amos 4: 8 water, but they were not **s**
Mic 6:14 You shall eat, but not be **s**
Hab 2: 5 is like death, and cannot be **s**

SATISFIES (*see* SATISFY)
Ps 103: 5 Who **s** your mouth with good
Ps 107: 9 For He **s** the longing soul, And

SATISFY (*see* SATISFACTION, SATISFIED, SATISFIES, SATISFYING, UNSATISFIED)
Job 38:27 To **s** the desolate waste, and
Job 38:39 or **s** the appetite of the
Ps 90:14 **s** us early with Your mercy,
Ps 91:16 With long life I will **s** him
Ps 132:15 I will **s** her poor with bread
Ps 145:16 **s** the desire of every living
Prov 5:19 let her breasts **s** you at all
Prov 6:30 a thief if he steals to **s**
Is 55: 2 wages for what does not **s**
Is 58:10 **s** the afflicted soul, then
Is 58:11 **s** your soul in drought, and
Ezek 7:19 they will not **s** their souls
Mark 8: 4 How can one **s** these people

SATISFYING (*see* SATISFY)
Prov 13:25 eats to the **s** of his soul

SATRAPS
Ezra 8:36 king's orders to the king's **s**
Esth 3:12 to the king's **s**, to the
Esth 8: 9 commanded, to the Jews, the **s**
Esth 9: 3 of the provinces, the **s**, the
Dan 3: 2 word to gather together the **s**
Dan 3: 3 So the **s**, the administrators,
Dan 3:27 And the **s**, administrators,
Dan 6: 1 one hundred and twenty **s**, to
Dan 6: 2 that the **s** might give account
Dan 6: 3 above the governors and **s**,
Dan 6: 4 **s** sought to find some charge
Dan 6: 6 **s** thronged before the king,
Dan 6: 7 the administrators and **s**, the

SATURATED (*see* SATURATES)
Is 34: 7 their dust **s** with fatness

SATURATES (*see* SATURATED)
Job 37:11 He **s** the thick clouds

SAUL (*see* PAUL, SAUL'S, SHAUL)
Gen 36:37 **S** of Rehoboth-by-the-River
Gen 36:38 When **S** died, Baal-Hanan the
1Sa 9: 2 he had a son whose name was **S**
1Sa 9: 3 And Kish said to his son **S**
1Sa 9: 5 **S** said to his servant who was
1Sa 9: 7 Then **S** said to his servant,
1Sa 9: 8 the servant answered **S** again
1Sa 9:10 Then **S** said to his servant,
1Sa 9:15 his ear the day before **S** came
1Sa 9:17 And when Samuel saw **S**, the
1Sa 9:18 Then **S** drew near to Samuel in
1Sa 9:19 And Samuel answered **S** and
1Sa 9:21 And **S** answered and said,
1Sa 9:22 Then Samuel took **S** and his
1Sa 9:24 upper part and set it before **S**
1Sa 9:24 So **S** ate with Samuel that
1Sa 9:25 Samuel spoke with **S** on the
1Sa 9:26 to **S** on the top of the house
1Sa 9:26 **S** arose, and both of them went
1Sa 9:27 of the city, Samuel said to **S**
1Sa 10:11 Is **S** also among the prophets
1Sa 10:12 Is **S** also among the prophets
1Sa 10:16 So **S** said to his uncle, "He
1Sa 10:21 **S** the son of Kish was chosen
1Sa 10:26 **S** also went home to Gibeah
1Sa 11: 4 came to Gibeah of **S** and told
1Sa 11: 5 Now there was **S**, coming
1Sa 11: 5 and **S** said, "What troubles
1Sa 11: 6 **S** when he heard this news
1Sa 11: 7 does not go out with **S** and
1Sa 11:11 day, that **S** put the people in
1Sa 11:12 said, "Shall **S** reign over us
1Sa 11:13 But **S** said, "Not a man shall
1Sa 11:15 there they made **S** king before
1Sa 11:15 before the LORD, and there **S**
1Sa 13: 1 **S** reigned one year
1Sa 13: 2 **S** chose for himself three
1Sa 13: 2 were with **S** in Michmash and in
1Sa 13: 3 Then **S** blew the trumpet
1Sa 13: 4 Israel heard it said that **S**
1Sa 13: 4 together to **S** at Gilgal
1Sa 13: 7 As for **S**, he was still in
1Sa 13: 9 So **S** said, "Bring a burnt
1Sa 13:10 **S** went out to meet him, that
1Sa 13:11 And **S** said, "When I saw
1Sa 13:13 And Samuel said to **S**, "You
1Sa 13:15 **S** numbered the people who
1Sa 13:16 **S**, Jonathan his son, and the
1Sa 13:22 of the people who were with **S**
1Sa 13:22 But they were found with **S**
1Sa 14: 1 that Jonathan the son of **S**
1Sa 14: 2 And **S** was sitting in the
1Sa 14:16 Now the watchmen of **S** in
1Sa 14:17 Then **S** said to the people who
1Sa 14:18 And **S** said to Ahijah,
1Sa 14:19 while **S** talked to the priest,
1Sa 14:19 so **S** said to the priest,
1Sa 14:20 Then **S** and all the people who
1Sa 14:21 Israelites who were with **S**
1Sa 14:24 for **S** had placed the people
1Sa 14:33 Then they told **S**, saying
1Sa 14:34 And **S** said, "Disperse
1Sa 14:35 Then **S** built an altar to the
1Sa 14:36 And **S** said, "Let us go down
1Sa 14:37 So **S** asked counsel of God,
1Sa 14:38 And **S** said, "Come over here
1Sa 14:40 And the people said to **S**
1Sa 14:41 Therefore **S** said to the LORD
1Sa 14:41 So **S** and Jonathan were taken
1Sa 14:42 And **S** said,
1Sa 14:43 Then **S** said to Jonathan
1Sa 14:44 And **S** answered, "God do so
1Sa 14:45 But the people said to **S**
1Sa 14:46 Then **S** returned from pursuing
1Sa 14:47 So **S** established his
1Sa 14:49 the sons of **S** were Jonathan
1Sa 14:51 Kish was the father of **S**, and
1Sa 14:52 Philistines all the days of **S**
1Sa 14:52 when **S** saw any strong man or
1Sa 15: 1 Samuel also said to **S**, "The
1Sa 15: 4 So **S** gathered the people
1Sa 15: 5 **S** came to a city of Amalek,
1Sa 15: 6 Then **S** said to the Kenites,
1Sa 15: 7 **S** attacked the Amalekites,
1Sa 15: 9 But **S** and the people spared
1Sa 15:11 that I have set up **S** as king
1Sa 15:12 in the morning to meet **S**, it
1Sa 15:12 **S** went to Carmel, and indeed,
1Sa 15:13 Samuel went to **S**, and **S** said
1Sa 15:13 to **S**, and **S** said to him,
1Sa 15:15 And **S** said, "They have
1Sa 15:16 Then Samuel said to **S**, "Be
1Sa 15:20 And **S** said to Samuel,
1Sa 15:24 Then **S** said to Samuel, "I
1Sa 15:26 But Samuel said to **S**, "I
1Sa 15:27 **S** seized the edge of his robe
1Sa 15:31 So Samuel turned back after **S**
1Sa 15:31 and **S** worshiped the LORD
1Sa 15:34 **S** went up to his house at
1Sa 15:34 to his house at Gibeah of **S**
1Sa 15:35 **S** until the day of his death
1Sa 15:35 Samuel mourned for **S**, and the
1Sa 15:35 had made **S** king over Israel
1Sa 16: 1 How long will you mourn for **S**
1Sa 16: 2 If **S** hears it, he will kill
1Sa 16:14 of the LORD departed from **S**
1Sa 16:17 So **S** said to his servants,
1Sa 16:19 Therefore **S** sent messengers
1Sa 16:20 them by his son David to **S**
1Sa 16:21 So David came to **S** and stood
1Sa 16:22 Then **S** sent to Jesse, saying,
1Sa 16:23 spirit from God was upon **S**
1Sa 16:23 Then **S** would become refreshed
1Sa 17: 2 And **S** and the men of Israel
1Sa 17: 8 and you the servants of **S**
1Sa 17:11 When **S** and all Israel heard
1Sa 17:12 in years, in the days of **S**
1Sa 17:13 to follow **S** to the battle
1Sa 17:14 the three oldest followed **S**
1Sa 17:15 returned from **S** to feed his
1Sa 17:19 Now **S** and they and all the men
1Sa 17:31 they reported them to **S**
1Sa 17:32 Then David said to **S**, "Let
1Sa 17:33 And **S** said to David,
1Sa 17:34 But David said to **S**, "Your
1Sa 17:37 And **S** said to David,
1Sa 17:38 So **S** clothed David with his
1Sa 17:39 And David said to **S**, "I
1Sa 17:55 Now when **S** saw David going
1Sa 17:57 brought him before **S** with the
1Sa 17:58 And **S** said to him,
1Sa 18: 1 he had finished speaking to **S**
1Sa 18: 2 **S** took him that day, and would
1Sa 18: 5 went out wherever **S** sent him
1Sa 18: 5 **S** set him over the men of war
1Sa 18: 6 and dancing, to meet King **S**
1Sa 18: 7 **S** has slain his thousands, and
1Sa 18: 8 Then **S** was very angry, and the
1Sa 18: 9 So **S** eyed David from that day
1Sa 18:10 spirit from God came upon **S**
1Sa 18:11 **S** cast the spear, for he said
1Sa 18:12 Now **S** was afraid of David,
1Sa 18:12 him, but had departed from **S**
1Sa 18:13 Therefore **S** removed him from
1Sa 18:15 when **S** saw that he behaved
1Sa 18:17 Then **S** said to David, "Here
1Sa 18:17 For **S** thought, "Let my hand
1Sa 18:18 So David said to **S**, "Who am
1Sa 18:20 And they told **S**, and the thing
1Sa 18:21 So **S** said, "I will give her
1Sa 18:21 Therefore **S** said to David a
1Sa 18:22 **S** commanded his servants,
1Sa 18:24 And the servants of **S** told him
1Sa 18:25 Then **S** said, "Thus you shall
1Sa 18:25 But **S** thought to make
1Sa 18:27 Then **S** gave him Michal his
1Sa 18:28 Thus **S** saw and knew that the
1Sa 18:29 **S** was still more afraid of
1Sa 18:29 So **S** became David's enemy
1Sa 18:30 than all the servants of **S**
1Sa 19: 1 Now **S** spoke to Jonathan his
1Sa 19: 2 My father **S** seeks to kill you
1Sa 19: 4 well of David to **S** his father
1Sa 19: 6 So **S** heeded the voice of
1Sa 19: 6 of Jonathan, and **S** swore,

1Sa 19: 7 Jonathan brought David to S
1Sa 19: 9 from the LORD came upon S as
1Sa 19:10 Then S sought to pin David to
1Sa 19:11 S also sent messengers to
1Sa 19:14 So when S sent messengers to
1Sa 19:15 Then S sent the messengers
1Sa 19:17 Then S said to Michal, "Why
1Sa 19:17 And Michal answered S, "He
1Sa 19:18 all that S had done to him
1Sa 19:19 Now it was told S, saying
1Sa 19:20 Then S sent messengers to
1Sa 19:20 came upon the messengers of S
1Sa 19:21 And when S was told, he sent
1Sa 19:21 Then S sent messengers again
1Sa 19:24 Is S also among the prophets
1Sa 20:26 Nevertheless S did not say
1Sa 20:27 S said to Jonathan his son,
1Sa 20:28 So Jonathan answered S
1Sa 20:32 answered S his father, and
1Sa 20:33 Then S cast a spear at him to
1Sa 21: 7 of S was there that day,
1Sa 21: 7 herdsmen who belonged to S
1Sa 21:10 fled that day from before S
1Sa 21:11 S has slain his thousands,
1Sa 22: 6 When S heard that David and
1Sa 22: 6 now S was staying in Gibeah
1Sa 22: 7 then S said to his servants
1Sa 22: 9 set over the servants of S
1Sa 22:12 And S said, "Hear now, son
1Sa 22:13 Then S said to him, "Why
1Sa 22:21 that S had killed the LORD's
1Sa 22:22 that he would surely tell S
1Sa 23: 7 S was told that David had
1Sa 23: 7 So S said, "God has
1Sa 23: 8 Then S called all the people
1Sa 23: 9 When David knew that S
1Sa 23:10 has certainly heard that S
1Sa 23:11 Will S come down, as Your
1Sa 23:12 and my men into the hand of S
1Sa 23:13 Then it was told S that David
1Sa 23:14 S sought him every day, but
1Sa 23:15 So David saw that S had come
1Sa 23:17 for the hand of S my father
1Sa 23:17 Even my father S knows that
1Sa 23:19 came up to S at Gibeah,
1Sa 23:21 And S said, "Blessed are you
1Sa 23:24 and went to Ziph before S
1Sa 23:25 When S and his men went to
1Sa 23:25 when S heard that, he pursued
1Sa 23:26 Then S went on one side of
1Sa 23:26 to get away from S, for S
1Sa 23:27 But a messenger came to S
1Sa 23:28 Therefore S returned from
1Sa 24: 1 when S had returned from
1Sa 24: 2 Then S took three thousand
1Sa 24: 3 S went in to attend to his
1Sa 24: 7 allow them to rise against S
1Sa 24: 7 S got up from the cave and
1Sa 24: 8 the cave, and called out to S
1Sa 24: 8 when S looked behind him,
1Sa 24: 9 And David said to S
1Sa 24:16 words to S, that S said
1Sa 24:16 S lifted his voice and wept
1Sa 24:22 So David swore to S
1Sa 24:22 S went home, but David and his
1Sa 25:44 But S had given Michal his
1Sa 26: 1 Ziphites came to S at Gibeah
1Sa 26: 2 Then S arose and went down to
1Sa 26: 3 S encamped in the hill of
1Sa 26: 3 he saw that S came after him
1Sa 26: 4 that S had indeed come
1Sa 26: 5 place where S had encamped
1Sa 26: 5 saw the place where S lay
1Sa 26: 5 Now S lay within the camp,
1Sa 26: 6 down with me to S in the camp
1Sa 26: 7 there S lay sleeping within
1Sa 26:17 Then S knew David's voice, and
1Sa 26:21 Then S said, "I have sinned
1Sa 26:25 Then S said to David, "May
1Sa 26:25 and S returned to his place
1Sa 27: 1 someday by the hand of S
1Sa 27: 1 S will despair of me, to seek
1Sa 27: 4 it was told S that David had
1Sa 28: 3 S had put the mediums and the
1Sa 28: 4 So S gathered all Israel
1Sa 28: 5 When S saw the army of the
1Sa 28: 6 when S inquired of the LORD,
1Sa 28: 7 Then S said to his servants,
1Sa 28: 8 So S disguised himself and put
1Sa 28: 9 you know what S has done
1Sa 28:10 S swore to her by the LORD,
1Sa 28:12 And the woman spoke to S,
1Sa 28:12 For you are S
1Sa 28:13 And the woman said to S, "I
1Sa 28:14 And S perceived that it was
1Sa 28:15 Now Samuel said to S, "Why
1Sa 28:15 And S answered, "I am deeply
1Sa 28:20 Then immediately S fell full
1Sa 28:21 And the woman came to S and
1Sa 28:25 So she brought it before S
1Sa 29: 3 servant of S king of Israel
1Sa 29: 5 S has slain his thousands,
1Sa 31: 2 followed hard after S and his
1Sa 31: 3 became intense against S
1Sa 31: 4 Then S said to his
1Sa 31: 4 Therefore S took a sword and
1Sa 31: 5 saw that S was dead, he also
1Sa 31: 6 So S, his three sons, his
1Sa 31: 7 of Israel had fled and that S
1Sa 31: 8 the slain, that they found S
1Sa 31:11 the Philistines had done to S
1Sa 31:12 night, and took the body of S
2Sa 1: 1 to pass after the death of S
2Sa 1: 4 are fallen and dead, and S and
2Sa 1: 5 How do you know that S and
2Sa 1: 6 on Mount Gilboa, there was S
2Sa 1:12 and fasted until evening for S
2Sa 1:17 with this lamentation over S
2Sa 1:21 The shield of S, not anointed
2Sa 1:22 the sword of S did not return
2Sa 1:23 S and Jonathan were beloved
2Sa 1:24 of Israel, weep over S, who
2Sa 2: 4 were the ones who buried S
2Sa 2: 5 kindness to your lord, to S
2Sa 2: 7 for your master S is dead
2Sa 2: 8 took Ishbosheth the son of S
2Sa 2:12 of Ishbosheth the son of S
2Sa 2:15 of Ishbosheth the son of S
2Sa 3: 1 war between the house of S
2Sa 3: 1 and the house of S grew weaker
2Sa 3: 6 war between the house of S
2Sa 3: 6 his hold on the house of S
2Sa 3: 7 S had a concubine, whose name
2Sa 3: 8 to the house of S your father
2Sa 3:10 kingdom from the house of S
2Sa 4: 4 old when the news about S
2Sa 4: 8 the son of S your enemy, who
2Sa 4: 8 lord the king this day of S
2Sa 4:10 S is dead,' thinking to have
2Sa 5: 2 when S was king over us, you
2Sa 6:20 of S came out to meet David
2Sa 6:23 Michal the daughter of S had
2Sa 7:15 from him, as I took it from S
2Sa 9: 1 who is left of the house of S
2Sa 9: 2 of S whose name was Ziba
2Sa 9: 3 someone of the house of S
2Sa 9: 6 son of Jonathan, the son of S
2Sa 9: 7 land of S your grandfather
2Sa 9: 9 son all that belonged to S
2Sa 12: 7 you from the hand of S
2Sa 16: 5 the family of the house of S
2Sa 16: 8 the blood of the house of S
2Sa 19:17 the servant of the house of S
2Sa 19:24 S came down to meet the king
2Sa 21: 1 It is because of S and his
2Sa 21: 2 but S had sought to kill them
2Sa 21: 4 gold from S or from his house
2Sa 21: 6 the LORD in Gibeah of S, whom
2Sa 21: 7 son of Jonathan, the son of S
2Sa 21: 7 and Jonathan the son of S
2Sa 21: 8 of Aiah, whom she bore to S
2Sa 21: 8 of Michal the daughter of S
2Sa 21:11 of Aiah, the concubine of S
2Sa 21:12 went and took the bones of S
2Sa 21:12 had struck down S in Gilboa
2Sa 21:13 he brought up the bones of S
2Sa 21:14 They buried the bones of S
2Sa 22: 1 and from the hand of S
1Ch 1:48 S of Rehoboth-by-the-River
1Ch 1:49 When S died, Baal-Hanan the
1Ch 5:10 Now in the days of S they
1Ch 8:33 Ner begot Kish, Kish begot S
1Ch 8:33 S begot Jonathan, Malchishua,
1Ch 9:39 Ner begot Kish, Kish begot S
1Ch 9:39 S begot Jonathan, Malchishua,
1Ch 10: 2 followed hard after S and his
1Ch 10: 3 became intense against S
1Ch 10: 4 Then S said to his
1Ch 10: 4 Therefore S took a sword and
1Ch 10: 5 saw that S was dead, he also
1Ch 10: 6 So S and his three sons died,
1Ch 10: 7 that they had fled and that S
1Ch 10: 8 the slain, that they found S
1Ch 10:11 the Philistines had done to S
1Ch 10:12 arose and took the body of S
1Ch 10:13 So S died for his
1Ch 11: 2 past, even when S was king
1Ch 12: 1 from S the son of Kish
1Ch 12:19 to battle against S
1Ch 12:19 He may defect to his master S
1Ch 12:23 over the kingdom of S to him
1Ch 12:29 of Benjamin, kinsmen of S
1Ch 12:29 loyal to the house of S)
1Ch 13: 3 at it since the days of S
1Ch 15:29 that Michal the daughter of S
1Ch 26:28 S the son of Kish, Abner the
Is 10:29 afraid, Gibeah of S has fled
Acts 7:58 feet of a young man named S
Acts 8: 1 Now S was consenting to his
Acts 8: 3 As for S, he made havoc of
Acts 9: 1 Then S, still breathing
Acts 9: 4 S, S, why are you persecuting
Acts 9: 8 Then S arose from the ground,
Acts 9:11 for one called S of Tarsus
Acts 9:17 Brother S, the Lord Jesus,
Acts 9:19 Then S spent some days with
Acts 9:22 But S increased all the more
Acts 9:24 their plot became known to S
Acts 9:26 when S had come to Jerusalem,
Acts 11:25 departed for Tarsus to seek S
Acts 11:30 by the hands of Barnabas and S
Acts 12:25 S returned from Jerusalem
Acts 13: 1 with Herod the tetrarch, and S
Acts 13: 2 S for the work to which I
Acts 13: 7 man called for Barnabas and S
Acts 13: 9 Then S, who also is called
Acts 13:21 gave them S the son of Kish
Acts 22: 7 voice saying to me, 'S, S
Acts 22:13 and said to me, 'Brother S
Acts 26:14 the Hebrew language, 'S, S

SAUL'S (*see* SAUL)
1Sa 9: 3 of Kish, S father, were lost
1Sa 10:14 Then S uncle said to him and
1Sa 10:15 And S uncle said, "Tell me,
1Sa 14:50 The name of S wife was
1Sa 14:50 Abner the son of Ner, S uncle
1Sa 16:15 And S servants said to him,
1Sa 18: 5 in the sight of S servants
1Sa 18:10 there was a spear in S hand
1Sa 18:19 S daughter, should have been
1Sa 18:20 S daughter, loved David
1Sa 18:23 So S servants spoke those
1Sa 18:28 Michal, S daughter, loved him
1Sa 19: 1 S son, delighted much in
1Sa 19:10 slipped away from S presence
1Sa 20:25 arose, and Abner sat by S side
1Sa 20:30 Then S anger was aroused
1Sa 23:16 S son, arose and went to David
1Sa 24: 4 cut off a corner of S robe
1Sa 24: 5 him because he had cut S robe
1Sa 26:12 and the jug of water by S head
1Sa 31: 2 and Malchishua, S sons
2Sa 1: 2 that a man came from S camp
2Sa 2: 8 of Ner, commander of S army
2Sa 2:10 S son, was forty years old
2Sa 3:13 S daughter, when you come to
2Sa 3:14 to Ishbosheth, S son, saying,
2Sa 4: 1 when S son heard that Abner
2Sa 4: 2 Now S son had two men who
2Sa 4: 4 S son, had a son who was lame
2Sa 6:16 S daughter, looked through a
2Sa 9: 9 S servant, and said to him,
1Ch 10: 2 and Malchishua, S sons
1Ch 12: 2 were of Benjamin, S brethren

SAVAGE
Acts 20:29 that after my departure s

SAVE (*see* SALVATION, SAVED, SAVES, SAVING)
Gen 45: 7 to s your lives by a great
Gen 50:20 day, to s many people alive
Ex 1:22 daughter you shall s alive
Deut 20: 4 your enemies, to s you
Deut 22:27 but there was no one to s her
Deut 28:29 and no one shall s you
Josh 10: 6 s us and help us, for all the
Josh 22:22 LORD, do not s us this day
Judg 6:14 you shall s Israel from the
Judg 6:15 O my Lord, how can I s Israel
Judg 6:31 Would you s him
Judg 6:36 If You will s Israel by my

Judg 6:37 You will s Israel by my hand
Judg 7: 7 men who lapped I will s you
Judg 10: 1 Abimelech there arose to s
1Sa 4: 3 may s us from the hand of our
1Sa 7: 8 that He may s us from the
1Sa 9:16 that he may s My people from
1Sa 10:27 How can this man s us
1Sa 11: 3 if there is no one to s us
1Sa 17:47 LORD does not s with sword
1Sa 19:11 If you do not s your life
1Sa 23: 2 the Philistines, and s Keilah
1Sa 27:11 David would s neither man nor
2Sa 3:18 I will s My people Israel
2Sa 22: 3 You s me from violence
2Sa 22:28 You will s the humble people
2Sa 22:42 but there was none to s
1Ki 1:12 that you may s your own life
2Ki 16: 7 s me from the hand of the
2Ki 19:19 s us from his hand, that all
2Ki 19:34 to s it for My own sake and
1Ch 16:35 S us, O God of our salvation
2Ch 20: 9 and You will hear and s
Neh 6:11 into the temple to s his life
Job 20:20 he will not s anything he
Job 22:29 then He will s the humble
Job 40:14 your own right hand can s you
Ps 3: 7 S me, O my God
Ps 6: 4 s me for Your mercies' sake
Ps 7: 1 S me from all those who
Ps 17: 7 O You who s those who trust
Ps 18:27 For You will s the humble
Ps 18:41 but there was none to s them
Ps 20: 9 S, LORD! May the King
Ps 22:21 S Me from the lion's mouth And
Ps 28: 9 S Your people, And bless Your
Ps 31: 2 A fortress of defense to s me
Ps 31:16 S me for Your mercies' sake
Ps 37:40 s them, Because they trust in
Ps 44: 3 Nor did their own arm s them
Ps 44: 6 bow, Nor shall my sword s me
Ps 54: 1 S me, O God, by Your name,
Ps 55:16 God, And the LORD shall s me
Ps 57: 3 send from heaven and s me
Ps 59: 2 s me from bloodthirsty men
Ps 60: 5 S with Your right hand, and
Ps 69: 1 S me, O God! For the waters
Ps 69:35 For God will s Zion And build
Ps 71: 2 Your ear to me, and s me
Ps 71: 3 given the commandment to s me
Ps 72: 4 He will s the children of the
Ps 72:13 will s the souls of the needy
Ps 80: 2 strength, And come and s us
Ps 86: 2 S Your servant who trusts in
Ps 86:16 s the son of Your maidservant
Ps 106:47 S us, O LORD our God, And
Ps 108: 6 S with Your right hand, and
Ps 109:26 s me according to Your mercy,
Ps 109:31 poor, To s him from those who
Ps 118:25 S now, I pray, O LORD
Ps 119:94 I am Yours, s me
Ps 119:146 S me, and I will keep Your
Ps 138: 7 And Your right hand will s me
Ps 145:19 will hear their cry and s them
Prov 20:22 the LORD, and He will s you
Is 25: 9 for Him, and He will s us
Is 33:22 our King; He will s us
Is 35: 4 He will come and s you
Is 37:20 s us from his hand, that all
Is 37:35 to s it for My own sake and
Is 38:20 The LORD was ready to s me
Is 45:20 pray to a god that cannot s
Is 46: 7 nor s him out of his trouble
Is 47:13 s you from these things that
Is 47:15 no one shall s you
Is 49:25 and I will s your children
Is 59: 1 shortened, that it cannot s
Is 63: 1 in righteousness, mighty to s
Jer 2:27 they will say, 'Arise and s us
Jer 2:28 if they can s you in the time
Jer 11:12 but they will not s them at
Jer 14: 9 a mighty one who cannot s
Jer 15:20 for I am with you to s you
Jer 17:14 s me, and I shall be saved,
Jer 30:10 I will s you from afar, and
Jer 30:11 says the LORD, 'to s you
Jer 31: 7 s Your people, the remnant of
Jer 42:11 to s you and deliver you from
Jer 46:27 I will s you from afar, and
Jer 48: 6 Flee, s your lives
Jer 51: 6 and every one s his life

Lam 4:17 a nation that could not s us
Ezek 3:18 way, to s his life, that same
Ezek 13:22 his wicked way to s his life
Ezek 33: 5 takes warning will s his life
Ezek 34:22 therefore I will s My flock
Hos 1: 7 will s them by the LORD their
Hos 1: 7 will not s them by bow, nor
Hos 13:10 that he may s you in all your
Hos 14: 3 Assyria shall not s us, we
Mic 6:14 away, but shall not s them
Hab 1: 2 And You will not s
Zeph 3:17 midst, the Mighty One, will s
Zeph 3:19 I will s the lame, and gather
Zech 8: 7 I will s My people from the
Zech 8:13 of Israel, so I will s you
Zech 9:16 God will s them in that day
Zech 10: 6 I will s the house of Joseph
Zech 12: 7 The LORD will s the tents of
Matt 1:21 for He will s His people from
Matt 8:25 Him, saying, "Lord, s us
Matt 14:30 out, saying, "Lord, s me
Matt 16:25 to s his life will lose it
Matt 18:11 come to s that which was lost
Matt 27:40 it in three days, s Yourself
Matt 27:42 Himself He cannot s
Matt 27:49 if Elijah will come to s Him
Mark 3: 4 do evil, to s life or to kill
Mark 8:35 to s his life will lose it
Mark 8:35 and the gospel's will s it
Mark 15:30 s Yourself, and come down from
Mark 15:31 Himself He cannot s
Luke 6: 9 to s life or to destroy it
Luke 9:24 to s his life will lose it
Luke 9:24 life for My sake will s it
Luke 9:56 men's lives but to s them
Luke 17:33 Whoever seeks to s his life
Luke 19:10 and to s that which was lost
Luke 23:35 let Him s Himself if He is
Luke 23:37 King of the Jews, s Yourself
Luke 23:39 the Christ, s Yourself and us
John 12:27 Father, s Me from this hour'
John 12:47 the world but to s the world
Acts 27:43 centurion, wanting to s Paul
Rom 11:14 my flesh and s some of them
1Co 1:21 to s those who believe
1Co 7:16 you will s your husband
1Co 7:16 whether you will s your wife
1Co 9:22 I might by all means s some
1Ti 1:15 into the world to s sinners
1Ti 4:16 this you will s both yourself
Heb 5: 7 was able to s Him from death
Heb 7:25 He is also able to s to the
Jas 1:21 which is able to s your souls
Jas 2:14 Can faith s him
Jas 4:12 Lawgiver, who is able to s
Jas 5:15 of faith will s the sick, and
Jas 5:20 way will s a soul from death
Jude 23 but others s with fear,

SAVED (*see* SAVE)
Gen 47:25 said, "You have s our lives
Ex 1:17 but s the male children alive
Ex 1:18 s the male children alive
Ex 14:30 So the LORD s Israel that day
Num 10: 9 and you will be s from your
Deut 33:29 a people s by the LORD, the
Judg 7: 2 saying, 'My own hand has s me
Judg 21:14 had s alive of the women of
1Sa 10:19 who Himself s you out of all
1Sa 14:23 So the LORD s Israel that day
1Sa 23: 5 So David s the inhabitants of
2Sa 19: 5 who today have s your life
2Sa 19: 9 The king s us from the hand
2Sa 22: 4 so shall I be s from my
2Ki 14:27 but He s them by the hand of
1Ch 11:14 the LORD s them by a great
2Ch 32:22 Thus the LORD s Hezekiah and
Neh 9:27 gave them deliverers who s
Job 26: 2 How have you s the arm that
Ps 18: 3 So shall I be s from my
Ps 33:16 No king is s by the multitude
Ps 34: 6 s him out of all his troubles
Ps 44: 7 But You have s us from our
Ps 80: 3 to shine, And we shall be s
Ps 80: 7 to shine, And we shall be s
Ps 80:19 to shine, And we shall be s
Ps 106: 8 Nevertheless He s them for
Ps 106:10 He s them from the hand of
Ps 107:13 And He s them out of their
Ps 107:19 And He s them out of their
Ps 116: 6 I was brought low, and He s me

Prov 28:18 walks blamelessly will be s
Is 30:15 and rest you shall be s
Is 43:12 I have declared and s, I have
Is 45:17 be s by the LORD with an
Is 45:22 Look to Me, and be s, all you
Is 63: 9 Angel of His Presence s them
Is 64: 5 and we need to be s
Jer 4:14 wickedness, that you may be s
Jer 8:20 is ended, and we are not s
Jer 17:14 save me, and I shall be s, for
Jer 23: 6 In His days Judah will be s
Jer 30: 7 but he shall be s out of it
Jer 33:16 In those days Judah will be s
Joel 2:32 name of the LORD shall be s
Matt 10:22 endures to the end will be s
Matt 19:25 Who then can be s
Matt 24:13 endures to the end shall be s
Matt 24:22 no flesh would be s
Matt 27:42 He s others; Himself He
Mark 10:26 Who then can be s
Mark 13:13 endures to the end shall be s
Mark 13:20 days, no flesh would be s
Mark 15:31 themselves, "He s others
Mark 16:16 and is baptized will be s
Luke 1:71 should be s from our enemies
Luke 7:50 Your faith has s you
Luke 8:12 they should believe and be s
Luke 13:23 Lord, are there few who are s
Luke 18:26 Who then can be s
Luke 18:42 your faith has s you
Luke 23:35 saying, "He s others
John 3:17 world through Him might be s
John 5:34 things that you may be s
John 10: 9 enters by Me, he will be s
Acts 2:21 name of the LORD shall be s
Acts 2:40 Be s from this perverse
Acts 2:47 daily those who were being s
Acts 4:12 men by which we must be s
Acts 11:14 all your household will be s
Acts 15: 1 of Moses, you cannot be s
Acts 15:11 Jesus Christ we shall be s in
Acts 16:30 Sirs, what must I do to be s
Acts 16:31 Christ, and you will be s, you
Acts 27:20 be s was finally given up
Acts 27:31 in the ship, you cannot be s
Rom 5: 9 we shall be s from wrath
Rom 5:10 we shall be s by His life
Rom 8:24 For we were s in this hope,
Rom 9:27 sea, the remnant will be s
Rom 10: 1 Israel is that they may be s
Rom 10: 9 from the dead, you will be s
Rom 10:13 name of the LORD shall be s
Rom 11:26 And so all Israel will be s
1Co 1:18 s it is the power of God
1Co 3:15 but he himself will be s, yet
1Co 5: 5 be s in the day of the Lord
1Co 10:33 of many, that they may be s
1Co 15: 2 by which also you are s, if
2Co 2:15 among those who are being s
Eph 2: 5 (by grace you have been s)
Eph 2: 8 you have been s through faith
1Th 2:16 Gentiles that they may be s
2Th 2:10 truth, that they might be s
1Ti 2: 4 who desires all men to be s
1Ti 2:15 be s in childbearing if they
2Ti 1: 9 who has s us and called us
Tit 3: 5 to His mercy He s us, through
1Pe 3:20 souls, were s through water
1Pe 4:18 righteous one is scarcely s
2Pe 2: 5 but s Noah, one of eight
Jude 5 having s the people out of
Rev 21:24 are s shall walk in its light

SAVES (*see* SAVE)
1Sa 14:39 who s Israel, though it be in
Job 5:15 But He s the needy from the
Ps 7:10 Who s the upright in heart
Ps 20: 6 that the LORD s His anointed
Ps 34:18 s such as have a contrite
1Pe 3:21 an antitype which now s us

SAVING (*see* SAVE)
Gen 19:19 have shown me by s my life
1Sa 14: 6 LORD from s by many or by few
Ps 20: 6 His holy heaven With the s
Ps 28: 8 He is the s refuge of His
Heb 10:39 believe to the s of the soul
Heb 11: 7 for the s of his household

SAVIOR (*see* SAVIORS)
2Sa 22: 3 my S, You save me from
Ps 106:21 They forgot God their S, Who
Is 19:20 and He will send them a S
Is 43: 3 Holy One of Israel, your S
Is 43:11 and besides Me there is no s
Is 45:15 O God of Israel, the S
Is 45:21 besides Me, a just God and a S
Is 49:26 that I, the LORD, am your S
Is 60:16 that I, the LORD, am your S
Is 63: 8 So He became their S
Jer 14: 8 his S in time of trouble, why
Hos 13: 4 for there is no s besides Me
Luke 1:47 has rejoiced in God my S
Luke 2:11 day in the city of David a S
John 4:42 Christ, the S of the world
Acts 5:31 right hand to be Prince and S
Acts 13:23 God raised up for Israel a S
Eph 5:23 and He is the S of the body
Phil 3:20 also eagerly wait for the S
1Ti 1: 1 the commandment of God our S
1Ti 2: 3 in the sight of God our S
1Ti 4:10 God, who is the S of all men
2Ti 1:10 of our S Jesus Christ, who
Tit 1: 3 the commandment of God our S
Tit 1: 4 the Lord Jesus Christ our S
Tit 2:10 of God our S in all things
Tit 2:13 great God and S Jesus Christ,
Tit 3: 4 God our S toward man appeared
Tit 3: 6 through Jesus Christ our S
2Pe 1: 1 of our God and S Jesus Christ
2Pe 1:11 of our Lord and S Jesus Christ
2Pe 2:20 and S Jesus Christ, they are
2Pe 3: 2 the apostles of the Lord and S
2Pe 3:18 of our Lord and S Jesus Christ
1Jn 4:14 the Son as S of the world
Jude 25 to God our S, who alone is

SAVIORS (*see* SAVIOR)
Obad 21 Then s shall come to Mount

SAVOR (*see* SAVORY)
Amos 5:21 and I do not s your sacred

SAVORY (*see* SAVOR, UNSAVORY)
Gen 27: 4 And make me s food, such as I
Gen 27: 7 make s food for me, that I
Gen 27: 9 I will make s food from them
Gen 27:14 and his mother made s food
Gen 27:17 Then she gave the s food and
Gen 27:31 He also had made s food, and

SAW (*see* PREFACE)

SAW* (*see* SAWS)
Is 10:15 Or shall the s magnify itself

SAWN (*see* PREFACE)

SAWS (*see* SAW*)
2Sa 12:31 and put them to work with s
1Ki 7: 9 hewn to size, trimmed with s
1Ch 20: 3 and put them to work with s
Is 10:15 against him who s with it

SAY (*see* PREFACE)

SAYING (*see* PREFACE)

SAYINGS (*see* PREFACE)

SAYS (*see* PREFACE)

SCAB (*see* SCABS)
Lev 13: 2 of his body a swelling, a s
Lev 13: 6 it is only a s, and he shall
Lev 13: 7 But if the s should at all
Lev 13: 8 s has indeed spread on the
Lev 14:56 for a swelling and a s and a
Lev 21:20 in his eye, or eczema or s
Deut 28:27 with tumors, with the s, and
Is 3:17 a s the crown of the head of

SCABBARD
Jer 47: 6 Put yourself up into your s

SCABS (*see* SCAB)
Lev 22:22 have an ulcer or eczema or s

SCALES
Lev 11: 9 in the water has fins and s
Lev 11:10 that do not have fins and s
Lev 11:12 water does not have fins or s
Deut 14: 9 eat all that have fins and s
Deut 14:10 fins and s you shall not eat
Job 41:15 His rows of s are his pride,
Prov 21:22 A wise man s the city of the
Is 40:12 Weighed the mountains in s
Ezek 29: 4 rivers to stick to your s
Ezek 29: 4 rivers will stick to your s
Hos 12: 7 deceitful s are in his hand
Acts 9:18 his eyes something like s
Rev 6: 5 had a pair of s in his hand

SCALL
Lev 13:30 It is a s, a leprosy of the
Lev 13:31 looks at the sore of the s
Lev 13:31 the sore of the s seven days
Lev 13:32 and indeed if the s has not
Lev 13:32 the s does not appear deeper
Lev 13:33 but the s he shall not shave
Lev 13:33 has the s another seven days
Lev 13:34 priest shall look at the s
Lev 13:34 and indeed if the s has not
Lev 13:35 But if the s should at all
Lev 13:36 indeed if the s has spread
Lev 13:37 But if the s appears to be at
Lev 13:37 up in it, the s has healed
Lev 14:54 law for any leprous sore and s

SCALP
Ps 68:21 The hairy s of the one who

SCAN
Zech 4:10 eyes of the LORD, which s to

SCAPEGOAT
Lev 16: 8 and the other lot for the s
Lev 16:10 the lot fell to be the s
Lev 16:10 as the s into the wilderness
Lev 16:26 the s shall wash his clothes

SCAR
Lev 13:23 it is the s of the boil
Lev 13:28 for it is the s from the burn

SCARCELY
Gen 27:30 Jacob had s gone out from the
Song 3: 4 S had I passed by them, when
Is 40:24 S shall they be planted,
Is 40:24 s shall they be sown,
Is 40:24 s shall their stock take root
Acts 14:18 s restrain the multitudes
Rom 5: 7 For s for a righteous man
1Pe 4:18 the righteous one is s saved

SCARCITY
Deut 8: 9 you will eat bread without s

SCARE
Job 7:14 then You s me with dreams and

SCARLET
Gen 38:28 the midwife took a s thread
Gen 38:30 had the s thread on his hand
Ex 25: 4 s yarn, fine linen thread, and
Ex 26: 1 and blue and purple and s yarn
Ex 26:31 s yarn, and fine linen thread
Ex 26:36 s yarn, and fine linen thread,
Ex 27:16 s yarn, and fine linen thread,
Ex 28: 5 and s thread, and fine linen,
Ex 28: 6 and s thread, and fine linen
Ex 28: 8 and s thread, and fine linen
Ex 28:15 s thread, and of fine linen
Ex 28:33 s yarn, all around its hem,
Ex 35: 6 s yarn, fine linen thread, and
Ex 35:23 was found blue and purple and s
Ex 35:25 spun, of blue and purple and s
Ex 35:35 maker, in blue and purple and s
Ex 36: 8 and blue and purple and s yarn
Ex 36:35 s yarn, and fine linen thread
Ex 36:37 s yarn, and fine linen thread,
Ex 38:18 s yarn, and fine linen thread
Ex 38:23 s yarn, and fine linen thread
Ex 39: 1 s thread they made garments
Ex 39: 2 s thread, and of fine linen
Ex 39: 3 with the blue and purple and s
Ex 39: 5 and s thread, and fine linen
Ex 39: 8 and s thread, and fine linen
Ex 39:24 of blue and purple and s and
Ex 39:29 s thread, woven as the LORD
Lev 14: 4 and clean birds, cedar wood, s
Lev 14: 6 it, the cedar wood and the s
Lev 14:49 two birds, cedar wood, s
Lev 14:51 cedar wood, the hyssop, the s
Lev 14:52 wood, the hyssop, and the s
Num 4: 8 spread over them a s cloth
Num 19: 6 cedar wood and hyssop and s
Josh 2:18 you bind this line of s cord
Josh 2:21 she bound the s cord in the
2Sa 1:24 Saul, who clothed you in s
Prov 31:21 household is clothed with s
Song 4: 3 lips are like a strand of s
Is 1:18 Though your sins are like s
Lam 4: 5 up in s embrace ash heaps
Nah 2: 3 red, the valiant men are in s
Matt 27:28 Him and put a s robe on Him
Heb 9:19 water, s wool, and hyssop, and
Rev 17: 3 a s beast which was full of
Rev 17: 4 was arrayed in purple and s
Rev 18:12 linen and purple, silk and s
Rev 18:16 in fine linen, purple, and s

SCARVES
Is 3:18 the jingling anklets, the s

SCATTER (*see* SCATTERED, SCATTERING, SCATTERS)
Gen 49: 7 in Jacob and s them in Israel
Ex 9: 8 let Moses s it toward the
Lev 26:33 I will s you among the
Num 16:37 s the fire some distance away
Deut 4:27 the LORD will s you among the
Deut 28:64 Then the LORD will s you
1Ki 14:15 will s them beyond the River,
Neh 1: 8 I will s you among the
Ps 59:11 S them by Your power, And
Ps 68:30 S the peoples who delight in
Ps 106:27 And to s them in the lands
Ps 144: 6 forth lightning and s them
Is 28:25 s the cummin, plant the wheat
Is 41:16 and the whirlwind shall s them
Jer 9:16 I will s them also among the
Jer 13:24 Therefore I will s them like
Jer 18:17 I will s them as with an east
Jer 23: 1 s the sheep of My pasture
Jer 49:32 I will s to all winds those
Jer 49:36 s them toward all those winds
Ezek 5: 2 you shall s in the wind
Ezek 5:10 I will s to all the winds
Ezek 5:12 I will s another third to all
Ezek 6: 5 and I will s your bones all
Ezek 10: 2 and s them over the city
Ezek 12:14 I will s to every wind all
Ezek 12:15 LORD, when I s them among the
Ezek 20:23 that I would s them among the
Ezek 22:15 I will s you among the
Ezek 29:12 I will s the Egyptians among
Ezek 30:23 I will s the Egyptians among
Ezek 30:26 I will s the Egyptians among
Dan 4:14 off its leaves and s its fruit
Hab 3:14 out like a whirlwind to s me
Zech 1:21 the land of Judah to s it
Mark 4:26 should s seed on the ground

SCATTERED (*see* SCATTER)
Gen 11: 4 lest we be s abroad over the
Gen 11: 8 So the LORD s them abroad
Gen 11: 9 from there the LORD s them
Ex 5:12 So the people were s abroad
Ex 9:10 Moses s them toward heaven
Ex 32:20 he s it on the water and made
Num 10:35 Let Your enemies be s, and let
Deut 30: 3 the LORD your God has s you
1Sa 11:11 those who survived were s
1Sa 13: 8 and the people were s from him
1Sa 13:11 the people were s from me
2Sa 18: 8 For the battle there was s
2Sa 22:15 He sent out arrows and s them
1Ki 22:17 all Israel s on the mountains
2Ki 25: 5 All his army was s from him
2Ch 18:16 all Israel s on the mountains
2Ch 34: 4 s it on the graves of those
Esth 3: 8 There is a certain people s
Job 4:11 the cubs of the lioness are s
Job 18:15 Brimstone is s on his
Job 38:24 east wind s over the earth
Ps 18:14 and s the foe, Lightnings in
Ps 44:11 have s us among the nations
Ps 53: 5 For God has s the bones of
Ps 68: 1 arise, Let His enemies be s
Ps 68:14 the Almighty s kings in it
Ps 89:10 You have s Your enemies with
Ps 92: 9 of iniquity shall be s
Ps 141: 7 Our bones are s at the mouth
Is 33: 3 up, the nations shall be s
Jer 3:13 have s your charms to alien
Jer 10:21 all their flocks shall be s
Jer 23: 2 You have s My flock, driven
Jer 30:11 nations where I have s you
Jer 31:10 He who s Israel will gather
Jer 40:15 gathered to you would be s
Jer 50:17 Israel is like s sheep
Jer 52: 8 All his army was s from him
Lam 4: 1 s at the head of every street

Lam 4:16 The face of the LORD s them
Ezek 6: 8 when you are s through the
Ezek 11:16 although I have s them among
Ezek 11:17 where you have been s, and I
Ezek 17:21 shall be s to every wind
Ezek 20:34 the countries where you are s
Ezek 20:41 where you have been s
Ezek 28:25 peoples among whom they are s
Ezek 29:13 among whom they were s
Ezek 34: 5 So they were s because there
Ezek 34: 5 of the field when they were s
Ezek 34: 6 My flock was s over the whole
Ezek 34:12 day he is among his s sheep
Ezek 34:12 where they were s on a cloudy
Ezek 34:21 your horns, and s them abroad,
Ezek 36:19 So I s them among the nations
Ezek 46:18 may be s from his property
Joel 3: 2 whom they have s among the
Nah 3:18 Your people are s on the
Hab 3: 6 everlasting mountains were s
Zech 1:19 the horns that have s Judah
Zech 1:21 are the horns that s Judah
Zech 7:14 But I s them with a whirlwind
Zech 13: 7 and the sheep will be s
Matt 9:36 because they were weary and s
Matt 25:24 where you have not s seed
Matt 25:26 where I have not s seed
Matt 26:31 sheep of the flock will be s
Mark 14:27 and the sheep will be s
Luke 1:51 he has s the proud in the
John 11:52 of God who were s abroad
John 16:32 now come, that you will be s
Acts 5:36 and all who obeyed him were s
Acts 8: 1 they were all s throughout
Acts 8: 4 Therefore those who were s
Acts 11:19 Now those who were s after
1Co 10: 5 were s in the wilderness
Jas 1: 1 tribes which are s abroad

SCATTERING (*see* SCATTER)
Job 37: 9 cold from the s winds of the
Is 30:30 of a devouring fire, with s

SCATTERS (*see* SCATTER)
Job 36:30 He s his light upon it, and
Job 37:11 He s His bright clouds
Ps 147:16 He s the frost like ashes
Prov 11:24 There is one who s, yet
Prov 20: 8 s all evil with his eyes
Is 24: 1 and s abroad its inhabitants
Nah 2: 1 He who s has come up before
Matt 12:30 not gather with Me s abroad
Luke 11:23 who does not gather with Me s
John 10:12 catches the sheep and s them

SCENT (*see* SCENTED)
Job 14: 9 yet at the s of water it will
Song 4:10 the s of your perfumes than
Jer 48:11 him, and his s has not changed
Hos 14: 7 Their s shall be like the

SCENTED (*see* SCENT)
Ps 45: 8 garments are s with myrrh
Song 5:13 spices, like banks of s herbs

SCEPTER (*see* SCEPTERS)
Gen 49:10 The s shall not depart from
Num 24:17 A S shall rise out of Israel,
Esth 4:11 king holds out the golden s
Esth 5: 2 golden s that was in his hand
Esth 5: 2 and touched the top of the s
Esth 8: 4 the golden s toward Esther
Ps 45: 6 A s of righteousness is the
Ps 45: 6 is the s of Your kingdom
Ps 125: 3 For the s of wickedness shall
Is 14: 5 wicked, the s of the rulers
Ezek 19:14 a s for ruling
Ezek 21:10 it despises the s of My son
Ezek 21:13 the sword despises even the s
Ezek 21:13 The s shall be no more,"
Amos 1: 5 holds the s from Beth Eden
Amos 1: 8 who holds the s from Ashkelon
Zech 10:11 the s of Egypt shall depart
Heb 1: 8 a s of righteousness
Heb 1: 8 is the s of Your Kingdom

SCEPTERS (*see* SCEPTER)
Ezek 19:11 branches for s of rulers

SCEVA
Acts 19:14 there were seven sons of S

SCHEDULE
1Ch 24: 3 to the s of their service
1Ch 24:19 This was the s of their

SCHEME (*see* SCHEMED, SCHEMER, SCHEMES)
Esth 8: 3 the s which he had devised
Ps 26:10 whose hands is a sinister s
Ps 31:13 They s to take away my life
Ps 64: 6 We have perfected a shrewd s
Ps 140: 8 Do not further his wicked s
Mic 7: 3 so they s together

SCHEMED (*see* SCHEME)
2Sa 14:13 Why then have you s such a

SCHEMER (*see* SCHEME)
Prov 24: 8 to do evil will be called a s
Is 32: 7 the schemes of the s are evil

SCHEMES (*see* SCHEME)
Num 25:18 harassed you with their s by
Job 21:27 the s with which you would
Ps 37: 7 who brings wicked s to pass
Eccl 7:29 they have sought out many s
Is 32: 7 Also the s of the schemer are
Jer 11:19 they had devised s against me
Lam 3:60 all their s against me
Lam 3:61 LORD, all their s against me,
Dan 8:23 Who understands sinister s

SCHISM
1Co 12:25 should be no s in the body

SCHOLARS
Eccl 12:11 and the words of s are like

SCHOOL
Acts 19: 9 daily in the s of Tyrannus

SCOFF (*see* SCOFFED, SCOFFER, SCOFFING)
Ps 73: 8 They s and speak wickedly
Prov 9:12 for yourself, and if you s
Hab 1:10 They s at kings, and princes

SCOFFED (*see* SCOFF)
2Ch 36:16 s at His prophets, until the

SCOFFER (*see* SCOFF, SCOFFERS)
Prov 9: 7 He who reproves a s gets
Prov 9: 8 Do not reprove a s, lest he
Prov 13: 1 but a s does not listen to
Prov 14: 6 A s seeks wisdom and does not
Prov 15:12 A s does not love one who
Prov 17:21 He who begets a s does so to
Prov 19:25 Strike a s, and the simple
Prov 21:11 When the s is punished, the
Prov 21:24 S" is his name
Prov 22:10 Cast out the s, and contention
Prov 24: 9 the s is an abomination to

SCOFFERS (*see* SCOFFER)
Prov 19:29 Judgments are prepared for s
Prov 29: 8 S ensnare a city, but wise
Hos 7: 5 stretched out his hand with s
2Pe 3: 3 that s will come in the last

SCOFFING (*see* SCOFF)
Gen 21: 9 she had borne to Abraham, s

SCORCH (*see* SCORCHED, SCORCHING)
Is 43: 2 nor shall the flame s you
Rev 16: 8 to him to s men with fire

SCORCHED (*see* SCORCH)
Ezek 20:47 to the north shall be s by it
Matt 13: 6 the sun was up they were s
Mark 4: 6 when the sun was up it was s
Rev 16: 9 men were s with great heat,

SCORCHING (*see* SCORCH)
Deut 28:22 fever, with the sword, with s

SCORN (*see* SCORNED, SCORNERS, SCORNFUL, SCORNING, SCORNS)
2Ki 19:21 you, laughed you to s
2Ch 30:10 but they laughed them to s
Neh 2:19 of it, they laughed us to s
Job 12: 4 blameless who is laughed to s
Job 16:20 My friends s me
Job 22:19 the innocent laugh them to s
Job 34: 7 Job, who drinks s like water
Ps 22: 7 who see Me laugh Me to s
Ps 44:13 to our neighbors, A s and a
Ps 79: 4 to our neighbors, A s and
Ps 123: 4 s of those who are at ease
Is 37:22 you, laughed you to s
Jer 48:27 him, You shake your head in s
Ezek 23:32 you shall be laughed to s
Matt 9:24 And they laughed Him to s
Mark 5:40 And they laughed Him to s
Luke 8:53 And they laughed Him to s,

SCORNED (*see* SCORN)
Lam 1:11 LORD, and consider, for I am s
Ezek 16:31 harlot, because you s payment
Hab 1:10 and princes are s by them

SCORNERS (*see* SCORN)
Prov 1:22 For s delight in their

SCORNFUL (*see* SCORN, SCORNFULLY)
Ps 1: 1 Nor sits in the seat of the s
Prov 3:34 Surely He scorns the s, but
Is 28:14 word of the LORD, you s men
Is 29:20 the s one is consumed, and all

SCORNFULLY (*see* SCORNFUL)
Deut 32:15 s esteemed the Rock of his

SCORNING (*see* SCORN)
Prov 1:22 scorners delight in their s

SCORNS (*see* SCORN)
Job 39: 7 he s the tumult of the city
Job 39:18 she s the horse and its rider
Prov 3:34 Surely He s the scornful, but
Prov 19:28 witness s justice, and the
Prov 30:17 s obedience to his mother,

SCORPION (*see* SCORPIONS)
Luke 11:12 an egg, will he offer him a s
Rev 9: 5 of a s when it strikes a man

SCORPIONS (*see* SCORPION)
Deut 8:15 were fiery serpents and s and
Ezek 2: 6 with you and you dwell among s
Luke 10:19 to trample on serpents and s
Rev 9: 3 as the s of the earth have
Rev 9:10 They had tails like s, and

SCOUNDREL (*see* SCOUNDRELS)
1Sa 25:17 For he is such a s that one
1Sa 25:25 my lord regard this s Nabal

SCOUNDRELS (*see* SCOUNDREL)
1Ki 21:10 and seat two men, s, before
1Ki 21:13 And two men, s, came in and sat
1Ki 21:13 the s witnessed against him,

SCOURED
Lev 6:28 pot, it shall be both s and

SCOURGE (*see* SCOURGED, SCOURGES, SCOURGING)
Job 5:21 from the s of the tongue, and
Job 9:23 If the s slays suddenly, He
Is 10:26 of hosts will stir up a s for
Is 28:15 overflowing s passes through
Is 28:18 overflowing s passes through
Matt 10:17 s you in their synagogues
Matt 20:19 the Gentiles to mock and to s
Matt 23:34 you will s in your synagogues
Mark 10:34 s Him, and spit on Him, and
Luke 18:33 And they will s Him and put
Acts 22:25 you to s a man who is a Roman

SCOURGED (*see* SCOURGE)
Job 30: 8 they were s from the land
Matt 27:26 and when he had s Jesus, he
Mark 15:15 Jesus, after he had s Him
John 19: 1 Pilate took Jesus and s Him

SCOURGES (*see* SCOURGE)
Josh 23:13 s on your sides and thorns in
1Ki 12:11 I will chastise you with s
1Ki 12:14 I will chastise you with s
2Ch 10:11 I will chastise you with s
2Ch 10:14 I will chastise you with s
Heb 12: 6 s every son whom He receives

SCOURGING (*see* SCOURGE, SCOURGINGS)
Lev 19:20 for this there shall be s
Acts 22:24 he should be examined under s

SCOURGINGS (*see* SCOURGING)
Heb 11:36 had trial of mockings and s

SCRAPE (*see* SCRAPED)
Lev 14:41 the dust that they s off they
Num 5:23 he shall s them off into the
Job 2: 8 a potsherd with which to s
Ezek 26: 4 I will also s her dust from

SCRAPED (*see* SCRAPE)
Lev 14:41 the house to be s inside, all
Lev 14:43 after he has s the house

SCRATCHED
1Sa 21:13 s on the doors of the gate,

SCREECH
Lev 11:17 the fisher owl, and the s owl
Deut 14:16 the little owl, the s owl

SCREEN
Ex 26:36 You shall make a s for the
Ex 26:37 you shall make for the s five
Ex 27:16 be a s twenty cubits long
Ex 35:15 the s for the door at the
Ex 35:17 the s for the gate of the
Ex 36:37 He also made a s for the
Ex 38:18 The s for the gate of the
Ex 39:38 the s for the tabernacle door
Ex 39:40 the s for the court gate, its
Ex 40: 5 put up the s for the door of
Ex 40: 8 hang up the s at the court
Ex 40:28 He hung up the s at the door
Ex 40:33 hung up the s of the court
Num 3:25 the s for the door of the
Num 3:26 the s for the door of the
Num 3:31 which they ministered, the s
Num 4:25 the s for the door of the
Num 4:26 the s for the door of the

SCRIBE (*see* SCRIBE'S, SCRIBES)
2Sa 8:17 Seraiah was the s
2Sa 20:25 Sheva was s
2Ki 12:10 the chest, that the king's s
2Ki 18:18 the household, Shebna the s
2Ki 18:37 the household, Shebna the s
2Ki 19: 2 the household, Shebna the s
2Ki 22: 3 the king sent Shaphan the s
2Ki 22: 8 priest said to Shaphan the s
2Ki 22: 9 So Shaphan the s went to the
2Ki 22:10 Shaphan the s showed the king
2Ki 22:12 of Michaiah, Shaphan the s
2Ki 25:19 the principal s of the army
1Ch 18:16 Shavsha was the s
1Ch 24: 6 And the s, Shemaiah the son of
1Ch 27:32 counselor, a wise man, and a s
2Ch 24:11 much money, that the king's s
2Ch 26:11 as prepared by Jeiel the s
2Ch 34:15 and said to Shaphan the s, "I
2Ch 34:18 Shaphan the s told the king
2Ch 34:20 son of Micah, Shaphan the s
Ezra 4: 8 Shimshai the s wrote a letter
Ezra 4: 9 the commander, Shimshai the s
Ezra 4:17 commander, to Shimshai the s
Ezra 4:23 before Rehum, Shimshai the s
Ezra 7: 6 he was a skilled s in the Law
Ezra 7:11 gave Ezra the priest, the s
Ezra 7:12 a s of the Law of the God of
Ezra 7:21 the s of the Law of the God
Neh 8: 1 they told Ezra the s to bring
Neh 8: 4 So Ezra the s stood on a
Neh 8: 9 Ezra the priest and s, and the
Neh 8:13 were gathered to Ezra the s
Neh 12:26 and of Ezra the priest, the s
Neh 12:36 Ezra the s went before them
Neh 13:13 the priest and Zadok the s
Is 33:18 Where is the s?
Is 36: 3 the household, Shebna the s
Is 36:22 the household, Shebna the s
Is 37: 2 the household, Shebna the s
Jer 8: 8 Look, the false pen of the s
Jer 36:10 the son of Shaphan the s, in
Jer 36:12 Elishama the s, Delaiah the
Jer 36:20 the chamber of Elishama the s
Jer 36:26 Abdeel, to seize Baruch the s
Jer 36:32 and gave it to Baruch the s
Jer 37:15 the house of Jonathan the s
Jer 37:20 the house of Jonathan the s
Jer 52:25 the principal s of the army
Matt 8:19 Then a certain s came and said
Matt 13:52 Therefore every s instructed
Mark 12:32 So the s said to Him, "Well
1Co 1:20 Where is the s?

SCRIBE'S (*see* SCRIBE)
Jer 36:12 house, into the s chamber
Jer 36:21 from Elishama the s chamber
Jer 36:23 king cut it with the s knife

SCRIBES (*see* SCRIBE)
1Ki 4: 3 Ahijah, the sons of Shisha, s
1Ch 2:55 the families of the s who
2Ch 34:13 And some of the Levites were s
Esth 3:12 Then the king's s were called
Esth 8: 9 So the king's s were called
Matt 2: 4 s of the people together, he
Matt 5:20 the righteousness of the s
Matt 7:29 authority, and not as the s
Matt 9: 3 at once some of the s said
Matt 12:38 Then some of the s and
Matt 15: 1 Then the s and Pharisees who
Matt 16:21 elders and chief priests and s
Matt 17:10 Why then do the s say that
Matt 20:18 the chief priests and to the s
Matt 21:15 s saw the wonderful things
Matt 23: 2 The s and the Pharisees sit in
Matt 23:13 But woe to you, s and
Matt 23:14 Woe to you, s and Pharisees,
Matt 23:15 Woe to you, s and Pharisees,
Matt 23:23 Woe to you, s and Pharisees,
Matt 23:25 Woe to you, s and Pharisees,
Matt 23:27 Woe to you, s and Pharisees,
Matt 23:29 Woe to you, s and Pharisees,
Matt 23:34 you prophets, wise men, and s
Matt 26: 3 Then the chief priests, the s
Matt 26:57 the high priest, where the s
Matt 27:41 also mocking with the s and
Mark 1:22 authority, and not as the s
Mark 2: 6 But some of the s were
Mark 2:16 And when the s and Pharisees
Mark 3:22 And the s who came down from
Mark 7: 1 some of the s came together
Mark 7: 5 the Pharisees and s asked Him,
Mark 8:31 elders and chief priests and s
Mark 9:11 Why do the s say that Elijah
Mark 9:14 and s disputing with them
Mark 9:16 And He asked the s, "What are
Mark 10:33 the chief priests and to the s
Mark 11:18 And the s and chief priests
Mark 11:27 the chief priests, the s
Mark 12:28 Then one of the s came, and
Mark 12:35 How is it that the s say that
Mark 12:38 Beware of the s, who desire
Mark 14: 1 the s sought how they might
Mark 14:43 the chief priests and the s
Mark 14:53 priests, the elders, and the s
Mark 15: 1 with the elders and s and the
Mark 15:31 also, together with the s
Luke 5:21 And the s and the Pharisees
Luke 5:30 But their s and the Pharisees
Luke 6: 7 And the s and Pharisees
Luke 9:22 elders and chief priests and s
Luke 11:44 Woe to you, s and Pharisees,
Luke 11:53 these things to them, the s
Luke 15: 2 and s murmured, saying,
Luke 19:47 But the chief priests, the s
Luke 20: 1 the chief priests and the s
Luke 20:19 the s that very hour sought
Luke 20:39 Then some of the s answered
Luke 20:46 Beware of the s, who desire
Luke 22: 2 the s sought how they might
Luke 22:66 both chief priests and s,
Luke 23:10 s stood and vehemently accused
John 8: 3 Then the s and Pharisees
Acts 4: 5 their rulers, elders, and s
Acts 6:12 people, the elders, and the s
Acts 23: 9 And the s who were of the

SCRIPT
Ezra 4: 7 was written in Aramaic s, and
Esth 1:22 to each province in its own s
Esth 3:12 province according to its s
Esth 8: 9 every province in its own s
Esth 8: 9 and to the Jews in their own s

SCRIPTURE (*see* SCRIPTURES)
Dan 10:21 is noted in the S of Truth
Mark 12:10 Have you not read this S
Mark 15:28 So the S was fulfilled which
Luke 4:21 Today this S is fulfilled in
John 2:22 and they believed the S and the
John 7:38 as the S has said, out of his
John 7:42 Has not the S said that the
John 10:35 (and the S cannot be broken),
John 13:18 but that the S may be
John 17:12 that the S might be fulfilled
John 19:24 be," that the S might be
John 19:28 that the S might be fulfilled
John 19:36 the S should be fulfilled
John 19:37 And again another S says
John 20: 9 yet they did not know the S
Acts 1:16 this S had to be fulfilled,
Acts 8:32 The place in the S which he
Acts 8:35 mouth, and beginning at this S
Rom 4: 3 For what does the S say
Rom 9:17 For the S says to Pharaoh,
Rom 10:11 For the S says, "Whoever
Rom 11: 2 what the S says of Elijah
Gal 3: 8 And the S, foreseeing that God
Gal 3:22 But the S has confined all
Gal 4:30 what does the S say
1Ti 5:18 For the S says, "You shall
2Ti 3:16 All S is given by inspiration
Jas 2: 8 royal law according to the S
Jas 2:23 the S was fulfilled which
Jas 4: 5 think that the S says in vain
1Pe 2: 6 it is also contained in the S
2Pe 1:20 of S is of any private

SCRIPTURES (*see* SCRIPTURE)
Matt 21:42 Did you never read in the S
Matt 22:29 not knowing the S nor the
Matt 26:54 then could the S be fulfilled
Matt 26:56 S of the prophets might be
Mark 12:24 the S nor the power of God
Mark 14:49 But the S must be fulfilled
Luke 24:27 to them in all the S the
Luke 24:32 while He opened the S to us
Luke 24:45 they might comprehend the S
John 5:39 You search the S, for in them
Acts 17: 2 reasoned with them from the S
Acts 17:11 searched the S daily to find
Acts 18:24 man and mighty in the S, came
Acts 18:28 showing from the S that Jesus
Rom 1: 2 His prophets in the Holy S
Rom 15: 4 comfort of the S might have
Rom 16:26 by the prophetic S has been
1Co 15: 3 our sins according to the S
1Co 15: 4 third day according to the S
2Ti 3:15 you have known the Holy S
2Pe 3:16 do also the rest of the S

SCROLL
Ezra 6: 2 a s was found, and in it a
Ps 40: 7 In the s of the Book it is
Is 8: 1 Take a large s, and write on
Is 30: 8 a tablet, and note it on a s
Is 34: 4 shall be rolled up like a s
Jer 36: 2 Take a s of a book and write
Jer 36: 4 Baruch wrote on a s of a book
Jer 36: 6 read from the s which you
Jer 36:14 Take in your hand the s from
Jer 36:14 Neriah took the s in his hand
Jer 36:20 but they stored the s in the
Jer 36:21 sent Jehudi to bring the s
Jer 36:23 until all the s was consumed
Jer 36:25 the king not to burn the s
Jer 36:27 the king had burned the s
Jer 36:28 Take yet another s, and write
Jer 36:28 that were in the first s
Jer 36:29 You have burned this s,
Jer 36:32 Then Jeremiah took another s
Ezek 2: 9 a s of a book was in it
Ezek 3: 1 eat this s, and go, speak to
Ezek 3: 2 and He caused me to eat that s
Ezek 3: 3 with this s that I give you
Zech 5: 1 eyes, and saw there a flying s
Zech 5: 2 I see a flying s
Zech 5: 3 what is on this side of the s
Rev 5: 1 the throne a s written inside
Rev 5: 2 Who is worthy to open the s
Rev 5: 3 earth was able to open the s
Rev 5: 4 worthy to open and read the s
Rev 5: 5 has prevailed to open the s
Rev 5: 7 took the s out of the right
Rev 5: 8 Now when He had taken the s
Rev 5: 9 You are worthy to take the s
Rev 6:14 as a s when it is rolled up

SCRUPLES
Rom 15: 1 bear with the s of the weak

SCULPTURED
Ps 144:12 as pillars, S in palace style

SCUM
Ezek 24: 6 to the pot whose s is in it
Ezek 24: 6 whose s is not gone from it
Ezek 24:11 that its s may be consumed
Ezek 24:12 her great s has not gone from
Ezek 24:12 Let her s be in the fire

SCYTHIAN
Col 3:11 uncircumcised, barbarian, S

SEA (*see* SEACOAST, SEAFARING, SEAGULL, SEAMEN, SEAS, SEASHORE)
Gen 1:21 God created great s creatures
Gen 1:26 over the fish of the s, over
Gen 1:28 over the fish of the s, over
Gen 9: 2 and on all the fish of the s

Gen 14: 3 Siddim (that is, the Salt S)
Gen 32:12 as the sand of the s, which
Gen 41:49 grain, as the sand of the s
Gen 49:13 dwell by the haven of the s
Ex 10:19 and blew them into the Red S
Ex 13:18 the wilderness of the Red S
Ex 14: 2 between Migdol and the s,
Ex 14: 2 shall camp before it by the s
Ex 14: 9 by the s beside Pi Hahiroth
Ex 14:16 out your hand over the s and
Ex 14:16 through the midst of the s
Ex 14:21 out his hand over the s
Ex 14:21 the LORD caused the s to go
Ex 14:21 made the s into dry land, and
Ex 14:22 of the s on the dry ground
Ex 14:23 them into the midst of the s
Ex 14:26 out your hand over the s,
Ex 14:27 out his hand over the s
Ex 14:27 the s returned to its full
Ex 14:27 in the midst of the s
Ex 14:28 came into the s after them
Ex 14:29 land in the midst of the s
Ex 15: 1 He has thrown into the s
Ex 15: 4 army He has cast into the s
Ex 15: 4 also are drowned in the Red S
Ex 15: 8 in the heart of the s
Ex 15:10 Your wind, the s covered them
Ex 15:19 and his horsemen into the s
Ex 15:19 the waters of the s upon them
Ex 15:19 land in the midst of the s
Ex 15:21 He has thrown into the s
Ex 15:22 brought Israel from the Red S
Ex 20:11 heavens and the earth, the s
Ex 23:31 the Red S to the S of the
Num 11:22 s be gathered together for
Num 11:31 it brought quail from the s
Num 13:29 the Canaanites dwell by the s
Num 14:25 by the Way of the Red S
Num 21: 4 Hor by the Way of the Red S
Num 33: 8 of the s into the wilderness
Num 33:10 Elim and camped by the Red S
Num 33:11 They moved from the Red S
Num 34: 3 to the end of the Salt S
Num 34: 5 and it shall end at the S
Num 34: 6 have the Great S for a border
Num 34: 7 From the Great S you shall
Num 34:11 side of the S of Chinnereth
Num 34:12 and it shall end at the Salt S
Deut 1:40 by the Way of the Red S
Deut 2: 1 of the Way of the Red S, as
Deut 3:17 S of the Arabah (the Salt S)
Deut 4:49 as far as the S of the Arabah
Deut 11: 4 Red S overflow them as they
Deut 11:24 even to the Western S, shall
Deut 30:13 Nor is it beyond the s, that
Deut 30:13 Who will go over the s for us
Deut 34: 2 Judah as far as the Western S
Josh 1: 4 to the Great S toward the
Josh 2:10 up the water of the Red S for
Josh 3:16 S of the Arabah, the Salt S
Josh 4:23 your God did to the Red S
Josh 5: 1 Canaanites who were by the s
Josh 9: 1 of the Great S toward Lebanon
Josh 12: 3 Jordan plain from the S of
Josh 12: 3 S of the Arabah (the Salt S)
Josh 13:27 edge of the S of Chinnereth
Josh 15: 2 at the shore of the Salt S
Josh 15: 4 and the border ended at the s
Josh 15: 5 east border was the Salt S as
Josh 15: 5 began at the bay of the s at
Josh 15:11 and the border ended at the s
Josh 15:12 the coastline of the Great S
Josh 15:46 from Ekron to the s, all that
Josh 15:47 Egypt and the Great S with its
Josh 16: 3 and it ended at the s
Josh 16: 6 the s on the north side of
Josh 16: 8 Kanah, and it ended at the s
Josh 17: 9 and it ended at the s
Josh 17:10 and the s was its border
Josh 18:19 the north bay at the Salt S
Josh 19:29 ended at the s by the region
Josh 23: 4 far as the Great S westward
Josh 24: 6 Egypt, and you came to the s
Josh 24: 6 and horsemen to the Red S
Josh 24: 7 brought the s upon them, and
Judg 11:16 as far as the Red S and came
2Sa 17:11 is by the s for multitude
2Sa 22:16 channels of the s were seen
1Ki 4:20 sand by the s in multitude
1Ki 5: 9 down from Lebanon to the s
1Ki 5: 9 s to the place you indicate
1Ki 7:23 he made the S of cast bronze
1Ki 7:24 all the way around the S
1Ki 7:25 the S was set upon them, and
1Ki 7:39 He set the S on the right
1Ki 7:44 S, and twelve oxen under the S
1Ki 9:26 on the shore of the Red S
1Ki 9:27 fleet, seamen who knew the s
1Ki 10:22 at s with the fleet of Hiram
1Ki 18:43 Go up now, look toward the s
1Ki 18:44 hand, rising out of the s
2Ki 14:25 Hamath to the S of the Arabah
2Ki 16:17 he took down the S from the
2Ki 25:13 the bronze S that were in the
2Ki 25:16 The two pillars, one S, and
1Ch 16:32 Let the s roar, and all its
1Ch 18: 8 Solomon made the bronze S
2Ch 2:16 to you in rafts by s to Joppa
2Ch 4: 2 he made the S of cast bronze
2Ch 4: 3 all the way around the S
2Ch 4: 4 the S was set upon them, and
2Ch 4: 6 but the S was for the priests
2Ch 4:10 He set the S on the right
2Ch 4:15 one S and twelve oxen under it
2Ch 8:18 and servants who knew the s
2Ch 20: 2 against you from beyond the s
Ezra 3: 7 Lebanon to the s at Joppa
Neh 9: 9 heard their cry by the Red S
Neh 9:11 You divided the s before them
Neh 9:11 of the s on the dry land
Esth 10: 1 and on the islands of the s
Job 6: 3 than the sand of the s
Job 7:12 Am I a s, or a s serpent,
Job 9: 8 treads on the waves of the s
Job 11: 9 earth and broader than the s
Job 12: 8 and the fish of the s will
Job 14:11 water disappears from the s
Job 26:12 stirs up the s with His power
Job 28:14 the s says, It is not with
Job 36:30 and covers the depths of the s
Job 38: 8 who shut in the s with doors
Job 38:16 entered the springs of the s
Job 41:31 he makes the s like a pot of
Ps 8: 8 the fish of the s That pass
Ps 33: 7 of the s together as a heap
Ps 46: 2 into the midst of the s
Ps 66: 6 He turned the s into dry land
Ps 68:22 back from the depths of the s
Ps 72: 8 dominion also from s to s
Ps 74:13 You divided the s by Your
Ps 74:13 the s serpents in the waters
Ps 77:19 Your way was in the s, Your
Ps 78:13 He divided the s and caused
Ps 78:53 But the s overwhelmed their
Ps 80:11 sent out her boughs to the S
Ps 89: 9 You rule the raging of the s
Ps 89:25 will set his hand over the s
Ps 93: 4 the mighty waves of the s
Ps 95: 5 The s is His, for He made it
Ps 96:11 Let the s roar, and all its
Ps 98: 7 Let the s roar, and all its
Ps 104:25 This great and wide s, In
Ps 106: 7 rebelled by the s—the Red S
Ps 106: 9 He rebuked the Red S also
Ps 106:22 Awesome things by the Red S
Ps 107:23 who go down to the s in ships
Ps 107:25 lifts up the waves of the s
Ps 114: 3 The s saw it and fled
Ps 114: 5 What ails you, O s, that you
Ps 136:13 who divided the Red S in two
Ps 136:15 and his army in the Red S, For
Ps 139: 9 the uttermost parts of the s
Ps 146: 6 made heaven and earth, The s
Ps 148: 7 earth, You great s creatures
Prov 8:29 assigned to the s its limit
Prov 23:34 down in the midst of the s
Prov 30:19 a ship in the midst of the s
Eccl 1: 7 All the rivers run into the s
Eccl 1: 7 yet the s is not full
Is 5:30 like the roaring of the s
Is 9: 1 her, by the way of the s,
Is 10:22 be as the sand of the s, yet
Is 10:26 as His rod was on the s, so
Is 11: 9 as the waters cover the s
Is 11:11 and the islands of the s
Is 11:15 the tongue of the S of Egypt
Is 16: 8 out, they are gone over the s
Is 18: 2 which sends ambassadors by s
Is 19: 5 waters will fail from the s
Is 21: 1 the Wilderness of the S
Is 23: 2 who cross the s have filled
Is 23: 4 for the s has spoken
Is 23: 4 the strength of the s
Is 23:11 out His hand over the s, He
Is 24:14 shall cry aloud from the s
Is 24:15 in the coastlands of the s
Is 27: 1 the reptile that is in the s
Is 42:10 you who go down to the s
Is 43:16 who makes a way in the s
Is 48:18 like the waves of the s
Is 50: 2 with My rebuke I dry up the s
Is 51:10 the One who dried up the s
Is 51:10 s a road for the redeemed to
Is 51:15 who divided the s whose waves
Is 57:20 are like the troubled s, when
Is 60: 5 the abundance of the s shall
Is 63:11 s with the shepherd of His
Jer 5:22 sand as the bound of the s
Jer 6:23 their voice roars like the s
Jer 25:22 which are across the s
Jer 27:19 the pillars, concerning the S
Jer 31:35 by night, Who disturbs the s
Jer 33:22 the sand of the s measured
Jer 46:18 and as Carmel by the s, so he
Jer 48:32 plants have gone over the s
Jer 48:32 they reach to the s of Jazer
Jer 49:21 noise is heard at the Red S
Jer 49:23 There is trouble on the s
Jer 50:42 voice shall roar like the s
Jer 51:36 I will dry up her s and make
Jer 51:42 The s has come up over
Jer 52:17 the bronze S that were in the
Jer 52:20 The two pillars, one S, the
Lam 2:13 ruin is spread wide as the s
Ezek 26: 3 as the s causes its waves to
Ezek 26: 5 nets in the midst of the s
Ezek 26:16 s will come down from their
Ezek 26:17 city, who was strong at s
Ezek 26:18 by the s are troubled at your
Ezek 27: 3 at the entrance of the s,
Ezek 27: 9 all the ships of the s and
Ezek 27:29 all the pilots of the s will
Ezek 27:32 in the midst of the s
Ezek 27:33 When your wares went out by s
Ezek 38:20 so that the fish of the s
Ezek 39:11 who pass by east of the s
Ezek 47: 8 the valley, and enters the s
Ezek 47: 8 When it reaches the s, its
Ezek 47:10 as the fish of the Great S
Ezek 47:15 from the Great S, by the road
Ezek 47:17 be from the S to Hazar Enan
Ezek 47:18 the eastern side of the s
Ezek 47:19 the brook to the Great S
Ezek 47:20 side shall be the Great S
Ezek 48:28 the brook to the Great S
Dan 7: 2 were stirring up the Great S
Dan 7: 3 beasts came up from the s
Hos 1:10 shall be as the sand of the s
Hos 4: 3 of the s will be taken away
Joel 2:20 his face toward the eastern s
Joel 2:20 his back toward the western s
Amos 5: 8 calls for the waters of the s
Amos 8:12 shall wander from s to s
Amos 9: 3 sight at the bottom of the s
Amos 9: 6 calls for the waters of the s
Jon 1: 4 out a great wind on the s
Jon 1: 4 was a mighty tempest on the s
Jon 1: 5 was in the ship into the s
Jon 1: 9 God of heaven, who made the s
Jon 1:11 that the s may be calm for us
Jon 1:11 for the s was growing more
Jon 1:12 me up and throw me into the s
Jon 1:12 then the s will become calm
Jon 1:13 for the s continued to grow
Jon 1:15 Jonah and threw him into the s
Jon 1:15 the s ceased from its raging
Mic 7:12 to the River, from s to s
Mic 7:19 sins into the depths of the s
Nah 1: 4 He rebukes the s and makes it
Nah 3: 8 whose rampart was like the s
Nah 3: 8 whose wall was like the s
Hab 1:14 make men like fish of the s
Hab 2:14 as the waters cover the s
Hab 3: 8 was Your wrath against the s
Hab 3:15 the s with Your horses,
Zeph 1: 3 heavens, the fish of the s
Hag 2: 6 shake heaven and earth, the s
Zech 9: 4 destroy her power in the s
Zech 9:10 shall be 'from s to s, and
Zech 10:11 through the s with affliction

Zech 10:11 and strike the waves of the s
Zech 14: 8 of them toward the eastern s
Zech 14: 8 of them toward the western s
Matt 4:13 Capernaum, which is by the s
Matt 4:15 of Naphtali, the way of the s
Matt 4:18 walking by the S of Galilee
Matt 4:18 casting a net into the s
Matt 8:24 great tempest arose on the s
Matt 8:26 and rebuked the winds and the s
Matt 8:27 the winds and the s obey Him
Matt 8:32 the steep place into the s
Matt 13: 1 of the house and sat by the s
Matt 13:47 that was cast into the s and
Matt 14:24 now in the middle of the s
Matt 14:25 to them, walking on the s
Matt 14:26 saw Him walking on the s,
Matt 15:29 skirted the S of Galilee
Matt 17:27 we offend them, go to the s
Matt 18: 6 drowned in the depth of the s
Matt 21:21 removed and be cast into the s
Matt 23:15 s to win one proselyte, and
Mark 1:16 He walked by the S of Galilee
Mark 1:16 casting a net into the s
Mark 2:13 He went out again by the s
Mark 3: 7 with His disciples to the s
Mark 4: 1 He began to teach by the s
Mark 4: 1 a boat and sat in it on the s
Mark 4: 1 was on the land facing the s
Mark 4:39 the wind, and said to the s
Mark 4:41 the wind and the s obey Him
Mark 5: 1 to the other side of the s
Mark 5:13 the steep place into the s
Mark 5:13 and drowned in the s
Mark 5:21 and He was by the s
Mark 6:47 was in the middle of the s
Mark 6:48 to them, walking on the s
Mark 6:49 they saw Him walking on the s
Mark 7:31 Decapolis to the S of Galilee
Mark 9:42 and he were thrown into the s
Mark 11:23 removed and be cast into the s
Luke 17: 2 and he were thrown into the s
Luke 17: 6 roots and be planted in the s
Luke 21:25 with perplexity, the s and
John 6: 1 went over the S of Galilee
John 6: 1 which is the S of Tiberias
John 6:16 disciples went down to the s
John 6:17 and went over the s toward
John 6:18 Then the s arose because a
John 6:19 saw Jesus walking on the s
John 6:22 on the other side of the s
John 6:25 on the other side of the s
John 21: 1 at the S of Tiberias, and in
John 21: 7 it), and plunged into the s
Acts 4:24 made heaven and earth and the s
Acts 7:36 of Egypt, and in the Red S
Acts 10: 6 whose house is by the s
Acts 10:32 of Simon, a tanner, by the s
Acts 14:15 the heaven, the earth, the s
Acts 17:14 Paul away, to go to the s
Acts 27: 2 of Adramyttium, we put to s
Acts 27: 4 we had put to s from there
Acts 27: 5 the s which is off Cilicia
Acts 27:13 purpose, putting out to s
Acts 27:27 up and down in the Adriatic S
Acts 27:30 let down the skiff into the s
Acts 27:38 out the wheat into the s
Acts 27:40 anchors and left them in the s
Acts 28: 4 though he has escaped the s
Rom 9:27 be as the sand of the s, the
1Co 10: 1 all passed through the s
1Co 10: 2 in the cloud and in the s,
2Co 11:26 in perils in the s, in
Heb 11:29 the Red S as by dry land,
Jas 1: 6 like a wave of the s driven
Jas 3: 7 reptile and creature of the s
Jude 13 raging waves of the s,
Rev 4: 6 throne there was a s of glass
Rev 5:13 earth and such as are in the s
Rev 7: 1 blow on the earth, on the s
Rev 7: 2 to harm the earth and the s
Rev 7: 3 Do not harm the earth, the s
Rev 8: 8 fire was thrown into the s
Rev 8: 8 a third of the s became blood
Rev 8: 9 creatures in the s died, and a
Rev 10: 2 set his right foot on the s
Rev 10: 5 whom I saw standing on the s
Rev 10: 6 that are in it, and the s and
Rev 10: 8 the angel who stands on the s
Rev 12:12 of the earth and the s
Rev 13: 1 I stood on the sand of the s
Rev 13: 1 beast rising up out of the s
Rev 14: 7 made heaven and earth, the s
Rev 15: 2 I saw something like a s of
Rev 15: 2 standing on the s of glass
Rev 16: 3 poured out his bowl on the s
Rev 16: 3 living creature in the s died
Rev 18:17 and as many as trade on the s
Rev 18:19 all who had ships on the s
Rev 18:21 and threw it into the s,
Rev 20: 8 is as the sand of the s
Rev 20:13 The s gave up the dead who
Rev 21: 1 Also there was no more s

SEACOAST (*see* SEA)
Deut 1: 7 in the South and on the s
2Ch 8:17 Ezion Geber and Elath on the s
Ezek 25:16 destroy the remnant of the s
Zeph 2: 5 to the inhabitants of the s
Zeph 2: 6 The s shall be pastures, with
Luke 6:17 and from the s of Tyre and

SEAFARING (*see* SEA)
Ezek 26:17 O one inhabited by s men

SEAGULL (*see* SEA)
Lev 11:16 the short-eared owl, the s
Deut 14:15 the short-eared owl, the s

SEAH (*see* SEAHS)
2Ki 7: 1 s of fine flour shall be sold
2Ki 7:16 So a s of fine flour was sold
2Ki 7:18 and a s of fine flour for a

SEAHS (*see* SEAH)
1Sa 25:18 five s of roasted grain, one
1Ki 18:32 enough to hold two s of seed
2Ki 7: 1 two s of barley for a shekel,
2Ki 7:16 two s of barley for a shekel,
2Ki 7:18 Two s of barley for a shekel,

SEAL (*see* SEALED, SEALING, SEALS)
1Ki 21: 8 name, sealed them with his s
Neh 9:38 Levites and our priests s it
Neh 10: 1 their s on the document were
Esth 8: 8 s it with the king's signet
Job 38:14 on form like clay under a s
Job 41:15 shut up tightly as with a s
Song 8: 6 Set me as a s upon your heart
Song 8: 6 as a s upon your arm
Is 8:16 S the law among my disciples
Jer 32:44 s them, and take witnesses, in
Ezek 28:12 You were the s of perfection,
Dan 8:26 therefore s up the vision,
Dan 9:24 to s up vision and prophecy,
Dan 12: 4 s the book until the time of
John 6:27 Father has set His s on Him
Rom 4:11 a s of the righteousness of
1Co 9: 2 For you are the s of my
2Ti 2:19 of God stands, having this s
Rev 6: 3 When He opened the second s
Rev 6: 5 When He opened the third s
Rev 6: 7 When He opened the fourth s
Rev 6: 9 When He opened the fifth s
Rev 6:12 when He opened the sixth s
Rev 7: 2 having the s of the living
Rev 8: 1 When He opened the seventh s
Rev 9: 4 men who do not have the s of
Rev 10: 4 S up the things which the
Rev 20: 3 set a s on him, so that he
Rev 22:10 Do not s the words of the

SEALED (*see* SEAL)
Deut 32:34 Me, s up among My treasures
1Ki 21: 8 s them with his seal, and sent
Esth 3:12 s with the king's signet ring
Esth 8: 8 s with the king's signet ring
Esth 8:10 s it with the king's signet
Job 14:17 is s up in a bag, and You
Song 4:12 spring shut up, a fountain s
Is 29:11 the words of a book that is s
Is 29:11 I cannot, for it is s
Jer 32:10 and s it, took witnesses, and
Jer 32:11 deed, both that which was s
Jer 32:14 this purchase deed which is s
Dan 6:17 the king s it with his own
Dan 12: 9 s till the time of the end
Rom 15:28 have s to them this fruit, I
2Co 1:22 who also has s us and given us
Eph 1:13 you were s with the Holy
Eph 4:30 by whom you were s for the
Rev 5: 1 the back, s with seven seals
Rev 7: 3 or the trees till we have s
Rev 7: 4 number of those who were s
Rev 7: 4 the children of Israel were s
Rev 7: 5 Judah twelve thousand were s
Rev 7: 5 Reuben twelve thousand were s
Rev 7: 5 of Gad twelve thousand were s
Rev 7: 6 Asher twelve thousand were s
Rev 7: 6 twelve thousand were s
Rev 7: 6 twelve thousand were s
Rev 7: 7 Simeon twelve thousand were s
Rev 7: 7 Levi twelve thousand were s
Rev 7: 7 twelve thousand were s
Rev 7: 8 twelve thousand were s
Rev 7: 8 Joseph twelve thousand were s
Rev 7: 8 twelve thousand were s

SEALING (*see* SEAL)
Matt 27:66 s the stone and setting the

SEALS (*see* SEAL)
Job 9: 7 He s off the stars
Job 33:16 men, and s their instruction
Job 37: 7 He s the hand of every man,
Rev 5: 1 the back, sealed with seven s
Rev 5: 2 the scroll and to loose its s
Rev 5: 5 and to loose its seven s
Rev 5: 9 the scroll, and to open its s
Rev 6: 1 the Lamb opened one of the s

SEAM (*see* SEAMS)
Ex 28:27 right at the s above the
Ex 39:20 right at the s above the
John 19:23 Now the tunic was without s

SEAMEN (*see* SEA)
1Ki 9:27 s who knew the sea, to work

SEAMS (*see* SEAM)
Ezek 27: 9 were in you to caulk your s

SEANCE
1Sa 28: 8 Please conduct a s for me

SEARCH (*see* SEARCHED, SEARCHES, SEARCHING)
Num 10:33 to s out a resting place for
Deut 1:22 let them s out the land for
Deut 1:33 to s out a place for you to
Deut 13:14 s out, and ask diligently
Josh 2: 2 Israel to s out the country
Josh 2: 3 come to s out all the country
Judg 18: 2 to spy out the land and s it
Judg 18: 2 to them, "Go, s the land
1Sa 23:23 land, that I will s for him
2Sa 5:17 went up to s for David
2Sa 10: 3 servants to you to s the city
1Ki 20: 6 and they shall s your house
2Ki 2:16 go and s for your master, lest
2Ki 10:23 S and see that no servants of
1Ch 14: 8 went up to s for David
1Ch 19: 3 servants not come to you to s
Ezra 4:15 that s may be made in the
Ezra 4:19 a s has been made, and it was
Ezra 5:17 let a s be made in the king's
Ezra 6: 1 a s was made in the archives,
Job 3:21 s for it more than hidden
Job 10: 6 my iniquity and s out my sin,
Job 11: 7 Can you s out the deep things
Job 38:16 you walked in s of the depths
Ps 44:21 Would not God s this out
Ps 77: 6 And my spirit makes diligent s
Ps 139:23 S me, O God, and know my
Prov 2: 4 and s for her as for hidden
Prov 23:30 who go in s of mixed wine
Prov 25: 2 of kings is to s out a matter
Eccl 1:13 s out by wisdom concerning
Eccl 7:25 my heart to know, to s and
Is 34:16 S from the book of the LORD,
Jer 2:34 have not found it by secret s
Jer 17:10 s the heart, I test the mind,
Jer 29:13 when you s for Me with all
Lam 3:40 Let us s out and examine our
Ezek 34: 8 My shepherds s for My flock
Ezek 34:11 I Myself will s for My sheep
Ezek 39:14 with the help of a s party
Ezek 39:14 months they will make a s
Ezek 39:15 The s party will pass through
Amos 9: 3 Carmel, from there I will s
Zeph 1:12 I will s Jerusalem with lamps
Matt 2: 8 s diligently for the young
John 5:39 You s the Scriptures, for in
John 7:52 S and look, for no prophet has

SEARCHED (*see* SEARCH)
Gen 31:34 Laban s all about the tent
Gen 31:35 he s but did not find the
Gen 31:37 you have s all my things,

Gen 44:12 So he s, and he began with the
2Sa 17:20 And when they had s and could
2Ki 2:17 they s for three days but did
2Ch 22: 9 Then he s for Ahaziah
Job 5:27 Behold, this we have s out
Job 28:27 it, indeed, He s it out
Job 29:16 I s out the case that I did
Job 32:11 while you s out what to say
Ps 139: 1 O LORD, You have s me and
Eccl 2: 3 I s in my heart how to
Jer 31:37 of the earth s out beneath
Jer 46:23 Though it cannot be s,
Ezek 20: 6 that I had s out for them
Obad 6 Oh, how Esau shall be s out
Mark 1:36 who were with Him s for Him
Acts 12:19 But when Herod had s for him
Acts 17:11 s the Scriptures daily to
1Pe 1:10 s diligently, who prophesied

SEARCHES (*see* SEARCH)
1Ch 28: 9 for the LORD s all hearts
Job 13: 9 it be well when He s you out
Job 28: 3 s every recess for ore in the
Job 39: 8 he s after every green thing
Prov 28:11 has understanding s him out
Rom 8:27 Now He who s the hearts knows
1Co 2:10 For the Spirit s all things
Rev 2:23 that I am He who s the minds

SEARCHING (*see* SEARCH, SEARCHINGS)
Prov 20:27 s all the inner depths of his
Is 40:28 There is no s of His
Ezek 34: 6 one was seeking or s for them
1Pe 1:11 s what, or what manner of

SEARCHINGS (*see* SEARCHING)
Judg 5:16 Reuben have great s of heart

SEARED
Prov 6:28 coals, and his feet not be s
1Ti 4: 2 conscience s with a hot iron

SEAS (*see* SEA)
Gen 1:10 of the waters He called S
Gen 1:22 and fill the waters in the s
Lev 11: 9 whether in the s or in the
Lev 11:10 But all in the s or in the
Deut 33:19 of the abundance of the s
Neh 9: 6 and all things on it, the s
Ps 8: 8 through the paths of the s
Ps 24: 2 He has founded it upon the s
Ps 65: 5 earth, And of the far-off s
Ps 65: 7 who still the noise of the s
Ps 69:34 and earth praise Him, The s
Ps 78:27 fowl like the sand of the s
Ps 135: 6 heaven and in earth, In the s
Is 17:12 noise like the roar of the s
Jer 15: 8 more than the sand of the s
Ezek 27: 4 are in the midst of the s
Ezek 27:25 in the midst of the s
Ezek 27:26 you in the midst of the s
Ezek 27:27 the s on the day of your ruin
Ezek 27:34 when you are broken by the s
Ezek 28: 2 gods, in the midst of the s
Ezek 28: 8 slain in the midst of the s
Ezek 32: 2 are like a monster in the s
Dan 11:45 of his palace between the s
Jon 2: 3 deep, into the heart of the s
Acts 27:41 a place where two s met, they

SEASHORE (*see* SEA)
Gen 22:17 as the sand which is on the s
Ex 14:30 the Egyptians dead on the s
Josh 11: 4 that is on the s in multitude
Judg 5:17 Asher continued at the s, and
Judg 7:12 sand by the s in multitude
1Sa 13: 5 is on the s in multitude
1Ki 4:29 heart like the sand on the s
Jer 47: 7 Ashkelon and against the s
Heb 11:12 as the sand which is by the s

SEASON (*see* SEASONED, SEASONS)
Ex 13:10 in its s from year to year
Lev 2:13 you shall s with salt
Lev 26: 4 I will give you rain in its s
Num 13:20 Now the time was the s of
Deut 11:14 rain for your land in its s
Deut 28:12 rain to your land in its s
Ezra 10:13 it is the s for heavy rain,
Job 5:26 of grain ripens in its s
Job 38:32 bring out Mazzaroth in its s
Ps 1: 3 forth its fruit in its s,
Ps 4: 7 in the s that their grain
Ps 22: 2 And in the night s, and am not
Ps 104:27 give them their food in due s
Ps 145:15 give them their food in due s
Prov 15:23 and a word spoken in due s
Eccl 3: 1 To everything there is a s
Is 50: 4 word in s to him who is weary
Jer 5:24 and the latter, in its s
Jer 33:20 be day and night in their s
Ezek 34:26 to come down in their s
Dan 7:12 lives were prolonged for a s
Hos 2: 9 time and My new wine in its s
Hos 9:10 the fig tree in its first s
Matt 24:45 to give them food in due s
Mark 9:50 its flavor, how will you s it
Mark 11:13 for it was not the s for figs
Luke 12:42 portion of food in due s
Luke 13: 1 There were present at that s
Gal 6: 9 for in due s we shall reap if
2Ti 4: 2 ready in s and out of s

SEASONED (*see* SEASON)
Matt 5:13 its flavor, how shall it be s
Mark 9:49 everyone will be s with fire
Mark 9:49 sacrifice will be s with salt
Luke 14:34 its flavor, how shall it be s
Col 4: 6 s with salt, that you may

SEASONS (*see* SEASON)
Gen 1:14 and let them be for signs and s
Ps 16: 7 instructs me in the night s
Ps 104:19 He appointed the moon for s
Ezek 45:17 at all the appointed s of the
Dan 2:21 He changes the times and the s
Matt 21:41 to him the fruits in their s
Acts 1: 7 for you to know times or s
Acts 14:17 from heaven and fruitful s
Gal 4:10 observe days and months and s
1Th 5: 1 concerning the times and the s

SEAT (*see* SEATED, SEATING, SEATS)
Ex 25:17 make a mercy s of pure gold
Ex 25:18 the two ends of the mercy s
Ex 25:19 of one piece with the mercy s
Ex 25:20 the mercy s with their wings
Ex 25:20 shall be toward the mercy s
Ex 25:21 the mercy s on top of the ark
Ex 25:22 you from above the mercy s
Ex 26:34 mercy s upon the ark of the
Ex 30: 6 before the mercy s that is
Ex 31: 7 the mercy s that is on it, and
Ex 35:12 its poles, with the mercy s
Ex 37: 6 made the mercy s of pure gold
Ex 37: 7 the two ends of the mercy s
Ex 37: 8 of one piece with the mercy s
Ex 37: 9 the mercy s with their wings
Ex 37: 9 were toward the mercy s
Ex 39:35 its poles, and the mercy s
Ex 40:20 put the mercy s on top of the
Lev 16: 2 before the mercy s which is
Lev 16: 2 the cloud above the mercy s
Lev 16:13 s that is on the Testimony
Lev 16:14 the mercy s on the east side
Lev 16:14 before the mercy s he shall
Lev 16:15 and sprinkle it on the mercy s
Lev 16:15 and before the mercy s
Num 7:89 s that was on the ark of the
Judg 3:20 So he arose from his s
1Sa 1: 9 the s by the doorpost of the
1Sa 4:13 sitting on a s by the wayside
1Sa 4:18 God, that Eli fell off the s
1Sa 20:18 because your s will be empty
1Sa 20:25 Now the king sat on his s
1Sa 20:25 times, on a s by the wall
1Ki 10:19 side of the place of the s
1Ki 21: 9 and s Naboth with high honor
1Ki 21:10 s two men, scoundrels, before
2Ki 25:28 gave him a more prominent s
1Ch 28:11 and the place of the mercy s
2Ch 9:18 side of the place of the s
Esth 3: 1 and set his s above all the
Job 23: 3 that I might come to His s
Job 29: 7 when I took my s in the open
Ps 1: 1 sits in the s of the scornful
Ps 113: 8 That He may s him with
Prov 9:14 on a s by the highest places
Song 3:10 its s of purple, its interior
Jer 52:32 gave him a more prominent s
Ezek 8: 3 where the s of the image of
Ezek 28: 2 a god, I sit in the s of gods
Amos 6: 3 who cause the s of violence
Matt 23: 2 the Pharisees sit in Moses' s
Matt 27:19 was sitting on the judgment s
John 19:13 sat down in the judgment s in
Acts 18:12 brought him to the judgment s
Acts 18:16 them from the judgment s
Acts 18:17 him before the judgment s
Acts 25: 6 sitting on the judgment s
Acts 25:10 stand at Caesar's judgment s
Acts 25:17 day I sat on the judgment s
Rom 14:10 the judgment s of Christ
2Co 5:10 the judgment s of Christ,
Heb 9: 5 overshadowing the mercy s

SEATED (*see* SEAT)
1Ki 16:11 as he was s on his throne
1Ki 21:12 and s Naboth with high honor
Job 36: 7 for He has s them forever, and
Dan 7: 9 and the Ancient of Days was s
Dan 7:10 The court was s, and the books
Dan 7:26 But the court shall be s
Matt 5: 1 when He was s His disciples
Eph 1:20 s Him at His right hand in
Heb 8: 1 who is s at the right hand of

SEATING (*see* SEAT)
1Ki 10: 5 the s of his servants, the
2Ch 9: 4 the s of his servants, the

SEATS (*see* SEAT)
Matt 21:12 the s of those who sold doves
Matt 23: 6 the best s in the synagogues,
Mark 11:15 the s of those who sold doves
Mark 12:39 the best s in the synagogues,
Luke 11:43 the best s in the synagogues
Luke 20:46 the best s in the synagogues,

SEBA (*see* SHEBA)
Gen 10: 7 The sons of Cush were S,
1Ch 1: 9 The sons of Cush were S,
Ps 72:10 Sheba and S Will offer gifts
Is 43: 3 Ethiopia and S in your place

SECACAH
Josh 15:61 Beth Arabah, Middin, S,

SECHU
1Sa 19:22 the great well that is at S

SECLUSION
2Sa 20: 3 the house, and put them in s

SECOND
Gen 1: 8 and the morning were the s day
Gen 2:13 name of the s river is Gihon
Gen 4:19 the name of the s was Zillah
Gen 6:16 shall make it with lower, s
Gen 7:11 Noah's life, in the s month
Gen 8:14 And in the s month, on the
Gen 22:15 a s time out of heaven,
Gen 30: 7 again and bore Jacob a s son
Gen 30:12 Zilpah bore Jacob a s son
Gen 32:19 So he commanded the s, the
Gen 41: 5 He slept and dreamed a s time
Gen 41:43 in the s chariot which he had
Gen 41:52 the name of the s he called
Gen 43:10 have returned this s time
Ex 2:13 And when he went out the s day
Ex 16: 1 s month after they departed
Ex 25:35 same, a knob under the s two
Ex 26: 4 other curtain of the s set
Ex 26: 5 is on the end of the s set
Ex 26:10 of the curtain of the s set
Ex 26:20 And for the s side of the
Ex 28:18 the s row shall be a
Ex 36:11 other curtain of the s set
Ex 36:12 on the end of the s set
Ex 36:17 of the curtain of the s set
Ex 37:21 same, a knob under the s two
Ex 39:11 the s row, a turquoise, a
Ex 40:17 the first month of the s year
Lev 5:10 he shall offer the s as a
Lev 8:22 And he brought the s ram, the
Lev 13:58 it shall be washed a s time
Num 1: 1 the first day of the s month
Num 1: 1 in the s year after they had
Num 1:18 the first day of the s month
Num 2:16 shall be the s to break camp
Num 7:18 On the s day Nethaneel the
Num 9: 1 s year after they had come
Num 9:11 fourteenth day of the s month
Num 10: 6 sound the advance the s time
Num 10:11 s month, in the s year
Num 29:17 On the s day present twelve
Josh 5: 2 of Israel again the s time
Josh 6:14 the s day they marched around
Josh 10:32 who took it on the s day
Josh 19: 1 The s lot came out for Simeon

Judg 6:25 the s bull of seven years old
Judg 6:26 and take the s bull and offer
Judg 6:28 the s bull was being offered
Judg 20:24 of Benjamin on the s day
Judg 20:25 them from Gibeah on the s day
1Sa 8: 2 Joel, and the name of his s
1Sa 18:21 Saul said to David a s time
1Sa 20:27 the s day of the month, that
1Sa 20:34 ate no food the s day of the
1Sa 26: 8 have to strike him a s time
2Sa 3: 3 his s, Chileab, by Abigail
2Sa 14:29 when he sent again the s time
1Ki 6: 1 of Ziv, which is the s month
1Ki 9: 2 to Solomon the s time, as He
1Ki 15:25 king over Israel in the s
1Ki 18:34 Do it a s time,"
1Ki 18:34 and they did it a s time
1Ki 19: 7 the LORD came back the s time
2Ki 1:17 in the s year of Jehoram the
2Ki 9:19 Then he sent out a s horseman
2Ki 10: 6 he wrote a s letter to them
2Ki 14: 1 In the s year of Joash the
2Ki 15:32 In the s year of Pekah the
2Ki 19:29 in the s year what springs
2Ki 22:14 in Jerusalem in the S Quarter
2Ki 23: 4 the priests of the s order
2Ki 25:17 The s pillar was the same,
2Ki 25:18 Zephaniah the s priest, and
1Ch 2:13 his firstborn, Abinadab the s
1Ch 3: 1 the s, Daniel, by Abigail the
1Ch 3:15 the s Jehoiakim, the third
1Ch 6:28 firstborn, and Abijah the s
1Ch 8: 1 his firstborn, Ashbel the s
1Ch 8:39 his firstborn, Jeush the s
1Ch 12: 9 Ezer the first, Obadiah the s
1Ch 15:18 their brethren of the s rank
1Ch 23:11 was the first and Zizah the s
1Ch 23:19 was the first, Amariah the s
1Ch 23:20 the first and Jesshiah the s
1Ch 24: 7 Jehoiarib, the s to Jedaiah,
1Ch 24:23 was the first, Amariah the s
1Ch 25: 9 the s for Gedaliah, him with
1Ch 26: 2 the firstborn, Jediael the s
1Ch 26: 4 firstborn, Jehozabad the s
1Ch 26:11 Hilkiah the s, Tebaliah the
1Ch 27: 4 Over the division of the s
1Ch 29:22 son of David king the s time
2Ch 3: 2 on the s day of the s month
2Ch 27: 5 paid him this amount in the s
2Ch 28: 7 Elkanah who was s to the king
2Ch 30: 2 the Passover in the s month
2Ch 30:13 Bread in the s month
2Ch 30:15 fourteenth day of the s month
2Ch 34:22 in Jerusalem in the S Quarter
2Ch 35:24 put him in the s chariot that
Ezra 3: 8 in the s month of the s year
Ezra 4:24 was discontinued until the s
Neh 8:13 Now on the s day the heads of
Neh 11: 9 of Senuah was s over the city
Neh 11:17 Bakbukiah the s among his
Esth 2:14 to the s house of the women
Esth 2:19 gathered together a s time
Esth 7: 2 And on the s day, at the
Esth 9:29 this s letter about Purim
Esth 10: 3 Jew was s to King Ahasuerus
Job 42:14 the name of the s Keziah
Eccl 4:15 they were with the s youth
Is 11:11 set His hand again the s time
Is 37:30 the s year what springs from
Jer 1:13 LORD came to me the s time
Jer 13: 3 LORD came to me the s time
Jer 33: 1 came to Jeremiah a s time
Jer 41: 4 on the s day after he had
Jer 52:22 The s pillar, with
Jer 52:24 Zephaniah the s priest, and
Ezek 10:14 the s face the face of a man,
Ezek 43:22 On the s day you shall offer
Dan 2: 1 Now in the s year of
Dan 7: 5 suddenly another beast, a s
Jon 3: 1 LORD came to Jonah the s time
Nah 1: 9 will not rise up a s time
Zeph 1:10 a wailing from the S Quarter
Hag 1: 1 In the s year of King Darius,
Hag 1:15 in the s year of King Darius
Hag 2:10 in the s year of Darius, the
Zech 1: 1 month of the s year of Darius
Zech 1: 7 in the s year of Darius, the
Zech 6: 2 with the s chariot black
Mal 2:13 this is the s thing you do
Matt 21:30 Then he came to the s and said
Matt 22:26 Likewise the s also, and the
Matt 22:39 And the s is like it
Matt 26:42 He went away again a s time
Mark 12:21 the s took her, and he died
Mark 12:31 And the s, like it, is this
Mark 14:72 a s time the rooster crowed
Luke 6: 1 Now it happened on the s
Luke 12:38 he should come in the s watch
Luke 19:18 the s came, saying, 'Master,
Luke 20:30 the s took her as wife, and he
John 3: 4 Can he enter a s time into
John 4:54 This again is the s sign that
John 21:16 He said to him again a s time
Acts 7:13 the s time Joseph was made
Acts 10:15 spoke to him again the s time
Acts 12:10 the s guard posts, they came
Acts 13:33 also written in the s Psalm
1Co 12:28 s prophets, third teachers,
1Co 15:47 the s Man is the Lord from
2Co 1:15 you might have a s benefit
2Co 13: 2 if I were present the s time
Tit 3:10 the first and s admonition,
Heb 8: 7 have been sought for a s
Heb 9: 3 and behind the s veil, the
Heb 9: 7 But into the s part the high
Heb 9:28 Him He will appear a s time
Heb 10: 9 that He may establish the s
2Pe 3: 1 I now write to you this s
Rev 2:11 not be hurt by the s death
Rev 4: 7 the s living creature like a
Rev 6: 3 When He opened the s seal
Rev 6: 3 I heard the s living creature
Rev 8: 8 Then the s angel sounded
Rev 11:14 The s woe is past
Rev 16: 3 Then the s angel poured out
Rev 20: 6 Over such the s death has no
Rev 20:14 This is the s death
Rev 21: 8 which is the s death
Rev 21:19 the s sapphire, the third

SECRET (*see* SECRETLY, SECRETS)
Deut 27:15 craftsman, and sets it up in s
Deut 29:29 The s things belong to the
Judg 3:19 I have a s message for you, O
Judg 16: 9 So the s of his strength was
1Sa 19: 2 morning, and stay in a s place
Neh 6:10 who was a s informer
Ps 10: 8 In the s places he murders
Ps 17:12 lion lurking in s places
Ps 18:11 He made darkness His s place
Ps 19:12 Cleanse me from s faults
Ps 25:14 The s of the LORD is with
Ps 27: 5 In the s place of His
Ps 31:20 You shall hide them in the s
Ps 64: 2 Hide me from the s counsel of
Ps 64: 4 shoot in s at the blameless
Ps 81: 7 you in the s place of thunder
Ps 90: 8 Our s sins in the light of
Ps 91: 1 He who dwells in the s place
Ps 139:15 You, When I was made in s
Prov 3:32 but His s counsel is with the
Prov 9:17 bread eaten in s is pleasant
Prov 21:14 A gift in s pacifies anger,
Prov 25: 9 not disclose the s to another
Eccl 12:14 including every s thing,
Song 2:14 in the s places of the cliff,
Is 3:17 will uncover their s parts
Is 45: 3 and hidden riches of s places
Is 45:19 I have not spoken in s, in a
Is 48:16 in s from the beginning
Jer 2:34 have not found it by s search
Jer 13:17 will weep in s for your pride
Jer 23:24 hide himself in s places, so
Jer 49:10 I have uncovered his s places
Ezek 7:22 they will defile My s place
Ezek 28: 3 there is no s that can be
Dan 2:18 of heaven concerning this s
Dan 2:19 Then the s was revealed to
Dan 2:22 He reveals deep and s things
Dan 2:27 The s which the king has
Dan 2:30 this s has not been revealed
Dan 2:47 since you could reveal this s
Dan 4: 9 no s troubles you, explain to
Amos 3: 7 His s to His servants the
Hab 3:14 feasting on the poor in s
Matt 6: 4 charitable deed may be in s
Matt 6: 4 in s will Himself reward you
Matt 6: 6 Father who is in the s place
Matt 6: 6 in s will reward you openly
Matt 6:18 Father who is in the s place
Matt 6:18 in s will reward you openly
Matt 13:35 s from the foundation of the
Mark 4:22 s but that it should come to
Luke 8:17 For nothing is s that will
Luke 11:33 puts it in a s place or under
John 7: 4 s while he himself seeks to
John 7:10 openly, but as it were in s
John 18:20 and in s I have said nothing
Rom 16:25 kept s since the world began
Eph 5:12 which are done by them in s

SECRETLY (*see* SECRET)
Gen 31:27 Why did you flee away s, and
Deut 13: 6 s entices you, saying, 'Let
Deut 27:24 who attacks his neighbor s
Deut 28:57 for she will eat them s for
Josh 2: 1 from Acacia Grove to spy s
Judg 9:31 messengers to Abimelech s
1Sa 18:22 Communicate with David s, and
1Sa 24: 4 s cut off a corner of Saul's
2Sa 12:12 For you did it s, but I will
2Ki 17: 9 s did against the LORD their
Job 4:12 a word was s brought to me
Job 13:10 you if you s show partiality
Job 31:27 my heart has been s enticed
Ps 10: 8 His eyes are s fixed on the
Ps 10: 9 He lies in wait s, as a lion
Ps 11: 2 That they may shoot s at the
Ps 31: 4 which they have s laid for me
Ps 31:20 You shall keep them s in a
Ps 64: 5 They talk of laying snares s
Ps 101: 5 Whoever s slanders his
Ps 142: 3 have s set a snare for me
Prov 1:11 Let us lurk s for the
Prov 1:18 They lurk s for their own
Jer 37:17 king asked him s in his house
Jer 38:16 the king swore s to Jeremiah
Jer 40:15 spoke s to Gedaliah in Mizpah
Matt 1:19 was minded to put her away s
Matt 2: 7 when he had s called the wise
John 11:28 s called Mary her sister,
John 19:38 a disciple of Jesus, but s
Acts 6:11 Then they s induced men to
Acts 16:37 And now do they put us out s
Gal 2: 4 because of false brethren s
2Pe 2: 1 you, who will s bring in

SECRETS (*see* SECRET)
Job 11: 6 show you the s of wisdom
Ps 44:21 He knows the s of the heart
Prov 11:13 A talebearer reveals s, but
Prov 20:19 as a talebearer reveals s
Dan 2:28 a God in heaven who reveals s
Dan 2:29 He who reveals s has made
Dan 2:47 of kings, and a revealer of s
Rom 2:16 the s of men by Jesus Christ
1Co 14:25 thus the s of his heart are

SECT
Acts 5:17 is the s of the Sadducees)
Acts 15: 5 But some of the s of the
Acts 24: 5 of the s of the Nazarenes
Acts 24:14 the Way which they call a s
Acts 26: 5 s of our religion I lived a
Acts 28:22 for concerning this s, we

SECTION
Neh 3:11 repaired another s, as well
Neh 3:19 repaired another s in front
Neh 3:20 repaired the other s, from
Neh 3:21 of Koz, repaired another s
Neh 3:24 of Henadad repaired another s
Neh 3:27 Tekoites repaired another s
Neh 3:30 of Zalaph, repaired another s

SECUNDUS
Acts 20: 4 S of the Thessalonians, and

SECURE (*see* SECURED, SECURELY, SECURES, SECURITY)
Judg 8:11 army while the camp felt s
Judg 18: 7 of the Sidonians, quiet and s
Judg 18:10 you will come to a s people
Judg 18:27 a people who were quiet and s
2Sa 23: 5 ordered in all things and s
Job 11:18 And you would be s, because
Job 12: 6 those who provoke God are s
Job 21:23 being wholly at ease and s
Prov 1:33 dwell safely, and will be s
Prov 11:15 who hates being surety is s
Is 22:23 him as a peg in a s place
Is 22:25 the s place will be removed
Is 32:18 in s dwellings, and in quiet
Matt 27:64 be made s until the third day

Ps 119:155 they do not s Your statutes
Ps 119:176 S Your servant, For I do not
Ps 122: 9 our God I will s your good
Prov 1:28 they will s me diligently,
Prov 2: 4 If you s her as silver, and
Prov 7:15 diligently to s your face
Prov 8:17 those who s me diligently
Prov 21: 6 fantasy of those who s death
Prov 23:35 that I may s another drink
Prov 25:27 so to s one's own glory is
Prov 28: 5 but those who s the LORD
Prov 29:10 but the just s his well-being
Prov 29:26 Many s the ruler's favor, but
Eccl 1:13 And I set my heart to s and
Eccl 7:25 s out wisdom and the reason of
Song 3: 2 I will s the one I love
Song 6: 1 that we may s him with you
Is 1:17 s justice, reprove the
Is 8:19 S those who are mediums and
Is 8:19 not a people s their God
Is 8:19 Should they s the dead on
Is 9:13 nor do they s the LORD of
Is 10:31 inhabitants of Gebim s refuge
Is 11:10 for the Gentiles shall s Him
Is 26: 9 within me I will s You early
Is 29:15 Woe to those who s deep to
Is 31: 1 One of Israel, nor s the LORD
Is 41:12 You shall s them and not find
Is 41:17 the poor and needy s water
Is 45:19 seed of Jacob, 'S Me in vain'
Is 51: 1 you who s the LORD
Is 55: 6 S the LORD while He may be
Is 58: 2 Yet they s Me daily, and
Is 65: 1 by those who did not s Me
Jer 2:24 All those who s her will not
Jer 2:33 beautify your way to s love
Jer 4:30 they will s your life
Jer 5: 1 s in her open places if you
Jer 11:21 of Anathoth who s your life
Jer 19: 7 of those who s their lives
Jer 19: 9 those who s their lives shall
Jer 21: 7 of those who s their life
Jer 22:25 hand of those who s your life
Jer 26:19 LORD and s the LORD's favor
Jer 29: 7 s the peace of the city where
Jer 29:13 And you will s Me and find Me,
Jer 30:14 they do not s you
Jer 34:20 of those who s their life
Jer 34:21 of those who s their life
Jer 38: 4 For this man does not s the
Jer 38:16 of these men who s your life
Jer 44:30 hand of those who s his life
Jer 45: 5 do you s great things for
Jer 45: 5 Do not s them
Jer 46:26 of those who s their lives
Jer 49:37 before those who s their life
Jer 50: 4 come, and s the LORD their God
Lam 1:11 her people sigh, they s bread
Ezek 7:25 they will s peace, but there
Ezek 7:26 then they will s a vision
Ezek 34:11 for My sheep and s them out
Ezek 34:12 so will I s out My sheep and
Ezek 34:16 I will s what was lost and
Dan 2:18 that they might s mercies
Hos 2: 7 yes, she will s them, but not
Hos 3: 5 s the LORD their God and David
Hos 5: 6 they shall go to s the LORD
Hos 5:15 Then they will s My face
Hos 5:15 they will diligently s Me
Hos 7:10 God, nor s Him for all this
Hos 10:12 for it is time to s the LORD
Amos 5: 4 S Me and live
Amos 5: 5 But do not s Bethel, nor
Amos 5: 6 S the LORD and live, lest He
Amos 5:14 S good and not evil, that you
Nah 3: 7 Where shall I s comforters
Nah 3:11 you also will s refuge from
Zeph 2: 3 S the LORD, all you meek of
Zeph 2: 3 S righteousness, s humility
Zech 8:21 LORD, and s the LORD of hosts
Zech 8:22 to s the LORD of hosts in
Zech 11:16 nor s the young, nor heal
Zech 12: 9 s to destroy all the nations
Mal 2: 7 people should s the law from
Mal 3: 1 And the Lord, whom you s, will
Matt 2:13 for Herod will s the young
Matt 6:32 these things the Gentiles s
Matt 6:33 But s first the kingdom of
Matt 7: 7 s, and you will find
Matt 18:12 go to the mountains to s the
Matt 28: 5 for I know that you s Jesus
Mark 8:12 does this generation s a sign
Mark 16: 6 You s Jesus of Nazareth, who
Luke 11: 9 s, and you will find
Luke 12:29 do not s what you should eat
Luke 12:30 nations of the world s after
Luke 12:31 But s the kingdom of God, and
Luke 13:24 will s to enter and will not
Luke 15: 8 s diligently until she finds
Luke 19:10 the Son of Man has come to s
Luke 24: 5 Why do you s the living among
John 1:38 What do you s?
John 4:27 What do You s?
John 5:30 because I do not s My own
John 5:44 do not s the honor that comes
John 6:26 I say to you, you s Me, not
John 7:19 Why do you s to kill Me
John 7:25 not He whom they s to kill
John 7:34 You will s Me and not find Me,
John 7:36 that He said, 'You will s Me
John 8:21 going away, and you will s Me
John 8:37 but you s to kill Me, because
John 8:40 But now you s to kill Me, a
John 8:50 And I do not s My own glory
John 13:33 You will s Me
John 18: 8 Therefore, if you s Me, let
Acts 6: 3 s out from among you seven
Acts 10:21 Yes, I am he whom you s
Acts 11:25 departed for Tarsus to s Saul
Acts 15:17 of mankind may s the LORD
Acts 17:27 that they should s the Lord
Rom 2: 7 in doing good s for glory
Rom 9:32 they did not s it by faith
Rom 10:20 by those who did not s Me
Rom 11: 3 am left, and they s my life"
1Co 1:22 and Greeks s after wisdom
1Co 7:27 Do not s to be loosed
1Co 7:27 Do not s a wife
1Co 10:24 Let no one s his own, but
1Co 13: 5 rudely, does not s its own
1Co 14:12 church that you s to excel
2Co 12:14 for I do not s yours, but you
2Co 13: 3 since you s a proof of Christ
Gal 1:10 Or do I s to please men
Gal 2:17 while we s to be justified by
Phil 2:21 For all s their own, not the
Phil 4:17 Not that I s the gift, but I
Phil 4:17 gift, but I s the fruit that
Col 3: 1 s those things which are
1Th 2: 6 Nor did we s glory from men,
Heb 11: 6 of those who diligently s Him
Heb 11:14 that they s a homeland
Heb 13:14 but we s the one to come
1Pe 3:11 let him s peace and pursue it
Rev 9: 6 those days men will s death

SEEKING (*see* SEEK)
Gen 37:15 What are you s?
Gen 37:16 he said, "I am s my brothers
Num 16:10 are you s the priesthood also
Num 35:23 not his enemy or s his harm
Judg 14: 4 that He was s an occasion to
Judg 18: 1 tribe of the Danites was s an
2Sa 3:17 In time past you were s for
Esth 10: 3 s the good of his people and
Job 24: 5 work, s diligently for food
Ps 119:82 My eyes fail from s Your word
Ps 119:123 fail from s Your salvation
Is 16: 5 and s justice and hastening
Ezek 34: 6 no one was s or searching for
Dan 8:15 and was s the meaning, that
Amos 8:12 s the word of the LORD, but
Matt 12:43 places, s rest, and finds none
Matt 12:46 outside, s to speak with Him
Matt 12:47 outside, s to speak with You
Matt 13:45 a merchant s beautiful pearls
Mark 3:32 brothers are outside s You
Mark 8:11 s from Him a sign from heaven
Luke 2:45 returned to Jerusalem, s Him
Luke 11:24 through dry places, s rest
Luke 11:54 s to catch Him in something
Luke 13: 6 and he came s fruit on it and
Luke 13: 7 come s fruit on this fig tree
John 4:23 for the Father is s such to
John 6:24 and came to Capernaum, s Jesus
John 7:20 Who is s to kill You
John 18: 4 Whom are you s?
John 18: 7 Whom are you s?
John 20:15 Whom are you s?
Acts 10:19 Behold, three men are s you
Acts 13: 8 s to turn the proconsul away
Acts 13:11 he went around s someone to
Acts 21:31 as they were s to kill him
Acts 27:30 And as the sailors were s to
Rom 10: 3 and s to establish their own
1Co 10:33 not s my own profit, but the
1Pe 5: 8 lion, s whom he may devour

SEEKS (*see* SEEK)
Deut 22: 2 you until your brother s it
1Sa 19: 2 My father Saul s to kill you
1Sa 20: 1 father, that he s my life
1Sa 22:23 who s my life s your life
1Sa 23:10 Saul s to come to Keilah to
1Sa 24: 9 Indeed David s your harm'
2Sa 16:11 from my own body s my life
1Ki 20: 7 and see how this man s trouble
2Ki 5: 7 see how he s a quarrel with
Ps 37:32 righteous, And s to slay him
Prov 11:27 diligently s good finds favor
Prov 11:27 will come to him who s evil
Prov 14: 6 A scoffer s wisdom and does
Prov 15:14 has understanding s knowledge
Prov 17: 9 covers a transgression s love
Prov 17:11 An evil man s only rebellion
Prov 17:19 exalts his gate s destruction
Prov 18: 1 himself s his own desire
Prov 18:15 ear of the wise s knowledge
Prov 31:13 She s wool and flax, and
Eccl 7:28 still s but I cannot find
Is 40:20 He s for himself a skillful
Jer 5: 1 who s the truth, and I will
Jer 30:17 no one s her
Lam 3:25 Him, to the soul who s Him
Ezek 34:12 As a shepherd s out his flock
Mic 7: 3 gifts, the judge s a bribe
Mal 2:15 He s godly offspring
Matt 7: 8 receives, and he who s finds
Matt 12:39 generation s after a sign
Matt 16: 4 generation s after a sign
Luke 11:10 receives, and he who s finds
Luke 11:29 It s a sign, and no sign will
Luke 17:33 Whoever s to save his life
John 7: 4 himself s to be known openly
John 7:18 from himself s his own glory
John 7:18 but He who s the glory of the
John 8:50 there is One who s and judges
Rom 3:11 there is none who s after God
Rom 11: 7 has not obtained what it s

SEEM (*see* PREFACE)

SEEMED (*see* PREFACE)

SEEMS (*see* PREFACE)

SEEN
Gen 7: 1 because I have s that you are
Gen 8: 5 tops of the mountains were s
Gen 9:14 shall be s in the cloud
Gen 16:13 I also here s Him who sees me
Gen 26:28 We have certainly s that the
Gen 31:12 for I have s all that Laban
Gen 31:42 God has s my affliction and
Gen 32:30 For I have s God face to face
Gen 33:10 inasmuch as I have s your
Gen 33:10 I had s the face of God, and
Gen 41:19 s in all the land of Egypt
Gen 44:28 and I have not s him since
Gen 45:13 and of all that you have s
Gen 46:30 die, since I have s your face
Ex 3: 7 I have surely s the
Ex 3: 9 I have also s the oppression
Ex 3:16 and s what is done to you in
Ex 10: 6 your fathers' fathers have s
Ex 13: 7 bread shall be s among you
Ex 13: 7 nor shall leaven be s among
Ex 16: 8 This shall be s when the LORD
Ex 19: 4 You have s what I did to the
Ex 20:22 You have s that I have
Ex 32: 9 I have s this people, and
Ex 33:23 but My face shall not be s
Ex 34: 3 let no man be s throughout
Lev 5: 1 whether he has s or known of
Lev 13: 7 after he has been s by the
Lev 13: 7 he shall be s by the priest
Num 14:14 are s face to face and that
Num 14:22 these men who have s My glory
Num 23:21 nor has He s wickedness in
Num 27:13 And when you have s it, you
Deut 1:28 moreover we have s the sons
Deut 3:21 Your eyes have s all that
Deut 4: 3 Your eyes have s what the
Deut 4: 9 the things your eyes have s

Deut 5:24 We have s this day that God
Deut 9:13 I have s this people, and
Deut 10:21 things which your eyes have s
Deut 11: 2 who have not s the chastening
Deut 11: 7 but your eyes have s every
Deut 16: 4 no leaven shall be s among
Deut 21: 7 blood, nor have our eyes s it
Deut 29: 2 You have s all that the LORD
Deut 29: 3 trials which your eyes have s
Deut 33: 9 mother, 'I have not s them'
Josh 23: 3 You have s all that the LORD
Judg 2: 7 who had s all the great works
Judg 5: 8 was s among forty thousand in
Judg 6:22 For I have s the Angel of the
Judg 9:48 What you have s me do, make
Judg 13:22 die, because we have s God
Judg 14: 2 I have s a woman in Timnah of
Judg 18: 9 For we have s the land, and
Judg 19:30 or s from the day that the
1Sa 6:16 of the Philistines had s it
1Sa 16:18 I have s a son of Jesse the
1Sa 17:25 Have you s this man who has
1Sa 23:22 is, and who has s him there
1Sa 24:10 this day your eyes have s
2Sa 17:17 not be s coming into the city
2Sa 18:21 tell the king what you have s
2Sa 22:11 He was s upon the wings of
2Sa 22:16 channels of the sea were s
1Ki 6:18 there was no stone to be s
1Ki 8: 8 be s from the holy place, in
1Ki 8: 8 could not be s from outside
1Ki 10: 4 s all the wisdom of Solomon
1Ki 10:12 the like been s to this day
1Ki 13:12 For his sons had s which
1Ki 20:13 Have you s all this great
2Ki 20: 5 prayer, I have s your tears
2Ki 20:15 have they s in your house
2Ki 20:15 They have s all that is in my
2Ki 23:24 were s in the land of Judah
1Ch 29:17 with joy I have s Your people
2Ch 5: 9 be s from the holy place, in
2Ch 5: 9 could not be s from outside
2Ch 9: 3 had s the wisdom of Solomon
2Ch 9:11 were none such as these s
Ezra 3:12 who had s the first temple,
Esth 9:26 what they had s concerning
Job 4: 8 Even as I have s, those who
Job 5: 3 I have s the foolish taking
Job 8:18 saying, 'I have not s you
Job 10:18 perished and no eye had s me
Job 13: 1 Behold, my eye has s all this
Job 15:17 what I have s I will declare,
Job 20: 7 those who have s him will say
Job 27:12 Surely all of you have s it
Job 28: 7 nor has the falcon's eye s it
Job 31:19 if I have s anyone perish for
Job 33:21 out which once were not s
Job 36:25 Everyone has s it
Job 38:17 Or have you s the doors of
Job 38:22 or have you s the treasury of
Ps 10:14 But You have s it, for You
Ps 18:15 the channels of waters were s
Ps 35:21 Our eyes have s it
Ps 35:22 This You have s, O LORD
Ps 37:25 Yet I have not s the
Ps 37:35 I have s the wicked in great
Ps 48: 8 So we have s In the city of
Ps 54: 7 my eye has s its desire upon
Ps 55: 9 For I have s violence and
Ps 68:24 They have s Your procession,
Ps 90:15 years in which we have s evil
Ps 92:11 My eye also has s my desire
Ps 98: 3 s the salvation of our God
Ps 119:96 I have s the consummation of
Prov 25: 7 prince, whom your eyes have s
Eccl 1:14 I have s all the works that
Eccl 3:10 I have s the God-given task
Eccl 4: 3 who has not s the evil work
Eccl 5:13 which I have s under the sun
Eccl 5:18 Here is what I have s
Eccl 6: 1 which I have s under the sun
Eccl 6: 5 Though it has not s the sun
Eccl 6: 6 but has not s goodness
Eccl 7:15 I have s all things in my
Eccl 8: 9 All this I have s, and applied
Eccl 9:13 I have also s under the sun
Eccl 10: 5 evil I have s under the sun
Eccl 10: 7 I have s servants on horses,
Song 3: 3 Have you s the one I love
Is 6: 5 for my eyes have s the King
Is 9: 2 darkness have s a great light
Is 16:12 when it is s that Moab is
Is 38: 5 prayer, I have s your tears
Is 39: 4 have they s in your house
Is 39: 4 They have s all that is in my
Is 44:16 I am warm, I have s the fire
Is 47: 3 yes, your shame will be s
Is 57:18 I have s his ways, and will
Is 58: 3 they say, 'and You have not s
Is 60: 2 His glory will be s upon you
Is 64: 4 nor has the eye s any God
Is 66: 8 Who has s such things
Is 66:19 heard My fame nor s My glory
Jer 1:12 You have s well, for I am
Jer 3: 6 Have you s what backsliding
Jer 7:11 Behold, I, even I, have s it
Jer 12: 3 you have s me, and You have
Jer 13:27 I have s your adulteries and
Jer 23:13 And I have s folly in the
Jer 23:14 Also I have s a horrible
Jer 44: 2 You have s all the calamity
Jer 46: 5 Why have I s them dismayed and
Lam 1: 8 they have s her nakedness
Lam 1:10 for she has s the nations
Lam 2:14 prophets have s for you false
Lam 2:16 have found it, we have s it
Lam 3: 1 I am the man who has s
Lam 3:59 You have s how I am wronged
Lam 3:60 You have s all their
Ezek 8:12 have you s what the elders of
Ezek 8:15 Have you s this, O son of man
Ezek 8:17 Have you s this, O son of man
Ezek 10:22 I had s by the River Chebar
Ezek 11:24 that I had s went up from me
Ezek 13: 3 own spirit and have s nothing
Ezek 13: 7 Have you not s a futile
Ezek 19:11 was s in her height amid the
Ezek 47: 6 Son of man, have you s this
Dan 2:26 me the dream which I have s
Dan 4: 9 of my dream that I have s
Dan 4:11 it could be s to the ends of
Dan 4:18 King Nebuchadnezzar, have s
Dan 4:20 which could be s by all the
Dan 8: 6 which I had s standing beside
Dan 8:15 had s the vision and was
Dan 9:21 whom I had s in the vision at
Hos 6:10 I have s a horrible thing in
Zech 9: 8 for now I have s with My eyes
Zech 9:14 the LORD will be s over them
Matt 2: 2 For we have s His star in the
Matt 2: 9 had s in the East went before
Matt 6: 1 before men, to be s by them
Matt 6: 5 that they may be s by men
Matt 9:33 It was never s like this in
Matt 23: 5 works they do to be s by men
Mark 9: 9 no one the things they had s
Mark 16:11 alive and had been s by her
Mark 16:14 had s Him after He had risen
Luke 1:22 had s a vision in the temple
Luke 2:17 Now when they had s Him, they
Luke 2:20 that they had heard and s, as
Luke 2:26 he had s the Lord's Christ
Luke 2:30 my eyes have s Your salvation
Luke 5:26 We have s strange things
Luke 7:22 John the things you have s
Luke 8:36 They also who had s it told
Luke 9:36 any of the things they had s
Luke 10:24 you see, and have not s it
Luke 11:44 like graves which are not s
Luke 19:37 the mighty works they had s
Luke 24:23 saying that they had also s a
Luke 24:37 supposed they had s a spirit
John 1:18 No one has s God at any time
John 1:34 And I have s and testified that
John 3:11 and testify what We have s
John 3:21 his deeds may be clearly s
John 3:32 And what He has s and heard,
John 4:45 having s all the things He
John 5:37 at any time, nor s His form
John 6:14 when they had s the sign that
John 6:36 to you that you have s Me
John 6:46 that anyone has s the Father
John 6:46 He has s the Father
John 8:38 what I have s with My Father
John 8:38 you have s with your father
John 8:57 old, and have You s Abraham
John 9: 8 had s that he was blind said
John 9:37 You have both s Him and it is
John 11:45 had s the things Jesus did,
John 14: 7 know Him and have s Him
John 14: 9 has s Me has s the Father
John 15:24 but now they have s and also
John 19:35 he who has s has testified,
John 20:18 that she had s the Lord, and
John 20:25 to him, "We have s the Lord
John 20:29 Thomas, because you have s Me
John 20:29 are those who have not s and
Acts 1: 3 being s by them during forty
Acts 4:20 the things which we have s
Acts 7:34 I have certainly s the
Acts 7:44 to the pattern that he had s
Acts 9:12 in a vision he has s a man
Acts 9:27 he had s the Lord on the road
Acts 10:17 vision which he had s meant
Acts 11:13 he told us how he had s an
Acts 11:23 had s the grace of God, he
Acts 13:31 He was s for many days by
Acts 16:10 Now after he had s the vision
Acts 16:40 when they had s the brethren
Acts 21:29 (For they had previously s
Acts 22:15 to all men of what you have s
Acts 26:16 the things which you have s
Rom 1:20 attributes are clearly s,
Rom 8:24 hope that is s is not hope
1Co 2: 9 Eye has not s, nor ear heard,
1Co 9: 1 Have I not s Jesus Christ our
1Co 15: 5 and that He was s by Cephas
1Co 15: 6 After that He was s by over
1Co 15: 7 After that He was s by James
1Co 15: 8 of all He was s by me also
2Co 4:18 at the things which are s
2Co 4:18 at the things which are not s
2Co 4:18 which are s are temporary
2Co 4:18 which are not s are eternal
Col 2: 1 not s my face in the flesh
Col 2:18 things which he has not s
1Ti 3:16 s by angels, preached among
1Ti 6:16 whom no man has s or can see
Heb 11: 1 the evidence of things not s
Heb 11: 3 are s were not made of things
Heb 11: 7 warned of things not yet s
Heb 11:13 but having s them afar off
Jas 5:11 s the end intended by the
1Pe 1: 8 whom having not s you love
1Jn 1: 1 which we have s with our eyes
1Jn 1: 2 was manifested, and we have s
1Jn 1: 3 that which we have s and heard
1Jn 3: 6 neither s Him nor known Him
1Jn 4:12 No one has s God at any time
1Jn 4:14 And we have s and testify that
1Jn 4:20 his brother whom he has s
1Jn 4:20 he love God whom he has not s
3Jn 11 who does evil has not s God
Rev 1:19 the things which you have s
Rev 11:19 covenant was s in His temple

SEER (*see* SEER'S, SEERS)
1Sa 9: 9 Come, let us go to the s"
1Sa 9: 9 was formerly called a s
1Sa 9:11 Is the s here
1Sa 9:19 I am the s
2Sa 15:27 Are you not a s?
2Sa 24:11 to the prophet Gad, David's s
2Ki 17:13 His prophets, namely every s
1Ch 9:22 Samuel the s had appointed
1Ch 21: 9 LORD spoke to Gad, David's s
1Ch 25: 5 king's s in the words of God
1Ch 26:28 And all that Samuel the s,
1Ch 29:29 in the book of Samuel the s
1Ch 29:29 and in the book of Gad the s
2Ch 9:29 in the visions of Iddo the s
2Ch 12:15 and of Iddo the s concerning
2Ch 16: 7 at that time Hanani the s
2Ch 16:10 Then Asa was angry with the s
2Ch 19: 2 the s went out to meet him
2Ch 29:25 of David, of Gad the king's s
2Ch 29:30 of David and of Asaph the s
2Ch 35:15 and Jeduthun the king's s
Amos 7:12 Go, you s! Flee to the land

SEER'S (*see* SEER)
1Sa 9:18 tell me, where is the s house

SEERS (*see* SEER)
2Ch 33:18 the words of the s who spoke
Is 29:10 your heads, namely, the s
Is 30:10 Who say to the s, "Do not
Mic 3: 7 So the s shall be ashamed, and

SEES (*see* PREFACE)

SEGUB
1Ki 16:34 son S he set up its gates
1Ch 2:21 and she bore him S
1Ch 2:22 S begot Jair, who had

SEIR
Gen 14: 6 in their mountain of S, as
Gen 32: 3 his brother in the land of S
Gen 33:14 until I come to my lord in S
Gen 33:16 that day on his way to S
Gen 36: 8 So Esau dwelt in Mount S
Gen 36: 9 of the Edomites in Mount S
Gen 36:20 These were the sons of S the
Gen 36:21 of the Horites, the sons of S
Gen 36:30 their chiefs in the land of S
Num 24:18 S also, his enemies, shall be
Deut 1: 2 of Mount S to Kadesh Barnea
Deut 1:44 you back from S to Hormah
Deut 2: 1 skirted Mount S for many days
Deut 2: 4 of Esau, who live in S
Deut 2: 5 S to Esau as a possession
Deut 2: 8 of Esau who dwell in S, away
Deut 2:12 Horites formerly dwelt in S
Deut 2:22 of Esau, who dwelt in S, when
Deut 2:29 of Esau who dwell in S and the
Deut 33: 2 and dawned on them from S
Josh 11:17 Halak and the ascent to S,
Josh 12: 7 Halak and the ascent to S,
Josh 15:10 from Baalah to Mount S,
Josh 24: 4 the mountains of S to possess
Judg 5: 4 when You went out from S
1Ch 1:38 The sons of S were Lotan,
1Ch 4:42 of Simeon, went to Mount S
2Ch 20:10 of Ammon, Moab, and Mount S
2Ch 20:22 of Ammon, Moab, and Mount S
2Ch 20:23 of Mount S to utterly kill
2Ch 20:23 end of the inhabitants of S
2Ch 25:11 thousand of the people of S
2Ch 25:14 the gods of the people of S
Is 21:11 He calls to me out of S
Ezek 25: 8 Because Moab and S say, 'Look
Ezek 35: 2 set your face against Mount S
Ezek 35: 3 Behold, O Mount S, I am
Ezek 35: 7 make Mount S most desolate
Ezek 35:15 shall be desolate, O Mount S

SEIRAH
Judg 3:26 stone images and escaped to S

SEIZE (*see* SEIZED, SEIZES)
Josh 8: 7 s the city, for the LORD your
Judg 7:24 and s from them the watering
1Ki 18:40 S the prophets of Baal
Job 3: 6 that night, may darkness s it
Job 24: 2 they s flocks violently and
Ps 55:15 Let death s them
Ps 109:11 creditor s all that he has
Is 10: 6 to s the spoil, to take the
Is 22:17 man, and will surely s you
Jer 13:21 Will not pangs s you, like a
Jer 20: 5 s them, and carry them to
Jer 36:26 to s Baruch the scribe and
Ezek 14: 5 that I may s the house of
Dan 11:21 s the kingdom by intrigue
Mic 2: 2 also houses, and s them
Hab 1:10 up mounds of earth and s it
Zech 14:13 Everyone will s the hand of
Matt 21:38 kill him and s his inheritance
Matt 26:48 s Him
Matt 26:55 temple, and you did not s Me
Luke 20:20 they might s on His words
Luke 22:53 you did not try to s Me
John 10:39 they sought again to s Him
John 11:57 it, that they might s Him
Acts 12: 3 further to s Peter also

SEIZED (*see* SEIZE)
Gen 21:25 Abimelech's servants had s
Judg 3:28 s the fords of the Jordan
Judg 7:24 s the watering places as far
Judg 12: 5 The Gileadites s the fords of
1Sa 15:27 Saul s the edge of his robe,
1Ki 18:40 So they s them
2Ki 11:16 So they s her
2Ch 8: 3 went to Hamath Zobah and s it
2Ch 23:15 So they s her
Job 20:19 he has violently s a house
Is 33:14 has s the hypocrites
Jer 26: 8 and all the people s him,
Jer 37:13 he s Jeremiah the prophet,
Jer 37:14 So Irijah s Jeremiah and
Jer 49:24 to flee, and fear has s her
Jer 51:41 of the whole earth is s
Mic 4: 9 For pangs have s you like a
Matt 22: 6 And the rest s his servants,
Luke 8:29 For it had often s him, and he
Luke 8:37 for they were s with great
Acts 6:12 s him, and brought him to the
Acts 16:19 profit was gone, they s Paul
Acts 19:29 one accord, having s Gaius
Acts 21:30 s Paul, and dragged him out of
Acts 23:27 This man was s by the Jews
Acts 24: 6 we s him, and wanted to judge
Acts 26:21 the Jews s me in the temple

SEIZES (*see* SEIZE)
Deut 22:28 he s her and lies with her, and
Deut 25:11 and s him by the genitals,
Mark 9:18 And wherever he s him, he
Luke 9:39 And behold, a spirit s him

SELA
Judg 1:36 Ascent of Akrabbim, from S
2Ki 14: 7 took S by war, and called its
Is 16: 1 from S to the wilderness, to
Is 42:11 Let the inhabitants of S sing

SELDOM
Prov 25:17 S set foot in your neighbor's

SELECT (*see* SELECTED)
Gen 41:33 let Pharaoh s a discerning and
Ex 18:21 Moreover you shall s from all
Num 14: 4 Let us s a leader and return
Judg 20:15 numbered seven hundred s men
Judg 20:16 s men who were left-handed
Judg 20:34 ten thousand s men from all

SELECTED (*see* SELECT)
2Ch 2: 2 Solomon s seventy thousand

SELED
1Ch 2:30 The sons of Nadab were S and
1Ch 2:30 S died without children

SELEUCIA
Acts 13: 4 Spirit, they went down to S

SELF (*see* PREFACE)

SELF-CONDEMNED
Tit 3:11 is warped and sinning, being s

SELF-CONFIDENT
Prov 14:16 but a fool rages and is s

SELF-CONTROL
Acts 24:25 about righteousness, s, and
1Co 7: 5 you because of your lack of s
1Co 7: 9 but if they cannot exercise s
Gal 5:23 gentleness, s. Against such
1Ti 2:15 love, and holiness, with s
2Ti 3: 3 slanderers, without s,
2Pe 1: 6 to knowledge s
2Pe 1: 6 to s perseverance, to

SELF-CONTROLLED
Tit 1: 8 sober-minded, just, holy, s

SELF-IMPOSED
Col 2:23 of wisdom in s religion,

SELF-INDULGENCE
Matt 23:25 are full of extortion and s

SELFISH
2Co 12:20 s ambitions, backbitings,
Gal 5:20 s ambitions, dissensions,
Phil 1:16 preach Christ from s ambition
Phil 2: 3 through s ambition or conceit

SELF-SEEKING
Rom 2: 8 but to those who are s and do
Jas 3:14 and s in your hearts, do not
Jas 3:16 s exist, confusion and every

SELF-SUFFICIENCY
Job 20:22 In his s he will be in

SELF-WILL
Gen 49: 6 in their s they hamstrung an

SELF-WILLED
Tit 1: 7 as a steward of God, not s
2Pe 2:10 They are presumptuous, s

SELL (*see* SELLER, SELLING, SELLS, SOLD)
Gen 25:31 S me your birthright as of
Gen 37:27 Come and let us s him to the
Gen 47:22 they did not s their lands
Ex 21: 8 to s her to a foreign people
Ex 21:35 then they shall s the live ox
Lev 25:14 if you s anything to your
Lev 25:15 of crops he shall s to you
Deut 2:28 You shall s me food for
Deut 14:21 eat it, or you may s it to a
Deut 21:14 shall not s her for money
Judg 4: 9 for the LORD will s Sisera
2Ki 4: 7 s the oil and pay your debt
Neh 5: 8 will you even s your brethren
Neh 10:31 grain to s on the Sabbath day
Ps 44:12 You s Your people for naught,
Prov 23:23 Buy the truth, and do not s it
Ezek 30:12 s the land into the hand of
Ezek 48:14 they shall not s or exchange
Joel 3: 8 I will s your sons and your
Joel 3: 8 and they will s them to the
Amos 2: 6 because they s the righteous
Amos 8: 5 be past, that we may s grain
Amos 8: 6 even s the bad wheat
Zech 11: 5 those who s them say
Matt 19:21 s what you have and give to
Matt 25: 9 but go rather to those who s
Mark 10:21 s whatever you have and give
Luke 12:33 S what you have and give alms
Luke 18:22 S all that you have and
Luke 22:36 let him s his garment and buy
Jas 4:13 spend a year there, buy and s
Rev 13:17 and that no one may buy or s

SELLER (*see* SELL, SELLERS)
Is 24: 2 with the buyer, so with the s
Ezek 7:12 rejoice, nor the s mourn, for
Ezek 7:13 For the s shall not return to
Acts 16:14 She was a s of purple from

SELLERS (*see* SELLER)
Neh 13:20 and s of all kinds of wares

SELLING (*see* SELL)
Neh 13:15 which they were s provisions

SELLS (*see* SELL)
Ex 21: 7 if a man s his daughter to be
Ex 21:16 s him, or if he is found in
Ex 22: 1 and slaughters it or s it
Lev 25:16 for he s to you according to
Lev 25:29 And if a man s a house in a
Lev 25:39 s himself to you, you shall
Lev 25:47 s himself to the stranger or
Deut 24: 7 and mistreats him or s him
Prov 11:26 on the head of him who s it
Prov 31:24 s them, and supplies sashes
Nah 3: 4 who s nations through her
Matt 13:44 s all that he has and buys

SELVEDGE
Ex 26: 4 curtain on the s of one set
Ex 36:11 curtain on the s of one set

SEMACHIAH
1Ch 26: 7 Elihu and S were able men

SEMEI (*see* SHEMAAH)
Luke 3:26 of Mattathiah, the son of S

SEMEN
Lev 15:16 any man has an emission of s
Lev 15:17 leather on which there is s
Lev 15:18 and there is an emission of s
Lev 15:32 and for him who emits s and is
Lev 22: 4 who has had an emission of s

SENAAH (*see* HASSENAAH)
Ezra 2:35 the people of S, three
Neh 7:38 the children of S, three

SEND (*see* SENDING, SENDS, SENT)
Gen 18:16 them to s them on the way
Gen 24: 7 He will s His angel before
Gen 24:40 will s His angel with you and
Gen 24:54 S me away to my master
Gen 24:56 s me away so that I may go to
Gen 27:45 then I will s and bring you
Gen 30:25 S me away, that I may go to
Gen 37:13 Come, I will s you to them
Gen 38:17 I will s you a young goat
Gen 38:17 me a pledge till you s it
Gen 42: 4 But Jacob did not s Joseph's
Gen 42:16 S one of you, and let him
Gen 43: 4 If you s our brother with us,
Gen 43: 5 But if you will not s him
Gen 43: 8 S the lad with me, and we will
Ex 3:10 I will s you to Pharaoh that
Ex 4:13 Lord, please s by the hand of
Ex 4:13 of whomever else You may s

Ex 7: 2 that he must s the children
Ex 8:21 I will s swarms of flies on
Ex 9:14 for at this time I will s all
Ex 9:19 Therefore s now and gather
Ex 12:33 that they might s them out of
Ex 23:20 I s an Angel before you to
Ex 23:27 I will s My fear before you,
Ex 23:28 I will s hornets before you,
Ex 33: 2 I will s My Angel before you,
Ex 33:12 know whom You will s with me
Lev 16:21 and shall s it away into the
Lev 26:22 I will also s wild beasts
Lev 26:25 I will s pestilence among you
Lev 26:36 I will s faintness into their
Num 13: 2 S men to spy out the land of
Num 13: 2 fathers you shall s a man
Num 22:37 Did I not earnestly s to you
Num 31: 4 Israel you shall s to the war
Deut 1:22 Let us s men before us, and
Deut 7:20 the LORD your God will s the
Deut 11:15 I will s grass in your fields
Deut 15:13 when you s him away free from
Deut 15:18 you s him away free from you
Deut 19:12 elders of his city shall s
Deut 28:20 The LORD will s on you
Deut 28:48 the LORD will s against you
Deut 32:24 I will also s against them
Josh 1:16 wherever you s us we will go
Josh 18: 4 each tribe, and I will s them
1Sa 5:11 S away the ark of the God of
1Sa 6: 2 we should s it to its place
1Sa 6: 3 If you s away the ark of the
1Sa 6: 3 of Israel, do not s it empty
1Sa 6: 8 Then s it away, and let it go
1Sa 9:16 about this time I will s you
1Sa 9:26 that I may s you on your way
1Sa 11: 3 that we may s messengers to
1Sa 12:17 LORD, and He will s thunder
1Sa 16:11 S and bring him
1Sa 16:19 S me your son David, who is
1Sa 20:12 David, and I do not s to you
1Sa 20:13 s you away, that you may go
1Sa 20:21 and there I will s a lad,
1Sa 20:31 Now therefore, s and bring him
1Sa 21: 2 the business on which I s you
2Sa 11: 6 S me Uriah the Hittite
2Sa 14:29 to s him to the king, but he
2Sa 14:32 so that I may s you to the
2Sa 15:36 and by them you shall s me
2Sa 17:16 s quickly and tell David,
1Ki 8:44 enemy, wherever You s them
1Ki 18: 1 I will s rain on the earth
1Ki 18:19 Now therefore, s and gather
1Ki 20: 6 but I will s my servants to
1Ki 20:34 I will s you away with this
2Ki 2:16 You shall not s anyone
2Ki 2:17 he said, "S them out
2Ki 4:22 Please s me one of the young
2Ki 5: 5 I will s a letter to the king
2Ki 6:13 see where he is, that I may s
2Ki 7:13 so let us s them and see
2Ki 9:17 s him to meet them, and let
2Ki 15:37 to s Rezin king of Syria and
2Ki 17:27 S there one of the priests
2Ki 19: 7 Surely I will s a spirit upon
1Ch 13: 2 let us s out to our brethren
2Ch 2: 7 Therefore s me at once a man
2Ch 2: 8 Also s me cedar and cypress and
2Ch 2:15 let him s to his servants
2Ch 6:27 s rain on Your land which You
2Ch 6:34 enemies, wherever You s them
2Ch 7:13 or s pestilence among My
Ezra 5:17 and let the king s us his
Neh 2: 5 I ask that you s me to Judah
Neh 2: 6 it pleased the king to s me
Neh 8:10 s portions to those for whom
Neh 8:12 to s portions and rejoice
Job 1: 4 his appointed day, and would s
Job 1: 5 course, that Job would s and
Job 14:20 his countenance and s him away
Job 21:11 They s forth their little
Job 38:35 Can you s out lightnings,
Ps 20: 2 May He s you help from the
Ps 43: 3 Oh, s out Your light and Your
Ps 57: 3 He shall s from heaven and
Ps 57: 3 God shall s forth His mercy
Ps 104:30 You s forth Your Spirit, they
Ps 110: 2 The LORD shall s the rod of
Ps 118:25 I pray, s now prosperity
Prov 10:26 sluggard to those who s him
Prov 22:21 truth to those who s to you
Prov 25:13 messenger to those who s him
Is 6: 8 Whom shall I s, and who will
Is 6: 8 I said, "Here am I! S me."
Is 10: 6 I will s him against an
Is 10:16 will s leanness among his fat
Is 16: 1 S the lamb to the ruler of
Is 19:20 He will s them a Savior and a
Is 32:20 who s out freely the feet of
Is 37: 7 Surely I will s a spirit upon
Is 42:19 deaf as My messenger whom I s
Is 43:14 your sake I will s to Babylon
Is 66:19 I will s to the nations
Jer 1: 7 go to all to whom I s you
Jer 2:10 see, s to Kedar and consider
Jer 8:17 I will s serpents among you,
Jer 9:16 I will s a sword after them
Jer 9:17 s for skillful wailing women,
Jer 14:15 in My name, whom I did not s
Jer 16:16 I will s for many fishermen,
Jer 16:16 I will s for many hunters
Jer 23:32 Yet I did not s them or
Jer 24:10 And I will s the sword, the
Jer 25: 9 behold, I will s and take all
Jer 25:15 the nations, to whom I s you
Jer 25:16 that I will s among them
Jer 25:27 which I will s among you
Jer 27: 3 s them to the king of Edom,
Jer 29:17 I will s on them the sword,
Jer 29:31 S to all those in captivity,
Jer 42: 6 LORD our God to whom we s you
Jer 43:10 Behold, I will s and bring
Jer 48:12 LORD, "That I shall s him
Jer 49:37 I will s the sword after them
Jer 51: 2 I will s winnowers to Babylon
Lam 4:22 He will no longer s you into
Ezek 5:16 When I s against them the
Ezek 5:16 which I will s to destroy you
Ezek 5:17 So I will s against you
Ezek 7: 3 I will s My anger against you
Ezek 14:13 s famine on it, and cut off
Ezek 14:19 Or if I s a pestilence into
Ezek 14:21 more it shall be when I s My
Ezek 28:23 For I will s pestilence upon
Ezek 39: 6 I will s fire on Magog and on
Hos 8:14 but I will s fire upon his
Joel 2:19 I will s you grain and new
Amos 1: 4 But I will s a fire into the
Amos 1: 7 But I will s a fire upon the
Amos 1:10 But I will s a fire upon the
Amos 1:12 But I will s a fire upon
Amos 2: 2 But I will s a fire upon Moab
Amos 2: 5 but I will s a fire upon
Amos 5:27 Therefore I will s you into
Amos 8:11 That I will s a famine on the
Zech 5: 4 I will s out the curse,"
Mal 2: 2 I will s a curse upon you, and
Mal 3: 1 I s My messenger, and he will
Mal 4: 5 I will s you Elijah the
Matt 9:38 to s out laborers into His
Matt 10:16 I s you out as sheep in the
Matt 11:10 I s My messenger before Your
Matt 13:41 of Man will s out His angels
Matt 14:15 S the multitudes away, that
Matt 15:23 S her away, for she cries out
Matt 15:32 want to s them away hungry
Matt 21: 3 and immediately he will s them
Matt 23:34 I s you prophets, wise men,
Matt 24:31 He will s His angels with a
Mark 1: 2 I s My messenger before Your
Mark 3:14 that He might s them out to
Mark 5:10 not s them out of the country
Mark 5:12 S us to the swine, that we
Mark 6: 7 began to s them out two by
Mark 6:36 S them away, that they may go
Mark 8: 3 if I s them away hungry to
Mark 11: 3 immediately he will s it here
Mark 13:27 And then He will s His angels
Luke 7:27 I s My messenger before Your
Luke 9:12 S the multitude away, that
Luke 10: 2 to s out laborers into His
Luke 10: 3 I s you out as lambs among
Luke 11:49 I will s them prophets and
Luke 12:49 I came to s fire on the earth
Luke 16:24 s Lazarus that he may dip the
Luke 16:27 that you would s him to my
Luke 20:13 I will s my beloved son
Luke 21:16 they will s some of you to
Luke 24:49 I s the Promise of My Father
John 3:17 For God did not s His Son
John 13:20 whomever I s receives Me
John 14:26 the Father will s in My name
John 15:26 whom I shall s to you from
John 16: 7 I depart, I will s Him to you
John 20:21 has sent Me, I also s you
Acts 3:20 that He may s Jesus Christ,
Acts 7:34 come, I will s you to Egypt
Acts 10: 5 Now s men to Joppa
Acts 10: 5 s for Simon whose surname is
Acts 10:32 S therefore to Joppa and call
Acts 11:13 S men to Joppa, and call for
Acts 11:29 determined to s relief to the
Acts 15:22 to s chosen men of their own
Acts 15:25 to s chosen men to you with
Acts 22:21 for I will s you far from
Acts 25:21 till I could s him to Caesar
Acts 25:25 Augustus, I decided to s him
Acts 25:27 unreasonable to s a prisoner
Acts 26:17 Gentiles, to whom I now s you
1Co 1:17 did not s me to baptize, but
1Co 16: 3 I will s to bear your gift to
1Co 16: 6 you, that you may s me on my
1Co 16:11 But s him on his journey in
Phil 2:19 to s Timothy to you shortly
Phil 2:23 I hope to s him at once, as
Phil 2:25 to s to you Epaphroditus, my
2Th 2:11 will s them strong delusion
Tit 3:12 When I s Artemas to you, or
Tit 3:13 S Zenas the lawyer and Apollos
Jas 3:11 Does a spring s forth fresh
3Jn 6 If you s them forward on
Rev 1:11 s it to the seven churches
Rev 11:10 and s gifts to one another,

SENDING (*see* SEND)
1Sa 16: 1 I am s you to Jesse the
2Sa 13:16 This evil of s me away is
2Ki 1: 6 s to inquire of Baal-Zebub
2Ch 36:15 and s them, because He had
Esth 9:19 for s presents to one another
Esth 9:22 of s presents to one another
Ps 78:49 By s angels of destruction
Is 27: 8 by s it away, you contended
Jer 7:25 rising up early and s them
Jer 25: 4 and s them, but you have not
Jer 26: 5 and s them (but you have not
Jer 29:19 rising up early and s them
Jer 35:15 s them, saying, 'Turn now
Jer 44: 4 early and s them, saying,
Ezek 2: 3 I am s you to the children of
Ezek 2: 4 I am s you to them, and you
Ezek 17:15 by s his ambassadors to Egypt
Rom 8: 3 God did by s His own Son in
Col 4: 8 I am s him to you for this
Phm 12 I am s him back

SENDS (*see* SEND)
Deut 24: 1 and s her out of his house,
Deut 24: 3 s her out of his house, or if
1Ki 17:14 the LORD s rain on the earth
2Ki 5: 7 that this man s a man to me
Job 5:10 and s waters on the fields
Job 12:15 if He s them out, they
Job 37: 3 He s it forth under the whole
Ps 68:33 He s out His voice, a mighty
Ps 104:10 He s the springs into the
Ps 147:15 He s out His command to the
Ps 147:18 He s out His word and melts
Prov 26: 6 He who s a message by the
Song 1:12 my spikenard s forth its
Is 18: 2 which s ambassadors by sea,
Jer 42: 5 the LORD your God s us by you
Matt 5:45 s rain on the just and on the
Matt 12:20 till He s forth justice to
Luke 14:32 he s a delegation and asks

SENEH
1Sa 14: 4 and the name of the other S

SENIR
Deut 3: 9 and the Amorites call it S)
1Ch 5:23 to Baal Hermon, that is, to S
Song 4: 8 of Amana, from the top of S
Ezek 27: 5 planks of fir trees from S

SENNACHERIB
2Ki 18:13 S king of Assyria came up
2Ki 19:16 and hear the words of S, which
2Ki 19:20 S king of Assyria I have
2Ki 19:36 So S king of Assyria departed
2Ch 32: 1 S king of Assyria came and
2Ch 32: 2 Hezekiah saw that S had come
2Ch 32: 9 After this S king of Assyria

2Ch 32:10 Thus says S king of Assyria
2Ch 32:22 hand of S the king of Assyria
Is 36: 1 S king of Assyria came up
Is 37:17 and hear all the words of S
Is 37:21 Me against S king of Assyria
Is 37:37 So S king of Assyria departed

SENSE (*see* SENSED, SENSELESS, SENSES, SENSIBLY)
Neh 8: 8 and they gave the s, and helped
Hos 7:11 like a silly dove, without s
Heb 11:19 him in a figurative s

SENSED (*see* SENSE)
Acts 27:27 about midnight the sailors s

SENSELESS (*see* SENSE)
Ps 49:10 the s person perish, And leave
Ps 92: 6 A s man does not know, Nor
Ps 94: 8 you s among the people

SENSES (*see* SENSE)
2Ti 2:26 that they may come to their s
Heb 5:14 s exercised to discern both

SENSIBLY (*see* SENSE)
Prov 26:16 seven men who can answer s

SENSITIVE (*see* SENSITIVITY)
Deut 28:54 The man among you who is s

SENSITIVITY (*see* SENSITIVE)
Deut 28:56 of her delicateness and s,

SENSUAL
Jas 3:15 from above, but is earthly, s
Jude 19 These are s persons, who

SENT (*see* SEND)
Gen 3:23 therefore the LORD God s him
Gen 8: 7 Then he s out a raven, which
Gen 8: 8 He also s out from himself a
Gen 8:10 again he s the dove out from
Gen 8:12 s out the dove, which did not
Gen 12:20 they s him away, with his
Gen 19:13 the LORD has s us to destroy
Gen 19:29 s Lot out of the midst of the
Gen 20: 2 And Abimelech king of Gerar s
Gen 21:14 boy to Hagar, and s her away
Gen 24:59 So they s away Rebekah their
Gen 25: 6 living he s them eastward
Gen 26:27 me and have s me away from you
Gen 26:29 and have s you away in peace
Gen 26:31 Isaac s them away, and they
Gen 27:42 So she s and called Jacob her
Gen 28: 5 So Isaac s Jacob away, and he
Gen 28: 6 s him away to Padan Aram to
Gen 31: 4 So Jacob s and called Rachel
Gen 31:27 for I might have s you away
Gen 31:42 have s me away empty-handed
Gen 32: 3 Then Jacob s messengers
Gen 32: 5 I have s to tell my lord,
Gen 32:18 a present s to my lord Esau
Gen 32:23 s them over the brook
Gen 32:23 and s over what he had
Gen 37:14 So he s him out of the
Gen 37:32 Then they s the tunic of many
Gen 38:20 Judah s the young goat by the
Gen 38:23 for I s this young goat and
Gen 38:25 she s to her father-in-law,
Gen 41: 8 spirit was troubled, and he s
Gen 41:14 Then Pharaoh s and called
Gen 44: 3 dawned, the men were s away
Gen 45: 5 for God s me before you to
Gen 45: 7 And God s me before you to
Gen 45: 8 it was not you who s me here
Gen 45:23 And he s to his father these
Gen 45:24 So he s his brothers away, and
Gen 45:27 Joseph had s to carry him
Gen 46: 5 Pharaoh had s to carry him
Gen 46:28 Then he s Judah before him to
Gen 50:16 So they s messengers to
Ex 2: 5 she s her maid to get it
Ex 3:12 sign to you that I have s you
Ex 3:13 your fathers has s me to you
Ex 3:14 Israel, 'I AM has s me to you
Ex 3:15 God of Jacob, has s me to you
Ex 4:28 of the LORD who had s him
Ex 5:22 Why is it You have s me
Ex 7:16 the Hebrews has s me to you
Ex 9: 7 Then Pharaoh s, and indeed,
Ex 9:23 and the LORD s thunder and hail
Ex 9:27 And Pharaoh s and called for
Ex 15: 7 You s forth Your wrath which
Ex 18: 2 wife, after he had s her back
Ex 24: 5 Then he s young men of the
Num 13: 3 So Moses s them from the
Num 13:16 Moses s to spy out the land
Num 13:17 So Moses s them to spy out
Num 13:27 to the land where you s us
Num 14:36 the men whom Moses s to spy
Num 16:12 Moses s to call Dathan and
Num 16:28 know that the LORD has s me
Num 16:29 then the LORD has not s me
Num 20:14 Now Moses s messengers from
Num 20:16 s the Angel and brought us up
Num 21: 6 So the LORD s fiery serpents
Num 21:21 Then Israel s messengers to
Num 21:32 Then Moses s to spy out Jazer
Num 22: 5 Then he s messengers to
Num 22:10 of Moab, has s to me, saying,
Num 22:15 Then Balak again s princes
Num 22:40 he s some to Balaam and to the
Num 24:12 messengers whom you s to me
Num 31: 6 Then Moses s them to the war,
Num 31: 6 he s them to the war with
Num 32: 8 I s them away from Kadesh
Deut 2:26 And I s messengers from the
Deut 9:23 when the LORD s you from
Deut 34:11 wonders which the LORD s him
Josh 2: 1 Nun s out two men from Acacia
Josh 2: 3 king of Jericho s to Rahab
Josh 2:21 And she s them away, and they
Josh 6:17 hid the messengers that we s
Josh 6:25 Joshua s to spy out Jericho
Josh 7: 2 Now Joshua s men from Jericho
Josh 7:22 So Joshua s messengers, and
Josh 8: 3 valor and s them away by night
Josh 8: 9 Joshua therefore s them out
Josh 10: 3 king of Jerusalem s to Hoham
Josh 10: 6 the men of Gibeon s to Joshua
Josh 11: 1 that he s to Jobab king of
Josh 14: 7 the servant of the LORD s me
Josh 14:11 on the day that Moses s me
Josh 22: 6 s them away, and they went to
Josh 22: 7 when Joshua s them away to
Josh 22:13 s Phinehas the son of Eleazar
Josh 24: 5 Also I s Moses and Aaron, and
Josh 24: 9 make war against Israel, and s
Josh 24:12 I s the hornet before you
Judg 1:23 s men to spy out Bethel
Judg 3:15 s tribute to Eglon king of
Judg 3:18 he s away the people who had
Judg 4: 6 Then she s and called for
Judg 5:15 so was Barak s into the
Judg 6: 8 that the LORD s a prophet to
Judg 6:14 Have I not s you
Judg 6:35 he s messengers throughout
Judg 6:35 He also s messengers to Asher
Judg 7: 8 he s away all the rest of
Judg 7:24 Then Gideon s messengers
Judg 9:23 God s a spirit of ill will
Judg 9:31 he s messengers to Abimelech
Judg 11:12 Now Jephthah s messengers to
Judg 11:14 So Jephthah again s
Judg 11:17 Then Israel s messengers to
Judg 11:17 they s to the king of Moab
Judg 11:19 Then Israel s messengers to
Judg 11:28 words which Jephthah s him
Judg 11:38 he s her away for two months
Judg 13: 8 whom You s come to us again
Judg 16:18 told her all his heart, she s
Judg 18: 2 So the children of Dan s five
Judg 19:29 and s her throughout all the
Judg 20: 6 and s her throughout all the
Judg 20:12 s men through all the tribe
Judg 21:10 So the congregation s out
Judg 21:13 s word to the children of
1Sa 4: 4 So the people s to Shiloh
1Sa 5: 8 Therefore they s and gathered
1Sa 5:10 Therefore they s the ark of
1Sa 5:11 So they s and gathered
1Sa 6:21 So they s messengers to the
1Sa 10:25 Samuel s all the people away,
1Sa 11: 7 s them throughout all the
1Sa 12: 8 LORD, then the LORD s Moses
1Sa 12:11 the LORD s Jerubbaal, Bedan,
1Sa 12:18 LORD, and the LORD s thunder
1Sa 13: 2 rest of the people he s away
1Sa 15: 1 The LORD s me to anoint you
1Sa 15:18 Now the LORD s you on a
1Sa 15:20 on which the LORD s me, and
1Sa 16:12 So he s and brought him in
1Sa 16:19 Therefore Saul s messengers
1Sa 16:20 s them by his son David to
1Sa 16:22 Then Saul s to Jesse, saying,
1Sa 17:31 and he s for him
1Sa 18: 5 went out wherever Saul s him
1Sa 19:11 Saul also s messengers to
1Sa 19:14 So when Saul s messengers to
1Sa 19:15 Then Saul s the messengers
1Sa 19:17 s my enemy away, so that he
1Sa 19:20 Then Saul s messengers to
1Sa 19:21 he s other messengers, and
1Sa 19:21 Then Saul s messengers again
1Sa 20:22 for the LORD has s you away
1Sa 22:11 Then the king s to call
1Sa 25: 5 David s ten young men
1Sa 25:14 David s messengers from the
1Sa 25:25 men of my lord whom you s
1Sa 25:32 who s you this day to meet me
1Sa 25:39 And David s and proposed to
1Sa 25:40 David s us to you, to ask you
1Sa 26: 4 David therefore s out spies
1Sa 30:26 he s some of the spoil to the
1Sa 31: 9 s word throughout the land of
2Sa 2: 5 So David s messengers to the
2Sa 3:12 Then Abner s messengers on
2Sa 3:14 So David s messengers to
2Sa 3:15 And Ishbosheth s and took her
2Sa 3:21 So David s Abner away, and
2Sa 3:22 Hebron, for he had s him away
2Sa 3:23 he s him away, and he has gone
2Sa 3:24 why is it that you s him away
2Sa 3:26 he s messengers after Abner,
2Sa 5:11 of Tyre s messengers to David
2Sa 8:10 then Toi s Joram his son to
2Sa 9: 5 Then King David s and brought
2Sa 10: 2 So David s by the hand of
2Sa 10: 3 he has s comforters to you
2Sa 10: 3 Has David not rather s his
2Sa 10: 4 buttocks, and s them away
2Sa 10: 5 he s to meet them, because
2Sa 10: 6 David, the people of Ammon s
2Sa 10: 7 he s Joab and all the army of
2Sa 10:16 Then Hadadezer s and brought
2Sa 11: 1 to battle, that David s Joab
2Sa 11: 3 So David s and inquired about
2Sa 11: 4 Then David s messengers, and
2Sa 11: 5 so she s and told David, and
2Sa 11: 6 Then David s to Joab, saying,
2Sa 11: 6 And Joab s Uriah to David
2Sa 11:14 s it by the hand of Uriah
2Sa 11:18 Then Joab s and told David all
2Sa 11:22 all that Joab had s by him
2Sa 11:27 mourning was over, David s
2Sa 12: 1 Then the LORD s Nathan to
2Sa 12:25 And He s word by the hand of
2Sa 12:27 Joab s messengers to David,
2Sa 13: 7 David s home to Tamar, saying
2Sa 14: 2 Joab s to Tekoa and brought
2Sa 14:29 Therefore Absalom s for Joab
2Sa 14:29 when he s again the second
2Sa 14:32 I s to you, saying, "Come
2Sa 15:10 Then Absalom s spies
2Sa 15:12 Then Absalom s for Ahithophel
2Sa 18: 2 Then David s out one third of
2Sa 18:29 When Joab s the king's
2Sa 19:11 Then King David s to Zadok
2Sa 19:14 so that they s this word to
2Sa 22:15 He s out arrows and scattered
2Sa 22:17 He s from above, He took me,
2Sa 24:13 take back to Him who s me
2Sa 24:15 So the LORD s a plague upon
1Ki 1:44 The king has s with him Zadok
1Ki 1:53 So King Solomon s them to
1Ki 2:25 So King Solomon s by the hand
1Ki 2:29 Then Solomon s Benaiah the
1Ki 2:36 Then the king s and called for
1Ki 2:42 Then the king s and called for
1Ki 5: 1 Now Hiram king of Tyre s his
1Ki 5: 2 Then Solomon s to Hiram,
1Ki 5: 8 Then Hiram s to Solomon,
1Ki 5: 8 the message which you s me
1Ki 5:14 he s them to Lebanon, ten
1Ki 7:13 Now King Solomon s and
1Ki 8:66 day he s the people away
1Ki 9:14 Then Hiram s the king one
1Ki 9:27 Then Hiram s his servants
1Ki 12: 3 that they s and called him
1Ki 12:18 Then King Rehoboam s
1Ki 12:20 they s for him and called him
1Ki 14: 6 For I have been s to you with
1Ki 15:18 King Asa s them to Ben-Hadad
1Ki 15:19 I have s you a present of

1Ki 15:20 s the captains of his armies
1Ki 18:10 not s someone to hunt for you
1Ki 18:20 So Ahab s for all the
1Ki 19: 2 Then Jezebel s a messenger to
1Ki 20: 2 Then he s messengers into the
1Ki 20: 5 Indeed I have s to you,
1Ki 20: 7 for he s to me for my wives,
1Ki 20: 9 All that you s for to your
1Ki 20:10 Then Ben-Hadad s to him and
1Ki 20:17 Ben-Hadad s out a patrol, and
1Ki 20:34 treaty with him and s him away
1Ki 21: 8 s the letters to the elders
1Ki 21:11 did as Jezebel had s to them
1Ki 21:11 which she had s to them
1Ki 21:14 Then they s to Jezebel,
2Ki 1: 2 so he s messengers and said to
2Ki 1: 6 return to the king who s you
2Ki 1: 9 Then the king s to him a
2Ki 1:11 Then he s to him another
2Ki 1:13 he s a third captain of fifty
2Ki 1:16 Because you have s messengers
2Ki 2: 2 LORD has s me on to Bethel
2Ki 2: 4 LORD has s me on to Jericho
2Ki 2: 6 for the LORD has s me on to
2Ki 2:17 Therefore they s fifty men
2Ki 3: 7 and s to Jehoshaphat king of
2Ki 5: 6 you, that I have s Naaman my
2Ki 5: 8 that he s to the king, saying
2Ki 5:10 Elisha s a messenger to him,
2Ki 5:22 My master has s me, saying
2Ki 6: 9 the man of God s to the king
2Ki 6:10 s someone to the place of
2Ki 6:14 Therefore he s horses and
2Ki 6:23 he s them away and they went
2Ki 6:32 the king s a man ahead of him
2Ki 6:32 has s someone to take away my
2Ki 7:14 and the king s them in the
2Ki 8: 9 king of Syria has s me to you
2Ki 9:19 Then he s out a second
2Ki 10: 1 s them to Samaria, to the
2Ki 10: 5 the sons, s to Jehu, saying,
2Ki 10: 7 and s them to him at Jezreel
2Ki 10:21 Then Jehu s throughout all
2Ki 11: 4 the seventh year Jehoiada s
2Ki 12:18 and s them to Hazael king of
2Ki 14: 8 Then Amaziah s messengers to
2Ki 14: 9 Jehoash king of Israel s to
2Ki 14: 9 s to the cedar that was in
2Ki 14:19 but they s after him to
2Ki 16: 7 So Ahaz s messengers to
2Ki 16: 8 s it as a present to the king
2Ki 16:10 King Ahaz s to Urijah the
2Ki 16:11 King Ahaz had s from Damascus
2Ki 17: 4 for he had s messengers to So
2Ki 17:13 and which I s to you by My
2Ki 17:25 the LORD s lions among them
2Ki 17:26 He has s lions among them
2Ki 18:14 s to the king of Assyria at
2Ki 18:17 king of Assyria s the Tartan
2Ki 18:27 Has my master s me to your
2Ki 19: 2 Then he s Eliakim, who was
2Ki 19: 4 the king of Assyria has s to
2Ki 19: 9 So he again s messengers to
2Ki 19:16 which he has s to reproach
2Ki 19:20 the son of Amoz s to Hezekiah
2Ki 20:12 s letters and a present to
2Ki 22: 3 that the king s Shaphan the
2Ki 22:15 Tell the man who s you to me
2Ki 22:18 who s you to inquire of the
2Ki 23: 1 Then the king s them to
2Ki 23:16 And he s and took the bones out
2Ki 24: 2 And the LORD s against him
2Ki 24: 2 He s them against Judah to
1Ch 8: 8 after he had s away Hushim
1Ch 10: 9 s word throughout the land of
1Ch 12:19 s him away by counsel, saying
1Ch 14: 1 of Tyre s messengers to David
1Ch 18:10 he s Hadoram his son to King
1Ch 19: 2 So David s messengers to
1Ch 19: 3 he has s comforters to you
1Ch 19: 4 buttocks, and s them away
1Ch 19: 5 he s to meet them, because
1Ch 19: 6 and the people of Ammon s a
1Ch 19: 8 he s Joab and all the army of
1Ch 19:16 they s messengers and brought
1Ch 21:12 take back to Him who s me
1Ch 21:14 So the LORD s a plague upon
1Ch 21:15 God s an angel to Jerusalem
2Ch 2: 3 Then Solomon s to Hiram king
2Ch 2: 3 s him cedars to build himself
2Ch 2:11 which he s to Solomon
2Ch 2:13 now I have s a skillful man,
2Ch 7:10 he s the people away to their
2Ch 8:18 Hiram s him ships by the hand
2Ch 10: 3 Then they s for him and called
2Ch 10:18 Then King Rehoboam s
2Ch 16: 2 s to Ben-Hadad king of Syria,
2Ch 16: 3 I have s you silver and gold
2Ch 16: 4 s the captains of his armies
2Ch 17: 7 of his reign he s his leaders
2Ch 17: 8 And with them he s Levites
2Ch 24:19 Yet He s prophets to them, to
2Ch 24:23 s all their spoil to the king
2Ch 25:15 He s him a prophet who said
2Ch 25:17 and s to Joash the son of
2Ch 25:18 Joash king of Israel s to
2Ch 25:18 s to the cedar that was in
2Ch 25:27 but they s after him to
2Ch 28:16 s to the kings of Assyria to
2Ch 30: 1 Hezekiah s to all Israel and
2Ch 32: 9 s his servants to Jerusalem
2Ch 32:21 Then the LORD s an angel who
2Ch 32:31 whom they s to him to inquire
2Ch 34: 8 he s Shaphan the son of
2Ch 34:23 Tell the man who s you to Me
2Ch 34:26 who s you to inquire of the
2Ch 34:29 Then the king s and gathered
2Ch 35:21 But he s messengers to him,
2Ch 36:15 s warnings to them by His
Ezra 4:11 of the letter that they s him
Ezra 4:14 therefore we have s and
Ezra 4:17 Then the king s an answer
Ezra 4:18 The letter which you s to us
Ezra 5: 6 of the letter that Tattenai s
Ezra 5: 7 They s a letter to him, in
Ezra 6:13 to what King Darius had s
Ezra 7:14 you are being s by the king
Ezra 8:16 Then I s for Eliezer, Ariel,
Neh 2: 9 Now the king had s captains
Neh 6: 2 Sanballat and Geshem s to me
Neh 6: 3 So I s messengers to them,
Neh 6: 4 But they s me this message
Neh 6: 5 Then Sanballat s his servant
Neh 6: 8 Then I s to him, saying, "No
Neh 6:12 that God had not s him at all
Neh 6:17 s many letters to Tobiah, and
Neh 6:19 Tobiah s letters to frighten
Esth 1:22 Then he s letters to all the
Esth 3:13 And the letters were s by
Esth 4: 4 Then she s garments to clothe
Esth 5:10 himself and went home, and he s
Esth 8:10 and s letters by couriers on
Esth 9:20 s letters to all the Jews who
Esth 9:30 Mordecai s letters to all the
Job 22: 9 You have s widows away empty,
Ps 18:14 He s out His arrows and
Ps 18:16 He s from above, He took me
Ps 68: 9 s a plentiful rain, Whereby
Ps 77:17 The skies s out a sound
Ps 78:25 He s them food to the full
Ps 78:45 He s swarms of flies among
Ps 80:11 She s out her boughs to the
Ps 105:17 He s a man before them
Ps 105:20 The king s and released him,
Ps 105:26 He s Moses His servant, And
Ps 105:28 He s darkness, and made it
Ps 106:15 But s leanness into their
Ps 107:20 He s His word and healed them,
Ps 111: 9 He has s redemption to His
Ps 135: 9 He s signs and wonders into
Prov 9: 3 She has s out her maidens,
Prov 17:11 will be s against him
Is 9: 8 The LORD s a word against
Is 20: 1 the king of Assyria s him
Is 36: 2 Then the king of Assyria s
Is 36:12 Has my master s me to your
Is 37: 2 Then he s Eliakim, who was
Is 37: 4 the king of Assyria has s to
Is 37: 9 he s messengers to Hezekiah,
Is 37:17 who has s to reproach the
Is 37:21 the son of Amoz s to Hezekiah
Is 39: 1 s letters and a present to
Is 48:16 GOD and His Spirit have s Me
Is 55:11 in the thing for which I s it
Is 57: 9 you s your messengers far off
Is 61: 1 He has s Me to heal the
Jer 7:25 I have even s to you all My
Jer 14: 3 Their nobles have s their
Jer 14:14 I have not s them, commanded
Jer 19:14 LORD had s him to prophesy
Jer 21: 1 s to him Pashhur the son of
Jer 23:21 I have not s these prophets,
Jer 23:38 and I have s to you, saying,
Jer 24: 5 whom I have s out of this
Jer 25: 4 the LORD has s to you all His
Jer 25:17 to whom the LORD had s me
Jer 26: 5 the prophets whom I s to you
Jer 26:12 The LORD s me to prophesy
Jer 26:15 has s me to you to speak all
Jer 26:22 the king s men to Egypt
Jer 27:15 for I have not s them," says
Jer 28: 9 one whom the LORD has truly s
Jer 28:15 the LORD has not s you, but
Jer 29: 1 s from Jerusalem to the
Jer 29: 3 The letter was s by the hand
Jer 29: 3 king of Judah s to Babylon
Jer 29: 9 I have not s them, says the
Jer 29:19 LORD, which I s to them by My
Jer 29:20 whom I have s from Jerusalem
Jer 29:25 You have s letters in your
Jer 29:28 For he has s to us in Babylon
Jer 29:31 to you, and I have not s him
Jer 35:15 I have also s to you all My
Jer 36:14 Therefore all the princes s
Jer 36:21 So the king s Jehudi to bring
Jer 37: 3 Zedekiah the king s Jehucal
Jer 37: 7 who s you to Me to inquire of
Jer 37:17 then Zedekiah the king s and
Jer 38:14 Then Zedekiah the king s and
Jer 39:13 of the guard s Nebushasban
Jer 39:14 then they s someone to take
Jer 40:14 has s Ishmael the son of
Jer 42: 9 to whom you s me to present
Jer 42:20 you s me to the LORD your God
Jer 42:21 which He has s you by me
Jer 43: 1 their God had s him to them
Jer 43: 2 our God has not s you to say
Jer 44: 4 However I have s to you all
Jer 49:14 has been s to the nations
Lam 1:13 From above He has s fire into
Ezek 3: 5 For you are not s to a people
Ezek 3: 6 had I s you to them, they
Ezek 13: 6 But the LORD has not s them
Ezek 20:28 There they also s up their
Ezek 23:16 and s messengers to them in
Ezek 23:40 Furthermore you s for men to
Ezek 23:40 to whom a messenger was s
Ezek 31: 4 s out rivulets to all the
Ezek 31: 5 of water, as it s them out
Ezek 39:28 who s them into captivity
Dan 3: 2 King Nebuchadnezzar s word to
Dan 3:28 who s His Angel and delivered
Dan 5:24 of the hand were s from Him
Dan 6:22 My God s His angel and shut
Dan 10:11 for I have now been s to you
Hos 5:13 to Assyria and s to King Jareb
Joel 2:25 army which I s among you
Amos 4:10 I s among you a plague after
Amos 7:10 the priest of Bethel s to
Obad 1 has been s among the nations
Jon 1: 4 But the LORD s out a great
Mic 6: 4 I s before you Moses, Aaron,
Hag 1:12 the LORD their God had s him
Zech 1:10 the LORD has s to walk to
Zech 2: 8 He s Me after glory, to the
Zech 2: 9 the LORD of hosts has s Me
Zech 2:11 LORD of hosts has s Me to you
Zech 4: 9 LORD of hosts has s Me to you
Zech 6:15 LORD of hosts has s Me to you
Zech 7: 2 when the people s Sherezer
Zech 7:12 s by His Spirit through the
Mal 2: 4 s this commandment to you
Matt 2: 8 he s them to Bethlehem and
Matt 2:16 he s forth and put to death
Matt 10: 5 These twelve Jesus s out and
Matt 10:40 Me receives Him who s Me
Matt 11: 2 he s two of his disciples
Matt 13:36 Then Jesus s the multitude
Matt 14:10 So he s and had John beheaded
Matt 14:22 while He s the multitudes
Matt 14:23 when He had s the multitudes
Matt 14:35 Him, they s out into all that
Matt 15:24 I was not s except to the
Matt 15:39 He s away the multitude, got
Matt 20: 2 he s them into his vineyard
Matt 21: 1 then Jesus s two disciples,
Matt 21:34 he s his servants to the
Matt 21:36 Again he s other servants,
Matt 21:37 of all he s his son to them
Matt 22: 3 s out his servants to call

Matt 22: 4 he s out other servants,
Matt 22: 7 And he s out his armies,
Matt 22:16 they s to Him their disciples
Matt 23:37 stones those who are s to her
Matt 27:19 seat, his wife s to him,
Mark 1:43 him and s him away at once
Mark 3:31 outside they s to Him,
Mark 6:17 For Herod himself had s and
Mark 6:27 the king s an executioner
Mark 6:45 while He s the multitude away
Mark 6:46 And when He had s them away
Mark 8: 9 And He s them away
Mark 8:26 He s him away to his house,
Mark 9:37 not Me but Him who s Me
Mark 11: 1 He s out two of His disciples
Mark 12: 2 he s a servant to the
Mark 12: 3 and s him away empty-handed
Mark 12: 4 Again he s them another
Mark 12: 4 s him away shamefully treated
Mark 12: 5 And again he s another, and him
Mark 12: 6 he also s him to them last,
Mark 12:13 Then they s to Him some of
Mark 14:13 So He s out two of His
Luke 1:19 and was s to speak to you and
Luke 1:26 s by God to a city of Galilee
Luke 1:53 the rich He has s away empty
Luke 4:18 He has s Me to heal the
Luke 4:26 Elijah s except to Zarephath
Luke 4:43 this purpose I have been s
Luke 7: 3 he s elders of the Jews to
Luke 7: 6 the centurion s friends to
Luke 7:10 And those who were s,
Luke 7:19 him, s them to Jesus, saying,
Luke 7:20 the Baptist has s us to You
Luke 8:38 But Jesus s him away, saying,
Luke 9: 2 He s them to preach the
Luke 9:48 Me receives Him who s Me
Luke 9:52 s messengers before His face
Luke 10: 1 s them two by two before His
Luke 10:16 Me rejects Him who s Me
Luke 13:34 stones those who are s to her
Luke 14:17 s his servant at supper time
Luke 15:15 he s him into his fields to
Luke 19:14 s a delegation after him,
Luke 19:29 Olivet, that He s two of His
Luke 19:32 So those who were s departed
Luke 20:10 he s a servant to the
Luke 20:10 and s him away empty-handed
Luke 20:11 Again he s another servant
Luke 20:11 and s him away empty-handed
Luke 20:12 And again he s a third
Luke 20:20 s spies who pretended to be
Luke 22: 8 He s Peter and John, saying,
Luke 22:35 When I s you without money
Luke 23: 7 he s Him to Herod, who was
Luke 23:11 robe, and s Him back to Pilate
Luke 23:15 for I s you back to him
John 1: 6 There was a man s from God
John 1: 8 but was s to bear witness of
John 1:19 John, when the Jews s priests
John 1:22 an answer to those who s us
John 1:24 Now those who were s were
John 1:33 but He who s me to baptize
John 3:28 I have been s before Him
John 3:34 For He whom God has s speaks
John 4:34 do the will of Him who s Me
John 4:38 I s you to reap that for
John 5:23 honor the Father who s Him
John 5:24 believes in Him who s Me has
John 5:30 will of the Father who s Me
John 5:33 You have s to John, and he has
John 5:36 Me, that the Father has s Me
John 5:37 the Father Himself, who s Me
John 5:38 in you, because whom He s
John 6:29 you believe in Him whom He s
John 6:38 but the will of Him who s Me
John 6:39 will of the Father who s Me
John 6:40 is the will of Him who s Me
John 6:44 the Father who s Me draws him
John 6:57 As the living Father s Me
John 7:16 is not Mine, but His who s Me
John 7:18 of the One who s Him is true
John 7:28 but He who s Me is true,
John 7:29 for I am from Him, and He s Me
John 7:32 the chief priests s officers
John 7:33 and then I go to Him who s Me
John 8:16 I am with the Father who s Me
John 8:18 the Father who s Me bears
John 8:26 you, but He who s Me is true
John 8:29 And He who s Me is with Me
John 8:42 I come of Myself, but He s Me
John 9: 4 Him who s Me while it is day
John 9: 7 (which is translated, S)
John 10:36 s into the world, 'You are
John 11: 3 the sisters s to Him, saying,
John 11:42 may believe that You s Me
John 12:44 not in Me but in Him who s Me
John 12:45 who sees Me sees Him who s Me
John 12:49 but the Father who s Me gave
John 13:16 nor is he who is s greater
John 13:16 than he who s him
John 13:20 Me receives Him who s Me
John 14:24 but the Father's who s Me
John 15:21 they do not know Him who s Me
John 16: 5 now I go away to Him who s Me
John 17: 3 Jesus Christ whom You have s
John 17: 8 have believed that You s Me
John 17:18 As You s Me into the world
John 17:18 I also have s them into the
John 17:21 may believe that You s Me
John 17:23 may know that You have s Me
John 17:25 have known that You s Me
John 18:24 Then Annas s Him bound to
John 20:21 As the Father has s Me, I
Acts 3:26 Jesus, s Him to bless you, in
Acts 5:21 s to the prison to have them
Acts 7:12 he s out our fathers first
Acts 7:14 Then Joseph s and called his
Acts 7:35 the one God s to be a ruler
Acts 8:14 they s Peter and John to them,
Acts 9:17 has s me that you may receive
Acts 9:30 and s him out to Tarsus
Acts 9:38 there, they s two men to him,
Acts 10: 8 to them, he s them to Joppa
Acts 10:17 the men who had been s from
Acts 10:20 for I have s them
Acts 10:21 been s to him from Cornelius
Acts 10:29 as soon as I was s for
Acts 10:29 what reason have you s for me
Acts 10:33 So I s to you immediately, and
Acts 10:36 The word which God s to the
Acts 11:11 was, having been s to me from
Acts 11:22 they s out Barnabas to go as
Acts 11:30 s it to the elders by the
Acts 12:11 that the Lord has s His angel
Acts 13: 3 on them, they s them away
Acts 13: 4 So, being s out by the Holy
Acts 13:15 of the synagogue s to them
Acts 13:26 of this salvation has been s
Acts 15: 3 being s on their way by the
Acts 15:27 We have therefore s Judas
Acts 15:30 So when they were s off, they
Acts 15:33 a time, they were s back with
Acts 16:35 magistrates s the officers
Acts 16:36 have s to let you go
Acts 17:10 brethren immediately s Paul
Acts 17:14 the brethren s Paul away, to
Acts 19:22 So he s into Macedonia two of
Acts 19:31 s to him pleading that he
Acts 20:17 From Miletus he s to Ephesus
Acts 23:30 I s him immediately to you,
Acts 24:24 he s for Paul and heard him
Acts 24:26 Therefore he s for him more
Acts 28:28 has been s to the Gentiles
Rom 10:15 they preach unless they are s
1Co 4:17 I have s Timothy to you, who
2Co 8:18 And we have s with him the
2Co 8:22 And we have s with them our
2Co 9: 3 Yet I have s the brethren,
2Co 12:17 any of those whom I s to you
2Co 12:18 and s our brother with him
Gal 4: 4 God s forth His Son, born of
Gal 4: 6 God has s forth the Spirit of
Eph 6:22 whom I have s to you for this
Phil 2:28 Therefore I s him the more
Phil 4:16 Thessalonica you s aid once
Phil 4:18 things which were s from you
1Th 3: 2 s Timothy, our brother and
1Th 3: 5 I s to know your faith, lest
2Ti 4:12 Tychicus I have s to Ephesus
Heb 1:14 s forth to minister for those
Jas 2:25 and s them out another way
1Pe 1:12 the Holy Spirit s from heaven
1Pe 2:14 as to those who are s by him
1Jn 4: 9 us, that God has s His only
1Jn 4:10 us and s His Son to be the
1Jn 4:14 s the Son as Savior of the
Rev 1: 1 And He s and signified it by
Rev 5: 6 God s out into all the earth
Rev 22: 6 s His angel to show His
Rev 22:16 have s My angel to testify to

SENTENCE
Deut 17: 9 upon you the s of judgment
Deut 17:10 s which they pronounce upon
Deut 17:11 According to the s of the law
Deut 17:11 or to the left from the s
Eccl 8:11 Because the s against an evil
Dan 4:17 the s by the word of the holy
Luke 23:24 So Pilate gave s that it
2Co 1: 9 Yes, we had the s of death in

SENUAH (*see* HASSENUAH)
Neh 11: 9 Judah the son of S was second

SEORIM
1Ch 24: 8 to Harim, the fourth to S

SEPARATE (*see* SEPARATED, SEPARATES, SEPARATING, SEPARATION)
Gen 13: 9 Please s from me
Gen 49:26 who was s from his brothers
Ex 33:16 So we shall be s, Your people
Lev 15:31 Thus you shall s the
Lev 22: 2 that they s themselves from
Num 6: 2 to s himself to the LORD,
Num 6: 3 he shall s himself from wine
Num 8:14 Thus you shall s the Levites
Num 16:21 S yourselves from among this
Deut 19: 2 you shall s three cities for
Deut 19: 7 You shall s three cities for
Deut 29:21 the LORD would s him from all
Deut 33:16 who was s from his brothers
Josh 16: 9 The s cities for the children
Ezra 10:11 s yourselves from the peoples
Ezek 42:20 to s the holy areas from the
Matt 13:49 s the wicked from among the
Matt 19: 6 together, let not man s
Matt 25:32 and He will s them one from
Mark 10: 9 together, let not man s
Acts 13: 2 Now s to Me Barnabas and Saul
Rom 8:35 Who shall s us from the love
Rom 8:39 shall be able to s us from
2Co 6:17 out from among them and be s
Heb 7:26 s from sinners, and has become

SEPARATED (*see* SEPARATE)
Gen 10: 5 were s into their lands,
Gen 13:11 And they s from each other
Gen 13:14 after Lot had s from him
Gen 25:23 shall be s from your body
Gen 30:40 Then Jacob s the lambs, and
Lev 20:24 God, who has s you from the
Lev 20:25 which I have s from you as
Lev 20:26 have s you from the peoples,
Num 6: 5 he s himself to the LORD, he
Num 16: 9 s you from the congregation
Num 31:42 which Moses s from the men
Deut 10: 8 At that time the LORD s the
Deut 32: 8 when He s the sons of Adam,
Judg 4:11 Moses, had s himself from the
1Ki 8:53 For You s them from among all
2Ki 2:11 of fire, and s the two of them
1Ch 25: 1 the captains of the army s
Ezra 6:21 s themselves from the filth
Ezra 8:24 Then I s twelve of the
Ezra 9: 1 and the Levites have not s
Ezra 10: 8 he himself would be s from
Neh 4:19 we are s far from one another
Neh 9: 2 lineage s themselves from all
Neh 10:28 and all those who had s
Neh 13: 3 that they s all the mixed
Prov 19: 4 the poor is s from his friend
Is 56: 3 s me from His people"
Is 59: 2 have s you from your God
Hos 9:10 s themselves to that shame
Rom 1: 1 s to the gospel of God
Gal 1:15 who s me from my mother's
Gal 2:12 s himself, fearing those who

SEPARATES (*see* SEPARATE)
Num 6: 6 All the days that he s
Prov 16:28 a whisperer s the best of
Prov 17: 9 matter s the best of friends
Ezek 14: 7 who s himself from Me and sets

SEPARATING (*see* SEPARATE)
Ezek 41:12 s courtyard at its western
Ezek 41:13 and the s courtyard with the
Ezek 41:14 including the s courtyard
Ezek 41:15 it, facing the s courtyard
Ezek 42: 1 was opposite the s courtyard
Ezek 42:10 opposite the s courtyard
Ezek 42:13 are opposite the s courtyard

SEPARATION (*see* SEPARATE)
Num 6: 4 All the days of his **s** he
Num 6: 5 **s** no razor shall come upon
Num 6: 7 because his **s** to God is on
Num 6: 8 All the days of his **s** he
Num 6:12 to the LORD the days of his **s**
Num 6:12 because his **s** was defiled
Num 6:13 days of his **s** are fulfilled
Num 6:21 LORD the offering for his **s**
Num 6:21 according to the law of his **s**

SEPHAR
Gen 10:30 from Mesha as you go toward **S**

SEPHARAD
Obad 20 of Jerusalem who are in **S**

SEPHARVAIM
2Ki 17:24 Ava, Hamath, and from **S**, and
2Ki 17:31 and Anammelech, the gods of **S**
2Ki 18:34 Where are the gods of **S** and
2Ki 19:13 and the king of the city of **S**
Is 36:19 Where are the gods of **S**
Is 37:13 and the king of the city of **S**

SEPHARVITES
2Ki 17:31 the **S** burned their children

SEPULCHER
Is 22:16 that you have hewn a **s** here
Is 22:16 who hews himself a **s** on high

SERAH (*see* SARAH, TIMNATH SERAH)
Gen 46:17 Ishuah, Isui, Beriah, and **S**
Num 26:46 the daughter of Asher was **S**
1Ch 7:30 Beriah, and their sister **S**

SERAIAH (*see* SHAVSHA)
2Sa 8:17 **S** was the scribe
2Ki 25:18 guard took **S** the chief priest
2Ki 25:23 **S** the son of Tanhumeth the
1Ch 4:13 of Kenaz were Othniel and **S**
1Ch 4:14 **S** begot Joab the father of
1Ch 4:35 of Joshibiah, the son of **S**
1Ch 6:14 Azariah begot **S**
1Ch 6:14 and **S** begot Jehozadak
Ezra 2: 2 were Jeshua, Nehemiah, **S**,
Ezra 7: 1 of Persia, Ezra the son of **S**
Neh 10: 2 **S**, Azariah, Jeremiah,
Neh 11:11 **S** the son of Hilkiah, the son
Neh 12: 1 **S**, Jeremiah, Ezra,
Neh 12:12 of **S**, Meraiah
Jer 36:26 son, **S** the son of Azriel, and
Jer 40: 8 **S** the son of Tanhumeth, the
Jer 51:59 commanded **S** the son of Neriah
Jer 51:59 And **S** was the quartermaster
Jer 51:61 And Jeremiah said to **S**, When
Jer 52:24 guard took **S** the chief priest

SERAPHIM
Is 6: 2 Above it stood **s**
Is 6: 6 Then one of the **s** flew to me

SERED
Gen 46:14 The sons of Zebulun were **S**
Num 26:26 of **S**, the family of the

SERGIUS
Acts 13: 7 **S** Paulus, an intelligent man

SERIOUS
Deut 15:21 or blind or has any **s** defect
Deut 28:59 and **s** and prolonged sicknesses
1Ki 17:17 his sickness was so **s** that
2Ch 21:14 people with a **s** affliction
Neh 5: 7 After **s** thought, I rebuked
Acts 25: 7 and laid many **s** complaints
1Pe 4: 7 therefore be **s** and watchful in

SERPENT (*see* SERPENT'S, SERPENTS)
Gen 3: 1 Now the **s** was more cunning
Gen 3: 2 And the woman said to the **s**
Gen 3: 4 And the **s** said to the woman,
Gen 3:13 The **s** deceived me, and I ate
Gen 3:14 So the LORD God said to the **s**
Gen 49:17 Dan shall be a **s** by the way
Ex 4: 3 the ground, and it became a **s**
Ex 7: 9 Pharaoh, and let it become a **s**
Ex 7:10 servants, and it became a **s**
Ex 7:15 rod which was turned to a **s**
Num 21: 8 Make a fiery **s**, and set it on
Num 21: 9 So Moses made a bronze **s**, and
Num 21: 9 if a **s** had bitten anyone,
Num 21: 9 he looked at the bronze **s**
2Ki 18: 4 bronze **s** that Moses had made
Neh 2:13 the Valley Gate to the **S** Well
Job 7:12 Am I a sea, or a sea **s**, that
Job 26:13 hand pierced the fleeing **s**
Ps 58: 4 is like the poison of a **s**
Ps 91:13 the **s** you shall trample under
Ps 140: 3 their tongues like a **s**
Prov 23:32 at the last it bites like a **s**
Prov 30:19 air, the way of a **s** on a rock
Eccl 10: 8 a wall will be bitten by a **s**
Eccl 10:11 A **s** may bite when it is not
Is 14:29 will be a fiery flying **s**
Is 27: 1 Leviathan the fleeing **s**,
Is 27: 1 Leviathan that twisted **s**
Is 30: 6 the viper and fiery flying **s**
Is 51: 9 Rahab apart, and wounded the **s**
Jer 46:22 Her noise shall go like a **s**
Amos 5:19 on the wall, and a **s** bit him
Amos 9: 3 there I will command the **s**
Mic 7:17 shall lick the dust like a **s**
Matt 7:10 a fish, will he give him a **s**
Luke 11:11 him a **s** instead of a fish
John 3:14 up the **s** in the wilderness
2Co 11: 3 as the **s** deceived Eve by his
Rev 12: 9 that **s** of old, called the
Rev 12:14 from the presence of the **s**
Rev 12:15 So the **s** spewed water out of
Rev 20: 2 that **s** of old, who is the

SERPENT'S (*see* SERPENT)
Is 14:29 for out of the **s** roots will
Is 65:25 and dust shall be the **s** food

SERPENTS (*see* SERPENT)
Ex 7:12 his rod, and they became **s**
Num 21: 6 sent fiery **s** among the people
Num 21: 7 He take away the **s** from us
Deut 8:15 in which were fiery **s** and
Deut 32:24 the poison of **s** of the dust
Deut 32:33 Their wine is the poison of **s**
Ps 74:13 of the sea **s** in the waters
Jer 8:17 I will send **s** among you,
Matt 10:16 Therefore be wise as **s** and
Matt 23:33 **S**, brood of vipers
Mark 16:18 they will take up **s**
Luke 10:19 the authority to trample on **s**
1Co 10: 9 and were destroyed by **s**
Rev 9:19 for their tails are like **s**

SERUG
Gen 11:20 thirty-two years, and begot **S**
Gen 11:21 After he begot **S**, Reu lived
Gen 11:22 **S** lived thirty years, and
Gen 11:23 **S** lived two hundred years, and
1Ch 1:26 **S**, Nahor, Terah,
Luke 3:35 the son of **S**, the son of Reu,

SERVANT (*see* MAIDSERVANT, MANSERVANT, SERVANT'S, SERVANTS, SERVE)
Gen 9:25 a **s** of servants he shall be
Gen 9:26 Shem, and may Canaan be his **s**
Gen 9:27 and may Canaan be his **s**
Gen 18: 3 do not pass on by Your **s**
Gen 18: 5 as you have come to your **s**
Gen 19:19 your **s** has found favor in
Gen 24: 2 to the oldest **s** of his house
Gen 24: 5 And the **s** said to him,
Gen 24: 9 So the **s** put his hand under
Gen 24:10 Then the **s** took ten of his
Gen 24:14 appointed for Your **s** Isaac
Gen 24:17 the **s** ran to meet her and said
Gen 24:34 I am Abraham's **s**
Gen 24:52 when Abraham's **s** heard their
Gen 24:53 Then the **s** brought out
Gen 24:59 and her nurse, and Abraham's **s**
Gen 24:61 So the **s** took Rebekah and
Gen 24:65 for she had said to the **s**
Gen 24:65 And the **s** said, "It is my
Gen 24:66 And the **s** told Isaac all the
Gen 26:24 for My **s** Abraham's sake
Gen 32: 4 Esau, 'Thus your **s** Jacob says
Gen 32:10 which You have shown Your **s**
Gen 32:18 say, 'They are your **s** Jacob's
Gen 32:20 your **s** Jacob is behind us
Gen 33: 5 has graciously given your **s**
Gen 33:14 lord go on ahead before his **s**
Gen 39:17 The Hebrew **s** whom you
Gen 39:19 Your **s** did to me after this
Gen 41:12 a **s** of the captain of the
Gen 43:28 Your **s** our father is in good
Gen 44:18 please let your **s** speak a
Gen 44:18 anger burn against your **s**
Gen 44:24 went up to your **s** my father
Gen 44:27 Then your **s** my father said to
Gen 44:30 I come to your **s** my father
Gen 44:31 **s** our father with sorrow to
Gen 44:32 For your **s** became surety for
Gen 44:33 please let your **s** remain
Ex 4:10 You have spoken to Your **s**
Ex 12:44 But every man's **s** who is
Ex 12:45 a hired **s** shall not eat it
Ex 14:31 the LORD and His **s** Moses
Ex 21: 2 If you buy a Hebrew **s**, he
Ex 21: 5 But if the **s** plainly says, 'I
Ex 21:20 if a man beats his **s** or his
Ex 21:26 man strikes the eye of his **s**
Ex 33:11 but his **s** Joshua the son of
Lev 22:10 with the priest, or a hired **s**
Lev 25: 6 for you and your **s**, for your
Lev 25: 6 maidservant and your hired **s**
Lev 25:40 But as a hired **s** and a
Lev 25:50 the time of a hired **s** for him
Lev 25:53 with him as a yearly hired **s**
Num 11:11 Why have You afflicted Your **s**
Num 12: 7 Not so with My **s** Moses
Num 12: 8 to speak against My **s** Moses
Num 14:24 But My **s** Caleb, because he
Deut 3:24 to show Your **s** Your greatness
Deut 15:17 and he shall be your **s** forever
Deut 15:18 **s** in serving you six years
Deut 24:14 oppress a hired **s** who is poor
Deut 34: 5 So Moses the **s** of the LORD
Josh 1: 1 of Moses the **s** of the LORD
Josh 1: 2 Moses My **s** is dead
Josh 1: 7 Moses My **s** commanded you
Josh 1:13 the word which Moses the **s** of
Josh 1:15 which Moses the LORD's **s** gave
Josh 5:14 does my Lord say to His **s**
Josh 8:31 as Moses the **s** of the LORD
Josh 8:33 as Moses the **s** of the LORD
Josh 9:24 **s** Moses to give you all the
Josh 11:12 as Moses the **s** of the LORD
Josh 11:15 had commanded Moses his **s**
Josh 12: 6 These Moses the **s** of the LORD
Josh 12: 6 Moses the **s** of the LORD had
Josh 13: 8 as Moses the **s** of the LORD
Josh 14: 7 **s** of the LORD sent me from
Josh 18: 7 which Moses the **s** of the LORD
Josh 22: 2 kept all that Moses the **s** of
Josh 22: 4 which Moses the **s** of the LORD
Josh 22: 5 the law which Moses the **s** of
Josh 24:29 Nun, the **s** of the LORD, died,
Judg 2: 8 the **s** of the LORD, died when
Judg 7:10 to the camp with Purah your **s**
Judg 7:11 **s** to the outpost of the armed
Judg 15:18 by the hand of Your **s**
Judg 19: 3 bring her back, having his **s**
Judg 19: 9 he and his concubine and his **s**
Judg 19:11 the **s** said to his master,
Judg 19:13 So he said to his **s**, "Come,
Judg 19:19 young man who is with your **s**
Ruth 2: 5 Then Boaz said to his **s** who
Ruth 2: 6 So the **s** who was in charge of
1Sa 2:13 the priest's **s** would come
1Sa 2:15 the priest's **s** would come
1Sa 3: 9 Speak, LORD, for Your **s** hears
1Sa 3:10 Speak, for Your **s** hears
1Sa 9: 5 to his **s** who was with him
1Sa 9: 7 Then Saul said to his **s**
1Sa 9: 8 the **s** answered Saul again and
1Sa 9:10 Then Saul said to his **s**
1Sa 9:22 Samuel took Saul and his **s**
1Sa 9:27 Tell the **s** to go on ahead of
1Sa 10:14 uncle said to him and his **s**
1Sa 17:32 your **s** will go and fight with
1Sa 17:34 Your **s** used to keep his
1Sa 17:36 Your **s** has killed both lion
1Sa 17:58 I am the son of your **s** Jesse
1Sa 19: 4 the king sin against his **s**
1Sa 20: 7 is well,' your **s** will be safe
1Sa 20: 8 shall deal kindly with your **s**
1Sa 20: 8 for you have brought your **s**
1Sa 22: 8 stirred up my **s** against me
1Sa 22:15 king impute anything to his **s**
1Sa 22:15 For your **s** knew nothing of
1Sa 23:10 Your **s** has certainly heard
1Sa 23:11 down, as Your **s** has heard
1Sa 23:11 Israel, I pray, tell Your **s**
1Sa 25:39 and has kept His **s** from evil
1Sa 25:41 a **s** to wash the feet of the
1Sa 26:18 my lord thus pursue his **s**
1Sa 26:19 king hear the words of his **s**
1Sa 27: 5 For why should your **s** dwell
1Sa 27:12 he will be my **s** forever

1Sa 28: 2 you know what your s can do
1Sa 29: 3 the s of Saul king of Israel,
1Sa 29: 8 s as long as I have been with
1Sa 30:13 from Egypt, s of an Amalekite
2Sa 3:18 By the hand of My s David
2Sa 7: 5 Go and tell My s David, 'Thus
2Sa 7: 8 shall you say to My s David
2Sa 7:20 You, Lord GOD, know Your s
2Sa 7:21 to make Your s know them
2Sa 7:25 have spoken concerning Your s
2Sa 7:26 let the house of Your s David
2Sa 7:27 have revealed this to Your s
2Sa 7:27 Therefore Your s found it in
2Sa 7:28 this goodness to Your s
2Sa 7:29 to bless the house of Your s
2Sa 7:29 of Your s be blessed forever
2Sa 9: 2 there was a s of the house of
2Sa 9: 6 Here is your s
2Sa 9: 8 What is your s, that you
2Sa 9: 9 king called to Ziba, Saul's s
2Sa 9:11 the king has commanded his s
2Sa 9:11 so will your s do
2Sa 11:21 Your s Uriah the Hittite is
2Sa 11:24 your s Uriah the Hittite is
2Sa 13:17 called his s who attended him
2Sa 13:18 his s put her out and bolted
2Sa 13:24 your s has sheepshearers
2Sa 13:24 his servants go with your s
2Sa 13:35 as your s said, so it is
2Sa 14:19 For your s Joab commanded me,
2Sa 14:20 s Joab has done this thing
2Sa 14:22 Today your s knows that I
2Sa 14:22 the request of his s
2Sa 15: 2 Your s is from such and such a
2Sa 15: 8 For your s vowed a vow while
2Sa 15:21 there also your s will be
2Sa 15:34 to Absalom, I will be your s
2Sa 15:34 your father's s previously
2Sa 15:34 so I will now also be your s
2Sa 16: 1 Ziba the s of Mephibosheth
2Sa 18:29 When Joab sent the king's s
2Sa 18:29 and me your s
2Sa 19:17 Ziba the s of the house of
2Sa 19:19 s did on the day that my lord
2Sa 19:20 For I, your s, know that I
2Sa 19:26 O king, my s deceived me
2Sa 19:26 For your s said, 'I will
2Sa 19:26 king,' because your s is lame
2Sa 19:27 your s to my lord the king
2Sa 19:28 Yet you set your s among
2Sa 19:35 Can your s taste what I eat
2Sa 19:35 Why then should your s be a
2Sa 19:36 Your s will go a little way
2Sa 19:37 let your s turn back again
2Sa 19:37 But here is your s Chimham
2Sa 24:10 away the iniquity of Your s
2Sa 24:21 lord the king come to his s
1Ki 1:19 but Solomon your s he has not
1Ki 1:26 invited me, even me your s
1Ki 1:26 Jehoiada, nor your s Solomon
1Ki 1:27 your s who should sit on the
1Ki 1:51 his s to death with the sword
1Ki 2:38 has said, so your s will do
1Ki 3: 6 to your s David my father
1Ki 3: 7 You have made Your s king
1Ki 3: 8 Your s is in the midst of
1Ki 3: 9 Therefore give to Your s an
1Ki 8:24 Your s David my father
1Ki 8:25 Your s David my father,
1Ki 8:26 to Your s David my father
1Ki 8:28 regard the prayer of Your s
1Ki 8:28 the prayer which Your s is
1Ki 8:29 s makes toward this place
1Ki 8:30 the supplication of Your s
1Ki 8:52 to the supplication of Your s
1Ki 8:53 by the hand of Your s Moses
1Ki 8:56 promised through His s Moses
1Ki 8:59 maintain the cause of His s
1Ki 8:66 LORD had done for His s David
1Ki 11:11 from you and give it to your s
1Ki 11:13 for the sake of my s David
1Ki 11:26 Then Solomon's s, Jeroboam
1Ki 11:32 for the sake of My s David
1Ki 11:34 for the sake of My s David
1Ki 11:36 that My s David may always
1Ki 11:38 as My s David did, then I
1Ki 12: 7 If you will be a s to these
1Ki 14: 8 have not been as My s David
1Ki 14:18 His s Ahijah the prophet
1Ki 15:29 by His s Ahijah the Shilonite
1Ki 16: 9 Now his s Zimri, commander of
1Ki 18: 9 your s into the hand of Ahab
1Ki 18:12 But I your s have feared the
1Ki 18:36 Israel, and that I am Your s
1Ki 18:43 and said to his s, "Go up now
1Ki 19: 3 to Judah, and left his s there
1Ki 20: 9 s the first time I will do
1Ki 20:32 Your s Ben-Hadad says
1Ki 20:39 Your s went out into the
1Ki 20:40 while your s was busy here and
2Ki 4: 1 Your s my husband is dead, and
2Ki 4: 1 that your s feared the LORD
2Ki 4:12 Then he said to Gehazi his s
2Ki 4:19 So he said to a s, "Carry
2Ki 4:24 a donkey, and said to her s
2Ki 4:25 that he said to his s Gehazi
2Ki 4:38 and he said to his s, "Put on
2Ki 4:43 his s said, "What? Shall I
2Ki 5: 6 have sent Naaman my s to you
2Ki 5:15 take a gift from your s
2Ki 5:17 please let your s be given
2Ki 5:17 for your s will no longer
2Ki 5:18 may the LORD pardon your s
2Ki 5:18 pardon your s in this thing
2Ki 5:20 the s of Elisha the man of
2Ki 5:25 Your s did not go anywhere
2Ki 6:15 when the s of the man of God
2Ki 6:15 And his s said to him,
2Ki 8: 4 the s of the man of God,
2Ki 8:13 But what is your s
2Ki 8:19 for the sake of his s David
2Ki 9: 4 the s of the prophet, went to
2Ki 9:36 by His s Elijah the Tishbite
2Ki 10:10 what He spoke by His s Elijah
2Ki 14:25 s Jonah the son of Amittai
2Ki 16: 7 I am your s and your son
2Ki 18:12 all that Moses the s of the
2Ki 19:34 sake and for My s David's sake
2Ki 20: 6 and for the sake of My s David
2Ki 21: 8 My s Moses commanded them
2Ki 22:12 and Asaiah a s of the king,
2Ki 25: 8 a s of the king of Babylon,
1Ch 2:34 s whose name was Jarha
1Ch 2:35 to Jarha his s as wife, and
1Ch 6:49 the s of God had commanded
1Ch 16:13 O seed of Israel His s, you
1Ch 17: 4 Go and tell My s David, 'Thus
1Ch 17: 7 shall you say to My s David
1Ch 17:18 You for the honor of Your s
1Ch 17:18 For You know Your s
1Ch 17:23 have spoken concerning Your s
1Ch 17:24 let the house of Your s David
1Ch 17:25 have told Your s that You
1Ch 17:25 Therefore Your s has found it
1Ch 17:26 this goodness to Your s
1Ch 17:27 to bless the house of Your s
1Ch 21: 8 away the iniquity of Your s
2Ch 1: 3 which Moses the s of the LORD
2Ch 6:15 Your s David my father
2Ch 6:16 Your s David my father,
2Ch 6:17 have spoken to Your s David
2Ch 6:19 regard the prayer of Your s
2Ch 6:19 Your s is praying before You
2Ch 6:20 s prays toward this place
2Ch 6:21 the supplications of Your s
2Ch 6:42 the mercies of Your s David
2Ch 13: 6 the s of Solomon the son of
2Ch 24: 6 of Moses the s of the LORD
2Ch 24: 9 the s of God had imposed on
2Ch 32:16 God and against His s Hezekiah
2Ch 34:20 and Asaiah a s of the king,
Neh 1: 6 s which I pray before You now
Neh 1: 7 You commanded Your s Moses
Neh 1: 8 You commanded Your s Moses
Neh 1:11 to the prayer of Your s, and
Neh 1:11 let Your s prosper this day,
Neh 2: 5 if your s has found favor in
Neh 4:22 man and his s stay at night in
Neh 6: 5 sent his s to me as before
Neh 9:14 by the hand of Moses Your s
Neh 10:29 given by Moses the s of God
Job 1: 8 Have you considered My s Job
Job 2: 3 Have you considered My s Job
Job 3:19 the s is free from his master
Job 7: 2 Like a s who earnestly
Job 19:16 I call my s, but he gives no
Job 41: 4 you take him as a s forever
Job 42: 7 is right, as My s Job has
Job 42: 8 and seven rams, go to My s Job
Job 42: 8 My s Job shall pray for you
Job 42: 8 is right, as My s Job has
Ps 19:11 by them Your s is warned, And
Ps 19:13 Keep back Your s also from
Ps 27: 9 not turn Your s away in anger
Ps 31:16 Your face shine upon Your s
Ps 35:27 in the prosperity of His s
Ps 69:17 hide Your face from Your s
Ps 78:70 He also chose David His s
Ps 86: 2 Save Your s who trusts in You
Ps 86: 4 Rejoice the soul of Your s
Ps 86:16 Give Your strength to Your s
Ps 89: 3 I have sworn to My s David
Ps 89:20 I have found My s David
Ps 89:39 the covenant of Your s
Ps 105: 6 O seed of Abraham His s, You
Ps 105:26 He sent Moses His s, And
Ps 105:42 promise, And Abraham His s
Ps 109:28 But let Your s rejoice
Ps 116:16 O LORD, truly I am Your s
Ps 116:16 I am Your s, the son of Your
Ps 119:17 Deal bountifully with Your s
Ps 119:23 But Your s meditates on Your
Ps 119:38 Establish Your word to Your s
Ps 119:49 Remember the word to Your s
Ps 119:65 have dealt well with Your s
Ps 119:76 to Your word to Your s
Ps 119:84 many are the days of Your s
Ps 119:122 Be surety for Your s for good
Ps 119:124 Deal with Your s according to
Ps 119:125 I am Your s
Ps 119:135 Your face shine upon Your s
Ps 119:140 Therefore Your s loves it
Ps 119:176 Seek Your s, For I do not
Ps 132:10 For Your s David's sake, Do
Ps 136:22 A heritage to Israel His s
Ps 143: 2 into judgment with Your s
Ps 143:12 For I am Your s
Ps 144:10 His s From the deadly sword
Prov 11:29 the fool will be s to the
Prov 12: 9 who is slighted but has a s
Prov 14:35 favor is toward a wise s, but
Prov 17: 2 A wise s will rule over a son
Prov 19:10 much less for a s to rule
Prov 22: 7 borrower is s to the lender
Prov 29:19 A s will not be corrected by
Prov 29:21 He who pampers his s from
Prov 30:10 not malign a s to his master
Prov 30:22 for a s when he reigns, a
Eccl 7:21 you hear your s cursing you
Is 20: 3 Just as My s Isaiah has
Is 22:20 that I will call My s Eliakim
Is 24: 2 as with the s, so with his
Is 37:35 sake and for My s David's sake
Is 41: 8 But you, Israel, are My s
Is 41: 9 and said to You, 'You are My s
Is 42: 1 My S whom I uphold, My Elect
Is 42:19 Who is blind but My s, or
Is 42:19 and blind as the LORD's s
Is 43:10 My s whom I have chosen, that
Is 44: 1 Yet hear now, O Jacob My s
Is 44: 2 Fear not, O Jacob My s
Is 44:21 And Israel, for you are My s
Is 44:21 have formed you, you are My s
Is 44:26 confirms the word of His s
Is 48:20 LORD has redeemed His s Jacob
Is 49: 3 He said to me, 'You are My s
Is 49: 5 Me from the womb to be His S
Is 49: 6 S to raise up the tribes of
Is 49: 7 abhors, to the S of rulers
Is 50:10 Who obeys the voice of His S
Is 52:13 My S shall deal prudently, He
Is 53:11 S shall justify many, for He
Jer 2:14 Is Israel a s
Jer 25: 9 the king of Babylon, My s
Jer 27: 6 the king of Babylon, My s
Jer 30:10 O My s Jacob,' says the LORD,
Jer 33:21 be broken with David My s
Jer 33:22 the descendants of David My s
Jer 33:26 of Jacob and David My s, so
Jer 43:10 the king of Babylon, My s
Jer 46:27 O My s Jacob, and do not be
Jer 46:28 Do not fear, O Jacob My s
Ezek 28:25 which I gave to My s Jacob
Ezek 34:23 he shall feed them—My s David
Ezek 34:24 My s David a prince among
Ezek 37:24 David My s shall be king over
Ezek 37:25 I have given to Jacob My s
Ezek 37:25 My s David shall be their
Dan 6:20 s of the living God, has your
Dan 9:11 in the Law of Moses the s of

Dan 9:17 hear the prayer of Your s
Dan 10:17 For how can this s of my lord
Hag 2:23 take you, Zerubbabel My s
Zech 3: 8 forth My S the BRANCH
Mal 1: 6 his father, and a s his master
Mal 4: 4 the Law of Moses, My s, which
Matt 8: 6 Lord, my s is lying at home
Matt 8: 8 word, and my s will be healed
Matt 8: 9 and to my s, 'Do this,' and he
Matt 8:13 his s was healed that same
Matt 10:24 nor a s above his master
Matt 10:25 and a s like his master
Matt 12:18 My S whom I have chosen, my
Matt 18:26 The s therefore fell down
Matt 18:27 Then the master of that s was
Matt 18:28 But that s went out and found
Matt 18:29 So his fellow s fell down at
Matt 18:32 said to him, 'You wicked s
Matt 18:33 compassion on your fellow s
Matt 20:26 among you, let him be your s
Matt 23:11 among you shall be your s
Matt 24:45 then is a faithful and wise s
Matt 24:46 is that s whom his master
Matt 24:48 But if that evil s says in
Matt 24:50 the master of that s will
Matt 25:21 Well done, good and faithful s
Matt 25:23 Well done, good and faithful s
Matt 25:26 to him, 'You wicked and lazy s
Matt 25:30 cast the unprofitable s into
Matt 26:51 struck the s of the high
Matt 26:69 a s girl came to him, saying,
Mark 9:35 be last of all and s of all
Mark 10:43 among you shall be your s
Mark 12: 2 sent a s to the vinedressers
Mark 12: 4 Again he sent them another s
Mark 14:47 and struck the s of the high
Mark 14:66 one of the s girls of the
Mark 14:69 the s girl saw him again, and
Luke 1:54 He has helped His s Israel
Luke 1:69 in the house of His s David
Luke 2:29 Your s depart in peace,
Luke 7: 2 And a certain centurion's s
Luke 7: 3 Him to come and heal his s
Luke 7: 7 word, and my s will be healed
Luke 7: 8 and to my s, 'Do this,' and he
Luke 7:10 found the s well who had been
Luke 12:43 Blessed is that s whom his
Luke 12:45 But if that s says in his
Luke 12:46 the master of that s will
Luke 12:47 that s who knew his master's
Luke 14:17 sent his s at supper time to
Luke 14:21 So that s came and reported
Luke 14:21 being angry, said to his s
Luke 14:22 the s said, 'Master, it is
Luke 14:23 Then the master said to the s
Luke 16:13 No s can serve two masters
Luke 17: 7 having a s plowing or tending
Luke 17: 9 Does he thank that s because
Luke 19:17 to him, 'Well done, good s
Luke 19:22 will judge you, you wicked s
Luke 20:10 sent a s to the vinedressers
Luke 20:11 Again he sent another s
Luke 22:50 the s of the high priest and
Luke 22:56 And a certain s girl, seeing
John 12:26 I am, there My s will be also
John 13:16 a s is not greater than his
John 15:15 for a s does not know what
John 15:20 A s is not greater than his
John 18:10 and struck the high priest's s
John 18:17 Then the s girl who kept the
Acts 3:13 glorified His S Jesus, whom
Acts 3:26 having raised up His S Jesus
Acts 4:25 of Your s David have said
Acts 4:27 against Your holy S Jesus
Acts 4:30 the name of Your holy S Jesus
Rom 1: 1 a s of Jesus Christ, called
Rom 14: 4 are you to judge another's s
Rom 15: 8 Jesus Christ has become a s
Rom 16: 1 who is a s of the church in
1Co 9:19 I have made myself a s to all
Gal 1:10 I would not be a s of Christ
Phil 2: 7 taking the form of a s, and
Col 1: 7 Epaphras, our dear fellow s
Col 4: 7 a fellow s in the Lord, will
Col 4:12 a s of Christ, greets you,
2Ti 2:24 And a s of the Lord must not
Tit 1: 1 a s of God and an apostle of
Heb 3: 5 in all His house as a s, for
Jas 1: 1 a s of God and of the Lord
2Pe 1: 1 Simon Peter, a s and apostle
Jude 1 Jude, a s of Jesus Christ, and
Rev 1: 1 it by His angel to His s John
Rev 15: 3 the s of God, and the song of
Rev 19:10 I am your fellow s, and of
Rev 22: 9 For I am your fellow s, and of

SERVANT'S (*see* SERVANT)
Gen 19: 2 turn in to your s house and
Ex 21:27 if he knocks out his s tooth
2Sa 7:19 have also spoken of Your s
1Ch 17:17 have also spoken of Your s
1Ch 17:19 O LORD, for Your s sake, and
Is 45: 4 For Jacob My s sake, and
John 18:10 The s name was Malchus

SERVANTS (*see* SERVANT, SERVANTS')
Gen 9:25 a servant of s he shall be to
Gen 12:16 donkeys, male and female s
Gen 14:14 eighteen trained s who were
Gen 14:15 he and his s attacked them and
Gen 20: 8 the morning, called all his s
Gen 20:14 oxen, and male and female s
Gen 21:25 Abimelech's s had seized
Gen 24:35 and gold, male and female s
Gen 26:14 herds and a great number of s
Gen 26:15 s had dug in the days of
Gen 26:19 Also Isaac's s dug in the
Gen 26:25 and there Isaac's s dug a well
Gen 26:32 same day that Isaac's s came
Gen 27:37 I have given to him as s
Gen 30:43 flocks, female and male s, and
Gen 32: 5 flocks, and male and female s
Gen 32:16 them to the hand of his s
Gen 32:16 by itself, and said to his s
Gen 40:20 he made a feast for all his s
Gen 40:20 the chief baker among his s
Gen 41:10 Pharaoh was angry with his s
Gen 41:37 and in the eyes of all his s
Gen 41:38 And Pharaoh said to his s
Gen 42:10 but your s have come to buy
Gen 42:11 your s are not spies
Gen 42:13 Your s are twelve brothers,
Gen 44: 7 your s should do such a thing
Gen 44: 9 of your s it is found, let
Gen 44:16 out the iniquity of your s
Gen 44:19 My lord asked his s, saying
Gen 44:21 Then you said to your s
Gen 44:23 But you said to your s
Gen 44:31 So your s will bring down the
Gen 45:16 pleased Pharaoh and his s well
Gen 47: 3 Your s are shepherds, both we
Gen 47: 4 land, because your s have no
Gen 47: 4 please let your s dwell in
Gen 47:19 our land will be s of Pharaoh
Gen 47:25 and we will be Pharaoh's s
Gen 50: 2 Joseph commanded his s the
Gen 50: 7 went up all the s of Pharaoh
Gen 50:17 s of the God of your father
Gen 50:18 Behold, we are your s
Ex 5:15 you dealing thus with your s
Ex 5:16 is no straw given to your s
Ex 5:16 And indeed your s are beaten
Ex 5:21 and in the sight of his s, to
Ex 7:10 Pharaoh and before his s, and
Ex 7:20 and in the sight of his s
Ex 8: 3 into the houses of your s
Ex 8: 4 your people, and on all your s
Ex 8: 9 intercede for you, for your s
Ex 8:11 from your houses, from your s
Ex 8:21 of flies on you and your s
Ex 8:29 from Pharaoh, from his s, and
Ex 8:31 from Pharaoh, from his s, and
Ex 9:14 your very heart, and on your s
Ex 9:20 the s of Pharaoh made his s
Ex 9:20 of Pharaoh made his s and his
Ex 9:21 word of the LORD left his s
Ex 9:30 But as for you and your s, I
Ex 9:34 his heart, he and his s
Ex 10: 1 heart and the hearts of his s
Ex 10: 6 the houses of all your s
Ex 10: 7 Then Pharaoh's s said to him
Ex 11: 3 in the sight of Pharaoh's s
Ex 11: 8 all these your s shall come
Ex 12:30 in the night, he, all his s
Ex 14: 5 his s was turned against the
Ex 32:13 Isaac, and Israel, Your s
Lev 25:42 For they are My s, whom I
Lev 25:55 of Israel are s to Me
Lev 25:55 they are My s whom I brought
Num 22:18 and said to the s of Balak
Num 22:22 and his two s were with him
Num 31:49 Your s have taken a count of
Num 32: 4 and your s have livestock
Num 32: 5 to your s as a possession
Num 32:25 Your s will do as my lord
Num 32:27 but your s will cross over,
Num 32:31 the LORD has said to your s
Deut 9:27 Remember Your s, Abraham,
Deut 29: 2 to Pharaoh and to all his s
Deut 32:36 and have compassion on His s
Deut 32:43 avenge the blood of His s
Deut 34:11 Pharaoh, before all his s
Josh 9: 8 We are your s
Josh 9: 9 far country your s have come
Josh 9:11 We are your s
Josh 9:24 your s that the LORD your God
Josh 10: 6 Do not forsake your s
Judg 3:24 Eglon's s came to look, and to
Judg 6:27 took ten men from among his s
1Sa 4: 9 not become s of the Hebrews
1Sa 8:14 groves, and give them to his s
1Sa 8:15 give it to his officers and s
1Sa 8:17 And you will be his s
1Sa 9: 3 take one of the s with you
1Sa 12:19 Pray for your s to the LORD
1Sa 16:15 And Saul's s said to him,
1Sa 16:16 our master now command your s
1Sa 16:17 So Saul said to his s
1Sa 16:18 Then one of the s answered
1Sa 17: 8 and you the s of Saul
1Sa 17: 9 me, then we will be your s
1Sa 17: 9 him, then you shall be our s
1Sa 18: 5 also in the sight of Saul's s
1Sa 18:22 And Saul commanded his s
1Sa 18:22 in you, and all his s love you
1Sa 18:23 So Saul's s spoke those words
1Sa 18:24 And the s of Saul told him,
1Sa 18:26 So when his s told David
1Sa 18:30 wisely than all the s of Saul
1Sa 19: 1 his son and to all his s, that
1Sa 21: 7 Now a certain man of the s of
1Sa 21:11 the s of Achish said to him,
1Sa 21:14 Then Achish said to his s
1Sa 22: 6 all his s standing about him
1Sa 22: 7 to his s who stood about him
1Sa 22: 9 was set over the s of Saul
1Sa 22:14 who among all your s is so
1Sa 22:17 But the s of the king would
1Sa 24: 7 his s with these words, and
1Sa 25: 8 comes to your hand to your s
1Sa 25:10 Then Nabal answered David's s
1Sa 25:10 There are many s nowadays who
1Sa 25:19 And she said to her s, "Go on
1Sa 25:40 when the s of David had come
1Sa 25:41 the feet of the s of my lord
1Sa 28: 7 Then Saul said to his s
1Sa 28: 7 And his s said to him,
1Sa 28:23 But his s, together with
1Sa 28:25 it before Saul and his s, and
1Sa 29:10 s who have come with you
2Sa 2:12 the s of Ishbosheth the son
2Sa 2:13 the s of David, went out and
2Sa 2:15 and twelve from the s of David
2Sa 2:17 beaten before the s of David
2Sa 2:30 of David's s nineteen men
2Sa 2:31 But the s of David had struck
2Sa 3:22 At that moment the s of David
2Sa 3:38 Then the king said to his s
2Sa 6:20 eyes of the maids of his s
2Sa 8: 2 the Moabites became David's s
2Sa 8: 6 the Syrians became David's s
2Sa 8: 7 to the s of Hadadezer, and
2Sa 8:14 the Edomites became David's s
2Sa 9:10 and your sons and your s,
2Sa 9:10 had fifteen sons and twenty s
2Sa 9:12 Ziba were s of Mephibosheth
2Sa 10: 2 sent by the hand of his s to
2Sa 10: 2 David's s came into the land
2Sa 10: 3 s to you to search the city
2Sa 10: 4 Hanun took David's s, shaved
2Sa 10:19 s to Hadadezer saw that they
2Sa 11: 1 his s with him, and all Israel
2Sa 11: 9 with all the s of his lord
2Sa 11:11 the s of my lord are encamped
2Sa 11:13 bed with the s of his lord
2Sa 11:17 people of the s of David fell
2Sa 11:24 shot from the wall at your s
2Sa 11:24 some of the king's s are dead
2Sa 12:18 the s of David were afraid to
2Sa 12:19 that his s were whispering
2Sa 12:19 Therefore David said to his s

2Sa 12:21 Then his s said to him
2Sa 13:24 his s go with your servant
2Sa 13:28 Absalom had commanded his s
2Sa 13:29 So the s of Absalom did to
2Sa 13:31 all his s stood by with their
2Sa 13:36 all his s wept very bitterly
2Sa 14:30 So he said to his s, "See,
2Sa 14:30 Absalom's s set the field on
2Sa 14:31 Why have your s set my field
2Sa 15:14 his s who were with him at
2Sa 15:15 the king's s said to the king
2Sa 15:15 We are your s, ready to do
2Sa 15:18 Then all his s passed before
2Sa 16: 6 at all the s of King David
2Sa 16:11 said to Abishai and all his s
2Sa 17:20 when Absalom's s came to the
2Sa 18: 7 there before the s of David
2Sa 18: 9 Absalom met the s of David
2Sa 19: 5 s who today have saved your
2Sa 19: 6 regard neither princes nor s
2Sa 19: 7 and speak comfort to your s
2Sa 19:14 Return, you and all your s
2Sa 19:17 sons and his twenty s with him
2Sa 20: 6 Take your lord's s and pursue
2Sa 21:15 his s with him went down and
2Sa 21:22 David and by the hand of his s
2Sa 24:20 and his s coming toward him
1Ki 1: 2 Therefore his s said to him
1Ki 1: 9 men of Judah, the king's s
1Ki 1:33 with you the s of your lord
1Ki 1:47 moreover the king's s have
1Ki 3:15 and made a feast for all his s
1Ki 5: 1 of Tyre sent his s to Solomon
1Ki 5: 6 and my s will be with your s
1Ki 5: 6 s according to whatever you
1Ki 5: 9 My s shall bring them down
1Ki 8:23 mercy with Your s who walk
1Ki 8:32 and act and judge Your s,
1Ki 8:36 and forgive the sin of Your s
1Ki 9:22 they were men of war and his s
1Ki 9:27 sent his s with the fleet
1Ki 9:27 to work with the s of Solomon
1Ki 10: 5 table, the seating of his s
1Ki 10: 8 men and happy are these your s
1Ki 10:13 her own country, she and her s
1Ki 11:17 of his father's s with him
1Ki 12: 7 they will be your s forever
1Ki 15:18 them into the hand of his s
1Ki 20: 6 but I will send my s to you
1Ki 20: 6 house and the houses of your s
1Ki 20:12 post, that he said to his s
1Ki 20:23 Then the s of the king of
1Ki 20:31 And his s said to him,
1Ki 22: 3 king of Israel said to his s
1Ki 22:49 Let my s go with your s
2Ki 1:13 s of yours be precious in
2Ki 2:16 fifty strong men with your s
2Ki 3:11 one of the s of the king of
2Ki 5:13 his s came near and spoke to
2Ki 5:23 handed them to two of his s
2Ki 5:26 and oxen, male and female s
2Ki 6: 3 consent to go with your s
2Ki 6: 8 and he took counsel with his s
2Ki 6:11 and he called his s and said to
2Ki 6:12 And one of his s said, "None,
2Ki 7:12 in the night and said to his s
2Ki 7:13 And one of his s answered and
2Ki 9: 7 blood of My s the prophets
2Ki 9: 7 of all the s of the LORD, at
2Ki 9:11 out to the s of his master
2Ki 9:28 And his s carried him in the
2Ki 10: 5 We are your s, we will do all
2Ki 10:19 prophets of Baal, all his s
2Ki 10:23 see that no s of the LORD are
2Ki 12:20 And his s arose and made a
2Ki 12:21 the son of Shomer, his s,
2Ki 14: 5 that he executed his s who
2Ki 17:13 to you by My s the prophets
2Ki 17:23 by all His s the prophets
2Ki 18:24 of the least of my master's s
2Ki 18:26 Please speak to your s in the
2Ki 19: 5 So the s of King Hezekiah
2Ki 19: 6 with which the s of the king
2Ki 21:10 spoke by His s the prophets
2Ki 21:23 Then the s of Amon conspired
2Ki 22: 9 Your s have gathered the
2Ki 23:30 Then his s moved his body in
2Ki 24: 2 spoken by His s the prophets
2Ki 24:10 At that time the s of
2Ki 24:11 as his s were besieging it
2Ki 24:12 of Judah, his mother, his s
2Ki 25:24 of the s of the Chaldeans
1Ch 18: 2 the Moabites became David's s
1Ch 18: 6 the Syrians became David's s
1Ch 18: 7 were on the s of Hadadezer
1Ch 18:13 the Edomites became David's s
1Ch 19: 2 the s of David came to Hanun
1Ch 19: 3 Did his s not come to you to
1Ch 19: 4 Hanun took David's s, shaved
1Ch 19:19 when the s of Hadadezer saw
1Ch 19:19 with David and became his s
1Ch 20: 8 David and by the hand of his s
1Ch 21: 3 are they not all my lord's s
2Ch 2: 8 for I know that your s have
2Ch 2: 8 my s will be with your s
2Ch 2:10 indeed I will give to your s
2Ch 2:15 of, let him send to his s
2Ch 6:14 mercy with Your s who walk
2Ch 6:23 and act, and judge Your s,
2Ch 6:27 and forgive the sin of Your s
2Ch 8: 9 of Israel s for his work
2Ch 8:18 his s, and s who knew the sea
2Ch 8:18 They went with the s of
2Ch 9: 4 table, the seating of his s
2Ch 9: 7 men and happy are these your s
2Ch 9:10 Also, the s of Hiram and the
2Ch 9:10 the s of Solomon, who brought
2Ch 9:12 her own country, she and her s
2Ch 9:21 Tarshish with the s of Huram
2Ch 10: 7 they will be your s forever
2Ch 12: 8 they will be his s, that they
2Ch 24:25 his own s conspired against
2Ch 25: 3 that he executed his s who
2Ch 32: 9 his s to Jerusalem (but he
2Ch 32:16 his s spoke even more against
2Ch 33:24 Then his s conspired against
2Ch 34:16 to your s they are doing
2Ch 35:23 and the king said to his s
2Ch 35:24 His s therefore took him out
2Ch 36:20 where they became s to him
Ezra 2:55 The sons of Solomon's s
Ezra 2:58 s were three hundred and
Ezra 2:65 their male and female s, of
Ezra 4:11 your s the men of the region
Ezra 5:11 We are the s of the God of
Ezra 7:24 or s of this house of God
Ezra 8:17 us s for the house of our God
Ezra 9:11 by Your s the prophets,
Neh 1: 6 the children of Israel Your s
Neh 1:10 Now these are Your s and Your
Neh 1:11 to the prayer of Your s who
Neh 2:20 therefore we His s will arise
Neh 4:16 that half of my s worked at
Neh 4:23 neither I, my brethren, my s
Neh 5:10 with my brethren and my s
Neh 5:15 even their s bore rule over
Neh 5:16 All my s were gathered there
Neh 7:57 The children of Solomon's s
Neh 7:60 the children of Solomon's s
Neh 7:67 their male and female s, of
Neh 9:10 Pharaoh, against all his s
Neh 9:36 Here we are, s today
Neh 9:36 things, here we are, s in it
Neh 11: 3 and descendants of Solomon's s
Neh 13:19 some of my s at the gates
Esth 1: 3 for all his officials and s
Esth 2: 2 Then the king's s who
Esth 2:18 for all his officials and s
Esth 3: 2 all the king's s who were
Esth 3: 3 Then the king's s who were
Esth 4:11 All the king's s and the
Esth 5:11 officials and s of the king
Esth 6: 3 the king's s who attended him
Esth 6: 5 The king's s said to him,
Job 1:15 s with the edge of the sword
Job 1:16 burned up the sheep and the s
Job 1:17 killed the s with the edge of
Job 4:18 If He puts no trust in His s
Ps 34:22 redeems the soul of His s
Ps 69:36 of His s shall inherit it
Ps 79: 2 The dead bodies of Your s
Ps 79:10 of Your s which has been shed
Ps 89:50 Lord, the reproach of Your s
Ps 90:13 And have compassion on Your s
Ps 90:16 Your work appear to Your s
Ps 102:14 For Your s take pleasure in
Ps 102:28 of Your s will continue, And
Ps 105:25 To deal craftily with His s
Ps 113: 1 O s of the LORD, Praise the
Ps 119:91 For all are Your s
Ps 123: 2 as the eyes of s look to the
Ps 134: 1 All you s of the LORD, Who by
Ps 135: 1 Him, O you s of the LORD
Ps 135: 9 Upon Pharaoh and all his s
Ps 135:14 will have compassion on His s
Prov 29:12 lies, all his s become wicked
Eccl 2: 7 I acquired male and female s
Eccl 2: 7 and had s born in my house
Eccl 10: 7 I have seen s on horses,
Eccl 10: 7 walk on the ground like s
Is 14: 2 will possess them for s and
Is 36: 9 of the least of my master's s
Is 36:11 Please speak to your s in the
Is 37: 5 So the s of King Hezekiah
Is 37: 6 with which the s of the king
Is 37:24 By your s you have reproached
Is 54:17 heritage of the s of the LORD
Is 56: 6 name of the LORD, to be His s
Is 61: 6 call you the S of our God
Is 65: 9 it, and My s shall dwell there
Is 65:13 My s shall eat, but you shall
Is 65:13 My s shall drink, but you
Is 65:13 My s shall rejoice, but you
Is 65:14 My s shall sing for joy of
Is 65:15 call His s by another name
Is 66:14 LORD shall be known to His s
Jer 7:25 to you all My s the prophets
Jer 21: 7 Zedekiah king of Judah, his s
Jer 22: 2 of David, you and your s and
Jer 22: 4 in chariots, accompanied by s
Jer 25: 4 to you all His s the prophets
Jer 25:19 Pharaoh king of Egypt, his s
Jer 26: 5 to heed the words of My s the
Jer 29:19 to them by My s the prophets
Jer 35:15 to you all My s the prophets
Jer 36:24 the king nor any of his s who
Jer 36:31 and his s for their iniquity
Jer 37: 2 But neither he nor his s nor
Jer 37:18 against you, against your s
Jer 44: 4 to you all My s the prophets
Jer 46:26 Babylon and the hand of his s
Lam 5: 8 S rule over us
Ezek 38:17 My s the prophets of Israel
Ezek 46:17 inheritance to one of his s
Dan 1:12 test your s for ten days, and
Dan 1:13 see fit, so deal with your s
Dan 2: 4 Tell your s the dream, and we
Dan 2: 7 the king tell his s the dream
Dan 3:26 s of the Most High God, come
Dan 3:28 delivered His s who trusted
Dan 9: 6 we heeded Your s the prophets
Dan 9:10 us by His s the prophets
Amos 3: 7 secret to His s the prophets
Zech 1: 6 I commanded My s the prophets
Zech 2: 9 become spoil for their s
Matt 13:27 So the s of the owner came and
Matt 13:28 The s said to him, 'Do you
Matt 14: 2 and said to his s, "This is
Matt 18:23 to settle accounts with his s
Matt 18:28 s who owed him a hundred
Matt 18:31 So when his fellow s saw what
Matt 21:34 near, he sent his s to the
Matt 21:35 the vinedressers took his s
Matt 21:36 Again he sent other s, more
Matt 22: 3 sent out his s to call those
Matt 22: 4 Again, he sent out other s
Matt 22: 6 And the rest seized his s,
Matt 22: 8 Then he said to his s, 'The
Matt 22:10 So those s went out into the
Matt 22:13 Then the king said to the s
Matt 24:49 begins to beat his fellow s
Matt 25:14 country, who called his own s
Matt 25:19 time the lord of those s came
Matt 26:58 sat with the s to see the end
Mark 1:20 in the boat with the hired s
Mark 13:34 and gave authority to his s
Mark 14:54 And he sat with the s and
Luke 12:37 are those s whom the master
Luke 12:38 them so, blessed are those s
Luke 15:17 hired s have bread enough
Luke 15:19 me like one of your hired s
Luke 15:22 But the father said to his s
Luke 15:26 So he called one of the s
Luke 17:10 say, 'We are unprofitable s
Luke 19:13 So he called ten of his s
Luke 19:15 he then commanded these s
John 2: 5 His mother said to the s
John 2: 9 the s who had drawn the water
John 4:51 his s met him and told him,
John 15:15 No longer do I call you s

John 18:18 And the s and officers who had
John 18:26 One of the s of the high
John 18:36 My s would fight, so that I
Acts 4:29 grant to Your s that with all
Acts 10: 7 called two of his household s
Acts 16:17 These men are the s of the
1Co 4: 1 as s of Christ and stewards of
2Co 4: 5 ourselves your s for Jesus'
Eph 6: 5 S, be obedient to those who
Eph 6: 6 but as s of Christ, doing the
Phil 1: 1 s of Jesus Christ, To all the
Col 3:22 S, obey in all things your
Col 4: 1 give your s what is just and
1Ti 6: 1 Let as many s as are under
Tit 2: 9 Exhort s to be obedient to
1Pe 2:16 for vice, but as s of God
1Pe 2:18 S, be submissive to your
Rev 1: 1 God gave Him to show His s
Rev 2:20 beguile My s to commit sexual
Rev 6:11 the number of their fellow s
Rev 7: 3 the s of our God on their
Rev 10: 7 to His s the prophets
Rev 11:18 reward Your s the prophets
Rev 19: 2 blood of His s shed by her
Rev 19: 5 Praise our God, all you His s
Rev 22: 3 it, and His s shall serve Him
Rev 22: 6 His s the things which must

SERVANTS' (*see* SERVANTS)
Gen 46:34 Your s occupation has been
Ex 8:24 of Pharaoh, into his s houses
Is 63:17 Return for Your s sake, the
Is 65: 8 so will I do for My s sake

SERVE (*see* SERVANT, SERVED, SERVES, SERVICE, SERVING, SERVITUDE)
Gen 15:13 is not theirs, and will s them
Gen 15:14 whom they s I will judge
Gen 25:23 the older shall s the younger
Gen 27:29 Let peoples s you, and nations
Gen 27:40 and you shall s your brother
Gen 29:15 therefore s me for nothing
Gen 29:18 I will s you seven years for
Gen 29:27 the service which you will s
Gen 43:31 and said, "S the bread
Ex 1:13 of Israel s with rigor
Ex 1:14 made them s was with rigor
Ex 3:12 you shall s God on this
Ex 4:23 My son go that he may s Me
Ex 7:16 that they may s Me in the
Ex 8: 1 people go, that they may s Me
Ex 8:20 people go, that they may s Me
Ex 9: 1 people go, that they may s Me
Ex 9:13 people go, that they may s Me
Ex 10: 3 people go, that they may s Me
Ex 10: 7 go, that they may s the LORD
Ex 10: 8 Go, s the LORD your God
Ex 10:11 s the LORD, for that is what
Ex 10:24 and said, "Go, s the LORD
Ex 10:26 of them to s the LORD our God
Ex 10:26 s the LORD until we arrive
Ex 12:31 s the LORD as you have said
Ex 14:12 that we may s the Egyptians
Ex 14:12 s the Egyptians than that we
Ex 20: 5 bow down to them nor s them
Ex 21: 2 servant, he shall s six years
Ex 21: 6 and he shall s him forever
Ex 23:24 nor s them, nor do according
Ex 23:25 So you shall s the LORD your
Ex 23:33 For if you s their gods, it
Lev 25:39 compel him to s as a slave
Lev 25:40 shall s you until the Year of
Num 3: 6 priest, that they may s him
Num 4:26 so shall they s
Num 4:37 all who might s in the
Num 4:41 of all who might s in the
Num 16: 9 the congregation to s them
Num 18: 2 s you while you and your sons
Num 18: 7 and you shall s
Deut 4:19 s them, which the LORD your
Deut 4:28 And there you will s gods, the
Deut 5: 9 bow down to them nor s them
Deut 6:13 s Him, and shall take oaths in
Deut 7: 4 following Me, to s other gods
Deut 7:16 nor shall you s their gods
Deut 8:19 s them and worship them, I
Deut 10:12 to s the LORD your God with
Deut 10:20 you shall s Him, and to Him
Deut 11:13 s Him with all your heart and
Deut 11:16 s other gods and worship them,
Deut 12:30 these nations s their gods
Deut 13: 2 not known, and let us s them
Deut 13: 4 His voice, and you shall s Him
Deut 13: 6 s other gods,' which you have
Deut 13:13 s other gods," gods whom you
Deut 18: 7 then he may s in the name of
Deut 19:17 judges who s in those days
Deut 20:11 tribute to you, and s you
Deut 28:14 go after other gods to s them
Deut 28:36 there you shall s other gods
Deut 28:47 Because you did not s the
Deut 28:48 you shall s your enemies,
Deut 28:64 there you shall s other gods
Deut 29:18 s the gods of these nations,
Deut 30:17 worship other gods and s them,
Deut 31:20 turn to other gods and s them
Josh 22: 5 to s Him with all your heart
Josh 23: 7 you shall not s them nor bow
Josh 24:14 s Him in sincerity and in
Josh 24:14 S the LORD
Josh 24:15 evil to you to s the LORD
Josh 24:15 this day whom you will s,
Josh 24:15 my house, we will s the LORD
Josh 24:16 the LORD to s other gods
Josh 24:18 We also will s the LORD, for
Josh 24:19 You cannot s the LORD, for He
Josh 24:20 s foreign gods, then He will
Josh 24:21 No, but we will s the LORD
Josh 24:22 LORD for yourselves, to s Him
Josh 24:24 The LORD our God we will s
Judg 2:19 to s them and bow down to them
Judg 9:28 Shechem, that we should s him
Judg 9:28 S the men of Hamor the father
Judg 9:28 but why should we s him
Judg 9:38 that we should s him
Judg 10: 6 the LORD and did not s Him
1Sa 7: 3 for the LORD, and s Him only
1Sa 11: 1 with us, and we will s you
1Sa 12:10 our enemies, and we will s You
1Sa 12:14 s Him and obey His voice, and
1Sa 12:20 but s the LORD with all your
1Sa 12:24 s Him in truth with all your
1Sa 17: 9 shall be our servants and s us
1Sa 26:19 saying, 'Go, s other gods
2Sa 15: 8 then I will s the LORD
2Sa 16:19 Furthermore, whom should I s
2Sa 16:19 Should I not s in the
2Sa 22:44 I have not known shall s me
1Ki 9: 6 s other gods and worship them,
1Ki 12: 4 put on us, and we will s you
1Ki 12: 7 s them, and answer them, and
2Ki 4:41 S it to the people, that they
2Ki 10:18 but Jehu will s him much
2Ki 17:35 nor bow down to them nor s
2Ki 18: 7 of Assyria and did not s him
2Ki 25:24 s the king of Babylon, and it
1Ch 26:12 to s in the house of the LORD
1Ch 28: 9 s Him with a loyal heart and
2Ch 7:19 s other gods, and worship them
2Ch 8:14 s before the priests) as the
2Ch 10: 4 put on us, and we will s you
2Ch 23: 6 and those of the Levites who s
2Ch 29:11 to s Him, and that you should
2Ch 30: 8 s the LORD your God, that the
2Ch 31: 2 and peace offerings, to s, to
2Ch 33:16 commanded Judah to s the LORD
2Ch 34:33 s the LORD their God
2Ch 35: 3 Now s the LORD your God and
Job 21:15 that we should s Him
Job 36:11 s Him, they shall spend their
Job 39: 9 wild ox be willing to s you
Ps 2:11 S the LORD with fear, And
Ps 18:43 I have not known shall s me
Ps 22:30 A posterity shall s Him
Ps 72:11 All nations shall s Him
Ps 97: 7 to shame who s carved images
Ps 100: 2 S the LORD with gladness
Ps 101: 6 a perfect way, He shall s me
Ps 102:22 the kingdoms, to s the LORD
Is 14: 3 in which you were made to s
Is 19:23 will s with the Assyrians
Is 43:23 you to s with grain offerings
Is 56: 6 to s Him, and to love the name
Is 60:12 will not s you shall perish
Jer 5:19 so you shall s aliens in a
Jer 11:10 after other gods to s them
Jer 13:10 after other gods to s them
Jer 16:13 you shall s other gods day
Jer 17: 4 I will cause you to s your
Jer 25: 6 go after other gods to s them
Jer 25:11 these nations shall s the
Jer 27: 6 have also given him to s him
Jer 27: 7 So all nations shall s him
Jer 27: 7 kings shall make him s them
Jer 27: 8 and kingdom which will not s
Jer 27: 9 You shall not s the king of
Jer 27:11 s him, I will let them remain
Jer 27:12 s him and his people, and live
Jer 27:13 not s the king of Babylon
Jer 27:14 You shall not s the king of
Jer 27:17 s the king of Babylon, and
Jer 28:14 nations, that they may s
Jer 28:14 and they shall s him
Jer 30: 9 But they shall s the LORD
Jer 35:15 go after other gods to s them
Jer 40: 9 be afraid to s the Chaldeans
Jer 40: 9 s the king of Babylon, and it
Jer 40:10 s the Chaldeans who come to
Jer 44: 3 to s other gods whom they did
Ezek 20:39 s every one of you his idols
Ezek 20:40 them in the land, shall s Me
Dan 1: 4 who had ability to s in the
Dan 1: 5 they might s before the king
Dan 3:12 They do not s your gods or
Dan 3:14 that you do not s my gods or
Dan 3:17 our God whom we s is able to
Dan 3:18 that we do not s your gods
Dan 3:28 that they should not s nor
Dan 6:16 whom you s continually, He
Dan 6:20 whom you s continually, been
Dan 7:14 and languages should s Him
Dan 7:27 and all dominions shall s
Zeph 3: 9 to s Him with one accord
Mal 3:14 said, 'It is vain to s God
Mal 3:18 one who does not s Him
Matt 4:10 God, and Him only you shall s
Matt 6:24 No one can s two masters
Matt 6:24 You cannot s God and mammon
Matt 20:28 come to be served, but to s
Mark 10:45 come to be served, but to s
Luke 1:74 might s Him without fear,
Luke 4: 8 God, and Him only you shall s
Luke 10:40 sister has left me to s alone
Luke 12:37 eat, and will come and s them
Luke 16:13 No servant can s two masters
Luke 16:13 You cannot s God and mammon
Luke 17: 8 s me till I have eaten and
Acts 6: 2 the word of God and s tables
Acts 7: 7 out and s Me in this place
Acts 27:23 to whom I belong and whom I s
Rom 1: 9 whom I s with my spirit in
Rom 7: 6 so that we should s in the
Rom 7:25 I myself s the law of God
Rom 9:12 The older shall s the younger
Rom 16:18 not s our Lord Jesus Christ
1Co 7:35 and that you may s the Lord
1Co 9:13 and those who s at the altar
Gal 3:19 purpose then does the law s
Gal 5:13 through love s one another
Col 3:24 for you s the Lord Christ
1Th 1: 9 from idols to s the living
1Ti 3:10 then let them s as deacons
1Ti 6: 2 but rather s them because
2Ti 1: 3 God, whom I s with a pure
Heb 8: 5 who s the copy and shadow of
Heb 9:14 works to s the living God
Heb 12:28 grace, by which we may s God
Heb 13:10 who s the tabernacle have no
Rev 7:15 s Him day and night in His
Rev 22: 3 and His servants shall s Him

SERVED (*see* SERVE)
Gen 14: 4 years they s Chedorlaomer
Gen 29:20 So Jacob s seven years for
Gen 29:25 not for Rachel that I s you
Gen 29:30 he s with Laban still another
Gen 30:26 for whom I have s you, and let
Gen 30:29 You know how I have s you
Gen 31: 6 my might I have s your father
Gen 31:41 I s you fourteen years for
Gen 39: 4 favor in his sight, and s him
Gen 40: 4 with them, and he s them
Deut 12: 2 shall dispossess s their gods
Deut 17: 3 s other gods and worshiped
Deut 29:26 s other gods and worshiped
Josh 23:16 s other gods, and bowed down
Josh 24: 2 and they s other gods
Josh 24:14 s on the other side of the
Josh 24:15 s that were on the other side
Josh 24:31 Israel s the LORD all the
Judg 2: 7 So the people s the LORD all
Judg 2:11 of the LORD, and s the Baals

Judg 2:13 and **s** Baal and the Ashtoreths
Judg 3: 6 and they **s** their gods
Judg 3: 7 and **s** the Baals and Asherahs
Judg 3: 8 and the children of Israel **s**
Judg 3:14 So the children of Israel **s**
Judg 10: 6 **s** the Baals and the Ashtoreths
Judg 10:10 our God and **s** the Baals
Judg 10:13 forsaken Me and **s** other gods
Judg 10:16 from among them and **s** the
1Sa 7: 4 and **s** the LORD only
1Sa 8: 8 forsaken Me and **s** other gods
1Sa 12:10 **s** the Baals and Ashtoreths
2Sa 10:19 peace with Israel and **s** them
2Sa 16:19 As I have **s** in your father's
1Ki 1: 4 cared for the king, and **s** him
1Ki 4:21 **s** Solomon all the days of his
1Ki 9: 9 and worshiped them and **s** them
1Ki 16:31 and **s** Baal and worshiped him
1Ki 19:21 and followed Elijah, and **s** him
1Ki 22:53 for he **s** Baal and worshiped
2Ki 4:40 Then they **s** it to the men to
2Ki 10:18 Ahab **s** Baal a little, but
2Ki 17:12 for they **s** idols, of which
2Ki 17:16 the host of heaven, and **s** Baal
2Ki 17:33 LORD, yet **s** their own gods
2Ki 17:41 yet **s** their carved images
2Ki 21: 3 the host of heaven and **s** them
2Ki 21:21 and he **s** the idols
2Ki 21:21 that his father had **s**
1Ch 6:32 and they **s** in their office
1Ch 27: 1 **s** the king in every matter of
1Ch 28: 1 the divisions who **s** the king
2Ch 7:22 and worshiped them and **s** them
2Ch 17:19 These **s** the king, besides
2Ch 22: 8 brothers who **s** Ahaziah, that
2Ch 24:18 and **s** wooden images and idols
2Ch 33: 3 the host of heaven and **s** them
2Ch 33:22 Manasseh had made, and **s** them
Neh 9:35 For they have not **s** You in
Esth 1: 7 And they **s** drinks in golden
Esth 1:10 seven eunuchs who **s** in the
Ps 106:36 They **s** their idols, Which
Ps 137: 8 repays you as you have **s** us
Eccl 5: 9 himself is **s** from the field
Jer 5:19 **s** foreign gods in your land,
Jer 8: 2 loved and which they have **s**
Jer 16:11 other gods and have **s** them
Jer 22: 9 other gods and **s** them
Jer 25:14 kings shall be **s** by them also
Jer 34:14 when he has **s** you six years,
Jer 52:12 who **s** the king of Babylon,
Dan 1:19 therefore they **s** before the
Hos 12:12 Israel **s** for a spouse, and for
Matt 8:15 Then she arose and **s** them
Matt 20:28 of Man did not come to be **s**
Mark 1:31 And she **s** them
Mark 10:45 of Man did not come to be **s**
Luke 2:37 but **s** God with fastings and
Luke 4:39 she arose and **s** them
John 12: 2 and Martha **s**, but Lazarus was
Acts 13:36 David, after he had **s** his own
Rom 1:25 **s** the creature rather than
Gal 4: 8 you **s** those which by nature
Phil 2:22 he **s** with me in the gospel
1Ti 3:13 For those who have **s** well as

SERVES (*see* SERVE)
Deut 15:12 **s** you six years, then in the
Ps 73: 6 Therefore pride **s** as their
Mal 3:17 spares his own son who **s** him
Mal 3:18 wicked, between one who **s** God
Luke 22:26 and he who governs as he who **s**
Luke 22:27 at the table, or he who **s**
Luke 22:27 am among you as the One who **s**
John 12:26 If anyone **s** Me, let him
John 12:26 If anyone **s** Me, him My Father
Rom 14:18 For he who **s** Christ in these

SERVICE (*see* SERVE, SERVICES)
Gen 29:27 **s** which you will serve with
Gen 30:26 for you know my **s** which I
Ex 1:14 all manner of **s** in the field
Ex 1:14 All their **s** in which they
Ex 12:25 that you shall keep this **s**
Ex 12:26 What do you mean by this **s**
Ex 13: 5 keep this **s** in this month
Ex 27:19 the tabernacle for all its **s**
Ex 30:16 the **s** of the tabernacle of
Ex 35:21 of meeting, for all its **s**
Ex 35:24 wood for any work of the **s**
Ex 36: 1 for the **s** of the sanctuary
Ex 36: 3 the **s** of making the sanctuary
Ex 36: 5 more than enough for the **s** of
Ex 38:21 for the **s** of the Levites, by
Ex 39:40 for the **s** of the tabernacle
Num 4: 3 all who enter the **s** to do the
Num 4: 4 This is the **s** of the sons of
Num 4: 9 vessels, with which they **s** it
Num 4:12 take all the utensils of **s**
Num 4:19 appoint each of them to his **s**
Num 4:23 who enter to perform the **s**
Num 4:24 This is the **s** of the families
Num 4:26 the furnishings for their **s**
Num 4:27 all the **s** of the sons of the
Num 4:27 their tasks and all their **s**
Num 4:28 This is the **s** of the families
Num 4:30 the **s** to do the work of the
Num 4:31 their **s** for the tabernacle of
Num 4:32 furnishings and all their **s**
Num 4:33 This is the **s** of the families
Num 4:33 as all their **s** for the
Num 4:35 everyone who entered the **s**
Num 4:39 everyone who entered the **s**
Num 4:43 everyone who entered the **s**
Num 4:47 who came to do the work of **s**
Num 4:49 each according to his **s** and
Num 7: 5 every man according to his **s**
Num 7: 7 Gershon, according to their **s**
Num 7: 8 Merari, according to their **s**
Num 7: 9 was the **s** of the holy things
Num 8:15 **s** the tabernacle of meeting
Num 8:24 perform **s** in the work of the
Num 18: 7 to you as a gift for **s**, but
Josh 22:27 that we may perform the **s** of
2Sa 9: 2 And he said, "At your **s**!"
1Ki 10: 5 the **s** of his waiters and their
1Ki 12: 4 burdensome **s** of your father
1Ch 6:31 David appointed over the **s** of
1Ch 6:48 of **s** of the tabernacle of the
1Ch 9:13 of the **s** of the house of God
1Ch 9:19 charge of the work of the **s**
1Ch 23:24 **s** of the house of the LORD
1Ch 23:26 any of the articles for its **s**
1Ch 23:28 **s** of the house of the LORD
1Ch 23:28 and the work of the **s** of the
1Ch 24: 3 to the schedule of their **s**
1Ch 24:19 **s** for coming into the house
1Ch 25: 1 **s** some of the sons of Asaph
1Ch 25: 1 according to their **s** was
1Ch 25: 6 for the **s** of the house of God
1Ch 26:30 LORD, and in the **s** of the king
1Ch 28:13 for all the work of the **s** of
1Ch 28:13 for all the articles of **s** in
1Ch 28:14 used in every kind of **s**
1Ch 28:14 used in every kind of **s**
1Ch 28:20 all the work for the **s** of the
1Ch 28:21 all the **s** of the house of God
1Ch 28:21 for every kind of **s**
2Ch 8:14 of the priests for their **s**
2Ch 9: 4 the **s** of his waiters and their
2Ch 10: 4 burdensome **s** of your father
2Ch 12: 8 My **s** from the **s** of the
2Ch 24:12 who did the work of the **s** of
2Ch 29:35 So the **s** of the house of the
2Ch 31: 2 each man according to his **s**
2Ch 31:16 portion for the work of his **s**
2Ch 31:21 in the **s** of the house of God
2Ch 34:13 who did work in any kind of **s**
2Ch 35: 2 encouraged them for the **s** of
2Ch 35:10 So the **s** was prepared, and the
2Ch 35:16 So all the **s** of the LORD was
Ezra 6:18 over the **s** of God in
Ezra 7:19 **s** of the house of your God
Ezra 8:20 for the **s** of the Levites, two
Neh 10:32 of a shekel for the **s** of the
Neh 11:22 of the **s** of the house of God
Neh 13:30 and the Levites, each to his **s**
Job 7: 1 of hard **s** for man on earth
Job 14:14 days of my hard **s** I will wait
Ps 104:14 vegetation for the **s** of man
Jer 22:13 neighbor's **s** without wages
Luke 1:23 days of his **s** were completed
John 16: 2 think that he offers God **s**
Rom 9: 4 the **s** of God, and the promises
Rom 12: 1 which is your reasonable **s**
Rom 15:31 that my **s** for Jerusalem may
2Co 9:12 the administration of this **s**
Eph 6: 7 with good will doing **s**, as to
Phil 2:17 **s** of your faith, I am glad and
Phil 2:30 lacking in your **s** toward me
Heb 9: 1 had ordinances of divine **s**
Heb 9: 9 **s** perfect in regard to the
Rev 2:19 I know your works, love, **s**

SERVICES (*see* SERVICE)
2Ch 7: 6 priests attended to their **s**
Neh 13:14 house of my God, and for its **s**
Heb 9: 6 tabernacle, performing the **s**

SERVING (*see* SERVE, SERVINGS)
Gen 43:34 but Benjamin's **s** was five
Ex 14: 5 have let Israel go from **s** us
Ex 38: 8 the bronze mirrors of the **s**
Num 4:24 of the Gershonites, in **s** and
Deut 15:18 servant in **s** you six years
1Ki 1:15 the Shunammite was **s** the king
1Ch 9:28 in charge of the **s** vessels
2Ch 11:14 from **s** as priests to the LORD
2Ch 24:14 of the LORD, articles for **s**
Eccl 11: 2 Give a **s** to seven, and also to
Ezek 20:32 countries, **s** wood and stone
Luke 1: 8 that while he was **s** as priest
Luke 10:40 was distracted with much **s**
Luke 15:29 many years I have been **s** you
Acts 20:19 **s** the Lord with all humility,
Acts 26: 7 tribes, earnestly **s** God night
Rom 12:11 fervent in spirit, **s** the Lord
Tit 3: 3 **s** various lusts and pleasures,
1Pe 5: 2 you, **s** as overseers, not by
Jude 12 fear, **s** only themselves

SERVINGS (*see* SERVING)
Gen 43:34 Then he took **s** to them from

SERVITUDE (*see* SERVE)
Lam 1: 3 under affliction and hard **s**

SET (*see* PREFACE)

SETH
Gen 4:25 she bore a son and named him **S**
Gen 4:26 And as for **S**, to him also a
Gen 5: 3 his image, and named him **S**
Gen 5: 4 After he begot **S**, the days of
Gen 5: 6 **S** lived one hundred and five
Gen 5: 7 **S** lived eight hundred and
Gen 5: 8 days of **S** were nine hundred
1Ch 1: 1 Adam, **S**, Enosh,
Luke 3:38 the son of Enos, the son of **S**

SETHUR
Num 13:13 Asher, **S** the son of Michael

SETS (*see* PREFACE)

SETTING (*see* PREFACE)

SETTINGS (*see* PREFACE)

SETTLE (*see* SETTLED, SETTLEMENTS, SETTLING)
Deut 29:20 in this book would **s** on him
Job 3: 5 may a cloud **s** on it
Ps 65:10 abundantly, You **s** its furrows
Is 14: 1 and **s** them in their own land
Ezek 32: 4 cause to **s** on you all the
Zech 9: 6 mixed race shall **s** in Ashdod
Matt 18:23 **s** accounts with his servants
Matt 18:24 he had begun to **s** accounts
Luke 12:58 along the way to **s** with him
Luke 21:14 Therefore **s** it in your hearts
1Pe 5:10 strengthen, and **s** you

SETTLED (*see* SETTLE)
Num 9:17 the place where the cloud **s**
Num 10:12 then the cloud **s** down in the
Deut 21: 5 and every assault shall be **s**
Judg 9:24 sons of Jerubbaal might be **s**
1Ch 5: 9 Eastward they **s** as far as the
2Ch 8: 2 he **s** the children of Israel
Ezra 4:10 **s** in the cities of Samaria and
Job 29:22 my speech **s** on them as dew
Ps 94:17 would soon have **s** in silence
Ps 119:89 Your word is **s** in heaven
Prov 8:25 Before the mountains were **s**
Is 13:20 nor will it be **s** from
Jer 48:11 he has **s** on his dregs, and has
Zeph 1:12 men who are **s** in complacency
Matt 25:19 came and **s** accounts with them

SETTLEMENTS (*see* SETTLE)
Gen 25:16 by their towns and their **s**
1Ch 6:54 their **s** in their territory

SETTLING (*see* SETTLE)
Num 22: 5 earth, and are **s** next to me

Neh 7:67 of whom there were s thousand
Neh 7:68 Their horses were s hundred
Neh 7:69 six thousand s hundred and
Neh 8:18 And they kept the feast s days
Esth 1: 5 king made a feast lasting s
Esth 1:10 s eunuchs who served in the
Esth 1:14 the s princes of Persia and
Esth 2: 9 Then s choice maidservants
Job 1: 2 s sons and three daughters
Job 2:13 with him on the ground s days
Job 2:13 s nights, and no one spoke a
Job 5:19 in s no evil shall touch you
Job 42: 8 take for yourselves s bulls
Job 42: 8 s rams, go to My servant Job,
Job 42:13 He also had s sons and three
Ps 12: 6 of earth, Purified s times
Ps 119:164 S times a day I praise You,
Prov 6:16 s are an abomination to Him
Prov 9: 1 has hewn out her s pillars
Prov 24:16 man may fall s times and rise
Prov 26:16 wiser in his own eyes than s
Prov 26:25 for there are s abominations
Eccl 11: 2 Give a serving to s, and also
Is 4: 1 in that day s women shall
Is 11:15 and strike it in the s streams
Is 30:26 as the light of s days, in
Jer 15: 9 languishes who has borne s
Jer 34:14 At the end of s years let
Jer 52:25 s men of the king's close
Jer 52:30 captive of the Jews s hundred
Ezek 3:15 astonished among them s days
Ezek 3:16 s days that the word of the
Ezek 39: 9 fires with them for s years
Ezek 39:12 For s months the house of
Ezek 39:14 At the end of s months they
Ezek 40:22 it was ascended by s steps
Ezek 40:26 S steps led up to it, and its
Ezek 41: 3 of the entrance, s cubits
Ezek 43:25 Every day for s days you
Ezek 43:26 S days they shall make
Ezek 44:26 shall count s days for him
Ezek 45:21 Passover, a feast of s days
Ezek 45:23 On the s days of the feast he
Ezek 45:23 s bulls and s rams without
Ezek 45:23 blemish, daily for s days
Ezek 45:25 shall do likewise for s days
Dan 3:19 s times more than it was
Dan 4:16 let s times pass over him
Dan 4:23 till s times pass over him'
Dan 4:25 s times shall pass over you,
Dan 4:32 s times shall pass over you,
Dan 9:25 there shall be s weeks and
Mic 5: 5 raise against him s shepherds
Zech 3: 9 upon the stone are s eyes
Zech 4: 2 on the stand s lamps with
Zech 4: 2 s pipes to the s lamps
Zech 4:10 for these s rejoice to see
Matt 12:45 and takes with him s other
Matt 15:34 S, and a few little fish
Matt 15:36 And He took the s loaves and
Matt 15:37 they took up s large baskets
Matt 16:10 Nor the s loaves of the four
Matt 18:21 forgive him? Up to s times?
Matt 18:22 not say to you, up to s times
Matt 18:22 but up to seventy times s
Matt 22:25 there were with us s brothers
Matt 22:28 wife of the s will she be
Mark 8: 5 And they said, "S."
Mark 8: 6 And He took the s loaves and
Mark 8: 8 they took up s large baskets
Mark 8:20 when I broke the s for the
Mark 8:20 And they said, "S."
Mark 12:20 Now there were s brothers
Mark 12:22 So the s had her and left no
Mark 12:23 For all s had her as wife
Mark 16: 9 of whom He had cast s demons
Luke 2:36 s years from her virginity
Luke 8: 2 out of whom had come s demons
Luke 11:26 and takes with him s other
Luke 17: 4 against you s times in a day
Luke 17: 4 s times in a day returns to
Luke 20:29 Now there were s brothers
Luke 20:31 and in like manner the s also
Luke 20:33 For all s had her as wife
Luke 24:13 which was about s miles from
Acts 6: 3 you s men of good reputation
Acts 13:19 And when He had destroyed s
Acts 19:14 there were s sons of Sceva
Acts 20: 6 Troas, where we stayed s days
Acts 21: 4 we stayed there s days
Acts 21: 8 who was one of the s, and
Acts 21:27 when the s days were almost
Acts 28:14 to stay with them s days
Rom 11: 4 s thousand men who have not
Heb 11:30 were encircled for s days
Rev 1: 4 to the s churches which are
Rev 1: 4 from the s Spirits who are
Rev 1:11 send it to the s churches
Rev 1:12 I saw s golden lampstands
Rev 1:13 and in the midst of the s
Rev 1:16 had in His right hand s stars
Rev 1:20 The mystery of the s stars
Rev 1:20 and the s golden lampstands
Rev 1:20 The s stars are
Rev 1:20 the angels of the s churches
Rev 1:20 the s lampstands which
Rev 1:20 you saw are the s churches
Rev 2: 1 says He who holds the s stars
Rev 2: 1 of the s golden lampstands
Rev 3: 1 who has the s Spirits of God
Rev 3: 1 Spirits of God and the s stars
Rev 4: 5 there were s lamps of fire
Rev 4: 5 which are the s Spirits of
Rev 5: 1 the back, sealed with s seals
Rev 5: 5 and to loose its s seals
Rev 5: 6 having s horns and s eyes
Rev 5: 6 which are the s Spirits of
Rev 8: 2 I saw the s angels who stand
Rev 8: 2 to them were given s trumpets
Rev 8: 6 So the s angels who
Rev 8: 6 had the s trumpets prepared
Rev 10: 3 out, s thunders uttered their
Rev 10: 4 Now when the s thunders
Rev 10: 4 which the s thunders uttered
Rev 11:13 In the earthquake s thousand
Rev 12: 3 red dragon having s heads
Rev 12: 3 and s diadems on his heads
Rev 13: 1 of the sea, having s heads
Rev 15: 1 s angels having the s last
Rev 15: 6 s angels having the s
Rev 15: 7 creatures gave to the s
Rev 15: 7 s golden bowls full of the
Rev 15: 8 enter the temple till the s
Rev 15: 8 the s angels were completed
Rev 16: 1 temple saying to the s angels
Rev 17: 1 Then one of the s angels who
Rev 17: 1 who had the s bowls came and
Rev 17: 3 of blasphemy, having s heads
Rev 17: 7 her, which has the s heads
Rev 17: 9 The s heads are s
Rev 17:10 There are also s kings
Rev 17:11 the eighth, and is of the s
Rev 21: 9 Then one of the s angels who
Rev 21: 9 the s last plagues came to me

SEVENFOLD

Gen 4:15 shall be taken on him s
Gen 4:24 If Cain shall be avenged s
Ps 79:12 s into their bosom Their
Prov 6:31 is found, he must restore s
Is 30:26 light of the sun will be s

SEVENTEEN (*see* SEVENTEENTH)

Gen 37: 2 being s years old, was
Gen 47:28 in the land of Egypt s years
1Ki 14:21 He reigned s years in
2Ki 13: 1 Samaria, and reigned s years
1Ch 7:11 there were s thousand two
2Ch 12:13 and he reigned s years in
Ezra 2:39 of Harim, one thousand and s
Neh 7:42 of Harim, one thousand and s
Jer 32: 9 s shekels of silver

SEVENTEENTH (*see* SEVENTEEN)

Gen 7:11 the s day of the month, on
Gen 8: 4 the s day of the month, on
1Ki 22:51 Israel in Samaria in the s
2Ki 16: 1 In the s year of Pekah the
1Ch 24:15 the s to Hezir, the
1Ch 25:24 the s for Joshbekashah, his

SEVENTH (*see* SEVEN)

Gen 2: 2 on the s day God ended His
Gen 2: 2 He rested on the s day from
Gen 2: 3 Then God blessed the s day
Gen 8: 4 the ark rested in the s month
Ex 12:15 the first day until the s day
Ex 12:16 on the s day there shall be a
Ex 13: 6 on the s day there shall be a
Ex 16:26 gather it, but on the s day
Ex 16:27 out on the s day to gather
Ex 16:29 out of his place on the s day
Ex 16:30 people rested on the s day
Ex 20:10 but the s day is the Sabbath
Ex 20:11 in them, and rested the s day
Ex 21: 2 in the s he shall go out free
Ex 23:11 but the s year you shall let
Ex 23:12 on the s day you shall rest,
Ex 24:16 on the s day He called to
Ex 31:15 but the s is the Sabbath of
Ex 31:17 on the s day He rested and was
Ex 34:21 but on the s day you shall
Ex 35: 2 but the s day shall be a holy
Lev 13: 5 look at him on the s day
Lev 13: 6 at him again on the s day
Lev 13:27 look at him on the s day
Lev 13:32 on the s day the priest shall
Lev 13:34 On the s day the priest shall
Lev 13:51 at the plague on the s day
Lev 14: 9 But on the s day he shall
Lev 14:39 shall come again on the s day
Lev 16:29 In the s month, on the tenth
Lev 23: 3 but the s day is a Sabbath of
Lev 23: 8 The s day shall be a holy
Lev 23:16 the day after the s Sabbath
Lev 23:24 In the s month, on the first
Lev 23:27 s month shall be the Day of
Lev 23:34 The fifteenth day of this s
Lev 23:39 fifteenth day of the s month
Lev 23:41 celebrate it in the s month
Lev 25: 4 but in the s year there
Lev 25: 9 the tenth day of the s month
Lev 25:20 shall we eat in the s year
Num 6: 9 on the s day he shall shave
Num 7:48 On the s day Elishama the son
Num 19:12 the third day and on the s day
Num 19:12 the third day and on the s day
Num 19:19 the third day and on the s day
Num 19:19 on the s day he shall purify
Num 28:25 on the s day you shall have a
Num 29: 1 And in the s month, on the
Num 29: 7 On the tenth day of this s
Num 29:12 s month you shall have a holy
Num 29:32 On the s day present seven
Num 31:19 the third day and on the s day
Num 31:24 your clothes on the s day
Deut 5:14 but the s day is the Sabbath
Deut 15: 9 heart, saying, 'The s year
Deut 15:12 then in the s year you shall
Deut 16: 8 on the s day there shall be a
Josh 6: 4 But the s day you shall march
Josh 6:15 s day that they rose early
Josh 6:16 the s time it was so, when
Josh 19:40 The s lot came out for the
Judg 14:15 the s day that they said to
Judg 14:17 it happened on the s day that
Judg 14:18 the s day before the sun went
2Sa 12:18 Then on the s day it came to
1Ki 8: 2 Ethanim, which is the s month
1Ki 18:44 it came to pass the s time
1Ki 20:29 So it was that on the s day
2Ki 11: 4 In the s year Jehoiada sent
2Ki 12: 1 In the s year of Jehu,
2Ki 18: 9 which was the s year of
2Ki 25: 8 on the s day of the month
2Ki 25:25 Now it happened in the s
1Ch 2:15 the sixth, and David the s
1Ch 12:11 Attai the sixth, Eliel the s
1Ch 24:10 the s to Hakkoz, the eighth
1Ch 25:14 the s for Jesharelah, his
1Ch 26: 3 the sixth, Eljehoenai the s
1Ch 26: 5 the sixth, Issachar the s
1Ch 27:10 The s captain for the s month
2Ch 5: 3 which was in the s month
2Ch 7:10 s month he sent the people
2Ch 23: 1 In the s year Jehoiada
2Ch 31: 7 they finished in the s month
Ezra 3: 1 when the s month had come, and
Ezra 3: 6 s month they began to offer
Ezra 7: 7 the s year of King Artaxerxes
Ezra 7: 8 was in the s year of the king
Neh 7:73 When the s month came, the
Neh 8: 2 the first day of the s month
Neh 8:14 the feast of the s month,
Neh 10:31 forego the s year's produce
Esth 1:10 On the s day, when the heart
Esth 2:16 in the s year of his reign
Jer 28:17 the same year in the s month
Jer 41: 1 s month that Ishmael the son
Jer 52:28 in the s year, three thousand
Ezek 20: 1 It came to pass in the s year
Ezek 30:20 on the s day of the month,

Ezek 45:20 on the s day of the month for
Ezek 45:25 In the s month, on the
Hag 2: 1 In the s month, on the
Zech 7: 5 s months during those seventy
Zech 8:19 the fifth, the fast of the s
Matt 22:26 and the third, even to the s
John 4:52 Yesterday at the s hour the
Heb 4: 4 of the s day in this way
Heb 4: 4 God rested on the s day from
Jude 14 the s from Adam, prophesied
Rev 8: 1 When He opened the s seal
Rev 10: 7 the sounding of the s angel
Rev 11:15 Then the s angel sounded
Rev 16:17 Then the s angel poured out
Rev 21:20 the s chrysolite, the eighth

SEVENTY
Gen 5:12 Cainan lived s years, and
Gen 11:26 Now Terah lived s years, and
Gen 46:27 who went to Egypt were s
Gen 50: 3 mourned for him s days
Ex 1: 5 descendants of Jacob were s
Ex 15:27 of water and s palm trees
Ex 24: 1 s of the elders of Israel, and
Ex 24: 9 s of the elders of Israel,
Ex 38:29 of bronze was s talents and
Num 7:13 one silver bowl of s shekels
Num 7:19 one silver bowl of s shekels
Num 7:25 one silver bowl of s shekels
Num 7:31 one silver bowl of s shekels
Num 7:37 one silver bowl of s shekels
Num 7:43 one silver bowl of s shekels
Num 7:49 one silver bowl of s shekels
Num 7:55 one silver bowl of s shekels
Num 7:61 one silver bowl of s shekels
Num 7:67 one silver bowl of s shekels
Num 7:73 one silver bowl of s shekels
Num 7:79 one silver bowl of s shekels
Num 7:85 and each bowl s shekels
Num 11:16 Gather to Me s men of the
Num 11:24 he gathered the s men of the
Num 11:25 the same upon the s elders
Num 33: 9 of water and s palm trees
Deut 10:22 down to Egypt with s persons
Judg 1: 7 S kings with their thumbs and
Judg 8:30 Gideon had s sons who were
Judg 9: 2 that all s of the sons of
Judg 9: 4 So they gave him s shekels of
Judg 9: 5 the s sons of Jerubbaal, on
Judg 9:18 and killed his s sons on one
Judg 9:24 s sons of Jerubbaal might be
Judg 9:56 by killing his s brothers
Judg 12:14 who rode on s young donkeys
1Sa 6:19 s men of the people, and the
2Sa 24:15 From Dan to Beersheba s
1Ki 5:15 Solomon had s thousand who
2Ki 10: 1 Now Ahab had s sons in
2Ki 10: 6 s persons, were with the
2Ki 10: 7 sons and slaughtered s persons
1Ch 21: 5 s thousand men who drew the
1Ch 21:14 s thousand men of Israel fell
2Ch 2: 2 Solomon selected s thousand
2Ch 2:18 he made s thousand of them
2Ch 29:32 brought was s bulls, one
2Ch 36:21 Sabbath, to fulfill s years
Ezra 8: 7 Athaliah, and with him s males
Ezra 8:14 Zabbud, and with them s males
Ps 90:10 days of our lives are s years
Is 23:15 will be forgotten s years
Is 23:15 At the end of s years it will
Is 23:17 be, at the end of s years
Jer 25:11 the king of Babylon s years
Jer 25:12 when s years are completed,
Jer 29:10 After s years are completed
Ezek 8:11 there stood before them s men
Ezek 41:12 western end was s cubits wide
Dan 9: 2 that He would accomplish s
Dan 9:24 S weeks are determined for
Zech 1:12 You were angry these s years
Zech 7: 5 months during those s years
Matt 18:22 but up to s times seven
Luke 10: 1 Lord appointed s others also
Luke 10:17 Then the s returned with joy,
Acts 23:23 s horsemen, and two hundred

SEVENTY-FIVE
Gen 12: 4 Abram was s years old when he
Gen 25: 7 one hundred and s years
Ex 38:25 s shekels, according to the
Ex 38:28 s shekels he made hooks for
Num 31:32 hundred and s thousand sheep,
Num 31:37 sheep was six hundred and s
Ezra 2: 5 of Arah, seven hundred and s
Esth 9:16 killed s thousand of their
Acts 7:14 relatives to him, s people

SEVENTY-FOUR
Num 1:27 were s thousand six hundred
Num 2: 4 at s thousand six hundred
Ezra 2:40 of the sons of Hodaviah, s
Neh 7:43 of the children of Hodevah, s

SEVENTY-SEVEN
Gen 5:31 were seven hundred and s years
Judg 8:14 Succoth and its elders, s men
Ezra 8:35 s lambs, and twelve male goats

SEVENTY-SEVENFOLD
Gen 4:24 sevenfold, then Lamech s

SEVENTY-SIX
Num 26:22 s thousand five hundred
Acts 27:37 and s persons on the ship

SEVENTY-THREE
Num 3:43 thousand two hundred and s
Num 3:46 s of the firstborn of the
Ezra 2:36 of Jeshua, nine hundred and s
Neh 7:39 of Jeshua, nine hundred and s

SEVENTY-TWO
Num 31:33 s thousand cattle,
Num 31:38 the LORD's tribute was s
Ezra 2: 3 two thousand one hundred and s
Ezra 2: 4 three hundred and s
Neh 7: 8 two thousand one hundred and s
Neh 7: 9 three hundred and s
Neh 11:19 gates, were one hundred and s

SEVER
Is 2:22 S yourselves from such a man,

SEVERAL (*see* PREFACE)

SEVERE (*see* SEVERELY, SEVERITY)
Gen 12:10 the famine was s in the land
Gen 41:31 for it will be very s
Gen 41:56 the famine became s in the
Gen 41:57 the famine was s in all lands
Gen 43: 1 the famine was s in the land
Gen 47: 4 for the famine is s in the
Gen 47:13 for the famine was very s
Gen 47:20 the famine was s upon them
Ex 9: 3 will be a very s pestilence
Ex 10:14 They were very s
Deut 6:22 before our eyes, great and s
Deut 28:22 with s burning fever, with
Deut 28:35 and on the legs with s boils
1Ki 18: 2 and there was a s famine in
2Ki 25: 3 the famine had become so s in
2Ch 16:12 and his malady was very s
2Ch 21:19 so he died in s pain
Ps 71:20 s troubles, Shall revive me
Eccl 5:13 There is a s evil which I
Eccl 5:16 And this also is a s evil,
Is 27: 1 day the LORD with His s sword
Jer 10:19 My wound is s
Jer 14:17 stroke, with a very s blow
Jer 30:12 is incurable, your wound is s
Jer 52: 6 the famine had become so s in
Ezek 14:21 four s judgments on Jerusalem
Nah 3:19 no healing, your wound is s
Luke 15:14 there arose a s famine in
2Co 2: 5 not to be too s

SEVERELY (*see* SEVERE)
Judg 10: 9 that Israel was s distressed
1Sa 1: 6 her rival also provoked her s
1Sa 28:21 and saw that he was s troubled
1Sa 31: 3 and he was s wounded by the
2Ch 24:25 (for they left him s wounded)
2Ch 35:23 me away, for I am s wounded
Ps 38: 8 I am feeble and s broken
Ps 44:19 But You have s broken us in
Ps 55: 4 My heart is s pained within
Ps 118:18 The LORD has chastened me s
Is 64:12 peace, and afflict us very s
Matt 15:22 My daughter is s
Matt 17:15 is an epileptic and suffers s
Acts 4:17 let us s threaten them, that

SEVERITY (*see* SEVERE)
Rom 11:22 the goodness and s of God
Rom 11:22 on those who fell, s

SEW (*see* SEWED, SEWN, SEWS)
Eccl 3: 7 time to tear, and a time to s
Ezek 13:18 Woe to the women who s magic

SEWED (*see* SEW)
Gen 3: 7 they s fig leaves together and

SEWN (*see* SEW)
Job 16:15 I have s sackcloth over my

SEWS (*see* SEW)
Mark 2:21 No one s a piece of unshrunk

SEXUAL (*see* SEXUALLY)
Matt 5:32 s immorality causes her to
Matt 19: 9 wife, except for s immorality
Acts 15:20 from s immorality, from
Acts 15:29 and from s immorality
Acts 21:25 and from s immorality
Rom 1:29 s immorality, wickedness,
1Co 5: 1 is s immorality among you
1Co 5: 1 such s immorality as is not
1Co 6:13 Now the body is not for s
1Co 6:18 Flee s immorality
1Co 6:18 body, but he who commits s
1Co 7: 2 because of s immorality, let
1Co 10: 8 let us commit s immorality
1Th 4: 3 abstain from s immorality
Jude 7 over to s immorality and gone
Rev 2:14 and to commit s immorality
Rev 2:20 to commit s immorality and to
Rev 2:21 to repent of her s immorality
Rev 9:21 s immorality or their thefts

SEXUALLY (*see* SEXUAL)
1Co 5: 9 company with s immoral people
1Co 5:10 did not mean with the s
Rev 21: 8 s immoral, sorcerers,
Rev 22:15 s immoral and murderers and

SHAALABBIN (*see* SHAALBIM)
Josh 19:42 S, Aijalon, Jethlah,

SHAALBIM (*see* SHAALABBIN, SHAALBONITE)
Judg 1:35 Heres, in Aijalon, and in S
1Ki 4: 9 Ben-Deker, in Makaz, S, Beth

SHAALBONITE (*see* SHAALBIM)
2Sa 23:32 Eliahba the S (of the sons of
1Ch 11:33 the Baharumite, Eliahba the S

SHAALIM
1Sa 9: 4 passed through the land of S

SHAAPH
1Ch 2:47 Geshan, Pelet, Ephah, and S
1Ch 2:49 She also bore S the father of

SHAARAIM (*see* SHARAIM, SHARUHEN, SHILHIM)
1Sa 17:52 fell along the road to S,
1Ch 4:31 Susim, Beth Biri, and at S

SHAASHGAZ
Esth 2:14 women, to the custody of S

SHABBETHAI
Ezra 10:15 and S the Levite gave them
Neh 8: 7 Sherebiah, Jamin, Akkub, S
Neh 11:16 S and Jozabad, of the heads of

SHACKLES
Mark 5: 4 had often been bound with s
Mark 5: 4 and the s broken in pieces
Luke 8:29 guard, bound with chains and s

SHADE (*see* SHADED)
Judg 9:15 come and take shelter in my s
Job 7: 2 who earnestly desires the s
Job 40:22 trees cover him with their s
Ps 121: 5 The LORD is your s at your
Song 2: 3 I sat down in his s with
Is 4: 6 for s in the daytime from the
Is 25: 4 the storm, a s from the heat
Dan 4:12 of the field found s under it
Hos 4:13 because their s is good
Jon 4: 5 and sat under it in the s,
Jon 4: 6 that it might be s for his
Mark 4:32 the air may nest under its s

SHADED (*see* SHADE)
Ezek 31: 3 branches that s the forest

SHADOW (*see* SHADOWED, SHADOWS)
Gen 19: 8 come under the s of my roof
2Ki 20: 9 shall the s go forward ten
2Ki 20:10 the s to go down ten degrees
2Ki 20:10 but let the s go backward ten
2Ki 20:11 He brought the s ten degrees

1Ch 29:15 our days on earth are as a s
Job 3: 5 and the s of death claim it
Job 8: 9 our days on earth are a s
Job 10:21 darkness and the s of death,
Job 10:22 as the s of death, without
Job 12:22 and brings the s of death to
Job 14: 2 He flees like a s and does not
Job 16:16 my eyelids is the s of death
Job 24:17 to them as the s of death
Job 24:17 the terrors of the s of death
Job 28: 3 darkness and the s of death
Job 34:22 There is no darkness nor s of
Job 38:17 the doors of the s of death
Ps 17: 8 me under the s of Your wings
Ps 23: 4 the valley of the s of death
Ps 36: 7 under the s of Your wings
Ps 39: 6 man walks about like a s
Ps 44:19 us with the s of death
Ps 57: 1 in the s of Your wings I will
Ps 63: 7 Therefore in the s of Your
Ps 80:10 hills were covered with its s
Ps 91: 1 under the s of the Almighty
Ps 102:11 are like a s that lengthens
Ps 107:10 in the s of death, Bound in
Ps 107:14 and the s of death, And broke
Ps 109:23 I am gone like a s when it
Ps 144: 4 His days are like a passing s
Eccl 6:12 life which he passes like a s
Eccl 8:13 his days, which are as a s
Is 9: 2 in the land of the s of death
Is 16: 3 make your s like the night in
Is 25: 5 as heat in the s of a cloud
Is 30: 2 and to trust in the s of Egypt
Is 30: 3 trust in the s of Egypt shall
Is 32: 2 as the s of a great rock in a
Is 34:15 and gather them under her s
Is 38: 8 bring the s on the sundial
Is 49: 2 in the s of His hand He has
Is 51:16 you with the s of My hand
Jer 2: 6 the s of death, through a
Jer 13:16 turns it into the s of death
Jer 48:45 the s of Heshbon because of
Lam 4:20 Under his s we shall live
Ezek 17:23 in the s of its branches they
Ezek 31: 6 in its s all great nations
Ezek 31:12 have gone from under its s
Hos 14: 7 under his s shall return
Amos 5: 8 he turns the s of death into
Matt 4:16 s of death light has dawned
Luke 1:79 the s of death, to guide our
Acts 5:15 that at least the s of Peter
Col 2:17 which are a s of things to
Heb 8: 5 s of the heavenly things, as
Heb 10: 1 having a s of the good things
Jas 1:17 no variation or s of turning

SHADOWED (*see* SHADOW)
Is 18: 1 Woe to the land s with

SHADOWS (*see* SHADOW)
Judg 9:36 him, "You see the s of the
Job 17: 7 and all my members are like s
Song 2:17 the s flee away, turn, my
Song 4: 6 the s flee away, I will go my
Jer 6: 4 for the s of the evening are
Ezek 31:17 in its s among the nations

SHADRACH (*see* HANANIAH)
Dan 1: 7 to Hananiah, S
Dan 2:49 the king, and he set S,
Dan 3:12 S, Meshach, and Abed-Nego
Dan 3:13 gave the command to bring S
Dan 3:14 Is it true, S, Meshach, and
Dan 3:16 S, Meshach, and Abed-Nego
Dan 3:19 on his face changed toward S
Dan 3:20 were in his army to bind S
Dan 3:22 those men who took up S,
Dan 3:23 And these three men, S,
Dan 3:26 S, Meshach, and Abed-Nego,
Dan 3:26 Then S, Meshach, and
Dan 3:28 Blessed be the God of S,
Dan 3:29 amiss against the God of S
Dan 3:30 Then the king promoted S,

SHAFT (*see* SHAFTS)
Ex 25:31 Its s, its branches, its
Ex 37:17 Its s, its branches, its
Num 8: 4 from its s to its flowers it
2Sa 5: 8 up by way of the water s and
2Sa 21:19 the s of whose spear was like
2Sa 23: 7 the s of a spear, and they
1Ch 20: 5 the s of whose spear was like
Job 28: 4 open a s away from people
Is 49: 2 Me, and made Me a polished s

SHAFTS (*see* SHAFT)
Ps 7:13 makes His arrows into fiery s

SHAGEH
1Ch 11:34 the son of S the Hararite

SHAHARAIM
1Ch 8: 8 And S begot children in the

SHAHAZIMAH
Josh 19:22 border reached to Tabor, S

SHAKE (*see* SHAKEN, SHAKES, SHAKING, SHOOK)
Judg 16:20 other times, and s myself free
Neh 5:13 So may God s out each man
Job 4:14 which made all my bones s
Job 15:33 He will s off his unripe
Job 16: 4 you, and s my head at you
Job 17: 3 he who will s hands with me
Ps 22: 7 lip, they s the head, saying,
Ps 46: 3 mountains s with its swelling
Ps 69:23 their loins s continually
Ps 109:25 at me, they s their heads
Is 2:19 when He arises to s the earth
Is 2:21 when He arises to s the earth
Is 10:32 he will s his fist at the
Is 11:15 s His fist over the River
Is 13:13 I will s the heavens, and the
Is 33: 9 Carmel s off their fruits
Is 52: 2 S yourself from the dust,
Is 64: 1 might s at Your presence
Jer 18:16 be astonished and s his head
Jer 23: 9 all my bones s
Jer 48:27 him, You s your head in scorn
Lam 2:15 s their heads at the daughter
Ezek 26:10 your walls will s at the
Ezek 26:15 Will the coastlands not s at
Ezek 27:28 The common-land will s at the
Ezek 29: 7 and made all their loins s
Ezek 31:16 I made the nations s at the
Ezek 38:20 earth shall s at My presence
Joel 3:16 the heavens and earth will s
Amos 9: 1 that the thresholds may s
Nah 2:10 heart melts, and the knees s
Zeph 2:15 her shall hiss and s his fist
Hag 2: 6 little while) I will s heaven
Hag 2: 7 I will s all nations, and they
Hag 2:21 I will s heaven and earth
Zech 2: 9 For surely I will s My hand
Matt 10:14 s off the dust from your feet
Mark 6:11 s off the dust under your
Luke 6:48 that house, and could not s it
Luke 9: 5 s off the very dust from your
Heb 12:26 Yet once more I s not only

SHAKEN (*see* SHAKE)
Lev 26:36 the sound of a s leaf shall
1Ki 14:15 as a reed is s in the water
2Ki 19:21 s her head behind your back
Neh 5:13 Even thus may he be s out
Job 16:12 by my neck, and s me to pieces
Job 34:20 the people are s and pass away
Job 38:13 and the wicked be s out of it
Ps 18: 7 hills also quaked and were s
Ps 109:23 I am s off like a locust
Ps 112: 6 Surely he will never be s
Prov 6: 1 if you have s hands in pledge
Is 6: 4 s by the voice of him who
Is 24:18 of the earth are s
Is 24:19 the earth is s exceedingly
Is 37:22 s her head behind your back
Nah 3:12 if they are s, they fall into
Matt 11: 7 A reed s by the wind
Matt 24:29 of the heavens will be s
Mark 13:25 powers in heaven will be s
Luke 6:38 s together, and running over
Luke 7:24 A reed s by the wind
Luke 21:26 powers of heaven will be s
Acts 2:25 hand, that I may not be s
Acts 4:31 were assembled together was s
Acts 16:26 of the prison were s
1Th 3: 3 be s by these afflictions
2Th 2: 2 not to be soon s in mind or
Heb 12:27 those things that are being s
Heb 12:27 which cannot be s may remain
Heb 12:28 a kingdom which cannot be s
Rev 6:13 when it is s by a mighty wind

SHAKES (*see* SHAKE)
Job 9: 6 He s the earth out of its
Ps 29: 8 of the LORD s the wilderness
Ps 29: 8 The LORD s the Wilderness of
Prov 17:18 s hands in a pledge, and
Prov 22:26 those who s hands in a pledge
Jer 49:21 The earth s at the noise of
Ezek 21:21 he s the arrows, he consults

SHAKING (*see* SHAKE)
Ps 44:14 A s of the head among the
Ps 60: 2 its breaches, for it is s
Is 17: 6 like the s of an olive tree,
Is 24:13 like the s of an olive tree

SHALISHA
1Sa 9: 4 and through the land of S, but

SHALL (*see* PREFACE)

SHALLECHETH
1Ch 26:16 Gate, with the S Gate on the

SHALLUM (*see* JEHOAHAZ, MESHELEMIAH, SHELEMIAH, SHILLEM)
2Ki 15:10 Then S the son of Jabesh
2Ki 15:13 S the son of Jabesh became
2Ki 15:14 struck S the son of Jabesh in
2Ki 15:15 Now the rest of the acts of S
2Ki 22:14 the wife of S the son of
1Ch 2:40 Sismai, and Sismai begot S
1Ch 2:41 S begot Jekamiah, and
1Ch 3:15 Zedekiah, and the fourth S
1Ch 4:25 S his son, Mibsam his son, and
1Ch 6:12 Zadok, and Zadok begot S
1Ch 6:13 S begot Hilkiah, and Hilkiah
1Ch 7:13 Jahziel, Guni, Jezer, and S
1Ch 9:17 And the gatekeepers were S
1Ch 9:17 S was the chief
1Ch 9:19 S the son of Kore, the son of
1Ch 9:31 firstborn of S the Korahite
2Ch 28:12 Jehizkiah the son of S, and
2Ch 34:22 the wife of S the son of
Ezra 2:42 the sons of S, the sons of
Ezra 7: 2 the son of S, the son of
Ezra 10:24 S, Telem, and Uri
Ezra 10:42 S, Amariah, and Joseph
Neh 3:12 next to him was S the son of
Neh 7:45 the children of S, the
Jer 22:11 S the son of Josiah, king of
Jer 32: 7 Hanameel the son of S your
Jer 35: 4 of Maaseiah the son of S, the

SHALLUN
Neh 3:15 S the son of Col-Hozeh,

SHALMAI
Ezra 2:46 sons of Hagab, the sons of S

SHALMAN (*see* SHALMANESER)
Hos 10:14 shall be plundered as S

SHALMANESER (*see* SHALMAN)
2Ki 17: 3 S king of Assyria came up
2Ki 18: 9 that S king of Assyria came

SHAMA
1Ch 11:44 Uzzia the Ashterathite, S

SHAMARIAH
2Ch 11:19 Jeush, S, and Zaham

SHAMBLES
Joel 1:17 clods, storehouses are in s

SHAME (*see* SHAMED, SHAMEFACED, SHAMEFUL, SHAMELESSLY, SHAMES)
Ex 32:25 them, to their s among their
Judg 18: 7 put them to s for anything
1Sa 20:30 son of Jesse to your own s
1Sa 20:30 to the s of your mother's
2Sa 13:13 And I, where could I take my s
Job 8:22 you will be clothed with s
Ps 4: 2 Will you turn my glory to s
Ps 14: 6 You s the counsel of the poor
Ps 35: 4 Let those be put to s and
Ps 35:26 Let them be clothed with s
Ps 40:15 appalled because of their s
Ps 44: 7 have put to s those who hated
Ps 44: 9 cast us off and put us to s
Ps 44:15 the s of my face has covered
Ps 53: 5 You have put them to s,
Ps 69: 7 S has covered my face
Ps 69:19 You know my reproach, my s
Ps 70: 3 back because of their s, Who
Ps 71: 1 Let me never be put to s
Ps 71:24 brought to s Who seek my hurt

Ps 83:16 Fill their faces with s, That
Ps 83:17 Yes, let them be put to s
Ps 89:45 You have covered him with s
Ps 97: 7 Let all be put to s who serve
Ps 109:29 my accusers be clothed with s
Ps 119:31 O LORD, do not put me to s
Ps 129: 5 who hate Zion Be put to s
Ps 132:18 enemies I will clothe with s
Prov 3:35 but s shall be the legacy of
Prov 9: 7 a scoffer gets s for himself
Prov 10: 5 harvest is a son who causes s
Prov 11: 2 pride comes, then comes s
Prov 12: 4 but she who causes s is like
Prov 12:16 but a prudent man covers s
Prov 13: 5 is loathsome and comes to s
Prov 13:18 and s will come to him who
Prov 14:35 is against him who causes s
Prov 17: 2 rule over a son who causes s
Prov 18:13 it, it is folly and s to him
Prov 19:26 mother is a son who causes s
Prov 25: 8 neighbor has put you to s
Prov 25:10 he who hears it expose your s
Prov 29:15 brings s to his mother
Is 20: 4 uncovered, to the s of Egypt
Is 22:18 chariots shall be the s of
Is 30: 3 of Pharaoh shall be your s
Is 30: 5 be help or benefit, but a s
Is 47: 3 yes, your s will be seen
Is 50: 6 I did not hide My face from s
Is 54: 4 for you will not be put to s
Is 54: 4 forget the s of your youth
Is 61: 7 Instead of your s you shall
Jer 3:24 For s has devoured the labor
Jer 3:25 We lie down in our s, and our
Jer 7:19 to the s of their own faces
Jer 10:14 put to s by the graven image
Jer 13:26 face, that your s may appear
Jer 17:18 but do not let me be put to s
Jer 20:18 should be consumed with s
Jer 23:40 upon you, and a perpetual s
Jer 46:12 nations have heard of your s
Jer 48:39 has turned her back with s
Jer 51:17 put to s by the carved image
Jer 51:51 S has covered our faces, for
Ezek 7:18 s will be on every face,
Ezek 16:52 sisters, bear your own s also
Ezek 16:52 also, and bear your own s,
Ezek 16:54 that you may bear your own s
Ezek 16:63 anymore because of your s
Ezek 32:24 now they bear their s with
Ezek 32:25 yet they bear their s with
Ezek 32:30 in s at the terror which they
Ezek 32:30 bear their s with those who
Ezek 34:29 land, nor bear the s of the
Ezek 36: 6 borne the s of the nations
Ezek 36: 7 you shall bear their own s
Ezek 39:26 after they have borne their s
Ezek 44:13 but they shall bear their s
Dan 9: 7 to You, but to us s of face
Dan 9: 8 Lord, to us belongs s of face
Dan 12: 2 everlasting life, some to s
Hos 4: 7 change their glory into s
Hos 9:10 themselves to that s
Hos 10: 6 Ephraim shall receive s, and
Joel 2:26 shall never be put to s
Joel 2:27 shall never be put to s
Obad 10 s shall cover you, and you
Mic 1:11 Pass by in naked s, you
Mic 7:10 s will cover her who said to
Nah 3: 5 and the kingdoms your s
Hab 2:16 with s instead of glory
Hab 2:16 utter s will be on your glory
Zeph 3: 5 But the unjust knows no s
Zeph 3:19 land where they were put to s
Zech 10: 5 on horses shall be put to s
Luke 13:17 His adversaries were put to s
Luke 14: 9 then you begin with s to take
Acts 5:41 to suffer s for His name
Rom 9:33 on Him will not be put to s
Rom 10:11 on Him will not be put to s
1Co 1:27 world to put to s the wise
1Co 1:27 of the world to put to s the
1Co 4:14 write these things to s you
1Co 6: 5 I say this to your s
1Co 11:22 and s those who have nothing
1Co 15:34 I speak this to your s
2Co 4: 2 the hidden things of s, not
2Co 11:21 To our s, I say that we were
Phil 3:19 and whose glory is in their s
Heb 6: 6 God, and put Him to an open s
Heb 12: 2 the cross, despising the s
1Pe 2: 6 will by no means be put to s
Jude 13 sea, foaming up their own s
Rev 3:18 that the s of your nakedness
Rev 16:15 walk naked and they see his s

SHAMED (*see* SHAME)
Gen 38:23 for herself, lest we be s
Num 12:14 would she not be s seven days
Is 33: 9 and languishes, Lebanon is s
Jer 48: 1 is plundered, Kirjathaim is s
Jer 48: 1 the high stronghold is s and
Jer 48:20 Moab is s, for he is broken
Jer 49:23 Hamath and Arpad are s, for
Jer 50: 2 Babylon is taken, Bel is s
Zeph 3:11 be s for any of your deeds in

SHAMEFACED (*see* SHAME)
2Ch 32:21 So he returned s to his own

SHAMEFUL (*see* SHAME, SHAMEFULLY)
Deut 22:14 and charges her with s conduct
Deut 22:17 charged her with s conduct
Jer 11:13 set up altars to that s thing
Hab 2:10 You gave s counsel to your
Rom 1:27 with men committing what is s
1Co 11: 6 But if it is s for a woman to
1Co 14:35 for it is s for women to
Eph 5:12 For it is s even to speak of

SHAMEFULLY (*see* SHAMEFUL)
1Sa 20:34 his father had treated him s
Hos 2: 5 who conceived them has done s
Mark 12: 4 and sent him away s treated
Luke 20:11 beat him also, treated him s

SHAMELESSLY (*see* SHAME)
2Sa 6:20 fellows s uncovers himself

SHAMER (*see* SHOMER)
1Ch 6:46 the son of Bani, the son of S

SHAMES (*see* SHAME)
Prov 28: 7 of gluttons s his father

SHAMGAR
Judg 3:31 After him was S the son of
Judg 5: 6 In the days of S, son of

SHAMHUTH (*see* SHAMMOTH)
1Ch 27: 8 month was S the Izrahite

SHAMIR
Josh 15:48 S, Jattir, Sochoh,
Judg 10: 1 and he dwelt in S in the
Judg 10: 2 and he died and was buried in S
1Ch 24:24 of the sons of Michah, S

SHAMMA (*see* SHAMMAH, SHAMMOTH)
1Ch 7:37 Bezer, Hod, S, Shilshah,

SHAMMAH (*see* SHAMMA, SHIMEA, SHIMEI)
Gen 36:13 Nahath, Zerah, S, and Mizzah
Gen 36:17 Nahath, Chief Zerah, Chief S
1Sa 16: 9 Then Jesse made S pass by
1Sa 17:13 him Abinadab, and the third S
2Sa 23:11 after him was S the son of
2Sa 23:25 S the Harodite, Elika the
2Sa 23:33 S the Hararite, Ahiam the son
1Ch 1:37 Reuel were Nahath, Zerah, S

SHAMMAI
1Ch 2:28 The sons of Onam were S and
1Ch 2:28 The sons of S were Nadab and
1Ch 2:32 of Jada, the brother of S
1Ch 2:44 of Jorkoam, and Rekem begot S
1Ch 2:45 And the son of S was Maon, and
1Ch 4:17 Mered's wife bore Miriam, S

SHAMMOTH (*see* SHAMHUTH, SHAMMA)
1Ch 11:27 S the Harorite, Helez the

SHAMMUA (*see* SHEMAIAH, SHIMEA, SHIMEI)
Num 13: 4 Reuben, S the son of Zaccur
2Sa 5:14 S, Shobab, Nathan, Solomon,
1Ch 14: 4 S, Shobab, Nathan, Solomon,
Neh 11:17 and Abda the son of S, the
Neh 12:18 of Bilgah, S

SHAMSHERAI
1Ch 8:26 S, Shehariah, Athaliah,

SHAN
1Sa 31:10 body to the wall of Beth S
1Sa 31:12 sons from the wall of Beth S
2Sa 21:12 from the street of Beth S

SHAPE (*see* SHAPED)
1Ki 6:25 were of the same size and s
1Ki 7:19 hall were in the s of lilies
1Ki 7:22 were in the s of lilies
1Ki 7:37 mold, one measure, and one s
Rev 9: 7 the s of the locusts was like

SHAPED (*see* SHAPE)
1Ki 7:26 its brim was s like the brim
1Ki 7:31 s like a pedestal, one and a
2Ch 4: 5 its brim was s like the brim
Acts 17:29 or stone, something s by art

SHAPHAM
1Ch 5:12 S the next, then Jaanai and

SHAPHAN
2Ki 22: 3 the king sent S the scribe
2Ki 22: 8 priest said to S the scribe
2Ki 22: 8 And Hilkiah gave the book to S
2Ki 22: 9 So S the scribe went to the
2Ki 22:10 Then S the scribe showed the
2Ki 22:10 S read it before the king
2Ki 22:12 priest, Ahikam the son of S
2Ki 22:12 S the scribe, and Asaiah a
2Ki 22:14 the priest, Ahikam, Achbor, S
2Ki 25:22 son of Ahikam, the son of S
2Ch 34: 8 he sent S the son of Azaliah,
2Ch 34:15 and said to S the scribe,
2Ch 34:15 And Hilkiah gave the book to S
2Ch 34:16 So S carried the book to the
2Ch 34:18 Then S the scribe told the
2Ch 34:18 S read it before the king
2Ch 34:20 Hilkiah, Ahikam the son of S
2Ch 34:20 S the scribe, and Asaiah a
Jer 26:24 son of S was with Jeremiah
Jer 29: 3 hand of Elasah the son of S
Jer 36:10 the son of S the scribe, in
Jer 36:11 son of Gemariah, the son of S
Jer 36:12 Achbor, Gemariah the son of S
Jer 39:14 son of Ahikam, the son of S
Jer 40: 5 son of Ahikam, the son of S
Jer 40: 9 son of Ahikam, the son of S
Jer 40:11 son of Ahikam, the son of S
Jer 41: 2 son of Ahikam, the son of S
Jer 43: 6 son of Ahikam, the son of S
Ezek 8:11 stood Jaazaniah the son of S

SHAPHAT
Num 13: 5 of Simeon, S the son of Hori
1Ki 19:16 Elisha the son of S of Abel
1Ki 19:19 and found Elisha the son of S
2Ki 3:11 Elisha the son of S is here
2Ki 6:31 son of S remains on him today
1Ch 3:22 Igal, Bariah, Neariah, and S
1Ch 5:12 then Jaanai and S in Bashan,
1Ch 27:29 S the son of Adlai was over

SHAPHIR
Mic 1:11 shame, you inhabitant of S

SHARAI
Ezra 10:40 Machnadebai, Shashai, S,

SHARAIM (*see* SHAARAIM)
Josh 15:36 S, Adithaim, Gederah, and

SHARAR (*see* SACAR)
2Sa 23:33 the son of S the Hararite

SHARD (*see* SHARDS)
Is 30:14 a s to take fire from the

SHARDS (*see* SHARD)
Ezek 23:34 it, you shall break its s

SHARE (*see* SHARED, SHARES, SHARING)
1Sa 30:24 they shall s alike
Prov 14:10 a stranger does not s its joy
Prov 17: 2 will s an inheritance among
Eccl 9: 6 s in anything done under the
Is 58: 7 Is it not to s your bread
Hab 1:16 by them their s is sumptuous
Gal 6: 6 him who is taught the word s
Eph 4:16 which every part does its s
1Ti 5:22 nor s in other people's sins
1Ti 6:18 ready to give, willing to s
2Ti 1: 8 but s with me in the
Heb 13:16 not forget to do good and to s
Rev 18: 4 lest you s in her sins, and

SHARED (*see* SHARE)
Prov 21: 9 than in a house s with a
Prov 25:24 than in a house s with a
Phil 4:14 that you s in my distress
Phil 4:15 no church s with me

Heb 2:14 likewise s in the same, that

SHARES (*see* SHARE)
2Sa 19:43 We have ten s in the king
2Jn 11 him s in his evil deeds

SHAREZER (*see* SHEREZER)
2Ki 19:37 S struck him down with the
Is 37:38 S his sons struck him down

SHARING (*see* SHARE)
2Co 9:13 for your liberal s with them
Phm 6 that the s of your faith may

SHARON (*see* SHARONITE)
1Ch 5:16 of S within their borders
1Ch 27:29 over the herds that fed in S
Song 2: 1 I am the rose of S, and the
Is 33: 9 S is like a wilderness, and
Is 35: 2 the excellence of Carmel and S
Is 65:10 S shall be a fold of flocks,
Acts 9:35 S saw him and turned to the

SHARONITE (*see* SHARON)
1Ch 27:29 Shitrai the S was over the

SHARP (*see* SHARPER, SHARPLY, SHARPNESS)
Ex 4:25 Then Zipporah took a s stone
1Sa 14: 4 there was a s rock on one
1Sa 14: 4 a s rock on the other side
2Sa 2:16 called the Field of S Swords
Job 41:30 are like s potsherds
Ps 45: 5 Your arrows are s in the
Ps 52: 2 destruction, Like a s razor
Ps 57: 4 And their tongue a s sword
Ps 120: 4 S arrows of the warrior, With
Prov 5: 4 s as a two-edged sword
Prov 25:18 a club, a sword, and a s arrow
Is 5:28 Whose arrows are s, and all
Is 41:15 threshing sledge with s teeth
Is 49: 2 made My mouth like a s sword
Ezek 5: 1 son of man, take a s sword
Acts 15:39 the contention became so s
Rev 1:16 went a s two-edged sword, and
Rev 2:12 who has the s two-edged sword
Rev 14:14 and in His hand a s sickle
Rev 14:17 he also having a s sickle
Rev 14:18 to him who had the s sickle
Rev 14:18 Thrust in your s sickle and
Rev 19:15 of His mouth goes a s sword

SHARPEN (*see* SHARPENED, SHARPENING, SHARPENS)
1Sa 13:20 to s each man's plowshare
Ps 7:12 back, He will s His sword
Ps 64: 3 Who s their tongue like a
Ps 140: 3 They s their tongues like a
Eccl 10:10 and one does not s the edge

SHARPENED (*see* SHARPEN)
Ezek 21: 9 A sword, a sword is s and
Ezek 21:10 S to make a dreadful
Ezek 21:11 this sword is s, and it is

SHARPENING (*see* SHARPEN)
1Sa 13:21 the charge for a s was a pim

SHARPENS (*see* SHARPEN)
Job 16: 9 my adversary s His gaze on me
Prov 27:17 As iron s iron, so a man
Prov 27:17 so a man s the countenance of

SHARPER (*see* SHARP)
Mic 7: 4 is s than a thorn hedge
Heb 4:12 s than any two-edged sword,

SHARPLY (*see* SHARP)
Judg 8: 1 And they reprimanded him s
Mark 14: 5 And they criticized her s
Tit 1:13 Therefore rebuke them s, that

SHARPNESS (*see* SHARP)
2Co 13:10 being present I should use s

SHARUHEN (*see* SHAARAIM, SHILHIM)
Josh 19: 6 Beth Lebaoth, and S

SHASHAI
Ezra 10:40 Machnadebai, S, Sharai,

SHASHAK
1Ch 8:14 Ahio, S, Jeremoth,
1Ch 8:25 and Penuel were the sons of S

SHATTER (*see* SHATTERED, SHATTERS)
Hos 2:18 I will s from the earth, to

SHATTERED (*see* SHATTER)
Job 16:12 was at ease, but He has s me
Eccl 12: 6 or the pitcher s at the
Is 8: 9 Be s, O you peoples, and be
Dan 12: 7 people has been completely s

SHATTERS (*see* SHATTER)
Dan 2:40 in pieces and s all things

SHAUL (*see* SAUL, SHAULITES)
Gen 46:10 Ohad, Jachin, Zohar, and S
Ex 6:15 and S the son of a Canaanite
Num 26:13 of S, the family of the
1Ch 4:24 Jamin, Jarib, Zerah, and S
1Ch 6:24 Uzziah his son, and S his son

SHAULITES (*see* SHAUL)
Num 26:13 of Shaul, the family of the S

SHAVE (*see* SHAVED, SHAVEN)
Lev 13:33 he shall s himself
Lev 13:33 but the scall he shall not s
Lev 14: 8 s off all his hair, and wash
Lev 14: 9 s all the hair off his head
Lev 14: 9 all his hair he shall s off
Lev 19:27 You shall not s around the
Lev 21: 5 nor shall they s the edges of
Num 6: 9 then he shall s his head on
Num 6: 9 the seventh day he shall s it
Num 6:18 Then the Nazirite shall s
Num 8: 7 let them s all their body, and
Deut 14: 1 not cut yourselves nor s the
Deut 21:12 and she shall s her head and
Judg 16:19 had him s off the seven locks
Is 7:20 will s with a hired razor
Ezek 27:31 they will s themselves
Ezek 44:20 Nor shall they s their heads
Acts 21:24 that they may s their heads

SHAVED (*see* SHAVE)
Gen 41:14 and he s, changed his clothing
Num 6:19 he has s his consecrated hair
2Sa 10: 4 s off half of their beards,
1Ch 19: 4 s them, and cut off their
Job 1:20 s his head, and he fell to the
Jer 41: 5 men with their beards s and
1Co 11: 5 same as if her head were s
1Co 11: 6 for a woman to be shorn or s

SHAVEH (*see* SHAVEH KIRIATHAIM)
Gen 14:17 at the Valley of S (that is

SHAVEH KIRIATHAIM (*see* SHAVEH)
Gen 14: 5 Zuzim in Ham, the Emim in S

SHAVEN (*see* SHAVE)
Judg 16:17 If I am s, then my strength
Judg 16:22 again after it had been s

SHAVSHA (*see* SERAIAH, SHEVA, SHISHA)
1Ch 18:16 S was the scribe

SHAWL
Ruth 3:15 Bring the s that is on you and

SHE (*see* PREFACE)

SHEAF (*see* SHEAVES)
Gen 37: 7 my s arose and also stood
Gen 37: 7 around and bowed down to my s
Lev 23:10 then you shall bring a s of
Lev 23:11 wave the s before the LORD
Lev 23:12 that day, when you wave the s
Lev 23:15 the s of the wave offering
Deut 24:19 forget a s in the field, you
Job 5:26 as a s of grain ripens in its

SHEAL
Ezra 10:29 Malluch, Adaiah, Jashub, S

SHEALTIEL
1Ch 3:17 were Assir, S his son,
Ezra 3: 2 and Zerubbabel the son of S
Ezra 3: 8 Zerubbabel the son of S,
Ezra 5: 2 So Zerubbabel the son of S
Neh 12: 1 with Zerubbabel the son of S
Hag 1: 1 to Zerubbabel the son of S
Hag 1:12 Then Zerubbabel the son of S
Hag 1:14 of Zerubbabel the son of S
Hag 2: 2 to Zerubbabel the son of S
Hag 2:23 My servant, the son of S,'
Matt 1:12 to Babylon, Jeconiah begot S
Matt 1:12 and S begot Zerubbabel
Luke 3:27 of Zerubbabel, the son of S

SHEAR (*see* SHEARER, SHEARING, SHORN)
Gen 31:19 Laban had gone to s his sheep
Gen 38:13 up to Timnah to s his sheep
Deut 15:19 nor s the firstborn of your

SHEARER (*see* SHEAR, SHEARERS)
Acts 8:32 a lamb silent before its s

SHEARERS (*see* SHEARER)
1Sa 25: 7 I have heard that you have s
1Sa 25:11 that I have killed for my s
Is 53: 7 sheep before its s is silent

SHEARIAH
1Ch 8:38 Azrikam, Bocheru, Ishmael, S
1Ch 9:44 Azrikam, Bocheru, Ishmael, S

SHEARING (*see* SHEAR)
1Sa 25: 2 he was s his sheep in Carmel
1Sa 25: 4 that Nabal was s his sheep

SHEAR-JASHUB (*see* JASHUB)
Is 7: 3 S your son, at the end of the

SHEATH
1Sa 17:51 sword and drew it out of its s
2Sa 20: 8 fastened in its s at his hips
1Ch 21:27 returned his sword to its s
Ezek 21: 3 draw My sword out of its s
Ezek 21: 4 its s against all flesh from
Ezek 21: 5 drawn My sword out of its s
Ezek 21:30 Return it to its s
John 18:11 Put your sword into the s

SHEAVES (*see* SHEAF)
Gen 37: 7 were, binding s in the field
Gen 37: 7 and indeed your s stood all
Ruth 2: 7 after the reapers among the s
Ruth 2:15 her glean even among the s
Neh 13:15 the Sabbath, and bringing in s
Job 24:10 away the s from the hungry
Ps 126: 6 Bringing his s with him
Ps 129: 7 his hand, Nor he who binds s
Amos 2:13 down that is full of s
Mic 4:12 like s to the threshing floor
Zech 12: 6 like a fiery torch in the s

SHEBA (*see* SEBA, SHEBAH)
Gen 10: 7 and the sons of Raamah were S
Gen 10:28 Obal, Abimael, S,
Gen 25: 3 Jokshan begot S and Dedan
Josh 19: 2 inheritance Beersheba (S)
2Sa 20: 1 whose name was S the son of
2Sa 20: 2 followed S the son of Bichri
2Sa 20: 6 Now S the son of Bichri will
2Sa 20: 7 to pursue S the son of Bichri
2Sa 20:10 pursued S the son of Bichri
2Sa 20:13 to pursue S the son of Bichri
2Sa 20:14 together and also went after S
2Sa 20:21 S the son of Bichri by name,
2Sa 20:22 head of S the son of Bichri
1Ki 10: 1 of S heard of the fame of
1Ki 10: 4 when the queen of S had seen
1Ki 10:10 of S gave to King Solomon
1Ki 10:13 queen of S all she desired
1Ch 1: 9 The sons of Raama were S and
1Ch 1:22 Ebal, Abimael, S,
1Ch 1:32 The sons of Jokshan were S
1Ch 5:13 Michael, Meshullam, S, Jorai,
2Ch 9: 1 of S heard of the fame of
2Ch 9: 3 when the queen of S had seen
2Ch 9: 9 of S gave to King Solomon
2Ch 9:12 queen of S all she desired
Job 6:19 travelers of S hope for them
Ps 72:10 The kings of S and Seba Will
Ps 72:15 the gold of S will be given
Is 60: 6 all those from S shall come
Jer 6:20 Me comes frankincense from S
Ezek 27:22 The merchants of S and Raamah
Ezek 27:23 Eden, the merchants of S
Ezek 38:13 S, Dedan, the merchants of

SHEBAH (*see* SHEBA)
Gen 26:33 So he called it S

SHEBAM (*see* SHIBMAH)
Num 32: 3 Nimrah, Heshbon, Elealeh, S

SHEBANIAH (*see* SHECANIAH, SHECHANIAH)
1Ch 15:24 S, Joshaphat, Nethaneel,
Neh 9: 4 Then Jeshua, Bani, Kadmiel, S
Neh 9: 5 Sherebiah, Hodijah, S, and
Neh 10: 4 Hattush, S, Malluch,
Neh 10:10 S, Hodijah, Kelita, Pelaiah,
Neh 10:12 Zaccur, Sherebiah, S,
Neh 12:14 of S, Joseph

SHEBARIM
Josh 7: 5 before the gate as far as **S**

SHEBAT
Zech 1: 7 month, which is the month **S**

SHEBER
1Ch 2:48 Caleb's concubine, bore **S**

SHEBNA
2Ki 18:18 **S** the scribe, and Joah the son
2Ki 18:26 Eliakim the son of Hilkiah, **S**
2Ki 18:37 **S** the scribe, and Joah the son
2Ki 19: 2 **S** the scribe, and the elders
Is 22:15 proceed to this steward, to **S**
Is 36: 3 **S** the scribe, and Joah the son
Is 36:11 Then Eliakim, **S**, and Joah said
Is 36:22 **S** the scribe, and Joah the son
Is 37: 2 **S** the scribe, and the elders

SHEBUEL (*see* SHUBAEL)
1Ch 23:16 of Gershon, **S** was the first
1Ch 25: 4 Bukkiah, Mattaniah, Uzziel, **S**
1Ch 26:24 **S** the son of Gershom, the son

SHECANIAH (*see* SHEBANIAH, SHECHANIAH)
1Ch 24:11 to Jeshua, the tenth to **S**
2Ch 31:15 Shemaiah, Amariah, and **S**, his
Ezra 8: 3 of the sons of **S**, of the sons

SHECHANIAH (*see* SHEBANIAH, SHECANIAH)
1Ch 3:21 of Obadiah, and the sons of **S**
1Ch 3:22 The son of **S** was Shemaiah
Ezra 8: 5 of the sons of **S**,
Ezra 10: 2 **S** the son of Jehiel, one of
Neh 3:29 him Shemaiah the son of **S**
Neh 6:18 of **S** the son of Arah, and his
Neh 12: 3 **S**, Rehum, Meremoth,

SHECHEM (*see* SHECHEMITES, SHECHEM'S, SYCHAR)
Gen 12: 6 the land to the place of **S**
Gen 33:18 came safely to the city of **S**
Gen 34: 2 when **S** the son of Hamor the
Gen 34: 4 So **S** spoke to his father
Gen 34: 6 Then Hamor the father of **S**
Gen 34: 8 The soul of my son **S** longs
Gen 34:11 Then **S** said to her father and
Gen 34:13 the sons of Jacob answered **S**
Gen 34:18 words pleased Hamor and **S**,
Gen 34:20 **S** his son came to the gate of
Gen 34:24 heeded Hamor and **S** his son
Gen 34:26 **S** his son with the edge of
Gen 35: 4 terebinth tree which was by **S**
Gen 37:12 their father's flock in **S**
Gen 37:13 feeding the flock in **S**
Gen 37:14 of Hebron, and he went to **S**
Num 26:31 of **S**, the family of the
Josh 17: 2 of Asriel, the children of **S**
Josh 17: 7 that lies east of **S**
Josh 20: 7 **S** in the mountains of Ephraim
Josh 21:21 For they gave them **S** with its
Josh 24: 1 all the tribes of Israel to **S**
Josh 24:25 statute and an ordinance in **S**
Josh 24:32 of Egypt, they buried at **S**
Josh 24:32 **S** for one hundred pieces of
Judg 8:31 was in **S** also bore him a son
Judg 9: 1 son of Jerubbaal went to **S**
Judg 9: 2 hearing of all the men of **S**
Judg 9: 3 hearing of all the men of **S**
Judg 9: 6 all the men of **S** gathered
Judg 9: 6 at the pillar that was in **S**
Judg 9: 7 Listen to me, you men of **S**
Judg 9:18 king over the men of **S**,
Judg 9:20 and devour the men of **S** and
Judg 9:20 fire come from the men of **S**
Judg 9:23 Abimelech and the men of **S**
Judg 9:23 and the men of **S** dealt
Judg 9:24 them, and on the men of **S**, who
Judg 9:25 And the men of **S** set men in
Judg 9:26 brothers and went over to **S**
Judg 9:26 and the men of **S** put their
Judg 9:28 Who is Abimelech, and who is **S**
Judg 9:28 men of Hamor the father of **S**
Judg 9:31 his brothers have come to **S**
Judg 9:34 against **S** in four companies
Judg 9:39 out, leading the men of **S**
Judg 9:41 they would not dwell in **S**
Judg 9:46 the tower of **S** had heard that
Judg 9:47 of **S** were gathered together
Judg 9:49 people of the tower of **S** died
Judg 9:57 **S** God returned on their own
Judg 21:19 that goes up from Bethel to **S**
1Ki 12: 1 Now Rehoboam went to **S**, for
1Ki 12: 1 gone to **S** to make him king
1Ki 12:25 Then Jeroboam built **S** in the
1Ch 6:67 **S** with its common-lands, in
1Ch 7:19 sons of Shemida were Ahian, **S**
1Ch 7:28 west Gezer and its towns, and **S**
2Ch 10: 1 And Rehoboam went to **S**, for
2Ch 10: 1 gone to **S** to make him king
Ps 60: 6 I will divide **S** And measure
Ps 108: 7 I will divide **S** And measure
Jer 41: 5 that certain men came from **S**
Hos 6: 9 murder on the way to **S**
Acts 7:16 they were carried back to **S**
Acts 7:16 of Hamor, the father of **S**

SHECHEMITES (*see* SHECHEM)
Num 26:31 Shechem, the family of the **S**

SHECHEM'S (*see* SHECHEM)
Gen 33:19 **S** father, for one hundred
Gen 34:26 and took Dinah from **S** house

SHED (*see* SHEDDER, SHEDDING, SHEDS)
Gen 9: 6 by man his blood shall be **s**
Gen 37:22 **S** no blood, but cast him into
Lev 17: 4 He has **s** blood
Num 35:33 for the blood that is **s** on it
Num 35:33 by the blood of him who **s** it
Deut 19:10 lest innocent blood be **s** in
Deut 21: 7 hands have not **s** this blood
1Sa 25:31 have **s** blood without cause
1Ki 2: 5 And he **s** the blood of war in
1Ki 2:31 innocent blood which Joab **s**
2Ki 21:16 Moreover Manasseh **s** very
2Ki 24: 4 innocent blood that he had **s**
1Ch 22: 8 You have **s** much blood and
1Ch 22: 8 because you have **s** much blood
1Ch 28: 3 a man of war and have **s** blood
Ps 79: 3 have **s** like water all around
Ps 79:10 servants which has been **s**
Ps 106:38 **s** innocent blood, Even the
Prov 1:11 let us lie in wait to **s** blood
Prov 1:16 and they make haste to **s** blood
Prov 6:17 hands that **s** innocent blood,
Is 59: 7 haste to **s** innocent blood
Jer 7: 6 do not **s** innocent blood in
Jer 22: 3 nor **s** innocent blood in this
Lam 4:13 who **s** in her midst the blood
Ezek 16:38 wedlock or **s** blood are judged
Ezek 22: 4 by the blood which you have **s**
Ezek 22: 6 his power to **s** blood in you
Ezek 22:12 they take bribes to **s** blood
Ezek 22:27 to **s** blood, to destroy people
Ezek 23:45 manner of women who **s** blood
Ezek 33:25 toward your idols, and **s** blood
Ezek 35: 5 and have **s** the blood of the
Ezek 36:18 blood they had **s** on the land
Joel 3:19 for they have **s** innocent
Matt 23:35 blood **s** on the earth, from
Matt 26:28 which is **s** for many for the
Mark 14:24 covenant, which is **s** for many
Luke 11:50 **s** from the foundation of the
Luke 22:20 My blood, which is **s** for you
Acts 22:20 of Your martyr Stephen was **s**
Rom 3:15 feet are swift to **s** blood
Rev 16: 6 For they have **s** the blood of
Rev 19: 2 of His servants **s** by her

SHEDDER (*see* SHED)
Ezek 18:10 is a robber or a **s** of blood

SHEDDING (*see* SHED)
Jer 22:17 for **s** innocent blood, and
Heb 9:22 without **s** of blood there is

SHEDEUR
Num 1: 5 Reuben, Elizur the son of **S**
Num 2:10 shall be Elizur the son of **S**
Num 7:30 day Elizur the son of **S**,
Num 7:35 of Elizur the son of **S**
Num 10:18 army was Elizur the son of **S**

SHEDS (*see* SHED)
Gen 9: 6 Whoever **s** man's blood, by man
Ezek 22: 3 The city **s** blood in her own

SHEEP (*see* SHEEPBREEDER, SHEEPFOLD, SHEEP'S, SHEEPSHEARERS, SHEEPSKINS)
Gen 4: 2 Now Abel was a keeper of **s**
Gen 12:16 He had **s**, oxen, male donkeys,
Gen 20:14 Then Abimelech took **s**, oxen,
Gen 21:27 So Abraham took **s** and oxen
Gen 29: 2 three flocks of **s** lying by it
Gen 29: 3 the well's mouth, water the **s**
Gen 29: 6 Rachel is coming with the **s**
Gen 29: 7 Water the **s**, and go and feed
Gen 29: 8 then we water the **s**
Gen 29: 9 came with her father's **s**, for
Gen 29:10 the **s** of Laban his mother's
Gen 30:32 all the speckled and spotted **s**
Gen 31:19 Laban had gone to shear his **s**
Gen 34:28 They took their **s**, their oxen
Gen 38:13 up to Timnah to shear his **s**
Ex 9: 3 on the oxen, and on the **s**
Ex 12: 5 from the **s** or from the goats
Ex 20:24 your peace offerings, your **s**
Ex 22: 1 If a man steals an ox or a **s**
Ex 22: 1 an ox and four **s** for a **s**
Ex 22: 4 it is an ox or donkey or **s**
Ex 22: 9 concerns an ox, a donkey, a **s**
Ex 22:10 neighbor a donkey, an ox, a **s**
Ex 22:30 do with your oxen and your **s**
Ex 34:19 livestock, whether ox or **s**
Lev 1:10 of the **s** or of the goats
Lev 7:23 any fat, of ox or **s** or goat
Lev 22:19 from the cattle, from the **s**
Lev 22:21 from the cattle or the **s**, it
Lev 22:27 When a bull or a **s** or a goat
Lev 27:26 whether it is an ox or **s**, it
Num 18:17 a cow, the firstborn of a **s**
Num 22:40 Then Balak offered oxen and **s**
Num 27:17 like **s** which have no shepherd
Num 31:28 cattle, the donkeys, and the **s**
Num 31:30 cattle, the donkeys, and the **s**
Num 31:32 and seventy-five thousand **s**
Num 31:36 thousand five hundred **s**
Num 31:37 of the **s** was six hundred and
Num 31:43 thousand five hundred **s**,
Num 32:24 ones and folds for your **s**, and
Num 32:36 cities, and folds for **s**
Deut 14: 4 the ox, the **s**, the goat,
Deut 14: 5 antelope, and the mountain **s**
Deut 14:26 for oxen or **s**, for wine or
Deut 17: 1 or **s** which has any blemish or
Deut 18: 3 whether it is bull or **s**
Deut 18: 4 first of the fleece of your **s**
Deut 22: 1 ox or his **s** going astray, and
Deut 28:31 your **s** shall be given to your
Josh 6:21 woman, young and old, ox and **s**
Josh 7:24 his oxen, his donkeys, his **s**
Judg 6: 4 neither **s** nor ox nor donkey
1Sa 8:17 will take a tenth of your **s**
1Sa 14:32 on the spoil, and took **s**, oxen
1Sa 14:34 man's ox and every man's **s**
1Sa 15: 3 and nursing child, ox and **s**
1Sa 15: 9 Agag and the best of the **s**
1Sa 15:14 bleating of the **s** in my ears
1Sa 15:15 spared the best of the **s** and
1Sa 15:21 people took of the plunder, **s**
1Sa 16:11 and there he is, keeping the **s**
1Sa 16:19 son David, who is with the **s**
1Sa 17:15 his father's **s** at Bethlehem
1Sa 17:20 left the **s** with a keeper, and
1Sa 17:28 those few **s** in the wilderness
1Sa 17:34 used to keep his father's **s**
1Sa 22:19 infants, oxen and donkeys and **s**
1Sa 25: 2 He had three thousand **s** and a
1Sa 25: 2 was shearing his **s** in Carmel
1Sa 25: 4 that Nabal was shearing his **s**
1Sa 25:16 were with them keeping the **s**
1Sa 25:18 five **s** already dressed, five
1Sa 27: 9 alive, but took away the **s**
2Sa 6:13 sacrificed oxen and fatted **s**
2Sa 7: 8 from following the **s**, to be
2Sa 17:29 honey and curds, **s** and cheese
2Sa 24:17 but these **s**, what have they
1Ki 1: 9 And Adonijah sacrificed **s** and
1Ki 1:19 and **s** in abundance, and has
1Ki 1:25 and **s** in abundance, and has
1Ki 4:23 pastures, and one hundred **s**
1Ki 8: 5 before the ark, sacrificing **s**
1Ki 8:63 hundred and twenty thousand **s**
1Ki 22:17 as **s** that have no shepherd
2Ki 5:26 olive groves and vineyards, **s**
1Ch 5:21 and fifty thousand of their **s**
1Ch 12:40 **s** abundantly, for there was
1Ch 17: 7 from following the **s**, that
1Ch 21:17 but these **s**, what have they
2Ch 5: 6 the ark, were sacrificing **s**
2Ch 7: 5 hundred and twenty thousand **s**
2Ch 14:15 enclosures, and carried off **s**
2Ch 15:11 seven thousand **s** from the
2Ch 18: 2 and Ahab killed **s** and oxen in
2Ch 18:16 as **s** that have no shepherd
2Ch 29:33 bulls and three thousand **s**

2Ch 30:24 bulls and seven thousand s
2Ch 30:24 bulls and ten thousand s
2Ch 31: 6 the tithe of oxen and s
Neh 3: 1 priests and built the S Gate
Neh 3:32 corner, as far as the S Gate
Neh 5:18 was one ox and six choice s
Neh 12:39 Hundred, as far as the S Gate
Job 1:16 heaven and burned up the s
Job 31:20 with the fleece of my s
Job 42:12 he had fourteen thousand s
Ps 8: 7 All s and oxen
Ps 44:11 up like s intended for food
Ps 44:22 as s for the slaughter
Ps 49:14 Like s they are laid in the
Ps 74: 1 against the s of Your pasture
Ps 78:52 own people go forth like s
Ps 79:13 s of Your pasture, Will give
Ps 95: 7 pasture, And the s of His hand
Ps 100: 3 and the s of His pasture
Ps 119:176 gone astray like a lost s
Ps 144:13 That our s may bring forth
Song 4: 2 are like a flock of shorn s
Song 6: 6 teeth are like a flock of s
Is 7:21 alive a young cow and two s
Is 7:25 oxen and a place for s to roam
Is 13:14 as a s that no man takes up
Is 22:13 slaying oxen and killing s
Is 43:23 s for your burnt offerings
Is 53: 6 All we like s have gone
Is 53: 7 as a s before its shearers is
Jer 12: 3 out like s for the slaughter
Jer 13:20 to you, your beautiful s
Jer 23: 1 scatter the s of My pasture
Jer 50: 6 My people have been lost s
Jer 50:17 Israel is like scattered s
Ezek 34: 6 My s wandered through all the
Ezek 34:10 them to cease feeding the s
Ezek 34:11 I Myself will search for My s
Ezek 34:12 he is among his scattered s
Ezek 34:12 so will I seek out My s and
Ezek 34:17 shall judge between s and s
Ezek 34:20 between the fat and the lean s
Ezek 34:22 I will judge between s and s
Hos 12:12 and for a wife he tended s
Joel 1:18 even the flocks of s suffer
Mic 2:12 together like s of the fold
Mic 5: 8 young lion among flocks of s
Zech 10: 2 people wend their way like s
Zech 13: 7 and the s will be scattered
Matt 9:36 like s having no shepherd
Matt 10: 6 lost s of the house of Israel
Matt 10:16 I send you out as s in the
Matt 12:11 there among you who has one s
Matt 12:12 value then is a man than a s
Matt 15:24 lost s of the house of Israel
Matt 18:12 If a man has a hundred s, and
Matt 18:13 s than over the ninety-nine
Matt 25:32 divides his s from the goats
Matt 25:33 And He will set the s on His
Matt 26:31 the s of the flock will be
Mark 6:34 like s not having a shepherd
Mark 14:27 and the s will be scattered
Luke 15: 4 of you, having a hundred s
Luke 15: 6 found my s which was lost
Luke 17: 7 servant plowing or tending s
John 2:14 those who sold oxen and s and
John 2:15 out of the temple, with the s
John 5: 2 by the S Gate a pool, which
John 10: 2 door is the shepherd of the s
John 10: 3 and the s hear his voice
John 10: 3 and he calls his own s by name
John 10: 4 when he brings out his own s
John 10: 4 the s follow him, for they
John 10: 7 you, I am the door of the s
John 10: 8 but the s did not hear them
John 10:11 gives His life for the s
John 10:12 one who does not own the s
John 10:12 wolf coming and leaves the s
John 10:12 and the wolf catches the s
John 10:13 and does not care about the s
John 10:14 and I know My s, and am known
John 10:15 I lay down My life for the s
John 10:16 other s I have which are not
John 10:26 because you are not of My s
John 10:27 My s hear My voice, and I know
John 21:16 He said to him, "Tend My s."
John 21:17 said to him, "Feed My s.
Acts 8:32 He was led as a s to the
Rom 8:36 as s for the slaughter
Heb 13:20 that great Shepherd of the s
1Pe 2:25 you were like s going astray
Rev 18:13 flour and wheat, cattle and s

SHEEPBREEDER (*see* SHEEP)
2Ki 3: 4 Mesha king of Moab was a s

SHEEPFOLD (*see* SHEEP, SHEEPFOLDS)
2Sa 7: 8 I took you from the s, from
1Ch 17: 7 I took you from the s, from
John 10: 1 not enter the s by the door

SHEEPFOLDS (*see* SHEEPFOLD)
Num 32:16 We will build s here for our
Judg 5:16 Why did you sit among the s
1Sa 24: 3 he came to the s by the road
Ps 68:13 you lie down among the s, Yet
Ps 78:70 And took him from the s
Is 13:20 shepherds make their s there

SHEEP'S (*see* SHEEP)
Matt 7:15 who come to you in s clothing

SHEEPSHEARERS (*see* SHEEP)
Gen 38:12 and went up to his s at Timnah
2Sa 13:23 Absalom had s in Baal Hazor
2Sa 13:24 note, your servant has s

SHEEPSKINS (*see* SHEEP)
Heb 11:37 They wandered about in s and

SHEERAH (*see* UZZEN SHEERAH)
1Ch 7:24 Now his daughter was S, who

SHEET (*see* SHEETS)
Acts 10:11 and an object like a great s
Acts 11: 5 descending like a great s

SHEETS (*see* SHEET)
Ex 39: 3 beat the gold into thin s

SHEHARIAH
1Ch 8:26 Shamsherai, S, Athaliah,

SHEKEL (*see* SHEKELS)
Gen 24:22 nose ring weighing half a s
Ex 30:13 half a s according to the s
Ex 30:13 (a s is twenty gerahs)
Ex 30:15 not give less than half a s
Ex 30:24 to the s of the sanctuary
Ex 38:24 to the s of the sanctuary
Ex 38:25 to the s of the sanctuary
Ex 38:26 a s, according to the s
Lev 5:15 to the s of the sanctuary
Lev 27: 3 to the s of the sanctuary
Lev 27:25 to the s of the sanctuary
Lev 27:25 twenty gerahs to the s
Num 3:47 of the s of the sanctuary
Num 3:47 the s of twenty gerahs
Num 3:50 to the s of the sanctuary
Num 7:13 to the s of the sanctuary
Num 7:19 to the s of the sanctuary
Num 7:25 to the s of the sanctuary
Num 7:31 to the s of the sanctuary
Num 7:37 to the s of the sanctuary
Num 7:43 to the s of the sanctuary
Num 7:49 to the s of the sanctuary
Num 7:55 to the s of the sanctuary
Num 7:61 to the s of the sanctuary
Num 7:67 to the s of the sanctuary
Num 7:73 to the s of the sanctuary
Num 7:79 to the s of the sanctuary
Num 7:85 to the s of the sanctuary
Num 7:86 to the s of the sanctuary
Num 18:16 to the s of the sanctuary
1Sa 9: 8 one fourth of a s of silver
2Ki 7: 1 flour shall be sold for a s
2Ki 7: 1 two seahs of barley for a s
2Ki 7:16 fine flour was sold for a s
2Ki 7:16 two seahs of barley for a s
2Ki 7:18 Two seahs of barley for a s
2Ki 7:18 a seah of fine flour for a s
Neh 10:32 yearly one-third of a s for
Ezek 45:12 The s shall be twenty gerahs
Amos 8: 5 the s large, falsifying the

SHEKELS (*see* SHEKEL)
Gen 23:15 four hundred s of silver
Gen 23:16 four hundred s of silver
Gen 24:22 wrists weighing ten s of gold
Gen 37:28 for twenty s of silver
Ex 21:32 master thirty s of silver
Ex 30:23 five hundred s of liquid
Ex 30:23 (two hundred and fifty s), two
Ex 30:23 fifty s of sweet-smelling
Ex 30:24 five hundred s of cassia,
Ex 38:24 and seven hundred and thirty s
Ex 38:25 hundred and seventy-five s
Ex 38:28 seventy-five s he made hooks
Ex 38:29 two thousand four hundred s
Lev 5:15 with your valuation in s of
Lev 27: 3 shall be fifty s of silver
Lev 27: 4 valuation shall be thirty s
Lev 27: 5 for a male shall be twenty s
Lev 27: 5 and for a female ten s
Lev 27: 6 shall be five s of silver
Lev 27: 6 shall be three s of silver
Lev 27: 7 valuation shall be fifteen s
Lev 27: 7 and for a female ten s
Lev 27:16 valued at fifty s of silver
Num 3:47 you shall take five s for
Num 3:50 three hundred and sixty-five s
Num 7:13 was one hundred and thirty s
Num 7:13 one silver bowl of seventy s
Num 7:14 one gold pan of ten s, full
Num 7:19 was one hundred and thirty s
Num 7:19 one silver bowl of seventy s
Num 7:20 one gold pan of ten s, full
Num 7:25 was one hundred and thirty s
Num 7:25 one silver bowl of seventy s
Num 7:26 one gold pan of ten s, full
Num 7:31 was one hundred and thirty s
Num 7:31 one silver bowl of seventy s
Num 7:32 one gold pan of ten s, full
Num 7:37 was one hundred and thirty s
Num 7:37 one silver bowl of seventy s
Num 7:38 one gold pan of ten s, full
Num 7:43 was one hundred and thirty s
Num 7:43 one silver bowl of seventy s
Num 7:44 one gold pan of ten s, full
Num 7:49 was one hundred and thirty s
Num 7:49 one silver bowl of seventy s
Num 7:50 one gold pan of ten s, full
Num 7:55 was one hundred and thirty s
Num 7:55 one silver bowl of seventy s
Num 7:56 one gold pan of ten s, full
Num 7:61 was one hundred and thirty s
Num 7:61 one silver bowl of seventy s
Num 7:62 one gold pan of ten s, full
Num 7:67 was one hundred and thirty s
Num 7:67 one silver bowl of seventy s
Num 7:68 one gold pan of ten s, full
Num 7:73 was one hundred and thirty s
Num 7:73 one silver bowl of seventy s
Num 7:74 one gold pan of ten s, full
Num 7:79 was one hundred and thirty s
Num 7:79 one silver bowl of seventy s
Num 7:80 one gold pan of ten s, full
Num 7:85 one hundred and thirty s and
Num 7:85 and each bowl seventy s
Num 7:85 two thousand four hundred s
Num 7:86 incense weighed ten s apiece
Num 7:86 one hundred and twenty s
Num 18:16 for five s of silver,
Num 31:52 seven hundred and fifty s
Deut 22:19 him one hundred s of silver
Deut 22:29 father fifty s of silver, and
Josh 7:21 two hundred s of silver, and
Josh 7:21 of gold weighing fifty s, I
Judg 8:26 seven hundred s of gold,
Judg 9: 4 So they gave him seventy s of
Judg 17: 2 The eleven hundred s of
Judg 17: 3 s of silver to his mother
Judg 17: 4 took two hundred s of silver
Judg 17:10 you ten s of silver per year
1Sa 17: 5 was five thousand s of bronze
1Sa 17: 7 weighed six hundred s
2Sa 14:26 s according to the king's
2Sa 18:11 given you ten s of silver
2Sa 18:12 s of silver in my hand, I
2Sa 21:16 spear was three hundred s
2Sa 24:24 oxen for fifty s of silver
1Ki 10:16 six hundred s of gold went
1Ki 10:29 cost six hundred s of silver
2Ki 5: 5 six thousand s of gold, and
2Ki 6:25 sold for eighty s of silver
2Ki 6:25 for five s of silver
2Ki 15:20 each man fifty s of silver
1Ch 21:25 gave Ornan six hundred s of
2Ch 1:17 for six hundred s of silver
2Ch 3: 9 the nails was fifty s of gold
2Ch 9:15 six hundred s of hammered
2Ch 9:16 three hundred s of gold went
Neh 5:15 besides forty s of silver
Ps 119:72 Than thousands of s of gold
Is 7:23 worth a thousand s of silver
Jer 32: 9 seventeen s of silver

Ezek 4:10 be by weight, twenty s a day
Ezek 45:12 twenty s, twenty-five s
Ezek 45:12 fifteen s shall be your mina
Hos 3: 2 for fifteen s of silver, and .

SHELAH
Gen 38: 5 a son, and called his name **S**
Gen 38:11 house till my son **S** is grown
Gen 38:14 for she saw that **S** was grown
Gen 38:26 did not give her to **S** my son
Gen 46:12 of Judah were Er, Onan, **S**
Num 26:20 of **S**, the family of the
1Ch 1:18 Arphaxad begot **S**
1Ch 1:18 and **S** begot Eber
1Ch 1:24 Shem, Arphaxad, **S**,
1Ch 2: 3 of Judah were Er, Onan, and **S**
1Ch 4:21 The sons of **S** the son of
Neh 3:15 of **S** by the King's Garden
Luke 3:35 the son of Eber, the son of **S**

SHELANITES
Num 26:20 Shelah, the family of the **S**

SHELEMIAH (*see* MESHELEMIAH, SHALLUM)
1Ch 26:14 for the East Gate fell to **S**
Ezra 10:39 **S**, Nathan, Adaiah,
Ezra 10:41 Azareel, **S**, Shemariah,
Neh 3:30 him Hananiah the son of **S**
Neh 13:13 the storehouse **S** the priest
Jer 36:14 of Nethaniah, the son of **S**
Jer 36:26 **S** the son of Abdeel, to seize
Jer 37: 3 sent Jehucal the son of **S**
Jer 37:13 name was Irijah the son of **S**
Jer 38: 1 Pashhur, Jucal the son of **S**

SHELEPH
Gen 10:26 Joktan begot Almodad, **S**,
1Ch 1:20 Joktan begot Almodad, **S**,

SHELESH
1Ch 7:35 Helem were Zophah, Imna, **S**

SHELOMI
Num 34:27 of Asher, Ahihud the son of **S**

SHELOMITH (*see* SHELOMOTH)
Lev 24:11 was **S** the daughter of Dibri
1Ch 3:19 Hananiah, **S** their sister,
1Ch 23: 9 **S**, Haziel, and Haran
1Ch 23:18 of Izhar, **S** was the first
1Ch 26:25 Zichri his son, and **S** his son
1Ch 26:26 This **S** and his brethren were
1Ch 26:28 was under the hand of **S** and
2Ch 11:20 him Abijah, Attai, Ziza, and **S**
Ezra 8:10 of the sons of **S**,

SHELOMOTH (*see* SHELOMITH)
1Ch 24:22 Of the Izharites, **S**
1Ch 24:22 of the sons of **S**, Jahath

SHELTER (*see* SHELTERED, SHELTERS)
Judg 9:15 come and take s in my shade
Job 18:14 from the s of his tent, and
Job 24: 8 around the rock for want of s
Ps 61: 3 For You have been a s for me
Ps 61: 4 trust in the s of Your wings
Ps 143: 9 In You I take s
Is 4: 6 for a s from storm and rain
Is 16: 4 be a s to them from the face
Joel 3:16 will be a s for His people
Jon 4: 5 There he made himself a s
Acts 27: 4 sailed under the s of Cyprus
Acts 27: 7 we sailed under the s of
Acts 27:16 running under the s of an

SHELTERED (*see* SHELTER)
Ps 83: 3 together against Your s ones

SHELTERS (*see* SHELTER)
Deut 33:12 Who s him all the day long
Zeph 2: 6 with s for shepherds and folds

SHELUMIEL
Num 1: 6 **S** the son of Zurishaddai
Num 2:12 be **S** the son of Zurishaddai
Num 7:36 On the fifth day **S** the son of
Num 7:41 of **S** the son of Zurishaddai
Num 10:19 was **S** the son of Zurishaddai

SHEM
Gen 5:32 years old, and Noah begot **S**
Gen 6:10 **S**, Ham, and Japheth
Gen 7:13 day Noah and Noah's sons, **S**
Gen 9:18 went out of the ark were **S**
Gen 9:23 But **S** and Japheth took a
Gen 9:26 be the LORD, the God of **S**
Gen 9:27 he dwell in the tents of **S**
Gen 10: 1 **S**, Ham, and Japheth
Gen 10:21 children were born also to **S**
Gen 10:22 The sons of **S** were Elam,
Gen 10:31 These were the sons of **S**,
Gen 11:10 This is the genealogy of **S**
Gen 11:10 **S** was one hundred years old,
Gen 11:11 **S** lived five hundred years,
1Ch 1: 4 Noah, **S**, Ham, and Japheth
1Ch 1:17 The sons of **S** were Elam,
1Ch 1:24 **S**, Arphaxad, Shelah,
Luke 3:36 son of Arphaxad, the son of **S**

SHEMA (*see* SHEMAIAH, SHEMARIAH)
Josh 15:26 Amam, **S**, Moladah,
1Ch 2:43 Korah, Tappuah, Rekem, and **S**
1Ch 2:44 **S** begot Raham the father of
1Ch 5: 8 the son of Azaz, the son of **S**
1Ch 8:13 and Beriah and **S**, who were
Neh 8: 4 hand, stood Mattithiah, **S**

SHEMAAH (*see* SEMEI)
1Ch 12: 3 the sons of **S** the Gibeathite

SHEMAIAH (*see* SHAMMUA, SHEMA, SHIMEI)
1Ki 12:22 God came to **S** the man of God
1Ch 3:22 The son of Shechaniah was **S**
1Ch 3:22 The sons of **S** were Hattush,
1Ch 4:37 son of Shimri, the son of **S**
1Ch 5: 4 sons of Joel were **S** his son
1Ch 9:14 **S** the son of Hasshub, the son
1Ch 9:16 Obadiah the son of **S**, the son
1Ch 15: 8 **S** the chief, and two hundred
1Ch 15:11 for Uriel, Asaiah, Joel, **S**
1Ch 24: 6 **S** the son of Nethaneel, one
1Ch 26: 4 were **S** the firstborn,
1Ch 26: 6 Also to **S** his son were sons
1Ch 26: 7 The sons of **S** were Othni,
2Ch 11: 2 LORD came to **S** the man of God
2Ch 12: 5 Then **S** the prophet came to
2Ch 12: 7 word of the LORD came to **S**
2Ch 12:15 in the book of **S** the prophet
2Ch 17: 8 **S**, Nethaniah, Zebadiah,
2Ch 29:14 and of the sons of Jeduthun, **S**
2Ch 31:15 Eden, Miniamin, Jeshua, **S**
2Ch 35: 9 also Conaniah, his brothers **S**
Ezra 8:13 Eliphelet, Jeiel, and **S**
Ezra 8:16 I sent for Eliezer, Ariel, **S**
Ezra 10:21 Maaseiah, Elijah, **S**, Jehiel,
Ezra 10:31 Ishijah, Malchijah, **S**,
Neh 3:29 After him **S** the son of
Neh 6:10 house of **S** the son of Delaiah
Neh 10: 8 Maaziah, Bilgai, and **S**
Neh 11:15 **S** the son of Hasshub, the son
Neh 12: 6 **S**, Joiarib, Jedaiah,
Neh 12:18 of **S**, Jehonathan
Neh 12:34 Judah, Benjamin, **S**, Jeremiah,
Neh 12:35 son of Jonathan, the son of **S**
Neh 12:36 and his brethren, **S**, Azarel,
Neh 12:42 also Maaseiah, **S**, Eleazar,
Jer 26:20 son of **S** of Kirjath Jearim
Jer 29:24 speak to **S** the Nehelamite
Jer 29:31 concerning **S** the Nehelamite
Jer 29:31 Because **S** has prophesied to
Jer 29:32 Behold, I will punish **S** the
Jer 36:12 scribe, Delaiah the son of **S**

SHEMARIAH (*see* SHEMA)
1Ch 12: 5 Eluzai, Jerimoth, Bealiah, **S**
Ezra 10:32 Benjamin, Malluch, and **S**
Ezra 10:41 Azareel, Shelemiah, **S**,

SHEMEBER
Gen 14: 2 **S** king of Zeboiim, and the

SHEMED
1Ch 8:12 were Eber, Misham, and **S**, who

SHEMER
1Ki 16:24 the hill of Samaria from **S**
1Ki 16:24 Samaria, after the name of **S**
1Ch 7:34 The sons of **S** were Ahi,

SHEMIDA (*see* SHEMIDAITES)
Num 26:32 of **S**, the family of the
Josh 17: 2 Hepher, and the children of **S**
1Ch 7:19 And the sons of **S** were Ahian

SHEMIDAITES (*see* SHEMIDA)
Num 26:32 Shemida, the family of the **S**

SHEMINITH
1Ch 15:21 to direct with harps on the **S**

SHEMIRAMOTH
1Ch 15:18 Zechariah, Ben, Jaaziel, **S**
1Ch 15:20 Zechariah, Aziel, **S**, Jehiel,
1Ch 16: 5 him Zechariah, then Jeiel, **S**
2Ch 17: 8 Zebadiah, Asahel, **S**,

SHEMUEL (*see* SAMUEL)
Num 34:20 Simeon, **S** the son of Ammihud
1Ch 7: 2 Jeriel, Jahmai, Jibsam, and **S**

SHEN
1Sa 7:12 set it up between Mizpah and **S**

SHENAZZAR
1Ch 3:18 and Malchiram, Pedaiah, **S**,

SHEOL
2Sa 22: 6 sorrows of **S** surrounded me
Job 11: 8 Deeper than **S**—what can you
Job 17:16 go down to the gates of **S**
Job 26: 6 **S** is naked before Him, and
Ps 16:10 will not leave my soul in **S**
Ps 18: 5 sorrows of **S** surrounded me
Ps 86:13 my soul from the depths of **S**
Ps 116: 3 the pangs of **S** laid hold of
Prov 1:12 us swallow them alive like **S**
Is 5:14 Therefore **S** has enlarged
Is 14:11 pomp is brought down to **S**
Is 14:15 shall be brought down to **S**
Is 28:15 with **S** we are in agreement
Is 28:18 with **S** will not stand
Is 38:10 I shall go to the gates of **S**
Is 38:18 For **S** cannot thank You, death
Is 57: 9 and debased yourself even to **S**
Jon 2: 2 out of the belly of **S** I cried

SHEPHAM
Num 34:10 border from Hazar Enan to **S**
Num 34:11 border shall go down from **S**

SHEPHATIAH
2Sa 3: 4 fifth, **S** the son of Abital
1Ch 3: 3 the fifth, **S**, by Abital
1Ch 9: 8 Meshullam the son of **S**, the
1Ch 12: 5 Shemariah, and **S** the Haruphite
1Ch 27:16 **S** the son of Maachah
2Ch 21: 2 Azaryahu, Michael, and **S**
Ezra 2: 4 the people of **S**, three
Ezra 2:57 the sons of **S**, the sons of
Ezra 8: 8 of the sons of **S**, Zebadiah
Neh 7: 9 the children of **S**, three
Neh 7:59 the children of **S**, the
Neh 11: 4 son of Amariah, the son of **S**
Jer 38: 1 Now **S** the son of Mattan,

SHEPHER
Num 33:23 and camped at Mount **S**
Num 33:24 They moved from Mount **S** and

SHEPHERD (*see* SHEPHERDED, SHEPHERDESS, SHEPHERD'S, SHEPHERDS)
Gen 46:34 for every s is an abomination
Gen 49:24 of Jacob (from there is the **S**
Num 27:17 be like sheep which have no s
2Sa 5: 2 You shall s My people Israel
2Sa 7: 7 to s My people Israel, saying
1Ki 22:17 as sheep that have no s
1Ch 11: 2 You shall s My people Israel
1Ch 17: 6 I commanded to s My people
2Ch 18:16 as sheep that have no s
Ps 23: 1 The LORD is my s
Ps 28: 9 **S** them also, And bear them up
Ps 78:71 To s Jacob His people, And
Ps 80: 1 O **S** of Israel, You who lead
Eccl 12:11 nails, given by one **S**
Is 40:11 will feed His flock like a s
Is 44:28 says of Cyrus, He is My s
Is 63:11 sea with the s of His flock
Jer 17:16 being a s who follows You
Jer 31:10 and keep him as a s does his
Jer 43:12 as a s puts on his garment,
Jer 49:19 And who is that s who will
Jer 50:44 and who is that s who will
Jer 51:23 I will break in pieces the s
Ezek 34: 5 because there was no s
Ezek 34: 8 field, because there was no s
Ezek 34:12 As a s seeks out his flock on
Ezek 34:23 establish one s over them
Ezek 34:23 shall feed them and be their s
Ezek 37:24 and they shall all have one s
Amos 3:12 As a s takes from the mouth
Mic 7:14 **S** Your people with Your staff
Zech 10: 2 trouble because there is no s
Zech 11:15 the implements of a foolish s

Zech 11:16 a s in the land who will not
Zech 11:17 Woe to the worthless s, who
Zech 13: 7 Awake, O sword, against My S
Zech 13: 7 Strike the S, and the sheep
Matt 2: 6 who will s My people Israel
Matt 9:36 like sheep having no s
Matt 25:32 as a s divides his sheep from
Matt 26:31 I will strike the S, and the
Mark 6:34 like sheep not having a s
Mark 14:27 I will strike the S, and the
John 10: 2 door is the s of the sheep
John 10:11 I am the good s
John 10:11 The good s gives His life for
John 10:12 is a hireling and not the s
John 10:14 I am the good s
John 10:16 will be one flock and one s
Acts 20:28 to s the church of God which
Heb 13:20 that great S of the sheep,
1Pe 2:25 have now returned to the S
1Pe 5: 2 S the flock of God which is
1Pe 5: 4 and when the Chief S appears
Rev 7:17 of the throne will s them

SHEPHERDED (*see* SHEPHERD)
Ps 78:72 So he s them according to the

SHEPHERDESS (*see* SHEPHERD)
Gen 29: 9 sheep, for she was a s

SHEPHERD'S (*see* SHEPHERD)
1Sa 17:40 brook, and put them in a s bag
Is 38:12 taken from me like a s tent

SHEPHERDS (*see* SHEPHERD, SHEPHERDS')
Gen 46:32 And the men are s, for their
Gen 47: 3 Your servants are s, both we
Ex 2:17 Then the s came and drove them
Ex 2:19 us from the hand of the s
Num 14:33 your sons shall be s in the
1Sa 25: 7 Your s were with us, and we
2Ki 10:12 way, at Beth Eked of the S
Is 13:20 nor will the s make their
Is 31: 4 of s is summoned against him
Is 56:11 And they are s who cannot
Jer 3:15 I will give you s according
Jer 6: 3 The s with their flocks shall
Jer 10:21 For the s have become
Jer 23: 1 Woe to the s who destroy and
Jer 23: 2 the s who feed My people
Jer 23: 4 I will set up s over them who
Jer 25:34 Wail, s, and cry
Jer 25:35 the s will have no way to
Jer 25:36 A voice of the cry of the s
Jer 33:12 again be a habitation of s
Jer 50: 6 Their s have led them astray
Ezek 34: 2 against the s of Israel,
Ezek 34: 2 says the Lord GOD to the s
Ezek 34: 2 Woe to the s of Israel who
Ezek 34: 2 Should not the s feed the
Ezek 34: 7 Therefore, you s, hear the
Ezek 34: 8 nor did My s search for My
Ezek 34: 8 but the s fed themselves and
Ezek 34: 9 therefore, O s, hear the
Ezek 34:10 Behold, I am against the s
Ezek 34:10 the s shall feed themselves
Amos 1: 2 the pastures of the s mourn
Mic 5: 5 raise against him seven s
Nah 3:18 Your s slumber, O king of
Zeph 2: 6 pastures, with shelters for s
Zech 10: 3 is kindled against the s, and
Zech 11: 3 is the sound of wailing s
Zech 11: 5 and their s do not pity them
Zech 11: 8 the three s in one month
Luke 2: 8 s living out in the fields
Luke 2:15 that the s said to one
Luke 2:18 which were told them by the s
Luke 2:20 Then the s returned,

SHEPHERDS' (*see* SHEPHERDS)
Song 1: 8 goats beside the s tents

SHEPHI (*see* SHEPHO)
1Ch 1:40 were Alian, Manahath, Ebal, S

SHEPHO (*see* SHEPHI)
Gen 36:23 Alvan, Manahath, Ebal, S, and

SHEPHUPHAN (*see* SHUPHAM, SHUPPIM)
1Ch 8: 5 Gera, S, and Huram

SHEREBIAH
Ezra 8:18 the son of Israel, namely S
Ezra 8:24 S, Hashabiah, and ten of their
Neh 8: 7 Also Jeshua, Bani, S, Jamin,
Neh 9: 4 Kadmiel, Shebaniah, Bunni, S
Neh 9: 5 Kadmiel, Bani, Hashabniah, S
Neh 10:12 Zaccur, S, Shebaniah,
Neh 12: 8 Jeshua, Binnui, Kadmiel, S
Neh 12:24 the Levites were Hashabiah, S

SHERESH
1Ch 7:16 The name of his brother was S

SHEREZER (*see* SHAREZER)
Zech 7: 2 when the people sent S, with

SHESHACH (*see* BABYLON)
Jer 25:26 Also the king of S shall
Jer 51:41 Oh, how S is taken

SHESHAI
Num 13:22 Ahiman, S, and Talmai, the
Josh 15:14 S, Ahiman, and Talmai, the
Judg 1:10 And they killed S, Ahiman,

SHESHAN (*see* SHESHAN'S)
1Ch 2:31 Ishi, the son of Ishi was S
1Ch 2:34 Now S had no sons, only
1Ch 2:34 S had an Egyptian servant
1Ch 2:35 S gave his daughter to Jarha

SHESHAN'S (*see* SHESHAN)
1Ch 2:31 Sheshan, and S child was Ahlai

SHESHBAZZAR (*see* ZERUBBABEL)
Ezra 1: 8 out to S the prince of Judah
Ezra 1:11 All these S took with the
Ezra 5:14 were given to one named S
Ezra 5:16 Then the same S came and laid

SHETHAR
Esth 1:14 to him being Carshena, S,

SHETHAR-BAZNAI
Ezra 5: 6 region beyond the River, and S

SHETHAR-BOZENAI
Ezra 5: 3 region beyond the River and S

SHETHAR-BOZNAI
Ezra 6: 6 region beyond the River, and S
Ezra 6:13 region beyond the River, S

SHEVA (*see* SHAVSHA)
2Sa 20:25 S was scribe
1Ch 2:49 S the father of Machbenah and

SHIBBOLETH (*see* SIBBOLETH)
Judg 12: 6 Then say, 'S'!" And he would

SHIBMAH (*see* SHEBAM)
Num 32:38 names being changed) and S

SHICRON
Josh 15:11 the border went around to S

SHIELD (*see* SHIELD-BEARER, SHIELDS)
Gen 15: 1 I am your s, your exceedingly
Deut 33:29 the s of your help and the
Judg 5: 8 not a s or spear was seen
1Sa 17:41 bore the s went before him
2Sa 1:21 For the s of the mighty is
2Sa 1:21 The s of Saul, not anointed
2Sa 22: 3 in Him I will trust, my s
2Sa 22:31 he is a s to all who trust in
2Sa 22:36 me the s of Your salvation
1Ki 10:16 of gold went into each s
1Ki 10:17 of gold went into each s
2Ki 19:32 nor come before it with s
1Ch 5:18 men, men able to bear s and
1Ch 12: 8 battle, who could handle s
1Ch 12:24 children of Judah bearing s
1Ch 12:34 thirty-seven thousand with s
2Ch 9:15 gold went into each s
2Ch 9:16 of gold went into each s
2Ch 17:17 men armed with bow and s
2Ch 25: 5 who could handle spear and s
Job 15:26 with his strong, embossed s
Ps 3: 3 are a s for me, My glory and
Ps 5:12 will surround him as with a s
Ps 18: 2 My s and the horn of my
Ps 18:30 He is a s to all who trust in
Ps 18:35 me the s of Your salvation
Ps 28: 7 LORD is my strength and my s
Ps 33:20 He is our help and our s
Ps 35: 2 Take hold of s and buckler, And
Ps 59:11 bring them down, O Lord our s
Ps 76: 3 the arrows of the bow, The s
Ps 84: 9 O God, behold our s, And look
Ps 84:11 the LORD God is a sun and s
Ps 89:18 For our s belongs to the LORD
Ps 91: 4 His truth shall be your s
Ps 115: 9 He is their help and their s
Ps 115:10 He is their help and their s
Ps 115:11 He is their help and their s
Ps 119:114 are my hiding place and my s
Ps 144: 2 tower and my deliverer, My s
Prov 2: 7 He is a s to those who walk
Prov 30: 5 He is a s to those who put
Is 21: 5 you princes, anoint the s
Is 22: 6 and Kir uncovered the s
Is 37:33 nor come before it with s
Jer 46: 3 Order the buckler and s, and
Jer 46: 9 the Libyans who handle the s
Ezek 23:24 array against you buckler, s
Ezek 27:10 they hung s and helmet in you
Ezek 38: 5 with them, all of them with s
Eph 6:16 taking the s of faith with

SHIELD-BEARER (*see* SHIELD)
1Sa 17: 7 and a s went before him

SHIELDS (*see* SHIELD)
2Sa 8: 7 David took the s of gold that
1Ki 10:16 large s of hammered gold
1Ki 10:17 hundred s of hammered gold
1Ki 14:26 gold s which Solomon had made
1Ki 14:27 made bronze s in their place
2Ki 11:10 s which had belonged to King
1Ch 18: 7 David took the s of gold that
2Ch 9:15 large s of hammered gold
2Ch 9:16 hundred s of hammered gold
2Ch 11:12 Also in every city he put s
2Ch 12: 9 gold s which Solomon had made
2Ch 12:10 King Rehoboam made bronze s
2Ch 14: 8 men from Judah who carried s
2Ch 14: 8 thousand men who carried s
2Ch 23: 9 small s which had been King
2Ch 26:14 them, for the entire army, s
2Ch 32: 5 weapons and s in abundance
2Ch 32:27 stones, for spices, for s
Neh 4:16 half held the spears, the s
Ps 47: 9 For the s of the earth belong
Song 4: 4 bucklers, all s of mighty men
Jer 51:11 arrows bright! Gather the s!
Ezek 27:11 they hung their s on your
Ezek 38: 4 company with bucklers and s
Ezek 39: 9 burn the weapons, both the s
Nah 2: 3 The s of his mighty men are

SHIFTED (*see* SHIFTS)
1Sa 14:23 the battle s to Beth Aven

SHIFTS (*see* SHIFTED)
1Ki 5:14 ten thousand a month in s

SHIGIONOTH
Hab 3: 1 of Habakkuk the prophet, on S

SHIHOR (*see* SHIHOR LIBNATH, SIHOR)
1Ch 13: 5 from S in Egypt to as far as
Is 23: 3 great waters the grain of S

SHIHOR LIBNATH (*see* SHIHOR)
Josh 19:26 westward, along the Brook S

SHILHI
1Ki 22:42 was Azubah the daughter of S
2Ch 20:31 was Azubah the daughter of S

SHILHIM (*see* SHAARAIM, SHARUHEN)
Josh 15:32 Lebaoth, S, Ain, and Rimmon

SHILLEM (*see* SHALLUM, SHILLEMITES)
Gen 46:24 Jahzeel, Guni, Jezer, and S
Num 26:49 of S, the family of the

SHILLEMITES (*see* SHILLEM)
Num 26:49 Shillem, the family of the S

SHILOAH (*see* SILOAM)
Is 8: 6 waters of S that flow softly

SHILOH (*see* SHILONI, SHILONITE, TAANATH SHILOH)
Gen 49:10 his feet, until S comes
Josh 18: 1 assembled together at S, and
Josh 18: 8 you here before the LORD in S
Josh 18: 9 to Joshua at the camp in S
Josh 18:10 for them in S before the LORD
Josh 19:51 by lot in S before the LORD
Josh 21: 2 at S in the land of Canaan
Josh 22: 9 the children of Israel at S
Josh 22:12 S to go to war against them
Judg 18:31 the house of God was in S
Judg 21:12 brought them to the camp at S
Judg 21:19 yearly feast of the LORD in S
Judg 21:21 S come out to perform their
Judg 21:21 from the daughters of S
1Sa 1: 3 to the LORD of hosts in S

2Ch 20:36 to make s to go to Tarshish
2Ch 20:36 and they made the s in Ezion
2Ch 20:37 Then the s were wrecked, so
Job 9:26 They pass by like swift s
Ps 48: 7 As when You break the s of
Ps 104:26 There the s sail about
Ps 107:23 who go down to the sea in s
Prov 31:14 She is like the merchant s
Is 2:16 upon all the s of Tarshish
Is 23: 1 Wail, you s of Tarshish
Is 23:14 Wail, you s of Tarshish
Is 33:21 sail, nor majestic s pass by
Is 43:14 who rejoice in their s
Is 60: 9 the s of Tarshish will come
Ezek 27: 9 all the s of the sea and their
Ezek 27:25 The s of Tarshish were
Ezek 27:29 will come down from their s
Ezek 30: 9 Me in s to make the careless
Dan 11:30 For s from Cyprus shall come
Dan 11:40 horsemen, and with many s
Jas 3: 4 Look also at s
Rev 8: 9 third of the s were destroyed
Rev 18:19 in which all who had s on the

SHIPWRECK (*see* SHIP, SHIPWRECKED)
1Ti 1:19 the faith have suffered s

SHIPWRECKED (*see* SHIPWRECK)
2Co 11:25 three times I was s

SHISHA (*see* SHAVSHA)
1Ki 4: 3 and Ahijah, the sons of S,

SHISHAK
1Ki 11:40 to S king of Egypt, and was in
1Ki 14:25 that S king of Egypt came up
2Ch 12: 2 that S king of Egypt came up
2Ch 12: 5 in Jerusalem because of S
2Ch 12: 5 left you in the hand of S
2Ch 12: 7 on Jerusalem by the hand of S
2Ch 12: 9 So S king of Egypt came up

SHITRAI
1Ch 27:29 S the Sharonite was over the

SHIZA
1Ch 11:42 Adina the son of S the

SHOA
Ezek 23:23 all the Chaldeans, Pekod, S

SHOBAB
2Sa 5:14 Shammua, S, Nathan, Solomon,
1Ch 2:18 Jesher, S, and Ardon
1Ch 3: 5 Shimea, S, Nathan, and
1Ch 14: 4 Shammua, S, Nathan, Solomon,

SHOBACH (*see* SHOPHACH)
2Sa 10:16 And S the commander of
2Sa 10:18 struck S the commander of

SHOBAI
Ezra 2:42 of Hatita, and the sons of S
Neh 7:45 of Hatita, the children of S

SHOBAL
Gen 36:20 Lotan, S, Zibeon, Anah,
Gen 36:23 These were the sons of S
Gen 36:29 Chief Lotan, Chief S, Chief
1Ch 1:38 sons of Seir were Lotan, S
1Ch 1:40 The sons of S were Alian,
1Ch 2:50 were S the father of Kirjath
1Ch 2:52 And S the father of Kirjath
1Ch 4: 1 Hezron, Carmi, Hur, and S
1Ch 4: 2 the son of S begot Jahath

SHOBEK
Neh 10:24 Hallohesh, Pilha, S,

SHOBI
2Sa 17:27 that S the son of Nahash from

SHOCKS
Judg 15: 5 and burned up both the s and

SHOD (*see* UNSHOD)
Eph 6:15 having s your feet with the

SHOE
Ps 60: 8 Over Edom I will cast My s
Ps 108: 9 Over Edom I will cast My s

SHOHAM
1Ch 24:27 by Jaaziah were Beno, S,

SHOMER (*see* SHAMER, SHIMRITH)
2Ki 12:21 and Jehozabad the son of S
1Ch 7:32 And Heber begot Japhlet, S

SHONE (*see* SHINE)
Ex 34:29 s while he talked with Him
Ex 34:30 the skin of his face s, and
Ex 34:35 the skin of Moses' face s
Deut 33: 2 He s forth from Mount Paran,
Job 29: 3 when His lamp s upon my head
Ezek 43: 2 the earth s with His glory
Matt 17: 2 His face s like the sun, and
Luke 2: 9 of the Lord s around them
Acts 9: 3 suddenly a light s around him
Acts 12: 7 and a light s in the prison
Acts 22: 6 light from heaven s around me
2Co 4: 6 out of darkness who has s in

SHOOK (*see* SHAKE)
1Sa 4: 5 so loudly that the earth s
2Sa 22: 8 Then the earth s and trembled
2Sa 22: 8 of heaven moved and s, because
Neh 5:13 Then I s out the fold of my
Ps 18: 7 Then the earth s and trembled
Ps 68: 8 The earth s; The heavens also
Ps 77:18 The earth trembled and s
Is 14:16 tremble, who s kingdoms,
Is 23:11 the sea, He s the kingdoms
Is 64: 3 down, the mountains s at Your
Matt 28: 4 the guards s for fear of him,
Acts 13:51 But they s off the dust from
Acts 18: 6 he s his garments and said to
Acts 28: 5 But he s off the creature
Heb 12:26 whose voice then s the earth

SHOOT (*see* SHOOTING, SHOOTS, SHOT)
1Sa 20:20 Then I will s three arrows to
1Sa 20:36 find the arrows which I s
2Sa 11:20 they would s from the wall
2Ki 9:27 S him also in the chariot
2Ki 13:17 Then Elisha said, "S"
2Ki 19:32 nor s an arrow there, nor
1Ch 5:18 sword, to s with the bow, and
2Ch 26:15 to s arrows and large stones
Job 41:19 sparks of fire s out
Ps 11: 2 That they may s secretly at
Ps 22: 7 They s out the lip, they
Ps 64: 3 their bows to s their arrows
Ps 64: 4 That they may s in secret at
Ps 64: 4 Suddenly they s at him and do
Ps 64: 7 But God shall s at them with
Ps 144: 6 S out Your arrows and destroy
Is 37:33 nor s an arrow there, nor
Jer 50:14 s at her, spare no arrows,
Ezek 36: 8 you shall s forth your

SHOOTING (*see* SHOOT)
1Ch 12: 2 and s arrows with the bow

SHOOTS (*see* SHOOT)
Job 14: 7 its tender s will not cease
Ezek 17: 6 branches, and put forth s
Mark 4:32 s out large branches, so that

SHOPHACH (*see* SHOBACH)
1Ch 19:16 River, and S the commander of
1Ch 19:18 killed S the commander of the

SHOPHAN (*see* ZAPHON)
Num 32:35 Atroth and S and Jazer and

SHORE (*see* SHORES)
Josh 15: 2 at the s of the Salt Sea,
1Ki 9:26 Elath on the s of the Red Sea
Ezek 27:29 their ships and stand on the s
Matt 13: 2 multitude stood on the s
Matt 13:48 it was full, they drew to s
John 21: 4 come, Jesus stood on the s
Acts 21: 5 And we knelt down on the s
Acts 27:40 to the wind and made for s

SHORES (*see* SHORE)
Zeph 2:11 all the s of the nations

SHORN (*see* SHEAR)
Song 4: 2 of s sheep which have come up
1Co 11: 6 covered, let her also be s
1Co 11: 6 for a woman to be s or shaved

SHORT (*see* SHORTEN, SHORTER, SHORTLY)
Ex 39:28 s trousers of fine linen,
Lev 22:23 any limb too long or too s
2Ki 5:19 from him a s distance
Job 20: 5 triumphing of the wicked is s
Ps 89:47 Remember how s my time is
Is 28:20 For the bed is too s for a
Mic 6:10 and the s measure that is an
Luke 19: 3 for he was of s stature
Rom 3:23 fall s of the glory of God,
Rom 9:28 cut it s in righteousness,
Rom 9:28 make a s work upon the earth
1Co 1: 7 so that you come s in no gift
1Co 7:29 say, brethren, the time is s
1Th 2:17 you for a s time in presence
Heb 4: 1 you seem to have come s of it
Heb 12:15 fall s of the grace of God
Rev 12:12 he knows that he has a s time
Rev 17:10 he must continue a s time

SHORT-EARED
Lev 11:16 the ostrich, the s owl, the
Deut 14:15 the ostrich, the s owl, the

SHORTENED (*see* SHORT)
Num 11:23 Has the LORD's arm been s
Job 18: 7 steps of his strength are s
Ps 89:45 days of his youth You have s
Ps 102:23 He s my days
Prov 10:27 years of the wicked will be s
Is 50: 2 Is My hand s at all that it
Is 59: 1 the LORD's hand is not s
Ezek 42: 6 was s more than the lower
Matt 24:22 And unless those days were s
Matt 24:22 sake those days will be s
Mark 13:20 the Lord had s those days
Mark 13:20 whom He chose, He s the days

SHORTER (*see* SHORT)
Ezek 42: 5 Now the upper chambers were s

SHORTLY (*see* SHORT)
Gen 41:32 God will s bring it to pass
Jer 27:16 now s be brought back from
Acts 25: 4 he himself was going there s
Rom 16:20 crush Satan under your feet s
1Co 4:19 But I will come to you s, if
Phil 2:19 to send Timothy to you s,
Phil 2:24 I myself shall also come s
1Ti 3:14 I hope to come to you s
Heb 13:23 I shall see you if he comes s
2Pe 1:14 knowing that s I must put off
3Jn 14 but I hope to see you s, and
Rev 1: 1 which must s take place
Rev 22: 6 which must s take place

SHORTSIGHTED
2Pe 1: 9 who lacks these things is s

SHOT (*see* SHOOT)
Gen 40:10 budded, its blossoms s forth
Gen 49:23 him, s at him and hated him
Ex 19:13 be stoned or s with an arrow
Num 21:30 But we have s at them
1Sa 20:20 it, as though I s at a target
1Sa 20:36 ran, he s an arrow beyond him
1Sa 20:37 was which Jonathan had s,
2Sa 11:24 The archers s from the wall
2Ki 9:24 s Jehoram between his arms
2Ki 13:17 said, "Shoot"; and he s
2Ch 35:23 And the archers s King Josiah
Jer 9: 8 tongue is an arrow s out

SHOULD (*see* PREFACE)

SHOULDER (*see* SHOULDERS)
Gen 21:14 and putting it on her s, he
Gen 24:15 out with her pitcher on her s
Gen 24:45 out with her pitcher on her s
Gen 24:46 her pitcher down from her s
Gen 49:15 he bowed his s to bear a
Ex 28: 7 It shall have two s straps
Ex 28:25 put them on the s straps of
Ex 28:27 put them on the two s straps
Ex 39: 4 They made s straps for it to
Ex 39:18 put them on the s straps of
Ex 39:20 put them on the two s straps
Num 6:19 take the boiled s of the ram
Deut 18: 3 give to the priest the s, the
Josh 4: 5 you take up a stone on his s
Judg 9:48 took it and laid it on his s
Job 31:22 let my arm fall from my s
Job 31:36 I would carry it on my s, and
Ps 81: 6 I removed his s from the
Is 9: 4 burden and the staff of his s
Is 9: 6 government will be upon His s
Is 10:27 be taken away from your s
Is 11:14 shall fly down upon the s of
Is 22:22 of David I will lay on his s
Is 46: 7 They bear it on the s, they
Ezek 12: 7 them on my s in their sight
Ezek 12:12 on his s at twilight and go
Ezek 24: 4 piece, The thigh and the s
Ezek 29:18 bald, and every s rubbed raw

Ezek 34:21 have pushed with side and s

SHOULDERS (*see* SHOULDER)
Gen 9:23 laid it on both their s, and
Ex 12:34 in their clothes on their s
Ex 28:12 s of the ephod as memorial
Ex 28:12 on his two s as a memorial
Ex 39: 7 them on the s of the ephod
Num 7: 9 which they carried on their s
Deut 33:12 he shall dwell between His s
Judg 16: 3 bar and all, put them on his s
1Sa 9: 2 From his s upward he was
1Sa 10:23 the people from his s upward
1Sa 17: 6 bronze javelin between his s
1Ch 15:15 the ark of God on their s
2Ch 35: 3 longer be a burden on your s
Neh 3: 5 nobles did not put their s to
Neh 9:29 And they shrugged their s
Is 14:25 burden removed from their s
Is 49:22 shall be carried on their s
Ezek 12: 6 you shall bear them on your s
Ezek 29: 7 you broke and tore all their s
Zech 7:11 to heed, shrugged their s
Matt 23: 4 bear, and lay them on men's s
Luke 15: 5 found it, he lays it on his s

SHOUT (*see* SHOUTED, SHOUTING, SHOUTS)
Ex 32:18 of those who s in victory
Num 23:21 the s of a King is among them
Josh 6: 5 shall s with a great s
Josh 6:10 You shall not s or make any
Josh 6:10 the day I say to you, 'S
Josh 6:10 Then you shall s
Josh 6:16 S, for the LORD has given you
Josh 6:20 people shouted with a great s
1Sa 4: 6 heard the noise of the s,
1Sa 4: 6 the sound of this great s in
1Ki 22:36 a s went throughout the army,
2Ch 13:15 the men of Judah gave a s
Ezra 3:11 people shouted with a great s
Ezra 3:13 s of joy from the noise of
Ezra 3:13 people shouted with a loud s
Job 3: 7 May no joyful s come into it
Ps 5:11 Let them ever s for joy,
Ps 32:11 s for joy, all you upright in
Ps 33: 3 skillfully with a s of joy
Ps 35:27 Let them s for joy and be glad
Ps 47: 1 S to God with the voice of
Ps 47: 5 God has gone up with a s, The
Ps 60: 8 s in triumph because of Me
Ps 65:13 They s for joy, they also
Ps 66: 1 Make a joyful s to God, all
Ps 81: 1 Make a joyful s to the God of
Ps 95: 1 Let us s joyfully to the Rock
Ps 95: 2 Let us s joyfully to Him with
Ps 98: 4 S joyfully to the LORD, all
Ps 98: 6 S joyfully before the LORD,
Ps 100: 1 Make a joyful s to the LORD
Ps 132: 9 And let Your saints s for joy
Ps 132:16 saints shall s aloud for joy
Eccl 9:17 the s of a ruler of fools
Is 12: 6 Cry out and s, O inhabitant of
Is 42:11 let them s from the top of
Is 42:13 shall cry out, yes, s aloud
Is 44:23 S, you lower parts of the
Jer 25:30 He will give a s, as those
Jer 31: 7 and s among the chief of the
Jer 50:15 S against her all around
Jer 51:14 shall lift up a s against you
Lam 3: 8 Even when I cry and s, He
Zeph 3:14 S, O Israel! Be glad
Zech 9: 9 S, O daughter of Jerusalem
Gal 4:27 Break forth and s, you who do
1Th 4:16 descend from heaven with a s

SHOUTED (*see* SHOUT)
Ex 32:17 noise of the people as they s
Lev 9:24 all the people saw it, they s
Josh 6:20 So the people s when the
Josh 6:20 the people s with a great
1Sa 4: 5 all Israel s so loudly that
1Sa 10:24 So all the people s and said
1Sa 17:52 of Israel and Judah arose and s
2Ch 13:15 and as the men of Judah s, it
Ezra 3:11 people s with a great shout
Ezra 3:12 yet many s aloud for joy,
Ezra 3:13 for the people s with a loud
Job 30: 5 they s at them as at a thief
Job 38: 7 all the sons of God s for joy
Jer 20: 8 I s, "Violence and plunder
Luke 23:21 But they s, saying, "Crucify
Acts 22:24 why they s so against him

SHOUTING (*see* SHOUT)
Judg 15:14 came s against him
1Sa 17:20 the fight and s for the battle
2Sa 6:15 up the ark of the LORD with s
1Ch 15:28 covenant of the LORD with s
2Ch 15:14 with a loud voice, with s
Job 39:25 the thunder of captains and s
Prov 11:10 the wicked perish, there is s
Is 16:10 singing, nor will there be s
Is 16:10 I have made their s cease
Jer 20:16 the morning and the s at noon,
Jer 48:33 one will tread with joyous s
Jer 48:33 not joyous s
Ezek 21:22 to lift the voice with s
Amos 1:14 amid s in the day of battle,
Amos 2: 2 shall die with tumult, with s
Acts 12:22 And the people kept s, "The

SHOUTS (*see* SHOUT)
Job 39: 7 not heed the s of the driver
Ps 78:65 man who s because of wine
Zech 4: 7 forth the capstone with s of

SHOVEL (*see* SHOVELS)
Is 30:24 has been winnowed with the s

SHOVELS (*see* SHOVEL)
Ex 27: 3 receive its ashes, and its s
Ex 38: 3 the pans, the s, the basins,
Num 4:14 firepans, the forks, the s
1Ki 7:40 made the lavers and the s and
1Ki 7:45 the pots, the s, and the bowls
2Ki 25:14 took away the pots, the s
2Ch 4:11 Huram made the pots and the s
2Ch 4:16 also the pots, the s, the
Jer 52:18 took away the pots, the s

SHOW (*see* SHOWED, SHOWING, SHOWN, SHOWS)
Gen 12: 1 to a land that I will s you
Gen 24:12 and s kindness to my master
Gen 40:14 and please s kindness to me
Ex 7: 9 S a miracle for yourselves,'
Ex 9:16 that I may s My power in you,
Ex 10: 1 that I may s these signs of
Ex 18:20 s them the way in which they
Ex 23: 3 You shall not s partiality to
Ex 25: 9 According to all that I s you
Ex 33:13 s me now Your way, that I may
Ex 33:18 Please, s me Your glory
Num 16: 5 the LORD will s who is His
Deut 1:17 You shall not s partiality
Deut 1:33 to s you the way you should
Deut 3:24 GOD, You have begun to s Your
Deut 7: 2 with them nor s mercy to them
Deut 13:17 s you mercy, have compassion
Deut 16:19 you shall not s partiality
Deut 28:50 nor s favor to the young
Deut 32: 7 your father, and he will s you
Josh 2:12 that you also will s kindness
Josh 5: 6 not s them the land which the
Judg 1:24 Please s us the entrance to
Judg 1:24 city, and we will s you mercy
Judg 4:22 I will s you the man whom you
Judg 6:17 then s me a sign that it is
Judg 8:35 nor did they s kindness to
1Sa 8: 9 s them the behavior of the
1Sa 9: 6 perhaps he can s us the way
1Sa 10: 8 and s you what you should do
1Sa 14: 8 we will s ourselves to them
1Sa 14:12 and we will s you something
1Sa 16: 3 I will s you what you shall
1Sa 20:14 you shall not only s me the
2Sa 2: 6 now may the LORD s kindness
2Sa 3: 8 Today I s loyalty to the
2Sa 9: 1 that I may s him kindness for
2Sa 9: 3 to whom I may s the kindness
2Sa 9: 7 fear, for I will surely s you
2Sa 10: 2 I will s kindness to Hanun
2Sa 15:25 back and s me both it and His
2Sa 22:26 You will s Yourself merciful
2Sa 22:26 You will s Yourself blameless
2Sa 22:27 pure You will s Yourself pure
2Sa 22:27 You will s Yourself shrewd
1Ki 2: 7 But s kindness to the sons of
2Ki 6:11 Will you not s me which of us
2Ki 20:13 that Hezekiah did not s them
1Ch 19: 2 I will s kindness to Hanun
2Ch 16: 9 to s Himself strong on behalf
Neh 9:19 to s them light, and the way
Esth 1:11 in order to s her beauty to
Esth 4: 8 that he might s it to Esther
Job 10: 2 s me why You contend with me
Job 10:16 again You s Yourself awesome
Job 11: 6 that He would s you the
Job 13: 8 Will you s partiality for Him
Job 13:10 if you secretly s partiality
Job 32:21 pray, s partiality to anyone
Job 33:23 to s man His uprightness,
Job 36: 2 I will s you that there are
Ps 4: 6 say, "Who will s us any good
Ps 16:11 You will s me the path of
Ps 17: 7 S Your marvelous
Ps 18:25 You will s Yourself merciful
Ps 18:25 You will s Yourself blameless
Ps 18:26 pure You will s Yourself pure
Ps 18:26 You will s Yourself shrewd
Ps 25: 4 S me Your ways, O LORD
Ps 25:14 He will s them His covenant
Ps 50:23 I will s the salvation of God
Ps 51:15 my mouth shall s forth Your
Ps 79:13 We will s forth Your praise
Ps 82: 2 s partiality to the wicked
Ps 85: 7 S us Your mercy, O LORD, And
Ps 86:17 S me a sign for good, That
Ps 91:16 him, And s him My salvation
Ps 102:14 And s favor to her dust
Ps 109:16 did not remember to s mercy
Prov 18: 5 It is not good to s
Prov 24:23 It is not good to s
Prov 28:21 To s partiality is not good,
Is 27:11 them will s them no favor
Is 30:30 s the descent of His arm,
Is 39: 2 that Hezekiah did not s them
Is 41:22 and s us what will happen
Is 41:22 let them s the former things,
Is 41:23 S the things that are to come
Is 43: 9 this, and s us former things
Is 44: 7 let them s these to them
Is 46: 8 this, and s yourselves men
Is 49: 9 in darkness, 'S yourselves
Jer 16:10 when you s this people all
Jer 16:13 where I will not s you favor
Jer 18:17 I will s them the back and not
Jer 32:18 You s lovingkindness to
Jer 33: 3 s you great and mighty things,
Jer 42: 3 may s us the way in which we
Jer 42:12 I will s you mercy, that he
Jer 50:42 cruel and shall not s mercy
Jer 51:31 to s the king of Babylon that
Lam 3:32 yet He will s compassion
Lam 4:16 nor s favor to the elders
Ezek 22: 2 s her all her abominations
Ezek 33:31 their mouth they s much love
Ezek 37:18 Will you not s us what you
Ezek 38:18 My fury will s in My face
Ezek 40: 4 mind on everything I s you
Ezek 40: 4 so that I might s them to you
Dan 6:13 does not s due regard for you
Dan 11:30 and s regard for those who
Joel 2:30 And I will s wonders in the
Mic 7:15 I will s them marvelous
Nah 3: 5 I will s the nations your
Hab 1: 3 Why do You s me iniquity, and
Zech 1: 9 I will s you what they are
Zech 7: 9 s mercy and compassion
Matt 8: 4 s yourself to the priest, and
Matt 16: 1 s them a sign from heaven
Matt 16:21 to s to His disciples that He
Matt 22:19 S Me the tax money
Matt 24: 1 to s Him the buildings of the
Matt 24:24 s great signs and wonders, so
Mark 1:44 s yourself to the priest, and
Mark 13:22 s signs and wonders to deceive
Mark 14:15 Then he will s you a large
Luke 5:14 s yourself to the priest, and
Luke 6:47 I will s you whom he is like
Luke 12: 5 But I will s you whom you
Luke 17:14 s yourselves to the priests
Luke 20:21 and You do not s personal
Luke 20:24 S Me a denarius
Luke 22:12 Then he will s you a large
John 2:18 What sign do You s to us,
John 5:20 He will s Him greater works
John 7: 4 s Yourself to the world
John 14: 8 s us the Father, and it is
John 14: 9 you say, 'S us the Father'
Acts 1:24 s which of these two You have
Acts 2:19 I will s wonders in heaven
Acts 7: 3 to a land that I will s you
Acts 9:16 For I will s him how many
Rom 2:15 who s the work of the law

Acts 28: 8 of Publius lay s of a fever
1Co 11:30 s among you, and many sleep
Phil 2:26 you had heard that he was s
Phil 2:27 he was s almost unto death
2Ti 4:20 I have left in Miletus s
Jas 5:14 Is anyone among you s
Jas 5:15 of faith will save the s, and

SICKBED (*see* SICK)
Ps 41: 3 You will sustain him on his s
Rev 2:22 I will cast her into a s, and

SICKLE
Deut 16: 9 to put the s to the grain
Deut 23:25 but you shall not use a s on
1Sa 13:20 his mattock, his ax, and his s
Jer 50:16 handles the s at harvest time
Joel 3:13 Put in the s, for the harvest
Mark 4:29 immediately he puts in the s
Rev 14:14 and in His hand a sharp s
Rev 14:15 Thrust in Your s and reap, for
Rev 14:16 thrust in His s on the earth
Rev 14:17 he also having a sharp s
Rev 14:18 to him who had the sharp s
Rev 14:18 Thrust in your sharp s and
Rev 14:19 thrust his s into the earth

SICKNESS (*see* SICK, SICKNESSES)
Ex 23:25 I will take s away from the
Lev 20:18 with a woman during her s
Deut 7:15 will take away from you all s
Deut 28:61 Also every s and every plague,
1Ki 8:37 plague or whatever s there is
1Ki 17:17 his s was so serious that
2Ch 6:28 plague or whatever s there is
2Ch 21:15 come out by reason of the s
2Ch 21:19 came out because of his s
Prov 18:14 a man will sustain him in s
Eccl 5:17 and he has much sorrow and s
Is 38: 9 and had recovered from his s
Hos 5:13 When Ephraim saw his s, and
Matt 4:23 and healing all kinds of s
Matt 9:35 kingdom, and healing every s
Matt 10: 1 and to heal all kinds of s
John 11: 4 This s is not unto death, but

SICKNESSES (*see* SICKNESS)
Deut 28:59 and serious and prolonged s
Deut 29:22 the s which the LORD has laid
Matt 8:17 our infirmities and bore our s
Mark 3:15 and to have power to heal s

SIDDIM
Gen 14: 3 in the Valley of S (that is
Gen 14: 8 in battle in the Valley of S
Gen 14:10 Now the Valley of S was full

SIDE (*see* SIDED, SIDES)
Gen 6:16 the door of the ark in its s
Ex 2: 5 walked along the river's s
Ex 17:12 his hands, one on one s,
Ex 17:12 and the other on the other s
Ex 25:12 two rings shall be on one s
Ex 25:12 and two rings on the other s
Ex 25:32 of the lampstand out of one s
Ex 25:32 lampstand out of the other s
Ex 26:13 And a cubit on one s
Ex 26:13 and a cubit on the other s
Ex 26:13 of the tabernacle, on this s
Ex 26:13 on this s and on that s
Ex 26:18 twenty boards for the south s
Ex 26:20 And for the second s of
Ex 26:20 the tabernacle, the north s
Ex 26:22 For the far s of the
Ex 26:26 on one s of the tabernacle
Ex 26:27 the other s of the tabernacle
Ex 26:27 of the s of the tabernacle
Ex 26:27 for the far s westward
Ex 26:35 from the table on the s of
Ex 26:35 put the table on the north s
Ex 27: 9 For the south s there shall
Ex 27: 9 hundred cubits long for one s
Ex 27:11 the length of the north s
Ex 27:12 of the court on the west s
Ex 27:13 east s shall be fifty cubits
Ex 27:14 The hangings on one s of the
Ex 27:15 And on the other s shall be
Ex 28:26 on the inner s of the ephod
Ex 32:15 on the one s and on the other
Ex 32:26 Whoever is on the LORD's s
Ex 32:27 man put his sword on his s
Ex 36:23 twenty boards for the south s
Ex 36:25 And for the other s of
Ex 36:25 the tabernacle, the north s
Ex 36:27 For the west s of the
Ex 36:31 on one s of the tabernacle
Ex 36:32 the other s of the tabernacle
Ex 36:32 on the far s westward
Ex 37: 3 two rings on one s, and two
Ex 37: 3 rings on the other s of it
Ex 37: 8 cherub at one end on this s
Ex 37: 8 at the other end on that s
Ex 37:18 of the lampstand out of one s
Ex 37:18 lampstand out of the other s
Ex 38: 9 made the court on the south s
Ex 38:11 On the north s the hangings
Ex 38:12 And on the west s there were
Ex 38:13 For the east s the hangings
Ex 38:14 The hangings of one s of the
Ex 38:15 the other s of the court gate
Ex 38:15 on this s and that were
Ex 39:19 on the inward s of the ephod
Ex 40:22 on the north s of the
Ex 40:24 table, on the south s of the
Lev 1:11 s of the altar before the
Lev 1:15 out at the s of the altar
Lev 1:16 the altar on the east s, into
Lev 5: 9 on the s of the altar, and the
Lev 16:14 the mercy seat on the east s
Num 2: 3 On the east s, toward the
Num 2:10 On the south s shall be the
Num 2:18 On the west s shall be the
Num 2:25 s according to their armies
Num 3:29 the south s of the tabernacle
Num 3:35 the north s of the tabernacle
Num 10: 5 east s shall then begin their
Num 10: 6 s shall begin their journey
Num 11:31 a day's journey on this s
Num 11:31 day's journey on the other s
Num 21:13 on the other s of the Arnon
Num 22: 1 s of the Jordan across from
Num 22:24 this s and a wall on that s
Num 32:19 on the other s of the Jordan
Num 32:19 this eastern s of the Jordan
Num 32:32 us on this s of the Jordan
Num 34: 4 turn from the southern s of
Num 34:11 Riblah on the east s of Ain
Num 34:11 reach to the eastern s of the
Num 34:15 on this s of the Jordan,
Num 35: 5 east s two thousand cubits
Num 35: 5 on the south s two thousand
Num 35: 5 on the west s two thousand
Num 35: 5 on the north s two thousand
Num 35:14 on this s of the Jordan, and
Deut 1: 1 this s of the Jordan in the
Deut 1: 5 On this s of the Jordan in
Deut 3: 8 were on this s of the Jordan
Deut 3:17 as far as the east s of the
Deut 4:41 on this s of the Jordan,
Deut 4:46 on this s of the Jordan, in
Deut 4:47 were on this s of the Jordan
Deut 4:49 all the plain on the east s
Deut 11:30 on the other s of the Jordan
Josh 1:14 you on this s of the Jordan
Josh 1:15 s of the Jordan toward the
Josh 2:10 on the other s of the Jordan
Josh 5: 1 on the west s of the Jordan
Josh 7: 2 Aven, on the east s of Bethel
Josh 7: 7 on the other s of the Jordan
Josh 8: 9 and Ai, on the west s of Ai
Josh 8:11 camped on the north s of Ai
Josh 8:12 Ai, on the west s of the city
Josh 8:22 this s and some on that s
Josh 8:33 stood on either s of the ark
Josh 9: 1 were on this s of the Jordan
Josh 12: 1 s of the Jordan toward the
Josh 12: 7 on this s of the Jordan, on
Josh 13:27 on the other s of the Jordan
Josh 13:32 on the other s of the Jordan
Josh 14: 3 on the other s of the Jordan
Josh 15: 3 s of the Ascent of Akrabbim
Josh 15: 3 the south s of Kadesh Barnea
Josh 15: 7 on the south s of the valley
Josh 15:10 passed along to the s of
Josh 15:11 to the s of Ekron northward
Josh 16: 5 inheritance on the east s was
Josh 16: 6 on the north s of Michmethath
Josh 17: 5 on the other s of the Jordan
Josh 17: 9 on the north s of the brook
Josh 18:12 north s began at the Jordan
Josh 18:12 the s of Jericho on the north
Josh 18:13 to the s of Luz (which is
Josh 18:13 south s of Lower Beth Horon
Josh 18:14 the west s to the south, from
Josh 18:14 This was the west s
Josh 18:15 The south s began at the end
Josh 18:16 to the s of the Jebusite city
Josh 18:18 toward the north s of Arabah
Josh 18:19 to the north s of Beth Hoglah
Josh 18:20 was its border on the east s
Josh 19:14 on the north s of Hannathon
Josh 19:34 Zebulun on the south s
Josh 19:34 and Asher on the west s
Josh 20: 8 on the other s of the Jordan,
Josh 22: 4 on the other s of the Jordan
Josh 22: 7 on this s of the Jordan,
Josh 22:11 on the s occupied by the
Josh 24: 2 dwelt on the other s of the
Josh 24: 3 from the other s of the River
Josh 24: 8 on the other s of the Jordan
Josh 24:14 on the other s of the River
Josh 24:15 on the other s of the River
Josh 24:30 on the north s of Mount Gaash
Judg 2: 3 shall be thorns in your s
Judg 2: 9 on the north s of Mount Gaash
Judg 7: 1 s of them by the hill of
Judg 7:18 on every s of the whole camp
Judg 7:25 on the other s of the Jordan
Judg 8:34 all their enemies on every s
Judg 10: 8 who were on the other s of
Judg 11:18 came to the east s of the
Judg 11:18 on the other s of the Arnon
Judg 21:19 on the east s of the highway
1Sa 4:18 backward by the s of the gate
1Sa 6: 8 offering in a chest by its s
1Sa 12:11 of your enemies on every s
1Sa 14: 1 that is on the other s
1Sa 14: 4 was a sharp rock on one s
1Sa 14: 4 a sharp rock on the other s
1Sa 14:40 You be on one s, and my son
1Sa 14:40 and I will be on the other s
1Sa 14:47 all his enemies on every s
1Sa 17: 3 stood on a mountain on one s
1Sa 17: 3 on a mountain on the other s
1Sa 20:20 three arrows to the s of it
1Sa 20:21 arrows are on this s of you
1Sa 20:25 and Abner sat by Saul's s
1Sa 23:26 went on one s of the mountain
1Sa 23:26 the other s of the mountain
1Sa 26:13 went over to the other s, and
1Sa 31: 7 on the other s of the valley
1Sa 31: 7 on the other s of the Jordan
2Sa 2:13 one on one s of the pool and
2Sa 2:13 on the other s of the pool
2Sa 2:16 his sword in his opponent's s
2Sa 24: 5 on the right s of the town
1Ki 3:20 and took my son from my s,
1Ki 4:12 far as the other s of Jokneam
1Ki 4:24 s of the River from Tiphsah
1Ki 4:24 kings on this s of the River
1Ki 4:24 on every s all around him
1Ki 5: 3 fought against him on every s
1Ki 5: 4 has given me rest on every s
1Ki 6: 5 Thus he made s chambers all
1Ki 6: 8 on the right s of the temple
1Ki 6:10 he built s chambers against
1Ki 7:39 on the right s of the house
1Ki 7:39 on the left s of the house
1Ki 7:39 s of the house toward the
1Ki 7:49 gold, five on the right s
1Ki 10:19 were armrests on either s of
1Ki 10:20 one on each s of the six
2Ki 3:22 the other s as red as blood
2Ki 9:32 Who is on my s
2Ki 11:11 king, from the right s of the
2Ki 11:11 to the left s of the temple
2Ki 12: 9 on the right s as one comes
2Ki 16:14 the north s of the new altar
1Ch 4:39 as the east s of the valley
1Ch 5: 9 this s of the River Euphrates
1Ch 6:78 on the other s of the Jordan,
1Ch 6:78 on the east s of the Jordan,
1Ch 12:18 we are on your s, O son of
1Ch 12:37 the other s of the Jordan
1Ch 18:17 ministers at the king's s
1Ch 22:18 not given you rest on every s
1Ch 26:30 of Israel on the west s of
2Ch 4: 6 and put five on the right s
2Ch 4: 7 temple, five on the right s
2Ch 4: 8 temple, five on the right s
2Ch 4:10 He set the Sea on the right s
2Ch 9:18 were armrests on either s of
2Ch 9:19 one on each s of the six

2Ch 11:12 Judah and Benjamin on his s
2Ch 14: 7 has given us rest on every s
2Ch 23:10 hand, from the right s of the
2Ch 23:10 to the left s of the temple
2Ch 32:22 and guided them on every s
2Ch 32:30 west s of the City of David
2Ch 33:14 David on the west s of Gihon
Neh 4:18 girded at his s as he built
Job 1:10 all that he has on every s
Job 18:11 frighten him on every s, and
Job 18:12 destruction is ready at his s
Job 19:10 He breaks me down on every s
Ps 12: 8 The wicked prowl on every s
Ps 31:13 Fear is on every s
Ps 65:12 hills rejoice on every s
Ps 71:21 And comfort me on every s
Ps 91: 7 A thousand may fall at your s
Ps 118: 6 The LORD is on my s
Ps 124: 1 the LORD who was on our s
Ps 124: 2 the LORD who was on our s
Eccl 4: 1 on the s of their oppressors
Is 60: 4 shall be nursed at your s
Jer 6:25 the enemy, fear is on every s
Jer 20:10 mocking: "Fear on every s!"
Jer 49:29 to them, 'Fear is on every s
Ezek 1:10 face of a lion on the right s
Ezek 1:10 face of an ox on the left s
Ezek 1:23 had two which covered one s
Ezek 1:23 the other s of the body
Ezek 4: 4 Lie also on your left s, and
Ezek 4: 6 lie again on your right s
Ezek 4: 8 s to another till you have
Ezek 4: 9 days that you lie on your s
Ezek 9: 2 a writer's inkhorn at his s
Ezek 9: 3 the writer's inkhorn at his s
Ezek 9:11 who had the inkhorn at his s
Ezek 10: 3 s of the temple when the man
Ezek 11:23 is on the east s of the city
Ezek 19: 8 from the provinces on every s
Ezek 23:22 them against you from every s
Ezek 28:23 sword against her on every s
Ezek 34:21 you have pushed with s and
Ezek 36: 3 swallowed you up on every s
Ezek 37:21 will gather them from every s
Ezek 40:10 three gate chambers on one s
Ezek 40:10 size on this s and that s
Ezek 40:12 chambers, one cubit on this s
Ezek 40:12 and one cubit on that s
Ezek 40:12 were six cubits on this s
Ezek 40:12 and six cubits on that s
Ezek 40:18 was by the s of the gateways
Ezek 40:21 chambers, three on this s
Ezek 40:21 and three on that s
Ezek 40:26 on this s and one on that s
Ezek 40:34 on this s and on that s
Ezek 40:37 on this s and on that s
Ezek 40:39 were two tables on this s
Ezek 40:39 and two tables on that s
Ezek 40:40 At the outer s of the
Ezek 40:40 and on the other s of the
Ezek 40:41 Four tables were on this s
Ezek 40:41 and four tables on that s
Ezek 40:41 by the s of the gateway,
Ezek 40:44 the s of the northern gateway
Ezek 40:44 the s of the southern gateway
Ezek 40:48 five cubits on this s and
Ezek 40:48 five cubits on that s
Ezek 40:48 was three cubits on this s
Ezek 40:48 and three cubits on that s
Ezek 40:49 the doorposts, one on this s
Ezek 40:49 and another on that s
Ezek 41: 1 six cubits wide on one s
Ezek 41: 1 cubits wide on the other s
Ezek 41: 2 the s walls of the entrance
Ezek 41: 2 were five cubits on this s
Ezek 41: 2 and five cubits on the other s
Ezek 41: 5 The width of each s chamber
Ezek 41: 5 was four cubits on every s
Ezek 41: 6 The s chambers were in three
Ezek 41: 6 for the s chambers all around
Ezek 41: 7 the s chambers became wider
Ezek 41: 8 foundation of the s chambers
Ezek 41: 9 s chambers was five cubits
Ezek 41: 9 the s chambers of the temple
Ezek 41:10 around the temple on every s
Ezek 41:11 The doors of the s chambers
Ezek 41:15 one s and on the other s
Ezek 41:19 toward a palm tree on one s
Ezek 41:19 a palm tree on the other s
Ezek 41:26 frames and palm trees on one s
Ezek 41:26 also on the s chambers of the
Ezek 42: 9 the entrance on the east s
Ezek 42:16 He measured the east s with
Ezek 42:17 He measured the north s, five
Ezek 42:18 He measured the south s, five
Ezek 42:19 He came around to the west s
Ezek 45: 7 shall have a portion on one s
Ezek 45: 7 westward on the west s and
Ezek 45: 7 and eastward on the east s
Ezek 45: 7 the length shall be s by s
Ezek 46:19 was at the s of the gate,
Ezek 47: 1 the right s of the temple
Ezek 47: 2 running out on the right s
Ezek 47: 7 were very many trees on one s
Ezek 47:12 bank of the river, on this s
Ezek 47:17 This is the north s
Ezek 47:18 On the east s you shall mark
Ezek 47:18 the eastern s of the sea
Ezek 47:18 This is the east s
Ezek 47:19 The south s, toward the South
Ezek 47:19 This is the south s, toward
Ezek 47:20 The west s shall be the Great
Ezek 47:20 This is the west s
Ezek 48: 1 from its east to its west s
Ezek 48: 2 from the east s to the west
Ezek 48: 3 from the east s to the west
Ezek 48: 4 from the east s to the west
Ezek 48: 5 from the east s to the west
Ezek 48: 6 from the east s to the west
Ezek 48: 7 from the east s to the west
Ezek 48: 8 from the east s to the west
Ezek 48: 8 from the east s to the west
Ezek 48:16 the north s four thousand
Ezek 48:16 the south s four thousand
Ezek 48:16 the east s four thousand five
Ezek 48:16 the west s four thousand five
Ezek 48:21 to the prince, on one s and on
Ezek 48:23 from the east s to the west
Ezek 48:24 from the east s to the west
Ezek 48:25 from the east s to the west
Ezek 48:26 from the east s to the west
Ezek 48:27 from the east s to the west
Ezek 48:28 border of Gad, on the south s
Ezek 48:30 On the north s, measuring
Ezek 48:32 on the east s, four thousand
Ezek 48:33 on the south s, measuring
Ezek 48:34 on the west s, four thousand
Dan 7: 5 It was raised up on one s
Dan 10: 4 as I was by the s of the
Obad 11 that you stood on the other s
Jon 4: 5 sat on the east s of the city
Nah 2:10 much pain is in every s, and
Zech 5: 3 is on this s of the scroll
Zech 5: 3 to what is on that s of it
Matt 8:18 to depart to the other s
Matt 8:28 He had come to the other s
Matt 14:22 go before Him to the other s
Matt 16: 5 had come to the other s, they
Mark 4:35 us cross over to the other s
Mark 5: 1 to the other s of the sea
Mark 5:21 again by boat to the other s
Mark 6:45 go before Him to the other s
Mark 8:13 departed to the other s
Mark 9:40 is not against us is on our s
Mark 10: 1 by the other s of the Jordan
Mark 16: 5 robe sitting on the right s
Luke 1:11 standing on the right s of
Luke 8:22 to the other s of the lake
Luke 10:31 he passed by on the other s
Luke 10:32 and passed by on the other s
Luke 19:43 and close you in on every s
John 6:22 s of the sea saw that there
John 6:25 Him on the other s of the sea
John 19:18 with Him, one on either s
John 19:34 pierced His s with a spear
John 20:20 them His hands and His s
John 20:25 and put my hand into His s
John 20:27 here, and put it into My s
John 21: 6 on the right s of the boat
Acts 12: 7 and he struck Peter on the s
2Co 4: 8 are hard pressed on every s
2Co 7: 5 we were troubled on every s
Rev 22: 2 on either s of the river, was

SIDED (*see* SIDE)
Acts 14: 4 part s with the Jews, and part

SIDES (*see* SIDE)
Ex 25:14 the rings on the s of the ark
Ex 25:32 shall come out of its s
Ex 26:13 over the s of the tabernacle
Ex 27: 7 two s of the altar to bear it
Ex 30: 3 top, its s all around, and its
Ex 30: 4 the molding on both its s
Ex 30: 4 shall place them on its two s
Ex 32:15 were written on both s
Ex 37: 5 the rings at the s of the ark
Ex 37:18 branches came out of its s
Ex 37:26 top, its s all around, and its
Ex 37:27 by its two corners on both s
Ex 38: 7 rings on the s of the altar
Lev 19:27 around the s of your head
Num 33:55 your eyes and thorns in your s
Josh 23:13 to you, and scourges on your s
2Ki 11: 8 surround the king on all s
2Ch 23: 7 surround the king on all s
Ps 48: 2 Zion on the s of the north
Ps 141: 6 by the s of the cliff, And
Is 14:13 the farthest s of the north
Is 66:12 on her s shall you be carried
Jer 48:28 in the s of the cave's mouth
Jer 49:32 their calamity from all its s
Jer 51:31 his city is taken on all s
Jer 52:23 pomegranates on the s
Ezek 1: 8 their wings on their four s
Ezek 39:17 all s to My sacrificial meal
Ezek 41:22 length, and its s were of wood
Ezek 41:26 on the s of the vestibule
Ezek 42:20 He measured it on the four s
Ezek 43:17 fourteen wide on its four s
Heb 9: 4 overlaid on all s with gold

SIDON (*see* SIDONIANS)
Gen 10:15 Canaan begot **S** his firstborn,
Gen 10:19 from **S** as you go toward Gerar
Gen 49:13 and his border shall adjoin **S**
Josh 11: 8 and chased them to Greater **S**
Josh 19:28 and Kanah, as far as Greater **S**
Judg 1:31 Acco or the inhabitants of **S**
Judg 10: 6 gods of Syria, the gods of **S**
Judg 18:28 because it was far from **S**
2Sa 24: 6 to Dan Jaan and around to **S**
1Ki 17: 9 Zarephath, which belongs to **S**
1Ch 1:13 Canaan begot **S**, his firstborn
Ezra 3: 7 and oil to the people of **S**
Is 23: 2 coastland, you merchants of **S**
Is 23: 4 Be ashamed, O **S**
Is 23:12 virgin daughter of **S**
Jer 25:22 of Tyre, all the kings of **S**
Jer 27: 3 of Tyre, and the king of **S**
Jer 47: 4 **S** every helper who remains
Ezek 27: 8 Inhabitants of **S** and Arvad
Ezek 28:21 man, set your face toward **S**
Ezek 28:22 Behold, I am against you, O **S**
Joel 3: 4 to do with Me, O Tyre and **S**
Zech 9: 2 on it, and against Tyre and **S**
Matt 11:21 had been done in Tyre and **S**
Matt 11:22 **S** in the day of judgment than
Matt 15:21 to the region of Tyre and **S**
Mark 3: 8 and those from Tyre and **S**, a
Mark 7:24 to the region of Tyre and **S**
Mark 7:31 from the region of Tyre and **S**
Luke 4:26 Zarephath, in the region of **S**
Luke 6:17 the seacoast of Tyre and **S**
Luke 10:13 had been done in Tyre and **S**
Luke 10:14 **S** at the judgment than for
Acts 12:20 with the people of Tyre and **S**
Acts 27: 3 the next day we landed at **S**

SIDONIANS (*see* SIDON)
Deut 3: 9 (the **S** call Hermon Sirion, and
Josh 13: 4 to the **S** as far as Aphek, to
Josh 13: 6 Misrephoth, and all the **S**
Judg 3: 3 all the Canaanites, the **S**
Judg 10:12 Also the **S** and Amalekites and
Judg 18: 7 in the manner of the **S**,
Judg 18: 7 They were far from the **S**, and
1Ki 5: 6 to cut timber like the **S**
1Ki 11: 1 Ammonites, Edomites, **S**, and
1Ki 11: 5 the goddess of the **S**, and
1Ki 11:33 the goddess of the **S**, Chemosh
1Ki 16:31 of Ethbaal, king of the **S**
2Ki 23:13 the abomination of the **S**, for
1Ch 22: 4 for the **S** and those from Tyre
Ezek 32:30 all of them, and all the **S**

SIEGE (*see* SIEGEWORKS)
Deut 20:19 cut them down to use in the s
Deut 28:53 God has given you, in the s
Deut 28:55 he has nothing left in the s
Deut 28:57 lack of all things in the s
2Sa 20:15 and they cast up a s mound
1Ki 15:27 Israel laid s to Gibbethon

2Ki 19:32 nor build a s mound against
2Ki 25: 1 they built a s wall against
2Ch 32: 9 laid s against Lachish), to
2Ch 32:10 remain under s in Jerusalem
Is 29: 3 I will lay s against you with
Is 37:33 nor build a s mound against
Jer 19: 9 flesh of his friend in the s
Jer 32:24 Look, the s mounds
Jer 33: 4 fortify against the s mounds
Jer 37:11 s of Jerusalem for fear of
Jer 52: 4 they built a s wall against
Ezek 4: 2 Lay s against it, build a s
Ezek 4: 3 and you shall lay s against it
Ezek 4: 7 toward the s of Jerusalem
Ezek 4: 8 have ended the days of your s
Ezek 5: 2 days of the s are finished
Ezek 17:17 when they heap up a s mound
Ezek 21:22 gates, to heap up a s mound
Ezek 24: 2 s against Jerusalem this very
Ezek 26: 8 heap up a s mound against you
Dan 11:15 shall come and build a s mound
Mic 5: 1 He has laid s against us
Nah 3:14 Draw your water for the s
Zech 12: 2 when they lay s against Judah

SIEGEWORKS (*see* SIEGE)
Deut 20:20 to build s against the city
Is 29: 3 and I will raise s against you

SIEVE (*see* SIFT)
Is 30:28 with the s of futility
Amos 9: 9 as grain is sifted in a s

SIFT (*see* SIEVE, SIFTED, SIFTS)
Is 30:28 to s the nations with the
Amos 9: 9 will s the house of Israel
Luke 22:31 that he may s you as wheat

SIFTED (*see* SIFT)
Amos 9: 9 as grain is s in a sieve

SIFTS (*see* SIFT)
Prov 20:26 A wise king s out the wicked,

SIGH (*see* SIGHED, SIGHING, SIGHS)
Ps 90: 9 We finish our years like a s
Is 24: 7 all the merry-hearted s
Lam 1: 4 her priests s, her virgins
Lam 1:11 All her people s, they seek
Lam 1:21 They have heard that I s,
Ezek 9: 4 foreheads of the men who s
Ezek 21: 6 S therefore, son of man, with
Ezek 21: 6 and s with bitterness before
Ezek 24:17 S in silence, make no

SIGHED (*see* SIGH)
Mark 7:34 looking up to heaven, He s
Mark 8:12 But He s deeply in His spirit

SIGHING (*see* SIGH)
Job 3:24 For my s comes before I eat,
Ps 12: 5 for the s of the needy, Now I
Ps 31:10 grief, And my years with s
Ps 38: 9 my s is not hidden from You
Is 21: 2 All its s I have made to
Is 35:10 sorrow and s shall flee away
Is 51:11 sorrow and s shall flee away
Jer 45: 3 I fainted in my s, and I find
Lam 3:56 not hide Your ear from my s
Ezek 21: 7 say to you, 'Why are you s

SIGHS (*see* SIGH)
Lam 1: 8 yes, she s and turns away
Lam 1:22 for my s are many, and my

SIGHT (*see* SIGHTED, SIGHTS)
Gen 2: 9 that is pleasant to the s
Gen 18: 3 now found favor in Your s
Gen 19:19 has found favor in your s
Gen 21:11 s because of his son
Gen 21:12 your s because of the lad or
Gen 23: 4 may bury my dead out of my s
Gen 23: 8 I bury my dead out of my s
Gen 32: 5 I may find favor in your s
Gen 33: 8 favor in the s of my lord
Gen 33:10 now found favor in your s
Gen 33:15 favor in the s of my lord
Gen 38: 7 wicked in the s of the LORD
Gen 39: 4 Joseph found favor in his s
Gen 39:21 He gave him favor in the s of
Gen 47:18 is nothing left in the s of
Gen 47:25 favor in the s of my lord
Gen 47:29 I have found favor in your s
Ex 3: 3 aside and see this great s
Ex 3:21 in the s of the Egyptians
Ex 4:30 signs in the s of the people
Ex 5:21 abhorrent in the s of Pharaoh
Ex 5:21 in the s of his servants, to
Ex 7:20 in the s of Pharaoh
Ex 7:20 and in the s of his servants
Ex 9: 8 heavens in the s of Pharaoh
Ex 11: 3 in the s of the Egyptians
Ex 11: 3 Egypt, in the s of Pharaoh's
Ex 11: 3 and in the s of the people
Ex 12:36 in the s of the Egyptians
Ex 15:26 and do what is right in His s
Ex 17: 6 Moses did so in the s of the
Ex 19:11 in the s of all the people
Ex 24:17 The s of the glory of the
Ex 33:12 have also found grace in My s
Ex 33:13 I have found grace in Your s
Ex 33:13 I may find grace in Your s
Ex 33:16 I have found grace in Your s
Ex 33:17 you have found grace in My s
Ex 34: 9 I have found grace in Your s
Ex 40:38 in the s of all the house of
Lev 10:19 accepted in the s of the LORD
Lev 20:17 off in the s of their people
Lev 25:53 with rigor over him in your s
Lev 26:45 Egypt in the s of the nations
Num 11:11 I not found favor in Your s
Num 11:15 I have found favor in Your s
Num 13:33 grasshoppers in our own s
Num 13:33 and so we were in their s
Num 19: 5 shall be burned in his s
Num 20:27 the s of all the congregation
Num 25: 6 woman in the s of Moses
Num 25: 6 and in the s of all the
Num 27:19 and inaugurate him in their s
Num 32: 5 we have found favor in your s
Num 32:13 in the s of the LORD was gone
Num 33: 3 in the s of all the Egyptians
Deut 4: 6 the s of the peoples who will
Deut 4:25 do evil in the s of the LORD
Deut 6:18 and good in the s of the LORD
Deut 9:18 wickedly in the s of the LORD
Deut 12:25 is right in the s of the LORD
Deut 12:28 right in the s of the LORD
Deut 17: 2 in the s of the LORD your God
Deut 21: 9 is right in the s of the LORD
Deut 25: 3 be humiliated in your s
Deut 28:34 of the s which your eyes see
Deut 28:67 because of the s which your
Deut 31: 7 to him in the s of all Israel
Deut 31:29 do evil in the s of the LORD
Deut 34:12 in the s of all Israel
Josh 3: 7 you in the s of all Israel
Josh 4:14 Joshua in the s of all Israel
Josh 10:12 and he said in the s of Israel
Josh 23: 5 and drive them out of your s
Josh 24:17 those great signs in our s
Judg 2:11 did evil in the s of the LORD
Judg 3: 7 did evil in the s of the LORD
Judg 3:12 did evil in the s of the LORD
Judg 3:12 evil in the s of the LORD
Judg 4: 1 did evil in the s of the LORD
Judg 6: 1 did evil in the s of the LORD
Judg 6:17 I have found favor in Your s
Judg 6:21 LORD departed out of his s
Judg 10: 6 did evil in the s of the LORD
Judg 13: 1 did evil in the s of the LORD
Ruth 2: 2 in whose s I may find favor
Ruth 2:13 Let me find favor in your s
1Sa 1:18 find favor in your s
1Sa 12:17 done in the s of the LORD
1Sa 15:19 do evil in the s of the LORD
1Sa 16:22 he has found favor in my s
1Sa 18: 5 in the s of all the people
1Sa 18: 5 and also in the s of Saul's
1Sa 29: 6 in the army is good in my s
1Sa 29: 9 in my s as an angel of God
2Sa 6:22 and will be humble in my own s
2Sa 7:19 was a small thing in Your s
2Sa 12: 9 the LORD, to do evil in His s
2Sa 12:11 wives in the s of this sun
2Sa 13: 5 and prepare the food in my s
2Sa 13: 6 of cakes for me in my s, that
2Sa 13: 8 it, made cakes in his s, and
2Sa 14:22 I have found favor in your s
2Sa 16: 4 I may find favor in your s
2Sa 16:22 in the s of all Israel
1Ki 9: 7 name I will cast out of My s
1Ki 11: 6 did evil in the s of the LORD
1Ki 11:19 favor in the s of Pharaoh
1Ki 11:38 and do what is right in My s
1Ki 14:22 did evil in the s of the LORD
1Ki 15:26 did evil in the s of the LORD
1Ki 15:34 did evil in the s of the LORD
1Ki 16: 7 s of the LORD in provoking
1Ki 16:19 evil in the s of the LORD
1Ki 16:30 did evil in the s of the LORD
1Ki 21:20 do evil in the s of the LORD
1Ki 21:25 in the s of the LORD, because
1Ki 22:52 did evil in the s of the LORD
2Ki 1:13 yours be precious in your s
2Ki 1:14 now be precious in your s
2Ki 3: 2 did evil in the s of the LORD
2Ki 3:18 thing in the s of the LORD
2Ki 8:18 did evil in the s of the LORD
2Ki 8:27 did evil in the s of the LORD
2Ki 10: 5 Do what is good in your s
2Ki 10:30 doing what is right in My s
2Ki 12: 2 did what was right in the s
2Ki 13: 2 did evil in the s of the LORD
2Ki 13:11 did evil in the s of the LORD
2Ki 14: 3 right in the s of the LORD
2Ki 14:24 did evil in the s of the LORD
2Ki 15: 3 right in the s of the LORD
2Ki 15: 9 did evil in the s of the LORD
2Ki 15:18 did evil in the s of the LORD
2Ki 15:24 did evil in the s of the LORD
2Ki 15:28 did evil in the s of the LORD
2Ki 15:34 right in the s of the LORD
2Ki 16: 2 in the s of the LORD his God
2Ki 17: 2 did evil in the s of the LORD
2Ki 17:17 do evil in the s of the LORD
2Ki 17:18 and removed them from His s
2Ki 17:20 He had cast them from His s
2Ki 17:23 removed Israel out of His s
2Ki 18: 3 right in the s of the LORD
2Ki 20: 3 done what was good in Your s
2Ki 21: 2 did evil in the s of the LORD
2Ki 21: 6 evil in the s of the LORD
2Ki 21:15 they have done evil in My s
2Ki 21:16 evil in the s of the LORD
2Ki 21:20 did evil in the s of the LORD
2Ki 22: 2 right in the s of the LORD
2Ki 23:27 also remove Judah from My s
2Ki 23:32 did evil in the s of the LORD
2Ki 23:37 did evil in the s of the LORD
2Ki 24: 3 His s because of the sins of
2Ki 24: 9 did evil in the s of the LORD
2Ki 24:19 did evil in the s of the LORD
1Ch 2: 3 wicked in the s of the LORD
1Ch 17:17 was a small thing in Your s
1Ch 19:13 LORD do what is good in His s
1Ch 22: 8 blood on the earth in My s
1Ch 28: 8 in the s of all Israel, the
1Ch 29:25 in the s of all Israel, and
2Ch 7:20 name I will cast out of My s
2Ch 20:32 right in the s of the LORD
2Ch 21: 6 did evil in the s of the LORD
2Ch 22: 4 did evil in the s of the LORD
2Ch 24: 2 did what was right in the s
2Ch 25: 2 right in the s of the LORD
2Ch 26: 4 right in the s of the LORD
2Ch 27: 2 right in the s of the LORD
2Ch 28: 1 right in the s of the LORD
2Ch 29: 2 right in the s of the LORD
2Ch 32:23 s of all nations thereafter
2Ch 33: 2 did evil in the s of the LORD
2Ch 33: 6 evil in the s of the LORD
2Ch 33:22 did evil in the s of the LORD
2Ch 34: 2 right in the s of the LORD
2Ch 36: 5 he did evil in the s of the
2Ch 36: 9 did evil in the s of the LORD
2Ch 36:12 in the s of the LORD his God
Ezra 9: 9 the s of the kings of Persia
Neh 1:11 mercy in the s of this man
Neh 2: 5 has found favor in your s
Neh 8: 5 in the s of all the people
Esth 2:15 in the s of all who saw her
Esth 2:17 favor in his s more than all
Esth 5: 2 that she found favor in his s
Esth 5: 8 favor in the s of the king
Esth 7: 3 I have found favor in your s
Esth 8: 5 I have found favor in his s
Job 15:15 heavens are not pure in His s
Job 18: 3 regarded as stupid in your s
Job 19:15 I am an alien in their s
Job 21: 8 with them in their s, and
Job 25: 5 stars are not pure in His s
Job 33:21 His flesh wastes away from s
Job 34:26 men in the open s of others
Job 41: 9 overwhelmed at the s of him

SIGNPOSTS (*see* SIGN)
Jer 31:21 Set up s, make landmarks

SIGNS (*see* SIGN)
Gen 1:14 and let them be for s and
Ex 4: 9 not believe even these two s
Ex 4:17 with which you shall do the s
Ex 4:28 and all the s which He had
Ex 4:30 Then he did the s in the
Ex 7: 3 heart, and multiply My s and My
Ex 10: 1 these s of Mine before him
Ex 10: 2 My s which I have done among
Num 14:11 with all the s which I have
Num 14:22 the s which I did in Egypt and
Deut 4:34 nation, by trials, by s, by
Deut 6:22 and the LORD showed s and
Deut 7:19 which your eyes saw, the s
Deut 11: 3 His s and His acts which He
Deut 26: 8 with great terror and with s
Deut 29: 3 your eyes have seen, the s
Deut 34:11 in all the s and wonders which
Josh 24:17 those great s in our sight
1Sa 10: 7 when these s come to you,
1Sa 10: 9 all those s came to pass that
Neh 9:10 You showed s and wonders
Job 21:29 And do you not know their s
Ps 65: 8 parts are afraid of Your s
Ps 74: 4 set up their banners for s
Ps 74: 9 We do not see our s
Ps 78:43 When He worked His s in Egypt
Ps 105:27 performed His s among them
Ps 135: 9 He sent s and wonders into the
Is 8:18 We are for s and wonders in
Is 44:25 the s of the babblers, and
Jer 10: 2 dismayed at the s of heaven
Jer 32:20 You have set s and wonders in
Jer 32:21 of the land of Egypt with s
Dan 4: 2 it good to declare the s and
Dan 4: 3 How great are His s, and how
Dan 6:27 and rescues, and He works s
Matt 16: 3 discern the s of the times
Matt 24:24 will arise and show great s
Mark 13:22 prophets will rise and show s
Mark 16:17 these s will follow those who
Mark 16:20 through the accompanying s
Luke 1:62 So they made s to his father
Luke 21:11 sights and great s from heaven
Luke 21:25 And there will be s in the sun
John 2:11 This beginning of s Jesus did
John 2:23 they saw the s which He did
John 3: 2 for no one can do these s
John 4:48 Unless you people see s and
John 6: 2 because they saw His s which
John 6:26 Me, not because you saw the s
John 7:31 will He do more s than these
John 11:47 For this Man works many s
John 12:37 done so many s before them
John 20:30 s in the presence of His
Acts 2:19 and s in the earth beneath
Acts 2:22 s which God did through Him
Acts 2:43 and s were done through the
Acts 4:30 Your hand to heal, and that s
Acts 5:12 hands of the apostles many s
Acts 6: 8 wonders and s among the people
Acts 7:36 s in the land of Egypt, and in
Acts 8:13 miracles and s which were done
Acts 14: 3 word of His grace, granting s
Rom 15:19 in mighty s and wonders, by
2Co 12:12 Truly the s of an apostle
2Co 12:12 with all perseverance, in s
2Th 2: 9 of Satan, with all power, s
Heb 2: 4 bearing witness both with s
Rev 13:13 He performs great s, so that
Rev 13:14 s which he was granted to do
Rev 16:14 of demons, performing s,
Rev 19:20 who worked s in his presence

SIHON
Num 21:21 to S king of the Amorites
Num 21:23 But S would not allow Israel
Num 21:23 So S gathered all his people
Num 21:26 of S king of the Amorites
Num 21:27 let the city of S be repaired
Num 21:28 a flame from the city of S
Num 21:29 to S king of the Amorites
Num 21:34 did to S king of the Amorites
Num 32:33 the kingdom of S king of the
Deut 1: 4 after he had killed S king of
Deut 2:24 into your hand S the Amorite
Deut 2:26 Kedemoth to S king of Heshbon
Deut 2:30 But S king of Heshbon would
Deut 2:31 See, I have begun to give S
Deut 2:32 Then S and all his people came
Deut 3: 2 did to S king of the Amorites
Deut 3: 6 them, as we did to S king of
Deut 4:46 in the land of S king of the
Deut 29: 7 S king of Heshbon and Og king
Deut 31: 4 do to them as He did to S
Josh 2:10 other side of the Jordan, S
Josh 9:10 to S king of Heshbon, and Og
Josh 12: 2 S king of the Amorites, who
Josh 12: 5 border of S king of Heshbon
Josh 13:10 all the cities of S king of
Josh 13:21 all the kingdom of S king of
Josh 13:21 Reba, who were princes of S
Josh 13:27 kingdom of S king of Heshbon
Judg 11:19 to S king of the Amorites
Judg 11:20 But S did not trust Israel
Judg 11:20 So S gathered all his people
Judg 11:21 God of Israel delivered S
1Ki 4:19 in the country of S king of
Neh 9:22 possession of the land of S
Ps 135:11 S king of the Amorites, Og
Ps 136:19 S king of the Amorites, For
Jer 48:45 a flame from the midst of S

SIHOR (*see* SHIHOR)
Josh 13: 3 from S, which is east of
Jer 2:18 to drink the waters of S

SIKKUTH
Amos 5:26 You also carried S your king

SILAS
Acts 15:22 was also named Barsabas, and S
Acts 15:27 therefore sent Judas and S
Acts 15:32 Now Judas and S, themselves
Acts 15:34 good to S to remain there
Acts 15:40 but Paul chose S and departed,
Acts 16:19 gone, they seized Paul and S
Acts 16:25 S were praying and singing
Acts 16:29 trembling before Paul and S
Acts 17: 4 women, joined Paul and S
Acts 17:10 and S away by night to Berea
Acts 17:14 but both S and Timothy
Acts 17:15 and receiving a command for S
Acts 18: 5 When S and Timothy had come

SILENCE (*see* SILENCED, SILENCING, SILENT)
Judg 3:19 He said, "Keep s!" And all
Job 4:16 there was s
Job 29:21 and kept s for my counsel
Job 31:34 of families, so that I kept s
Ps 8: 2 That You may s the enemy
Ps 31:18 the lying lips be put to s
Ps 35:22 Do not keep s. O Lord,
Ps 39: 2 I was mute with s, I held my
Ps 94:17 would soon have settled in s
Ps 115:17 Nor any who go down into s
Eccl 3: 7 a time to keep s, and a time
Is 41: 1 Keep s before Me, O
Is 47: 5 Sit in s, and go into darkness
Is 65: 6 I will not keep s, but will
Jer 8:14 LORD our God has put us to s
Lam 2:10 sit on the ground and keep s
Ezek 24:17 Sigh in s, make no mourning
Amos 8: 3 shall throw them out in s
Hab 2:20 the earth keep s before Him
Acts 21:40 And when there was a great s
1Ti 2:11 in s with all submission
1Ti 2:12 over a man, but to be in s
1Pe 2:15 to s the ignorance of foolish
Rev 8: 1 there was s in heaven for

SILENCED (*see* SILENCE)
Neh 5: 8 Then they were s and found
Lam 3:53 They s my life in the pit and
Matt 22:34 that He had s the Sadducees

SILENCING (*see* SILENCE)
Jer 51:55 s her loud voice, though her

SILENT (*see* SILENCE, SILENTLY)
Gen 24:21 her, remained s so as to know
1Sa 2: 9 wicked shall be s in darkness
2Ki 2: 3 Yes, I know; keep s!"
2Ki 2: 5 Yes, I know; keep s!"
2Ki 7: 9 of good news, and we remain s
Esth 4:14 completely s at this time
Job 13: 5 Oh, that you would be s, and
Job 16: 6 and though I remain s, how am
Ps 22: 2 the night season, and am not s
Ps 28: 1 Do not be s to me, Lest, if
Ps 28: 1 me, Lest, if You are s to me
Ps 30:12 praise to You and not be s
Ps 31:17 Let them be s in the grave
Ps 32: 3 When I kept s, my bones grew
Ps 39:12 Do not be s at my tears
Ps 50: 3 come, and shall not keep s
Ps 50:21 you have done, and I kept s
Ps 58: 1 righteousness, you s ones
Ps 83: 1 Do not keep s, O God
Ps 109: 1 Do not keep s, O God of my
Is 53: 7 before its shearers is s, so
Is 62: 6 of the LORD, do not keep s
Jer 8:14 cities, and let us be s there
Lam 3:28 Let him sit alone and keep s
Amos 5:13 prudent keep s at that time
Hab 2:19 to s stone, "Arise
Zeph 1: 7 Be s in the presence of the
Zech 2:13 Be s, all flesh, before the
Matt 26:63 But Jesus kept s
Mark 3: 4 But they kept s
Mark 9:34 But they kept s, for on the
Mark 14:61 But He kept s and answered
Luke 14: 4 But they kept s
Luke 19:40 that if these should keep s
Luke 20:26 at His answer and kept s
Acts 8:32 and like a lamb s before its
Acts 11:18 these things they became s
Acts 12:17 them with his hand to keep s
Acts 15:12 Then all the multitude kept s
Acts 15:13 And after they had become s
Acts 18: 9 but speak, and do not keep s
Acts 22: 2 they kept all the more s
1Co 14:28 let him keep s in church
1Co 14:30 sits by, let the first keep s
1Co 14:34 women keep s in the churches

SILENTLY (*see* SILENT)
Ps 62: 1 Truly my soul s waits for God
Ps 62: 5 wait s for God alone, For my

SILK
Ezek 16:10 linen and covered you with s
Ezek 16:13 clothing was of fine linen, s
Rev 18:12 fine linen and purple, s and

SILLA
2Ki 12:20 Millo, which goes down to S

SILLY
Jer 4:22 They are s children, and they
Hos 7:11 Ephraim also is like a s dove

SILOAM (*see* SHILOAH)
Luke 13: 4 on whom the tower in S fell
John 9: 7 Go, wash in the pool of S"
John 9:11 to me, "Go to the pool of S

SILVANUS
2Co 1:19 by me, S, and Timothy
1Th 1: 1 Paul, S, and Timothy, To the
2Th 1: 1 Paul, S, and Timothy, To the
1Pe 5:12 By S, our faithful brother as

SILVER (*see* SILVER-HAIRED, SILVERSMITH)
Gen 13: 2 very rich in livestock, in s
Gen 20:16 a thousand pieces of s
Gen 23:15 four hundred shekels of s
Gen 23:16 the s for Ephron which he had
Gen 23:16 four hundred shekels of s
Gen 24:35 given him flocks and herds, s
Gen 24:53 brought out jewelry of s,
Gen 37:28 for twenty shekels of s
Gen 44: 2 Also put my cup, the s cup
Gen 44: 8 How then could we steal s or
Gen 45:22 three hundred pieces of s
Ex 3:22 near her house, articles of s
Ex 11: 2 her neighbor, articles of s
Ex 12:35 the Egyptians articles of s
Ex 20:23 gods of s or gods of gold you
Ex 21:32 master thirty shekels of s
Ex 25: 3 gold, s, and bronze
Ex 26:19 of s under the twenty boards
Ex 26:21 and their forty sockets of s
Ex 26:25 with their sockets of s
Ex 26:32 gold, upon four sockets of s
Ex 27:10 and their bands shall be of s
Ex 27:11 pillars and their bands of s
Ex 27:17 court shall have bands of s
Ex 27:17 their hooks shall be of s
Ex 31: 4 works, to work in gold, in s
Ex 35: 5 gold, s, and bronze
Ex 35:24 of s or bronze brought the
Ex 35:32 works, to work in gold and s
Ex 36:24 Forty sockets of s he made to
Ex 36:26 and their forty sockets of s
Ex 36:30 sixteen sockets of s

Ex 36:36 four sockets of s for them
Ex 38:10 and their bands were of s
Ex 38:11 and their bands were of s
Ex 38:12 and their bands were of s
Ex 38:17 and their bands were of s, and
Ex 38:17 of their capitals was of s
Ex 38:17 of the court had bands of s
Ex 38:19 their hooks were of s, and the
Ex 38:19 and their bands was of s
Ex 38:25 the s from those who were
Ex 38:27 of s were cast the sockets of
Lev 5:15 valuation in shekels of s
Lev 27: 3 shall be fifty shekels of s
Lev 27: 6 shall be five shekels of s
Lev 27: 6 shall be three shekels of s
Lev 27:16 valued at fifty shekels of s
Num 7:13 offering was one s platter
Num 7:13 one s bowl of seventy shekels
Num 7:19 he offered one s platter, the
Num 7:19 one s bowl of seventy shekels
Num 7:25 offering was one s platter
Num 7:25 one s bowl of seventy shekels
Num 7:31 offering was one s platter
Num 7:31 one s bowl of seventy shekels
Num 7:37 offering was one s platter
Num 7:37 one s bowl of seventy shekels
Num 7:43 offering was one s platter
Num 7:43 one s bowl of seventy shekels
Num 7:49 offering was one s platter
Num 7:49 one s bowl of seventy shekels
Num 7:55 offering was one s platter
Num 7:55 one s bowl of seventy shekels
Num 7:61 offering was one s platter
Num 7:61 one s bowl of seventy shekels
Num 7:67 offering was one s platter
Num 7:67 one s bowl of seventy shekels
Num 7:73 offering was one s platter
Num 7:73 one s bowl of seventy shekels
Num 7:79 offering was one s platter
Num 7:79 one s bowl of seventy shekels
Num 7:84 twelve s platters
Num 7:84 twelve s bowls, and
Num 7:85 Each s platter weighed one
Num 7:85 All the s of the vessels
Num 10: 2 Make two s trumpets for
Num 18:16 for five shekels of s,
Num 22:18 give me his house full of s
Num 24:13 give me his house full of s
Num 31:22 Only the gold, the s, the
Deut 7:25 the s or gold that is on them
Deut 8:13 flocks multiply, and your s
Deut 17:17 shall he greatly multiply s
Deut 22:19 him one hundred shekels of s
Deut 22:29 father fifty shekels of s
Deut 29:17 wood and stone and s and gold)
Josh 6:19 But all the s and gold, and
Josh 6:24 Only the s and gold, and the
Josh 7:21 two hundred shekels of s
Josh 7:21 my tent, with the s under it
Josh 7:22 his tent, with the s under it
Josh 7:24 Achan the son of Zerah, the s
Josh 22: 8 very much livestock, with s
Josh 24:32 for one hundred pieces of s
Judg 5:19 they took no spoils of s
Judg 9: 4 of s from the temple of
Judg 16: 5 eleven hundred pieces of s
Judg 17: 2 of s that were taken from you
Judg 17: 2 here is the s with me
Judg 17: 3 shekels of s to his mother
Judg 17: 3 s from my hand to the LORD
Judg 17: 4 returned the s to his mother
Judg 17: 4 took two hundred shekels of s
Judg 17:10 you ten shekels of s per year
1Sa 2:36 down to him for a piece of s
1Sa 9: 8 one fourth of a shekel of s
2Sa 8:10 with him articles of s,
2Sa 8:11 to the LORD, along with the s
2Sa 18:11 given you ten shekels of s
2Sa 18:12 shekels of s in my hand, I
2Sa 21: 4 We will have no s or gold
2Sa 24:24 oxen for fifty shekels of s
1Ki 7:51 the s and the gold and the
1Ki 10:21 not one was of s, for this
1Ki 10:22 ships came bringing gold, s
1Ki 10:25 articles of s and gold,
1Ki 10:27 The king made s as common in
1Ki 10:29 cost six hundred shekels of s
1Ki 15:15 s and gold and utensils
1Ki 15:18 Then Asa took all the s and
1Ki 15:19 have sent you a present of s
1Ki 16:24 Shemer for two talents of s
1Ki 20: 3 Your s and your gold are mine
1Ki 20: 5 shall deliver to me your s
1Ki 20: 7 my wives, my children, my s
1Ki 20:39 you shall pay a talent of s
2Ki 5: 5 with him ten talents of s
2Ki 5:22 give them a talent of s and
2Ki 5:23 two talents of s in two bags
2Ki 6:25 sold for eighty shekels of s
2Ki 6:25 for five shekels of s
2Ki 7: 8 drank, and carried from it s
2Ki 12:13 house of the LORD basins of s
2Ki 12:13 of gold, or articles of s
2Ki 14:14 And he took all the gold and s
2Ki 15:19 Pul a thousand talents of s
2Ki 15:20 each man fifty shekels of s
2Ki 16: 8 And Ahaz took the s and gold
2Ki 18:14 three hundred talents of s
2Ki 18:15 Hezekiah gave him all the s
2Ki 20:13 the s and gold, the spices and
2Ki 23:33 of one hundred talents of s
2Ki 23:35 So Jehoiakim gave the s and
2Ki 23:35 he exacted the s and gold from
2Ki 25:15 made of solid gold and solid s
1Ch 18:10 kinds of articles of gold, s
1Ch 18:11 to the LORD, along with the s
1Ch 19: 6 of s to hire for themselves
1Ch 22:14 and one million talents of s
1Ch 22:16 Of gold and s and bronze and
1Ch 28:14 also s for all articles of s
1Ch 28:15 the lampstands of s by weight
1Ch 28:16 and s for the tables of s
1Ch 28:17 for the s bowls, s by weight
1Ch 29: 2 gold, s for things of s,
1Ch 29: 3 special treasure of gold and s
1Ch 29: 4 thousand talents of refined s
1Ch 29: 5 and the s for things of s
1Ch 29: 7 ten thousand talents of s
2Ch 1:15 Also the king made s and gold
2Ch 1:17 for six hundred shekels of s
2Ch 2: 7 skillful to work in gold and s
2Ch 2:14 skilled to work in gold and s
2Ch 5: 1 the s and the gold and all the
2Ch 9:14 brought gold and s to Solomon
2Ch 9:20 Not one was of s, for this
2Ch 9:21 ships came, bringing gold, s
2Ch 9:24 articles of s and gold,
2Ch 9:27 The king made s as common in
2Ch 15:18 s and gold and utensils
2Ch 16: 2 Then Asa brought s and gold
2Ch 16: 3 Here, I have sent you s and
2Ch 17:11 presents and s as tribute
2Ch 21: 3 gave them great gifts of s
2Ch 24:14 and vessels of gold and s
2Ch 25: 6 for one hundred talents of s
2Ch 25:24 And he took all the gold and s
2Ch 27: 5 year one hundred talents of s
2Ch 32:27 made himself treasuries for s
2Ch 36: 3 of one hundred talents of s
Ezra 1: 4 of his place help him with s
Ezra 1: 6 them with articles of s and
Ezra 1: 9 one thousand s platters,
Ezra 1:10 ten s basins of a similar
Ezra 1:11 s were five thousand four
Ezra 2:69 five thousand minas of s
Ezra 5:14 s articles of the house of
Ezra 6: 5 s articles of the house of
Ezra 7:15 you are to carry the s and
Ezra 7:16 and whereas all the s and gold
Ezra 7:18 to do with the rest of the s
Ezra 7:22 to one hundred talents of s
Ezra 8:25 and weighed out to them the s
Ezra 8:26 hundred and fifty talents of s
Ezra 8:26 s articles weighing one
Ezra 8:28 and the s and the gold are a
Ezra 8:30 and the Levites received the s
Ezra 8:33 Now on the fourth day the s
Neh 5:15 besides forty shekels of s
Neh 7:71 thousand two hundred s minas
Neh 7:72 two thousand s minas, and
Esth 1: 6 linen and purple on s rods
Esth 1: 6 s on a mosaic pavement of
Esth 3: 9 s into the hands of those who
Job 3:15 filled their houses with s
Job 22:25 your gold and your precious s
Job 27:16 he heaps up s like dust, and
Job 27:17 innocent will divide the s
Job 28: 1 Surely there is a mine for s
Job 28:15 nor can s be weighed for its
Job 42:11 one gave him a piece of s
Ps 12: 6 Like s tried in a furnace of
Ps 66:10 refined us as s is refined
Ps 68:13 of a dove covered with s, And
Ps 68:30 himself with pieces of s
Ps 105:37 also brought them out with s
Ps 115: 4 Their idols are s and gold,
Ps 119:72 of shekels of gold and s
Ps 135:15 idols of the nations are s
Prov 2: 4 If you seek her as s, and
Prov 3:14 better than the profits of s
Prov 8:10 my instruction, and not s, and
Prov 8:19 and my revenue than choice s
Prov 10:20 of the righteous is choice s
Prov 16:16 is to be chosen rather than s
Prov 17: 3 The refining pot is for s
Prov 22: 1 loving favor rather than s
Prov 25: 4 Take away the dross from s
Prov 25:11 of gold in settings of s
Prov 26:23 covered with s dross
Prov 27:21 The refining pot is for s
Eccl 2: 8 I also gathered for myself s
Eccl 5:10 He who loves s will not be
Eccl 5:10 satisfied with s; nor he
Eccl 12: 6 before the s cord is loosed
Song 1:11 of gold with studs of s
Song 3:10 He made its pillars of s, its
Song 8: 9 upon her a battlement of s
Song 8:11 fruit a thousand pieces of s
Is 1:22 Your s has become dross, your
Is 2: 7 Their land is also full of s
Is 2:20 will cast away his idols of s
Is 7:23 worth a thousand shekels of s
Is 13:17 them, who will not regard s
Is 30:22 of your graven images of s
Is 31: 7 throw away his idols of s
Is 39: 2 the s and gold, the spices and
Is 40:19 silversmith casts s chains
Is 46: 6 and weigh s in the balance
Is 48:10 refined you, but not as s
Is 60: 9 your sons from afar, their s
Is 60:17 of iron I will bring s,
Jer 6:30 will call them rejected s
Jer 10: 4 They decorate it with s and
Jer 10: 9 S is beaten into plates
Jer 32: 9 seventeen shekels of s
Jer 52:19 and whatever was of solid s
Ezek 7:19 their s into the streets, and
Ezek 7:19 their s and their gold will
Ezek 16:13 were adorned with gold and s
Ezek 16:17 jewelry from My gold and My s
Ezek 22:18 they have become dross from s
Ezek 22:20 As men gather s, bronze,
Ezek 22:22 As s is melted in the midst
Ezek 27:12 They gave you s, iron, tin,
Ezek 28: 4 and s into your treasuries
Ezek 38:13 take booty, to carry away s
Dan 2:32 gold, its chest and arms of s
Dan 2:35 the clay, the bronze, the s
Dan 2:45 the bronze, the clay, the s
Dan 5: 2 s vessels which his father
Dan 5: 4 praised the gods of gold and s
Dan 5:23 have praised the gods of s
Dan 11: 8 their precious articles of s
Dan 11:38 he shall honor with gold and s
Dan 11:43 the treasures of gold and s
Hos 2: 8 and oil, and multiplied her s
Hos 3: 2 for fifteen shekels of s, and
Hos 8: 4 From their s and gold they
Hos 9: 6 possess their valuables of s
Hos 13: 2 images, idols of their s,
Joel 3: 5 because you have taken My s
Amos 2: 6 they sell the righteous for s
Amos 8: 6 we may buy the poor for s
Nah 2: 9 Take spoil of s
Hab 2:19 it is overlaid with gold and s
Zeph 1:18 Neither their s nor their
Hag 2: 8 The s is Mine, and the gold
Zech 6:11 Take the s and gold, make an
Zech 9: 3 heaped up s like the dust, and
Zech 11:12 my wages thirty pieces of s
Zech 11:13 I took the thirty pieces of s
Zech 13: 9 refine them as s is refined
Zech 14:14 gold, s, and apparel in great
Mal 3: 3 a refiner and a purifier of s
Mal 3: 3 and purge them as gold and s
Matt 10: 9 gold nor s nor copper in your
Matt 26:15 out to him thirty pieces of s
Matt 27: 3 of s to the chief priests
Matt 27: 5 the pieces of s in the temple
Matt 27: 6 priests took the s pieces

Matt 27: 9 took the thirty pieces of **s**
Luke 15: 8 woman, having ten **s** coins
Acts 3: 6 **S** and gold I do not have, but
Acts 17:29 is like gold or **s** or stone
Acts 19:19 fifty thousand pieces of **s**
Acts 19:24 who made **s** shrines of Diana,
Acts 20:33 no one's **s** or gold or apparel
1Co 3:12 this foundation with gold, **s**
2Ti 2:20 not only vessels of gold and **s**
Jas 5: 3 and **s** are corroded, and their
1Pe 1:18 like **s** or gold, from your
Rev 9:20 demons, and idols of gold, **s**
Rev 18:12 merchandise of gold and **s**,

SILVER-HAIRED (*see* SILVER)
Prov 16:31 The **s** head is a crown of

SILVERSMITH (*see* SILVER)
Judg 17: 4 silver and gave them to the **s**
Prov 25: 4 will go to the **s** for jewelry
Is 40:19 the **s** casts silver chains
Acts 19:24 man named Demetrius, a **s**, who

SIMEON (*see* NIGER, SHIMEON, SIMEONITES)
Gen 29:33 And she called his name **S**
Gen 34:25 two of the sons of Jacob, **S**
Gen 34:30 Then Jacob said to **S** and Levi,
Gen 35:23 Jacob's firstborn, and **S**,
Gen 42:24 he took **S** from them and bound
Gen 42:36 **S** is no more, and you want to
Gen 43:23 Then he brought **S** out to them
Gen 46:10 The sons of **S** were Jemuel
Gen 48: 5 as Reuben and **S**, they shall be
Gen 49: 5 **S** and Levi are brothers
Ex 1: 2 Reuben, **S**, Levi, and Judah
Ex 6:15 And the sons of **S** were Jemuel
Ex 6:15 These are the families of **S**
Num 1: 6 from **S**, Shelumiel the son of
Num 1:22 From the children of **S**, their
Num 1:23 of **S** were fifty-nine thousand
Num 2:12 him shall be the tribe of **S**
Num 2:12 leader of the children of **S**
Num 7:36 leader of the children of **S**
Num 10:19 of **S** was Shelumiel the son of
Num 13: 5 from the tribe of **S**, Shaphat
Num 26:12 The sons of **S** according to
Num 34:20 tribe of the children of **S**
Deut 27:12 **S**, Levi, Judah, Issachar,
Josh 19: 1 The second lot came out for **S**
Josh 19: 1 tribe of the children of **S**
Josh 19: 8 tribe of the children of **S**
Josh 19: 9 of the children of **S** was
Josh 19: 9 of **S** had their inheritance
Josh 21: 4 of Judah, from the tribe of **S**
Josh 21: 9 of **S** these cities which are
Judg 1: 3 Judah said to **S** his brother
Judg 1: 3 And **S** went with him
Judg 1:17 Judah went with his brother **S**
1Ch 2: 1 Reuben, **S**, Levi, Judah,
1Ch 4:24 The sons of **S** were Nemuel
1Ch 4:42 hundred men of the sons of **S**
1Ch 6:65 tribe of the children of **S**
1Ch 12:25 of the children of **S**, mighty
2Ch 15: 9 from Ephraim, Manasseh, and **S**
2Ch 34: 6 of Manasseh, Ephraim, and **S**
Ezek 48:24 **S** shall have one portion
Ezek 48:25 by the border of **S**, from the
Ezek 48:33 one gate for **S**, one gate for
Luke 2:25 in Jerusalem whose name was **S**
Luke 2:34 Then **S** blessed them, and said
Luke 3:30 the son of **S**, the son of
Acts 13: 1 **S** who was called Niger,
Rev 7: 7 of the tribe of **S** twelve

SIMEONITES (*see* SIMEON)
Num 25:14 a father's house among the **S**
Num 26:14 are the families of the **S**
1Ch 27:16 over the **S**, Shephatiah the

SIMILAR
Num 6: 3 himself from wine and **s** drink
Num 6: 3 nor vinegar made from **s** drink
Deut 14:26 or sheep, for wine or **s** drink
Deut 29: 6 you drunk wine or **s** drink
Judg 13: 4 not to drink wine or **s** drink
Judg 13: 7 Now drink no wine or **s** drink
Judg 13:14 may she drink wine or **s** drink
Ezra 1:10 ten silver basins of a **s** kind
Jer 36:32 added to them many **s** words
Acts 19:25 the workers of **s** occupation
Jude 7 them in a **s** manner to these

SIMILITUDE
Jas 3: 9 been made in the **s** of God

SIMMER
Ezek 24: 5 well, and let the cuts **s** in it

SIMON (*see* BAR-JONAH, CEPHAS, NIGER, PETER, SIMON'S)
Matt 4:18 **S** called Peter, and Andrew his
Matt 10: 2 first, **S**, who is called Peter
Matt 10: 4 **S** the Canaanite, and Judas
Matt 13:55 His brothers James, Joses, **S**
Matt 16:16 **S** Peter answered and said,
Matt 16:17 **S** Bar-Jonah, for flesh and
Matt 17:25 What do you think, **S**
Matt 26: 6 at the house of **S** the leper
Matt 27:32 a man of Cyrene, **S** by name
Mark 1:16 the Sea of Galilee, He saw **S**
Mark 1:29 they entered the house of **S**
Mark 1:36 And **S** and those who were with
Mark 3:16 **S**, to whom He gave the name
Mark 3:18 Thaddaeus, **S** the Canaanite
Mark 6: 3 of James, Joses, Judas, and **S**
Mark 14: 3 at the house of **S** the leper
Mark 14:37 **S**, are you sleeping
Mark 15:21 **S** a Cyrenian, the father of
Luke 5: 4 speaking, He said to **S**
Luke 5: 5 But **S** answered and said to Him
Luke 5: 8 When **S** Peter saw it, he fell
Luke 5:10 who were partners with **S**
Luke 5:10 And Jesus said to **S**, "Do not
Luke 6:14 **S**, whom He also named Peter,
Luke 6:15 and **S** called the Zealot
Luke 7:40 **S**, I have something to say to
Luke 7:43 **S** answered and said, "I
Luke 7:44 to the woman and said to **S**
Luke 22:31 **S**, **S**! Indeed, Satan has asked
Luke 23:26 **S** a Cyrenian, who was coming
Luke 24:34 indeed, and has appeared to **S**
John 1:40 was Andrew, **S** Peter's brother
John 1:41 first found his own brother **S**
John 1:42 You are **S** the son of Jonah
John 6: 8 **S** Peter's brother, said to
John 6:68 Then **S** Peter answered Him,
John 6:71 Judas Iscariot, the son of **S**
John 13: 6 Then He came to **S** Peter
John 13: 9 **S** Peter said to Him, "Lord,
John 13:24 **S** Peter therefore motioned to
John 13:26 Judas Iscariot, the son of **S**
John 13:36 **S** Peter said to Him, "Lord,
John 18:10 Then **S** Peter, having a sword,
John 18:15 **S** Peter followed Jesus, and so
John 18:25 Now **S** Peter stood and warmed
John 20: 2 she ran and came to **S** Peter
John 20: 6 Then **S** Peter came, following
John 21: 2 **S** Peter, Thomas called
John 21: 3 **S** Peter said to them, "I am
John 21: 7 Now when **S** Peter heard that
John 21:11 **S** Peter went up and dragged
John 21:15 Jesus said to **S** Peter
John 21:15 **S**, son of Jonah, do you love
John 21:16 **S**, son of Jonah, do you love
John 21:17 **S**, son of Jonah, do you love
Acts 1:13 of Alphaeus and **S** the Zealot
Acts 8: 9 was a certain man called **S**
Acts 8:13 Then **S** himself also believed
Acts 8:18 Now when **S** saw that through
Acts 8:24 Then **S** answered and said
Acts 9:43 many days in Joppa with **S**
Acts 10: 5 send for **S** whose surname is
Acts 10: 6 He is lodging with **S**, a
Acts 10:18 called and asked whether **S**
Acts 10:32 to Joppa and call **S** here,
Acts 10:32 is lodging in the house of **S**
Acts 11:13 call for **S** whose surname is
Acts 15:14 **S** has declared how God at the
2Pe 1: 1 **S** Peter, a servant and apostle

SIMON'S (*see* SIMON)
Mark 1:30 But **S** wife's mother lay sick
Luke 4:38 synagogue and entered **S** house
Luke 4:38 But **S** wife's mother was sick
Luke 5: 3 one of the boats, which was **S**
John 12: 4 **S** son, who would betray Him,
John 13: 2 **S** son, to betray Him,
Acts 10:17 had made inquiry for **S** house

SIMPLE (*see* SIMPLICITY, SIMPLY)
Job 5: 2 man, and envy slays a **s** one
Ps 19: 7 is sure, making wise the **s**
Ps 116: 6 The LORD preserves the **s**
Ps 119:130 gives understanding to the **s**
Prov 1: 4 to give prudence to the **s**
Prov 1:22 you **s** ones, will you love
Prov 1:32 away of the **s** will slay them
Prov 7: 7 and saw among the **s**, I
Prov 8: 5 O you **s** ones, understand
Prov 9: 4 Whoever is **s**, let him turn in
Prov 9:13 she is **s**, and knows nothing
Prov 9:16 Whoever is **s**, let him turn in
Prov 14:15 The **s** believes every word,
Prov 14:18 The **s** inherit folly, but the
Prov 19:25 and the **s** will become wary
Prov 21:11 punished, the **s** is made wise
Prov 22: 3 himself, but the **s** pass on
Prov 27:12 the **s** pass on and are punished
Rom 16:18 deceive the hearts of the **s**
Rom 16:19 is good, and **s** concerning evil

SIMPLICITY (*see* SIMPLE)
Prov 1:22 simple ones, will you love **s**
Acts 2:46 with gladness and **s** of heart,
2Co 1:12 ourselves in the world in **s**
2Co 11: 3 from the **s** that is in Christ

SIMPLY (*see* SIMPLE)
Lev 16: 2 at **s** any time into the Holy

SIN (*see* SINFUL, SINNED, SINNER, SINNING, SINS)
Gen 4: 7 do well, **s** lies at the door
Gen 18:20 and because their **s** is very
Gen 20: 9 me and on my kingdom a great **s**
Gen 31:36 What is my **s**, that you have
Gen 39: 9 wickedness, and **s** against God
Gen 42:22 Do not **s** against the boy'
Gen 50:17 of your brothers and their **s**
Ex 10:17 forgive my **s** only this once
Ex 20:20 you, so that you may not **s**
Ex 23:33 they make you **s** against Me
Ex 29:14 It is a **s** offering
Ex 29:36 as a **s** offering for atonement
Ex 30:10 the **s** offering of atonement
Ex 32:21 so great a **s** upon them
Ex 32:30 You have sinned a great **s**
Ex 32:30 can make atonement for your **s**
Ex 32:31 people have sinned a great **s**
Ex 32:32 if You will forgive their **s**
Ex 32:34 upon them for their **s**
Ex 34: 7 and transgression and **s**, by no
Ex 34: 9 pardon our iniquity and our **s**
Lev 4: 3 offer to the LORD for his **s**
Lev 4: 3 blemish as a **s** offering
Lev 4: 8 of the bull as the **s** offering
Lev 4:14 when the **s** which they have
Lev 4:14 offer a young bull for the **s**
Lev 4:20 with the bull as a **s** offering
Lev 4:21 It is a **s** offering for the
Lev 4:23 or if his **s** which he has
Lev 4:24 It is a **s** offering
Lev 4:25 **s** offering with his finger
Lev 4:26 for him concerning his **s**, and
Lev 4:28 or if his **s** which he has
Lev 4:28 for his **s** which he has sinned
Lev 4:29 on the head of the **s** offering
Lev 4:29 kill the **s** offering in the
Lev 4:32 a lamb as his **s** offering, he
Lev 4:33 on the head of the **s** offering
Lev 4:33 slay it as a **s** offering at
Lev 4:34 **s** offering with his finger
Lev 4:35 his **s** that he has committed
Lev 5: 6 for his **s** which he has sinned
Lev 5: 6 of the goats as a **s** offering
Lev 5: 6 for him concerning his **s**
Lev 5: 7 one as a **s** offering and the
Lev 5: 8 is for the **s** offering first
Lev 5: 9 some of the blood of the **s**
Lev 5: 9 It is a **s** offering
Lev 5:10 for his **s** which he has sinned
Lev 5:11 of fine flour as a **s** offering
Lev 5:11 on it, for it is a **s** offering
Lev 5:12 It is a **s** offering
Lev 5:13 for his **s** that he has sinned
Lev 6:17 holy, like the **s** offering
Lev 6:25 is the law of the **s** offering
Lev 6:25 the **s** offering shall be
Lev 6:26 offers it for **s** shall eat it
Lev 6:30 But no **s** offering from which
Lev 7: 7 is like the **s** offering
Lev 7:37 the **s** offering, the trespass
Lev 8: 2 oil, a bull as the **s** offering
Lev 8:14 the bull for the **s** offering
Lev 8:14 the bull for the **s** offering
Lev 9: 2 a young bull as a **s** offering

Lev 9: 3 of the goats as a s offering
Lev 9: 7 altar, offer your s offering
Lev 9: 8 the calf of the s offering
Lev 9:10 s offering he burned on the
Lev 9:15 which was the s offering for
Lev 9:15 killed it and offered it for s
Lev 9:22 from offering the s offering
Lev 10:16 the goat of the s offering
Lev 10:17 s offering in a holy place
Lev 10:19 have offered their s offering
Lev 10:19 eaten the s offering today
Lev 12: 6 a turtledove as a s offering
Lev 12: 8 and the other as a s offering
Lev 14:13 where he kills the s offering
Lev 14:13 for as the s offering is the
Lev 14:19 shall offer the s offering
Lev 14:22 one shall be a s offering
Lev 14:31 the one as a s offering and
Lev 15:15 them, the one as a s offering
Lev 15:30 offer the one as a s offering
Lev 16: 3 a young bull as a s offering
Lev 16: 5 of the goats as a s offering
Lev 16: 6 the bull as a s offering,
Lev 16: 9 and offer it as a s offering
Lev 16:11 the bull of the s offering
Lev 16:11 the s offering which is for
Lev 16:15 the goat of the s offering
Lev 16:25 The fat of the s offering he
Lev 16:27 The bull for the s offering
Lev 16:27 the goat for the s offering
Lev 19:17 not bear s because of him
Lev 19:22 for his s which he has done
Lev 19:22 the s which he has done shall
Lev 20:20 They shall bear their s
Lev 22: 9 lest they bear s for it and
Lev 23:19 of the goats as a s offering
Lev 24:15 his God shall bear his s
Num 5: 6 any s that men commit in
Num 5: 7 the s which he has done
Num 6:11 offer one as a s offering
Num 6:14 blemish as a s offering, one
Num 6:16 LORD and offer his s offering
Num 7:16 of the goats as a s offering
Num 7:22 of the goats as a s offering
Num 7:28 of the goats as a s offering
Num 7:34 of the goats as a s offering
Num 7:40 of the goats as a s offering
Num 7:46 of the goats as a s offering
Num 7:52 of the goats as a s offering
Num 7:58 of the goats as a s offering
Num 7:64 of the goats as a s offering
Num 7:70 of the goats as a s offering
Num 7:76 of the goats as a s offering
Num 7:82 of the goats as a s offering
Num 7:87 goats as a s offering twelve
Num 8: 8 young bull as a s offering
Num 8:12 offer one as a s offering
Num 9:13 that man shall bear his s
Num 12:11 do not lay this s on us, in
Num 15:22 if you s unintentionally, and
Num 15:24 of the goats as a s offering
Num 15:25 their s offering before the
Num 15:25 LORD, for their unintended s
Num 15:27 first year as a s offering
Num 16:22 of all flesh, shall one man s
Num 18: 9 every s offering and every
Num 18:22 of meeting, lest they bear s
Num 18:32 shall bear no s because of it
Num 19: 9 it is for purifying from s
Num 19:17 burnt for purification from s
Num 27: 3 but he died in his own s
Num 28:15 one kid of the goats as a s
Num 28:22 also one goat as a s offering
Num 29: 5 of the goats as a s offering
Num 29:11 of the goats as a s offering
Num 29:11 besides the s offering for
Num 29:16 of the goats as a s offering
Num 29:19 of the goats as a s offering
Num 29:22 also one goat as a s offering
Num 29:25 of the goats as a s offering
Num 29:28 also one goat as a s offering
Num 29:31 also one goat as a s offering
Num 29:34 also one goat as a s offering
Num 29:38 also one goat as a s offering
Num 32:23 be sure your s will find you
Deut 9:18 because of all your s which
Deut 9:21 Then I took your s, the calf
Deut 9:27 their wickedness or their s
Deut 15: 9 you, and it become s among you
Deut 19:15 or any s that he commits
Deut 20:18 you s against the LORD your
Deut 21:22 committed a s worthy of death
Deut 22:26 woman no s worthy of death
Deut 23:21 you, and it would be s to you
Deut 23:22 it shall not be s to you
Deut 24: 4 you shall not bring s on the
Deut 24:15 the LORD, and it be s to you
Deut 24:16 be put to death for his own s
1Sa 2:17 Therefore the s of the young
1Sa 12:23 s against the LORD in ceasing
1Sa 14:34 do not s against the LORD by
1Sa 14:38 and see what this s was today
1Sa 15:23 is as the s of witchcraft
1Sa 15:25 therefore, please pardon my s
1Sa 19: 4 Let not the king s against
1Sa 19: 5 Why then will you s against
1Sa 20: 1 and what is my s before your
2Sa 12:13 LORD also has put away your s
1Ki 8:34 forgive the s of Your people
1Ki 8:35 turn from their s because You
1Ki 8:36 and forgive the s of Your
1Ki 8:46 When they s against You (for
1Ki 8:46 is no one who does not s)
1Ki 12:30 Now this thing became a s
1Ki 13:34 this thing was the s of the
1Ki 14:16 sinned and who made Israel s
1Ki 15:26 in his s by which
1Ki 15:26 he had made Israel s
1Ki 15:30 by which he had made Israel s
1Ki 15:34 in his s by which
1Ki 15:34 he had made Israel s
1Ki 16: 2 have made My people Israel s
1Ki 16:13 which they had made Israel s
1Ki 16:19 and in his s which he had
1Ki 16:19 committed to make Israel s
1Ki 16:26 in his s by which
1Ki 16:26 he had made Israel s
1Ki 17:18 to bring my s to remembrance
1Ki 21:22 Me to anger, and made Israel s
1Ki 22:52 Nebat, who had made Israel s
2Ki 3: 3 Nebat, who had made Israel s
2Ki 10:29 Nebat, who had made Israel s
2Ki 10:31 who had made Israel s
2Ki 12:16 and the money from the s
2Ki 13: 2 Nebat, who had made Israel s
2Ki 13: 6 who had made Israel s, but
2Ki 13:11 Nebat, who had made Israel s
2Ki 14: 6 be put to death for his own s
2Ki 14:24 Nebat, who had made Israel s
2Ki 15: 9 Nebat, who had made Israel s
2Ki 15:18 Nebat, who had made Israel s
2Ki 15:24 Nebat, who had made Israel s
2Ki 15:28 Nebat, who had made Israel s
2Ki 17:21 and made them commit a great s
2Ki 21:11 made Judah s with his idols)
2Ki 21:16 besides his s
2Ki 21:16 with which he made Judah s
2Ki 21:17 and the s that he committed
2Ki 23:15 of Nebat, who made Israel s
2Ch 6:25 forgive the s of Your people
2Ch 6:26 turn from their s because You
2Ch 6:27 and forgive the s of Your
2Ch 6:36 When they s against You (for
2Ch 6:36 is no one who does not s)
2Ch 7:14 and will forgive their s and
2Ch 25: 4 shall die for his own s
2Ch 29:21 and seven male goats for a s
2Ch 29:23 s offering before the king
2Ch 29:24 as a s offering to make an
2Ch 29:24 the s offering be made for
2Ch 33:19 his entreaty, and all his s
Ezra 6:17 and as a s offering for all
Ezra 8:35 male goats as a s offering
Neh 4: 5 do not let their s be blotted
Neh 6:13 afraid and act that way and s
Neh 10:33 for the s offerings to make
Neh 13:26 of Israel s by these things
Neh 13:26 women caused even him to s
Job 1:22 In all this Job did not s nor
Job 2:10 Job did not s with his lips
Job 10: 6 iniquity and search out my s
Job 10:14 If I s, then You mark me, and
Job 13:23 know my transgression and my s
Job 14:16 but do not watch over my s
Job 31:30 not allowed my mouth to s by
Job 34:37 he adds rebellion to his s
Job 35: 6 If you s, what do you
Ps 4: 4 Be angry, and do not s
Ps 32: 1 forgiven, Whose s is covered
Ps 32: 5 I acknowledged my s to You
Ps 32: 5 forgave the iniquity of my s
Ps 38: 3 in my bones Because of my s
Ps 38:18 will be in anguish over my s
Ps 39: 1 ways, Lest I s with my tongue
Ps 40: 6 and s offering You did not
Ps 51: 2 And cleanse me from my s
Ps 51: 3 And my s is ever before me
Ps 51: 5 in s my mother conceived me
Ps 59: 3 my transgression nor for my s
Ps 59:12 For the s of their mouth and
Ps 85: 2 You have covered all their s
Ps 109: 7 And let his prayer become s
Ps 109:14 let not the s of his mother
Ps 119:11 I might not s against You
Prov 5:22 caught in the cords of his s
Prov 10:16 the wages of the wicked to s
Prov 10:19 of words s is not lacking
Prov 14: 9 Fools mock at s, but among
Prov 14:34 but s is a reproach to any
Prov 20: 9 clean, I am pure from my s"
Prov 21: 4 plowing of the wicked are s
Prov 24: 9 devising of foolishness is s
Eccl 5: 6 mouth cause your flesh to s
Eccl 7:20 who does good and does not s
Is 3: 9 they declare their s as Sodom
Is 5:18 and s as if with a cart rope
Is 6: 7 taken away, and your s purged
Is 27: 9 fruit of taking away his s
Is 30: 1 that they may add s to s
Is 31: 7 s, which your own hands have
Is 53:10 His soul an offering for s
Is 53:12 and He bore the s of many
Jer 16:10 Or what is our s that we have
Jer 16:18 for their iniquity and their s
Jer 17: 1 The s of Judah is written
Jer 17: 3 your high places of s within
Jer 18:23 out their s from Your sight
Jer 31:34 their s I will remember no
Jer 32:35 to cause Judah to s
Jer 36: 3 their iniquity and their s
Jer 51: 5 s against the Holy One of
Lam 4: 6 punishment of the s of Sodom
Ezek 3:20 he shall die in his s, and
Ezek 3:21 the righteous should not s
Ezek 3:21 and he does not s
Ezek 18:24 the s which he has committed,
Ezek 33:14 die,' if he turns from his s
Ezek 40:39 the s offering, and the
Ezek 42:13 the s offering, and the
Ezek 43:19 a s offering to the priests
Ezek 43:21 the bull of the s offering
Ezek 43:22 blemish for a s offering
Ezek 43:25 a goat for a s offering
Ezek 44:27 he must offer his s offering
Ezek 44:29 the s offering, and the
Ezek 45:17 shall prepare the s offering
Ezek 45:19 the blood of the s offering
Ezek 45:22 land a bull for a s offering
Ezek 45:23 goats daily for a s offering
Ezek 45:25 according to the s offering
Ezek 46:20 the s offering, and where they
Dan 9:20 praying, and confessing my s
Dan 9:20 the s of my people Israel, and
Hos 4: 8 eat up the s of My people
Hos 8:11 has made many altars for s
Hos 10: 8 the s of Israel, shall be
Hos 12: 8 in me no iniquity that is s
Hos 13: 2 Now they s more and more, and
Hos 13:12 his s is stored up
Amos 8:14 who swear by the s of Samaria
Mic 1:13 of s to the daughter of Zion)
Mic 3: 8 and to Israel his s
Mic 6: 7 my body for the s of my soul
Zech 13: 1 of Jerusalem, for s and for
Matt 5:29 right eye causes you to s
Matt 5:30 right hand causes you to s
Matt 12:31 I say to you, every s and
Matt 18: 6 ones who believe in Me to s
Matt 18: 8 hand or foot causes you to s
Matt 18: 9 if your eye causes you to s
Matt 18:21 shall my brother s against me
Mark 9:43 And if your hand makes you s
Mark 9:45 And if your foot makes you s
Mark 9:47 And if your eye makes you s
John 1:29 takes away the s of the world
John 5:14 S no more, lest a worse thing
John 8: 7 He who is without s among you
John 8:11 go and s no more
John 8:21 Me, and will die in your s
John 8:34 commits s is a slave of s

John 8:46 Which of you convicts Me of s
John 9:41 blind, you would have no s
John 9:41 Therefore your s remains
John 15:22 to them, they would have no s
John 15:22 have no excuse for their s
John 15:24 did, they would have no s
John 16: 8 will convict the world of s
John 16: 9 of s, because they do not
John 19:11 Me to you has the greater s
Acts 7:60 not charge them with this s
Rom 3: 9 that they are all under s
Rom 3:20 the law is the knowledge of s
Rom 4: 8 the LORD shall not impute s
Rom 5:12 one man s entered the world
Rom 5:12 and death through s
Rom 5:13 the law s was in the world
Rom 5:13 but s is not imputed when
Rom 5:20 But where s abounded, grace
Rom 5:21 so that as s reigned in death
Rom 6: 1 Shall we continue in s that
Rom 6: 2 to s live any longer in it
Rom 6: 6 that the body of s might be
Rom 6: 6 no longer be slaves of s
Rom 6: 7 died has been freed from s
Rom 6:10 He died to s once for all
Rom 6:11 to be dead indeed to s, but
Rom 6:12 Therefore do not let s reign
Rom 6:13 of unrighteousness to s, but
Rom 6:14 For s shall not have dominion
Rom 6:15 Shall we s because we are not
Rom 6:16 obey, whether of s to death
Rom 6:17 though you were slaves of s
Rom 6:18 having been set free from s
Rom 6:20 For when you were slaves of s
Rom 6:22 having been set free from s
Rom 6:23 For the wages of s is death
Rom 7: 7 Is the law s?
Rom 7: 7 s except through the law
Rom 7: 8 But s, taking opportunity by
Rom 7: 8 apart from the law s was dead
Rom 7: 9 came, s revived and I died
Rom 7:11 For s, taking occasion by the
Rom 7:13 s, that it might appear s
Rom 7:13 good, so that s through the
Rom 7:14 but I am carnal, sold under s
Rom 7:17 it, but s that dwells in me
Rom 7:20 it, but s that dwells in me
Rom 7:23 of s which is in my members
Rom 7:25 with the flesh the law of s
Rom 8: 2 me free from the law of s
Rom 8: 3 sinful flesh, on account of s
Rom 8: 3 He condemned s in the flesh
Rom 8:10 the body is dead because of s
Rom 14:23 is not from faith is s
1Co 6:18 Every s that a man does is
1Co 7:36 he does not s
1Co 8:12 But when you thus s against
1Co 8:12 you s against Christ
1Co 15:34 to righteousness, and do not s
1Co 15:56 The sting of death is s, and
1Co 15:56 the strength of s is the law
2Co 5:21 knew no s to be s for us
2Co 11: 7 Did I commit s in abasing
Gal 2:17 therefore a minister of s
Gal 3:22 has confined all under s,
Eph 4:26 Be angry, and do not s"
2Th 2: 3 the man of s is revealed, the
Heb 3:13 the deceitfulness of s
Heb 4:15 as we are, yet without s
Heb 9:26 s by the sacrifice of Himself
Heb 9:28 a second time, apart from s
Heb 10: 6 sacrifices for s You had no
Heb 10: 8 offerings for s You did not
Heb 10:18 no longer an offering for s
Heb 10:26 For if we s willfully after
Heb 11:25 the passing pleasures of s
Heb 12: 1 and the s which so easily
Heb 12: 4 bloodshed, striving against s
Heb 13:11 by the high priest for s, are
Jas 1:15 it gives birth to s
Jas 1:15 and s, when it is full-grown,
Jas 2: 9 show partiality, you commit s
Jas 4:17 not do it, to him it is s
1Pe 2:22 Who committed no s, nor was
1Pe 4: 1 the flesh has ceased from s
2Pe 2:14 and that cannot cease from s
1Jn 1: 7 Son cleanses us from all s
1Jn 1: 8 If we say that we have no s
1Jn 2: 1 to you, that you may not s
1Jn 3: 4 Whoever commits s also
1Jn 3: 4 and s is lawlessness
1Jn 3: 5 sins, and in Him there is no s
1Jn 3: 6 abides in Him does not s
1Jn 3: 9 been born of God does not s
1Jn 3: 9 and he cannot s, because he
1Jn 5:16 a s which does not lead to
1Jn 5:16 commit s not leading to death
1Jn 5:16 There is s leading to death
1Jn 5:17 All unrighteousness is s, and
1Jn 5:17 there is s not leading to
1Jn 5:18 is born of God does not s

SIN*
Ex 16: 1 came to the Wilderness of S
Ex 17: 1 from the Wilderness of S,
Num 33:11 camped in the Wilderness of S
Num 33:12 from the Wilderness of S and
Ezek 30:15 I will pour My fury on S, the
Ezek 30:16 S shall have great pain, no

SINAI (*see* HOREB)
Ex 16: 1 which is between Elim and S
Ex 19: 1 came to the Wilderness of S
Ex 19: 2 had come to the Desert of S
Ex 19:11 S in the sight of all the
Ex 19:18 Now Mount S was completely in
Ex 19:20 LORD came down upon Mount S
Ex 19:23 cannot come up to Mount S
Ex 24:16 of the LORD rested on Mount S
Ex 31:18 speaking with him on Mount S
Ex 34: 2 up in the morning to Mount S
Ex 34: 4 morning and went up Mount S
Ex 34:29 came down from Mount S
Ex 34:32 spoken with him on Mount S
Lev 7:38 commanded Moses on Mount S
Lev 7:38 LORD in the Wilderness of S
Lev 25: 1 spoke to Moses on Mount S
Lev 26:46 on Mount S by the hand of
Lev 27:34 children of Israel on Mount S
Num 1: 1 Moses in the Wilderness of S
Num 1:19 them in the Wilderness of S
Num 3: 1 spoke with Moses on Mount S
Num 3: 4 LORD in the Wilderness of S
Num 3:14 Moses in the Wilderness of S
Num 9: 1 Moses in the Wilderness of S
Num 9: 5 in the Wilderness of S
Num 10:12 of S on their journeys
Num 26:64 Israel in the Wilderness of S
Num 28: 6 at Mount S for a sweet aroma
Num 33:15 camped in the Wilderness of S
Num 33:16 from the Wilderness of S and
Deut 33: 2 The LORD came from S, and
Judg 5: 5 before the LORD, this S,
Neh 9:13 came down also on Mount S
Ps 68: 8 S itself was moved at the
Ps 68:17 Lord is among them as in S
Acts 7:30 in the wilderness of Mount S
Acts 7:38 who spoke to him on Mount S
Gal 4:24 the one from Mount S which
Gal 4:25 Hagar is Mount S in Arabia

SINCE (*see* PREFACE)

SINCERE (*see* SINCERELY, SINCERITY)
2Co 6: 6 the Holy Spirit, by s love,
Phil 1:10 excellent, that you may be s
1Ti 1: 5 conscience, and from s faith,
1Pe 1:22 in s love of the brethren

SINCERELY (*see* SINCERE)
Phil 1:16 from selfish ambition, not s
Phil 2:20 who will s care for your

SINCERITY (*see* SINCERE)
Josh 24:14 fear the LORD, serve Him in s
Judg 9:16 s in making Abimelech king,
Judg 9:19 s with Jerubbaal and with his
1Co 5: 8 the unleavened bread of s
2Co 1:12 in simplicity and godly s, not
2Co 2:17 but as of s, but as from God,
2Co 8: 8 the s of your love by the
Eph 6: 5 in s of heart, as to Christ
Eph 6:24 our Lord Jesus Christ in s
Col 3:22 but in s of heart, fearing

SINEW (*see* SINEWS)
Is 48: 4 and your neck was an iron s

SINEWS (*see* SINEW)
Job 10:11 me together with bones and s
Job 40:17 the s of his thighs are
Ezek 37: 6 I will put s on you and bring
Ezek 37: 8 Indeed, as I looked, the s

SINFUL (*see* SIN)
Gen 13:13 wicked and s against the LORD
Num 32:14 place, a brood of s men, to
Is 1: 4 s nation, a people laden with
Amos 9: 8 Lord GOD are on the s kingdom
Mark 8:38 s generation, of him the Son
Luke 5: 8 from me, for I am a s man
Luke 24: 7 into the hands of s men, and
Rom 7:13 might become exceedingly s
Rom 8: 3 in the likeness of s flesh

SING (*see* SANG, SINGER, SINGING, SINGS, SONG, SUNG)
Ex 15: 1 I will s to the LORD, for He
Ex 15:21 S to the LORD, for He has
Ex 32:18 of those who s that I hear
Num 21:17 all of you s to it
Judg 5: 3 I, even I, will s to the LORD
Judg 5: 3 I will s praise to the LORD
Judg 5:12 Awake, awake, s a song
1Sa 21:11 Did they not s of him to one
2Sa 22:50 and s praises to Your name
1Ch 16: 9 S to Him, s psalms to Him
1Ch 16:23 S to the LORD, all the earth
2Ch 20:21 who should s to the LORD, and
2Ch 20:22 Now when they began to s and
2Ch 29:30 commanded the Levites to s
Job 21:12 They s to the tambourine and
Job 29:13 widow's heart to s for joy
Ps 7:17 will s praise to the name of
Ps 9: 2 I will s praise to Your name,
Ps 9:11 S praises to the LORD, who
Ps 13: 6 I will s to the LORD, Because
Ps 18:49 And s praises to Your name
Ps 21:13 We will s and praise Your
Ps 27: 6 I will s, yes, I will s
Ps 30: 4 S praise to the LORD, You
Ps 30:12 my glory may s praise to You
Ps 33: 3 S to Him a new song
Ps 47: 6 S praises to God, s praises
Ps 47: 6 God, s praises! S praises
Ps 47: 6 s praises!
Ps 47: 7 S praises with understanding
Ps 51:14 my tongue shall s aloud of
Ps 57: 7 I will s and give praise
Ps 57: 9 I will s to You among the
Ps 59:16 But I will s of Your power
Ps 59:16 I will s aloud of Your mercy
Ps 59:17 my Strength, I will s praises
Ps 61: 8 So I will s praise to Your
Ps 65:13 shout for joy, they also s
Ps 66: 2 S out the honor of His name
Ps 66: 4 You And s praises to You
Ps 66: 4 They shall s praises to Your
Ps 67: 4 nations be glad and s for joy
Ps 68: 4 S to God, s praises to His
Ps 68:32 S to God, you kingdoms of the
Ps 68:32 s praises to the Lord, Selah
Ps 71:22 To You I will s with the harp
Ps 71:23 rejoice when I s to You, And
Ps 75: 9 I will s praises to the God
Ps 81: 1 S aloud to God our strength
Ps 89: 1 I will s of the mercies of
Ps 92: 1 to s praises to Your name, O
Ps 95: 1 Oh come, let us s to the LORD
Ps 96: 1 Oh, s to the LORD a new song
Ps 96: 1 S to the LORD, all the earth
Ps 96: 2 S to the LORD, bless His name
Ps 98: 1 Oh, s to the LORD a new song
Ps 98: 4 song, rejoice, and s praises
Ps 98: 5 S to the LORD with the harp,
Ps 101: 1 I will s of mercy and justice
Ps 101: 1 You, O LORD, I will s praises
Ps 104:12 They s among the branches
Ps 104:33 I will s to the LORD as long
Ps 104:33 I will s praise to my God
Ps 105: 2 S to Him, s psalms to Him
Ps 108: 1 I will s and give praise, even
Ps 108: 3 I will s praises to You among
Ps 135: 3 S praises to His name, for it
Ps 137: 3 S us one of the songs of Zion
Ps 137: 4 How shall we s the LORD's
Ps 138: 1 gods I will s praises to You
Ps 138: 5 they shall s of the ways of
Ps 144: 9 I will s a new song to You, O
Ps 144: 9 I will s praises to You,
Ps 145: 7 shall s of Your righteousness
Ps 146: 2 I will s praises to my God
Ps 147: 1 For it is good to s praises
Ps 147: 7 S to the LORD with
Ps 147: 7 S praises on the harp to our

Ps 149: 1 S to the LORD a new song, And
Ps 149: 3 Let them s praises to Him
Ps 149: 5 Let them s aloud on their
Is 5: 1 Now let me s to my
Is 12: 5 S to the LORD, For He has
Is 23:16 s many songs, that you may be
Is 24:14 up their voice, they shall s
Is 26:19 Awake and s, you who dwell in
Is 27: 2 In that day s to her, "A
Is 35: 6 and the tongue of the dumb s
Is 38:20 therefore we will s my songs
Is 42:10 S to the LORD a new song, and
Is 42:11 Let the inhabitants of Sela s
Is 44:23 S, O heavens, for the LORD
Is 49:13 S, O heavens! Be joyful
Is 52: 8 voices they shall s together
Is 52: 9 s together, you waste places
Is 54: 1 S, O barren, you who have not
Is 65:14 shall s for joy of heart, but
Jer 20:13 S to the LORD! Praise the
Jer 31: 7 S with gladness for Jacob, and
Jer 31:12 and s in the height of Zion,
Jer 51:48 shall s joyously over Babylon
Hos 2:15 she shall s there, as in the
Zeph 2:14 voice shall s in the windows
Zeph 3:14 S, O daughter of Zion
Zech 2:10 S and rejoice, O daughter of
Rom 15: 9 Gentiles, and s to Your name
1Co 14:15 I will s with the spirit, and
1Co 14:15 and I will also s with the
Heb 2:12 I will s praise to You
Jas 5:13 Let him s psalms
Rev 15: 3 they s the song of Moses, the

SINGED
Dan 3:27 not s nor were their garments

SINGER (*see* SING, SINGERS)
1Ch 6:33 Kohathites were Heman the s

SINGERS (*see* SINGER)
1Ki 10:12 and stringed instruments for s
1Ch 9:33 These are the s, heads of the
1Ch 15:16 their brethren to be the s
1Ch 15:19 the s, Heman, Asaph, and
1Ch 15:27 who bore the ark, the s, and
1Ch 15:27 the music master with the s
2Ch 5:12 and the Levites who were the s
2Ch 5:13 s were as one, to make one
2Ch 9:11 and stringed instruments for s
2Ch 23:13 also the s with instruments
2Ch 29:28 the s sang, and the trumpeters
2Ch 35:15 And the s, the sons of Asaph,
Ezra 2:41 The s: the sons of Asaph
Ezra 2:65 two hundred men and women s
Ezra 2:70 some of the people, the s
Ezra 7: 7 priests, the Levites, the s
Ezra 7:24 of the priests, Levites, s
Ezra 10:24 Also of the s: Eliashib
Neh 7: 1 when the gatekeepers, the s
Neh 7:44 The s: the children of Asaph
Neh 7:67 and forty-five men and women s
Neh 7:73 the gatekeepers, the s, some
Neh 10:28 the gatekeepers, the s, the
Neh 10:39 the gatekeepers and the s are
Neh 11:22 Asaph, the s in charge of the
Neh 11:23 portion should be for the s
Neh 12:28 the sons of the s gathered
Neh 12:29 for the s had built
Neh 12:42 The s sang loudly with
Neh 12:45 Both the s and the gatekeepers
Neh 12:46 there were chiefs of the s
Neh 12:47 gave the portions for the s
Neh 13: 5 be given to the Levites and s
Neh 13:10 the s who did the work had
Ps 68:25 The s went before, the
Ps 87: 7 Both the s and the players on
Eccl 2: 8 I acquired male and female s
Ezek 40:44 for the s in the inner court

SINGING (*see* SING)
1Sa 18: 6 all the cities of Israel, s
2Sa 19:35 of s men and s women
1Ch 13: 8 with all their might, with s
2Ch 23:18 with rejoicing and with s
2Ch 30:21 s to the LORD, accompanied by
2Ch 35:25 And to this day all the s men
2Ch 35:25 the s women speak of Josiah
Neh 12:27 both with thanksgivings and s
Ps 100: 2 before His presence with s
Ps 126: 2 And our tongue with s
Song 2:12 the time of s has come, and
Is 14: 7 they break forth into s
Is 16:10 vineyards there will be no s
Is 35: 2 rejoice, even with joy and s
Is 35:10 and come to Zion with s, with
Is 44:23 break forth into s, you
Is 48:20 With a voice of s, declare,
Is 49:13 And break out in s, O
Is 51:11 and come to Zion with s, with
Is 54: 1 Break forth into s, and cry
Is 55:12 break forth into s before you
Zeph 3:17 will rejoice over you with s
Acts 16:25 and s hymns to God, and the
Eph 5:19 hymns and spiritual songs, s
Col 3:16 s with grace in your hearts

SINGLE (*see* SINGLENESS, SINGULAR)
2Ch 28:25 in every s city of Judah he
2Ch 31:19 their cities, in every s city

SINGLENESS (*see* SINGLE)
2Ch 30:12 them s of heart to do the

SINGS (*see* SING)
Prov 25:20 is one who s songs to a heavy
Prov 29: 6 snared, but the righteous s

SINGULAR (*see* SINGLE)
Ezek 7: 5 A disaster, a s disaster

SINIM
Is 49:12 and these from the land of S

SINISTER
Ps 26:10 In whose hands is a s scheme
Dan 8:23 Who understands s schemes

SINITE
Gen 10:17 Hivite, the Arkite, and the S
1Ch 1:15 Hivite, the Arkite, and the S

SINK (*see* SANK, SINKING, SINKS, SUNK)
Ps 69: 2 I s in deep mire, Where there
Ps 69:14 of the mire, And let me not s
Jer 51:64 say, "Thus Babylon shall s
Matt 14:30 beginning to s he cried out
Luke 5: 7 so that they began to s
Luke 9:44 Let these words s down into

SINKING (*see* SINK)
Acts 20: 9 who was s into a deep sleep

SINKS (*see* SINK)
Lam 3:20 remembers and s within me

SINNED (*see* SIN)
Ex 9:27 to them, "I have s this time
Ex 9:34 had ceased, he s yet more
Ex 10:16 I have s against the LORD
Ex 32:30 You have s a great sin
Ex 32:31 people have s a great sin
Ex 32:33 Whoever has s against Me, I
Lev 4: 3 he has s a young bull without
Lev 4:14 they have s becomes known
Lev 4:22 When a ruler has s, and done
Lev 4:23 has s comes to his knowledge
Lev 4:28 has s comes to his knowledge
Lev 4:28 for his sin which he has s
Lev 5: 5 that he has s in that thing
Lev 5: 6 for his sin which he has s
Lev 5:10 for his sin which he has s
Lev 5:11 then he who s shall bring for
Lev 5:13 has s in any of these matters
Lev 6: 4 it shall be, because he has s
Num 6:11 because he s by reason of the
Num 12:11 and in which we have s
Num 14:40 has promised, for we have s
Num 16:38 who s against their own souls
Num 21: 7 We have s, for we have spoken
Num 22:34 I have s, for I did not know
Num 32:23 you have s against the LORD
Deut 1:41 We have s against the LORD
Deut 9:16 you had s against the LORD
Josh 7:11 Israel has s, and they have
Josh 7:20 Indeed I have s against the
Judg 10:10 We have s against You,
Judg 10:15 to the LORD, We have s!
Judg 11:27 I have not s against you, but
1Sa 7: 6 We have s against the LORD
1Sa 12:10 the LORD, and said, "We have s
1Sa 15:24 I have s, for I have
1Sa 15:30 Then he said, "I have s
1Sa 19: 4 he has not s against you, and
1Sa 24:11 and I have not s against you
1Sa 26:21 Then Saul said, "I have s
2Sa 12:13 I have s against the LORD
2Sa 19:20 servant, know that I have s
2Sa 24:10 I have s greatly in what I
2Sa 24:17 Surely I have s, and I have
1Ki 8:33 they have s against You, and
1Ki 8:35 they have s against You, when
1Ki 8:47 captive, saying, "We have s
1Ki 8:50 people who have s against You
1Ki 14:16 the sins of Jeroboam, who s
1Ki 15:30 of Jeroboam, which he had s
1Ki 16:13 his son, by which they had s
1Ki 16:19 of the sins which he had s in
1Ki 18: 9 How have I s, that you are
2Ki 17: 7 s against the LORD their God
1Ch 21: 8 I have s greatly, because I
1Ch 21:17 I am the one who has s and
2Ch 6:24 they have s against You, and
2Ch 6:26 they have s against You, when
2Ch 6:37 captivity, saying, "We have s
2Ch 6:39 people who have s against You
Neh 1: 6 which we have s against You
Neh 1: 6 my father's house and I have s
Neh 9:29 but s against Your judgments,
Job 1: 5 It may be that my sons have s
Job 7:20 Have I s? What have I done
Job 8: 4 your sons have s against Him
Job 24:19 the grave those who have s
Job 33:27 at men and says, "I have s
Job 35: 3 I have, more than if I had s
Ps 41: 4 for I have s against You
Ps 51: 4 You, You only, have I s, And
Ps 78:17 But they s even more against
Ps 78:32 In spite of this they still s
Ps 106: 6 We have s with our fathers,
Is 42:24 He against whom we have s
Is 43:27 Your first father s, and your
Is 64: 5 indeed angry, for we have s
Jer 2:35 you say, "I have not s
Jer 3:25 For we have s against the
Jer 8:14 because we have s against the
Jer 14: 7 many, we have s against You
Jer 14:20 for we have s against You
Jer 33: 8 which they have s against Me
Jer 33: 8 by which they have s and by
Jer 40: 3 have s against the LORD, and
Jer 44:23 you have s against the LORD
Jer 50: 7 they have s against the LORD
Jer 50:14 for she has s against the
Lam 1: 8 Jerusalem has s grievously
Lam 5: 7 Our fathers s and are no more,
Lam 5:16 Woe to us, for we have s
Ezek 28:16 violence within, and you s
Ezek 37:23 places in which they have s
Ezek 45:20 has s unintentionally or in
Dan 9: 5 we have s and committed
Dan 9: 8 because we have s against You
Dan 9:11 because we have s against Him
Dan 9:15 we have s, we have done
Hos 4: 7 the more they s against Me
Hos 10: 9 you have s from the days of
Mic 7: 9 because I have s against Him
Hab 2:10 and s against your soul
Zeph 1:17 they have s against the LORD
Matt 27: 4 I have s by betraying
Luke 15:18 I have s against heaven and
Luke 15:21 I have s against heaven and in
John 9: 2 Rabbi, who s, this man or his
John 9: 3 this man nor his parents s
Rom 2:12 For as many as have s without
Rom 2:12 as many as have s in the law
Rom 3:23 for all have s and fall short
Rom 5:12 to all men, because all s
Rom 5:14 s according to the likeness
Rom 5:16 came through the one who s
1Co 7:28 you do marry, you have not s
1Co 7:28 virgin marries, she has not s
2Co 12:21 for many who have s before
2Co 13: 2 to those who have s before
Heb 3:17 Was it not with those who s
2Pe 2: 4 not spare the angels who s
1Jn 1:10 If we say that we have not s
1Jn 3: 8 for the devil has s from the

SINNER (*see* SIN, SINNERS)
Prov 11:31 much more the wicked and the s
Prov 13: 6 wickedness overthrows the s
Prov 13:22 of the s is stored up for the
Eccl 2:26 but to the s He gives the
Eccl 7:26 but the s shall be taken by
Eccl 8:12 Though a s does evil a
Eccl 9: 2 As is the good, so is the s
Eccl 9:18 but one s destroys much good
Is 65:20 but the s being one hundred

Luke 7:37 woman in the city who was a **s**
Luke 7:39 touching Him, for she is a **s**
Luke 15: 7 one **s** who repents than over
Luke 15:10 of God over one **s** who repents
Luke 18:13 God be merciful to me a **s**
Luke 19: 7 a guest with a man who is a **s**
John 9:16 who is a **s** do such miracles
John 9:24 We know that this Man is a **s**
John 9:25 Whether He is a **s** or not I do
Rom 3: 7 am I also still judged as a **s**
Jas 5:20 know that he who turns a **s**
1Pe 4:18 the ungodly and the **s** appear

SINNERS (*see* SINNER)
1Sa 15:18 Go, and utterly destroy the **s**
Ps 1: 1 Nor stands in the path of **s**
Ps 1: 5 Nor **s** in the congregation of
Ps 25: 8 He teaches **s** in the way
Ps 26: 9 my soul together with **s**, Nor
Ps 51:13 **s** shall be converted to You
Ps 104:35 May **s** be consumed from the
Prov 1:10 son, if **s** entice you, do not
Prov 13:21 Evil pursues **s**, but to the
Prov 23:17 Do not let your heart envy **s**
Is 1:28 of **s** shall be together, and
Is 13: 9 He will destroy its **s** from it
Is 33:14 The **s** in Zion are afraid
Amos 9:10 All the **s** of My people shall
Matt 9:10 **s** came and sat down with Him
Matt 9:11 eat with tax collectors and **s**
Matt 9:13 to call the righteous, but **s**
Matt 11:19 friend of tax collectors and **s**
Matt 26:45 betrayed into the hands of **s**
Mark 2:15 and **s** also sat together with
Mark 2:16 with the tax collectors and **s**
Mark 2:16 with tax collectors and **s**
Mark 2:17 to call the righteous, but **s**
Mark 14:41 betrayed into the hands of **s**
Luke 5:30 with tax collectors and **s**
Luke 5:32 to call the righteous, but **s**
Luke 6:32 For even **s** love those who
Luke 6:33 For even **s** do the same
Luke 6:34 For even **s** lend to **s** to
Luke 7:34 friend of tax collectors and **s**
Luke 13: 2 **s** than all other Galileans
Luke 13: 4 **s** than all other men who
Luke 15: 1 the **s** drew near to Him to
Luke 15: 2 This man receives **s** and eats
John 9:31 know that God does not hear **s**
Rom 5: 8 in that while we were still **s**
Rom 5:19 disobedience many were made **s**
Gal 2:15 and not **s** of the Gentiles,
Gal 2:17 we ourselves also are found **s**
1Ti 1: 9 for the ungodly and for **s**
1Ti 1:15 came into the world to save **s**
Heb 7:26 undefiled, separate from **s**
Heb 12: 3 from **s** against Himself, lest
Jas 4: 8 Cleanse your hands, you **s**
Jude 15 **s** have spoken against Him

SINNING (*see* SIN)
Gen 20: 6 you from **s** against Me
1Sa 14:33 the people are **s** against the
Hos 8:11 become for him altars for **s**
1Ti 5:20 Those who are **s** rebuke in the
Tit 3:11 such a person is warped and **s**
1Jn 5:16 **s** a sin which does not lead

SINS (*see* SIN)
Lev 4: 2 If a person **s**
Lev 4: 3 if the anointed priest **s**
Lev 4:13 of Israel **s** unintentionally
Lev 4:27 **s** unintentionally by doing
Lev 5: 1 If a person **s** in hearing the
Lev 5:15 **s** unintentionally in regard
Lev 5:17 If a person **s**, and commits any
Lev 6: 2 If a person **s** and commits a
Lev 6: 3 a man may do in which he **s**
Lev 16:16 for all their **s**
Lev 16:21 concerning all their **s**,
Lev 16:30 all your **s** before the LORD
Lev 16:34 of Israel, for all their **s**
Lev 26:18 seven times more for your **s**
Lev 26:21 plagues, according to your **s**
Lev 26:24 yet seven times for your **s**
Lev 26:28 you seven times for your **s**
Num 15:27 if a person **s** unintentionally
Num 15:28 person who **s** unintentionally
Num 15:28 when he **s** unintentionally
Num 15:29 for him who **s** unintentionally
Num 16:26 be consumed in all their **s**
Josh 24:19 transgressions nor your **s**
1Sa 2:25 If one man **s** against another,
1Sa 2:25 But if a man **s** against the
1Sa 12:19 we have added to all our **s**
1Ki 8:31 When anyone **s** against his
1Ki 14:16 because of the **s** of Jeroboam
1Ki 14:22 their **s** which they committed
1Ki 15: 3 in all the **s** of his father
1Ki 15:30 because of the **s** of Jeroboam
1Ki 16: 2 Me to anger with their **s**,
1Ki 16:13 for all the **s** of Baasha and
1Ki 16:13 the **s** of Elah his son, by
1Ki 16:19 because of the **s** which he had
1Ki 16:31 the **s** of Jeroboam the son of
2Ki 3: 3 he persisted in the **s** of
2Ki 10:29 the **s** of Jeroboam the son of
2Ki 10:31 depart from the **s** of Jeroboam
2Ki 13: 2 followed the **s** of Jeroboam
2Ki 13: 6 did not depart from the **s** of
2Ki 13:11 the **s** of Jeroboam the son of
2Ki 14:24 the **s** of Jeroboam the son of
2Ki 15: 9 the **s** of Jeroboam the son of
2Ki 15:18 all his days from the **s** of
2Ki 15:24 the **s** of Jeroboam the son of
2Ki 15:28 the **s** of Jeroboam the son of
2Ki 17:22 **s** of Jeroboam which he did
2Ki 24: 3 because of the **s** of Manasseh
2Ch 6:22 If anyone **s** against his
2Ch 28:13 You intend to add to our **s**
Neh 1: 6 confess the **s** of the children
Neh 9: 2 stood and confessed their **s**
Neh 9:37 set over us, because of our **s**
Job 13:23 many are my iniquities and **s**
Ps 19:13 also from presumptuous **s**
Ps 25: 7 remember the **s** of my youth
Ps 25:18 my pain, And forgive all my **s**
Ps 51: 9 Hide Your face from my **s**, And
Ps 69: 5 my **s** are not hidden from You
Ps 79: 9 provide atonement for our **s**
Ps 90: 8 Our secret **s** in the light of
Ps 103:10 with us according to our **s**
Prov 8:36 but he who **s** against me
Prov 10:12 strife, but love covers all **s**
Prov 14:21 who despises his neighbor **s**
Prov 19: 2 he **s** who hastens with his
Prov 20: 2 anger **s** against his own life
Prov 28:13 covers his **s** will not prosper
Is 1:18 Though your **s** are like
Is 38:17 all my **s** behind Your back
Is 40: 2 hand double for all her **s**
Is 43:24 have burdened Me with your **s**
Is 43:25 and I will not remember your **s**
Is 44:22 and like a cloud, your **s**
Is 58: 1 and the house of Jacob their **s**
Is 59: 2 your **s** have hidden His face
Is 59:12 and our **s** testify against us
Jer 5:25 your **s** have withheld good
Jer 14:10 now, and punish their **s**
Jer 15:13 price, because of all your **s**
Jer 30:14 because your **s** have increased
Jer 30:15 because your **s** have increased
Jer 50:20 and the **s** of Judah, but they
Lam 3:39 for the punishment of his **s**
Lam 4:13 Because of the **s** of her
Lam 4:22 He will uncover your **s**
Ezek 14:13 when a land **s** against Me by
Ezek 16:51 did not commit half of your **s**
Ezek 16:52 also, because the **s** which you
Ezek 18: 4 the soul who **s** shall die
Ezek 18:14 a son who sees all the **s**
Ezek 18:20 The soul who **s** shall die
Ezek 18:21 his **s** which he has committed
Ezek 21:24 all your doings your **s** appear
Ezek 23:49 pay for your idolatrous **s**
Ezek 33:10 our **s** lie upon us, and we pine
Ezek 33:12 in the day that he **s**
Ezek 33:16 None of his **s** which he has
Dan 4:27 break off your **s** by being
Dan 9:16 because for our **s**, and for the
Dan 9:24 to make an end of **s**, to make
Hos 8:13 iniquity and punish their **s**
Hos 9: 9 He will punish their **s**
Amos 5:12 and your mighty **s**
Mic 1: 5 for the **s** of the house of
Mic 6:13 desolate because of your **s**
Mic 7:19 You will cast all our **s** into
Matt 1:21 save His people from their **s**
Matt 3: 6 Jordan, confessing their **s**
Matt 9: 2 your **s** are forgiven you
Matt 9: 5 Your **s** are forgiven you,' or
Matt 9: 6 power on earth to forgive **s**"
Matt 18:15 if your brother **s** against you
Matt 26:28 many for the remission of **s**
Mark 1: 4 for the remission of **s**
Mark 1: 5 River, confessing their **s**
Mark 2: 5 Son, your **s** are forgiven you
Mark 2: 7 can forgive **s** but God alone
Mark 2: 9 Your **s** are forgiven you,' or
Mark 2:10 power on earth to forgive **s**"
Mark 3:28 all **s** will be forgiven the
Mark 4:12 and their **s** be forgiven them
Luke 1:77 by the remission of their **s**
Luke 3: 3 for the remission of **s**,
Luke 5:20 Man, your **s** are forgiven you
Luke 5:21 can forgive **s** but God alone
Luke 5:23 Your **s** are forgiven you,' or
Luke 5:24 power on earth to forgive **s**"
Luke 7:47 Therefore I say to you, her **s**
Luke 7:48 to her, "Your **s** are forgiven
Luke 7:49 is this who even forgives **s**
Luke 11: 4 and forgive us our **s**, for we
Luke 17: 3 If your brother **s** against you
Luke 17: 4 if he **s** against you seven
Luke 24:47 and remission of **s** should be
John 8:24 that you will die in your **s**
John 8:24 am He, you will die in your **s**
John 9:34 You were completely born in **s**
John 20:23 If you forgive the **s** of any
John 20:23 if you retain the **s** of any
Acts 2:38 Christ for the remission of **s**
Acts 3:19 that your **s** may be blotted
Acts 5:31 to Israel and forgiveness of **s**
Acts 10:43 will receive remission of **s**
Acts 13:38 to you the forgiveness of **s**
Acts 22:16 baptized, and wash away your **s**
Acts 26:18 may receive forgiveness of **s**
Rom 3:25 the **s** that were previously
Rom 4: 7 and whose **s** are covered
Rom 7: 5 the passions of **s** which were
Rom 11:27 when I take away their **s**
1Co 6:18 **s** against his own body
1Co 15: 3 that Christ died for our **s**
1Co 15:17 you are still in your **s**
Gal 1: 4 who gave Himself for our **s**
Eph 1: 7 blood, the forgiveness of **s**
Eph 2: 1 were dead in trespasses and **s**
Col 1:14 blood, the forgiveness of **s**
Col 2:11 body of the **s** of the flesh
1Th 2:16 up the measure of their **s**
1Ti 5:22 nor share in other people's **s**
1Ti 5:24 Some men's **s** are clearly
2Ti 3: 6 women loaded down with **s**, led
Heb 1: 3 had by Himself purged our **s**
Heb 2:17 for the **s** of the people
Heb 5: 1 gifts and sacrifices for **s**
Heb 5: 3 for himself, to offer for **s**
Heb 7:27 first for His own **s** and then
Heb 8:12 unrighteousness, and their **s**
Heb 9: 7 for the people's **s** committed
Heb 9:28 once to bear the **s** of many
Heb 10: 2 no more consciousness of **s**
Heb 10: 3 is a reminder of **s** every year
Heb 10: 4 and goats could take away **s**
Heb 10:11 which can never take away **s**
Heb 10:12 one sacrifice for **s** forever
Heb 10:17 Their **s** and their lawless
Heb 10:26 remains a sacrifice for **s**
Jas 5:15 And if he has committed **s**, he
Jas 5:20 and cover a multitude of **s**
1Pe 2:24 who Himself bore our **s** in His
1Pe 2:24 that we, having died to **s**
1Pe 3:18 also suffered once for **s**, the
1Pe 4: 8 will cover a multitude of **s**
2Pe 1: 9 he was purged from his old **s**
1Jn 1: 9 If we confess our **s**, He is
1Jn 1: 9 and just to forgive us our **s**
1Jn 2: 1 And if anyone **s**, we have an
1Jn 2: 2 is the propitiation for our **s**
1Jn 2:12 because your **s** are forgiven
1Jn 3: 5 manifested to take away our **s**
1Jn 3: 6 Whoever **s** has neither seen
1Jn 3: 8 He who **s** is of the devil, for
1Jn 4:10 be the propitiation for our **s**
Rev 1: 5 from our **s** in His own blood
Rev 18: 4 lest you share in her **s**, and
Rev 18: 5 For her **s** have reached to

SION (*see* SIRION, ZION)
Deut 4:48 even to Mount **S** (that is

SIPHMOTH
1Sa 30:28 in Aroer, those who were in S

SIPPAI (*see* SAPH)
1Ch 20: 4 the Hushathite killed S, who

SIR (*see* SIRS)
Gen 43:20 O s, we indeed came down the
Matt 13:27 owner came and said to him, "S
Matt 21:30 he answered and said, 'I go, s
Matt 27:63 S, we remember, while He was
Luke 13: 8 answered and said to him, 'S
John 4:11 S, You have nothing to draw
John 4:15 S, give me this water, that I
John 4:19 S, I perceive that You are a
John 4:49 S, come down before my child
John 5: 7 S, I have no man to put me
John 12:21 S, we wish to see Jesus
John 20:15 S, if You have carried Him
Rev 7:14 said to him, "S, you know."

SIRAH
2Sa 3:26 him back from the well of S

SIRION (*see* HERMON, SION)
Deut 3: 9 (the Sidonians call Hermon S
Ps 29: 6 and S like a young wild ox

SIRS (*see* SIR)
Acts 16:30 S, what must I do to be saved

SISERA
Judg 4: 2 commander of his army was S
Judg 4: 7 against you I will deploy S
Judg 4: 9 for the LORD will sell S into
Judg 4:12 they reported to S that Barak
Judg 4:13 So S gathered together all
Judg 4:14 delivered S into your hand
Judg 4:15 And the LORD routed S and all
Judg 4:15 S alighted from his chariot
Judg 4:16 all the army of S fell by the
Judg 4:17 S had fled away on foot to
Judg 4:18 And Jael went out to meet S
Judg 4:22 And then, as Barak pursued S
Judg 4:22 into her tent, there lay S
Judg 5:20 courses fought against S
Judg 5:26 she pounded S, she pierced
Judg 5:28 The mother of S looked
Judg 5:30 for S, plunder of dyed
1Sa 12: 9 sold them into the hand of S
Ezra 2:53 sons of Barkos, the sons of S
Neh 7:55 of Barkos, the children of S
Ps 83: 9 as with Midian, As with S

SISMAI
1Ch 2:40 Eleasah begot S
1Ch 2:40 and S begot Shallum

SISTER (*see* SISTER-IN-LAW, SISTER'S, SISTERS)
Gen 4:22 And the s of Tubal-Cain was
Gen 12:13 Please say you are my s, that
Gen 12:19 did you say, 'She is my s',
Gen 20: 2 his wife, "She is my s."
Gen 20: 5 not say to me, 'She is my s'
Gen 20:12 But indeed she is truly my s
Gen 24:30 the words of his s Rebekah
Gen 24:59 sent away Rebekah their s
Gen 24:60 Our s, may you become the
Gen 25:20 the s of Laban the Syrian
Gen 26: 7 And he said, "She is my s"
Gen 26: 9 could you say, 'She is my s'
Gen 28: 9 the s of Nebajoth, to be his
Gen 30: 1 children, Rachel envied her s
Gen 30: 8 I have wrestled with my s
Gen 34:13 he had defiled Dinah their s
Gen 34:14 to give our s to one who is
Gen 34:27 because their s had been
Gen 34:31 he treat our s like a harlot
Gen 36: 3 daughter, s of Nebajoth
Gen 36:22 Lotan's s was Timna
Gen 46:17 Beriah, and Serah, their s
Ex 2: 4 his s stood afar off, to know
Ex 2: 7 Then his s said to Pharaoh's
Ex 6:20 Jochebed, his father's s, as
Ex 6:23 s of Nahshon, as wife
Ex 15:20 the s of Aaron, took the
Lev 18: 9 The nakedness of your s, the
Lev 18:11 she is your s—you shall not
Lev 18:12 nakedness of your father's s
Lev 18:13 nakedness of your mother's s
Lev 18:18 a woman as a rival to her s
Lev 20:17 If a man takes his s, his
Lev 20:19 nakedness of your mother's s
Lev 20:19 nor of your father's s
Lev 21: 3 also his virgin s who is
Num 6: 7 for his brother or his s
Num 25:18 a leader of Midian, their s
Num 26:59 and Moses and their s Miriam
Deut 27:22 the one who lies with his s
Judg 15: 2 her younger s better than she
2Sa 13: 1 son of David had a lovely s
2Sa 13: 2 s Tamar that he became sick
2Sa 13: 4 Tamar, my brother Absalom's s
2Sa 13: 5 Please let my s Tamar come
2Sa 13: 6 Please let Tamar my s come
2Sa 13:11 Come, lie with me, my s
2Sa 13:20 But now hold your peace, my s
2Sa 13:22 he had forced his s Tamar
2Sa 13:32 that he forced his s Tamar
2Sa 17:25 s of Zeruiah, Joab's mother
1Ki 11:19 as wife the s of his own wife
1Ki 11:19 is, the s of Queen Tahpenes
1Ki 11:20 Then the s of Tahpenes bore
2Ki 11: 2 s of Ahaziah, took Joash the
1Ch 1:39 Lotan's s was Timna
1Ch 3: 9 concubines, and Tamar their s
1Ch 3:19 Hananiah, Shelomith their s
1Ch 4: 3 of their s was Hazelelponi
1Ch 4:19 the s of Naham, were the
1Ch 7:15 as his wife the s of Huppim
1Ch 7:18 His s Hammoleketh bore Ishhod
1Ch 7:30 Beriah, and their s Serah
1Ch 7:32 Hotham, and their s Shua
2Ch 22:11 for she was the s of Ahaziah)
Job 17:14 You are my mother and my s
Prov 7: 4 You are my s," and call
Song 4: 9 have ravished my heart, my s
Song 4:10 How fair is your love, my s
Song 4:12 A garden enclosed is my s
Song 5: 1 have come to my garden, my s
Song 5: 2 Open for me, my s, my love,
Song 8: 8 We have a little s, and she
Song 8: 8 our s in the day when she is
Jer 3: 7 treacherous s Judah saw it
Jer 3: 8 s Judah did not fear, but
Jer 3:10 all this her treacherous s
Jer 22:18 my brother!' or 'Alas, my s
Ezek 16:45 you are the s of your sisters
Ezek 16:46 Your elder s is Samaria, who
Ezek 16:46 and your younger s, who dwells
Ezek 16:48 neither your s Sodom nor her
Ezek 16:49 the iniquity of your s Sodom
Ezek 16:56 For your s Sodom was not a
Ezek 22:11 another in you violates his s
Ezek 23: 4 the elder and Oholibah her s
Ezek 23:11 Now although her s Oholibah
Ezek 23:18 alienated Myself from her s
Ezek 23:31 walked in the way of your s
Ezek 23:33 The cup of your s Samaria
Ezek 44:25 for brother or unmarried s
Matt 12:50 in heaven is My brother and s
Mark 3:35 of God is My brother and My s
Luke 10:39 she had a s called Mary, who
Luke 10:40 do You not care that my s has
John 11: 1 town of Mary and her s Martha
John 11: 5 Jesus loved Martha and her s
John 11:28 and secretly called Mary her s
John 11:39 the s of him who was dead,
John 19:25 His mother, and His mother's s
Rom 16: 1 I commend to you Phoebe our s
Rom 16:15 and Julia, Nereus and his s
1Co 7:15 a brother or a s is not under
Jas 2:15 If a brother or s is naked
2Jn 13 of your elect s greet you

SISTER-IN-LAW (*see* SISTER)
Ruth 1:15 your s has gone back to her
Ruth 1:15 return after your s

SISTER'S (*see* SISTER)
Gen 24:30 the bracelets on his s wrists
Gen 29:13 report about Jacob his s son
Lev 20:17 has uncovered his s nakedness
Ezek 23:11 corrupt than her s harlotry
Ezek 23:32 You shall drink of your s cup
Acts 23:16 when Paul's s son heard of

SISTERS (*see* SISTER)
Josh 2:13 my mother, my brothers, my s
1Ch 2:16 Now their s were Zeruiah and
Job 1: 4 invite their three s to eat
Job 42:11 all his brothers, all his s
Ezek 16:45 you are the sister of your s
Ezek 16:51 have justified your s by all
Ezek 16:52 You who judged your s, bear
Ezek 16:52 because you justified your s
Ezek 16:55 When your s, Sodom and her
Ezek 16:61 your older and your younger s
Hos 2: 1 My people,' and to your s
Matt 13:56 And His s, are they not all
Matt 19:29 left houses or brothers or s
Mark 6: 3 are not His s here with us
Mark 10:29 left house or brothers or s
Mark 10:30 houses and brothers and s and
Luke 14:26 and children, brothers and s
John 11: 3 Therefore the s sent to Him
1Ti 5: 2 as mothers, the younger as s

SISTRUMS
2Sa 6: 5 on tambourines, on s, and on

SIT (*see* SAT, SITS, SITTING)
Gen 27:19 please arise, s and eat of my
Ex 18:14 Why do you alone s, and all
Num 32: 6 go to war while you s here
Deut 6: 7 them when you s in your house
Deut 11:19 them when you s in your house
Deut 23:13 when you s down outside, you
Deut 33: 3 they s down at Your feet
Judg 4: 5 she would s under the palm
Judg 5:10 who s in judges' attire, and
Judg 5:16 Why did you s among the
Ruth 3:18 S still, my daughter, until
Ruth 4: 1 aside, friend, s down here
Ruth 4: 2 city, and said, "S down here
1Sa 9:22 had them s in the place of
1Sa 16:11 For we will not s down till
1Sa 20: 5 to s with the king to eat
1Ki 1:13 he shall s on my throne"
1Ki 1:17 and he shall s on my throne
1Ki 1:20 s on the throne of my lord
1Ki 1:24 and he shall s on my throne'
1Ki 1:27 your servant who should s on
1Ki 1:30 he shall s on my throne in my
1Ki 1:35 s on my throne, and he shall
1Ki 1:48 who has given one to s on my
1Ki 3: 6 him a son to s on his throne
1Ki 8:20 s on the throne of Israel, as
1Ki 8:25 not fail to have a man s
2Ki 7: 4 And if we s here, we die also
2Ki 10:30 your sons shall s on the
2Ki 15:12 Your sons shall s on the
2Ki 18:27 to the men who s on the wall
1Ch 28: 5 to s on the throne of the
2Ch 6:10 s on the throne of Israel, as
2Ch 6:16 not fail to have a man s
Ps 26: 5 will not s with the wicked
Ps 50:20 You s and speak against your
Ps 69:12 Those who s in the gate speak
Ps 110: 1 S at My right hand, Till I
Ps 119:23 Princes also s and speak
Ps 127: 2 To s up late, To eat the
Ps 132:12 also shall s upon your throne
Prov 23: 1 When you s down to eat with a
Eccl 10: 6 while the rich s in a lowly
Is 3:26 shall s on the ground
Is 14:13 I will also s on the mount of
Is 16: 5 One will s on it in truth, in
Is 36:12 to the men who s on the wall
Is 42: 7 those who s in darkness from
Is 47: 1 and s in the dust, O virgin
Is 47: 1 s on the ground without a
Is 47: 5 S in silence, and go into
Is 47: 8 I shall not s as a widow, nor
Is 47:14 by, nor a fire to s before
Is 52: 2 arise, and s down, O Jerusalem
Is 65: 4 Who s among the graves, and
Jer 8:14 Why do we s still
Jer 13:13 kings who s on David's throne
Jer 13:18 s down, for your rule shall
Jer 15:17 I did not s in the assembly
Jer 16: 8 of feasting to s with them
Jer 22: 2 you who s on the throne of
Jer 22: 4 kings who s on the throne of
Jer 33:17 shall never lack a man to s
Jer 36:15 S down now, and read it in our
Jer 36:30 to s on the throne of David
Jer 48:18 your glory, and s in thirst
Lam 2:10 of Zion s on the ground and
Lam 3:28 Let him s alone and keep
Ezek 26:16 they will s on the ground,
Ezek 28: 2 I s in the seat of gods, in
Ezek 33:31 do, they s before you as My
Ezek 44: 3 he may s in it to eat bread
Joel 3:12 I will s to judge all the
Mic 4: 4 shall s under his vine and
Mic 7: 8 when I s in darkness, the

Zech 3: 8 companions who **s** before you
Zech 6:13 bear the glory, and shall **s**
Zech 8: 4 old women shall again **s** in
Mal 3: 3 He will **s** as a refiner and a
Matt 8:11 **s** down with Abraham, Isaac,
Matt 14:19 to **s** down on the grass
Matt 15:35 to **s** down on the ground
Matt 19:28 will also **s** on twelve thrones
Matt 20:21 these two sons of mine may **s**
Matt 20:23 but to **s** on My right hand and
Matt 22:44 **S** at My right hand, till I
Matt 23: 2 the Pharisees **s** in Moses'
Matt 25:31 then He will **s** on the throne
Matt 26:36 **S** here while I go and pray
Mark 6:39 them to make them all **s** down
Mark 8: 6 to **s** down on the ground
Mark 10:37 Grant us that we may **s**, one
Mark 10:40 but to **s** on My right hand and
Mark 12:36 **S** at My right hand, till I
Mark 14:32 **S** here while I pray
Luke 1:79 to those who **s** in darkness
Luke 9:14 Make them **s** down in groups of
Luke 9:15 so, and made them all **s** down
Luke 12:37 have them **s** down to eat, and
Luke 13:29 **s** down in the kingdom of God
Luke 14: 8 do not **s** down in the best
Luke 14:10 **s** down in the lowest place,
Luke 14:10 who **s** at the table with you
Luke 14:28 does not **s** down first and
Luke 14:31 does not **s** down first and
Luke 16: 6 **s** down quickly and write fifty
Luke 17: 7 at once and **s** down to eat'
Luke 20:42 Lord, "**s** at My right hand,
Luke 22:30 and **s** on thrones judging the
Luke 22:69 the Son of Man will **s** on the
John 6:10 Make the people **s** down
Acts 2:30 the Christ to **s** on his throne
Acts 2:34 Lord, "**S** at My right hand,
Acts 8:31 to come up and **s** with him
Acts 23: 3 For you **s** to judge me
Eph 2: 6 made us **s** together in the
Heb 1:13 **S** at My right hand, Till I
Jas 2: 3 You **s** here in a good place,"
Jas 2: 3 **S** here at my footstool,"
Rev 3:21 to **s** with Me on My throne
Rev 18: 7 I **s** as queen, and am no widow
Rev 19:18 and of those who **s** on them

SITE (*see* SITES)
Ezra 5:15 temple **s** that is in Jerusalem
Ezra 5:15 be rebuilt on its former **s**
Ezra 6: 7 this house of God on its **s**

SITES (*see* SITE)
2Ch 33:19 the **s** where he built high

SITNAH
Gen 26:21 So he called its name **S**

SITS (*see* SIT)
Ex 11: 5 Pharaoh who **s** on his throne
Lev 15: 4 which he **s** shall be unclean
Lev 15: 6 He who **s** on anything on
Lev 15:20 she **s** on shall be unclean
Lev 15:23 or on anything on which she **s**
Lev 15:26 whatever she **s** on shall be
Deut 17:18 when he **s** on the throne of
1Ki 1:46 Also Solomon **s** on the throne
Esth 6:10 who **s** within the king's gate
Ps 1: 1 Nor **s** in the seat of the
Ps 2: 4 He who **s** in the heavens shall
Ps 10: 8 He **s** in the lurking places of
Ps 29:10 the LORD **s** as King forever
Ps 47: 8 God **s** on His holy throne
Prov 9:14 For she **s** at the door of her
Prov 20: 8 A king who **s** on the throne of
Prov 31:23 when he **s** among the elders of
Is 28: 6 to him who **s** in judgment, and
Is 40:22 It is He who **s** above the
Jer 29:16 who **s** on the throne of David
Lam 1: 1 How lonely **s** the city that
Matt 19:28 when the Son of Man **s** on the
Matt 23:22 of God and by Him who **s** on it
Luke 22:27 he who **s** at the table, or he
Luke 22:27 it not he who **s** at the table
1Co 14:30 revealed to another who **s** by
2Th 2: 4 so that he **s** as God in the
Rev 4: 9 to Him who **s** on the throne
Rev 4:10 Him who **s** on the throne and
Rev 5:13 be to Him who **s** on the throne
Rev 6:16 of Him who **s** on the throne
Rev 7:10 our God who **s** on the throne
Rev 7:15 He who **s** on the throne will
Rev 17: 1 harlot who **s** on many waters
Rev 17: 9 on which the woman **s**
Rev 17:15 you saw, where the harlot **s**

SITTING (*see* SIT)
Gen 18: 1 as he was **s** in the tent door
Gen 19: 1 and Lot was **s** in the gate of
Deut 22: 6 with the mother **s** on the
Judg 3:20 he was **s** upstairs in his cool
Judg 13: 9 as she was **s** in the field
1Sa 1: 9 Now Eli the priest was **s** on
1Sa 4:13 **s** on a seat by the wayside
1Sa 14: 2 Saul was **s** in the outskirts
2Sa 18:24 Now David was **s** between the
2Sa 19: 8 is the king, **s** in the gate
1Ki 13:14 and found him **s** under an oak
1Ki 22:19 saw the LORD **s** on His throne
2Ki 1: 9 was, **s** on the top of a hill
2Ki 4:38 prophets were **s** before him
2Ki 6:32 But Elisha was **s** in his house
2Ki 6:32 and the elders were **s** with him
2Ki 7: 3 Why are we **s** here until we
2Ki 9: 5 the captains of the army **s**
2Ch 18:18 saw the LORD **s** on His throne
Neh 2: 6 (the queen also **s** beside him)
Esth 5:13 the Jew **s** at the king's gate
Ps 139: 2 You know my **s** down and my
Is 6: 1 I saw the Lord **s** on a throne
Jer 17:25 princes **s** on the throne of
Jer 22:30 **s** on the throne of David, and
Jer 36:12 there all the princes were **s**
Jer 36:22 Now the king was **s** in the
Jer 38: 7 When the king was **s** at the
Lam 3:63 Look at their **s** down and their
Ezek 8: 1 elders of Judah **s** before me
Ezek 8:14 women were **s** there weeping
Zech 5: 7 this is a woman **s** inside the
Matt 9: 9 Matthew **s** at the tax office
Matt 11:16 **s** in the marketplaces and
Matt 20:30 two blind men **s** by the road
Matt 21: 5 **s** on a donkey, a colt, the
Matt 26:64 **s** at the right hand of the
Matt 27:19 While he was **s** on the
Matt 27:36 **S** down, they kept watch over
Matt 27:61 Mary, **s** opposite the tomb
Mark 2: 6 of the scribes were **s** there
Mark 2:14 Alphaeus **s** at the tax office
Mark 3:32 a multitude was **s** around Him
Mark 5:15 and had the legion, **s** and
Mark 14:62 **s** at the right hand of the
Mark 16: 5 robe **s** on the right side
Luke 2:46 temple, **s** in the midst of the
Luke 5:17 and teachers of the law **s** by
Luke 5:27 Levi, **s** at the tax office
Luke 7:32 children **s** in the marketplace
Luke 8:35 **s** at the feet of Jesus,
Luke 10:13 ago, **s** in sackcloth and ashes
John 6:11 the disciples to those **s** down
John 11:20 but Mary was **s** in the house
John 12:15 coming, **s** on a donkey's colt
John 19:29 full of sour wine was **s** there
John 20:12 she saw two angels in white **s**
Acts 2: 2 whole house where they were **s**
Acts 8:28 And **s** in his chariot, he was
Acts 14: 8 strength in his feet was **s**
Acts 25: 6 **s** on the judgment seat, he
Col 3: 1 **s** at the right hand of God
Rev 4: 4 I saw twenty-four elders **s**
Rev 17: 3 I saw a woman **s** on a scarlet

SITUATED (*see* SITUATION)
Gen 47:11 Joseph **s** his father and his
Ezek 27: 3 Tyre, "You who are **s** at the
Ezek 46:19 there, a place was **s** at their
Nah 3: 8 Amon that was **s** by the River

SITUATION (*see* SITUATED)
2Ki 2:19 notice, the **s** of this city is

SIVAN
Esth 8: 9 which is the month of **S**, on

SIX (*see* SIXTH)
Gen 7: 6 Noah was **s** hundred years old
Gen 7:11 In the **s** hundredth year of
Gen 8:13 came to pass in the **s** hundred
Gen 30:20 I have borne him **s** sons
Gen 31:41 **s** years for your flock, and
Ex 12:37 about **s** hundred thousand men
Ex 14: 7 he took **s** hundred choice
Ex 16:26 **S** days you shall gather it,
Ex 20: 9 **S** days you shall labor and do
Ex 20:11 For in **s** days the LORD made
Ex 21: 2 he shall serve **s** years
Ex 23:10 **S** years you shall sow your
Ex 23:12 **S** days you shall do your work
Ex 24:16 the cloud covered it **s** days
Ex 25:32 **s** branches shall come out of
Ex 25:33 so for the **s** branches that
Ex 25:35 according to the **s** branches
Ex 26: 9 **s** curtains by themselves, and
Ex 26:22 you shall make **s** boards
Ex 28:10 **s** of their names on one stone
Ex 28:10 the remaining **s** names on the
Ex 31:15 Work shall be done for **s** days
Ex 31:17 for in **s** days the LORD made
Ex 34:21 **S** days you shall work, but on
Ex 35: 2 Work shall be done for **s** days
Ex 36:16 and **s** curtains by themselves
Ex 36:27 tabernacle he made **s** boards
Ex 37:18 **s** branches came out of its
Ex 37:19 so for the **s** branches coming
Ex 37:21 according to the **s** branches
Ex 38:26 above, for **s** hundred and three
Lev 23: 3 **S** days shall work be done,
Lev 24: 6 **s** in a row, on the pure table
Lev 25: 3 **S** years you shall sow your
Lev 25: 3 **s** years you shall prune your
Num 1:25 forty-five thousand **s** hundred
Num 1:27 thousand **s** hundred
Num 1:46 were numbered were **s** hundred
Num 2: 4 thousand **s** hundred
Num 2:15 forty-five thousand **s** hundred
Num 2:31 thousand **s** hundred
Num 2:32 of the forces were **s** hundred
Num 3:28 **s** hundred keeping charge of
Num 3:34 were **s** thousand two hundred
Num 4:40 were two thousand **s** hundred
Num 7: 3 **s** covered carts and twelve
Num 11:21 are **s** hundred thousand men on
Num 26:41 forty-five thousand **s** hundred
Num 26:51 **s** hundred and one thousand
Num 31:32 was **s** hundred and seventy-five
Num 31:37 of the sheep was **s** hundred
Num 35: 6 appoint **s** cities of refuge
Num 35:13 you shall have **s** cities of
Num 35:15 These **s** cities shall be for
Deut 5:13 **S** days you shall labor and do
Deut 15:12 to you and serves you **s** years
Deut 15:18 in serving you **s** years
Deut 16: 8 **S** days you shall eat
Josh 6: 3 This you shall do **s** days
Josh 6:14 So they did **s** days
Josh 15:59 **s** cities with their villages
Josh 15:62 **s** cities with their villages
Judg 3:31 who killed **s** hundred men of
Judg 12: 7 judged Israel **s** years
Judg 18:11 **s** hundred men of the family
Judg 18:16 The **s** hundred men armed with
Judg 18:17 of the gate with the **s**
Judg 20:47 But **s** hundred men turned and
Ruth 3:15 it, he measured **s** ephahs of
Ruth 3:17 These **s** ephahs of barley he
1Sa 13: 5 and **s** thousand horsemen, and
1Sa 13:15 with him, about **s** hundred men
1Sa 14: 2 him were about **s** hundred men
1Sa 17: 4 whose height was **s** cubits
1Sa 17: 7 weighed **s** hundred shekels
1Sa 23:13 about **s** hundred, arose and
1Sa 27: 2 went over with the **s** hundred
1Sa 30: 9 the **s** hundred men who were
2Sa *2:11 was seven years and **s** months
2Sa 5: 5 **s** months, and in Jerusalem he
2Sa 6:13 of the LORD had gone **s** paces
2Sa 15:18 **s** hundred men who had
2Sa 21:20 who had **s** fingers on each
2Sa 21:20 hand and **s** toes on each foot,
1Ki 6: 6 the middle was **s** cubits wide
1Ki 10:14 Solomon yearly was **s** hundred
1Ki 10:16 **s** hundred shekels of gold
1Ki 10:19 The throne had **s** steps, and
1Ki 10:20 on each side of the **s** steps
1Ki 10:29 imported from Egypt cost **s**
1Ki 11:16 (because for **s** months Joab
1Ki 16:23 **S** years he reigned in Tirzah
2Ki 5: 5 **s** thousand shekels of gold,
2Ki 11: 3 house of the LORD for **s** years
2Ki 13:19 have struck five or **s** times
2Ki 15: 8 Israel in Samaria **s** months
1Ch 3: 4 These **s** were born to him in
1Ch 3: 4 **s** months, and in Jerusalem he
1Ch 3:22 **s** in all

1Ch 4:27 sixteen sons and s daughters
1Ch 7: 2 twenty-two thousand s hundred
1Ch 8:38 Azel had s sons whose names
1Ch 9: 6 s hundred and ninety
1Ch 9:44 Azel had s sons whose names
1Ch 12:24 s thousand eight hundred
1Ch 12:26 Levi four thousand s hundred
1Ch 12:35 thousand s hundred
1Ch 20: 6 s on each hand and s on each
1Ch 21:25 So David gave Ornan s hundred
1Ch 23: 4 s thousand were officers and
1Ch 25: 3 Hashabiah, and Mattithiah, s
1Ch 26:17 On the east were s Levites
2Ch 1:17 from Egypt a chariot for s
2Ch 2: 2 three thousand s hundred to
2Ch 2:17 thousand s hundred
2Ch 2:18 and three thousand s hundred
2Ch 3: 8 He overlaid it with s hundred
2Ch 9:13 Solomon yearly was s hundred
2Ch 9:15 s hundred shekels of hammered
2Ch 9:18 The throne had s steps, with
2Ch 9:19 on each side of the s steps
2Ch 22:12 the house of God for s years
2Ch 26:12 was two thousand s hundred
2Ch 29:33 things were s hundred bulls
2Ch 35: 8 s hundred from the flock, and
Ezra 2:10 Bani, s hundred and forty-two
Ezra 2:11 s hundred and twenty-three
Ezra 2:13 s hundred and sixty-six
Ezra 2:26 Geba, s hundred and
Ezra 2:35 three thousand s hundred
Ezra 2:60 s hundred and fifty-two
Ezra 2:67 and their donkeys s thousand
Ezra 8:26 into their hand s hundred
Neh 5:18 was one ox and s choice sheep
Neh 7:10 Arah, s hundred and fifty-two
Neh 7:15 s hundred and forty-eight
Neh 7:16 s hundred and twenty-eight
Neh 7:18 s hundred and sixty-seven
Neh 7:20 Adin, s hundred and fifty-five
Neh 7:30 Geba, s hundred and
Neh 7:62 s hundred and forty-two
Neh 7:69 and donkeys s thousand seven
Esth 2:12 s months with oil of myrrh,
Esth 2:12 s months with perfumes and
Job 5:19 deliver you in s troubles
Job 42:12 sheep, s thousand camels, one
Prov 6:16 These s things the LORD hates
Is 6: 2 each one had s wings
Jer 34:14 he has served you s years
Jer 52:30 were four thousand s hundred
Ezek 9: 2 suddenly s men came from the
Ezek 40: 5 a measuring rod s cubits long
Ezek 40:12 were s cubits on this side
Ezek 40:12 and s cubits on that side
Ezek 41: 1 s cubits wide on one side and
Ezek 41: 1 s cubits wide on the other
Ezek 41: 3 the entrance, s cubits high
Ezek 41: 5 wall of the temple, s cubits
Ezek 41: 8 rod, that is, s cubits high
Ezek 46: 1 be shut the s working days
Ezek 46: 4 be s lambs without blemish
Ezek 46: 6 blemish, s lambs, and a ram
Dan 3: 1 cubits and its width s cubits
Matt 17: 1 Now after s days Jesus took
Mark 9: 2 Now after s days Jesus took
Luke 4:25 and s months, and there was a
Luke 13:14 There are s days on which men
John 2: 6 there s waterpots of stone
John 12: 1 s days before the Passover,
Acts 11:12 Moreover these s brethren
Acts 18:11 s months, teaching the word
Jas 5:17 for three years and s months
Rev 4: 8 each having s wings, were
Rev 14:20 thousand s hundred furlongs

SIXTEEN (*see* SIXTEENTH)
Gen 46:18 she bore to Jacob: s persons
Ex 26:25 s sockets
Ex 36:30 s sockets of silver
Num 31:40 The persons were s thousand
Num 31:46 and s thousand persons
Num 31:52 was s thousand seven hundred
Josh 15:41 s cities with their villages
Josh 19:22 s cities with their villages
2Ki 13:10 Samaria, and reigned s years
2Ki 14:21 who was s years old, and made
2Ki 15: 2 He was s years old when he
2Ki 15:33 and he reigned s years in
2Ki 16: 2 and he reigned s years in
1Ch 4:27 Shimei had s sons and six
1Ch 24: 4 s heads of their fathers'
2Ch 13:21 sons and s daughters
2Ch 26: 1 who was s years old, and made
2Ch 26: 3 Uzziah was s years old when
2Ch 27: 1 and he reigned s years in
2Ch 27: 8 and he reigned s years in
2Ch 28: 1 and he reigned s years in

SIXTEENTH (*see* SIXTEEN)
1Ch 24:14 to Bilgah, the s to Immer,
1Ch 25:23 the s for Hananiah, his sons
2Ch 29:17 on the s day of the first

SIXTH (*see* SIX)
Gen 1:31 and the morning were the s day
Gen 30:19 again and bore Jacob a s son
Ex 16: 5 it shall be on the s day that
Ex 16:22 And so it was, on the s day
Ex 16:29 He gives you on the s day
Ex 26: 9 you shall double over the s
Lev 25:21 blessing on you in the s year
Num 7:42 On the s day Eliasaph the son
Num 29:29 On the s day present eight
Josh 19:32 The s lot came out to the
2Sa 3: 5 and the s, Ithream, by David's
2Ki 18:10 In the s year of Hezekiah,
1Ch 2:15 Ozem the s, and David the
1Ch 3: 3 the s, Ithream, by his wife
1Ch 12:11 Attai the s, Eliel the
1Ch 24: 9 Malchijah, the s to Mijamin,
1Ch 25:13 the s for Bukkiah, his sons
1Ch 26: 3 the fifth, Jehohanan the s
1Ch 26: 5 Ammiel the s, Issachar the
1Ch 27: 9 The s captain for the s month
Ezra 6:15 which was in the s year of
Neh 3:30 the s son of Zalaph, repaired
Ezek 8: 1 the s year, in the s month
Ezek 46:14 a s of an ephah, and a third
Hag 1: 1 King Darius, in the s month
Hag 1:15 day of the s month, in the
Matt 20: 5 Again he went out about the s
Matt 27:45 Now from the s hour until the
Mark 15:33 Now when the s hour had come,
Luke 1:26 Now in the s month the angel
Luke 1:36 this is now the s month for
Luke 23:44 And it was about the s hour
John 4: 6 It was about the s hour
John 19:14 Passover, and about the s hour
Acts 10: 9 to pray, about the s hour
Rev 6:12 when He opened the s seal
Rev 9:13 Then the s angel sounded
Rev 9:14 saying to the s angel who had
Rev 16:12 Then the s angel poured out
Rev 21:20 the s sardius, the seventh

SIXTY
Gen 25:26 Isaac was s years old when
Lev 27: 3 years old up to s years old
Lev 27: 7 if from s years old and above,
Num 7:88 rams s, the male goats s
Num 7:88 lambs in their first year s
Num 26:27 s thousand five hundred
Deut 3: 4 s cities, all the region of
Josh 13:30 which are in Bashan, s cities
2Sa 2:31 hundred and s men who died
1Ki 4:13 s large cities with walls and
1Ki 4:22 fine flour, s kors of meal,
1Ki 6: 2 LORD, its length was s cubits
2Ki 25:19 s men of the people of the
1Ch 2:21 when he was s years old
1Ch 2:23 Kenath and its towns—s towns
1Ch 5:18 s valiant men, men able to
1Ch 9:13 thousand seven hundred and s
2Ch 3: 3 The length was s cubits (by
2Ch 11:21 and s concubines, and begot
2Ch 11:21 sons and s daughters
2Ch 12: 3 s thousand horsemen, and
Ezra 2: 9 of Zaccai, seven hundred and s
Ezra 2:64 thousand three hundred and s
Ezra 6: 3 laid, its height s cubits
Ezra 6: 3 and its width s cubits
Ezra 8:10 him one hundred and s males
Ezra 8:13 and with them s males
Neh 7:14 of Zaccai, seven hundred and s
Neh 7:66 thousand three hundred and s
Song 3: 7 with s valiant men around it,
Song 6: 8 There are s queens and eighty
Jer 52:25 s men of the people of the
Ezek 40:14 s cubits high, and the court
Dan 3: 1 whose height was s cubits
Matt 13: 8 some a hundredfold, some s
Matt 13:23 some a hundredfold, some s
Mark 4: 8 some thirtyfold, some s, and
Mark 4:20 some thirtyfold, some s, and
1Ti 5: 9 Do not let a widow under s
Rev 11: 3 s days, clothed in sackcloth
Rev 12: 6 two hundred and s days

SIXTY-EIGHT
1Ch 16:38 Obed-Edom with his s brethren
Neh 11: 6 four hundred and s valiant men

SIXTY-FIVE
Gen 5:15 Mahalaleel lived s years, and
Gen 5:21 Enoch lived s years, and begot
Gen 5:23 were three hundred and s years
Num 3:50 s shekels, according to the
Is 7: 8 Within s years Ephraim will

SIXTY-FOUR
Num 26:25 s thousand three hundred
Num 26:43 were s thousand four hundred

SIXTY-NINE
Gen 5:27 were nine hundred and s years

SIXTY-ONE
Num 31:34 s thousand donkeys,
Num 31:39 the LORD's tribute was s
Ezra 2:69 work s thousand gold drachmas

SIXTY-SEVEN
Neh 7:18 of Adonikam, six hundred and s
Neh 7:19 of Bigvai, two thousand and s
Neh 7:72 minas, and s priestly garments

SIXTY-SIX
Gen 46:26 wives, were s persons in all
Lev 12: 5 of her purification s days
1Ki 10:14 hundred and s talents of gold,
2Ch 9:13 hundred and s talents of gold,
Ezra 2:13 of Adonikam, six hundred and s

SIXTY-TWO
Gen 5:18 and s years, and begot Enoch
Gen 5:20 were nine hundred and s years
Num 1:39 were s thousand seven hundred
Num 2:26 at s thousand seven hundred
1Ch 26: 8 for the work: s of Obed-Edom
Dan 5:31 being about s years old
Dan 9:25 be seven weeks and s weeks
Dan 9:26 after the s weeks Messiah

SIZE (*see* SIZES)
Ex 36: 9 curtains were all the same s
Ex 36:15 curtains were the same s
1Ki 6:25 cherubim were of the same s
1Ki 7: 9 of costly stones hewn to s
1Ki 7:11 were costly stones, hewn to s
Ezek 40:10 the three were all the same s
Ezek 40:10 of the same s on this side
Ezek 46:22 four corners were the same s

SIZES (*see* SIZE)
1Ch 23:29 all kinds of measures and s

SKIES (*see* SKY)
2Sa 22:12 and thick clouds of the s
Job 37:18 have you spread out the s
Job 37:21 when it is bright in the s
Ps 18:11 And thick clouds of the s
Ps 77:17 The s sent out a sound
Is 45: 8 above, and let the s pour down
Jer 51: 9 and is lifted up to the s

SKIFF
Acts 27:16 Clauda, we secured the s with
Acts 27:30 let down the s into the sea
Acts 27:32 cut away the ropes of the s

SKILL (*see* SKILLED, SKILLFUL, UNSKILLED)
Ex 35:35 He has filled them with s to
1Ki 5: 6 has s to cut timber like the
1Ki 7:14 s in working with all kinds
2Ch 2: 7 who has s to engrave with the
2Ch 2: 8 that your servants have s to
Ps 137: 5 my right hand forget her s
Eccl 2:21 with wisdom, knowledge, and s
Eccl 9:11 nor favor to men of s
Dan 1:17 s in all literature and wisdom
Dan 9:22 to give you s to understand
Hos 13: 2 silver, according to their s

SKILLED (*see* SKILL)
2Ch 2:14 s to work in gold and silver,
Ezra 7: 6 he was a s scribe in the Law

SKILLFUL (*see* SKILL, SKILLFULLY, SKILLFULNESS)
Gen 25:27 And Esau was a s hunter, a man
Ex 35:10 All who are s among you
1Sa 16:16 who is a s player on the harp
1Sa 16:18 who is s in playing, a mighty
1Ch 5:18 s in war, who went to war
1Ch 15:22 the music, because he was s
1Ch 22:15 all types of s men for every
1Ch 25: 7 of the LORD, all who were s
2Ch 2: 7 once a man s to work in gold
2Ch 2: 7 the s men who are with me in
2Ch 2:13 And now I have sent a s man
2Ch 2:14 given to him, with your s men
2Ch 2:14 with the s men of my lord
2Ch 26:15 Jerusalem, invented by s men
2Ch 34:12 all of whom were s with
Eccl 4: 4 every s work a man is envied
Song 7: 1 of the hands of a s workman
Is 3: 3 the s artisan, and the expert
Is 40:20 He seeks for himself a s
Jer 9:17 send for s wailing women,
Jer 10: 9 are all the work of s men
Ezek 21:31 men who are s to destroy
Amos 5:16 and s lamenters to wailing

SKILLFULLY (*see* SKILLFUL)
Ex 28: 4 a s woven tunic, a turban, and
Ex 28:39 You shall s weave the tunic
Ps 33: 3 Play s with a shout of joy
Ps 58: 5 charmers, Charming ever so s
Ps 139:15 s wrought in the lowest parts
Prov 30:28 the spider s grasps with its

SKILLFULNESS (*see* SKILLFUL)
Ps 78:72 them by the s of his hands

SKIN (*see* SKINNED, SKINS, SMOOTH-SKINNED)
Gen 3:21 the LORD God made tunics of s
Gen 21:14 and took bread and a s of water
Gen 21:15 water in the s was used up
Gen 21:19 and filled the s with water
Ex 22:27 it is his garment for his s
Ex 29:14 flesh of the bull, with its s
Ex 34:29 s of his face shone while he
Ex 34:30 the s of his face shone, and
Ex 34:35 that the s of Moses' face
Lev 1: 6 he shall s the burnt offering
Lev 7: 8 shall have for himself the s
Lev 11:32 wood or clothing or s or sack
Lev 13: 2 When a man has on the s of
Lev 13: 2 it becomes on the s of his
Lev 13: 3 the sore on the s of the body
Lev 13: 3 deeper than the s of his body
Lev 13: 4 is white on the s of his body
Lev 13: 4 to be deeper than the s, and
Lev 13: 5 sore has not spread on the s
Lev 13: 6 sore has not spread on the s
Lev 13: 7 at all spread over the s,
Lev 13: 8 has indeed spread on the s
Lev 13:10 swelling on the s is white
Lev 13:11 leprosy on the s of his body
Lev 13:12 breaks out all over the s
Lev 13:12 the leprosy covers all the s
Lev 13:18 body develops a boil in the s
Lev 13:20 appears deeper than the s
Lev 13:21 it is not deeper than the s
Lev 13:22 at all spread over the s,
Lev 13:24 a burn on its s by fire, and
Lev 13:25 it appears deeper than the s
Lev 13:26 it is not deeper than the s
Lev 13:27 has at all spread over the s
Lev 13:28 and has not spread on the s
Lev 13:30 it appears deeper than the s
Lev 13:31 not appear deeper than the s
Lev 13:32 not appear deeper than the s
Lev 13:34 has not spread over the s
Lev 13:34 not appear deeper than the s
Lev 13:35 the s after his cleansing
Lev 13:36 scall has spread over the s
Lev 13:38 spots on the s of the body
Lev 13:39 s of the body are dull white
Lev 13:39 spot that grows on the s
Lev 13:43 leprosy on the s of the body
Num 6: 4 the grapevine, from seed to s
1Sa 1:24 a s of wine, and brought him
1Sa 10: 3 another carrying a s of wine
1Sa 16:20 a s of wine, and a young goat,
2Sa 16: 1 summer fruits, and a s of wine
2Ch 29:34 so that they could not s all
Job 2: 4 LORD and said, "S for s
Job 7: 5 my s is cracked and breaks out
Job 10:11 clothe me with s and flesh, and
Job 16:15 have sewn sackcloth over my s
Job 18:13 It devours patches of his s
Job 19:20 My bone clings to my s and to
Job 19:20 escaped by the s of my teeth
Job 19:26 after my s is destroyed, this
Job 30:30 My s grows black and falls
Job 41: 7 you fill his s with harpoons
Ps 102: 5 My bones cling to my s
Is 18: 2 a nation tall and smooth of s
Is 18: 7 a people tall and smooth of s
Jer 13:23 s or the leopard its spots
Lam 3: 4 He has aged my flesh and my s
Lam 4: 8 their s clings to their bones
Lam 5:10 Our s is hot as an oven,
Ezek 16:10 gave you sandals of badger s
Ezek 37: 6 upon you, cover you with s
Ezek 37: 8 and the s covered them over
Mic 3: 2 who strip the s from My
Mic 3: 3 flay their s from them,

SKINNED (*see* SKIN)
2Ch 35:11 the Levites s the animals

SKINS (*see* SKIN)
Gen 27:16 she put the s of the kids of
Ex 25: 5 s dyed red, badger s, and
Ex 26:14 rams' s dyed red for the tent
Ex 26:14 of badger s above that
Ex 35: 7 s dyed red, badger s, and
Ex 35:23 red s of rams, and badger
Ex 35:23 s of rams, and badger s
Ex 36:19 the tent of rams' s dyed red
Ex 36:19 of badger s above that
Ex 39:34 covering of rams' s dyed red
Ex 39:34 the covering of badger s
Lev 16:27 burn in the fire their s,
Num 4: 6 on it a covering of badger s
Num 4: 8 with a covering of badger s
Num 4:10 in a covering of badger s
Num 4:11 with a covering of badger s
Num 4:12 with a covering of badger s
Num 4:14 on it a covering of badger s
Num 4:25 of badger s that is on it
1Sa 25:18 two s of wine, five sheep

SKIP (*see* SKIPPED, SKIPPING)
Ps 29: 6 makes them also s like a calf

SKIPPED (*see* SKIP)
Ps 114: 4 The mountains s like rams
Ps 114: 6 that you s like rams

SKIPPING (*see* SKIP)
Song 2: 8 mountains, s upon the hills

SKIRT (*see* SKIRTED, SKIRTS)
Is 47: 2 your veil, take off the s

SKIRTED (*see* SKIRT)
Deut 2: 1 we s Mount Seir for many days
Deut 2: 3 You have s this mountain
Matt 15:29 s the Sea of Galilee, and went

SKIRTS (*see* SKIRT)
Jer 2:34 Also on your s is found the
Jer 13:22 your s have been uncovered
Jer 13:26 uncover your s over your face
Lam 1: 9 Her uncleanness is in her s
Nah 3: 5 lift your s over your face

SKULL
Judg 9:53 head and crushed his s
2Ki 9:35 no more of her than the s
Matt 27:33 that is to say, Place of a S
Mark 15:22 is translated, Place of a S
John 19:17 place called the Place of a S

SKY (*see* SKIES)
1Ki 18:45 s became black with clouds
Ps 89:37 the faithful witness in the s
Amos 9: 6 builds His layers in the s
Matt 16: 2 weather, for the s is red'
Matt 16: 3 today, for the s is red and
Matt 16: 3 to discern the face of the s
Luke 12:56 can discern the face of the s
Heb 11:12 stars of the s in multitude
Rev 6:14 Then the s receded as a

SLABS
1Ch 29: 2 and marble s in abundance

SLACK (*see* SLACKEN, SLACKNESS)
Deut 7:10 He will not be s with him who
Prov 10: 4 with a s hand becomes poor
2Pe 3: 9 The Lord is not s concerning

SLACKEN (*see* SLACK)
2Ki 4:24 do not s the pace for me

SLACKNESS (*see* SLACK)
2Pe 3: 9 His promise, as some count s

SLAIN (*see* SLAY)
Gen 34:27 sons of Jacob came upon the s
Lev 14:51 in the blood of the s bird
Num 19:16 field touches one who is s by
Num 19:18 one who touched a bone, the s
Num 23:24 and drinks the blood of the s
Num 31:19 and whoever has touched any s
Deut 21: 1 If anyone is found s, lying
Deut 21: 2 the distance from the s man
Deut 21: 3 the s man will take a heifer
Deut 21: 6 s man shall wash their hands
Deut 32:42 with the blood of the s and
Josh 11: 6 all of them s before Israel
Judg 15:16 I have s a thousand men
1Sa 18: 7 Saul has s his thousands, and
1Sa 21:11 Saul has s his thousands, and
1Sa 29: 5 Saul has s his thousands, and
1Sa 31: 1 and fell s on Mount Gilboa
1Sa 31: 8 came to strip the s, that
2Sa 1:19 is s on your high places
2Sa 1:22 From the blood of the s, from
2Sa 1:25 Jonathan was s in your high
1Ki 11:15 had gone up to bury the s
2Ki 11:20 for they had s Athaliah with
1Ch 10: 1 and fell s on Mount Gilboa
1Ch 10: 8 came to strip the s, that
2Ch 13:17 choice men of Israel fell s
2Ch 23:21 for they had s Athaliah with
Job 39:30 and where the s are, there it
Ps 62: 3 You shall be s, all of you,
Ps 88: 5 Like the s who lie in the
Ps 89:10 in pieces, as one who is s
Prov 7:26 all who were s by her were
Prov 22:13 I shall be s in the streets
Is 10: 4 they shall fall among the s
Is 14:19 garment of those who are s
Is 14:20 your land and s your people
Is 22: 2 Your s men are not s with
Is 26:21 and will no more cover her s
Is 27: 7 Or has He been s according to
Is 27: 7 of those who were s by Him
Is 34: 3 Also their s shall be thrown
Is 66:16 the s of the LORD shall be
Jer 9: 1 day and night for the s of the
Jer 14:18 those s with the sword
Jer 18:21 their young men be s by the
Jer 25:33 at that day the s of the LORD
Jer 41: 9 of the men whom he had s,
Jer 41: 9 filled it with the s
Jer 51: 4 Thus the s shall fall in the
Jer 51:47 all her s shall fall in her
Jer 51:49 the s of Israel to fall, so
Jer 51:49 so at Babylon the s of all
Lam 2: 4 He has s all who were
Lam 2:20 prophet be s in the sanctuary
Lam 2:21 You have s them in the day of
Lam 3:43 You have s and not pitied
Lam 4: 9 Those s by the sword are
Ezek 6: 4 your s men before your idols
Ezek 6: 7 The s shall fall in your
Ezek 6:13 when their s men are among
Ezek 9: 7 and fill the courts with the s
Ezek 11: 6 your s in this city, and you
Ezek 11: 6 filled its streets with the s
Ezek 11: 7 Your s whom you have laid in
Ezek 16:21 that you have s My children
Ezek 21:29 the s whose day has come,
Ezek 23:39 For after they had s their
Ezek 26: 6 shall be s by the sword
Ezek 28: 8 s in the midst of the seas
Ezek 30: 4 when the s fall in Egypt, and
Ezek 30:11 and fill the land with the s
Ezek 31:17 with those s by the sword
Ezek 31:18 with those s by the sword
Ezek 32:20 midst of those s by the sword
Ezek 32:21 uncircumcised, s by the sword
Ezek 32:22 all around her, all of them s
Ezek 32:23 her grave, all of them s,
Ezek 32:24 her grave, all of them s,
Ezek 32:25 her bed in the midst of the s
Ezek 32:25 uncircumcised, s by the sword
Ezek 32:25 was put in the midst of the s
Ezek 32:26 s by the sword, though they
Ezek 32:28 lie with those s by the sword
Ezek 32:29 those who were s by the sword

Ezek 32:30 the s in shame at the terror
Ezek 32:30 with those s by the sword
Ezek 32:31 s by the sword," says the
Ezek 32:32 with those s by the sword
Ezek 35: 8 fill its mountains with the s
Ezek 35: 8 are s by the sword shall fall
Ezek 37: 9 breath, and breathe on these s
Dan 5:30 king of the Chaldeans, was s
Dan 7:11 watched till the beast was s
Dan 11:26 and many shall fall down s
Hos 6: 5 I have s them by the words of
Nah 3: 3 There is a multitude of s
Zeph 2:12 you shall be s by My sword
Acts 5:36 He was s, and all who obeyed
Heb 11:37 were s with the sword
Rev 5: 6 Lamb as though it had been s
Rev 5: 9 for You were s, and have
Rev 5:12 who was s to receive power
Rev 6: 9 been s for the word of God
Rev 13: 8 Book of Life of the Lamb s
Rev 18:24 all who were s on the earth

SLANDER (*see* SLANDERED, SLANDERER, SLANDEROUSLY, SLANDERS)
Ps 31:13 For I hear the s of many
Ps 50:20 You s your own mother's son
Prov 10:18 whoever spreads s is a fool
Ezek 22: 9 men who s to cause bloodshed

SLANDERED (*see* SLANDER)
2Sa 19:27 he has s your servant to my
Ezek 36: 3 talkers and s by the people"

SLANDERER (*see* SLANDER, SLANDERERS)
Ps 140:11 Let not a s be established in

SLANDERERS (*see* SLANDERER)
Jer 6:28 stubborn rebels, walking as s
Jer 9: 4 neighbor will walk with s
1Ti 3:11 wives must be reverent, not s
2Ti 3: 3 unloving, unforgiving, s,
Tit 2: 3 reverent in behavior, not s

SLANDEROUSLY (*see* SLANDER)
Rom 3: 8 as we are s reported and as

SLANDERS (*see* SLANDER)
Ps 101: 5 secretly s his neighbor, Him

SLAPS
Matt 5:39 But whoever s you on your

SLASH
Hos 11: 6 sword shall s in his cities

SLAUGHTER (*see* SLAUGHTERED, SLAUGHTERS)
Gen 43:16 s an animal and make ready
Deut 12:15 However, you may s and eat
Deut 12:21 then you may s from your herd
Josh 10:10 them with a great s at Gibeon
Josh 10:20 them with a very great s,
Judg 11:33 Keramim, with a very great s
Judg 15: 8 hip and thigh with a great s
1Sa 4:10 There was a very great s, and
1Sa 4:17 a great s among the people
1Sa 6:19 the people with a great s
1Sa 14:14 That first s which Jonathan
1Sa 14:30 s among the Philistines
1Sa 14:34 sheep, s them here, and eat
1Sa 17:57 from the s of the Philistine
1Sa 18: 6 from the s of the Philistine
2Sa 1: 1 from the s of the Amalekites
2Sa 17: 9 say, "There is a s among the
2Sa 18: 7 a great s of twenty thousand
1Ki 20:21 the Syrians with a great s
2Ch 13:17 struck them with a great s
2Ch 25:14 from the s of the Edomites
2Ch 28: 5 defeated him with a great s
2Ch 30:17 s of the Passover lambs for
2Ch 35: 6 So s the Passover offerings,
Esth 9: 5 stroke of the sword, with s
Ps 44:22 accounted as sheep for the s
Prov 7:22 her, as an ox goes to the s
Prov 24:11 back those stumbling to the s
Is 10:26 s of Midian at the rock of
Is 14:21 Prepare s for his children
Is 27: 7 s of those who were slain by
Is 30:25 in the day of the great s
Is 34: 2 has given them over to the s
Is 34: 6 a great s in the land of Edom
Is 53: 7 He was led as a lamb to the s
Is 65:12 shall all bow down to the s
Jer 7:32 Hinnom, but the Valley of S
Jer 11:19 docile lamb brought to the s
Jer 12: 3 them out like sheep for the s
Jer 12: 3 prepare them for the day of s
Jer 19: 6 Hinnom, but the Valley of S
Jer 25:34 For the days of your s and
Jer 48:15 men have gone down to the s
Jer 50:27 let them go down to the s
Jer 51:40 them down like lambs to the s
Ezek 21:10 to make a dreadful s,
Ezek 21:15 it is grasped for s
Ezek 21:22 rams, to call for a s, to
Ezek 21:28 is drawn, polished for s, for
Ezek 26:15 when s is made in the midst
Ezek 34: 3 you s the fatlings, but you
Hos 5: 2 are deeply involved in s,
Obad 9 of Esau may be cut off by s
Zech 11: 4 Feed the flock for s,
Zech 11: 5 whose owners s them and feel
Zech 11: 7 So I fed the flock for s, in
Acts 8:32 was led as a sheep to the s
Rom 8:36 accounted as sheep for the s
Heb 7: 1 from the s of the kings and
Jas 5: 5 your hearts as in a day of s

SLAUGHTERED (*see* SLAUGHTER)
Num 11:22 flocks and herds be s for them
Num 19: 3 and it shall be s before him
Deut 28:31 shall be s before your eyes
1Sa 1:25 Then they s a bull, and
1Sa 14:32 and s them on the ground
1Sa 14:34 him that night, and s it there
1Ki 19:21 s them and boiled their flesh,
2Ki 10: 7 s seventy persons, put their
2Ch 30:15 Then they s the Passover
2Ch 35: 1 they s the Passover lambs on
2Ch 35:11 they s the Passover offerings
Ezra 6:20 they s the Passover lambs for
Prov 9: 2 she has s her meat, she has
Lam 2:21 day of Your anger, you have s
Ezek 40:41 which they s the sacrifices
Ezek 40:42 they s the burnt offering
Acts 7:42 Did you offer Me s animals

SLAUGHTERS (*see* SLAUGHTER)
Ex 22: 1 s it or sells it, he shall

SLAVE (*see* SLAVERY, SLAVES)
Gen 44:10 it is found shall be my s
Gen 44:17 was found, he shall be my s
Gen 44:33 of the lad as a s to my lord
Lev 25:39 compel him to serve as a s
Deut 5:15 were a s in the land of Egypt
Deut 15:15 were a s in the land of Egypt
Deut 16:12 that you were a s in Egypt
Deut 23:15 s who has escaped from his
Deut 24:18 that you were a s in Egypt
Deut 24:22 were a s in the land of Egypt
Ps 105:17 who was sold as a s
Jer 2:14 is he a homeborn s
Jer 34: 9 set free his male and female s
Lam 1: 1 the provinces has become a s
Matt 20:27 among you, let him be your s
Mark 10:44 to be first shall be s of all
John 8:34 commits sin is a s of sin
John 8:35 a s does not abide in the
Acts 16:16 prayer, that a certain s girl
1Co 7:21 Were you called while a s
1Co 7:22 a s is the Lord's freedman
1Co 7:22 while free is Christ's s
Gal 3:28 there is neither s nor free
Gal 4: 1 not differ at all from a s
Gal 4: 7 are no longer a s but a son
Eph 6: 8 whether he is a s or free
Col 3:11 s nor free, but Christ is all
Phm 16 as a s but more than a s
Rev 6:15 the mighty men, every s and
Rev 13:16 rich and poor, free and s, to
Rev 19:18 of all people, free and s,

SLAVERY (*see* SLAVE)
Neh 5: 5 are brought into s already

SLAVES (*see* SLAVE)
Gen 43:18 us, to take us as s with our
Gen 44: 9 we also will be my lord's s
Gen 44:16 here we are, my lord's s,
Gen 49:15 burden, and became a band of s
Lev 25:42 they shall not be sold as s
Lev 25:44 female s whom you may have
Lev 25:44 you may buy male and female s
Lev 25:46 shall be your permanent s
Lev 26:13 you should not be their s
Deut 6:21 We were s of Pharaoh in
Deut 28:68 enemies as male and female s
Josh 9:23 shall be freed from being s
1Ki 2:39 that two s of Shimei ran away
1Ki 2:39 Look, your s are in Gath
1Ki 2:40 Achish at Gath to seek his s
1Ki 2:40 and brought his s from Gath
2Ki 4: 1 take my two sons to be his s
2Ch 28:10 to be your male and female s
Ezra 9: 9 For we were s
Neh 5: 5 sons and our daughters to be s
Esth 7: 4 been sold as male and female s
Jer 34:10 set free his male and female s
Jer 34:11 the male and female s return
Jer 34:11 as male and female s
Jer 34:16 back his male and female s
Jer 34:16 to be your male and female s
Rom 6: 6 should no longer be s of sin
Rom 6:16 present yourselves s to obey
Rom 6:16 that one's s whom you obey
Rom 6:17 that though you were s of sin
Rom 6:18 you became s of righteousness
Rom 6:19 members as s of uncleanness
Rom 6:19 as s of righteousness for
Rom 6:20 For when you were s of sin
Rom 6:22 and having become s of God
1Co 7:23 do not become s of men
1Co 12:13 or Greeks, whether s or free
2Pe 2:19 are s of corruption

SLAY (*see* SLAIN, SLAYER, SLAYING, SLAYS, SLEW)
Gen 18:25 to s the righteous with the
Gen 20: 4 will You s a righteous nation
Gen 22:10 took the knife to s his son
Lev 4:33 s it as a sin offering at the
Deut 27:25 bribe to s an innocent person
2Ki 11:15 and s with the sword whoever
2Ch 23:14 and s with the sword whoever
Job 13:15 Though He s me, yet will I
Job 20:16 the viper's tongue will s him
Ps 34:21 Evil shall s the wicked, And
Ps 37:14 To s those who are of upright
Ps 37:32 righteous, And seeks to s him
Ps 59:11 Do not s them, lest my people
Ps 94: 6 They s the widow and the
Ps 109:16 man, That he might even s the
Ps 139:19 that You would s the wicked
Prov 1:32 of the simple will s them
Is 11: 4 lips He shall s the wicked
Is 14:30 and it will s your remnant
Is 27: 1 He will s the reptile that is
Is 65:15 for the Lord GOD will s you
Jer 5: 6 from the forest shall s them
Jer 15: 3 the sword to s, the dogs to
Jer 18:23 which is against me, to s me
Jer 20: 4 and s them with the sword
Jer 29:21 he shall s them before your
Jer 33: 5 men whom I will s in My anger
Jer 50:27 S all her bulls, let them go
Ezek 9: 6 Utterly s old and young men,
Ezek 23:47 they shall s their sons and
Ezek 26: 8 He will s with the sword
Ezek 26:11 he will s your people by the
Ezek 40:39 side, on which to s the burnt
Ezek 44:11 they shall s the burnt
Hos 2: 3 land, and s her with thirst
Amos 2: 3 s all its princes with him,"
Amos 9: 1 I will s the last of them
Amos 9: 4 the sword, and it shall s them
Hab 1:17 continue to s nations without
Luke 19:27 them, and s them before me

SLAYER (*see* SLAY)
Josh 20: 3 that the s who kills any
Josh 20: 5 deliver the s into his hand
Josh 20: 6 Then the s may return and come
Josh 21:13 (a city of refuge for the s)
Josh 21:21 (a city of refuge for the s)
Josh 21:27 (a city of refuge for the s)
Josh 21:32 (a city of refuge for the s)
Josh 21:38 (a city of refuge for the s)
Ezek 21:11 given into the hand of the s

SLAYING (*see* SLAY)
Josh 8:24 s all the inhabitants of Ai
Josh 10:20 of s them with a very great
Is 22:13 s oxen and killing sheep,
Is 57: 5 s the children in the valleys

SLAYS (*see* SLAY)
Job 5: 2 man, and envy s a simple one
Job 9:23 If the scourge s suddenly
Is 66: 3 a bull is as if he s a man

Ezek 21:14 it is the sword that s, the
Ezek 21:14 sword that s the great men
Ezek 28: 9 say before him who s you, "I
Ezek 28: 9 in the hand of him who s you

SLEDGE
Is 28:27 threshed with a threshing s
Is 41:15 threshing s with sharp teeth

SLEEK
Jer 5:28 have grown fat, they are s

SLEEP (*see* SLEEPER, SLEEPING, SLEEPLESSNESS, SLEEPS, SLEPT)
Gen 2:21 a deep s to fall on Adam, and
Gen 15:12 a deep s fell upon Abram
Gen 28:11 lay down in that place to s
Gen 28:16 Then Jacob awoke from his s
Gen 31:40 my s departed from my eyes
Ex 22:27 What will he s in
Deut 24:13 that he may s in his own
Judg 16:14 But he awoke from his s
Judg 16:19 lulled him to s on her knees
Judg 16:20 So he awoke from his s, and
1Sa 3: 3 Samuel was lying down to s
1Sa 26:12 because a deep s from the
Esth 6: 1 night the king could not s
Job 4:13 when deep s falls on men,
Job 14:12 nor be roused from their s
Job 33:15 when deep s falls upon men,
Ps 4: 8 both lie down in peace, and s
Ps 13: 3 Lest I s the s of death
Ps 44:23 Why do You s, O Lord
Ps 76: 5 They have sunk into their s
Ps 76: 6 horse were cast into a dead s
Ps 78:65 Lord awoke as one out of s
Ps 90: 5 They are like a s
Ps 121: 4 Shall neither slumber nor s
Ps 127: 2 For so He gives His beloved s
Ps 132: 4 I will not give s to my eyes
Prov 3:24 down and your s will be sweet
Prov 4:16 For they do not s unless they
Prov 4:16 their s is taken away unless
Prov 6: 4 Give no s to your eyes, nor
Prov 6: 9 will you rise from your s
Prov 6:10 A little s, a little slumber,
Prov 6:10 folding of the hands to s
Prov 6:22 when you s, they will keep
Prov 19:15 casts one into a deep s, and
Prov 20:13 Do not love s, lest you come
Prov 24:33 a little s, a little slumber,
Eccl 5:12 The s of a laboring man is
Eccl 5:12 rich will not permit him to s
Eccl 8:16 one sees no s day or night
Song 5: 2 I s, but my heart is awake
Is 5:27 No one will slumber or s
Is 14:18 s in glory, everyone in his
Is 29:10 on you the spirit of deep s
Jer 31:26 and my s was sweet to me
Jer 51:39 and s a perpetual s and
Jer 51:57 shall s a perpetual s
Ezek 34:25 wilderness and s in the woods
Dan 2: 1 troubled that his s left him
Dan 6:18 Also his s went from him
Dan 8:18 I was in a deep s with my
Dan 10: 9 I was in a deep s on my face
Dan 12: 2 many of those who s in the
Zech 4: 1 who is wakened out of his s
Matt 1:24 Joseph, being aroused from s
Mark 4:27 should s by night and rise by
Luke 9:32 with him were heavy with s
Luke 22:46 said to them, "Why do you s
John 11:13 about taking rest in s
Acts 16:27 of the prison, awaking from s
Acts 20: 9 who was sinking into a deep s
Acts 20: 9 He was overcome by s
Rom 13:11 high time to awake out of s
1Co 11:30 and sick among you, and many s
1Co 15:51 We shall not all s, but we
Eph 5:14 Awake, you who s, arise from
1Th 4:14 with Him those who s in Jesus
1Th 5: 6 Therefore let us not s, as
1Th 5: 7 For those who s, s at night
1Th 5:10 us, that whether we wake or s

SLEEPER (*see* SLEEP, SLEEPERS)
Jon 1: 6 What do you mean, s

SLEEPERS (*see* SLEEPER)
Song 7: 9 moving gently the lips of s

SLEEPING (*see* SLEEP)
1Sa 26: 7 there Saul lay s within the
1Ki 18:27 a journey, or perhaps he is s
Is 56:10 s, lying down, loving to
Matt 9:24 the girl is not dead, but s
Matt 26:45 Are you still s and resting
Mark 5:39 The child is not dead, but s
Mark 13:36 suddenly, he find you s
Mark 14:37 Then He came and found them s
Mark 14:37 Simon, are you s
Mark 14:41 Are you still s and resting
Luke 8:52 she is not dead, but s
Luke 22:45 He found them s from sorrow
Acts 12: 6 out, that night Peter was s

SLEEPLESSNESS (*see* SLEEP)
2Co 6: 5 in tumults, in labors, in s
2Co 11:27 in s often, in hunger and

SLEEPS (*see* SLEEP)
Prov 10: 5 but he who s in harvest is a
Hos 7: 6 their baker s all night
John 11:11 Our friend Lazarus s, but I
John 11:12 if he s he will get well

SLEEVE (*see* SLEEVES)
Zech 8:23 grasp the s of a Jewish man

SLEEVES (*see* SLEEVE)
Ezek 13:18 sew magic charms on their s

SLEPT (*see* SLEEP)
Gen 2:21 to fall on Adam, and he s
Gen 41: 5 He s and dreamed a second time
2Sa 11: 9 But Uriah s at the door of
1Ki 3:20 while your maidservant s
1Ki 19: 5 lay and s under a broom tree,
Ps 3: 5 I lay down and s
Matt 13:25 but while men s, his enemy
Matt 25: 5 they all slumbered and s
Matt 28:13 and stole Him away while we s

SLEW (*see* SLAY)
Gen 49: 6 in their anger they s a man
Ps 78:31 s the stoutest of them, And
Ps 78:34 When He s them, then they
Ps 135:10 nations And s mighty kings
Ps 136:18 s famous kings, For His mercy
Ezek 23:10 and s her with the sword

SLICED
2Ki 4:39 s them into the pot of stew,

SLIDDEN (*see* SLIDE)
Jer 8: 5 then has this people s back

SLIDE (*see* SLIDDEN)
Ps 37:31 None of his steps shall s

SLIGHTED
Prov 12: 9 who is s but has a servant

SLIGHTLY
Jer 6:14 the hurt of My people s,
Jer 8:11 the daughter of My people s

SLING (*see* SLINGERS, SLINGS, SLINGSTONES, SLUNG)
Judg 20:16 every one could s a stone at
1Sa 17:40 had, and his s was in his hand
1Sa 17:50 over the Philistine with a s
1Sa 25:29 your enemies He shall s out
1Sa 25:29 as from the pocket of a s
Prov 26: 8 s is he who gives honor to a
Zech 9:15 and subdue with s stones

SLINGERS (*see* SLING)
2Ki 3:25 However the s surrounded and

SLINGS (*see* SLING)
2Ch 26:14 bows, and s to cast stones

SLINGSTONES (*see* SLING)
Job 41:28 s become like stubble to him

SLIP (*see* SLIPPED, SLIPPERY, SLIPS)
Deut 32:35 foot shall s in due time
2Sa 22:37 so my feet did not s
1Ki 20:42 Because you have let s out
Job 12: 5 ready for those whose feet s
Ps 17: 5 That my footsteps may not s
Ps 18:36 So that my feet did not s
Ps 26: 1 I shall not s

SLIPPED (*see* SLIP)
1Sa 19:10 but he s away from Saul's
Ps 73: 2 My steps had nearly s

SLIPPERY (*see* SLIP)
Ps 35: 6 Let their way be dark and s
Ps 73:18 You set them in s places
Jer 23:12 shall be to them like s ways

SLIPS (*see* SLIP)
Deut 19: 5 the head s from the handle and
Ps 38:16 over me, Lest, when my foot s
Ps 94:18 My foot s," Your mercy, O

SLOOPS
Is 2:16 and upon all the beautiful s

SLOPE (*see* SLOPES)
Num 21:15 and the s of the brooks that
Josh 15: 8 of Hinnom to the southern s

SLOPES (*see* SLOPE)
Deut 3:17 Sea), below the s of Pisgah
Deut 4:49 Arabah, below the s of Pisgah
Josh 10:40 lowland and the wilderness s
Josh 12: 3 below the s of Pisgah
Josh 12: 8 in the Jordan plain, in the s
Josh 13:20 the s of Pisgah, and Beth

SLOTHFUL (*see* SLOTHFULNESS)
Prov 12:24 but the s will be put to
Prov 12:27 The s man does not roast what
Prov 15:19 The way of the s man is like
Prov 18: 9 He who is s in his work is a
Prov 19:24 A s man buries his hand in
Prov 21:25 The desire of the s kills him
Prov 22:13 The s man says, "There is a
Prov 24:30 I went by the field of the s
Prov 26:13 The s man says, "There is a
Prov 26:14 so does the s turn on his bed
Prov 26:15 The s man buries his hand in

SLOTHFULNESS (*see* SLOTHFUL)
Prov 19:15 S casts one into a deep sleep

SLOW (*see* SLOWLY)
Ex 4:10 s of speech and s of tongue
Neh 9:17 s to anger, abundant in
Ps 103: 8 S to anger, and abounding in
Ps 145: 8 S to anger and great in mercy
Prov 14:29 He who is s to wrath has
Prov 15:18 but he who is s to anger
Prov 16:32 He who is s to anger is
Prov 19:11 of a man makes him s to anger
Joel 2:13 s to anger, and of great
Jon 4: 2 s to anger and abundant in
Nah 1: 3 the LORD is s to anger and
Luke 24:25 s of heart to believe in all
Jas 1:19 s to speak, s to wrath

SLOWLY (*see* SLOW)
Gen 33:14 I will lead on s at a pace
Acts 27: 7 we had sailed s many days

SLUGGARD
Prov 6: 6 Go to the ant, you s
Prov 6: 9 long will you slumber, O s
Prov 10:26 so is the s to those who send
Prov 13: 4 the soul of a s desires, and
Prov 20: 4 The s will not plow because
Prov 26:16 The s is wiser in his own

SLUGGISH
Heb 6:12 that you do not become s, but

SLUMBER (*see* SLUMBERED, SLUMBERING)
Ps 121: 3 He who keeps you will not s
Ps 121: 4 Shall neither s nor sleep
Ps 132: 4 to my eyes Or s to my eyelids
Prov 6: 4 eyes, nor s to your eyelids
Prov 6: 9 How long will you s, O
Prov 6:10 A little sleep, a little s
Prov 24:33 a little sleep, a little s
Is 5:27 them, No one will s or sleep
Is 56:10 lying down, loving to s
Nah 3:18 Your shepherds s, O king of
2Pe 2: 3 their destruction does not s

SLUMBERED (*see* SLUMBER)
Matt 25: 5 was delayed, they all s and

SLUMBERING (*see* SLUMBER)
Job 33:15 men, while s on their beds,

SLUNG (*see* SLING)
1Sa 17:49 and he s it and struck the

SMALL (*see* SMALLER, SMALLEST)
Gen 19:11 house with blindness, both s
Gen 30:15 Is it a s matter that you
Ex 12: 4 is too s for the lamb, let
Ex 16:14 was a s round substance, as

Ex 18:22 you, but every s matter they
Ex 18:26 every s case themselves
Num 16: 9 Is it a s thing to you that
Num 16:13 Is it a s thing that you have
Num 26:54 to a s tribe you shall give a
Num 32:41 went and took its s towns, and
Deut 1:17 you shall hear the s as well
Deut 9:21 it and ground it very s, until
Deut 25:14 measures, a large and a s
1Sa 5: 9 the men of the city, both s
1Sa 20: 2 or s without first telling me
1Sa 30: 2 were there, from s to great
1Sa 30:19 either s or great, sons or
2Sa 7:19 yet this was a s thing in
2Sa 17:13 not one s stone found there
1Ki 2:20 I desire one s petition of
1Ki 8:64 too s to receive the burnt
1Ki 17:13 but make me a s cake from it
1Ki 18:44 as s as a man's hand, rising
1Ki 19:12 the fire a still s voice
1Ki 22:31 Fight with no one s or great
2Ki 4:10 let us make a s upper room on
2Ki 6: 1 with you is too s for us
2Ki 23: 2 and all the people, both s
2Ki 25:26 And all the people, s and great
1Ch 17:17 yet this was a s thing in
1Ch 25: 8 the s as well as the great,
1Ch 26:13 the s as well as the great,
2Ch 15:13 whether s or great, whether
2Ch 18:30 Fight with no one s or great
2Ch 23: 9 s shields which had been King
2Ch 24:24 came with a s company of men
2Ch 31:15 to the great as well as the s
2Ch 34:30 and all the people, great and s
2Ch 36:18 the house of God, great and s
Neh 9:32 s before You that has come
Esth 1: 5 the citadel, from great to s
Esth 1:20 husbands, both great and s
Job 3:19 The s and great are there, and
Job 8: 7 Though your beginning was s
Job 15:11 of God too s for you, and the
Job 26:14 how s a whisper we hear of
Ps 104:25 things, Living things both s
Ps 115:13 who fear the LORD, Both s
Ps 119:141 I am s and despised, Yet I do
Prov 24:10 adversity, your strength is s
Is 1: 9 left to us a very s remnant
Is 7:13 Is it a s thing for you to
Is 16:14 and the remnant will be very s
Is 22:24 all vessels of s quantity
Is 40:15 are counted as the s dust on
Is 41:15 the mountains and beat them s
Is 49: 6 It is too s a thing that You
Is 49:19 be too s for the inhabitants
Is 49:20 The place is too s for me
Is 60:22 and a s one a strong nation
Jer 16: 6 the s shall die in this land
Jer 30:19 them, and they shall not be s
Jer 44:28 Yet a s number who escape
Jer 49:15 will make you s among nations
Ezek 5: 3 also take a s number of them
Ezek 16:20 acts of harlotry a s matter
Dan 11:23 with a s number of people
Amos 7: 2 Jacob may stand, for he is s
Amos 7: 5 Jacob may stand, for he is s
Amos 8: 5 Making the ephah s and the
Obad 2 I will make you s among the
Zech 4:10 despised the day of s things
Mark 3: 9 a s boat should be kept ready
Mark 8: 7 And they had a few s fish
John 6: 9 two s fish, but what are they
Acts 12:18 there was no s stir among the
Acts 15: 2 Barnabas had no s dissension
Acts 19:24 brought no s profit to the
Acts 26:22 I stand, witnessing both to s
Acts 27:20 no s tempest beat on us, all
1Co 4: 3 very s thing that I should be
Jas 3: 4 s rudder wherever the pilot
Rev 11:18 those who fear Your name, s
Rev 13:16 And he causes all, both s and
Rev 19: 5 and those who fear Him, both s
Rev 19:18 people, free and slave, both s
Rev 20:12 And I saw the dead, s and great

SMALLER (*see* SMALL)
Num 26:54 shall give a s inheritance
Num 26:56 between the larger and the s
Num 33:54 to the s you shall give a
Num 33:54 shall give a s inheritance
Num 35: 8 from the s you shall give few
Ezek 43:14 from the s ledge to the
Mark 4:31 is s than all the seeds on

SMALLEST (*see* SMALL)
1Sa 9:21 of the s of the tribes of
Amos 9: 9 yet not the s grain shall
1Co 6: 2 to judge the s matters

SMELL (*see* SMELLED, SMELLING, SMELLS)
Gen 27:27 and he smelled the s of his
Gen 27:27 the s of my son is like the
Gen 27:27 s of a field which the LORD
Ex 30:38 makes any like it, to s it
Lev 26:31 I will not s the fragrance of
Deut 4:28 see nor hear nor eat nor s
Ps 115: 6 they have, but they do not s
Song 2:13 tender grapes give a good s
Is 3:24 Instead of a sweet s there
Dan 3:27 the s of fire was not on them

SMELLED (*see* SMELL)
Gen 8:21 the LORD s a soothing aroma
Gen 27:27 and he s the smell of his

SMELLING (*see* SMELL)
1Co 12:17 hearing, where would be the s

SMELLS (*see* SMELL)
Job 39:25 He s the battle from afar,

SMELTED (*see* SMELTER)
Job 28: 2 and copper is s from ore

SMELTER (*see* SMELTED)
Jer 6:29 the s refines in vain, for

SMILE
1Sa 2: 1 I s at my enemies, because I
Job 9:27 off my sad face and wear a s

SMITE (*see* SMITTEN)
Ex 8: 2 I will s all your territory

SMITHS
2Ki 24:14 and all the craftsmen and s
2Ki 24:16 thousand, and craftsmen and s
Jer 24: 1 Judah with the craftsmen and s
Jer 29: 2 and the s had departed from

SMITTEN (*see* SMITE)
Is 53: 4 s by God, and afflicted

SMOKE (*see* SMOKING)
Gen 19:28 the s of the land which went
Gen 19:28 up like the s of a furnace
Ex 19:18 Sinai was completely in s
Ex 19:18 Its s ascended like the s
Josh 8:20 the s of the city ascended to
Josh 8:21 and that the s of the city
Judg 20:38 of s rise up from the city
Judg 20:40 the city in a column of s
Judg 20:40 city going up in s to heaven
2Sa 22: 9 S went up from His nostrils,
Job 41:20 S goes out of his nostrils,
Ps 18: 8 S went up from His nostrils,
Ps 37:20 Into s they shall vanish away
Ps 68: 2 As s is driven away, So drive
Ps 74: 1 Why does Your anger s against
Ps 102: 3 my days are consumed like s
Ps 104:32 touches the hills, and they s
Ps 119:83 become like a wineskin in s
Ps 144: 5 mountains, and they shall s
Prov 10:26 and s to the eyes, so is the
Song 3: 6 wilderness like pillars of s
Is 4: 5 s by day and the shining of a
Is 6: 4 the house was filled with s
Is 9:18 shall mount up like rising s
Is 14:31 for s will come from the
Is 34:10 its s shall ascend forever
Is 51: 6 will vanish away like s, the
Is 65: 5 These are s in My nostrils,
Hos 13: 3 and like s from a chimney
Joel 2:30 blood and fire and pillars of s
Nah 2:13 will burn your chariots in s
Acts 2:19 blood and fire and vapor of s
Rev 8: 4 the s of the incense, with
Rev 9: 2 s arose out of the pit
Rev 9: 2 like the s of a great furnace
Rev 9: 2 because of the s of the pit
Rev 9: 3 Then out of the s locusts
Rev 9:17 of their mouths came fire, s
Rev 9:18 by the fire and the s and the
Rev 14:11 And the s of their torment
Rev 15: 8 with s from the glory of God
Rev 18: 9 they see the s of her burning
Rev 18:18 they saw the s of her burning
Rev 19: 3 her s rises up forever and

SMOKING (*see* SMOKE)
Gen 15:17 behold, there was a s oven
Ex 20:18 trumpet, and the mountain s
Is 7: 4 two stubs of s firebrands
Is 42: 3 s flax He will not quench
Matt 12:20 s flax He will not quench,

SMOOTH (*see* SMOOTHER, SMOOTHLY, SMOOTHS, SMOOTH-SKINNED)
Gen 27:16 on the s part of his neck
1Sa 17:40 five s stones from the brook
Ps 27:11 LORD, And lead me in a s path
Is 18: 2 and s of skin, to a people
Is 18: 7 s of skin, and from a people
Is 30:10 speak to us s things,
Is 40: 4 and the rough places s
Is 57: 6 Among the s stones of the
Jer 12: 6 they speak s words to you
Luke 3: 5 and the rough ways made s
Rom 16:18 and by s words and flattering

SMOOTHER (*see* SMOOTH)
Ps 55:21 his mouth were s than butter
Prov 5: 3 and her mouth is s than oil

SMOOTHLY (*see* SMOOTH)
Prov 23:31 cup, when it swirls around s
Song 7: 9 goes down s for my beloved

SMOOTHS (*see* SMOOTH)
Is 41: 7 and he who s with the hammer

SMOOTH-SKINNED (*see* SKIN, SMOOTH)
Gen 27:11 a hairy man, and I am a s man

SMYRNA
Rev 1:11 to Ephesus, to S, to Pergamos
Rev 2: 8 of the church in S write

SNAIL
Ps 58: 8 Let them be like a s which

SNAKE (*see* SNAKES)
Is 34:15 There the arrow s shall make

SNAKES (*see* SNAKE)
Mic 7:17 holes like s of the earth

SNARE (*see* SNARED, SNARES)
Ex 10: 7 shall this man be a s to us
Ex 23:33 it will surely be a s to you
Ex 34:12 lest it be a s in your midst
Deut 7:16 for that will be a s to you
Judg 2: 3 gods shall be a s to you
Judg 8:27 It became a s to Gideon and to
1Sa 18:21 that she may be a s to him
1Sa 28: 9 do you lay a s for my life
Job 5: 5 a s snatches their substance
Job 18: 8 feet, and he walks into a s
Job 18: 9 heel, and a s lays hold of him
Job 40:24 one pierces his nose with a s
Job 41: 1 or s his tongue with a line
Ps 69:22 table become a s before them
Ps 91: 3 you from the s of the fowler
Ps 106:36 Which became a s to them
Ps 119:110 wicked have laid a s for me
Ps 124: 7 from the s of the fowlers
Ps 124: 7 The s is broken, and we have
Ps 140: 5 proud have hidden a s for me
Ps 142: 3 have secretly set a s for me
Prov 7:23 As a bird hastens to the s
Prov 18: 7 lips are the s of his soul
Prov 20:25 It is a s for a man to devote
Prov 22:25 ways and set a s for your soul
Prov 29:25 The fear of man brings a s
Eccl 9:12 net, like birds caught in a s
Is 8:14 a s to the inhabitants of
Is 24:17 pit and the s are upon you, O
Is 24:18 pit shall be caught in the s
Is 29:21 lay a s for him who reproves
Jer 48:43 the s shall be upon you, O
Jer 48:44 pit shall be caught in the s
Jer 50:23 I have laid a s for you
Lam 3:47 and a s have come upon us,
Ezek 12:13 and he shall be caught in My s
Ezek 17:20 and he shall be taken in My s
Hos 5: 1 you have been a s to Mizpah
Hos 9: 8 a fowler's s in all his ways
Amos 3: 5 fall into a s on the earth
Amos 3: 5 Will a s spring up from the
Luke 21:35 For it will come as a s on
Rom 11: 9 Let their table become a s
1Ti 3: 7 and the s of the devil
1Ti 6: 9 fall into temptation and a s
2Ti 2:26 escape the s of the devil,

SNARED (*see* SNARE)
Deut 7:25 lest you be s by it
Ps 9:16 The wicked is s in the work
Prov 6: 2 you are s by the words of
Prov 29: 6 an evil man is s, but the
Eccl 9:12 of men are s in an evil time
Is 8:15 shall fall and be broken, be s
Is 28:13 backward, and be broken and s
Is 42:22 all of them are s in holes

SNARES (*see* SNARE)
Josh 23:13 But they shall be s and traps
2Sa 22: 6 the s of death confronted me
Job 22:10 Therefore s are all around
Ps 18: 5 The s of death confronted me
Ps 38:12 who seek my life lay s for me
Ps 64: 5 talk of laying s secretly
Ps 141: 9 Keep me from the s which they
Prov 13:14 one away from the s of death
Prov 14:27 life, to avoid the s of death
Prov 22: 5 and s are in the way of the
Eccl 7:26 the woman whose heart is s
Eccl 9:14 and built great s around it
Jer 5:26 lie in wait as one who sets s
Jer 18:22 me, and hidden s for my feet

SNATCH (*see* SNATCHES)
Job 24: 9 Some s the fatherless from
Is 9:20 he shall s on the right hand
John 10:28 anyone s them out of My hand
John 10:29 no one is able to s them out

SNATCHES (*see* SNATCH)
Job 5: 5 a snare s their substance
Matt 13:19 s away what was sown in his

SNEER (*see* SNEERED, SNEERS)
Mal 1:13 you s at it," says the LORD

SNEERED (*see* SNEER)
Luke 23:35 even the rulers with them s

SNEERS (*see* SNEER)
Ps 10: 5 all his enemies, he s at them

SNEEZED (*see* SNEEZINGS)
2Ki 4:35 then the child s seven times

SNEEZINGS (*see* SNEEZED)
Job 41:18 His s flash forth light, and

SNIFFED (*see* SNIFFS)
Jer 14: 6 they s at the wind like

SNIFFS (*see* SNIFFED)
Jer 2:24 that s at the wind in her

SNORTING
Job 39:20 His majestic s strikes terror
Jer 8:16 The s of His horses was heard

SNOUT
Prov 11:22 a ring of gold in a swine's s

SNOW (*see* SNOW-WATER, SNOWY)
Ex 4: 6 his hand was leprous, like s
Num 12:10 became leprous, as white as s
2Ki 5:27 leprous, as white as s
Job 6:16 and into which the s vanishes
Job 9:30 If I wash myself with s water
Job 24:19 and heat consume the s waters
Job 37: 6 For He says to the s, "Be on
Job 38:22 you entered the treasury of s
Ps 51: 7 and I shall be whiter than s
Ps 68:14 It was white as s in Zalmon
Ps 147:16 He gives s like wool
Ps 148: 8 Fire and hail, s and clouds
Prov 25:13 Like the cold of s in time of
Prov 26: 1 As s in summer and rain in
Prov 31:21 afraid of s for her household
Is 1:18 they shall be as white as s
Is 55:10 the s from heaven, and do not
Lam 4: 7 were brighter than s and
Dan 7: 9 His garment was white as s
Matt 28: 3 and his clothing as white as s
Mark 9: 3 exceedingly white, like s
Rev 1:14 like wool, as white as s, and

SNOW-WATER (*see* SNOW)
Jer 18:14 a man leave the s of Lebanon

SNOWY (*see* SNOW)
2Sa 23:20 the midst of a pit on a s day
1Ch 11:22 the midst of a pit on a s day

SO (*see* PREFACE)

SO*
2Ki 17: 4 he had sent messengers to S

SOAKED
Is 34: 7 land shall be s with blood

SOAP
Job 9:30 and cleanse my hands with s
Jer 2:22 with lye, and use much s, yet
Mal 3: 2 fire And like fuller's s

SOBER (*see* SOBERLY, SOBER-MINDED)
Deut 29:19 could be included with the s
1Th 5: 6 do, but let us watch and be s
1Th 5: 8 us who are of the day be s
Tit 2: 2 that the older men be s,
1Pe 1:13 the loins of your mind, be s
1Pe 5: 8 Be s, be vigilant

SOBERLY (*see* SOBER)
Rom 12: 3 to think, but to think s, as
Tit 2:12 lusts, we should live s,

SOBER-MINDED (*see* SOBER)
1Ti 3: 2 of one wife, temperate, s
Tit 1: 8 a lover of what is good, s
Tit 2: 6 exhort the young men to be s

SO-CALLED
1Co 8: 5 For even if there are s gods

SOCHOH
Josh 15:48 Shamir, Jattir, S,
1Sa 17: 1 were gathered together at S
1Sa 17: 1 they encamped between S and
1Ki 4:10 to him belonged S and all the
1Ch 4:18 Gedor, Heber the father of S
2Ch 11: 7 Beth Zur, S, Adullam,
2Ch 28:18 S with its villages, Timnah

SOCKET (*see* SOCKETS)
Gen 32:25 He touched the s of his hip
Gen 32:25 the s of Jacob's hip was out
Gen 32:32 shrank, which is on the hip s
Gen 32:32 the s of Jacob's hip in the
Ex 38:27 one talent for each s
Job 31:22 let my arm be torn from the s

SOCKETS (*see* SOCKET)
Ex 26:19 You shall make forty s of
Ex 26:19 two s under one board for its
Ex 26:19 two s under another board for
Ex 26:21 and their forty s of silver
Ex 26:21 two s under one board, and
Ex 26:21 two s under another board
Ex 26:25 their s of silver—sixteen s
Ex 26:25 two s under one board, and
Ex 26:25 two s under another board
Ex 26:32 gold, upon four s of silver
Ex 26:37 five s of bronze for them
Ex 27:10 their twenty s shall be of
Ex 27:11 and their twenty s of bronze
Ex 27:12 ten pillars and their ten s
Ex 27:14 pillars and their three s
Ex 27:15 pillars and their three s
Ex 27:16 have four pillars and four s
Ex 27:17 silver and their s of bronze
Ex 27:18 thread, and its s of bronze
Ex 35:11 bars, its pillars, and its s
Ex 35:17 court, its pillars, their s
Ex 36:24 Forty s of silver he made to
Ex 36:24 two s under one board for its
Ex 36:24 two s under another board for
Ex 36:26 and their forty s of silver
Ex 36:26 two s under one board and
Ex 36:26 two s under another board
Ex 36:30 were eight boards and their s
Ex 36:30 sixteen s of silver
Ex 36:30 two s under every board
Ex 36:36 he cast four s of silver for
Ex 36:38 their five s were of bronze
Ex 38:10 them, with twenty bronze s
Ex 38:11 and their twenty bronze s
Ex 38:12 ten pillars and their ten s
Ex 38:14 pillars and their three s,
Ex 38:15 pillars and their three s
Ex 38:17 The s for the pillars were of
Ex 38:19 with their four s of bronze
Ex 38:27 cast the s of the sanctuary
Ex 38:27 one hundred s from the
Ex 38:30 the s for the door of the
Ex 38:31 the s for the court all
Ex 39:33 bars, its pillars, and its s
Ex 39:40 court, its pillars and its s
Ex 40:18 tabernacle, fastened its s
Num 3:36 its bars, its pillars, its s
Num 3:37 all around, with their s,
Num 4:31 its bars, its pillars, its s
Num 4:32 around the court with their s
Zech 14:12 shall dissolve in their s

SOCOH
Josh 15:35 Jarmuth, Adullam, S, Azekah,

SODA
Prov 25:20 weather, and like vinegar on s

SODI
Num 13:10 Zebulun, Gaddiel the son of S

SODOM (*see* SODOMITES)
Gen 10:19 then as you go toward S,
Gen 13:10 (before the LORD destroyed S
Gen 13:12 his tent even as far as S
Gen 13:13 But the men of S were
Gen 14: 2 made war with Bera king of S
Gen 14: 8 And the king of S, the king of
Gen 14:10 and the kings of S and
Gen 14:11 they took all the goods of S
Gen 14:12 brother's son who dwelt in S
Gen 14:17 the king of S went out to
Gen 14:21 the king of S said to Abram
Gen 14:22 Abram said to the king of S
Gen 18:16 from there and looked toward S
Gen 18:20 Because the outcry against S
Gen 18:22 from there and went toward S
Gen 18:26 said, "If I find in S fifty
Gen 19: 1 came to S in the evening, and
Gen 19: 1 was sitting in the gate of S
Gen 19: 4 men of the city, the men of S
Gen 19:24 rained brimstone and fire on S
Gen 19:28 Then he looked toward S and
Deut 29:23 like the overthrow of S and
Deut 32:32 vine is of the vine of S and
Is 1: 9 we would have become like S
Is 1:10 of the LORD, you rulers of S
Is 3: 9 they declare their sin as S
Is 13:19 be as when God overthrew S
Jer 23:14 All of them are like S to Me
Jer 49:18 As in the overthrow of S and
Jer 50:40 As God overthrew S and
Lam 4: 6 punishment of the sin of S
Ezek 16:46 to the south of you, is S
Ezek 16:48 neither your sister S nor her
Ezek 16:49 the iniquity of your sister S
Ezek 16:53 captives, the captives of S
Ezek 16:55 When your sisters, S and her
Ezek 16:56 For your sister S was not a
Amos 4:11 of you, as God overthrew S
Zeph 2: 9 Surely Moab shall be like S
Matt 10:15 tolerable for the land of S
Matt 11:23 in you had been done in S
Matt 11:24 tolerable for the land of S
Mark 6:11 will be more tolerable for S
Luke 10:12 Day for S than for that city
Luke 17:29 went out of S it rained fire
Rom 9:29 we would have become like S
2Pe 2: 6 and turning the cities of S
Jude 7 as S and Gomorrah, and the
Rev 11: 8 which spiritually is called S

SODOMITES (*see* SODOM)
1Co 6: 9 nor homosexuals, nor s,
1Ti 1:10 for fornicators, for s, for

SOFT (*see* SOFTER, SOFTLY)
Ps 65:10 You make it s with showers,
Prov 15: 1 A s answer turns away wrath,
Matt 11: 8 A man clothed in s garments
Matt 11: 8 those who wear s clothing are
Luke 7:25 A man clothed in s garments

SOFTER (*see* SOFT)
Ps 55:21 His words were s than oil

SOFTLY (*see* SOFT)
Judg 4:21 went s to him and drove the
Ruth 3: 7 and she came s, uncovered his
Job 41: 3 Will he speak s to you
Is 8: 6 waters of Shiloah that flow s
Acts 27:13 When the south wind blew s

SOIL
2Ch 26:10 in Carmel, for he loved the s
Job 14:19 wash away the s of the earth
Is 28:24 Does he keep turning his s
Ezek 17: 8 in good s by many waters, to
Ezek 26:12 your s in the midst of the

Heb 5:14 But **s** food belongs to those

SOLITARILY (*see* SOLITARY)
Mic 7:14 who dwell **s** in a woodland, in

SOLITARY (*see* SOLITARILY)
Ps 68: 6 God sets the **s** in families
Mark 1:35 out and departed to a **s** place

SOLOMON (*see* JEDIDIAH, SOLOMON'S)
2Sa 5:14 Shammua, Shobab, Nathan, **S**
2Sa 12:24 son, and he called his name **S**
1Ki 1:10 mighty men, or **S** his brother
1Ki 1:11 to Bathsheba the mother of **S**
1Ki 1:12 and the life of your son **S**
1Ki 1:13 Assuredly your son **S** shall
1Ki 1:17 Assuredly **S** your son shall
1Ki 1:19 but **S** your servant he has not
1Ki 1:21 my son **S** will be counted as
1Ki 1:26 Jehoiada, nor your servant **S**
1Ki 1:30 Assuredly **S** your son shall
1Ki 1:33 have **S** my son ride on my own
1Ki 1:34 and say, "Long live King **S**
1Ki 1:37 even so may He be with **S**
1Ki 1:38 had **S** ride on King David's
1Ki 1:39 the tabernacle and anointed **S**
1Ki 1:39 Long live King **S**
1Ki 1:43 King David has made **S** king
1Ki 1:46 Also **S** sits on the throne of
1Ki 1:47 of **S** better than your name
1Ki 1:50 Now Adonijah was afraid of **S**
1Ki 1:51 And it was told **S**, saying
1Ki 1:51 Adonijah is afraid of King **S**
1Ki 1:51 Let King **S** swear to me today
1Ki 1:52 Then **S** said, "If he proves
1Ki 1:53 So King **S** sent them to bring
1Ki 1:53 and fell down before King **S**
1Ki 1:53 **S** said to him, "Go to your
1Ki 2: 1 die, and he charged **S** his son
1Ki 2:12 Then **S** sat on the throne of
1Ki 2:13 to Bathsheba the mother of **S**
1Ki 2:17 Please speak to King **S**, for
1Ki 2:19 therefore went to King **S**, to
1Ki 2:22 King **S** answered and said to
1Ki 2:23 Then King **S** swore by the LORD
1Ki 2:25 So King **S** sent by the hand of
1Ki 2:27 So **S** removed Abiathar from
1Ki 2:29 And King **S** was told,
1Ki 2:29 Then **S** sent Benaiah the son
1Ki 2:41 **S** was told that Shimei had
1Ki 2:45 But King **S** shall be blessed,
1Ki 2:46 established in the hand of **S**
1Ki 3: 1 Now **S** made a treaty with
1Ki 3: 3 **S** loved the LORD, walking in
1Ki 3: 4 **S** offered a thousand burnt
1Ki 3: 5 to **S** in a dream by night
1Ki 3: 6 And **S** said: "You have shown
1Ki 3:10 that **S** had asked this thing
1Ki 3:15 Then **S** awoke; and indeed it
1Ki 4: 1 So King **S** was king over all
1Ki 4: 7 **S** had twelve governors over
1Ki 4:11 the daughter of **S** as wife
1Ki 4:15 the daughter of **S** as wife
1Ki 4:21 So **S** reigned over all
1Ki 4:21 served **S** all the days of his
1Ki 4:25 Beersheba, all the days of **S**
1Ki 4:26 **S** had forty thousand stalls
1Ki 4:27 provided food for King **S**
1Ki 4:29 And God gave **S** wisdom and
1Ki 4:34 came to hear the wisdom of **S**
1Ki 5: 1 Tyre sent his servants to **S**
1Ki 5: 2 Then **S** sent to Hiram, saying
1Ki 5: 7 Hiram heard the words of **S**
1Ki 5: 8 Then Hiram sent to **S**, saying
1Ki 5:10 So Hiram gave **S** cedar and
1Ki 5:11 **S** gave Hiram twenty thousand
1Ki 5:11 Thus **S** gave to Hiram year by
1Ki 5:12 So the LORD gave **S** wisdom
1Ki 5:12 was peace between Hiram and **S**
1Ki 5:13 Then King **S** raised up a labor
1Ki 5:15 **S** had seventy thousand who
1Ki 6: 2 King **S** built for the LORD
1Ki 6:11 word of the LORD came to **S**
1Ki 6:14 So **S** built the temple and
1Ki 6:21 So **S** overlaid the inside of
1Ki 7: 1 But **S** took thirteen years to
1Ki 7: 8 **S** also made a house like this
1Ki 7:13 Now King **S** sent and brought
1Ki 7:14 So he came to King **S** and did
1Ki 7:40 **S** on the house of the LORD
1Ki 7:45 **S** for the house of the LORD
1Ki 7:47 And **S** did not weigh all the
1Ki 7:48 **S** had all the furnishings
1Ki 7:51 **S** had done for the house of
1Ki 7:51 **S** brought in the things which
1Ki 8: 1 Now **S** assembled the elders of
1Ki 8: 1 to King **S** in Jerusalem, that
1Ki 8: 2 **S** at the feast in the month
1Ki 8: 5 Also King **S**, and all the
1Ki 8:12 Then **S** spoke: "The LORD said
1Ki 8:22 Then **S** stood before the altar
1Ki 8:54 when **S** had finished praying
1Ki 8:63 And **S** offered a sacrifice of
1Ki 8:65 At that time **S** held a feast
1Ki 9: 1 when **S** had finished building
1Ki 9: 2 appeared to **S** the second time
1Ki 9:10 when **S** had built the two
1Ki 9:11 had supplied **S** with cedar
1Ki 9:11 that King **S** then gave Hiram
1Ki 9:12 cities which **S** had given him
1Ki 9:15 force which King **S** raised
1Ki 9:17 **S** built Gezer, Lower Beth
1Ki 9:19 the storage cities that **S** had
1Ki 9:19 whatever **S** desired to build
1Ki 9:21 from these **S** raised forced
1Ki 9:22 **S** made no forced laborers
1Ki 9:24 which **S** had built for her
1Ki 9:25 Now three times a year **S**
1Ki 9:26 King **S** also built a fleet of
1Ki 9:27 work with the servants of **S**
1Ki 9:28 and brought it to King **S**
1Ki 10: 1 **S** concerning the name of the
1Ki 10: 2 and when she came to **S**, she
1Ki 10: 3 So **S** answered all her
1Ki 10: 4 had seen all the wisdom of **S**
1Ki 10:10 queen of Sheba gave to King **S**
1Ki 10:13 And King **S** gave the queen of
1Ki 10:13 besides what **S** had given her
1Ki 10:14 to **S** yearly was six hundred
1Ki 10:16 King **S** made two hundred large
1Ki 10:21 as nothing in the days of **S**
1Ki 10:23 So King **S** surpassed all the
1Ki 10:24 of **S** to hear his wisdom,
1Ki 10:26 And **S** gathered chariots and
1Ki 10:28 **S** had horses imported from
1Ki 11: 1 But King **S** loved many foreign
1Ki 11: 2 **S** clung to these in love
1Ki 11: 4 so, when **S** was old, that his
1Ki 11: 5 For **S** went after Ashtoreth
1Ki 11: 6 **S** did evil in the sight of
1Ki 11: 7 Then **S** built a high place for
1Ki 11: 9 the LORD became angry with **S**
1Ki 11:11 Therefore the LORD said to **S**
1Ki 11:14 up an adversary against **S**
1Ki 11:25 **S** (besides the trouble that
1Ki 11:27 **S** had built the Millo and
1Ki 11:28 and **S**, seeing that the young
1Ki 11:31 kingdom out of the hand of **S**
1Ki 11:40 **S** therefore sought to kill
1Ki 11:40 in Egypt until the death of **S**
1Ki 11:41 Now the rest of the acts of **S**
1Ki 11:41 in the book of the acts of **S**
1Ki 11:42 the period that **S** reigned in
1Ki 11:43 Then **S** rested with his
1Ki 12: 2 from the presence of King **S**
1Ki 12: 6 father **S** while he still lived
1Ki 12:21 to Rehoboam the son of **S**
1Ki 12:23 to Rehoboam the son of **S**,
1Ki 14:21 the son of **S** reigned in Judah
1Ki 14:26 gold shields which **S** had made
2Ki 21: 7 to David and to **S** his son,
2Ki 23:13 which **S** king of Israel had
2Ki 24:13 **S** king of Israel had made in
2Ki 25:16 which **S** had made for the
1Ch 3: 5 Shimea, Shobab, Nathan, and **S**
1Ch 6:10 that **S** built in Jerusalem)
1Ch 6:32 until **S** had built the house
1Ch 14: 4 Shammua, Shobab, Nathan, **S**
1Ch 18: 8 with which **S** made the bronze
1Ch 22: 5 said, "**S** my son is young and
1Ch 22: 6 Then he called for his son **S**
1Ch 22: 7 And David said to **S**
1Ch 22: 9 His name shall be **S**, for I
1Ch 22:17 of Israel to help **S** his son
1Ch 23: 1 he made his son **S** king over
1Ch 28: 5 sons) He has chosen my son **S**
1Ch 28: 6 It is your son **S** who shall
1Ch 28: 9 As for you, my son **S**, know
1Ch 28:11 Then David gave his son **S** the
1Ch 28:20 And David said to his son **S**
1Ch 29: 1 My son **S**, whom alone God has
1Ch 29:19 give my son **S** a loyal heart
1Ch 29:22 they made **S** the son of David
1Ch 29:23 Then **S** sat on the throne of
1Ch 29:24 themselves to King **S**
1Ch 29:25 So the LORD exalted **S**
1Ch 29:28 and **S** his son reigned in his
2Ch 1: 1 Now **S** the son of David was
2Ch 1: 2 **S** spoke to all Israel, to the
2Ch 1: 3 Then **S**, and all the
2Ch 1: 5 **S** and the congregation sought
2Ch 1: 6 **S** went up there to the bronze
2Ch 1: 7 that night God appeared to **S**
2Ch 1: 8 And **S** said to God: "You have
2Ch 1:11 And God said to **S**: "Because
2Ch 1:13 So **S** came to Jerusalem from
2Ch 1:14 And **S** gathered chariots and
2Ch 1:16 **S** had horses imported from
2Ch 2: 1 Then **S** determined to build a
2Ch 2: 2 **S** selected seventy thousand
2Ch 2: 3 Then **S** sent to Hiram king of
2Ch 2:11 writing, which he sent to **S**
2Ch 2:17 Then **S** numbered all the
2Ch 3: 1 Now **S** began to build the
2Ch 3: 3 is the foundation which **S**
2Ch 4:11 King **S** for the house of God
2Ch 4:16 **S** for the house of the LORD
2Ch 4:18 **S** had all these articles made
2Ch 4:19 Thus **S** had all the
2Ch 5: 1 So all the work that **S** had
2Ch 5: 1 **S** brought in all the things
2Ch 5: 2 Now **S** assembled the elders of
2Ch 5: 6 Also King **S**, and all the
2Ch 6: 1 Then **S** said: "The LORD said
2Ch 6:12 Then **S** stood before the
2Ch 6:13 (for **S** had made a bronze
2Ch 7: 1 Now when **S** had finished
2Ch 7: 5 King **S** offered a sacrifice of
2Ch 7: 7 Furthermore **S** consecrated the
2Ch 7: 7 the bronze altar which **S** had
2Ch 7: 8 At that time **S** kept the feast
2Ch 7:10 had done for David, for **S**
2Ch 7:11 Thus **S** finished the house of
2Ch 7:11 **S** successfully accomplished
2Ch 7:12 LORD appeared to **S** by night
2Ch 8: 1 in which **S** had built the
2Ch 8: 2 which Hiram had given to **S**
2Ch 8: 2 **S** built them; and he settled
2Ch 8: 3 **S** went to Hamath Zobah and
2Ch 8: 6 the storage cities that **S** had
2Ch 8: 6 all that **S** desired to build
2Ch 8: 8 from these **S** raised forced
2Ch 8: 9 But **S** did not make the
2Ch 8:10 of the officials of King **S**
2Ch 8:11 Now **S** brought the daughter of
2Ch 8:12 Then **S** offered burnt
2Ch 8:16 Now all the work of **S** was
2Ch 8:17 Then **S** went to Ezion Geber and
2Ch 8:18 the servants of **S** to Ophir
2Ch 8:18 and brought it to King **S**
2Ch 9: 1 Sheba heard of the fame of **S**
2Ch 9: 1 to test **S** with hard questions
2Ch 9: 1 and when she came to **S**, she
2Ch 9: 2 So **S** answered all her
2Ch 9: 2 nothing so difficult for **S**
2Ch 9: 3 had seen the wisdom of **S**, the
2Ch 9: 9 queen of Sheba gave to King **S**
2Ch 9:10 of Hiram and the servants of **S**
2Ch 9:12 Now King **S** gave to the queen
2Ch 9:13 to **S** yearly was six hundred
2Ch 9:14 brought gold and silver to **S**
2Ch 9:15 King **S** made two hundred large
2Ch 9:20 as nothing in the days of **S**
2Ch 9:22 So King **S** surpassed all the
2Ch 9:23 of **S** to hear his wisdom,
2Ch 9:25 **S** had four thousand stalls
2Ch 9:28 horses to **S** from Egypt and
2Ch 9:29 Now the rest of the acts of **S**
2Ch 9:30 **S** reigned in Jerusalem over
2Ch 9:31 Then **S** rested with his
2Ch 10: 2 the presence of **S** the king)
2Ch 10: 6 father **S** while he still lived
2Ch 11: 3 to Rehoboam the son of **S**,
2Ch 11:17 of **S** strong for three years
2Ch 11:17 of David and **S** for three years
2Ch 12: 9 gold shields which **S** had made
2Ch 13: 6 the servant of **S** the son of
2Ch 13: 7 against Rehoboam the son of **S**
2Ch 30:26 time of **S** the son of David
2Ch 33: 7 to David and to **S** his son,
2Ch 35: 3 which **S** the son of David,
2Ch 35: 4 instruction of **S** his son

Num 2:20 be Gamaliel the s of Pedahzur
Num 2:22 be Abidan the s of Gideoni
Num 2:25 Ahiezer the s of Ammishaddai
Num 2:27 be Pagiel the s of Ocran
Num 2:29 shall be Ahira the s of Enan
Num 3:24 was Eliasaph the s of Lael
Num 3:30 was Elizaphan the s of Uzziel
Num 3:32 Eleazar the s of Aaron the
Num 3:35 was Zuriel the s of Abihail
Num 4:16 duty of Eleazar the s of
Num 4:28 the s of Aaron the priest
Num 4:33 the s of Aaron the priest
Num 7: 8 the s of Aaron the priest
Num 7:12 Nahshon the s of Amminadab
Num 7:17 of Nahshon the s of Amminadab
Num 7:18 day Nethaneel the s of Zuar
Num 7:23 of Nethaneel the s of Zuar
Num 7:24 day Eliab the s of Helon,
Num 7:29 of Eliab the s of Helon
Num 7:30 day Elizur the s of Shedeur
Num 7:35 of Elizur the s of Shedeur
Num 7:36 the s of Zurishaddai, leader
Num 7:41 the s of Zurishaddai
Num 7:42 day Eliasaph the s of Deuel
Num 7:47 of Eliasaph the s of Deuel
Num 7:48 day Elishama the s of Ammihud
Num 7:53 of Elishama the s of Ammihud
Num 7:54 Gamaliel the s of Pedahzur
Num 7:59 of Gamaliel the s of Pedahzur
Num 7:60 day Abidan the s of Gideoni
Num 7:65 of Abidan the s of Gideoni
Num 7:66 Ahiezer the s of Ammishaddai
Num 7:71 Ahiezer the s of Ammishaddai
Num 7:72 day Pagiel the s of Ocran
Num 7:77 of Pagiel the s of Ocran
Num 7:78 day Ahira the s of Enan,
Num 7:83 of Ahira the s of Enan
Num 10:14 Nahshon the s of Amminadab
Num 10:15 was Nethaneel the s of Zuar
Num 10:16 was Eliab the s of Helon
Num 10:18 was Elizur the s of Shedeur
Num 10:19 the s of Zurishaddai
Num 10:20 was Eliasaph the s of Deuel
Num 10:22 was Elishama the s of Ammihud
Num 10:23 Gamaliel the s of Pedahzur
Num 10:24 was Abidan the s of Gideoni
Num 10:25 Ahiezer the s of Ammishaddai
Num 10:26 was Pagiel the s of Ocran
Num 10:27 was Ahira the s of Enan
Num 10:29 the s of Reuel the Midianite
Num 11:28 So Joshua the s of Nun,
Num 13: 4 Shammua the s of Zaccur
Num 13: 5 Simeon, Shaphat the s of Hori
Num 13: 6 Caleb the s of Jephunneh
Num 13: 7 Igal the s of Joseph
Num 13: 8 Ephraim, Hoshea the s of Nun
Num 13: 9 Palti the s of Raphu
Num 13:10 Gaddiel the s of Sodi
Num 13:11 Manasseh, Gaddi the s of Susi
Num 13:12 Dan, Ammiel the s of Gemalli
Num 13:13 Sethur the s of Michael
Num 13:14 Nahbi the s of Vophsi
Num 13:15 of Gad, Geuel the s of Machi
Num 13:16 called Hoshea the s of Nun
Num 14: 6 And Joshua the s of Nun and
Num 14: 6 Caleb the s of Jephunneh, who
Num 14:30 for Caleb the s of Jephunneh
Num 14:30 and Joshua the s of Nun, you
Num 14:38 But Joshua the s of Nun
Num 14:38 and Caleb the s of Jephunneh
Num 16: 1 Now Korah the s of Izhar
Num 16: 1 s of Kohath, the s of Levi
Num 16: 1 On the s of Peleth, sons of
Num 16:37 the s of Aaron the priest, to
Num 20:25 Take Aaron and Eleazar his s
Num 20:26 and put them on Eleazar his s
Num 20:28 and put them on Eleazar his s
Num 22: 2 Now Balak the s of Zippor saw
Num 22: 4 Balak the s of Zippor was
Num 22: 5 the s of Beor at Pethor,
Num 22:10 Balak the s of Zippor, king
Num 22:16 says Balak the s of Zippor
Num 23:18 Listen to me, s of Zippor
Num 23:19 lie, nor a s of man, that He
Num 24: 3 of Balaam the s of Beor, the
Num 24:15 of Balaam the s of Beor, and
Num 25: 7 Phinehas the s of Eleazar
Num 25: 7 the s of Aaron the priest,
Num 25:11 Phinehas the s of Eleazar
Num 25:11 the s of Aaron the priest,
Num 25:14 was Zimri the s of Salu, a
Num 26: 1 Eleazar the s of Aaron the
Num 26: 8 And the s of Pallu was Eliab
Num 26:33 Now Zelophehad the s of
Num 26:65 Caleb the s of Jephunneh and
Num 26:65 and Joshua the s of Nun
Num 27: 1 of Zelophehad the s of Hepher
Num 27: 1 s of Gilead, the s of Machir
Num 27: 1 the s of Manasseh, from the
Num 27: 1 of Manasseh the s of Joseph
Num 27: 4 family because he had no s
Num 27: 8 If a man dies and has no s
Num 27:18 Joshua the s of Nun with you
Num 31: 6 the s of Eleazar the priest
Num 31: 8 Balaam the s of Beor they
Num 32:12 Caleb the s of Jephunneh, the
Num 32:12 and Joshua the s of Nun, for
Num 32:28 to Joshua the s of Nun, and
Num 32:33 of Manasseh the s of Joseph
Num 32:39 s of Manasseh went to Gilead
Num 32:40 to Machir the s of Manasseh
Num 32:41 Also Jair the s of Manasseh
Num 34:17 priest and Joshua the s of Nun
Num 34:19 Caleb the s of Jephunneh
Num 34:20 Shemuel the s of Ammihud
Num 34:21 Elidad the s of Chislon
Num 34:22 of Dan, Bukki the s of Jogli
Num 34:23 Hanniel the s of Ephod,
Num 34:24 Kemuel the s of Shiphtan
Num 34:25 Elizaphan the s of Parnach
Num 34:26 Paltiel the s of Azzan
Num 34:27 Ahihud the s of Shelomi
Num 34:28 Pedahel the s of Ammihud
Num 36: 1 of Gilead the s of Machir
Num 36: 1 the s of Manasseh, of the
Num 36:12 of Manasseh the s of Joseph
Deut 1:31 you, as a man carries his s
Deut 1:36 Caleb the s of Jephunneh
Deut 1:38 but Joshua the s of Nun, who
Deut 3:14 Jair the s of Manasseh took
Deut 5:14 you, nor your s, nor your
Deut 6: 2 I command you, you and your s
Deut 6:20 When your s asks you in time
Deut 6:21 then you shall say to your s
Deut 7: 3 give your daughter to their s
Deut 7: 3 their daughter for your s
Deut 8: 5 that as a man chastens his s
Deut 10: 6 Eleazar his s ministered as
Deut 11: 6 of Eliab, the s of Reuben
Deut 12:18 God chooses, you and your s
Deut 13: 6 the s of your mother, your
Deut 13: 6 your s or your daughter, the
Deut 16:11 LORD your God, you and your s
Deut 16:14 in your feast, you and your s
Deut 18:10 his s or his daughter pass
Deut 21:15 if the firstborn s is of her
Deut 21:16 on the s of the loved wife in
Deut 21:16 to the s of the unloved, who
Deut 21:17 he shall acknowledge the s of
Deut 21:18 rebellious s who will not
Deut 21:20 This s of ours is stubborn
Deut 23: 4 the s of Beor from Pethor of
Deut 25: 5 one of them dies and has no s
Deut 25: 6 s which she bears will
Deut 28:56 of her bosom, and to her s
Deut 31:23 Joshua the s of Nun, and said,
Deut 32:44 came with Joshua the s of Nun
Deut 34: 9 Now Joshua the s of Nun was
Josh 1: 1 spoke to Joshua the s of Nun
Josh 2: 1 Now Joshua the s of Nun sent
Josh 2:23 came to Joshua the s of Nun
Josh 6: 6 So Joshua the s of Nun called
Josh 7: 1 for Achan the s of Carmi
Josh 7: 1 s of Zabdi, the s of Zerah
Josh 7:18 man, and Achan the s of Carmi
Josh 7:18 s of Zabdi, the s of Zerah
Josh 7:19 My s, I beg you, give glory
Josh 7:24 took Achan the s of Zerah
Josh 13:22 sword Balaam the s of Beor
Josh 13:31 of Machir the s of Manasseh
Josh 14: 1 priest, Joshua the s of Nun
Josh 14: 6 Caleb the s of Jephunneh the
Josh 14:13 the s of Jephunneh as an
Josh 14:14 inheritance of Caleb the s of
Josh 15: 6 of Bohan the s of Reuben
Josh 15: 8 up by the Valley of the S of
Josh 15:13 Now to Caleb the s of
Josh 15:17 So Othniel the s of Kenaz
Josh 17: 2 the s of Joseph according to
Josh 17: 3 Zelophehad the s of Hepher
Josh 17: 3 s of Gilead, the s of Machir
Josh 17: 3 the s of Manasseh, had no
Josh 17: 4 before Joshua the s of Nun
Josh 18:16 the Valley of the S of Hinnom
Josh 18:17 of Bohan the s of Reuben
Josh 19:49 them to Joshua the s of Nun
Josh 19:51 priest, Joshua the s of Nun
Josh 21: 1 to Joshua the s of Nun, and
Josh 21:12 the s of Jephunneh as his
Josh 22:13 s of Eleazar the priest to
Josh 22:20 Did not Achan the s of Zerah
Josh 22:31 Then Phinehas the s of
Josh 22:32 Phinehas the s of Eleazar the
Josh 24: 9 Then Balak the s of Zippor
Josh 24: 9 called Balaam the s of Beor
Josh 24:29 that Joshua the s of Nun, the
Josh 24:33 Eleazar the s of Aaron died
Josh 24:33 belonged to Phinehas his s
Judg 1:13 And Othniel the s of Kenaz
Judg 2: 8 Now Joshua the s of Nun, the
Judg 3: 9 Othniel the s of Kenaz,
Judg 3:11 Othniel the s of Kenaz died
Judg 3:15 Ehud the s of Gera, the
Judg 3:31 was Shamgar the s of Anath
Judg 4: 6 called for Barak the s of
Judg 4:12 to Sisera that Barak the s of
Judg 5: 1 Barak the s of Abinoam sang
Judg 5: 6 s of Anath, in the days of
Judg 5:12 captives away, O s of Abinoam
Judg 6:11 while his s Gideon threshed
Judg 6:29 Gideon the s of Joash has
Judg 6:30 Bring out your s, that he may
Judg 7:14 of Gideon the s of Joash, a
Judg 8:13 Then Gideon the s of Joash
Judg 8:18 one resembled the s of a king
Judg 8:22 over us, both you and your s
Judg 8:23 nor shall my s rule over you
Judg 8:29 Jerubbaal the s of Joash went
Judg 8:31 in Shechem also bore him a s
Judg 8:32 Now Gideon the s of Joash
Judg 9: 1 Abimelech the s of Jerubbaal
Judg 9: 5 s of Jerubbaal was left,
Judg 9:18 the s of his maidservant,
Judg 9:26 Now Gaal the s of Ebed came
Judg 9:28 Then Gaal the s of Ebed said
Judg 9:28 Is he not the s of Jerubbaal
Judg 9:30 words of Gaal the s of Ebed
Judg 9:31 Gaal the s of Ebed and his
Judg 9:35 When Gaal the s of Ebed went
Judg 9:57 of Jotham the s of Jerubbaal
Judg 10: 1 Israel Tola the s of Puah
Judg 10: 1 the s of Dodo, a man of
Judg 11: 1 but he was the s of a harlot
Judg 11: 2 for you are the s of another
Judg 11:25 than Balak the s of Zippor
Judg 11:34 he had neither s nor daughter
Judg 12:13 Abdon the s of Hillel the
Judg 12:15 Then Abdon the s of Hillel
Judg 13: 3 shall conceive and bear a s
Judg 13: 5 shall conceive and bear a s
Judg 13: 7 shall conceive and bear a s
Judg 13:24 So the woman bore a s and
Judg 17: 2 be blessed by the LORD, my s
Judg 17: 3 my hand to the LORD for my s
Judg 18:30 and Jonathan the s of Gershom
Judg 18:30 the s of Manasseh, and his
Judg 20:28 and Phinehas the s of Eleazar
Judg 20:28 the s of Aaron, stood before
Ruth 4:13 conception, and she bore a s
Ruth 4:17 There is a s born to Naomi
1Sa 1: 1 was Elkanah the s of Jeroham
1Sa 1: 1 s of Elihu, the s of Tohu
1Sa 1: 1 the s of Zuph, an Ephraimite
1Sa 1:20 Hannah conceived and bore a s
1Sa 1:23 nursed her s until she had
1Sa 3: 6 I did not call, my s
1Sa 3:16 and said, "Samuel, my s!"
1Sa 4:16 What happened, my s
1Sa 4:20 fear, for you have borne a s
1Sa 7: 1 consecrated Eleazar his s to
1Sa 9: 1 name was Kish the s of Abiel
1Sa 9: 1 the s of Zeror
1Sa 9: 1 the s of Bechorath
1Sa 9: 1 the s of Aphiah, a Benjamite,
1Sa 9: 2 he had a s whose name was
1Sa 9: 3 And Kish said to his s Saul
1Sa 10: 2 What shall I do about my s
1Sa 10:11 has come upon the s of Kish
1Sa 10:21 Saul the s of Kish was chosen
1Sa 13:16 Saul, Jonathan his s, and the

1Sa 13:22 with Saul and Jonathan his s
1Sa 14: 1 s of Saul said to the young
1Sa 14: 3 Ahijah the s of Ahitub,
1Sa 14: 3 s of Phinehas, the s of Eli
1Sa 14:39 though it be in Jonathan my s
1Sa 14:40 my s Jonathan and I will be on
1Sa 14:42 lots between my s Jonathan
1Sa 14:50 army was Abner the s of Ner
1Sa 14:51 of Abner was the s of Abiel
1Sa 16:18 I have seen a s of Jesse the
1Sa 16:19 Send me your s David, who is
1Sa 16:20 them by his s David to Saul
1Sa 17:12 Now David was the s of that
1Sa 17:17 Jesse said to his s David
1Sa 17:55 Abner, whose s is this youth
1Sa 17:56 Inquire whose s this young
1Sa 17:58 Whose s are you, young man
1Sa 17:58 I am the s of your servant
1Sa 19: 1 Saul spoke to Jonathan his s
1Sa 19: 1 but Jonathan, Saul's s,
1Sa 20:27 Saul said to Jonathan his s
1Sa 20:27 Why has the s of Jesse not
1Sa 20:30 him, "You s of a perverse,
1Sa 20:30 that you have chosen the s of
1Sa 20:31 For as long as the s of Jesse
1Sa 22: 7 Will the s of Jesse give
1Sa 22: 8 my s has made a covenant
1Sa 22: 8 with the s of Jesse
1Sa 22: 8 s has stirred up my servant
1Sa 22: 9 I saw the s of Jesse going to
1Sa 22: 9 to Ahimelech the s of Ahitub
1Sa 22:11 the s of Ahitub, and all his
1Sa 22:12 said, "Hear now, s of Ahitub
1Sa 22:13 the s of Jesse, in that you
1Sa 22:20 of Ahimelech the s of Ahitub
1Sa 23: 6 when Abiathar the s of
1Sa 23:16 Then Jonathan, Saul's s,
1Sa 24:16 this your voice, my s David
1Sa 25: 8 servants and to your s David
1Sa 25:10 and who is the s of Jesse
1Sa 25:44 wife, to Palti the s of Laish
1Sa 26: 5 lay, and Abner the s of Ner
1Sa 26: 6 to Abishai the s of Zeruiah
1Sa 26:14 and to Abner the s of Ner,
1Sa 26:17 that your voice, my s David
1Sa 26:21 Return, my s David
1Sa 26:25 you be blessed, my s David
1Sa 27: 2 him to Achish the s of Maoch
1Sa 30: 7 the priest, Ahimelech's s
2Sa 1: 4 Jonathan his s are dead also
2Sa 1: 5 and Jonathan his s are dead
2Sa 1:12 Saul and for Jonathan his s
2Sa 1:13 I am the s of an alien, an
2Sa 1:17 Saul and over Jonathan his s
2Sa 2: 8 But Abner the s of Ner,
2Sa 2: 8 took Ishbosheth the s of Saul
2Sa 2:10 Ishbosheth, Saul's s, was
2Sa 2:12 Now Abner the s of Ner, and
2Sa 2:12 of Ishbosheth the s of Saul
2Sa 2:13 Joab the s of Zeruiah, and the
2Sa 2:15 of Ishbosheth the s of Saul
2Sa 3: 3 Absalom the s of Maacah, the
2Sa 3: 4 Adonijah the s of Haggith
2Sa 3: 4 Shephatiah the s of Abital
2Sa 3:14 to Ishbosheth, Saul's s,
2Sa 3:15 from Paltiel the s of Laish
2Sa 3:23 Abner the s of Ner came to
2Sa 3:25 s of Ner came to deceive you
2Sa 3:28 blood of Abner the s of Ner
2Sa 3:37 to kill Abner the s of Ner
2Sa 4: 1 And when Saul's s heard that
2Sa 4: 2 Now Saul's s had two men who
2Sa 4: 4 Jonathan, Saul's s, had a s
2Sa 4: 8 the s of Saul your enemy, who
2Sa 7:14 Father, and he shall be My s
2Sa 8: 3 Hadadezer the s of Rehob,
2Sa 8:10 Joram his s to King David
2Sa 8:12 of Hadadezer the s of Rehob
2Sa 8:16 Joab the s of Zeruiah was
2Sa 8:16 Jehoshaphat the s of Ahilud
2Sa 8:17 Zadok the s of Ahitub and
2Sa 8:17 Ahimelech the s of Abiathar
2Sa 8:18 Benaiah the s of Jehoiada was
2Sa 9: 3 king, "There is still a s of
2Sa 9: 4 of Machir the s of Ammiel
2Sa 9: 5 of Machir the s of Ammiel
2Sa 9: 6 the s of Jonathan
2Sa 9: 6 the s of Saul, had come to
2Sa 9: 9 s all that belonged to Saul
2Sa 9:10 that your master's s may have
2Sa 9:10 Mephibosheth your master's s
2Sa 9:12 young s whose name was Micha
2Sa 10: 1 Hanun his s reigned in his
2Sa 10: 2 to Hanun the s of Nahash, as
2Sa 11:21 the s of Jerubbesheth
2Sa 11:27 his wife and bore him a s
2Sa 12:24 So she bore a s, and he called
2Sa 13: 1 the s of David had a lovely
2Sa 13: 1 Amnon the s of David loved
2Sa 13: 3 was Jonadab the s of Shimeah
2Sa 13: 4 Why are you, the king's s
2Sa 13:25 No, my s, let us not all go
2Sa 13:32 Then Jonadab the s of Shimeah
2Sa 13:37 to Talmai the s of Ammihud
2Sa 13:37 mourned for his s every day
2Sa 14: 1 So Joab the s of Zeruiah
2Sa 14:11 lest they destroy my s
2Sa 14:11 not one hair of your s shall
2Sa 14:16 me and my s together from the
2Sa 15:27 sons with you, Ahimaaz your s
2Sa 15:27 and Jonathan the s of Abiathar
2Sa 15:36 two sons, Ahimaaz, Zadok's s
2Sa 15:36 and Jonathan, Abiathar's s
2Sa 16: 3 And where is your master's s
2Sa 16: 5 name was Shimei the s of Gera
2Sa 16: 8 the hand of Absalom your s
2Sa 16: 9 Then Abishai the s of Zeruiah
2Sa 16:11 See how my s who came from my
2Sa 16:19 in the presence of his s
2Sa 17:25 This Amasa was the s of a man
2Sa 17:27 that Shobi the s of Nahash
2Sa 17:27 Machir the s of Ammiel from
2Sa 18: 2 of Abishai the s of Zeruiah
2Sa 18:12 my hand against the king's s
2Sa 18:18 I have no s to keep my name
2Sa 18:19 Ahimaaz the s of Zadok said
2Sa 18:20 because the king's s is dead
2Sa 18:22 Ahimaaz the s of Zadok said
2Sa 18:22 Why will you run, my s, since
2Sa 18:27 of Ahimaaz the s of Zadok
2Sa 18:33 O my s Absalom
2Sa 18:33 my s, my s Absalom
2Sa 18:33 O Absalom my s, my s
2Sa 18:33 O Absalom my s, my s
2Sa 19: 2 The king is grieved for his s
2Sa 19: 4 loud voice, O my s Absalom
2Sa 19: 4 O Absalom, my s, my s
2Sa 19:16 And Shimei the s of Gera, a
2Sa 19:18 Now Shimei the s of Gera fell
2Sa 19:21 But Abishai the s of Zeruiah
2Sa 19:24 Now Mephibosheth the s of
2Sa 20: 1 was Sheba the s of Bichri
2Sa 20: 1 inheritance in the s of Jesse
2Sa 20: 2 Sheba the s of Bichri
2Sa 20: 6 Now Sheba the s of Bichri
2Sa 20: 7 pursue Sheba the s of Bichri
2Sa 20:10 pursued Sheba the s of Bichri
2Sa 20:13 pursue Sheba the s of Bichri
2Sa 20:21 Sheba the s of Bichri by name
2Sa 20:22 head of Sheba the s of Bichri
2Sa 20:23 Benaiah the s of Jehoiada was
2Sa 20:24 Jehoshaphat the s of Ahilud
2Sa 21: 7 s of Jonathan, the s of Saul
2Sa 21: 7 and Jonathan the s of Saul
2Sa 21: 8 Adriel the s of Barzillai the
2Sa 21:12 the bones of Jonathan his s
2Sa 21:13 of Jonathan his s from there
2Sa 21:14 Jonathan his s in the country
2Sa 21:17 But Abishai the s of Zeruiah
2Sa 21:19 where Elhanan the s of
2Sa 21:21 Jonathan the s of Shimeah
2Sa 23: 1 says David the s of Jesse
2Sa 23: 9 him was Eleazar the s of Dodo
2Sa 23:11 the s of Agee the Hararite
2Sa 23:18 the s of Zeruiah, was chief
2Sa 23:20 Benaiah was the s of Jehoiada
2Sa 23:20 the s of a valiant man from
2Sa 23:22 Benaiah the s of Jehoiada did
2Sa 23:24 Elhanan the s of Dodo of
2Sa 23:26 Ira the s of Ikkesh the
2Sa 23:29 Heleb the s of Baanah (the
2Sa 23:29 Ittai the s of Ribai from
2Sa 23:33 Ahiam the s of Sharar the
2Sa 23:34 Eliphelet the s of Ahasbai
2Sa 23:34 the s of the Maacathite,
2Sa 23:34 Eliam the s of Ahithophel the
2Sa 23:36 Igal the s of Nathan of Zobah
2Sa 23:37 of Joab the s of Zeruiah)
1Ki 1: 5 Now Adonijah the s of Haggith
1Ki 1: 7 with Joab the s of Zeruiah
1Ki 1: 8 Benaiah the s of Jehoiada
1Ki 1:11 s of Haggith has become king
1Ki 1:12 and the life of your s Solomon
1Ki 1:13 Assuredly your s Solomon
1Ki 1:17 your s shall reign after me
1Ki 1:21 my s Solomon will be counted
1Ki 1:26 nor Benaiah the s of Jehoiada
1Ki 1:30 your s shall be king after me
1Ki 1:32 and Benaiah the s of Jehoiada
1Ki 1:33 have Solomon my s ride on my
1Ki 1:36 Benaiah the s of Jehoiada
1Ki 1:38 Benaiah the s of Jehoiada
1Ki 1:42 the s of Abiathar the priest
1Ki 1:44 Benaiah the s of Jehoiada
1Ki 2: 1 and he charged Solomon his s
1Ki 2: 5 the s of Zeruiah did to me
1Ki 2: 5 Israel, to Abner the s of Ner
1Ki 2: 5 and Amasa the s of Jether
1Ki 2: 8 with you Shimei the s of Gera
1Ki 2:13 Now Adonijah the s of Haggith
1Ki 2:22 and for Joab the s of Zeruiah
1Ki 2:25 of Benaiah the s of Jehoiada
1Ki 2:29 Benaiah the s of Jehoiada
1Ki 2:32 Abner the s of Ner, the
1Ki 2:32 and Amasa the s of Jether
1Ki 2:34 So Benaiah the s of Jehoiada
1Ki 2:35 s of Jehoiada in his place
1Ki 2:39 to Achish the s of Maachah
1Ki 2:46 Benaiah the s of Jehoiada
1Ki 3: 6 him a s to sit on his throne
1Ki 3:19 this woman's s died in the
1Ki 3:20 took my s from my side, while
1Ki 3:21 in the morning to nurse my s
1Ki 3:21 he was not my s whom I had
1Ki 3:22 But the living one is my s
1Ki 3:22 and the dead one is your s
1Ki 3:22 But the dead one is your s
1Ki 3:22 and the living one is my s
1Ki 3:23 The one says, This is my s
1Ki 3:23 and your s is the dead one'
1Ki 3:23 But your s is the dead one,
1Ki 3:23 and my s is the living one
1Ki 3:26 Then the woman whose s was
1Ki 3:26 with compassion for her s
1Ki 4: 2 Azariah the s of Zadok, the
1Ki 4: 3 Jehoshaphat the s of Ahilud
1Ki 4: 4 Benaiah the s of Jehoiada
1Ki 4: 5 Azariah the s of Nathan, over
1Ki 4: 5 Zabud the s of Nathan, a
1Ki 4: 6 and Adoniram the s of Abda
1Ki 4:12 Baana the s of Ahilud, in
1Ki 4:13 of Jair the s of Manasseh
1Ki 4:14 Ahinadab the s of Iddo, in
1Ki 4:16 Baanah the s of Hushai, in
1Ki 4:17 Jehoshaphat the s of Paruah
1Ki 4:18 Shimei the s of Elah, in
1Ki 4:19 Geber the s of Uri, in the
1Ki 5: 5 father David, saying, "Your s
1Ki 5: 7 wise s over this great people
1Ki 7:14 He was the s of a widow from
1Ki 8:19 build the house, but your s
1Ki 11:12 it out of the hand of your s
1Ki 11:13 s for the sake of my servant
1Ki 11:20 bore him Genubath his s, whom
1Ki 11:23 Rezon the s of Eliadah, who
1Ki 11:26 Jeroboam the s of Nebat, an
1Ki 11:36 And to his s I will give one
1Ki 11:43 Rehoboam his s reigned in his
1Ki 12: 2 when Jeroboam the s of Nebat
1Ki 12:15 to Jeroboam the s of Nebat
1Ki 12:16 inheritance in the s of Jesse
1Ki 12:21 to Rehoboam the s of Solomon
1Ki 12:23 to Rehoboam the s of Solomon
1Ki 14: 1 the s of Jeroboam became sick
1Ki 14: 5 ask you something about her s
1Ki 14:20 Then Nadab his s reigned in
1Ki 14:21 Rehoboam the s of Solomon
1Ki 14:31 Then Abijam his s reigned in
1Ki 15: 1 King Jeroboam the s of Nebat
1Ki 15: 4 by setting up his s after him
1Ki 15: 8 Then Asa his s reigned in his
1Ki 15:18 Ben-Hadad the s of Tabrimmon
1Ki 15:18 the s of Hezion, king of
1Ki 15:24 his s reigned in his place
1Ki 15:25 Now Nadab the s of Jeroboam
1Ki 15:27 Then Baasha the s of Ahijah
1Ki 15:33 Baasha the s of Ahijah became
1Ki 16: 1 came to Jehu the s of Hanani
1Ki 16: 3 of Jeroboam the s of Nebat
1Ki 16: 6 Then Elah his s reigned in

1Ki 16: 7 by the prophet Jehu the s of
1Ki 16: 8 Elah the s of Baasha became
1Ki 16:13 and the sins of Elah his s
1Ki 16:21 Tibni the s of Ginath, to
1Ki 16:22 Tibni the s of Ginath
1Ki 16:26 of Jeroboam the s of Nebat
1Ki 16:28 Then Ahab his s reigned in
1Ki 16:29 Ahab the s of Omri became
1Ki 16:29 Ahab the s of Omri reigned
1Ki 16:30 Now Ahab the s of Omri did
1Ki 16:31 of Jeroboam the s of Nebat
1Ki 16:34 with his youngest s Segub he
1Ki 16:34 through Joshua the s of Nun
1Ki 17:12 prepare it for myself and my s
1Ki 17:13 some for yourself and your s
1Ki 17:17 s of the woman who owned the
1Ki 17:18 remembrance, and to kill my s
1Ki 17:19 Give me your s
1Ki 17:20 I lodge, by killing her s
1Ki 17:23 said, "See, your s lives
1Ki 19:16 the s of Nimshi as king over
1Ki 19:16 Elisha the s of Shaphat of
1Ki 19:19 found Elisha the s of Shaphat
1Ki 21:22 of Jeroboam the s of Nebat
1Ki 21:22 of Baasha the s of Ahijah
1Ki 21:29 but in the days of his s I
1Ki 22: 8 man, Micaiah the s of Imlah
1Ki 22: 9 the s of Imlah quickly
1Ki 22:11 Now Zedekiah the s of
1Ki 22:24 Then Zedekiah the s of
1Ki 22:26 city and to Joash the king's s
1Ki 22:40 Then Ahaziah his s reigned in
1Ki 22:41 Now Jehoshaphat the s of Asa
1Ki 22:49 Then Ahaziah the s of Ahab
1Ki 22:50 Then Jehoram his s reigned in
1Ki 22:51 Ahaziah the s of Ahab became
1Ki 22:52 of Jeroboam the s of Nebat
2Ki 1:17 Because he had no s, Jehoram
2Ki 1:17 Jehoram the s of Jehoshaphat
2Ki 3: 1 Now Jehoram the s of Ahab
2Ki 3: 3 of Jeroboam the s of Nebat
2Ki 3:11 Elisha the s of Shaphat is
2Ki 3:27 Then he took his eldest s who
2Ki 4: 6 full, that she said to her s
2Ki 4:14 Actually, she has no s, and
2Ki 4:16 year you shall embrace a s
2Ki 4:17 bore a s when the appointed
2Ki 4:28 Did I ask a s of my lord
2Ki 4:36 Pick up your s
2Ki 4:37 then she picked up her s and
2Ki 6:28 said to me, 'Give your s,
2Ki 6:28 and we will eat my s tomorrow
2Ki 6:29 So we boiled my s, and ate him
2Ki 6:29 on the next day, 'Give your s
2Ki 6:29 but she has hidden her s
2Ki 6:31 s of Shaphat remains on him
2Ki 6:32 Do you see how this s of a
2Ki 8: 1 s he had restored to life
2Ki 8: 5 s he had restored to life
2Ki 8: 5 this is her s whom Elisha
2Ki 8: 9 Your s Ben-Hadad king of
2Ki 8:16 year of Joram the s of Ahab
2Ki 8:16 Jehoram the s of Jehoshaphat
2Ki 8:24 Then Ahaziah his s reigned in
2Ki 8:25 year of Joram the s of Ahab
2Ki 8:25 Ahaziah the s of Jehoram
2Ki 8:28 the s of Ahab to war against
2Ki 8:29 And Ahaziah the s of Jehoram
2Ki 8:29 the s of Ahab in Jezreel,
2Ki 9: 2 for Jehu the s of Jehoshaphat
2Ki 9: 2 the s of Nimshi, and go in and
2Ki 9: 9 of Jeroboam the s of Nebat
2Ki 9: 9 of Baasha the s of Ahijah
2Ki 9:14 So Jehu the s of Jehoshaphat,
2Ki 9:14 the s of Nimshi, conspired
2Ki 9:20 of Jehu the s of Nimshi, for
2Ki 9:29 year of Joram the s of Ahab
2Ki 10:15 met Jehonadab the s of Rechab
2Ki 10:23 Jehonadab the s of Rechab
2Ki 10:29 of Jeroboam the s of Nebat
2Ki 10:35 Then Jehoahaz his s reigned
2Ki 11: 1 saw that her s was dead, she
2Ki 11: 2 took Joash the s of Ahaziah
2Ki 11: 4 and showed them the king's s
2Ki 11:12 he brought out the king's s
2Ki 12:21 Jozachar the s of Shimeath
2Ki 12:21 and Jehozabad the s of Shomer
2Ki 12:21 Then Amaziah his s reigned in
2Ki 13: 1 of Joash the s of Ahaziah
2Ki 13: 1 Jehoahaz the s of Jehu became
2Ki 13: 2 of Jeroboam the s of Nebat
2Ki 13: 3 of Ben-Hadad the s of Hazael
2Ki 13: 9 Then Joash his s reigned in
2Ki 13:10 Jehoash the s of Jehoahaz
2Ki 13:11 of Jeroboam the s of Nebat
2Ki 13:24 Then Ben-Hadad his s reigned
2Ki 13:25 Jehoash the s of Jehoahaz
2Ki 13:25 the s of Hazael, the cities
2Ki 14: 1 of Joash the s of Jehoahaz
2Ki 14: 1 Amaziah the s of Joash, king
2Ki 14: 8 to Jehoash the s of Jehoahaz
2Ki 14: 8 the s of Jehu, king of Israel
2Ki 14: 9 daughter to my s as wife'
2Ki 14:13 the s of Jehoash
2Ki 14:13 the s of Ahaziah, at Beth
2Ki 14:16 Then Jeroboam his s reigned
2Ki 14:17 Amaziah the s of Joash, king
2Ki 14:17 of Jehoash the s of Jehoahaz
2Ki 14:23 of Amaziah the s of Joash
2Ki 14:23 Jeroboam the s of Joash,
2Ki 14:24 of Jeroboam the s of Nebat
2Ki 14:25 Jonah the s of Amittai, the
2Ki 14:27 of Jeroboam the s of Joash
2Ki 14:29 Then Zechariah his s reigned
2Ki 15: 1 Azariah the s of Amaziah
2Ki 15: 5 Jotham the king's s was over
2Ki 15: 7 Then Jotham his s reigned in
2Ki 15: 8 Zechariah the s of Jeroboam
2Ki 15: 9 of Jeroboam the s of Nebat
2Ki 15:10 Then Shallum the s of Jabesh
2Ki 15:13 Shallum the s of Jabesh
2Ki 15:14 For Menahem the s of Gadi
2Ki 15:14 and struck Shallum the s of
2Ki 15:17 Menahem the s of Gadi became
2Ki 15:18 of Jeroboam the s of Nebat
2Ki 15:22 Then Pekahiah his s reigned
2Ki 15:23 Pekahiah the s of Menahem
2Ki 15:24 of Jeroboam the s of Nebat
2Ki 15:25 Then Pekah the s of Remaliah
2Ki 15:27 Pekah the s of Remaliah
2Ki 15:28 of Jeroboam the s of Nebat
2Ki 15:30 Then Hoshea the s of Elah led
2Ki 15:30 Pekah the s of Remaliah, and
2Ki 15:30 of Jotham the s of Uzziah
2Ki 15:32 of Pekah the s of Remaliah
2Ki 15:32 Jotham the s of Uzziah, king
2Ki 15:37 and Pekah the s of Remaliah
2Ki 15:38 Then Ahaz his s reigned in
2Ki 16: 1 of Pekah the s of Remaliah
2Ki 16: 1 Ahaz the s of Jotham, king of
2Ki 16: 3 indeed he made his s pass
2Ki 16: 5 Pekah the s of Remaliah, king
2Ki 16: 7 I am your servant and your s
2Ki 16:20 Then Hezekiah his s reigned
2Ki 17: 1 Hoshea the s of Elah became
2Ki 17:21 Jeroboam the s of Nebat king
2Ki 18: 1 year of Hoshea the s of Elah
2Ki 18: 1 that Hezekiah the s of Ahaz
2Ki 18: 9 year of Hoshea the s of Elah
2Ki 18:18 Eliakim the s of Hilkiah
2Ki 18:18 and Joah the s of Asaph, the
2Ki 18:26 Then Eliakim the s of Hilkiah
2Ki 18:37 Then Eliakim the s of Hilkiah
2Ki 18:37 and Joah the s of Asaph, the
2Ki 19: 2 the prophet, the s of Amoz
2Ki 19:20 Then Isaiah the s of Amoz
2Ki 19:37 Then Esarhaddon his s reigned
2Ki 20: 1 the s of Amoz, went to him and
2Ki 20:12 the s of Baladan, king of
2Ki 20:21 Then Manasseh his s reigned
2Ki 21: 6 Also he made his s pass
2Ki 21: 7 to David and to Solomon his s
2Ki 21:18 Then his s Amon reigned in
2Ki 21:24 s Josiah king in his place
2Ki 21:26 Then Josiah his s reigned in
2Ki 22: 3 the s of Azaliah
2Ki 22: 3 the s of Meshullam, to the
2Ki 22:12 Ahikam the s of Shaphan,
2Ki 22:12 Achbor the s of Michaiah,
2Ki 22:14 of Shallum the s of Tikvah
2Ki 22:14 the s of Harhas, keeper of
2Ki 23:10 the Valley of the S of Hinnom
2Ki 23:10 his s or his daughter pass
2Ki 23:15 which Jeroboam the s of Nebat
2Ki 23:30 took Jehoahaz the s of Josiah
2Ki 23:34 Necho made Eliakim the s of
2Ki 24: 6 Then Jehoiachin his s reigned
2Ki 25:22 made Gedaliah the s of Ahikam
2Ki 25:22 the s of Shaphan, governor
2Ki 25:23 Ishmael the s of Nethaniah,
2Ki 25:23 Johanan the s of Careah,
2Ki 25:23 Seraiah the s of Tanhumeth
2Ki 25:23 and Jaazaniah the s of a
2Ki 25:25 Ishmael the s of Nethaniah
2Ki 25:25 the s of Elishama, of the
1Ch 1:41 The s of Anah was Dishon
1Ch 1:43 Bela the s of Beor, and the
1Ch 1:44 died, Jobab the s of Zerah of
1Ch 1:46 died, Hadad the s of Bedad
1Ch 1:49 Baal-Hanan the s of Achbor
1Ch 2: 7 The s of Carmi was Achar, the
1Ch 2: 8 The s of Ethan was Azariah
1Ch 2:18 Caleb the s of Hezron begot
1Ch 2:31 The s of Appaim was Ishi, the
1Ch 2:31 the s of Ishi was Sheshan, and
1Ch 2:45 the s of Shammai was Maon, and
1Ch 3: 2 Absalom the s of Maacah, the
1Ch 3: 2 Adonijah the s of Haggith
1Ch 3:10 Solomon's s was Rehoboam
1Ch 3:10 Abijah was his s, Asa his s
1Ch 3:10 his s, Jehoshaphat his s
1Ch 3:11 Joram his s, Ahaziah his s,
1Ch 3:11 Ahaziah his s, Joash his s
1Ch 3:12 Amaziah his s
1Ch 3:12 Azariah his s, Jotham his s
1Ch 3:13 Ahaz his s, Hezekiah his s
1Ch 3:13 Manasseh his s
1Ch 3:14 Amon his s, and Josiah his s
1Ch 3:16 Jehoiakim were Jeconiah his s
1Ch 3:16 and Zedekiah his s
1Ch 3:17 were Assir, Shealtiel his s
1Ch 3:22 The s of Shechaniah was
1Ch 4: 2 Reaiah the s of Shobal begot
1Ch 4: 8 of Aharhel the s of Harum
1Ch 4:15 the s of Jephunneh were Iru
1Ch 4:15 The s of Elah was Kenaz
1Ch 4:21 The sons of Shelah the s of
1Ch 4:25 Shallum his s, Mibsam his s
1Ch 4:25 and Mishma his s
1Ch 4:26 Hamuel his s, Zacchur his s
1Ch 4:26 and Shimei his s
1Ch 4:34 and Joshah the s of Amaziah
1Ch 4:35 Jehu the s of Joshibiah, the
1Ch 4:35 s of Seraiah, the s of Asiel
1Ch 4:37 s of Shiphi, the s of Allon
1Ch 4:37 s of Jedaiah, the s of Shimri
1Ch 4:37 the s of Shemaiah
1Ch 5: 1 the s of Israel, so that the
1Ch 5: 4 of Joel were Shemaiah his s
1Ch 5: 4 Gog his s, Shimei his s
1Ch 5: 5 Micah his s, Reaiah his s,
1Ch 5: 5 Reaiah his s, Baal his s
1Ch 5: 6 and Beerah his s, whom
1Ch 5: 8 and Bela the s of Azaz
1Ch 5: 8 s of Shema, the s of Joel
1Ch 5:14 of Abihail the s of Huri
1Ch 5:14 the s of Jaroah
1Ch 5:14 the s of Gilead
1Ch 5:14 the s of Michael
1Ch 5:14 the s of Jeshishai
1Ch 5:14 s of Jahdo, the s of Buz
1Ch 5:15 Ahi the s of Abdiel
1Ch 5:15 the s of Guni, was chief of
1Ch 6:20 Of Gershon were Libni his s
1Ch 6:20 Jahath his s, Zimmah his s
1Ch 6:21 Joah his s, Iddo his s,
1Ch 6:21 Zerah his s
1Ch 6:21 and Jeatherai his s
1Ch 6:22 Kohath were Amminadab his s
1Ch 6:22 Korah his s, Assir his s
1Ch 6:23 Elkanah his s, Ebiasaph his s
1Ch 6:23 Ebiasaph his s, Assir his s
1Ch 6:24 Tahath his s, Uriel his s,
1Ch 6:24 Uriel his s, Uzziah his s
1Ch 6:24 and Shaul his s
1Ch 6:26 Zophai his s, Nahath his s
1Ch 6:27 Eliab his s, Jeroham his s,
1Ch 6:27 and Elkanah his s
1Ch 6:29 were Mahli, Libni his s,
1Ch 6:29 Shimei his s, Uzzah his s
1Ch 6:30 Shimea his s, Haggiah his s
1Ch 6:30 and Asaiah his s
1Ch 6:33 s of Joel, the s of Samuel,
1Ch 6:34 the s of Elkanah
1Ch 6:34 the s of Jeroham
1Ch 6:34 s of Eliel, the s of Toah,
1Ch 6:35 the s of Zuph
1Ch 6:35 the s of Elkanah
1Ch 6:35 s of Mahath, the s of Amasai
1Ch 6:36 the s of Elkanah

1Ch 6:36 the s of Joel
1Ch 6:36 the s of Azariah
1Ch 6:36 the s of Zephaniah
1Ch 6:37 the s of Tahath
1Ch 6:37 the s of Assir
1Ch 6:37 s of Ebiasaph, the s of Korah
1Ch 6:38 the s of Izhar, the s of
1Ch 6:38 the s of Kohath, the s of
1Ch 6:38 s of Levi, the s of Israel
1Ch 6:39 was Asaph the s of Berachiah
1Ch 6:39 the s of Shimea
1Ch 6:40 the s of Michael
1Ch 6:40 the s of Baaseiah
1Ch 6:40 the s of Malchijah
1Ch 6:41 the s of Ethni
1Ch 6:41 s of Zerah, the s of Adaiah
1Ch 6:42 the s of Ethan, the s of
1Ch 6:42 s of Ethan, the s of Zimmah
1Ch 6:42 of Zimmah, the s of Shimei,
1Ch 6:43 the s of Jahath
1Ch 6:43 s of Gershon, the s of Levi
1Ch 6:44 were Ethan the s of Kishi
1Ch 6:44 s of Abdi, the s of Malluch
1Ch 6:45 the s of Hashabiah
1Ch 6:45 s of Amaziah, the s of Hilkiah
1Ch 6:46 the s of Amzi
1Ch 6:46 s of Bani, the s of Shamer,
1Ch 6:47 the s of Mahli
1Ch 6:47 the s of Mushi
1Ch 6:47 s of Merari, the s of Levi
1Ch 6:50 Eleazar his s, Phinehas his s
1Ch 6:50 Abishua his s
1Ch 6:51 Bukki his s, Uzzi his s,
1Ch 6:51 Zerahiah his s
1Ch 6:52 Meraioth his s, Amariah his s
1Ch 6:52 Ahitub his s
1Ch 6:53 Zadok his s, and Ahimaaz his s
1Ch 6:56 to Caleb the s of Jephunneh
1Ch 7: 3 The s of Uzzi was Izrahiah,
1Ch 7:10 The s of Jediael was Bilhan,
1Ch 7:12 and Hushim was the s of Aher
1Ch 7:16 the wife of Machir bore a s
1Ch 7:17 The s of Ulam was Bedan
1Ch 7:17 s of Machir, the s of Manasseh
1Ch 7:20 were Shuthelah, Bered his s
1Ch 7:20 Tahath his s, Eladah his s
1Ch 7:20 Tahath his s
1Ch 7:21 Zabad his s, Shuthelah his s
1Ch 7:23 she conceived and bore a s
1Ch 7:25 and Rephah was his s, as well
1Ch 7:25 and Telah his s, Tahan his s
1Ch 7:26 Laadan his s, Ammihud his s
1Ch 7:26 Elishama his s
1Ch 7:27 Nun his s, and Joshua his s
1Ch 7:29 of Joseph, the s of Israel
1Ch 8:30 And his firstborn s was Abdon
1Ch 8:34 The s of Jonathan was
1Ch 8:37 Raphah his s, Eleasah his s
1Ch 8:37 and Azel his s
1Ch 9: 4 Uthai the s of Ammihud
1Ch 9: 4 s of Omri, the
1Ch 9: 4 the s of Bani, of the descendants
1Ch 9: 4 of Perez, the s of Judah
1Ch 9: 7 Sallu the s of Meshullam
1Ch 9: 7 the s of Hodaviah
1Ch 9: 7 the s of Hassenuah
1Ch 9: 8 Ibneiah the s of Jeroham
1Ch 9: 8 s of Uzzi, the s of Michri
1Ch 9: 8 Meshullam the s of Shephatiah
1Ch 9: 8 s of Reuel, the s of Ibnijah
1Ch 9:11 Azariah the s of Hilkiah
1Ch 9:11 the s of Meshullam
1Ch 9:11 the s of Zadok
1Ch 9:11 the s of Meraioth
1Ch 9:11 the s of Ahitub, the officer
1Ch 9:12 Adaiah the s of Jeroham
1Ch 9:12 s of Pashur, the s of Malchijah
1Ch 9:12 Maasai the s of Adiel
1Ch 9:12 the s of Jahzerah
1Ch 9:12 the s of Meshullam
1Ch 9:12 the s of Meshillemith
1Ch 9:12 the s of Immer
1Ch 9:14 Shemaiah the s of Hasshub
1Ch 9:14 the s of Azrikam
1Ch 9:14 the s of Hashabiah
1Ch 9:15 and Mattaniah the s of Micah
1Ch 9:15 s of Zichri, the s of Asaph
1Ch 9:16 Obadiah the s of Shemaiah
1Ch 9:16 s of Galal, the s of Jeduthun
1Ch 9:16 and Berechiah the s of Asa
1Ch 9:16 the s of Elkanah, who lived
1Ch 9:19 Shallum the s of Kore
1Ch 9:19 the s of Ebiasaph
1Ch 9:19 the s of Korah, and his
1Ch 9:20 Phinehas the s of Eleazar had
1Ch 9:21 Zechariah the s of
1Ch 9:36 His firstborn s was Abdon
1Ch 9:40 The s of Jonathan was
1Ch 9:43 begot Binea, Rephaiah his s
1Ch 9:43 Eleasah his s, and Azel his s
1Ch 10:14 over to David the s of Jesse
1Ch 11: 6 Joab the s of Zeruiah went up
1Ch 11:11 Jashobeam the s of a
1Ch 11:12 him was Eleazar the s of Dodo
1Ch 11:22 Benaiah was the s of Jehoiada
1Ch 11:22 the s of a valiant man from
1Ch 11:24 the s of Jehoiada had done
1Ch 11:26 Elhanan the s of Dodo of
1Ch 11:28 Ira the s of Ikkesh the
1Ch 11:30 Heled the s of Baanah the
1Ch 11:31 Ithai the s of Ribai of
1Ch 11:34 Jonathan the s of Shageh the
1Ch 11:35 Ahiam the s of Sacar the
1Ch 11:35 Hararite, Eliphal the s of Ur
1Ch 11:37 Naarai the s of Ezbai,
1Ch 11:38 Nathan, Mibhar the s of Hagri
1Ch 11:39 of Joab the s of Zeruiah)
1Ch 11:41 Hittite, Zabad the s of Ahlai
1Ch 11:42 Adina the s of Shiza the
1Ch 11:43 Hanan the s of Maachah,
1Ch 11:45 Jediael the s of Shimri, and
1Ch 12: 1 from Saul the s of Kish
1Ch 12:18 on your side, O s of Jesse
1Ch 15:17 appointed Heman the s of Joel
1Ch 15:17 Asaph the s of Berechiah
1Ch 15:17 Ethan the s of Kushaiah
1Ch 16:38 Obed-Edom the s of Jeduthun
1Ch 17:13 Father, and he shall be My s
1Ch 18:10 Hadoram his s to King David
1Ch 18:12 Moreover Abishai the s of
1Ch 18:15 Joab the s of Zeruiah was
1Ch 18:15 Jehoshaphat the s of Ahilud
1Ch 18:16 Zadok the s of Ahitub and
1Ch 18:16 Abimelech the s of Abiathar
1Ch 18:17 Benaiah the s of Jehoiada was
1Ch 19: 1 his s reigned in his place
1Ch 19: 2 to Hanun the s of Nahash,
1Ch 20: 5 Elhanan the s of Jair killed
1Ch 20: 7 Jonathan the s of Shimea
1Ch 22: 5 Solomon my s is young and
1Ch 22: 6 he called for his s Solomon
1Ch 22: 7 My s, as for me, it was in my
1Ch 22: 9 a s shall be born to you, who
1Ch 22:10 My name, and he shall be My s
1Ch 22:11 Now, my s, may the LORD be
1Ch 22:17 Israel to help Solomon his s
1Ch 23: 1 he made his s Solomon king
1Ch 24: 6 Shemaiah the s of Nethaneel
1Ch 24: 6 Ahimelech the s of Abiathar
1Ch 24:26 the s of Jaaziah, Beno
1Ch 24:29 the s of Kish, Jerahmeel
1Ch 26: 1 Meshelemiah the s of Kore
1Ch 26: 6 Also to Shemaiah his s were
1Ch 26:14 cast lots for his s Zechariah
1Ch 26:24 Shebuel the s of Gershom
1Ch 26:24 the s of Moses, was overseer
1Ch 26:25 Eliezer were Rehabiah his s
1Ch 26:25 Rehabiah his s, Jeshaiah his s
1Ch 26:25 Jeshaiah his s, Joram his s
1Ch 26:25 Zichri his s
1Ch 26:25 his s, and Shelomith his s
1Ch 26:28 the seer, Saul the s of Kish
1Ch 26:28 Abner the s of Ner
1Ch 26:28 Joab the s of Zeruiah had
1Ch 27: 2 Jashobeam the s of Zabdiel
1Ch 27: 5 the s of Jehoiada the priest,
1Ch 27: 6 division was Ammizabad his s
1Ch 27: 7 and Zebadiah his s after him
1Ch 27: 9 the s of Ikkesh the Tekoite
1Ch 27:16 was Eliezer the s of Zichri
1Ch 27:16 Shephatiah the s of Maachah
1Ch 27:17 Hashabiah the s of Kemuel
1Ch 27:18 Omri the s of Michael
1Ch 27:19 Ishmaiah the s of Obadiah
1Ch 27:19 Jerimoth the s of Azriel
1Ch 27:20 Hoshea the s of Azaziah
1Ch 27:20 Joel the s of Pedaiah
1Ch 27:21 Iddo the s of Zechariah
1Ch 27:21 Jaasiel the s of Abner
1Ch 27:22 Dan, Azarel the s of Jeroham
1Ch 27:24 Joab the s of Zeruiah began a
1Ch 27:25 Azmaveth the s of Adiel was
1Ch 27:25 Jehonathan the s of Uzziah
1Ch 27:26 Ezri the s of Chelub was over
1Ch 27:29 Shaphat the s of Adlai was
1Ch 27:32 Jehiel the s of Hachmoni was
1Ch 27:34 was Jehoiada the s of Benaiah
1Ch 28: 5 my s Solomon to sit on the
1Ch 28: 6 It is your s Solomon who
1Ch 28: 6 I have chosen him to be My s
1Ch 28: 9 my s Solomon, know the God of
1Ch 28:11 Then David gave his s Solomon
1Ch 28:20 David said to his s Solomon
1Ch 29: 1 My s Solomon, whom alone
1Ch 29:19 give my s Solomon a loyal
1Ch 29:22 they made Solomon the s of
1Ch 29:26 Thus David the s of Jesse
1Ch 29:28 Solomon his s reigned in his
2Ch 1: 1 Now Solomon the s of David
2Ch 1: 5 that Bezaleel the s of Uri
2Ch 1: 5 the s of Hur, had made, he
2Ch 2:12 has given King David a wise s
2Ch 2:14 (the s of a woman of the
2Ch 6: 9 but your s who will come
2Ch 9:29 Jeroboam the s of Nebat
2Ch 9:31 Rehoboam his s reigned in his
2Ch 10: 2 s of Nebat heard it (he was
2Ch 10:15 to Jeroboam the s of Nebat
2Ch 10:16 inheritance in the s of Jesse
2Ch 11: 3 to Rehoboam the s of Solomon
2Ch 11:17 and made Rehoboam the s of
2Ch 11:18 of Jerimoth the s of David
2Ch 11:18 of Eliah the s of Jesse
2Ch 11:22 the s of Maacah as chief, to
2Ch 12:16 Then Abijah his s reigned in
2Ch 13: 6 Yet Jeroboam the s of Nebat
2Ch 13: 6 of Solomon the s of David
2Ch 13: 7 Rehoboam the s of Solomon
2Ch 14: 1 Then Asa his s reigned in his
2Ch 15: 1 upon Azariah the s of Oded
2Ch 17: 1 his s reigned in his place
2Ch 17:16 was Amasiah the s of Zichri
2Ch 18: 7 He is Micaiah the s of Imla
2Ch 18: 8 Micaiah the s of Imla quickly
2Ch 18:10 Now Zedekiah the s of
2Ch 18:23 Then Zedekiah the s of
2Ch 18:25 city and to Joash the king's s
2Ch 19: 2 Jehu the s of Hanani the seer
2Ch 19:11 and Zebadiah the s of Ishmael
2Ch 20:14 Jahaziel the s of Zechariah
2Ch 20:14 the s of Benaiah
2Ch 20:14 the s of Jeiel
2Ch 20:14 the s of Mattaniah, a Levite
2Ch 20:34 book of Jehu the s of Hanani
2Ch 20:37 But Eliezer the s of Dodavah
2Ch 21: 1 Then Jehoram his s reigned in
2Ch 21:17 so that there was not a s
2Ch 22: 1 youngest s king in his place
2Ch 22: 1 So Ahaziah the s of Jehoram
2Ch 22: 5 went with Jehoram the s of
2Ch 22: 6 And Azariah the s of Jehoram
2Ch 22: 6 the s of Ahab in Jezreel,
2Ch 22: 7 against Jehu the s of Nimshi
2Ch 22: 9 he is the s of Jehoshaphat,
2Ch 22:10 saw that her s was dead, she
2Ch 22:11 took Joash the s of Ahaziah
2Ch 23: 1 Azariah the s of Jeroham,
2Ch 23: 1 Ishmael the s of Jehohanan,
2Ch 23: 1 Azariah the s of Obed,
2Ch 23: 1 Maaseiah the s of Adaiah
2Ch 23: 1 and Elishaphat the s of Zichri
2Ch 23: 3 the king's s shall reign, as
2Ch 23:11 they brought out the king's s
2Ch 24:20 the s of Jehoiada the priest
2Ch 24:22 done to him, but killed his s
2Ch 24:26 Zabad the s of Shimeath the
2Ch 24:26 Jehozabad the s of Shimrith
2Ch 24:27 Then Amaziah his s reigned in
2Ch 25:17 to Joash the s of Jehoahaz
2Ch 25:17 the s of Jehu, king of Israel
2Ch 25:18 daughter to my s as wife'
2Ch 25:23 the s of Joash
2Ch 25:23 the s of Jehoahaz
2Ch 25:25 Amaziah the s of Joash, king
2Ch 25:25 of Joash the s of Jehoahaz
2Ch 26:21 Then Jotham his s was over
2Ch 26:22 Isaiah the s of Amoz wrote
2Ch 26:23 Then Jotham his s reigned
2Ch 27: 9 Then Ahaz his s reigned in
2Ch 28: 3 the Valley of the S of Hinnom

2Ch 28: 6 For Pekah the s of Remaliah
2Ch 28: 7 killed Maaseiah the king's s
2Ch 28:12 Azariah the s of Johanan
2Ch 28:12 the s of Meshillemoth
2Ch 28:12 Jehizkiah the s of Shallum
2Ch 28:12 and Amasa the s of Hadlai
2Ch 28:27 Then Hezekiah his s reigned
2Ch 29:12 Mahath the s of Amasai and
2Ch 29:12 Joel the s of Azariah, of the
2Ch 29:12 of Merari, Kish the s of Abdi
2Ch 29:12 Azariah the s of Jehalelel
2Ch 29:12 Joah the s of Zimmah and Eden
2Ch 29:12 Zimmah and Eden the s of Joah
2Ch 30:26 of Solomon the s of David
2Ch 31:14 Kore the s of Imnah the
2Ch 32:20 the s of Amoz, prayed and
2Ch 32:32 the s of Amoz, and in the book
2Ch 32:33 Then Manasseh his s reigned
2Ch 33: 6 the Valley of the S of Hinnom
2Ch 33: 7 to David and to Solomon his s
2Ch 33:20 Then his s Amon reigned in
2Ch 33:25 s Josiah king in his place
2Ch 34: 8 sent Shaphan the s of Azaliah
2Ch 34: 8 and Joah the s of Joahaz the
2Ch 34:20 Ahikam the s of Shaphan,
2Ch 34:20 Abdon the s of Micah
2Ch 34:22 of Shallum the s of Tokhath
2Ch 34:22 the s of Hasrah, keeper of
2Ch 35: 3 which Solomon the s of David
2Ch 35: 4 instruction of Solomon his s
2Ch 36: 1 took Jehoahaz the s of Josiah
2Ch 36: 8 Then Jehoiachin his s reigned
Ezra 3: 2 Then Jeshua the s of Jozadak
Ezra 3: 2 Zerubbabel the s of Shealtiel
Ezra 3: 8 Zerubbabel the s of Shealtiel
Ezra 3: 8 Jeshua the s of Jozadak, and
Ezra 5: 1 and Zechariah the s of Iddo
Ezra 5: 2 Zerubbabel the s of Shealtiel
Ezra 5: 2 Jeshua the s of Jozadak rose
Ezra 6:14 and Zechariah the s of Iddo
Ezra 7: 1 Ezra the s of Seraiah
Ezra 7: 1 s of Azariah, the s of Hilkiah
Ezra 7: 2 the s of Shallum
Ezra 7: 2 s of Zadok, the s of Ahitub
Ezra 7: 3 the s of Amariah
Ezra 7: 3 the s of Azariah
Ezra 7: 3 the s of Meraioth
Ezra 7: 4 the s of Zerahiah
Ezra 7: 4 s of Uzzi, the s of Bukki,
Ezra 7: 5 the s of Abishua
Ezra 7: 5 the s of Phinehas
Ezra 7: 5 the s of Eleazar
Ezra 7: 5 the s of Aaron the chief
Ezra 8: 4 Elihoenai the s of Zerahiah
Ezra 8: 6 Ebed the s of Jonathan, and
Ezra 8: 7 Jeshaiah the s of Athaliah
Ezra 8: 8 Zebadiah the s of Michael
Ezra 8: 9 Joab, Obadiah the s of Jehiel
Ezra 8:11 Zechariah the s of Bebai
Ezra 8:12 Johanan the s of Hakkatan
Ezra 8:18 sons of Mahli the s of Levi
Ezra 8:18 the s of Israel, namely
Ezra 8:33 the s of Uriah the priest
Ezra 8:33 was Eleazar the s of Phinehas
Ezra 8:33 Jozabad the s of Jeshua and
Ezra 8:33 and Noadiah the s of Binnui
Ezra 10: 2 And Shechaniah the s of Jehiel
Ezra 10: 6 Jehohanan the s of Eliashib
Ezra 10:15 Only Jonathan the s of Asahel
Ezra 10:15 and Jahaziah the s of Tikvah
Ezra 10:18 of Jeshua the s of Jozadak
Neh 1: 1 Nehemiah the s of Hachaliah
Neh 3: 2 Zaccur the s of Imri built
Neh 3: 4 them Meremoth the s of Urijah
Neh 3: 4 the s of Koz, made repairs
Neh 3: 4 Meshullam the s of Berechiah
Neh 3: 4 the s of Meshezabeel, made
Neh 3: 4 the s of Baana made repairs
Neh 3: 6 Jehoiada the s of Paseah and
Neh 3: 6 Meshullam the s of Besodeiah
Neh 3: 8 him Uzziel the s of Harhaiah
Neh 3: 9 to them Rephaiah the s of Hur
Neh 3:10 Next to them Jedaiah the s of
Neh 3:10 next to him Hattush the s of
Neh 3:11 Malchijah the s of Harim and
Neh 3:11 Hashub the s of Pahath-Moab
Neh 3:12 Shallum the s of Hallohesh
Neh 3:14 Malchijah the s of Rechab
Neh 3:15 Shallun the s of Col-Hozeh,
Neh 3:16 him Nehemiah the s of Azbuk
Neh 3:17 under Rehum the s of Bani
Neh 3:18 under Bavai the s of Henadad
Neh 3:19 to him Ezer the s of Jeshua
Neh 3:20 the s of Zabbai diligently
Neh 3:21 him Meremoth the s of Urijah
Neh 3:21 the s of Koz, repaired
Neh 3:23 Azariah the s of Maaseiah
Neh 3:23 the s of Ananiah, made
Neh 3:24 After him Binnui the s of
Neh 3:25 Palal the s of Uzai made
Neh 3:25 After him Pedaiah the s of
Neh 3:29 After them Zadok the s of
Neh 3:29 Shemaiah the s of Shechaniah
Neh 3:30 Hananiah the s of Shelemiah
Neh 3:30 Hanun, the sixth s of Zalaph
Neh 3:30 After him Meshullam the s of
Neh 6:10 of Shemaiah the s of Delaiah
Neh 6:10 the s of Mehetabeel, who was
Neh 6:18 of Shechaniah the s of Arah
Neh 6:18 his s Jehohanan had married
Neh 6:18 Meshullam the s of Berechiah
Neh 8:17 the days of Joshua the s of
Neh 10: 1 the s of Hacaliah, and
Neh 10: 9 Jeshua the s of Azaniah,
Neh 11: 4 Athaiah the s of Uzziah
Neh 11: 4 the s of Zechariah
Neh 11: 4 the s of Amariah
Neh 11: 4 the s of Shephatiah
Neh 11: 4 the s of Mahalaleel
Neh 11: 5 and Maaseiah the s of Baruch
Neh 11: 5 the s of Col-Hozeh
Neh 11: 5 the s of Hazaiah
Neh 11: 5 the s of Adaiah
Neh 11: 5 the s of Joiarib
Neh 11: 5 the s of Zechariah
Neh 11: 5 the s of Shiloni
Neh 11: 7 Sallu the s of Meshullam
Neh 11: 7 the s of Joed, the s of
Neh 11: 7 the s of Pedaiah
Neh 11: 7 the s of Kolaiah
Neh 11: 7 the s of Maaseiah
Neh 11: 7 s of Ithiel, the s of Jeshaiah
Neh 11: 9 Joel the s of Zichri was
Neh 11: 9 Judah the s of Senuah was
Neh 11:10 Jedaiah the s of Joiarib
Neh 11:11 Seraiah the s of Hilkiah
Neh 11:11 the s of Meshullam
Neh 11:11 the s of Zadok
Neh 11:11 the s of Meraioth
Neh 11:11 the s of Ahitub, was the
Neh 11:12 and Adaiah the s of Jeroham
Neh 11:12 the s of Pelaliah
Neh 11:12 the s of Amzi
Neh 11:12 the s of Zechariah
Neh 11:12 the s of Pashhur
Neh 11:12 the s of Malchijah
Neh 11:13 and Amashai the s of Azareel
Neh 11:13 the s of Ahzai
Neh 11:13 the s of Meshillemoth
Neh 11:13 the s of Immer
Neh 11:14 the s of one of the great men
Neh 11:15 Shemaiah the s of Hasshub
Neh 11:15 the s of Azrikam
Neh 11:15 the s of Hashabiah
Neh 11:15 the s of Bunni
Neh 11:17 and Mattaniah the s of Micha
Neh 11:17 s of Zabdi, the s of Asaph
Neh 11:17 Abda the s of Shammua, the
Neh 11:17 s of Galal, the s of Jeduthun
Neh 11:22 was Uzzi the s of Bani, the
Neh 11:22 the s of Hashabiah
Neh 11:22 the s of Mattaniah
Neh 11:22 the s of Micha, of the sons
Neh 11:24 the s of Meshezabeel
Neh 11:24 of Zerah the s of Judah, was
Neh 12: 1 Zerubbabel the s of Shealtiel
Neh 12:17 the s of Minjamin
Neh 12:23 of Johanan the s of Eliashib
Neh 12:24 and Jeshua the s of Kadmiel
Neh 12:26 of Joiakim the s of Jeshua
Neh 12:26 the s of Jozadak, and in the
Neh 12:35 Zechariah the s of Jonathan
Neh 12:35 the s of Shemaiah
Neh 12:35 the s of Mattaniah
Neh 12:35 the s of Michaiah
Neh 12:35 s of Zaccur, the s of Asaph
Neh 12:45 of David and Solomon his s
Neh 13:13 was Hanan the s of Zaccur
Neh 13:13 of Zaccur, the s of Mattaniah
Neh 13:28 the s of Eliashib the high
Esth 2: 5 was Mordecai the s of Jair
Esth 2: 5 the s of Shimei
Esth 2: 5 the s of Kish, a Benjamite
Esth 3: 1 the s of Hammedatha the
Esth 3:10 the s of Hammedatha the
Esth 8: 5 the s of Hammedatha the
Esth 9:10 of Haman the s of Hammedatha
Esth 9:24 the s of Hammedatha the
Job 18:19 He has neither s nor
Job 25: 6 a s of man, who is a worm
Job 32: 2 the s of Barachel the Buzite,
Job 32: 6 the s of Barachel the Buzite,
Job 35: 8 your righteousness a s of man
Ps 2: 7 said to Me, You are My S
Ps 2:12 Kiss the S, lest He be angry,
Ps 8: 4 the s of man that You visit
Ps 50:20 slander your own mother's s
Ps 72: 1 righteousness to the king's S
Ps 72:20 the s of Jesse are ended
Ps 80:17 Upon the s of man whom You
Ps 86:16 And save the s of Your
Ps 89:22 him, Nor the s of wickedness
Ps 116:16 the s of Your maidservant
Ps 144: 3 Or the s of man, that You are
Ps 146: 3 in princes, Nor in a s of man
Prov 1: 1 of Solomon the s of David
Prov 1: 8 My s, hear the instruction of
Prov 1:10 My s, if sinners entice you,
Prov 1:15 my s, do not walk in the way
Prov 2: 1 My s, if you receive my words
Prov 3: 1 My s, do not forget my law,
Prov 3:11 My s, do not despise the
Prov 3:12 the s in whom he delights
Prov 3:21 My s, let them not depart
Prov 4: 3 When I was my father's s,
Prov 4:10 Hear, my s, and receive my
Prov 4:20 My s, give attention to my
Prov 5: 1 My s, pay attention to my
Prov 5:20 For why should you, my s, be
Prov 6: 1 My s, if you become surety
Prov 6: 3 So do this, my s, and deliver
Prov 6:20 My s, keep your father's
Prov 7: 1 My s, keep my words, and
Prov 10: 1 A wise s makes a glad father,
Prov 10: 1 but a foolish s is the grief
Prov 10: 5 gathers in summer is a wise s
Prov 10: 5 is a s who causes shame
Prov 13: 1 A wise s heeds his father's
Prov 13:24 spares his rod hates his s
Prov 15:20 A wise s makes a father glad,
Prov 17: 2 over a s who causes shame
Prov 17:25 A foolish s is a grief to his
Prov 19:13 A foolish s is the ruin of
Prov 19:18 Chasten your s while there is
Prov 19:26 is a s who causes shame and
Prov 19:27 to instruction, my s, and you
Prov 23:15 My s, if your heart is wise,
Prov 23:19 Hear, my s, and be wise
Prov 23:26 My s, give me your heart, and
Prov 24:13 My s, eat honey because it is
Prov 24:21 My s, fear the LORD and the
Prov 27:11 My s, be wise, and make my
Prov 28: 7 the law is a discerning s
Prov 29:17 Correct your s, and he will
Prov 29:21 have him as a s in the end
Prov 30: 1 words of Agur the s of Jakeh
Prov 31: 2 What, my s?
Prov 31: 2 And what, s of my womb
Prov 31: 2 And what, s of my vows
Eccl 1: 1 the s of David, king in
Eccl 4: 8 he has neither s nor brother
Eccl 5:14 when he begets a s, there is
Eccl 10:17 your king is the s of nobles
Eccl 12:12 And further, my s, be
Is 1: 1 of Isaiah the s of Amoz,
Is 2: 1 the s of Amoz saw concerning
Is 7: 1 days of Ahaz the s of Jotham
Is 7: 1 the s of Uzziah, king of
Is 7: 1 Pekah the s of Remaliah, king
Is 7: 3 you and Shear-Jashub your s
Is 7: 4 Syria, and the s of Remaliah
Is 7: 5 the s of Remaliah have taken
Is 7: 6 over them, the s of Tabeel"
Is 7: 9 of Samaria is Remaliah's s
Is 7:14 shall conceive and bear a S
Is 8: 2 priest and Zechariah the s of
Is 8: 3 and she conceived and bore a s
Is 8: 6 in Rezin and in Remaliah's s
Is 9: 6 is born, unto us a S is given
Is 13: 1 Isaiah the s of Amoz saw

Ezek 47: 6 **S** of man, have you seen this
Dan 3:25 fourth is like the **S** of God
Dan 5:22 But you his **s**, Belshazzar,
Dan 7:13 behold, One like the **S** of Man
Dan 8:17 **s** of man, that the vision
Dan 9: 1 of Darius the **s** of Ahasuerus
Hos 1: 1 came to Hosea the **s** of Beeri
Hos 1: 1 of Jeroboam the **s** of Joash
Hos 1: 3 she conceived and bore him a **s**
Hos 1: 8 she conceived and bore a **s**
Hos 11: 1 and out of Egypt I called My **s**
Hos 13:13 He is an unwise **s**, for he
Joel 1: 1 came to Joel the **s** of Pethuel
Amos 1: 1 of Jeroboam the **s** of Joash
Amos 7:14 nor was I a **s** of a prophet,
Amos 8:10 like mourning for an only **s**
Jon 1: 1 to Jonah the **s** of Amittai
Mic 6: 5 what Balaam the **s** of Beor
Mic 7: 6 For **s** dishonors father,
Zeph 1: 1 to Zephaniah the **s** of Cushi
Zeph 1: 1 the **s** of Gedaliah
Zeph 1: 1 the **s** of Amariah
Zeph 1: 1 the **s** of Hezekiah
Zeph 1: 1 days of Josiah the **s** of Amon
Hag 1: 1 Zerubbabel the **s** of Shealtiel
Hag 1: 1 to Joshua the **s** of Jehozadak
Hag 1:12 Zerubbabel the **s** of Shealtiel
Hag 1:12 Joshua the **s** of Jehozadak,
Hag 1:14 Zerubbabel the **s** of Shealtiel
Hag 1:14 of Joshua the **s** of Jehozadak
Hag 2: 2 Zerubbabel the **s** of Shealtiel
Hag 2: 2 to Joshua the **s** of Jehozadak
Hag 2: 4 **s** of Jehozadak, the high
Hag 2:23 the **s** of Shealtiel,' says the
Zech 1: 1 Zechariah the **s** of Berechiah
Zech 1: 1 the **s** of Iddo the prophet,
Zech 1: 7 Zechariah the **s** of Berechiah
Zech 1: 7 the **s** of Iddo the prophet
Zech 6:10 of Josiah the **s** of Zephaniah
Zech 6:11 of Joshua the **s** of Jehozadak
Zech 6:14 and Hen the **s** of Zephaniah
Zech 12:10 as one mourns for his only **s**
Mal 1: 6 A **s** honors his father, and a
Mal 3:17 his own **s** who serves him
Matt 1: 1 **S** of David, the **S** of Abraham
Matt 1:20 **s** of David, do not be afraid
Matt 1:21 And she will bring forth a **S**
Matt 1:23 be with child, and bear a **S**
Matt 1:25 brought forth her firstborn **S**
Matt 2:15 Out of Egypt I called My **S**
Matt 3:17 This is My beloved **S**, in whom
Matt 4: 3 If You are the **S** of God,
Matt 4: 6 If You are the **S** of God,
Matt 4:21 James the **s** of Zebedee, and
Matt 7: 9 if his **s** asks for bread, will
Matt 8:20 but the **S** of Man has nowhere
Matt 8:29 with You, Jesus, You **S** of God
Matt 9: 2 **S**, be of good cheer
Matt 9: 6 **S** of Man has power on earth
Matt 9:27 **S** of David, have mercy on us
Matt 10: 2 James the **s** of Zebedee, and
Matt 10: 3 James the **s** of Alphaeus, and
Matt 10:23 before the **S** of Man comes
Matt 10:37 he who loves **s** or daughter
Matt 11:19 The **S** of Man came eating and
Matt 11:27 no one knows the **S** except the
Matt 11:27 know the Father except the **S**
Matt 11:27 he to whom the **S** wills to
Matt 12: 8 For the **S** of Man is Lord even
Matt 12:23 Could this be the **S** of David
Matt 12:32 a word against the **S** of Man
Matt 12:40 so will the **S** of Man be three
Matt 13:37 the good seed is the **S** of Man
Matt 13:41 The **S** of Man will send out
Matt 13:55 Is this not the carpenter's **s**
Matt 14:33 Truly You are the **S** of God
Matt 15:22 on me, O Lord, **S** of David
Matt 16:13 say that I, the **S** of Man, am
Matt 16:16 the **S** of the living God
Matt 16:27 For the **S** of Man will come in
Matt 16:28 the **S** of Man coming in His
Matt 17: 5 This is My beloved **S**, in whom
Matt 17: 9 **S** of Man is risen from the
Matt 17:12 Likewise the **S** of Man is also
Matt 17:15 Lord, have mercy on my **s**, for
Matt 17:22 The **S** of Man is about to be
Matt 18:11 For the **S** of Man has come to
Matt 19:28 when the **S** of Man sits on the
Matt 20:18 the **S** of Man will be betrayed
Matt 20:28 just as the **S** of Man did not
Matt 20:30 on us, O Lord, **S** of David
Matt 20:31 on us, O Lord, **S** of David
Matt 21: 9 Hosanna to the **S** of David
Matt 21:15 Hosanna to the **S** of David
Matt 21:28 came to the first and said, '**S**
Matt 21:37 of all he sent his **s** to them
Matt 21:37 They will respect my **s**
Matt 21:38 the vinedressers saw the **s**
Matt 22: 2 arranged a marriage for his **s**
Matt 22:42 Whose **S** is He?
Matt 22:42 said to Him, "The **S** of David
Matt 22:45 Him Lord,' how is He his **S**
Matt 23:15 a **s** of hell as yourselves
Matt 23:35 **s** of Berechiah, whom you
Matt 24:27 the coming of the **S** of Man be
Matt 24:30 Then the sign of the **S** of Man
Matt 24:30 they will see the **S** of Man
Matt 24:37 the coming of the **S** of Man be
Matt 24:39 the coming of the **S** of Man be
Matt 24:44 for the **S** of Man is coming at
Matt 25:13 which the **S** of Man is coming
Matt 25:31 When the **S** of Man comes in
Matt 26: 2 and the **S** of Man will be
Matt 26:24 The **S** of Man goes as it is
Matt 26:24 whom the **S** of Man is betrayed
Matt 26:45 and the **S** of Man is being
Matt 26:63 are the Christ, the **S** of God
Matt 26:64 hereafter you will see the **S**
Matt 27:40 If You are the **S** of God, come
Matt 27:43 He said, 'I am the **S** of God
Matt 27:54 Truly this was the **S** of God
Matt 28:19 of the Father and of the **S**
Mark 1: 1 of Jesus Christ, the **S** of God
Mark 1:11 You are My beloved **S**, in whom
Mark 1:19 He saw James the **s** of Zebedee
Mark 2: 5 **S**, your sins are forgiven you
Mark 2:10 **S** of Man has power on earth
Mark 2:14 He saw Levi the **s** of Alphaeus
Mark 2:28 Therefore the **S** of Man is
Mark 3:11 You are the **S** of God
Mark 3:17 James the **s** of Zebedee and
Mark 3:18 James the **s** of Alphaeus,
Mark 5: 7 Jesus, **S** of the Most High God
Mark 6: 3 the **S** of Mary, and brother of
Mark 8:31 to teach them that the **S** of
Mark 8:38 of him the **S** of Man also will
Mark 9: 7 This is My beloved **S**
Mark 9: 9 till the **S** of Man had risen
Mark 9:12 concerning the **S** of Man, that
Mark 9:17 Teacher, I brought You my **s**
Mark 9:31 them, 'The **S** of Man is being
Mark 10:33 and the **S** of Man will be
Mark 10:45 For even the **S** of Man did not
Mark 10:46 the **s** of Timaeus, sat by the
Mark 10:47 **S** of David, have mercy on me
Mark 10:48 **S** of David, have mercy on me
Mark 12: 6 Therefore still having one **s**
Mark 12: 6 They will respect my **s**
Mark 12:35 the Christ is the **S** of David
Mark 12:37 how is He then his **S**
Mark 13:26 Then they will see the **S** of
Mark 13:32 angels in heaven, nor the **S**
Mark 14:21 The **S** of Man indeed goes just
Mark 14:21 whom the **S** of Man is betrayed
Mark 14:41 behold, the **S** of Man is being
Mark 14:61 Christ, the **S** of the Blessed
Mark 14:62 you will see the **S** of Man
Mark 15:39 this Man was the **S** of God
Luke 1:13 Elizabeth will bear you a **s**
Luke 1:31 your womb and bring forth a **S**
Luke 1:32 called the **S** of the Highest
Luke 1:35 will be called the **S** of God
Luke 1:36 conceived a **s** in her old age
Luke 1:57 and she brought forth a **s**
Luke 2: 7 brought forth her firstborn **S**
Luke 2:48 **S**, why have You done this to
Luke 3: 2 the **s** of Zacharias in the
Luke 3:22 You are My beloved **S**
Luke 3:23 was supposed) the **s** of Joseph
Luke 3:23 **s** of Joseph, the **s** of Heli,
Luke 3:24 the **s** of Matthat
Luke 3:24 the **s** of Levi
Luke 3:24 the **s** of Melchi
Luke 3:24 **s** of Janna, the **s** of Joseph
Luke 3:25 the **s** of Mattathiah
Luke 3:25 the **s** of Amos
Luke 3:25 the **s** of Nahum
Luke 3:25 **s** of Esli, the **s** of Naggai,
Luke 3:26 the **s** of Maath
Luke 3:26 the **s** of Mattathiah
Luke 3:26 the **s** of Semei
Luke 3:26 **s** of Joseph, the **s** of Judah
Luke 3:27 the **s** of Joannas
Luke 3:27 the **s** of Rhesa
Luke 3:27 the **s** of Zerubbabel
Luke 3:27 **s** of Shealtiel, the **s** of Neri
Luke 3:28 the **s** of Melchi
Luke 3:28 the **s** of Addi
Luke 3:28 the **s** of Cosam
Luke 3:28 **s** of Elmodam, the **s** of Er,
Luke 3:29 the **s** of Jose
Luke 3:29 the **s** of Eliezer
Luke 3:29 the **s** of Jorim
Luke 3:29 **s** of Matthat, the **s** of Levi
Luke 3:30 the **s** of Simeon
Luke 3:30 the **s** of Judah
Luke 3:30 the **s** of Joseph
Luke 3:30 **s** of Jonan, the **s** of Eliakim
Luke 3:31 the **s** of Melea
Luke 3:31 the **s** of Menan
Luke 3:31 the **s** of Mattathah
Luke 3:31 **s** of Nathan, the **s** of David
Luke 3:32 the **s** of Jesse, the **s** of
Luke 3:32 the **s** of Obed, the **s** of
Luke 3:32 the **s** of Boaz, the **s** of
Luke 3:32 **s** of Salmon, the **s** of Nahshon
Luke 3:33 the **s** of Amminadab
Luke 3:33 the **s** of Ram
Luke 3:33 the **s** of Hezron
Luke 3:33 **s** of Perez, the **s** of Judah,
Luke 3:34 the **s** of Jacob
Luke 3:34 the **s** of Isaac
Luke 3:34 the **s** of Abraham
Luke 3:34 **s** of Terah, the **s** of Nahor,
Luke 3:35 the **s** of Serug
Luke 3:35 the **s** of Reu
Luke 3:35 the **s** of Peleg
Luke 3:35 **s** of Eber, the **s** of Shelah,
Luke 3:36 the **s** of Cainan
Luke 3:36 the **s** of Arphaxad
Luke 3:36 the **s** of Shem
Luke 3:36 **s** of Noah, the **s** of Lamech,
Luke 3:37 the **s** of Methuselah, the **s**
Luke 3:37 the **s** of Enoch, the **s** of
Luke 3:37 the **s** of Jared, the **s** of
Luke 3:37 the **s** of Mahalalel, the **s**
Luke 3:37 the **s** of Cainan
Luke 3:38 **s** of Enos, the **s** of Seth
Luke 3:38 the **s** of Adam, the **s** of God
Luke 4: 3 If You are the **S** of God,
Luke 4: 9 If You are the **S** of God,
Luke 4:22 Is this not Joseph's **s**
Luke 4:41 are the Christ, the **S** of God
Luke 5:24 **S** of Man has power on earth
Luke 6: 5 The **S** of Man is also Lord of
Luke 6:15 James the **s** of Alphaeus, and
Luke 6:16 Judas the **s** of James, and
Luke 6:22 evil, for the **S** of Man's sake
Luke 7:12 out, the only **s** of his mother
Luke 7:34 The **S** of Man has come eating
Luke 8:28 Jesus, **S** of the Most High God
Luke 9:22 The **S** of Man must suffer many
Luke 9:26 of him the **S** of Man will be
Luke 9:35 This is My beloved **S**
Luke 9:38 I implore You, look on my **s**
Luke 9:41 Bring your **s** here
Luke 9:44 for the **S** of Man is about to
Luke 9:56 For the **S** of Man did not come
Luke 9:58 but the **S** of Man has nowhere
Luke 10: 6 if a **s** of peace is there,
Luke 10:22 who the **S** is but the Father
Luke 10:22 who the Father is but the **S**
Luke 10:22 the **S** wills to reveal Him
Luke 11:11 If a **s** asks for bread from
Luke 11:30 so also the **S** of Man will be
Luke 12: 8 him the **S** of Man also will
Luke 12:10 a word against the **S** of Man
Luke 12:40 for the **S** of Man is coming at
Luke 12:53 will be divided against **s**
Luke 12:53 and **s** against father, mother
Luke 15:13 the younger **s** gathered all
Luke 15:19 worthy to be called your **s**
Luke 15:21 the **s** said to him, 'Father, I
Luke 15:21 worthy to be called your **s**
Luke 15:24 for this my **s** was dead and is
Luke 15:25 Now his older **s** was in the
Luke 15:30 soon as this **s** of yours came
Luke 15:31 And he said to him, '**S**, you
Luke 16:25 But Abraham said, '**S**,
Luke 17:22 of the days of the **S** of Man

Luke 17:24 so also the S of Man will be
Luke 17:26 in the days of the S of Man
Luke 17:30 when the S of Man is revealed
Luke 18: 8 when the S of Man comes, will
Luke 18:31 S of Man will be accomplished
Luke 18:38 S of David, have mercy on me
Luke 18:39 S of David, have mercy on me
Luke 19: 9 he also is a s of Abraham
Luke 19:10 for the S of Man has come to
Luke 20:13 I will send my beloved s
Luke 20:41 that the Christ is David's S
Luke 20:44 how is He then his S
Luke 21:27 Then they will see the S of
Luke 21:36 to stand before the S of Man
Luke 22:22 truly the S of Man goes as it
Luke 22:48 the S of Man with a kiss
Luke 22:69 Hereafter the S of Man will
Luke 22:70 Are You then the S of God
Luke 24: 7 saying, 'The S of Man must be
John 1:18 The only begotten S, who is
John 1:34 that this is the S of God
John 1:42 You are Simon the s of Jonah
John 1:45 of Nazareth, the s of Joseph
John 1:49 Rabbi, You are the S of God
John 1:51 descending upon the S of Man
John 3:13 the S of Man who is in heaven
John 3:14 even so must the S of Man be
John 3:16 He gave His only begotten S
John 3:17 For God did not send His S
John 3:18 of the only begotten S of God
John 3:35 The Father loves the S, and
John 3:36 in the S has everlasting life
John 3:36 the S shall not see life, but
John 4: 5 Jacob gave to his s Joseph
John 4:46 whose s was sick at Capernaum
John 4:47 to come down and heal his s
John 4:50 Go your way; your s lives
John 4:51 him, saying, "Your s lives
John 4:53 said to him, "Your s lives
John 5:19 you, the S can do nothing of
John 5:19 does, the S also does in like
John 5:20 For the Father loves the S
John 5:21 even so the S gives life to
John 5:22 all judgment to the S,
John 5:23 the S just as they honor the
John 5:23 S does not honor the Father
John 5:25 the voice of the S of God
John 5:26 so He has granted the S to
John 5:27 because He is the S of Man
John 6:27 which the S of Man will give
John 6:40 that everyone who sees the S
John 6:42 the s of Joseph, whose father
John 6:53 eat the flesh of the S of Man
John 6:62 S of Man ascend where He was
John 6:69 the S of the living God
John 6:71 the s of Simon, for it was he
John 8:28 When you lift up the S of Man
John 8:35 but a s abides forever
John 8:36 if the S makes you free, you
John 9:19 Is this your s, who you say
John 9:20 We know that this is our s
John 9:35 you believe in the S of God
John 10:36 I said, 'I am the S of God'
John 11: 4 God, that the S of God may be
John 11:27 the S of God, who is to come
John 12: 4 Judas Iscariot, Simon's s
John 12:23 S of Man should be glorified
John 12:34 The S of Man must be lifted
John 12:34 Who is this S of Man
John 13: 2 of Judas Iscariot, Simon's s
John 13:26 Iscariot, the s of Simon
John 13:31 Now the S of Man is glorified
John 14:13 may be glorified in the S
John 17: 1 Glorify Your S
John 17: 1 that Your S also may glorify
John 17:12 except the s of perdition
John 19: 7 He made Himself the S of God
John 19:26 Woman, behold your s
John 20:31 Christ, the S of God, and that
John 21:15 s of Jonah, do you love Me
John 21:16 s of Jonah, do you love Me
John 21:17 s of Jonah, do you love Me
Acts 1:13 James the s of Alphaeus and
Acts 1:13 and Judas the s of James
Acts 4:36 S of Encouragement), a Levite
Acts 7:21 brought him up as her own s
Acts 7:56 the S of Man standing at the
Acts 8:37 Jesus Christ is the S of God
Acts 9:20 that He is the S of God
Acts 13:10 you s of the devil, you enemy
Acts 13:21 gave them Saul the s of Kish
Acts 13:22 found David the s of Jesse
Acts 13:33 You are My S, today I have
Acts 16: 1 the s of a certain Jewish
Acts 23: 6 Pharisee, the s of a Pharisee
Acts 23:16 when Paul's sister's s heard
Rom 1: 3 concerning His S Jesus Christ
Rom 1: 4 to be the S of God with power
Rom 1: 9 spirit in the gospel of His S
Rom 5:10 through the death of His S
Rom 8: 3 S in the likeness of sinful
Rom 8:29 to the image of His S, that
Rom 8:32 who did not spare His own S
Rom 9: 9 come and Sarah shall have a s
1Co 1: 9 into the fellowship of His S
1Co 4:17 faithful s in the Lord, who
1Co 15:28 then the S Himself will also
2Co 1:19 For the S of God, Jesus
Gal 1:16 to reveal His S in me, that I
Gal 2:20 live by faith in the S of God
Gal 4: 4 come, God sent forth His S
Gal 4: 6 of His S into your hearts
Gal 4: 7 are no longer a slave but a s
Gal 4: 7 if a s, then an heir of God
Gal 4:30 out the bondwoman and her s
Gal 4:30 for the s of the bondwoman
Gal 4:30 with the s of the freewoman
Eph 4:13 the knowledge of the S of God
Phil 2:22 that as a s with his father
Col 1:13 kingdom of the S of His love
1Th 1:10 to wait for His S from heaven
2Th 2: 3 revealed, the s of perdition,
1Ti 1: 2 my true s in the faith
1Ti 1:18 s Timothy, according to the
2Ti 1: 2 To Timothy, my beloved s
2Ti 2: 1 You therefore, my s, be
Tit 1: 4 my true s in our common faith
Phm 10 to you for my s Onesimus,
Heb 1: 2 days spoken to us by His S
Heb 1: 5 You are My S, today I have
Heb 1: 5 and He shall be to Me a S"
Heb 1: 8 But to the S He says
Heb 2: 6 or the s of man that You take
Heb 3: 6 but Christ as a S over His
Heb 4:14 heavens, Jesus the S of God
Heb 5: 5 You are My S, today I have
Heb 5: 8 though He was a S, yet He
Heb 6: 6 for themselves the S of God
Heb 7: 3 but made like the S of God
Heb 7:28 appoints the S who has been
Heb 10:29 the S of God underfoot,
Heb 11:17 up his only begotten s,
Heb 11:24 the s of Pharaoh's daughter
Heb 12: 5 My s, do not despise the
Heb 12: 6 and scourges every s whom He
Heb 12: 7 for what s is there whom a
Jas 2:21 Isaac his s on the altar
1Pe 5:13 and so does Mark my s
2Pe 1:17 This is My beloved S, in whom
2Pe 2:15 way of Balaam the s of Beor
1Jn 1: 3 and with His S Jesus Christ
1Jn 1: 7 S cleanses us from all sin
1Jn 2:22 denies the Father and the S
1Jn 2:23 Whoever denies the S does not
1Jn 2:23 the S has the Father also
1Jn 2:24 you also will abide in the S
1Jn 3: 8 For this purpose the S of God
1Jn 3:23 name of His S Jesus Christ
1Jn 4: 9 begotten S into the world
1Jn 4:10 us and sent His S to be the
1Jn 4:14 the S as Savior of the world
1Jn 4:15 that Jesus is the S of God
1Jn 5: 5 that Jesus is the S of God
1Jn 5: 9 He has testified of His S
1Jn 5:10 He who believes in the S of
1Jn 5:10 that God has given of His S
1Jn 5:11 and this life is in His S
1Jn 5:12 He who has the S has life
1Jn 5:12 he who does not have the S of
1Jn 5:13 in the name of the S of God
1Jn 5:13 in the name of the S of God
1Jn 5:20 that the S of God has come
1Jn 5:20 true, in His S Jesus Christ
2Jn 3 the S of the Father, in truth
2Jn 9 has both the Father and the S
Rev 1:13 One like the S of Man,
Rev 2:18 things says the S of God, who
Rev 14:14 sat One like the S of Man
Rev 21: 7 his God and he shall be My s

SONG (*see* SING, SONGS)
Ex 15: 1 sang this s to the LORD, and
Ex 15: 2 The LORD is my strength and s
Num 21:17 Then Israel sang this s
Deut 31:19 down this s for yourselves
Deut 31:19 that this s may be a witness
Deut 31:21 that this s will testify
Deut 31:22 wrote this s the same day
Deut 31:30 this s until they were ended
Deut 32:44 this s in the hearing of the
Judg 5:12 Awake, awake, sing a s
2Sa 1:18 of Judah the S of the Bow
2Sa 22: 1 the LORD the words of this s
1Ch 6:31 over the service of s in the
2Ch 29:27 the s of the LORD also began,
Ps 28: 7 with my s I will praise Him
Ps 33: 3 Sing to Him a new s
Ps 40: 3 has put a new s in my mouth
Ps 42: 8 night His s shall be with me
Ps 69:12 I am the s of the drunkards
Ps 69:30 the name of God with a s, And
Ps 77: 6 remembrance my s in the night
Ps 81: 2 Raise a s and strike the
Ps 96: 1 Oh, sing to the LORD a new s
Ps 98: 1 Oh, sing to the LORD a new s
Ps 98: 4 Break forth in s, rejoice, and
Ps 118:14 The LORD is my strength and s
Ps 137: 3 captive required of us a s
Ps 137: 4 LORD's s In a foreign land
Ps 144: 9 I will sing a new s to You
Ps 149: 1 Sing to the LORD a new s, And
Eccl 7: 5 a man to hear the s of fools
Song 1: 1 The s of songs, which is
Is 5: 1 sing to my Well-beloved a s
Is 12: 2 LORD, is my strength and my s
Is 23:15 as in the s of the harlot
Is 24: 9 shall not drink wine with a s
Is 25: 5 the s of the terrible ones
Is 26: 1 In that day this s will be
Is 30:29 You shall have a s as in the
Is 42:10 Sing to the LORD a new s, and
Lam 3:14 their taunting s all the day
Lam 3:63 I am their taunting s
Ezek 33:32 to them as a very lovely s of
Rev 5: 9 And they sang a new s, saying
Rev 14: 3 a new s before the throne
Rev 14: 3 that s except the hundred
Rev 15: 3 And they sing the s of Moses
Rev 15: 3 the s of the Lamb, saying

SONGS (*see* SONG)
Gen 31:27 sent you away with joy and s
1Ki 4:32 his s were one thousand and
1Ch 25: 7 in the s of the LORD, all who
Neh 12:46 s of praise and thanksgiving
Job 35:10 Who gives s in the night,
Ps 32: 7 me with s of deliverance
Ps 119:54 been my s In the house of my
Ps 137: 3 Sing us one of the s of Zion
Prov 25:20 who sings s to a heavy heart
Song 1: 1 The song of s, which is
Is 23:16 sweet melody, sing many s
Is 24:16 of the earth we have heard s
Is 38:20 s with stringed instruments
Ezek 26:13 an end to the sound of your s
Amos 5:23 from Me the noise of your s
Amos 8: 3 the s of the temple shall be
Amos 8:10 all your s into lamentation
Eph 5:19 and hymns and spiritual s,
Col 3:16 and hymns and spiritual s,

SON-IN-LAW (*see* SON, SONS-IN-LAW)
Gen 19:12 S, your sons, your daughters,
Judg 15: 6 the s of the Timnite, because
Judg 19: 5 woman's father said to his s
1Sa 18:18 I should be s to the king
1Sa 18:21 You shall be my s today
1Sa 18:22 become the king's s
1Sa 18:23 light thing to be a king's s
1Sa 18:26 well to become the king's s
1Sa 18:27 he might become the king's s
1Sa 22:14 as David, who is the king's s
2Ki 8:27 for he was the s of the house
Neh 6:18 him, because he was the s of
Neh 13:28 was a s of Sanballat the

SON'S (*see* SON)
Gen 24:51 her be your master's s wife
Gen 27:25 and I will eat of my s game
Gen 27:31 arise and eat of his s game
Gen 30:14 me some of your s mandrakes
Gen 30:15 take away my s mandrakes also

Lev 10: 6 to Eleazar and Ithamar, his s
Lev 10: 9 you, nor your s with you
Lev 10:12 Ithamar, his s who were left
Lev 10:14 in a clean place, you, your s
Lev 10:16 the s of Aaron who were left,
Lev 13: 2 to one of his s the priests
Lev 16: 1 death of the two s of Aaron
Lev 17: 2 Speak to Aaron, to his s, and
Lev 21: 1 the s of Aaron, and say to
Lev 21:24 told it to Aaron and his s
Lev 22: 2 Speak to Aaron and his s, that
Lev 22:18 Speak to Aaron and his s, and
Lev 24: 9 shall be for Aaron and his s
Lev 26:29 shall eat the flesh of your s
Num 1:10 from the s of Joseph
Num 1:32 From the s of Joseph, the
Num 3: 2 the names of the s of Aaron
Num 3: 3 the names of the s of Aaron
Num 3: 9 the Levites to Aaron and his s
Num 3:10 shall appoint Aaron and his s
Num 3:17 These were the s of Levi by
Num 3:18 of the s of Gershon by their
Num 3:19 And the s of Kohath by their
Num 3:20 And the s of Merari by their
Num 3:38 were Moses, Aaron, and his s
Num 3:48 redeemed, to Aaron and his s
Num 3:51 money to Aaron and his s,
Num 4: 2 Take a census of the s of
Num 4: 4 This is the service of the s
Num 4: 5 his s shall come, and they
Num 4:15 his s have finished covering
Num 4:15 then the s of Kohath shall
Num 4:15 of meeting which the s of
Num 4:19 his s shall go in and appoint
Num 4:22 a census of the s of Gershon
Num 4:27 his s shall assign all the
Num 4:27 of the s of the Gershonites
Num 4:28 of the s of Gershon in the
Num 4:29 As for the s of Merari, you
Num 4:33 families of the s of Merari
Num 4:34 congregation numbered the s
Num 4:38 numbered of the s of Gershon
Num 4:41 families of the s of Gershon
Num 4:42 of the families of the s of
Num 4:45 families of the s of Merari
Num 6:23 Speak to Aaron and his s,
Num 7: 7 he gave to the s of Gershon
Num 7: 8 he gave to the s of Merari
Num 7: 9 But to the s of Kohath he
Num 8:13 Levites before Aaron and his s
Num 8:19 his s from among the children
Num 8:22 meeting before Aaron and his s
Num 10: 8 The s of Aaron, the priests,
Num 10:17 the s of Gershon
Num 10:17 and the s of Merari set out,
Num 14:33 your s shall be shepherds in
Num 16: 1 and Abiram the s of Eliab, and
Num 16: 1 Peleth, s of Reuben, took men
Num 16: 7 yourselves, you s of Levi
Num 16: 8 Hear now, you s of Levi
Num 16:10 the s of Levi, with you
Num 16:12 and Abiram the s of Eliab, but
Num 16:27 with their wives, their s
Num 18: 1 You and your s and your
Num 18: 1 your s with you shall bear
Num 18: 2 your s are with you before
Num 18: 7 your s with you shall attend
Num 18: 8 as a portion to you and your s
Num 18: 9 most holy for you and your s
Num 18:11 given them to you, and your s
Num 18:19 I have given to you and your s
Num 21:29 has given his s as fugitives
Num 21:35 So they defeated him, his s
Num 22: 5 land of the s of his people
Num 24:17 destroy all the s of tumult
Num 26: 9 The s of Eliab were Nemuel,
Num 26:12 The s of Simeon according to
Num 26:15 The s of Gad according to
Num 26:18 are the families of the s of
Num 26:19 The s of Judah were Er and
Num 26:20 the s of Judah according to
Num 26:21 And the s of Perez were
Num 26:23 The s of Issachar according
Num 26:26 The s of Zebulun according to
Num 26:28 The s of Joseph according to
Num 26:29 The s of Manasseh
Num 26:30 These are the s of Gilead
Num 26:33 the son of Hepher had no s
Num 26:35 These are the s of Ephraim
Num 26:36 these are the s of Shuthelah
Num 26:37 the s of Ephraim according to
Num 26:37 These are the s of Joseph
Num 26:38 The s of Benjamin according
Num 26:40 the s of Bela were Ard and
Num 26:41 These are the s of Benjamin
Num 26:42 These are the s of Dan
Num 26:44 The s of Asher according to
Num 26:45 Of the s of Beriah
Num 26:47 are the families of the s of
Num 26:48 The s of Naphtali according
Num 27: 3 and he had no s
Num 34:23 from the s of Joseph
Num 36: 1 families of the s of Joseph
Num 36: 3 are married to any of the s
Num 36: 5 What the tribe of the s of
Num 36:11 were married to the s of
Deut 1:28 the s of the Anakim there
Deut 2:33 so we defeated him, his s
Deut 7: 4 your s away from following Me
Deut 11: 6 and Abiram the s of Eliab, the
Deut 12:12 LORD your God, you and your s
Deut 12:31 for they burn even their s
Deut 18: 5 LORD, him and his s forever
Deut 21: 5 the s of Levi, shall come
Deut 21:16 his possessions to his s,
Deut 23:17 one of the s of Israel
Deut 28:32 Your s and your daughters
Deut 28:41 You shall beget s and
Deut 28:53 own body, the flesh of your s
Deut 31: 9 the s of Levi, who bore the
Deut 32: 8 He separated the s of Adam
Deut 32:19 of the provocation of His s
Deut 33:24 Asher is most blessed of s
Josh 5: 2 circumcise the s of Israel
Josh 5: 3 circumcised the s of Israel
Josh 5: 7 s whom He raised up in their
Josh 7:24 the wedge of gold, his s
Josh 15:14 three s of Anak from there
Josh 17: 3 the son of Manasseh, had no s
Josh 17: 6 an inheritance among his s
Josh 17: 6 s had the land of Gilead
Josh 24:32 the s of Hamor the father of
Judg 1:20 there the three s of Anak
Judg 3: 6 their daughters to their s
Judg 4: 6 men of the s of Naphtali and
Judg 4: 6 and of the s of Zebulun
Judg 8:19 brothers, the s of my mother
Judg 8:30 Gideon had seventy s who were
Judg 9: 2 that all seventy of the s of
Judg 9: 5 the seventy s of Jerubbaal,
Judg 9:18 his seventy s on one stone
Judg 9:24 s of Jerubbaal might be
Judg 10: 4 Now he had thirty s who rode
Judg 11: 2 Gilead's wife bore s
Judg 11: 2 and when his wife's s grew up
Judg 12: 9 He had thirty s
Judg 12: 9 from elsewhere for his s
Judg 12:14 He had forty s and thirty
Judg 14:16 riddle to the s of my people
Judg 14:17 riddle to the s of her people
Judg 17: 5 he consecrated one of his s
Judg 17:11 like one of his s to him
Judg 18:30 his s were priests to the
Ruth 1: 1 he and his wife and his two s
Ruth 1: 2 of his two s were Mahlon and
Ruth 1: 3 and she was left, and her two s
Ruth 1: 5 the woman survived her two s
Ruth 1:11 Are there still s in my womb
Ruth 1:12 tonight and should also bear s
Ruth 4:15 is better to you than seven s
1Sa 1: 3 Also the two s of Eli, Hophni
1Sa 1: 4 his wife and to all her s and
1Sa 1: 8 not better to you than ten s
1Sa 2:12 Now the s of Eli were corrupt
1Sa 2:21 she conceived and bore three s
1Sa 2:22 his s did to all Israel, and
1Sa 2:24 No, my s! For it is not
1Sa 2:29 honor your s more than Me, to
1Sa 2:34 will come upon your two s
1Sa 3:13 because his s made themselves
1Sa 4: 4 And the two s of Eli, Hophni
1Sa 4:11 and the two s of Eli, Hophni
1Sa 4:17 Also your two s, Hophni and
1Sa 8: 1 made his s judges over Israel
1Sa 8: 3 But his s did not walk in his
1Sa 8: 5 your s do not walk in your
1Sa 8:11 He will take your s and
1Sa 12: 2 and look, my s are with you
1Sa 14:49 Now the s of Saul were
1Sa 16: 1 Myself a king among his s
1Sa 16: 5 he sanctified Jesse and his s
1Sa 16:10 of his s pass before Samuel
1Sa 17:12 was Jesse, and who had eight s
1Sa 17:13 The three oldest s of Jesse
1Sa 17:13 The names of his three s who
1Sa 22:20 Now one of the s of Ahimelech
1Sa 28:19 you and your s will be with me
1Sa 30: 3 and their wives, their s, and
1Sa 30: 6 grieved, every man for his s
1Sa 30:19 s or daughters, spoil or
1Sa 31: 2 hard after Saul and his s
1Sa 31: 2 and Malchishua, Saul's s
1Sa 31: 6 So Saul, his three s, his
1Sa 31: 7 his s were dead, they forsook
1Sa 31: 8 his three s fallen on Mount
1Sa 31:12 the bodies of his s from the
2Sa 2:18 Now the three s of Zeruiah
2Sa 3: 2 S were born to David in
2Sa 3:39 the s of Zeruiah, are too
2Sa 4: 2 Rechab, the s of Rimmon the
2Sa 4: 5 Then the s of Rimmon the
2Sa 4: 9 brother, the s of Rimmon the
2Sa 5:13 Also more s and daughters were
2Sa 6: 3 the s of Abinadab, drove the
2Sa 7:10 nor shall the s of wickedness
2Sa 7:14 the blows of the s of men
2Sa 8:18 and David's s were chief
2Sa 9:10 You therefore, and your s and
2Sa 9:10 Now Ziba had fifteen s and
2Sa 9:11 like one of the king's s
2Sa 13:23 invited all the king's s
2Sa 13:27 all the king's s go with him
2Sa 13:29 Then all the king's s arose
2Sa 13:30 has killed all the king's s
2Sa 13:32 the young men, the king's s
2Sa 13:33 all the king's s are dead
2Sa 13:35 Look, the king's s are coming
2Sa 13:36 that the king's s indeed came
2Sa 14: 6 your maidservant had two s
2Sa 14:27 To Absalom were born three s
2Sa 15:27 peace, and your two s with you
2Sa 15:36 there with them their two s
2Sa 16:10 do with you, you s of Zeruiah
2Sa 19: 5 life, the lives of your s
2Sa 19:17 of Saul, and his fifteen s
2Sa 19:22 you s of Zeruiah, that you
2Sa 21: 8 the two s of Rizpah the
2Sa 21: 8 and the five s of Michal the
2Sa 21:16 was one of the s of the giant
2Sa 21:18 was one of the s of the giant
2Sa 23: 6 But the s of rebellion shall
2Sa 23:32 (of the s of Jashen),
1Ki 1: 9 his brothers, the king's s
1Ki 1:19 invited all the s of the king
1Ki 1:25 has invited all the king's s
1Ki 2: 4 If your s take heed to their
1Ki 2: 7 But show kindness to the s of
1Ki 4: 3 the s of Shisha, scribes
1Ki 4:31 and Darda, the s of Mahol
1Ki 8:25 only if your s take heed to
1Ki 8:39 hearts of all the s of men)
1Ki 9: 6 But if you or your s at all
1Ki 11:20 among the s of Pharaoh
1Ki 12:31 who were not of the s of Levi
1Ki 13:11 his s came and told him all
1Ki 13:12 For his s had seen which
1Ki 13:13 Then he said to his s
1Ki 13:27 And he spoke to his s, saying,
1Ki 13:31 him, that he spoke to his s
1Ki 18:31 the tribes of the s of Jacob
1Ki 20:35 Now a certain man of the s of
2Ki 2: 3 the s of the prophets who
2Ki 2: 5 the s of the prophets who
2Ki 2: 7 fifty men of the s of the
2Ki 2:15 Now when the s of the
2Ki 4: 1 s of the prophets cried out
2Ki 4: 1 my two s to be his slaves
2Ki 4: 4 the door behind you and your s
2Ki 4: 5 the door behind her and her s
2Ki 4: 7 and your s live on the rest
2Ki 4:38 Now the s of the prophets
2Ki 4:38 for the s of the prophets
2Ki 5:22 now two young men of the s of
2Ki 6: 1 the s of the prophets said to
2Ki 8:19 lamp to him and his s forever
2Ki 9: 1 one of the s of the prophets
2Ki 9:26 Naboth and the blood of his s
2Ki 10: 1 Ahab had seventy s in Samaria
2Ki 10: 1 to those who reared Ahab's s
2Ki 10: 2 your master's s are with you

2Ki 10: 3 qualified of your master's s
2Ki 10: 5 and those who reared the s
2Ki 10: 6 of the men, your master's s
2Ki 10: 6 Now the king's s, seventy
2Ki 10: 7 that they took the king's s
2Ki 10: 8 the heads of the king's s
2Ki 10:13 to greet the s of the king
2Ki 10:13 the s of the queen mother
2Ki 10:30 your s shall sit on the
2Ki 11: 2 s who were being murdered
2Ki 15:12 Your s shall sit on the
2Ki 17:17 And they caused their s and
2Ki 19:37 that his s Adrammelech and
2Ki 20:18 take away some of your s who
2Ki 25: 7 Then they killed the s of
1Ch 1: 5 The s of Japheth were Gomer,
1Ch 1: 6 The s of Gomer were Ashkenaz,
1Ch 1: 7 The s of Javan were Elishah,
1Ch 1: 8 The s of Ham were Cush,
1Ch 1: 9 The s of Cush were Seba,
1Ch 1: 9 The s of Raama were Sheba and
1Ch 1:17 The s of Shem were Elam,
1Ch 1:19 To Eber were born two s
1Ch 1:23 these were the s of Joktan
1Ch 1:28 The s of Abraham were Isaac
1Ch 1:31 These were the s of Ishmael
1Ch 1:32 Now the s born to Keturah,
1Ch 1:32 The s of Jokshan were Sheba
1Ch 1:33 The s of Midian were Ephah,
1Ch 1:34 The s of Isaac were Esau and
1Ch 1:35 The s of Esau were Eliphaz,
1Ch 1:36 the s of Eliphaz were Teman,
1Ch 1:37 The s of Reuel were Nahath,
1Ch 1:38 The s of Seir were Lotan,
1Ch 1:39 the s of Lotan were Hori and
1Ch 1:40 The s of Shobal were Alian,
1Ch 1:40 The s of Zibeon were Ajah and
1Ch 1:41 The s of Dishon were Hamran,
1Ch 1:42 The s of Ezer were Bilhan,
1Ch 1:42 The s of Dishan were Uz and
1Ch 2: 1 These were the s of Israel
1Ch 2: 3 The s of Judah were Er, Onan,
1Ch 2: 4 All the s of Judah were five
1Ch 2: 5 The s of Perez were Hezron and
1Ch 2: 6 The s of Zerah were Zimri,
1Ch 2: 9 Also the s of Hezron who were
1Ch 2:16 the s of Zeruiah were Abishai
1Ch 2:18 Now these were her s
1Ch 2:23 the s of Machir the father of
1Ch 2:25 The s of Jerahmeel, the
1Ch 2:27 The s of Ram, the firstborn
1Ch 2:28 The s of Onam were Shammai
1Ch 2:28 The s of Shammai were Nadab
1Ch 2:30 The s of Nadab were Seled and
1Ch 2:32 The s of Jada, the brother of
1Ch 2:33 The s of Jonathan were Peleth
1Ch 2:33 These were the s of Jerahmeel
1Ch 2:34 Now Sheshan had no s, only
1Ch 2:42 the s of Mareshah the father
1Ch 2:43 The s of Hebron were Korah,
1Ch 2:47 the s of Jahdai were Regem,
1Ch 2:50 The s of Hur, the firstborn
1Ch 2:54 The s of Salma were Bethlehem
1Ch 3: 1 Now these were the s of David
1Ch 3: 9 These were all the s of David
1Ch 3: 9 besides the s of the
1Ch 3:15 The s of Josiah were Johanan
1Ch 3:16 The s of Jehoiakim were
1Ch 3:17 the s of Jeconiah were Assir,
1Ch 3:19 The s of Pedaiah were
1Ch 3:19 The s of Zerubbabel were
1Ch 3:21 The s of Hananiah were
1Ch 3:21 the s of Rephaiah
1Ch 3:21 the s of Arnan
1Ch 3:21 the s of Obadiah
1Ch 3:21 and the s of Shechaniah
1Ch 3:22 The s of Shemaiah were
1Ch 3:23 The s of Neariah were
1Ch 3:24 The s of Elioenai were
1Ch 4: 1 The s of Judah were Perez,
1Ch 4: 3 These were the s of the
1Ch 4: 4 These were the s of Hur, the
1Ch 4: 6 These were the s of Naarah
1Ch 4: 7 The s of Helah were Zereth,
1Ch 4:13 The s of Kenaz were Othniel
1Ch 4:13 The s of Othniel were Hathath
1Ch 4:15 The s of Caleb the son of
1Ch 4:16 The s of Jahaleleel were Ziph
1Ch 4:17 The s of Ezrah were Jether,
1Ch 4:18 these were the s of Bithiah
1Ch 4:19 The s of Hodiah's wife, the
1Ch 4:20 the s of Shimon were Amnon,
1Ch 4:20 the s of Ishi were Zoheth and
1Ch 4:21 The s of Shelah the son of
1Ch 4:24 The s of Simeon were Nemuel,
1Ch 4:26 the s of Mishma were Hamuel
1Ch 4:27 Shimei had sixteen s and six
1Ch 4:42 men of the s of Simeon, went
1Ch 4:42 and Uzziel, the s of Ishi
1Ch 5: 1 Now the s of Reuben the
1Ch 5: 1 was given to the s of Joseph
1Ch 5: 3 the s of Reuben the firstborn
1Ch 5: 4 The s of Joel were Shemaiah
1Ch 5:18 The s of Reuben, the Gadites,
1Ch 6: 1 The s of Levi were Gershon,
1Ch 6: 2 The s of Kohath were Amram,
1Ch 6: 3 the s of Aaron were Nadab,
1Ch 6:16 The s of Levi were Gershon,
1Ch 6:17 the names of the s of Gershon
1Ch 6:18 The s of Kohath were Amram,
1Ch 6:19 The s of Merari were Mahli and
1Ch 6:22 The s of Kohath were
1Ch 6:25 The s of Elkanah were Amasai
1Ch 6:26 the s of Elkanah were Zophai
1Ch 6:28 The s of Samuel were Joel the
1Ch 6:29 The s of Merari were Mahli,
1Ch 6:33 who ministered with their s
1Ch 6:33 Of the s of the Kohathites
1Ch 6:44 the s of Merari, on the left
1Ch 6:49 his s offered sacrifices on
1Ch 6:50 Now these are the s of Aaron
1Ch 6:54 by lot to the s of Aaron, of
1Ch 6:57 to the s of Aaron they gave
1Ch 6:62 And to the s of Gershon,
1Ch 6:63 To the s of Merari,
1Ch 6:66 s of Kohath were given cities
1Ch 6:70 the family of the s of Kohath
1Ch 6:71 half-tribe of Manasseh the s
1Ch 7: 1 The s of Issachar were Tola,
1Ch 7: 2 The s of Tola were Uzzi,
1Ch 7: 2 The s of Tola were mighty men
1Ch 7: 3 and the s of Izrahiah were
1Ch 7: 4 for they had many wives and s
1Ch 7: 6 The s of Benjamin were Bela,
1Ch 7: 7 The s of Bela were Ezbon,
1Ch 7: 8 The s of Becher were Zemirah,
1Ch 7: 8 All these are the s of Becher
1Ch 7:10 the s of Bilhan were Jeush,
1Ch 7:11 All these s of Jediael were
1Ch 7:12 and Huppim were the s of Ir
1Ch 7:13 The s of Naphtali were
1Ch 7:13 and Shallum, the s of Bilhah
1Ch 7:16 and his s were Ulam and Rakem
1Ch 7:19 the s of Shemida were Ahian,
1Ch 7:20 The s of Ephraim were
1Ch 7:30 The s of Asher were Imnah,
1Ch 7:31 The s of Beriah were Heber and
1Ch 7:33 The s of Japhlet were Pasach,
1Ch 7:34 The s of Shemer were Ahi,
1Ch 7:35 the s of his brother Helem
1Ch 7:36 The s of Zophah were Suah,
1Ch 7:38 The s of Jether were
1Ch 7:39 The s of Ulla were Arah,
1Ch 8: 3 The s of Bela were Addar,
1Ch 8: 6 And these are the s of Ehud
1Ch 8:10 These were his s, heads of
1Ch 8:12 The s of Elpaal were Eber,
1Ch 8:16 and Joha were the s of Beriah
1Ch 8:18 and Jobab were the s of Elpaal
1Ch 8:21 Shimrath were the s of Shimei
1Ch 8:25 Penuel were the s of Shashak
1Ch 8:27 Zichri were the s of Jeroham
1Ch 8:35 The s of Micah were Pithon,
1Ch 8:38 Azel had six s whose names
1Ch 8:38 All these were the s of Azel
1Ch 8:39 the s of Eshek his brother
1Ch 8:40 The s of Ulam were mighty men
1Ch 8:40 They had many s and grandsons,
1Ch 8:40 These were all s of Benjamin
1Ch 9: 5 Asaiah the firstborn and his s
1Ch 9: 6 Of the s of Zerah
1Ch 9: 7 Of the s of Benjamin
1Ch 9:14 Hashabiah, of the s of Merari
1Ch 9:30 some of the s of the priests
1Ch 9:32 of their brethren of the s of
1Ch 9:41 The s of Micah were Pithon,
1Ch 9:44 Azel had six s whose names
1Ch 9:44 these were the s of Azel
1Ch 10: 2 hard after Saul and his s
1Ch 10: 2 and Malchishua, Saul's s
1Ch 10: 6 So Saul and his three s died
1Ch 10: 7 his s were dead, they forsook
1Ch 10: 8 his s fallen on Mount Gilboa
1Ch 10:12 Saul and the bodies of his s
1Ch 11:34 the s of Hashem the Gizonite,
1Ch 11:44 Jeiel the s of Hotham the
1Ch 11:46 and Joshaviah the s of Elnaam
1Ch 12: 3 Joash, the s of Shemaah the
1Ch 12: 3 and Pelet the s of Azmaveth
1Ch 12: 7 Zebadiah the s of Jeroham of
1Ch 12:14 These were from the s of Gad
1Ch 14: 3 and David begot more s and
1Ch 15: 5 of the s of Kohath, Uriel the
1Ch 15: 6 of the s of Merari, Asaiah
1Ch 15: 7 of the s of Gershom, Joel the
1Ch 15: 8 of the s of Elizaphan,
1Ch 15: 9 of the s of Hebron, Eliel the
1Ch 15:10 of the s of Uzziel, Amminadab
1Ch 15:17 the s of Merari, Ethan the
1Ch 16:42 Now the s of Jeduthun were
1Ch 17: 9 nor shall the s of wickedness
1Ch 17:11 you, who will be of your s
1Ch 18:17 and David's s were chief
1Ch 20: 4 was one of the s of the giant
1Ch 21:20 his four s who were with him
1Ch 23: 6 divisions among the s of Levi
1Ch 23: 8 The s of Laadan
1Ch 23: 9 The s of Shimei
1Ch 23:10 And the s of Shimei
1Ch 23:10 were the four s of Shimei
1Ch 23:11 and Beriah did not have many s
1Ch 23:12 The s of Kohath
1Ch 23:13 The s of Amram
1Ch 23:13 his s forever, that he should
1Ch 23:14 Now the s of Moses the man of
1Ch 23:15 The s of Moses were Gershon
1Ch 23:16 Of the s of Gershon, Shebuel
1Ch 23:17 And Eliezer had no other s
1Ch 23:17 but the s of Rehabiah were
1Ch 23:18 Of the s of Izhar, Shelomith
1Ch 23:19 Of the s of Hebron, Jeriah
1Ch 23:20 Of the s of Uzziel, Michah
1Ch 23:21 The s of Merari were Mahli and
1Ch 23:21 The s of Mahli were Eleazar
1Ch 23:22 And Eleazar died, and had no s
1Ch 23:22 the s of Kish, took them as
1Ch 23:23 The s of Mushi were Mahli,
1Ch 23:24 These were the s of Levi by
1Ch 23:28 s of Aaron in the service of
1Ch 23:32 the needs of the s of Aaron
1Ch 24: 1 divisions of the s of Aaron
1Ch 24: 1 The s of Aaron were Nadab,
1Ch 24: 3 Zadok of the s of Eleazar
1Ch 24: 3 Ahimelech of the s of Ithamar
1Ch 24: 4 more leaders found of the s
1Ch 24: 4 than of the s of Ithamar, and
1Ch 24: 4 Among the s of Eleazar there
1Ch 24: 4 houses among the s of Ithamar
1Ch 24: 5 from the s of Eleazar
1Ch 24: 5 and from the s of Ithamar
1Ch 24:20 Now the rest of the s of Levi
1Ch 24:20 of the s of Amram, Shubael
1Ch 24:20 of the s of Shubael, Jehdeiah
1Ch 24:21 of the s of Rehabiah, the
1Ch 24:22 of the s of Shelomoth, Jahath
1Ch 24:23 Of the s of Hebron, Jeriah
1Ch 24:24 Of the s of Uzziel, Michah
1Ch 24:24 of the s of Michah, Shamir
1Ch 24:25 of the s of Isshiah,
1Ch 24:26 The s of Merari were Mahli and
1Ch 24:27 The s of Merari by Jaaziah
1Ch 24:28 Eleazar, who had no s
1Ch 24:30 Also the s of Mushi were
1Ch 24:30 These were the s of the
1Ch 24:31 brothers the s of Aaron did
1Ch 25: 1 some of the s of Asaph, of
1Ch 25: 2 Of the s of Asaph
1Ch 25: 2 the s of Asaph were under the
1Ch 25: 3 Jeduthun, the s of Jeduthun
1Ch 25: 4 Of Heman, the s of Heman
1Ch 25: 5 All these were the s of Heman
1Ch 25: 5 For God gave Heman fourteen s
1Ch 25: 9 him with his brethren and s
1Ch 25:10 the third for Zaccur, his s
1Ch 25:11 the fourth for Jizri, his s
1Ch 25:12 fifth for Nethaniah, his s
1Ch 25:13 the sixth for Bukkiah, his s
1Ch 25:14 seventh for Jesharelah, his s
1Ch 25:15 eighth for Jeshaiah, his s
1Ch 25:16 ninth for Mattaniah, his s

1Ch 25:17 the tenth for Shimei, his s
1Ch 25:18 eleventh for Azarel, his s
1Ch 25:19 twelfth for Hashabiah, his s
1Ch 25:20 thirteenth for Shubael, his s
1Ch 25:21 for Mattithiah, his s and his
1Ch 25:22 fifteenth for Jeremoth, his s
1Ch 25:23 sixteenth for Hananiah, his s
1Ch 25:24 for Joshbekashah, his s and
1Ch 25:25 eighteenth for Hanani, his s
1Ch 25:26 for Mallothi, his s and his
1Ch 25:27 twentieth for Eliathah, his s
1Ch 25:28 for Hothir, his s and his
1Ch 25:29 for Giddalti, his s and his
1Ch 25:30 for Mahazioth, his s and his
1Ch 25:31 for Romamti-Ezer, his s and
1Ch 26: 1 of Kore, of the s of Asaph
1Ch 26: 2 the s of Meshelemiah were
1Ch 26: 4 Moreover the s of Obed-Edom
1Ch 26: 6 s born who governed their
1Ch 26: 7 The s of Shemaiah were Othni,
1Ch 26: 8 were of the s of Obed-Edom
1Ch 26: 8 they and their s
1Ch 26: 9 And Meshelemiah had s and
1Ch 26:10 the children of Merari, had s
1Ch 26:11 all the s and brethren of
1Ch 26:15 and to his s the storehouse
1Ch 26:19 among the s of Korah
1Ch 26:19 and among the s of Merari
1Ch 26:21 The s of Laadan, the
1Ch 26:22 The s of Jehieli, Zetham and
1Ch 26:29 his s performed duties as
1Ch 27:32 was with the king's s
1Ch 28: 1 of the king and of his s, with
1Ch 28: 4 among the s of my father, He
1Ch 28: 5 s (for the LORD has given me
1Ch 29:24 also all the s of King David,
2Ch 5:12 and Jeduthun, with their s
2Ch 6:16 only if your s take heed to
2Ch 6:30 the hearts of the s of men)
2Ch 11:14 his s had rejected them from
2Ch 11:21 and begot twenty-eight s and
2Ch 11:23 of his s throughout all the
2Ch 13: 5 forever, to him and his s, by
2Ch 13: 8 in the hand of the s of David
2Ch 13: 9 LORD, the s of Aaron, and the
2Ch 13:10 the LORD are the s of Aaron
2Ch 13:21 wives, and begot twenty-two s
2Ch 20:14 a Levite of the s of Asaph
2Ch 21: 2 the s of Jehoshaphat
2Ch 21: 2 all these were the s of
2Ch 21: 7 to him and to his s forever
2Ch 21:17 king's house, and also his s
2Ch 21:17 the youngest of his s
2Ch 22: 1 had killed all the older s
2Ch 22: 8 the s of Ahaziah's brothers
2Ch 22:11 s who were being murdered
2Ch 23: 3 has said of the s of David
2Ch 23:11 his s anointed him, and said,
2Ch 24: 3 him two wives, and he had s
2Ch 24: 7 For the s of Athaliah, that
2Ch 24:25 the s of Jehoiada the priest
2Ch 24:27 Now concerning his s, and the
2Ch 26:18 the s of Aaron, who are
2Ch 28: 8 two hundred thousand women, s
2Ch 29: 9 and our s, our daughters, and
2Ch 29:11 My s, do not be negligent now
2Ch 29:12 of the s of the Kohathites
2Ch 29:12 of the s of Merari, Kish the
2Ch 29:13 of the s of Elizaphan, Shimri
2Ch 29:13 of the s of Asaph, Zechariah
2Ch 29:14 of the s of Heman, Jehiel and
2Ch 29:14 and of the s of Jeduthun,
2Ch 29:21 the s of Aaron, to offer them
2Ch 31:18 ones and their wives, their s
2Ch 31:19 Also for the s of Aaron the
2Ch 32:33 upper tombs of the s of David
2Ch 33: 6 Also he caused his s to pass
2Ch 34:12 of the s of Merari, and
2Ch 34:12 of the s of the Kohathites,
2Ch 35:14 the s of Aaron, were busy in
2Ch 35:14 the priests, the s of Aaron
2Ch 35:15 the s of Asaph, were in their
2Ch 36:20 his s until the reign of the
Ezra 2:36 the s of Jedaiah, of the
Ezra 2:37 the s of Immer, one thousand
Ezra 2:38 the s of Pashhur, one
Ezra 2:39 the s of Harim, one thousand
Ezra 2:40 the s of Jeshua and Kadmiel,
Ezra 2:40 of the s of Hodaviah,
Ezra 2:41 the s of Asaph, one hundred
Ezra 2:42 The s of the gatekeepers
Ezra 2:42 s of Shallum, the s of Ater
Ezra 2:42 s of Talmon, the s of Akkub
Ezra 2:42 the s of Hatita
Ezra 2:42 the s of Shobai, one hundred
Ezra 2:43 the s of Ziha
Ezra 2:43 the s of Hasupha
Ezra 2:43 the s of Tabbaoth
Ezra 2:44 the s of Keros
Ezra 2:44 s of Siaha, the s of Padon
Ezra 2:45 the s of Lebanah
Ezra 2:45 s of Hagabah, the s of Akkub
Ezra 2:46 the s of Hagab
Ezra 2:46 s of Shalmai, the s of Hanan
Ezra 2:47 the s of Giddel, the s of
Ezra 2:47 s of Gahar, the s of Reaiah
Ezra 2:48 the s of Rezin
Ezra 2:48 s of Nekoda, the s of Gazzam
Ezra 2:49 the s of Uzza
Ezra 2:49 s of Paseah, the s of Besai
Ezra 2:50 the s of Asnah
Ezra 2:50 s of Meunim, the s of Nephusim
Ezra 2:51 the s of Bakbuk
Ezra 2:51 s of Hakupha, the s of Harhur
Ezra 2:52 the s of Bazluth
Ezra 2:52 s of Mehida, the s of Harsha
Ezra 2:53 s of Barkos, the s of Sisera
Ezra 2:53 the s of Tamah
Ezra 2:54 of Neziah, and the s of Hatipha
Ezra 2:55 The s of Solomon's servants
Ezra 2:55 the s of Sotai
Ezra 2:55 s of Sophereth, the s of Peruda
Ezra 2:56 s of Jaala, the s of Darkon
Ezra 2:56 the s of Giddel
Ezra 2:57 the s of Shephatiah
Ezra 2:57 the s of Hattil
Ezra 2:57 the s of Pochereth of Zebaim,
Ezra 2:57 and the s of Ami
Ezra 2:60 s of Delaiah, the s of Tobiah
Ezra 2:60 the s of Nekoda, six hundred
Ezra 2:61 and of the s of the priests
Ezra 2:61 s of Habaiah, the s of Koz
Ezra 2:61 the s of Barzillai, who took
Ezra 3: 9 Then Jeshua with his s and
Ezra 3: 9 brothers, Kadmiel with his s
Ezra 3: 9 the s of Judah, arose as one
Ezra 3: 9 s of Henadad with their s
Ezra 3:10 the s of Asaph, with cymbals,
Ezra 6:10 the life of the king and his s
Ezra 7:23 realm of the king and his s
Ezra 8: 2 of the s of Phinehas, Gershom
Ezra 8: 2 of the s of Ithamar, Daniel
Ezra 8: 2 of the s of David, Hattush
Ezra 8: 3 of the s of Shecaniah,
Ezra 8: 3 of the s of Parosh, Zechariah
Ezra 8: 4 of the s of Pahath-Moab,
Ezra 8: 5 of the s of Shechaniah,
Ezra 8: 6 of the s of Adin, Ebed the
Ezra 8: 7 of the s of Elam, Jeshaiah
Ezra 8: 8 of the s of Shephatiah,
Ezra 8: 9 of the s of Joab, Obadiah the
Ezra 8:10 of the s of Shelomith,
Ezra 8:11 of the s of Bebai, Zechariah
Ezra 8:12 of the s of Azgad, Johanan
Ezra 8:13 of the last s of Adonikam
Ezra 8:14 also of the s of Bigvai,
Ezra 8:15 none of the s of Levi there
Ezra 8:18 of the s of Mahli the son of
Ezra 8:18 namely Sherebiah, with his s
Ezra 8:19 Jeshaiah of the s of Merari
Ezra 8:19 his brothers and their s,
Ezra 9: 2 for themselves and their s
Ezra 9:12 as wives for their s, nor
Ezra 9:12 their daughters to your s
Ezra 10: 2 Jehiel, one of the s of Elam
Ezra 10:18 among the s of the priests
Ezra 10:18 of the s of Jeshua the son of
Ezra 10:20 Also of the s of Immer
Ezra 10:21 of the s of Harim
Ezra 10:22 of the s of Pashhur
Ezra 10:25 of the s of Parosh
Ezra 10:26 of the s of Elam
Ezra 10:27 of the s of Zattu
Ezra 10:28 of the s of Bebai
Ezra 10:29 of the s of Bani
Ezra 10:30 of the s of Pahath-Moab
Ezra 10:31 of the s of Harim
Ezra 10:33 of the s of Hashum
Ezra 10:34 of the s of Bani
Ezra 10:43 of the s of Nebo
Neh 3: 3 Also the s of Hassenaah built
Neh 4:14 for your brethren, your s
Neh 5: 2 We, our s, and our daughters
Neh 5: 5 indeed we are forcing our s
Neh 10: 9 Binnui of the s of Henadad
Neh 10:28 of God, their wives, their s
Neh 10:30 their daughters for our s
Neh 10:36 bring the firstborn of our s
Neh 11: 6 All the s of Perez who dwelt
Neh 11: 7 these are the s of Benjamin
Neh 11:22 Micha, of the s of Asaph, the
Neh 12:23 The s of Levi, the heads of
Neh 12:28 the s of the singers gathered
Neh 12:35 the priests' s with trumpets
Neh 13:25 daughters as wives to their s
Neh 13:25 for your s or yourselves
Neh 13:28 And one of the s of Joiada
Esth 9:10 the ten s of Haman the son of
Esth 9:12 and the ten s of Haman
Esth 9:13 let Haman's ten s be hanged
Esth 9:14 and they hanged Haman's ten s
Esth 9:25 his s should be hanged on the
Job 1: 2 And seven s and three daughters
Job 1: 4 Now his s would go and feast
Job 1: 5 may be that my s have sinned
Job 1: 6 the s of God came to present
Job 1:13 there was a day when his s
Job 1:18 Your s and daughters were
Job 2: 1 the s of God came to present
Job 5: 4 His s are far from safety,
Job 8: 4 If your s have sinned against
Job 14:21 His s come to honor, and he
Job 30: 8 s of fools, yes, s of vile men
Job 38: 7 all the s of God shouted for
Job 42:13 He also had seven s and three
Ps 4: 2 O you s of men, Will you turn
Ps 11: 4 His eyelids test the s of men
Ps 12: 1 from among the s of men
Ps 12: 8 is exalted among the s of men
Ps 21:10 from among the s of men
Ps 31:19 the presence of the s of men
Ps 33:13 He sees all the s of men
Ps 45: 2 are fairer than the s of men
Ps 45:16 Your fathers shall be Your s
Ps 57: 4 I lie among the s of men Who
Ps 58: 1 judge uprightly, you s of men
Ps 66: 5 His doing toward the s of men
Ps 77:15 The s of Jacob and Joseph
Ps 89: 6 Who among the s of the mighty
Ps 89:30 If his s forsake My law And do
Ps 106:37 They even sacrificed their s
Ps 106:38 Even the blood of their s
Ps 132:12 If your s will keep My
Ps 132:12 Their s also shall sit upon
Ps 137: 7 against the s of Edom The day
Ps 144:12 That our s may be as plants
Ps 145:12 To make known to the s of men
Prov 8: 4 my voice is to the s of men
Prov 8:31 delight was with the s of men
Prov 15:11 the hearts of the s of men
Eccl 1:13 God has given to the s of man
Eccl 2: 3 s of men to do under heaven
Eccl 2: 8 the delights of the s of men
Eccl 3:10 task with which the s of men
Eccl 3:18 the estate of the s of men
Eccl 3:19 the s of men also happens to
Eccl 3:21 the spirit of the s of men
Eccl 8:11 therefore the heart of the s
Eccl 9: 3 the s of men are full of evil
Eccl 9:12 so the s of men are snared in
Song 1: 6 My mother's s were angry with
Song 2: 3 so is my beloved among the s
Is 37:38 Sharezer his s struck him
Is 39: 7 take away some of your s who
Is 43: 6 Bring My s from afar, and My
Is 45:11 to come concerning My s
Is 49:17 Your s shall make haste
Is 49:22 bring your s in their arms
Is 51:18 the s she has brought forth
Is 51:18 all the s she has brought up
Is 51:20 Your s have fainted, they lie
Is 52:14 form more than the s of men
Is 56: 5 a name better than that of s
Is 56: 6 Also the s of the foreigner
Is 57: 3 you s of the sorceress, you
Is 60: 4 your s shall come from afar,
Is 60: 9 to bring your s from afar
Is 60:10 The s of foreigners shall
Is 60:14 Also the s of those who
Is 61: 5 the s of the foreigner shall

Is 62: 5 so shall your s marry you
Is 62: 8 the s of the foreigner shall
Jer 3:24 and their herds, their s and
Jer 5:17 and your bread, which your s
Jer 6:21 the s together shall fall on
Jer 7:31 of Hinnom, to burn their s
Jer 11:22 die by the sword, their s
Jer 13:14 the s together," says the
Jer 14:16 their s nor their daughters
Jer 16: 2 wife, nor shall you have s or
Jer 16: 3 the LORD concerning the s
Jer 19: 5 to burn their s with fire for
Jer 19: 9 to eat the flesh of their s
Jer 29: 6 Take wives and beget s and
Jer 29: 6 and take wives for your s and
Jer 29: 6 so that they may bear s and
Jer 32:19 all the ways of the s of men
Jer 32:35 of Hinnom, to cause their s
Jer 35: 3 his brothers and all his s
Jer 35: 4 of the s of Hanan the son of
Jer 35: 5 the s of the house of the
Jer 35: 6 drink no wine, you nor your s
Jer 35: 8 days, we, our wives, our s
Jer 35:14 which he commanded his s
Jer 35:16 Surely the s of Jonadab the
Jer 39: 6 king of Babylon killed the s
Jer 40: 8 and Jonathan the s of Kareah
Jer 40: 8 Tanhumeth, the s of Ephai the
Jer 48:45 the head of the s of tumult
Jer 48:46 for your s have been taken
Jer 49: 1 Has Israel no s?
Jer 52:10 king of Babylon killed the s
Lam 4: 2 The precious s of Zion,
Ezek 5:10 eat their s in your midst
Ezek 5:10 s shall eat their fathers
Ezek 14:16 neither s nor daughters
Ezek 14:18 neither s nor daughters, but
Ezek 14:22 will be brought out, both s
Ezek 16:20 Moreover you took your s and
Ezek 20:31 make your s pass through the
Ezek 23: 4 were Mine, and they bore s
Ezek 23:10 nakedness, took away her s
Ezek 23:25 they shall take your s and
Ezek 23:37 their s whom they bore to Me
Ezek 23:47 they shall slay their s and
Ezek 24:21 and your s and daughters whom
Ezek 24:25 they set their minds, their s
Ezek 40:46 these are the s of Zadok,
Ezek 40:46 from the s of Levi
Ezek 44:15 the s of Zadok, who kept
Ezek 46:16 inheritance to any of his s
Ezek 46:16 it shall belong to his s
Ezek 46:17 shall belong to his s
Ezek 46:18 his s from his own property
Ezek 48:11 the priests of the s of Zadok
Dan 1: 6 of the s of Judah were Daniel
Dan 5:21 was driven from the s of men
Dan 10:16 the s of men touched my lips
Dan 11:10 However his s shall stir up
Dan 12: 1 over the s of your people
Hos 1:10 You are the s of the living
Hos 11:10 roars, then His s shall come
Joel 1:12 away from the s of men
Joel 2:28 your s and your daughters
Joel 3: 8 I will sell your s and your
Amos 2:11 up some of your s as prophets
Amos 7:17 your s and daughters shall
Mic 5: 7 man nor wait for the s of men
Zech 9:13 s, O Zion, against your s
Mal 3: 3 He will purify the s of Levi
Mal 3: 6 not consumed, O s of Jacob
Matt 5: 9 they shall be called s of God
Matt 5:45 that you may be s of your
Matt 8:12 But the s of the kingdom will
Matt 12:27 whom do your s cast them out
Matt 13:38 are the s of the kingdom, but
Matt 13:38 are the s of the wicked one
Matt 17:25 from their own s or from
Matt 17:26 Then the s are free
Matt 20:20 s came to Him with her s
Matt 20:21 these two s of mine may sit
Matt 21:28 A man had two s, and he came
Matt 23:31 yourselves that you are s of
Matt 26:37 the two s of Zebedee, and He
Matt 27:56 and the mother of Zebedee's s
Mark 3:17 that is, "S of Thunder"
Mark 3:28 will be forgiven the s of men
Mark 10:35 the s of Zebedee, came to Him
Luke 5:10 the s of Zebedee, who were
Luke 6:35 you will be s of the Highest
Luke 11:19 whom do your s cast them out
Luke 15:11 A certain man had two s
Luke 16: 8 For the s of this world are
Luke 16: 8 than the s of light
Luke 20:34 The s of this age marry and
Luke 20:36 angels and are s of God
Luke 20:36 being s of the resurrection
John 4:12 it himself, as well as his s
John 12:36 you may become s of light
John 21: 2 the s of Zebedee, and two
Acts 2:17 your s and your daughters
Acts 3:25 You are s of the prophets, and
Acts 7:16 of money from the s of Hamor
Acts 7:29 of Midian, where he had two s
Acts 13:26 s of the family of Abraham,
Acts 19:14 there were seven s of Sceva
Rom 8:14 of God, these are s of God
Rom 8:19 the revealing of the s of God
Rom 9:26 be called s of the living God
2Co 6:18 to you, and you shall be My s
Gal 3: 7 are of faith are s of Abraham
Gal 3:26 For you are all s of God
Gal 4: 5 receive the adoption as s
Gal 4: 6 And because you are s, God has
Gal 4:22 that Abraham had two s
Eph 1: 5 us to adoption as s by Jesus
Eph 2: 2 in the s of disobedience,
Eph 3: 5 made known to the s of men
Eph 5: 6 upon the s of disobedience
Col 3: 6 upon the s of disobedience
1Th 5: 5 s of light and s of the day
Heb 2:10 in bringing many s to glory
Heb 7: 5 who are of the s of Levi, who
Heb 11:21 each of the s of Joseph, and
Heb 12: 5 which speaks to you as to s
Heb 12: 7 God deals with you as with s
Heb 12: 8 you are illegitimate and not s

SONS' (*see* SONS)
Gen 6:18 and your s wives with you
Gen 7: 7 his s wives, went into the
Gen 8:16 sons and your s wives with you
Gen 8:18 wife and his s wives with him
Gen 46: 7 his s sons, his daughters and
Gen 46: 7 his s daughters, and all his
Gen 46:26 body, besides Jacob's s wives
Ex 29:21 and his s garments with him
Ex 29:29 shall be his s after him, to
Ex 39:41 his s garments, to minister
Lev 2: 3 shall be Aaron's and his s
Lev 2:10 shall be Aaron's and his s
Lev 7:31 shall be Aaron's and his s
Lev 8:27 hands and in his s hands, and
Lev 10:13 it is your due and your s due
Lev 10:14 are your due and your s due
Lev 10:15 your s with you, by a statute

SONS-IN-LAW (*see* SON-IN-LAW)
Gen 19:14 went out and spoke to his s
Gen 19:14 But to his s he seemed to

SOON (*see* SOONER)
Gen 18:33 s as He had finished speaking
Gen 26:10 One of the people might s
Gen 27:30 as s as Isaac had finished
Gen 44: 3 As s as the morning dawned,
Ex 2:18 that you have come so s today
Ex 9:29 As s as I have gone out of
Ex 32:19 as s as he came near the camp
Deut 4:26 day, that you will s utterly
Josh 2: 7 as s as those who pursued
Josh 2:11 as s as we heard these things
Josh 3:13 as s as the soles of the feet
Josh 8:19 they ran as s as he had
Josh 8:29 as s as the sun was down,
Judg 8:33 as s as Gideon was dead, that
Judg 9:33 as s as the sun is up in the
Judg 9:33 as s as he and the people who
1Sa 9:13 As s as you come into the
1Sa 13:10 as s as he had finished
1Sa 20:41 Now as s as the lad had gone,
1Sa 29:10 as s as you are up early in
2Sa 13:36 was, as s as he had finished
2Sa 15:10 As s as you hear the sound of
2Sa 22:45 as s as they hear, they obey
1Ki 16:11 as s as he was seated on his
1Ki 18:12 as s as I am gone from you,
1Ki 20:36 as s as you depart from me, a
1Ki 20:36 as s as he left him, a lion
2Ki 10: 2 Now as s as this letter comes
2Ki 10:25 as s as he had made an end of
2Ki 14: 5 as s as the kingdom was
2Ch 31: 5 As s as the commandment was
Job 32:22 my Maker would s take me away
Ps 18:44 As s as they hear of me they
Ps 37: 2 For they shall s be cut down
Ps 58: 3 astray as s as they are born
Ps 81:14 I would s subdue their
Ps 90:10 For it is s cut off, and we
Ps 94:17 My soul would s have settled
Ps 106:13 They s forgot His works
Is 66: 8 For as s as Zion travailed,
Ezek 7: 8 you I will s pour out My fury
Ezek 23:16 As s as her eyes saw them,
Matt 21:20 the fig tree wither away so s
Mark 1:29 Now as s as they had come out
Mark 1:42 As s as He had spoken,
Mark 5:36 As s as Jesus heard the word
Mark 9:39 a miracle in My name can s
Mark 11: 2 as s as you have entered it
Mark 14:45 And as s as He had come,
Luke 1:23 was, as s as the days of his
Luke 1:44 as s as the voice of your
Luke 8: 6 and as s as it sprang up, it
Luke 15:30 But as s as this son of
Luke 22:66 As s as it was day, the
Luke 23: 7 And as s as he knew that He
John 11:20 as s as she heard that Jesus
John 11:29 As s as she heard that, she
John 16:21 but as s as she has given
John 21: 9 as s as they had come to land
Acts 10:29 as s as I was sent for
Acts 12:18 as s as it was day, there was
Gal 1: 6 you are turning away so s
Phil 2:23 as s as I see how it goes
2Th 2: 2 not to be s shaken in mind or
Rev 12: 4 her Child as s as it was born

SOONER (*see* SOON)
Heb 13:19 may be restored to you the s
Jas 1:11 For no s has the sun risen

SOOT
Lam 4: 8 appearance is blacker than s

SOOTHED (*see* SOOTHING)
Is 1: 6 bound up, or s with ointment

SOOTHING (*see* SOOTHED)
Gen 8:21 And the LORD smelled a s aroma

SOOTHSAYER (*see* SOOTHSAYERS, SOOTHSAYING)
Deut 18:10 practices witchcraft, or a s
Josh 13:22 Balaam the son of Beor, the s

SOOTHSAYERS (*see* SOOTHSAYER)
Deut 18:14 will dispossess listened to s
Is 2: 6 they are s like the
Jer 27: 9 your dreamers, your s, or
Jer 50:36 A sword is against the s, and
Dan 2:27 the s cannot declare to the
Dan 4: 7 the s came in, and I told them
Dan 5: 7 the Chaldeans, and the s
Dan 5:11 astrologers, Chaldeans, and s
Mic 5:12 hand, and you shall have no s

SOOTHSAYING (*see* SOOTHSAYER)
Lev 19:26 you practice divination or s
2Ki 17:17 practiced witchcraft and s
2Ki 21: 6 through the fire, practiced s
2Ch 33: 6 he practiced s, used

SOPATER (*see* SOSIPATER)
Acts 20: 4 S of Berea accompanied him to

SOPHERETH
Ezra 2:55 sons of Sotai, the sons of S
Neh 7:57 of Sotai, the children of S

SORCERER (*see* SORCERERS, SORCERY)
Deut 18:10 who interprets omens, or a s
Acts 13: 6 they found a certain s, a
Acts 13: 8 But Elymas the s (for so his

SORCERERS (*see* SORCERER)
Ex 7:11 called the wise men and the s
Is 19: 3 the mediums and the s
Jer 27: 9 your soothsayers, or your s
Dan 2: 2 the astrologers, the s, and
Mal 3: 5 be a swift witness against s
Rev 21: 8 sexually immoral, s,
Rev 22:15 But outside are dogs and s

SORCERESS (*see* SORCERY)
Ex 22:18 shall not permit a s to live
Is 57: 3 come here, you sons of the s

Song 5: 6 I s him, but I could not find
Is 62:12 and you shall be called S Out
Is 65: 1 I was s by those who did not
Is 65:10 for My people who have s Me
Jer 8: 2 walked, which they have s
Jer 10:21 and have not s the LORD
Jer 26:21 the king s to put him to
Jer 44:30 his enemy who s his life
Jer 50:20 iniquity of Israel shall be s
Lam 1:19 while they s food to restore
Ezek 22:30 So I s for a man among them
Ezek 26:21 though you are s for, you
Ezek 34: 4 away, nor s what was lost
Dan 2:13 and they s Daniel and his
Dan 6: 4 satraps s to find some charge
Hos 12: 4 he wept, and s favor from Him
Obad 6 treasures shall be s after
Zeph 1: 6 LORD, and have not s the LORD
Matt 2:20 for those who s the young
Matt 21:46 But when they s to lay hands
Matt 26:16 So from that time he s
Matt 26:59 and all the council s false
Mark 11:18 s how they might destroy Him
Mark 12:12 they s to lay hold of Him,
Mark 14: 1 the scribes s how they might
Mark 14:11 So he s how he might
Mark 14:55 all the council s testimony
Luke 2:44 s Him among their relatives
Luke 2:48 and I have s You anxiously
Luke 2:49 Why is it that you s Me
Luke 4:42 And the crowd s Him and came
Luke 5:18 they s to bring him in and lay
Luke 6:19 multitude s to touch Him, for
Luke 9: 9 And he s to see Him
Luke 11:16 s from Him a sign from heaven
Luke 19: 3 he s to see who Jesus was,
Luke 19:47 the people s to destroy Him
Luke 20:19 hour s to lay hands on Him
Luke 22: 2 the scribes s how they might
Luke 22: 6 s opportunity to betray Him
John 5:16 s to kill Him, because He had
John 5:18 Therefore the Jews s all the
John 7: 1 the Jews s to kill Him
John 7:11 Then the Jews s Him at the
John 7:30 Then they s to take Him
John 10:39 Therefore they s again to
John 11: 8 the Jews s to stone You, and
John 11:56 Then they s Jesus, and spoke
John 19:12 on Pilate s to release Him
Acts 13: 7 s to hear the word of God
Acts 16:10 immediately we s to go to
Acts 17: 5 s to bring them out to the
2Ti 1:17 he s me out very diligently
Heb 8: 7 have been s for a second
Heb 12:17 though he s it diligently

SOUL (*see* SOUL'S, SOULS)
Gen 19:20 and my s shall live
Gen 27: 4 eat, that my s may bless you
Gen 27:19 that your s may bless me
Gen 27:25 so that my s may bless you
Gen 27:31 that your s may bless me
Gen 34: 3 His s was strongly attracted
Gen 34: 8 The s of my son Shechem longs
Gen 35:18 as her s was departing (for
Gen 42:21 his s when he pleaded with us
Gen 49: 6 Let not my s enter their
Lev 17:11 makes atonement for the s
Lev 23:29 of s on that same day, he
Lev 26:11 and My s shall not abhor you
Lev 26:15 or if your s abhors My
Lev 26:30 and My s shall abhor you
Lev 26:43 because their s abhorred My
Num 21: 4 the s of the people became
Num 21: 5 our s loathes this worthless
Num 30:13 binding oath to afflict her s
Deut 4:29 your heart and with all your s
Deut 6: 5 your heart, with all your s
Deut 10:12 your heart and with all your s
Deut 11:13 your heart and with all your s
Deut 11:18 in your heart and in your s
Deut 13: 3 your heart and with all your s
Deut 13: 6 friend who is as your own s
Deut 26:16 your heart and with all your s
Deut 28:65 failing eyes, and anguish of s
Deut 30: 2 your heart and with all your s
Deut 30: 6 your heart and with all your s
Deut 30:10 your heart and with all your s
Josh 22: 5 your heart and with all your s
Judg 5:21 O my s, march on in strength
Judg 10:16 His s could no longer endure
Judg 16:16 so that his s was vexed to
1Sa 1:10 And she was in bitterness of s
1Sa 1:15 out my s before the LORD
1Sa 1:26 As your s lives, my lord, I
1Sa 17:55 As your s lives, O king, I do
1Sa 18: 1 that the s of Jonathan
1Sa 18: 1 was knit to the s of David
1Sa 18: 1 loved him as his own s
1Sa 18: 3 he loved him as his own s
1Sa 20: 3 LORD lives and as your s lives
1Sa 20:17 him as he loved his own s
1Sa 23:20 desire of your s to come down
1Sa 25:26 LORD lives and as your s lives
1Sa 30: 6 him, because the s of all the
2Sa 5: 8 who are hated by David's s)
2Sa 11:11 you live, and as your s lives
1Ki 2: 4 heart and with all their s
1Ki 8:48 with all their s in the land
1Ki 17:21 child's s come back to him
1Ki 17:22 the s of the child came back
2Ki 2: 2 lives, and as your s lives
2Ki 2: 4 lives, and as your s lives
2Ki 2: 6 lives, and as your s lives
2Ki 4:27 for her s is in deep distress
2Ki 4:30 lives, and as your s lives
2Ki 23: 3 all his heart and all his s
2Ki 23:25 all his heart, with all his s
1Ch 22:19 your s to seek the LORD your
2Ch 6:38 with all their s in the land
2Ch 15:12 heart and with all their s
2Ch 15:15 sought Him with all their s
2Ch 34:31 all his heart and all his s
Job 3:20 and life to the bitter of s
Job 6: 7 My s refuses to touch them
Job 7:11 in the bitterness of my s
Job 7:15 so that my s chooses
Job 10: 1 My s loathes life
Job 10: 1 in the bitterness of my s
Job 14:22 and his s will mourn over it
Job 16: 4 if your s were in my soul's
Job 19: 2 long will you torment my s
Job 21:25 in the bitterness of his s
Job 23:13 And whatever His s desires
Job 27: 2 who has made my s bitter
Job 30:16 And now my s is poured out
Job 30:25 Has not my s grieved for the
Job 31:30 asking for a curse on his s)
Job 33:18 keeps back his s from the Pit
Job 33:20 and his s succulent food
Job 33:22 his s draws near the Pit, and
Job 33:28 He will redeem his s from
Job 33:30 bring back his s from the Pit
Ps 6: 3 My s also is greatly troubled
Ps 11: 1 How can you say to my s
Ps 11: 5 loves violence His s hates
Ps 13: 2 shall I take counsel in my s
Ps 16: 2 O my s, you have said to the
Ps 16:10 will not leave my s in Sheol
Ps 19: 7 is perfect, converting the s
Ps 23: 3 He restores my s
Ps 24: 4 lifted up his s to an idol
Ps 25: 1 You, O LORD, I lift up my s
Ps 25:20 Oh, keep my s, and deliver me
Ps 26: 9 Do not gather my s together
Ps 30: 3 my s up from the grave
Ps 31: 7 known my s in adversities
Ps 31: 9 away with grief, Yes, my s
Ps 33:19 To deliver their s from death
Ps 33:20 Our s waits for the LORD
Ps 34: 2 My s shall make its boast in
Ps 34:22 redeems the s of His servants
Ps 35: 3 Say to my s, "I am your
Ps 35: 9 my s shall be joyful in the
Ps 35:12 good, To the sorrow of my s
Ps 41: 4 Heal my s, for I have sinned
Ps 42: 1 brooks, So pants my s for You
Ps 42: 2 My s thirsts for God, for the
Ps 42: 4 I pour out my s within me
Ps 42: 5 Why are you cast down, O my s
Ps 42: 6 my s is cast down within me
Ps 42:11 Why are you cast down, O my s
Ps 43: 5 Why are you cast down, O my s
Ps 44:25 For our s is bowed down to
Ps 49:15 But God will redeem my s from
Ps 55:18 He has redeemed my s in peace
Ps 56:13 delivered my s from death
Ps 57: 1 For my s trusts in You
Ps 57: 4 My s is among lions
Ps 57: 6 My s is bowed down
Ps 62: 1 Truly my s silently waits for
Ps 62: 5 My s, wait silently for God
Ps 63: 1 My s thirsts for You
Ps 63: 5 My s shall be satisfied as
Ps 63: 8 My s follows close behind You
Ps 66: 9 Who keeps our s among the
Ps 66:16 what He has done for my s
Ps 69:10 chastened my s with fasting
Ps 69:18 Draw near to my s, and redeem
Ps 71:23 when I sing to You, And my s
Ps 77: 2 My s refused to be comforted
Ps 78:50 not spare their s from death
Ps 84: 2 My s longs, yes, even faints
Ps 86: 4 Rejoice the s of Your servant
Ps 86: 4 You, O Lord, I lift up my s
Ps 86:13 You have delivered my s from
Ps 88: 3 For my s is full of troubles,
Ps 88:14 why do You cast off my s
Ps 94:17 My s would soon have settled
Ps 94:19 Your comforts delight my s
Ps 103: 1 Bless the LORD, O my s
Ps 103: 2 Bless the LORD, O my s, And
Ps 103:22 Bless the LORD, O my s
Ps 104: 1 Bless the LORD, O my s
Ps 104:35 Bless the LORD, O my s
Ps 106:15 sent leanness into their s
Ps 107: 5 Their s fainted in them
Ps 107: 9 He satisfies the longing s
Ps 107: 9 the hungry s with goodness
Ps 107:18 Their s abhorred all manner
Ps 107:26 Their s melts because of
Ps 116: 4 I implore You, deliver my s
Ps 116: 7 Return to your rest, O my s
Ps 116: 8 delivered my s from death
Ps 119:20 My s breaks with longing For
Ps 119:25 My s clings to the dust
Ps 119:28 My s melts from heaviness
Ps 119:81 My s faints for Your
Ps 119:129 Therefore my s keeps them
Ps 119:167 My s keeps Your testimonies,
Ps 119:175 Let my s live, and it shall
Ps 120: 2 Deliver my s, O LORD, from
Ps 120: 6 My s has dwelt too long With
Ps 121: 7 He shall preserve your s
Ps 123: 4 Our s is exceedingly filled
Ps 124: 4 would have gone over our s
Ps 124: 5 Would have gone over our s
Ps 124: 7 Our s has escaped as a bird
Ps 130: 5 my s waits, And in His word I
Ps 130: 6 My s waits for the Lord More
Ps 131: 2 I have calmed and quieted my s
Ps 131: 2 child is my s within me
Ps 138: 3 me bold with strength in my s
Ps 139:14 that my s knows very well
Ps 141: 8 Do not leave my s destitute
Ps 142: 4 No one cares for my s
Ps 142: 7 Bring my s out of prison,
Ps 143: 3 the enemy has persecuted my s
Ps 143: 6 My s longs for You like a
Ps 143: 8 For I lift up my s to You
Ps 143:11 sake bring my s out of
Ps 143:12 all those who afflict my s
Ps 146: 1 Praise the LORD, O my s
Prov 2:10 is pleasant to your s,
Prov 3:22 they will be life to your s
Prov 6:32 does so destroys his own s
Prov 8:36 against me wrongs his own s
Prov 10: 3 the righteous s to famish
Prov 11:17 man does good for his own s
Prov 11:25 The generous s will be made
Prov 13: 2 but the s of the unfaithful
Prov 13: 4 the s of a sluggard desires,
Prov 13: 4 but the s of the diligent
Prov 13:19 is sweet to the s, but it is
Prov 13:25 to the satisfying of his s
Prov 15:32 despises his own s, but he
Prov 16:17 keeps his way preserves his s
Prov 16:24 honeycomb, sweetness to the s
Prov 18: 7 lips are the snare of his s
Prov 19: 2 a s to be without knowledge
Prov 19: 8 gets wisdom loves his own s
Prov 19:16 the commandment keeps his s
Prov 21:10 The s of the wicked desires
Prov 21:23 keeps his s from troubles
Prov 22: 5 he who guards his s will be
Prov 22:23 plunder the s of those who
Prov 22:25 and set a snare for your s
Prov 23:14 and deliver his s from hell
Prov 24:12 he who keeps your s, does He
Prov 24:14 of wisdom be to your s
Prov 25:13 the s of his masters

Prov 25:25 As cold water to a weary s
Prov 27: 7 A satisfied s loathes the
Prov 27: 7 but to a hungry s every
Prov 29:17 will give delight to your s
Eccl 2:24 that his s should enjoy good
Eccl 6: 3 but his s is not satisfied
Eccl 6: 7 yet the s is not satisfied
Eccl 7:28 which my s still seeks but I
Song 6:12 my s had made me as the
Is 1:14 appointed feasts my s hates
Is 3: 9 Woe to their s
Is 10:18 of his fruitful field, both s
Is 19:10 wages will be troubled of s
Is 26: 8 of our s is for Your name
Is 26: 9 With my s I have desired You
Is 29: 8 and his s is still empty
Is 29: 8 faint, and his s still craves
Is 38:15 in the bitterness of my s
Is 38:17 s from the pit of corruption
Is 42: 1 One in whom My s delights
Is 44:20 and he cannot deliver his s
Is 53:10 When You make His s an
Is 53:11 see the travail of His s, and
Is 53:12 poured out His s unto death
Is 55: 2 let your s delight itself in
Is 55: 3 Hear, and your s shall live
Is 58: 5 for a man to afflict his s
Is 58:10 extend your s to the hungry
Is 58:10 and satisfy the afflicted s
Is 58:11 and satisfy your s in drought
Is 61:10 my s shall be joyful in my
Is 66: 3 their s delights in their
Jer 4:19 O my s, my s! I am pained
Jer 4:19 O my s, my s
Jer 4:19 you have heard, O my s, the
Jer 4:31 for my s is weary because of
Jer 6: 8 lest My s depart from you
Jer 12: 7 of My s into the hand of her
Jer 13:17 my s will weep in secret for
Jer 14:19 Has Your s loathed Zion
Jer 31:14 I will satiate the s of the
Jer 31:25 I have satiated the weary s
Jer 31:25 replenished every sorrowful s
Jer 32:41 all My heart and with all My s
Jer 38:17 then your s shall live
Jer 38:20 you, and your s shall live
Jer 50:19 his s shall be satisfied on
Lam 1:20 distress; my s is troubled
Lam 3:17 moved my s far from peace
Lam 3:20 My s still remembers and sinks
Lam 3:24 is my portion," says my s
Lam 3:25 Him, to the s who seeks Him
Lam 3:51 to my s because of all the
Lam 3:58 pleaded the case for my s
Ezek 3:19 but you have delivered your s
Ezek 3:21 will have delivered your s
Ezek 18: 4 the s of the father as well
Ezek 18: 4 as the s of the son is Mine
Ezek 18: 4 the s who sins shall die
Ezek 18:20 The s who sins shall die
Ezek 24:21 eyes, the delight of your s
Ezek 33: 9 but you have delivered your s
Jon 2: 5 encompassed me, even to my s
Jon 2: 7 When my s fainted within me,
Mic 6: 7 my body for the sin of my s
Mic 7: 1 fruit which my s desires
Hab 2: 4 his s is not upright in him
Hab 2:10 and sinned against your s
Zech 11: 8 My s loathed them,
Zech 11: 8 and their s also abhorred me
Matt 10:28 body but cannot kill the s
Matt 10:28 who is able to destroy both s
Matt 12:18 in whom My s is well pleased
Matt 16:26 world, and loses his own s
Matt 16:26 give in exchange for his s
Matt 22:37 your heart, with all your s
Matt 26:38 My s is exceedingly sorrowful
Mark 8:36 world, and loses his own s
Mark 8:37 give in exchange for his s
Mark 12:30 your heart, with all your s
Mark 12:33 understanding, with all the s
Mark 14:34 My s is exceedingly sorrowful
Luke 1:46 My s magnifies the Lord,
Luke 2:35 through your own s also),
Luke 10:27 your heart, with all your s
Luke 12:19 And I will say to my s
Luke 12:19 S, you have many goods laid
Luke 12:20 This night your s will be
John 12:27 Now My s is troubled, and what
Acts 2:27 will not leave my s in Hades
Acts 2:31 that His s was not left in
Acts 2:43 Then fear came upon every s
Acts 3:23 s who will not hear that
Acts 4:32 were of one heart and one s
Rom 2: 9 on every s of man who does
Rom 13: 1 Let every s be subject to the
2Co 1:23 God as witness against my s
1Th 5:23 and may your whole spirit, s
Heb 4:12 even to the division of s
Heb 6:19 we have as an anchor of the s
Heb 10:38 my s has no pleasure in him
Heb 10:39 to the saving of the s
Jas 5:20 way will save a s from death
1Pe 2:11 lusts which war against the s
2Pe 2: 8 tormented his righteous s
3Jn 2 just as your s prospers
Rev 18:14 the fruit that your s longed

SOUL'S (*see* SOUL)
Job 16: 4 your soul were in my s place

SOULS (*see* SOUL)
Lev 16:29 you shall afflict your s
Lev 16:31 and you shall afflict your s
Lev 17:11 to make atonement for your s
Lev 23:27 you shall afflict your s, and
Lev 23:32 and you shall afflict your s
Num 16:38 sinned against their own s
Num 29: 7 You shall afflict your s
Josh 23:14 in all your s that not one
Job 24:12 the s of the wounded cry out
Ps 49: 8 of their s is costly, And it
Ps 72:13 will save the s of the needy
Ps 97:10 preserves the s of His saints
Prov 11:30 and he who wins s is wise
Prov 14:25 A true witness delivers s
Is 57:16 and the s which I have made
Is 58: 3 Why have we afflicted our s
Jer 6:16 you will find rest for your s
Jer 31:12 their s shall be like a
Jer 38:16 lives, who made our very s
Ezek 7:19 they will not satisfy their s
Ezek 13:18 of every height to hunt s
Ezek 13:18 you hunt the s of My people
Ezek 13:20 you hunt s there like birds
Ezek 13:20 your arms, and let the s go
Ezek 13:20 the s you hunt like birds
Ezek 18: 4 Behold, all s are Mine
Matt 11:29 you will find rest for your s
Luke 21:19 your patience possess your s
Acts 2:41 thousand s were added to them
Acts 14:22 the s of the disciples,
Acts 15:24 with words, unsettling your s
2Co 12:15 spend and be spent for your s
Heb 12: 3 and discouraged in your s
Heb 13:17 for they watch out for your s
Jas 1:21 which is able to save your s
1Pe 1: 9 the salvation of your s
1Pe 1:22 your s in obeying the truth
1Pe 2:25 and Overseer of your s
1Pe 3:20 which a few, that is, eight s
1Pe 4:19 their s to Him in doing good
2Pe 2:14 sin, beguiling unstable s
Rev 6: 9 I saw under the altar the s
Rev 18:13 and bodies and s of men
Rev 20: 4 I saw the s of those who had

SOUND (*see* SOUNDED, SOUNDING, SOUNDNESS, SOUNDS)
Gen 3: 8 they heard the s of the LORD
Ex 19:16 the s of the trumpet was very
Ex 20:18 the s of the trumpet, and the
Ex 28:35 its s will be heard when he
Lev 25: 9 to s on the tenth day of the
Lev 25: 9 to s throughout all your land
Lev 26:36 the s of a shaken leaf shall
Num 10: 5 When you s the advance, the
Num 10: 6 When you s the advance the
Num 10: 6 they shall s the call for
Num 10: 7 blow, but not s the advance
Num 10: 9 then you shall s an alarm
Deut 1:34 heard the s of your words
Deut 4:12 You heard the s of the words
Josh 6: 5 you hear the s of the trumpet
Josh 6:20 heard the s of the trumpet
1Sa 4: 6 What does the s of this great
1Sa 4:14 What does the s of this
2Sa 5:24 be, when you hear the s of
2Sa 6:15 with the s of the trumpet
2Sa 15:10 you hear the s of the trumpet
1Ki 1:40 seemed to split with their s
1Ki 1:41 Joab heard the s of the horn
1Ki 14: 6 when Ahijah heard the s of
1Ki 18:41 for there is the s of
2Ki 6:32 Is not the s of his master's
2Ki 7:10 one was there, not a human s
1Ch 14:15 when you hear a s of marching
1Ch 15:19 were to s the cymbals of
1Ch 15:28 with the s of the horn, with
1Ch 16:42 to s aloud with trumpets and
2Ch 5:13 to make one s to be heard in
2Ch 13:12 to s the alarm against you
Ezra 3:13 and the s was heard afar off
Neh 4:20 you hear the s of the trumpet
Job 21:12 rejoice to the s of the flute
Job 26: 3 you declared s advice to many
Job 33: 8 heard the s of your words
Job 34:16 listen to the s of my words
Ps 47: 5 LORD with the s of a trumpet
Ps 77:17 The skies sent out a s
Ps 89:15 people who know the joyful s
Ps 92: 3 the harp, With harmonious s
Ps 98: 5 the harp and the s of a psalm,
Ps 98: 6 trumpets and the s of a horn
Ps 102: 5 Because of the s of my
Ps 150: 3 Him with the s of the trumpet
Prov 2: 7 He stores up s wisdom for the
Prov 3:21 keep s wisdom and discretion
Prov 8:14 Counsel is mine, and s wisdom
Prov 14:30 A s heart is life to the body
Eccl 12: 4 and the s of grinding is low
Eccl 12: 4 rises up at the s of a bird
Is 14:11 and the s of your stringed
Is 30:19 to you at the s of your cry
Is 66: 6 The s of noise from the city
Jer 4:19 the s of the trumpet, the
Jer 4:21 hear the s of the trumpet
Jer 6:17 to the s of the trumpet
Jer 8:16 the s of the neighing of His
Jer 25:10 the s of the millstones and
Jer 42:14 nor hear the s of the trumpet
Jer 50:22 A s of battle is in the land,
Jer 51:54 The s of a cry comes from
Ezek 10: 5 the s of the wings of the
Ezek 23:42 The s of a carefree multitude
Ezek 26:13 an end to the s of your songs
Ezek 26:13 the s of your harps shall be
Ezek 26:15 shake at the s of your fall
Ezek 27:28 will shake at the s of the
Ezek 31:16 shake at the s of its fall
Ezek 33: 4 hears the s of the trumpet
Ezek 33: 5 He heard the s of the
Ezek 43: 2 was like the s of many waters
Dan 3: 5 you hear the s of the horn
Dan 3: 7 heard the s of the horn,
Dan 3:10 who hears the s of the horn
Dan 3:15 you hear the s of the horn
Dan 7:11 s of the pompous words which
Dan 10: 6 the s of his words like the
Dan 10: 9 I heard the s of his words
Dan 10: 9 while I heard the s of his
Joel 2: 1 and s an alarm in My holy
Amos 2: 2 with shouting and trumpet s
Amos 6: 5 who chant to the s of
Zeph 1:10 The s of a mournful cry from
Zech 11: 3 There is the s of wailing
Zech 11: 3 There is the s of roaring
Matt 6: 2 do not s a trumpet before you
Matt 24:31 with a great s of a trumpet
Luke 15:27 he has received him safe and s
John 3: 8 and you hear the s of it, but
Acts 2: 2 there came a s from heaven
Acts 2: 6 And when this s occurred, the
Rom 10:18 Their s has gone out to all
1Co 14: 7 or harp, when they make a s
1Co 14: 8 trumpet makes an uncertain s
1Co 15:52 For the trumpet will s, and
2Co 5:13 or if we are of s mind, it is
1Ti 1:10 is contrary to s doctrine
2Ti 1: 7 and of love and of a s mind
2Ti 1:13 Hold fast the pattern of s
2Ti 4: 3 will not endure s doctrine
Tit 1: 9 by s doctrine, both to exhort
Tit 1:13 they may be s in the faith
Tit 2: 1 are proper for s doctrine
Tit 2: 2 s in faith, in love, in
Tit 2: 8 s speech that cannot be
Heb 12:19 the s of a trumpet and the
Rev 1:15 voice as the s of many waters
Rev 8: 6 prepared themselves to s
Rev 8:13 angels who are about to s
Rev 9: 9 the s of their wings was like

Rev 9: 9 the s of chariots with many
Rev 10: 7 angel, when he is about to s
Rev 14: 2 I heard the s of harpists
Rev 18:22 The s of harpists, musicians,
Rev 18:22 the s of a millstone shall
Rev 19: 6 as the s of many waters
Rev 19: 6 and as the s of mighty

SOUNDED (*see* SOUND)
Ex 19:19 blast of the trumpet s long
1Sa 20:12 When I have s out my father
2Ch 7: 6 The priests s trumpets
2Ch 13:14 the priests s the trumpets
2Ch 29:28 sang, and the trumpeters s
Neh 4:18 the one who s the trumpet was
Job 39:24 because the trumpet has s
Luke 1:44 of your greeting s in my ears
1Th 1: 8 word of the Lord has s forth
Rev 8: 7 The first angel s
Rev 8: 8 Then the second angel s
Rev 8:10 Then the third angel s
Rev 8:12 Then the fourth angel s
Rev 9: 1 Then the fifth angel s
Rev 9:13 Then the sixth angel s
Rev 11:15 Then the seventh angel s

SOUNDING (*see* SOUND, SOUNDINGS)
2Ch 5:12 priests s with trumpets
2Ch 13:12 His priests with s trumpets
Ps 150: 5 Him with high s cymbals
1Co 13: 1 I have become as s brass or a
Rev 10: 7 of the s of the seventh angel

SOUNDINGS (*see* SOUNDING)
Acts 27:28 And they took s and found it to
Acts 27:28 farther, they took s again

SOUNDNESS (*see* SOUND)
Ps 38: 3 There is no s in my flesh
Ps 38: 7 And there is no s in my flesh
Is 1: 6 the head, there is no s in it
Acts 3:16 s in the presence of you all

SOUNDS (*see* SOUND)
Ex 19:13 When the trumpet s long,
Job 15:21 Dreadful s are in his ears
1Co 14: 7 make a distinction in the s

SOUR
Job 20:14 food in his stomach turns s
Is 18: 5 the s grape is ripening in
Jer 31:29 fathers have eaten s grapes
Jer 31:30 man who eats the s grapes
Ezek 18: 2 fathers have eaten s grapes
Matt 27:34 they gave Him s wine mingled
Matt 27:48 sponge, filled it with s wine
Mark 15:36 a sponge full of s wine, put
Luke 23:36 coming and offering Him s wine
John 19:29 Now a vessel full of s wine
John 19:29 filled a sponge with s wine
John 19:30 Jesus had received the s wine

SOURCE
2Ki 2:21 out to the s of the water
Job 28: 6 stones are the s of sapphires

SOUTH (*see* SOUTHERN, SOUTHWARD)
Gen 12: 9 going on still toward the S
Gen 13: 1 and Lot with him, to the S
Gen 13: 3 from the S as far as Bethel
Gen 20: 1 journeyed from there to the S
Gen 24:62 Roi, for he dwelt in the S
Gen 28:14 east, to the north and the s
Ex 26:18 twenty boards for the s side
Ex 26:35 the tabernacle toward the s
Ex 27: 9 For the s side there shall be
Ex 36:23 twenty boards for the s side
Ex 38: 9 made the court on the s side
Ex 40:24 table, on the s side of the
Num 2:10 On the s side shall be the
Num 3:29 the s side of the tabernacle
Num 10: 6 the s side shall begin their
Num 13:17 Go up this way into the S
Num 13:22 And they went up through the S
Num 13:29 dwell in the land of the S
Num 21: 1 Canaanite, who dwelt in the S
Num 33:40 who dwelt in the S in the
Num 34: 4 be on the s of Kadesh Barnea
Num 35: 5 on the s side two thousand
Deut 1: 7 and in the lowland, in the S
Deut 3:27 the west, the north, the s
Deut 33:23 possess the west and the s
Deut 34: 3 the S, and the plain of the
Josh 10:40 the mountain country and the S
Josh 11: 2 in the plain s of Chinneroth,
Josh 11:16 mountain country, all the S
Josh 12: 8 the wilderness, and in the S
Josh 13: 4 from the s, all the land of
Josh 15: 3 ascended on the s side of
Josh 15: 7 which is on the s side of the
Josh 15:19 have given me land in the S
Josh 15:21 the border of Edom in the S
Josh 17: 7 the border went along s to
Josh 18: 5 in their territory on the s
Josh 18:13 s side of Lower Beth Horon
Josh 18:14 around the west side to the s
Josh 18:15 The s side began at the end
Josh 18:16 of the Jebusite city on the s
Josh 18:19 at the s end of the Jordan
Josh 19: 8 Baalath Beer, Ramah of the S
Josh 19:34 Zebulun on the s side and
Judg 1: 9 in the mountains, in the S
Judg 1:15 have given me land in the S
Judg 1:16 which lies in the S near Arad
Judg 21:19 to Shechem, and s of Lebonah
1Sa 20:41 from a place toward the s
1Sa 23:19 which is on the s of Jeshimon
1Sa 23:24 plain on the s of Jeshimon
1Sa 30: 1 Amalekites had invaded the S
1Sa 30:27 who were in Ramoth of the S
2Sa 24: 7 Then they went out to S Judah
1Ki 7:25 three looking toward the s
2Ki 23:13 which were on the s of the
1Ch 9:24 the east, west, north, and s
1Ch 26:15 to Obed-Edom the S Gate, and
1Ch 26:17 on the s four each day, and
2Ch 4: 4 three looking toward the s
2Ch 28:18 of the S of Judah, and had
Job 9: 9 and the chambers of the s
Job 37: 9 of the s comes the whirlwind
Job 37:17 the earth by the s wind
Job 39:26 spread its wings toward the s
Ps 75: 6 from the west nor from the s
Ps 78:26 He brought in the s wind
Ps 89:12 The north and the s, You have
Ps 107: 3 From the north and from the s
Ps 126: 4 LORD, As the streams in the S
Eccl 1: 6 The wind goes toward the s
Eccl 11: 3 falls to the s or the north
Song 4:16 O north wind, and come, O s
Is 21: 1 in the S pass through, so it
Is 30: 6 against the beasts of the S
Is 43: 6 And to the s, 'Do not keep
Jer 13:19 of the S shall be shut up
Jer 17:26 the mountains and from the S
Jer 32:44 and in the cities of the S
Jer 33:13 in the cities of the S, in
Ezek 10: 3 were standing on the s side
Ezek 16:46 who dwells to the s of you
Ezek 20:46 set your face toward the s
Ezek 20:46 preach against the s and
Ezek 20:46 the forest land, the S,
Ezek 20:47 and say to the forest of the S
Ezek 20:47 all faces from the s to the
Ezek 21: 4 all flesh from s to north
Ezek 40: 2 on it toward the s was
Ezek 40:24 he brought me toward the s
Ezek 40:24 there a gateway was facing s
Ezek 40:27 on the inner court, facing s
Ezek 40:27 to gateway toward the s, one
Ezek 40:44 one facing s at the side of
Ezek 40:45 This chamber which faces s is
Ezek 41:11 north and another toward the s
Ezek 42:12 chambers that were facing s
Ezek 42:13 the s chambers, which are
Ezek 42:18 He measured the s side, five
Ezek 46: 9 go out by way of the s gate
Ezek 46: 9 enters by way of the s gate
Ezek 47: 1 of the temple, s of the altar
Ezek 47:19 The s side, toward the S,
Ezek 47:19 The s side, toward the S
Ezek 47:19 the s side, toward the S
Ezek 48:10 on the s twenty-five thousand
Ezek 48:16 the s side four thousand five
Ezek 48:17 to the s two hundred and fifty
Ezek 48:28 the s side, toward the S
Ezek 48:33 on the s side, measuring four
Dan 8: 9 great toward the s, toward
Dan 11: 5 of the S shall become strong
Dan 11: 6 S shall go to the king of the
Dan 11: 9 kingdom of the king of the S
Dan 11:11 the king of the S shall be
Dan 11:14 up against the king of the S
Dan 11:15 the forces of the S shall not
Dan 11:25 of the S with a great army
Dan 11:25 the king of the S shall be
Dan 11:29 return and go toward the s
Dan 11:40 of the S shall attack him
Obad 19 The inhabitants of the S
Obad 20 possess the cities of the S
Zech 6: 6 going toward the s country
Zech 7: 7 and prosperous, and the S and
Zech 9:14 go with whirlwinds from the s
Zech 14: 4 and half of it toward the s
Zech 14:10 Geba to Rimmon s of Jerusalem
Matt 12:42 The queen of the S will rise
Luke 11:31 The queen of the S will rise
Luke 12:55 when you see the s wind blow
Luke 13:29 west, from the north and the s
Acts 8:26 go toward the s along the
Acts 27:13 When the s wind blew softly,
Acts 28:13 after one day the s wind blew
Rev 21:13 north, three gates on the s

SOUTHEAST
1Ki 7:39 of the house toward the s
2Ch 4:10 on the right side, to the s

SOUTHERN (*see* SOUTH)
Num 34: 3 Your s border shall be from
Num 34: 3 then your s border shall
Num 34: 4 the s side of the Ascent of
Josh 15: 1 was the extreme s boundary
Josh 15: 2 their s border began at the
Josh 15: 3 the s side of the Ascent of
Josh 15: 4 This shall be your s border
Josh 15: 8 s slope of the Jebusite city
Josh 18:19 This was the s boundary
1Sa 27:10 Against the s area of Judah,
1Sa 27:10 or against the s area of the
1Sa 27:10 or against the s area of the
1Sa 30:14 the s area of the Cherethites
1Sa 30:14 and of the s area of Caleb
Ezek 40:28 court through the s gateway
Ezek 40:28 he measured the s gateway
Ezek 40:44 at the side of the s gateway
Ezek 47:20 from the s boundary until one

SOUTHWARD (*see* SOUTH)
Gen 13:14 northward, s, eastward, and
Josh 12: 3 s below the slopes of Pisgah
Josh 15: 1 s was the extreme southern
Josh 15: 2 from the bay that faces s
Josh 17: 9 Brook Kanah, s to the brook
Josh 17:10 S it was Ephraim's, northward
Josh 18:13 of Luz (which is Bethel) s
Josh 18:14 that lies before Beth Horon s
1Sa 14: 5 the other s opposite Gibeah
Dan 8: 4 westward, northward, and s

SOUTHWEST
Acts 27:12 of Crete opening toward the s

SOVEREIGNTY
1Sa 14:47 established his s over Israel

SOW (*see* SOWED, SOWER, SOWING, SOWN, SOWS)
Gen 47:23 you, and you shall s the land
Ex 23:10 years you shall s your land
Lev 19:19 You shall not s your field
Lev 25: 3 years you shall s your field
Lev 25: 4 You shall neither s your
Lev 25:11 in it you shall neither s nor
Lev 25:20 since we shall not s nor
Lev 25:22 you shall s in the eighth
Lev 26:16 you shall s your seed in vain
Deut 22: 9 You shall not s your vineyard
2Ki 19:29 also in the third year s and
Job 4: 8 and s trouble reap the same
Job 31: 8 Then let me s, and another eat
Ps 107:37 s fields and plant vineyards,
Ps 126: 5 Those who s in tears Shall
Eccl 11: 4 observes the wind will not s
Eccl 11: 6 In the morning s your seed
Is 28:24 keep plowing all day to s
Is 28:25 does he not s the black
Is 30:23 with which you s the ground
Is 32:20 you who s beside all waters
Is 37:30 also in the third year s and
Jer 4: 3 and do not s among thorns
Jer 31:27 that I will s the house of
Jer 35: 7 s seed, plant a vineyard, nor
Hos 2:23 Then I will s her for Myself
Hos 8: 7 They s the wind, and reap the
Hos 10:12 S for yourselves
Mic 6:15 You shall s, but not reap

Zech 10: 9 I will s them among the
Matt 6:26 for they neither s nor reap
Matt 13: 3 Behold, a sower went out to s
Matt 13:27 did you not s good seed in
Mark 4: 3 Behold, a sower went out to s
Luke 8: 5 sower went out to s his seed
Luke 12:24 for they neither s nor reap
Luke 19:21 and reap what you did not s
Luke 19:22 and reaping what I did not s
1Co 15:36 what you s is not made alive
1Co 15:37 And what you s, you do not s
2Pe 2:22 a s, having washed, to her

SOWED (*see* sow)
Gen 26:12 Then Isaac s in that land, and
Deut 11:10 come, where you s your seed
Judg 9:45 the city and s it with salt
Matt 13: 4 And as he s, some seed fell by
Matt 13:24 who s good seed in his field
Matt 13:25 s tares among the wheat and
Matt 13:31 a man took and s in his field,
Matt 13:39 The enemy who s them is the
Mark 4: 4 And it happened, as he s, that
Luke 8: 5 And as he s, some fell by the

SOWER (*see* sow)
Is 55:10 it may give seed to the s
Jer 50:16 Cut off the s from Babylon,
Matt 13: 3 Behold, a s went out to sow
Matt 13:18 hear the parable of the s
Mark 4: 3 Behold, a s went out to sow
Mark 4:14 The s sows the word
Luke 8: 5 A s went out to sow his seed
2Co 9:10 He who supplies seed to the s

SOWING (*see* sow)
Lev 26: 5 shall last till the time of s
Ps 126: 6 weeping, Bearing seed for s

SOWN (*see* sow)
Ex 23:16 which you have s in the field
Lev 11:37 seed which is to be s, it
Deut 21: 4 which is neither plowed nor s
Deut 22: 9 of the seed which you have s
Deut 29:23 it is not s, nor does it bear
Judg 6: 3 it was, whenever Israel had s
Ps 97:11 Light is s for the righteous,
Is 19: 7 everything s by the River,
Is 40:24 scarcely shall they be s
Is 61:11 are s in it to spring forth
Jer 2: 2 in a land that was not s
Jer 12:13 They have s wheat but reaped
Ezek 36: 9 and you shall be tilled and s
Hag 1: 6 You have s much, and bring in
Matt 13:19 away what was s in his heart
Matt 25:24 reaping where you have not s
Matt 25:26 I reap where I have not s
Mark 4:15 wayside where the word is s
Mark 4:15 that was s in their hearts
Mark 4:16 ones s on stony ground who
Mark 4:18 are the ones s among thorns
Mark 4:20 are the ones s on good ground
Mark 4:31 when it is s on the ground,
Mark 4:32 but when it is s, it grows up
1Co 9:11 If we have s spiritual things
1Co 15:42 The body is s in corruption,
1Co 15:43 It is s in dishonor, it is
1Co 15:43 It is s in weakness, it is
1Co 15:44 It is s a natural body, it is
2Co 9:10 multiply the seed you have s
Jas 3:18 fruit of righteousness is s

SOWS (*see* sow)
Prov 6:14 continually, he s discord
Prov 6:19 and one who s discord among
Prov 11:18 work, but to him who s
Prov 16:28 A perverse man s strife, and a
Prov 22: 8 He who s iniquity will reap
Amos 9:13 of grapes him who s seed
Matt 13:37 He who s the good seed is the
Mark 4:14 The sower s the word
John 4:36 life, that both he who s and
John 4:37 One s and another reaps
2Co 9: 6 He who s sparingly will also
2Co 9: 6 he who s bountifully will
Gal 6: 7 for whatever a man s, that he
Gal 6: 8 For he who s to his flesh
Gal 6: 8 but he who s to the Spirit

SPACE (*see* SPACIOUS)
Lev 25:30 within the s of a full year
Josh 3: 4 shall be a s between you and
1Ki 7:36 there was a clear s on each
Job 26: 7 out the north over empty s
Jer 28:11 the s of two full years
Ezek 40: 7 was a s of five cubits
Ezek 40:12 There was a s in front of the
Ezek 41:17 from the s above the door,
Ezek 41:20 floor to the s above the door
Ezek 42: 5 the galleries took away s
Ezek 45: 2 around it for an open s

SPACIOUS (*see* SPACE)
Neh 7: 4 Now the city was large and s
Jer 22:14 a wide house with s chambers

SPAIN
Rom 15:24 whenever I journey to S, I
Rom 15:28 I shall go by way of you to S

SPAN (*see* SPANNED)
Ex 28:16 a s shall be its length
Ex 28:16 and a s shall be its width
Ex 39: 9 a s was its length and a s
1Sa 17: 4 height was six cubits and a s
Is 38:12 My life s is gone, taken from
Is 40:12 measured heaven with a s
Ezek 43:13 all around its edge of one s

SPANNED (*see* SPAN)
2Ch 3:13 s twenty cubits overall

SPARE (*see* SPARED, SPARES, SPARING, SPARINGLY)
Gen 18:24 and not s it for the fifty
Gen 18:26 then I will s all the place
Deut 13: 8 him, nor shall you s him or
Deut 29:20 The LORD would not s him
Josh 2:13 s my father, my mother, my
1Sa 15: 3 they have, and do not s them
1Ki 20:31 perhaps he will s your life
Neh 13:22 and s me according to the
Job 2: 6 in your hand, but s his life
Job 6:10 let Him not s, for I have not
Job 27:22 against him and does not s
Ps 72:13 He will s the poor and needy,
Ps 78:50 He did not s their soul from
Prov 6:34 therefore he will not s in
Prov 21:26 righteous gives and does not s
Is 9:19 no man shall s his brother
Is 13:18 their eye will not s children
Is 30:14 He shall not s
Is 54: 2 do not s; lengthen your
Is 58: 1 Cry aloud, s not
Jer 13:14 not pity nor s nor have mercy
Jer 21: 7 He shall not s them, or have
Jer 50:14 her, s no arrows, for she has
Jer 51: 3 Do not s her young men
Ezek 5:11 My eye will not s, nor will I
Ezek 7: 4 My eye will not s you, nor
Ezek 7: 9 My eye will not s, nor will
Ezek 8:18 My eye will not s nor will I
Ezek 9: 5 do not let your eye s, nor
Ezek 9:10 also, My eye will neither s
Ezek 12:16 But I will s a few of their
Ezek 24:14 not hold back, nor will I s
Joel 2:17 S Your people, O LORD, and do
Mal 3:17 I will s them as a man spares
Luke 15:17 have bread enough and to s
Rom 8:32 He who did not s His own Son
Rom 11:21 For if God did not s the
Rom 11:21 He may not s you either
1Co 7:28 the flesh, but I would s you
2Co 1:23 that to s you I came no more
2Co 13: 2 if I come again I will not s
2Pe 2: 4 For if God did not s the
2Pe 2: 5 did not s the ancient world,

SPARED (*see* SPARE)
Josh 6:25 Joshua s Rahab the harlot,
1Sa 15: 9 But Saul and the people s Agag
1Sa 15:15 for the people s the best of
1Sa 24:10 But my eye s you, and I said
2Sa 8: 4 except that he s enough of
2Sa 21: 7 But the king s Mephibosheth
2Ki 5:20 my master has s Naaman this
1Ch 18: 4 except that he s enough of
Ezek 20:17 Nevertheless My eye s them

SPARES (*see* SPARE)
Job 20:13 though he s it and does not
Prov 13:24 He who s his rod hates his
Prov 17:27 who has knowledge s his words
Mal 3:17 s his own son who serves him

SPARING (*see* SPARE)
Acts 20:29 in among you, not s the flock

SPARINGLY (*see* SPARE)
2Co 9: 6 who sows s will also reap s

SPARK (*see* SPARKS)
Is 1:31 and the work of it as a s

SPARKLED (*see* SPARKLES)
Ezek 1: 7 They s like the color of

SPARKLES (*see* SPARKLED)
Prov 23:31 when it s in the cup, when it

SPARKS (*see* SPARK)
Job 5: 7 trouble, as the s fly upward
Job 41:19 s of fire shoot out
Is 50:11 encircle yourselves with s
Is 50:11 in the s you have kindled

SPARROW (*see* SPARROWS)
Ps 84: 3 Even the s has found a home,
Ps 102: 7 And am like a s alone on the
Prov 26: 2 Like a flitting s, like a

SPARROWS (*see* SPARROW)
Matt 10:29 Are not two s sold for a
Matt 10:31 are of more value than many s
Luke 12: 6 Are not five s sold for two
Luke 12: 7 are of more value than many s

SPAT (*see* SPIT)
Matt 26:67 Then they s in His face and
Matt 27:30 Then they s on Him, and took
Mark 7:33 fingers in his ears, and He s
Mark 15:19 head with a reed and s on Him
John 9: 6 He s on the ground and made

SPATTERED
2Ki 9:33 of her blood s on the wall

SPEAK (*see* SPEAKER, SPEAKING, SPEAKS, SPEECH, SPOKE, SPOKEN)
Gen 18:27 upon myself to s to the Lord
Gen 18:30 Lord be angry, and I will s
Gen 18:31 upon myself to s to the Lord
Gen 18:32 and I will s but once more
Gen 24:33 And he said, "S on
Gen 24:50 we cannot s to you either bad
Gen 27: 6 father s to Esau your brother
Gen 31:24 Be careful that you s to
Gen 31:29 Be careful that you s to
Gen 32: 4 S thus to my lord Esau, 'Thus
Gen 32:19 In this manner you shall s to
Gen 34: 6 out to Jacob to s with him
Gen 37: 4 could not s peaceably to him
Gen 42:22 Did I not s to you, saying
Gen 44:16 What shall we s
Gen 44:18 please let your servant s a
Gen 50: 4 please s in the hearing of
Ex 4:14 I know that he can s well
Ex 4:15 Now you shall s to him and put
Ex 5:23 to Pharaoh to s in Your name
Ex 6:11 s to Pharaoh king of Egypt,
Ex 6:29 S to Pharaoh king of Egypt
Ex 7: 2 You shall s all that I
Ex 7: 2 brother shall s to Pharaoh
Ex 11: 2 S now in the hearing of the
Ex 12: 3 S to all the congregation of
Ex 14: 2 S to the children of Israel,
Ex 16:12 S to them, saying, 'At
Ex 19: 6 s to the children of Israel
Ex 19: 9 may hear when I s with you
Ex 20:19 You s with us, and we will
Ex 20:19 but let not God s with us
Ex 23:22 His voice and do all that I s
Ex 25: 2 S to the children of Israel,
Ex 25:22 I will s with you from above
Ex 28: 3 So you shall s to all who are
Ex 29:42 I will meet you to s with you
Ex 30:31 you shall s to the children
Ex 31:13 S also to the children of
Ex 32:12 Why should the Egyptians s
Ex 34:34 before the LORD to s with Him
Ex 34:34 s to the children of Israel
Ex 34:35 he went in to s with Him
Lev 1: 2 S to the children of Israel,
Lev 4: 2 S to the children of Israel,
Lev 6:25 S to Aaron and to his sons,
Lev 7:23 S to the children of Israel,
Lev 7:29 S to the children of Israel,
Lev 9: 3 of Israel you shall s, saying
Lev 11: 2 S to the children of Israel,
Lev 12: 2 S to the children of Israel,

Lev 15: 2 S to the children of Israel,
Lev 17: 2 S to Aaron, to his sons, and
Lev 18: 2 S to the children of Israel,
Lev 19: 2 S to all the congregation of
Lev 21: 1 S to the priests, the sons of
Lev 21:17 S to Aaron, saying
Lev 22: 2 S to Aaron and his sons, that
Lev 22:18 S to Aaron and his sons, and to
Lev 23: 2 S to the children of Israel,
Lev 23:10 S to the children of Israel,
Lev 23:24 S to the children of Israel,
Lev 23:34 S to the children of Israel,
Lev 24:15 Then you shall s to the
Lev 25: 2 S to the children of Israel,
Lev 27: 2 S to the children of Israel,
Num 5: 6 S to the children of Israel
Num 5:12 S to the children of Israel,
Num 6: 2 S to the children of Israel,
Num 6:23 S to Aaron and his sons,
Num 7:89 of meeting to s with Him, he
Num 8: 2 S to Aaron, and say to him
Num 9:10 S to the children of Israel,
Num 12: 6 and I s to him in a dream
Num 12: 8 I s with him face to face,
Num 12: 8 to s against My servant Moses
Num 14:15 heard of Your fame will s
Num 15: 2 S to the children of Israel,
Num 15:18 S to the children of Israel,
Num 15:38 S to the children of Israel
Num 16:24 S to the congregation, saying
Num 17: 2 S to the children of Israel,
Num 18:26 S thus to the Levites, and say
Num 19: 2 S to the children of Israel,
Num 20: 8 S to the rock before their
Num 21:27 those who s in proverbs say
Num 22:20 the word which I s to you
Num 22:35 only the word that I s to you
Num 22:35 to you, that you shall s
Num 22:38 in my mouth, that I must s
Num 23: 5 to Balak, and thus you shall s
Num 23:12 Must I not take heed to s
Num 23:16 to Balak, and thus you shall s
Num 24:12 Did I not also s to your
Num 24:13 the LORD says, that I must s'
Num 27: 7 of Zelophehad s what is right
Num 27: 8 you shall s to the children
Num 33:51 S to the children of Israel,
Num 35:10 S to the children of Israel,
Deut 3:26 S no more to Me of this
Deut 5: 1 judgments which I s in your
Deut 5:31 and I will s to you all the
Deut 11: 2 I do not s with your children
Deut 18:18 He shall s to them all that I
Deut 18:20 to s a word in My name, which
Deut 18:20 I have not commanded him to s
Deut 20: 2 approach and s to the people
Deut 20: 5 shall s to the people, saying
Deut 20: 8 shall s further to the people
Deut 25: 8 shall call him and s to him
Deut 27:14 shall s with a loud voice
Deut 31:28 that I may s these words in
Deut 32: 1 ear, O heavens, and I will s
Josh 4:10 Joshua to s to the people
Josh 20: 2 S to the children of Israel,
Josh 22:24 may s to our descendants,
Judg 5:10 S, you who ride on white
Judg 6:39 and let me s just once more
Judg 9: 2 Please s in the hearing of
Judg 19: 3 to s kindly to her and bring
Judg 19:30 it, take counsel, and s up
1Sa 3: 9 you, that you must say, 'S
1Sa 3:10 S, for Your servant hears
1Sa 9:21 then do you s like this to me
1Sa 15:16 And he said to him, "S on
1Sa 19: 3 I will s with my father about
1Sa 25:17 that one cannot s to him
1Sa 25:24 maidservant s in your ears
2Sa 3:19 Then Abner also went to s in
2Sa 3:27 gate to s with him privately
2Sa 13:13 please s to the king
2Sa 14: 3 and s to him in this manner
2Sa 14:12 let your maidservant s
2Sa 14:15 I have come to s of this
2Sa 14:15 I will now s to the king
2Sa 14:18 let my lord the king s
2Sa 17: 6 If not, s up
2Sa 19: 7 s comfort to your servants
2Sa 19:11 S to the elders of Judah,
2Sa 19:29 Why do you s anymore of your
2Sa 20:16 nearby, that I may s with you

1Ki 2:17 Please s to King Solomon, for
1Ki 2:18 I will s for you to the king
1Ki 2:19 to s to him for Adonijah
1Ki 12: 7 s good words to them, then
1Ki 12:10 Thus you should s to this
1Ki 12:23 S to Rehoboam the son of
1Ki 21:19 You shall s to him, saying
1Ki 21:19 And you shall s to him,
1Ki 22:13 of them, and s encouragement
1Ki 22:14 says to me, that I will s
1Ki 22:24 LORD go from me to s to you
2Ki 4:13 Do you want me to s on your
2Ki 6:12 that you s in your bedroom
2Ki 18:20 You s of having counsel and
2Ki 18:26 Please s to your servants in
2Ki 18:26 do not s to us in Hebrew in
2Ki 18:27 to you to s these words, and
2Ki 19:10 Thus you shall s to Hezekiah
2Ki 22:18 manner you shall s to him
1Ch 17:15 so did Nathan s to David
2Ch 10: 7 s good words to them, they
2Ch 10:10 Thus you should s to the
2Ch 11: 3 S to Rehoboam the son of
2Ch 18:12 of them, and s encouragement
2Ch 18:13 my God says, that I will s
2Ch 18:23 LORD go from me to s to you
2Ch 32:17 to s against Him, saying,
2Ch 34:26 manner you shall s to him
2Ch 35:25 the singing women s of Josiah
Neh 13:24 could not s the language of
Esth 1:22 s in the language of his own
Job 2:10 You s as one of the foolish
Job 7:11 I will s in the anguish of my
Job 8: 2 long will you s these things
Job 9:35 Then I would s and not fear
Job 10: 1 I will s in the bitterness of
Job 11: 5 But oh, that God would s, and
Job 12: 8 or s to the earth, and it will
Job 13: 3 But I would s to the Almighty
Job 13: 7 Will you s wickedly for God,
Job 13:13 peace with me, and let me s
Job 13:22 or let me s, then You respond
Job 16: 4 I also could s as you do, if
Job 16: 6 Though I s, my grief is not
Job 18: 2 and afterward we will s
Job 19:18 I arise, and they s against me
Job 21: 3 Bear with me that I may s
Job 27: 4 my lips will not s wickedness
Job 29:22 my words they did not s again
Job 32: 4 Elihu had waited to s to Job
Job 32: 7 I said, 'Age should s, and
Job 32:16 because they did not s,
Job 32:20 I will s, that I may find
Job 33:14 For God may s in one way, or
Job 33:31 hold your peace, and I will s
Job 33:32 s, for I desire to justify
Job 34:33 therefore s what you know
Job 36: 2 words to s on God's behalf
Job 37:20 He be told that I wish to s
Job 37:20 If a man were to s, surely he
Job 41: 3 Will he s softly to you
Job 42: 4 Listen, please, and let me s
Ps 2: 5 Then He shall s to them in
Ps 5: 6 destroy those who s falsehood
Ps 12: 2 They s idly everyone with his
Ps 12: 2 lips and a double heart they s
Ps 17:10 their mouths they s proudly
Ps 28: 3 Who s peace to their
Ps 31:18 Which s insolent things
Ps 35:20 For they do not s peace, But
Ps 35:28 my tongue shall s of Your
Ps 38:12 seek my hurt s of destruction
Ps 40: 5 s of them, They are more than
Ps 41: 5 My enemies s evil of me
Ps 49: 3 My mouth shall s wisdom, And
Ps 50: 7 O My people, and I will s
Ps 50:20 sit and s against your brother
Ps 51: 4 may be found just when You s
Ps 58: 1 Do you indeed s righteousness
Ps 59:12 cursing and lying which they s
Ps 63:11 who s lies shall be stopped
Ps 69:12 sit in the gate s against me
Ps 71:10 For my enemies s against me
Ps 73: 8 and s wickedly concerning
Ps 73: 8 They s loftily
Ps 73:15 I will s thus," Behold, I
Ps 75: 5 Do not s with a stiff neck
Ps 77: 4 so troubled that I cannot s
Ps 85: 8 hear what God the LORD will s
Ps 85: 8 For He will s peace To His

Ps 94: 4 speech, and s insolent things
Ps 109:20 to those who s evil against
Ps 115: 5 mouths, but they do not s
Ps 119:23 sit and s against me, But Your
Ps 119:46 I will s of Your testimonies
Ps 119:172 tongue shall s of Your word
Ps 120: 7 But when I s, they are for
Ps 127: 5 But shall s with their
Ps 135:16 mouths, but they do not s
Ps 139:20 For they s against You
Ps 145: 6 Men shall s of the might of
Ps 145:11 They shall s of the glory of
Ps 145:21 My mouth shall s the praise
Prov 6:22 awake, they will s with you
Prov 8: 6 for I will s of excellent
Prov 8: 7 for my mouth will s truth
Prov 21:28 hears him will s endlessly
Prov 23: 9 Do not s in the hearing of a
Prov 23:16 when your lips s right things
Eccl 3: 7 keep silence, and a time to s
Is 8:10 s the word, but it will not
Is 8:20 If they do not s according to
Is 14:10 They all shall s and say to
Is 19:18 will s the language of Canaan
Is 28:11 He will s to this people,
Is 29: 4 you shall s out of the ground
Is 30:10 s to us smooth things,
Is 32: 4 will be ready to s plainly
Is 32: 6 person will s foolishness
Is 36: 5 I say you s of having counsel
Is 36:11 Please s to your servants in
Is 36:11 do not s to us in Hebrew in
Is 36:12 to you to s these words, and
Is 37:10 Thus you shall s to Hezekiah
Is 40: 2 S comfort to Jerusalem, and
Is 40:27 Why do you say, O Jacob, and s
Is 41: 1 come near, then let them s
Is 45:19 s righteousness, I declare
Is 50: 4 that I should know how to s a
Is 56: 3 joined himself to the LORD s
Is 59: 4 in empty words and s lies
Is 63: 1 I who s in righteousness,
Jer 1: 6 Behold, I cannot s, for I am
Jer 1: 7 I command you, you shall s
Jer 1:17 s to them all that I command
Jer 4:12 now I will also s judgment
Jer 5: 5 and s to them, for they have
Jer 5:14 Because you s this word,
Jer 6:10 To whom shall I s and give
Jer 7:22 For I did not s to your
Jer 7:27 Therefore you shall s all
Jer 8: 6 but they do not s aright
Jer 9: 5 and will not s the truth
Jer 9: 5 taught their tongue to s lies
Jer 9:22 S, "Thus says the LORD
Jer 10: 5 a palm tree, and they cannot s
Jer 11: 2 s to the men of Judah and to
Jer 12: 6 even though they s smooth
Jer 13:12 you shall s to them this word
Jer 18: 7 The instant I s concerning a
Jer 18: 9 the instant I s concerning a
Jer 18:11 s to the men of Judah and to
Jer 18:20 before You to s good for them
Jer 19: 5 which I did not command or s
Jer 20: 9 nor s anymore in His name
Jer 22: 1 Judah, and there s this word,
Jer 23:16 they s a vision of their own
Jer 23:28 let him s My word faithfully
Jer 26: 2 s to all the cities of Judah,
Jer 26: 2 I command you to s to them
Jer 26: 8 him to s to all the people
Jer 26:15 to s all these words in your
Jer 27: 9 who s to you, saying,
Jer 27:14 of the prophets who s to you
Jer 28: 7 word that I s in your hearing
Jer 29:24 You shall also s to Shemaiah
Jer 32: 4 shall s with him face to face
Jer 34: 2 s to Zedekiah king of Judah
Jer 34: 3 he shall s with you face to
Jer 35: 2 s to them, and bring them into
Jer 38:20 of the LORD which I s to you
Jer 39:16 Go and s to Ebed-Melech the
Jer 40:16 for you s falsely concerning
Jer 43: 2 to Jeremiah, "You s falsely
Jer 48:27 For whenever you s of him
Ezek 2: 1 your feet, and I will s to you
Ezek 2: 7 You shall s My words to them,
Ezek 3: 1 go, s to the house of Israel
Ezek 3: 4 and s with My words to them
Ezek 3:10 all My words that I s to you

Ezek 3:11 s to them and tell them, 'Thus
Ezek 3:18 nor s to warn the wicked from
Ezek 3:27 But when I s with you, I will
Ezek 11: 5 S! 'Thus says the LORD
Ezek 12:25 I s, and the word
Ezek 12:25 which I s will come
Ezek 12:28 word which I s will be done
Ezek 14: 4 Therefore s to them, and say
Ezek 14: 9 is induced to s anything, I
Ezek 17: 2 s a parable to the house of
Ezek 20: 3 s to the elders of Israel, and
Ezek 20:27 s to the house of Israel, and
Ezek 20:49 me, 'Does he not s parables
Ezek 24:21 S to the house of Israel,
Ezek 24:27 you shall s and no longer be
Ezek 29: 3 S, and say, 'Thus says the
Ezek 29:21 mouth to s in their midst
Ezek 32:21 among the mighty Shall s to
Ezek 33: 2 s to the children of your
Ezek 33: 8 and you do not s to warn the
Ezek 33:30 and they s to one another,
Ezek 37:18 of your people s to you,
Ezek 39:17 S to every sort of bird and
Dan 2: 9 you have agreed to s lying
Dan 7:25 He shall s pompous words
Dan 10:11 the words that I s to you
Dan 10:19 Let my lord s, for you have
Dan 11:27 they shall s lies at the same
Dan 11:36 shall s blasphemies against
Hos 1: 2 the LORD began to s by Hosea
Hos 2:14 and s comfort to her
Mic 2:11 and s a lie, saying, 'I will
Hab 2: 3 but at the end it will s, and
Zeph 3:13 and s no lies, nor shall a
Hag 2: 2 S now to Zerubbabel the son
Hag 2:21 S to Zerubbabel, governor of
Zech 2: 4 s to this young man, saying
Zech 6:12 Then s to him, saying, 'Thus
Zech 8:16 s each man the truth to his
Zech 9:10 He shall s peace to the
Zech 10: 2 For the idols s delusion
Matt 8: 8 But only s a word, and my
Matt 10:19 how or what you should s
Matt 10:19 that hour what you should s
Matt 10:20 for it is not you who s, but
Matt 10:27 in the dark, s in the light
Matt 12:34 being evil, s good things
Matt 12:36 for every idle word men may s
Matt 12:46 seeking to s with Him
Matt 12:47 seeking to s with You
Matt 13:10 Why do You s to them in
Matt 13:13 Therefore I s to them in
Matt 13:34 parable He did not s to them
Matt 16:11 not s to you concerning bread
Mark 1:34 did not allow the demons to s
Mark 2: 7 Why does this Man s
Mark 4:34 parable He did not s to them
Mark 7:37 deaf to hear and the mute to s
Mark 9:39 soon afterward s evil of Me
Mark 12: 1 Then He began to s to them in
Mark 13:11 premeditate what you will s
Mark 13:11 you in that hour, s that
Mark 13:11 for it is not you who s, but
Mark 14:71 know this Man of whom you s
Mark 16:17 they will s with new tongues
Luke 1:19 God, and was sent to s to you
Luke 1:20 not able to s until the day
Luke 1:22 out, he could not s to them
Luke 4:41 them, did not allow them to s
Luke 6:26 when all men s well of you
Luke 7:15 was dead sat up and began to s
Luke 7:24 He began to s to the
Luke 12:41 do You s this parable only to
John 1:37 The two disciples heard him s
John 1:40 of the two who heard John s
John 3:11 We s what We know and testify
John 4:26 her, "I who s to you am He
John 6:63 The words that I s to you are
John 7:17 I s on My own authority
John 8:26 I s to the world those things
John 8:28 taught Me, I s these things
John 8:38 I s what I have seen with My
John 9:21 He will s for himself
John 12:49 should say and what I should s
John 12:50 Therefore, whatever I s, just
John 12:50 Father has told Me, so I s
John 13:18 I do not s concerning all of
John 14:10 The words that I s to you I
John 14:10 do not s on My own authority
John 16:13 for He will not s on His own
John 16:13 whatever He hears He will s
John 16:25 longer s to you in figurative
John 17:13 these things I s in the world
Acts 2: 4 began to s with other tongues
Acts 2: 6 them s in his own language
Acts 2: 7 not all these who s Galileans
Acts 2:29 let me s freely to you of the
Acts 4:17 that from now on they s to no
Acts 4:18 commanded them not to s at
Acts 4:20 For we cannot but s the
Acts 4:29 boldness they may s Your word
Acts 5:20 s to the people all the words
Acts 5:40 not s in the name of Jesus
Acts 6:11 to say, "We have heard him s
Acts 6:13 s blasphemous words against
Acts 10:32 he comes, he will s to you
Acts 10:46 heard them s with tongues
Acts 11:15 And as I began to s, the Holy
Acts 17:19 doctrine is of which you s
Acts 18: 9 Do not be afraid, but s, and
Acts 18:26 So he began to s boldly in
Acts 21:37 commander, "May I s to you
Acts 21:37 Can you s Greek?
Acts 21:39 permit me to s to the people
Acts 23: 5 You shall not s evil of the
Acts 24:10 had nodded to him to s,
Acts 26: 1 permitted to s for yourself
Acts 26:25 but s the words of truth and
Acts 26:26 before whom I also s freely
Acts 28:20 s with you, because for the
Rom 3: 5 I s as a man
Rom 6:19 I s in human terms because of
Rom 7: 1 brethren (for I s to those
Rom 11:13 For I s to you Gentiles
Rom 15:18 to s of any of those things
1Co 1:10 that you all s the same thing
1Co 2: 6 we s wisdom among those who
1Co 2: 7 But we s the wisdom of God in
1Co 2:13 These things we also s, not
1Co 3: 1 could not s to you as to
1Co 10:15 I s as to wise men
1Co 12:30 Do all s with tongues
1Co 13: 1 Though I s with the tongues
1Co 14: 2 does not s to men but to God
1Co 14: 6 s to you either by revelation
1Co 14:18 I thank my God I s with
1Co 14:19 rather s five words with my
1Co 14:21 lips I will s to this people
1Co 14:23 all s with tongues, and there
1Co 14:28 let him s to himself and to
1Co 14:29 Let two or three prophets s
1Co 14:34 they are not permitted to s
1Co 14:35 for women to s in church
1Co 14:39 not forbid to s with tongues
1Co 15:34 I s this to your shame
2Co 2:17 we s in the sight of God in
2Co 4:13 also believe and therefore s
2Co 6:13 the same (I s as to children)
2Co 8: 8 I s not by commandment, but I
2Co 11:17 What I s, I s not according
2Co 11:21 I s foolishly—I am bold
2Co 11:23 I s as a fool—I am more
2Co 12: 6 for I will s the truth
2Co 12:19 We s before God in Christ
Gal 3:15 I s in the manner of men
Eph 4:25 each one s truth with his
Eph 5:12 s of those things which are
Eph 5:32 but I s concerning Christ and
Eph 6:20 s boldly, as I ought to s
Phil 1:14 to s the word without fear
Phil 4:11 Not that I s in regard to
Col 4: 3 to s the mystery of Christ,
Col 4: 4 it manifest, as I ought to s
1Th 2: 2 we were bold in our God to s
1Th 2: 4 with the gospel, even so we s
1Th 2:16 forbidding us to s to the
1Ti 5:14 adversary to s reproachfully
Tit 2: 1 s the things which are proper
Tit 2:15 S these things, exhort, and
Tit 3: 2 to s evil of no one, to be
Heb 2: 5 world to come, of which we s
Heb 6: 9 though we s in this manner
Heb 7: 9 through Abraham, so to s,
Heb 9: 5 we cannot now s in detail
Jas 1:19 be swift to hear, slow to s
Jas 2:12 So s and so do as those who
Jas 4:11 Do not s evil of one another,
1Pe 2:12 that when they s against you
1Pe 4:11 let him s as the oracles of
2Pe 2:10 to s evil of dignitaries,
2Pe 2:12 s evil of the things they do
2Pe 2:18 For when they s great
1Jn 4: 5 Therefore they s as of the
2Jn 12 s face to face, that our joy
3Jn 14 and we shall s face to face
Jude 8 and s evil of dignitaries
Jude 10 But these s evil of whatever
Rev 13:15 of the beast should both s

SPEAKER (*see* SPEAK)
Acts 14:12 because he was the chief s

SPEAKING (*see* SPEAK)
Gen 18:33 had finished s with Abraham
Gen 24:15 before he had finished s
Gen 24:45 I had finished s in my heart
Gen 29: 9 he was still s with them,
Ex 31:18 of s with him on Mount Sinai
Ex 34:33 had finished s with them, he
Lev 5: 4 s thoughtlessly with his lips
Num 7:89 he heard the voice of One s
Num 16:31 as he finished s all these
Deut 4:33 God s out of the midst of the
Deut 5:26 s from the midst of the fire
Deut 11:19 s of them when you sit in
Deut 20: 9 have finished s to the people
Deut 32:45 Moses finished s all these
Judg 15:17 was, when he had finished s
Ruth 1:18 her, she stopped s to her
1Sa 18: 1 he had finished s to Saul
1Sa 24:16 s these words to Saul, that
2Sa 13:36 as soon as he had finished s
1Ki 1:42 While he was still s, there
Esth 10: 3 s peace to all his kindred
Job 1:16 While he was still s, another
Job 1:17 While he was still s, another
Job 1:18 While he was still s, another
Job 4: 2 can withhold himself from s
Ps 34:13 And your lips from s guile
Ps 52: 3 rather than s righteousness
Ps 58: 3 soon as they are born, s lies
Is 58: 9 the finger, and s wickedness,
Is 58:13 nor s your own words,
Is 59:13 God, s oppression and revolt,
Is 65:24 and while they are still s
Jer 7:13 to you, rising up early and s
Jer 25: 3 to you, rising early and s
Jer 26: 7 the people heard Jeremiah s
Jer 26: 8 of s all that the LORD had
Jer 35:14 to you, rising early and s
Jer 38: 4 by s such words to them
Jer 38:27 So they stopped s with him
Jer 43: 1 s to all the people all the
Ezek 1:28 and I heard a voice of One s
Ezek 43: 6 Then I heard Him s to me from
Dan 7: 8 and a mouth s pompous words
Dan 7:11 words which the horn was s
Dan 8:13 Then I heard a holy one s
Dan 8:13 to that certain one who was s
Dan 8:18 Now, as he was s with me, I
Dan 9:20 Now while I was s, praying,
Dan 9:21 yes, while I was s in prayer
Dan 10:11 While he was s this word to
Matt 15:31 when they saw the mute s, the
Matt 17: 5 While he was still s, behold,
Matt 21:45 that He was s of them
Matt 26:47 And while He was still s,
Mark 5:35 While He was still s, some
Mark 14:43 while He was still s, Judas,
Luke 5: 4 Now when He had stopped s
Luke 8:49 While He was still s, someone
Luke 22:47 And while He was still s,
Luke 22:60 while he was still s, the
John 2:21 But He was s of the temple of
John 11:13 they thought that He was s
John 16:29 See, now You are s plainly
John 18:34 Are you s for yourself on
John 19:10 Are You not s to me
Acts 1: 3 s of the things pertaining to
Acts 2:11 we hear them s in our own
Acts 10:44 Peter was still s these words
Acts 13:43 s to them, persuaded them to
Acts 14: 3 s boldly in the Lord, who was
Acts 14: 9 This man heard Paul s
Acts 20: 9 and as Paul continued s, he
Acts 20:30 s perverse things, to draw
Acts 26:14 I heard a voice s to me and
1Co 12: 3 known to you that no one s by
1Co 14: 6 I come to you s with tongues
1Co 14: 9 you will be s into the air
2Co 13: 3 a proof of Christ s in me

Eph 4:15 s the truth in love, may grow
Eph 4:31 evil s be put away from you,
Eph 5:19 s to one another in psalms and
1Ti 2: 7 I am s the truth in Christ and
1Ti 4: 2 s lies in hypocrisy, having
1Pe 2: 1 envy, and all evil s,
1Pe 3:10 and his lips from s guile
1Pe 4: 4 of dissipation, s evil of you
2Pe 2:16 a dumb donkey s with a man's
2Pe 3:16 s in them of these things, in
Rev 4: 1 was like a trumpet s with me
Rev 13: 5 given a mouth s great things

SPEAKS (*see* SPEAK)
Gen 45:12 it is my mouth that s to you
Ex 7: 9 When Pharaoh s to you, saying
Ex 33:11 as a man s to his friend
Num 22: 8 to you, as the LORD s to me
Num 23:26 saying, 'All that the LORD s
Num 36: 5 the sons of Joseph s is right
Deut 5:24 this day that God s with man
Deut 18:19 which He s in My name, I will
Deut 18:20 or who s in the name of other
Deut 18:22 when a prophet s in the name
2Sa 14:13 For the king s this thing as
1Ki 20: 5 Thus s Ben-Hadad, saying
Job 2:10 as one of the foolish women s
Job 17: 5 He who s flattery to his
Job 33: 2 my tongue s in my mouth
Job 34:35 Job s without knowledge, his
Ps 12: 3 tongue that s proud things
Ps 15: 2 And s the truth in his heart
Ps 37:30 of the righteous s wisdom
Ps 41: 6 to see me, he s vain words
Ps 144: 8 Whose mouth s vain words, And
Ps 144:11 Whose mouth s vain words
Prov 1:21 in the city she s her words
Prov 2:12 the man who s perverse things
Prov 6:19 a false witness who s lies
Prov 12:17 He who s truth declares
Prov 12:18 There is one who s like the
Prov 14:25 a deceitful witness s lies
Prov 16:13 love him who s what is right
Prov 19: 5 he who s lies will not escape
Prov 19: 9 he who s lies shall perish
Prov 26:25 when he s kindly, do not
Is 9:17 and every mouth s folly
Is 32: 7 even when the needy s justice
Is 33:15 s uprightly, he who despises
Is 52: 6 that day that I am He who s
Jer 9: 8 it s deceit; one s peaceably
Jer 10: 1 word which the LORD s to you
Jer 28: 2 Thus s the LORD of hosts, the
Jer 29:25 Thus s the LORD of hosts, the
Jer 30: 2 Thus s the LORD God of Israel
Lam 3:37 Who is he who s and it comes
Ezek 10: 5 of Almighty God when He s
Dan 3:29 or language which s anything
Amos 5:10 abhor the one who s uprightly
Hag 1: 2 Thus s the LORD of hosts,
Matt 10:20 of your Father who s in you
Matt 12:32 Anyone who s a word against
Matt 12:32 but whoever s against the
Matt 12:34 of the heart the mouth s
Luke 5:21 Who is this who s blasphemies
Luke 6:45 of the heart his mouth s
Luke 12:10 anyone who s a word against
John 3:31 is earthly and s of the earth
John 3:34 has sent s the words of God
John 7:18 He who s from himself seeks
John 7:26 He s boldly, and they say
John 8:44 When he s a lie,
John 8:44 he s from his own resources,
John 19:12 a king s against Caesar
Rom 10: 6 of faith s in this way, "Do
1Co 14: 2 For he who s in a tongue does
1Co 14: 2 in the spirit he s mysteries
1Co 14: 3 who prophesies s edification
1Co 14: 4 He who s in a tongue edifies
1Co 14: 5 than he who s with tongues
1Co 14:11 be a foreigner to him who s
1Co 14:11 he who s will be a foreigner
1Co 14:13 Therefore let him who s in a
1Co 14:27 If anyone s in a tongue, let
Heb 11: 4 it he being dead still s
Heb 12: 5 which s to you as to sons
Heb 12:24 blood of sprinkling that s
Heb 12:25 you do not refuse Him who s
Heb 12:25 from Him who s from heaven
Jas 4:11 He who s evil of a brother and
Jas 4:11 s evil of the law and judges
1Pe 4:11 If anyone s, let him speak as

SPEAR (*see* SPEARHEAD, SPEARMEN, SPEARS)
Josh 8:18 Stretch out the s that is in
Josh 8:18 the s that he had in his hand
Josh 8:26 which he stretched out the s
Judg 5: 8 not a shield or s was seen
1Sa 13:22 s found in the hand of any of
1Sa 17: 7 Now the staff of his s was
1Sa 17:45 to me with a sword, with a s
1Sa 17:47 does not save with sword and s
1Sa 18:10 there was a s in Saul's hand
1Sa 18:11 And Saul cast the s, for he
1Sa 19: 9 house with his s in his hand
1Sa 19:10 David to the wall with the s
1Sa 19:10 he drove the s into the wall
1Sa 20:33 Then Saul cast a s at him to
1Sa 21: 8 here on hand a s or a sword
1Sa 22: 6 with his s in his hand, and
1Sa 26: 7 camp, with his s stuck in the
1Sa 26: 8 strike him at once with the s
1Sa 26:11 But please, take now the s
1Sa 26:12 So David took the s and the
1Sa 26:16 now see where the king's s is
1Sa 26:22 Here is the king's s
2Sa 1: 6 was Saul, leaning on his s
2Sa 2:23 with the blunt end of the s
2Sa 2:23 so that the s came out of his
2Sa 21:16 s was three hundred shekels
2Sa 21:19 the shaft of whose s was like
2Sa 23: 7 with iron and the shaft of a s
2Sa 23:18 He lifted his s against three
2Sa 23:21 Egyptian had a s in his hand
2Sa 23:21 wrested the s out of the
2Sa 23:21 and killed him with his own s
1Ch 11:11 he had lifted up his s
1Ch 11:20 He had lifted up his s
1Ch 11:23 been a s like a weaver's beam
1Ch 11:23 wrested the s out of the
1Ch 11:23 and killed him with his own s
1Ch 12: 8 who could handle shield and s
1Ch 12:24 of Judah bearing shield and s
1Ch 12:34 thousand with shield and s
1Ch 20: 5 the shaft of whose s was like
2Ch 25: 5 go to war, who could handle s
Job 39:23 against him, the glittering s
Job 41:26 nor does s, dart, or javelin
Ps 35: 3 Also draw out the s, And stop
Ps 46: 9 the bow and cuts the s in two
Jer 6:23 will lay hold on bow and s
Nah 3: 3 bright sword and glittering s
Hab 3:11 shining of Your glittering s
John 19:34 pierced His side with a s

SPEARHEAD (*see* SPEAR)
1Sa 17: 7 and his iron s weighed six

SPEARMEN (*see* SPEAR)
Acts 23:23 and two hundred s to go to

SPEARS (*see* SPEAR)
1Sa 13:19 the Hebrews make swords or s
2Sa 18:14 he took three s in his hand
2Ki 11:10 captains of hundreds the s
2Ch 11:12 city he put shields and s, and
2Ch 14: 8 who carried shields and s, and
2Ch 23: 9 captains of hundreds the s
2Ch 26:14 the entire army, shields, s
Neh 4:13 with their swords, their s
Neh 4:16 the other half held the s
Neh 4:21 the s from daybreak until the
Job 41: 7 or his head with fishing s
Ps 57: 4 on fire, Whose teeth are s
Is 2: 4 their s into pruning hooks
Jer 46: 4 your helmets, polish the s
Ezek 39: 9 and arrows, the javelins and s
Joel 3:10 and your pruninghooks into s
Mic 4: 3 their s into pruning hooks
Nah 2: 3 and the s are brandished

SPECIAL
Ex 19: 5 then you shall be a s
Deut 7: 6 a s treasure above all the
Deut 14: 2 a s treasure above all the
Deut 26:18 you to be His s people, just
1Ch 29: 3 my own s treasure of gold and
Ps 135: 4 Israel for His s treasure
Eccl 2: 8 the s treasures of kings and
Mark 7: 3 wash their hands in a s way
Tit 2:14 for Himself His own s people
1Pe 2: 9 holy nation, His own s people

SPECIES
Gen 7: 3 to keep the s alive on the

SPECIFICALLY (*see* SPECIFY)
Lev 13:38 body, s white bright spots,

SPECIFIED (*see* SPECIFY)
Neh 12:44 s by the Law for the priests
Dan 9: 2 s by the word of the LORD

SPECIFY (*see* SPECIFICALLY, SPECIFIED)
Acts 25:27 not to s the charges against

SPECK
Matt 7: 3 the s in your brother's eye
Matt 7: 4 remove the s out of your eye'
Matt 7: 5 s out of your brother's eye
Luke 6:41 the s in your brother's eye
Luke 6:42 let me remove the s that is
Luke 6:42 s that is in your brother's

SPECKLED
Gen 30:32 removing from there all the s
Gen 30:32 spotted and s among the goats
Gen 30:33 every one that is not s and
Gen 30:35 the male goats that were s
Gen 30:35 the female goats that were s
Gen 30:39 brought forth streaked, s
Gen 31: 8 The s shall be your wages,'
Gen 31: 8 then all the flocks bore s
Gen 31:10 the flocks were streaked, s
Gen 31:12 on the flocks are streaked, s
Jer 12: 9 is to Me like a s vulture

SPECTACLE (*see* SPECTACULAR)
Nah 3: 6 you vile, and make you a s
1Co 4: 9 been made a s to the world
Col 2:15 He made a public s of them
Heb 10:33 made a s both by reproaches

SPECTACULAR (*see* SPECTACLE)
2Sa 23:21 killed an Egyptian, a s man

SPEECH (*see* SPEAK, SPEECHES, SPEECHLESS)
Gen 4:23 of Lamech, listen to my s
Gen 11: 1 had one language and one s
Gen 11: 7 understand one another's s
Ex 4:10 but I am slow of s and slow of
Deut 32: 2 my s distill as the dew, as
1Sa 16:18 a man of war, prudent in s
1Ki 3:10 the s pleased the LORD, that
Job 12:20 the trusted ones of s, and
Job 13:17 Listen diligently to my s
Job 21: 2 Listen carefully to my s, and
Job 24:25 and make my s worth nothing
Job 29:22 my s settled on them as dew
Job 33: 1 But please, Job, hear my s
Ps 17: 6 Your ear to me, and hear my s
Ps 19: 2 Day unto day utters s, And
Ps 19: 3 There is no s nor language
Ps 94: 4 They utter s, and speak
Prov 7:21 With her enticing s she
Prov 17: 7 Excellent s is not becoming
Is 28:23 my voice, listen and hear my s
Is 29: 4 your s shall be low, out of
Is 29: 4 your s shall whisper out of
Is 32: 9 daughters, give ear to my s
Is 33:19 people, a people of obscure s
Jer 31:23 this s in the land of Judah
Ezek 3: 5 to a people of unfamiliar s
Ezek 3: 6 many people of unfamiliar s
Hab 3: 2 O LORD, I have heard your s
Matt 26:73 because your s betrays you
Mark 7:32 and had an impediment in his s
Mark 14:70 Galilean, and your s shows it
John 8:43 do you not understand My s
John 16:29 and using no figure of s
Rom 16:18 and flattering s deceive the
1Co 2: 1 s or of wisdom declaring to
1Co 2: 4 And my s and my preaching
2Co 3:12 we use great boldness of s
2Co 7: 4 my boldness of s toward you
2Co 8: 7 in faith, in s, in knowledge,
2Co 10:10 weak, and his s contemptible
2Co 11: 6 though I am untrained in s
Col 4: 6 Let your s always be with
Tit 2: 8 sound s that cannot be

SPEECHES (*see* SPEECH)
Job 6:26 the s of a desperate one,
Job 15: 3 or by s with which he can do

SPEECHLESS (*see* SPEECH)
Prov 31: 8 Open your mouth for the **s**
Dan 10:15 toward the ground and became **s**
Matt 22:12 And he was **s**
Luke 1:22 to them and remained **s**
Acts 9: 7 journeyed with him stood **s**

SPEED (*see* SPEEDILY, SPEEDY)
Is 5:19 Let Him make **s** and hasten His
Is 5:26 surely they shall come with **s**
Acts 17:15 to come to him with all **s**

SPEEDILY (*see* SPEED)
Gen 44:11 Then each man **s** let down his
1Sa 27: 1 **s** escape to the land of the
2Sa 17:16 but **s** cross over, lest the
Ezra 7:26 judgment be executed **s** on him
Ps 31: 2 Your ear to me, Deliver me **s**
Ps 69:17 I am in trouble; Hear me **s**
Ps 79: 8 mercies come **s** to meet us
Ps 102: 2 day that I call, answer me **s**
Ps 143: 7 Answer me **s**, O LORD
Eccl 8:11 evil work is not executed **s**
Is 58: 8 healing shall spring forth **s**
Jer 46: 5 They have **s** fled, And did not
Joel 3: 4 and **s** I will return your
Luke 18: 8 that He will avenge them **s**

SPEEDY (*see* SPEED)
Zeph 1:18 for He will make **s** riddance

SPELLS
Deut 18:11 or one who conjures **s**, or a

SPELT
Ex 9:32 the **s** were not struck, for
Is 28:25 place, and the **s** in its place
Ezek 4: 9 beans, lentils, millet, and **s**

SPEND (*see* SPENT)
Gen 19: 2 **s** the night, and wash your
Gen 19: 2 but we will **s** the night in
Deut 14:26 you shall **s** that money for
Deut 32:23 I will **s** My arrows upon them
Judg 19: 9 please **s** the night
Judg 19:10 not willing to **s** that night
Judg 19:13 **s** the night in Gibeah or in
Judg 19:15 into his house to **s** the night
Judg 19:20 only do not **s** the night in
Judg 20: 4 to Benjamin, to **s** the night
2Sa 17:16 Do not **s** this night in the
Neh 13:21 Why do you **s** the night around
Job 21:13 They **s** their days in wealth,
Job 24: 7 They **s** the night naked,
Job 36:11 they shall **s** their days in
Is 55: 2 Why do you **s** money for what
Is 65: 4 and **s** the night in the tombs
Ezek 6:12 Thus will I **s** My fury upon
Ezek 7: 8 fury, and **s** My anger upon you
Luke 10:35 and whatever more you **s**, when
Acts 20:16 not have to **s** time in Asia
1Co 16: 6 or even **s** the winter with you
2Co 12:15 And I will very gladly **s** and be
Tit 3:12 decided to **s** the winter there
Jas 4: 3 that you may **s** it on your
Jas 4:13 **s** a year there, buy and sell,

SPENT (*see* SPEND)
Lev 26:20 strength shall be **s** in vain
Deut 1:46 to the days that you **s** there
Judg 19:11 Jebus, and the day was far **s**
1Ki 19: 9 **s** the night in that place
Job 7: 6 and are **s** without hope
Ps 31:10 For my life is **s** with grief
Is 49: 4 I have **s** my strength for
Ezek 5:13 Thus shall My anger be **s**
Ezek 5:13 when I have **s** My fury upon
Dan 6:18 palace and **s** the night fasting
Mark 5:26 She had **s** all that she had and
Mark 6:35 And when the day was now far **s**
Luke 8:43 who had **s** all her livelihood
Luke 15:14 But when he had **s** all, there
Luke 24:29 evening, and the day is far **s**
Acts 9:19 Then Saul **s** some days with
Acts 17:21 foreigners who were there **s**
Acts 18:23 After he had **s** some time
Acts 26: 4 youth, which was **s** from the
Acts 27: 9 Now when much time had been **s**
Rom 13:12 The night is far **s**, the day
2Co 12:15 spend and be **s** for your souls
1Pe 4: 3 For we have **s** enough of our

SPEW (*see* SPEWED)
Rev 3:16 I will **s** you out of My mouth

SPEWED (*see* SPEW)
Rev 12:15 So the serpent **s** water out of
Rev 12:16 dragon had **s** out of his mouth

SPHERE
2Co 10:13 the **s** which God appointed us
2Co 10:13 a **s** which especially includes
2Co 10:14 ourselves beyond our **s** (thus
2Co 10:15 enlarged by you in our **s**,
2Co 10:16 man's **s** of accomplishment

SPICE (*see* SPICED, SPICES)
Song 5: 1 gathered my myrrh with my **s**

SPICED (*see* SPICE)
Song 8: 2 cause you to drink of **s** wine

SPICES (*see* SPICE)
Gen 37:25 with their camels, bearing **s**
Gen 43:11 balm and a little honey, **s**
Ex 25: 6 **s** for the anointing oil and
Ex 30:23 take for yourself quality **s**
Ex 30:34 Take sweet **s**, stacte and
Ex 30:34 with these sweet **s**
Ex 35: 8 **s** for the anointing oil and
Ex 35:28 and **s** and oil for the light,
Ex 37:29 the pure incense of sweet **s**
1Ki 10: 2 with camels that bore **s**,
1Ki 10:10 **s** in great abundance, and
1Ki 10:10 came such abundance of **s** as
1Ki 10:25 and gold, garments, armor, **s**
2Ki 20:13 the silver and gold, the **s**
1Ch 9:29 oil and the incense and the **s**
1Ch 9:30 made the ointment of the **s**
2Ch 9: 1 retinue, camels that bore **s**
2Ch 9: 9 **s** in great abundance, and
2Ch 9: 9 there never were any **s** such
2Ch 9:24 and gold, garments, armor, **s**
2Ch 16:14 bed which was filled with **s**
2Ch 32:27 for precious stones, for **s**
Song 4:10 of your perfumes than all **s**
Song 4:14 aloes, with all the chief **s**
Song 4:16 that its **s** may flow out
Song 5:13 cheeks are like a bed of **s**
Song 6: 2 his garden, to the beds of **s**
Song 8:14 stag on the mountains of **s**
Is 39: 2 the silver and gold, the **s**
Ezek 24:10 the meat well, Mix in the **s**
Ezek 27:22 for your wares the choicest **s**
Mark 16: 1 of James, and Salome bought **s**
Luke 23:56 they returned and prepared **s**
Luke 24: 1 the **s** which they had prepared
John 19:40 in strips of linen with the **s**

SPIDER (*see* SPIDER'S)
Prov 30:28 the **s** skillfully grasps with

SPIDER'S (*see* SPIDER)
Job 8:14 and whose trust is a **s** web
Is 59: 5 eggs and weave the **s** web

SPIED (*see* SPY)
Num 13:21 up and **s** out the land from the
Num 13:32 the land which they had **s** out
Num 14: 6 those who had **s** out the land
Num 14:34 in which you **s** out the land
Deut 1:24 Valley of Eshcol, and **s** it out
Josh 6:22 men who had **s** out the country
Josh 7: 2 the men went up and **s** out Ai
2Ki 13:21 they **s** a band of raiders

SPIES (*see* SPY)
Gen 42: 9 said to them, "You are **s**!
Gen 42:11 your servants are not **s**
Gen 42:14 to you, saying, "You are **s**
Gen 42:16 of Pharaoh, surely you are **s**
Gen 42:30 took us for **s** of the country
Gen 42:31 honest men; we are not **s**
Gen 42:34 shall know that you are not **s**
Num 13:32 which we have gone as **s** is a
Josh 6:23 men who had been **s** went in
Judg 1:24 when the **s** saw a man coming
Judg 18: 8 Then the **s** came back to their
1Sa 26: 4 David therefore sent out **s**
2Sa 15:10 Then Absalom sent **s**
Job 39:29 From there it **s** out the prey
Luke 20:20 sent **s** who pretended to be
Heb 11:31 had received the **s** with peace

SPIKENARD
Song 1:12 table, my **s** sends forth its
Song 4:13 fruits, fragrant henna with **s**
Song 4:14 **s** and saffron, calamus and
Mark 14: 3 flask of very costly oil of **s**
John 12: 3 pound of very costly oil of **s**

SPILLED
2Sa 14:14 like water **s** on the ground
Matt 9:17 break, the wine is **s**, and the
Mark 2:22 the wineskins, the wine is **s**
Luke 5:37 burst the wineskins and be **s**

SPIN (*see* SPUN)
Matt 6:28 they neither toil nor **s**
Luke 12:27 they neither toil nor **s**

SPINDLE
Prov 31:19 and her hand holds the **s**

SPIRIT (*see* HOLY, SPIRITS)
Gen 1: 2 the **S** of God was hovering
Gen 6: 3 My **S** shall not strive with
Gen 7:22 the breath of the **s** of life
Gen 41: 8 that his **s** was troubled, and
Gen 41:38 a man in whom is the **S** of God
Gen 45:27 the **s** of Jacob their father
Ex 6: 9 because of anguish of **s** and
Ex 28: 3 filled with the **s** of wisdom
Ex 31: 3 filled him with the **S** of God
Ex 35:21 everyone whose **s** was willing
Ex 35:31 filled him with the **S** of God
Num 5:14 if the **s** of jealousy comes
Num 5:14 or if the **s** of jealousy comes
Num 5:30 or when the **s** of jealousy
Num 11:17 of the **S** that is upon you
Num 11:25 took of the **S** that was upon
Num 11:25 when the **S** rested upon them,
Num 11:26 And the **S** rested upon them
Num 11:29 would put His **S** upon them
Num 14:24 he has a different **s** in him
Num 24: 2 the **S** of God came upon him
Num 27:18 you, a man in whom is the **S**
Deut 2:30 LORD your God hardened his **s**
Deut 34: 9 was full of the **s** of wisdom
Josh 5: 1 there was no **s** in them any
Judg 3:10 The **S** of the LORD came upon
Judg 6:34 But the **S** of the LORD came
Judg 9:23 God sent a **s** of ill will
Judg 11:29 Then the **S** of the LORD came
Judg 13:25 the **S** of the LORD began to
Judg 14: 6 And the **S** of the LORD came
Judg 14:19 Then the **S** of the LORD came
Judg 15:14 Then the **S** of the LORD came
Judg 15:19 his **s** returned, and he revived
1Sa 1:15 I am a woman of sorrowful **s**
1Sa 10: 6 Then the **S** of the LORD will
1Sa 10:10 then the **S** of God came upon
1Sa 11: 6 Then the **S** of God came upon
1Sa 16:13 the **S** of the LORD came upon
1Sa 16:14 But the **S** of the LORD
1Sa 16:14 a distressing **s** from the LORD
1Sa 16:15 a distressing **s** from God is
1Sa 16:16 **s** from God is upon you, and
1Sa 16:23 whenever the **s** from God was
1Sa 16:23 and the distressing **s** would
1Sa 18:10 **s** from God came upon Saul
1Sa 19: 9 Now the distressing **s** from
1Sa 19:20 the **S** of God came upon the
1Sa 19:23 Then the **S** of God was upon
1Sa 28:13 I saw a **s** ascending out of
2Sa 23: 2 The **S** of the LORD spoke by me
1Ki 10: 5 there was no more **s** in her
1Ki 18:12 that the **S** of the LORD will
1Ki 21: 5 Why is your **s** so sullen that
1Ki 22:21 Then a **s** came forward and
1Ki 22:22 be a lying **s** in the mouth of
1Ki 22:23 The LORD has put a lying **s** in
1Ki 22:24 Which way did the **s** from the
2Ki 2: 9 portion of your **s** be upon me
2Ki 2:15 The **s** of Elijah rests on
2Ki 2:16 lest perhaps the **S** of the
2Ki 19: 7 I will send a **s** upon him, and
1Ch 5:26 the **s** of Pul king of Assyria
1Ch 12:18 Then the **S** came upon Amasai,
1Ch 28:12 for all that he had by the **S**
2Ch 9: 4 there was no more **s** in her
2Ch 15: 1 Now the **S** of God came upon
2Ch 18:20 Then a **s** came forward and
2Ch 18:21 be a lying **s** in the mouth of
2Ch 18:22 lying **s** in the mouth of these
2Ch 18:23 Which way did the **s** from the

2Ch 20:14 Then the S of the LORD came
2Ch 21:16 the s of the Philistines and
2Ch 24:20 Then the S of God came upon
2Ch 36:22 the s of Cyrus king of Persia
Ezra 1: 1 the s of Cyrus king of Persia
Neh 9:20 Your good S to instruct them
Neh 9:30 by Your S in Your prophets
Job 4:15 Then a s passed before my
Job 6: 4 my s drinks in their poison
Job 7:11 speak in the anguish of my s
Job 10:12 Your care has preserved my s
Job 15:13 you turn your s against God
Job 17: 1 My s is broken, my days are
Job 20: 3 the s of my understanding
Job 26: 4 And whose s came from you
Job 26:13 By His S He adorned the
Job 32: 8 But there is a s in man, and
Job 32:18 the s within me compels me
Job 33: 4 The S of God has made me, and
Job 34:14 gather to Himself His S and
Ps 31: 5 Into Your hand I commit my s
Ps 32: 2 in whose s there is no guile
Ps 34:18 such as have a contrite s
Ps 51:10 renew a steadfast s within me
Ps 51:11 not take Your Holy S from me
Ps 51:12 me with Your generous S
Ps 51:17 of God are a broken s, A
Ps 76:12 cut off the s of princes
Ps 77: 3 and my s was overwhelmed
Ps 77: 6 my s makes diligent search
Ps 78: 8 whose s was not faithful to
Ps 104:30 You send forth Your S, they
Ps 106:33 they rebelled against His S
Ps 139: 7 Where can I go from Your S
Ps 142: 3 When my s was overwhelmed
Ps 143: 4 Therefore my s is overwhelmed
Ps 143: 7 My s fails! Do not hide
Ps 143:10 my God; Your S is good
Ps 146: 4 His s departs, he returns to
Prov 1:23 I will pour out my s on you
Prov 11:13 faithful s conceals a matter
Prov 15: 4 in it breaks the s
Prov 15:13 of the heart the s is broken
Prov 16:18 a haughty s before a fall
Prov 16:19 of a humble s with the lowly
Prov 16:32 he who rules his s than he
Prov 17:22 but a broken s dries the
Prov 17:27 understanding is of a calm s
Prov 18:14 The s of a man will sustain
Prov 18:14 but who can bear a broken s
Prov 20:27 The s of a man is the lamp of
Prov 25:28 has no rule over his own s is
Prov 29:23 humble in s will retain honor
Eccl 3:21 Who knows the s of the sons
Eccl 3:21 the s of the beast, which
Eccl 7: 8 the patient in s is better
Eccl 7: 8 than the proud in s
Eccl 7: 9 hasten in your s to be angry
Eccl 8: 8 the s to retain the s
Eccl 10: 4 If the s of the ruler rises
Eccl 12: 7 the s will return to God who
Is 4: 4 by the s of judgment and by
Is 4: 4 and by the s of burning,
Is 11: 2 The S of the LORD shall rest
Is 11: 2 upon Him, the S of wisdom and
Is 11: 2 the S of counsel and might,
Is 11: 2 the S of knowledge and of the
Is 19: 3 The s of Egypt will fail in
Is 19:14 a perverse s in her midst
Is 26: 9 by my s within me I will seek
Is 28: 6 for a s of justice to him who
Is 29:10 on you the s of deep sleep
Is 29:24 These also who erred in s
Is 30: 1 devise plans, but not of My S
Is 31: 3 horses are flesh, and not s
Is 32:15 until the S is poured upon us
Is 34:16 and His S has gathered them
Is 37: 7 I will send a s upon him, and
Is 38:16 things is the life of my s
Is 40:13 directed the S of the LORD
Is 42: 1 I have put My S upon Him
Is 42: 5 s to those who walk on it
Is 44: 3 I will pour My S on your
Is 48:16 GOD and His S have sent Me
Is 54: 6 forsaken and grieved in s,
Is 57:15 has a contrite and humble s
Is 57:15 to revive the s of the humble
Is 57:16 for the s would fail before
Is 59:19 the S of the LORD will lift
Is 59:21 My S who is upon you, and My
Is 61: 1 The S of the Lord GOD is upon
Is 61: 3 praise for the s of heaviness
Is 63:10 and grieved His Holy S
Is 63:11 put His Holy S within them
Is 63:14 the S of the LORD causes him
Is 65:14 heart, and wail for grief of s
Is 66: 2 is poor and of a contrite s
Jer 51:11 s of the kings of the Medes
Ezek 1:12 wherever the s wanted to go
Ezek 1:20 Wherever the s wanted to go
Ezek 1:20 because there the s went
Ezek 1:20 them, for the s of the living
Ezek 1:21 them, for the s of the living
Ezek 2: 2 Then the S entered me when He
Ezek 3:12 Then the S lifted me up, and I
Ezek 3:14 So the S lifted me up and took
Ezek 3:14 in the heat of my s
Ezek 3:24 Then the S entered me and set
Ezek 8: 3 the S lifted me up between
Ezek 10:17 up, for the s of the living
Ezek 11: 1 Then the S lifted me up and
Ezek 11: 5 Then the S of the LORD fell
Ezek 11:19 will put a new s within them
Ezek 11:24 Then the S took me up and
Ezek 11:24 by the S of God into Chaldea
Ezek 13: 3 who follow their own s and
Ezek 18:31 a new heart and a new s
Ezek 21: 7 every s will faint, and all
Ezek 36:26 and put a new s within you
Ezek 36:27 I will put My S within you
Ezek 37: 1 me out in the S of the LORD
Ezek 37:14 I will put My S in you, and
Ezek 39:29 My S on the house of Israel
Ezek 43: 5 The S lifted me up and brought
Dan 2: 1 his s was so troubled that
Dan 2: 3 my s is anxious to know the
Dan 4: 8 in him is the S of the Holy
Dan 4: 9 because I know that the S of
Dan 4:18 for the S of the Holy God is
Dan 5:11 whom is the S of the Holy God
Dan 5:12 Inasmuch as an excellent s
Dan 5:14 that the S of God is in you,
Dan 5:20 his s was hardened in pride,
Dan 6: 3 an excellent s was in him
Dan 7:15 in my s within my body, and
Hos 4:12 For the s of harlotry has
Hos 5: 4 for the s of harlotry is in
Joel 2:28 pour out My S on all flesh
Joel 2:29 pour out My S in those days
Mic 2: 7 Is the S of the LORD
Mic 2:11 man should walk in a false s
Mic 3: 8 of power by the S of the LORD
Hag 1:14 s of Zerubbabel the son of
Hag 1:14 the s of Joshua the son of
Hag 1:14 the s of all the remnant of
Hag 2: 5 so My S remains among you
Zech 4: 6 nor by power, but by My S
Zech 6: 8 to My S in the north country
Zech 7:12 of hosts had sent by His S
Zech 12: 1 forms the s of man within him
Zech 12:10 of Jerusalem the S of grace
Zech 13: 2 the unclean s to depart from
Mal 2:15 having a remnant of the S
Mal 2:15 Therefore take heed to your s
Mal 2:16 Therefore take heed to your s
Matt 1:18 with child of the Holy S
Matt 1:20 in her is of the Holy S
Matt 3:11 baptize you with the Holy S
Matt 3:16 Him, and He saw the S of God
Matt 4: 1 Jesus was led up by the S
Matt 5: 3 Blessed are the poor in s
Matt 10:20 but the S of your Father who
Matt 12:18 I will put My S upon Him, and
Matt 12:28 out demons by the S of God
Matt 12:31 S will not be forgiven men
Matt 12:32 speaks against the Holy S
Matt 12:43 When an unclean s goes out of
Matt 22:43 David in the S call Him 'Lord
Matt 26:41 The s indeed is willing, but
Matt 27:50 loud voice, yielded up His s
Matt 28:19 of the Son and of the Holy S
Mark 1: 8 baptize you with the Holy S
Mark 1:10 the S descending upon Him
Mark 1:12 immediately the S drove Him
Mark 1:23 synagogue with an unclean s
Mark 1:26 And when the unclean s had
Mark 2: 8 His s that they reasoned thus
Mark 3:29 Holy S never has forgiveness
Mark 3:30 He has an unclean s
Mark 5: 2 tombs a man with an unclean s
Mark 5: 8 out of the man, unclean s
Mark 7:25 an unclean s heard about Him
Mark 8:12 But He sighed deeply in His s
Mark 9:17 You my son, who has a mute s
Mark 9:20 the s convulsed him, and he
Mark 9:25 He rebuked the unclean s
Mark 9:25 You deaf and dumb s, I
Mark 9:26 Then the s cried out,
Mark 12:36 himself said by the Holy S
Mark 13:11 you who speak, but the Holy S
Mark 14:38 The s truly is ready, but the
Luke 1:15 be filled with the Holy S
Luke 1:17 also go before Him in the s
Luke 1:35 The Holy S will come upon you
Luke 1:41 was filled with the Holy S
Luke 1:47 my s has rejoiced in God my
Luke 1:67 was filled with the Holy S
Luke 1:80 grew and became strong in s
Luke 2:25 and the Holy S was upon him
Luke 2:26 S that he would not see death
Luke 2:27 came by the S into the temple
Luke 2:40 grew and became strong in s
Luke 3:16 baptize you with the Holy S
Luke 3:22 And the Holy S descended in
Luke 4: 1 being filled with the Holy S
Luke 4: 1 was led by the S into the
Luke 4:14 the power of the S to Galilee
Luke 4:18 The S of the LORD is upon Me,
Luke 4:33 had a s of an unclean demon
Luke 8:29 s to come out of the man
Luke 8:55 Then her s returned, and she
Luke 9:39 behold, a s seizes him, and he
Luke 9:42 Jesus rebuked the unclean s
Luke 9:55 what manner of s you are of
Luke 10:21 hour Jesus rejoiced in the S
Luke 11:13 Holy S to those who ask Him
Luke 11:24 When an unclean s goes out of
Luke 12:10 blasphemes against the Holy S
Luke 12:12 For the Holy S will teach you
Luke 13:11 s of infirmity eighteen years
Luke 23:46 Your hands I commend My s
Luke 24:37 and supposed they had seen a s
Luke 24:39 for a s does not have flesh
John 1:32 I saw the S descending from
John 1:33 whom you see the S descending
John 1:33 who baptizes with the Holy S
John 3: 5 one is born of water and the S
John 3: 6 is born of the S is s
John 3: 8 everyone who is born of the S
John 3:34 not give the S by measure
John 4:23 will worship the Father in s
John 4:24 God is S, and those who
John 4:24 worship Him must worship in s
John 6:63 It is the S who gives life
John 6:63 that I speak to you are s
John 7:39 He spoke concerning the S
John 7:39 for the Holy S was not yet
John 11:33 weeping, He groaned in the s
John 13:21 things, He was troubled in s
John 14:17 even the S of truth, whom the
John 14:26 But the Helper, the Holy S
John 15:26 the S of truth who proceeds
John 16:13 the S of truth, has come, He
John 19:30 His head, He gave up His s
John 20:22 Receive the Holy S
Acts 1: 2 S had given commandments to
Acts 1: 5 Holy S not many days from now
Acts 1: 8 the Holy S has come upon you
Acts 1:16 which the Holy S spoke before
Acts 2: 4 all filled with the Holy S
Acts 2: 4 as the S gave them utterance
Acts 2:17 pour out of My S on all flesh
Acts 2:18 pour out My S in those days
Acts 2:33 the promise of the Holy S
Acts 2:38 the gift of the Holy S
Acts 4: 8 Peter, filled with the Holy S
Acts 4:31 all filled with the Holy S
Acts 5: 3 heart to lie to the Holy S
Acts 5: 9 to test the S of the Lord
Acts 5:32 so also is the Holy S whom
Acts 6: 3 full of the Holy S and wisdom
Acts 6: 5 full of faith and the Holy S
Acts 6:10 and the S by which he spoke
Acts 7:51 You always resist the Holy S
Acts 7:55 he, being full of the Holy S
Acts 7:59 Lord Jesus, receive my s
Acts 8:15 they might receive the Holy S
Acts 8:17 and they received the Holy S
Acts 8:18 hands the Holy S was given
Acts 8:19 hands may receive the Holy S

Acts 8:29 Then the **S** said to Philip,
Acts 8:39 the **S** of the Lord caught
Acts 9:17 and be filled with the Holy **S**
Acts 9:31 in the comfort of the Holy **S**
Acts 10:19 vision, the **S** said to him,
Acts 10:38 of Nazareth with the Holy **S**
Acts 10:44 the Holy **S** fell upon all
Acts 10:45 the gift of the Holy **S** had
Acts 10:47 the Holy **S** just as we have
Acts 11:12 Then the **S** told me to go with
Acts 11:15 the Holy **S** fell upon them, as
Acts 11:16 be baptized with the Holy **S**
Acts 11:24 good man, full of the Holy **S**
Acts 11:28 showed by the **S** that there
Acts 13: 2 and fasted, the Holy **S** said
Acts 13: 4 being sent out by the Holy **S**
Acts 13: 9 Paul, filled with the Holy **S**
Acts 13:52 with joy and with the Holy **S**
Acts 15: 8 Holy **S** just as He did to us
Acts 15:28 it seemed good to the Holy **S**
Acts 16: 6 **S** to preach the word in Asia
Acts 16: 7 but the **S** did not permit them
Acts 16:16 with a **s** of divination met us
Acts 16:18 turned and said to the **s**, "I
Acts 17:16 his **s** was provoked within him
Acts 18: 5 Paul was constrained by the **S**
Acts 18:25 and being fervent in **s**, he
Acts 19: 2 the Holy **S** when you believed
Acts 19: 2 whether there is a Holy **S**
Acts 19: 6 the Holy **S** came upon them, and
Acts 19:15 And the evil **s** answered and
Acts 19:16 the evil **s** was leaped on them
Acts 19:21 Paul purposed in the **S**, when
Acts 20:22 bound in the **s** to Jerusalem
Acts 20:23 except that the Holy **S**
Acts 20:28 among which the Holy **S** has
Acts 21: 4 **S** not to go up to Jerusalem
Acts 21:11 Thus says the Holy **S**, 'So
Acts 23: 8 and no angel or **s**
Acts 23: 9 but if a **s** or an angel has
Acts 28:25 The Holy **S** spoke rightly
Rom 1: 4 to the **S** of holiness, by the
Rom 1: 9 whom I serve with my **s** in the
Rom 2:29 that of the heart, in the **S**
Rom 5: 5 Holy **S** who was given to us
Rom 7: 6 serve in the newness of the **S**
Rom 8: 1 flesh, but according to the **S**
Rom 8: 2 For the law of the **S** of life
Rom 8: 4 flesh but according to the **S**
Rom 8: 5 the **S**, the things of the **S**
Rom 8: 9 not in the flesh but in the **S**
Rom 8: 9 if indeed the **S** of God dwells
Rom 8: 9 does not have the **S** of Christ
Rom 8:10 but the **S** is life because of
Rom 8:11 But if the **S** of Him who
Rom 8:11 His **S** who dwells in you
Rom 8:13 but if by the **S** you put to
Rom 8:14 as are led by the **S** of God
Rom 8:15 **s** of bondage again to fear
Rom 8:15 but you received the **S** of
Rom 8:16 The **S** Himself bears witness
Rom 8:16 with our **s** that we are
Rom 8:23 have the firstfruits of the **S**
Rom 8:26 Likewise the **S** also helps in
Rom 8:26 but the **S** Himself makes
Rom 8:27 what the mind of the **S** is
Rom 9: 1 me witness in the Holy **S**,
Rom 11: 8 has given them a **s** of stupor
Rom 12:11 in diligence, fervent in **s**
Rom 14:17 and peace and joy in the Holy **S**
Rom 15:13 by the power of the Holy **S**
Rom 15:16 sanctified by the Holy **S**
Rom 15:19 by the power of the **S** of God
Rom 15:30 and through the love of the **S**
1Co 2: 4 but in demonstration of the **S**
1Co 2:10 them to us through His **S**
1Co 2:10 For the **S** searches all things
1Co 2:11 **s** of the man which is in him
1Co 2:11 of God except the **S** of God
1Co 2:12 not the **s** of the world
1Co 2:12 but the **S** who is from God,
1Co 2:13 but which the Holy **S** teaches
1Co 2:14 the things of the **S** of God
1Co 3:16 that the **S** of God dwells in
1Co 4:21 in love and a **s** of gentleness
1Co 5: 3 in body but present in **s**,
1Co 5: 4 together, along with my **s**
1Co 5: 5 that his **s** may be saved in
1Co 6:11 Jesus and by the **S** of our God
1Co 6:17 to the Lord is one **s** with Him
1Co 6:19 of the Holy **S** who is in you
1Co 6:20 God in your body and in your **s**
1Co 7:34 be holy both in body and in **s**
1Co 7:40 I also have the **S** of God
1Co 12: 3 **S** of God calls Jesus accursed
1Co 12: 3 is Lord except by the Holy **S**
1Co 12: 4 of gifts, but the same **S**
1Co 12: 7 **S** is given to each one for
1Co 12: 8 word of wisdom through the **S**
1Co 12: 8 knowledge through the same **S**
1Co 12: 9 another faith by the same **S**
1Co 12: 9 of healings by the same **S**
1Co 12:11 the same **S** works all these
1Co 12:13 For by one **S** we were all
1Co 12:13 been made to drink into one **S**
1Co 14: 2 in the **s** he speaks mysteries
1Co 14:14 a tongue, my **s** prays, but my
1Co 14:15 I will pray with the **s**, and I
1Co 14:15 I will sing with the **s**, and I
1Co 14:16 if you bless with the **s**, how
1Co 15:45 Adam became a life-giving **s**
1Co 16:18 For they refreshed my **s** and
2Co 1:22 given us the **S** in our hearts
2Co 2:13 I had no rest in my **s**,
2Co 3: 3 by the **S** of the living God
2Co 3: 6 of the letter but of the **S**
2Co 3: 6 kills, but the **S** gives life
2Co 3: 8 of the **S** not be more glorious
2Co 3:17 Now the Lord is the **S**
2Co 3:17 where the **S** of the Lord is,
2Co 3:18 just as by the **S** of the Lord
2Co 4:13 we have the same **s** of faith
2Co 5: 5 given us the **S** as a guarantee
2Co 6: 6 by kindness, by the Holy **S**
2Co 7: 1 filthiness of the flesh and **s**
2Co 7:13 Titus, because his **s** has been
2Co 11: 4 if you receive a different **s**
2Co 12:18 Did we not walk in the same **s**
2Co 13:14 of the Holy **S** be with you all
Gal 3: 2 Did you receive the **S** by the
Gal 3: 3 Having begun in the **S**, are
Gal 3: 5 He who supplies the **S** to you
Gal 3:14 of the **S** through faith
Gal 4: 6 God has sent forth the **S** of
Gal 4:29 was born according to the **S**
Gal 5: 5 For we through the **S** eagerly
Gal 5:16 Walk in the **S**, and you shall
Gal 5:17 the flesh lusts against the **S**
Gal 5:17 and the **S** against the flesh
Gal 5:18 But if you are led by the **S**
Gal 5:22 the fruit of the **S** is love
Gal 5:25 If we live in the **S**, let us
Gal 5:25 let us also walk in the **S**
Gal 6: 1 a one in a **s** of gentleness
Gal 6: 8 but he who sows to the **S** will
Gal 6: 8 the **S** reap everlasting life
Gal 6:18 Jesus Christ be with your **s**
Eph 1:13 with the Holy **S** of promise
Eph 1:17 give to you the **s** of wisdom
Eph 2: 2 the **s** who now works in the
Eph 2:18 access by one **S** to the Father
Eph 2:22 a habitation of God in the **S**
Eph 3: 5 by the **S** to His holy apostles
Eph 3:16 His **S** in the inner man,
Eph 4: 3 of the **S** in the bond of peace
Eph 4: 4 There is one body and one **S**
Eph 4:23 renewed in the **s** of your mind
Eph 4:30 not grieve the Holy **S** of God
Eph 5: 9 of the **S** is in all goodness
Eph 5:18 but be filled with the **S**,
Eph 6:17 and the sword of the **S**, which
Eph 6:18 and supplication in the **S**,
Phil 1:19 of the **S** of Jesus Christ,
Phil 1:27 that you stand fast in one **s**
Phil 2: 1 if any fellowship of the **S**
Phil 3: 3 who worship God in the **S**
Col 1: 8 to us your love in the **S**
Col 2: 5 flesh, yet I am with you in **s**
1Th 1: 5 in power, and in the Holy **S**
1Th 1: 6 with joy of the Holy **S**,
1Th 4: 8 has also given us His Holy **S**
1Th 5:19 Do not quench the **S**
1Th 5:23 and may your whole **s**, soul, and
2Th 2: 2 either by **s** or by word or by
2Th 2:13 sanctification by the **S** and
1Ti 3:16 the flesh, justified in the **S**
1Ti 4: 1 Now the **S** expressly says that
1Ti 4:12 in conduct, in love, in **s**
2Ti 1: 7 has not given us a **s** of fear
2Ti 1:14 the Holy **S** who dwells in us
2Ti 4:22 Jesus Christ be with your **s**
Tit 3: 5 and renewing of the Holy **S**
Phm 25 Jesus Christ be with your **s**
Heb 2: 4 and gifts of the Holy **S**,
Heb 3: 7 Therefore, as the Holy **S** says
Heb 4:12 to the division of soul and **s**
Heb 6: 4 partakers of the Holy **S**,
Heb 9: 8 the Holy **S** indicating this,
Heb 9:14 **S** offered Himself without
Heb 10:15 the Holy **S** also witnesses to
Heb 10:29 and insulted the **S** of grace
Jas 2:26 body without the **s** is dead
Jas 4: 5 The **S** who dwells in us yearns
1Pe 1: 2 in sanctification of the **S**
1Pe 1:11 the **S** of Christ who was in
1Pe 1:12 the Holy **S** sent from heaven
1Pe 1:22 the truth through the **S** in
1Pe 3: 4 of a gentle and quiet **s**, which
1Pe 3:18 flesh but made alive by the **S**
1Pe 4: 6 according to God in the **s**
1Pe 4:14 for the **S** of glory and of God
2Pe 1:21 they were moved by the Holy **S**
1Jn 3:24 by the **S** whom He has given us
1Jn 4: 1 do not believe every **s**, but
1Jn 4: 2 By this you know the **S** of God
1Jn 4: 2 Every **s** that confesses that
1Jn 4: 3 every **s** that does not confess
1Jn 4: 3 And this is the **s** of the
1Jn 4: 6 **s** of truth and the **s** of error
1Jn 4:13 He has given us of His **S**
1Jn 5: 6 it is the **S** who bears witness
1Jn 5: 6 because the **S** is truth
1Jn 5: 7 the Word, and the Holy **S**
1Jn 5: 8 the **S**, the water, and the
Jude 19 divisions, not having the **S**
Jude 20 faith, praying in the Holy **S**
Rev 1:10 I was in the **S** on the Lord's
Rev 2: 7 the **S** says to the churches
Rev 2:11 the **S** says to the churches
Rev 2:17 the **S** says to the churches
Rev 2:29 the **S** says to the churches
Rev 3: 6 the **S** says to the churches
Rev 3:13 the **S** says to the churches
Rev 3:22 the **S** says to the churches
Rev 4: 2 Immediately I was in the **S**
Rev 14:13 Yes," says the **S**, "that
Rev 17: 3 in the **S** into the wilderness
Rev 18: 2 a prison for every foul **s**
Rev 19:10 of Jesus is the **s** of prophecy
Rev 21:10 me away in the **S** to a great
Rev 22:17 And the **S** and the bride say

SPIRITIST (*see* SPIRITISTS)
Deut 18:11 spells, or a medium, or a **s**

SPIRITISTS (*see* SPIRITIST)
1Sa 28: 3 and the **s** out of the land
1Sa 28: 9 and the **s** from the land
2Ki 21: 6 witchcraft, and consulted **s**
2Ki 23:24 who consulted mediums and **s**
2Ch 33: 6 and consulted mediums and **s**

SPIRITS (*see* SPIRIT)
Lev 19:31 to mediums and familiar **s**
Lev 20: 6 after mediums and familiar **s**
Lev 20:27 medium, or who has familiar **s**
Num 16:22 the God of the **s** of all flesh
Num 27:16 the God of the **s** of all flesh
Ezra 1: 5 those whose **s** God had moved
Ps 104: 4 Who makes His angels **s**, His
Prov 16: 2 but the LORD weighs the **s**
Zech 6: 5 These are four **s** of heaven
Matt 8:16 He cast out the **s** with a word
Matt 10: 1 them power over unclean **s**
Matt 12:45 **s** more wicked than himself
Mark 1:27 commands even the unclean **s**
Mark 3:11 And the unclean **s**, whenever
Mark 5:13 Then the unclean **s** went out
Mark 6: 7 them power over unclean **s**
Luke 4:36 He commands the unclean **s**
Luke 6:18 were tormented with unclean **s**
Luke 7:21 afflictions, and evil **s**
Luke 8: 2 who had been healed of evil **s**
Luke 10:20 that the **s** are subject to you
Luke 11:26 **s** more wicked than himself
Acts 5:16 were tormented by unclean **s**
Acts 8: 7 For unclean **s**, crying with a
Acts 19:12 the evil **s** went out of them
Acts 19:13 over those who had evil **s**
1Co 12:10 to another discerning of **s**
1Co 14:32 the **s** of the prophets are
1Ti 4: 1 giving heed to deceiving **s**

Heb 1: 7 Who makes His angels **s** and His
Heb 1:14 they not all ministering **s**
Heb 12: 9 subjection to the Father of **s**
Heb 12:23 to the **s** of just men made
1Pe 3:19 preached to the **s** in prison
1Jn 4: 1 every spirit, but test the **s**
Rev 1: 4 and from the seven **S** who are
Rev 3: 1 He who has the seven **S** of God
Rev 4: 5 which are the seven **S** of God
Rev 5: 6 which are the seven **S** of God
Rev 16:13 I saw three unclean **s** like
Rev 16:14 For they are **s** of demons,

SPIRITUAL (*see* SPIRITUALLY)
Hos 9: 7 the **s** man is insane, Because
Rom 1:11 may impart to you some **s** gift
Rom 7:14 For we know that the law is **s**
Rom 15:27 partakers of their **s** things
1Co 2:13 comparing **s** things with **s**
1Co 2:15 But he who is **s** judges all
1Co 3: 1 not speak to you as to **s**
1Co 9:11 we have sown **s** things for you
1Co 10: 3 all ate the same **s** food,
1Co 10: 4 and all drank the same **s** drink
1Co 10: 4 For they drank of that **s** Rock
1Co 12: 1 Now concerning **s** gifts,
1Co 14: 1 love, and desire **s** gifts, but
1Co 14:12 you are zealous for **s** gifts
1Co 14:37 himself to be a prophet or **s**
1Co 15:44 body, it is raised a **s** body
1Co 15:44 body, and there is a **s** body
1Co 15:46 the **s** is not first, but the
1Co 15:46 natural, and afterward the **s**
Gal 6: 1 you who are **s** restore such a
Eph 1: 3 **s** blessing in the heavenly
Eph 5:19 **s** songs, singing and making
Eph 6:12 against **s** hosts of wickedness
Col 1: 9 all wisdom and **s** understanding
Col 3:16 **s** songs, singing with grace
1Pe 2: 5 are being built up a **s** house
1Pe 2: 5 to offer up **s** sacrifices

SPIRITUALLY (*see* SPIRITUAL)
Rom 8: 6 but to be **s** minded is life and
1Co 2:14 because they are **s** discerned
Rev 11: 8 city which **s** is called Sodom

SPIT (*see* SPAT, SPITS, SPITTING)
Num 12:14 father had but **s** in her face
Deut 25: 9 **s** in his face, and answer and
Job 17: 6 one in whose face men **s**
Job 30:10 not hesitate to **s** in my face
Jer 51:34 delicacies, he has **s** me out
Mark 8:23 And when He had **s** on his eyes
Mark 10:34 Him, and **s** on Him, and kill Him
Mark 14:65 Then some began to **s** on Him
Luke 18:32 mocked and insulted and **s** upon

SPITE (*see* SPITEFUL)
Ezra 10: 2 hope in Israel in **s** of this
Neh 5:18 yet in **s** of this I did not
Ps 78:32 In **s** of this they still

SPITEFUL (*see* SPITE, SPITEFULLY)
Prov 17: 4 listens eagerly to a **s** tongue
Ezek 25:15 took vengeance with a **s** heart
Ezek 36: 5 **s** minds, in order to plunder

SPITEFULLY (*see* SPITEFUL)
Matt 5:44 pray for those who **s** use you
Matt 22: 6 his servants, treated them **s**
Luke 6:28 pray for those who **s** use you
1Th 2: 2 were **s** treated at Philippi,

SPITS (*see* SPIT)
Lev 15: 8 **s** on him who is clean, then

SPITTING (*see* SPIT)
Is 50: 6 hide My face from shame and **s**

SPLENDID (*see* SPLENDIDLY)
Rev 18:14 **s** have gone from you, and you

SPLENDIDLY (*see* SPLENDID)
Ezek 38: 4 all **s** clothed, a great

SPLENDOR
Esth 1: 4 and the **s** of his excellent
Job 37:22 from the north as golden **s**
Job 40:10 yourself with majesty and **s**
Ps 37:20 Like the **s** of the meadows,
Ps 145: 5 glorious **s** of Your majesty
Prov 20:29 the **s** of old men is their
Lam 1: 6 Zion all her **s** has departed
Ezek 16:14 it was perfect through My **s**
Ezek 27:10 they gave **s** to you
Ezek 28: 7 your wisdom, and defile your **s**
Ezek 28:17 wisdom for the sake of your **s**
Dan 2:31 whose **s** was excellent, stood
Dan 4:36 my honor and **s** returned to me

SPLINT
Ezek 30:21 nor a **s** put on to bind it, to

SPLINTERED (*see* SPLINTERS)
Ps 105:33 And **s** the trees of their

SPLINTERS (*see* SPLINTERED)
Ps 29: 5 Yes, the LORD **s** the cedars of

SPLIT (*see* SPLITS)
Gen 22: 3 he **s** the wood for the burnt
Lev 1:17 Then he shall **s** it at its
Num 16:31 that the ground **s** apart under
Deut 14: 6 the hoof **s** into two parts
Judg 5:26 she pierced his head, she **s**
Judg 15:19 So God **s** the hollow place
1Sa 6:14 So they **s** the wood of the
1Ki 1:40 seemed to **s** with their sound
1Ki 13: 3 the altar shall **s** apart, and
1Ki 13: 5 The altar also was **s** apart
Ps 78:15 He **s** the rocks in the
Is 24:19 broken, the earth is **s** open
Is 48:21 He also **s** the rock, and the
Ezek 30:16 pain, no shall be **s** open, and
Mic 1: 4 the valleys will **s** like wax
Zech 14: 4 of Olives shall be **s** in two
Matt 27:51 quaked, and the rocks were **s**

SPLITS (*see* SPLIT)
Eccl 10: 9 them, and he who **s** wood may

SPOIL (*see* SPOILER, SPOILS)
Gen 49:27 night he shall divide the **s**
Ex 15: 9 overtake, I will divide the **s**
Num 31: 9 took as **s** all their cattle,
Num 31:11 And they took all the **s** and all
Num 31:12 the **s** to Moses, to Eleazar
Num 31:53 (The men of war had taken **s**
Deut 2:35 with the **s** of the cities
Deut 3: 7 the **s** of the cities we took
Deut 20:14 is in the city, all its **s**
Josh 8: 2 Only its **s** and its cattle you
Josh 8:27 the **s** of that city Israel
Josh 11:14 all the **s** of these cities and
Josh 22: 8 Divide the **s** of your enemies
Judg 5:30 not finding and dividing the **s**
1Sa 14:30 eaten freely today of the **s**
1Sa 14:32 And the people rushed on the **s**
1Sa 15:19 did you swoop down on the **s**
1Sa 30:16 because of all the great **s**
1Sa 30:19 **s** or anything which they had
1Sa 30:20 This is David's **s**
1Sa 30:22 the **s** that we have recovered
1Sa 30:26 he sent some of the **s** to the
1Sa 30:26 **s** of the enemies of the LORD
2Sa 3:22 and brought much **s** with them
2Sa 8:12 from the **s** of Hadadezer the
2Sa 12:30 the **s** of the city in great
2Ki 3:23 now therefore, Moab, to the **s**
1Ch 20: 2 the **s** of the city in great
2Ch 14:13 they carried away very much **s**
2Ch 14:14 exceedingly much **s** in them
2Ch 15:11 the **s** which they had brought
2Ch 20:25 came to take away their **s**
2Ch 20:25 three days gathering the **s**
2Ch 24:23 sent all their **s** to the king
2Ch 25:13 in them, and took much **s**
2Ch 28: 8 took away much **s** from them
2Ch 28: 8 and brought the **s** to Samaria
2Ch 28:14 the **s** before the leaders and
2Ch 28:15 from the **s** they clothed all
Job 30:22 You **s** my success
Ps 44:10 have taken **s** for themselves
Ps 68:12 remains at home divides the **s**
Prov 1:13 shall fill our houses with **s**
Prov 16:19 divide the **s** with the proud
Song 2:15 little foxes that **s** the vines
Is 8: 4 and the **s** of Samaria will be
Is 9: 3 when they divide the **s**
Is 10: 6 him charge, to seize the **s**
Is 53:12 divide the **s** with the strong
Ezek 7:21 the wicked of the earth as **s**
Ezek 29:19 her wealth, carry off her **s**
Dan 11:24 among them the plunder, **s**
Hos 7: 1 of robbers takes **s** outside
Nah 2: 9 **s** of silver! Take **s** of gold
Zech 2: 9 they shall become **s** for their
Zech 14: 1 your **s** will be divided in

SPOILER (*see* SPOIL)
Is 16: 4 them from the face of the **s**
Is 54:16 have created the **s** to destroy

SPOILS (*see* SPOIL)
Josh 7:21 When I saw among the **s** a
Judg 5:19 they took no **s** of silver
1Ch 26:27 Some of the **s** won in battles
Luke 11:22 he trusted, and divides his **s**
Heb 7: 4 Abraham gave a tenth of the **s**

SPOKE (*see* SPEAK)
Gen 8:15 Then God **s** to Noah, saying,
Gen 9: 8 Then God **s** to Noah and to his
Gen 16:13 name of the LORD who **s** to her
Gen 18:29 Then he **s** to Him yet again and
Gen 19:14 **s** to his sons-in-law, who had
Gen 21:22 army, **s** to Abraham, saying,
Gen 22: 7 But Isaac **s** to Abraham his
Gen 23: 3 **s** to the sons of Heth, saying
Gen 23: 8 And he **s** with them, saying,
Gen 23:13 he **s** to Ephron in the hearing
Gen 24: 7 who **s** to me and swore to me,
Gen 24:30 Thus the man **s** to me," that
Gen 27: 5 when Isaac **s** to Esau his son
Gen 27: 6 So Rebekah **s** to Jacob her son
Gen 31:11 of God **s** to me in a dream
Gen 31:29 father **s** to me last night
Gen 34: 3 **s** kindly to the young woman
Gen 34: 4 So Shechem **s** to his father
Gen 34: 8 But Hamor **s** with them, saying
Gen 34:13 **s** deceitfully, because he had
Gen 34:20 **s** with the men of their city,
Gen 35:15 place where God **s** with him
Gen 39:10 as she **s** to Joseph day by day
Gen 39:14 house and **s** to them, saying,
Gen 39:17 Then she **s** to him with words
Gen 39:19 words which his wife **s** to him
Gen 41: 9 the chief butler **s** to Pharaoh
Gen 42: 7 to them and **s** roughly to them
Gen 42:14 It is as I **s** to you, saying
Gen 42:23 for he **s** to them through an
Gen 42:30 of the land **s** roughly to us
Gen 42:37 Then Reuben **s** to his father,
Gen 43: 3 But Judah **s** to him, saying
Gen 43:27 the old man of whom you **s**
Gen 43:29 brother of whom you **s** to me
Gen 44: 6 he **s** to them these same words
Gen 46: 2 Then God **s** to Israel in the
Gen 47: 5 Then Pharaoh **s** to Joseph,
Gen 49:28 what their father **s** to them
Gen 50: 4 Joseph **s** to the household of
Gen 50:17 wept when they **s** to him
Gen 50:21 them and **s** kindly to them
Ex 1:15 **s** to the Hebrew midwives, of
Ex 4:30 Aaron **s** all the words which
Ex 5:10 and **s** to the people, saying,
Ex 6: 2 God **s** to Moses and said to him
Ex 6: 9 So Moses **s** thus to the
Ex 6:10 And the LORD **s** to Moses,
Ex 6:12 And Moses **s** before the LORD,
Ex 6:13 Then the LORD **s** to Moses and
Ex 6:27 These are the ones who **s** to
Ex 6:28 **s** to Moses in the land of
Ex 6:29 that the LORD **s** to Moses,
Ex 7: 7 old when they **s** to Pharaoh
Ex 7: 8 Then the LORD **s** to Moses and
Ex 7:19 Then the LORD **s** to Moses
Ex 8: 1 And the LORD **s** to Moses, "Go
Ex 8: 5 Then the LORD **s** to Moses
Ex 12: 1 Now the LORD **s** to Moses and
Ex 13: 1 Then the LORD **s** to Moses,
Ex 14: 1 Now the LORD **s** to Moses,
Ex 15: 1 this song to the LORD, and **s**
Ex 16: 9 Then Moses **s** to Aaron, "Say
Ex 16:10 pass, as Aaron **s** to the whole
Ex 16:11 And the LORD **s** to Moses,
Ex 19:19 louder and louder, Moses **s**
Ex 19:25 to the people and **s** to them
Ex 20: 1 God **s** all these words, saying
Ex 25: 1 Then the LORD **s** to Moses,
Ex 30:11 Then the LORD **s** to Moses,
Ex 30:17 Then the LORD **s** to Moses,
Ex 30:22 Moreover the LORD **s** to Moses
Ex 31: 1 Then the LORD **s** to Moses,
Ex 31:12 And the LORD **s** to Moses,
Ex 33:11 So the LORD **s** to Moses face
Ex 35: 4 And Moses **s** to all the
Ex 36: 5 and they **s** to Moses, saying,
Ex 40: 1 Then the LORD **s** to Moses,
Lev 1: 1 **s** to him from the tabernacle

Lev 4: 1 Now the LORD s to Moses,
Lev 5:14 Then the LORD s to Moses,
Lev 6: 1 And the LORD s to Moses,
Lev 6: 8 Then the LORD s to Moses,
Lev 6:19 And the LORD s to Moses,
Lev 6:24 And the LORD s to Moses,
Lev 7:22 And the LORD s to Moses,
Lev 7:28 Then the LORD s to Moses,
Lev 8: 1 And the LORD s to Moses,
Lev 10: 3 This is what the LORD s,
Lev 10: 8 Then the LORD s to Aaron,
Lev 10:12 Then Moses s to Aaron, and to
Lev 11: 1 And the LORD s to Moses and
Lev 12: 1 Then the LORD s to Moses,
Lev 13: 1 And the LORD s to Moses and
Lev 14: 1 Then the LORD s to Moses,
Lev 14:33 And the LORD s to Moses and
Lev 15: 1 And the LORD s to Moses and
Lev 16: 1 Now the LORD s to Moses after
Lev 17: 1 And the LORD s to Moses,
Lev 18: 1 Then the LORD s to Moses,
Lev 19: 1 And the LORD s to Moses,
Lev 20: 1 Then the LORD s to Moses,
Lev 21:16 And the LORD s to Moses,
Lev 22: 1 Then the LORD s to Moses,
Lev 22:17 And the LORD s to Moses,
Lev 22:26 And the LORD s to Moses,
Lev 23: 1 And the LORD s to Moses,
Lev 23: 9 And the LORD s to Moses,
Lev 23:23 Then the LORD s to Moses,
Lev 23:26 And the LORD s to Moses,
Lev 23:33 Then the LORD s to Moses,
Lev 24: 1 Then the LORD s to Moses,
Lev 24:13 And the LORD s to Moses,
Lev 24:23 Then Moses s to the children
Lev 25: 1 the LORD s to Moses on Mount
Lev 27: 1 Now the LORD s to Moses,
Num 1: 1 Now the LORD s to Moses in
Num 2: 1 And the LORD s to Moses and
Num 3: 1 Moses when the LORD s with
Num 3: 5 And the LORD s to Moses,
Num 3:11 Then the LORD s to Moses,
Num 3:14 Then the LORD s to Moses in
Num 3:44 Then the LORD s to Moses,
Num 4: 1 Then the LORD s to Moses and
Num 4:17 Then the LORD s to Moses and
Num 4:21 Then the LORD s to Moses,
Num 5: 1 And the LORD s to Moses,
Num 5: 4 as the LORD s to Moses, so
Num 5: 5 Then the LORD s to Moses,
Num 5:11 And the LORD s to Moses,
Num 6: 1 Then the LORD s to Moses,
Num 6:22 And the LORD s to Moses,
Num 7: 4 Then the LORD s to Moses,
Num 7:89 thus He s to him
Num 8: 1 And the LORD s to Moses,
Num 8: 5 Then the LORD s to Moses,
Num 8:23 Then the LORD s to Moses,
Num 9: 1 Now the LORD s to Moses in
Num 9: 9 Then the LORD s to Moses,
Num 10: 1 And the LORD s to Moses,
Num 11:25 and s to him, and took of the
Num 12: 1 Aaron s against Moses because
Num 13: 1 And the LORD s to Moses,
Num 14: 7 and they s to all the
Num 14:26 Then the LORD s to Moses and
Num 15: 1 And the LORD s to Moses,
Num 15:17 Again the LORD s to Moses
Num 15:37 Again the LORD s to Moses
Num 16: 5 and he s to Korah and all his
Num 16:20 And the LORD s to Moses and
Num 16:23 So the LORD s to Moses,
Num 16:26 he s to the congregation,
Num 16:36 Then the LORD s to Moses,
Num 16:44 And the LORD s to Moses,
Num 17: 1 And the LORD s to Moses,
Num 17: 6 So Moses s to the children of
Num 17:12 children of Israel s to Moses
Num 18: 8 And the LORD s to Aaron
Num 18:25 Then the LORD s to Moses,
Num 19: 1 Now the LORD s to Moses and
Num 20: 3 contended with Moses and s
Num 20: 7 Then the LORD s to Moses,
Num 20:12 Then the LORD s to Moses and
Num 20:23 And the LORD s to Moses and
Num 21: 5 the people s against God and
Num 22: 7 s to him the words of Balak
Num 25:10 Then the LORD s to Moses,
Num 25:16 Then the LORD s to Moses,
Num 26: 1 that the LORD s to Moses
Num 26: 3 Eleazar the priest s with
Num 26:52 Then the LORD s to Moses,
Num 27: 6 And the LORD s to Moses,
Num 27:15 Then Moses s to the LORD,
Num 28: 1 Now the LORD s to Moses,
Num 30: 1 Then Moses s to the heads of
Num 31: 1 And the LORD s to Moses,
Num 31: 3 So Moses s to the people,
Num 31:25 And the LORD s to Moses,
Num 32: 2 s to Moses, to Eleazar the
Num 32:25 children of Reuben s to Moses
Num 33:50 Now the LORD s to Moses in
Num 34: 1 Then the LORD s to Moses,
Num 34:16 And the LORD s to Moses,
Num 35: 1 the LORD s to Moses in the
Num 35: 9 Then the LORD s to Moses,
Num 36: 1 s before Moses and before the
Deut 1: 1 are the words which Moses s
Deut 1: 3 that Moses s to the children
Deut 1: 6 LORD our God s to us in Horeb
Deut 1: 9 And I s to you at that time,
Deut 1:43 So I s to you
Deut 2: 1 Red Sea, as the LORD s to me
Deut 2: 2 And the LORD s to me, saying
Deut 2:17 that the LORD s to me, saying
Deut 4:12 the LORD s to you out of the
Deut 4:15 saw no form when the LORD s
Deut 4:45 s to the children of Israel
Deut 5:22 LORD s to all your assembly
Deut 5:28 your words when you s to me
Deut 9:13 Furthermore the LORD s to me
Deut 13: 2 he s to you comes to pass
Deut 27: 9 s to all Israel, saying,
Deut 31: 1 s these words to all Israel
Deut 31:30 Then Moses s in the hearing
Deut 32:44 s all the words of this song
Deut 32:48 Then the LORD s to Moses that
Josh 1: 1 s to Joshua the son of Nun
Josh 1:12 tribe of Manasseh Joshua s
Josh 3: 6 Then Joshua s to the priests,
Josh 4: 1 that the LORD s to Joshua
Josh 4:15 Then the LORD s to Joshua
Josh 4:21 Then he s to the children of
Josh 7: 2 Bethel, and s to them, saying,
Josh 9:11 of our country s to us,
Josh 9:22 and he s to them, saying,
Josh 10:12 Then Joshua s to the LORD in
Josh 14:10 ever since the LORD s this
Josh 14:12 which the LORD s in that day
Josh 17:14 of Joseph s to Joshua, saying
Josh 17:17 And Joshua s to the house of
Josh 20: 1 The LORD also s to Joshua
Josh 20: 2 of which I s to you through
Josh 21: 2 they s to them at Shiloh in
Josh 22: 8 and s to them, saying,
Josh 22:15 they s with them, saying,
Josh 22:30 and the children of Manasseh s
Josh 22:33 they s no more of going
Josh 23:14 your God s concerning you
Josh 24:27 of the LORD which He s to us
Judg 2: 4 LORD s these words to all the
Judg 8: 8 s to them in the same way
Judg 8: 9 So he also s to the men of
Judg 9: 1 s with them and with all the
Judg 9: 3 his mother's brothers s all
Judg 9:37 So Gaal s again and said
Judg 11:11 and Jephthah s all his words
Judg 13:11 the Man who s to this woman
Judg 15:13 So they s to him, saying
Judg 19:22 They s to the master of the
1Sa 1:13 Now Hannah s in her heart
1Sa 7: 3 Then Samuel s to all the
1Sa 9: 9 to inquire of God, he s thus
1Sa 9:17 the man of whom I s to you
1Sa 9:25 Samuel s with Saul on the top
1Sa 17:23 he s according to the same
1Sa 17:26 Then David s to the men who
1Sa 17:28 heard when he s to the men
1Sa 17:31 which David s were heard,
1Sa 18:23 So Saul's servants s those
1Sa 18:24 In this manner David s
1Sa 19: 1 Now Saul s to Jonathan his
1Sa 19: 4 Now Jonathan s well of David
1Sa 25: 9 they s to Nabal according to
1Sa 25:40 Carmel, they s to her saying,
1Sa 28:12 And the woman s to Saul,
1Sa 28:17 for Himself as He s by me
1Sa 28:21 the words which you s to me
1Sa 30: 6 the people s of stoning him
2Sa 3:19 Abner also s in the hearing
2Sa 5: 1 came to David at Hebron and s
2Sa 5: 6 land, who s to David, saying,
2Sa 7:17 vision, so Nathan s to David
2Sa 12:18 we s to him, and he would not
2Sa 13:22 And Absalom s to his brother
2Sa 14: 4 woman of Tekoa s to the king
2Sa 17: 6 to Absalom, Absalom s to him
2Sa 20:18 Then she s, saying, "They
2Sa 21: 2 the Gibeonites and s to them
2Sa 22: 1 Then David s to the LORD the
2Sa 23: 2 Spirit of the LORD s by me
2Sa 23: 3 the Rock of Israel s to me
2Sa 24:17 Then David s to the LORD when
1Ki 1:11 So Nathan s to Bathsheba the
1Ki 2: 4 word which He s concerning me
1Ki 2:27 word of the LORD which He s
1Ki 3:22 Thus they s before the king
1Ki 3:26 son was living s to the king
1Ki 4:32 He s three thousand proverbs,
1Ki 4:33 Also he s of trees, from the
1Ki 4:33 he s also of animals, of
1Ki 5: 5 as the LORD s to my father
1Ki 6:12 you, which I s to your father
1Ki 8:12 Then Solomon s: "The LORD
1Ki 8:15 who s with His mouth to my
1Ki 8:20 fulfilled His word which He s
1Ki 8:53 as You s by the hand of Your
1Ki 10: 2 she s with him about all that
1Ki 12: 3 and s to Rehoboam, saying,
1Ki 12: 7 And they s to him, saying,
1Ki 12:10 grown up with him s to him
1Ki 12:14 he s to them according to the
1Ki 13:18 an angel s to me by the word
1Ki 13:26 of the LORD which He s to him
1Ki 13:27 he s to his sons, saying,
1Ki 13:31 that he s to his sons, saying
1Ki 14:18 word of the LORD which He s
1Ki 16:12 which He s against Baasha by
1Ki 17:16 the LORD which He s by Elijah
1Ki 20:28 s to the king of Israel, and
1Ki 21: 2 So Ahab s to Naboth, saying,
1Ki 21: 6 Because I s to Naboth the
1Ki 21:23 Jezebel the LORD also s,
1Ki 22:13 gone to call Micaiah s to him
1Ki 22:20 So one s in this manner,
1Ki 22:20 and another s in that manner
2Ki 1: 9 And he s to him: "Man of God
2Ki 2:22 saying of Elisha which he s
2Ki 5:13 near and s to him, and said,
2Ki 7:17 who s when the king came down
2Ki 8: 1 Then Elisha s to the woman
2Ki 9:12 Thus and thus he s to me,
2Ki 9:36 which He s by His servant
2Ki 10:10 s concerning the house of
2Ki 10:10 He s by His servant Elijah
2Ki 10:17 the LORD which He s to Elijah
2Ki 15:12 the LORD which He s to Jehu
2Ki 17:26 So they s to the king of
2Ki 18:28 a loud voice in Hebrew, and s
2Ki 21:10 the LORD s by His servants
2Ki 22:14 And they s with her
2Ki 22:19 what I s against this place
2Ki 25:28 He s kindly to him, and gave
1Ch 15:16 Then David s to the leaders
1Ch 21: 9 And the LORD s to Gad, David's
2Ch 1: 2 Solomon s to all Israel, to
2Ch 6: 4 with His hands what He s with
2Ch 6:10 fulfilled His word which He s
2Ch 9: 1 she s with him about all that
2Ch 10: 3 and s to Rehoboam, saying,
2Ch 10: 7 And they s to him, saying,
2Ch 10:10 grown up with him s to him
2Ch 10:14 he s to them according to the
2Ch 18:12 gone to call Micaiah s to him
2Ch 18:19 And one s in this manner
2Ch 18:19 and another s in that manner
2Ch 30: 6 and s according to the
2Ch 32:16 And his servants s even more
2Ch 32:19 they s against the God of
2Ch 32:24 He s to him and gave him a
2Ch 33:10 the LORD s to Manasseh and his
2Ch 33:18 s to him in the name of the
2Ch 34:22 they s to her to that effect
2Ch 36:12 who s from the mouth of the
Ezra 5: 3 to them and s thus to them
Ezra 5: 9 elders, and s thus to them
Ezra 10: 2 Elam, s up and said to Ezra,
Neh 4: 2 he s before his brethren and
Neh 9:13 s with them from heaven, and
Neh 13:24 s the language of Ashdod, and

Neh 13:24 Judah, but s according to the
Esth 3: 4 when they s to him daily and
Esth 4:10 Then Esther s to Hathach, and
Esth 7: 9 who s good on the king's
Esth 8: 3 Now Esther s again to the
Job 2:13 no one s a word to him, for
Job 3: 2 And Job s, and said
Ps 33: 9 For He s, and it was done
Ps 39: 3 Then I s with my tongue
Ps 78:19 Yes, they s against God
Ps 89:19 Then You s in a vision to
Ps 99: 7 He s to them in the cloudy
Ps 105:31 He s, and there came swarms of
Ps 105:34 He s, and locusts came, Young
Ps 106:33 So that he s rashly with his
Ps 116:10 I believed, therefore I s
Song 2:10 My beloved s, and said to me
Song 5: 6 went out to him when he s
Is 7:10 the LORD s again to Ahaz,
Is 8: 5 The LORD also s to me again
Is 8:11 For the LORD s thus to me
Is 20: 2 s by Isaiah the son of Amoz
Is 65:12 when I s, you did not hear,
Is 66: 4 when I s they did not hear
Jer 7:13 I s to you, rising up early
Jer 20: 8 For when I s, I cried out
Jer 22:21 I s to you in your prosperity
Jer 25: 2 s to all the people of Judah
Jer 26:11 the prophets s to the princes
Jer 26:12 Then Jeremiah s to all the
Jer 26:17 s to all the assembly of the
Jer 26:18 s to all the people of Judah,
Jer 27:12 I also s to Zedekiah king of
Jer 27:16 Also I s to the priests and to
Jer 28: 1 s to me in the house of the
Jer 28: 5 Then the prophet Jeremiah s
Jer 28:11 Hananiah s in the presence of
Jer 30: 4 the LORD s concerning Israel
Jer 31:20 For though I s against him
Jer 34: 6 Then Jeremiah the prophet s
Jer 36: 2 from the day I s to you,
Jer 37: 2 He s by the prophet Jeremiah
Jer 38: 8 and s to the king, saying
Jer 40:15 s secretly to Gedaliah in
Jer 43: 2 and all the proud men s,
Jer 44:20 Then Jeremiah s to all the
Jer 45: 1 that Jeremiah the prophet s
Jer 46:13 The word that the LORD s to
Jer 50: 1 the LORD s against Babylon
Jer 51:12 done what He s against the
Jer 52:32 he s kindly to him and gave
Ezek 2: 2 entered me when He s to me
Ezek 2: 2 and I heard Him who s to me
Ezek 3:24 and s with me and said to me
Ezek 10: 2 He s to the man clothed with
Ezek 11:25 So I s to those in captivity
Ezek 24:18 So I s to the people in the
Dan 2: 4 Then the Chaldeans s to the
Dan 3: 9 They s and said to King
Dan 3:14 Nebuchadnezzar s, saying to
Dan 3:19 Therefore he s and commanded
Dan 3:24 and he rose in haste and s,
Dan 3:26 burning fiery furnace and s
Dan 3:28 Nebuchadnezzar s, saying
Dan 4:19 So the king s, and said
Dan 4:30 The king s, saying, "Is not
Dan 5: 7 And the king s, saying to the
Dan 5:10 And the queen s, saying, "O
Dan 5:13 And the king s, and said to
Dan 6:12 and s concerning the king's
Dan 6:16 But the king s, saying to
Dan 6:20 The king s, saying to Daniel,
Dan 7: 2 Daniel s, saying, "I saw in
Dan 7:20 a mouth which s pompous words
Dan 9: 6 who s in Your name to our
Dan 9:12 which He s against us and
Dan 10:16 then I opened my mouth and s
Dan 10:19 So when he s to me I was
Hos 12: 4 Bethel, and there He s to us
Hos 13: 1 When Ephraim s, trembling, he
Jon 2:10 So the LORD s to the fish
Hag 1:13 s the LORD's message to the
Zech 1:14 So the angel who s with me
Zech 3: 4 s to those who stood before
Zech 4: 4 s to the angel who talked
Zech 6: 8 to me, and s to me, saying,
Mal 3:16 the LORD s to one another
Matt 9:18 While He s these things to
Matt 9:33 was cast out, the mute s
Matt 12:22 the blind and mute man both s
Matt 13: 3 Then He s many things to them
Matt 13:33 Another parable He s to them
Matt 13:34 Jesus s to the multitude in
Matt 14:27 immediately Jesus s to them
Matt 17:13 understood that He s to them
Matt 22: 1 s to them again by parables
Matt 23: 1 Then Jesus s to the
Matt 28:18 came and s to them, saying,
Mark 4:33 He s the word to them as they
Mark 7:35 was loosed, and he s plainly
Mark 8:32 He s this word openly
Mark 9:18 So I s to Your disciples,
Mark 11: 6 So they s to them just as
Mark 12:26 passage, how God s to him
Mark 14:31 But he s more vehemently,
Mark 14:39 prayed, and s the same words
Luke 1:42 Then she s out with a loud
Luke 1:55 As He s to our fathers, to
Luke 1:64 and his tongue loosed, and he s
Luke 1:70 as He s by the mouth of His
Luke 2:38 s of Him to all those who
Luke 2:50 statement which He s to them
Luke 4:36 s among themselves, saying,
Luke 5:36 Then He s a parable to them
Luke 6:39 And He s a parable to them
Luke 7:39 he s to himself, saying,
Luke 8: 4 every city, He s by a parable
Luke 9:11 s to them about the kingdom
Luke 9:31 s of His decease which He was
Luke 11:14 had gone out, that the mute s
Luke 11:27 as He s these things, that a
Luke 11:37 And as He s, a certain
Luke 12:16 Then He s a parable to them,
Luke 13: 6 He also s this parable
Luke 14: 3 s to the lawyers and Pharisees
Luke 15: 3 So He s this parable to them,
Luke 18: 1 Then He s a parable to them,
Luke 18: 9 Also He s this parable to
Luke 19:11 He s another parable, because
Luke 20: 2 and s to Him, saying,
Luke 21: 5 as some s of the temple, how
Luke 21:29 And He s to them a parable
Luke 22:65 blasphemously s against Him
Luke 24: 6 Remember how He s to you
Luke 24:44 I s to you while I was still
John 4:18 in that you s truly
John 4:50 the word that Jesus s to him
John 6:71 He s of Judas Iscariot, the
John 7:13 no one s openly of Him for
John 7:39 But this He s concerning the
John 7:46 No man ever s like this Man
John 8:12 Then Jesus s to them again,
John 8:20 words Jesus s in the treasury
John 8:27 He s to them of the Father
John 8:30 As He s these words, many
John 9:29 We know that God s to Moses
John 10: 6 the things which He s to them
John 10:41 s about this Man were true
John 11:13 Jesus s of his death, but
John 11:56 s among themselves as they
John 12:36 These things Jesus s, and
John 12:38 be fulfilled, which he s
John 12:41 he saw His glory and s of Him
John 13:22 perplexed about whom He s
John 13:24 ask who it was of whom He s
John 17: 1 Jesus s these words, lifted
John 18: 9 might be fulfilled which He s
John 18:16 s to her who kept the door,
John 18:20 I s openly to the world
John 18:32 might be fulfilled which He s
John 21:19 This He s, signifying by what
Acts 1:16 which the Holy Spirit s
Acts 2:31 s concerning the resurrection
Acts 4: 1 Now as they s to the people,
Acts 4:31 they s the word of God with
Acts 6:10 and the Spirit by which he s
Acts 7: 6 But God s in this way
Acts 7:38 with the Angel who s to him
Acts 8:26 angel of the Lord s to Philip
Acts 9:29 he s boldly in the name of
Acts 10: 7 when the angel who s to him
Acts 10:15 a voice s to him again the
Acts 11:20 Antioch, s to the Hellenists,
Acts 14: 1 so s that a great multitude
Acts 16:13 s to the women who met there
Acts 16:32 Then they s the word of the
Acts 18: 9 Now the Lord s to Paul in the
Acts 18:25 being fervent in spirit, he s
Acts 19: 6 and they s with tongues and
Acts 19: 8 s boldly for three months,
Acts 19: 9 but s evil of the Way before
Acts 20: 7 s to them and continued his
Acts 20:38 all for the words which he s
Acts 21:40 he s to them in the Hebrew
Acts 22: 2 he s to them in the Hebrew
Acts 22: 9 the voice of Him who s to me
Acts 28:19 when the Jews s against it
Acts 28:25 The Holy Spirit s rightly
1Co 13:11 I s as a child, I understood
1Co 14: 5 I wish you all s with tongues
2Co 4:13 I believed and therefore I s
2Co 7:14 But as we s all things to you
Heb 1: 1 in different ways s in time
Heb 7:14 Moses s nothing concerning
Heb 12:25 refused Him who s on earth
Jas 5:10 who s in the name of the Lord
2Pe 1:21 but holy men of God s as they
Rev 1:12 see the voice that s with me
Rev 10: 8 from heaven s to me again
Rev 13:11 a lamb and s like a dragon

SPOKEN (*see* SPEAK)
Gen 12: 4 as the LORD had s to him, and
Gen 18:19 Abraham what He has s to him
Gen 19:21 city for which you have s
Gen 21: 1 did for Sarah as He had s
Gen 21: 2 of which God had s to him
Gen 24:51 son's wife, as the LORD has s
Gen 28:15 done what I have s to you
Gen 41:28 which I have s to Pharaoh
Gen 44: 2 to the word that Joseph had s
Ex 4:10 You have s to Your servant
Ex 4:30 which the LORD had s to Moses
Ex 9:12 as the LORD had s to Moses
Ex 9:35 as the LORD had s by Moses
Ex 10:29 You have s well. I will
Ex 19: 8 the LORD has s we will do
Ex 32:13 I have s of I give to your
Ex 32:34 of which I have s to you
Ex 33:17 do this thing that you have s
Ex 34:32 all that the LORD had s with
Lev 10:11 has s to them by the hand of
Num 1:48 for the LORD had s to Moses
Num 12: 2 indeed s only through Moses
Num 12: 2 Has He not s through us also
Num 14:17 be great, just as You have s
Num 14:28 as you have s in My hearing
Num 14:35 I the LORD have s this
Num 15:22 which the LORD has s to Moses
Num 21: 7 for we have s against the
Num 23: 2 did just as Balaam had s, and
Num 23:17 What has the LORD s
Num 23:19 Or has He s, and will He not
Deut 1:21 of your fathers has s to you
Deut 5:28 which they have s to you
Deut 5:28 right in all that they have s
Deut 6:19 before you, as the LORD has s
Deut 9:10 words which the LORD had s to
Deut 10: 4 which the LORD had s to you
Deut 13: 5 because he has s in order to
Deut 18:17 What they have s is good
Deut 18:21 word which the LORD has not s
Deut 18:22 which the LORD has not s
Deut 18:22 the prophet has s it
Deut 26:19 your God, just as He has s
Deut 29:13 you, just as He has s to you
Josh 4: 8 as the LORD had s to Joshua
Josh 4:12 as Moses had s to them
Josh 6: 8 Joshua had s to the people
Josh 21:45 had s to the house of Israel
Ruth 2:13 me, and have s kindly to your
Ruth 4: 1 of whom Boaz had s came by
1Sa 1:16 and grief I have s until now
1Sa 3:12 I have s concerning his house
1Sa 20:23 which you and I have s of,
1Sa 25:30 that He has s concerning you
2Sa 2:27 God lives, unless you had s
2Sa 3:18 For the LORD has s of David
2Sa 6:22 of whom you have s, by them I
2Sa 7: 7 have I ever s a word to
2Sa 7:19 and You have also s of Your
2Sa 7:25 s concerning Your servant
2Sa 7:29 You, O Lord GOD, have s it
2Sa 14:19 that my lord the king has s
2Sa 17: 6 has s in this manner
1Ki 2:23 if Adonijah has not s this
1Ki 8:24 You have both s with Your
1Ki 8:26 which You have s to Your
1Ki 12: 9 this people who have s to me
1Ki 12:10 this people who have s to you
1Ki 12:15 word, which the LORD had s by

1Ki 13: 3 the sign which the LORD has s
1Ki 13:11 which he had s to the king
1Ki 14:11 for the LORD has s it
1Ki 15:29 of the LORD which He had s by
1Ki 16:34 which He had s through Joshua
1Ki 18:24 It is well s
1Ki 21: 4 the Jezreelite had s to him
1Ki 22:28 the LORD has not s by me
1Ki 22:38 of the LORD which He had s
2Ki 1:17 the LORD which Elijah had s
2Ki 7:18 man of God had s to the king
2Ki 14:25 which He had s through His
2Ki 19:21 the LORD has s concerning him
2Ki 20: 9 do the thing which He has s
2Ki 20:19 LORD which you have s is good
2Ki 24: 2 He had s by His servants the
1Ch 17: 6 have I ever s a word to any
1Ch 17:17 and You have also s of Your
1Ch 17:23 s concerning Your servant
1Ch 21:19 which he had s in the name of
2Ch 2:15 wine which my lord has s of
2Ch 6:15 You have both s with Your
2Ch 6:17 which You have s to Your
2Ch 10: 9 this people who have s to me
2Ch 10:10 the people who have s to you
2Ch 10:15 which He had s by the hand of
2Ch 18:27 the LORD has not s by me
2Ch 36:22 s by the mouth of Jeremiah
Ezra 1: 1 s by the mouth of Jeremiah
Ezra 8:22 because we had s to the king
Neh 2:18 words that he had s to me
Esth 6:10 undone of all that you have s
Job 15:11 the word s gently with you
Job 21: 3 may speak, and after I have s
Job 33: 8 you have s in my hearing, and
Job 40: 5 Once I have s, but I will not
Job 42: 7 LORD had s these words to Job
Job 42: 7 for you have not s of Me what
Job 42: 8 not s of Me what is right
Ps 50: 1 One, God the LORD, Has s and
Ps 60: 6 God has s in His holiness
Ps 62:11 God has s once, Twice I have
Ps 66:14 my mouth has s when I was in
Ps 87: 3 Glorious things are s of you
Ps 108: 7 God has s in His holiness
Ps 109: 2 They have s against me with a
Prov 15:23 a word s in due season, how
Prov 25:11 A word fitly s is like apples
Eccl 9:17 s quietly, should be heard
Song 8: 8 in the day when she is s for
Is 1: 2 For the LORD has s
Is 1:20 the mouth of the LORD has s
Is 16:13 s concerning Moab since that
Is 16:14 But now the LORD has s,
Is 21:17 LORD God of Israel has s it
Is 22:25 for the LORD has s
Is 23: 4 for the sea has s, the
Is 24: 3 for the LORD has s this word
Is 25: 8 for the LORD has s
Is 31: 4 For thus the LORD has s to me
Is 37:22 the LORD has s concerning him
Is 38: 7 do this thing which He has s
Is 38:15 He has both s to me, and He
Is 39: 8 LORD which you have s is good
Is 40: 5 the mouth of the LORD has s
Is 45:19 I have not s in secret, in a
Is 46:11 Indeed I have s it
Is 48:15 I, even I, have s
Is 48:16 I have not s in secret from
Is 58:14 The mouth of the LORD has s
Is 59: 3 your lips have s lies, your
Jer 3: 5 Behold, you have s and done
Jer 4:28 be black, because I have s
Jer 9:12 the mouth of the LORD has s
Jer 13:15 be proud, for the LORD has s
Jer 14:14 commanded them, nor s to them
Jer 18: 8 I have s turns from its evil
Jer 23:21 I have not s to them, yet
Jer 23:35 and, 'What has the LORD s
Jer 23:37 and, 'What has the LORD s
Jer 25: 3 and I have s to you, rising
Jer 26:16 For he has s to us in the
Jer 27:13 as the LORD has s against the
Jer 29:23 have s lying words in My name
Jer 30: 2 words that I have s to you
Jer 32:24 What You have s has happened
Jer 33:24 what these people have s,
Jer 35:14 But although I have s to you
Jer 35:17 because I have s to them but
Jer 36: 2 have s to you against Israel
Jer 36: 4 LORD which He had s to him
Jer 38: 1 had s to all the people,
Jer 44:16 s to us in the name of the
Jer 44:25 your wives have s with your
Jer 48: 8 destroyed, as the LORD has s
Jer 51:62 You have s against this place
Ezek 5:13 have s it in My zeal, when I
Ezek 5:15 I, the LORD, have s
Ezek 5:17 I, the LORD, have s
Ezek 13: 7 and have you not s false
Ezek 13: 7 LORD says,' but I have not s
Ezek 13: 8 Because you have s nonsense
Ezek 17:21 know that I, the LORD, have s
Ezek 17:24 I, the LORD, have s and have
Ezek 21:17 I, the LORD, have s
Ezek 21:32 for I the LORD have s
Ezek 22:14 I, the LORD, have s, and will
Ezek 22:28 GOD,' when the LORD had not s
Ezek 23:34 for I have s,' says the Lord
Ezek 24:14 I, the LORD, have s it
Ezek 26: 5 of the sea, for I have s,'
Ezek 26:14 for I the LORD have s,' says
Ezek 28:10 for I have s," says the Lord
Ezek 30:12 I, the LORD, have s
Ezek 34:24 I, the LORD, have s
Ezek 35:12 s against the mountains of
Ezek 36: 5 Surely I have s in My burning
Ezek 36: 6 I have s in My jealousy and My
Ezek 36:36 I, the LORD, have s it, and I
Ezek 37:14 that I, the LORD, have s it
Ezek 38:17 I have s in former days by My
Ezek 38:19 the fire of My wrath I have s
Ezek 39: 5 for I have s," says the Lord
Ezek 39: 8 is the day of which I have s
Dan 4:31 to you it is s
Dan 10:15 When he had s such words to
Hos 7:13 yet they have s lies against
Hos 10: 4 They have s words, swearing
Hos 12:10 I have also s by the prophets
Joel 3: 8 for the LORD has s
Amos 3: 1 the LORD has s against you
Amos 3: 8 The Lord GOD has s
Amos 5:14 be with you, as you have s
Obad 12 nor should you have s proudly
Obad 18 of Esau," for the LORD has s
Mic 4: 4 of the LORD of hosts has s
Mic 6:12 her inhabitants have s lies
Zech 13: 3 because you have s lies in
Mal 3:13 What have we s against You
Matt 1:22 be fulfilled which was s by
Matt 2:15 be fulfilled which was s by
Matt 2:17 was s by Jeremiah the prophet
Matt 2:23 which was s by the prophets
Matt 3: 3 For this is he who was s of
Matt 4:14 was s by Isaiah the prophet
Matt 8:17 was s by Isaiah the prophet
Matt 12:17 was s by Isaiah the prophet
Matt 13:35 which was s by the prophet
Matt 21: 4 which was s by the prophet
Matt 22:31 read what was s to you by God
Matt 24:15 s of by Daniel the prophet,
Matt 26:65 saying, "He has s blasphemy
Matt 27: 9 was s by Jeremiah the prophet
Matt 27:35 which was s by the prophet
Mark 1:42 As soon as He had s,
Mark 5:36 heard the word that was s
Mark 12:12 for they knew He had s the
Mark 12:32 You have s the truth, for
Mark 13:14 s of by Daniel the prophet,
Mark 14: 9 be s of as a memorial to her
Mark 16:19 after the Lord had s to them
Luke 2:33 things which were s of Him
Luke 2:34 sign which will be s against
Luke 12: 3 s in the dark will be heard
Luke 12: 3 what you have s in the ear in
Luke 18:34 know the things which were s
Luke 20:19 s this parable against them
Luke 20:39 Teacher, You have s well
Luke 24:25 all that the prophets have s
John 12:29 An angel has s to Him
John 12:48 the word that I have s will
John 12:49 For I have not s on My own
John 14:25 These things I have s to you
John 15: 3 word which I have s to you
John 15:11 These things I have s to you
John 15:22 s to them, they would have no
John 16: 1 These things I have s to you
John 16:25 These things I have s to you
John 16:33 These things I have s to you
John 18: 1 When Jesus had s these words
John 18:23 If I have s evil, bear
John 20:18 that He had s these things to
John 21:19 And when He had s this, He
Acts 1: 9 when He had s these things
Acts 2:16 was s by the prophet Joel
Acts 3:21 which God has s by the mouth
Acts 3:24 who follow, as many as have s
Acts 8: 6 heeded the things s by Philip
Acts 8:24 you have s may come upon me
Acts 9:27 road, and that He had s to him
Acts 13:34 to corruption, He has s thus
Acts 13:40 lest what has been s in the
Acts 13:45 opposed the things s by Paul
Acts 13:46 God should be s to you first
Acts 16: 2 He was well s of by the
Acts 16:14 to heed the things s by Paul
Acts 23: 9 or an angel has s to him, let
Acts 27:11 than by the things s by Paul
Acts 28:21 reported or s any evil of you
Acts 28:22 it is s against everywhere
Acts 28:24 by the things which were s
Rom 1: 8 all, that your faith is s of
Rom 4:18 according to what was s
Rom 14:16 let your good be s of as evil
1Co 10:30 why am I evil s of for the
1Co 14: 9 will it be known what is s
2Co 6:11 We have s openly to you, our
Heb 1: 2 last days s to us by His Son
Heb 2: 2 For if the word s through
Heb 2: 3 began to be s by the Lord
Heb 3: 5 which would be s afterward
Heb 4: 4 For He has s in a certain
Heb 4: 8 have s of another day
Heb 7:13 s belongs to another tribe
Heb 9:19 For when Moses had s every
Heb 12:19 not be s to them anymore
Heb 13: 7 who have s the word of God to
2Pe 3: 2 of the words which were s
Jude 15 sinners have s against Him
Jude 17 the words which were s before

SPOKES

1Ki 7:33 pins, their rims, their s

SPOKESMAN

Ex 4:16 shall be your s to the people
Job 33: 6 I am as your s before God

SPONGE

Matt 27:48 one of them ran and took a s
Mark 15:36 filled a s full of sour wine,
John 19:29 they filled a s with sour

SPOONS

2Ki 25:14 shovels, the trimmers, the s
2Ch 24:14 for serving and offering, s
Jer 52:18 trimmers, the bowls, the s
Jer 52:19 pots, the lampstands, the s

SPORT

Prov 10:23 do evil is like s to a fool

SPOT (*see* SPOTS, SPOTTED, UNSPOTTED)

Lev 13: 2 a scab, or a bright s, and it
Lev 13: 4 But if the bright s is white
Lev 13:10 there is a s of raw flesh in
Lev 13:19 white swelling or a bright s
Lev 13:23 But if the bright s stays in
Lev 13:24 the burn becomes a bright s
Lev 13:25 the bright s has turned white
Lev 13:26 white hairs in the bright s
Lev 13:28 But if the bright s stays in
Lev 13:39 it is a white s that grows on
Lev 14:56 and a scab and a bright s,
2Sa 2:23 down there and died on the s
Job 11:15 lift up your face without s
Job 31: 7 or if any s adheres to my
Song 4: 7 love, and there is no s in you
Eph 5:27 not having s or wrinkle or
1Ti 6:14 this commandment without s
Heb 9:14 Himself without s to God,
1Pe 1:19 without blemish and without s
2Pe 3:14 by Him in peace, without s

SPOTS (*see* SPOT)

Lev 13:38 s on the skin of the body
Lev 13:38 specifically white bright s
Lev 13:39 indeed if the bright s on the
Jer 13:23 his skin or the leopard its s
2Pe 2:13 They are s and blemishes,
Jude 12 These are s in your love

SPOTTED (*see* SPOT)
Gen 30:32 s sheep, and all the brown
Gen 30:32 among the lambs, and the s
Gen 30:33 s among the goats, and brown
Gen 30:35 goats that were speckled and s
Gen 30:35 goats that were speckled and s
Gen 30:39 streaked, speckled, and s

SPOUSE
Song 4: 8 with me from Lebanon, my s
Song 4: 9 my heart, my sister, my s
Song 4:10 is your love, my sister, my s
Song 4:11 Your lips, O my s, drip as
Song 4:12 enclosed is my sister, my s
Song 5: 1 to my garden, my sister, my s
Hos 12:12 Israel served for a s, and for

SPOUT
Amos 7:16 do not s against the house of

SPRANG (*see* SPRING)
Gen 41: 6 east wind, s up after them
Gen 41:23 east wind, s up after them
Matt 13: 5 they immediately s up because
Matt 13: 7 thorns, and the thorns s up
Mark 4: 5 immediately it s up because
Mark 4: 8 and yielded a crop that s up
Luke 8: 6 and as soon as it s up, it
Luke 8: 7 and the thorns s up with it
Luke 8: 8 s up, and yielded a crop a

SPREAD (*see* SPREADING, SPREADS)
Gen 28:14 you shall s abroad to the
Ex 9:29 I will s out my hands to the
Ex 9:33 s out his hands to the LORD
Ex 37: 9 The cherubim s out their
Ex 40:19 he s out the tent over the
Lev 13: 5 sore has not s on the skin
Lev 13: 6 sore has not s on the skin
Lev 13: 7 should at all s over the skin
Lev 13: 8 scab has indeed s on the skin
Lev 13:22 should at all s over the skin
Lev 13:23 in one place, and has not s
Lev 13:27 it has at all s over the skin
Lev 13:28 has not s on the skin, but
Lev 13:32 indeed if the scall has not s
Lev 13:34 scall has not s over the skin
Lev 13:35 all s over the skin after his
Lev 13:36 the scall has s over the skin
Lev 13:51 plague has s in the garment
Lev 13:53 has not s in the garment,
Lev 13:55 though the plague has not s
Lev 14:39 indeed if the plague has s on
Lev 14:44 the plague has s in the house
Lev 14:48 not s in the house after the
Num 4: 6 s over that a cloth entirely
Num 4: 7 they shall s a blue cloth
Num 4: 8 They shall s over them a
Num 4:11 they shall s a blue cloth
Num 4:13 and s a purple cloth over it
Num 4:14 they shall s on it a covering
Num 11:32 and they s them out for
Deut 22:17 they shall s the cloth before
Josh 6:27 his fame s throughout all the
Judg 8:25 they s out a garment, and each
Judg 20:37 the men in ambush s out and
1Sa 30:16 s out over all the land,
2Sa 17:19 s a covering over the well's
2Sa 17:19 and s ground grain on it
2Sa 21:10 s it for herself on the rock,
2Sa 22:43 the streets, and I s them out
1Ki 6:32 he s gold on the cherubim and
1Ki 8: 7 For the cherubim s their two
1Ki 8:22 s out his hands toward heaven
1Ki 8:54 with his hands s up to heaven
2Ki 8:15 s it over his face so that he
2Ki 19:14 LORD, and s it before the LORD
1Ch 28:18 cherubim that s their wings
2Ch 5: 8 For the cherubim s their
2Ch 6:12 of Israel, and s out his hands
2Ch 6:13 s out his hands toward heaven
2Ch 26: 8 His fame s as far as the
2Ch 26:15 So his fame s far and wide,
Ezra 9: 5 s out my hands to the LORD my
Esth 9: 4 his fame s throughout all the
Job 8:16 his branches s out in his
Job 29:19 My root is s out to the
Job 37:18 have you s out the skies,
Job 39:26 s its wings toward the south
Ps 105:39 He s a cloud for a covering,
Ps 140: 5 They have s a net by the
Ps 143: 6 I s out my hands to You
Prov 1:17 in vain the net is s in the
Prov 7:16 I have s my bed with tapestry
Is 1:15 When you s out your hands, I
Is 14:11 the maggot is s under you
Is 19: 8 who s nets on the waters
Is 25: 7 that is s over all nations
Is 25:11 He will s out His hands in
Is 33:23 they could not s the sail
Is 37:14 LORD, and s it before the LORD
Is 42: 5 Who s forth the earth and that
Is 58: 5 to s out sackcloth and ashes
Jer 8: 2 They shall s them before the
Jer 43:10 he will s his royal pavilion
Jer 48:40 and s his wings over Moab
Jer 49:22 and s His wings over Bozrah
Lam 1:10 The adversary has s his hand
Lam 1:13 He has s a net for my feet and
Lam 2:13 ruin is s wide as the sea
Ezek 1:23 their wings s out straight
Ezek 2:10 Then He s it before me
Ezek 12:13 I will also s My net over him
Ezek 16: 8 so I s My wing over you and
Ezek 17:20 I will s My net over him, and
Ezek 19: 8 side, and s their net over him
Ezek 27: 7 was what you s for your sail
Ezek 32: 3 I will therefore s My net
Hos 5: 1 to Mizpah and a net s on Tabor
Hos 7:12 go, I will s My net on them
Hos 14: 6 His branches shall s
Joel 2: 2 clouds s over the mountains
Zech 1:17 My cities shall again s out
Zech 2: 6 for I have s you abroad like
Mal 2: 3 s refuse on your faces, the
Matt 9:31 they s the news about Him in
Matt 21: 8 And a very great multitude s
Matt 21: 8 trees and s them on the road
Mark 1:28 And immediately His fame s
Mark 1:45 and to s the matter, so that
Mark 11: 8 many s their garments on the
Mark 11: 8 trees and s them on the road
Luke 19:36 they s their clothes on the
Acts 6: 7 And the word of God s, and the
Acts 13:49 s throughout all the region
Rom 5:12 and thus death s to all men
2Co 4:15 having s through the many,
2Ti 2:17 message will s like cancer

SPREADING (*see* SPREAD)
Lev 13:57 of leather, it is a s plague
Deut 32:11 s out its wings, taking them
Job 36:29 understand the s of clouds
Ps 37:35 s himself like a native green
Ezek 17: 6 and became a s vine of low
Ezek 26: 5 s nets in the midst of the
Ezek 26:14 shall be a place for s nets
Ezek 47:10 be places for s their nets

SPREADS (*see* SPREAD)
1Ki 8:38 s out his hands toward this
2Ch 6:29 s out his hands to this house
Job 9: 8 He alone s out the heavens,
Job 26: 9 and s His cloud over it
Job 41:30 he s pointed marks in the
Prov 10:18 whoever s slander is a fool
Prov 29: 5 neighbor s a net for his feet
Is 25:11 swims s out his hands to swim
Is 40:22 s them out like a tent to
Is 44:24 Who s abroad the earth by
Jer 4:31 who s her hands, saying, 'Woe
Jer 17: 8 which s out its roots by the
Lam 1:17 Zion s out her hands, but
Acts 4:17 But so that it s no further

SPRIGS
Is 18: 5 off the s with pruning hooks

SPRING (*see* SPRANG, SPRINGING, SPRINGS, WATERSPRINGS, WELLSPRING)
Gen 16: 7 s of water in the wilderness
Gen 16: 7 by the s on the way to Shur
Lev 11:36 Nevertheless a s or a cistern
Num 21:17 S up, O well
Josh 18:15 and went out to the s of the
2Sa 11: 1 to pass in the s of the year
1Ki 20:22 for in the s of the year the
1Ki 20:26 in the s of the year, that
2Ki 3:19 and stop up every s of water
2Ki 13:20 the land in the s of the year
1Ch 20: 1 in the s of the year, at the
2Ch 24:23 So it happened in the s of
Job 5: 6 trouble s from the ground
Job 29:23 mouth wide as for the s rain
Job 38:27 cause to s forth the growth
Ps 84: 6 of Baca, They make it a s
Ps 85:11 Truth shall s out of the
Ps 92: 7 the wicked s up like grass
Prov 4:23 for out of it s the issues of
Prov 25:26 the wicked is like a murky s
Song 4:12 a s shut up, a fountain
Is 42: 9 before they s forth I tell
Is 43:19 thing, now it shall s forth
Is 44: 4 They will s up among the
Is 45: 8 righteousness s up together
Is 58: 8 shall s forth speedily, and
Is 58:11 and like a s of water, whose
Is 61:11 are sown in it to s forth
Is 61:11 praise to s forth before all
Ezek 17: 9 All of its s leaves will
Ezek 29:21 house of Israel to s forth
Hos 13:15 Then his s shall become dry,
Amos 3: 5 Will a snare s up from the
Jas 3:11 Does a s send forth fresh
Jas 3:12 Thus no s can yield both salt

SPRINGING (*see* SPRING)
2Sa 23: 4 grass s out of the earth, by
Joel 2:22 the open pastures are s up
John 4:14 s up into everlasting life
Heb 12:15 bitterness s up cause trouble

SPRINGS (*see* SPRING)
Num 33: 9 Elim were twelve s of water
Deut 8: 7 of water, of fountains and s
Josh 15:19 give me also s of water
Josh 15:19 upper s and the lower s
Judg 1:15 give me also s of water
Judg 1:15 Caleb gave her the upper s
1Ki 4:33 hyssop that s out of the wall
1Ki 18: 5 land to all the s of water
2Ki 3:25 stopped up all the s of water
2Ki 19:29 year what s from the same
2Ch 32: 3 to stop the water from the s
2Ch 32: 4 who stopped all the s and the
Job 38:16 you entered the s of the sea
Ps 87: 7 say, "All my s are in you
Ps 104:10 He sends the s into the
Is 35: 7 the thirsty land s of water
Is 37:30 year what s from the same
Is 41:18 and the dry land s of water
Is 49:10 even by the s of water He
Jer 51:36 up her sea and make her s dry
Hos 10: 4 Thus judgment s up like
Rev 8:10 rivers and on the s of water
Rev 14: 7 earth, the sea and s of water
Rev 16: 4 s of water, and they became

SPRINKLE (*see* SPRINKLED, SPRINKLES, SPRINKLING, SPRINKLING-BOWLS)
Ex 29:16 s it all around on the altar
Ex 29:20 s the blood all around on the
Ex 29:21 and s it on Aaron and on his
Lev 1: 5 s the blood all around on the
Lev 1:11 shall s its blood all around
Lev 3: 2 shall s the blood all around
Lev 3: 8 and Aaron's sons shall s its
Lev 3:13 the sons of Aaron shall s its
Lev 4: 6 s some of the blood seven
Lev 4:17 s it seven times before the
Lev 5: 9 Then he shall s some of the
Lev 7: 2 And its blood he shall s all
Lev 14: 7 he shall s it seven times on
Lev 14:16 shall s some of the oil with
Lev 14:27 Then the priest shall s with
Lev 14:51 and s the house seven times
Lev 16:14 s it with his finger on the
Lev 16:14 the mercy seat he shall s
Lev 16:15 s it on the mercy seat and
Lev 16:19 Then he shall s some of the
Lev 17: 6 the priest shall s the blood
Num 8: 7 S water of purification on
Num 18:17 You shall s their blood on
Num 19: 4 s some of its blood seven
Num 19:18 s it on the tent, on all the
Num 19:19 The clean person shall s the
2Ki 16:15 s on it all the blood of the
Is 52:15 So shall He s many nations
Ezek 36:25 Then I will s clean water on

SPRINKLED (*see* SPRINKLE)
Ex 24: 6 the blood he s on the altar
Ex 24: 8 s it on the people, and said,
Lev 6:27 its blood is s on any garment
Lev 6:27 wash that on which it was s
Lev 8:11 He s some of it on the altar

Lev 8:19 Then he s the blood all
Lev 8:24 Moses s the blood all around
Lev 8:30 and s it on Aaron, on his
Lev 9:12 which he s all around on the
Lev 9:18 which he s all around on the
Num 19:13 purification was not s on him
Num 19:20 has not been s on him
2Ki 16:13 and s the blood of his peace
2Ch 29:22 blood and s it on the altar
2Ch 29:22 and s the blood on the altar
2Ch 29:22 and s the blood on the altar
2Ch 30:16 the priests s the blood which
2Ch 35:11 the priests s the blood with
Job 2:12 s dust on his head toward
Is 63: 3 their blood is s upon My
Heb 9:19 s both the book itself and all
Heb 9:21 Then likewise he s with blood
Heb 10:22 having our hearts s from an

SPRINKLES (*see* SPRINKLE)
Lev 7:14 who s the blood of the peace
Num 19:21 He who s the water of

SPRINKLING (*see* SPRINKLE)
Ezek 43:18 on it, and for s blood on it
Heb 9:13 s the unclean, sanctifies for
Heb 11:28 the s of blood, lest he who
Heb 12:24 to the blood of s that speaks
1Pe 1: 2 and s of the blood of Jesus

SPRINKLING-BOWLS (*see* SPRINKLE)
2Ki 12:13 basins of silver, trimmers, s

SPROUT (*see* SPROUTED)
Job 14: 7 down, that it will s again
Mark 4:27 by day, and the seed should s

SPROUTED (*see* SPROUT)
Num 17: 8 of the house of Levi, had s
Matt 13:26 But when the grain had s and

SPUN (*see* SPIN)
Ex 35:25 s yarn with their hands, and
Ex 35:25 and brought what they had s
Ex 35:26 wisdom s yarn of goats' hair

SPUR
Is 9:11 him, and s his enemies on,

SPURNED
Deut 32:19 He s them, because of the
Lam 2: 6 indignation He has s the king
Lam 2: 7 The Lord has s His altar, He

SPY (*see* SPIED, SPIES, SPYING)
Num 13: 2 Send men to s out the land of
Num 13:16 Moses sent to s out the land
Num 13:17 So Moses sent them to s out
Num 14: 7 land we passed through to s
Num 14:36 Moses sent to s out the land
Num 14:38 who went to s out the land
Num 21:32 Moses sent to s out Jazer
Josh 2: 1 Acacia Grove to s secretly
Josh 6:25 Joshua sent to s out Jericho
Josh 7: 2 Go up and s out the country
Josh 14: 7 Barnea to s out the land, and
Judg 1:23 sent men to s out Bethel
Judg 18: 2 to s out the land and search
Judg 18:14 to s out the country of Laish
Judg 18:17 to s out the land went up
2Sa 10: 3 to s it out, and to overthrow
1Ch 19: 3 and to s out the land
Gal 2: 4 to s out our liberty which we

SPYING (*see* SPY)
Num 13:25 they returned from s out the

SQUADS
Acts 12: 4 delivered him to four s of

SQUANDERS
Prov 21:20 wise, but a foolish man s it

SQUARE (*see* SQUARES)
Gen 19: 2 spend the night in the open s
Ex 27: 1 the altar shall be s
Ex 28:16 It shall be doubled into a s
Ex 30: 2 it shall be s
Ex 37:25 it was s
Ex 38: 1 it was s
Ex 39: 9 breastplate s by doubling it
Judg 19:15 in the open s of the city
Judg 19:17 in the open s of the city
Judg 19:20 spend the night in the open s
1Ki 7:31 but the panels were s, not
2Ch 29: 4 gathered them in the East S
2Ch 32: 6 the open s of the city gate
Ezra 10: 9 open s of the house of God
Neh 8: 1 as one man in the open s that
Neh 8: 3 s that was in front of the
Neh 8:16 in the open s of the Water
Neh 8:16 in the open s of the Gate of
Esth 4: 2 He went as far as the s in
Esth 4: 6 s that was in front of the
Esth 6: 9 horseback through the city s
Esth 6:11 horseback through the city s
Job 29: 7 I took my seat in the open s
Prov 7:12 at times in the open s,
Ezek 41:21 of the temple were s, and so
Ezek 43:16 wide, s at its four corners
Ezek 45: 2 be a s plot for the sanctuary
Rev 21:16 the city is laid out as a s

SQUARES (*see* SQUARE)
Prov 1:20 her voice in the open s
Song 3: 2 in the s I will seek the one

SQUEEZED
Judg 6:38 s the fleece together, he

STABBED
2Sa 3:27 there s him in the stomach,
2Sa 4: 6 they s him in the stomach

STABILITY
Is 33: 6 will be the s of your times

STABLE
Ezek 25: 5 make Rabbah a s for camels

STACHYS
Rom 16: 9 fellow worker in Christ, and S

STACKED
Ex 22: 6 in thorns, so that s grain

STACTE
Ex 30:34 Take sweet spices, s and

STAFF (*see* STAFFS)
Gen 32:10 over this Jordan with my s
Gen 38:18 your s that is in your hand
Gen 38:25 the signet and cord, and s
Ex 12:11 feet, and your s in your hand
Ex 21:19 about outside with his s,
Num 22:27 struck the donkey with his s
Judg 5:14 who bear the recruiter's s
Judg 6:21 of the s that was in His hand
1Sa 17: 7 Now the s of his spear was
1Sa 17:40 he took his s in his hand
2Sa 3:29 who leans on a s or falls by
2Sa 23:21 he went down to him with a s
2Ki 4:29 take my s in your hand, and be
2Ki 4:29 but lay my s on the face of
2Ki 4:31 laid the s on the face of the
2Ki 18:21 in the s of this broken reed
1Ch 11:23 he went down to him with a s
Ps 23: 4 Your rod and Your s, they
Is 9: 4 the s of his shoulder, the
Is 10: 5 the s in whose hand is My
Is 10:15 or as if a s could lift up,
Is 10:24 and lift up his s against you
Is 14: 5 broken the s of the wicked
Is 30:32 the s of punishment passes
Is 36: 6 in the s of this broken reed
Jer 48:17 How the strong s is broken
Ezek 29: 6 a s of reed to the house of
Hos 4:12 and their s informs them
Mic 7:14 Your people with Your s, the
Zech 8: 4 each one with his s in his
Zech 11:10 And I took my s, Beauty, and
Zech 11:14 Then I cut in two my other s
Mark 6: 8 for the journey except a s
Heb 11:21 leaning on the top of his s

STAFFS (*see* STAFF)
Zech 11: 7 I took for myself two s
Matt 10:10 tunics, nor sandals, nor s
Luke 9: 3 neither s nor bag nor bread

STAG
Song 2: 9 like a gazelle or a young s
Song 2:17 young s upon the mountains of
Song 8:14 like a gazelle or a young s

STAGGER (*see* STAGGERED, STAGGERS)
Job 12:25 and He makes them s like a
Ps 107:27 s like a drunken man, And are
Is 29: 9 they s, but not with
Jer 25:16 And they will drink and s and go

STAGGERED (*see* STAGGER)
Lam 5:13 boys s under loads of wood

STAGGERS (*see* STAGGER)
Is 19:14 a drunken man s in his vomit

STAINED
Is 63: 3 and I have s all My robes

STAIRS (*see* STAIRWAY)
1Ki 6: 8 They went up by s to the
Neh 3:15 as far as the s that go down
Neh 9: 4 stood on the s of the Levites
Neh 12:37 they went up the s of the
Ezek 40: 6 and he went up its s and
Acts 21:35 And when he reached the s, he
Acts 21:40 Paul stood on the s and

STAIRWAY (*see* STAIRS)
Neh 12:37 on the s of the wall, beyond

STAKES
Is 33:20 not one of its s will ever be
Is 54: 2 cords, and strengthen your s

STALK (*see* STALKS)
Gen 41: 5 of grain came up on one s
Gen 41:22 seven heads came up on one s
Hos 8: 7 The s has no bud

STALKS (*see* STALK)
Josh 2: 6 them with the s of flax,

STALL (*see* STALL-FED, STALLS)
Amos 6: 4 from the midst of the s
Luke 13:15 ox or his donkey from the s

STALL-FED (*see* STALL)
Mal 4: 2 out and grow fat like s calves

STALLIONS
Jer 5: 8 were like well-fed lusty s

STALLS (*see* STALL)
1Ki 4:26 s of horses for his chariots
2Ch 9:25 four thousand s for horses
2Ch 32:28 s for all kinds of livestock,
Hab 3:17 and there be no herd in the s

STAMMERERS (*see* STAMMERING)
Is 32: 4 the tongue of the s will be

STAMMERING (*see* STAMMERERS)
Is 28:11 For with s lips and another
Is 33:19 of a s tongue that you cannot

STAMP (*see* STAMPED, STAMPING)
Ezek 6:11 s your feet, and say, 'Alas,

STAMPED (*see* STAMP)
Ezek 25: 6 s your feet, and rejoiced in

STAMPING (*see* STAMP)
Jer 47: 3 At the noise of the s hooves

STAND (*see* STANDING, STANDS, STOOD)
Gen 19: 9 And they said, "S back
Gen 24:13 I s here by the well of water
Gen 24:31 Why do you s outside
Gen 24:43 I s by the well of water
Ex 3: 5 where you s is holy ground
Ex 7:15 you shall s by the river's
Ex 8:20 s before Pharaoh as he comes
Ex 8:21 the ground on which they s
Ex 9:11 the magicians could not s
Ex 9:13 s before Pharaoh, and say to
Ex 14:13 S still, and see the salvation
Ex 17: 6 I will s before you there on
Ex 17: 9 Tomorrow I will s on the top
Ex 18:14 all the people s before you
Ex 18:19 S before God for the people,
Ex 33:21 and you shall s on the rock
Lev 18:23 Nor shall any woman s before
Lev 19:16 nor shall you take a s
Lev 26:37 to s before your enemies
Lev 27:14 values it, so it shall s
Lev 27:17 to your valuation it shall s
Num 1: 5 the men who shall s with you
Num 5:18 Then the priest shall s the
Num 5:30 then he shall s the woman
Num 8:13 And you shall s the Levites
Num 9: 8 S still, that I may hear what
Num 11:16 that they may s there with
Num 16: 9 to s before the congregation
Num 22:22 s in the way as an adversary
Num 22:32 come out to s against you
Num 23: 3 S by your burnt offering, and
Num 23:15 S here by your burnt offering
Num 27:21 He shall s before Eleazar the

Num 30: 4 then all her vows shall s
Num 30: 4 she has bound herself shall s
Num 30: 5 she has bound herself shall s
Num 30: 7 hears, then her vows shall s
Num 30: 7 she bound herself shall s
Num 30: 9 herself, shall s against her
Num 30:11 then all her vows shall s
Num 30:11 she bound herself shall s
Num 30:12 binding her, it shall not s
Deut 5:31 s here by Me, and I will speak
Deut 7:24 no one shall be able to s
Deut 9: 2 said, 'Who can s before the
Deut 10: 8 LORD, to s before the LORD to
Deut 11:25 be able to s against you
Deut 18: 5 out of all your tribes to s
Deut 18: 7 who s there before the LORD
Deut 19:17 shall s before the LORD,
Deut 24:11 You shall s outside, and the
Deut 27:12 These shall s on Mount
Deut 27:13 these shall s on Mount Ebal
Deut 29:10 All of you s today before the
Josh 1: 5 No man shall be able to s
Josh 3: 8 you shall s in the Jordan
Josh 3:13 and they shall s as a heap
Josh 5:15 the place where you s is holy
Josh 7:12 of Israel could not s before
Josh 7:13 you cannot s before your
Josh 10: 8 of them shall s before you
Josh 10:12 Sun, s still over Gibeon
Josh 23: 9 to s against you to this day
Judg 2:14 longer s before their enemies
Judg 4:20 S at the door of the tent, and
1Sa 6:20 Who is able to s before this
1Sa 9:27 But you s here awhile, that I
1Sa 12: 7 s still, that I may reason
1Sa 12:16 Now therefore, s and see this
1Sa 14: 9 then we will s still in our
1Sa 16:22 Please let David s before me
1Sa 19: 3 s beside my father in the
2Sa 1: 9 me again, 'Please s over me
2Sa 2:25 took their s on top of a hill
2Sa 15: 2 s beside the way to the gate
2Sa 18:30 said, "Turn aside and s here
1Ki 1: 2 let her s before the king, and
1Ki 10: 8 who s continually before you
1Ki 17: 1 Israel lives, before whom I s
1Ki 18:15 hosts lives, before whom I s
1Ki 19:11 s on the mountain before the
2Ki 3:14 hosts lives, before whom I s
2Ki 5:11 surely come out to me, and s
2Ki 5:16 LORD lives, before whom I s
2Ki 10: 4 kings could not s up to him
2Ki 10: 4 how then can we s
2Ki 23: 3 took their s for the covenant
1Ch 23:30 to s every morning to thank
2Ch 9: 7 who s continually before you
2Ch 11:13 Israel took their s with him
2Ch 20: 9 we will s before this temple
2Ch 20:17 s still and see the salvation
2Ch 29:11 chosen you to s before Him
2Ch 34:32 Benjamin take their s for it
2Ch 35: 5 s in the holy place according
Ezra 9:15 though no one can s before
Ezra 10:13 we are not able to s outside
Ezra 10:14 of our entire congregation s
Neh 7: 3 and while they s guard, let
Neh 9: 5 S up and bless the LORD your
Esth 3: 4 Mordecai's words would s
Esth 5: 9 that he did not s or tremble
Job 8:15 his house, but it does not s
Job 19:25 He shall s at last on the
Job 30:20 I s up, and You regard me
Job 30:28 I s up in the congregation and
Job 33: 5 before me; take your s
Job 37:14 s still and consider the
Job 39:24 nor does he s firm, because
Job 41:10 then is able to s against Me
Ps 1: 5 shall not s in the judgment
Ps 5: 5 shall not s in Your sight
Ps 10: 1 Why do You s afar off, O LORD
Ps 20: 8 we have risen and s upright
Ps 24: 3 Or who may s in His holy
Ps 30: 7 made my mountain s strong
Ps 33: 8 of the world s in awe of Him
Ps 35: 2 buckler, And s up for my help
Ps 38:11 my friends s aloof from my
Ps 38:11 And my kinsmen s afar off
Ps 76: 7 who may s in Your presence
Ps 78:13 the waters s up like a heap
Ps 89:28 shall s firm with him
Ps 94:16 Who will s up for me against
Ps 109: 6 let an accuser s at his right
Ps 109:31 For He shall s at the right
Ps 111: 8 They s fast forever and ever,
Ps 130: 3 O Lord, who could s
Ps 134: 1 Who by night s in the house
Ps 135: 2 You who s in the house of the
Ps 147:17 Who can s before His cold
Prov 8: 2 She takes her s on the top of
Prov 12: 7 house of the righteous will s
Prov 19:21 LORD's counsel—that will s
Prov 22:29 He will s before kings
Prov 22:29 he will not s before unknown
Prov 25: 6 and do not s in the place of
Prov 27: 4 is able to s before jealousy
Eccl 8: 3 Do not take your s for an
Is 7: 7 It shall not s, nor shall it
Is 8:10 the word, but it will not s
Is 11:10 who shall s as a banner to
Is 14:24 have purposed, so it shall s
Is 21: 8 I s continually on the
Is 27: 9 and incense altars do not s up
Is 28:18 with Sheol will not s
Is 32: 8 and by generosity he shall s
Is 44:11 together, let them s up
Is 46:10 saying, 'My counsel shall s
Is 47:12 S now with your enchantments
Is 47:13 monthly prognosticators s up
Is 48:13 to them, they s up together
Is 50: 8 Let us s together
Is 51:17 S up, O Jerusalem, you who
Is 61: 5 Strangers shall s and feed
Jer 6:16 S in the ways and see, and ask
Jer 7: 2 S in the gate of the LORD's
Jer 7:10 s before Me in this house
Jer 15:19 you shall s before Me
Jer 17:19 s in the gate of the children
Jer 26: 2 S in the court of the LORD's
Jer 35:19 a man to s before Me forever
Jer 44:28 shall know whose words will s
Jer 44:29 s against you for adversity
Jer 46: 4 S forth with your helmets,
Jer 46:14 S fast and prepare yourselves
Jer 46:15 They did not s because the
Jer 46:21 They did not s, for the day
Jer 48:19 Aroer, s by the way and watch
Jer 51:50 Do not s still
Ezek 2: 1 s on your feet, and I will
Ezek 13: 5 for the house of Israel to s
Ezek 17:14 his covenant it might s
Ezek 22:30 s in the gap before Me on
Ezek 27:29 their ships and s on the shore
Ezek 44:11 they shall s before them to
Ezek 44:15 they shall s before Me to
Ezek 44:24 they shall s as judges, and
Ezek 46: 2 outside, and s by the gatepost
Ezek 47:10 be that fishermen will s by
Dan 2:44 and it shall s forever
Dan 7: 4 made to s on two feet like a
Dan 10:11 s upright, for I have now
Dan 11: 6 he nor his authority shall s
Dan 11:16 and no one shall s against him
Dan 11:16 He shall s in the Glorious
Dan 11:17 but she shall not s with him
Dan 11:25 but he shall not s, for they
Dan 12: 1 that time Michael shall s up
Amos 2:15 He shall not s who handles
Amos 7: 2 Oh, that Jacob may s, for he
Amos 7: 5 Oh, that Jacob may s, for he
Mic 1:11 Its place to s is taken away
Mic 5: 4 And He shall s and feed His
Nah 1: 6 Who can s before His
Hab 2: 1 I will s my watch and set
Zech 3: 7 walk among these who s here
Zech 4: 2 on the s seven lamps with
Zech 4:14 who s beside the Lord of the
Zech 11:16 nor feed those that still s
Zech 14: 4 will s on the Mount of Olives
Zech 14:12 while they s on their feet
Mal 3: 2 who can s when He appears
Matt 12:25 against itself will not s
Matt 12:26 How then will his kingdom s
Mark 3:24 itself, that kingdom cannot s
Mark 3:25 itself, that house cannot s
Mark 3:26 and is divided, he cannot s
Mark 11:25 And whenever you s praying
Luke 6: 8 hand, "Arise and s here
Luke 11:18 how will his kingdom s
Luke 13:25 and you begin to s outside
Luke 21:36 to s before the Son of Man
John 8:44 and does not s in the truth,
Acts 1:11 why do you s gazing up into
Acts 4:26 of the earth took their s
Acts 5:20 s in the temple and speak to
Acts 7:33 where you s is holy ground
Acts 8:38 the chariot to s still
Acts 10:26 lifted him up, saying, "S up
Acts 14:10 S up straight on your feet
Acts 25:10 I s at Caesar's judgment seat
Acts 26: 6 And now I s and am judged for
Acts 26:16 But rise and s on your feet
Acts 26:22 from God, to this day I s
Rom 5: 2 into this grace in which we s
Rom 9:11 according to election might s
Rom 11:20 broken off, and you s by faith
Rom 14: 4 Indeed, he will be made to s
Rom 14: 4 for God is able to make him s
Rom 14:10 For we shall all s before the
1Co 15: 1 received and in which you s
1Co 15:30 why do we s in jeopardy every
1Co 16:13 s fast in the faith, be brave
2Co 1:24 for by faith you s
Gal 5: 1 S fast therefore in the
Eph 6:11 that you may be able to s
Eph 6:13 day, and having done all, to s
Eph 6:14 S therefore, having girded
Phil 1:27 that you s fast in one spirit
Phil 4: 1 crown, so s fast in the Lord,
Col 4:12 that you may s perfect and
1Th 3: 8 if you s fast in the Lord
2Th 2:15 s fast and hold the traditions
Jas 2: 3 man, "You s there," or,
1Pe 5:12 grace of God in which you s
Rev 3:20 I s at the door and knock
Rev 6:17 has come, and who is able to s
Rev 8: 2 seven angels who s before God
Rev 18:15 will s at a distance for fear

STANDARD (*see* STANDARDS)
Num 1:52 camp, everyone by his own s
Num 2: 2 shall camp by his own s,
Num 2: 3 those of the s of the forces
Num 2:10 s of the forces with Reuben
Num 2:18 s of the forces with Ephraim
Num 2:25 The s of the forces with Dan
Num 10:14 The s of the camp of the
Num 10:18 the s of the camp of Reuben
Num 10:22 And the s of the camp of the
Num 10:25 Then the s of the camp of the
Deut 3:11 according to the s cubit
2Sa 14:26 according to the king's s
Is 49:22 set up My s for the peoples
Is 59:19 will lift up a s against him
Jer 4: 6 Set up the s toward Zion
Jer 4:21 How long will I see the s
Jer 50: 2 Proclaim, and set up a s
Jer 51:12 Set up the s on the walls of

STANDARDS (*see* STANDARD)
Num 2:17 in his place, by their s
Num 2:31 break camp last, with their s
Num 2:34 so they camped by their s

STANDING (*see* STAND)
Gen 18: 2 three men were s by him
Ex 22: 6 s grain, or the field is
Ex 26:15 of acacia wood, s upright
Ex 33:10 s at the tabernacle door, and
Ex 36:20 of acacia wood, s upright
Num 22:23 s in the way with His drawn
Num 22:31 s in the way with His drawn
Num 23: 6 s by his burnt offering, he
Num 23:17 s by his burnt offering, and
Deut 23:25 into your neighbor's s grain
Deut 23:25 on your neighbor's s grain
Judg 15: 5 s grain of the Philistines
Judg 15: 5 the s grain, as well as the
1Sa 19:20 Samuel s as leader over them,
1Sa 22: 6 all his servants s about him
1Ki 8:14 congregation of Israel was s
1Ki 13:25 and the lion s by the corpse
1Ki 13:28 and the lion s by the corpse
1Ki 22:19 all the host of heaven s by
2Ki 11:14 s by a pillar according to
1Ch 21:16 of the LORD s between earth
2Ch 18:18 of heaven s on His right hand
2Ch 23:13 there was the king s by his
Neh 8: 5 for he was s above all the
Esth 5: 2 Queen Esther s in the court
Esth 6: 5 is there, s in the court
Esth 7: 9 is s at the house of Haman
Ps 69: 2 mire, Where there is no s

Ps 122: 2 have been s Within your gates
Lam 2: 4 S like an enemy, He has bent
Ezek 10: 3 Now the cherubim were s on
Dan 8: 3 s beside the river, was a ram
Dan 8: 6 I had seen s beside the river
Amos 9: 1 I saw the Lord s by the altar
Zech 3: 1 s before the Angel of the
Zech 3: 1 Satan s at his right hand to
Zech 3: 3 and was s before the Angel
Matt 6: 5 to pray s in the synagogues
Matt 12:47 Your brothers are s outside
Matt 16:28 there are some s here who
Matt 20: 3 and saw others s idle in the
Matt 20: 6 out and found others s idle
Matt 20: 6 you been s here idle all day
Matt 24:15 s in the holy place"
Mark 3:31 s outside they sent to Him,
Mark 9: 1 s here who will not taste
Mark 13:14 s where it ought not" (let
Luke 1:11 s on the right side of the
Luke 5: 2 saw two boats s by the lake
Luke 8:20 Your brothers are s outside
Luke 9:27 there are some s here who
Luke 18:13 s afar off, would not so much
John 6:22 s on the other side of the
John 8: 9 and the woman s in the midst
John 11:42 who are s by I said this,
John 19:26 disciple whom He loved s by
John 20:14 around and saw Jesus s there
Acts 2:14 s up with the eleven, raised
Acts 4:14 had been healed s with them
Acts 5:23 the guards s outside before
Acts 5:25 in prison are s in the temple
Acts 7:55 Jesus s at the right hand of
Acts 7:56 the Son of Man s at the right
Acts 11:13 seen an angel s in his house
Acts 22:20 I also was s by consenting to
Acts 24:21 s among them, 'Concerning the
1Ti 3:13 for themselves a good s and
Heb 9: 8 first tabernacle was still s
Jas 5: 9 the Judge is s at the door
2Pe 3: 5 the earth s out of water and
Rev 4: 1 a door s open in heaven
Rev 7: 1 things I saw four angels s at
Rev 7: 9 s before the throne and before
Rev 10: 5 angel whom I saw s on the sea
Rev 11: 4 the two lampstands s before
Rev 14: 1 a Lamb s on Mount Zion, and
Rev 15: 2 s on the sea of glass, having
Rev 18:10 s at a distance for fear of
Rev 19:17 I saw an angel s in the sun
Rev 20:12 s before God, and books were

STANDS (*see* STAND)
Num 14:14 that Your cloud s above them
Num 35:12 may not die until he s before
Deut 1:38 who s before you, he shall go
Deut 17:12 not heed the priest who s to
Deut 25: 8 and if he s firm and says, 'I
Deut 29:15 but also with him who s here
Josh 20: 4 s at the entrance of the gate
Josh 20: 6 s before the congregation for
Josh 22:19 where the LORD's tabernacle s
Job 6:29 my righteousness still s
Job 38:14 seal, and s out like a garment
Ps 1: 1 Nor s in the path of sinners,
Ps 26:12 My foot s in an even place
Ps 33:11 counsel of the LORD s forever
Ps 45: 9 At Your right hand s the
Ps 82: 1 God s in the congregation of
Ps 119:161 But my heart s in awe of Your
Eccl 4:15 youth who s in his place
Song 2: 9 behold, he s behind our wall
Is 3:13 The LORD s up to plead,
Is 3:13 and s to judge the people
Is 40: 8 the word of our God s forever
Is 46: 7 set it in its place, and it s
Is 59:14 and righteousness s afar off
Ezek 21:21 For the king of Babylon s at
Dan 12: 1 the great prince who s watch
Luke 1:19 who s in the presence of God,
John 1:26 but there s One among you
John 3:29 of the bridegroom, who s and
Acts 4:10 by Him this man s here before
Rom 14: 4 his own master he s or falls
1Co 7:37 Nevertheless he who s
1Co 10:12 let him who thinks he s take
2Ti 2:19 the solid foundation of God s
Heb 10:11 every priest s ministering
Rev 10: 8 of the angel who s on the sea

STANDSTILL
Lev 13:37 scall appears to be at a s

STANK (*see* STINK)
Ex 7:21 the river died, the river s
Ex 8:14 in heaps, and the land s
Ex 16:20 and it bred worms and s

STAR (*see* STARGAZERS, STARS)
Num 24:17 A S shall come out of Jacob
Amos 5:26 the s of your gods, which you
Matt 2: 2 have seen His s in the East
Matt 2: 7 them what time the s appeared
Matt 2: 9 the s which they had seen in
Matt 2:10 When they saw the s, they
Acts 7:43 the s of your god Remphan,
1Co 15:41 for one s differs from
1Co 15:41 from another s in glory
2Pe 1:19 the morning s rises in your
Rev 2:28 I will give him the morning s
Rev 8:10 a great s fell from heaven,
Rev 8:11 the name of the s is Wormwood
Rev 9: 1 I saw a s fallen from heaven
Rev 22:16 the Bright and Morning S

STARE
2Ki 8:11 in a s until he was ashamed
Ps 22:17 They look and s at Me

STARGAZERS (*see* STAR)
Is 47:13 now the astrologers, the s

STARS (*see* STAR)
Gen 1:16 He made the s also
Gen 15: 5 count the s if you are able
Gen 22:17 as the s of the heaven and as
Gen 26: 4 multiply as the s of heaven
Gen 37: 9 the eleven s bowed down to me
Ex 32:13 as the s of heaven
Deut 1:10 today, as the s of heaven in
Deut 4:19 the sun, the moon, and the s
Deut 10:22 the s of heaven in multitude
Deut 28:62 the s of heaven in multitude
Judg 5:20 the s from their courses
1Ch 27:23 like the s of the heavens
Neh 4:21 daybreak until the s appeared
Neh 9:23 children as the s of heaven
Job 3: 9 May the s of its morning be
Job 9: 7 He seals off the s
Job 22:12 And see the highest s, how
Job 25: 5 the s are not pure in His
Job 38: 7 the morning s sang together
Ps 8: 3 fingers, The moon and the s
Ps 136: 9 s to rule by night, For His
Ps 147: 4 He counts the number of the s
Ps 148: 3 Him, all you s of light
Eccl 12: 2 the light, the moon and the s
Is 13:10 For the s of heaven and their
Is 14:13 my throne above the s of God
Jer 31:35 the s for a light by night,
Ezek 32: 7 heavens, and make its s dark
Dan 8:10 some of the s to the ground,
Dan 12: 3 like the s forever and ever
Joel 2:10 dark, and the s diminish their
Joel 3:15 the s will diminish their
Obad 4 you set your nest among the s
Nah 3:16 more than the s of heaven
Matt 24:29 the s will fall from heaven,
Mark 13:25 the s of heaven will fall, and
Luke 21:25 sun, in the moon, and in the s
Acts 27:20 nor s appeared for many days
1Co 15:41 and another glory of the s
Heb 11:12 the s of the sky in multitude
Jude 13 wandering s for whom is
Rev 1:16 had in His right hand seven s
Rev 1:20 The mystery of the seven s
Rev 1:20 The seven s are the angels of
Rev 2: 1 the seven s in His right hand
Rev 3: 1 Spirits of God and the seven s
Rev 6:13 the s of heaven fell to the
Rev 8:12 the moon, and a third of the s
Rev 12: 1 head a garland of twelve s
Rev 12: 4 a third of the s of heaven

START (*see* STARTED, STARTING, STARTS)
Prov 20: 3 any fool can s a quarrel

STARTED (*see* START)
Num 10:13 So they s out for the first
Ezek 24: 2 the king of Babylon s his

STARTING (*see* START)
Num 33: 2 Now Moses wrote down the s
Num 33: 2 according to their s points

STARTLED
Ruth 3: 8 midnight that the man was s
Hab 3: 6 He looked and s the nations

STARTS (*see* START)
Prov 17:14 contention before a quarrel s

STARVED (*see* STARVING)
Job 18:12 His strength is s, and

STARVING (*see* STARVED)
Prov 6:30 satisfy himself when he is s

STATE (*see* STATEMENT)
Ps 39: 5 at his best s is but vapor
Ps 136:23 remembered us in our lowly s
Ps 144:15 people who are in such a s
Prov 27:23 to know the s of your flocks
Is 43:26 s your case, that you may be
Ezek 16:55 return to their former s
Ezek 16:55 return to their former s,
Ezek 16:55 will return to your former s
Matt 12:45 the last s of that man is
Luke 1:48 lowly s of His maidservant
Luke 11:26 the last s of that man is
Acts 23:30 to s before you the charges
Phil 2:19 encouraged when I know your s
Phil 2:20 sincerely care for your s
Phil 4:11 learned in whatever s I am

STATELY
Prov 30:29 yes, four which are s in walk
Ezek 23:41 You sat on a s couch, with a

STATEMENT (*see* STATE)
Luke 2:50 the s which He spoke to them
Acts 24:21 this one s which I cried out

STATION (*see* STATIONED)
Neh 7: 3 Jerusalem, one at his watch s
Zech 6: 5 who go out from their s

STATIONED (*see* STATION)
Judg 16:25 And they s him between the
2Sa 23:12 But he s himself in the
1Ki 10:26 whom he s in the chariot
1Ch 11:14 But they s themselves in the
2Ch 1:14 whom he s in the chariot
2Ch 9:25 he s in the chariot cities
2Ch 29:25 Then he s the Levites in the

STATURE
Num 13:32 saw in it are men of great s
1Sa 2:26 And the child Samuel grew in s
1Sa 16: 7 or at the height of his s
2Sa 21:20 there was a man of great s
1Ch 20: 6 there was a man of great s
Song 7: 7 This s of yours is like a
Is 10:33 those of high s will be hewn
Is 45:14 and of the Sabeans, men of s
Ezek 17: 6 a spreading vine of low s
Ezek 19:11 She towered in s above the
Ezek 31: 3 the forest, and of high s
Matt 6:27 can add one cubit to his s
Luke 2:52 increased in wisdom and s, and
Luke 12:25 can add one cubit to his s
Luke 19: 3 crowd, for he was of short s
Eph 4:13 to the measure of the s of

STATUS
Deut 21:16 s on the son of the loved

STATUTE (*see* STATUTES)
Ex 15:25 There He made a s and an
Ex 27:21 It shall be a s forever to
Ex 28:43 It shall be a s forever to
Ex 29: 9 be theirs for a perpetual s
Ex 29:28 and his sons by a s forever
Ex 30:21 it shall be a s forever to
Lev 3:17 This shall be a perpetual s
Lev 6:18 It shall be a s forever in
Lev 6:22 It is a s forever to the LORD
Lev 7:34 of Israel by a s forever
Lev 7:36 by a s forever throughout
Lev 10: 9 It shall be a s forever
Lev 10:15 by a s forever, as the LORD
Lev 16:29 shall be a s forever for you
Lev 16:31 It is a s forever
Lev 16:34 be an everlasting s for you
Lev 17: 7 This shall be a s forever for
Lev 23:14 it shall be a s forever
Lev 23:21 It shall be a s forever in

STEPPED (*see* STEP)
Luke 8:27 when He s out on the land,
John 5: 4 then whoever s in first,

STEPS (*see* STEP)
Ex 20:26 you go up by s to My altar
1Ki 10:12 the king made s of the almug
1Ki 10:19 The throne had six s, and the
1Ki 10:20 one on each side of the six s
2Ki 9:13 under him on the top of the s
2Ch 9:18 The throne had six s, with a
2Ch 9:19 one on each side of the six s
Job 14:16 For now You number my s, but
Job 18: 7 The s of his strength are
Job 23:11 foot has held fast to His s
Job 29: 6 when my s were bathed with
Job 31: 4 my ways, and count all my s
Job 31:37 to Him the number of my s
Job 34:21 of man, and He sees all his s
Ps 17: 5 Uphold my s in Your paths,
Ps 17:11 now surrounded us in our s
Ps 37:23 The s of a good man are
Ps 37:31 None of his s shall slide
Ps 40: 2 a rock, And established my s
Ps 44:18 Nor have our s departed from
Ps 56: 6 They hide, they mark my s
Ps 57: 6 have prepared a net for my s
Ps 73: 2 My s had nearly slipped
Ps 119:133 Direct my s by Your word, And
Ps 140: 4 purposed to make my s stumble
Prov 4:12 your s will not be hindered,
Prov 5: 5 death, her s lay hold of hell
Prov 14:15 man considers well his s
Prov 16: 9 but the LORD directs his s
Prov 20:24 A man's s are of the LORD
Is 26: 6 poor and the s of the needy
Jer 10:23 who walks to direct his own s
Lam 4:18 They tracked our s so that we
Ezek 40:22 it was ascended by seven s
Ezek 40:26 Seven s led up to it, and its
Ezek 40:31 going up to it were eight s
Ezek 40:34 going up to it were eight s
Ezek 40:37 going up to it were eight s
Ezek 40:49 by the s which led up to it
Ezek 41: 7 of the temple ascended like s
Ezek 43:17 its s face toward the east
John 5: 7 another s down before me
Rom 4:12 the s of the faith which our
2Co 12:18 Did we not walk in the same s
1Pe 2:21 that you should follow His s

STERN (*see* STERNLY, STERNNESS)
Mark 4:38 But He was in the s, asleep
Acts 27:29 four anchors from the s, and
Acts 27:41 but the s was being broken up

STERNLY (*see* STERN)
Matt 9:30 Jesus s warned them, saying,
Mark 3:12 But He s warned them that

STERNNESS (*see* STERN)
Eccl 8: 1 the s of his face is changed

STEW
Gen 25:29 Now Jacob cooked a s
Gen 25:30 feed me with that same red s
Gen 25:34 Esau bread and s of lentils
2Ki 4:38 boil s for the sons of the
2Ki 4:39 sliced them into the pot of s
2Ki 4:40 as they were eating the s
Hag 2:12 edge he touches bread or s

STEWARD (*see* STEWARDS, STEWARDSHIP)
Gen 43:16 he said to the s of his house
Gen 43:19 to the s of Joseph's house
Gen 44: 1 commanded the s of his house
Gen 44: 4 far off, Joseph said to his s
1Ki 16: 9 s of his house in Tirzah
Is 22:15 Go, proceed to this s, to
Dan 1:11 the s whom the chief of the
Dan 1:16 Thus the s took away their
Matt 20: 8 of the vineyard said to his s
Luke 8: 3 the wife of Chuza, Herod's s
Luke 12:42 is that faithful and wise s
Luke 16: 1 certain rich man who had a s
Luke 16: 2 for you can no longer be s
Luke 16: 3 Then the s said within
Luke 16: 8 unjust s because he had dealt
Tit 1: 7 blameless, as a s of God, not

STEWARDS (*see* STEWARD)
1Ch 28: 1 the s over all the substance
1Co 4: 1 s of the mysteries of God
1Co 4: 2 s that one be found faithful
Gal 4: 2 s until the time appointed by
1Pe 4:10 as good s of the manifold

STEWARDSHIP (*see* STEWARD)
Luke 16: 2 Give an account of your s
Luke 16: 3 is taking the s away from me
Luke 16: 4 when I am put out of the s
1Co 9:17 have been entrusted with a s
Col 1:25 s from God which was given to

STICK (*see* STICKS, STUCK)
2Ki 6: 6 So he cut off a s, and threw
Job 33:21 his bones s out which once
Job 41:17 they s together and cannot be
Is 28:27 cummin is beaten out with a s
Is 57: 4 mouth and s out the tongue
Ezek 29: 4 rivers to s to your scales
Ezek 29: 4 rivers will s to your scales
Ezek 37:16 man, take a s for yourself and
Ezek 37:16 Then take another s and write
Ezek 37:16 the s of Ephraim, and for all
Ezek 37:17 for yourself into one s, and
Ezek 37:19 I will take the s of Joseph
Ezek 37:19 with it, with the s of Judah
Ezek 37:19 and make them one s

STICKS (*see* STICK)
Num 15:32 s on the Sabbath day
Num 15:33 s brought him to Moses and
1Sa 17:43 that you come to me with s
1Ki 17:10 a widow was there gathering s
1Ki 17:12 couple of s that I may go in
Prov 18:24 who s closer than a brother
Ezek 37:20 the s on which you write will
Acts 28: 3 had gathered a bundle of s

STIFF (*see* STIFFENED)
Deut 31:27 your rebellion and your s neck
Ps 75: 5 Do not speak with a s neck
Jer 17:23 ear, but made their neck s

STIFFENED (*see* STIFF, STIFF-NECKED)
2Ki 17:14 but s their necks, like the
2Ch 36:13 but he s his neck and hardened
Neh 9:29 s their necks, and would not
Jer 7:26 their ear, but s their neck
Jer 19:15 because they have s their

STIFF-NECKED (*see* STIFFENED)
Ex 32: 9 and indeed it is a s people
Ex 33: 3 way for you are a s people
Ex 33: 5 Israel, 'You are a s people
Ex 34: 9 even though we are a s people
Deut 9: 6 for you are a s people
Deut 9:13 and indeed they are a s people
Deut 10:16 your heart, and be s no longer

STIFFNECKED
2Ch 30: 8 Now do not be s, as your
Acts 7:51 You s and uncircumcised in

STILL
Gen 12: 9 going on s toward the South
Gen 18:22 but Abraham s stood before
Gen 25: 6 while he was s living he sent
Gen 29: 7 Look, it is s high day
Gen 29: 9 Now while he was s speaking
Gen 29:27 with me s another seven years
Gen 29:30 Laban s another seven years
Gen 31:14 Is there s any portion or
Gen 37: 9 he dreamed s another dream
Gen 43: 6 you had s another brother
Gen 43: 7 Is your father s alive
Gen 43:27 Is he s alive?
Gen 43:28 he is s alive
Gen 44:14 house, and he was s there
Gen 45: 3 does my father s live
Gen 45: 6 there are s five years in
Gen 45:11 for there are s five years of
Gen 45:26 Joseph is s alive, and he is
Gen 45:26 And Jacob's heart stood s
Gen 45:28 Joseph my son is s alive
Gen 46:30 face, because you are s alive
Ex 4:18 see whether they are s alive
Ex 9: 2 let them go, and s hold them,
Ex 14:13 Stand s, and see the salvation
Ex 15:16 they will be as s as a stone
Lev 25:51 If there are s many years
Num 9: 8 Stand s, that I may hear what
Num 9:10 he may s keep the LORD's
Num 11:33 was s between their teeth
Num 19:13 his uncleanness is s on him
Num 32:14 to increase s more the fierce
Deut 5:24 with man; yet he s lives
Josh 3:16 down from upstream stood s
Josh 7:26 stones, s there to this day
Josh 10:12 Sun, stand s over Gibeon
Josh 10:13 So the sun stood s, and the
Josh 10:13 So the sun stood s in the
Judg 3:25 s he had not opened the doors
Judg 5:27 he sank, he fell, he lay s
Judg 6:24 To this day it is s in Ophrah
Judg 7: 4 The people are s too many
Judg 8: 4 exhausted but s in pursuit
Judg 8:20 because he was s a youth
Ruth 1:11 Are there s sons in my womb,
Ruth 3:18 Sit s, my daughter, until you
1Sa 12: 7 Now therefore, stand s, that
1Sa 12:25 But if you s do wickedly, you
1Sa 13: 7 he was s in Gilgal, and all
1Sa 14: 9 we will stand s in our place
1Sa 18:29 Saul was s more afraid of
1Sa 20:14 of the LORD while I s live
1Sa 26:25 things and also s prevail
2Sa 1: 9 but my life s remains in me
2Sa 2:23 fell down and died, stood s
2Sa 2:28 and all the people stood s
2Sa 3:35 eat food while it was s day
2Sa 9: 1 Is there s anyone who is left
2Sa 9: 3 Is there not s someone of the
2Sa 9: 3 There is s a son of Jonathan
2Sa 12:18 while the child was s alive
2Sa 12:22 While the child was s alive
2Sa 14:32 better for me to be there s
2Sa 18:14 while he was s alive in the
2Sa 18:30 So he turned aside and stood s
2Sa 19:28 I s to cry out anymore to the
2Sa 20:12 that all the people stood s
1Ki 1:14 while you are s talking there
1Ki 1:22 while she was s talking with
1Ki 1:42 While he was s speaking,
1Ki 11:17 Hadad was s a little child
1Ki 12: 2 heard it (he was s in Egypt
1Ki 12: 6 Solomon while he s lived, and
1Ki 19:12 the fire a s small voice
1Ki 20:32 Is he s alive
1Ki 22: 7 Is there not s a prophet of
1Ki 22: 8 There is s one man, Micaiah
2Ki 6:33 while he was s talking with
2Ki 12: 3 the people s sacrificed and
2Ki 14: 4 and the people s sacrificed
2Ki 15: 4 the people s sacrificed and
2Ki 15:35 the people s sacrificed and
2Ki 25: 4 though the Chaldeans were s
1Ch 12: 1 at Ziklag while he was s a
2Ch 10: 6 Solomon while he s lived,
2Ch 18: 6 Is there not s a prophet of
2Ch 18: 7 There is s one man by whom we
2Ch 20:17 Position yourselves, stand s
2Ch 27: 2 But s the people acted
2Ch 33:17 s sacrificed on the high
2Ch 34: 3 reign, while he was s young
Neh 8:11 Be s, for the day is holy
Esth 6:14 While they were s talking
Job 1:16 While he was s speaking,
Job 1:17 While he was s speaking,
Job 1:18 While he was s speaking,
Job 2: 3 And s he holds fast to his
Job 2: 9 him, "Do you s hold to your
Job 3:13 For now I would have lain s
Job 4:16 it stood s, but I could not
Job 6:10 Then I would s have comfort
Job 6:29 my righteousness s stands
Job 20:13 but s keeps it in his mouth,
Job 32:16 speak, because they stood s
Job 37:14 stand s and consider the
Ps 4: 4 heart on your bed, and be s
Ps 23: 2 leads me beside the s waters
Ps 46:10 Be s, and know that I am God
Ps 65: 7 You who s the noise of the
Ps 68:21 s goes on in His trespasses
Ps 69: 4 nothing, I s must restore it
Ps 76: 8 The earth feared and was s
Ps 78:30 food was s in their mouths
Ps 78:32 spite of this they s sinned
Ps 83: 1 Your peace, And do not be s
Ps 84: 4 They will s be praising You
Ps 89: 9 its waves rise, You s them
Ps 92:14 They shall s bear fruit in
Ps 107:29 So that its waves are s
Ps 139:18 When I awake, I am s with You
Ps 141: 5 For s my prayer is against
Prov 9: 9 man, and he will be s wiser
Eccl 4: 2 the living who are s alive

Eccl 7:28 which my soul s seeks but I
Eccl 12: 9 wise, he s taught the people
Is 5:25 His hand is stretched out s
Is 9:12 His hand is stretched out s
Is 9:17 His hand is stretched out s
Is 9:21 His hand is stretched out s
Is 10: 4 His hand is stretched out s
Is 14: 1 and will s choose Israel, and
Is 23: 2 Be s, you inhabitants of the
Is 28: 4 up while it is s in his hand
Is 29: 8 and his soul is s empty
Is 29: 8 faint, and his soul s craves
Is 42:14 a long time, I have been s
Is 65:24 and while they are s speaking
Jer 8:14 Why do we sit s
Jer 13:27 Will you s not be made clean
Jer 31:20 I earnestly remember him s
Jer 33: 1 while he was s shut up in the
Jer 42:10 If you will s abide in this
Jer 47: 6 your scabbard, rest and be s
Jer 51:50 Do not stand s
Lam 3:20 My soul s remembers and sinks
Lam 4:17 S our eyes failed us,
Ezek 1:24 and when they stood s, they
Ezek 7:13 though he may s be alive
Ezek 10:17 s, the wheels stood s
Ezek 16:28 them and s were not satisfied
Ezek 17:15 a covenant and s be delivered
Ezek 17:18 s did all these things, he
Ezek 28: 9 Will you s say before him who
Dan 4:31 While the word was s in the
Dan 11:27 for the end will s be at the
Dan 11:35 because it is s for the
Hos 11:12 but Judah s walks with God,
Amos 4: 7 you, when there were s three
Jon 4: 2 when I was s in my country
Hab 3:11 sun and moon stood s in their
Hag 2:19 Is the seed s in the barn
Zech 11:16 nor feed those that s stand
Zech 13: 3 that if anyone s prophesies
Matt 12:46 While He was s talking to the
Matt 15:16 Are you also s without
Matt 17: 5 While he was s speaking,
Matt 19:20 What do I s lack
Matt 20:32 So Jesus stood s and called
Matt 26:45 Are you s sleeping and resting
Matt 26:47 And while He was s speaking
Matt 27:63 while He was s alive, how
Mark 4:39 to the sea, "Peace, be s!"
Mark 5:35 While He was s speaking, some
Mark 8:17 Is your heart s hardened
Mark 10:49 So Jesus stood s and
Mark 12: 6 Therefore s having one son,
Mark 14:41 Are you s sleeping and resting
Mark 14:43 while He was s speaking,
Mark 15: 5 But Jesus s answered nothing,
Luke 7:14 those who carried him stood s
Luke 8:49 While He was s speaking,
Luke 9:42 And as he was s coming, the
Luke 14:20 S another said, 'I have
Luke 14:22 commanded, and s there is room
Luke 14:32 other is s a great way off
Luke 15:20 when he was s a great way off
Luke 18:22 him, "You s lack one thing
Luke 18:40 So Jesus stood s and
Luke 22:37 must s be accomplished in Me
Luke 22:47 And while He was s speaking
Luke 22:60 while he was s speaking, the
Luke 24: 6 you when He was s in Galilee
Luke 24:41 But while they s did not
Luke 24:44 to you while I was s with you
John 4:35 There are s four months and
John 16:12 I s have many things to say
John 20: 1 early, while it was s dark
Acts 8:38 the chariot to stand s
Acts 9: 1 s breathing threats and murder
Acts 10:44 While Peter was s speaking
Acts 18:18 So Paul s remained a good
Rom 3: 7 why am I also s judged as a
Rom 4:11 he had while s uncircumcised
Rom 4:12 had while s uncircumcised
Rom 5: 6 we were s without strength
Rom 5: 8 that while we were s sinners
Rom 8:24 for why does one s hope for
Rom 9:19 Why does He s find fault
1Co 3: 2 even now you are s not able
1Co 3: 3 for you are s carnal
1Co 15:17 you are s in your sins
2Co 1:10 that He will s deliver us
Gal 1:10 For if I s pleased men, I
Gal 5:11 if I s preach circumcision,
Gal 5:11 why do I s suffer persecution
Phil 1: 9 your love may abound s more
2Th 2: 5 remember that when I was s
Heb 7:10 for he was s in the loins of
Heb 9: 8 tabernacle was s standing
Heb 11: 4 it he being dead s speaks
Heb 11:36 S others had trial of
Rev 9:12 s two more woes are coming
Rev 10: 1 I saw s another mighty angel
Rev 22:11 unjust, let him be unjust s
Rev 22:11 filthy, let him be filthy s
Rev 22:11 let him be righteous s
Rev 22:11 is holy, let him be holy s

STILLBORN
Job 3:16 I not hidden like a s child
Ps 58: 8 Like a s child of a woman,
Eccl 6: 3 I say that a s child is

STING (*see* STINGS)
1Co 15:55 O Death, where is your s
1Co 15:56 The s of death is sin, and the

STINGS (*see* STING)
Prov 23:32 a serpent, and s like a viper
Rev 9:10 there were s in their tails

STINK (*see* STANK)
Ex 7:18 shall die, the river shall s
Ex 16:24 and it did not s, nor were
Is 50: 2 their fish s because there is

STIR (*see* STIRRED, STIRRING, STIRS)
Job 41:10 that he would dare s him up
Ps 35:23 S up Yourself, and awake to my
Ps 78:38 did not s up all His wrath
Ps 80: 2 S up Your strength, And come
Song 2: 7 do not s up nor awaken love
Song 3: 5 do not s up nor awaken love
Song 8: 4 do not s up nor awaken love
Is 10:26 the LORD of hosts will s up a
Is 13:17 I will s up the Medes against
Is 42:13 He shall s up His zeal like a
Ezek 23:22 I will s up your lovers
Dan 11: 2 he shall s up all against the
Dan 11:10 his sons shall s up strife
Dan 11:10 his fortress and s up strife
Dan 11:25 He shall s up his power and
Acts 12:18 there was no small s among
2Ti 1: 6 Therefore I remind you to s
Heb 10:24 another in order to s up love
2Pe 1:13 to s you up by reminding you,
2Pe 3: 1 I s up your pure minds by way

STIRRED (*see* STIR)
Ex 35:21 came whose heart was s, and
Ex 35:26 s with wisdom spun yarn of
Ex 36: 2 everyone whose heart was s
1Sa 22: 8 to me that my son has s up my
1Sa 26:19 If the LORD has s you up
1Ki 21:25 Jezebel his wife s him up
1Ch 5:26 So the God of Israel s up the
2Ch 21:16 Moreover the LORD s up
2Ch 36:22 the LORD s up the spirit of
Ezra 1: 1 the LORD s up the spirit of
Ps 39: 2 And my sorrow was s up
Dan 11:25 be s up to battle with a very
Hos 11: 8 My sympathy is s
Hag 1:14 So the LORD s up the spirit
Mark 15:11 chief priests s up the crowd
John 5: 4 the pool and s up the water
John 5: 7 pool when the water is s up
Acts 6:12 they s up the people, the
Acts 13:50 But the Jews s up the devout
Acts 14: 2 Jews s up the Gentiles and
Acts 17:13 there also and s up the crowds
Acts 21:27 s up the whole crowd and laid
2Co 9: 2 and your zeal has s up the

STIRRING (*see* STIR)
Dan 7: 2 were s up the Great Sea
Hos 7: 4 he ceases s the fire after
John 5: 4 after the s of the water, was

STIRS (*see* STIR)
Deut 32:11 As an eagle s up its nest
Job 17: 8 the innocent s himself up
Job 26:12 He s up the sea with His
Prov 10:12 Hatred s up strife, but love
Prov 15: 1 but a harsh word s up anger
Prov 15:18 A wrathful man s up strife
Prov 28:25 of a proud heart s up strife
Prov 29:22 An angry man s up strife, and
Is 14: 9 it s up the dead for you, all
Is 64: 7 who s himself up to take hold
Luke 23: 5 He s up the people, teaching

STOCK (*see* STOCKS)
Is 3: 1 Jerusalem and from Judah the s
Is 40:24 scarcely shall their s take
Phil 3: 5 of the s of Israel, of the

STOCKS (*see* STOCK)
Job 13:27 You put my feet in the s, and
Job 33:11 He puts my feet in the s, He
Prov 7:22 to the correction of the s
Jer 20: 2 put him in the s that were in
Jer 20: 3 brought Jeremiah out of the s
Jer 29:26 put him in prison and in the s
Acts 16:24 fastened their feet in the s

STOIC
Acts 17:18 S philosophers encountered

STOLE (*see* STEAL, STOLEN)
Gen 31:20 And Jacob s away, unknown to
2Sa 15: 6 So Absalom s the hearts of
2Sa 19: 3 the people s back into the
2Ki 11: 2 s him away from among the
2Ch 22:11 s him away from among the
Matt 28:13 s Him away while we slept
Eph 4:28 Let him who s steal no longer

STOLEN (*see* STOLE)
Gen 30:33 lambs, will be considered s
Gen 31:19 Rachel had s the household
Gen 31:26 that you have s away unknown
Gen 31:32 know that Rachel had s them
Gen 31:39 s by day or s by night
Gen 40:15 For indeed I was s away from
Ex 22: 7 and it is s out of the man's
Ex 22:12 it is s from him, he shall
Lev 6: 4 shall restore what he has s
Josh 7:11 things, and have both s and
2Sa 19:41 s you away and brought the
2Sa 21:12 had s them from the street of
Ps 69: 4 Though I have s nothing, I
Prov 9:17 S water is sweet, and bread
Ezek 33:15 gives back what he has s
Obad 5 would they not have s till
Mal 1:13 And you bring the s, the lame,

STOMACH (*see* STOMACH'S, STOMACHS)
Num 5:22 the curse go into your s, and
Deut 18: 3 the cheeks, and the s
2Sa 2:23 Abner struck him in the s
2Sa 3:27 and there stabbed him in the s
2Sa 4: 6 and they stabbed him in the s
2Sa 20:10 struck him with it in the s
Job 20:14 his food in his s turns sour
Job 20:23 he is about to fill his s
Job 40:16 his power is in his s muscles
Prov 13:25 but the s of the wicked shall
Prov 18:20 A man's s shall be satisfied
Jer 51:34 he has filled his s with my
Ezek 3: 3 fill your s with this scroll
Matt 15:17 the mouth goes into the s
Mark 7:19 not enter his heart but his s
Luke 15:16 his s with the pods that the
1Co 6:13 Foods for the s and the
1Co 6:13 the s for foods, but God will
Rev 10: 9 and it will make your s bitter
Rev 10:10 eaten it, my s became bitter

STOMACH'S (*see* STOMACH)
1Ti 5:23 a little wine for your s sake

STOMACHS (*see* STOMACH)
Ezek 7:19 their souls, nor fill their s

STONE (*see* STONECUTTERS, STONED, STONE'S, STONES, STONING, STONY)
Gen 2:12 and the onyx s are there
Gen 11: 3 They had brick for s, and
Gen 28:18 took the s that he had put at
Gen 28:22 this s which I have set as a
Gen 29: 2 A large s was on the well's
Gen 29: 3 they would roll the s from
Gen 29: 3 put the s back in its place
Gen 29: 8 they have rolled the s from
Gen 29:10 rolled the s from the well's
Gen 31:45 So Jacob took a s and set it
Gen 35:14 with him, a pillar of s
Gen 49:24 Shepherd, the S of Israel),
Ex 4:25 Then Zipporah took a sharp s
Ex 7:19 of wood and vessels of s
Ex 8:26 eyes, then will they not s us
Ex 15: 5 sank to the bottom like a s

Ex 15:16 they will be as still as a s
Ex 17: 4 They are almost ready to s me
Ex 17:12 so they took a s and put it
Ex 20:25 if you make Me an altar of s
Ex 20:25 shall not build it of hewn s
Ex 21:18 with a s or with his fist
Ex 24:10 a paved work of sapphire s
Ex 24:12 I will give you tablets of s
Ex 28:10 six of their names on one s
Ex 28:10 six names on the other s,
Ex 28:11 the work of an engraver in s
Ex 31:18 the Testimony, tablets of s
Ex 34: 1 Cut two tablets of s like the
Ex 34: 4 of s like the first ones
Ex 34: 4 his hand the two tablets of s
Lev 20: 2 land shall s him with stones
Lev 20:27 they shall s them with stones
Lev 24:14 all the congregation s him
Lev 24:16 shall certainly s him, the
Lev 26: 1 up an engraved s in your land
Num 14:10 said to s them with stones
Num 15:35 all the congregation shall s
Num 35:17 him with a s in the hand, by
Num 35:23 or uses a s, by which a man
Deut 4:13 them on two tablets of s
Deut 4:28 of men's hands, wood and s
Deut 5:22 them on two tablets of s and
Deut 9: 9 to receive the tablets of s
Deut 9:10 to me two tablets of s
Deut 9:11 gave me the two tablets of s
Deut 10: 1 tablets of s like the first
Deut 10: 3 tablets of s like the first
Deut 13:10 you shall s him with stones
Deut 17: 5 shall s to death that man or
Deut 21:21 s him to death with stones
Deut 22:21 s her to death with stones
Deut 22:24 you shall s them to death
Deut 28:36 serve other gods—wood and s
Deut 28:64 have known—wood and s
Deut 29:17 wood and s and silver and gold)
Josh 4: 5 take up a s on his shoulder
Josh 15: 6 the border went up to the s
Josh 18:17 descended to the s of Bohan
Josh 24:26 And he took a large s, and set
Josh 24:27 this s shall be a witness to
Judg 3:19 turned back from the s images
Judg 3:26 and passed beyond the s images
Judg 9: 5 sons of Jerubbaal, on one s
Judg 9:18 his seventy sons on one s
Judg 20:16 sling a s at a hair's breadth
1Sa 6:14 a large s was there
1Sa 6:15 and put them on the large s
1Sa 6:18 even as far as the large s of
1Sa 6:18 which s remains to this day
1Sa 7:12 Then Samuel took a s and set
1Sa 14:33 roll a large s to me this day
1Sa 17:49 in his bag and took out a s
1Sa 17:49 so that the s sank into his
1Sa 17:50 with a sling and a s, and
1Sa 20:19 and remain by the s Ezel
1Sa 25:37 him, and he became like a s
2Sa 17:13 not one small s found there
2Sa 20: 8 large s which is in Gibeon
1Ki 1: 9 cattle by the s of Zoheleth
1Ki 5:15 quarried s in the mountains
1Ki 6: 7 was built with s finished at
1Ki 6:18 there was no s to be seen
1Ki 6:36 with three rows of hewn s
1Ki 8: 9 of s which Moses put there at
1Ki 21:10 and s him, that he may die
2Ki 3:25 each man threw a s on every
2Ki 12:12 for buying timber and hewn s
2Ki 19:18 of men's hands—wood and s
2Ki 22: 6 hewn s to repair the house
1Ch 22:14 s also, and you may add to
1Ch 22:15 hewers and workers of s and
2Ch 2: 2 to quarry s in the mountains
2Ch 2:14 and silver, bronze and iron, s
2Ch 2:18 hewers of s in the mountain
2Ch 34:11 and builders to buy hewn s
Neh 4: 3 will break down their s wall
Neh 9:11 as a s into the mighty waters
Job 38:30 The waters harden like s, and
Job 41:24 His heart is as hard as s
Ps 91:12 dash your foot against a s
Ps 118:22 The s which the builders
Prov 17: 8 precious s in the eyes of its
Prov 24:31 its s wall was broken down
Prov 26: 8 Like one who binds a s in a
Prov 26:27 he who rolls a s will have it
Prov 27: 3 A s is heavy and sand is
Is 8:14 but a s of stumbling and a
Is 28:16 I lay in Zion a s for a
Is 28:16 for a foundation, a tried s
Is 37:19 of men's hands—wood and s
Jer 2:27 You are my father,' and to a s
Jer 51:26 a s for a corner nor a s
Jer 51:63 that you shall tie a s to it
Lam 3: 9 blocked my ways with hewn s
Ezek 1:26 appearance like a sapphire s
Ezek 3: 9 Like adamant s, harder than
Ezek 10: 1 something like a sapphire s
Ezek 10: 9 have the color of a beryl s
Ezek 16:40 they shall s you with stones
Ezek 20:32 countries, serving wood and s
Ezek 23:47 shall s them with stones and
Ezek 28:13 every precious s was your
Ezek 36:26 heart of s out of your flesh
Ezek 40:42 hewn s for the burnt offering
Dan 2:34 You watched while a s was cut
Dan 2:35 the s that struck the image
Dan 2:45 as you saw that the s was cut
Dan 5: 4 bronze and iron, wood and s
Dan 5:23 bronze and iron, wood and s
Dan 6:17 Then a s was brought and laid
Amos 5:11 have built houses of hewn s
Hab 2:11 For the s will cry out from
Hab 2:19 to silent s, 'Arise
Hag 2:15 from before s was laid upon
Hag 2:15 s in the temple of the LORD
Zech 3: 9 the s that I have laid before
Zech 3: 9 upon the s are seven eyes
Zech 12: 3 very heavy s for all peoples
Matt 4: 6 dash your foot against a s
Matt 7: 9 for bread, will give him a s
Matt 21:42 The s which the builders
Matt 21:44 on this s will be broken
Matt 24: 2 not one s shall be left here
Matt 27:60 he rolled a large s against
Matt 27:66 tomb secure, sealing the s
Matt 28: 2 back the s from the door, and
Mark 12:10 The s which the builders
Mark 13: 2 Not one s shall be left upon
Mark 15:46 rolled a s against the door
Mark 16: 3 Who will roll away the s from
Mark 16: 4 they saw that the s had been
Luke 4: 3 God, command this s to become
Luke 4:11 dash Your foot against a s
Luke 11:11 you, will he give him a s
Luke 19:44 in you one s upon another
Luke 20: 6 all the people will s us
Luke 20:17 The s which the builders
Luke 20:18 on that s will be broken
Luke 21: 6 s shall be left upon another
Luke 24: 2 But they found the s rolled
John 1:42 (which is translated, A S)
John 2: 6 set there six waterpots of s
John 8: 7 him throw a s at her first
John 10:31 took up stones again to s Him
John 10:32 of those works do you s Me
John 10:33 a good work we do not s You
John 11: 8 the Jews sought to s You, and
John 11:38 a cave, and a s lay against it
John 11:39 Take away the s
John 11:41 Then they took away the s
John 20: 1 saw that the s had been taken
Acts 4:11 This is the s which was
Acts 14: 5 rulers, to abuse and s them,
Acts 17:29 is like gold or silver or s
Rom 9:32 stumbled at that stumbling s
Rom 9:33 I lay in Zion a stumbling s
2Co 3: 3 not on tablets of s but on
1Pe 2: 4 to Him as to a living s,
1Pe 2: 7 The s which the builders
1Pe 2: 8 A s of stumbling and a rock of
Rev 2:17 And I will give him a white s
Rev 2:17 on the s a new name written
Rev 4: 3 a sardius s in appearance
Rev 9:20 of gold, silver, brass, s
Rev 18:21 up a s like a great millstone
Rev 21:11 precious s, like a jasper s

STONECUTTERS (*see* STONE)
2Ki 12:12 and to masons and s, and for

STONED (*see* STONE)
Ex 19:13 be s or shot with an arrow
Ex 21:28 then the ox shall surely be s
Ex 21:29 or a woman, the ox shall be s
Ex 21:32 silver, and the ox shall be s
Lev 24:23 cursed, and s him with stones
Num 15:36 s him with stones, and he died
Josh 7:25 all Israel s him with stones
Josh 7:25 they had s them with stones
1Ki 12:18 but all Israel s him with
1Ki 21:13 s him with stones, so that he
1Ki 21:14 Naboth has been s and is dead
1Ki 21:15 heard that Naboth had been s
2Ch 10:18 of Israel s him with stones
2Ch 24:21 of the king they s him with
Matt 21:35 one, killed one, and s another
John 8: 5 us that such should be s
Acts 5:26 people, lest they should be s
Acts 7:58 him out of the city and s him
Acts 7:59 And they s Stephen as he was
Acts 14:19 the multitudes, they s Paul
2Co 11:25 with rods; once I was s;
Heb 11:37 They were s, they were sawn
Heb 12:20 it shall be s or thrust

STONE'S (*see* STONE)
Luke 22:41 from them about a s throw

STONES (*see* STONE)
Gen 28:11 one of the s of that place
Gen 31:46 to his brethren, "Gather s."
Gen 31:46 And they took s and made a
Ex 25: 7 onyx s, and s to be set
Ex 28: 9 you shall take two onyx s
Ex 28:11 you shall engrave the two s
Ex 28:12 you shall put the two s on
Ex 28:12 s for the sons of Israel
Ex 28:17 s in it, four rows of s
Ex 28:21 the s shall have the names of
Ex 35: 9 onyx s, and s to be set
Ex 35:27 The rulers brought onyx s
Ex 35:27 s, and the s to be set
Ex 39: 6 And they set onyx s, enclosed
Ex 39: 7 that they should be s for a
Ex 39:10 they set in it four rows of s
Ex 39:14 There were twelve s according
Lev 14:40 the s in which is the plague
Lev 14:42 Then they shall take other s
Lev 14:42 them in the place of those s
Lev 14:43 after he has taken away the s
Lev 14:45 break down the house, its s
Lev 20: 2 land shall stone him with s
Lev 20:27 they shall stone them with s
Lev 24:23 cursed, and stoned him with s
Num 14:10 said to stone them with s
Num 15:35 him with s outside the camp
Num 15:36 the camp and stoned him with s
Num 33:52 destroy all their engraved s
Deut 8: 9 a land whose s are iron and
Deut 13:10 him with s until he dies,
Deut 17: 5 that man or woman with s
Deut 21:21 stone him to death with s
Deut 22:21 stone her to death with s
Deut 22:24 stone them to death with s
Deut 27: 2 set up for yourselves large s
Deut 27: 4 Ebal you shall set up these s
Deut 27: 5 LORD your God, an altar of s
Deut 27: 6 s the altar of the LORD your
Deut 27: 8 s all the words of this law
Josh 4: 3 yourselves twelve s from here
Josh 4: 6 What do these s mean to you
Josh 4: 7 And these s shall be for a
Josh 4: 8 took up twelve s from the
Josh 4: 9 Then Joshua set up twelve s
Josh 4:20 those twelve s which they
Josh 4:21 saying, 'What are these s
Josh 7:25 all Israel stoned him with s
Josh 7:25 they had stoned them with s
Josh 7:26 over him a great heap of s
Josh 8:29 over it a great heap of s
Josh 8:31 an altar of whole s over
Josh 8:32 he wrote on the s a copy of
Josh 10:18 Roll large s against the
Josh 10:27 and laid large s against the
1Sa 17:40 five smooth s from the brook
2Sa 12:30 of gold, with precious s
2Sa 16: 6 And he threw s at David and at
2Sa 16:13 threw s at him and kicked up
2Sa 18:17 very large heap of s over him
1Ki 5:17 them to quarry large s,
1Ki 5:17 costly s, and hewn s
1Ki 5:18 and s to build the temple
1Ki 7: 9 were of costly s hewn to size
1Ki 7:10 was of costly s, large s
1Ki 7:11 And above were costly s, hewn
1Ki 7:12 with three rows of hewn s
1Ki 10: 2 very much gold, and precious s

1Ki 10:10 abundance, and precious **s**
1Ki 10:11 wood and precious **s** from Ophir
1Ki 10:27 as common in Jerusalem as **s**
1Ki 12:18 all Israel stoned him with **s**
1Ki 15:22 And they took away the **s** and
1Ki 18:31 And Elijah took twelve **s**,
1Ki 18:32 Then with the **s** he built an
1Ki 18:38 and the wood and the **s** and the
1Ki 21:13 the city and stoned him with **s**
2Ki 3:19 good piece of land with **s**
2Ki 3:25 intact the **s** of Kir Haraseth
2Ki 16:17 and put it on a pavement of **s**
1Ch 12: 2 hand and the left in hurling **s**
1Ch 20: 2 there were precious **s** in it
1Ch 22: 2 masons to cut hewn **s** to build
1Ch 29: 2 onyx **s**, **s** to be set
1Ch 29: 2 set, glistening **s** of various
1Ch 29: 2 all kinds of precious **s**, and
1Ch 29: 8 whoever had precious **s** gave
2Ch 1:15 as common in Jerusalem as **s**
2Ch 3: 6 with precious **s** for beauty
2Ch 9: 1 in abundance, and precious **s**
2Ch 9: 9 abundance, and precious **s**
2Ch 9:10 algum wood and precious **s**
2Ch 9:27 as common in Jerusalem as **s**
2Ch 10:18 of Israel stoned him with **s**
2Ch 16: 6 and they carried away the **s**
2Ch 24:21 **s** in the court of the house
2Ch 26:14 bows, and slings to cast **s**
2Ch 26:15 to shoot arrows and large **s**
2Ch 32:27 for gold, for precious **s**
Ezra 5: 8 is being built with heavy **s**
Ezra 6: 4 with three rows of heavy **s**
Neh 4: 2 Will they revive the **s** from
Neh 4: 2 **s** that are burned
Job 5:23 with the **s** of the field, and
Job 6:12 my strength the strength of **s**
Job 8:17 and look for a place in the **s**
Job 14:19 As water wears away **s**, and as
Job 22:24 among the **s** of the brooks
Job 28: 6 its **s** are the source of
Ps 102:14 take pleasure in her **s**, And
Eccl 3: 5 a time to cast away **s**
Eccl 3: 5 and a time to gather **s**
Eccl 10: 9 He who quarries **s** may be hurt
Is 5: 2 it up and cleared out its **s**
Is 9:10 we will rebuild with hewn **s**
Is 14:19 go down to the **s** of the pit
Is 27: 9 all the **s** of the altar like
Is 34:11 and the **s** of emptiness
Is 54:11 I will lay your **s** with
Is 54:12 all your walls of precious **s**
Is 57: 6 Among the smooth **s** of the
Is 60:17 wood, bronze, and instead of **s**
Is 62:10 Take out the **s**, lift up a
Jer 3: 9 and committed adultery with **s**
Jer 43: 9 Take large **s** in your hand, and
Jer 43:10 these **s** that I have hidden
Lam 3:53 in the pit and threw **s** at me
Lam 4: 1 The **s** of the sanctuary are
Ezek 16:40 they shall stone you with **s**
Ezek 23:47 shall stone them with **s** and
Ezek 26:12 they will lay your **s**, your
Ezek 27:22 all kinds of precious **s**, and
Ezek 28:14 forth in the midst of fiery **s**
Ezek 28:16 from the midst of the fiery **s**
Ezek 46:23 building **s** all around in them
Ezek 46:23 the rows of **s** all around
Dan 11:38 and silver, with precious **s**
Mic 1: 6 down her **s** into the valley
Zech 5: 4 it, with its timber and **s**
Zech 9:15 devour and subdue with sling **s**
Matt 3: 9 to Abraham from these **s**
Matt 4: 3 that these **s** become bread
Matt 23:37 **s** those who are sent to her
Mark 5: 5 out and cutting himself with **s**
Mark 12: 4 and at him they threw **s**,
Mark 13: 1 Teacher, see what manner of **s**
Luke 3: 8 to Abraham from these **s**
Luke 13:34 **s** those who are sent to her
Luke 19:40 the **s** would immediately cry
Luke 21: 5 was adorned with beautiful **s**
John 8:59 took up **s** to throw at Him
John 10:31 took up **s** again to stone Him
1Co 3:12 with gold, silver, precious **s**
2Co 3: 7 written and engraved on **s**
1Pe 2: 5 you also, as living **s**, are
Rev 17: 4 with gold and precious **s** and
Rev 18:12 of gold and silver, precious **s**
Rev 18:16 with gold and precious **s** and
Rev 21:19 with all kinds of precious **s**

STONING (*see* STONE)
1Sa 30: 6 for the people spoke of **s** him

STONY (*see* STONE)
Ezek 11:19 take the **s** heart out of their
Matt 13: 5 Some fell on **s** places, where
Matt 13:20 received the seed on **s** places
Mark 4: 5 Some fell on **s** ground, where
Mark 4:16 the ones sown on **s** ground who

STOOD (*see* STAND)
Gen 18: 8 he **s** by them under the tree
Gen 18:22 still **s** before the LORD
Gen 19:27 he had **s** before the LORD
Gen 23: 3 Then Abraham **s** up from before
Gen 23: 7 Then Abraham **s** up and bowed
Gen 24:30 there he **s** by the camels at
Gen 28:13 behold, the LORD **s** above it
Gen 37: 7 sheaf arose and also **s** upright
Gen 37: 7 your sheaves **s** all around
Gen 41: 1 and behold, he **s** by the river
Gen 41: 3 **s** by the other cows on the
Gen 41:17 in my dream I **s** on the bank
Gen 41:46 he **s** before Pharaoh king of
Gen 43:15 and they **s** before Joseph
Gen 45: 1 before all those who **s** by him
Gen 45: 1 So no one **s** with him while
Gen 45:26 And Jacob's heart **s** still
Ex 2: 4 And his sister **s** afar off, to
Ex 2:17 but Moses **s** up and helped them
Ex 5:20 Aaron who **s** there to meet
Ex 9:10 **s** before Pharaoh, and Moses
Ex 14:19 before them and **s** behind them
Ex 15: 8 the floods **s** upright like a
Ex 18:13 the people **s** before Moses
Ex 19:17 they **s** at the foot of the
Ex 20:18 they trembled and **s** afar off
Ex 20:21 So the people **s** afar off, but
Ex 32:26 then Moses **s** in the entrance
Ex 33: 8 each man **s** at his tent door
Ex 33: 9 and **s** at the door of the
Ex 34: 5 cloud and **s** with him there, and
Lev 9: 5 near and **s** before the LORD
Num 12: 5 cloud and **s** in the door of the
Num 16:18 it, and **s** at the door of the
Num 16:27 **s** at the door of their tents,
Num 16:48 he **s** between the dead and the
Num 22:24 **s** in a narrow path between
Num 22:26 **s** in a narrow place where
Num 22:34 You **s** in the way against me
Num 27: 2 they **s** before Moses, before
Deut 4:10 concerning the day you **s**
Deut 4:11 **s** at the foot of the mountain
Deut 5: 5 I **s** between the LORD and you
Deut 31:15 the pillar of cloud **s** above
Josh 3:16 down from upstream **s** still
Josh 3:17 **s** firm on dry ground in the
Josh 4: 3 the priests' feet **s** firm
Josh 4: 9 the ark of the covenant **s**
Josh 4:10 priests who bore the ark **s** in
Josh 5:13 a Man **s** opposite him with His
Josh 8:33 **s** on either side of the ark
Josh 10:13 So the sun **s** still, and the
Josh 10:13 So the sun **s** still in the
Josh 11:13 cities that **s** on their mounds
Josh 20: 9 he **s** before the congregation
Josh 21:44 their enemies **s** against them
Judg 6:31 said to all who **s** against him
Judg 7:21 every man **s** in his place all
Judg 9: 7 **s** on top of Mount Gerizim, and
Judg 9:35 **s** in the entrance to the city
Judg 9:44 **s** at the entrance of the gate
Judg 18:16 **s** by the entrance of the gate
Judg 18:17 The priest **s** at the entrance
Judg 19: 5 morning, and he **s** to depart
Judg 19: 7 And when the man **s** to depart
Judg 19: 9 And when the man **s** to depart
Judg 20:28 **s** before it in those days),
1Sa 1:26 the woman who **s** by you here
1Sa 3:10 Then the LORD came and **s** and
1Sa 4:20 who **s** by her said to her
1Sa 6:14 of Beth Shemesh, and **s** there
1Sa 10:23 when he **s** among the people,
1Sa 16:21 came to Saul and **s** before him
1Sa 17: 3 The Philistines **s** on a
1Sa 17: 3 Israel **s** on a mountain on the
1Sa 17: 8 Then he **s** and cried out to the
1Sa 17:26 spoke to the men who **s** by him
1Sa 17:51 **s** over the Philistine, took
1Sa 22: 7 his servants who **s** about him
1Sa 22:17 to the guards who **s** about him
1Sa 26:13 **s** on the top of a hill afar
2Sa 1:10 So I **s** over him and killed him
2Sa 2:23 fell down and died, **s** still
2Sa 2:28 and all the people **s** still
2Sa 13:31 all his servants **s** by with
2Sa 18: 4 So the king **s** beside the
2Sa 18:30 So he turned aside and **s** still
2Sa 20:11 of Joab's men **s** near Amasa
2Sa 20:12 that all the people **s** still
2Sa 20:15 city, and it **s** by the rampart
1Ki 1:28 presence and **s** before the king
1Ki 3:15 and **s** before the ark of the
1Ki 3:16 to the king, and **s** before him
1Ki 7:25 It **s** on twelve oxen
1Ki 8:22 Then Solomon **s** before the
1Ki 8:55 Then he **s** and blessed all the
1Ki 10:19 and two lions **s** beside the
1Ki 10:20 Twelve lions **s** there, one on
1Ki 12: 6 consulted the elders who **s**
1Ki 12: 8 up with him, who **s** before him
1Ki 13: 1 Jeroboam **s** by the altar to
1Ki 13:24 road, and the donkey **s** by it
1Ki 13:24 the lion also **s** by the corpse
1Ki 19:13 **s** in the entrance of the cave
1Ki 22:21 **s** before the LORD, and said
2Ki 2: 7 **s** facing them at a distance,
2Ki 2: 7 two of them **s** by the Jordan
2Ki 2:13 **s** by the bank of the Jordan
2Ki 3:21 and they **s** at the border
2Ki 4:12 called her, she **s** before him
2Ki 4:15 her, she **s** in the doorway
2Ki 5: 9 he **s** at the door of the house
2Ki 5:15 and came and **s** before him
2Ki 5:25 in and **s** before his master
2Ki 8: 9 and **s** before him, and said,
2Ki 9:17 Now a watchman **s** on the tower
2Ki 10: 9 that he went out and **s**, and
2Ki 11:11 Then the escorts **s**, every man
2Ki 13:21 he revived and **s** on his feet
2Ki 18:17 **s** by the aqueduct from the
2Ki 18:28 Then the Rabshakeh **s** and
2Ki 23: 3 Then the king **s** by a pillar
1Ch 6:39 who **s** at his right hand, was
1Ch 21: 1 Now Satan **s** up against Israel
1Ch 21:15 the angel of the LORD **s** by
2Ch 3:13 They **s** on their feet, and they
2Ch 4: 4 It **s** on twelve oxen
2Ch 5:12 **s** at the east end of the
2Ch 6: 3 the congregation of Israel **s**
2Ch 6:12 Then Solomon **s** before the
2Ch 6:13 he **s** on it, knelt down on his
2Ch 7: 6 them, while all Israel **s**
2Ch 9:18 and two lions **s** beside the
2Ch 9:19 Twelve lions **s** there, one on
2Ch 10: 6 consulted the elders who **s**
2Ch 10: 8 up with him, who **s** before him
2Ch 13: 4 Then Abijah **s** on Mount
2Ch 18:20 **s** before the LORD, and said
2Ch 20: 5 Then Jehoshaphat **s** in the
2Ch 20:13 children, **s** before the LORD
2Ch 20:19 **s** up to praise the LORD God
2Ch 20:20 they went out, Jehoshaphat **s**
2Ch 20:23 and Moab **s** up against the
2Ch 24:20 who **s** above the people, and
2Ch 28:12 **s** up against those who came
2Ch 29:26 The Levites **s** with the
2Ch 30:16 They **s** in their place
2Ch 34:31 Then the king **s** in his place
2Ch 35:10 the priests **s** in their places
Ezra 3:10 LORD, the priests **s** in their
Ezra 10:10 Then Ezra the priest **s** up
Neh 8: 4 So Ezra the scribe **s** on a
Neh 8: 4 **s** Mattithiah, Shema, Anaiah,
Neh 8: 5 it, all the people **s** up
Neh 8: 7 the people **s** in their place
Neh 9: 2 and they **s** and confessed their
Neh 9: 3 they **s** up in their place and
Neh 9: 4 Chenani **s** on the stairs of
Neh 12: 9 **s** across from them in their
Neh 12:40 choirs **s** in the house of God
Esth 5: 1 **s** in the inner court of the
Esth 7: 7 but Haman **s** before Queen
Esth 8: 4 arose and **s** before the king,
Job 4:15 the hair on my body **s** up
Job 4:16 it **s** still, but I could not
Job 29: 8 hid, and the aged arose and **s**
Job 32:16 speak, because they **s** still
Ps 33: 9 He commanded, and it **s** fast
Ps 104: 6 The waters **s** above the

Ps 106:23 s before Him in the breach
Ps 106:30 Then Phinehas s up and
Is 6: 2 Above it s seraphim
Is 36: 2 he s by the aqueduct from the
Is 36:13 Then the Rabshakeh s and
Jer 14: 6 the wild donkeys s in the
Jer 15: 1 Samuel s before Me, yet My
Jer 18:20 Remember that I s before You
Jer 19:14 and he s in the court of the
Jer 23:18 For who has s in the counsel
Jer 23:22 if they had s in My counsel
Jer 28: 5 of all the people who s in
Jer 36:21 princes who s beside the king
Jer 44:15 with all the women who s by
Jer 48:45 Those who fled s under the
Ezek 1:21 when those s, these s
Ezek 1:21 when those s, these s
Ezek 1:24 and when they s still, they
Ezek 1:25 whenever they s, they let
Ezek 3:23 the glory of the LORD s there
Ezek 8:11 there s before them seventy
Ezek 8:11 in their midst s Jaazaniah
Ezek 9: 2 s beside the bronze altar
Ezek 10: 6 in and s beside the wheels
Ezek 10:17 When the cherubim s still
Ezek 10:17 still, the wheels s still
Ezek 10:18 temple and s over the cherubim
Ezek 10:19 they s at the door of the
Ezek 11:23 s on the mountain, which is
Ezek 37:10 and s upon their feet, an
Ezek 40: 3 hand, and he s in the gateway
Ezek 43: 6 while a man s beside me
Dan 2: 2 came and s before the king
Dan 2:31 was excellent, s before you
Dan 3: 3 they s before the image that
Dan 7:10 ten thousand s before Him
Dan 7:16 near to one of those who s by
Dan 8:15 that suddenly there s before
Dan 8:17 So he came near where I s
Dan 8:18 touched me, and s me upright
Dan 8:22 the four that s up in its
Dan 10:11 word to me, I s trembling
Dan 10:16 saying to him who s before me
Dan 11: 1 s up to confirm and strengthen
Dan 12: 5 there s two others, one on
Hos 10: 9 There they s
Amos 7: 7 the Lord s on a wall made
Obad 11 that you s on the other side
Obad 14 You should not have s at the
Hab 3: 6 He s and measured the earth
Hab 3:11 sun and moon s still in their
Zech 1: 8 it s among the myrtle trees
Zech 1:10 And the man who s among the
Zech 1:11 who s among the myrtle trees,
Zech 3: 4 to those who s before Him
Zech 3: 5 And the Angel of the LORD s by
Matt 2: 9 s over where the young Child
Matt 12:46 mother and brothers s outside
Matt 13: 2 multitude s on the shore
Matt 20:32 So Jesus s still and called
Matt 26:73 those who s by came to him
Matt 27:11 Now Jesus s before the
Matt 27:47 Some of those who s there
Mark 10:49 So Jesus s still and commanded
Mark 11: 5 some of those who s there
Mark 14:47 one of those who s by drew
Mark 14:60 high priest s up in the midst
Mark 14:69 to say to those who s by
Mark 14:70 who s by said to Peter again
Mark 15:35 Some of those who s by, when
Mark 15:39 who s opposite Him, saw that
Luke 2: 9 of the Lord s before them
Luke 4:16 Sabbath day, and s up to read
Luke 4:39 So He s over her and rebuked
Luke 5: 1 God, that He s by the Lake of
Luke 6: 8 And he arose and s
Luke 6:17 s on a level place with a
Luke 7:14 those who carried him s still
Luke 7:38 and s at His feet behind Him
Luke 9:32 and the two men who s with Him
Luke 10:25 behold, a certain lawyer s up
Luke 17:12 were lepers, who s afar off
Luke 18:11 The Pharisee s and prayed thus
Luke 18:40 So Jesus s still and commanded
Luke 19: 8 Then Zacchaeus s and said to
Luke 19:24 And he said to those who s by
Luke 23:10 chief priests and scribes s
Luke 23:35 And the people s looking on
Luke 23:49 s at a distance, watching
Luke 24: 4 two men s by them in shining
Luke 24:36 Jesus Himself s in the midst
John 1:35 day, John s with two of his
John 7:37 day of the feast, Jesus s
John 11:56 as they s in the temple
John 12:29 Therefore the people who s by
John 18: 5 Him, also s with them
John 18:16 But Peter s at the door
John 18:18 made a fire of coals s there
John 18:18 Peter s with them and warmed
John 18:22 one of the officers who s by
John 18:25 Now Simon Peter s and warmed
John 19:25 Now there s by the cross of
John 20:11 But Mary s outside by the
John 20:19 s in the midst, and said to
John 20:26 and s in the midst, and said,
John 21: 4 come, Jesus s on the shore
Acts 1:10 two men s by them in white
Acts 1:15 in those days Peter s up in
Acts 3: 8 So he, leaping up, s and
Acts 5:34 Then one in the council s up
Acts 9: 7 with him s speechless,
Acts 9:39 the widows s by him weeping
Acts 10:17 house, and s before the gate
Acts 10:30 a man s before me in bright
Acts 11:11 three men s before the house
Acts 11:28 s up and showed by the Spirit
Acts 12: 7 an angel of the Lord s by him
Acts 12:14 that Peter s before the gate
Acts 13:16 Then Paul s up, and motioning
Acts 16: 9 A man of Macedonia s and
Acts 17:22 Then Paul s in the midst of
Acts 21:40 Paul s on the stairs and
Acts 22:13 and he s and said to me
Acts 22:25 to the centurion who s by
Acts 23: 2 s by him to strike him on the
Acts 23: 4 And those who s by said, "Do
Acts 23:11 night the Lord s by him and
Acts 24:20 while I s before the council
Acts 25: 7 down from Jerusalem s about
Acts 25:18 When the accusers s up, they
Acts 26:30 these things, the king s up
Acts 27:21 then Paul s in the midst of
Acts 27:23 For there s by me this night
2Ti 4:16 defense no one s with me, but
2Ti 4:17 But the Lord s with me and
Rev 5: 6 s a Lamb as though it had
Rev 7:11 all the angels s around the
Rev 8: 3 came and s at the altar
Rev 11: 1 And the angel s, saying
Rev 11:11 and they s on their feet, and
Rev 12: 4 the dragon s before the woman
Rev 13: 1 Then I s on the sand of the
Rev 18:17 on the sea, s at a distance

STOOP (*see* STOOPED, STOOPING, STOOPS)
Is 46: 2 They s, they bow down
Mark 1: 7 I am not worthy to s down

STOOPED (*see* STOOP)
1Sa 24: 8 David s with his face to the
1Sa 28:14 he s with his face to the
Hos 11: 4 I s and fed them
John 8: 6 But Jesus s down and wrote on
John 8: 8 And again He s down and wrote
John 20:11 and as she wept she s down

STOOPING (*see* STOOP)
Luke 24:12 and s down, he saw the linen
John 20: 5 s down and looking in, saw the

STOOPS (*see* STOOP)
Is 46: 1 Bel bows down, Nebo s

STOP (*see* STOPPED, STOPS, UNSTOPPED)
2Ki 3:19 s up every spring of water,
2Ch 32: 3 commanders to s the water
Neh 5:10 Please, let us s this usury
Job 38:11 here your proud waves must s
Ps 35: 3 And s those who pursue me
Prov 17:14 therefore s contention before
Prov 20: 3 for a man to s striving,
Ezek 45: 9 s dispossessing My people,"
2Co 11:10 no one shall s me from this

STOPPED (*see* STOP)
Gen 8: 2 windows of heaven were also s
Gen 26:15 Now the Philistines had s up
Gen 26:18 for the Philistines had s
Gen 29:35 Then she s bearing
Gen 30: 9 saw that she had s bearing
Gen 41:49 the sea, until he s counting
Lev 15: 3 or his body is s up by his
Num 16:48 so the plague was s
Num 16:50 meeting, for the plague had s
Num 25: 8 So the plague was s among the
Josh 10:13 stood still, and the moon s
Ruth 1:18 her, she s speaking to her
2Sa 15:17 him, and s at the outskirts
1Ki 15:21 that he s building Ramah, and
2Ki 3:25 they s up all the springs of
2Ki 13:18 he struck three times, and s
2Ch 16: 5 that he s building Ramah and
2Ch 32: 4 who s all the springs and the
2Ch 32:30 This same Hezekiah also s the
Neh 12:39 they s by the Gate of the
Ps 63:11 who speak lies shall be s
Ps 106:30 And so the plague was s
Jer 38:27 So they s speaking with him,
Jer 43: 1 when Jeremiah had s speaking
Jer 44:18 But since we s burning
Zech 7:11 s their ears so that they
Luke 5: 4 Now when He had s speaking
Luke 8:44 her flow of blood s
Acts 7:57 s their ears, and ran at him
Acts 21:32 soldiers, they s beating Paul
Rom 3:19 that every mouth may be s
Tit 1:11 whose mouths must be s, who
Heb 11:33 s the mouths of lions,

STOPS (*see* STOP)
1Ki 18:44 go down before the rain s you
Ps 58: 4 the deaf cobra that s its ear
Ps 107:42 And all iniquity s its mouth
Is 33:15 who s his ears from hearing

STORAGE (*see* STORE)
1Ki 9:19 all the s cities that Solomon
2Ch 8: 4 all the s cities which he
2Ch 8: 6 all the s cities that Solomon
2Ch 16: 4 all the s cities of Naphtali
2Ch 17:12 and s cities in Judah

STORE (*see* STORAGE, STORED, STOREHOUSE, STOREROOMS, STORES, STORING)
Gen 41:35 and s up grain under the
Num 19: 9 s them outside the camp in a
Deut 14:28 s it up within your gates
Deut 32:34 this not laid up in s with Me
1Ch 27:28 Joash was over the s of oil
Job 36:13 in heart s up wrath
Prov 10:14 Wise people s up knowledge,
Is 3: 1 from Judah the stock and the s
Amos 3:10 Who s up violence and robbery
Luke 12:17 I have no room to s my crops
Luke 12:18 there I will s all my crops
2Pe 3: 7 kept in s by the same word

STORED (*see* STORE)
2Ki 5:24 and s them away in the house
Ezra 6: 1 treasures were s in Babylon
Neh 13: 5 had s the grain offerings
Prov 13:22 is s up for the righteous
Jer 36:20 but they s the scroll in the
Hos 13:12 his sin is s up

STOREHOUSE (*see* STORE, STOREHOUSES)
1Ch 26:15 Gate, and to his sons the s
1Ch 26:17 day, and for the s two by two
Neh 10:38 God, to the rooms of the s
Neh 12:44 of the s for the offerings
Neh 13:12 new wine and the oil to the s
Neh 13:13 the s Shelemiah the priest
Mal 3:10 all the tithes into the s
Luke 12:24 which have neither s nor barn

STOREHOUSES (*see* STOREHOUSE)
Gen 41:56 and Joseph opened all the s
Deut 28: 8 the blessing on you in your s
1Ch 27:25 was over the s in the field
2Ch 32:28 s for the harvest of grain,
Ps 33: 7 He lays up the deep in s
Jer 50:26 open her s; cast her up
Joel 1:17 the clods, s are in shambles

STOREROOMS (*see* STORE)
Neh 10:37 to the s of the house of our
Neh 10:39 to the s where the articles
Neh 12:25 watch at the s of the gates
Neh 13: 4 the s of the house of our God

STORES (*see* STORE)
2Ch 11:11 and s of food, oil, and wine
Prov 2: 7 He s up sound wisdom for the

STORIES (*see* STORY)
Ezek 41: 6 side chambers were in three s
Ezek 41:16 all around their three s
Ezek 42: 3 against gallery in three s

Ezek 42: 5 and middle **s** of the building
Ezek 42: 6 For they were in three **s** and

STORING (*see* STORE)
1Co 16: 2 **s** up as he may prosper, that
1Ti 6:19 **s** up for themselves a good

STORK (*see* STORK'S)
Lev 11:19 the **s**, the heron after its
Deut 14:18 the **s**, the heron after its
Ps 104:17 The **s** has her home in the fir
Jer 8: 7 Even the **s** in the heavens
Zech 5: 9 wings like the wings of a **s**

STORK'S (*see* STORK)
Job 39:13 and pinions like the kindly **s**

STORM (*see* STORMY, WINDSTORM)
Job 21:18 chaff that a **s** carries away
Job 26:12 He breaks up the **s**
Job 30:14 the ruinous **s** they roll along
Job 36:33 also, concerning the rising **s**
Ps 55: 8 my escape From the windy **s**
Ps 83:15 And frighten them with Your **s**
Ps 107:29 He calms the **s**, So that its
Prov 1:27 your terror comes like a **s**
Is 4: 6 and for a shelter from **s** and
Is 25: 4 distress, a refuge from the **s**
Is 25: 4 is as a **s** against the wall
Is 28: 2 of hail and a destroying **s**
Is 29: 6 and great noise, with **s** and
Ezek 38: 9 will ascend, coming like a **s**
Nah 1: 3 in the whirlwind and in the **s**

STORMY (*see* STORM)
Ps 107:25 commands and raises the **s** wind
Ps 148: 8 **S** wind, fulfilling His word
Ezek 13:11 a **s** wind shall tear it down
Ezek 13:13 I will cause a **s** wind to

STORY (*see* STORIES)
1Ki 6: 8 **s** was on the right side of
1Ki 6: 8 up by stairs to the middle **s**
Ezek 41: 6 thirty chambers in each **s**
Ezek 41: 7 one went up from **s** to **s**
Ezek 41: 7 **s** to the highest by way of
Acts 20: 9 he fell down from the third **s**

STOUT (*see* STOUTEST, STOUTHEARTED)
Judg 3:29 of Moab, all **s** men of valor

STOUTEST (*see* STOUT)
Ps 78:31 them, And slew the **s** of them

STOUTHEARTED (*see* STOUT)
1Ch 12:33 **s** men who could keep ranks
Ps 76: 5 The **s** were plundered

STOVE
Lev 11:35 it is an oven or cooking **s**

STRAGGLERS
Deut 25:18 all the **s** at your rear, when

STRAIGHT
Josh 6: 5 go up every man **s** before him
Josh 6:20 every man **s** before him, and
1Sa 6:12 headed **s** for the road to Beth
Ps 5: 8 Make Your way **s** before my
Prov 4:25 Let your eyes look **s** ahead
Prov 9:15 by, who go **s** on their way
Eccl 1:15 is crooked cannot be made **s**
Eccl 7:13 for who can make **s** what He
Is 40: 3 make **s** in the desert a
Is 40: 4 places shall be made **s**, and
Is 42:16 them, and crooked places **s**
Is 45: 2 and make the crooked places **s**
Jer 31: 9 in a **s** way in which they
Jer 31:39 line shall again extend **s**
Ezek 1: 7 Their legs were **s**, and the
Ezek 1: 9 but each one went **s** forward
Ezek 1:12 And each one went **s** forward
Ezek 1:23 their wings spread out **s**, one
Ezek 10:22 They each went **s** forward
Amos 4: 3 each one **s** ahead of her, and
Matt 3: 3 of the LORD, make His paths **s**
Mark 1: 3 of the LORD, make His paths **s**
Luke 3: 4 of the LORD, make His paths **s**
Luke 3: 5 places shall be made **s** and the
Luke 13:13 and immediately she was made **s**
John 1:23 Make **s** the way of the LORD,"
Acts 9:11 and go to the street called **S**
Acts 13:10 the **s** ways of the Lord
Acts 14:10 Stand up **s** on your feet
Acts 16:11 Troas, we ran a **s** course to
Acts 21: 1 running a **s** course we came to
Heb 12:13 make **s** paths for your feet,

STRAIGHTFORWARD
Gal 2:14 not **s** about the truth of the

STRAIN (*see* STRAINING)
Matt 23:24 who **s** out a gnat and swallow a

STRAINING (*see* STRAIN)
Mark 6:48 Then He saw them **s** at rowing

STRAITS
Deut 28:53 desperate **s** in which your
Deut 28:55 desperate **s** in which your
Deut 28:57 desperate **s** in which your
Lam 1: 3 overtake her in dire **s**

STRAND
Judg 16: 9 as a **s** of yarn breaks when it
Song 4: 3 lips are like a **s** of scarlet

STRANGE (*see* STRANGER)
Ex 30: 9 not offer **s** incense on it
2Ki 19:24 I have dug and drunk **s** water
Ps 114: 1 from a people of **s** language
Prov 23:33 Your eyes will see **s** things
Jer 18:14 be forsaken for **s** waters
Hos 8:12 were considered a **s** thing
Luke 5:26 We have seen **s** things today
Acts 17:20 some **s** things to our ears
Heb 13: 9 with various and **s** doctrines
1Pe 4: 4 they think it **s** that you do
1Pe 4:12 do not think it **s** concerning
1Pe 4:12 you, as though some **s** thing
Jude 7 and gone after **s** flesh, are

STRANGER (*see* STRANGE, STRANGER'S, STRANGERS)
Gen 17: 8 the land in which you are a **s**
Gen 17:12 **s** who is not your descendant
Gen 17:27 or bought with money from a **s**
Gen 28: 4 the land in which you are a **s**
Gen 37: 1 land where his father was a **s**
Gen 42: 7 but he acted as a **s** to them
Ex 2:22 I have been a **s** in a foreign
Ex 12:19 whether he is a **s** or a native
Ex 12:48 when a **s** sojourns with you and
Ex 12:49 for the **s** who sojourns among
Ex 18: 3 I have been a **s** in a foreign
Ex 20:10 nor your **s** who is within your
Ex 22:21 mistreat a **s** nor oppress him
Ex 23: 9 you shall not oppress a **s**
Ex 23: 9 for you know the heart of a **s**
Ex 23:12 and the **s** may be refreshed
Ex 29:33 but a **s** shall not eat them,
Lev 16:29 or a **s** who sojourns among you
Lev 17:12 nor shall any **s** who sojourns
Lev 17:15 of your own country or a **s**
Lev 18:26 any **s** who sojourns among you
Lev 19:10 them for the poor and the **s**
Lev 19:33 if a **s** sojourns with you in
Lev 19:34 But the **s** who dwells among
Lev 23:22 for the poor and for the **s**
Lev 24:16 the **s** as well as him who is
Lev 24:22 have the same law for the **s**
Lev 25: 6 for the **s** who sojourns with
Lev 25:35 like a **s** or a sojourner, that
Lev 25:47 Now if a sojourner or **s**
Lev 25:47 sells himself to the **s** or
Num 9:14 if a **s** sojourns among you, and
Num 9:14 one ordinance, both for the **s**
Num 15:14 if a **s** sojourns with you, or
Num 15:15 for the **s** who sojourns with
Num 15:15 so shall the **s** be before the
Num 15:16 for the **s** who sojourns with
Num 15:26 the **s** who sojourns among them
Num 15:29 for the **s** who sojourns among
Num 15:30 he is native-born or a **s**,
Num 19:10 to the **s** who sojourns among
Num 35:15 children of Israel, for the **s**
Deut 1:16 or the **s** who is with him
Deut 5:14 nor your **s** who is within your
Deut 10:18 and the widow, and loves the **s**
Deut 10:19 Therefore love the **s**, for you
Deut 14:29 with you, and the **s** and the
Deut 16:11 is within your gates, the **s**
Deut 16:14 and the Levite, the **s** and the
Deut 24:17 due the **s** or the fatherless
Deut 24:19 it shall be for the **s**, the
Deut 24:20 it shall be for the **s**, the
Deut 24:21 it shall be for the **s**, the
Deut 25: 5 to a **s** outside the family
Deut 26:11 and the **s** who is among you
Deut 26:12 given it to the Levite, the **s**
Deut 26:13 them to the Levite, the **s**
Deut 27:19 the justice due the **s**, the
Deut 29:11 also the **s** who is in your
Deut 31:12 and the **s** who is within your
Josh 8:33 the **s** as well as he who was
Josh 20: 9 for the **s** who sojourned among
Job 19:15 maidservants, count me as a **s**
Ps 39:12 For I am a **s** with You, A
Ps 69: 8 become a **s** to my brothers
Ps 94: 6 They slay the widow and the **s**
Ps 119:19 I am a **s** in the earth
Prov 6: 1 hands in pledge for a **s**,
Prov 11:15 for a **s** will suffer for it
Prov 14:10 a **s** does not share its joy
Prov 20:16 of one who is surety for a **s**
Prov 27: 2 a **s**, and not your own lips
Prov 27:13 of him who is surety for a **s**
Jer 7: 6 if you do not oppress the **s**
Jer 14: 8 You be like a **s** in the land
Jer 22: 3 and do no violence to the **s**
Ezek 22: 7 they have oppressed the **s**
Ezek 22:29 they wrongfully oppress the **s**
Ezek 47:23 whatever tribe the **s** sojourns
Matt 25:35 I was a **s** and you took Me in
Matt 25:38 When did we see You a **s** and
Matt 25:43 I was a **s** and you did not
Matt 25:44 or a **s** or naked or sick or in
Luke 24:18 You the only **s** in Jerusalem
John 10: 5 will by no means follow a **s**

STRANGER'S (*see* STRANGER)
Lev 25:47 to a member of the **s** family

STRANGERS (*see* STRANGER)
Gen 15:13 be **s** in a land that is not
Gen 31:15 we not considered **s** by him
Gen 36: 7 were **s** could not support them
Ex 6: 4 in which they were **s**
Ex 22:21 for you were **s** in the land of
Ex 23: 9 because you were **s** in the
Lev 17: 8 or of the **s** who sojourn among
Lev 17:10 or of the **s** who sojourn among
Lev 17:13 or of the **s** who sojourn among
Lev 19:34 for you were **s** in the land of
Lev 20: 2 or of the **s** who sojourn in
Lev 22:18 Israel, or of the **s** in Israel
Lev 25:23 for you are **s** and sojourners
Lev 25:45 the **s** who sojourn among you
Deut 10:19 for you were **s** in the land of
Josh 8:35 the **s** who were living among
1Ch 16:19 indeed very few, and **s** in it
Ps 54: 3 For **s** have risen up against
Ps 105:12 Indeed very few, and **s** in it
Ps 109:11 And let **s** plunder his labor
Ps 146: 9 The LORD watches over the **s**
Prov 5:17 own, and not for **s** with you
Is 1: 7 **s** devour your land in your
Is 1: 7 desolate, as overthrown by **s**
Is 5:17 of the fat ones **s** shall eat
Is 14: 1 The **s** will be joined with
Is 61: 5 **S** shall stand and feed your
Jer 51:51 for **s** have come into the
Ezek 7:21 plunder into the hands of **s**
Ezek 11: 9 you into the hands of **s**, and
Ezek 14: 7 or of the **s** who sojourn in
Ezek 16:32 who takes **s** instead of her
Ezek 28: 7 I will bring **s** against you
Ezek 47:22 for the **s** who sojourn among
Obad 11 in the day that **s** carried
Matt 17:25 from their own sons or from **s**
Matt 17:26 Peter said to Him, "From **s**."
Matt 27: 7 potter's field, to bury **s** in
John 10: 5 do not know the voice of **s**
Acts 13:17 as **s** in the land of Egypt
Eph 2:12 and **s** from the covenants of
Eph 2:19 you are no longer **s** and
1Ti 5:10 children, if she has lodged **s**
Heb 11:13 and confessed that they were **s**
Heb 13: 2 Do not forget to entertain **s**
3Jn 5 do for the brethren and for **s**

STRANGLED (*see* STRANGLING)
Acts 15:20 immorality, from things **s**
Acts 15:29 from blood, from things **s**
Acts 21:25 from blood, from things **s**

STRANGLING (*see* STRANGLED)
Job 7:15 so that my soul chooses **s**

STRAP (*see* STRAPS)
Gen 14:23 from a thread to a sandal **s**
Is 5:27 nor the **s** of their sandals be
Mark 1: 7 I, whose sandal **s** I am not

Ps 37:39 He is their s in the time of
Ps 38:10 My heart pants, my s fails me
Ps 39:13 from me, that I may regain s
Ps 43: 2 For You are the God of my s
Ps 46: 1 God is our refuge and s, A
Ps 52: 7 who did not make God his s
Ps 54: 1 And vindicate me by Your s
Ps 59: 9 O You his S, I will wait for
Ps 59:17 To You, O my S, I will sing
Ps 62: 7 The rock of my s, And my
Ps 65: 6 the mountains by His s, Being
Ps 68:28 God has commanded your s
Ps 68:34 Ascribe s to God
Ps 68:34 And His s is in the clouds
Ps 68:35 of Israel is He who gives s
Ps 71: 9 forsake me when my s fails
Ps 71:16 go in the s of the Lord GOD
Ps 71:18 Your s to this generation
Ps 73: 4 death, But their s is firm
Ps 73:26 But God is the s of my heart
Ps 74:13 You divided the sea by Your s
Ps 77:14 Your s among the peoples
Ps 78: 4 praises of the LORD, And His s
Ps 78:51 The first of their s in the
Ps 78:61 And delivered His s into
Ps 80: 2 and Manasseh, Stir up Your s
Ps 81: 1 Sing aloud to God our s
Ps 84: 5 is the man whose s is in You
Ps 84: 7 They go from s to s
Ps 86:16 Give Your s to Your servant,
Ps 88: 4 I am like a man who has no s
Ps 89:17 You are the glory of their s
Ps 90:10 if by reason of s they are
Ps 93: 1 He has girded Himself with s
Ps 96: 6 S and beauty are in His
Ps 96: 7 Give to the LORD glory and s
Ps 99: 4 The King's s also loves
Ps 102:23 He weakened my s in the way
Ps 103:20 His angels, Who excel in s
Ps 105: 4 Seek the LORD and His s
Ps 105:36 The first of all their s
Ps 110: 2 the rod of Your s out of Zion
Ps 118:14 The LORD is my s and song, And
Ps 132: 8 You and the ark of Your s
Ps 138: 3 me bold with s in my soul
Ps 140: 7 the s of my salvation, You
Ps 147:10 delight in the s of the horse
Prov 3: 8 flesh, and s to your bones
Prov 8:14 I am understanding, I have s
Prov 10:29 the LORD is s for the upright
Prov 14: 4 comes by the s of an ox
Prov 20:29 glory of young men is their s
Prov 24: 5 man of knowledge increases s
Prov 24:10 of adversity, your s is small
Prov 31: 3 Do not give your s to women
Prov 31:17 She girds herself with s, and
Prov 31:25 S and honor are her clothing
Eccl 9:16 Wisdom is better than s
Eccl 10:10 edge, then he must use more s
Eccl 10:17 for s and not for drunkenness
Is 10:13 By the s of my hand I have
Is 12: 2 For YAH, the LORD, is my s
Is 23: 4 the s of the sea, saying,
Is 23:10 there is no more s
Is 23:14 for your s is laid waste
Is 25: 4 You have been a s to the poor
Is 25: 4 poor, a s to the needy in his
Is 26: 4 the LORD, is everlasting s
Is 27: 5 Or let him take hold of My s
Is 28: 6 for s to those who turn back
Is 30: 2 in the s of Pharaoh, and to
Is 30: 3 Therefore the s of Pharaoh
Is 30:15 and confidence shall be your s
Is 33: 6 times, and the s of salvation
Is 36: 5 having counsel and s for war
Is 37: 3 but there is no s to bring
Is 40: 9 lift up your voice with s
Is 40:26 might and the s of His power
Is 40:29 have no might He increases s
Is 40:31 the LORD shall renew their s
Is 41: 1 let the people renew their s
Is 42:25 His anger and the s of battle
Is 44:12 it with the s of his arms
Is 44:12 he is hungry, and his s fails
Is 45:24 I have righteousness and s
Is 49: 4 I have spent my s for nothing
Is 49: 5 and My God shall be My s)
Is 51: 9 Awake, awake, put on s, O arm
Is 52: 1 Put on your s, O Zion
Is 62: 8 hand and by the arm of His s
Is 63: 1 in the greatness of His s
Is 63: 6 down their s to the earth
Is 63:15 Where are Your zeal and Your s
Jer 16:19 O LORD, my s and my fortress,
Jer 17: 5 in man and makes flesh his s
Jer 51:53 fortify the height of her s
Lam 1: 6 that flee without s before
Lam 1:14 He made my s fail
Lam 3:18 My s and my hope Have
Ezek 30:15 fury on Sin, the s of Egypt
Ezek 30:18 her arrogant s shall cease in
Ezek 33:28 her arrogant s shall cease
Dan 2:37 given you a kingdom, power, s
Dan 2:41 yet the s of the iron shall
Dan 10: 8 and no s remained in me
Dan 10: 8 in me, and I retained no s
Dan 10:16 me, and I have retained no s
Dan 10:17 no s remains in me now, nor
Dan 11: 2 by his s, through his riches,
Dan 11:15 shall have no s to resist
Dan 11:17 the s of his whole kingdom
Hos 7: 9 Aliens have devoured his s
Hos 12: 3 in his s he struggled with
Joel 2:22 and the vine yield their s
Joel 3:16 and the s of the children of
Amos 3:11 he shall sap your s from you
Amos 6:13 for ourselves by our own s
Mic 5: 4 flock in the s of the LORD
Nah 3: 9 Ethiopia and Egypt were her s
Hab 3:19 The LORD God is my s
Hag 2:22 I will destroy the s of the
Zech 12: 5 of Jerusalem are my s in the
Mark 12:30 your mind, and with all your s
Mark 12:33 the soul, and with all the s
Luke 1:51 He has shown s with His arm
Luke 10:27 your soul, with all your s
Acts 3: 7 and ankle bones received s
Acts 9:22 increased all the more in s
Acts 14: 8 a certain man without s in
Rom 5: 6 when we were still without s
1Co 15:56 and the s of sin is the law
2Co 1: 8 beyond measure, above s, so
2Co 12: 9 for My s is made perfect in
Heb 11:11 received s to conceive seed
Rev 1:16 like the sun shining in its s
Rev 3: 8 for you have a little s, have
Rev 5:12 and riches and wisdom, and s
Rev 12:10 Now salvation, and s, and the
Rev 14:10 full s into the cup of His

STRENGTHEN (*see* STRENGTH, STRENGTHENED, STRENGTHENING, STRENGTHENS)
Deut 3:28 and encourage him and s him
Judg 16:28 S me, I pray, just this once,
2Sa 11:25 S your attack against the
1Ki 20:22 said to him, "Go, s yourself
2Ki 15:19 to s the kingdom in his hand
Ezra 6:22 to s their hands in the work
Neh 6: 9 therefore, O God, s my hands
Job 16: 5 But I would s you with my
Ps 20: 2 And s you out of Zion
Ps 27:14 And He shall s your heart
Ps 31:24 He shall s your heart, All
Ps 41: 3 The LORD will s him on his
Ps 68:28 S, O God, what You have done
Ps 89:21 Also My arm shall s him
Ps 119:28 S me according to Your word
Is 22:21 robe and s him with your belt
Is 30: 2 to s themselves in the
Is 33:23 they could not s their mast
Is 35: 3 S the weak hands, and make
Is 41:10 I will s you, yes, I will
Is 54: 2 your cords, and s your stakes
Is 58:11 in drought, and s your bones
Jer 23:14 they also s the hands of
Ezek 7:13 no one will s himself who
Ezek 16:49 neither did she s the hand of
Ezek 30:24 I will s the arms of the
Ezek 30:25 Thus I will s the arms of
Ezek 34:16 the broken and s what was sick
Dan 11: 1 stood up to confirm and s him
Amos 2:14 strong shall not s his power
Nah 2: 1 S your flanks! Fortify your
Zech 10: 6 I will s the house of Judah,
Zech 10:12 So I will s them in the LORD,
Luke 22:32 to Me, s your brethren
Heb 12:12 Therefore s the hands which
1Pe 5:10 while, perfect, establish, s
Rev 3: 2 s the things which remain,

STRENGTHENED (*see* STRENGTHEN)
Gen 48: 2 Israel s himself and sat up on
Judg 3:12 So the LORD s Eglon king of
Judg 7:11 your hands shall be s to go
1Sa 23:16 woods and s his hand in God
1Sa 30: 6 But David s himself in the
2Sa 2: 7 let your hands be s, and be
1Ch 11:10 who s themselves with him in
2Ch 1: 1 of David was s in his kingdom
2Ch 11:17 So they s the kingdom of
2Ch 12: 1 and had s himself, that he
2Ch 12:13 So King Rehoboam s himself in
2Ch 13: 7 s themselves against Rehoboam
2Ch 17: 1 and s himself against Israel
2Ch 21: 4 he s himself and killed all
2Ch 23: 1 year Jehoiada s himself, and
2Ch 25:11 Then Amaziah s himself, and
2Ch 26: 8 for he s himself exceedingly
2Ch 32: 5 he s himself, built up all
2Ch 32: 8 And the people were s by the
Job 4: 3 and you have s weak hands
Job 4: 4 you have s the feeble knees
Ps 52: 7 s himself in his wickedness
Ps 147:13 For He has s the bars of your
Prov 8:28 when He s the fountains of
Ezek 13:22 you have s the hands of the
Ezek 34: 4 The weak you have not s, nor
Dan 10:18 of a man touched me and s me
Dan 10:19 when he spoke to me I was s
Dan 10:19 lord speak, for you have s me
Dan 11: 6 with him who s her in those
Hos 7:15 s their arms, yet they devise
Acts 9:19 had received food, he was s
Acts 15:32 with many words and s them
Acts 16: 5 churches were s in the faith
Rom 4:20 but was s in faith, giving
Eph 3:16 to be s with might through
Col 1:11 s with all might, according
2Ti 4:17 s me, so that the message

STRENGTHENING (*see* STRENGTHEN)
2Sa 3: 6 that Abner was s his hold on
Luke 22:43 to Him from heaven, s Him
Acts 14:22 s the souls of the disciples,
Acts 15:41 and Cilicia, s the churches
Acts 18:23 in order, s all the disciples

STRENGTHENS (*see* STRENGTHEN)
Ps 104:15 And bread which s man's heart
Prov 31:17 with strength, and s her arms
Eccl 7:19 Wisdom s the wise more than
Phil 4:13 through Christ who s me

STRENUOUSLY
Ezek 29:18 army to labor s against Tyre

STRETCH (*see* STRETCHED, STRETCHES, STRETCHING)
Ex 3:20 So I will s out My hand and
Ex 7: 5 when I s out My hand on Egypt
Ex 7:19 and s out your hand over the
Ex 8: 5 S out your hand with your
Ex 8:16 S out your rod, and strike
Ex 9:22 S out your hand toward heaven
Ex 10:12 S out your hand over the land
Ex 10:21 S out your hand toward heaven
Ex 14:16 s out your hand over the sea
Ex 14:26 S out your hand over the sea,
Ex 25:20 And the cherubim shall s out
Num 24: 6 Like valleys that s out, like
Josh 8:18 S out the spear that is in
1Sa 24: 6 to s out my hand against him,
1Sa 24:10 I will not s out my hand
1Sa 26: 9 for who can s out his hand
1Sa 26:11 s out my hand against the
1Sa 26:23 but I would not s out my hand
2Ki 21:13 I will s over Jerusalem the
Job 1:11 s out Your hand and touch all
Job 2: 5 But s out Your hand now, and
Job 11:13 s out your hands toward Him
Job 30:24 Surely He would not s out His
Ps 68:31 s out her hands to God
Ps 104: 2 Who s out the heavens like a
Ps 138: 7 You will s out Your hand
Ps 144: 7 S out Your hand from above
Is 28:20 short for a man to s out on
Is 34:11 He shall s out over it the
Is 54: 2 let them s out the curtains
Jer 6:12 for I will s out My hand
Jer 15: 6 Therefore I will s out My
Jer 51:25 I will s out My hand against
Ezek 6:14 So I will s out My hand

Ezek 14: 9 I will **s** out My hand against
Ezek 14:13 I will **s** out My hand against
Ezek 25: 7 I will **s** out My hand against
Ezek 25:13 I will also **s** out My hand
Ezek 25:16 I will **s** out My hand against
Ezek 35: 3 I will **s** out My hand against
Ezek 38:12 to **s** out your hand against
Dan 11:42 He shall **s** out his hand
Amos 6: 4 **s** out on your couches, eat
Zeph 1: 4 I will **s** out My hand against
Zeph 2:13 And He will **s** out His hand
Matt 12:13 to the man, "**S** out your hand
Mark 3: 5 to the man, "**S** out your hand
Luke 6:10 to the man, "**S** out your hand
John 21:18 you will **s** out your hands, and

STRETCHED (*see* STRETCH)
Gen 22:10 Abraham **s** out his hand and
Gen 48:14 Then Israel **s** out his right
Ex 8: 6 So Aaron **s** out his hand over
Ex 8:17 For Aaron **s** out his hand with
Ex 9:15 Now if I had **s** out My hand
Ex 9:23 Moses **s** out his rod toward
Ex 10:13 So Moses **s** out his rod over
Ex 10:22 So Moses **s** out his hand
Ex 14:21 Then Moses **s** out his hand
Ex 14:27 Moses **s** out his hand over the
Ex 15:12 You **s** out Your right hand
Josh 8:18 Joshua **s** out the spear that
Josh 8:19 soon as he had **s** out his hand
Josh 8:26 with which he **s** out the spear
Judg 5:26 She **s** her hand to the tent
1Sa 14:27 therefore he **s** out the end of
2Sa 24:16 when the angel **s** out His hand
1Ki 6:21 He **s** gold chains across the
1Ki 6:27 they **s** out the wings of the
1Ki 13: 4 that he **s** out his hand from
1Ki 13: 4 which he **s** out toward him,
1Ki 17:21 he **s** himself out on the child
2Ki 4:34 he **s** himself out on the child
2Ki 4:35 up and **s** himself out on him
1Ch 21:16 sword **s** out over Jerusalem
Job 38: 5 Or who **s** the line upon it
Ps 44:20 God, Or **s** out our hands to a
Ps 77: 2 My hand was **s** out in the
Ps 88: 9 I have **s** out my hands to You
Prov 1:24 I have **s** out my hand and no
Is 5:25 he has **s** out His hand against
Is 5:25 but His hand is **s** out still
Is 9:12 but His hand is **s** out still
Is 9:17 but His hand is **s** out still
Is 9:21 but His hand is **s** out still
Is 10: 4 but His hand is **s** out still
Is 14:26 is **s** out over all the nations
Is 14:27 His hand is **s** out, and who
Is 16: 8 Her branches are **s** out, they
Is 23:11 He **s** out His hand over the
Is 42: 5 **s** them out, Who spread forth
Is 45:12 My hands that **s** out the
Is 48:13 hand has **s** out the heavens
Is 51:13 Who **s** out the heavens and laid
Is 65: 2 I have **s** out My hands all day
Jer 10:12 has **s** out the heavens at His
Jer 51:15 and **s** out the heaven by His
Lam 2: 8 He has **s** out a line
Ezek 1:11 Their wings were **s** upward
Ezek 1:22 **s** out over their heads
Ezek 2: 9 there was a hand **s** out to me
Ezek 8: 3 He **s** out the form of a hand,
Ezek 10: 7 the cherub **s** out his hand
Ezek 16:27 I **s** out My hand against you,
Ezek 17: 7 **s** its branches toward him,
Hos 7: 5 He **s** out his hand with
Zech 1:16 shall be **s** out over Jerusalem
Matt 12:13 And he **s** it out, and it was
Matt 12:49 He **s** out His hand toward His
Matt 14:31 Jesus **s** out His hand and
Matt 26:51 with Jesus **s** out his hand
Mark 3: 5 he **s** it out, and his hand was
Acts 12: 1 that time Herod the king **s**
Acts 26: 1 So Paul **s** out his hand and
Rom 10:21 I have **s** out My hands to a

STRETCHES (*see* STRETCH)
Job 15:25 for he **s** out his hand against
Job 26: 7 He **s** out the north over empty
Prov 31:19 She **s** out her hands to the
Is 31: 3 When the LORD **s** out His hand
Is 40:22 Who **s** out the heavens like a
Is 44:13 The craftsman **s** out his rule
Is 44:24 Who **s** out the heavens all

Ezek 30:25 he **s** it out against the land
Zech 12: 1 who **s** out the heavens, lays

STRETCHING (*see* STRETCH)
Is 8: 8 the **s** out of his wings will
Acts 4:30 by **s** out Your hand to heal,

STRICKEN
1Sa 5:12 die were **s** with the tumors
Ps 102: 4 My heart is **s** and withered
Is 1: 5 Why should you be **s** again
Is 5:25 **s** them, and the hills trembled
Is 16: 7 surely they are **s**
Is 24:12 left, and the gate is **s** with
Is 53: 4 yet we esteemed Him **s**,
Is 53: 8 of My people He was **s**
Jer 5: 3 You have **s** them, but they
Jer 14:19 Why have You **s** us so that
Lam 4: 9 **s** for lack of the fruits of
Hos 6: 1 He has **s**, but He will bind us
Hos 9:16 Ephraim is **s**, their root is

STRICTER (*see* STRICTEST, STRICTLY, STRICTNESS)
Jas 3: 1 we shall receive a **s** judgment

STRICTEST (*see* STRICTER)
Acts 26: 5 that according to the **s** sect

STRICTLY (*see* STRICTER)
Deut 2:27 I will keep **s** to the road
1Sa 14:28 Your father **s** charged the
Mark 1:43 He **s** warned him and sent him
Mark 5:43 But He commanded them **s** that
Luke 9:21 He **s** warned and commanded
Acts 5:28 Did we not **s** command you not

STRICTNESS (*see* STRICTER)
Acts 22: 3 to the **s** of our fathers' law

STRIFE
Gen 13: 7 And there was **s** between the
Gen 13: 8 let there be no **s** between you
Num 27:14 of Zin, during the **s** of the
Ps 31:20 From the **s** of tongues
Ps 55: 9 violence and **s** in the city
Ps 80: 6 made us a **s** to our neighbors
Ps 106:32 Him also at the waters of **s**
Prov 10:12 Hatred stirs up **s**, but love
Prov 15:18 A wrathful man stirs up **s**
Prov 16:28 A perverse man sows **s**, and a
Prov 17: 1 house full of feasting with **s**
Prov 17:14 The beginning of **s** is like
Prov 17:19 loves transgression loves **s**
Prov 22:10 yes, **s** and reproach will cease
Prov 26:20 is no talebearer, **s** ceases
Prov 26:21 a contentious man to kindle **s**
Prov 28:25 of a proud heart stirs up **s**
Prov 29:22 An angry man stirs up **s**, and a
Prov 30:33 forcing of wrath produces **s**
Is 58: 4 Indeed you fast for **s** and
Jer 15:10 you have borne me, a man of **s**
Dan 11:10 his sons shall stir up **s**, and
Dan 11:10 to his fortress and stir up **s**
Hab 1: 3 there is **s**, and contention
Rom 1:29 full of envy, murder, **s**,
Rom 13:13 and lewdness, not in **s** and envy
1Co 3: 3 For where there are envy, **s**
Phil 1:15 Christ even from envy and **s**
1Ti 6: 4 from which come envy, **s**,
2Ti 2:23 knowing that they generate **s**

STRIKE (*see* STRIKES, STRIKING, STRUCK)
Ex 3:20 **s** Egypt with all My wonders
Ex 7:17 I will **s** the waters which are
Ex 8:16 **s** the dust of the land, so
Ex 12:12 will **s** all the firstborn in
Ex 12:13 when I **s** the land of Egypt
Ex 12:22 and **s** the lintel and the two
Ex 12:23 through to **s** the Egyptians
Ex 12:23 into your houses to **s** you
Ex 17: 6 and you shall **s** the rock, and
Num 14:12 I will **s** them with the
Deut 13:15 you shall surely **s** the
Deut 20:13 you shall **s** every male in it
Deut 28:22 The LORD will **s** you with
Deut 28:27 The LORD will **s** you with the
Deut 28:28 The LORD will **s** you with
Deut 28:35 The LORD will **s** you in the
Deut 33:11 **s** the loins of those who rise
Judg 20:31 They began to **s** down and kill
Judg 20:39 Now Benjamin had begun to **s**
Judg 21:10 **s** the inhabitants of Jabesh
1Sa 17:46 into my hand, and I will **s** you

1Sa 22:17 to **s** the priests of the LORD
1Sa 26: 8 let me **s** him at once with the
1Sa 26: 8 have to **s** him a second time
1Sa 26:10 lives, the LORD shall **s** him
2Sa 2:22 Why should I **s** you to the
2Sa 5:24 will go out before you to **s**
2Sa 13:28 when I say to you, '**S** Amnon
2Sa 15:14 **s** the city with the edge of
2Sa 17: 2 and I will **s** only the king
2Sa 18:11 why did you not **s** him there
2Sa 20:10 and he did not **s** him again
1Ki 2:29 saying, "Go, **s** him down
1Ki 2:31 **s** him down and bury him, that
1Ki 14:15 For the LORD will **s** Israel
1Ki 20:35 of the LORD, "**S** me, please
1Ki 20:35 And the man refused to **s** him
1Ki 20:37 man, and said, "**S** me, please
2Ki 6:18 **S** this people, I pray, with
2Ki 9: 7 You shall **s** down the house
2Ki 13:17 for you must **s** the Syrians at
2Ki 13:18 of Israel, "**S** the ground"
2Ki 13:19 But now you will **s** Syria only
1Ch 14:15 has gone out before you to **s**
2Ch 21:14 the LORD will **s** your people
Job 16:10 they **s** me reproachfully on
Job 36:32 and commands it to **s**
Ps 81: 2 **s** the timbrel, The pleasant
Ps 121: 6 sun shall not **s** you by day
Ps 141: 5 Let the righteous **s** me
Prov 17:26 nor to **s** princes for their
Prov 19:25 **S** a scoffer, and the simple
Is 3:17 therefore the Lord will **s**
Is 10:24 He shall **s** you with a rod and
Is 11: 4 He shall **s** the earth with the
Is 11:15 **s** it in the seven streams, and
Is 19:22 will **s** Egypt, He will **s**
Is 49:10 heat nor sun shall **s** them
Is 58: 4 and to **s** with the fist of
Jer 21: 6 I will **s** the inhabitants of
Jer 21: 7 he shall **s** them with the edge
Jer 43:11 he shall **s** the land of Egypt
Jer 46:13 come and **s** the land of Egypt
Jer 49:28 king of Babylon shall **s**
Ezek 5: 2 **s** around it with the sword,
Ezek 21:12 therefore **s** your thigh
Ezek 21:14 and **s** your hands together
Ezek 32:15 when I **s** all who dwell in it,
Amos 9: 1 **S** the doorposts, that the
Mic 5: 1 they will **s** the judge of
Zech 10:11 and **s** the waves of the sea
Zech 12: 4 I will **s** every horse with
Zech 12: 4 will **s** every horse of the
Zech 13: 7 **S** the Shepherd, and the sheep
Zech 14:12 with which the LORD will **s**
Mal 4: 6 and **s** the earth with a curse
Matt 26:31 I will **s** the Shepherd, and
Mark 14:27 I will **s** the Shepherd, and
Luke 22:49 shall we **s** with the sword
John 18:23 but if well, why do you **s** Me
Acts 23: 2 by him to **s** him on the mouth
Acts 23: 3 God will **s** you, you
Rev 7:16 the sun shall not **s** them, nor
Rev 11: 6 and to **s** the earth with all
Rev 19:15 it He should **s** the nations

STRIKES (*see* STRIKE)
Ex 21:12 He who **s** a man so that he
Ex 21:15 he who **s** his father or his
Ex 21:18 one **s** the other with a stone
Ex 21:26 if a man **s** the eye of his
Num 35:16 But if he **s** him with an iron
Num 35:17 if he **s** him with a stone in
Num 35:18 Or if he **s** him with a wooden
Num 35:21 or in enmity he **s** him with
Deut 19: 5 **s** his neighbor so that he
Deut 19:11 **s** him mortally, so that he
Job 34:26 He **s** them as wicked men in
Job 39:20 majestic snorting **s** terror
Is 9:13 do not turn to Him who **s** them
Is 41: 7 inspired him who **s** the anvil
Lam 3:30 cheek to the one who **s** him
Ezek 7: 9 know that I am the LORD who **s**
Zech 14:18 plague with which the LORD **s**
Luke 6:29 To him who **s** you on the one
2Co 11:20 if one **s** you on the face
Rev 9: 5 of a scorpion when it **s** a man

STRIKING (*see* STRIKE)
Ex 2:13 Why are you **s** your companion
2Sa 24:17 angel who was **s** the people
Mic 6:13 also make you sick by **s** you

Acts 27:41 But s a place where two seas

STRING (*see* STRINGED, STRINGS)
Ps 11: 2 ready their arrow on the s
Ps 21:12 on Your s toward their faces

STRINGED (*see* STRING)
1Sa 10: 5 place with a s instrument
2Sa 6: 5 harps, on s instruments, on
1Ki 10:12 s instruments for singers
1Ch 13: 8 harps, on s instruments, on
1Ch 15:16 s instruments, harps, and
1Ch 15:28 music with s instruments and
1Ch 16: 5 Jeiel with s instruments and
1Ch 25: 1 s instruments, and cymbals
1Ch 25: 6 s instruments, and harps, for
2Ch 5:12 s instruments and harps, and
2Ch 9:11 s instruments for singers
2Ch 20:28 with s instruments and harps
2Ch 29:25 with s instruments, and with
Neh 12:27 and s instruments and harps
Ps 150: 4 Praise Him with s instruments
Is 14:11 sound of your s instruments
Is 38:20 we will sing my songs with s
Amos 5:23 melody of your s instruments
Amos 6: 5 to the sound of s instruments
Hab 3:19 With my s instruments

STRINGS (*see* STRING)
1Ch 15:20 with s according to Alamoth
Ps 33: 2 with an instrument of ten s
Ps 92: 3 On an instrument of ten s
Ps 144: 9 On a harp of ten s I will
Is 5:12 The harp and the s, the

STRIP (*see* STRIPPED, STRIPS)
Num 20:26 s Aaron of his garments and
1Sa 31: 8 came to s the slain, that
1Ch 10: 8 came to s the slain, that
Is 32:11 s yourselves, make yourselves
Ezek 16:39 They shall also s you of your
Ezek 23:26 They shall also s you of your
Dan 4:14 s off its leaves and scatter
Hos 2: 3 Lest I s her naked and expose
Mic 3: 2 who s the skin from My people

STRIPE (*see* STRIPES)
Ex 21:25 wound for wound, s for s

STRIPES (*see* STRIPE)
Ps 89:32 rod, And their iniquity with s
Prov 20:30 as do s the inner depths of
Is 53: 5 and by His s we are healed
Luke 12:47 shall be beaten with many s
Luke 12:48 committed things worthy of s
Acts 16:23 they had laid many s on them
Acts 16:33 the night and washed their s
2Co 6: 5 in s, in imprisonments, in
2Co 11:23 in s above measure, in
2Co 11:24 I received forty s minus one
1Pe 2:24 by whose s you were healed

STRIPPED (*see* STRIP)
Gen 37:23 that they s Joseph of his
Ex 33: 6 Israel s themselves of their
Num 20:28 Moses s Aaron of his garments
1Sa 19:24 he also s off his clothes and
1Sa 31: 9 s off his armor, and sent word
2Ki 18:16 At that time Hezekiah s the
1Ch 10: 9 And they s him and took his
2Ch 20:25 jewelry, which they s off for
Job 19: 9 He has s me of my glory, and
Job 22: 6 s the naked of their clothing
Joel 1: 7 he has s it bare and thrown it
Mic 1: 8 wail and howl, I will go s
Matt 27:28 And they s Him and put a
Luke 10:30 who s him of his clothing,

STRIPS (*see* STRIP)
Gen 30:37 trees, peeled white s in them
Ps 29: 9 birth, And s the forests bare
John 19:40 bound it in s of linen with

STRIVE (*see* STRIVES, STRIVING, STRIVINGS)
Gen 6: 3 shall not s with man forever
Judg 11:25 Did he ever s against Israel
Ps 35: 1 with those who s with me
Ps 103: 9 He will not always s with us
Prov 3:30 Do not s with a man without
Is 41:11 those who s with you shall
Is 45: 9 Let the potsherd s with the
Luke 13:24 S to enter through the narrow
Acts 24:16 I myself always s to have a
Rom 15:30 that you s together with me
2Ti 2:14 to s about words to no profit

STRIVES (*see* STRIVE)
Is 45: 9 to him who s with his Maker

STRIVING (*see* STRIVE)
Prov 20: 3 honorable for a man to stop s
Eccl 2:22 for the s of his heart with
Phil 1:27 with one mind s together for
Col 1:29 s according to His working
Heb 12: 4 to bloodshed, s against sin

STRIVINGS (*see* STRIVE)
2Sa 22:44 me from the s of my people
Ps 18:43 me from the s of the people
Tit 3: 9 and s about the law

STROKE
Deut 19: 5 his hand swings a s with the
Esth 9: 5 with the s of the sword, with
Is 14: 6 in wrath with a continual s
Is 30:26 heals the s of their wound
Jer 14:17 been broken with a mighty s
Ezek 24:16 of your eyes with one s

STRONG (*see* STRONGER, STRONGEST, STRONGLY)
Gen 49:14 Issachar is a s donkey, lying
Gen 49:24 s by the hands of the Mighty
Ex 6: 1 For with a s hand he will let
Ex 6: 1 with a s hand he will drive
Ex 10:19 turned a very s west wind
Ex 13: 9 for with a s hand the LORD
Ex 14:21 the sea to go back by a s
Num 13:18 who dwell in it are s or weak
Num 13:28 who dwell in the land are s
Num 20:20 many men and with a s hand
Deut 2:36 was not one city too s for us
Deut 11: 8 you today, that you may be s
Deut 31: 6 Be s and of good courage, do
Deut 31: 7 Be s and of good courage, for
Deut 31:23 Be s and of good courage
Josh 1: 6 Be s and of good courage, for
Josh 1: 7 Only be s and very courageous,
Josh 1: 9 Be s and of good courage
Josh 1:18 Only be s and of good courage
Josh 10:25 be s and of good courage, for
Josh 14:11 As yet I am as s this day as
Josh 17:13 the children of Israel grew s
Josh 17:18 have iron chariots and are s
Josh 23: 9 before you great and s nations
Judg 1:28 to pass, when Israel was s
Judg 9:51 But there was a s tower in
Judg 14:14 out of the s came something
Judg 18:26 that they were too s for him
1Sa 4: 9 Be s and conduct yourselves
1Sa 14:52 when Saul saw any s man or
2Sa 10:11 the Syrians are too s for me
2Sa 10:11 of Ammon are too s for you
2Sa 10:12 let us be s for our people and
2Sa 15:12 And the conspiracy grew s, for
2Sa 16:21 who are with you will be s
2Sa 22:18 delivered me from my s enemy
2Sa 22:18 for they were too s for me
1Ki 2: 2 be s, therefore, and prove
1Ki 8:42 great name and Your s hand
1Ki 19:11 great and s wind tore into the
2Ki 2:16 there are fifty s men with
2Ki 24:16 one thousand, all who were s
1Ch 19:12 the Syrians are too s for me
1Ch 19:12 of Ammon are too s for you
1Ch 19:13 let us be s for our people and
1Ch 22:13 Be s and of good courage
1Ch 28:10 be s, and do it
1Ch 28:20 Be s and of good courage, and
2Ch 11:12 spears, and made them very s
2Ch 11:17 of Solomon s for three years
2Ch 15: 7 But you, be s and do not let
2Ch 16: 9 to show Himself s on behalf
2Ch 25: 8 Be s in battle
2Ch 26:15 helped till he became s
2Ch 26:16 But when he was s his heart
2Ch 32: 7 Be s and courageous
Ezra 9:12 prosperity, that you may be s
Neh 1:10 power, and by Your s hand
Neh 9:25 And they took s cities and a
Job 8: 2 your mouth be like a s wind
Job 9:19 of strength, indeed He is s
Job 15:26 against Him with his s,
Job 33:19 with s pain in many of his
Job 37:18 s as a cast metal mirror
Job 39: 4 they grow s with grain
Ps 18:17 delivered me from my s enemy
Ps 18:17 For they were too s for me
Ps 19: 5 rejoices like a s man to run
Ps 22:12 S bulls of Bashan have
Ps 24: 8 The LORD s and mighty, The
Ps 30: 7 have made my mountain stand s
Ps 31:21 kindness in a s city
Ps 35:10 from him who is too s for him
Ps 38:19 are vigorous, and they are s
Ps 60: 9 will bring me into the s city
Ps 61: 3 And a s tower from the enemy
Ps 71: 3 Be my s habitation, To which
Ps 71: 7 many, But You are my s refuge
Ps 80:15 that You made s for Yourself
Ps 80:17 whom You made s for Yourself
Ps 89:13 S is Your hand, and high is
Ps 108:10 will bring me into the s city
Ps 136:12 With a s hand, and with an
Prov 7:26 were slain by her were s men
Prov 10:15 man's wealth is his s city
Prov 14:26 LORD there is s confidence
Prov 18:10 name of the LORD is a s tower
Prov 18:11 man's wealth is his s city
Prov 18:19 harder to win than a s city
Prov 21:14 behind the back, s wrath
Prov 24: 5 A wise man is s, yes, a man
Prov 30:25 the ants are a people not s
Prov 31: 6 Give s drink to him who is
Eccl 9:11 nor the battle to the s, nor
Eccl 12: 3 and the s men bow down
Song 8: 6 for love is as s as death
Is 1:31 The s shall be as tinder, and
Is 8: 7 the waters of the River, s
Is 8:11 thus to me with a s hand, and
Is 17: 9 In that day his s cities will
Is 24: 9 s drink is bitter to those
Is 25: 3 Therefore the s people will
Is 26: 1 We have a s city
Is 27: 1 His severe sword, great and s
Is 28: 2 s one, like a tempest of hail
Is 28:22 lest your bonds be made s
Is 31: 1 because they are very s, but
Is 35: 4 Be s, do not fear
Is 40:10 GOD shall come with a s hand
Is 41:21 Bring forth your s reasons
Is 53:12 divide the spoil with the s
Is 60:22 and a small one a s nation
Jer 4:12 a wind too s for these will
Jer 8:16 of the neighing of His s ones
Jer 21: 5 hand and with a s arm, even in
Jer 32:21 and wonders, with a s hand
Jer 47: 3 hooves of his s horses, at
Jer 48:14 mighty and s men for the war'
Jer 48:17 How the s staff is broken,
Jer 49:19 the habitation of the s
Jer 50:34 Their Redeemer is s
Jer 50:44 the habitation of the s
Jer 51:12 make the guard s, set up the
Ezek 3: 8 face s against their faces
Ezek 3: 8 your forehead s against their
Ezek 3:14 of the LORD was s upon me
Ezek 7:24 the pomp of the s to cease
Ezek 19:11 She had s branches for
Ezek 19:12 Her s branches were broken and
Ezek 19:14 so that she has no s branch
Ezek 22:14 or can your hands remain s
Ezek 26:11 your s pillars will fall to
Ezek 26:17 city, who was s at sea, she
Ezek 27:24 in s twined cords, which were
Ezek 30:21 to make it s enough to hold a
Ezek 30:22 his arms, both the s one and
Ezek 31:17 and those who were its s arm
Ezek 32:21 The s among the mighty Shall
Ezek 34:16 will destroy the fat and the s
Dan 2:40 kingdom shall be as s as iron
Dan 2:42 the kingdom shall be partly s
Dan 4:11 The tree grew and became s
Dan 4:20 saw, which grew and became s
Dan 4:22 who have grown and become s
Dan 7: 7 and terrible, exceedingly s
Dan 8: 8 but when he became s, the
Dan 10:19 be s, yes, be s
Dan 11: 5 of the South shall become s
Dan 11:23 become s with a small number
Dan 11:32 who know their God shall be s
Joel 1: 6 come up against My land, s
Joel 2: 2 a people come, great and s
Joel 2: 5 like a s people set in battle
Joel 2:11 for s is the One who executes
Joel 3:10 let the weak say, 'I am s
Amos 2: 9 and he was as s as the oaks
Amos 2:14 the s shall not strengthen

Hab 3:13 You s the head from the house
Hag 2:17 I s you with blight and
Matt 26:51 s the servant of the high
Matt 26:67 others s Him with the palms
Matt 26:68 Who is the one who s You
Matt 27:30 the reed and s Him on the head
Mark 14:47 s the servant of the high
Mark 14:65 the officers s Him with the
Mark 15:19 Then they s Him on the head
Luke 22:50 one of them s the servant of
Luke 22:64 they s Him on the face and
Luke 22:64 Who is it that s You
John 18:10 s the high priest's servant,
John 18:22 the officers who stood by s
John 19: 3 they s Him with their hands
Acts 7:24 and s down the Egyptian
Acts 12: 7 he s Peter on the side and
Acts 12:23 an angel of the Lord s him
Acts 23: 3 to be s contrary to the law
Acts 27:17 the Syrtis Sands, they s sail
2Co 4: 9 s down, but not destroyed
Rev 8:12 And a third of the sun was s

STRUCTURE
Ezek 40: 2 like the s of a city
Ezek 40: 5 the width of the wall s, one
Ezek 41: 7 s increased as one went up

STRUGGLE (*see* STRUGGLED, STRUGGLING)
Judg 12: 2 I were in a great s with the
Heb 10:32 a great s with sufferings

STRUGGLED (*see* STRUGGLE)
Gen 25:22 But the children s together
Gen 32:28 for you have s with God and
Hos 12: 3 in his strength he s with God
Hos 12: 4 Yes, he s with the Angel and

STRUGGLING (*see* STRUGGLE)
Ezek 16: 6 saw you s in your own blood,
Ezek 16:22 and bare, s in your blood

STUBBLE
Ex 5:12 to gather s instead of straw
Ex 15: 7 which consumed them like s
Job 13:25 And will You pursue dry s
Job 41:28 become like s to him
Is 5:24 as the fire devours the s
Is 33:11 you shall bring forth s
Is 40:24 will take them away like s
Is 41: 2 sword, as driven s to his bow
Is 47:14 Behold, they shall be as s
Jer 13:24 s that passes away by the
Joel 2: 5 fire that devours the s, like
Obad 18 the house of Esau shall be s
Nah 1:10 devoured like s fully dried
Mal 4: 1 all who do wickedly will be s

STUBBORN (*see* STUBBORN-HEARTED, STUBBORNLY, STUBBORNNESS)
Ex 13:15 when Pharaoh was s about
Deut 21:18 If a man has a s and
Deut 21:20 city, 'This son of ours is s
Judg 2:19 doings nor from their s way
Ps 78: 8 be like their fathers, A s
Ps 81:12 over to their own s heart
Jer 6:28 They are all s rebels,
Ezek 2: 4 are impudent and s children
Hos 4:16 Israel is s like a s calf;

STUBBORN-HEARTED (*see* STUBBORN)
Is 46:12 Listen to Me, you s, who are

STUBBORNLY (*see* STUBBORN)
Job 15:26 running s against Him with

STUBBORNNESS (*see* STUBBORN)
Deut 9:27 look on the s of this people
1Sa 15:23 s is as iniquity and idolatry
Jer 3:17 the s of their evil heart

STUBS
Is 7: 4 two s of smoking firebrands

STUCK (*see* STICK)
1Sa 26: 7 camp, with his spear s in the
2Sa 23:10 and his hand s to the sword
Job 29:10 their tongue s to the roof of
Acts 27:41 and the prow s fast and

STUDENT
1Ch 25: 8 great, the teacher with the s

STUDIED (*see* STUDY)
Ps 111: 2 S by all who have pleasure in
John 7:15 know letters, having never s

STUDIES (*see* STUDY)
Prov 15:28 the righteous s how to answer

STUDS
Song 1:11 of gold with s of silver

STUDY (*see* STUDIED, STUDIES)
Eccl 12:12 much s is wearisome to the

STUFF
Josh 7:11 also put it among their own s

STUMBLE (*see* STUMBLED, STUMBLES, STUMBLING, STUMBLINGBLOCK)
Lev 26:37 They shall s over one another
Ps 64: 8 So He will make them s over
Ps 119:165 And nothing causes them to s
Ps 140: 4 purposed to make my steps s
Prov 3:23 way, and your foot will not s
Prov 4:12 when you run, you will not s
Prov 4:19 do not know what makes them s
Is 5:27 will be weary or s among them
Is 8:15 And many among them shall s
Is 28: 7 in vision, they s in judgment
Is 59:10 we s at noonday as at
Is 63:13 that they might not s
Jer 13:16 before your feet s on the
Jer 18:15 themselves to s in their ways
Jer 20:11 my persecutors will s, and
Jer 31: 9 way in which they shall not s
Jer 46: 6 they will s and fall toward
Jer 50:32 The most proud shall s and
Ezek 14: 3 them to s into iniquity
Ezek 14: 4 causes him to s into iniquity
Ezek 14: 7 causes him to s into iniquity
Ezek 21:15 heart may melt and many may s
Ezek 36:15 your nation to s anymore,"
Dan 11:19 but he shall s and fall, and
Hos 4: 5 you shall s in the day
Hos 4: 5 shall s with you in the night
Hos 5: 5 Ephraim s in their iniquity
Hos 14: 9 but transgressors s in them
Nah 2: 5 they s in their walk
Nah 3: 3 they s over the corpses
Mal 2: 8 caused many to s at the law
Matt 26:31 to s because of Me this night
Matt 26:33 are made to s because of You
Matt 26:33 I will never be made to s
Mark 4:17 sake, immediately they s
Mark 9:42 ones who believe in Me to s
Mark 14:27 to s because of Me this night
Mark 14:29 Even if all are made to s
John 11: 9 in the day, he does not s
John 16: 1 you should not be made to s
1Co 8:13 if food makes my brother s
1Co 8:13 lest I make my brother s
2Co 11:29 Who is made to s, and I do not
Jas 2:10 yet s in one point, he is
Jas 3: 2 For we all s in many things
Jas 3: 2 If anyone does not s in word
1Pe 2: 8 They s, being disobedient
2Pe 1:10 these things you will never s

STUMBLED (*see* STUMBLE)
1Sa 2: 4 those who s are girded with
2Sa 6: 6 hold of it, for the oxen s
1Ch 13: 9 hold the ark, for the oxen s
Ps 27: 2 My enemies and foes, They s
Ps 73: 2 for me, my feet had almost s
Is 3: 8 For Jerusalem s, and Judah is
Jer 46:12 man has s against the mighty
Hos 14: 1 for you have s because of
Rom 9:32 For they s at that stumbling
Rom 11:11 have they s that they should

STUMBLES (*see* STUMBLE)
Prov 24:17 your heart be glad when he s
Hos 5: 5 Judah also s with them
Matt 13:21 of the word, immediately he s
John 11:10 one walks in the night, he s
Rom 14:21 by which your brother s or is

STUMBLING (*see* STUMBLE)
Job 4: 4 have upheld him who was s
Prov 24:11 and hold back those s to the
Is 8:14 a sanctuary, but a stone of s
Is 57:14 take the s block out of the
Jer 6:21 I will lay s blocks before
Jer 20:10 watched for my s, saying
Ezek 3:20 I lay a s block before him,
Ezek 7:19 their s block of iniquity
Zeph 1: 3 the s blocks along with the
Rom 9:32 they stumbled at that s stone
Rom 9:33 I lay in Zion a s stone and
Rom 11: 9 a s block and a recompense to
Rom 14:13 not to put a s block or a
1Co 1:23 to the Jews a s block and to
1Co 8: 9 liberty of yours become a s
1Pe 2: 8 A stone of s and a rock of
1Jn 2:10 is no cause for s in him
Jude 24 is able to keep you from s
Rev 2:14 a s block before the children

STUMBLINGBLOCK (*see* STUMBLE)
Lev 19:14 nor put a s before the blind,

STUMP
Job 14: 8 its s may die in the ground,
Is 6:13 whose s remains when it is
Is 6:13 the holy seed shall be its s
Dan 4:15 Nevertheless leave the s and
Dan 4:23 destroy it, but leave its s
Dan 4:26 the command to leave the s

STUPID
Job 18: 3 regarded as s in your sight
Prov 12: 1 but he who hates reproof is s
Prov 30: 2 I am more s than any man, and

STUPOR
Rom 11: 8 has given them a spirit of s

STYLE
Ps 144:12 Sculptured in palace s

SUAH
1Ch 7:36 The sons of Zophah were S

SUBDUE (*see* SUBDUED, SUBDUES)
Gen 1:28 fill the earth and s it
1Ch 17:10 Also I will s all your
Ps 47: 3 He will s the peoples under
Ps 81:14 I would soon s their enemies,
Is 45: 1 to s nations before him and
Dan 7:24 ones, and shall s three kings
Mic 7:19 us, and will s our iniquities
Zech 9:15 devour and s with sling stones
Phil 3:21 to s all things to Himself

SUBDUED (*see* SUBDUE)
Num 32:22 the land is s before the LORD
Num 32:29 and the land is s before you
Deut 20:20 war with you, until it is s
Josh 18: 1 And the land was s before them
Judg 3:30 So Moab was s that day under
Judg 4:23 So on that day God s Jabin
Judg 8:28 Thus Midian was s before the
Judg 11:33 were s before the children of
1Sa 7:13 So the Philistines were s
2Sa 8: 1 the Philistines and s them
2Sa 8:11 the nations which he had s
2Sa 22:40 you have s under me those who
2Ki 18: 8 He s the Philistines, as far
1Ch 18: 1 s them, and took Gath and its
1Ch 20: 4 And they were s
1Ch 22:18 the land is s before the LORD
2Ch 13:18 of Israel were s at that time
Neh 9:24 you s before them the
Ps 18:39 You have s under me those who
Heb 11:33 who through faith s kingdoms

SUBDUES (*see* SUBDUE)
2Sa 22:48 who s the people under me,
Ps 18:47 me, And s the peoples under me
Ps 144: 2 Who s my people under me

SUBJECT (*see* SUBJECTED, SUBJECTION)
Gen 30:33 when the s of my wages comes
Mark 3:29 but is s to eternal
Luke 2:51 was s to them, but His mother
Luke 10:17 are s to us in Your name
Luke 10:20 that the spirits are s to you
Rom 8: 7 for it is not s to the law of
Rom 13: 1 soul be s to the governing
Rom 13: 5 Therefore you must be s, not
1Co 14:32 are s to the prophets
1Co 15:28 all things are made s to Him
1Co 15:28 Son Himself will also be s to
Eph 5:24 as the church is s to Christ
Col 2:20 world, do you s yourselves to
Tit 3: 1 Remind them to be s to rulers
Heb 2:15 their lifetime s to bondage
1Pe 3:22 having been made s to Him

SUBJECTED (*see* SUBJECT)
Rom 8:20 creation was s to futility
Rom 8:20 of Him who s it in hope

SUBJECTION (*see* SUBJECT)
Ps 106:42 into s under their hand
Jer 34:11 brought them into s as male
Jer 34:16 and brought them back into s
1Co 9:27 my body and bring it into s
Heb 2: 5 we speak, in s to angels
Heb 2: 8 things in s under his feet
Heb 2: 8 He put all in s under him
Heb 12: 9 in s to the Father of spirits

SUBMISSION (*see* SUBMIT)
Ps 81:15 LORD would pretend s to Him
Gal 2: 5 not yield s even for an hour
1Ti 2:11 learn in silence with all s
1Ti 3: 4 in s with all reverence

SUBMISSIVE (*see* SUBMIT)
1Co 14:34 but they are to be s, as the
Heb 13:17 who rule over you, and be s
1Pe 2:18 be s to your masters with all
1Pe 3: 1 be s to your own husbands,
1Pe 3: 5 being s to their own husbands
1Pe 5: 5 Yes, all of you be s to one

SUBMIT (*see* SUBMISSION, SUBMISSIVE, SUBMITS, SUBMITTED, SUBMITTING)
Gen 16: 9 s yourself under her hand
Deut 33:29 Your enemies shall s to you
2Sa 22:45 The foreigners s to me
Ps 18:44 The foreigners s to me
Ps 66: 3 shall s themselves to You
1Co 16:16 that you also s to such, and
Eph 5:22 s to your own husbands, as to
Col 3:18 s to your own husbands, as is
Jas 4: 7 Therefore s to God
1Pe 2:13 Therefore s yourselves to
1Pe 5: 5 s yourselves to your elders

SUBMITS (*see* SUBMIT)
Ps 68:30 Till everyone s himself with

SUBMITTED (*see* SUBMIT)
1Ch 29:24 s themselves to King Solomon
Rom 10: 3 have not s to the

SUBMITTING (*see* SUBMIT)
Eph 5:21 s to one another in the fear

SUBSIDE (*see* SUBSIDED)
Amos 8: 8 s like the River of Egypt
Amos 9: 5 s like the River of Egypt

SUBSIDED (*see* SUBSIDE)
Gen 8: 1 the earth, and the waters s
Esth 2: 1 the wrath of King Ahasuerus s
Esth 7:10 Then the king's wrath s

SUBSTANCE
Ex 16:14 was a small round s, as fine
Deut 11: 6 all the s that was in their
Deut 33:11 Bless his s, LORD, and accept
1Ch 28: 1 the stewards over all the s
Job 5: 5 and a snare snatches their s
Ps 17:14 of their s for their babes
Ps 139:16 Your eyes saw my s, being yet
Prov 6:31 up all the s of his house
Obad 13 their s in the day of their
Mic 4:13 their s to the Lord of the
Luke 8: 3 provided for Him from their s
Col 2:17 come, but the s is of Christ
Heb 11: 1 Now faith is the s of things

SUBSTITUTE
Lev 27:10 He shall not s it or

SUBVERT
Job 8: 3 Does God s judgment
Lam 3:36 or s a man in his cause
Tit 1:11 who s whole households,

SUCCEED (*see* SUCCEEDED, SUCCEEDING, SUCCEEDS, SUCCESS)
Num 14:41 For this will not s
Deut 25: 6 s to the name of his dead
Jer 32: 5 Chaldeans, you shall not s"'

SUCCEEDED (*see* SUCCEED)
Ezek 16:13 beautiful, and s to royalty
Acts 24:27 years Porcius Festus s Felix

SUCCEEDING (*see* SUCCEED)
Lev 21:17 descendants in s generations

SUCCEEDS (*see* SUCCEED)
Prov 30:23 who s her mistress
Eccl 2:12 can the man do who s the king

SUCCESS (*see* SUCCEED, SUCCESSFUL)
Gen 24:12 please give me s this day
Josh 1: 8 and then you will have good s
2Ki 14:10 Glory in your s, and stay at
Job 6:13 And is s driven from me
Job 30:22 You spoil my s
Eccl 10:10 but wisdom brings s

SUCCESSFUL (*see* SUCCESS, SUCCESSFULLY)
Gen 39: 2 Joseph, and he was a s man

SUCCESSFULLY (*see* SUCCESSFUL)
2Ch 7:11 Solomon s accomplished all
Mic 7: 3 That they may s do evil with

SUCCESSIVE
Gen 32:16 distance between s droves
Joel 2: 2 even for many s generations

SUCCOTH
Gen 33:17 And Jacob journeyed to S,
Gen 33:17 name of the place is called S
Ex 12:37 journeyed from Rameses to S
Ex 13:20 took their journey from S
Num 33: 5 from Rameses and camped at S
Num 33: 6 They departed from S and
Josh 13:27 Beth Haram, Beth Nimrah, S
Judg 8: 5 Then he said to the men of S
Judg 8: 6 And the leaders of S said
Judg 8: 8 the men of S had answered him
Judg 8:14 a young man of the men of S
Judg 8:14 down for him the leaders of S
Judg 8:15 Then he came to the men of S
Judg 8:16 them he taught the men of S
1Ki 7:46 cast in clay molds, between S
2Ch 4:17 cast in clay molds, between S
Ps 60: 6 measure out the Valley of S
Ps 108: 7 measure out the Valley of S

SUCCOTH BENOTH
2Ki 17:30 The men of Babylon made S

SUCCULENT
Job 33:20 bread, and his soul s food

SUCH (*see* PREFACE)

SUCHATHITES
1Ch 2:55 the Shimeathites, and the S

SUCK (*see* SUCKLING)
Job 20:16 He will s the poison of
Job 39:30 Its young ones s up blood

SUCKLING (*see* SUCK)
1Sa 7: 9 And Samuel took a s lamb and

SUDDEN (*see* SUDDENLY)
Job 22:10 you, and s fear troubles you,
Prov 3:25 Do not be afraid of s terror
1Th 5: 3 then s destruction comes

SUDDENLY (*see* SUDDEN)
Gen 41: 2 S there came up out of the
Gen 41: 5 s seven heads of grain came
Gen 41:18 S seven cows came up out of
Gen 41:22 s seven heads came up on one
Num 6: 9 anyone dies very s beside him
Num 12: 4 S the LORD said to Moses,
Num 12:10 s Miriam became leprous, as
Num 16:42 s the cloud covered it, and
Num 35:22 pushes him s without enmity
Deut 7: 4 against you and destroy you s
Josh 10: 9 therefore came upon them s
Josh 11: 7 them s by the waters of Merom
Judg 19:22 s certain men of the city,
2Sa 15:14 depart, lest he overtake us s
1Ki 11:22 that s you seek to go to your
1Ki 18: 7 on his way, s Elijah met him
1Ki 19: 5 s an angel touched him, and
1Ki 19:13 s a voice came to him, and
1Ki 20:13 S a prophet approached Ahab
2Ki 2:11 that s a chariot of fire
2Ki 3:20 that s water came by way of
2Ki 13:21 that s they spied a band of
2Ch 29:36 the events took place so s
Job 1:19 and s a great wind came from
Job 5: 3 but s I cursed his habitation
Job 9:23 If the scourge slays s, He
Ps 6:10 turn back and be ashamed s
Ps 64: 4 S they shoot at him and do not
Ps 64: 7 S they shall be wounded
Prov 6:15 his calamity shall come s
Prov 6:15 s he shall be broken without
Prov 24:22 their calamity will rise s
Prov 29: 1 will s be destroyed, and that
Eccl 9:12 when it falls s upon them
Is 29: 5 it shall be in an instant, s
Is 30:13 wall, whose breaking comes s
Is 47:11 shall come upon you s, which
Is 48: 3 S I did them, and they came to
Jer 4:20 S my tents are plundered, and
Jer 6:26 plunderer will s come upon us
Jer 15: 8 and terror to fall on them s
Jer 18:22 You bring a troop s upon them
Jer 49:19 but I will s make him run
Jer 50:44 make them s run away from her
Jer 51: 8 Babylon has s fallen and been
Ezek 9: 2 And s six men came from the
Ezek 37: 7 was a noise, and s a rattling
Dan 7: 5 s another beast, a second,
Dan 8: 5 s a male goat came from the
Dan 8:15 that s there stood before me
Dan 10:10 Then, s, a hand touched me,
Dan 10:16 And s, one having the likeness
Hab 2: 7 not your creditors rise up s
Mal 3: 1 will s come to His temple,
Matt 3:17 s a voice came from heaven,
Matt 8:24 s a great tempest arose on
Matt 8:29 s they cried out, saying,
Matt 8:32 s the whole herd of swine ran
Matt 9:20 And s, a woman who had a flow
Matt 17: 5 s a voice came out of the
Matt 26:51 And s, one of those who were
Mark 9: 8 S, when they had looked
Mark 13:36 lest, coming s, he find you
Luke 2:13 s there was with the angel a
Luke 9:38 S a man from the multitude
Luke 9:39 seizes him, and he s cries out
Acts 2: 2 s there came a sound from
Acts 9: 3 s a light shone around him
Acts 16:26 S there was a great
Acts 22: 6 s a great light from heaven
Acts 28: 6 swell up or s fall down dead

SUE (*see* SUIT)
Matt 5:40 If anyone wants to s you and

SUFFER (*see* SUFFERED, SUFFERING, SUFFERS)
Ex 23:26 No one shall s miscarriage or
Job 24:11 winepresses, yet s thirst
Ps 34:10 young lions lack and s hunger
Ps 88:15 I s Your terrors
Prov 11:15 for a stranger will s for it
Prov 19:15 an idle person will s hunger
Prov 19:19 great wrath will s punishment
Dan 6: 2 that the king would s no loss
Joel 1:18 of sheep s your punishment
Matt 16:21 s many things from the elders
Matt 17:12 about to s at their hands
Mark 8:31 Son of Man must s many things
Mark 9:12 that He must s many things
Luke 9:22 Son of Man must s many things
Luke 17:25 first He must s many things
Luke 22:15 Passover with you before I s
Luke 24:46 necessary for the Christ to s
Acts 3:18 that the Christ would s, He
Acts 5:41 to s shame for His name
Acts 7:24 And seeing one of them s wrong
Acts 9:16 he must s for My name's sake
Acts 17: 3 that the Christ had to s and
Acts 26:23 that the Christ would s, that
Rom 8:17 if indeed we s with Him,
1Co 3:15 is burned, he will s loss
1Co 12:26 all the members s with it
2Co 1: 6 sufferings which we also s
2Co 7: 9 that you might s loss from us
Gal 5:11 why do I still s persecution
Gal 6:12 only that they may not s
Phil 1:29 but also to s for His sake,
Phil 4:12 both to abound and to s need
1Th 3: 4 that we would s tribulation
2Th 1: 5 of God, for which you also s
1Ti 4:10 s reproach, because we trust
2Ti 1:12 reason I also s these things
2Ti 2: 9 for which I s trouble as an
2Ti 3:12 Jesus will s persecution
Heb 9:26 He then would have had to s
Heb 11:25 choosing rather to s
1Pe 2:20 and s for it, if you take it
1Pe 3:14 But even if you should s for
1Pe 3:17 to s for doing good than for
1Pe 4:15 none of you s as a murderer
1Pe 4:19 Therefore let those who s
Rev 2:10 which you are about to s

SUFFERED (*see* SUFFER)
Jer 15:15 for Your sake I have **s** rebuke
Matt 27:19 Man, for I have **s** many things
Mark 5:26 had **s** many things from many
Luke 13: 2 because they **s** such things
Luke 24:26 Christ to have **s** these things
Acts 28: 5 into the fire and **s** no harm
2Co 7:12 the sake of him who **s** wrong
Gal 3: 4 Have you **s** so many things in
Phil 3: 8 for whom I have **s** the loss of
1Th 2: 2 even after we had **s** before
1Th 2:14 For you also **s** the same
1Ti 1:19 the faith have **s** shipwreck
Heb 2:18 For in that He Himself has **s**
Heb 5: 8 by the things which He **s**
Heb 13:12 own blood, **s** outside the gate
1Pe 2:21 because Christ also **s** for us
1Pe 2:23 when He **s**, He did not
1Pe 3:18 Christ also **s** once for sins
1Pe 4: 1 since Christ **s** for us in the
1Pe 4: 1 for he who has **s** in the flesh
1Pe 5:10 after you have **s** a while

SUFFERING (*see* SUFFER, SUFFERINGS)
Lam 3:51 my eyes bring **s** to my soul
Acts 1: 3 Himself alive after His **s** by
Heb 2: 9 for the **s** of death crowned
Jas 5:10 the Lord, as an example of **s**
Jas 5:13 Is anyone among you **s**
1Pe 2:19 endures grief, **s** wrongfully
Jude 7 **s** the vengeance of eternal

SUFFERINGS (*see* SUFFERING)
Job 9:28 I am afraid of all my **s**
Rom 8:18 For I consider that the **s** of
2Co 1: 5 For as the **s** of Christ abound
2Co 1: 6 same **s** which we also suffer
2Co 1: 7 as you are partakers of the **s**
Phil 3:10 and the fellowship of His **s**
Col 1:24 I now rejoice in my **s** for you
2Ti 1: 8 but share with me in the **s**
Heb 2:10 salvation perfect through **s**
Heb 10:32 a great struggle with **s**
1Pe 1:11 beforehand the **s** of Christ
1Pe 4:13 you partake of Christ's **s**
1Pe 5: 1 a witness of the **s** of Christ
1Pe 5: 9 knowing that the same **s** are

SUFFERS (*see* SUFFER)
Matt 11:12 kingdom of heaven **s** violence
Matt 17:15 is an epileptic and **s** severely
1Co 12:26 And if one member **s**, all the
1Co 13: 4 Love **s** long and is kind
1Pe 4:16 Yet if anyone **s** as a

SUFFICIENCY (*see* SUFFICIENT)
2Co 3: 5 but our **s** is from God,
2Co 9: 8 having all **s** in all things

SUFFICIENT (*see* SUFFICIENCY, SUFFICIENTLY)
Ex 36: 7 the material they had was **s**
Num 35:30 but one witness is not **s**
Deut 15: 8 lend him **s** for his need,
Deut 33: 7 let his hands be **s** for him
2Ch 30: 3 because a **s** number of priests
Is 40:16 And Lebanon is not **s** to burn
Is 40:16 nor its beasts **s** for a burnt
Matt 6:34 **S** for the day is its own
John 6: 7 of bread is not **s** for them
John 14: 8 the Father, and it is **s** for us
2Co 2: 6 majority is **s** for such a man
2Co 2:16 who is **s** for these things
2Co 3: 5 Not that we are **s** of
2Co 3: 6 who also made us **s** as
2Co 12: 9 My grace is **s** for you, for My

SUFFICIENTLY (*see* SUFFICIENT)
Is 23:18 before the LORD, to eat **s**

SUGGEST (*see* SUGGESTED)
Esth 5:14 in the morning **s** to the king
Esth 6: 4 of the king's palace to **s**
Acts 23:15 **s** to the commander that he be

SUGGESTED (*see* SUGGEST)
Esth 6:10 and the horse, as you have **s**

SUIT (*see* SUE)
Judg 17:10 year, a **s** of clothes, and your
2Sa 15: 4 everyone who has any **s** or

SUITABLE
Lev 16:21 by the hand of a **s** man
Acts 27:12 harbor was not **s** to winter in

SUKKIIM
2Ch 12: 3 the Lubim and the **S** and the

SULFUR
Rev 9:17 hyacinth blue, and **s** yellow

SULLEN
1Ki 20:43 of Israel went to his house **s**
1Ki 21: 4 So Ahab went into his house **s**
1Ki 21: 5 so **s** that you eat no food

SUM (*see* SUMMED)
Gen 25: 7 This is the **s** of the years of
Ex 21:30 imposed on him a **s** of money
2Sa 24: 9 Then Joab gave the **s** of the
1Ch 21: 5 Then Joab gave the **s** of the
Esth 4: 7 the **s** of money that Haman had
Ps 139:17 How great is the **s** of them
Matt 28:12 they gave a large **s** of money
Acts 7:16 a **s** of money from the sons of
Acts 22:28 With a large **s** I obtained

SUMMED (*see* SUM)
Rom 13: 9 are all **s** up in this saying,

SUMMER
Gen 8:22 cold and heat, and winter and **s**
2Sa 16: 1 raisins, one hundred **s** fruits
2Sa 16: 2 **s** fruit for the young men to
Ps 32: 4 turned into the drought of **s**
Ps 74:17 You have made **s** and winter
Prov 6: 8 her supplies in the **s**, and
Prov 10: 5 gathers in **s** is a wise son
Prov 26: 1 As snow in **s** and rain in
Prov 30:25 prepare their food in the **s**
Is 16: 9 fallen over your **s** fruits
Is 18: 6 birds of prey will **s** on them
Is 28: 4 the first fruit before the **s**
Jer 8:20 the **s** is ended, and we are not
Jer 40:10 **s** fruit and oil, put them in
Jer 40:12 wine and **s** fruit in abundance
Jer 48:32 has fallen on your **s** fruit
Dan 2:35 from the **s** threshing floors
Amos 3:15 house along with the **s** house
Amos 8: 1 Behold, a basket of **s** fruit
Amos 8: 2 A basket of **s** fruit
Mic 7: 1 those who gather **s** fruits
Zech 14: 8 in both **s** and winter it shall
Matt 24:32 you know that **s** is near
Mark 13:28 you know that **s** is near
Luke 21:30 yourselves that **s** is now near

SUMMON (*see* SUMMONED, SUMMONING)
Acts 10:22 angel to **s** you to his house
Acts 25: 3 him, that he would **s** him to

SUMMONED (*see* SUMMON)
2Ch 36:10 King Nebuchadnezzar **s** him
Is 31: 4 of shepherds is **s** against him
Acts 6: 2 Then the twelve **s** the

SUMMONING (*see* SUMMON)
Mark 15:44 **s** the centurion, he asked him

SUMPTUOUS (*see* SUMPTUOUSLY)
Hab 1:16 by them their share is **s** and

SUMPTUOUSLY (*see* SUMPTUOUS)
Luke 16:19 linen and fared **s** every day

SUN (*see* SUNDIAL, SUNRISE, SUNSET, SUNSHINE)
Gen 15:12 Now when the **s** was going down
Gen 15:17 when the **s** went down and it
Gen 19:23 The **s** had risen upon the
Gen 28:11 night, because the **s** had set
Gen 32:31 over Penuel the **s** rose on him
Gen 37: 9 And this time, the **s**, the moon
Ex 16:21 when the **s** became hot, it
Ex 17:12 until the going down of the **s**
Ex 22: 3 If the **s** has risen on him,
Ex 22:26 to him before the **s** goes down
Lev 22: 7 when the **s** goes down he shall
Num 2: 3 toward the rising of the **s**
Num 25: 4 before the LORD, out in the **s**
Deut 4:19 heaven, and when you see the **s**
Deut 4:41 toward the rising of the **s**
Deut 4:47 toward the rising of the **s**
Deut 11:30 Jordan, toward the setting **s**
Deut 16: 6 at the going down of the **s**
Deut 17: 3 either the **s** or moon or any
Deut 23:11 and when the **s** sets, he may
Deut 24:13 again when the **s** goes down
Deut 24:15 not let the **s** go down on it,
Deut 33:14 the precious fruits of the **s**
Josh 1: 4 the going down of the **s**,
Josh 8:29 And as soon as the **s** was down
Josh 10:12 **S**, stand still over Gibeon
Josh 10:13 So the **s** stood still, and the
Josh 10:13 So the **s** stood still in the
Josh 10:27 the **s** that Joshua commanded
Josh 12: 1 toward the rising of the **s**
Judg 5:31 who love Him be like the **s**
Judg 9:33 as soon as the **s** is up in the
Judg 14:18 day before the **s** went down
Judg 19:14 the **s** went down on them near
1Sa 11: 9 by the time the **s** is hot
2Sa 2:24 the **s** was going down when
2Sa 3:35 else till the **s** goes down
2Sa 12:11 wives in the sight of this **s**
2Sa 12:12 all Israel, before the **s**
2Sa 23: 4 the morning when the **s** rises
1Ki 22:36 as the **s** was going down, a
2Ki 3:22 and the **s** was shining on the
2Ki 23: 5 incense to Baal, to the **s**
2Ki 23:11 Judah had dedicated to the **s**
2Ki 23:11 chariots of the **s** with fire
Neh 7: 3 be opened until the **s** is hot
Job 8:16 He grows green in the **s**, and
Job 9: 7 He commands the **s**, and it does
Job 30:28 mourning, but not in the **s**
Job 31:26 observed the **s** when it shines
Ps 19: 4 set a tabernacle for the **s**
Ps 50: 1 of the **s** to its going down
Ps 58: 8 that they may not see the **s**
Ps 72: 5 fear You As long as the **s**
Ps 72:17 continue as long as the **s**
Ps 74:16 prepared the light and the **s**
Ps 84:11 For the LORD God is a **s** and
Ps 89:36 his throne as the **s** before Me
Ps 104:19 The **s** knows its going down
Ps 104:22 When the **s** arises, they
Ps 113: 3 the **s** to its going down The
Ps 121: 6 The **s** shall not strike you by
Ps 136: 8 The **s** to rule by day, For His
Ps 148: 3 Praise Him, **s** and moon
Prov 4:18 just is like the shining **s**
Eccl 1: 3 in which he toils under the **s**
Eccl 1: 5 The **s** also rises
Eccl 1: 5 the **s** goes down, and hastens
Eccl 1: 9 is nothing new under the **s**
Eccl 1:14 that are done under the **s**
Eccl 2:11 was no profit under the **s**
Eccl 2:17 the **s** was grievous to me, for
Eccl 2:18 I had toiled under the **s**,
Eccl 2:19 shown myself wise under the **s**
Eccl 2:20 I had toiled under the **s**
Eccl 2:22 he has toiled under the **s**
Eccl 3:16 Moreover I saw under the **s**
Eccl 4: 1 that is done under the **s**
Eccl 4: 3 work that is done under the **s**
Eccl 4: 7 and I saw vanity under the **s**
Eccl 4:15 living who walk under the **s**
Eccl 5:13 which I have seen under the **s**
Eccl 5:18 **s** all the days of his life
Eccl 6: 1 which I have seen under the **s**
Eccl 6: 5 seen the **s** or known anything
Eccl 6:12 happen after him under the **s**
Eccl 7:11 to those who see the **s**
Eccl 8: 9 work that is done under the **s**
Eccl 8:15 under the **s** than to eat,
Eccl 8:15 God gives him under the **s**
Eccl 8:17 work that is done under the **s**
Eccl 9: 3 all that is done under the **s**
Eccl 9: 6 in anything done under the **s**
Eccl 9: 9 He has given you under the **s**
Eccl 9: 9 which you perform under the **s**
Eccl 9:11 and saw under the **s** that
Eccl 9:13 I have also seen under the **s**
Eccl 10: 5 evil I have seen under the **s**
Eccl 11: 7 for the eyes to behold the **s**
Eccl 12: 2 while the **s** and the light, the
Song 1: 6 because the **s** has tanned me
Song 6:10 as the moon, clear as the **s**
Is 13:10 the **s** will be darkened in its
Is 24:23 be disgraced and the **s** ashamed
Is 30:26 will be as the light of the **s**
Is 30:26 the light of the **s** will be
Is 38: 8 the **s** on the sundial of Ahaz
Is 38: 8 So the **s** returned ten
Is 41:25 from the rising of the **s** he
Is 45: 6 **s** to its setting that there

Is 49:10 neither heat nor s shall
Is 59:19 from the rising of the s
Is 60:19 The s shall no longer be your
Is 60:20 Your s shall no longer go
Jer 8: 2 spread them before the s and
Jer 15: 9 her s has gone down while it
Jer 31:35 Who gives the s for a light
Ezek 8:16 the s toward the east
Ezek 32: 7 will cover the s with a cloud
Dan 6:14 down of the s to deliver him
Joel 2:10 the s and moon grow dark, and
Joel 2:31 The s shall be turned into
Joel 3:15 The s and moon will grow dark,
Amos 8: 9 make the s go down at noon
Jon 4: 8 it happened, when the s arose
Jon 4: 8 the s beat on Jonah's head,
Mic 3: 6 the s shall go down on the
Nah 3:17 but when the s rises they
Hab 3:11 The s and moon stood still in
Mal 1:11 For from the rising of the s
Mal 4: 2 the S of Righteousness shall
Matt 5:45 makes His s rise on the evil
Matt 13: 6 But when the s was up they
Matt 13:43 the s in the kingdom of their
Matt 17: 2 His face shone like the s
Matt 24:29 days the s will be darkened
Mark 1:32 evening, when the s had set
Mark 4: 6 But when the s was up it was
Mark 13:24 the s will be darkened, and
Mark 16: 2 the tomb when the s had risen
Luke 4:40 Now when the s was setting
Luke 21:25 there will be signs in the s
Luke 23:45 Then the s was darkened, and
Acts 2:20 The s shall be turned into
Acts 13:11 not seeing the s for a time
Acts 26:13 heaven, brighter than the s
Acts 27:20 Now when neither s nor stars
1Co 15:41 There is one glory of the s
Eph 4:26 do not let the s go down on
Jas 1:11 For no sooner has the s risen
Rev 1:16 the s shining in its strength
Rev 6:12 and the s became black as
Rev 7:16 the s shall not strike them,
Rev 8:12 a third of the s was struck
Rev 9: 2 And the s and the air were
Rev 10: 1 head, his face was like the s
Rev 12: 1 a woman clothed with the s
Rev 16: 8 poured out his bowl on the s
Rev 19:17 an angel standing in the s
Rev 21:23 s or of the moon to shine in
Rev 22: 5 no lamp nor light of the s

SUNDIAL (*see* SUN)
2Ki 20:11 gone down on the s of Ahaz
Is 38: 8 bring the shadow on the s
Is 38: 8 with the sun on the s of Ahaz

SUNG (*see* SING)
Job 36:24 His work, of which men have s
Is 26: 1 be s in the land of Judah
Matt 26:30 And when they had s a hymn
Mark 14:26 And when they had s a hymn

SUNK (*see* SINK)
Ps 9:15 The nations have s down in
Ps 76: 5 They have s into their sleep
Jer 38:22 your feet have s in the mire
Lam 2: 9 Her gates have s into the

SUNRISE (*see* SUN)
Num 21:11 is east of Moab, toward the s
Num 34:15 eastward, toward the s
Josh 1:15 of the Jordan toward the s
Josh 13: 5 and all Lebanon, toward the s
Josh 19:12 the s along the border of
Josh 19:27 toward the s to Beth Dagon
Josh 19:34 by the Jordan toward the s

SUNSET (*see* SUN)
2Ch 18:34 about the time of s he died

SUNSHINE (*see* SUN)
Is 18: 4 place like clear heat in s

SUPERFLUOUS
2Co 9: 1 it is s for me to write to

SUPERVISE (*see* SUPERVISED)
2Ch 34:12 sons of the Kohathites, to s

SUPERVISED (*see* SUPERVISE)
1Ki 5:16 who s the people who labored

SUPH
Deut 1: 1 in the plain opposite S,

SUPHAH
Num 21:14 Waheb in S, the brooks of the

SUPPER
Luke 14:12 When you give a dinner or a s
Luke 14:16 A certain man gave a great s
Luke 14:17 sent his servant at s time to
Luke 14:24 were invited shall taste my s
Luke 17: 8 Prepare something for my s
Luke 22:20 He also took the cup after s
John 12: 2 There they made Him a s
John 13: 2 And s being ended, the devil
John 13: 4 rose from s and laid aside His
John 21:20 leaned on His breast at the s
1Co 11:20 it is not to eat the Lord's S
1Co 11:21 his own s ahead of others
1Co 11:25 He also took the cup after s
Rev 19: 9 to the marriage s of the Lamb
Rev 19:17 for the s of the great God

SUPPLANT (*see* SUPPLANTED)
Jer 9: 4 every brother will utterly s

SUPPLANTED (*see* SUPPLANT)
Gen 27:36 For he has s me these two

SUPPLICATION (*see* SUPPLICATIONS)
1Sa 13:12 I have not made s to the LORD
1Ki 8:28 of Your servant and his s, O
1Ki 8:30 hear the s of Your servant
1Ki 8:33 make s to You in this temple,
1Ki 8:38 whatever s is made by anyone,
1Ki 8:45 their prayer and their s, and
1Ki 8:47 make s to You in the land of
1Ki 8:49 place their prayer and their s
1Ki 8:52 open to the s of Your servant
1Ki 8:52 the s of Your people Israel,
1Ki 8:54 s to the LORD, that he arose
1Ki 8:59 I have made s before the LORD
1Ki 9: 3 your s that you have made
2Ch 6:19 of Your servant and his s, O
2Ch 6:24 make s before You in this
2Ch 6:29 whatever s is made by anyone,
2Ch 6:35 their prayer and their s, and
2Ch 6:37 make s to You in the land of
2Ch 33:13 his entreaty, heard his s
Esth 4: 8 to the king to make s to him
Job 8: 5 make your s to the Almighty,
Ps 6: 9 The LORD has heard my s
Ps 30: 8 And to the LORD I made s
Ps 55: 1 not hide Yourself from my s
Ps 119:170 Let my s come before You
Ps 142: 1 voice to the LORD I make my s
Is 45:14 They will make s to you,
Jer 36: 7 their s before the LORD, and
Dan 6:11 and making s before his God
Dan 9:20 presenting my s before the
Zech 12:10 the Spirit of grace and s
Acts 1:14 one accord in prayer and s
Eph 6:18 and s in the Spirit, being
Eph 6:18 and s for all the saints
Phil 4: 6 in everything by prayer and s

SUPPLICATIONS (*see* SUPPLICATION)
2Ch 6:21 hear the s of Your servant
2Ch 6:39 place their prayer and their s
Job 41: 3 Will he make many s to you
Ps 28: 2 of my s When I cry to You
Ps 28: 6 has heard the voice of my s
Ps 31:22 my s When I cried out to You
Ps 86: 6 attend to the voice of my s
Ps 116: 1 He has heard My voice and my s
Ps 130: 2 To the voice of my s
Ps 140: 6 Hear the voice of my s, O
Ps 143: 1 O LORD, Give ear to my s
Jer 3:21 s of the children of Israel
Jer 31: 9 and with s I will lead them
Dan 9: 3 make request by prayer and s
Dan 9:17 of Your servant, and his s
Dan 9:18 s before You because of our
Dan 9:23 your s the command went out
1Ti 2: 1 I exhort first of all that s
1Ti 5: 5 in God and continues in s and
Heb 5: 7 had offered up prayers and s

SUPPLIED (*see* SUPPLY)
1Ki 9:11 Tyre had s Solomon with cedar
Acts 12:20 was s with food by the king's
1Co 16:17 lacking on your part they s
2Co 11: 9 who came from Macedonia s
2Pe 1:11 s to you abundantly into the

SUPPLIES (*see* SUPPLY)
1Sa 17:22 David left his s in the hand
1Sa 25:13 two hundred stayed with the s
1Sa 30:24 part be who stays by the s
2Sa 19:32 had provided the king with s
Prov 6: 8 provides her s in the summer,
Prov 31:24 s sashes for the merchants
2Co 9:10 Now may He who s seed to the
2Co 9:12 s the needs of the saints
Gal 3: 5 Therefore He who s the Spirit
Eph 4:16 by what every joint s,
1Pe 4:11 with the ability which God s

SUPPLY (*see* SUPPLIED, SUPPLIES, SUPPLYING)
Ex 1:11 built for Pharaoh s cities
Lev 26:26 have cut off your s of bread
Deut 15:14 you shall s him liberally
1Sa 17:22 in the hand of the s keeper
2Sa 12:27 have taken the city's water s
1Ki 4:27 There was no lack in their s
1Ch 27:27 vineyards for the s of wine
Is 3: 1 store, the whole s of bread
Is 3: 1 bread and the whole s of water
Ezek 4:16 the s of bread in Jerusalem
Ezek 5:16 and cut off your s of bread
Ezek 14:13 I will cut off its s of bread
2Co 8:14 abundance may s their lack
2Co 8:14 also may s your lack
2Co 9:10 sower, and bread for food, s
Phil 1:19 the s of the Spirit of Jesus
Phil 2:30 to s what was lacking in your
Phil 4:19 my God shall s all your need

SUPPLYING (*see* SUPPLY)
Ps 144:13 full, S all kinds of produce

SUPPORT (*see* SUPPORTED, SUPPORTING, SUPPORTS)
Gen 13: 6 land was not able to s them
Gen 36: 7 not s them because of their
Judg 16:26 pillars which s the temple
2Sa 22:19 but the LORD was my s
1Ki 6: 6 so that the s beams would not
2Ch 31: 4 contribute s for the priests
Ezra 4:14 we receive s from the palace
Ezra 8:36 So they gave s to the people
Ezra 10:15 the Levite gave them s
Ps 18:18 But the LORD was my s
Song 3:10 its s of gold, its seat of
Acts 20:35 that you must s the weak
Rom 11:18 that you do not s the root

SUPPORTED (*see* SUPPORT)
Ex 17:12 Hur s his hands, one on one
Judg 16:29 pillars which s the temple
2Sa 20: 3 s them, but did not go in to
Ezek 41: 6 around, that they might be s

SUPPORTING (*see* SUPPORT)
Ezek 41: 7 because their s ledges in the

SUPPORTS (*see* SUPPORT)
1Ki 7:30 and its four feet had s
1Ki 7:30 Under the laver were s of
1Ki 7:34 there were four s at the four
1Ki 7:34 its s were part of the cart
Rom 11:18 the root, but the root s you

SUPPOSE (*see* SUPPOSED, SUPPOSING)
Gen 18:24 S there were fifty righteous
Gen 18:28 S there were five less than
Gen 18:29 S there should be forty found
Gen 18:30 S thirty should be found
Gen 18:31 S twenty should be found
Gen 18:32 S ten should be found there
Ex 4: 1 But s they will not believe
Ex 4: 1 s they say, 'The LORD has not
2Sa 13:32 Let not my lord s that they
Luke 7:43 I s the one whom he forgave
Luke 12:51 Do you s that I came to give
Luke 13: 2 Do you s that these Galileans
John 21:25 one, I s that even the world
Acts 2:15 these are not drunk, as you s
1Co 7:26 I s therefore that this is
1Ti 6: 5 who s that godliness is a
Heb 10:29 worse punishment, do you s
Jas 1: 7 man s that he will receive

SUPPOSED (*see* SUPPOSE)
Matt 20:10 came, they s that they would
Mark 6:49 they s it was a ghost, and
Luke 3:23 being (as was s) the son of
Luke 24:37 and s they had seen a spirit
Acts 7:25 For he s that his brethren

Acts 21:29 whom they s that Paul had
Acts 25:18 him of such things as I s

SUPPOSING (*see* SUPPOSE)
Luke 2:44 but s Him to have been in the
John 20:15 s Him to be the gardener,
Acts 14:19 of the city, s him to be dead
Acts 16:27 s the prisoners had fled,
Acts 27:13 s that they had obtained
Phil 1:16 s to add affliction to my

SUPPRESS
Rom 1:18 of men, who s the truth in

SUPREME
1Pe 2:13 whether to the king as s

SUR
2Ki 11: 6 shall be at the gate of S

SURE (*see* SURETY)
Ex 3:19 But I am s that the king of
Num 28:19 Be s they are without blemish
Num 28:31 Be s they are without
Num 29: 8 Be s they are without blemish
Num 32:23 be s your sin will find you
Deut 12:23 Only be s that you do not eat
1Sa 2:35 I will build him a s house
1Sa 20: 7 angry, then be s that evil is
1Sa 23:22 Please go and find out for s
2Sa 1:10 because I was s that he could
Neh 9:38 this, we make a s covenant
Job 24:22 up, but no man is s of life
Ps 19: 7 testimony of the LORD is s
Ps 93: 5 Your testimonies are very s
Ps 111: 7 All His precepts are s
Prov 11:18 will be a s reward
Is 28:16 cornerstone, a s foundation
Is 33:16 him, his water will be s
Is 55: 3 the s mercies of David
Dan 2:45 and its interpretation is s
Hos 5: 9 Israel I make known what is s
John 16:30 Now we are s that You know
Acts 13:34 you the s mercies of David
Rom 4:16 might be s to all the seed
Heb 6:19 an anchor of the soul, both s
2Pe 1:10 your calling and election s
2Pe 1:19 prophetic word made more s

SURELY (*see* PREFACE)

SURETY (*see* SURE)
Gen 43: 9 I myself will be s for him
Gen 44:32 For your servant became s for
Ps 119:122 Be s for Your servant for
Prov 6: 1 son, if you become s for your
Prov 11:15 He who is s for a stranger
Prov 11:15 who hates being s is secure
Prov 17:18 and becomes s for his friend
Prov 20:16 one who is s for a stranger
Prov 22:26 of those who is s for debts
Prov 27:13 him who is s for a stranger
Prov 27:13 when he is s for a seductress
Heb 7:22 a s of a better covenant

SURFACE
Gen 7:18 about on the s of the waters
Gen 8:13 indeed the s of the ground
Ex 16:14 on the s of the wilderness,
Num 11:31 above the s of the ground
1Ki 7:20 by the convex s which was
2Ki 9:37 refuse on the s of the field
Job 38:30 the s of the deep is frozen
Prov 24:31 its s was covered with
Is 24: 1 it waste, distorts its s and
Is 25: 7 on this mountain the s of the
Is 28:25 When he has leveled its s
Dan 8: 5 across the s of the whole

SURNAME (*see* SURNAMED)
Matt 10: 3 whose s was Thaddaeus
Acts 10: 5 for Simon whose s is Peter
Acts 10:18 Simon, whose s was Peter, was
Acts 10:32 Simon here, whose s is Peter
Acts 11:13 for Simon whose s is Peter
Acts 12:12 of John whose s was Mark,
Acts 12:25 them John whose s was Mark

SURNAMED (*see* SURNAME)
Luke 22: 3 s Iscariot, who was numbered
Acts 1:23 Barsabas, who was s Justus

SURPASS (*see* SURPASSED, SURPASSES, SURPASSING)
Jer 5:28 yes, they s the deeds of the
Ezek 32:19 Whom do you s in beauty

SURPASSED (*see* SURPASS)
1Ki 10:23 So King Solomon s all the
2Ch 9:22 So King Solomon s all the

SURPASSES (*see* SURPASS)
Phil 4: 7 which s all understanding,

SURPASSING (*see* SURPASS)
2Sa 1:26 s the love of women

SURPRISE (*see* SURPRISED, SURPRISINGLY)
Judg 3:24 came to look, and to their s
Judg 7:13 To my s, a loaf of barley
Judg 14: 5 Now to his s, a young lion
2Ki 7: 5 to their s no one was there
2Ch 13:14 to their s the battle line

SURPRISED (*see* SURPRISE)
Jer 48:41 and the strongholds are s

SURPRISINGLY (*see* SURPRISE)
Gen 42:35 that s each man's bundle of
1Sa 14:17 they had called the roll, s
2Ki 7:10 s no one was there, not a

SURRENDER (*see* SURRENDERED)
2Ki 7: 4 let us s to the army of the
Jer 38:17 If you surely s to the king
Jer 38:18 But if you do not s to the
Jer 38:21 But if you refuse to s, this
Jer 38:23 they shall s all your wives

SURRENDERED (*see* SURRENDER)
Deut 32:30 them, and the LORD had s them
Jer 38:22 be s to the king of Babylon's

SURROUND (*see* SURROUNDED, SURROUNDING, SURROUNDS)
Josh 7: 9 s us, and cut off our name
2Ki 11: 8 But you shall s the king on
2Ch 23: 7 the Levites shall s the king
Job 16:13 His archers s me
Job 40:22 willows by the brook s him
Ps 5:12 With favor You will s him as
Ps 7: 7 of the peoples shall s You
Ps 17: 9 my deadly enemies who s me
Ps 32: 7 You shall s me with songs of
Ps 32:10 the LORD, mercy shall s him
Ps 97: 2 Clouds and darkness s Him
Ps 125: 2 As the mountains s Jerusalem
Ps 140: 9 the head of those who s me
Ps 142: 7 The righteous shall s me, For
Lam 2:22 day the terrors that s me
Hab 1: 4 the wicked s the righteous
Luke 19:43 you, s you and close you in on

SURROUNDED (*see* SURROUND)
Gen 19: 4 every quarter, s the house
Gen 41:48 of the fields which s them
Judg 16: 2 they s the place and lay in
Judg 19:22 s the house and beat on the
Judg 20: 5 s the house at night because
Judg 20:43 They s the Benjamites and
2Sa 18:15 bore Joab's armor s Absalom
2Sa 22: 6 the sorrows of Sheol s me
2Ki 3:25 However the slingers s and
2Ki 6:14 came by night and s the city
2Ki 8:21 the Edomites who had s him
2Ch 18:31 they s him to attack
2Ch 21: 9 the Edomites who had s him
Job 19: 6 me, and has s me with His net
Ps 17:11 They have now s us in our
Ps 18: 5 The sorrows of Sheol s me
Ps 22:12 Many bulls have s Me
Ps 22:16 For dogs have s Me
Ps 40:12 innumerable evils have s me
Ps 109: 3 They have also s me with
Ps 118:10 All nations s me, But in the
Ps 118:11 s me, Yes, they s me
Ps 118:12 They s me like bees
Lam 3: 5 s me with bitterness and woe
Hos 7: 2 their own deeds have s them
Jon 2: 3 the seas, and the floods s me
Luke 21:20 you see Jerusalem s by armies
John 10:24 Then the Jews s Him and said
Heb 12: 1 since we are s by so great a
Rev 20: 9 s the camp of the saints and

SURROUNDING (*see* SURROUND)
Gen 23:17 were within all the s borders
Num 32:33 the cities of the s country
Num 34:12 land with its s boundaries
Deut 21: 2 the slain man to the s cities
Josh 21:11 with the common-land s it
Josh 21:42 had its common-land s it
1Sa 14:21 the camp from the s country
1Ki 4:31 fame was in all the s nations
2Ki 6:15 s the city with horses and
1Ch 6:55 with its s common-lands
1Ch 11: 8 from the Millo to the s area
Ezek 43:12 The whole area s the
Joel 3:12 to judge all the s nations
Zech 12: 2 to all the s peoples, when
Zech 12: 6 s peoples on the right hand
Zech 14:14 And the wealth of all the s
Matt 14:35 out into all that s region
Mark 6:36 may go into the s country
Mark 6:55 through that whole s region
Luke 4:14 out through all the s region
Luke 4:37 every place in the s region
Luke 7:17 all Judea and all the s region
Luke 8:37 the s region of the Gadarenes
Luke 9:12 they may go into the s towns
Acts 5:16 the s cities to Jerusalem
Acts 14: 6 Lycaonia, and to the s region

SURROUNDS (*see* SURROUND)
Ps 49: 5 the iniquity at my heels s me
Ps 89: 8 Your faithfulness also s You
Ps 125: 2 So the LORD s His people From

SURVEY (*see* SURVEYOR'S)
Josh 18: 4 land, s it according to their
Josh 18: 6 You shall therefore s the
Josh 18: 6 bring the s here to me, that
Josh 18: 8 those who went to s the land
Josh 18: 8 s it, and come back to me,
Josh 18: 9 and wrote the s in a book in
Ps 78:55 them an inheritance by s, And
Amos 7:17 shall be divided by s line

SURVEYOR'S (*see* SURVEY)
Jer 31:39 The s line shall again extend
Zech 1:16 a s line shall be stretched

SURVIVAL (*see* SURVIVE)
Acts 27:34 for this is for your s,

SURVIVE (*see* SURVIVAL, SURVIVED, SURVIVOR)
Job 27:15 Those who s him shall be
Jer 44:14 there shall escape or s, lest
Ezek 7:16 Those who s will escape and

SURVIVED (*see* SURVIVE)
Ruth 1: 5 so the woman s her two sons
1Sa 11:11 those who s were scattered
Neh 1: 2 who had s the captivity, and
Jer 31: 2 The people who s the sword

SURVIVOR (*see* SURVIVE, SURVIVORS)
Num 21:35 until there was no s left him
Ezra 9:14 would be no remnant or s
Lam 2:22 there was no refugee or s
Obad 18 and no s shall remain of the

SURVIVORS (*see* SURVIVOR)
Deut 3: 3 until he had no s remaining
Judg 5:13 Then the s came down, the
Judg 21:17 for the s of Benjamin, that a
Neh 1: 3 The s who are left from the

SUSANNA
Luke 8: 3 Chuza, Herod's steward, and S

SUSI
Num 13:11 Manasseh, Gaddi the son of S

SUSPICIONS
1Ti 6: 4 strife, reviling, evil s

SUSTAIN (*see* SUSTAINED, SUSTAINS, SUSTENANCE)
Ps 41: 3 You will s him on his sickbed
Ps 55:22 the LORD, And He shall s you
Prov 18:14 a man will s him in sickness
Song 2: 5 S me with cakes of raisins,

SUSTAINED (*see* SUSTAIN)
Gen 27:37 grain and wine I have s him
Neh 9:21 Forty years You s them in the
Ps 3: 5 I awoke, for the LORD s me
Ps 89:43 have not s him in the battle
Is 59:16 own righteousness, it s Him
Is 63: 5 and My own fury, it s Me

SUSTAINS (*see* SUSTAIN)
Lev 17:14 Its blood s its life

SUSTENANCE (*see* SUSTAIN)
Judg 6: 4 and leave no s for Israel,
Judg 17:10 a suit of clothes, and your s
Acts 7:11 and our fathers found no s

SWADDLING
Job 38: 9 and thick darkness its s band
Ezek 16: 4 salt nor swathed in s cloths
Luke 2: 7 and wrapped Him in s cloths
Luke 2:12 a Babe wrapped in s cloths

SWALLOW (*see* SWALLOWED, SWALLOWS)
Num 16:34 Lest the earth s us up also
2Sa 20:19 Why would you s up the
2Sa 20:20 that I should s up or destroy
Job 7:19 me alone till I s my saliva
Job 20:18 and will not s it down
Ps 21: 9 The LORD shall s them up in
Ps 56: 1 O God, for man would s me up
Ps 57: 3 the one who would s me up
Ps 69:15 me, Nor let the deep s me up
Ps 84: 3 the s a nest for herself,
Prov 1:12 let us s them alive like
Prov 26: 2 sparrow, like a flying s, so
Eccl 10:12 lips of a fool shall s him up
Is 25: 8 He will s up death forever,
Is 38:14 Like a crane or a s, so I
Jer 8: 7 the s observe the time of
Hos 8: 7 produce, aliens would s it up
Amos 8: 4 you who s up the needy, and
Obad 16 yes, they shall drink, and s
Jon 1:17 a great fish to s Jonah
Matt 23:24 out a gnat and s a camel

SWALLOWED (*see* SWALLOW)
Ex 7:12 Aaron's rod s up their rods
Ex 15:12 the earth s them
Num 16:32 and s them up, with their
Num 26:10 s them up together with Korah
Deut 11: 6 s them up, their households,
2Sa 17:16 who are with him be s up
Job 37:20 surely he would be s up
Ps 35:25 We have s him up
Ps 106:17 and s Dathan, And covered the
Ps 124: 3 they would have s us alive
Is 28: 7 they are s up by wine, they
Is 49:19 those who s you up will be
Jer 51:34 he has s me up like a monster
Jer 51:44 of his mouth what he has s
Lam 2: 2 The Lord has s up and has not
Lam 2: 5 He has s up Israel
Lam 2: 5 He has s up all her palaces
Lam 2:16 We have s her up
Ezek 36: 3 s you up on every side, so
Hos 8: 8 Israel is s up
1Co 15:54 Death is s up in victory
2Co 2: 7 be s up with too much sorrow
2Co 5: 4 mortality may be s up by life
Rev 12:16 and s up the flood which the

SWALLOWS (*see* SWALLOW)
Num 16:30 and s them up with all that
Job 20:15 He s down riches and vomits

SWAMPS
Ezek 47:11 But its s and marshes will not

SWARM (*see* SWARMING, SWARMS)
Judg 14: 8 a s of bees and honey were in

SWARMING (*see* SWARM)
Joel 1: 4 left, the s locust has eaten
Joel 1: 4 what the s locust left, the
Joel 2:25 that the s locust has eaten
Nah 3:15 like the s locusts
Nah 3:17 commanders are like s locusts

SWARMS (*see* SWARM)
Ex 8:21 I will send s of flies on you
Ex 8:21 shall be full of s of flies
Ex 8:22 that no s of flies shall be
Ex 8:24 Thick s of flies came into
Ex 8:24 because of the s of flies
Ex 8:29 LORD, that the s of flies may
Ex 8:31 He removed the s of flies
Ps 78:45 He sent s of flies among them
Ps 105:31 and there came s of flies
Amos 7: 1 He formed locust s at the

SWATHED
Ezek 16: 4 nor s in swaddling cloths

SWAY (*see* SWAYED)
Judg 9: 9 and men, and go to s over trees
Judg 9:11 fruit, and go to s over trees
Judg 9:13 and men, and go to s over trees
1Jn 5:19 under the s of the wicked one

SWAYED (*see* SWAY)
2Sa 19:14 So he s the hearts of all the

SWEAR (*see* SWEARING, SWEARS, SWORE, SWORN)
Gen 21:23 s to me by God that you will
Gen 21:24 Abraham said, "I will s."
Gen 24: 3 I will make you s by the LORD
Gen 24:37 Now my master made me s,
Gen 25:33 S to me as of this day
Gen 47:31 Then he said, "S to me
Gen 50: 5 My father made me s, saying,
Gen 50: 6 your father, as he made you s
Lev 19:12 you shall not s by My name
Josh 2:12 s to me by the LORD, since I
Josh 2:17 which you have made us s,
Josh 2:20 your oath which you made us s
Josh 23: 7 nor cause anyone to s by them
Judg 15:12 S to me that you will not
1Sa 24:21 Therefore s now to me by the
1Sa 30:15 S to me by God that you will
2Sa 19: 7 For I s by the LORD, if you
1Ki 1:13 s to your maidservant, saying
1Ki 1:51 Let King Solomon s to me
1Ki 2:42 I not make you s by the LORD
1Ki 22:16 s that you tell me nothing
2Ch 18:15 s that you tell me nothing
2Ch 36:13 had made him s an oath by God
Ezra 10: 5 all Israel s an oath that
Neh 13:25 hair, and made them s by God
Ps 102: 8 me s an oath against me
Is 19:18 and s by the LORD of hosts
Is 48: 1 who s by the name of the LORD
Is 65:16 shall s by the God of truth
Jer 4: 2 And you shall s, 'The LORD
Jer 5: 2 lives,' surely they s falsely
Jer 7: 9 s falsely, burn incense to
Jer 12:16 to s by My name, 'As the LORD
Jer 12:16 taught My people to s by Baal
Jer 22: 5 I s by Myself," says the
Hos 4:15 nor s an oath, saying, 'As
Amos 8:14 Those who s by the sin of
Zeph 1: 5 s oaths by the LORD, but who
Zeph 1: 5 but who also s by Milcom
Matt 5:33 old, 'You shall not s falsely
Matt 5:34 I say to you, do not s at all
Matt 5:36 Nor shall you s by your head
Matt 26:74 Then he began to curse and s
Mark 14:71 But he began to curse and s
Heb 3:18 to whom did He s that they
Heb 6:13 because He could s by no one
Heb 6:16 men indeed s by the greater
Jas 5:12 all, my brethren, do not s

SWEARING (*see* SWEAR)
Hos 4: 2 By s and lying, killing and
Hos 10: 4 words, s falsely in making a

SWEARS (*see* SWEAR)
Lev 5: 4 Or if a person s, speaking
Lev 6: 3 concerning it, and s falsely
Num 30: 2 or s an oath to bind himself
Ps 15: 4 He who s to his own hurt and
Ps 63:11 Everyone who s by Him shall
Prov 29:24 he s to tell the truth, but
Is 65:16 he who s in the earth shall
Zech 5: 4 one who s falsely by My name
Matt 23:16 Whoever s by the temple, it
Matt 23:16 but whoever s by the gold of
Matt 23:18 Whoever s by the altar, it
Matt 23:18 but whoever s by the gift
Matt 23:20 he who s by the altar,
Matt 23:20 s by it and by all things on
Matt 23:21 He who s by the temple,
Matt 23:21 s by it and by Him who dwells
Matt 23:22 he who s by heaven
Matt 23:22 s by the throne of God and by

SWEAT
Gen 3:19 In the s of your face you
Ezek 44:18 with anything that causes s
Luke 22:44 His s became like great drops

SWEEP (*see* SWEEPS, SWEPT)
Is 14:23 I will s it with the broom of
Is 28:17 the hail will s away the
Luke 15: 8 a lamp, s the house, and seek

SWEEPS (*see* SWEEP)
Job 27:21 it s him out of his place

SWEET (*see* SWEETER, SWEETLY, SWEETNESS, SWEET-SMELLING)
Ex 15:25 the waters were made s
Ex 25: 6 oil and for the s incense
Ex 29:18 it is a s aroma, an offering
Ex 29:25 as a s aroma before the LORD
Ex 29:41 in the morning, for a s aroma
Ex 30: 7 on it s incense every morning
Ex 30:34 Take s spices, stacte and
Ex 30:34 with these s spices
Ex 31:11 s incense for the holy place
Ex 35: 8 oil and for the s incense
Ex 35:15 the s incense, and the screen
Ex 35:28 oil, and for the s incense
Ex 37:29 the pure incense of s spices
Ex 39:38 oil, and the s incense
Ex 40:27 he burned s incense on it, as
Lev 1: 9 fire, a s aroma to the LORD
Lev 1:13 fire, a s aroma to the LORD
Lev 1:17 fire, a s aroma to the LORD
Lev 2: 2 fire, a s aroma to the LORD
Lev 2: 9 fire, a s aroma to the LORD
Lev 2:12 on the altar for a s aroma
Lev 3: 5 fire, a s aroma to the LORD
Lev 3:16 made by fire for a s aroma
Lev 4: 7 of s incense before the LORD
Lev 4:31 for a s aroma to the LORD
Lev 6:15 it on the altar for a s aroma
Lev 6:21 for a s aroma to the LORD
Lev 8:21 burnt sacrifice for a s aroma
Lev 8:28 offerings for a s aroma
Lev 16:12 full of s incense beaten fine
Lev 17: 6 fat for a s aroma to the LORD
Lev 23:13 to the LORD, for a s aroma
Lev 23:18 for a s aroma to the LORD
Lev 26:31 fragrance of your s aromas
Num 4:16 the s incense, the daily
Num 15: 3 to make a s aroma to the LORD
Num 15: 7 wine as a s aroma to the LORD
Num 15:10 fire, a s aroma to the LORD
Num 15:13 fire, a s aroma to the LORD
Num 15:14 a s aroma to the LORD, just
Num 15:24 as a s aroma to the LORD,
Num 18:17 for a s aroma to the LORD
Num 28: 2 by fire as a s aroma to Me
Num 28: 6 at Mount Sinai for a s aroma
Num 28: 8 fire, a s aroma to the LORD
Num 28:13 a burnt offering of s aroma
Num 28:24 as a s aroma to the LORD
Num 28:27 as a s aroma to the LORD
Num 29: 2 as a s aroma to the LORD
Num 29: 6 as a s aroma, an offering
Num 29: 8 to the LORD as a s aroma
Num 29:13 fire as a s aroma to the LORD
Num 29:36 fire as a s aroma to the LORD
Judg 14:14 the strong came something s
2Sa 23: 1 and the s psalmist of Israel
2Ch 2: 4 to burn before Him s incense
2Ch 13:11 burnt sacrifices and s incense
Ezra 6:10 may offer sacrifices of s
Neh 8:10 way, eat the fat, drink the s
Job 20:12 Though evil is s in his mouth
Job 21:33 the valley shall be s to him
Ps 55:14 We took s counsel together,
Ps 66:15 With the s aroma of rams
Ps 104:34 May my meditation be s to Him
Ps 119:103 How s are Your words to my
Ps 141: 6 hear my words, for they are s
Prov 3:24 down and your sleep will be s
Prov 9:17 Stolen water is s, and bread
Prov 13:19 accomplished is s to the soul
Prov 20:17 by deceit is s to a man, but
Prov 24:13 which is s to your taste
Prov 27: 7 soul every bitter thing is s
Eccl 5:12 sleep of a laboring man is s
Eccl 11: 7 Truly the light is s, and it
Song 2: 3 his fruit was s to my taste
Song 2:14 for your voice is s, and your
Song 5:16 His mouth is most s, yes, he
Is 3:24 Instead of a s smell there
Is 5:20 for s, and s for bitter
Is 23:16 make s melody, sing many
Is 43:24 Me no s cane with money, nor
Is 49:26 own blood as with s wine
Jer 6:20 s cane from a far country
Jer 6:20 nor your sacrifices s to Me
Jer 31:26 and my sleep was s to me
Ezek 6:13 oak, wherever they offered s
Ezek 16:19 it before them as s incense
Ezek 20:28 also sent up their s aroma

Ezek 20:41 I will accept you as a s
Amos 9:13 shall drip with s wine, and
Mic 6:15 and make s wine, but not drink
Rev 10: 9 but it will be as s as honey
Rev 10:10 it was as s as honey in my

SWEETER (*see* SWEET)
Judg 14:18 What is s than honey
Ps 19:10 S also than honey and the
Ps 119:103 s than honey to my mouth

SWEETLY (*see* SWEET)
Job 24:20 the worm should feed s on him

SWEETNESS (*see* SWEET)
Judg 9:11 to them, 'Should I cease my s
Prov 16:21 and s of the lips increases
Prov 16:24 s to the soul and health to
Prov 27: 9 the s of a man's friend does
Ezek 3: 3 in my mouth like honey in s

SWEET-SMELLING (*see* SWEET)
Ex 30:23 half as much s cinnamon (two
Ex 30:23 and fifty shekels of s cane
Eph 5: 2 to God for a s aroma
Phil 4:18 you, a s aroma, an acceptable

SWELL (*see* SWELLING, SWOLLEN)
Num 5:21 thigh rot and your belly s
Num 5:22 stomach, and make your belly s
Num 5:27 bitter, and her belly will s
Deut 8: 4 your foot s these forty years
Neh 9:21 out and their feet did not s
Is 60: 5 your heart shall s with joy
Amos 8: 8 of it shall s like the River
Amos 9: 5 of it shall s like the River
Acts 28: 6 expecting that he would s up

SWELLING (*see* SWELL)
Lev 13: 2 on the skin of his body a s
Lev 13:10 indeed if the s on the skin
Lev 13:10 a spot of raw flesh in the s
Lev 13:19 a white s or a bright spot
Lev 13:28 it is a s from the burn
Lev 13:43 indeed if the s of the sore
Lev 14:56 for a s and a scab and a bright
Ps 46: 3 mountains shake with its s
2Pe 2:18 great s words of emptiness
Jude 16 and they mouth great s words

SWEPT (*see* SWEEP)
Judg 5:21 torrent of Kishon s them away
1Sa 12:25 wickedly, you shall be s away
Job 22:16 were s away by a flood
Jer 46:15 are your valiant men s away
Dan 11:22 be s away from before him
Dan 11:26 his army shall be s away, and
Matt 12:44 comes, he finds it empty, s
Luke 11:25 when he comes, he finds it s

SWIFT (*see* SWIFTER, SWIFTLY)
Deut 28:49 as s as the eagle flies, a
1Ch 12: 8 were as s as gazelles on the
Esth 8:10 horses bred from s steeds
Job 9:26 They pass by like s ships
Job 24:18 They should be s on the face
Prov 6:18 feet that are s in running to
Eccl 9:11 The race is not to the s, nor
Is 18: 2 s messengers, to a nation
Is 19: 1 the LORD rides on a s cloud
Is 30:16 We will ride on s horses"
Is 30:16 who pursue you shall be s
Jer 2:23 You are a s dromedary
Jer 8: 7 and the turtledove, the s, and
Jer 46: 6 Do not let the s flee away
Joel 2: 4 like s steeds, so they run
Amos 2:14 shall perish from the s, the
Amos 2:15 bow, the s of foot shall not
Mic 1:13 to the s steeds (She was the
Mal 3: 5 I will be a s witness against
Rom 3:15 feet are s to shed blood
Jas 1:19 let every man be s to hear
2Pe 2: 1 on themselves s destruction

SWIFTER (*see* SWIFT)
2Sa 1:23 they were s than eagles, they
Job 7: 6 My days are s than a weaver's
Job 9:25 my days are s than a runner
Jer 4:13 His horses are s than eagles
Lam 4:19 Our pursuers were s than the
Hab 1: 8 also are s than leopards, and

SWIFTLY (*see* SWIFT)
Ps 147:15 His word runs very s
Is 5:26 they shall come with speed, s
Dan 9:21 being caused to fly s,
Joel 3: 4 you retaliate against Me, s

SWIM (*see* SWIMS)
Ps 6: 6 All night I make my bed s
Is 25:11 spreads out his hands to s
Ezek 47: 5 water in which one must s
Acts 27:42 any of them should s away
Acts 27:43 that those who could s should

SWIMS (*see* SWIM)
Is 25:11 s spreads out his hands to

SWINE (*see* SWINE'S)
Lev 11: 7 and the s, though it divides
Deut 14: 8 Also the s is unclean for you
Matt 7: 6 nor cast your pearls before s
Matt 8:30 was a herd of many s feeding
Matt 8:31 to go away into the herd of s
Matt 8:32 they went into the herd of s
Matt 8:32 of s ran violently down the
Mark 5:11 Now a large herd of s was
Mark 5:12 Send us to the s, that we may
Mark 5:13 entered the s (there were
Mark 5:14 Now those who fed the s fled
Mark 5:16 and about the s
Luke 8:32 Now a herd of many s was
Luke 8:33 of the man and entered the s
Luke 15:15 him into his fields to feed s
Luke 15:16 with the pods that the s ate

SWINE'S (*see* SWINE)
Prov 11:22 a ring of gold in a s snout
Is 65: 4 who eat s flesh, and the broth
Is 66: 3 as if he offers s blood
Is 66:17 in the midst, eating s flesh

SWING (*see* SWINGS)
Job 28: 4 they s to and fro

SWINGS (*see* SWING)
Deut 19: 5 his hand s a stroke with the

SWIRL (*see* SWIRLS)
Job 37:12 they s about, being turned by

SWIRLS (*see* SWIRL)
Prov 23:31 when it s around smoothly

SWOLLEN (*see* SWELL)
Ps 124: 5 Then the s waters Would have

SWOON
Lam 2:12 as they s like the wounded

SWOOP (*see* SWOOPING)
1Sa 15:19 Why did you s down on the

SWOOPING (*see* SWOOP)
Job 9:26 like an eagle s on its prey

SWORD (*see* SWORDS)
Gen 3:24 and a flaming s which turned
Gen 27:40 By your s you shall live, and
Gen 31:26 captives taken with the s
Gen 34:25 brothers, each took his s
Gen 34:26 son with the edge of the s
Gen 48:22 hand of the Amorite with my s
Ex 5: 3 with pestilence or with the s
Ex 5:21 to put a s in their hand to
Ex 15: 9 I will draw my s, my hand
Ex 17:13 people with the edge of the s
Ex 18: 4 me from the s of Pharaoh")
Ex 22:24 and I will kill you with the s
Ex 32:27 man put his s on his side
Lev 26: 6 the s will not go through
Lev 26: 7 fall by the s before you
Lev 26: 8 fall by the s before you
Lev 26:25 I will bring a s against you
Lev 26:33 and draw out a s after you
Lev 26:36 as though fleeing from a s
Lev 26:37 as it were before a s, when
Num 14: 3 to this land to fall by the s
Num 14:43 and you shall fall by the s
Num 19:16 slain by a s or who has died
Num 20:18 out against you with the s
Num 21:24 him with the edge of the s
Num 22:23 with His drawn s in His hand
Num 22:29 there were a s in my hand
Num 22:31 with His drawn s in His hand
Num 31: 8 they also killed with the s
Deut 13:15 city with the edge of the s
Deut 13:15 with the edge of the s
Deut 20:13 in it with the edge of the s
Deut 28:22 burning fever, with the s
Deut 32:25 The s shall destroy outside
Deut 32:41 If I whet My glittering s
Deut 32:42 My s shall devour flesh, with
Deut 33:29 help and the s of your majesty
Josh 5:13 with His s drawn in His hand
Josh 6:21 with the edge of the s
Josh 8:24 s until they were consumed
Josh 8:24 it with the edge of the s
Josh 10:11 of Israel killed with the s
Josh 10:28 king with the edge of the s
Josh 10:30 in it with the edge of the s
Josh 10:32 in it with the edge of the s
Josh 10:35 it with the edge of the s
Josh 10:37 it with the edge of the s
Josh 10:39 them with the edge of the s
Josh 11:10 and struck its king with the s
Josh 11:11 in it with the edge of the s
Josh 11:12 struck with the edge of the s
Josh 11:14 s until they had destroyed
Josh 13:22 the s Balaam the son of Beor
Josh 19:47 it with the edge of the s
Josh 24:12 with your s or with your bow
Judg 1: 8 it with the edge of the s
Judg 1:25 city with the edge of the s
Judg 4:15 edge of the s before Barak
Judg 4:16 fell by the edge of the s
Judg 7:14 is nothing else but the s of
Judg 7:18 say, 'The s of the LORD and of
Judg 7:20 The s of the LORD and of
Judg 7:22 man's s against his companion
Judg 8:10 men who drew the s had fallen
Judg 8:20 youth would not draw his s
Judg 9:54 Draw your s and kill me, lest
Judg 18:27 them with the edge of the s
Judg 20: 2 foot soldiers who drew the s
Judg 20:15 thousand men who drew the s
Judg 20:17 thousand men who drew the s
Judg 20:25 all these drew the s
Judg 20:35 all these drew the s
Judg 20:37 city with the edge of the s
Judg 20:46 thousand men who drew the s
Judg 20:48 down with the edge of the s
Judg 21:10 Gilead with the edge of the s
1Sa 13:22 that there was neither s nor
1Sa 14:20 and indeed every man's s was
1Sa 15: 8 people with the edge of the s
1Sa 15:33 As your s has made women
1Sa 17:39 fastened his s to his armor
1Sa 17:45 You come to me with a s, with
1Sa 17:47 the LORD does not save with s
1Sa 17:50 But there was no s in the
1Sa 17:51 the Philistine, took his s
1Sa 18: 4 with his armor, even to his s
1Sa 21: 8 here on hand a spear or a s
1Sa 21: 8 my s nor my weapons with me
1Sa 21: 9 said, "The s of Goliath the
1Sa 22:10 gave him the s of Goliath the
1Sa 22:13 have given him bread and a s
1Sa 22:19 struck with the edge of the s
1Sa 22:19 with the edge of the s
1Sa 25:13 Every man gird on his s
1Sa 25:13 So every man girded on his s
1Sa 25:13 and David also girded on his s
1Sa 31: 4 Draw your s, and thrust me
1Sa 31: 4 Therefore Saul took a s and
1Sa 31: 5 dead, he also fell on his s
2Sa 1:12 they had fallen by the s
2Sa 1:22 the s of Saul did not return
2Sa 2:16 head and thrust his s in his
2Sa 2:26 Shall the s devour forever
2Sa 3:29 on a staff or falls by the s
2Sa 11:25 for the s devours one as well
2Sa 12: 9 Uriah the Hittite with the s
2Sa 12: 9 the s of the people of Ammon
2Sa 12:10 the s shall never depart from
2Sa 15:14 city with the edge of the s
2Sa 18: 8 that day than the s devoured
2Sa 20: 8 on it was a belt with a s
2Sa 20:10 the s that was in Joab's hand
2Sa 21:16 who was bearing a new s,
2Sa 23:10 and his hand stuck to the s
2Sa 24: 9 valiant men who drew the s
1Ki 1:51 servant to death with the s
1Ki 2: 8 put you to death with the s
1Ki 2:32 he, and killed them with the s
1Ki 3:24 Bring me a s
1Ki 3:24 brought a s before the king
1Ki 19: 1 all the prophets with the s
1Ki 19:10 Your prophets with the s

1Ki 19:14 Your prophets with the s
1Ki 19:17 escapes the s of Hazael, Jehu
1Ki 19:17 escapes from the s of Jehu
2Ki 6:22 taken captive with your s
2Ki 8:12 men you will kill with the s
2Ki 10:25 them with the edge of the s
2Ki 11:15 and slay with the s whoever
2Ki 11:20 the s in the king's house
2Ki 19: 7 fall by the s in his own land
2Ki 19:37 struck him down with the s
1Ch 5:18 men able to bear shield and s
1Ch 10: 4 Draw your s, and thrust me
1Ch 10: 4 Therefore Saul took a s and
1Ch 10: 5 dead, he also fell on his s
1Ch 21: 5 thousand men who drew the s
1Ch 21: 5 thousand men who drew the s
1Ch 21:12 by your foes with the s of
1Ch 21:12 three days the s of the LORD
1Ch 21:16 a drawn s stretched out over
1Ch 21:27 returned his s to its sheath
1Ch 21:30 s of the angel of the LORD
2Ch 20: 9 comes upon us, such as the s
2Ch 21: 4 all his brothers with the s
2Ch 23:14 and slay with the s whoever
2Ch 23:21 had slain Athaliah with the s
2Ch 29: 9 fathers have fallen by the s
2Ch 32:21 him down with the s there
2Ch 36:17 the s in the house of their
2Ch 36:20 s he carried away to Babylon
Ezra 9: 7 kings of the lands, to the s
Neh 4:18 s girded at his side as he
Esth 9: 5 with the stroke of the s,
Job 1:15 with the edge of the s
Job 1:17 with the edge of the s
Job 5:15 He saves the needy from the s
Job 5:20 war from the power of the s
Job 15:22 and he watches for the s
Job 19:29 of the s for yourselves
Job 19:29 the punishment of the s, that
Job 27:14 multiplied, it is for the s
Job 33:18 life from perishing by the s
Job 36:12 they shall perish by the s
Job 39:22 does he turn back from the s
Job 40:19 made him can bring near His s
Job 41:26 Though the s reaches him, it
Ps 7:12 back, He will sharpen His s
Ps 17:13 from the wicked with Your s
Ps 22:20 Deliver Me from the s, My
Ps 37:14 The wicked have drawn the s
Ps 37:15 Their s shall enter their own
Ps 44: 3 of the land by their own s
Ps 44: 6 bow, Nor shall my s save me
Ps 45: 3 Gird Your s upon Your thigh,
Ps 57: 4 And their tongue a sharp s
Ps 63:10 They shall fall by the s
Ps 64: 3 sharpen their tongue like a s
Ps 76: 3 the bow, The shield and the s
Ps 78:62 gave His people over to the s
Ps 78:64 Their priests fell by the s
Ps 89:43 turned back the edge of his s
Ps 144:10 His servant From the deadly s
Ps 149: 6 a two-edged s in their hand,
Prov 5: 4 sharp as a two-edged s
Prov 12:18 like the piercings of a s
Prov 25:18 neighbor is like a club, a s
Song 3: 8 every man has his s on his
Is 1:20 shall be devoured by the s"
Is 2: 4 not lift up s against nation
Is 3:25 Your men shall fall by the s
Is 13:15 captured will fall by the s
Is 14:19 thrust through with a s, who
Is 21:15 the swords, from the drawn s
Is 22: 2 men are not slain with the s
Is 27: 1 the LORD with His severe s
Is 31: 8 shall fall by a s not of man
Is 31: 8 and a s not of mankind shall
Is 31: 8 But he shall flee from the s
Is 34: 5 For My s shall be bathed in
Is 34: 6 The s of the LORD is filled
Is 37: 7 fall by the s in his own land
Is 37:38 struck him down with the s
Is 41: 2 them as the dust to his s
Is 49: 2 made My mouth like a sharp s
Is 51:19 and destruction, famine and s
Is 65:12 I will number you for the s
Is 66:16 by His s the LORD will judge
Jer 2:30 Your s has devoured your
Jer 4:10 whereas the s reaches to the
Jer 5:12 nor shall we see s or famine
Jer 5:17 which you trust, with the s
Jer 6:25 Because of the s of the enemy
Jer 9:16 I will send a s after them
Jer 11:22 young men shall die by the s
Jer 12:12 for the s of the LORD shall
Jer 14:12 I will consume them by the s
Jer 14:13 You shall not see the s
Jer 14:15 did not send, and who say, S
Jer 14:15 By s and famine those
Jer 14:16 of the famine and the s
Jer 14:18 those slain with the s
Jer 15: 2 and such as are for the s, to
Jer 15: 2 are for the s, to the s
Jer 15: 3 the s to slay, the dogs to
Jer 15: 9 to the s before their enemies
Jer 16: 4 shall be consumed by the s
Jer 18:21 blood by the force of the s
Jer 18:21 be slain by the s in battle
Jer 19: 7 by the s before their enemies
Jer 20: 4 by the s of their enemies
Jer 20: 4 and slay them with the s
Jer 21: 7 from the pestilence and the s
Jer 21: 7 them with the edge of the s
Jer 21: 9 this city shall die by the s
Jer 24:10 And I will send the s, the
Jer 25:16 go mad because of the s that
Jer 25:27 because of the s which I will
Jer 25:29 for I will call for a s on
Jer 25:31 those who are wicked to the s
Jer 26:23 who killed him with the s
Jer 27: 8 says the LORD, 'with the s
Jer 27:13 you and your people, by the s
Jer 29:17 I will send on them the s
Jer 29:18 I will pursue them with the s
Jer 31: 2 the s found grace in the
Jer 32:24 against it, because of the s
Jer 32:36 the king of Babylon by the s
Jer 33: 4 the siege mounds and the s
Jer 34: 4 You shall not die by the s
Jer 34:17 to the s, to pestilence, and
Jer 38: 2 this city shall die by the s
Jer 39:18 you shall not fall by the s
Jer 41: 2 son of Shaphan, with the s
Jer 42:16 the s which you feared shall
Jer 42:17 They shall die by the s, by
Jer 42:22 that you shall die by the s
Jer 43:11 to the s those appointed for
Jer 43:11 those appointed for the s
Jer 44:12 shall be consumed by the s
Jer 44:12 to the greatest, by the s
Jer 44:13 punished Jerusalem, by the s
Jer 44:18 have been consumed by the s
Jer 44:27 shall be consumed by the s
Jer 44:28 s shall return from the land
Jer 46:10 The s shall devour
Jer 46:14 for the s devours all around
Jer 46:16 from the oppressing s
Jer 47: 6 O you s of the LORD, how long
Jer 48: 2 The s shall pursue you
Jer 48:10 keeps back his s from blood
Jer 49:37 I will send the s after them
Jer 50:16 s everyone shall turn to his
Jer 50:35 A s is against the Chaldeans,
Jer 50:36 A s is against the
Jer 50:36 A s is against her mighty men
Jer 50:37 A s is against their horses,
Jer 50:37 A s is against her treasures,
Jer 51:50 You who have escaped the s
Lam 1:20 Outside the s bereaves, at
Lam 2:21 men have fallen by the s
Lam 4: 9 Those slain by the s are
Lam 5: 9 because of the s in the
Ezek 5: 1 son of man, take a sharp s
Ezek 5: 2 strike around it with the s
Ezek 5: 2 I will draw out a s after them
Ezek 5:12 fall by the s all around you
Ezek 5:12 will draw out a s after them
Ezek 5:17 will bring the s against you
Ezek 6: 3 I, will bring a s against you
Ezek 6: 8 the s among the nations, when
Ezek 6:11 For they shall fall by the s
Ezek 6:12 is near shall fall by the s
Ezek 7:15 The s is outside, and the
Ezek 7:15 the field will die by the s
Ezek 11: 8 You have feared the s
Ezek 11: 8 and I will bring a s upon you
Ezek 11:10 You shall fall by the s
Ezek 12:14 draw out the s after them
Ezek 12:16 a few of their men from the s
Ezek 14:17 if I bring a s on that land
Ezek 14:17 and say, 'S, go
Ezek 14:21 the s and famine and wild
Ezek 17:21 troops shall fall by the s
Ezek 21: 3 I will draw My s out of its
Ezek 21: 4 therefore My s shall go out
Ezek 21: 5 have drawn My s out of its
Ezek 21: 9 A s, a s is sharpened and
Ezek 21:11 this s is sharpened, and it is
Ezek 21:12 Terrors including the s will
Ezek 21:13 what if the s despises even
Ezek 21:14 let the s do double damage
Ezek 21:14 it is the s that slays,
Ezek 21:14 the s that slays the great
Ezek 21:15 the s against all their gates
Ezek 21:19 s of the king of Babylon to
Ezek 21:20 the s to go to Rabbah of the
Ezek 21:28 A s, a s is drawn,
Ezek 23:10 and slew her with the s
Ezek 23:25 remnant shall fall by the s
Ezek 24:21 behind shall fall by the s
Ezek 25:13 Dedan shall fall by the s
Ezek 26: 6 shall be slain by the s
Ezek 26: 8 He will slay with the s your
Ezek 26:11 slay your people by the s
Ezek 28:23 s against her on every side
Ezek 29: 8 I will bring a s upon you
Ezek 30: 4 The s shall come upon Egypt,
Ezek 30: 5 shall fall with them by the s
Ezek 30: 6 her shall fall by the s,"
Ezek 30:17 Pi Beseth shall fall by the s
Ezek 30:21 it strong enough to hold a s
Ezek 30:22 I will make the s fall out of
Ezek 30:24 and put My s in his hand
Ezek 30:25 when I put My s into the hand
Ezek 31:17 it, with those slain by the s
Ezek 31:18 with those slain by the s
Ezek 32:10 I brandish My s before them
Ezek 32:11 The s of the king of Babylon
Ezek 32:20 midst of those slain by the s
Ezek 32:20 She is delivered to the s
Ezek 32:21 uncircumcised, slain by the s
Ezek 32:22 them slain, fallen by the s
Ezek 32:23 them slain, fallen by the s
Ezek 32:24 them slain, fallen by the s
Ezek 32:25 uncircumcised, slain by the s
Ezek 32:26 uncircumcised, slain by the s
Ezek 32:28 lie with those slain by the s
Ezek 32:29 those who were slain by the s
Ezek 32:30 with those slain by the s
Ezek 32:31 all his army, slain by the s
Ezek 32:32 with those slain by the s
Ezek 33: 2 I bring the s upon a land
Ezek 33: 3 when he sees the s coming
Ezek 33: 4 take warning, if the s comes
Ezek 33: 6 watchman sees the s coming
Ezek 33: 6 and the s comes and takes any
Ezek 33:26 You rely on your s, you
Ezek 33:27 the ruins shall fall by the s
Ezek 35: 5 of the s at the time of their
Ezek 35: 8 are slain by the s shall fall
Ezek 38: 8 those brought back from the s
Ezek 38:21 I will call for a s against
Ezek 38:21 Every man's s will be against
Ezek 39:23 and they all fell by the s
Dan 11:33 days they shall fall by s
Hos 1: 7 nor by s or battle, by horses
Hos 2:18 s of battle I will shatter
Hos 7:16 s for the cursings of their
Hos 11: 6 And the s shall slash in his
Hos 13:16 They shall fall by the s
Amos 1:11 his brother with the s, and
Amos 4:10 young men I killed with a s
Amos 7: 9 the s against the house of
Amos 7:11 Jeroboam shall die by the s
Amos 7:17 daughters shall fall by the s
Amos 9: 1 the last of them with the s
Amos 9: 4 there I will command the s
Amos 9:10 My people shall die by the s
Mic 4: 3 not lift up s against nation
Mic 5: 6 the s the land of Assyria
Mic 6:14 I will give over to the s
Nah 2:13 the s shall devour your young
Nah 3: 3 Horsemen charge with bright s
Nah 3:15 you, the s will cut you off
Zeph 2:12 you shall be slain by My s
Hag 2:22 one by the s of his brother
Zech 9:13 like the s of a mighty man
Zech 11:17 A s shall be against his arm
Zech 13: 7 Awake, O s, against My
Matt 10:34 come to bring peace but a s
Matt 26:51 out his hand and drew his s

Matt 26:52 Put your **s** in its place, for
Matt 26:52 for all who take the **s**
Matt 26:52 will perish by the **s**
Mark 14:47 those who stood by drew his **s**
Luke 2:35 a **s** will pierce through your
Luke 21:24 fall by the edge of the **s**
Luke 22:36 and he who has no **s**, let him
Luke 22:49 shall we strike with the **s**
John 18:10 Then Simon Peter, having a **s**
John 18:11 Put your **s** into the sheath
Acts 12: 2 brother of John with the **s**
Acts 16:27 had fled, drew his **s** and was
Rom 8:35 or nakedness, or peril, or **s**
Rom 13: 4 does not bear the **s** in vain
Eph 6:17 the **s** of the Spirit, which is
Heb 4:12 sharper than any two-edged **s**
Heb 11:34 escaped the edge of the **s**
Heb 11:37 were slain with the **s**
Rev 1:16 went a sharp two-edged **s**, and
Rev 2:12 who has the sharp two-edged **s**
Rev 2:16 them with the **s** of My mouth
Rev 6: 4 was given to him a great **s**
Rev 6: 8 of the earth, to kill with **s**
Rev 13:10 he who kills with the **s**
Rev 13:10 must be killed with the **s**
Rev 13:14 who was wounded by the **s** and
Rev 19:15 of His mouth goes a sharp **s**
Rev 19:21 **s** which proceeded from the

SWORDS (*see* SWORD)
1Sa 13:19 the Hebrews make **s** or spears
2Sa 2:16 called the Field of Sharp **S**
2Ki 3:23 kings have surely struck **s**
2Ki 3:26 seven hundred men who drew **s**
Neh 4:13 their families, with their **s**
Ps 55:21 oil, Yet they were drawn **s**
Ps 59: 7 **S** are in their lips
Prov 30:14 whose teeth are like **s**, and
Song 3: 8 They all hold **s**, being expert
Is 2: 4 beat their **s** into plowshares
Is 21:15 For they fled from the **s**,
Ezek 16:40 you through with their **s**
Ezek 21:16 **S** at the ready
Ezek 23:47 and execute them with their **s**
Ezek 28: 7 and they shall draw their **s**
Ezek 30:11 draw their **s** against Egypt
Ezek 32:12 By the **s** of the mighty
Ezek 32:27 their **s** under their heads
Ezek 38: 4 all of them handling **s**
Joel 3:10 Beat your plowshares into **s**
Mic 4: 3 beat their **s** into plowshares
Matt 26:47 with a great multitude with **s**
Matt 26:55 as against a robber, with **s**
Mark 14:43 with a great multitude with **s**
Mark 14:48 as against a robber, with **s**
Luke 22:38 Lord, look, here are two **s**
Luke 22:52 as against a robber, with **s**

SWORE (*see* SWEAR)
Gen 21:31 two of them **s** an oath there
Gen 24: 7 **s** to me, saying, 'To your
Gen 24: 9 and **s** to him concerning this
Gen 25:33 So he **s** to him, and sold his
Gen 26: 3 I **s** to Abraham your father
Gen 26:31 **s** an oath with one another
Gen 31:53 Jacob **s** by the Fear of his
Gen 47:31 And he **s** to him
Gen 50:24 land of which He **s** to Abraham
Ex 6: 8 which I **s** to give to Abraham
Ex 13: 5 which He **s** to your fathers to
Ex 13:11 as He **s** to you and your
Ex 32:13 to whom You **s** by Your own
Ex 33: 1 land of which I **s** to Abraham
Num 11:12 which You **s** to their fathers'
Num 14:16 land which He **s** to give them
Num 14:23 of which I **s** to their fathers
Num 14:30 enter the land which I **s** I
Num 32:10 day, and He **s** an oath, saying,
Num 32:11 land of which I **s** to Abraham
Deut 1: 8 the LORD **s** to your fathers
Deut 1:35 I **s** to give to your fathers
Deut 4:21 **s** that I would not cross over
Deut 4:31 fathers which He **s** to them
Deut 6:10 of which He **s** to your fathers
Deut 6:18 the LORD **s** to your fathers
Deut 6:23 of which He **s** to our fathers
Deut 7: 8 which He **s** to your fathers
Deut 7:12 which He **s** to your fathers
Deut 7:13 in the land of which He **s** to
Deut 8: 1 the LORD **s** to your fathers
Deut 8:18 which He **s** to your fathers
Deut 9: 5 the LORD **s** to your fathers
Deut 10:11 I **s** to their fathers to give
Deut 11: 9 LORD **s** to give your fathers
Deut 11:21 **s** to your fathers to give
Deut 13:17 just as He **s** to your fathers,
Deut 19: 8 as He **s** to your fathers, and
Deut 26: 3 **s** to our fathers to give us
Deut 26:15 just as You **s** to our fathers,
Deut 28:11 the land of which the LORD **s**
Deut 30:20 the LORD **s** to your fathers
Deut 31:20 of which I **s** to their fathers
Deut 31:21 of which I **s** to give them
Deut 31:23 the land of which I **s** to them
Deut 34: 4 of which I **s** to give Abraham
Josh 1: 6 the land which I **s** to their
Josh 5: 6 to whom the LORD **s** that He
Josh 6:22 that she has, as you **s** to her
Josh 9:15 of the congregation **s** to them
Josh 9:20 the oath which we **s** to them
Josh 14: 9 So Moses **s** on that day,
Judg 2: 1 of which I **s** to your fathers
1Sa 19: 6 voice of Jonathan, and Saul **s**
1Sa 24:22 So David **s** to Saul
1Sa 28:10 Saul **s** to her by the LORD,
2Sa 19:23 And the king **s** to him
2Sa 21:17 the men of David **s** to him
1Ki 1:17 you **s** by the LORD your God to
1Ki 1:30 just as I **s** to you by the
1Ki 2: 8 and I **s** to him by the LORD,
1Ki 2:23 King Solomon **s** by the LORD
Ezra 10: 5 So they **s** an oath
Ps 89:49 Which You **s** to David in Your
Ps 95:11 So I **s** in My wrath, 'They
Ps 132: 2 How he **s** to the LORD, And
Jer 32:22 land, of which You **s** to their
Jer 38:16 king **s** secretly to Jeremiah
Ezek 16: 8 I **s** an oath to you and entered
Dan 12: 7 **s** by Him who lives forever,
Mark 6:23 He also **s** to her, "Whatever
Luke 1:73 the oath which He **s** to our
Heb 3:11 So I **s** in My wrath, 'They
Heb 4: 3 So I **s** in My wrath, They
Heb 6:13 one greater, He **s** by Himself,
Rev 10: 6 **s** by Him who lives forever and

SWORN (*see* SWEAR)
Gen 22:16 By Myself I have **s**, says the
Ex 17:16 Because the LORD has **s**
Lev 6: 5 about which he has **s** falsely
Deut 2:14 as the LORD had **s** to them
Deut 28: 9 just as He has **s** to you, if
Deut 29:13 and just as He has **s** to your
Deut 31: 7 **s** to their fathers to give
Josh 5: 6 **s** to their fathers that He
Josh 9:18 of the congregation had **s** to
Josh 9:19 We have **s** to them by the LORD
Josh 21:43 **s** to give to their fathers
Josh 21:44 He had **s** to their fathers
Judg 2:15 and as the LORD had **s** to them
Judg 21: 1 had **s** an oath at Mizpah,
Judg 21: 7 seeing we have **s** by the LORD
Judg 21:18 of Israel have **s** an oath,
1Sa 3:14 therefore I have **s** to the
1Sa 20:42 since we have both **s** in the
2Sa 3: 9 as the LORD has **s** to him
2Sa 21: 2 had **s** protection to them, but
2Ch 15:15 for they had **s** with all their
Neh 9:15 which You had **s** to give them
Ps 24: 4 to an idol, Nor **s** deceitfully
Ps 89: 3 I have **s** to My servant David
Ps 89:35 Once I have **s** by My holiness
Ps 110: 4 The LORD has **s** And will not
Ps 119:106 I have **s** and confirmed That I
Ps 132:11 The LORD has **s** in truth to
Is 14:24 The LORD of hosts has **s**,
Is 45:23 I have **s** by Myself
Is 54: 9 for as I have **s** that the
Is 54: 9 so have I **s** that I would not
Is 62: 8 The LORD has **s** by His right
Jer 5: 7 **s** by those that are not gods
Jer 11: 5 I have **s** to your fathers, to
Jer 44:26 I have **s** by My great name,'
Jer 49:13 For I have **s** by Myself,"
Jer 51:14 of hosts has **s** by Himself
Ezek 21:23 who have **s** oaths with them
Amos 4: 2 GOD has **s** by His holiness
Amos 6: 8 The Lord GOD has **s** by Himself
Amos 8: 7 The LORD has **s** by the pride
Mic 7:20 which You have **s** to our
Hab 3: 9 oaths were **s** over Your arrows
Acts 2:30 knowing that God had **s** with
Acts 7:17 which God had **s** to Abraham
Heb 7:21 The LORD has **s** and will not

SYCAMORE (*see* SYCAMORES)
1Ch 27:28 the **s** trees that were in the
Ps 78:47 And their **s** trees with frost
Amos 7:14 and a tender of **s** fruit
Luke 19: 4 up into a **s** tree to see Him

SYCAMORES (*see* SYCAMORE)
1Ki 10:27 **s** which are in the lowland
2Ch 1:15 **s** which are in the lowland
2Ch 9:27 **s** which are in the lowland
Is 9:10 the **s** are cut down, but we

SYCHAR (*see* SHECHEM)
John 4: 5 of Samaria which is called **S**

SYENE
Ezek 29:10 and desolate, from Migdol to **S**
Ezek 30: 6 From Migdol to **S** those within

SYMBOL (*see* SYMBOLIC, SYMBOLS)
1Co 11:10 a **s** of authority on her head

SYMBOLIC (*see* SYMBOL)
Gal 4:24 which things are **s**
Heb 9: 9 It was **s** for the present time

SYMBOLS (*see* SYMBOL)
Hos 12:10 I have given **s** through the

SYMPATHIZE (*see* SYMPATHY)
Heb 4:15 cannot **s** with our weaknesses

SYMPATHY (*see* SYMPATHIZE)
Hos 11: 8 My **s** is stirred

SYMPHONY
Dan 3: 5 in **s** with all kinds of music,
Dan 3: 7 in **s** with all kinds of music,
Dan 3:10 in **s** with all kinds of music,
Dan 3:15 in **s** with all kinds of music,

SYNAGOGUE (*see* SYNAGOGUE'S, SYNAGOGUES)
Matt 12: 9 there, He went into their **s**
Matt 13:54 He taught them in their **s**
Mark 1:21 the Sabbath He entered the **s**
Mark 1:23 **s** with an unclean spirit
Mark 1:29 as they had come out of the **s**
Mark 3: 1 And He entered the **s** again
Mark 5:22 of the rulers of the **s** came
Mark 5:36 He said to the ruler of the **s**
Mark 5:38 house of the ruler of the **s**
Mark 6: 2 He began to teach in the **s**
Luke 4:16 He went into the **s** on the
Luke 4:20 in the **s** were fixed on Him
Luke 4:28 Then all those in the **s**, when
Luke 4:33 Now in the **s** there was a man
Luke 4:38 Now He arose from the **s** and
Luke 6: 6 also, that He entered the **s**
Luke 7: 5 nation, and has built us a **s**
Luke 8:41 and he was a ruler of the **s**
Luke 13:14 But the ruler of the **s**
John 6:59 **s** as He taught in Capernaum
John 9:22 he would be put out of the **s**
John 12:42 should be put out of the **s**
Acts 6: 9 from what is called the **S** of
Acts 13:14 and went into the **s** on the
Acts 13:15 rulers of the **s** sent to them
Acts 13:42 the Jews went out of the **s**
Acts 14: 1 together to the **s** of the Jews
Acts 17: 1 there was a **s** of the Jews
Acts 17:10 went into the **s** of the Jews
Acts 17:17 in the **s** with the Jews and
Acts 18: 4 in the **s** every Sabbath, and
Acts 18: 7 house was next door to the **s**
Acts 18: 8 Crispus, the ruler of the **s**
Acts 18:17 Sosthenes, the ruler of the **s**
Acts 18:19 but he himself entered the **s**
Acts 18:26 to speak boldly in the **s**
Acts 19: 8 And he went into the **s** and
Acts 22:19 that in every **s** I imprisoned
Acts 26:11 them often in every **s** and
Rev 2: 9 are not, but are a **s** of Satan
Rev 3: 9 make those of the **s** of Satan

SYNAGOGUE'S (*see* SYNAGOGUE)
Mark 5:35 ruler of the **s** house who said
Luke 8:49 from the ruler of the **s** house

SYNAGOGUES (*see* SYNAGOGUE)
Matt 4:23 Galilee, teaching in their **s**
Matt 6: 2 as the hypocrites do in the **s**
Matt 6: 5 to pray standing in the **s**
Matt 9:35 villages, teaching in their **s**

Matt 10:17 and scourge you in their **s**
Matt 23: 6 the best seats in the **s**,
Matt 23:34 you will scourge in your **s**
Mark 1:39 **s** throughout all Galilee, and
Mark 12:39 the best seats in the **s**, and
Mark 13: 9 you will be beaten in the **s**
Luke 4:15 And He taught in their **s**,
Luke 4:44 preaching in the **s** of Galilee
Luke 11:43 love the best seats in the **s**
Luke 12:11 when they bring you to the **s**
Luke 13:10 one of the **s** on the Sabbath
Luke 20:46 the best seats in the **s**, and
Luke 21:12 delivering you up to the **s**
John 16: 2 will put you out of the **s**
John 18:20 I always taught in **s** and in
Acts 9: 2 from him to the **s** of Damascus
Acts 9:20 preached the Christ in the **s**
Acts 13: 5 of God in the **s** of the Jews
Acts 15:21 read in the **s** every Sabbath
Acts 24:12 either in the **s** or in the

SYNTYCHE
Phil 4: 2 I implore **S** to be of the same

SYRACUSE
Acts 28:12 And landing at **S**, we stayed

SYRIA (*see* ARAM, SYRIAN, SYRIA'S)
Judg 10: 6 the Ashtoreths, the gods of **S**
2Sa 8: 6 garrisons in **S** of Damascus
2Sa 8:12 from **S**, from Moab, from the
2Sa 15: 8 while I dwelt at Geshur in **S**
1Ki 10:29 Hittites and the kings of **S**
1Ki 11:25 Israel, and reigned over **S**
1Ki 15:18 the son of Hezion, king of **S**
1Ki 19:15 anoint Hazael as king over **S**
1Ki 20: 1 of **S** gathered all his forces
1Ki 20:20 and Ben-Hadad the king of **S**
1Ki 20:22 of the year the king of **S**
1Ki 20:23 of the king of **S** said to him
1Ki 22: 1 passed without war between **S**
1Ki 22: 3 of the hand of the king of **S**
1Ki 22:31 Now the king of **S** had
2Ki 5: 1 of the army of the king of **S**
2Ki 5: 1 LORD had given victory to **S**
2Ki 5: 5 So the king of **S** said, "Go
2Ki 6: 8 Now the king of **S** was making
2Ki 6:11 of **S** was greatly troubled by
2Ki 6:24 of **S** gathered all his army
2Ki 8: 7 Ben-Hadad king of **S** was sick
2Ki 8: 9 king of **S** has sent me to you
2Ki 8:13 you will become king over **S**
2Ki 8:28 king of **S** at Ramoth Gilead
2Ki 8:29 against Hazael king of **S**
2Ki 9:14 against Hazael king of **S**
2Ki 9:15 fought with Hazael king of **S**
2Ki 12:17 Now Hazael king of **S** went up
2Ki 12:18 sent them to Hazael king of **S**
2Ki 13: 3 the hand of Hazael king of **S**
2Ki 13: 4 the king of **S** oppressed them
2Ki 13: 7 for the king of **S** had
2Ki 13:17 arrow of deliverance from **S**
2Ki 13:19 **S** till you had destroyed it
2Ki 13:19 strike **S** only three times
2Ki 13:22 Hazael king of **S** oppressed
2Ki 13:24 Now Hazael king of **S** died
2Ki 15:37 began to send Rezin king of **S**
2Ki 16: 5 Then Rezin king of **S** and Pekah
2Ki 16: 6 of **S** captured Elath for **S**
2Ki 16: 7 the hand of the king of **S**
1Ch 2:23 **S** took from them the towns of
1Ch 18: 6 garrisons in **S** of Damascus
2Ch 1:17 Hittites and the kings of **S**
2Ch 16: 2 sent to Ben-Hadad king of **S**
2Ch 16: 7 have relied on the king of **S**
2Ch 16: 7 the army of the king of **S** has
2Ch 18:30 Now the king of **S** had
2Ch 20: 2 from beyond the sea, from **S**
2Ch 22: 5 king of **S** at Ramoth Gilead
2Ch 22: 6 against Hazael king of **S**
2Ch 24:23 army of **S** came up against him
2Ch 28: 5 the hand of the king of **S**
2Ch 28:23 of the kings of **S** help them
Is 7: 1 Judah, that Rezin king of **S**
Is 7: 4 fierce anger of Rezin and **S**
Is 7: 5 Because **S**, Ephraim, and the
Is 7: 8 For the head of **S** is Damascus
Is 17: 3 Damascus, and the remnant of **S**
Ezek 16:57 of the daughters of **S** and all
Ezek 27:16 **S** was your merchant because
Hos 12:12 fled to the country of **S**
Amos 1: 5 the people of **S** shall go
Matt 4:24 fame went throughout all **S**
Luke 2: 2 Quirinius was governing **S**
Acts 15:23 of the Gentiles in Antioch, **S**
Acts 15:41 And he went through **S** and
Acts 18:18 the brethren and sailed for **S**
Acts 20: 3 as he was about to sail to **S**
Acts 21: 3 it on the left, sailed to **S**
Gal 1:21 I went into the regions of **S**

SYRIAN (*see* SYRIA, SYRIANS, SYRO-PHOENICIAN)
Gen 25:20 Bethuel the **S** of Padan Aram
Gen 25:20 the sister of Laban the **S**
Gen 28: 5 the son of Bethuel the **S**, the
Gen 31:20 away, unknown to Laban the **S**
Gen 31:24 the **S** in a dream by night
Deut 26: 5 My father was a **S**, about to
2Ki 5:20 has spared Naaman this **S**,
2Ki 6:23 So the bands of **S** raiders
2Ki 7: 5 the outskirts of the **S** camp
2Ki 7:10 We went to the **S** camp, and
2Ki 7:14 the direction of the **S** army
1Ch 7:14 his **S** concubine bore him
1Ch 19: 6 from **S** Maachah, and from
Luke 4:27 cleansed except Naaman the **S**

SYRIANS (*see* SYRIAN)
2Sa 8: 5 When the **S** of Damascus came
2Sa 8: 5 twenty-two thousand of the **S**
2Sa 8: 6 the **S** became David's servants
2Sa 8:13 **S** in the Valley of Salt
2Sa 10: 6 hired the **S** of Beth Rehob and
2Sa 10: 6 and the **S** of Zoba, twenty
2Sa 10: 8 the **S** of Zoba, Rehob, Ish-Tob
2Sa 10: 9 in battle array against the **S**
2Sa 10:11 If the **S** are too strong for
2Sa 10:13 for the battle against the **S**
2Sa 10:14 saw that the **S** were fleeing
2Sa 10:15 Now when the **S** saw that they
2Sa 10:16 brought out the **S** who were
2Sa 10:17 And the **S** set themselves in
2Sa 10:18 Then the **S** fled before Israel
2Sa 10:18 thousand horsemen of the **S**
2Sa 10:19 So the **S** were afraid to help
1Ki 20:20 so the **S** fled, and Israel
1Ki 20:21 killed the **S** with a great
1Ki 20:26 that Ben-Hadad mustered the **S**
1Ki 20:27 goats, while the **S** filled the
1Ki 20:28 Because the **S** have said
1Ki 20:29 soldiers of the **S** in one day
1Ki 22:11 **S** until they are destroyed
1Ki 22:35 in his chariot, facing the **S**
2Ki 5: 2 the **S** had gone out on raids,
2Ki 6: 9 for the **S** are coming down
2Ki 6:18 So when the **S** came down to
2Ki 7: 4 to the army of the **S**
2Ki 7: 5 to go to the camp of the **S**
2Ki 7: 6 of the **S** to hear the noise of
2Ki 7:12 what the **S** have done to us
2Ki 7:15 and weapons which the **S** had
2Ki 7:16 plundered the tents of the **S**
2Ki 8:28 and the **S** wounded Joram
2Ki 8:29 the **S** had inflicted on him at
2Ki 9:15 **S** had inflicted on him when
2Ki 13: 5 from under the hand of the **S**
2Ki 13:17 the **S** at Aphek till you have
2Ki 24: 2 of Chaldeans, bands of **S**,
1Ch 18: 5 When the **S** of Damascus came
1Ch 18: 5 twenty-two thousand of the **S**
1Ch 18: 6 the **S** became David's servants
1Ch 19:10 in battle array against the **S**
1Ch 19:12 If the **S** are too strong for
1Ch 19:14 for the battle against the **S**
1Ch 19:15 saw that the **S** were fleeing
1Ch 19:16 Now when the **S** saw that they
1Ch 19:16 brought the **S** who were beyond
1Ch 19:17 in battle array against the **S**
1Ch 19:18 Then the **S** fled before Israel
1Ch 19:18 foot soldiers of the **S**, and
1Ch 19:19 So the **S** were not willing to
2Ch 18:10 **S** until they are destroyed
2Ch 18:34 facing the **S** until evening
2Ch 22: 5 and the **S** wounded Joram
2Ch 24:24 For the army of the **S** came
Is 9:12 the **S** before and the
Jer 35:11 for fear of the army of the **S**
Amos 9: 7 Caphtor, and the **S** from Kir

SYRIA'S (*see* SYRIA)
Is 7: 2 **S** forces are deployed in

SYRO-PHOENICIAN (*see* SYRIAN)
Mark 7:26 a **S** by birth, and she kept

SYRTIS
Acts 27:17 run aground on the **S** Sands

T

TAANACH (*see* TANACH)
Josh 12:21 the king of **T**, one
Josh 17:11 towns, the inhabitants of **T**
Judg 1:27 Shean and its villages, or **T**
Judg 5:19 kings of Canaan fought in **T**
1Ki 4:12 Baana the son of Ahilud, in **T**
1Ch 7:29 Beth Shean and its towns, **T**

TAANATH SHILOH (*see* SHILOH)
Josh 16: 6 went around eastward to **T**

TABBAOTH
Ezra 2:43 of Hasupha, the sons of **T**
Neh 7:46 of Hasupha, the children of **T**

TABBATH
Judg 7:22 border of Abel Meholah, by **T**

TABEEL
Ezra 4: 7 also, Bishlam, Mithredath, **T**
Is 7: 6 over them, the son of **T**"

TABERAH
Num 11: 3 the name of the place **T**,
Deut 9:22 Also at **T** and Massah and

TABERNACLE (*see* TABERNACLES)
Ex 25: 9 that is, the pattern of the **t**
Ex 26: 1 **t** with ten curtains woven of
Ex 26: 6 so that it may be one **t**
Ex 26: 7 hair, to be a tent over the **t**
Ex 26:12 hang over the back of the **t**
Ex 26:13 hang over the sides of the **t**
Ex 26:15 for the **t** you shall make the
Ex 26:17 for all the boards of the **t**
Ex 26:18 make the boards for the **t**
Ex 26:20 for the second side of the **t**
Ex 26:22 For the far side of the **t**
Ex 26:23 the two back corners of the **t**
Ex 26:26 boards on one side of the **t**
Ex 26:27 on the other side of the **t**
Ex 26:27 boards of the side of the **t**
Ex 26:30 And you shall raise up the **t**
Ex 26:35 of the **t** toward the south
Ex 26:36 screen for the door of the **t**
Ex 27: 9 also make the court of the **t**
Ex 27:19 of the **t** for all its service
Ex 27:21 In the **t** of meeting, outside
Ex 28:43 come into the **t** of meeting
Ex 29: 4 the door of the **t** of meeting
Ex 29:10 before the **t** of meeting, and
Ex 29:11 the door of the **t** of meeting
Ex 29:30 days, when he enters the **t** of
Ex 29:32 the door of the **t** of meeting
Ex 29:42 at the door of the **t** of
Ex 29:43 the **t** shall be sanctified by
Ex 29:44 sanctify the **t** of meeting
Ex 30:16 service of the **t** of meeting
Ex 30:18 it between the **t** of meeting
Ex 30:20 they go into the **t** of meeting
Ex 30:26 shall anoint the **t** of meeting
Ex 30:36 the **t** of meeting where I will
Ex 31: 7 the **t** of meeting, the ark of
Ex 31: 7 and all the furniture of the **t**
Ex 33: 7 and called it the **t** of meeting
Ex 33: 7 to the **t** of meeting which was
Ex 33: 8 Moses went out to the **t**, that
Ex 33: 8 until he had gone into the **t**
Ex 33: 9 when Moses entered the **t**
Ex 33: 9 and stood at the door of the **t**
Ex 33:10 cloud standing at the **t** door
Ex 33:11 did not depart from the **t**
Ex 35:11 the **t**, its tent, its
Ex 35:15 door at the entrance of the **t**
Ex 35:18 the pegs of the **t**, the pegs
Ex 35:21 the work of the **t** of meeting
Ex 36: 8 them who worked on the **t** made
Ex 36:13 that it might be one **t**
Ex 36:14 hair for the tent over the **t**
Ex 36:20 For the **t** he made boards of
Ex 36:22 for all the boards of the **t**
Ex 36:23 And he made boards for the **t**

Ex 36:25 for the other side of the **t**
Ex 36:27 of the **t** he made six boards
Ex 36:28 the two back corners of the **t**
Ex 36:31 boards on one side of the **t**
Ex 36:32 on the other side of the **t**
Ex 36:32 **t** on the far side westward
Ex 36:37 made a screen for the **t** door
Ex 38: 8 the door of the **t** of meeting
Ex 38:20 All the pegs of the **t**, and of
Ex 38:21 is the inventory of the **t**
Ex 38:21 the **t** of the Testimony, which
Ex 38:30 the door of the **t** of meeting
Ex 38:31 gate, all the pegs for the **t**
Ex 39:32 Thus all the work of the **t** of
Ex 39:33 they brought the **t** to Moses
Ex 39:38 the screen for the **t** door
Ex 39:40 for the service of the **t**, for
Ex 40: 2 the **t** of the tent of meeting
Ex 40: 5 screen for the door of the **t**
Ex 40: 6 the **t** of the tent of meeting
Ex 40: 7 between the **t** of meeting and
Ex 40: 9 oil, and anoint the **t** and all
Ex 40:12 the door of the **t** of meeting
Ex 40:17 that the **t** was raised up
Ex 40:18 So Moses raised up the **t**,
Ex 40:19 out the tent over the **t** and
Ex 40:21 he brought the ark into the **t**
Ex 40:22 the table in the **t** of meeting
Ex 40:22 on the north side of the **t**
Ex 40:24 lampstand in the **t** of meeting
Ex 40:24 on the south side of the **t**
Ex 40:26 put the gold altar in the **t**
Ex 40:28 screen at the door of the **t**
Ex 40:29 the **t** of the tent of meeting
Ex 40:30 between the **t** of meeting and
Ex 40:32 went into the **t** of meeting
Ex 40:33 up the court all around the **t**
Ex 40:34 covered the **t** of meeting, and
Ex 40:34 of the LORD filled the **t**
Ex 40:35 to enter the **t** of meeting
Ex 40:35 of the LORD filled the **t**
Ex 40:36 was taken up from above the **t**
Ex 40:38 LORD was above the **t** by day
Lev 1: 1 to him from the **t** of meeting
Lev 1: 3 will at the door of the **t** of
Lev 1: 5 the door of the **t** of meeting
Lev 3: 2 the door of the **t** of meeting
Lev 3: 8 it before the **t** of meeting
Lev 3:13 it before the **t** of meeting
Lev 4: 4 **t** of meeting before the LORD
Lev 4: 5 bring it to the **t** of meeting
Lev 4: 7 which is in the **t** of meeting
Lev 4: 7 the door of the **t** of meeting
Lev 4:14 it before the **t** of meeting
Lev 4:16 blood to the **t** of meeting
Lev 4:18 which is in the **t** of meeting
Lev 4:18 the door of the **t** of meeting
Lev 6:16 in the court of the **t** of
Lev 6:26 the court of the **t** of meeting
Lev 6:30 brought into the **t** of meeting
Lev 8: 3 the door of the **t** of meeting
Lev 8: 4 the door of the **t** of meeting
Lev 8:10 oil, and anointed the **t** and all
Lev 8:31 the door of the **t** of meeting
Lev 8:33 **t** of meeting for seven days
Lev 8:35 door of the **t** of meeting day
Lev 9: 5 before the **t** of meeting
Lev 9:23 went into the **t** of meeting
Lev 10: 7 the door of the **t** of meeting
Lev 10: 9 you go into the **t** of meeting
Lev 12: 6 the door of the **t** of meeting
Lev 14:11 the door of the **t** of meeting
Lev 14:23 the door of the **t** of meeting
Lev 15:14 the door of the **t** of meeting
Lev 15:29 the door of the **t** of meeting
Lev 15:31 My **t** that is among them
Lev 16: 7 the door of the **t** of meeting
Lev 16:16 so he shall do for the **t** of
Lev 16:17 shall be no man in the **t** of
Lev 16:20 the **t** of meeting, and the
Lev 16:23 come into the **t** of meeting
Lev 16:33 for the **t** of meeting and for
Lev 17: 4 the door of the **t** of meeting
Lev 17: 4 LORD before the **t** of the LORD
Lev 17: 5 the door of the **t** of meeting
Lev 17: 6 the door of the **t** of meeting
Lev 17: 9 the door of the **t** of meeting
Lev 19:21 the door of the **t** of meeting
Lev 24: 3 in the **t** of meeting, Aaron
Lev 26:11 I will set My **t** among you
Num 1: 1 in the **t** of meeting, on the
Num 1:50 over the **t** of the Testimony
Num 1:50 they shall carry the **t** and all
Num 1:50 to it and camp around the **t**
Num 1:51 when the **t** is to go forward,
Num 1:51 when the **t** is to be set up,
Num 1:53 around the **t** of the Testimony
Num 1:53 of the **t** of the Testimony
Num 2: 2 from the **t** of meeting
Num 2:17 Then the **t** of meeting shall
Num 3: 7 before the **t** of meeting, to
Num 3: 7 to do the work of the **t**
Num 3: 8 of the **t** of meeting, and to
Num 3: 8 to do the work of the **t**
Num 3:23 to camp behind the **t** westward
Num 3:25 **t** of meeting included the **t**
Num 3:25 the door of the **t** of meeting
Num 3:26 court which are around the **t**
Num 3:29 on the south side of the **t**
Num 3:35 on the north side of the **t**
Num 3:36 included the boards of the **t**
Num 3:38 camp before the **t** on the east
Num 3:38 before the **t** of meeting
Num 4: 3 the work in the **t** of meeting
Num 4: 4 of Kohath in the **t** of meeting
Num 4:15 **t** of meeting which the sons
Num 4:16 the oversight of all the **t**
Num 4:23 the work in the **t** of meeting
Num 4:25 of the **t** and the **t** of meeting
Num 4:25 the door of the **t** of meeting
Num 4:26 court which are around the **t**
Num 4:28 Gershon in the **t** of meeting
Num 4:30 the work of the **t** of meeting
Num 4:31 service for the **t** of meeting
Num 4:31 the boards of the **t**, its bars
Num 4:33 service for the **t** of meeting
Num 4:35 for work in the **t** of meeting
Num 4:37 serve in the **t** of meeting
Num 4:39 for work in the **t** of meeting
Num 4:41 serve in the **t** of meeting
Num 4:43 for work in the **t** of meeting
Num 4:47 burdens in the **t** of meeting
Num 5:17 that is on the floor of the **t**
Num 6:10 the door of the **t** of meeting
Num 6:13 the door of the **t** of meeting
Num 6:18 the door of the **t** of meeting
Num 7: 1 had finished setting up the **t**
Num 7: 3 presented them before the **t**
Num 7: 5 the work of the **t** of meeting
Num 7:89 **t** of meeting to speak with
Num 8: 9 before the **t** of meeting, and
Num 8:15 to service the **t** of meeting
Num 8:19 of Israel in the **t** of meeting
Num 8:22 the **t** of meeting before Aaron
Num 8:24 the work of the **t** of meeting
Num 8:26 brethren in the **t** of meeting
Num 9:15 day that the **t** was raised up
Num 9:15 the cloud covered the **t**
Num 9:15 morning it was above the **t**
Num 9:17 was taken up from above the **t**
Num 9:18 the **t** they remained encamped
Num 9:19 long, many days above the **t**
Num 9:20 was above the **t** a few days
Num 9:22 cloud remained above the **t**
Num 10: 3 the door of the **t** of meeting
Num 10:11 above the **t** of the Testimony
Num 10:17 Then the **t** was taken down
Num 10:17 set out, carrying the **t**
Num 10:21 (The **t** would be prepared for
Num 11:16 them to the **t** of meeting,
Num 11:24 and placed them around the **t**
Num 11:26 who had not gone out to the **t**
Num 12: 4 three, to the **t** of meeting
Num 12: 5 and stood in the door of the **t**
Num 12:10 departed from above the **t**
Num 14:10 **t** of meeting before all the
Num 16: 9 the work of the **t** of the LORD
Num 16:18 the **t** of meeting with Moses
Num 16:19 the door of the **t** of meeting
Num 16:42 toward the **t** of meeting
Num 16:43 came before the **t** of meeting
Num 16:50 the door of the **t** of meeting
Num 17: 4 the **t** of meeting before the
Num 17: 7 the LORD in the **t** of witness
Num 17: 8 went into the **t** of witness
Num 17:13 the **t** of the LORD must die
Num 18: 2 you before the **t** of witness
Num 18: 3 and all the needs of the **t**
Num 18: 4 the needs of the **t** of meeting
Num 18: 4 for all the work of the **t**
Num 18: 6 the work of the **t** of meeting
Num 18:21 the work of the **t** of meeting
Num 18:22 come near the **t** of meeting
Num 18:23 the work of the **t** of meeting
Num 18:31 your work in the **t** of meeting
Num 19: 4 in front of the **t** of meeting
Num 19:13 defiles the **t** of the LORD
Num 20: 6 the door of the **t** of meeting
Num 25: 6 the door of the **t** of meeting
Num 27: 2 doorway of the **t** of meeting
Num 31:30 charge of the **t** of the LORD
Num 31:47 charge of the **t** of the LORD
Num 31:54 and brought it into the **t** of
Deut 31:14 in the **t** of meeting, that I
Deut 31:14 in the **t** of meeting
Deut 31:15 at the **t** in a pillar of cloud
Deut 31:15 stood above the door of the **t**
Josh 18: 1 set up the **t** of meeting there
Josh 19:51 the door of the **t** of meeting
Josh 22:19 where the LORD's **t** stands
Josh 22:29 our God which is before His **t**
1Sa 1: 9 doorpost of the **t** of the LORD
1Sa 2:22 the door of the **t** of meeting
1Sa 3: 3 **t** of the LORD where the ark
2Sa 6:17 place in the midst of the **t**
2Sa 7: 6 about in a tent and in a **t**
1Ki 1:39 took a horn of oil from the **t**
1Ki 2:28 fled to the **t** of the LORD
1Ki 2:29 has fled to the **t** of the LORD
1Ki 2:30 went to the **t** of the LORD
1Ki 8: 4 the **t** of meeting, and all the
1Ki 8: 4 that were in the **t**
1Ch 6:32 place of the **t** of meeting
1Ch 6:48 of the **t** of the house of God
1Ch 9:19 service, gatekeepers of the **t**
1Ch 9:21 the door of the **t** of meeting
1Ch 9:23 the LORD, the house of the **t**
1Ch 16: 1 **t** that David had erected for
1Ch 16:39 before the **t** of the LORD at
1Ch 17: 5 and from one **t** to another
1Ch 21:29 For the **t** of the LORD and the
1Ch 23:26 shall no longer carry the **t**
1Ch 23:32 the needs of the **t** of meeting
2Ch 1: 3 for the **t** of meeting with God
2Ch 1: 5 put before the **t** of the LORD
2Ch 1: 6 which was at the **t** of meeting
2Ch 1:13 from before the **t** of meeting
2Ch 5: 5 the **t** of meeting, and all the
2Ch 5: 5 that were in the **t**
2Ch 24: 6 Israel, for the **t** of witness
Ps 15: 1 Lord, who may abide in Your **t**
Ps 19: 4 He has set a **t** for the sun
Ps 27: 5 of His **t** He shall hide me
Ps 27: 6 sacrifices of joy in His **t**
Ps 43: 3 Your holy hill And to Your **t**
Ps 46: 4 of the **t** of the Most High
Ps 61: 4 will abide in Your **t** forever
Ps 76: 2 In Salem also is His **t**, And
Ps 78:60 He forsook the **t** of Shiloh
Ps 84: 1 How lovely is Your **t**, O LORD
Ps 132: 7 Let us go into His **t**
Is 4: 6 there will be a **t** for shade
Is 16: 5 in the **t** of David, judging and
Is 33:20 a **t** that will not be taken
Lam 2: 6 He has done violence to His **t**
Ezek 37:27 My **t** also shall be with them
Ezek 41: 1 the width of the **t**
Amos 9:11 will raise up The **t** of David
Acts 7:43 you took up the **t** of Moloch
Acts 7:44 had the **t** of witness in the
Acts 15:16 will rebuild the **t** of David
Heb 8: 2 of the true **t** which the Lord
Heb 8: 5 he was about to make the **t**
Heb 9: 2 For a **t** was prepared
Heb 9: 3 the part of the **t** which is
Heb 9: 6 into the first part of the **t**
Heb 9: 8 first **t** was still standing
Heb 9:11 more perfect **t** not made with
Heb 9:21 with blood both the **t** and all
Heb 13:10 the **t** have no right to eat
Rev 13: 6 to blaspheme His name, His **t**
Rev 15: 5 the temple of the **t** of the
Rev 21: 3 the **t** of God is with men, and

TABERNACLES (*see* TABERNACLE)
Lev 23:34 **T** for seven days to the LORD
Deut 16:13 the Feast of **T** seven days
Deut 16:16 Weeks, and at the Feast of **T**
Deut 31:10 of release, at the Feast of **T**
2Ch 8:13 of Weeks, and the Feast of **T**
Ezra 3: 4 They also kept the Feast of **T**

Zech 14:16 and to keep the Feast of **T**
Zech 14:18 up to keep the Feast of **T**
Zech 14:19 up to keep the Feast of **T**
Matt 17: 4 let us make here three **t**
Mark 9: 5 and let us make three **t**
Luke 9:33 and let us make three **t**
John 7: 2 Jews' Feast of **T** was at hand

TABITHA (*see* DORCAS)
Acts 9:36 a certain disciple named **T**
Acts 9:40 body he said, "**T**, arise."

TABLE (*see* TABLES)
Ex 25:23 also make a **t** of acacia wood
Ex 25:27 for the poles to bear the **t**
Ex 25:28 that the **t** may be carried
Ex 25:30 on the **t** before Me always
Ex 26:35 set the **t** outside the veil
Ex 26:35 from the **t** on the side of the
Ex 26:35 put the **t** on the north side
Ex 30:27 the **t** and all its utensils,
Ex 31: 8 the **t** and its utensils, the
Ex 35:13 the **t** and its poles, all its
Ex 37:10 He made the **t** of acacia wood
Ex 37:14 for the poles to bear the **t**
Ex 37:15 of acacia wood to bear the **t**
Ex 37:16 utensils which were on the **t**
Ex 39:36 the **t**, all its utensils, and
Ex 40: 4 You shall bring in the **t** and
Ex 40:22 He put the **t** in the
Ex 40:24 of meeting, across from the **t**
Lev 24: 6 on the pure **t** before the LORD
Num 3:31 duty included the ark, the **t**
Num 4: 7 On the **t** of showbread they
Judg 1: 7 gather their food under my **t**
1Sa 20:29 has not come to the king's **t**
1Sa 20:34 from the **t** in fierce anger
2Sa 9: 7 eat bread at my **t** continually
2Sa 9:10 eat bread at my **t** always
2Sa 9:11 he shall eat at my **t** like one
2Sa 9:13 continually at the king's **t**
2Sa 19:28 those who eat at your own **t**
1Ki 2: 7 among those who eat at your **t**
1Ki 4:27 who came to King Solomon's **t**
1Ki 7:48 the **t** of gold on which was
1Ki 10: 5 the food on his **t**, the
1Ki 13:20 as they sat at the **t**, that
1Ki 18:19 who eat at Jezebel's **t**
2Ki 4:10 a bed for him there, and a **t**
1Ch 28:16 of the showbread, for each **t**
2Ch 9: 4 the food on his **t**, the
2Ch 13:11 in order on the pure **t**, and
2Ch 29:18 the **t** of the showbread with
Neh 5:17 were at my **t** one hundred and
Job 36:16 what is set on your **t** would
Ps 23: 5 You prepare a **t** before me in
Ps 69:22 Let their **t** become a snare
Ps 78:19 prepare a **t** in the wilderness
Ps 128: 3 plants All around your **t**
Prov 9: 2 she has also furnished her **t**
Song 1:12 While the king is at his **t**
Is 21: 5 Prepare the **t**, set a watchman
Is 65:11 who prepare a **t** for Gad, and
Ezek 23:41 with a **t** prepared before it,
Ezek 39:20 be filled at My **t** with horses
Ezek 41:22 This is the **t** that is before
Ezek 44:16 near My **t** to minister to Me
Dan 11:27 speak lies at the same **t**
Mal 1: 7 saying, 'The **t** of the LORD is
Mal 1:12 The **t** of the LORD is defiled
Matt 9:10 sat at the **t** in the house
Matt 14: 9 who sat with him at the **t**
Matt 15:27 fall from their masters' **t**
Matt 26: 7 His head as He sat at the **t**
Mark 7:28 the **t** eat from the children's
Mark 14: 3 the leper, as He sat at the **t**
Mark 16:14 eleven as they sat at the **t**
Luke 7:37 the **t** in the Pharisee's house
Luke 7:49 those who sat at the **t** with
Luke 14:10 who sit at the **t** with you
Luke 14:15 **t** with Him heard these things
Luke 16:21 fell from the rich man's **t**
Luke 22:21 betrayer is with Me on the **t**
Luke 22:27 greater, he who sits at the **t**
Luke 22:27 it not he who sits at the **t**
Luke 22:30 drink at My **t** in My kingdom,
Luke 24:30 as He sat at the **t** with them
John 12: 2 who sat at the **t** with Him
John 13:28 But no one at the **t** knew for
Rom 11: 9 Let their **t** become a snare and
1Co 10:21 partake of the Lord's **t**
1Co 10:21 and of the **t** of demons
Heb 9: 2 was the lampstand, the **t**, and

TABLES (*see* TABLE)
1Ch 28:16 for the **t** of the showbread
1Ch 28:16 and silver for the **t** of silver
2Ch 4: 8 He also made ten **t**, and placed
2Ch 4:19 and the **t** on which was the
Is 28: 8 For all **t** are full of vomit
Ezek 40:39 were two **t** on this side and
Ezek 40:39 two **t** on that side, on which
Ezek 40:40 northern gateway, were two **t**
Ezek 40:40 of the gateway were two **t**
Ezek 40:41 Four **t** were on this side and
Ezek 40:41 four **t** on that side, by the
Ezek 40:41 eight **t** on which they
Ezek 40:42 There were also four **t** of
Ezek 40:43 the sacrifices was on the **t**
Matt 21:12 and overturned the **t** of the
Mark 11:15 and overturned the **t** of the
John 2:15 money and overturned the **t**
Acts 6: 2 the word of God and serve **t**

TABLET (*see* TABLETS)
Prov 3: 3 them on the **t** of your heart
Prov 7: 3 them on the **t** of your heart
Is 30: 8 write it before them on a **t**
Jer 17: 1 on the **t** of their heart, and
Ezek 4: 1 son of man, take a clay **t**
Luke 1:63 And he asked for a writing **t**

TABLETS (*see* TABLET)
Ex 24:12 and I will give you **t** of stone
Ex 31:18 Moses two **t** of the Testimony
Ex 31:18 **t** of stone, written with the
Ex 32:15 the two **t** of the Testimony
Ex 32:15 The **t** were written on both
Ex 32:16 Now the **t** were the work of
Ex 32:16 of God engraved on the **t**
Ex 32:19 and he cast the **t** out of his
Ex 34: 1 Cut two **t** of stone like the
Ex 34: 1 I will write on these **t** the
Ex 34: 1 the first **t** which you broke
Ex 34: 4 So he cut two **t** of stone like
Ex 34: 4 his hand the two **t** of stone
Ex 34:28 He wrote on the **t** the words
Ex 34:29 the two **t** of the Testimony
Deut 4:13 wrote them on two **t** of stone
Deut 5:22 wrote them on two **t** of stone
Deut 9: 9 to receive the **t** of stone
Deut 9: 9 the **t** of the covenant which
Deut 9:10 LORD delivered to me two **t** of
Deut 9:11 gave me the two **t** of stone
Deut 9:11 the **t** of the covenant
Deut 9:15 the two **t** of the covenant
Deut 9:17 Then I took the two **t** and
Deut 10: 1 Hew for yourself two **t** of
Deut 10: 2 I will write on the **t** the
Deut 10: 2 that were on the first **t**,
Deut 10: 3 hewed two **t** of stone like the
Deut 10: 3 having the two **t** in my hand
Deut 10: 4 He wrote on the **t** according
Deut 10: 5 put the **t** in the ark which I
1Ki 8: 9 **t** of stone which Moses put
2Ch 5:10 **t** which Moses put there at
Hab 2: 2 vision and make it plain on **t**
2Co 3: 3 God, not on **t** of stone
2Co 3: 3 but on **t** of flesh
Heb 9: 4 and the **t** of the covenant

TABOR (*see* AZNOTH TABOR, CHISLOTH TABOR)
Josh 19:22 And the border reached to **T**
Judg 4: 6 and deploy troops at Mount **T**
Judg 4:12 had gone up to Mount **T**
Judg 4:14 Mount **T** with ten thousand men
Judg 8:18 they whom you killed at **T**
1Sa 10: 3 to the terebinth tree of **T**
1Ch 6:77 and **T** with its common-lands
Ps 89:12 **T** and Hermon rejoice in Your
Jer 46:18 Surely as **T** is among the
Hos 5: 1 Mizpah and a net spread on **T**

TABRIMMON
1Ki 15:18 to Ben-Hadad the son of **T**

TACHMONITE (*see* HACHMONITE)
2Sa 23: 8 Josheb-Basshebeth the **T**,

TACKLE
Is 33:23 your **t** is loosed, they could
Acts 27:19 **t** overboard with our own

TADMOR
1Ki 9:18 **T** in the wilderness, in the
2Ch 8: 4 He also built **T** in the

TAHAN (*see* TAHANITES)
Num 26:35 of **T**, the family of the
1Ch 7:25 and Telah his son, **T** his son,

TAHANITES (*see* TAHAN)
Num 26:35 of Tahan, the family of the **T**

TAHATH
Num 33:26 Makheloth and camped at **T**
Num 33:27 They departed from **T** and
1Ch 6:24 **T** his son, Uriel his son,
1Ch 6:37 the son of **T**, the son of
1Ch 7:20 **T** his son, Eladah his son,
1Ch 7:20 Eladah his son, **T** his son,

TAHPANHES (*see* TAHPENES, TEHAPHNEHES)
Jer 2:16 **T** have broken the crown of
Jer 43: 7 And they went as far as **T**
Jer 43: 8 LORD came to Jeremiah in **T**
Jer 43: 9 to Pharaoh's house in **T**
Jer 44: 1 who dwell at Migdol, at **T**
Jer 46:14 Proclaim in Noph and in **T**

TAHPENES (*see* TAHPANHES)
1Ki 11:19 is, the sister of Queen **T**
1Ki 11:20 Then the sister of **T** bore him
1Ki 11:20 whom **T** weaned in Pharaoh's

TAHREA (*see* TAREA)
1Ch 9:41 Micah were Pithon, Melech, **T**

TAHTIM HODSHI
2Sa 24: 6 to Gilead and to the land of **T**

TAIL (*see* TAILS)
Ex 4: 4 hand and take it by the **t**"
Ex 29:22 the fat of the ram, the fat **t**
Lev 3: 9 and the whole fat **t** which he
Lev 7: 3 The fat **t** and the fat that
Lev 8:25 he took the fat and the fat **t**
Lev 9:19 the fatty **t**, what covers the
Deut 28:13 you the head and not the **t**
Deut 28:44 head, and you shall be the **t**
Judg 15: 4 turned the foxes **t** to **t**
Judg 15: 4 turned the foxes **t** to **t**
Job 40:17 He moves his **t** like a cedar
Is 9:14 **t** from Israel, palm branch and
Is 9:15 who teaches lies, he is the **t**
Is 19:15 Egypt, which the head or **t**
Rev 12: 4 His **t** drew a third of the

TAILS (*see* TAIL)
Judg 15: 4 torch between each pair of **t**
Rev 9:10 They had **t** like scorpions, and
Rev 9:10 there were stings in their **t**
Rev 9:19 in their mouth and in their **t**
Rev 9:19 for their **t** are like serpents

TAKE (*see* TAKEN, TAKES, TAKING, TOOK)
Gen 3:22 **t** also of the tree of life,
Gen 6:21 you shall **t** for yourself of
Gen 7: 2 You shall **t** with you seven
Gen 12:19 **t** her and go your way
Gen 13: 9 If you **t** the left, then I
Gen 14:21 and **t** the goods for yourself
Gen 14:23 that I will **t** nothing, from a
Gen 14:23 that I will not **t** anything
Gen 14:24 let them **t** their portion
Gen 19:12 **t** them out of this place
Gen 19:15 **t** your wife and your two
Gen 21:30 You will **t** these seven ewe
Gen 22: 2 **T** now your son, your only son
Gen 23:13 **t** it from me and I will bury
Gen 24: 3 that you will not **t** a wife
Gen 24: 4 **t** a wife for my son Isaac
Gen 24: 5 Must I **t** your son back to the
Gen 24: 6 do not **t** my son back there
Gen 24: 7 you shall **t** a wife for my son
Gen 24: 8 only do not **t** my son back
Gen 24:37 You shall not **t** a wife for
Gen 24:38 and **t** a wife for my son
Gen 24:40 you shall **t** a wife for my son
Gen 24:48 me in the way of truth to **t**
Gen 24:51 **t** her and go, and let her be
Gen 27: 3 please **t** your weapons, your
Gen 27:10 Then you shall **t** it to your
Gen 28: 1 You shall not **t** a wife from
Gen 28: 2 **t** yourself a wife from there
Gen 28: 6 **t** himself a wife from there
Gen 28: 6 You shall not **t** a wife from
Gen 30:15 Would you **t** away my son's

Gen 31:31 Perhaps you would **t** your
Gen 31:32 of yours and **t** it with you
Gen 31:50 or if you **t** other wives
Gen 33:11 **t** my blessing that is brought
Gen 33:12 said, "Let us **t** our journey
Gen 34: 9 **t** our daughters to yourselves
Gen 34:16 we will **t** your daughters to
Gen 34:17 then we will **t** our daughter
Gen 34:21 Let us **t** their daughters to
Gen 38:23 Let her **t** them for herself,
Gen 42:33 **t** food for the famine of your
Gen 42:36 you want to **t** Benjamin away
Gen 43:11 **T** some of the best fruits of
Gen 43:12 **T** double money in your hand,
Gen 43:12 **t** back in your hand the money
Gen 43:13 **T** your brother also, and arise
Gen 43:16 **T** these men to my home, and
Gen 43:18 to **t** us as slaves with our
Gen 44:29 But if you **t** this one also
Gen 45:19 **T** carts out of the land of
Ex 2: 9 **T** this child away and nurse
Ex 3: 5 **T** your sandals off your feet,
Ex 4: 4 **t** it by the tail" (and he
Ex 4: 9 that you shall **t** water from
Ex 4: 9 the water which you **t** from
Ex 4:17 you shall **t** this rod in your
Ex 5: 4 why do you **t** the people from
Ex 6: 7 I will **t** you as My people,
Ex 7: 9 **T** your rod and cast it before
Ex 7:15 you shall **t** in your hand
Ex 7:19 **T** your rod and stretch out
Ex 8: 8 the LORD that He may **t** away
Ex 9: 8 **T** for yourselves handfuls of
Ex 10:17 that He may **t** away from me
Ex 10:26 For we must **t** some of them to
Ex 10:28 **T** heed to yourself and see my
Ex 12: 3 shall **t** for himself a lamb
Ex 12: 4 **t** it according to the number
Ex 12: 5 You may **t** it from the sheep
Ex 12: 7 And they shall **t** some of the
Ex 12:21 out and **t** lambs for yourselves
Ex 12:22 you shall **t** a bunch of hyssop
Ex 12:32 Also **t** your flocks and your
Ex 13:22 He did not **t** away the pillar
Ex 15:14 sorrow will **t** hold of the
Ex 15:15 trembling will **t** hold of them
Ex 16:16 let every man **t** for those who
Ex 16:33 **T** a pot and put an omer of
Ex 17: 5 **t** with you some of the elders
Ex 17: 5 Also **t** in your hand your rod
Ex 19:12 **T** heed to yourselves that
Ex 20: 7 You shall not **t** the name of
Ex 21:14 you shall **t** him from My altar
Ex 22:26 If you ever **t** your neighbor's
Ex 23: 8 And you shall **t** no bribe, for
Ex 23:25 I will **t** sickness away from
Ex 25: 2 heart you shall **t** My offering
Ex 25: 3 which you shall **t** from them
Ex 28: 1 Now **t** Aaron your brother, and
Ex 28: 5 They shall **t** the gold and blue
Ex 28: 9 Then you shall **t** two onyx
Ex 29: 1 **T** one young bull and two rams
Ex 29: 5 Then you shall **t** the garments
Ex 29: 7 you shall **t** the anointing oil
Ex 29:12 You shall **t** some of the blood
Ex 29:13 you shall **t** all the fat that
Ex 29:15 You shall also **t** one ram, and
Ex 29:16 ram, and you shall **t** its blood
Ex 29:19 shall also **t** the other ram
Ex 29:20 **t** some of its blood and put it
Ex 29:21 you shall **t** some of the blood
Ex 29:22 Also you shall **t** the fat of
Ex 29:26 Then you shall **t** the breast
Ex 29:31 you shall **t** the ram of the
Ex 30:12 When you **t** the census of the
Ex 30:16 you shall **t** the atonement
Ex 30:23 Also **t** for yourself quality
Ex 30:34 **T** sweet spices, stacte and
Ex 33: 5 **t** off your ornaments, that I
Ex 33:23 Then I will **t** away My hand,
Ex 34: 9 and **t** us as Your inheritance
Ex 34:12 **T** heed to yourself, lest you
Ex 34:16 you **t** of his daughters for
Ex 34:34 he would **t** the veil off until
Ex 35: 5 **T** from among you an offering
Ex 40: 9 you shall **t** the anointing oil
Lev 2: 2 one of whom shall **t** from it
Lev 2: 9 Then the priest shall **t** from
Lev 4: 5 **t** some of the bull's blood
Lev 4: 8 He shall **t** from it all the
Lev 4:19 He shall **t** all the fat from
Lev 4:25 The priest shall **t** some of
Lev 4:30 Then the priest shall **t** some
Lev 4:34 The priest shall **t** some of
Lev 5:12 and the priest shall **t** his
Lev 6:10 **t** up the ashes of the burnt
Lev 6:11 Then he shall **t** off his
Lev 6:15 He shall **t** from it his
Lev 8: 2 **T** Aaron and his sons with him,
Lev 9: 2 **T** for yourself a young bull
Lev 9: 3 **T** a kid of the goats as a
Lev 10:12 **T** the grain offering that
Lev 14: 4 to **t** for him who is to be
Lev 14: 6 living bird, he shall **t** it
Lev 14:10 **t** two male lambs without
Lev 14:12 priest shall **t** one male lamb
Lev 14:14 The priest shall **t** some of
Lev 14:15 the priest shall **t** some of
Lev 14:21 then he shall **t** one male lamb
Lev 14:24 the priest shall **t** the lamb
Lev 14:25 the priest shall **t** some of
Lev 14:40 shall command that they **t**
Lev 14:42 they shall **t** other stones
Lev 14:42 he shall **t** other mortar and
Lev 14:49 And he shall **t**, to cleanse the
Lev 14:51 he shall **t** the cedar wood,
Lev 15:14 **t** for himself two turtledoves
Lev 15:29 **t** for herself two turtledoves
Lev 16: 5 And he shall **t** from the
Lev 16: 7 He shall **t** the two goats and
Lev 16:12 Then he shall **t** a censer full
Lev 16:14 He shall **t** some of the blood
Lev 16:18 shall **t** some of the blood of
Lev 16:23 shall **t** off the linen
Lev 18:17 nor shall you **t** her son's
Lev 18:18 Nor shall you **t** a woman as a
Lev 19:16 nor shall you **t** a stand
Lev 19:18 You shall not **t** vengeance
Lev 21: 7 They shall not **t** a wife who
Lev 21: 7 nor shall they **t** a woman
Lev 21:13 And he shall **t** a wife in her
Lev 21:14 but he shall **t** a virgin of
Lev 23:40 you shall **t** for yourselves on
Lev 24: 5 you shall **t** fine flour and
Lev 24:14 **T** outside the camp him who
Lev 25:36 **T** no usury or interest from
Lev 25:46 And you may **t** them as an
Num 1: 2 **T** a census of all the
Num 1:49 nor **t** a census of them among
Num 1:51 the Levites shall **t** it down
Num 3:40 **t** the number of their names
Num 3:41 you shall **t** the Levites for
Num 3:45 **T** the Levites instead of all
Num 3:47 you shall **t** five shekels for
Num 3:47 you shall **t** them in the
Num 4: 2 **T** a census of the sons of
Num 4: 5 and they shall **t** down the
Num 4: 9 they shall **t** a blue cloth and
Num 4:12 Then they shall **t** all the
Num 4:13 Also they shall **t** away the
Num 4:22 Also **t** a census of the sons
Num 5:17 The priest shall **t** holy
Num 5:17 **t** some of the dust that is on
Num 5:25 shall **t** the grain offering of
Num 5:26 the priest shall **t** a handful
Num 6: 2 to **t** the vow of a Nazirite
Num 6:18 shall **t** the hair from his
Num 6:19 the priest shall **t** the boiled
Num 8: 6 **T** the Levites from among the
Num 8: 8 Then let them **t** a young bull
Num 8: 8 you shall **t** another young
Num 11:17 I will **t** of the Spirit that
Num 13:30 **t** possession, for we are well
Num 16: 3 them, You **t** too much upon
Num 16: 6 **T** censers, Korah and all your
Num 16: 7 You **t** too much upon
Num 16:17 Each of you **t** his censer and
Num 16:46 **T** a censer and put fire in it
Num 16:46 on it, and **t** it quickly to the
Num 18:26 When you **t** from the children
Num 19: 3 that he may **t** it outside the
Num 19: 4 Eleazar the priest shall **t**
Num 19: 6 the priest shall **t** cedar wood
Num 19:17 **t** some of the ashes of the
Num 19:18 A clean person shall **t** hyssop
Num 20: 8 **T** the rod; you and your
Num 20:25 **T** Aaron and Eleazar his son,
Num 21: 7 pray to the LORD that He **t**
Num 23:12 Must I not **t** heed to speak
Num 23:27 I will **t** you to another place
Num 25: 4 **T** all the leaders of the
Num 26: 2 **T** a census of all the
Num 26: 4 **T** a census of the people from
Num 27:18 **T** Joshua the son of Nun with
Num 31: 2 **T** vengeance for the children
Num 31: 3 **t** vengeance for the LORD on
Num 31:29 **t** it from their half, and give
Num 31:30 shall **t** one of every fifty
Num 32: 5 do not **t** us over the Jordan
Num 32:23 you do not do so, then **t** note
Num 34:18 you shall **t** one leader of
Num 35:31 Moreover you shall **t** no
Num 35:32 you shall **t** no ransom for him
Deut 1: 7 **t** your journey, and go to the
Deut 1:40 and **t** your journey into the
Deut 2:24 **t** your journey, and cross over
Deut 3: 4 which we did not **t** from them
Deut 4: 2 nor **t** anything from it, that
Deut 4: 9 Only **t** heed to yourself, and
Deut 4:15 **T** careful heed to yourselves,
Deut 4:19 **t** heed, lest you lift your
Deut 4:23 **T** heed to yourselves, lest
Deut 4:34 **t** for Himself a nation from
Deut 5:11 You shall not **t** the name of
Deut 6:13 shall **t** oaths in His name
Deut 7: 3 nor **t** their daughter for your
Deut 7:15 the LORD will **t** away from you
Deut 7:25 nor **t** it for yourselves, lest
Deut 10:20 fast, and **t** oaths in His name
Deut 11:16 **T** heed to yourselves, lest
Deut 12: 6 There you shall **t** your burnt
Deut 12:13 **T** heed to yourself that you
Deut 12:19 **T** heed to yourself that you
Deut 12:26 vowed offerings, you shall **t**
Deut 12:30 **t** heed to yourself that you
Deut 12:32 add to it nor **t** away from it
Deut 14:25 **t** the money in your hand, and
Deut 15:17 then you shall **t** an awl and
Deut 16:19 nor **t** a bribe, for a bribe
Deut 20:19 making war against it to **t** it
Deut 21: 3 to the slain man will **t** a
Deut 21:10 hand, and you **t** them captive,
Deut 21:11 would **t** her for your wife,
Deut 21:19 mother shall **t** hold of him
Deut 22: 6 you shall not **t** the mother
Deut 22: 7 **t** the young for yourself,
Deut 22:15 of the young woman shall **t**
Deut 22:18 of that city shall **t** that man
Deut 22:30 A man shall not **t** his
Deut 24: 4 not **t** her back to be his wife
Deut 24: 6 No man shall **t** the lower or
Deut 24: 8 **T** heed in an outbreak of
Deut 24:17 nor **t** a widow's garment as a
Deut 25: 5 **t** her as his wife, and perform
Deut 25: 7 want to **t** his brother's wife
Deut 25: 8 says, 'I do not want to **t** her
Deut 26: 2 that you shall **t** some of the
Deut 26: 4 Then the priest shall **t** the
Deut 27: 9 **T** heed and listen, O Israel
Deut 28:68 the LORD will **t** you back to
Deut 31:26 **T** this Book of the Law, and
Josh 3: 6 **T** up the ark of the covenant
Josh 3:12 **t** for yourselves twelve men
Josh 4: 2 **T** for yourselves twelve men
Josh 4: 3 **T** for yourselves twelve
Josh 4: 5 each one of you **t** up a stone
Josh 5:15 **T** your sandal off your foot,
Josh 6: 6 **T** up the ark of the covenant,
Josh 6:18 you **t** of the accursed things
Josh 7:13 your enemies until you **t** away
Josh 8: 1 **t** all the people of war with
Josh 8: 2 its cattle you shall **t** as
Josh 8:29 **t** his corpse down from the
Josh 9:11 **T** provisions with you for
Josh 20: 4 they shall **t** him into the
Josh 22: 5 But **t** diligent heed to do the
Josh 22:19 and **t** possession among us
Josh 23:11 Therefore **t** diligent heed to
Judg 4: 6 **t** with you ten thousand men
Judg 6:20 **T** the meat and the unleavened
Judg 6:25 **T** your father's young bull,
Judg 6:26 **t** the second bull and offer a
Judg 9:15 come and **t** shelter in my shade
Judg 9:31 secretly, saying, "**T** note
Judg 11: 9 If you **t** me back home to
Judg 11:15 Israel did not **t** away the
Judg 12: 6 Then they would **t** him and kill
Judg 14:15 us in order to **t** what is ours
Judg 15: 2 Please, **t** her instead
Judg 15: 7 I will surely **t** revenge on

Judg 16:28 one blow t vengeance on the
Judg 19:15 for no one would t them into
Judg 19:18 who will t me into his house
Judg 19:30 it, t counsel, and speak up
Judg 20:10 We will t ten men out of
Judg 21:22 because we did not t a wife
Ruth 2:10 you should t notice of me
Ruth 3: 9 T your maidservant under your
1Sa 1:22 then I will t him, that he
1Sa 2:14 and the priest would t for
1Sa 2:15 for he will not t boiled meat
1Sa 2:16 then you may t as much as
1Sa 2:16 if not, I will t it by force
1Sa 6: 7 t two milk cows which have
1Sa 6: 7 t their calves home, away
1Sa 6: 8 Then t the ark of the LORD and
1Sa 6:21 come down and t it up with you
1Sa 8:11 He will t your sons and
1Sa 8:13 He will t your daughters to
1Sa 8:14 he will t the best of your
1Sa 8:15 He will t a tenth of your
1Sa 8:16 he will t your menservants and
1Sa 8:17 He will t a tenth of your
1Sa 9: 3 t one of the servants with
1Sa 12:13 t note, the LORD has set a
1Sa 16: 2 T a heifer with you, and say
1Sa 16:23 that David would t a harp
1Sa 17:17 T now for your brothers an
1Sa 17:46 you and t your head from you
1Sa 18:25 to t vengeance on the king's
1Sa 19:14 sent messengers to t David
1Sa 19:19 T note, David is at Naioth in
1Sa 19:20 sent messengers to t David
1Sa 21: 9 If you will t that, t it
1Sa 23:23 and t knowledge of all the
1Sa 23:26 David and his men to t them
1Sa 24: 1 told him, saying, "T note
1Sa 24:11 Yet you hunt my life to t it
1Sa 25:11 Shall I then t my bread and my
1Sa 25:39 Abigail, to t her as his wife
1Sa 26:11 t now the spear and the jug of
1Sa 30:15 Can you t me down to this
1Sa 30:15 I will t you down to this
2Sa 2:21 and t his armor for yourself
2Sa 12: 4 who refused to t from his own
2Sa 12:11 I will t your wives before
2Sa 12:28 t it, lest I t the city and
2Sa 13:13 I, where could I t my shame
2Sa 13:20 do not t this thing to heart
2Sa 13:33 king t the thing to his heart
2Sa 14:14 God does not t away a life
2Sa 15: 5 his hand and t him and kiss him
2Sa 15:20 and t your brethren back
2Sa 16: 9 me go over and t off his head
2Sa 18:19 t the news to the king, how
2Sa 18:20 You shall not t the news this
2Sa 18:20 day, for you shall t the news
2Sa 18:20 But today you shall t no news
2Sa 19:19 the king should t it to heart
2Sa 19:30 Rather, let him t it all,
2Sa 20: 6 T your lord's servants and
2Sa 24:10 t away the iniquity of Your
2Sa 24:13 t back to Him who sent me
2Sa 24:22 Let my lord the king t and
1Ki 1:33 T with you the servants of
1Ki 1:33 mule, and t him down to Gihon
1Ki 2: 4 If your sons t heed to their
1Ki 2:31 that you may t away from me
1Ki 5: 9 then you can t them away
1Ki 8:25 your sons t heed to their way
1Ki 8:31 and is forced to t an oath
1Ki 8:46 they t them captive to the
1Ki 11:31 T for yourself ten pieces,
1Ki 11:34 However I will not t the
1Ki 11:35 But I will t the kingdom out
1Ki 11:37 So I will t you, and you
1Ki 14: 3 Also t with you ten loaves,
1Ki 14:10 I will t away the remnant of
1Ki 16: 3 surely I will t away the
1Ki 19: 4 t my life, for I am no better
1Ki 19:10 and they seek to t my life
1Ki 19:14 and they seek to t my life
1Ki 20: 6 put in their hands and t it
1Ki 20:18 out for peace, t them alive
1Ki 20:18 out for war, t them alive
1Ki 20:22 t note, and see what you
1Ki 20:41 Then he hastened to t the
1Ki 21:10 Then t him out, and stone him
1Ki 21:15 t possession of the vineyard
1Ki 21:16 went down to t possession of
1Ki 21:18 down to t possession of it
1Ki 21:21 I will t away your posterity,
1Ki 22: 3 but we hesitate to t it out
1Ki 22:26 T Micaiah, and return him to
1Ki 22:28 T heed, all you people
1Ki 22:34 t me out of the battle, for I
2Ki 2: 1 t up Elijah into heaven by a
2Ki 2: 3 t away your master from over
2Ki 2: 5 t away your master from over
2Ki 4: 1 to t my two sons to be his
2Ki 4:29 t my staff in your hand, and
2Ki 5:15 please t a gift from your
2Ki 5:16 And he urged him to t it
2Ki 5:20 him and t something from him
2Ki 5:23 said, "Please, t two talents
2Ki 6: 2 let every man t a beam from
2Ki 6:32 someone to t away my head
2Ki 7:13 let several men t five of the
2Ki 8: 8 T a present in your hand, and
2Ki 9: 1 t this flask of oil in your
2Ki 9: 2 and t him to an inner room
2Ki 9: 3 Then t the flask of oil, and
2Ki 9:13 man hastened to t his garment
2Ki 9:26 Now therefore, t and throw him
2Ki 10: 6 t the heads of the men, your
2Ki 10:14 And he said, "T them alive
2Ki 11:15 T her outside under guard, and
2Ki 12: 5 the priests t it themselves
2Ki 12: 7 do not t any more money from
2Ki 13:15 him, "T a bow and some arrows
2Ki 13:18 he said, "T the arrows"
2Ki 18:32 t you away to a land like
2Ki 19:30 shall again t root downward
2Ki 20: 7 said, "T a lump of figs
2Ki 20:18 they shall t away some of
1Ch 7:21 down to t away their cattle
1Ch 17:13 I will not t My mercy away
1Ch 21: 8 t away the iniquity of Your
1Ch 21:12 what answer I should t back
1Ch 21:23 T it to yourself, and let my
1Ch 21:24 for I will not t what is
1Ch 22:13 if you t care to fulfill the
1Ch 27:23 But David did not t the
2Ch 6:16 your sons t heed to their way
2Ch 6:22 and is forced to t an oath
2Ch 6:36 they t them captive to a land
2Ch 12:11 then they would t them back
2Ch 18:25 T Micaiah, and return him to
2Ch 18:27 T heed, all you people
2Ch 18:33 t me out of the battle, for I
2Ch 19: 6 T heed to what you are doing,
2Ch 19: 7 t care and do it, for there is
2Ch 19:11 And t notice
2Ch 20:25 came to t away their spoil
2Ch 23:14 T her outside under guard, and
2Ch 32:18 that they might t the city
2Ch 34:32 Benjamin t their stand for it
2Ch 35:23 T me away, for I am severely
Ezra 4:22 T heed now that you do not
Ezra 5:15 to him, 'T these articles
Ezra 9:12 nor t their daughters to your
Neh 6: 7 let us t counsel together
Neh 10:30 nor t their daughters for our
Neh 13:25 nor t their daughters for
Esth 2:13 whatever she desired to t
Esth 4: 4 t his sackcloth away from him
Esth 6:10 t the robe and the horse, as
Job 7:21 and t away my iniquity
Job 9:34 Let Him t His rod away from
Job 10:20 that I may t a little comfort
Job 11:18 you, and t your rest in safety
Job 13:14 Why do I t my flesh in my
Job 23: 6 But He would t note of me
Job 23:10 But He knows the way that I t
Job 24: 3 they t the widow's ox as a
Job 24: 9 and t a pledge from the poor
Job 24:10 they t away the sheaves from
Job 30:16 of affliction t hold of me
Job 30:17 and my gnawing pains t no rest
Job 32:22 my Maker would soon t me away
Job 33: 5 t your stand
Job 36:17 and justice t hold of you
Job 36:18 beware lest He t you away
Job 36:21 T heed, do not turn to
Job 38:13 that it might t hold of the
Job 38:20 that you may t it to its
Job 41: 4 Will you t him as a servant
Job 42: 8 t for yourselves seven bulls
Ps 2: 2 the rulers t counsel together
Ps 13: 2 How long shall I t counsel in
Ps 15: 3 Nor does he t up a reproach
Ps 15: 5 Nor does he t a bribe against
Ps 16: 4 Nor t up their names on my
Ps 27:10 the LORD will t care of me
Ps 28: 3 Do not t me away with the
Ps 31:13 While they t counsel together
Ps 31:13 They scheme to t away my life
Ps 35: 2 T hold of shield and buckler,
Ps 50: 9 I will not t a bull from your
Ps 50:16 Or t My covenant in your
Ps 51:11 do not t Your Holy Spirit
Ps 52: 5 He shall t you away, and pluck
Ps 58: 9 He shall t them away as with
Ps 69:20 looked for someone to t pity
Ps 69:24 wrathful anger t hold of them
Ps 71:10 my life t counsel together
Ps 71:11 t him, for there is none to
Ps 74:11 T it out of Your bosom and
Ps 80: 9 And caused it to t deep root
Ps 83:12 Let us t for ourselves The
Ps 89:33 I will not utterly t from him
Ps 91: 4 His wings you shall t refuge
Ps 102:14 For Your servants t pleasure
Ps 102:24 Do not t me away in the midst
Ps 104:29 You t away their breath, they
Ps 109: 8 And let another t his office
Ps 116:13 I will t up the cup of
Ps 119:43 And t not the word of truth
Ps 139: 9 If I t the wings of the
Ps 139:20 Your enemies t Your name in
Ps 141: 8 In You I t refuge
Ps 143: 9 In You I t shelter
Ps 144: 2 and the One in whom I t refuge
Ps 144: 3 that You t knowledge of him
Prov 3:18 to those who t hold of her
Prov 4:13 T firm hold of instruction,
Prov 6:27 can a man t fire to his bosom
Prov 7:18 let us t our fill of love
Prov 7:23 not know it would t his life
Prov 20:16 T the garment of one who is
Prov 22:27 why should he t away your bed
Prov 25: 4 T away the dross from silver,
Prov 25: 5 T away the wicked from before
Prov 27:13 T the garment of him who is
Eccl 5:15 he shall t nothing from his
Eccl 7: 2 the living will t it to heart
Eccl 7:21 Also do not t to heart
Eccl 8: 3 Do not t your stand for an
Song 7: 8 I will t hold of its branches
Is 1:24 t vengeance on My enemies
Is 1:25 and t away all your alloy
Is 3:18 Lord will t away the finery
Is 4: 1 women shall t hold of one man
Is 4: 1 name, to t away our reproach
Is 5: 5 I will t away its hedge, and
Is 5:23 and t away justice from the
Is 7: 4 T heed, and be quiet
Is 8: 1 T a large scroll, and write on
Is 8: 2 I will t for Myself faithful
Is 8:10 T counsel together, but it
Is 10: 2 to t what is right from the
Is 10: 6 to t the prey, and to tread
Is 13: 8 sorrows will t hold of them
Is 14: 2 Then people will t them and
Is 14: 2 they will t them captive
Is 14: 4 that you will t up this
Is 14:32 people shall t refuge in it
Is 16: 3 T counsel, execute judgment
Is 18: 4 I will t My rest, and I will
Is 18: 5 and t away and cut down the
Is 20: 2 t your sandals off your feet
Is 23:16 T a harp, go about the city,
Is 25: 8 of His people He will t away
Is 27: 5 Or let him t hold of My
Is 27: 6 cause to t root in Jacob
Is 28:19 as it goes out it will t you
Is 30: 1 Who t counsel, but not of Me,
Is 30:14 to t fire from the hearth
Is 30:14 or to t water from the
Is 33:23 the lame t the prey
Is 36:17 t you away to a land like
Is 37:31 shall again t root downward
Is 38:21 Let them t a lump of figs, and
Is 39: 7 they shall t away some of
Is 40:14 With whom did He t counsel
Is 40:24 stock t root in the earth
Is 40:24 the whirlwind will t them
Is 42:25 yet he did not t it to heart
Is 44:15 for he will t some of it
Is 45:21 let them t counsel together

Is 45:23 every tongue shall t an oath
Is 47: 2 T the millstones and grind
Is 47: 2 t off the skirt, uncover the
Is 47: 3 I will t vengeance, and I will
Is 47: 7 so that you did not t these
Is 49: 1 t heed, you peoples from afar
Is 57:13 away, a breath will t them
Is 57:14 t the stumbling block out of
Is 58: 2 they t delight in approaching
Is 58: 3 our souls, and You t no notice
Is 58: 9 If you t away the yoke from
Is 62:10 T out the stones, lift up a
Is 64: 7 himself up to t hold of You
Is 66:21 I will also t some of them
Jer 2:18 now why t the road to Egypt,
Jer 2:18 Or why t the road to Assyria,
Jer 3:14 I will t you, one from a city
Jer 4: 4 t away the foreskins of your
Jer 4: 6 T refuge
Jer 5:10 T away her branches, for they
Jer 7:29 t up a lamentation on the
Jer 9: 4 Everyone t heed to his
Jer 9:10 I will t up a weeping and
Jer 9:18 t up a wailing for us, that
Jer 13: 4 T the sash that you acquired,
Jer 13: 6 t from there the sash which I
Jer 15:15 and t vengeance for me on my
Jer 15:15 Do not t me away in Your
Jer 15:19 If you t out the precious
Jer 16: 2 You shall not t a wife, nor
Jer 17:21 T heed to yourselves, and bear
Jer 18:22 they have dug a pit to t me
Jer 19: 1 t some of the elders of the
Jer 20:10 we will t our revenge on him
Jer 25: 9 t all the families of the
Jer 25:10 Moreover I will t from them
Jer 25:15 T this wine cup of fury from
Jer 25:28 if they refuse to t the cup
Jer 27:20 king of Babylon did not t
Jer 29: 6 T wives and beget sons and
Jer 29: 6 t wives for your sons and give
Jer 32: 3 of Babylon, and he shall t it
Jer 32:14 T these deeds, both this
Jer 32:24 have come to the city to t it
Jer 32:25 for money, and t witnesses"
Jer 32:28 of Babylon, and he shall t it
Jer 32:44 t witnesses, in the land of
Jer 33:26 so that I will not t any of
Jer 34:22 t it and burn it with fire
Jer 36: 2 T a scroll of a book and write
Jer 36:14 T in your hand the scroll
Jer 36:28 T yet another scroll, and
Jer 37: 8 t it and burn it with fire
Jer 38: 3 army, which shall t it
Jer 38:10 T from here thirty men with
Jer 39:12 T him and look after him, and
Jer 39:14 then they sent someone to t
Jer 39:14 that he should t him home
Jer 43: 9 T large stones in your hand,
Jer 44:12 I will t the remnant of Judah
Jer 46:11 and t balm, O virgin, the
Jer 49: 2 shall t possession of his
Jer 49:29 flocks they shall t away
Jer 49:29 They shall t for themselves
Jer 50:15 T vengeance on her
Jer 51: 8 T balm for her pain
Jer 51:26 They shall not t from you a
Jer 51:36 case and t vengeance for you
Ezek 4: 1 t a clay tablet and lay it
Ezek 4: 3 Moreover t for yourself an
Ezek 4: 9 Also t for yourself wheat,
Ezek 5: 1 t a sharp sword
Ezek 5: 1 t it as a barber's razor, and
Ezek 5: 1 then t balances to weigh and
Ezek 5: 2 then you shall t one-third
Ezek 5: 3 You shall also t a small
Ezek 5: 4 Then t some of them again and
Ezek 10: 6 T fire from among the wheels,
Ezek 11:18 and they will t away all its
Ezek 11:19 and t the stony heart out of
Ezek 16:39 t your beautiful jewelry, and
Ezek 17:22 I will t also one of the
Ezek 19: 1 Moreover t up a lamentation
Ezek 21:26 turban, and t off the crown
Ezek 22:12 In you they t bribes to shed
Ezek 22:12 you t usury and increase
Ezek 23:25 they shall t your sons and
Ezek 23:26 t away your beautiful jewelry
Ezek 23:29 t away all you have worked
Ezek 24: 5 t the choice of the flock
Ezek 24: 8 t vengeance, I have set her
Ezek 24:16 I t away from you the desire
Ezek 24:25 t from them their stronghold
Ezek 26:16 and t off their embroidered
Ezek 26:17 they will t up a lamentation
Ezek 27: 2 t up a lamentation for Tyre,
Ezek 27:32 they will t up a lamentation
Ezek 28:12 t up a lamentation for the
Ezek 29:19 he shall t away her wealth,
Ezek 30: 4 they t away her wealth, and
Ezek 32: 2 man, t up a lamentation for
Ezek 33: 2 the people of the land t a
Ezek 33: 4 trumpet and does not t warning
Ezek 33: 5 but did not t warning
Ezek 36:12 they shall t possession of
Ezek 36:24 For I will t you from among
Ezek 36:26 I will t the heart of stone
Ezek 37:16 t a stick for yourself and
Ezek 37:16 Then t another stick and
Ezek 37:19 Surely I will t the stick of
Ezek 37:21 Surely I will t the children
Ezek 38:12 to t plunder and to t booty
Ezek 38:13 Have you come to t plunder
Ezek 38:13 gathered your army to t booty
Ezek 38:13 to t away livestock and goods,
Ezek 38:13 to t great plunder
Ezek 39:10 They will not t wood from the
Ezek 43:20 You shall t some of its
Ezek 43:21 also t the bull of the sin
Ezek 44:19 they shall t off their
Ezek 44:22 They shall not t as wife a
Ezek 44:22 woman, but t virgins of the
Ezek 45:18 you shall t a young bull
Ezek 45:19 The priest shall t some of
Ezek 46:18 not t any of the people's
Dan 2:24 t me before the king, and I
Dan 6:23 t Daniel up out of the den
Dan 7:26 and they shall t away his
Dan 11:15 mound, and t a fortified city
Dan 11:18 coastlands, and shall t many
Dan 11:31 then they shall t away the
Hos 1: 2 t yourself a wife of harlotry
Hos 1: 6 I will utterly t them away
Hos 2: 9 t away my grain in its time
Hos 2: 9 will t back My wool and My
Hos 2:17 For I will t from her mouth
Hos 5: 1 T heed, O house of Israel
Hos 5:14 I will t them away, and no one
Hos 11: 4 t the yoke from their neck
Hos 14: 2 T words with you, and return
Hos 14: 2 to Him, 'T away all iniquity
Amos 4: 2 t you away with fishhooks
Amos 5: 1 word which I t up against you
Amos 5:11 and t grain taxes from him,
Amos 5:12 afflict the just and t bribes
Amos 5:23 T away from Me the noise of
Amos 6:10 to t them out of the house
Amos 9: 2 there my hand shall t them
Amos 9: 3 there I will search and t them
Jon 4: 3 please t my life from me, for
Mic 2: 2 and t them by violence, also
Mic 2: 4 In that day one shall t up a
Nah 1: 2 the LORD will t vengeance on
Nah 2: 9 T spoil of silver
Nah 2: 9 T spoil of gold
Hab 1:15 They t up all of them with a
Hab 2: 6 Shall not all these t up a
Zeph 3:11 for then I will t away from
Hag 1: 8 that I may t pleasure in it
Hag 2:23 LORD of hosts, 'I will t you
Zech 2:12 the LORD will t possession of
Zech 3: 4 T away the filthy garments
Zech 6:11 T the silver and gold, make an
Zech 9: 7 I will t away the blood from
Zech 11:15 t for yourself the implements
Zech 14:21 and t them and cook in them
Mal 2: 2 if you will not t it to heart
Mal 2: 2 you do not t it to heart
Mal 2: 3 one will t you away with it
Mal 2:15 Therefore t heed to your
Mal 2:16 Therefore t heed to your
Matt 1:20 do not be afraid to t to you
Matt 2:13 t the young Child and His
Matt 2:20 t the young Child and His
Matt 5:40 t away your tunic, let him
Matt 6: 1 T heed that you do not do
Matt 9: 6 t up your bed, and go to your
Matt 10:38 he who does not t his cross
Matt 11:12 and the violent t it by force
Matt 11:29 T My yoke upon you and learn
Matt 15:26 It is not good to t the
Matt 16: 5 they had forgotten to t bread
Matt 16: 6 T heed and beware of the
Matt 16:24 t up his cross, and follow Me
Matt 17:25 the earth t customs or taxes
Matt 17:27 and t the fish that comes up
Matt 17:27 t that and give it to them for
Matt 18:10 T heed that you do not
Matt 18:16 t with you one or two more,
Matt 20:14 T what is yours and go your
Matt 22:13 t him away, and cast him into
Matt 24: 4 T heed that no one deceives
Matt 24:17 t anything out of his house
Matt 25:28 Therefore t the talent from
Matt 25:38 t You in, or naked and clothe
Matt 25:43 and you did not t Me in, naked
Matt 26: 4 and plotted to t Jesus by
Matt 26:26 T, eat; this is My body
Matt 26:52 for all who t the sword will
Matt 26:55 with swords and clubs to t Me
Mark 2: 9 Arise, t up your bed and walk'
Mark 2:11 t up your bed, and go your way
Mark 4:24 them, "T heed what you hear
Mark 6: 8 He commanded them to t
Mark 7:27 to t the children's bread
Mark 8:14 had forgotten to t bread, and
Mark 8:15 T heed, beware of the leaven
Mark 8:19 of fragments did you t up
Mark 8:20 of fragments did you t up
Mark 8:34 t up his cross, and follow Me
Mark 10:21 t up the cross, and follow Me
Mark 12:19 his brother should t his wife
Mark 13: 5 T heed that no one deceives
Mark 13:15 nor enter to t anything out
Mark 13:23 But t heed; see, I have told
Mark 13:30 till all these things t place
Mark 13:33 T heed, watch and pray
Mark 14: 1 they might t Him by trickery
Mark 14:22 T, eat; this is My body
Mark 14:36 T this cup away from Me
Mark 14:44 t Him and lead Him away safely
Mark 14:48 with swords and clubs to t Me
Mark 14:49 teaching, and you did not t Me
Mark 15:23 to drink, but He did not t it
Mark 15:24 what every man should t
Mark 15:36 will come to t Him down
Mark 16:18 they will t up serpents
Luke 1:20 the day these things t place
Luke 1:25 to t away my reproach among
Luke 5:24 t up your bed, and go to your
Luke 8:18 Therefore t heed how you hear
Luke 9: 3 T nothing for the journey,
Luke 9:23 and t up his cross daily, and
Luke 10:35 said to him, 'T care of him
Luke 11:35 Therefore t heed that the
Luke 12:15 them, "T heed and beware of
Luke 12:19 t your ease; eat, drink
Luke 14: 9 shame to t the lowest place
Luke 16: 6 T your bill, and sit down
Luke 16: 7 T your bill, and write eighty
Luke 17: 3 T heed to yourselves
Luke 17:31 not come down to t them away
Luke 19:24 T the mina from him, and give
Luke 20:28 his brother should t his wife
Luke 21: 7 things are about to t place
Luke 21: 8 T heed that you not be
Luke 21:34 But t heed to yourselves,
Luke 22:17 T this and divide it among
Luke 22:36 has a money bag, let him t it
John 2: 8 t it to the master of the
John 2:16 doves, "T these things away
John 5: 8 Rise, t up your bed and walk
John 5:11 to me, 'T up your bed and walk
John 5:12 you, 'T up your bed and walk'
John 6:15 t Him by force to make Him
John 7:30 Then they sought to t Him
John 7:32 sent officers to t Him
John 7:44 some of them wanted to t Him
John 10:17 My life that I may t it again
John 10:18 and I have power to t it again
John 11:39 said, "T away the stone
John 11:48 and t away both our place and
John 12: 6 he used to t what was put in
John 16:14 for He will t of what is Mine
John 16:15 I said that He will t of Mine
John 16:22 joy no one will t from you
John 17:15 t them out of the world, but
John 18:31 You t Him and judge Him
John 19: 6 You t Him and crucify Him, for
John 19:38 t away the body of Jesus

John 20:15 Him, and I will t Him away
Acts 1:20 and, 'Let another t his office
Acts 1:25 to t part in this ministry and
Acts 5:35 t heed to yourselves what you
Acts 7:33 T your sandals off your feet,
Acts 15:14 visited the Gentiles to t out
Acts 15:37 t with them John called Mark
Acts 15:38 that they should not t with
Acts 20:13 intending to t Paul on board
Acts 20:28 Therefore t heed to
Acts 21:24 T them and be purified with
Acts 22:26 T care what you do, for this
Acts 23:10 t him by force from among
Acts 23:17 T this young man to the
Acts 27:22 And now I urge you to t heart
Acts 27:25 Therefore t heart, men, for I
Acts 27:33 implored them all to t food
Acts 27:34 I urge you to t nourishment
Rom 11:27 when I t away their sins
1Co 3:10 But let each one t heed how
1Co 6:15 Shall I then t the members of
1Co 9: 5 to t along a believing wife
1Co 10:12 he stands t heed lest he fall
1Co 11:24 T, eat; this is My body
2Co 2:11 should t advantage of us
2Co 12:10 Therefore I t pleasure in
2Co 12:17 Did I t advantage of you by
2Co 12:18 Did Titus t advantage of you
Eph 6:13 Therefore t up the whole
Eph 6:17 t the helmet of salvation, and
Col 4:17 T heed to the ministry which
1Th 4: 6 no one should t advantage of
1Ti 3: 5 how will he t care of the
1Ti 4:16 T heed to yourself and to the
Heb 2: 6 of man that You t care of him
Heb 10: 4 and goats could t away sins
Heb 10:11 which can never t away sins
Jas 5:10 t the prophets, who spoke in
1Pe 2:20 faults, you t it patiently
1Pe 2:20 if you t it patiently, this
1Jn 3: 5 manifested to t away our sins
Rev 1: 1 which must shortly t place
Rev 1:19 which will t place after this
Rev 3:11 that no one may t your crown
Rev 4: 1 which must t place after this
Rev 5: 9 are worthy to t the scroll
Rev 6: 4 it to t peace from the earth
Rev 10: 8 t the little book which is
Rev 10: 9 T and eat it
Rev 22: 6 which must shortly t place
Rev 22:17 let him t the water of life
Rev 22:19 God shall t away his part

TAKEN (*see* TAKE)
Gen 2:22 had t from man He made into a
Gen 2:23 because she was t out of Man
Gen 3:19 for out of it you were t
Gen 3:23 ground from which he was t
Gen 4:15 shall be t on him sevenfold
Gen 12:15 the woman was t to Pharaoh's
Gen 12:19 I might have t her as my wife
Gen 14:14 his brother was t captive
Gen 18:27 ashes have t it upon myself
Gen 18:31 I have t it upon myself to
Gen 20: 3 of the woman whom you have t
Gen 27:35 and has t away your blessing
Gen 27:36 he has t away my blessing
Gen 30:15 you have t away my husband
Gen 30:23 God has t away my reproach
Gen 31: 1 Jacob has t away all that was
Gen 31: 9 So God has t away the
Gen 31:16 t from our father are really
Gen 31:26 captives t with the sword
Gen 31:34 Now Rachel had t the
Gen 39: 1 had been t down to Egypt
Gen 39: 1 who had t him down there
Ex 14:11 have you t us away to die in
Ex 25:15 they shall not be t from it
Ex 40:36 cloud was t up from above the
Ex 40:37 But if the cloud was not t up
Ex 40:37 till the day that it was t up
Lev 4:10 as it was t from the bull of
Lev 7:34 the heave offering I have t
Lev 14:43 after he has t away the
Lev 24: 8 being t from the children of
Num 3:12 I Myself have t the Levites
Num 8:16 I have t them for Myself
Num 8:18 I have t the Levites instead
Num 9:17 cloud was t up from above the
Num 9:21 cloud was t up in the morning
Num 9:21 whenever the cloud was t up
Num 9:22 but when it was t up, they
Num 10:11 cloud was t up from above the
Num 10:17 the tabernacle was t down
Num 16:15 I have not t one donkey from
Num 18: 6 I Myself have t your brethren
Num 21:26 had t all his land from his
Num 31:26 up the plunder that was t
Num 31:32 which the men of war had t
Num 31:49 Your servants have t a count
Num 31:53 (The men of war had t spoil
Num 36: 3 their inheritance will be t
Num 36: 3 so it will be t from the lot
Num 36: 4 t away from the inheritance
Deut 4:20 But the LORD has t you and
Deut 24: 5 When a man has t a new wife
Deut 24: 5 to his wife whom he has t
Deut 28:31 t away from before you, and
Josh 1:15 they also have t possession
Josh 7:11 For they have even t some of
Josh 7:15 is t with the accursed thing
Josh 7:16 and the tribe of Judah was t
Josh 7:17 man by man, and Zabdi was t
Josh 7:18 of the tribe of Judah, was t
Josh 8: 8 be, when you have t the city
Josh 8:21 the ambush had t the city
Josh 10: 1 heard how Joshua had t Ai
Judg 14: 9 he had t the honey out of the
Judg 15: 6 because he has t his wife
Judg 17: 2 silver that were t from you
Judg 18:24 You have t away my gods which
1Sa 7:14 t from Israel were restored
1Sa 12: 3 Whose ox have I t
1Sa 12: 3 or whose donkey have I t
1Sa 12: 4 nor have you t anything from
1Sa 14:24 before I have t vengeance on
1Sa 14:41 So Saul and Jonathan were t
1Sa 14:42 So Jonathan was t
1Sa 21: 6 been t from before the LORD
1Sa 21: 6 on the day when it was t away
1Sa 30: 2 had t captive the women and
1Sa 30: 3 daughters had been t captive
1Sa 30: 5 Carmelite, had been t captive
1Sa 30:16 had t from the land of the
1Sa 30:19 which they had t from them
2Sa 12: 9 you have t his wife to be
2Sa 12:10 have t the wife of Uriah the
2Sa 12:27 I have t the city's water
2Sa 18:18 Absalom in his lifetime had t
2Sa 23: 6 they cannot be t with hands
1Ki 1:51 he has t hold of the horns of
1Ki 7: 8 whom he had t as wife
1Ki 9:16 t Gezer and burned it with
1Ki 16:18 Zimri saw that the city was t
1Ki 18: 4 LORD, that Obadiah had t one
1Ki 21:19 murdered and also t possession
1Ki 22:43 high places were not t away
2Ki 2: 9 before I am t away from you
2Ki 2:10 see me when I am t from you
2Ki 2:16 of the LORD has t him up and
2Ki 4:20 When he had t him and brought
2Ki 6:22 t captive with your sword
2Ki 12: 3 high places were not t away
2Ki 13:25 the cities which he had t out
2Ki 14: 4 high places were not t away
2Ki 18:10 king of Israel, Samaria was t
2Ki 18:22 altars Hezekiah has t away
2Ki 24: 7 t all that belonged to the
1Ch 22:14 Indeed I have t much trouble
1Ch 24: 6 father's house t for Eleazar
2Ch 15: 8 the cities which he had t in
2Ch 17: 2 which Asa his father had t
2Ch 20:33 high places were not t away
2Ch 28:11 whom you have t captive from
2Ch 28:18 had t Beth Shemesh, Aijalon,
2Ch 32:12 t away His high places and His
Ezra 1: 7 had t from Jerusalem and put
Ezra 5:14 which Nebuchadnezzar had t
Ezra 6: 5 t back to the temple which is
Ezra 9: 2 For they have t some of their
Ezra 10: 2 have t pagan wives from the
Ezra 10:10 have t pagan wives, adding to
Ezra 10:14 have t pagan wives come at
Ezra 10:17 the men who had t pagan wives
Ezra 10:18 t pagan wives the following
Ezra 10:44 All these had t pagan wives
Esth 2: 8 was t to the king's palace
Esth 2:15 who had t her as his daughter
Esth 2:16 So Esther was t to King
Esth 8: 2 which he had t from Haman
Job 1:21 gave, and the LORD has t away
Job 16:12 He also has t me by my neck,
Job 19: 9 and t the crown from my head
Job 22: 6 For you have t pledges from
Job 24:24 they are t out of the way
Job 27: 2 who has t away my justice, and
Job 28: 2 Iron is t from the earth, and
Job 34: 5 but God has t away my justice
Job 34:20 the mighty are t away without
Job 35:15 nor t much notice of folly,
Ps 44:10 have t spoil for themselves
Ps 59:12 them even be t in their pride
Ps 83: 3 They have t crafty counsel
Ps 85: 3 You have t away all Your
Ps 119:53 Indignation has t hold of me
Ps 119:111 have t as a heritage forever
Prov 4:16 their sleep is t away unless
Prov 6: 2 you are t by the words of
Prov 7:20 He has t a bag of money with
Prov 11: 6 will be t by their own lust
Eccl 3:14 to it, and nothing t from it
Eccl 7:26 the sinner shall be t by her
Eccl 9:12 Like fish t in a cruel net,
Song 5: 3 I have t off my robe
Is 6: 6 had t with the tongs from the
Is 6: 7 your iniquity is t away, and
Is 7: 5 t evil counsel against you
Is 8: 4 be t away before the king of
Is 8:15 and be broken, be snared and t
Is 10:27 be t away from your shoulder
Is 10:29 they have t up lodging at
Is 16:10 Gladness is t away, and joy
Is 21: 3 pangs have t hold of me, like
Is 23: 8 Who has t this counsel
Is 33:20 that will not be t down
Is 36: 7 altars Hezekiah has t away
Is 38:12 t from me like a shepherd's
Is 41: 9 You whom I have t from the
Is 49:24 the prey be t from the mighty
Is 49:25 of the mighty shall be t away
Is 51:22 I have t out of your hand the
Is 52: 5 people are t away for nothing
Is 53: 8 He was t from prison and from
Is 57: 1 merciful men are t away,
Is 57: 1 righteous is t away from evil
Is 57:11 Me, nor t it to your heart
Is 64: 6 like the wind, have t us away
Jer 6:11 shall be t with the wife, the
Jer 6:24 Anguish has t hold of us,
Jer 8: 9 they are dismayed and t
Jer 8:21 astonishment has t hold of me
Jer 12: 2 them, yes, they have t root
Jer 13:17 flock has been t captive
Jer 16: 5 for I have t away My peace
Jer 29:22 of them a curse shall be t up
Jer 34: 3 hand, but shall surely be t
Jer 38:23 but shall be t by the hand of
Jer 38:28 the day that Jerusalem was t
Jer 38:28 there when Jerusalem was t
Jer 40: 1 when he had t him bound in
Jer 40:10 your cities that you have t
Jer 48: 1 Kirjathaim is shamed and t
Jer 48: 7 you also shall be t
Jer 48:33 and gladness are t from the
Jer 48:41 Kerioth is t, and the
Jer 48:46 your sons have been t captive
Jer 49:20 that He has t against Edom
Jer 49:24 sorrows have t her like a
Jer 49:30 has t counsel against you
Jer 50: 2 Say, 'Babylon is t, Bel is
Jer 50:43 anguish has t hold of him
Jer 50:45 that He has t against Babylon
Jer 51:31 his city is t on all sides
Jer 51:41 Oh, how Sheshach is t
Jer 51:56 and her mighty men are t
Ezek 15: 3 Is wood t from it to make any
Ezek 16:17 You have also t your
Ezek 17:20 and he shall be t in My snare
Ezek 18: 8 usury nor t any increase, but
Ezek 18:13 exacted usury or t increase
Ezek 21:23 that they may be t
Ezek 21:24 you shall be t in hand
Ezek 22:25 they have t treasure and
Ezek 33: 6 he is t away in his iniquity
Ezek 36: 3 you are t up by the lips of
Dan 5: 2 t from the temple which had
Dan 5: 3 been t from the temple of the
Dan 6:23 So Daniel was t up out of the
Dan 7:12 had their dominion t away
Dan 8:11 daily sacrifices were t away
Dan 11:12 When he has t away the

Dan 12:11 the daily sacrifice is **t** away
Hos 4: 3 of the sea will be **t** away
Joel 3: 5 because you have **t** My silver
Amos 2: 8 altar on clothes **t** in pledge
Amos 3:12 be **t** out who dwell in Samaria
Amos 6:13 Have we not **t** Karnaim for
Mic 1:11 to stand is **t** away from you
Mic 2: 9 have **t** away My glory forever
Zeph 3:15 The LORD has **t** away your
Zech 14: 2 the city shall be **t**, the
Matt 9:15 will be **t** away from them, and
Matt 13:12 has will be **t** away from him
Matt 16: 7 is because we have **t** no bread
Matt 21:43 of God will be **t** from you
Matt 24:40 one will be **t** and the other
Matt 24:41 one will be **t** and the other
Matt 25:29 what he has will be **t** away
Matt 27:59 And when Joseph had **t** the body
Matt 28:12 **t** counsel, they gave a large
Mark 2:20 will be **t** away from them, and
Mark 4:25 has will be **t** away from him
Mark 6:41 when He had **t** the five loaves
Mark 9:36 when He had **t** him in His arms
Luke 1: 1 Inasmuch as many have **t** in
Luke 5: 9 of fish which they had **t**
Luke 5:35 will be **t** away from them
Luke 5:36 was **t** out of the new does not
Luke 8:18 to have will be **t** from him
Luke 9:17 fragments were **t** up by them
Luke 10:42 will not be **t** away from her
Luke 11:52 For you have **t** away the key
Luke 17:34 the one will be **t** and the
Luke 17:35 the one will be **t** and the
Luke 17:36 the one will be **t** and the
Luke 19: 8 if I have **t** anything from
Luke 19:26 has will be **t** away from him
John 2:20 It has **t** forty-six years to
John 13:12 **t** His garments, and sat down
John 19:31 and that they might be **t** away
John 20: 1 had been **t** away from the tomb
John 20: 2 They have **t** away the Lord out
John 20:13 they have **t** away my Lord, and
Acts 1: 2 the day in which He was **t** up
Acts 1: 9 they watched, He was **t** up
Acts 1:11 who was **t** up from you into
Acts 1:22 day when He was **t** up from us
Acts 2:23 you have **t** by lawless hands,
Acts 8:33 His justice was **t** away
Acts 8:33 His life is **t** from the earth
Acts 10:16 And the object was **t** up into
Acts 17: 9 So when they had **t** security
Acts 18:18 Cenchrea, for he had **t** a vow
Acts 20: 9 third story and was **t** up dead
Acts 21: 6 When we had **t** our leave of
Acts 21:23 four men who have **t** a vow
Acts 21:34 him to be **t** into the barracks
Acts 25:26 after the examination has **t**
Acts 27:17 When they had **t** it on board
Rom 9: 6 word of God has **t** no effect
1Co 5: 2 be **t** away from among you
2Co 3:14 the veil is **t** away in Christ
2Co 3:16 the Lord, the veil is **t** away
Col 2:14 He has **t** it out of the way,
1Th 2:17 having been **t** away from you
2Th 2: 7 until He is **t** out of the way
1Ti 5: 9 old be **t** into the number, and
2Ti 2:26 having been **t** captive by him
Heb 5: 1 For every priest **t** from among
Rev 5: 8 Now when He had **t** the scroll
Rev 11:17 You have **t** Your great power

TAKES (*see* TAKE)
Gen 27:46 if Jacob **t** a wife of the
Ex 20: 7 who **t** His name in vain
Ex 21:10 If he **t** another wife, he
Lev 20:17 If a man **t** his sister, his
Lev 20:21 If a man **t** his brother's
Num 6:21 to the vow which he **t**, so he
Num 30: 6 But if indeed she **t** a husband
Deut 5:11 who **t** His name in vain
Deut 10:17 no partiality nor **t** a bribe
Deut 22:13 If any man **t** a wife, and goes
Deut 24: 1 When a man **t** a wife and
Deut 24: 6 for he **t** one's living in
Deut 27:25 Cursed is the one who **t** a
Deut 32:41 My hand **t** hold on judgment, I
Josh 7:14 **t** shall come according to
Josh 7:14 **t** shall come by households
Josh 7:14 LORD **t** shall come man by man
Josh 15:16 and **t** it, to him I will give
Judg 1:12 **t** it, to him I will give my
Judg 11:24 God **t** possession of before us
1Sa 17:26 and **t** away the reproach from
1Ki 8:31 **t** an oath before Your altar
1Ki 14:10 as one **t** away refuse until it
1Ki 20:11 like the one who **t** it off
2Ch 6:22 **t** an oath before Your altar
Job 9:12 If He **t** away, who can hinder
Job 12:20 **t** away the discernment of the
Job 12:24 He **t** away the understanding
Job 18: 9 The net **t** him by the heel, and
Job 21: 6 trembling **t** hold of my flesh
Job 27: 8 much, if God **t** away his life
Job 38:14 It **t** on form like clay under
Job 40:24 Though he **t** it in his eyes,
Ps 5: 4 who **t** pleasure in wickedness
Ps 137: 9 Happy shall he be who **t** and
Ps 147:10 He **t** no pleasure in the legs
Ps 147:11 The LORD **t** pleasure in those
Ps 149: 4 For the LORD **t** pleasure in
Prov 1:19 It **t** away the life of its
Prov 8: 2 She **t** her stand on the top of
Prov 16:32 spirit than he who **t** a city
Prov 25:20 Like one who **t** away a garment
Prov 26:17 one who **t** a dog by the ears
Eccl 2:23 the night his heart **t** no rest
Eccl 9: 2 he who **t** an oath as he who
Is 3: 1 **t** away from Jerusalem and from
Is 3: 6 When a man **t** hold of his
Is 13:14 as a sheep that no man **t** up
Is 44:14 and **t** the cypress and the oak
Is 51:18 nor is there any who **t** her by
Is 57: 1 and no man **t** it to heart
Is 59: 8 whoever **t** that way shall not
Jer 12:11 because no one **t** it to heart
Ezek 16:32 who **t** strangers instead of
Ezek 33: 4 **t** him away, his blood shall
Ezek 33: 5 But he who **t** warning will
Ezek 33: 6 **t** any person from among them,
Hos 7: 1 of robbers **t** spoil outside
Amos 3:12 As a shepherd **t** from the
Matt 12:45 and **t** with him seven other
Mark 4:15 **t** away the word that was sown
Luke 6:29 And from him who **t** away your
Luke 6:30 And from him who **t** away your
Luke 8:12 **t** away the word out of their
Luke 11:22 he **t** from him all his armor
Luke 11:26 and **t** with him seven other
John 1:29 The Lamb of God who **t** away
John 10:18 No one **t** it from Me, but I
John 15: 2 does not bear fruit He **t** away
1Co 11:21 each one **t** his own supper
2Co 11:20 if one **t** from you, if one
Heb 5: 4 And no man **t** this honor to
Heb 10: 9 He **t** away the first that He
Rev 22:19 if anyone **t** away from the

TAKING (*see* TAKE)
Deut 32:11 **t** them up, carrying them on
Judg 4: 9 you in the journey you are **t**
2Ch 19: 7 partiality, nor **t** of bribes
Job 5: 3 have seen the foolish **t** root
Job 5: 5 **t** it even from the thorns, and
Ps 119: 9 By **t** heed according to Your
Is 27: 9 the fruit of **t** away his sin
Jer 50:46 At the noise of the **t** of
Ezek 25:12 house of Judah by **t** vengeance
Hos 11: 3 to walk, **t** them by their arms
Mark 15:43 **t** courage, went in to Pilate
Luke 4: 5 **t** Him up on a high mountain,
Luke 16: 3 For my master is **t** the
John 11:13 about **t** rest in sleep
Rom 7: 8 But sin, **t** opportunity by the
Rom 7:11 **t** occasion by the commandment
2Co 2:13 but **t** my leave of them, I
2Co 11: 8 **t** wages from them to minister
Eph 6:16 **t** the shield of faith with
Phil 2: 7 **t** the form of a servant, and
Col 2:18 **t** delight in false humility
2Th 1: 8 in flaming fire **t** vengeance
3Jn 7 **t** nothing from the Gentiles

TALEBEARER (*see* TALES)
Lev 19:16 as a **t** among your people
Prov 11:13 A **t** reveals secrets, but he
Prov 18: 8 The words of a **t** are like
Prov 20:19 about as a **t** reveals secrets
Prov 26:20 and where there is no **t**,
Prov 26:22 The words of a **t** are like

TALENT (*see* TALENTS)
Ex 25:39 be made of a **t** of pure gold
Ex 37:24 Of a **t** of pure gold he made
Ex 38:27 one **t** for each socket
2Sa 12:30 Its weight was a **t** of gold
1Ki 20:39 you shall pay a **t** of silver
2Ki 5:22 give them a **t** of silver and
2Ki 23:33 of silver and a **t** of gold
1Ch 20: 2 found it to weigh a **t** of gold
2Ch 36: 3 of silver and a **t** of gold
Matt 25:24 had received the one **t** came
Matt 25:25 and hid your **t** in the ground
Matt 25:28 Therefore take the **t** from him
Rev 16:21 about the weight of a **t**

TALENTS (*see* TALENT)
Ex 38:24 offering, was twenty-nine **t**
Ex 38:25 was one hundred **t** and one
Ex 38:27 from the hundred **t** of silver
Ex 38:27 sockets from the hundred **t**
Ex 38:29 of bronze was seventy **t** and
1Ki 9:14 hundred and twenty **t** of gold
1Ki 9:28 twenty **t** of gold from there,
1Ki 10:10 twenty **t** of gold, spices in
1Ki 10:14 and sixty-six **t** of gold,
1Ki 16:24 Shemer for two **t** of silver
2Ki 5: 5 took with him ten **t** of silver
2Ki 5:23 Please, take two **t**
2Ki 5:23 bound two **t** of silver in two
2Ki 15:19 Pul a thousand **t** of silver
2Ki 18:14 three hundred **t** of silver
2Ki 18:14 and thirty **t** of gold
2Ki 23:33 of one hundred **t** of silver
1Ch 19: 6 **t** of silver to hire for
1Ch 22:14 hundred thousand **t** of gold
1Ch 22:14 and one million **t** of silver
1Ch 29: 4 three thousand **t** of gold, of
1Ch 29: 4 seven thousand **t** of refined
1Ch 29: 7 house of God five thousand **t**
1Ch 29: 7 ten thousand **t** of silver
1Ch 29: 7 eighteen thousand **t** of bronze
1Ch 29: 7 hundred thousand **t** of iron
2Ch 3: 8 six hundred **t** of fine gold
2Ch 8:18 fifty **t** of gold from there,
2Ch 9: 9 twenty **t** of gold, spices in
2Ch 9:13 and sixty-six **t** of gold,
2Ch 25: 6 for one hundred **t** of silver
2Ch 25: 9 we do about the hundred **t**
2Ch 27: 5 year one hundred **t** of silver
2Ch 36: 3 of one hundred **t** of silver
Ezra 7:22 up to one hundred **t** of silver
Ezra 8:26 fifty **t** of silver, silver
Ezra 8:26 weighing one hundred **t**
Ezra 8:26 one hundred **t** of gold,
Esth 3: 9 I will pay ten thousand **t** of
Matt 18:24 who owed him ten thousand **t**
Matt 25:15 And to one he gave five **t**, to
Matt 25:16 had received the five **t** went
Matt 25:16 them, and made another five **t**
Matt 25:20 who had received five **t** came
Matt 25:20 and brought five other **t**
Matt 25:20 you delivered to me five **t**
Matt 25:20 five more **t** besides them
Matt 25:22 who had received two **t** came
Matt 25:22 you delivered to me two **t**
Matt 25:22 two more **t** besides them
Matt 25:28 give it to him who has ten **t**

TALES (*see* TALEBEARER)
Luke 24:11 seemed to them like idle **t**

TALITHA
Mark 5:41 **T**, cumi," which is

TALK (*see* PREFACE)

TALKED (*see* PREFACE)

TALKERS
Ezek 36: 3 are taken up by the lips of **t**
Tit 1:10 insubordinate, both idle **t**

TALKING (*see* PREFACE)

TALKS (*see* PREFACE)

TALL (*see* TALLER)
Deut 2:10 numerous and **t** as the Anakim
Deut 2:21 numerous and **t** as the Anakim
Deut 9: 2 a people great and **t**, the
2Ki 19:23 I will cut down its **t** cedars
1Ch 11:23 great height, five cubits **t**
Is 18: 2 messengers, to a nation **t**
Is 18: 7 LORD of hosts from a people **t**
Is 37:24 I will cut down its **t** cedars

TALLER (*see* TALL)
Deut 1:28 are greater and **t** than we
1Sa 9: 2 was **t** than any of the people
1Sa 10:23 he was **t** than any of the

TALMAI
Num 13:22 Ahiman, Sheshai, and **T**, the
Josh 15:14 Sheshai, Ahiman, and **T**, the
Judg 1:10 killed Sheshai, Ahiman, and **T**
2Sa 3: 3 of Maacah, the daughter of **T**
2Sa 13:37 went to **T** the son of Ammihud,
1Ch 3: 2 of Maacah, the daughter of **T**

TALMON
1Ch 9:17 were Shallum, Akkub, **T**,
Ezra 2:42 sons of Ater, the sons of **T**
Neh 7:45 of Ater, the children of **T**
Neh 11:19 the gatekeepers, Akkub, **T**
Neh 12:25 Obadiah, Meshullam, **T**, and

TAMAH
Ezra 2:53 sons of Sisera, the sons of **T**
Neh 7:55 of Sisera, the children of **T**

TAMAR (*see* BAAL TAMAR, HAZAZON TAMAR)
Gen 38: 6 firstborn, and her name was **T**
Gen 38:11 Then Judah said to **T** his
Gen 38:11 And **T** went and dwelt in her
Gen 38:13 And it was told **T**, saying
Gen 38:24 **T** your daughter-in-law has
Ruth 4:12 whom **T** bore to Judah, because
2Sa 13: 1 sister, whose name was **T**
2Sa 13: 2 sister **T** that he became sick
2Sa 13: 4 I love **T**, my brother
2Sa 13: 5 Please let my sister **T** come
2Sa 13: 6 Please let **T** my sister come
2Sa 13: 7 And David sent home to **T**,
2Sa 13: 8 So **T** went to her brother
2Sa 13:10 Then Amnon said to **T**, "Bring
2Sa 13:10 **T** took the cakes which she
2Sa 13:19 Then **T** put ashes on her head,
2Sa 13:20 So **T** remained desolate in
2Sa 13:22 he had forced his sister **T**
2Sa 13:32 that he forced his sister **T**
2Sa 14:27 one daughter whose name was **T**
1Ch 2: 4 And **T**, his daughter-in-law,
1Ch 3: 9 concubines, and **T** their sister
Ezek 47:19 shall be from **T** to the waters
Ezek 48:28 the border shall be from **T** to
Matt 1: 3 begot Perez and Zerah by **T**

TAMARISK
Gen 21:33 planted a **t** tree in Beersheba
1Sa 22: 6 under a **t** tree in Ramah, with
1Sa 31:13 under the **t** tree at Jabesh
1Ch 10:12 under the **t** tree at Jabesh

TAMBOURINE (*see* TAMBOURINES)
1Sa 10: 5 a stringed instrument, a **t**
Job 21:12 They sing to the **t** and harp,
Is 5:12 harp and the strings, the **t**
Is 24: 8 The mirth of the **t** ceases

TAMBOURINES (*see* TAMBOURINE)
1Sa 18: 6 to meet King Saul, with **t**
2Sa 6: 5 on stringed instruments, on **t**
1Ch 13: 8 on stringed instruments, on **t**
Is 30:32 on him, it will be with **t**
Jer 31: 4 again be adorned with your **t**

TAME (*see* TAMED)
Mark 5: 4 neither could anyone **t** him
Jas 3: 8 But no man can **t** the tongue

TAMED (*see* TAME)
Jas 3: 7 and creature of the sea, is **t**
Jas 3: 7 and has been **t** by mankind

TAMMUZ
Ezek 8:14 sitting there weeping for **T**

TANACH (*see* TAANACH)
Josh 21:25 **T** with its common-land and

TANGLED
Nah 1:10 For while **t** like thorns, and

TANHUMETH
2Ki 25:23 the son of **T** the Netophathite
Jer 40: 8 Kareah, Seraiah the son of **T**

TANNED
Song 1: 6 because the sun has **t** me

TANNER
Acts 9:43 days in Joppa with Simon, a **t**
Acts 10: 6 He is lodging with Simon, a **t**
Acts 10:32 in the house of Simon, a **t**

TAPESTRY
Ex 35:35 and the **t** maker, in blue and
Prov 7:16 I have spread my bed with **t**
Prov 31:22 She makes **t** for herself

TAPHATH
1Ki 4:11 he had **T** the daughter of

TAPPUAH (*see* BETH TAPPUAH, EN TAPPUAH)
Josh 12:17 the king of **T**, one
Josh 15:34 Zanoah, En Gannim, **T**, Enam,
Josh 16: 8 The border went out from **T**
Josh 17: 8 Manasseh had the land of **T**
Josh 17: 8 but **T** on the border of
1Ch 2:43 sons of Hebron were Korah, **T**

TARALAH
Josh 18:27 Rekem, Irpeel, **T**,

TAREA (*see* TAHREA)
1Ch 8:35 Micah were Pithon, Melech, **T**

TARES
Matt 13:25 sowed **t** among the wheat and
Matt 13:26 then the **t** also appeared
Matt 13:27 How then does it have **t**
Matt 13:29 while you gather up the **t** you
Matt 13:30 First gather together the **t**
Matt 13:36 parable of the **t** of the field
Matt 13:38 but the **t** are the sons of the
Matt 13:40 as the **t** are gathered and

TARGET
1Sa 20:20 it, as though I shot at a **t**
Job 7:20 Why have You set me as Your **t**
Job 16:12 He has set me up for His **t**
Lam 3:12 me up as a **t** for the arrow

TARPELITES
Ezra 4: 9 the Apharsathchites, the **T**

TARRIES (*see* TARRY)
Judg 5:28 Why **t** the clatter of his
Hab 2: 3 Though it **t**, wait for it

TARRY (*see* TARRIES)
Gen 45: 9 come down to me, do not **t**
Jer 14: 8 turns aside to **t** for a night
Mic 5: 7 that **t** for no man nor wait
Hab 2: 3 surely come, it will not **t**
Luke 24:49 but **t** in the city of
1Co 16: 8 But I will **t** in Ephesus until
Heb 10:37 will come and will not **t**

TARSHISH (*see* THARSHISH)
Gen 10: 4 sons of Javan were Elishah, **T**
2Ch 9:21 the king's ships went to **T**
2Ch 20:36 him to make ships to go to **T**
2Ch 20:37 they were not able to go to **T**
Esth 1:14 Carshena, Shethar, Admatha, **T**
Ps 48: 7 ships of **T** With an east wind
Ps 72:10 The kings of **T** and of the
Is 2:16 upon all the ships of **T**, and
Is 23: 1 Wail, you ships of **T**
Is 23: 6 Cross over to **T**
Is 23:10 the River, O daughter of **T**
Is 23:14 Wail, you ships of **T**
Is 60: 9 and the ships of **T** will come
Is 66:19 to **T** and Pul and Lud, who draw
Jer 10: 9 it is brought from **T**, and gold
Ezek 27:12 **T** was your merchant because
Ezek 27:25 The ships of **T** were carriers
Ezek 38:13 Dedan, the merchants of **T**
Jon 1: 3 to **T** from the presence of the
Jon 1: 3 and found a ship going to **T**
Jon 1: 3 to go with them to **T** from the
Jon 4: 2 I fled previously to **T**

TARSHISHAH
1Ch 1: 7 sons of Javan were Elishah, **T**

TARSUS
Acts 9:11 for one called Saul of **T**, for
Acts 9:30 Caesarea and sent him out to **T**
Acts 11:25 departed for **T** to seek Saul
Acts 21:39 I am a Jew from **T**, in Cilicia
Acts 22: 3 born in **T** of Cilicia, but

TARTAK
2Ki 17:31 the Avites made Nibhaz and **T**

TARTAN
2Ki 18:17 king of Assyria sent the **T**
Is 20: 1 year that **T** came to Ashdod

TASK (*see* TASKMASTERS, TASKS)
Ex 5:14 your **t** in making brick both
Num 4:19 them to his service and his **t**
Num 4:49 service and according to his **t**
Neh 13:13 their **t** was to distribute to
Eccl 1:13 this grievous **t** God has given
Eccl 3:10 I have seen the God-given **t**

TASKMASTERS (*see* MASTERS, TASK)
Ex 1:11 Therefore they set **t** over
Ex 3: 7 their cry because of their **t**
Ex 5: 6 commanded the **t** of the people
Ex 5:10 the **t** of the people and their
Ex 5:13 the **t** forced them to hurry,
Ex 5:14 whom Pharaoh's **t** had set over

TASKS (*see* TASK)
Num 4:27 the Gershonites, all their **t**
Num 4:27 all their **t** as their duty

TASSEL (*see* TASSELS)
Num 15:39 And you shall have the **t**, that

TASSELS (*see* TASSEL)
Num 15:38 Tell them to make **t** on the
Num 15:38 in the **t** of the corners
Deut 22:12 You shall make **t** on the four

TASTE (*see* TASTED, TASTES, TASTY)
Ex 16:31 the **t** of it was like wafers
Num 11: 8 its **t** was like the **t** of
2Sa 3:35 if I **t** bread or anything else
2Sa 19:35 Can your servant **t** what I eat
Job 6: 6 Or is there any **t** in the
Job 6:30 Cannot my **t** discern the
Job 12:11 words and the mouth **t** its food
Ps 34: 8 Oh, **t** and see that the LORD is
Ps 119:103 sweet are Your words to my **t**
Prov 24:13 which is sweet to your **t**
Song 2: 3 his fruit was sweet to my **t**
Jer 48:11 Therefore his **t** remained in
Jon 3: 7 herd nor flock, **t** anything
Matt 16:28 **t** death till they see the Son
Mark 9: 1 not **t** death till they see the
Luke 9:27 not **t** death till they see the
Luke 14:24 invited shall **t** my supper
John 8:52 word he shall never **t** death
Col 2:21 Do not touch, do not **t**, do
Heb 2: 9 might **t** death for everyone

TASTED (*see* TASTE)
1Sa 14:24 So none of the people **t** food
1Sa 14:29 I **t** a little of this honey
1Sa 14:43 I only **t** a little honey with
Dan 5: 2 While he **t** the wine,
Matt 27:34 But when He had **t** it, He
John 2: 9 had **t** the water that was made
Heb 6: 4 have **t** the heavenly gift, and
Heb 6: 5 have **t** the good word of God
1Pe 2: 3 if indeed you have **t** that the

TASTES (*see* TASTE)
Job 34: 3 words as the palate **t** food

TASTY (*see* TASTE)
Prov 18: 8 talebearer are like **t** trifles
Prov 26:22 talebearer are like **t** trifles

TATTENAI
Ezra 5: 3 At the same time **T** the
Ezra 5: 6 of the letter that **T** sent
Ezra 6: 6 Now therefore, **T**, governor of
Ezra 6:13 Then **T**, governor of the

TATTOO
Lev 19:28 dead, nor **t** any marks on you

TAUGHT (*see* TEACH)
Deut 4: 5 Surely I have **t** you statutes
Deut 31:22 and **t** it to the children of
Judg 3: 2 Israel might be **t** to know war
Judg 8:16 with them he **t** the men of
2Ki 17:28 **t** them how they should fear
2Ch 17: 9 So they **t** in Judah, and had
2Ch 17: 9 of Judah and **t** the people
2Ch 30:22 to all the Levites who **t** the
2Ch 35: 3 the Levites who **t** all Israel
Neh 8: 9 the Levites who **t** the people
Ps 71:17 You have **t** me from my youth
Ps 119:102 For You Yourself have **t** me
Prov 4: 4 He also **t** me, and said to me
Prov 4:11 I have **t** you in the way of
Prov 31: 1 which his mother **t** him
Eccl 12: 9 wise, he still **t** the people
Is 29:13 their fear toward Me is **t** by
Is 40:13 or as His counselor has **t** Him

Is 40:14 **t** Him in the path of justice
Is 40:14 Who **t** Him knowledge, and
Is 54:13 shall be **t** by the LORD, and
Jer 2:33 Therefore you have also **t** the
Jer 9: 5 they have **t** their tongue to
Jer 9:14 which their fathers **t** them
Jer 12:16 as they **t** My people to swear
Jer 13:21 For you have **t** them to be
Jer 28:16 because you have **t** rebellion
Jer 29:32 because he has **t** rebellion
Jer 32:33 though I **t** them, rising up
Ezek 23:48 may be **t** not to practice your
Hos 11: 3 I **t** Ephraim to walk, taking
Zech 13: 5 for a man **t** me to keep cattle
Matt 5: 2 His mouth and **t** them, saying
Matt 7:29 for He **t** them as one having
Matt 13:54 He **t** them in their synagogue,
Mark 1:21 He entered the synagogue and **t**
Mark 1:22 for He **t** them as one having
Mark 2:13 came to Him, and He **t** them
Mark 4: 2 Then He **t** them many things by
Mark 6:30 had done and what they had **t**
Mark 9:31 For He **t** His disciples and
Mark 10: 1 accustomed, He **t** them again
Mark 11:17 Then He **t**, saying to them
Mark 12:35 while He **t** in the temple,
Luke 4:15 He **t** in their synagogues,
Luke 5: 3 **t** the multitudes from the
Luke 6: 6 He entered the synagogue and **t**
Luke 11: 1 as John also **t** his disciples
Luke 13:26 and You **t** in our streets
Luke 20: 1 as He **t** the people in the
John 6:45 And they shall all be **t** by God
John 6:59 as He **t** in Capernaum
John 7:14 went up into the temple and **t**
John 7:28 as He **t** in the temple, saying
John 8: 2 and He sat down and **t** them
John 8:20 as He **t** in the temple
John 8:28 but as My Father **t** Me, I
John 18:20 I always **t** in synagogues and
Acts 4: 2 that they **t** the people and
Acts 5:21 early in the morning and **t**
Acts 11:26 and **t** a great many people
Acts 15: 1 from Judea and **t** the brethren,
Acts 18:25 **t** accurately the things of
Acts 20:20 **t** you publicly and from house
Acts 22: 3 **t** according to the strictness
Gal 1:12 it from man, nor was I **t** it
Gal 6: 6 Let him who is **t** the word
Eph 4:21 Him and have been **t** by Him
Col 2: 7 the faith, as you have been **t**
1Th 4: 9 for you yourselves are **t** by
2Th 2:15 traditions which you were **t**
Tit 1: 9 word as he has been **t**, that
1Jn 2:27 lie, and just as it has **t** you
Rev 2:14 Balaam, who **t** Balak to put a

TAUNT (*see* TAUNTING, TAUNTS, TAUNT-SONG)
Jer 24: 9 a reproach and a byword, a **t**
Ezek 5:15 it shall be a reproach, a **t**

TAUNTING (*see* TAUNT)
Lam 3:14 and their **t** song all the day
Lam 3:63 I am their **t** song
Hab 2: 6 a **t** riddle against him, and

TAUNTS (*see* TAUNT)
Ezek 36:15 the **t** of the nations anymore

TAUNT-SONG (*see* TAUNT)
Job 30: 9 And now I am their **t**

TAX (*see* TAXED, TAXES)
Ezra 4:13 they will not pay **t**, tribute
Ezra 4:20 and **t**, tribute, and custom were
Ezra 7:24 not be lawful to impose **t**
Neh 5: 4 for the king's **t** on our lands
Matt 5:46 Do not even the **t** collectors
Matt 5:47 Do not even the **t** collectors
Matt 9: 9 sitting at the **t** office
Matt 9:10 many **t** collectors and sinners
Matt 9:11 Teacher eat with **t** collectors
Matt 10: 3 and Matthew the **t** collector
Matt 11:19 a friend of **t** collectors
Matt 17:24 the temple **t** came to Peter
Matt 17:24 Teacher not pay the temple **t**
Matt 18:17 a heathen and a **t** collector
Matt 21:31 say to you that **t** collectors
Matt 21:32 but **t** collectors and harlots
Matt 22:19 Show Me the **t** money
Mark 2:14 sitting at the **t** office, and
Mark 2:15 that many **t** collectors and
Mark 2:16 eating with the **t** collectors
Mark 2:16 and drinks with **t** collectors
Luke 3:12 Then **t** collectors also came
Luke 5:27 saw a **t** collector named Levi,
Luke 5:27 sitting at the **t** office
Luke 5:29 great number of **t** collectors
Luke 5:30 and drink with **t** collectors
Luke 7:29 Him, even the **t** collectors
Luke 7:34 a friend of **t** collectors
Luke 15: 1 Then all the **t** collectors
Luke 18:10 and the other a **t** collector
Luke 18:11 or even as this **t** collector
Luke 18:13 the **t** collector, standing
Luke 19: 2 who was a chief **t** collector

TAXED (*see* TAX)
2Ki 23:35 but he **t** the land to give

TAXES (*see* TAX)
Ezra 6: 8 **t** on the region beyond the
Dan 11:20 **t** on the glorious kingdom
Amos 5:11 poor and take grain **t** from him
Matt 17:25 the earth take customs or **t**
Matt 22:17 it lawful to pay **t** to Caesar
Mark 12:14 it lawful to pay **t** to Caesar
Luke 20:22 us to pay **t** to Caesar or not
Luke 23: 2 forbidding to pay **t** to Caesar
Rom 13: 6 of this you also pay **t**, for
Rom 13: 7 **t** to whom **t** are due,
Rom 13: 7 **t** to whom **t** are due,

TEACH (*see* TAUGHT, TEACHER, TEACHES, TEACHING, UNTAUGHT)
Ex 4:12 and **t** you what you shall say
Ex 4:15 I will **t** you what you shall
Ex 18:20 you shall **t** them the statutes
Ex 24:12 written, that you may **t** them
Ex 35:34 in his heart the ability to **t**
Lev 10:11 that you may **t** the children
Lev 14:57 to **t** when it is unclean and
Deut 4: 1 which I **t** you to observe,
Deut 4: 9 **t** them to your children and
Deut 4:10 and that they may **t** their
Deut 4:14 that time to **t** you statutes
Deut 5:31 which you shall **t** them, that
Deut 6: 1 God has commanded to **t** you
Deut 6: 7 you shall **t** them diligently
Deut 11:19 You shall **t** them to your
Deut 20:18 lest they **t** you to do
Deut 24: 8 the Levites, shall **t** you
Deut 31:19 and **t** it to the children of
Deut 33:10 They shall **t** Jacob Your
Judg 13: 8 **t** us what we shall do for the
1Sa 12:23 but I will **t** you the good and
2Sa 1:18 and he told them to **t** the
1Ki 8:36 that You may **t** them the good
2Ki 17:27 let him **t** them the rituals of
2Ch 6:27 that You may **t** them the good
2Ch 17: 7 to **t** in the cities of Judah
Ezra 7:10 to **t** statutes and ordinances
Ezra 7:25 **t** those who do not know them
Job 6:24 **T** me, and I will hold my
Job 8:10 Will they not **t** you and tell
Job 12: 7 beasts, and they will **t** you
Job 12: 8 the earth, and it will **t** you
Job 21:22 Can anyone **t** God knowledge,
Job 27:11 I will **t** you about the hand
Job 32: 7 of years should **t** wisdom
Job 33:33 peace, and I will **t** you wisdom
Job 34:32 **t** me what I do not see
Job 37:19 **T** us what we should say to
Ps 25: 4 **T** me Your paths
Ps 25: 5 **t** me, For You are the God of
Ps 25:12 Him shall He **t** in the way He
Ps 27:11 **T** me Your way, O LORD, And
Ps 32: 8 **t** you in the way you should
Ps 34:11 I will **t** you the fear of the
Ps 45: 4 shall **t** You awesome things
Ps 51:13 Then I will **t** transgressors
Ps 86:11 **T** me Your way, O LORD
Ps 90:12 So **t** us to number our days,
Ps 94:12 O LORD, And **t** out of Your law,
Ps 105:22 And **t** his elders wisdom
Ps 119:12 **T** me Your statutes
Ps 119:26 **T** me Your statutes
Ps 119:33 **T** me, O LORD, the way of Your
Ps 119:64 **T** me Your statutes
Ps 119:66 **T** me good judgment and
Ps 119:68 **T** me Your statutes
Ps 119:108 LORD, And **t** me Your
Ps 119:124 mercy, And **t** me Your statutes
Ps 119:135 And **t** me Your statutes
Ps 119:171 For You **t** me Your statutes
Ps 132:12 which I shall **t** them, Their
Ps 143:10 **T** me to do Your will, For You
Prov 9: 9 **t** a just man, and he will
Is 2: 3 he will **t** us His ways, and we
Is 28: 9 Whom will he **t** knowledge
Jer 9:20 **t** your daughters wailing, and
Jer 31:34 every man **t** his neighbor, and
Ezek 44:23 they shall **t** My people the
Dan 1: 4 they might **t** the language
Mic 3:11 bribe, her priests **t** for pay
Mic 4: 2 He will **t** us His ways, and we
Hab 2:19 It shall **t**
Matt 11: 1 He departed from there to **t**
Matt 22:16 **t** the way of God in truth
Mark 4: 1 He began to **t** by the sea
Mark 6: 2 come, He began to **t** in the
Mark 6:34 So He began to **t** them many
Mark 8:31 He began to **t** them that the
Mark 12:14 but **t** the way of God in truth
Luke 11: 1 **t** us to pray, as John also
Luke 12:12 For the Holy Spirit will **t**
Luke 20:21 **t** rightly, and You do not show
Luke 20:21 but **t** the way of God truly
John 7:35 the Greeks and **t** the Greeks
John 14:26 He will **t** you all things, and
Acts 1: 1 Jesus began both to do and **t**
Acts 4:18 nor **t** in the name of Jesus
Acts 5:28 you not to **t** in this name
Acts 16:21 they **t** customs which are not
Acts 21:21 **t** all the Jews who are among
Rom 2:21 You, therefore, who **t** another
Rom 2:21 do you not **t** yourself
1Co 4:17 as I **t** everywhere in every
1Co 11:14 **t** you that if a man has long
1Co 14:19 that I may **t** others also,
1Ti 1: 3 that they **t** no other doctrine
1Ti 2:12 I do not permit a woman to **t**
1Ti 3: 2 hospitable, able to **t**
1Ti 4:11 These things command and **t**
1Ti 6: 2 **T** and exhort these things
2Ti 2: 2 will be able to **t** others also
2Ti 2:24 be gentle to all, able to **t**
Heb 5:12 to **t** you again the first
Heb 8:11 of them shall **t** his neighbor
1Jn 2:27 do not need that anyone **t** you
Rev 2:20 herself a prophetess, to **t**

TEACHER (*see* TEACH, TEACHERS)
1Ch 25: 8 great, the **t** with the student
Hab 2:18 a **t** of lies, that the maker
Matt 8:19 **T**, I will follow You wherever
Matt 9:11 Why does your **T** eat with tax
Matt 10:24 A disciple is not above his **t**
Matt 10:25 that he be like his **t**, and a
Matt 12:38 **T**, we want to see a sign from
Matt 17:24 Does your **T** not pay the
Matt 19:16 Good **T**, what good thing shall
Matt 22:16 **T**, we know that You are true,
Matt 22:24 **T**, Moses said that if a man
Matt 22:36 **T**, which is the great
Matt 23: 8 for One is your **T**, the Christ
Matt 23:10 for One is your **T**, the Christ
Matt 26:18 and say to him, 'The **T** says
Mark 4:38 **T**, do You not care that we
Mark 5:35 Why trouble the **T** any further
Mark 9:17 **T**, I brought You my son, who
Mark 9:38 **T**, we saw someone who does
Mark 10:17 Good **T**, what shall I do that
Mark 10:20 **T**, all these I have observed
Mark 10:35 **T**, we want You to do for us
Mark 12:14 **T**, we know that You are true,
Mark 12:19 **T**, Moses wrote to us that if
Mark 12:32 Well said, **T**
Mark 13: 1 **T**, see what manner of stones
Mark 14:14 of the house, 'The **T** says
Luke 3:12 **T**, what shall we do
Luke 6:40 A disciple is not above his **t**
Luke 6:40 trained will be like his **t**
Luke 7:40 And he said, "**T**, say it."
Luke 8:49 Do not trouble the **T**
Luke 9:38 **T**, I implore You, look on my
Luke 10:25 **T**, what shall I do to inherit
Luke 11:45 **T**, by saying these things You
Luke 12:13 **T**, tell my brother to divide
Luke 18:18 Good **T**, what shall I do to
Luke 19:39 **T**, rebuke Your disciples
Luke 20:21 **T**, we know that You say and
Luke 20:28 **T**, Moses wrote to us that if
Luke 20:39 **T**, You have spoken well
Luke 21: 7 **T**, but when will these things
Luke 22:11 house, 'The **T** says to you,

John 1:38 to say, when translated, **T**),
John 3: 2 You are a **t** come from God
John 3:10 Are you the **t** of Israel, and
John 8: 4 **T**, this woman was caught in
John 11:28 The **T** has come and is calling
John 13:13 You call me **T** and Lord, and
John 13:14 If I then, your Lord and **T**
John 20:16 (which is to say, **T**)
Acts 5:34 a **t** of the law held in
Rom 2:20 a **t** of babes, having the form
1Ti 2: 7 a **t** of the Gentiles in faith
2Ti 1:11 and a **t** of the Gentiles

TEACHERS (*see* TEACHER)
Ps 119:99 understanding than all my **t**
Prov 5:13 not obeyed the voice of my **t**
Is 30:20 yet your **t** will not be moved
Is 30:20 your eyes shall see your **t**
Matt 23:10 And do not be called **t**
Luke 2:46 sitting in the midst of the **t**
Luke 5:17 **t** of the law sitting by, who
Acts 13: 1 were certain prophets and **t**
1Co 12:28 second prophets, third **t**
1Co 12:29 Are all **t**
Eph 4:11 and some pastors and **t**,
1Ti 1: 7 desiring to be **t** of the law
2Ti 4: 3 will heap up for themselves **t**
Tit 2: 3 much wine, **t** of good things
Heb 5:12 this time you ought to be **t**
Jas 3: 1 let not many of you become **t**
2Pe 2: 1 will be false **t** among you

TEACHES (*see* TEACH)
2Sa 22:35 He **t** my hands to make war, so
Job 15: 5 your iniquity **t** your mouth
Job 35:11 Who **t** us more than the beasts
Job 36:22 who **t** like Him
Ps 18:34 He **t** my hands to make war, So
Ps 25: 8 Therefore He **t** sinners in the
Ps 25: 9 And the humble He **t** His way
Ps 94:10 He who **t** man knowledge
Prov 16:23 heart of the wise **t** his mouth
Is 9:15 the prophet who **t** lies, he is
Is 28:26 right judgment, his God **t** him
Is 48:17 God, Who **t** you to profit, Who
Matt 5:19 **t** men so, shall be called
Matt 5:19 **t** them, he shall be called
Acts 21:28 This is the man who **t** all men
Rom 12: 7 he who **t**, in teaching
1Co 2:13 **t** but which the Holy Spirit **t**
Gal 6: 6 good things with him who **t**
1Ti 6: 3 If anyone **t** otherwise and does
1Jn 2:27 **t** you concerning all things

TEACHING (*see* TEACH)
Deut 32: 2 Let my **t** drop as the rain, my
2Ch 15: 3 true God, without a **t** priest
Jer 32:33 **t** them, yet they have not
Matt 4:23 **t** in their synagogues,
Matt 7:28 were astonished at His **t**,
Matt 9:35 **t** in their synagogues,
Matt 15: 9 Me, **t** as doctrines the
Matt 21:23 confronted Him as He was **t**
Matt 22:33 they were astonished at His **t**
Matt 26:55 **t** in the temple, and you did
Matt 28:20 **t** them to observe all things
Mark 1:22 they were astonished at His **t**
Mark 4: 2 and said to them in His **t**
Mark 6: 6 the villages in a circuit, **t**
Mark 7: 7 Me, **t** as doctrines the
Mark 11:18 were astonished at His **t**
Mark 12:38 Then He said to them in His **t**
Mark 14:49 with you in the temple **t**, and
Luke 4:31 was **t** them on the Sabbaths
Luke 4:32 they were astonished at His **t**
Luke 5:17 on a certain day, as He was **t**
Luke 13:10 Now He was **t** in one of the
Luke 13:22 the cities and villages, **t**
Luke 19:47 He was **t** daily in the temple
Luke 21:37 He was **t** in the temple, but
Luke 23: 5 **t** throughout all Judea,
John 9:34 born in sins, and are you **t** us
Acts 5:25 in the temple and **t** the people
Acts 5:42 house, they did not cease **t**
Acts 13:12 at the **t** of the Lord
Acts 15:35 also remained in Antioch, **t**
Acts 18:11 **t** the word of God among them
Acts 28:31 **t** the things which concern
Rom 12: 7 he who teaches, in **t**
1Co 14: 6 by prophesying, or by **t**
1Co 14:26 of you has a psalm, has a **t**
Col 1:28 **t** every man in all wisdom,
Col 3:16 you richly in all wisdom, **t**
2Ti 4: 2 with all longsuffering and **t**
Tit 1:11 **t** things which they ought not
Tit 2:12 **t** us that, denying

TEAR (*see* TEARING, TEARS, TORE, TORN)
Ex 28:32 mail, so that it does not **t**
Ex 39:23 so that it would not **t**
Lev 10: 6 your heads nor **t** your clothes
Lev 13:56 then he shall **t** it out of the
Lev 21:10 his head nor **t** his clothes
Judg 2: 2 you shall **t** down their altars
Judg 6:25 **t** down the altar of Baal that
Judg 8: 7 then I will **t** your flesh with
Judg 8: 9 I will **t** down this tower
2Sa 3:31 him, "**T** your clothes, gird
1Ki 11:11 I will surely **t** the kingdom
1Ki 11:12 but I will **t** it out of the
1Ki 11:13 However I will not **t** away the
1Ki 11:31 I will **t** the kingdom out of
Job 18: 4 You who **t** yourself in anger,
Ps 7: 2 Lest they **t** me like a lion,
Ps 17:12 that is eager to **t** his prey
Ps 50:22 Lest I **t** you in pieces, And
Eccl 3: 7 a time to **t**, and a time to sew
Jer 36:24 nor did they **t** their garments
Ezek 13:11 a stormy wind shall **t** it down
Ezek 13:20 I will **t** them from your arms,
Ezek 13:21 I will also **t** off your veils
Ezek 23:34 and **t** at your own breasts
Hos 5:14 I, even I, will **t** them and go
Hos 13: 8 I will **t** open their rib cage,
Hos 13: 8 The wild beast shall **t** them
Zech 11:16 and **t** their hooves in pieces
Matt 7: 6 and turn and **t** you in pieces
Matt 9:16 and the **t** is made worse
Mark 2:21 old, and the **t** is made worse
Luke 5:36 otherwise the new makes a **t**
John 19:24 Let us not **t** it, but cast
Rev 7:17 away every **t** from their eyes
Rev 21: 4 away every **t** from their eyes

TEARING (*see* TEAR)
Ezek 22:25 a roaring lion **t** the prey
Ezek 22:27 are like wolves **t** the prey

TEARS (*see* TEAR)
Deut 33:20 **t** the arm and the crown of his
2Ki 20: 5 prayer, I have seen your **t**
Esth 8: 3 and implored him with **t** to
Job 16: 9 He **t** me in His wrath, and
Job 16:20 my eyes pour out **t** to God
Ps 6: 6 I drench my couch with my **t**
Ps 39:12 Do not be silent at my **t**
Ps 42: 3 My **t** have been my food day and
Ps 56: 8 Put my **t** into Your bottle
Ps 80: 5 fed them with the bread of **t**
Ps 80: 5 And given them **t** to drink in
Ps 116: 8 from death, My eyes from **t**
Ps 126: 5 Those who sow in **t** Shall reap
Eccl 4: 1 The **t** of the oppressed, but
Is 16: 9 I will drench you with my **t**
Is 25: 8 wipe away **t** from all faces
Is 38: 5 prayer, I have seen your **t**
Jer 9: 1 and my eyes a fountain of **t**
Jer 9:18 that our eyes may run with **t**
Jer 13:17 bitterly and run down with **t**
Jer 14:17 Let my eyes flow with **t** night
Jer 31:16 weeping, and your eyes from **t**
Lam 1: 2 her **t** are on her cheeks
Lam 2:11 My eyes fail with **t**, my heart
Lam 2:18 let **t** run down like a river
Ezek 24:16 nor shall your **t** run down
Mic 5: 8 and **t** in pieces, and none can
Mal 2:13 the altar of the LORD with **t**
Mark 9:24 cried out and said with **t**
Luke 7:38 to wash His feet with her **t**
Luke 7:44 has washed My feet with her **t**
Acts 20:19 all humility, with many **t**
Acts 20:31 everyone night and day with **t**
2Co 2: 4 I wrote to you, with many **t**
2Ti 1: 4 you, being mindful of your **t**
Heb 5: 7 **t** to Him who was able to save
Heb 12:17 sought it diligently with **t**

TEBAH
Gen 22:24 name was Reumah, also bore **T**

TEBALIAH
1Ch 26:11 **T** the third, Zechariah the

TEBETH
Esth 2:16 which is the month of **T**, in

TEDIOUS
Acts 24: 4 not to be **t** to you any
Phil 3: 1 same things to you is not **t**

TEEMING
Ps 104:25 are innumerable **t** things,

TEETH (*see* TOOTH)
Gen 49:12 and his **t** whiter than milk
Num 11:33 was still between their **t**
Deut 32:24 against them the **t** of beasts
Job 4:10 the **t** of the young lions are
Job 13:14 do I take my flesh in my **t**
Job 16: 9 He gnashes at me with His **t**
Job 19:20 escaped by the skin of my **t**
Job 29:17 plucked the victim from his **t**
Job 41:14 his terrible **t** all around
Ps 3: 7 broken the **t** of the ungodly
Ps 35:16 gnashed at me with their **t**
Ps 37:12 And gnashes at him with his **t**
Ps 57: 4 Whose **t** are spears and arrows,
Ps 58: 6 Break their **t** in their mouth,
Ps 112:10 He will gnash his **t** and melt
Ps 124: 6 given us as prey to their **t**
Prov 10:26 As vinegar to the **t** and smoke
Prov 30:14 whose **t** are like swords, and
Song 4: 2 Your **t** are like a flock of
Song 6: 6 Your **t** are like a flock of
Is 41:15 threshing sledge with sharp **t**
Jer 31:29 the children's **t** are set on
Jer 31:30 his **t** shall be set on edge
Lam 2:16 they hiss and gnash their **t**
Lam 3:16 also broken my **t** with gravel
Ezek 18: 2 the children's **t** are set on
Dan 7: 5 in its mouth between its **t**
Dan 7: 7 It had huge iron **t**
Dan 7:19 dreadful, with its **t** of iron
Joel 1: 6 his **t** are the **t** of a lion
Amos 4: 6 of **t** in all your cities
Mic 3: 5 while they chew with their **t**
Zech 9: 7 from between his **t**
Matt 8:12 be weeping and gnashing of **t**
Matt 13:42 be wailing and gnashing of **t**
Matt 13:50 be wailing and gnashing of **t**
Matt 22:13 be weeping and gnashing of **t**
Matt 24:51 be weeping and gnashing of **t**
Matt 25:30 be weeping and gnashing of **t**
Mark 9:18 at the mouth, gnashes his **t**
Luke 13:28 be weeping and gnashing of **t**
Acts 7:54 gnashed at him with their **t**
Rev 9: 8 **t** were like lions' **t**

TEHAPHNEHES (*see* TAHPANHES)
Ezek 30:18 At **T** the day shall also be

TEHINNAH
1Ch 4:12 **T** the father of Ir-Nahash

TEKEL
Dan 5:25 MENE, MENE, **T**,
Dan 5:27 **T**: You have been weighed

TEKOA (*see* TEKOITE)
2Sa 14: 2 And Joab sent to **T** and brought
2Sa 14: 4 woman of **T** spoke to the king
2Sa 14: 9 the woman of **T** said to the
1Ch 2:24 him Ashhur the father of **T**
1Ch 4: 5 the father of **T** had two wives
2Ch 11: 6 he built Bethlehem, Etam, **T**
2Ch 20:20 out into the Wilderness of **T**
Jer 6: 1 Blow the trumpet in **T**, and set
Amos 1: 1 was among the herdsmen of **T**

TEKOITE (*see* TEKOA, TEKOITES)
2Sa 23:26 Ira the son of Ikkesh the **T**
1Ch 11:28 Ira the son of Ikkesh the **T**
1Ch 27: 9 Ira the son of Ikkesh the **T**

TEKOITES (*see* TEKOITE)
Neh 3: 5 to them the **T** made repairs
Neh 3:27 After them the **T** repaired

TEL ABIB
Ezek 3:15 I came to the captives at **T**

TELAH
1Ch 7:25 **T** his son, Tahan his son,

TELAIM (*see* TELEM)
1Sa 15: 4 and numbered them in **T**, two

TELASSAR
2Ki 19:12 people of Eden who were in T
Is 37:12 people of Eden who were in T

TELEM (*see* TELAIM)
Josh 15:24 Ziph, T, Bealoth,
Ezra 10:24 Shallum, T, and Uri

TEL HARSHA
Ezra 2:59 who came up from Tel Melah, T
Neh 7:61 who came up from Tel Melah, T

TELL (*see* PREFACE)

TELLING (*see* PREFACE)

TELLS (*see* PREFACE)

TEL MELAH
Ezra 2:59 the ones who came up from T
Neh 7:61 the ones who came up from T

TEMA
Gen 25:15 Hadar, T, Jetur, Naphish, and
1Ch 1:30 Dumah, Massa, Hadad, T,
Job 6:19 The caravans of T look, the
Is 21:14 inhabitants of the land of T
Jer 25:23 Dedan, T, Buz, and all who are

TEMAN (*see* TEMANITE)
Gen 36:11 And the sons of Eliphaz were T
Gen 36:15 son of Esau, were Chief T
Gen 36:42 Chief Kenaz, Chief T, Chief
1Ch 1:36 And the sons of Eliphaz were T
1Ch 1:53 Chief Kenaz, Chief T, Chief
Jer 49: 7 Is wisdom no more in T
Jer 49:20 against the inhabitants of T
Ezek 25:13 and make it desolate from T
Amos 1:12 But I will send a fire upon T
Obad 9 Then your mighty men, O T
Hab 3: 3 God came from T, the Holy One

TEMANITE (*see* TEMAN, TEMANITES)
Job 2:11 Eliphaz the T, Bildad the
Job 4: 1 Then Eliphaz the T answered
Job 15: 1 Then Eliphaz the T answered
Job 22: 1 Then Eliphaz the T answered
Job 42: 7 LORD said to Eliphaz the T
Job 42: 9 So Eliphaz the T and Bildad

TEMANITES (*see* TEMANITE)
Gen 36:34 of the T reigned in his place
1Ch 1:45 of the T reigned in his place

TEMENI
1Ch 4: 6 bore him Ahuzzam, Hepher, T

TEMPERATE
1Co 9:25 the prize is t in all things
1Ti 3: 2 the husband of one wife, t
1Ti 3:11 reverent, not slanderers, t
Tit 2: 2 men be sober, reverent, t

TEMPEST (*see* TEMPEST-TOSSED, TEMPESTUOUS)
Job 9:17 For He crushes me with a t
Job 27:20 a t steals him away in the
Ps 55: 8 From the windy storm and t
Ps 83:15 So pursue them with Your t
Is 28: 2 one, like a t of hail and a
Is 29: 6 great noise, with storm and t
Is 30:30 fire, with scattering, t, and
Is 32: 2 wind, and a cover from the t
Is 54:11 afflicted one, tossed with t
Amos 1:14 and a t in the day of the
Jon 1: 4 was a mighty t on the sea
Jon 1:12 this great t is because of me
Matt 8:24 a great t arose on the sea
Acts 27:20 no small t beat on us, all
Heb 12:18 to blackness and darkness and t
2Pe 2:17 water, clouds carried by a t

TEMPEST-TOSSED (*see* TEMPEST)
Acts 27:18 because we were exceedingly t

TEMPESTUOUS (*see* TEMPEST)
Ps 50: 3 be very t all around Him
Jon 1:11 the sea was growing more t
Jon 1:13 to grow more t against them
Acts 27:14 a t head wind arose, called

TEMPLE (*see* TEMPLES)
Judg 4:21 and drove the peg into his t
Judg 4:22 dead with the peg in his t
Judg 5:26 split and struck through his t
Judg 9: 4 from the t of Baal-Berith
Judg 9:46 of the t of the god Berith
Judg 16:26 pillars which support the t
Judg 16:27 Now the t was full of men and
Judg 16:29 pillars which supported the t
Judg 16:30 the t fell on the lords and
1Sa 5: 2 it into the t of Dagon and set
1Sa 5: 5 t tread on the threshold of
1Sa 31: 9 it in the t of their idols
1Sa 31:10 in the t of the Ashtoreths
2Sa 22: 7 He heard my voice from His t
1Ki 5:17 lay the foundation of the t
1Ki 5:18 and stones to build the t
1Ki 6: 5 the t he built chambers all
1Ki 6: 5 against the walls of the t
1Ki 6: 6 around the outside of the t
1Ki 6: 6 into the walls of the t
1Ki 6: 7 And the t, when it was being
1Ki 6: 7 t while it was being built
1Ki 6: 8 on the right side of the t
1Ki 6: 9 So he built the t and finished
1Ki 6: 9 he paneled the t with beams
1Ki 6:10 chambers against the entire t
1Ki 6:10 to the t with cedar beams
1Ki 6:12 Concerning this t which you
1Ki 6:14 So Solomon built the t and
1Ki 6:15 of the t with cedar boards
1Ki 6:15 from the floor of the t to
1Ki 6:15 the t with planks of cypress
1Ki 6:16 room at the rear of the t
1Ki 6:17 And in front of it the t
1Ki 6:18 The inside of the t was cedar
1Ki 6:19 inner sanctuary inside the t
1Ki 6:21 of the t with pure gold
1Ki 6:22 The whole t he overlaid with
1Ki 6:22 he had finished all the t
1Ki 6:29 the walls of the t all around
1Ki 6:30 And the floor of the t he
1Ki 7:12 and the vestibule of the t
1Ki 7:21 by the vestibule of the t
1Ki 7:50 of the main hall of the t
1Ki 8: 6 the inner sanctuary of the t
1Ki 8:27 this t which I have built
1Ki 8:29 be open toward this t night
1Ki 8:31 before Your altar in this t
1Ki 8:33 supplication to You in this t
1Ki 8:38 out his hands toward this t
1Ki 8:42 comes and prays toward this t
1Ki 8:43 this t which I have built is
1Ki 8:44 toward the t which I have
1Ki 8:48 the t which I have built for
1Ki 9:25 So he finished the t
1Ki 16:32 for Baal in the t of Baal
2Ki 5:18 my master goes into the t of
2Ki 5:18 I bow down in the t of Rimmon
2Ki 5:18 I bow down in the t of Rimmon
2Ki 10:21 they came into the t of Baal
2Ki 10:21 the t of Baal was full from
2Ki 10:23 went into the t of Baal, and
2Ki 10:25 inner room of the t of Baal
2Ki 10:26 pillars out of the t of Baal
2Ki 10:27 and tore down the t of Baal
2Ki 11:10 were in the t of the LORD
2Ki 11:11 from the right side of the t
2Ki 11:11 to the left side of the t
2Ki 11:11 by the altar and the t
2Ki 11:13 into the t of the LORD
2Ki 11:18 land went to the t of Baal
2Ki 12: 5 repair the damages of the t
2Ki 12: 6 repaired the damages of the t
2Ki 12: 7 repaired the damages of the t
2Ki 12: 7 the damages of the t
2Ki 12: 8 repair the damages of the t
2Ki 12:12 was paid out to repair the t
2Ki 16:14 LORD, from the front of the t
2Ki 16:18 which they had built in the t
2Ki 18:16 doors of the t of the LORD
2Ki 19:37 in the t of Nisroch his god
2Ki 23: 4 of the t of the LORD all the
2Ki 24:13 had made in the t of the LORD
1Ch 6:10 the t that Solomon built in
1Ch 10: 9 news in the t of their idols
1Ch 10:10 armor in the t of their gods
1Ch 10:10 his head in the t of Dagon
1Ch 29: 1 because the t is not for man
1Ch 29:19 to build the t for which I
2Ch 2: 1 determined to build a t for
2Ch 2: 4 I am building a t for the
2Ch 2: 5 the t which I build will be
2Ch 2: 6 who is able to build Him a t
2Ch 2: 6 that I should build Him a t
2Ch 2: 9 for the t which I am about to
2Ch 2:12 will build a t for the LORD
2Ch 3:15 the t two pillars thirty-five
2Ch 3:17 up the pillars before the t
2Ch 4: 7 design, and set them in the t
2Ch 4: 8 and placed them in the t,
2Ch 4:22 of the main hall of the t
2Ch 5: 7 the inner sanctuary of the t
2Ch 6: 7 a t for the name of the LORD
2Ch 6: 8 to build a t for My name, you
2Ch 6: 9 shall build the t for My name
2Ch 6:10 I have built the t for the
2Ch 6:18 this t which I have built
2Ch 6:20 may be open toward this t day
2Ch 6:22 before Your altar in this t
2Ch 6:24 before You in this t,
2Ch 6:32 they come and pray in this t
2Ch 6:33 this t which I have built is
2Ch 6:34 toward the t which I have
2Ch 6:38 toward the t which I have
2Ch 7: 1 of the LORD filled the t
2Ch 7: 3 glory of the LORD on the t
2Ch 20: 9 we will stand before this t
2Ch 20: 9 (for Your name is in this t)
2Ch 23: 9 that were in the t of God
2Ch 23:10 from the right side of the t
2Ch 23:10 to the left side of the t
2Ch 23:10 by the altar and by the t, all
2Ch 23:12 people in the t of the LORD
2Ch 23:17 people went to the t of Baal
2Ch 26:16 his God by entering the t of
2Ch 27: 2 not enter the t of the LORD)
2Ch 29:16 that they found in the t of
2Ch 32:21 gone into the t of his god
2Ch 34: 8 had purged the land and the t
2Ch 35:20 Josiah had prepared the t
2Ch 36: 7 put them in his t at Babylon
Ezra 1: 7 and put in the t of his gods
Ezra 3: 6 the t of the LORD had not yet
Ezra 3:10 of the t of the LORD, the
Ezra 3:12 men, who had seen the first t
Ezra 3:12 t was laid before their eyes
Ezra 4: 1 t of the LORD God of Israel
Ezra 5: 3 commanded you to build this t
Ezra 5: 8 to the t of the great God,
Ezra 5: 9 commanded you to build this t
Ezra 5:11 we are rebuilding the t that
Ezra 5:12 who destroyed this t and
Ezra 5:14 had taken from the t that was
Ezra 5:14 carried into the t of Babylon
Ezra 5:14 took from the t of Babylon
Ezra 5:15 carry them to the t site that
Ezra 6: 5 took from the t which is in
Ezra 6: 5 taken back to the t which is
Ezra 6:15 Now the t was finished on the
Neh 2: 8 which pertains to the t, for
Neh 6:10 house of God, within the t
Neh 6:10 us close the doors of the t
Neh 6:11 into the t to save his life
Ps 5: 7 worship toward Your holy t
Ps 11: 4 The LORD is in His holy t
Ps 18: 6 He heard my voice from His t
Ps 27: 4 LORD, And to inquire in His t
Ps 29: 9 And in His t everyone says,
Ps 48: 9 In the midst of Your t
Ps 65: 4 of Your house, Of Your holy t
Ps 68:29 of Your t at Jerusalem, Kings
Ps 79: 1 Your holy t they have defiled
Ps 138: 2 worship toward Your holy t
Is 6: 1 of His robe filled the t
Is 15: 2 he has gone up to the t and
Is 44:28 shall be built," and to the t
Is 64:11 Our holy and beautiful t,
Is 66: 6 A voice from the t
Jer 7: 4 The t of the LORD
Jer 7: 4 the t of the LORD
Jer 7: 4 the t of the LORD are these
Jer 24: 1 set before the t of the LORD
Jer 26:18 the mountain of the t like
Jer 50:28 God, the vengeance of His t
Jer 51:11 LORD, the vengeance for His t
Ezek 8:16 the door of the t of the LORD
Ezek 8:16 toward the t of the LORD and
Ezek 9: 3 to the threshold of the t
Ezek 9: 6 elders who were before the t
Ezek 9: 7 Defile the t, and fill the
Ezek 10: 3 of the t when the man went in
Ezek 10: 4 over the threshold of the t
Ezek 10:18 from the threshold of the t
Ezek 40: 5 around the outside of the t
Ezek 40:45 who have charge of the t
Ezek 40:47 altar was in front of the t

TEMPLES (*see* TEMPLE)

TEMPORARY

TEMPT (*see* TEMPTATION, TEMPTED, TEMPTER)

TEMPTATION (*see* TEMPT, TEMPTATIONS)

TEMPTATIONS (*see* TEMPTATION)

TEMPTED (*see* TEMPT)

TEMPTER (*see* TEMPT)

TEN (*see* TENS, TENTH)

Gen 18: 6 hastened into the **t** to Sarah
Gen 18: 9 Here, in the **t**
Gen 18:10 **t** door which was behind him
Gen 24:67 her into his mother Sarah's **t**
Gen 26:17 pitched his **t** in the Valley
Gen 26:25 and he pitched his **t** there
Gen 31:25 his **t** in the mountains, and
Gen 31:33 Jacob's **t**, into Leah's **t**
Gen 31:33 Leah's **t** and entered Rachel's **t**
Gen 31:34 the **t** but did not find them
Gen 33:18 he pitched his **t** before the
Gen 33:19 where he had pitched his **t**
Gen 35:21 and pitched his **t** beyond the
Ex 16:16 for those who are in his **t**
Ex 18: 7 and they went into the **t**
Ex 26: 7 to be a **t** over the tabernacle
Ex 26: 9 at the forefront of the **t**
Ex 26:11 and couple the **t** together
Ex 26:12 of the curtains of the **t**, the
Ex 26:13 of the curtains of the **t**,
Ex 26:14 skins dyed red for the **t**, and
Ex 33: 7 Moses took his **t** and pitched
Ex 33: 8 each man stood at his **t** door
Ex 33:10 each man in his **t** door
Ex 35:11 the tabernacle, its **t**, its
Ex 36:14 for the **t** over the tabernacle
Ex 36:18 to couple the **t** together,
Ex 36:19 the **t** of rams' skins dyed red
Ex 39:32 the **t** of meeting was finished
Ex 39:33 tabernacle to Moses, the **t**
Ex 39:40 for the **t** of meeting
Ex 40: 2 of the **t** of meeting
Ex 40: 6 of the **t** of meeting
Ex 40:19 he spread out the **t** over the
Ex 40:19 of the **t** on top of it, as the
Ex 40:29 of the **t** of meeting, and
Lev 14: 8 stay outside his **t** seven days
Num 3:25 the **t** with its covering, the
Num 9:15 the **t** of the Testimony
Num 11:10 everyone at the door of his **t**
Num 19:14 law when a man dies in a **t**
Num 19:14 All who come into the **t** and
Num 19:14 all who are in the **t** shall be
Num 19:18 water, sprinkle it on the **t**
Num 25: 8 the man of Israel into the **t**
Josh 7:21 earth in the midst of my **t**
Josh 7:22 and they ran to the **t**
Josh 7:22 there it was, hidden in his **t**
Josh 7:23 them from the midst of the **t**
Josh 7:24 his donkeys, his sheep, his **t**
Judg 4:11 and pitched his **t** near the
Judg 4:17 away on foot to the **t** of Jael
Judg 4:18 aside with her into the **t**
Judg 4:20 Stand at the door of the **t**
Judg 4:21 Heber's wife, took a **t** peg
Judg 4:22 And when he went into her **t**
Judg 5:26 her hand to the **t** peg, her
Judg 7: 8 of Israel, every man to his **t**
Judg 7:13 it came to a **t** and struck it
Judg 7:13 and the **t** collapsed
Judg 20: 8 None of us will go to his **t**
1Sa 4:10 and every man fled to his **t**
1Sa 13: 2 sent away, every man to his **t**
1Sa 17:54 but he put his armor in his **t**
2Sa 7: 2 God dwells inside **t** curtains
2Sa 7: 6 but have moved about in a **t**
2Sa 16:22 So they pitched a **t** for
2Sa 18:17 fled, everyone to his **t**
2Sa 19: 8 of Israel had fled to his **t**
2Sa 20:22 the city, every man to his **t**
2Ki 7: 8 camp, they went into one **t**
2Ki 7: 8 back and entered another **t**
2Ki 14:12 and every man fled to his **t**
1Ch 15: 1 of God, and pitched a **t** for it
1Ch 17: 1 the LORD is under **t** curtains
1Ch 17: 5 but have gone from **t** to **t**
2Ch 1: 4 a **t** for it at Jerusalem
2Ch 25:22 and every man fled to his **t**
Job 5:24 know that your **t** is in peace
Job 18: 6 The light is dark in his **t**
Job 18:14 from the shelter of his **t**
Job 18:15 They dwell in his **t** who are
Job 19:12 they encamp all around my **t**
Job 20:26 with him who is left in his **t**
Job 21:28 And where is the **t**, the
Job 29: 4 counsel of God was over my **t**
Job 31:31 the men of my **t** have not said
Ps 78:60 The **t** which He had placed
Ps 78:67 He rejected the **t** of Joseph
Prov 14:11 but the **t** of the upright will
Is 38:12 from me like a shepherd's **t**
Is 40:22 them out like a **t** to dwell in
Is 54: 2 Enlarge the place of your **t**
Jer 10:20 My **t** is plundered, and all my
Jer 10:20 no one to pitch my **t** anymore
Jer 37:10 rise up, every man in his **t**
Lam 2: 4 on the **t** of the daughter of
Zech 10: 4 from him the **t** peg, from him
2Co 5: 1 if our earthly house, this **t**
2Co 5: 4 we who are in this **t** groan
2Pe 1:13 as long as I am in this **t**
2Pe 1:14 shortly I must put off my **t**

TENTH (*see* TEN)
Gen 8: 5 continually until the **t** month
Gen 8: 5 In the **t** month, on the first
Gen 28:22 I will surely give a **t** to You
Ex 12: 3 On the **t** day of this month
Lev 16:29 on the **t** day of the month,
Lev 23:27 Also the **t** day of this
Lev 25: 9 **t** day of the seventh month
Lev 27:32 the **t** one shall be holy to
Num 7:66 On the **t** day Ahiezer the son
Num 18:26 to the LORD, a **t** of the tithe
Num 29: 7 On the **t** day of this seventh
Deut 23: 2 even to the **t** generation none
Deut 23: 3 even to the **t** generation none
Josh 4:19 the **t** day of the first month
1Sa 8:15 will take a **t** of your grain
1Sa 8:17 will take a **t** of your sheep
2Ki 25: 1 of his reign, in the **t** month
2Ki 25: 1 on the **t** day of the month,
1Ch 12:13 Jeremiah the **t**, and Machbanai
1Ch 24:11 Jeshua, the **t** to Shecaniah,
1Ch 25:17 the **t** for Shimei, his sons and
1Ch 27:13 **t** captain for the **t** month
Ezra 10:16 on the first day of the **t**
Neh 10:38 Levites shall bring up a **t** of
Esth 2:16 royal palace, in the **t** month
Is 6:13 But yet a **t** will be in it, and
Jer 32: 1 from the LORD in the **t** year
Jer 39: 1 king of Judah, in the **t** month
Jer 52: 4 of his reign, in the **t** month
Jer 52: 4 on the **t** day of the month,
Jer 52:12 on the **t** day of the month
Ezek 20: 1 on the **t** day of the month,
Ezek 24: 1 ninth year, in the **t** month
Ezek 24: 1 on the **t** day of the month,
Ezek 29: 1 **t** year, in the **t** month
Ezek 33:21 our captivity, in the **t** month
Ezek 40: 1 on the **t** day of the month, in
Zech 8:19 seventh, and the fast of the **t**
John 1:39 (now it was about the **t** hour)
Heb 7: 2 Abraham gave a **t** part of all
Heb 7: 4 gave a **t** of the spoils
Rev 11:13 and a **t** of the city fell
Rev 21:20 topaz, the **t** chrysoprase, the

TENTMAKERS (*see* TENT)
Acts 18: 3 for by occupation they were **t**

TENTS (*see* TENT)
Gen 4:20 of those who dwell in **t** and
Gen 9:27 may he dwell in the **t** of Shem
Gen 13: 5 had flocks and herds and **t**
Gen 25:27 was a mild man, dwelling in **t**
Gen 31:33 and into the two maids' **t**
Num 1:52 of Israel shall pitch their **t**
Num 9:17 of Israel would pitch their **t**
Num 16:24 Get away from the **t** of Korah
Num 16:26 the **t** of these wicked men
Num 16:27 from around the **t** of Korah
Num 16:27 stood at the door of their **t**
Num 24: 5 How lovely are your **t**, O
Deut 1:27 and you murmured in your **t**
Deut 1:33 place for you to pitch your **t**
Deut 5:30 Return to your **t**
Deut 11: 6 up, their households, their **t**
Deut 16: 7 shall turn and go to your **t**
Deut 33:18 out, and Issachar in your **t**
Josh 22: 4 return and go to your **t** and to
Josh 22: 6 away, and they went to their **t**
Josh 22: 7 sent them away to their **t**
Josh 22: 8 with much riches to your **t**
Judg 5:24 is she among women in **t**
Judg 6: 5 their livestock and their **t**
Judg 8:11 in **t** on the east of Nobah
1Sa 17:53 and they plundered their **t**
2Sa 11:11 and Judah are dwelling in **t**
2Sa 20: 1 every man to his **t**, O Israel
1Ki 8:66 and went to their **t** joyful
1Ki 12:16 To your **t**, O Israel
1Ki 12:16 So Israel departed to their **t**
2Ki 7: 7 their **t**, their horses, and
2Ki 7:10 donkeys tied, and the **t** intact
2Ki 7:16 out and plundered the **t** of the
2Ki 8:21 his people fled to their **t**
2Ki 13: 5 dwelt in their **t** as before
1Ch 4:41 and they attacked their **t** and
1Ch 5:10 and they dwelt in their **t**
2Ch 7:10 the people away to their **t**
2Ch 10:16 Every man to your **t**, O Israel
2Ch 10:16 Israel departed to their **t**
Job 11:14 wickedness dwell in your **t**
Job 12: 6 The **t** of robbers prosper, and
Job 15:34 will consume the **t** of bribery
Job 22:23 iniquity far from your **t**
Ps 69:25 Let no one dwell in their **t**
Ps 78:51 strength in the **t** of Ham
Ps 78:55 of Israel dwell in their **t**
Ps 83: 6 The **t** of Edom and the
Ps 84:10 dwell in the **t** of wickedness
Ps 106:25 But murmured in their **t**, And
Ps 118:15 Is in the **t** of the righteous
Ps 120: 5 I dwell among the **t** of Kedar
Song 1: 5 like the **t** of Kedar, like
Song 1: 8 goats beside the shepherds' **t**
Is 13:20 the Arabian pitch **t** there
Jer 4:20 Suddenly my **t** are plundered,
Jer 6: 3 **t** against her all around
Jer 30:18 the captivity of Jacob's **t**
Jer 35: 7 days you shall dwell in **t**
Jer 35:10 But we have dwelt in **t**, and
Jer 49:29 Their **t** and their flocks they
Dan 11:45 he shall plant the **t** of his
Hos 9: 6 thorns shall be in their **t**
Hos 12: 9 again make you dwell in **t**
Hab 3: 7 I saw the **t** of Cushan in
Zech 12: 7 save the **t** of Judah first
Mal 2:12 **t** of Jacob the man who does
Heb 11: 9 dwelling in **t** with Isaac

TERAH
Gen 11:24 twenty-nine years, and begot **T**
Gen 11:25 After he begot **T**, Nahor lived
Gen 11:26 Now **T** lived seventy years, and
Gen 11:27 genealogy of **T**: **T** begot Abram
Gen 11:28 father **T** in his native land
Gen 11:31 **T** took his son Abram and his
Gen 11:32 So the days of **T** were two
Gen 11:32 years, and **T** died in Haran
Num 33:27 from Tahath and camped at **T**
Num 33:28 They moved from **T** and camped
Josh 24: 2 Your fathers, including **T**
1Ch 1:26 Serug, Nahor, **T**,
Luke 3:34 son of Abraham, the son of **T**

TERAPHIM
Hos 3: 4 pillar, without ephod or **t**

TEREBINTH (*see* TEREBINTHS)
Gen 12: 6 as far as the **t** tree of Moreh
Gen 13:18 dwelt by the **t** trees of Mamre
Gen 14:13 for he dwelt by the **t** trees
Gen 18: 1 him by the **t** trees of Mamre
Gen 35: 4 Jacob hid them under the **t**
Gen 35: 8 below Bethel under the **t** tree
Deut 11:30 beside the **t** trees of Moreh
Josh 19:33 from the **t** tree in Zaanannim
Judg 4:11 near the **t** tree at Zaanaim
Judg 6:11 sat under the **t** tree which
Judg 6:19 out to Him under the **t** tree
Judg 9: 6 Abimelech king beside the **t**
Judg 9:37 from the Diviners' **T** Tree
1Sa 10: 3 come to the **t** tree of Tabor
2Sa 18: 9 boughs of a great **t** tree
2Sa 18: 9 and his head caught in the **t**
2Sa 18:10 Absalom hanging in a **t** tree
2Sa 18:14 in the midst of the **t** tree
Is 1:29 of the **t** trees which you have
Is 1:30 be as a **t** whose leaf fades
Is 6:13 as a **t** tree or as an oak,

TEREBINTHS (*see* TEREBINTH)
Hos 4:13 under oaks, poplars, and **t**

TERESH
Esth 2:21 king's eunuchs, Bigthan and **T**
Esth 6: 2 had told of Bigthana and **T**

TERMED (*see* TERMS)
Is 62: 4 shall no longer be **t** Forsaken
Is 62: 4 land any more be **t** Desolate

TERMS (*see* TERMED)
Job 34:33 repay it according to your t
Rom 6:19 I speak in human t because of

TERRACE
Ezek 17: 7 from the garden t where it
Ezek 17:10 in the garden t where it grew
Ezek 41: 9 so also the remaining t by
Ezek 41:11 side chambers opened on the t
Ezek 41:11 the width of the t was five

TERRESTRIAL
1Co 15:40 celestial bodies and t bodies
1Co 15:40 the glory of the t is another

TERRIBLE (*see* TERROR)
Deut 1:19 t wilderness which you saw on
Deut 7:15 you with none of the t
Deut 8:15 t wilderness, in which were
Job 41:14 with his t teeth all around
Is 13:11 low the haughtiness of the t
Is 18: 2 to a people t from their
Is 18: 7 from a people t from their
Is 21: 1 the desert, from a t land
Is 25: 3 the city of the t nations
Is 25: 4 for the blast of the t ones
Is 25: 5 the song of the t ones will
Is 29: 5 the multitude of the t ones
Is 29:20 For the t one is brought to
Is 49:25 prey of the t be delivered
Jer 15:21 you from the grip of the t
Ezek 5:16 the t arrows of famine which
Ezek 28: 7 the most t of the nations
Ezek 30:11 the most t of the nations,
Ezek 31:12 the most t of the nations,
Ezek 32:12 the most t of the nations
Dan 7: 7 a fourth beast, dreadful and t
Joel 2:11 the LORD is great and very t
Joel 2:31 great and t day of the LORD
Hab 1: 7 They are t and dreadful

TERRIFIED (*see* TERRIFY)
Deut 1:29 I said to you, 'Do not be t
Deut 7:21 You shall not be t of them
Deut 20: 3 or be t because of them
Esth 7: 6 So Haman was t before the
Job 21: 6 Even when I remember I am t
Job 23:15 Therefore I am t at His
Ps 90: 7 And by Your wrath we are t
Jer 51:32 fire, and the men of war are t
Luke 21: 9 and commotions, do not be t
Luke 24:37 But they were t and frightened
Phil 1:28 and not in any way t by your

TERRIFIES (*see* TERRIFY)
Deut 28:67 the fear which t your heart
Job 23:16 weak, and the Almighty t me

TERRIFY (*see* TERRIFIED, TERRIFIES, TERRIFYING)
Job 3: 5 the blackness of the day t it
Job 7:14 dreams and t me with visions,
Job 9:34 do not let dread of Him t me
Job 33: 7 no fear of me will t you, nor
Zech 1:21 are coming to t them, to cast
2Co 10: 9 I seem to t you by letters

TERRIFYING (*see* TERRIFY)
Heb 12:21 so t was the sight that Moses

TERRITORIES (*see* TERRITORY)
2Sa 21: 5 in any of the t of Israel
2Ch 11:13 from all their t the priests
2Ch 11:23 throughout all the t of Judah
Jer 15:13 your sins, throughout your t

TERRITORY (*see* TERRITORIES)
Ex 8: 2 smite all your t with frogs
Ex 10: 4 bring locusts into your t
Ex 10:14 rested on all the t of Egypt
Ex 10:19 locust in all the t of Egypt
Num 20:17 we have passed through your t
Num 20:21 Israel passage through his t
Num 21:22 we have passed through your t
Num 21:23 Israel to pass through his t
Num 22:36 Arnon, the boundary of the t
Deut 2: 4 the t of your brethren, the
Deut 11:24 Western Sea, shall be your t
Deut 16: 4 in all your t for seven days
Deut 19: 3 t of your land which the LORD
Deut 19: 8 LORD your God enlarges your t
Deut 28:40 trees throughout all your t
Josh 1: 4 of the sun, shall be your t
Josh 12: 4 Og king of Bashan and his t
Josh 13: 2 all the t of the Philistines
Josh 13:16 Their t was from Aroer, which
Josh 13:25 Their t was Jazer, and all the
Josh 13:30 Their t was from Mahanaim,
Josh 17: 7 the t of Manasseh was from
Josh 17:10 Manasseh's t was adjoining
Josh 18: 5 in their t on the south, and
Josh 18: 5 in their t on the north
Josh 18:11 the t of their lot came out
Josh 19:18 their t went to Jezreel, and
Josh 19:25 their t included Helkath,
Josh 19:33 enclosing the t from the
Josh 19:41 the t of their inheritance
Judg 1: 3 up with me to my allotted t
Judg 1: 3 with you to your allotted t
Judg 1:18 Judah took Gaza with its t
Judg 1:18 Ashkelon with its t
Judg 1:18 and Ekron with its t
Judg 11:20 Israel to pass through his t
Judg 11:22 of all the t of the Amorites
Judg 18: 2 of their family from their t
Judg 19:29 all the t of Israel
Judg 20: 6 the t of the inheritance of
1Sa 5: 6 tumors, both Ashdod and its t
1Sa 6: 9 goes up the road to its own t
1Sa 7:13 anymore into the t of Israel
1Sa 7:14 Israel recovered its t from
1Sa 10: 2 the t of Benjamin at Zelzah
1Sa 11: 3 to all the t of Israel
1Sa 11: 7 them throughout all the t of
1Sa 30:14 in the t which belongs to
2Sa 8: 3 his t at the River Euphrates
1Ki 1: 3 all the t of Israel, and found
2Ki 10:32 them in all the t of Israel
2Ki 14:25 He restored the t of Israel
2Ki 15:16 all who were there, and its t
2Ki 18: 8 as far as Gaza and its t,
1Ch 4:10 me indeed, and enlarge my t
1Ch 6:54 their settlements in their t
1Ch 6:66 t from the tribe of Ephraim
1Ch 21:12 all the t of Israel
Job 38:20 that you may take it to its t
Ps 105:31 flies, And lice in all their t
Ps 105:33 the trees of their t
Is 20: 6 this t will say in that day
Is 56:11 his own gain, from his own t
Ezek 25: 9 I will clear the t of Moab of
Ezek 33: 2 land take a man from their t
Ezek 45: 1 throughout its t all around
Amos 1:13 they might enlarge their t
Amos 6: 2 their t greater than your t
Amos 7: 4 great deep and devoured the t
Mal 1: 4 be called the T of Wickedness

TERROR (*see* TERRIBLE, TERRORS)
Gen 35: 5 the t of God was upon the
Lev 26:16 will even appoint t over you
Deut 26: 8 arm, with great t and with
Deut 32:25 there shall be t within for
Deut 34:12 all the great t which Moses
Josh 2: 9 that the t of you has fallen
Job 6:21 you are nothing, you see t
Job 31:23 from God is a t to me, and
Job 39:20 majestic snorting strikes t
Ps 91: 5 be afraid of the t by night
Prov 1:26 I will mock when your t comes
Prov 1:27 when your t comes like a
Prov 3:25 Do not be afraid of sudden t
Is 2:10 from the t of the LORD and the
Is 2:19 from the t of the LORD and the
Is 2:21 from the t of the LORD and the
Is 10:33 will lop off the bough with t
Is 19:17 of Judah will be a t to Egypt
Is 28:19 it will be a t just to
Is 33:18 Your heart will meditate on t
Is 54:14 and from t, for it shall not
Jer 15: 8 t to fall on them suddenly
Jer 17:17 Do not be a t to me
Jer 20: 4 will make you a t to yourself
Jer 32:21 arm, and with great t
Ezek 26:17 their t to be on all her
Ezek 26:21 I will make you a t, and you
Ezek 32:23 who caused t in the land of
Ezek 32:24 who caused their t in the
Ezek 32:25 though their t was caused in
Ezek 32:26 though they caused their t in
Ezek 32:27 because of the t of the
Ezek 32:30 the slain in shame at the t
Ezek 32:32 For I have caused My t in the
Dan 10: 7 but a great t fell upon them,
Hos 11: 9 and I will not come with t
Rom 13: 3 are not a t to good works
2Co 5:11 the t of the Lord, we
1Pe 3: 6 and are not afraid with any t

TERRORS (*see* TERROR)
Deut 4:34 arm, and by great t, according
Job 6: 4 the t of God are arrayed
Job 18:11 T frighten him on every side,
Job 18:14 him before the king of t
Job 20:25 T come upon him
Job 24:17 they are in the t of the
Job 27:20 T overtake him like a flood
Job 30:15 T are turned upon me
Ps 55: 4 the t of death have fallen
Ps 73:19 are utterly consumed with t
Ps 88:15 I suffer Your t
Ps 88:16 Your t have cut me off
Eccl 12: 5 of height, and of t in the way
Lam 2:22 day the t that surround me
Ezek 21:12 T including the sword will be

TERTIUS
Rom 16:22 I, T, who wrote this epistle,

TERTULLUS
Acts 24: 1 and a certain orator named T
Acts 24: 2 upon, T began his accusation,

TEST (*see* TESTED, TESTING, TESTS)
Ex 16: 4 every day, that I may t them
Ex 20:20 for God has come to t you
Num 14:22 and have put Me to the t now
Deut 8: 2 t you, to know what was in
Deut 8:16 you and that He might t you
Judg 2:22 through them I may t Israel
Judg 3: 1 that He might t Israel by
Judg 3: 4 that He might t Israel by
Judg 6:39 Let me t, I pray, just once
Judg 7: 4 I will t them for you there
1Ki 10: 1 she came to t him with hard
1Ch 29:17 that You t the heart and have
2Ch 9: 1 she came to Jerusalem to t
2Ch 32:31 from him, in order to t him
Job 7:18 and t him every moment
Job 12:11 Does not the ear t words and
Ps 11: 4 His eyelids t the sons of men
Eccl 2: 1 now, I will t you with mirth
Is 7:12 ask, nor will I t the LORD
Jer 6:27 you may know and t their way
Jer 17:10 I t the mind, even to give
Jer 20:12 You who t the righteous, and
Dan 1:12 Please t your servants for
Zech 13: 9 and t them as gold is tested
Matt 22:18 Why do you t Me, you
Mark 12:15 Why do you t Me
Luke 14:19 oxen, and I am going to t them
Luke 20:23 Why do you t Me
John 6: 6 But this He said to t him
Acts 5: 9 to t the Spirit of the Lord
Acts 15:10 why do you t God by putting a
1Co 3:13 the fire will t each one's
2Co 2: 9 that I might put you to the t
1Th 5:21 T all things
1Jn 4: 1 but t the spirits, whether
Rev 3:10 to t those who dwell on the

TESTAMENT (*see* TESTATOR)
2Co 3:14 in the reading of the Old T
Heb 9:16 For where there is a t, there
Heb 9:17 For a t is in force after men

TESTATOR (*see* TESTAMENT)
Heb 9:16 be the death of the t
Heb 9:17 at all while the t lives

TESTED (*see* TEST)
Gen 22: 1 things that God t Abraham
Gen 42:15 In this manner you shall be t
Gen 42:16 that your words may be t to
Ex 15:25 And there He t them,
Deut 33: 8 whom You t at Massah, and with
1Sa 17:39 walk, for he had not t them
1Sa 17:39 these, for I have not t them
Job 23:10 when He has t me, I shall
Ps 17: 3 You have t my heart
Ps 78:18 they t God in their heart By
Ps 78:56 Yet they t and provoked the
Ps 95: 9 When your fathers t Me
Ps 105:19 The word of the LORD t him
Ps 106:14 And t God in the desert
Is 48:10 I have t you in the furnace
Jer 12: 3 You have t my heart toward
Dan 1:14 matter, and t them ten days
Zech 13: 9 and test them as gold is t
Luke 10:25 stood up and t Him, saying,

Heb 3: 9 where your fathers t Me,
Heb 11:17 faith Abraham, when he was t
1Pe 1: 7 though it is t by fire, may
Rev 2: 2 you have t those who say they
Rev 2:10 prison, that you may be t

TESTIFIED (*see* TESTIFY)
Deut 19:18 who has t falsely against his
Ruth 1:21 the LORD has t against me
2Sa 1:16 own mouth has t against you
2Ki 17:13 Yet the LORD t against Israel
2Ki 17:15 which He had t against them
2Ch 24:19 they t against them, but they
Neh 9:26 who t against them to turn
Neh 9:29 and t against them, that You
Neh 9:30 t against them by Your Spirit
Neh 9:34 with which You t against them
John 1:34 t that this is the Son of God
John 3:26 Jordan, to whom you have t
John 4:39 the word of the woman who t
John 4:44 For Jesus Himself t that a
John 5:37 who sent Me, has t of Me
John 13:21 was troubled in spirit, and t
John 19:35 And he who has seen has t, and
Acts 2:40 And with many other words he t
Acts 8:25 So when they had t and
Acts 18: 5 t to the Jews that Jesus is
Acts 23:11 for as you have t for Me in
Acts 28:23 solemnly t of the kingdom of
1Co 15:15 because we have t of God that
1Th 4: 6 we also forewarned you and t
1Ti 2: 6 for all, to be t in due time,
Heb 2: 6 But one t in a certain place,
1Pe 1:11 t beforehand the sufferings
1Jn 5: 9 God which He has t of His Son
3Jn 3 t of the truth that is in you

TESTIFIES (*see* TESTIFY)
Hos 5: 5 pride of Israel t to his face
Hos 7:10 pride of Israel t to his face
John 3:32 has seen and heard, that He t
John 21:24 who t of these things, and
Acts 20:23 Holy Spirit t in every city
Heb 7:17 For He t
Rev 22:20 He who t to these things says

TESTIFY (*see* TESTIFIED, TESTIFIES, TESTIFYING)
Ex 23: 2 nor shall you t in a dispute
Deut 8:19 I t against you this day that
Deut 19:16 rises against any man to t
Deut 31:21 that this song will t against
Deut 32:46 which I t among you today
Job 15: 6 your own lips t against you
Ps 50: 7 and I will t against you
Is 59:12 You, and our sins t against us
Jer 14: 7 our iniquities t against us
Amos 3:13 t against the house of Jacob,
Mic 6: 3 T against Me
Matt 26:62 that these men t against You
Matt 27:13 things they t against You
Mark 14:60 is it these men t against You
Mark 15: 4 things they t against You
Luke 16:28 that he may t to them, lest
John 2:25 that anyone should t of man
John 3:11 t what We have seen, and you
John 5:39 these are they which t of Me
John 7: 7 I t of it that its works are
John 15:26 the Father, He will t of Me
Acts 10:42 to t that it is He who was
Acts 20:24 to t to the gospel of the
Acts 20:26 Therefore I t to you this day
Acts 26: 5 if they were willing to t
Gal 5: 3 I t again to every man who
Eph 4:17 and t in the Lord, that you
1Jn 4:14 t that the Father has sent
Rev 22:16 have sent My angel to t to
Rev 22:18 For I t to everyone who hears

TESTIFYING (*see* TESTIFY)
Acts 20:21 t to Jews, and also to Greeks,
Heb 11: 4 righteous, God t of his gifts
1Pe 5:12 t that this is the true grace

TESTIMONIES (*see* TESTIMONY)
Deut 4:45 These are the t, the statutes
Deut 6:17 of the LORD your God, His t
Deut 6:20 What is the meaning of the t
1Ki 2: 3 His judgments, and His t, as
2Ki 17:15 His t which He had testified
2Ki 23: 3 His commandments and His t
1Ch 29:19 commandments and Your t
2Ch 34:31 His commandments and His t
Neh 9:34 commandments and Your t
Ps 25:10 as keep His covenant and His t
Ps 78:56 God, And did not keep His t
Ps 93: 5 Your t are very sure
Ps 99: 7 They kept His t and the
Ps 119: 2 are those who keep His t, Who
Ps 119:14 rejoiced in the way of Your t
Ps 119:22 For I have kept Your t
Ps 119:24 Your t also are my delight And
Ps 119:31 I cling to Your t
Ps 119:36 Incline my heart to Your t
Ps 119:46 of Your t also before kings
Ps 119:59 And turned my feet to Your t
Ps 119:79 to me, Those who know Your t
Ps 119:95 But I will consider Your t
Ps 119:99 For Your t are my meditation
Ps 119:111 Your t I have taken as a
Ps 119:119 Therefore I love Your t
Ps 119:125 That I may know Your t
Ps 119:129 Your t are wonderful
Ps 119:138 Your t, which You have
Ps 119:144 of Your t is everlasting
Ps 119:146 me, and I will keep Your t
Ps 119:152 Concerning Your t, I have
Ps 119:157 Yet I do not turn from Your t
Ps 119:167 My soul keeps Your t, And I
Ps 119:168 keep Your precepts and Your t
Jer 44:23 in His statutes or in His t
Mark 14:56 but their t did not agree

TESTIMONY (*see* TESTIMONIES)
Ex 16:34 Aaron laid it up before the T
Ex 25:16 the T which I will give you
Ex 25:21 the T that I will give you
Ex 25:22 which are on the ark of the T
Ex 26:33 the ark of the T in there
Ex 26:34 ark of the T in the Most Holy
Ex 27:21 veil which is before the T
Ex 30: 6 is before the ark of the T
Ex 30: 6 mercy seat that is over the T
Ex 30:26 meeting and the ark of the T
Ex 30:36 the T in the tabernacle of
Ex 31: 7 of meeting, the ark of the T
Ex 31:18 Moses two tablets of the T
Ex 32:15 of the T were in his hand
Ex 34:29 the two tablets of the T were
Ex 38:21 the tabernacle of the T,
Ex 39:35 ark of the T with its poles
Ex 40: 3 put in it the ark of the T
Ex 40: 5 before the ark of the T, and
Ex 40:20 He took the T and put it into
Ex 40:21 off the ark of the T, as the
Lev 16:13 mercy seat that is on the T
Lev 24: 3 Outside the veil of the T
Num 1:50 over the tabernacle of the T
Num 1:53 the tabernacle of the T, that
Num 1:53 of the tabernacle of the T
Num 4: 5 the ark of the T with it
Num 7:89 that was on the ark of the T
Num 9:15 tabernacle, the tent of the T
Num 10:11 above the tabernacle of the T
Num 17: 4 of meeting before the T,
Num 17:10 Aaron's rod back before the T
Num 35:30 death on the t of witnesses
Num 35:30 t against a person for the
Deut 17: 6 be put to death on the t of
Deut 17: 6 death on the t of one witness
Josh 4:16 who bear the ark of the T to
2Ki 11:12 on him, and gave him the T
2Ch 23:11 crown on him, gave him the T
Ps 19: 7 The t of the LORD is sure,
Ps 78: 5 He established a t in Jacob
Ps 81: 5 established in Joseph for a t
Ps 119:88 may keep the t of Your mouth
Ps 122: 4 To the T of Israel, To give
Ps 132:12 My t which I shall teach them
Is 8:16 Bind up the t, Seal the law
Is 8:20 To the law and to the t
Matt 8: 4 commanded, as a t to them
Matt 10:18 as a t to them and to the
Matt 26:59 the council sought false t
Mark 1:44 commanded, as a t to them
Mark 6:11 your feet as a t against them
Mark 13: 9 for My sake, for a t to them
Mark 14:55 and all the council sought t
Mark 14:59 even then did their t agree
Luke 5:14 as a t to them, just as Moses
Luke 9: 5 your feet as a t against them
Luke 21:13 for you as an occasion for t
Luke 22:71 What further t do we need
John 1:19 Now this is the t of John
John 3:32 and no one receives His t
John 3:33 He who has received His t has
John 5:34 I do not receive t from man
John 8:17 that the t of two men is true
John 19:35 testified, and his t is true
John 21:24 and we know that his t is true
Acts 13:22 king, to whom also He gave t
Acts 22:12 having a good t with all the
Acts 22:18 receive your t concerning Me
1Co 1: 6 even as the t of Christ was
1Co 2: 1 declaring to you the t of God
2Co 1:12 the t of our conscience that
2Th 1:10 because our t among you was
1Ti 3: 7 he must have a good t among
2Ti 1: 8 ashamed of the t of our Lord
Tit 1:13 This t is true
Heb 3: 5 for a t of those things which
Heb 10:28 t of two or three witnesses
Heb 11: 2 the elders obtained a good t
Heb 11: 5 his translation he had this t
Heb 11:39 a good t through faith, did
1Jn 5:10 he has not believed the t
1Jn 5:11 And this is the t
3Jn 12 has a good t from all, and
3Jn 12 you know that our t is true
Rev 1: 2 to the t of Jesus Christ, and
Rev 1: 9 for the t of Jesus Christ
Rev 6: 9 for the t which they held
Rev 11: 7 Now when they finish their t
Rev 12:11 and by the word of their t
Rev 12:17 have the t of Jesus Christ
Rev 15: 5 of the t in heaven was opened
Rev 19:10 who have the t of Jesus
Rev 19:10 For the t of Jesus is the

TESTING (*see* TEST)
Deut 13: 3 is t you to know whether you
Jer 11:20 t the mind and the heart, let
Ezek 21:13 Because it is a t, and what if
Matt 16: 1 t Him asked that He would
Matt 19: 3 Him, t Him, and saying to Him,
Matt 22:35 a question, t Him, and saying,
Mark 8:11 Him a sign from heaven, t Him
Mark 10: 2 t Him
Luke 11:16 t Him, sought from Him a sign
John 8: 6 t Him, that they might have
2Co 8: 8 but I am t the sincerity of
Jas 1: 3 knowing that the t of your

TESTS (*see* TEST)
Job 34: 3 For the ear t words as the
Ps 7: 9 righteous God t the hearts
Ps 11: 5 The LORD t the righteous, But
Prov 17: 3 but the LORD t the hearts
Eccl 3:18 God t them, that they may see
1Th 2: 4 men, but God who t our hearts

TETRARCH
Matt 14: 1 the t heard the report about
Luke 3: 1 Herod being t of Galilee
Luke 3: 1 brother Philip t of Iturea
Luke 3: 1 and Lysanias t of Abilene,
Luke 3:19 But Herod the t, being
Luke 9: 7 Now Herod the t heard of all
Acts 13: 1 brought up with Herod the t

THADDAEUS (*see* JUDAS, LEBBAEUS)
Matt 10: 3 whose surname was T
Mark 3:18 James the son of Alphaeus, T

THAHASH
Gen 22:24 also bore Tebah, Gaham, T

THAN (*see* PREFACE)

THANK (*see* THANKED, THANKFUL, THANKING, THANKS)
1Ch 16: 4 LORD, to commemorate, to t
1Ch 16: 7 his brethren, to t the LORD
1Ch 23:30 to stand every morning to t
1Ch 29:13 God, we t You and praise Your
2Ch 29:31 t offerings into the house of
2Ch 29:31 t offerings, and as many as
2Ch 33:16 and t offerings on it, and
Is 38:18 For Sheol cannot t You, death
Dan 2:23 I t You and praise You, O God
Matt 11:25 I t You, Father, Lord of
Luke 17: 9 Does he t that servant
Luke 18:11 I t You that I am not like
John 11:41 I t You that You have heard
Rom 1: 8 I t my God through Jesus
Rom 7:25 I t God
1Co 1: 4 I t my God always concerning
1Co 1:14 I t God that I baptized none

1Co 14:18 I **t** my God I speak with
Phil 1: 3 I **t** my God upon every
1Th 2:13 we also **t** God without ceasing
2Th 1: 3 We are bound to **t** God always
1Ti 1:12 I **t** Christ Jesus our Lord who
2Ti 1: 3 I **t** God, whom I serve with a
Phm 4 I **t** my God, making mention of

THANKED (*see* THANK)
2Sa 14:22 bowed himself, and **t** the king
Acts 28:15 he **t** God and took courage
Rom 6:17 But God be **t** that though you

THANKFUL (*see* THANK, THANKFULNESS, UNTHANKFUL)
Ps 100: 4 Be **t** to Him, and bless His
Rom 1:21 Him as God, nor were **t**, but
Col 3:15 called in one body; and be **t**

THANKFULNESS (*see* THANKFUL)
Acts 24: 3 most noble Felix, with all **t**

THANKING (*see* THANK)
2Ch 5:13 and **t** the LORD, and when they

THANKS (*see* THANK, THANKSGIVING)
2Sa 22:50 I will give **t** to You, O LORD,
1Ch 16: 8 Oh, give **t** to the LORD
1Ch 16:34 give **t** to the LORD, for He is
1Ch 16:35 to give **t** to Your holy name,
1Ch 16:41 name, to give **t** to the LORD,
1Ch 25: 3 with a harp to give **t** and to
2Ch 31: 2 to serve, to give **t**, and to
Ezra 3:11 and giving **t** to the LORD
Neh 12:24 them, to praise and give **t**
Ps 6: 5 the grave who will give You **t**
Ps 18:49 I will give **t** to You, O LORD,
Ps 30: 4 give **t** at the remembrance of
Ps 30:12 I will give **t** to You forever
Ps 35:18 I will give You **t** in the
Ps 75: 1 We give **t** to You, O God
Ps 75: 1 we give **t**! For Your wondrous
Ps 79:13 Will give You **t** forever
Ps 92: 1 is good to give **t** to the LORD
Ps 97:12 give **t** at the remembrance of
Ps 105: 1 Oh, give **t** to the LORD
Ps 106: 1 give **t** to the LORD, for He is
Ps 106:47 To give **t** to Your holy name,
Ps 107: 1 give **t** to the LORD, for He is
Ps 107: 8 give **t** to the LORD for His
Ps 107:15 give **t** to the LORD for His
Ps 107:21 give **t** to the LORD for His
Ps 107:31 give **t** to the LORD for His
Ps 118: 1 give **t** to the LORD, for He is
Ps 118:29 give **t** to the LORD, for He is
Ps 119:62 I will rise to give **t** to You
Ps 122: 4 To give **t** to the name of the
Ps 136: 1 give **t** to the LORD, for He is
Ps 136: 2 give **t** to the God of gods
Ps 136: 3 give **t** to the Lord of lords
Ps 136:26 give **t** to the God of heaven
Ps 140:13 shall give **t** to Your name
Dan 6:10 gave **t** before his God, as was
Matt 15:36 loaves and the fish and gave **t**
Matt 26:27 He took the cup, and gave **t**
Mark 8: 6 the seven loaves and gave **t**
Mark 14:23 when He had given **t** He gave
Luke 2:38 she gave **t** to the Lord, and
Luke 17:16 at His feet, giving Him **t**
Luke 22:17 He took the cup, and gave **t**
Luke 22:19 And He took bread, gave **t** and
John 6:11 and when He had given **t** He
John 6:23 after the Lord had given **t**
Acts 27:35 gave **t** to God in the presence
Rom 14: 6 the Lord, for he gives God **t**
Rom 14: 6 does not eat, and gives God **t**
Rom 16: 4 to whom not only I give **t**
1Co 10:30 But if I partake with **t**, why
1Co 10:30 the food over which I give **t**
1Co 11:24 and when He had given **t**, He
1Co 14:16 Amen" at your giving of **t**
1Co 14:17 For you indeed give **t** well
1Co 15:57 But **t** be to God, who gives us
2Co 1:11 that **t** may be given by many
2Co 2:14 Now **t** be to God who always
2Co 8:16 But **t** be to God who puts the
2Co 9:15 **T** be to God for His
Eph 1:16 not cease to give **t** for you
Eph 5: 4 but rather giving of **t**
Eph 5:20 giving **t** always for all
Col 1: 3 We give **t** to the God and
Col 1:12 giving **t** to the Father who
Col 3:17 giving **t** to God the Father
1Th 1: 2 We give **t** to God always for
1Th 3: 9 For what **t** can we render to
1Th 5:18 in everything give **t**
2Th 2:13 give **t** to God always for you
1Ti 2: 1 giving of **t** be made for all
Heb 13:15 lips, giving **t** to His name
Rev 4: 9 and **t** to Him who sits on the
Rev 11:17 We give You **t**, O Lord God

THANKSGIVING (*see* THANKS, THANKSGIVINGS)
Lev 7:12 If he offers it for a **t**,
Lev 7:12 with the sacrifice of **t**,
Lev 7:13 of **t** of his peace offering
Lev 7:15 of his peace offering for **t**
Lev 22:29 a sacrifice of **t** to the LORD
Neh 11:17 who began the **t** with prayer
Neh 12: 8 who led the **t** psalms, he and
Neh 12:31 appointed two large **t** choirs
Neh 12:38 The other **t** choir went the
Neh 12:40 So the two **t** choirs stood in
Neh 12:46 songs of praise and **t** to God
Ps 26: 7 proclaim with the voice of **t**
Ps 50:14 Offer to God **t**, And pay your
Ps 69:30 And will magnify Him with **t**
Ps 95: 2 before His presence with **t**
Ps 100: 4 Enter into His gates with **t**
Ps 107:22 sacrifice the sacrifices of **t**
Ps 116:17 to You the sacrifice of **t**
Ps 147: 7 Sing to the LORD with **t**
Is 51: 3 will be found in it, **t** and the
Jer 30:19 out of them shall proceed **t**
Amos 4: 5 a sacrifice of **t** with leaven
Jon 2: 9 to You with the voice of **t**
2Co 4:15 may cause **t** to abound to the
2Co 9:11 which causes **t** through us to
Phil 4: 6 and supplication, with **t**, let
Col 2: 7 abounding in it with **t**
Col 4: 2 being vigilant in it with **t**
1Ti 4: 3 with **t** by those who believe
1Ti 4: 4 if it is received with **t**
Rev 7:12 and glory and wisdom, **t** and

THANKSGIVINGS (*see* THANKSGIVING)
Neh 12:27 with gladness, both with **t**
2Co 9:12 through many **t** to God,

THARSHISH (*see* TARSHISH)
1Ch 7:10 Ehud, Chenaanah, Zethan, **T**

THAT (*see* PREFACE)

THE (*see* PREFACE)

THEATER
Acts 19:29 into the **t** with one accord
Acts 19:31 would not venture into the **t**

THEBEZ
Judg 9:50 Then Abimelech went to **T**
Judg 9:50 and he encamped against **T**
2Sa 11:21 wall, so that he died in **T**

THEFT (*see* THEFTS)
Ex 22: 3 he shall be sold for his **t**
Ex 22: 4 If the **t** is certainly found

THEFTS (*see* THEFT)
Matt 15:19 adulteries, fornications, **t**
Mark 7:22 **t**, covetousness, wickedness,
Rev 9:21 sexual immorality or their **t**

THEIR (*see* PREFACE)

THEIRS (*see* PREFACE)

THE-LORD-IS-MY-BANNER (*see* LORD)
Ex 17:15 altar and called its name, **T**

THE-LORD-SHALOM (*see* LORD)
Judg 6:24 to the LORD, and called it **T**

THE-LORD-WILL-PROVIDE (*see* LORD)
Gen 22:14 the name of the place, **T**

THEM (*see* PREFACE)

THEME
Ps 45: 1 is overflowing with a good **t**

THEMSELVES (*see* PREFACE)

THEN (*see* PREFACE)

THEOPHILUS
Luke 1: 3 account, most excellent **T**
Acts 1: 1 former account I made, O **T**

THERE (*see* PREFACE)

THEREAFTER (*see* PREFACE)

THEREBY (*see* PREFACE)

THEREFORE (*see* PREFACE)

THEREIN (*see* PREFACE)

THESE (*see* PREFACE)

THESSALONIANS (*see* THESSALONICA)
Acts 20: 4 and Secundus of the **T**, and
1Th 1: 1 of the **T** in God the Father
2Th 1: 1 of the **T** in God our Father

THESSALONICA (*see* THESSALONIANS)
Acts 17: 1 and Apollonia, they came to **T**
Acts 17:11 fair-minded than those in **T**
Acts 17:13 But when the Jews from **T**
Acts 27: 2 a Macedonian of **T**, was with
Phil 4:16 For even in **T** you sent aid
2Ti 4:10 world, and has departed for **T**

THEUDAS
Acts 5:36 For some time ago **T** rose up

THEY (*see* PREFACE)

THICK (*see* THICKER, THICKLY, THICKNESS)
Ex 8:24 **T** swarms of flies came into
Ex 10:22 there was **t** darkness in all
Ex 19: 9 I come to you in the **t** cloud
Ex 19:16 a **t** cloud on the mountain
Ex 20:21 the **t** darkness where God was
Deut 4:11 cloud, and **t** darkness
Deut 5:22 the **t** darkness, with a loud
Deut 32:15 you grew fat, you grew **t**, you
2Sa 18: 9 The mule went under the **t**
2Sa 22:12 and **t** clouds of the skies
1Ki 7:26 It was a handbreadth **t**
2Ki 8:15 day that he took a **t** cloth
2Ch 4: 5 It was a handbreadth **t**
Job 22:14 **T** clouds cover Him, so that
Job 26: 8 up the water in His **t** clouds
Job 37:11 He saturates the **t** clouds
Job 38: 9 **t** darkness its swaddling band
Ps 18:11 And **t** clouds of the skies
Ps 18:12 Him, His **t** clouds passed with
Ps 74: 5 up Axes among the **t** trees
Is 44:22 blotted out, like a **t** cloud
Ezek 6:13 tree, and under every **t** oak
Ezek 8:11 a **t** cloud of incense went up
Ezek 19:11 stature above the **t** branches
Ezek 20:28 high hills and all the **t** trees
Ezek 31: 3 top was among the **t** boughs
Ezek 31:10 its top among the **t** boughs
Ezek 31:14 their tops among the **t** boughs
Ezek 41:12 was five cubits **t** all around
Joel 2: 2 **t** darkness, like the morning
Zeph 1:15 day of clouds and **t** darkness,
Zech 11: 2 for the **t** forest has come

THICKER (*see* THICK)
1Ki 12:10 be **t** than my father's waist
2Ch 10:10 be **t** than my father's waist

THICKET (*see* THICKETS)
Gen 22:13 caught in a **t** by its horns
Jer 4: 7 lion has come up from his **t**

THICKETS (*see* THICKET)
1Sa 13: 6 the people hid in caves, in **t**
Is 9:18 kindle in the **t** of the forest
Is 10:34 He will cut down the **t** of the
Jer 4:29 They shall go into **t** and climb

THICKLY (*see* THICK)
Luke 11:29 were **t** gathered together, He

THICKNESS (*see* THICK)
Jer 52:21 and its **t** was four fingers
Ezek 41: 9 The **t** of the outer wall of
Ezek 42:10 **t** of the wall of the court

THIEF (*see* THIEVES)
Ex 22: 2 If the **t** is found breaking in
Ex 22: 7 if the **t** is found, he shall
Ex 22: 8 If the **t** is not found, then
Job 24:14 in the night he is like a **t**
Job 30: 5 shouted at them as at a **t**
Ps 50:18 When you saw a **t**, you
Prov 6:30 a **t** if he steals to satisfy
Prov 29:24 with a **t** hates his own life
Jer 2:26 As the **t** is ashamed when he
Hos 7: 1 the **t** comes in
Joel 2: 9 enter at the windows like a **t**

Zech 5: 3 Every t shall be expelled,'
Zech 5: 4 enter the house of the t and
Matt 24:43 what hour the t would come
Luke 12:33 where no t approaches nor
Luke 12:39 what hour the t would come
John 10: 1 other way, the same is a t
John 10:10 The t does not come except to
John 12: 6 poor, but because he was a t
1Th 5: 2 so comes as a t in the night
1Th 5: 4 should overtake you as a t
1Pe 4:15 you suffer as a murderer, a t
2Pe 3:10 will come as a t in the night
Rev 3: 3 I will come upon you as a t
Rev 16:15 Behold, I am coming as a t

THIEVES (*see* THIEF)
Is 1:23 and companions of t
Jer 7:11 a den of t in your eyes
Jer 48:27 Was he found among t
Jer 49: 9 If t by night, would they not
Obad 5 If t had come to you, if
Matt 6:19 where t break in and steal
Matt 6:20 where t do not break in and
Matt 21:13 you have made it a 'den of t
Mark 11:17 you have made it a 'den of t
Luke 10:30 to Jericho, and fell among t
Luke 10:36 to him who fell among the t
Luke 19:46 you have made it a 'den of t
John 10: 8 who ever came before Me are t
1Co 6:10 nor t, nor covetous, nor

THIGH (*see* THIGHS)
Gen 24: 2 put your hand under my t
Gen 24: 9 the t of Abraham his master
Gen 47:29 put your hand under my t, and
Ex 29:22 the right t (for it is a ram
Ex 29:27 the t of the heave offering
Lev 7:32 Also the right t you shall
Lev 7:33 have the right t for his part
Lev 7:34 the t of the heave offering I
Lev 8:25 and their fat, and the right t
Lev 8:26 on the fat and on the right t
Lev 9:21 the right t Aaron waved as a
Lev 10:14 the t of the heave offering
Lev 10:15 The t of the heave offering
Num 5:21 the LORD makes your t rot
Num 5:22 belly swell and your t rot
Num 5:27 her t will rot, and the woman
Num 6:20 the t of the heave offering
Num 18:18 and the right t are yours
Judg 3:16 his clothes on his right t
Judg 3:21 the dagger from his right t
Judg 15: 8 and t with a great slaughter
1Sa 9:24 up the t with its upper part
Ps 45: 3 Gird Your sword upon Your t
Song 3: 8 his t because of fear in the
Is 47: 2 off the skirt, uncover the t
Jer 31:19 I struck myself on the t
Ezek 21:12 therefore strike your t
Ezek 24: 4 it, every good piece, The t
Rev 19:16 and on His t a name written

THIGHS (*see* THIGH)
Ex 28:42 reach from the waist to the t
Job 40:17 of his t are tightly knit
Song 7: 1 of your t are like jewels
Dan 2:32 its belly and t of bronze,

THIN (*see* THINNER)
Gen 41: 6 Then behold, seven t heads
Gen 41: 7 the seven t heads devoured
Gen 41:23 seven heads, withered, t
Gen 41:24 And the t heads devoured the
Gen 41:27 And the seven t and ugly cows
Ex 39: 3 beat the gold into t sheets
Lev 13:30 there is in it t yellow hair

THING (*see* PREFACE)

THINGS (*see* PREFACE)

THINK (*see* THINKING, THINKS, THOUGHT)
Num 36: 6 them marry whom they t best
Deut 9: 4 Do not t in your heart, after
2Sa 10: 3 Do you t that David really
2Sa 13:33 to t that all the king's sons
2Sa 18:27 I t the running of the first
1Ch 19: 3 Do you t that David really
2Ch 13: 8 now you t to withstand the
Esth 4:13 Do not t in your heart that
Job 35: 2 Do you t this is right
Job 41:32 one would t the deep had
Is 10: 7 so, nor does his heart t so
Jer 29:11 thoughts that I t toward you
Zech 8:17 let none of you t evil in
Matt 3: 9 do not t to say to yourselves
Matt 5:17 Do not t that I came to
Matt 6: 7 For they t that they will be
Matt 9: 4 Why do you t evil in your
Matt 10:34 Do not t that I came to bring
Matt 17:25 What do you t, Simon
Matt 18:12 What do you t
Matt 21:28 But what do you t
Matt 22:17 us, therefore, what do You t
Matt 22:42 What do you t about the
Matt 26:53 Or do you t that I cannot now
Matt 26:66 What do you t
Mark 14:64 What do you t
Luke 7: 7 t myself worthy to come to
Luke 10:36 you t was neighbor to him who
Luke 13: 4 do you t that they were worse
Luke 13:16 t of it—for eighteen years
Luke 17: 9 were commanded him? I t not
John 5:39 for in them you t you have
John 5:45 Do not t that I shall accuse
John 11:56 What do you t
John 16: 2 t that he offers God service
Acts 13:25 he said, 'Who do you t I am
Acts 17:29 we ought not to t that the
Acts 26: 2 I t myself happy, King
Acts 28:22 to hear from you what you t
Rom 2: 3 And do you t this, O man, you
Rom 12: 3 you, not to t of himself more
Rom 12: 3 highly than he ought to t
Rom 12: 3 but to t soberly, as God has
1Co 4: 6 to t beyond what is written
1Co 4: 9 For I t that God has
1Co 7:40 I t I also have the Spirit of
1Co 12:23 we t to be less honorable
2Co 3: 5 t of anything as being from
2Co 10: 2 who t of us as if we walked
2Co 11:16 again, let no one t me a fool
2Co 12: 6 lest anyone should t of me
2Co 12:19 do you t that we excuse
Eph 3:20 above all that we ask or t
Phil 1: 7 for me to t this of you all
Phil 3:15 in anything you t otherwise
Jas 4: 5 Or do you t that the
1Pe 4: 4 they t it strange that you do
1Pe 4:12 Beloved, do not t it strange
2Pe 1:13 I t it is right, as long as I

THINKING (*see* THINK)
2Sa 4:10 t to have brought good news,
2Sa 5: 6 the lame will repel you," t
2Ch 32: 1 t to win them over to himself

THINKS (*see* THINK)
Ps 40:17 Yet the LORD t upon me
Prov 23: 7 for as he t in his heart, so
1Co 7:36 But if any man t he is
1Co 8: 2 if anyone t that he knows
1Co 10:12 Therefore let him who t he
1Co 13: 5 is not provoked, t no evil
1Co 14:37 If anyone t himself to be a
Gal 6: 3 For if anyone t himself to be
Phil 3: 4 If anyone else t he may have
Jas 1:26 among you t he is religious

THINNER (*see* THIN)
2Sa 13: 4 son, becoming t day after day

THIRD (*see* THIRDS, THREE)
Gen 1:13 and the morning were the t day
Gen 2:14 The name of the t river is
Gen 6:16 lower, second, and t decks
Gen 22: 4 Then on the t day Abraham
Gen 31:22 Laban was told on the t day
Gen 32:19 commanded the second, the t
Gen 34:25 it came to pass on the t day
Gen 40:20 it came to pass on the t day
Gen 42:18 Joseph said to them the t day
Gen 50:23 children to the t generation
Ex 19: 1 In the t month after the
Ex 19:11 them be ready for the t day
Ex 19:11 For on the t day the LORD
Ex 19:15 Be ready for the t day
Ex 19:16 it came to pass on the t day
Ex 20: 5 on the children to the t and
Ex 25:35 and a knob under the t two
Ex 28:19 the t row, a jacinth, an
Ex 34: 7 children's children to the t
Ex 37:21 and a knob under the t two
Ex 39:12 the t row, a jacinth, an
Lev 7:17 the t day must be burned with
Lev 7:18 is eaten at all on the t day
Lev 19: 6 any remains until the t day
Lev 19: 7 is eaten at all on the t day
Num 2:24 shall be the t to break camp
Num 7:24 On the t day Eliab the son of
Num 14:18 on the children to the t and
Num 19:12 with the water on the t day
Num 19:12 purify himself on the t day
Num 19:19 the unclean on the t day and
Num 29:20 On the t day present eleven
Num 31:19 and your captives on the t day
Deut 5: 9 upon the children to the t
Deut 14:28 At the end of every t year
Deut 23: 8 The children of the t
Deut 26:12 your increase in the t year
Josh 9:17 to their cities on the t day
Josh 19:10 The t lot came out for the
Judg 20:30 of Benjamin on the t day, and
1Sa 3: 8 Samuel again the t time
1Sa 17:13 Abinadab, and the t Shammah
1Sa 19:21 messengers again the t time
1Sa 20: 5 until the t day at evening
1Sa 20:12 tomorrow, or the t day, and
1Sa 30: 1 came to Ziklag, on the t day
2Sa 1: 2 on the t day, behold, it
2Sa 3: 3 the t, Absalom the son of
2Sa 18: 2 one t of the people under the
2Sa 18: 2 Joab, one t under the hand of
2Sa 18: 2 one t under the hand of Ittai
1Ki 3:18 the t day after I had given
1Ki 6: 6 the t was seven cubits wide
1Ki 6: 8 and from the middle to the t
1Ki 12:12 came to Rehoboam the t day
1Ki 12:12 Come back to me the t day
1Ki 15:28 Baasha killed him in the t
1Ki 15:33 In the t year of Asa king of
1Ki 18: 1 came to Elijah, in the t year
1Ki 18:34 Do it a t time,"
1Ki 18:34 and they did it a t time
1Ki 22: 2 came to pass, in the t year
2Ki 1:13 he sent a t captain of fifty
2Ki 1:13 the t captain of fifty went
2Ki 18: 1 t year of Hoshea the son of
2Ki 19:29 also in the t year sow and
2Ki 20: 5 On the t day you shall go up
2Ki 20: 8 house of the LORD the t day
1Ch 2:13 the second, Shimea the t,
1Ch 3: 2 the t, Absalom the son of
1Ch 3:15 the t Zedekiah, and the fourth
1Ch 8: 1 the second, Aharah the t,
1Ch 8:39 second, and Eliphelet the t
1Ch 12: 9 the second, Eliab the t,
1Ch 23:19 the second, Jahaziel the t
1Ch 24: 8 the t to Harim, the fourth to
1Ch 24:23 the second, Jahaziel the t
1Ch 25:10 the t for Zaccur, his sons and
1Ch 26: 2 the second, Zebadiah the t
1Ch 26: 4 the second, Joah the t, Sacar
1Ch 26:11 the second, Tebaliah the t
1Ch 27: 5 The t captain of the army
1Ch 27: 5 for the t month was Benaiah
2Ch 10:12 came to Rehoboam on the t day
2Ch 10:12 Come back to me the t day
2Ch 15:10 at Jerusalem in the t month
2Ch 17: 7 Also in the t year of his
2Ch 27: 5 in the second and t years also
2Ch 31: 7 In the t month they began
Ezra 6:15 t day of the month of Adar
Esth 1: 3 that in the t year of his
Esth 5: 1 Now it happened on the t day
Esth 8: 9 at that time, in the t month
Job 42:14 name of the t Keren-Happuch
Is 37:30 also in the t year sow and
Jer 38:14 brought to him at the t
Ezek 5:12 another t to all the winds
Ezek 10:14 the t the face of a lion, and
Ezek 21:14 The t time let the sword do
Ezek 31: 1 eleventh year, in the t month
Ezek 46:14 and a t of a hin of oil to
Dan 1: 1 In the t year of the reign of
Dan 2:39 a t kingdom of bronze, which
Dan 5: 7 he shall be the t ruler in
Dan 5:16 shall be the t ruler in the
Dan 5:29 be the t ruler in the kingdom
Dan 8: 1 In the t year of the reign of
Dan 10: 1 In the t year of Cyrus king
Hos 6: 2 on the t day He will raise us
Zech 6: 3 with the t chariot white
Zech 13: 8 but one t shall be left in it
Zech 13: 9 the one t through the fire
Matt 16:21 and be raised again the t day

Matt 17:23 the t day He will be raised
Matt 20: 3 he went out about the t hour
Matt 20:19 the t day He will rise again
Matt 22:26 the second also, and the t
Matt 26:44 again, and prayed the t time
Matt 27:64 made secure until the t day
Mark 9:31 He will rise the t day
Mark 10:34 the t day He will rise again
Mark 12:21 And the t likewise
Mark 14:41 Then He came the t time and
Mark 15:25 Now it was the t hour, and
Luke 9:22 and be raised the t day
Luke 12:38 watch, or come in the t watch
Luke 13:32 and the t day I shall be
Luke 18:33 the t day He will rise again
Luke 20:12 And again he sent a t
Luke 20:31 Then the t took her, and in
Luke 23:22 And he said to them the t time
Luke 24: 7 and the t day rise again
Luke 24:21 today is the t day since
Luke 24:46 rise from the dead the t day
John 2: 1 On the t day there was a
John 21:14 This is now the t time Jesus
John 21:17 He said to him the t time
John 21:17 He said to him the t time
Acts 2:15 is only the t hour of the day
Acts 10:40 God raised up on the t day
Acts 20: 9 he fell down from the t story
Acts 23:23 at the t hour of the night
Acts 27:19 On the t day we threw the
1Co 12:28 t teachers, after that
1Co 15: 4 the t day according to the
2Co 12: 2 was caught up to the t heaven
2Co 12:14 Now for the t time I am ready
2Co 13: 1 This will be the t time I am
Rev 4: 7 the t living creature had a
Rev 6: 5 When He opened the t seal
Rev 6: 5 I heard the t living creature
Rev 8: 7 a t of the trees were burned
Rev 8: 8 a t of the sea became blood
Rev 8: 9 a t of the living creatures
Rev 8: 9 and a t of the ships were
Rev 8:10 Then the t angel sounded
Rev 8:10 it fell on a t of the rivers
Rev 8:11 and a t of the waters became
Rev 8:12 a t of the sun was struck,
Rev 8:12 a t of the moon
Rev 8:12 a t of the stars
Rev 8:12 so that a t of them were
Rev 8:12 a t of the day did not shine,
Rev 9:15 to kill a t of mankind
Rev 9:18 a t of mankind was killed
Rev 11:14 the t woe is coming quickly
Rev 12: 4 His tail drew a t of the
Rev 14: 9 Then a t angel followed them,
Rev 16: 4 Then the t angel poured out
Rev 21:19 the t chalcedony, the fourth

THIRDS (*see* THIRD)
Zech 13: 8 That two t in it shall be cut

THIRST (*see* THIRSTED, THIRSTS, THIRSTY)
Ex 17: 3 and our livestock with t
Deut 28:48 against you, in hunger, in t
Judg 15:18 and now shall I die of t and
2Ch 32:11 over to die by famine and by t
Neh 9:15 out of the rock for their t
Neh 9:20 gave them water for their t
Job 24:11 winepresses, yet suffer t
Ps 69:21 for my t they gave me vinegar
Ps 104:11 wild donkeys quench their t
Is 5:13 multitude dried up with t
Is 41:17 and their tongues fail for t
Is 48:21 they did not t when He led
Is 49:10 shall neither hunger nor t
Is 50: 2 is no water, and die of t
Jer 2:25 unshod, and your throat from t
Jer 48:18 from your glory, and sit in t
Lam 4: 4 the roof of its mouth for t
Hos 2: 3 dry land, and slay her with t
Amos 8:11 nor a t for water, but of
Amos 8:13 young men shall faint from t
Matt 5: 6 t for righteousness, for they
John 4:13 of this water will t again
John 4:14 I shall give him will never t
John 4:15 this water, that I may not t
John 6:35 believes in Me shall never t
John 19:28 be fulfilled, said, "I t!"
1Co 4:11 hour we both hunger and t, and
2Co 11:27 often, in hunger and t, in
Rev 7:16 hunger anymore nor t anymore

THIRSTED (*see* THIRST)
Ex 17: 3 the people t there for water,

THIRSTS (*see* THIRST)
Ps 42: 2 My soul t for God, for the
Ps 63: 1 My soul t for You
Is 55: 1 Everyone who t, come to the
John 7:37 If anyone t, let him come to
Rom 12:20 if he t, give him a drink
Rev 21: 6 of life freely to him who t
Rev 22:17 And let him who t come

THIRSTY (*see* THIRST)
Deut 8:15 t land where there was no
Judg 4:19 water to drink, for I am t
Judg 15:18 Then he became very t
Ruth 2: 9 And when you are t, go to the
2Sa 17:29 weary and t in the wilderness
Ps 63: 1 and t land Where there is no
Ps 107: 5 Hungry and t, Their soul
Ps 143: 6 longs for You like a t land
Prov 25:21 and if he is t, give him water
Is 21:14 bring water to him who is t
Is 29: 8 or as when a t man dreams
Is 32: 6 the drink of the t to fail
Is 35: 7 the t land springs of water
Is 44: 3 pour water on him who is t
Is 65:13 drink, but you shall be t
Ezek 19:13 in a dry and t land
Matt 25:35 I was t and you gave Me drink
Matt 25:37 You hungry and feed You, or t
Matt 25:42 I was t and you gave Me no
Matt 25:44 did we see You hungry or t or

THIRTEEN (*see* THIRTEENTH)
Gen 17:25 Ishmael his son was t years
Num 29:13 t young bulls, two rams, and
Num 29:14 ephah for each of the t bulls
Josh 19: 6 t cities and their villages
Josh 21: 4 had t cities by lot from the
Josh 21: 6 had t cities by lot from the
Josh 21:19 were t cities with their
Josh 21:33 were t cities with their
1Ki 7: 1 But Solomon took t years to
1Ch 6:60 among their families were t
1Ch 6:62 they gave t cities from the
1Ch 26:11 and brethren of Hosah were t
Ezek 40:11 length of the gate, t cubits

THIRTEENTH (*see* THIRTEEN)
Gen 14: 4 in the t year they rebelled
1Ch 24:13 the t to Huppah, the
1Ch 25:20 the t for Shubael, his sons
Esth 3:12 the t day of the first month
Esth 3:13 on the t day of the twelfth
Esth 8:12 on the t day of the twelfth
Esth 9: 1 month of Adar, on the t day
Esth 9:17 This was on the t day of the
Esth 9:18 together on the t day, as
Jer 1: 2 in the t year of his reign
Jer 25: 3 From the t year of Josiah the

THIRTIETH (*see* THIRTY)
Ezek 1: 1 it came to pass in the t year

THIRTY (*see* THIRTIETH)
Gen 5: 3 t years, and begot a son in
Gen 5: 5 were nine hundred and t years
Gen 5:16 t years, and begot sons and
Gen 6:15 and its height t cubits
Gen 11:14 Salah lived t years, and begot
Gen 11:17 t years, and begot sons and
Gen 11:18 Peleg lived t years, and begot
Gen 11:22 Serug lived t years, and begot
Gen 18:30 Suppose t should be found
Gen 18:30 not do it if I find t there
Gen 32:15 t milk camels with their
Gen 41:46 Joseph was t years old when
Gen 47: 9 are one hundred and t years
Ex 12:40 was four hundred and t years
Ex 12:41 the four hundred and t years
Ex 21:32 master t shekels of silver
Ex 26: 8 curtain shall be t cubits
Ex 36:15 of each curtain was t cubits
Ex 38:24 t shekels, according to the
Lev 27: 4 valuation shall be t shekels
Num 4: 3 from t years old and above,
Num 4:23 From t years old and above,
Num 4:30 From t years old and above,
Num 4:35 from t years old and above,
Num 4:39 from t years old and above,
Num 4:40 two thousand six hundred and t
Num 4:43 from t years old and above,
Num 4:47 from t years old and above,
Num 7:13 t shekels, and one silver bowl
Num 7:19 t shekels, and one silver bowl
Num 7:25 t shekels, and one silver bowl
Num 7:31 t shekels, and one silver bowl
Num 7:37 t shekels, and one silver bowl
Num 7:43 t shekels, and one silver bowl
Num 7:49 t shekels, and one silver bowl
Num 7:55 t shekels, and one silver bowl
Num 7:61 t shekels, and one silver bowl
Num 7:67 t shekels, and one silver bowl
Num 7:73 t shekels, and one silver bowl
Num 7:79 t shekels, and one silver bowl
Num 7:85 and t shekels and each bowl
Num 20:29 mourned for Aaron t days
Num 26: 7 thousand seven hundred and t
Num 26:51 thousand seven hundred and t
Num 31:39 The donkeys were t thousand
Num 31:45 t thousand five hundred
Deut 34: 8 in the plains of Moab t days
Josh 8: 3 and Joshua chose t thousand
Judg 10: 4 t sons who rode on t donkeys
Judg 10: 4 they also had t towns, which
Judg 12: 9 He had t sons
Judg 12: 9 he gave away t daughters in
Judg 12: 9 brought in t daughters from
Judg 12:14 and t grandsons, who rode on
Judg 14:11 saw him, that they brought t
Judg 14:12 give you t linen garments
Judg 14:12 and t changes of clothing
Judg 14:13 give me t linen garments
Judg 14:13 and t changes of clothing
Judg 14:19 killed t of their men, took
Judg 20:31 field, about t men of Israel
Judg 20:39 kill about t of the men of
1Sa 4:10 and there fell of Israel t
1Sa 9:22 there were about t persons
1Sa 11: 8 the men of Judah t thousand
1Sa 13: 5 t thousand chariots and six
2Sa 5: 4 David was t years old when he
2Sa 6: 1 men of Israel, t thousand
2Sa 23:13 Then three of the t chief men
2Sa 23:23 was more honored than the t
2Sa 23:24 of Joab was one of the t
1Ki 4:22 day was t kors of fine flour
1Ki 5:13 force was t thousand men
1Ki 6: 2 and its height t cubits
1Ki 7: 2 and its height t cubits, with
1Ki 7: 6 cubits, and its width t cubits
1Ki 7:23 a line of t cubits measured
2Ki 18:14 silver and t talents of gold
1Ch 11:15 Now three of the t chief men
1Ch 11:25 was more honored than the t
1Ch 11:42 Reubenites) and t with him,
1Ch 12: 4 among the t, and over the t
1Ch 15: 7 hundred and t of his brethren
1Ch 23: 3 from the age of t years and
1Ch 27: 6 who was mighty among the t
1Ch 27: 6 and was over the t
2Ch 4: 2 a line of t cubits measured
2Ch 24:15 and t years old when he died
2Ch 35: 7 to the number of t thousand
Ezra 1: 9 t gold platters, one thousand
Ezra 1:10 t gold basins, four hundred
Ezra 2:35 thousand six hundred and t
Neh 7:38 thousand nine hundred and t
Neh 7:70 and t priestly garments
Esth 4:11 in to the king these t days
Jer 38:10 Take from here t men with you
Ezek 40:17 t chambers faced the pavement
Ezek 41: 6 t chambers in each story
Ezek 46:22 forty cubits long and t wide
Dan 6: 7 any god or man for t days
Dan 6:12 any god or man within t days
Zech 11:12 my wages t pieces of silver
Zech 11:13 So I took the t pieces of
Matt 13: 8 some sixty, some t
Matt 13:23 some sixty, some t
Matt 26:15 out to him t pieces of silver
Matt 27: 3 brought back the t pieces of
Matt 27: 9 they took the t pieces of
Luke 3:23 at about t years of age,
John 2: 6 twenty or t gallons apiece
Gal 3:17 t years later, cannot annul

THIRTY-EIGHT (*see* THIRTY-EIGHTH)
Deut 2:14 of the Zered was t years,
1Ch 23: 3 males was t thousand
Neh 7:45 of Shobai, one hundred and t
John 5: 5 who had an infirmity t years

Dan 2:29 t came to your mind while on
Dan 2:30 may know the t of your heart
Dan 4: 5 and the t on my bed and the
Dan 4:19 a time, and his t troubled him
Dan 5: 6 his t troubled him, so that
Dan 5:10 Do not let your t trouble you
Dan 7:28 my t greatly troubled me, and
Mic 4:12 do not know the t of the LORD
Matt 9: 4 But Jesus, knowing their t
Matt 12:25 But Jesus knew their t, and
Matt 15:19 of the heart proceed evil t
Mark 7:21 heart of men, proceed evil t
Luke 2:35 that the t of many hearts may
Luke 5:22 when Jesus perceived their t
Luke 6: 8 But He knew their t, and said
Luke 11:17 But He, knowing their t, said
Rom 1:21 but became futile in their t
Rom 2:15 between themselves their t
1Co 3:20 LORD knows the t of the wise
Heb 4:12 and is a discerner of the t
Jas 2: 4 and become judges with evil t

THOUSAND (*see* THOUSANDS)
Gen 20:16 brother a t pieces of silver
Ex 12:37 six hundred t men on foot
Ex 32:28 And about three t men of the
Ex 38:25 and one t seven hundred and
Ex 38:26 for six hundred and three t
Ex 38:28 from the one t seven hundred
Ex 38:29 two t four hundred shekels
Lev 26: 8 you shall put ten t to flight
Num 1:21 were forty-six t five hundred
Num 1:23 fifty-nine t three hundred
Num 1:25 were forty-five t six hundred
Num 1:27 seventy-four t six hundred
Num 1:29 fifty-four t four hundred
Num 1:31 fifty-seven t four hundred
Num 1:33 were forty t five hundred
Num 1:35 were thirty-two t two hundred
Num 1:37 thirty-five t four hundred
Num 1:39 sixty-two t seven hundred
Num 1:41 were forty-one t five hundred
Num 1:43 fifty-three t four hundred
Num 1:46 three t five hundred and fifty
Num 2: 4 at seventy-four t six hundred
Num 2: 6 at fifty-four t four hundred
Num 2: 8 at fifty-seven t four hundred
Num 2: 9 eighty-six t four hundred
Num 2:11 at forty-six t five hundred
Num 2:13 at fifty-nine t three hundred
Num 2:15 at forty-five t six hundred
Num 2:16 fifty-one t four hundred and
Num 2:19 at forty t five hundred
Num 2:21 at thirty-two t two hundred
Num 2:23 at thirty-five t four hundred
Num 2:24 and eight t one hundred
Num 2:26 at sixty-two t seven hundred
Num 2:28 at forty-one t five hundred
Num 2:30 at fifty-three t four hundred
Num 2:31 and fifty-seven t six hundred
Num 2:32 three t five hundred and fifty
Num 3:22 were seven t five hundred
Num 3:28 above, there were eight t six
Num 3:34 above, were six t two hundred
Num 3:39 and above, were twenty-two t
Num 3:43 were twenty-two t two hundred
Num 3:50 money, one t three hundred and
Num 4:36 were two t seven hundred and
Num 4:40 were two t six hundred and
Num 4:44 were three t two hundred
Num 4:48 were eight t five hundred
Num 7:85 two t four hundred shekels
Num 11:21 are six hundred t men on foot
Num 16:49 were fourteen t seven hundred
Num 25: 9 the plague were twenty-four t
Num 26: 7 forty-three t seven hundred
Num 26:14 twenty-two t two hundred
Num 26:18 forty t five hundred
Num 26:22 seventy-six t five hundred
Num 26:25 sixty-four t three hundred
Num 26:27 sixty t five hundred
Num 26:34 fifty-two t seven hundred
Num 26:37 thirty-two t five hundred
Num 26:41 were forty-five t six hundred
Num 26:43 sixty-four t four hundred
Num 26:47 fifty-three t four hundred
Num 26:50 forty-five t four hundred
Num 26:51 one t seven hundred and thirty
Num 26:62 of them were twenty-three t
Num 31: 4 A t from each tribe of all
Num 31: 5 Israel one t from each tribe
Num 31: 5 twelve t armed for war
Num 31: 6 war, one t from each tribe
Num 31:32 and seventy-five t sheep,
Num 31:33 seventy-two t cattle,
Num 31:34 sixty-one t donkeys,
Num 31:35 thirty-two t persons in all,
Num 31:36 thirty-seven t five hundred
Num 31:38 The cattle were thirty-six t
Num 31:39 were thirty t five hundred
Num 31:40 The persons were sixteen t
Num 31:43 thirty-seven t five hundred
Num 31:44 thirty-six t cattle,
Num 31:45 thirty t five hundred donkeys
Num 31:46 and sixteen t persons
Num 31:52 was sixteen t seven hundred
Num 35: 4 outward a t cubits all around
Num 35: 5 on the east side two t cubits
Num 35: 5 the south side two t cubits
Num 35: 5 on the west side two t cubits
Num 35: 5 the north side two t cubits
Deut 1:11 a t times more numerous than
Deut 7: 9 mercy for a t generations
Deut 32:30 How could one chase a t
Deut 32:30 and two put ten t to flight
Josh 3: 4 about two t cubits by measure
Josh 4:13 About forty t prepared for
Josh 7: 3 two or three t men go up and
Josh 7: 4 So about three t men went up
Josh 8: 3 thirty t mighty men of valor
Josh 8:12 So he took about five t men
Josh 8:25 men and women, were twelve t
Josh 23:10 man of you shall chase a t
Judg 1: 4 killed ten t men at Bezek
Judg 3:29 about ten t men of Moab, all
Judg 4: 6 take with you ten t men of
Judg 4:10 he went up with ten t men
Judg 4:14 with ten t men following him
Judg 5: 8 seen among forty t in Israel
Judg 7: 3 twenty-two t of the people
Judg 7: 3 returned, and ten t remained
Judg 8:10 them, about fifteen t men
Judg 8:10 twenty t men who drew the
Judg 8:26 t seven hundred shekels of
Judg 9:49 Shechem died, about a t men
Judg 12: 6 time forty-two t Ephraimites
Judg 15:11 Then three t men of Judah
Judg 15:15 it, and killed a t men with it
Judg 15:16 a donkey I have slain a t men
Judg 16:27 there were about three t men
Judg 20: 2 four hundred t foot soldiers
Judg 20:10 a hundred out of every t
Judg 20:10 a t out of every ten t
Judg 20:15 numbered twenty-six t men who
Judg 20:17 numbered four hundred t men
Judg 20:21 t men of the Israelites
Judg 20:25 t more of the children of
Judg 20:34 ten t select men from all
Judg 20:35 that day twenty-five t one
Judg 20:44 eighteen t men of Benjamin
Judg 20:45 they cut down five t of them
Judg 20:45 and killed two t of them
Judg 20:46 t men who drew the sword
Judg 21:10 sent out there twelve t of
1Sa 4: 2 who killed about four t men
1Sa 4:10 Israel thirty t foot soldiers
1Sa 6:19 He struck fifty t and seventy
1Sa 11: 8 Israel were three hundred t
1Sa 11: 8 and the men of Judah thirty t
1Sa 13: 2 himself three t men of Israel
1Sa 13: 2 Two t were with Saul in
1Sa 13: 2 a t were with Jonathan in
1Sa 13: 5 thirty t chariots and
1Sa 13: 5 six t horsemen, and people as
1Sa 15: 4 two hundred t foot soldiers
1Sa 15: 4 and ten t men of Judah
1Sa 17: 5 was five t shekels of bronze
1Sa 17:18 to the captain of their t
1Sa 18:13 made him his captain over a t
1Sa 24: 2 Then Saul took three t chosen
1Sa 25: 2 three t sheep and a t goats
1Sa 26: 2 having three t chosen men of
2Sa 6: 1 men of Israel, thirty t
2Sa 8: 4 took from him one t chariots
2Sa 8: 4 and twenty t foot soldiers
2Sa 8: 5 twenty-two t of the Syrians
2Sa 8:13 from killing eighteen t
2Sa 10: 6 Zoba, twenty t foot soldiers
2Sa 10: 6 and from King Maacah one t
2Sa 10: 6 and from Ish-Tob twelve t men
2Sa 10:18 and forty t horsemen of the
2Sa 17: 1 let me choose twelve t men
2Sa 18: 3 you are worth ten t of us now
2Sa 18: 7 t men took place there that
2Sa 18:12 a t shekels of silver in my
2Sa 19:17 There were a t men of
2Sa 24: 9 in Israel eight hundred t
2Sa 24: 9 Judah were five hundred t men
2Sa 24:15 t men of the people died
1Ki 3: 4 Solomon offered a t burnt
1Ki 4:26 Solomon had forty t stalls of
1Ki 4:26 and twelve t horsemen
1Ki 4:32 He spoke three t proverbs
1Ki 4:32 and his songs were one t and
1Ki 5:11 t kors of wheat as food for
1Ki 5:13 labor force was thirty t men
1Ki 5:14 ten t a month in shifts
1Ki 5:15 seventy t who carried burdens
1Ki 5:15 eighty t who quarried stone
1Ki 5:16 besides three t three hundred
1Ki 7:26 It contained two t baths
1Ki 8:63 the LORD, twenty-two t bulls
1Ki 8:63 one hundred and twenty t sheep
1Ki 10:26 he had one t four hundred
1Ki 10:26 twelve t horsemen, whom he
1Ki 12:21 eighty t chosen men who were
1Ki 19:18 reserved seven t in Israel
1Ki 20:15 the children of Israel—seven t
1Ki 20:29 t foot soldiers of the
1Ki 20:30 t of the men who were left
2Ki 3: 4 of Israel one hundred t lambs
2Ki 3: 4 wool of one hundred t rams
2Ki 5: 5 six t shekels of gold, and ten
2Ki 13: 7 and ten t foot soldiers
2Ki 14: 7 He killed ten t Edomites in
2Ki 15:19 Pul a t talents of silver
2Ki 18:23 I will give you two t horses
2Ki 19:35 one hundred and eighty-five t
2Ki 24:14 ten t captives, and all the
2Ki 24:16 All the valiant men, seven t
2Ki 24:16 and craftsmen and smiths, one t
1Ch 5:18 forty-four t seven hundred
1Ch 5:21 fifty t of their camels, two
1Ch 5:21 fifty t of their sheep
1Ch 5:21 and two t of their donkeys
1Ch 5:21 one hundred t of their men
1Ch 7: 2 was twenty-two t six hundred
1Ch 7: 4 were thirty-six t troops of
1Ch 7: 5 eighty-seven t in all
1Ch 7: 7 genealogies, twenty-two t
1Ch 7: 9 twenty t two hundred mighty
1Ch 7:11 there were seventeen t two
1Ch 7:40 their number was twenty-six t
1Ch 9:13 one t seven hundred and sixty
1Ch 12:14 and the greatest was over a t
1Ch 12:24 six t eight hundred armed for
1Ch 12:25 for war, seven t one hundred
1Ch 12:26 of Levi four t six hundred
1Ch 12:27 him three t seven hundred
1Ch 12:29 Saul, three t (until then the
1Ch 12:30 twenty t eight hundred,
1Ch 12:31 of Manasseh eighteen t, who
1Ch 12:33 t who went out to battle,
1Ch 12:34 of Naphtali one t captains
1Ch 12:34 thirty-seven t with shield
1Ch 12:35 twenty-eight t six hundred
1Ch 12:36 battle formation, forty t
1Ch 12:37 twenty t armed for battle
1Ch 16:15 for a t generations,
1Ch 18: 4 took from him one t chariots
1Ch 18: 4 seven t horsemen
1Ch 18: 4 and twenty t foot soldiers
1Ch 18: 5 twenty-two t of the Syrians
1Ch 18:12 t Edomites in the Valley of
1Ch 19: 6 a t talents of silver to hire
1Ch 19: 7 thirty-two t chariots, with
1Ch 19:18 killed seven t charioteers
1Ch 19:18 forty t foot soldiers of the
1Ch 21: 5 t men who drew the sword, and
1Ch 21: 5 seventy t men who drew the
1Ch 21:14 seventy t men of Israel fell
1Ch 22:14 one hundred t talents of gold
1Ch 23: 3 males was thirty-eight t
1Ch 23: 4 twenty-four t were to look
1Ch 23: 4 six t were officers and judges
1Ch 23: 5 four t were gatekeepers, and
1Ch 23: 5 four t praised the LORD with
1Ch 26:30 one t seven hundred able men,
1Ch 26:32 his brethren were two t seven
1Ch 27: 1 division having twenty-four t
1Ch 27: 2 division were twenty-four t

1Ch 27: 4 division were twenty-four **t**
1Ch 27: 5 division were twenty-four **t**
1Ch 27: 7 division were twenty-four **t**
1Ch 27: 8 division were twenty-four **t**
1Ch 27: 9 division were twenty-four **t**
1Ch 27:10 division were twenty-four **t**
1Ch 27:11 division were twenty-four **t**
1Ch 27:12 division were twenty-four **t**
1Ch 27:13 division were twenty-four **t**
1Ch 27:14 division were twenty-four **t**
1Ch 27:15 division were twenty-four **t**
1Ch 29: 4 three **t** talents of gold, of
1Ch 29: 4 seven **t** talents of refined
1Ch 29: 7 house of God five **t** talents
1Ch 29: 7 ten **t** darics of gold
1Ch 29: 7 ten **t** talents of silver,
1Ch 29: 7 eighteen **t** talents of bronze,
1Ch 29: 7 one hundred **t** talents of iron
1Ch 29:21 a **t** rams, a **t** lambs,
1Ch 29:21 a **t** lambs, with their drink
2Ch 1: 6 offered a **t** burnt offerings
2Ch 1:14 he had one **t** four hundred
2Ch 1:14 twelve **t** horsemen, whom he
2Ch 2: 2 seventy **t** men to bear burdens
2Ch 2: 2 eighty **t** to quarry stone in
2Ch 2: 2 and three **t** six hundred to
2Ch 2:10 twenty **t** kors of ground wheat
2Ch 2:10 twenty **t** kors of barley,
2Ch 2:10 twenty **t** baths of wine,
2Ch 2:10 and twenty **t** baths of oil
2Ch 2:17 and fifty-three **t** six hundred
2Ch 2:18 he made seventy **t** of them
2Ch 2:18 eighty **t** hewers of stone in
2Ch 2:18 three **t** six hundred overseers
2Ch 4: 5 It contained three **t** baths
2Ch 7: 5 of twenty-two **t** bulls and one
2Ch 7: 5 one hundred and twenty **t** sheep
2Ch 9:25 Solomon had four **t** stalls for
2Ch 9:25 twelve **t** horsemen whom he
2Ch 11: 1 eighty **t** chosen men who were
2Ch 12: 3 sixty **t** horsemen, and people
2Ch 13: 3 four hundred **t** choice men
2Ch 13: 3 eight hundred **t** choice men
2Ch 13:17 so five hundred **t** choice men
2Ch 14: 8 an army of three hundred **t**
2Ch 14: 8 and eighty **t** men who carried
2Ch 15:11 seven **t** sheep from the spoil
2Ch 17:11 seven **t** seven hundred rams and
2Ch 17:11 seven **t** seven hundred male
2Ch 17:14 hundred **t** mighty men of valor
2Ch 17:15 him two hundred and eighty **t**
2Ch 17:16 hundred **t** mighty men of valor
2Ch 17:17 hundred **t** men armed with bow
2Ch 17:18 eighty **t** prepared for war
2Ch 25: 5 be three hundred **t** choice men
2Ch 25: 6 **t** mighty men of valor from
2Ch 25:11 killed ten **t** of the people of
2Ch 25:12 captive another ten **t** alive
2Ch 25:13 Horon, killed three **t** in them
2Ch 26:12 valor was two **t** six hundred
2Ch 26:13 seven **t** five hundred, that
2Ch 27: 5 ten **t** kors of wheat, and ten **t**
2Ch 28: 6 twenty **t** in Judah in one day,
2Ch 28: 8 brethren two hundred **t** women
2Ch 29:33 bulls and three **t** sheep
2Ch 30:24 **t** bulls and seven **t** sheep
2Ch 30:24 **t** bulls and ten **t** sheep
2Ch 35: 7 to the number of thirty **t**
2Ch 35: 7 as well as three **t** cattle
2Ch 35: 8 **t** six hundred from the flock
2Ch 35: 9 five **t** from the flock and five
Ezra 1: 9 one **t** silver platters,
Ezra 1:10 kind, and one **t** other articles
Ezra 1:11 were five **t** four hundred
Ezra 2: 3 Parosh, two **t** one hundred and
Ezra 2: 6 two **t** eight hundred and twelve
Ezra 2: 7 of Elam, one **t** two hundred and
Ezra 2:12 Azgad, one **t** two hundred and
Ezra 2:14 the people of Bigvai, two **t**
Ezra 2:31 Elam, one **t** two hundred and
Ezra 2:35 three **t** six hundred and thirty
Ezra 2:37 the sons of Immer, one **t** and
Ezra 2:38 Pashhur, one **t** two hundred and
Ezra 2:39 the sons of Harim, one **t** and
Ezra 2:64 was forty-two **t** three hundred
Ezra 2:65 were seven **t** three hundred
Ezra 2:67 donkeys six **t** seven hundred
Ezra 2:69 sixty-one **t** gold drachmas
Ezra 2:69 five **t** minas of silver, and
Ezra 8:27 basins worth a **t** drachmas

Neh 3:13 repaired a **t** cubits of the
Neh 7: 8 Parosh, two **t** one hundred and
Neh 7:11 Joab, two **t** eight hundred and
Neh 7:12 of Elam, one **t** two hundred and
Neh 7:17 Azgad, two **t** three hundred and
Neh 7:19 the children of Bigvai, two **t**
Neh 7:34 Elam, one **t** two hundred and
Neh 7:38 three **t** nine hundred and
Neh 7:40 the children of Immer, one **t**
Neh 7:41 Pashhur, one **t** two hundred and
Neh 7:42 the children of Harim, one **t**
Neh 7:66 was forty-two **t** three hundred
Neh 7:67 were seven **t** three hundred
Neh 7:69 donkeys six **t** seven hundred
Neh 7:70 treasury one **t** gold drachmas
Neh 7:71 work twenty **t** gold drachmas
Neh 7:71 and two **t** two hundred silver
Neh 7:72 was twenty **t** gold drachmas
Neh 7:72 two **t** silver minas, and
Esth 3: 9 I will pay ten **t** talents of
Esth 9:16 **t** of their enemies
Job 1: 3 were seven **t** sheep
Job 1: 3 three **t** camels, five hundred
Job 9: 3 Him one time out of a **t**
Job 33:23 a mediator, one among a **t**
Job 42:12 for he had fourteen **t** sheep
Job 42:12 six **t** camels
Job 42:12 one **t** yoke of oxen
Job 42:12 and one **t** female donkeys
Ps 50:10 And the cattle on a **t** hills
Ps 68:17 chariots of God are twenty **t**
Ps 84:10 courts is better than a **t**
Ps 90: 4 For a **t** years in Your sight
Ps 91: 7 A **t** may fall at your side
Ps 91: 7 And ten **t** at your right hand
Ps 105: 8 for a **t** generations,
Eccl 6: 6 he lives a **t** years twice over
Eccl 7:28 man among a **t** I have found
Song 4: 4 on which hang a **t** bucklers
Song 5:10 and ruddy, chief among ten **t**
Song 8:11 fruit a **t** pieces of silver
Song 8:12 You, O Solomon, may have a **t**
Is 7:23 be a **t** vines worth a **t**
Is 7:23 worth a **t** shekels of silver
Is 30:17 One **t** shall flee at the
Is 36: 8 I will give you two **t** horses
Is 37:36 one hundred and eighty-five **t**
Is 60:22 A little one shall become a **t**
Jer 52:28 in the seventh year, three **t**
Jer 52:30 were four **t** six hundred
Ezek 45: 1 shall be twenty-five **t** cubits
Ezek 45: 1 and the width ten **t**
Ezek 45: 3 **t** cubits long and ten **t** wide
Ezek 45: 5 twenty-five **t** cubits long
Ezek 45: 5 ten **t** wide shall belong to
Ezek 45: 6 an area five **t** cubits wide
Ezek 45: 6 and twenty-five **t** long
Ezek 47: 3 he measured one **t** cubits
Ezek 47: 4 Again he measured one **t** and
Ezek 47: 4 Again he measured one **t** and
Ezek 47: 5 Again he measured one **t**, and
Ezek 48: 8 twenty-five **t** cubits in width
Ezek 48: 9 **t** cubits in length
Ezek 48: 9 and ten **t** in width
Ezek 48:10 **t** cubits in length
Ezek 48:10 on the west ten **t** in width
Ezek 48:10 on the east ten **t** in width
Ezek 48:10 south twenty-five **t** in length
Ezek 48:13 **t** cubits in length and ten **t**
Ezek 48:13 length shall be twenty-five **t**
Ezek 48:13 and its width ten **t**
Ezek 48:15 The five **t** cubits in width
Ezek 48:15 the edge of the twenty-five **t**
Ezek 48:16 four **t** five hundred cubits
Ezek 48:16 side four **t** five hundred, the
Ezek 48:16 east side four **t** five hundred
Ezek 48:16 west side four **t** five hundred
Ezek 48:18 shall be ten **t** cubits to the
Ezek 48:18 the east and ten **t** to the west
Ezek 48:20 shall be twenty-five **t** cubits
Ezek 48:20 by twenty-five **t** cubits,
Ezek 48:21 next to the twenty-five **t**
Ezek 48:21 **t** as far as the western
Ezek 48:30 measuring four **t** five hundred
Ezek 48:32 four **t** five hundred cubits,
Ezek 48:33 measuring four **t** five hundred
Ezek 48:34 four **t** five hundred cubits
Ezek 48:35 shall be eighteen **t** cubits
Dan 5: 1 feast for a **t** of his lords
Dan 5: 1 wine in the presence of the **t**

Dan 7:10 a **t** thousands ministered to
Dan 7:10 **t** times ten **t** stood before Him
Dan 8:14 For two **t** three hundred days
Dan 12:11 shall be one **t** two hundred
Dan 12:12 to the one **t** three hundred
Amos 5: 3 a **t** shall have a hundred left
Jon 4:11 twenty **t** persons who cannot
Mic 6: 7 rams or ten **t** rivers of oil
Matt 14:21 eaten were about five **t** men
Matt 15:38 those who ate were four **t** men
Matt 16: 9 the five loaves of the five **t**
Matt 16:10 seven loaves of the four **t**
Matt 18:24 who owed him ten **t** talents
Mark 5:13 (there were about two **t**)
Mark 6:44 loaves were about five **t** men
Mark 8: 9 had eaten were about four **t**
Mark 8:19 five loaves for the five **t**
Mark 8:20 the seven for the four **t**, how
Luke 9:14 there were about five **t** men
Luke 14:31 ten **t** to meet him who comes
Luke 14:31 against him with twenty **t**
John 6:10 down, in number about five **t**
Acts 2:41 that day about three **t** souls
Acts 4: 4 men came to be about five **t**
Acts 19:19 fifty **t** pieces of silver
Acts 21:38 led the four **t** assassins out
Rom 11: 4 reserved for Myself seven **t**
1Co 4:15 ten **t** instructors in Christ
1Co 10: 8 one day twenty-three **t** fell
1Co 14:19 than ten **t** words in a tongue
2Pe 3: 8 Lord one day is as a **t** years
2Pe 3: 8 and a **t** years as one day
Rev 5:11 was ten **t** times ten **t**
Rev 7: 4 and forty-four **t** of all the
Rev 7: 5 of Judah twelve **t** were sealed
Rev 7: 5 Reuben twelve **t** were sealed
Rev 7: 5 of Gad twelve **t** were sealed
Rev 7: 6 of Asher twelve **t** were sealed
Rev 7: 6 Naphtali twelve **t** were sealed
Rev 7: 6 Manasseh twelve **t** were sealed
Rev 7: 7 Simeon twelve **t** were sealed
Rev 7: 7 of Levi twelve **t** were sealed
Rev 7: 7 Issachar twelve **t** were sealed
Rev 7: 8 Zebulun twelve **t** were sealed
Rev 7: 8 Joseph twelve **t** were sealed
Rev 7: 8 Benjamin twelve **t** were sealed
Rev 11: 3 prophesy one **t** two hundred
Rev 11:13 seven **t** men were killed, and
Rev 12: 6 her there one **t** two hundred
Rev 14: 1 one hundred and forty-four **t**
Rev 14: 3 and forty-four **t** who were
Rev 14:20 for one **t** six hundred
Rev 20: 2 and bound him for a **t** years
Rev 20: 3 the **t** years were finished
Rev 20: 4 with Christ for a **t** years
Rev 20: 5 the **t** years were finished
Rev 20: 6 reign with Him a **t** years
Rev 20: 7 Now when the **t** years have
Rev 21:16 the reed: twelve **t** furlongs

THOUSANDS (*see* THOUSAND)
Gen 24:60 mother of **t** of ten **t**
Ex 18:21 over them to be rulers of **t**
Ex 18:25 rulers of **t**, rulers of
Ex 20: 6 but showing mercy to **t**, to
Ex 34: 7 keeping mercy for **t**,
Num 10:36 LORD, to the many **t** of Israel
Num 31:14 with the captains over **t**
Num 31:48 who were over **t** of the army
Num 31:48 the captains of **t**
Num 31:52 LORD, from the captains of **t**
Num 31:54 gold from the captains of **t**
Deut 1:15 heads over you, leaders of **t**
Deut 5:10 but showing mercy to **t**, to
Deut 33: 2 He came with ten **t** of saints
Deut 33:17 they are the ten **t** of Ephraim
Deut 33:17 and they are the **t** of Manasseh
1Sa 8:12 appoint captains over his **t**
1Sa 18: 7 Saul has slain his **t**
1Sa 18: 7 and David his ten **t**
1Sa 18: 8 have ascribed to David ten **t**
1Sa 18: 8 me they have ascribed but **t**
1Sa 21:11 Saul has slain his **t**
1Sa 21:11 and David his ten **t**
1Sa 22: 7 and make you all captains of **t**
1Sa 29: 2 in review by hundreds and by **t**
1Sa 29: 5 Saul has slain his **t**, and
1Sa 29: 5 and David his ten **t**'
2Sa 18: 1 him, and set captains of **t**
2Sa 18: 4 went out by hundreds and by **t**
1Ch 12:20 captains of the **t** who were

1Ch 13: 1 with the captains of t and
1Ch 15:25 the captains over t went to
1Ch 26:26 houses, the captains over t
1Ch 27: 1 houses, the captains of t
1Ch 28: 1 the king, the captains over t
1Ch 29: 6 of Israel, the captains of t
2Ch 1: 2 Israel, to the captains of t
2Ch 17:14 Of Judah, the captains of t
2Ch 25: 5 set over them captains of t
Ps 3: 6 ten t of people Who have set
Ps 68:17 thousand, Even t of t
Ps 119:72 me Than t of shekels of gold
Ps 144:13 our sheep may bring forth t
Ps 144:13 And ten t in our fields
Jer 32:18 You show lovingkindness to t
Dan 7:10 a thousand t ministered to
Dan 11:12 he will cast down tens of t
Mic 5: 2 little among the t of Judah
Mic 6: 7 t of rams or ten thousand
Jude 14 with ten t of His saints,
Rev 5:11 thousand, and t of t,

THREAD (*see* THREADS)
Gen 14:23 from a t to a sandal strap,
Gen 38:28 the midwife took a scarlet t
Gen 38:30 had the scarlet t on his hand
Ex 25: 4 and scarlet yarn, fine linen t
Ex 26: 1 woven of fine linen t, and
Ex 26:31 scarlet yarn, and fine linen t
Ex 26:36 scarlet yarn, and fine linen t
Ex 27: 9 court woven of fine linen t
Ex 27:16 scarlet yarn, and fine linen t
Ex 27:18 cubits, woven of fine linen t
Ex 28: 5 blue and purple and scarlet t
Ex 28: 6 scarlet t, and fine linen t
Ex 28: 8 scarlet t, and fine linen t
Ex 28:15 t, and of fine linen t
Ex 28:39 the tunic of fine linen t
Ex 35: 6 and scarlet yarn, fine linen t
Ex 36: 8 woven of fine linen t, and
Ex 36:35 scarlet yarn, and fine linen t
Ex 36:37 scarlet yarn, and fine linen t
Ex 38:18 scarlet yarn, and fine linen t
Ex 38:23 scarlet yarn, and fine linen t
Ex 39: 1 scarlet t they made garments
Ex 39: 2 t, and of fine linen t
Ex 39: 3 and scarlet and fine linen t
Ex 39: 5 scarlet t, and fine linen t
Ex 39: 8 scarlet t, and fine linen t
Ex 39:24 and scarlet and fine linen t
Ex 39:29 blue and purple and scarlet t
Num 15:38 and to put a blue t in the
Judg 16:12 them off his arms like a t

THREADS (*see* THREAD)
Ex 39: 3 thin sheets and cut it into t

THREAT (*see* THREATEN, THREATS)
Job 41:29 laughs at the t of javelins
Is 30:17 shall flee at the t of one
Is 30:17 at the t of five you shall

THREATEN (*see* THREAT, THREATENED, THREATENING)
Acts 4:17 let us severely t them, that
1Pe 2:23 He suffered, He did not t

THREATENED (*see* THREATEN)
Acts 4:21 when they had further t them

THREATENING (*see* THREATEN)
Matt 16: 3 for the sky is red and t
Eph 6: 9 things to them, giving up t

THREATS (*see* THREAT)
Is 8:12 nor be afraid of their t
Zeph 2: 8 made arrogant t against their
Zeph 2:10 made arrogant t against the
Acts 4:29 Now, Lord, look on their t
Acts 9: 1 Then Saul, still breathing t
1Pe 3:14 do not be afraid of their t

THREE (*see* THIRD, THREE-DAY, THREE-PRONGED, THREE-YEAR-OLD)
Gen 5:22 with God t hundred years, and
Gen 5:23 days of Enoch were t hundred
Gen 6:10 And Noah begot t sons
Gen 6:15 ark shall be t hundred cubits
Gen 7:13 the t wives of his sons with
Gen 9:19 These t were the sons of Noah
Gen 9:28 after the flood t hundred
Gen 11:13 t years, and begot sons and
Gen 11:15 t years, and begot sons and
Gen 14:14 he armed his t hundred and
Gen 18: 2 t men were standing by him
Gen 18: 6 make ready t measures of fine
Gen 29: 2 there were t flocks of sheep
Gen 29:34 I have borne him t sons
Gen 30:36 Then he put t days' journey
Gen 38:24 about t months after, that
Gen 40:10 in the vine were t branches
Gen 40:12 The t branches are t days
Gen 40:13 Now within t days Pharaoh
Gen 40:16 there I had t white baskets
Gen 40:18 The t baskets are t days
Gen 40:19 Within t days Pharaoh will
Gen 42:17 all together in prison t days
Gen 45:22 but to Benjamin he gave t
Ex 2: 2 child, she hid him t months
Ex 3:18 let us go t days' journey
Ex 5: 3 let us go t days' journey
Ex 8:27 We will go t days' journey
Ex 10:22 all the land of Egypt t days
Ex 10:23 from his place for t days
Ex 15:22 And they went t days in the
Ex 21:11 does not do these t for her
Ex 23:14 T times you shall keep a
Ex 23:17 T times in the year all your
Ex 25:32 t branches of the lampstand
Ex 25:32 t branches of the lampstand
Ex 25:33 T bowls shall be made like
Ex 25:33 and t bowls made like almond
Ex 27: 1 its height shall be t cubits
Ex 27:14 cubits, with their t pillars
Ex 27:14 and their t sockets
Ex 27:15 cubits, with their t pillars
Ex 27:15 and their t sockets
Ex 32:28 about t thousand men of the
Ex 34:23 T times in the year all your
Ex 34:24 your God t times in the year
Ex 37:18 t branches of the lampstand
Ex 37:18 t branches of the lampstand
Ex 37:19 There were t bowls made like
Ex 37:19 and t bowls made like almond
Ex 38: 1 and its height was t cubits
Ex 38:14 long, with their t pillars
Ex 38:14 and their t sockets
Ex 38:15 cubits, with their t pillars
Ex 38:15 and their t sockets
Ex 38:26 t thousand, five hundred and
Lev 19:23 T years it shall be as
Lev 25:21 produce enough for t years
Lev 27: 6 shall be t shekels of silver
Num 1:23 fifty-nine thousand t hundred
Num 1:46 t thousand five hundred and
Num 2:13 fifty-nine thousand t hundred
Num 2:32 t thousand five hundred and
Num 3:50 money, one thousand t hundred
Num 4:44 were t thousand two hundred
Num 10:33 LORD on a journey of t days
Num 10:33 them for the t days' journey
Num 12: 4 Come out, you t, to the
Num 12: 4 So the t came out
Num 22:28 have struck me these t times
Num 22:32 your donkey these t times
Num 22:33 aside from Me these t times
Num 24:10 blessed them these t times
Num 26:25 sixty-four thousand t hundred
Num 31:36 war, was in number t hundred
Num 31:43 congregation was t hundred
Num 33: 8 went t days' journey in the
Num 35:14 You shall appoint t cities
Num 35:14 t cities you shall appoint in
Deut 4:41 Then Moses set apart t cities
Deut 16:16 T times a year all your males
Deut 17: 6 of two or t witnesses, but he
Deut 19: 2 you shall separate t cities
Deut 19: 3 and divide into t parts the
Deut 19: 7 t cities for yourself
Deut 19: 9 then you shall add t more
Deut 19: 9 for yourself besides these t
Deut 19:15 by the mouth of two or t
Josh 1:11 for within t days you will
Josh 2:16 Hide there t days, until the
Josh 2:22 stayed there t days until the
Josh 3: 2 So it was, after t days, that
Josh 7: 3 two or t thousand men go up
Josh 7: 4 So about t thousand men went
Josh 9:16 happened at the end of t days
Josh 15:14 Caleb drove out the t sons of
Josh 17:11 t hilly regions
Josh 18: 4 you t men for each tribe, and
Josh 21:32 t cities
Judg 1:20 from there the t sons of Anak
Judg 7: 6 mouth, was t hundred men
Judg 7: 7 By the t hundred men who
Judg 7: 8 retained those t hundred men
Judg 7:16 t hundred men into t companies
Judg 7:20 Then the t companies blew the
Judg 7:22 When the t hundred blew the
Judg 8: 4 the t hundred men who were
Judg 9:22 reigned over Israel t years
Judg 9:43 divided them into t companies
Judg 11:26 for t hundred years, why did
Judg 14:14 Now for t days they could
Judg 15: 4 and caught t hundred foxes
Judg 15:11 Then t thousand men of Judah
Judg 16:15 have mocked me these t times
Judg 16:27 were about t thousand men
Judg 19: 4 and he stayed with him t days
1Sa 1:24 with t bulls, one ephah of
1Sa 2:21 she conceived and bore t sons
1Sa 9:20 that were lost t days ago
1Sa 10: 3 There t men going up to God
1Sa 10: 3 one carrying t young goats
1Sa 10: 3 carrying t loaves of bread
1Sa 11: 8 were t hundred thousand, and
1Sa 11:11 put the people in t companies
1Sa 13: 2 t thousand men of Israel
1Sa 13:17 Philistines in t companies
1Sa 17:13 The t oldest sons of Jesse
1Sa 17:13 The names of his t sons who
1Sa 17:14 the t oldest followed Saul
1Sa 20:19 when you have stayed t days
1Sa 20:20 Then I will shoot t arrows to
1Sa 20:41 ground, and bowed down t times
1Sa 21: 5 about t days since I came out
1Sa 24: 2 Then Saul took t thousand
1Sa 25: 2 He had t thousand sheep and a
1Sa 26: 2 having t thousand chosen men
1Sa 30:12 drunk any water for t days
1Sa 30:12 for t days and t nights
1Sa 30:13 because t days ago I fell
1Sa 31: 6 his t sons, his armorbearer,
1Sa 31: 8 his t sons fallen on Mount
2Sa 2:18 Now the t sons of Zeruiah
2Sa 2:31 t hundred and sixty men who
2Sa 6:11 the Gittite t months
2Sa 13:38 Geshur, and was there t years
2Sa 14:27 To Absalom were born t sons
2Sa 18:14 he took t spears in his hand
2Sa 20: 4 of Judah for me within t days
2Sa 21: 1 the days of David for t years
2Sa 21:16 spear was t hundred shekels
2Sa 23: 9 one of the t mighty men with
2Sa 23:13 Then t of the thirty chief
2Sa 23:16 So the t mighty men broke
2Sa 23:17 were done by the t mighty men
2Sa 23:18 was chief of another t
2Sa 23:18 spear against t hundred men
2Sa 23:18 and won a name among these t
2Sa 23:19 he not the most honored of t
2Sa 23:19 did not attain to the first t
2Sa 23:22 won a name among t mighty
2Sa 23:23 did not attain to the first t
2Sa 24:12 I offer you t things
2Sa 24:13 Or shall you flee t months
2Sa 24:13 Or shall there be t days'
1Ki 2:39 at the end of t years, that
1Ki 4:32 He spoke t thousand proverbs,
1Ki 5:16 besides t thousand t hundred
1Ki 6:36 with t rows of hewn stone
1Ki 7: 4 with beveled frames in t rows
1Ki 7: 4 opposite window in t tiers
1Ki 7: 5 opposite window in t tiers
1Ki 7:12 with t rows of hewn stones
1Ki 7:25 t looking toward the north,
1Ki 7:25 t looking toward the west,
1Ki 7:25 t looking toward the south,
1Ki 7:25 t looking toward the east
1Ki 7:27 width, and t cubits its height
1Ki 9:25 Now t times a year Solomon
1Ki 10:17 He also made t hundred
1Ki 10:17 t minas of gold went into
1Ki 10:22 Once every t years the
1Ki 11: 3 and t hundred concubines
1Ki 12: 5 Depart for t days, then come
1Ki 15: 2 He reigned t years in
1Ki 17:21 out on the child t times, and
1Ki 22: 1 Now t years passed without
2Ki 2:17 they searched for t days but
2Ki 3:10 t kings together to deliver
2Ki 3:13 t kings together to deliver
2Ki 9:32 two or t eunuchs looked out

2Ki 13:18 so he struck t times, and
2Ki 13:19 strike Syria only t times
2Ki 13:25 T times Joash defeated him and
2Ki 17: 5 and besieged it for t years
2Ki 18:10 at the end of t years they
2Ki 18:14 Hezekiah king of Judah t
2Ki 23:31 and he reigned t months in
2Ki 24: 1 became his vassal for t years
2Ki 24: 8 reigned in Jerusalem t months
2Ki 25:17 of the capital was t cubits
2Ki 25:18 priest, and the t doorkeepers
1Ch 2: 3 These t were born to him by
1Ch 2:16 Abishai, Joab, and Asahel—t
1Ch 3:23 t in all
1Ch 7: 6 t in all
1Ch 10: 6 his t sons died, and all his
1Ch 11:11 his spear against t hundred
1Ch 11:12 was one of the t mighty men
1Ch 11:15 Now t of the thirty chief men
1Ch 11:18 So the t broke through the
1Ch 11:19 were done by the t mighty men
1Ch 11:20 Joab was chief of another t
1Ch 11:20 spear against t hundred men
1Ch 11:20 and won a name among these t
1Ch 11:21 Of the t he was more honored
1Ch 11:21 did not attain to the first t
1Ch 11:24 won a name among t mighty
1Ch 11:25 did not attain to the first t
1Ch 12:27 with him t thousand seven
1Ch 12:29 t thousand (until then the
1Ch 12:39 were there with David t days
1Ch 13:14 in his house t months
1Ch 21:10 I offer you t things
1Ch 21:12 either t years of famine
1Ch 21:12 or t months to be defeated by
1Ch 21:12 or else for t days the sword
1Ch 23: 8 t in all
1Ch 23: 9 t in all
1Ch 23:23 t in all
1Ch 25: 5 fourteen sons and t daughters
1Ch 29: 4 t thousand talents of gold,
2Ch 2: 2 t thousand six hundred to
2Ch 2:18 and t thousand six hundred
2Ch 4: 4 t looking toward the north,
2Ch 4: 4 t looking toward the west,
2Ch 4: 4 t looking toward the south,
2Ch 4: 4 t looking toward the east
2Ch 4: 5 It contained t thousand baths
2Ch 6:13 t cubits high, and had set it
2Ch 8:13 the t appointed yearly feasts
2Ch 9:16 He also made t hundred
2Ch 9:16 t hundred shekels of gold
2Ch 9:21 Once every t years the
2Ch 10: 5 Come back to me after t days
2Ch 11:17 of Solomon strong for t years
2Ch 11:17 David and Solomon for t years
2Ch 13: 2 He reigned t years in
2Ch 14: 8 Asa had an army of t hundred
2Ch 14: 9 t hundred chariots, and he
2Ch 17:14 with him t hundred thousand
2Ch 20:25 they were t days gathering
2Ch 25: 5 found them to be t hundred
2Ch 25:13 killed t thousand in them, and
2Ch 26:13 hand was an army of t hundred
2Ch 29:33 bulls and t thousand sheep
2Ch 31:16 those males from t years old
2Ch 35: 7 as well as t thousand cattle
2Ch 35: 8 flock, and t hundred cattle
2Ch 36: 2 and he reigned t months in
2Ch 36: 9 reigned in Jerusalem t months
Ezra 2: 4 t hundred and seventy-two
Ezra 2:17 t hundred and twenty-three
Ezra 2:32 of Harim, t hundred and twenty
Ezra 2:34 t hundred and forty-five
Ezra 2:35 t thousand six hundred and
Ezra 2:58 servants were t hundred and
Ezra 2:64 forty-two thousand t hundred
Ezra 2:65 were seven thousand t hundred
Ezra 6: 4 with t rows of heavy stones
Ezra 8: 5 and with him t hundred males
Ezra 8:15 and we camped there t days
Ezra 8:32 and stayed there t days
Ezra 10: 8 would not come within t days
Ezra 10: 9 at Jerusalem within t days
Neh 2:11 Jerusalem and was there t days
Neh 7: 9 t hundred and seventy-two
Neh 7:17 Azgad, two thousand t hundred
Neh 7:22 t hundred and twenty-eight
Neh 7:23 t hundred and twenty-four
Neh 7:35 of Harim, t hundred and twenty
Neh 7:36 t hundred and forty-five
Neh 7:38 t thousand nine hundred and
Neh 7:60 were t hundred and ninety-two
Neh 7:66 forty-two thousand t hundred
Neh 7:67 were seven thousand t hundred
Esth 4:16 eat nor drink for t days,
Esth 9:15 and killed t hundred men at
Job 1: 2 t daughters were born to him
Job 1: 4 invite their t sisters to eat
Job 1:17 The Chaldeans formed t bands
Job 2:11 Now when Job's t friends
Job 32: 1 So these t men ceased
Job 32: 3 Also against his t friends
Job 32: 5 in the mouth of these t men
Job 33:29 in fact, t times with a man,
Job 42:13 had seven sons and t daughters
Prov 30:15 There are t things that are
Prov 30:18 There are t things which are
Prov 30:21 For t things the earth is
Prov 30:29 There are t things which are
Is 16:14 Within t years, as the years
Is 17: 6 two or t olives at the top of
Is 19:24 will be one of t with Egypt
Is 20: 3 barefoot t years for a sign
Jer 36:23 had read t or four columns
Jer 52:24 priest, and the t doorkeepers
Jer 52:28 t thousand and twenty-three
Ezek 4: 5 t hundred and ninety days
Ezek 4: 9 t hundred and ninety days, you
Ezek 14:14 Though these t men, Noah,
Ezek 14:16 though these t men were in it
Ezek 14:18 though these t men were in it
Ezek 40:10 t gate chambers on one side
Ezek 40:10 on one side and t on the other
Ezek 40:10 the t were all the same size
Ezek 40:21 t on this side and t on that
Ezek 40:48 was t cubits on this side
Ezek 40:48 and t cubits on that side
Ezek 41: 6 chambers were in t stories
Ezek 41:16 their t stories opposite the
Ezek 41:22 t cubits high, and its length
Ezek 42: 3 against gallery in t stories
Ezek 42: 6 For they were in t stories
Ezek 48:31 the t gates northward
Ezek 48:32 five hundred cubits, t gates
Ezek 48:33 five hundred cubits, t gates
Ezek 48:34 cubits with their t gates
Dan 1: 5 t years of training for them,
Dan 3:23 And these t men, Shadrach,
Dan 3:24 Did we not cast t men bound
Dan 6: 2 t governors, of whom Daniel
Dan 6:10 on his knees t times that day
Dan 6:13 his petition t times a day
Dan 7: 5 and had t ribs in its mouth
Dan 7: 8 before whom t of the first
Dan 7:20 came up, before which t fell
Dan 7:24 ones, and shall subdue t kings
Dan 8:14 two thousand t hundred days
Dan 10: 2 was mourning t full weeks
Dan 10: 3 all, till t whole weeks were
Dan 11: 2 t more kings will arise in
Dan 12:12 to the one thousand t hundred
Amos 1: 3 For t transgressions of
Amos 1: 6 For t transgressions of Gaza,
Amos 1: 9 For t transgressions of Tyre,
Amos 1:11 For t transgressions of Edom,
Amos 1:13 For t transgressions of the
Amos 2: 1 For t transgressions of Moab,
Amos 2: 4 For t transgressions of Judah
Amos 2: 6 For t transgressions of
Amos 4: 4 your tithes every t days
Amos 4: 7 still t months to the harvest
Amos 4: 8 So two or t cities wandered
Jon 1:17 t days and t nights
Zech 11: 8 I dismissed the t shepherds
Matt 12:40 For as Jonah was t days and
Matt 12:40 t nights in the belly of the
Matt 12:40 will the Son of Man be t days
Matt 12:40 t nights in the heart of the
Matt 13:33 hid in t measures of meal
Matt 15:32 now continued with Me t days
Matt 17: 4 us make here t tabernacles
Matt 18:16 by the mouth of two or t
Matt 18:20 For where two or t are
Matt 26:34 you will deny Me t times
Matt 26:61 God and to build it in t days
Matt 26:75 you will deny Me t times
Matt 27:40 temple and build it in t days
Matt 27:63 After t days I will rise
Mark 8: 2 have now been with Me t days
Mark 8:31 and after t days rise again
Mark 9: 5 and let us make t tabernacles
Mark 14: 5 more than t hundred denarii
Mark 14:30 you will deny Me t times
Mark 14:58 within t days I will build
Mark 14:72 you will deny Me t times
Mark 15:29 temple and build it in t days
Luke 1:56 with her about t months, and
Luke 2:46 Now so it was that after t
Luke 4:25 heaven was shut up t years
Luke 9:33 and let us make t tabernacles
Luke 10:36 So which of these t do you
Luke 11: 5 Friend, lend me t loaves
Luke 12:52 t against two
Luke 12:52 and two against t
Luke 13: 7 Look, for t years I have come
Luke 13:21 hid in t measures of meal
Luke 22:34 deny t times that you know Me
Luke 22:61 you will deny Me t times
John 2:19 in t days I will raise it up
John 2:20 You raise it up in t days
John 6:19 rowed about t or four miles
John 12: 5 sold for t hundred denarii
John 13:38 you have denied Me t times
Acts 2:41 that day about t thousand
Acts 5: 7 Now it was about t hours
Acts 7:20 father's house for t months
Acts 9: 9 he was t days without sight,
Acts 10:16 This was done t times
Acts 10:19 Behold, t men are seeking you
Acts 11:10 Now this was done t times
Acts 11:11 t men stood before the house
Acts 17: 2 for t Sabbaths reasoned with
Acts 19: 8 and spoke boldly for t months
Acts 20: 3 and stayed t months
Acts 20:31 remember that for t years I
Acts 25: 1 after t days he went up from
Acts 28: 7 us courteously for t days
Acts 28:11 After t months we sailed in
Acts 28:12 at Syracuse, we stayed t days
Acts 28:15 far as Appii Forum and T Inns
Acts 28:17 it came to pass after t days
1Co 13:13 faith, hope, love, these t
1Co 14:27 there be two or at the most t
1Co 14:29 Let two or t prophets speak,
2Co 11:25 T times I was beaten with
2Co 11:25 t times I was shipwrecked
2Co 12: 8 I pleaded with the Lord t
2Co 13: 1 By the mouth of two or t
Gal 1:18 Then after t years I went up
1Ti 5:19 from two or t witnesses
Heb 10:28 of two or t witnesses
Heb 11:23 was hidden t months by his
Jas 5:17 rain on the land for t years
1Jn 5: 7 For there are t who bear
1Jn 5: 7 and these t are one
1Jn 5: 8 there are t that bear witness
1Jn 5: 8 and these t agree as one
Rev 6: 6 and t quarts of barley for a
Rev 8:13 of the trumpet of the t
Rev 9:18 By these t plagues a third of
Rev 11: 9 will see their dead bodies t
Rev 11:11 Now after the t and a half
Rev 16:13 I saw t unclean spirits like
Rev 16:19 city was divided into t parts
Rev 21:13 t gates on the east
Rev 21:13 t gates on the north
Rev 21:13 t gates on the south
Rev 21:13 and t gates on the west

THREE-DAY (*see* THREE)
Jon 3: 3 city, a t journey in extent

THREEFOLD
Eccl 4:12 and a t cord is not quickly

THREE-PRONGED (*see* THREE)
1Sa 2:13 servant would come with a t

THREE-TENTHS
Lev 14:10 t of an ephah of fine flour
Num 15: 9 bull a grain offering of t of
Num 28:12 t of an ephah of fine flour
Num 28:20 t of an ephah you shall offer
Num 28:28 t of an ephah for each bull,
Num 29: 3 t of an ephah for the bull,
Num 29: 9 t of an ephah for the bull,
Num 29:14 t of an ephah for each of the

THREE-YEAR-OLD (*see* THREE)
Gen 15: 9 Bring Me a t heifer
Gen 15: 9 a t female goat, a t ram,
Is 15: 5 flee to Zoar, like a t heifer

Jer 48:34 to Horonaim, like a **t** heifer

THRESH (*see* THRESHED, THRESHES, THRESHING, THRESHINGFLOOR)
Is 27:12 that day that the LORD will **t**
Is 28:28 he does not **t** it forever,
Is 41:15 you shall **t** the mountains and
Jer 51:33 when it is time to **t** her
Hos 10:11 heifer that loves to **t** grain
Mic 4:13 Arise and **t**, O daughter of

THRESHED (*see* THRESH)
Judg 6:11 while his son Gideon **t** wheat
Is 28:27 not **t** with a threshing sledge
Amos 1: 3 because they have **t** Gilead

THRESHES (*see* THRESH)
1Co 9:10 he who **t** in hope should be

THRESHING (*see* THRESH)
Gen 50:10 came to the **t** floor of Atad
Gen 50:11 at the **t** floor of Atad, they
Lev 26: 5 Your **t** shall last till the
Num 15:20 heave offering of the **t** floor
Num 18:27 were the grain of the **t** floor
Num 18:30 as the produce of the **t** floor
Deut 15:14 your flock, from your **t** floor
Deut 16:13 gathered from your **t** floor
Judg 6:37 fleece of wool on the **t** floor
Ruth 3: 2 barley tonight at the **t** floor
Ruth 3: 3 and go down to the **t** floor
Ruth 3: 6 she went down to the **t** floor
Ruth 3:14 the woman came to the **t** floor
1Sa 23: 1 they are robbing the **t** floors
2Sa 24:16 by the **t** floor of Araunah the
2Sa 24:18 on the **t** floor of Araunah the
2Sa 24:21 To buy the **t** floor from you,
2Sa 24:22 **t** implements and the yokes of
2Sa 24:24 So David bought the **t** floor
1Ki 22:10 at a **t** floor at the entrance
2Ki 6:27 From the **t** floor or from the
2Ki 13: 7 made them like the dust at **t**
1Ch 13: 9 they came to Chidon's **t** floor
1Ch 21:15 of the LORD stood by the **t**
1Ch 21:18 **t** floor of Ornan the Jebusite
1Ch 21:20 but Ornan continued **t** wheat
1Ch 21:21 he went out from the **t** floor
1Ch 21:22 me the place of this **t** floor
1Ch 21:23 the **t** implements for wood, and
1Ch 21:28 had answered him on the **t**
2Ch 3: 1 David had prepared on the **t**
2Ch 18: 9 they sat at a **t** floor at the
Job 39:12 and gather it to your **t** floor
Prov 20:26 brings the **t** wheel over them
Is 21:10 Oh, my **t** and the grain of my
Is 28:27 not threshed with a **t** sledge
Is 41:15 new **t** sledge with sharp teeth
Jer 50:11 fat like a heifer **t** grain
Jer 51:33 of Babylon is like a **t** floor
Dan 2:35 from the summer **t** floors
Hos 9: 1 for reward on every **t** floor
Hos 9: 2 The **t** floor and the winepress
Hos 13: 3 blown off from a **t** floor and
Joel 2:24 The **t** floors shall be full of
Mic 4:12 like sheaves to the **t** floor
Matt 3:12 thoroughly purge His **t** floor
Luke 3:17 thoroughly purge His **t** floor

THRESHINGFLOOR (*see* THRESH)
2Sa 6: 6 when they came to Nachon's **t**

THRESHOLD (*see* THRESHOLDS)
Judg 19:27 house with her hands on the **t**
1Sa 5: 4 were broken off on the **t**
1Sa 5: 5 **t** of Dagon in Ashdod to this
1Ki 14:17 came to the **t** of the house
Ezek 9: 3 been, to the **t** of the temple
Ezek 10: 4 over the **t** of the temple
Ezek 10:18 from the **t** of the temple and
Ezek 40: 6 measured the **t** of the gateway
Ezek 40: 6 the other **t** was one rod wide
Ezek 40: 7 the **t** of the gateway by the
Ezek 41:16 three stories opposite the **t**
Ezek 43: 8 set their **t** by My **t**
Ezek 46: 2 worship at the **t** of the gate
Ezek 47: 1 flowing from under the **t** of
Zeph 1: 9 all those who leap over the **t**
Zeph 2:14 desolation shall be at the **t**

THRESHOLDS (*see* THRESHOLD)
Amos 9: 1 that the **t** may shake, and

THREW (*see* THROW)
Ex 7:12 For every man **t** down his rod
Deut 9:17 **t** them out of my two hands and
Deut 9:21 I **t** its dust into the brook
Judg 8:25 and each man **t** into it the
Judg 15:17 that he **t** the jawbone from
2Sa 16: 6 he **t** stones at David and at
2Sa 16:13 **t** stones at him and kicked up
2Sa 20:12 **t** a garment over him, when he
2Sa 20:22 Bichri, and **t** it out to Joab
1Ki 19:19 by him and **t** his mantle on him
2Ki 3:25 each man **t** a stone on every
2Ki 6: 6 off a stick, and **t** it in there
2Ki 9:33 So they **t** her down, and some
2Ki 10:25 and the officers **t** them out
2Ki 23: 6 **t** its ashes on the graves of
2Ki 23:12 **t** their dust into the Brook
2Ch 31: 1 **t** down the high places and the
Neh 9:11 You **t** into the deep, as a
Neh 13: 8 therefore I **t** all the
Lam 3:53 in the pit and **t** stones at me
Jon 1: 5 **t** the cargo that was in the
Jon 1:15 **t** him into the sea, and the
Zech 5: 8 **t** the lead cover over its
Zech 11:13 **t** them into the house of the
Matt 13:48 vessels, but **t** the bad away
Matt 18:30 **t** him into prison till he
Matt 27: 5 Then he **t** down the pieces of
Mark 11: 7 **t** their garments on it, and He
Mark 12: 4 and at him they **t** stones,
Mark 12:42 **t** in two mites, which make a
Luke 9:42 coming, the demon **t** him down
Luke 19:35 they **t** their own garments on
Acts 16:23 they **t** them into prison,
Acts 22:23 and **t** dust into the air,
Acts 27:19 On the third day we **t** the
Acts 27:38 **t** out the wheat into the sea
Rev 8: 5 altar, and **t** it to the earth
Rev 12: 4 heaven and **t** them to the earth
Rev 14:19 **t** it into the great winepress
Rev 18:19 they **t** dust on their heads and
Rev 18:21 **t** it into the sea, saying,

THRIVE
Ezek 16: 7 I made you **t** like a plant in
Ezek 17: 9 Will it **t**
Ezek 17:10 it is planted, will it **t**
Dan 8:24 and shall prosper and **t**
Zech 9:17 shall make the young men **t**

THROAT
Ps 5: 9 Their **t** is an open tomb
Ps 69: 3 My **t** is dry
Ps 115: 7 they mutter through their **t**
Prov 23: 2 put a knife to your **t** if you
Jer 2:25 unshod, and your **t** from thirst
Matt 18:28 on him and took him by the **t**
Rom 3:13 Their **t** is an open tomb

THRONE (*see* THRONES)
Gen 41:40 only in regard to the **t** will
Ex 11: 5 of Pharaoh who sits on his **t**
Ex 12:29 his **t** to the firstborn of the
Deut 17:18 sits on the **t** of his kingdom
1Sa 2: 8 them inherit the **t** of glory
2Sa 3:10 set up the **t** of David over
2Sa 7:13 I will establish the **t** of his
2Sa 7:16 Your **t** shall be established
2Sa 14: 9 king and his **t** be guiltless
1Ki 1:13 me, and he shall sit on my **t**"
1Ki 1:17 me, and he shall sit on my **t**
1Ki 1:20 them who will sit on the **t** of
1Ki 1:24 me, and he shall sit on my **t**'
1Ki 1:27 who should sit on the **t** of my
1Ki 1:30 shall sit on my **t** in my place
1Ki 1:35 he shall come and sit on my **t**
1Ki 1:37 make his **t** greater than the
1Ki 1:37 the **t** of my lord King David
1Ki 1:46 sits on the **t** of the kingdom
1Ki 1:47 may He make his **t** greater
1Ki 1:47 **t** greater than your **t**
1Ki 1:48 one to sit on my **t** this day
1Ki 2: 4 lack a man on the **t** of Israel
1Ki 2:12 on the **t** of his father David
1Ki 2:19 to her, and sat down on his **t**
1Ki 2:19 had a **t** set for the king's
1Ki 2:24 set me on the **t** of David my
1Ki 2:33 upon his house and his **t**,
1Ki 2:45 and the **t** of David shall be
1Ki 3: 6 him a son to sit on his **t**
1Ki 5: 5 set on your **t** in your place
1Ki 7: 7 Then he made a hall for the **t**
1Ki 8:20 and sit on the **t** of Israel
1Ki 8:25 before Me on the **t** of Israel
1Ki 9: 5 then I will establish the **t**
1Ki 9: 5 have a man on the **t** of Israel
1Ki 10: 9 you on the **t** of Israel
1Ki 10:18 king made a great **t** of ivory
1Ki 10:19 The **t** had six steps, and the
1Ki 10:19 the top of the **t** was round at
1Ki 16:11 as he was seated on his **t**
1Ki 22:10 robes, sat each on his **t**, at
1Ki 22:19 saw the LORD sitting on His **t**
2Ki 10: 3 set him on his father's **t**
2Ki 10:30 the **t** of Israel to the fourth
2Ki 11:19 he sat on the **t** of the kings
2Ki 13:13 Then Jeroboam sat on his **t**
2Ki 15:12 the **t** of Israel to the fourth
1Ch 17:12 will establish his **t** forever
1Ch 17:14 his **t** shall be established
1Ch 22:10 I will establish the **t** of his
1Ch 28: 5 son Solomon to sit on the **t**
1Ch 29:23 Then Solomon sat on the **t** of
2Ch 6:10 and sit on the **t** of Israel
2Ch 6:16 before Me on the **t** of Israel
2Ch 7:18 the **t** of your kingdom, as I
2Ch 9: 8 setting you on His **t** to be
2Ch 9:17 king made a great **t** of ivory
2Ch 9:18 The **t** had six steps, with a
2Ch 9:18 which were fastened to the **t**
2Ch 18: 9 robes, sat each on his **t**
2Ch 18:18 saw the LORD sitting on His **t**
2Ch 23:20 king on the **t** of the kingdom
Esth 1: 2 sat on the **t** of his kingdom
Esth 5: 1 royal **t** in the royal house
Job 26: 9 He covers the face of His **t**
Job 36: 7 they are on the **t** with kings
Ps 9: 4 You sat on the **t** judging in
Ps 9: 7 prepared His **t** for judgment
Ps 11: 4 The LORD's **t** is in heaven
Ps 45: 6 Your **t**, O God, is forever and
Ps 47: 8 God sits on His holy **t**
Ps 89: 4 And build up your **t** to all
Ps 89:14 are the foundation of Your **t**
Ps 89:29 his **t** as the days of heaven
Ps 89:36 his **t** as the sun before Me
Ps 89:44 cast his **t** down to the ground
Ps 93: 2 Your **t** is established from of
Ps 94:20 Shall the **t** of iniquity,
Ps 97: 2 are the foundation of His **t**
Ps 103:19 established His **t** in heaven
Ps 132:11 I will set upon your **t** the
Ps 132:12 sit upon your **t** forevermore
Prov 16:12 for a **t** is established by
Prov 20: 8 A king who sits on the **t** of
Prov 20:28 he upholds his **t**
Prov 25: 5 his **t** will be established in
Prov 29:14 his **t** will be established
Is 6: 1 I saw the Lord sitting on a **t**
Is 9: 7 no end, upon the **t** of David
Is 14:13 I will exalt my **t** above the
Is 16: 5 In mercy the **t** will be
Is 22:23 **t** to his father's house
Is 47: 1 sit on the ground without a **t**
Is 66: 1 Heaven is My **t**, and earth is
Jer 1:15 each one set his **t** at the
Jer 3:17 be called The **T** of the LORD
Jer 13:13 kings who sit on David's **t**
Jer 14:21 disgrace the **t** of Your glory
Jer 17:12 A glorious high **t** from the
Jer 17:25 sitting on the **t** of David
Jer 22: 2 you who sit on the **t** of David
Jer 22: 4 who sit on the **t** of David
Jer 22:30 sitting on the **t** of David
Jer 29:16 who sits on the **t** of David
Jer 33:17 the **t** of the house of Israel
Jer 33:21 have a son to reign on his **t**
Jer 36:30 one to sit on the **t** of David
Jer 43:10 will set his **t** above these
Jer 49:38 I will set My **t** in Elam, and
Lam 5:19 Your **t** from generation to
Ezek 1:26 heads was the likeness of a **t**
Ezek 1:26 on the likeness of the **t** was
Ezek 10: 1 of the likeness of a **t**
Ezek 43: 7 this is the place of My **t**
Dan 5:20 was deposed from his kingly **t**
Dan 7: 9 His **t** was a fiery flame, its
Jon 3: 6 and he arose from his **t** and
Hag 2:22 overthrow the **t** of kingdoms
Zech 6:13 and shall sit and rule on His **t**
Zech 6:13 He shall be a priest on His **t**
Matt 5:34 by heaven, for it is God's **t**

Matt 19:28 sits on the **t** of His glory
Matt 23:22 swears by the **t** of God and by
Matt 25:31 sit on the **t** of His glory
Luke 1:32 Him the **t** of His father David
Acts 2:30 up the Christ to sit on his **t**
Acts 7:49 Heaven is My **t**, and earth is
Acts 12:21 royal apparel, sat on his **t**
Heb 1: 8 Your **t**, O God, is forever and
Heb 4:16 come boldly to the **t** of grace
Heb 8: 1 the **t** of the Majesty in the
Heb 12: 2 right hand of the **t** of God
Rev 1: 4 Spirits who are before His **t**
Rev 2:13 you dwell, where Satan's **t** is
Rev 3:21 grant to sit with Me on My **t**
Rev 3:21 down with My Father on His **t**
Rev 4: 2 a **t** set in heaven
Rev 4: 2 and One sat on the **t**
Rev 4: 3 was a rainbow around the **t**
Rev 4: 4 Around the **t** were twenty-four
Rev 4: 5 And from the **t** proceeded
Rev 4: 5 of fire burning before the **t**
Rev 4: 6 Before the **t** there was a sea
Rev 4: 6 And in the midst of the **t**
Rev 4: 6 and around the **t**
Rev 4: 9 to Him who sits on the **t**, who
Rev 4:10 before Him who sits on the **t**
Rev 4:10 their crowns before the **t**
Rev 5: 1 the **t** a scroll written inside
Rev 5: 6 behold, in the midst of the **t**
Rev 5: 7 hand of Him who sat on the **t**
Rev 5:11 of many angels around the **t**
Rev 5:13 be to Him who sits on the **t**
Rev 6:16 face of Him who sits on the **t**
Rev 7: 9 standing before the **t** and
Rev 7:10 to our God who sits on the **t**
Rev 7:11 the angels stood around the **t**
Rev 7:11 on their faces before the **t**
Rev 7:15 they are before the **t** of God
Rev 7:15 He who sits on the **t** will
Rev 7:17 of the **t** will shepherd them
Rev 8: 3 altar which was before the **t**
Rev 12: 5 caught up to God and to His **t**
Rev 13: 2 gave him his power, his **t**
Rev 14: 3 were a new song before the **t**
Rev 14: 5 fault before the **t** of God
Rev 16:10 bowl on the **t** of the beast
Rev 16:17 temple of heaven, from the **t**
Rev 19: 4 God who sat on the **t**, saying,
Rev 19: 5 Then a voice came from the **t**
Rev 20:11 Then I saw a great white **t**
Rev 21: 5 Then He who sat on the **t** said
Rev 22: 1 proceeding from the **t** of God
Rev 22: 3 more curse, but the **t** of God

THRONES (*see* THRONE)
Ps 122: 5 For **t** are set there for
Ps 122: 5 The **t** of the house of David
Is 14: 9 their **t** all the kings of the
Ezek 26:16 will come down from their **t**
Dan 7: 9 I watched till **t** were put in
Matt 19:28 Me will also sit on twelve **t**
Luke 1:52 down the mighty from their **t**
Luke 22:30 sit on **t** judging the twelve
Col 1:16 whether **t** or dominions or
Rev 4: 4 the throne were twenty-four **t**
Rev 4: 4 on the **t** I saw twenty-four
Rev 11:16 their **t** fell on their faces
Rev 20: 4 And I saw **t**, and they sat on

THRONG (*see* THRONGED, THRONGING)
Ps 55:14 to the house of God in the **t**
Jer 31: 8 a great **t** shall return there
Luke 8:45 Master, the multitudes **t** You

THRONGED (*see* THRONG)
Dan 6: 6 satraps **t** before the king, and
Mark 5:24 followed Him and **t** Him
Luke 8:42 He went, the multitudes **t** Him

THRONGING (*see* THRONG)
Mark 5:31 You see the multitude **t** You

THROUGH (*see* PREFACE)

THROUGHOUT (*see* PREFACE)

THROW (*see* THREW, THROWING, THROWN, THROWS)
Ex 22:31 you shall **t** it to the dogs
2Sa 20:15 the wall to **t** it down
2Ki 9:25 **t** him into the tract of the
2Ki 9:26 **t** him on the plot of ground,
2Ki 9:33 Then he said, "**T** her down
2Ch 20:11 **t** us out of Your possession
Eccl 3: 6 to keep, and a time to **t** away
Is 22:17 the LORD will **t** you away
Is 30:22 You will **t** them away as an
Is 31: 7 **t** away his idols of silver
Jer 1:10 to **t** down, to build and to
Jer 10:18 I will **t** out at this time the
Jer 31:28 to **t** down, to destroy, and to
Jer 51:63 **t** it out into the Euphrates
Lam 2:10 they **t** dust on their heads and
Ezek 5: 4 **t** them into the midst of the
Ezek 7:19 They will **t** their silver
Ezek 16:39 and they shall **t** down your
Ezek 20: 7 **t** away the abominations which
Ezek 28: 8 They shall **t** you down into
Ezek 43:24 priests shall **t** salt on them
Amos 8: 3 They shall **t** them out in
Jon 1:12 me up and **t** me into the sea
Mic 5:11 **t** down all your strongholds
Zech 11:13 to me, "**T** it to the potter"
Mal 1: 4 may build, but I will **t** down
Matt 4: 6 Son of God, **t** Yourself down
Matt 15:26 and **t** it to the little dogs
Mark 7:27 and **t** it to the little dogs
Luke 4: 9 **t** Yourself down from here
Luke 4:29 that they might **t** Him down
Luke 12:58 the officer **t** you into prison
Luke 14:35 dunghill, but men **t** it out
Luke 22:41 from them about a stone's **t**
John 8: 7 you, let him **t** a stone at her
John 8:59 took up stones to **t** at Him
John 15: 6 **t** them into the fire, and they
Rev 2:10 the devil is about to **t** some

THROWING (*see* THROW)
Num 35:23 **t** it at him without seeing
Mark 10:50 **t** aside his garment, he rose

THROWN (*see* THROW)
Ex 15: 1 rider He has **t** into the sea
Ex 15:21 rider He has **t** into the sea
2Sa 20:21 his head will be **t** to you
1Ki 13:24 his corpse was **t** on the road
1Ki 13:25 saw the corpse **t** on the road
1Ki 13:28 his corpse **t** on the road, and
2Ki 7:15 had **t** away in their haste
Is 16: 2 bird **t** out of the nest
Is 34: 3 their slain shall be **t** out
Jer 31:40 up or **t** down anymore forever
Jer 50:15 fallen, her walls are **t** down
Lam 2: 2 He has **t** down in His wrath
Lam 2:17 He has **t** down and has not
Ezek 15: 4 it is **t** into the fire for
Ezek 16: 5 but you were **t** out into the
Ezek 38:20 The mountains shall be **t** down
Joel 1: 7 stripped it bare and **t** it away
Nah 1: 6 the rocks are **t** down by Him
Matt 3:10 cut down and **t** into the fire
Matt 5:13 for nothing but to be **t** out
Matt 5:25 and you are **t** into prison
Matt 6:30 tomorrow is **t** into the oven,
Matt 7:19 cut down and **t** into the fire
Matt 24: 2 that shall not be **t** down
Mark 9:22 often he has **t** him both into
Mark 9:42 and he were **t** into the sea
Mark 13: 2 that shall not be **t** down
Mark 14:51 having a linen cloth **t** around
Luke 3: 9 cut down and **t** into the fire
Luke 4:35 had **t** him in their midst, it
Luke 12:28 tomorrow is **t** into the oven,
Luke 17: 2 he were **t** into the sea, than
Luke 21: 6 that shall not be **t** down
Luke 23:19 who had been **t** into prison
Luke 23:25 murder had been **t** into prison
John 3:24 not yet been **t** into prison
Acts 16:37 and have **t** us into prison
Rev 8: 7 and they were **t** to the earth
Rev 8: 8 with fire was **t** into the sea
Rev 18:21 city Babylon shall be **t** down

THROWS (*see* THROW)
Num 35:22 or **t** anything at him without
Prov 26:18 a madman who **t** firebrands
Mark 9:18 he seizes him, he **t** him down

THRUST
Ex 21:29 But if the ox tended to **t**
Ex 21:36 ox tended to **t** in time past
Num 25: 8 **t** both of them through, the
Deut 15:17 **t** it through his ear to the
Deut 33:27 He will **t** out the enemy from
Judg 3:21 thigh, and **t** it into his belly
Judg 9:54 his young man **t** him through
1Sa 2:14 Then he would **t** it into the
1Sa 31: 4 **t** me through with it, lest
1Sa 31: 4 and **t** me through and abuse me
2Sa 2:16 **t** his sword in his opponent's
2Sa 18:14 and **t** them through Absalom's
2Sa 23: 6 shall all be as thorns **t** away
1Ch 10: 4 **t** me through with it, lest
2Ch 26:20 so they **t** him out of that
Is 13:15 is found will be **t** through
Is 14:19 **t** through with a sword, who
Jer 51: 4 and those **t** through in her
Lam 1:14 His hands, and **t** upon my neck
Ezek 16:40 and **t** you through with their
Ezek 21:16 Swords at the ready! **T** right
Ezek 21:16 Set your blade! **T** left
Hab 3:14 You **t** through with his own
Zech 5: 8 he **t** her down into the basket
Zech 13: 3 shall **t** him through when he
Luke 4:29 up and **t** Him out of the city
Luke 10:15 will be **t** down to Hades
Luke 13:28 of God, and yourselves **t** out
Heb 12:20 or **t** through with an arrow
Rev 14:15 **T** in Your sickle and reap, for
Rev 14:16 **t** in His sickle on the earth
Rev 14:18 **T** in your sharp sickle and
Rev 14:19 So the angel **t** his sickle

THUMB (*see* THUMBS)
Ex 29:20 on the **t** of their right hand
Lev 8:23 on the **t** of his right hand,
Lev 14:14 on the **t** of his right hand,
Lev 14:17 on the **t** of his right hand,
Lev 14:25 on the **t** of his right hand,
Lev 14:28 on the **t** of the right hand,

THUMBS (*see* THUMB)
Lev 8:24 on the **t** of their right hands
Judg 1: 6 caught him and cut off his **t**
Judg 1: 7 Seventy kings with their **t**

THUMMIM (*see* URIM)
Ex 28:30 of judgment the Urim and the **T**
Lev 8: 8 and the **T** in the breastplate
Deut 33: 8 Let Your **T** and Your Urim be
Ezra 2:63 consult with the Urim and **T**
Neh 7:65 consult with the Urim and **T**

THUNDER (*see* THUNDERBOLT, THUNDERED, THUNDERING, THUNDEROUS, THUNDERS)
Ex 9:23 and the LORD sent **t** and hail,
Ex 9:29 the **t** will cease, and there
Ex 9:33 then the **t** and the hail ceased
Ex 9:34 the **t** had ceased, he sinned
1Sa 2:10 heaven He will **t** against them
1Sa 7:10 **t** upon the Philistines that
1Sa 12:17 the LORD, and He will send **t**
1Sa 12:18 the LORD, and the LORD sent **t**
Job 26:14 But the **t** of His power who
Job 36:29 clouds, the **t** from His canopy
Job 36:33 His **t** declares it, the cattle
Job 37: 2 the **t** of His voice, and the
Job 39:19 you clothed his neck with **t**
Job 39:25 the **t** of captains and shouting
Job 40: 9 Or can you **t** with a voice
Ps 77:18 The voice of Your **t** was in
Ps 81: 7 you in the secret place of **t**
Ps 104: 7 of Your **t** they hastened away
Is 29: 6 by the LORD of hosts with **t**
Mark 3:17 Sons of **T**"
Rev 6: 1 saying with a voice like **t**
Rev 14: 2 and like the voice of loud **t**

THUNDERBOLT (*see* THUNDER)
Job 28:26 the rain, and a path for the **t**
Job 38:25 water, or a path for the **t**

THUNDERED (*see* THUNDER)
1Sa 7:10 But the LORD **t** with a loud
2Sa 22:14 The LORD **t** from heaven, and
Ps 18:13 The LORD also **t** in the
John 12:29 heard it said that it had **t**

THUNDERING (*see* THUNDER, THUNDERINGS)
Ex 9:28 there may be no more mighty **t**

THUNDERINGS (*see* THUNDERING)
Ex 19:16 morning, that there were **t**
Ex 20:18 the people witnessed the **t**
Rev 4: 5 proceeded lightnings, **t**, and
Rev 8: 5 And there were noises, **t**,
Rev 11:19 were lightnings, noises, **t**
Rev 16:18 And there were noises and **t**
Rev 19: 6 and as the sound of mighty **t**

Judg 21:24 departed from there at that **t**
1Sa 1: 4 And whenever the **t** came for
1Sa 1:20 of **t** that Hannah conceived
1Sa 3: 2 And it came to pass at that **t**
1Sa 3: 8 Samuel again the third **t**
1Sa 4:20 about the **t** of her death the
1Sa 7: 2 in Kirjath Jearim a long **t**
1Sa 9:13 for about this **t** you will
1Sa 9:16 Tomorrow about this **t** I will
1Sa 9:24 for until this **t** it has been
1Sa 11: 9 by the **t** the sun is hot, you
1Sa 13: 8 to the **t** set by Samuel
1Sa 14:18 of God here" (for at that **t**
1Sa 14:21 the Philistines before that **t**
1Sa 18:19 happened at the **t** when Merab
1Sa 18:21 Saul said to David a second **t**
1Sa 19:21 messengers again the third **t**
1Sa 20:35 at the **t** appointed with David
1Sa 22: 4 the **t** that David was in the
1Sa 25:16 all the **t** we were with them
1Sa 26: 8 have to strike him a second **t**
1Sa 27: 7 Now the **t** that David dwelt in
1Sa 27:11 **t** he dwelt in the country of
2Sa 2:11 the **t** that David was king in
2Sa 3:17 In **t** past you were seeking
2Sa 5: 2 in **t** past, when Saul was king
2Sa 7: 6 dwelt in a house since the **t**
2Sa 7:11 since the **t** that I commanded
2Sa 11: 1 at the **t** when kings go out to
2Sa 14: 2 a long **t** for the dead
2Sa 14:29 he sent again the second **t**
2Sa 17: 7 given is not good at this **t**
2Sa 20: 5 **t** which David had appointed
2Sa 23: 8 eight hundred men at one **t**
2Sa 23:13 men went down at harvest **t**
2Sa 24:15 morning till the appointed **t**
1Ki 1: 6 him at any **t** by saying, "Why
1Ki 2:26 put you to death at this **t**
1Ki 2:26 **t** my father was afflicted
1Ki 8:65 At that **t** Solomon held a
1Ki 9: 2 to Solomon the second **t**, as
1Ki 11:29 Now it happened at that **t**
1Ki 14: 1 At that **t** Abijah the son of
1Ki 15:23 But in the **t** of his old age
1Ki 18:29 the **t** of the offering of the
1Ki 18:34 Do it a second **t**
1Ki 18:34 and they did it a second **t**
1Ki 18:34 Do it a third **t**
1Ki 18:34 and they did it a third **t**
1Ki 18:36 at the **t** of the offering of
1Ki 18:44 it came to pass the seventh **t**
1Ki 19: 2 them by tomorrow about this **t**
1Ki 19: 7 LORD came back the second **t**
1Ki 20: 6 to you tomorrow about this **t**
1Ki 20: 9 servant the first **t** I will do
2Ki 3: 6 went out of Samaria at that **t**
2Ki 4:16 About this **t** next year you
2Ki 4:17 when the appointed **t** had come
2Ki 5:26 Is it **t** to receive money and
2Ki 7: 1 Tomorrow about this **t** a seah
2Ki 7:18 this **t** in the gate of Samaria
2Ki 8:22 And Libnah revolted at that **t**
2Ki 10: 6 at Jezreel by this **t** tomorrow
2Ki 16: 6 At that **t** Rezin king of Syria
2Ki 18:16 At that **t** Hezekiah stripped
2Ki 20:12 At that **t** Berodach-Baladan
2Ki 24:10 At that **t** the servants of
1Ch 9:20 officer over them in **t** past
1Ch 9:25 from **t** to **t** for seven days
1Ch 11: 2 in **t** past, even when Saul was
1Ch 11:11 killed by him at one **t**
1Ch 12:22 For at that **t** they came to
1Ch 15:13 you did not do it the first **t**
1Ch 17: 5 **t** that I brought up Israel
1Ch 17:10 since the **t** that I commanded
1Ch 20: 1 at the **t** kings go out to
1Ch 20: 4 at which **t** Sibbechai the
1Ch 21:28 At that **t**, when David saw
1Ch 21:29 were at that **t** at the high
1Ch 29:22 of David king the second **t**
2Ch 7: 8 At that **t** Solomon kept the
2Ch 13:18 Israel were subdued at that **t**
2Ch 15: 3 For a long **t** Israel has been
2Ch 15:11 at that **t** seven hundred bulls
2Ch 16: 7 at that **t** Hanani the seer
2Ch 16:10 some of the people at that **t**
2Ch 18:34 about the **t** of sunset he died
2Ch 21:10 At that **t** Libnah revolted
2Ch 21:19 happened in the course of **t**
2Ch 24:11 So it was, at that **t**, when
2Ch 25:27 After the **t** that Amaziah
2Ch 28:16 At the same **t** King Ahaz sent
2Ch 28:22 Now in the **t** of his distress
2Ch 30: 3 could not keep it at that **t**
2Ch 30: 5 **t** in the prescribed manner
2Ch 30:26 for since the **t** of Solomon
2Ch 35:17 kept the Passover at that **t**
Ezra 5: 3 At the same **t** Tattenai the
Ezra 5:16 from that **t** even until now it
Ezra 8:34 was written down at that **t**
Neh 2: 6 and I set him a **t**
Neh 4:16 So it was, from that **t** on
Neh 4:22 At the same **t** I also said to
Neh 5:14 from the **t** that I was
Neh 6: 1 left in it (though at that **t**
Neh 6: 5 to me as before, the fifth **t**
Neh 9:27 in the **t** of their trouble,
Neh 12:44 And at the same **t** some were
Neh 13:21 From that **t** on they came no
Esth 2:19 gathered together a second **t**
Esth 4:14 completely silent at this **t**
Esth 4:14 kingdom for such a **t** as this
Esth 8: 9 scribes were called at that **t**
Esth 9: 1 the **t** came for the king's
Esth 9:27 according to the prescribed **t**
Esth 9:31 of Purim at their appointed **t**
Job 7: 1 Is there not a **t** of hard
Job 9: 3 Him one **t** out of a thousand
Job 14:13 You would appoint me a set **t**
Job 15:32 be accomplished before his **t**
Job 22:16 were cut down before their **t**
Job 38:23 reserved for the **t** of trouble
Job 39: 1 Do you know the **t** when the
Job 39: 2 Or do you know the **t** when
Ps 21: 9 oven in the **t** of Your anger
Ps 27: 5 For in the **t** of trouble He
Ps 32: 6 In a **t** when You may be found
Ps 37:19 not be ashamed in the evil **t**
Ps 37:39 strength in the **t** of trouble
Ps 41: 1 deliver him in **t** of trouble
Ps 69:13 O LORD, in the acceptable **t**
Ps 71: 9 me off in the **t** of old age
Ps 75: 2 When I choose the proper **t**
Ps 78:38 many a **t** He turned His anger
Ps 81: 3 at the **t** of the New Moon, At
Ps 89:47 Remember how short my **t** is
Ps 102:13 For the **t** to favor her
Ps 102:13 Yes, the set **t**, has come
Ps 105:19 Until the **t** that his word
Ps 113: 2 of the LORD From this **t** forth
Ps 115:18 the LORD From this **t** forth
Ps 119:126 It is **t** for You to act, O
Ps 121: 8 coming in From this **t** forth
Ps 125: 2 His people From this **t** forth
Ps 129: 1 Many a **t** they have afflicted
Ps 129: 2 Many a **t** they have afflicted
Ps 131: 3 in the LORD From this **t** forth
Prov 25:13 in **t** of harvest is a faithful
Prov 25:19 in an unfaithful man in **t** of
Prov 31:25 shall rejoice in **t** to come
Eccl 3: 1 a **t** for every purpose under
Eccl 3: 2 **t** to be born, and a **t** to die
Eccl 3: 2 a **t** to plant
Eccl 3: 2 a **t** to pluck what is planted
Eccl 3: 3 a **t** to kill, and a **t** to heal
Eccl 3: 3 a **t** to break down
Eccl 3: 3 and a **t** to build up
Eccl 3: 4 **t** to weep, and a **t** to laugh
Eccl 3: 4 **t** to mourn, and a **t** to dance
Eccl 3: 5 a **t** to cast away stones
Eccl 3: 5 and a **t** to gather stones
Eccl 3: 5 a **t** to embrace
Eccl 3: 5 a **t** to refrain from embracing
Eccl 3: 6 a **t** to gain, and a **t** to lose
Eccl 3: 6 a **t** to lose; a **t** to keep
Eccl 3: 7 a **t** to tear, and a **t** to sew
Eccl 3: 7 a **t** to keep silence
Eccl 3: 7 and a **t** to speak
Eccl 3: 8 **t** to love, and a **t** to hate
Eccl 3: 8 **t** of war, and a **t** of peace
Eccl 3:11 everything beautiful in its **t**
Eccl 3:17 for there shall be a **t** there
Eccl 7:17 should you die before your **t**
Eccl 8: 5 man's heart discerns both **t**
Eccl 8: 6 for every matter there is a **t**
Eccl 8: 9 There is a **t** in which one man
Eccl 9:11 but **t** and chance happen to
Eccl 9:12 man also does not know his **t**
Eccl 9:12 men are snared in an evil **t**
Eccl 10:17 princes feast at the proper **t**
Song 2:12 the **t** of singing has come, and
Is 9: 7 justice from that **t** forward
Is 11:11 **t** to recover the remnant of
Is 13:22 Her **t** is near to come, and her
Is 16:13 concerning Moab since that **t**
Is 18: 7 In that **t** a present will be
Is 20: 2 at the same **t** the LORD spoke
Is 26:17 near the **t** of her delivery
Is 30: 8 that it may be for **t** to come
Is 33: 2 also in the **t** of trouble
Is 39: 1 At that **t** Merodach-Baladan
Is 41:27 The first **t** I said to Zion
Is 42:14 I have held My peace a long **t**
Is 42:23 and hear for the **t** to come
Is 44: 8 I not told you from that **t**
Is 45:21 declared this from ancient **t**
Is 45:21 Who has told it from that **t**
Is 48: 6 hear new things from this **t**
Is 48:16 from the **t** that it was, I was
Is 49: 8 acceptable **t** I have heard You
Is 59:21 from this **t** and forevermore
Is 60:22 LORD, will hasten it in its **t**
Is 66: 9 I bring to the **t** of birth
Jer 1:13 LORD came to me the second **t**
Jer 2:24 in her **t** of mating, who can
Jer 2:27 But in the **t** of their trouble
Jer 2:28 you in the **t** of your trouble
Jer 3: 4 you not from this **t** cry to Me
Jer 3:17 At that **t** Jerusalem shall be
Jer 4:11 At that **t** it will be said to
Jer 6:15 at the **t** I punish them, they
Jer 8: 1 At that **t**," says the LORD
Jer 8: 7 observe the **t** of their coming
Jer 8:12 in the **t** of their punishment
Jer 8:15 for a **t** of health, and there
Jer 10:15 in the **t** of their punishment
Jer 10:18 I will throw out at this **t**
Jer 11:12 all in the **t** of their trouble
Jer 11:14 the **t** that they cry out to Me
Jer 13: 3 LORD came to me the second **t**
Jer 14: 8 his Savior in **t** of trouble
Jer 14:19 and for the **t** of healing, and
Jer 15:11 you in the **t** of adversity
Jer 15:11 and in the **t** of affliction
Jer 18:23 them in the **t** of Your anger
Jer 27: 7 until the **t** of his land comes
Jer 30: 7 and it is the **t** of Jacob's
Jer 31: 1 At the same **t**," says the
Jer 33: 1 came to Jeremiah a second **t**
Jer 33:15 at that **t** I will cause to
Jer 39:10 and fields at the same **t**
Jer 46:17 has passed by the appointed **t**
Jer 46:21 the **t** of their punishment
Jer 49: 8 the **t** that I will punish him
Jer 50: 4 In those days and in that **t**
Jer 50:16 the sickle at harvest **t**
Jer 50:20 In those days and in that **t**
Jer 50:27 the **t** of their punishment
Jer 50:31 the **t** that I will punish you
Jer 51: 6 for this is the **t** of the
Jer 51:18 in the **t** of their punishment
Jer 51:33 when it is **t** to thresh her
Jer 51:33 the **t** of her harvest will
Lam 3: 3 turned His hand against me **t**
Lam 3: 3 **t** again throughout the day
Lam 5:20 and forsake us for so long a **t**
Ezek 4:10 from **t** to **t** you shall eat
Ezek 4:11 from **t** to **t** you shall
Ezek 7: 7 The **t** has come, a day of
Ezek 7:12 The **t** has come, the day draws
Ezek 11: 3 The **t** is not near to build
Ezek 16: 8 your **t** was the **t** of love
Ezek 16:57 It was like the **t** of the
Ezek 21:14 The third **t** let the sword do
Ezek 22: 3 midst, that her **t** may come
Ezek 30: 3 clouds, the **t** of the Gentiles
Ezek 35: 5 at the **t** of their calamity
Ezek 38:18 come to pass at the same **t**
Dan 1: 5 so that at the end of that **t**
Dan 2: 8 certain that you would gain **t**
Dan 2: 9 me till the **t** has changed
Dan 2:16 asked the king to give him **t**
Dan 3: 5 that at the **t** you hear the
Dan 3: 7 So at that **t**, when all the
Dan 3: 8 Therefore at that **t** certain
Dan 3:15 **t** you hear the sound of the
Dan 4:19 was astonished for a **t**, and
Dan 4:34 And at the end of the **t** I,
Dan 4:36 At the same **t** my reason
Dan 7:12 prolonged for a season and a **t**

Dan 7:22 the t came for the saints to
Dan 7:25 a t and times and half a t
Dan 8: 1 appeared to me the first t
Dan 8:17 refers to the t of the end
Dan 8:19 latter t of the indignation
Dan 8:19 appointed t the end shall be
Dan 8:23 And in the latter t of their
Dan 9:21 reached me about the t of the
Dan 10: 1 but the appointed t was long
Dan 11:24 strongholds, but only for a t
Dan 11:27 still be at the appointed t
Dan 11:29 appointed t he shall return
Dan 11:35 white, until the t of the end
Dan 11:35 is still for the appointed t
Dan 11:40 At the t of the end the king
Dan 12: 1 At that t Michael shall stand
Dan 12: 1 there shall be a t of trouble
Dan 12: 1 was a nation, even to that t
Dan 12: 1 at that t your people shall
Dan 12: 4 book until the t of the end
Dan 12: 7 a t, times, and half a t
Dan 12: 9 sealed till the t of the end
Dan 12:11 from the t that the daily
Hos 2: 9 take away my grain in its t
Hos 10:12 for it is t to seek the LORD,
Joel 3: 1 in those days and at that t
Amos 5:13 prudent keep silent at that t
Amos 5:13 for it is an evil t
Jon 3: 1 came to Jonah the second t
Mic 2: 3 for this is an evil t
Mic 3: 4 His face from them at that t
Mic 5: 3 until the t that she who is
Nah 1: 9 will not rise up a second t
Hab 2: 3 is yet for an appointed t
Zeph 1:12 at that t that I will search
Zeph 3:19 at that t I will deal with
Zeph 3:20 At that t I will bring you
Zeph 3:20 even at the t I gather you
Hag 1: 2 The t has not come
Hag 1: 2 the t that the LORD's house
Hag 1: 4 Is it t for you yourselves to
Zech 10: 1 in the t of the latter rain
Zech 14: 7 But at evening t it shall
Matt 1:11 his brothers about the t they
Matt 2: 7 them what t the star appeared
Matt 2:16 according to the t which he
Matt 4:17 From that t Jesus began to
Matt 8:29 to torment us before the t
Matt 11:25 At that t Jesus answered and
Matt 12: 1 At that t Jesus went through
Matt 13:30 at the t of harvest I will
Matt 14: 1 At that t Herod the tetrarch
Matt 16:21 From that t Jesus began to
Matt 18: 1 At that t the disciples came
Matt 24:21 of the world until this t
Matt 25:19 After a long t the lord of
Matt 26:16 So from that t he sought
Matt 26:18 says, "My t is at hand
Matt 26:42 He went away again a second t
Matt 26:44 again, and prayed the third t
Mark 1:15 The t is fulfilled, and the
Mark 4:17 and so endure only for a t
Mark 6:31 did not even have t to eat
Mark 10:30 a hundredfold now in this t
Mark 13:19 God created until this t, nor
Mark 13:33 you do not know when the t is
Mark 14:41 Then He came the third t and
Mark 14:72 a second t the rooster crowed
Mark 15:44 He had been dead for some t
Luke 1:20 be fulfilled in their own t
Luke 1:57 full t came for her to be
Luke 4: 5 of the world in a moment of t
Luke 4:13 from Him until an opportune t
Luke 4:27 the t of Elisha the prophet
Luke 7:45 My feet since the t I came in
Luke 8:13 in t of temptation fall away
Luke 8:27 who had demons for a long t
Luke 9:51 when the t had come for Him
Luke 12:56 it you do not discern this t
Luke 13:35 the t comes when you say
Luke 14:17 t to say to those who were
Luke 15:29 your commandment at any t
Luke 16:16 Since that t the kingdom of
Luke 18:30 times more in this present t
Luke 19:44 know the t of your visitation
Luke 20: 9 a far country for a long t
Luke 21: 8 and, 'The t has drawn near
Luke 23: 7 also in Jerusalem at that t
Luke 23: 8 for a long t to see Him,
Luke 23:22 he said to them the third t

John 1:18 No one has seen God at any t
John 3: 4 Can he enter a second t into
John 5: 4 at a certain t into the pool
John 5: 6 in that condition a long t
John 5:35 you were willing for a t to
John 5:37 heard His voice at any t, nor
John 6:66 From that t many of His
John 7: 6 My t has not yet come, but
John 7: 6 but your t is always ready
John 7: 8 for My t has not yet fully
John 11:39 by this t there is a stench,
John 16: 2 the t is coming that whoever
John 16: 4 you, that when the t comes
John 16:25 but the t is coming when I
John 21:14 This is now the third t Jesus
John 21:16 said to him again a second t
John 21:17 He said to him the third t
John 21:17 He said to him the third t
Acts 1: 6 will You at this t restore
Acts 1:21 t that the Lord Jesus went in
Acts 5:36 For some t ago Theudas rose
Acts 7:13 the second t Joseph was made
Acts 7:17 But when the t of the promise
Acts 7:20 At this t Moses was born, and
Acts 8: 1 At that t a great persecution
Acts 8:11 his sorceries for a long t
Acts 10:15 to him again the second t
Acts 11: 8 has at any t entered my mouth
Acts 12: 1 Now about that t Herod the
Acts 13:11 not seeing the sun for a t
Acts 13:18 Now for a t of about forty
Acts 14: 3 they stayed there a long t
Acts 14:28 a long t with the disciples
Acts 15:33 they had stayed there for a t
Acts 17:21 t in nothing else but either
Acts 18:20 to stay a longer t with them
Acts 18:23 he had spent some t there
Acts 19:22 stayed in Asia for a t
Acts 19:23 about that t there arose a
Acts 20:16 not have to spend t in Asia
Acts 21:26 at which t an offering should
Acts 21:38 not the Egyptian who some t
Acts 24:25 t I will call for you
Acts 27: 9 Now when much t had been
Acts 28: 6 they had looked for a long t
Rom 3:26 present t His righteousness
Rom 5: 6 in due t Christ died for the
Rom 8:18 t are not worthy to be
Rom 9: 9 At this t I will come and
Rom 11: 5 at this present t there is a
Rom 13:11 And do this, knowing the t
Rom 13:11 that now it is high t to
1Co 4: 5 judge nothing before the t
1Co 7: 5 except with consent for a t
1Co 7:29 the t is short, so that from
1Co 15: 8 as by one born out of due t
1Co 16:12 unwilling to come at this t
1Co 16:12 when he has a convenient t
2Co 6: 2 acceptable t I have heard you
2Co 6: 2 Behold, now is the accepted t
2Co 8:14 that now at this t your
2Co 9: 5 to go to you ahead of t, and
2Co 12:14 Now for the third t I am
2Co 13: 1 third t I am coming to you
2Co 13: 2 I were present the second t
Gal 4: 2 and stewards until the t
Gal 4: 4 fullness of the t had come
Gal 5:21 as I also told you in t past
Eph 2:12 that at that t you were
Eph 5:16 redeeming the t, because the
Col 4: 5 are outside, redeeming the t
1Th 2: 5 For neither at any t did we
1Th 2:17 you for a short t in presence
1Th 2:18 even I, Paul, t and again
2Th 2: 6 may be revealed in his own t
1Ti 2: 6 all, to be testified in due t
1Ti 6:15 He will manifest in His own t
1Ti 6:19 foundation for the t to come
2Ti 1: 9 Christ Jesus before t began
2Ti 4: 3 For the t will come when they
2Ti 4: 6 the t of my departure is at
Tit 1: 2 lie, promised before t began
Tit 1: 3 but has in due t manifested
Heb 1: 1 t past to the fathers by the
Heb 4: 7 Today," after such a long t
Heb 4:16 grace to help in t of need
Heb 5:12 For though by this t you
Heb 9: 9 present t in which both gifts
Heb 9:10 until the t of reformation
Heb 9:28 Him He will appear a second t

Heb 10:13 from that t waiting till His
Heb 11:32 For the t would fail me to
Jas 4:14 that appears for a little t
1Pe 1: 5 to be revealed in the last t
1Pe 1:11 what, or what manner of t
1Pe 1:17 yourselves throughout the t
1Pe 4: 2 t in the flesh for the lusts
1Pe 4:17 For the t has come for
1Pe 5: 6 He may exalt you in due t
2Pe 2: 3 for a long t their judgment
1Jn 4:12 No one has seen God at any t
Jude 18 be mockers in the last t who
Rev 1: 3 for the t is near
Rev 2:21 I gave her t to repent of her
Rev 11:18 the t of the dead, that they
Rev 12:12 knows that he has a short t
Rev 12:14 a t and times and half a t
Rev 14:15 for the t has come for You to
Rev 17:10 he must continue a short t
Rev 22:10 book, for the t is at hand

TIMES (*see* TIME)
Gen 27:36 has supplanted me these two t
Gen 31: 7 me and changed my wages ten t
Gen 31:41 have changed my wages ten t
Gen 33: 3 himself to the ground seven t
Gen 43:34 t as much as any of theirs
Ex 18:22 judge the people at all t
Ex 18:26 judged the people at all t
Ex 21:29 with its horn in t past, and
Ex 23:14 Three t you shall keep a
Ex 23:17 Three t in the year all your
Ex 34:23 Three t in the year all your
Ex 34:24 your God three t in the year
Lev 4: 6 blood seven t before the LORD
Lev 4:17 it seven t before the LORD
Lev 8:11 of it on the altar seven t
Lev 14: 7 seven t on him who is to be
Lev 14:16 seven t before the LORD
Lev 14:27 hand seven t before the LORD
Lev 14:51 and sprinkle the house seven t
Lev 16:14 blood with his finger seven t
Lev 16:19 on it with his finger seven t
Lev 23: 4 proclaim at their appointed t
Lev 25: 8 yourself, seven t seven years
Lev 26:18 seven t more for your sins
Lev 26:21 on you seven t more plagues
Lev 26:24 you yet seven t for your sins
Lev 26:28 you seven t for your sins
Num 14:22 to the test now these ten t
Num 19: 4 some of its blood seven t
Num 22:28 have struck me these three t
Num 22:32 your donkey these three t
Num 22:33 aside from Me these three t
Num 24: 1 he did not go as at other t
Num 24:10 blessed them these three t
Deut 1:11 t more numerous than you are
Deut 2:10 had dwelt there in t past
Deut 16:16 Three t a year all your males
Josh 6: 4 march around the city seven t
Josh 6:15 seven t in the same manner
Josh 6:15 around the city seven t
Josh 24: 2 side of the River in old t
Judg 16:15 have mocked me these three t
Judg 16:20 go out as before, at other t
Judg 20:30 Gibeah as at the other t
Judg 20:31 the people, as at the other t
Ruth 4: 7 former t in Israel concerning
1Sa 3:10 stood and called as at other t
1Sa 18:10 with his hand, as at other t
1Sa 19: 7 in his presence as in t past
1Sa 20:25 on his seat, as at other t
1Sa 20:41 ground, and bowed down three t
2Sa 20:18 They used to talk in former t
1Ki 9:25 Now three t a year Solomon
1Ki 17:21 out on the child three t, and
1Ki 18:43 And seven t he said,
1Ki 22:16 How many t shall I make you
2Ki 4:35 the child sneezed seven t
2Ki 5:10 and wash in the Jordan seven t
2Ki 5:14 dipped seven t in the Jordan,
2Ki 13:18 so he struck three t, and
2Ki 13:19 have struck five or six t
2Ki 13:19 strike Syria only three t
2Ki 13:25 Three t Joash defeated him and
2Ki 19:25 From ancient t that I formed
1Ch 12:32 had understanding of the t
1Ch 21: 3 hundred t more than they are
2Ch 15: 5 in those t there was no peace
2Ch 18:15 How many t shall I make you
Ezra 4:15 within the city in former t

Ezra 4:19 **t** has made insurrection
Ezra 10:14 wives come at appointed **t**
Neh 4:12 came, that they told us ten **t**
Neh 6: 4 sent me this message four **t**
Neh 9:28 many **t** You delivered them
Neh 10:34 the appointed **t** year by year
Neh 13:31 firstfruits at appointed **t**
Esth 1:13 **t** (for this was the king's
Job 19: 3 These ten **t** you have
Job 24: 1 Since **t** are not hidden from
Job 33:29 in fact, three **t** with a man,
Ps 9: 9 A refuge in **t** of trouble
Ps 10: 1 hide Yourself in **t** of trouble
Ps 12: 6 of earth, Purified seven **t**
Ps 31:15 My **t** are in Your hand
Ps 34: 1 will bless the LORD at all **t**
Ps 62: 8 Trust in Him at all **t**, you
Ps 77: 5 old, The years of ancient **t**
Ps 106: 3 does righteousness at all **t**
Ps 106:43 Many **t** He delivered them
Ps 119:20 For Your judgments at all **t**
Ps 119:164 Seven **t** a day I praise You,
Prov 5:19 breasts satisfy you at all **t**
Prov 7:12 At **t** she was outside,
Prov 7:12 at **t** in the open square,
Prov 17:17 A friend loves at all **t**, and a
Prov 24:16 man may fall seven **t** and rise
Eccl 1:10 been in ancient **t** before us
Eccl 7:22 For many **t**, also, your own
Eccl 8:12 sinner does evil a hundred **t**
Is 14:31 be alone in his appointed **t**
Is 33: 6 be the stability of your **t**
Is 37:26 from ancient **t** that I formed
Is 41:26 and former **t**, that we may say,
Is 46:10 from ancient **t** things that
Jer 8: 7 heavens knows her appointed **t**
Ezek 12:27 and he prophesies of **t** far off
Ezek 36:11 you inhabited as in former **t**
Dan 1:20 he found them ten **t** better
Dan 2:21 And He changes the **t** and the
Dan 3:19 **t** more than it was usually
Dan 4:16 let seven **t** pass over him
Dan 4:23 till seven **t** pass over him'
Dan 4:25 seven **t** shall pass over you,
Dan 4:32 seven **t** shall pass over you,
Dan 6:10 on his knees three **t** that day
Dan 6:13 his petition three **t** a day
Dan 7:10 ten thousand **t** ten thousand
Dan 7:25 and shall intend to change **t**
Dan 7:25 into his hand for a time and **t**
Dan 9:25 wall, even in troublesome **t**
Dan 11: 6 strengthened her in those **t**
Dan 11:14 in those **t** many shall rise up
Dan 12: 7 it shall be for a time, **t**
Matt 16: 3 discern the signs of the **t**
Matt 18:21 Up to seven **t**
Matt 18:22 not say to you, up to seven **t**
Matt 18:22 but up to seventy **t** seven
Matt 26:34 you will deny Me three **t**
Matt 26:75 you will deny Me three **t**
Mark 14:30 you will deny Me three **t**
Mark 14:72 you will deny Me three **t**
Luke 17: 4 against you seven **t** in a day
Luke 17: 4 seven **t** in a day returns to
Luke 18:30 **t** more in this present time
Luke 21:24 the **t** of the Gentiles are
Luke 22:34 deny three **t** that you know Me
Luke 22:61 you will deny Me three **t**
John 13:38 you have denied Me three **t**
Acts 1: 7 It is not for you to know **t**
Acts 3:19 so that **t** of refreshing may
Acts 3:21 the **t** of restoration of all
Acts 10:16 This was done three **t**
Acts 11:10 Now this was done three **t**
Acts 17:26 their preappointed **t** and the
Acts 17:30 these **t** of ignorance God
2Co 11:24 From the Jews five **t** I
2Co 11:25 Three **t** I was beaten with
2Co 11:25 three **t** I was shipwrecked
2Co 12: 8 **t** that it might depart from
Eph 1:10 of the fullness of the **t** He
1Th 5: 1 But concerning the **t** and the
1Ti 4: 1 says that in latter **t** some
2Ti 3: 1 days perilous **t** will come
Heb 1: 1 God, who at various **t** and in
1Pe 1:20 in these last **t** for you
1Pe 3: 5 in this manner, in former **t**
Rev 5:11 ten thousand **t** ten thousand
Rev 12:14 is nourished for a time and **t**

TIMNA (*see* TIMNAH)
Gen 36:12 Now **T** was the concubine of
Gen 36:22 Lotan's sister was **T**
1Ch 1:36 and by **T**, Amalek
1Ch 1:39 Lotan's sister was **T**

TIMNAH (*see* TIMNA, TIMNATH, TIMNITE)
Gen 36:40 Chief **T**, Chief Alvah, Chief
Gen 38:12 up to his sheepshearers at **T**
Gen 38:13 is going up to **T** to shear his
Gen 38:14 which was on the way to **T**
Josh 15:10 Shemesh, and passed on to **T**
Josh 15:57 Kain, Gibeah, and **T**
Josh 19:43 Elon, **T**, Ekron,
Judg 14: 1 Now Samson went down to **T**
Judg 14: 1 and saw a woman in **T** of the
Judg 14: 2 I have seen a woman in **T** of
Judg 14: 5 down to **T** with his father
Judg 14: 5 and came to the vineyards of **T**
1Ch 1:51 chiefs of Edom were Chief **T**
2Ch 28:18 **T** with its villages, and Gimzo

TIMNATH HERES (*see* HERES, TIMNATH, TIMNATH SERAH)
Judg 2: 9 of his inheritance at **T**, in

TIMNATH SERAH (*see* SERAH, TIMNATH HERES)
Josh 19:50 **T** in the mountains of Ephraim
Josh 24:30 of his inheritance at **T**,

TIMNITE (*see* TIMNAH)
Judg 15: 6 the son-in-law of the **T**,

TIMON
Acts 6: 5 Philip, Prochorus, Nicanor, **T**

TIMOTHY
Acts 16: 1 disciple was there, named **T**
Acts 17:14 Silas and **T** remained there
Acts 17:15 **T** to come to him with all
Acts 18: 5 **T** had come from Macedonia,
Acts 19:22 who ministered to him, **T** and
Acts 20: 4 and Gaius of Derbe, and **T**, and
Rom 16:21 **T**, my fellow worker, and
1Co 4:17 reason I have sent **T** to you
1Co 16:10 Now if **T** comes, see that he
2Co 1: 1 **T** our brother, To the church
2Co 1:19 by me, Silvanus, and **T**
Phil 1: 1 Paul and **T**, servants of Jesus
Phil 2:19 to send **T** to you shortly,
Col 1: 1 of God, and **T** our brother,
1Th 1: 1 Paul, Silvanus, and **T**, To the
1Th 3: 2 and sent **T**, our brother and
1Th 3: 6 But now that **T** has come to us
2Th 1: 1 Paul, Silvanus, and **T**, To the
1Ti 1: 2 To **T**, my true son in the
1Ti 1:18 charge I commit to you, son **T**
1Ti 6:20 **T**! Guard what was committed
2Ti 1: 2 To **T**, my beloved son
Phm 1 **T** our brother, To Philemon
Heb 13:23 brother **T** has been set free

TIN
Num 31:22 the bronze, the iron, the **t**
Ezek 22:18 they are all bronze, **t**, iron,
Ezek 22:20 **t** into the midst of a furnace
Ezek 27:12 They gave you silver, iron, **t**

TINDER
Is 1:31 The strong shall be as **t**, and

TINGLE
1Sa 3:11 everyone who hears it will **t**
2Ki 21:12 of it, both his ears will **t**
Jer 19: 3 hears of it, his ears will **t**

TIP (*see* TIPS)
Ex 29:20 put it on the **t** of the right
Ex 29:20 on the **t** of the right ear of
Lev 8:23 put it on the **t** of Aaron's
Lev 14:14 priest shall put it on the **t**
Lev 14:17 shall put some on the **t** of
Lev 14:25 put it on the **t** of the right
Lev 14:28 that is in his hand on the **t**
1Ki 6:24 ten cubits from the **t** of one
1Ki 6:24 wing to the **t** of the other
Jer 48:12 who will **t** him over and empty
Luke 16:24 the **t** of his finger in water

TIPHSAH
1Ki 4:24 the River from **T** even to Gaza
2Ki 15:16 Tirzah, Menahem attacked **T**

TIPS (*see* TIP)
Lev 8:24 on the **t** of their right ears

TIRAS
Gen 10: 2 Javan, Tubal, Meshech, and **T**
1Ch 1: 5 Javan, Tubal, Meshech, and **T**

TIRATHITES
1Ch 2:55 who dwelt at Jabez were the **T**

TIRED
Deut 25:18 at your rear, when you were **t**

TIRHAKAH
2Ki 19: 9 concerning **T** king of Ethiopia
Is 37: 9 concerning **T** king of Ethiopia

TIRHANAH
1Ch 2:48 concubine, bore Sheber and **T**

TIRIA
1Ch 4:16 were Ziph, Ziphah, **T**, and

TIRZAH
Num 26:33 Noah, Hoglah, Milcah, and **T**
Num 27: 1 Noah, Hoglah, Milcah, and **T**
Num 36:11 for Mahlah, **T**, Hoglah, Milcah
Josh 12:24 the king of **T**, one
Josh 17: 3 Noah, Hoglah, Milcah, and **T**
1Ki 14:17 and departed, and came to **T**
1Ki 15:21 Ramah, and remained in **T**
1Ki 15:33 king over all Israel in **T**
1Ki 16: 6 fathers and was buried in **T**
1Ki 16: 8 and reigned two years in **T**
1Ki 16: 9 against him as he was in **T**
1Ki 16: 9 steward of his house in **T**
1Ki 16:15 had reigned in **T** seven days
1Ki 16:17 Gibbethon, and they besieged **T**
1Ki 16:23 Six years he reigned in **T**
2Ki 15:14 son of Gadi went up from **T**
2Ki 15:16 Then from **T**, Menahem
Song 6: 4 you are as beautiful as **T**

TISHBITE
1Ki 17: 1 And Elijah the **T**, of the
1Ki 21:17 the LORD came to Elijah the **T**
1Ki 21:28 the LORD came to Elijah the **T**
2Ki 1: 3 the LORD said to Elijah the **T**
2Ki 1: 8 It is Elijah the **T**
2Ki 9:36 by His servant Elijah the **T**

TITHE (*see* TITHES, TITHING)
Gen 14:20 And he gave him a **t** of all
Lev 27:30 And all the **t** of the land,
Lev 27:32 concerning the **t** of the herd
Num 18:26 to the LORD, a tenth of the **t**
Deut 12:17 **t** of your grain or your new
Deut 14:22 You shall truly **t** all the
Deut 14:23 the **t** of your grain and your
Deut 14:24 are not able to carry the **t**
Deut 14:28 the **t** of your produce of that
Deut 26:12 laying aside all the **t** of
Deut 26:13 the holy **t** from my house, and
2Ch 31: 5 the **t** of everything
2Ch 31: 6 Judah, brought the **t** of oxen
2Ch 31: 6 also the **t** of holy things
Neh 13:12 brought the **t** of the grain
Matt 23:23 For you pay **t** of mint and
Luke 11:42 For you **t** mint and rue and all

TITHES (*see* TITHE)
Lev 27:31 at all to redeem any of his **t**
Num 18:21 children of Levi all the **t** in
Num 18:24 For the **t** of the children of
Num 18:26 the children of Israel the **t**
Num 18:28 to the LORD from all your **t**
Deut 12: 6 your sacrifices, your **t**, the
Deut 12:11 your sacrifices, your **t**, the
2Ch 31:12 in the offerings, the **t**, and
Neh 10:37 to bring the **t** of our land to
Neh 10:37 the **t** in all our farming
Neh 10:38 when the Levites receive **t**
Neh 10:38 the **t** to the house of our God
Neh 12:44 the firstfruits, and the **t**
Neh 13: 5 the **t** of grain, the new wine
Amos 4: 4 your **t** every three days
Mal 3: 8 In **t** and offerings
Mal 3:10 Bring all the **t** into the
Luke 18:12 I give **t** of all that I
Heb 7: 5 a commandment to receive **t**
Heb 7: 6 them received **t** from Abraham
Heb 7: 8 Here mortal men receive **t**
Heb 7: 9 Even Levi, who receives **t**
Heb 7: 9 paid **t** through Abraham, so to

TITHING (*see* TITHE)
Deut 26:12 year, which is the year of **t**

TITLE
John 19:19 Now Pilate wrote a **t** and put
John 19:20 many of the Jews read this **t**

TITTLE
Matt 5:18 one jot or one **t** will by no
Luke 16:17 for one **t** of the law to fail

TITUS
2Co 2:13 I did not find **T** my brother
2Co 7: 6 us by the coming of **T**,
2Co 7:13 more for the joy of **T**,
2Co 7:14 boasting to **T** was found true
2Co 8: 6 So we urged **T**, that as he had
2Co 8:16 for you into the heart of **T**
2Co 8:23 If anyone inquires about **T**
2Co 12:18 I urged **T**, and sent our
2Co 12:18 Did **T** take advantage of you
Gal 2: 1 and also took **T** with me
Gal 2: 3 Yet not even **T** who was with
2Ti 4:10 for Galatia, **T** for Dalmatia
Tit 1: 4 To **T**, my true son in our

TIZITE
1Ch 11:45 and Joha his brother, the **T**

TO (*see* PREFACE)

TOAH (*see* TOHU)
1Ch 6:34 son of Eliel, the son of **T**

TOB (*see* ISH-TOB, TOBADONIJAH)
Judg 11: 3 and dwelt in the land of **T**
Judg 11: 5 Jephthah from the land of **T**

TOBADONIJAH (*see* TOB)
2Ch 17: 8 Adonijah, Tobijah, and **T**

TOBIAH (*see* TOBIJAH)
Ezra 2:60 of Delaiah, the sons of **T**
Neh 2:10 **T** the Ammonite official heard
Neh 2:19 **T** the Ammonite official, and
Neh 4: 3 Now **T** the Ammonite was
Neh 4: 7 happened, when Sanballat, **T**
Neh 6: 1 it happened when Sanballat, **T**
Neh 6:12 prophecy against me because **T**
Neh 6:14 My God, remember **T** and
Neh 6:17 Judah sent many letters to **T**
Neh 6:17 the letters of **T** came to them
Neh 6:19 **T** sent letters to frighten me
Neh 7:62 of Delaiah, the children of **T**
Neh 13: 4 of our God, was allied with **T**
Neh 13: 7 that Eliashib had done for **T**
Neh 13: 8 goods of **T** out of the room

TOBIJAH (*see* TOBIAH)
2Ch 17: 8 Jehonathan, Adonijah, **T**, and
Zech 6:10 from Heldai, **T**, and Jedaiah,
Zech 6:14 of the LORD for Helem, **T**,

TOCHEN
1Ch 4:32 were Etam, Ain, Rimmon, **T**

TODAY (*see* TODAY'S)
Gen 21:26 nor had I heard of it until **t**
Gen 30:32 pass through all your flock **t**
Gen 40: 7 Why do you look so sad **t**
Gen 42:13 youngest is with our father **t**
Ex 2:18 that you have come so soon **t**
Ex 5:14 brick both yesterday and **t**
Ex 14:13 He will accomplish for you **t**
Ex 14:13 the Egyptians whom you see **t**
Ex 16:23 Bake what you will bake **t**
Ex 16:25 Eat that **t**, for **t** is a
Ex 16:25 **t** you will not find it in the
Ex 19:10 the people and sanctify them **t**
Ex 32:29 yourselves **t** to the LORD,
Lev 9: 4 for **t** the LORD will appear to
Lev 10:19 had eaten the sin offering **t**
Deut 1:10 you, and here you are **t**, as
Deut 1:39 who **t** have no knowledge of
Deut 4: 4 the LORD your God are alive **t**
Deut 4:40 which I command you **t**, that
Deut 5: 1 I speak in your hearing **t**
Deut 5: 3 with us, those who are here **t**
Deut 6: 6 you **t** shall be in your heart
Deut 7:11 which I command you **t**, to
Deut 8: 1 which I command you **t** you
Deut 8:11 which I command you **t**,
Deut 9: 1 to cross over the Jordan **t**
Deut 9: 3 Therefore understand **t** that
Deut 10:13 I command you **t** for your good
Deut 11: 2 Know **t** that I do not speak
Deut 11: 8 which I command you **t**, that
Deut 11:13 which I command you **t**, to
Deut 11:26 I set before you **t** a blessing
Deut 11:27 God which I command you **t**
Deut 11:28 the way which I command you **t**
Deut 11:32 which I set before you **t**
Deut 12: 8 all do as we are doing here **t**
Deut 13:18 which I command you **t**, to do
Deut 15: 5 which I command you **t**
Deut 15:15 I command you this thing **t**
Deut 19: 9 them, which I command you **t**
Deut 20: 3 **T** you are on the verge of
Deut 26: 3 I declare **t** to the LORD your
Deut 26:17 **T** you have proclaimed the
Deut 26:18 Also **t** the LORD has
Deut 27: 1 which I command you **t**
Deut 27: 4 stones, which I command you **t**
Deut 27:10 which I command you **t**
Deut 28: 1 which I command you **t**, that
Deut 28:13 God, which I command you **t**
Deut 28:15 which I command you **t**, that
Deut 29:10 All of you stand **t** before the
Deut 29:12 your God makes with you **t**
Deut 29:13 you **t** as a people for Himself
Deut 29:15 us **t** before the LORD our God
Deut 29:15 him who is not here with us **t**
Deut 29:18 away **t** from the LORD our God
Deut 30: 2 to all that I command you **t**
Deut 30: 8 which I command you **t**
Deut 30:11 which I command you **t**, it is
Deut 30:15 I have set before you **t** life
Deut 30:16 in that I command you **t** to
Deut 30:18 I announce to you **t** that you
Deut 30:19 as witnesses **t** against you
Deut 31: 2 hundred and twenty years old **t**
Deut 31:21 of their behavior **t**, even
Deut 31:27 If **t**, while I am yet alive
Deut 32:46 which I testify among you **t**
Josh 22:18 if you rebel **t** against the
Judg 21: 3 that **t** there should be one
Judg 21: 6 is cut off from Israel **t**
Ruth 2:19 Where have you gleaned **t**
Ruth 2:19 with whom I worked **t** is Boaz
1Sa 4: 3 us **t** before the Philistines
1Sa 4:16 I fled **t** from the battle line
1Sa 9:12 for **t** he came to this city,
1Sa 9:12 people **t** on the high place
1Sa 9:19 for you shall eat with me **t**
1Sa 10: 2 you have departed from me **t**
1Sa 10:19 But you have **t** rejected your
1Sa 11:13 this day, for **t** the LORD has
1Sa 12:17 Is **t** not the wheat harvest
1Sa 14:30 **t** of the spoil of their
1Sa 14:38 and see what this sin was **t**
1Sa 15:28 kingdom of Israel from you **t**
1Sa 18:21 You shall be my son-in-law **t**
1Sa 20:27 to eat, either yesterday or **t**
1Sa 24:10 **t** into my hand in the cave
1Sa 26:23 delivered you into my hand **t**
1Sa 27:10 Where have you made a raid **t**
2Sa 3: 8 **T** I show loyalty to the house
2Sa 3: 8 you charge me **t** with a fault
2Sa 3:39 And I am weak **t**, though
2Sa 6:20 was the king of Israel **t**,
2Sa 6:20 uncovering himself **t** in the
2Sa 11:12 Wait here **t** also, and tomorrow
2Sa 14:22 **T** your servant knows that I
2Sa 15:20 wander up and down with us **t**
2Sa 16: 3 **T** the house of Israel will
2Sa 18:20 But **t** you shall take no news,
2Sa 19: 5 **T** you have disgraced all your
2Sa 19: 5 who **t** have saved your life
2Sa 19: 6 For you have declared **t** that
2Sa 19: 6 for **t** I perceive that if
2Sa 19: 6 lived and all of us had died **t**
2Sa 19:20 the first to come **t** of all
2Sa 19:22 should be adversaries to me **t**
2Sa 19:22 be put to death **t** in Israel
2Sa 19:22 that **t** I am king over Israel
2Sa 19:35 I am **t** eighty years old
1Ki 1:25 For he has gone down **t**, and
1Ki 1:51 me **t** that he will not put his
1Ki 2:24 shall be put to death **t**
1Ki 8:28 is praying before You **t**
1Ki 12: 7 a servant to these people **t**
1Ki 18:15 present myself to him **t**
1Ki 20:13 deliver it into your hand **t**
1Ki 22: 5 for the word of the LORD **t**
2Ki 2: 3 your master from over you **t**
2Ki 2: 5 your master from over you **t**
2Ki 4:23 Why are you going to him **t**
2Ki 6:28 son, that we may eat him **t**
2Ki 6:31 of Shaphat remains on him **t**
2Ch 18: 4 for the word of the LORD **t**
Neh 9:36 Here we are, servants **t**
Esth 5: 4 Haman come **t** to the banquet
Job 23: 2 Even **t** my complaint is bitter
Ps 2: 7 My Son, **T** I have begotten You
Ps 95: 7 **T**, if you will hear His voice
Prov 7:14 **t** I have paid my vows
Prov 22:19 I have instructed you **t**, even
Is 56:12 tomorrow will be as **t**, and
Zech 9:12 Even **t** I declare that I will
Matt 6:30 of the field, which **t** is, and
Matt 16: 3 It will be foul weather **t**
Matt 21:28 go, work **t** in my vineyard
Matt 27:19 **t** in a dream because of Him
Mark 14:30 I say to you that **t**, even
Luke 4:21 **T** this Scripture is fulfilled
Luke 5:26 We have seen strange things **t**
Luke 12:28 which **t** is in the field and
Luke 13:32 out demons and perform cures **t**
Luke 13:33 Nevertheless I must journey **t**
Luke 19: 5 for **t** I must stay at your
Luke 19: 9 **T** salvation has come to this
Luke 23:43 you, **t** you will be with Me in
Luke 24:21 **t** is the third day since
Acts 13:33 My Son, **t** I have begotten You
Acts 22: 3 toward God as you all are **t**
Acts 26: 2 because **t** I shall answer for
Acts 26:29 but also all who hear me **t**
Acts 27:33 **T** is the fourteenth day you
Heb 1: 5 Son, **t** I have begotten You"
Heb 3: 7 **T**, if you will hear His voice
Heb 3:13 **T**," lest any of you be
Heb 3:15 **T**, if you will hear His voice
Heb 4: 7 **T**," after such a long time,
Heb 4: 7 **T**, if you will hear His voice
Heb 5: 5 My Son, **t** I have begotten You
Heb 13: 8 is the same yesterday, **t**, and
Jas 4:13 **T** or tomorrow we will go to

TODAY'S (*see* TODAY)
Esth 9:13 according to **t** decree, and let
Acts 19:40 in question for **t** uproar,

TOE (*see* TOES)
Ex 29:20 on the big **t** of their right
Lev 8:23 on the big **t** of his right
Lev 14:14 on the big **t** of his right
Lev 14:17 on the big **t** of his right
Lev 14:25 on the big **t** of his right
Lev 14:28 on the big **t** of his right

TOES (*see* TOE)
Lev 8:24 on the big **t** of their right
Judg 1: 6 cut off his thumbs and big **t**
Judg 1: 7 big **t** cut off used to gather
2Sa 21:20 hand and six **t** on each foot,
1Ch 20: 6 with twenty-four fingers and **t**
Dan 2:41 Whereas you saw the feet and **t**
Dan 2:42 as the **t** of the feet were

TOGARMAH
Gen 10: 3 were Ashkenaz, Riphath, and **T**
1Ch 1: 6 were Ashkenaz, Diphath, and **T**
Ezek 27:14 Those from the house of **T**
Ezek 38: 6 the house of **T** from the far

TOGETHER (*see* PREFACE)

TOHU (*see* NAHATH, TOAH)
1Sa 1: 1 son of Elihu, the son of **T**

TOI (*see* TOU)
2Sa 8: 9 When **T** king of Hamath heard
2Sa 8:10 then **T** sent Joram his son to
2Sa 8:10 for Hadadezer had wars with **T**

TOIL (*see* TOILED, TOILS)
Gen 3:17 in **t** you shall eat of it all
Gen 5:29 the **t** of our hands, because
Gen 41:51 has made me forget all my **t**
Eccl 4: 4 Again, I saw that for all **t**
Eccl 4: 6 hands full, together with **t**
Eccl 4: 8 For whom do I **t** and deprive
Matt 6:28 they neither **t** nor spin
Luke 12:27 they neither **t** nor spin
2Co 11:27 in weariness and **t**, in
1Th 2: 9 brethren, our labor and **t**
2Th 3: 8 **t** night and day, that we might

TOILED (*see* TOIL)
Eccl 2:11 on the labor in which I had t
Eccl 2:18 which I had t under the sun
Eccl 2:19 all my labor in which I t
Eccl 2:20 which I had t under the sun
Eccl 2:22 which he has t under the sun
Luke 5: 5 we have t all night and caught

TOILS (*see* TOIL)
Eccl 1: 3 in which he t under the sun
Eccl 5:18 all his labor in which he t

TOKEN
Josh 2:12 house, and give me a true t

TOKHATH
2Ch 34:22 wife of Shallum the son of T

TOLA (*see* TOLAITES)
Gen 46:13 The sons of Issachar were T
Num 26:23 of T, the family of the
Judg 10: 1 save Israel T the son of Puah
1Ch 7: 1 The sons of Issachar were T
1Ch 7: 2 The sons of T were Uzzi,
1Ch 7: 2 The sons of T were mighty men

TOLAD (*see* EL TOLAD)
1Ch 4:29 Bilhah, Ezem, T,

TOLAITES (*see* TOLA)
Num 26:23 of Tola, the family of the T

TOLD (*see* PREFACE)

TOLERABLE
Matt 10:15 it will be more t for the
Matt 11:22 it will be more t for Tyre
Matt 11:24 t for the land of Sodom in
Mark 6:11 it will be more t for Sodom
Luke 10:12 t in that Day for Sodom than
Luke 10:14 it will be more t for Tyre

TOMB (*see* TOMBS)
Judg 8:32 was buried in the t of Joash
Judg 16:31 and Eshtaol in the t of his
1Sa 10: 2 t in the territory of
2Sa 2:32 buried him in his father's t
2Sa 4:12 buried it in the t of Abner
2Sa 17:23 was buried in his father's t
2Sa 21:14 in the t of Kish his father
1Ki 13:22 come to the t of your fathers
1Ki 13:30 laid the corpse in his own t
1Ki 13:31 then bury me in the t where
2Ki 9:28 buried him in his t with his
2Ki 13:21 the man in the t of Elisha
2Ki 21:26 he was buried in his t in the
2Ki 23:17 It is the t of the man of God
2Ki 23:30 and buried him in his own t
2Ch 16:14 They buried him in his own t
Job 21:32 and a vigil kept over the t
Ps 5: 9 Their throat is an open t
Is 22:16 who carves a t for himself in
Jer 5:16 quiver is like an open t
Matt 27:60 laid it in his new t which he
Matt 27:60 against the door of the t
Matt 27:61 Mary, sitting opposite the t
Matt 27:64 t be made secure until the
Matt 27:66 went and made the t secure
Matt 28: 1 other Mary came to see the t
Matt 28: 8 quickly from the t with fear
Mark 6:29 his corpse and laid it in a t
Mark 15:46 he laid Him in a t which had
Mark 15:46 against the door of the t
Mark 16: 2 they came to the t when the
Mark 16: 3 from the door of the t for us
Mark 16: 5 And entering the t, they saw a
Mark 16: 8 quickly and fled from the t
Luke 23:53 laid it in a t that was hewn
Luke 23:55 after, and they observed the t
Luke 24: 1 came to the t bringing the
Luke 24: 2 stone rolled away from the t
Luke 24: 9 Then they returned from the t
Luke 24:12 Peter arose and ran to the t
Luke 24:22 who arrived at the t early
Luke 24:24 were with us went to the t
John 11:17 been in the t four days
John 11:31 going to the t to weep there
John 11:38 in Himself, came to the t
John 12:17 called Lazarus out of his t
John 19:41 and in the garden a new t in
John 19:42 Day, for the t was nearby
John 20: 1 Magdalene came to the t early
John 20: 1 been taken away from the t
John 20: 2 away the Lord out of the t
John 20: 3 and were going to the t
John 20: 4 Peter and came to the t first
John 20: 6 him, and went into the t
John 20: 8 who came to the t first,
John 20:11 outside by the t weeping, and
John 20:11 down and looked into the t
Acts 2:29 his t is with us to this day
Acts 7:16 laid in the t that Abraham
Acts 13:29 the tree and laid Him in a t
Rom 3:13 Their throat is an open t

TOMBS (*see* TOMB)
2Ki 23:16 he saw the t that were there
2Ki 23:16 took the bones out of the t
2Ch 21:20 but not in the t of the kings
2Ch 24:25 him in the t of the kings
2Ch 28:27 the t of the kings of Israel
2Ch 32:33 upper t of the sons of David
2Ch 35:24 one of the t of his fathers
Neh 2: 3 the place of my fathers' t
Neh 2: 5 to the city of my fathers' t
Neh 3:16 in front of the t of David
Is 65: 4 and spend the night in the t
Matt 8:28 men, coming out of the t,
Matt 23:27 t which indeed appear
Matt 23:29 build the t of the prophets
Mark 5: 2 the t a man with an unclean
Mark 5: 3 had his dwelling among the t
Mark 5: 5 in the mountains and in the t
Luke 8:27 live in a house but in the t
Luke 11:47 build the t of the prophets
Luke 11:48 them, and you build their t

TOMORROW
Ex 8:10 So he said, "T."
Ex 8:23 T this sign shall be
Ex 8:29 may depart t from Pharaoh
Ex 9: 5 T the LORD will do this thing
Ex 9:18 t about this time I will
Ex 10: 4 t I will bring locusts into
Ex 16:23 T is a Sabbath rest, a holy
Ex 17: 9 T I will stand on the top of
Ex 19:10 and sanctify them today and t
Ex 32: 5 T is a feast to the LORD
Num 11:18 Sanctify yourselves for t
Num 14:25 t turn and move out into the
Num 16: 5 T morning the LORD will show
Num 16: 7 in them before the LORD t
Num 16:16 T, you and all your company be
Josh 3: 5 for t the LORD will do
Josh 7:13 Sanctify yourselves for t
Josh 11: 6 for t about this time I will
Josh 22:18 that t He will be angry with
Judg 19: 9 T go your way early, so that
Judg 20:28 for t I will deliver them
1Sa 9:16 T about this time I will send
1Sa 9:19 t I will let you go and will
1Sa 11: 9 T, by the time the sun is
1Sa 11:10 T we will come out to you, and
1Sa 19:11 tonight, t you will be killed
1Sa 20: 5 Indeed t is the New Moon, and
1Sa 20:12 out my father sometime t, or
1Sa 20:18 to David, "T is the New Moon
1Sa 28:19 t you and your sons will be
2Sa 11:12 and t I will let you depart
1Ki 19: 2 of them by t about this time
1Ki 20: 6 to you t about this time, and
2Ki 6:28 and we will eat my son t
2Ki 7: 1 T about this time a seah of
2Ki 7:18 shall be sold t about this
2Ki 10: 6 me at Jezreel by this time t
2Ch 20:16 T go down against them
2Ch 20:17 t go out against them, for
Esth 5: 8 t I will do as the king has
Esth 5:12 t I am again invited by her,
Esth 9:13 are in Shushan to do again t
Prov 3:28 t I will give it," when you
Prov 27: 1 Do not boast about t, for you
Is 22:13 us eat and drink, for t we die
Is 56:12 t will be as today, and much
Matt 6:30 t is thrown into the oven,
Matt 6:34 do not worry about t
Matt 6:34 for t will worry about its
Luke 12:28 t is thrown into the oven,
Luke 13:32 and perform cures today and t
Luke 13:33 I must journey today, t, and
Acts 23:15 he be brought down to you t
Acts 23:20 Paul down to the council t
Acts 25:22 T," he said, "you shall
1Co 15:32 us eat and drink, for t we die
Jas 4:13 Today or t we will go to such
Jas 4:14 not know what will happen t

TONE
Gal 4:20 you now and to change my t

TONGS
Is 6: 6 with the t from the altar
Is 44:12 the t works one in the coals

TONGUE (*see* TONGUES)
Ex 4:10 slow of speech and slow of t
Ex 11: 7 Israel shall a dog move its t
Josh 10:21 No one moved his t against
Judg 7: 5 from the water with his t
2Sa 23: 2 me, and His word was on my t
Esth 7: 4 I would have held my t,
Job 5:21 from the scourge of the t
Job 6:24 Teach me, and I will hold my t
Job 6:30 Is there injustice on my t
Job 13:19 If now I hold my t, I perish
Job 15: 5 choose the t of the crafty
Job 20:12 and he hides it under his t
Job 20:16 the viper's t will slay him
Job 27: 4 nor my t utter deceit
Job 29:10 their t stuck to the roof of
Job 33: 2 my t speaks in my mouth
Job 41: 1 or snare his t with a line
Ps 5: 9 They flatter with their t
Ps 10: 7 Under his t is trouble and
Ps 12: 3 And the t that speaks proud
Ps 12: 4 With our t we will prevail
Ps 15: 3 does not backbite with his t
Ps 22:15 And My t clings to My jaws
Ps 34:13 Keep your t from evil, And
Ps 35:28 And my t shall speak of Your
Ps 37:30 And his t talks of justice
Ps 39: 1 my ways, Lest I sin with my t
Ps 39: 3 Then I spoke with my t
Ps 45: 1 My t is the pen of a ready
Ps 50:19 evil, And your t frames deceit
Ps 51:14 my t shall sing aloud of Your
Ps 52: 2 Your t devises destruction,
Ps 52: 4 words, You deceitful t
Ps 57: 4 And their t a sharp sword
Ps 64: 3 sharpen their t like a sword
Ps 64: 8 them stumble over their own t
Ps 66:17 And He was extolled with my t
Ps 71:24 My t also shall talk of Your
Ps 73: 9 their t walks through the
Ps 78:36 they lied to Him with their t
Ps 109: 2 against me with a lying t
Ps 119:172 My t shall speak of Your word
Ps 120: 2 lips And from a deceitful t
Ps 120: 3 be done to you, You false t
Ps 126: 2 And our t with singing
Ps 137: 6 Let my t cling to the roof of
Ps 139: 4 there is not a word on my t
Prov 6:17 A proud look, a lying t,
Prov 6:24 flattering t of a seductress
Prov 10:20 The t of the righteous is
Prov 10:31 perverse t will be cut out
Prov 12:18 sword, but the t of the wise
Prov 12:19 but a lying t is but for a
Prov 15: 2 The t of the wise uses
Prov 15: 4 A wholesome t is a tree of
Prov 16: 1 of the t is from the LORD
Prov 17: 4 eagerly to a spiteful t
Prov 17:20 a perverse t falls into evil
Prov 18:21 are in the power of the t
Prov 21: 6 treasures by a lying t is the
Prov 21:23 and t keeps his soul from
Prov 25:15 and a gentle t breaks a bone
Prov 25:23 and a backbiting t an angry
Prov 26:28 A lying t hates those who are
Prov 28:23 he who flatters with the t
Prov 31:26 and on her t is the law of
Song 4:11 and milk are under your t
Is 3: 8 is fallen, because their t
Is 11:15 the t of the Sea of Egypt
Is 28:11 another t He will speak to
Is 30:27 His t like a devouring fire
Is 32: 4 the t of the stammerers will
Is 33:19 of a stammering t that you
Is 35: 6 and the t of the dumb sing
Is 45:23 every t shall take an oath
Is 50: 4 given Me the t of the learned
Is 54:17 every t which rises against
Is 57: 4 wide mouth and stick out the t
Is 59: 3 lies, your t has muttered
Jer 9: 5 taught their t to speak lies
Jer 9: 8 Their t is an arrow shot out
Jer 18:18 let us attack him with the t
Lam 4: 4 The t of the infant clings to

Ezek 3:26 I will make your t cling to
Hos 7:16 for the cursings of their t
Amos 6:10 Hold your t! For we dare not
Mic 6:12 their t is deceitful in their
Hab 1:13 hold Your t when the wicked
Zeph 3:13 nor shall a deceitful t be
Mark 7:33 and He spat and touched his t
Mark 7:35 of his t was loosed, and he
Luke 1:64 his t loosed, and he spoke,
Luke 16:24 finger in water and cool my t
Acts 2:26 rejoiced, and my t was glad
Rom 14:11 every t shall confess to God
1Co 14: 2 For he who speaks in a t does
1Co 14: 4 speaks in a t edifies himself
1Co 14: 9 unless you utter by the t
1Co 14:13 let him who speaks in a t
1Co 14:14 For if I pray in a t, my
1Co 14:19 ten thousand words in a t
1Co 14:26 has a teaching, has a t, has
1Co 14:27 If anyone speaks in a t, let
Phil 2:11 that every t should confess
Jas 1:26 does not bridle his t but
Jas 3: 5 Even so the t is a little
Jas 3: 6 the t is a fire, a world of
Jas 3: 6 The t is so set among our
Jas 3: 8 But no man can tame the t
1Pe 3:10 him refrain his t from evil
1Jn 3:18 us not love in word or in t
Rev 5: 9 blood out of every tribe and t
Rev 13: 7 given him over every tribe, t
Rev 14: 6 to every nation, tribe, t

TONGUES (*see* TONGUE)

Ps 31:20 pavilion From the strife of t
Ps 55: 9 O Lord, and divide their t
Ps 68:23 the t of your dogs may have
Ps 140: 3 their t like a serpent
Is 41:17 their t fail for thirst, I,
Is 66:18 will gather all nations and t
Jer 9: 3 have bent their t for lies
Jer 23:31 who use their t and say, He
Zech 14:12 their t shall dissolve in
Mark 16:17 they will speak with new t
Acts 2: 3 appeared to them divided t
Acts 2: 4 began to speak with other t
Acts 2:11 them speaking in our own t
Acts 10:46 they heard them speak with t
Acts 19: 6 them, and they spoke with t
Rom 3:13 with their t they have
1Co 12:10 another different kinds of t
1Co 12:10 the interpretation of t
1Co 12:28 varieties of t
1Co 12:30 Do all speak with t
1Co 13: 1 I speak with the t of men
1Co 13: 8 whether there are t, they
1Co 14: 5 I wish you all spoke with t
1Co 14: 5 than he who speaks with t
1Co 14: 6 I come to you speaking with t
1Co 14:18 with t more than you all
1Co 14:21 With men of other t and other
1Co 14:22 Therefore t are for a sign,
1Co 14:23 place, and all speak with t
1Co 14:39 do not forbid to speak with t
Rev 7: 9 tribes, peoples, and t,
Rev 10:11 many peoples, nations, t, and
Rev 11: 9 from the peoples, tribes, t
Rev 16:10 they gnawed their t because
Rev 17:15 multitudes, nations, and t

TONIGHT

Gen 19: 5 are the men who came to you t
Gen 19:34 us make him drink wine t also
Gen 30:15 he will lie with you t for
Num 22: 8 Lodge here t, and I will bring
Num 22:19 please, you also stay here t
Josh 2: 2 men have come here t from the
Josh 4: 3 place where you lodge t
Ruth 1:12 if I should have a husband t
Ruth 3: 2 t at the threshing floor
1Sa 19:11 you do not save your life t
2Sa 17: 1 will arise and pursue David t

TOO (*see* PREFACE)

TOOK (*see* TAKE)

Gen 2:15 Then the LORD God t the man
Gen 2:21 and He t one of his ribs, and
Gen 3: 6 she t of its fruit and ate
Gen 4:19 Then Lamech t for himself two
Gen 5:24 and he was not, for God t him
Gen 6: 2 they t wives for themselves
Gen 8: 9 t her, and drew her into the
Gen 8:20 t of every clean animal and of
Gen 9:23 Japheth t a garment, laid it
Gen 11:29 Then Abram and Nahor t wives
Gen 11:31 Terah t his son Abram and his
Gen 12: 5 Then Abram t Sarai his wife
Gen 14:11 Then they t all the goods of
Gen 14:12 They also t Lot, Abram's
Gen 16: 3 wife, t Hagar her maid, the
Gen 17:23 So Abraham t Ishmael his son,
Gen 18: 7 t a tender and good calf, gave
Gen 18: 8 So he t butter and milk and the
Gen 19:16 the men t hold of his hand,
Gen 20: 2 king of Gerar sent and t Sarah
Gen 20:14 Then Abimelech t sheep, oxen,
Gen 21:14 t bread and a skin of water
Gen 21:21 his mother t a wife for him
Gen 21:27 So Abraham t sheep and oxen
Gen 22: 3 t two of his young men with
Gen 22: 6 So Abraham t the wood of the
Gen 22: 6 he t the fire in his hand, and
Gen 22:10 t the knife to slay his son
Gen 22:13 t the ram, and offered it up
Gen 24: 7 who t me from my father's
Gen 24:10 Then the servant t ten of his
Gen 24:22 that the man t a golden nose
Gen 24:61 So the servant t Rebekah and
Gen 24:65 So she t a veil and covered
Gen 24:67 he t Rebekah and she became
Gen 25: 1 Abraham again t a wife, and
Gen 25:20 old when he t Rebekah as wife
Gen 25:26 his hand t hold of Esau's
Gen 26:34 old, he t as wives Judith the
Gen 27:15 Then Rebekah t the choice
Gen 27:36 He t away my birthright, and
Gen 28: 9 t Mahalath the daughter of
Gen 28:11 he t one of the stones of
Gen 28:18 t the stone that he had put
Gen 29:23 that he t Leah his daughter
Gen 30: 9 she t Zilpah her maid and gave
Gen 30:37 Now Jacob t for himself rods
Gen 31:23 Then he t his brethren with
Gen 31:45 So Jacob t a stone and set it
Gen 31:46 they t stones and made a heap,
Gen 32:13 t what came to his hand as a
Gen 32:22 and t his two wives, his two
Gen 32:23 He t them, sent them over the
Gen 33:11 And he urged him, and he t it
Gen 34: 2 he t her and lay with her, and
Gen 34:25 each t his sword and came
Gen 34:26 t Dinah from Shechem's house,
Gen 34:28 They t their sheep, their
Gen 34:29 and their wives they t captive
Gen 36: 2 Esau t his wives from the
Gen 36: 6 Then Esau t his wives, his
Gen 37:24 Then they t him and cast him
Gen 37:28 And they t Joseph to Egypt
Gen 37:31 So they t Joseph's tunic,
Gen 38: 6 Then Judah t a wife for Er
Gen 38:14 So she t off her widow's
Gen 38:28 and the midwife t a scarlet
Gen 39:20 Then Joseph's master t him
Gen 40:11 I t the grapes and pressed
Gen 41:42 Then Pharaoh t his signet
Gen 42:24 And he t Simeon from them and
Gen 42:30 t us for spies of the country
Gen 43:15 So the men t that present and
Gen 43:15 they t double money in their
Gen 43:34 Then he t servings to them
Gen 46: 1 So Israel t his journey with
Gen 46: 6 So they t their livestock and
Gen 47: 2 he t five men from among his
Gen 48: 1 he t with him his two sons,
Gen 48:13 Joseph t them both, Ephraim
Gen 48:17 so he t hold of his father's
Gen 48:22 which I t from the hand of
Gen 50:25 Then Joseph t an oath from
Ex 2: 1 t as wife a daughter of Levi
Ex 2: 3 she t an ark of bulrushes for
Ex 2: 9 So the woman t the child
Ex 4: 6 bosom, and when he t it out
Ex 4:20 Then Moses t his wife and his
Ex 4:20 Moses t the rod of God in his
Ex 4:25 Then Zipporah t a sharp stone
Ex 6:20 Now Amram t for himself
Ex 6:23 Aaron t to himself Elisheba,
Ex 6:25 son, t for himself one of the
Ex 9:10 Then they t ashes from the
Ex 10:19 which t the locusts away and
Ex 12:34 So the people t their dough
Ex 13:19 Moses t the bones of Joseph
Ex 13:20 So they t their journey from
Ex 14: 6 and t his people with him
Ex 14: 7 Also, he t six hundred choice
Ex 14:25 He t off their chariot wheels
Ex 15:20 t the timbrel in her hand
Ex 17:12 so they t a stone and put it
Ex 18: 2 t Zipporah, Moses' wife,
Ex 18:12 t a burnt offering and
Ex 24: 6 Moses t half the blood and put
Ex 24: 7 Then he t the Book of the
Ex 24: 8 Moses t the blood, sprinkled
Ex 32:20 Then he t the calf which they
Ex 33: 7 Moses t his tent and pitched
Ex 34: 4 and he t in his hand the two
Ex 40:20 He t the Testimony and put it
Lev 8:10 Then Moses t the anointing
Lev 8:15 Then he t the blood, and put
Lev 8:16 Then he t all the fat that
Lev 8:23 he t some of its blood and put
Lev 8:25 Then he t the fat and the fat
Lev 8:26 LORD he t one unleavened cake
Lev 8:28 Then Moses t them from their
Lev 8:29 Moses t the breast and waved
Lev 8:30 Then Moses t some of the
Lev 9:15 t the goat, which was the sin
Lev 9:17 t a handful of it, and burned
Lev 10: 1 each t his censer and put fire
Lev 24:23 they t outside the camp him
Num 1:17 Aaron t these men who had
Num 3:49 So Moses t the redemption
Num 3:50 of Israel he t the money, one
Num 7: 6 So Moses t the carts and the
Num 11:25 t of the Spirit that was upon
Num 16: 1 Peleth, sons of Reuben, t men
Num 16:18 So every man t his censer
Num 16:39 priest t the bronze censers
Num 16:47 Then Aaron t it as Moses
Num 17: 9 looked, and each man t his rod
Num 20: 9 So Moses t the rod from
Num 21: 1 and t some of them prisoners
Num 21:24 t possession of his land from
Num 21:25 So Israel t all these cities,
Num 21:32 they t its villages and drove
Num 21:35 they t possession of his land
Num 22:22 the Angel of the LORD t His
Num 22:41 next day, that Balak t Balaam
Num 23: 7 he t up his oracle and said
Num 23:11 I t you to curse my enemies,
Num 23:18 Then he t up his oracle and
Num 23:28 So Balak t Balaam to the top
Num 24: 3 Then he t up his oracle and
Num 24:15 Then he t up his oracle and
Num 24:20 he t up his oracle and said
Num 24:21 he t up his oracle and said
Num 24:23 Then he t up his oracle and
Num 25: 7 and t a javelin in his hand
Num 27:22 He t Joshua and set him before
Num 31: 9 the children of Israel t all
Num 31: 9 t as spoil all their cattle,
Num 31:11 they t all the spoil and all
Num 31:27 those who t part in the war
Num 31:47 Moses t one of every fifty
Num 32:39 t it, and dispossessed the
Num 32:41 t its small towns, and called
Num 32:42 t Kenath and its villages, and
Deut 1:15 So I t the heads of your
Deut 1:23 so I t twelve of your men,
Deut 1:25 They also t some of the fruit
Deut 1:34 angry, and t an oath, saying,
Deut 2:14 the time we t to come from
Deut 2:34 We t all his cities at that
Deut 2:35 We t only the livestock as
Deut 2:35 of the cities which we t
Deut 3: 4 we t all his cities at that
Deut 3: 7 we t as booty for ourselves
Deut 3: 8 at that time we t the land
Deut 3:14 t all the region of Argob
Deut 4:47 they t possession of his land
Deut 9:17 Then I t the two tablets and
Deut 9:21 Then I t your sin, the calf
Deut 22:14 I t this woman, and when I
Deut 24: 3 dies who t her to be his wife
Deut 29: 8 We t their land and gave it as
Josh 2: 4 Then the woman t the two men
Josh 3: 6 So they t up the ark of the
Josh 4: 8 t up twelve stones from the
Josh 4:20 they t out of the Jordan,
Josh 6:12 the priests t up the ark of
Josh 6:20 him, and they t the city
Josh 7: 1 t of the accursed things

Josh 7:17 and he t the family of the
Josh 7:21 I coveted them and t them
Josh 7:23 they t them from the midst of
Josh 7:24 t Achan the son of Zerah, the
Josh 8:12 So he t about five thousand
Josh 8:19 t it, and hastened to set the
Josh 8:23 the king of Ai they t alive
Josh 8:27 t as booty for themselves
Josh 9: 4 they t old sacks on their
Josh 9:12 This bread of ours we t hot
Josh 9:14 Then the men of Israel t some
Josh 10:27 they t them down from the
Josh 10:28 On that day Joshua t Makkedah
Josh 10:32 who t it on the second day,
Josh 10:35 They t it on that day and
Josh 10:37 And they t it and struck it
Josh 10:39 And he t it and its king and all
Josh 10:42 land Joshua t at one time
Josh 11:10 t Hazor, and struck its king
Josh 11:12 and all their kings, Joshua t
Josh 11:14 the children of Israel t as
Josh 11:16 So Joshua t all this land
Josh 11:19 the others they t in battle
Josh 11:23 So Joshua t the whole land,
Josh 15:17 the brother of Caleb, t it
Josh 16: 4 Ephraim, t their inheritance
Josh 19:47 fight against Leshem and t it
Josh 19:47 t possession of it, and dwelt
Josh 21:43 they t possession of it and
Josh 24: 3 Then I t your father Abraham
Josh 24:26 he t a large stone, and set it
Judg 1: 8 against Jerusalem and t it
Judg 1:13 Caleb's younger brother, t it
Judg 1:18 Also Judah t Gaza with its
Judg 3: 6 they t their daughters to be
Judg 3:13 t possession of the city of
Judg 3:21 t the dagger from his right
Judg 3:25 Therefore they t the key and
Judg 4:21 t a tent peg and t a hammer
Judg 5:19 they t no spoils of silver
Judg 6:27 So Gideon t ten men from
Judg 7: 8 So the people t provisions
Judg 8:12 he t the two kings of Midian,
Judg 8:16 he t the elders of the city,
Judg 8:21 t the crescent ornaments that
Judg 9:43 So he t his people, divided
Judg 9:45 he t the city and killed the
Judg 9:48 Abimelech t an ax in his hand
Judg 9:48 and t it and laid it on his
Judg 9:50 against Thebez and t it
Judg 11:13 Because Israel t away my land
Judg 11:22 They t possession of all the
Judg 12: 3 I t my life in my hands and
Judg 13:19 So Manoah t the young goat
Judg 14: 9 He t some of it in his hands
Judg 14:19 t their apparel, and gave the
Judg 15: 4 and he t torches, turned the
Judg 15:15 t it, and killed a thousand
Judg 16: 3 t hold of the doors of the
Judg 16:12 Therefore Delilah t new ropes
Judg 16:21 Then the Philistines t him
Judg 16:29 And Samson t hold of the two
Judg 16:31 t him, and brought him up and
Judg 17: 2 the silver with me; I t it
Judg 17: 4 Then his mother t two hundred
Judg 18:17 they t the carved image, the
Judg 18:18 t the graven image, the ephod
Judg 18:20 he t the ephod, the household
Judg 18:20 t his place among the people
Judg 18:27 So they t the things Micah
Judg 19: 1 He t for himself a concubine
Judg 19:25 So the man t his concubine and
Judg 19:29 his house he t a knife, laid
Judg 20: 6 So I t hold of my concubine,
Judg 21:23 they t themselves enough
Ruth 1: 4 Now they t wives of the women
Ruth 2:18 Then she t it up and went into
Ruth 2:19 the one who t notice of you
Ruth 4: 2 he t ten men of the elders of
Ruth 4: 7 one man t off his sandal and
Ruth 4: 8 So he t off his sandal
Ruth 4:13 So Boaz t Ruth and she became
Ruth 4:16 Then Naomi t the child and
1Sa 1:24 she t him up with her, with
1Sa 5: 1 Philistines t the ark of God
1Sa 5: 2 Philistines t the ark of God
1Sa 5: 3 So they t Dagon and set it in
1Sa 6:10 they t two milk cows and
1Sa 6:15 The Levites t down the ark of
1Sa 7: 1 t the ark of the LORD, and
1Sa 7: 9 Samuel t a suckling lamb and
1Sa 7:12 Then Samuel t a stone and set
1Sa 8: 3 gain, t bribes, and perverted
1Sa 9:22 Then Samuel t Saul and his
1Sa 9:24 So the cook t up the thigh
1Sa 10: 1 Then Samuel t a flask of oil
1Sa 11: 7 So he t a yoke of oxen and cut
1Sa 14:32 t sheep, oxen, and calves, and
1Sa 14:52 man, he t him for himself
1Sa 15: 8 He also t Agag king of the
1Sa 15:21 the people t of the plunder
1Sa 16:13 Then Samuel t the horn of oil
1Sa 16:20 Jesse t a donkey loaded with
1Sa 17:20 t the things and went as Jesse
1Sa 17:34 t a lamb out of the flock,
1Sa 17:39 So David t them off
1Sa 17:40 Then he t his staff in his
1Sa 17:49 in his bag and t out a stone
1Sa 17:51 t his sword and drew it out of
1Sa 17:54 And David t the head of the
1Sa 17:57 the Philistine, Abner t him
1Sa 18: 2 Saul t him that day, and would
1Sa 18: 4 Jonathan t off the robe that
1Sa 19: 5 For he t his life in his
1Sa 19:13 Michal t an image and laid it
1Sa 20: 3 Then David t an oath again,
1Sa 21:12 Now David t these words to
1Sa 23: 5 and t away their livestock
1Sa 24: 2 Then Saul t three thousand
1Sa 25:18 t two hundred loaves of bread
1Sa 25:43 David also t Ahinoam of
1Sa 26:12 So David t the spear and the
1Sa 27: 9 but t away the sheep, the
1Sa 28:24 she t flour and kneaded it, and
1Sa 30:20 Then David t all the flocks
1Sa 31: 4 Therefore Saul t a sword and
1Sa 31:12 t the body of Saul and the
1Sa 31:13 Then they t their bones and
2Sa 1:10 I t the crown that was on his
2Sa 1:11 Then David t hold of his own
2Sa 2: 8 t Ishbosheth the son of Saul
2Sa 2:25 t their stand on top of a
2Sa 2:32 Then they t up Asahel and
2Sa 3:15 t her from her husband, from
2Sa 3:27 Joab t him aside in the gate
2Sa 3:35 day, David t an oath, saying,
2Sa 3:36 all the people t note of it
2Sa 4: 4 and his nurse t him up and fled
2Sa 4: 7 t his head, and were all night
2Sa 4:12 But they t the head of
2Sa 5: 7 Nevertheless David t the
2Sa 5:13 David t more concubines and
2Sa 6: 6 t hold of it, for the oxen
2Sa 6:10 but David t it aside into the
2Sa 7: 8 I t you from the sheepfold,
2Sa 7:15 as I t it from Saul, whom I
2Sa 8: 1 David t Metheg Ammah from
2Sa 8: 4 David t from him one thousand
2Sa 8: 7 David t the shields of gold
2Sa 8: 8 King David t a large amount
2Sa 10: 4 Therefore Hanun t David's
2Sa 11: 4 sent messengers, and t her
2Sa 12: 4 but he t the poor man's lamb
2Sa 12:26 of Ammon, and t the royal city
2Sa 12:29 fought against it, and t it
2Sa 12:30 Then he t their king's crown
2Sa 13: 8 Then she t flour and kneaded
2Sa 13: 9 she t the pan and placed them
2Sa 13:10 Tamar t the cakes which she
2Sa 13:11 he t hold of her and said to
2Sa 17:19 Then the woman t and spread a
2Sa 18: 7 men t place there that day
2Sa 18:14 he t three spears in his hand
2Sa 18:17 they t Absalom and cast him
2Sa 20: 3 the king t the ten women, his
2Sa 20: 9 Joab t Amasa by the beard
2Sa 21: 8 So the king t Armoni and
2Sa 21:10 daughter of Aiah t sackcloth
2Sa 21:12 t the bones of Saul, and the
2Sa 22:17 He sent from above, He t me
2Sa 23:16 t it and brought it to David
1Ki 1:29 And the king t an oath and said
1Ki 1:38 mule, and t him to Gihon
1Ki 1:39 Then Zadok the priest t a
1Ki 1:50 t hold of the horns of the
1Ki 2:28 t hold of the horns of the
1Ki 3:20 t my son from my side, while
1Ki 4:15 he also t Basemath the
1Ki 7: 1 But Solomon t thirteen years
1Ki 8: 3 and the priests t up the ark
1Ki 8:47 of those who t them captive
1Ki 8:50 those who t them captive,
1Ki 11:18 they t men with them from
1Ki 11:30 Then Ahijah t hold of the new
1Ki 12:28 Therefore the king t counsel
1Ki 13:29 the prophet t up the corpse
1Ki 14:26 he t away the treasures of
1Ki 14:26 he t away everything
1Ki 14:26 He also t away all the gold
1Ki 15:18 Then Asa t all the silver and
1Ki 15:22 they t away the stones and
1Ki 16:31 that he t as wife Jezebel the
1Ki 17:19 So he t him out of her arms
1Ki 17:23 Elijah t the child and brought
1Ki 18:10 here,' he t an oath from the
1Ki 18:26 So they t the bull which was
1Ki 18:31 And Elijah t twelve stones,
1Ki 19:21 him, and t a yoke of oxen and
1Ki 20:34 t from your father I will
1Ki 21:13 Then they t him outside the
2Ki 2: 8 Now Elijah t his mantle,
2Ki 2:12 he t hold of his own clothes
2Ki 2:13 He also t up the mantle of
2Ki 2:14 Then he t the mantle of
2Ki 3:26 he t with him seven hundred
2Ki 3:27 Then he t his eldest son who
2Ki 5: 5 t with him ten talents of
2Ki 5:24 he t them from their hand, and
2Ki 6: 7 reached out his hand and t it
2Ki 6: 8 and he t counsel with his
2Ki 7:14 Therefore they t two chariots
2Ki 8: 9 and t a present with him, of
2Ki 8:15 day that he t a thick cloth
2Ki 10: 7 that they t the king's sons
2Ki 10:14 So they t them alive, and
2Ki 10:15 he t him up to him into the
2Ki 10:31 But Jehu t no heed to walk in
2Ki 11: 2 t Joash the son of Ahaziah,
2Ki 11: 4 t an oath from them in the
2Ki 11: 9 Each of them t his men who
2Ki 11:19 Then he t the captains of
2Ki 12: 9 Jehoiada the priest t a chest
2Ki 12:17 fought against Gath, and t it
2Ki 12:18 Jehoash king of Judah t all
2Ki 13:15 So he t himself a bow and
2Ki 13:18 the arrows"; so he t them
2Ki 14: 7 t Sela by war, and called its
2Ki 14:14 he t all the gold and silver,
2Ki 14:21 the people of Judah t Azariah
2Ki 15:29 t Ijon, Abel Beth Maachah,
2Ki 16: 8 Ahaz t the silver and gold
2Ki 16: 9 and t it, carried its people
2Ki 16:17 he t down the Sea from the
2Ki 17: 6 the king of Assyria t Samaria
2Ki 17:24 they t possession of Samaria
2Ki 18:10 end of three years they t it
2Ki 18:13 cities of Judah and t them
2Ki 20: 7 So they t and laid it on the
2Ki 23: 3 all the people t their stand
2Ki 23:16 t the bones out of the tombs
2Ki 23:19 Then Josiah also t away all
2Ki 23:30 And the people of the land t
2Ki 23:34 Pharaoh t Jehoahaz and went to
2Ki 24:12 of his reign, t him prisoner
2Ki 25: 6 So they t the king and brought
2Ki 25: 7 fetters, and t him to Babylon
2Ki 25:14 They also t away the pots,
2Ki 25:15 captain of the guard t away
2Ki 25:18 t Seraiah the chief priest
2Ki 25:19 He also t out of the city an
2Ki 25:20 t these and brought them to
2Ki 25:24 Gedaliah t an oath before
1Ch 2:19 Caleb t Ephrath as his wife,
1Ch 2:23 Syria t from them the towns
1Ch 4:18 of Pharaoh, whom Mered t
1Ch 5:21 Then they t away their
1Ch 5:26 He t them to Halah, Habor,
1Ch 7:15 Machir t as his wife the
1Ch 9:28 in and t them out by count
1Ch 10: 4 Therefore Saul t a sword and
1Ch 10: 9 t his head and his armor, and
1Ch 10:12 t the body of Saul and the
1Ch 11: 5 Nevertheless David t the
1Ch 11:18 t it and brought it to David
1Ch 13:13 but t it aside into the house
1Ch 14: 3 Then David t more wives in
1Ch 17: 7 I t you from the sheepfold,
1Ch 17:13 as I t it from him who was
1Ch 18: 1 t Gath and its towns from the
1Ch 18: 4 David t from him one thousand

1Ch 18: 7 David t the shields of gold
1Ch 19: 4 Therefore Hanun t David's
1Ch 20: 2 Then David t their king's
1Ch 23:22 sons of Kish, t them as wives
2Ch 5: 4 and the Levites t up the ark
2Ch 11:13 Israel t their stand with him
2Ch 11:18 Then Rehoboam t for himself
2Ch 11:20 After her he t Maacah the
2Ch 11:21 for he t eighteen wives and
2Ch 12: 4 he t the fortified cities of
2Ch 12: 9 t away the treasures of the
2Ch 12: 9 he t everything
2Ch 13:19 Jeroboam and t cities from him
2Ch 15: 8 he t courage, and removed the
2Ch 15:14 Then they t an oath before
2Ch 16: 6 Then King Asa t all Judah
2Ch 17: 6 his heart t delight in the
2Ch 22:11 t Joash the son of Ahaziah,
2Ch 23: 8 each man t his men who were
2Ch 23:20 Then he t the captains of
2Ch 24: 3 Jehoiada t for him two wives,
2Ch 24:11 t it and returned it to its
2Ch 25:12 Judah t captive another ten
2Ch 25:13 in them, and t much spoil
2Ch 25:17 king of Judah t counsel and
2Ch 25:24 he t all the gold and silver,
2Ch 26: 1 the people of Judah t Uzziah
2Ch 28: 8 they also t away much spoil
2Ch 28:15 t the captives, and from the
2Ch 28:21 For Ahaz t part of the
2Ch 29:16 And the Levites t it out and
2Ch 29:36 since the events t place so
2Ch 30:14 t away the altars that were
2Ch 30:14 they t away all the incense
2Ch 32: 3 he t counsel with his leaders
2Ch 33:11 who t Manasseh with hooks,
2Ch 33:15 He t away the foreign gods and
2Ch 35:24 His servants therefore t him
2Ch 36: 1 t Jehoahaz the son of Josiah
2Ch 36: 4 Necho t Jehoahaz his brother
2Ch 36:10 t him to Babylon, with the
2Ch 36:18 all these he t to Babylon
Ezra 1:11 All these Sheshbazzar t with
Ezra 2:61 who t a wife of the daughters
Ezra 4:10 and noble Osnapper t captive
Ezra 5:14 those King Cyrus t from the
Ezra 6: 5 which Nebuchadnezzar t from
Neh 2: 1 that I t the wine and gave it
Neh 4:23 followed me t off our clothes
Neh 4:23 t them off for washing
Neh 5:15 t from them bread and wine,
Neh 7:63 who t a wife of the daughters
Neh 9:22 So they t possession of the
Neh 9:25 they t strong cities and a
Esth 2: 7 Mordecai t her as his own
Esth 3:10 So the king t his signet ring
Esth 6:11 So Haman t the robe and the
Esth 8: 2 So the king t off his signet
Job 1:15 raided them and t them away
Job 1:17 t them away, yes, and killed
Job 2: 8 he t for himself a potsherd
Job 29: 7 when I t my seat in the open
Ps 18:16 He sent from above, He t me
Ps 22: 9 He who t Me out of the womb
Ps 48: 6 Fear t hold of them there, And
Ps 55:14 We t sweet counsel together,
Ps 71: 6 You are He who t me out of my
Ps 78:70 t him from the sheepfolds
Ps 99: 8 Though You t vengeance on
Prov 7: 8 he t the path to her house
Prov 12:27 roast what he t in hunting
Song 5: 7 walls t my veil away from me
Is 20: 1 against Ashdod and t it,
Is 36: 1 cities of Judah and t them
Jer 13: 7 I t the sash from the place
Jer 25:17 Then I t the cup from the
Jer 28: 3 king of Babylon t away from
Jer 28:10 t the yoke off the prophet
Jer 31:32 I t them by the hand to bring
Jer 32:10 t witnesses, and weighed the
Jer 32:11 So I t the purchase deed,
Jer 32:23 t possession of it, but they
Jer 35: 3 Then I t Jaazaniah the son of
Jer 36:14 t the scroll in his hand and
Jer 36:21 he t it from Elishama the
Jer 36:32 Then Jeremiah t another
Jer 37:17 the king sent and t him out
Jer 38: 6 So they t Jeremiah and cast
Jer 38:11 So Ebed-Melech t the men with
Jer 38:11 t from there old clothes and
Jer 40: 2 of the guard t Jeremiah and
Jer 40: 9 t an oath before them and
Jer 41:12 they t all the men and went to
Jer 41:16 t from Mizpah all the rest of
Jer 43: 5 t all the remnant of Judah
Jer 50:33 all who t them captive have
Jer 52: 9 So they t the king and brought
Jer 52:11 t him to Babylon, and put him
Jer 52:18 They also t away the pots,
Jer 52:19 captain of the guard t away
Jer 52:24 t Seraiah the chief priest
Jer 52:25 He also t out of the city an
Jer 52:26 captain of the guard t these
Ezek 3:14 up and t me away, and I went in
Ezek 3:21 live because he t warning
Ezek 8: 3 t me by a lock of my hair
Ezek 10: 7 t some of it and put it into
Ezek 10: 7 clothed with linen, who t it
Ezek 11:24 Then the Spirit t me up and
Ezek 16:16 You t some of your garments
Ezek 16:18 You t your embroidered
Ezek 16:20 Moreover you t your sons and
Ezek 16:37 with whom you t pleasure, all
Ezek 16:50 therefore I t them away as I
Ezek 17: 3 t from the cedar the highest
Ezek 17: 5 Then he t some of the seed of
Ezek 17:12 t its king and princes, and led
Ezek 17:13 he t the king's offspring,
Ezek 17:13 He also t away the mighty of
Ezek 19: 5 she t another of her cubs and
Ezek 23:10 t away her sons and daughters,
Ezek 23:13 both t the same way
Ezek 25:15 t vengeance with a spiteful
Ezek 27: 5 they t a cedar from Lebanon
Ezek 29: 7 When they t hold of you with
Ezek 40: 1 and He t me there
Ezek 40: 2 In the visions of God He t me
Ezek 40: 3 He t me there, and behold,
Ezek 42: 5 because the galleries t away
Dan 1:16 Thus the steward t away their
Dan 3:22 those men who t up Shadrach
Dan 5:20 they t his glory from him
Hos 1: 3 and t Gomer the daughter of
Hos 12: 3 He t his brother by the heel
Hos 13:11 and t him away in My wrath
Amos 1: 6 because they t captive the
Amos 7:15 Then the LORD t me as I
Zech 11: 7 I t for myself two staffs
Zech 11:10 I t my staff, Beauty, and cut
Zech 11:13 So I t the thirty pieces of
Matt 1:24 him and t to him his wife,
Matt 2:14 he t the young Child and His
Matt 2:21 t the young Child and His
Matt 4: 5 Then the devil t Him up into
Matt 4: 8 the devil t Him up on an
Matt 8:17 He Himself t our infirmities
Matt 9:25 t her by the hand, and the
Matt 12:14 t counsel against Him, how
Matt 13:31 a mustard seed, which a man t
Matt 13:33 like leaven, which a woman t
Matt 14:12 t away the body and buried it,
Matt 14:19 He t the five loaves and the
Matt 14:20 they t up twelve baskets full
Matt 15:36 He t the seven loaves and the
Matt 15:37 they t up seven large baskets
Matt 16: 9 and how many baskets you t up
Matt 16:10 many large baskets you t up
Matt 16:22 Then Peter t Him aside and
Matt 17: 1 after six days Jesus t Peter
Matt 18:28 t him by the throat, saying
Matt 20:17 t the twelve disciples aside
Matt 21:35 vinedressers t his servants
Matt 21:46 because they t Him for a
Matt 24:39 t them all away, so also will
Matt 25: 1 ten virgins who t their lamps
Matt 25: 3 were foolish t their lamps
Matt 25: 3 and t no oil with them
Matt 25: 4 but the wise t oil in their
Matt 25:35 was a stranger and you t Me in
Matt 26:26 were eating, Jesus t bread
Matt 26:27 Then He t the cup, and gave
Matt 26:37 He t with Him Peter and the
Matt 26:50 laid hands on Jesus and t Him
Matt 27: 1 and elders of the people t
Matt 27: 6 priests t the silver pieces
Matt 27: 7 they t counsel and bought with
Matt 27: 9 they t the thirty pieces of
Matt 27:24 he t water and washed his
Matt 27:27 soldiers of the governor t
Matt 27:30 t the reed and struck Him on
Matt 27:31 they t the robe off Him, put
Matt 27:48 t a sponge, filled it with
Matt 28:15 So they t the money and did as
Mark 1:31 t her by the hand and lifted
Mark 2:12 t up the bed, and went out in
Mark 4:36 they t Him along in the boat
Mark 5:40 He t the father and the mother
Mark 5:41 Then He t the child by the
Mark 6:29 t away his corpse and laid it
Mark 6:43 they t up twelve baskets full
Mark 7:33 And He t him aside from the
Mark 8: 6 He t the seven loaves and gave
Mark 8: 8 they t up seven large baskets
Mark 8:23 So He t the blind man by the
Mark 8:32 Peter t Him aside and began to
Mark 9: 2 after six days Jesus t Peter
Mark 9:27 But Jesus t him by the hand
Mark 9:36 Then He t a little child and
Mark 10:16 He t them up in His arms, put
Mark 10:32 Then He t the twelve aside
Mark 12: 3 And they t him and beat him and
Mark 12: 8 And they t him and killed him
Mark 12:20 The first t a wife
Mark 12:21 And the second t her, and he
Mark 14:22 were eating, Jesus t bread
Mark 14:23 Then He t the cup, and when He
Mark 14:33 He t Peter, James, and John
Mark 14:46 their hands on Him and t Him
Mark 15:20 they t the purple off Him,
Mark 15:46 t Him down, and wrapped Him
Luke 2: 2 This census first t place
Luke 2:28 he t Him up in his arms and
Luke 5:25 t up what he had been lying
Luke 6: 4 went into the house of God, t
Luke 8:54 t her by the hand and called,
Luke 9:10 And He t them and went aside
Luke 9:16 Then He t the five loaves and
Luke 9:28 sayings, that He t Peter,
Luke 9:47 t a little child and set him
Luke 10:34 to an inn, and t care of him
Luke 10:35 he t out two denarii, gave
Luke 13:19 a mustard seed, which a man t
Luke 13:21 like leaven, which a woman t
Luke 14: 4 He t him and healed him, and
Luke 18:31 Then He t the twelve aside and
Luke 20:29 And the first t a wife, and
Luke 20:30 the second t her as wife, and
Luke 20:31 Then the third t her, and in
Luke 22:17 Then He t the cup, and gave
Luke 22:19 He t bread, gave thanks and
Luke 22:20 Likewise He also t the cup
Luke 23:53 Then he t it down, wrapped it
Luke 24:30 with them, that He t bread
Luke 24:43 And He t it and ate in their
John 2: 8 And they t it
John 5: 9 well, t up his bed, and walked
John 6:11 Jesus t the loaves, and when
John 8:59 Then they t up stones to
John 10:31 Then the Jews t up stones
John 11:41 Then they t away the stone
John 12: 3 Then Mary t a pound of very
John 12:10 But the chief priests t
John 12:13 t branches of palm trees and
John 13: 4 t a towel and girded Himself
John 19: 1 So then Pilate t Jesus and
John 19:16 So they t Jesus and led Him
John 19:23 t His garments and made four
John 19:27 t her to his own home
John 19:38 came and t the body of Jesus
John 19:40 Then they t the body of Jesus
John 21:13 t the bread and gave it to
Acts 3: 7 he t him by the right hand and
Acts 4:26 of the earth t their stand
Acts 5:33 and t counsel to kill them
Acts 7:21 Pharaoh's daughter t him away
Acts 7:43 you t up the tabernacle of
Acts 9:25 the disciples t him by night
Acts 9:27 But Barnabas t him and brought
Acts 12:25 they also t with them John
Acts 13:29 they t Him down from the tree
Acts 15:39 And so Barnabas t Mark and
Acts 16: 3 he t him and circumcised him
Acts 16:33 he t them the same hour of
Acts 17: 5 t some of the evil men from
Acts 17:19 And they t him and brought him
Acts 18:17 all the Greeks t Sosthenes
Acts 18:17 But Gallio t no notice of
Acts 18:18 Then he t leave of the
Acts 18:21 but t leave of them, saying,
Acts 18:26 they t him aside and explained

Acts 19:13 t it upon themselves to call
Acts 20:14 we t him on board and came to
Acts 21:11 he t Paul's belt, bound his
Acts 21:26 Then Paul t the men, and the
Acts 21:32 He immediately t soldiers
Acts 21:33 t him, and commanded him to
Acts 23:18 So he t him and brought him to
Acts 23:19 commander t him by the hand
Acts 23:31 t Paul and brought him by
Acts 24: 7 with great violence t him out
Acts 27:28 they t soundings and found it
Acts 27:28 they t soundings again and
Acts 27:35 he t bread and gave thanks to
Acts 27:36 and also t food themselves
Acts 28:15 he thanked God and t courage
1Co 11:23 which He was betrayed t bread
1Co 11:25 also t the cup after supper
Gal 2: 1 and also t Titus with me
Heb 8: 9 I t them by the hand to lead
Heb 9:19 he t the blood of calves and
Rev 5: 7 t the scroll out of the right
Rev 8: 5 Then the angel t the censer
Rev 10:10 I t the little book out of
Rev 18:21 Then a mighty angel t up a

TOOL
Ex 20:25 for if you use your t on it
Ex 32: 4 it with an engraving t, and
Deut 27: 5 not use any iron t on them
Josh 8:31 no man has wielded any iron t
1Ki 6: 7 or chisel or any iron t was

TOOTH (*see* TEETH)
Ex 21:24 t for t, hand for hand,
Ex 21:24 eye for eye, t for t,
Ex 21:27 he knocks out his servant's t
Ex 21:27 or his maidservant's t
Ex 21:27 go free for the sake of his t
Lev 24:20 eye for eye, t for t
Deut 19:21 t for t, hand for hand,
Prov 25:19 of trouble is like a bad t
Matt 5:38 for an eye and a t for a t

TOP (*see* TOPMOST, TOPS)
Gen 11: 4 a tower whose t is in the
Gen 28:12 and its t reached to heaven
Gen 28:18 and poured oil on t of it
Ex 17: 9 I will stand on the t of the
Ex 17:10 went up to the t of the hill
Ex 19:20 on the t of the mountain
Ex 19:20 to the t of the mountain, and
Ex 24:17 a consuming fire on the t of
Ex 25:21 mercy seat on t of the ark
Ex 26:24 together at the t by one ring
Ex 30: 3 And you shall overlay its t
Ex 34: 2 on the t of the mountain
Ex 36:29 together at the t by one ring
Ex 37:26 its t, its sides all around,
Ex 40:19 of the tent on t of it, as
Ex 40:20 mercy seat on t of the ark
Num 14:40 and went up to the t of the
Num 20:28 on the t of the mountain
Num 21:20 to the t of Pisgah which
Num 23: 9 For from the t of the rocks I
Num 23:14 to the t of Pisgah, and built
Num 23:28 took Balaam to the t of Peor
Deut 3:27 Go up to the t of Pisgah
Deut 28:35 foot to the t of your head
Deut 34: 1 to the t of Pisgah, which is
Josh 15: 8 t of the mountain that lies
Josh 15: 9 t of the hill to the fountain
Judg 6:26 to the LORD your God on t of
Judg 9: 7 stood on t of Mount Gerizim,
Judg 9:51 went up to the t of the tower
Judg 16: 3 carried them to the t of the
1Sa 9:25 Saul on the t of the house
1Sa 9:26 to Saul on the t of the house
1Sa 26:13 stood on the t of a hill afar
2Sa 2:25 their stand on t of a hill
2Sa 15:32 come to the t of the mountain
2Sa 16: 1 past the t of the mountain
2Sa 16:22 Absalom on the t of the house
1Ki 7:17 were on t of the pillars
1Ki 7:18 the capitals that were on t
1Ki 7:19 t of the pillars in the hall
1Ki 7:29 frames was a pedestal on t
1Ki 7:31 inside the crown at the t was
1Ki 7:35 On the t of the cart, at the
1Ki 7:35 on the t of the cart, its
1Ki 7:41 were on t of the two pillars
1Ki 7:41 were on t of the pillars
1Ki 7:42 were on t of the pillars)
1Ki 10:19 the t of the throne was round
1Ki 18:42 went up to the t of Carmel
2Ki 1: 9 sitting on the t of a hill
2Ki 9:13 him on the t of the steps
2Ch 3:15 t of each of them was five
2Ch 3:16 put them on t of the pillars
2Ch 4:12 were on t of the two pillars
2Ch 4:12 were on t of the pillars
2Ch 25:12 them to the t of the rock
2Ch 25:12 down from the t of the rock
Esth 5: 2 touched the t of the scepter
Ps 72:16 On the t of the mountains
Prov 8: 2 on the t of the high hill
Prov 23:34 who lies at the t of the mast
Song 4: 8 Look from the t of Amana,
Song 4: 8 from the t of Senir
Is 2: 2 on the t of the mountains
Is 17: 6 the t of the uppermost bough
Is 30:17 as a pole on t of a mountain
Is 42:11 from the t of the mountains
Ezek 24: 7 she set it on t of a rock
Ezek 24: 8 set her blood on t of a rock
Ezek 26: 4 make her like the t of a rock
Ezek 26:14 make you like the t of a rock
Ezek 31: 3 its t was among the thick
Ezek 31:10 it set its t among the thick
Amos 1: 2 and the t of Carmel withers
Amos 9: 3 themselves on t of Carmel
Mic 4: 1 on the t of the mountains
Zech 4: 2 gold with a bowl on t of it
Matt 27:51 torn in two from t to bottom
Mark 15:38 torn in two from t to bottom
John 19:23 woven from the t in one piece
Heb 11:21 leaning on the t of his staff

TOPAZ
Ex 28:17 row shall be a sardius, a t
Ex 39:10 a row with a sardius, a t
Job 28:19 The t of Ethiopia cannot
Ezek 28:13 the sardius, t, and diamond,
Rev 21:20 the eighth beryl, the ninth t

TOPHEL
Deut 1: 1 Suph, between Paran, T, Laban

TOPHET (*see* TOPHETH)
Is 30:33 For T was established of old,
Jer 7:31 built the high places of T
Jer 7:32 it will no more be called T
Jer 7:32 for they will bury in T until
Jer 19: 6 shall no more be called T or
Jer 19:11 they shall bury them in T
Jer 19:12 and make this city like T
Jer 19:13 defiled like the place of T
Jer 19:14 Then Jeremiah came from T

TOPHETH (*see* TOPHET)
2Ki 23:10 And he defiled T, which is in

TOPMOST (*see* TOP)
Ezek 17: 4 cropped off its t young twig
Ezek 17:22 I will crop off from the t of

TOPPLE
Jer 10: 4 hammers so that it will not t

TOPS (*see* TOP)
Gen 8: 5 the t of the mountains were
Judg 9:25 him on the t of the mountains
Judg 9:36 from the t of the mountains
2Sa 5:24 the t of the mulberry trees
1Ki 7:16 to set on the t of the
1Ki 7:22 The t of the pillars were in
1Ch 14:15 the t of the mulberry trees
Is 15: 3 on the t of their houses and
Ezek 31:14 nor set their t among the

TORCH (*see* TORCHES)
Gen 15:17 and a burning t that passed
Judg 15: 4 put a t between each pair of
Zech 12: 6 like a fiery t in the sheaves
Rev 8:10 from heaven, burning like a t

TORCHES (*see* TORCH)
Judg 7:16 and t inside the pitchers
Judg 7:20 they held the t in their left
Judg 15: 4 and he took t, turned the
Judg 15: 5 When he had set the t on fire
Ezek 1:13 and like the appearance of t
Dan 10: 6 his eyes like t of fire, his
Nah 2: 3 flaming t in the day of his
Nah 2: 4 they seem like t, they run
John 18: 3 came there with lanterns, t

TORE (*see* TEAR)
Gen 37:29 and he t his clothes
Gen 37:34 Then Jacob t his clothes, put
Gen 44:13 Then they t their clothes, and
Num 14: 6 out the land, t their clothes
Josh 7: 6 Then Joshua t his clothes
Judg 8:17 Then he t down the tower of
Judg 11:35 that he t his clothes, and
Judg 14: 6 he t the lion apart as one
1Sa 15:27 the edge of his robe, and it t
2Sa 1:11 t them, and so did all the men
2Sa 13:19 t her robe of many colors
2Sa 13:31 t his garments and lay on the
1Ki 11:30 and t it into twelve pieces
1Ki 14: 8 t the kingdom away from the
1Ki 19:11 and strong wind t into the
1Ki 21:27 that he t his clothes and put
2Ki 2:12 and t them into two pieces
2Ki 5: 7 that he t his clothes and said
2Ki 6:30 woman, that he t his clothes
2Ki 10:27 t down the temple of Baal and
2Ki 11:14 Athaliah t her clothes and
2Ki 11:18 temple of Baal, and t it down
2Ki 17:21 For He t Israel from the
2Ki 19: 1 it, that he t his clothes,
2Ki 22:11 Law, that he t his clothes
2Ki 22:19 you t your clothes and wept
2Ki 23: 7 Then he t down the ritual
2Ch 23:13 So Athaliah t her clothes
2Ch 23:17 temple of Baal, and t it down
2Ch 34:19 Law, that he t his clothes
2Ch 34:27 you t your clothes and wept
Ezra 9: 3 I t my garment and my robe, and
Esth 4: 1 he t his clothes and put on
Job 1:20 t his robe and shaved his head
Job 2:12 and each one t his robe and
Ps 35:15 They t at me and did not cease
Is 37: 1 it, that he t his clothes,
Ezek 29: 7 and t all their shoulders
Amos 1:11 his anger t perpetually, and
Nah 2:12 The lion t in pieces enough
Matt 26:65 the high priest t his clothes
Mark 14:63 the high priest t his clothes
Acts 14:14 they t their clothes and ran
Acts 16:22 the magistrates t off their
Acts 22:23 t off their clothes and threw

TORMENT (*see* TORMENTED, TORMENTS)
Judg 16:19 Then she began to t him, and
Job 19: 2 How long will you t my soul
Is 50:11 you shall lie down in t
Matt 8:29 here to t us before the time
Mark 5: 7 by God that You do not t me
Luke 8:28 I beg You, do not t me
Luke 16:28 also come to this place of t
1Jn 4:18 fear, because fear involves t
Rev 9: 5 but to t them for five months
Rev 9: 5 months. And their t was like
Rev 14:11 of their t ascends forever
Rev 18: 7 the same measure give her t
Rev 18:10 a distance for fear of her t
Rev 18:15 a distance for fear of her t

TORMENTED (*see* TORMENT)
Matt 8: 6 home paralyzed, dreadfully t
Luke 6:18 were t with unclean spirits
Luke 16:24 for I am t in this flame
Luke 16:25 he is comforted and you are t
Acts 5:16 those who were t by unclean
Heb 11:37 being destitute, afflicted, t
2Pe 2: 8 t his righteous soul from day
Rev 11:10 t those who dwell on the
Rev 14:10 And he shall be t with fire
Rev 20:10 And they will be t day and

TORMENTS (*see* TORMENT)
Matt 4:24 with various diseases and t
Luke 16:23 And being in t in Hades, he

TORN (*see* TEAR)
Gen 31:39 That which was t by beasts I
Gen 37:33 doubt Joseph is t to pieces
Gen 44:28 Surely he is t to pieces"
Ex 22:13 If it is t to pieces by an
Ex 22:13 not make good what was t
Ex 22:31 is t by beasts in the field
Lev 7:24 of what is t by wild animals
Lev 13:45 is, his clothes shall be t
Lev 17:15 or what was t by beasts,
Lev 22: 8 dies naturally or is t by
Lev 22:24 or crushed, or t or cut
Josh 9: 4 donkeys, old wineskins t and

Josh 9:13 were new, and see, they are **t**
Judg 6:28 was the altar of Baal, **t** down
Judg 6:30 because he has **t** down the
Judg 6:31 his altar has been **t** down
Judg 6:32 he has **t** down his altar
Judg 14: 6 have **t** apart a young goat
1Sa 4:12 to Shiloh with his clothes **t**
1Sa 15:28 The LORD has **t** the kingdom of
1Sa 28:17 For the LORD has **t** the
2Sa 1: 2 camp with his clothes **t** and
2Sa 13:31 stood by with their clothes **t**
2Sa 15:32 to meet him with his robe **t**
1Ki 13:26 to the lion, which has **t** him
1Ki 13:28 the corpse nor **t** the donkey
1Ki 19:10 **t** down Your altars, and killed
1Ki 19:14 **t** down Your altars, and killed
2Ki 5: 8 of Israel had **t** his clothes
2Ki 5: 8 Why have you **t** your clothes
2Ki 18:37 Hezekiah with their clothes **t**
Ezra 9: 5 having **t** my garment and my
Job 31:22 let my arm be **t** from the
Is 36:22 Hezekiah with their clothes **t**
Jer 5: 6 there shall be **t** in pieces
Jer 41: 5 shaved and their clothes **t**
Lam 3:11 my ways and **t** me in pieces
Ezek 4:14 of itself or was **t** by beasts
Ezek 44:31 or was **t** by wild animals
Hos 6: 1 for He has **t**, but He will
Matt 27:51 **t** in two from top to bottom
Mark 15:38 **t** in two from top to bottom
Luke 23:45 of the temple was **t** in two
Rom 11: 3 and **t** down Your altars, and I

TORRENT (*see* TORRENTS)
Judg 5:21 The **t** of Kishon swept them
Judg 5:21 ancient **t**, the **t** of Kishon
Prov 27: 4 Wrath is cruel and anger a **t**

TORRENTS (*see* TORRENT)
Job 14:19 as **t** wash away the soil of

TORSO
1Sa 5: 4 only the **t** of Dagon was left

TORTURED (*see* TORTURERS)
Heb 11:35 And others were **t**, not

TORTURERS (*see* TORTURED)
Matt 18:34 delivered him to the **t** until

TOSS (*see* TOSSED, TOSSING)
Is 22:18 and **t** you like a ball into a
Jer 5:22 And though its waves **t** to and

TOSSED (*see* TOSS)
Is 54:11 one, **t** with tempest, and not
Matt 14:24 **t** by the waves, for the wind
Eph 4:14 **t** to and fro and carried about
Jas 1: 6 sea driven and **t** by the wind

TOSSING (*see* TOSS)
Job 7: 4 had my fill of **t** till dawn

TOTAL (*see* TOTALED, TOTALLY)
2Ch 26:12 The **t** number of chief
Job 20:26 **T** darkness is reserved for
Prov 5:14 I was on the verge of **t** ruin

TOTALED (*see* TOTAL)
Acts 19:19 it **t** fifty thousand pieces of

TOTALLY (*see* TOTAL)
Zech 11:17 right eye shall be **t** blinded

TOTTER (*see* TOTTERING)
Is 19: 1 Egypt will **t** at His presence
Is 24:20 and shall **t** like a hut
Is 40:20 carved image that will not **t**
Is 41: 7 pegs, that it might not **t**

TOTTERING (*see* TOTTER)
Ps 62: 3 a leaning wall and a **t** fence

TOU (*see* TOI)
1Ch 18: 9 When **T** king of Hamath heard
1Ch 18:10 had been at war with **T**)

TOUCH (*see* TOUCHED, TOUCHES, TOUCHING)
Gen 3: 3 eat it, nor shall you **t** it
Gen 20: 6 I did not let you **t** her
Ex 19:12 to the mountain or **t** its base
Ex 19:13 Not a hand shall **t** him, but
Lev 11: 8 carcasses you shall not **t**
Lev 12: 4 She shall not **t** any hallowed
Num 4:15 shall not **t** any holy thing
Num 16:26 **T** nothing of theirs, lest you
Deut 14: 8 or **t** their dead carcasses
Josh 9:19 therefore, we may not **t** them
Ruth 2: 9 the young men not to **t** you
2Sa 14:10 and he shall not **t** you anymore
2Sa 18:12 Beware lest anyone **t** the
1Ch 16:22 Do not **t** My anointed ones, and
Job 1:11 **t** all that he has, and he will
Job 2: 5 **t** his bone and his flesh, and
Job 5:19 in seven no evil shall **t** you
Job 6: 7 My soul refuses to **t** them
Ps 105:15 Do not **t** My anointed ones, And
Ps 144: 5 **T** the mountains, and they
Is 52:11 there, **t** no unclean thing
Jer 12:14 who **t** the inheritance which I
Lam 4:14 no one would **t** their garments
Lam 4:15 go away, go away, do not **t** us
Matt 9:21 If only I may **t** His garment
Matt 14:36 only **t** the hem of His garment
Mark 3:10 pressed about Him to **t** Him
Mark 5:28 If only I may **t** His clothes
Mark 6:56 Him that they might just **t**
Mark 8:22 Him, and begged Him to **t** him
Mark 10:13 to Him, that He might **t** them
Luke 6:19 multitude sought to **t** Him
Luke 11:46 you yourselves do not **t** the
Luke 18:15 to Him that He might **t** them
1Co 7: 1 for a man not to **t** a woman
2Co 6:17 Do not **t** what is unclean, and
Col 2:21 Do not **t**, do not taste, do
Heb 11:28 the firstborn should **t** them
1Jn 5:18 the wicked one does not **t** him

TOUCHED (*see* TOUCH)
Gen 26:29 harm, since we have not **t** you
Gen 32:25 He **t** the socket of his hip
Gen 32:32 because He **t** the socket of
Lev 22: 6 the person who has **t** any
Num 19:18 or on the one who **t** a bone
Num 31:19 and whoever has **t** any slain
Josh 4:18 priests' feet **t** the dry land
Judg 6:21 **t** the meat and the unleavened
1Sa 10:26 him, whose hearts God had **t**
1Ki 6:27 wing of the one **t** one wall
1Ki 6:27 other cherub **t** the other wall
1Ki 6:27 their wings **t** each other in
1Ki 19: 5 tree, suddenly an angel **t** him
1Ki 19: 7 time, and **t** him, and said,
2Ki 13:21 **t** the bones of Elisha, he
Esth 5: 2 and **t** the top of the scepter
Is 6: 7 he **t** my mouth with it, and
Is 6: 7 Behold, this has **t** your lips
Jer 1: 9 **t** my mouth, and the LORD said
Ezek 1: 9 Their wings **t** one another
Ezek 1:11 of each one **t** one another
Ezek 3:13 creatures that **t** one another
Dan 8:18 but he **t** me, and stood me
Dan 10:10 Then, suddenly, a hand **t** me
Dan 10:16 of the sons of men **t** my lips
Dan 10:18 the likeness of a man **t** me
Matt 8: 3 His hand and **t** him, saying,
Matt 8:15 He **t** her hand, and the fever
Matt 9:20 and **t** the hem of His garment
Matt 9:29 Then He **t** their eyes, saying,
Matt 14:36 as many as **t** it were made
Matt 17: 7 Jesus came and **t** them and said,
Matt 20:34 compassion and **t** their eyes
Mark 1:41 and **t** him, and said to him,
Mark 5:27 in the crowd and **t** His garment
Mark 5:30 and said, "Who **t** My clothes
Mark 5:31 You, and You say, 'Who **t** Me
Mark 6:56 as many as **t** Him were made
Mark 7:33 and He spat and **t** his tongue
Luke 5:13 His hand and **t** him, saying,
Luke 7:14 **t** the open coffin, and those
Luke 8:44 **t** the border of His garment
Luke 8:45 And Jesus said, "Who **t** Me?
Luke 8:45 You, and You say, 'Who **t** Me
Luke 8:46 Somebody **t** Me, for I
Luke 8:47 the reason she had **t** Him and
Luke 22:51 He **t** his ear and healed him
Heb 12:18 to the mountain that may be **t**

TOUCHES (*see* TOUCH)
Gen 26:11 He who **t** this man or his wife
Ex 19:12 Whoever **t** the mountain shall
Ex 29:37 Whatever **t** the altar must be
Ex 30:29 whatever **t** them must be holy
Lev 5: 2 Or if a person **t** any unclean
Lev 5: 3 Or if he **t** human uncleanness
Lev 6:18 Everyone who **t** them must be
Lev 6:27 Everyone who **t** its flesh
Lev 7:19 The flesh that **t** any unclean
Lev 7:21 who **t** any unclean thing, such
Lev 11:24 whoever **t** the carcass of any
Lev 11:26 Everyone who **t** it shall be
Lev 11:27 Whoever **t** any such carcass
Lev 11:31 Whoever **t** them when they are
Lev 11:36 but whatever **t** any such
Lev 11:39 he who **t** its carcass shall be
Lev 15: 5 whoever **t** his bed shall wash
Lev 15: 7 he who **t** the body of him who
Lev 15:10 Whoever **t** anything that was
Lev 15:11 he who has the discharge **t**
Lev 15:12 discharge **t** shall be broken
Lev 15:19 and whoever **t** her shall be
Lev 15:21 Whoever **t** her bed shall wash
Lev 15:22 whoever **t** anything that she
Lev 15:23 which she sits, when he **t** it
Lev 15:27 Whoever **t** those things shall
Lev 22: 4 And whoever **t** anything made
Lev 22: 5 or whoever **t** any creeping
Num 19:11 He who **t** the dead body of
Num 19:13 Whoever **t** the body of anyone
Num 19:16 Whoever in the open field **t**
Num 19:21 and he who **t** the water of
Num 19:22 person **t** shall be unclean
Num 19:22 the person who **t** it shall be
Judg 16: 9 of yarn breaks when it **t** fire
2Sa 23: 7 But the man who **t** them must
Job 4: 5 it **t** you, and you are troubled
Ps 104:32 He **t** the hills, and they smoke
Prov 6:29 whoever **t** her shall not be
Ezek 17:10 when the east wind **t** it
Amos 9: 5 He who **t** the earth and it
Hag 2:12 the edge he **t** bread or stew
Hag 2:13 of a dead body **t** any of these
Zech 2: 8 he who **t** you **t** the apple
Heb 12:20 as a beast **t** the mountain

TOUCHING (*see* TOUCH)
2Ch 3:11 **t** the wall of the room, and
2Ch 3:11 **t** the wing of the other
2Ch 3:12 **t** the wall of the room, and
2Ch 3:12 **t** the wing of the other
Dan 8: 5 earth, without **t** the ground
Luke 7:39 of woman this is who is **t** Him

TOWARD (*see* PREFACE)

TOWEL
John 13: 4 aside His garments, took a **t**
John 13: 5 to wipe them with the **t** with

TOWER (*see* TOWERED, TOWERS, WATCHTOWER)
Gen 11: 4 and a **t** whose top is in the
Gen 11: 5 the **t** which the sons of men
Gen 35:21 his tent beyond the **t** of Eder
Judg 8: 9 I will tear down this **t**
Judg 8:17 he tore down the **t** of Penuel
Judg 9:46 **t** of Shechem had heard that
Judg 9:47 that all the men of the **t** of
Judg 9:49 of the **t** of Shechem died,
Judg 9:51 was a strong **t** in the city
Judg 9:51 went up to the top of the **t**
Judg 9:52 came as far as the **t** and
Judg 9:52 of the **t** to burn it with fire
2Sa 22:51 He is the **t** of salvation to
2Ki 9:17 stood on the **t** in Jezreel
Neh 3: 1 far as the **T** of the Hundred
Neh 3: 1 as far as the **T** of Hananeel
Neh 3:11 as well as the **T** of the Ovens
Neh 3:25 on the **t** which projects from
Neh 3:26 east, and on the projecting **t**
Neh 3:27 to the great projecting **t**
Neh 12:38 going past the **T** of the Ovens
Neh 12:39 the **T** of Hananeal
Neh 12:39 the **T** of the Hundred, as far
Ps 61: 3 a strong **t** from the enemy
Ps 144: 2 and my fortress, My high **t**
Prov 18:10 of the LORD is a strong **t**
Song 4: 4 neck is like the **t** of David
Song 7: 4 Your neck is like an ivory **t**
Song 7: 4 Your nose is like the **t** of
Is 2:15 upon every high **t**, and upon
Is 5: 2 He built a **t** in its midst, and
Is 21: 5 set a watchman in the **t**, eat
Jer 31:38 **T** of Hananeel to the Corner
Mic 4: 8 And you, O **t** of the flock, the
Zech 9: 3 for Tyre built herself a **t**
Zech 14:10 from the **T** of Hananeel to the
Matt 21:33 winepress in it and built a **t**
Mark 12: 1 for the wine vat and built a **t**
Luke 13: 4 on whom the **t** in Siloam fell
Luke 14:28 you, intending to build a **t**

TOWERED (*see* TOWER)
Ezek 19:11 She t in stature above the

TOWERS (*see* TOWER)
2Ch 14: 7 make walls around them, and t
2Ch 26: 9 Uzziah built t in Jerusalem
2Ch 26:10 Also he built t in the desert
2Ch 26:15 skillful men, to be on the t
2Ch 27: 4 he built fortresses and t
2Ch 32: 5 broken, raised it up to the t
Ps 48:12 all around her. Count her t
Song 8:10 a wall, and my breasts like t
Is 23:13 They set up its t, they
Is 30:25 slaughter, when the t fall
Is 32:14 t will become lairs forever,
Is 33:18 Where is he who counts the t
Ezek 26: 4 of Tyre and break down her t
Ezek 26: 9 he will break down your t
Ezek 27:11 men of Gammad were in your t
Zeph 1:16 cities and against the high t

TOWN (*see* TOWNS)
Josh 13: 9 the t that is in the midst of
Ruth 3:11 of my t know that you are a
1Sa 16: 4 the elders of the t trembled
1Sa 23: 7 entering a t that has gates
1Sa 27: 5 in some t in the country,
2Sa 24: 5 t which is in the midst of
Hab 2:12 who builds a t with bloodshed
Matt 10:11 whatever city or t you enter
Mark 8:23 hand and led him out of the t
Mark 8:26 Neither go into the t
Mark 8:26 nor tell anyone in the t
Luke 5:17 out of every t of Galilee
John 7:42 and from the t of Bethlehem,
John 11: 1 the t of Mary and her sister
John 11:30 had not yet come into the t

TOWNS (*see* TOWN)
Gen 25:16 were their names, by their t
Num 32:41 went and took its small t, and
Deut 3: 5 besides a great many rural t
Josh 13:30 all the t of Jair which are
Josh 15:45 Ekron, with its t and villages
Josh 15:47 Ashdod with its t and villages
Josh 15:47 Gaza with its t
Josh 17:11 had Beth Shean and its t,
Josh 17:11 Ibleam and its t
Josh 17:11 inhabitants of Dor and its t
Josh 17:11 of En Dor and its t, the
Josh 17:11 of Taanach and its t, and the
Josh 17:11 of Megiddo and its t
Josh 17:16 are of Beth Shean and its t
Judg 10: 4 they also had thirty t, which
1Ki 4:13 to him belonged the t of Jair
1Ch 2:23 took from them the t of Jair
1Ch 2:23 Kenath and its t—sixty t
1Ch 7:28 were Bethel and its t
1Ch 7:28 to the west Gezer and its t
1Ch 7:28 and Shechem and its t
1Ch 7:28 as far as Ayyah and its t
1Ch 7:29 were Beth Shean and its t,
1Ch 7:29 Taanach and its t
1Ch 7:29 Megiddo and its t
1Ch 7:29 and its t, Dor and its t
1Ch 8:12 built Ono and Lod with its t
1Ch 18: 1 its t from the hand of the
Esth 9:19 t celebrated the fourteenth
Jer 19:15 on all her t all the doom
Zech 2: 4 inhabited as t without walls
Mark 1:38 Let us go into the next t
Mark 8:27 to the t of Caesarea Philippi
Luke 9: 6 and went through the t,
Luke 9:12 may go into the surrounding t

TRACE
Dan 2:35 that no t of them was found
Zeph 1: 4 I will cut off every t of

TRACHONITIS
Luke 3: 1 of Iturea and the region of T

TRACKED
Lam 4:18 They t our steps so that we

TRACT
2Ki 9:25 throw him into the t of the

TRADE (*see* TRADED, TRADER, TRADING)
Gen 34:10 Dwell and t in it, and acquire
Gen 34:21 dwell in the land and t in it
Gen 42:34 you, and you may t in the land
Ezek 17: 4 and carried it to a land of t
Ezek 28: 5 in t you have increased your
Amos 8: 5 that we may t our wheat
Acts 18: 3 because he was of the same t
Acts 19:25 have our prosperity by this t
Acts 19:27 So not only is this t of ours
Rev 18:17 and as many as t on the sea

TRADED (*see* TRADE)
Ezek 27:14 t for your wares with horses
Ezek 27:17 They t for your merchandise
Ezek 27:21 They t with you in lambs,
Ezek 27:22 They t for your wares the
Matt 25:16 t with them, and made another

TRADER (*see* TRADE, TRADERS)
Ezek 16:29 as far as the land of the t

TRADERS (*see* TRADER)
Gen 37:28 Then Midianite t passed by
1Ki 10:15 from the income of t, from
2Ch 9:14 merchants and t brought
Is 23: 8 whose t are the honorable of
Ezek 27:13 Tubal, and Meshech were your t
Ezek 27:15 The men of Dedan were your t
Ezek 27:17 land of Israel were your t

TRADING (*see* TRADE)
Ezek 28:16 your t you became filled with
Ezek 28:18 by the iniquity of your t
Luke 19:15 every man had gained by t

TRADITION (*see* TRADITIONS)
Matt 15: 2 the t of the elders
Matt 15: 3 of God because of your t
Matt 15: 6 of God of no effect by your t
Mark 7: 3 holding the t of the elders
Mark 7: 5 to the t of the elders, but
Mark 7: 8 of God, you hold the t of men
Mark 7: 9 God, that you may keep your t
Mark 7:13 of no effect through your t
Col 2: 8 according to the t of men
2Th 3: 6 not according to the t which
1Pe 1:18 by t from your fathers,

TRADITIONS (*see* TRADITION)
1Co 11: 2 keep the t as I delivered
Gal 1:14 for the t of my fathers
2Th 2:15 hold the t which you were

TRAGEDY
1Ki 17:20 have You also brought t on
1Ch 7:23 because t had come upon his

TRAIN (*see* TRAINED, TRAINING, TRAINS, UNTRAINED)
Prov 22: 6 T up a child in the way he
Is 6: 1 the t of His robe filled the

TRAINED (*see* TRAIN)
Gen 14:14 eighteen t servants who were
1Ch 12: 8 men t for battle, who could
Hos 10:11 Ephraim is a t heifer that
Luke 6:40 t will be like his teacher
Heb 12:11 those who have been t by it
2Pe 2:14 They have a heart t in

TRAINING (*see* TRAIN)
Dan 1: 5 and three years of t for them
Eph 6: 4 but bring them up in the t

TRAINS (*see* TRAIN)
Ps 144: 1 Who t my hands for war, And

TRAITOR (*see* TRAITORS)
Luke 6:16 Iscariot who also became a t

TRAITORS (*see* TRAITOR)
2Ti 3: 4 t, headstrong, haughty,

TRAMP
Gen 49:19 Gad, a troop shall t upon him

TRAMPLE (*see* TRAMPLED, TRAMPLING)
Ps 7: 5 Yes, let him t my life to the
Ps 44: 5 t those who rise up against
Ps 91:13 you shall t under foot
Is 1:12 your hand, to t My courts
Ezek 26:11 he will t all your streets
Dan 7:23 t it and break it in pieces
Mal 4: 3 You shall t the wicked, for
Matt 7: 6 lest they t them under their
Luke 10:19 authority to t on serpents

TRAMPLED (*see* TRAMPLE)
Judg 20:43 easily t them down as far as
2Ki 7:17 But the people t him in the
2Ki 7:20 for the people t him in the
2Ki 9:33 and he t her under foot
2Ki 14: 9 passed by and t the thistle
2Ch 25:18 passed by and t the thistle
Is 5: 5 wall, and it shall be t down
Is 25:10 Moab shall be t down under
Is 25:10 as straw is t down for the
Is 28: 3 Ephraim, will be t under foot
Is 28:18 then you will be t down by it
Is 63: 3 anger, and t them in My fury
Lam 1:15 The Lord has t underfoot all
Lam 1:15 The Lord t as in a winepress
Ezek 34:19 you have t with your feet
Dan 7:19 t the residue with its feet
Dan 8: 7 down to the ground and t him
Dan 8:10 to the ground, and t them
Dan 8:13 the host to be t under foot
Hos 4:14 do not understand will be t
Mic 7:10 now she will be t down like
Hab 3:12 you t the nations in anger
Matt 5:13 out and t under foot by men
Luke 8: 5 and it was t down, and the
Luke 12: 1 so that they t one another
Luke 21:24 And Jerusalem will be t by
Heb 10:29 t the Son of God underfoot
Rev 14:20 was t outside the city, and

TRAMPLING (*see* TRAMPLE)
Dan 7: 7 t the residue with its feet

TRANCE
Acts 10:10 made ready, he fell into a t
Acts 11: 5 in a t I saw a vision, an
Acts 22:17 the temple, that I was in a t

TRANSFER (*see* TRANSFERRED)
2Sa 3:10 to t the kingdom from the

TRANSFERRED (*see* TRANSFER)
1Co 4: 6 have figuratively t to myself

TRANSFIGURED
Matt 17: 2 and was t before them
Mark 9: 2 and He was t before them

TRANSFORM (*see* TRANSFORMED, TRANSFORMING, TRANSFORMS)
2Co 11:15 t themselves into ministers
Phil 3:21 who will t our lowly body

TRANSFORMED (*see* TRANSFORM)
Rom 12: 2 but be t by the renewing of
2Co 3:18 are being t into the same

TRANSFORMING (*see* TRANSFORM)
2Co 11:13 t themselves into apostles of

TRANSFORMS (*see* TRANSFORM)
2Co 11:14 For Satan himself t himself

TRANSGRESS (*see* TRANSGRESSED, TRANSGRESSES, TRANSGRESSING, TRANSGRESSION, TRANSGRESSOR)
Num 14:41 Now why do you t the command
1Sa 2:24 You make the LORD's people t
2Ch 24:20 Why do you t the
Esth 3: 3 Why do you t the king's
Ps 17: 3 that my mouth shall not t
Prov 8:29 would not t His command, when
Prov 16:10 mouth must not t in judgment
Prov 28:21 a piece of bread a man will t
Jer 2:20 and you said, 'I will not t
Ezek 20:38 and those who t against Me
Amos 4: 4 Come to Bethel and t, at
Zeph 3:11 in which you t against Me
Matt 15: 2 Why do Your disciples t the
Matt 15: 3 them, "Why do you also t the

TRANSGRESSED (*see* TRANSGRESS)
Deut 26:13 I have not t Your
Josh 7:11 they have also t My covenant
Josh 7:15 because he has t the covenant
Josh 23:16 When you have t the covenant
Judg 2:20 has t My covenant which I
1Sa 15:24 for I have t the commandment
1Ki 8:50 which they have t against You
2Ki 18:12 but t His covenant and all
1Ch 2: 7 who t in the accursed thing
2Ch 12: 2 they had t against the LORD
2Ch 26:16 for he t against the LORD his
2Ch 36:14 priests and the people t more
Ezra 10:10 You have t and have taken
Ezra 10:13 us who have t in this matter
Is 24: 5 because they have t the laws
Is 43:27 mediators have t against Me
Is 66:24 the men who have t against Me
Jer 2: 8 the rulers also t against Me
Jer 2:29 You all have t against Me
Jer 3:13 that you have t against the

Jer 33: 8 which they have **t** against Me
Jer 34:18 men who have **t** My covenant
Lam 3:42 We have **t** and rebelled
Ezek 2: 3 their fathers have **t** against
Dan 9:11 all Israel has **t** Your law
Hos 6: 7 like men they **t** the covenant
Hos 7:13 they have **t** against Me
Hos 8: 1 they have **t** My covenant and
Luke 15:29 I never **t** your commandment at

TRANSGRESSES (*see* TRANSGRESS)
Hab 1:11 his mind changes, and he **t**
Hab 2: 5 Indeed, because he **t** by wine
2Jn 9 Whoever **t** and does not abide

TRANSGRESSING (*see* TRANSGRESS)
Deut 17: 2 your God, in **t** His covenant,
Neh 13:27 **t** against our God by marrying
Is 59:13 in **t** and lying against the

TRANSGRESSION (*see* TRANSGRESS, TRANSGRESSIONS)
Ex 34: 7 forgiving iniquity and **t** and
Num 14:18 forgiving iniquity and **t**
2Ch 29:19 in his **t** we have prepared
Ezra 9: 4 because of the **t** of those who
Job 7:21 then do You not pardon my **t**
Job 8: 4 cast them away for their **t**
Job 13:23 Make me know my **t** and my sin
Job 14:17 My **t** is sealed up in a bag,
Job 33: 9 I am pure, without **t**
Job 34: 6 though I am without **t**
Ps 19:13 shall be innocent of great **t**
Ps 32: 1 is he whose **t** is forgiven
Ps 36: 1 the **t** of the wicked
Ps 59: 3 Not for my **t** nor for my sin,
Ps 89:32 visit their **t** with the rod
Ps 107:17 Fools, because of their **t**
Prov 12:13 ensnared by the **t** of his lips
Prov 17: 9 He who covers a **t** seeks love
Prov 17:19 He who loves **t** loves strife
Prov 19:11 to his glory to overlook a **t**
Prov 28: 2 Because of the **t** of a land
Prov 28:24 It is no **t**," the same is
Prov 29: 6 By **t** an evil man is snared,
Prov 29:16 are multiplied, **t** increases
Prov 29:22 and a furious man abounds in **t**
Is 24:20 its **t** shall be heavy upon it,
Is 57: 4 Are you not children of **t**
Is 58: 1 tell My people their **t**, and
Is 59:20 who turn from **t** in Jacob,"
Ezek 33:12 him in the day of his **t**
Dan 8:12 Because of **t**, an army was
Dan 8:13 and the **t** of desolation, the
Dan 9:24 holy city, to finish the **t**
Amos 4: 4 at Gilgal multiply **t**
Mic 1: 5 this is for the **t** of Jacob
Mic 1: 5 What is the **t** of Jacob
Mic 3: 8 to declare to Jacob his **t**
Mic 6: 7 I give my firstborn for my **t**
Mic 7:18 passing over the **t** of the
Acts 1:25 from which Judas by **t** fell
Rom 4:15 there is no law there is no **t**
Rom 5:14 the likeness of the **t** of Adam
1Ti 2:14 being deceived, fell into **t**
Heb 2: 2 proved steadfast, and every **t**

TRANSGRESSIONS (*see* TRANSGRESSION)
Ex 23:21 for He will not pardon your **t**
Lev 16:16 Israel, and because of their **t**
Lev 16:21 of Israel, and all their **t**
Josh 24:19 forgive your **t** nor your sins
1Ki 8:50 all their **t** which they have
Job 31:33 I have covered my **t** as Adam
Job 35: 6 if your **t** are multiplied,
Job 36: 9 them their work and their **t**
Ps 5:10 in the multitude of their **t**
Ps 25: 7 sins of my youth, nor my **t**
Ps 32: 5 will confess my **t** to the LORD
Ps 39: 8 Deliver me from all my **t**
Ps 51: 1 tender mercies, Blot out my **t**
Ps 51: 3 For I acknowledge my **t**, And
Ps 65: 3 As for our **t**, You will
Ps 103:12 has He removed our **t** from us
Is 43:25 out your **t** for My own sake
Is 44:22 like a thick cloud, your **t**
Is 50: 1 for your **t** your mother has
Is 53: 5 But He was wounded for our **t**
Is 53: 8 for the **t** of My people He was
Is 59:12 For our **t** are multiplied
Is 59:12 for our **t** are with us, and as
Jer 5: 6 because their **t** are many
Lam 1: 5 of the multitude of her **t**
Lam 1:14 The yoke of my **t** was bound
Lam 1:22 have done to me for all my **t**
Ezek 14:11 anymore with all their **t**, but
Ezek 18:22 None of the **t** which he has
Ezek 18:28 all the **t** which he committed
Ezek 18:30 and turn from all your **t**, so
Ezek 18:31 **t** which you have committed
Ezek 21:24 in that your **t** are uncovered,
Ezek 33:10 If our **t** and our sins lie upon
Ezek 37:23 nor with any of their **t**
Ezek 39:24 according to their **t** I have
Hos 10:10 I bind them for their two **t**
Amos 1: 3 For three **t** of Damascus, and
Amos 1: 6 For three **t** of Gaza, and for
Amos 1: 9 For three **t** of Tyre, and for
Amos 1:11 For three **t** of Edom, and for
Amos 1:13 For three **t** of the people of
Amos 2: 1 For three **t** of Moab, and for
Amos 2: 4 For three **t** of Judah, and for
Amos 2: 6 For three **t** of Israel, and for
Amos 3:14 I punish Israel for their **t**
Amos 5:12 For I know your manifold **t**
Mic 1:13 for the **t** of Israel were
Gal 3:19 It was added because of **t**
Heb 9:15 **t** under the first covenant

TRANSGRESSOR (*see* TRANSGRESS, TRANSGRESSORS)
Prov 26:10 his hire and the **t** his wages
Is 48: 8 were called a **t** from the womb
Rom 2:27 are a **t** of the law
Gal 2:18 destroyed, I make myself a **t**
Jas 2:11 have become a **t** of the law

TRANSGRESSORS (*see* TRANSGRESSOR)
Ps 37:38 But the **t** shall be destroyed
Ps 51:13 Then I will teach **t** Your ways
Ps 59: 5 be merciful to any wicked **t**
Is 1:28 The destruction of **t** and of
Is 46: 8 recall to mind, O you **t**
Is 53:12 and He was numbered with the **t**
Is 53:12 made intercession for the **t**
Dan 8:23 when the **t** have reached their
Hos 14: 9 them, but **t** stumble in them
Mark 15:28 He was numbered with the **t**
Luke 22:37 He was numbered with the **t**
Jas 2: 9 are convicted by the law as **t**

TRANSLATED (*see* TRANSLATION)
Ezra 4: 7 **t** into the Aramaic language
Matt 1:23 name Immanuel," which is **t**
Mark 5:41 Talitha, cumi," which is **t**
Mark 15:22 place Golgotha, which is **t**
Mark 15:34 which is **t**, "My God, My
John 1:38 (which is to say, when **t**
John 1:41 the Messiah" (which is **t**
John 1:42 called Cephas" (which is **t**
John 9: 7 pool of Siloam" (which is **t**
Acts 4:36 is **t** Son of Encouragement)
Acts 9:36 Tabitha, which is **t** Dorcas
Acts 13: 8 his name is **t**) withstood them
Col 1:13 **t** us into the kingdom of the
Heb 7: 2 part of all, first being **t**
Heb 11: 5 By faith Enoch was **t** so that
Heb 11: 5 found because God had **t** him"

TRANSLATION (*see* TRANSLATED)
Heb 11: 5 for before his **t** he had this

TRANSPARENT
Rev 21:21 was pure gold, like **t** glass

TRAP (*see* TRAPPED, TRAPS)
Job 18:10 and a **t** for him in the road
Ps 69:22 them, And their well-being a **t**
Is 8:14 the houses of Israel, as a **t**
Jer 5:26 they set a **t**
Amos 3: 5 where there is no **t** for it
Obad 7 bread shall lay a **t** for you
Rom 11: 9 table become a snare and a **t**

TRAPPED (*see* TRAP)
Jer 50:24 You have indeed been **t**, O
Ezek 19: 4 he was **t** in their pit, and
Ezek 19: 8 he was **t** in their pit

TRAPS (*see* TRAP)
Josh 23:13 **t** to you, and scourges on your
Ps 140: 5 They have set **t** for me
Ps 141: 9 from the **t** of the workers of

TRAVAIL (*see* TRAVAILED, TRAVAILS)
Ps 48: 6 And pain, as of a woman in **t**
Is 53:11 shall see the **t** of His soul
Gal 4:27 and shout, you who do not **t**

TRAVAILED (*see* TRAVAIL)
Gen 35:16 Rachel **t** in childbirth, and
Is 54: 1 you who have not **t** with child
Is 66: 7 Before she **t**, she gave birth
Is 66: 8 For as soon as Zion **t**, she

TRAVAILS (*see* TRAVAIL)
Ps 7:14 the wicked **t** with iniquity,

TRAVEL (*see* TRAVELED, TRAVELER, TRAVELING)
1Ki 2:42 **t** anywhere, you shall surely
Neh 9:12 the road which they should **t**
Job 21:29 asked those who **t** the road
Prov 4:15 Avoid it, do not **t** on it
Matt 23:15 For you **t** land and sea to win
Acts 19:29 Paul's **t** companions
2Co 8:19 to **t** with us with this gift
Rev 18:17 shipmaster, all who **t** by ship

TRAVELED (*see* TRAVEL)
1Sa 31:12 **t** all night, and took the body
Acts 11:19 Stephen **t** as far as Phoenicia

TRAVELER (*see* TRAVEL, TRAVELERS)
Judg 19:17 he saw the **t** in the open
2Sa 12: 4 a **t** came to the rich man, who
Job 31:32 opened my doors to the **t**)

TRAVELERS (*see* TRAVELER)
Judg 5: 6 the **t** walked along the byways
Job 6:19 the **t** of Sheba hope for them
Ezek 39:11 and it will obstruct **t**,

TRAVELING (*see* TRAVEL)
1Ki 10:15 that from the **t** merchants
2Ch 9:14 besides what the **t** merchants
Is 21:13 lodge, O you **t** companies of
Is 63: 1 **t** in the greatness of His
Matt 25:14 like a man **t** to a far country
Luke 24:13 two of them were **t** that same

TRAVERSE (*see* TRAVERSING)
Prov 8:20 I **t** the way of righteousness,

TRAVERSING (*see* TRAVERSE)
Ezek 27:19 your wares, **t** back and forth

TRAYS
Ex 25:38 their **t** shall be of pure gold
Ex 37:23 and its **t** of pure gold
Num 4: 9 its wick-trimmers, its **t**

TREACHEROUS (*see* TREACHEROUSLY, TREACHERY)
Ps 119:158 I see the **t**, and am disgusted,
Is 21: 2 the **t** dealer deals
Is 24:16 The **t** dealers have dealt
Is 24:16 the **t** dealers have dealt very
Jer 3: 7 her **t** sister Judah saw it
Jer 3: 8 yet her **t** sister Judah did
Jer 3:10 yet for all this her **t** sister
Jer 3:11 more righteous than **t** Judah
Jer 9: 2 an assembly of **t** men
Zeph 3: 4 are insolent, **t** people

TREACHEROUSLY (*see* TREACHEROUS)
Judg 9:23 dealt **t** with Abimelech,
1Sa 14:33 You have dealt **t**
Ps 25: 3 who deal **t** without cause
Is 21: 2 treacherous dealer deals **t**
Is 24:16 dealers have dealt **t**, indeed,
Is 24:16 dealers have dealt very **t**
Is 33: 1 and you who deal **t**, though
Is 33: 1 have not dealt **t** with you
Is 33: 1 you make an end of dealing **t**
Is 33: 1 they will deal **t** with you
Is 48: 8 that you would deal very **t**
Jer 3:20 as a wife **t** departs from her
Jer 3:20 so have you dealt **t** with Me
Jer 5:11 have dealt very **t** with Me
Jer 12: 1 are those happy who deal so **t**
Jer 12: 6 they have dealt **t** with you
Lam 1: 2 friends have dealt **t** with her
Hos 5: 7 have dealt **t** with the LORD
Hos 6: 7 There they dealt **t** with Me
Hab 1:13 You look on those who deal **t**
Mal 2:10 Why do we deal **t** with one
Mal 2:11 Judah has dealt **t**, and an
Mal 2:14 with whom you have dealt **t**
Mal 2:15 let none deal **t** with the wife

Mal 2:16 that you do not deal t
Acts 7:19 This man dealt t with our

TREACHERY (*see* TREACHEROUS)
Josh 22:16 What t is this that you have
Josh 22:22 or if in t against the LORD,
Josh 22:31 this t against the LORD
2Ki 9:23 to Ahaziah, "T, Ahaziah!"

TREAD (*see* TREADER, TREADING, TREADS)
Deut 11:25 upon all the land where you t
Deut 33:29 you shall t down their high
Josh 1: 3 will t upon I have given you
1Sa 5: 5 come into Dagon's temple t on
Job 24:11 t winepresses, yet suffer
Job 40:12 t down the wicked in their
Ps 60:12 who shall t down our enemies
Ps 91:13 You shall t upon the lion and
Ps 108:13 who shall t down our enemies
Is 10: 6 to t them down like the mire
Is 14:25 My mountains t him under foot
Is 16:10 No treaders will t out wine
Is 26: 6 The foot shall t it down
Jer 25:30 as those who t the grapes
Jer 48:33 no one will t with joyous
Ezek 34:18 that you must t down with
Amos 5:11 because you t down the poor
Mic 1: 3 t on the high places of the
Mic 6:15 you shall t the olives, but
Nah 3:14 into the clay and t the mortar
Zech 10: 5 who t down their enemies in
Rev 11: 2 they will t the holy city

TREADER (*see* TREAD, TREADERS)
Amos 9:13 the t of grapes him who sows

TREADERS (*see* TREADER)
Is 16:10 No t will tread out wine in

TREADING (*see* TREAD)
Neh 13:15 I saw in Judah some people t
Is 18: 2 t down, whose land the rivers
Is 18: 7 t down, whose land the rivers
Is 22: 5 t down and perplexity by the

TREADS (*see* TREAD)
Deut 11:24 of your foot t shall be yours
Deut 25: 4 ox while it t out the grain
Job 9: 8 t on the waves of the sea
Is 41:25 mortar, as the potter t clay
Is 63: 2 one who t in the winepress
Amos 4:13 who t the high places of the
Mic 5: 5 when he t in our palaces,
Mic 5: 6 when he t within our borders
Mic 5: 8 passes through, both t down
1Co 9: 9 ox while it t out the grain
1Ti 5:18 ox while it t out the grain
Rev 19:15 He Himself t the winepress of

TREASON
1Ki 16:20 the t he committed, are they
2Ki 11:14 and cried out, "T! T!"
2Ch 23:13 clothes and said, "T! T!"
Ezek 17:20 try him there for the t which

TREASURE (*see* TREASURED, TREASURER, TREASURES, TREASURING, TREASURY)
Gen 43:23 has given you t in your sacks
Ex 19: 5 t to Me above all people
Deut 7: 6 a special t above all the
Deut 14: 2 a special t above all the
Deut 28:12 will open to you His good t
1Ch 29: 3 my own special t of gold
Ezra 5:17 be made in the king's t house
Ps 17:14 You fill with Your hidden t
Ps 119:162 word As one who finds great t
Ps 135: 4 Israel for His special t
Prov 2: 1 t my commands within you,
Prov 7: 1 and t my commands within you
Prov 15: 6 the righteous there is much t
Prov 15:16 than great t with trouble
Prov 21:20 There is desirable t, and oil
Is 33: 6 the fear of the LORD is His t
Ezek 22:25 they have taken t and precious
Dan 1: 2 into the t house of his god
Nah 2: 9 There is no end of t, Or
Matt 6:21 For where your t is, there
Matt 12:35 t of his heart brings forth
Matt 12:35 t brings forth evil things
Matt 13:44 is like t hidden in a field
Matt 13:52 out of his t things new and
Matt 19:21 and you will have t in heaven
Mark 10:21 and you will have t in heaven
Luke 6:45 t of his heart brings forth
Luke 6:45 t of his heart brings forth
Luke 12:21 he who lays up t for himself
Luke 12:33 a t in the heavens that does
Luke 12:34 For where your t is, there
Luke 18:22 and you will have t in heaven
2Co 4: 7 But we have this t in earthen
Jas 5: 3 heaped up t in the last days

TREASURED (*see* TREASURE)
Job 23:12 I have t the words of His
Is 23:18 it will not be t nor laid up

TREASURER (*see* TREASURE, TREASURERS)
Ezra 1: 8 the hand of Mithredath the t
Rom 16:23 the t of the city, greets you

TREASURERS (*see* TREASURER)
Ezra 7:21 the t who are in the region
Neh 13:13 I appointed as t over the
Dan 3: 2 the counselors, the t, the
Dan 3: 3 the counselors, the t, the

TREASURES (*see* TREASURE)
Deut 32:34 with Me, sealed up among My t
Deut 33:19 and of t hidden in the sand
1Ki 14:26 he took away the t of the
1Ki 14:26 the t of the king's house
2Ki 20:13 them all the house of his t
2Ki 20:13 that was found among his t
2Ki 20:15 there is nothing among my t
2Ki 24:13 out from there all the t of
2Ki 24:13 the t of the king's house, and
2Ch 12: 9 took away the t of the house
2Ch 12: 9 the t of the king's house
2Ch 25:24 the t of the king's house, and
2Ch 28:21 For Ahaz took part of the t
2Ch 36:18 the t of the house of the
2Ch 36:18 the t of the king and of his
Ezra 6: 1 where the t were stored in
Job 3:21 for it more than hidden t
Job 20:26 is reserved for his t
Prov 2: 4 for her as for hidden t
Prov 10: 2 t of wickedness profit
Prov 21: 6 Getting t by a lying tongue
Eccl 2: 8 and the special t of kings
Is 2: 7 and there is no end to their t
Is 30: 6 and their t on the humps of
Is 39: 2 them the house of his t
Is 39: 2 that was found among his t
Is 39: 4 there is nothing among my t
Is 45: 3 give you the t of darkness
Jer 15:13 your t I will give as plunder
Jer 17: 3 your wealth, all your t, and
Jer 20: 5 all the t of the kings of
Jer 41: 8 us, for we have t of wheat
Jer 48: 7 in your works and your t, you
Jer 49: 4 Who trusted in her t, saying,
Jer 50:37 A sword is against her t, and
Jer 51:13 by many waters, abundant in t
Dan 11:43 have power over the t of gold
Obad 6 How his hidden t shall be
Mic 6:10 Are there yet the t of
Matt 2:11 when they had opened their t
Matt 6:19 up for yourselves t on earth
Matt 6:20 up for yourselves t in heaven
Col 2: 3 hidden all the t of wisdom
Heb 11:26 riches than the t in Egypt

TREASURIES (*see* TREASURY)
1Ki 7:51 he put them in the t of the
1Ki 15:18 t of the house of the LORD
1Ki 15:18 the t of the king's house, and
2Ki 12:18 t of the house of the LORD
2Ki 14:14 in the t of the king's house,
2Ki 16: 8 in the t of the king's house,
2Ki 18:15 in the t of the king's house
1Ch 9:26 and t of the house of God
1Ch 26:20 the t of the house of God
1Ch 26:20 over the t of the dedicated
1Ch 26:22 were over the t of the house
1Ch 26:24 Moses, was overseer of the t
1Ch 26:26 the t of the dedicated things
1Ch 27:25 Adiel was over the king's t
1Ch 28:11 vestibule, its houses, its t
1Ch 28:12 of the t of the house of God,
1Ch 28:12 of the t for the dedicated
2Ch 5: 1 he put them in the t of the
2Ch 8:15 matter or concerning the t
2Ch 16: 2 gold from the t of the house
2Ch 32:27 he made himself t for silver
Esth 3: 9 to bring it into the king's t
Esth 4: 7 king's t to destroy the Jews
Ps 135: 7 brings the wind out of His t
Prov 8:21 that I may fill their t
Is 10:13 and have robbed their t
Jer 10:13 brings the wind out of His t
Jer 51:16 brings the wind out of His t
Ezek 28: 4 gold and silver into your t

TREASURING (*see* TREASURE)
Rom 2: 5 t up for yourself wrath in

TREASURY (*see* TREASURE, TREASURIES)
Josh 6:19 come into the t of the LORD
Josh 6:24 they put into the t of the
1Ch 29: 8 stones gave them to the t of
Ezra 2:69 they gave to the t for the
Ezra 4:13 and the king's t will be
Ezra 6: 4 be paid from the king's t
Ezra 7:20 pay for it from the king's t
Neh 7:70 The governor gave to the t
Neh 7:71 t of the work twenty thousand
Job 38:22 you entered the t of snow
Job 38:22 have you seen the t of hail
Jer 38:11 house of the king under the t
Hos 13:15 He shall plunder the t of
Matt 27: 6 lawful to put them into the t
Mark 12:41 Now Jesus sat opposite the t
Mark 12:41 people put money into the t
Mark 12:43 those who have given to the t
Luke 21: 1 their gifts into the t,
John 8:20 words Jesus spoke in the t
Acts 8:27 who had charge of all her t

TREAT (*see* TREATED, TREATS)
Gen 32:12 I will surely t you well
Gen 34:31 Should he t our sister like a
Num 10:29 us, and we will t you well
Num 11:15 If You t me like this, please
Deut 21:14 you shall not t her brutally
Zech 8:11 But now I will not t the

TREATED (*see* TREAT)
Gen 12:16 He t Abram well for her sake
1Sa 20:34 father had t him shamefully
2Ch 30: 9 your children will be t with
Ps 119:78 For they t me wrongfully with
Matt 22: 6 t them spitefully, and killed
Mark 9:12 things and be t with contempt
Mark 12: 4 and sent him away shamefully t
Luke 20:11 t him shamefully, and sent him
Luke 23:11 t Him with contempt and
Acts 27: 3 Julius t Paul kindly and gave
1Th 2: 2 were spitefully t at Philippi
Heb 10:33 of those who were so t

TREATS (*see* TREAT)
Deut 27:16 Cursed is the one who t his
Job 39:16 She t her young harshly, as

TREATY
1Ki 3: 1 Now Solomon made a t with
1Ki 5:12 two of them made a t together
1Ki 15:19 Let there be a t between you
1Ki 15:19 break your t with Baasha king
1Ki 20:34 send you away with this t
1Ki 20:34 So he made a t with him
2Ch 16: 3 Let there be a t between you
2Ch 16: 3 break your t with Baasha king

TREE (*see* TREES)
Gen 1:11 the fruit t that yields fruit
Gen 1:12 and the t that yields fruit,
Gen 1:29 every t whose fruit yields
Gen 2: 9 the LORD God made every t
Gen 2: 9 The t of life was also in the
Gen 2: 9 the t of the knowledge of
Gen 2:16 Of every t of the garden you
Gen 2:17 but of the t of the knowledge
Gen 3: 1 eat of every t of the garden'
Gen 3: 3 but of the fruit of the t
Gen 3: 6 that the t was good for food
Gen 3: 6 a t desirable to make one
Gen 3:11 Have you eaten from the t of
Gen 3:12 with me, she gave me of the t
Gen 3:17 and have eaten from the t of
Gen 3:22 and take also of the t of life
Gen 3:24 the way to the t of life
Gen 12: 6 as the terebinth t of Moreh
Gen 18: 4 rest yourselves under the t
Gen 18: 8 them under the t as they ate
Gen 21:33 a tamarisk t in Beersheba
Gen 35: 4 t which was by Shechem
Gen 35: 8 Bethel under the terebinth t
Gen 40:19 from you and hang you on a t
Ex 9:25 broke every t of the field
Ex 10: 5 they shall eat every t which

Ex 15:25 and the LORD showed him a **t**
Lev 27:30 land or of the fruit of the **t**
Deut 12: 2 hills and under every green **t**
Deut 16:21 not plant for yourself any **t**
Deut 19: 5 with the ax to cut down the **t**
Deut 20:19 for the **t** of the field is
Deut 21:22 death, and you hang him on a **t**
Deut 21:23 not remain overnight on the **t**
Deut 22: 6 in any **t** or on the ground,
Josh 8:29 hanged on a **t** until evening
Josh 8:29 his corpse down from the **t**
Josh 19:33 the terebinth **t** in Zaanannim
Judg 4: 5 **t** of Deborah between Ramah
Judg 4:11 the terebinth **t** at Zaanaim
Judg 6:11 **t** which was in Ophrah, which
Judg 6:19 to Him under the terebinth **t**
Judg 9: 6 **t** at the pillar that was in
Judg 9: 8 And they said to the olive **t**
Judg 9: 9 But the olive **t** said to them
Judg 9:10 the trees said to the fig **t**
Judg 9:11 But the fig **t** said to them
Judg 9:37 the Diviners' Terebinth **T**
1Sa 10: 3 to the terebinth **t** of Tabor
1Sa 14: 2 **t** which is in Migron
1Sa 22: 6 under a tamarisk **t** in Ramah
1Sa 31:13 the tamarisk **t** at Jabesh, and
2Sa 18: 9 boughs of a great terebinth **t**
2Sa 18:10 hanging in a terebinth **t**
2Sa 18:14 the midst of the terebinth **t**
1Ki 4:25 under his vine and his fig **t**
1Ki 4:33 from the cedar **t** of Lebanon
1Ki 14:23 hill and under every green **t**
1Ki 19: 4 and sat down under a broom **t**
1Ki 19: 5 lay and slept under a broom **t**
2Ki 3:19 shall cut down every good **t**
2Ki 6: 5 as one was cutting down a **t**
2Ki 16: 4 hills, and under every green **t**
2Ki 17:10 hill and under every green **t**
2Ki 18:31 every one from his own fig **t**
1Ch 10:12 the tamarisk **t** at Jabesh, and
2Ch 28: 4 hills, and under every green **t**
Job 14: 7 For there is hope for a **t**
Job 15:33 his blossom like an olive **t**
Job 19:10 hope He has uprooted like a **t**
Job 24:20 should be broken like a **t**
Job 30: 4 broom **t** roots for their food
Ps 1: 3 He shall be like a **t** Planted
Ps 37:35 himself like a native green **t**
Ps 52: 8 olive **t** in the house of God
Ps 92:12 shall flourish like a palm **t**
Ps 120: 4 With coals of the broom **t**
Prov 3:18 She is a **t** of life to those
Prov 11:30 the righteous is a **t** of life
Prov 13:12 comes, it is a **t** of life
Prov 15: 4 tongue is a **t** of life, but
Prov 27:18 the fig **t** will eat its fruit
Eccl 11: 3 if a **t** falls to the south or
Eccl 11: 3 the place where the **t** falls
Eccl 12: 5 when the almond **t** blossoms
Song 2: 3 Like an apple **t** among the
Song 2:13 The fig **t** puts forth her
Song 7: 7 of yours is like a palm **t**
Song 7: 8 I will go up to the palm **t**
Song 8: 5 you under the apple **t**
Is 6:13 as a terebinth **t** or as an oak
Is 17: 6 the shaking of an olive **t**
Is 24:13 the shaking of an olive **t**
Is 34: 4 as fruit falling from a fig **t**
Is 36:16 every one from his own fig **t**
Is 40:20 chooses a **t** that will not rot
Is 41:19 the cedar and the acacia **t**
Is 41:19 the myrtle and the oil **t**
Is 41:19 in the desert the cypress **t**
Is 41:19 pine and the box **t** together,
Is 44:23 O forest, and every **t** in it
Is 55:13 shall come up the cypress **t**
Is 55:13 shall come up the myrtle **t**
Is 56: 3 Here I am, a dry **t**
Is 57: 5 with gods under every green **t**
Is 60:13 and the box **t** together, to
Is 65:22 for as the days of a **t**, so
Jer 1:11 I see a branch of an almond **t**
Jer 2:20 every green **t** you lay down
Jer 2:27 Saying to a **t**, 'You are my
Jer 3: 6 and under every green **t**, and
Jer 3:13 deities under every green **t**
Jer 8:13 vine, nor figs on the fig **t**
Jer 10: 3 for one cuts a **t** from the
Jer 10: 5 are upright, like a palm **t**
Jer 11:16 your name, green Olive **T**,
Jer 11:19 destroy the **t** with its fruit
Jer 17: 8 a **t** planted by the waters
Ezek 6:13 under every green **t**, and
Ezek 17: 5 and set it like a willow **t**
Ezek 17:24 have brought down the high **t**
Ezek 17:24 and exalted the low **t**
Ezek 17:24 dried up the green **t**
Ezek 17:24 and made the dry **t** flourish
Ezek 20:47 it shall devour every green **t**
Ezek 20:47 and every dry **t** in you
Ezek 31: 8 no **t** in the garden of God was
Ezek 31:14 that no **t** which drinks water
Ezek 41:18 a palm **t** between cherub and
Ezek 41:19 toward a palm **t** on one side
Ezek 41:19 a palm **t** on the other side
Dan 4:10 A **t** in the midst of the earth
Dan 4:11 The **t** grew and became strong
Dan 4:14 Chop down the **t** and cut off
Dan 4:20 The **t** that you saw, which
Dan 4:23 and saying, 'Chop down the **t**
Dan 4:26 the stump and roots of the **t**
Hos 9:10 the fig **t** in its first season
Hos 14: 6 shall be like an olive **t**, and
Hos 14: 8 I am like a green cypress **t**
Joel 1: 7 My vine, and ruined My fig **t**
Joel 1:12 up, and the fig **t** has withered
Joel 1:12 pomegranate **t**, the palm **t**
Joel 1:12 and the apple **t**
Joel 2:22 up, and the **t** bears its fruit
Joel 2:22 the fig **t** and the vine yield
Mic 4: 4 his vine and under his fig **t**
Hab 3:17 Though the fig **t** may not
Hag 2:19 As yet the vine, the fig **t**
Hag 2:19 the olive **t** have not yielded
Zech 3:10 his vine and under his fig **t**
Matt 3:10 Therefore every **t** which does
Matt 7:17 every good **t** bears good fruit
Matt 7:17 but a bad **t** bears bad fruit
Matt 7:18 A good **t** cannot bear bad
Matt 7:18 nor can a bad **t** bear good
Matt 7:19 Every **t** that does not bear
Matt 12:33 Either make the **t** good and its
Matt 12:33 good, or else make the **t** bad
Matt 12:33 for a **t** is known by its fruit
Matt 13:32 than the herbs and becomes a **t**
Matt 21:19 And seeing a fig **t** by the road
Matt 21:19 the fig **t** withered away
Matt 21:20 How did the fig **t** wither away
Matt 21:21 do what was done to the fig **t**
Matt 24:32 this parable from the fig **t**
Mark 11:13 afar a fig **t** having leaves
Mark 11:20 they saw the fig **t** dried up
Mark 11:21 The fig **t** which You cursed
Mark 13:28 this parable from the fig **t**
Luke 3: 9 Therefore every **t** which does
Luke 6:43 For a good **t** does not bear
Luke 6:43 nor does a bad **t** bear good
Luke 6:44 For every **t** is known by its
Luke 13: 6 fig **t** planted in his vineyard
Luke 13: 7 seeking fruit on this fig **t**
Luke 13:19 it grew and became a large **t**
Luke 17: 6 can say to this mulberry **t**
Luke 19: 4 into a sycamore **t** to see Him
Luke 21:29 Look at the fig **t**, and all the
John 1:48 when you were under the fig **t**
John 1:50 I saw you under the fig **t**
Acts 5:30 murdered by hanging on a **t**
Acts 10:39 they killed by hanging on a **t**
Acts 13:29 they took Him down from the **t**
Rom 11:17 and you, being a wild olive **t**
Rom 11:17 and fatness of the olive **t**
Rom 11:24 **t** which is wild by nature
Rom 11:24 to nature into a good olive **t**
Rom 11:24 into their own olive **t**
Gal 3:13 everyone who hangs on a **t**")
Jas 3:12 Can a fig **t**, my brethren,
1Pe 2:24 sins in His own body on the **t**
Rev 2: 7 to eat from the **t** of life
Rev 6:13 as a fig **t** drops its late
Rev 7: 1 on the sea, or on any **t**
Rev 9: 4 or any green thing, or any **t**
Rev 22: 2 the river, was the **t** of life
Rev 22: 2 each **t** yielding its fruit
Rev 22: 2 the leaves of the **t** were for
Rev 22:14 the right to the **t** of life

TREES (*see* TREE)
Gen 3: 2 fruit of the **t** of the garden
Gen 3: 8 God among the **t** of the garden
Gen 13:18 by the terebinth **t** of Mamre
Gen 14:13 **t** of Mamre the Amorite,
Gen 18: 1 by the terebinth **t** of Mamre
Gen 23:17 all the **t** that were in the
Gen 30:37 of the almond and chestnut **t**
Ex 10:15 all the fruit of the **t** which
Ex 10:15 nothing green on the **t** or on
Ex 15:27 of water and seventy palm **t**
Lev 19:23 all kinds of **t** for food, then
Lev 23:40 day the fruit of beautiful **t**
Lev 23:40 branches of palm **t**
Lev 23:40 the boughs of leafy **t**
Lev 26: 4 and the **t** of the field shall
Lev 26:20 nor shall the **t** of the land
Num 33: 9 of water and seventy palm **t**
Deut 6:11 olive **t** which you did not
Deut 8: 8 and barley, of vines and fig **t**
Deut 11:30 the terebinth **t** of Moreh
Deut 20:19 **t** by wielding an ax against
Deut 20:20 **t** which you know are not **t**
Deut 24:20 When you beat your olive **t**
Deut 28:40 olive **t** throughout all your
Deut 28:42 shall consume all your **t** and
Deut 34: 3 Jericho, the city of palm **t**
Josh 10:26 and hanged them on five **t**
Josh 10:26 on the **t** until evening
Josh 10:27 took them down from the **t**
Judg 9: 8 The **t** once went forth to
Judg 9: 9 and men, and go to sway over **t**
Judg 9:10 Then the **t** said to the fig
Judg 9:11 fruit, and go to sway over **t**
Judg 9:12 Then the **t** said to the vine
Judg 9:13 and men, and go to sway over **t**
Judg 9:14 Then all the **t** said to the
Judg 9:15 And the bramble said to the **t**
Judg 9:48 cut down a bough from the **t**
2Sa 5:11 to David, and cedar **t**, and
2Sa 5:23 in front of the mulberry **t**
2Sa 5:24 in the tops of the mulberry **t**
1Ki 4:33 Also he spoke of **t**, from the
1Ki 6:29 figures of cherubim, palm **t**
1Ki 6:32 figures of cherubim, palm **t**
1Ki 6:32 the cherubim and on the palm **t**
1Ki 6:35 he carved cherubim, palm **t**
1Ki 7:36 cherubim, lions, and palm **t**
2Ki 3:25 and cut down all the good **t**
2Ki 6: 4 the Jordan, they cut down **t**
2Ki 19:23 and its choice cypress **t**
1Ch 14: 1 to David, and cedar **t**, with
1Ch 14:14 in front of the mulberry **t**
1Ch 14:15 in the tops of the mulberry **t**
1Ch 16:33 Then the **t** of the woods shall
1Ch 22: 4 and cedar **t** in abundance
1Ch 27:28 Gederite was over the olive **t**
1Ch 27:28 the sycamore **t** that were in
2Ch 3: 5 gold, and he carved palm **t**
2Ch 9:27 he made cedar **t** as abundant
2Ch 28:15 Jericho, the city of palm **t**
Neh 8:15 branches, branches of oil **t**
Neh 8:15 and branches of leafy **t**, to
Neh 9:25 and fruit **t** in abundance
Neh 10:35 of all fruit of all **t**, year
Neh 10:37 the fruit from all kinds of **t**
Job 40:21 He lies under the lotus **t**
Job 40:22 The lotus **t** cover him with
Ps 74: 5 up Axes among the thick **t**
Ps 78:47 their sycamore **t** with frost
Ps 96:12 Then all the **t** of the woods
Ps 104:16 The **t** of the LORD are full of
Ps 104:17 has her home in the fir **t**
Ps 105:33 vines also, and their fig **t**
Ps 105:33 splintered the **t** of their
Ps 148: 9 Fruitful **t** and all cedars
Eccl 2: 5 all kinds of fruit **t** in them
Eccl 2: 6 the growing **t** of the grove
Song 2: 3 tree among the **t** of the woods
Song 4:14 with all **t** of frankincense,
Is 1:29 **t** which you have desired
Is 7: 2 people were moved as the **t** of
Is 10:19 Then the rest of the **t** of his
Is 14: 8 cypress **t** rejoice over you
Is 37:24 and its choice cypress **t**
Is 44:14 among the **t** of the forest
Is 55:12 all the **t** of the field shall
Is 61: 3 be called **t** of righteousness
Jer 3: 9 adultery with stones and **t**
Jer 5:17 up your vines and your fig **t**
Jer 6: 6 Hew down **t**, and build a mound
Jer 7:20 on the **t** of the field and on
Jer 17: 2 the green **t** on the high hills
Ezek 15: 2 is among the **t** of the forest
Ezek 15: 6 among the **t** of the forest

Ezek 17:24 all the t of the field shall
Ezek 20:28 high hills and all the thick t
Ezek 27: 5 planks of fir t from Senir
Ezek 31: 4 to all the t of the field
Ezek 31: 5 above all the t of the field
Ezek 31: 8 the fir t were not like its
Ezek 31: 8 the chestnut t were not like
Ezek 31: 9 so that all the t of Eden
Ezek 31:14 So that no t by the waters
Ezek 31:15 all the t of the field wilted
Ezek 31:16 and all the t of Eden, the
Ezek 31:18 To which of the t in Eden
Ezek 31:18 t of Eden to the depths of
Ezek 34:27 Then the t of the field shall
Ezek 36:30 multiply the fruit of your t
Ezek 40:16 on each gatepost were palm t
Ezek 40:22 archways, and also its palm t
Ezek 40:26 and it had palm t on its
Ezek 40:31 palm t were on its gateposts,
Ezek 40:34 palm t were on its gateposts
Ezek 40:37 palm t were on its gateposts
Ezek 41:18 made with cherubim and palm t
Ezek 41:20 and palm t were carved
Ezek 41:25 palm t were carved on the
Ezek 41:26 palm t on one side and on the
Ezek 47: 7 were very many t on one side
Ezek 47:12 all kinds of t used for food
Hos 2:12 her vines and her fig t, of
Joel 1:12 all the t of the field are
Joel 1:19 burned all the t of the field
Amos 4: 9 fig t, and your olive t
Nah 3:12 are fig t with ripened figs
Zech 1: 8 the myrtle t in the hollow
Zech 1:10 among the myrtle t answered
Zech 1:11 who stood among the myrtle t
Zech 4: 3 Two olive t are by it, one at
Zech 4:11 What are these two olive t
Zech 11: 2 the mighty t are ruined
Matt 3:10 is laid to the root of the t
Matt 21: 8 cut down branches from the t
Mark 8:24 I see men like t, walking
Mark 11: 8 leafy branches from the t
Luke 3: 9 is laid to the root of the t
Luke 21:29 at the fig tree, and all the t
John 12:13 took branches of palm t and
Jude 12 late autumn t without fruit,
Rev 7: 3 or the t till we have sealed
Rev 8: 7 third of the t were burned up
Rev 11: 4 These are the two olive t

TREMBLE (*see* TREMBLED, TREMBLES, TREMBLING)
Deut 2:25 the report of you, and shall t
Deut 20: 3 and do not t or be terrified
1Ch 16:30 T before Him, all the earth
Ezra 10: 3 and of those who t at the
Esth 5: 9 did not stand or t before him
Job 9: 6 its place, and its pillars t
Job 26: 5 The dead t, those under the
Job 26:11 The pillars of heaven t, and
Ps 60: 2 You have made the earth t
Ps 96: 9 T before Him, all the earth
Ps 99: 1 Let the peoples t
Ps 114: 7 T, O earth, at the presence
Eccl 12: 3 the keepers of the house t
Is 14:16 the man who made the earth t
Is 32:11 T, you women who are at ease
Is 64: 2 may t at Your presence
Is 66: 5 LORD, you who t at His word
Jer 5:22 Will you not t at My
Jer 10:10 At His wrath the earth will t
Jer 33: 9 t for all the goodness and all
Jer 51:29 And the land will t and sorrow
Ezek 7:27 of the common people will t
Ezek 26:16 ground, t every moment, and be
Ezek 26:18 Now the coastlands t on the
Ezek 32:10 they shall t every moment,
Dan 6:26 of my kingdom men must t and
Dan 10:10 which made me t on my knees
Joel 2: 1 the inhabitants of the land t
Joel 2:10 before them, the heavens t
Amos 8: 8 Shall the land not t for this
Jas 2:19 the demons believe—and t!

TREMBLED (*see* TREMBLE)
Gen 27:33 Then Isaac t exceedingly, and
Ex 19:16 people who were in the camp t
Ex 20:18 the people saw it, they t
Judg 5: 4 field of Edom, the earth t
1Sa 4:13 for his heart t for the ark
1Sa 14:15 and the raiders also t
1Sa 16: 4 of the town t at his coming
1Sa 28: 5 and his heart t greatly
2Sa 22: 8 Then the earth shook and t
Ezra 9: 4 Then everyone who t at the
Ps 18: 7 Then the earth shook and t
Ps 77:16 The depths also t
Ps 77:18 The earth t and shook
Is 5:25 stricken them, and the hills t
Jer 4:24 mountains, and indeed they t
Jer 8:16 The whole land t at the sound
Dan 5:19 nations, and languages t and
Hab 3: 7 of the land of Midian t
Hab 3:10 The mountains saw You and t
Hab 3:16 When I heard, my body t
Hab 3:16 I t in myself, that I might
Mark 16: 8 from the tomb, for they t
Acts 7:32 And Moses t and dared not look

TREMBLES (*see* TREMBLE)
Job 37: 1 At this also my heart t, and
Ps 97: 4 The earth sees and t
Ps 104:32 looks on the earth, and it t
Ps 119:120 My flesh t for fear of You,
Is 66: 2 spirit, and who t at My word
Jer 50:46 taking of Babylon the earth t

TREMBLING (*see* TREMBLE)
Ex 15:15 t will take hold of them
Deut 28:65 LORD will give you a t heart
1Sa 13: 7 all the people followed him t
1Sa 14:15 there was t in the camp, in
1Sa 14:15 so that it was a very great t
Ezra 10: 9 t because of this matter and
Job 4:14 fear came upon me, and t,
Job 21: 6 and t takes hold of my flesh
Ps 2:11 with fear, And rejoice with t
Ps 55: 5 and t have come upon me, And
Is 51:17 the dregs of the cup of t
Is 51:22 out of your hand the cup of t
Jer 30: 5 We have heard a voice of t
Ezek 12:18 and drink your water with t
Ezek 26:16 will clothe themselves with t
Dan 10:11 this word to me, I stood t
Hos 11:10 shall come t from the west
Hos 11:11 they shall come t like a bird
Hos 13: 1 When Ephraim spoke, t, he
Mark 5:33 But the woman, fearing and t
Luke 8:47 was not hidden, she came t
Acts 9: 6 So he, t and astonished, said,
Acts 16:29 fell down t before Paul and
1Co 2: 3 in fear, and in much t
2Co 7:15 fear and t you received him
Eph 6: 5 to the flesh, with fear and t
Phil 2:12 own salvation with fear and t
Heb 12:21 I am exceedingly afraid and t

TRENCH
1Ki 18:32 he made a t around the altar
1Ki 18:35 also filled the t with water
1Ki 18:38 the water that was in the t

TRESPASS (*see* TRESPASSED, TRESPASSES)
Gen 31:36 What is my t
Gen 50:17 the t of your brothers and
Gen 50:17 forgive the t of the servants
Ex 22: 9 For any kind of t, whether it
Lev 5: 6 he shall bring his t offering
Lev 5: 7 LORD, for his t which he has
Lev 5:15 If a person commits a t, and
Lev 5:15 his t offering a ram without
Lev 5:15 sanctuary, as a t offering
Lev 5:16 the ram of the t offering
Lev 5:18 valuation, as a t offering
Lev 5:19 It is a t offering
Lev 6: 2 commits a t against the LORD
Lev 6: 5 on the day of his t offering
Lev 6: 6 he shall bring his t offering
Lev 6: 6 as a t offering, to the
Lev 6:17 offering and the t offering
Lev 7: 1 this is the law of the t
Lev 7: 2 shall kill the t offering
Lev 7: 5 It is a t offering
Lev 7: 7 The t offering is like the
Lev 7:37 offering, the t offering, the
Lev 14:12 and offer it as a t offering
Lev 14:13 so is the t offering
Lev 14:14 the blood of the t offering
Lev 14:17 the blood of the t offering
Lev 14:21 as a t offering to be waved
Lev 14:24 the lamb of the t offering
Lev 14:25 the lamb of the t offering
Lev 14:25 the blood of the t offering
Lev 14:28 the blood of the t offering
Lev 19:21 he shall bring his t offering
Lev 19:21 a ram as a t offering
Lev 19:22 t offering before the LORD
Lev 22:16 of t when they eat their holy
Num 5: 7 for his t in full value plus
Num 6:12 first year as a t offering
Num 18: 9 every t offering which they
Num 31:16 to t against the LORD in the
Josh 7: 1 of Israel committed a t
Josh 22:20 a t in the accursed thing
1Sa 6: 3 it to Him with a t offering
1Sa 6: 4 What is the t offering which
1Sa 6: 8 are returning to Him as a t
1Sa 6:17 as a t offering to the LORD
1Sa 25:28 Please forgive the t of your
2Ki 12:16 money from the t offerings
2Ch 19:10 lest they t against the LORD
2Ch 24:18 Jerusalem because of their t
2Ch 33:19 entreaty, and all his sin and t
Ezra 9: 2 has been foremost in this t
Ezra 10:19 the flock as their t offering
Ezek 40:39 offering, and the t offering
Ezek 42:13 offering, and the t offering
Ezek 44:29 offering, and the t offering
Ezek 46:20 shall boil the t offering
Gal 6: 1 a man is overtaken in any t

TRESPASSED (*see* TRESPASS)
Lev 5:19 certainly t against the LORD
Deut 32:51 because you t against Me
2Ch 26:18 the sanctuary, for you have t
2Ch 29: 6 For our fathers have t and
2Ch 30: 7 who t against the LORD God of
2Ch 33:23 but Amon t more and more
Ezra 10: 2 We have t against our God, and

TRESPASSES (*see* TRESPASS)
Lev 6: 7 may have done in which he t
Ps 68:21 who still goes on in His t
Matt 6:14 if you forgive men their t
Matt 6:15 do not forgive men their t
Matt 6:15 your Father forgive your t
Matt 18:35 not forgive his brother his t
Mark 11:25 may also forgive you your t
Mark 11:26 in heaven forgive your t
2Co 5:19 not imputing their t to them
Eph 2: 1 alive, who were dead in t
Eph 2: 5 even when we were dead in t
Col 2:13 And you, being dead in your t
Col 2:13 having forgiven you all t
Jas 5:16 Confess your t to one another

TRESSES
Song 7: 5 king is held captive by its t

TRIAL (*see* TRIALS)
Ps 95: 8 as in the day of t in the
2Co 8: 2 that in a great t of
Gal 4:14 my t which was in my flesh
Heb 3: 8 in the day of t in the
Heb 11:36 others had t of mockings and
1Pe 4:12 fiery t which is to try you
Rev 3:10 t which shall come upon the

TRIALS (*see* TRIAL)
Deut 4:34 midst of another nation, by t
Deut 7:19 the great t which your eyes
Deut 29: 3 the great t which your eyes
Luke 22:28 continued with Me in My t
Acts 20:19 t which happened to me by the
Jas 1: 2 when you fall into various t
1Pe 1: 6 been grieved by various t

TRIBAL (*see* TRIBE)
Ezek 45: 7 with one of the t portions
Ezek 48:21 adjacent to the t portions

TRIBE (*see* TRIBAL, TRIBES)
Ex 31: 2 son of Hur, of the t of Judah
Ex 31: 6 of Ahisamach, of the t of Dan
Ex 35:30 son of Hur, of the t of Judah
Ex 35:34 of Ahisamach, of the t of Dan
Ex 38:22 of the t of Judah, made all
Ex 38:23 of Ahisamach, of the t of Dan
Lev 24:11 of Dibri, of the t of Dan
Num 1: 4 shall be a man from every t
Num 1:21 t of Reuben were forty-six
Num 1:23 who were numbered of the t of
Num 1:25 the t of Gad were forty-five
Num 1:27 who were numbered of the t of
Num 1:29 who were numbered of the t of
Num 1:31 who were numbered of the t of
Num 1:33 the t of Ephraim were forty

Judg 20:12 Then the t of Israel sent men
Judg 21: 5 t of Israel who did not come
Judg 21: 8 t of Israel who did not come
Judg 21:15 a void in the t of Israel
1Sa 2:28 t of Israel to be My priest
1Sa 9:21 smallest of the t of Israel
1Sa 10:19 before the LORD by your t
1Sa 10:20 the t of Israel to come near
1Sa 15:17 not head of the t of Israel
2Sa 5: 1 Then all the t of Israel came
2Sa 7: 7 anyone from the t of Israel
2Sa 15:10 all the t of Israel, saying,
2Sa 19: 9 all the t of Israel, saying,
2Sa 20:14 all the t of Israel to Abel
2Sa 24: 2 all the t of Israel, from Dan
1Ki 8: 1 and all the heads of the t
1Ki 11:31 and will give ten t to you
1Ki 11:32 out of all the t of Israel)
1Ki 11:35 ten t
1Ki 14:21 out of all the t of Israel
1Ki 18:31 of the t of the sons of Jacob
2Ki 21: 7 out of all the t of Israel
1Ch 27:16 over the t of Israel
1Ch 27:22 leaders of the t of Israel
1Ch 28: 1 the officers of the t and the
1Ch 29: 6 leaders of the t of Israel
2Ch 5: 2 and all the heads of the t
2Ch 11:16 from all the t of Israel,
2Ch 12:13 out of all the t of Israel
2Ch 33: 7 out of all the t of Israel
Ezra 6:17 the number of the t of Israel
Ps 78:55 made the t of Israel dwell in
Ps 105:37 was none feeble among His t
Ps 122: 4 Where the t go up
Ps 122: 4 The t of the LORD, To the
Is 19:13 who are the mainstay of its t
Is 49: 6 to raise up the t of Jacob
Is 63:17 the t of Your inheritance
Ezek 37:19 and the t of Israel, his
Ezek 45: 8 Israel, according to their t
Ezek 47:13 among the twelve t of Israel
Ezek 47:21 according to the t of Israel
Ezek 47:22 you among the t of Israel
Ezek 48: 1 these are the names of the t
Ezek 48:19 from all the t of Israel
Ezek 48:23 As for the rest of the t,
Ezek 48:29 among the t of Israel, and
Ezek 48:31 named after the t of Israel)
Hos 5: 9 among the t of Israel I make
Zech 9: 1 all the t of Israel are on
Matt 19:28 the twelve t of Israel
Matt 24:30 then all the t of the earth
Luke 22:30 the twelve t of Israel
Acts 26: 7 To this promise our twelve t
Jas 1: 1 To the twelve t which are
Rev 1: 7 all the t of the earth will
Rev 7: 4 thousand of all the t of the
Rev 7: 9 number, of all nations, t
Rev 11: 9 those from the peoples, t
Rev 21:12 t of the children of Israel

TRIBULATION (*see* TRIBULATIONS)
1Sa 26:24 Him deliver me out of all t
Matt 13:21 For when t or persecution
Matt 24: 9 they will deliver you up to t
Matt 24:21 then there will be great t
Matt 24:29 Immediately after the t of
Mark 4:17 when t or persecution arises
Mark 13:19 in those days there will be t
Mark 13:24 in those days, after that t
John 16:33 In the world you will have t
Rom 2: 9 t and anguish, on every soul
Rom 5: 3 knowing that t produces
Rom 8:35 Shall t, or distress, or
Rom 12:12 in hope, patient in t,
2Co 1: 4 who comforts us in all our t
2Co 7: 4 joyful in all our t
1Th 3: 4 you that we would suffer t
2Th 1: 6 with t those who trouble you
Rev 1: 9 brother and companion in t
Rev 2: 9 I know your works, t, and
Rev 2:10 and you will have t ten days
Rev 2:22 with her into great t, unless
Rev 7:14 who come out of the great t

TRIBULATIONS (*see* TRIBULATION)
1Sa 10:19 your adversities and your t
Acts 14:22 We must through many t enter
Acts 20:23 that chains and t await me
Rom 5: 3 that, but we also glory in t
2Co 6: 4 in much patience, in t, in
Eph 3:13 lose heart at my t for you
2Th 1: 4 and t that you endure,
Heb 10:33 both by reproaches and t, and

TRIBUTE
Num 31:28 levy a t for the LORD on the
Num 31:37 the LORD's t of the sheep was
Num 31:38 the LORD's t was seventy-two
Num 31:39 the LORD's t was sixty-one
Num 31:40 of which the LORD's t was
Num 31:41 So Moses gave the t which was
Deut 16:10 the LORD your God with the t
Deut 20:11 be placed under t to you, and
Judg 1:28 put the Canaanites under t
Judg 1:30 them, and were put under t
Judg 1:33 were put under t to them
Judg 1:35 they were put under t
Judg 3:15 sent t to Eglon king of Moab
Judg 3:17 So he brought the t to Eglon
Judg 3:18 had finished presenting the t
Judg 3:18 people who had carried the t
2Sa 8: 2 servants, and brought t
2Sa 8: 6 servants, and brought t
1Ki 4:21 They brought t and served
2Ki 17: 3 vassal, and paid him t money
2Ki 17: 4 brought no t to the king of
2Ki 23:33 he imposed on the land a t of
1Ch 18: 2 servants, and brought t
1Ch 18: 6 servants, and brought t
2Ch 17:11 presents and silver as t
2Ch 26: 8 Ammonites brought t to Uzziah
2Ch 36: 3 he imposed on the land a t of
Ezra 4:13 they will not pay tax, t
Ezra 4:20 and tax, t, and custom were
Ezra 7:24 be lawful to impose tax, t
Esth 10: 1 imposed t on the land and on

TRICKERY
Is 25:11 with the t of their hands
Matt 26: 4 and plotted to take Jesus by t
Mark 14: 1 how they might take Him by t
Eph 4:14 of doctrine, by the t of men

TRICKLING
Job 28:11 He dams up the streams from t

TRIED (*see* TRY)
1Sa 17:39 he t to walk, for he had not
Ezra 4: 4 t to discourage the people of
Esth 8: 7 on the gallows because he t
Job 34:36 that Job were t to the utmost
Ps 12: 6 Like silver t in a furnace of
Ps 17: 3 You have t me and have found
Is 28:16 a t stone, a precious
Matt 3:14 John t to prevent Him, saying
Luke 4:42 t to keep Him from leaving
Acts 9:26 t to reconcile them, saying
Acts 9:26 he t to join the disciples
Acts 16: 7 they t to go into Bithynia,
Acts 24: 6 He even t to profane the
Acts 26:21 in the temple and t to kill me
Gal 1:13 measure and t to destroy it
Gal 1:23 which he once t to destroy

TRIFLES
Prov 18: 8 a talebearer are like tasty t
Prov 26:22 a talebearer are like tasty t

TRIM (*see* TRIMMED, TRIMMERS)
Deut 21:12 shave her head and t her nails

TRIMMED (*see* TRIM)
2Sa 19:24 feet, nor t his mustache, nor
1Ki 7: 9 t with saws, inside and out,
Ezek 44:20 shall keep their hair well t
Matt 25: 7 arose and t their lamps

TRIMMERS (*see* TRIM)
1Ki 7:50 the basins, the t, the bowls,
2Ki 12:13 the LORD basins of silver, t
2Ki 25:14 the pots, the shovels, the t
2Ch 4:22 the t, the bowls, the ladles,
Jer 52:18 the pots, the shovels, the t

TRIUMPH (*see* TRIUMPHED, TRIUMPHING, TRIUMPHS)
Gen 49:19 him, but he shall t at last
2Sa 1:20 of the uncircumcised t
1Ch 16:35 name, to t in Your praise
Ps 25: 2 Let not my enemies t over me
Ps 41:11 my enemy does not t over me
Ps 47: 1 to God with the voice of t
Ps 60: 8 shout in t because of Me
Ps 92: 4 I will t in the works of Your
Ps 94: 3 How long will the wicked t
Ps 106:47 name, And to t in Your praise
Ps 108: 9 Over Philistia I will t
2Co 2:14 leads us in t in Christ, and

TRIUMPHED (*see* TRIUMPH)
Ex 15: 1 LORD, for He has t gloriously
Ex 15:21 LORD, for He has t gloriously

TRIUMPHING (*see* TRIUMPH)
Job 20: 5 That the t of the wicked is
Col 2:15 of them, t over them in it

TRIUMPHS (*see* TRIUMPH)
Jas 2:13 Mercy t over judgment

TRIVIAL
1Ki 16:31 as though it had been a t
2Ki 3:18 this is but a t thing in the
Ezek 8:17 Is it a t thing to the house

TROAS
Acts 16: 8 by Mysia, they came down to T
Acts 16:11 Therefore, sailing from T
Acts 20: 5 ahead, waited for us at T
Acts 20: 6 in five days joined them at T
2Co 2:12 when I came to T to preach
2Ti 4:13 Carpus at T when you come

TROD (*see* TRODDEN)
Judg 9:27 and t them, and made merry
2Sa 22:43 I t them like dirt in the
Job 22:15 way which wicked men have t

TRODDEN (*see* TROD)
Josh 14: 9 land where your foot has t
Job 28: 8 The proud lions have not t it
Is 14:19 like a corpse t under foot
Is 63: 3 I have t the winepress alone,
Is 63: 3 For I have t them in My anger
Is 63: 6 I have t down the peoples in
Is 63:18 have t down Your sanctuary
Jer 12:10 they have t My portion under

TROGYLLIUM
Acts 20:15 at Samos and stayed at T

TROOP (*see* TROOPS)
Gen 30:11 Then Leah said, "A t comes
Gen 49:19 a t shall tramp upon him, but
1Sa 30: 8 Shall I pursue this t
1Sa 30:15 you take me down to this t
1Sa 30:15 will take you down to this t
1Sa 30:23 the t that came against us
2Sa 22:30 by You I can run against a t
2Sa 23:11 gathered together into a t
2Sa 23:13 the t of Philistines encamped
1Ch 12:18 made them captains of the t
Ps 18:29 by You I can run against a t
Jer 18:22 when You bring a t suddenly

TROOPS (*see* TROOP)
Judg 4: 6 Go and deploy t at Mount Tabor
2Sa 3:23 all the t that were with him
2Sa 4: 2 men who were captains of t
1Ch 7: 4 were thirty-six thousand t of
2Ch 14:10 and they set the t in battle
2Ch 17: 2 And he placed t in all the
2Ch 25: 9 have given to the t of Israel
2Ch 25:10 t that had come to him from
Job 19:12 His t come together and build
Prov 30:31 a king whose t are with him
Jer 5: 7 by t in the harlots' houses
Ezek 12:14 him to help him, and all his t
Ezek 17:21 his t shall fall by the sword
Ezek 38: 6 Gomer and all its t
Ezek 38: 6 the far north and all its t
Ezek 38: 9 a cloud, you and all your t
Ezek 38:22 rain down on him, on his t
Ezek 39: 4 of Israel, you and all your t
Dan 11:15 Even his choice t shall have
Mic 5: 1 Now gather yourself in t, O
Mic 5: 1 in t, O daughter of t
Hab 3:16 will invade them with his t
John 18: 3 received a detachment of t
John 18:12 Then the detachment of t and
Acts 23:27 with the t I rescued him,

TROPHIMUS
Acts 20: 4 and Tychicus and T of Asia
Acts 21:29 T the Ephesian with him in
2Ti 4:20 but T I have left in Miletus

TROUBLE (*see* TROUBLED, TROUBLEMAKING, TROUBLER, TROUBLES, TROUBLESOME, TROUBLING)

Ex 5:19 were in t after it was said
Ex 5:22 You brought t on this people
Josh 6:18 of Israel a curse, and t it
Josh 7:25 The LORD will t you this day
Judg 11:35 You are among those who t me
1Ki 11:25 the t that Hadad caused)
1Ki 20: 7 and see how this man seeks t
2Ki 14:10 with t so that you fall
2Ki 19: 3 This day is a day of t, and
1Ch 22:14 Indeed I have taken much t to
2Ch 15: 4 but when in their t they
2Ch 25:19 why should you meddle with t
2Ch 29: 8 and He has given them up to t
2Ch 32:18 t them, that they might take
Neh 9:27 and in the time of their t
Neh 9:32 do not let all the t seem
Job 3:26 I have no rest, for t comes
Job 4: 8 and sow t reap the same
Job 5: 6 nor does t spring from the
Job 5: 7 yet man is born to t, as the
Job 14: 1 is of few days and full of t
Job 15:24 T and anguish make him afraid
Job 15:35 They conceive t and bring
Job 27: 9 his cry when t comes upon him
Job 30:25 not wept for him who was in t
Job 34:29 who then can make t
Job 38:23 reserved for the time of t
Ps 3: 1 they have increased who t me
Ps 7:14 with iniquity, Conceives t
Ps 7:16 His t shall return upon his
Ps 9: 9 A refuge in times of t
Ps 9:13 Consider my t from those who
Ps 10: 1 hide Yourself in times of t
Ps 10: 7 Under his tongue is t and
Ps 10:14 seen it, for You observe t
Ps 13: 4 Lest those who t me rejoice
Ps 20: 1 answer you in the day of t
Ps 22:11 far from Me, For t is near
Ps 27: 5 For in the time of t He shall
Ps 31: 7 For You have considered my t
Ps 31: 9 on me, O LORD, for I am in t
Ps 32: 7 You shall preserve me from t
Ps 37:39 strength in the time of t
Ps 41: 1 will deliver him in time of t
Ps 46: 1 A very present help in t
Ps 50:15 Call upon Me in the day of t
Ps 54: 7 has delivered me out of all t
Ps 55: 3 For they bring down t upon me
Ps 55:10 t are also in the midst of it
Ps 59:16 And refuge in the day of my t
Ps 60:11 Give us help from t, For vain
Ps 66:14 has spoken when I was in t
Ps 69:17 Your servant, For I am in t
Ps 73: 5 are not in t as other men
Ps 77: 2 In the day of my t I sought
Ps 78:49 Wrath, indignation, and t
Ps 81: 7 You called in t, and I
Ps 86: 7 In the day of my t I will
Ps 91:15 I will be with him in t
Ps 102: 2 from me in the day of my t
Ps 107: 6 out to the LORD in their t
Ps 107:13 out to the LORD in their t
Ps 107:19 out to the LORD in their t
Ps 107:26 Their soul melts because of t
Ps 107:28 out to the LORD in their t
Ps 108:12 Give us help from t, For vain
Ps 116: 3 I found t and sorrow
Ps 119:143 T and anguish have overtaken
Ps 138: 7 I walk in the midst of t, You
Ps 142: 2 I declare before Him my t
Ps 143:11 sake bring my soul out of t
Prov 3:25 nor of t from the wicked when
Prov 10:10 winks with the eye causes t
Prov 11: 8 righteous is delivered from t
Prov 11:27 but t will come to him who
Prov 12:13 righteous will come through t
Prov 12:21 No grave t will overtake the
Prov 13:17 wicked messenger falls into t
Prov 15: 6 revenue of the wicked is t
Prov 15:16 than great treasure with t
Prov 25:19 time of t is like a bad tooth
Is 1:14 they are a t to Me, I am
Is 7: 6 t it, and let us make a gap in
Is 8:22 look to the earth, and see t
Is 17:14 Then behold, at eventide, t
Is 22: 5 For it is a day of t and
Is 26:16 in t they have visited You,
Is 30: 6 Through a land of t and
Is 33: 2 also in the time of t
Is 37: 3 This day is a day of t and
Is 46: 7 nor save him out of his t
Is 47:11 And t shall fall upon you
Is 65:23 bring forth children for t
Jer 2:27 time of their t they will say
Jer 2:28 you in the time of your t
Jer 8:15 of health, and there was t
Jer 11:12 at all in the time of their t
Jer 11:14 out to Me because of their t
Jer 14: 8 his Savior in time of t, why
Jer 14:19 of healing, and there was t
Jer 15: 4 I will hand them over to t
Jer 24: 9 I will deliver them to t
Jer 29:18 and I will deliver them to t
Jer 30: 7 it is the time of Jacob's t
Jer 34:17 I will deliver you to t among
Jer 44:17 were well-off, and saw no t
Jer 49:23 There is t on the sea
Lam 1:21 my enemies have heard of my t
Ezek 7: 7 has come, a day of t is near
Ezek 23:46 them, give them up to t and
Ezek 32: 9 I will also t the hearts of
Dan 4:19 or its interpretation t you
Dan 5:10 not let your thoughts t you
Dan 11:44 east and the north shall t him
Dan 12: 1 And there shall be a time of t
Jon 1: 7 cause this t has come upon us
Jon 1: 8 whose cause is this t upon us
Nah 1: 7 a stronghold in the day of t
Hab 1: 3 and cause me to see t
Hab 3:16 I might rest in the day of t
Zeph 1:15 is a day of wrath, a day of t
Zech 10: 2 they are in t because there
Matt 6:34 for the day is its own t
Matt 26:10 Why do you t the woman
Mark 5:35 Why t the Teacher any further
Mark 14: 6 Why do you t her
Luke 7: 6 do not t Yourself, for I am
Luke 8:49 Do not t the Teacher
Luke 11: 7 within and say, 'Do not t me
Acts 7:11 great t came over all the
Acts 15:19 not t those from among the
Acts 16:20 Jews, exceedingly t our city
Acts 20:10 Do not t yourselves, for his
1Co 7:28 such will have t in the flesh
2Co 1: 4 those who are in any t, with
2Co 1: 8 of our t which came to us in
Gal 1: 7 but there are some who t you
Gal 5:12 who t you would even cut
Gal 6:17 From now on let no one t me
2Th 1: 6 tribulation those who t you
2Ti 2: 9 I suffer t as an evildoer
Heb 12:15 springing up cause t, and by
Jas 1:27 orphans and widows in their t

TROUBLED (*see* TROUBLE)
Gen 34:30 You have t me by making me
Gen 41: 8 morning that his spirit was t
Gen 45:24 do not become t along the way
Ex 14:24 and He t the army of the
Josh 7:25 Why have you t us
1Sa 14:29 My father has t the land
1Sa 16:14 spirit from the LORD t him
1Sa 24: 5 that David's heart t him
1Sa 28:21 and saw that he was severely t
2Sa 4: 1 heart, and all Israel was t
1Ki 18:18 I have not t Israel, but you
2Ki 6:11 was greatly t by this thing
2Ch 15: 6 for God t them with every
Ezra 4: 4 They t them in building,
Job 4: 5 it touches you, and you are t
Ps 6: 2 heal me, for my bones are t
Ps 6: 3 My soul also is greatly t
Ps 6:10 be ashamed and greatly t
Ps 30: 7 You hid Your face, and I was t
Ps 38: 6 I am t, I am bowed down
Ps 46: 3 its waters roar and be t,
Ps 48: 5 They were t, they hastened
Ps 77: 3 I remembered God, and was t
Ps 77: 4 I am so t that I cannot speak
Ps 104:29 hide Your face, they are t
Is 8:12 of their threats, nor be t
Is 19:10 make wages will be t of soul
Is 32:10 and some days you will be t
Is 32:11 be t, you complacent ones
Is 57:20 the wicked are like the t sea
Lam 1:20 in distress; my soul is t
Lam 2:11 with tears, my heart is t
Ezek 26:18 sea are t at your departure
Ezek 27:35 their countenance will be t
Dan 2: 1 his spirit was so t that his
Dan 4: 5 the visions of my head t me
Dan 4:19 a time, and his thoughts t him
Dan 5: 6 and his thoughts t him, so
Dan 5: 9 King Belshazzar was greatly t
Dan 7:15 the visions of my head t me
Dan 7:28 my thoughts greatly t me
Matt 2: 3 heard these things, he was t
Matt 14:26 on the sea, they were t,
Matt 24: 6 See that you are not t
Mark 6:50 they all saw Him and were t
Mark 13: 7 rumors of wars, do not be t
Mark 14:33 with Him, and He began to be t
Luke 1:12 Zacharias saw him, he was t
Luke 1:29 she was t at his saying, and
Luke 10:41 and t about many things
Luke 24:38 Why are you t
John 11:33 in the spirit and was t
John 12:27 Now My soul is t, and what
John 13:21 He was t in spirit, and
John 14: 1 Let not your heart be t
John 14:27 Let not your heart be t,
Acts 15:24 from us have t you with words
Acts 17: 8 And they t the crowd and the
2Co 7: 5 but we were t on every side
2Th 1: 7 to give you who are t rest
2Th 2: 2 be soon shaken in mind or t
1Pe 3:14 of their threats, nor be t

TROUBLEMAKING (*see* TROUBLE)
Prov 24: 2 and their lips talk of t

TROUBLER (*see* TROUBLE)
1Ki 18:17 Is that you, O t of Israel
1Ch 2: 7 Achar, the t of Israel, who

TROUBLES (*see* TROUBLE)
Deut 31:17 t shall befall them, so that
Deut 31:21 t have come upon them, that
1Sa 11: 5 What t the people, that they
2Sa 14: 5 said to her, "What t you?"
Job 5:19 He shall deliver you in six t
Job 22:10 you, and sudden fear t you
Ps 25:17 The t of my heart have
Ps 25:22 O God, Out of all their t
Ps 34: 6 And saved him out of all his t
Ps 34:17 them out of all their t
Ps 71:20 shown me great and severe t
Ps 88: 3 For my soul is full of t, And
Prov 11:17 who is cruel t his own flesh
Prov 11:29 He who t his own house will
Prov 15:27 for gain t his own house, but
Prov 21:23 tongue keeps his soul from t
Is 65:16 the former t are forgotten
Dan 4: 9 is in you, and no secret t you
Mark 13: 8 and there will be famines and t
Luke 18: 5 widow t me I will avenge her
Acts 7:10 him out of all his t, and gave
Gal 5:10 but he who t you shall bear

TROUBLESOME (*see* TROUBLE)
Deut 28:25 you shall become t to all the
Dan 9:25 and the wall, even in t times

TROUBLING (*see* TROUBLE)
1Sa 16:15 spirit from God is t you
2Ki 6:28 What is t you
Job 3:17 There the wicked cease from t
Ezek 32: 2 t the waters with your feet,

TROUGH (*see* TROUGHS)
Gen 24:20 her pitcher into the t, ran
Prov 14: 4 no oxen are, the t is clean

TROUGHS (*see* TROUGH)
Gen 30:38 in the watering t where the
Ex 2:16 they filled the t to water

TROUSERS
Ex 28:42 t to cover their nakedness
Ex 39:28 linen, short t of fine linen,
Lev 6:10 his linen t he shall put on
Lev 16: 4 and the linen t on his body
Ezek 44:18 and linen t on their bodies
Dan 3:21 bound in their coats, their t

TRUDGING
Deut 2: 7 He knows your t through this

TRUE (*see* TRULY, TRUTH, UNTRUE)
Deut 13:14 And if it is indeed t and
Deut 17: 4 And if it is indeed t and
Deut 22:20 But if the thing is t, and
Josh 2:12 house, and give me a t token
Ruth 3:12 Now it is t that I am your
2Sa 7:28 are God, and Your words are t

1Ki 8:26 Israel, let Your word come **t**
1Ki 10: 6 It was a **t** report which I
2Ch 6:17 Israel, let Your word come **t**
2Ch 9: 5 It was a **t** report which I
2Ch 15: 3 has been without the **t** God
2Ch 31:20 **t** before the LORD his God
Neh 9:13 and **t** laws, good statutes and
Job 5:27 it is **t**. Hear it, and know
Ps 19: 9 judgments of the LORD are **t**
Prov 14:25 A **t** witness delivers souls,
Jer 10:10 But the LORD is the **t** God
Jer 42: 5 Let the LORD be a **t** and
Ezek 18: 8 executed **t** judgment between
Dan 3:14 Is it **t**, Shadrach, Meshach,
Dan 3:24 to the king, T, O king."
Dan 6:12 The thing is **t**, according to
Dan 8:26 mornings which was told is **t**
Dan 10: 1 The message was **t**, but the
Zech 7: 9 Execute **t** justice, show
Matt 15:27 **T**, Lord, yet even the little
Matt 22:16 we know that You are **t**, and
Mark 12:14 we know that You are **t**, and
Luke 16:11 to your trust the **t** riches
John 1: 9 That was the **t** Light which
John 3:33 has certified that God is **t**
John 4:23 when the **t** worshipers will
John 4:37 For in this the saying is **t**
John 5:31 Myself, My witness is not **t**
John 5:32 which He witnesses of Me is **t**
John 6:32 you the **t** bread from heaven
John 7:18 of the One who sent Him is **t**
John 7:28 but He who sent Me is **t**,
John 8:13 Your witness is not **t**
John 8:14 of Myself, My witness is **t**
John 8:16 I do judge, My judgment is **t**
John 8:17 the testimony of two men is **t**
John 8:26 you, but He who sent Me is **t**
John 10:41 spoke about this Man were **t**
John 15: 1 I am the **t** vine, and My Father
John 17: 3 may know You, the only **t** God
John 19:35 and his testimony is **t**
John 21:24 know that his testimony is **t**
Rom 3: 4 let God be **t** but every man a
2Co 6: 8 as deceivers, and yet **t**
2Co 7:14 boasting to Titus was found **t**
Eph 4:24 righteousness and **t** holiness
Phil 4: 3 **t** companion, help these women
Phil 4: 8 whatever things are **t**,
1Th 1: 9 to serve the living and **t** God,
1Ti 1: 2 my **t** son in the faith
Tit 1: 4 my **t** son in our common faith
Tit 1:13 This testimony is **t**
Heb 8: 2 of the **t** tabernacle which the
Heb 9:24 which are copies of the **t**
Heb 10:22 let us draw near with a **t**
1Pe 5:12 **t** grace of God in which you
2Pe 2:22 according to the **t** proverb
1Jn 2: 8 you, which thing is **t** in Him
1Jn 2: 8 and the **t** light is already
1Jn 2:27 all things, and is **t**, and is
1Jn 5:20 that we may know Him who is **t**
1Jn 5:20 and we are in Him who is **t**
1Jn 5:20 This is the **t** God and eternal
3Jn 12 know that our testimony is **t**
Rev 3: 7 He who is holy, He who is **t**
Rev 3:14 **T** Witness, the Beginning of
Rev 6:10 How long, O Lord, holy and **t**
Rev 15: 3 **t** are Your ways, O King of
Rev 16: 7 Even so, Lord God Almighty, **t**
Rev 19: 2 For **t** and righteous are His
Rev 19: 9 These are the **t** sayings of
Rev 19:11 him was called Faithful and **T**
Rev 21: 5 Write, for these words are **t**
Rev 22: 6 These words are faithful and **t**

TRULY (*see* TRUE)
Gen 20:12 But indeed she is **t** my sister
Gen 24:49 **t** with my master, tell me
Gen 42:21 We are **t** guilty concerning
Gen 47:29 and deal kindly and **t** with me
Gen 48:19 but **t** his younger brother
Num 13:27 It **t** flows with milk and honey
Num 14:21 but **t**, as I live, all the
Num 30:12 But if her husband **t** made
Deut 14:22 You shall **t** tithe all the
Deut 21:16 who is **t** the firstborn
Josh 2:14 deal kindly and **t** with you
Josh 2:24 **T** the LORD has delivered all
1Sa 20: 3 But **t**, as the LORD lives and
1Sa 21: 5 **T**, women have been kept from
2Ki 19:17 **T**, LORD, the kings of Assyria
Job 9: 2 **T** I know it is so, but how
Job 33: 6 **T** I am as your spokesman
Job 36: 4 For **t** my words are not false
Ps 62: 1 **T** my soul silently waits for
Ps 73: 1 **T** God is good to Israel, To
Ps 116:16 O LORD, **t** I am Your servant
Eccl 7:29 **T**, this only I have found
Eccl 9: 3 **T** the hearts of the sons of
Eccl 11: 7 **T** the light is sweet, and it
Is 5: 9 **T**, many houses shall be
Is 37:18 **T**, LORD, the kings of Assyria
Is 45:15 **T** You are God, who hide
Jer 3:23 **T**, in vain is salvation hoped
Jer 3:23 **T**, in the LORD our God is the
Jer 10:19 **T** this is an infirmity, and I
Jer 26:15 for **t** the LORD has sent me to
Jer 28: 9 one whom the LORD has **t** sent
Dan 2:47 **T** your God is the God of gods
Mic 3: 8 But **t** I am full of power by
Matt 9:37 The harvest **t** is plentiful,
Matt 14:33 **T** You are the Son of God
Matt 17:11 Elijah **t** is coming first and
Matt 27:54 **T** this was the Son of God
Mark 14:38 The spirit **t** is ready, but
Mark 15:39 **T** this Man was the Son of God
Luke 4:25 But I tell you **t**, many widows
Luke 9:27 But I tell you **t**, there are
Luke 10: 2 The harvest **t** is great, but
Luke 12:44 **T**, I say to you that he will
Luke 20:21 but teach the way of God **t**
Luke 21: 3 **T** I say to you that this poor
Luke 22:22 **t** the Son of Man goes as it
John 4:18 in that you spoke **t**
John 6:14 This is **t** the Prophet who is
John 7:26 that this is **t** the Christ
John 7:40 said, "**T** this is the Prophet
John 20:30 **t** Jesus did many other signs
Acts 1: 5 for John **t** baptized with
Acts 3:22 For Moses **t** said to the
Acts 4:27 For **t** against Your holy
Acts 17:30 **T**, these times of ignorance
1Co 5: 7 since you **t** are unleavened
1Co 14:25 that God is **t** among you
2Co 12:12 **T** the signs of an apostle
Gal 3:21 **t** righteousness would have
Heb 11:15 **t** if they had called to mind
1Jn 1: 3 **t** our fellowship is with the
1Jn 2: 5 word, **t** the love of God is

TRUMPET (*see* TRUMPETERS, TRUMPETS)
Ex 19:13 When the **t** sounds long, they
Ex 19:16 sound of the **t** was very loud
Ex 19:19 blast of the **t** sounded long
Ex 20:18 flashes, the sound of the **t**
Lev 25: 9 Then you shall cause the **t**
Lev 25: 9 you shall make the **t** to sound
Josh 6: 5 you hear the sound of the **t**
Josh 6:20 heard the sound of the **t**, and
Judg 3:27 that he blew the **t** in the
Judg 6:34 then he blew the **t**, and the
Judg 7:16 he put a **t** into every man's
Judg 7:18 When I blow the **t**, I and all
1Sa 13: 3 Then Saul blew the **t**
2Sa 2:28 So Joab blew a **t**
2Sa 6:15 and with the sound of the **t**
2Sa 15:10 you hear the sound of the **t**
2Sa 18:16 Then Joab blew the **t**, and the
2Sa 20: 1 And he blew a **t**, and said
2Sa 20:22 Then he blew a **t**, and they
Neh 4:18 sounded the **t** was beside me
Neh 4:20 you hear the sound of the **t**
Job 39:24 because the **t** has sounded
Job 39:25 At the blast of the **t** he says
Ps 47: 5 LORD with the sound of a **t**
Ps 81: 3 Blow the **t** at the time of the
Ps 150: 3 Him with the sound of the **t**
Is 18: 3 and when he blows a **t**, you
Is 27:13 the great **t** will be blown
Is 58: 1 lift up your voice like a **t**
Jer 4: 5 Blow the **t** in the land
Jer 4:19 O my soul, the sound of the **t**
Jer 4:21 and hear the sound of the **t**
Jer 6: 1 Blow the **t** in Tekoa, and set
Jer 6:17 listen to the sound of the **t**
Jer 42:14 nor hear the sound of the **t**
Jer 51:27 blow the **t** among the nations
Ezek 7:14 They have blown the **t** and
Ezek 33: 3 the land, if he blows the **t**
Ezek 33: 4 hears the sound of the **t** and
Ezek 33: 5 He heard the sound of the **t**
Ezek 33: 6 coming and does not blow the **t**
Hos 5: 8 in Gibeah, the **t** in Ramah
Hos 8: 1 Set the **t** to your mouth
Joel 2: 1 Blow the **t** in Zion, and sound
Joel 2:15 Blow the **t** in Zion,
Amos 2: 2 with shouting and **t** sound
Amos 3: 6 If a **t** is blown in a city,
Zeph 1:16 a day of **t** and alarm against
Zech 9:14 The Lord GOD will blow the **t**
Matt 6: 2 do not sound a **t** before you
Matt 24:31 with a great sound of a **t**
1Co 14: 8 For if the **t** makes an
1Co 15:52 of an eye, at the last **t**
1Co 15:52 For the **t** will sound, and the
1Th 4:16 and with the **t** of God
Heb 12:19 and the sound of a **t** and the
Rev 1:10 me a loud voice, as of a **t**
Rev 4: 1 was like a **t** speaking with me
Rev 8:13 **t** of the three angels who are
Rev 9:14 the sixth angel who had the **t**

TRUMPETERS (*see* TRUMPET)
2Ki 11:14 and the **t** were by the king
2Ch 5:13 it came to pass, when the **t**
2Ch 23:13 and the **t** were by the king
2Ch 29:28 sang, and the **t** sounded
Rev 18:22 **t** shall not be heard in you

TRUMPETS (*see* TRUMPET)
Lev 23:24 a memorial of blowing of **t**
Num 10: 2 two silver **t** for yourself
Num 10: 8 the priests, shall blow the **t**
Num 10: 9 sound an alarm with the **t**
Num 10:10 you shall blow the **t** over
Num 29: 1 it is a day of blowing the **t**
Num 31: 6 and the signal **t** in his hand
Josh 6: 4 priests shall bear seven **t** of
Josh 6: 4 the priests shall blow the **t**
Josh 6: 6 seven priests bear seven **t** of
Josh 6: 8 **t** of rams' horns before the
Josh 6: 8 LORD advanced and blew the **t**
Josh 6: 9 the priests who blew the **t**
Josh 6: 9 continued blowing the **t**
Josh 6:13 **t** of rams' horns before the
Josh 6:13 and blew with the **t**
Josh 6:13 continued blowing the **t**
Josh 6:16 when the priests blew the **t**
Josh 6:20 when the priests blew the **t**
Judg 7: 8 and their **t** in their hands
Judg 7:18 then you also blow the **t** on
Judg 7:19 and they blew the **t** and broke
Judg 7:20 three companies blew the **t**
Judg 7:20 the **t** in their right hands
Judg 7:22 the three hundred blew the **t**
2Ki 9:13 and they blew **t**, saying
2Ki 11:14 were rejoicing and blowing **t**
2Ki 12:13 trimmers, sprinkling-bowls, **t**
1Ch 13: 8 on cymbals, and with **t**
1Ch 15:24 were to blow the **t** before the
1Ch 15:28 the sound of the horn, with **t**
1Ch 16: 6 the **t** before the ark of the
1Ch 16:42 to sound aloud with **t** and
2Ch 5:12 priests sounding with **t**
2Ch 5:13 up their voice with the **t**
2Ch 7: 6 sounded **t** opposite them,
2Ch 13:12 His priests with sounding **t**
2Ch 13:14 and the priests sounded the **t**
2Ch 15:14 voice, with shouting and **t**
2Ch 20:28 instruments and harps and **t**
2Ch 23:13 land, rejoicing and blowing **t**
2Ch 29:26 and the priests with the **t**
2Ch 29:27 LORD also began, with the **t**
Ezra 3:10 stood in their apparel with **t**
Neh 12:35 of the priests' sons with **t**
Neh 12:41 and Hananiah, with **t**
Ps 98: 6 With **t** and the sound of a horn
Rev 8: 2 and to them were given seven **t**
Rev 8: 6 **t** prepared themselves to

TRUST (*see* TRUSTED, TRUSTING, TRUSTS, TRUSTWORTHY)
Deut 28:52 walls, in which you **t**, come
Judg 11:20 But Sihon did not **t** Israel
2Sa 22: 3 my strength, in Him I will **t**
2Sa 22:31 a shield to all who **t** in Him
2Ki 18:19 is this in which you **t**
2Ki 18:20 And in whom do you **t**, that you
2Ki 18:21 of Egypt to all who **t** in him
2Ki 18:22 We **t** in the LORD our God,'
2Ki 18:24 and put your **t** in Egypt for
2Ki 18:30 make you **t** in the LORD,
2Ki 19:10 God in whom you **t** deceive you
1Ch 5:20 they put their **t** in Him

2Ch 32:10 In what do you t, that you
Job 4:18 If He puts no t in His
Job 8:14 whose t is a spider's web
Job 13:15 He slay me, yet will I t Him
Job 15:15 God puts no t in His saints
Job 15:31 Let him not t in futile
Job 39:11 Will you t him because his
Job 39:12 Will you t him to bring home
Ps 2:12 those who put their t in Him
Ps 4: 5 And put your t in the LORD
Ps 5:11 who put their t in You
Ps 7: 1 my God, in You I put my t
Ps 9:10 name will put their t in You
Ps 11: 1 In the LORD I put my t
Ps 16: 1 O God, for in You I put my t
Ps 17: 7 O You who save those who t in
Ps 18: 2 my strength, in whom I will t
Ps 18:30 a shield to all who t in Him
Ps 20: 7 Some t in chariots, and some
Ps 22: 9 You made Me t when I was on
Ps 25: 2 O my God, I t in You
Ps 25:20 for I put my t in You
Ps 31: 1 In You, O LORD, I put my t
Ps 31: 6 But I t in the LORD
Ps 31:14 as for me, I t in You, O LORD
Ps 31:19 t in You In the presence of
Ps 34:22 none of those who t in Him
Ps 36: 7 t under the shadow of Your
Ps 37: 3 T in the LORD, and do good
Ps 37: 5 T also in Him, And He shall
Ps 37:40 them, Because they t in Him
Ps 40: 3 fear, And will t in the LORD
Ps 40: 4 man who makes the LORD his t
Ps 44: 6 For I will not t in my bow
Ps 49: 6 Those who t in their wealth
Ps 52: 8 I t in the mercy of God
Ps 55:23 But I will t in You
Ps 56: 3 I am afraid, I will t in You
Ps 56: 4 word), In God I have put my t
Ps 56:11 In God I have put my t
Ps 61: 4 I will t in the shelter of
Ps 62: 8 T in Him at all times, you
Ps 62:10 Do not t in oppression, Nor
Ps 64:10 glad in the LORD, and t in Him
Ps 71: 1 In You, O LORD, I put my t
Ps 71: 5 You are my t from my youth
Ps 73:28 I have put my t in the Lord
Ps 78:22 did not t in His salvation
Ps 91: 2 My God, in Him I will t
Ps 115: 9 O Israel, t in the LORD
Ps 115:10 house of Aaron, t in the LORD
Ps 115:11 fear the LORD, t in the LORD
Ps 118: 8 It is better to t in the LORD
Ps 118: 9 It is better to t in the LORD
Ps 119:42 me, For I t in Your word
Ps 125: 1 Those who t in the LORD Are
Ps 143: 8 morning, For in You do I t
Ps 146: 3 Do not put your t in princes
Prov 3: 5 T in the LORD with all your
Prov 22:19 So that your t may be in the
Prov 30: 5 those who put their t in Him
Is 12: 2 God is my salvation, I will t
Is 26: 4 T in the LORD forever, for in
Is 30: 2 to t in the shadow of Egypt
Is 30: 3 and t in the shadow of Egypt
Is 30:12 t in oppression and perversity
Is 31: 1 who t in chariots because
Is 36: 4 is this in which you t
Is 36: 5 Now in whom do you t, that
Is 36: 6 of Egypt to all who t in him
Is 36: 7 We t in the LORD our God,'
Is 36: 9 and put your t in Egypt for
Is 36:15 make you t in the LORD,
Is 37:10 God in whom you t deceive you
Is 42:17 who t in carved images, who
Is 50:10 Let him t in the name of the
Is 51: 5 Me, and on My arm they will t
Is 57:13 But he who puts his t in Me
Is 59: 4 they t in empty words and
Jer 5:17 cities, in which you t, with
Jer 7: 4 Do not t in these lying words
Jer 7: 8 you t in lying words that
Jer 7:14 by My name, in which you t
Jer 9: 4 and do not t any brother
Jer 28:15 make this people t in a lie
Jer 29:31 has caused you to t in a lie
Jer 39:18 you have put your t in Me
Jer 46:25 Pharaoh and those who t in him
Jer 49:11 and let your widows t in Me
Amos 6: 1 t in Mount Samaria, notable
Mic 2: 8 garment from those who t you
Mic 7: 5 Do not t in a friend
Nah 1: 7 He knows those who t in Him
Hab 2:18 of its mold should t in it
Zeph 3:12 they shall t in the name of
Matt 12:21 in His name Gentiles will t
Mark 10:24 who t in riches to enter the
Luke 16:11 to your t the true riches
John 5:45 Moses, in whom you t
2Co 1: 9 that we should not t in
2Co 1:10 in whom we t that He will
2Co 1:13 Now I t you will understand,
2Co 3: 4 we have such t through Christ
2Co 5:11 I also t are well-known in
2Co 13: 6 But I t that you will know
Phil 2:19 But I t in the Lord Jesus to
Phil 2:24 But I t in the Lord that I
1Ti 1:11 which was committed to my t
1Ti 4:10 because we t in the living
1Ti 6:17 nor to t in uncertain riches
1Ti 6:20 what was committed to your t
Phm 22 for I t that through your
Heb 2:13 I will put My t in Him

TRUSTED (*see* TRUST)
2Ki 18: 5 He t in the LORD God of
1Ch 9:22 them to their t office
1Ch 9:26 For in this t office were
1Ch 9:31 had the t office over the
Job 12:20 deprives the t ones of speech
Ps 13: 5 But I have t in Your mercy
Ps 22: 4 Our fathers t in You
Ps 22: 4 They t, and You delivered them
Ps 22: 5 They t in You, and were not
Ps 22: 8 He t in the LORD, let Him
Ps 26: 1 I have also t in the LORD
Ps 28: 7 My heart t in Him, and I am
Ps 33:21 Because we have t in His holy
Ps 41: 9 familiar friend in whom I t
Ps 52: 7 But t in the abundance of his
Prov 21:22 brings down the t stronghold
Is 47:10 For you have t in your
Jer 2:37 has rejected your t allies
Jer 12: 5 land of peace, in which you t
Jer 13:25 Me and t in falsehood
Jer 48: 7 you have t in your works and
Jer 49: 4 Who t in her treasures,
Ezek 16:15 But you t in your own beauty,
Dan 3:28 His servants who t in Him
Hos 10:13 because you t in your own way
Zeph 3: 2 she has not t in the LORD
Matt 27:43 He t in God; let Him
Luke 11:22 all his armor in which he t
Luke 18: 9 who t in themselves that they
Eph 1:12 that we who first t in Christ
Eph 1:13 In Him you also t, after you
1Pe 3: 5 the holy women who t in God

TRUSTING (*see* TRUST)
2Ki 18:21 You are t in the staff of
Ps 112: 7 is steadfast, t in the LORD
Is 36: 6 You are t in the staff of

TRUSTS (*see* TRUST)
Ps 21: 7 For the king t in the LORD
Ps 32:10 But he who t in the LORD,
Ps 34: 8 is the man who t in Him
Ps 57: 1 For my soul t in You
Ps 84:12 is the man who t in You
Ps 86: 2 Your servant who t in You
Ps 115: 8 So is everyone who t in them
Ps 135:18 So is everyone who t in them
Prov 11:28 He who t in his riches will
Prov 16:20 whoever t in the LORD, happy
Prov 28:25 but he who t in the LORD will
Prov 28:26 He who t in his own heart is
Prov 29:25 but whoever t in the LORD
Prov 31:11 of her husband safely t her
Is 26: 3 on You, because he t in You
Jer 17: 5 is the man who t in man and
Jer 17: 7 is the man who t in the LORD
Ezek 33:13 live, but he t in his own
1Ti 5: 5 t in God and continues in

TRUSTWORTHY (*see* TRUST, UNTRUSTWORTHY)
1Co 7:25 Lord in His mercy has made t

TRUTH (*see* TRUE, TRUTHFUL)
Gen 24:27 and His t toward my master
Gen 24:48 had led me in the way of t to
Gen 32:10 of all the t which You have
Gen 42:16 whether there is any t in you
Ex 18:21 such as fear God, men of t
Ex 34: 6 and abounding in goodness and t
Deut 32: 4 ways are justice, a God of t
Josh 24:14 Him in sincerity and in t, and
Judg 9:15 If in t you anoint me as
Judg 9:16 if you have acted in t and
Judg 9:19 if then you have acted in t
1Sa 12:24 serve Him in t with all your
2Sa 2: 6 show kindness and t to you
2Sa 15:20 Mercy and t be with you
1Ki 2: 4 Me in t with all their heart
1Ki 3: 6 he walked before You in t
1Ki 17:24 LORD in your mouth is the t
1Ki 22:16 the t in the name of the LORD
2Ki 20: 3 I have walked before You in t
2Ki 20:19 and t at least in my days
2Ch 18:15 the t in the name of the LORD
Esth 9:30 with words of peace and t
Ps 15: 2 speaks the t in his heart
Ps 25: 5 Lead me in Your t and teach me
Ps 25:10 of the LORD are mercy and t
Ps 26: 3 And I have walked in Your t
Ps 30: 9 Will it declare Your t
Ps 31: 5 redeemed me, O LORD God of t
Ps 33: 4 And all His work is done in t
Ps 40:10 and Your t From the great
Ps 40:11 Your t continually preserve
Ps 43: 3 send out Your light and Your t
Ps 45: 4 prosperously because of t
Ps 51: 6 You desire t in the inward
Ps 54: 5 Cut them off in Your t
Ps 57: 3 send forth His mercy and His t
Ps 57:10 And Your t unto the clouds
Ps 60: 4 be displayed because of the t
Ps 61: 7 Oh, prepare mercy and t, which
Ps 69:13 Hear me in the t of Your
Ps 85:10 Mercy and t have met together
Ps 85:11 T shall spring out of the
Ps 86:11 I will walk in Your t
Ps 86:15 and abundant in mercy and t
Ps 89:14 and t go before Your face
Ps 89:49 You swore to David in Your t
Ps 91: 4 His t shall be your shield and
Ps 96:13 And the peoples with His t
Ps 100: 5 And His t endures to all
Ps 108: 4 Your t reaches to the clouds
Ps 111: 8 and ever, And are done in t
Ps 115: 1 mercy, And because of Your t
Ps 117: 2 the t of the LORD endures
Ps 119:30 I have chosen the way of t
Ps 119:43 And take not the word of t
Ps 119:142 And Your law is t
Ps 119:151 all Your commandments are t
Ps 119:160 entirety of Your word is t
Ps 132:11 LORD has sworn in t to David
Ps 138: 2 Your lovingkindness and Your t
Ps 145:18 To all who call upon Him in t
Ps 146: 6 Who keeps t forever,
Prov 3: 3 not mercy and t forsake you
Prov 8: 7 for my mouth will speak t
Prov 12:17 He who speaks t declares
Prov 14:22 t belong to those who devise
Prov 16: 6 t atonement is provided for
Prov 20:28 t preserve the king, and by
Prov 22:21 certainty of the words of t
Prov 22:21 you may answer words of t to
Prov 23:23 Buy the t, and do not sell it,
Prov 29:14 who judges the poor with t
Prov 29:24 he swears to tell the t, but
Eccl 12:10 words of t
Is 10:20 the Holy One of Israel, in t
Is 16: 5 and One will sit on it in t
Is 25: 1 of old are faithfulness and t
Is 26: 2 keeps the t may enter in
Is 38: 3 I have walked before You in t
Is 38:18 pit cannot hope for Your t
Is 38:19 known Your t to the children
Is 39: 8 will be peace and t in my days
Is 42: 3 bring forth justice for t
Is 43: 9 hear and say, "It is t."
Is 48: 1 of Israel, but not in t or in
Is 59: 4 nor does any plead for t
Is 59:14 for t is fallen in the street
Is 59:15 So t fails, and he who departs
Is 61: 8 I will direct their work in t
Is 65:16 bless himself in the God of t
Is 65:16 shall swear by the God of t
Jer 4: 2 swear, 'The LORD lives,' in t
Jer 5: 1 judgment, who seeks the t
Jer 5: 3 are not Your eyes on the t

Jer 7:28 T has perished and has been
Jer 9: 3 for the t on the earth
Jer 9: 5 and will not speak the t
Jer 33: 6 the abundance of peace and t
Dan 4:37 all of whose works are t
Dan 7:16 asked him the t of all this
Dan 7:19 the t about the fourth beast
Dan 8:12 he cast t down to the ground
Dan 9:13 and understand Your t
Dan 10:21 noted in the Scripture of T
Dan 11: 2 And now I will tell you the t
Hos 4: 1 There is no t or mercy or
Mic 7:20 You will give t to Jacob and
Zech 8: 3 shall be called the City of T
Zech 8: 8 and I will be their God, in t
Zech 8:16 man the t to his neighbor
Zech 8:16 judgment in your gates for t
Zech 8:19 Therefore love t and peace
Mal 2: 6 The law of t was in his mouth
Matt 22:16 and teach the way of God in t
Mark 5:33 Him and told Him the whole t
Mark 12:14 but teach the way of God in t
Mark 12:32 You have spoken the t, for
John 1:14 Father, full of grace and t
John 1:17 t came through Jesus Christ
John 3:21 does the t comes to the light
John 4:23 the Father in spirit and t
John 4:24 must worship in spirit and t
John 5:33 he has bore witness to the t
John 8:32 And you shall know the t, and
John 8:32 the t shall make you free
John 8:40 the t which I heard from God
John 8:44 and does not stand in the t
John 8:44 because there is no t in him
John 8:45 But because I tell the t, you
John 8:46 And if I tell the t, why do
John 14: 6 I am the way, the t, and the
John 14:17 even the Spirit of t, whom
John 15:26 the Spirit of t who proceeds
John 16: 7 Nevertheless I tell you the t
John 16:13 when He, the Spirit of t
John 16:13 He will guide you into all t
John 17:17 Sanctify them by Your t
John 17:17 Your word is t
John 17:19 may be sanctified by the t
John 18:37 should bear witness to the t
John 18:37 is of the t hears My voice
John 18:38 said to Him, "What is t?"
John 19:35 that he is telling the t, so
Acts 10:34 In t I perceive that God
Acts 21:34 the t because of the tumult
Acts 26:25 but speak the words of t
Rom 1:18 of men, who suppress the t in
Rom 1:25 who exchanged the t of God
Rom 2: 2 of God is according to t
Rom 2: 8 and do not obey the t, but
Rom 2:20 of knowledge and t in the law
Rom 3: 7 For if the t of God has
Rom 9: 1 I tell the t in Christ, I am
Rom 15: 8 circumcision for the t of God
1Co 5: 8 bread of sincerity and t
1Co 13: 6 but rejoices in the t
2Co 4: 2 the t commending ourselves to
2Co 6: 7 by the word of t, by the
2Co 7:14 spoke all things to you in t
2Co 11:10 As the t of Christ is in me,
2Co 12: 6 for I will speak the t
2Co 13: 8 can do nothing against the t
2Co 13: 8 but for the t
Gal 2: 5 that the t of the gospel
Gal 2:14 about the t of the gospel
Gal 3: 1 you should not obey the t
Gal 4:16 because I tell you the t
Gal 5: 7 you from obeying the t
Eph 1:13 after you heard the word of t
Eph 4:15 but, speaking the t in love
Eph 4:21 by Him, as the t is in Jesus
Eph 4:25 each one speak t with his
Eph 5: 9 righteousness, and t),
Eph 6:14 girded your waist with t,
Phil 1:18 whether in pretense or in t
Col 1: 5 word of the t of the gospel
Col 1: 6 and knew the grace of God in t
1Th 2:13 of men, but as it is in t
2Th 2:10 not receive the love of the t
2Th 2:12 the t but had pleasure in
2Th 2:13 the Spirit and belief in the t
1Ti 2: 4 to the knowledge of the t
1Ti 2: 7 I am speaking the t in Christ
1Ti 2: 7 of the Gentiles in faith and t
1Ti 3:15 the pillar and ground of the t
1Ti 4: 3 who believe and know the t
1Ti 6: 5 minds and destitute of the t
2Ti 2:15 dividing the word of t
2Ti 2:18 have strayed concerning the t
2Ti 2:25 so that they may know the t
2Ti 3: 7 to the knowledge of the t
2Ti 3: 8 so do these also resist the t
2Ti 4: 4 their ears away from the t
Tit 1: 1 the t which is according to
Tit 1:14 of men who turn from the t
Heb 10:26 the knowledge of the t, there
Jas 1:18 us forth by the word of t
Jas 3:14 boast and lie against the t
Jas 5:19 among you wanders from the t
1Pe 1:22 the t through the Spirit in
2Pe 1:12 established in the present t
2Pe 2: 2 way of t will be blasphemed
1Jn 1: 6 lie and do not practice the t
1Jn 1: 8 and the t is not in us
1Jn 2: 4 liar, and the t is not in him
1Jn 2:21 because you do not know the t
1Jn 2:21 and that no lie is of the t
1Jn 3:18 tongue, but in deed and in t
1Jn 3:19 we know that we are of the t
1Jn 4: 6 this we know the spirit of t
1Jn 5: 6 because the Spirit is t
2Jn 1 children, whom I love in t
2Jn 1 those who have known the t
2Jn 2 because of the t which abides
2Jn 3 the Son of the Father, in t
2Jn 4 of your children walking in t
3Jn 1 Gaius, whom I love in t
3Jn 3 of the t that is in you
3Jn 3 just as you walk in the t
3Jn 4 that my children walk in t
3Jn 8 fellow workers for the t
3Jn 12 all, and from the t itself

TRUTHFUL (*see* TRUTH, TRUTHFULLY)
Prov 12:19 The t lip shall be

TRUTHFULLY (*see* TRUTHFUL)
Prov 12:22 who deal t are His delight

TRY (*see* TRIED, TRYING)
Deut 4:34 Or did God ever t to go and
Ps 26: 2 T my mind and my heart
Ps 139:23 T me, and know my anxieties
Jer 9: 7 I will refine them and t them
Jer 23:27 who t to make My people
Ezek 17:20 t him there for the treason
Luke 22:53 you did not t to seize Me
Gal 6:12 these t to compel you to be
1Pe 4:12 fiery trial which is to t you
1Jn 2:26 those who t to deceive you

TRYING (*see* TRY)
Gen 19:11 weary t to find the door
Neh 6: 9 all were t to make us afraid

TRYPHENA
Rom 16:12 Greet T and Tryphosa, who

TRYPHOSA
Rom 16:12 Greet Tryphena and T, who

TUBAL (*see* TUBAL-CAIN)
Gen 10: 2 Magog, Madai, Javan, T
1Ch 1: 5 Magog, Madai, Javan, T
Is 66:19 Lud, who draw the bow, and T
Ezek 27:13 Javan, T, and Meshech were
Ezek 32:26 There are Meshech and T and all
Ezek 38: 2 prince of Rosh, Meshech, and T
Ezek 38: 3 prince of Rosh, Meshech, and T
Ezek 39: 1 prince of Rosh, Meshech, and T

TUBAL-CAIN (*see* TUBAL,)
Gen 4:22 for Zillah, she also bore T
Gen 4:22 And the sister of T was Naamah

TUMBLED
Judg 7:13 a loaf of barley bread t into

TUMORS
Deut 28:27 the boils of Egypt, with t
1Sa 5: 6 them and struck them with t
1Sa 5: 9 great, and t broke out on them
1Sa 5:12 die were stricken with the t
1Sa 6: 4 Five golden t and five golden
1Sa 6: 5 shall make images of your t
1Sa 6:11 rats and the images of their t
1Sa 6:17 gold t which the Philistines

TUMULT (*see* TUMULTS, TUMULTUOUS)
Num 24:17 and destroy all the sons of t
1Sa 4:14 does the sound of this t mean
2Sa 18:29 your servant, I saw a great t
2Ki 19:28 your t have come up to My
Job 39: 7 he scorns the t of the city
Ps 65: 7 And the t of the peoples
Ps 74:23 The t of those who rise up
Ps 83: 2 behold, Your enemies make a t
Is 33: 3 At the noise of the t the
Is 37:29 your t have come up to My
Jer 11:16 t He has kindled fire on it
Jer 48:45 of the head of the sons of t
Ezek 1:24 a t like the noise of an army
Ezek 22: 5 you as infamous and full of t
Hos 10:14 Therefore t shall arise among
Amos 2: 2 Moab shall die with t, with
Matt 27:24 rather that a t was rising
Mark 5:38 of the synagogue, and saw a t
Acts 21:34 the truth because of the t
Acts 24:18 with a multitude nor with t

TUMULTS (*see* TUMULT)
Amos 3: 9 see great t in her midst, and
2Co 6: 5 in imprisonments, in t, in
2Co 12:20 whisperings, conceits, t

TUMULTUOUS (*see* TUMULT)
Is 13: 4 A t noise of the kingdoms of
Is 22: 2 a t city, a joyous city

TUNIC (*see* TUNICS)
Gen 37: 3 made him a t of many colors
Gen 37:23 they stripped Joseph of his t
Gen 37:23 the t of many colors that was
Gen 37:31 So they took Joseph's t,
Gen 37:31 dipped the t in the blood
Gen 37:32 sent the t of many colors
Gen 37:32 it is your son's t or not
Gen 37:33 It is my son's t
Ex 28: 4 a robe, a skillfully woven t
Ex 28:39 the t of fine linen thread
Ex 29: 5 put the t on Aaron, and the
Lev 8: 7 And he put the t on him,
Lev 16: 4 He shall put the holy linen t
Matt 5:40 sue you and take away your t
Luke 6:29 do not withhold your t either
John 19:23 soldier a part, and also the t
John 19:23 Now the t was without seam,

TUNICS (*see* TUNIC)
Gen 3:21 the LORD God made t of skin
Ex 28:40 Aaron's sons you shall make t
Ex 29: 8 his sons and put t on them
Ex 39:27 They made t, artistically
Ex 40:14 sons and clothe them with t
Lev 8:13 put t on them, girded them
Lev 10: 5 by their t out of the camp
Matt 10:10 for your journey, nor two t
Mark 6: 9 and not to put on two t
Luke 3:11 He who has two t, let him
Luke 9: 3 and do not have two t apiece
Acts 9:39 by him weeping, showing the t

TUNNEL
2Ki 20:20 and how he made a pool and a t
2Ch 32:30 brought the water by t to the

TURBAN (*see* TURBANS)
Ex 28: 4 a skillfully woven tunic, a t
Ex 28:37 cord, that it may be on the t
Ex 28:37 be on the front of the t
Ex 28:39 make the t of fine linen, and
Ex 29: 6 shall put the t on his head
Ex 29: 6 put the holy crown on the t
Ex 39:28 a t of fine linen, exquisite
Ex 39:31 to fasten it above on the t
Lev 8: 9 And he put the t on his head
Lev 8: 9 Also on the t, on its front,
Lev 16: 4 with the linen t he shall be
Job 29:14 was like a robe and a t
Ezek 21:26 Remove the t, and take off
Ezek 24:17 bind your t on your head, and
Zech 3: 5 put a clean t on his head
Zech 3: 5 put a clean t on his head

TURBANS (*see* TURBAN)
Is 3:23 the fine linen, the t, and the
Ezek 23:15 flowing t on their heads, all
Ezek 24:23 Your t shall be on your
Ezek 44:18 have linen t on their heads
Dan 3:21 their trousers, their t, and

TURMOIL
2Ch 15: 5 but great **t** was on all the
Job 20: 2 because of the **t** within me
Job 30:27 My heart is in **t** and cannot
Ps 38: 8 because of the **t** of my heart

TURN (*see* TURNED, TURNING, TURNS, UNTURNED)
Gen 19: 2 please **t** in to your servant's
Gen 24:49 that I may **t** to the right
Ex 3: 3 I will now **t** aside and see
Ex 14: 2 of Israel, that they **t** and
Ex 23: 2 in a dispute so as to **t** aside
Ex 23:27 enemies **t** their backs to you
Ex 32:12 **T** from Your fierce wrath, and
Lev 19: 4 Do not **t** to idols, nor make
Num 14:25 tomorrow **t** and move out into
Num 20:17 we will not **t** aside to the
Num 21:22 We will not **t** aside into
Num 22:23 to **t** her back onto the road
Num 22:26 where there was no way to **t**
Num 22:34 displeases You, I will **t** back
Num 25: 4 LORD may **t** away from Israel
Num 32:15 For if you **t** away from
Num 34: 4 your border shall **t** from the
Num 34: 5 the border shall **t** from
Deut 1: 7 **T** and take your journey, and
Deut 1:40 But as for you, **t** and take
Deut 2: 3 this mountain long enough; **t**
Deut 2:27 I will **t** neither to the right
Deut 4:30 when you **t** to the LORD your
Deut 5:32 you shall not **t** aside to the
Deut 7: 4 For they will **t** your sons
Deut 11:16 you **t** aside and serve other
Deut 11:28 God, but **t** aside from the way
Deut 13: 5 he has spoken in order to **t**
Deut 13:17 that the LORD may **t** from the
Deut 16: 7 and in the morning you shall **t**
Deut 17:11 you shall not **t** aside to the
Deut 17:17 lest his heart **t** away
Deut 17:20 that he may not **t** aside from
Deut 23:13 you shall dig with it and **t**
Deut 23:14 among you, and **t** away from you
Deut 28:14 So you shall not **t** aside from
Deut 30:10 if you **t** to the LORD your God
Deut 31:20 they will **t** to other gods
Deut 31:29 **t** aside from the way which I
Josh 1: 7 do not **t** from it to the right
Josh 22:16 to **t** away this day from
Josh 22:18 you must **t** away this day from
Josh 22:23 to **t** from following the LORD
Josh 22:29 **t** from following the LORD
Josh 23: 6 lest you **t** aside from it to
Josh 24:20 foreign gods, then He will **t**
Judg 4:18 **T** aside, my lord, **t** aside
Judg 7: 3 fearful and afraid, let him **t**
Judg 19:11 let us **t** aside into this city
Judg 19:12 We will not **t** aside here into
Judg 20: 8 any of us **t** back to his house
Judg 20:39 of Israel would **t** in battle
Ruth 1:11 said, "**T** back, my daughters
Ruth 1:12 **T** back, my daughters, go your
Ruth 1:16 or to **t** back from following
Ruth 3:18 how the matter will **t** out
1Sa 6:12 did not **t** aside to the right
1Sa 12:20 yet do not **t** aside from
1Sa 12:21 And do not **t** aside
1Sa 22:17 **T** and kill the priests of the
1Sa 22:18 You **t** and kill the priests
2Sa 1:22 of Jonathan did not **t** back
2Sa 2:19 in going he did not **t** to the
2Sa 2:21 **T** aside to your right hand or
2Sa 2:21 But Asahel would not **t**
2Sa 2:22 **T** aside from following me
2Sa 2:23 he refused to **t** aside
2Sa 14:19 no one can **t** to the right
2Sa 15:31 **t** the counsel of Ahithophel
2Sa 18:30 said, "**T** aside and stand here
2Sa 19:37 let your servant **t** back again
2Sa 22:38 neither did I **t** back again
1Ki 2: 3 that you do and wherever you **t**
1Ki 8:33 when they **t** back to You and
1Ki 8:35 **t** from their sin because You
1Ki 9: 6 at all **t** from following Me
1Ki 11: 2 For surely they will **t** away
1Ki 12:15 for the **t** of affairs was from
1Ki 12:27 will **t** back to their lord
1Ki 13:33 did not **t** from his evil way
1Ki 17: 3 **t** eastward, and hide by the
1Ki 22:34 **T** around and take me out of
1Ki 22:43 He did not **t** aside from them,
2Ki 4:10 to us, he can **t** in there
2Ki 9:18 **T** around and follow me
2Ki 9:19 **T** around and follow me
2Ki 10:29 However Jehu did not **t** away
2Ki 17:13 **T** from your evil ways, and
2Ki 18:14 **t** away from me
2Ki 19:28 I will **t** you back by the way
2Ki 22: 2 he did not **t** aside to the
2Ki 23:26 the LORD did not **t** from the
1Ch 12:23 came to David at Hebron to **t**
2Ch 6:26 **t** from their sin because You
2Ch 6:42 do not **t** away the face of
2Ch 7:14 **t** from their wicked ways,
2Ch 7:19 But if you **t** away and forsake
2Ch 10:15 for the **t** of affairs was from
2Ch 18:31 moved them to **t** away from him
2Ch 18:33 **T** around and take me out of
2Ch 20:32 and did not **t** aside from it,
2Ch 29:10 wrath may **t** away from us
2Ch 30: 8 His wrath may **t** away from you
2Ch 30: 9 will not **t** His face from you
2Ch 34: 2 he did not **t** aside to the
2Ch 35:22 Josiah would not **t** his face
2Ch 36:10 At the **t** of the year King
Neh 4: 4 **t** their reproach on their own
Neh 4:12 From whatever place you **t**
Neh 9:26 them to **t** them to Yourself
Neh 9:35 nor did they **t** from their
Esth 2:12 Each young woman's **t** came to
Esth 2:15 Now when the **t** came for
Job 5: 1 of the holy ones will you **t**
Job 6:18 paths of their way **t** aside
Job 6:29 **T** now, let there be no
Job 6:29 **t** again, my righteousness
Job 10: 9 will You **t** me into dust again
Job 15:13 that you **t** your spirit
Job 24:18 so that no one would **t** into
Job 33:17 In order to **t** man from his
Job 36:10 that they **t** from iniquity
Job 36:21 do not **t** to iniquity, for you
Job 39:22 nor does he **t** back from the
Ps 4: 2 Will you **t** my glory to shame
Ps 6:10 Let them **t** back and be ashamed
Ps 7:12 If he does not **t** back, He
Ps 9: 3 When my enemies **t** back, They
Ps 18:37 Neither did I **t** back again
Ps 21:12 will make them **t** their back
Ps 22:27 **t** to the LORD, And all the
Ps 25:16 **T** Yourself to me, and have
Ps 27: 9 Do not **t** Your servant away in
Ps 40: 4 nor such as **t** aside to lies
Ps 44:10 You make us **t** back from the
Ps 56: 9 Then my enemies will **t** back
Ps 69:16 **T** to me according to the
Ps 80:18 we will not **t** back from You
Ps 81:14 And **t** My hand against their
Ps 85: 8 let them not **t** back to folly
Ps 86:16 **t** to me, and have mercy on me
Ps 90: 3 You **t** man to destruction, And
Ps 106:23 To **t** away His wrath, lest He
Ps 119:37 **T** away my eyes from looking
Ps 119:39 **T** away my reproach which I
Ps 119:51 Yet I do not **t** aside from
Ps 119:79 those who fear You **t** to me
Ps 119:157 Yet I do not **t** from Your
Ps 125: 5 As for such as **t** aside to
Ps 132:10 Do not **t** away the face of
Ps 132:11 He will not **t** from it
Prov 1:23 **T** at my reproof
Prov 4: 5 nor **t** away from the words of
Prov 4:15 **t** away from it and pass on
Prov 4:27 Do not **t** to the right or the
Prov 7:25 heart **t** aside to her ways
Prov 9: 4 is simple, let him **t** in here
Prov 9:16 simple, let him **t** in here"
Prov 13:14 to **t** one away from the snares
Prov 15:24 that he may **t** away from hell
Prov 24:18 He **t** away His wrath from him
Prov 26:14 the slothful **t** on his bed
Prov 29: 8 but wise men **t** away wrath
Prov 30:30 and does not **t** away from any
Song 2:17 and the shadows flee away, **t**
Song 6: 5 **T** your eyes away from me, for
Is 1:25 I will **t** My hand against you,
Is 9:13 For the people do not **t** to
Is 13:14 every man will **t** to his own
Is 14:27 out, and who will **t** it back
Is 19: 6 The rivers will **t** foul, and
Is 22:18 He will surely **t** violently
Is 28: 6 for strength to those who **t**
Is 29:21 **t** aside the just for a thing
Is 30:11 **t** aside from the path, cause
Is 30:21 whenever you **t** to the right
Is 30:21 or whenever you **t** to the left
Is 37:29 I will **t** you back by the way
Is 50: 5 rebellious, nor did I **t** away
Is 58:13 If you **t** away your foot from
Is 59:20 Zion, and to those who **t** from
Jer 2:24 of mating, who can **t** her away
Jer 2:35 His anger shall **t** from me
Jer 3:19 and not **t** away from Me
Jer 4:28 nor will I **t** back from it
Jer 8: 4 Will one **t** away and not return
Jer 15: 5 Or who will **t** aside to ask
Jer 18:20 to **t** away Your wrath from
Jer 21: 4 I will **t** back the weapons of
Jer 23:20 **t** back until He has executed
Jer 26: 3 **t** from his evil way, that I
Jer 31:13 for I will **t** their mourning
Jer 31:21 **T** back, O virgin of Israel,
Jer 31:21 **t** back to these your cities
Jer 31:39 then it shall **t** toward Goath
Jer 32:40 that I will not **t** away from
Jer 35:15 **T** now everyone from his evil
Jer 36: 3 may **t** from his evil way, that
Jer 36: 7 everyone will **t** from his evil
Jer 44: 5 to **t** from their wickedness
Jer 49: 8 **t** back, dwell in the depths,
Jer 50:16 shall **t** to his own people
Lam 3:35 to **t** aside the justice due a
Lam 3:40 ways, and **t** back to the LORD
Lam 5:21 **T** us back to You, O LORD, and
Ezek 1: 9 did not **t** when they went, but
Ezek 1:12 they did not **t** when they went
Ezek 1:17 they did not **t** aside when
Ezek 3:19 and he does not **t** from his
Ezek 4: 8 you so that you cannot **t** from
Ezek 7:13 and it shall not **t** back
Ezek 7:22 I will **t** My face from them,
Ezek 8: 6 Now **t** again, you will see
Ezek 8:13 **T** again, and you will see
Ezek 8:15 **T** again, you will see greater
Ezek 10:11 they did not **t** aside when
Ezek 10:11 They did not **t** aside when
Ezek 10:16 did not **t** from beside them
Ezek 13:22 so that he does not **t** from
Ezek 14: 6 **t** away from your idols, and
Ezek 14: 6 **t** your faces away from all
Ezek 18:23 he should **t** from his ways
Ezek 18:30 Repent, and **t** from all your
Ezek 18:32 Therefore **t** and live
Ezek 33: 9 the wicked to **t** from his way
Ezek 33: 9 he does not **t** from his way,
Ezek 33:11 the wicked **t** from his way
Ezek 33:11 **T**, **t** from your evil ways
Ezek 36: 9 for you, and I will **t** to you
Ezek 38: 4 I will **t** you around, put
Ezek 39: 2 I will **t** you around and lead
Dan 9:13 God, that we might **t** from our
Dan 11:18 After this he shall **t** his
Dan 11:18 he shall **t** back on him
Dan 11:19 Then he shall **t** his face
Dan 12: 3 and those who **t** many to
Joel 2:12 **T** to me with all your heart,
Joel 2:14 Who knows if He will **t** and
Amos 1: 3 four, I will not **t** away its
Amos 1: 6 four, I will not **t** away its
Amos 1: 8 I will **t** My hand against
Amos 1: 9 four, I will not **t** away its
Amos 1:11 four, I will not **t** away its
Amos 1:13 four, I will not **t** away its
Amos 2: 1 four, I will not **t** away its
Amos 2: 4 four, I will not **t** away its
Amos 2: 6 four, I will not **t** away its
Amos 5: 7 you who **t** justice to wormwood
Amos 8:10 I will **t** your feasts into
Jon 3: 8 let every one **t** from his evil
Jon 3: 9 Who can tell if God will **t**
Jon 3: 9 **t** away from His fierce anger,
Hag 2:17 yet you did not **t** to Me,'
Zech 1: 4 **T** now from your evil ways and
Zech 13: 7 then I will **t** My hand against
Mal 3: 5 those who **t** away an alien
Mal 4: 6 he will **t** the hearts of the
Matt 5:39 **t** the other to him also
Matt 5:42 borrow from you do not **t** away
Matt 7: 6 them under their feet, and **t**
Matt 13:15 with their heart and **t**, so
Mark 4:12 lest they should **t**, and their
Luke 1:16 And he will **t** many of the

Acts 7:39 hearts they t back to Egypt
Acts 7:42 Then God t and gave them up to
Acts 9:35 saw him and t to the Lord
Acts 11:21 believed and t to the Lord
Acts 16:18 But Paul, greatly annoyed, t
Acts 17: 6 These who have t the world
Acts 19:26 t away many people, saying
Phil 1:12 to me have actually t out for
1Th 1: 9 how you t to God from idols
1Ti 1: 6 have t aside to idle talk,
1Ti 5:15 already t aside after Satan
2Ti 1:15 in Asia have t away from me
2Ti 4: 4 and be t aside to fables
Heb 11:34 t to flight the armies of the
Jas 3: 4 they are t by a very small
Jas 4: 9 laughter be t to mourning
Rev 1:12 Then I t to see the voice
Rev 1:12 having t I saw seven golden

TURNING (*see* TURN)
2Ki 21:13 wiping it and t it upside down
2Ch 36:13 t to the LORD God of Israel
Prov 1:32 For the t away of the simple
Is 28:24 Does he keep t his soil and
Jer 31:19 Surely, after my t, I
Hos 5: 4 deeds toward t to their God
Luke 23:28 But Jesus, t to them, said,
John 21:20 t around, saw the disciple
Acts 3:26 in t away every one of you
Acts 9:40 And t to the body he said,
Acts 15:19 the Gentiles who are t to God
Gal 1: 6 I marvel that you are t away
Jas 1:17 no variation or shadow of t
2Pe 2: 6 and t the cities of Sodom and

TURNS (*see* TURN)
Gen 27:44 your brother's fury t away
Gen 27:45 anger t away from you, and he
Lev 13:16 t white again, he shall come
Lev 20: 6 person who t after mediums
Deut 29:18 whose heart t away today from
Deut 30:17 But if your heart t away so
Josh 7: 8 shall I say when Israel t its
Job 20:14 food in his stomach t sour
Job 23: 9 when He t to the right hand,
Ps 107:33 He t rivers into a wilderness
Ps 107:35 He t a wilderness into pools
Ps 146: 9 the wicked He t upside down
Prov 15: 1 A soft answer t away wrath
Prov 17: 8 wherever he t, he prospers
Prov 21: 1 He t it wherever He wishes
Prov 26:14 As a door t on its hinges, so
Prov 28: 9 One who t away his ear from
Eccl 1: 6 and t around to the north
Is 44:25 Who t wise men backward, and
Jer 13:16 He t it into the shadow of
Jer 14: 8 like a wayfaring man who t
Jer 18: 8 I have spoken t from its evil
Jer 23:14 so that no one t back from
Jer 49:24 t to flee, and fear has seized
Lam 1: 8 yes, she sighs and t away
Ezek 3:20 when a righteous man t from
Ezek 18:21 But if a wicked man t from
Ezek 18:24 But when a righteous man t
Ezek 18:26 When a righteous man t away
Ezek 18:27 when a wicked man t away from
Ezek 18:28 and t away from all the
Ezek 33:12 that he t from his wickedness
Ezek 33:14 if he t from his sin and does
Ezek 33:18 When the righteous t from his
Ezek 33:19 wicked t from his wickedness
Amos 5: 8 he t the shadow of death into
Nah 2: 8 but no one t back
2Co 3:16 when one t to the Lord, the
Jas 5:19 truth, and someone t him back,
Jas 5:20 let him know that he who t a

TURQUOISE
Ex 28:18 the second row shall be a t
Ex 39:11 the second row, a t, a
Esth 1: 6 pavement of alabaster, t, and
Ezek 28:13 onyx, and jasper, sapphire, t

TURTLEDOVE (*see* TURTLEDOVES)
Gen 15: 9 a three-year-old ram, a t
Lev 12: 6 or a t as a sin offering, to
Ps 74:19 of Your t to the wild beast
Song 2:12 the voice of the t is heard
Jer 8: 7 and the t, the swift, and the

TURTLEDOVES (*see* TURTLEDOVE)
Lev 1:14 of t or young pigeons
Lev 5: 7 two t or two young pigeons
Lev 5:11 two t or two young pigeons
Lev 12: 8 two t or two young pigeons
Lev 14:22 two t or two young pigeons,
Lev 14:30 one of the t or young pigeons
Lev 15:14 two t or two young pigeons
Lev 15:29 two t or two young pigeons
Num 6:10 day he shall bring two t or
Luke 2:24 A pair of t or two young

TUSKS
Ezek 27:15 They brought you ivory t and

TUTOR
Gal 3:24 our t to bring us to Christ
Gal 3:25 we are no longer under a t

TWELFTH (*see* TWELVE)
Num 7:78 On the t day Ahira the son of
1Ki 19:19 him, and he was with the t
2Ki 8:25 In the t year of Joram the
2Ki 17: 1 In the t year of Ahaz king of
2Ki 25:27 king of Judah, in the t month
1Ch 24:12 to Eliashib, the t to Jakim,
1Ch 25:19 the t for Hashabiah, his sons
1Ch 27:15 t captain for the t month
2Ch 34: 3 in the t year he began to
Ezra 8:31 the t day of the first month
Esth 3: 7 Nisan, in the t year of King
Esth 3: 7 until it fell on the t month
Esth 3:13 thirteenth day of the t month
Esth 8:12 thirteenth day of the t month
Esth 9: 1 Now in the t month, that is,
Jer 52:31 king of Judah, in the t month
Ezek 29: 1 on the t day of the month,
Ezek 32: 1 t year, in the t month
Ezek 32:17 to pass also in the t year
Ezek 33:21 the t year of our captivity
Rev 21:20 jacinth, and the t amethyst

TWELVE (*see* TWELFTH)
Gen 5: 8 were nine hundred and t years
Gen 14: 4 T years they served
Gen 17:20 He shall beget t princes, and
Gen 25:16 t princes according to their
Gen 35:22 Now the sons of Jacob were t
Gen 42:13 Your servants are t brothers
Gen 42:32 We are t brothers, sons of
Gen 49:28 are the t tribes of Israel
Ex 15:27 there were t wells of water
Ex 24: 4 and t pillars according
Ex 24: 4 to the t tribes of Israel
Ex 28:21 t according to their names,
Ex 28:21 be according to the t tribes
Ex 39:14 There were t stones according
Ex 39:14 according to the t tribes
Lev 24: 5 flour and bake t cakes with it
Num 1:44 t men, each one representing
Num 7: 3 t oxen, a cart for every two
Num 7:84 t silver platters
Num 7:84 t silver bowls
Num 7:84 and t gold pans
Num 7:86 The t gold pans full of
Num 7:87 offering were t young bulls
Num 7:87 the rams t
Num 7:87 lambs in their first year t
Num 7:87 the goats as a sin offering t
Num 17: 2 their fathers' houses—t rods
Num 17: 6 their fathers' houses, t rods
Num 29:17 day present t young bulls
Num 31: 5 t thousand armed for war
Num 33: 9 At Elim were t springs of
Deut 1:23 so I took t of your men, one
Josh 3:12 take for yourselves t men
Josh 4: 2 t men from the people, one
Josh 4: 3 yourselves t stones from here
Josh 4: 4 Then Joshua called the t men
Josh 4: 8 took up t stones from the
Josh 4: 9 Then Joshua set up t stones
Josh 4:20 those t stones which they
Josh 8:25 men and women, were t
Josh 18:24 t cities with their villages
Josh 19:15 t cities with their villages
Josh 21: 7 to their families had t
Josh 21:40 were by their lot t cities
Judg 19:29 dismembered her into t pieces
Judg 21:10 t thousand of their most
2Sa 2:15 t from Benjamin, followers of
2Sa 2:15 t from the servants of David
2Sa 10: 6 from Ish-Tob t thousand men
2Sa 17: 1 let me choose t thousand men
1Ki 4: 7 Solomon had t governors over
1Ki 4:26 and t thousand horsemen
1Ki 7:15 a line of t cubits measured
1Ki 7:25 It stood on t oxen
1Ki 7:44 Sea, and t oxen under the Sea
1Ki 10:20 T lions stood there, one on
1Ki 10:26 t thousand horsemen, whom he
1Ki 11:30 him, and tore it into t pieces
1Ki 16:23 Israel, and reigned t years
1Ki 18:31 And Elijah took t stones,
1Ki 19:19 who was plowing with t yoke
2Ki 3: 1 of Judah, and reigned t years
2Ki 21: 1 Manasseh was t years old when
1Ch 6:63 they gave t cities from the
1Ch 9:22 were two hundred and t
1Ch 15:10 hundred and t of his brethren
1Ch 25: 9 with his brethren and sons, t
1Ch 25:10 his sons and his brethren, t
1Ch 25:11 his sons and his brethren, t
1Ch 25:12 his sons and his brethren, t
1Ch 25:13 his sons and his brethren, t
1Ch 25:14 his sons and his brethren, t
1Ch 25:15 his sons and his brethren, t
1Ch 25:16 his sons and his brethren, t
1Ch 25:17 his sons and his brethren, t
1Ch 25:18 his sons and his brethren, t
1Ch 25:19 his sons and his brethren, t
1Ch 25:20 his sons and his brethren, t
1Ch 25:21 his sons and his brethren, t
1Ch 25:22 his sons and his brethren, t
1Ch 25:23 his sons and his brethren, t
1Ch 25:24 his sons and his brethren, t
1Ch 25:25 his sons and his brethren, t
1Ch 25:26 his sons and his brethren, t
1Ch 25:27 his sons and his brethren, t
1Ch 25:28 his sons and his brethren, t
1Ch 25:29 his sons and his brethren, t
1Ch 25:30 his sons and his brethren, t
1Ch 25:31 his sons and his brethren, t
2Ch 1:14 t thousand horsemen, whom he
2Ch 4: 4 It stood on t oxen
2Ch 4:15 one Sea and t oxen under it
2Ch 9:19 T lions stood there, one on
2Ch 9:25 t thousand horsemen whom he
2Ch 12: 3 with t hundred chariots,
2Ch 33: 1 Manasseh was t years old when
Ezra 2: 6 thousand eight hundred and t
Ezra 2:18 of Jorah, one hundred and t
Ezra 6:17 for all Israel t male goats
Ezra 8:24 Then I separated t of the
Ezra 8:35 t bulls for all Israel,
Ezra 8:35 and t male goats as a sin
Neh 5:14 t years, neither I nor my
Neh 7:24 of Hariph, one hundred and t
Esth 2:12 t months' preparation,
Jer 52:20 the t bronze bulls which were
Jer 52:21 a measuring line of t cubits
Ezek 43:16 altar hearth is t cubits long
Ezek 43:16 t wide, square at its four
Ezek 47:13 among the t tribes of Israel
Dan 4:29 At the end of the t months he
Matt 9:20 for t years came from behind
Matt 10: 1 called His t disciples to Him
Matt 10: 2 of the t apostles are these
Matt 10: 5 These t Jesus sent out and
Matt 11: 1 commanding His t disciples
Matt 14:20 they took up t baskets full
Matt 19:28 Me will also sit on t thrones
Matt 19:28 judging the t tribes of
Matt 20:17 took the t disciples aside on
Matt 26:14 Then one of the t, called
Matt 26:20 come, He sat down with the t
Matt 26:47 behold, Judas, one of the t
Matt 26:53 more than t legions of angels
Mark 3:14 Then He appointed t, that
Mark 4:10 those around Him with the t
Mark 5:25 a flow of blood for t years
Mark 5:42 for she was t years of age
Mark 6: 7 And He called the t to Him
Mark 6:43 they took up t baskets full
Mark 8:19 They said to Him, "T."
Mark 9:35 And He sat down, called the t
Mark 10:32 He took the t aside again
Mark 11:11 out to Bethany with the t
Mark 14:10 Judas Iscariot, one of the t
Mark 14:17 evening He came with the t
Mark 14:20 It is one of the t, who dips
Mark 14:43 speaking, Judas, one of the t
Luke 2:42 And when He was t years old

Luke 6:13 from them He chose t whom He
Luke 8: 1 And the t were with Him,
Luke 8:42 daughter about t years of age
Luke 8:43 a flow of blood for t years
Luke 9: 1 His t disciples together and
Luke 9:12 the t came and said to Him,
Luke 9:17 t baskets of the leftover
Luke 18:31 Then He took the t aside and
Luke 22: 3 who was numbered among the t
Luke 22:14 and the t apostles with Him
Luke 22:30 the t tribes of Israel
Luke 22:47 called Judas, one of the t
John 6:13 filled t baskets with the
John 6:67 Then Jesus said to the t
John 6:70 Did I not choose you, the t
John 6:71 Him, being one of the t
John 11: 9 Are there not t hours in the
John 20:24 called Didymus, one of the t
Acts 6: 2 Then the t summoned the
Acts 7: 8 Jacob begot the t patriarchs
Acts 19: 7 the men were about t in all
Acts 24:11 t days since I went up to
Acts 26: 7 To this promise our t tribes
1Co 15: 5 seen by Cephas, then by the t
Jas 1: 1 To the t tribes which are
Rev 7: 5 Judah t thousand were sealed
Rev 7: 5 Reuben t thousand were sealed
Rev 7: 5 of the tribe of Gad t
Rev 7: 6 Asher t thousand were sealed
Rev 7: 6 t thousand were sealed
Rev 7: 6 t thousand were sealed
Rev 7: 7 Simeon t thousand were sealed
Rev 7: 7 Levi t thousand were sealed
Rev 7: 7 t thousand were sealed
Rev 7: 8 t thousand were sealed
Rev 7: 8 Joseph t thousand were sealed
Rev 7: 8 t thousand were sealed
Rev 12: 1 her head a garland of t stars
Rev 21:12 and high wall with t gates
Rev 21:12 t angels at the gates, and
Rev 21:12 t tribes of the children of
Rev 21:14 of the city had t foundations
Rev 21:14 of the t apostles of the Lamb
Rev 21:16 t thousand furlongs
Rev 21:21 t gates were t pearls
Rev 22: 2 of life, which bore t fruits

TWENTIETH (*see* TWENTY)
Num 10:11 the t day of the second month
1Ki 15: 9 In the t year of Jeroboam
2Ki 15:30 t year of Jotham the son of
1Ch 24:16 the t to Jehezekel,
1Ch 25:27 the t for Eliathah, his sons
Ezra 10: 9 on the t day of the month
Neh 1: 1 of Chislev, in the t year
Neh 2: 1 Nisan, in the t year of King
Neh 5:14 from the t year until the

TWENTY (*see* TWENTIETH)
Gen 6: 3 be one hundred and t years
Gen 18:31 Suppose t should be found
Gen 18:31 destroy it for the sake of t
Gen 31:38 These t years I have been
Gen 31:41 been in your house t years
Gen 32:14 t male goats
Gen 32:14 two hundred ewes and t rams,
Gen 32:15 t female donkeys and ten foals
Gen 37:28 for t shekels of silver
Ex 26:18 t boards for the south side
Ex 26:19 of silver under the t boards
Ex 26:20 side, there shall be t boards
Ex 27:10 its t pillars and
Ex 27:10 their t sockets shall be of
Ex 27:11 long, with its t pillars and
Ex 27:11 their t sockets of bronze, and
Ex 27:16 be a screen t cubits long
Ex 30:13 (a shekel is t gerahs)
Ex 30:14 from t years old and above,
Ex 36:23 t boards for the south side
Ex 36:24 made to go under the t boards
Ex 36:25 north side, he made t boards
Ex 38:10 There were t pillars for them
Ex 38:10 with t bronze sockets
Ex 38:11 long, with t pillars
Ex 38:11 and their t bronze sockets
Ex 38:18 The length was t cubits, and
Ex 38:26 numbering from t years old
Lev 27: 3 t years old up to sixty years
Lev 27: 5 years old up to t years old
Lev 27: 5 for a male shall be t shekels
Lev 27:25 t gerahs to the shekel
Num 1: 3 from t years old and above
Num 1:18 from t years old and above,
Num 1:20 from t years old and above,
Num 1:22 from t years old and above,
Num 1:24 from t years old and above,
Num 1:26 from t years old and above,
Num 1:28 from t years old and above,
Num 1:30 from t years old and above,
Num 1:32 from t years old and above,
Num 1:34 from t years old and above,
Num 1:36 from t years old and above,
Num 1:38 from t years old and above,
Num 1:40 from t years old and above,
Num 1:42 from t years old and above,
Num 1:45 from t years old and above,
Num 3:47 the shekel of t gerahs
Num 7:86 one hundred and t shekels
Num 11:19 nor ten days, nor t days,
Num 14:29 from t years old and above
Num 18:16 sanctuary, which is t gerahs
Num 26: 2 of Israel from t years old
Num 26: 4 the people from t years old
Num 32:11 from t years old and above,
Deut 31: 2 hundred and t years old today
Deut 34: 7 and t years old when he died
Judg 4: 3 and for t years he harshly
Judg 8:10 t thousand men who drew the
Judg 11:33 as far as Minnith—t cities
Judg 15:20 he judged Israel t years in
Judg 16:31 He had judged Israel t years
1Sa 7: 2 it was there t years
1Sa 14:14 t men within about half an
2Sa 3:20 t men with him came to David
2Sa 8: 4 and t thousand foot soldiers
2Sa 9:10 fifteen sons and t servants
2Sa 10: 6 t thousand foot soldiers
2Sa 18: 7 and a great slaughter of t
2Sa 19:17 and his t servants with him
2Sa 24: 8 end of nine months and t days
1Ki 4:23 t oxen from the pastures, and
1Ki 5:11 Solomon gave Hiram t thousand
1Ki 5:11 and t kors of pressed oil
1Ki 6: 2 was sixty cubits, its width t
1Ki 6: 3 was t cubits long across the
1Ki 6:20 sanctuary was t cubits long
1Ki 6:20 t cubits wide
1Ki 6:20 and t cubits high
1Ki 8:63 hundred and t thousand sheep
1Ki 9:10 at the end of t years, when
1Ki 9:11 Hiram t cities in the land of
1Ki 9:14 hundred and t talents of gold
1Ki 9:28 t talents of gold from there,
1Ki 10:10 t talents of gold, spices in
2Ki 4:42 t loaves of barley bread, and
2Ki 15:27 Samaria, and reigned t years
2Ki 16: 2 Ahaz was t years old when he
1Ch 7: 9 t thousand two hundred mighty
1Ch 12:30 t thousand eight hundred,
1Ch 12:37 t thousand armed for battle
1Ch 15: 5 hundred and t of his brethren
1Ch 15: 6 hundred and t of his brethren
1Ch 18: 4 and t thousand foot soldiers
1Ch 23:24 LORD, from the age of t years
1Ch 23:27 numbered from t years old
1Ch 27:23 number of those t years old
2Ch 2:10 t thousand kors of ground
2Ch 2:10 t thousand kors of barley,
2Ch 2:10 t thousand baths of wine
2Ch 2:10 and t thousand baths of oil
2Ch 3: 3 and the width t cubits
2Ch 3: 4 was t cubits long across the
2Ch 3: 4 height was one hundred and t
2Ch 3: 8 width of the house, t cubits
2Ch 3: 8 and its width t cubits
2Ch 3:11 t cubits in overall length
2Ch 3:13 spanned t cubits overall
2Ch 4: 1 t cubits was its length,
2Ch 4: 1 t cubits its width, and ten
2Ch 5:12 and t priests sounding with
2Ch 7: 5 hundred and t thousand sheep
2Ch 8: 1 to pass at the end of t years
2Ch 9: 9 t talents of gold, spices in
2Ch 25: 5 them from t years old and
2Ch 28: 1 Ahaz was t years old when he
2Ch 28: 6 t thousand in Judah in one
2Ch 31:17 the Levites from t years old
Ezra 2:32 of Harim, three hundred and t
Ezra 2:67 thousand seven hundred and t
Ezra 3: 8 the Levites from t years old
Ezra 8:19 brothers and their sons, t men
Ezra 8:20 two hundred and t Nethinim
Ezra 8:27 t gold basins worth a
Neh 7:35 of Harim, three hundred and t
Neh 7:69 thousand seven hundred and t
Neh 7:71 work t thousand gold drachmas
Neh 7:72 was t thousand gold drachmas
Ps 68:17 of God are t thousand, Even
Ezek 4:10 be by weight, t shekels a day
Ezek 40:49 of the vestibule was t cubits
Ezek 41: 2 and its width, t cubits
Ezek 41: 4 measured the length, t cubits
Ezek 41: 4 width, t cubits, beyond the
Ezek 41:10 of t cubits all around the
Ezek 42: 3 the inner court of t cubits
Ezek 45: 5 they shall have t chambers as
Ezek 45:12 The shekel shall be t gerahs
Ezek 45:12 t shekels, twenty-five
Dan 6: 1 t satraps, to be over the
Jon 4:11 t thousand persons who cannot
Hag 2:16 came to a heap of t ephahs
Hag 2:16 the press, there were but t
Zech 5: 2 Its length is t cubits and its
Luke 14:31 against him with t thousand
John 2: 6 Jews, containing t or thirty
Acts 1:15 a hundred and t), and said,
Acts 27:28 and found it to be t fathoms

TWENTY-CUBIT
1Ki 6:16 Then he built the t room at

TWENTY-EIGHT
Ex 26: 2 curtain shall be t cubits
Ex 36: 9 of each curtain was t cubits
2Ki 10:36 Israel in Samaria was t years
1Ch 12:35 t thousand six hundred
2Ch 11:21 concubines, and begot t sons
Ezra 2:23 of Anathoth, one hundred and t
Ezra 2:41 of Asaph, one hundred and t
Ezra 8:11 of Bebai, and with him t males
Neh 7:16 of Bebai, six hundred and t
Neh 7:22 of Hashum, three hundred and t
Neh 7:27 of Anathoth, one hundred and t
Neh 11: 8 and Sallai, nine hundred and t
Neh 11:14 valor, were one hundred and t

TWENTY-FIFTH (*see* TWENTY-FIVE)
Neh 6:15 t day of the month of Elul
Jer 52:31 on the t day of the month,
Ezek 40: 1 In the t year of our

TWENTY-FIRST (*see* TWENTY-ONE)
Ex 12:18 until the t day of the month
1Ch 24:17 the t to Jachin, the
1Ch 25:28 the t for Hothir, his sons and
Hag 2: 1 on the t day of the month,

TWENTY-FIVE (*see* TWENTY-FIFTH)
Num 8:24 From t years old and above one
Judg 20:35 day t thousand one hundred
Judg 20:46 t thousand men who drew the
1Ki 22:42 and he reigned t years in
2Ki 14: 2 He was t years old when he
2Ki 15:33 He was t years old when he
2Ki 18: 2 He was t years old when he
2Ki 23:36 Jehoiakim was t years old
2Ch 20:31 and he reigned t years in
2Ch 25: 1 Amaziah was t years old when
2Ch 27: 1 Jotham was t years old when
2Ch 27: 8 He was t years old when he
2Ch 29: 1 king when he was t years old
2Ch 36: 5 Jehoiakim was t years old
Ezra 2:33 and Ono, seven hundred and t
Ezek 8:16 were about t men with their
Ezek 11: 1 door of the gate were t men
Ezek 40:13 the width was t cubits, as
Ezek 40:21 cubits and its width t cubits
Ezek 40:25 cubits and its width t cubits
Ezek 40:29 cubits long and t cubits wide
Ezek 40:30 t cubits long and five cubits
Ezek 40:33 cubits long and t cubits wide
Ezek 40:36 cubits and its width t cubits
Ezek 45: 1 shall be t thousand cubits
Ezek 45: 3 t thousand cubits long and ten
Ezek 45: 5 An area t thousand cubits
Ezek 45: 6 t thousand long, adjacent to
Ezek 45:12 t shekels, and fifteen shekels
Ezek 48: 8 t thousand cubits in width,
Ezek 48: 9 t thousand cubits in length
Ezek 48:10 on the north t thousand
Ezek 48:10 on the south t thousand in
Ezek 48:13 t thousand cubits in length
Ezek 48:13 length shall be t thousand
Ezek 48:15 the edge of the t thousand

Ezek 48:20 shall be **t** thousand cubits by
Ezek 48:20 by **t** thousand cubits
Ezek 48:21 next to the **t** thousand cubits
Ezek 48:21 and westward next to the **t**

TWENTY-FOUR (*see* TWENTY-FOURTH)
Num 7:88 peace offerings were **t** bulls
Num 25: 9 in the plague were **t** thousand
2Sa 21:20 on each foot, **t** in number
1Ki 15:33 in Tirzah, and reigned **t** years
1Ch 20: 6 with **t** fingers and toes, six
1Ch 23: 4 **t** thousand were to look after
1Ch 27: 1 division having **t** thousand
1Ch 27: 2 his division were **t** thousand
1Ch 27: 4 his division were **t** thousand
1Ch 27: 5 his division were **t** thousand
1Ch 27: 7 his division were **t** thousand
1Ch 27: 8 his division were **t** thousand
1Ch 27: 9 his division were **t** thousand
1Ch 27:10 his division were **t** thousand
1Ch 27:11 his division were **t** thousand
1Ch 27:12 his division were **t** thousand
1Ch 27:13 his division were **t** thousand
1Ch 27:14 his division were **t** thousand
1Ch 27:15 his division were **t** thousand
Neh 7:23 of Bezai, three hundred and **t**
Rev 4: 4 the throne were **t** thrones
Rev 4: 4 I saw **t** elders sitting,
Rev 4:10 the **t** elders fall down before
Rev 5: 8 the **t** elders fell down before
Rev 5:14 the **t** elders fell down and
Rev 11:16 the **t** elders who sat before
Rev 19: 4 And the **t** elders and the four

TWENTY-FOURTH (*see* TWENTY-FOUR)
1Ch 24:18 to Delaiah, the **t** to Maaziah
1Ch 25:31 the **t** for Romamti-Ezer, his
Neh 9: 1 Now on the **t** day of this
Dan 10: 4 Now on the **t** day of the first
Hag 1:15 on the **t** day of the sixth
Hag 2:10 On the **t** day of the ninth
Hag 2:18 from the **t** day of the ninth
Hag 2:20 on the **t** day of the month
Zech 1: 7 On the **t** day of the eleventh

TWENTY-NINE
Gen 11:24 Nahor lived **t** years, and begot
Ex 38:24 was **t** talents and seven
Josh 15:32 all the cities are **t**, with
2Ki 14: 2 and he reigned **t** years in
2Ki 18: 2 and he reigned **t** years in
2Ch 25: 1 and he reigned **t** years in
2Ch 29: 1 old, and he reigned **t** years in
Ezra 1: 9 silver platters, **t** knives,

TWENTY-ONE (*see* TWENTY-FIRST)
2Ki 24:18 Zedekiah was **t** years old when
2Ch 36:11 Zedekiah was **t** years old when
Ezra 2:26 and Geba, six hundred and **t**
Neh 7:30 and Geba, six hundred and **t**
Neh 7:37 and Ono, seven hundred and **t**
Jer 52: 1 Zedekiah was **t** years old when
Dan 10:13 of Persia withstood me **t** days

TWENTY-SECOND
1Ch 24:17 to Jachin, the **t** to Gamul,
1Ch 25:29 the **t** for Giddalti, his sons

TWENTY-SEVEN (*see* TWENTY-SEVENTH)
Gen 23: 1 lived one hundred and **t** years
1Ki 20:30 then a wall fell on **t**
Esth 1: 1 one hundred and **t** provinces),
Esth 8: 9 **t** provinces in all, to every
Esth 9:30 **t** provinces of the kingdom of

TWENTY-SEVENTH (*see* TWENTY-SEVEN)
Gen 8:14 on the **t** day of the month,
1Ki 16:10 killed him in the **t** year of
1Ki 16:15 In the **t** year of Asa king of
2Ki 15: 1 In the **t** year of Jeroboam
2Ki 25:27 on the **t** day of the month,
Ezek 29:17 it came to pass in the **t** year

TWENTY-SIX (*see* TWENTY-SIXTH)
Judg 20:15 of Benjamin numbered **t**
1Ch 7:40 their number was **t** thousand

TWENTY-SIXTH (*see* TWENTY-SIX)
1Ki 16: 8 In the **t** year of Asa king of

TWENTY-THIRD (*see* TWENTY-THREE)
2Ki 12: 6 by the **t** year of King Jehoash
2Ki 13: 1 In the **t** year of Joash the
1Ch 24:18 the **t** to Delaiah, the
1Ch 25:30 the **t** for Mahazioth, his sons
2Ch 7:10 On the **t** day of the seventh
Esth 8: 9 month of Sivan, on the **t** day
Jer 25: 3 this is the **t** year in which
Jer 52:30 in the **t** year of

TWENTY-THREE (*see* TWENTY-THIRD)
Num 26:62 of them were **t** thousand,
Num 33:39 **t** years old when he died on
Judg 10: 2 He judged Israel **t** years
2Ki 23:31 Jehoahaz was **t** years old when
1Ch 2:22 who had **t** cities in the land
2Ch 36: 2 Jehoahaz was **t** years old when
Ezra 2:11 of Bebai, six hundred and **t**
Ezra 2:17 of Bezai, three hundred and **t**
Ezra 2:19 of Hashum, two hundred and **t**
Ezra 2:21 Bethlehem, one hundred and **t**
Ezra 2:28 and Ai, two hundred and **t**
Neh 7:32 and Ai, one hundred and **t**
Jer 52:28 three thousand and **t** Jews
1Co 10: 8 in one day **t** thousand fell

TWENTY-TWO
Num 3:39 old and above, were **t** thousand
Num 3:43 were **t** thousand two hundred
Num 26:14 **t** thousand two hundred
Josh 19:30 **t** cities with their villages
Judg 7: 3 And **t** thousand of the people
Judg 10: 3 and he judged Israel **t** years
Judg 20:21 ground **t** thousand men of the
2Sa 8: 5 David killed **t** thousand of
1Ki 8:63 LORD, **t** thousand bulls and one
1Ki 14:20 Jeroboam reigned was **t** years
1Ki 16:29 Israel in Samaria **t** years
2Ki 8:26 Ahaziah was **t** years old when
2Ki 21:19 Amon was **t** years old when he
1Ch 7: 2 was **t** thousand six hundred
1Ch 7: 7 **t** thousand and thirty-four
1Ch 12:28 his father's house **t** captains
1Ch 18: 5 David killed **t** thousand of
2Ch 7: 5 sacrifice of **t** thousand bulls
2Ch 13:21 wives, and begot **t** sons and
2Ch 33:21 Amon was **t** years old when he
Ezra 2:12 one thousand two hundred and **t**
Ezra 2:27 of Michmas, one hundred and **t**
Neh 7:17 thousand three hundred and **t**
Neh 7:31 of Michmas, one hundred and **t**
Neh 11:12 house were eight hundred and **t**

TWICE
Gen 41:32 **t** because the thing is
Ex 16: 5 it shall be **t** as much as they
Ex 16:22 they gathered **t** as much bread
Num 20:11 the rock **t** with his rod
1Sa 18:11 David escaped his presence **t**
1Ki 11: 9 who had appeared to him **t**
2Ki 6:10 there, not just once or **t**
Neh 13:20 outside Jerusalem once or **t**
Job 33:29 God works all these things, **t**
Job 40: 5 yes, **t**, but I will proceed no
Job 42:10 **t** as much as he had before
Ps 62:11 once, **T** I have heard this
Eccl 6: 6 lives a thousand years **t** over
Matt 23:15 you make him **t** as much a son
Mark 14:30 before the rooster crows **t**
Mark 14:72 Before the rooster crows **t**
Luke 18:12 I fast **t** a week
Jude 12 **t** dead, pulled up by the

TWIG (*see* TWIGS)
Ezek 17: 4 off its topmost young **t** and
Hos 10: 7 cut off like a **t** on the water

TWIGS (*see* TWIG)
Ezek 17:22 of its young **t** a tender one

TWILIGHT
Ex 12: 6 of Israel shall kill it at **t**
Ex 16:12 At **t** you shall eat meat, and
Ex 29:39 lamb you shall offer at **t**
Ex 29:41 lamb you shall offer at **t**
Ex 30: 8 Aaron lights the lamps at **t**
Lev 23: 5 at **t** is the LORD's Passover
Num 9: 3 day of this month, at **t**, you
Num 9: 5 day of the first month, at **t**
Num 9:11 day of the second month, at **t**
Deut 16: 4 at **t** remain overnight until
Deut 16: 6 sacrifice the Passover at **t**
Josh 5:10 day of the month at **t** on the
1Sa 30:17 **t** until the evening of the
2Ki 7: 5 they rose at **t** to go to the
2Ki 7: 7 they arose and fled at **t**, and
Job 24:15 the adulterer waits for the **t**
Prov 7: 9 in the **t**, in the evening, in
Is 59:10 we stumble at noonday as at **t**
Ezek 12: 6 and carry them out at **t**
Ezek 12: 7 I brought them out at **t**, and I
Ezek 12:12 on his shoulder at **t** and go

TWIN (*see* TWINS)
Acts 28:11 figurehead was the **T** Brothers

TWINED
Ezek 27:24 apparel, in strong **t** cords

TWINKLING
1Co 15:52 in the **t** of an eye, at the

TWINS (*see* TWIN)
Gen 25:24 there were **t** in her womb
Gen 38:27 behold, **t** were in her womb
Song 4: 2 every one of which bears **t**
Song 4: 5 **t** of a gazelle, which feed
Song 6: 6 every one bears **t**, and none is
Song 7: 3 two fawns, **t** of a gazelle

TWIST (*see* TWISTED, TWISTS)
Ps 56: 5 All day they **t** my words
2Pe 3:16 and unstable **t** to their own

TWISTED (*see* TWIST)
Is 27: 1 Leviathan that **t** serpent
Matt 27:29 When they had **t** a crown of
Mark 15:17 they **t** a crown of thorns, put
John 19: 2 the soldiers **t** a crown of

TWISTS (*see* TWIST)
Deut 16:19 **t** the words of the righteous
Prov 19: 3 of a man **t** his way, and his

TWO (*see* TWO-EDGED)
Gen 1:16 Then God made **t** great lights
Gen 4:19 took for himself **t** wives
Gen 6:19 all flesh you shall bring **t**
Gen 6:20 **t** of every kind will come to
Gen 7: 2 **t** each of animals that are
Gen 7: 9 **t** by **t** they went into the
Gen 7:15 the ark to Noah, **t** by **t**
Gen 9:22 told his **t** brothers outside
Gen 10:25 To Eber were born **t** sons
Gen 11:10 begot Arphaxad **t** years after
Gen 11:19 Reu, Peleg lived **t** hundred
Gen 11:21 Serug, Reu lived **t** hundred
Gen 11:23 Serug lived **t** hundred years,
Gen 11:32 days of Terah were **t** hundred
Gen 15:10 these to Him and cut them in **t**
Gen 15:10 he did not cut the birds in **t**
Gen 19: 1 Now the **t** angels came to
Gen 19: 8 I have **t** daughters who have
Gen 19:15 your **t** daughters who are here
Gen 19:16 the hands of his **t** daughters
Gen 19:30 his **t** daughters were with him
Gen 19:30 his **t** daughters dwelt in a
Gen 21:27 the **t** of them made a covenant
Gen 21:31 because the **t** of them swore
Gen 22: 3 took **t** of his young men with
Gen 22: 6 the **t** of them went together
Gen 22: 8 the **t** of them went together
Gen 24:22 **t** bracelets for her wrists
Gen 25:23 **T** nations are in your womb,
Gen 25:23 **t** peoples shall be separated
Gen 27: 9 bring me from there **t** choice
Gen 27:36 supplanted me these **t** times
Gen 29:16 Now Laban had **t** daughters
Gen 31:33 into the **t** maids' tents, but
Gen 31:41 years for your **t** daughters
Gen 32: 7 and camels, into **t** companies
Gen 32:10 now I have become **t** companies
Gen 32:14 **t** hundred female goats and
Gen 32:14 **t** hundred ewes and twenty rams
Gen 32:22 night and took his **t** wives
Gen 32:22 his **t** maidservants, and his
Gen 33: 1 Rachel, and the **t** maidservants
Gen 34:25 that **t** of the sons of Jacob,
Gen 40: 2 was angry with his **t** officers
Gen 41: 1 at the end of **t** full years
Gen 41:50 to Joseph were born **t** sons
Gen 42:37 Kill my **t** sons if I do not
Gen 44:27 that my wife bore me **t** sons
Gen 45: 6 For these **t** years the famine
Gen 46:27 him in Egypt were **t** persons
Gen 48: 1 he took with him his **t** sons
Gen 48: 5 And now your **t** sons, Ephraim
Gen 49:14 lying down between **t** burdens
Ex 2:13 **t** Hebrew men were fighting,
Ex 4: 9 believe even these **t** signs
Ex 12: 7 and put it on the **t** doorposts
Ex 12:22 and the **t** doorposts with the

Ex 12:23 on the t doorposts, the LORD
Ex 16:22 bread, t omers for each one
Ex 16:29 sixth day bread for t days
Ex 18: 3 with her t sons, of whom the
Ex 18: 6 wife and her t sons with her
Ex 21:21 he remains alive a day or t
Ex 25:10 t and a half cubits shall be
Ex 25:12 t rings shall be on one side,
Ex 25:12 t rings on the other side
Ex 25:17 t and a half cubits shall be
Ex 25:18 you shall make t cherubim of
Ex 25:18 the t ends of the mercy seat
Ex 25:19 the t ends of it of one piece
Ex 25:22 from between the t cherubim
Ex 25:23 t cubits shall be its length,
Ex 25:35 first t branches of the same
Ex 25:35 second t branches of the same
Ex 25:35 third t branches of the same
Ex 26:17 T tenons shall be in each
Ex 26:19 t sockets under one board
Ex 26:19 for its t tenons
Ex 26:19 t sockets under another board
Ex 26:19 for its t tenons
Ex 26:21 t sockets under one board, and
Ex 26:21 t sockets under another board
Ex 26:23 you shall also make t boards
Ex 26:23 for the t back corners of the
Ex 26:24 shall be for the t corners
Ex 26:25 t sockets under one board, and
Ex 26:25 t sockets under another board
Ex 27: 7 the poles shall be on the t
Ex 28: 7 It shall have t shoulder
Ex 28: 7 straps joined at its t edges
Ex 28: 9 you shall take t onyx stones
Ex 28:11 you shall engrave the t
Ex 28:12 you shall put the t stones on
Ex 28:12 before the LORD on his t
Ex 28:14 you shall make t chains of
Ex 28:23 you shall make t rings of
Ex 28:23 put the t rings on the t ends
Ex 28:24 Then you shall put the t
Ex 28:24 chains of gold in the t rings
Ex 28:25 the other t ends of the
Ex 28:25 t braided chains you shall
Ex 28:25 fasten to the t settings, and
Ex 28:26 shall make t rings of gold
Ex 28:26 put them on the t ends of the
Ex 28:27 t other rings of gold you
Ex 28:27 them on the t shoulder straps
Ex 29: 1 and t rams without blemish,
Ex 29: 3 with the bull and the t rams
Ex 29:13 the t kidneys and the fat that
Ex 29:22 the t kidneys and the fat on
Ex 29:38 t lambs of the first year,
Ex 30: 2 t cubits shall be its height
Ex 30: 4 T gold rings you shall make
Ex 30: 4 place them on its t sides
Ex 30:23 (t hundred and fifty shekels)
Ex 30:23 t hundred and fifty shekels of
Ex 31:18 He gave Moses t tablets of
Ex 32:15 and the t tablets of the
Ex 34: 1 Cut t tablets of stone like
Ex 34: 4 So he cut t tablets of stone
Ex 34: 4 hand the t tablets of stone
Ex 34:29 (and the t tablets of the
Ex 36:22 Each board had t tenons for
Ex 36:24 t sockets under one board for
Ex 36:24 one board for its t tenons
Ex 36:24 t sockets under another
Ex 36:24 board for its t tenons
Ex 36:26 t sockets under one board and
Ex 36:26 t sockets under another board
Ex 36:28 He also made t boards
Ex 36:28 for the t back corners of the
Ex 36:29 of them for the t corners
Ex 36:30 t sockets under every board
Ex 37: 1 t and a half cubits was its
Ex 37: 3 t rings on one side
Ex 37: 3 t rings on the other side of
Ex 37: 6 t and a half cubits was its
Ex 37: 7 He made t cherubim of beaten
Ex 37: 7 the t ends of the mercy seat
Ex 37: 8 t ends of one piece with the
Ex 37:10 t cubits was its length, a
Ex 37:21 first t branches of the same
Ex 37:21 second t branches of the same
Ex 37:21 third t branches of the same
Ex 37:25 and t cubits was its height
Ex 37:27 He made t rings of gold for
Ex 37:27 by its t corners on both
Ex 38:29 and t thousand four hundred
Ex 39: 4 together at its t edges
Ex 39:16 They also made t settings of
Ex 39:16 t gold rings
Ex 39:16 put the t rings on the t ends
Ex 39:17 they put the t braided chains
Ex 39:17 chains of gold in the t rings
Ex 39:18 The t ends of the t braided
Ex 39:18 fastened in the t settings
Ex 39:19 they made t rings of gold and
Ex 39:19 put them on the t ends of the
Ex 39:20 They made t other gold rings
Ex 39:20 them on the t shoulder straps
Lev 3: 4 the t kidneys and the fat
Lev 3:10 the t kidneys and the fat
Lev 3:15 the t kidneys and the fat
Lev 4: 9 the t kidneys and the fat
Lev 5: 7 t turtledoves or t young
Lev 5:11 t turtledoves or t young
Lev 7: 4 the t kidneys and the fat
Lev 8: 2 t rams, and a basket of
Lev 8:16 the t kidneys with their fat,
Lev 8:25 the t kidneys and their fat,
Lev 12: 5 she shall be unclean t weeks
Lev 12: 8 she may bring t turtledoves
Lev 12: 8 or t young pigeons
Lev 14: 4 is to be cleansed t living
Lev 14:10 eighth day he shall take t
Lev 14:22 t turtledoves or t young
Lev 14:49 t birds, cedar wood, scarlet,
Lev 15:14 t turtledoves or t young
Lev 15:29 t turtledoves or t young
Lev 16: 1 death of the t sons of Aaron
Lev 16: 5 of the children of Israel t
Lev 16: 7 He shall take the t goats
Lev 16: 8 cast lots for the t goats
Lev 23:17 t wave loaves of two-tenths
Lev 23:18 one young bull, and t rams
Lev 23:19 t male lambs of the first
Lev 23:20 the LORD, with the t lambs
Lev 24: 6 You shall set them in t rows
Num 1:35 thirty-two thousand t hundred
Num 2:21 thirty-two thousand t hundred
Num 3:34 were six thousand t hundred
Num 3:43 twenty-two thousand t hundred
Num 3:46 redemption of the t hundred
Num 4:36 were t thousand seven hundred
Num 4:40 were t thousand six hundred
Num 4:44 were three thousand t hundred
Num 6:10 t turtledoves or t young
Num 6:10 bring t turtledoves or t
Num 7: 3 for every t of the leaders
Num 7: 7 T carts and four oxen he gave
Num 7:17 t oxen, five rams, five male
Num 7:23 t oxen, five rams, five male
Num 7:29 t oxen, five rams, five male
Num 7:35 t oxen, five rams, five male
Num 7:41 t oxen, five rams, five male
Num 7:47 t oxen, five rams, five male
Num 7:53 t oxen, five rams, five male
Num 7:59 t oxen, five rams, five male
Num 7:65 t oxen, five rams, five male
Num 7:71 t oxen, five rams, five male
Num 7:77 t oxen, five rams, five male
Num 7:83 t oxen, five rams, five male
Num 7:85 t thousand four hundred
Num 7:89 from between the t cherubim
Num 9:22 Whether it was t days, a
Num 10: 2 Make t silver trumpets for
Num 11:19 nor t days, nor five days,
Num 11:26 But t men had remained in the
Num 11:31 and about t cubits above the
Num 13:23 between t of them on a pole
Num 16: 2 t hundred and fifty leaders of
Num 16:17 t hundred and fifty censers
Num 16:35 and consumed the t hundred
Num 22:22 his t servants were with him
Num 26:10 the fire devoured t hundred
Num 26:14 twenty-two thousand t hundred
Num 28: 3 t male lambs in their first
Num 28: 9 on the Sabbath day t lambs in
Num 28:11 t young bulls, one ram, and
Num 28:19 t young bulls, one ram, and
Num 28:27 t young bulls, one ram, and
Num 29:13 t rams, and fourteen lambs in
Num 29:14 for each of the t rams,
Num 29:17 t rams, fourteen lambs in
Num 29:20 t rams, fourteen lambs in
Num 29:23 t rams, and fourteen lambs in
Num 29:26 t rams, and fourteen lambs in
Num 29:29 t rams, and fourteen lambs in
Num 29:32 t rams, and fourteen lambs in
Num 31:27 the plunder into t parts,
Num 34:15 The t tribes and the
Num 35: 5 east side t thousand cubits
Num 35: 5 south side t thousand cubits
Num 35: 5 west side t thousand cubits
Num 35: 5 north side t thousand cubits
Deut 3: 8 t kings of the Amorites who
Deut 3:21 God has done to these t kings
Deut 4:13 them on t tablets of stone
Deut 4:47 t kings of the Amorites, who
Deut 5:22 them on t tablets of stone
Deut 9:10 me t tablets of stone written
Deut 9:11 me the t tablets of stone
Deut 9:15 the t tablets of the covenant
Deut 9:15 were in my t hands
Deut 9:17 Then I took the t tablets
Deut 9:17 threw them out of my t hands
Deut 10: 1 Hew for yourself t tablets
Deut 10: 3 hewed t tablets of stone like
Deut 10: 3 having the t tablets in my
Deut 14: 6 the hoof split into t parts
Deut 17: 6 of t or three witnesses, but
Deut 19:15 by the mouth of t or three
Deut 21:15 If a man has t wives, one
Deut 25:11 If t men fight together, and
Deut 32:30 t put ten thousand to flight,
Josh 2: 1 the son of Nun sent out t men
Josh 2: 4 Then the woman took the t men
Josh 2:10 what you did to the t kings
Josh 2:23 So the t men returned,
Josh 3: 4 about t thousand cubits by
Josh 6:22 t men who had spied out the
Josh 7: 3 up, but let about t or three
Josh 7:21 t hundred shekels of silver,
Josh 9:10 and all that He did to the t
Josh 14: 3 inheritance of the t tribes
Josh 14: 4 of Joseph were t tribes
Josh 15:60 t cities with their villages
Josh 21:16 cities from those t tribes
Josh 21:25 common-land: t cities
Josh 21:27 common-land: t cities
Josh 24:12 you, also the t kings of the
Judg 5:30 to every man a girl or t
Judg 5:30 t pieces of dyed embroidery
Judg 7:25 they captured t princes of
Judg 8:12 he took the t kings of Midian
Judg 9:44 the other t companies rushed
Judg 11:37 let me alone for t months
Judg 11:38 he sent her away for t months
Judg 11:39 it was so at the end of t
Judg 15:13 bound him with t new ropes
Judg 16: 3 the t gateposts, pulled them
Judg 16:28 the Philistines for my t eyes
Judg 16:29 of the t middle pillars which
Judg 17: 4 Then his mother took t
Judg 19: 6 the t of them ate and drank
Judg 19:10 were the t saddled donkeys
Judg 20:45 killed t thousand of them
Ruth 1: 1 he and his wife and his t sons
Ruth 1: 2 of his t sons were Mahlon
Ruth 1: 3 she was left, and her t sons
Ruth 1: 5 the woman survived her t sons
Ruth 1: 7 her t daughters-in-law with
Ruth 1: 8 to her t daughters-in-law
Ruth 1:19 Now the t of them went until
Ruth 4:11 the t who built the house of
1Sa 1: 2 And he had t wives
1Sa 1: 3 Also the t sons of Eli,
1Sa 2:21 three sons and t daughters
1Sa 2:34 will come upon your t sons
1Sa 4: 4 the t sons of Eli, Hophni and
1Sa 4:11 the t sons of Eli, Hophni and
1Sa 4:17 Also your t sons, Hophni and
1Sa 6: 7 take t milk cows which have
1Sa 6:10 they took t milk cows and
1Sa 10: 2 today, you will find t men by
1Sa 10: 4 give you t loaves of bread,
1Sa 11:11 so that no t of them were
1Sa 13: 1 reigned t years over Israel
1Sa 13: 2 T thousand were with Saul in
1Sa 14:49 the names of his t daughters
1Sa 15: 4 t hundred thousand foot
1Sa 18:27 killed t hundred men of the
1Sa 23:18 So the t of them made a
1Sa 25:13 t hundred stayed with the
1Sa 25:18 and took t hundred loaves of
1Sa 25:18 t skins of wine, five sheep
1Sa 25:18 t hundred cakes of figs, and

1Sa 27: 3 and David with his t wives
1Sa 28: 8 and he went, and t men with him
1Sa 30: 5 And David's t wives, Ahinoam
1Sa 30:10 for t hundred stayed behind,
1Sa 30:12 figs and t clusters of raisins
1Sa 30:18 and David rescued his t wives
1Sa 30:21 Now David came to the t
2Sa 1: 1 had stayed t days in Ziklag
2Sa 2: 2 his t wives also, Ahinoam the
2Sa 2:10 Israel, and he reigned t years
2Sa 4: 2 Now Saul's son had t men who
2Sa 8: 2 With t lines he measured off
2Sa 12: 1 There were t men in one city,
2Sa 13:23 after t full years, that
2Sa 14: 6 your maidservant had t sons
2Sa 14: 6 the t fought with each other
2Sa 14:26 the hair of his head at t
2Sa 14:28 Absalom dwelt t full years in
2Sa 15:11 with Absalom went t hundred
2Sa 15:27 your t sons with you, Ahimaaz
2Sa 15:36 there with them their t sons
2Sa 16: 1 on them t hundred loaves of
2Sa 18:24 sitting between the t gates
2Sa 21: 8 the t sons of Rizpah the
2Sa 23:20 He had killed t lion-like
1Ki 2: 5 me, and what he did to the t
1Ki 2:32 down t men more righteous
1Ki 2:39 that t slaves of Shimei ran
1Ki 3:16 Then t women who were harlots
1Ki 3:18 except the t of us in the
1Ki 3:25 Divide the living child in t
1Ki 5:12 the t of them made a treaty
1Ki 5:14 Lebanon and t months at home
1Ki 6:23 made t cherubim of olive wood
1Ki 6:32 The t doors were of olive
1Ki 6:34 the t doors were of cypress
1Ki 6:34 t panels comprised one
1Ki 6:34 t panels comprised the other
1Ki 7:15 he cast t pillars of bronze,
1Ki 7:16 Then he made t capitals of
1Ki 7:18 t rows of pomegranates above
1Ki 7:20 on the t pillars also had
1Ki 7:20 there were t hundred such
1Ki 7:24 buds were cast in t rows when
1Ki 7:26 It contained t thousand baths
1Ki 7:41 the t pillars
1Ki 7:41 the t bowl-shaped capitals
1Ki 7:41 were on top of the t pillars
1Ki 7:41 the t networks covering the
1Ki 7:41 t bowl-shaped capitals which
1Ki 7:42 pomegranates for the t
1Ki 7:42 for the t networks (t rows
1Ki 7:42 to cover the t bowl-shaped
1Ki 8: 7 the cherubim spread their t
1Ki 8: 9 in the ark except the t
1Ki 9:10 had built the t houses, the
1Ki 10:16 King Solomon made t hundred
1Ki 10:19 and t lions stood beside the
1Ki 11:29 the t were alone in the field
1Ki 12:28 made t calves of gold, and
1Ki 15:25 reigned over Israel t years
1Ki 16: 8 reigned t years in Tirzah
1Ki 16:21 were divided into t parts
1Ki 16:24 for t talents of silver
1Ki 18:21 you falter between t opinions
1Ki 18:23 let them give us t bulls
1Ki 18:32 to hold t seahs of seed
1Ki 20:15 and there were t hundred and
1Ki 20:27 like t little flocks of goats
1Ki 21:10 and seat t men, scoundrels,
1Ki 21:13 t men, scoundrels, came in and
1Ki 22:51 reigned t years over Israel
2Ki 1:14 and burned up the first t
2Ki 2: 6 So the t of them went on
2Ki 2: 7 while the t of them stood by
2Ki 2: 8 so that the t of them crossed
2Ki 2:11 and separated the t of them
2Ki 2:12 and tore them into t pieces
2Ki 2:24 t female bears came out of
2Ki 4: 1 is coming to take my t sons
2Ki 4:33 the door behind the t of them
2Ki 5:17 given t mule-loads of earth
2Ki 5:22 just now t young men of the
2Ki 5:22 and t changes of garments
2Ki 5:23 Please, take t talents
2Ki 5:23 t talents of silver in t bags
2Ki 5:23 with t changes of garments,
2Ki 5:23 and handed them to t of his
2Ki 7: 1 and t seahs of barley for a
2Ki 7:14 Therefore they took t
2Ki 7:16 and t seahs of barley for a
2Ki 7:18 T seahs of barley for a
2Ki 9:32 t or three eunuchs looked out
2Ki 10: 4 t kings could not stand up to
2Ki 10: 8 Lay them in t heaps at the
2Ki 11: 7 The t contingents of you who
2Ki 15:23 Samaria, and reigned t years
2Ki 17:16 t calves, made a wooden image
2Ki 18:23 give you t thousand horses
2Ki 21: 5 the host of heaven in the t
2Ki 21:19 and he reigned t years in
2Ki 23:12 Manasseh had made in the t
2Ki 25: 4 of the gate between t walls
2Ki 25:16 The t pillars, one Sea, and
1Ch 1:19 To Eber were born t sons
1Ch 4: 5 father of Tekoa had t wives
1Ch 5:21 t hundred and fifty thousand
1Ch 5:21 t thousand of their donkeys
1Ch 7: 9 twenty thousand t hundred
1Ch 7:11 were seventeen thousand t
1Ch 9:22 as gatekeepers were t hundred
1Ch 11:21 honored than the other t men
1Ch 11:22 He had killed t lion-like
1Ch 12:32 their chiefs were t hundred
1Ch 15: 6 t hundred and twenty of his
1Ch 15: 8 t hundred of his brethren
1Ch 25: 7 was t hundred and eighty-eight
1Ch 26:17 for the storehouse t by t
1Ch 26:18 highway and t at the Parbar
1Ch 26:32 his brethren were t thousand
2Ch 3:10 Holy Place he made t cherubim
2Ch 3:15 t pillars thirty-five cubits
2Ch 4: 3 The oxen were cast in t rows
2Ch 4:12 the t pillars and the
2Ch 4:12 were on top of the t pillars
2Ch 4:12 t networks covering the t
2Ch 4:13 for the t networks (t rows
2Ch 4:13 to cover the t bowl-shaped
2Ch 5:10 in the ark except the t
2Ch 8:10 t hundred and fifty, who ruled
2Ch 9:15 King Solomon made t hundred
2Ch 9:18 and t lions stood beside the
2Ch 14: 8 and from Benjamin t hundred
2Ch 17:15 and with him t hundred and
2Ch 17:16 with him t hundred thousand
2Ch 17:17 with him t hundred thousand
2Ch 21:19 after the end of t years
2Ch 24: 3 Jehoiada took for him t wives
2Ch 26:12 was t thousand six hundred
2Ch 28: 8 t hundred thousand women,
2Ch 29:32 rams, and t hundred lambs
2Ch 33: 5 the host of heaven in the t
2Ch 33:21 and he reigned t years in
2Ch 35: 8 t thousand six hundred from
Ezra 2: 3 t thousand one hundred and
Ezra 2: 6 t thousand eight hundred and
Ezra 2: 7 Elam, one thousand t hundred
Ezra 2:12 Azgad, one thousand t hundred
Ezra 2:14 t thousand and fifty-six
Ezra 2:19 t hundred and twenty-three
Ezra 2:28 t hundred and twenty-three
Ezra 2:31 Elam, one thousand t hundred
Ezra 2:38 one thousand t hundred and
Ezra 2:65 they had t hundred men and
Ezra 2:66 their mules t hundred and
Ezra 6:17 t hundred rams, four hundred
Ezra 8: 4 and with him t hundred males
Ezra 8: 9 Jehiel, and with him t hundred
Ezra 8:20 t hundred and twenty Nethinim
Ezra 8:27 t vessels of fine polished
Ezra 10:13 the work of one or t days
Neh 7: 8 t thousand one hundred and
Neh 7:11 t thousand eight hundred and
Neh 7:12 Elam, one thousand t hundred
Neh 7:17 t thousand three hundred and
Neh 7:19 t thousand and sixty-seven
Neh 7:34 Elam, one thousand t hundred
Neh 7:41 one thousand t hundred and
Neh 7:67 and they had t hundred and
Neh 7:68 their mules t hundred and
Neh 7:71 t thousand t hundred silver
Neh 7:72 t thousand silver minas, and
Neh 11:13 were t hundred and forty-two
Neh 11:18 the holy city were t hundred
Neh 12:31 wall, and appointed t large
Neh 12:40 So the t thanksgiving choirs
Esth 2:21 t of the king's eunuchs,
Esth 6: 2 t of the king's eunuchs, the
Esth 9:27 these t days every year,
Job 13:20 Only t things do not do to me
Job 42: 7 your t friends, for you have
Ps 46: 9 bow and cuts the spear in t
Ps 107:16 And cut the bars of iron in t
Ps 136:13 who divided the Red Sea in t
Prov 24:22 the ruin those t can bring
Prov 30: 7 T things I request of You
Prov 30:15 The leech has t daughters
Eccl 4: 9 T are better than one,
Eccl 4:11 if t lie down together, they
Eccl 4:12 another, t can withstand him
Song 4: 5 Your t breasts are like t
Song 4: 5 t breasts are like t fawns
Song 7: 3 t breasts are like t fawns
Song 8:12 who keep its fruit t hundred
Is 6: 2 with t he covered his face,
Is 6: 2 with t he covered his feet,
Is 6: 2 and with t he flew
Is 7: 4 be fainthearted for these t
Is 7:21 alive a young cow and t sheep
Is 17: 6 t or three olives at the top
Is 22:11 a reservoir between the t
Is 36: 8 give you t thousand horses
Is 47: 9 But these t things shall come
Is 51:19 These t things have come to
Jer 2:13 people have committed t evils
Jer 3:14 t from a family, and I will
Jer 24: 1 there were t baskets of figs
Jer 28: 3 Within t full years I will
Jer 28:11 the space of t full years
Jer 33:24 The t families which the
Jer 34:18 when they cut the calf in t
Jer 39: 4 the gate between the t walls
Jer 52: 7 the gate between the t walls
Jer 52:20 The t pillars, one Sea, the
Ezek 1:11 t wings of each one touched
Ezek 1:11 and t covered their bodies
Ezek 1:23 Each one had t which covered
Ezek 1:23 each one had t which covered
Ezek 21:19 appoint for yourself t ways
Ezek 21:21 at the fork of the t roads
Ezek 23: 2 of man, there were t women
Ezek 35:10 These t nations and
Ezek 35:10 these t countries shall be
Ezek 37:22 shall no longer be t nations
Ezek 37:22 divided into t kingdoms again
Ezek 40: 9 and the gateposts, t cubits
Ezek 40:39 were t tables on this side
Ezek 40:39 t tables on that side, on
Ezek 40:40 gateway, were t tables
Ezek 40:40 of the gateway were t tables
Ezek 41: 3 the doorposts, t cubits
Ezek 41:18 Each cherub had t faces,
Ezek 41:22 high, and its length t cubits
Ezek 41:23 and the sanctuary had t doors
Ezek 41:24 The doors had t panels apiece
Ezek 41:24 t folding panels
Ezek 41:24 t panels for one door and
Ezek 41:24 t panels for the other door
Ezek 43:14 to the lower ledge, t cubits
Ezek 45:15 from a flock of t hundred
Ezek 47:13 Joseph shall have t portions
Ezek 48:17 to the north t hundred and
Ezek 48:17 to the south t hundred and
Ezek 48:17 fifty, to the east t hundred
Ezek 48:17 and to the west t hundred
Dan 7: 4 to stand on t feet like a man
Dan 8: 3 was a ram which had t horns
Dan 8: 3 and the t horns were high
Dan 8: 6 to the ram that had t horns
Dan 8: 7 the ram, and broke his t horns
Dan 8:14 For t thousand three hundred
Dan 8:20 you saw, having the t horns
Dan 12: 5 and there stood t others, one
Dan 12:11 be one thousand t hundred
Hos 6: 2 After t days He will revive
Hos 10:10 for their t transgressions
Amos 1: 1 t years before the earthquake
Amos 3: 3 can t walk together, unless
Amos 3:12 from the mouth of a lion t
Amos 4: 8 So t or three cities wandered
Zech 4: 3 T olive trees are by it, one
Zech 4:11 What are these t olive trees
Zech 4:12 him, "What are these t olive
Zech 4:12 t gold pipes from which the
Zech 4:14 These are the t anointed ones
Zech 5: 9 looked, and there were t women
Zech 6: 1 from between t mountains, and
Zech 11: 7 I took for myself t staffs
Zech 11:10 staff, Beauty, and cut it in t
Zech 11:14 Then I cut in t my other

Zech 13: 8 That **t** thirds in it shall be
Zech 14: 4 of Olives shall be split in **t**
Matt 2:16 from **t** years old and under,
Matt 4:18 saw **t** brothers, Simon called
Matt 4:21 He saw **t** other brothers,
Matt 5:41 to go one mile, go with him **t**
Matt 6:24 No one can serve **t** masters
Matt 8:28 Gergesenes, there met Him **t**
Matt 9:27 **t** blind men followed Him,
Matt 10:10 nor **t** tunics, nor sandals,
Matt 10:29 Are not **t** sparrows sold for a
Matt 11: 2 he sent **t** of his disciples
Matt 14:17 only five loaves and **t** fish
Matt 14:19 the **t** fish, and looking up to
Matt 18: 8 having **t** hands or **t** feet
Matt 18: 9 rather than having **t** eyes
Matt 18:16 take with you one or **t** more
Matt 18:16 that by the mouth of **t** or
Matt 18:19 if **t** of you agree on earth
Matt 18:20 For where **t** or three are
Matt 19: 5 the **t** shall become one flesh'
Matt 19: 6 are no longer **t** but one flesh
Matt 20:21 Grant that these **t** sons of
Matt 20:24 against the **t** brothers
Matt 20:30 **t** blind men sitting by the
Matt 21: 1 then Jesus sent **t** disciples
Matt 21:28 A man had **t** sons, and he came
Matt 21:31 Which of the **t** did the will
Matt 22:40 On these **t** commandments hang
Matt 24:40 Then **t** men will be in the
Matt 24:41 **T** women will be grinding at
Matt 24:51 and will cut him in **t** and
Matt 25:15 five talents, to another **t**
Matt 25:17 who had received **t** gained **t**
Matt 25:22 had received **t** talents came
Matt 25:22 you delivered to me **t** talents
Matt 25:22 I have gained **t** more talents
Matt 26: 2 You know that after **t** days is
Matt 26:37 the **t** sons of Zebedee, and He
Matt 26:60 But at last **t** false witnesses
Matt 27:21 Which of the **t** do you want me
Matt 27:38 Then **t** robbers were crucified
Matt 27:51 torn in **t** from top to bottom
Mark 5:13 (there were about **t** thousand)
Mark 6: 7 to send them out **t** by **t**
Mark 6: 9 and not to put on **t** tunics
Mark 6:37 buy **t** hundred denarii worth
Mark 6:38 they said, "Five, and **t** fish
Mark 6:41 the **t** fish, He looked up to
Mark 6:41 the **t** fish He divided among
Mark 9:43 maimed, than having **t** hands
Mark 9:45 life lame, than having **t** feet
Mark 9:47 one eye, than having **t** eyes
Mark 10: 8 the **t** shall become one flesh'
Mark 10: 8 so then they are no longer **t**
Mark 11: 1 Olives, He sent out **t** of His
Mark 12:42 came and threw in **t** mites,
Mark 14: 1 After **t** days it was the
Mark 14:13 So He sent out **t** of His
Mark 15:27 they also crucified **t** robbers
Mark 15:38 torn in **t** from top to bottom
Mark 16:12 to **t** of them as they walked
Luke 2:24 or **t** young pigeons
Luke 3:11 He who has **t** tunics, let him
Luke 5: 2 saw **t** boats standing by the
Luke 7:19 calling **t** of his disciples to
Luke 7:41 creditor who had **t** debtors
Luke 9: 3 do not have **t** tunics apiece
Luke 9:13 **t** fish, unless we go and buy
Luke 9:16 the **t** fish, and looking up to
Luke 9:30 **t** men talked with Him, who
Luke 9:32 the **t** men who stood with Him
Luke 10: 1 sent them **t** by **t** before His
Luke 10:35 he took out **t** denarii, gave
Luke 12: 6 sold for **t** copper coins
Luke 12:46 and will cut him in **t** and
Luke 12:52 three against **t**, and **t**
Luke 15:11 A certain man had **t** sons
Luke 16:13 servant can serve **t** masters
Luke 17:34 will be **t** men in one bed
Luke 17:35 **T** women will be grinding
Luke 17:36 **T** men will be in the field
Luke 18:10 **T** men went up to the temple
Luke 19:29 Olivet, that He sent **t** of His
Luke 21: 2 poor widow putting in **t** mites
Luke 22:38 Lord, look, here are **t** swords
Luke 23:32 There were also **t** others,
Luke 23:45 of the temple was torn in **t**
Luke 24: 4 **t** men stood by them in
Luke 24:13 **t** of them were traveling that
John 1:35 day, John stood with **t** of his
John 1:37 The **t** disciples heard him
John 1:40 One of the **t** who heard John
John 4:40 and He stayed there **t** days
John 4:43 Now after the **t** days He
John 6: 7 **T** hundred denarii worth of
John 6: 9 **t** small fish, but what are
John 8:17 testimony of **t** men is true
John 11: 6 He stayed **t** more days in the
John 11:18 Jerusalem, about **t** miles away
John 19:18 **t** others with Him, one on
John 20:12 she saw **t** angels in white
John 21: 2 **t** others of His disciples
John 21: 8 but about **t** hundred cubits),
Acts 1:10 **t** men stood by them in white
Acts 1:23 And they proposed **t**
Acts 1:24 of these **t** You have chosen
Acts 7:26 to **t** of them as they were
Acts 7:29 Midian, where he had **t** sons
Acts 9:38 they sent **t** men to him,
Acts 10: 7 Cornelius called **t** of his
Acts 12: 6 **t** chains between **t** soldiers
Acts 19:10 And this continued for **t** years
Acts 19:22 So he sent into Macedonia **t**
Acts 19:34 cried out for about **t** hours
Acts 21:33 him to be bound with **t** chains
Acts 23:23 And he called for **t** centurions
Acts 23:23 Prepare **t** hundred soldiers,
Acts 23:23 **t** hundred spearmen to go to
Acts 24:27 But after **t** years Porcius
Acts 27:37 And in all we were **t** hundred
Acts 27:41 a place where **t** seas met,
Acts 28:30 Then Paul dwelt **t** whole years
1Co 6:16 The **t**," He says, "shall
1Co 14:27 let there be **t** or at the most
1Co 14:29 Let **t** or three prophets speak
2Co 13: 1 By the mouth of **t** or three
Gal 4:22 that Abraham had **t** sons
Gal 4:24 For these are the **t** covenants
Eph 2:15 one new man from the **t**, thus
Eph 5:31 the **t** shall become one flesh
Phil 1:23 am hard pressed between the **t**
1Ti 5:19 from **t** or three witnesses
Heb 6:18 that by **t** immutable things,
Heb 10:28 of **t** or three witnesses
Heb 11:37 stoned, they were sawn in **t**
Rev 9:12 still **t** more woes are coming
Rev 9:16 was **t** hundred million, and I
Rev 11: 3 give power to my **t** witnesses
Rev 11: 3 one thousand **t** hundred and
Rev 11: 4 These are the **t** olive trees
Rev 11: 4 the **t** lampstands standing
Rev 11:10 because these **t** prophets
Rev 12: 6 there one thousand **t** hundred
Rev 12:14 **t** wings of a great eagle,
Rev 13:11 he had **t** horns like a lamb and
Rev 19:20 These **t** were cast alive into

TWO-EDGED (*see* TWO)
Ps 149: 6 And a **t** sword in their hand,
Prov 5: 4 wormwood, sharp as a **t** sword
Heb 4:12 and sharper than any **t** sword
Rev 1:16 mouth went a sharp **t** sword
Rev 2:12 He who has the sharp **t** sword

TWO-TENTHS
Lev 23:13 **t** of an ephah of fine flour
Lev 23:17 wave loaves of **t** of an ephah
Lev 24: 5 **T** of an ephah shall be in
Num 15: 6 **t** of an ephah of fine flour
Num 28: 9 **t** of an ephah of fine flour
Num 28:12 **t** of an ephah of fine flour
Num 28:20 for a bull, and **t** for a ram
Num 28:28 each bull, **t** for the one ram,
Num 29: 3 for the bull, **t** for the ram,
Num 29: 9 the bull, **t** for the one ram,
Num 29:14 **t** for each of the two rams,

TYCHICUS
Acts 20: 4 of Derbe, and Timothy, and **T**
Eph 6:21 affairs and how I am doing, **T**
Col 4: 7 **T**, who is a beloved brother,
2Ti 4:12 And **T** I have sent to Ephesus
Tit 3:12 I send Artemas to you, or **T**

TYPE (*see* TYPES)
Rom 5:14 who is a **t** of Him who was to

TYPES (*see* TYPE)
1Ch 22:15 all **t** of skillful men for

TYRANNUS
Acts 19: 9 daily in the school of **T**

TYRE
Josh 19:29 and to the fortified city of **T**
2Sa 5:11 Then Hiram king of **T** sent
2Sa 24: 7 came to the stronghold of **T**
1Ki 5: 1 Now Hiram king of **T** sent his
1Ki 7:13 sent and brought Hiram from **T**
1Ki 7:14 and his father was a man of **T**
1Ki 9:11 (Hiram the king of **T** had
1Ki 9:12 Then Hiram went from **T** to see
1Ch 14: 1 Now Hiram king of **T** sent
1Ch 22: 4 those from **T** brought much
2Ch 2: 3 sent to Hiram king of **T**,
2Ch 2:11 Then Hiram king of **T** answered
2Ch 2:14 and his father was a man of **T**)
Ezra 3: 7 **T** to bring cedar logs from
Neh 13:16 Men of **T** dwelt there also,
Ps 45:12 the daughter of **T** will be
Ps 83: 7 with the inhabitants of **T**
Ps 87: 4 Behold, O Philistia and **T**,
Is 23: 1 The burden against **T**
Is 23: 5 in agony at the report of **T**
Is 23: 8 taken this counsel against **T**
Is 23:15 to pass in that day that **T**
Is 23:15 to **T** as in the song of the
Is 23:17 that the LORD will visit **T**
Jer 25:22 all the kings of **T**, all the
Jer 27: 3 the Ammonites, the king of **T**
Jer 47: 4 to cut off from **T** and Sidon
Ezek 26: 2 because **T** has said against
Ezek 26: 3 Behold, I am against you, O **T**
Ezek 26: 4 shall destroy the walls of **T**
Ezek 26: 7 against **T** from the north
Ezek 26:15 Thus says the Lord GOD to **T**
Ezek 27: 2 take up a lamentation for **T**
Ezek 27: 3 and say to **T**, 'You who are
Ezek 27: 3 O **T**, you have said, 'I am
Ezek 27: 8 your own wise men, O **T**, were
Ezek 27:32 for you, 'What city is like **T**
Ezek 28: 2 man, say to the prince of **T**
Ezek 28:12 lamentation for the king of **T**
Ezek 29:18 labor strenuously against **T**
Ezek 29:18 army received wages from **T**
Hos 9:13 Just as I saw Ephraim like **T**
Joel 3: 4 have you to do with Me, O **T**
Amos 1: 9 For three transgressions of **T**
Amos 1:10 a fire upon the wall of **T**
Zech 9: 2 borders on it, and against **T**
Zech 9: 3 for **T** built herself a tower,
Matt 11:21 in you had been done in **T**
Matt 11:22 will be more tolerable for **T**
Matt 15:21 departed to the region of **T**
Mark 3: 8 and those from **T** and Sidon, a
Mark 7:24 and went to the region of **T**
Mark 7:31 from the region of **T** and Sidon
Luke 6:17 and from the seacoast of **T**
Luke 10:13 in you had been done in **T**
Luke 10:14 will be more tolerable for **T**
Acts 12:20 angry with the people of **T**
Acts 21: 3 to Syria, and landed at **T**
Acts 21: 7 finished our voyage from **T**

U

UCAL
Prov 30: 1 to Ithiel and **U**

UEL
Ezra 10:34 Maadai, Amram, **U**,

UGLINESS (*see* UGLY)
Gen 41:19 such **u** as I have never seen

UGLY (*see* UGLINESS)
Gen 41: 3 them out of the river, **u** and
Gen 41: 4 And the **u** and gaunt cows ate up
Gen 41:19 up after them, poor and very **u**
Gen 41:20 **u** cows ate up the first seven
Gen 41:21 just as **u** as at the beginning
Gen 41:27 **u** cows which came up after

ULAI
Dan 8: 2 that I was by the River **U**
Dan 8:16 between the banks of the **U**

ULAM
1Ch 7:16 Sheresh, and his sons were **U**
1Ch 7:17 The son of **U** was Bedan
1Ch 8:39 brother were **U** his firstborn
1Ch 8:40 The sons of **U** were mighty men

ULCER
Lev 22:22 or have an **u** or eczema or

ULLA
1Ch 7:39 The sons of **U** were Arah,

UMMAH
Josh 19:30 Also **U**, Aphek, and Rehob

UNABLE
Deut 7:22 you will be **u** to destroy them
Luke 19:48 and were **u** to do anything

UNAFRAID
Rom 13: 3 want to be **u** of the authority

UNAPPROACHABLE
1Ti 6:16 dwelling in **u** light, whom no

UNAWARE
Rom 1:13 Now I do not want you to be **u**
1Co 10: 1 I do not want you to be **u**

UNBELIEF (*see* BELIEF, UNBELIEVING)
Matt 13:58 there because of their **u**
Matt 17:20 Because of your **u**
Mark 6: 6 marveled because of their **u**
Mark 9:24 Lord, I believe; help my **u**!
Mark 16:14 and He rebuked their **u** and
Rom 3: 3 Will their **u** make the
Rom 4:20 the promise of God through **u**
Rom 11:20 Because of **u** they were broken
Rom 11:23 if they do not continue in **u**
1Ti 1:13 I did it ignorantly in **u**
Heb 3:12 of **u** in departing from the
Heb 3:19 not enter in because of **u**

UNBELIEVER (*see* BELIEVER, UNBELIEVERS)
1Co 7:15 But if the **u** departs, let him
1Co 14:24 an **u** or an uninformed person
2Co 6:15 part has a believer with an **u**
1Ti 5: 8 faith and is worse than an **u**

UNBELIEVERS (*see* UNBELIEVER)
Luke 12:46 him his portion with the **u**
1Co 6: 6 brother, and that before **u**
1Co 14:22 to those who believe but to **u**
1Co 14:22 **u** but for those who believe
1Co 14:23 those who are uninformed or **u**
2Co 6:14 yoked together with **u**

UNBELIEVING (*see* UNBELIEF)
John 20:27 Do not be **u**, but believing
Acts 14: 2 But the **u** Jews stirred up the
1Co 7:14 For the **u** husband is
1Co 7:14 the **u** wife is sanctified by
Tit 1:15 defiled and **u** nothing is pure
Rev 21: 8 But the cowardly, **u**,

UNCERTAIN (*see* CERTAIN, UNCERTAINTY)
Acts 25:20 And because I was **u** of such
1Co 14: 8 the trumpet makes an **u** sound
1Ti 6:17 nor to trust in **u** riches but

UNCERTAINTY (*see* UNCERTAIN)
1Co 9:26 I run thus: not with **u**

UNCHANGEABLE (*see* CHANGE)
Heb 7:24 forever, has an **u** priesthood

UNCIRCUMCISED (*see* CIRCUMCISE, UNCIRCUMCISION)
Gen 17:14 the **u** male child, who is not
Gen 34:14 our sister to one who is **u**
Ex 6:12 heed me, for I am of **u** lips
Ex 6:30 Behold, I am of **u** lips, and
Ex 12:48 For no **u** person shall eat it
Lev 19:23 shall count their fruit as **u**
Lev 19:23 years it shall be as **u** to you
Lev 26:41 if their **u** hearts are humbled
Josh 5: 7 for they were **u**, because they
Judg 14: 3 a wife from the **u** Philistines
Judg 15:18 fall into the hand of the **u**
1Sa 14: 6 to the garrison of these **u**
1Sa 17:26 For who is this **u** Philistine
1Sa 17:36 this **u** Philistine will be
1Sa 31: 4 it, lest these **u** men come
2Sa 1:20 daughters of the **u** triumph
1Ch 10: 4 it, lest these **u** men come
Is 52: 1 For the **u** and the unclean
Jer 6:10 Indeed their ear is **u**, and
Jer 9:25 are circumcised with the **u**
Jer 9:26 For all these nations are **u**
Jer 9:26 of Israel are **u** in the heart
Ezek 28:10 the **u** by the hand of aliens
Ezek 31:18 lie in the midst of the **u**
Ezek 32:19 Go down, be placed with the **u**
Ezek 32:21 down, they lie with the **u**
Ezek 32:24 who have gone down **u** to the
Ezek 32:25 all around it, all of them **u**
Ezek 32:26 around it, all of them **u**,
Ezek 32:27 who are fallen of the **u**, who
Ezek 32:28 broken in the midst of the **u**
Ezek 32:29 they shall lie with the **u**
Ezek 32:30 they lie **u** with those slain
Ezek 32:32 the **u** with those slain by the
Ezek 44: 7 **u** in heart and **u** in flesh
Ezek 44: 9 **u** in heart or **u** in flesh
Hab 2:16 and be exposed as **u**
Acts 7:51 and **u** in heart and ears
Acts 11: 3 You went in to **u** men and ate
Rom 2:26 if an **u** man keeps the
Rom 2:27 And will not the physically **u**
Rom 3:30 faith and the **u** through faith
Rom 4: 9 only, or upon the **u** also
Rom 4:10 he was circumcised, or **u**
Rom 4:10 circumcised, but while **u**
Rom 4:11 which he had while still **u**
Rom 4:11 believe, though they are **u**
Rom 4:12 Abraham had while still **u**
1Co 7:18 Let him not become **u**
1Co 7:18 Was anyone called while **u**
Gal 2: 7 **u** had been committed to me
Col 3:11 nor Jew, circumcised nor **u**

UNCIRCUMCISION (*see* UNCIRCUMCISED)
Rom 2:25 circumcision has become **u**
Rom 2:26 will not his **u** be counted as
1Co 7:19 **u** is nothing, but keeping the
Gal 5: 6 nor **u** avails anything, but
Gal 6:15 nor **u** avails anything, but a
Eph 2:11 who are called **U** by what is
Col 2:13 the **u** of your flesh, He has

UNCLE (*see* UNCLE'S)
Lev 10: 4 sons of Uzziel the **u** of Aaron
Lev 25:49 or his **u** or his uncle's son
1Sa 10:14 Then Saul's **u** said to him
1Sa 10:15 And Saul's **u** said, "Tell me,
1Sa 10:16 So Saul said to his **u**, "He
1Sa 14:50 the son of Ner, Saul's **u**
2Ki 24:17 Mattaniah, Jehoiachin's **u**
1Ch 27:32 Also Jehonathan, David's **u**
Esth 2:15 of Abihail the **u** of Mordecai
Jer 32: 7 your **u** will come to you,
Jer 32: 9 the son of my **u** who was in

UNCLEAN (*see* CLEAN, UNCLEANNESS)
Gen 7: 2 each of animals that are **u**
Gen 7: 8 beasts, of beasts that are **u**
Lev 5: 2 a person touches any **u** thing
Lev 5: 2 is the carcass of an **u** beast
Lev 5: 2 or the carcass of **u** livestock
Lev 5: 2 carcass of **u** creeping things
Lev 5: 2 from him, he also shall be **u**
Lev 7:19 **u** thing shall not be eaten
Lev 7:20 to the LORD, while he is **u**
Lev 7:21 who touches any **u** thing, such
Lev 7:21 any **u** beast
Lev 7:21 or any abominable **u** thing
Lev 10:10 holy and unholy, and between **u**
Lev 11: 4 cloven hooves, is **u** to you
Lev 11: 5 cloven hooves, is **u** to you
Lev 11: 6 cloven hooves, is **u** to you
Lev 11: 7 not chew the cud, is **u** to you
Lev 11: 8 They are **u** to you
Lev 11:24 By these you shall become **u**
Lev 11:24 them shall be **u** until evening
Lev 11:25 clothes and be **u** until evening
Lev 11:26 not chew the cud, is **u** to you
Lev 11:26 who touches it shall be **u**
Lev 11:27 all fours, those are **u** to you
Lev 11:27 shall be **u** until evening
Lev 11:28 clothes and be **u** until evening
Lev 11:28 It is **u** to you
Lev 11:29 These also shall be **u** to you
Lev 11:31 These are **u** to you among all
Lev 11:31 dead shall be **u** until evening
Lev 11:32 when they are dead shall be **u**
Lev 11:32 it shall be **u** until evening
Lev 11:33 whatever is in it shall be **u**
Lev 11:34 which water falls becomes **u**
Lev 11:34 be drunk from it becomes **u**
Lev 11:35 such carcass falls shall be **u**
Lev 11:35 are **u**, and shall be **u** to you
Lev 11:36 any such carcass becomes **u**
Lev 11:38 on it, it becomes **u** to you
Lev 11:39 shall be **u** until evening
Lev 11:40 clothes and be **u** until evening
Lev 11:40 clothes and be **u** until evening
Lev 11:43 make yourselves **u** with them
Lev 11:47 To distinguish between the **u**
Lev 12: 2 she shall be **u** seven days
Lev 12: 2 impurity she shall be **u**
Lev 12: 5 then she shall be **u** two weeks
Lev 13: 3 at him, and pronounce him **u**
Lev 13: 8 priest shall pronounce him **u**
Lev 13:11 priest shall pronounce him **u**
Lev 13:11 not isolate him, for he is **u**
Lev 13:14 appears on him, he shall be **u**
Lev 13:15 and pronounce him to be **u**
Lev 13:15 for the raw flesh is **u**
Lev 13:20 priest shall pronounce him **u**
Lev 13:22 priest shall pronounce him **u**
Lev 13:25 priest shall pronounce him **u**
Lev 13:27 priest shall pronounce him **u**
Lev 13:30 priest shall pronounce him **u**
Lev 13:36 for yellow hair. He is **u**
Lev 13:44 a leprous man. He is **u**
Lev 13:44 shall surely pronounce him **u**
Lev 13:45 mustache, and cry, '**U**! **U**!'
Lev 13:46 He shall be **u**
Lev 13:46 he has the sore he shall be **u**
Lev 13:46 He is **u**, and he shall dwell
Lev 13:51 an active leprosy. It is **u**
Lev 13:55 has not spread, it is **u**, and
Lev 13:59 it clean or to pronounce it **u**
Lev 14:36 the house may not be made **u**
Lev 14:40 an **u** place outside the city
Lev 14:41 an **u** place outside the city
Lev 14:44 leprosy in the house. It is **u**
Lev 14:45 the city to an **u** place
Lev 14:46 up shall be **u** until evening
Lev 14:57 to teach when it is **u** and when
Lev 15: 2 his body, his discharge is **u**
Lev 15: 4 Every bed is **u** on which he
Lev 15: 4 on which he sits shall be **u**
Lev 15: 5 water, and be **u** until evening
Lev 15: 6 water, and be **u** until evening
Lev 15: 7 water, and be **u** until evening
Lev 15: 8 water, and be **u** until evening
Lev 15: 9 discharge rides shall be **u**
Lev 15:10 him shall be **u** until evening
Lev 15:10 water, and be **u** until evening
Lev 15:11 water, and be **u** until evening
Lev 15:16 water, and be **u** until evening
Lev 15:17 water, and be **u** until evening
Lev 15:18 water, and be **u** until evening
Lev 15:19 her shall be **u** until evening
Lev 15:20 her impurity shall be **u**
Lev 15:20 that she sits on shall be **u**
Lev 15:21 water, and be **u** until evening
Lev 15:22 water, and be **u** until evening
Lev 15:23 he shall be **u** until evening
Lev 15:24 him, he shall be **u** seven days
Lev 15:24 on which he lies shall be **u**
Lev 15:25 all the days of her **u**
Lev 15:25 She shall be **u**
Lev 15:26 she sits on shall be **u**, as
Lev 15:27 those things shall be **u**
Lev 15:27 water, and be **u** until evening
Lev 15:32 emits semen and is **u** thereby,
Lev 15:33 who lies with her who is **u**
Lev 17:15 water, and be **u** until evening
Lev 20:21 wife, it is an **u** thing
Lev 20:25 between clean beasts and **u**
Lev 20:25 between **u** birds and clean
Lev 20:25 have separated from you as **u**
Lev 22: 4 anything made **u** by a corpse
Lev 22: 5 by which he would be made **u**
Lev 22: 5 by whom he would become **u**
Lev 22: 6 shall be **u** until evening, and
Lev 27:11 If it is an **u** beast which
Lev 27:27 And if it is an **u** beast, then
Num 6: 7 **u** even for his father or his
Num 9:10 is **u** because of a dead body
Num 18:15 the firstborn of **u** animals
Num 19: 7 shall be **u** until evening
Num 19: 8 and shall be **u** until evening
Num 19:10 and be **u** until evening
Num 19:11 anyone shall be **u** seven days
Num 19:13 He shall be **u**, because the
Num 19:14 tent shall be **u** seven days
Num 19:15 no cover fastened on it, is **u**

Num 19:16 grave, shall be **u** seven days
Num 19:17 for an **u** person they shall
Num 19:19 the **u** on the third day and on
Num 19:20 But the man who is **u** and does
Num 19:20 sprinkled on him; he is **u**
Num 19:21 shall be **u** until evening
Num 19:22 **u** person touches shall be **u**
Num 19:22 it shall be **u** until evening
Deut 12:15 the **u** and the clean may eat of
Deut 12:22 the **u** and the clean alike may
Deut 14: 7 they are **u** for you
Deut 14: 8 Also the swine is **u** for you
Deut 14:10 it is **u** for you
Deut 14:19 thing that flies is **u** for you
Deut 15:22 the **u** and the clean person
Deut 23:10 **u** by some occurrence in the
Deut 23:14 may see no **u** thing among you
Deut 26:14 any of it for any **u** use, nor
Josh 22:19 land of your possession is **u**
Judg 13: 4 and not to eat any **u** thing
Judg 13: 7 drink, nor eat anything **u**
Judg 13:14 drink, nor eat anything **u**
1Sa 20:26 he is **u**, surely he is **u**
2Ch 23:19 was in any way **u** should enter
Ezra 9:11 to possess is an **u** land, with
Job 14: 4 a clean thing out of an **u**
Eccl 9: 2 the good, the clean, and the **u**
Is 6: 5 Because I am a man of **u** lips
Is 6: 5 midst of a people of **u** lips
Is 30:22 throw them away as an **u** thing
Is 35: 8 The **u** shall not pass over it,
Is 52: 1 the **u** shall no longer come to
Is 52:11 from there, touch no **u** thing
Is 64: 6 we are all like an **u** thing
Lam 1:17 become an **u** thing among them
Lam 4:15 Go away, **u**
Ezek 20:26 I pronounced them **u** because
Ezek 22:26 the difference between the **u**
Ezek 44:23 them to discern between the **u**
Hos 9: 3 shall eat **u** things in Assyria
Hag 2:13 If one who is **u** because of a
Hag 2:13 any of these, will it be **u**
Hag 2:13 It shall be **u**
Hag 2:14 and what they offer there is **u**
Zech 13: 2 the **u** spirit to depart from
Matt 10: 1 them power over **u** spirits
Matt 12:43 When an **u** spirit goes out of
Mark 1:23 synagogue with an **u** spirit
Mark 1:26 And when the **u** spirit had
Mark 1:27 commands even the **u** spirits
Mark 3:11 the **u** spirits, whenever they
Mark 3:30 He has an **u** spirit
Mark 5: 2 tombs a man with an **u** spirit
Mark 5: 8 Come out of the man, **u** spirit
Mark 5:13 Then the **u** spirits went out
Mark 6: 7 them power over **u** spirits
Mark 7:25 an **u** spirit heard about Him
Mark 9:25 He rebuked the **u** spirit,
Luke 4:33 had a spirit of an **u** demon
Luke 4:36 He commands the **u** spirits
Luke 6:18 were tormented with **u** spirits
Luke 8:29 For He had commanded the **u**
Luke 9:42 Jesus rebuked the **u** spirit
Luke 11:24 When an **u** spirit goes out of
Acts 5:16 were tormented by **u** spirits
Acts 8: 7 For **u** spirits, crying with a
Acts 10:14 eaten anything common or **u**
Acts 10:28 not call any man common or **u**
Acts 11: 8 For nothing common or **u** has
Rom 14:14 there is nothing **u** of itself
Rom 14:14 considers anything to be **u**
Rom 14:14 to him it is **u**
1Co 7:14 your children would be **u**, but
2Co 6:17 Do not touch what is **u**, and I
Eph 5: 5 **u** person, nor covetous man,
Heb 9:13 of a heifer, sprinkling the **u**
Rev 16:13 I saw three **u** spirits like
Rev 18: 2 spirit, and a cage for every **u**

UNCLEANNESS (*see* UNCLEAN, UNCLEANNESSES)
Lev 5: 3 Or if he touches human **u**
Lev 5: 3 whatever sort of **u** it is with
Lev 7:21 thing, such as human **u**, any
Lev 14:19 is to be cleansed from his **u**
Lev 15: 3 this shall be his **u** in regard
Lev 15: 3 by his discharge, it is his **u**
Lev 15:26 as the **u** of her impurity
Lev 15:30 for the discharge of her **u**
Lev 15:31 of Israel from their **u**, lest
Lev 15:31 their **u** when they defile My
Lev 16:16 because of the **u** of the
Lev 16:16 them in the midst of their **u**
Lev 16:19 sanctify it from the **u** of the
Lev 22: 3 LORD, while he has **u** upon him
Lev 22: 5 whatever his **u** may be
Num 5:19 **u** while under your husband's
Num 19:13 his **u** is still on him
Deut 24: 1 he has found some **u** in her
Ezra 9:11 with the **u** of the peoples of
Lam 1: 9 Her **u** is in her skirts
Ezek 36:17 Me their way was like the **u**
Ezek 39:24 According to their **u** and
Zech 13: 1 Jerusalem, for sin and for **u**
Matt 23:27 of dead men's bones and all **u**
Rom 1:24 God also gave them up to **u**
Rom 6:19 your members as slaves of **u**
2Co 12:21 and have not repented of the **u**
Gal 5:19 adultery, fornication, **u**,
Eph 4:19 to work all **u** with greediness
Eph 5: 3 all **u** or covetousness, let it
Col 3: 5 fornication, **u**, passion, evil
1Th 2: 3 did not come from deceit or **u**
1Th 4: 7 For God did not call us to **u**
2Pe 2:10 to the flesh in the lust of **u**

UNCLEANNESSES (*see* UNCLEANNESS)
Ezek 36:29 deliver you from all your **u**

UNCLE'S (*see* UNCLE)
Lev 20:20 If a man lies with his **u** wife
Lev 20:20 has uncovered his **u** nakedness
Lev 25:49 or his **u** son may redeem him
Esth 2: 7 his **u** daughter, for she had
Jer 32: 8 Then Hanameel my **u** son came
Jer 32:12 presence of Hanameel my **u** son

UNCLOTHED (*see* CLOTHE)
2Co 5: 4 not because we want to be **u**

UNCONDEMNED (*see* CONDEMN)
Acts 16:37 **u** Romans, and have thrown us
Acts 22:25 a man who is a Roman, and **u**

UNCOVER (*see* COVER, UNCOVERED, UNCOVERING, UNCOVERS)
Lev 10: 6 Do not **u** your heads nor tear
Lev 18: 6 to him, to **u** his nakedness
Lev 18: 7 your mother you shall not **u**
Lev 18: 7 you shall not **u** her nakedness
Lev 18: 8 father's wife you shall not **u**
Lev 18: 9 nakedness you shall not **u**
Lev 18:10 nakedness you shall not **u**
Lev 18:11 you shall not **u** her nakedness
Lev 18:12 You shall not **u** the
Lev 18:13 You shall not **u** the
Lev 18:14 You shall not **u** the
Lev 18:15 You shall not **u** the
Lev 18:15 you shall not **u** her nakedness
Lev 18:16 You shall not **u** the
Lev 18:17 You shall not **u** the
Lev 18:17 daughter, to **u** her nakedness
Lev 18:18 to **u** her nakedness while the
Lev 18:19 not approach a woman to **u** her
Lev 20:19 You shall not **u** the
Lev 20:19 for that would **u** his near of
Lev 21:10 shall not **u** his head nor tear
Num 5:18 **u** the woman's head, and put
Deut 22:30 wife, nor **u** his father's bed
Ruth 3: 4 in, **u** his feet, and lie down
Is 3:17 the LORD will **u** their secret
Is 47: 2 **u** the thigh, pass through the
Jer 13:26 Therefore I will **u** your
Lam 4:22 He will **u** your sins
Ezek 16:37 will **u** your nakedness to them
Ezek 22:10 In you men **u** their fathers'
Hos 2:10 Now I will **u** her lewdness in
Mic 1: 6 and I will **u** her foundations

UNCOVERED (*see* UNCOVER)
Gen 9:21 and became **u** in his tent
Lev 20:11 has **u** his father's nakedness
Lev 20:17 He has **u** his sister's
Lev 20:18 she has **u** the flow of her
Lev 20:20 wife, he has **u** his uncle's
Lev 20:21 He has **u** his brother's
Deut 27:20 because he has **u** his father's
Ruth 3: 7 **u** his feet, and lay down
2Sa 22:16 of the world were **u**, at the
2Ki 17: 4 And the king of Assyria **u** a
Ps 18:15 world were **u** At Your rebuke
Is 20: 4 with their buttocks **u**, to
Is 22: 6 horsemen, and Kir **u** the shield
Is 47: 3 Your nakedness shall be **u**
Is 57: 8 for you have **u** yourself to
Jer 13:22 your skirts have been **u**, your
Jer 49:10 I have **u** his secret places,
Lam 2:14 they have not **u** your iniquity
Ezek 4: 7 your arm shall be **u**, and you
Ezek 13:14 that its foundation will be **u**
Ezek 16:36 and your nakedness **u** in your
Ezek 16:57 before your wickedness was **u**
Ezek 21:24 your transgressions are **u**
Ezek 23:10 They **u** her nakedness, took
Ezek 23:18 harlotry and **u** her nakedness
Ezek 23:29 of your harlotry shall be **u**
Hos 7: 1 the iniquity of Ephraim was **u**
Mark 2: 4 they **u** the roof where He was
1Co 11: 5 her head **u** dishonors her head
1Co 11:13 pray to God with her head **u**

UNCOVERING (*see* UNCOVER)
2Sa 6:20 **u** himself today in the eyes

UNCOVERS (*see* UNCOVER)
Lev 20:18 and **u** her nakedness, he has
2Sa 6:20 fellows shamelessly **u** himself
Job 12:22 He **u** deep things out of

UNDEFILED (*see* DEFILE)
Ps 119: 1 Blessed are the **u** in the way
Heb 7:26 us, who is holy, harmless, **u**
Heb 13: 4 among all, and the bed **u**
Jas 1:27 **u** religion before God and the
1Pe 1: 4 incorruptible and **u** and that

UNDER (*see* PREFACE)

UNDERFOOT
Lam 1:15 The Lord has trampled **u** all
Heb 10:29 has trampled the Son of God **u**

UNDERGIRD
Acts 27:17 used cables to **u** the ship

UNDERGROUND
Ezek 31: 4 **u** waters gave it height, with

UNDERMINE
Job 6:27 and you **u** your friend

UNDERNEATH (*see* PREFACE)

UNDERSIDES
Job 41:30 His **u** are like sharp

UNDERSTAND (*see* UNDERSTANDING, UNDERSTANDS, UNDERSTOOD)
Gen 11: 7 that they may not **u** one
Gen 41:15 of you that you can **u** a dream
Num 16:30 then you will **u** that these
Deut 9: 3 Therefore **u** today that the
Deut 9: 6 Therefore **u** that the LORD
Deut 28:49 whose language you will not **u**
2Ki 18:26 Aramaic language, for we **u** it
1Ch 28:19 the LORD made me **u** in writing
Neh 8: 3 women and those who could **u**
Neh 8: 7 the people to **u** the Law
Neh 8: 8 helped them to **u** the reading
Neh 8:13 in order to **u** the words of
Job 6:24 cause me to **u** wherein I have
Job 15: 9 What do you **u** that is not in
Job 23: 5 **u** what He would say to me
Job 26:14 of His power who can **u**
Job 32: 9 do the aged always **u** justice
Job 36:29 can anyone **u** the spreading of
Job 42: 3 have uttered what I did not **u**
Ps 14: 2 To see if there are any who **u**
Ps 19:12 Who can **u** his errors
Ps 49:20 is in honor, yet does not **u**
Ps 53: 2 To see if there are any who **u**
Ps 73:16 When I thought how to **u** this
Ps 81: 5 a language that I did not **u**
Ps 82: 5 do not know, nor do they **u**
Ps 92: 6 know, Nor does a fool **u** this
Ps 94: 7 Nor does the God of Jacob **u**
Ps 94: 8 **U**, you senseless among the
Ps 106: 7 Egypt did not **u** Your wonders
Ps 107:43 things, And they will **u** the
Ps 119:27 Make me **u** the way of Your
Ps 119:100 I **u** more than the ancients,
Ps 139: 2 You **u** my thought afar off
Prov 1: 6 to **u** a proverb and an enigma,
Prov 2: 5 then you will **u** the fear of
Prov 2: 9 Then you will **u** righteousness
Prov 8: 5 **u** prudence, and you fools, be
Prov 14: 8 the prudent is to **u** his way
Prov 20:24 then can a man **u** his own way
Prov 28: 5 Evil men do not **u** justice
Prov 28: 5 those who seek the LORD **u** all
Prov 29: 7 does not **u** such knowledge

Prov 30:18 yes, four which I do not **u**
Is 6: 9 Keep on hearing, but do not **u**
Is 6:10 **u** with their heart, and return
Is 28: 9 will he make to **u** the message
Is 28:19 a terror just to **u** the report
Is 32: 4 of the rash will **u** knowledge
Is 33:19 tongue that you cannot **u**
Is 36:11 Aramaic language, for we **u** it
Is 41:20 **u** together, that the hand of
Is 43:10 believe Me, and **u** that I am He
Is 44:18 They do not know nor **u**
Is 44:18 hearts, so that they cannot **u**
Is 56:11 are shepherds who cannot **u**
Jer 5:15 nor can you **u** what they say
Jer 9:12 the wise man who may **u** this
Jer 23:20 days you will **u** it perfectly
Ezek 3: 6 whose words you cannot **u**
Dan 1: 4 knowledge and quick to **u**, who
Dan 8:16 make this man **u** the vision
Dan 8:17 **U**, son of man, that the
Dan 9:13 iniquities and **u** Your truth
Dan 9:22 forth to give you skill to **u**
Dan 9:23 the matter, and **u** the vision
Dan 9:25 Know therefore and **u**, that
Dan 10:11 **u** the words that I speak to
Dan 10:12 that you set your heart to **u**
Dan 10:14 **u** what will happen to your
Dan 11:33 who **u** shall instruct many
Dan 12: 8 Although I heard, I did not **u**
Dan 12:10 and none of the wicked shall **u**
Dan 12:10 but the wise shall **u**
Hos 4:14 who do not **u** will be trampled
Hos 14: 9 Let him **u** these things
Mic 4:12 nor do they **u** His counsel
Matt 13:13 do not hear, nor do they **u**
Matt 13:14 you will hear and shall not **u**
Matt 13:15 should **u** with their heart
Matt 13:19 the kingdom, and does not **u** it
Matt 15:10 said to them, "Hear and **u**
Matt 15:17 Do you not yet **u** that
Matt 16: 9 Do you not yet **u**, or remember
Matt 16:11 How is it you do not **u** that I
Matt 24:15 (whoever reads, let him **u**)
Mark 4:12 they may hear and not **u**
Mark 4:13 Do you not **u** this parable
Mark 4:13 will you **u** all the parables
Mark 7:14 Hear Me, everyone, and **u**
Mark 8:17 Do you not yet perceive nor **u**
Mark 8:21 How is it you do not **u**
Mark 9:32 they did not **u** this saying
Mark 13:14 not" (let the reader **u**)
Mark 14:68 I neither know nor **u** what you
Luke 2:50 But they did not **u** the
Luke 8:10 and hearing they may not **u**
Luke 9:45 they did not **u** this saying
John 6:60 a hard saying; who can **u** it
John 8:27 They did not **u** that He spoke
John 8:43 Why do you not **u** My speech
John 10: 6 but they did not **u** the things
John 12:16 not **u** these things at first
John 12:40 **u** with their heart, lest they
John 13: 7 I am doing you do not **u** now
Acts 7:25 his hand, but they did not **u**
Acts 8:30 Do you **u** what you are reading
Acts 28:26 you will hear, and shall not **u**
Acts 28:27 should **u** with their heart
Rom 7:15 what I am doing, I do not **u**
Rom 15:21 who have not heard shall **u**
1Co 13: 2 and **u** all mysteries and all
1Co 14: 9 by the tongue words easy to **u**
1Co 14:16 he does not **u** what you say
2Co 1:13 you than what you read or **u**
2Co 1:13 Now I trust you will **u**, even
Eph 3: 4 you may **u** my knowledge in the
Eph 5:17 but **u** what the will of the
Heb 11: 3 By faith we **u** that the worlds
2Pe 2:12 of the things they do not **u**
2Pe 3:16 are some things hard to **u**

UNDERSTANDING (*see* UNDERSTAND)
Ex 31: 3 of God, in wisdom, in **u**, in
Ex 35:31 Spirit of God, in wisdom and **u**
Ex 36: 1 the LORD has put wisdom and **u**
Deut 1:13 Choose wise, **u**, and
Deut 4: 6 your **u** in the sight of the
Deut 4: 6 nation is a wise and **u** people
Deut 32:28 nor is there any **u** in them
1Sa 25: 3 And she was a woman of good **u**
1Ki 3: 9 give to Your servant an **u**
1Ki 3:11 yourself **u** to discern justice
1Ki 3:12 **u** heart, so that there has
1Ki 4:29 wisdom and exceedingly great **u**
1Ki 7:14 was filled with wisdom and **u**
1Ch 12:32 who had **u** of the times, to
1Ch 22:12 the LORD give you wisdom and **u**
2Ch 2:12 endowed with prudence and **u**
2Ch 2:13 skillful man, endowed with **u**
2Ch 26: 5 who had **u** in the visions of
Ezra 8:16 Joiarib and Elnathan, men of **u**
Ezra 8:18 they brought us a man of **u**
Neh 8: 2 and all who could hear with **u**
Neh 10:28 who had knowledge and **u**),
Job 12: 3 But I have **u** as well as you
Job 12:12 and with length of days, **u**
Job 12:13 strength, He has counsel and **u**
Job 12:24 He takes away the **u** of the
Job 17: 4 hidden their heart from **u**
Job 18: 2 Gain **u**, and afterward we will
Job 20: 3 the spirit of my **u** causes me
Job 26:12 by His **u** He breaks up the
Job 28:12 And where is the place of **u**
Job 28:20 And where is the place of **u**
Job 28:28 and to depart from evil is **u**
Job 32: 8 of the Almighty gives him **u**
Job 34:10 listen to me, you men of **u**
Job 34:16 If you have **u**, hear this
Job 34:34 Men of **u** say to me, wise men
Job 36: 5 He is mighty in strength of **u**
Job 38: 4 Tell Me, if you have **u**
Job 38:36 who has given **u** to the heart
Job 39:17 and did not endow her with **u**
Ps 32: 9 the mule, Which have no **u**
Ps 47: 7 Sing praises with **u**
Ps 49: 3 of my heart shall bring **u**
Ps 111:10 A good **u** have all those who
Ps 119:34 Give me **u**, and I shall keep
Ps 119:73 Give me **u**, that I may learn
Ps 119:99 I have more **u** than all my
Ps 119:104 Through Your precepts I get **u**
Ps 119:125 Give me **u**, That I may know
Ps 119:130 It gives **u** to the simple
Ps 119:144 Give me **u**, and I shall live
Ps 119:169 Give me **u** according to Your
Ps 147: 5 His **u** is infinite
Prov 1: 2 to perceive the words of **u**
Prov 1: 5 a man of **u** will attain wise
Prov 2: 2 and apply your heart to **u**
Prov 2: 3 and lift up your voice for **u**
Prov 2: 6 mouth come knowledge and **u**
Prov 2:11 **U** will keep you,
Prov 3: 5 and lean not on your own **u**
Prov 3:13 and the man who gains **u**
Prov 3:19 by **u** He established the
Prov 4: 1 and give attention to know **u**
Prov 4: 5 Get wisdom! Get **u**!
Prov 4: 7 And in all your getting, get **u**
Prov 5: 1 lend your ear to my **u**,
Prov 6:32 adultery with a woman lacks **u**
Prov 7: 4 and call **u** your nearest kin,
Prov 7: 7 a young man devoid of **u**,
Prov 8: 1 out, and **u** lift up her voice
Prov 8: 5 you fools, be of an **u** heart
Prov 8:14 I am **u**, I have strength
Prov 9: 4 As for him who lacks **u**, she
Prov 9: 6 live, and go in the way of **u**
Prov 9:10 of the Holy One is **u**
Prov 9:16 and as for him who lacks **u**
Prov 10:13 on the lips of him who has **u**
Prov 10:13 of him who is devoid of **u**
Prov 10:23 but a man of **u** has wisdom
Prov 11:12 but a man of **u** holds his
Prov 12:11 frivolity is devoid of **u**
Prov 13:15 Good **u** gains favor, but the
Prov 14:29 is slow to wrath has great **u**
Prov 14:33 in the heart of him who has **u**
Prov 15:14 him who has **u** seeks knowledge
Prov 15:21 but a man of **u** walks
Prov 15:32 he who heeds reproof gets **u**
Prov 16:16 And to get **u** is to be chosen
Prov 16:22 **U** is a wellspring of life to
Prov 17:18 A man devoid of **u** shakes
Prov 17:24 in the sight of him who has **u**
Prov 17:27 and a man of **u** is of a calm
Prov 18: 2 A fool has no delight in **u**
Prov 19: 8 he who keeps **u** will find good
Prov 19:25 reprove one who has **u**, and he
Prov 20: 5 but a man of **u** will draw it
Prov 21:16 the way of **u** will rest in the
Prov 21:30 There is no wisdom or **u** or
Prov 23: 4 because of your own **u**, cease
Prov 23:23 wisdom and instruction and **u**
Prov 24: 3 and by **u** it is established
Prov 24:30 of the man devoid of **u**
Prov 28: 2 but by a man of **u** and
Prov 28:11 who has **u** searches him out
Prov 28:16 A ruler who lacks **u** is a
Prov 30: 2 and do not have the **u** of a man
Eccl 9:11 wise, nor riches to men of **u**
Is 11: 2 the Spirit of wisdom and **u**
Is 27:11 For it is a people of no **u**
Is 29:14 the **u** of their prudent men
Is 29:16 who formed it, He has no **u**"?
Is 29:24 in spirit will come to **u**, and
Is 40:14 and showed Him the way of **u**
Is 40:28 is no searching of His **u**
Is 44:19 there knowledge nor **u** to say
Jer 3:15 feed you with knowledge and **u**
Jer 4:22 children, and they have no **u**
Jer 5:21 O foolish people, without **u**
Jer 51:15 out the heaven by His **u**
Ezek 28: 4 your **u** you have gained riches
Dan 1:17 Daniel had **u** in all visions
Dan 1:20 and **u** about which the king
Dan 2:21 knowledge to those who have **u**
Dan 4:34 and my **u** returned to me
Dan 5:11 of your father, light and **u**
Dan 5:12 spirit, knowledge, **u**,
Dan 5:14 is in you, and that light and **u**
Dan 10: 1 and had **u** of the vision
Dan 11:35 some of those of **u** shall fall
Obad 8 **u** from the mountains of Esau
Matt 15:16 Are you also still without **u**
Mark 7:18 Are you thus without **u** also
Mark 12:33 all the heart, with all the **u**
Luke 1: 3 having had perfect **u** of all
Luke 2:47 Him were astonished at His **u**
Luke 24:45 And He opened their **u**, that
1Co 1:19 nothing the **u** of the prudent
1Co 14:14 prays, but my **u** is unfruitful
1Co 14:15 I will also pray with the **u**
1Co 14:15 I will also sing with the **u**
1Co 14:19 speak five words with my **u**
1Co 14:20 do not be children in **u**
1Co 14:20 be babes, but in **u** be mature
Eph 1:18 the eyes of your **u** being
Eph 4:18 having their **u** darkened,
Phil 4: 7 of God, which surpasses all **u**
Col 1: 9 in all wisdom and spiritual **u**
Col 2: 2 of the full assurance of **u**
1Ti 1: 7 **u** neither what they say nor
2Ti 2: 7 Lord give you **u** in all things
Jas 3:13 Who is wise and **u** among you
1Pe 3: 7 dwell with them with **u**,
1Jn 5:20 has come and has given us an **u**
Rev 13:18 Let him who has **u** calculate

UNDERSTANDS (*see* UNDERSTAND)
1Ch 28: 9 and **u** all the intent of the
Job 28:23 God **u** its way, and He knows
Prov 8: 9 are all plain to him who **u**
Prov 14: 6 is easy to him who **u**
Prov 29:19 for though he **u**, he will not
Jer 9:24 glory in this, that he **u** and
Dan 8:23 Who **u** sinister schemes
Matt 13:23 **u** it, who indeed bears fruit
Rom 3:11 there is none who **u**
1Co 14: 2 but to God, for no one **u** him

UNDERSTOOD (*see* UNDERSTAND)
Gen 42:23 not know that Joseph **u** them
Deut 32:29 were wise, that they **u** this
1Sa 4: 6 Then they **u** that the ark of
1Sa 26: 4 **u** that Saul had indeed come
2Sa 3:37 all Israel **u** that day that it
Neh 8:12 because they **u** the words that
Esth 1:13 said to the wise men who **u**
Job 13: 1 My ear has heard and **u** it
Ps 73:17 Then I **u** their end
Eccl 1:16 My heart has **u** great wisdom
Is 40:21 Have you not **u** from the
Dan 8:27 the vision, but no one **u** it
Dan 9: 2 **u** by the books the number of
Dan 10: 1 and he **u** the message, and had
Matt 13:51 Have you **u** all these things
Matt 16:12 Then they **u** that He did not
Matt 17:13 Then the disciples **u** that He
Mark 6:52 had not **u** about the loaves
Luke 18:34 But they **u** none of these
Acts 7:25 his brethren would have **u**
Acts 23:34 when he **u** that he was from
Rom 1:20 being **u** by the things that
1Co 13:11 I **u** as a child, I thought as

2Co 1:14 also you have **u** us in part)

UNDERTAKE
Is 38:14 **u** for me

UNDESIRABLE (*see* DESIRE)
Zeph 2: 1 gather together, O **u** nation,

UNDIGNIFIED
2Sa 6:22 will be even more **u** than this

UNDISCERNING (*see* DISCERN)
Rom 1:31 **u**, untrustworthy, unloving,

UNDO (*see* UNDONE)
Is 58: 6 to **u** the heavy burdens, to

UNDONE (*see* UNDO)
Josh 11:15 He left nothing **u** of all that
Esth 6:10 Leave nothing **u** of all that
Is 6: 5 Woe is me, for I am **u**
Matt 23:23 without leaving the others **u**
Luke 11:42 without leaving the others **u**

UNDULY
Eccl 5:20 For he will not dwell **u** on

UNEDUCATED
Acts 4:13 and perceived that they were **u**

UNEQUALLY (*see* EQUAL)
2Co 6:14 Do not be **u** yoked together

UNEXPECTEDLY (*see* EXPECT)
Gen 38:29 that his brother came out **u**
Ps 35: 8 destruction come upon him **u**
Luke 21:34 and that Day come on you **u**

UNFAITHFUL (*see* FAITHFUL, UNFAITHFULLY, UNFAITHFULNESS)
Lev 26:40 in which they were **u** to Me
1Ch 5:25 they were **u** to the God of
2Ch 28:19 continually **u** to the LORD
2Ch 28:22 increasingly **u** to the LORD
Neh 1: 8 Moses, saying, If you are **u**
Prov 2:22 the **u** will be uprooted from
Prov 11: 3 of the **u** will destroy them
Prov 11: 6 but the **u** will be taken by
Prov 13: 2 of the **u** feeds on violence
Prov 13:15 but the way of the **u** is hard
Prov 21:18 and the **u** for the upright
Prov 23:28 and increases the **u** among men
Prov 25:19 Confidence in an **u** man in
Ezek 20:27 Me, by being **u** to Me
Ezek 39:23 because they were **u** to Me
Ezek 39:26 in which they were **u** to Me

UNFAITHFULLY (*see* UNFAITHFUL)
Num 5:12 and behaves **u** toward him,
Num 5:27 behaved **u** toward her husband,
Ps 78:57 acted **u** like their fathers

UNFAITHFULNESS (*see* UNFAITHFUL)
Lev 26:40 with their **u** in which they
Num 5: 6 commit in **u** against the LORD
1Ch 9: 1 to Babylon because of their **u**
1Ch 10:13 So Saul died for his **u** which
Ezek 14:13 against Me by persistent **u**
Ezek 15: 8 they have persisted in **u**,'
Ezek 18:24 because of the **u** of which he
Ezek 39:26 all their **u** in which they
Dan 9: 7 because of the **u** which they

UNFAMILIAR (*see* FAMILIAR)
Ezek 3: 5 sent to a people of **u** speech
Ezek 3: 6 to many people of **u** speech

UNFANNED (*see* FAN)
Job 20:26 an **u** fire will consume him

UNFORGIVING (*see* FORGIVE)
Rom 1:31 untrustworthy, unloving, **u**
2Ti 3: 3 unloving, **u**, slanderers,

UNFORMED (*see* FORM)
Ps 139:16 saw my substance, being yet **u**

UNFRUITFUL (*see* FRUITFUL)
Matt 13:22 the word, and he becomes **u**
Mark 4:19 the word, and it becomes **u**
1Co 14:14 but my understanding is **u**
Eph 5:11 with the **u** works of darkness
Tit 3:14 needs, that they may not be **u**
2Pe 1: 8 nor **u** in the knowledge of our

UNGODLINESS (*see* UNGODLY)
2Sa 22: 5 me, the floods of **u** made me
Ps 18: 4 And the floods of **u** made me
Is 32: 6 to practice **u**, to utter error
Rom 1:18 from heaven against all **u**
Rom 11:26 will turn away **u** from Jacob
2Ti 2:16 they will increase to more **u**
Tit 2:12 teaching us that, denying **u**

UNGODLY (*see* GODLY, UNGODLINESS)
Job 16:11 God has delivered me to the **u**
Ps 1: 1 not in the counsel of the **u**
Ps 1: 4 The **u** are not so, But are
Ps 1: 5 Therefore the **u** shall not
Ps 1: 6 the way of the **u** shall perish
Ps 3: 7 broken the teeth of the **u**
Ps 35:16 With **u** mockers at feasts They
Ps 43: 1 my cause against an **u** nation
Ps 73:12 Behold, these are the **u**, Who
Prov 16:27 An **u** man digs up evil, and it
Is 10: 6 send him against an **u** nation
Rom 4: 5 on Him who justifies the **u**
Rom 5: 6 time Christ died for the **u**
1Ti 1: 9 and insubordinate, for the **u**
1Pe 4:18 saved, where will the **u** and
2Pe 2: 5 flood on the world of the **u**
2Pe 2: 6 who afterward would live **u**
2Pe 3: 7 and perdition of **u** men
Jude 4 **u** men, who turn the grace of
Jude 15 all, to convict all who are **u**
Jude 15 their **u** deeds which they have
Jude 15 have committed in an **u** way
Jude 15 all the harsh things which **u**
Jude 18 to their own **u** lusts

UNHEARD (*see* HEAR)
John 9:32 **u** of that anyone opened the

UNHOLY (*see* HOLY)
Lev 10:10 distinguish between holy and **u**
Ezek 22:26 between the holy and **u**, nor
Ezek 44:23 between the holy and the **u**
1Ti 1: 9 and for sinners, for the **u**
2Ti 3: 2 to parents, unthankful, **u**

UNINFORMED
1Co 14:16 the place of the **u** say Amen
1Co 14:23 who are **u** or unbelievers,
1Co 14:24 or an **u** person comes in, he

UNINHABITED (*see* INHABIT)
Lev 16:22 their iniquities to an **u** land
Ezek 29:11 and it shall be **u** forty years
Ezek 35: 9 and your cities shall be **u**

UNINTENDED (*see* INTEND, UNINTENTIONAL)
Num 15:25 the LORD, for their **u** sin

UNINTENTIONAL (*see* UNINTENDED, UNINTENTIONALLY)
Num 15:25 forgiven them, for it was **u**

UNINTENTIONALLY (*see* UNINTENTIONAL)
Lev 4: 2 If a person sins **u** against
Lev 4:13 congregation of Israel sins **u**
Lev 4:22 done something **u** against any
Lev 4:27 of the common people sins **u**
Lev 5:15 sins **u** in regard to the holy
Lev 22:14 man eats the holy offering **u**
Num 15:22 And if you sin **u**, and do not
Num 15:24 if it is **u** committed, without
Num 15:26 all the people did it **u**
Num 15:27 And if a person sins **u**, then
Num 15:28 for the person who sins **u**
Num 15:28 when he sins **u** before the
Num 15:29 one law for him who sins **u**
Deut 4:42 who kills his neighbor **u**
Deut 19: 4 Whoever kills his neighbor **u**
Josh 20: 3 or **u** may flee there
Josh 20: 5 he struck his neighbor **u**, but
Ezek 45:20 has sinned **u** or in ignorance

UNIQUE
Job 23:13 But He is **u**, and who can make

UNIT
2Sa 2:25 behind Abner and became a **u**

UNITE (*see* UNITED, UNITY)
Ps 86:11 **U** my heart to fear Your name

UNITED (*see* UNITE)
Gen 49: 6 honor be **u** to their assembly
Judg 20:11 city, **u** together as one man
1Ch 12:17 my heart will be **u** with you
Rom 6: 5 For if we have been **u**

UNITY (*see* UNITE)
Job 10: 8 fashioned me, an intricate **u**
Ps 133: 1 to dwell together in **u**
Eph 4: 3 endeavoring to keep the **u** of
Eph 4:13 come to the **u** of the faith

UNJUST (*see* JUST, UNJUSTLY)
Ps 43: 1 from the deceitful and **u** man
Prov 11: 7 and the hope of the **u** perishes
Prov 29:27 An **u** man is an abomination to
Zeph 3: 5 But the **u** knows no shame
Matt 5:45 rain on the just and on the **u**
Luke 16: 8 the **u** steward because he had
Luke 16:10 he who is **u** in what is least
Luke 16:10 is **u** also in much
Luke 18: 6 Hear what the **u** judge said
Luke 18:11 extortioners, **u**, adulterers,
Acts 24:15 both of the just and the **u**
Rom 3: 5 Is God **u** who inflicts wrath
Heb 6:10 For God is not **u** to forget
1Pe 3:18 for sins, the just for the **u**
2Pe 2: 9 and to reserve the **u** under
Rev 22:11 He who is **u**, let him be **u**

UNJUSTLY (*see* UNJUST)
Ps 82: 2 How long will you judge **u**
Is 26:10 of uprightness he will deal **u**

UNKNOWN (*see* KNOW)
Gen 31:20 **u** to Laban the Syrian, in
Gen 31:26 you have stolen away **u** to me
Prov 22:29 will not stand before **u** men
Acts 17:23 inscription: to the **u** God
2Co 6: 9 as **u**, and yet well-known
Gal 1:22 and I was **u** by face to the

UNLAWFUL (*see* LAWFUL)
Acts 10:28 You know how **u** it is for a

UNLEAVENED (*see* LEAVEN)
Gen 19: 3 a feast, and baked **u** bread
Ex 12: 8 with **u** bread and with bitter
Ex 12:15 days you shall eat **u** bread
Ex 12:17 observe the Feast of **U** Bread
Ex 12:18 you shall eat **u** bread, until
Ex 12:20 you shall eat **u** bread
Ex 12:39 they baked **u** cakes of the
Ex 13: 6 days you shall eat **u** bread
Ex 13: 7 **U** bread shall be eaten seven
Ex 23:15 keep the Feast of **U** Bread
Ex 23:15 you shall eat **u** bread seven
Ex 29: 2 **u** bread, **u** cakes mixed with
Ex 29: 2 **u** wafers anointed with oil
Ex 29:23 from the basket of the **u**
Ex 34:18 The Feast of **U** Bread you
Ex 34:18 days you shall eat **u** bread
Lev 2: 4 it shall be **u** cakes of fine
Lev 2: 4 or **u** wafers anointed with oil
Lev 2: 5 it shall be of fine flour, **u**
Lev 6:16 with **u** bread it shall be
Lev 7:12 **u** cakes mixed with oil,
Lev 7:12 **u** wafers anointed with oil,
Lev 8: 2 rams, and a basket of **u** bread
Lev 8:26 from the basket of **u** bread
Lev 8:26 the LORD he took one **u** cake
Lev 23: 6 Feast of **U** Bread to the LORD
Lev 23: 6 days you must eat **u** bread
Num 6:15 a basket of **u** bread, cakes
Num 6:15 **u** wafers anointed with oil,
Num 6:17 with the basket of **u** bread
Num 6:19 one **u** cake from the basket,
Num 6:19 one **u** wafer, and put them upon
Num 9:11 shall eat it with **u** bread
Num 28:17 **u** bread shall be eaten for
Deut 16: 3 you shall eat **u** bread with it
Deut 16: 8 days you shall eat **u** bread
Deut 16:16 at the Feast of **U** Bread, at
Josh 5:11 **u** bread and parched grain on
Judg 6:19 and **u** bread from an ephah of
Judg 6:20 the **u** bread and lay them on
Judg 6:21 the meat and the **u** bread
Judg 6:21 the meat and the **u** bread
1Sa 28:24 it, and baked **u** bread from it
2Ki 23: 9 but they ate **u** bread among
1Ch 23:29 offering, with the **u** cakes
2Ch 8:13 the Feast of **U** Bread, the
2Ch 30:13 to keep the Feast of **U** Bread
2Ch 30:21 **U** Bread seven days with great
2Ch 35:17 and the Feast of **U** Bread for
Ezra 6:22 And they kept the Feast of **U**
Ezek 45:21 **u** bread shall be eaten
Matt 26:17 day of the Feast of the **U**
Mark 14: 1 and the Feast of **U** Bread
Mark 14:12 on the first day of **U** Bread
Luke 22: 1 Feast of **U** Bread drew near
Luke 22: 7 Then came the Day of **U** Bread
Acts 12: 3 during the Days of **U** Bread

Acts 20: 6 after the Days of **U** Bread
1Co 5: 7 lump, since you truly are **u**
1Co 5: 8 but with the **u** bread of

UNLESS (*see* PREFACE)

UNLIFTED (*see* LIFT)
2Co 3:14 **u** in the reading of the Old

UNLIKE (*see* LIKE)
2Co 3:13 **u** Moses, who put a veil over

UNLOAD (*see* LOAD, UNLOADED)
Acts 21: 3 the ship was to **u** her cargo

UNLOADED (*see* UNLOAD)
Gen 24:32 he **u** the camels, and provided

UNLOVED (*see* LOVE, UNLOVING)
Gen 29:31 the LORD saw that Leah was **u**
Gen 29:33 LORD has heard that I am **u**
Deut 21:15 one loved and the other **u**
Deut 21:15 both the loved and the **u**, and
Deut 21:15 son is of her who is **u**,
Deut 21:16 to the son of the **u**, who is
Deut 21:17 **u** wife as the firstborn by

UNLOVING (*see* UNLOVED)
Rom 1:31 untrustworthy, **u**,
2Ti 3: 3 **u**, unforgiving, slanderers,

UNMARRIED (*see* MARRY)
Ezek 44:25 for brother or **u** sister may
1Co 7: 8 But I say to the **u** and to the
1Co 7:11 let her remain **u** or be
1Co 7:32 He who is **u** cares for the
1Co 7:34 The **u** woman cares about the

UNMERCIFUL (*see* MERCIFUL)
Rom 1:31 unloving, unforgiving, **u**

UNMINDFUL (*see* MIND)
Deut 32:18 Rock who begot you, you are **u**

UNNI
1Ch 15:18 Shemiramoth, Jehiel, **U**,
1Ch 15:20 Aziel, Shemiramoth, Jehiel, **U**
Neh 12: 9 Also Bakbukiah and **U**, their

UNNOTICED (*see* NOTICE)
Jude 4 certain men have crept in **u**

UNPREPARED (*see* PREPARE)
2Co 9: 4 come with me and find you **u**

UNPRESENTABLE (*see* PRESENT)
1Co 12:23 and our **u** parts have greater

UNPROFITABLE (*see* PROFITABLE, UNPROFITABLENESS)
Job 15: 3 Should he reason with **u** talk
Jer 16:19 worthlessness and **u** things
Matt 25:30 cast the **u** servant into the
Luke 17:10 say, 'We are **u** servants
Rom 3:12 they have together become **u**
Tit 3: 9 for they are **u** and useless
Phm 11 who once was **u** to you, but
Heb 13:17 for that would be **u** for you

UNPROFITABLENESS (*see* UNPROFITABLE)
Heb 7:18 because of its weakness and **u**

UNPUNISHED (*see* PUNISH)
Prov 11:21 the wicked will not go **u**
Prov 16: 5 join forces, none will go **u**
Prov 17: 5 at calamity will not go **u**
Prov 19: 5 A false witness will not go **u**
Prov 19: 9 A false witness will not go **u**
Prov 28:20 to be rich will not go **u**
Jer 25:29 and should you be utterly **u**
Jer 25:29 You shall not be **u**, for I
Jer 30:11 not let you go altogether **u**
Jer 46:28 I will not leave you wholly **u**
Jer 49:12 one who will altogether go **u**
Jer 49:12 You shall not go **u**, but you

UNQUENCHABLE (*see* QUENCH)
Matt 3:12 burn up the chaff with **u** fire
Luke 3:17 He will burn with **u** fire

UNREASONABLE (*see* REASONABLE)
Acts 25:27 to me **u** to send a prisoner
2Th 3: 2 we may be delivered from **u**

UNRECOGNIZED (*see* RECOGNIZE)
Lam 4: 8 they go **u** in the streets

UNRELIABLE (*see* RELY)
Jer 15:18 be to me like an **u** stream

UNRESTRAINED (*see* RESTRAIN)
Ex 32:25 were **u** (for Aaron had not

UNRIGHTEOUS (*see* RIGHTEOUS, UNRIGHTEOUSLY, UNRIGHTEOUSNESS)
Ex 23: 1 the wicked to be an **u** witness
Job 27: 7 up against me like the **u**
Ps 71: 4 Out of the hand of the **u**
Is 10: 1 to those who decree **u** decrees
Is 55: 7 and the **u** man his thoughts
Luke 16: 9 for yourselves by **u** mammon
Luke 16:11 been faithful in the **u** mammon
1Co 6: 1 go to law before the **u**, and
1Co 6: 9 the **u** will not inherit the
2Th 2:10 with all **u** deception among

UNRIGHTEOUSLY (*see* UNRIGHTEOUS)
Deut 25:16 things, and all who behave **u**

UNRIGHTEOUSNESS (*see* UNRIGHTEOUS)
Ps 92:15 rock, and there is no **u** in Him
Jer 22:13 him who builds his house by **u**
Zeph 3: 5 in her midst, he will do no **u**
Zeph 3:13 of Israel shall do no **u** and
John 7:18 is true, and no **u** is in Him
Rom 1:18 all ungodliness and **u** of men
Rom 1:18 who suppress the truth in **u**
Rom 1:29 being filled with all **u**,
Rom 2: 8 obey the truth, but obey **u**
Rom 3: 5 But if our **u** demonstrates the
Rom 6:13 as instruments of **u** to sin
Rom 9:14 Is there **u** with God
2Th 2:12 truth but had pleasure in **u**
Heb 8:12 I will be merciful to their **u**
2Pe 2:13 will receive the wages of **u**
2Pe 2:15 who loved the wages of **u**
1Jn 1: 9 and to cleanse us from all **u**
1Jn 5:17 All **u** is sin, and there is sin

UNRIPE (*see* RIPE)
Job 15:33 off his **u** grape like a vine

UNRULY
1Th 5:14 warn those who are **u**,
Jas 3: 8 It is an **u** evil, full of

UNSATISFIED (*see* SATISFY)
Is 32: 6 LORD, to keep the hungry **u**

UNSAVORY (*see* SAVORY)
Job 6:30 Cannot my taste discern the **u**

UNSEARCHABLE
Job 5: 9 Who does great things, and **u**
Ps 145: 3 And His greatness is **u**
Prov 25: 3 so the heart of kings is **u**
Rom 11:33 How **u** are His judgments and
Eph 3: 8 the **u** riches of Christ,

UNSETTLING
Acts 15:24 **u** your souls, saying, 'You

UNSHOD (*see* SHOD)
Jer 2:25 your foot from being **u**, and

UNSHRUNK
Matt 9:16 No one puts a piece of **u**
Mark 2:21 No one sews a piece of **u**

UNSKILLED (*see* SKILL)
Heb 5:13 of milk is **u** in the word of

UNSPOTTED (*see* SPOT)
Jas 1:27 keep oneself **u** from the world

UNSTABLE
Gen 49: 4 **U** as water, you shall not
Ps 82: 5 of the earth are **u**
Prov 5: 6 her ways are **u**
Jas 1: 8 man, **u** in all his ways
2Pe 2:14 from sin, beguiling **u** souls
2Pe 3:16 and **u** twist to their own

UNSTOPPED (*see* STOP)
Is 35: 5 ears of the deaf shall be **u**

UNTAUGHT (*see* TEACH)
2Pe 3:16 which those who are **u** and

UNTEMPERED
Ezek 13:10 they plaster it with **u** mortar
Ezek 13:11 who plaster it with **u** mortar
Ezek 13:14 have plastered with **u** mortar
Ezek 13:15 plastered it with **u** mortar
Ezek 22:28 plastered them with **u** mortar

UNTENDED (*see* TEND)
Lev 25: 5 the grapes of your **u** vine
Lev 25:11 the grapes of your **u** vine

UNTHANKFUL (*see* THANKFUL)
Luke 6:35 For He is kind to the **u** and
2Ti 3: 2 disobedient to parents, **u**

UNTIL (*see* PREFACE)

UNTO (*see* PREFACE)

UNTRAINED (*see* TRAIN)
Jer 31:18 was chastised, like an **u** bull
Acts 4:13 and **u** men, they marveled
2Co 11: 6 Even though I am **u** in speech

UNTRUE (*see* TRUE)
Ps 73:15 I would have been **u** to the

UNTRUSTWORTHY (*see* TRUSTWORTHY)
Rom 1:31 undiscerning, **u**, unloving,

UNTURNED (*see* TURN)
Hos 7: 8 Ephraim is a cake **u**

UNUSUAL (*see* USUAL)
Is 28:21 to pass His act, His **u** act
Acts 19:11 Now God worked **u** miracles by
Acts 28: 2 natives showed us **u** kindness

UNVEILED (*see* VEIL)
2Co 3:18 But we all, with **u** face,

UNWALLED
Esth 9:19 in the **u** towns celebrated the
Ezek 38:11 against a land of **u** villages

UNWASHED (*see* WASH)
Matt 15:20 but to eat with **u** hands does
Mark 7: 2 is, with **u** hands, they found
Mark 7: 5 but eat bread with **u** hands

UNWILLING (*see* WILLING)
1Sa 15: 9 were **u** to utterly destroy
1Co 16:12 but he was quite **u** to come at

UNWISE (*see* WISE)
Deut 32: 6 LORD, O foolish and **u** people
Hos 13:13 He is an **u** son, for he should
Rom 1:14 both to wise and to **u**
Eph 5:17 Therefore do not be **u**, but

UNWITTINGLY
Heb 13: 2 have **u** entertained angels

UNWORTHY (*see* WORTHY)
Acts 13:46 it, and judge yourselves **u** of
1Co 6: 2 you, are you **u** to judge the
1Co 11:27 an **u** manner will be guilty of
1Co 11:29 and drinks in an **u** manner eats

UP (*see* PREFACE)

UPBRAID
Matt 11:20 Then He began to **u** the cities

UPHARSIN (*see* PERES)
Dan 5:25 MENE, MENE, TEKEL, **U**

UPHAZ
Jer 10: 9 from Tarshish, and gold from **U**
Dan 10: 5 was girded with gold of **U**

UPHELD (*see* UPHOLD)
Job 4: 4 Your words have **u** him who was
Ps 71: 6 I have been **u** from my birth
Is 46: 3 who have been **u** by Me from
Zeph 2: 3 earth, who have **u** His justice

UPHOLD (*see* UPHELD, UPHOLDING, UPHOLDS)
Job 8:20 nor will He **u** the evildoers
Ps 17: 5 **U** my steps in Your paths,
Ps 41:12 You **u** me in my integrity, And
Ps 51:12 And **u** me with Your generous
Ps 54: 4 is with those who **u** my life
Ps 119:116 **U** me according to Your word,
Is 41:10 you, I will **u** you with My
Is 42: 1 My Servant whom I **u**, My Elect
Is 63: 5 that there was no one to **u**
Ezek 30: 6 Those who **u** Egypt shall fall,
1Th 5:14 **u** the weak, be patient with

UPHOLDING (*see* UPHOLD)
Heb 1: 3 **u** all things by the word of

UPHOLDS (*see* UPHOLD)
Ps 37:17 But the LORD **u** the righteous
Ps 37:24 For the LORD **u** him with His
Ps 63: 8 Your right hand **u** me
Ps 145:14 The LORD **u** all who fall, And

Prov 20:28 he **u** his throne
Dan 10:21 (No one **u** me against these,

UPLIFTED (*see* LIFT)
Acts 13:17 with an **u** arm He brought them

UPON (*see* PREFACE)

UPPER (*see* UPPERMOST)
Deut 24: 6 or the **u** millstone in pledge
Josh 15:19 So he gave her the **u** springs
Josh 16: 5 Addar as far as **U** Beth Horon
Judg 1:15 Caleb gave her the **u** springs
Judg 3:23 of the **u** room behind him and
Judg 3:24 of the **u** room were locked
Judg 3:25 the doors of the **u** room
Judg 9:53 an **u** millstone on Abimelech's
1Sa 9:24 up the thigh with its **u** part
1Ki 17:19 carried him to the **u** room
1Ki 17:23 the **u** room into the house
2Ki 1: 2 of his **u** room in Samaria, and
2Ki 4:10 a small **u** room on the wall
2Ki 4:11 and he turned in to the **u** room
2Ki 15:35 He built the **U** Gate of the
2Ki 18:17 the aqueduct from the **u** pool
2Ki 23:12 the **u** chamber of Ahaz, which
1Ch 7:24 **U** Beth Horon and Uzzen
1Ch 28:11 its **u** chambers, its inner
2Ch 3: 9 overlaid the **u** area with gold
2Ch 8: 5 He built **U** Beth Horon and
2Ch 23:20 they went through the **U** Gate
2Ch 27: 3 He built the **U** Gate of the
2Ch 32:30 the water outlet of **U** Gihon
2Ch 32:33 and they buried him in the **u**
Neh 3:25 projects from the king's **u**
Neh 3:31 as far as the **u** room at the
Neh 3:32 between the **u** room at the
Ps 104: 3 His **u** chambers in the waters
Ps 104:13 the hills from His **u** chambers
Is 7: 3 the aqueduct from the **u** pool
Is 36: 2 the aqueduct from the **u** pool
Jer 36:10 in the **u** court at the entry
Ezek 9: 2 the direction of the **u** gate
Ezek 42: 5 Now the **u** chambers were
Ezek 42: 6 therefore the **u** level was
Dan 6:10 And in his **u** room, with his
Mark 14:15 will show you a large **u** room
Luke 22:12 you a large, furnished **u** room
Acts 1:13 the **u** room where they were
Acts 9:37 they laid her in an **u** room
Acts 9:39 brought him to the **u** room
Acts 19: 1 passed through the **u** regions
Acts 20: 8 in the **u** room where they were

UPPERMOST (*see* UPPER)
Gen 40:17 In the **u** basket there were
Is 17: 6 at the top of the **u** bough
Is 17: 9 an **u** branch, which they left

UPRAISED (*see* RAISE)
Job 38:15 and the **u** arm is broken

UPRIGHT (*see* UPRIGHTLY, UPRIGHTNESS)
Gen 37: 7 sheaf arose and also stood **u**
Ex 15: 8 floods stood **u** like a heap
Ex 26:15 of acacia wood, standing **u**
Ex 36:20 of acacia wood, standing **u**
Lev 26:13 your yoke and made you walk **u**
Deut 32: 4 righteous and **u** is He
1Sa 29: 6 LORD lives, you have been **u**
Job 1: 1 that man was blameless and **u**
Job 1: 8 **u** man, one who fears God and
Job 2: 3 **u** man, one who fears God and
Job 4: 7 where were the **u** ever cut off
Job 8: 6 if you were pure and **u**, surely
Job 17: 8 **U** men are astonished at this,
Job 23: 7 There the **u** could reason with
Job 33: 3 My words come from my **u** heart
Ps 7:10 God, Who saves the **u** in heart
Ps 11: 2 secretly at the **u** in heart
Ps 11: 7 His countenance beholds the **u**
Ps 17: 2 look on the things that are **u**
Ps 20: 8 But we have risen and stand **u**
Ps 25: 8 Good and **u** is the LORD
Ps 32:11 for joy, all you **u** in heart
Ps 33: 1 from the **u** is beautiful
Ps 36:10 to the **u** in heart
Ps 37:14 those who are of **u** conduct
Ps 37:18 LORD knows the days of the **u**
Ps 37:37 man, and observe the **u**
Ps 49:14 The **u** shall have dominion
Ps 64:10 And all the **u** in heart shall
Ps 92:15 To declare that the LORD is **u**
Ps 94:15 And all the **u** in heart will
Ps 97:11 gladness for the **u** in heart
Ps 111: 1 In the assembly of the **u**
Ps 112: 2 of the **u** will be blessed
Ps 112: 4 Unto the **u** there arises light
Ps 119:137 LORD, And **u** are Your
Ps 125: 4 who are **u** in their hearts
Ps 140:13 The **u** shall dwell in Your
Prov 2: 7 up sound wisdom for the **u**
Prov 2:21 For the **u** will dwell in the
Prov 3:32 secret counsel is with the **u**
Prov 10:29 LORD is strength for the **u**
Prov 11: 3 of the **u** will guide them, but
Prov 11: 6 of the **u** will deliver them
Prov 11:11 of the **u** the city is exalted
Prov 12: 6 of the **u** will deliver them
Prov 14: 9 sin, but among the **u** there is
Prov 14:11 tent of the **u** will flourish
Prov 15: 8 of the **u** is His delight
Prov 15:19 the way of the **u** is a highway
Prov 16:17 The highway of the **u** is to
Prov 21:18 and the unfaithful for the **u**
Prov 21:29 his face, but as for the **u**
Prov 28:10 Whoever causes the **u** to go
Prov 29:27 he who is **u** in the way is an
Eccl 7:29 that God made man **u**, but they
Eccl 12:10 and what was written was **u**
Is 26: 7 O Most **U**, You weigh the path
Jer 10: 5 They are **u**, like a palm tree,
Dan 8:18 he touched me, and stood me **u**
Dan 10:11 I speak to you, and stand **u**
Dan 11:17 kingdom, and **u** ones with him
Mic 7: 2 there is no one **u** among men
Mic 7: 4 the most **u** is sharper than a
Hab 2: 4 his soul is not **u** in him

UPRIGHTLY (*see* UPRIGHT)
Ps 15: 2 He who walks **u**, And works
Ps 58: 1 Do you judge **u**, you sons of
Ps 75: 2 proper time, I will judge **u**
Ps 84:11 From those who walk **u**
Prov 2: 7 a shield to those who walk **u**
Prov 15:21 man of understanding walks **u**
Is 33:15 walks righteously and speaks **u**
Amos 5:10 abhor the one who speaks **u**
Mic 2: 7 do good to him who walks **u**

UPRIGHTNESS (*see* UPRIGHT)
Deut 9: 5 **u** of your heart that you go
1Ki 3: 6 and in **u** of heart with You
1Ki 9: 4 in integrity of heart and in **u**
1Ch 29:17 heart and have pleasure in **u**
1Ch 29:17 in the **u** of my heart I have
Job 33:23 a thousand, to show man His **u**
Ps 9: 8 judgment for the peoples in **u**
Ps 25:21 **u** preserve me, For I wait for
Ps 111: 8 And are done in truth and **u**
Ps 119: 7 praise You with **u** of heart
Ps 143:10 Lead me in the land of **u**
Prov 2:13 of **u** to walk in the ways of
Prov 14: 2 walks in his **u** fears the LORD
Prov 17:26 to strike princes for their **u**
Is 26: 7 The way of the just is **u**
Is 26:10 in the land of **u** he will deal
Is 57: 2 each one walking in his **u**

UPROAR
1Ki 1:41 is the city in such a noisy **u**
1Ki 1:45 so that the city is in an **u**
Matt 26: 5 be an **u** among the people
Mark 14: 2 there be an **u** of the people
Acts 17: 5 mob, set all the city in an **u**
Acts 19:40 in question for today's **u**
Acts 20: 1 After the **u** had ceased, Paul
Acts 21:31 all Jerusalem was in an **u**

UPROOT (*see* UPROOTED, UPROOTS)
1Ki 14:15 He will **u** Israel from this
2Ch 7:20 then I will **u** them from My
Ps 52: 5 **u** you from the land of the
Matt 13:29 also **u** the wheat with them

UPROOTED (*see* UPROOT)
Deut 29:28 the LORD **u** them from their
Job 18:14 He is **u** from the shelter of
Job 19:10 My hope He has **u** like a tree
Prov 2:22 unfaithful will be **u** from it
Dan 11: 4 for his kingdom shall be **u**
Zeph 2: 4 noonday, and Ekron shall be **u**
Matt 15:13 has not planted will be **u**

UPROOTS (*see* UPROOT)
Ps 80:13 boar out of the woods **u** it

UPSIDE
2Ki 21:13 it and turning it **u** down
Ps 146: 9 of the wicked He turns **u** down
Acts 17: 6 **u** down have come here too

UPSTAIRS
Judg 3:20 to him (now he was sitting **u**

UPSTREAM
Josh 3:13 waters that come down from **u**
Josh 3:16 came down from **u** stood still

UPWARD
Gen 7:20 prevailed fifteen cubits **u**
Judg 1:36 of Akrabbim, from Sela, and **u**
1Sa 9: 2 From his shoulders **u** he was
1Sa 10:23 people from his shoulders **u**
2Ki 19:30 downward, and bear fruit **u**
Job 5: 7 trouble, as the sparks fly **u**
Prov 15:24 of life winds **u** for the wise
Eccl 3:21 the sons of men, which goes **u**
Is 8:21 king and their God, and look **u**
Is 37:31 downward, and bear fruit **u**
Is 38:14 my eyes fail from looking **u**
Ezek 1:11 Their wings were stretched **u**
Ezek 1:27 and **u** I saw, as it were, the
Ezek 8: 2 and from His waist and **u**, like
Ezek 43:15 extending **u** from the hearth
Phil 3:14 goal for the prize of the **u**

UR
Gen 11:28 land, in **U** of the Chaldeans
Gen 11:31 went out with them from **U** of
Gen 15: 7 you out of **U** of the Chaldeans
1Ch 11:35 Eliphal the son of **U**,
Neh 9: 7 him out of **U** of the Chaldees

URBANUS
Rom 16: 9 Greet **U**, our fellow worker in

URGE (*see* URGED)
2Ki 18:23 I **u** you, give a pledge to my
Is 36: 8 I **u** you, give a pledge to my
Acts 27:22 now I **u** you to take heart,
Acts 27:34 Therefore I **u** you to take
Rom 16:17 Now I **u** you, brethren, note
1Co 4:16 Therefore I **u** you, imitate me
1Co 16:15 I **u** you, brethren
2Co 2: 8 Therefore I **u** you to reaffirm
Gal 4:12 I **u** you to become as I am,
Phil 4: 3 I **u** you also, true companion,
1Th 4: 1 Finally then, brethren, we **u**
1Th 4:10 But we **u** you, brethren, that
1Th 5:12 And we **u** you, brethren, to
1Ti 6:13 I **u** you in the sight of God
Heb 13:19 I especially **u** you to do this

URGED (*see* URGE)
Gen 19:15 the angels **u** Lot to hurry,
Gen 33:11 And he **u** him, and he took it
Ex 12:33 And the Egyptians **u** the people
Judg 1:14 that she **u** him to ask her
Judg 19: 7 his father-in-law **u** him
1Sa 24:10 and someone **u** me to kill you
1Sa 28:23 with the woman, **u** him
2Sa 13:25 Then he **u** him, but he would
2Sa 13:27 But Absalom **u** him
2Ki 2:17 But when they **u** him till he
2Ki 5:16 he **u** him to take it, but he
2Ki 5:23 And he **u** him, and bound two
Matt 15:23 came and **u** Him, saying,
John 4:31 meantime His disciples **u** Him
John 4:40 they **u** Him to stay with them
1Co 16:12 I strongly **u** him to come to
2Co 8: 6 So we **u** Titus, that as he had
2Co 12:18 I **u** Titus, and sent our
1Ti 1: 3 As I **u** you when I went into

URGENCY (*see* URGENT)
2Co 8: 4 imploring us with much **u** that

URGENT (*see* URGENCY)
Dan 2:15 the decree from the king so **u**
Dan 3:22 the king's command was **u**, and
Tit 3:14 good works, to meet **u** needs

URI
Ex 31: 2 by name Bezaleel the son of **U**
Ex 35:30 by name Bezaleel the son of **U**
Ex 38:22 Bezaleel the son of **U**, the
1Ki 4:19 Geber the son of **U**, in the
1Ch 2:20 And Hur begot **U**
1Ch 2:20 and **U** begot Bezaleel

2Ch 1: 5 that Bezaleel the son of **U**
Ezra 10:24 Shallum, Telem, and **U**

URIAH (*see* URIAH'S, URIJAH)
2Sa 11: 3 the wife of **U** the Hittite
2Sa 11: 6 Send me **U** the Hittite
2Sa 11: 6 And Joab sent **U** to David
2Sa 11: 7 When **U** had come to him, David
2Sa 11: 8 And David said to **U**, "Go down
2Sa 11: 8 So **U** departed from the
2Sa 11: 9 But **U** slept at the door of
2Sa 11:10 **U** did not go down to his
2Sa 11:10 his house," David said to **U**
2Sa 11:11 And **U** said to David,
2Sa 11:12 Then David said to **U**, "Wait
2Sa 11:12 So **U** remained in Jerusalem
2Sa 11:14 and sent it by the hand of **U**
2Sa 11:15 Set **U** in the forefront of the
2Sa 11:16 that he assigned **U** to a place
2Sa 11:17 and **U** the Hittite died also
2Sa 11:21 Your servant **U** the Hittite
2Sa 11:24 your servant **U** the Hittite is
2Sa 11:26 When the wife of **U** heard that
2Sa 11:26 that **U** her husband was dead
2Sa 12: 9 You have killed **U** the Hittite
2Sa 12:10 have taken the wife of **U** the
2Sa 23:39 and **U** the Hittite
1Ki 15: 5 the matter of **U** the Hittite
1Ch 11:41 **U** the Hittite, Zabad the son
Ezra 8:33 the son of **U** the priest, and
Is 8: 2 **U** the priest and Zechariah the
Matt 1: 6 who had been the wife of **U**

URIAH'S (*see* URIAH)
2Sa 12:15 that **U** wife bore to David

URIEL
1Ch 6:24 **U** his son, Uzziah his son, and
1Ch 15: 5 **U** the chief, and one hundred
1Ch 15:11 for **U**, Asaiah, Joel, Shemaiah
2Ch 13: 2 the daughter of **U** of Gibeah

URIJAH (*see* URIAH)
2Ki 16:10 and King Ahaz sent to **U** the
2Ki 16:11 Then **U** the priest built an
2Ki 16:11 So **U** the priest made it
2Ki 16:15 Ahaz commanded **U** the priest
2Ki 16:16 Thus did **U** the priest,
Neh 3: 4 to them Meremoth the son of **U**
Neh 3:21 him Meremoth the son of **U**
Neh 8: 4 Mattithiah, Shema, Anaiah, **U**
Jer 26:20 **U** the son of Shemaiah of
Jer 26:21 but when **U** heard it, he was
Jer 26:23 And they brought **U** from Egypt

URIM (*see* THUMMIM)
Ex 28:30 breastplate of judgment the **U**
Lev 8: 8 on him, and he put the **U** and
Num 27:21 him by the judgment of the **U**
Deut 33: 8 Your **U** be with Your holy one,
1Sa 28: 6 or by **U** or by the prophets
Ezra 2:63 could consult with the **U** and
Neh 7:65 could consult with the **U** and

US (*see* PREFACE)

USE (*see* PREFACE)

USED (*see* PREFACE)

USEFUL
Ezek 15: 4 Is it **u** for any work
Ezek 15: 5 How much less will it be **u**
2Ti 2:21 **u** for the Master, prepared
2Ti 4:11 you, for he is **u** to me for
Heb 6: 7 bears herbs **u** for those by

USELESS
Is 40:23 the judges of the earth **u**
Is 44: 9 image, all of them are **u**, and
1Ti 6: 5 **u** wranglings of men of
Tit 3: 9 they are unprofitable and **u**
Jas 1:26 this one's religion is **u**

USES (*see* PREFACE)

USING (*see* PREFACE)

USUAL (*see* UNUSUAL, USUALLY)
Lev 14:32 cannot afford the **u** cleansing
Lev 15:25 beyond her **u** time of impurity

USUALLY (*see* USUAL)
Dan 3:19 more than it was **u** heated

USURY
Lev 25:36 Take no **u** or interest from
Lev 25:37 not lend him your money for **u**
Neh 5: 7 exacting **u** from his brother
Neh 5:10 Please, let us stop this **u**
Ps 15: 5 not put out his money at **u**
Prov 28: 8 his possessions by **u** and
Ezek 18: 8 if he has not exacted **u** nor
Ezek 18:13 exacted **u** or taken increase
Ezek 18:17 and not received **u** or increase
Ezek 22:12 you take **u** and increase

UTENSILS
Ex 25:39 pure gold, with all these **u**
Ex 27: 3 make all its **u** of bronze
Ex 27:19 All the **u** of the tabernacle
Ex 30:27 the table and all its **u**, the
Ex 30:27 the lampstand and its **u**, and
Ex 30:28 burnt offering with all its **u**
Ex 31: 8 the table and its **u**
Ex 31: 8 pure lampstand with all its **u**
Ex 31: 9 burnt offering with all its **u**
Ex 35:13 table and its poles, all its **u**
Ex 35:14 for the light, its **u**, its
Ex 35:16 grating, its poles, all its **u**
Ex 37:16 the **u** which were on the table
Ex 37:24 he made it, with all its **u**
Ex 38: 3 made all the **u** for the altar
Ex 38: 3 all its **u** he made of bronze
Ex 38:30 and all the **u** for the altar,
Ex 39:36 the table, all its **u**, and the
Ex 39:37 set in order), all its **u**, and
Ex 39:39 its poles, and all its **u**
Ex 39:40 all the **u** for the service of
Ex 40: 9 shall hallow it and all its **u**
Ex 40:10 burnt offering and all its **u**
Lev 8:11 the altar and all its **u**, and
Num 3:31 the **u** of the sanctuary with
Num 3:36 pillars, its sockets, its **u**
Num 4:10 its **u** in a covering of badger
Num 4:12 they shall take all the **u** of
Num 4:14 and all the **u** of the altar
Num 7: 1 and the altar and all its **u**
1Ki 15:15 silver and gold and **u**
2Ki 25:14 all the bronze **u** with which
2Ch 15:18 silver and gold and **u**
Jer 52:18 all the bronze **u** with which

UTHAI
1Ch 9: 4 **U** the son of Ammihud, the son
Ezra 8:14 also of the sons of Bigvai, **U**

UTMOST (*see* UTTERMOST)
Gen 49:26 up to the **u** bound of the
Job 34:36 that Job were tried to the **u**
2Ti 4:21 Do your **u** to come before

UTTER (*see* UTTERANCE, UTTERED, UTTERING, UTTERS)
1Ki 20:42 I appointed to **u** destruction
Job 8:10 and **u** words from their heart
Job 27: 4 nor my tongue **u** deceit
Job 33: 3 my lips **u** pure knowledge
Ps 78: 2 I will **u** dark sayings of old,
Ps 94: 4 They **u** speech, and speak
Ps 106: 2 Who can **u** the mighty acts of
Ps 119:171 My lips shall **u** praise, For
Ps 145: 7 They shall **u** the memory of
Prov 14: 5 a false witness will **u** lies
Prov 23:33 heart will **u** perverse things
Eccl 5: 2 let not your heart **u** anything
Is 32: 6 to **u** error against the LORD,
Is 48:20 **u** it even to the end of the
Jer 1:16 I will **u** My judgments against
Jer 25:30 **u** His voice from His holy
Ezek 24: 3 **u** a parable to the rebellious
Joel 3:16 **u** His voice from Jerusalem
Mic 2:10 you, even with **u** destruction
Nah 1: 8 make an **u** end of its place
Nah 1: 9 He will make an **u** end of it
Hab 2:16 **u** shame will be on your glory
Zech 14:11 shall there be **u** destruction
Matt 13:35 I will **u** things which have
Mark 3:28 blasphemies they may **u**
1Co 6: 7 it is already an **u** failure
1Co 14: 9 unless you **u** by the tongue
2Co 12: 4 is not lawful for a man to **u**

UTTERANCE (*see* UTTER)
Lev 5: 1 in hearing the **u** of an oath
Num 24: 3 The **u** of Balaam the son of
Num 24: 3 the **u** of the man whose eyes
Num 24: 4 the **u** of him who hears the
Num 24:15 The **u** of Balaam the son of
Num 24:15 the **u** of the man whose eyes
Num 24:16 the **u** of him who hears the
Num 30: 6 by her vows or by a rash **u**
Prov 30: 1 Agur the son of Jakeh, his **u**
Prov 31: 1 the **u** which his mother taught
Acts 2: 4 as the Spirit gave them **u**
1Co 1: 5 in everything by Him in all **u**
Eph 6:19 that **u** may be given to me,

UTTERED (*see* UTTER)
Num 30: 8 what she **u** with her lips, by
2Sa 22:14 and the Most High **u** His voice
Job 26: 4 To whom have you **u** words
Job 42: 3 Therefore I have **u** what I
Ps 18:13 And the Most High **u** His voice
Ps 46: 6 He **u** His voice, the earth
Ps 66:14 Which my lips have **u** And my
Jer 48:34 Jahaz they have **u** their voice
Jer 51:55 the noise of their voice is **u**
Hab 3:10 The deep **u** its voice, and
Rom 8:26 groanings which cannot be **u**
Rev 10: 3 seven thunders **u** their voices
Rev 10: 4 seven thunders **u** their voices
Rev 10: 4 which the seven thunders **u**

UTTERING (*see* UTTER)
Is 59:13 **u** from the heart words of

UTTERLY
Ex 17:14 that I will **u** blot out the
Ex 22:17 If her father **u** refuses to
Ex 22:20 only, he shall be **u** destroyed
Ex 23:24 but you shall **u** overthrow
Lev 26:44 to **u** destroy them and break My
Num 17:13 Shall we all **u** die
Num 21: 2 then I will **u** destroy their
Num 21: 3 and they **u** destroyed them and
Deut 2:34 we **u** destroyed the men, women
Deut 3: 6 we **u** destroyed them, as we
Deut 3: 6 **u** destroying the men, women,
Deut 4:26 that you will soon **u** perish
Deut 4:26 it, but will be **u** destroyed
Deut 7: 2 them and **u** destroy them
Deut 7:26 but you shall **u** detest it
Deut 7:26 and **u** abhor it, for it is an
Deut 12: 2 You shall **u** destroy all the
Deut 13:15 **u** destroying it, all that is
Deut 20:17 but you shall **u** destroy them
Deut 31:29 you will become **u** corrupt
Josh 2:10 and Og, whom you **u** destroyed
Josh 6:21 they **u** destroyed all that was
Josh 8:26 until he had **u** destroyed all
Josh 10: 1 Ai and had **u** destroyed it
Josh 10:28 He **u** destroyed them
Josh 10:35 in it he **u** destroyed that day
Josh 10:37 but **u** destroyed it and all the
Josh 10:39 **u** destroyed all the people
Josh 10:40 but **u** destroyed all that
Josh 11:11 the sword, **u** destroying them
Josh 11:12 He **u** destroyed them, as Moses
Josh 11:20 that He might **u** destroy them
Josh 11:21 Joshua **u** destroyed them with
Josh 17:13 but did not **u** drive them out
Judg 1:17 Zephath, and **u** destroyed it
Judg 21:11 You shall **u** destroy every
1Sa 15: 3 **u** destroy all that they have,
1Sa 15: 8 **u** destroyed all the people
1Sa 15: 9 unwilling to **u** destroy them
1Sa 15: 9 that they **u** destroyed
1Sa 15:15 the rest we have **u** destroyed
1Sa 15:18 **u** destroy the sinners, the
1Sa 15:20 I have **u** destroyed the
1Sa 15:21 should have been **u** destroyed
1Sa 27:12 his people Israel **u** abhor him
2Sa 23: 7 they shall be **u** burned with
2Ki 19:11 lands by **u** destroying them
1Ch 4:41 **u** destroyed them, as it is to
2Ch 20:23 of Mount Seir to **u** kill and
2Ch 31: 1 until they had **u** destroyed
2Ch 32:14 **u** destroyed that could
Neh 9:31 great mercy You did not **u**
Ps 37:24 he shall not be **u** cast down
Ps 73:19 They are **u** consumed with
Ps 89:33 I will not **u** take from him
Ps 119: 8 Oh, do not forsake me **u**
Ps 119:43 of truth **u** out of my mouth
Song 8: 7 house, it would be **u** despised
Is 2:18 the idols He shall **u** abolish
Is 6:11 a man, the land is **u** desolate
Is 11:15 The LORD will **u** destroy the
Is 24: 3 **u** plundered, for the LORD has

Is 34: 2 He has **u** destroyed them, He
Is 37:11 lands by **u** destroying them
Is 40:30 and the young men shall **u** fall
Is 56: 3 The LORD has **u** separated me
Is 60:12 nations shall be **u** ruined
Jer 9: 4 every brother will **u** supplant
Jer 12:17 I will **u** pluck up and destroy
Jer 14:19 Have You **u** rejected Judah
Jer 23:39 will **u** forget you and forsake
Jer 25: 9 will **u** destroy them, and make
Jer 25:29 and should you be **u** unpunished
Jer 50:21 **u** destroy them," says the
Jer 50:26 of ruins, and destroy her **u**
Jer 51: 3 **u** destroy all her army
Jer 51:58 of Babylon shall be **u** broken
Lam 5:22 unless You have **u** rejected us
Ezek 9: 6 **U** slay old and young men,
Ezek 17:10 will it not **u** wither when the
Ezek 29:10 the land of Egypt **u** waste
Hos 1: 6 but I will **u** take them away
Hos 10:15 of Israel shall be cut off **u**
Amos 9: 8 yet I will not **u** destroy the
Mic 2: 4 We are **u** destroyed
Nah 1:15 he is **u** cut off
Hab 1: 5 be **u** astounded
Zeph 1: 2 I will **u** consume all things
Acts 3:23 be **u** destroyed from among the
2Pe 2:12 will **u** perish in their own
Rev 18: 8 she will be **u** burned with

UTTERMOST (*see* UTMOST)
Ps 139: 9 dwell in the **u** parts of the
1Th 2:16 has come upon them to the **u**
Heb 7:25 the **u** those who come to God

UTTERS (*see* UTTER)
Ps 19: 2 Day unto day **u** speech, And
Jer 10:13 When He **u** His voice, there is
Jer 51:16 When He **u** His voice
Amos 1: 2 **u** His voice from Jerusalem
Mic 7: 3 and the great man **u** his evil

UZ
Gen 10:23 The sons of Aram were **U**, Hul,
Gen 36:28 sons of Dishan: **U** and Aran
1Ch 1:17 Arphaxad, Lud, Aram, **U**, Hul,
1Ch 1:42 The sons of Dishan were **U**
Job 1: 1 was a man in the land of **U**
Jer 25:20 the kings of the land of **U**
Lam 4:21 who dwell in the land of **U**

UZAI
Neh 3:25 Palal the son of **U** made

UZAL
Gen 10:27 Hadoram, **U**, Diklah,
1Ch 1:21 Hadoram, **U**, Diklah,

UZZA (*see* UZZAH)
2Ki 21:18 own house, in the garden of **U**
2Ki 21:26 his tomb in the garden of **U**
1Ch 8: 7 He begot **U** and Ahihud
1Ch 13: 7 the house of Abinadab, and **U**
1Ch 13: 9 **U** put out his hand to hold
1Ch 13:10 LORD was aroused against **U**
1Ch 13:11 the LORD's outbreak against **U**
1Ch 13:11 is called Perez **U** to this day
Ezra 2:49 the sons of **U**, the sons of
Neh 7:51 of Gazzam, the children of **U**

UZZAH (*see* UZZA)
2Sa 6: 3 and **U** and Ahio, the sons of
2Sa 6: 6 **U** put out his hand to the ark
2Sa 6: 7 LORD was aroused against **U**
2Sa 6: 8 the LORD's outbreak against **U**
1Ch 6:29 Shimei his son, **U** his son,

UZZEN SHEERAH (*see* SHEERAH)
1Ch 7:24 and Upper Beth Horon and **U**

UZZI
1Ch 6: 5 begot Bukki, and Bukki begot **U**
1Ch 6: 6 **U** begot Zerahiah, and Zerahiah
1Ch 6:51 **U** his son, Zerahiah his son,
1Ch 7: 2 The sons of Tola were **U**,
1Ch 7: 3 The son of **U** was Izrahiah, and
1Ch 7: 7 sons of Bela were Ezbon, **U**
1Ch 9: 8 Elah the son of **U**, the son of
Ezra 7: 4 son of Zerahiah, the son of **U**
Neh 11:22 was **U** the son of Bani, the
Neh 12:19 of Jedaiah, **U**
Neh 12:42 Shemaiah, Eleazar, **U**,

UZZIA
1Ch 11:44 **U** the Ashterathite, Shama and

UZZIAH
2Ki 15:13 year of **U** king of Judah
2Ki 15:30 year of Jotham the son of **U**
2Ki 15:32 Israel, Jotham the son of **U**
2Ki 15:34 that his father **U** had done
1Ch 6:24 **U** his son, and Shaul his son
1Ch 27:25 Jehonathan the son of **U** was
2Ch 26: 1 the people of Judah took **U**
2Ch 26: 3 **U** was sixteen years old when
2Ch 26: 8 brought tribute to **U**
2Ch 26: 9 **U** built towers in Jerusalem
2Ch 26:11 Moreover **U** had an army of
2Ch 26:14 Then **U** prepared for them, for
2Ch 26:18 And they withstood King **U**, and
2Ch 26:18 It is not for you, **U**, to burn
2Ch 26:19 Then **U** became furious
2Ch 26:21 King **U** was a leper until the
2Ch 26:22 Now the rest of the acts of **U**
2Ch 26:23 So **U** rested with his fathers,
2Ch 27: 2 to all that his father **U** had
Ezra 10:21 Shemaiah, Jehiel, and **U**
Neh 11: 4 Athaiah the son of **U**, the son
Is 1: 1 and Jerusalem in the days of **U**
Is 6: 1 In the year that King **U** died
Is 7: 1 son of Jotham, the son of **U**
Hos 1: 1 of Beeri, in the days of **U**
Amos 1: 1 the days of **U** king of Judah
Zech 14: 5 the days of **U** king of Judah
Matt 1: 8 begot Joram, and Joram begot **U**
Matt 1: 9 **U** begot Jotham, Jotham begot

UZZIEL (*see* UZZIELITES)
Ex 6:18 Amram, Izhar, Hebron, and **U**
Ex 6:22 the sons of **U** were Mishael,
Lev 10: 4 the sons of **U** the uncle of
Num 3:19 Amram, Izehar, Hebron, and **U**
Num 3:30 was Elizaphan the son of **U**
1Ch 4:42 Neariah, Rephaiah, and **U**, the
1Ch 6: 2 Amram, Izhar, Hebron, and **U**
1Ch 6:18 Amram, Izhar, Hebron, and **U**
1Ch 7: 7 of Bela were Ezbon, Uzzi, **U**
1Ch 15:10 of the sons of **U**, Amminadab
1Ch 23:12 Amram, Izhar, Hebron, and **U**
1Ch 23:20 Of the sons of **U**, Michah was
1Ch 24:24 Of the sons of **U**, Michah
1Ch 25: 4 Bukkiah, Mattaniah, **U**,
2Ch 29:14 of Jeduthun, Shemaiah and **U**
Neh 3: 8 Next to him **U** the son of

UZZIELITES (*see* UZZIEL)
Num 3:27 and the family of the **U**
1Ch 26:23 the Hebronites, and the **U**

V

VAGABOND (*see* VAGABONDS)
Gen 4:12 a **v** you shall be on the earth
Gen 4:14 a **v** on the earth, and it will

VAGABONDS (*see* VAGABOND)
Ps 109:10 his children continually be **v**

VAIN (*see* VAINLY)
Ex 20: 7 of the LORD your God in **v**
Ex 20: 7 who takes His name in **v**
Lev 26:16 you shall sow your seed in **v**
Lev 26:20 strength shall be spent in **v**
Deut 5:11 of the LORD your God in **v**
Deut 5:11 who takes His name in **v**
1Sa 25:21 Surely in **v** I have protected
2Ki 18:20 but they are **v** words
Job 9:29 why then do I labor in **v**
Job 35:16 Job opens his mouth in **v**
Job 39:16 her labor is in **v**, without
Job 41: 9 hope of overcoming him is **v**
Ps 2: 1 And the people plot a **v** thing
Ps 31: 6 those who regard **v** idols
Ps 33:17 A horse is a **v** hope for
Ps 39: 6 they busy themselves in **v**
Ps 41: 6 to see me, he speaks **v** words
Ps 60:11 For **v** is the help of man
Ps 73:13 I have cleansed my heart in **v**
Ps 108:12 For **v** is the help of man
Ps 127: 1 They labor in **v** who build it
Ps 127: 1 The watchman stays awake in **v**
Ps 127: 2 It is **v** for you to rise up
Ps 139:20 enemies take Your name in **v**
Ps 144: 8 Whose mouth speaks **v** words
Ps 144:11 Whose mouth speaks **v** words
Prov 1:17 in **v** the net is spread in the
Prov 31:30 is deceitful and beauty is **v**
Eccl 6:12 all the days of his **v** life
Eccl 9: 9 love all the days of your **v**
Is 30: 7 the Egyptians shall help in **v**
Is 36: 5 but they are **v** words
Is 45:18 Who did not create it in **v**
Is 45:19 seed of Jacob, 'Seek Me in **v**'
Is 49: 4 I said, 'I have labored in **v**
Is 49: 4 strength for nothing and in **v**
Is 65:23 They shall not labor in **v**
Jer 2:30 In **v** I have chastened your
Jer 3:23 in **v** is salvation hoped for
Jer 4:30 in **v** you will make yourself
Jer 6:29 the smelter refines in **v**, for
Jer 46:11 In **v** you will use many
Jer 50: 9 none shall return in **v**
Jer 51:58 the people will labor in **v**
Ezek 6:10 in **v** that I would bring this
Ezek 21:29 while they see **v** visions for
Hab 2:13 nations weary themselves in **v**
Zech 10: 2 they comfort in **v**
Mal 1:10 kindle fire on My altar in **v**
Mal 3:14 said, 'It is **v** to serve God
Matt 6: 7 do not use **v** repetitions as
Matt 15: 9 And in **v** they worship Me,
Mark 7: 7 And in **v** they worship Me,
Acts 4:25 and the people plot **v** things
Acts 14:15 **v** things to the living God
Rom 13: 4 does not bear the sword in **v**
1Co 15: 2 unless you believed in **v**
1Co 15:10 grace toward me was not in **v**
1Co 15:14 then our preaching is **v** and
1Co 15:14 and your faith is also **v**
1Co 15:58 labor is not in **v** in the Lord
2Co 6: 1 receive the grace of God in **v**
2Co 9: 3 be in **v** in this respect, that
Gal 2: 2 I might run, or had run, in **v**
Gal 2:21 law, then Christ died in **v**
Gal 3: 4 suffered so many things in **v**
Gal 3: 4 if indeed it was in **v**
Gal 4:11 I have labored for you in **v**
Phil 2:16 run in **v** or labored in **v**
1Th 2: 1 coming to you was not in **v**
1Th 3: 5 and our labor might be in **v**
1Ti 6:20 **v** babblings and contradictions
2Ti 2:16 **v** babblings, for they will
Jas 4: 5 that the Scripture says in **v**

VAINLY (*see* VAIN)
Ps 62:10 Nor **v** hope in robbery
Lam 4:17 us, watching **v** for our help
Col 2:18 **v** puffed up by his fleshly

VAJEZATHA
Esth 9: 9 Arisai, Aridai, and **V**

VALIANT (*see* VALIANTLY)
Judg 21:10 thousand of their most **v** men
1Sa 10:26 **v** men went with him, whose
1Sa 14:52 any strong man or any **v** man
1Sa 18:17 Only be **v** for me, and fight
1Sa 31:12 all the **v** men arose and
2Sa 2: 7 be strengthened, and be **v**
2Sa 11:16 he knew there were **v** men
2Sa 13:28 Be courageous and **v**
2Sa 17:10 And even he who is **v**, whose
2Sa 17:10 who are with him are **v** men
2Sa 23:20 the son of a **v** man from
2Sa 24: 9 **v** men who drew the sword, and
2Ki 24:16 All the **v** men, seven thousand
1Ch 5:18 seven hundred and sixty **v** men
1Ch 10:12 all the **v** men arose and took
1Ch 11:22 the son of a **v** man from
1Ch 12:28 man, a **v** warrior, and from his
1Ch 28: 1 with the officials, the **v** men
2Ch 13: 3 with an army of **v** warriors
2Ch 26:17 of the LORD, who were **v** men
2Ch 28: 6 Judah in one day, all **v** men
Neh 11: 6 hundred and sixty-eight **v** men
Song 3: 7 with sixty **v** men around it,
Song 3: 7 of the **v** of Israel
Is 5:22 wine, woe to men **v** for mixing
Is 10:13 the inhabitants like a **v** man
Is 33: 7 Surely their **v** ones shall cry
Jer 9: 3 They are not **v** for the truth
Jer 46:15 Why are your **v** men swept away
Nah 2: 3 red, the **v** men are in scarlet
Heb 11:34 became **v** in battle, turned to

VALIANTLY (*see* VALIANT)
Num 24:18 while Israel does v
Ps 60:12 Through God we will do v, For
Ps 108:13 Through God we will do v, For
Ps 118:15 right hand of the LORD does v
Ps 118:16 right hand of the LORD does v

VALLEY (*see* VALLEYS)
Gen 14: 3 in the V of Siddim (that is
Gen 14: 8 in battle in the V of Siddim
Gen 14:10 Now the V of Siddim was full
Gen 14:17 at the V of Shaveh
Gen 14:17 (that is, the King's V),
Gen 26:17 his tent in the V of Gerar
Gen 26:19 Isaac's servants dug in the v
Gen 37:14 him out of the V of Hebron
Num 13:23 they came to the V of Eshcol
Num 13:24 was called the V of Eshcol
Num 14:25 the Canaanites dwell in the v
Num 21:12 and camped in the V of Zered
Num 21:20 in the v that is in the
Num 32: 9 went up to the V of Eshcol
Deut 1:24 and came to the V of Eshcol
Deut 2:13 cross over the V of the Zered
Deut 2:13 over the V of the Zered
Deut 2:14 over the V of the Zered was
Deut 3:29 in the v opposite Beth Peor
Deut 4:46 in the v opposite Beth Peor,
Deut 21: 4 to a v with flowing water
Deut 21: 4 heifer's neck there in the v
Deut 21: 6 neck was broken in the v
Deut 34: 3 the plain of the V of Jericho
Deut 34: 6 He buried him in a v in the
Josh 7:24 them to the V of Achor
Josh 7:26 the V of Achor to this day
Josh 8:11 there was a v between them
Josh 8:13 night into the midst of the v
Josh 10:12 and Moon, in the V of Aijalon
Josh 11: 8 to the V of Mizpah eastward
Josh 11:17 the V of Lebanon below Mount
Josh 12: 7 from Baal Gad in the V of
Josh 13:19 on the mountain of the v,
Josh 13:27 in the v Beth Haram, Beth
Josh 15: 7 Debir from the V of Achor
Josh 15: 7 is on the south side of the v
Josh 15: 8 the border went up by the V
Josh 15: 8 the V of Hinnom westward,
Josh 15: 8 of the V of Rephaim northward
Josh 17:16 the v have chariots of iron
Josh 17:16 who are of the V of Jezreel
Josh 18:16 the V of the Son of Hinnom
Josh 18:16 which is in the V of the
Josh 18:16 descended to the V of Hinnom
Josh 19:14 ended in the V of Jiphthah El
Josh 19:27 to the V of Jiphthah El, then
Judg 1:34 them to come down to the v
Judg 5:15 into the v under his command
Judg 6:33 encamped in the V of Jezreel
Judg 7: 1 by the hill of Moreh in the v
Judg 7: 8 Midian was below him in the v
Judg 7:12 East, were lying in the v as
Judg 16: 4 a woman in the V of Sorek
Judg 18:28 It was in the v that belongs
1Sa 6:13 their wheat harvest in the v
1Sa 13:18 the V of Zeboim toward the
1Sa 15: 5 and lay in wait in the v
1Sa 17: 2 encamped in the V of Elah
1Sa 17: 3 side, with a v between them
1Sa 17:19 Israel were in the V of Elah
1Sa 17:52 far as the entrance of the v
1Sa 21: 9 you killed in the V of Elah
1Sa 31: 7 on the other side of the v
2Sa 5:18 in the V of Rephaim
2Sa 5:22 in the V of Rephaim
2Sa 8:13 Syrians in the V of Salt
2Sa 18:18 which is in the King's V
2Sa 23:13 encamped in the V of Rephaim
2Ki 2:16 some mountain or into some v
2Ki 3:16 Make this v full of ditches
2Ki 3:17 yet that v shall be filled
2Ki 14: 7 Edomites in the V of Salt
2Ki 23:10 which is in the V of the Son
1Ch 4:39 far as the east side of the v
1Ch 10: 7 the v saw that they had fled
1Ch 11:15 encamped in the V of Rephaim
1Ch 14: 9 a raid on the V of Rephaim
1Ch 14:13 again made a raid on the v
1Ch 18:12 Edomites in the V of Salt
2Ch 14:10 in battle array in the V of
2Ch 20:26 in the V of Berachah, for
2Ch 20:26 that place was called The V
2Ch 25:11 he went to the V of Salt
2Ch 26: 9 Corner Gate, at the V Gate
2Ch 28: 3 in the V of the Son of Hinnom
2Ch 33: 6 in the V of the Son of Hinnom
2Ch 33:14 west side of Gihon, in the v
2Ch 35:22 to fight in the V of Megiddo
Neh 2:13 V Gate to the Serpent Well
Neh 2:15 went up in the night by the v
Neh 2:15 back and entered by the V Gate
Neh 3:13 of Zanoah repaired the V Gate
Neh 11:30 Beersheba to the V of Hinnom
Neh 11:35 Ono, and the V of Craftsmen
Job 21:33 The clods of the v shall be
Job 39:21 He paws in the v, and rejoices
Ps 23: 4 the v of the shadow of death
Ps 60: 6 measure out the V of Succoth
Ps 84: 6 pass through the V of Baca
Ps 108: 7 measure out the V of Succoth
Prov 30:17 of the v will pick it out
Song 6:11 to see the verdure of the v
Is 17: 5 of grain in the V of Rephaim
Is 22: 1 against the V of Vision
Is 22: 5 of hosts in the V of Vision
Is 28: 4 at the head of the verdant v
Is 28:21 angry as in the V of Gibeon
Is 40: 4 Every v shall be exalted, and
Is 63:14 a beast goes down into the v
Is 65:10 the V of Achor a place for
Jer 2:23 See your way in the v
Jer 7:31 which is in the V of the Son
Jer 7:32 or the V of the Son of Hinnom
Jer 7:32 but the V of Slaughter
Jer 19: 2 go out to the V of the Son of
Jer 19: 6 or the V of the Son of Hinnom
Jer 19: 6 but the V of Slaughter
Jer 21:13 you, O inhabitant of the v
Jer 31:40 And the whole v of the dead
Jer 32:35 in the V of the Son of Hinnom
Jer 47: 5 with the remnant of their v
Jer 48: 8 The v also shall perish, and
Jer 49: 4 the valleys, your flowing v
Ezek 37: 1 me down in the midst of the v
Ezek 37: 2 were very many in the open v
Ezek 39:11 the v of those who pass by
Ezek 39:11 call it the V of Hamon Gog
Ezek 39:15 it in the V of Hamon Gog
Ezek 47: 8 region, goes down into the v
Hos 1: 5 of Israel in the V of Jezreel
Hos 2:15 the V of Achor as a door of
Joel 3: 2 down to the V of Jehoshaphat
Joel 3:12 up to the V of Jehoshaphat
Joel 3:14 in the v of decision
Joel 3:14 is near in the v of decision
Joel 3:18 and water the V of Acacias
Amos 1: 5 inhabitant from the V of Aven
Amos 6:14 Hamath to the V of the Arabah
Mic 1: 6 down her stones into the v
Zech 14: 4 west, making a very large v
Zech 14: 5 flee through My mountain v
Zech 14: 5 for the mountain v shall
Luke 3: 5 Every v shall be filled and

VALLEYS (*see* VALLEY)
Num 24: 6 Like v that stretch out, like
Deut 8: 7 springs, that flow out of v
Deut 11:11 is a land of hills and v,
1Ki 20:28 but He is not God of the v
1Ch 12:15 to flight all those in the v
1Ch 27:29 the herds that were in the v
Job 30: 6 live in the clefts of the v
Job 39:10 will he plow the v behind you
Ps 65:13 The v also are covered with
Ps 104: 8 They went down into the v
Ps 104:10 sends the springs into the v
Song 2: 1 Sharon, and the lily of the v
Is 7:19 will rest in the desolate v
Is 22: 7 v shall be full of chariots
Is 28: 1 at the head of the verdant v
Is 41:18 in the midst of the v
Is 57: 5 slaying the children in the v
Jer 49: 4 Why do you glory in the v
Ezek 6: 3 to the ravines, and to the v
Ezek 7:16 mountains like doves of the v
Ezek 31:12 the mountains and in all the v
Ezek 32: 5 fill the v with your carcass
Ezek 34:13 mountains of Israel, in the v
Ezek 35: 8 on your hills and in your v
Ezek 36: 4 the hills, the rivers, the v
Ezek 36: 6 hills, the rivers, and the v
Mic 1: 4 the v will split like wax

VALOR
Deut 3:18 All you men of v shall cross
Josh 1:14 all your mighty men of v
Josh 6: 2 king, and the mighty men of v
Josh 8: 3 thousand mighty men of v and
Josh 10: 7 and all the mighty men of v
Judg 3:29 of Moab, all stout men of v
Judg 6:12 with you, you mighty man of v
Judg 11: 1 was a mighty man of v, but he
Judg 18: 2 men of v from Zorah and
Judg 20:44 all these were men of v
Judg 20:46 all these were men of v
1Sa 16:18 in playing, a mighty man of v
1Ki 11:28 was a mighty man of v
2Ki 5: 1 He was also a mighty man of v
2Ki 24:14 and all the mighty men of v
1Ch 5:24 They were mighty men of v
1Ch 7: 2 men of v in their generations
1Ch 7: 5 Issachar were mighty men of v
1Ch 7: 7 thirty-four mighty men of v
1Ch 7: 9 two hundred mighty men of v
1Ch 7:11 of v fit to go out for war
1Ch 7:40 choice men, mighty men of v
1Ch 8:40 of Ulam were mighty men of v
1Ch 12: 8 wilderness, mighty men of v
1Ch 12:21 they were all mighty men of v
1Ch 12:25 mighty men of v fit for war
1Ch 12:30 hundred, mighty men of v,
1Ch 28: 1 and all the mighty men of v
2Ch 13: 3 choice men, mighty men of v
2Ch 14: 8 these were mighty men of v
2Ch 17:13 men of war, mighty men of v
2Ch 17:14 thousand mighty men of v
2Ch 17:16 thousand mighty men of v
2Ch 17:17 Eliada a mighty man of v, and
2Ch 25: 6 thousand mighty men of v from
2Ch 26:12 men of v was two thousand six
2Ch 32:21 down every mighty man of v
Neh 11:14 brethren, mighty men of v
Dan 3:20 certain mighty men of v who

VALUABLE (*see* VALUABLES, VALUE)
Lam 4: 2 v as fine gold, how they are

VALUABLES (*see* VALUABLE)
2Ch 20:25 of v on the dead bodies, and
Lam 1:11 they have given their v for
Hos 9: 6 possess their v of silver

VALUATION (*see* VALUATIONS, VALUE)
Lev 5:15 with your v in shekels of
Lev 5:18 from the flock, with your v
Lev 6: 6 from the flock, with your v
Lev 27: 2 the LORD, according to your v
Lev 27: 3 if your v is of a male from
Lev 27: 3 then your v shall be fifty
Lev 27: 4 then your v shall be thirty
Lev 27: 5 then your v for a male shall
Lev 27: 6 then your v for a male shall
Lev 27: 6 for a female your v shall be
Lev 27: 7 then your v shall be fifteen
Lev 27: 8 he is too poor to pay your v
Lev 27:13 must add one-fifth to your v
Lev 27:15 of the money of your v to it
Lev 27:16 then your v shall be
Lev 27:17 to your v it shall stand
Lev 27:18 shall be deducted from your v
Lev 27:19 of the money of your v to it
Lev 27:23 to him the worth of your v
Lev 27:23 he shall give your v on that
Lev 27:27 redeem it according to your v
Lev 27:27 be sold according to your v
Num 18:16 old, according to your v, for

VALUATIONS (*see* VALUATION)
Lev 27:25 all your v shall be according

VALUE (*see* VALUABLE, VALUATION, VALUED, VALUES)
Lev 6: 5 He shall restore its full v
Lev 27: 8 priest shall set a v for him
Lev 27: 8 vowed, the priest shall v him
Lev 27:12 priest shall set a v for it
Lev 27:12 priest, v it, so it shall be
Lev 27:14 priest shall set a v for it
Num 5: 7 full v plus one-fifth of it
Job 28:13 Man does not know its v, Nor
Matt 6:26 you not of more v than they
Matt 10:31 you are of more v than many
Matt 12:12 Of how much more v then is a
Matt 27: 9 the v of Him who was priced,
Luke 12: 7 you are of more v than many
Luke 12:24 Of how much more v are you

Acts 19:19 they counted up the v of them
Col 2:23 but are of no v against the

VALUED (*see* VALUE)
Lev 27:16 of barley seed shall be v at
1Sa 26:24 as your life was v much this
1Sa 26:24 so let my life be v much in
Job 28:16 It cannot be v in the gold of
Job 28:19 nor can it be v in pure gold
Prov 27:21 a man is v by what others say

VALUES (*see* VALUE)
Lev 27:14 as the priest v it, so it

VANIAH
Ezra 10:36 V, Meremoth, Eliashib,

VANISH (*see* VANISHED, VANISHES)
Job 6:17 hot, they v from their place
Ps 37:20 of the meadows, shall v
Ps 37:20 Into smoke they shall v away
Is 51: 6 will v away like smoke, the
1Co 13: 8 is knowledge, it will v away
Heb 8:13 old is ready to v away

VANISHED (*see* VANISH)
Jer 49: 7 Has their wisdom v
Luke 24:31 and He v from their sight

VANISHES (*see* VANISH)
Job 6:16 ice, and into which the snow v
Job 7: 9 v away, so he who goes down
Jas 4:14 a little time and then v away

VANITIES (*see* VANITY)
Eccl 1: 2 Vanity of v," says the
Eccl 1: 2 Vanity of v, all is vanity
Eccl 12: 8 Vanity of v," says the

VANITY (*see* VANITIES)
Eccl 1: 2 V of vanities," says the
Eccl 1: 2 V of vanities, all is v
Eccl 1:14 and indeed, all is v and
Eccl 2: 1 but surely, this also was v
Eccl 2:11 and indeed all was v and
Eccl 2:15 This also is v
Eccl 2:17 grievous to me, for all is v
Eccl 2:19 This also is v
Eccl 2:21 This also is v and a great
Eccl 2:23 This also is v
Eccl 2:26 This also is v and grasping
Eccl 3:19 over beasts, for all is v
Eccl 4: 4 This also is v and grasping
Eccl 4: 7 and I saw v under the sun
Eccl 4: 8 This also is v and a grave
Eccl 4:16 Surely this also is v and
Eccl 5: 7 and many words there is also v
Eccl 5:10 This also is v
Eccl 6: 2 This is v, and it is an evil
Eccl 6: 4 for it comes in v and departs
Eccl 6: 9 This also is v and grasping
Eccl 6:11 many things that increase v
Eccl 7: 6 This also is v
Eccl 7:15 all things in my days of v
Eccl 8:10 This also is v
Eccl 8:14 There is a v which occurs on
Eccl 8:14 I said that this also is v
Eccl 9: 9 the sun, all your days of v
Eccl 11: 8 All that is coming is v
Eccl 11:10 for childhood and youth are v
Eccl 12: 8 V of vanities," says the
Eccl 12: 8 All is v
Is 5:18 draw iniquity with cords of v
Hos 12:11 surely they are v

VANQUISH (*see* VANQUISHED)
Job 32:13 God will v him, not man

VANQUISHED (*see* VANQUISH)
2Sa 22:15 lightning bolts, and He v them
Ps 18:14 in abundance, and He v them

VAPOR (*see* VAPORS)
Ps 39: 5 at his best state is but v
Ps 39:11 Surely every man is v
Ps 62: 9 men of low degree are a v
Ps 62: 9 are altogether lighter than v
Acts 2:19 blood and fire and v of smoke
Jas 4:14 It is even a v that appears

VAPORS (*see* VAPOR)
Ps 135: 7 He causes the v to ascend
Jer 10:13 He causes the v to ascend
Jer 51:16 He causes the v to ascend

VARIATION (*see* VARIETIES)
Jas 1:17 is no v or shadow of turning

VARIETIES (*see* VARIATION, VARIOUS)
1Co 12:28 administrations, v of tongues

VARIOUS (*see* VARIETIES)
1Ch 29: 2 glistening stones of v colors
2Ch 16:14 v ingredients prepared in a
Ezek 17: 3 full of feathers of v colors
Matt 4:24 afflicted with v diseases
Matt 24: 7 and earthquakes in v places
Mark 1:34 who were sick with v diseases
Mark 13: 8 be earthquakes in v places
Luke 4:40 v diseases brought them to
Luke 21:11 great earthquakes in v places
2Ti 3: 6 sins, led away by v lusts
Tit 3: 3 deceived, serving v lusts
Heb 1: 1 God, who at v times and in
Heb 2: 4 with v miracles, and gifts of
Heb 9:10 v washings, and fleshly
Heb 13: 9 not be carried about with v
Jas 1: 2 when you fall into v trials
1Pe 1: 6 have been grieved by v trials

VASHTI
Esth 1: 9 Queen V also made a feast for
Esth 1:11 to bring Queen V before the
Esth 1:12 But Queen V refused to come
Esth 1:15 What shall we do to Queen V
Esth 1:16 Queen V has not only wronged
Esth 1:17 commanded Queen V
Esth 1:19 that V shall come no more
Esth 2: 1 subsided, he remembered V
Esth 2: 4 king be queen instead of V
Esth 2:17 made her queen instead of V

VASSAL
2Ki 17: 3 and Hoshea became his v, and
2Ki 24: 1 became his v for three years

VAST
Prov 16: 8 than v revenues without

VAT (*see* VATS)
Hag 2:16 v to draw out fifty baths
Mark 12: 1 dug a place for the wine v

VATS (*see* VAT)
Prov 3:10 your v will overflow with new
Joel 2:24 the v shall overflow with new
Joel 3:13 is full, the v overflow

VEGETABLE (*see* VEGETABLES, VEGETATION)
Deut 11:10 it by foot, as a v garden
1Ki 21: 2 I may have it for a v garden

VEGETABLES (*see* VEGETABLE)
Dan 1:12 and let them give us v to eat
Dan 1:16 were to drink, and gave them v
Rom 14: 2 he who is weak eats only v

VEGETATION (*see* VEGETABLE)
Ps 104:14 v for the service of man,
Ps 105:35 up all the v in their land
Is 42:15 hills, and dry up all their v

VEHEMENT (*see* VEHEMENTLY)
Song 8: 6 of fire, a most v flame
Jon 4: 8 God prepared a v east wind
2Co 7:11 what v desire, what zeal,
Heb 5: 7 with v cries and tears to Him

VEHEMENTLY (*see* VEHEMENT)
Mark 14:31 But he spoke more v, "If I
Luke 6:48 the stream beat v against
Luke 6:49 which the stream beat v
Luke 11:53 began to assail Him v, and to
Luke 23:10 stood and v accused Him

VEIL (*see* UNVEILED, VEILED, VEILS)
Gen 24:65 So she took a v and covered
Gen 38:14 covered herself with a v
Gen 38:19 away, and laid aside her v
Ex 26:31 shall make a v woven of blue
Ex 26:33 hang the v from the clasps
Ex 26:33 in there, behind the v
Ex 26:33 The v shall be a divider for
Ex 26:35 set the table outside the v
Ex 27:21 outside the v which is before
Ex 30: 6 v that is before the ark of
Ex 34:33 them, he put a v on his face
Ex 34:34 he would take the v off until
Ex 34:35 put the v on his face again
Ex 35:12 and the v of the covering
Ex 36:35 he made a v woven of blue and
Ex 38:27 and the bases of the v
Ex 39:34 and the v of the covering
Ex 40: 3 off the ark with the v
Ex 40:21 hung up the v of the covering
Ex 40:22 the tabernacle, outside the v
Ex 40:26 of meeting in front of the v
Lev 4: 6 in front of the v of the
Lev 4:17 the LORD, in front of the v
Lev 16: 2 the Holy Place inside the v
Lev 16:12 and bring it inside the v
Lev 16:15 bring its blood inside the v
Lev 21:23 the v or approach the altar
Lev 24: 3 Outside the v of the
Num 4: 5 take down the covering v and
Num 18: 7 at the altar and behind the v
2Ch 3:14 And he made the v of blue and
Song 4: 1 dove's eyes behind your v
Song 4: 3 your v are like a piece of
Song 5: 7 walls took my v away from me
Song 6: 7 your temples behind your v
Is 25: 7 the v that is spread over all
Is 47: 2 Remove your v, take off the
Matt 27:51 the v of the temple was torn
Mark 15:38 Then the v of the temple was
Luke 23:45 the v of the temple was torn
2Co 3:13 who put a v over his face so
2Co 3:14 v remains unlifted in the
2Co 3:14 because the v is taken away
2Co 3:15 read, a v lies on their heart
2Co 3:16 the Lord, the v is taken away
Heb 6:19 the Presence behind the v
Heb 9: 3 and behind the second v, the
Heb 10:20 for us, through the v, that

VEILED (*see* VEIL)
Lam 3:65 Give them a v heart
2Co 4: 3 But even if our gospel is v
2Co 4: 3 it is v to those who are

VEILS (*see* VEIL)
Song 1: 7 v herself by the flocks of
Is 3:19 the bracelets, and the v
Ezek 13:18 and make v for the heads of
Ezek 13:21 I will also tear off your v

VENGEANCE (*see* VENGEFULLY)
Gen 4:15 Cain, v shall be taken on him
Lev 19:18 You shall not take v, nor
Lev 26:25 execute the v of My covenant
Num 31: 2 Take v for the children of
Num 31: 3 take v for the LORD on Midian
Deut 32:35 V is Mine, and recompense
Deut 32:41 I will render v to My enemies
Deut 32:43 render v to His adversaries
Judg 16:28 I may with one blow take v on
1Sa 14:24 I have taken v on my enemies
1Sa 18:25 to take v on the king's
Ps 58:10 rejoice when he sees the v
Ps 94: 1 O LORD God, to whom v belongs
Ps 94: 1 O God, to whom v belongs,
Ps 99: 8 You took v on their deeds
Ps 149: 7 To execute v on the nations,
Prov 6:34 not spare in the day of v
Is 1:24 and take v on My enemies
Is 34: 8 it is the day of the LORD's v
Is 35: 4 your God will come with v
Is 47: 3 I will take v, and I will not
Is 59:17 garments of v for clothing
Is 61: 2 and the day of v of our God
Is 63: 4 the day of v is in My heart
Jer 11:20 let me see Your v on them
Jer 15:15 me, and take v for me on my
Jer 20:12 let me see Your v on them
Jer 46:10 Lord GOD of hosts, a day of v
Jer 50:15 for it is the v of the LORD
Jer 50:15 Take v on her
Jer 50:28 the v of the LORD our God
Jer 50:28 our God, the v of His temple
Jer 51: 6 is the time of the LORD's v
Jer 51:11 it is the v of the LORD, the
Jer 51:11 LORD, the v for His temple
Jer 51:36 your case and take v for you
Lam 3:60 You have seen all their v
Ezek 24: 8 may raise up fury and take v
Ezek 25:12 house of Judah by taking v
Ezek 25:14 I will lay My v on Edom by
Ezek 25:14 and they shall know My v,"
Ezek 25:15 took v with a spiteful heart,
Ezek 25:17 great v on them with furious
Ezek 25:17 when I lay My v upon them
Mic 5:15 And I will execute v in anger
Nah 1: 2 take v on His adversaries
Luke 21:22 For these are the days of v

Rom 12:19 V is Mine, I will repay,"
2Th 1: 8 in flaming fire taking v on
Heb 10:30 Him who said, "V is Mine
Jude 7 suffering the v of eternal

VENGEFULLY (*see* VENGEANCE)
Ezek 25:15 the Philistines dealt v and

VENOM
Deut 32:33 and the cruel v of cobras
Job 20:14 it becomes cobra v within him

VENT (*see* VENTS)
Job 32:19 is like wine that has no v

VENTS (*see* VENT)
Prov 29:11 A fool v all his feelings,

VENTURE
Deut 28:56 who would not v to set the
Acts 19:31 would not v into the theater

VERDANT (*see* VERDURE)
Is 28: 1 at the head of the v valleys
Is 28: 4 at the head of the v valley

VERDURE (*see* VERDANT)
Song 6:11 to see the v of the valley

VERGE
Deut 20: 2 you are on the v of battle
Deut 20: 3 Today you are on the v of
Prov 5:14 I was on the v of total ruin,

VERIFIED
Gen 42:20 so your words will be v, and

VERITY
Ps 111: 7 The works of His hands are v

VERMILION
Jer 22:14 cedar and painting it with v
Ezek 23:14 of Chaldeans portrayed in v

VERY (*see* PREFACE)

VESSEL (*see* VESSELS)
Lev 6:28 But the earthen v in which
Lev 11:33 Any earthen v into which any
Lev 11:34 in such a v, any edible food
Lev 14: 5 earthen v over running water
Lev 14:50 earthen v over running water
Lev 15:12 The v of earth that he who
Lev 15:12 and every v of wood shall be
Num 5:17 holy water in an earthen v
Num 19:15 and every open v, which has
Num 19:17 shall be put on them in a v
1Sa 21: 5 sanctified in the v this day
2Ki 4: 6 Bring me another v
2Ki 4: 6 There is not another v
Esth 1: 7 each v being different from
Ps 2: 9 in pieces like a potter's v
Ps 31:12 I am like a broken v
Is 30:14 breaking of the potter's v
Is 66:20 an offering in a clean v into
Jer 18: 4 the v that he made of clay
Jer 18: 4 made it again into another v
Jer 19:11 as one breaks a potter's v
Jer 22:28 Is he a v in which is no
Jer 25:34 shall fall like a precious v
Jer 32:14 and put them in an earthen v
Jer 48:11 been emptied from v to v
Jer 48:38 a v in which is no pleasure
Jer 51:34 he has made me an empty v
Ezek 4: 9 put them into one v, and make
Ezek 15: 3 peg from it to hang any v on
Hos 8: 8 like a v in which there is no
Luke 8:16 covers it with a v or puts it
John 19:29 Now a v full of sour wine was
Acts 9:15 for he is a chosen v of Mine
Rom 9:21 lump to make one v for honor
1Th 4: 4 his own v in sanctification
2Ti 2:21 he will be a v for honor
1Pe 3: 7 the wife, as to the weaker v

VESSELS (*see* VESSEL)
Gen 43:11 fruits of the land in your v
Ex 7:19 v of wood and v of stone
Num 4: 9 its trays, and all its oil v
Num 7:85 All the silver of the v
Num 19:18 it on the tent, on all the v
Josh 6:19 and v of bronze and iron, are
Josh 6:24 the v of bronze and iron, they
Ruth 2: 9 you are thirsty, go to the v
1Sa 9: 7 bread in our v is all gone
1Sa 21: 5 the v of the young men are
2Sa 17:28 beds and basins, earthen v
1Ki 10:21 drinking v were of gold, and
1Ki 10:21 all the v of the House of the
2Ki 4: 3 borrow v from everywhere,
2Ki 4: 3 empty v; do not gather
2Ki 4: 4 then pour it into all those v
2Ki 4: 5 who brought the v to her
2Ki 4: 6 when the v were full, that
1Ch 9:28 in charge of the serving v
2Ch 9:20 drinking v were of gold, and
2Ch 9:20 all the v of the House of the
2Ch 24:14 spoons and v of gold and silver
Ezra 8:27 two v of fine polished bronze
Esth 1: 7 served drinks in golden v
Is 18: 2 sea, even in v of reed on the
Is 22:24 all v of small quantity, from
Is 52:11 who bear the v of the LORD
Is 65: 4 things is in their v
Jer 14: 3 returned with their v empty
Jer 27:16 the v of the LORD's house
Jer 27:18 that the v which are left in
Jer 27:19 the remainder of the v that
Jer 27:21 concerning the v that remain
Jer 28: 3 all the v of the LORD's house
Jer 28: 6 to bring back the v of the
Jer 40:10 and oil, put them in your v
Jer 48:12 tip him over and empty his v
Jer 49:29 their curtains, All their v
Ezek 27:13 lives and v of bronze for your
Dan 5: 2 silver v which his father
Dan 5: 3 v that had been taken from
Dan 5:23 They have brought the v of
Matt 13:48 and gathered the good into v
Matt 25: 4 in their v with their lamps
Mark 7: 4 of cups, pitchers, copper v
Rom 9:22 the v of wrath prepared for
Rom 9:23 His glory on the v of mercy
2Co 4: 7 this treasure in earthen v
2Ti 2:20 there are not only v of gold
Heb 9:21 all the v of the ministry
Rev 2:27 as the potter's v shall be

VESTIBULE (*see* VESTIBULES)
1Ki 6: 3 The v in front of the
1Ki 7:12 LORD and the v of the temple
1Ki 7:21 by the v of the temple
1Ch 28:11 Solomon the plans for the v
2Ch 3: 4 the v that was in front of
2Ch 8:12 he had built before the v
2Ch 15: 8 was before the v of the LORD
2Ch 29: 7 shut up the doors of the v
2Ch 29:17 came to the v of the LORD
Ezek 40: 7 of the gateway by the v of
Ezek 40: 8 the v of the inside gate, one
Ezek 40: 9 measured the v of the gateway
Ezek 40: 9 The v of the gate was on the
Ezek 40:15 gate to the front of the v of
Ezek 40:39 In the v of the gateway were
Ezek 40:40 At the outer side of the v
Ezek 40:40 the v of the gateway were two
Ezek 40:48 me to the v of the temple
Ezek 40:48 the doorposts of the v, five
Ezek 40:49 of the v was twenty cubits
Ezek 41:25 on the front of the v outside
Ezek 41:26 other, on the sides of the v
Ezek 44: 3 way of the v of the gateway
Ezek 46: 2 v of that gateway from the
Ezek 46: 8 way of the v of that gateway

VESTIBULES (*see* VESTIBULE)
Ezek 40:16 around, and likewise in the v

VESTMENTS
2Ki 10:22 Bring out v for all the
2Ki 10:22 So he brought out v for them

VEXED
Judg 16:16 that his soul was v to death
Ps 73:21 And I was v in my mind

VICE
1Pe 2:16 your liberty as a cloak for v

VICINITY
2Ki 9:10 Jezebel in the v of Jezreel

VICTIM (*see* VICTIMS)
Deut 19: 6 not hated the v in time past
Job 29:17 plucked the v from his teeth
Prov 23:28 also lies in wait as for a v
Nah 3: 1 Its v never departs

VICTIMS (*see* VICTIM)
Num 14: 3 and children should become v
Num 14:31 whom you said would be v
Deut 1:39 who you say will be v, who
2Ki 21:14 and they shall become v of

VICTORIES (*see* VICTORY)
Ps 44: 4 Command v for Jacob

VICTORY (*see* VICTORIES)
Ex 32:18 voice of those who shout in v
2Sa 19: 2 So the v that day was turned
2Sa 23:10 about a great v that day
2Sa 23:12 LORD brought about a great v
2Ki 5: 1 the LORD had given v to Syria
1Ch 29:11 the power and the glory, the v
Ps 98: 1 arm have gained Him the v
Matt 12:20 He sends forth justice to v
1Co 15:54 Death is swallowed up in v
1Co 15:55 O Hades, where is your v
1Co 15:57 who gives us the v through
1Jn 5: 4 And this is the v that has
Rev 15: 2 who have the v over the beast

VIEW (*see* VIEWED)
Gen 20:10 What did you have in v, that
Deut 32:49 v the land of Canaan, which I
Josh 2: 1 Go, v the land, especially

VIEWED (*see* VIEW)
Neh 2:13 and v the walls of Jerusalem
Neh 2:15 by the valley, and v the wall
Ps 102:19 heaven the LORD v the earth

VIGIL (*see* VIGILANT)
Job 21:32 and a v kept over the tomb

VIGILANT (*see* VIGIL)
Col 4: 2 in prayer, being v in it with
1Pe 5: 8 Be sober, be v

VIGOR (*see* VIGOROUS)
Deut 34: 7 dim nor his natural v abated
Job 20:11 are full of his youthful v
Job 30: 2 Their v has perished
Dan 10: 8 for my v was turned to

VIGOROUS (*see* VIGOR, VIGOROUSLY)
Ps 38:19 But my enemies are v, and they

VIGOROUSLY (*see* VIGOROUS)
Acts 18:28 for he v refuted the Jews

VILE (*see* VILENESS)
Judg 19:24 man do not do such a v thing
1Sa 3:13 his sons made themselves v
Job 30: 8 of fools, yes, sons of v men
Job 40: 4 Behold, I am v
Ps 15: 4 In whose eyes a v person is
Jer 15:19 out the precious from the v
Lam 1: 8 therefore she has become v
Dan 11:21 place shall arise a v person
Nah 1:14 dig your grave, for you are v
Nah 3: 6 filth upon you, make you v
Rom 1:26 gave them up to v passions

VILENESS (*see* VILE)
Judg 20:10 the v that they have done in
Ps 12: 8 When v is exalted among the

VILLAGE (*see* VILLAGERS, VILLAGES)
Judg 5: 7 V life ceased, it ceased in
Matt 21: 2 Go into the v opposite you,
Mark 11: 2 Go into the v opposite you
Luke 8: 1 went through every city and v
Luke 9:52 went, they entered a v of the
Luke 9:56 And they went to another v
Luke 10:38 that He entered a certain v
Luke 17:12 as He entered a certain v
Luke 19:30 Go into the v opposite you,
Luke 24:13 same day to a v called Emmaus
Luke 24:28 the v where they were going

VILLAGERS (*see* VILLAGE)
Judg 5:11 acts for His v in Israel

VILLAGES (*see* VILLAGE)
Lev 25:31 However the houses of v
Num 21:25 in Heshbon and in all its v
Num 21:32 and they took its v and drove
Num 32:42 went and took Kenath and its v
Deut 2:23 who dwelt in v as far as Gaza
Josh 13:23 the cities and their v
Josh 13:28 the cities and their v
Josh 15:32 are twenty-nine, with their v
Josh 15:36 fourteen cities with their v
Josh 15:41 sixteen cities with their v

Josh 15:44 nine cities with their v
Josh 15:45 Ekron, with its towns and v
Josh 15:46 lay near Ashdod, with their v
Josh 15:47 Ashdod with its towns and v
Josh 15:47 Gaza with its towns and v
Josh 15:51 eleven cities with their v
Josh 15:54 nine cities with their v
Josh 15:57 ten cities with their v
Josh 15:59 six cities with their v
Josh 15:60 two cities with their v
Josh 15:62 six cities with their v
Josh 16: 9 all the cities with their v
Josh 18:24 twelve cities with their v
Josh 18:28 fourteen cities with their v
Josh 19: 6 thirteen cities and their v
Josh 19: 7 four cities and their v
Josh 19: 8 and all the v that were all
Josh 19:15 twelve cities with their v
Josh 19:16 these cities with their v
Josh 19:22 sixteen cities with their v
Josh 19:23 the cities and their v
Josh 19:30 cities with their v
Josh 19:31 these cities with their v
Josh 19:38 nineteen cities with their v
Josh 19:39 the cities and their v
Josh 19:48 these cities with their v
Josh 21:12 its v they gave to Caleb the
Judg 1:27 of Beth Shean and its v
Judg 1:27 or Taanach and its v
Judg 1:27 inhabitants of Dor and its v
Judg 1:27 of Ibleam and its v, or the
Judg 1:27 of Megiddo and its v
Judg 11:26 dwelt in Heshbon and its v
Judg 11:26 in Aroer and its v
1Sa 6:18 fortified cities and country v
1Ch 4:32 And their v were Etam, Ain,
1Ch 4:33 all the v that were around
1Ch 5:16 Gilead, in Bashan and in its v
1Ch 6:56 its v they gave to Caleb the
1Ch 9:16 who lived in the v of the
1Ch 9:22 their genealogy, in their v
1Ch 9:25 their brethren in their v had
1Ch 27:25 in the cities, in the v, and
2Ch 13:19 Bethel with its v
2Ch 13:19 Jeshanah with its v
2Ch 13:19 and Ephrain with its v
2Ch 28:18 Gederoth, Sochoh with its v
2Ch 28:18 Timnah with its v
2Ch 28:18 and Gimzo with its v
Neh 6: 2 of the v in the plain of Ono
Neh 11:25 And as for the v with their
Neh 11:25 in Kirjath Arba and its v,
Neh 11:25 Dibon and its v
Neh 11:25 Jekabzeel and its v
Neh 11:27 Shual, and Beersheba and its v
Neh 11:28 in Ziklag and Meconah and its v
Neh 11:30 Zanoah, Adullam, and their v
Neh 11:30 in Azekah and its v
Neh 11:31 Aija, and Bethel, and their v
Neh 12:28 Jerusalem, from the v of the
Neh 12:29 v all around Jerusalem
Esth 9:19 v who dwelt in the unwalled
Ps 10: 8 the lurking places of the v
Song 7:11 let us lodge in the v
Is 42:11 the v that Kedar inhabits
Jer 49: 2 her v shall be burned with
Ezek 26: 6 Also her daughter v which
Ezek 26: 8 your daughter v in the fields
Ezek 38:11 against a land of unwalled v
Hab 3:14 own arrows the head of his v
Matt 9:35 about all the cities and v
Matt 14:15 that they may go into the v
Mark 6: 6 went about the v in a circuit
Mark 6:36 the surrounding country and v
Mark 6:56 Wherever He entered, into v
Luke 13:22 went through the cities and v
Acts 8:25 in many v of the Samaritans

VINDICATE (*see* VINDICATED, VINDICATES, VINDICATION)
Ps 26: 1 V me, O LORD, For I have
Ps 35:24 V me, O LORD my God,
Ps 43: 1 V me, O God, And plead my
Ps 54: 1 And v me by Your strength

VINDICATED (*see* VINDICATE)
Job 11: 2 a man full of talk be v
Job 13:18 I know that I shall be v

VINDICATES (*see* VINDICATE)
Gen 20:16 indeed this v you before all

VINDICATION (*see* VINDICATE)
Ps 17: 2 Let my v come from Your
Ps 35:23 up Yourself, and awake to my v
2Co 7:11 desire, what zeal, what v

VINE (*see* GRAPEVINE, VINEDRESSER, VINES, VINEYARD)
Gen 40: 9 in my dream a v was before me
Gen 40:10 in the v were three branches
Gen 49:11 Binding his donkey to the v
Gen 49:11 donkey's colt to the choice v
Lev 25: 5 the grapes of your untended v
Lev 25:11 the grapes of your untended v
Deut 32:32 v is of the v of Sodom
Judg 9:12 Then the trees said to the v
Judg 9:13 But the v said to them
Judg 13:14 that comes from the v, nor
1Ki 4:25 safely, each man under his v
2Ki 4:39 herbs, and found a wild v, and
2Ki 18:31 one of you eat from his own v
Job 15:33 off his unripe grape like a v
Ps 80: 8 have brought a v out of Egypt
Ps 80:14 and see, And visit this v
Ps 128: 3 shall be like a fruitful v In
Song 6:11 see whether the v had budded
Song 7: 8 be like clusters of the v
Song 7:12 us see if the v has budded
Is 5: 2 it with the choicest v
Is 16: 8 languish, and the v of Sibmah
Is 16: 9 I will bewail the v of Sibmah
Is 24: 7 the v languishes, all the
Is 32:12 fields, for the fruitful v
Is 34: 4 as the leaf falls from the v
Is 36:16 one of you eat from his own v
Jer 2:21 I had planted you a noble v
Jer 2:21 plant of an alien v
Jer 6: 9 as a v the remnant of Israel
Jer 8:13 shall be no grapes on the v
Jer 48:32 O v of Sibmah! I will weep
Ezek 15: 2 man, how is the wood of the v
Ezek 15: 2 the v branch which is among
Ezek 15: 6 Like the wood of the v among
Ezek 17: 6 a spreading v of low stature
Ezek 17: 6 So it became a v, Brought
Ezek 17: 7 this v bent its roots toward
Ezek 17: 8 fruit, and become a majestic v
Ezek 19:10 like a v in your bloodline
Hos 10: 1 Israel empties his v
Hos 14: 7 grain, and grow like the v
Joel 1: 7 He has laid waste My v, and
Joel 1:12 The v has dried up, and the
Joel 2:22 the v yield their strength
Mic 4: 4 shall sit under his v and
Nah 2: 2 and ruined their v branches
Hag 2:19 As yet the v, the fig tree,
Zech 3:10 his neighbor under his v and
Zech 8:12 the v shall give its fruit,
Mal 3:11 nor shall the v fail to bear
Matt 26:29 v from now on until that day
Mark 14:25 drink of the fruit of the v
Luke 22:18 v until the kingdom of God
John 15: 1 I am the true v, and My Father
John 15: 4 unless it abides in the v
John 15: 5 I am the v, you are the
Rev 14:18 of the v of the earth, for
Rev 14:19 gathered the v of the earth

VINEDRESSER (*see* VINE, VINEDRESSERS)
John 15: 1 vine, and My Father is the v

VINEDRESSERS (*see* VINEDRESSER)
2Ki 25:12 of the poor of the land as v
2Ch 26:10 and v in the mountains and in
Is 61: 5 be your plowmen and your v
Jer 52:16 of the poor of the land as v
Joel 1:11 you farmers, wail, you v
Matt 21:33 And he leased it to v and went
Matt 21:34 he sent his servants to the v
Matt 21:35 the v took his servants, beat
Matt 21:38 But when the v saw the son
Matt 21:40 what will he do to those v
Matt 21:41 v who will render to him the
Mark 12: 1 And he leased it to v and went
Mark 12: 2 he sent a servant to the v
Mark 12: 2 of the vineyard from the v
Mark 12: 7 But those v said among
Mark 12: 9 He will come and destroy the v
Luke 20: 9 a vineyard, leased it to v
Luke 20:10 he sent a servant to the v
Luke 20:10 But the v beat him and sent
Luke 20:14 But when the v saw him, they
Luke 20:16 will come and destroy those v

VINEGAR
Num 6: 3 he shall drink neither v made
Num 6: 3 nor v made from similar drink
Ruth 2:14 your piece of bread in the v
Ps 69:21 they gave me v to drink
Prov 10:26 As v to the teeth and smoke to
Prov 25:20 like v on soda, is one who

VINES (*see* VINE)
Num 20: 5 or figs or v or pomegranates
Deut 8: 8 land of wheat and barley, of v
Ps 78:47 destroyed their v with hail
Ps 105:33 He struck their v also, and
Song 2:13 the v with the tender grapes
Song 2:15 little foxes that spoil the v
Song 2:15 for our v have tender grapes
Is 7:23 there could be a thousand v
Jer 5:17 they shall eat up your v and
Jer 31: 5 You shall yet plant v on the
Hos 2:12 And I will destroy her v and
Hab 3:17 nor fruit be on the v

VINEYARD (*see* VINE, VINEYARDS)
Gen 9:20 a farmer, and he planted a v
Ex 22: 5 a field or v to be grazed
Ex 22: 5 and the best of his own v
Ex 23:11 you shall do with your v and
Lev 19:10 And you shall not glean your v
Lev 19:10 gather every grape of your v
Lev 25: 3 years you shall prune your v
Lev 25: 4 your field nor prune your v
Deut 20: 6 is there who has planted a v
Deut 22: 9 You shall not sow your v with
Deut 22: 9 fruit of your v be defiled
Deut 23:24 come into your neighbor's v
Deut 24:21 gather the grapes of your v
Deut 28:30 you shall plant a v, but
1Ki 21: 1 had a v which was in Jezreel
1Ki 21: 2 Give me your v, that I may
1Ki 21: 2 give you a v better than it
1Ki 21: 6 Give me your v for money
1Ki 21: 6 give you another v for it
1Ki 21: 6 I will not give you my v
1Ki 21: 7 I will give you the v of
1Ki 21:15 take possession of the v of
1Ki 21:16 v of Naboth the Jezreelite
1Ki 21:18 in the v of Naboth, where he
Job 24: 6 glean in the v of the wicked
Ps 80:15 the v which Your right hand
Prov 24:30 by the v of the man devoid of
Prov 31:16 her profits she plants a v
Song 1: 6 but my own v I have not kept
Song 8:11 Solomon had a v at Baal Hamon
Song 8:11 he leased the v to keepers
Song 8:12 My own v is before me
Is 1: 8 is left as a booth in a v
Is 3:14 For you have eaten up the v
Is 5: 1 of my Beloved regarding His v
Is 5: 1 my Well-beloved has a v On a
Is 5: 3 please, between Me and My v
Is 5: 4 v that I have not done in it
Is 5: 5 you what I will do to My v
Is 5: 7 For the v of the LORD of
Is 5:10 For ten acres of v shall
Is 27: 2 to her, A v of red wine
Jer 12:10 rulers have destroyed My v
Jer 35: 7 a house, sow seed, plant a v
Jer 35: 9 nor do we have v, field, or
Mic 1: 6 places for planting a v
Matt 20: 1 to hire laborers for his v
Matt 20: 2 day, he sent them into his v
Matt 20: 4 them, 'You also go into the v
Matt 20: 7 them, 'You also go into the v
Matt 20: 8 the owner of the v said to
Matt 21:28 Son, go, work today in my v
Matt 21:33 landowner who planted a v
Matt 21:39 him, and cast him out of the v
Matt 21:40 when the owner of the v comes
Matt 21:41 and lease his v to other
Mark 12: 1 A man planted a v and set a
Mark 12: 2 the v from the vinedressers
Mark 12: 8 him and cast him out of the v
Mark 12: 9 will the owner of the v do
Mark 12: 9 and give the v to others
Luke 13: 6 a fig tree planted in his v
Luke 13: 7 said to the keeper of his v
Luke 20: 9 A certain man planted a v
Luke 20:10 some of the fruit of the v

Luke 20:13 Then the owner of the v said
Luke 20:15 So they cast him out of the v
Luke 20:15 the owner of the v do to them
Luke 20:16 and give the v to others
1Co 9: 7 Who plants a v and does not

VINEYARDS (*see* VINEYARD)
Num 16:14 us inheritance of fields and v
Num 20:17 not pass through fields or v
Num 21:22 turn aside into fields or v
Num 22:24 a narrow path between the v
Deut 6:11 which you did not dig, v and
Deut 28:39 You shall plant v and tend
Josh 24:13 you eat of the v and olive
Judg 9:27 gathered grapes from their v
Judg 14: 5 and came to the v of Timnah
Judg 15: 5 grain, as well as the v and
Judg 21:20 Go, lie in wait in the v,
Judg 21:21 then come out from the v
1Sa 8:14 best of your fields, your v
1Sa 22: 7 every one of you fields and v
2Ki 5:26 clothing, olive groves and v
2Ki 18:32 wine, a land of bread and v
2Ki 19:29 year sow and reap, plant v
1Ch 27:27 the Ramathite was over the v
1Ch 27:27 the v for the supply of wine
Neh 5: 3 have mortgaged our lands and v
Neh 5: 4 king's tax on our lands and v
Neh 5: 5 other men have our lands and v
Neh 5:11 day, their lands, their v
Neh 9:25 cisterns already dug, v,
Job 24:18 turn into the way of their v
Ps 107:37 And sow fields and plant v,
Eccl 2: 4 houses, and planted myself v
Song 1: 6 made me the keeper of the v
Song 1:14 blooms in the v of En Gedi
Song 7:12 Let us get up early to the v
Is 16:10 in the v there will be no
Is 36:17 wine, a land of bread and v
Is 37:30 year sow and reap, plant v
Is 65:21 they shall plant v and eat
Jer 32:15 v shall be possessed again in
Jer 39:10 had nothing, and gave them v
Ezek 28:26 build houses, and plant v
Hos 2:15 give her her v from there
Amos 4: 9 gardens increased, your v
Amos 5:11 you have planted pleasant v
Amos 5:17 In all v there shall be
Amos 9:14 they shall plant v and drink
Zeph 1:13 they shall plant v, but not

VINTAGE (*see* VINTAGE-TIME)
Lev 26: 5 shall last till the time of v
Lev 26: 5 the v shall last till the
Judg 8: 2 better than the v of Abiezer
1Sa 8:15 tenth of your grain and your v
Is 24:13 of grapes when the v is done
Is 32:10 for the v will fail, the
Jer 48:32 your summer fruit and your v
Mic 7: 1 like those who glean v grapes

VINTAGE-TIME (*see* VINTAGE)
Matt 21:34 Now when v drew near, he sent
Mark 12: 2 Now at v he sent a servant to
Luke 20:10 Now at v he sent a servant to

VIOLATE (*see* VIOLATED, VIOLATES)
Ezek 22:10 in you they v women who are

VIOLATED (*see* VIOLATE)
Gen 34: 2 her and lay with her, and v her
Ezek 22:26 Her priests have v My law

VIOLATES (*see* VIOLATE)
Ezek 22:11 another in you v his sister

VIOLENCE (*see* VIOLENT)
Gen 6:11 the earth was filled with v
Gen 6:13 is filled with v through them
2Sa 22: 3 my Savior, You save me from v
Job 16:17 although no v is in my hands,
Ps 11: 5 who loves v His soul hates
Ps 27:12 me, And such as breathe out v
Ps 55: 9 tongues, For I have seen v
Ps 58: 2 You weigh out the v of your
Ps 72:14 life from oppression and v
Ps 73: 6 V covers them like a garment
Prov 4:17 and drink the wine of v
Prov 10: 6 but v covers the mouth of the
Prov 10:11 but v covers the mouth of the
Prov 13: 2 of the unfaithful feeds on v
Prov 21: 7 The v of the wicked will
Prov 24: 2 for their heart devises v
Prov 26: 6 off his own feet and drinks v
Is 53: 9 because He had done no v
Is 59: 6 and the act of v is in their
Is 60:18 V shall no longer be heard in
Jer 6: 7 V and plundering are heard in
Jer 20: 8 I shouted, "V and plunder!"
Jer 22: 3 do no v to the stranger, the
Jer 22:17 and practicing oppression and v
Jer 51:35 Let the v done to me and my
Jer 51:46 v in the land, ruler against
Lam 2: 6 He has done v to His
Ezek 7:11 V has risen up into a rod of
Ezek 7:23 and the city is full of v
Ezek 8:17 have filled the land with v
Ezek 12:19 because of the v of all those
Ezek 18: 7 has robbed no one by v, but
Ezek 18:12 poor and needy, robbed by v
Ezek 18:16 a pledge, nor robbed by v
Ezek 18:18 robbed his brother by v, and
Ezek 28:16 became filled with v within
Ezek 45: 9 Remove v and plundering,
Joel 3:19 because of v against the
Amos 3:10 the LORD, Who store up v
Amos 6: 3 the seat of v to come near
Obad 10 For your v against your
Jon 3: 8 from the v that is in his
Mic 2: 2 fields and take them by v,
Mic 6:12 her rich men are full of v
Hab 1: 2 even cry out to You, V!"
Hab 1: 3 plundering and v are before me
Hab 1: 9 They all come for v
Hab 2: 8 the v of the land and the city
Hab 2:17 For the v done to Lebanon
Hab 2:17 the v of the land and the city
Zeph 1: 9 their masters' houses with v
Zeph 3: 4 they have done v to the law
Mal 2:16 covers one's garment with v
Matt 11:12 kingdom of heaven suffers v
Acts 5:26 and brought them without v
Acts 21:35 because of the v of the mob
Acts 24: 7 with great v took him out of
Acts 27:41 up by the v of the waves
Heb 11:34 quenched the v of fire,
Rev 18:21 Thus with v the great city

VIOLENT (*see* VIOLENCE, VIOLENTLY)
2Sa 22:49 delivered me from the v man
Ps 7:16 his v dealing shall come down
Ps 18:48 delivered me from the v man
Ps 86:14 a mob of v men have sought my
Ps 140: 1 Preserve me from v men,
Ps 140: 4 Preserve me from v men, Who
Ps 140:11 Let evil hunt the v man to
Prov 16:29 A v man entices his neighbor,
Eccl 5: 8 the v perversion of justice
Jer 23:19 a v whirlwind
Dan 11:14 also certain v men of your
Matt 11:12 and the v take it by force
Acts 14: 5 when a v attempt was made by
Rom 1:30 backbiters, haters of God, v
1Ti 3: 3 not given to wine, not v, not
Tit 1: 7 not given to wine, not v

VIOLENTLY (*see* VIOLENT)
Deut 28:31 your donkey shall be v taken
Job 20:19 he has v seized a house which
Job 24: 2 they seize flocks v and feed
Ps 118:13 You pushed me v, that I might
Is 22:17 LORD will throw you away v
Is 22:18 He will surely turn v and toss
Is 24:19 The earth is v broken, the
Jer 23:19 It will fall v on the head of
Jer 30:23 it will fall v on the head of
Matt 8:32 v down the steep place into
Mark 5:13 the herd ran v down the steep
Luke 8:33 the herd ran v down the steep

VIPER (*see* VIPER'S, VIPERS)
Gen 49:17 a v by the path, that bites
Prov 23:32 a serpent, and stings like a v
Is 14:29 roots will come forth a v
Is 30: 6 the lioness and lion, the v
Is 59: 5 is crushed a v breaks out
Acts 28: 3 a v came out because of the

VIPER'S (*see* VIPER)
Job 20:16 the v tongue will slay him
Is 11: 8 put his hand in the v den

VIPERS (*see* VIPER)
Is 59: 5 They hatch v' eggs and weave
Jer 8:17 v which cannot be charmed, and
Matt 3: 7 he said to them, Brood of v!
Matt 12:34 Brood of v! How can you,
Matt 23:33 Serpents, brood of v
Luke 3: 7 Brood of v! Who warned you

VIRGIN (*see* VIRGINITY, VIRGIN'S)
Gen 24:16 very beautiful to behold, a v
Gen 24:43 the v comes out to draw water
Ex 22:16 if a man entices a v who is
Lev 21: 3 also his v sister who is
Lev 21:14 but he shall take a v of his
Deut 22:14 her I found she was not a v
Deut 22:17 your daughter was not a v
Deut 22:19 a bad name on a v of Israel
Deut 22:23 a v is betrothed to a husband
Deut 22:28 a young woman who is a v, who
Deut 32:25 within for the young man and v
Judg 19:24 Look, here is my v daughter
2Sa 13: 2 for she was a v
2Sa 13:18 for the king's v daughters
1Ki 1: 2 Let a young woman, a v, be
2Ki 19:21 The v, the daughter of Zion,
2Ch 36:17 compassion on young man or v
Prov 30:19 and the way of a man with a v
Is 7:14 the v shall conceive and bear
Is 23:12 O you oppressed v daughter of
Is 37:22 The v, the daughter of Zion,
Is 47: 1 dust, O v daughter of Babylon
Is 62: 5 as a young man marries a v
Jer 2:32 Can a v forget her ornaments,
Jer 14:17 for the v daughter of my
Jer 18:13 The v of Israel has done a
Jer 31: 4 be rebuilt, O v of Israel
Jer 31:13 Then shall the v rejoice in
Jer 31:21 O v of Israel, turn back to
Jer 46:11 to Gilead and take balm, O v
Lam 1:15 the v daughter of Judah
Lam 2:13 you, O v daughter of Zion
Ezek 23: 3 their v bosom was there
Ezek 23: 8 with her, pressed her v bosom
Joel 1: 8 Lament like a v girded with
Amos 5: 2 The v of Israel has fallen
Matt 1:23 a v shall be with child, and
Luke 1:27 to a v betrothed to a man
Acts 21: 9 Now this man had four v
1Co 7:28 if a v marries, she has not
1Co 7:34 between a wife and a v
1Co 7:36 improperly toward his v, if
1Co 7:37 heart that he will keep his v
2Co 11: 2 you as a chaste v to Christ

VIRGINITY (*see* VIRGIN)
Lev 21:13 he shall take a wife in her v
Deut 22:15 of the young woman's v to the
Deut 22:17 evidences of my daughter's v
Deut 22:20 evidences of v are not found
Judg 11:37 the mountains and bewail my v
Judg 11:38 and bewailed her v on the
Luke 2:36 seven years from her v

VIRGIN'S (*see* VIRGIN)
Luke 1:27 The v name was Mary

VIRGINS (*see* VIRGIN)
Ex 22:17 to the bride-price of v
Judg 21:12 v who had not known a man
Esth 2: 2 Let beautiful young v be
Esth 2: 3 v to Shushan the citadel,
Esth 2:17 his sight more than all the v
Esth 2:19 When v were gathered together
Ps 45:14 The v, her companions who
Song 1: 3 therefore the v love you
Song 6: 8 and v without number
Is 23: 4 young men, nor bring up v
Lam 1: 4 her v are afflicted, and she
Lam 1:18 my v and my young men have
Lam 2:10 The v of Jerusalem bow their
Lam 2:21 my v and my young men have
Ezek 44:22 but take v of the descendants
Amos 8:13 In that day the fair v and
Matt 25: 1 to ten v who took their lamps
Matt 25: 7 Then all those v arose and
Matt 25:11 the other v came also, saying
1Co 7:25 Now concerning v: I have no
Rev 14: 4 with women, for they are v

VIRTUE (*see* VIRTUOUS)
Phil 4: 8 report, if there is any v
2Pe 1: 3 who called us by glory and v
2Pe 1: 5 your faith v, to v knowledge

VIRTUOUS (*see* VIRTUE)
Ruth 3:11 know that you are a v woman
Prov 31:10 Who can find a v wife

VISAGE (*see* VISION)
Is 52:14 so His v was marred more than

VISIBLE (*see* VISION)
Col 1:16 and that are on earth, v and
Heb 11: 3 made of things which are v

VISION (*see* VISAGE, VISIBLE, VISIONS)
Gen 15: 1 the LORD came to Abram in a v
Num 12: 6 Myself known to him in a v
Num 24: 4 of God, who sees the v of the
Num 24:16 High, who sees the v of the
1Sa 3:15 was afraid to tell Eli the v
2Sa 7:17 and according to all this v
1Ch 17:15 and according to all this v
2Ch 32:32 the v of Isaiah the prophet
Job 20: 8 away like a v of the night
Job 33:15 in a v of the night, when
Ps 89:19 spoke in a v to Your holy one
Is 1: 1 The v of Isaiah the son of
Is 21: 2 a distressing v is declared
Is 22: 1 against the Valley of V
Is 22: 5 of hosts in the Valley of V
Is 28: 7 they err in v, they stumble
Is 29: 7 be as a dream of a night v
Is 29:11 The whole v has become to you
Jer 14:14 prophesy to you a false v
Jer 23:16 they speak a v of their own
Lam 2: 9 find no v from the LORD
Ezek 7:13 for the v concerns the whole
Ezek 7:26 will seek a v from a prophet
Ezek 8: 4 like the v that I saw in the
Ezek 11:24 and brought me in a v by the
Ezek 11:24 the v that I had seen went up
Ezek 12:22 prolonged, and every v fails'
Ezek 12:23 and the fulfillment of every v
Ezek 12:24 v or flattering divination
Ezek 12:27 The v that he sees is for
Ezek 13: 7 Have you not seen a futile v
Ezek 43: 3 of the v which I saw
Ezek 43: 3 like the v which I saw when I
Ezek 43: 3 v which I saw by the River
Dan 2:19 to Daniel in a night v
Dan 7: 2 I saw in my v by night, and
Dan 8: 1 Belshazzar a v appeared to me
Dan 8: 2 I saw in the v, and it so
Dan 8: 2 I saw in the v that I was by
Dan 8:13 How long will the v be,
Dan 8:15 I, Daniel, had seen the v
Dan 8:16 this man understand the v
Dan 8:17 that the v refers to the time
Dan 8:26 And the v of the evenings and
Dan 8:26 therefore seal up the v, for
Dan 8:27 I was astonished by the v
Dan 9:21 in the v at the beginning
Dan 9:23 matter, and understand the v
Dan 9:24 righteousness, to seal up v
Dan 10: 1 and had understanding of the v
Dan 10: 7 And I, Daniel, alone saw the v
Dan 10: 7 with me did not see the v
Dan 10: 8 alone when I saw this great v
Dan 10:14 for the v refers to many days
Dan 10:16 because of the v my sorrows
Dan 11:14 in fulfillment of the v, but
Obad 1 The v of Obadiah
Mic 3: 6 shall have night without v
Nah 1: 1 The book of the v of Nahum
Hab 2: 2 Write the v and make it plain
Hab 2: 3 For the v is yet for an
Zech 13: 4 of his v when he prophesies
Matt 17: 9 Tell the v to no one until
Luke 1:22 he had seen a v in the temple
Luke 24:23 a v of angels who said He was
Acts 9:10 to him the Lord said in a v
Acts 9:12 And in a v he has seen a man
Acts 10: 3 a v an angel of God coming in
Acts 10:17 v which he had seen meant
Acts 10:19 Peter thought about the v
Acts 11: 5 and in a trance I saw a v, an
Acts 12: 9 but thought he was seeing a v
Acts 16: 9 a v appeared to Paul in the
Acts 16:10 Now after he had seen the v
Acts 18: 9 to Paul in the night by a v
Acts 26:19 disobedient to the heavenly v
Rev 9:17 I saw the horses in the v

VISIONS (*see* VISION)
Gen 46: 2 Israel in the v of the night
2Ch 9:29 in the v of Iddo the seer
2Ch 26: 5 understanding in the v of God
Job 4:13 from the v of the night, when
Job 7:14 dreams and terrify me with v
Lam 2:14 for you false and deceptive v
Ezek 1: 1 were opened and I saw v of God
Ezek 8: 3 brought me in v of God to
Ezek 13:16 who see v of peace for her
Ezek 21:29 while they see vain v for you
Ezek 22:28 mortar, seeing false v, and
Ezek 40: 2 In the v of God He took me
Ezek 43: 3 The v were like the vision
Dan 1:17 had understanding in all v
Dan 2:28 the v of your head upon your
Dan 4: 5 the v of my head troubled me
Dan 4: 9 explain to me the v of my
Dan 4:10 These were the v of my head
Dan 4:13 I saw in the v of my head
Dan 7: 1 v of his head while on his
Dan 7: 7 this I saw in the night v
Dan 7:13 I was watching in the night v
Dan 7:15 the v of my head troubled me
Hos 12:10 and have multiplied v
Joel 2:28 your young men shall see v
Acts 2:17 your young men shall see v
2Co 12: 1 I will come to v and

VISIT (*see* VISITATION, VISITED, VISITING, VISITORS)
Gen 50:24 but God will surely v you
Gen 50:25 God will surely v you, and you
Ex 13:19 God will surely v you, and you
Ex 32:34 day when I v for punishment
Ex 32:34 I will v punishment upon them
Lev 18:25 therefore I v the punishment
1Ki 22: 2 down to v the king of Israel
2Ch 18: 2 down to v Ahab in Samaria
Job 5:24 You shall v your habitation
Job 7:18 that You should v him every
Ps 8: 4 the son of man that You v him
Ps 65: 9 You v the earth and water it,
Ps 80:14 heaven and see, And v this vine
Ps 89:32 Then I will v their
Ps 106: 4 v me with Your salvation,
Is 23:17 that the LORD will v Tyre
Jer 3:16 it, nor shall they v it, nor
Jer 15:15 v me, and take vengeance for
Jer 27:22 until the day that I v them
Jer 29:10 at Babylon, I will v you and
Jer 32: 5 he shall be until I v him
Amos 3:14 I will also v destruction on
Zech 10: 3 of hosts will v His flock
Matt 25:43 in prison and you did not v Me
Acts 7:23 his heart to v his brethren
Acts 15:36 v our brethren in every city
Acts 24:23 to provide for or v him
Jas 1:27 to v orphans and widows in

VISITATION (*see* VISIT)
Luke 19:44 not know the time of your v
1Pe 2:12 glorify God in the day of v

VISITED (*see* VISIT)
Gen 21: 1 the LORD v Sarah as He had
Gen 38: 1 v a certain Adullamite whose
Ex 3:16 I have surely v you and seen
Ex 4:31 had v the children of Israel
Num 16:29 men, or if they are v by the
Judg 15: 1 it happened that Samson v his
Ruth 1: 6 v His people in giving them
1Sa 2:21 And the LORD v Hannah, so that
Ps 17: 3 You have v me in the night
Prov 19:23 he will not be v with evil
Is 26:16 in trouble they have v You
Ezek 38: 8 After many days you will be v
Matt 25:36 I was sick and you v Me
Luke 1:68 God of Israel, for He has v
Luke 1:78 from on high has v us
Luke 7:16 and, "God has v His people
Acts 15:14 how God at the first v the

VISITING (*see* VISIT)
Ex 20: 5 v the iniquity of the fathers
Ex 34: 7 v the iniquity of the fathers
Num 14:18 v the iniquity of the fathers
Deut 5: 9 v the iniquity of the fathers

VISITORS (*see* VISIT)
Acts 2:10 v from Rome, both Jews and

VITALITY
Ps 32: 4 My v was turned into the

VOICE (*see* VOICES)
Gen 3:10 I heard Your v in the garden,
Gen 3:17 heeded the v of your wife
Gen 4:10 The v of your brother's blood
Gen 4:23 Adah and Zillah, hear my v
Gen 16: 2 Abram heeded the v of Sarai
Gen 21:12 said to you, listen to her v
Gen 21:16 opposite him, and lifted her v
Gen 21:17 And God heard the v of the lad
Gen 21:17 for God has heard the v of
Gen 22:18 because you have obeyed My v
Gen 26: 5 because Abraham obeyed My v
Gen 27: 8 obey my v according to what I
Gen 27:13 only obey my v, and go, get
Gen 27:22 The v is Jacob's v, but
Gen 27:38 And Esau lifted up his v
Gen 27:43 therefore, my son, obey my v
Gen 29:11 Rachel, and lifted up his v
Gen 30: 6 and He has also heard my v
Gen 39:14 and I cried out with a loud v
Gen 39:15 he heard that I lifted my v
Gen 39:18 it happened, as I lifted my v
Ex 3:18 Then they will heed your v
Ex 4: 1 believe me or listen to my v
Ex 4: 9 signs, or listen to your v
Ex 5: 2 obey His v to let Israel go
Ex 15:26 the v of the LORD your God
Ex 18:19 Listen now to my v
Ex 18:24 So Moses heeded the v of his
Ex 19: 5 if you will indeed obey My v
Ex 19:19 and God answered him by v
Ex 23:21 Beware of Him and obey His v
Ex 23:22 But if you indeed obey His v
Ex 24: 3 people answered with one v
Ex 32:18 It is not the v of those who
Ex 32:18 nor is it the v of those who
Ex 32:18 but the v of those who sing
Num 7:89 Him, he heard the v of One
Num 14:22 and have not heeded My v,
Num 20:16 to the LORD, He heard our v
Num 21: 3 listened to the v of Israel
Deut 1:45 to your v nor give ear to you
Deut 4:12 you only heard a v
Deut 4:30 LORD your God and obey His v
Deut 4:33 any people ever hear the v of
Deut 4:36 heaven He let you hear His v
Deut 5:22 thick darkness, with a loud v
Deut 5:23 when you heard the v from the
Deut 5:24 we have heard His v from the
Deut 5:25 if we hear the v of the LORD
Deut 5:26 v of the living God speaking
Deut 5:28 the v of your words when you
Deut 5:28 I have heard the v of the
Deut 8:20 to the v of the LORD your God
Deut 9:23 believe Him nor obey His v
Deut 13: 4 commandments and obey His v
Deut 13:18 to the v of the LORD your God
Deut 15: 5 the v of the LORD your God
Deut 18:16 the v of the LORD my God, nor
Deut 21:18 son who will not obey the v
Deut 21:18 father or the v of his mother
Deut 21:20 he will not obey our v
Deut 26: 7 and the LORD heard our v and
Deut 26:14 I have obeyed the v of the
Deut 26:17 and that you will obey His v
Deut 27:10 you shall obey the v of the
Deut 27:14 shall speak with a loud v
Deut 28: 1 the v of the LORD your God
Deut 28: 2 the v of the LORD your God
Deut 28:15 the v of the LORD your God
Deut 28:45 the v of the LORD your God
Deut 28:62 the v of the LORD your God
Deut 30: 2 LORD your God and obey His v
Deut 30: 8 again obey the v of the LORD
Deut 30:10 if you obey the v of the LORD
Deut 30:20 God, that you may obey His v
Deut 33: 7 the v of Judah, and bring him
Josh 5: 6 not obey the v of the LORD
Josh 6:10 or make any noise with your v
Josh 10:14 LORD heeded the v of a man
Josh 22: 2 have obeyed my v in all that
Josh 24:24 serve, and His v we will obey
Judg 2: 2 But you have not obeyed My v
Judg 2: 4 the people lifted up their v
Judg 2:20 and has not heeded My v,
Judg 6:10 But you have not obeyed My v
Judg 9: 7 Gerizim, and lifted his v and
Judg 13: 9 listened to the v of Manoah
Judg 18: 3 the v of the young Levite
Judg 18:25 Do not let your v be heard
Judg 20:13 to the v of their brethren
1Sa 1:13 but her v was not heard
1Sa 2:25 heed the v of their father
1Sa 8: 7 Heed the v of the people in
1Sa 8: 9 Now therefore, heed their v

1Sa 8:19 to obey the v of Samuel
1Sa 8:22 Heed their v, and make them a
1Sa 12: 1 Indeed I have heeded your v
1Sa 12:14 and serve Him and obey His v
1Sa 12:15 do not obey the v of the LORD
1Sa 15: 1 heed the v of the words of
1Sa 15:19 not obey the v of the LORD
1Sa 15:20 have obeyed the v of the LORD
1Sa 15:22 in obeying the v of the LORD
1Sa 15:24 the people and obeyed their v
1Sa 19: 6 Saul heeded the v of Jonathan
1Sa 24:16 Is this your v, my son David
1Sa 24:16 And Saul lifted his v and
1Sa 25:35 See, I have heeded your v
1Sa 26:17 Then Saul knew David's v, and
1Sa 26:17 Is that your v, my son David
1Sa 26:17 It is my v, my lord, O king
1Sa 28:12 she cried out with a loud v
1Sa 28:18 you did not obey the v of the
1Sa 28:21 maidservant has obeyed your v
1Sa 28:22 heed also the v of your
1Sa 28:23 and he heeded their v
2Sa 3:32 and the king lifted up his v
2Sa 12:18 and he would not heed our v
2Sa 13:14 he would not heed her v
2Sa 13:36 and they lifted up their v
2Sa 15:23 country wept with a loud v
2Sa 19: 4 king cried out with a loud v
2Sa 19:35 longer the v of singing men
2Sa 22: 7 He heard my v from His temple
2Sa 22:14 the Most High uttered His v
1Ki 8:55 of Israel with a loud v,
1Ki 17:22 LORD heard the v of Elijah
1Ki 18:26 But there was no v
1Ki 18:29 But there was no v
1Ki 19:12 the fire a still small v
1Ki 19:13 suddenly a v came to him, and
1Ki 20:25 And he listened to their v
1Ki 20:36 not obeyed the v of the LORD
2Ki 4:31 was neither v nor hearing
2Ki 10: 6 me, and if you will obey my v
2Ki 18:12 the v of the LORD their God
2Ki 18:28 out with a loud v in Hebrew
2Ki 19:22 whom have you raised your v
1Ch 15:16 by raising the v with
2Ch 5:13 up their v with the trumpets
2Ch 15:14 before the LORD with a loud v
2Ch 30:27 people, and their v was heard
2Ch 32:18 v in Hebrew to the people of
Ezra 3:12 wept with a loud v when the
Ezra 10:12 and said with a loud v, "Yes
Neh 9: 4 loud v to the LORD their God
Job 3:18 hear the v of the oppressor
Job 4:10 the v of the fierce lion, and
Job 4:16 then I heard a v saying
Job 9:16 that He was listening to my v
Job 29:10 the v of nobles was hushed,
Job 30:31 my flute to the v of those
Job 37: 2 the thunder of His v, and the
Job 37: 4 After it a v roars
Job 37: 4 thunders with His majestic v
Job 37: 4 them when His v is heard
Job 37: 5 marvelously with His v
Job 38:34 lift up your v to the clouds
Job 40: 9 you thunder with a v like His
Ps 3: 4 I cried to the LORD with my v
Ps 5: 2 Give heed to the v of my cry
Ps 5: 3 My v You shall hear in the
Ps 6: 8 has heard the v of my weeping
Ps 18: 6 He heard my v from His temple
Ps 18:13 the Most High uttered His v
Ps 19: 3 Where their v is not heard
Ps 26: 7 with the v of thanksgiving
Ps 27: 7 O LORD, when I cry with my v
Ps 28: 2 Hear the v of my
Ps 28: 6 the v of my supplications
Ps 29: 3 The v of the LORD is over the
Ps 29: 4 The v of the LORD is powerful
Ps 29: 4 The v of the LORD is full of
Ps 29: 5 The v of the LORD breaks the
Ps 29: 7 The v of the LORD divides the
Ps 29: 8 The v of the LORD shakes the
Ps 29: 9 The v of the LORD makes the
Ps 31:22 v of my supplications When I
Ps 42: 4 of God, With the v of joy
Ps 44:16 Because of the v of him who
Ps 46: 6 He uttered His v, the earth
Ps 47: 1 to God with the v of triumph
Ps 55: 3 Because of the v of the enemy
Ps 55:17 aloud, And He shall hear my v
Ps 58: 5 not heed the v of charmers
Ps 64: 1 Hear my v, O God, in my
Ps 66: 8 make the v of His praise to
Ps 66:19 to the v of my prayer
Ps 68:33 sends out His v, a mighty v
Ps 74:23 forget the v of Your enemies
Ps 77: 1 I cried out to God with my v
Ps 77: 1 To God with my v
Ps 77:18 The v of Your thunder was in
Ps 81:11 My people would not heed My v
Ps 86: 6 And attend to the v of my
Ps 93: 3 floods have lifted up their v
Ps 95: 7 Today, if you will hear His v
Ps 103:20 Heeding the v of His word
Ps 104: 7 At the v of Your thunder they
Ps 106:25 not heed the v of the LORD
Ps 116: 1 because He has heard My v
Ps 118:15 The v of rejoicing and
Ps 119:149 Hear my v according to Your
Ps 130: 2 Lord, hear my v
Ps 130: 2 To the v of my supplications
Ps 140: 6 Hear the v of my
Ps 141: 1 Give ear to my v when I cry
Ps 142: 1 cry out to the LORD with my v
Ps 142: 1 With my v to the LORD I make
Prov 1:20 she raises her v in the open
Prov 2: 3 and lift up your v for
Prov 5:13 obeyed the v of my teachers
Prov 8: 1 understanding lift up her v
Prov 8: 4 my v is to the sons of men
Prov 27:14 his friend with a loud v,
Eccl 5: 3 a fool's v is known by his
Eccl 10:20 of the air may carry your v
Song 2: 8 The v of my beloved
Song 2:12 the v of the turtledove is
Song 2:14 let me hear your v
Song 2:14 for your v is sweet, and your
Song 5: 2 it is the v of my beloved
Song 8:13 companions listen for your v
Is 6: 4 by the v of him who cried out
Is 6: 8 I heard the v of the Lord
Is 10:30 Lift up your v, O daughter of
Is 13: 2 raise your v to them
Is 15: 4 their v shall be heard as far
Is 24:14 They shall lift up their v
Is 28:23 Give ear and hear my v, listen
Is 29: 4 Your v shall be like a
Is 30:30 His glorious v to be heard
Is 30:31 For through the v of the LORD
Is 31: 4 v nor be disturbed by their
Is 32: 9 who are at ease, hear my v
Is 36:13 out with a loud v in Hebrew
Is 37:23 whom have you raised your v
Is 40: 3 The v of one crying in the
Is 40: 6 The v said, "Cry out
Is 40: 9 lift up your v with strength,
Is 42: 2 not cry out, nor raise His v
Is 42: 2 nor cause His v to be heard
Is 42:11 and its cities lift up their v
Is 48:20 With a v of singing, declare,
Is 50:10 Who obeys the v of His
Is 51: 3 and the v of melody
Is 58: 1 lift up your v like a trumpet
Is 58: 4 to make your v heard on high
Is 65:19 the v of weeping shall no
Is 65:19 in her, nor the v of crying
Is 66: 6 A v from the temple
Is 66: 6 The v of the LORD, Who fully
Jer 3:13 and you have not obeyed My v
Jer 3:21 A v was heard on the desolate
Jer 3:25 the v of the LORD our God
Jer 4:15 For a v declares from Dan and
Jer 4:16 raise their v against the
Jer 4:31 For I have heard a v as of a
Jer 4:31 the v of the daughter of Zion
Jer 6:23 their v roars like the sea
Jer 7:23 them, saying, 'Obey My v, and
Jer 7:28 that does not obey the v of
Jer 7:34 of Jerusalem the v of mirth
Jer 7:34 the v of gladness
Jer 7:34 the v of the bridegroom and
Jer 7:34 and the v of the bride
Jer 8:19 The v, the cry of the
Jer 9:10 men hear the v of the cattle
Jer 9:13 them, and have not obeyed My v
Jer 9:19 For a v of wailing is heard
Jer 10:13 When He utters His v, there
Jer 11: 4 furnace, saying, 'Obey My v
Jer 11: 7 saying, "Obey My v."
Jer 16: 9 the v of mirth and
Jer 16: 9 the v of gladness
Jer 16: 9 the v of the bridegroom and
Jer 16: 9 and the v of the bride
Jer 18:10 so that it does not obey My v
Jer 18:19 listen to the v of those who
Jer 22:20 and lift up your v in Bashan
Jer 22:21 that you did not obey My v
Jer 25:10 take from them the v of mirth
Jer 25:10 the v of gladness
Jer 25:10 the v of the bridegroom and
Jer 25:10 the v of the bride, the sound
Jer 25:30 utter His v from His holy
Jer 25:36 A v of the cry of the
Jer 26:13 obey the v of the LORD your
Jer 30: 5 have heard a v of trembling
Jer 30:19 the v of those who make merry
Jer 31:15 A v was heard in Ramah,
Jer 31:16 Refrain your v from weeping
Jer 32:23 Your v or walked in Your law
Jer 33:11 the v of joy and
Jer 33:11 the v of gladness
Jer 33:11 the v of the bridegroom and
Jer 33:11 the v of the bride
Jer 33:11 the v of those who will say
Jer 35: 8 the v of Jonadab the son of
Jer 38:20 obey the v of the LORD which
Jer 40: 3 the LORD, and not obeyed His v
Jer 42: 6 we will obey the v of the
Jer 42: 6 the v of the LORD our God
Jer 42:13 disobeying the v of the LORD
Jer 42:21 the v of the LORD your God
Jer 43: 4 not obey the v of the LORD
Jer 43: 7 not obey the v of the LORD
Jer 44:23 have not obeyed the v of the
Jer 48: 3 a v of crying shall be from
Jer 48:34 they have uttered their v
Jer 50:28 The v of those who flee and
Jer 50:42 Their v shall roar like the
Jer 51:16 When He utters His v
Jer 51:55 and silencing her loud v,
Jer 51:55 noise of their v is uttered
Lam 3:56 You have heard my v
Ezek 1:24 like the v of the Almighty, a
Ezek 1:25 A v came from above the
Ezek 1:28 I heard a v of One speaking
Ezek 3:12 me a great thunderous v
Ezek 8:18 cry in My ears with a loud v
Ezek 9: 1 in my hearing with a loud v
Ezek 10: 5 like the v of Almighty God
Ezek 11:13 face and cried with a loud v
Ezek 19: 9 that his v should no longer
Ezek 21:22 to lift the v with shouting,
Ezek 27:30 their v heard because of you
Ezek 33:32 of one who has a pleasant v
Ezek 43: 2 His v was like the sound of
Dan 4:31 mouth, a v fell from heaven
Dan 6:20 with a lamenting v to Daniel
Dan 8:16 I heard a man's v between the
Dan 9:10 the v of the LORD our God
Dan 9:11 so as not to obey Your v
Dan 9:14 we have not obeyed His v
Dan 10: 6 like the v of a multitude
Joel 2:11 The LORD gives v before His
Joel 3:16 utter His v from Jerusalem
Amos 1: 2 utters His v from Jerusalem
Jon 2: 2 I cried, and You heard my v
Jon 2: 9 with the v of thanksgiving
Mic 6: 1 and let the hills hear your v
Mic 6: 9 The LORD's v cries to the
Nah 2: 7 her as with the v of doves
Nah 2:13 and the v of your messengers
Hab 3:10 The deep uttered its v, and
Hab 3:16 my lips quivered at the v
Zeph 2:14 their v shall sing in the
Zeph 3: 2 She has not obeyed His v, she
Hag 1:12 obeyed the v of the LORD
Zech 6:15 the v of the LORD your God
Matt 2:18 A v was heard in Ramah,
Matt 3: 3 The v of one crying in the
Matt 3:17 suddenly a v came from heaven
Matt 12:19 hear His v in the streets
Matt 17: 5 suddenly a v came out of the
Matt 27:46 Jesus cried out with a loud v
Matt 27:50 cried out again with a loud v
Mark 1: 3 The v of one crying in the
Mark 1:11 Then a v came from heaven,
Mark 1:26 and cried out with a loud v
Mark 5: 7 And he cried out with a loud v
Mark 9: 7 a v came out of the cloud,
Mark 15:34 Jesus cried out with a loud v

Mark 15:37 Jesus cried out with a loud v
Luke 1:42 she spoke out with a loud v
Luke 1:44 as soon as the v of your
Luke 3: 4 The v of one crying in the
Luke 3:22 a v came from heaven which
Luke 4:33 And he cried out with a loud v
Luke 8:28 Him, and with a loud v said
Luke 9:35 Then a v came out of the
Luke 9:36 when the v had ceased, Jesus
Luke 11:27 from the crowd raised her v
Luke 17:15 with a loud v glorified God,
Luke 19:37 praise God with a loud v for
Luke 23:46 had cried out with a loud v
John 1:23 I am 'The v of one crying in
John 3:29 because of the bridegroom's v
John 5:25 hear the v of the Son of God
John 5:28 in the graves will hear His v
John 5:37 heard His v at any time, nor
John 10: 3 and the sheep hear his v
John 10: 4 him, for they know his v
John 10: 5 not know the v of strangers
John 10:16 bring, and they will hear My v
John 10:27 My sheep hear My v, and I know
John 11:43 He cried with a loud v
John 12:28 Then a v came from heaven,
John 12:30 This v did not come because
John 18:37 is of the truth hears My v
Acts 2:14 with the eleven, raised his v
Acts 4:24 they raised their v to God
Acts 7:31 the v of the Lord came to him
Acts 7:57 they cried out with a loud v
Acts 7:60 and cried out with a loud v
Acts 8: 7 spirits, crying with a loud v
Acts 9: 4 and heard a v saying to him,
Acts 9: 7 hearing a v but seeing no one
Acts 10:13 And a v came to him,
Acts 10:15 a v spoke to him again the
Acts 11: 7 I heard a v saying to me
Acts 11: 9 But the v answered me again
Acts 12:14 When she recognized Peter's v
Acts 12:22 The v of a god and not of a
Acts 14:10 said with a loud v, "Stand
Acts 16:28 But Paul called with a loud v
Acts 19:34 all with one v cried out for
Acts 22: 7 heard a v saying to me, 'Saul
Acts 22: 9 the v of Him who spoke to me
Acts 22:14 and hear the v of His mouth
Acts 26:14 I heard a v speaking to me and
Acts 26:24 Festus said with a loud v
1Th 4:16 with the v of an archangel,
Heb 3: 7 Today, if you will hear His v
Heb 3:15 Today, if you will hear His v
Heb 4: 7 Today, if you will hear His v
Heb 12:19 the v of words, so that those
Heb 12:26 whose v then shook the earth
2Pe 1:17 glory when such a v came to
2Pe 1:18 we heard this v which came
2Pe 2:16 speaking with a man's v
Rev 1:10 and I heard behind me a loud v
Rev 1:12 see the v that spoke with me
Rev 1:15 His v as the sound of many
Rev 3:20 If anyone hears My v and opens
Rev 4: 1 the first v which I heard was
Rev 5: 2 proclaiming with a loud v
Rev 5:11 I heard the v of many angels
Rev 5:12 saying with a loud v
Rev 6: 1 saying with a v like thunder
Rev 6: 6 I heard a v in the midst of
Rev 6: 7 I heard the v of the fourth
Rev 6:10 And they cried with a loud v
Rev 7: 2 he cried with a loud v to the
Rev 7:10 and crying out with a loud v
Rev 8:13 heaven, saying with a loud v
Rev 9:13 I heard a v from the four
Rev 10: 3 and cried with a loud v, as
Rev 10: 4 but I heard a v from heaven
Rev 10: 8 Then the v which I heard from
Rev 11:12 And they heard a loud v from
Rev 12:10 a loud v saying in heaven
Rev 14: 2 I heard a v from heaven, like
Rev 14: 2 like the v of many waters, and
Rev 14: 2 like the v of loud thunder
Rev 14: 7 saying with a loud v, "Fear
Rev 14: 9 them, saying with a loud v
Rev 14:13 Then I heard a v from heaven
Rev 14:15 crying with a loud v to Him
Rev 16: 1 Then I heard a loud v from
Rev 16:17 and a loud v came out of the
Rev 18: 2 cried mightily with a loud v
Rev 18: 4 I heard another v from heaven
Rev 18:23 the v of bridegroom and bride
Rev 19: 1 v of a great multitude in
Rev 19: 5 Then a v came from the throne
Rev 19: 6 the v of a great multitude,
Rev 19:17 and he cried with a loud v
Rev 21: 3 I heard a loud v from heaven

VOICES (*see* VOICE)
Num 14: 1 lifted up their v and cried,
Judg 21: 2 They lifted up their v and
Ruth 1: 9 and they lifted up their v
Ruth 1:14 Then they lifted up their v
1Sa 11: 4 the people lifted up their v
1Sa 30: 4 with him lifted up their v
2Ch 20:19 God of Israel with v loud
Job 2:12 him, they lifted their v and
Is 52: 8 shall lift up their v, with
Is 52: 8 with their v they shall sing
Luke 17:13 And they lifted up their v
Luke 23:23 demanding with loud v that He
Luke 23:23 the v of these men and of the
Acts 13:27 Him, nor even the v of the
Acts 14:11 had done, they raised their v
Acts 22:22 and then they raised their v
Rev 4: 5 lightnings, thunderings, and v
Rev 10: 3 thunders uttered their v
Rev 10: 4 thunders uttered their v, I
Rev 11:15 there were loud v in heaven

VOID
Gen 1: 2 earth was without form, and v
Num 30: 8 he shall make v her vow which
Num 30:12 v on the day he heard them
Num 30:12 her husband has made them v
Num 30:13 or her husband may make it v
Num 30:15 v after he has heard them
Deut 32:28 are a nation v of counsel
Judg 21:15 a v in the tribes of Israel
Ps 119:126 have regarded Your law as v
Is 55:11 it shall not return to Me v
Jer 4:23 it was without form, and v
Jer 19: 7 I will make v the counsel of
Rom 3:31 Do we then make v the law
Rom 4:14 are heirs, faith is made v
1Co 9:15 should make my boasting v

VOLUME
Lev 19:35 of length, weight, or v
Heb 10: 7 in the v of the book it is

VOLUNTARILY (*see* VOLUNTARY)
Deut 23:23 for you v vowed to the LORD

VOLUNTARY (*see* VOLUNTARILY, VOLUNTEER)
Lev 7:16 is a vow or a v offering, it
Ezek 46:12 v burnt offering or
Ezek 46:12 v peace offering to the LORD
Phm 14 compulsion, as it were, but v

VOLUNTEER (*see* VOLUNTARY, VOLUNTEERS)
Ezra 7:13 who v to go up to Jerusalem,

VOLUNTEERS (*see* VOLUNTEER)
Ps 110: 3 Your people shall be v In the

VOMIT (*see* VOMITED, VOMITS)
Lev 18:28 lest the land v you out also
Lev 20:22 to dwell may not v you out
Prov 23: 8 you have eaten, you will v up
Prov 25:16 you be filled with it and v
Prov 26:11 As a dog returns to his own v
Is 19:14 drunken man staggers in his v
Is 28: 8 For all tables are full of v
Jer 25:27 Drink, be drunk, and v
Jer 48:26 Moab shall wallow in his v
2Pe 2:22 A dog returns to his own v

VOMITED (*see* VOMIT)
Lev 18:28 as it v out the nations that
Jon 2:10 and it v Jonah onto dry land

VOMITS (*see* VOMIT)
Lev 18:25 it, and the land v out its
Job 20:15 riches and v them up again

VOPHSI
Num 13:14 Naphtali, Nahbi the son of V

VOTE
Acts 26:10 I cast my v against them

VOW (*see* VOWED, VOWING, VOWS)
Gen 28:20 Then Jacob made a v, saying,
Gen 31:13 and where you made a v to Me
Lev 7:16 of his offering is a v or a
Lev 22:21 to the LORD, to fulfill his v
Lev 22:23 but for a v it shall not be
Lev 27: 2 v certain persons to the LORD
Num 6: 2 to take the v of a Nazirite
Num 6: 5 All the days of the v of his
Num 6:21 to the v which he takes, so
Num 15: 3 to fulfill a v or as a
Num 15: 8 as a sacrifice to fulfill a v
Num 21: 2 Israel made a v to the LORD
Num 30: 2 If a man vows a v to the LORD
Num 30: 3 a woman vows a v to the LORD
Num 30: 4 and her father hears her v
Num 30: 8 void her v which she vowed
Num 30: 9 But any v of a widow or a
Num 30:13 Every v and every binding oath
Deut 12:11 which you v to the LORD
Deut 12:17 of your offerings which you v
Deut 23:21 When you make a v to the LORD
Judg 11:30 Jephthah made a v to the LORD
Judg 11:39 he carried out his v with her
1Sa 1:11 Then she made a v and said
1Sa 1:21 the yearly sacrifice and his v
1Sa 20:17 again caused David to v,
2Sa 15: 7 pay the v which I vowed to
2Sa 15: 8 For your servant vowed a v
Ps 65: 1 And to You the v shall be
Eccl 5: 4 When you make a v to God, do
Eccl 5: 5 better not to v than to v
Is 19:21 will make a v to the LORD
Mal 1:14 flock a male, and makes a v
Acts 18:18 for he had taken a v
Acts 21:23 four men who have taken a v

VOWED (*see* VOW)
Lev 27: 8 to the ability of him who v
Num 29:39 (besides your v offerings
Num 30: 8 make void her vow which she v
Num 30:10 If she v in her husband's
Deut 12: 6 hand, your v offerings, your
Deut 12:26 your v offerings, you shall
Deut 23:18 your God for any v offering
Deut 23:23 for you voluntarily v to the
Judg 11:39 vow with her which he had v
2Sa 15: 7 the vow which I v to the LORD
2Sa 15: 8 For your servant v a vow
Ps 132: 2 v to the Mighty God of Jacob
Eccl 5: 4 Pay what you have v
Jon 2: 9 I will pay what I have v

VOWING (*see* VOW)
Deut 23:22 But if you abstain from v

VOWS (*see* VOW)
Lev 22:18 sacrifice for any of his v or
Lev 23:38 gifts, besides all your v
Num 6:21 v to the LORD the offering
Num 30: 2 If a man v a vow to the LORD,
Num 30: 3 Or if a woman v a vow to the
Num 30: 4 then all her v shall stand
Num 30: 5 then none of her v nor her
Num 30: 6 while bound by her v or by a
Num 30: 7 then her v shall stand, and
Num 30:11 then all her v shall stand
Num 30:12 her lips concerning her v or
Num 30:14 then he confirms all her v or
Job 22:27 you, and you will pay your v
Ps 22:25 I will pay My v before those
Ps 50:14 pay your v to the Most High
Ps 56:12 V made to You are binding
Ps 61: 5 You, O God, have heard my v
Ps 61: 8 That I may daily perform my v
Ps 66:13 I will pay You my v,
Ps 76:11 Make v to the LORD your God,
Ps 116:14 I will pay my v to the LORD
Ps 116:18 I will pay my v to the LORD
Prov 7:14 today I have paid my v
Prov 20:25 afterward to reconsider his v
Prov 31: 2 And what, son of my v
Jer 44:25 our v that we have made, to
Jer 44:25 will surely fulfill your v
Jer 44:25 and perform your v
Jon 1:16 to the LORD and made v
Nah 1:15 feasts, perform your v

VOYAGE
Acts 21: 7 had finished our v from Tyre
Acts 27:10 I perceive that this v will

VULTURE (*see* VULTURES)
Lev 11:13 the eagle, the v, the buzzard
Lev 11:18 the jackdaw, and the carrion v
Deut 14:12 the eagle, the v, the buzzard
Deut 14:17 the jackdaw, the carrion v
Jer 12: 9 is to Me like a speckled v

VULTURES (*see* VULTURE)
Gen 15:11 when the v came down on the
Jer 12: 9 the v all around are against

WAFER (*see* WAFERS)
Ex 29:23 one w from the basket of the
Lev 8:26 anointed with oil, and one w
Num 6:19 basket, and one unleavened w

WAFERS (*see* WAFER)
Ex 16:31 it was like w made with honey
Ex 29: 2 unleavened w anointed with
Lev 2: 4 or unleavened w anointed with
Lev 7:12 unleavened w anointed with
Num 6:15 unleavened w anointed with

WAGE (*see* WAGES)
Prov 20:18 by wise counsel w war
Prov 24: 6 you will w your own war, and
Mal 3: 5 those who exploit w earners
1Ti 1:18 you may w the good warfare

WAGES (*see* WAGE)
Gen 29:15 me, what should your w be
Gen 30:28 Name me your w, and I will
Gen 30:32 and these shall be my w
Gen 30:33 of my w comes before you
Gen 31: 7 me and changed my w ten times
Gen 31: 8 The speckled shall be your w
Gen 31: 8 The streaked shall be your w
Gen 31:41 have changed my w ten times
Ex 2: 9 me, and I will give you your w
Lev 19:13 The w of him who is hired
Deut 24:15 day you shall give him his w
1Ki 5: 6 I will pay you w for your
Job 7: 2 who eagerly looks for his w
Prov 10:16 the w of the wicked to sin
Prov 26:10 and the transgressor his w
Is 19:10 All who make w will be
Is 55: 2 and your w for what does not
Jer 22:13 neighbor's service without w
Ezek 29:18 his army received w from Tyre
Ezek 29:19 will be the w for his army
Hag 1: 6 and he who earns w
Hag 1: 6 earns w to put into a bag
Zech 8:10 no w for man nor any hire for
Zech 11:12 to you, give me my w
Zech 11:12 my w thirty pieces of silver
Matt 20: 8 laborers and give them their w
Luke 3:14 and be content with your w
Luke 10: 7 laborer is worthy of his w
John 4:36 And he who reaps receives w
Acts 1:18 field with the w of iniquity
Rom 4: 4 the w are not counted as
Rom 6:23 For the w of sin is death,
2Co 11: 8 taking w from them to
1Ti 5:18 laborer is worthy of his w
Jas 5: 4 Indeed the w of the laborers
2Pe 2:13 and will receive the w of
2Pe 2:15 of Beor, who loved the w of

WAGGING
Matt 27:39 blasphemed Him, w their heads
Mark 15:29 Him, w their heads and saying,

WAGONS
Ezek 23:24 against you with chariots, w
Ezek 26:10 noise of the horsemen, the w

WAHEB
Num 21:14 W in Suphah, the brooks of

WAIFS
Lam 5: 3 We have become orphans and w

WAIL (*see* WAILED, WAILING)
Is 13: 6 W, for the day of the LORD is
Is 14:31 W, O gate! Cry, O city!
Is 15: 2 Moab will w over Nebo and over
Is 15: 3 their streets everyone will w
Is 16: 7 Moab shall w for Moab
Is 16: 7 everyone shall w
Is 23: 1 W, you ships of Tarshish
Is 23: 6 w, you inhabitants of the
Is 23:14 W, you ships of Tarshish
Is 52: 5 rule over them make them w
Is 65:14 and w for grief of spirit
Jer 4: 8 with sackcloth, lament and w
Jer 25:34 W, shepherds, and cry
Jer 47: 2 of the land shall w
Jer 48:20 W and cry! Tell it in Arnon
Jer 48:31 Therefore I will w for Moab
Jer 48:36 shall w like flutes for Moab
Jer 48:36 w for the men of Kir Heres
Jer 48:39 They shall w: 'How she is
Jer 49: 3 W, O Heshbon, for Ai is
Jer 51: 8 W for her! Take balm for her
Ezek 21:12 Cry and w, son of man
Ezek 30: 2 W, 'Woe to the day
Ezek 32:18 w over the multitude of Egypt
Joel 1: 5 and w, all you drinkers of
Joel 1:11 Be ashamed, you farmers, w
Joel 1:13 w, you who minister before
Mic 1: 8 Therefore I will w and howl, I
Zeph 1:11 W, you inhabitants of Maktesh
Zech 11: 2 W, O cypress, for the cedar
Zech 11: 2 W, O oaks of Bashan, for the

WAILED (*see* WAIL)
Hos 7:14 when they w upon their beds
Mark 5:38 and those who wept and w

WAILING (*see* WAIL)
Esth 4: 3 with fasting, weeping, and w
Is 15: 8 Moab, its w to Eglaim and its
Is 15: 8 Eglaim and its w to Beer Elim
Jer 9:10 w for the mountains, and for
Jer 9:17 and send for skillful w women
Jer 9:18 haste and take up a w for us
Jer 9:19 For a voice of w is heard
Jer 9:20 teach your daughters w, and
Jer 25:36 a w of the leaders to the
Ezek 7:11 nor shall there be w for them
Ezek 27:31 of heart and bitter w
Ezek 27:32 In their w for you they will
Amos 5:16 shall be w in all streets
Amos 5:16 and skillful lamenters to w
Amos 5:17 vineyards there shall be w
Amos 8: 3 temple shall be w in that day
Mic 1: 8 I will make a w like the
Zeph 1:10 a w from the Second Quarter,
Zech 11: 3 is the sound of w shepherds
Matt 9:23 players and the noisy crowd w
Matt 13:42 There will be w and gnashing
Matt 13:50 There will be w and gnashing
Rev 18:15 of her torment, weeping and w
Rev 18:19 and cried out, weeping and w

WAIST (*see* WAISTS)
Gen 37:34 put sackcloth on his w, and
Ex 12:11 with a belt on your w, your
Ex 28:42 from the w to the thighs
1Ki 2: 5 belt that was around his w
1Ki 12:10 be thicker than my father's w
2Ki 1: 8 a leather belt around his w
2Ch 10:10 be thicker than my father's w
Job 12:18 And binds their w with a belt
Job 15:27 made his w heavy with fat,
Song 7: 2 Your w is a heap of wheat set
Is 11: 5 the belt of His w
Jer 13: 1 sash, and put it around your w
Jer 13: 2 LORD, and put it around my w
Jer 13: 4 which is around your w, and
Jer 13:11 sash clings to the w of a man
Ezek 1:27 from the appearance of His w
Ezek 1:27 from the appearance of His w
Ezek 8: 2 from the appearance of His w
Ezek 8: 2 and from His w and upward, like
Ezek 47: 4 the water came up to my w
Dan 10: 5 whose w was girded with gold
Amos 8:10 bring sackcloth on every w
Matt 3: 4 a leather belt around his w
Mark 1: 6 a leather belt around his w
Luke 12:35 Let your w be girded and your
Eph 6:14 girded your w with truth,

WAISTS (*see* WAIST)
1Ki 20:31 us put sackcloth around our w
1Ki 20:32 wore sackcloth around their w
Is 32:11 and gird sackcloth on your w
Ezek 23:15 with belts around their w

WAIT (*see* WAITED, WAITERS, WAITING, WAITS)
Ex 12:39 out of Egypt and could not w
Ex 21:13 But if he did not lie in w
Ex 24:14 W here for us until we come
Num 35:20 hatred or, while lying in w
Num 35:22 at him without lying in w
Deut 19:11 neighbor, lies in w for him
Judg 6:18 I will w until you come back
Judg 9:32 you, and lie in w in the field
Judg 9:34 laid in w against Shechem in
Judg 9:35 with him rose from lying in w
Judg 9:43 and laid in w in the field
Judg 16: 2 lay in w for him all night at
Judg 16: 9 Now there were men lying in w
Judg 16:12 And there were men lying in w
Judg 21:20 lie in w in the vineyards,
Ruth 1:13 would you w for them till
1Sa 1:23 w until you have weaned him
1Sa 10: 8 Seven days you shall w, till
1Sa 14: 9 W until we come to you,'
1Sa 15: 2 how he laid w for him on the
1Sa 15: 5 and lay in w in the valley
1Sa 22: 8 against me, to lie in w, as
1Sa 22:13 rise against me, to lie in w
2Sa 10: 5 W at Jericho until your
2Sa 11:12 W here today also, and
2Sa 15:28 I will w in the plains of the
2Ki 6:33 why should I w for the LORD
2Ki 7: 9 If we w until morning light,
1Ch 19: 5 W at Jericho until your
Job 14:14 of my hard service I will w
Job 17:13 If I w for the grave as my
Job 35:14 Him, and you must w for Him
Job 38:40 in their lairs to lie in w
Ps 10: 9 He lies in w secretly, as a
Ps 10: 9 He lies in w to catch the
Ps 25: 5 On You I w all the day
Ps 25:21 preserve me, For I w for You
Ps 27:14 W on the LORD
Ps 27:14 W, I say, on the LORD
Ps 37: 7 LORD, and w patiently for Him
Ps 37: 9 But those who w on the LORD
Ps 37:34 W on the LORD, And keep His
Ps 39: 7 And now, Lord, what do I w for
Ps 52: 9 saints I will w on Your name
Ps 56: 6 they lie in w for my life
Ps 59: 3 they lie in w for my life
Ps 59: 9 Strength, I will w for You
Ps 62: 5 w silently for God alone, For
Ps 69: 3 fail while I w for my God
Ps 69: 6 Let not those who w for You
Ps 71:10 those who lie in w for my
Ps 104:27 These all w for You, That You
Ps 106:13 They did not w for His
Ps 119:95 The wicked w for me to
Ps 130: 5 I w for the LORD, my soul
Prov 1:11 let us lie in w to shed blood
Prov 1:18 but they lie in w for their
Prov 12: 6 Lie in w for blood," but the
Prov 20:22 w for the LORD, and He will
Prov 23:28 lies in w as for a victim
Prov 24:15 Do not lie in w, O wicked man
Is 8:17 I will w on the LORD, Who
Is 30:18 Therefore the LORD will w
Is 30:18 are all those who w for Him
Is 40:31 But those who w on the LORD
Is 42: 4 shall w for His law
Is 49:23 not be ashamed who w for Me
Is 51: 5 the coastlands will w upon Me
Is 60: 9 the coastlands shall w for Me
Jer 5:26 they lie in w as one who sets
Jer 9: 8 but in his heart he lies in w
Jer 14:22 Therefore we will w for You
Lam 3:10 to me like a bear lying in w
Lam 3:25 good to those who w for Him
Lam 3:26 w quietly for the salvation
Lam 4:19 and lay in w for us in the
Hos 6: 9 of robbers lie in w for a man
Hos 7: 6 an oven, while they lie in w
Hos 12: 6 w on your God continually
Mic 5: 7 man nor w for the sons of men
Mic 7: 2 They all lie in w for blood
Mic 7: 7 I will w for the God of my
Hab 2: 3 Though it tarries, w for it
Zeph 3: 8 Therefore w for Me," says
Luke 11:54 lying in w for Him, and
Luke 12:36 men who w for their master
Acts 1: 4 but to w for the Promise of
Acts 23:21 of them lie in w for him, men
Acts 23:30 the Jews lay in w for the man
Rom 8:25 then we eagerly w for it with
1Co 11:33 to eat, w for one another
Gal 5: 5 eagerly w for the hope of
Eph 4:14 they lie in w to deceive,
Phil 3:20 also eagerly w for the Savior
1Th 1:10 to w for His Son from heaven,
Heb 9:28 To those who eagerly w for

WAITED (*see* WAIT)
Gen 8:10 he w yet another seven days,
Gen 8:12 So he w yet another seven
Gen 49:18 I have w for your salvation,
Judg 3:25 So they w till they were
1Sa 13: 8 Then he w seven days,
1Sa 25: 9 in the name of David, and w
1Ki 20:38 w for the king by the road,
2Ki 5: 2 She w on Naaman's wife
Job 29:21 Men listened to me and w, and
Job 29:23 They w for me as for the rain
Job 30:26 when I w for light, then came
Job 32: 4 Elihu had w to speak to Job
Job 32:11 Indeed I w for your words, I
Job 32:16 And I have w, because they did
Ps 40: 1 I w patiently for the LORD
Is 25: 9 we have w for Him, and He will
Is 25: 9 we have w for Him
Is 26: 8 O LORD, we have w for You
Is 33: 2 we have w for You
Lam 2:16 this is the day we have w for
Ezek 19: 5 When she saw that she w,
Luke 1:21 the people w for Zacharias,
Acts 10: 7 who w on him continually
Acts 17:16 Now while Paul w for them at
Acts 20: 5 ahead, w for us at Troas
Acts 27:33 the fourteenth day you have w
Heb 11:10 for he w for the city which
1Pe 3:20 of God w in the days of Noah

WAITERS (*see* WAIT)
1Ki 10: 5 the service of his w and
2Ch 9: 4 the service of his w and

WAITING (*see* WAIT)
Prov 8:34 w at the posts of my doors
Mark 15:43 who was himself w for the
Luke 2:25 w for the Consolation of
Luke 8:40 for they were all w for Him
Luke 23:51 who himself was also w for
John 5: 3 w for the moving of the water
Acts 10:24 Now Cornelius was w for them
Acts 22:16 And now why are you w
Acts 23:21 w for the promise from you
Rom 8:23 eagerly w for the adoption,
1Co 1: 7 eagerly w for the revelation
1Co 16:11 for I am w for him with the
Heb 10:13 from that time w till His
Jas 5: 7 w patiently for it until it

WAITS (*see* WAIT)
Job 24:15 adulterer w for the twilight
Ps 25: 3 let no one who w on You be
Ps 33:20 Our soul w for the LORD
Ps 62: 1 my soul silently w for God
Ps 130: 5 wait for the LORD, my soul w
Ps 130: 6 My soul w for the Lord More
Prov 27:18 so he who w on his master
Is 64: 4 for the one who w for Him
Dan 12:12 Blessed is he who w, and comes
Rom 8:19 of the creation eagerly w for
Jas 5: 7 See how the farmer w for the

WAKE (*see* WAKENED)
Job 41:32 leaves a shining w behind him
Joel 3: 9 W up the mighty men, let all
John 11:11 but I go that I may w him up
1Th 5:10 that whether we w or sleep

WAKENED (*see* WAKE)
Joel 3:12 Let the nations be w, and come
Zech 4: 1 w me, as a man who is w

WALK (*see* WALKED, WALKING, WALKS)
Gen 13:17 w in the land through its
Gen 17: 1 w before Me and be blameless
Gen 24:40 The LORD, before whom I w
Ex 16: 4 they will w in My law or not
Ex 18:20 the way in which they must w
Lev 18: 3 nor shall you w in their
Lev 18: 4 My ordinances, to w in them
Lev 20:23 And you shall not w in the
Lev 26: 3 If you w in My statutes and
Lev 26:12 I will w among you and be your
Lev 26:13 yoke and made you w upright
Lev 26:21 if you w contrary to Me, and
Lev 26:23 by Me, but w contrary to Me,
Lev 26:24 I also will w contrary to you
Lev 26:27 Me, but w contrary to Me,
Lev 26:28 then I also will w contrary
Deut 5:33 You shall w in all the ways
Deut 6: 7 when you w by the way, when
Deut 8: 6 to w in His ways and to fear
Deut 10:12 to w in all His ways and to
Deut 11:19 when you w by the way, when
Deut 11:22 to w in all His ways, and to
Deut 13: 4 You shall w after the LORD
Deut 13: 5 your God commanded you to w
Deut 19: 9 to w always in His ways, then
Deut 26:17 that you will w in His ways
Deut 28: 9 your God and w in His ways
Deut 29:19 peace, even though I w in the
Deut 30:16 to w in His ways, and to keep
Josh 18: 8 w through the land, survey it
Josh 22: 5 to w in all His ways, to keep
Judg 2:22 to w in them as their fathers
Judg 5:10 and who w along the road
1Sa 2:30 would w before Me forever'
1Sa 2:35 he shall w before My anointed
1Sa 8: 3 sons did not w in his ways
1Sa 8: 5 sons do not w in your ways
1Sa 17:39 his armor, and he tried to w
1Sa 17:39 I cannot w with these, for I
1Ki 2: 3 to w in His ways, to keep His
1Ki 2: 4 to w before Me in truth with
1Ki 3:14 So if you w in My ways, to
1Ki 6:12 if you w in My statutes,
1Ki 6:12 and w in them, then I will
1Ki 8:23 with Your servants who w
1Ki 8:25 that they w before Me as you
1Ki 8:36 way in which they should w
1Ki 8:58 to w in all His ways, and to
1Ki 8:61 to w in His statutes and keep
1Ki 9: 4 Now if you w before Me as
1Ki 11:38 w in My ways, and do what is
1Ki 16:31 a trivial thing for him to w
2Ki 10:31 But Jehu took no heed to w in
2Ki 21:22 did not w in the way of the
2Ch 6:14 with Your servants who w
2Ch 6:16 to w in My law as you have
2Ch 6:27 way in which they should w
2Ch 6:31 to w in Your ways as long as
2Ch 7:17 if you w before Me as your
Neh 5: 9 Should you not w in the fear
Neh 10:29 an oath to w in God's Law,
Ps 23: 4 though I w through the valley
Ps 26:11 me, I will w in my integrity
Ps 48:12 W about Zion, And go all
Ps 56:13 That I may w before God In
Ps 78:10 They refused to w in His law
Ps 81:12 To w in their own counsels
Ps 81:13 Israel would w in My ways
Ps 82: 5 They w about in darkness
Ps 84:11 From those who w uprightly
Ps 86:11 I will w in Your truth
Ps 89:15 They w, O LORD, in the light
Ps 89:30 do not w in My judgments,
Ps 101: 2 I will w within my house with
Ps 115: 7 they have, but they do not w
Ps 116: 9 I will w before the LORD In
Ps 119: 1 Who w in the law of the LORD
Ps 119: 3 They w in His ways
Ps 119:35 Make me w in the path of Your
Ps 119:45 I will w at liberty, For I
Ps 138: 7 Though I w in the midst of
Ps 142: 3 In the way in which I w They
Ps 143: 8 the way in which I should w
Prov 1:15 do not w in the way with them
Prov 2: 7 to those who w uprightly
Prov 2:13 to w in the ways of darkness
Prov 2:20 so you may w in the way of
Prov 3:23 Then you will w safely in
Prov 4:12 When you w, your steps will
Prov 4:14 do not w in the way of evil
Prov 6:28 Can one w on hot coals, and
Prov 30:29 four which are stately in w
Eccl 4:15 living who w under the sun
Eccl 5: 1 W prudently when you go to
Eccl 6: 8 who knows how to w before the
Eccl 10: 7 while princes w on the ground
Eccl 11: 9 w in the ways of your heart,
Is 2: 3 and we shall w in His paths
Is 2: 5 let us w in the light of the
Is 3:16 w with outstretched necks and
Is 8:11 me that I should not w in the
Is 30: 2 Who w to go down to Egypt, and
Is 30:21 w in it," whenever you turn
Is 35: 9 the redeemed shall w there
Is 38:15 I shall w carefully all my
Is 40:31 and not be weary, they shall w
Is 42: 5 spirit to those who w on it
Is 42:24 they would not w in His ways
Is 43: 2 When you w through the fire,
Is 45:14 they shall w behind you, they
Is 50:11 w in the light of your fire
Is 51:23 down, that we may w over you
Is 51:23 street, for those who w over
Is 59: 9 but we w in blackness
Is 65: 2 who w in a way that is not
Jer 3:17 they shall w no more after
Jer 3:18 w with the house of Israel
Jer 6:16 the good way is, and w in it
Jer 6:16 said, 'We will not w in it
Jer 6:25 the field, nor w by the way
Jer 7: 6 or w after other gods to your
Jer 7: 9 w after other gods whom you
Jer 7:23 w in all the ways that I have
Jer 9: 4 will w with slanderers
Jer 13:10 who w in the imagination of
Jer 13:10 w after other gods to serve
Jer 18:12 So we will w according to our
Jer 18:15 to w in pathways and not on a
Jer 23:14 commit adultery and w in lies
Jer 26: 4 to w in My law which I have
Jer 31: 9 I will cause them to w by the
Jer 42: 3 the way in which we should w
Lam 3: 2 made me w in darkness and not
Lam 4:18 we could not w in our streets
Ezek 11:20 that they may w in My
Ezek 11:21 w after the heart of their
Ezek 16:47 You did not w in their ways
Ezek 20:13 they did not w in My statutes
Ezek 20:16 did not w in My statutes, but
Ezek 20:18 Do not w in the statutes of
Ezek 20:19 W in My statutes, keep My
Ezek 20:21 they did not w in My statutes
Ezek 36:12 I will cause men to w on you
Ezek 36:27 cause you to w in My statutes
Ezek 37:24 shall also w in My judgments
Ezek 42: 4 was a w ten cubits wide, at a
Ezek 42:11 There was a w in front of
Ezek 42:12 was a door in front of the w
Dan 4:37 those who w in pride He is
Dan 9:10 to w in His laws, which He
Hos 11: 3 I taught Ephraim to w, taking
Hos 11:10 They shall w after the LORD
Hos 14: 9 the righteous w in them, but
Amos 3: 3 can two w together, unless
Jon 3: 4 the city on the first day's w
Mic 2: 3 nor shall you w haughtily
Mic 2:11 If a man should w in a false
Mic 4: 2 and we shall w in His paths
Mic 4: 5 For all people w each in the
Mic 4: 5 but we will w in the name of
Mic 6: 8 to w humbly with your God
Mic 6:16 you w in their counsels, that
Nah 2: 5 they stumble in their w
Hab 3:19 He will make me w on my high
Zeph 1:17 they shall w like blind men,
Zech 1:10 the LORD has sent to w to
Zech 3: 7 If you will w in My ways
Zech 3: 7 I will give you places to w
Zech 6: 7 to go, that they might w to
Zech 6: 7 w to and fro throughout the
Zech 10:12 the LORD, and they shall w up
Matt 9: 5 you,' or to say, 'Arise and w'
Matt 11: 5 their sight and the lame w
Mark 2: 9 Arise, take up your bed and w'
Mark 7: 5 Why do Your disciples not w
Luke 5:23 or to say, 'Rise up and w'
Luke 7:22 the blind see, the lame w
Luke 11:44 the men who w over them are
Luke 20:46 who desire to w in long robes
Luke 24:17 with one another as you w
John 5: 8 Rise, take up your bed and w
John 5:11 to me, 'Take up your bed and w
John 5:12 you, 'Take up your bed and w'
John 7: 1 He did not want to w in Judea
John 8:12 Me shall not w in darkness
John 12:35 W while you have the light,
Acts 3: 6 of Nazareth, rise up and w
Acts 3:12 we had made this man w
Acts 14:16 to w in their own ways
Acts 21:21 their children nor to w
Acts 21:24 you yourself also w orderly
Rom 4:12 but who also w in the steps
Rom 6: 4 should w in newness of life
Rom 8: 1 who do not w according to the
Rom 8: 4 w according to the flesh but
Rom 13:13 Let us w properly, as in the
1Co 7:17 called each one, so let him w
2Co 5: 7 For we w by faith, not by
2Co 6:16 dwell in them and w among

2Co 10: 3 For though we **w** in the flesh
2Co 12:18 Did we not **w** in the same
2Co 12:18 Did we not **w** in the same
Gal 5:16 **W** in the Spirit, and you shall
Gal 5:25 let us also **w** in the Spirit
Gal 6:16 as many as **w** according to
Eph 2:10 that we should **w** in them
Eph 4: 1 Lord, beseech you to have a **w**
Eph 4:17 that you should no longer **w**
Eph 4:17 as the rest of the Gentiles **w**
Eph 5: 2 **w** in love, as Christ also has
Eph 5: 8 **W** as children of light
Eph 5:15 then that you **w** circumspectly
Phil 3:16 let us **w** by the same rule,
Phil 3:17 and note those who so **w**, as
Phil 3:18 For many **w**, of whom I have
Col 1:10 have a **w** worthy of the Lord
Col 2: 6 Jesus the Lord, so **w** in Him,
Col 4: 5 **W** in wisdom toward those who
1Th 2:12 that you would have a **w**
1Th 4: 1 from us how you ought to **w**
1Th 4:12 that you may **w** properly
2Th 3:11 that there are some who **w**
2Pe 2:10 and especially those who **w**
1Jn 1: 6 **w** in darkness, we lie and do
1Jn 1: 7 But if we **w** in the light as
1Jn 2: 6 also to **w** just as He walked
2Jn 6 that we **w** according to His
2Jn 6 beginning, you should **w** in it
3Jn 3 just as you **w** in the truth
3Jn 4 that my children **w** in truth
Jude 18 **w** according to their own
Rev 3: 4 they shall **w** with Me in white
Rev 9:20 neither see nor hear nor **w**
Rev 16:15 his garments, lest he **w** naked
Rev 21:24 saved shall **w** in its light

WALKED (*see* WALK)
Gen 5:22 Enoch **w** with God three
Gen 5:24 And Enoch **w** with God
Gen 6: 9 Noah **w** with God
Gen 48:15 fathers Abraham and Isaac **w**
Ex 2: 5 And her maidens **w** along the
Ex 14:29 the children of Israel had **w**
Lev 26:40 also have **w** contrary to Me
Lev 26:41 also have **w** contrary to them
Deut 1:36 giving the land on which he **w**
Josh 5: 6 Israel **w** forty years in the
Judg 2:17 way in which their fathers **w**
Judg 5: 6 the travelers **w** along the
Judg 11:16 they **w** through the wilderness
1Sa 12: 2 I have **w** before you from my
2Sa 7: 7 **w** with all the children of
2Sa 11: 2 **w** on the roof of the king's
1Ki 3: 6 because he **w** before You in
1Ki 3:14 as your father David **w**, then
1Ki 8:25 Me as you have **w** before Me
1Ki 9: 4 Me as your father David **w**
1Ki 11:33 have not **w** in My ways to do
1Ki 15: 3 he **w** in all the sins of his
1Ki 15:26 **w** in the way of his father,
1Ki 15:34 **w** in the way of Jeroboam, and
1Ki 16: 2 and you have **w** in the way of
1Ki 16:26 For he **w** in all the ways of
1Ki 22:43 he **w** in all the ways of his
1Ki 22:52 **w** in the way of his father and
2Ki 4:35 **w** back and forth in the house,
2Ki 8:18 he **w** in the way of the kings
2Ki 8:27 he **w** in the way of the house
2Ki 13: 6 Israel sin, but **w** in them
2Ki 13:11 but he **w** in them
2Ki 16: 3 But he **w** in the way of the
2Ki 17: 8 had **w** in the statutes of the
2Ki 17:19 God, but **w** in the statutes of
2Ki 17:22 For the children of Israel **w**
2Ki 20: 3 how I have **w** before You in
2Ki 21:21 So he **w** in all the ways that
2Ki 21:21 ways that his father had **w**
2Ki 22: 2 and **w** in all the ways of his
2Ch 6:16 law as you have **w** before Me
2Ch 7:17 Me as your father David **w**
2Ch 11:17 because they **w** in the way of
2Ch 17: 3 because he **w** in the former
2Ch 17: 4 **w** in His commandments and not
2Ch 20:32 he **w** in the way of his father
2Ch 21: 6 he **w** in the way of the kings
2Ch 21:12 Because you have not **w** in the
2Ch 21:13 but have **w** in the ways of the
2Ch 22: 3 He also **w** in the ways of the
2Ch 22: 5 He also **w** in their counsel,
2Ch 28: 2 For he **w** in the ways of the
2Ch 34: 2 **w** in the ways of his father
Job 29: 3 light I **w** through darkness
Job 31: 5 If I have **w** with falsehood,
Job 31: 7 or my heart **w** after my eyes,
Job 38:16 Or have you **w** in search of
Ps 26: 1 For I have **w** in my integrity
Ps 26: 3 And I have **w** in Your truth
Ps 55:14 **w** to the house of God in the
Is 9: 2 The people who **w** in darkness
Is 20: 3 My servant Isaiah has **w** naked
Is 38: 3 how I have **w** before You in
Jer 2: 8 **w** after things that do not
Jer 7:24 but **w** in the counsels and in
Jer 8: 2 and after which they have **w**
Jer 9:13 voice, nor **w** according to it,
Jer 9:14 but they have **w** according to
Jer 11: 8 ear, but everyone **w** in the
Jer 16:11 they have **w** after other gods
Jer 32:23 Your voice or **w** in Your law
Jer 44:10 they have not **w** in My law or
Jer 44:23 of the LORD or **w** in His law
Ezek 5: 6 and they have not **w** in My
Ezek 5: 7 have not **w** in My statutes,
Ezek 11:12 for you have not **w** in My
Ezek 18: 9 if he has **w** in My statutes and
Ezek 18:17 judgments and **w** in My statutes
Ezek 23:31 You have **w** in the way of
Ezek 28:14 you **w** back and forth in the
Hos 5:11 willingly **w** by human precept
Amos 2: 4 after which their fathers **w**
Nah 2:11 young lions, where the lion **w**
Hab 3:15 You **w** through the sea with
Zech 1:11 We have **w** to and fro
Zech 6: 7 So they **w** to and fro
Mal 2: 6 He **w** with Me in peace and
Mal 3:14 that we have **w** as mourners
Matt 14:29 he **w** on the water to go to
Mark 1:16 as He **w** by the Sea of Galilee
Mark 5:42 the girl arose and **w**, for she
Mark 16:12 form to two of them as they **w**
John 1:36 And looking at Jesus as He **w**
John 5: 9 well, took up his bed, and **w**
John 6:66 back and **w** with Him no more
John 7: 1 things Jesus **w** in Galilee
John 10:23 Jesus **w** in the temple, in
John 11:54 **w** openly among the Jews, but
John 21:18 and **w** where you wished
Acts 3: 8 So he, leaping up, stood and **w**
Acts 14: 8 womb, who had never **w**
Acts 14:10 And he leaped and **w**
2Co 10: 2 we **w** according to the flesh
Eph 2: 2 in which you once **w** according
Col 3: 7 once **w** when you lived in them
1Pe 4: 3 when we **w** in licentiousness,
1Jn 2: 6 also to walk just as He **w**

WALKING (*see* WALK)
Gen 3: 8 **w** in the garden in the cool
Gen 24:65 Who is this man **w** in the
1Sa 12: 2 is the king, **w** before you
1Ki 3: 3 **w** in the statutes of his
1Ki 16:19 in **w** in the way of Jeroboam,
Job 1: 7 on the earth, and from **w** back
Job 2: 2 on the earth, and from **w** back
Is 3:16 necks and wanton eyes, **w** and
Is 20: 2 did so, **w** naked and barefoot
Is 57: 2 each one **w** in his uprightness
Jer 6:28 rebels, **w** as slanderers
Lam 5:18 with foxes **w** about on it
Dan 3:25 **w** in the midst of the fire
Dan 4:29 **w** about the royal palace of
Matt 4:18 **w** by the Sea of Galilee, saw
Matt 14:25 went to them, **w** on the sea
Matt 14:26 saw Him **w** on the sea, they
Matt 15:31 made whole, the lame **w**
Mark 6:48 **w** on the sea, and would have
Mark 6:49 they saw Him **w** on the sea
Mark 8:24 I see men like trees, **w**
Mark 11:27 as He was **w** in the temple,
Luke 1: 6 **w** in all the commandments and
John 6:19 they saw Jesus **w** on the sea
Acts 3: 8 **w**, leaping, and praising God
Acts 3: 9 And all the people saw him **w**
Acts 9:31 **w** in the fear of the Lord and
Rom 14:15 you are no longer **w** in love
2Co 4: 2 not **w** in craftiness nor
2Pe 3: 3 **w** according to their own
2Jn 4 of your children **w** in truth
Jude 16 **w** according to their own

WALKS (*see* WALK)
Ex 21:19 and **w** about outside with his
Deut 23:14 For the LORD your God **w** in
Job 18: 8 feet, and he **w** into a snare
Job 22:14 and He **w** above the circle of
Job 34: 8 and **w** with wicked men
Ps 1: 1 Blessed is the man Who **w** not
Ps 15: 2 He who **w** uprightly, And works
Ps 39: 6 Surely every man **w** about like
Ps 73: 9 their tongue **w** through the
Ps 91: 6 pestilence that **w** in darkness
Ps 101: 6 He who **w** in a perfect way, He
Ps 104: 3 Who **w** on the wings of the
Ps 128: 1 the LORD, Who **w** in His ways
Prov 6:12 man, **w** with a perverse mouth
Prov 10: 9 **w** with integrity **w** securely
Prov 13:20 He who **w** with wise men will
Prov 14: 2 He who **w** in his uprightness
Prov 15:21 of understanding **w** uprightly
Prov 19: 1 Better is the poor who **w** in
Prov 20: 7 man **w** in his integrity
Prov 28: 6 Better is the poor who **w** in
Prov 28:18 Whoever **w** blamelessly will be
Prov 28:26 but whoever **w** wisely will be
Eccl 2:14 but the fool **w** in darkness
Eccl 10: 3 when a fool **w** along the way
Is 33:15 He who **w** righteously and
Is 35: 8 Whoever **w** the road, although
Is 50:10 Who **w** in darkness and has no
Jer 10:23 it is not in man who **w** to
Jer 16:12 each one **w** according to the
Jer 23:17 to everyone who **w** according
Ezek 33:15 **w** in the statutes of life
Hos 11:12 but Judah still **w** with God
Mic 2: 7 good to him who **w** uprightly
John 11: 9 If anyone **w** in the day, he
John 11:10 But if one **w** in the night, he
John 12:35 he who **w** in darkness does not
2Th 3: 6 brother who **w** disorderly and
1Pe 5: 8 your adversary the devil **w**
1Jn 2:11 **w** in darkness, and does not
Rev 2: 1 who **w** in the midst of the

WALKWAYS
2Ch 9:11 the king made **w** of the algum

WALL (*see* WALLED, WALLS)
Gen 49:22 his branches run over the **w**
Ex 14:22 the waters were a **w** to them
Ex 14:29 the waters were a **w** to them
Lev 14:37 appear to be deep in the **w**
Lev 25:31 no **w** around them shall be
Num 22:24 with a **w** on this side
Num 22:24 and a **w** on that side
Num 22:25 pushed herself against the **w**
Num 22:25 Balaam's foot against the **w**
Num 35: 4 the **w** of the city outward a
Josh 2:15 her house was on the city **w**
Josh 2:15 she dwelt on the **w**
Josh 6: 5 then the **w** of the city will
Josh 6:20 that the **w** fell down flat
1Sa 18:11 pin David to the **w** with it
1Sa 19:10 David to the **w** with the spear
1Sa 19:10 he drove the spear into the **w**
1Sa 20:25 times, on a seat by the **w**
1Sa 25:16 They were a **w** to us both by
1Sa 31:10 body to the **w** of Beth Shan
1Sa 31:12 sons from the **w** of Beth Shan
2Sa 11:20 they would shoot from the **w**
2Sa 11:21 a millstone on him from the **w**
2Sa 11:21 Why did you go near the **w**
2Sa 11:24 from the **w** at your servants
2Sa 18:24 roof over the gate, to the **w**
2Sa 20:15 the **w** to throw it down
2Sa 20:21 be thrown to you over the **w**
2Sa 22:30 by my God I can leap over a **w**
1Ki 3: 1 the **w** all around Jerusalem
1Ki 4:33 that springs out of the **w**
1Ki 6: 5 Against the **w** of the temple
1Ki 6:27 wing of the one touched one **w**
1Ki 6:27 cherub touched the other **w**
1Ki 6:31 were one-fifth of the **w**
1Ki 6:33 wood, one-fourth of the **w**
1Ki 9:15 the **w** of Jerusalem, Hazor,
1Ki 20:30 then a **w** fell on twenty-seven
1Ki 21:23 Jezebel by the **w** of Jezreel
2Ki 3:27 a burnt offering upon the **w**
2Ki 4:10 a small upper room on the **w**
2Ki 6:26 was passing by on the **w**, a
2Ki 6:30 and as he passed by on the **w**
2Ki 9:33 her blood spattered on the **w**

2Ki 14:13 broke down the w of Jerusalem
2Ki 18:26 the people who are on the w
2Ki 18:27 to the men who sit on the w
2Ki 20: 2 turned his face toward the w
2Ki 25: 1 they built a siege w against
2Ki 25: 4 Then the city w was broken
2Ch 3:11 touching the w of the room
2Ch 3:12 touching the w of the room
2Ch 25:23 broke down the w of Jerusalem
2Ch 26: 6 and broke down the w of Gath
2Ch 26: 6 the w of Jabneh
2Ch 26: 6 and the w of Ashdod
2Ch 26: 9 the corner buttress of the w
2Ch 27: 3 extensively on the w of Ophel
2Ch 32: 5 up all the w that was broken
2Ch 32: 5 and built another w outside
2Ch 32:18 Jerusalem who were on the w
2Ch 33:14 After this he built a w
2Ch 36:19 broke down the w of Jerusalem
Ezra 5: 3 this temple and finish this w
Ezra 9: 9 and to give us a w in Judah
Neh 1: 3 The w of Jerusalem is also
Neh 2: 8 to the temple, for the city w
Neh 2:15 the valley, and viewed the w
Neh 2:17 us build the w of Jerusalem
Neh 3: 8 as far as the Broad W
Neh 3:13 a thousand cubits of the w as
Neh 3:15 repaired the w of the Pool of
Neh 3:27 and as far as the w of Ophel
Neh 4: 1 that we were rebuilding the w
Neh 4: 3 will break down their stone w
Neh 4: 6 So we built the w
Neh 4: 6 and the entire w was joined
Neh 4:10 are not able to build the w
Neh 4:13 the lower parts of the w, at
Neh 4:15 all of us returned to the w
Neh 4:17 Those who built on the w, and
Neh 4:19 far from one another on the w
Neh 5:16 continued the work on this w
Neh 6: 1 that I had rebuilt the w, and
Neh 6: 6 you are rebuilding the w
Neh 6:15 So the w was finished on the
Neh 7: 1 when the w was built and I had
Neh 12:27 w of Jerusalem they sought
Neh 12:30 people, the gates, and the w
Neh 12:31 leaders of Judah up on the w
Neh 12:31 the w toward the Refuse Gate
Neh 12:37 on the stairway of the w
Neh 12:38 half of the people on the w
Neh 12:38 Ovens as far as the Broad W
Neh 13:21 spend the night around the w
Ps 18:29 by my God I can leap over a w
Ps 62: 3 all of you, Like a leaning w
Prov 18:11 and like a high w in his own
Prov 24:31 its stone w was broken down
Eccl 10: 8 whoever breaks through a w
Song 2: 9 he stands behind our w
Song 8: 9 If she is a w, we will build
Song 8:10 I am a w, and my breasts like
Is 2:15 and upon every fortified w
Is 5: 5 and break down its w, and it
Is 7: 6 a gap in its w for ourselves
Is 22:10 broke down to fortify the w
Is 25: 4 is as a storm against the w
Is 30:13 to fall, a bulge in a high w
Is 36:11 the people who are on the w
Is 36:12 to the men who sit on the w
Is 38: 2 turned his face toward the w
Is 59:10 for the w like the blind, and
Jer 15:20 people a fortified bronze w
Jer 49:27 a fire in the w of Damascus
Jer 51:44 the w of Babylon shall fall
Jer 52: 4 they built a siege w against
Jer 52: 7 Then the city w was broken
Lam 2: 8 the w of the daughter of Zion
Lam 2: 8 the rampart and w to lament
Lam 2:18 O w of the daughter of Zion,
Ezek 4: 2 build a siege w against it
Ezek 4: 3 it as an iron w between you
Ezek 8: 7 there was a hole in the w
Ezek 8: 8 Son of man, dig into the w"
Ezek 8: 8 and when I dug into the w,
Ezek 12: 5 through the w in their sight
Ezek 12: 7 through the w with my hand
Ezek 12:12 w to carry them out through
Ezek 13: 5 w for the house of Israel to
Ezek 13:10 and one builds a boundary w
Ezek 13:12 when the w has fallen, will
Ezek 13:14 the w you have plastered with
Ezek 13:15 accomplish My wrath on the w
Ezek 13:15 The w is no more, nor those
Ezek 17:17 build a w to cut off many
Ezek 21:22 siege mound, and to build a w
Ezek 22:30 them who would make a w
Ezek 23:14 at men portrayed on the w
Ezek 26: 8 build a w against you, and
Ezek 38:20 every w shall fall to the
Ezek 40: 5 Now there was a w all around
Ezek 40: 5 the width of the w structure
Ezek 41: 5 measured the w of the temple
Ezek 41: 6 to the w of the temple
Ezek 41: 7 supporting ledges in the w of
Ezek 41: 9 w of the side chambers was
Ezek 41:10 the w chambers was a width of
Ezek 41:12 the w of the building was
Ezek 41:17 on every w all around, inside
Ezek 41:20 on the w of the sanctuary,
Ezek 42: 7 a w which was outside ran
Ezek 42:10 the w of the court toward the
Ezek 42:12 of the w toward the east
Ezek 42:20 it had a w all around, five
Ezek 43: 8 with a w between them and Me,
Dan 5: 5 of the w of the king's palace
Dan 9:25 be built again, and the w,
Hos 2: 6 w her in, so that she cannot
Joel 2: 7 they climb the w like men of
Joel 2: 9 the city, they run on the w
Amos 1: 7 a fire upon the w of Gaza
Amos 1:10 a fire upon the w of Tyre
Amos 1:14 a fire in the w of Rabbah
Amos 5:19 leaned his hand on the w
Amos 7: 7 the Lord stood on a w made
Nah 3: 8 sea, whose w was like the sea
Hab 2:11 stone will cry out from the w
Zech 2: 5 will be a w of fire all
Acts 9:25 the w in a large basket
Acts 23: 3 strike you, you whitewashed w
2Co 11:33 through a window in the w
Eph 2:14 w of division between us,
Rev 21:12 high w with twelve gates, and
Rev 21:14 Now the w of the city had
Rev 21:15 the city, its gates, and its w
Rev 21:17 Then he measured its w
Rev 21:18 of its w was of jasper
Rev 21:19 the foundations of the w of

WALLED (*see* WALL)
Lev 25:29 man sells a house in a w city
Lev 25:30 in the w city shall belong

WALLOW (*see* WALLOWED, WALLOWING)
Jer 48:26 Moab shall w in his vomit, and

WALLOWED (*see* WALLOW)
2Sa 20:12 But Amasa w in his blood in
Mark 9:20 and he fell on the ground and w

WALLOWING (*see* WALLOW)
2Pe 2:22 washed, to her w in the mire

WALLS (*see* WALL)
Lev 14:37 if the plague is on the w of
Lev 14:39 spread on the w of the house
Deut 3: 5 were fortified with high w
Deut 28:52 your high and fortified w, in
1Ki 4:13 sixty large cities with w
1Ki 6: 5 against the w of the temple,
1Ki 6: 6 into the w of the temple
1Ki 6:15 he built the inside w of the
1Ki 6:29 Then he carved all the w of
2Ki 25: 4 way of the gate between two w
2Ki 25:10 the w of Jerusalem all around
1Ch 29: 4 overlay the w of the houses
2Ch 3: 7 the beams and doorposts, its w
2Ch 3: 7 he carved cherubim on the w
2Ch 8: 5 fortified cities with w,
2Ch 14: 7 make w around them, and
Ezra 4:12 city, and are finishing its w
Ezra 4:13 the w completed, they will
Ezra 4:16 and its w are completed, the
Ezra 5: 8 timber is being laid in the w
Ezra 5: 9 temple and to finish these w
Neh 2:13 viewed the w of Jerusalem
Neh 4: 7 the w of Jerusalem were being
Job 24:11 press out oil within their w
Ps 51:18 Build the w of Jerusalem
Ps 55:10 they go around it on its w
Ps 122: 7 Peace be within your w,
Prov 25:28 a city broken down, without w
Song 5: 7 the keepers of the w took my
Is 22: 5 breaking down the w and of
Is 22:11 w for the water of the old
Is 25:12 of your w He will bring down
Is 26: 1 will appoint salvation for w
Is 49:16 your w are continually before
Is 54:12 all your w of precious stones
Is 56: 5 house and within My w a place
Is 60:10 shall build up your w, and
Is 60:18 shall call your w Salvation
Is 62: 6 I have set watchmen on your w
Jer 1:15 against all its w all around
Jer 1:18 bronze w against the whole
Jer 5:10 Go up on her w and destroy,
Jer 21: 4 who besiege you outside the w
Jer 39: 4 by the gate between the two w
Jer 39: 8 broke down the w of Jerusalem
Jer 49: 3 and run to and fro by the w
Jer 50:15 fallen, her w are thrown down
Jer 51:12 standard on the w of Babylon
Jer 51:58 The broad w of Babylon shall
Jer 52: 7 of the gate between the two w
Jer 52:14 the w of Jerusalem all around
Lam 2: 7 He has given up the w of her
Ezek 8:10 portrayed all around on the w
Ezek 26: 4 shall destroy the w of Tyre
Ezek 26: 9 battering rams against your w
Ezek 26:10 your w will shake at the
Ezek 26:12 they will break down your w
Ezek 27:11 were on your w all around
Ezek 27:11 shields on your w all around
Ezek 33:30 about you beside the w and in
Ezek 38:11 of them dwelling without w
Ezek 41: 2 the side w of the entrance
Ezek 41:13 its w was one hundred cubits
Ezek 41:25 as they were carved on the w
Amos 4: 3 will go out through broken w
Mic 7:11 when your w are to be built
Nah 2: 5 they make haste to her w, and
Zech 2: 4 inhabited as towns without w
Heb 11:30 By faith the w of Jericho

WANDER (*see* WANDERED, WANDERERS, WANDERING, WANDERS)
Gen 20:13 when God caused me to w from
Num 32:13 and He made them w in the
Deut 27:18 the blind to w off the road
Judg 11:37 w on the mountains and bewail
2Sa 15:20 Should I make you w up and
2Ki 21: 8 w anymore from the land which
Job 12:24 makes them w in a pathless
Job 38:41 and w about for lack of food
Ps 55: 7 Indeed, I would w far off
Ps 59:15 They w up and down for food,
Ps 107:40 And causes them to w in the
Ps 119:10 Oh, let me not w from Your
Is 47:15 they shall w each one to his
Jer 14:10 Thus they have loved to w
Jer 49: 5 will gather those who w off
Amos 8:12 They shall w from sea to sea,

WANDERED (*see* WANDER)
Gen 21:14 and w in the Wilderness of
Josh 14:10 Israel w in the wilderness
Ps 107: 4 They w in the wilderness in a
Is 16: 8 and w through the wilderness
Lam 4:14 They w blind in the streets
Lam 4:15 When they fled and w, those
Ezek 34: 6 My sheep w through all the
Amos 4: 8 So two or three cities w to
Heb 11:37 They w about in sheepskins and
Heb 11:38 They w in deserts and

WANDERERS (*see* WANDER)
Hos 9:17 they shall be w among the

WANDERING (*see* WANDER, WANDERINGS)
Gen 37:15 there he was, w in the field
Eccl 6: 9 the eyes than the w of desire
Is 16: 2 For it shall be as a w bird
Is 49:21 a captive, and w to and fro
1Ti 5:13 w about from house to house,
Jude 13 w stars for whom is reserved

WANDERINGS (*see* WANDERING)
Ps 56: 8 You number my w

WANDERS (*see* WANDER)
Job 15:23 He w about for bread, saying,
Prov 21:16 A man who w from the way of
Prov 27: 8 Like a bird that w from its
Prov 27: 8 is a man who w from his place
Jas 5:19 among you w from the truth

WANE
Is 17: 4 the glory of Jacob will w

WANT (*see* WANTED, WANTING, WANTS)
Gen 42:36 you w to take Benjamin away
Lev 27:20 not w to redeem the field
Deut 25: 7 But if the man does not w to
Deut 25: 8 I do not w to take her,'
Ruth 3:13 But if he does not w to
2Ki 4:13 Do you w me to speak on your
Job 24: 8 the rock for w of shelter
Job 30: 3 They are gaunt from w and
Ps 23: 1 I shall not w
Ps 34: 9 There is no w to those who
Prov 13:25 of the wicked shall be in w
Prov 24:34 and your w like an armed man
Matt 7:12 whatever you w men to do to
Matt 12:38 we w to see a sign from You
Matt 13:28 Do you w us then to go and
Matt 15:32 I do not w to send them away
Matt 19:17 But if you w to enter into
Matt 19:21 If you w to be perfect, go,
Matt 20:32 What do you w Me to do for
Matt 26:17 Where do You w us to prepare
Matt 27:17 Whom do you w me to release
Matt 27:21 do you w me to release to you
Mark 6:22 Ask me whatever you w, and I
Mark 6:25 I w you to give me at once
Mark 6:26 he did not w to refuse her
Mark 9:30 He did not w anyone to know
Mark 10:35 we w You to do for us
Mark 10:36 What do you w Me to do for
Mark 10:51 What do you w Me to do for
Mark 14:12 Where do You w us to go and
Mark 15: 9 Do you w me to release to you
Mark 15:12 What then do you w me to do
Luke 6:31 just as you w men to do to
Luke 9:54 do You w us to command fire
Luke 15:14 land, and he began to be in w
Luke 16:26 so that those who w to pass
Luke 18:41 What do you w Me to do for
Luke 19:27 who did not w me to reign
Luke 22: 9 Where do You w us to prepare
John 5: 6 Do you w to be made well
John 6:67 Do you also w to go away
John 7: 1 for He did not w to walk in
John 8:44 of your father you w to do
John 9:27 Why do you w to hear it again
John 9:27 Do you also w to become His
John 18:39 Do you therefore w me to
Acts 7:28 Do you w to kill me as you
Acts 9: 6 Lord, what do You w me to do
Acts 17:18 does this babbler w to say
Acts 17:20 Therefore we w to know what
Acts 18:15 for I do not w to be a judge
Rom 1:13 Now I do not w you to be
Rom 13: 3 Do you w to be unafraid of
Rom 16:19 but I w you to be wise in
1Co 4:21 What do you w
1Co 7:32 But I w you to be without
1Co 10: 1 I do not w you to be unaware
1Co 10:20 and I do not w you to have
1Co 11: 3 But I w you to know that the
1Co 12: 1 I do not w you to be ignorant
1Co 14:35 if they w to learn something,
2Co 1: 8 For we do not w you to be
2Co 5: 4 not because we w to be
Gal 1: 7 w to pervert the gospel of
Gal 3: 2 This only I w to learn from
Gal 4:17 they w to exclude you, that
Phil 1:12 But I w you to know, brethren
Col 2: 1 For I w you to know what a
1Th 4:13 But I do not w you to be
Tit 3: 8 and these things I w you to
Jas 2:20 But do you w to know, O
Jude 5 But I w to remind you, though

WANTED (*see* WANT)
1Ki 9: 1 desire which he w to do,
Ezek 1:12 wherever the spirit w to go
Ezek 1:20 Wherever the spirit w to go
Matt 14: 5 although he w to put him to
Matt 18:23 is like a certain king who w
Matt 23:37 How often I w to gather your
Mark 3:13 to Him those He Himself w
Mark 6:19 w to kill him, but she could
Mark 7:24 w no one to know it, but He
Luke 13:34 How often I w to gather your
John 1:43 day Jesus w to go to Galilee
John 6:11 the fish, as much as they w
John 7:44 some of them w to take Him
Acts 10:10 very hungry and w to eat
Acts 16: 3 Paul w to have him go on with
Acts 19:30 when Paul w to go in to the
Acts 19:33 w to make his defense to the
Acts 22:30 day, because he w to know for
Acts 23:28 when I w to know the reason
Acts 24: 6 w to judge him according to
Acts 28:18 w to let me go, because there
1Th 2:18 Therefore we w to come to you
Phm 14 consent I w to do nothing
Heb 12:17 when he w to inherit the

WANTING (*see* WANT)
Dan 5:27 in the balances, and found w
Matt 1:19 not w to make her a public
Mark 15:15 w to gratify the crowd,
Luke 10:29 w to justify himself, said to
Acts 24:27 w to do the Jews a favor,
Acts 25: 9 w to do the Jews a favor,
Acts 27:43 w to save Paul, kept them
Rom 9:22 w to show His wrath and to

WANTON
Is 3:16 w eyes, walking and mincing as
1Ti 5:11 to grow w against Christ,

WANTS (*see* WANT)
Ex 12:48 w to keep the Passover to the
Lev 27:13 But if he w at all to redeem
Lev 27:15 it w to redeem his house,
Lev 27:31 If a man w at all to redeem
Ezek 46: 5 as much as he w to give, as
Ezek 46: 7 as much as he w to give for
Ezek 46:11 as much as he w to give for
Matt 5:40 If anyone w to sue you and
Matt 5:42 from him who w to borrow from
Luke 13:31 here, for Herod w to kill You
John 7:17 If anyone w to do His will,
Jas 4: 4 Whoever therefore w to be a
Rev 11: 5 if anyone w to harm them,
Rev 11: 5 if anyone w to harm them, he

WAR (*see* WARFARE, WAR-HORSES, WARRED, WARRING, WARRIOR, WARS)
Gen 14: 2 that they made w with Bera
Ex 1:10 it happen, in the event of w
Ex 13:17 their minds when they see w
Ex 15: 3 The LORD is a man of w
Ex 17:16 the LORD will have w with
Ex 32:17 is a noise of w in the camp
Num 1: 3 are able to go to w in Israel
Num 1:20 all who were able to go to w
Num 1:22 all who were able to go to w
Num 1:24 all who were able to go to w
Num 1:26 all who were able to go to w
Num 1:28 all who were able to go to w
Num 1:30 all who were able to go to w
Num 1:32 all who were able to go to w
Num 1:34 all who were able to go to w
Num 1:36 all who were able to go to w
Num 1:38 all who were able to go to w
Num 1:40 all who were able to go to w
Num 1:42 all who were able to go to w
Num 1:45 able to go to w in Israel
Num 10: 9 When you go to w in your land
Num 26: 2 are able to go to w in Israel
Num 31: 3 some of yourselves for the w
Num 31: 4 you shall send to the w
Num 31: 5 twelve thousand armed for w
Num 31: 6 Then Moses sent them to the w
Num 31: 6 he sent them to the w with
Num 31:21 priest said to the men of w
Num 31:27 those who took part in the w
Num 31:28 of w who went out to battle
Num 31:32 which the men of w had taken
Num 31:36 those who had gone out to w
Num 31:49 w who are under our command
Num 31:53 (The men of w had taken spoil
Num 32: 6 go to w while you sit here
Num 32:20 before the LORD for the w
Num 32:27 over, every man armed for w
Deut 1:41 girded on his weapons of w
Deut 2:14 generation of the men of w
Deut 2:16 when all the men of w had
Deut 4:34 by signs, by wonders, by w
Deut 20:12 but would make w against you
Deut 20:19 while making w against it to
Deut 20:20 city that makes w with you
Deut 21:10 When you go out to w against
Deut 24: 5 to w or be charged with any
Josh 4:13 for w crossed over before the
Josh 5: 4 were males, all the men of w
Josh 5: 6 the people who were men of w
Josh 6: 3 the city, all you men of w
Josh 8: 1 all the people of w with you
Josh 8: 3 arose, and all the people of w
Josh 8:11 all the people of w who were
Josh 10: 5 Gibeon and made w against it
Josh 10: 7 all the people of w with him
Josh 10:24 men of w who went with him
Josh 11: 7 all the people of w with him
Josh 11:18 Joshua made w a long time
Josh 11:23 Then the land rested from w
Josh 14:11 so now is my strength for w
Josh 14:15 Then the land had rest from w
Josh 17: 1 because he was a man of w
Josh 22:12 to go to w against them
Josh 24: 9 Moab, arose to make w against
Judg 3: 2 might be taught to know w
Judg 3:10 He went out to w, and the LORD
Judg 5: 8 then there was w in the gates
Judg 11: 4 Ammon made w against Israel
Judg 11: 5 Ammon made w against Israel
Judg 18:11 armed with weapons of w
Judg 18:16 armed with their weapons of w
Judg 18:17 were armed with weapons of w
Judg 20:17 all of these were men of w
Judg 21:22 wife for any of them in the w
1Sa 8:12 some to make his weapons of w
1Sa 14:52 Now there was fierce w with
1Sa 16:18 man of valor, a man of w,
1Sa 17:33 he a man of w from his youth
1Sa 18: 5 set him over the men of w
1Sa 18:30 the Philistines went out to w
1Sa 19: 8 And there was w again
1Sa 23: 8 all the people together for w
1Sa 28: 1 their armies together for w
1Sa 28:15 Philistines make w against me
2Sa 1:27 and the weapons of w perished
2Sa 3: 1 Now there was a long w
2Sa 3: 6 while there was w between the
2Sa 11: 7 doing, and how the w prospered
2Sa 11:18 the things concerning the w
2Sa 11:19 matters of the w to the king
2Sa 17: 8 and your father is a man of w
2Sa 21:15 were at w again with Israel
2Sa 22:35 He teaches my hands to make w
1Ki 2: 5 the blood of w in peacetime
1Ki 2: 5 put the blood of w on his
1Ki 9:22 because they were men of w
1Ki 14:19 of Jeroboam, how he made w
1Ki 14:30 there was w between Rehoboam
1Ki 15: 6 there was w between Rehoboam
1Ki 15: 7 there was w between Abijam
1Ki 15:16 Now there was w between Asa
1Ki 15:32 there was w between Asa and
1Ki 20: 1 Samaria, and made w against it
1Ki 20:18 if they have come out for w
1Ki 22: 1 without w between Syria and
1Ki 22:15 shall we go to w against
1Ki 22:45 he showed, and how he made w
2Ki 6: 8 was making w against Israel
2Ki 8:28 to w against Hazael king of
2Ki 13:25 of Jehoahaz his father by w
2Ki 14: 7 of Salt, and took Sela by w
2Ki 14:28 his might, how he made w, and
2Ki 16: 5 up to Jerusalem to make w
2Ki 18:20 counsel and strength for w
2Ki 19: 9 come out to make w with you
2Ki 24:16 who were strong and fit for w
2Ki 25: 4 and all the men of w fled at
2Ki 25:19 had charge of the men of w
1Ch 5:10 they made w with the Hagrites
1Ch 5:18 skillful in w, who went to w
1Ch 5:19 They made w with the Hagrites
1Ch 5:22 dead, because the w was God's
1Ch 7: 4 of the army ready for w
1Ch 7:11 of valor fit to go out for w
1Ch 12: 1 mighty men, helpers in the w
1Ch 12:23 that were equipped for the w
1Ch 12:24 eight hundred armed for w
1Ch 12:25 mighty men of valor fit for w
1Ch 12:33 in w with all weapons of w
1Ch 12:36 those who could go out to w
1Ch 12:37 every kind of weapon of w
1Ch 12:38 All these men of w, who could
1Ch 18:10 had been at w with Tou)
1Ch 20: 4 it happened afterward that w
1Ch 20: 5 Again there was w with the
1Ch 20: 6 Yet again there was w at Gath
1Ch 28: 3 you have been a man of w and
2Ch 8: 9 Some were men of w, captains
2Ch 13: 2 there was w between Abijah and
2Ch 14: 6 he had no w in those years,
2Ch 15:19 there was no more w until the

2Ch 17:10 make w against Jehoshaphat
2Ch 17:13 and the men of w, mighty men
2Ch 17:18 thousand prepared for w
2Ch 18: 3 we will be with you in the w
2Ch 18: 5 Shall we go to w against
2Ch 18:14 shall we go to w against
2Ch 22: 5 make w against Hazael king of
2Ch 25: 5 choice men, able to go to w
2Ch 26: 6 out and made w against the
2Ch 26:11 went out to w by companies
2Ch 26:13 that made w with mighty power
2Ch 28:12 those who came from the w
2Ch 32: 2 to make w against Jerusalem
2Ch 35:21 the house with which I have w
Job 5:20 in w from the power of the
Job 10:17 changes and w are ever with me
Job 38:23 for the day of battle and w
Ps 18:34 He teaches my hands to make w
Ps 27: 3 Though w should rise against
Ps 55:21 But w was in his heart
Ps 68:30 the peoples who delight in w
Ps 120: 7 when I speak, they are for w
Ps 140: 2 gather together for w
Ps 144: 1 Who trains my hands for w
Prov 20:18 by wise counsel wage w
Prov 24: 6 you will wage your own w, and
Eccl 3: 8 a time of w, and a time of
Eccl 8: 8 is no discharge in that w
Eccl 9:18 is better than weapons of w
Song 3: 8 swords, being expert in w
Is 2: 4 shall they learn w anymore
Is 3: 2 mighty man and the man of w
Is 3:25 and your mighty in the w
Is 7: 1 to make w against it, but
Is 21:15 and from the distress of w
Is 36: 5 counsel and strength for w
Is 37: 9 come out to make w with you
Is 41:12 Those who w against you shall
Is 42:13 up His zeal like a man of w
Jer 4:19 the trumpet, the alarm of w
Jer 6: 4 Prepare w against her
Jer 6:23 as men of w set in array
Jer 21: 2 of Babylon makes w against us
Jer 21: 4 of w that are in your hands
Jer 28: 8 of w and disaster and
Jer 38: 4 of w who remain in this city
Jer 39: 4 and all the men of w saw them
Jer 41: 3 found there, the men of w
Jer 41:16 the mighty men of w and the
Jer 42:14 Egypt where we shall see no w
Jer 48:14 and strong men for the w'
Jer 49: 2 to be heard an alarm of w in
Jer 49:26 all the men of w shall be cut
Jer 50:30 all her men of w shall be cut
Jer 51:20 My battle-ax and weapons of w
Jer 51:32 the men of w are terrified
Jer 52: 7 and all the men of w fled
Jer 52:25 had charge of the men of w
Ezek 17:17 company do anything in the w
Ezek 27:10 were in your army as men of w
Ezek 27:27 your men of w who are in you
Ezek 32:27 hell with their weapons of w
Ezek 39:20 men and with all the men of w
Dan 7:21 making w against the saints
Dan 9:26 And till the end of the w
Joel 2: 7 climb the wall like men of w
Joel 3: 9 Prepare for w! Wake up the
Joel 3: 9 all the men of w draw near
Mic 2: 8 by, like men returned from w
Mic 3: 5 But who prepare w against him
Mic 4: 3 shall they learn w any more
Luke 14:31 king, going to make w against
Luke 23:11 Then Herod, with his men of w
1Co 9: 7 Who ever goes to w at his own
2Co 10: 3 we do not w according to the
Jas 4: 1 that w in your members
Jas 4: 2 You fight and w
1Pe 2:11 which w against the soul,
Rev 11: 7 pit will make w against them
Rev 12: 7 And w broke out in heaven
Rev 12:17 he went to make w with the
Rev 13: 4 is able to make w with him
Rev 13: 7 him to make w with the saints
Rev 17:14 will make w with the Lamb
Rev 19:11 He judges and makes w
Rev 19:19 gathered together to make w

WARDROBE
2Ki 10:22 to the one in charge of the w
2Ki 22:14 of Harhas, keeper of the w
2Ch 34:22 of Hasrah, keeper of the w

WARES
Neh 10:31 peoples of the land bring w
Neh 13:20 sellers of all kinds of w
Jer 10:17 up your w from the land, O
Ezek 27:14 traded for your w with horses
Ezek 27:16 gave you for your w emeralds
Ezek 27:19 Dan and Javan paid for your w
Ezek 27:22 your w the choicest spices
Ezek 27:27 Your riches, w, and
Ezek 27:33 When your w went out by sea,
Mark 11:16 to carry w through the temple

WARFARE (*see* WAR)
Is 40: 2 to her, that her w is ended
2Co 10: 4 For the weapons of our w are
1Ti 1:18 them you may wage the good w
2Ti 2: 4 No one engaged in w entangles

WAR-HORSES (*see* HORSE, WAR)
Ezek 23:24 with chariots, wagons, and w

WARM (*see* WARMED, WARMING, WARMS)
1Ki 1: 1 him, but he could not get w
1Ki 1: 2 our lord the king may be w
2Ki 4:34 flesh of the child became w
Job 6:17 When it is w, they cease to
Eccl 4:11 together, they will keep w
Eccl 4:11 but how can one be w alone
Is 44:15 take some of it and w himself
Is 44:16 I am w, I have seen the fire
Hag 1: 6 yourselves, but no one is w

WARMED (*see* WARM)
Job 31:20 and if he was not w with the
Is 47:14 not be a coal to be w by, nor
Mark 14:54 and w himself at the fire
John 18:18 cold, and they w themselves
John 18:18 stood with them and w himself
John 18:25 Peter stood and w himself
Jas 2:16 Depart in peace, be w and

WARMING (*see* WARM)
Mark 14:67 when she saw Peter w himself

WARMS (*see* WARM)
Job 39:14 ground, and w them in the dust
Is 44:16 he even w himself and says

WARN (*see* WARNED, WARNING, WARNS)
Ex 19:21 w the people, lest they break
1Ki 2:42 and w you, saying, 'Know for
2Ch 19:10 ordinances, you shall w them
Ezek 3:18 nor speak to w the wicked
Ezek 3:19 if you w the wicked, and he
Ezek 3:21 Nevertheless if you w the
Ezek 33: 7 My mouth and w them for Me
Ezek 33: 8 you do not speak to w the
Ezek 33: 9 Nevertheless if you w the
Acts 20:31 not cease to w everyone night
1Co 4:14 my beloved children I w you
1Th 5:14 w those who are unruly,

WARNED (*see* WARN)
Gen 43: 3 The man solemnly w us, saying
Ex 19:23 for You w us, saying, 'Set
2Ki 6:10 Thus he w him, and he was
Neh 13:15 I w them about the day on
Neh 13:21 So I w them, and said to them,
Ps 19:11 by them Your servant is w
Ezek 33: 6 and the people are not w, and
Matt 2:12 being divinely w in a dream
Matt 2:22 being w by God in a dream, he
Matt 3: 7 Who has w you to flee from
Matt 9:30 And Jesus sternly w them,
Matt 12:16 He w them not to make Him
Matt 20:31 Then the multitude w them
Mark 1:43 And He strictly w him and sent
Mark 3:12 But He sternly w them that
Mark 10:48 Then many w him to be quiet
Luke 3: 7 Who w you to flee from the
Luke 9:21 And He strictly w and
Luke 18:39 Then those who went before w
Heb 11: 7 being divinely w of things

WARNING (*see* WARN, WARNINGS)
Jer 6:10 whom shall I speak and give w
Ezek 3:17 mouth, and give them w from
Ezek 3:18 die,' and you give him no w
Ezek 3:20 you did not give him w, he
Ezek 3:21 surely live because he took w
Ezek 33: 4 trumpet and does not take w
Ezek 33: 5 trumpet, but did not take w
Ezek 33: 5 But he who takes w will save
Col 1:28 w every man and teaching every

WARNINGS (*see* WARNING)
2Ch 36:15 w to them by His messengers

WARNS (*see* WARN)
Ezek 33: 3 the trumpet and w the people,

WARP (*see* WARPED)
Lev 13:48 whether it is in the w or
Lev 13:49 in the w or in the woof, or
Lev 13:51 either in the w or in the
Lev 13:52 the plague, whether w or woof
Lev 13:53 either in the w or in the
Lev 13:56 of the w or out of the woof
Lev 13:57 either in the w or in the
Lev 13:58 either w or woof, or whatever
Lev 13:59 either in the w or woof, or

WARPED (*see* WARP)
Is 47:10 and your knowledge have w you
Tit 3:11 that such a person is w and

WARRED (*see* WAR)
Num 31: 7 they w against the Midianites

WARRING (*see* WAR)
2Ki 19: 8 of Assyria w against Libnah
Is 37: 8 of Assyria w against Libnah
Rom 7:23 w against the law of my mind,

WARRIOR (*see* WAR, WARRIOR'S, WARRIORS)
1Ch 12:28 a young man, a valiant w
Job 16:14 He runs at me like a w
Ps 120: 4 Sharp arrows of the w, With
Ps 127: 4 arrows in the hand of a w
Jer 50: 9 be like those of an expert w

WARRIOR'S (*see* WARRIOR)
Is 9: 5 For every w sandal from the

WARRIORS (*see* WARRIOR)
1Ki 12:21 chosen men who were w, to
1Ch 11:26 Also the mighty w were Asahel
2Ch 11: 1 chosen men who were w, to
2Ch 13: 3 with an army of valiant w
Ezek 32:12 By the swords of the mighty w

WARS (*see* WAR)
Num 21:14 the Book of the W of the LORD
Judg 3: 1 known any of the w in Canaan
2Sa 8:10 for Hadadezer had w with Toi
1Ki 5: 3 w which were fought against
1Ch 22: 8 blood and have made great w
2Ch 12:15 there were w between
2Ch 16: 9 from now on you shall have w
2Ch 27: 7 acts of Jotham, and all his w
Ps 46: 9 He makes w cease to the end
Matt 24: 6 hear of w and rumors of w
Mark 13: 7 hear of w and rumors of w
Luke 21: 9 But when you hear of w and
Jas 4: 1 Where do w and fights come

WARY
Prov 19:25 and the simple will become w

WAS (*see* PREFACE)

WASH (*see* UNWASHED, WASHED, WASHES, WASHING, WASHPOT)
Gen 18: 4 and w your feet, and rest
Gen 19: 2 the night, and w your feet
Gen 24:32 and water to w his feet and
Ex 2: 5 to w herself at the river
Ex 19:10 and let them w their clothes
Ex 29: 4 you shall w them with water
Ex 29:17 w its entrails and its legs,
Ex 30:19 his sons shall w their hands
Ex 30:20 LORD, they shall w with water
Ex 30:21 So they shall w their hands
Ex 40:12 meeting and w them with water
Lev 1: 9 but he shall w its entrails
Lev 1:13 but he shall w the entrails
Lev 6:27 you shall w that on which it
Lev 11:25 of them shall w his clothes
Lev 11:28 carcass shall w his clothes
Lev 11:40 carcass shall w his clothes
Lev 11:40 carcass shall w his clothes
Lev 13: 6 he shall w his clothes and be
Lev 13:34 He shall w his clothes and be
Lev 13:54 shall command that they w the
Lev 13:58 if you w the garment, either
Lev 14: 8 cleansed shall w his clothes
Lev 14: 8 w himself in water, that he
Lev 14: 9 He shall w his clothes and
Lev 14: 9 w his body in water, and he
Lev 14:47 the house shall w his clothes
Lev 14:47 the house shall w his clothes

Lev 15: 5 his bed shall w his clothes
Lev 15: 6 sat shall w his clothes and
Lev 15: 7 discharge shall w his clothes
Lev 15: 8 then he shall w his clothes
Lev 15:10 things shall w his clothes
Lev 15:11 he shall w his clothes and
Lev 15:13 w his clothes, and bathe his
Lev 15:16 then he shall w all his body
Lev 15:21 her bed shall w his clothes
Lev 15:22 sat on shall w his clothes
Lev 15:27 he shall w his clothes and
Lev 16: 4 he shall w his body in water
Lev 16:24 And he shall w his body with
Lev 16:26 scapegoat shall w his clothes
Lev 16:28 them shall w his clothes and
Lev 17:15 he shall both w his clothes
Lev 17:16 does not w or bathe his body
Num 8: 7 let them w their clothes, and
Num 19: 7 priest shall w his clothes
Num 19: 8 shall w his clothes in water
Num 19:10 heifer shall w his clothes
Num 19:19 w his clothes, and bathe in
Num 19:21 shall w his clothes
Num 31:24 you shall w your clothes on
Deut 21: 6 to the slain man shall w
Deut 23:11 that he shall w himself with
Ruth 3: 3 Therefore w yourself and
1Sa 25:41 a servant to w the feet of
2Sa 11: 8 to your house and w your feet
2Ki 5:10 w in the Jordan seven times,
2Ki 5:12 Could I not w in them and be
2Ki 5:13 then, when he says to you, 'W
2Ch 4: 6 on the left, to w in them
2Ch 4: 6 offering they would w in them
2Ch 4: 6 was for the priests to w in
Job 9:30 If I w myself with snow water
Job 14:19 as torrents w away the soil
Ps 26: 6 I will w my hands in
Ps 51: 2 W me thoroughly from my
Ps 51: 7 W me, and I shall be whiter
Ps 58:10 He shall w his feet in the
Is 1:16 W yourselves, make yourselves
Jer 2:22 For though you w yourself
Jer 4:14 w your heart from wickedness,
Matt 6:17 your head and w your face,
Matt 15: 2 For they do not w their hands
Mark 7: 3 w their hands in a special
Mark 7: 4 they do not eat unless they w
Luke 7:38 she began to w His feet with
John 9: 7 w in the pool of Siloam"
John 9:11 Go to the pool of Siloam and w
John 13: 5 began to w the disciples'
John 13: 8 You shall never w my feet
John 13: 8 If I do not w you, you have
John 13:10 needs only to w his feet, but
John 13:14 feet, you also ought to w one
Acts 22:16 w away your sins, calling on

WASHED (*see* WASH)
Gen 43:24 water, and they w their feet
Gen 43:31 Then he w his face and came
Gen 49:11 he w his garments in wine, and
Ex 19:14 and they w their clothes
Ex 40:31 his sons w their hands and
Ex 40:32 came near the altar, they w
Lev 8: 6 his sons and w them with water
Lev 8:21 Then he w the entrails and the
Lev 9:14 he w the entrails and the legs
Lev 13:55 plague after it has been w
Lev 13:58 it shall be w a second time
Lev 15:17 it shall be w with water
Num 8:21 themselves and w their clothes
Judg 19:21 they w their feet, and ate and
2Sa 12:20 arose from the ground, w and
2Sa 19:24 nor w his clothes, from the
1Ki 22:38 Then someone w the chariot at
Ps 73:13 And w my hands in innocence
Prov 30:12 eyes, yet is not w from its
Song 5: 3 I have w my feet
Song 5:12 w with milk, and fitly set
Is 4: 4 When the Lord has w away the
Ezek 16: 4 nor were you w in water to
Ezek 16: 9 Then I w you in water
Ezek 16: 9 I thoroughly w off your blood
Ezek 23:40 And you w yourself for them,
Ezek 40:38 where they w the burnt
Matt 27:24 and w his hands before the
Luke 7:44 but she has w My feet with
Luke 11:38 had not first w before dinner
John 9: 7 So he went and w, and came
John 9:11 So I went and w, and I
John 9:15 put clay on my eyes, and I w
John 13:12 So when He had w their feet
John 13:14 have w your feet, you also
Acts 9:37 When they had w her, they
Acts 16:33 the night and w their stripes
1Co 6:11 But you were w, but you were
1Ti 5:10 if she has w the saints' feet
Heb 10:22 our bodies w with pure water
2Pe 2:22 a sow, having w, to her
Rev 1: 5 w us from our sins in His own
Rev 7:14 w their robes and made them

WASHES (*see* WASH)
Lev 22: 6 he w his body with water

WASHING (*see* WASH, WASHINGS)
Ex 30:18 base also of bronze, for w
Ex 40:30 and put water there for w
Lev 13:56 plague has faded after w it
Neh 4:23 everyone took them off for w
Song 4: 2 which have come up from the w
Song 6: 6 which have come up from the w
Mark 7: 4 and hold, like the w of cups
Mark 7: 8 the w of pitchers and cups, and
Luke 5: 2 them and were w their nets
John 13: 6 Lord, are You w my feet
Eph 5:26 and cleanse it with the w of
Tit 3: 5 through the w of regeneration

WASHINGS (*see* WASHING)
Heb 9:10 foods and drinks, various w

WASHPOT (*see* POT, WASH)
Ps 60: 8 Moab is My w
Ps 108: 9 Moab is My w

WASTE (*see* WASTED, WASTELAND, WASTES, WASTING)
Lev 26:31 I will lay your cities w and
Lev 26:33 be desolate and your cities w
Lev 26:39 w away in their iniquity in
Lev 26:39 with them, they shall w away
Num 21:30 Then we laid w as far as
2Ki 18:27 and drink their own w with you
2Ki 19:17 have laid w the nations and
Neh 2: 3 of my fathers' tombs, lies w
Neh 2:17 are in, how Jerusalem lies w
Job 30: 3 the wilderness, desolate and w
Job 38:27 To satisfy the desolate w
Ps 31:10 iniquity, And my bones w away
Ps 79: 7 laid w his dwelling place
Ps 91: 6 that lays w at noonday
Prov 13:23 lack of justice there is w
Prov 23: 8 up, and w your pleasant words
Is 5: 6 I will lay it w
Is 5:17 in the w places of the fat
Is 6:11 Until the cities are laid w
Is 15: 1 night Ar of Moab is laid w
Is 15: 1 night Kir of Moab is laid w
Is 23: 1 For it is laid w, so that
Is 23:14 for your strength is laid w
Is 24: 1 the earth empty and makes it w
Is 33: 8 The highways lie w, the
Is 34:10 to generation it shall lie w
Is 36:12 and drink their own w with you
Is 37:18 have laid w all the nations
Is 42:15 I will lay w the mountains and
Is 44:26 I will raise up her w places
Is 49:17 those who laid you w shall go
Is 49:19 For your w and desolate places
Is 51: 3 will comfort all her w places
Is 52: 9 you w places of Jerusalem
Is 58:12 shall build the old w places
Is 64:11 pleasant things are laid w
Jer 2:15 they made his land w
Jer 4: 7 Your cities will be laid w
Jer 27:17 should this city be laid w
Jer 46:19 For Noph shall be w and be
Jer 49:13 a desolation, a reproach, a w
Jer 50:21 W and utterly destroy them,"
Ezek 4:12 of human w in their sight
Ezek 4:15 cow dung instead of human w
Ezek 4:17 and w away because of their
Ezek 5:14 Moreover I will make you a w
Ezek 6: 6 the cities shall be laid w
Ezek 6: 6 your altars may be laid w
Ezek 12:20 are inhabited shall be laid w
Ezek 19: 7 and laid w their cities
Ezek 26: 2 she is laid w
Ezek 29: 9 shall become desolate and w
Ezek 29:10 the land of Egypt utterly w
Ezek 29:12 the cities that are laid w
Ezek 30: 7 of the cities that are laid w
Ezek 30:12 I will make the land w, and
Ezek 35: 4 I shall lay your cities w
Ezek 38:12 the w places that are again
Hos 4: 3 who dwells there will w away
Joel 1: 7 He has laid w My vine, and
Amos 7: 9 of Israel shall be laid w
Amos 9:14 they shall build the w cities
Mic 5: 6 They shall w with the sword
Nah 2:10 She is empty, desolate, and w
Nah 3: 7 and say, 'Nineveh is laid w
Mal 1: 3 laid w his mountains and his
Matt 26: 8 To what purpose is this w

WASTED (*see* WASTE)
Deut 32:24 They shall be w with hunger
Is 19: 5 sea, and the river will be w
Jer 44: 6 and they are w and desolate, as
Ezek 36:35 and the w, desolate, and ruined
Joel 1:10 The field is w, the land
Mark 14: 4 Why was this fragrant oil w
Luke 15:13 there w his possessions with

WASTELAND (*see* WASTE)
Num 21:20 which looks down on the w
Num 23:28 of Peor, that overlooks the w
Deut 32:10 in a desert land and in the w
Is 35: 1 the w shall be glad for them,

WASTES (*see* WASTE)
Job 33:21 His flesh w away from sight,
Ps 6: 7 My eye w away because of
Ps 31: 9 My eye w away with grief, Yes
Ps 88: 9 My eye w away because of
Prov 29: 3 of harlots w his wealth
Is 10:18 be as when a sick man w away
Jer 49:13 cities shall be perpetual w
Ezek 36: 4 the valleys, the desolate w

WASTING (*see* WASTE)
Lev 26:16 you, w disease and fever which
Is 59: 7 w and destruction are in their
Is 60:18 neither w nor destruction
Luke 16: 1 that this man was w his goods

WATCH (*see* WATCHED, WATCHER, WATCHES, WATCHFUL, WATCHING, WATCHMAN, WATCHTOWER)
Gen 31:49 May the LORD w between you
Ex 14:24 to pass, in the morning w
Num 4:20 w while the holy things are
Deut 2: 4 Therefore w yourselves
Judg 7:17 w, and when I come to the edge
Judg 7:19 the beginning of the middle w
Judg 7:19 just as they had posted the w
Judg 21:21 and w; and just when the
1Sa 6: 9 And w: if it goes up
1Sa 11:11 of the camp in the morning w
1Sa 19:11 to David's house to w him
2Sa 13:28 W now, when Amnon's heart is
2Sa 13:34 was keeping w lifted his eyes
2Sa 20:21 W, his head will be thrown to
2Ki 11: 5 w over the king's house,
2Ki 11: 6 shall keep the w of the house
2Ki 11: 7 w of the house of the LORD
2Ch 23: 4 be keeping w over the doors
2Ch 23: 6 shall keep the w of the LORD
Ezra 8:29 W and keep them until you
Neh 4: 9 we set a w against them day
Neh 7: 3 one at his w station and
Neh 12:25 gatekeepers keeping the w at
Job 13:27 and w closely all my paths
Job 14:16 but do not w over my sin
Ps 90: 4 And like a w in the night
Ps 130: 6 those who w for the morning
Ps 130: 6 those who w for the morning
Ps 141: 3 Keep w over the door of my
Prov 15: 3 keeping w on the evil and the
Is 29:20 all who w for iniquity are
Jer 5: 6 a leopard will w over their
Jer 31:28 so I will w over them to
Jer 44:27 I will w over them for
Jer 48:19 Aroer, stand by the way and w
Dan 12: 1 w over the sons of your
Nah 2: 1 Man the fort! W the road!
Hab 1: 5 Look among the nations and w
Hab 2: 1 I will stand my w and set
Hab 2: 1 w to see what He will say to
Matt 14:25 Now in the fourth w of the
Matt 24:42 W therefore, for you do not
Matt 25:13 W therefore, for you know
Matt 26:38 Stay here and w with Me
Matt 26:40 could you not w with Me one
Matt 26:41 W and pray, lest you enter

Matt 27:36 they kept w over Him there
Mark 6:48 about the fourth w of the
Mark 13: 9 But w out for yourselves, for
Mark 13:33 Take heed, w and pray
Mark 13:34 the doorkeeper to w
Mark 13:35 W therefore, for you do not
Mark 13:37 I say to all: W!
Mark 14:34 Stay here and w
Mark 14:37 Could you not w one hour
Mark 14:38 W and pray, lest you enter
Luke 2: 8 keeping w over their flock by
Luke 12:38 should come in the second w
Luke 12:38 or come in the third w
Luke 21:36 W therefore, and pray always
Acts 20:31 Therefore w, and remember
1Co 16:13 W, stand fast in the faith,
1Th 5: 6 as others do, but let us w
Heb 13:17 for they w out for your souls
Rev 3: 3 Therefore if you will not w

WATCHED (*see* WATCH)
Ex 33: 8 w Moses until he had gone
Judg 16:27 women on the roof who w while
1Sa 1:12 LORD, that Eli w her mouth
Job 29: 2 the days when God w over me
Jer 20:10 w for my stumbling, saying
Jer 31:28 that as I have w over them to
Lam 4:17 in our watching we w for a
Ezek 10: 2 And he went in as I w
Dan 2:34 You w while a stone was cut
Dan 7: 4 I w till its wings were
Dan 7: 9 I w till thrones were put in
Dan 7:11 I w then because of the sound
Dan 7:11 I w till the beast was slain,
Matt 24:43 would come, he would have w
Mark 3: 2 they w Him closely, whether
Luke 6: 7 and Pharisees w Him closely,
Luke 12:39 would come, he would have w
Luke 14: 1 that they w Him closely
Luke 20:20 So they w Him, and sent spies
Acts 1: 9 these things, while they w
Acts 9:24 they w the gates day and night

WATCHER (*see* WATCH, WATCHERS)
Job 7:20 I done to You, O w of men
Dan 4:13 on my bed, and there was a w
Dan 4:23 inasmuch as the king saw a w

WATCHERS (*see* WATCHER)
Jer 4:16 that w come from a far
Dan 4:17 is by the decree of the w

WATCHES (*see* WATCH)
Job 15:22 and he w for the sword
Job 33:11 the stocks, He w all my paths
Ps 37:32 The wicked w the righteous,
Ps 63: 6 on You in the night w
Ps 119:148 are awake through the night w
Ps 146: 9 The LORD w over the strangers
Prov 31:27 She w over the ways of her
Eccl 5: 8 for high official w over high
Lam 2:19 at the beginning of the w
Rev 16:15 Blessed is he who w, and keeps

WATCHFUL (*see* WATCH)
2Ki 6:10 warned him, and he was w there
Eph 6:18 being w to this end with all
2Ti 4: 5 But you be w in all things,
1Pe 4: 7 serious and w in your prayers
Rev 3: 2 Be w, and strengthen the

WATCHING (*see* WATCH)
1Sa 4:13 on a seat by the wayside w
1Ki 20:33 w to see whether any sign of
Prov 8:34 w daily at my gates, waiting
Lam 4:17 us, w vainly for our help
Lam 4:17 in our w we watched for a
Dan 2:31 You, O king, were w
Dan 7:13 I was w in the night visions,
Dan 7:21 I was w; and the same horn
Zech 11:11 of the flock, who were w me
Luke 12:37 when he comes, will find w
Luke 23:49 at a distance, w these things

WATCHMAN (*see* WATCH, WATCHMAN'S, WATCHMEN)
2Sa 18:24 the w went up to the roof
2Sa 18:25 Then the w cried out and told
2Sa 18:26 Then the w saw another man
2Sa 18:26 and the w called to the
2Sa 18:27 So the w said, "I think the
2Ki 9:17 Now a w stood on the tower in
2Ki 9:18 And the w reported, saying,
2Ki 9:20 And the w reported, saying,
1Ch 26:16 w opposite w
Job 27:18 like a booth which a w makes
Ps 127: 1 The w stays awake in vain
Is 21: 5 set a w in the tower, eat and
Is 21: 6 Go, set a w, let him declare
Is 21:11 W, what of the night
Is 21:11 W, what of the night
Is 21:12 The w said, "The morning
Ezek 3:17 I have made you a w for the
Ezek 33: 2 territory and make him their w
Ezek 33: 6 But if the w sees the sword
Ezek 33: 7 I have made you a w for the
Hos 9: 8 The w of Ephraim is with my
Mic 7: 4 the day of your w and your

WATCHMAN'S (*see* WATCHMAN)
Ezek 33: 6 I will require at the w hand

WATCHMEN (*see* WATCHMAN)
1Sa 14:16 Now the w of Saul in Gibeah
Song 3: 3 The w who go about the city
Song 5: 7 The w who went about the city
Is 52: 8 Your w shall lift up their
Is 56:10 His w are blind, they are all
Is 62: 6 I have set w on your walls, O
Jer 6:17 I set w over you, saying
Jer 31: 6 shall be a day when the w
Jer 51:12 guard strong, set up the w

WATCHTOWER (*see* TOWER, WATCH)
2Ki 17: 9 from w to fortified city
2Ki 18: 8 from w to fortified city
Is 21: 8 on the w in the daytime

WATER (*see* WATERCOURSES, WATERED, WATERFALLS, WATERING, WATERLESS, WATERPOOLS, WATERPOT, WATERS, WATERSPRINGS)
Gen 2:10 out of Eden to w the garden
Gen 16: 7 spring of w in the wilderness
Gen 18: 4 let a little w be brought
Gen 21:14 and took bread and a skin of w
Gen 21:15 the w in the skin was used up
Gen 21:19 eyes, and she saw a well of w
Gen 21:19 and filled the skin with w
Gen 21:25 because of a well of w which
Gen 24:11 a well of w at evening time
Gen 24:11 when women go out to draw w
Gen 24:13 I stand here by the well of w
Gen 24:13 city are coming out to draw w
Gen 24:17 a little w from your pitcher
Gen 24:19 I will draw w for your camels
Gen 24:20 back to the well to draw w
Gen 24:32 w to wash his feet and the
Gen 24:43 I stand by the well of w
Gen 24:43 virgin comes out to draw w
Gen 24:43 Please give me a little w
Gen 24:45 down to the well and drew w
Gen 26:18 dug again the wells of w
Gen 26:19 a well of running w there
Gen 26:20 saying, "The w is ours
Gen 26:32 We have found w
Gen 29: 3 w the sheep, and put the stone
Gen 29: 7 W the sheep, and go and feed
Gen 29: 8 then we w the sheep
Gen 36:24 the w in the wilderness as he
Gen 37:24 there was no w in it
Gen 43:24 Joseph's house and gave them w
Gen 49: 4 Unstable as w, you shall not
Ex 2:10 I drew him out of the w
Ex 2:16 And they came and drew w, and
Ex 2:16 to w their father's flock
Ex 2:19 he also drew enough w for us
Ex 4: 9 shall take w from the river
Ex 4: 9 the w which you take from the
Ex 7:15 when he goes out to the w
Ex 7:18 to drink the w of the river
Ex 7:19 and over all their pools of w
Ex 7:21 not drink the w of the river
Ex 7:24 the river for w to drink,
Ex 7:24 not drink the w of the river
Ex 8:20 as he comes out to the w
Ex 12: 9 raw, nor boiled at all with w
Ex 15:22 the wilderness and found no w
Ex 15:27 there were twelve wells of w
Ex 17: 1 but there was no w for the
Ex 17: 2 Give us w, that we may drink
Ex 17: 3 people thirsted there for w
Ex 17: 6 w will come out of it, that
Ex 20: 4 is in the w under the earth
Ex 23:25 bless your bread and your w
Ex 29: 4 and you shall wash them with w
Ex 30:18 And you shall put w in it,
Ex 30:19 and their feet in w from it
Ex 30:20 LORD, they shall wash with w
Ex 32:20 and he scattered it on the w
Ex 34:28 neither ate bread nor drank w
Ex 40: 7 and the altar, and put w in it
Ex 40:12 meeting and wash them with w
Ex 40:30 and put w there for washing
Ex 40:31 and their feet with w from it
Lev 1: 9 entrails and its legs with w
Lev 1:13 entrails and the legs with w
Lev 6:28 both scoured and rinsed in w
Lev 8: 6 sons and washed them with w
Lev 8:21 the entrails and the legs in w
Lev 11: 9 eat of all that are in the w
Lev 11: 9 whatever in the w has fins
Lev 11:10 all that move in the w or any
Lev 11:10 thing which is in the w, they
Lev 11:12 Whatever in the w does not
Lev 11:32 is done, it must be put in w
Lev 11:34 which w falls becomes unclean
Lev 11:36 in which there is plenty of w
Lev 11:38 But if any w is put on the
Lev 14: 5 earthen vessel over running w
Lev 14: 6 was killed over the running w
Lev 14: 8 hair, and wash himself in w
Lev 14: 9 clothes and wash his body in w
Lev 14:50 earthen vessel over running w
Lev 14:51 bird and in the running w, and
Lev 14:52 of the bird and the running w
Lev 15: 5 his clothes and bathe in w
Lev 15: 6 his clothes and bathe in w
Lev 15: 7 his clothes and bathe in w
Lev 15: 8 his clothes and bathe in w
Lev 15:10 his clothes and bathe in w
Lev 15:11 has not rinsed his hands in w
Lev 15:11 his clothes and bathe in w
Lev 15:12 of wood shall be rinsed in w
Lev 15:13 bathe his body in running w
Lev 15:16 shall wash all his body in w
Lev 15:17 it shall be washed with w
Lev 15:18 they both shall bathe in w
Lev 15:21 his clothes and bathe in w
Lev 15:22 his clothes and bathe in w
Lev 15:27 his clothes and bathe in w
Lev 16: 4 he shall wash his body in w
Lev 16:24 body with w in a holy place
Lev 16:26 and bathe his body in w, and
Lev 16:28 and bathe his body in w, and
Lev 17:15 his clothes and bathe in w
Lev 22: 6 he washes his body with w
Num 5:17 holy w in an earthen vessel
Num 5:17 and put it into the w
Num 5:18 bitter w that brings a curse
Num 5:19 bitter w that brings a curse
Num 5:22 may this w that causes the
Num 5:23 them off into the bitter w
Num 5:24 bitter w that brings a curse
Num 5:24 the w that brings the curse
Num 5:26 make the woman drink the w
Num 5:27 he has made her drink the w
Num 5:27 that the w that brings a
Num 8: 7 Sprinkle w of purification on
Num 19: 7 clothes, he shall bathe in w
Num 19: 8 clothes in w, bathe in w
Num 19: 9 for the w of purification
Num 19:12 with the w on the third day
Num 19:13 because the w of purification
Num 19:17 running w shall be put on
Num 19:18 hyssop and dip it in the w
Num 19:19 his clothes, and bathe in w
Num 19:20 The w of purification has not
Num 19:21 He who sprinkles the w of
Num 19:21 and he who touches the w of
Num 20: 2 Now there was no w for the
Num 20: 5 nor is there any w to drink
Num 20: 8 eyes, and it will yield its w
Num 20: 8 thus you shall bring w for
Num 20:10 Must we bring w for you out
Num 20:11 w came out abundantly, and the
Num 20:13 This was the w of Meribah
Num 20:17 will we drink w from wells
Num 20:19 livestock drink any of your w
Num 20:24 My word at the w of Meribah
Num 21: 5 For there is no food and no w
Num 21:16 and I will give them w
Num 21:22 will not drink w from wells
Num 24: 7 He shall pour w from his
Num 31:23 with the w of purification
Num 31:23 fire you shall put through w

Num 33: 9 Elim were twelve springs of **w**
Num 33:14 where there was no **w** for the
Deut 2: 6 you shall also buy **w** from
Deut 2:28 give me **w** for money, that I
Deut 4:18 is in the **w** beneath the earth
Deut 5: 8 is in the **w** under the earth
Deut 8: 7 land, a land of brooks of **w**
Deut 8:15 land where there was no **w**
Deut 8:15 who brought **w** for you out of
Deut 9: 9 neither ate bread nor drank **w**
Deut 9:18 neither ate bread nor drank **w**
Deut 10: 7 a land of rivers of **w**
Deut 11:11 which drinks **w** from the rain
Deut 12:16 pour it on the earth like **w**
Deut 12:24 pour it on the earth like **w**
Deut 15:23 pour it on the ground like **w**
Deut 21: 4 to a valley with flowing **w**
Deut 23: 4 **w** on the road when you came
Deut 23:11 he shall wash himself with **w**
Deut 29:11 to the one who draws your **w**
Josh 2:10 how the LORD dried up the **w**
Josh 3: 8 edge of the **w** of the Jordan
Josh 3:15 **w** (for the Jordan overflows
Josh 7: 5 melted and became like **w**
Josh 9:21 and **w** carriers for all the
Josh 9:23 **w** carriers for the house of
Josh 9:27 and **w** carriers for the
Josh 15: 9 fountain of the **w** of Nephtoah
Josh 15:19 give me also springs of **w**
Judg 1:15 give me also springs of **w**
Judg 4:19 give me a little **w** to drink
Judg 5: 4 the clouds also poured **w**
Judg 5:25 He asked for **w**, she gave milk
Judg 6:38 the fleece, a bowl full of **w**
Judg 7: 4 bring them down to the **w**, and
Judg 7: 5 the people down to the **w**
Judg 7: 5 from the **w** with his tongue
Judg 7: 6 on their knees to drink **w**
Judg 15:19 and **w** came out, and he drank
1Sa 7: 6 together at Mizpah, drew **w**
1Sa 9:11 women going out to draw **w**
1Sa 25:11 I then take my bread and my **w**
1Sa 26:11 the jug of **w** that are by his
1Sa 26:12 the jug of **w** by Saul's head,
1Sa 26:16 the jug of **w** that was by his
1Sa 30:11 ate, and they let him drink **w**
1Sa 30:12 drunk any **w** for three days
2Sa 5: 8 up by way of the **w** shaft and
2Sa 5:20 me, like a breakthrough of **w**
2Sa 12:27 taken the city's **w** supply
2Sa 14:14 become like **w** spilled on the
2Sa 17:20 have gone over the **w** brook
2Sa 17:21 and cross over the **w** quickly
2Sa 23:15 give me a drink of the **w** from
2Sa 23:16 drew **w** from the well of
1Ki 13: 8 nor drink **w** in this place
1Ki 13: 9 not eat bread, nor drink **w**
1Ki 13:16 **w** with you in this place
1Ki 13:17 eat bread nor drink **w** there
1Ki 13:18 he may eat bread and drink **w**
1Ki 13:19 in his house, and drank **w**
1Ki 13:22 drank **w** in the place of which
1Ki 13:22 Eat no bread and drink no **w**
1Ki 14:15 as a reed is shaken in the **w**
1Ki 17:10 bring me a little **w** in a cup
1Ki 18: 4 had fed them with bread and **w**
1Ki 18: 5 land to all the springs of **w**
1Ki 18:13 and fed them with bread and **w**
1Ki 18:33 Fill four waterpots with **w**
1Ki 18:35 So the **w** ran all around the
1Ki 18:35 also filled the trench with **w**
1Ki 18:38 it licked up the **w** that was
1Ki 19: 6 baked on coals, and a jar of **w**
1Ki 22:27 **w** of affliction, until I come
2Ki 2: 8 rolled it up, and struck the **w**
2Ki 2:14 from him, and struck the **w**
2Ki 2:14 when he also had struck the **w**
2Ki 2:19 but the **w** is bad, and the
2Ki 2:21 out to the source of the **w**
2Ki 2:21 I have healed this **w**
2Ki 2:22 So the **w** remains healed to
2Ki 3: 9 there was no **w** for the army
2Ki 3:11 who poured **w** on the hands of
2Ki 3:17 valley shall be filled with **w**
2Ki 3:19 and stop up every spring of **w**
2Ki 3:20 that suddenly **w** came by way
2Ki 3:20 and the land was filled with **w**
2Ki 3:22 the sun was shining on the **w**
2Ki 3:22 the Moabites saw the **w** on the
2Ki 3:25 up all the springs of **w** and
2Ki 6: 5 iron ax head fell into the **w**
2Ki 6:22 **w** before them, that they may
2Ki 8:15 thick cloth and dipped it in **w**
2Ki 19:24 I have dug and drunk strange **w**
2Ki 20:20 and brought **w** into the city
1Ch 11:17 would give me a drink of **w**
1Ch 11:18 drew **w** from the well of
1Ch 14:11 hand like a breakthrough of **w**
2Ch 18:26 and **w** of affliction until I
2Ch 32: 3 commanders to stop the **w** from
2Ch 32: 4 Assyria come and find much **w**
2Ch 32:30 the **w** outlet of Upper Gihon
2Ch 32:30 brought the **w** by tunnel to
Ezra 10: 6 he ate no bread and drank no **w**
Neh 3:26 of the **W** Gate toward the east
Neh 8: 1 was in front of the **W** Gate
Neh 8: 3 the **W** Gate from morning until
Neh 8:16 the open square of the **W** Gate
Neh 9:15 brought them **w** out of the
Neh 9:20 gave them **w** for their thirst
Neh 12:37 as far as the **W** Gate eastward
Neh 13: 2 of Israel with bread and **w**
Job 3:24 my groanings pour out like **w**
Job 8:11 the reeds flourish without **w**
Job 9:30 If I wash myself with snow **w**
Job 14: 9 at the scent of **w** it will bud
Job 14:11 As **w** disappears from the sea,
Job 14:19 As **w** wears away stones, and as
Job 15:16 Who drinks iniquity like **w**
Job 22: 7 given the weary **w** to drink
Job 22:11 an abundance of **w** covers you
Job 26: 8 He binds up the **w** in His
Job 34: 7 Job, who drinks scorn like **w**
Job 36:27 For He draws up drops of **w**
Job 38:25 channel for the overflowing **w**
Job 38:34 abundance of **w** may cover you
Ps 1: 3 Planted by the rivers of **w**
Ps 22:14 I am poured out like **w**, And
Ps 42: 1 deer pants for the **w** brooks
Ps 63: 1 land Where there is no **w**
Ps 65: 9 **w** it, You greatly enrich it
Ps 65: 9 The river of God is full of **w**
Ps 65:10 You **w** its ridges abundantly,
Ps 66:12 through fire and through **w**
Ps 72: 6 Like showers that **w** the earth
Ps 77:17 The clouds poured out **w**
Ps 79: 3 like **w** all around Jerusalem
Ps 88:17 around me all day long like **w**
Ps 105:41 the rock, and **w** gushed out
Ps 107:35 a wilderness into pools of **w**
Ps 109:18 let it enter his body like **w**
Ps 114: 8 the rock into a pool of **w**
Ps 119:136 Rivers of **w** run down from my
Prov 5:15 Drink **w** from your own cistern
Prov 5:15 running **w** from your own well
Prov 5:16 streams of **w** in the streets
Prov 8:24 no fountains abounding with **w**
Prov 9:17 Stolen **w** is sweet, and bread
Prov 17:14 of strife is like releasing **w**
Prov 20: 5 heart of man is like deep **w**
Prov 21: 1 LORD, like the rivers of **w**
Prov 25:21 thirsty, give him **w** to drink
Prov 25:25 As cold **w** to a weary soul, so
Prov 27:19 As in **w** face reveals face, so
Prov 30:16 that is not satisfied with **w**
Eccl 2: 6 to **w** the growing trees of the
Is 1:22 dross, your wine mixed with **w**
Is 1:30 and as a garden that has no **w**
Is 3: 1 and the whole supply of **w**
Is 12: 3 with joy you will draw **w** from
Is 14:23 and marshes of muddy **w**
Is 21:14 bring **w** to him who is thirsty
Is 22:11 for the **w** of the old pool
Is 27: 3 keep it, I **w** it every moment
Is 30:14 or to take **w** from the cistern
Is 30:20 the **w** of affliction, yet your
Is 32: 2 as rivers of **w** in a dry place
Is 33:16 given him, his **w** will be sure
Is 35: 7 the thirsty land springs of **w**
Is 37:25 I have dug and drunk **w**, and
Is 41:17 the poor and needy seek **w**
Is 41:18 the wilderness a pool of **w**
Is 41:18 and the dry land springs of **w**
Is 44: 3 For I will pour **w** on him who
Is 44:12 he drinks no **w** and is faint
Is 49:10 of **w** He will guide them
Is 50: 2 stink because there is no **w**
Is 55:10 but **w** the earth, and make it
Is 58:11 garden, and like a spring of **w**
Is 63:12 dividing the **w** before them to
Is 64: 2 as fire causes **w** to boil
Jer 2:13 cisterns that can hold no **w**
Jer 6: 7 As a fountain wells up with **w**
Jer 8:14 given us **w** of gall to drink,
Jer 9:15 give them **w** of gall to drink
Jer 9:18 and our eyelids gush with **w**
Jer 13: 1 waist, but do not put it in **w**
Jer 14: 3 have sent their lads for **w**
Jer 14: 3 to the cisterns and found no **w**
Jer 23:15 make them drink the **w** of gall
Jer 38: 6 in the dungeon there was no **w**
Lam 1:16 eye, my eye overflows with **w**
Lam 2:19 pour out your heart like **w**
Lam 3:48 overflow with rivers of **w** for
Lam 5: 4 We pay for the **w** we drink
Ezek 4:11 shall also drink **w** by measure
Ezek 4:16 and shall drink **w** by measure
Ezek 4:17 that they may lack bread and **w**
Ezek 7:17 knee will be as weak as **w**
Ezek 12:18 drink your **w** with trembling
Ezek 12:19 and drink their **w** with dread
Ezek 16: 4 washed in **w** to cleanse you
Ezek 16: 9 Then I washed you in **w**
Ezek 17: 7 planted, that he might **w** it
Ezek 21: 7 all knees will be weak as **w**
Ezek 24: 3 it on, and also pour **w** into it
Ezek 26:12 soil in the midst of the **w**
Ezek 31: 5 because of the abundance of **w**
Ezek 31:14 that no tree which drinks **w**
Ezek 31:16 of Lebanon, all that drink **w**
Ezek 32: 6 I will also **w** the land with
Ezek 36:25 will sprinkle clean **w** on you
Ezek 47: 1 and there was **w**, flowing from
Ezek 47: 1 the **w** was flowing from under
Ezek 47: 2 and there was **w**, running out
Ezek 47: 3 the **w** came up to my ankles
Ezek 47: 4 the **w** came up to my knees
Ezek 47: 4 the **w** came up to my waist
Ezek 47: 5 for the **w** was too deep, **w**
Ezek 47: 5 **w** in which one must swim, a
Ezek 47: 8 This **w** flows toward the
Ezek 47:12 because their **w** flows from
Dan 1:12 to eat and **w** to drink
Hos 2: 5 who give me my bread and my **w**
Hos 5:10 out my wrath on them like **w**
Hos 10: 7 cut off like a twig on the **w**
Joel 1:20 for the **w** brooks are dried up
Joel 3:18 Judah shall be flooded with **w**
Joel 3:18 and **w** the Valley of Acacias
Amos 4: 8 to another city to drink **w**
Amos 5:24 let justice run down like **w**
Amos 8:11 of bread, nor a thirst for **w**
Jon 3: 7 not let them eat, or drink **w**
Nah 2: 8 of old was like a pool of **w**
Nah 3:14 Draw your **w** for the siege
Hab 3:10 of the **w** passed by
Matt 3:11 you with **w** unto repentance
Matt 3:16 up immediately from the **w**
Matt 8:32 the sea, and perished in the **w**
Matt 10:42 ones only a cup of cold **w** in
Matt 14:28 me to come to You on the **w**
Matt 14:29 on the **w** to go to Jesus
Matt 17:15 the fire and often into the **w**
Matt 27:24 tumult was rising, he took **w**
Mark 1: 8 I indeed baptized you with **w**
Mark 1:10 coming up from the **w**, He saw
Mark 9:22 into the **w** to destroy him
Mark 9:41 cup of **w** to drink in My name
Mark 14:13 you carrying a pitcher of **w**
Luke 3:16 I indeed baptize you with **w**
Luke 7:44 you gave Me no **w** for My feet
Luke 8:23 and they were filling with **w**
Luke 8:24 wind and the raging of the **w**
Luke 8:25 commands even the winds and **w**
Luke 13:15 and lead it away to **w** it
Luke 16:24 the tip of his finger in **w**
Luke 22:10 you carrying a pitcher of **w**
John 1:26 I baptize with **w**, but there
John 1:31 I came baptizing with **w**
John 1:33 to baptize with **w** said to me
John 2: 7 Fill the waterpots with **w**
John 2: 9 the **w** that was made wine, and
John 2: 9 who had drawn the **w** knew)
John 3: 5 you, unless one is born of **w**
John 3:23 there was much **w** there
John 4: 7 of Samaria came to draw **w**
John 4:10 would have given you living **w**
John 4:11 then do You get that living **w**
John 4:13 of this **w** will thirst again
John 4:14 but whoever drinks of the **w**

John 4:14 But the w that I shall give
John 4:14 of w springing up into
John 4:15 Sir, give me this w, that I
John 4:46 where He had made the w wine
John 5: 3 for the moving of the w
John 5: 4 the pool and stirred up the w
John 5: 4 after the stirring of the w
John 5: 7 pool when the w is stirred up
John 7:38 will flow rivers of living w
John 13: 5 He poured w into a basin and
John 19:34 blood and w came out
Acts 1: 5 John truly baptized with w
Acts 8:36 the road, they came to some w
Acts 8:36 See, here is w
Acts 8:38 eunuch went down into the w
Acts 8:39 they came up out of the w
Acts 10:47 Can anyone forbid w, that
Acts 11:16 John indeed baptized with w
Eph 5:26 the washing of w by the word
1Ti 5:23 No longer drink only w, but
Heb 9:19 of calves and goats, with w
Heb 10:22 our bodies washed with pure w
Jas 3:11 a spring send forth fresh w
Jas 3:12 spring can yield both salt w
1Pe 3:20 souls, were saved through w
2Pe 2:17 These are wells without w
2Pe 3: 5 standing out of w and in the w
2Pe 3: 6 being flooded with w
1Jn 5: 6 This is He who came by w and
1Jn 5: 6 not only by w, but by w
1Jn 5: 8 the Spirit, the w, and the
Jude 12 they are clouds without w
Rev 8:10 rivers and on the springs of w
Rev 8:11 and many men died from the w
Rev 12:15 So the serpent spewed w out
Rev 14: 7 the sea and springs of w
Rev 16: 4 on the rivers and springs of w
Rev 16:12 its w was dried up, so that
Rev 21: 6 w of life freely to him who
Rev 22: 1 me a pure river of w of life
Rev 22:17 him take the w of life freely

WATERCOURSES (*see* WATER)
Is 44: 4 grass like willows by the w

WATERED (*see* WATER)
Gen 2: 6 and w the whole face of the
Gen 13:10 that it was well w everywhere
Gen 29: 2 that well they w the flocks
Gen 29:10 and w the flock of Laban his
Ex 2:17 helped them, and w their flock
Ex 2:19 water for us and w the flock
Deut 11:10 w it by foot, as a vegetable
Prov 11:25 waters will also be w himself
Is 58:11 you shall be like a w garden
1Co 3: 6 I planted, Apollos w, but God

WATERFALLS (*see* WATER)
Ps 42: 7 deep at the noise of Your w

WATERING (*see* WATER)
Gen 30:38 in the w troughs where the
Judg 5:11 archers, among the w places
Judg 7:24 seize from them the w places
Judg 7:24 seized the w places as far as

WATERLESS (*see* WATER)
Zech 9:11 prisoners free from the w pit

WATERPOOLS (*see* POOL, WATER)
Eccl 2: 6 I made myself w from which to

WATERPOT (*see* POT, WATER, WATERPOTS)
John 4:28 The woman then left her w

WATERPOTS (*see* WATERPOT)
1Ki 18:33 Fill four w with water, and
John 2: 6 were set there six w of stone
John 2: 7 them, "Fill the w with water

WATERS (*see* WATER)
Gen 1: 2 over the face of the w
Gen 1: 6 in the midst of the w, and let
Gen 1: 6 divide the w from the w
Gen 1: 7 and divided the w which were
Gen 1: 7 the w which were above the
Gen 1: 9 Let the w under the heavens
Gen 1:10 of the w He called Seas
Gen 1:20 Let the w abound with an
Gen 1:21 with which the w abounded
Gen 1:22 fill the w in the seas, and
Gen 6:17 the flood of w on the earth
Gen 7: 6 flood of w was on the earth
Gen 7: 7 because of the w of the flood
Gen 7:10 w of the flood were on the
Gen 7:17 The w increased and lifted up
Gen 7:18 The w prevailed and greatly
Gen 7:18 about on the surface of the w
Gen 7:19 the w prevailed exceedingly
Gen 7:20 The w prevailed fifteen
Gen 7:24 the w prevailed on the earth
Gen 8: 1 the earth, and the w subsided
Gen 8: 3 the w receded continually
Gen 8: 3 and fifty days the w decreased
Gen 8: 5 the w decreased continually
Gen 8: 7 fro until the w had dried up
Gen 8: 8 to see if the w had abated
Gen 8: 9 for the w were on the face of
Gen 8:11 and Noah knew that the w had
Gen 8:13 that the w were dried up from
Gen 9:11 cut off by the w of the flood
Gen 9:15 the w shall never again
Ex 7:17 I will strike the w which are
Ex 7:19 your hand over the w of Egypt
Ex 7:20 struck the w that were in the
Ex 7:20 all the w that were in the
Ex 8: 6 his hand over the w of Egypt
Ex 14:21 land, and the w were divided
Ex 14:22 the w were a wall to them on
Ex 14:26 that the w may come back upon
Ex 14:28 Then the w returned and
Ex 14:29 the w were a wall to them on
Ex 15: 8 the w were gathered together
Ex 15:10 like lead in the mighty w
Ex 15:19 the w of the sea upon them
Ex 15:23 not drink the w of Marah, for
Ex 15:25 and when he cast it into the w
Ex 15:25 the w were made sweet
Ex 15:27 so they camped there by the w
Lev 11:46 creature that moves in the w
Num 24: 6 like cedars beside the w
Num 24: 7 his seed shall be in many w
Num 27:14 Me at the w before their eyes
Num 27:14 (These are the w of Meribah
Deut 11: 4 how He made the w of the Red
Deut 14: 9 eat of all that are in the w
Deut 32:51 at the w of Meribah Kadesh
Deut 33: 8 contended at the w of Meribah
Josh 3:13 rest in the w of the Jordan
Josh 3:13 that the w of the Jordan
Josh 3:13 the w that come down from
Josh 3:16 that the w which came down
Josh 3:16 So the w that went down into
Josh 4: 7 w of the Jordan were cut off
Josh 4: 7 the w of the Jordan were cut
Josh 4:18 that the w of the Jordan
Josh 4:23 w of the Jordan before you
Josh 5: 1 w of the Jordan from before
Josh 11: 5 camped together at the w of
Josh 11: 7 suddenly by the w of Merom
Josh 15: 7 toward the w of En Shemesh
Josh 16: 1 to the w of Jericho on the
Josh 18:15 spring of the w of Nephtoah
Judg 5:19 Taanach, by the w of Megiddo
2Sa 22:12 canopies around Him, dark w
2Sa 22:17 me, He drew me out of many w
2Ki 5:12 than all the w of Israel
2Ki 18:31 the w of his own cistern
Neh 9:11 as a stone into the mighty w
Job 5:10 and sends w on the fields
Job 11:16 remember it as w that have
Job 12:15 If He withholds the w, they
Job 24:18 be swift on the face of the w
Job 24:19 and heat consume the snow w
Job 26: 5 tremble, those under the w
Job 26:10 horizon on the face of the w
Job 28:25 and mete out the w by measure
Job 29:19 root is spread out to the w
Job 37:10 and the broad w are frozen
Job 38:30 The w harden like stone, and
Ps 18:11 canopy around Him was dark w
Ps 18:15 the channels of w were seen
Ps 18:16 He drew me out of many w
Ps 23: 2 leads me beside the still w
Ps 24: 2 And established it upon the w
Ps 29: 3 of the LORD is over the w
Ps 29: 3 The LORD is over many w
Ps 32: 6 w They shall not come near
Ps 33: 7 He gathers the w of the sea
Ps 46: 3 Though its w roar and be
Ps 58: 7 as w which run continually
Ps 69: 1 For the w have come up to my
Ps 69: 2 I have come into deep w,
Ps 69:14 hate me, And out of the deep w
Ps 73:10 w of a full cup are drained
Ps 74:13 of the sea serpents in the w
Ps 77:16 The w saw You, O God
Ps 77:16 The w saw You, they were
Ps 77:19 sea, Your path in the great w
Ps 78:13 He made the w stand up like a
Ps 78:16 caused w to run down like
Ps 78:20 So that the w gushed out
Ps 81: 7 you at the w of Meribah
Ps 93: 4 Than the noise of many w,
Ps 104: 3 His upper chambers in the w
Ps 104: 6 The w stood above the
Ps 104:13 He w the hills from His upper
Ps 105:29 He turned their w into blood
Ps 106:11 The w covered their enemies
Ps 106:32 Him also at the w of strife
Ps 107:23 Who do business on great w
Ps 114: 8 flint into a fountain of w
Ps 124: 4 Then the w would have
Ps 124: 5 Then the swollen w Would have
Ps 136: 6 out the earth above the w
Ps 144: 7 and deliver me out of great w
Ps 147:18 wind to blow, and the w flow
Ps 148: 4 And you w above the heavens
Prov 8:29 so that the w would not
Prov 11:25 he who w will also be watered
Prov 18: 4 of a man's mouth are deep w
Prov 30: 4 has bound the w in a garment
Eccl 11: 1 Cast your bread upon the w
Song 4:15 gardens, a well of living w
Song 5:12 like doves by the rivers of w
Song 8: 7 Many w cannot quench love,
Is 8: 6 w of Shiloah that flow softly
Is 8: 7 over them the w of the River
Is 11: 9 LORD as the w cover the sea
Is 15: 6 For the w of Nimrim will be
Is 15: 9 For the w of Dimon will be
Is 17:12 like the rushing of mighty w
Is 17:13 like the rushing of many w
Is 18: 2 in vessels of reed on the w
Is 19: 5 The w will fail from the sea,
Is 19: 8 who spread nets on the w
Is 22: 9 the w of the lower pool
Is 23: 3 And on great w the grain of
Is 28: 2 flood of mighty w overflowing
Is 28:17 and the w will overflow the
Is 30:25 hill rivers and streams of w
Is 32:20 are you who sow beside all w
Is 35: 6 For w shall burst forth in
Is 36:16 the w of his own cistern
Is 40:12 Who has measured the w in the
Is 43: 2 When you pass through the w
Is 43:16 a path through the mighty w
Is 43:20 because I give w in the
Is 48:21 He caused the w to flow from
Is 48:21 the rock, and the w gushed out
Is 51:10 sea, the w of the great deep
Is 54: 9 is like the w of Noah to Me
Is 54: 9 the w of Noah would no longer
Is 55: 1 who thirsts, come to the w
Is 57:20 whose w cast up mire and dirt
Is 58:11 of water, whose w do not fail
Jer 2:13 Me, the fountain of living w
Jer 2:18 to drink the w of Sihor
Jer 2:18 to drink the w of the River
Jer 9: 1 Oh, that my head were w, and
Jer 10:13 multitude of w in the heavens
Jer 15:18 stream, as w that fail
Jer 17: 8 like a tree planted by the w
Jer 17:13 the fountain of living w
Jer 18:14 Will the cold flowing w be
Jer 18:14 be forsaken for strange w
Jer 31: 9 to walk by the rivers of w
Jer 46: 7 whose w move like the rivers
Jer 46: 8 its w move like the rivers
Jer 47: 2 w rise out of the north, and
Jer 48:34 for the w of Nimrim also
Jer 50:38 A drought is against her w
Jer 51:13 O you who dwell by many w
Jer 51:16 multitude of w in the heavens
Jer 51:55 her waves roar like great w
Lam 3:54 The w flowed over my head
Ezek 1:24 like the noise of many w
Ezek 17: 5 he placed it by abundant w
Ezek 17: 8 in good soil by many w, to
Ezek 19:10 bloodline, Planted by the w
Ezek 19:10 of branches because of many w
Ezek 26:19 you, and great w cover you,
Ezek 27:26 brought you into many w, but
Ezek 27:34 seas in the depths of the w
Ezek 31: 4 The w made it grow

Ezek 31: 4 underground **w** gave it height,
Ezek 31: 7 roots reached to abundant **w**
Ezek 31:14 by the **w** may ever again exalt
Ezek 31:15 the great **w** were held back
Ezek 32: 2 troubling the **w** with your
Ezek 32:13 from beside its great **w**
Ezek 32:14 I will make their **w** clear
Ezek 34:18 to have drunk of the clear **w**
Ezek 43: 2 was like the sound of many **w**
Ezek 47: 3 he brought me through the **w**
Ezek 47: 4 and brought me through the **w**
Ezek 47: 8 the sea, its **w** are healed
Ezek 47: 9 because these **w** go there
Ezek 47:19 to the **w** of Meribah by Kadesh
Ezek 48:28 to the **w** of Meribah by Kadesh
Dan 12: 6 was above the **w** of the river
Dan 12: 7 was above the **w** of the river
Amos 5: 8 He calls for the **w** of the sea
Amos 9: 6 calls for the **w** of the sea
Jon 2: 5 The **w** encompassed me, even to
Mic 1: 4 like **w** poured down a steep
Nah 3: 8 that had the **w** around her
Hab 2:14 LORD, as the **w** cover the sea
Hab 3:15 through the heap of great **w**
Zech 14: 8 **w** shall flow from Jerusalem
1Co 3: 7 is anything, nor he who **w**
1Co 3: 8 he who **w** are one, and each one
2Co 11:26 often, in perils of **w**, in
Rev 1:15 voice as the sound of many **w**
Rev 7:17 them to living fountains of **w**
Rev 8:11 and a third of the **w** became
Rev 11: 6 they have power over **w** to
Rev 14: 2 like the voice of many **w**
Rev 16: 5 the angel of the **w** saying
Rev 17: 1 harlot who sits on many **w**
Rev 17:15 The **w** which you saw, where
Rev 19: 6 as the sound of many **w** and as

WATERSPRINGS (*see* SPRING, WATER)
Ps 107:33 And the **w** into dry ground
Ps 107:35 of water, And dry land into **w**

WAVE (*see* WAVED, WAVES, WAVING, WAVY)
Ex 29:24 you shall **w** them as a **w**
Ex 29:24 a **w** offering before the LORD
Ex 29:26 and **w** it as a **w** offering
Ex 29:27 the **w** offering which is waved
Lev 7:30 a **w** offering before the LORD
Lev 7:34 the breast of the **w** offering
Lev 8:27 waved them as a **w** offering
Lev 8:29 and waved it as a **w** offering
Lev 9:21 thigh Aaron waved as a **w**
Lev 10:14 The breast of the **w** offering
Lev 10:15 the breast of the **w** offering
Lev 10:15 to offer as a **w** offering
Lev 14:12 **w** them as a **w** offering
Lev 14:24 the priest shall **w** them as a
Lev 14:24 a **w** offering before the LORD
Lev 23:11 He shall **w** the sheaf before
Lev 23:11 Sabbath the priest shall **w** it
Lev 23:12 when you **w** the sheaf, a male
Lev 23:15 the sheaf of the **w** offering
Lev 23:17 from your habitations two **w**
Lev 23:20 The priest shall **w** them with
Lev 23:20 of the firstfruits as a **w**
Num 5:25 shall **w** the offering before
Num 6:20 the priest shall **w** them as a
Num 6:20 a **w** offering before the LORD
Num 6:20 the breast of the **w** offering
Num 8:11 as though a **w** offering from
Num 8:13 a **w** offering to the LORD
Num 8:15 them, as though a **w** offering
Num 8:21 as though a **w** offering before
Num 18:11 with all the **w** offerings of
Num 18:18 yours, just as the **w** breast
2Ki 5:11 **w** his hand over the place, and
Job 39:13 of the ostrich **w** proudly, but
Ps 72:16 fruit shall **w** like Lebanon
Is 13: 2 **w** your hand, that they may
Jas 1: 6 is like a **w** of the sea driven

WAVED (*see* WAVE)
Ex 29:27 the wave offering which is **w**
Lev 7:30 that the breast may be **w** as a
Lev 8:27 **w** them as a wave offering
Lev 8:29 and **w** it as a wave offering
Lev 9:21 the right thigh Aaron **w** as a
Lev 14:21 a trespass offering to be **w**

WAVER (*see* WAVERED, WAVERING)
Rom 4:20 He did not **w** at the promise

WAVERED (*see* WAVER)
Is 21: 4 My heart **w**, fearfulness

WAVERING (*see* WAVER)
Heb 10:23 of our hope without **w**, for He

WAVES (*see* WAVE)
2Sa 22: 5 When the **w** of death
Job 9: 8 and treads on the **w** of the sea
Job 38:11 here your proud **w** must stop
Ps 42: 7 All Your **w** and billows have
Ps 65: 7 seas, The noise of their **w**
Ps 88: 7 afflicted me with all Your **w**
Ps 89: 9 When its **w** rise, You still
Ps 93: 3 The floods lift up their **w**
Ps 93: 4 Than the mighty **w** of the sea
Ps 107:25 lifts up the **w** of the sea
Ps 107:29 So that its **w** are still
Is 19:16 of hosts, which He **w** over it
Is 48:18 like the **w** of the sea
Is 51:15 the sea whose **w** roared
Jer 5:22 And though its **w** toss to and
Jer 31:35 its **w** roar (the LORD of hosts
Jer 51:42 with the multitude of its **w**
Jer 51:55 though her **w** roar like great
Ezek 26: 3 sea causes its **w** to come up
Jon 2: 3 and Your **w** passed over me
Zech 10:11 and strike the **w** of the sea
Matt 8:24 boat was covered with the **w**
Matt 14:24 of the sea, tossed by the **w**
Mark 4:37 the **w** beat into the boat, so
Luke 21:25 the sea and the **w** roaring
Acts 27:41 up by the violence of the **w**
Jude 13 raging **w** of the sea, foaming

WAVING (*see* WAVE)
Is 19:16 fear because of the **w** of the

WAVY (*see* WAVE)
Song 5:11 his locks are **w**, and black as

WAX
Ps 22:14 My heart is like **w**
Ps 68: 2 As **w** melts before the fire,
Ps 97: 5 The mountains melt like **w** at
Mic 1: 4 split like **w** before the fire

WAY (*see* WAYS, WAYSIDE)
Gen 3:24 sword which turned every **w**
Gen 3:24 to guard the **w** to the tree of
Gen 6:12 their **w** on the earth
Gen 12:19 take her and go your **w**
Gen 14:11 provisions, and went their **w**
Gen 16: 7 the spring on the **w** to Shur
Gen 18:16 them to send them on the **w**
Gen 18:19 they keep the **w** of the LORD
Gen 18:33 So the LORD went His **w** as
Gen 19: 2 rise early and go on your **w**
Gen 24:27 As for me, being on the **w**
Gen 24:40 with you and prosper your **w**
Gen 24:42 prosper the **w** in which I go
Gen 24:48 in the **w** of truth to take the
Gen 24:56 the LORD has prospered my **w**
Gen 24:62 from the **w** of Beer Lahai Roi
Gen 25:22 all is well, why am I this **w**
Gen 25:34 drank, arose, and went his **w**
Gen 28:20 me in this **w** that I am going
Gen 32: 1 So Jacob went on his **w**, and
Gen 33:16 that day on his **w** to Seir
Gen 35: 3 me in the **w** which I have gone
Gen 35:19 and was buried on the **w** to
Gen 37:25 on their **w** to carry them down
Gen 38:14 which was on the **w** to Timnah
Gen 38:16 he turned to her by the **w**
Gen 42:38 along the **w** in which you go
Gen 45:24 become troubled along the **w**
Gen 46:28 before him the **w** to Goshen
Gen 48: 7 the land of Canaan on the **w**
Gen 48: 7 on the **w** to Ephrath (that is
Gen 49:17 shall be a serpent by the **w**
Ex 2:12 he looked this **w** and that **w**
Ex 4:24 And it came to pass on the **w**
Ex 13:17 them by **w** of the land of the
Ex 13:18 by **w** of the wilderness of the
Ex 13:21 pillar of cloud to lead the **w**
Ex 18: 8 had come upon them on the **w**
Ex 18:20 show them the **w** in which they
Ex 18:27 he went his **w** to his own land
Ex 22:23 If you afflict them in any **w**
Ex 23:20 you to keep you in the **w** and
Ex 32: 8 the **w** which I commanded them
Ex 33: 3 lest I consume you on the **w**
Ex 33:13 sight, show me now Your **w**
Lev 7:24 may be used in any other **w**
Lev 20: 4 **w** hide their eyes from the
Num 6:23 This is the **w** you shall
Num 13:17 Go up this **w** into the South,
Num 14:25 by the **W** of the Red Sea
Num 21: 4 Hor by the **W** of the Red Sea
Num 21: 4 very discouraged on the **w**
Num 21:33 and went up by the **w** to Bashan
Num 22:22 LORD took His stand in the **w**
Num 22:23 **w** with His drawn sword in His
Num 22:23 turned aside out of the **w**
Num 22:26 place where there was no **w** to
Num 22:31 **w** with His drawn sword in His
Num 22:32 because your **w** is perverse
Num 22:34 You stood in the **w** against me
Num 24:25 Balak also went his **w**
Deut 1: 2 by **w** of Mount Seir to Kadesh
Deut 1:19 which you saw on the **w** to the
Deut 1:22 back word to us of the **w** by
Deut 1:31 in all the **w** that you went
Deut 1:33 who went in the **w** before you
Deut 1:33 show you the **w** you should go
Deut 1:40 by the **W** of the Red Sea
Deut 2: 1 of the **W** of the Red Sea, as
Deut 2: 8 passed by **w** of the Wilderness
Deut 6: 7 house, when you walk by the **w**
Deut 8: 2 **w** these forty years in the
Deut 9:12 turned aside from the **w** which
Deut 9:16 from the **w** which the LORD had
Deut 11:19 house, when you walk by the **w**
Deut 11:28 but turn aside from the **w**
Deut 12:31 the LORD your God in that **w**
Deut 13: 5 to entice you from the **w** in
Deut 17:16 shall not return that **w** again
Deut 19: 6 him, because the **w** is long
Deut 22: 6 to be before you along the **w**
Deut 24: 9 God did to Miriam on the **w**
Deut 25:17 Amalek did to you on the **w** as
Deut 25:18 how he met you on the **w** and
Deut 28: 7 come out against you one **w**
Deut 28:25 go out one **w** against them
Deut 28:68 by the **w** of which I said to
Deut 31:29 turn aside from the **w** which I
Josh 1: 8 will make your **w** prosperous
Josh 2:16 Afterward you may go your **w**
Josh 2:22 sought them all along the **w**
Josh 3: 4 the **w** by which you must go
Josh 3: 4 have not passed this **w** before
Josh 5: 4 in the wilderness on the **w**
Josh 5: 5 in the wilderness on the **w** as
Josh 5: 7 not been circumcised on the **w**
Josh 8:15 them, and fled by the **w** of the
Josh 8:20 to flee this **w** or that **w**
Josh 23:14 going the **w** of all the earth
Josh 24:17 us in all the **w** that we went
Judg 2:17 the **w** in which their fathers
Judg 2:19 nor from their stubborn **w**
Judg 8: 8 spoke to them in the same **w**
Judg 9:25 passed by them along that **w**
Judg 17: 9 I am on my **w** to find a place
Judg 18: 6 LORD be with you on your **w**
Judg 18:22 When they were a good **w** from
Judg 18:26 children of Dan went their **w**
Judg 19: 5 bread, and afterward go your **w**
Judg 19: 9 Tomorrow go your **w** early, so
Judg 19:14 passed by and went their **w**
Judg 19:27 house and went out to go his **w**
Ruth 1: 7 they went on the **w** to return
Ruth 1:12 back, my daughters, go your **w**
1Sa 1:18 So the woman went her **w**
1Sa 9: 6 us the **w** that we should go
1Sa 9: 8 man of God, to tell us our **w**
1Sa 9:14 on his **w** up to the high place
1Sa 9:26 that I may send you on your **w**
1Sa 12:23 you the good and the right **w**
1Sa 15: 2 **w** when he came up from Egypt
1Sa 15: 7 Havilah all the **w** to Shur
1Sa 20:22 go your **w**, for the LORD has
1Sa 24: 7 the cave and went on his **w**
1Sa 26:25 So David went on his **w**, and
1Sa 28:22 when you go on your **w**
1Sa 30: 2 them away and went their **w**
2Sa 4: 6 all the **w** into the house, as
2Sa 5: 8 up by **w** of the water shaft
2Sa 13:30 while they were on the **w**
2Sa 15: 2 beside the **w** to the gate
2Sa 15:23 the **w** of the wilderness
2Sa 18:23 Ahimaaz ran by **w** of the plain

2Sa 19:36 servant will go a little w
2Sa 22:31 As for God, His w is perfect
2Sa 22:33 and He makes my w perfect
1Ki 1:49 arose, and each one went his w
1Ki 2: 2 I go the w of all the earth
1Ki 2: 4 sons take heed to their w
1Ki 7:24 all the w around the Sea
1Ki 8:25 sons take heed to their w
1Ki 8:32 bringing his w on his head
1Ki 8:36 w in which they should walk
1Ki 11:29 Shilonite met him on the w
1Ki 13: 9 return by the same w you came
1Ki 13:10 So he went another w and did
1Ki 13:10 by the w he came to Bethel
1Ki 13:12 to them, "Which w did he go
1Ki 13:12 w the man of God went who
1Ki 13:17 by going the w you came
1Ki 13:26 him back from the w heard it
1Ki 13:33 did not turn from his evil w
1Ki 15:26 walked in the w of his father
1Ki 15:34 walked in the w of Jeroboam
1Ki 16: 2 walked in the w of Jeroboam
1Ki 16:19 walking in the w of Jeroboam
1Ki 18: 6 Ahab went one w by himself
1Ki 18: 6 went another w by himself
1Ki 18: 7 Now as Obadiah was on his w
1Ki 19:15 Go, return on your w to the
1Ki 22:22 LORD said to him, 'In what w
1Ki 22:24 Which w did the spirit from
1Ki 22:52 walked in the w of his father
1Ki 22:52 in the w of his mother and in
1Ki 22:52 in the w of Jeroboam the son
2Ki 2: 8 and it was divided this w and
2Ki 2:14 water, it was divided this w
2Ki 3: 8 Which w shall we go up
2Ki 3: 8 By w of the Wilderness of
2Ki 3:20 water came by w of Edom, and
2Ki 4:29 in your hand, and be on your w
2Ki 6:19 This is not the w, nor is
2Ki 8:18 he walked in the w of the
2Ki 8:27 he walked in the w of the
2Ki 10:12 On the w, at Beth Eked of the
2Ki 11:16 she went by w of the horses'
2Ki 11:19 went by w of the gate of the
2Ki 16: 3 But he walked in the w of the
2Ki 19:28 back by the w which you came
2Ki 19:33 By the w that he came, by the
2Ki 21:22 not walk in the w of the LORD
2Ki 25: 4 by w of the gate between two
2Ki 25: 4 king went by w of the plain
2Ch 4: 3 all the w around the Sea
2Ch 6:16 sons take heed to their w
2Ch 6:23 his w on his own head, and
2Ch 6:27 w in which they should walk
2Ch 11:17 they walked in the w of David
2Ch 18:20 LORD said to him, 'In what w
2Ch 18:23 Which w did the spirit from
2Ch 20:32 he walked in the w of his
2Ch 21: 6 he walked in the w of the
2Ch 21:13 the w of the kings of Israel
2Ch 23:15 she went by w of the entrance
2Ch 23:19 in any w unclean should enter
2Ch 32:13 of those lands in any w able
Ezra 8:21 from Him the right w for us
Neh 6:13 be afraid and act that w and
Neh 8:10 Go your w, eat the fat, drink
Neh 8:12 people went their w to eat
Neh 9:19 and the w they should go
Neh 12:38 choir went the opposite w
Esth 4:17 Then Mordecai went his w and
Job 3:23 to a man whose w is hidden
Job 6:18 paths of their w turn aside
Job 8:19 this is the joy of His w
Job 16:22 I shall go the w of no return
Job 17: 9 righteous will hold to his w
Job 19: 8 He has fenced up my w, so
Job 21:31 condemns his w to his face
Job 22:15 Will you keep to the old w
Job 23:10 He knows the w that I take
Job 23:11 I have kept His w and not
Job 24:18 into the w of their vineyards
Job 24:24 out of the w like all others
Job 28:23 God understands its w, and He
Job 29:25 I chose the w for them, and
Job 31: 7 my step has turned from the w
Job 33:14 For God may speak in one w
Job 34:11 a reward according to his w
Job 36:23 Who has assigned Him His w
Job 38:19 Where is the w to the
Job 38:24 By what w is light diffused,

Ps 1: 6 knows the w of the righteous
Ps 1: 6 But the w of the ungodly
Ps 2:12 angry, And you perish in the w
Ps 5: 8 Make Your w straight before
Ps 18:30 As for God, His w is perfect
Ps 18:32 And makes my w perfect
Ps 25: 8 He teaches sinners in the w
Ps 25: 9 the humble He teaches His w
Ps 25:12 He teach in the w He chooses
Ps 27:11 Teach me Your w, O LORD, And
Ps 32: 8 you in the w you should go
Ps 35: 6 Let their w be dark and
Ps 36: 4 in a w that is not good
Ps 37: 5 Commit your w to the LORD
Ps 37: 7 of him who prospers in his w
Ps 37:23 LORD, And He delights in his w
Ps 37:34 on the LORD, And keep His w
Ps 44:18 steps departed from Your w
Ps 49:13 This is the w of those who
Ps 67: 2 That Your w may be known on
Ps 77:13 Your w, O God, is in the
Ps 77:19 Your w was in the sea, Your
Ps 80:12 pass by the w pluck her fruit
Ps 86:11 Teach me Your w, O LORD
Ps 89:41 who pass by the w plunder him
Ps 101: 2 behave wisely in a perfect w
Ps 101: 6 He who walks in a perfect w
Ps 102:23 weakened my strength in the w
Ps 107: 4 wilderness in a desolate w
Ps 107: 7 led them forth by the right w
Ps 107:40 where there is no w
Ps 119: 1 are the undefiled in the w
Ps 119: 9 can a young man cleanse his w
Ps 119:14 in the w of Your testimonies
Ps 119:27 the w of Your precepts
Ps 119:29 Remove from me the w of lying
Ps 119:30 I have chosen the w of truth
Ps 119:32 I will run in the w of Your
Ps 119:33 the w of Your statutes, And I
Ps 119:37 And revive me in Your w
Ps 119:101 my feet from every evil w
Ps 119:104 I hate every false w
Ps 119:128 I hate every false w
Ps 139:24 there is any wicked w in me
Ps 139:24 lead me in the w everlasting
Ps 142: 3 In the w in which I walk They
Ps 143: 8 Cause me to know the w in
Ps 146: 9 But the w of the wicked He
Prov 1:15 not walk in the w with them
Prov 1:31 eat the fruit of their own w
Prov 2: 8 preserves the w of His saints
Prov 2:12 you from the w of evil, from
Prov 2:20 may walk in the w of goodness
Prov 3:23 will walk safely in your w
Prov 4:11 taught you in the w of wisdom
Prov 4:14 do not walk in the w of evil
Prov 4:19 The w of the wicked is like
Prov 5: 8 Remove your w far from her,
Prov 6:23 instruction are the w of life
Prov 7:27 Her house is the w to hell
Prov 8: 2 the high hill, beside the w
Prov 8:13 and arrogance and the evil w
Prov 8:20 I traverse the w of
Prov 8:22 me at the beginning of His w
Prov 9: 6 go in the w of understanding
Prov 9:15 who go straight on their w
Prov 10:17 is in the w of life, but he
Prov 10:29 The w of the LORD is strength
Prov 11: 5 will direct his w aright, but
Prov 12:15 The w of a fool is right in
Prov 12:26 for the w of the wicked leads
Prov 12:28 In the w of righteousness is
Prov 13: 6 him whose w is blameless, but
Prov 13:15 but the w of the unfaithful
Prov 14: 8 is to understand his w, but
Prov 14:12 There is a w which seems
Prov 14:12 but its end is the w of death
Prov 15: 9 The w of the wicked is an
Prov 15:10 is for him who forsakes the w
Prov 15:19 The w of the slothful man is
Prov 15:19 but the w of the upright is a
Prov 15:24 The w of life winds upward
Prov 16: 9 A man's heart plans his w
Prov 16:17 he who keeps his w preserves
Prov 16:25 There is a w that seems right
Prov 16:25 but its end is the w of death
Prov 16:29 leads him in a w that is not
Prov 16:31 in the w of righteousness
Prov 19: 3 of a man twists his w, and his
Prov 20:14 but when he has gone his w

Prov 20:24 a man understand his own w
Prov 21: 2 Every w of a man is right in
Prov 21: 8 The w of a guilty man is
Prov 21:16 w of understanding will rest
Prov 21:29 upright, he establishes his w
Prov 22: 5 are in the w of the perverse
Prov 22: 6 a child in the w he should go
Prov 23:19 and guide your heart in the w
Prov 28:10 to go astray in an evil w
Prov 29:27 w is an abomination to the
Prov 30:19 the w of an eagle in the air,
Prov 30:19 the w of a serpent on a rock,
Prov 30:19 the w of a ship in the midst
Prov 30:19 the w of a man with a virgin
Prov 30:20 This is the w of an
Eccl 10: 3 when a fool walks along the w
Eccl 11: 5 what is the w of the wind
Eccl 12: 5 and of terrors in the w
Song 4: 6 away, I will go my w to the
Is 3:12 destroy the w of your paths
Is 8:11 walk in the w of this people
Is 9: 1 by the w of the sea, beyond
Is 15: 5 for in the w of Horonaim they
Is 26: 7 The w of the just is
Is 26: 8 in the w of Your judgments, O
Is 28: 7 drink are out of the w
Is 28: 7 they are out of the w through
Is 30:11 Get out of the w, turn aside
Is 30:21 This is the w, walk in it,"
Is 37:29 back by the w which you came
Is 37:34 By the w that he came, by the
Is 40: 3 Prepare the w of the LORD
Is 40:14 and showed Him the w of
Is 40:27 My w is hidden from the LORD,
Is 41: 3 passed safely by the w that
Is 42:16 by a w they did not know
Is 43:16 who makes a w in the sea
Is 48:15 him, and his w will prosper
Is 48:17 you by the w you should go
Is 53: 6 every one, to his own w
Is 55: 7 Let the wicked forsake his w
Is 56:11 they all look to their own w
Is 57:10 in the length of your w
Is 57:14 Prepare the w, take the
Is 57:14 out of the w of My people
Is 57:17 in the w of his heart
Is 59: 8 The w of peace they have not
Is 59: 8 whoever takes that w shall
Is 62:10 Prepare the w for the people
Is 65: 2 who walk in a w that is not
Jer 2:17 God when He led you in the w
Jer 2:23 See your w in the valley
Jer 2:33 beautify your w to seek love
Jer 2:36 so much to change your w
Jer 3:21 they have perverted their w
Jer 4: 7 of nations is on his w
Jer 5: 4 do not know the w of the LORD
Jer 5: 5 have known the w of the LORD
Jer 6:16 paths, where the good w is
Jer 6:25 the field, nor walk by the w
Jer 6:27 you may know and test their w
Jer 10: 2 learn the w of the Gentiles
Jer 10:23 I know the w of man is not in
Jer 12: 1 Why does the w of the wicked
Jer 18:11 now every one from his evil w
Jer 21: 8 w of life and the w of death
Jer 23:12 Therefore their w shall be to
Jer 23:22 turned them from their evil w
Jer 25: 5 now everyone of his evil w
Jer 25:35 will have no w to flee, nor
Jer 26: 3 and turn from his evil w, that
Jer 28:11 prophet Jeremiah went his w
Jer 31: 9 in a straight w in which they
Jer 31:21 the w in which you went
Jer 32:39 give them one heart and one w
Jer 35:15 now everyone from his evil w
Jer 36: 3 may turn from his evil w,
Jer 36: 7 will turn from his evil w
Jer 39: 4 by w of the king's garden, by
Jer 39: 4 he went out by w of the plain
Jer 41:17 they went on their w to Egypt
Jer 42: 3 the w in which we should walk
Jer 48:19 of Aroer, stand by the w and
Jer 50: 5 They shall ask the w to Zion
Jer 52: 7 w of the gate between the two
Jer 52: 7 they went by w of the plain
Ezek 3:18 the wicked from his wicked w
Ezek 3:19 nor from his wicked w, he
Ezek 7:27 to them according to their w
Ezek 13:22 his wicked w to save his life

Ezek 18:25 The w of the Lord is not
Ezek 18:25 is it not My w which is fair,
Ezek 18:29 The w of the Lord is not
Ezek 23:13 both took the same w
Ezek 23:31 in the w of your sister
Ezek 33: 8 to warn the wicked from his w
Ezek 33: 9 the wicked to turn from his w
Ezek 33: 9 he does not turn from his w
Ezek 33:11 the wicked turn from his w
Ezek 33:17 The w of the LORD is not
Ezek 33:17 But it is their w which is
Ezek 33:20 The w of the LORD is not
Ezek 36:17 to Me their w was like the
Ezek 41: 7 by w of the middle one
Ezek 42: 1 by the w toward the north
Ezek 42:12 the w directly in front of
Ezek 43: 2 came from the w of the east
Ezek 43: 4 by w of the gate which faces
Ezek 44: 3 he shall enter by w of the
Ezek 44: 3 gateway, and go out the same w
Ezek 44: 4 Then He brought me by w of
Ezek 46: 2 by w of the vestibule of that
Ezek 46: 8 he shall go in by w of the
Ezek 46: 8 gateway, and go out the same w
Ezek 46: 9 whoever enters by w of the
Ezek 46: 9 go out by w of the south gate
Ezek 46: 9 whoever enters by w of the
Ezek 46: 9 go out by w of the north gate
Ezek 46: 9 He shall not return by w of
Ezek 47: 2 me out by w of the north gate
Ezek 48:35 All the w around shall be
Dan 12: 9 Go your w, Daniel, for the
Dan 12:13 you, go your w till the end
Hos 2: 6 hedge up your w with thorns
Hos 6: 9 murder on the w to Shechem
Hos 10:13 you trusted in your own w
Amos 2: 7 pervert the w of the humble
Amos 8:14 As the w of Beersheba lives
Jon 3: 8 one turn from his evil w and
Jon 3:10 they turned from their evil w
Nah 1: 3 has His w in the whirlwind
Zech 10: 2 wend their w like sheep
Mal 1: 2 In what w have You loved us
Mal 1: 6 In what w have we despised
Mal 1: 7 In what w have we defiled
Mal 2: 8 you have departed from the w
Mal 2:17 In what w have we wearied Him
Mal 3: 1 will prepare the w before Me
Mal 3: 7 In what w shall we return
Mal 3: 8 In what w have we robbed You
Matt 2:12 their own country another w
Matt 3: 3 Prepare the w of the LORD
Matt 4:15 the w of the sea, beyond the
Matt 5:24 the altar, and go your w
Matt 5:25 you are on the w with him
Matt 7:13 broad is the w that leads to
Matt 7:14 and difficult is the w which
Matt 8: 4 but go your w, show yourself
Matt 8:13 Go your w; and as you have
Matt 8:28 that no one could pass that w
Matt 8:30 Now a good w off from them
Matt 10: 5 go into the w of the Gentiles
Matt 11:10 prepare Your w before You
Matt 13:25 among the wheat and went his w
Matt 15:32 lest they faint on the w
Matt 20:14 what is yours and go your w
Matt 21:32 you in the w of righteousness
Matt 22:16 teach the w of God in truth
Matt 22:22 and left Him and went their w
Matt 27:65 go your w, make it as secure
Mark 1: 2 prepare Your w before You
Mark 1: 3 Prepare the w of the LORD
Mark 1:44 but go your w, show yourself
Mark 2:11 and go your w to your house
Mark 7: 3 their hands in a special w
Mark 7:29 For this saying go your w
Mark 8: 3 they will faint on the w
Mark 10:21 Go your w, sell whatever you
Mark 10:52 Go your w; your faith has
Mark 11: 4 So they went their w, and
Mark 12:14 but teach the w of God in
Luke 1:79 our feet into the w of peace
Luke 3: 4 Prepare the w of the LORD
Luke 4:30 midst of them, He went His w
Luke 7:27 prepare Your w before You
Luke 8:39 And he went his w and
Luke 10: 3 Go your w; behold, I send
Luke 12:58 the w to settle with him,
Luke 13:11 could in no w raise herself
Luke 14:32 other is still a great w off
Luke 15:20 he was still a great w off
Luke 17:19 Arise, go your w
Luke 19: 4 He was going to pass that w
Luke 20:21 but teach the w of God truly
Luke 22: 4 So he went his w and conferred
John 1:23 straight the w of the LORD
John 4:28 went her w into the city, and
John 4:50 Go your w; your son lives
John 4:50 to him, and he went his w
John 10: 1 but climbs up some other w
John 11:28 these things, she went her w
John 14: 4 you know, and the w you know
John 14: 5 and how can we know the w
John 14: 6 I am the w, the truth, and the
John 18: 8 seek Me, let these go their w
John 21: 1 in this w He showed Himself
Acts 4:21 finding no w of punishing
Acts 7: 6 But God spoke in this w
Acts 8:39 and he went on his w rejoicing
Acts 9: 2 found any who were of the W
Acts 9:17 And Ananias went his w and
Acts 15: 3 sent on their w by the church
Acts 16:17 to us the w of salvation
Acts 18:25 in the w of the Lord
Acts 18:26 explained to him the w of God
Acts 19: 9 of the W before the multitude
Acts 19:23 a great commotion about the W
Acts 20:35 I have shown you in every w
Acts 21: 5 we departed and went on our w
Acts 22: 4 this W to the death, binding
Acts 24:14 that according to the W which
Acts 24:22 accurate knowledge of the W
Rom 1:10 now at last I may find a w in
Rom 3: 2 Much in every w
Rom 3:12 have all gone out of the w
Rom 3:17 the w of peace they have not
Rom 10: 6 of faith speaks in this w
Rom 14:13 to fall in our brother's w
Rom 15:24 helped on my w there by you
Rom 15:28 I shall go by w of you to
1Co 9:24 Run in such a w that you may
1Co 10:13 also make the w of escape
1Co 12:31 I show you a more excellent w
1Co 16: 7 wish to see you now on the w
2Co 1:16 to pass by w of you to
2Co 1:16 by you on my w to Judea
Phil 1:18 Only that in every w, whether
Phil 1:28 not in any w terrified by
Col 2:14 He has taken it out of the w
1Th 3:11 Christ, direct our w to you
2Th 2: 7 He is taken out of the w
2Th 3:16 you peace always in every w
Heb 4: 4 of the seventh day in this w
Heb 9: 8 that the w into the Holiest
Heb 10:20 living w which He consecrated
Jas 2:25 and sent them out another w
Jas 5:20 from the error of his w will
2Pe 2: 2 because of whom the w of
2Pe 2:15 have forsaken the right w
2Pe 2:15 following the w of Balaam the
2Pe 2:21 known the w of righteousness
2Pe 3: 1 pure minds by w of reminder)
Jude 11 have gone in the w of Cain
Jude 15 committed in an ungodly w
Rev 16:12 so that the w of the kings

WAYFARING

2Sa 12: 4 the w man who had come to him
Is 33: 8 lie waste, the w man ceases
Jer 9: 2 a lodging place for w men
Jer 14: 8 like a w man who turns aside

WAYS (*see* WAY)

Deut 5:33 You shall walk in all the w
Deut 8: 6 your God, to walk in His w
Deut 10:12 God, to walk in all His w
Deut 11:22 God, to walk in all His w
Deut 19: 9 and to walk always in His w
Deut 26:17 that you will walk in His w
Deut 28: 7 and flee before you seven w
Deut 28: 9 your God and walk in His w
Deut 28:25 and flee seven w before them
Deut 28:29 shall not prosper in your w
Deut 30:16 your God, to walk in His w
Deut 32: 4 for all His w are justice
Josh 22: 5 God, to walk in all His w
Judg 2:22 will keep the w of the LORD
1Sa 8: 3 sons did not walk in his w
1Sa 8: 5 sons do not walk in your w
1Sa 18:14 behaved wisely in all his w
2Sa 22:22 I have kept the w of the LORD
1Ki 2: 3 to walk in His w, to keep His
1Ki 3:14 So if you walk in My w, to
1Ki 8:39 according to all his w, whose
1Ki 8:58 Himself, to walk in all His w
1Ki 11:33 have not walked in My w to do
1Ki 11:38 I command you, walk in My w
1Ki 16:26 the w of Jeroboam the son of
1Ki 22:43 all the w of his father Asa
2Ki 17:13 Turn from your evil w, and
2Ki 21:21 So he walked in all the w
2Ki 22: 2 walked in all the w of his
2Ch 6:30 according to all his w, whose
2Ch 6:31 to walk in Your w as long as
2Ch 7:14 and turn from their wicked w
2Ch 13:22 of the acts of Abijah, his w
2Ch 17: 3 former w of his father David
2Ch 17: 6 delight in the w of the LORD
2Ch 21:12 w of Jehoshaphat your father
2Ch 21:12 or in the w of Asa king of
2Ch 22: 3 in the w of the house of Ahab
2Ch 27: 6 his w before the LORD his God
2Ch 27: 7 and all his wars and his w
2Ch 28: 2 For he walked in the w of the
2Ch 28:26 rest of his acts and all his w
2Ch 34: 2 walked in the w of his father
Esth 5:11 all the w in which the king
Job 4: 6 integrity of your w your hope
Job 13:15 defend my own w before Him
Job 21:14 the knowledge of Your w
Job 22: 3 you make your w blameless
Job 22:28 so light will shine on your w
Job 24:13 they do not know its w nor
Job 24:23 yet His eyes are on their w
Job 26:14 are the mere edges of His w
Job 30:12 me their w of destruction
Job 31: 4 Does He not see my w, and
Job 34:21 His eyes are on the w of man
Job 34:27 not consider any of His w
Job 40:19 is the first of the w of God
Ps 10: 5 His w are always prospering
Ps 18:21 I have kept the w of the LORD
Ps 25: 4 Show me Your w, O LORD
Ps 39: 1 I will guard my w, Lest I sin
Ps 51:13 teach transgressors Your w
Ps 81:13 Israel would walk in My w
Ps 91:11 To keep you in all your w
Ps 95:10 And they do not know My w
Ps 103: 7 He made known His w to Moses
Ps 119: 3 They walk in His w
Ps 119: 5 that my w were directed To
Ps 119:15 And contemplate Your w
Ps 119:26 I have declared my w, and You
Ps 119:59 I thought about my w, And
Ps 119:168 For all my w are before You
Ps 125: 5 turn aside to their crooked w
Ps 128: 1 the LORD, Who walks in His w
Ps 138: 5 sing of the w of the LORD
Ps 139: 3 are acquainted with all my w
Ps 145:17 is righteous in all His w
Prov 1:19 So are the w of everyone who
Prov 2:13 to walk in the w of darkness
Prov 2:15 whose w are crooked, and who
Prov 3: 6 in all your w acknowledge Him
Prov 3:17 Her w are w of
Prov 3:17 Her w are w of
Prov 3:31 and choose none of his w
Prov 4:26 let all your w be established
Prov 5: 6 her w are unstable
Prov 5:21 For the w of man are before
Prov 6: 6 Consider her w and be wise,
Prov 7:25 heart turn aside to her w
Prov 8:32 are those who keep my w
Prov 10: 9 his w will become known
Prov 11:20 in their w are His delight
Prov 14: 2 in his w despises Him
Prov 14:14 will be filled with his own w
Prov 16: 2 All the w of a man are pure
Prov 16: 7 When a man's w please the
Prov 17:23 to pervert the w of justice
Prov 19:16 is careless of his w will die
Prov 22:25 lest you learn his w and set a
Prov 23:26 and let your eyes observe my w
Prov 28: 6 than one perverse in his w
Prov 28:18 in his w will fall at once
Prov 31: 3 nor your w to that which
Prov 31:27 over the w of her household
Eccl 11: 9 walk in the w of your heart,
Is 2: 3 he will teach us His w, and we
Is 2: 6 are filled with eastern w
Is 42:24 they would not walk in His w

Is 45:13 and I will direct all his **w**
Is 55: 8 nor are your **w** My **w**,"
Is 55: 9 My **w** higher than your **w**
Is 57:18 I have seen his **w**, and will
Is 58: 2 and delight to know My **w**, as
Is 58:13 Him, not doing your own **w**
Is 59: 8 is no justice in their **w**
Is 63:17 You made us stray from Your **w**
Is 64: 5 who remembers You in Your **w**
Is 64: 5 in these **w** we continue
Is 66: 3 they have chosen their own **w**
Jer 2:23 breaking loose in her **w**,
Jer 2:33 the wicked women your **w**
Jer 4:18 Your **w** and your doings have
Jer 6:16 Stand in the **w** and see, and ask
Jer 7: 3 Amend your **w** and your doings,
Jer 7: 5 you thoroughly amend your **w**
Jer 7:23 walk in all the **w** that I have
Jer 12:16 learn the **w** of My people, to
Jer 15: 7 do not return from their **w**
Jer 16:17 My eyes are on all their **w**
Jer 17:10 every man according to his **w**
Jer 18:11 his evil way, and make your **w**
Jer 18:15 to stumble in their **w**, from
Jer 23:12 be to them like slippery **w**
Jer 26:13 Now therefore, amend your **w**
Jer 32:19 all the **w** of the sons of men
Jer 32:19 everyone according to his **w**
Lam 3: 9 blocked my **w** with hewn stone
Lam 3:11 He has turned aside my **w** and
Lam 3:40 search out and examine our **w**
Ezek 7: 3 judge you according to your **w**
Ezek 7: 4 but I will repay your **w**, and
Ezek 7: 8 judge you according to your **w**
Ezek 7: 9 repay you according to your **w**
Ezek 14:22 you, and you will see their **w**
Ezek 14:23 you, when you see their **w**
Ezek 16:47 You did not walk in their **w**
Ezek 16:47 than they in all your **w**
Ezek 16:61 Then you will remember your **w**
Ezek 18:23 he should turn from his **w**
Ezek 18:25 your **w** which are not fair
Ezek 18:29 is it not My **w** which are fair
Ezek 18:29 your **w** which are not fair
Ezek 18:30 every one according to his **w**
Ezek 20:43 you shall remember your **w**
Ezek 20:44 **w** nor according to your
Ezek 21:19 appoint for yourself two **w**
Ezek 24:14 according to your **w** and
Ezek 28:15 your **w** from the day you were
Ezek 33:11 Turn, turn from your evil **w**
Ezek 33:20 of you according to his own **w**
Ezek 36:17 defiled it by their own **w**
Ezek 36:19 them according to their **w**
Ezek 36:31 you will remember your evil **w**
Ezek 36:32 and confounded for your own **w**
Dan 4:37 are truth, and His **w** justice
Dan 5:23 His hand and owns all your **w**
Hos 4: 9 will punish them for their **w**
Hos 9: 8 a fowler's snare in all his **w**
Hos 12: 2 Jacob according to his **w**
Hos 14: 9 For the **w** of the LORD are
Mic 4: 2 He will teach us His **w**, and we
Hab 3: 6 His **w** are everlasting
Hag 1: 5 Consider your **w**
Hag 1: 7 Consider your **w**
Zech 1: 4 Turn now from your evil **w**
Zech 1: 6 do to us, according to our **w**
Zech 3: 7 If you will walk in My **w**
Mal 2: 9 you have not kept My **w** but
Matt 22: 5 light of it and went their **w**
Luke 1:76 of the Lord to prepare His **w**
Luke 3: 5 and the rough **w** made smooth
Acts 2:28 known to me the **w** of life
Acts 13:10 the straight **w** of the Lord
Acts 13:18 their **w** in the wilderness
Acts 14:16 to walk in their own **w**
Acts 28:10 also honored us in many **w**
Rom 3:16 and misery are in their **w**
Rom 11:33 and His **w** past finding out
1Co 4:17 remind you of my **w** in Christ
2Ti 1:18 many **w** he ministered to me at
Heb 1: 1 in different **w** spoke in time
Heb 3:10 and they have not known My **w**
Jas 1: 8 man, unstable in all his **w**
2Pe 2: 2 follow their destructive **w**
Rev 15: 3 Just and true are Your **w**, O

WAYSIDE (*see* WAY)
1Sa 4:13 on a seat by the **w** watching
Ps 110: 7 drink of the brook by the **w**
Ps 140: 5 have spread a net by the **w**
Matt 13: 4 some seed fell by the **w**
Matt 13:19 he who received seed by the **w**
Mark 4: 4 that some seed fell by the **w**
Mark 4:15 the **w** where the word is sown
Luke 8: 5 he sowed, some fell by the **w**
Luke 8:12 Those by the **w** are the ones

WE (*see* PREFACE)

WEAK (*see* WEAKENS, WEAKER, WEAKNESS)
Gen 33:13 knows that the children are **w**
Num 13:18 dwell in it are strong or **w**
Judg 16: 7 dried, then I shall become **w**
Judg 16:11 used, then I shall become **w**
Judg 16:17 leave me, and I shall become **w**
2Sa 3:39 I am **w** today, though anointed
2Sa 17: 2 him while he is weary and **w**
2Ch 15: 7 and do not let your hands be **w**
2Ch 36:17 virgin, on the aged or the **w**
Job 4: 3 you have strengthened **w** hands
Job 23:16 For God made my heart **w**, and
Ps 6: 2 on me, O LORD, for I am **w**
Ps 109:24 My knees are **w** through
Is 14:10 you also become as **w** as we
Is 35: 3 Strengthen the **w** hands, and
Is 40:29 He gives power to the **w**, and
Ezek 7:17 knee will be as **w** as water
Ezek 21: 7 all knees will be **w** as water
Ezek 34: 4 The **w** you have not
Ezek 34:21 butted all the **w** ones with
Joel 3:10 let the **w** say, 'I am strong
Zeph 3:16 Zion, let not your hands be **w**
Matt 26:41 willing, but the flesh is **w**
Mark 14:38 is ready, but the flesh is **w**
Acts 20:35 that you must support the **w**
Rom 4:19 And not being **w** in faith, he
Rom 8: 3 it was **w** through the flesh
Rom 14: 1 one who is **w** in the faith
Rom 14: 2 but he who is **w** eats only
Rom 14:21 or is offended or is made **w**
Rom 15: 1 with the scruples of the **w**
1Co 1:27 God has chosen the **w** things
1Co 4:10 We are **w**, but you are strong
1Co 8: 7 and their conscience, being **w**
1Co 8: 9 block to those who are **w**
1Co 8:10 conscience of him who is **w** be
1Co 8:11 shall the **w** brother perish
1Co 8:12 and wound their **w** conscience
1Co 9:22 to the **w** I became as **w**,
1Co 9:22 **w**, that I might win the **w**
1Co 11:30 For this reason many are **w**
2Co 10:10 but his bodily presence is **w**
2Co 11:21 that we were too **w** for that
2Co 11:29 Who is **w**, and I am not **w**
2Co 12:10 For when I am **w**, then I am
2Co 13: 3 me, who is not **w** toward you
2Co 13: 4 For we also are **w** in Him, but
2Co 13: 9 For we are glad when we are **w**
Gal 4: 9 that you turn again to the **w**
1Th 5:14 fainthearted, uphold the **w**

WEAKENED (*see* WEAKENS)
Neh 6: 9 hands will be **w** in the work
Ps 102:23 He **w** my strength in the way
Is 14:12 ground, you who **w** the nations

WEAKENS (*see* WEAK, WEAKENED)
Jer 38: 4 for thus he **w** the hands of

WEAKER (*see* WEAK, WEAKEST)
2Sa 3: 1 house of Saul grew **w** and **w**
1Co 12:22 seem to be **w** are necessary
1Pe 3: 7 the wife, as to the **w** vessel

WEAKEST (*see* WEAKER)
Judg 6:15 my clan is the **w** in Manasseh

WEAKNESS (*see* WEAK, WEAKNESSES)
Rom 6:19 of the **w** of your flesh
1Co 1:25 the **w** of God is stronger than
1Co 2: 3 I was with you in **w**, in fear,
1Co 15:43 It is sown in **w**, it is raised
2Co 12: 9 strength is made perfect in **w**
2Co 13: 4 though He was crucified in **w**
Heb 5: 2 he himself is also beset by **w**
Heb 7:18 commandment because of its **w**
Heb 7:28 high priests men who have **w**
Heb 11:34 out of **w** were made strong,

WEAKNESSES (*see* WEAKNESS)
Rom 8:26 Spirit also helps in our **w**
Heb 4:15 cannot sympathize with our **w**

WEALTH (*see* WEALTHY)
Gen 31: 1 he has acquired all this **w**
Gen 34:29 and all their **w**
Deut 8:17 my hand have gained me this **w**
Deut 8:18 who gives you power to get **w**
Ruth 2: 1 husband's, a man of great **w**
2Ch 1:11 or **w** or honor or the life of
2Ch 1:12 I will give you riches and **w**
Job 6:22 a bribe for me from your **w**'
Job 15:29 rich, nor will his **w** continue
Job 20:10 his hands will restore his **w**
Job 21:13 They spend their days in **w**
Job 31:25 because my **w** was great, and
Ps 49: 6 Those who trust in their **w**
Ps 49:10 And leave their **w** to others
Ps 112: 3 **W** and riches will be in his
Prov 5:10 aliens be filled with your **w**
Prov 8:21 who love me to inherit **w**,
Prov 10:15 The rich man's **w** is his
Prov 13:11 **W** gained by dishonesty will
Prov 13:22 but the **w** of the sinner is
Prov 18:11 The rich man's **w** is his
Prov 19: 4 **W** makes many friends, but the
Prov 29: 3 of harlots wastes his **w**
Eccl 5:19 God has given riches and **w**
Eccl 6: 2 God has given riches and **w**
Song 8: 7 love all the **w** of his house
Is 60: 5 the **w** of the Gentiles shall
Is 60:11 to you the **w** of the Gentiles
Jer 15:13 Your **w** and your treasures I
Jer 17: 3 I will give as plunder your **w**
Jer 20: 5 all the **w** of this city, all
Ezek 29:19 he shall take away her **w**,
Ezek 30: 4 and they take away her **w**, and
Hos 12: 8 I have found **w** for myself
Nah 2: 9 Or **w** of every desirable prize
Zech 14:14 the **w** of all the surrounding
Rev 18:19 the sea became rich by her **w**

WEALTHY (*see* WEALTH)
2Ki 15:20 Israel, from all the very **w**
Jer 49:31 go up to the **w** nation that
Rev 3:17 I am rich, have become **w**

WEANED
Gen 21: 8 So the child grew and was **w**
Gen 21: 8 the same day that Isaac was **w**
1Sa 1:22 go up until the child is **w**
1Sa 1:23 wait until you have **w** him
1Sa 1:23 her son until she had **w** him
1Sa 1:24 Now when she had **w** him, she
1Ki 11:20 whom Tahpenes **w** in Pharaoh's
Ps 131: 2 soul, Like a **w** child with his
Ps 131: 2 Like a **w** child is my soul
Is 11: 8 the **w** child shall put his
Is 28: 9 Those just **w** from milk
Hos 1: 8 Now when she had **w**

WEAPON (*see* WEAPONS)
Num 35:18 him with a wooden hand **w**, by
1Ch 12:37 with every kind of **w** of war
2Ch 23:10 man with his **w** in his hand
Neh 4:17 and with the other held a **w**
Job 20:24 He will flee from the iron **w**
Is 54:17 no **w** formed against you shall
Ezek 9: 1 with a deadly **w** in his hand

WEAPONS (*see* WEAPON)
Gen 27: 3 therefore, please take your **w**
Deut 1:41 had girded on his **w** of war
Judg 18:11 Eshtaol, armed with **w** of war
Judg 18:16 men armed with their **w** of war
Judg 18:17 who were armed with **w** of war
1Sa 8:12 and some to make his **w** of war
1Sa 20:40 gave his **w** to his lad, and
1Sa 21: 8 my sword nor my **w** with me
2Sa 1:27 and the **w** of war perished
2Ki 7:15 and **w** which the Syrians had
2Ki 10: 2 a fortified city also, and **w**
2Ki 11: 8 man with his **w** in his hand
2Ki 11:11 man with his **w** in his hand
1Ch 12:33 in war with all **w** of war,
2Ch 23: 7 man with his **w** in his hand
2Ch 32: 5 the City of David, and made **w**
Eccl 9:18 is better than **w** of war
Is 13: 5 and His **w** of indignation, to
Jer 21: 4 I will turn back the **w** of war
Jer 22: 7 you, everyone with his **w**
Jer 50:25 out the **w** of His indignation

Jer 51:20 are My battle-ax and **w** of war
Ezek 32:27 to hell with their **w** of war
Ezek 39: 9 and set on fire and burn the **w**
Ezek 39:10 will make fires with the **w**
Joel 2: 8 when they lunge between the **w**
John 18: 3 with lanterns, torches, and **w**
2Co 10: 4 For the **w** of our warfare are

WEAR (*see* WEARING, WEARS, WORE, WORN)
Ex 18:18 will surely **w** yourselves out
Lev 21:10 consecrated to **w** the garments
Deut 8: 4 garments did not **w** out on you
Deut 22: 5 A woman shall not **w** anything
Deut 22:11 You shall not **w** a garment of
1Sa 2:28 and to **w** an ephod before Me
Neh 9:21 their clothes did not **w** out
Job 9:27 my sad face and **w** a smile,'
Job 27:17 it up, but the just will **w** it
Is 4: 1 own food and **w** our own apparel
Zech 13: 4 they will not **w** a robe of
Matt 6:31 or 'What shall we **w**
Matt 11: 8 those who **w** soft clothing are
Mark 6: 9 but to **w** sandals, and not to
Luke 9:12 When the day began to **w** away

WEARIED (*see* WEARY)
Is 43:23 nor **w** you with incense
Is 43:24 sins, you have **w** Me with your
Is 47:13 You are **w** in the multitude of
Is 57:10 You are **w** in the length of
Jer 12: 5 footmen, and they have **w** you
Jer 12: 5 which you trusted, they **w** you
Ezek 24:12 She has **w** herself with lies,
Mic 6: 3 and how have I **w** you
Mal 2:17 You have **w** the LORD with your
Mal 2:17 In what way have we **w** Him
John 4: 6 being **w** from His journey, sat

WEARIES (*see* WEARY)
Prov 26:15 it **w** him to bring it back to
Eccl 10:15 The labor of fools **w** them

WEARINESS (*see* WEARY)
Mal 1:13 You also say, 'Oh, what a **w**
2Co 11:27 in **w** and toil, in

WEARING (*see* WEAR)
1Sa 2:18 as a child, **w** a linen ephod
1Sa 14: 3 in Shiloh, was **w** an ephod
2Sa 6:14 David was **w** a linen ephod
Esth 1:11 **w** her royal crown, in order
John 19: 5 **w** the crown of thorns and the
Jas 2: 3 to the one **w** the fine clothes
1Pe 3: 3 of **w** gold, or of putting on

WEARISOME (*see* WEARY)
Job 7: 3 **w** nights have been appointed
Eccl 12:12 much study is **w** to the flesh

WEARS (*see* WEAR)
Job 14:19 As water **w** away stones, and as

WEARY (*see* WEARIED, WEARIES, WEARINESS, WEARISOME)
Gen 19:11 so that they became **w** trying
Gen 25:29 from the field, and he was **w**
Gen 25:30 same red stew, for I am **w**
Gen 27:46 I am **w** of my life because of
Deut 25:18 when you were tired and **w**
Josh 7: 3 Do not **w** all the people there
Judg 4:21 for he was fast asleep and **w**
Judg 8:15 give bread to your **w** men
1Sa 30:10 who were so **w** that they could
1Sa 30:21 **w** that they could not follow
2Sa 16:14 who were with him became **w**
2Sa 17: 2 come upon him while he is **w**
2Sa 17:29 The people are hungry and **w**
2Sa 23:10 until his hand was **w**, and his
Job 3:17 and there the **w** are at rest
Job 4: 2 with you, will you become **w**
Job 4: 5 comes upon you, and you are **w**
Job 22: 7 given the **w** water to drink
Ps 6: 6 I am **w** with my groaning
Ps 68: 9 inheritance, When it was **w**
Ps 69: 3 I am **w** with my crying
Prov 25:17 lest he become **w** of you and
Prov 25:25 As cold water to a **w** soul
Is 1:14 to Me, I am **w** of bearing them
Is 5:27 No one will be **w** or stumble
Is 7:13 small thing for you to **w** men
Is 7:13 but will you **w** my God also
Is 16:12 Moab is **w** on the high place
Is 28:12 you may cause the **w** to rest
Is 32: 2 of a great rock in a **w** land
Is 40:28 neither faints nor is **w**
Is 40:30 youths shall faint and be **w**
Is 40:31 they shall run and not be **w**
Is 43:22 and you have been **w** of Me, O
Is 46: 1 a burden to the **w** beast
Is 50: 4 in season to him who is **w**
Jer 2:24 her will not **w** themselves
Jer 4:31 for my soul is **w** because of
Jer 6:11 I am **w** of holding it in
Jer 9: 5 and **w** themselves to commit
Jer 15: 6 I am **w** of relenting
Jer 20: 9 I was **w** of holding it back,
Jer 31:25 I have satiated the **w** soul
Jer 51:58 and they shall be **w**
Jer 51:64 And they shall be **w**
Hab 2:13 nations **w** themselves in vain
Matt 9:36 for them, because they were **w**
Luke 18: 5 her continual coming she **w** me
Gal 6: 9 let us not grow **w** while doing
2Th 3:13 do not grow **w** in doing good
Heb 12: 3 Himself, lest you become **w**
Rev 2: 3 sake and have not become **w**

WEATHER
Prov 25:20 away a garment in cold **w**, and
Matt 16: 2 you say, 'It will be fair **w**
Matt 16: 3 It will be foul **w** today
Luke 12:55 say, 'There will be hot **w**'

WEAVE (*see* WEAVER, WOVE, WOVEN)
Ex 26: 1 of cherubim you shall **w** them
Ex 28:39 You shall skillfully **w** the
Judg 16:13 If you **w** the seven locks of
Is 19: 9 those who **w** fine fabric will
Is 59: 5 eggs and **w** the spider's web

WEAVER (*see* WEAVE, WEAVER'S)
Ex 26:36 linen thread, made by a **w**
Ex 27:16 linen thread, made by a **w**
Ex 35:35 and fine linen, and of the **w**
Ex 36:37 linen thread, made by a **w**
Ex 38:23 a **w** in blue and purple and
Is 38:12 have cut off my life like a **w**

WEAVER'S (*see* WEAVER)
1Sa 17: 7 his spear was like a **w** beam
2Sa 21:19 whose spear was like a **w** beam
1Ch 11:23 been a spear like a **w** beam
1Ch 20: 5 whose spear was like a **w** beam
Job 7: 6 are swifter than a **w** shuttle

WEB (*see* WEBS)
Judg 16:13 head into the **w** of the loom"
Judg 16:14 batten and the **w** from the loom
Job 8:14 whose trust is a spider's **w**
Is 59: 5 eggs and weave the spider's **w**

WEBS (*see* WEB)
Is 59: 6 Their **w** will not become

WEDDING (*see* WEDLOCK)
Matt 22: 3 who were invited to the **w**
Matt 22: 4 Come to the **w**
Matt 22: 8 The **w** is ready, but those
Matt 22: 9 as you find, invite to the **w**
Matt 22:10 the **w** hall was filled with
Matt 22:11 did not have on a **w** garment
Matt 22:12 in here without a **w** garment
Matt 25:10 went in with him to the **w**
Luke 12:36 he will return from the **w**
Luke 14: 8 by anyone to a **w** feast, do
John 2: 1 was a **w** in Cana of Galilee
John 2: 2 were invited to the **w**

WEDGE
Josh 7:21 a **w** of gold weighing fifty
Josh 7:24 the **w** of gold, his sons, his
Is 13:12 than the golden **w** of Ophir

WEDLOCK (*see* WEDDING)
Ezek 16:38 you as women who break **w** or

WEEDS
Job 31:40 wheat, and **w** instead of barley
Jon 2: 5 **w** were wrapped around my
Zeph 2: 9 overrun with **w** and saltpits,

WEEK (*see* WEEKS)
Gen 29:27 Fulfill her **w**, and we will
Gen 29:28 did so and fulfilled her **w**
Dan 9:27 covenant with many for one **w**
Dan 9:27 **w** He shall bring an end to
Matt 28: 1 day of the **w** began to dawn
Mark 16: 2 on the first day of the **w**
Mark 16: 9 on the first day of the **w**
Luke 18:12 I fast twice a **w**
Luke 24: 1 Now on the first day of the **w**
John 20: 1 On the first day of the **w**
John 20:19 being the first day of the **w**
Acts 20: 7 Now on the first day of the **w**
1Co 16: 2 the **w** let each one of you lay

WEEKS (*see* WEEK)
Ex 34:22 shall observe the Feast of **W**
Lev 12: 5 she shall be unclean two **w**
Num 28:26 the LORD at your Feast of **W**
Deut 16: 9 count seven **w** for yourself
Deut 16: 9 begin to count the seven **w**
Deut 16:10 **W** to the LORD your God with
Deut 16:16 Bread, at the Feast of **W**, and
2Ch 8:13 Bread, the Feast of **W**, and the
Jer 5:24 appointed **w** of the harvest
Dan 9:24 Seventy **w** are determined for
Dan 9:25 be seven **w** and sixty-two **w**
Dan 9:26 after the sixty-two **w** Messiah
Dan 10: 2 was mourning three full **w**
Dan 10: 3 three whole **w** were fulfilled

WEEP (*see* WEEPING, WEEPS, WEPT)
Gen 23: 2 for Sarah and to **w** for her
Gen 43:30 and sought somewhere to **w**
Num 11:13 For they **w** all over me,
1Sa 1: 8 Hannah, why do you **w**
1Sa 11: 5 the people, that they **w**
1Sa 30: 4 they had no more power to **w**
2Sa 1:24 **w** over Saul, who clothed you
Neh 8: 9 do not mourn nor **w**
Job 27:15 and their widows shall not **w**
Job 30:31 to the voice of those who **w**
Job 31:38 me, and its furrows **w** together
Eccl 3: 4 a time to **w**, and a time to
Is 15: 2 to the high places to **w**
Is 22: 4 from me, I will **w** bitterly
Is 30:19 you shall **w** no more
Is 33: 7 of peace shall **w** bitterly
Jer 9: 1 of tears, that I might **w** day
Jer 13:17 my soul will **w** in secret for
Jer 13:17 my eyes will **w** bitterly and
Jer 22:10 **W** not for the dead, nor
Jer 22:10 but **w** bitterly for him who
Jer 48:32 I will **w** for you with the
Lam 1:16 For these things I **w**
Ezek 24:16 you shall neither mourn nor **w**
Ezek 24:23 you shall neither mourn nor **w**
Ezek 27:31 **w** for you with bitterness of
Joel 1: 5 Awake, you drunkards, and **w**
Joel 2:17 **w** between the porch and the
Mic 1:10 **w** not at all in Beth Aphrah,
Zech 7: 3 Should I **w** in the fifth month
Mark 5:39 make this commotion and **w**
Luke 6:21 Blessed are you who **w** now
Luke 6:25 now, For you shall mourn and **w**
Luke 7:13 said to her, "Do not **w**."
Luke 7:32 to you, and you did not **w**
Luke 8:52 Do not **w**; she is not dead
Luke 23:28 of Jerusalem, do not **w** for Me
Luke 23:28 but **w** for yourselves and for
John 11:31 going to the tomb to **w** there
John 16:20 I say to you that you will **w**
Rom 12:15 and **w** with those who **w**
1Co 7:30 those who **w**
1Co 7:30 as though they did not **w**
Jas 4: 9 Lament and mourn and **w**
Jas 5: 1 Come now, you rich, **w** and howl
Rev 5: 5 elders said to me, "Do not **w**.
Rev 18: 9 luxuriously with her will **w**
Rev 18:11 merchants of the earth will **w**

WEEPING (*see* WEEP)
Num 11:10 **w** throughout their families
Num 25: 6 who were **w** at the door of the
Deut 34: 8 So the days of **w** and mourning
2Sa 3:16 her to Bahurim, **w** behind her
2Sa 15:30 and went up, **w** as they went up
2Sa 19: 1 Behold, the king is **w** and
2Ki 8:12 Why is my lord **w**
Ezra 3:13 noise of the **w** of the people
Ezra 10: 1 and while he was confessing, **w**
Esth 4: 3 the Jews, with fasting, **w**
Job 16:16 My face is flushed from **w**
Ps 6: 8 has heard the voice of my **w**
Ps 30: 5 **W** may endure for a night, But
Ps 102: 9 And mingled my drink with **w**
Ps 126: 6 who continually goes forth **w**
Is 5: 7 righteousness, but behold, a **w**
Is 15: 3 will wail, **w** bitterly
Is 15: 5 Luhith they will go up with **w**
Is 16: 9 Sibmah, with the **w** of Jazer

Is 22:12 GOD of hosts called for w
Is 65:19 the voice of w shall no
Jer 3:21 on the desolate heights, w
Jer 9:10 I will take up a w and wailing
Jer 31: 9 They shall come with w, and
Jer 31:15 lamentation and bitter w,
Jer 31:15 Rachel w for her children,
Jer 31:16 Refrain your voice from w
Jer 41: 6 meet them, w as he went along
Jer 48: 5 they ascend with continual w
Jer 48:32 for you with the w of Jazer
Jer 50: 4 with continual w they shall
Ezek 8:14 sitting there w for Tammuz
Joel 2:12 heart, with fasting, with w
Mal 2:13 the LORD with tears, with w
Matt 2:18 in Ramah, lamentation, w, and
Matt 2:18 Rachel w for her children,
Matt 8:12 There will be w and gnashing
Matt 22:13 there will be w and gnashing
Matt 24:51 There shall be w and gnashing
Matt 25:30 There will be w and gnashing
Luke 7:38 at His feet behind Him w
Luke 13:28 There will be w and gnashing
John 11:33 when Jesus saw her w, and the
John 11:33 the Jews who came with her w
John 20:11 stood outside by the tomb w
John 20:13 Woman, why are you w
John 20:15 Woman, why are you w
Acts 9:39 all the widows stood by him w
Acts 21:13 What do you mean by w and
Phil 3:18 often, and now tell you even w
Rev 18:15 for fear of her torment, w
Rev 18:19 their heads and cried out, w

WEEPS (*see* WEEP)
Lam 1: 2 She w bitterly in the night,

WEIGH (*see* WEIGHED, WEIGHING, WEIGHS, WEIGHT)
1Ki 7:47 Solomon did not w all the
1Ch 20: 2 found it to w a talent of
Ezra 8:29 keep them until you w them
Ps 58: 2 You w out the violence of
Is 26: 7 You w the path of the just
Is 46: 6 and w silver in the balance
Ezek 5: 1 then take balances to w and

WEIGHED (*see* WEIGH)
Gen 23:16 Abraham w out the silver for
Num 7:85 silver platter w one hundred
Num 7:85 w two thousand four hundred
Num 7:86 incense w ten shekels apiece
Num 7:86 of the pans w one hundred
1Sa 2: 3 and by Him actions are w
1Sa 17: 7 and his iron spearhead w six
2Sa 14:26 he w the hair of his head at
Ezra 8:25 w out to them the silver, the
Ezra 8:26 I even w into their hand six
Ezra 8:33 the articles were w in the
Job 6: 2 that my grief were fully w
Job 28:15 can silver be w for its price
Job 31: 6 Let me be w in a just balance
Ps 62: 9 If they are w in the balances
Is 40:12 W the mountains in scales and
Jer 32: 9 and w out to him the money
Jer 32:10 w the money in the balances
Dan 5:27 You have been w in the
Amos 2:13 I am w down by you
Amos 2:13 as a cart is w down that is
Zech 11:12 So they w out for my wages
Luke 21:34 be w down with carousing,

WEIGHING (*see* WEIGH)
Gen 24:22 nose ring w half a shekel
Gen 24:22 wrists w ten shekels of gold
Josh 7:21 wedge of gold w fifty shekels
Ezra 8:26 silver articles w one hundred

WEIGHS (*see* WEIGH)
Prov 16: 2 but the LORD w the spirits
Prov 21: 2 but the LORD w the hearts
Prov 24:12 this," does not He who w the
Is 33:18 Where is he who w

WEIGHT (*see* WEIGH, WEIGHTIER, WEIGHTS, WEIGHTY)
Gen 43:21 his sack, our money in full w
Lev 19:35 in measurement of length, w
Lev 26:26 back to you your bread by w
Num 7:13 the w of which was one
Num 7:19 the w of which was one
Num 7:25 the w of which was one
Num 7:31 the w of which was one
Num 7:37 the w of which was one
Num 7:43 the w of which was one
Num 7:49 the w of which was one
Num 7:55 the w of which was one
Num 7:61 the w of which was one
Num 7:67 the w of which was one
Num 7:73 the w of which was one
Num 7:79 the w of which was one
Deut 25:15 have a perfect and just w, a
Judg 8:26 Now the w of the gold
1Sa 17: 5 the w of the coat was five
2Sa 12:30 Its w was a talent of gold,
2Sa 21:16 the w of whose bronze spear
1Ki 7:47 the w of the bronze was not
1Ki 10:14 The w of gold that came to
1Ch 21:25 of gold by w for the place
1Ch 28:14 He gave gold by w for things
1Ch 28:14 all articles of silver by w
1Ch 28:15 the w for the lampstands of
1Ch 28:15 by w for each lampstand and
1Ch 28:15 the lampstands of silver by w
1Ch 28:16 by w he gave gold for the
1Ch 28:17 gave gold by w for every bowl
1Ch 28:17 silver by w for every bowl
1Ch 28:18 refined gold by w for the
2Ch 3: 9 The w of the nails was fifty
2Ch 4:18 the w of the bronze was not
2Ch 9:13 The w of gold that came to
Ezra 8:30 the gold and the articles by w
Ezra 8:34 the number and w of everything
Ezra 8:34 All the w was written down at
Job 28:25 to establish a w for the wind
Prov 11: 1 but a just w is His delight
Prov 16:11 A just w and balance are the
Ezek 4:10 which you eat shall be by w
Ezek 4:16 they shall eat bread by w
2Co 4:17 and eternal w of glory,
Heb 12: 1 let us lay aside every w
Rev 16:21 about the w of a talent

WEIGHTIER (*see* WEIGHT)
Matt 23:23 the w matters of the law

WEIGHTS (*see* WEIGHT)
Lev 19:36 have just balances, just w
Deut 25:13 have in your bag differing w
Prov 16:11 all the w in the bag are His
Prov 20:10 Diverse w and diverse measures
Prov 20:23 Diverse w are an abomination
Mic 6:11 with the bag of deceitful w

WEIGHTY (*see* WEIGHT)
Prov 27: 3 A stone is heavy and sand is w
2Co 10:10 are w and powerful, but his

WELCOME (*see* WELCOMED)
Acts 28: 2 a fire and made us all w,
Col 4:10 if he comes to you, w him),

WELCOMED (*see* WELCOME)
Luke 8:40 that the multitude w Him
Luke 10:38 Martha w Him into her house
1Th 2:13 you w it not as the word of

WELFARE
Esth 2:11 to learn of Esther's w and
Jer 38: 4 not seek the w of this people

WELL (*see* PREFACE)

WELL* (*see* WELL'S, WELLS, WELLSPRING)
Gen 16:14 Therefore the w was called
Gen 21:19 eyes, and she saw a w of water
Gen 21:25 Abimelech because of a w of
Gen 21:30 that I have dug this w
Gen 24:11 a w of water at evening time
Gen 24:13 stand here by the w of water
Gen 24:16 And she went down to the w
Gen 24:20 back to the w to draw water
Gen 24:29 ran out to the man by the w
Gen 24:42 And this day I came to the w
Gen 24:43 I stand by the w of water
Gen 24:45 and she went down to the w
Gen 26:19 found a w of running water
Gen 26:20 called the name of the w Esek
Gen 26:21 Then they dug another w, and
Gen 26:22 from there and dug another w
Gen 26:25 Isaac's servants dug a w
Gen 26:32 the w which they had dug, and
Gen 29: 2 and saw a w in the field
Gen 29: 2 for out of that w they
Gen 49:22 a fruitful bough by a w
Ex 2:15 and he sat down by a w
Num 21:16 which is the w where the LORD
Num 21:17 Spring up, O w! All of you sing
Num 21:18 the w the leaders sank, dug
1Sa 19:22 the great w that is at Sechu
2Sa 3:26 him back from the w of Sirah
2Sa 17:18 who had a w in his court
2Sa 17:21 they came up out of the w
2Sa 23:15 water from the w of Bethlehem
2Sa 23:16 drew water from the w of
1Ch 11:17 water from the w of Bethlehem
1Ch 11:18 drew water from the w of
Neh 2:13 Valley Gate to the Serpent W
Prov 5:15 running water from your own w
Prov 10:11 the righteous is a w of life
Song 4:15 a w of living waters, and
John 4: 6 Now Jacob's w was there
John 4: 6 journey, sat thus by the w
John 4:11 draw with, and the w is deep
John 4:12 Jacob, who gave us the w, and

WELL-ADVANCED (*see* ADVANCE)
Gen 18:11 and Sarah were old, w in age
Gen 24: 1 Now Abraham was old, w in age

WELL-ADVISED (*see* ADVISE)
Prov 13:10 but with the w is wisdom

WELL-BEING
Gen 43:27 he asked them about their w
Ex 18: 7 each other about their w, and
Neh 2:10 w of the children of Israel
Job 20:21 therefore his w will not last
Ps 69:22 them, And their w a trap
Prov 29:10 but the just seek his w
Lam 3:38 High that woe and w proceed
1Co 10:24 but each one the other's w

WELL-BELOVED (*see* BELOVED)
Is 5: 1 to my W a song of my Beloved
Is 5: 1 my W has a vineyard On a very

WELL-DRIVEN (*see* DRIVE)
Eccl 12:11 of scholars are like w nails

WELL-FED (*see* FEED)
Jer 5: 8 They were like w lusty

WELL-KNOWN (*see* KNOW, KNOWN)
Mark 6:14 for His name had become w
2Co 5:11 but we are w to God, and I
2Co 5:11 I also trust are w in your
2Co 6: 9 as unknown, and yet w

WELL-LADEN (*see* LADEN)
Ps 144:14 That our oxen may be w

WELL-OFF
Jer 44:17 we had plenty of food, were w

WELL-ORDERED (*see* ORDER)
2Ch 8:16 was w from the day of the

WELL-RECEIVED (*see* RECEIVE)
Esth 10: 3 w by the multitude of his

WELL-REFINED (*see* REFINE)
Is 25: 6 of w wines on the lees

WELL'S (*see* WELL*)
Gen 29: 2 stone was on the w mouth
Gen 29: 3 the stone from the w mouth
Gen 29: 3 in its place on the w mouth
Gen 29: 8 the stone from the w mouth
Gen 29:10 the stone from the w mouth
2Sa 17:19 a covering over the w mouth

WELLS (*see* WELL*, WELLSPRING)
Gen 26:15 had stopped up all the w
Gen 26:18 And Isaac dug again the w of
Ex 15:27 there were twelve w of water
Num 20:17 will we drink water from w
Num 21:22 will not drink water from w
Deut 6:11 hewn-out w which you did not
Deut 10: 6 w of Bene Jaakan to Moserah
2Ch 26:10 He dug many w, for he had
Is 12: 3 water from the w of salvation
Jer 6: 7 As a fountain w up with water
Jer 6: 7 so she w up with her
2Pe 2:17 These are w without water,

WELL-SET
Is 3:24 instead of w hair, baldness

WELLSPRING (*see* SPRING, WELL*, WELLS, WELLSPRINGS)
Prov 16:22 Understanding is a w of life
Prov 18: 4 the w of wisdom is a flowing

WELLSPRINGS (*see* WELLSPRING)
Is 48: 1 forth from the w of Judah

WELL-WATERED (*see* WATER)
Jer 31:12 shall be like a w garden, and

WEND
Zech 10: 2 people w their way like sheep

WENT (*see* PREFACE)

WEPT (*see* WEEP)
Gen 21:16 him, and lifted her voice and w
Gen 27:38 Esau lifted up his voice and w
Gen 29:11 and lifted up his voice and w
Gen 33: 4 neck and kissed him, and they w
Gen 37:35 Thus his father w for him
Gen 42:24 himself away from them and w
Gen 43:30 into his chamber and w there
Gen 45: 2 he w aloud, and the Egyptians
Gen 45:14 brother Benjamin's neck and w
Gen 45:14 and Benjamin w on his neck
Gen 45:15 w over them, and after that
Gen 46:29 w on his neck a good while
Gen 50: 1 w over him, and kissed him
Gen 50:17 Joseph w when they spoke to
Ex 2: 6 child, and behold, the baby w
Num 11: 4 of Israel also w again and
Num 11:18 for you have w in the hearing
Num 11:20 have w before Him, saying,
Num 14: 1 and the people w that night
Deut 1:45 w before the LORD, but the
Deut 34: 8 the children of Israel w for
Judg 2: 4 lifted up their voice and w
Judg 14:16 Then Samson's wife w on him
Judg 14:17 Now she had w on him the
Judg 20:23 up and w before the LORD until
Judg 20:26 came to the house of God and w
Judg 21: 2 their voices and w bitterly,
Ruth 1: 9 lifted up their voices and w
Ruth 1:14 up their voices and w again
1Sa 1: 7 therefore she w and did not
1Sa 1:10 to the LORD and w in anguish
1Sa 11: 4 lifted up their voices and w
1Sa 20:41 they w together, but David
1Sa 24:16 And Saul lifted his voice and w
1Sa 30: 4 lifted up their voices and w
2Sa 1:12 And they mourned and w and
2Sa 3:32 w at the grave of Abner, and
2Sa 3:32 and all the people w
2Sa 3:34 the people w over him again
2Sa 12:21 w for the child while he was
2Sa 12:22 still alive, I fasted and w
2Sa 13:36 lifted up their voice and w
2Sa 13:36 his servants w very bitterly
2Sa 15:23 all the country w with a loud
2Sa 15:30 of Olives, and w as he went up
2Sa 18:33 chamber over the gate, and w
2Ki 8:11 and the man of God w
2Ki 13:14 w over his face, and said,
2Ki 20: 3 And Hezekiah w bitterly
2Ki 22:19 and w before Me, I also have
2Ch 34:27 and w before Me, I also have
Ezra 3:12 w with a loud voice when the
Ezra 10: 1 the people w very bitterly
Neh 1: 4 words, that I sat down and w
Neh 8: 9 For all the people w, when
Job 2:12 they lifted their voices and w
Job 30:25 Have I not w for him who was
Ps 69:10 When I w and chastened my soul
Ps 137: 1 we w When we remembered
Is 38: 3 And Hezekiah w bitterly
Hos 12: 4 he w, and sought favor from
Matt 26:75 he went out and w bitterly
Mark 5:38 saw a tumult and those who w
Mark 14:72 he thought about it, he w
Mark 16:10 Him, as they mourned and w
Luke 8:52 Now all w and mourned for her
Luke 19:41 He saw the city and w over it,
Luke 22:62 Peter went out and w bitterly
John 11:35 Jesus w
John 20:11 as she w she stooped down and
Acts 20:37 Then they all w freely, and
Rev 5: 4 So I w much, because no one

WERE (*see* PREFACE)

WEST (*see* WESTERN, WESTWARD)
Gen 12: 8 his tent with Bethel on the w
Gen 28:14 shall spread abroad to the w
Ex 10:19 turned a very strong w wind
Ex 27:12 w side shall be hangings of
Ex 36:27 For the w side of the
Ex 38:12 And on the w side there were
Num 2:18 On the w side shall be the
Num 35: 5 on the w side two thousand
Deut 3:27 lift your eyes toward the w
Deut 33:23 of the LORD, possess the w
Josh 5: 1 on the w side of the Jordan
Josh 8: 9 and Ai, on the w side of Ai
Josh 8:12 on the w side of the city
Josh 8:13 guard on the w of the city
Josh 11: 2 the heights of Dor on the w
Josh 11: 3 in the east and in the w, the
Josh 12: 7 side of the Jordan, on the w
Josh 15:12 The w border was the
Josh 18:14 the w side to the south, from
Josh 18:14 This was the w side
Josh 18:15 the border extended on the w
Josh 19:11 border went toward the w and
Josh 19:34 side and Asher on the w side
Judg 18:12 it is, w of Kirjath Jearim
1Ki 7:25 three looking toward the w
1Ch 7:28 east Naaran, to the w Gezer
1Ch 9:24 the east, w, north, and south
1Ch 12:15 to the east and to the w
1Ch 26:16 lot came out for the W Gate
1Ch 26:18 As for the Parbar on the w
1Ch 26:30 w side of the Jordan for all
2Ch 4: 4 three looking toward the w
2Ch 32:30 w side of the City of David
2Ch 33:14 David on the w side of Gihon
Job 18:20 Those in the w are astonished
Ps 75: 6 from the w nor from the south
Ps 103:12 far as the east is from the w
Ps 107: 3 From the east and from the w
Is 11:14 the Philistines toward the w
Is 43: 5 and gather you from the w
Is 49:12 Those from the north and the w
Is 59:19 name of the LORD from the w
Ezek 42:19 He came around to the w side
Ezek 45: 7 westward on the w side and
Ezek 45: 7 from the w border to the east
Ezek 47:20 The w side shall be the Great
Ezek 47:20 This is the w side
Ezek 48: 1 from its east to its w side
Ezek 48: 2 from the east side to the w
Ezek 48: 3 from the east side to the w
Ezek 48: 4 from the east side to the w
Ezek 48: 5 from the east side to the w
Ezek 48: 6 from the east side to the w
Ezek 48: 7 from the east side to the w
Ezek 48: 8 from the east side to the w
Ezek 48: 8 from the east side to the w
Ezek 48:10 on the w ten thousand in
Ezek 48:16 the w side four thousand five
Ezek 48:17 to the w two hundred and fifty
Ezek 48:18 east and ten thousand to the w
Ezek 48:23 from the east side to the w
Ezek 48:24 from the east side to the w
Ezek 48:25 from the east side to the w
Ezek 48:26 from the east side to the w
Ezek 48:27 from the east side to the w
Ezek 48:34 on the w side, four thousand
Dan 8: 5 a male goat came from the w
Hos 11:10 come trembling from the w
Zech 8: 7 and from the land of the w
Zech 14: 4 split in two, from east to w
Matt 8:11 many will come from east and w
Matt 24:27 the east and flashes to the w
Luke 12:54 a cloud rising out of the w
Luke 13:29 come from the east and the w
Rev 21:13 and three gates on the w

WESTERN (*see* WEST)
Num 34: 6 As for the w border, you
Num 34: 6 this shall be your w border
Deut 11:24 Euphrates, even to the W Sea
Deut 34: 2 of Judah as far as the W Sea
Ezek 41:12 w end was seventy cubits wide
Ezek 46:19 at their extreme w end
Ezek 48:21 as far as the w border,
Joel 2:20 and his back toward the w sea
Zech 14: 8 half of them toward the w sea

WESTWARD (*see* WEST)
Gen 13:14 southward, eastward, and w
Ex 26:22 far side of the tabernacle, w
Ex 26:27 for the far side w
Ex 36:32 tabernacle on the far side w
Num 3:23 camp behind the tabernacle w
Josh 15: 8 before the Valley of Hinnom w
Josh 15:10 Then the border turned w from
Josh 16: 3 went down w to the boundary
Josh 16: 8 Tappuah w to the Brook Kanah
Josh 18:12 up through the mountains w
Josh 19:26 it reached to Mount Carmel w
Josh 19:34 extended w to Aznoth Tabor
Josh 22: 7 on this side of the Jordan, w
Josh 23: 4 as far as the Great Sea w
Ezek 45: 7 extending w on the west side
Ezek 48:21 w next to the twenty-five
Dan 8: 4 I saw the ram pushing w,

WET
Job 24: 8 They are w with the showers
Dan 4:15 let it be w with the dew of
Dan 4:23 let it be w with the dew of
Dan 4:25 They shall w you with the dew
Dan 4:33 his body was w with the dew
Dan 5:21 his body was w with the dew

WHAT (*see* PREFACE)

WHATEVER (*see* PREFACE)

WHEAT
Gen 30:14 went in the days of w harvest
Ex 9:32 But the w and the spelt were
Ex 29: 2 shall make them of w flour)
Ex 34:22 the firstfruits of w harvest
Deut 8: 8 a land of w and barley, of
Deut 32:14 and goats, with the choicest w
Judg 6:11 threshed w in the winepress
Judg 15: 1 in the time of w harvest
Ruth 2:23 barley harvest and w harvest
1Sa 6:13 their w harvest in the valley
1Sa 12:17 Is today not the w harvest
2Sa 4: 6 the house, as though to get w
2Sa 17:28 basins, earthen vessels and w
1Ki 5:11 twenty thousand kors of w as
1Ch 21:20 Ornan continued threshing w
1Ch 21:23 the w for the grain offering
2Ch 2:10 thousand kors of ground w
2Ch 2:15 Now therefore, the w, the
2Ch 27: 5 ten thousand kors of w, and
Ezra 6: 9 of the God of heaven, w, salt
Ezra 7:22 silver, one hundred kors of w
Job 31:40 thistles grow instead of w
Ps 81:16 also with the finest of w
Ps 147:14 fills you with the finest w
Song 7: 2 of w set about with lilies
Is 28:25 cummin, plant the w in rows
Jer 12:13 They have sown w but reaped
Jer 23:28 What is the chaff to the w
Jer 31:12 for w and new wine and oil, for
Jer 41: 8 for we have treasures of w
Ezek 4: 9 Also take for yourself w,
Ezek 27:17 your merchandise w of Minnith
Ezek 45:13 of an ephah from a homer of w
Joel 1:11 you vinedressers, for the w
Joel 2:24 floors shall be full of w
Amos 8: 5 that we may trade our w
Amos 8: 6 even sell the bad w
Matt 3:12 gather His w into the barn
Matt 13:25 and sowed tares among the w
Matt 13:29 also uproot the w with them
Matt 13:30 but gather the w into my barn
Luke 3:17 gather the w into His barn
Luke 16: 7 A hundred measures of w
Luke 22:31 that he may sift you as w
John 12:24 unless a grain of w falls
Acts 27:38 threw out the w into the sea
1Co 15:37 perhaps w or some other grain
Rev 6: 6 A quart of w for a denarius,
Rev 18:13 wine and oil, fine flour and w

WHEEL (*see* WHEELS)
1Ki 7:32 The height of a w was one
1Ki 7:33 workmanship of a chariot w
Prov 20:26 the threshing w over them
Eccl 12: 6 or the w broken at the well
Jer 18: 3 making something at the w
Ezek 1:15 a w was on the earth beside
Ezek 1:16 a w in the middle of a w
Ezek 10: 9 one w by one cherub and
Ezek 10: 9 and another w by each other
Ezek 10:10 a w in the middle of a w
Ezek 10:13 called in my hearing, "W."

WHEELS (*see* WHEEL)
Ex 14:25 He took off their chariot w
1Ki 7:30 Every cart had four bronze w
1Ki 7:32 the panels were the four w
1Ki 7:32 and the axles of the w were
1Ki 7:33 The workmanship of the w was
Is 5:28 and their w like a whirlwind

Jer 47: 3 at the rumbling of his **w**
Ezek 1:16 The appearance of the **w** and
Ezek 1:19 went, the **w** went beside them
Ezek 1:19 earth, the **w** were lifted up
Ezek 1:20 the **w** were lifted together
Ezek 1:20 living creatures was in the **w**
Ezek 1:21 the **w** were lifted up together
Ezek 1:21 living creatures was in the **w**
Ezek 3:13 noise of the **w** beside them
Ezek 10: 2 Go in among the **w**, under the
Ezek 10: 6 Take fire from among the **w**
Ezek 10: 6 went in and stood beside the **w**
Ezek 10: 9 were four **w** by the cherubim
Ezek 10: 9 the **w** appeared to have the
Ezek 10:12 the **w** that the four had, were
Ezek 10:13 As for the **w**, they were
Ezek 10:16 went, the **w** went beside them
Ezek 10:16 the same **w** also did not turn
Ezek 10:17 the **w** stood still, and when
Ezek 10:19 out, the **w** were beside them
Ezek 11:22 with the **w** beside them, and
Dan 7: 9 flame, its **w** a burning fire
Nah 3: 2 and the noise of rattling **w**

WHELP (*see* WHELPS)
Gen 49: 9 Judah is a lion's **w**
Deut 33:22 Dan is a lion's **w**

WHELPS (*see* WHELP)
Jer 51:38 shall growl like lions' **w**

WHEN (*see* PREFACE)

WHENCE (*see* PREFACE)

WHENEVER (*see* PREFACE)

WHERE (*see* PREFACE)

WHEREAS (*see* PREFACE)

WHEREBY (*see* PREFACE)

WHEREIN (*see* PREFACE)

WHEREOF (*see* PREFACE)

WHEREUPON (*see* PREFACE)

WHEREVER (*see* PREFACE)

WHET
Deut 32:41 If I **w** My glittering sword,

WHETHER (*see* PREFACE)

WHICH (*see* PREFACE)

WHICHEVER (*see* PREFACE)

WHILE (*see* PREFACE)

WHIP (*see* WHIPS)
Prov 26: 3 A **w** for the horse, a bridle
Nah 3: 2 The noise of a **w** and the noise
John 2:15 When He had made a **w** of cords

WHIPS (*see* WHIP)
1Ki 12:11 father chastised you with **w**
1Ki 12:14 father chastised you with **w**
2Ch 10:11 father chastised you with **w**
2Ch 10:14 father chastised you with **w**

WHIRLING (*see* WHIRLS)
2Sa 6:16 leaping and **w** before the LORD
1Ch 15:29 a window, saw King David **w**
Ps 83:13 make them like the **w** dust

WHIRLS (*see* WHIRLING)
Eccl 1: 6 the wind **w** about continually,

WHIRLWIND (*see* WHIRLWINDS)
2Ki 2: 1 up Elijah into heaven by a **w**
2Ki 2:11 went up by a **w** into heaven
Job 37: 9 of the south comes the **w**, and
Job 38: 1 answered Job out of the **w**
Job 40: 6 answered Job out of the **w**
Ps 58: 9 take them away as with a **w**
Ps 77:18 of Your thunder was in the **w**
Prov 1:27 destruction comes like a **w**
Prov 10:25 When the **w** passes by, the
Is 5:28 and their wheels like a **w**
Is 17:13 a rolling thing before the **w**
Is 40:24 the **w** will take them away
Is 41:16 and the **w** shall scatter them
Is 66:15 with His chariots, like a **w**
Jer 4:13 and his chariots like a **w**
Jer 23:19 a **w** of the LORD has gone
Jer 23:19 a violent **w**
Jer 25:32 a great **w** shall be raised up
Jer 30:23 the **w** of the LORD goes forth
Jer 30:23 with fury, a continuing **w**
Ezek 1: 4 a **w** was coming out of the
Dan 11:40 come against him like a **w**
Hos 8: 7 sow the wind, and reap the **w**
Amos 1:14 a tempest in the day of the **w**
Nah 1: 3 the LORD has His way in the **w**
Hab 3:14 out like a **w** to scatter me
Zech 7:14 **w** among all the nations which

WHIRLWINDS (*see* WHIRLWIND)
Is 21: 1 As **w** in the South pass
Zech 9:14 and go with **w** from the south

WHISPER (*see* WHISPERER, WHISPERING)
Job 4:12 and my ear received a **w** of it
Job 26:14 how small a **w** we hear of Him
Ps 41: 7 All who hate me **w** together
Is 8:19 mediums and wizards, who **w**
Is 29: 4 shall **w** out of the dust

WHISPERER (*see* WHISPER, WHISPERERS)
Prov 16:28 a **w** separates the best of

WHISPERERS (*see* WHISPERER)
Rom 1:29 they are **w**,

WHISPERING (*see* WHISPER, WHISPERINGS)
2Sa 12:19 saw that his servants were **w**
Lam 3:62 their **w** against me all the

WHISPERINGS (*see* WHISPERING)
2Co 12:20 ambitions, backbitings, **w**

WHISTLE
Is 5:26 will **w** to them from the end
Is 7:18 **w** for the fly that is in the
Zech 10: 8 I will **w** for them and gather

WHITE (*see* REDDISH-WHITE, WHITEN, WHITER, WHITEWASH)
Gen 30:35 one that had some **w** in it
Gen 30:37 peeled **w** strips in them, and
Gen 30:37 exposed the **w** which was in
Gen 40:16 there I had three **w** baskets
Ex 16:31 it was like **w** coriander seed,
Lev 11:18 the **w** owl, the jackdaw, and
Lev 13: 3 hair on the sore has turned **w**
Lev 13: 4 is **w** on the skin of his body
Lev 13: 4 and its hair has not turned **w**
Lev 13:10 the swelling on the skin is **w**
Lev 13:10 and it has turned the hair **w**
Lev 13:13 It has all turned **w**
Lev 13:16 changes and turns **w** again, he
Lev 13:17 if the sore has turned **w**,
Lev 13:19 a **w** swelling or a bright spot
Lev 13:20 and its hair has turned **w**
Lev 13:21 there are no **w** hairs in it
Lev 13:24 spot, reddish-white or **w**,
Lev 13:25 the bright spot has turned **w**
Lev 13:26 indeed there are no **w** hairs
Lev 13:38 specifically **w** bright spots
Lev 13:39 skin of the body are dull **w**
Lev 13:39 it is a **w** spot that grows on
Num 12:10 became leprous, as **w** as snow
Deut 14:16 the screech owl, the **w** owl
Judg 5:10 you who ride on **w** donkeys
2Ki 5:27 leprous, as **w** as snow
2Ch 5:12 the altar, clothed in **w** linen
Esth 1: 6 There were **w** and blue linen
Esth 1: 6 of alabaster, turquoise, and **w**
Esth 8:15 in royal apparel of blue and **w**
Job 6: 6 any taste in the **w** of an egg
Job 41:32 think the deep had **w** hair
Ps 68:14 It was **w** as snow in Zalmon
Eccl 9: 8 Let your garments always be **w**
Song 5:10 My beloved is **w** and ruddy,
Is 1:18 they shall be as **w** as snow
Ezek 27:18 wine of Helbon and with **w** wool
Dan 7: 9 His garment was **w** as snow
Dan 11:35 purge them, and make them **w**
Dan 12:10 shall be purified, made **w**
Joel 1: 7 its branches are made **w**
Zech 1: 8 red, sorrel, and **w**
Zech 6: 3 the third chariot **w** horses
Zech 6: 6 the **w** are going after them,
Matt 5:36 make one hair **w** or black
Matt 17: 2 became as **w** as the light
Matt 28: 3 and his clothing as **w** as snow
Mark 9: 3 became shining, exceedingly **w**
Mark 16: 5 **w** robe sitting on the right
Luke 9:29 altered, and His robe became **w**
John 4:35 are already **w** for harvest
John 20:12 saw two angels in **w** sitting
Acts 1:10 stood by them in **w** apparel
Rev 1:14 and His hair were **w** like wool
Rev 1:14 as **w** as snow, and His eyes
Rev 2:17 And I will give him a **w** stone
Rev 3: 4 they shall walk with Me in **w**
Rev 3: 5 be clothed in **w** garments, and
Rev 3:18 **w** garments, that you may be
Rev 4: 4 sitting, clothed in **w** robes
Rev 6: 2 looked, and behold, a **w** horse
Rev 6:11 a **w** robe was given to each of
Rev 7: 9 Lamb, clothed with **w** robes
Rev 7:13 are these arrayed in **w** robes
Rev 7:14 made them **w** in the blood of
Rev 14:14 a **w** cloud, and on the cloud
Rev 19:11 opened, and behold, a **w** horse
Rev 19:14 clothed in fine linen, **w**
Rev 19:14 followed Him on **w** horses
Rev 20:11 Then I saw a great **w** throne

WHITEN (*see* WHITE)
Mark 9: 3 launderer on earth can **w** them

WHITER (*see* WHITE)
Gen 49:12 and his teeth **w** than milk
Ps 51: 7 me, and I shall be **w** than snow
Lam 4: 7 than snow and **w** than milk

WHITEWASH (*see* WHITE, WHITEWASHED)
Deut 27: 2 stones, and **w** them with lime
Deut 27: 4 you shall **w** them with lime

WHITEWASHED (*see* WHITEWASH)
Matt 23:27 For you are like **w** tombs
Acts 23: 3 will strike you, you **w** wall

WHO (*see* PREFACE)

WHOEVER (*see* PREFACE)

WHOLE (*see* WHOLE-HEARTED, WHOLESOME, WHOLLY)
Gen 2: 6 watered the **w** face of the
Gen 2:11 the **w** land of Havilah, where
Gen 2:13 the **w** land of Cush
Gen 7:19 the **w** heaven were covered
Gen 8: 9 on the face of the **w** earth
Gen 9:19 from these the **w** earth was
Gen 11: 1 Now the **w** earth had one
Gen 11: 4 over the face of the **w** earth
Gen 13: 9 Is not the **w** land before you
Ex 9:25 the **w** land of Egypt, all that
Ex 10:15 the face of the **w** earth, so
Ex 12: 6 Then the **w** assembly of the
Ex 16: 2 Then the **w** congregation of
Ex 16: 3 this **w** assembly with hunger
Ex 16:10 to the **w** congregation of the
Ex 19:18 the **w** mountain quaked greatly
Ex 29:18 burn the **w** ram on the altar
Lev 3: 9 the **w** fat tail which he shall
Lev 4:12 the **w** bull he shall carry
Lev 4:13 Now if the **w** congregation of
Lev 8:21 burned the **w** ram on the altar
Lev 10: 6 the **w** house of Israel, bewail
Lev 25:29 a **w** year after it is sold
Num 3: 7 needs and the needs of the **w**
Num 8: 9 shall gather together the **w**
Num 11: 6 but now our **w** being is dried
Num 11:20 but for a **w** month, until it
Num 11:21 they may eat for a **w** month
Num 14: 2 the **w** congregation said to
Num 15:24 that the **w** congregation shall
Num 15:25 for the **w** congregation of the
Num 15:26 the **w** congregation of the
Num 20: 1 the **w** congregation, came into
Num 20:22 the **w** congregation, journeyed
Deut 2:25 nations under the **w** heaven
Deut 4:19 the **w** heaven as a heritage
Deut 27: 6 You shall build with **w** stones
Deut 29:23 The **w** land is brimstone,
Deut 33:10 a **w** burnt sacrifice on Your
Josh 3:15 during the **w** time of harvest)
Josh 8:31 an altar of **w** stones over
Josh 10:13 to go down for about a **w** day
Josh 11:23 So Joshua took the **w** land
Josh 18: 1 Then the **w** congregation of
Josh 22:12 the **w** congregation of the
Josh 22:16 Thus says the **w** congregation
Josh 22:18 the **w** congregation of Israel
Judg 7:14 Midian and the **w** camp
Judg 7:18 on every side of the **w** camp
Judg 7:21 the **w** army ran and cried out
Judg 7:22 throughout the **w** camp
Judg 8:12 and routed the **w** army
Judg 18: 1 their **w** inheritance among the
Judg 19: 2 and was there four **w** months

Judg 20:37 struck the w city with the
Judg 20:40 there was the w city going up
Judg 21:13 Then the w congregation sent
1Sa 7: 9 and offered it as a w burnt
2Sa 3:19 and the w house of Benjamin
2Sa 6:19 among the w multitude of
2Sa 14: 7 now the w family has risen up
2Sa 18: 8 the face of the w countryside
1Ki 6:22 The w temple he overlaid with
1Ki 8:14 blessed the w congregation of
1Ki 11:13 not tear away the w kingdom
1Ki 11:34 the w kingdom out of his hand
1Ki 12: 3 the w congregation of Israel
2Ki 9: 8 For the w house of Ahab
2Ch 6: 3 blessed the w congregation of
2Ch 16: 9 and fro throughout the w earth
2Ch 30:23 Then the w assembly agreed to
2Ch 30:25 The w congregation of Judah
2Ch 31:18 the w company of them
2Ch 33: 8 them, according to the w law
Ezra 2:64 The w congregation together
Neh 7:66 Altogether the w congregation
Neh 8:17 So the w congregation of
Esth 3: 6 the w kingdom of Ahasuerus
Job 5:18 wounds, but His hands make w
Job 28:24 and sees under the w heavens
Job 34:13 Him over the w world
Job 37: 3 it forth under the w heaven
Job 37:12 on the face of the w earth
Ps 9: 1 You, O LORD, with my w heart
Ps 48: 2 The joy of the w earth, Is
Ps 51:19 offering and w burnt offering
Ps 72:19 let the w earth be filled
Ps 97: 5 of the Lord of the w earth
Ps 111: 1 the LORD with my w heart, In
Ps 119: 2 Who seek Him with the w heart
Ps 119:10 With my w heart I have sought
Ps 119:34 observe it with my w heart
Ps 119:58 Your favor with my w heart
Ps 119:69 Your precepts with my w heart
Ps 119:145 I cry out with my w heart
Ps 138: 1 praise You with my w heart
Prov 1:12 them alive like Sheol, and w
Prov 26:26 before the w congregation
Eccl 12:13 conclusion of the w matter
Eccl 12:13 for this is the w duty of man
Is 1: 5 The w head is sick
Is 1: 5 and the w heart faints
Is 3: 1 the w supply of bread and the
Is 3: 1 and the w supply of water
Is 6: 3 the w earth is full of His
Is 13: 5 to destroy the w land
Is 14: 7 The w earth is at rest and
Is 14:26 purposed against the w earth
Is 28:22 even upon the w earth
Is 29:11 The w vision has become to
Is 54: 5 called the God of the w earth
Jer 1:18 walls against the w land
Jer 3:10 turned to Me with her w heart
Jer 4:20 for the w land is plundered
Jer 4:27 The w land shall be desolate
Jer 4:29 The w city shall flee from
Jer 7:15 the w posterity of Ephraim
Jer 8:16 The w land trembled at the
Jer 12:11 the w land is made desolate,
Jer 13:11 caused the w house of Israel
Jer 13:11 the w house of Judah to cling
Jer 15:10 of contention to the w earth
Jer 19:11 which cannot be made w again
Jer 24: 7 to Me with their w heart
Jer 25:11 And this w land shall be a
Jer 31:40 And the w valley of the dead
Jer 35: 3 the w house of the Rechabites
Jer 37:10 w army of the Chaldeans who
Jer 45: 4 up, that is, this w land
Jer 50:23 How the hammer of the w earth
Jer 51:41 of the w earth is seized
Jer 51:47 her w land shall be ashamed,
Lam 2:15 the joy of the w earth'
Ezek 7:12 wrath is on their w multitude
Ezek 7:13 concerns the w multitude, and
Ezek 10:12 And their w body, with their
Ezek 15: 5 Indeed, when it was w, no
Ezek 32: 4 the beasts of the w earth
Ezek 34: 6 over the w face of the earth
Ezek 35:14 The w earth will rejoice when
Ezek 37:11 are the w house of Israel
Ezek 39:25 on the w house of Israel
Ezek 43:11 they may keep its w design
Ezek 43:12 The w area surrounding the
Ezek 45: 6 to the w house of Israel
Dan 2:35 and filled the w earth
Dan 2:48 the w province of Babylon
Dan 6: 1 to be over the w kingdom
Dan 6: 3 setting him over the w realm
Dan 7:23 and shall devour the w earth
Dan 7:27 kingdoms under the w heaven
Dan 8: 5 the surface of the w earth
Dan 9:12 for under the w heaven such
Dan 10: 3 all, till three w weeks were
Dan 11:17 the strength of his w kingdom
Amos 1: 6 they took captive the w
Amos 1: 9 up the w captivity to Edom
Amos 3: 1 against the w family which I
Mic 4:13 to the Lord of the w earth
Zeph 1:18 but the w land shall be
Zech 4:10 and fro throughout the w earth
Zech 4:14 the Lord of the w earth
Zech 5: 3 over the face of the w earth
Mal 3: 9 robbed Me, even this w nation
Matt 5:29 than for your w body to be
Matt 5:30 than for your w body to be
Matt 6:22 your w body will be full of
Matt 6:23 your w body will be full of
Matt 8:32 suddenly the w herd of swine
Matt 8:34 the w city came out to meet
Matt 12:13 restored as w as the other
Matt 13: 2 the w multitude stood on the
Matt 15:31 speaking, the maimed made w
Matt 16:26 if he gains the w world, and
Matt 26:13 is preached in the w world
Matt 27:27 and gathered the w garrison
Mark 1:33 And the w city was gathered
Mark 3: 5 restored as w as the other
Mark 4: 1 the w multitude was on the
Mark 5:33 Him and told Him the w truth
Mark 6:55 ran through that w
Mark 8:36 a man if he gains the w world
Mark 12:33 all the w burnt offerings
Mark 12:44 she had, her w livelihood
Mark 14: 9 throughout the w world, what
Mark 15: 1 and scribes and the w council
Mark 15:16 together the w garrison
Mark 15:33 w land until the ninth hour
Luke 1:10 the w multitude of the people
Luke 6:10 restored as w as the other
Luke 6:19 the w multitude sought to
Luke 8:37 Then the w multitude of the
Luke 8:39 the w city what great things
Luke 9:25 a man if he gains the w world
Luke 11:34 your w body also is full of
Luke 11:36 If then your w body is full
Luke 11:36 the w body will be full of
Luke 19:37 the w multitude of the
Luke 21:35 on the face of the w earth
Luke 23: 1 Then the w multitude of them
Luke 23:48 the w crowd who came together
John 4:53 believed, and his w household
John 11:50 not that the w nation should
Acts 2: 2 it filled the w house where
Acts 4:10 man stands here before you w
Acts 6: 5 pleased the w multitude
Acts 11:26 So it was that for a w year
Acts 13:44 w city came together to hear
Acts 15:22 and elders, with the w church
Acts 19:29 So the w city was filled with
Acts 20:27 to you the w counsel of God
Acts 21:27 stirred up the w crowd and
Acts 25:24 the w assembly of the Jews
Acts 28:30 Then Paul dwelt two w years
Rom 1: 8 of throughout the w world
Rom 8:22 that the w creation groans
Rom 16:23 and the host of the w church
1Co 5: 6 leaven leavens the w lump
1Co 12:17 If the w body were an eye,
1Co 12:17 If the w were hearing, where
1Co 14:23 Therefore if the w church
Gal 5: 3 is a debtor to keep the w law
Gal 5: 9 leaven leavens the w lump
Eph 2:21 in whom the w building, being
Eph 3:15 from whom the w family in
Eph 4:16 from whom the w body, joined
Eph 6:11 Put on the w armor of God,
Eph 6:13 take up the w armor of God
Phil 1:13 evident to the w palace guard
1Th 5:23 and may your w spirit, soul,
Tit 1:11 who subvert w households
Jas 2:10 whoever shall keep the w law
Jas 3: 2 also to bridle the w body
Jas 3: 3 us, and we turn their w body
Jas 3: 6 that it defiles the w body
1Jn 2: 2 only but also for the w world
1Jn 5:19 the w world lies under the
Rev 3:10 shall come upon the w world
Rev 12: 9 who deceives the w world
Rev 16:14 the earth and of the w world

WHOLE-HEARTED (*see* HEART, WHOLE)
Ezek 36: 5 as a possession, with w joy

WHOLESOME (*see* WHOLE)
Prov 15: 4 A w tongue is a tree of life,
1Ti 6: 3 does not consent to w words

WHOLLY (*see* WHOLE)
Lev 6:22 It shall be w burned
Lev 6:23 the priest shall be w burned
Lev 19: 9 you shall not w reap the
Lev 23:22 you shall not w reap the
Num 8:16 For they are w given to Me
Num 32:11 they have not w followed Me
Num 32:12 for they have w followed the
Deut 1:36 because he w followed the
Josh 14: 8 but I w followed the LORD my
Josh 14: 9 because you have w followed
Josh 14:14 because he w followed the
Judg 17: 3 I had w dedicated the silver
Job 21:23 being w at ease and secure
Jer 13:19 it shall be w carried away
Jer 42:15 If you w set your faces to
Jer 46:28 not leave you w unpunished
Jer 50:13 but she shall be w desolate

WHOM (*see* PREFACE)

WHOMEVER (*see* PREFACE)

WHOSE (*see* PREFACE)

WHY (*see* PREFACE)

WICK (*see* WICK-TRIMMERS)
Is 43:17 they are quenched like a w)

WICKED (*see* WICKEDLY, WICKEDNESS)
Gen 13:13 of Sodom were exceedingly w
Gen 18:23 the righteous with the w
Gen 18:25 slay the righteous with the w
Gen 18:25 righteous should be as the w
Gen 38: 7 was w in the sight of the
Ex 9:27 and my people and I are w
Ex 23: 1 the w to be an unrighteous
Ex 23: 7 For I will not justify the w
Lev 20:17 nakedness, it is a w thing
Num 16:26 from the tents of these w men
Deut 15: 9 be a w thought in your heart
Deut 17: 2 w in the sight of the LORD
Deut 17: 5 has committed that w thing
Deut 23: 9 yourself from every w thing
Deut 25: 1 righteous and condemn the w
Deut 25: 2 if the w man deserves to be
Judg 20: 3 how did this w deed happen
1Sa 1:16 your maidservant a w woman
1Sa 2: 9 but the w shall be silent in
1Sa 24:13 proceeds from the w
1Sa 30:22 Then all the w and worthless
2Sa 3:34 as a man falls before w men
2Sa 4:11 when w men have killed a
1Ki 8:32 servants, condemning the w
2Ki 17:11 they did w things to provoke
1Ch 2: 3 was w in the sight of the
2Ch 6:23 w by bringing his way on his
2Ch 7:14 and turn from their w ways
2Ch 19: 2 Should you help the w and love
2Ch 24: 7 that w woman, had broken into
Neh 9:35 they turn from their w works
Esth 7: 6 and enemy is this w Haman
Esth 9:25 by letter that this w plot
Job 3:17 There the w cease from
Job 8:22 of the w will come to nothing
Job 9:22 the blameless and the w
Job 9:24 given into the hand of the w
Job 10: 3 shine on the counsel of the w
Job 10: 7 You know that I am not w, and
Job 10:15 If I am w, woe to me
Job 11:20 the eyes of the w will fail
Job 15:20 the w man writhes with pain
Job 16:11 me over to the hands of the w
Job 18: 5 of the w indeed goes out, and
Job 18:21 are the dwellings of the w
Job 20: 5 triumphing of the w is short
Job 20:29 portion from God for a w man
Job 21: 7 Why do the w live and become
Job 21:16 of the w is far from me
Job 21:17 is the lamp of the w put out

Job 21:28 the dwelling place of the w
Job 21:30 For the w are reserved for
Job 22:15 old way which w men have trod
Job 22:18 of the w is far from me
Job 24: 6 in the vineyard of the w
Job 27: 7 May my enemy be like the w
Job 27:13 portion of a w man with God
Job 29:17 I broke the fangs of the w
Job 31: 3 it not destruction for the w
Job 34: 8 iniquity, and walks with w men
Job 34:18 and to nobles, You are w'
Job 34:26 He strikes them as w men in
Job 34:36 are like those of w men
Job 36: 6 preserve the life of the w
Job 36:17 with the judgment due the w
Job 38:13 the w be shaken out of it
Job 38:15 From the w their light is
Job 40:12 down the w in their place
Ps 7: 9 of the w come to an end, But
Ps 7:11 is angry with the w every day
Ps 7:14 the w travails with iniquity,
Ps 9: 5 You have destroyed the w
Ps 9:16 The w is snared in the work
Ps 9:17 The w shall be turned into
Ps 10: 2 The w in his pride persecutes
Ps 10: 3 For the w boasts of his
Ps 10: 4 The w in his proud
Ps 10:13 Why do the w renounce God
Ps 10:15 Break the arm of the w and the
Ps 11: 2 The w bend their bow, They
Ps 11: 5 the righteous, But the w and
Ps 11: 6 Upon the w He will rain coals
Ps 12: 8 The w prowl on every side,
Ps 17: 9 From the w who oppress me,
Ps 17:13 from the w with Your sword
Ps 22:16 of the w has enclosed Me
Ps 26: 5 And will not sit with the w
Ps 27: 2 When the w came against me To
Ps 28: 3 not take me away with the w
Ps 31:17 Let the w be ashamed
Ps 32:10 sorrows shall be to the w
Ps 34:21 Evil shall slay the w, And
Ps 36: 1 the transgression of the w
Ps 36:11 hand of the w drive me away
Ps 37: 7 who brings w schemes to pass
Ps 37:10 and the w shall be no more
Ps 37:12 The w plots against the just,
Ps 37:14 The w have drawn the sword
Ps 37:16 than the riches of many w
Ps 37:17 arms of the w shall be broken
Ps 37:20 But the w shall perish
Ps 37:21 The w borrows and does not
Ps 37:28 of the w shall be cut off
Ps 37:32 The w watches the righteous,
Ps 37:34 When the w are cut off, you
Ps 37:35 seen the w in great power
Ps 37:38 of the w shall be cut off
Ps 37:40 shall deliver them from the w
Ps 39: 1 While the w are before me
Ps 50:16 But to the w God says
Ps 55: 3 of the oppression of the w
Ps 58: 3 The w are estranged from the
Ps 58:10 feet in the blood of the w
Ps 59: 5 to any w transgressors
Ps 64: 2 the secret counsel of the w
Ps 68: 2 So let the w perish at the
Ps 71: 4 God, out of the hand of the w
Ps 73: 3 I saw the prosperity of the w
Ps 75: 4 deal boastfully,' And to the w
Ps 75: 8 all the w of the earth Drain
Ps 75:10 of the w I will also cut off
Ps 82: 2 And show partiality to the w
Ps 82: 4 them from the hand of the w
Ps 91: 8 And see the reward of the w
Ps 92: 7 When the w spring up like
Ps 92:11 the w Who rise up against me
Ps 94: 3 LORD, how long will the w
Ps 94: 3 How long will the w triumph
Ps 94:13 the pit is dug for the w
Ps 97:10 them out of the hand of the w
Ps 101: 3 set nothing w before my eyes
Ps 101: 8 destroy all the w of the land
Ps 104:35 earth, And the w be no more
Ps 106:18 The flame burned up the w
Ps 109: 2 For the mouth of the w and the
Ps 109: 6 Set a w man over him, And let
Ps 112:10 The w will see it and be
Ps 112:10 desire of the w shall perish
Ps 119:53 hold of me Because of the w
Ps 119:61 cords of the w have bound me
Ps 119:95 The w wait for me to destroy
Ps 119:110 The w have laid a snare for
Ps 119:119 You put away all the w of the
Ps 119:155 Salvation is far from the w
Ps 129: 4 in pieces the cords of the w
Ps 139:19 Oh, that You would slay the w
Ps 139:24 if there is any w way in me
Ps 140: 4 LORD, from the hands of the w
Ps 140: 8 O LORD, the desires of the w
Ps 140: 8 Do not further his w scheme
Ps 141: 4 To practice w works With men
Ps 141: 5 is against the deeds of the w
Ps 141:10 Let the w fall into their own
Ps 145:20 But all the w He will destroy
Ps 146: 9 But the way of the w He turns
Ps 147: 6 He casts the w down to the
Prov 2:14 in the perversity of the w
Prov 2:22 but the w will be cut off
Prov 3:25 from the w when it comes
Prov 3:33 LORD is on the house of the w
Prov 4:14 not enter the path of the w
Prov 4:19 The way of the w is like
Prov 5:22 iniquities entrap the w man
Prov 6:12 person, a w man, walks with a
Prov 6:18 a heart that devises w plans
Prov 9: 7 he who rebukes a w man gets
Prov 10: 3 away the desire of the w
Prov 10: 6 covers the mouth of the w
Prov 10: 7 the name of the w will rot
Prov 10:11 covers the mouth of the w
Prov 10:16 the wages of the w to sin
Prov 10:20 of the w is worth little
Prov 10:24 The fear of the w will come
Prov 10:25 the w is no more, but the
Prov 10:27 of the w will be shortened
Prov 10:28 of the w will perish
Prov 10:30 but the w will not inhabit
Prov 10:32 of the w what is perverse
Prov 11: 5 but the w will fall by his
Prov 11: 7 When a w man dies, his
Prov 11: 8 and it comes to the w instead
Prov 11:10 and when the w perish, there
Prov 11:11 by the mouth of the w
Prov 11:18 The w man does deceptive work
Prov 11:21 the w will not go unpunished
Prov 11:23 expectation of the w is wrath
Prov 11:31 earth, how much more the w
Prov 12: 2 but a man of w devices He
Prov 12: 5 of the w are deceitful
Prov 12: 6 The words of the w are, "Lie
Prov 12: 7 The w are overthrown and are
Prov 12:10 mercies of the w are cruel
Prov 12:12 The w covet the catch of evil
Prov 12:13 The w is ensnared by the
Prov 12:21 but the w shall be filled
Prov 12:26 of the w leads them astray
Prov 13: 5 but a w man is loathsome and
Prov 13: 9 lamp of the w will be put out
Prov 13:17 A w messenger falls into
Prov 13:25 of the w shall be in want
Prov 14:11 The house of the w will be
Prov 14:17 and a man of w intentions is
Prov 14:19 the w at the gates of the
Prov 14:32 The w is banished in his
Prov 15: 6 revenue of the w is trouble
Prov 15: 8 The sacrifice of the w is an
Prov 15: 9 The way of the w is an
Prov 15:26 The thoughts of the w are an
Prov 15:28 of the w pours forth evil
Prov 15:29 The LORD is far from the w
Prov 16: 4 even the w for the day of
Prov 17:15 He who justifies the w, and he
Prov 17:23 A w man accepts a bribe
Prov 18: 3 When the w comes, contempt
Prov 18: 5 to show partiality to the w
Prov 19:28 of the w devours iniquity
Prov 20:26 A wise king sifts out the w
Prov 21: 4 the plowing of the w are sin
Prov 21: 7 of the w will destroy them
Prov 21:10 soul of the w desires evil
Prov 21:12 considers the house of the w
Prov 21:12 overthrowing the w for their
Prov 21:18 The w shall be a ransom for
Prov 21:27 of the w is an abomination
Prov 21:27 he brings it with w intent
Prov 21:29 A w man hardens his face, but
Prov 24:15 O w man, against the dwelling
Prov 24:16 but the w shall fall by
Prov 24:19 nor be envious of the w
Prov 24:20 lamp of the w will be put out
Prov 24:24 He who says to the w, You
Prov 24:25 the w will have delight, and a
Prov 25: 5 Take away the w from before
Prov 25:26 the w is like a murky spring
Prov 26:23 Fervent lips with a w heart
Prov 28: 1 The w flee when no one
Prov 28: 4 forsake the law praise the w
Prov 28:12 but when the w arise, men
Prov 28:15 a charging bear is a w ruler
Prov 28:28 When the w arise, men hide
Prov 29: 2 but when a w man rules, the
Prov 29: 7 but the w does not understand
Prov 29:12 all his servants become w
Prov 29:16 When the w are multiplied,
Prov 29:27 is an abomination to the w
Eccl 3:17 judge the righteous and the w
Eccl 7:15 there is a w man who prolongs
Eccl 7:17 Do not be overly w, nor be
Eccl 8:10 Then I saw the w buried, who
Eccl 8:13 will not be well with the w
Eccl 8:14 to the work of the w
Eccl 8:14 there are w men to whom it
Eccl 9: 2 to the righteous and the w
Is 3:11 Woe to the w! It shall be ill
Is 5:23 who justify the w for a bribe
Is 11: 4 His lips He shall slay the w
Is 13:11 and the w for their iniquity
Is 14: 5 has broken the staff of the w
Is 26:10 Let grace be shown to the w
Is 32: 7 he devises w plans to destroy
Is 48:22 says the LORD, "for the w."
Is 53: 9 made His grave with the w
Is 55: 7 Let the w forsake his way, and
Is 57:20 But the w are like the
Is 57:21 says my God, "for the w."
Jer 2:33 taught the w women your ways
Jer 5:26 My people are found w men
Jer 5:28 surpass the deeds of the w
Jer 6:29 for the w are not drawn off
Jer 12: 1 does the way of the w prosper
Jer 15:21 you from the hand of the w
Jer 17: 9 all things, and desperately w
Jer 23:19 on the head of the w
Jer 25:31 those who are w to the sword
Jer 30:23 on the head of the w
Ezek 3:18 When I say to the w, 'You
Ezek 3:18 the w from his w way
Ezek 3:18 that same w man shall die in
Ezek 3:19 Yet, if you warn the w, and he
Ezek 3:19 nor from his w way, he shall
Ezek 7:21 and to the w of the earth as
Ezek 8: 9 see the w abominations which
Ezek 11: 2 give w counsel in this city,
Ezek 13:22 the hands of the w, so that
Ezek 13:22 his w way to save his life
Ezek 18:20 the w shall be upon himself
Ezek 18:21 But if a w man turns from all
Ezek 18:23 at all that the w should die
Ezek 18:24 that the w man does, shall he
Ezek 18:27 when a w man turns away from
Ezek 20:44 not according to your w ways
Ezek 21: 3 both righteous and w from you
Ezek 21: 4 and w from you, therefore My
Ezek 21:25 w prince of Israel, whose day
Ezek 21:29 you on the necks of the w
Ezek 30:12 land into the hand of the w
Ezek 33: 8 When I say to the w, 'O
Ezek 33: 8 O w man, you shall surely
Ezek 33: 8 to warn the w from his way
Ezek 33: 8 that w man shall die in his
Ezek 33: 9 if you warn the w to turn
Ezek 33:11 in the death of the w, but
Ezek 33:11 but that the w turn from his
Ezek 33:12 for the wickedness of the w
Ezek 33:14 Again, when I say to the w
Ezek 33:15 if the w restores the pledge,
Ezek 33:19 But when the w turns from his
Dan 12:10 but the w shall do wickedly
Dan 12:10 and none of the w shall
Mic 6:10 in the house of the w, and the
Mic 6:11 those with the w balances
Nah 1: 3 will not at all acquit the w
Nah 1:11 the LORD, a w counselor
Nah 1:15 For the w one shall no more
Hab 1: 4 For the w surround the
Hab 1:13 w devours one more rightous
Hab 3:13 head from the house of the w
Zeph 1: 3 blocks along with the w
Mal 3:18 the righteous and the w,
Mal 4: 3 You shall trample the w, for

Matt 12:45 spirits more **w** than himself
Matt 12:45 be with this **w** generation
Matt 13:19 it, then the **w** one comes and
Matt 13:38 are the sons of the **w** one
Matt 13:49 separate the **w** from among the
Matt 16: 4 A **w** and adulterous generation
Matt 18:32 said to him, 'You **w** servant
Matt 21:41 destroy those **w** men miserably
Matt 25:26 and said to him, 'You **w** and
Luke 11:26 spirits more **w** than himself
Luke 19:22 will judge you, you **w** servant
Acts 18:14 of wrongdoing or **w** crimes
1Co 5:13 from yourselves that **w** person
Eph 6:16 the fiery darts of the **w** one
Col 1:21 in your mind by **w** works, yet
2Th 3: 2 from unreasonable and **w** men
2Pe 2: 7 the filthy conduct of the **w**
2Pe 3:17 away with the error of the **w**
1Jn 2:13 you have overcome the **w** one
1Jn 2:14 you have overcome the **w** one
1Jn 3:12 as Cain who was of the **w** one
1Jn 5:18 the **w** one does not touch him
1Jn 5:19 under the sway of the **w** one

WICKEDLY (*see* WICKED)
Gen 19: 7 my brethren, do not do so **w**
Deut 9:18 you committed in doing **w** in
Judg 19:23 I beg you, do not act so **w**
1Sa 12:25 But if you still do **w**, you
2Sa 22:22 have not **w** departed from my
2Sa 24:17 have sinned, and I have done **w**
2Ki 21:11 (he has acted more **w** than all
2Ch 6:37 done wrong, and have acted **w**'
2Ch 20:35 of Israel, who acted very **w**
2Ch 22: 3 mother counseled him to do **w**
Neh 9:33 but we have done **w**
Job 13: 7 Will you speak **w** for God, and
Job 34:12 Surely God will never do **w**
Ps 18:21 have not **w** departed from my
Ps 73: 8 speak **w** concerning oppression
Ps 106: 6 iniquity, We have done **w**
Ps 139:20 For they speak against You **w**
Dan 9: 5 iniquity, we have done **w** and
Dan 9:15 have sinned, we have done **w**
Dan 11:32 Those who do **w** against the
Dan 12:10 but the wicked shall do **w**
Mal 4: 1 all who do **w** will be stubble

WICKEDNESS (*see* WICKED)
Gen 6: 5 the **w** of man was great in the
Gen 39: 9 then can I do this great **w**
Lev 18:17 near of kin to her. It is **w**
Lev 19:29 and the land become full of **w**
Lev 20:14 woman and her mother, it is **w**
Lev 20:14 there may be no **w** among you
Num 23:21 nor has He seen **w** in Israel
Deut 9: 4 but it is because of the **w** of
Deut 9: 5 but because of the **w** of these
Deut 9:27 or on their **w** or their sin,
Deut 13:11 do such **w** as this among you
Deut 28:20 because of the **w** of your
Judg 9:56 God repaid the **w** of Abimelech
Judg 20:12 What is this **w** that has
1Sa 12:17 and see that your **w** is great
1Sa 12:20 You have done all this **w**
1Sa 24:13 **W** proceeds from the wicked
1Sa 25:39 **w** of Nabal on his own head
2Sa 3:39 evildoer according to his **w**
2Sa 7:10 of **w** oppress them anymore
1Ki 1:52 but if **w** is found in him, he
1Ki 2:44 all the **w** that you did to my
1Ki 2:44 your **w** on your own head
1Ki 8:47 wrong, we have committed **w**'
1Ki 21:25 do **w** in the sight of the LORD
1Ch 17: 9 of **w** oppress them anymore
Job 11:11 He sees **w** also
Job 11:14 would not let **w** dwell in your
Job 22: 5 Is not your **w** great, And your
Job 24:20 **w** should be broken like a
Job 27: 4 my lips will not speak **w**, nor
Job 31:11 For that would be **w**
Job 34:10 far be it from God to do **w**
Job 35: 8 Your **w** affects a man such as
Ps 5: 4 a God who takes pleasure in **w**
Ps 7: 9 let the **w** of the wicked come
Ps 10:15 Seek out his **w** until You find
Ps 28: 4 according to the **w** of their
Ps 36: 3 The words of his mouth are **w**
Ps 36: 4 He devises **w** on his bed
Ps 45: 7 love righteousness and hate **w**
Ps 52: 7 strengthened himself in his **w**
Ps 55:15 For **w** is in their dwellings
Ps 58: 2 No, in heart you work **w**
Ps 84:10 dwell in the tents of **w**
Ps 89:22 Nor the son of **w** afflict him
Ps 94:23 cut them off in their own **w**
Ps 101: 4 I will not know **w**
Ps 107:34 For the **w** of those who dwell
Ps 119:150 draw near who follow after **w**
Ps 125: 3 For the scepter of **w** shall
Prov 4:17 For they eat the bread of **w**
Prov 8: 7 **w** is an abomination to my
Prov 10: 2 treasures of **w** profit nothing
Prov 11: 5 wicked will fall by his own **w**
Prov 12: 3 A man is not established by **w**
Prov 13: 6 but **w** overthrows the sinner
Prov 14:32 wicked is banished in his **w**
Prov 16:12 for kings to commit **w**, for a
Prov 21:12 the wicked for their **w**
Prov 26:26 his **w** will be revealed before
Prov 30:20 I have done no **w**
Eccl 3:16 of judgment, **w** was there
Eccl 7:15 prolongs his life in his **w**
Eccl 7:25 to know the **w** of folly, even
Eccl 8: 8 **w** will not deliver those who
Is 9:18 For **w** burns as the fire
Is 47:10 you have trusted in your **w**
Is 58: 4 to strike with the fist of **w**
Is 58: 6 to loose the bonds of **w**, to
Is 58: 9 of the finger, and speaking **w**
Jer 1:16 them concerning all their **w**
Jer 2:19 Your own **w** will correct you,
Jer 3: 2 your harlotries and your **w**
Jer 4:14 wash your heart from **w**, that
Jer 4:18 This is your **w**, Because it is
Jer 6: 7 so she wells up with her **w**
Jer 7:12 of the **w** of My people Israel
Jer 8: 6 No man repented of his **w**,
Jer 12: 4 For the **w** of those who dwell
Jer 14:16 I will pour their **w** on them
Jer 14:20 acknowledge, O LORD, our **w**
Jer 22:22 and humiliated for all your **w**
Jer 23:11 My house I have found their **w**
Jer 23:14 no one turns back from his **w**
Jer 33: 5 all for whose **w** I have hidden
Jer 44: 3 because of their **w** which
Jer 44: 5 ear to turn from their **w**, to
Jer 44: 9 the **w** of your fathers, the
Jer 44: 9 the **w** of the kings of Judah,
Jer 44: 9 **w** of their wives, your own **w**
Jer 44: 9 the **w** of your wives, which
Lam 1:22 Let all their **w** come before
Ezek 3:19 he does not turn from his **w**
Ezek 5: 6 doing **w** more than the nations
Ezek 7:11 has risen up into a rod of **w**
Ezek 16:23 it was so, after all your **w**
Ezek 16:57 before your **w** was uncovered
Ezek 18:20 the **w** of the wicked shall be
Ezek 18:27 from the **w** which he committed
Ezek 31:11 have driven it out for its **w**
Ezek 33:12 as for the **w** of the wicked,
Ezek 33:12 day that he turns from his **w**
Ezek 33:19 the wicked turns from his **w**
Hos 7: 1 and the **w** of Samaria
Hos 7: 2 that I remember all their **w**
Hos 7: 3 make a king glad with their **w**
Hos 9:15 All their **w** is in Gilgal, for
Hos 10:13 You have plowed **w**
Hos 10:15 because of your great **w**
Joel 3:13 for their **w** is great
Jon 1: 2 for their **w** has come up
Mic 6:10 **w** in the house of the wicked
Nah 3:19 not your **w** passed continually
Hab 1:13 evil, and cannot look on **w**
Zech 5: 8 This is **W**
Mal 1: 4 be called the Territory of **W**
Mal 3:15 those who do **w** are raised up
Matt 22:18 But Jesus perceived their **w**
Mark 7:22 thefts, covetousness, **w**,
Luke 11:39 part is full of greed and **w**
Acts 8:22 therefore of this your **w**, and
Rom 1:29 sexual immorality, **w**,
1Co 5: 8 the leaven of malice and **w**
Eph 6:12 of **w** in the heavenly places
Jas 1:21 filthiness and overflow of **w**

WICK-TRIMMERS (*see* WICK)
Ex 25:38 And its **w** and their trays shall
Ex 37:23 made its seven lamps, its **w**
Num 4: 9 light, with its lamps, its **w**
1Ki 7:49 and the lamps and the **w** of gold
2Ch 4:21 the **w** of gold, of purest gold

WIDE (*see* WIDELY, WIDER, WIDTH)
Num 24: 4 down, with eyes opened **w**
Num 24:16 down, with eyes opened **w**
Deut 15: 8 shall open your hand **w** to him
Deut 15:11 your hand **w** to your brother
1Ki 6: 6 chamber was five cubits **w**
1Ki 6: 6 the middle was six cubits **w**
1Ki 6: 6 the third was seven cubits **w**
1Ki 6:20 cubits long, twenty cubits **w**
2Ch 26:15 So his fame spread far and **w**
Job 29:23 **w** as for the spring rain
Ps 31: 8 have set my feet in a **w** place
Ps 35:21 their mouth **w** against me, And
Ps 81:10 Open your mouth **w**, and I will
Ps 104:25 great and **w** sea, In which are
Prov 13: 3 but he who opens **w** his lips
Is 57: 4 whom do you make a **w** mouth
Jer 22:14 a **w** house with spacious
Lam 2:13 ruin is spread **w** as the sea
Ezek 23:32 cup, the deep and **w** one
Ezek 40: 6 gateway, which was one rod **w**
Ezek 40: 6 other threshold was one rod **w**
Ezek 40: 7 was one rod long and one rod **w**
Ezek 40:29 long and twenty-five cubits **w**
Ezek 40:30 cubits long and five cubits **w**
Ezek 40:33 long and twenty-five cubits **w**
Ezek 40:42 long, one cubit and a half **w**
Ezek 40:43 were hooks, a handbreadth **w**
Ezek 40:47 long and one hundred cubits **w**
Ezek 41: 1 six cubits **w** on one side and
Ezek 41: 1 six cubits **w** on the other
Ezek 41:12 end was seventy cubits **w**
Ezek 42: 4 was a walk ten cubits **w**, at
Ezek 42:11 as **w** as the others, and all
Ezek 42:20 cubits long and five hundred **w**
Ezek 43:13 one cubit high and one cubit **w**
Ezek 43:16 twelve cubits long, twelve **w**
Ezek 43:17 fourteen **w** on its four sides,
Ezek 45: 3 cubits long and ten thousand **w**
Ezek 45: 5 ten thousand **w** shall belong
Ezek 45: 6 area five thousand cubits **w**
Ezek 46:22 forty cubits long and thirty **w**
Mic 7:11 the decree shall go far and **w**
Nah 3:13 are **w** open for your enemies
Matt 7:13 for **w** is the gate and broad is
2Co 6:11 to you, our heart is **w** open

WIDELY (*see* WIDE)
Mark 7:36 the more **w** they proclaimed it
Luke 2:17 they made **w** known the saying

WIDER (*see* WIDE)
Ezek 41: 7 chambers became **w** all around

WIDESPREAD
1Sa 3: 1 there was no **w** revelation

WIDOW (*see* WIDOWHOOD, WIDOW'S, WIDOWS)
Gen 38:11 Remain a **w** in your father's
Ex 22:22 any **w** or fatherless child
Lev 21:14 A **w** or a divorced woman or a
Lev 22:13 daughter is a **w** or divorced
Num 30: 9 But any vow of a **w** or a
Deut 10:18 for the fatherless and the **w**
Deut 14:29 the **w** who are within your
Deut 16:11 the **w** who are among you, at
Deut 16:14 and the fatherless and the **w**
Deut 24:19 the fatherless, and the **w**
Deut 24:20 the fatherless, and the **w**
Deut 24:21 the fatherless, and the **w**
Deut 25: 5 the **w** of the dead man shall
Deut 26:12 the fatherless, and the **w**
Deut 26:13 the fatherless, and the **w**
Deut 27:19 the fatherless, and **w**
1Sa 27: 3 the Carmelitess, Nabal's **w**
1Sa 30: 5 Abigail the **w** of Nabal the
2Sa 2: 2 Abigail the **w** of Nabal the
2Sa 3: 3 by Abigail the **w** of Nabal the
2Sa 14: 5 Indeed I am a **w**, my husband
1Ki 7:14 He was the son of a **w** from
1Ki 11:26 mother's name was Zeruah, a **w**
1Ki 17: 9 I have commanded a **w** there to
1Ki 17:10 city, indeed a **w** was there
1Ki 17:20 on the **w** with whom I lodge
Job 24:21 and does no good for the **w**
Job 31:16 the eyes of the **w** to fail
Job 31:18 mother's womb I guided the **w**)
Ps 94: 6 They slay the **w** and the
Ps 109: 9 fatherless, And his wife a **w**
Ps 146: 9 relieves the fatherless and **w**
Prov 15:25 the boundary of the **w**

Is 1:17 fatherless, plead for the **w**
Is 1:23 of the **w** come before them
Is 47: 8 I shall not sit as a **w**, nor
Jer 7: 6 the fatherless, and the **w**
Jer 22: 3 the fatherless, or the **w**
Lam 1: 1 How like a **w** is she, Who was
Ezek 22: 7 the fatherless and the **w**
Ezek 44:22 wife a **w** or a divorced woman
Zech 7:10 the **w** or the fatherless, the
Mark 12:42 Then one poor **w** came and
Mark 12:43 **w** has put in more than all
Luke 2:37 this woman was a **w** of about
Luke 4:26 Sidon, to a woman who was a **w**
Luke 7:12 and she was a **w**
Luke 18: 3 there was a **w** in that city
Luke 18: 5 yet because this **w** troubles
Luke 21: 2 poor **w** putting in two mites
Luke 21: 3 **w** has put in more than all
1Ti 5: 4 But if any **w** has children or
1Ti 5: 5 Now she who is really a **w**
1Ti 5: 9 Do not let a **w** under sixty
Rev 18: 7 I sit as queen, and am no **w**

WIDOWHOOD (*see* WIDOW)
Gen 38:19 put on the garments of her **w**
2Sa 20: 3 of their death, living in **w**
Is 47: 9 the loss of children, and **w**
Is 54: 4 reproach of your **w** anymore

WIDOW'S (*see* WIDOW)
Gen 38:14 she took off her **w** garments
Deut 24:17 nor take a **w** garment as a
Job 24: 3 they take the **w** ox as a
Job 29:13 I caused the **w** heart to sing

WIDOWS (*see* WIDOW, WIDOWS')
Ex 22:24 your wives shall be **w**, and
Job 22: 9 You have sent **w** away empty
Job 27:15 and their **w** shall not weep,
Ps 68: 5 fatherless, a defender of **w**
Ps 78:64 their **w** made no lamentation
Is 9:17 on their fatherless and **w**
Is 10: 2 that **w** may be their prey, and
Jer 15: 8 Their **w** will be increased to
Jer 18:21 let their wives become **w** and
Jer 49:11 and let your **w** trust in Me
Lam 5: 3 waifs, our mothers are like **w**
Ezek 22:25 have made many **w** in her midst
Ezek 44:22 of Israel, or **w** of priests
Mal 3: 5 who exploit wage earners and **w**
Luke 4:25 many **w** were in Israel in the
Acts 6: 1 because their **w** were
Acts 9:39 And all the **w** stood by him
Acts 9:41 he had called the saints and **w**
1Co 7: 8 to the unmarried and to the **w**
1Ti 5: 3 Honor **w** who are really **w**
1Ti 5:11 But refuse the younger **w**
1Ti 5:14 that the younger **w** marry,
1Ti 5:16 believing man or woman has **w**
1Ti 5:16 those who are really **w**
Jas 1:27 **w** in their trouble, and to

WIDOWS' (*see* WIDOWS)
Matt 23:14 For you devour **w** houses, and
Mark 12:40 who devour **w** houses, and for a
Luke 20:47 who devour **w** houses, and for a

WIDTH (*see* WIDE)
Gen 6:15 its **w** fifty cubits, and its
Gen 13:17 through its length and its **w**
Ex 25:10 a cubit and a half its **w**, and
Ex 25:17 and a cubit and a half its **w**
Ex 25:23 be its length, a cubit its **w**
Ex 26: 2 the **w** of each curtain four
Ex 26: 8 the **w** of each curtain four
Ex 26:16 shall be the **w** of each board
Ex 27:12 along the **w** of the court on
Ex 27:13 The **w** of the court on the
Ex 27:18 the **w** fifty throughout, and
Ex 28:16 and a span shall be its **w**
Ex 30: 2 its length and a cubit its **w**
Ex 36: 9 the **w** of each curtain four
Ex 36:15 the **w** of each curtain four
Ex 36:21 the **w** of each board a cubit
Ex 37: 1 a cubit and a half its **w**, and
Ex 37: 6 and a cubit and a half its **w**
Ex 37:10 was its length, a cubit its **w**
Ex 37:25 was a cubit and its **w** a cubit
Ex 38: 1 length and five cubits its **w**
Ex 38:18 along its **w** was five cubits
Ex 39: 9 a span its **w** when doubled
Deut 3:11 length and four cubits its **w**
1Ki 6: 2 its **w** twenty, and its height
1Ki 6: 3 its **w** extended ten cubits
1Ki 7: 2 its **w** fifty cubits, and its
1Ki 7: 6 and its **w** thirty cubits
1Ki 7:27 each cart, four cubits its **w**
2Ch 3: 3 and the **w** twenty cubits
2Ch 3: 4 across the **w** of the house
2Ch 3: 8 to the **w** of the house, twenty
2Ch 3: 8 and its **w** twenty cubits
2Ch 4: 1 length, twenty cubits its **w**
Ezra 6: 3 cubits and its **w** sixty cubits,
Ezek 40: 5 he measured the **w** of the wall
Ezek 40:11 He measured the **w** of the
Ezek 40:13 the **w** was twenty-five cubits,
Ezek 40:19 Then he measured the **w** from
Ezek 40:20 measured its length and its **w**
Ezek 40:21 and its **w** twenty-five cubits
Ezek 40:25 and its **w** twenty-five cubits
Ezek 40:36 and its **w** twenty-five cubits
Ezek 40:48 and the **w** of the gateway was
Ezek 40:49 and the **w** eleven cubits
Ezek 41: 1 the **w** of the tabernacle
Ezek 41: 2 The **w** of the entryway was ten
Ezek 41: 2 forty cubits, and its **w**,
Ezek 41: 3 the **w** of the entrance, seven
Ezek 41: 4 and the **w**, twenty cubits,
Ezek 41: 5 The **w** of each side chamber
Ezek 41: 7 therefore the **w** of the
Ezek 41:10 the wall chambers was a **w** of
Ezek 41:11 the **w** of the terrace was five
Ezek 41:14 also the **w** of the eastern
Ezek 42: 2 (the **w** was fifty cubits), was
Ezek 43:14 the **w** of the ledge, one cubit
Ezek 43:14 the **w** of the ledge, one cubit
Ezek 45: 1 cubits, and the **w** ten thousand
Ezek 48: 8 thousand cubits in **w**, and in
Ezek 48: 9 length and ten thousand in **w**
Ezek 48:10 on the west ten thousand in **w**
Ezek 48:10 on the east ten thousand in **w**
Ezek 48:13 length and ten thousand in **w**
Ezek 48:13 and its **w** ten thousand
Ezek 48:15 cubits in **w** that remain,
Dan 3: 1 cubits and its **w** six cubits
Zech 2: 2 to see what is its **w** and what
Zech 5: 2 cubits and its **w** ten cubits
Eph 3:18 all the saints what is the **w**

WIELD (*see* WIELDED, WIELDING)
Is 10:15 As if a rod could **w** itself

WIELDED (*see* WIELD)
Josh 8:31 no man has **w** any iron tool

WIELDING (*see* WIELD)
Deut 20:19 trees by **w** an ax against them

WIFE (*see* WIFE'S, WIVES)
Gen 2:24 mother and be joined to his **w**
Gen 2:25 both naked, the man and his **w**
Gen 3: 8 his **w** hid themselves from the
Gen 3:17 heeded the voice of your **w**
Gen 3:21 and his **w** the LORD God made
Gen 4: 1 Now Adam knew Eve his **w**, and
Gen 4:17 And Cain knew his **w**, and she
Gen 4:25 And Adam knew his **w** again,
Gen 6:18 you, your sons, your **w**, and
Gen 7: 7 So Noah, with his sons, his **w**
Gen 7:13 and Japheth, and Noah's **w**
Gen 8:16 out of the ark, you and your **w**
Gen 8:18 out, and his sons and his **w**
Gen 11:29 name of Abram's **w** was Sarai
Gen 11:29 and the name of Nahor's **w**
Gen 11:31 Sarai, his son Abram's **w**, and
Gen 12: 5 Then Abram took Sarai his **w**
Gen 12:11 that he said to Sarai his **w**
Gen 12:12 will say, 'This is his **w**'
Gen 12:17 because of Sarai, Abram's **w**
Gen 12:18 tell me that she was your **w**
Gen 12:19 might have taken her as my **w**
Gen 12:19 Now therefore, here is your **w**
Gen 12:20 sent him away, with his **w**
Gen 13: 1 up from Egypt, he and his **w**
Gen 16: 1 Now Sarai, Abram's **w**, had
Gen 16: 3 Then Sarai, Abram's **w**, took
Gen 16: 3 her husband Abram to be his **w**
Gen 17:15 As for Sarai your **w**, you
Gen 17:19 Sarah your **w** shall bear you a
Gen 18: 9 Where is Sarah your **w**
Gen 18:10 Sarah your **w** shall have a son
Gen 19:15 Arise, take your **w** and your
Gen 19:26 But his **w** looked back behind
Gen 20: 2 Abraham said of Sarah his **w**
Gen 20: 3 taken, for she is a man's **w**
Gen 20: 7 restore the man's **w**
Gen 20:11 kill me on account of my **w**
Gen 20:12 and she became my **w**
Gen 20:14 restored Sarah his **w** to him
Gen 20:17 God healed Abimelech, his **w**
Gen 20:18 because of Sarah, Abraham's **w**
Gen 21:21 his mother took a **w** for him
Gen 23:19 Abraham buried Sarah his **w** in
Gen 24: 3 take a **w** for my son from the
Gen 24: 4 take a **w** for my son Isaac
Gen 24: 7 you shall take a **w** for my son
Gen 24:15 the **w** of Nahor, Abraham's
Gen 24:36 Sarah my master's **w** bore a
Gen 24:37 take a **w** for my son from the
Gen 24:38 and take a **w** for my son
Gen 24:40 you shall take a **w** for my son
Gen 24:51 her be your master's son's **w**
Gen 24:67 Rebekah and she became his **w**
Gen 25: 1 Abraham again took a **w**, and
Gen 25:10 was buried, and Sarah his **w**
Gen 25:20 old when he took Rebekah as **w**
Gen 25:21 with the LORD for his **w**,
Gen 25:21 and Rebekah his **w** conceived
Gen 26: 7 place asked him about his **w**
Gen 26: 7 She is my **w**," because he
Gen 26: 8 endearment to Rebekah his **w**
Gen 26: 9 Quite obviously she is your **w**
Gen 26:10 soon have lain with your **w**
Gen 26:11 his **w** shall surely be put to
Gen 27:46 if Jacob takes a **w** of the
Gen 28: 1 You shall not take a **w** from
Gen 28: 2 take yourself a **w** from there
Gen 28: 6 take himself a **w** from there
Gen 28: 6 You shall not take a **w** from
Gen 28: 9 to be his **w** in addition to
Gen 29:21 Give me my **w**, for my days are
Gen 29:28 his daughter Rachel as **w** also
Gen 30: 4 gave him Bilhah her maid as **w**
Gen 30: 9 and gave her to Jacob as **w**
Gen 34: 4 me this young woman as a **w**
Gen 34: 8 Please give her to him as a **w**
Gen 34:12 me the young woman as a **w**
Gen 36:10 the son of Adah the **w** of Esau
Gen 36:10 son of Basemath the **w** of Esau
Gen 36:12 the sons of Adah, Esau's **w**
Gen 36:13 sons of Basemath, Esau's **w**
Gen 36:14 sons of Aholibamah, Esau's **w**
Gen 36:17 sons of Basemath, Esau's **w**
Gen 36:18 sons of Aholibamah, Esau's **w**
Gen 36:18 from Aholibamah, Esau's **w**
Gen 38: 6 Then Judah took a **w** for Er
Gen 38: 8 Go in to your brother's **w**
Gen 38: 9 he went in to his brother's **w**
Gen 38:12 daughter of Shua, Judah's **w**
Gen 38:14 was not given to him as a **w**
Gen 39: 7 things that his master's **w**
Gen 39: 8 and said to his master's **w**
Gen 39: 9 you, because you are his **w**
Gen 39:19 which his **w** spoke to him,
Gen 41:45 And he gave him as a **w** Asenath
Gen 44:27 that my **w** bore me two sons
Gen 46:19 The sons of Rachel, Jacob's **w**
Gen 49:31 Abraham and Sarah his **w**
Gen 49:31 buried Isaac and Rebekah his **w**
Ex 2: 1 took as **w** a daughter of Levi
Ex 4:20 Then Moses took his **w** and his
Ex 6:20 his father's sister, as **w**
Ex 6:23 sister of Nahshon, as **w**
Ex 6:25 the daughters of Putiel as **w**
Ex 18: 2 took Zipporah, Moses' **w**,
Ex 18: 5 sons and his **w** to Moses in the
Ex 18: 6 am coming to you with your **w**
Ex 20:17 not covet your neighbor's **w**
Ex 21: 3 then his **w** shall go out with
Ex 21: 4 his master has given him a **w**
Ex 21: 4 him sons or daughters, the **w**
Ex 21: 5 says, 'I love my master, my **w**
Ex 21:10 If he takes another **w**, he
Ex 22:16 for her to be his **w**
Lev 18: 8 **w** you shall not uncover
Lev 18:14 You shall not approach his **w**
Lev 18:15 she is your son's **w**
Lev 18:16 nakedness of your brother's **w**
Lev 18:20 with your neighbor's **w**, to
Lev 20:10 adultery with another man's **w**
Lev 20:10 with his neighbor's **w**, the
Lev 20:11 **w** has uncovered his father's
Lev 20:20 a man lies with his uncle's **w**
Lev 20:21 a man takes his brother's **w**
Lev 21: 7 take a **w** who is a harlot or a

Lev 21:13 And he shall take a w in her
Lev 21:14 virgin of his own people as w
Num 5:12 If any man's w goes astray
Num 5:14 he becomes jealous of his w
Num 5:14 he becomes jealous of his w
Num 5:15 bring his w to the priest
Num 5:29 the law of jealousy, when a w
Num 5:30 he becomes jealous of his w
Num 26:59 The name of Amram's w was
Num 30:16 Moses, between a man and his w
Num 36: 8 of Israel shall be the w of
Deut 5:21 not covet your neighbor's w
Deut 13: 6 the w of your bosom, or your
Deut 21:11 and would take her for your w
Deut 21:13 and she shall be your w
Deut 21:16 on the son of the loved w in
Deut 21:17 the son of the unloved w as
Deut 22:13 If any man takes a w, and goes
Deut 22:16 my daughter to this man as w
Deut 22:19 And she shall be his w
Deut 22:24 he humbled his neighbor's w
Deut 22:29 she shall be his w because he
Deut 22:30 shall not take his father's w
Deut 24: 1 When a man takes a w and
Deut 24: 2 and becomes another man's w
Deut 24: 3 dies who took her to be his w
Deut 24: 4 w after she has been defiled
Deut 24: 5 When a man has taken a new w
Deut 24: 5 to his w whom he has taken
Deut 25: 5 in to her, take her as his w
Deut 25: 7 want to take his brother's w
Deut 25: 7 then let his brother's w go
Deut 25: 9 then his brother's w shall
Deut 25:11 the w of one draws near to
Deut 27:20 who lies with his father's w
Deut 28:30 You shall betroth a w, but
Deut 28:54 toward the w of his bosom, and
Josh 15:16 give Achsah my daughter as w
Josh 15:17 him Achsah his daughter as w
Judg 1:12 give my daughter Achsah as w
Judg 1:13 him his daughter Achsah as w
Judg 4: 4 the w of Lapidoth, was
Judg 4:17 the w of Heber the Kenite
Judg 4:21 Then Jael, Heber's w, took a
Judg 5:24 the w of Heber the Kenite
Judg 11: 2 Gilead's w bore sons
Judg 13: 2 his w was barren and had no
Judg 13:11 arose and followed his w
Judg 13:19 Manoah and his w looked on
Judg 13:20 his w saw this, they fell on
Judg 13:21 no more to Manoah and his w
Judg 13:22 And Manoah said to his w, "We
Judg 13:23 Then his w said to him, "If
Judg 14: 2 get her for me as a w
Judg 14: 3 must go and get a w from the
Judg 14:15 that they said to Samson's w
Judg 14:16 Then Samson's w wept on him
Judg 14:20 Samson's w was given to his
Judg 15: 1 his w with a young goat
Judg 15: 1 Let me go in to my w, into
Judg 15: 6 because he has taken his w
Judg 21: 1 daughter to Benjamin as a w
Judg 21:18 one who gives a w to Benjamin
Judg 21:21 and every man catch a w for
Judg 21:22 because we did not take a w
Ruth 1: 1 country of Moab, he and his w
Ruth 1: 2 the name of his w was Naomi
Ruth 4: 5 the w of the dead, to raise
Ruth 4:10 the w of Mahlon
Ruth 4:10 I have acquired as my w, to
Ruth 4:13 took Ruth and she became his w
1Sa 1: 4 portions to Peninnah his w
1Sa 1:19 Elkanah knew Hannah his w
1Sa 2:20 would bless Elkanah and his w
1Sa 4:19 daughter-in-law, Phinehas' w
1Sa 14:50 The name of Saul's w was
1Sa 18:17 I will give her to you as a w
1Sa 18:19 Adriel the Meholathite as a w
1Sa 18:27 Michal his daughter as a w
1Sa 19:11 And Michal, David's w, told
1Sa 25: 3 and the name of his w Abigail
1Sa 25:14 men told Abigail, Nabal's w
1Sa 25:37 and his w had told him these
1Sa 25:39 Abigail, to take her as his w
1Sa 25:40 to ask you to become his w
1Sa 25:42 of David, and became his w
1Sa 25:44 his daughter, David's w, to
1Sa 30:22 except for every man's w
2Sa 3: 5 Ithream, by David's w Eglah
2Sa 3:14 Give me my w Michal, whom I
2Sa 11: 3 the w of Uriah the Hittite
2Sa 11:11 and drink, and to lie with my w
2Sa 11:26 When the w of Uriah heard
2Sa 11:27 house, and she became his w
2Sa 12: 9 taken his w to be your w
2Sa 12:10 have taken the w of Uriah the
2Sa 12:10 the Hittite to be your w
2Sa 12:15 that Uriah's w bore to David
2Sa 12:24 comforted Bathsheba his w
1Ki 2:17 Abishag the Shunammite as w
1Ki 2:21 to Adonijah your brother as w
1Ki 4:11 the daughter of Solomon as w
1Ki 4:15 the daughter of Solomon as w
1Ki 7: 8 whom he had taken as w
1Ki 9:16 to his daughter, Solomon's w
1Ki 11:19 as w the sister of his own w
1Ki 14: 2 And Jeroboam said to his w
1Ki 14: 2 you as the w of Jeroboam, and
1Ki 14: 4 And Jeroboam's w did so
1Ki 14: 5 Here is the w of Jeroboam
1Ki 14: 6 Come in, w of Jeroboam
1Ki 14:17 Then Jeroboam's w arose and
1Ki 16:31 that he took as w Jezebel the
1Ki 21: 5 But Jezebel his w came to him
1Ki 21: 7 Jezebel his w said to him
1Ki 21:25 Jezebel his w stirred him up
2Ki 5: 2 She waited on Naaman's w
2Ki 8:18 daughter of Ahab was his w
2Ki 14: 9 your daughter to my son as w'
2Ki 22:14 the w of Shallum the son of
1Ch 2:18 children by Azubah, his w
1Ch 2:19 Caleb took Ephrath as his w
1Ch 2:24 Hezron's w Abijah bore him
1Ch 2:26 Jerahmeel had another w,
1Ch 2:29 the name of the w of Abishur
1Ch 2:35 to Jarha his servant as w
1Ch 3: 3 Ithream, by his w Eglah
1Ch 4:17 And Mered's w bore Miriam,
1Ch 4:18 (His w Jehudijah bore Jered
1Ch 4:19 The sons of Hodiah's w, the
1Ch 7:15 Machir took as his w the
1Ch 7:16 (Maachah the w of Machir bore
1Ch 7:23 And when he went in to his w
1Ch 8: 9 By Hodesh his w he begot
2Ch 8:11 My w shall not dwell in the
2Ch 11:18 took for himself as w
2Ch 21: 6 the daughter of Ahab as a w
2Ch 22:11 the w of Jehoiada the priest
2Ch 25:18 your daughter to my son as w'
2Ch 34:22 the w of Shallum the son of
Ezra 2:61 who took a w of the daughters
Neh 7:63 who took a w of the daughters
Esth 5:10 his friends and his w Zeresh
Esth 5:14 Then his w Zeresh and all his
Esth 6:13 When Haman told his w Zeresh
Esth 6:13 his w Zeresh said to him,
Job 2: 9 Then his w said to him, "Do
Job 19:17 breath is offensive to my w
Job 31:10 Then let my w grind for
Ps 109: 9 fatherless, And his w a widow
Ps 128: 3 Your w shall be like a
Prov 5:18 with the w of your youth
Prov 6:29 goes in to his neighbor's w
Prov 12: 4 an excellent w is the crown
Prov 18:22 He who finds a w finds a good
Prov 19:13 the contentions of a w are a
Prov 19:14 but a prudent w is from the
Prov 31:10 Who can find a virtuous w
Eccl 9: 9 Live joyfully with the w whom
Is 54: 6 like a youthful w when you
Jer 3: 1 say, 'If a man divorces his w
Jer 3:20 as a w treacherously departs
Jer 5: 8 after his neighbor's w
Jer 6:11 shall be taken with the w
Jer 16: 2 You shall not take a w, nor
Ezek 16:32 You are an adulterous w, who
Ezek 18: 6 nor defiled his neighbor's w
Ezek 18:11 or defiled his neighbor's w
Ezek 18:15 Nor defiled his neighbor's w
Ezek 22:11 with his neighbor's w
Ezek 24:18 and at evening my w died
Ezek 44:22 They shall not take as w a
Hos 1: 2 take yourself a w of harlotry
Hos 2: 2 for she is not My w, nor am I
Hos 12:12 and for a w he tended sheep
Amos 7:17 Your w shall be a harlot in
Mal 2:14 the w of your youth, with
Mal 2:14 and your w by covenant
Mal 2:15 with the w of his youth
Matt 1: 6 who had been the w of Uriah
Matt 1:20 to take to you Mary your w
Matt 1:24 him and took to him his w,
Matt 5:31 said, 'Whoever divorces his w
Matt 5:32 his w for any reason except
Matt 14: 3 his brother Philip's w
Matt 18:25 that he be sold, with his w
Matt 19: 3 his w for just any reason
Matt 19: 5 mother and be joined to his w
Matt 19: 9 you, whoever divorces his w
Matt 19:10 case of the man with his w
Matt 19:29 or w or children or lands
Matt 22:24 his brother shall marry his w
Matt 22:25 left his w to his brother
Matt 22:28 whose w of the seven will she
Matt 27:19 his w sent to him, saying,
Mark 6:17 his brother Philip's w
Mark 6:18 you to have your brother's w
Mark 10: 2 for a man to divorce his w
Mark 10: 7 mother and be joined to his w
Mark 10:11 Whoever divorces his w and
Mark 10:29 or w or children or lands
Mark 12:19 dies, and leaves his w behind
Mark 12:19 his brother should take his w
Mark 12:20 The first took a w
Mark 12:23 rise, whose w will she be
Mark 12:23 For all seven had her as w
Luke 1: 5 His w was of the daughters of
Luke 1:13 your w Elizabeth will bear
Luke 1:18 and my w is well advanced in
Luke 1:24 his w Elizabeth conceived
Luke 2: 5 with Mary, his betrothed w
Luke 3:19 his brother Philip's w, and
Luke 8: 3 and Joanna the w of Chuza,
Luke 14:20 said, 'I have married a w
Luke 14:26 hate his father and mother, w
Luke 16:18 Whoever divorces his w and
Luke 17:32 Remember Lot's w
Luke 18:29 or brothers or w or children
Luke 20:28 brother dies, having a w, and
Luke 20:28 his brother should take his w
Luke 20:29 And the first took a w, and
Luke 20:30 And the second took her as w
Luke 20:33 whose w does she become
Luke 20:33 For all seven had her as w
John 19:25 Mary the w of Clopas, and Mary
Acts 5: 1 Ananias, with Sapphira his w
Acts 5: 2 his w also being aware of it,
Acts 5: 7 later when his w came in, not
Acts 18: 2 come from Italy with his w
Acts 24:24 came with his w Drusilla, who
1Co 5: 1 that a man has his father's w
1Co 7: 2 let each man have his own w
1Co 7: 3 his w the affection due her
1Co 7: 3 also the w to her husband
1Co 7: 4 The w does not have authority
1Co 7: 4 his own body, but the w does
1Co 7:10 A w is not to depart from her
1Co 7:11 is not to divorce his w
1Co 7:12 has a w who does not believe
1Co 7:14 is sanctified by the w, and
1Co 7:14 w, and the unbelieving w is
1Co 7:16 For how do you know, O w,
1Co 7:16 whether you will save your w
1Co 7:27 Are you bound to a w
1Co 7:27 Are you loosed from a w
1Co 7:27 Do not seek a w
1Co 7:33 how he may please his w
1Co 7:34 is a difference between a w
1Co 7:39 A w is bound by law as long
1Co 9: 5 to take along a believing w
Eph 5:23 the husband is head of the w
Eph 5:28 who loves his w loves himself
Eph 5:31 mother and be joined to his w
Eph 5:33 so love his own w as himself
Eph 5:33 and let the w see that she
1Ti 3: 2 the husband of one w,
1Ti 3:12 be the husbands of one w,
1Ti 5: 9 she has been the w of one man
Tit 1: 6 the husband of one w, having
1Pe 3: 7 giving honor to the w, as to
Rev 19: 7 His w has made herself ready
Rev 21: 9 you the bride, the Lamb's w

WIFE'S (*see* WIFE)
Gen 3:20 Adam called his w name Eve
Gen 19:16 his w hand, and the hands of
Gen 36:39 His w name was Mehetabel, the
Lev 18:11 of your father's w daughter
Judg 11: 2 when his w sons grew up, they
1Ch 1:50 His w name was Mehetabel the
1Ch 8:29 whose w name was Maacah,

1Ch 9:35 whose w name was Maacah,
Matt 8:14 He saw his w mother lying
Mark 1:30 But Simon's w mother lay sick
Luke 4:38 But Simon's w mother was sick

WILD

Gen 16:12 He shall be a w man
Gen 37:20 Some w beast has devoured
Gen 37:33 A w beast has devoured him
Lev 7:24 of what is torn by w animals
Lev 26:22 also send w beasts among you
Num 23:22 He has strength like a w ox
Num 24: 8 he has strength like a w ox
Deut 14: 5 the w goat, the mountain goat
Deut 33:17 like the horns of the w ox
1Sa 17:46 the w beasts of the earth,
1Sa 24: 2 on the Rocks of the W Goats
2Sa 2:18 fleet of foot as a w gazelle
2Ki 4:39 herbs, and found a w vine, and
2Ki 4:39 it a lap full of w gourds
2Ki 14: 9 a w beast that was in Lebanon
2Ch 25:18 a w beast that was in Lebanon
Job 6: 5 Does the w donkey bray when
Job 11:12 when a w donkey's colt is
Job 24: 5 like w donkeys in the desert,
Job 39: 1 w mountain goats bear young
Job 39: 5 Who set the w donkey free
Job 39: 9 Will the w ox be willing to
Job 39:10 Can you bind the w ox in the
Job 39:15 or that a w beast may break
Ps 22:21 from the horns of the w oxen
Ps 29: 6 and Sirion like a young w ox
Ps 50:11 the w beasts of the field are
Ps 74:19 turtledove to the w beast
Ps 80:13 And the w beast of the field
Ps 92:10 You have exalted like a w ox
Ps 104:11 The w donkeys quench their
Ps 104:18 hills are for the w goats
Is 5: 2 but it brought forth w grapes
Is 5: 4 did it bring forth w grapes
Is 13:21 But w beasts of the desert
Is 13:21 And w goats will caper there
Is 23:13 it for w beasts of the desert
Is 32:14 forever, a joy of w donkeys
Is 34: 7 The w oxen shall come down
Is 34:14 The w beasts of the desert
Is 34:14 the w goat shall bleat to its
Jer 2:24 A w donkey used to the
Jer 14: 6 the w donkeys stood in the
Jer 50:39 Therefore the w desert beasts
Ezek 5:17 and w beasts, and they will
Ezek 14:15 If I cause w beasts to pass
Ezek 14:21 and w beasts and pestilence
Ezek 34:25 cause w beasts to cease from
Ezek 44:31 or was torn by w animals
Dan 5:21 was with the w donkeys
Hos 8: 9 like a w donkey alone by
Hos 13: 8 The w beast shall tear them
Matt 3: 4 food was locusts and w honey
Mark 1: 6 and he ate locusts and w honey
Mark 1:13 and was with the w beasts
Acts 10:12 w beasts, creeping things, and
Acts 11: 6 w beasts, creeping things, and
Rom 11:17 being a w olive tree, were
Rom 11:24 tree which is w by nature

WILDERNESS

Gen 14: 6 El Paran, which is by the w
Gen 16: 7 by a spring of water in the w
Gen 21:14 in the W of Beersheba
Gen 21:20 and he grew and dwelt in the w
Gen 21:21 He dwelt in the W of Paran
Gen 36:24 w as he pastured the donkeys
Gen 37:22 this pit which is in the w
Ex 3:18 days' journey into the w,
Ex 4:27 Go into the w to meet Moses
Ex 5: 1 hold a feast to Me in the w
Ex 7:16 they may serve Me in the w"
Ex 8:27 days' journey into the w and
Ex 8:28 to the LORD your God in the w
Ex 13:18 way of the w of the Red Sea
Ex 13:20 in Etham at the edge of the w
Ex 14: 3 the w has closed them in
Ex 14:11 taken us away to die in the w
Ex 14:12 that we should die in the w
Ex 15:22 went out into the W of Shur
Ex 15:22 they went three days in the w
Ex 16: 1 Israel came to the W of Sin
Ex 16: 2 Moses and Aaron in the w
Ex 16: 3 brought us out into this w to
Ex 16:10 that they looked toward the w
Ex 16:14 on the surface of the w, was
Ex 16:32 with which I fed you in the w
Ex 17: 1 journey from the W of Sin
Ex 18: 5 and his wife to Moses in the w
Ex 19: 1 they came to the W of Sinai
Ex 19: 2 of Sinai, and camped in the w
Lev 7:38 to the LORD in the W of Sinai
Lev 16:10 as the scapegoat into the w
Lev 16:21 w by the hand of a suitable
Lev 16:22 release the goat in the w
Num 1: 1 to Moses in the W of Sinai
Num 1:19 them in the W of Sinai
Num 3: 4 the LORD in the W of Sinai
Num 3:14 to Moses in the W of Sinai
Num 9: 1 to Moses in the W of Sinai
Num 9: 5 twilight, in the W of Sinai
Num 10:12 W of Sinai on their journeys
Num 10:12 down in the W of Paran
Num 10:31 how we are to camp in the w
Num 12:16 and camped in the W of Paran
Num 13: 3 W of Paran according to the
Num 13:21 the W of Zin as far as Rehob
Num 13:26 of Israel in the W of Paran
Num 14: 2 if only we had died in this w
Num 14:16 He killed them in the w
Num 14:22 I did in Egypt and in the w
Num 14:25 move out into the w by the
Num 14:29 Me shall fall in this w, all
Num 14:32 shall fall in this w
Num 14:33 in the w forty years, and bear
Num 14:33 are consumed in the w
Num 14:35 In this w they shall be
Num 15:32 of Israel were in the w, they
Num 16:13 and honey, to kill us in the w
Num 20: 1 came into the W of Zin in the
Num 20: 4 of the LORD into this w, that
Num 21: 5 out of Egypt to die in the w
Num 21:11 in the w which is east of
Num 21:13 Arnon, which is in the w that
Num 21:18 And from the w they went to
Num 21:23 out against Israel in the w
Num 24: 1 he set his face toward the w
Num 26:64 of Israel in the W of Sinai
Num 26:65 shall surely die in the w
Num 27: 3 Our father died in the w
Num 27:14 For in the W of Zin, during
Num 27:14 at Kadesh in the W of Zin
Num 32:13 wander in the w forty years
Num 32:15 again leave them in the w
Num 33: 6 which is on the edge of the w
Num 33: 8 midst of the sea into the w
Num 33: 8 journey in the W of Etham
Num 33:11 Sea and camped in the W of Sin
Num 33:12 journeyed from the W of Sin
Num 33:15 and camped in the W of Sinai
Num 33:16 moved from the W of Sinai
Num 33:36 and camped in the W of Zin
Num 34: 3 border shall be from the W of
Deut 1: 1 side of the Jordan in the w
Deut 1:19 terrible w which you saw on
Deut 1:31 in the w where you saw how
Deut 1:40 w by the Way of the Red Sea
Deut 2: 1 journeyed into the w of the
Deut 2: 7 trudging through this great w
Deut 2: 8 by way of the W of Moab
Deut 2:26 W of Kedemoth to Sihon king
Deut 4:43 Bezer in the w on the plateau
Deut 8: 2 these forty years in the w
Deut 8:15 that great and terrible w, in
Deut 8:16 fed you in the w with manna
Deut 9: 7 your God to wrath in the w
Deut 9:28 out to kill them in the w
Deut 11: 5 the w until you came to this
Deut 11:24 from the w and Lebanon, from
Deut 29: 5 led you forty years in the w
Deut 32:10 in the wasteland, a howling w
Deut 32:51 Kadesh, in the W of Zin,
Josh 1: 4 From the w and this Lebanon as
Josh 5: 4 had died in the w on the way
Josh 5: 5 w on the way as they came out
Josh 5: 6 walked forty years in the w
Josh 8:15 and fled by the way of the w
Josh 8:20 people who had fled to the w
Josh 8:24 in the w where they pursued
Josh 10:40 the w slopes, and all their
Josh 12: 8 in the slopes, in the w, and
Josh 14:10 Israel wandered in the w
Josh 15: 1 W of Zin southward was the
Josh 15:61 In the w
Josh 16: 1 to the w that goes up from
Josh 18:12 ended at the W of Beth Aven
Josh 20: 8 Bezer in the w on the plain
Josh 24: 7 dwelt in the w a long time
Judg 1:16 of Judah into the W of Judah
Judg 8: 7 with the thorns of the w and
Judg 8:16 the city, and thorns of the w
Judg 11:16 the w as far as the Red Sea
Judg 11:18 they went along through the w
Judg 11:22 and from the w to the Jordan
Judg 20:42 in the direction of the w
Judg 20:45 fled toward the w to the rock
Judg 20:47 fled toward the w to the rock
1Sa 4: 8 with all the plagues in the w
1Sa 13:18 Valley of Zeboim toward the w
1Sa 17:28 left those few sheep in the w
1Sa 23:14 in strongholds in the w, and
1Sa 23:14 mountains in the W of Ziph
1Sa 23:15 David was in the W of Ziph in
1Sa 23:24 his men were in the W of Maon
1Sa 23:25 and stayed in the W of Maon
1Sa 23:25 David in the W of Maon
1Sa 24: 1 David is in the W of En Gedi
1Sa 25: 1 went down to the W of Paran
1Sa 25: 4 When David heard in the w
1Sa 25:14 the w to greet our master
1Sa 25:21 that this fellow has in the w
1Sa 26: 2 and went down to the W of Ziph
1Sa 26: 2 seek David in the W of Ziph
1Sa 26: 3 But David stayed in the w
1Sa 26: 3 came after him into the w
2Sa 2:24 the road to the W of Gibeon
2Sa 15:23 over toward the way of the w
2Sa 15:28 w until word comes from you
2Sa 16: 2 are faint in the w to drink
2Sa 17:16 night in the plains of the w
2Sa 17:29 and weary and thirsty in the w
1Ki 2:34 in his own house in the w
1Ki 9:18 Baalath, and Tadmor in the w
1Ki 19: 4 a day's journey into the w
1Ki 19:15 your way to the W of Damascus
2Ki 3: 8 By way of the W of Edom
1Ch 5: 9 the w this side of the River
1Ch 6:78 Bezer in the w with its
1Ch 12: 8 at the stronghold in the w
1Ch 21:29 which Moses had made in the w
2Ch 1: 3 of the LORD had made in the w
2Ch 8: 4 He also built Tadmor in the w
2Ch 20:16 brook before the W of Jeruel
2Ch 20:20 went out into the W of Tekoa
2Ch 20:24 to a place overlooking the w
2Ch 24: 9 imposed on Israel in the w
Neh 9:19 did not forsake them in the w
Neh 9:21 You sustained them in the w
Job 1:19 wind came from across the w
Job 12:24 them wander in a pathless w
Job 24: 5 The w yields food for them and
Job 30: 3 famine, fleeing late to the w
Job 38:26 A w in which there is no man
Job 39: 6 Whose home I have made the w
Ps 29: 8 of the LORD shakes the w
Ps 29: 8 LORD shakes the W of Kadesh
Ps 55: 7 far off, And remain in the w
Ps 65:12 drop on the pastures of the w
Ps 68: 7 You marched through the w
Ps 72: 9 in the w will bow before Him
Ps 74:14 the people inhabiting the w
Ps 78:15 He split the rocks in the w
Ps 78:17 the Most High in the w
Ps 78:19 God prepare a table in the w
Ps 78:40 they provoked Him in the w
Ps 78:52 them in the w like a flock
Ps 95: 8 in the day of trial in the w
Ps 102: 6 I am like a pelican of the w
Ps 106: 9 the depths, As through the w
Ps 106:14 lusted exceedingly in the w
Ps 106:26 To overthrow them in the w
Ps 107: 4 in the w in a desolate way
Ps 107:33 He turns rivers into a w, And
Ps 107:35 He turns a w into pools of
Ps 107:40 the w where there is no way
Ps 136:16 led His people through the w
Prov 21:19 is better to dwell in the w
Song 3: 6 the w like pillars of smoke
Song 8: 5 is this coming up from the w
Is 14:17 who made the world as a w
Is 16: 1 the land, from Sela to the w
Is 16: 8 and wandered through the w
Is 21: 1 against the W of the Sea
Is 27:10 forsaken and left like a w
Is 32:15 and the w becomes a fruitful

Is 32:16 justice will dwell in the **w**
Is 33: 9 Sharon is like a **w**, and Bashan
Is 35: 1 The **w** and the wasteland shall
Is 35: 6 shall burst forth in the **w**
Is 40: 3 voice of one crying in the **w**
Is 41:18 make the **w** a pool of water
Is 41:19 will plant in the **w** the cedar
Is 42:11 Let the **w** and its cities lift
Is 43:19 even make a road in the **w**
Is 43:20 I give waters in the **w** and
Is 50: 2 sea, I make the rivers a **w**
Is 51: 3 He will make her **w** like Eden
Is 63:13 the deep, as a horse in the **w**
Is 64:10 cities are a **w**, Zion is a **w**
Jer 2: 2 you went after Me in the **w**
Jer 2: 6 Who led us through the **w**
Jer 2:24 A wild donkey used to the **w**
Jer 2:31 Have I been a **w** to Israel
Jer 3: 2 them like an Arabian in the **w**
Jer 4:11 heights blows in the **w** toward
Jer 4:26 the fruitful land was a **w**
Jer 9: 2 that I had in the **w** a lodging
Jer 9:10 of the **w** a lamentation,
Jer 9:12 perish and burn up like a **w**
Jer 9:26 corners, who dwell in the **w**
Jer 12:10 pleasant portion a desolate **w**
Jer 12:12 the desolate heights in the **w**
Jer 13:24 away by the wind of the **w**
Jer 17: 6 the parched places in the **w**
Jer 22: 6 I surely will make you a **w**
Jer 23:10 places of the **w** are dried up
Jer 31: 2 sword found grace in the **w**
Jer 48: 6 be like the juniper in the **w**
Jer 50:12 of the nations shall be a **w**
Jer 51:43 desolation, a dry land and a **w**
Lam 4: 3 like ostriches in the **w**
Lam 4:19 lay in wait for us in the **w**
Lam 5: 9 because of the sword in the **w**
Ezek 6:14 than the **w** toward Diblah, in
Ezek 19:13 now she is planted in the **w**
Ezek 20:10 and brought them into the **w**
Ezek 20:13 rebelled against Me in the **w**
Ezek 20:13 out My fury on them in the **w**
Ezek 20:15 in an oath to them in the **w**
Ezek 20:17 make an end of them in the **w**
Ezek 20:18 to their children in the **w**
Ezek 20:21 anger against them in the **w**
Ezek 20:23 in an oath to those in the **w**
Ezek 20:35 you into the **w** of the peoples
Ezek 20:36 in the **w** of the land of Egypt
Ezek 23:42 were brought from the **w** with
Ezek 29: 5 I will leave you in the **w**
Ezek 34:25 will dwell safely in the **w**
Hos 2: 3 born, and make her like a **w**
Hos 2:14 will bring her into the **w**
Hos 9:10 Israel like grapes in the **w**
Hos 13: 5 I knew you in the **w**, in the
Hos 13:15 LORD shall come up from the **w**
Joel 2: 3 and behind them a desolate **w**
Joel 3:19 and Edom a desolate **w**,
Amos 2:10 you forty years through the **w**
Amos 5:25 in the **w** forty years, O house
Zeph 2:13 a desolation, as dry as the **w**
Mal 1: 3 for the jackals of the **w**
Matt 3: 1 preaching in the **w** of Judea
Matt 3: 3 voice of one crying in the **w**
Matt 4: 1 up by the Spirit into the **w**
Matt 11: 7 you go out into the **w** to see
Matt 15:33 in the **w** to fill such a great
Mark 1: 3 voice of one crying in the **w**
Mark 1: 4 John came baptizing in the **w**
Mark 1:12 Spirit drove Him into the **w**
Mark 1:13 was there in the **w** forty days
Mark 8: 4 with bread here in the **w**
Luke 3: 2 the son of Zacharias in the **w**
Luke 3: 4 voice of one crying in the **w**
Luke 4: 1 led by the Spirit into the **w**
Luke 5:16 often withdrew into the **w**
Luke 7:24 you go out into the **w** to see
Luke 8:29 by the demon into the **w**
Luke 15: 4 the ninety-nine in the **w**, and
John 1:23 voice of one crying in the **w**
John 3:14 up the serpent in the **w**, even
John 6:49 ate the manna in the **w**, and
John 11:54 into the country near the **w**
Acts 7:30 bush, in the **w** of Mount Sinai
Acts 7:36 Sea, and in the **w** forty years
Acts 7:38 in the congregation in the **w**
Acts 7:42 during forty years in the **w**
Acts 7:44 of witness in the **w**, as He
Acts 13:18 up with their ways in the **w**
Acts 21:38 assassins out into the **w**
1Co 10: 5 were scattered in the **w**
2Co 11:26 the city, in perils in the **w**
Heb 3: 8 in the day of trial in the **w**
Heb 3:17 whose corpses fell in the **w**
Rev 12: 6 the woman fled into the **w**
Rev 12:14 fly into the **w** to her place
Rev 17: 3 away in the Spirit into the **w**

WILES
Eph 6:11 against the **w** of the devil

WILL (*see* PREFACE)

WILL* (*see* WILLED, WILLFULLY, WILLING, WILLS)
Lev 1: 3 own free **w** at the door of the
Lev 19: 5 offer it of your own free **w**
Lev 22:19 offer of your own free **w** a
Lev 22:29 offer it of your own free **w**
Ezra 7:18 to the **w** of your God
Ps 27:12 me to the **w** of my adversaries
Ps 40: 8 I delight to do Your **w**, O my
Ps 143:10 Teach me to do Your **w**, For
Ezek 16:27 gave you up to the **w** of those
Dan 4:35 His **w** in the army of heaven
Dan 8: 4 but he did according to his **w**
Dan 11: 3 and do according to his **w**
Dan 11:16 do according to his own **w**
Dan 11:36 do according to his own **w**
Matt 6:10 Your **w** be done on earth as it
Matt 7:21 but he who does the **w** of My
Matt 12:50 For whoever does the **w** of My
Matt 18:14 Even so it is not the **w** of
Matt 21:31 two did the **w** of his father
Matt 26:42 I drink it, Your **w** be done
Mark 3:35 the **w** of God is My brother
Luke 11: 2 Your **w** be done On earth as it
Luke 12:47 who knew his master's **w**, and
Luke 12:47 or do according to his **w**,
Luke 22:42 Father, if it is Your **w**,
Luke 23:25 he delivered Jesus to their **w**
John 1:13 nor of the **w** of the flesh,
John 4:34 do the **w** of Him who sent Me
John 5:30 I do not seek My own **w** but
John 6:38 heaven, not to do My own **w**
John 6:38 but the **w** of Him who sent Me
John 6:39 This is the **w** of the Father
John 6:40 this is the **w** of Him who sent
John 7:17 If anyone wants to do His **w**
John 9:31 of God and does His **w**, He
Acts 13:22 heart, who will do all My **w**
Acts 13:36 generation by the **w** of God
Acts 21:14 The **w** of the Lord be done
Acts 22:14 that you should know His **w**
Rom 1:10 the **w** of God to come to you
Rom 2:18 and know His **w**, and approve
Rom 9:19 For who has resisted His **w**
Rom 12: 2 and perfect **w** of God
Rom 15:32 you with joy by the **w** of God
1Co 1: 1 Christ through the **w** of God
1Co 7:37 but has power over his own **w**
2Co 1: 1 Jesus Christ by the **w** of God
2Co 8: 5 and then to us by the **w** of God
Gal 1: 4 according to the **w** of our God
Eph 1: 1 Jesus Christ by the **w** of God
Eph 1: 5 to the good pleasure of His **w**
Eph 1: 9 to us the mystery of His **w**
Eph 1:11 to the counsel of His **w**,
Eph 5:17 what the **w** of the Lord is
Eph 6: 6 doing the **w** of God from the
Col 1: 1 Jesus Christ by the **w** of God
Col 1: 9 of His **w** in all wisdom and
Col 4:12 complete in all the **w** of God
1Th 4: 3 For this is the **w** of God,
1Th 5:18 for this is the **w** of God in
2Ti 1: 1 Jesus Christ by the **w** of God
2Ti 2:26 captive by him to do his **w**
Heb 2: 4 according to His own **w**
Heb 10: 7 to do Your **w**, O God
Heb 10: 9 I have come to do Your **w**
Heb 10:10 By that **w** we have been
Heb 10:36 you have done the **w** of God
Heb 13:21 every good work to do His **w**
1Pe 2:15 For this is the **w** of God,
1Pe 3:17 better, if it is the **w** of God
1Pe 4: 2 of men, but for the **w** of God
1Pe 4: 3 doing the **w** of the Gentiles
1Pe 4:19 **w** of God commit their souls
2Pe 1:21 never came by the **w** of man
1Jn 2:17 but he who does the **w** of God
1Jn 5:14 anything according to His **w**

WILLED (*see* WILL*, WILLS)
Col 1:27 To them God **w** to make known

WILLFULLY (*see* WILL*, WILLS)
Heb 10:26 For if we sin **w** after we have
2Pe 3: 5 For this they **w** forget

WILLING (*see* UNWILLING, WILL*, WILLINGLY, WILLINGNESS, WILLS)
Gen 24: 5 the woman will not be **w** to
Gen 24: 8 woman is not **w** to follow you
Ex 35: 5 Whoever is of a **w** heart, let
Ex 35:21 everyone whose spirit was **w**
Ex 35:22 as many as had a **w** heart
Ex 35:29 women whose hearts were **w** to
Lev 26:21 are not **w** to obey Me, I will
Judg 19:10 was not **w** to spend that night
1Ch 19:19 So the Syrians were not **w** to
1Ch 28: 9 loyal heart and with a **w** mind
1Ch 28:21 every **w** craftsman will be
1Ch 29: 5 Who then is **w** to consecrate
2Ch 29:31 of a **w** heart brought burnt
Job 39: 9 the wild ox be **w** to serve you
Is 1:19 If you are **w** and obedient, you
Matt 8: 2 Lord, if You are **w**, You can
Matt 8: 3 I am **w**; be cleansed
Matt 11:14 if you are **w** to receive it,
Matt 22: 3 and they were not **w** to come
Matt 23:37 her wings, but you were not **w**
Matt 26:15 What are you **w** to give me if
Matt 26:41 The spirit indeed is **w**, but
Mark 1:40 If You are **w**, You can make me
Mark 1:41 I am **w**; be cleansed
Luke 5:12 Lord, if You are **w**, You can
Luke 5:13 I am **w**; be cleansed
Luke 13:34 her wings, but you were not **w**
John 5:35 and you were **w** for a time to
John 5:40 But you are not **w** to come to
Acts 18:21 return again to you, God **w**
Acts 25: 9 said, "Are you **w** to go up to
Acts 25:20 he was **w** to go to Jerusalem
Acts 26: 5 if they were **w** to testify
1Co 7:12 she is **w** to live with him,
1Co 7:13 if he is **w** to live with her,
2Co 8: 3 ability, they were freely **w**
2Co 8:12 if there is first a **w** mind
1Ti 6:18 ready to give, **w** to share,
Jas 3:17 **w** to yield, full of mercy and
2Pe 3: 9 not **w** that any should perish

WILLINGLY (*see* WILLING)
Ex 25: 2 it **w** with his heart you shall
Deut 15: 8 **w** lend him sufficient for his
Judg 5: 2 when the people **w** offer
Judg 5: 9 themselves **w** with the people
1Ch 29: 6 the king's work, offered **w**
1Ch 29: 9 for they had offered **w**,
1Ch 29: 9 had offered **w** to the LORD
1Ch 29:14 be able to offer so **w** as this
1Ch 29:17 of my heart I have **w** offered
1Ch 29:17 here to offer **w** to You
2Ch 17:16 who **w** offered himself to the
2Ch 35: 8 leaders gave **w** to the people
Ezra 1: 6 all that was **w** offered
Ezra 3: 5 and those of everyone who **w**
Neh 11: 2 blessed all the men who **w**
Prov 31:13 and **w** works with her hands
Lam 3:33 For He does not afflict **w**
Hos 5:11 because he **w** walked by human
John 6:21 Then they **w** received Him into
Rom 8:20 subjected to futility, not **w**
1Co 9:17 For if I do this **w**, I have a
1Pe 5: 2 not by constraint but **w**, not

WILLINGNESS (*see* WILLING)
2Co 9: 2 for I know your **w**, about

WILLOW (*see* WILLOWS)
Ezek 17: 5 and set it like a **w** tree

WILLOWS (*see* WILLOW)
Lev 23:40 trees, and **w** of the brook
Job 40:22 the **w** by the brook surround
Ps 137: 2 Upon the **w** in the midst of it
Is 15: 7 away to the Brook of the **W**
Is 44: 4 like **w** by the watercourses

WILLS (*see* WILL*, WILLED, WILLFULLY, WILLING)
Matt 11:27 whom the Son **w** to reveal Him
Luke 10:22 whom the Son **w** to reveal Him

Rom 7:21 me, the one who w to do good
Rom 9:16 then it is not of him who w
Rom 9:18 He has mercy on whom He w
Rom 9:18 and whom He w He hardens
1Co 4:19 to you shortly, if the Lord w
1Co 12:11 each one individually as He w
Jas 4:15 If the Lord w, we shall live

WILTED (*see* WILTS)
Ezek 31:15 of the field w because of it

WILTS (*see* WILTED)
Nah 1: 4 and the flower of Lebanon w

WIN (*see* WINS, WON)
2Ch 32: 1 thinking to w them over to
Prov 18:19 to w than a strong city, and
Matt 23:15 sea to w one proselyte, and
1Co 9:19 all, that I might w the more
1Co 9:20 as a Jew, that I might w Jews
1Co 9:20 that I might w those who are
1Co 9:21 that I might w those who are
1Co 9:22 weak, that I might w the weak

WIND (*see* WINDS, WINDSTORM, WINDY)
Gen 8: 1 God made a w to pass over the
Gen 41: 6 heads, blighted by the east w
Gen 41:23 and blighted by the east w
Gen 41:27 w are seven years of famine
Ex 10:13 w on the land all that day
Ex 10:13 the east w brought the
Ex 10:19 turned a very strong west w
Ex 14:21 strong east w all that night
Ex 15:10 You blew with Your w, the sea
Num 11:31 Now a w went out from the
2Sa 22:11 seen upon the wings of the w
1Ki 18:45 became black with clouds and w
1Ki 19:11 and strong w tore into the
1Ki 19:11 but the LORD was not in the w
1Ki 19:11 after the w an earthquake,
2Ki 3:17 You shall not see w, nor
Job 1:19 suddenly a great w came from
Job 6:26 desperate one, which are as w
Job 8: 2 your mouth be like a strong w
Job 15: 2 fill himself with the east w
Job 16: 3 Shall words of w have an end
Job 21:18 are like straw before the w
Job 27:21 The east w carries him away,
Job 28:25 establish a weight for the w
Job 30:15 they pursue my honor as the w
Job 30:22 You lift me up to the w and
Job 37:17 the earth by the south w
Job 37:21 when the w has passed and
Job 38:24 or the east w scattered over
Ps 1: 4 chaff which the w drives away
Ps 11: 6 and brimstone and a burning w
Ps 18:10 flew upon the wings of the w
Ps 18:42 fine as the dust before the w
Ps 35: 5 be like chaff before the w
Ps 48: 7 of Tarshish With an east w
Ps 78:26 He caused an east w to blow
Ps 78:26 He brought in the south w
Ps 83:13 Like the chaff before the w
Ps 103:16 For the w passes over it, and
Ps 104: 3 walks on the wings of the w
Ps 107:25 and raises the stormy w, Which
Ps 135: 7 He brings the w out of His
Ps 147:18 He causes His w to blow, and
Ps 148: 8 Stormy w, fulfilling His word
Prov 11:29 own house will inherit the w
Prov 25:14 like clouds and w without rain
Prov 25:23 The north w brings forth rain
Prov 27:16 restrains her restrains the w
Prov 30: 4 gathered the w in His fists
Eccl 1: 6 The w goes toward the south,
Eccl 1: 6 the w whirls about
Eccl 1:14 vanity and grasping for the w
Eccl 1:17 also is grasping for the w
Eccl 2:11 vanity and grasping for the w
Eccl 2:17 vanity and grasping for the w
Eccl 2:26 vanity and grasping for the w
Eccl 4: 4 vanity and grasping for the w
Eccl 4: 6 toil and grasping for the w
Eccl 4:16 vanity and grasping for the w
Eccl 5:16 he who has labored for the w
Eccl 6: 9 vanity and grasping for the w
Eccl 11: 4 observes the w will not sow
Eccl 11: 5 know what is the way of the w
Song 4:16 Awake, O north w, and come, O
Is 7: 2 woods are moved with the w
Is 11:15 with His mighty w He will
Is 17:13 of the mountains before the w
Is 26:18 as it were, brought forth w
Is 27: 8 He removes it by His rough w
Is 27: 8 w in the day of the east w
Is 32: 2 as a hiding place from the w
Is 41:16 the w shall carry them away,
Is 41:29 their molded images are w
Is 57:13 But the w will carry them all
Is 64: 6 and our iniquities, like the w
Jer 2:24 sniffs at the w in her desire
Jer 4:11 A dry w of the desolate
Jer 4:12 a w too strong for these will
Jer 5:13 And the prophets become w, for
Jer 10:13 He brings the w out of His
Jer 13:24 by the w of the wilderness
Jer 14: 6 sniffed at the w like jackals
Jer 18:17 an east w before the enemy
Jer 22:22 The w shall eat up all your
Jer 51: 1 in Leb Kamai, a destroying w
Jer 51:16 He brings the w out of His
Ezek 5: 2 you shall scatter in the w
Ezek 12:14 I will scatter to every w all
Ezek 13:11 a stormy w shall tear it down
Ezek 13:13 I will cause a stormy w to
Ezek 17:10 when the east w touches it
Ezek 17:21 shall be scattered to every w
Ezek 19:12 the east w dried her fruit
Ezek 27:26 but the east w broke you in
Dan 2:35 the w carried them away so
Hos 4:19 The w has wrapped her up in
Hos 8: 7 They sow the w, and reap the
Hos 12: 1 Ephraim feeds on the w, and
Hos 12: 1 and pursues the east w
Hos 13:15 an east w shall come
Hos 13:15 the w of the LORD shall come
Amos 4:13 mountains, and creates the w
Jon 1: 4 sent out a great w on the sea
Jon 4: 8 prepared a vehement east w
Hab 1: 9 faces are set like the east w
Zech 5: 9 with the w in their wings
Matt 11: 7 A reed shaken by the w
Matt 14:24 waves, for the w was contrary
Matt 14:30 saw that the w was boisterous
Matt 14:32 into the boat, the w ceased
Mark 4:39 He arose and rebuked the w
Mark 4:39 the w ceased and there was a
Mark 4:41 can this be, that even the w
Mark 6:48 for the w was against them
Mark 6:51 boat to them, and the w ceased
Luke 7:24 A reed shaken by the w
Luke 8:24 He arose and rebuked the w
Luke 12:55 when you see the south w blow
John 3: 8 The w blows where it wishes,
John 6:18 because a great w was blowing
Acts 2: 2 as of a rushing mighty w
Acts 27: 7 the w not permitting us to
Acts 27:13 When the south w blew softly
Acts 27:14 a tempestuous head w arose
Acts 27:15 and could not head into the w
Acts 27:40 hoisted the mainsail to the w
Acts 28:13 one day the south w blew
Eph 4:14 with every w of doctrine, by
Jas 1: 6 sea driven and tossed by the w
Rev 6:13 it is shaken by a mighty w
Rev 7: 1 that the w should not blow on

WINDOW (*see* WINDOWS)
Gen 6:16 shall make a w for the ark
Gen 8: 6 that Noah opened the w of the
Gen 26: 8 looked through a w, and saw,
Josh 2:15 down by a rope through the w
Josh 2:18 w through which you let us
Josh 2:21 the scarlet cord in the w
Judg 5:28 Sisera looked through the w
1Sa 19:12 let David down through a w
2Sa 6:16 daughter, looked through a w
1Ki 7: 4 and w was opposite w in
1Ki 7: 5 and w was opposite w in
2Ki 9:30 head, and looked through a w
2Ki 9:32 And he looked up at the w, and
2Ki 13:17 Open the east w"
1Ch 15:29 of Saul, looking through a w
Prov 7: 6 For at the w of my house I
Ezek 40:16 There were beveled w frames
Ezek 41:16 and the beveled w frames
Ezek 41:26 There were beveled w frames
Acts 20: 9 in a w sat a certain young
2Co 11:33 through a w in the wall, and

WINDOWS (*see* WINDOW)
Gen 7:11 the w of heaven were opened
Gen 8: 2 the w of heaven were also
1Ki 6: 4 house w with beveled frames
1Ki 7: 4 There were w with beveled
2Ki 7: 2 LORD would make w in heaven
2Ki 7:19 LORD would make w in heaven
Eccl 12: 3 look through the w grow dim
Song 2: 9 he is looking through the w
Is 24:18 for the w from on high are
Jer 9:21 death has come through our w
Jer 22:14 chambers, and cut out w for it
Ezek 40:16 There were w all around on
Ezek 40:22 Its w and those of its
Ezek 40:25 There were w in it and in its
Ezek 40:25 all around like those w
Ezek 40:29 there were w in it and in its
Ezek 40:33 and there were w in it and in
Ezek 40:36 It had w all around
Ezek 41:16 wood from the ground to the w
Ezek 41:16 the w were covered
Dan 6:10 room, with his w open toward
Joel 2: 9 enter at the w like a thief
Zeph 2:14 voice shall sing in the w
Mal 3:10 open for you the w of heaven

WINDS (*see* WIND)
Job 37: 9 the scattering w of the north
Prov 15:24 The way of life w upward for
Jer 49:32 all w those in the farthest
Jer 49:36 w from the four quarters of
Jer 49:36 them toward all those w
Ezek 5:10 I will scatter to all the w
Ezek 5:12 another third to all the w
Ezek 37: 9 Come from the four w, O
Dan 7: 2 the four w of heaven were
Dan 8: 8 toward the four w of heaven
Dan 11: 4 toward the four w of heaven
Zech 2: 6 like the four w of heaven
Matt 7:25 the w blew and beat on that
Matt 7:27 the w blew and beat on that
Matt 8:26 He arose and rebuked the w
Matt 8:27 can this be, that even the w
Matt 24:31 His elect from the four w
Mark 13:27 His elect from the four w
Luke 8:25 For He commands even the w
Acts 27: 4 because the w were contrary
Jas 3: 4 and are driven by fierce w
Jude 12 water, carried about by the w
Rev 7: 1 the four w of the earth, that

WINDSTORM (*see* STORM, WIND)
Mark 4:37 And a great w arose, and the
Luke 8:23 a w came down on the lake, and

WINDY (*see* WIND)
Ps 55: 8 my escape From the w storm

WINE (*see* WINEBIBBER, WINEPRESS, WINES, WINESKIN, WINE-WORKERS)
Gen 9:21 Then he drank of the w and was
Gen 9:24 So Noah awoke from his w, and
Gen 14:18 Salem brought out bread and w
Gen 19:32 us make our father drink w
Gen 19:33 father drink w that night
Gen 19:34 make him drink w tonight also
Gen 19:35 drink w that night also
Gen 27:25 and he brought him w, and he
Gen 27:28 and plenty of grain and w
Gen 27:37 and w I have sustained him
Gen 49:11 he washed his garments in w
Gen 49:12 His eyes are darker than w
Ex 29:40 hin of w as a drink offering
Lev 10: 9 Do not drink w or
Lev 23:13 drink offering shall be of w
Num 6: 3 shall separate himself from w
Num 6: 3 from w nor vinegar made from
Num 6:20 that the Nazirite may drink w
Num 15: 5 one-fourth of a hin of w as a
Num 15: 7 of w as a sweet aroma to the
Num 15:10 offering half a hin of w as
Num 18:12 all the best of the new w
Num 28:14 be half a hin of w for a bull
Deut 7:13 your grain and your new w
Deut 11:14 in your grain, your new w
Deut 12:17 or your new w or your oil
Deut 14:23 of your grain and your new w
Deut 14:26 for w or similar drink, for
Deut 18: 4 of your grain and your new w
Deut 28:39 the w nor gather the grapes
Deut 28:51 you grain or new w or oil
Deut 29: 6 you drunk w or similar drink

Deut 32:14 and you drank w, the blood of
Deut 32:33 Their w is the poison of
Deut 32:38 drank the w of their drink
Deut 33:28 in a land of grain and new w
Judg 9:13 Should I cease my new w
Judg 13: 4 to drink w or similar drink
Judg 13: 7 Now drink no w or similar
Judg 13:14 she drink w or similar drink
Judg 19:19 and w for myself, for your
1Sa 1:14 Put your w away from you
1Sa 1:15 I have drunk neither w nor
1Sa 1:24 of flour, and a skin of w, and
1Sa 10: 3 another carrying a skin of w
1Sa 16:20 with bread, a skin of w, and a
1Sa 25:18 of bread, two skins of w,
1Sa 25:37 when the w had gone from
2Sa 13:28 Amnon's heart is merry with w
2Sa 16: 1 summer fruits, and a skin of w
2Sa 16: 2 the w for those who are faint
2Ki 18:32 a land of grain and new w
1Ch 9:29 over the fine flour and the w
1Ch 12:40 figs and cakes of raisins, w
1Ch 27:27 vineyards for the supply of w
2Ch 2:10 twenty thousand baths of w
2Ch 2:15 and the w which my lord has
2Ch 11:11 and stores of food, oil, and w
2Ch 31: 5 the firstfruits of grain and w
2Ch 32:28 for the harvest of grain, w
Ezra 6: 9 God of heaven, wheat, salt, w
Ezra 7:22 wheat, one hundred baths of w
Neh 2: 1 when w was before him
Neh 2: 1 that I took the w
Neh 5:11 money and the grain, the new w
Neh 5:15 and took from them bread and w
Neh 5:18 abundance of all kinds of w
Neh 10:37 all kinds of trees, the new w
Neh 10:39 of the grain, of the new w
Neh 13: 5 tithes of grain, the new w
Neh 13:12 of the grain and the new w
Neh 13:15 w presses on the Sabbath, and
Neh 13:15 and loading donkeys with w
Esth 1: 7 with royal w in abundance,
Esth 1:10 of the king was merry with w
Esth 5: 6 At the banquet of w the king
Esth 7: 2 day, at the banquet of w, the
Esth 7: 7 wrath from the banquet of w
Esth 7: 8 the place of the banquet of w
Job 1:13 drinking w in their oldest
Job 1:18 drinking w in their oldest
Job 32:19 is like w that has no vent
Ps 4: 7 their grain and w increased
Ps 60: 3 us drink the w of confusion
Ps 75: 8 is a cup, And the w is red
Ps 78:65 man who shouts because of w
Ps 104:15 w that makes glad the heart
Prov 3:10 vats will overflow with new w
Prov 4:17 and drink the w of violence
Prov 9: 2 her meat, she has mixed her w
Prov 9: 5 drink of the w which I have
Prov 20: 1 W is a mocker, intoxicating
Prov 21:17 he who loves w and oil will
Prov 23:30 who linger long at the w,
Prov 23:30 who go in search of mixed w
Prov 23:31 look on the w when it is red
Prov 31: 4 is not for kings to drink w
Prov 31: 6 w to those who are bitter of
Eccl 2: 3 to gratify my flesh with w
Eccl 9: 7 drink your w with a merry
Eccl 10:19 laughter, and w makes merry
Song 1: 2 your love is better than w
Song 1: 4 your love more than w
Song 4:10 better than w is your love
Song 5: 1 have drunk my w with my milk
Song 7: 9 of your mouth like the best w
Song 7: 9 The w goes down smoothly
Song 8: 2 you to drink of spiced w, of
Is 1:22 your w mixed with water
Is 5:11 night, till w inflames them
Is 5:12 and w are in their feasts
Is 5:22 to men mighty at drinking w
Is 16:10 tread out w in their presses
Is 22:13 eating meat and drinking w
Is 24: 7 The new w fails, the vine
Is 24: 9 shall not drink w with a song
Is 24:11 a crying for w in the streets
Is 27: 2 A vineyard of red w
Is 28: 1 those who are overcome with w
Is 28: 7 also have erred through w
Is 28: 7 they are swallowed up by w
Is 29: 9 are drunk, but not with w
Is 36:17 a land of grain and new w
Is 49:26 own blood as with sweet w
Is 51:21 and drunk but not with w
Is 55: 1 Yes, come, buy w and milk
Is 56:12 I will bring w, and we will
Is 62: 8 shall not drink your new w
Is 65: 8 As the new w is found in the
Jer 13:12 bottle shall be filled with w
Jer 13:12 bottle will be filled with w
Jer 23: 9 a man whom w has overcome
Jer 25:15 Take this w cup of fury from
Jer 31:12 for wheat and new w and oil,
Jer 35: 2 and give them w to drink
Jer 35: 5 Rechabites bowls full of w
Jer 35: 5 I said to them, "Drink w."
Jer 35: 6 We will drink no w, for
Jer 35: 6 saying, 'You shall drink no w
Jer 35: 8 to drink no w all our days,
Jer 35:14 his sons, not to drink w, are
Jer 40:10 But you, gather w and summer
Jer 40:12 at Mizpah, and gathered w and
Jer 48:33 I have caused w to fail from
Jer 51: 7 The nations drank her w
Lam 2:12 Where is grain and w
Ezek 27:18 with the w of Helbon and with
Ezek 44:21 No priest shall drink w when
Dan 1: 5 of the w which he drank, and
Dan 1: 8 nor with the w which he drank
Dan 1:16 the w that they were to drink
Dan 5: 1 drank w in the presence of
Dan 5: 2 While he tasted the w,
Dan 5: 4 They drank w, and praised the
Dan 5:23 have drunk w from them
Dan 10: 3 no meat or w came into my
Hos 2: 8 that I gave her grain, new w
Hos 2: 9 My new w in its season, and
Hos 2:22 answer With grain, with new w
Hos 4:11 Harlotry, w, and new w
Hos 7: 5 him sick, inflamed with w
Hos 7:14 together for grain and new w
Hos 9: 2 the new w shall fail in her
Hos 9: 4 They shall not offer w
Hos 14: 7 be like the w of Lebanon
Joel 1: 5 wail, all you drinkers of w
Joel 1: 5 because of the new w
Joel 1:10 the new w is dried up, the
Joel 2:19 will send you grain and new w
Joel 2:24 shall overflow with new w
Joel 3: 3 harlot, and sold a girl for w
Joel 3:18 shall drip with new w, the
Amos 2: 8 drink the w of the condemned
Amos 2:12 gave the Nazirites w to drink
Amos 4: 1 Bring w, let us drink
Amos 5:11 shall not drink w from them
Amos 6: 6 who drink w from bowls, and
Amos 9:13 shall drip with sweet w, and
Amos 9:14 and drink w from them
Mic 2:11 I will prophesy to you of w
Mic 6:15 sweet w, but not drink w
Hab 2: 5 because he transgresses by w
Zeph 1:13 but not drink their w
Hag 1:11 on the grain and the new w
Hag 2:12 w or oil, or any food, will
Hag 2:16 when one came to the w vat to
Zech 9:15 drink and roar as if with w
Zech 9:17 and new w the young women
Zech 10: 7 shall rejoice as if with w
Matt 9:17 put new w into old wineskins
Matt 9:17 the w is spilled, and the
Matt 9:17 But they put new w into new
Matt 27:34 they gave Him sour w mingled
Matt 27:48 sponge, filled it with sour w
Mark 2:22 no one puts new w into old
Mark 2:22 or else the new w bursts the
Mark 2:22 the w is spilled, and the
Mark 2:22 But new w must be put into
Mark 12: 1 it, dug a place for the w vat
Mark 15:23 Then they gave Him w mingled
Mark 15:36 a sponge full of sour w, put
Luke 1:15 neither w nor strong drink
Luke 5:37 no one puts new w into old
Luke 5:37 or else the new w will burst
Luke 5:38 But new w must be put into
Luke 5:39 And no one, having drunk old w
Luke 7:33 eating bread nor drinking w
Luke 10:34 wounds, pouring on oil and w
Luke 23:36 coming and offering Him sour w
John 2: 3 And when they ran out of w
John 2: 3 They have no w
John 2: 9 the water that was made w
John 2:10 beginning sets out the good w
John 2:10 kept the good w until now
John 4:46 where He had made the water w
John 19:29 of sour w was sitting there
John 19:29 filled a sponge with sour w
John 19:30 Jesus had received the sour w
Acts 2:13 They are full of new w
Rom 14:21 to eat meat nor drink w nor
Eph 5:18 And do not be drunk with w
1Ti 3: 3 not given to w, not violent,
1Ti 3: 8 not given to much w, not
1Ti 5:23 but use a little w for your
Tit 1: 7 not given to w, not violent,
Tit 2: 3 not given to much w,
Rev 6: 6 do not harm the oil and the w
Rev 14: 8 of the w of the wrath of her
Rev 14:10 of the w of the wrath of God
Rev 16:19 w of the fierceness of His
Rev 17: 2 with the w of her fornication
Rev 18: 3 of the w of the wrath of her
Rev 18:13 oil and frankincense, w and oil

WINEBIBBER (*see* WINE, WINEBIBBERS)
Matt 11:19 Look, a gluttonous man and a w
Luke 7:34 say, Look, a glutton and a w

WINEBIBBERS (*see* WINEBIBBER)
Prov 23:20 Do not mix with w, or with

WINEPRESS (*see* WINE, WINEPRESSES)
Num 18:27 and as the fullness of the w
Num 18:30 and as the produce of the w
Deut 15:14 floor, and from your w
Deut 16:13 floor and from your w
Judg 6:11 threshed wheat in the w, in
Judg 7:25 they killed at the w of Zeeb
2Ki 6:27 threshing floor or from the w
Is 5: 2 midst, and also made a w in it
Is 63: 2 like one who treads in the w
Is 63: 3 I have trodden the w alone
Lam 1:15 in a w the virgin daughter of
Hos 9: 2 the w Shall not feed them, and
Joel 3:13 for the w is full, the vats
Matt 21:33 around it, dug a w in it and
Rev 14:19 great w of the wrath of God
Rev 14:20 the w was trampled outside
Rev 14:20 and blood came out of the w
Rev 19:15 the w of the fierceness and

WINEPRESSES (*see* WINEPRESS)
Job 24:11 their walls, and tread w, yet
Jer 48:33 wine to fail from the w
Zech 14:10 of Hananeel to the king's w

WINES (*see* WINE)
Is 25: 6 a feast of w on the lees, of
Is 25: 6 of well-refined w on the lees

WINESKIN (*see* WINE, WINESKINS)
Ps 119:83 have become like a w in smoke

WINESKINS (*see* WINESKIN)
Josh 9: 4 old w torn and mended,
Josh 9:13 these w which we filled were
Job 32:19 is ready to burst like new w
Matt 9:17 put new wine into old w, or
Matt 9:17 or else the w break, the
Matt 9:17 spilled, and the w are ruined
Matt 9:17 they put new wine into new w
Mark 2:22 one puts new wine into old w
Mark 2:22 the new wine bursts the w
Mark 2:22 spilled, and the w are ruined
Mark 2:22 wine must be put into new w
Luke 5:37 one puts new wine into old w
Luke 5:37 the new wine will burst the w
Luke 5:37 and the w will be ruined
Luke 5:38 wine must be put into new w

WINE-WORKERS (*see* WINE)
Jer 48:12 him w who will tip him over

WING (*see* WINGED, WINGS)
Ruth 3: 9 your maidservant under your w
1Ki 6:24 One w of the cherub was five
1Ki 6:24 the other w of the cherub
1Ki 6:24 one w to the tip of the other
1Ki 6:27 w of the one touched one wall
1Ki 6:27 the w of the other cherub
2Ch 3:11 one w of the one cherub was
2Ch 3:11 the other w was five cubits,
2Ch 3:11 touching the w of the other
2Ch 3:12 one w of the other cherub was
2Ch 3:12 the other w also was five
2Ch 3:12 touching the w of the other
Is 10:14 was no one who moved his w

Ezek 16: 8 so I spread My **w** over you
Dan 9:27 and on the **w** of abominations

WINGED (*see* WING)
Gen 1:21 every **w** bird according to its
Deut 4:17 or the likeness of any **w** bird

WINGS (*see* WING)
Ex 19: 4 how I bore you on eagles' **w**
Ex 25:20 stretch out their **w** above
Ex 25:20 the mercy seat with their **w**
Ex 37: 9 spread out their **w** above, and
Ex 37: 9 the mercy seat with their **w**
Lev 1:17 he shall split it at its **w**
Deut 32:11 young, spreading out its **w**
Deut 32:11 up, carrying them on its **w**
Ruth 2:12 under whose **w** you have come
2Sa 22:11 seen upon the **w** of the wind
1Ki 6:27 they stretched out the **w** of
1Ki 6:27 their **w** touched each other in
1Ki 8: 6 under the **w** of the cherubim
1Ki 8: 7 **w** over the place of the ark
1Ch 28:18 cherubim that spread their **w**
2Ch 3:11 The **w** of the cherubim were
2Ch 3:13 The **w** of these cherubim
2Ch 5: 7 under the **w** of the cherubim
2Ch 5: 8 **w** over the place of the ark
Job 39:13 The **w** of the ostrich wave
Job 39:13 wave proudly, but are her **w**
Job 39:26 spread its **w** toward the south
Ps 17: 8 me under the shadow of Your **w**
Ps 18:10 flew upon the **w** of the wind
Ps 36: 7 under the shadow of Your **w**
Ps 55: 6 Oh, that I had **w** like a dove
Ps 57: 1 Your **w** I will make my refuge
Ps 61: 4 in the shelter of Your **w**
Ps 63: 7 of Your **w** I will rejoice
Ps 68:13 the **w** of a dove covered with
Ps 91: 4 under His **w** you shall take
Ps 104: 3 walks on the **w** of the wind
Ps 139: 9 If I take the **w** of the
Prov 23: 5 certainly make themselves **w**
Is 6: 2 each one had six **w**
Is 8: 8 **w** will fill the breadth of
Is 18: 1 land shadowed with buzzing **w**
Is 40:31 mount up with **w** like eagles
Jer 48: 9 Give **w** to Moab, that she may
Jer 48:40 and spread his **w** over Moab
Jer 49:22 and spread His **w** over Bozrah
Ezek 1: 6 faces, and each one had four **w**
Ezek 1: 8 their **w** on their four sides
Ezek 1: 8 of the four had faces and **w**
Ezek 1: 9 Their **w** touched one another
Ezek 1:11 Their **w** were stretched upward
Ezek 1:11 two **w** of each one touched one
Ezek 1:23 their **w** spread out straight
Ezek 1:24 I heard the noise of their **w**
Ezek 1:24 still, they let down their **w**
Ezek 1:25 stood, they let down their **w**
Ezek 3:13 the **w** of the living creatures
Ezek 10: 5 the sound of the **w** of the
Ezek 10: 8 of a man's hand under their **w**
Ezek 10:12 back, their hands, their **w**
Ezek 10:16 the cherubim lifted their **w**
Ezek 10:19 the cherubim lifted their **w**
Ezek 10:21 four faces and each one four **w**
Ezek 10:21 of a man was under their **w**
Ezek 11:22 cherubim lifted up their **w**
Ezek 17: 3 A great eagle with large **w**
Ezek 17: 7 great eagle with large **w** and
Dan 7: 4 like a lion, and had eagle's **w**
Dan 7: 4 till its **w** were plucked off
Dan 7: 6 on its back four **w** of a bird
Hos 4:19 has wrapped her up in its **w**
Zech 5: 9 with the wind in their **w**
Zech 5: 9 **w** like the **w** of a stork
Mal 4: 2 arise with healing in His **w**
Matt 23:37 her chicks under her **w**, but
Luke 13:34 gathers her brood under her **w**
Rev 4: 8 creatures, each having six **w**
Rev 9: 9 the sound of their **w** was like
Rev 12:14 given two **w** of a great eagle

WINK (*see* WINKS)
Job 15:12 and what do your eyes **w** at
Ps 35:19 Nor let them **w** with the eye

WINKS (*see* WINK)
Prov 6:13 he **w** with his eyes, he
Prov 10:10 He who **w** with the eye causes
Prov 16:30 He **w** his eye to devise

WINNOW (*see* WINNOWED, WINNOWERS, WINNOWING)
Is 41:16 You shall **w** them, the wind
Jer 15: 7 And I will **w** them with a
Jer 51: 2 to Babylon, who shall **w** her

WINNOWED (*see* WINNOW)
Is 30:24 which has been **w** with the

WINNOWERS (*see* WINNOW)
Jer 51: 2 And I will send **w** to Babylon

WINNOWING (*see* WINNOW)
Ruth 3: 2 he is **w** barley tonight at the
Jer 15: 7 a **w** fan in the gates of the
Matt 3:12 His **w** fan is in His hand, and
Luke 3:17 His **w** fan is in His hand, and

WINS (*see* WIN)
Prov 11:30 and he who **w** souls is wise

WINTER (*see* WINTERED)
Gen 8:22 and cold and heat, and **w** and
Ps 74:17 You have made summer and **w**
Prov 20: 4 will not plow because of **w**
Song 2:11 the **w** is past, the rain is
Is 18: 6 of the earth will **w** on them
Jer 36:22 **w** house in the ninth month
Amos 3:15 I will destroy the **w** house
Zech 14: 8 summer and **w** it shall occur
Matt 24:20 not be in **w** or on the Sabbath
Mark 13:18 your flight may not be in **w**
John 10:22 in Jerusalem, and it was **w**
Acts 27:12 was not suitable to **w** in, the
Acts 27:12 and northwest, and **w** there
1Co 16: 6 or even spend the **w** with you
2Ti 4:21 your utmost to come before **w**
Tit 3:12 decided to spend the **w** there

WINTERED (*see* WINTER)
Acts 28:11 which had **w** at the island

WIPE (*see* WIPED, WIPES, WIPING)
2Ki 21:13 I will **w** Jerusalem as one
Neh 13:14 do not **w** out my good deeds
Is 25: 8 and the Lord GOD will **w** away
Luke 10:11 to us we **w** off against you
John 13: 5 to **w** them with the towel with
Rev 7:17 God will **w** away every tear
Rev 21: 4 God will **w** away every tear

WIPED (*see* WIPE)
Prov 6:33 reproach will not be **w** away
Luke 7:38 **w** them with the hair of her
Luke 7:44 **w** them with the hair of her
John 11: 2 **w** His feet with her hair,
John 12: 3 and **w** His feet with her hair
Col 2:14 having **w** out the handwriting

WIPES (*see* WIPE)
2Ki 21:13 Jerusalem as one **w** a dish
Prov 30:20 eats and **w** her mouth, and says,

WIPING (*see* WIPE)
2Ki 21:13 **w** it and turning it upside

WISDOM (*see* WISE)
Ex 28: 3 filled with the spirit of **w**
Ex 31: 3 with the Spirit of God, in **w**
Ex 31: 6 I have put **w** in the hearts of
Ex 35:26 **w** spun yarn of goats' hair
Ex 35:31 with the Spirit of God, in **w**
Ex 36: 1 in whom the LORD has put **w**
Ex 36: 2 heart the LORD had put **w**,
Deut 4: 6 for this is your **w** and your
Deut 34: 9 was full of the spirit of **w**
2Sa 14:20 according to the **w** of the
2Sa 20:22 Then the woman in her **w** went
1Ki 2: 6 do according to your **w**, and do
1Ki 3:28 the **w** of God was in him to
1Ki 4:29 And God gave Solomon **w** and
1Ki 4:30 **w** excelled the **w** of all
1Ki 4:30 East and all the **w** of Egypt
1Ki 4:34 earth who had heard of his **w**
1Ki 4:34 came to hear the **w** of Solomon
1Ki 5:12 So the LORD gave Solomon **w**
1Ki 7:14 he was filled with **w** and
1Ki 10: 4 had seen all the **w** of Solomon
1Ki 10: 6 about your words and your **w**
1Ki 10: 7 Your **w** and prosperity exceed
1Ki 10: 8 before you and hear your **w**
1Ki 10:23 of the earth in riches and **w**
1Ki 10:24 of Solomon to hear his **w**,
1Ki 11:41 all that he did, and his **w**
1Ch 22:12 Only may the LORD give you **w**
2Ch 1:10 Now give me **w** and knowledge,
2Ch 1:11 but have asked **w** and
2Ch 1:12 **w** and knowledge are granted to
2Ch 9: 3 had seen the **w** of Solomon
2Ch 9: 5 about your words and your **w**
2Ch 9: 6 of your **w** was not told me
2Ch 9: 7 before you and hear your **w**
2Ch 9:22 of the earth in riches and **w**
2Ch 9:23 of Solomon to hear his **w**,
Ezra 7:25 according to your God-given **w**
Job 4:21 They die, even without **w**
Job 11: 6 show you the secrets of **w**
Job 12: 2 and **w** will die with you
Job 12:12 **W** is with aged men, and with
Job 12:13 With Him are **w** and strength,
Job 13: 5 silent, and it would be your **w**
Job 15: 8 Do you limit **w** to yourself
Job 26: 3 counseled one who has no **w**
Job 28:12 But where can **w** be found
Job 28:18 price of **w** is above rubies
Job 28:20 From where then does **w** come
Job 28:27 then He saw **w** and declared it
Job 28:28 fear of the Lord, that is **w**
Job 32: 7 of years should teach **w**
Job 32:13 you say, 'We have found **w**'
Job 33:33 peace, and I will teach you **w**
Job 34:35 his words are without **w**
Job 38:36 Who has put **w** in the mind
Job 38:37 can number the clouds by **w**
Job 39:17 because God deprived her of **w**
Job 39:26 Does the hawk fly by your **w**
Ps 37:30 of the righteous speaks **w**
Ps 49: 3 My mouth shall speak **w**, And
Ps 51: 6 You will make me to know **w**
Ps 90:12 That we may gain a heart of **w**
Ps 104:24 In **w** You have made them all
Ps 105:22 And teach his elders **w**
Ps 111:10 LORD is the beginning of **w**
Ps 136: 5 To Him who by **w** made the
Prov 1: 2 To know **w** and instruction, to
Prov 1: 3 receive the instruction of **w**
Prov 1: 7 but fools despise **w** and
Prov 1:20 **W** calls aloud outside
Prov 2: 2 you incline your ear to **w**
Prov 2: 6 For the LORD gives **w**
Prov 2: 7 up sound **w** for the upright
Prov 2:10 When **w** enters your heart, and
Prov 3:13 Happy is the man who finds **w**
Prov 3:19 The LORD by **w** founded the
Prov 3:21 keep sound **w** and discretion
Prov 4: 5 Get **w**! Get understanding!
Prov 4: 7 **W** is the principal thing
Prov 4: 7 therefore get **w**
Prov 4:11 taught you in the way of **w**
Prov 5: 1 My son, pay attention to my **w**
Prov 7: 4 Say to **w**, "You are my sister
Prov 8: 1 Does not **w** cry out, and
Prov 8:11 for **w** is better than rubies,
Prov 8:12 I, **w**, dwell with prudence, and
Prov 8:14 Counsel is mine, and sound **w**
Prov 9: 1 **W** has built her house, she
Prov 9:10 LORD is the beginning of **w**
Prov 10:13 **W** is found on the lips of him
Prov 10:21 but fools die for lack of **w**
Prov 10:23 a man of understanding has **w**
Prov 10:31 the righteous brings forth **w**
Prov 11: 2 but with the humble is **w**
Prov 11:12 He who is devoid of **w**
Prov 12: 8 commended according to his **w**
Prov 13:10 with the well-advised is **w**
Prov 14: 6 A scoffer seeks **w** and does not
Prov 14: 8 The **w** of the prudent is to
Prov 14:33 **W** rests quietly in the heart
Prov 15:33 LORD is the instruction of **w**
Prov 16:16 it is to get **w** than gold
Prov 17:16 fool the purchase price of **w**
Prov 17:24 **W** is in the sight of him who
Prov 18: 4 the wellspring of **w** is a
Prov 19: 8 He who gets **w** loves his own
Prov 21:30 There is no **w** or
Prov 23: 9 despise the **w** of your words
Prov 23:23 and do not sell it, also **w**
Prov 24: 3 Through **w** a house is built,
Prov 24: 7 **W** is too lofty for a fool
Prov 24:14 of **w** be to your soul
Prov 29: 3 Whoever loves **w** makes his
Prov 29:15 The rod and reproof give **w**
Prov 30: 3 I neither learned **w** nor have
Prov 31:26 She opens her mouth with **w**
Eccl 1:13 search out by **w** concerning
Eccl 1:16 have gained more **w** than all

Eccl 1:16 heart has understood great w
Eccl 1:17 And I set my heart to know w
Eccl 1:18 For in much w is much grief,
Eccl 2: 3 while guiding my heart with w
Eccl 2: 9 Also my w remained with me
Eccl 2:12 I turned myself to consider w
Eccl 2:13 Then I saw that w excels
Eccl 2:21 a man whose labor is with w
Eccl 2:26 For God gives w and knowledge
Eccl 7:11 W is good with an inheritance
Eccl 7:12 For w is a defense as money
Eccl 7:12 of knowledge is that w gives
Eccl 7:19 W strengthens the wise more
Eccl 7:23 All this I have proved by w
Eccl 7:25 know, to search and seek out w
Eccl 8: 1 A man's w makes his face
Eccl 8:16 I applied my heart to know w
Eccl 9:10 or device or knowledge or w
Eccl 9:13 This w I have also seen under
Eccl 9:15 he by his w delivered the
Eccl 9:16 W is better than strength
Eccl 9:16 the poor man's w is despised
Eccl 9:18 W is better than weapons of
Eccl 10: 1 folly to one respected for w
Eccl 10: 3 along the way, he lacks w
Eccl 10:10 but w brings success
Is 10:13 I have done it, and by my w
Is 11: 2 upon Him, the Spirit of w
Is 29:14 for the w of their wise men
Is 33: 6 W and knowledge will be the
Is 47:10 your w and your knowledge
Jer 8: 9 so what w do they have
Jer 9:23 the wise man glory in his w
Jer 10:12 the world by His w, And has
Jer 49: 7 Is w no more in Teman
Jer 49: 7 Has their w vanished
Jer 51:15 the world by His w, and
Ezek 28: 4 With your w and your
Ezek 28: 5 by your great w in trade you
Ezek 28: 7 against the beauty of your w
Ezek 28:12 seal of perfection, full of w
Ezek 28:17 you corrupted your w for the
Dan 1: 4 good-looking, gifted in all w
Dan 1:17 skill in all literature and w
Dan 1:20 And in all matters of w and
Dan 2:14 w Daniel answered Arioch, the
Dan 2:20 of God forever and ever, for w
Dan 2:21 He gives w to the wise And
Dan 2:23 you have given me w and might,
Dan 2:30 more w than anyone living
Dan 5:11 light and understanding and w
Dan 5:11 like the w of the gods, were
Dan 5:14 excellent w are found in you
Mic 6: 9 w shall see Your name
Matt 11:19 But w is justified by her
Matt 12:42 to hear the w of Solomon
Matt 13:54 Where did this Man get this w
Mark 6: 2 what w is this which is given
Luke 1:17 to the w of the just, to make
Luke 2:40 in spirit, filled with w
Luke 2:52 And Jesus increased in w and
Luke 7:35 But w is justified by all her
Luke 11:31 to hear the w of Solomon
Luke 11:49 Therefore the w of God also
Luke 21:15 w which all your adversaries
Acts 6: 3 full of the Holy Spirit and w
Acts 6:10 were not able to resist the w
Acts 7:10 w in the presence of Pharaoh,
Acts 7:22 in all the w of the Egyptians
Rom 11:33 of the riches both of the w
1Co 1:17 gospel, not with w of words
1Co 1:19 destroy the w of the wise
1Co 1:20 foolish the w of this world
1Co 1:21 For since, in the w of God
1Co 1:21 through w did not know God
1Co 1:22 sign, and Greeks seek after w
1Co 1:24 power of God and the w of God
1Co 1:30 who became for us w from God
1Co 2: 1 or of w declaring to you the
1Co 2: 4 persuasive words of human w
1Co 2: 5 w of men but in the power of
1Co 2: 6 we speak w among those who
1Co 2: 6 yet not the w of this age
1Co 2: 7 But we speak the w of God in
1Co 2: 7 the hidden w which God
1Co 2:13 not in words which man's w
1Co 3:19 For the w of this world is
1Co 12: 8 word of w through the Spirit
2Co 1:12 not with fleshly w but by the
Eph 1: 8 to abound toward us in all w
Eph 1:17 give to you the spirit of w
Eph 3:10 that now the manifold w of
Col 1: 9 of His will in all w and
Col 1:28 teaching every man in all w
Col 2: 3 hidden all the treasures of w
Col 2:23 have an appearance of w in
Col 3:16 dwell in you richly in all w
Col 4: 5 Walk in w toward those who
Jas 1: 5 If any of you lacks w, let
Jas 3:13 are done in the meekness of w
Jas 3:15 This w does not descend from
Jas 3:17 But the w that is from above
2Pe 3:15 to the w given to him, has
Rev 5:12 receive power and riches and w
Rev 7:12 Blessing and glory and w,
Rev 13:18 Here is w. Let him who has
Rev 17: 9 Here is the mind which has w

WISE (*see* UNWISE, WISDOM, WISELY, WISER, WISEST)

Gen 3: 6 tree desirable to make one w
Gen 41: 8 of Egypt and all its w men
Gen 41:33 w man, and set him over the
Gen 41:39 one as discerning and w as you
Ex 7:11 Pharaoh also called the w men
Deut 1:13 Choose w, understanding, and
Deut 1:15 the heads of your tribes, w
Deut 4: 6 this great nation is a w and
Deut 16:19 blinds the eyes of the w and
Deut 32:29 Oh, that they were w, that
2Sa 14: 2 brought from there a w woman
2Sa 14:20 but my lord is w, according
2Sa 20:16 Then a w woman cried out from
1Ki 2: 9 for you are a w man and know
1Ki 3:12 see, I have given you a w
1Ki 5: 7 for He has given David a w
1Ch 26:14 a w counselor, and his lot
1Ch 27:32 a w man, and a scribe
2Ch 2:12 has given King David a w son
Esth 1:13 the w men who understood the
Esth 6:13 happened to him, his w men
Job 5:13 He catches the w in their own
Job 9: 4 God is w in heart and mighty
Job 11:12 an empty-headed man will be w
Job 15: 2 Should a w man answer with
Job 15:18 what w men have told, not
Job 17:10 not find one w man among you
Job 22: 2 though he who is w may be
Job 32: 9 Great men are not always w
Job 34: 2 Hear my words, you w men
Job 34:34 to me, w men who listen to me
Job 37:24 to any who are w of heart
Ps 2:10 Now therefore, be w, O kings
Ps 19: 7 is sure, making w the simple
Ps 36: 3 He has ceased to be w and to
Ps 49:10 For he sees that w men die
Ps 94: 8 you fools, when will you be w
Ps 107:43 Whoever is w will observe
Prov 1: 5 A w man will hear and increase
Prov 1: 5 will attain w counsel,
Prov 1: 6 an enigma, the words of the w
Prov 3: 7 Do not be w in your own eyes
Prov 3:35 The w shall inherit glory,
Prov 6: 6 Consider her ways and be w
Prov 8:33 Hear instruction and be w, and
Prov 9: 8 rebuke a w man, and he will
Prov 9: 9 Give instruction to a w man
Prov 9:12 If you are w, you are w
Prov 10: 1 A w son makes a glad father,
Prov 10: 5 gathers in summer is a w son
Prov 10: 8 The w in heart will receive
Prov 10:14 W people store up knowledge,
Prov 10:19 who restrains his lips is w
Prov 11:29 be servant to the w of heart
Prov 11:30 and he who wins souls is w
Prov 12:15 but he who heeds counsel is w
Prov 12:18 of the w promotes health
Prov 13: 1 A w son heeds his father's
Prov 13:14 The law of the w is a
Prov 13:20 walks with w men will be w
Prov 14: 1 Every w woman builds her
Prov 14: 3 of the w will preserve them
Prov 14:16 A w man fears and departs from
Prov 14:24 of the w is their riches, but
Prov 14:35 favor is toward a w servant
Prov 15: 2 The tongue of the w uses
Prov 15: 7 The lips of the w disperse
Prov 15:12 him, nor will he go to the w
Prov 15:20 A w son makes a father glad,
Prov 15:24 life winds upward for the w
Prov 15:31 life will abide among the w
Prov 16:14 but a w man will appease it
Prov 16:21 The w in heart will be called
Prov 16:23 The heart of the w teaches
Prov 17: 2 A w servant will rule over a
Prov 17:10 is more effective for a w man
Prov 17:28 Even a fool is counted w when
Prov 18: 1 rages against all w judgment
Prov 18:15 and the ear of the w seeks
Prov 19:20 that you may be w in your
Prov 20: 1 is led astray by it is not w
Prov 20:18 by w counsel wage war
Prov 20:26 A w king sifts out the wicked
Prov 21:11 the simple is made w
Prov 21:11 but when the w is instructed,
Prov 21:20 oil in the dwelling of the w
Prov 21:22 A w man scales the city of
Prov 22:17 and hear the words of the w
Prov 23:15 My son, if your heart is w
Prov 23:19 Hear, my son, and be w
Prov 23:24 he who begets a w child will
Prov 24: 5 A w man is strong, yes, a man
Prov 24: 6 for by w counsel you will
Prov 24:23 things also belong to the w
Prov 25:12 ornament of fine gold is a w
Prov 26: 5 lest he be w in his own eyes
Prov 26:12 see a man w in his own eyes
Prov 27:11 My son, be w, and make my
Prov 28:11 rich man is w in his own eyes
Prov 29: 8 but w men turn away wrath
Prov 29: 9 If a w man contends with a
Prov 29:11 but a w man holds them back
Prov 30:24 but they are exceedingly w
Eccl 2:14 The w man's eyes are in his
Eccl 2:15 me, and why was I then more w
Eccl 2:16 w than of the fool forever
Eccl 2:16 and how does a w man die
Eccl 2:19 he will be a w man or a fool
Eccl 2:19 shown myself w under the sun
Eccl 4:13 and w youth than an old and
Eccl 6: 8 has the w man than the fool
Eccl 7: 4 The heart of the w is in the
Eccl 7: 5 to hear the rebuke of the w
Eccl 7: 7 destroys a w man's reason
Eccl 7:16 righteous, nor be overly w
Eccl 7:19 Wisdom strengthens the w more
Eccl 7:23 I will be w"
Eccl 8: 1 Who is like a w man
Eccl 8: 5 a w man's heart discerns both
Eccl 8:17 though a w man attempts to
Eccl 9: 1 that the righteous and the w
Eccl 9:11 strong, nor bread to the w
Eccl 9:15 was found in it a poor w man
Eccl 9:17 Words of the w, spoken
Eccl 10: 2 A w man's heart is at his
Eccl 10:12 The words of a w man's mouth
Eccl 12: 9 because the Preacher was w
Eccl 12:11 words of the w are like goads
Is 5:21 who are w in their own eyes
Is 19:11 Pharaoh's w counselors give
Is 19:11 I am the son of the w, the
Is 19:12 Where are your w men
Is 29:14 of their w men shall perish
Is 31: 2 Yet He also is w and will
Is 44:25 Who turns w men backward,
Jer 4:22 They are w to do evil, but to
Jer 8: 8 How can you say, 'We are w
Jer 8: 9 The w men are ashamed, they
Jer 9:12 Who is the w man who may
Jer 9:23 Let not the w man glory in
Jer 10: 7 for among all the w men of
Jer 18:18 nor counsel from the w, nor
Jer 50:35 her princes and her w men
Jer 51:57 w men, her governors, her
Ezek 27: 8 your own w men, O Tyre, were
Ezek 27: 9 and its w men were in you to
Dan 2:12 all the w men of Babylon
Dan 2:13 they began killing the w men
Dan 2:14 to kill the w men of Babylon
Dan 2:18 rest of the w men of Babylon
Dan 2:21 He gives wisdom to the w And
Dan 2:24 destroy the w men of Babylon
Dan 2:24 destroy the w men of Babylon
Dan 2:27 king has demanded, the w men
Dan 2:48 over all the w men of Babylon
Dan 4: 6 w men of Babylon before me
Dan 4:18 since all the w men of my
Dan 5: 7 spoke, saying to the w men of
Dan 5: 8 Now all the king's w men came
Dan 5:15 Now the w men, the
Dan 12: 3 Those who are w shall shine

Dan 12:10 but the **w** shall understand
Hos 14: 9 Who is **w**? Let him understand
Obad 8 destroy the **w** men from Edom
Zech 9: 2 Sidon, though they are very **w**
Matt 2: 1 **w** men from the East came to
Matt 2: 7 had secretly called the **w** men
Matt 2:16 he was deceived by the **w** men
Matt 2:16 had determined from the **w** men
Matt 7:24 I will liken him to a **w** man
Matt 10:16 Therefore be **w** as serpents
Matt 11:25 these things from the **w** and
Matt 23:34 prophets, **w** men, and scribes
Matt 24:45 **w** servant, whom his master
Matt 25: 2 Now five of them were **w**, and
Matt 25: 4 but the **w** took oil in their
Matt 25: 8 And the foolish said to the **w**
Matt 25: 9 But the **w** answered, saying
Luke 10:21 these things from the **w** and
Luke 12:42 **w** steward, whom his master
Rom 1:14 and to barbarians, both to **w**
Rom 1:22 Professing to be **w**, they
Rom 11:25 lest you should be **w** in your
Rom 12:16 Do not be **w** in your own
Rom 16:19 you to be **w** in what is good
Rom 16:27 to God, alone **w**, be glory
1Co 1:19 destroy the wisdom of the **w**
1Co 1:20 Where is the **w**
1Co 1:26 that not many **w** according to
1Co 1:27 world to put to shame the **w**
1Co 3:10 as a **w** master builder I have
1Co 3:18 you seems to be **w** in this age
1Co 3:18 a fool that he may become **w**
1Co 3:19 He catches the **w** in their own
1Co 3:20 knows the thoughts of the **w**
1Co 4:10 sake, but you are **w** in Christ
1Co 6: 5 is not a **w** man among you, not
1Co 10:15 I speak as to **w** men
2Co 10:12 among themselves, are not **w**
2Co 11:19 since you yourselves are **w**
Eph 5:15 not as fools but as **w**,
1Ti 1:17 to God who alone is **w**, be
2Ti 3:15 which are able to make you **w**
Jas 3:13 Who is **w** and understanding
Jude 25 our Savior, who alone is **w**

WISELY (*see* WISE)
Ex 1:10 come, let us deal **w** with them
1Sa 18: 5 Saul sent him, and behaved **w**
1Sa 18:14 David behaved **w** in all his
1Sa 18:15 saw that he behaved very **w**
1Sa 18:30 that David behaved more **w**
2Ch 11:23 He dealt **w**, and dispersed some
Ps 64: 9 For they shall **w** consider His
Ps 101: 2 I will behave **w** in a perfect
Prov 16:20 the word **w** will find good
Prov 21:12 The righteous God **w** considers
Prov 28:26 walks **w** will be delivered
Eccl 7:10 not inquire **w** concerning this
Mark 12:34 Jesus saw that he answered **w**

WISER (*see* WISE)
1Ki 4:31 For he was **w** than all men
Job 35:11 makes us **w** than the birds of
Ps 119:98 make me **w** than my enemies
Prov 9: 9 man, and he will be still **w**
Prov 26:16 The sluggard is **w** in his own
Ezek 28: 3 Behold, you are **w** than Daniel
1Co 1:25 of God is **w** than men, and the

WISEST (*see* WISE)
Judg 5:29 Her **w** ladies answered her,

WISH (*see* WISHED, WISHES, WISHING)
Gen 19: 8 you may do to them as you **w**
Gen 23: 8 If it is your **w** that I bury
Num 22:29 I **w** there were a sword in my
Josh 15:18 What do you **w**
Judg 1:14 What do you **w**
1Ki 1:16 What is your **w**
Esth 5: 3 What do you **w**, Queen Esther
Job 37:20 He be told that I **w** to speak
Ps 40:14 to dishonor Who **w** me evil
Ps 73: 7 have more than heart could **w**
Matt 17: 4 if You **w**, let us make here
Matt 20:14 I **w** to give to this last man
Matt 20:15 what I **w** with my own things
Matt 20:21 What do you **w**
Mark 14: 7 whenever you **w** you may do
Luke 4: 6 and I give it to whomever I **w**
Luke 12:49 and how I **w** it were already
John 12:21 Sir, we **w** to see Jesus
John 21:18 carry you where you do not **w**
Rom 9: 3 For I could **w** that I myself
1Co 4: 8 I could **w** you did reign, that
1Co 7: 7 For I **w** that all men were
1Co 14: 5 I **w** you all spoke with
1Co 16: 7 For I do not **w** to see you now
2Co 12:20 not find you such as I **w**, and
2Co 12:20 by you such as you do not **w**
Gal 5:12 I could **w** that those who
Gal 5:17 not do the things that you **w**
2Jn 12 I did not **w** to do so with
3Jn 10 and forbids those who **w** to
3Jn 13 but I do not **w** to write to
Rev 3:15 I could **w** you were cold or

WISHED (*see* WISH)
1Ki 13:33 whoever **w**, he consecrated him
Job 9: 3 If one **w** to contend with Him,
Dan 5:19 Whomever he **w**, he executed
Dan 5:19 whomever he **w**, he kept alive
Dan 5:19 whomever he **w**, he set up
Dan 5:19 and whomever he **w**, he put
Dan 7:19 Then I **w** to know the truth
Jon 4: 8 Then he **w** death for himself,
Matt 17:12 did to him whatever they **w**
Matt 27:15 one prisoner whom they **w**
Mark 9:13 did to him whatever they **w**
John 21:18 and walked where you **w**
Phm 13 whom I **w** to keep with me,

WISHES (*see* WISH)
Lev 27:19 the field ever **w** to redeem it
Prov 21: 1 He turns it wherever He **w**
John 3: 8 The wind blows where it **w**
1Co 7:36 must be, let him do what he **w**
1Co 7:39 to be married to whom she **w**

WISHING (*see* WISH)
Luke 23:20 **w** to release Jesus, again

WITCHCRAFT
Deut 18:10 fire, or one who practices **w**
1Sa 15:23 rebellion is as the sin of **w**
2Ki 9:22 Jezebel and her **w** are so many
2Ki 17:17 through the fire, practiced **w**
2Ki 21: 6 practiced soothsaying, used **w**
2Ch 33: 6 practiced soothsaying, used **w**

WITH (*see* PREFACE)

WITHDRAW (*see* WITHDRAWN, WITHDREW)
1Sa 14:19 to the priest, "**W** your hand
1Ki 15:19 so that he will **w** from me
2Ch 16: 3 so that he will **w** from me
Job 9:13 God will not **w** His anger, the
Job 13:21 **W** Your hand far from me, and
Job 36: 7 He does not **w** His eyes from
Ps 74:11 Why do You **w** Your hand, even
Is 60:20 nor shall your moon **w** itself
2Th 3: 6 that you **w** from every brother
1Ti 6: 5 From such **w** yourself

WITHDRAWN (*see* WITHDRAW)
2Sa 17:13 if he has **w** into a city, then
2Sa 24:21 may be **w** from the people
2Sa 24:25 the plague was **w** from Israel
1Ch 21:22 may be **w** from the people
2Ch 24:25 when they had **w** from him (for
Lam 2: 8 He has not **w** His hand from
Ezek 18: 8 but has **w** his hand from
Ezek 18:17 who has **w** his hand from the
Hos 5: 6 He has **w** Himself from them
Luke 22:41 He was **w** from them about a
John 5:13 who it was, for Jesus had **w**

WITHDREW (*see* WITHDRAW)
2Sa 20:22 they **w** from the city, every
2Ch 32:31 God **w** from him, in order to
Ezek 20:22 Nevertheless I **w** My hand and
Matt 12:15 knew it, He **w** from there
Mark 3: 7 But Jesus **w** with His
Luke 5:16 often **w** into the wilderness
Acts 19: 9 **w** the disciples, reasoning
Acts 22:29 to examine him **w** from him
Gal 2:12 but when they came, he **w** and

WITHER (*see* WITHERED, WITHERS)
Ps 1: 3 Whose leaf also shall not **w**
Ps 37: 2 grass, And **w** as the green herb
Ps 102:11 And I **w** away like grass
Is 19: 6 the reeds and rushes will **w**
Is 19: 7 sown by the River, will **w**
Is 40:24 blow on them, and they will **w**
Jer 12: 4 and the herbs of every field **w**
Ezek 17: 9 its fruit, and leave it to **w**
Ezek 17: 9 of its spring leaves will **w**
Ezek 17:10 will it not utterly **w** when
Ezek 17:10 It will **w** in the garden
Ezek 47:12 their leaves will not **w**, and
Nah 1: 4 Bashan and Carmel **w**, and the
Zech 11:17 his arm shall completely **w**
Matt 21:20 the fig tree **w** away so soon

WITHERED (*see* WITHER)
Gen 41:23 Then behold, seven heads, **w**
1Ki 13: 4 stretched out toward him, **w**
Ps 102: 4 and **w** like grass, So that I
Is 15: 6 the green grass has **w** away
Is 27:11 When its boughs are **w**, they
Ezek 19:12 branches were broken and **w**
Joel 1:12 up, and the fig tree has **w**
Joel 1:12 the trees of the field are **w**
Joel 1:12 surely joy has **w** away from
Joel 1:17 down, for the grain has **w**
Amos 4: 7 it did not rain the part **w**
Jon 4: 7 damaged the plant that it **w**
Matt 12:10 was a man who had a **w** hand
Matt 13: 6 they had no root they **w** away
Matt 21:19 the fig tree **w** away
Mark 3: 1 was there who had a **w** hand
Mark 3: 3 to the man who had the **w** hand
Mark 4: 6 it had no root it **w** away
Mark 11:21 which You cursed has **w** away
Luke 6: 6 there whose right hand was **w**
Luke 6: 8 to the man who had the **w** hand
Luke 8: 6 it **w** away because it lacked
John 15: 6 cast out as a branch and is **w**

WITHERS (*see* WITHER)
Job 8:12 it **w** before any other plant
Job 18:16 below, and his branch **w** above
Ps 90: 6 evening it is cut down and **w**
Ps 129: 6 Which **w** before it grows up,
Is 40: 7 The grass **w**, the flower fades
Is 40: 8 The grass **w**, the flower fades
Amos 1: 2 mourn, and the top of Carmel **w**
Jas 1:11 heat than it **w** the grass
1Pe 1:24 The grass **w**, and its flower

WITHHELD (*see* WITHHOLD)
Gen 11: 6 to do will be **w** from them
Gen 20: 6 For I also **w** you from sinning
Gen 22:12 you have not **w** your son, your
Gen 22:16 thing, and have not **w** your son
Gen 30: 2 who has **w** from you the fruit
Job 22: 7 you have **w** bread from the
Job 38:15 the wicked their light is **w**
Job 42: 2 of Yours can be **w** from You
Ps 21: 2 have not **w** the request of his
Jer 3: 3 the showers have been **w**, and
Jer 5:25 your sins have **w** good things
Ezek 18:16 nor **w** a pledge, nor robbed by
Joel 1:13 the drink offering are **w** from
Amos 4: 7 I also **w** rain from you, when
Amos 4: 7 I **w** rain from another city

WITHHOLD (*see* WITHHELD, WITHHOLDS)
Gen 23: 6 None of us will **w** from you
2Sa 13:13 for he will not **w** me from you
Neh 9:20 did not **w** Your manna from
Job 4: 2 but who can **w** himself from
Ps 40:11 Do not **w** Your tender mercies
Ps 84:11 will He **w** From those who walk
Prov 3:27 Do not **w** good from those to
Prov 23:13 Do not **w** correction from a
Eccl 2:10 I did not **w** my heart from any
Eccl 11: 6 evening do not **w** your hand
Jer 2:25 **W** your foot from being unshod
Hag 1:10 heavens above you **w** the dew
Luke 6:29 do not **w** your tunic either

WITHHOLDS (*see* WITHHOLD)
Job 12:15 If He **w** the waters, they dry
Prov 11:24 there is one who **w** more than
Prov 11:26 will curse him who **w** grain
Hag 1:10 dew, and the earth **w** its fruit

WITHIN (*see* PREFACE)

WITHOUT (*see* PREFACE)

WITHSTAND (*see* WITHSTOOD)
2Ch 13: 7 and could not **w** them
2Ch 13: 8 And now you think to **w** the
2Ch 20: 6 that no one is able to **w** You
Esth 9: 2 And no one could **w** them,
Eccl 4:12 by another, two can **w** him
Jer 49:19 that shepherd who will **w** Me
Jer 50:44 that shepherd who will **w** Me
Lam 1:14 those whom I am not able to **w**

Dan 8: 4 so that no beast could **w** him
Dan 8: 7 no power in the ram to **w** him
Dan 11:15 of the South shall not **w** him
Acts 11:17 who was I that I could **w** God
Eph 6:13 be able to **w** in the evil day

WITHSTOOD (*see* WITHSTAND)
2Ch 26:18 they **w** King Uzziah, and said
Dan 10:13 Persia **w** me twenty-one days
Acts 13: 8 name is translated) **w** them
Gal 2:11 I **w** him to his face, because

WITNESS (*see* EYEWITNESSES, WITNESSED, WITNESSES, WITNESSING)
Gen 21:30 that they may be my **w** that I
Gen 31:44 and let it be a **w** between you
Gen 31:48 This heap is a **w** between you
Gen 31:50 God is **w** between you and me
Gen 31:52 This heap is a **w**
Gen 31:52 and this pillar is a **w**, that
Ex 20:16 false **w** against your neighbor
Ex 23: 1 wicked to be an unrighteous **w**
Lev 5: 1 of an oath, and is a **w**,
Num 5:13 and there was no **w** against her
Num 17: 7 LORD in the tabernacle of **w**
Num 17: 8 went into the tabernacle of **w**
Num 18: 2 before the tabernacle of **w**
Num 35:30 but one **w** is not sufficient
Deut 4:26 earth to **w** against you this
Deut 5:20 false **w** against your neighbor
Deut 17: 6 on the testimony of one **w**
Deut 19:15 One **w** shall not rise against
Deut 19:16 If a false **w** rises against
Deut 19:18 if the **w** is a false **w**,
Deut 31:19 that this song may be a **w** for
Deut 31:21 testify against them as a **w**
Deut 31:26 be there as a **w** against you
Deut 31:28 and earth to **w** against them
Josh 22:27 it may be a **w** between you
Josh 22:28 but it is a **w** between you
Josh 22:34 of Gad called the altar, **W**
Josh 22:34 For it is a **w** between us that
Josh 24:27 this stone shall be a **w** to us
Josh 24:27 shall therefore be a **w** to you
Judg 11:10 LORD will be a **w** between us
1Sa 12: 3 **W** against me before the LORD
1Sa 12: 5 The LORD is **w** against you
1Sa 12: 5 and His anointed is **w** this day
1Sa 12: 5 they answered, "He is **w**."
1Sa 20:12 The LORD God of Israel is **w**
1Ki 21:10 him to bear **w** against him
2Ch 24: 6 for the tabernacle of **w**
Job 16: 8 up, and it is a **w** against me
Job 16: 8 me and bears **w** to my face
Job 16:19 even now my **w** is in heaven
Ps 89:37 the faithful **w** in the sky
Prov 6:19 a false **w** who speaks lies, and
Prov 12:17 righteousness, but a false **w**
Prov 14: 5 A faithful **w** does not lie,
Prov 14: 5 but a false **w** will utter lies
Prov 14:25 A true **w** delivers souls,
Prov 14:25 but a deceitful **w** speaks lies
Prov 19: 5 A false **w** will not go
Prov 19: 9 A false **w** will not go
Prov 19:28 disreputable **w** scorns justice
Prov 21:28 A false **w** shall perish, but
Prov 24:28 Do not be a **w** against your
Prov 25:18 A man who bears false **w**
Is 19:20 for a **w** to the LORD of hosts
Is 55: 4 him as a **w** to the people, a
Jer 29:23 Indeed I know, and am a **w**,
Jer 42: 5 faithful **w** between us, if we
Hos 12:10 through the **w** of the prophets
Mic 1: 2 Lord GOD be a **w** against you
Mal 2:14 LORD has been **w** between you
Mal 3: 5 a swift **w** against sorcerers
Matt 15:19 fornications, thefts, false **w**
Matt 19:18 You shall not bear false **w**
Matt 24:14 as a **w** to all the nations
Mark 10:19 steal,' 'Do not bear false **w**
Mark 14:56 many bore false **w** against Him
Mark 14:57 bore false **w** against Him,
Luke 4:22 So all bore **w** to Him, and
Luke 11:48 you bear **w** that you approve
Luke 18:20 steal,' 'Do not bear false **w**
John 1: 7 This man came for a **w**
John 1: 7 to bear **w** of the Light, that
John 1: 8 sent to bear **w** of that Light
John 1:15 John bore **w** of Him and cried
John 1:32 And John bore **w**, saying, "I
John 3:11 and you do not receive Our **w**
John 3:28 You yourselves bear me **w**,
John 5:31 If I bear **w** of Myself
John 5:31 My **w** is not true
John 5:32 is another who bears **w** of Me
John 5:32 I know that the **w** which He
John 5:33 he has bore **w** to the truth
John 5:36 have a greater **w** than John's
John 5:36 bear **w** of Me, that the Father
John 8:13 Him, "You bear **w** of Yourself
John 8:13 Your **w** is not true
John 8:14 Even if I bear **w** of Myself
John 8:14 My **w** is true, for I know
John 8:18 am One who bears **w** of Myself
John 8:18 who sent Me bears **w** of Me
John 10:25 name, they bear **w** of Me
John 12:17 him from the dead, bore **w**
John 15:27 And you also will bear **w**,
John 18:23 evil, bear **w** of the evil
John 18:37 I should bear **w** to the truth
Acts 1:22 one of these must become a **w**
Acts 4:33 power the apostles gave **w** to
Acts 7:44 of **w** in the wilderness, as He
Acts 10:43 Him all the prophets **w** that
Acts 14: 3 who was bearing **w** to the word
Acts 14:17 not leave Himself without **w**
Acts 22: 5 the high priest bears me **w**
Acts 22:15 For you will be His **w** to all
Acts 23:11 you must also bear **w** at Rome
Acts 26:16 a **w** both of the things which
Rom 1: 9 For God is my **w**, whom I serve
Rom 2:15 conscience also bearing **w**
Rom 8:16 The Spirit Himself bears **w**
Rom 9: 1 me **w** in the Holy Spirit,
Rom 10: 2 For I bear them **w** that they
Rom 13: 9 You shall not bear false **w**
2Co 1:23 call God as **w** against my soul
2Co 8: 3 For I bear **w** that according
Gal 4:15 For I bear you **w** that, if
Phil 1: 8 For God is my **w**, how greatly
Col 4:13 For I bear him **w** that he has
1Th 2: 5 God is **w**
Heb 2: 4 bearing **w** both with signs
Heb 11: 4 **w** that he was righteous, God
Jas 5: 3 will be a **w** against you and
1Pe 5: 1 and a **w** of the sufferings of
1Jn 1: 2 and we have seen, and bear **w**
1Jn 5: 6 it is the Spirit who bears **w**
1Jn 5: 7 three who bear **w** in heaven
1Jn 5: 8 three that bear **w** on earth
1Jn 5: 9 If we receive the **w** of men
1Jn 5: 9 the **w** of God is greater
1Jn 5: 9 for this is the **w** of God
1Jn 5:10 of God has the **w** in himself
3Jn 6 who have borne **w** of your love
3Jn 12 And we also bear **w**, and you
Rev 1: 2 who bore **w** to the word of God
Rev 1: 5 Jesus Christ, the faithful **w**
Rev 3:14 Amen, the Faithful and True **W**
Rev 20: 4 beheaded for their **w** to Jesus

WITNESSED (*see* WITNESS)
Ex 20:18 the people **w** the thunderings
1Ki 21:13 the scoundrels **w** against him
Rom 3:21 being **w** by the Law and the
1Ti 6:13 before Christ Jesus who **w** the
Heb 7: 8 of whom it is **w** that he lives

WITNESSES (*see* WITNESS)
Num 35:30 death on the testimony of **w**
Deut 17: 6 testimony of two or three **w**
Deut 17: 7 The hands of the **w** shall be
Deut 19:15 three **w** the matter shall be
Deut 30:19 earth as **w** today against you,
Josh 24:22 You are **w** against yourselves
Josh 24:22 And they said, "We are **w**."
Ruth 4: 9 You are **w** this day that I
Ruth 4:10 You are **w** this day
Ruth 4:11 elders, said, "We are **w**.
Job 10:17 You renew Your **w** against me
Ps 27:12 For false **w** have risen
Ps 35:11 Fierce **w** rise up
Is 3: 9 countenance **w** against them
Is 8: 2 Myself faithful **w** to record
Is 43: 9 Let them bring out their **w**
Is 43:10 You are My **w**," says the LORD
Is 43:12 therefore you are My **w**,"
Is 44: 8 You are My **w**
Is 44: 9 they are their own **w**
Jer 32:10 the deed and sealed it, took **w**
Jer 32:12 in the presence of the **w** who
Jer 32:25 field for money, and take **w**"
Jer 32:44 deeds and seal them, and take **w**
Matt 18:16 or three **w** every word may be
Matt 23:31 Therefore you are **w** against
Matt 26:60 many false **w** came forward
Matt 26:60 last two false **w** came forward
Matt 26:65 further need do we have of **w**
Mark 14:63 further need do we have of **w**
Luke 24:48 you are **w** of these things
John 5:32 which He **w** of Me is true
Acts 1: 8 and you shall be **w** to Me in
Acts 2:32 up, of which we are all **w**
Acts 3:15 the dead, of which we are **w**
Acts 5:32 we are His **w** to these things,
Acts 6:13 also set up false **w** who said
Acts 7:58 the **w** laid down their clothes
Acts 10:39 we are **w** of all things which
Acts 10:41 but to **w** chosen before by God
Acts 13:31 who are His **w** to the people
1Co 15:15 we are found false **w** of God
2Co 13: 1 three **w** every word shall be
1Th 2:10 You are **w**, and God also, how
1Ti 5:19 except from two or three **w**
1Ti 6:12 in the presence of many **w**
2Ti 2: 2 heard from me among many **w**
Heb 10:15 the Holy Spirit also **w** to us
Heb 10:28 testimony of two or three **w**
Heb 12: 1 by so great a cloud of **w**, let
Rev 11: 3 I will give power to my two **w**

WITNESSING (*see* WITNESS)
Acts 26:22 **w** both to small and great,

WITS'
Ps 107:27 man, And are at their **w** end

WIVES (*see* WIFE, WIVES')
Gen 4:19 Lamech took for himself two **w**
Gen 4:23 Then Lamech said to his **w**
Gen 4:23 O **w** of Lamech, listen to my
Gen 6: 2 they took **w** for themselves of
Gen 6:18 and your sons' **w** with you
Gen 7: 7 his wife, and his sons' **w**
Gen 7:13 the three **w** of his sons with
Gen 8:16 sons and your sons' **w** with you
Gen 8:18 wife and his sons' **w** with him
Gen 11:29 Then Abram and Nahor took **w**
Gen 26:34 old, he took as **w** Judith the
Gen 28: 9 in addition to the **w** he had
Gen 30:26 Give me my **w** and my children
Gen 31:17 his sons and his **w** on camels
Gen 31:50 other **w** besides my daughters
Gen 32:22 that night and took his two **w**
Gen 34:21 their daughters to us as **w**
Gen 34:29 their **w** they took captive
Gen 36: 2 Esau took his **w** from the
Gen 36: 6 Then Esau took his **w**, his
Gen 37: 2 of Zilpah, his father's **w**
Gen 45:19 your little ones and your **w**
Gen 46: 5 their little ones, and their **w**
Gen 46:26 body, besides Jacob's sons' **w**
Ex 19:15 do not come near your **w**
Ex 22:24 your **w** shall be widows, and
Ex 32: 2 are in the ears of your **w**
Num 14: 3 fall by the sword, that our **w**
Num 16:27 of their tents, with their **w**
Num 32:26 Our little ones, our **w**, our
Deut 3:19 But your **w**, your little ones
Deut 17:17 he multiply **w** for himself
Deut 21:15 If a man has two **w**, one loved
Deut 29:11 your little ones and your **w**
Josh 1:14 Your **w**, your little ones, and
Judg 3: 6 their daughters to be their **w**
Judg 8:30 offspring, for he had many **w**
Judg 21: 7 do for **w** for those who remain
Judg 21: 7 give them our daughters as **w**
Judg 21:16 do for **w** for those who remain
Judg 21:18 them **w** from our daughters
Judg 21:23 **w** for their number from those
Ruth 1: 4 Now they took **w** of the women
1Sa 1: 2 And he had two **w**
1Sa 25:43 and so both of them were his **w**
1Sa 27: 3 and David with his two **w**,
1Sa 30: 3 and their **w**, their sons, and
1Sa 30: 5 And David's two **w**, Ahinoam
1Sa 30:18 and David rescued his two **w**
2Sa 2: 2 up there, and his two **w** also
2Sa 5:13 **w** from Jerusalem, after he
2Sa 12: 8 your master's **w** into your
2Sa 12:11 take your **w** before your eyes
2Sa 12:11 he shall lie with your **w** in
2Sa 19: 5 the lives of your **w** and the
1Ki 11: 3 And he had seven hundred **w**

WIVES' (*see* WIVES)

WIZARDS

WOE (*see* WOEFUL, WOES)

WOEFUL (*see* WOE)

WOES (*see* WOE)

WOLF (*see* WOLVES)

WOLVES (*see* WOLF)

WOMAN (*see* WOMAN'S, WOMEN)

Lev 20:27 A man or a w who is a medium
Lev 21: 7 is a harlot or a defiled w
Lev 21: 7 nor shall they take a w
Lev 21:14 A widow or a divorced w or a
Lev 21:14 or a defiled w or a harlot
Lev 24:10 Now the son of an Israelite w
Num 5: 6 When a man or w commits any
Num 5:18 stand the w before the LORD
Num 5:19 under oath, and say to the w
Num 5:21 the priest shall put the w
Num 5:21 and he shall say to the w
Num 5:22 Then the w shall say
Num 5:24 he shall make the w drink the
Num 5:26 make the w drink the water
Num 5:27 the w will become a curse
Num 5:28 But if the w has not defiled
Num 5:30 stand the w before the LORD
Num 5:31 but that w shall bear her
Num 6: 2 When either a man or w
Num 12: 1 w whom he had married
Num 12: 1 he had married an Ethiopian w
Num 25: 6 w in the sight of Moses and in
Num 25: 8 and the w through her body
Num 25:14 killed with the Midianite w
Num 25:15 w who was killed was Cozbi
Num 30: 3 Or if a w vows a vow to the
Num 30: 9 of a widow or a divorced w
Num 31:17 kill every w who has known a
Deut 15:12 a Hebrew man, or a Hebrew w
Deut 17: 2 a man or a w who has been
Deut 17: 5 or w who has committed that
Deut 17: 5 that man or w with stones
Deut 20: 7 there who is betrothed to a w
Deut 21:11 the captives a beautiful w
Deut 22: 5 A w shall not wear anything
Deut 22:14 her, and says, 'I took this w
Deut 22:15 of the young w shall take
Deut 22:19 to the father of the young w
Deut 22:20 are not found for the young w
Deut 22:21 shall bring out the young w
Deut 22:22 with a w married to a husband
Deut 22:22 lay with the w, and the w
Deut 22:23 If a young w who is a virgin
Deut 22:24 the young w because she did
Deut 22:25 young w in the countryside
Deut 22:26 do nothing to the young w
Deut 22:26 there is in the young w no
Deut 22:27 betrothed young w cried out
Deut 22:28 a young w who is a virgin
Deut 28:56 delicate w among you, who
Deut 29:18 man or w or family or tribe
Josh 2: 4 Then the w took the two men
Josh 6:21 in the city, both man and w
Josh 6:22 and from there bring out the w
Judg 4: 9 Sisera into the hand of a w
Judg 9:53 But a certain w dropped an
Judg 9:54 say of me, 'A w killed him
Judg 11: 2 you are the son of another w
Judg 13: 3 of the LORD appeared to the w
Judg 13: 6 So the w came and told her
Judg 13: 9 Angel of God came to the w
Judg 13:10 Then the w ran in haste and
Judg 13:11 the Man who spoke to this w
Judg 13:13 to the w let her be careful
Judg 13:24 So the w bore a son and called
Judg 14: 1 and saw a w in Timnah of the
Judg 14: 2 I have seen a w in Timnah of
Judg 14: 3 Is there no w among the
Judg 14: 7 down and talked with the w
Judg 14:10 his father went down to the w
Judg 16: 4 a w in the Valley of Sorek
Judg 19: 3 father of the young w saw him
Judg 19:26 Then the w came as the day
Judg 20: 4 of the w who was murdered
Judg 21:11 every w who has known a man
Ruth 1: 5 so the w survived her two
Ruth 2: 5 Whose young w is this
Ruth 2: 6 It is the young Moabite w who
Ruth 3: 8 a w was lying at his feet
Ruth 3:11 that you are a virtuous w
Ruth 3:14 let it be known that the w
Ruth 4:11 The LORD make the w who is
Ruth 4:12 give you from this young w
1Sa 1:15 I am a w of sorrowful spirit
1Sa 1:16 your maidservant a wicked w
1Sa 1:18 So the w went her way and
1Sa 1:23 So the w stayed and nursed
1Sa 1:26 I am the w who stood by you
1Sa 2:20 you descendants from this w
1Sa 15: 3 But kill both man and w,
1Sa 20:30 of a perverse, rebellious w
1Sa 25: 3 And she was a w of good
1Sa 27: 9 left neither man nor w alive
1Sa 27:11 save neither man nor w alive
1Sa 28: 7 Find me a w who is a medium,
1Sa 28: 7 there is a w who is a medium
1Sa 28: 8 they came to the w by night
1Sa 28: 9 Then the w said to him
1Sa 28:11 Then the w said, "Whom shall
1Sa 28:12 When the w saw Samuel, she
1Sa 28:12 the w spoke to Saul, saying,
1Sa 28:13 And the w said to Saul,
1Sa 28:21 the w came to Saul and saw
1Sa 28:23 servants, together with the w
1Sa 28:24 Now the w had a fatted calf
2Sa 3: 8 a fault concerning this w
2Sa 11: 2 the roof he saw a w bathing
2Sa 11: 2 the w was very beautiful to
2Sa 11: 3 sent and inquired about the w
2Sa 11: 5 And the w conceived
2Sa 11:21 Was it not a w who cast a
2Sa 13:17 Put this w out, away from me,
2Sa 14: 2 brought from there a wise w
2Sa 14: 2 but act like a w who has been
2Sa 14: 4 when the w of Tekoa spoke to
2Sa 14: 8 Then the king said to the w
2Sa 14: 9 the w of Tekoa said to the
2Sa 14:12 Then the w said, "Please,
2Sa 14:13 And the w said: "Why then
2Sa 14:18 answered and said to the w
2Sa 14:18 And the w said, "Please, let
2Sa 14:19 And the w answered and said,
2Sa 14:27 She was a w of beautiful
2Sa 17:19 Then the w took and spread a
2Sa 17:20 came to the w at the house
2Sa 17:20 So the w said to them,
2Sa 20:16 Then a wise w cried out from
2Sa 20:17 come near to her, the w said,
2Sa 20:21 And the w said to Joab,
2Sa 20:22 Then the w in her wisdom went
1Ki 1: 2 Let a young w, a virgin, be
1Ki 1: 3 young w throughout all the
1Ki 1: 4 the young w was very lovely
1Ki 3:17 And one w said,
1Ki 3:17 O my lord, this w and I dwell
1Ki 3:18 that this w also gave birth
1Ki 3:22 Then the other w said, No
1Ki 3:22 And the first w said, No
1Ki 3:26 Then the w whose son was
1Ki 3:27 Give the first w the living
1Ki 14: 5 will pretend to be another w
1Ki 17:17 w who owned the house became
1Ki 17:24 Then the w said to Elijah,
2Ki 4: 1 A certain w of the wives of
2Ki 4: 8 where there was a notable w
2Ki 4:12 Call this Shunammite w
2Ki 4:17 the w conceived, and bore a
2Ki 4:25 there is the Shunammite w
2Ki 4:36 Call this Shunammite w
2Ki 6:26 a w cried out to him, saying,
2Ki 6:28 This w said to me, 'Give your
2Ki 6:30 king heard the words of the w
2Ki 8: 1 Then Elisha spoke to the w
2Ki 8: 2 So the w arose and did
2Ki 8: 3 that the w returned from the
2Ki 8: 5 that there was the w whose
2Ki 8: 5 lord, O king, this is the w
2Ki 8: 6 And when the king asked the w
2Ki 9:34 now, see to this accursed w
1Ch 16: 3 of Israel, both man and w, to
2Ch 2:14 (the son of a w of the
2Ch 15:13 or great, whether man or w
2Ch 24: 7 of Athaliah, that wicked w
Esth 2: 4 Then let the young w who
Esth 2: 7 The young w was lovely and
Esth 2: 9 Now the young w pleased him
Esth 2:13 each young w went to the king
Esth 4:11 know that any man or w who
Job 14: 1 is born of w is of few days
Job 15:14 And he who is born of a w,
Job 25: 4 he be pure who is born of a w
Job 31: 1 should I look upon a young w
Job 31: 9 heart has been enticed by a w
Ps 48: 6 pain, as of a w in travail,
Ps 58: 8 Like a stillborn child of a w
Ps 113: 9 He grants the barren w a home
Prov 2:16 you from the immoral w, from
Prov 5: 3 of an immoral w drip honey
Prov 5:20 be enraptured by an immoral w
Prov 6:24 to keep you from the evil w
Prov 6:32 with a w lacks understanding
Prov 7: 5 keep you from the immoral w
Prov 7:10 And there a w met him, with
Prov 9:13 A foolish w is clamorous
Prov 11:16 A gracious w retains honor,
Prov 11:22 so is a lovely w who lacks
Prov 14: 1 Every wise w builds her house
Prov 21: 9 shared with a contentious w
Prov 21:19 with a contentious and angry w
Prov 22:14 of an immoral w is a deep pit
Prov 25:24 shared with a contentious w
Prov 27:15 and a contentious w are alike
Prov 30:20 is the way of an adulterous w
Prov 30:23 a hateful w when she is
Prov 31:30 but a w who fears the LORD,
Eccl 7:26 the w whose heart is snares
Eccl 7:28 but a w among all these I
Is 13: 8 in pain as a w in childbirth
Is 21: 3 the pangs of a w in labor
Is 26:17 As a w with child is in pain
Is 42:14 I will cry like a w in labor
Is 45:10 Or to the w, 'What have you
Is 49:15 Can a w forget her nursing
Is 54: 1 the children of the married w
Is 54: 6 called you like a w forsaken
Jer 4:31 a voice as of a w in labor
Jer 6: 2 to a lovely and delicate w
Jer 6:24 us, pain as of a w in labor
Jer 13:21 seize you, like a w in labor
Jer 22:23 like the pain of a w in labor
Jer 30: 6 his loins like a w in labor
Jer 31: 8 the w with child and the one
Jer 31:22 a w shall encompass a man
Jer 34: 9 a Hebrew man or w
Jer 44: 7 to cut off from you man and w
Jer 48:41 heart of a w in birth pangs
Jer 49:22 heart of a w in birth pangs
Jer 49:24 taken her like a w in labor
Jer 50:43 pangs as of a w in childbirth
Jer 51:22 will break in pieces man and w
Ezek 18: 6 nor approached a w during her
Ezek 23:44 as men go in to a w who plays
Ezek 36:17 a w in her customary impurity
Ezek 44:22 wife a widow or a divorced w
Hos 3: 1 love a w who is loved by a
Hos 13:13 The sorrows of a w in
Mic 4: 9 seized you like a w in labor
Mic 4:10 Zion, like a w in birth pangs
Zech 5: 7 this is a w sitting inside
Matt 5:28 w to lust for her has already
Matt 5:32 whoever marries a w who is
Matt 9:20 a w who had a flow of blood
Matt 9:22 the w was made well from that
Matt 13:33 like leaven, which a w took
Matt 15:22 a w of Canaan came from that
Matt 15:28 O w, great is your faith
Matt 22:27 last of all the w died also
Matt 26: 7 a w came to Him having an
Matt 26:10 Why do you trouble the w
Matt 26:13 what this w has done will
Mark 5:25 Now a certain w had a flow of
Mark 5:33 But the w, fearing and
Mark 7:25 For a w whose young daughter
Mark 7:26 The w was a Greek, a
Mark 10:12 if a w divorces her husband
Mark 12:22 Last of all the w died also
Mark 14: 3 a w came having an alabaster
Mark 14: 9 what this w did will also be
Luke 2:37 this w was a widow of about
Luke 4:26 Sidon, to a w who was a widow
Luke 7:37 a w in the city who was a
Luke 7:39 what manner of w this is who
Luke 7:44 Then He turned to the w and
Luke 7:44 Do you see this w
Luke 7:45 but this w has not ceased to
Luke 7:46 but this w has anointed My
Luke 7:50 Then He said to the w, "Your
Luke 8:43 Now a w, having a flow of
Luke 8:47 Now when the w saw that she
Luke 10:38 and a certain w named Martha
Luke 11:27 that a certain w from the
Luke 13:11 there was a w who had a
Luke 13:12 W, you are loosed from your
Luke 13:16 So ought not this w, being a
Luke 13:21 like leaven, which a w took
Luke 15: 8 Or what w, having ten silver
Luke 20:32 Last of all the w died also
Luke 22:57 W, I do not know Him
John 2: 4 W, what does your concern
John 4: 7 A w of Samaria came to draw

John 4: 9 Then the w of Samaria said to
John 4: 9 drink from me, a Samaritan w
John 4:11 The w said to Him, "Sir, You
John 4:15 The w said to Him, "Sir,
John 4:17 The w answered and said, "I
John 4:19 The w said to Him, "Sir, I
John 4:21 W, believe Me, the hour is
John 4:25 The w said to Him, "I know
John 4:27 that He talked with a w
John 4:28 The w then left her waterpot,
John 4:39 word of the w who testified
John 4:42 Then they said to the w
John 8: 3 to Him a w caught in adultery
John 8: 4 this w was caught in adultery
John 8: 9 the w standing in the midst
John 8:10 up and saw no one but the w
John 8:10 W, where are those accusers
John 16:21 A w, when she is in labor,
John 19:26 W, behold your son
John 20:13 W, why are you weeping
John 20:15 W, why are you weeping
Acts 9:36 This w was full of good works
Acts 16: 1 certain Jewish w who believed
Acts 16:14 Now a certain w named Lydia
Acts 17:34 a w named Damaris, and others
Rom 1:27 the natural use of the w,
Rom 7: 2 For the w who has a husband
1Co 7: 1 for a man not to touch a w
1Co 7: 2 and let each w have her own
1Co 7:13 a w who has a husband who
1Co 7:34 The unmarried w cares about
1Co 11: 3 Christ, the head of w is man
1Co 11: 5 But every w who prays or
1Co 11: 6 For if a w is not covered,
1Co 11: 6 for a w to be shorn or shaved
1Co 11: 7 but w is the glory of man
1Co 11: 8 For man is not from w
1Co 11: 8 but w from man
1Co 11: 9 Nor was man created for the w
1Co 11: 9 but w for the man
1Co 11:10 For this reason the w ought
1Co 11:11 is man independent of w, nor
1Co 11:11 nor w independent of man, in
1Co 11:12 For as the w was from the man
1Co 11:12 the man also is through the w
1Co 11:13 Is it proper for a w to pray
1Co 11:15 But if a w has long hair, it
Gal 4: 4 forth His Son, born of a w
1Th 5: 3 labor pains upon a pregnant w
1Ti 2:11 Let a w learn in silence with
1Ti 2:12 I do not permit a w to teach
1Ti 2:14 but the w being deceived,
1Ti 5:16 believing man or w has widows
Rev 2:20 you allow that w Jezebel, who
Rev 12: 1 a w clothed with the sun,
Rev 12: 4 w who was ready to give birth
Rev 12: 6 Then the w fled into the
Rev 12:13 he persecuted the w who gave
Rev 12:14 But the w was given two wings
Rev 12:15 like a flood after the w,
Rev 12:16 But the earth helped the w
Rev 12:17 dragon was enraged with the w
Rev 17: 3 And I saw a w sitting on a
Rev 17: 4 The w was arrayed in purple
Rev 17: 6 And I saw the w, drunk with
Rev 17: 7 tell you the mystery of the w
Rev 17: 9 mountains on which the w sits
Rev 17:18 the w whom you saw is that

WOMAN'S (*see* WOMAN)
Gen 38:20 his pledge from the w hand
Ex 21:22 the w husband imposes on him
Lev 24:10 and this Israelite w son and a
Lev 24:11 And the Israelite w son
Num 5:18 the LORD, uncover the w head
Num 5:25 of jealousy from the w hand
Deut 22: 5 a man put on a w garment, for
Deut 22:15 the evidence of the young w
Deut 22:16 the young w father shall say
Deut 22:29 w father fifty shekels of
Judg 19: 4 the young w father, detained
Judg 19: 5 but the young w father said
Judg 19: 6 Then the young w father said
Judg 19: 8 but the young w father said
Judg 19: 9 the young w father, said to
1Ki 3:19 this w son died in the night,
Esth 2:12 Each young w turn came to go

WOMB (*see* WOMBS)
Gen 25:23 Two nations are in your w
Gen 25:24 there were twins in her w
Gen 29:31 was unloved, He opened her w
Gen 30: 2 from you the fruit of the w
Gen 30:22 to her and opened her w
Gen 38:27 behold, twins were in her w
Gen 49:25 of the breasts and of the w
Ex 13: 2 whatever opens the w among
Ex 13:12 the LORD all that open the w
Ex 13:15 all males that open the w
Ex 34:19 All that open the w are Mine
Num 3:12 the w among the children of
Num 8:16 instead of all who open the w
Num 12:12 comes out of his mother's w
Num 18:15 opens the w of all flesh,
Deut 7:13 bless the fruit of your w
Judg 13: 5 a Nazirite to God from the w
Judg 13: 7 the w to the day of his death
Judg 16:17 to God from my mother's w
Ruth 1:11 Are there still sons in my w
1Sa 1: 5 the LORD had closed her w
1Sa 1: 6 the LORD had closed her w
Job 1:21 I came from my mother's w
Job 3:10 up the doors of my mother's w
Job 3:11 perish when I came from the w
Job 10:18 You brought me out of the w
Job 10:19 from the w to the grave
Job 15:35 their w prepares deceit
Job 24:20 The w should forget him, the
Job 31:15 made me in the w make them
Job 31:15 same One fashion us in the w
Job 31:18 from my mother's w I guided
Job 38: 8 forth and issued from the w
Job 38:29 From whose w comes the ice
Ps 22: 9 He who took Me out of the w
Ps 22:10 From My mother's w You have
Ps 58: 3 are estranged from the w
Ps 71: 6 took me out of my mother's w
Ps 110: 3 from the w of the morning,
Ps 127: 3 fruit of the w is His reward
Ps 139:13 covered me in my mother's w
Prov 30:16 The grave, the barren w, the
Prov 31: 2 And what, son of my w
Eccl 5:15 he came from his mother's w
Eccl 11: 5 w of her who is with child
Is 13:18 no pity on the fruit of the w
Is 44: 2 you and formed you from the w
Is 44:24 He who formed you from the w
Is 46: 3 have been carried from the w
Is 48: 8 a transgressor from the w
Is 49: 1 LORD has called Me from the w
Is 49: 5 from the w to be His Servant
Is 49:15 on the son of her w
Is 66: 9 cause delivery shut up the w
Jer 1: 5 you in the w I knew you
Jer 20:17 he did not kill me from the w
Jer 20:17 her w always enlarged with me
Jer 20:18 forth from the w to see labor
Hos 9:14 Give them a miscarrying w
Hos 9:16 the beloved fruit of their w
Hos 12: 3 brother by the heel in the w
Matt 19:12 thus from their mother's w
Luke 1:15 even from his mother's w
Luke 1:31 you will conceive in your w
Luke 1:41 that the babe leaped in her w
Luke 1:42 is the fruit of your w
Luke 1:44 babe leaped in my w for joy
Luke 2:21 He was conceived in the w
Luke 2:23 Every male who opens the w
Luke 11:27 is the w that bore You, and
John 3: 4 time into his mother's w and
Acts 3: 2 his mother's w was carried
Acts 14: 8 a cripple from his mother's w
Rom 4:19 and the deadness of Sarah's w
Gal 1:15 me from my mother's w and

WOMBS (*see* WOMB)
Gen 20:18 w of the house of Abimelech
Luke 23:29 the w that never bore, and the

WOMEN (*see* WOMAN, WOMEN'S)
Gen 14:16 his goods, as well as the w
Gen 24:11 the time when w go out to
Gen 31:35 the manner of w is with me
Gen 33: 5 lifted his eyes and saw the w
Ex 1:16 of a midwife for the Hebrew w
Ex 1:19 Because the Hebrew w are not
Ex 1:19 are not like the Egyptian w
Ex 2: 7 for you from the Hebrew w
Ex 15:20 all the w went out after her
Ex 35:22 They came, both men and w, as
Ex 35:25 All the w who were gifted
Ex 35:26 all the w whose heart stirred
Ex 35:29 w whose hearts were willing
Ex 38: 8 mirrors of the serving w who
Lev 26:26 ten w shall bake your bread
Num 25: 1 harlotry with the w of Moab
Num 31: 9 all the w of Midian captive
Num 31:15 Have you kept all the w alive
Num 31:16 these w caused the children
Num 31:35 of w who had not known a man
Deut 2:34 utterly destroyed the men, w
Deut 3: 6 utterly destroying the men, w
Deut 20:14 But the w, the little ones,
Deut 31:12 the people together, men and w
Josh 8:25 fell that day, both men and w
Josh 8:35 of Israel, with the w, the
Judg 5:24 Most blessed among w is Jael
Judg 5:24 is she among w in tents
Judg 9:49 about a thousand men and w
Judg 9:51 the city, and all the men and w
Judg 16:27 temple was full of men and w
Judg 16:27 w on the roof who watched
Judg 21:10 of the sword, including the w
Judg 21:14 they gave them the w whom
Judg 21:14 of the w of Jabesh Gilead
Judg 21:16 since the w of Benjamin have
Judg 21:22 young w to them at this time
Ruth 1: 4 took wives of the w of Moab
Ruth 1:19 and the w said,
Ruth 2: 8 but stay close by my young w
Ruth 2:22 you go out with his young w
Ruth 2:23 close by the young w of Boaz
Ruth 3: 2 whose young w you were with,
Ruth 4:14 Then the w said to Naomi,
Ruth 4:17 neighbor w gave him a name
1Sa 2:22 how they lay with the w who
1Sa 4:20 w who stood by her said to
1Sa 9:11 they met some young w going
1Sa 15:33 sword has made w childless
1Sa 15:33 mother be childless among w
1Sa 18: 6 that the w had come out of
1Sa 18: 7 So the w sang as they danced,
1Sa 21: 4 least kept themselves from w
1Sa 21: 5 w have been kept from us
1Sa 22:19 of the sword, both men and w
1Sa 30: 2 and had taken captive the w
2Sa 1:26 surpassing the love of w
2Sa 6:19 of Israel, both the w and the
2Sa 15:16 But the king left ten w,
2Sa 19:35 of singing men and singing w
2Sa 20: 3 And the king took the ten w
1Ki 3:16 Then two w who were harlots
1Ki 11: 1 Solomon loved many foreign w
1Ki 11: 1 w of the Moabites, Ammonites,
2Ki 8:12 rip open their w with child
2Ki 15:16 all the w there who were with
2Ki 23: 7 where the w wove hangings for
2Ch 28: 8 two hundred thousand w, sons,
2Ch 35:25 the singing w speak of Josiah
Ezra 2:65 two hundred men and w singers
Ezra 10: 1 large congregation of men, w
Neh 7:67 forty-five men and w singers
Neh 8: 2 the congregation, of men and w
Neh 8: 3 midday, before the men and w
Neh 12:43 the w and the children also
Neh 13:23 who had married w of Ashdod
Neh 13:26 Nevertheless pagan w caused
Neh 13:27 our God by marrying pagan w
Esth 1: 9 w in the royal palace which
Esth 1:17 will become known to all w
Esth 2: 3 eunuch, custodian of the w
Esth 2: 8 and when many young w were
Esth 2: 8 Hegai the custodian of the w
Esth 2: 9 place in the house of the w
Esth 2:12 to the regulations for the w
Esth 2:12 for beautifying w
Esth 2:14 to the second house of the w
Esth 2:15 the custodian of the w,
Esth 2:17 more than all the other w
Esth 3:13 and old, little children and w
Esth 8:11 both little children and w
Job 2:10 one of the foolish w speaks
Job 42:15 no w so beautiful as the
Ps 45: 9 are among Your honorable w
Prov 31: 3 not give your strength to w
Song 1: 8 not know, O fairest among w
Song 5: 9 beloved, O fairest among w
Song 6: 1 gone, O fairest among w
Is 3:12 and w rule over them

Is 4: 1 in that day seven w shall
Is 19:16 that day Egypt will be like w
Is 27:11 the w come and set them on
Is 32: 9 you w who are at ease, hear
Is 32:10 be troubled, you complacent w
Is 32:11 you w who are at ease
Jer 2:33 taught the wicked w your ways
Jer 7:18 the w knead their dough, to
Jer 9:17 and call for the mourning w
Jer 9:17 send for skillful wailing w
Jer 9:20 the word of the LORD, O w
Jer 38:22 all the w who are left in the
Jer 38:22 princes, and those w shall say
Jer 40: 7 had committed to him men, w
Jer 41:16 mighty men of war and the w
Jer 43: 6 men, w, children, the king's
Jer 44:15 with all the w who stood by
Jer 44:19 The w also said, "And when we
Jer 44:20 the men, the w, and all the
Jer 44:24 the people and to all the w
Jer 50:37 and they will become like w
Jer 51:30 failed, they became like w
Lam 2:20 Should the w eat their
Lam 4:10 w have cooked their own
Lam 5:11 They ravished the w in Zion
Ezek 8:14 w were sitting there weeping
Ezek 9: 6 and little children and w
Ezek 13:18 Woe to the w who sew magic
Ezek 16:34 of other w in your harlotry
Ezek 16:38 I will judge you as w who
Ezek 16:41 on you in the sight of many w
Ezek 22:10 in you they violate w who are
Ezek 23: 2 Son of man, there were two w
Ezek 23:10 She became a byword among w
Ezek 23:44 and Oholibah, the lewd w
Ezek 23:45 manner of w who shed blood
Ezek 23:48 that all w may be taught not
Dan 11:17 daughter of w to destroy it
Dan 11:37 fathers nor the desire of w
Hos 13:16 their w with child ripped
Amos 1:13 the w with child in Gilead
Mic 2: 9 The w of My people you cast
Nah 3:13 people in your midst are w
Zech 5: 9 looked, and there were two w
Zech 8: 4 old w shall again sit in the
Zech 9:17 and new wine the young w
Zech 14: 2 rifled, and the w ravished
Matt 11:11 among those born of w there
Matt 14:21 five thousand men, besides w
Matt 15:38 four thousand men, besides w
Matt 24:41 Two w will be grinding at the
Matt 27:55 many w who followed Jesus
Matt 28: 5 answered and said to the w
Mark 15:40 There were also w looking on
Mark 15:41 many other w who came up with
Luke 1:28 blessed are you among w
Luke 1:42 Blessed are you among w, and
Luke 7:28 among those born of w there
Luke 8: 2 certain w who had been healed
Luke 17:35 Two w will be grinding
Luke 23:27 Him, and w who also mourned
Luke 23:49 the w who followed Him from
Luke 23:55 the w who had come with Him
Luke 24: 1 and certain other w with them
Luke 24:10 and the other w with them
Luke 24:22 certain w of our company, who
Luke 24:24 it just as the w had said
John 11:19 joined the w around Martha
Acts 1:14 and supplication, with the w
Acts 5:14 multitudes of both men and w
Acts 8: 3 and dragging off men and w
Acts 8:12 both men and w were baptized
Acts 9: 2 of the Way, whether men or w
Acts 13:50 up the devout and prominent w
Acts 16:13 spoke to the w who met there
Acts 17: 4 and not a few of the leading w
Acts 17:12 prominent w as well as men
Acts 22: 4 into prisons both men and w
Rom 1:26 For even their w exchanged
1Co 14:34 Let your w keep silent in the
1Co 14:35 for w to speak in church
Phil 4: 3 help these w who labored with
1Ti 2: 9 that the w adorn themselves
1Ti 2:10 but, which is proper for w
1Ti 5: 2 the older w as mothers, the
2Ti 3: 6 w loaded down with sins, led
Tit 2: 3 the older w likewise, that
Tit 2: 4 w to love their husbands, to
Heb 11:35 W received their dead raised
1Pe 3: 5 the holy w who trusted in God
Rev 14: 4 who were not defiled with w

WOMEN'S (*see* WOMEN)
Esth 2: 3 citadel, into the w quarters
Esth 2:11 the court of the w quarters
Esth 2:13 the w quarters to the king's
Rev 9: 8 They had hair like w hair

WON (*see* WIN)
2Sa 23:18 w a name among these three
2Sa 23:22 w a name among three mighty
1Ch 11:20 w a name among these three
1Ch 11:24 w a name among three mighty
1Ch 26:27 Some of the spoils w in
Matt 23:15 proselyte, and when he is w
1Pe 3: 1 may be w by the conduct of

WONDER (*see* WONDERED, WONDERFUL, WONDERING, WONDERS, WONDROUS)
Deut 13: 1 and he gives you a sign or a w
Deut 13: 2 the sign or the w of which he
Deut 28:46 be upon you for a sign and a w
2Ch 32:31 w that was done in the land
Ps 71: 7 I have become as a w to many
Is 20: 3 a w against Egypt and Ethiopia
Is 29: 9 Pause and w! Blind yourselves
Is 29:14 a marvelous work and a w
Jer 4: 9 and the prophets shall w
Acts 3:10 and they were filled with w
2Co 11:14 And no w! For Satan himself

WONDERED (*see* WONDER)
Is 59:16 man, and w that there was no
Is 63: 5 I w that there was no one to
Acts 5:24 they w what the outcome would
Acts 10:17 Now while Peter w within

WONDERFUL (*see* WONDER, WONDERFULLY)
Judg 13:18 ask My name, seeing it is w
2Sa 1:26 Your love to me was w,
2Ch 2: 9 to build shall be great and w
Job 42: 3 things too w for me, which I
Ps 40: 5 are Your w works Which You
Ps 78: 4 His w works that He has done
Ps 107: 8 And for His w works to the
Ps 107:15 And for His w works to the
Ps 107:21 And for His w works to the
Ps 107:31 And for His w works to the
Ps 111: 4 He has made His w works to be
Ps 119:129 Your testimonies are w
Ps 139: 6 knowledge is too w for me
Prov 30:18 things which are too w for me
Is 9: 6 And His name will be called W
Is 25: 1 for You have done w things
Is 28:29 hosts, Who is w in counsel and
Jer 21: 2 according to all His w works
Matt 21:15 scribes saw the w things that
Acts 2:11 tongues the w works of God

WONDERFULLY (*see* WONDERFUL)
Ps 139:14 for I am fearfully and w made

WONDERING (*see* WONDER)
Gen 24:21 w at her, remained silent so

WONDERS (*see* WONDER)
Ex 3:20 My w which I will do in its
Ex 4:21 see that you do all those w
Ex 7: 3 My w in the land of Egypt
Ex 11: 9 heed you, so that My w may be
Ex 11:10 all these w before Pharaoh
Ex 15:11 fearful in praises, doing w
Deut 4:34 by trials, by signs, by w
Deut 6:22 w before our eyes, great and
Deut 7:19 eyes saw, the signs and the w
Deut 26: 8 terror and with signs and w
Deut 29: 3 the signs, and those great w
Deut 34:11 w which the LORD sent him to
Josh 3: 5 the LORD will do w among you
1Ch 16:12 which He has done, His w and
1Ch 16:24 His w among all peoples
Neh 9:10 w against Pharaoh, against
Neh 9:17 w that You did among them
Job 9:10 out, yes, w without number
Ps 77:11 I will remember Your w of old
Ps 77:14 You are the God who does w
Ps 78:11 His w that He had shown them
Ps 78:43 His w in the field of Zoan
Ps 88:10 Will You work w for the dead
Ps 88:12 Shall Your w be known in the
Ps 89: 5 heavens will praise Your w
Ps 96: 3 His w among all peoples
Ps 105: 5 which He has done, His w, and
Ps 105:27 them, And w in the land of Ham
Ps 106: 7 did not understand Your w
Ps 107:24 LORD, And His w in the deep
Ps 135: 9 w into the midst of you, O
Ps 136: 4 To Him who alone does great w
Is 8:18 w in Israel From the LORD of
Jer 32:20 w in the land of Egypt, to
Jer 32:21 land of Egypt with signs and w
Dan 4: 2 w that the Most High God has
Dan 4: 3 signs, and how mighty His w
Dan 6:27 w in heaven and on earth, Who
Dan 12: 6 the fulfillment of these w be
Joel 2:30 I will show w in the heavens
Matt 7:22 and done many w in Your name
Matt 24:24 and show great signs and w, so
Mark 13:22 w to deceive, if possible,
John 4:48 you people see signs and w
Acts 2:19 I will show w in heaven above
Acts 2:22 by God to you by miracles, w
Acts 2:43 upon every soul, and many w
Acts 4:30 w may be done through the
Acts 5:12 w were done among the people
Acts 6: 8 faith and power, did great w
Acts 7:36 out, after he had shown w
Acts 14: 3 w to be done by their hands
Acts 15:12 w God had worked through
Rom 15:19 in mighty signs and w, by the
2Co 12:12 perseverance, in signs and w
2Th 2: 9 all power, signs, and lying w
Heb 2: 4 witness both with signs and w

WONDROUS (*see* WONDER, WONDROUSLY)
Judg 13:19 He did a w thing while Manoah
1Ch 16: 9 talk of all His w works
Job 37:14 consider the w works of God
Job 37:16 those w works of Him who is
Ps 26: 7 And tell of all Your w works
Ps 71:17 day I declare Your w works
Ps 72:18 Who only does w things
Ps 75: 1 For Your w works declare that
Ps 78:32 not believe in His w works
Ps 86:10 You are great, and do w things
Ps 105: 2 Talk of all His w works
Ps 106:22 W works in the land of Ham,
Ps 119:18 that I may see W things from
Ps 119:27 I meditate on Your w works
Ps 145: 5 majesty, And on Your w works
Zech 3: 8 you, for they are a w sign

WONDROUSLY (*see* WONDROUS)
Joel 2:26 God, who has dealt w with you

WOOD (*see* WOODCUTTERS, WOODEN, WOODPILE, WOODS)
Gen 22: 3 he split the w for the burnt
Gen 22: 6 So Abraham took the w of the
Gen 22: 7 Look, the fire and the w, but
Gen 22: 9 and placed the w in order
Gen 22: 9 him on the altar, upon the w
Ex 7:19 Egypt, both in vessels of w
Ex 25: 5 badger skins, and acacia w
Ex 25:10 shall make an ark of acacia w
Ex 25:13 shall make poles of acacia w
Ex 25:23 also make a table of acacia w
Ex 25:28 make the poles of acacia w
Ex 26:15 make the boards of acacia w
Ex 26:26 shall make bars of acacia w
Ex 26:32 acacia w overlaid with gold
Ex 26:37 five pillars of acacia w, and
Ex 27: 1 make an altar of acacia w
Ex 27: 6 the altar, poles of acacia w
Ex 30: 1 you shall make it of acacia w
Ex 30: 5 make the poles of acacia w
Ex 31: 5 for setting, in carving w
Ex 35: 7 badger skins, and acacia w
Ex 35:24 with whom was found acacia w
Ex 35:33 for setting, in carving w
Ex 36:20 he made boards of acacia w
Ex 36:31 And he made bars of acacia w
Ex 36:36 it four pillars of acacia w
Ex 37: 1 made the ark of acacia w
Ex 37: 4 He made poles of acacia w
Ex 37:10 He made the table of acacia w
Ex 37:15 of acacia w to bear the table
Ex 37:25 the incense altar of acacia w
Ex 37:28 he made the poles of acacia w
Ex 38: 1 of burnt offering of acacia w
Ex 38: 6 he made the poles of acacia w
Lev 1: 7 lay the w in order on the
Lev 1: 8 the fat in order on the w
Lev 1:12 w that is on the fire upon
Lev 1:17 on the w that is on the fire
Lev 3: 5 which is on the w that is on

Lev 4:12 and burn it on w with fire
Lev 6:12 burn w on it every morning
Lev 11:32 whether it is any item of w
Lev 14: 4 and clean birds, cedar w,
Lev 14: 6 he shall take it, the cedar w
Lev 14:49 the house, two birds, cedar w
Lev 14:51 and he shall take the cedar w
Lev 14:52 living bird, with the cedar w
Lev 15:12 every vessel of w shall be
Num 19: 6 the priest shall take cedar w
Num 31:20 hair, and everything made of w
Deut 4:28 the work of men's hands, w
Deut 10: 1 and make yourself an ark of w
Deut 10: 3 So I made an ark of acacia w
Deut 28:36 other gods—w and stone
Deut 28:64 have known—w and stone
Deut 29:11 w to the one who draws your
Deut 29:17 w and stone and silver and gold)
Judg 6:26 the w of the image which you
1Sa 6:14 they split the w of the cart
2Sa 6: 5 of instruments made of fir w
2Sa 24:22 the yokes of the oxen for w
1Ki 6:15 them on the inside with w
1Ki 6:23 made two cherubim of olive w
1Ki 6:31 he made doors of olive w
1Ki 6:32 The two doors were of olive w
1Ki 6:33 made doorposts of olive w
1Ki 6:34 two doors were of cypress w
1Ki 7:11 hewn to size, and cedar w
1Ki 10:11 great quantities of almug w
1Ki 10:12 made steps of the almug w for
1Ki 10:12 never again came such almug w
1Ki 18:23 in pieces, and lay it on the w
1Ki 18:23 bull, and lay it on the w, but
1Ki 18:33 And he put the w in order, cut
1Ki 18:33 pieces, and laid it on the w
1Ki 18:33 burnt sacrifice and on the w
1Ki 18:38 the burnt sacrifice, and the w
2Ki 19:18 men's hands—w and stone
1Ch 21:23 threshing implements for w
1Ch 22: 4 brought much cedar w to David
1Ch 29: 2 w for things of w, onyx
1Ch 29: 2 of iron, w for things of w
2Ch 2:14 bronze and iron, stone and w
2Ch 2:16 we will cut w from Lebanon,
2Ch 9:10 from Ophir, brought algum w
2Ch 9:11 w for the house of the LORD
Neh 8: 4 stood on a platform of w
Neh 10:34 for bringing the w offering
Neh 13:31 and to bringing the w offering
Job 41:27 straw, and bronze as rotten w
Prov 26:20 Where there is no w, the fire
Prov 26:21 coals, and w to fire, so is a
Eccl 10: 9 and he who splits w may be
Song 3: 9 Of the w of Lebanon Solomon
Is 10:15 lift up, as if it were not w
Is 30:33 its pyre is fire with much w
Is 37:19 men's hands—w and stone
Is 44:19 fall down before a block of w
Is 45:20 who carry the w of their
Is 60:17 bring silver, instead of w
Jer 5:14 mouth fire, and this people w
Jer 7:18 The children gather w, the
Jer 28:13 have broken the yokes of w
Jer 46:22 axes, like those who chop w
Lam 4: 8 it has become as dry as w
Lam 5: 4 and our w comes at a price
Lam 5:13 staggered under loads of w
Ezek 15: 2 man, how is the w of the vine
Ezek 15: 2 vine better than any other w
Ezek 15: 3 Is w taken from it to make
Ezek 15: 6 Like the w of the vine among
Ezek 20:32 in other countries, serving w
Ezek 21:10 of My son, As it does all w
Ezek 24:10 Heap on the w, kindle the
Ezek 39:10 They will not take w from the
Ezek 41:16 with w from the ground to the
Ezek 41:22 The altar was of w, three
Ezek 41:22 and its sides were of w
Dan 5: 4 and silver, bronze and iron, w
Dan 5:23 and gold, bronze and iron, w
Hab 2:19 Woe to him who says to w
Hag 1: 8 to the mountains and bring w
Luke 23:31 these things in the green w
1Co 3:12 silver, precious stones, w,
2Ti 2:20 gold and silver, but also of w
Rev 9:20 silver, brass, stone, and w
Rev 18:12 every kind of citron w,
Rev 18:12 of object of most precious w

WOODCUTTERS (*see* CUT, WOOD)
Josh 9:21 them live, but let them be w
Josh 9:23 w and water carriers for the
Josh 9:27 that day Joshua made them w

WOODED (*see* WOODS)
Josh 17:18 Although it is w, you shall

WOODEN (*see* WOOD)
Ex 34:13 and cut down their w images
Num 35:18 him with a w hand weapon, by
Deut 7: 5 and cut down their w images
Deut 12: 3 burn their w images with fire
Deut 16:21 as a w image, near the altar
Judg 6:25 cut down the w image that is
Judg 6:28 the w image that was beside
Judg 6:30 w image that was beside it
1Ki 14:15 they have made their w images
1Ki 14:23 w images on every high hill
1Ki 16:33 And Ahab made a w image
2Ki 13: 6 the w images also remained in
2Ki 17:10 w images on every high hill
2Ki 17:16 and two calves, made a w image
2Ki 18: 4 cut down the w images and
2Ki 21: 3 for Baal, and made a w image
2Ki 23: 6 he brought out the w image
2Ki 23: 7 wove hangings for the w image
2Ki 23:14 and cut down the w images, and
2Ki 23:15 powder, and burned the w
2Ch 14: 3 and cut down the w images
2Ch 17: 6 places and w images from Judah
2Ch 19: 3 the w images from the land
2Ch 24:18 fathers, and served w images
2Ch 31: 1 pieces, cut down the w images
2Ch 33: 3 the Baals, and made w images
2Ch 33:19 places and set up w images
2Ch 34: 3 the w images, the carved
2Ch 34: 4 and the w images, the carved
2Ch 34: 7 the w images, had beaten the
Is 17: 8 nor the w images nor the
Is 27: 9 when w images and incense
Jer 10: 8 a w idol is a worthless
Jer 17: 2 their w images by the green
Ezek 41:25 A w canopy was on the front
Hos 4:12 counsel from their w idols
Mic 5:14 I will pluck your w images

WOODLAND (*see* WOODS)
Mic 7:14 who dwell solitarily in a w

WOODPILE (*see* WOOD)
Zech 12: 6 Judah like a firepan in the w

WOODS (*see* WOOD, WOODED, WOODLAND)
Deut 19: 5 w with his neighbor to cut
1Sa 14:26 people had come into the w
1Sa 23:16 and went to David in the w
1Sa 23:18 And David stayed in the w, and
1Sa 23:19 us in strongholds in the w
2Sa 18: 6 was in the w of Ephraim
2Sa 18: 8 the w devoured more people
2Sa 18:17 him into a large pit in the w
2Ki 2:24 bears came out of the w and
1Ch 16:33 Then the trees of the w shall
Ps 80:13 boar out of the w uproots it
Ps 83:14 As the fire burns the w, And
Ps 96:12 the w will rejoice before the
Ps 132: 6 it in the fields of the w
Song 2: 3 tree among the trees of the w
Is 7: 2 the w are moved with the wind
Ezek 34:25 wilderness and sleep in the w

WOODSMAN
Is 14: 8 no w has come up against us

WOOF
Lev 13:48 warp or w of linen or wool
Lev 13:49 in the warp or in the w, or
Lev 13:51 in the warp or in the w, in
Lev 13:52 the plague, whether warp or w
Lev 13:53 in the warp or in the w, or
Lev 13:56 of the warp or out of the w
Lev 13:57 in the warp or in the w, or
Lev 13:58 the garment, either warp or w
Lev 13:59 either in the warp or w, or

WOOL (*see* WOOLEN)
Lev 13:48 warp or woof of linen or w
Lev 13:52 in w or in linen, or anything
Lev 13:59 in a garment of w or linen
Lev 19:19 linen and w come upon you
Deut 22:11 of different sorts, such as w
Judg 6:37 of w on the threshing floor
2Ki 3: 4 the w of one hundred thousand
Ps 147:16 He gives snow like w
Prov 31:13 She seeks w and flax, and
Is 1:18 crimson, they shall be as w
Is 51: 8 the worm will eat them like w
Ezek 27:18 of Helbon and with white w
Ezek 34: 3 clothe yourselves with the w
Ezek 44:17 no w shall come upon them
Dan 7: 9 of His head was like pure w
Hos 2: 5 my bread and my water, my w
Hos 2: 9 and will take back My w and My
Heb 9:19 goats, with water, scarlet w
Rev 1:14 and His hair were white like w

WOOLEN (*see* WOOL)
Lev 13:47 whether it is a w garment or

WORD (*see* WORD'S, WORDS)
Gen 15: 1 After these things the w of
Gen 15: 4 the w of the LORD came to him
Gen 30:34 it were according to your w
Gen 37:14 flocks, and bring back w to me
Gen 41:40 be ruled according to your w
Gen 44: 2 the w that Joseph had spoken
Gen 44:18 a w in my lord's hearing, and
Ex 8:10 Let it be according to your w
Ex 8:13 according to the w of Moses
Ex 8:31 according to the w of Moses
Ex 9:20 He who feared the w of the
Ex 9:21 the w of the LORD left his
Ex 12:35 according to the w of Moses
Ex 14:12 Is this not the w that we
Ex 32:28 according to the w of Moses
Lev 10: 7 according to the w of Moses
Num 3:16 to the w of the LORD, as he
Num 3:51 to the w of the LORD, as the
Num 4:45 numbered according to the w
Num 11:23 My w will befall you or not
Num 13:26 they brought back w to them
Num 14:20 pardoned, according to your w
Num 15:31 despised the w of the LORD
Num 20:24 My w at the water of Meribah
Num 22: 8 and I will bring back w to you
Num 22:18 the w of the LORD my God, to
Num 22:20 but only the w which I speak
Num 22:35 but only the w that I speak
Num 22:38 The w that God puts in my
Num 23: 5 put a w in Balaam's mouth
Num 23:16 put a w in his mouth, and said
Num 24:13 go beyond the w of the LORD
Num 27:21 at his w they shall go out,
Num 27:21 at his w they shall come in,
Num 30: 2 he shall not break his w
Num 36: 5 to the w of the LORD, saying
Deut 1:22 bring back w to us of the way
Deut 1:25 and they brought back w to us
Deut 4: 2 to the w which I command you
Deut 5: 5 to you the w of the LORD
Deut 8: 3 w that proceeds from the
Deut 9: 5 the w which the LORD swore to
Deut 18:20 to speak a w in My name,
Deut 18:21 the w which the LORD has not
Deut 21: 5 by their w every controversy
Deut 30:14 But the w is very near you,
Deut 32:47 by this w you shall prolong
Deut 33: 9 for they have observed Your w
Deut 34: 5 to the w of the LORD
Josh 1:13 Remember the w which Moses
Josh 6:10 nor shall any w proceed out
Josh 8:27 according to the w of the
Josh 8:35 There was not a w of all that
Josh 14: 6 You know the w which the LORD
Josh 14: 7 I brought back w to him as it
Josh 14:10 this w to Moses while Israel
Josh 19:50 According to the w of the
Josh 21:45 Not a w failed of any good
Josh 22: 9 w of the LORD by the hand of
Josh 22:32 and brought back w to them
Josh 23:14 not one w of them has failed
Judg 11:35 I have given my w to the LORD
Judg 11:36 have given your w to the LORD
Judg 21:13 w to the children of Benjamin
1Sa 1:23 let the LORD establish His w
1Sa 3: 1 the w of the LORD was rare in
1Sa 3: 7 nor was the w of the LORD yet
1Sa 3:21 Shiloh by the w of the LORD
1Sa 4: 1 the w of Samuel came to all
1Sa 9:27 announce to you the w of God
1Sa 15:10 Now the w of the LORD came to
1Sa 15:23 rejected the w of the LORD
1Sa 15:26 rejected the w of the LORD
1Sa 31: 9 sent w throughout the land of

2Sa 3:11 not answer Abner another w
2Sa 7: 4 that night that the w of the
2Sa 7: 7 have I ever spoken a w to
2Sa 7:25 the w which You have spoken
2Sa 12:25 And He sent w by the hand of
2Sa 14:12 another w to my lord the king
2Sa 14:17 The w of my lord the king
2Sa 15:28 of the wilderness until w
2Sa 19:14 they sent this w to the king
2Sa 22:31 the w of the LORD is proven
2Sa 23: 2 me, and His w was on my tongue
2Sa 24: 4 w prevailed against Joab and
2Sa 24:11 the w of the LORD came to the
2Sa 24:19 according to the w of Gad
1Ki 2: 4 the LORD may fulfill His w
1Ki 2:23 has not spoken this w against
1Ki 2:27 that he might fulfill the w
1Ki 2:30 brought back w to the king
1Ki 2:42 The w I have heard is good
1Ki 6:11 Then the w of the LORD came
1Ki 6:12 I will perform My w with you
1Ki 8:20 His w which He spoke
1Ki 8:26 let Your w come true, which
1Ki 8:56 one w of all His good promise
1Ki 12:15 that He might fulfill His w
1Ki 12:22 But the w of God came to
1Ki 12:24 they obeyed the w of the LORD
1Ki 12:24 to the w of the LORD
1Ki 13: 1 Bethel by the w of the LORD
1Ki 13: 2 altar by the w of the LORD
1Ki 13: 5 given by the w of the LORD
1Ki 13: 9 me by the w of the LORD,
1Ki 13:17 told by the w of the LORD
1Ki 13:18 to me by the w of the LORD
1Ki 13:20 that the w of the LORD came
1Ki 13:21 disobeyed the w of the LORD
1Ki 13:26 to the w of the LORD
1Ki 13:26 according to the w of the
1Ki 13:32 the w of the LORD against the
1Ki 14:18 according to the w of the
1Ki 15:29 according to the w of the
1Ki 16: 1 Then the w of the LORD came
1Ki 16: 7 also the w of the LORD came
1Ki 16:12 to the w of the LORD, which
1Ki 16:34 to the w of the LORD, which
1Ki 17: 1 these years, except at my w
1Ki 17: 2 Then the w of the LORD came
1Ki 17: 5 to the w of the LORD, for he
1Ki 17: 8 Then the w of the LORD came
1Ki 17:15 according to the w of Elijah
1Ki 17:16 according to the w of the
1Ki 17:24 that the w of the LORD in
1Ki 18: 1 after many days that the w of
1Ki 18:21 people answered him not a w
1Ki 18:31 to whom the w of the LORD had
1Ki 18:36 all these things at Your w
1Ki 19: 9 the w of the LORD came to him
1Ki 20: 9 and brought back w to him
1Ki 20:33 quickly grasped at this w
1Ki 20:35 neighbor by the w of the LORD
1Ki 21: 4 displeased because of the w
1Ki 21:17 Then the w of the LORD came
1Ki 21:28 the w of the LORD came to
1Ki 22: 5 for the w of the LORD today
1Ki 22:13 let your w be like the w
1Ki 22:19 hear the w of the LORD
1Ki 22:38 according to the w of the
2Ki 1:16 in Israel to inquire of His w
2Ki 1:17 died according to the w of
2Ki 3:12 The w of the LORD is with him
2Ki 4:44 to the w of the LORD
2Ki 6:18 according to the w of Elisha
2Ki 7: 1 Hear the w of the LORD
2Ki 7:16 to the w of the LORD
2Ki 9:26 to the w of the LORD
2Ki 9:36 This is the w of the LORD
2Ki 10:10 fall to the earth of the w of
2Ki 10:17 according to the w of the
2Ki 14:25 according to the w of the
2Ki 15:12 This was the w of the LORD
2Ki 18:28 Hear the w of the great king,
2Ki 18:36 peace and answered him not a w
2Ki 19:21 This is the w which the LORD
2Ki 20: 4 that the w of the LORD came
2Ki 20:16 Hear the w of the LORD
2Ki 20:19 The w of the LORD which you
2Ki 22: 9 the king, bringing the king w
2Ki 22:20 So they brought w to the king
2Ki 23:16 w of the LORD which the man
2Ki 24: 2 according to the w of the
1Ch 10: 9 sent w throughout the land of
1Ch 10:13 not keep the w of the LORD
1Ch 11: 3 according to the w of the
1Ch 11:10 according to the w of the
1Ch 12:23 to the w of the LORD
1Ch 15:15 to the w of the LORD
1Ch 16:15 the w which He commanded, for
1Ch 17: 3 that night that the w of God
1Ch 17: 6 have I ever spoken a w to any
1Ch 17:23 the w which You have spoken
1Ch 21: 4 w prevailed against Joab
1Ch 21: 6 them, for the king's w was
1Ch 21:19 David went up at the w of Gad
1Ch 22: 8 but the w of the LORD came to
2Ch 6:10 His w which He spoke, and I
2Ch 6:17 let Your w come true, which
2Ch 10:15 the LORD might fulfill His w
2Ch 11: 2 But the w of the LORD came to
2Ch 12: 7 the w of the LORD came to
2Ch 18: 4 for the w of the LORD today
2Ch 18:12 Therefore please let your w
2Ch 18:12 be like the w of one of them
2Ch 18:18 hear the w of the LORD
2Ch 30:12 leaders, at the w of the LORD
2Ch 34:16 the king, bringing the king w
2Ch 34:21 not kept the w of the LORD
2Ch 34:28 brought back w to the king
2Ch 35: 6 may do according to the w of
2Ch 36:21 to fulfill the w of the LORD
2Ch 36:22 that the w of the LORD spoken
Ezra 1: 1 that the w of the LORD spoken
Ezra 10: 5 would do according to this w
Neh 1: 8 the w that You commanded
Esth 1:21 according to the w of Memucan
Esth 7: 8 As the w left the king's
Job 2:13 and no one spoke a w to him
Job 4: 2 If one attempts a w with you
Job 4:12 Now a w was secretly brought
Job 15:11 the w spoken gently with you
Ps 17: 4 By the w of Your lips, I have
Ps 18:30 The w of the LORD is proven
Ps 33: 4 For the w of the LORD is
Ps 33: 6 By the w of the LORD the
Ps 56: 4 In God (I will praise His w)
Ps 56:10 In God (I will praise His w)
Ps 56:10 LORD (I will praise His w)
Ps 68:11 The Lord gave the w
Ps 89:34 Nor alter the w that has gone
Ps 103:20 in strength, who do His w
Ps 103:20 Heeding the voice of His w
Ps 105: 8 The w which He commanded,
Ps 105:19 time that his w came to pass
Ps 105:19 The w of the LORD tested him
Ps 105:28 did not rebel against His w
Ps 106:24 They did not believe His w
Ps 107:20 He sent His w and healed them,
Ps 119: 9 heed according to Your w
Ps 119:11 Your w I have hidden in my
Ps 119:16 I will not forget Your w
Ps 119:17 I may live and keep Your w
Ps 119:25 Revive me according to Your w
Ps 119:28 me according to Your w
Ps 119:38 Establish Your w to Your
Ps 119:41 salvation according to Your w
Ps 119:42 me, For I trust in Your w
Ps 119:43 And take not the w of truth
Ps 119:49 Remember the w to Your
Ps 119:50 For Your w has given me life
Ps 119:58 to me according to Your w
Ps 119:65 O LORD, according to Your w
Ps 119:67 astray, But now I keep Your w
Ps 119:74 I have hoped in Your w
Ps 119:76 to Your w to Your servant
Ps 119:81 But I hope in Your w
Ps 119:82 eyes fail from seeking Your w
Ps 119:89 Your w is settled in heaven
Ps 119:101 way, That I may keep Your w
Ps 119:105 Your w is a lamp to my feet
Ps 119:107 O LORD, according to Your w
Ps 119:114 I hope in Your w
Ps 119:116 Uphold me according to Your w
Ps 119:123 salvation And Your righteous w
Ps 119:133 Direct my steps by Your w
Ps 119:140 Your w is very pure
Ps 119:147 I hope in Your w
Ps 119:148 That I may meditate on Your w
Ps 119:154 Revive me according to Your w
Ps 119:158 they do not keep Your w
Ps 119:160 entirety of Your w is truth
Ps 119:161 heart stands in awe of Your w
Ps 119:162 I rejoice at Your w As one
Ps 119:169 according to Your w
Ps 119:170 me according to Your w
Ps 119:172 tongue shall speak of Your w
Ps 130: 5 waits, And in His w I do hope
Ps 138: 2 Your w above all Your name
Ps 139: 4 there is not a w on my tongue
Ps 147:15 His w runs very swiftly
Ps 147:18 He sends out His w and melts
Ps 147:19 He declares His w to Jacob
Ps 148: 8 Stormy wind, fulfilling His w
Prov 12:25 but a good w makes it glad
Prov 13:13 the w will be destroyed, but
Prov 14:15 The simple believes every w
Prov 15: 1 but a harsh w stirs up anger
Prov 15:23 a w spoken in due season, how
Prov 16:20 He who heeds the w wisely
Prov 25:11 A w fitly spoken is like
Prov 30: 5 Every w of God is pure
Eccl 8: 4 Where the w of a king is,
Is 1:10 Hear the w of the LORD, you
Is 2: 1 The w that Isaiah the son of
Is 2: 3 and the w of the LORD from
Is 5:24 despised the w of the Holy
Is 8:10 speak the w, but it will not
Is 8:20 not speak according to this w
Is 9: 8 LORD sent a w against Jacob
Is 16:13 This is the w which the LORD
Is 24: 3 the LORD has spoken this w
Is 28:13 But the w of the LORD was to
Is 28:14 hear the w of the LORD, you
Is 29:21 make a man an offender by a w
Is 30:12 Because you despise this w
Is 30:21 shall hear a w behind you
Is 36:21 peace and answered him not a w
Is 37:22 this is the w which the LORD
Is 38: 4 Then the w of the LORD came
Is 39: 5 Hear the w of the LORD of
Is 39: 8 The w of the LORD which you
Is 40: 8 but the w of our God stands
Is 41:28 of them, could answer a w
Is 44:26 confirms the w of His servant
Is 45:23 the w has gone out of My
Is 50: 4 a w in season to him who is
Is 55:11 So shall My w be that goes
Is 66: 2 and who trembles at My w
Is 66: 5 Hear the w of the LORD, you
Is 66: 5 you who tremble at His w
Jer 1: 2 to whom the w of the LORD
Jer 1: 4 Then the w of the LORD came
Jer 1:11 Moreover the w of the LORD
Jer 1:12 I am ready to perform My w
Jer 1:13 the w of the LORD came to me
Jer 2: 1 Moreover the w of the LORD
Jer 2: 4 Hear the w of the LORD, O
Jer 2:31 see the w of the LORD
Jer 5:13 for the w is not in them
Jer 5:14 Because you speak this w,
Jer 6:10 the w of the LORD is a
Jer 7: 1 The w that came to Jeremiah
Jer 7: 2 and proclaim there this w
Jer 7: 2 Hear the w of the LORD, all
Jer 8: 9 rejected the w of the LORD
Jer 9:20 Yet hear the w of the LORD
Jer 9:20 receive the w of His mouth
Jer 10: 1 Hear the w which the LORD
Jer 11: 1 The w that came to Jeremiah
Jer 13: 2 to the w of the LORD, and put
Jer 13: 3 the w of the LORD came to me
Jer 13: 8 Then the w of the LORD came
Jer 13:12 shall speak to them this w
Jer 14: 1 The w of the LORD that came
Jer 14:17 you shall say this w to them
Jer 15:16 Your w was to me the joy and
Jer 16: 1 The w of the LORD also came
Jer 17:15 Where is the w of the LORD
Jer 17:20 Hear the w of the LORD, you
Jer 18: 1 The w which came to Jeremiah
Jer 18: 5 Then the w of the LORD came
Jer 18:18 nor the w from the prophet
Jer 19: 3 Hear the w of the LORD, O
Jer 20: 8 Because the w of the LORD
Jer 20: 9 But His w was in my heart
Jer 21: 1 The w which came to Jeremiah
Jer 21:11 say, 'Hear the w of the LORD,
Jer 22: 1 Judah, and there speak this w
Jer 22: 2 Hear the w of the LORD, O
Jer 22:29 earth, hear the w of the LORD
Jer 23:18 has perceived and heard His w
Jer 23:18 Who has marked His w and

Jer 23:28 and he who has My w
Jer 23:28 let him speak My w faithfully
Jer 23:29 Is not My w like a fire
Jer 23:36 For every man's w will be his
Jer 23:38 Because you say this w
Jer 24: 4 Again the w of the LORD came
Jer 25: 1 The w that came to Jeremiah
Jer 25: 3 year in which the w of the
Jer 26: 1 this w came from the LORD,
Jer 26: 2 Do not diminish a w
Jer 27: 1 this w came to Jeremiah from
Jer 27:18 if the w of the LORD is with
Jer 28: 7 this w that I speak in your
Jer 28: 9 when the w of the prophet
Jer 28:12 Then the w of the LORD came
Jer 29:10 perform My good w toward you
Jer 29:20 hear the w of the LORD, all
Jer 29:30 Then the w of the LORD came
Jer 30: 1 The w that came to Jeremiah
Jer 31:10 Hear the w of the LORD, O
Jer 32: 1 The w that came to Jeremiah
Jer 32: 6 The w of the LORD came to me,
Jer 32: 8 to the w of the LORD, and said
Jer 32: 8 this was the w of the LORD
Jer 32:26 Then the w of the LORD came
Jer 33: 1 Moreover the w of the LORD
Jer 33:19 the w of the LORD came to
Jer 33:23 Moreover the w of the LORD
Jer 34: 1 The w which came to Jeremiah
Jer 34: 4 Yet hear the w of the LORD
Jer 34: 5 For I have pronounced the w
Jer 34: 8 This is the w that came to
Jer 34:12 Therefore the w of the LORD
Jer 35: 1 The w which came to Jeremiah
Jer 35:12 Then came the w of the LORD
Jer 36: 1 that this w came to Jeremiah
Jer 36:27 the w of the LORD came to
Jer 37: 6 the w of the LORD came to the
Jer 37:17 Is there any w from the LORD
Jer 38:21 this is the w that the LORD
Jer 39:15 Now the w of the LORD had
Jer 40: 1 The w that came to Jeremiah
Jer 42: 7 the w of the LORD came to
Jer 42:15 hear now the w of the LORD
Jer 43: 8 Then the w of the LORD came
Jer 44: 1 The w that came to Jeremiah
Jer 44:16 As for the w that you have
Jer 44:24 Hear the w of the LORD, all
Jer 44:26 hear the w of the LORD, all
Jer 45: 1 The w that Jeremiah the
Jer 46: 1 The w of the LORD which came
Jer 46:13 The w that the LORD spoke to
Jer 47: 1 The w of the LORD that came
Jer 49:34 The w of the LORD that came
Jer 50: 1 The w that the LORD spoke
Jer 51:59 The w which Jeremiah the
Lam 2:17 He has fulfilled His w which
Ezek 1: 3 the w of the LORD came
Ezek 3:16 the w of the LORD came to me
Ezek 3:17 hear a w from My mouth, and
Ezek 6: 1 Now the w of the LORD came to
Ezek 6: 3 hear the w of the Lord GOD
Ezek 7: 1 Moreover the w of the LORD
Ezek 11:14 Again the w of the LORD came
Ezek 12: 1 Now the w of the LORD came to
Ezek 12: 8 in the morning the w of the
Ezek 12:17 Moreover the w of the LORD
Ezek 12:21 the w of the LORD came to me,
Ezek 12:25 the w which I speak will come
Ezek 12:25 house, I will say the w and
Ezek 12:26 Again the w of the LORD came
Ezek 12:28 but the w which I speak will
Ezek 13: 1 the w of the LORD came to me,
Ezek 13: 2 Hear the w of the LORD
Ezek 13: 6 that the w may be confirmed
Ezek 14: 2 the w of the LORD came to me,
Ezek 14:12 The w of the LORD came again
Ezek 15: 1 Then the w of the LORD came
Ezek 16: 1 Again the w of the LORD came
Ezek 16:35 hear the w of the LORD
Ezek 17: 1 the w of the LORD came to me,
Ezek 17:11 Moreover the w of the LORD
Ezek 18: 1 The w of the LORD came to me
Ezek 20: 2 Then the w of the LORD came
Ezek 20:45 Furthermore the w of the LORD
Ezek 20:47 Hear the w of the LORD
Ezek 21: 1 the w of the LORD came to me,
Ezek 21: 8 Again the w of the LORD came
Ezek 21:18 The w of the LORD came to me
Ezek 22: 1 Moreover the w of the LORD
Ezek 22:17 The w of the LORD came to me,
Ezek 22:23 the w of the LORD came to me,
Ezek 23: 1 The w of the LORD came again
Ezek 24: 1 the w of the LORD came to me,
Ezek 24:15 Also the w of the LORD came
Ezek 24:20 The w of the LORD came to me,
Ezek 25: 1 The w of the LORD came to me,
Ezek 25: 3 Hear the w of the Lord GOD
Ezek 26: 1 that the w of the LORD came
Ezek 27: 1 The w of the LORD came again
Ezek 28: 1 The w of the LORD came to me
Ezek 28:11 Moreover the w of the LORD
Ezek 28:20 Then the w of the LORD came
Ezek 29: 1 the w of the LORD came to me,
Ezek 29:17 that the w of the LORD came
Ezek 30: 1 The w of the LORD came to me
Ezek 30:20 that the w of the LORD came
Ezek 31: 1 that the w of the LORD came
Ezek 32: 1 that the w of the LORD came
Ezek 32:17 that the w of the LORD came
Ezek 33: 1 Again the w of the LORD came
Ezek 33: 7 shall hear a w from My mouth
Ezek 33:23 Then the w of the LORD came
Ezek 33:30 hear what the w is that comes
Ezek 34: 1 the w of the LORD came to me,
Ezek 34: 7 hear the w of the LORD
Ezek 34: 9 hear the w of the LORD
Ezek 35: 1 Moreover the w of the LORD
Ezek 36: 1 hear the w of the LORD
Ezek 36: 4 hear the w of the Lord GOD
Ezek 36:16 Moreover the w of the LORD
Ezek 37: 4 bones, hear the w of the LORD
Ezek 37:15 Again the w of the LORD came
Ezek 38: 1 Now the w of the LORD came to
Dan 3: 2 sent w to gather together the
Dan 3:28 have frustrated the king's w
Dan 4:17 by the w of the holy ones
Dan 4:31 While the w was still in the
Dan 4:33 That very hour the w was
Dan 5:26 the interpretation of each w
Dan 9: 2 by the w of the LORD, given
Dan 10:11 he was speaking this w to me
Hos 1: 1 The w of the LORD that came
Hos 4: 1 Hear the w of the LORD, you
Joel 1: 1 The w of the LORD that came
Joel 2:11 is the One who executes His w
Amos 3: 1 Hear this w that the LORD has
Amos 4: 1 Hear this w, you cows of
Amos 5: 1 Hear this w which I take up
Amos 7:16 hear the w of the LORD
Amos 8:12 seeking the w of the LORD
Jon 1: 1 Now the w of the LORD came to
Jon 3: 1 Now the w of the LORD came to
Jon 3: 3 to the w of the LORD
Jon 3: 6 Then w came to the king of
Mic 1: 1 The w of the LORD that came
Mic 4: 2 and the w of the LORD from
Zeph 1: 1 The w of the LORD which came
Zeph 2: 5 The w of the LORD is against
Hag 1: 1 the w of the LORD came by
Hag 1: 3 Then the w of the LORD came
Hag 2: 1 the w of the LORD came by
Hag 2: 5 According to the w that I
Hag 2:10 the w of the LORD came by
Hag 2:20 again the w of the LORD came
Zech 1: 1 the w of the LORD came to
Zech 1: 7 the w of the LORD came to
Zech 4: 6 This is the w of the LORD to
Zech 4: 8 Moreover the w of the LORD
Zech 6: 9 Then the w of the LORD came
Zech 7: 1 the w of the LORD came to
Zech 7: 4 Then the w of the LORD of
Zech 7: 8 Then the w of the LORD came
Zech 8: 1 Again the w of the LORD of
Zech 8:18 Then the w of the LORD of
Zech 9: 1 The burden of the w of the
Zech 11:11 that it was the w of the LORD
Zech 12: 1 The burden of the w of the
Mal 1: 1 The burden of the w of the
Matt 2: 8 found Him, bring back w to me
Matt 2:13 there until I bring you w
Matt 4: 4 but by every w that proceeds
Matt 8: 8 But only speak a w, and my
Matt 8:16 cast out the spirits with a w
Matt 12:32 Anyone who speaks a w against
Matt 12:36 every idle w men may speak
Matt 13:19 hears the w of the kingdom
Matt 13:20 this is he who hears the w
Matt 13:21 arises because of the w,
Matt 13:22 thorns is he who hears the w
Matt 13:22 of riches choke the w, and he
Matt 13:23 ground is he who hears the w
Matt 15:23 But He answered her not a w
Matt 18:16 every w may be established
Matt 22:46 was able to answer Him a w
Matt 26:75 Peter remembered the w of
Matt 27:14 And He answered him not one w
Matt 28: 8 ran to bring His disciples w
Mark 2: 2 And He preached the w to them
Mark 4:14 The sower sows the w
Mark 4:15 wayside where the w is sown
Mark 4:15 takes away the w that was
Mark 4:16 who, when they hear the w
Mark 4:18 are the ones who hear the w
Mark 4:19 entering in choke the w, and
Mark 4:20 ground, those who hear the w
Mark 4:33 w to them as they were able
Mark 5:36 heard the w that was spoken
Mark 7:13 making the w of God of no
Mark 8:32 He spoke this w openly
Mark 9:10 kept this w to themselves
Mark 10:22 But he was sad at this w, and
Mark 14:72 Peter called to mind the w
Mark 16:20 confirming the w through the
Luke 1: 2 ministers of the w delivered
Luke 1:38 be to me according to your w
Luke 2:29 in peace, according to Your w
Luke 3: 2 the w of God came to John the
Luke 4: 4 alone, but by every w of God
Luke 4:32 for His w was with authority
Luke 4:36 saying, "What a w this is
Luke 5: 1 Him to hear the w of God,
Luke 5: 5 nevertheless at Your w I will
Luke 7: 7 But say the w, and my servant
Luke 8:11 The seed is the w of God
Luke 8:12 takes away the w out of their
Luke 8:13 hear, receive the w with joy
Luke 8:15 heard the w with a noble and
Luke 8:21 these who hear the w of God
Luke 10:39 at Jesus' feet and heard His w
Luke 11:28 those who hear the w of God
Luke 12:10 anyone who speaks a w against
Luke 22:61 remembered the w of the Lord
Luke 24:19 and w before God and all the
John 1: 1 In the beginning was the W
John 1: 1 the W was with God
John 1: 1 and the W was God
John 1:14 the W became flesh and dwelt
John 2:22 the w which Jesus had said
John 4:39 in Him because of the w of
John 4:41 believed because of His own w
John 4:50 the w that Jesus spoke to him
John 5:24 say to you, he who hears My w
John 5:38 not have His w abiding in you
John 8:31 If you abide in My w, you are
John 8:37 because My w has no place in
John 8:43 not able to listen to My w
John 8:51 if anyone keeps My w he shall
John 8:52 say, 'If anyone keeps My w he
John 8:55 I do know Him and keep His w
John 10:35 to whom the w of God came
John 12:38 that the w of Isaiah the
John 12:48 the w that I have spoken will
John 14:23 loves Me, he will keep My w
John 14:24 the w which you hear is not
John 15: 3 clean because of the w which
John 15:20 Remember the w that I said to
John 15:20 If they kept My w, they will
John 15:25 But this happened that the w
John 17: 6 Me, and they have kept Your w
John 17:14 I have given them Your w
John 17:17 Your w is truth
John 17:20 believe in Me through their w
Acts 2:41 received his w were baptized
Acts 4: 4 who heard the w believed
Acts 4:29 they may speak Your w,
Acts 4:31 they spoke the w of God with
Acts 6: 2 we should leave the w of God
Acts 6: 4 and to the ministry of the w
Acts 6: 7 the w of God spread, and the
Acts 8: 4 everywhere preaching the w
Acts 8:14 had received the w of God
Acts 8:25 and preached the w of the Lord
Acts 10:36 The w which God sent to the
Acts 10:37 that w you know, which was
Acts 10:44 all those who heard the w
Acts 11: 1 also received the w of God
Acts 11:16 remembered the w of the Lord
Acts 11:19 preaching the w to no one but
Acts 12:24 But the w of God grew and

Acts 13: 5 they preached the w of God in
Acts 13: 7 sought to hear the w of God
Acts 13:15 if you have any w of
Acts 13:26 God, to you the w of this
Acts 13:44 together to hear the w of God
Acts 13:46 It was necessary that the w
Acts 13:48 glorified the w of the Lord
Acts 13:49 the w of the Lord was being
Acts 14: 3 witness to the w of His grace
Acts 14:25 had preached the w in Perga
Acts 15: 7 hear the w of the gospel and
Acts 15:27 the same things by w of mouth
Acts 15:35 preaching the w of the Lord
Acts 15:36 preached the w of the Lord
Acts 16: 6 to preach the w in Asia
Acts 16:32 the w of the Lord to him and
Acts 17:11 the w with all readiness, and
Acts 17:13 learned that the w of God was
Acts 18:11 teaching the w of God among
Acts 19:10 heard the w of the Lord Jesus
Acts 19:20 So the w of the Lord grew
Acts 20:32 to the w of His grace, which
Acts 22:22 listened to him until this w
Acts 28:25 after Paul had said one w
Rom 9: 6 But it is not that the w of
Rom 9: 9 For this is the w of promise
Rom 10: 8 The w is near you, even in
Rom 10: 8 is, the w of faith which we
Rom 10:17 and hearing by the w of God
Rom 15:18 accomplished through me, in w
1Co 4:19 not the w of those who are
1Co 4:20 God is not in w but in power
1Co 12: 8 the w of wisdom through the
1Co 12: 8 to another the w of knowledge
1Co 14:36 Or did the w of God come
1Co 15: 2 if you hold fast that w which
2Co 1:18 our w to you was not Yes and
2Co 2:17 many, peddling the w of God
2Co 4: 2 the w of God deceitfully, but
2Co 5:19 to us the w of reconciliation
2Co 6: 7 by the w of truth, by the
2Co 10:11 that what we are in w by
2Co 13: 1 every w shall be established
Gal 5:14 the law is fulfilled in one w
Gal 6: 6 w share in all good things
Eph 1:13 you heard the w of truth, the
Eph 5:26 the washing of water by the w
Eph 6:17 Spirit, which is the w of God
Phil 1:14 to speak the w without fear
Phil 2:16 holding fast the w of life
Col 1: 5 you heard before in the w of
Col 1:25 you, to fulfill the w of God
Col 3:16 Let the w of Christ dwell in
Col 3:17 whatever you do in w or deed
Col 4: 3 open to us a door for the w
1Th 1: 5 did not come to you in w only
1Th 1: 6 the w in much affliction,
1Th 1: 8 For from you the w of the
1Th 2:13 when you received the w of
1Th 2:13 it not as the w of men, but
1Th 2:13 the w of God, which also
1Th 4:15 to you by the w of the Lord
2Th 2: 2 spirit or by w or by letter
2Th 2:15 whether by w or our epistle
2Th 2:17 establish you in every good w
2Th 3: 1 that the w of the Lord may
2Th 3:14 obey our w in this epistle
1Ti 4: 5 is sanctified by the w of God
1Ti 4:12 example to the believers in w
1Ti 5:17 those who labor in the w and
2Ti 2: 9 but the w of God is not
2Ti 2:15 dividing the w of truth
2Ti 4: 2 Preach the w! Be ready
Tit 1: 3 His w through preaching,
Tit 1: 9 w as he has been taught, that
Tit 2: 5 that the w of God may not be
Heb 1: 3 things by the w of His power
Heb 2: 2 For if the w spoken through
Heb 4: 2 but the w which they heard
Heb 4:12 For the w of God is living and
Heb 5:13 in the w of righteousness
Heb 6: 5 have tasted the good w of God
Heb 7:28 but the w of the oath, which
Heb 11: 3 were framed by the w of God
Heb 12:19 the w should not be spoken to
Heb 13: 7 spoken the w of God to you
Heb 13:22 brethren, bear with the w of
Jas 1:18 us forth by the w of truth
Jas 1:21 with meekness the implanted w
Jas 1:22 But be doers of the w, and not
Jas 1:23 anyone is a hearer of the w
Jas 3: 2 anyone does not stumble in w
1Pe 1:23 through the w of God which
1Pe 1:25 but the w of the LORD endures
1Pe 1:25 Now this is the w which by
1Pe 2: 2 desire the pure milk of the w
1Pe 2: 8 being disobedient to the w
1Pe 3: 1 obey the w, they, without a w
2Pe 1:19 prophetic w made more sure
2Pe 3: 5 that by the w of God the
2Pe 3: 7 kept in store by the same w
1Jn 1: 1 concerning the W of life
1Jn 1:10 a liar, and His w is not in us
1Jn 2: 5 But whoever keeps His w,
1Jn 2: 7 w which you heard from the
1Jn 2:14 the w of God abides in you,
1Jn 3:18 us not love in w or in tongue
1Jn 5: 7 the Father, the W, and the
Rev 1: 2 bore witness to the w of God
Rev 1: 9 Patmos for the w of God and
Rev 3: 8 strength, have kept My w, and
Rev 6: 9 been slain for the w of God
Rev 12:11 by the w of their testimony,
Rev 19:13 name is called The W of God
Rev 20: 4 to Jesus and for the w of God

WORD'S (*see* WORD)
2Sa 7:21 For Your w sake, and according
Mark 4:17 arises for the w sake,

WORDS (*see* WORD)
Gen 24:30 when he heard the w of his
Gen 24:52 servant heard their w, that
Gen 27:34 heard the w of his father
Gen 27:42 the w of Esau her older son
Gen 31: 1 heard the w of Laban's sons
Gen 34:18 And their w pleased Hamor and
Gen 37: 8 for his dreams and for his w
Gen 39:17 to him with w like these,
Gen 39:19 when his master heard the w
Gen 42:16 that your w may be tested to
Gen 42:20 so your w will be verified,
Gen 43: 7 told him according to these w
Gen 44: 6 he spoke to them these same w
Gen 44: 7 Why does my lord say these w
Gen 44:10 let it be according to your w
Gen 44:24 we told him the w of my lord
Gen 45:27 w which Joseph had said to
Gen 49:21 he gives goodly w
Ex 4:15 him and put the w in his mouth
Ex 4:28 w of the LORD who had sent
Ex 4:30 Aaron spoke all the w which
Ex 5: 9 let them not regard false w
Ex 19: 6 These are the w which you
Ex 19: 7 w which the LORD commanded
Ex 19: 8 w of the people to the LORD
Ex 19: 9 So Moses told the w of the
Ex 20: 1 And God spoke all these w,
Ex 23: 8 and perverts the w of the
Ex 24: 3 people all the w of the LORD
Ex 24: 3 All the w which the LORD has
Ex 24: 4 wrote all the w of the LORD
Ex 24: 8 you according to all these w
Ex 34: 1 the w that were on the first
Ex 34:27 Write these w, for according
Ex 34:27 to the tenor of these w I
Ex 34:28 tablets the w of the covenant
Ex 35: 1 These are the w which the
Num 11:24 the people the w of the LORD
Num 12: 6 Hear now My w
Num 14:39 Then Moses told these w to
Num 16:31 finished speaking all these w
Num 22: 7 spoke to him the w of Balak
Num 24: 4 of him who hears the w of God
Num 24:16 of him who hears the w of God
Deut 1: 1 These are the w which Moses
Deut 1:34 heard the sound of your w
Deut 2:26 with w of peace, saying,
Deut 4:10 and I will let them hear My w
Deut 4:12 You heard the sound of the w
Deut 4:36 you heard His w out of the
Deut 5:22 These w the LORD spoke to all
Deut 5:28 your w when you spoke to me
Deut 5:28 w of this people which they
Deut 6: 6 these w which I command you
Deut 9:10 on them were all the w which
Deut 10: 2 the w that were on the first
Deut 11:18 these w of mine in your heart
Deut 12:28 and obey all these w which I
Deut 13: 3 the w of that prophet or that
Deut 16:19 twists the w of the righteous
Deut 17:19 observe all the w of this law
Deut 18:18 will put My w in His mouth,
Deut 18:19 whoever will not hear My w
Deut 27: 3 on them all the w of this law
Deut 27: 8 stones all the w of this law
Deut 27:26 confirm all the w of this law
Deut 28:14 w which I command you this
Deut 28:58 the w of this law that are
Deut 29: 1 These are the w of the
Deut 29: 9 keep the w of this covenant
Deut 29:19 he hears the w of this curse
Deut 29:29 may do all the w of this law
Deut 31: 1 spoke these w to all Israel
Deut 31:12 observe all the w of this law
Deut 31:24 the w of this law in a book
Deut 31:28 these w in their hearing and
Deut 31:30 the w of this song until they
Deut 32: 1 O earth, the w of my mouth
Deut 32:44 spoke all the w of this song
Deut 32:45 all these w to all Israel
Deut 32:46 w which I testify among you
Deut 32:46 all the w of this law
Deut 33: 3 everyone receives Your w
Josh 1:18 and does not heed your w, in
Josh 2:21 According to your w, so be it
Josh 3: 9 hear the w of the LORD your
Josh 8:34 he read all the w of the law
Josh 22:30 heard the w that the children
Josh 24:26 Then Joshua wrote these w in
Josh 24:27 for it has heard all the w of
Judg 2: 4 w to all the children of
Judg 9: 3 these w concerning him in the
Judg 9:30 heard the w of Gaal the son
Judg 11:10 do not do according to your w
Judg 11:11 and Jephthah spoke all his w
Judg 11:28 the w which Jephthah sent him
Judg 13:12 Now let Your w come to pass
Judg 13:17 that when Your w come to pass
Judg 16:16 pestered him daily with her w
1Sa 3:19 let none of his w fall to the
1Sa 8:10 So Samuel told all the w of
1Sa 8:21 heard all the w of the people
1Sa 11: 5 they told him the w of the
1Sa 15: 1 voice of the w of the LORD
1Sa 15:24 of the LORD and your w,
1Sa 17:11 these w of the Philistine
1Sa 17:23 spoke according to the same w
1Sa 17:31 when the w which David spoke
1Sa 18:23 w in the hearing of David
1Sa 18:26 servants told David these w
1Sa 21:12 David took these w to heart
1Sa 24: 7 his servants with these w
1Sa 24: 9 to the w of men who say
1Sa 24:16 speaking these w to Saul,
1Sa 25: 9 these w in the name of David
1Sa 25:12 came and told him all these w
1Sa 25:24 ears, and hear the w of your
1Sa 26:19 hear the w of his servant
1Sa 28:20 because of the w of Samuel
1Sa 28:21 heeded the w which you spoke
2Sa 3: 8 angry at the w of Ishbosheth
2Sa 7:17 According to all these w and
2Sa 7:28 Your w are true, and You have
2Sa 14: 3 Joab put the w in her mouth
2Sa 14:19 he put all these w in the
2Sa 19:11 since the w of all Israel
2Sa 19:43 Yet the w of the men of
2Sa 19:43 the w of the men of Israel
2Sa 20:17 to him, "Hear the w of your
2Sa 22: 1 the LORD the w of this song
2Sa 23: 1 these are the last w of David
1Ki 1:14 after you and confirm your w
1Ki 3:12 have done according to your w
1Ki 5: 7 Hiram heard the w of Solomon
1Ki 8:59 And may these w of mine, with
1Ki 10: 6 in my own land about your w
1Ki 10: 7 believe the w until I came
1Ki 12: 7 them, and speak good w to them
1Ki 13:11 w which he had spoken to the
1Ki 21:27 was, when Ahab heard those w
1Ki 22:13 the w of the prophets with
2Ki 1: 7 meet you and told you these w
2Ki 6:12 the w that you speak in your
2Ki 6:30 king heard the w of the woman
2Ki 18:20 but they are vain w
2Ki 18:27 and to you to speak these w
2Ki 18:37 and told him the w of the
2Ki 19: 4 all the w of the Rabshakeh
2Ki 19: 4 will reprove the w which the
2Ki 19: 6 of the w which you have heard

2Ki 19:16 hear the w of Sennacherib,
2Ki 22:11 the w of the Book of the Law
2Ki 22:13 concerning the w of this book
2Ki 22:13 not obeyed the w of this book
2Ki 22:16 all the w of the book which
2Ki 22:18 Concerning the w which you
2Ki 23: 2 in their hearing all the w of
2Ki 23: 3 to perform the w of this
2Ki 23:16 who proclaimed these w
2Ki 23:24 the w of the law which were
1Ch 17:15 According to all these w and
1Ch 23:27 For by the last w of David
1Ch 25: 5 king's seer in the w of God
2Ch 9: 5 in my own land about your w
2Ch 9: 6 believe their w until I came
2Ch 10: 7 them, and speak good w to them
2Ch 11: 4 they obeyed the w of the LORD
2Ch 15: 8 And when Asa heard these w
2Ch 18:12 the w of the prophets with
2Ch 29:15 at the w of the LORD, to
2Ch 29:30 the LORD with the w of David
2Ch 32: 8 were strengthened by the w of
2Ch 33:18 the w of the seers who spoke
2Ch 34:19 king heard the w of the Law
2Ch 34:21 concerning the w of the book
2Ch 34:26 Concerning the w which you
2Ch 34:27 His w against this place and
2Ch 34:30 in their hearing all the w of
2Ch 34:31 soul, to perform the w of the
2Ch 35:22 did not heed the w of Necho
2Ch 36:16 of God, despised His w, and
Ezra 7:11 expert in the w of the
Ezra 9: 4 who trembled at the w of the
Neh 1: 1 The w of Nehemiah the son of
Neh 1: 4 it was, when I heard these w
Neh 2:18 also of the king's w that he
Neh 5: 6 heard their outcry and these w
Neh 6:19 me, and reported my w to him
Neh 8: 9 they heard the w of the Law
Neh 8:12 w that were declared to them
Neh 8:13 understand the w of the Law
Neh 9: 8 You have performed Your w
Esth 3: 4 Mordecai's w would stand
Esth 4: 9 told Esther the w of Mordecai
Esth 4:12 they told Mordecai Esther's w
Esth 9:26 of all the w of this letter
Esth 9:30 with w of peace and truth,
Job 4: 4 Your w have upheld him who
Job 6: 3 therefore my w have been rash
Job 6:10 the w of the Holy One
Job 6:25 How forceful are right w
Job 6:26 Do you intend to reprove my w
Job 8: 2 the w of your mouth be like a
Job 8:10 and utter w from their heart
Job 9:14 choose my w to reason with
Job 11: 2 multitude of w be answered
Job 12:11 Does not the ear test w and
Job 15:13 let such w go out of your
Job 16: 3 Shall w of wind have an end
Job 16: 4 I could heap up w against you
Job 18: 2 long till you put an end to w
Job 19: 2 and break me in pieces with w
Job 19:23 Oh, that my w were written
Job 21:34 you comfort me with empty w
Job 22:22 lay up His w in your heart
Job 23: 5 I would know the w which He
Job 23:12 I have treasured the w of His
Job 26: 4 To whom have you uttered w
Job 29:22 After my w they did not speak
Job 31:40 The w of Job are ended
Job 32:11 Indeed I waited for your w
Job 32:12 Job, or answered his w
Job 32:14 not directed his w against me
Job 32:14 not answer him with your w
Job 32:15 w escape them
Job 32:18 For I am full of w
Job 33: 1 speech, and listen to all my w
Job 33: 3 My w come from my upright
Job 33: 5 set your w in order before me
Job 33: 8 heard the sound of your w
Job 33:13 an accounting of any of His w
Job 34: 2 Hear my w, you wise men
Job 34: 3 For the ear tests w as the
Job 34:16 listen to the sound of my w
Job 34:35 his w are without wisdom
Job 34:37 multiplies his w against God
Job 35:16 he multiplies w without
Job 36: 2 w to speak on God's behalf
Job 36: 4 For truly my w are not false
Job 38: 2 by w without knowledge
Job 42: 7 had spoken these w to Job
Ps 5: 1 Give ear to my w, O LORD,
Ps 12: 6 w of the LORD are pure w
Ps 19: 4 their w to the end of the
Ps 19:14 Let the w of my mouth and the
Ps 22: 1 from the w of My groaning
Ps 36: 3 The w of his mouth are
Ps 41: 6 to see me, he speaks vain w
Ps 50:17 And cast My w behind you
Ps 52: 4 You love all devouring w, You
Ps 54: 2 Give ear to the w of my mouth
Ps 55:21 The w of his mouth were
Ps 55:21 His w were softer than oil,
Ps 56: 5 All day they twist my w
Ps 59:12 the w of their lips, Let them
Ps 64: 3 their arrows—bitter w
Ps 78: 1 ears to the w of my mouth
Ps 106:12 Then they believed His w
Ps 107:11 rebelled against the w of God
Ps 109: 3 me with w of hatred, And
Ps 119:57 said that I would keep Your w
Ps 119:103 sweet are Your w to my taste
Ps 119:130 of Your w gives light
Ps 119:139 enemies have forgotten Your w
Ps 138: 4 they hear the w of Your mouth
Ps 141: 6 the cliff, And they hear my w
Ps 144: 8 Whose mouth speaks vain w
Ps 144:11 Whose mouth speaks vain w
Prov 1: 2 to perceive the w of
Prov 1: 6 the w of the wise and their
Prov 1:21 in the city she speaks her w
Prov 1:23 I will make my w known to you
Prov 2: 1 My son, if you receive my w
Prov 2:16 who flatters with her w,
Prov 4: 4 Let your heart retain my w
Prov 4: 5 away from the w of my mouth
Prov 4:20 son, give attention to my w
Prov 5: 7 depart from the w of my mouth
Prov 6: 2 by the w of your own mouth
Prov 6: 2 taken by the w of your mouth
Prov 7: 1 My son, keep my w, and
Prov 7: 5 who flatters with her w
Prov 7:24 to the w of my mouth
Prov 8: 8 All the w of my mouth are
Prov 10:19 of w sin is not lacking, but
Prov 12: 6 The w of the wicked are
Prov 15:26 but the w of the pure are
Prov 16:24 Pleasant w are like a
Prov 17:27 has knowledge spares his w
Prov 18: 4 The w of a man's mouth are
Prov 18: 8 The w of a talebearer are
Prov 19: 7 He may pursue them with w
Prov 19:27 stray from the w of knowledge
Prov 22:12 the w of the faithless
Prov 22:17 hear the w of the wise, and
Prov 22:21 certainty of the w of truth
Prov 22:21 that you may answer w of
Prov 23: 8 up, and waste your pleasant w
Prov 23: 9 despise the wisdom of your w
Prov 23:12 your ears to w of knowledge
Prov 26:22 The w of a talebearer are
Prov 29:19 not be corrected by mere w
Prov 29:20 you see a man hasty in his w
Prov 30: 1 The w of Agur the son of
Prov 30: 6 Do not add to His w, lest He
Prov 31: 1 The w of King Lemuel, the
Eccl 1: 1 The w of the Preacher, the
Eccl 5: 2 therefore let your w be few
Eccl 5: 3 voice is known by his many w
Eccl 5: 7 many w there is also vanity
Eccl 9:16 and his w are not heard
Eccl 9:17 W of the wise, spoken quietly
Eccl 10:12 The w of a wise man's mouth
Eccl 10:13 the w of his mouth begin with
Eccl 10:14 A fool also multiplies w
Eccl 12:10 sought to find acceptable w
Eccl 12:10 was upright—w of truth
Eccl 12:11 The w of the wise are like
Eccl 12:11 the w of scholars are like
Is 29:11 w of a book that is sealed
Is 29:18 shall hear the w of the book
Is 31: 2 and will not call back His w
Is 32: 7 destroy the poor with lying w
Is 36: 5 but they are vain w
Is 36:12 and to you to speak these w
Is 36:13 Hear the w of the great king,
Is 36:22 and told him the w of the
Is 37: 4 hear the w of the Rabshakeh
Is 37: 4 will reprove the w which the
Is 37: 6 of the w which you have heard
Is 37:17 hear all the w of Sennacherib
Is 41:26 is no one who hears your w
Is 51:16 I have put My w in your mouth
Is 58:13 nor speaking your own w,
Is 59: 4 they trust in empty w and
Is 59:13 from the heart w of falsehood
Is 59:21 My w which I have put in your
Jer 1: 1 The w of Jeremiah the son of
Jer 1: 9 I have put My w in your mouth
Jer 3:12 proclaim these w toward the
Jer 5:14 I will make My w in your
Jer 6:19 they have not heeded My w
Jer 7: 4 Do not trust in these lying w
Jer 7: 8 in lying w that cannot profit
Jer 7:27 speak all these w to them
Jer 11: 2 Hear the w of this covenant,
Jer 11: 3 obey the w of this covenant
Jer 11: 6 Proclaim all these w in the
Jer 11: 6 Hear the w of this covenant
Jer 11: 8 all the w of this covenant
Jer 11:10 who refused to hear My w, and
Jer 12: 6 they speak smooth w to you
Jer 13:10 who refuse to hear My w, who
Jer 15:16 Your w were found, and I ate
Jer 16:10 show this people all these w
Jer 18: 2 I will cause you to hear My w
Jer 18:18 not give heed to any of his w
Jer 19: 2 proclaim there the w that I
Jer 19:15 that they might not hear My w
Jer 22: 5 if you will not hear these w
Jer 23: 9 and because of His holy w
Jer 23:16 to the w of the prophets who
Jer 23:22 caused My people to hear My w
Jer 23:30 who steal My w every one from
Jer 23:36 the w of the living God, the
Jer 25: 8 you have not heard My w,
Jer 25:13 My w which I have pronounced
Jer 25:30 against them all these w, and
Jer 26: 2 all the w that I command you
Jer 26: 5 to heed the w of My servants
Jer 26: 7 Jeremiah speaking these w in
Jer 26:12 all the w that you have heard
Jer 26:15 all these w in your hearing
Jer 26:20 to all the w of Jeremiah
Jer 26:21 all the princes, heard his w
Jer 27:12 according to all these w,
Jer 27:14 do not listen to the w of the
Jer 27:16 to the w of your prophets who
Jer 28: 6 the LORD perform your w which
Jer 29: 1 Now these are the w of the
Jer 29:19 they have not heeded My w
Jer 29:23 spoken lying w in My name
Jer 30: 2 w that I have spoken to you
Jer 30: 4 Now these are the w that the
Jer 34: 6 w to Zedekiah king of Judah
Jer 34:18 w of the covenant which they
Jer 35:13 instruction to obey My w
Jer 35:14 The w of Jonadab the son of
Jer 36: 2 write on it all the w that I
Jer 36: 4 all the w of the LORD which
Jer 36: 6 the w of the LORD, in the
Jer 36: 8 w of the LORD in the LORD's
Jer 36:10 read from the book the w of
Jer 36:11 heard all the w of the LORD
Jer 36:13 the w that he had heard when
Jer 36:16 when they had heard all the w
Jer 36:16 tell the king of all these w
Jer 36:17 how did you write all these w
Jer 36:18 his mouth all these w to me
Jer 36:20 told all the w in the hearing
Jer 36:24 who heard all these w
Jer 36:27 burned the scroll with the w
Jer 36:28 w that were in the first
Jer 36:32 of Jeremiah all the w of the
Jer 36:32 added to them many similar w
Jer 37: 2 the land gave heed to the w
Jer 38: 1 son of Malchiah heard the w
Jer 38: 4 by speaking such w to them
Jer 38:24 Let no one know of these w
Jer 38:27 w that the king had commanded
Jer 39:16 I will bring My w upon this
Jer 42: 4 your God according to your w
Jer 43: 1 the w of the LORD their God
Jer 43: 1 sent him to them, all these w
Jer 44:28 shall know whose w will stand
Jer 44:29 w will surely stand against
Jer 45: 1 these w in a book at the
Jer 51:60 all these w that are written
Jer 51:61 see it, and read all these w
Jer 51:64 far are the w of Jeremiah

Ezek 2: 6 them nor be afraid of their **w**
Ezek 2: 6 do not be afraid of their **w**
Ezek 2: 7 You shall speak My **w** to them
Ezek 3: 4 and speak with My **w** to them
Ezek 3: 6 whose **w** you cannot understand
Ezek 3:10 all My **w** that I speak to you
Ezek 12:28 None of My **w** will be
Ezek 33:31 people, and they hear your **w**
Ezek 33:32 for they hear your **w**, but
Ezek 35:13 multiplied your **w** against Me
Dan 2: 9 corrupt **w** before me till the
Dan 5:10 because of the **w** of the king
Dan 6:14 king, when he heard these **w**
Dan 7: 8 a mouth speaking pompous **w**
Dan 7:11 **w** which the horn was speaking
Dan 7:20 mouth which spoke pompous **w**
Dan 7:25 **w** against the Most High,
Dan 9:12 And He has confirmed His **w**
Dan 10: 6 the sound of his **w** like the
Dan 10: 9 I heard the sound of his **w**
Dan 10: 9 I heard the sound of his **w** I
Dan 10:11 understand the **w** that I speak
Dan 10:12 your God, your **w** were heard
Dan 10:12 I have come because of your **w**
Dan 10:15 he had spoken such **w** to me
Dan 12: 4 you, Daniel, shut up the **w**
Dan 12: 9 for the **w** are closed up and
Hos 6: 5 them by the **w** of My mouth
Hos 10: 4 They have spoken **w**, swearing
Hos 14: 2 Take **w** with you, and return to
Amos 1: 1 The **w** of Amos, who was among
Amos 7:10 is not able to bear all his **w**
Amos 8:11 of hearing the **w** of the LORD
Mic 2: 7 Do not My **w** do good to him
Hag 1:12 the **w** of Haggai the prophet,
Zech 1: 6 Yet surely My **w** and My
Zech 1:13 me, with good and comforting **w**
Zech 7: 7 you not have obeyed the **w**
Zech 7:12 the **w** which the LORD of hosts
Zech 8: 9 these **w** by the mouth of the
Mal 2:17 wearied the LORD with your **w**
Mal 3:13 Your **w** have been harsh
Matt 6: 7 be heard for their many **w**
Matt 10:14 receive you nor hear your **w**
Matt 12:37 For by your **w** you will be
Matt 12:37 and by your **w** you will be
Matt 22:22 When they had heard these **w**
Matt 24:35 but My **w** will by no means
Matt 26:44 third time, saying the same **w**
Mark 8:38 My **w** in this adulterous and
Mark 10:24 were astonished at His **w**
Mark 12:13 to catch Him in His **w**
Mark 13:31 but My **w** will by no means
Mark 14:39 prayed, and spoke the same **w**
Luke 1:20 you did not believe my **w**
Luke 3: 4 the **w** of Isaiah the prophet
Luke 4:22 marveled at the gracious **w**
Luke 9:26 is ashamed of Me and My **w**, of
Luke 9:44 Let these **w** sink down into
Luke 20:20 they might seize on His **w**
Luke 20:26 His **w** in the presence of the
Luke 21:33 but My **w** will by no means
Luke 23: 9 he questioned Him with many **w**
Luke 24: 8 And they remembered His **w**
Luke 24:11 their **w** seemed to them like
Luke 24:44 These are the **w** which I spoke
John 3:34 has sent speaks the **w** of God
John 5:47 how will you believe My **w**
John 6:63 The **w** that I speak to you are
John 6:68 You have the **w** of eternal
John 8:20 These **w** Jesus spoke in the
John 8:30 As He spoke these **w**, many
John 8:47 who is of God hears God's **w**
John 9:40 were with Him heard these **w**
John 10:21 These are not the **w** of one
John 12:47 And if anyone hears My **w** and
John 12:48 Me, and does not receive My **w**
John 14:10 The **w** that I speak to you I
John 14:24 love Me does not keep My **w**
John 15: 7 My **w** abide in you, you will
John 17: 1 Jesus spoke these **w**, lifted
John 17: 8 the **w** which You have given Me
John 18: 1 When Jesus had spoken these **w**
Acts 2:14 be known to you, and heed my **w**
Acts 2:22 Men of Israel, hear these **w**
Acts 2:40 many other **w** he testified
Acts 5: 5 Then Ananias, hearing these **w**
Acts 5:20 people all the **w** of this life
Acts 6:11 blasphemous **w** against Moses
Acts 6:13 **w** against this holy place
Acts 7:22 Egyptians, and was mighty in **w**
Acts 10:22 house, and to hear **w** from you
Acts 10:44 was still speaking these **w**
Acts 11:14 will tell you **w** by which you
Acts 13:42 **w** might be preached to them
Acts 15:15 And with this the **w** of the
Acts 15:24 us have troubled you with **w**
Acts 15:32 the brethren with many **w** and
Acts 16:36 reported these **w** to Paul,
Acts 16:38 these **w** to the magistrates
Acts 18:15 But if it is a question of **w**
Acts 20: 2 encouraged them with many **w**
Acts 20:35 remember the **w** of the Lord
Acts 20:38 all for the **w** which he spoke
Acts 24: 4 courtesy, a few **w** from us
Acts 26:25 but speak the **w** of truth
Acts 28:29 And when he had said these **w**
Rom 3: 4 may be justified in Your **w**
Rom 10:18 their **w** to the ends of the
Rom 16:18 own belly, and by smooth **w**
1Co 1:17 gospel, not with wisdom of **w**
1Co 2: 4 persuasive **w** of human wisdom
1Co 2:13 not in **w** which man's wisdom
1Co 14: 9 tongue **w** easy to understand
1Co 14:19 five **w** with my understanding
1Co 14:19 ten thousand **w** in a tongue
2Co 12: 4 and heard inexpressible **w**,
Eph 3: 3 (as I wrote before in a few **w**
Eph 5: 6 one deceive you with empty **w**
Col 2: 4 deceive you with persuasive **w**
1Th 2: 5 time did we use flattering **w**
1Th 4:18 one another with these **w**
1Ti 4: 6 nourished in the **w** of faith
1Ti 6: 3 not consent to wholesome **w**
1Ti 6: 3 even the **w** of our Lord Jesus
1Ti 6: 4 disputes and arguments over **w**
2Ti 1:13 **w** which you have heard from
2Ti 2:14 strive about **w** to no profit
2Ti 4:15 he has greatly resisted our **w**
Heb 12:19 a trumpet and the voice of **w**
Heb 13:22 have written to you in few **w**
2Pe 2: 3 exploit you with deceptive **w**
2Pe 2:18 great swelling **w** of emptiness
2Pe 3: 2 you may be mindful of the **w**
3Jn 10 against us with malicious **w**
Jude 16 they mouth great swelling **w**
Jude 17 remember the **w** which were
Rev 1: 3 hear the **w** of this prophecy
Rev 17:17 beast, until the **w** of God are
Rev 21: 5 Write, for these **w** are true
Rev 22: 6 These **w** are faithful and true
Rev 22: 7 the **w** of the prophecy of this
Rev 22: 9 who keep the **w** of this book
Rev 22:10 Do not seal the **w** of the
Rev 22:18 the **w** of the prophecy of this
Rev 22:19 the **w** of the book of this

WORE (*see* WEAR)
1Sa 22:18 men who **w** a linen ephod
2Sa 13:18 daughters **w** such apparel
1Ki 20:32 So they **w** sackcloth around
2Ki 1: 8 **w** a leather belt around his
1Ch 15:27 David also **w** a linen ephod
Neh 4:16 shields, the bows, and **w** armor
Luke 8:27 he **w** no clothes, nor did he

WORK (*see* WORKED, WORKER, WORKING, WORKMAN, WORK'S, WORKS)
Gen 2: 2 ended His **w** which He had done
Gen 2: 2 all His **w** which He had done
Gen 2: 3 His **w** which God had created
Gen 5:29 comfort us concerning our **w**
Gen 39:11 into the house to do his **w**
Ex 5: 4 take the people from their **w**
Ex 5: 9 Let more **w** be laid on the men
Ex 5:11 yet none of your **w** will be
Ex 5:13 Fulfill your **w**, your daily
Ex 5:18 Therefore go now and **w**
Ex 12:16 No manner of **w** shall be done
Ex 14:31 Thus Israel saw the great **w**
Ex 18:20 walk and the **w** they must do
Ex 20: 9 shall labor and do all your **w**
Ex 20:10 In it you shall do no **w**
Ex 23:12 Six days you shall do your **w**
Ex 24:10 a paved **w** of sapphire stone
Ex 25:18 of hammered **w** you shall make
Ex 25:31 shall be of hammered **w**
Ex 28:11 With the **w** of an engraver in
Ex 28:39 make the sash of woven **w**
Ex 31: 4 to **w** in gold, in silver, in
Ex 31: 5 and to **w** in all manner of
Ex 31:14 for whoever does any **w** on it
Ex 31:15 **W** shall be done for six days
Ex 31:15 Whoever does any **w** on the
Ex 32:16 the tablets were the **w** of God
Ex 34:10 shall see the **w** of the LORD
Ex 34:21 Six days you shall **w**, but on
Ex 35: 2 **W** shall be done for six days,
Ex 35: 2 Whoever does any **w** on it
Ex 35:21 the **w** of the tabernacle of
Ex 35:24 wood for any **w** of the service
Ex 35:29 all kinds of **w** which the LORD
Ex 35:32 to **w** in gold and silver and
Ex 35:33 and to **w** in all manner of
Ex 35:35 manner of **w** of the engraver
Ex 35:35 those who do every **w** and those
Ex 36: 1 of **w** for the service of the
Ex 36: 2 stirred, to come and do the **w**
Ex 36: 3 **w** of the service of making
Ex 36: 4 the **w** of the sanctuary came
Ex 36: 4 each from the **w** he was doing
Ex 36: 5 for the service of the **w**
Ex 36: 6 **w** for the offering of the
Ex 36: 7 for all the **w** to be done
Ex 37:17 of hammered **w** he made the
Ex 37:29 to the **w** of the perfumer
Ex 38:24 all the **w** of the holy place
Ex 39: 3 to **w** it in with the blue and
Ex 39:22 robe of the ephod of woven **w**
Ex 39:32 Thus all the **w** of the
Ex 39:42 of Israel did all the **w**
Ex 39:43 Moses looked over all the **w**
Ex 40:33 So Moses finished the **w**
Lev 11:32 it is, in which any **w** is done
Lev 16:29 do no **w** at all, whether a
Lev 23: 3 Six days shall **w** be done
Lev 23: 3 You shall do no **w** on it
Lev 23: 7 shall do no customary **w** on it
Lev 23: 8 shall do no customary **w** on it
Lev 23:21 shall do no customary **w** on it
Lev 23:25 shall do no customary **w** on it
Lev 23:28 you shall do no **w** on that
Lev 23:30 does any **w** on that same day
Lev 23:31 You shall do no manner of **w**
Lev 23:35 shall do no customary **w** on it
Lev 23:36 shall do no customary **w** on it
Num 3: 7 to do the **w** of the tabernacle
Num 3: 8 to do the **w** of the tabernacle
Num 3:26 to all the **w** relating to them
Num 3:31 all the **w** relating to them
Num 3:36 all the **w** relating to them,
Num 4: 3 do the **w** in the tabernacle of
Num 4:23 to do the **w** in the tabernacle
Num 4:30 do the **w** of the tabernacle of
Num 4:35 for **w** in the tabernacle of
Num 4:39 for **w** in the tabernacle of
Num 4:43 for **w** in the tabernacle of
Num 4:47 came to do the **w** of service
Num 4:47 the **w** of bearing burdens in
Num 7: 5 the **w** of the tabernacle of
Num 8: 4 its flowers it was hammered **w**
Num 8:11 may perform the **w** of the LORD
Num 8:19 to do the **w** for the children
Num 8:22 their **w** in the tabernacle of
Num 8:24 in the **w** of the tabernacle of
Num 8:25 must cease performing this **w**
Num 8:25 and shall **w** no more
Num 8:26 they themselves shall do no **w**
Num 10: 2 shall make them of hammered **w**
Num 16: 9 to do the **w** of the tabernacle
Num 18: 4 meeting, for all the **w** of the
Num 18: 6 to do the **w** of the tabernacle
Num 18:21 in return for the **w** which
Num 18:21 the **w** of the tabernacle of
Num 18:23 the **w** of the tabernacle of
Num 18:31 your **w** in the tabernacle of
Num 28:18 You shall do no customary **w**
Num 28:25 You shall do no customary **w**
Num 28:26 You shall do no customary **w**
Num 29: 1 You shall do no customary **w**
Num 29: 7 you shall not do any **w**
Num 29:12 You shall do no customary **w**
Num 29:35 You shall do no customary **w**
Deut 2: 7 you in all the **w** of your hand
Deut 4:28 the **w** of men's hands, wood and
Deut 5:13 shall labor and do all your **w**
Deut 5:14 In it you shall not do any **w**
Deut 14:29 may bless you in all the **w** of
Deut 15:19 you shall do no **w** with the
Deut 16: 8 You shall do no **w** on it
Deut 16:15 in all the **w** of your hands,

Deut 24:19 in all the w of your hands
Deut 27:15 the w of the hands of the
Deut 28:12 bless all the w of your hand
Deut 30: 9 in all the w of your hand
Deut 31:29 through the w of your hands
Deut 32: 4 is the Rock, His w is perfect
Deut 33:11 accept the w of his hands
Judg 2:10 the w which He had done for
Judg 13:12 boy's rule of life, and his w
Judg 19:16 his w in the field at evening
Ruth 2:12 The LORD repay your w, and a
Ruth 2:19 And where did you w
1Sa 8:16 donkeys, and put them to his w
1Sa 14: 6 that the LORD will w for us
2Sa 9:10 shall w the land for him, and
2Sa 12:31 and put them to w with saws
1Ki 5:16 people who labored in the w
1Ki 6:35 evenly on the carved w
1Ki 7:14 with all kinds of bronze w
1Ki 7:14 King Solomon and did all his w
1Ki 7:22 So the w of the pillars was
1Ki 7:29 were wreaths of plaited w
1Ki 7:40 finished doing all the w that
1Ki 7:51 Thus all the w that King
1Ki 9:23 who were over Solomon's w
1Ki 9:23 over the people who did the w
1Ki 9:27 to w with the servants of
1Ki 16: 7 anger with the w of his hands
2Ki 12:11 hands of those who did the w
2Ki 19:18 but the w of men's hands
2Ki 22: 5 the hand of those doing the w
2Ki 22: 5 house of the LORD doing the w
2Ki 22: 9 hand of those who do the w
1Ch 4:23 dwelt with the king for his w
1Ch 6:49 for all the w of the Most
1Ch 9:13 were very able men for the w
1Ch 9:19 of the w of the service,
1Ch 9:33 were employed in that w day
1Ch 16:37 as every day's w required
1Ch 20: 3 and put them to w with saws
1Ch 22:15 men for every kind of w
1Ch 23: 4 were to look after the w of
1Ch 23:24 who did the w for the service
1Ch 23:28 the w of the service of the
1Ch 23:32 w of the house of the LORD
1Ch 26: 8 men with strength for the w
1Ch 27:26 w of the field for tilling
1Ch 28:13 for all the w of the service
1Ch 28:20 the w for the service of the
1Ch 29: 1 the w is great, because the
1Ch 29: 5 for all kinds of w to be done
1Ch 29: 6 officers over the king's w
1Ch 29: 7 They gave for the w of the
2Ch 2: 7 a man skillful to w in gold
2Ch 2:14 Tyre), skilled to w in gold
2Ch 2:18 to make the people w
2Ch 4:11 w that he was to do for King
2Ch 5: 1 So all the w that Solomon had
2Ch 8: 9 of Israel servants for his w
2Ch 8:16 Now all the w of Solomon was
2Ch 15: 7 for your w shall be rewarded
2Ch 16: 5 Ramah and ceased his w
2Ch 24:12 it to those who did the w of
2Ch 24:13 the w was completed by them
2Ch 29:34 them until the w was ended
2Ch 31:16 for the w of his service, by
2Ch 31:17 and up according to their w
2Ch 31:21 in every w that he began in
2Ch 32:19 the w of men's hands
2Ch 34:12 the men did the w faithfully
2Ch 34:13 did w in any kind of service
Ezra 2:69 the w sixty-one thousand gold
Ezra 3: 8 to Jerusalem, began w and
Ezra 3: 8 above to oversee the w of the
Ezra 4:24 Thus the w of the house of
Ezra 5: 8 this w goes on diligently and
Ezra 6: 7 Let the w of this house of
Ezra 6:22 their hands in the w of the
Ezra 10:13 Nor is this the w of one or
Neh 2:16 or the others who did the w
Neh 2:18 their hands to do this good w
Neh 3: 5 to the w of their Lord
Neh 4: 6 the people had a mind to w
Neh 4:11 them and cause the w to cease
Neh 4:15 the wall, everyone to his w
Neh 4:19 The w is great and extensive,
Neh 4:21 So we labored in the w, and
Neh 5:16 continued the w on this wall
Neh 5:16 were gathered there for the w
Neh 6: 3 I am doing a great w, so that
Neh 6: 3 Why should the w cease while
Neh 6: 9 will be weakened in the w
Neh 6:16 this w was done by our God
Neh 7:70 fathers' houses gave to the w
Neh 7:71 of the w twenty thousand gold
Neh 10:33 all the w of the house of our
Neh 11:12 the w of the house were eight
Neh 13:10 the singers who did the w had
Esth 3: 9 hands of those who do the w
Esth 9: 3 all those doing the king's w
Job 1:10 blessed the w of his hands
Job 10: 3 despise the w of Your hands
Job 14:15 desire the w of Your hands
Job 24: 5 they go out to their w,
Job 34:11 repays man according to his w
Job 34:19 are all the w of His hands
Job 36: 9 then He tells them their w
Job 36:24 Remember to magnify His w
Job 37: 7 that all men may know His w
Ps 8: 3 the w of Your fingers, The
Ps 9:16 in the w of his own hands
Ps 28: 4 to the w of their hands
Ps 33: 4 all His w is done in truth
Ps 58: 2 No, in heart you w wickedness
Ps 62:12 each one according to his w
Ps 64: 9 And shall declare the w of God
Ps 74: 6 they break down its carved w
Ps 77:12 also meditate on all Your w
Ps 88:10 Will You w wonders for the
Ps 90:16 Let Your w appear to Your
Ps 90:17 establish the w of our hands
Ps 90:17 establish the w of our hands
Ps 92: 4 made me glad through Your w
Ps 95: 9 Me, though they saw My w
Ps 101: 3 I hate the w of those who
Ps 102:25 are the w of Your hands
Ps 104:23 Man goes out to his w And to
Ps 111: 3 His w is honorable and
Ps 115: 4 and gold, The w of men's hands
Ps 135:15 and gold, The w of men's hands
Ps 141: 4 works With men who w iniquity
Ps 143: 5 I muse on the w of Your hands
Prov 11:18 wicked man does deceptive w
Prov 16:11 weights in the bag are His w
Prov 18: 9 He who is slothful in his w
Prov 21: 8 for the pure, his w is right
Prov 22:29 see a man who excels in his w
Prov 24:27 Prepare your outside w, make
Prov 24:29 to the man according to his w
Eccl 2:17 I hated life because the w
Eccl 2:23 sorrowful, and his w grievous
Eccl 2:26 He gives the w of gathering
Eccl 3:11 out the w that God does from
Eccl 3:17 every purpose and for every w
Eccl 4: 3 who has not seen the evil w
Eccl 4: 4 every skillful w a man is
Eccl 5: 6 destroy the w of your hands
Eccl 7:13 Consider the w of God
Eccl 8: 9 applied my heart to every w
Eccl 8:11 w is not executed speedily
Eccl 8:14 to the w of the wicked
Eccl 8:14 to the w of the righteous
Eccl 8:17 then I saw all the w of God
Eccl 8:17 a man cannot find out the w
Eccl 9:10 for there is no w or device
Eccl 12:14 bring every w into judgment
Song 7: 1 the w of the hands of a
Is 1:31 and the w of it as a spark
Is 2: 8 they worship the w of their
Is 5:12 not regard the w of the LORD
Is 5:19 make speed and hasten His w
Is 10:12 all His w on Mount Zion and on
Is 17: 8 altars, the w of his hands
Is 19: 9 those who w in fine flax and
Is 19:14 Egypt to err in all her w
Is 19:15 will there be any w for Egypt
Is 19:25 and Assyria the w of My hands
Is 28:21 do His w, His awesome w
Is 29:14 marvelous w among this people
Is 29:14 a marvelous w
Is 29:23 the w of My hands, in his
Is 30:24 the young donkeys that w the
Is 31: 2 help of those who w iniquity
Is 32: 6 and his heart will w iniquity
Is 32:17 The w of righteousness will
Is 37:19 but the w of men's hands
Is 40:10 with Him, and His w before Him
Is 41:24 nothing, and your w is nothing
Is 43:13 I w, and who will reverse it
Is 45:11 concerning the w of My hands
Is 49: 4 the LORD, and my w with my
Is 54:16 forth an instrument for his w
Is 60:21 the w of My hands, that I may
Is 61: 8 will direct their w in truth
Is 62:11 with Him, and His w before Him
Is 64: 8 all we are the w of Your hand
Is 65: 7 former w into their bosom
Is 65:22 enjoy the w of their hands
Jer 10: 3 the w of the hands of the
Jer 10: 9 the w of the craftsman and of
Jer 10: 9 are all the w of skillful men
Jer 10:15 are futile, a w of errors
Jer 17:22 the Sabbath day, nor do any w
Jer 17:24 Sabbath day, to do no w in it
Jer 22:13 gives him nothing for his w
Jer 31:16 for your w shall be rewarded,
Jer 32:19 in counsel and mighty in w
Jer 32:30 with the w of their hands
Jer 48:10 the w of the LORD deceitfully
Jer 50:25 For this is the w of the Lord
Jer 50:29 Repay her according to her w
Jer 51:10 the w of the LORD our God
Jer 51:18 are futile, a w of errors
Lam 3:64 to the w of their hands
Lam 4: 2 the w of the hands of the
Ezek 15: 4 Is it useful for any w
Ezek 15: 5 will it be useful for any w
Ezek 44:14 of the temple, for all its w
Hos 13: 2 of it is the w of craftsmen
Hos 14: 3 anymore to the w of our hands
Mic 2: 1 And w out evil on their beds
Mic 5:13 worship the w of your hands
Hab 1: 5 For I will w a w in your
Hab 3: 2 revive Your w in the midst of
Zeph 2:14 He will lay bare the cedar w
Hag 2: 4 land,' says the LORD, 'and w
Hag 2:14 so is every w of their hands
Matt 14: 2 these powers are at w in him
Matt 21:28 go, w today in my vineyard
Matt 26:10 she has done a good w for Me
Mark 6: 5 He could do no mighty w there
Mark 6:14 these powers are at w in him
Mark 13:34 servants, and to each his w
Mark 14: 6 She has done a good w for Me
Luke 13:14 days on which men ought to w
John 4:34 sent Me, and to finish His w
John 6:28 that we may w the works of
John 6:29 This is the w of God, that
John 6:30 What w will You do
John 7:21 I did one w, and you all
John 9: 4 I must w the works of Him who
John 9: 4 is coming when no one can w
John 10:33 For a good w we do not stone
John 17: 4 I have finished the w which
Acts 5:38 this plan or this w is of men
Acts 13: 2 Saul for the w to which I
Acts 13:41 for I w a w in your days,
Acts 13:41 a w which you will by no
Acts 14:26 w which they had completed
Acts 15:38 not gone with them to the w
Rom 2:15 who show the w of the law
Rom 4: 5 not w but believes on Him who
Rom 7: 5 at w in our members to bear
Rom 8:28 we know that all things w
Rom 9:28 For He will finish the w and
Rom 9:28 make a short w upon the earth
Rom 11: 6 otherwise w is no longer w
Rom 14:20 Do not destroy the w of God
1Co 3:13 each one's w will become
1Co 3:13 fire will test each one's w
1Co 3:14 If anyone's w which he has
1Co 3:15 If anyone's w is burned, he
1Co 9: 1 Are you not my w in the Lord
1Co 15:58 in the w of the Lord, knowing
1Co 16:10 for he does the w of the Lord
2Co 9: 8 an abundance for every good w
Gal 6: 4 each one examine his own w
Eph 4:12 saints for the w of ministry
Eph 4:19 to w all uncleanness with
Phil 1: 6 w in you will complete it
Phil 2:12 w out your own salvation with
Phil 2:30 because for the w of Christ
Col 1:10 fruitful in every good w and
1Th 1: 3 ceasing your w of faith,
1Th 4:11 to w with your own hands, as
2Th 1:11 the w of faith with power,
2Th 2: 7 lawlessness is already at w
2Th 2:17 you in every good word and w
2Th 3:10 If anyone will not w, neither
2Th 3:12 that they w in quietness and

1Ti 3: 1 a bishop, he desires a good w
1Ti 5:10 followed every good w
2Ti 2:21 prepared for every good w
2Ti 3:17 equipped for every good w
2Ti 4: 5 do the w of an evangelist,
2Ti 4:18 deliver me from every evil w
Tit 1:16 disqualified for every good w
Tit 3: 1 to be ready for every good w
Heb 1:10 are the w of Your hands
Heb 6:10 not unjust to forget your w
Heb 13:21 every good w to do His will
Jas 1: 4 patience have its perfect w
Jas 1:25 hearer but a doer of the w
1Pe 1:17 according to each one's w
Rev 22:12 every one according to his w

WORKED (*see* WORK)
Ex 8:18 Now the magicians so w with
Ex 36: 8 artisans among them who w on
Deut 21: 3 a heifer which has not been w
Josh 9: 4 they w craftily, and went and
Ruth 2:19 with whom she had w, and said,
Ruth 2:19 with whom I w today is Boaz
1Sa 14:45 for he has w with God this
2Ki 12:11 builders who w on the house
2Ch 24:12 and also those who w in iron
2Ch 34:10 w in the house of the LORD
Neh 4:16 my servants w at construction
Neh 4:17 hand they w at construction
Neh 9:18 and w great provocations,
Neh 9:26 they w great provocations
Ps 78:43 When He w His signs in Egypt,
Ezek 23:29 take away all you have w for
Ezek 29:20 labor, because they w for Me
Dan 4: 2 Most High God has w for me
Hag 1:14 w on the house of the LORD of
Matt 20:12 last men have w only one hour
Acts 15:12 wonders God had w through
Acts 18: 3 he stayed with them and w
Acts 19:11 Now God w unusual miracles by
Gal 2: 8 (for He who w effectively in
Gal 2: 8 to the circumcised also w
Eph 1:20 which He w in Christ when He
2Th 3: 8 but w with labor and toil
Heb 11:33 w righteousness, obtained
2Jn 8 lose those things we w for
Rev 19:20 who w signs in his presence

WORKER (*see* WORK, WORKERS)
1Ki 7:14 was a man of Tyre, a bronze w
Eccl 3: 9 What profit has the w from
Matt 10:10 for a w is worthy of his food
Rom 16: 9 our fellow w in Christ, and
Rom 16:21 Timothy, my fellow w, and
2Co 8:23 and fellow w concerning you
Phil 2:25 my brother, fellow w, and
2Ti 2:15 a w who does not need to be

WORKERS (*see* WORKER)
1Ch 4:21 w of the house of Ashbea
1Ch 22:15 w of stone and timber, and all
Job 31: 3 for the w of iniquity
Job 34: 8 with the w of iniquity, and
Job 34:22 the w of iniquity may hide
Ps 5: 5 You hate all w of iniquity
Ps 6: 8 me, all you w of iniquity
Ps 14: 4 Have all the w of iniquity no
Ps 28: 3 with the w of iniquity, Who
Ps 36:12 There the w of iniquity have
Ps 37: 1 envious of the w of iniquity
Ps 53: 4 Have the w of iniquity no
Ps 59: 2 me from the w of iniquity
Ps 64: 2 of the w of iniquity,
Ps 92: 7 when all the w of iniquity
Ps 92: 9 All the w of iniquity shall
Ps 94: 4 All the w of iniquity boast
Ps 94:16 me against the w of iniquity
Ps 125: 5 away With the w of iniquity
Ps 141: 9 traps of the w of iniquity
Prov 10:29 come to the w of iniquity
Prov 21:15 come to the w of iniquity
Ezek 48:18 be food for the w of the city
Ezek 48:19 The w of the city, from all
Luke 13:27 Me, all you w of iniquity
Acts 19:25 the w of similar occupation
Rom 16: 3 my fellow w in Christ Jesus,
1Co 3: 9 For we are God's fellow w
1Co 12:29 Are all w of miracles
2Co 1:24 but are fellow w for your joy
2Co 6: 1 as w together with Him also
2Co 11:13 false apostles, deceitful w
Phil 3: 2 of dogs, beware of evil w
Phil 4: 3 and the rest of my fellow w
Col 4:11 These are my only fellow w
3Jn 8 become fellow w for the truth

WORKING (*see* WORK)
1Ki 7:14 skill in w with all kinds of
1Ch 22:16 Arise and begin w, and the LORD
Ezra 3: 9 those w on the house of God
Neh 4:22 by night and a w party by day
Ps 52: 2 a sharp razor, w deceitfully
Ps 74:12 W salvation in the midst of
Ezek 46: 1 shall be shut the six w days
Mark 16:20 the Lord w with them and
John 5:17 Father has been w until now
John 5:17 and I have been w
1Co 4:12 labor, w with our own hands
1Co 9: 6 no right to refrain from w
1Co 12:10 to another the w of miracles
2Co 4:12 So then death is w in us, but
2Co 4:17 is w for us a far more
Gal 5: 6 but faith w through love
Eph 1:19 according to the w of His
Eph 3: 7 the effective w of His power
Eph 4:16 w by which every part does
Eph 4:28 w with his hands what is good
Phil 3:21 according to the w by which
Col 1:29 striving according to His w
Col 2:12 through faith in the w of God
2Th 2: 9 according to the w of Satan
2Th 3:11 manner, not w at all, but are
Heb 13:21 will, w in you what is well
Jas 2:22 was w together with his works

WORKMAN (*see* WORK, WORKMANSHIP, WORKMEN)
Song 7: 1 of the hands of a skillful w
Is 40:19 The w molds a graven image,
Is 40:20 for himself a skillful w to
Jer 10: 3 work of the hands of the w
Hos 8: 6 a w made it, and it is not God

WORKMANSHIP (*see* WORKMAN)
Ex 28: 8 on it, shall be of the same w
Ex 28:15 woven according to the w of
Ex 31: 3 and in all manner of w,
Ex 31: 5 and to work in all manner of w
Ex 35:31 knowledge and all manner of w
Ex 35:33 in all manner of artistic w
Ex 39: 5 was on it was of the same w
Ex 39: 8 woven like the w of the ephod
Num 8: 4 Now this w of the lampstand
1Ki 7: 8 inside the hall, of like w
1Ki 7:33 The w of the wheels was like
1Ki 7:33 like the w of a chariot wheel
2Ki 16:10 according to all its w
1Ch 28:21 with you for all manner of w
Ezek 28:13 The w of your timbrels and
Eph 2:10 For we are His w, created in

WORKMEN (*see* WORKMAN, WORKMEN'S)
2Ki 12:14 But they gave that to the w
2Ki 12:15 the money to be paid to w
1Ch 22:15 Moreover there are w with you
1Ch 25: 1 the number of the w according
2Ch 24:13 So the w labored, and the work
2Ch 34:10 w who had the oversight of
2Ch 34:10 they gave it to the w who
2Ch 34:17 of the overseers and the w
Is 44:11 and the w, they are mere men

WORKMEN'S (*see* WORKMEN)
Judg 5:26 right hand to the w hammer

WORK'S (*see* WORK)
1Th 5:13 in love for their w sake

WORKS (*see* WORK)
Ex 23:24 nor do according to their w
Ex 31: 4 to design artistic w, to work
Ex 35:32 to design artistic w, to work
Ex 35:35 those who design artistic w
Num 16:28 has sent me to do all these w
Deut 3:24 can do anything like Your w
Deut 15:10 will bless you in all your w
Josh 24:31 who had known all the w of
Judg 2: 7 w of the LORD which He had
1Sa 8: 8 According to all the w which
1Sa 19: 4 because his w have been very
2Sa 12:31 cross over to the brick w
1Ki 13:11 told him all the w that the
2Ki 22:17 with all the w of their hands
1Ch 16: 9 talk of all His wondrous w
1Ch 16:12 marvelous w which He has done
1Ch 28:19 me, all the w of these plans
2Ch 20:37 the LORD has destroyed your w
2Ch 32:30 prospered in all his w
2Ch 34:25 with all the w of their hands
Neh 6:14 according to these their w
Neh 9:35 they turn from their wicked w
Job 23: 9 when He w on the left hand, I
Job 33:29 God w all these things, twice
Job 34:25 Therefore he knows their w
Job 37:14 the wondrous w of God
Job 37:16 those wondrous w of Him who
Ps 8: 6 over the w of Your hands
Ps 9: 1 tell of all Your marvelous w
Ps 14: 1 They have done abominable w
Ps 15: 2 w righteousness, And speaks
Ps 17: 4 Concerning the w of men, By
Ps 26: 7 tell of all Your wondrous w
Ps 28: 5 not regard the w of the LORD
Ps 33:15 He considers all their w
Ps 40: 5 are Your wonderful w Which
Ps 46: 8 behold the w of the LORD, Who
Ps 66: 3 How awesome are Your w
Ps 66: 5 Come and see the w of God
Ps 71:17 day I declare Your wondrous w
Ps 73:28 That I may declare all Your w
Ps 75: 1 For Your wondrous w declare
Ps 77:11 remember the w of the LORD
Ps 78: 4 His wonderful w that He has
Ps 78: 7 And not forget the w of God
Ps 78:11 And forgot His w And His
Ps 78:32 not believe in His wondrous w
Ps 86: 8 there any w like Your w
Ps 92: 4 in the w of Your hands
Ps 92: 5 O LORD, how great are Your w
Ps 101: 7 He who w deceit shall not
Ps 103:22 Bless the LORD, all His w
Ps 104:13 with the fruit of Your w
Ps 104:24 LORD, how manifold are Your w
Ps 104:31 May the LORD rejoice in His w
Ps 105: 2 Talk of all His wondrous w
Ps 105: 5 marvelous w which He has done
Ps 106:13 They soon forgot His w
Ps 106:22 Wondrous w in the land of Ham
Ps 106:35 Gentiles And learned their w
Ps 106:39 were defiled by their own w
Ps 107: 8 for His wonderful w to the
Ps 107:15 for His wonderful w to the
Ps 107:21 for His wonderful w to the
Ps 107:22 declare His w with rejoicing
Ps 107:24 They see the w of the LORD
Ps 107:31 for His wonderful w to the
Ps 111: 2 The w of the LORD are great,
Ps 111: 4 wonderful w to be remembered
Ps 111: 6 His people the power of His w
Ps 111: 7 The w of His hands are verity
Ps 118:17 And declare the w of the LORD
Ps 119:27 I meditate on Your wondrous w
Ps 138: 8 forsake the w of Your hands
Ps 139:14 Marvelous are Your w, And that
Ps 141: 4 To practice wicked w With men
Ps 143: 5 I meditate on all Your w
Ps 145: 4 praise Your w to another, And
Ps 145: 5 And on Your wondrous w
Ps 145: 9 mercies are over all His w
Ps 145:10 All Your w shall praise You,
Ps 145:17 ways, Gracious in all His w
Prov 8:22 His way, before His w of old
Prov 16: 3 Commit your w to the LORD
Prov 26:28 and a flattering mouth w ruin
Prov 31:13 willingly w with her hands
Prov 31:31 let her own w praise her in
Eccl 1:14 I have seen all the w that
Eccl 2: 4 I made my w great, I built
Eccl 2:11 the w that my hands had done
Eccl 3:22 should rejoice in his own w
Eccl 9: 1 their w are in the hand of
Eccl 9: 7 has already accepted your w
Eccl 11: 5 so you do not know the w of
Is 26:12 also done all our w in us
Is 29:15 and their w are in the dark
Is 41:29 their w are nothing
Is 44:12 the tongs w one in the coals
Is 44:12 w it with the strength of his
Is 57:12 your righteousness and your w
Is 59: 6 cover themselves with their w
Is 59: 6 their w are w of iniquity
Is 66:18 For I know their w and their
Jer 1:16 worshiped the w of their own
Jer 7:13 you have done all these w
Jer 8: 8 scribe certainly w falsehood
Jer 21: 2 to all His wonderful w, that

Jer 25: 6 with the w of your hands
Jer 25: 7 Me to anger with the w of
Jer 25:14 according to the w of their
Jer 44: 8 with the w of your hands,
Jer 48: 7 you have trusted in your w
Ezek 1:16 their w was like the color of
Ezek 1:16 The appearance of their w was
Ezek 6: 6 and your w may be abolished
Ezek 33:13 w shall be remembered
Dan 4:37 all of whose w are truth
Dan 6:27 and He w signs and wonders in
Dan 9:14 in all the w which He does
Amos 8: 7 never forget any of their w
Jon 3:10 Then God saw their w, that
Mic 6:16 all the w of Ahab's house are
Matt 5:16 that they may see your good w
Matt 11: 2 prison about the w of Christ
Matt 11:20 of His mighty w had been done
Matt 11:21 For if the mighty w which
Matt 11:23 for if the mighty w which
Matt 13:54 this wisdom and these mighty w
Matt 13:58 w there because of their
Matt 16:27 each according to his w
Matt 23: 3 not do according to their w
Matt 23: 5 But all their w they do to be
Mark 6: 2 Him, that such mighty w are
Mark 9:39 for no one who w a miracle in
Luke 10:13 For if the mighty w which
Luke 19:37 the mighty w they had seen
John 5:20 show Him greater w than these
John 5:36 for the w which the Father
John 5:36 the very w that I do
John 6:28 that we may work the w of God
John 7: 3 see the w that You are doing
John 7: 7 of it that its w are evil
John 8:39 you would do the w of Abraham
John 9: 3 but that the w of God should
John 9: 4 I must work the w of Him who
John 10:25 The w that I do in My
John 10:32 Many good w I have shown you
John 10:32 of those w do you stone Me
John 10:37 do not do the w of My Father
John 10:38 not believe Me, believe the w
John 11:47 For this Man w many signs
John 14:10 who dwells in Me does the w
John 14:11 the sake of the w themselves
John 14:12 the w that I do he will do
John 14:12 greater w than these he will
John 15:24 the w which no one else did
Acts 2:11 the wonderful w of God
Acts 7:41 rejoiced in the w of their
Acts 9:36 This woman was full of good w
Acts 10:35 w righteousness is accepted
Acts 15:18 from eternity are all His w
Acts 26:20 do w befitting repentance
Rom 2:10 everyone who w what is good
Rom 3:27 By what law? Of w?
Rom 4: 2 if Abraham was justified by w
Rom 4: 4 Now to him who w, the wages
Rom 4: 6 righteousness apart from w
Rom 9:11 not of w but of Him who calls
Rom 9:32 it were, by the w of the law
Rom 11: 6 then it is no longer of w
Rom 11: 6 But if it is of w, it is no
Rom 13: 3 are not a terror to good w
Rom 13:12 us cast off the w of darkness
1Co 12: 6 the same God who w all in all
1Co 12:11 the same Spirit w all these
1Co 16:16 to such, and to everyone who w
2Co 11:15 will be according to their w
Gal 2:16 w of the law but by faith in
Gal 2:16 and not by the w of the law
Gal 2:16 for by the w of the law no
Gal 3: 2 Spirit by the w of the law
Gal 3: 5 w miracles among you, does He
Gal 3: 5 He do it by the w of the law
Gal 3:10 w of the law are under the
Gal 5:19 Now the w of the flesh are
Eph 1:11 to the purpose of Him who w
Eph 2: 2 the spirit who now w in the
Eph 2: 9 not of w, lest anyone should
Eph 2:10 in Christ Jesus for good w
Eph 3:20 to the power that w in us
Eph 5:11 the unfruitful w of darkness
Phil 2:13 for it is God who w in you
Col 1:21 in your mind by wicked w, yet
Col 1:29 which w in me mightily
1Th 2:13 w in you who believe
1Ti 2:10 godliness, with good w
1Ti 5:10 well reported for good w
1Ti 5:25 the good w of some are
1Ti 6:18 that they be rich in good w
2Ti 1: 9 not according to our w, but
2Ti 4:14 repay him according to his w
Tit 1:16 but in w they deny Him, being
Tit 2: 7 to be a pattern of good w
Tit 2:14 people, zealous for good w
Tit 3: 5 not by w of righteousness
Tit 3: 8 be careful to maintain good w
Tit 3:14 also learn to maintain good w
Heb 2: 7 him over the w of Your hands
Heb 3: 9 Me, and saw My w forty years
Heb 4: 3 rest," although the w were
Heb 4: 4 seventh day from all His w"
Heb 4:10 his w as God did from His
Heb 6: 1 of repentance from dead w
Heb 9:14 w to serve the living God
Heb 10:24 to stir up love and good w
Jas 2:14 has faith but does not have w
Jas 2:17 itself, if it does not have w
Jas 2:18 You have faith, and I have w
Jas 2:18 me your faith without your w
Jas 2:18 show you my faith by my w
Jas 2:20 that faith without w is dead
Jas 2:21 our father justified by w
Jas 2:22 working together with his w
Jas 2:22 by w faith was made perfect
Jas 2:24 that a man is justified by w
Jas 2:25 by w when she received the
Jas 2:26 faith without w is dead also
Jas 3:13 by good conduct that his w
1Pe 2:12 by your good w which they
2Pe 3:10 the w that are in it will be
1Jn 3: 8 destroy the w of the devil
1Jn 3:12 Because his w were evil and
Rev 2: 2 I know your w, your labor,
Rev 2: 5 repent and do the first w, or
Rev 2: 9 I know your w, tribulation,
Rev 2:13 I know your w, and where you
Rev 2:19 I know your w, love, service,
Rev 2:19 and as for your w, the last
Rev 2:23 of you according to your w
Rev 2:26 keeps My w until the end, to
Rev 3: 1 I know your w, that you have
Rev 3: 2 your w perfect before God
Rev 3: 8 I know your w
Rev 3:15 I know your w, that you are
Rev 9:20 of the w of their hands, that
Rev 14:13 and their w follow them
Rev 15: 3 and marvelous are Your w
Rev 18: 6 her double according to her w
Rev 20:12 judged according to their w
Rev 20:13 each one according to his w

WORLD (*see* WORLDLY, WORLD'S, WORLDS)
1Sa 2: 8 and He has set the w upon them
2Sa 22:16 of the w were uncovered, at
1Ch 16:30 the w also is firmly
Job 18:18 and chased out of the w
Job 34:13 Him over the whole w
Ps 9: 8 judge the w in righteousness
Ps 17:14 From men of the w who have
Ps 18:15 the w were uncovered At Your
Ps 19: 4 words to the end of the w
Ps 22:27 ends of the w Shall remember
Ps 24: 1 and all its fullness, The w
Ps 33: 8 of the w stand in awe of Him
Ps 49: 1 all you inhabitants of the w
Ps 50:12 For the w is Mine, and all its
Ps 77:18 The lightnings lit up the w
Ps 89:11 The w and all its fullness,
Ps 90: 2 had formed the earth and the w
Ps 93: 1 Surely the w is established,
Ps 96:10 The w also is firmly
Ps 96:13 the w with righteousness, And
Ps 97: 4 His lightnings light the w
Ps 98: 7 and all its fullness, The w
Ps 98: 9 He shall judge the w, And the
Prov 8:26 or the primeval dust of the w
Prov 8:31 rejoicing in His inhabited w
Is 13:11 punish the w for its evil
Is 14:17 who made the w as a
Is 14:21 the face of the w with cities
Is 18: 3 All inhabitants of the w and
Is 23:17 all the kingdoms of the w on
Is 24: 4 the w languishes and fades
Is 26: 9 the inhabitants of the w will
Is 26:18 inhabitants of the w fallen
Is 27: 6 the face of the w with fruit
Is 34: 1 and all that is in it, the w
Is 38:11 the inhabitants of the w
Is 62:11 to the end of the w
Is 64: 4 the w men have not heard nor
Jer 10:12 the w by His wisdom, And has
Jer 25:26 all the kingdoms of the w
Jer 51:15 the w by His wisdom, and
Lam 4:12 and all inhabitants of the w
Nah 1: 5 at His presence, yes, the w
Matt 4: 8 Him all the kingdoms of the w
Matt 5:14 You are the light of the w
Matt 13:22 word, and the cares of this w
Matt 13:35 from the foundation of the w
Matt 13:38 The field is the w, the good
Matt 16:26 if he gains the whole w, and
Matt 18: 7 Woe to the w because of
Matt 24:14 the w as a witness to all the
Matt 24:21 of the w until this time, no,
Matt 25:34 from the foundation of the w
Matt 26:13 is preached in the whole w
Mark 4:19 and the cares of this w, the
Mark 8:36 a man if he gains the whole w
Mark 14: 9 throughout the whole w, what
Mark 16:15 Go into all the w and preach
Luke 1:70 have been since the w began
Luke 2: 1 the w should be registered
Luke 4: 5 of the w in a moment of time
Luke 9:25 a man if he gains the whole w
Luke 11:50 the w may be required of this
Luke 12:30 nations of the w seek after
Luke 16: 8 For the sons of this w are
John 1: 9 man who comes into the w
John 1:10 He was in the w
John 1:10 the w was made through Him,
John 1:10 and the w did not know Him
John 1:29 takes away the sin of the w
John 3:16 For God so loved the w that
John 3:17 the w to condemn the w
John 3:17 but that the w through Him
John 3:19 the light has come into the w
John 4:42 Christ, the Savior of the w
John 6:14 who is to come into the w
John 6:33 heaven and gives life to the w
John 6:51 give for the life of the w
John 7: 4 show Yourself to the w
John 7: 7 The w cannot hate you, but it
John 8:12 I am the light of the w
John 8:23 You are of this w
John 8:23 I am not of this w
John 8:26 I speak to the w those things
John 9: 5 As long as I am in the w, I
John 9: 5 I am the light of the w
John 9:32 Since the w began it has been
John 9:39 I have come into this w, that
John 10:36 sanctified and sent into the w
John 11: 9 he sees the light of this w
John 11:27 who is to come into the w
John 12:19 the w has gone after Him
John 12:25 w will keep it for eternal
John 12:31 Now is the judgment of this w
John 12:31 of this w will be cast out
John 12:46 come as a light into the w
John 12:47 the w but to save the w
John 13: 1 from this w to the Father
John 13: 1 His own who were in the w
John 14:17 whom the w cannot receive,
John 14:19 the w will see Me no more,
John 14:22 to us, and not to the w
John 14:27 not as the w gives do I give
John 14:30 the ruler of this w is coming
John 14:31 But that the w may know that
John 15:18 If the w hates you, you know
John 15:19 If you were of the w, the
John 15:19 the w would love its own
John 15:19 because you are not of the w
John 15:19 but I chose you out of the w
John 15:19 therefore the w hates you
John 16: 8 He will convict the w of sin
John 16:11 the ruler of this w is judged
John 16:20 but the w will rejoice
John 16:21 has been born into the w
John 16:28 and have come into the w
John 16:28 Again, I leave the w and go to
John 16:33 In the w you will have
John 16:33 cheer, I have overcome the w
John 17: 5 had with You before the w was
John 17: 6 have given Me out of the w
John 17: 9 I do not pray for the w but
John 17:11 Now I am no longer in the w
John 17:11 but these are in the w
John 17:12 I was with them in the w, I
John 17:13 these things I speak in the w

John 17:14 the w has hated them because
John 17:14 because they are not of the w
John 17:14 just as I am not of the w
John 17:15 should take them out of the w
John 17:16 They are not of the w
John 17:16 just as I am not of the w
John 17:18 As You sent Me into the w
John 17:18 have sent them into the w
John 17:21 that the w may believe that
John 17:23 that the w may know that You
John 17:24 the foundation of the w
John 17:25 The w has not known You, but
John 18:20 I spoke openly to the w
John 18:36 My kingdom is not of this w
John 18:36 If My kingdom were of this w
John 18:37 cause I have come into the w
John 21:25 I suppose that even the w
Acts 3:21 prophets since the w began
Acts 11:28 famine throughout all the w
Acts 17: 6 These who have turned the w
Acts 17:24 God, who made the w and
Acts 17:31 on which He will judge the w
Acts 19:27 all Asia and the w worship
Acts 24: 5 all the Jews throughout the w
Rom 1: 8 of throughout the whole w
Rom 1:20 w His invisible attributes
Rom 3: 6 then how will God judge the w
Rom 3:19 all the w may become guilty
Rom 4:13 w was not to Abraham or to
Rom 5:12 one man sin entered the w
Rom 5:13 the law sin was in the w, but
Rom 10:18 words to the ends of the w
Rom 11:12 fall is riches for the w, and
Rom 11:15 is the reconciling of the w
Rom 12: 2 do not be conformed to this w
Rom 16:25 kept secret since the w began
1Co 1:20 foolish the wisdom of this w
1Co 1:21 the w through wisdom did not
1Co 1:27 w to put to shame the wise
1Co 1:27 the weak things of the w to
1Co 1:28 and the base things of the w
1Co 2:12 not the spirit of the w, but
1Co 3:19 For the wisdom of this w is
1Co 3:22 or the w or life or death, or
1Co 4: 9 made a spectacle to the w
1Co 4:13 made as the filth of the w
1Co 5:10 immoral people of this w, or
1Co 5:10 would need to go out of the w
1Co 6: 2 the saints will judge the w
1Co 6: 2 if the w will be judged by
1Co 7:31 use this w as not misusing it
1Co 7:31 of this w is passing away
1Co 7:33 about the things of the w
1Co 7:34 about the things of the w
1Co 8: 4 an idol is nothing in the w
1Co 11:32 not be condemned with the w
1Co 14:10 kinds of languages in the w
2Co 1:12 in the w in simplicity and
2Co 5:19 reconciling the w to Himself
2Co 7:10 of the w produces death
Gal 4: 3 under the elements of the w
Gal 6:14 by whom the w has been
Gal 6:14 to me, and I to the w
Eph 1: 4 the foundation of the w, that
Eph 2: 2 to the course of this w,
Eph 2:12 hope and without God in the w
Eph 3:21 all ages, w without end
Phil 2:15 you shine as lights in the w
Col 1: 6 as it has also in all the w
Col 2: 8 the basic principles of the w
Col 2:20 the basic principles of the w
Col 2:20 as though living in the w
1Ti 1:15 into the w to save sinners
1Ti 3:16 believed on in the w,
1Ti 6: 7 brought nothing into this w
2Ti 4:10 having loved this present w
Heb 1: 6 the firstborn into the w, He
Heb 2: 5 He has not put the w to come
Heb 4: 3 from the foundation of the w
Heb 9:26 since the foundation of the w
Heb 10: 5 when He came into the w, He
Heb 11: 7 by which he condemned the w
Heb 11:38 of whom the w was not worthy
Jas 1:27 oneself unspotted from the w
Jas 2: 5 of this w to be rich in faith
Jas 3: 6 is a fire, a w of iniquity
Jas 4: 4 with the w is enmity with God
Jas 4: 4 w makes himself an enemy of
1Pe 1:20 the foundation of the w, but
1Pe 5: 9 by your brotherhood in the w
2Pe 1: 4 that is in the w through lust
2Pe 2: 5 did not spare the ancient w
2Pe 2: 5 flood on the w of the ungodly
2Pe 2:20 the pollutions of the w
2Pe 3: 6 by which the w that then
1Jn 2: 2 only but also for the whole w
1Jn 2:15 Do not love the w
1Jn 2:15 or the things in the w
1Jn 2:15 If anyone loves the w, the
1Jn 2:16 For all that is in the w
1Jn 2:16 of the Father but is of the w
1Jn 2:17 the w is passing away, and the
1Jn 3: 1 Therefore the w does not know
1Jn 3:13 brethren, if the w hates you
1Jn 4: 1 have gone out into the w
1Jn 4: 3 and is now already in the w
1Jn 4: 4 than he who is in the w
1Jn 4: 5 They are of the w
1Jn 4: 5 they speak as of the w
1Jn 4: 5 and the w hears them
1Jn 4: 9 only begotten Son into the w
1Jn 4:14 the Son as Savior of the w
1Jn 4:17 as He is, so are we in this w
1Jn 5: 4 born of God overcomes the w
1Jn 5: 4 that has overcome the w
1Jn 5: 5 Who is he who overcomes the w
1Jn 5:19 the whole w lies under the
2Jn 7 have gone out into the w who
Rev 3:10 shall come upon the whole w
Rev 11:15 The kingdoms of this w have
Rev 12: 9 who deceives the whole w
Rev 13: 3 And all the w marveled and
Rev 13: 8 from the foundation of the w
Rev 16:14 the earth and of the whole w
Rev 17: 8 from the foundation of the w

WORLDLY (*see* WORLD)
Tit 2:12 and w lusts, we should live

WORLD'S (*see* WORLD)
1Jn 3:17 But whoever has this w goods

WORLDS (*see* WORLD)
Heb 1: 2 whom also He made the w
Heb 11: 3 we understand that the w were

WORM (*see* WORMS)
Job 17:14 are my father,' and to the w
Job 24:20 the w should feed sweetly on
Job 25: 6 and a son of man, who is a w
Ps 22: 6 But I am a w, and no man
Is 41:14 not, you w Jacob, you men of
Is 51: 8 the w will eat them like wool
Is 66:24 For their w does not die, and
Jon 4: 7 the next day God prepared a w
Mark 9:44 where 'their w does not die
Mark 9:46 where 'their w does not die
Mark 9:48 where 'their w does not die

WORMS (*see* WORM)
Ex 16:20 until morning, and it bred w
Ex 16:24 nor were there any w in it
Deut 28:39 for the w shall eat them
Job 7: 5 My flesh is caked with w and
Job 21:26 in the dust, and w cover them
Is 14:11 under you, and w cover you
Acts 12:23 And he was eaten by w and died

WORMWOOD
Deut 29:18 root bearing bitterness or w
Prov 5: 4 in the end she is bitter as w
Jer 9:15 them, this people, with w
Jer 23:15 I will feed them with w, and
Lam 3:15 He has made me drink w
Lam 3:19 affliction and roaming, the w
Amos 5: 7 you who turn justice to w
Amos 6:12 fruit of righteousness into w
Rev 8:11 and the name of the star is W
Rev 8:11 third of the waters became w

WORN (*see* WEAR)
Deut 29: 5 clothes have not w out on you
Deut 29: 5 have not w out on your feet
Esth 6: 8 brought which the king has w
Job 16: 7 But now He has w me out

WORRIED (*see* WORRY)
1Sa 9: 5 donkeys and become w about us
Luke 10:41 Martha, Martha, you are w

WORRY (*see* WORRIED, WORRYING)
Matt 6:25 do not w about your life,
Matt 6:28 So why do you w about
Matt 6:31 Therefore do not w, saying
Matt 6:34 do not w about tomorrow
Matt 6:34 for tomorrow will w about its
Matt 10:19 do not w about how or what
Mark 13:11 up, do not w beforehand, or
Luke 12:11 do not w about how or what
Luke 12:22 do not w about your life,

WORRYING (*see* WORRY)
1Sa 10: 2 and is w about you, saying,
Matt 6:27 Which of you by w can add one
Luke 12:25 which of you by w can add one

WORSE (*see* PREFACE)

WORSHIP (*see* WORSHIPED, WORSHIPER, WORSHIPING, WORSHIPS)
Gen 22: 5 lad and I will go yonder and w
Ex 24: 1 of Israel, and w from afar
Ex 34:14 (for you shall w no other god
Deut 4:19 you feel driven to w them
Deut 8:19 w them, I testify against you
Deut 11:16 serve other gods and w them,
Deut 12: 4 You shall not w the LORD your
Deut 12:31 You shall not w the LORD your
Deut 26:10 w before the LORD your God
Deut 30:17 w other gods and serve them,
1Sa 1: 3 up from his city yearly to w
1Sa 15:25 me, that I may w the LORD
1Sa 15:30 that I may w the LORD your
1Ki 9: 6 serve other gods and w them,
1Ki 12:30 sin, for the people went to w
2Ki 5:18 temple of Rimmon to w there
2Ki 17:36 shall fear, Him you shall w
2Ki 18:22 You shall w before this
1Ch 16:29 w the LORD in the beauty of
2Ch 7:19 serve other gods, and w them,
2Ch 32:12 You shall w before one altar
Ps 5: 7 In fear of You I will w
Ps 22:27 nations Shall w before You
Ps 22:29 of the earth Shall eat and w
Ps 29: 2 W the LORD in the beauty of
Ps 45:11 He is your Lord, w Him
Ps 66: 4 All the earth shall w You
Ps 81: 9 Nor shall you w any foreign
Ps 86: 9 and w before You, O Lord, And
Ps 95: 6 Oh come, let us w and bow down
Ps 96: 9 w the LORD in the beauty of
Ps 97: 7 W Him, all you gods
Ps 99: 5 God, And w at His footstool
Ps 99: 9 God, And w at His holy hill
Ps 132: 7 Let us w at His footstool
Ps 138: 2 I will w toward Your holy
Is 2: 8 they w the work of their own
Is 2:20 made, each for himself to w
Is 27:13 shall w the LORD in the holy
Is 36: 7 You shall w before this
Is 46: 6 themselves, yes, they w
Is 49: 7 arise, princes also shall w
Is 66:23 shall come to w before Me
Jer 7: 2 at these gates to w the LORD
Jer 13:10 w them, shall be just like
Jer 25: 6 w them, and do not provoke Me
Jer 26: 2 which come to w in the LORD's
Jer 44:19 to w her, and pour out drink
Ezek 46: 2 He shall w at the threshold
Ezek 46: 3 w at the entrance to this
Ezek 46: 9 w shall go out by way of the
Dan 3: 5 w the gold image that King
Dan 3: 6 w shall be cast immediately
Dan 3:10 fall down and w the gold image
Dan 3:11 and w shall be cast into the
Dan 3:12 or w the gold image which you
Dan 3:14 w the gold image which I have
Dan 3:15 w the image which I have made
Dan 3:15 But if you do not w, you
Dan 3:18 nor will we w the gold image
Dan 3:28 w any god except their own
Mic 5:13 you shall no more w the work
Zeph 1: 5 those who w the host of
Zeph 1: 5 those who w and swear oaths by
Zeph 2:11 people shall w Him, each one
Zech 14:16 year to year to w the King
Zech 14:17 up to Jerusalem to w the King
Matt 2: 2 East and have come to w Him
Matt 2: 8 that I may come and w Him also
Matt 4: 9 if You will fall down and w me
Matt 4:10 You shall w the LORD your
Matt 15: 9 And in vain they w Me,
Mark 7: 7 And in vain they w Me,
Luke 4: 7 if You will w before me, all
Luke 4: 8 You shall w the LORD your
John 4:20 place where one ought to w
John 4:21 in Jerusalem, w the Father

John 4:22 You w what you do not know
John 4:22 we know what we w, for
John 4:23 will w the Father in spirit
John 4:23 is seeking such to w Him
John 4:24 who w Him must w in spirit
John 12:20 who came up to w at the feast
Acts 7:42 gave them up to w the host of
Acts 7:43 images which you made to w
Acts 8:27 and had come to Jerusalem to w
Acts 17:23 the objects of your w, I even
Acts 17:23 whom you w without knowing
Acts 18:13 to w God contrary to the law
Acts 19:27 whom all Asia and the world w
Acts 24:11 I went up to Jerusalem to w
Acts 24:14 so I w the God of my fathers,
1Co 14:25 on his face, he will w God
Phil 3: 3 who w God in the Spirit,
Col 2:18 w of angels, intruding into
Heb 1: 6 all the angels of God w Him
Rev 3: 9 w before your feet, and to
Rev 4:10 w Him who lives forever and
Rev 9:20 that they should not w demons
Rev 11: 1 altar, and those who w there
Rev 13: 8 dwell on the earth will w him
Rev 13:12 in it to w the first beast
Rev 13:15 w the image of the beast to
Rev 14: 7 and w Him who made heaven
Rev 14:11 who w the beast and his image,
Rev 15: 4 and w before You, for Your
Rev 19:10 I fell at his feet to w him
Rev 19:10 W God! For the testimony of
Rev 22: 8 I fell down to w before the
Rev 22: 9 words of this book. W God

WORSHIPED (*see* WORSHIP)
Gen 24:26 down his head and w the LORD
Gen 24:48 w the LORD, and blessed the
Gen 24:52 that he w the LORD, bowing
Ex 4:31 they bowed their heads and w
Ex 12:27 people bowed their heads and w
Ex 32: 8 w it and sacrificed to it, and
Ex 33:10 and all the people rose and w
Ex 34: 8 head toward the earth, and w
Deut 17: 3 w them, either the sun or
Deut 29:26 w them, gods that they did
Josh 5:14 on his face to the earth and w
Judg 7:15 its interpretation, that he w
1Sa 1:19 and w before the LORD, and
1Sa 1:28 So they w the LORD there
1Sa 15:31 Saul, and Saul w the LORD
2Sa 12:20 the house of the LORD and w
2Sa 15:32 the mountain, where he w God
1Ki 9: 9 and w them and served them
1Ki 11:33 w Ashtoreth the goddess of
1Ki 16:31 went and served Baal and w him
1Ki 22:53 w him, and provoked the LORD
2Ki 17:16 w all the host of heaven, and
2Ki 21: 3 he w all the host of heaven
2Ki 21:21 father had served, and w them
2Ch 7: 3 ground on the pavement, and w
2Ch 7:22 and w them and served them
2Ch 29:28 So all the congregation w
2Ch 29:29 present with him bowed and w
2Ch 29:30 they bowed their heads and w
2Ch 33: 3 he w all the host of heaven
Neh 8: 6 w the LORD with their faces
Neh 9: 3 and w the LORD their God
Job 1:20 and he fell to the ground and w
Ps 106:19 Horeb, And w the molded
Jer 1:16 and w the works of their own
Jer 8: 2 sought and which they have w
Jer 16:11 w them, and have forsaken Me
Jer 22: 9 w other gods and served them
Dan 3: 7 w the gold image which King
Matt 2:11 mother, and fell down and w
Matt 8: 2 leper came and w Him, saying,
Matt 9:18 ruler came and w Him, saying,
Matt 14:33 boat came and w Him, saying,
Matt 15:25 she came and w Him, saying,
Matt 28: 9 held Him by the feet and w Him
Matt 28:17 when they saw Him, they w Him
Mark 5: 6 from afar, he ran and w Him
Mark 15:19 bowing the knee, they w Him
Luke 24:52 And they w Him, and returned
John 4:20 Our fathers w on this
John 9:38 And he w Him
Acts 10:25 down at his feet and w him
Acts 16:14 city of Thyatira, who w God
Acts 17:25 Nor is He w with men's hands,
Acts 18: 7 named Justus, one who w God
Rom 1:25 of God for the lie, and w and
2Th 2: 4 is called God or that is w
Heb 11:21 of the sons of Joseph, and w
Rev 5:14 w Him who lives forever and
Rev 7:11 before the throne and w God,
Rev 11:16 fell on their faces and w God,
Rev 13: 4 So they w the dragon who gave
Rev 13: 4 they w the beast, saying,
Rev 16: 2 and those who w his image
Rev 19: 4 w God who sat on the throne,
Rev 19:20 and those who w his image
Rev 20: 4 who had not w the beast or

WORSHIPER (*see* WORSHIP, WORSHIPERS)
John 9:31 but if anyone is a w of God

WORSHIPERS (*see* WORSHIPER)
2Ki 10:19 of destroying the w of Baal
2Ki 10:21 all the w of Baal came, so
2Ki 10:22 for all the w of Baal
2Ki 10:23 and said to the w of Baal
2Ki 10:23 you, but only the w of Baal
Zeph 3:10 the rivers of Ethiopia my w
John 4:23 when the true w will worship
Acts 17:17 Jews and with the Gentile w
Heb 10: 2 For the w, once purged, would

WORSHIPING (*see* WORSHIP)
2Ki 19:37 as he was w in the temple of
2Ch 20:18 before the LORD, w the LORD
Is 37:38 as he was w in the house of
Ezek 8:16 they were w the sun toward

WORSHIPS (*see* WORSHIP)
Neh 9: 6 the host of heaven w You
Is 44:15 indeed he makes a god and w it
Is 44:17 w it, prays to it and says,
Rev 14: 9 If anyone w the beast and his

WORST (*see* PREFACE)

WORTH (*see* WORTHLESS)
Gen 23:15 the land is w four hundred
Lev 27:23 him the w of your valuation
Deut 15:18 for he has been w a double
2Sa 18: 3 But you are w ten thousand of
1Ki 21: 2 will give you its w in money
Ezra 8:27 twenty gold basins w a
Job 24:25 and make my speech w nothing
Prov 10:20 of the wicked is w little
Prov 31:10 For her w is far above rubies
Is 7:23 vines w a thousand shekels of
Mark 6:37 hundred denarii w of bread
John 6: 7 Two hundred denarii w of

WORTHIES (*see* WORTHY)
Nah 2: 5 He remembers his w

WORTHLESS (*see* WORTH, WORTHLESSNESS)
Num 21: 5 our soul loathes this w bread
Judg 9: 4 with which Abimelech hired w
Judg 11: 3 w men banded together with
1Sa 15: 9 But everything despised and w
1Sa 30:22 w men of those who went with
2Ch 13: 7 Then w rogues gathered to him
Job 13: 4 you are all w physicians
Job 34:18 to say to a king, 'You are w
Ps 119:37 eyes from looking at w things
Prov 6:12 A w person, a wicked man,
Is 40:17 by Him less than nothing and w
Is 41:29 Indeed they are all w
Jer 10: 8 a wooden idol is a w doctrine
Jer 14:14 a w thing, and the deceit of
Jer 18:15 burned incense to w idols
Jer 23:16 They make you w
Jon 2: 8 Those who regard w idols
Zech 11:17 Woe to the w shepherd, who

WORTHLESSNESS (*see* WORTHLESS)
Ps 4: 2 How long will you love w And
Jer 16:19 have inherited lies, w and

WORTHY (*see* UNWORTHY, WORTHIES)
Gen 32:10 I am not w of the least of
Deut 17: 6 Whoever is w of death shall
Deut 19: 6 though he was not w of death
Deut 21:22 committed a sin w of death
Deut 22:26 young woman no sin w of death
1Sa 26:16 LORD lives, you are w to die
2Sa 22: 4 LORD, who is w to be praised
1Ki 1:52 If he proves himself a w man
1Ki 2:26 for you are w of death
Job 31:11 be iniquity w of judgment
Job 31:28 be an iniquity w of judgment
Ps 18: 3 LORD, who is w to be praised
Matt 3: 8 bear fruits w of repentance
Matt 3:11 sandals I am not w to carry
Matt 8: 8 I am not w that You should
Matt 10:10 for a worker is w of his food
Matt 10:11 enter, inquire who in it is w
Matt 10:13 If the household is w, let
Matt 10:13 But if it is not w, let your
Matt 10:37 more than Me is not w of Me
Matt 10:37 more than Me is not w of Me
Matt 10:38 after Me is not w of Me
Matt 22: 8 who were invited were not w
Mark 1: 7 I am not w to stoop down and
Mark 14:64 Him to be w of death
Luke 3: 8 bear fruits w of repentance
Luke 3:16 strap I am not w to loose
Luke 7: 4 whom He should do this was w
Luke 7: 6 for I am not w that You
Luke 7: 7 think myself w to come to You
Luke 10: 7 the laborer is w of his wages
Luke 12:48 committed things w of stripes
Luke 15:19 I am no longer w to be called
Luke 15:21 am no longer w to be called
Luke 20:35 counted w to attain that age
Luke 21:36 that you may be counted w to
Luke 23:15 indeed nothing w of death has
John 1:27 strap I am not w to loose
Acts 5:41 that they were counted w to
Acts 13:25 feet I am not w to loose
Acts 23:29 him w of death or chains
Acts 25:11 committed anything w of death
Acts 25:25 committed nothing w of death
Acts 26:31 nothing w of death or chains
Rom 1:32 such things are w of death
Rom 8:18 not w to be compared with the
Rom 16: 2 in a manner w of the saints
1Co 15: 9 who am not w to be called an
Eph 4: 1 w of the calling with which
Phil 1:27 be w of the gospel of Christ
Col 1:10 may have a walk w of the Lord
1Th 2:12 w of God who calls you into
2Th 1: 5 w of the kingdom of God, for
2Th 1:11 count you w of this calling
1Ti 1:15 w of all acceptance, that
1Ti 4: 9 saying and w of all acceptance
1Ti 5:17 be counted w of double honor
1Ti 5:18 The laborer is w of his wages
1Ti 6: 1 own masters w of all honor
Heb 3: 3 w of more glory than Moses
Heb 10:29 will he be thought w who has
Heb 11:38 of whom the world was not w
3Jn 6 journey in a manner w of God
Rev 3: 4 Me in white, for they are w
Rev 4:11 You are w, O Lord, to receive
Rev 5: 2 Who is w to open the scroll
Rev 5: 4 no one was found w to open
Rev 5: 9 You are w to take the scroll,
Rev 5:12 W is the Lamb who was slain

WOULD (*see* PREFACE)

WOUND (*see* WOUNDED, WOUNDING, WOUNDS)
Ex 21:25 burn, w for w, stripe for
Ex 21:25 burn for burn, w for w
Deut 32:39 I w and I heal
1Ki 20:37 struck him, inflicting a w
1Ki 22:35 the w onto the floor of the
Job 16:14 breaks me with w upon w
Job 34: 6 My w is incurable, though I
Ps 68:21 But God will w the head of
Is 30:26 heals the stroke of their w
Jer 10:19 My w is severe
Jer 15:18 my w incurable, which refuses
Jer 30:12 incurable, your w is severe
Jer 30:14 you with the w of an enemy
Hos 5:13 sickness, and Judah saw his w
Hos 5:13 you, nor heal you of your w
Nah 3:19 no healing, your w is severe
1Co 8:12 w their weak conscience, you
Rev 13: 3 and his deadly w was healed
Rev 13:12 whose deadly w was healed

WOUNDED (*see* WOUND)
Judg 9:40 and many fell w, even to the
1Sa 17:52 the w of the Philistines fell
1Sa 31: 3 was severely w by the archers
2Sa 22:39 w them, so that they could
1Ki 22:34 out of the battle, for I am w
2Ki 8:28 and the Syrians w Joram
1Ch 10: 3 and he was w by the archers
2Ch 18:33 out of the battle, for I am w
2Ch 22: 5 and the Syrians w Joram
2Ch 24:25 for they left him severely w)

2Ch 35:23 me away, for I am severely **w**
Job 24:12 and the souls of the **w** cry out
Ps 18:38 I have **w** them, So that they
Ps 64: 7 Suddenly they shall be **w**
Ps 69:26 the grief of those You have **w**
Ps 109:22 And my heart is **w** within me
Prov 7:26 for she has cast down many **w**
Song 5: 7 They struck me, they **w** me
Is 51: 9 Rahab apart, and **w** the serpent
Is 53: 5 But He was **w** for our
Jer 30:14 for I have **w** you with the
Jer 37:10 only **w** men among them, they
Jer 51:52 her land the **w** shall groan
Lam 2:12 as they swoon like the **w** in
Ezek 26:15 of your fall, when the **w** cry
Ezek 28:23 the **w** shall be judged in her
Ezek 30:24 groanings of a mortally **w** man
Zech 13: 6 Those with which I was **w** in
Mark 12: 4 **w** him in the head, and sent
Luke 10:30 **w** him, and departed, leaving
Luke 20:12 they **w** him also and cast him
Acts 19:16 out of that house naked and **w**
Rev 13: 3 as if it had been mortally **w**
Rev 13:14 beast who was **w** by the sword

WOUNDING (*see* WOUND)
Gen 4:23 I have killed a man for **w** me

WOUNDS (*see* WOUND)
2Ki 8:29 the **w** which the Syrians had
2Ki 9:15 the **w** which the Syrians had
2Ch 22: 6 **w** which he had received at
Job 5:18 He **w**, but His hands make
Job 9:17 multiplies my **w** without cause
Ps 38: 5 My **w** are foul and festering
Ps 147: 3 And binds up their **w**
Prov 6:33 **W** and dishonor he will get, and
Prov 23:29 Who has **w** without cause
Prov 27: 6 are the **w** of a friend, but
Is 1: 6 is no soundness in it, but **w**
Jer 6: 7 Me continually are grief and **w**
Jer 30:17 to you and heal you of your **w**
Mic 1: 9 For her **w** are incurable
Zech 13: 6 are these **w** in your hands
Luke 10:34 went to him and bandaged his **w**

WOVE (*see* WEAVE)
Judg 16:14 So she **w** it tightly with the
2Ki 23: 7 where the women **w** hangings
2Ch 3:14 linen, and **w** cherubim into it

WOVEN (*see* WEAVE)
Ex 26: 1 with ten curtains **w** of fine
Ex 26:31 shall make a veil **w** of blue
Ex 26:31 It shall be **w** with an
Ex 26:36 **w** of blue and purple and
Ex 27: 9 court **w** of fine linen thread
Ex 27:16 long, **w** of blue and purple and
Ex 27:18 **w** of fine linen thread, and
Ex 28: 4 a robe, a skillfully **w** tunic
Ex 28: 6 linen thread, artistically **w**
Ex 28: 8 the intricately **w** band of the
Ex 28: 8 **w** of gold and blue and purple
Ex 28:15 Artistically **w** according to
Ex 28:27 **w** band of the ephod
Ex 28:28 **w** band of the ephod, and so
Ex 28:32 it shall have a **w** binding all
Ex 28:39 shall make the sash of **w** work
Ex 29: 5 **w** band of the ephod
Ex 36: 8 made ten curtains **w** of fine
Ex 36:35 And he made a veil **w** of blue
Ex 36:35 it was **w** with an artistic
Ex 36:37 door, **w** of blue and purple and
Ex 38: 9 court were **w** of fine linen
Ex 38:16 around were **w** of fine linen
Ex 38:18 of the court was **w** of blue
Ex 39: 5 the intricately **w** band of his
Ex 39: 5 **w** of gold and blue and purple
Ex 39: 8 artistically **w** like the
Ex 39:20 **w** band of the ephod
Ex 39:21 **w** band of the ephod
Ex 39:22 robe of the ephod of **w** work
Ex 39:23 with a **w** binding all around
Ex 39:27 artistically **w** of fine linen,
Ex 39:29 **w** as the LORD had commanded
Lev 8: 7 **w** band of the ephod, and with
Num 31:20 everything **w** of goats' hair,
Ps 45:13 Her clothing is **w** with gold
Lam 1:14 they were **w** together by His
John 19:23 **w** from the top in one piece

WRANGLINGS
1Ti 6: 5 useless **w** of men of corrupt

WRAP (*see* WRAPPED)
Job 8:17 His roots **w** around the rock
Is 28:20 he cannot **w** himself in it

WRAPPED (*see* WRAP)
Gen 38:14 **w** herself, and sat in an open
1Sa 21: 9 **w** in a cloth behind the ephod
1Ki 19:13 that he **w** his face in his
Hos 4:19 The wind has **w** her up in its
Jon 2: 5 weeds were **w** around my head
Matt 27:59 he **w** it in a clean linen
Mark 15:46 down, and **w** Him in the linen
Luke 2: 7 **w** Him in swaddling cloths, and
Luke 2:12 a Babe **w** in swaddling cloths
Luke 23:53 **w** it in linen, and laid it in
John 11:44 his face was **w** with a cloth
Acts 5: 6 **w** him up, carried him out, and

WRATH (*see* WRATHFUL)
Gen 49: 7 and their **w**, for it is cruel
Ex 15: 7 You sent forth Your **w** which
Ex 22:24 My **w** will become hot, and I
Ex 32:10 alone, that My **w** may burn hot
Ex 32:11 why does Your **w** burn hot
Ex 32:12 Turn from Your fierce **w**, and
Lev 10: 6 **w** come upon all the people
Num 1:53 that there may be no **w** on the
Num 11:33 the **w** of the LORD was aroused
Num 16:46 for **w** has gone out from the
Num 18: 5 **w** on the children of Israel
Num 25:11 has turned back My **w** from the
Deut 9: 7 God to **w** in the wilderness
Deut 9: 8 you provoked the LORD to **w**
Deut 9:22 you provoked the LORD to **w**
Deut 29:23 in His anger and His **w**
Deut 29:28 their land in anger, in **w**
Deut 32:27 not feared the **w** of the enemy
Josh 9:20 lest **w** be upon us because of
Josh 22:20 thing, and **w** fell on all the
1Sa 28:18 His fierce **w** upon Amalek,
2Sa 11:20 that the king's **w** rises, and
2Ki 22:13 for great is the **w** of the
2Ki 22:17 Therefore My **w** shall be
2Ki 23:26 the fierceness of His great **w**
1Ch 27:24 for **w** came upon Israel
2Ch 12: 7 My **w** shall not be poured out
2Ch 12:12 the **w** of the LORD turned from
2Ch 19: 2 Therefore the **w** of the LORD
2Ch 19:10 and **w** come upon you and your
2Ch 24:18 and **w** came upon Judah and
2Ch 28:11 for the fierce **w** of the LORD
2Ch 28:13 is fierce **w** against Israel
2Ch 29: 8 Therefore the **w** of the LORD
2Ch 29:10 that His fierce **w** may turn
2Ch 30: 8 His **w** may turn away from you
2Ch 32:25 therefore **w** was looming over
2Ch 32:26 so that the **w** of the LORD did
2Ch 34:21 for great is the **w** of the
2Ch 34:25 Therefore My **w** will be poured
2Ch 36:16 until the **w** of the LORD arose
Ezra 5:12 the God of heaven to **w**, He
Ezra 7:23 For why should there be **w**
Ezra 8:22 His **w** are against all those
Ezra 10:14 until the fierce **w** of our God
Neh 13:18 Yet you bring added **w** on
Esth 1:18 be excessive contempt and **w**
Esth 2: 1 when the **w** of King Ahasuerus
Esth 3: 5 Haman was filled with **w**
Esth 7: 7 **w** from the banquet of wine
Esth 7:10 Then the king's **w** subsided
Job 5: 2 For **w** kills a foolish man, and
Job 14:13 me until Your **w** is past, that
Job 16: 9 He tears me in His **w**, and
Job 19:11 also kindled His **w** against me
Job 19:29 for **w** brings the punishment
Job 20:23 cast on him the fury of His **w**
Job 20:28 flow away in the day of His **w**
Job 21:20 of the **w** of the Almighty
Job 21:30 brought out on the day of **w**
Job 32: 2 Then the **w** of Elihu, the son
Job 32: 2 his **w** was aroused because he
Job 32: 3 friends his **w** was aroused
Job 32: 5 three men, his **w** was aroused
Job 36:13 in heart store up **w**
Job 36:18 Because there is **w**, beware
Job 40:11 Disperse the rage of your **w**
Job 42: 7 My **w** is aroused against you
Ps 2: 5 shall speak to them in His **w**
Ps 2:12 When His **w** is kindled but a
Ps 21: 9 swallow them up in His **w**, And
Ps 37: 8 from anger, and forsake **w**
Ps 38: 1 do not rebuke me in Your **w**
Ps 55: 3 upon me, And in **w** they hate me
Ps 58: 9 As in His living and burning **w**
Ps 59:13 Consume them in **w**, consume
Ps 76:10 Surely the **w** of man shall
Ps 76:10 With the remainder of **w** You
Ps 78:31 The **w** of God came against
Ps 78:38 And did not stir up all His **w**
Ps 78:49 fierceness of His anger, **W**
Ps 79: 6 Pour out Your **w** on the
Ps 85: 3 have taken away all Your **w**
Ps 88: 7 Your **w** lies heavy upon me, And
Ps 88:16 Your fierce **w** has gone over
Ps 89:46 Will Your **w** burn like fire
Ps 90: 7 by Your **w** we are terrified
Ps 90: 9 have passed away in Your **w**
Ps 90:11 the fear of You, so is Your **w**
Ps 95:11 So I swore in My **w**, 'They
Ps 102:10 of Your indignation and Your **w**
Ps 106:23 breach, To turn away His **w**
Ps 106:40 Therefore the **w** of the LORD
Ps 110: 5 kings in the day of His **w**
Ps 124: 3 When their **w** was kindled
Ps 138: 7 Against the **w** of my enemies
Prov 11: 4 do not profit in the day of **w**
Prov 11:23 of the wicked is **w**
Prov 12:16 A fool's **w** is known at once,
Prov 14:29 He who is slow to **w** has great
Prov 14:35 but his **w** is against him who
Prov 15: 1 A soft answer turns away **w**
Prov 16:14 of death is the king's **w**, but
Prov 19:12 The king's **w** is like the
Prov 19:19 A man of great **w** will suffer
Prov 20: 2 The **w** of a king is like the
Prov 21:14 behind the back, strong **w**
Prov 24:18 He turn away His **w** from him
Prov 27: 3 but a fool's **w** is heavier
Prov 27: 4 **W** is cruel and anger a torrent
Prov 29: 8 but wise men turn away **w**
Prov 30:33 forcing of **w** produces strife
Is 9:19 Through the **w** of the LORD of
Is 10: 6 My **w** I will give him charge
Is 13: 9 comes, cruel, with both **w**
Is 13:13 in the **w** of the LORD of hosts
Is 14: 6 in **w** with a continual stroke
Is 16: 6 and his pride and his **w**
Is 54: 8 With a little **w** I hid My face
Is 60:10 for in My **w** I struck you, but
Jer 7:29 the generation of His **w**
Jer 10:10 At His **w** the earth will
Jer 18:20 to turn away Your **w** from them
Jer 21: 5 in anger and fury and great **w**
Jer 32:37 in My fury, and in great **w**
Jer 44: 8 to **w** with the works of your
Jer 48:30 I know his **w**," says the LORD
Jer 50:13 Because of the **w** of the LORD
Lam 2: 2 His **w** the strongholds of the
Lam 3: 1 by the rod of His **w**
Ezek 7:12 for **w** is on their whole
Ezek 7:14 For My **w** is on all their
Ezek 7:19 the day of the **w** of the LORD
Ezek 13:15 I accomplish My **w** on the wall
Ezek 21:31 you with the fire of My **w**
Ezek 22:21 on you with the fire of My **w**
Ezek 22:31 them with the fire of My **w**
Ezek 38:19 fire of My **w** I have spoken
Dan 11:36 the **w** has been accomplished
Hos 5:10 out my **w** on them like water
Hos 13:11 and took him away in My **w**
Amos 1:11 and he kept his **w** forever
Nah 1: 2 He reserves **w** for His enemies
Hab 3: 2 in **w** remember mercy
Hab 3: 8 was Your **w** against the sea,
Zeph 1:15 That day is a day of **w**, a day
Zeph 1:18 in the day of the LORD's **w**
Zech 7:12 Thus great **w** came from the
Zech 8:14 your fathers provoked Me to **w**
Matt 3: 7 to flee from the **w** to come
Luke 3: 7 to flee from the **w** to come
Luke 4:28 things, were filled with **w**
Luke 21:23 land and **w** upon this people
John 3:36 but the **w** of God abides on
Acts 19:28 this, they were full of **w**
Rom 1:18 For the **w** of God is revealed
Rom 2: 5 **w** in the day of **w** and
Rom 2: 8 indignation and **w**,
Rom 3: 5 Is God unjust who inflicts **w**
Rom 4:15 the law brings about **w**

Rom 5: 9 be saved from w through Him
Rom 9:22 if God, wanting to show His w
Rom 9:22 the vessels of w prepared for
Rom 12:19 but rather give place to w
Rom 13: 4 an avenger to execute w on
Rom 13: 5 not only because of w but
2Co 12:20 jealousies, outbursts of w
Gal 5:20 jealousies, outbursts of w
Eph 2: 3 were by nature children of w
Eph 4:26 let the sun go down on your w
Eph 4:31 Let all bitterness, w, anger,
Eph 5: 6 w of God comes upon the sons
Eph 6: 4 provoke your children to w
Col 3: 6 w of God is coming upon the
Col 3: 8 anger, w, malice, blasphemy,
1Th 1:10 us from the w to come
1Th 2:16 but w has come upon them to
1Th 5: 9 God did not appoint us to w
1Ti 2: 8 up holy hands, without w and
Heb 3:11 So I swore in My w, "They
Heb 4: 3 So I swore in My w, They
Heb 11:27 not fearing the w of the king
Jas 1:19 slow to speak, slow to w
Jas 1:20 for the w of man does not
Rev 6:16 and from the w of the Lamb
Rev 6:17 great day of His w has come
Rev 11:18 Your w has come, and the time
Rev 12:12 down to you, having great w
Rev 14: 8 of the w of her fornication
Rev 14:10 of the wine of the w of God
Rev 14:19 winepress of the w of God
Rev 15: 1 for in them the w of God is
Rev 15: 7 w of God who lives forever
Rev 16: 1 of the w of God on the earth
Rev 16:19 of the fierceness of His w
Rev 18: 3 of the w of her fornication
Rev 19:15 and w of Almighty God

WRATHFUL (*see* WRATH)
Ps 69:24 let Your w anger take hold of
Prov 15:18 A w man stirs up strife, but

WREATH (*see* WREATHS)
1Ki 7:30 of cast bronze beside each w

WREATHS (*see* WREATH)
1Ki 7:17 with w of chainwork, for the
1Ki 7:29 oxen were w of plaited work
1Ki 7:36 on each, with w all around
2Ch 3:16 He made w of chainwork, as in
2Ch 3:16 them on the w of chainwork

WRECKED
1Ki 22:48 ships were w at Ezion Geber
2Ch 20:37 Then the ships were w, so

WRESTED (*see* WRESTLE)
2Sa 23:21 staff, w the spear out of the
1Ch 11:23 staff, w the spear out of the

WRESTLE (*see* WRESTED, WRESTLED, WRESTLINGS)
Eph 6:12 For we do not w against flesh

WRESTLED (*see* WRESTLE)
Gen 30: 8 I have w with my sister, and
Gen 32:24 a Man w with him until the
Gen 32:25 out of joint as He w with him

WRESTLINGS (*see* WRESTLE)
Gen 30: 8 With great w I have wrestled

WRETCHED (*see* WRETCHEDNESS)
Rom 7:24 O w man that I am
Rev 3:17 and do not know that you are w

WRETCHEDNESS (*see* WRETCHED)
Num 11:15 and do not let me see my w

WRING (*see* WRINGING, WRUNG)
Lev 1:15 w off its head, and burn it on
Lev 5: 8 w off its head from its neck,

WRINGING (*see* WRING)
Prov 30:33 as w the nose produces blood,

WRINKLE
Eph 5:27 spot or w or any such thing

WRISTS
Gen 24:22 and two bracelets for her w
Gen 24:30 bracelets on his sister's w
Gen 24:47 and the bracelets on her w
Ezek 16:11 put bracelets on your w, and
Ezek 23:42 who put bracelets on their w

WRITE (*see* WRITER, WRITES, WRITING, WRITTEN, WROTE)
Ex 17:14 W this for a memorial in the
Ex 34: 1 I will w on these tablets the
Ex 34:27 W these words, for according
Num 5:23 w these curses in a book, and
Num 17: 2 W each man's name on his rod
Num 17: 3 you shall w Aaron's name on
Deut 6: 9 You shall w them on the
Deut 10: 2 I will w on the tablets the
Deut 11:20 And you shall w them on the
Deut 17:18 that he shall w for himself a
Deut 27: 3 You shall w on them all the
Deut 27: 8 you shall w very plainly on
Deut 31:19 w down this song for
Ezra 5:10 that we might w the names of
Neh 9:38 make a sure covenant, and w it
Esth 8: 8 You yourselves w a decree for
Job 13:26 For You w bitter things
Prov 3: 3 w them on the tablet of your
Prov 7: 3 w them on the tablet of your
Is 8: 1 and w on it with a man's pen
Is 10: 1 who w misfortune, which they
Is 10:19 that a child may w them
Is 30: 8 w it before them on a tablet,
Is 44: 5 another will w with his hand,
Jer 22:30 W this man down as childless
Jer 30: 2 W in a book for yourself all
Jer 31:33 and w it on their hearts
Jer 36: 2 w on it all the words that I
Jer 36:17 how did you w all these words
Jer 36:28 w on it all the former words
Ezek 24: 2 w down the name of the day,
Ezek 37:16 stick for yourself and w on it
Ezek 37:16 w on it, 'For Joseph, the
Ezek 37:20 the sticks on which you w
Ezek 43:11 W it down in their sight, so
Hab 2: 2 W the vision and make it plain
Mark 10: 4 to w a certificate of divorce
Luke 1: 3 first, to w to you an orderly
Luke 16: 6 sit down quickly and w fifty
Luke 16: 7 Take your bill, and w eighty
John 19:21 Do not w, 'The King of the
Acts 15:20 but that we w to them to
Acts 25:26 w to my lord concerning him
Acts 25:26 I may have something to w
1Co 4:14 I do not w these things to
1Co 14:37 that the things which I w to
2Co 9: 1 for me to w to you
2Co 13: 2 now being absent I w to those
2Co 13:10 Therefore I w these things
Gal 1:20 the things which I w to you
Phil 3: 1 For me to w the same things
1Th 4: 9 need that I should w to you
1Th 5: 1 need that I should w to you
2Th 3:17 in every epistle; so I w
1Ti 3:14 These things I w to you,
1Ti 3:15 I w so that you may know how
Phm 21 I w to you, knowing that you
Heb 8:10 and w them on their hearts
Heb 10:16 in their minds I will w them
2Pe 3: 1 I now w to you this second
1Jn 1: 4 these things we w to you that
1Jn 2: 1 these things I w to you,
1Jn 2: 7 I w no new commandment to
1Jn 2: 8 a new commandment I w to you
1Jn 2:12 I w to you, little children,
1Jn 2:13 I w to you, fathers, because
1Jn 2:13 I w to you, young men,
1Jn 2:13 I w to you, little children,
2Jn 12 many things to w to you, I
3Jn 13 I had many things to w, but I
3Jn 13 not wish to w to you with pen
Jude 3 to w to you concerning our
Jude 3 to w to you exhorting you to
Rev 1:11 w in a book and send it to the
Rev 1:19 W the things which you have
Rev 2: 1 of the church of Ephesus w
Rev 2: 8 of the church in Smyrna w
Rev 2:12 of the church in Pergamos w
Rev 2:18 of the church in Thyatira w
Rev 3: 1 of the church in Sardis w
Rev 3: 7 the church in Philadelphia w
Rev 3:12 I will w on him the name of
Rev 3:12 I will w on him My new name
Rev 3:14 church of the Laodiceans w
Rev 10: 4 voices, I was about to w
Rev 10: 4 uttered, and do not w them
Rev 14:13 W: 'Blessed are the dead
Rev 19: 9 W: 'Blessed are those
Rev 21: 5 W, for these words are true

WRITER (*see* WRITE, WRITER'S)
Ps 45: 1 is the pen of a ready w

WRITER'S (*see* WRITER)
Ezek 9: 2 had a w inkhorn at his side
Ezek 9: 3 who had the w inkhorn at his

WRITES (*see* WRITE)
Deut 24: 1 he w her a certificate of
Deut 24: 3 her and w her a certificate of
Rom 10: 5 For Moses w about the

WRITHE (*see* WRITHES)
Joel 2: 6 them the people w in pain

WRITHES (*see* WRITHE)
Job 15:20 the wicked man w with pain

WRITING (*see* WRITE, WRITINGS)
Ex 32:16 the w was the w of God
Deut 10: 4 according to the first w, the
Deut 31:24 when Moses had completed w
1Ch 28:19 LORD made me understand in w
2Ch 2:11 king of Tyre answered in w
2Ch 36:22 kingdom, and also put it in w
Ezra 1: 1 kingdom, and also put it in w
Is 38: 9 This is the w of Hezekiah
Ezek 2:10 there was w on the inside and
Dan 5: 7 Whoever reads this w, and
Dan 5: 8 but they could not read the w
Dan 5:15 that they should read this w
Dan 5:16 Now if you can read the w
Dan 5:17 I will read the w to the king
Dan 5:24 Him, and this w was written
Dan 6: 8 the decree and sign the w, so
Dan 6:10 knew that the w was signed
Luke 1:63 And he asked for a w tablet
John 19:19 And the w was: Jesus
2Co 1:13 For we are not w any other
Phm 19 Paul, am w with my own hand

WRITINGS (*see* WRITING)
John 5:47 if you do not believe his w

WRITTEN (*see* WRITE)
Ex 24:12 commandments which I have w
Ex 31:18 w with the finger of God
Ex 32:15 tablets were w on both sides
Ex 32:15 and on the other they were w
Ex 32:32 of Your book which You have w
Deut 9:10 w with the finger of God, and
Deut 28:58 law that are w in this book
Deut 28:61 which is not w in the book of
Deut 29:20 every curse that is w in this
Deut 29:21 are w in this Book of the Law
Deut 29:27 curse that is w in this book
Deut 30:10 His statutes which are w in
Josh 1: 8 to all that is w in it
Josh 8:31 as it is w in the Book of the
Josh 8:32 law of Moses, which he had w
Josh 8:34 is w in the Book of the Law
Josh 10:13 Is this not w in the Book of
Josh 23: 6 to do all that is w in the
2Sa 1:18 indeed it is w in the Book of
1Ki 2: 3 as it is w in the Law of
1Ki 11:41 are they not w in the book of
1Ki 14:19 indeed they are w in the book
1Ki 14:29 are they not w in the book of
1Ki 15: 7 are they not w in the book of
1Ki 15:23 are they not w in the book of
1Ki 15:31 are they not w in the book of
1Ki 16: 5 are they not w in the book of
1Ki 16:14 are they not w in the book of
1Ki 16:20 are they not w in the book of
1Ki 16:27 are they not w in the book of
1Ki 21:11 as it was w in the letters
1Ki 22:39 are they not w in the book of
1Ki 22:45 are they not w in the book of
2Ki 1:18 are they not w in the book of
2Ki 8:23 are they not w in the book of
2Ki 10:34 are they not w in the book of
2Ki 12:19 are they not w in the book of
2Ki 13: 8 are they not w in the book of
2Ki 13:12 are they not w in the book of
2Ki 14: 6 according to what is w in the
2Ki 14:15 are they not w in the book of
2Ki 14:18 are they not w in the book of
2Ki 14:28 are they not w in the book of
2Ki 15: 6 are they not w in the book of
2Ki 15:11 indeed they are w in the book
2Ki 15:15 indeed they are w in the book
2Ki 15:21 are they not w in the book of

2Ki 15:26 indeed they are w in the book
2Ki 15:31 indeed they are w in the book
2Ki 15:36 are they not w in the book of
2Ki 16:19 are they not w in the book of
2Ki 20:20 are they not w in the book of
2Ki 21:17 are they not w in the book of
2Ki 21:25 are they not w in the book of
2Ki 22:13 all that is w concerning us
2Ki 23: 3 that were w in this book
2Ki 23:21 as it is w in this Book of
2Ki 23:24 w in the book that Hilkiah
2Ki 23:28 are they not w in the book of
2Ki 24: 5 are they not w in the book of
1Ch 16:40 is w in the Law of the LORD
1Ch 29:29 indeed they are w in the book
2Ch 9:29 are they not w in the book of
2Ch 12:15 are they not w in the book of
2Ch 13:22 and his sayings are w in the
2Ch 16:11 are indeed w in the book of
2Ch 20:34 indeed they are w in the book
2Ch 23:18 as it is w in the Law of
2Ch 24:27 God, indeed they are w in the
2Ch 25: 4 but did as it is w in the Law
2Ch 25:26 indeed are they not w in the
2Ch 27: 7 indeed they are w in the book
2Ch 28:26 indeed they are w in the book
2Ch 30:18 contrary to what was w
2Ch 31: 3 as it is w in the Law of the
2Ch 31:16 old and up who were w in the
2Ch 31:17 to the priests who were w in
2Ch 31:18 and to all who were w in the
2Ch 32:32 indeed they are w in the
2Ch 33:18 indeed they are w in the book
2Ch 33:19 indeed they are w among the
2Ch 34:21 to all that is w in this book
2Ch 34:24 all the curses that are w in
2Ch 34:31 that were w in this book
2Ch 35: 4 following the w instruction
2Ch 35: 4 the w instruction of Solomon
2Ch 35:12 as it is w in the Book of
2Ch 35:25 they are w in the Laments
2Ch 35:26 according to what was w in
2Ch 35:27 indeed they are w in the book
2Ch 36: 8 indeed they are w in the book
Ezra 3: 2 it, as it is w in the Law of
Ezra 3: 4 of Tabernacles, as it is w
Ezra 4: 7 the letter was w in Aramaic
Ezra 5: 5 Then a w answer was returned
Ezra 5: 7 to him, in which was w thus
Ezra 6: 2 and in it a record was w thus
Ezra 6:18 as it is w in the Book of
Ezra 8:34 was w down at that time
Neh 6: 6 In it was w
Neh 7: 5 return, and found w in it
Neh 8:14 And they found w in the Law
Neh 8:15 to make booths, as it is w
Neh 10:34 our God as it is w in the Law
Neh 10:36 as it is w in the Law, and the
Neh 12:23 were w in the book of the
Neh 13: 1 in it was found w that no
Esth 2:23 it was w in the book of the
Esth 3: 9 let a decree be w that they
Esth 3:12 a decree was w according to
Esth 3:12 of King Ahasuerus it was w
Esth 4: 8 of the w decree for their
Esth 6: 2 it was found w that Mordecai
Esth 8: 5 let it be w to revoke the
Esth 8: 8 which is w in the king's name
Esth 8: 9 and it was w, according to all
Esth 9:23 as Mordecai had w to them
Esth 9:27 to the w instructions and
Esth 9:32 matters of Purim, and it was w
Esth 10: 2 are they not w in the book of
Job 19:23 Oh, that my words were w
Job 31:35 my Prosecutor had w a book
Ps 40: 7 of the Book it is w of me
Ps 69:28 not be w with the righteous
Ps 102:18 This will be w for the
Ps 139:16 in Your book they all were w
Ps 149: 9 on them the w judgment
Prov 22:20 Have I not w to you excellent
Eccl 12:10 and what was w was upright
Is 65: 6 Behold, it is w before Me
Jer 17: 1 Judah is w with a pen of iron
Jer 17:13 Me shall be w in the earth
Jer 25:13 all that is w in this book,
Jer 36: 6 you have w at my instruction
Jer 36:27 had w at the instruction of
Jer 36:29 Why have you w in it that
Jer 45: 1 when he had w these words in
Jer 51:60 that are w against Babylon
Ezek 2:10 w on it were lamentations and
Ezek 13: 9 nor be w in the record of the
Dan 5:24 Him, and this writing was w
Dan 5:25 is the inscription that was w
Dan 6: 9 Darius signed the w decree
Dan 9:11 and the oath w in the Law of
Dan 9:13 As it is w in the Law of
Dan 12: 1 who is found w in the book
Hos 8:12 I have w for him the great
Mal 3:16 w before Him for those who
Matt 2: 5 thus it is w by the prophet
Matt 4: 4 It is w, 'Man shall not live
Matt 4: 6 For it is w: 'He shall
Matt 4: 7 It is w again, 'You shall not
Matt 4:10 For it is w, 'You shall
Matt 11:10 this is he of whom it is w
Matt 21:13 It is w, 'My house shall be
Matt 26:24 of Man goes as it is w of Him
Matt 26:31 of Me this night, for it is w
Matt 27:37 the accusation w against Him
Mark 1: 2 As it is w in the Prophets
Mark 7: 6 of you hypocrites, as it is w
Mark 9:12 how is it w concerning the
Mark 9:13 wished, as it is w of him
Mark 11:17 Is it not w, 'My house shall
Mark 14:21 goes just as it is w of Him
Mark 14:27 of Me this night, for it is w
Mark 15:26 of His accusation was w above
Luke 2:23 (as it is w in the law of the
Luke 3: 4 as it is w in the book of the
Luke 4: 4 It is w, 'Man shall not live
Luke 4: 8 For it is w, 'You shall
Luke 4:10 For it is w: 'He shall give
Luke 4:17 the place where it was w
Luke 7:27 This is he of whom it is w
Luke 10:20 your names are w in heaven
Luke 10:26 him, "What is w in the law
Luke 18:31 all things that are w by the
Luke 19:46 It is w, 'My house is a house
Luke 20:17 What then is this that is w
Luke 21:22 which are w may be fulfilled
Luke 22:37 to you that this which is w
Luke 23:38 was w over Him in letters of
Luke 24:44 were w in the Law of Moses
Luke 24:46 Thus it is w, and thus it was
John 2:17 remembered that it was w
John 6:31 as it is w, 'He gave them
John 6:45 It is w in the prophets, 'And
John 8:17 It is also w in your law that
John 10:34 Is it not w in your law, 'I
John 12:14 as it is w:
John 12:16 these things were w about Him
John 15:25 which is w in their law
John 19:20 it was w in Hebrew, Greek, and
John 19:22 What I have w, I have w
John 19:22 What I have w, I have w
John 20:30 which are not w in this book
John 20:31 but these are w that you may
John 21:25 if they were w one by one
John 21:25 the books that would be w
Acts 1:20 For it is w in the book of
Acts 7:42 as it is w in the book of the
Acts 13:29 all that was w concerning Him
Acts 13:33 As it is also w in the second
Acts 15:15 agree, just as it is w
Acts 21:25 who believe, we have w and
Acts 23: 5 for it is w, 'You shall not
Acts 24:14 things which are w in the Law
Rom 1:17 as it is w, "The just shall
Rom 2:15 of the law w in their hearts
Rom 2:24 because of you," as it is w
Rom 2:27 who, even with your w code
Rom 3: 4 As it is w: "That You may
Rom 3:10 As it is w: "There is none
Rom 4:17 (as it is w, "I have made
Rom 4:23 Now it was not w for his sake
Rom 8:36 As it is w: "For Your sake
Rom 9:13 As it is w, "Jacob I have
Rom 9:33 As it is w: "Behold, I lay
Rom 10:15 As it is w: "How beautiful
Rom 11: 8 Just as it is w
Rom 11:26 will be saved, as it is w
Rom 12:19 for it is w, "Vengeance is
Rom 14:11 For it is w: "As I live
Rom 15: 3 but as it is w, "The
Rom 15: 4 For whatever things were w
Rom 15: 4 were w for our learning, that
Rom 15: 9 God for His mercy, as it is w
Rom 15:15 I have w more boldly to you
Rom 15:21 but as it is w: "To whom He
1Co 1:19 For it is w: "I will destroy
1Co 1:31 that, as it is w, "He who
1Co 2: 9 But as it is w: "Eye has not
1Co 3:19 For it is w, "He catches the
1Co 4: 6 not to think beyond what is w
1Co 5:11 But now I have w to you not
1Co 9: 9 For it is w in the law of
1Co 9:10 sakes, no doubt, this is w
1Co 9:15 nor have I w these things
1Co 10: 7 As it is w, "The people sat
1Co 10:11 and they were w for our
1Co 14:21 In the law it is w
1Co 15:45 And so it is w, "The first
1Co 15:54 to pass the saying that is w
2Co 3: 2 our epistle w in our hearts
2Co 3: 3 w not with ink but by the
2Co 3: 7 if the ministry of death, w
2Co 4:13 faith, according to what is w
2Co 8:15 As it is w, "He who gathered
2Co 9: 9 it is w: "He has dispersed
Gal 3:10 for it is w, "Cursed is
Gal 3:10 are w in the book of the law
Gal 3:13 a curse for us (for it is w
Gal 4:22 For it is w that Abraham had
Gal 4:27 For it is w: "Rejoice
Gal 6:11 w to you with my own hand
Heb 10: 7 of the book it is w of Me
Heb 13:22 for I have w to you in few
1Pe 1:16 because it is w, "Be holy,
1Pe 5:12 him, I have w to you briefly,
2Pe 3:15 given to him, has w to you,
1Jn 2:14 I have w to you, fathers,
1Jn 2:14 I have w to you, young men,
1Jn 2:21 I have not w to you because
1Jn 2:26 These things I have w to you
1Jn 5:13 These things I have w to you
Rev 1: 3 things which are w in it
Rev 2:17 on the stone a new name w
Rev 5: 1 the throne a scroll w inside
Rev 13: 8 whose names have not been w
Rev 14: 1 name w on their foreheads
Rev 17: 5 on her forehead a name was w
Rev 17: 8 whose names are not w in the
Rev 19:12 He had a name w that no one
Rev 19:16 robe and on His thigh a name w
Rev 20:12 which were w in the books
Rev 20:15 anyone not found w in the
Rev 21:12 names w on them, which are
Rev 21:27 but only those who are w in
Rev 22:18 that are w in this book
Rev 22:19 which are w in this book

WRONG (*see* WRONGDOING, WRONGED, WRONGFULLY, WRONGS)
Gen 16: 5 to Abram, "My w be upon you
Ex 2:13 said to the one who did the w
Num 5: 8 may be made for the w, the
Num 5: 8 the restitution for the w
2Sa 19:19 me, or remember what w your
1Ki 8:47 We have sinned and done w
2Ki 18:14 I have done w
1Ch 12:17 there is no w in my hands
1Ch 16:21 permitted no man to do them w
2Ch 6:37 have sinned, we have done w
Job 1:22 not sin nor charge God with w
Job 19: 7 If I cry out concerning w
Job 21:27 with which you would w me
Job 24:12 does not charge them with w
Job 36:23 has said, 'You have done w'
Ps 105:14 permitted no one to do them w
Jer 22: 3 Do no w and do no violence to
Jer 40: 4 But if it seems w for you to
Dan 6:22 I have done no w before you
Matt 20:13 Friend, I am doing you no w
Luke 23:41 this Man has done nothing w
Acts 7:24 seeing one of them suffer w
Acts 7:26 why do you w one another
Acts 7:27 neighbor w pushed him away
Acts 25:10 To the Jews I have done no w
1Co 6: 7 do you not rather accept w
1Co 6: 8 No, you yourselves do w and
2Co 7:12 of him who had done the w
2Co 7:12 sake of him who suffered w
2Co 12:13 Forgive me this w
Col 3:25 But he who does w will be
Col 3:25 for the w which he has done

WRONGDOING (*see* WRONG)
Deut 19:16 to testify against him of **w**
Acts 18:14 matter of **w** or wicked crimes
Acts 24:20 say if they found any **w** in me

WRONGED (*see* WRONG)
Num 5: 7 give it to the one he has **w**
Judg 11:27 you, but you **w** me by fighting
Esth 1:16 has not only **w** the king, but
Job 19: 3 ashamed that you have **w** me
Job 19: 6 Know then that God has **w** me
Lam 3:59 You have seen how I am **w**
2Co 7: 2 We have **w** no one, we have
Phm 18 But if he has **w** you or owes

WRONGFULLY (*see* WRONG)
Gen 43: 6 Why did you deal so **w** with me
Ps 35:19 over me who are **w** my enemies
Ps 38:19 who hate me **w** have multiplied
Ps 69: 4 me, Being my enemies **w**
Ps 119:78 treated me **w** with falsehood
Ps 119:86 They persecute me **w**
Ezek 22:29 they **w** oppress the stranger
1Pe 2:19 endures grief, suffering **w**

WRONGS (*see* WRONG)
Prov 8:36 against me **w** his own soul

WROTE (*see* WRITE)
Ex 24: 4 Moses **w** all the words of the
Ex 34:28 He **w** on the tablets the words
Ex 39:30 **w** on it an inscription like
Num 33: 2 Now Moses **w** down the starting
Deut 4:13 He **w** them on two tablets of
Deut 5:22 He **w** them on two tablets of
Deut 10: 4 He **w** on the tablets according
Deut 31: 9 So Moses **w** this law and
Deut 31:22 Therefore Moses **w** this song
Josh 8:32 he **w** on the stones a copy of
Josh 18: 9 **w** the survey in a book in
Josh 24:26 Then Joshua **w** these words in
Judg 8:14 he **w** down for him the leaders
1Sa 10:25 **w** it in a book and laid it up
2Sa 11:14 that David **w** a letter to Joab
2Sa 11:15 he **w** in the letter, saying,
1Ki 21: 8 So she **w** letters in Ahab's
1Ki 21: 9 she **w** in the letters, saying,
2Ki 10: 1 Jehu **w** letters and sent them
2Ki 10: 6 Then he **w** a second letter to
2Ki 17:37 which He **w** for you, you shall
1Ch 24: 6 **w** them down before the king,
2Ch 26:22 Isaiah the son of Amoz **w**
2Ch 30: 1 also **w** letters to Ephraim and
2Ch 32:17 He also **w** letters to revile
Ezra 4: 6 they **w** an accusation against
Ezra 4: 7 **w** to Artaxerxes king of
Ezra 4: 8 and Shimshai the scribe **w** a
Esth 8: 5 which he **w** to annihilate the
Esth 8:10 And he **w** in the name of King
Esth 9:20 Mordecai **w** these things and
Esth 9:29 Jew, **w** with full authority to
Jer 36: 4 Baruch **w** on a scroll of a
Jer 36:18 I **w** them with ink in the book
Jer 36:32 of Neriah, who **w** on it at the
Jer 51:60 So Jeremiah **w** in a book all
Dan 5: 5 **w** opposite the lampstand on
Dan 5: 5 the part of the hand that **w**
Dan 6:25 Then King Darius **w**
Dan 7: 1 Then he **w** down the dream,
Mark 10: 5 heart he **w** you this precept
Mark 12:19 Moses **w** to us that if a man's
Luke 1:63 for a writing tablet, and **w**
Luke 20:28 Moses **w** to us that if a man's
John 1:45 law, and also the prophets, **w**
John 5:46 for he **w** about Me
John 8: 6 and **w** on the ground with His
John 8: 8 down and **w** on the ground
John 19:19 Now Pilate **w** a title and put
John 21:24 things, and **w** these things
Acts 15:23 They **w** this letter by them
Acts 18:27 to Achaia, the brethren **w**
Acts 23:25 He **w** a letter in the
Rom 16:22 who **w** this epistle, greet you
1Co 5: 9 I **w** to you in my epistle not
1Co 7: 1 things of which you **w** to me
2Co 2: 3 I **w** this very thing to you,
2Co 2: 4 anguish of heart I **w** to you
2Co 2: 9 For to this end I also **w**,
2Co 7:12 although I **w** to you, I did
Eph 3: 3 (as I **w** before in a few words
2Jn 5 lady, not as though I **w** a new
3Jn 9 I **w** to the church, but

WROUGHT
Ps 139:15 skillfully **w** in the lowest
Ezek 27:19 **W** iron, cassia, and cane were

WRUNG (*see* WRING)
Judg 6:38 he **w** the dew out of the

YAH (*see* GOD)
Ps 68: 4 on the clouds, By His name **Y**
Is 12: 2 For **Y**, the LORD, is my
Is 26: 4 in the LORD forever, for in **Y**
Is 38:11 I shall not see **Y**, the LORD

YARN
Ex 25: 4 blue and purple and scarlet **y**
Ex 26: 1 blue and purple and scarlet **y**
Ex 26: 4 shall make loops of blue **y** on
Ex 26:31 blue and purple and scarlet **y**
Ex 26:36 blue and purple and scarlet **y**
Ex 27:16 blue and purple and scarlet **y**
Ex 28:33 blue and purple and scarlet **y**
Ex 35: 6 blue and purple and scarlet **y**
Ex 35:25 spun **y** with their hands, and
Ex 35:26 wisdom spun **y** of goats' hair
Ex 36: 8 blue and purple and scarlet **y**
Ex 36:11 He made loops of blue **y** on
Ex 36:35 blue and purple and scarlet **y**
Ex 36:37 blue and purple and scarlet **y**
Ex 38:18 blue and purple and scarlet **y**
Ex 38:23 blue and purple and scarlet **y**
Judg 16: 9 bowstrings as a strand of **y**

YEA
Ps 19:10 desired are they than gold, **Y**
Ps 23: 4 **Y**, though I walk through the
Ps 137: 1 Babylon, There we sat down, **y**

YEAR (*see* YEARLY, YEAR'S, YEARS)
Gen 7:11 hundredth **y** of Noah's life
Gen 8:13 in the six hundred and first **y**
Gen 14: 4 thirteenth **y** they rebelled
Gen 14: 5 the fourteenth **y** Chedorlaomer
Gen 17:21 you at this set time next **y**
Gen 26:12 in the same **y** a hundredfold
Gen 47:17 all their livestock that **y**
Gen 47:18 When that **y** had ended, they
Gen 47:18 they came to him the next **y**
Ex 12: 2 first month of the **y** to you
Ex 12: 5 a male of the first **y**
Ex 13:10 in its season from **y** to **y**
Ex 23:11 but the seventh **y** you shall
Ex 23:14 keep a feast to Me in the **y**
Ex 23:16 which is at the end of the **y**
Ex 23:17 Three times in the **y** all your
Ex 23:29 out from before you in one **y**
Ex 29:38 two lambs of the first **y**, day
Ex 30:10 upon its horns once a **y** with
Ex 30:10 once a **y** he shall make
Ex 34:23 Three times in the **y** all your
Ex 34:24 your God three times in the **y**
Ex 40:17 first month of the second **y**
Lev 9: 3 a lamb, both of the first **y**
Lev 12: 6 first **y** as a burnt offering
Lev 14:10 the first **y** without blemish
Lev 16:34 for all their sins, once a **y**
Lev 19:24 But in the fourth **y** all its
Lev 19:25 in the fifth **y** you may eat
Lev 23:12 a male lamb of the first **y**
Lev 23:18 seven lambs of the first **y**
Lev 23:19 **y** as a sacrifice of peace
Lev 23:41 LORD for seven days in the **y**
Lev 25: 4 but in the seventh **y** there
Lev 25: 5 for it is a **y** of rest for the
Lev 25:10 consecrate the fiftieth **y**
Lev 25:11 That fiftieth **y** shall be a
Lev 25:13 In this **Y** of Jubilee, each
Lev 25:20 shall we eat in the seventh **y**
Lev 25:21 on you in the sixth **y**, and it
Lev 25:22 you shall sow in the eighth **y**
Lev 25:22 old produce until the ninth **y**
Lev 25:28 it until the **Y** of Jubilee
Lev 25:29 a whole **y** after it is sold
Lev 25:29 within a full **y** he may redeem
Lev 25:30 within the space of a full **y**
Lev 25:33 released in the **Y** of Jubilee
Lev 25:40 you until the **Y** of Jubilee
Lev 25:50 from the **y** that he was sold
Lev 25:50 to him until the **Y** of Jubilee
Lev 25:52 years until the **Y** of Jubilee
Lev 25:54 released in the **Y** of Jubilee
Lev 27:17 field from the **Y** of Jubilee
Lev 27:18 remain till the **Y** of Jubilee
Lev 27:23 up to the **Y** of Jubilee, and he
Lev 27:24 In the **Y** of Jubilee the
Num 1: 1 in the second **y** after they
Num 6:12 **y** as a trespass offering
Num 6:14 **y** without blemish as a burnt
Num 6:14 **y** without blemish as a sin
Num 7:15 one male lamb in its first **y**
Num 7:17 male lambs in their first **y**
Num 7:21 one male lamb in its first **y**
Num 7:23 male lambs in their first **y**
Num 7:27 one male lamb in its first **y**
Num 7:29 male lambs in their first **y**
Num 7:33 one male lamb in its first **y**
Num 7:35 male lambs in their first **y**
Num 7:39 one male lamb in its first **y**
Num 7:41 male lambs in their first **y**
Num 7:45 one male lamb in its first **y**
Num 7:47 male lambs in their first **y**
Num 7:51 one male lamb in its first **y**
Num 7:53 male lambs in their first **y**
Num 7:57 one male lamb in its first **y**
Num 7:59 male lambs in their first **y**
Num 7:63 one male lamb in its first **y**
Num 7:65 male lambs in their first **y**
Num 7:69 one male lamb in its first **y**
Num 7:71 male lambs in their first **y**
Num 7:75 one male lamb in its first **y**
Num 7:77 male lambs in their first **y**
Num 7:81 one male lamb in its first **y**
Num 7:83 male lambs in their first **y**
Num 7:87 lambs in their first **y** twelve
Num 7:88 lambs in their first **y** sixty
Num 9: 1 first month of the second **y**
Num 9:22 month, or a **y** that the cloud
Num 10:11 second month, in the second **y**
Num 14:34 shall bear your guilt one **y**
Num 15:27 its first **y** as a sin offering
Num 28: 3 their first **y** without blemish
Num 28: 9 two lambs in their first **y**
Num 28:11 seven lambs in their first **y**
Num 28:14 the months of the **y**
Num 28:19 seven lambs in their first **y**
Num 28:27 seven lambs in their first **y**
Num 29: 2 seven lambs in their first **y**
Num 29: 8 seven lambs in their first **y**
Num 29:13 lambs in their first **y**
Num 29:17 their first **y** without blemish
Num 29:20 their first **y** without blemish
Num 29:23 lambs in their first **y**,
Num 29:26 their first **y** without blemish
Num 29:29 their first **y** without blemish
Num 29:32 their first **y** without blemish
Num 29:36 their first **y** without blemish
Num 33:38 **y** after the children of
Deut 1: 3 to pass in the fortieth **y**
Deut 11:12 from the beginning of the **y**
Deut 11:12 to the very end of the **y**
Deut 14:22 the field produces **y** by **y**
Deut 14:28 **y** you shall bring out the
Deut 14:28 of your produce of that **y**
Deut 15: 9 heart, saying, 'The seventh **y**
Deut 15: 9 the **y** of release, is at hand,
Deut 15:12 then in the seventh **y** you
Deut 15:20 **y** by **y** in the place which
Deut 16:16 Three times a **y** all your
Deut 24: 5 shall be free at home one **y**
Deut 26:12 your increase in the third **y**
Deut 26:12 which is the **y** of tithing
Deut 31:10 time in the **y** of release, at
Josh 5:12 of the land of Canaan that **y**
Judg 10: 8 From that **y** they harassed and
Judg 11:40 **y** to lament the daughter of
Judg 17:10 ten shekels of silver per **y**
1Sa 1: 7 **y** by **y**, when she went up
1Sa 2:19 bring it to him **y** by **y**
1Sa 7:16 He went from **y** to **y** on a
1Sa 13: 1 Saul reigned one **y**
1Sa 27: 7 Philistines was one full **y**
2Sa 11: 1 pass in the spring of the **y**
2Sa 14:26 at the end of every **y** he cut
2Sa 21: 1 for three years, **y** after **y**
1Ki 4: 7 for one month of the **y**
1Ki 5:11 gave to Hiram **y** by **y**
1Ki 6: 1 and eightieth **y** after the

1Ki 6: 1 in the fourth y of Solomon's
1Ki 6:37 In the fourth y the
1Ki 6:38 And in the eleventh y, in the
1Ki 9:25 Now three times a y Solomon
1Ki 10:25 at a set rate y by y
1Ki 14:25 in the fifth y of King
1Ki 15: 1 Now in the eighteenth y of
1Ki 15: 9 In the twentieth y of
1Ki 15:25 second y of Asa king of Judah
1Ki 15:28 third y of Asa king of Judah
1Ki 15:33 In the third y of Asa king of
1Ki 16: 8 In the twenty-sixth y of Asa
1Ki 16:10 y of Asa king of Judah, and
1Ki 16:15 y of Asa king of Judah, Zimri
1Ki 16:23 In the thirty-first y of Asa
1Ki 16:29 y of Asa king of Judah, Ahab
1Ki 18: 1 to Elijah, in the third y
1Ki 20:22 for in the spring of the y
1Ki 20:26 was, in the spring of the y
1Ki 22: 2 came to pass, in the third y
1Ki 22:41 y of Ahab king of Israel
1Ki 22:51 y of Jehoshaphat king of
2Ki 1:17 in the second y of Jehoram
2Ki 3: 1 y of Jehoshaphat king of
2Ki 4:16 About this time next y you
2Ki 8:16 Now in the fifth y of Joram
2Ki 8:25 In the twelfth y of Joram the
2Ki 8:26 he reigned one y in Jerusalem
2Ki 9:29 In the eleventh y of Joram
2Ki 11: 4 the seventh y Jehoiada sent
2Ki 12: 1 In the seventh y of Jehu,
2Ki 12: 6 y of King Jehoash, that the
2Ki 13: 1 In the twenty-third y of
2Ki 13:10 In the thirty-seventh y of
2Ki 13:20 land in the spring of the y
2Ki 14: 1 In the second y of Joash the
2Ki 14:23 In the fifteenth y of Amaziah
2Ki 15: 1 In the twenty-seventh y of
2Ki 15: 8 In the thirty-eighth y of
2Ki 15:13 y of Uzziah king of Judah
2Ki 15:17 In the thirty-ninth y of
2Ki 15:23 In the fiftieth y of Azariah
2Ki 15:27 In the fifty-second y of
2Ki 15:30 his place in the twentieth y
2Ki 15:32 In the second y of Pekah the
2Ki 16: 1 In the seventeenth y of Pekah
2Ki 17: 1 In the twelfth y of Ahaz king
2Ki 17: 4 as he had done y by y
2Ki 17: 6 In the ninth y of Hoshea, the
2Ki 18: 1 y of Hoshea the son of Elah
2Ki 18: 9 the fourth y of King Hezekiah
2Ki 18: 9 which was the seventh y of
2Ki 18:10 In the sixth y of Hezekiah
2Ki 18:10 the ninth y of Hoshea king of
2Ki 18:13 fourteenth y of King Hezekiah
2Ki 19:29 You shall eat this y such as
2Ki 19:29 in the second y what springs
2Ki 19:29 also in the third y sow and
2Ki 22: 3 eighteenth y of King Josiah
2Ki 23:23 y of King Josiah this
2Ki 24:12 in the eighth y of his reign
2Ki 25: 1 in the ninth y of his reign
2Ki 25: 2 eleventh y of King Zedekiah
2Ki 25: 8 (which was the nineteenth y
2Ki 25:27 y of the captivity of
2Ki 25:27 in the y that he began to
1Ch 20: 1 in the spring of the y, at
1Ch 26:31 In the fortieth y of the
1Ch 27: 1 all the months of the y, each
2Ch 3: 2 in the fourth y of his reign
2Ch 9:24 at a set rate y by y
2Ch 12: 2 in the fifth y of King
2Ch 13: 1 eighteenth y of King Jeroboam
2Ch 15:10 in the fifteenth y of the
2Ch 15:19 y of the reign of Asa
2Ch 16: 1 y of the reign of Asa, Baasha
2Ch 16:12 thirty-ninth y of his reign
2Ch 16:13 forty-first y of his reign
2Ch 17: 7 Also in the third y of his
2Ch 22: 2 he reigned one y in Jerusalem
2Ch 23: 1 In the seventh y Jehoiada
2Ch 24: 5 of your God from y to y
2Ch 24:23 in the spring of the y that
2Ch 27: 5 that y one hundred talents of
2Ch 29: 3 In the first y of his reign
2Ch 34: 3 in the eighth y of his reign
2Ch 34: 3 in the twelfth y he began to
2Ch 34: 8 the eighteenth y of his reign
2Ch 35:19 In the eighteenth y of the
2Ch 36:10 At the turn of the y King
2Ch 36:22 Now in the first y of Cyrus
Ezra 1: 1 Now in the first y of Cyrus
Ezra 3: 8 y of their coming to the
Ezra 4:24 until the second y of the
Ezra 5:13 in the first y of Cyrus king
Ezra 6: 3 In the first y of King Cyrus,
Ezra 6:15 which was in the sixth y of
Ezra 7: 7 seventh y of King Artaxerxes
Ezra 7: 8 in the seventh y of the king
Neh 1: 1 Chislev, in the twentieth y
Neh 2: 1 in the twentieth y of King
Neh 5:14 from the twentieth y until
Neh 5:14 y of King Artaxerxes, twelve
Neh 10:34 the appointed times y by y
Neh 10:35 y by y, to the house of
Neh 10:35 fruit of all trees, y by y
Neh 13: 6 y of Artaxerxes king of
Esth 1: 3 that in the third y of his
Esth 2:16 in the seventh y of his reign
Esth 3: 7 in the twelfth y of King
Esth 9:27 these two days every y,
Job 3: 6 among the days of the y, may
Ps 65:11 You crown the y with Your
Is 6: 1 In the y that King Uzziah
Is 14:28 in the y that King Ahaz died
Is 20: 1 In the y that Tartan came to
Is 21:16 Within a y, according to the
Is 21:16 to the y of a hired man, all
Is 29: 1 Add y to y
Is 32:10 In a y and some days you will
Is 34: 8 the y of recompense for the
Is 36: 1 y of King Hezekiah that
Is 37:30 You shall eat this y such as
Is 37:30 the second y what springs
Is 37:30 also in the third y sow and
Is 61: 2 the acceptable y of the LORD
Is 63: 4 the y of My redeemed has come
Jer 1: 2 the thirteenth y of his reign
Jer 1: 3 y of Zedekiah the son of
Jer 11:23 Anathoth, even the y of their
Jer 17: 8 anxious in the y of drought
Jer 23:12 the y of their punishment,"
Jer 25: 1 in the fourth y of Jehoiakim
Jer 25: 1 y of Nebuchadnezzar king of
Jer 25: 3 From the thirteenth y of
Jer 25: 3 y in which the word of the
Jer 28: 1 And it happened in the same y
Jer 28: 1 of Judah, in the fourth y
Jer 28:16 This y you shall die, because
Jer 28:17 same y in the seventh month
Jer 32: 1 y of Zedekiah king of Judah
Jer 32: 1 y of Nebuchadnezzar
Jer 36: 1 y of Jehoiakim the son of
Jer 36: 9 y of Jehoiakim the son of
Jer 39: 1 In the ninth y of Zedekiah
Jer 39: 2 In the eleventh y of Zedekiah
Jer 45: 1 in the fourth y of Jehoiakim
Jer 46: 2 defeated in the fourth y of
Jer 48:44 the y of their punishment
Jer 51:46 land (a rumor will come one y
Jer 51:46 in another y a rumor will
Jer 51:59 in the fourth y of his reign
Jer 52: 4 in the ninth y of his reign
Jer 52: 5 eleventh y of King Zedekiah
Jer 52:12 (which was the nineteenth y
Jer 52:28 in the seventh y, three
Jer 52:29 in the eighteenth y of
Jer 52:30 y of Nebuchadnezzar,
Jer 52:31 y of the captivity of
Jer 52:31 in the first y of his reign
Ezek 1: 1 to pass in the thirtieth y
Ezek 1: 2 fifth y of King Jehoiachin's
Ezek 4: 6 laid on you a day for each y
Ezek 8: 1 came to pass in the sixth y
Ezek 20: 1 came to pass in the seventh y
Ezek 24: 1 Again, in the ninth y, in the
Ezek 26: 1 to pass in the eleventh y
Ezek 29: 1 In the tenth y, in the tenth
Ezek 29:17 pass in the twenty-seventh y
Ezek 30:20 to pass in the eleventh y
Ezek 31: 1 to pass in the eleventh y
Ezek 32: 1 came to pass in the twelfth y
Ezek 32:17 to pass also in the twelfth y
Ezek 33:21 twelfth y of our captivity
Ezek 40: 1 y of our captivity
Ezek 40: 1 at the beginning of the y
Ezek 40: 1 in the fourteenth y after the
Ezek 46:13 the first y without blemish
Ezek 46:17 be his until the y of liberty
Dan 1: 1 In the third y of the reign
Dan 1:21 the first y of King Cyrus
Dan 2: 1 Now in the second y of
Dan 7: 1 In the first y of Belshazzar
Dan 8: 1 In the third y of the reign
Dan 9: 1 In the first y of Darius the
Dan 9: 2 in the first y of his reign I
Dan 10: 1 In the third y of Cyrus king
Dan 11: 1 Also in the first y of Darius
Mic 6: 6 with calves a y old
Hag 1: 1 In the second y of King
Hag 1:15 in the second y of King
Hag 2:10 in the second y of Darius
Zech 1: 1 of the second y of Darius
Zech 1: 7 in the second y of Darius
Zech 7: 1 Now in the fourth y of King
Zech 14:16 y to y to worship the King
Luke 2:41 every y at the Feast of the
Luke 3: 1 Now in the fifteenth y of the
Luke 4:19 the acceptable y of the LORD
Luke 13: 8 Sir, let it alone this y also
John 11:49 being high priest that y
John 11:51 y he prophesied that Jesus
John 18:13 who was high priest that y
Acts 11:26 y they assembled with the
Acts 18:11 And he continued there a y
2Co 8:10 were desiring to do a y ago
2Co 9: 2 that Achaia was ready a y ago
Heb 9: 7 priest went alone once a y
Heb 9:25 every y with blood of another
Heb 10: 1 offer continually y by y
Heb 10: 3 is a reminder of sins every y
Jas 4:13 such a city, spend a y there
Rev 9:15 hour and day and month and y

YEARLY (*see* YEAR)
Lev 25:53 with him as a y hired servant
Judg 21:19 there is a y feast of the
1Sa 1: 3 up from his city y to worship
1Sa 1:21 to the LORD the y sacrifice
1Sa 2:19 to offer the y sacrifice
1Sa 20: 6 for there is a y sacrifice
1Ki 10:14 to Solomon y was six hundred
2Ch 8:13 the three appointed y feasts
2Ch 9:13 to Solomon y was six hundred
Neh 10:32 to exact from ourselves y
Esth 9:21 celebrate y the fourteenth

YEARNED (*see* YEARNS)
Gen 43:30 Now his heart y for his
1Ki 3:26 for she y with compassion for
Song 5: 4 door, and my heart y for him

YEARNING (*see* YEARNS)
Is 63:15 the y of Your heart and Your

YEARNS (*see* YEARNED, YEARNING)
Job 19:27 How my heart y within me
Ps 12: 5 in the safety for which he y
Jer 31:20 therefore My heart y for him
Jas 4: 5 dwells in us y jealously"

YEAR'S (*see* YEAR)
Ex 34:22 of Ingathering at the y end
Neh 10:31 forego the seventh y produce

YEARS (*see* YEAR)
Gen 1:14 and seasons, and for days and y
Gen 5: 3 lived one hundred and thirty y
Gen 5: 4 of Adam were eight hundred y
Gen 5: 5 were nine hundred and thirty y
Gen 5: 6 lived one hundred and five y
Gen 5: 7 eight hundred and seven y, and
Gen 5: 8 were nine hundred and twelve y
Gen 5: 9 Enosh lived ninety y, and
Gen 5:10 eight hundred and fifteen y
Gen 5:11 were nine hundred and five y
Gen 5:12 Cainan lived seventy y, and
Gen 5:13 eight hundred and forty y, and
Gen 5:14 were nine hundred and ten y
Gen 5:15 Mahalaleel lived sixty-five y
Gen 5:16 eight hundred and thirty y
Gen 5:17 hundred and ninety-five y
Gen 5:18 one hundred and sixty-two y
Gen 5:19 Jared lived eight hundred y
Gen 5:20 nine hundred and sixty-two y
Gen 5:21 Enoch lived sixty-five y, and
Gen 5:22 with God three hundred y, and
Gen 5:23 three hundred and sixty-five y
Gen 5:25 one hundred and eighty-seven y
Gen 5:26 seven hundred and eighty-two y
Gen 5:27 nine hundred and sixty-nine y
Gen 5:28 one hundred and eighty-two y
Gen 5:30 five hundred and ninety-five y

Gen 5:31 hundred and seventy-seven y
Gen 5:32 Noah was five hundred y old
Gen 6: 3 be one hundred and twenty y
Gen 7: 6 Noah was six hundred y old
Gen 9:28 three hundred and fifty y
Gen 9:29 were nine hundred and fifty y
Gen 11:10 Shem was one hundred y old
Gen 11:10 two y after the flood
Gen 11:11 Shem lived five hundred y
Gen 11:12 Arphaxad lived thirty-five y
Gen 11:13 lived four hundred and three y
Gen 11:14 Salah lived thirty y, and
Gen 11:15 lived four hundred and three y
Gen 11:16 Eber lived thirty-four y, and
Gen 11:17 four hundred and thirty y, and
Gen 11:18 Peleg lived thirty y, and
Gen 11:19 lived two hundred and nine y
Gen 11:20 Reu lived thirty-two y, and
Gen 11:21 lived two hundred and seven y
Gen 11:22 Serug lived thirty y, and
Gen 11:23 Serug lived two hundred y
Gen 11:24 Nahor lived twenty-nine y
Gen 11:25 one hundred and nineteen y
Gen 11:26 Now Terah lived seventy y
Gen 11:32 were two hundred and five y
Gen 12: 4 Abram was seventy-five y old
Gen 14: 4 Twelve y they served
Gen 15:13 afflict them four hundred y
Gen 16: 3 ten y in the land of Canaan
Gen 16:16 Abram was eighty-six y old
Gen 17: 1 Abram was ninety-nine y old
Gen 17:17 man who is one hundred y old
Gen 17:17 Sarah, who is ninety y old
Gen 17:24 Abraham was ninety-nine y old
Gen 17:25 his son was thirteen y old
Gen 21: 5 y old when his son Isaac was
Gen 23: 1 one hundred and twenty-seven y
Gen 23: 1 these were the y of the life
Gen 25: 7 This is the sum of the y of
Gen 25: 7 one hundred and seventy-five y
Gen 25: 8 age, an old man and full of y
Gen 25:17 These were the y of the life
Gen 25:17 one hundred and thirty-seven y
Gen 25:20 Isaac was forty y old when he
Gen 25:26 Isaac was sixty y old when
Gen 26:34 When Esau was forty y old
Gen 29:18 I will serve you seven y for
Gen 29:20 served seven y for Rachel
Gen 29:27 with me still another seven y
Gen 29:30 Laban still another seven y
Gen 31:38 These twenty y I have been
Gen 31:41 been in your house twenty y
Gen 31:41 I served you fourteen y for
Gen 31:41 six y for your flock, and you
Gen 35:28 were one hundred and eighty y
Gen 37: 2 Joseph, being seventeen y old
Gen 41: 1 at the end of two full y
Gen 41:26 seven good cows are seven y
Gen 41:26 seven good heads are seven y
Gen 41:27 up after them are seven y
Gen 41:27 wind are seven y of famine
Gen 41:29 Indeed seven y of great
Gen 41:30 seven y of famine will arise
Gen 41:34 in the seven plentiful y
Gen 41:35 those good y that are coming
Gen 41:36 for the land for the seven y
Gen 41:46 Joseph was thirty y old when
Gen 41:47 y the ground brought forth
Gen 41:48 y which were in the land of
Gen 41:50 before the y of famine came
Gen 41:53 Then the seven y of plenty
Gen 41:54 the seven y of famine began
Gen 45: 6 For these two y the famine
Gen 45: 6 there are still five y in
Gen 45:11 are still five y of famine
Gen 47: 9 The days of the y of my
Gen 47: 9 are one hundred and thirty y
Gen 47: 9 the days of the y of my life
Gen 47: 9 y of the life of my fathers
Gen 47:28 the land of Egypt seventeen y
Gen 47:28 one hundred and forty-seven y
Gen 50:22 lived one hundred and ten y
Gen 50:26 one hundred and ten y old
Ex 6:16 the y of the life of Levi
Ex 6:18 the y of the life of Kohath
Ex 6:20 the y of the life of Amram
Ex 7: 7 And Moses was eighty y old
Ex 7: 7 Aaron eighty-three y old when
Ex 12:40 was four hundred and thirty y
Ex 12:41 the four hundred and thirty y
Ex 16:35 of Israel ate manna forty y
Ex 21: 2 servant, he shall serve six y
Ex 23:10 Six y you shall sow your land
Ex 30:14 numbered, from twenty y old
Ex 38:26 numbering from twenty y old
Lev 19:23 Three y it shall be as
Lev 25: 3 Six y you shall sow your
Lev 25: 3 six y you shall prune your
Lev 25: 8 sabbaths of y for yourself
Lev 25: 8 yourself, seven times seven y
Lev 25: 8 of the seven sabbaths of y
Lev 25: 8 shall be to you forty-nine y
Lev 25:15 y after the Jubilee you shall
Lev 25:15 y of crops he shall sell to
Lev 25:16 to the multitude of y you
Lev 25:16 of y you shall diminish its
Lev 25:16 number of the y of the crops
Lev 25:21 produce enough for three y
Lev 25:27 count the y since its sale
Lev 25:50 according to the number of y
Lev 25:51 are still many y remaining
Lev 25:52 y until the Year of Jubilee
Lev 25:52 according to his y he shall
Lev 25:54 he is not redeemed in these y
Lev 27: 3 is of a male from twenty y
Lev 27: 3 up to sixty y old
Lev 27: 5 and if from five y old
Lev 27: 5 up to twenty y old
Lev 27: 6 a month old up to five y old
Lev 27: 7 and if from sixty y old and
Lev 27:18 y that remain till the Year
Num 1: 3 from twenty y old and above
Num 1:18 of names, from twenty y old
Num 1:20 from twenty y old and above,
Num 1:22 from twenty y old and above,
Num 1:24 of names, from twenty y old
Num 1:26 of names, from twenty y old
Num 1:28 of names, from twenty y old
Num 1:30 of names, from twenty y old
Num 1:32 of names, from twenty y old
Num 1:34 of names, from twenty y old
Num 1:36 of names, from twenty y old
Num 1:38 of names, from twenty y old
Num 1:40 of names, from twenty y old
Num 1:42 of names, from twenty y old
Num 1:45 houses, from twenty y old
Num 4: 3 from thirty y old and above,
Num 4: 3 and above, even to fifty y old
Num 4:23 From thirty y old and above,
Num 4:23 even to fifty y old
Num 4:30 From thirty y old and above,
Num 4:30 even to fifty y old
Num 4:35 from thirty y old and above,
Num 4:35 even to fifty y old
Num 4:39 from thirty y old and above,
Num 4:39 even to fifty y old
Num 4:43 from thirty y old and above,
Num 4:43 even to fifty y old
Num 4:47 from thirty y old and above,
Num 4:47 even to fifty y old
Num 8:24 From twenty-five y old and
Num 8:25 at the age of fifty y they
Num 13:22 seven y before Zoan in Egypt
Num 14:29 number, from twenty y old
Num 14:33 in the wilderness forty y
Num 14:34 one year, namely forty y, and
Num 26: 2 of Israel from twenty y old
Num 26: 4 the people from twenty y old
Num 32:11 from Egypt, from twenty y old
Num 32:13 in the wilderness forty y
Num 33:39 twenty-three y old when he
Deut 2: 7 These forty y the LORD your
Deut 2:14 the Zered was thirty-eight y
Deut 8: 2 forty y in the wilderness
Deut 8: 4 your foot swell these forty y
Deut 15: 1 y you shall grant a release
Deut 15:12 to you and serves you six y
Deut 15:18 servant in serving you six y
Deut 29: 5 you forty y in the wilderness
Deut 31: 2 hundred and twenty y old today
Deut 31:10 At the end of every seven y
Deut 32: 7 old, consider the y of many
Deut 34: 7 twenty y old when he died
Josh 5: 6 forty y in the wilderness
Josh 13: 1 Joshua was old, advanced in y
Josh 13: 1 You are old, advanced in y
Josh 14: 7 I was forty y old when Moses
Josh 14:10 He said, these forty-five y
Josh 14:10 this day, eighty-five y old
Josh 24:29 one hundred and ten y old
Judg 2: 8 was one hundred and ten y old
Judg 3: 8 Cushan-Rishathaim eight y
Judg 3:11 the land had rest for forty y
Judg 3:14 Eglon king of Moab eighteen y
Judg 3:30 land had rest for eighty y
Judg 4: 3 and for twenty y he harshly
Judg 5:31 the land had rest for forty y
Judg 6: 1 hand of Midian for seven y
Judg 6:25 second bull of seven y old
Judg 8:28 forty y in the days of Gideon
Judg 9:22 reigned over Israel three y
Judg 10: 2 judged Israel twenty-three y
Judg 10: 3 he judged Israel twenty-two y
Judg 10: 8 of Israel for eighteen y
Judg 11:26 Arnon, for three hundred y
Judg 12: 7 Jephthah judged Israel six y
Judg 12: 9 He judged Israel seven y
Judg 12:11 He judged Israel ten y
Judg 12:14 He judged Israel eight y
Judg 13: 1 the Philistines for forty y
Judg 15:20 twenty y in the days of the
Judg 16:31 He had judged Israel twenty y
Ruth 1: 4 they dwelt there about ten y
1Sa 4:15 Eli was ninety-eight y old
1Sa 4:18 he had judged Israel forty y
1Sa 7: 2 it was there twenty y
1Sa 13: 1 had reigned two y over Israel
1Sa 17:12 man was old, advanced in y
1Sa 29: 3 me these days, or these y
2Sa 2:10 was forty y old when he began
2Sa 2:10 Israel, and he reigned two y
2Sa 2:11 house of Judah was seven y
2Sa 4: 4 He was five y old when the
2Sa 5: 4 David was thirty y old when
2Sa 5: 4 reign, and he reigned forty y
2Sa 5: 5 he reigned over Judah seven y
2Sa 5: 5 y over all Israel and Judah
2Sa 13:23 to pass, after two full y
2Sa 13:38 Geshur, and was there three y
2Sa 14:28 dwelt two full y in Jerusalem
2Sa 15: 7 y that Absalom said to the
2Sa 19:32 a very aged man, eighty y old
2Sa 19:35 I am today eighty y old
2Sa 21: 1 the days of David for three y
2Sa 24:13 Shall seven y of famine come
1Ki 1: 1 David was old, advanced in y
1Ki 2:11 over Israel was forty y
1Ki 2:11 seven y he reigned in Hebron,
1Ki 2:11 he reigned thirty-three y
1Ki 2:39 at the end of three y, that
1Ki 6:38 he was seven y in building it
1Ki 7: 1 y to build his own house
1Ki 9:10 at the end of twenty y, when
1Ki 10:22 Once every three y the
1Ki 11:42 over all Israel was forty y
1Ki 14:20 reigned was twenty-two y
1Ki 14:21 Rehoboam was forty-one y old
1Ki 14:21 seventeen y in Jerusalem, the
1Ki 15: 2 reigned three y in Jerusalem
1Ki 15:10 forty-one y in Jerusalem
1Ki 15:25 he reigned over Israel two y
1Ki 15:33 and reigned twenty-four y
1Ki 16: 8 and reigned two y in Tirzah
1Ki 16:23 Israel, and reigned twelve y
1Ki 16:23 Six y he reigned in Tirzah
1Ki 16:29 in Samaria twenty-two y
1Ki 17: 1 not be dew nor rain these y
1Ki 22: 1 Now three y passed without
1Ki 22:42 y old when he became king
1Ki 22:42 twenty-five y in Jerusalem
1Ki 22:51 and reigned two y over Israel
2Ki 3: 1 of Judah, and reigned twelve y
2Ki 8: 1 upon the land for seven y
2Ki 8: 2 of the Philistines seven y
2Ki 8: 3 pass, at the end of seven y
2Ki 8:17 He was thirty-two y old when
2Ki 8:17 reigned eight y in Jerusalem
2Ki 8:26 Ahaziah was twenty-two y old
2Ki 10:36 in Samaria was twenty-eight y
2Ki 11: 3 house of the LORD for six y
2Ki 11:21 Jehoash was seven y old when
2Ki 12: 1 reigned forty y in Jerusalem
2Ki 13: 1 and reigned seventeen y
2Ki 13:10 Samaria, and reigned sixteen y
2Ki 14: 2 He was twenty-five y old when
2Ki 14: 2 twenty-nine y in Jerusalem
2Ki 14:17 lived fifteen y after the
2Ki 14:21 who was sixteen y old, and
2Ki 14:23 and reigned forty-one y
2Ki 15: 2 He was sixteen y old when he

2Ki 15: 2 fifty-two y in Jerusalem
2Ki 15:17 and reigned ten y in Samaria
2Ki 15:23 in Samaria, and reigned two y
2Ki 15:27 Samaria, and reigned twenty y
2Ki 15:33 He was twenty-five y old when
2Ki 15:33 sixteen y in Jerusalem
2Ki 16: 2 Ahaz was twenty y old when he
2Ki 16: 2 sixteen y in Jerusalem
2Ki 17: 1 Samaria, and he reigned nine y
2Ki 17: 5 and besieged it for three y
2Ki 18: 2 He was twenty-five y old when
2Ki 18: 2 twenty-nine y in Jerusalem
2Ki 18:10 end of three y they took it
2Ki 20: 6 add to your days fifteen y
2Ki 21: 1 Manasseh was twelve y old
2Ki 21: 1 fifty-five y in Jerusalem
2Ki 21:19 Amon was twenty-two y old
2Ki 21:19 he reigned two y in Jerusalem
2Ki 22: 1 Josiah was eight y old when
2Ki 22: 1 thirty-one y in Jerusalem
2Ki 23:31 y old when he became king
2Ki 23:36 y old when he became king
2Ki 23:36 reigned eleven y in Jerusalem
2Ki 24: 1 became his vassal for three y
2Ki 24: 8 y old when he became king
2Ki 24:18 y old when he became king
2Ki 24:18 reigned eleven y in Jerusalem
1Ch 2:21 when he was sixty y old
1Ch 3: 4 There he reigned seven y and
1Ch 3: 4 he reigned thirty-three y
1Ch 21:12 either three y of famine
1Ch 23: 3 from the age of thirty y and
1Ch 23:24 from the age of twenty y
1Ch 23:27 numbered from twenty y old
1Ch 27:23 number of those twenty y old
1Ch 29:27 over Israel was forty y
1Ch 29:27 seven y he reigned in Hebron,
1Ch 29:27 thirty-three y he reigned in
2Ch 8: 1 pass at the end of twenty y
2Ch 9:21 Once every three y the
2Ch 9:30 over all Israel forty y
2Ch 11:17 of Solomon strong for three y
2Ch 11:17 David and Solomon for three y
2Ch 12:13 y old when he became king
2Ch 12:13 seventeen y in Jerusalem, the
2Ch 13: 2 reigned three y in Jerusalem
2Ch 14: 1 the land was quiet for ten y
2Ch 14: 6 he had no war in those y,
2Ch 18: 2 After some y he went down to
2Ch 20:31 He was thirty-five y old when
2Ch 20:31 twenty-five y in Jerusalem
2Ch 21: 5 Jehoram was thirty-two y old
2Ch 21: 5 reigned eight y in Jerusalem
2Ch 21:19 time, after the end of two y
2Ch 21:20 He was thirty-two y old when
2Ch 21:20 reigned in Jerusalem eight y
2Ch 22: 2 Ahaziah was forty-two y old
2Ch 22:12 in the house of God for six y
2Ch 24: 1 Joash was seven y old when he
2Ch 24: 1 reigned forty y in Jerusalem
2Ch 24:15 thirty y old when he died
2Ch 25: 1 y old when he became king
2Ch 25: 1 twenty-nine y in Jerusalem
2Ch 25: 5 them from twenty y old and
2Ch 25:25 lived fifteen y after the
2Ch 26: 1 Uzziah, who was sixteen y old
2Ch 26: 3 Uzziah was sixteen y old when
2Ch 26: 3 fifty-two y in Jerusalem
2Ch 27: 1 Jotham was twenty-five y old
2Ch 27: 1 sixteen y in Jerusalem
2Ch 27: 5 in the second and third y also
2Ch 27: 8 He was twenty-five y old when
2Ch 27: 8 sixteen y in Jerusalem
2Ch 28: 1 Ahaz was twenty y old when he
2Ch 28: 1 sixteen y in Jerusalem
2Ch 29: 1 when he was twenty-five y old
2Ch 29: 1 twenty-nine y in Jerusalem
2Ch 31:16 those males from three y old
2Ch 31:17 the Levites from twenty y old
2Ch 33: 1 Manasseh was twelve y old
2Ch 33: 1 fifty-five y in Jerusalem
2Ch 33:21 Amon was twenty-two y old
2Ch 33:21 he reigned two y in Jerusalem
2Ch 34: 1 Josiah was eight y old when
2Ch 34: 1 thirty-one y in Jerusalem
2Ch 36: 2 y old when he became king
2Ch 36: 5 y old when he became king
2Ch 36: 5 reigned eleven y in Jerusalem
2Ch 36: 9 Jehoiachin was eight y old
2Ch 36:11 y old when he became king
2Ch 36:11 reigned eleven y in Jerusalem
2Ch 36:21 Sabbath, to fulfill seventy y
Ezra 3: 8 the Levites from twenty y old
Ezra 5:11 that was built many y ago
Neh 5:14 of King Artaxerxes, twelve y
Neh 9:21 Forty y You sustained them in
Neh 9:30 Yet for many y You had
Job 10: 5 Are Your y like the days of a
Job 15:20 the number of y is hidden
Job 16:22 For when a few y are finished
Job 32: 4 they were y older than he
Job 32: 6 I am young in y, and you are
Job 32: 7 multitude of y should teach
Job 36:11 and their y in pleasures
Job 36:26 number of His y be discovered
Job 42:16 lived one hundred and forty y
Ps 31:10 grief, And my y with sighing
Ps 61: 6 His y as many generations
Ps 77: 5 old, The y of ancient times
Ps 77:10 But I will remember the y of
Ps 78:33 futility, And their y in fear
Ps 90: 4 For a thousand y in Your
Ps 90: 9 We finish our y like a sigh
Ps 90:10 of our lives are seventy y
Ps 90:10 of strength they are eighty y
Ps 90:15 the y in which we have seen
Ps 95:10 For forty y I was grieved
Ps 102:24 Your y are throughout all
Ps 102:27 And Your y will have no end
Prov 4:10 the y of your life will be
Prov 5: 9 and your y to the cruel one
Prov 9:11 y of life will be added to
Prov 10:27 but the y of the wicked will
Eccl 6: 3 children and lives many y, so
Eccl 6: 3 the days of his y are many
Eccl 6: 6 lives a thousand y twice over
Eccl 11: 8 But if a man lives many y
Eccl 12: 1 the y draw near when you say,
Is 7: 8 Within sixty-five y Ephraim
Is 16:14 Within three y, as the y
Is 20: 3 barefoot three y for a sign
Is 23:15 will be forgotten seventy y
Is 23:15 At the end of seventy y it
Is 23:17 be, at the end of seventy y
Is 38: 5 add to your days fifteen y
Is 38:10 of the remainder of my y
Is 38:15 my y in the bitterness of my
Is 65:20 shall die one hundred y old
Is 65:20 y old shall be accursed
Jer 25:11 the king of Babylon seventy y
Jer 25:12 when seventy y are completed,
Jer 28: 3 Within two full y I will
Jer 28:11 the space of two full y
Jer 29:10 After seventy y are completed
Jer 34:14 At the end of seven y let
Jer 34:14 when he has served you six y
Jer 52: 1 y old when he became king
Jer 52: 1 reigned eleven y in Jerusalem
Ezek 4: 5 you the y of their iniquity
Ezek 22: 4 come to the end of your y
Ezek 29:11 shall be uninhabited forty y
Ezek 29:12 shall be desolate forty y
Ezek 29:13 At the end of forty y I will
Ezek 38: 8 In the latter y you will come
Ezek 38:17 who prophesied for y in those
Ezek 39: 9 fires with them for seven y
Dan 1: 5 three y of training for them,
Dan 5:31 being about sixty-two y old
Dan 9: 2 y specified by the word of
Dan 9: 2 y in the desolations of
Dan 11: 6 at the end of some y they
Dan 11: 8 he shall continue more y than
Dan 11:13 of some y with a great army
Joel 2:25 y that the swarming locust
Amos 1: 1 two y before the earthquake
Amos 2:10 led you forty y through the
Amos 5:25 in the wilderness forty y
Hab 3: 2 work in the midst of the y
Hab 3: 2 midst of the y make it known
Zech 1:12 were angry these seventy y
Zech 7: 3 as I have done for so many y
Zech 7: 5 months during those seventy y
Mal 3: 4 days of old, as in former y
Matt 2:16 its districts, from two y old
Matt 9:20 for twelve y came from behind
Mark 5:25 a flow of blood for twelve y
Mark 5:42 for she was twelve y of age
Luke 1: 7 were both well advanced in y
Luke 1:18 my wife is well advanced in y
Luke 2:36 seven y from her virginity
Luke 2:37 widow of about eighty-four y
Luke 2:42 And when He was twelve y old
Luke 3:23 at about thirty y of age,
Luke 4:25 heaven was shut up three y
Luke 8:42 about twelve y of age, and she
Luke 8:43 a flow of blood for twelve y
Luke 12:19 many goods laid up for many y
Luke 13: 7 Look, for three y I have come
Luke 13:11 of infirmity eighteen y, and
Luke 13:16 for eighteen y, be loosed
Luke 15:29 Lo, these many y I have been
John 2:20 y to build this temple, and
John 5: 5 an infirmity thirty-eight y
John 8:57 You are not yet fifty y old
Acts 4:22 For the man was over forty y
Acts 7: 6 oppress them four hundred y
Acts 7:23 But when he was forty y old
Acts 7:30 And when forty y had passed
Acts 7:36 and in the wilderness forty y
Acts 7:42 forty y in the wilderness
Acts 9:33 had been bedridden eight y
Acts 13:18 y He put up with their ways
Acts 13:20 about four hundred and fifty y
Acts 13:21 of Benjamin, for forty y
Acts 19:10 And this continued for two y
Acts 20:31 y I did not cease to warn
Acts 24:10 many y a judge of this nation
Acts 24:17 Now after many y I came to
Acts 24:27 But after two y Porcius
Acts 28:30 y in his own rented house
Rom 4:19 he was about a hundred y old)
Rom 15:23 these many y to come to you
2Co 12: 2 in Christ who fourteen y ago
Gal 1:18 Then after three y I went up
Gal 2: 1 fourteen y I went up again to
Gal 3:17 hundred and thirty y later
Gal 4:10 and months and seasons and y
1Ti 5: 9 sixty y old be taken into the
Heb 1:12 same, and Your y will not fail
Heb 3: 9 Me, and saw My works forty y
Heb 3:17 whom was He angry forty y
Jas 5:17 rain on the land for three y
2Pe 3: 8 one day is as a thousand y
2Pe 3: 8 and a thousand y as one day
Rev 20: 2 and bound him for a thousand y
Rev 20: 3 the thousand y were finished
Rev 20: 4 with Christ for a thousand y
Rev 20: 5 the thousand y were finished
Rev 20: 6 reign with Him a thousand y
Rev 20: 7 the thousand y have expired

YELLOW
Lev 13:30 and there is in it thin y hair
Lev 13:32 and there is no y hair in it
Lev 13:36 need not seek for y hair
Ps 68:13 And her feathers with y gold
Rev 9:17 hyacinth blue, and sulfur y

YES (*see* PREFACE)

YESTERDAY
Ex 5:14 task in making brick both y
1Sa 20:27 to eat, either y or today
2Sa 15:20 In fact, you came only y
2Ki 9:26 Surely I saw y the blood of
Job 8: 9 for we are but of y, and know
Ps 90: 4 Are like y when it is past
John 4:52 Y at the seventh hour the
Acts 7:28 me as you did the Egyptian y
Heb 13: 8 Jesus Christ is the same y

YET (*see* PREFACE)

YIELD (*see* YIELDED, YIELDING, YIELDS)
Gen 4:12 it shall no longer y its
Gen 49:20 he shall y royal dainties
Lev 19:25 that it may y to you its
Lev 25:19 the land will y its fruit
Lev 26: 4 the land shall y its produce
Lev 26: 4 the field shall y their fruit
Lev 26:20 land shall not y its produce
Lev 26:20 of the land y their fruit
Num 20: 8 eyes, and it will y its water
Deut 11:17 the land y no produce, and you
Deut 22: 9 lest the y of the seed which
2Ch 30: 8 but y yourselves to the LORD
Job 40:20 the mountains y food for him
Ps 67: 6 earth shall y her increase
Ps 85:12 our land will y its increase
Ps 107:37 That they may y a fruitful
Prov 7:21 speech she caused him to y
Is 5:10 of vineyard shall y one bath
Is 5:10 of seed shall y one ephah

1Sa 25: 8 Therefore let my y men find
1Sa 25: 9 So when David's y men came
1Sa 25:12 So David's y men turned on
1Sa 25:14 Now one of the y men told
1Sa 25:25 did not see the y men of my
1Sa 25:27 the y men who follow my lord
1Sa 26:22 one of the y men come over
1Sa 30:13 I am a y man from Egypt,
1Sa 30:17 except four hundred y men who
2Sa 1: 5 to the y man who told him
2Sa 1: 6 the y man who told him said,
2Sa 1:13 to the y man who told him
2Sa 1:15 David called one of the y men
2Sa 2:14 Let the y men now arise and
2Sa 2:21 lay hold on one of the y men
2Sa 4:12 So David commanded his y men
2Sa 9:12 Mephibosheth had a y son
2Sa 13:32 have killed all the y men
2Sa 13:34 the y man who was keeping
2Sa 14:21 bring back the y man Absalom
2Sa 16: 2 fruit for the y men to eat
2Sa 18: 5 sake with the y man Absalom
2Sa 18:12 touch the y man Absalom
2Sa 18:15 ten y men who bore Joab's
2Sa 18:29 Is the y man Absalom safe
2Sa 18:32 Is the y man Absalom safe
2Sa 18:32 you harm, be as that y man is
1Ki 1: 2 Let a y woman, a virgin, be
1Ki 1: 3 y woman throughout all the
1Ki 1: 4 the y woman was very lovely
1Ki 11:28 seeing that the y man was
1Ki 12: 8 consulted the y men who had
1Ki 12:10 Then the y men who had grown
1Ki 12:14 to the counsel of the y men
1Ki 20:14 By the y leaders of the
1Ki 20:15 Then he mustered the y
1Ki 20:17 The y leaders of the
1Ki 20:19 Then these y leaders of the
2Ki 4:22 send me one of the y men and
2Ki 5: 2 a y girl from the land of
2Ki 5:22 just now two y men of the
2Ki 6:17 opened the eyes of the y man
2Ki 8:12 their y men you will kill
2Ki 9: 4 So the y man, the servant of
1Ch 12:28 a y man, a valiant warrior,
1Ch 22: 5 Solomon my son is y and
1Ch 29: 1 alone God has chosen, is y
2Ch 10: 8 consulted the y men who had
2Ch 10:10 Then the y men who had grown
2Ch 10:14 to the counsel of the y men
2Ch 13: 7 when Rehoboam was y
2Ch 13: 9 himself with a y bull and
2Ch 34: 3 reign, while he was still y
2Ch 35: 7 y goats from the flock, all
2Ch 36:17 who killed their y men with
2Ch 36:17 compassion on y man or virgin
Ezra 6: 9 y bulls, rams, and lambs for
Esth 2: 2 Let beautiful y virgins be
Esth 2: 3 y virgins to Shushan the
Esth 2: 4 Then let the y woman who
Esth 2: 7 The y woman was lovely and
Esth 2: 8 and when many y women were
Esth 2: 9 Now the y woman pleased him,
Esth 2:12 Each y woman's turn came to
Esth 2:13 each y woman went to the king
Esth 3:13 all the Jews, both y and old,
Job 1:19 and it fell on the y men, and
Job 4:10 of the y lions are broken
Job 19:18 Even y children despise me
Job 29: 8 the y men saw me and hid, and
Job 31: 1 should I look upon a y woman
Job 32: 6 I am y in years, and you are
Job 33:25 shall be y like a child's
Job 38:39 the appetite of the y lions
Job 38:41 when its y ones cry to God,
Job 39: 1 wild mountain goats bear y
Job 39: 2 the time when they bear y
Job 39: 3 they bring forth their y
Job 39: 4 Their y ones are healthy,
Job 39:16 She treats her y harshly, as
Job 39:30 Its y ones suck up blood
Ps 17:12 as a y lion lurking in secret
Ps 29: 6 and Sirion like a y wild ox
Ps 34:10 The y lions lack and suffer
Ps 37:25 I have been y, and now am old
Ps 58: 6 out the fangs of the y lions
Ps 78:63 The fire consumed their y men
Ps 78:71 that had y He brought him
Ps 84: 3 Where she may lay her y
Ps 91:13 The y lion and the serpent you
Ps 104:21 The y lions roar after their
Ps 105:34 Y locusts without number,
Ps 119: 9 How can a y man cleanse his
Ps 147: 9 And to the y ravens that cry
Ps 148:12 Both y men and maidens
Prov 1: 4 to the y man knowledge and
Prov 7: 7 the youths, a y man devoid of
Prov 20:29 The glory of y men is their
Prov 30:17 and the y eagles will eat it
Eccl 11: 9 O y man, in your youth, and
Song 2: 9 is like a gazelle or a y stag
Song 2:17 be like a gazelle or a y stag
Song 8:14 be like a gazelle or a y stag
Is 5:29 they will roar like y lions
Is 7:21 a man will keep alive a y cow
Is 9:17 have no joy in their y men
Is 11: 6 lie down with the y goat
Is 11: 6 the y lion and the fatling
Is 11: 7 their y ones shall lie down
Is 13:18 will dash the y men to pieces
Is 20: 4 the Ethiopians as captives, y
Is 23: 4 neither do I rear y men, nor
Is 30: 6 on the backs of y donkeys
Is 30:24 the y donkeys that work the
Is 31: 4 a y lion over his prey (when
Is 31: 8 his y men shall become forced
Is 34: 7 the y bulls with the mighty
Is 40:11 lead those who are with y
Is 40:30 the y men shall utterly fall,
Is 62: 5 For as a y man marries a
Jer 2:15 The y lions roared at him, and
Jer 6:11 assembly of y men together
Jer 9:21 and the y men
Jer 11:22 The y men shall die by the
Jer 15: 8 the mother of the y men, a
Jer 18:21 their y men be slain by the
Jer 31:12 for the y of the flock and the
Jer 31:13 in the dance, and the y men
Jer 48:15 Her chosen y men have gone
Jer 49:26 Therefore her y men shall
Jer 50:30 Therefore her y men shall
Jer 51: 3 Do not spare her y men
Jer 51:22 will break in pieces old and y
Jer 51:22 break in pieces the y man
Lam 1:15 against me to crush my y men
Lam 1:18 and my y men have gone into
Lam 2:19 the life of your y children
Lam 2:21 Y and old lie on the ground in
Lam 2:21 my y men have fallen by the
Lam 4: 3 breasts to nurse their y
Lam 4: 4 the y children ask for bread,
Lam 5:13 Y men ground at the
Lam 5:14 the y men from their music
Ezek 9: 6 and y men, maidens and little
Ezek 17: 4 off its topmost y twig and
Ezek 17:22 of its y twigs a tender one
Ezek 19: 2 among the y lions she
Ezek 19: 3 cubs, and he became a y lion
Ezek 19: 5 her cubs and made him a y lion
Ezek 19: 6 the lions, and became a y lion
Ezek 23: 6 all of them desirable y men
Ezek 23:12 all of them desirable y men
Ezek 23:23 all of them desirable y men
Ezek 30:17 The y men of Aven and Pi
Ezek 31: 6 field brought forth their y
Ezek 32: 2 You are like a y lion among
Ezek 36:11 they shall increase and bear y
Ezek 38:13 all their y lions will say to
Ezek 41:19 the face of a y lion toward a
Ezek 43:19 You shall give a y bull for
Ezek 43:23 it, you shall offer a y bull
Ezek 43:25 shall also prepare a y bull
Ezek 45:18 you shall take a y bull
Ezek 46: 6 be a y bull without blemish
Dan 1: 4 y men in whom there was no
Dan 1:10 the y men who are your age
Dan 1:13 the countenances of the y men
Dan 1:15 in flesh than all the y men
Dan 1:17 As for these four y men, God
Hos 5:14 like a y lion to the house of
Joel 2:28 your y men shall see visions
Amos 2:11 and some of your y men as
Amos 3: 4 Will a y lion cry out of his
Amos 4:10 your y men I killed with a
Amos 8:13 strong y men shall faint from
Mic 5: 8 like a y lion among flocks of
Nah 2:11 feeding place of the y lions
Nah 2:13 shall devour your y lions
Nah 3:10 her y children also were
Zech 2: 4 Run, speak to this y man,
Zech 9:17 shall make the y men thrive
Zech 9:17 and new wine the y women
Zech 11:16 are cut off, nor seek the y
Matt 2: 8 diligently for the y Child
Matt 2: 9 over where the y Child was
Matt 2:11 they saw the y Child with
Matt 2:13 Arise, take the y Child and
Matt 2:13 the y Child to destroy Him
Matt 2:14 he arose, he took the y Child
Matt 2:20 Arise, take the y Child and
Matt 2:20 the y Child's life are dead
Matt 2:21 he arose, took the y Child
Matt 19:20 The y man said to Him, "All
Matt 19:22 But when the y man heard that
Mark 7:25 For a woman whose y daughter
Mark 10:13 brought y children to Him
Mark 14:51 Now a certain y man followed
Mark 14:51 the y men laid hold of him,
Mark 16: 5 they saw a y man clothed in a
Luke 2:24 turtledoves or two y pigeons
Luke 7:14 Y man, I say to you, arise
Luke 15:29 you never gave me a y goat
John 12:14 when He had found a y donkey
Acts 2:17 your y men shall see visions,
Acts 5: 6 the y men arose and wrapped
Acts 5:10 the y men came in and found
Acts 7:58 feet of a y man named Saul
Acts 20: 9 certain y man named Eutychus
Acts 20:12 brought the y man in alive
Acts 23:17 Take this y man to the
Acts 23:18 me to bring this y man to you
Acts 23:22 let the y man depart, and
Tit 2: 4 the y women to love their
Tit 2: 6 Likewise exhort the y men to
1Jn 2:13 you, y men, because you have
1Jn 2:14 y men, because you are strong

YOUNGER (*see* YOUNG)
Gen 9:24 knew what his y son had done
Gen 19:31 the firstborn said to the y
Gen 19:34 the firstborn said to the y
Gen 19:35 the y arose and lay with him,
Gen 19:38 And the y, she also bore a son
Gen 25:23 the older shall serve the y
Gen 27:15 put them on Jacob her y son
Gen 27:42 and called Jacob her y son
Gen 29:16 the name of the y was Rachel
Gen 29:18 for Rachel your y daughter
Gen 29:26 to give the y before the
Gen 43:29 Is this your y brother of
Gen 48:14 Ephraim's head, who was the y
Gen 48:19 but truly his y brother shall
Judg 1:13 of Kenaz, Caleb's y brother
Judg 3: 9 of Kenaz, Caleb's y brother
Judg 15: 2 Is not her y sister better
1Sa 14:49 and the name of the y Michal
1Ch 24:31 did just as their y brethren
Job 30: 1 men y than I, whose fathers I
Ezek 16:46 your y sister, who dwells to
Ezek 16:61 your older and your y sisters
Luke 15:12 the y of them said to his
Luke 15:13 after, the y son gathered all
Luke 22:26 you, let him be as the y, and
John 21:18 I say to you, when you were y
Rom 9:12 The older shall serve the y
1Ti 5: 1 the y men as brothers,
1Ti 5: 2 the y as sisters, with all
1Ti 5:11 But refuse the y widows
1Ti 5:14 that the y widows marry, bear
1Pe 5: 5 Likewise you y people, submit

YOUNGEST (*see* YOUNG)
Gen 42:13 the y is with our father
Gen 42:15 your y brother comes here
Gen 42:20 bring your y brother to me
Gen 42:32 the y is with our father this
Gen 42:34 bring your y brother to me
Gen 43:33 the y according to his youth
Gen 44: 2 mouth of the sack of the y
Gen 44:12 oldest and left off with the y
Gen 44:23 Unless your y brother comes
Gen 44:26 if our y brother is with us,
Gen 44:26 our y brother is with us
Josh 6:26 with his y he shall set up
Judg 9: 5 But Jotham the y son of
1Sa 16:11 There remains yet the y, and
1Sa 17:14 David was the y
1Ki 16:34 with his y son Segub he set
2Ch 21:17 Jehoahaz, the y of his sons
2Ch 22: 1 his y son king in his place

YOUR (*see* PREFACE)

YOURS (*see* PREFACE)

YOURSELF (*see* PREFACE)

YOURSELVES (*see* PREFACE)

YOUTH (*see* YOUNG, YOUTHFUL, YOUTHS)
Gen 8:21 heart is evil from his y
Gen 43:33 youngest according to his y
Gen 46:34 from our y even till now,
Lev 22:13 father's house as in her y
Num 30: 3 her father's house in her y
Num 30:16 his daughter in her y in her
Judg 8:20 But the y would not draw
Judg 8:20 because he was still a y
1Sa 17:33 for you are but a y
1Sa 17:33 and he a man of war from his y
1Sa 17:42 for he was but a y, ruddy and
1Sa 17:55 Abner, whose son is this y
2Sa 19: 7 you from your y until now
1Ki 18:12 feared the LORD from my y
Job 13:26 the iniquities of my y
Job 31:18 (But from my y I reared him
Job 33:25 return to the days of his y
Job 36:14 They die in y, and their life
Ps 25: 7 not remember the sins of my y
Ps 71: 5 You are my trust from my y
Ps 71:17 You have taught me from my y
Ps 88:15 and ready to die from my y up
Ps 89:45 The days of his y You have
Ps 103: 5 So that your y is renewed
Ps 110: 3 You have the dew of Your y
Ps 127: 4 are the children of one's y
Ps 129: 1 have afflicted me from my y
Ps 129: 2 have afflicted me from my y
Ps 144:12 as plants grown up in their y
Prov 2:17 the companion of her y, and
Prov 5:18 with the wife of your y
Eccl 4:13 wise y than an old and foolish
Eccl 4:15 y who stands in his place
Eccl 11: 9 O young man, in your y, and
Eccl 11: 9 you in the days of your y
Eccl 11:10 for childhood and y are vanity
Eccl 12: 1 Creator in the days of your y
Is 47:12 you have labored from your y
Is 47:15 your merchants from your y
Is 54: 4 forget the shame of your y
Jer 1: 6 I cannot speak, for I am a y
Jer 1: 7 Do not say, 'I am a y,' for
Jer 2: 2 you, the kindness of your y
Jer 3: 4 You are the guide of my y
Jer 3:24 of our fathers from our y
Jer 3:25 from our y even to this day,
Jer 22:21 been your manner from your y
Jer 31:19 I bore the reproach of my y
Jer 32:30 evil before Me from their y
Jer 48:11 has been at ease from his y
Lam 3:27 man to bear the yoke in his y
Ezek 4:14 myself from my y till now
Ezek 16:22 remember the days of your y
Ezek 16:43 remember the days of your y
Ezek 16:60 you in the days of your y
Ezek 23: 3 committed harlotry in their y
Ezek 23: 8 for in her y they had lain
Ezek 23:19 remembrance the days of her y
Ezek 23:21 the lewdness of your y, when
Hos 2:15 as in the days of her y, as
Joel 1: 8 for the husband of her y
Zech 13: 5 me to keep cattle from my y
Mal 2:14 you and the wife of your y
Mal 2:15 with the wife of his y
Matt 19:20 things I have kept from my y
Mark 10:20 I have observed from my y
Luke 18:21 these I have kept from my y
Acts 26: 4 My manner of life from my y
1Co 7:36 is past the flower of her y
1Ti 4:12 Let no one despise your y

YOUTHFUL (*see* YOUTH)
Job 20:11 bones are full of his y vigor
Is 54: 6 like a y wife when you were
Ezek 23:21 because of your y breasts
2Ti 2:22 Flee also y lusts

YOUTHS (*see* YOUTH)
2Ki 2:23 some y came from the city and
2Ki 2:24 and mauled forty-two of the y
Prov 7: 7 I perceived among the y, a
Is 40:30 Even the y shall faint and be

Z

ZAANAIM (*see* ZAANANNIM)
Judg 4:11 near the terebinth tree at Z

ZAANAN (*see* ZENAN)
Mic 1:11 of Z does not go out

ZAANANNIM (*see* ZAANAIM)
Josh 19:33 from the terebinth tree in Z

ZAAVAN
Gen 36:27 Bilhan, Z, and Akan
1Ch 1:42 sons of Ezer were Bilhan, Z

ZABAD
1Ch 2:36 Nathan, and Nathan begot Z
1Ch 2:37 Z begot Ephlal, and Ephlal
1Ch 7:21 Z his son, Shuthelah his son,
1Ch 11:41 Hittite, Z the son of Ahlai,
2Ch 24:26 Z the son of Shimeath the
Ezra 10:27 Mattaniah, Jeremoth, Z, and
Ezra 10:33 Mattenai, Mattattah, Z,
Ezra 10:43 Jeiel, Mattithiah, Z, Zebina,

ZABBAI (*see* ZACCAI)
Ezra 10:28 Jehohanan, Hananiah, Z, and
Neh 3:20 of Z diligently repaired the

ZABBUD (*see* ZACCUR)
Ezra 8:14 sons of Bigvai, Uthai and Z

ZABDI (*see* ZACCHUR, ZACCUR)
Josh 7: 1 son of Carmi, the son of Z
Josh 7:17 man by man, and Z was taken
Josh 7:18 son of Carmi, the son of Z
1Ch 8:19 Jakim, Zichri, Z,
1Ch 27:27 Z the Shiphmite was over the
Neh 11:17 son of Micha, the son of Z

ZABDIEL
1Ch 27: 2 was Jashobeam the son of Z
Neh 11:14 Their overseer was Z the son

ZABUD
1Ki 4: 5 Z the son of Nathan, a priest

ZACCAI (*see* ZABBAI)
Ezra 2: 9 the people of Z, seven
Neh 7:14 the children of Z, seven

ZACCHAEUS
Luke 19: 2 named Z who was a chief tax
Luke 19: 5 Z, make haste and come down,
Luke 19: 8 Then Z stood and said to the

ZACCHUR (*see* ZABDI, ZACCUR)
1Ch 4:26 Z his son, and Shimei his son

ZACCUR (*see* ZABBUD, ZABDI, ZACCHUR, ZECHARIAH, ZICHRI)
Num 13: 4 Reuben, Shammua the son of Z
1Ch 24:27 Jaaziah were Beno, Shoham, Z
1Ch 25: 2 Z, Joseph, Nethaniah, and
1Ch 25:10 the third for Z, his sons and
Neh 3: 2 next to them Z the son of
Neh 10:12 Z, Sherebiah, Shebaniah,
Neh 12:35 son of Michaiah, the son of Z
Neh 13:13 them was Hanan the son of Z

ZACHARIAS (*see* ZECHARIAH)
Luke 1: 5 a certain priest named Z
Luke 1:12 And when Z saw him, he was
Luke 1:13 Do not be afraid, Z, for your
Luke 1:18 And Z said to the angel,
Luke 1:21 And the people waited for Z
Luke 1:40 and entered the house of Z
Luke 1:59 by the name of his father, Z
Luke 1:67 Now his father Z was filled
Luke 3: 2 son of Z in the wilderness

ZADOK (*see* ZADOK'S)
2Sa 8:17 Z the son of Ahitub and
2Sa 15:24 There was Z also, and all the
2Sa 15:25 Then the king said to Z
2Sa 15:27 also said to Z the priest
2Sa 15:29 Therefore Z and Abiathar
2Sa 15:35 And do you not have Z and
2Sa 15:35 house, you shall tell to Z
2Sa 17:15 Then Hushai said to Z and
2Sa 18:19 Ahimaaz the son of Z said
2Sa 18:22 son of Z said again to Joab
2Sa 18:27 of Ahimaaz the son of Z
2Sa 19:11 Then King David sent to Z
2Sa 20:25 Z and Abiathar were the
1Ki 1: 8 But Z the priest, Benaiah the
1Ki 1:26 nor Z the priest, nor Benaiah
1Ki 1:32 Call to me Z the priest,
1Ki 1:34 There let Z the priest and
1Ki 1:38 So Z the priest, Nathan the
1Ki 1:39 Then Z the priest took a horn
1Ki 1:44 sent with him Z the priest
1Ki 1:45 So Z the priest and Nathan the
1Ki 2:35 the king put Z the priest in
1Ki 4: 2 Azariah the son of Z, the
1Ki 4: 4 Z and Abiathar, the priests
2Ki 15:33 was Jerusha the daughter of Z
1Ch 6: 8 Ahitub begot Z
1Ch 6: 8 and Z begot Ahimaaz
1Ch 6:12 Ahitub begot Z, and Z
1Ch 6:12 Z, and Z begot Shallum
1Ch 6:53 Z his son, and Ahimaaz his son
1Ch 9:11 of Meshullam, the son of Z
1Ch 12:28 Z, a young man, a valiant
1Ch 15:11 And David called for Z and
1Ch 16:39 Z the priest and his brethren
1Ch 18:16 Z the son of Ahitub and
1Ch 24: 3 Then David with Z of the sons
1Ch 24: 6 Z the priest, Ahimelech the
1Ch 24:31 the presence of King David, Z
1Ch 27:17 over the Aaronites, Z
1Ch 29:22 the leader, and Z to be priest
2Ch 27: 1 Jerushah the daughter of Z
2Ch 31:10 priest, from the house of Z
Ezra 7: 2 son of Shallum, the son of Z
Neh 3: 4 Next to them Z the son of
Neh 3:29 After them Z the son of Immer
Neh 10:21 Meshezabeel, Z, Jaddua,
Neh 11:11 of Meshullam, the son of Z
Neh 13:13 and Z the scribe, and of the
Ezek 40:46 these are the sons of Z, from
Ezek 43:19 who are of the seed of Z
Ezek 44:15 the Levites, the sons of Z
Ezek 48:11 the priests of the sons of Z
Matt 1:14 Azor begot Z, Z begot Achim

ZADOK'S (*see* ZADOK)
2Sa 15:36 Ahimaaz, Z son, and Jonathan,

ZAHAM
2Ch 11:19 Jeush, Shamariah, and Z

ZAIR
2Ki 8:21 So Joram went to Z, and all

ZALAPH
Neh 3:30 and Hanun, the sixth son of Z

ZALMON (*see* ILAI)
Judg 9:48 Abimelech went up to Mount Z
2Sa 23:28 Z the Ahohite, Maharai the
Ps 68:14 it, It was white as snow in Z

ZALMONAH
Num 33:41 Mount Hor and camped at Z
Num 33:42 They departed from Z and

ZALMUNNA
Judg 8: 5 and I am pursuing Zebah and Z
Judg 8: 6 Z now in your hand, that we
Judg 8: 7 Z into my hand, then I will
Judg 8:10 Z were at Karkor, and their
Judg 8:12 and Z fled, he pursued them
Judg 8:12 kings of Midian, Zebah and Z
Judg 8:15 Here are Zebah and Z, about
Judg 8:15 Z now in your hand, that we
Judg 8:18 And he said to Zebah and Z
Judg 8:21 So Zebah and Z said,
Judg 8:21 arose and killed Zebah and Z
Ps 83:11 their princes like Zebah and Z

ZAMZUMMIM (*see* ZUZIM)
Deut 2:20 But the Ammonites call them Z

ZANOAH
Josh 15:34 Z, En Gannim, Tappuah,
Josh 15:56 Jezreel, Jokdeam, Z,
1Ch 4:18 and Jekuthiel the father of Z
Neh 3:13 the inhabitants of Z repaired
Neh 11:30 Z, Adullam, and their villages

ZAPHNATH-PAANEAH
Gen 41:45 called Joseph's name Z

ZAPHON (*see* SHOPHAN)
Josh 13:27 Beth Nimrah, Succoth, and Z
Judg 12: 1 crossed over toward Z, and

ZAREPHATH
1Ki 17: 9 Arise, go to **Z**, which belongs
1Ki 17:10 So he arose and went to **Z**
Obad 20 of the Canaanites as far as **Z**
Luke 4:26 was Elijah sent except to **Z**

ZARETAN
Josh 3:16 the city that is beside **Z**
1Ki 4:12 is beside **Z** below Jezreel
1Ki 7:46 molds, between Succoth and **Z**

ZARHITES (*see* ZERAH)
Num 26:13 of Zerah, the family of the **Z**
Num 26:20 of Zerah, the family of the **Z**
Josh 7:17 he took the family of the **Z**
Josh 7:17 family of the **Z** man by man
1Ch 27:11 the Hushathite, of the **Z**
1Ch 27:13 the Netophathite, of the **Z**

ZATTU
Ezra 2: 8 the people of **Z**, nine hundred
Ezra 10:27 of the sons of **Z**
Neh 7:13 the children of **Z**, eight
Neh 10:14 Parosh, Pahath-Moab, Elam, **Z**

ZAZA
1Ch 2:33 of Jonathan were Peleth and **Z**

ZEAL (*see* ZEALOT, ZEALOUS)
Num 25:11 zealous with My **z** among them
Num 25:11 children of Israel in My **z**
2Sa 21: 2 **z** for the children of Israel
2Ki 10:16 me, and see my **z** for the LORD
2Ki 19:31 The **z** of the LORD of hosts
Ps 69: 9 Because **z** for Your house has
Ps 119:139 My **z** has consumed me, Because
Is 9: 7 The **z** of the LORD of hosts
Is 37:32 The **z** of the LORD of hosts
Is 42:13 up His **z** like a man of war
Is 59:17 and was clad with **z** as a cloak
Is 63:15 Where are Your **z** and Your
Ezek 5:13 LORD, have spoken it in My **z**
Zech 1:14 and for Zion with great **z**
Zech 8: 2 zealous for Zion with great **z**
John 2:17 **Z** for Your house has eaten Me
Rom 10: 2 that they have a **z** for God
2Co 7: 7 your **z** for me, so that I
2Co 7:11 what vehement desire, what **z**
2Co 9: 2 your **z** has stirred up the
Phil 3: 6 concerning **z**, persecuting the
Col 4:13 that he has a great **z** for you

ZEALOT (*see* ZEAL)
Luke 6:15 and Simon called the **Z**
Acts 1:13 of Alphaeus and Simon the **Z**

ZEALOUS (*see* ZEAL, ZEALOUSLY)
Num 11:29 him, "Are you **z** for my sake
Num 25:11 because he was **z** with My zeal
Num 25:13 because he was **z** for his God
1Ki 19:10 I have been very **z** for the
1Ki 19:14 I have been very **z** for the
Joel 2:18 LORD will be **z** for His land
Zech 1:14 I am **z** for Jerusalem and for
Zech 8: 2 I am **z** for Zion with great
Zech 8: 2 great fervor I am **z** for her
Acts 21:20 and they are all **z** for the law
Acts 22: 3 was **z** toward God as you all
1Co 14:12 since you are **z** for spiritual
Gal 1:14 being more exceedingly **z** for
Gal 4:17 that you may be **z** for them
Gal 4:18 But it is good to be **z** in a
Tit 2:14 people, **z** for good works
Rev 3:19 Therefore be **z** and repent

ZEALOUSLY (*see* ZEALOUS)
Gal 4:17 They **z** court you, but for no

ZEBADIAH
1Ch 8:15 **Z**, Arad, Eder,
1Ch 8:17 **Z**, Meshullam, Hizki, Heber,
1Ch 12: 7 and **Z** the sons of Jeroham of
1Ch 26: 2 **Z** the third, Jathniel the
1Ch 27: 7 Joab, and **Z** his son after him
2Ch 17: 8 Shemaiah, Nethaniah, **Z**,
2Ch 19:11 **Z** the son of Ishmael, the
Ezra 8: 8 **Z** the son of Michael, and with
Ezra 10:20 Hanani and **Z**

ZEBAH
Judg 8: 5 exhausted, and I am pursuing **Z**
Judg 8: 6 Are the hands of **Z** and
Judg 8: 7 when the LORD has delivered **Z**
Judg 8:10 Now **Z** and Zalmunna were at
Judg 8:12 When **Z** and Zalmunna fled, he
Judg 8:12 the two kings of Midian, **Z**
Judg 8:15 Here are **Z** and Zalmunna,
Judg 8:15 saying, 'Are the hands of **Z**
Judg 8:18 And he said to **Z** and Zalmunna,
Judg 8:21 So **Z** and Zalmunna said, "Rise
Judg 8:21 So Gideon arose and killed **Z**
Ps 83:11 Yes, all their princes like **Z**

ZEBAIM
Ezra 2:57 the sons of Pochereth of **Z**
Neh 7:59 children of Pochereth of **Z**

ZEBEDEE (*see* ZEBEDEE'S)
Matt 4:21 brothers, James the son of **Z**
Matt 4:21 the boat with **Z** their father
Matt 10: 2 James the son of **Z**, and John
Matt 26:37 Peter and the two sons of **Z**
Mark 1:19 He saw James the son of **Z**
Mark 1:20 they left their father **Z** in
Mark 3:17 James the son of **Z** and John
Mark 10:35 James and John, the sons of **Z**
Luke 5:10 James and John, the sons of **Z**
John 21: 2 in Galilee, the sons of **Z**

ZEBEDEE'S (*see* ZEBEDEE)
Matt 20:20 Then the mother of **Z** sons
Matt 27:56 and the mother of **Z** sons

ZEBINA
Ezra 10:43 Jeiel, Mattithiah, Zabad, **Z**

ZEBOIIM (*see* ZEBOIM)
Gen 14: 2 of Admah, Shemeber king of **Z**
Gen 14: 8 king of Admah, the king of **Z**
Hos 11: 8 How can I set you like **Z**

ZEBOIM (*see* ZEBOIIM)
Gen 10:19 Gomorrah, Admah, and **Z**
Deut 29:23 and Gomorrah, Admah, and **Z**,
1Sa 13:18 of **Z** toward the wilderness
Neh 11:34 in Hadid, **Z**, Neballat

ZEBUDAH
2Ki 23:36 His mother's name was **Z** the

ZEBUL
Judg 9:28 and is not **Z** his officer
Judg 9:30 When **Z**, the ruler of the city
Judg 9:36 saw the people, he said to **Z**
Judg 9:36 But **Z** said to him,
Judg 9:38 Then **Z** said to him, "Where
Judg 9:41 and **Z** drove out Gaal and his

ZEBULUN (*see* ZEBULUNITE)
Gen 30:20 So she called his name **Z**
Gen 35:23 Levi, Judah, Issachar, and **Z**
Gen 46:14 The sons of **Z** were Sered,
Gen 49:13 **Z** shall dwell by the haven of
Ex 1: 3 Issachar, **Z**, and Benjamin
Num 1: 9 from **Z**, Eliab the son of
Num 1:30 From the children of **Z**, their
Num 1:31 numbered of the tribe of **Z**
Num 2: 7 shall come the tribe of **Z**
Num 2: 7 leader of the children of **Z**
Num 7:24 leader of the children of **Z**
Num 10:16 tribe of the children of **Z**
Num 13:10 from the tribe of **Z**, Gaddiel
Num 26:26 The sons of **Z** according to
Num 34:25 tribe of the children of **Z**
Deut 27:13 Reuben, Gad, Asher, **Z**, Dan,
Deut 33:18 And of **Z** he said
Deut 33:18 Rejoice, **Z**, in your going out
Josh 19:10 out for the children of **Z**
Josh 19:16 of the children of **Z**
Josh 19:27 and it reached to **Z** and to the
Josh 19:34 it adjoined **Z** on the south
Josh 21: 7 Gad, and from the tribe of **Z**
Josh 21:34 Levites, from the tribe of **Z**
Judg 1:30 Nor did **Z** drive out the
Judg 4: 6 Naphtali and of the sons of **Z**
Judg 4:10 And Barak called **Z** and
Judg 5:14 from **Z** those who bear the
Judg 5:18 **Z** is a people who jeopardized
Judg 6:35 sent messengers to Asher, **Z**
Judg 12:12 Aijalon in the country of **Z**
1Ch 2: 1 Levi, Judah, Issachar, **Z**
1Ch 6:63 Gad, and from the tribe of **Z**
1Ch 6:77 From the tribe of **Z** the rest
1Ch 12:33 of **Z** there were fifty
1Ch 12:40 as far away as Issachar and **Z**
1Ch 27:19 over **Z**, Ishmaiah the son of
2Ch 30:10 and Manasseh, as far as **Z**
2Ch 30:11 **Z** humbled themselves and came
2Ch 30:18 Manasseh, Issachar, and **Z**
Ps 68:27 company, The princes of **Z**
Is 9: 1 esteemed the land of **Z** and the
Ezek 48:26 **Z** shall have one portion
Ezek 48:27 by the border of **Z**, from the
Ezek 48:33 Issachar, and one gate for **Z**
Matt 4:13 the sea, in the regions of **Z**
Matt 4:15 The land of **Z** and the land of
Rev 7: 8 of the tribe of **Z** twelve

ZEBULUNITE (*see* ZEBULUN, ZEBULUNITES)
Judg 12:11 him, Elon the **Z** judged Israel
Judg 12:12 And Elon the **Z** died and was

ZEBULUNITES (*see* ZEBULUNITE)
Num 26:27 are the families of the **Z**

ZECHARIAH (*see* ZACCUR, ZACHARIAS)
2Ki 14:29 Then **Z** his son reigned in his
2Ki 15: 8 **Z** the son of Jeroboam reigned
2Ki 15:11 Now the rest of the acts of **Z**
2Ki 18: 2 was Abi the daughter of **Z**
1Ch 5: 7 the chief, Jeiel, and **Z**,
1Ch 9:21 **Z** the son of Meshelemiah was
1Ch 9:37 Gedor, Ahio, **Z**, and Mikloth
1Ch 15:18 **Z**, Ben, Jaaziel, Shemiramoth,
1Ch 15:20 **Z**, Aziel, Shemiramoth, Jehiel
1Ch 15:24 Nethaneel, Amasai, **Z**,
1Ch 16: 5 the chief, and next to him **Z**
1Ch 24:25 of the sons of Isshiah, **Z**
1Ch 26: 2 were **Z** the firstborn, Jediael
1Ch 26:11 the third, **Z** the fourth
1Ch 26:14 they cast lots for his son **Z**
1Ch 27:21 in Gilead, Iddo the son of **Z**
2Ch 17: 7 leaders, Ben-Hail, Obadiah, **Z**
2Ch 20:14 upon Jahaziel the son of **Z**
2Ch 21: 2 Azariah, Jehiel, **Z**, Azaryahu,
2Ch 24:20 **Z** the son of Jehoiada the
2Ch 26: 5 sought God in the days of **Z**
2Ch 29: 1 was Abijah the daughter of **Z**
2Ch 29:13 of the sons of Asaph, **Z** and
2Ch 34:12 of the sons of Merari, and **Z**
2Ch 35: 8 Hilkiah, **Z**, and Jehiel, rulers
Ezra 5: 1 **Z** the son of Iddo, prophets,
Ezra 6:14 prophet and **Z** the son of Iddo
Ezra 8: 3 of the sons of Parosh, **Z**
Ezra 8:11 **Z** the son of Bebai, and with
Ezra 8:16 Jarib, Elnathan, Nathan, **Z**
Ezra 10:26 Mattaniah, **Z**, Jehiel, Abdi,
Neh 8: 4 Hashum, Hashbadana, **Z**, and
Neh 11: 4 son of Uzziah, the son of **Z**
Neh 11: 5 son of Joiarib, the son of **Z**
Neh 11:12 the son of Amzi, the son of **Z**
Neh 12:16 of Iddo, **Z**
Neh 12:35 **Z** the son of Jonathan, the
Neh 12:41 Michaiah, Elioenai, **Z**, and
Is 8: 2 and **Z** the son of Jeberechiah
Zech 1: 1 to **Z** the son of Berechiah
Zech 1: 7 to **Z** the son of Berechiah
Zech 7: 1 word of the LORD came to **Z**
Zech 7: 8 word of the LORD came to **Z**
Matt 23:35 Abel to the blood of **Z**, son
Luke 11:51 of Abel to the blood of **Z** who

ZECHER
1Ch 8:31 Gedor, Ahio, **Z**,

ZEDAD
Num 34: 8 the border shall be toward **Z**
Ezek 47:15 to Hethlon, as one goes to **Z**

ZEDEKIAH (*see* MATTANIAH, ZEDEKIAH'S)
1Ki 22:11 Now **Z** the son of Chenaanah
1Ki 22:24 Then **Z** the son of Chenaanah
2Ki 24:17 and changed his name to **Z**
2Ki 24:18 **Z** was twenty-one years old
2Ki 24:20 Then **Z** rebelled against the
2Ki 25: 2 the eleventh year of King **Z**
2Ki 25: 7 the sons of **Z** before his eyes
2Ki 25: 7 eyes, put out the eyes of **Z**
1Ch 3:15 second Jehoiakim, the third **Z**
1Ch 3:16 Jeconiah his son and **Z** his son
2Ch 18:10 Now **Z** the son of Chenaanah
2Ch 18:23 Then **Z** the son of Chenaanah
2Ch 36:10 house of the LORD, and made **Z**
2Ch 36:11 **Z** was twenty-one years old
Neh 10: 1 the son of Hacaliah, and **Z**
Jer 1: 3 year of **Z** the son of Josiah
Jer 21: 1 from the LORD when King **Z**
Jer 21: 3 Thus you shall say to **Z**,
Jer 21: 7 will deliver **Z** king of Judah
Jer 24: 8 I give up **Z** the king of Judah
Jer 27: 3 Jerusalem to **Z** king of Judah
Jer 27:12 I also spoke to **Z** king of
Jer 28: 1 the reign of **Z** king of Judah

Jer 29: 3 whom **Z** king of Judah sent to
Jer 29:21 **Z** the son of Maaseiah, who
Jer 29:22 The LORD make you like **Z** and
Jer 32: 1 tenth year of **Z** king of Judah
Jer 32: 3 For **Z** king of Judah had shut
Jer 32: 4 **Z** king of Judah shall not
Jer 32: 5 he shall lead **Z** to Babylon
Jer 34: 2 speak to **Z** king of Judah and
Jer 34: 4 the LORD, O **Z** king of Judah
Jer 34: 6 spoke all these words to **Z**
Jer 34: 8 LORD, after King **Z** had made a
Jer 34:21 I will give **Z** king of Judah
Jer 36:12 **Z** the son of Hananiah, and all
Jer 37: 1 Then King **Z** the son of Josiah
Jer 37: 3 **Z** the king sent Jehucal the
Jer 37:17 then **Z** the king sent and took
Jer 37:18 Jeremiah said to King **Z**
Jer 37:21 Then **Z** the king commanded
Jer 38: 5 Then **Z** the king said, "Look,
Jer 38:14 Then **Z** the king sent and had
Jer 38:15 Then Jeremiah said to **Z**, "If
Jer 38:16 So **Z** the king swore secretly
Jer 38:17 Then Jeremiah said to **Z**
Jer 38:19 **Z** the king said to Jeremiah,
Jer 38:24 Then **Z** said to Jeremiah
Jer 39: 1 ninth year of **Z** king of Judah
Jer 39: 2 In the eleventh year of **Z**
Jer 39: 4 when **Z** the king of Judah and
Jer 39: 5 overtook **Z** in the plains of
Jer 39: 6 **Z** before his eyes in Riblah
Jer 44:30 as I gave **Z** king of Judah
Jer 49:34 the reign of **Z** king of Judah
Jer 51:59 when he went with **Z** the king
Jer 52: 1 **Z** was twenty-one years old
Jer 52: 3 Then **Z** rebelled against the
Jer 52: 5 the eleventh year of King **Z**
Jer 52: 8 they overtook **Z** in the plains
Jer 52:10 the sons of **Z** before his eyes
Jer 52:11 He also put out the eyes of **Z**

ZEDEKIAH'S (*see* ZEDEKIAH)
Jer 39: 7 Moreover he put out **Z** eyes

ZEEB
Judg 7:25 of the Midianites, Oreb and **Z**
Judg 7:25 Oreb, and **Z** they killed at the
Judg 7:25 killed at the winepress of **Z**
Judg 7:25 **Z** to Gideon on the other side
Judg 8: 3 princes of Midian, Oreb and **Z**
Ps 83:11 nobles like Oreb and like **Z**

ZELAH
Josh 18:28 **Z**, Eleph, Jebus (which is
2Sa 21:14 the country of Benjamin in **Z**

ZELEK
2Sa 23:37 **Z** the Ammonite, Naharai the
1Ch 11:39 **Z** the Ammonite, Naharai the

ZELOPHEHAD
Num 26:33 Now **Z** the son of Hepher had
Num 26:33 daughters of **Z** were Mahlah
Num 27: 1 of **Z** the son of Hepher, the
Num 27: 7 The daughters of **Z** speak what
Num 36: 2 brother **Z** to his daughters
Num 36: 6 concerning the daughters of **Z**
Num 36:10 so did the daughters of **Z**
Num 36:11 and Noah, the daughters of **Z**
Josh 17: 3 But **Z** the son of Hepher, the
1Ch 7:15 of Gilead's grandson was **Z**
1Ch 7:15 but **Z** begot only daughters

ZELZAH
1Sa 10: 2 territory of Benjamin at **Z**

ZEMARAIM (*see* ZEMARITE)
Josh 18:22 Beth Arabah, **Z**, Bethel,
2Ch 13: 4 Then Abijah stood on Mount **Z**

ZEMARITE (*see* ZEMARAIM)
Gen 10:18 the Arvadite, the **Z**, and the
1Ch 1:16 the Arvadite, the **Z**, and the

ZEMIRAH
1Ch 7: 8 The sons of Becher were **Z**

ZENAN (*see* ZAANAN)
Josh 15:37 **Z**, Hadashah, Migdal Gad,

ZENAS
Tit 3:13 Send **Z** the lawyer and Apollos

ZEPHANIAH
2Ki 25:18 **Z** the second priest, and the
1Ch 6:36 son of Azariah, the son of **Z**
Jer 21: 1 **Z** the son of Maaseiah, the
Jer 29:25 to **Z** the son of Maaseiah the
Jer 29:29 Now **Z** the priest read this
Jer 37: 3 **Z** the son of Maaseiah, the
Jer 52:24 **Z** the second priest, and the
Zeph 1: 1 came to **Z** the son of Cushi
Zech 6:10 house of Josiah the son of **Z**
Zech 6:14 Jedaiah, and Hen the son of **Z**

ZEPHATH (*see* HORMAH)
Judg 1:17 Canaanites who inhabited **Z**

ZEPHATHAH
2Ch 14:10 the Valley of **Z** at Mareshah

ZEPHI (*see* ZEPHO)
1Ch 1:36 Eliphaz were Teman, Omar, **Z**

ZEPHO (*see* ZEPHI)
Gen 36:11 Eliphaz were Teman, Omar, **Z**
Gen 36:15 Teman, Chief Omar, Chief **Z**

ZEPHON (*see* BAAL ZEPHON, ZEPHONITES, ZIPHION)
Num 26:15 of **Z**, the family of the

ZEPHONITES (*see* ZEPHON)
Num 26:15 Zephon, the family of the **Z**

ZER
Josh 19:35 cities are Ziddim, **Z**, Hammath

ZERAH (*see* EZRAHITE, ZARHITES, ZOHAR)
Gen 36:13 Nahath, **Z**, Shammah, and
Gen 36:17 Chief Nahath, Chief **Z**, Chief
Gen 36:33 Jobab the son of **Z** of Bozrah
Gen 38:30 And his name was called **Z**
Gen 46:12 **Z** (but Er and Onan died in the
Num 26:13 of **Z**, the family of the
Num 26:20 of **Z**, the family of the
Josh 7: 1 son of Zabdi, the son of **Z**
Josh 7:18 son of Zabdi, the son of **Z**
Josh 7:24 him, took Achan the son of **Z**
Josh 22:20 of **Z** commit a trespass in the
1Ch 1:37 sons of Reuel were Nahath, **Z**
1Ch 1:44 Jobab the son of **Z** of Bozrah
1Ch 2: 4 bore him Perez and **Z**
1Ch 2: 6 The sons of **Z** were Zimri,
1Ch 4:24 were Nemuel, Jamin, Jarib, **Z**
1Ch 6:21 **Z** his son, and Jeatherai his
1Ch 6:41 son of Ethni, the son of **Z**
1Ch 9: 6 Of the sons of **Z**
2Ch 14: 9 Then **Z** the Ethiopian came out
Neh 11:24 of **Z** the son of Judah, was
Matt 1: 3 and **Z** by Tamar, Perez begot

ZERAHIAH
1Ch 6: 6 Uzzi begot **Z**
1Ch 6: 6 and **Z** begot Meraioth
1Ch 6:51 son, Uzzi his son, **Z** his son,
Ezra 7: 4 the son of **Z**, the son of Uzzi
Ezra 8: 4 Elihoenai the son of **Z**, and

ZERED
Num 21:12 and camped in the Valley of **Z**
Deut 2:13 over the Valley of the **Z**
Deut 2:13 over the Valley of the **Z**
Deut 2:14 the **Z** was thirty-eight years

ZEREDA
1Ki 11:26 Nebat, an Ephraimite from **Z**

ZEREDAH
2Ch 4:17 molds, between Succoth and **Z**

ZERERAH
Judg 7:22 fled to Beth Acacia, toward **Z**

ZERESH
Esth 5:10 for his friends and his wife **Z**
Esth 5:14 Then his wife **Z** and all his
Esth 6:13 When Haman told his wife **Z**
Esth 6:13 and his wife **Z** said to him,

ZERETH
1Ch 4: 7 The sons of Helah were **Z**,

ZERETH SHAHAR (*see* SHAHAR)
Josh 13:19 **Z** on the mountain of the

ZERI
1Ch 25: 3 Gedaliah, **Z**, Jeshaiah, Shimei

ZEROR (*see* ZOHAR)
1Sa 9: 1 son of Abiel, the son of **Z**

ZERUAH
1Ki 11:26 whose mother's name was **Z**

ZERUBBABEL (*see* SHESHBAZZAR)
1Ch 3:19 The sons of Pedaiah were **Z**
1Ch 3:19 The sons of **Z** were Meshullam,
Ezra 2: 2 who came with **Z** were Jeshua
Ezra 3: 2 **Z** the son of Shealtiel and his
Ezra 3: 8 **Z** the son of Shealtiel,
Ezra 4: 2 they came to **Z** and the heads
Ezra 4: 3 But **Z** and Jeshua and the rest
Ezra 5: 2 So **Z** the son of Shealtiel and
Neh 7: 7 who came with **Z** were Jeshua
Neh 12: 1 with **Z** the son of Shealtiel
Neh 12:47 In the days of **Z** and in the
Hag 1: 1 to **Z** the son of Shealtiel
Hag 1:12 Then **Z** the son of Shealtiel,
Hag 1:14 of **Z** the son of Shealtiel
Hag 2: 2 Speak now to **Z** the son of
Hag 2: 4 Yet now be strong, **Z**,' says
Hag 2:21 Speak to **Z**, governor of Judah
Hag 2:23 you, **Z** My servant, the son of
Zech 4: 6 is the word of the LORD to **Z**
Zech 4: 7 Before **Z** you shall become a
Zech 4: 9 The hands of **Z** have laid the
Zech 4:10 plumb line in the hand of **Z**
Matt 1:12 and Shealtiel begot **Z**
Matt 1:13 **Z** begot Abiud, Abiud begot
Luke 3:27 son of Rhesa, the son of **Z**

ZERUIAH
1Sa 26: 6 and to Abishai the son of **Z**
2Sa 2:13 And Joab the son of **Z**, and the
2Sa 2:18 three sons of **Z** were there
2Sa 3:39 and these men, the sons of **Z**
2Sa 8:16 Joab the son of **Z** was over
2Sa 14: 1 So Joab the son of **Z**
2Sa 16: 9 the son of **Z** said to the king
2Sa 16:10 to do with you, you sons of **Z**
2Sa 17:25 of Nahash, sister of **Z**,
2Sa 18: 2 hand of Abishai the son of **Z**
2Sa 19:21 Abishai the son of **Z** answered
2Sa 19:22 to do with you, you sons of **Z**
2Sa 21:17 the son of **Z** came to his aid
2Sa 23:18 brother of Joab, the son of **Z**
2Sa 23:37 of Joab the son of **Z**),
1Ki 1: 7 with Joab the son of **Z** and
1Ki 2: 5 Joab the son of **Z** did to me
1Ki 2:22 and for Joab the son of **Z**
1Ch 2:16 Now their sisters were **Z** and
1Ch 2:16 the sons of **Z** were Abishai,
1Ch 11: 6 the son of **Z** went up first
1Ch 11:39 of Joab the son of **Z**),
1Ch 18:12 of **Z** killed eighteen thousand
1Ch 18:15 Joab the son of **Z** was over
1Ch 26:28 the son of **Z** had dedicated
1Ch 27:24 the son of **Z** began a census

ZETHAM
1Ch 23: 8 the first Jehiel, then **Z** and
1Ch 26:22 The sons of Jehieli, **Z** and

ZETHAN
1Ch 7:10 Benjamin, Ehud, Chenaanah, **Z**

ZETHAR
Esth 1:10 Harbona, Bigtha, Abagtha, **Z**

ZEUS
Acts 14:12 And Barnabas they called **Z**
Acts 14:13 Then the priest of **Z**, whose
Acts 19:35 image which fell down from **Z**

ZIA
1Ch 5:13 Sheba, Jorai, Jachan, **Z**, and

ZIBA
2Sa 9: 2 of Saul whose name was **Z**
2Sa 9: 2 Are you **Z**?"
2Sa 9: 3 And **Z** said to the king,
2Sa 9: 4 And **Z** said to the king,
2Sa 9: 9 And the king called to **Z**,
2Sa 9:10 Now **Z** had fifteen sons and
2Sa 9:11 Then **Z** said to the king
2Sa 9:12 house of **Z** were servants of
2Sa 16: 1 there was **Z** the servant of
2Sa 16: 2 And the king said to **Z**, "What
2Sa 16: 2 So **Z** said, "The donkeys
2Sa 16: 3 And **Z** said to the king,
2Sa 16: 4 So the king said to **Z**, "Here
2Sa 16: 4 **Z** said, "I humbly bow before
2Sa 19:17 **Z** the servant of the house of
2Sa 19:29 You and **Z** divide the land

ZIBEON
Gen 36: 2 the daughter of **Z** the Hivite
Gen 36:14 of Anah, the daughter of **Z**
Gen 36:20 Lotan, Shobal, **Z**, Anah,
Gen 36:24 These were the sons of **Z**
Gen 36:24 the donkeys of his father **Z**
Gen 36:29 Lotan, Chief Shobal, Chief **Z**
1Ch 1:38 of Seir were Lotan, Shobal, **Z**
1Ch 1:40 The sons of **Z** were Ajah and

ZIBIA
1Ch 8: 9 his wife he begot Jobab, **Z**

ZIBIAH
2Ki 12: 1 name was **Z** of Beersheba
2Ch 24: 1 name was **Z** of Beersheba

ZICHRI (*see* ZACCUR, ZITHRI)
Ex 6:21 were Korah, Nepheg, and **Z**
1Ch 8:19 Jakim, **Z**, Zabdi,
1Ch 8:23 Abdon, **Z**, Hanan,
1Ch 8:27 **Z** were the sons of Jeroham
1Ch 9:15 son of Micah, the son of **Z**
1Ch 26:25 **Z** his son, and Shelomith his
1Ch 27:16 was Eliezer the son of **Z**
2Ch 17:16 him was Amasiah the son of **Z**
2Ch 23: 1 and Elishaphat the son of **Z**
2Ch 28: 7 **Z**, a mighty man of Ephraim,
Neh 11: 9 Joel the son of **Z** was their
Neh 12:17 of Abijah, **Z**

ZIDDIM
Josh 19:35 And the fortified cities are **Z**

ZIHA
Ezra 2:43 the sons of **Z**, the sons of
Neh 7:46 the children of **Z**, the
Neh 11:21 And **Z** and Gishpa were over the

ZIKLAG
Josh 15:31 **Z**, Madmannah, Sansannah,
Josh 19: 5 **Z**, Beth Marcaboth, Hazar
1Sa 27: 6 So Achish gave him **Z** that day
1Sa 27: 6 Therefore **Z** has belonged to
1Sa 30: 1 David and his men came to **Z**
1Sa 30: 1 had invaded the South and **Z**
1Sa 30: 1 South and **Z**, attacked **Z**
1Sa 30:14 and we burned **Z** with fire
1Sa 30:26 Now when David came to **Z**, he
2Sa 1: 1 had stayed two days in **Z**,
2Sa 4:10 him and had him executed in **Z**
1Ch 4:30 Bethuel, Hormah, **Z**,
1Ch 12: 1 at **Z** while he was still a
1Ch 12:20 When he went to **Z**, those of
Neh 11:28 in **Z** and Meconah and its

ZILLAH
Gen 4:19 the name of the second was **Z**
Gen 4:22 And as for **Z**, she also bore
Gen 4:23 Adah and **Z**, hear my voice

ZILLETHAI
1Ch 8:20 Elienai, **Z**, Eliel,
1Ch 12:20 Michael, Jozabad, Elihu, and **Z**

ZILPAH
Gen 29:24 Laban gave his maid **Z** to his
Gen 30: 9 bearing, she took **Z** her maid
Gen 30:10 Leah's maid **Z** bore Jacob a
Gen 30:12 Leah's maid **Z** bore Jacob a
Gen 35:26 and the sons of **Z**, Leah's
Gen 37: 2 of Bilhah and the sons of **Z**
Gen 46:18 These were the sons of **Z**,

ZIMMAH
1Ch 6:20 Jahath his son, **Z** his son,
1Ch 6:42 son of Ethan, the son of **Z**
2Ch 29:12 Joah the son of **Z** and Eden

ZIMRAN
Gen 25: 2 And she bore him **Z**, Jokshan,
1Ch 1:32 Abraham's concubine, were **Z**

ZIMRI
Num 25:14 was **Z** the son of Salu, a
1Ki 16: 9 Now his servant **Z**, commander
1Ki 16:10 **Z** went in and struck him and
1Ki 16:12 Thus **Z** destroyed all the
1Ki 16:15 **Z** had reigned in Tirzah seven
1Ki 16:16 **Z** has conspired and also has
1Ki 16:18 when **Z** saw that the city was
1Ki 16:20 Now the rest of the acts of **Z**
2Ki 9:31 Is it peace, **Z**, murderer of
1Ch 2: 6 The sons of Zerah were **Z**,
1Ch 8:36 Alemeth, Azmaveth, and **Z**
1Ch 8:36 and **Z** begot Moza
1Ch 9:42 Alemeth, Azmaveth, and **Z**
1Ch 9:42 and **Z** begot Moza
Jer 25:25 all the kings of **Z**, all the

ZIN
Num 13:21 of **Z** as far as Rehob, near
Num 20: 1 of **Z** in the first month, and
Num 27:14 For in the Wilderness of **Z**
Num 27:14 Kadesh in the Wilderness of **Z**
Num 33:36 camped in the Wilderness of **Z**
Num 34: 3 of **Z** along the border of Edom
Num 34: 4 of Akrabbim, continue to **Z**
Deut 32:51 in the Wilderness of **Z**,
Josh 15: 1 **Z** southward was the extreme
Josh 15: 3 Akrabbim, passed along to **Z**

ZINA (*see* ZIZAH)
1Ch 23:10 Jahath, **Z**, Jeush, and Beriah

ZION (*see* SION, ZION'S)
2Sa 5: 7 the stronghold of **Z** (that is
1Ki 8: 1 the City of David, which is **Z**
2Ki 19:21 The virgin, the daughter of **Z**
2Ki 19:31 those who escape from Mount **Z**
1Ch 11: 5 the stronghold of **Z** (that is
2Ch 5: 2 the City of David, which is **Z**
Ps 2: 6 My King On My holy hill of **Z**
Ps 9:11 to the LORD, who dwells in **Z**
Ps 9:14 gates of the daughter of **Z**
Ps 14: 7 of Israel would come out of **Z**
Ps 20: 2 And strengthen you out of **Z**
Ps 48: 2 Is Mount **Z** on the sides of
Ps 48:11 Let Mount **Z** rejoice, Let the
Ps 48:12 Walk about **Z**, And go all
Ps 50: 2 Out of **Z**, the perfection of
Ps 51:18 in Your good pleasure to **Z**
Ps 53: 6 of Israel would come out of **Z**
Ps 65: 1 is awaiting You, O God, in **Z**
Ps 69:35 For God will save **Z** And build
Ps 74: 2 This Mount **Z** where You have
Ps 76: 2 And His dwelling place in **Z**
Ps 78:68 Judah, Mount **Z** which He loved
Ps 84: 7 them appears before God in **Z**
Ps 87: 2 **Z** More than all the dwellings
Ps 87: 5 And of **Z** it will be said,
Ps 97: 8 **Z** hears and is glad, And the
Ps 99: 2 The LORD is great in **Z**, And He
Ps 102:13 will arise and have mercy on **Z**
Ps 102:16 For the LORD shall build up **Z**
Ps 102:21 the name of the LORD in **Z**
Ps 110: 2 rod of Your strength out of **Z**
Ps 125: 1 in the LORD Are like Mount **Z**
Ps 126: 1 back the captivity of **Z**, We
Ps 128: 5 The LORD bless you out of **Z**
Ps 129: 5 who hate **Z** Be put to shame
Ps 132:13 For the LORD has chosen **Z**
Ps 133: 3 upon the mountains of **Z**
Ps 134: 3 and earth Bless you from **Z**
Ps 135:21 Blessed be the LORD out of **Z**
Ps 137: 1 wept When we remembered **Z**
Ps 137: 3 Sing us one of the songs of **Z**
Ps 146:10 Your God, O **Z**, to all
Ps 147:12 Praise your God, O **Z**
Ps 149: 2 Let the children of **Z** be
Song 3:11 Go forth, O daughters of **Z**
Is 1: 8 So the daughter of **Z** is left
Is 1:27 **Z** shall be redeemed with
Is 2: 3 For out of **Z** shall go forth
Is 3:16 daughters of **Z** are haughty
Is 3:17 head of the daughters of **Z**
Is 4: 3 pass that he who is left in **Z**
Is 4: 4 filth of the daughters of **Z**
Is 4: 5 dwelling place of Mount **Z**
Is 8:18 hosts, Who dwells in Mount **Z**
Is 10:12 all His work on Mount **Z** and on
Is 10:24 O My people, who dwell in **Z**
Is 10:32 mount of the daughter of **Z**
Is 12: 6 and shout, O inhabitant of **Z**
Is 14:32 That the LORD has founded **Z**
Is 16: 1 mount of the daughter of **Z**
Is 18: 7 the LORD of hosts, to Mount **Z**
Is 24:23 hosts will reign on Mount **Z**
Is 28:16 I lay in **Z** a stone for a
Is 29: 8 be, who fight against Mount **Z**
Is 30:19 shall dwell in **Z** at Jerusalem
Is 31: 4 down to fight for Mount **Z**
Is 31: 9 the LORD, whose fire is in **Z**
Is 33: 5 He has filled **Z** with justice
Is 33:14 The sinners in **Z** are afraid
Is 33:20 Look upon **Z**, the city of our
Is 34: 8 recompense for the cause of **Z**
Is 35:10 come to **Z** with singing, with
Is 37:22 The virgin, the daughter of **Z**
Is 37:32 those who escape from Mount **Z**
Is 40: 9 O **Z**, you who bring good
Is 41:27 The first time I said to **Z**
Is 46:13 I will place salvation in **Z**
Is 49:14 But **Z** said, "The LORD has
Is 51: 3 For the LORD will comfort **Z**
Is 51:11 come to **Z** with singing, with
Is 51:16 of the earth, and say to **Z**
Is 52: 1 Put on your strength, O **Z**
Is 52: 2 neck, O captive daughter of **Z**
Is 52: 7 salvation, who says to **Z**
Is 52: 8 when the LORD brings back **Z**
Is 59:20 The Redeemer will come to **Z**
Is 60:14 **Z** of the Holy One of Israel
Is 61: 3 console those who mourn in **Z**
Is 62:11 Say to the daughter of **Z**
Is 64:10 **Z** is a wilderness, Jerusalem
Is 66: 8 For as soon as **Z** travailed
Jer 3:14 and I will bring you to **Z**
Jer 4: 6 Set up the standard toward **Z**
Jer 4:31 of **Z** bewailing herself, who
Jer 6: 2 the daughter of **Z** to a lovely
Jer 6:23 against you, O daughter of **Z**
Jer 8:19 Is not the LORD in **Z**
Jer 9:19 of wailing is heard from **Z**
Jer 14:19 Has Your soul loathed **Z**
Jer 26:18 **Z** shall be plowed like a
Jer 30:17 this is **Z**; no one seeks her.
Jer 31: 6 Arise, and let us go up to **Z**
Jer 31:12 and sing in the height of **Z**
Jer 50: 5 They shall ask the way to **Z**
Jer 50:28 **Z** the vengeance of the LORD
Jer 51:10 let us declare in **Z** the work
Jer 51:24 have done in **Z** in your sight
Jer 51:35 the inhabitant of **Z** will say
Lam 1: 4 The roads to **Z** mourn because
Lam 1: 6 of **Z** all her splendor has
Lam 1:17 **Z** spreads out her hands, but
Lam 2: 1 **Z** with a cloud in His anger
Lam 2: 4 the tent of the daughter of **Z**
Lam 2: 6 Sabbaths to be forgotten in **Z**
Lam 2: 8 the wall of the daughter of **Z**
Lam 2:10 of **Z** sit on the ground and
Lam 2:13 you, O virgin daughter of **Z**
Lam 2:18 O wall of the daughter of **Z**
Lam 4: 2 The precious sons of **Z**,
Lam 4:11 He kindled a fire in **Z**, and it
Lam 4:22 accomplished, O daughter of **Z**
Lam 5:11 They ravished the women in **Z**
Lam 5:18 because of Mount **Z** which is
Joel 2: 1 Blow the trumpet in **Z**, and
Joel 2:15 Blow the trumpet in **Z**,
Joel 2:23 glad then, you children of **Z**
Joel 2:32 For in Mount **Z** and in
Joel 3:16 LORD also will roar from **Z**
Joel 3:17 God, dwelling in **Z** My holy
Joel 3:21 for the LORD dwells in **Z**
Amos 1: 2 The LORD roars from **Z**, and
Amos 6: 1 to you who are at ease in **Z**
Obad 17 But on Mount **Z** there shall be
Obad 21 **Z** to judge the mountains of
Mic 1:13 of sin to the daughter of **Z**)
Mic 3:10 Who build up **Z** with bloodshed
Mic 3:12 you **Z** shall be plowed like a
Mic 4: 2 For out of **Z** the law shall
Mic 4: 7 them in Mount **Z** From now on
Mic 4: 8 of the daughter of **Z**, to you
Mic 4:10 bring forth, O daughter of **Z**
Mic 4:11 and let our eye look upon **Z**
Mic 4:13 and thresh, O daughter of **Z**
Zeph 3:14 Sing, O daughter of **Z**
Zeph 3:16 **Z**, let not your hands be weak
Zech 1:14 and for **Z** with great zeal
Zech 1:17 the LORD will again comfort **Z**
Zech 2: 7 Up, **Z**! Escape, you who dwell
Zech 2:10 and rejoice, O daughter of **Z**
Zech 8: 2 zealous for **Z** with great zeal
Zech 8: 3 I will return to **Z**, and dwell
Zech 9: 9 greatly, O daughter of **Z**
Zech 9:13 and raised up your sons, O **Z**
Matt 21: 5 Tell the daughter of **Z**
John 12:15 Fear not, daughter of **Z**
Rom 9:33 I lay in **Z** a stumbling stone
Rom 11:26 Deliverer will come out of **Z**
Heb 12:22 But you have come to Mount **Z**
1Pe 2: 6 Behold, I lay in **Z** a chief
Rev 14: 1 a Lamb standing on Mount **Z**

ZION'S (*see* ZION)
Is 62: 1 For **Z** sake I will not hold My

ZIOR
Josh 15:54 Arba (which is Hebron), and **Z**

ZIPH (*see* ZIPHITES)
Josh 15:24 **Z**, Telem, Bealoth,
Josh 15:55 Maon, Carmel, **Z**, Juttah,
1Sa 23:14 in the Wilderness of **Z**
1Sa 23:15 Wilderness of **Z** in a forest
1Sa 23:24 and went to **Z** before Saul
1Sa 26: 2 down to the Wilderness of **Z**
1Sa 26: 2 David in the Wilderness of **Z**
1Ch 2:42 who was the father of **Z**, and
1Ch 4:16 The sons of Jahaleleel were **Z**
2Ch 11: 8 Gath, Mareshah, **Z**,

ZIPHAH
1Ch 4:16 of Jahaleleel were Ziph, **Z**

ZIPHION (*see* ZEPHON)
Gen 46:16 The sons of Gad were **Z**, Haggi

ZIPHITES (*see* ZIPH)
1Sa 23:19 Then the **Z** came up to Saul at
1Sa 26: 1 Now the **Z** came to Saul at

ZIPHRON
Num 34: 9 the border shall proceed to **Z**

ZIPPOR
Num 22: 2 Now Balak the son of **Z** saw
Num 22: 4 Balak the son of **Z** was king
Num 22:10 Balak the son of **Z**, king of
Num 22:16 Thus says Balak the son of **Z**
Num 23:18 Listen to me, son of **Z**
Josh 24: 9 Then Balak the son of **Z**,
Judg 11:25 than Balak the son of **Z**, king

ZIPPORAH
Ex 2:21 he gave **Z** his daughter to
Ex 4:25 Then **Z** took a sharp stone and
Ex 18: 2 Moses' father-in-law, took **Z**

ZITHRI (*see* ZICHRI)
Ex 6:22 were Mishael, Elzaphan, and **Z**

ZIV
1Ki 6: 1 Israel, in the month of **Z**
1Ki 6:37 was laid, in the month of **Z**

ZIZ
2Ch 20:16 come up by the ascent of **Z**

ZIZA (*see* ZIZAH)
1Ch 4:37 **Z** the son of Shiphi, the son
2Ch 11:20 she bore him Abijah, Attai, **Z**

ZIZAH (*see* ZINA, ZIZA)
1Ch 23:11 was the first and **Z** the second

ZOAN
Num 13:22 seven years before **Z** in Egypt
Ps 78:12 of Egypt, in the field of **Z**
Ps 78:43 His wonders in the field of **Z**
Is 19:11 the princes of **Z** are fools
Is 19:13 The princes of **Z** have become
Is 30: 4 For his princes were at **Z**
Ezek 30:14 desolate, set fire to **Z**, and

ZOAR
Gen 13:10 of Egypt as you go toward **Z**
Gen 14: 2 the king of Bela (that is, **Z**)
Gen 14: 8 is, **Z**) went out and joined
Gen 19:22 name of the city was called **Z**
Gen 19:23 the earth when Lot entered **Z**
Gen 19:30 Then Lot went up out of **Z**
Gen 19:30 he was afraid to dwell in **Z**
Deut 34: 3 of palm trees, as far as **Z**
Is 15: 5 his fugitives shall flee to **Z**
Jer 48:34 from **Z** to Horonaim, like a

ZOBA (*see* ZOBAH)
2Sa 10: 6 Rehob and the Syrians of **Z**
2Sa 10: 8 And the Syrians of **Z**, Rehob,

ZOBAH (*see* HAMATH ZOBAH, ZOBA)
1Sa 14:47 Edom, against the kings of **Z**
2Sa 8: 3 the son of Rehob, king of **Z**
2Sa 8: 5 to help Hadadezer king of **Z**
2Sa 8:12 the son of Rehob, king of **Z**
2Sa 23:36 Igal the son of Nathan of **Z**
1Ki 11:23 his lord, Hadadezer king of **Z**
1Ki 11:24 when David killed those of **Z**
1Ch 18: 3 king of **Z** as far as Hamath
1Ch 18: 5 to help Hadadezer king of **Z**
1Ch 18: 9 army of Hadadezer king of **Z**
1Ch 19: 6 Syrian Maachah, and from **Z**

ZOBEBAH
1Ch 4: 8 and Koz begot Anub, **Z**, and the

ZOHAR (*see* ZERAH, ZEROR)
Gen 23: 8 Ephron the son of **Z** for me
Gen 25: 9 the son of **Z** the Hittite,
Gen 46:10 Jamin, Ohad, Jachin, **Z**, and
Ex 6:15 Jamin, Ohad, Jachin, **Z**, and
1Ch 4: 7 sons of Helah were Zereth, **Z**

ZOHELETH
1Ki 1: 9 cattle by the stone of **Z**,

ZOHETH (*see* BEN-ZOHETH)
1Ch 4:20 And the sons of Ishi were **Z**

ZOPHAH
1Ch 7:35 of his brother Helem were **Z**
1Ch 7:36 The sons of **Z** were Suah,

ZOPHAI (*see* ZUPH)
1Ch 6:26 of Elkanah were **Z** his son

ZOPHAR
Job 2:11 Shuhite, and **Z** the Naamathite
Job 11: 1 Then **Z** the Naamathite
Job 20: 1 Then **Z** the Naamathite
Job 42: 9 **Z** the Naamathite went and did

ZOPHIM (*see* RAMATHAIM ZOPHIM)
Num 23:14 brought him to the field of **Z**

ZORAH (*see* ZORATHITES, ZORITES)
Josh 15:33 Eshtaol, **Z**, Ashnah,
Josh 19:41 of their inheritance was **Z**
Judg 13: 2 was a certain man from **Z**, of
Judg 13:25 him at Mahaneh Dan between **Z**
Judg 16:31 up and buried him between **Z**
Judg 18: 2 men of valor from **Z** and
Judg 18: 8 back to their brethren at **Z**
Judg 18:11 went from there, from **Z** and
2Ch 11:10 **Z**, Aijalon, and Hebron, which
Neh 11:29 in En Rimmon, **Z**, Jarmuth,

ZORATHITES (*see* ZORAH, ZORITES)
1Ch 2:53 From these came the **Z** and the
1Ch 4: 2 were the families of the **Z**

ZORITES (*see* ZORAH, ZORATHITES)
1Ch 2:54 of the Manahethites, and the **Z**

ZUAR
Num 1: 8 Nethaneel the son of **Z**
Num 2: 5 Nethaneel the son of **Z** shall
Num 7:18 day Nethaneel the son of **Z**
Num 7:23 of Nethaneel the son of **Z**
Num 10:15 was Nethaneel the son of **Z**

ZUPH (*see* ZOPHAI)
1Sa 1: 1 the son of Tohu, the son of **Z**
1Sa 9: 5 had come to the land of **Z**
1Ch 6:35 the son of **Z**, the son of

ZUR (*see* BETH ZUR)
Num 25:15 was Cozbi the daughter of **Z**
Num 31: 8 Evi, Rekem, **Z**, Hur, and Reba,
Josh 13:21 Evi, Rekem, **Z**, Hur, and Reba,
1Ch 8:30 son was Abdon, then **Z**, Kish,
1Ch 9:36 son was Abdon, then **Z**, Kish,

ZURIEL
Num 3:35 was **Z** the son of Abihail

ZURISHADDAI
Num 1: 6 Shelumiel the son of **Z**
Num 2:12 be Shelumiel the son of **Z**
Num 7:36 day Shelumiel the son of **Z**
Num 7:41 of Shelumiel the son of **Z**
Num 10:19 was Shelumiel the son of **Z**

ZUZIM (*see* ZAMZUMMIM)
Gen 14: 5 the **Z** in Ham, the Emim in